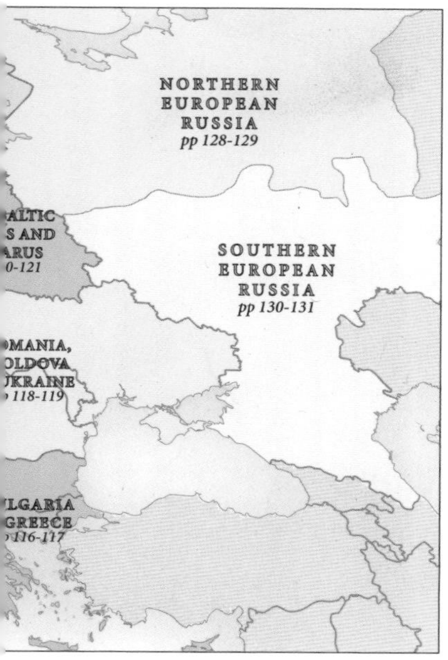
NORTHERN EUROPEAN RUSSIA
pp 128-129
SOUTHERN EUROPEAN RUSSIA
pp 130-131

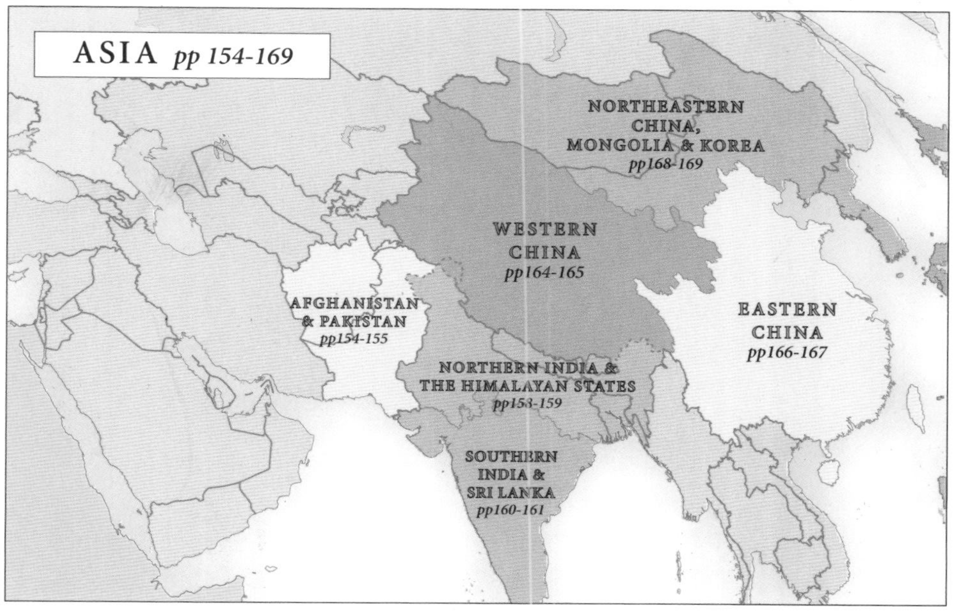
ASIA pp 154-169
NORTHEASTERN CHINA, MONGOLIA & KOREA
pp168-169
WESTERN CHINA
pp164-165
AFGHANISTAN & PAKISTAN
pp154-155
EASTERN CHINA
pp166-167
NORTHERN INDIA & THE HIMALAYAN STATES
pp158-159
SOUTHERN INDIA & SRI LANKA
pp160-161

Svalbard
p 94
THE RUSSIAN FEDERATION
pp125-127
pp 86-131
KAZAKHSTAN
pp150-151
ASIA
pp 132-179
(also see inset)
TURKEY & THE CAUCASUS
pp142-143
CENTRAL ASIA
pp152-153
MAINLAND EAST ASIA
pp 162-163
JAPAN
pp 170-172
Izu-shoto, Ogasawara-shoto and Kazan-retto
p 172
pp 122-124
Cyprus
pp 123-124
THE NEAR EAST
pp144-145
IRAN & THE GULF STATES
pp148-149
THE PACIFIC OCEAN
pp 198-200
Ryukyu Islands
p 172
Sakishima-shoto
p 172
pp 76-77
SOUTH ASIA
pp156-157
THE ARABIAN PENINSULA
pp146-147
Mariana Islands
p 196
Wake Island
p 201
Saipan
p 196
MICRONESIA
pp 196/201
AFRICA
pp 68-85
MAINLAND SOUTHEAST ASIA & THE PHILIPPINES
pp 177-179
Guam
p 196
Marshall Islands
p 201
Yap
p 196
Chuuk Islands
p 201
Pohnpei
p 201
Babeldaob
p 196
Majuro Atoll
p 201
EAST AFRICA
pp 82-83
Maldives
p 157
Palau
p 196
Micronesia
pp 196/201
Kosrae
p 201
Kiribati
p 203
CENTRAL AFRICA
pp 80-81
Nauru
p 201
Tarawa
p 202
MARITIME SOUTHEAST ASIA
pp 173-176
Seychelles
p 180
PAPUA NEW GUINEA & THE SOLOMON ISLANDS
pp 194-195
Comoro Islands
p 180
THE INDIAN OCEAN
pp 180-181
Santa Cruz Islands
p 195
Funafuti Atoll
p 202
Tuvalu
p 202
Madagascar
p 180
Vanuatu
p 197
SOUTHERN AFRICA
pp 84-85
Mauritius
p 181
Réunion
p 181
AUSTRALASIA & OCEANIA
pp 182-203
Fiji
p 197
MELANESIA
p 197
New Caledonia
p 197
AUSTRALIA
pp 188-189
SOUTHEAST AUSTRALIA
pp 190-191
NEW ZEALAND
pp 192-193
ANTARCTICA
pp 204-205

WORLD REFERENCE ATLAS

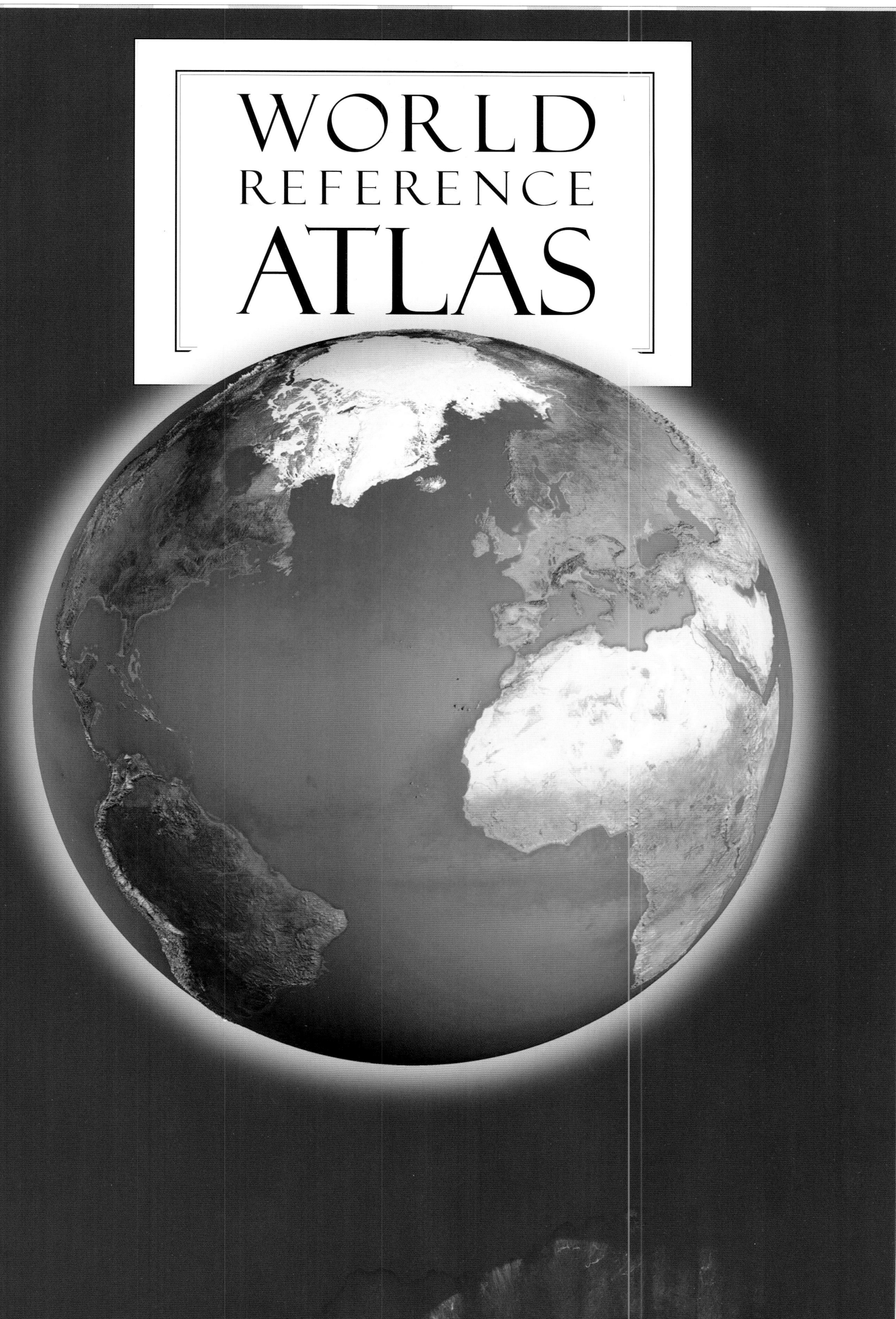

WORLD REFERENCE ATLAS

COVENT GARDEN BOOKS

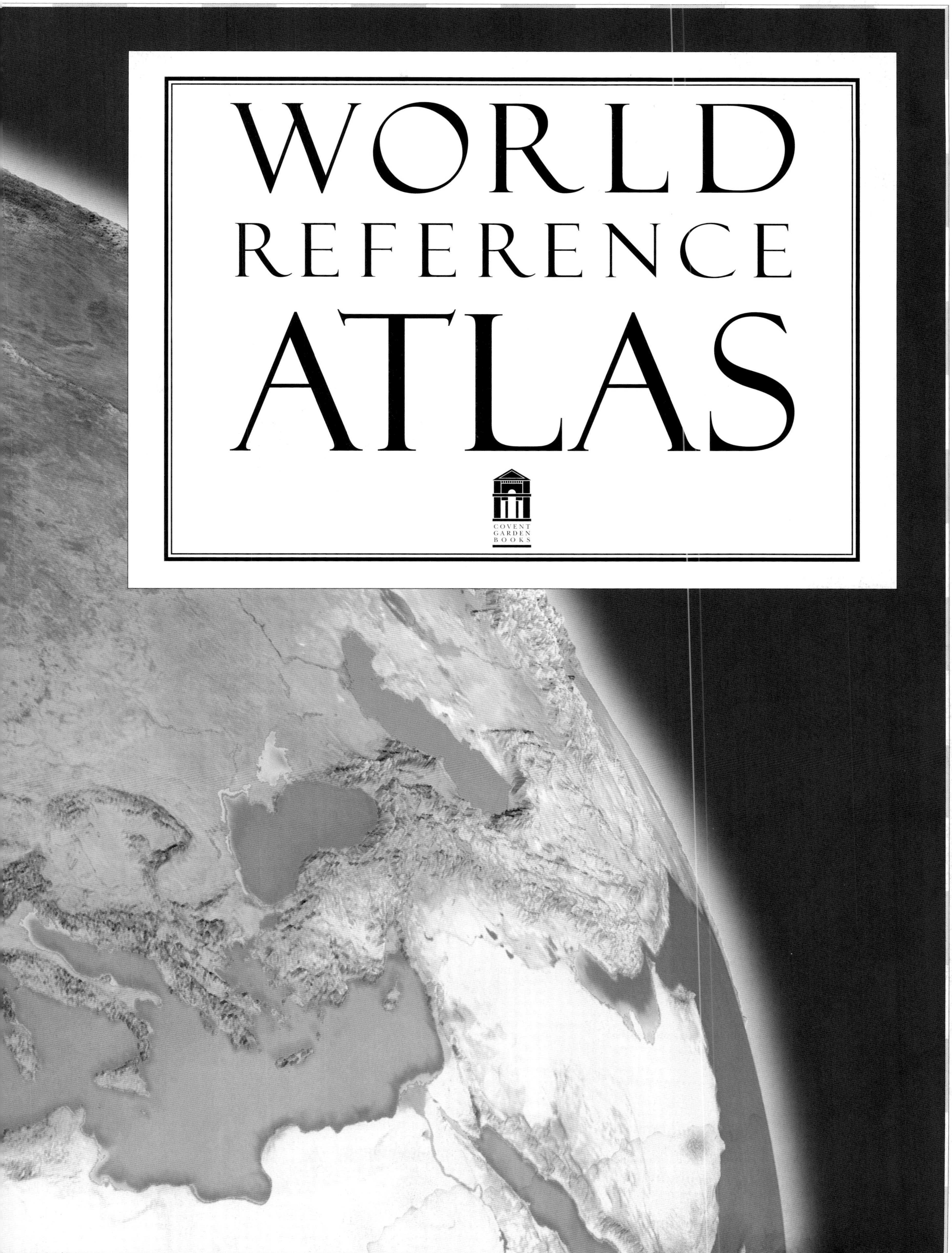

COVENT GARDEN BOOKS

GENERAL GEOGRAPHICAL CONSULTANTS

PHYSICAL GEOGRAPHY • Denys Brunsden, Emeritus Professor, Department of Geography, King's College, London

HUMAN GEOGRAPHY • Professor J Malcolm Wagstaff, Department of Geography, University of Southampton

PLACE NAMES • Caroline Burgess, Permanent Committee on Geographical Names, London

BOUNDARIES • International Boundaries Research Unit, Mountjoy Research Centre, University of Durham

DIGITAL MAPPING CONSULTANTS

DK Cartopia developed by George Galfalvi and XMap Ltd, London

Professor Jan-Peter Muller, Department of Photogrammetry and Surveying, University College, London

Cover globes, planets and information on the Solar System provided by Philip Eales and Kevin Tildsley, Planetary Visions Ltd, London

REGIONAL CONSULTANTS

NORTH AMERICA • Dr David Green, Department of Geography, King's College, London
Jim Walsh, Head of Reference, Wessell Library, Tufts University, Medford, Massachussetts

SOUTH AMERICA • Dr David Preston, School of Geography, University of Leeds

EUROPE • Dr Edward M Yates, formerly of the Department of Geography, King's College, London

AFRICA • Dr Philip Amis, Development Administration Group, University of Birmingham
Dr Ieuan Ll Griffiths, Department of Geography, University of Sussex
Dr Tony Binns, Department of Geography, University of Sussex

CENTRAL ASIA • Dr David Turnock, Department of Geography, University of Leicester

SOUTH AND EAST ASIA • Dr Jonathan Rigg, Department of Geography, University of Durham

AUSTRALASIA AND OCEANIA • Dr Robert Allison, Department of Geography, University of Durham

ACKNOWLEDGMENTS

Digital terrain data created by Eros Data Center, Sioux Falls, South Dakota, USA. Processed by GVS Images Inc, California, USA and Planetary Visions Ltd, London, UK • CIRCA Research and Reference Information, Cambridge, UK • Digitization by Robertson Research International, Swanley, UK • Peter Clark
British Isles maps generated from a dataset supplied by Map Marketing Ltd/European Map Graphics Ltd in combination with DK Cartopia copyright data

FOR THE THIRD EDITION

EDITOR-IN-CHIEF
Andrew Heritage

SENIOR CARTOGRAPHIC MANAGER
David Roberts

MANAGING CARTOGRAPHER
Roger Bullen

SENIOR CARTOGRAPHIC EDITOR
Simon Mumford

DIGITAL MAPPING SUPPLIERS
Encompass Graphics

CARTOGRAPHERS
Tony Chambers • Jan Clark • John Plumer • Rob Stokes • Julie Turner • Iorwerth Watkins • Peter Winfield

SENIOR EDITOR
Debra Clapson

SENIOR MANAGING ART EDITOR
Philip Lord

EDITORS
Wim Jenkins • Sam Atkinson

DESIGNERS
Karen Gregory, Carol Ann Davis, David Douglas

SYSTEMS COORDINATOR
Phil Rowles

INDEX GAZETTEER
Julia Lynch

PRODUCTION
Wendy Penn

DORLING KINDERSLEY CARTOGRAPHY

EDITOR-IN-CHIEF
Andrew Heritage

MANAGING CARTOGRAPHER
David Roberts

SENIOR CARTOGRAPHIC EDITOR
Roger Bullen

CARTOGRAPHERS
Pamela Alford • James Anderson • Sarah Baker-Ede • Caroline Bowie • Dale Buckton • Tony Chambers • Jan Clark • Bob Croser • Martin Darlison • Claire Ellam
Sally Gable • Jeremy Hepworth • Geraldine Horner • Chris Jackson • Christine Johnston • Julia Lunn • Michael Martin • James Mills-Hicks • Simon Mumford • John Plumer
John Scott • Ann Stephenson • Julie Turner • Jane Voss • Scott Wallace • Iorwerth Watkins • Bryony Webb • Alan Whitaker • Peter Winfield

DIGITAL MAPS CREATED IN DK CARTOPIA BY
Tom Coulson • Thomas Robertshaw
Philip Rowles • Rob Stokes

PLACENAMES DATABASE TEAM
Natalie Clarkson • Ruth Duxbury • Caroline Falce • John Featherstone • Dan Gardiner
Ciárán Hynes • Margaret Hynes • Helen Rudkin • Margaret Stevenson • Annie Wilson

DATABASE MANAGER
Simon Lewis

MANAGING EDITOR
Lisa Thomas

SENIOR MANAGING ART EDITOR
Philip Lord

EDITORS
Thomas Heath • Wim Jenkins • Jane Oliver • Siobhān Ryan • Elizabeth Wyse

DESIGNERS
Scott David • Carol Ann Davis • David Douglas • Rhonda Fisher • Karen Gregory • Nicola Liddiard

EDITORIAL RESEARCH
Helen Dangerfield • Andrew Rebeiro-Hargrave

ILLUSTRATIONS
Ciárán Hughes • Advanced Illustration, Congleton, UK

ADDITIONAL EDITORIAL ASSISTANCE
Debra Clapson • Robert Damon • Ailsa Heritage • Constance Novis • Jayne Parsons • Chris Whitwell

PICTURE RESEARCH
Melissa Albany • James Clarke • Anna Lord • Christine Rista • Sarah Moule • Louise Thomas

EDITORIAL DIRECTION • Louise Cavanagh

ART DIRECTION • Chez Picthall

First American Edition, 1997. Reprinted with revisions 1998, 1999. Third Edition (revised) 2003

This American Edition, 2004
04 05 10 9 8 7 6 5 4 3

Published in the United States by Dorling Kindersley Publishing, Inc., 375 Hudson Street, New York, New York 10014

see our complete catalog at

www.dk.com

A catalog record for this book is available from the Library of Congress

ISBN 0-7566-0481-8

Printed and bound by Mondadori, Italy.

Introduction

For many, the outstanding legacy of the twentieth century was the way in which the Earth shrank. As we enter the third millennium, it is increasingly important for us to have a clear vision of the world in which we live. The human population has increased fourfold since 1900. The last scraps of *terra incognita* – the polar regions and ocean depths – have been penetrated and mapped. New regions have been colonized, and previously hostile realms claimed for habitation. The advent of aviation technology and mass tourism allows many of us to travel farther, faster, and more frequently than ever before. In doing so we are given a bird's-eye view of the Earth's surface denied to our forebears.

At the same time, the amount of information about our world has grown enormously. Telecommunications can span the greatest distances in fractions of a second: our multimedia environment hurls uninterrupted streams of data at us, on the printed page, through the airwaves, and across our television and computer screens; events from all corners of the globe reach us instantaneously, and are witnessed as they unfold. Our sense of stability and certainty has been eroded; instead, we are aware that the world is in a constant state of flux and change. Natural disasters, man-made cataclysms, and conflicts between nations remind us daily of the enormity and fragility of our domain.

Our current "global" culture has made the need greater than ever before for everyone to possess an atlas. The *DK World Atlas* has been conceived to meet this need. At its core, like all atlases, it seeks to define where places are, to describe their main characteristics, and to locate them in relation to other places. Every attempt has been made to make the information on the maps as clear and accessible as possible. In addition, each page of the atlas provides a wealth of further information, bringing the maps to life. Using photographs, diagrams, "at-a-glance" maps, introductory texts, and captions, the atlas builds up a detailed portait of those features – cultural, political, economic, and geomorphological – which make each region unique, and which are also the main agents of change.

This Third Edition incorporates thousands of revisions and updates affecting every map and every page, and features a new typographic design for the maps; a further addition is the provision of longitude and latitude coordinates for every site in the Index-Gazetteer. Since its first publication in 1997 the *DK World Atlas* has proved extremely popular – going into 22 editions around the world – and has been translated into 13 languages, including Greek and Russian.

Andrew Heritage
Editor-in-Chief

CONTENTS

INTRODUCTION v

CONTENTS .... vi–vii

HOW TO USE THIS ATLAS .... viii–ix

THE WORLD TODAY

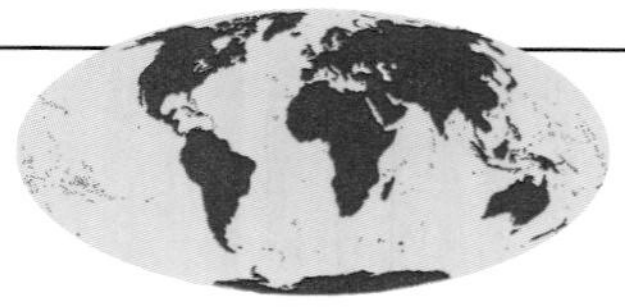

THE SOLAR SYSTEM .... x–xi

THE PHYSICAL WORLD .... xii–xiii

STRUCTURE OF THE EARTH ...... xiv–xv

SHAPING THE LANDSCAPE ...... xvi–xvii

THE WORLD'S OCEANS .... xviii–xix

THE GLOBAL CLIMATE .... xx–xxi

LIFE ON EARTH .... xxii–xxiii

POPULATION AND SETTLEMENT .... xxiv–xxv

THE ECONOMIC SYSTEM ...... xxvi–xxvii

THE POLITICAL WORLD ...... xxviii–xxix

STATES AND BOUNDARIES ...... xxx–xxxi

INTERNATIONAL DISPUTES xxxii

ATLAS OF THE WORLD

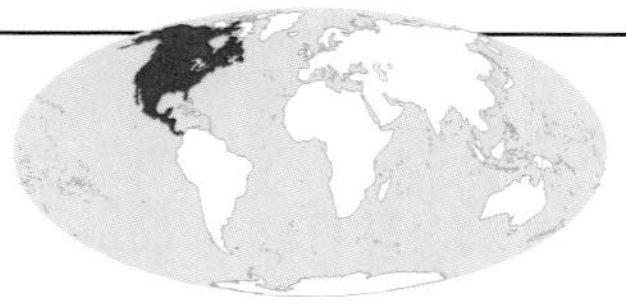

NORTH AMERICA

NORTH AMERICA 1

PHYSICAL NORTH AMERICA 2–3

POLITICAL NORTH AMERICA 4–5

NORTH AMERICAN RESOURCES 6–7

CANADA: WESTERN PROVINCES 8–9
Alberta, British Columbia, Manitoba, Saskatchewan, Yukon

CANADA: EASTERN PROVINCES 10–11
New Brunswick, Newfoundland & Labrador, Nova Scotia, Ontario, Prince Edward Island, Québec, St. Pierre & Miquelon

SOUTHEASTERN CANADA 12–13
Southern Ontario, Southern Québec

CANADA *(gatefold)* 14–16

UNITED STATES OF AMERICA *(gatefold)* .. 17–19

USA: NORTHEASTERN STATES 20–21
Connecticut, Maine, Massachussetts, New Hampshire, New Jersey, New York, Pennsylvania, Rhode Island, Vermont

USA: MID-EASTERN STATES 22–23
Delaware, District of Columbia, Kentucky, Maryland, North Carolina, South Carolina, Tennessee, Virginia, West Virginia

USA: SOUTHERN STATES 24–25
Alabama, Florida, Georgia, Louisiana, Mississippi

USA: TEXAS 26–27

USA: SOUTH MIDWESTERN STATES ... 28–29
Arkansas, Kansas, Missouri, Oklahoma

USA: NORTH MIDWESTERN STATES .. 30–31
Iowa, Minnesota, Nebraska, North Dakota, South Dakota

USA: GREAT LAKES STATES 32–33
Illinois, Indiana, Michigan, Ohio, Wisconsin

USA: NORTH MOUNTAIN STATES 34–35
Idaho, Montana, Oregon, Washington, Wyoming

USA: CALIFORNIA & NEVADA 36–37

USA: SOUTH MOUNTAIN STATES 38–39
Arizona, Colorado, New Mexico, Utah

USA: HAWAII & ALASKA 40–41

MEXICO 42–43

CENTRAL AMERICA 44–45
Belize, Costa Rica, El Salvador, Guatemala, Honduras, Nicaragua, Panama

THE CARIBBEAN 46–47
Anguilla, Antigua & Barbuda, Aruba, Bahamas, Barbados, British Virgin Islands, Cayman Islands, Cuba, Dominica, Dominican Republic, Grenada, Guadeloupe, Haiti, Jamaica, Martinique, Montserrat, Navassa Island, Netherlands Antilles, Puerto Rico, St. Kitts & Nevis, St. Lucia, St. Vincent & the Grenadines, Trinidad & Tobago, Turks & Caicos Islands, Virgin Islands (US)

SOUTH AMERICA

SOUTH AMERICA 48–49

PHYSICAL SOUTH AMERICA 50–51

POLITICAL SOUTH AMERICA 52–53

SOUTH AMERICAN RESOURCES 54–55

NORTHERN SOUTH AMERICA 56–57
Colombia, French Guiana, Guyana, Suriname, Venezuela

WESTERN SOUTH AMERICA 58–59
Bolivia, Ecuador, Peru

BRAZIL 60–61

EASTERN SOUTH AMERICA 62–63
Southeast Brazil, Northeast Argentina, Uruguay

SOUTHERN SOUTH AMERICA 64–65
Argentina, Chile, Paraguay

THE ATLANTIC OCEAN 66–67

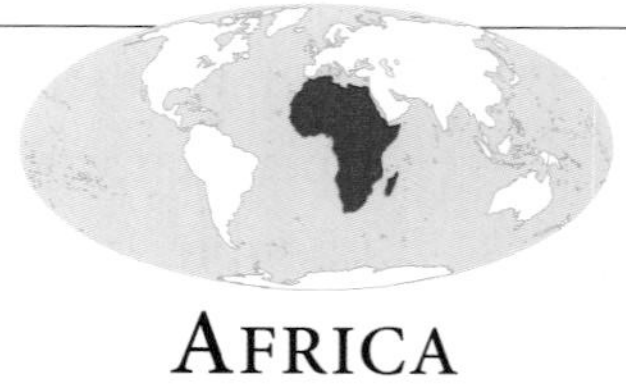

AFRICA

AFRICA 68–69

PHYSICAL AFRICA 70–71

POLITICAL AFRICA 72–73

AFRICAN RESOURCES 74–75

NORTH AFRICA 76–77
Algeria, Egypt, Libya, Morocco, Tunisia, Western Sahara

WEST AFRICA 78–79
Benin, Burkina, Cape Verde, Gambia, Ghana, Guinea, Guinea-Bissau, Ivory Coast, Liberia, Mali, Mauritania, Niger, Nigeria, Senegal, Sierra Leone, Togo

CENTRAL AFRICA 80–81
Cameroon, Central African Republic, Chad, Congo, Dem. Rep. Congo, Equatorial Guinea, Gabon, Sao Tome & Principe

EAST AFRICA 82–83
Burundi, Djibouti, Eritrea, Ethiopia, Kenya, Rwanda, Somalia, Sudan, Tanzania, Uganda

SOUTHERN AFRICA 84–85
Angola, Botswana, Lesotho, Malawi, Mozambique, Namibia, South Africa, Swaziland, Zambia, Zimbabwe

Europe

EUROPE 86–87

PHYSICAL EUROPE 88–89

POLITICAL EUROPE 90–91

EUROPEAN RESOURCES 92–93

SCANDINAVIA, FINLAND & ICELAND .. 94–95
Denmark, Finland, Iceland, Norway, Svalbard, Sweden

SOUTHERN SCANDINAVIA 96–97
Denmark, Faeroe Islands, Southern Norway, Southern Sweden

THE BRITISH ISLES 98–99
Channel Islands, Isle of Man, Ireland, United Kingdom

THE LOW COUNTRIES 100–101
Belgium, Luxembourg, Netherlands

GERMANY 102–103

FRANCE 104–105
France, Monaco

THE IBERIAN PENINSULA 106–107
Andorra, Gibraltar, Portugal, Spain

THE ITALIAN PENINSULA 108–109
Italy, San Marino, Vatican City

THE ALPINE STATES 110–111
Austria, Liechtenstein, Slovenia, Switzerland

CENTRAL EUROPE 112–113
Czech Republic, Hungary, Poland, Slovakia

SOUTHEAST EUROPE 114–115
Albania, Bosnia & Herzegovina, Croatia, Macedonia, Serbia & Montenegro (Yugoslavia)

BULGARIA & GREECE 116–117
(including European Turkey)

ROMANIA, MOLDOVA & UKRAINE 118–119

THE BALTIC STATES & BELARUS 120–121
Belarus, Estonia, Latvia, Lithuania, Kaliningrad

THE MEDITERRANEAN *(gatefold)* 122–124

THE RUSSIAN FEDERATION *(gatefold)* .. 125–127

NORTHERN EUROPEAN RUSSIA 128–129

SOUTHERN EUROPEAN RUSSIA 130–131

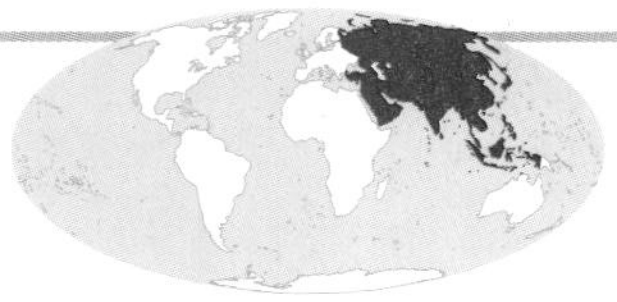

Asia

ASIA 132–133

ASIAN RESOURCES 134–135

POLITICAL ASIA .... 136 / 141

PHYSICAL ASIA *(gatefold)* 137–140

TURKEY & THE CAUCASUS 142–143
Armenia, Azerbaijan, Georgia, Turkey

THE NEAR EAST 144–145
Iraq, Israel, Jordan, Lebanon, Syria

THE ARABIAN PENINSULA 146–147
Bahrain, Kuwait, Oman, Qatar, Saudi Arabia, United Arab Emirates, Yemen

IRAN & THE GULF STATES 148–149
Bahrain, Iran, Kuwait, Qatar, United Arab Emirates

KAZAKHSTAN 150–151

CENTRAL ASIA 152–153
Kyrgyzstan, Tajikistan, Turkmenistan, Uzbekistan

AFGHANISTAN & PAKISTAN 154–155

SOUTH ASIA 156–157
Bangladesh, Bhutan, India, Maldives, Nepal, Pakistan, Sri Lanka

NORTHERN INDIA & THE HIMALAYAN STATES 158–159
Bangladesh, Bhutan, Nepal, Northern India

SOUTHERN INDIA & SRI LANKA 160–161

MAINLAND EAST ASIA 162–163
China, Mongolia, North Korea, South Korea, Taiwan

WESTERN CHINA 164–165

EASTERN CHINA 166–167
Eastern China, Taiwan

NORTHEASTERN CHINA, MONGOLIA & KOREA 168–169
Mongolia, Northeastern China, North Korea, South Korea

JAPAN *(gatefold)* 170–172

MARITIME SOUTHEAST ASIA *(gatefold)* . 173–176
Brunei, East Timor, Indonesia, Malaysia, Singapore

MAINLAND SOUTHEAST ASIA & THE PHILIPPINES *(gatefold)* 177–179
Cambodia, Laos, Myanmar, Paracel Islands, Philippines, Spratly Islands, Thailand, Vietnam

THE INDIAN OCEAN 180–181

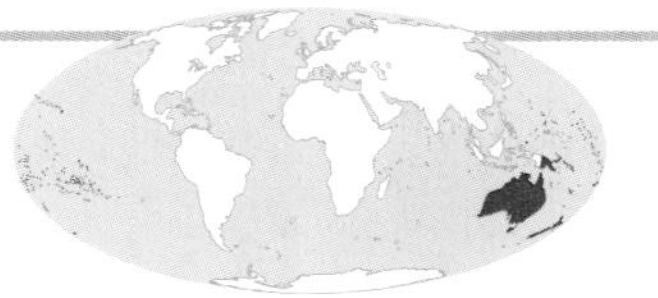

Australasia and Oceania

AUSTRALASIA & OCEANIA 182–183

POLITICAL AUSTRALASIA & OCEANIA 184–185

AUSTRALASIAN & OCEANIAN RESOURCES 186–187

AUSTRALIA 188–189

SOUTHEAST AUSTRALIA 190–191
New South Wales, South Australia, Tasmania, Victoria

NEW ZEALAND 192–193

PAPUA NEW GUINEA & THE SOLOMON ISLANDS 194–195

MICRONESIA .... 196 / 201
Guam, Marshall Islands, Micronesia, Nauru, Northern Mariana Islands, Palau, Wake Island

MELANESIA 197
Fiji, New Caledonia, Vanuatu

THE PACIFIC OCEAN *(gatefold)* 198–200

POLYNESIA 202–203
Cook Islands, Easter Island, French Polynesia, Kiribati, Niue, Pitcairn Islands, Tokelau, Tuvalu, Wallis & Futuna

ANTARCTICA 204–205

THE ARCTIC 206–207

INDEX-GAZETTEER

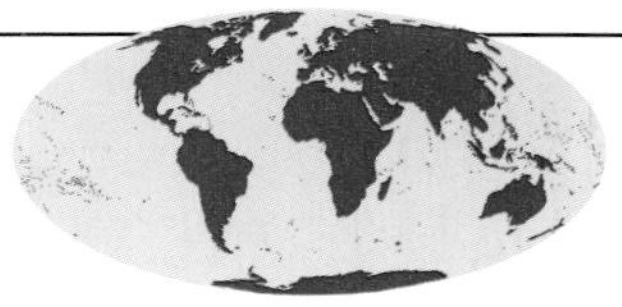

GEOGRAPHICAL COMPARISONS 208–209

COUNTRIES OF THE WORLD
including World Timezones 210–217

GEOGRAPHICAL NAMES 218

INDEX 219–353

CREDITS/ACKNOWLEDGEMENTS .. 353

SELECTED GLOSSARY 354

KEY TO REGIONAL MAPS

PHYSICAL FEATURES

elevation

6000m / 19,686ft
4000m / 13,124ft
3000m / 9843ft
2000m / 6562ft
1000m / 3281ft
500m / 1640ft
250m / 820ft
100m / 328ft
sea level
below sea level

▲ elevation above sea level (mountain height)

▲ volcano

✕ pass

▼ elevation below sea level (depression depth)

sand desert

lava flow

coastline

reef

atoll

sea depth

sea level
-250m / -820ft
-500m / -1640ft
-1000m / -3281ft
-2000m / -6562ft
-3000m / -9843ft

▲ seamount / guyot symbol

▼ undersea spot depth

DRAINAGE FEATURES

main river
secondary river
tertiary river
minor river
main seasonal river
secondary seasonal river
canal
waterfall
rapids
dam
perennial lake
seasonal lake
perennial salt lake
seasonal salt lake
reservoir
salt flat / salt pan
marsh / salt marsh
mangrove
wadi

○ spring / well / waterhole / oasis

ICE FEATURES

ice cap / sheet

ice shelf

glacier / snowfield

* * * * summer pack ice limit

winter pack ice limit

COMMUNICATIONS

highway

highway (under construction)

major road

minor road

→···← tunnel (road)

main line

minor line

→···← tunnel (railroad)

✈ international airport

BORDERS

full international border

undefined international border

disputed *de facto* border

disputed territorial claim border

indication of country extent (Pacific only)

indication of dependent territory extent (Pacific only)

demarcation/ cease-fire line

autonomous / federal region border

2nd order internal administrative border

3rd order internal administrative border

SETTLEMENTS

built-up area

settlement population symbols

▣ more than 5 million

▣ 1 million to 5 million

◉ 500,000 to 1 million

◎ 100,000 to 500,000

⊕ 50,000 to 100,000

○ 10,000 to 50,000

○ fewer than 10,000

▣ ● country/dependent territory capital city

▣ ● autonomous / federal region / 2nd order internal administrative center

▣ ● 3rd order internal administrative center

MISCELLANEOUS FEATURES

▫▫▫▫ ancient wall

◇ site of interest

⊚ scientific station

GRATICULE FEATURES

lines of latitude and longitude / Equator

Tropics / Polar circles

45° degrees of longitude / latitude

TYPOGRAPHIC KEY

PHYSICAL FEATURES

landscape features .. *Namib Desert*
Massif Central
ANDES

headland *Nordkapp*

elevation /
volcano / pass Mount Meru
4556 m

drainage features ... *Lake Geneva*

rivers / canals
spring / well /
waterhole / oasis /
waterfall /
rapids / dam *Mekong*

ice features *Vatnajökull*

sea features........... *Golfe de Lion*
Andaman Sea
INDIAN
OCEAN

undersea features ... *Barracuda Fracture Zone*

REGIONS

country................ **ARMENIA**

dependent territory
with parent state...... **NIUE (to NZ)**

region outside
feature area........... ANGOLA

autonomous /
federal region **MINAS GERAIS**

2nd order internal
administrative
region **MINSKAYA VOBLASTS'**

3rd order internal
administrative
region Vaucluse

cultural region....... New England

SETTLEMENTS

capital city............ **BEIJING**

dependent territory
capital city............ FORT-DE-FRANCE

other settlements.... **Chicago**
Adana
Tizi Ozou
Yonezawa
Farnham

MISCELLANEOUS

sites of interest /
miscellaneous........ Valley of the Kings

Tropics /
Polar circles.......... *Antarctic Circle*

HOW TO USE THIS ATLAS

THE ATLAS IS ORGANIZED BY CONTINENT, moving eastward from the International Dateline. The opening section describes the world's structure, systems, and its main features. The Atlas of the World that follows, is a continent-by-continent guide to today's world, starting with a comprehensive insight into the physical, political, and economic structure of each continent, followed by integrated mapping and descriptions of each region or country.

THE WORLD

THE INTRODUCTORY SECTION of the Atlas deals with every aspect of the planet, from physical structure to human geography, providing an overall picture of the world we live in. Complex topics such as the landscape of the Earth, climate, oceans, population, and economic patterns are clearly explained with the aid of maps and diagrams drawn from the latest information.

Diagrams
Photographs
Explanatory captions
GLOBAL MAPPING
Global information is shown in a variety of projections to give the reader a clear overview of each topic.
Supporting maps

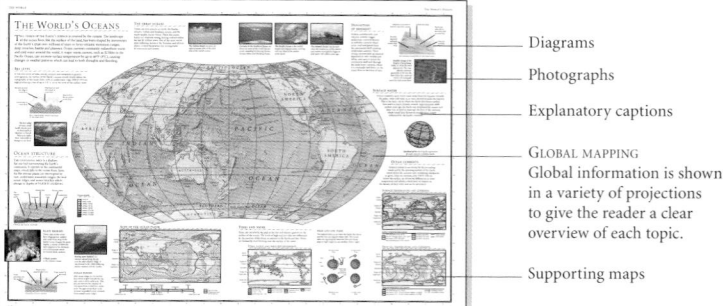

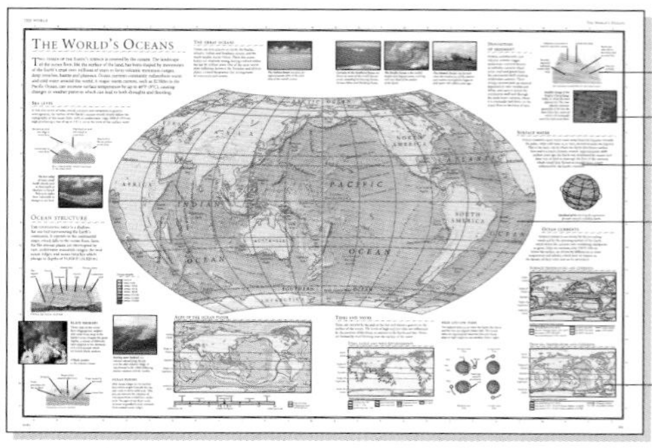

THE POLITICAL CONTINENT

THE POLITICAL PORTRAIT of the continent is a vital reference point for every continental section, showing the position of countries relative to one another, and the relationship between human settlement and geographic location. The complex mosaic of languages spoken in each continent is mapped, as is the effect of communications networks on the pattern of settlement.

Locator map
Introductory text
Communications map
Population map
POLITICAL MAP
All the countries in each continent are shown, with their political capitals and most populous cities.
Languages map

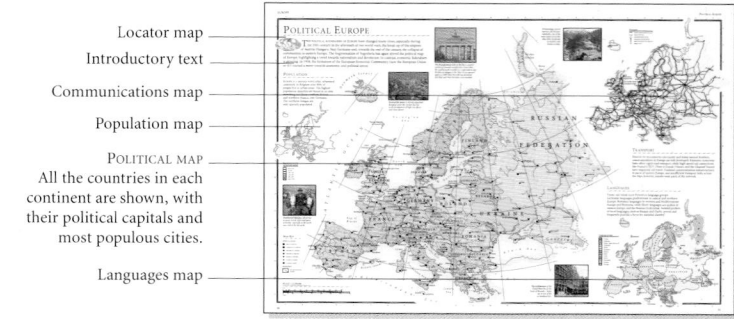

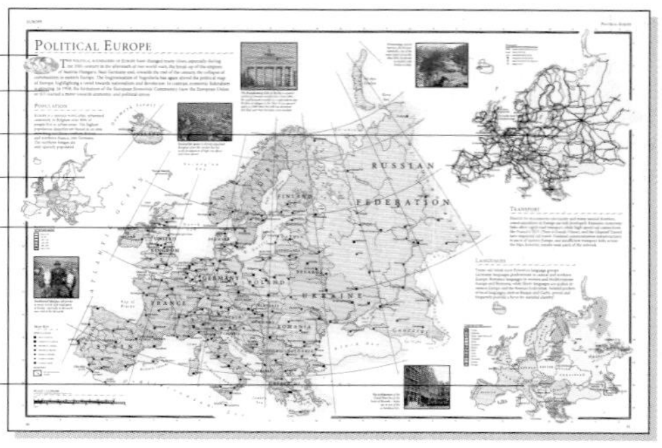

CONTINENTAL RESOURCES

THE EARTH'S RICH NATURAL RESOURCES, including oil, gas, minerals, and fertile land, have played a key role in the development of society. These pages show the location of minerals and agricultural resources on each continent, and how they have been instrumental in dictating industrial growth and the varieties of economic activity across the continent.

Mineral resources map
Environmental issues map
Land use map
Industry map
Comparative wealth map

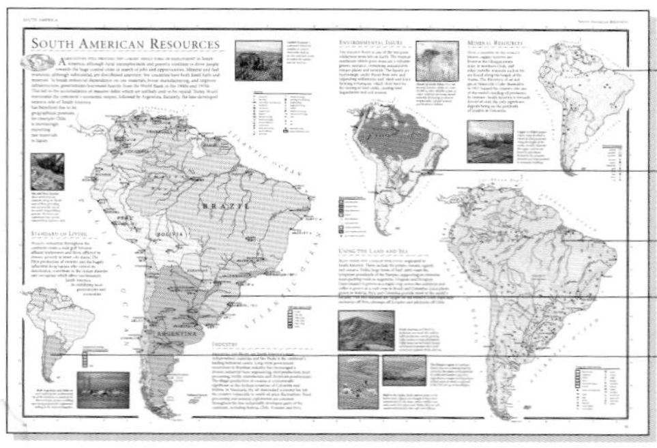

The Physical Continent

The astonishing variety of landforms, and the dramatic forces that created and continue to shape the landscape, are explained in the continental physical spread. Cross-sections, illustrations, and terrain maps highlight the different parts of the continent, showing how nature's forces have produced the landscapes we see today.

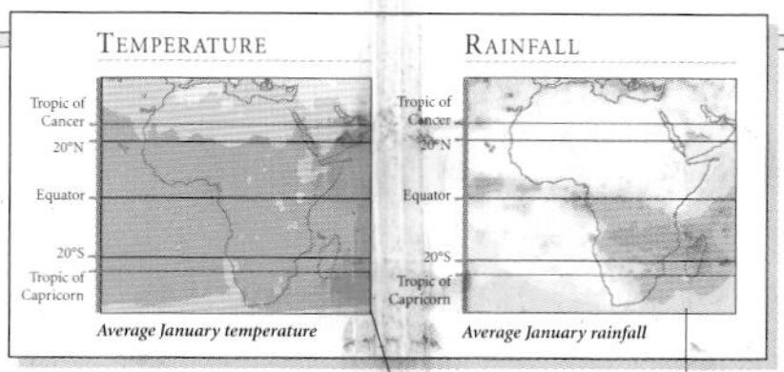

Climate charts
Rainfall and temperature charts clearly show the continental patterns of rainfall and temperature.

Climate map
Climatic regions vary across each continent. The map displays the differing climatic regions, as well as daily hours of sunshine at selected weather stations.

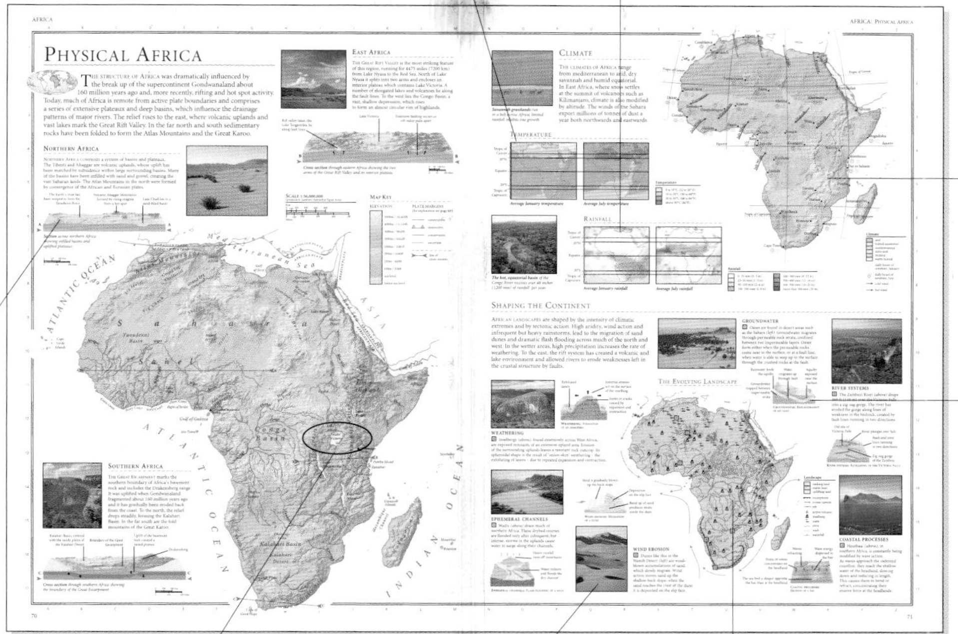

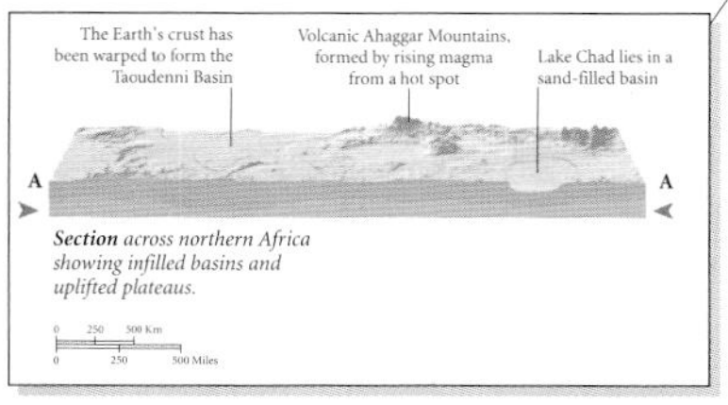

Cross-sections
Detailed cross-sections through selected parts of the continent show the underlying geomorphic structure.

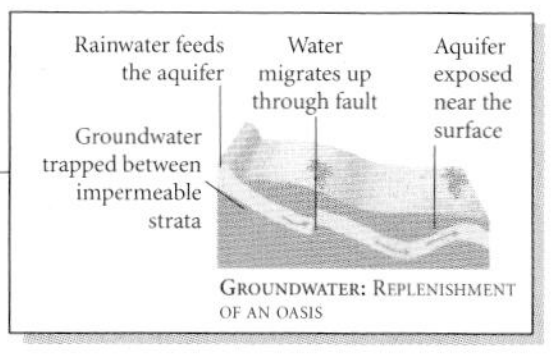

Landform diagrams
The complex formation of many typical landforms is summarized in these easy-to-understand illustrations.

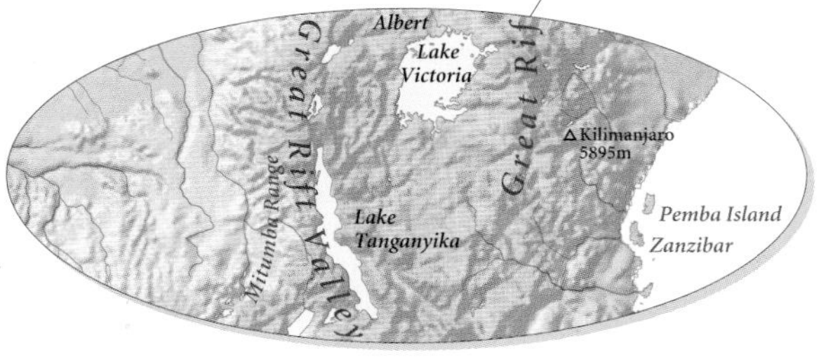

Main physical map
Detailed satellite data has been used to create an accurate and visually striking picture of the surface of the continent.

Photographs
A wide range of beautiful photographs bring the world's regions to life.

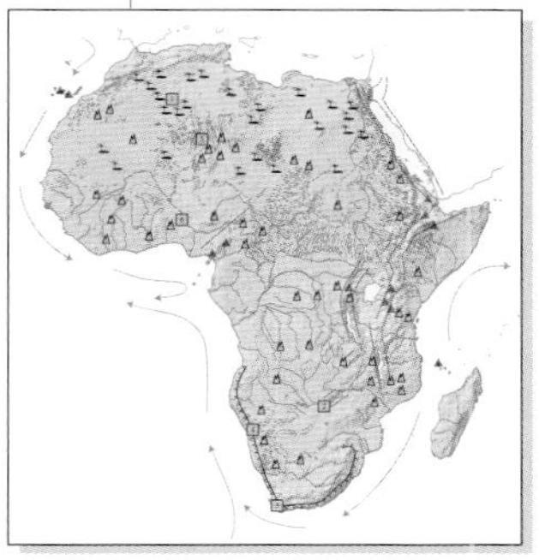

Landscape evolution map
The physical shape of each continent is affected by a variety of forces which continually sculpt and modify the landscape. This map shows the major processes which affect different parts of the continent.

Regional Mapping

The main body of the Atlas is a unique regional map set, with detailed information on the terrain, the human geography of the region and its infrastructure. Around the edge of the map, additional 'at-a-glance' maps, give an instant picture of regional industry, land use and agriculture. The detailed terrain map (shown in perspective), focuses on the main physical features of the region, and is enhanced by annotated illustrations, and photographs of the physical structure.

Regional Locator
This small map shows the location of each country in relation to its continent.

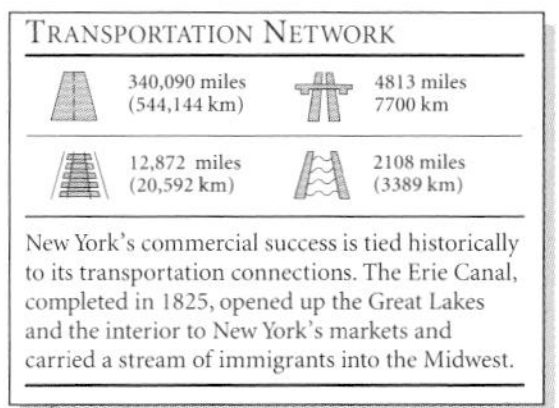

Transportation network
The differing extent of the transportation network for each region is shown here, along with key facts about the transportation system.

Key to main map
A key to the population symbols and land heights accompanies the main map.

World locator
This locates the continent in which the region is found on a small world map.

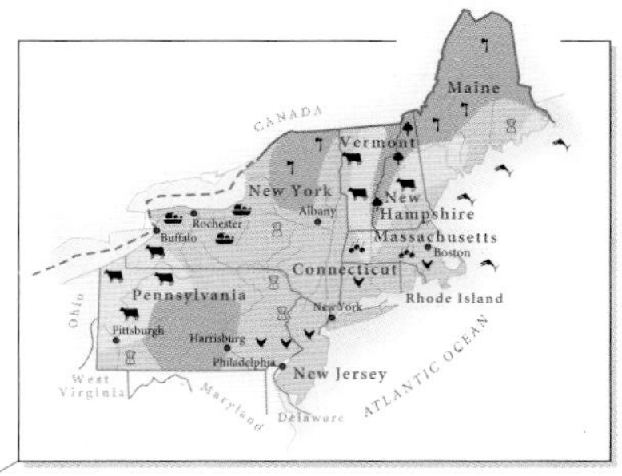

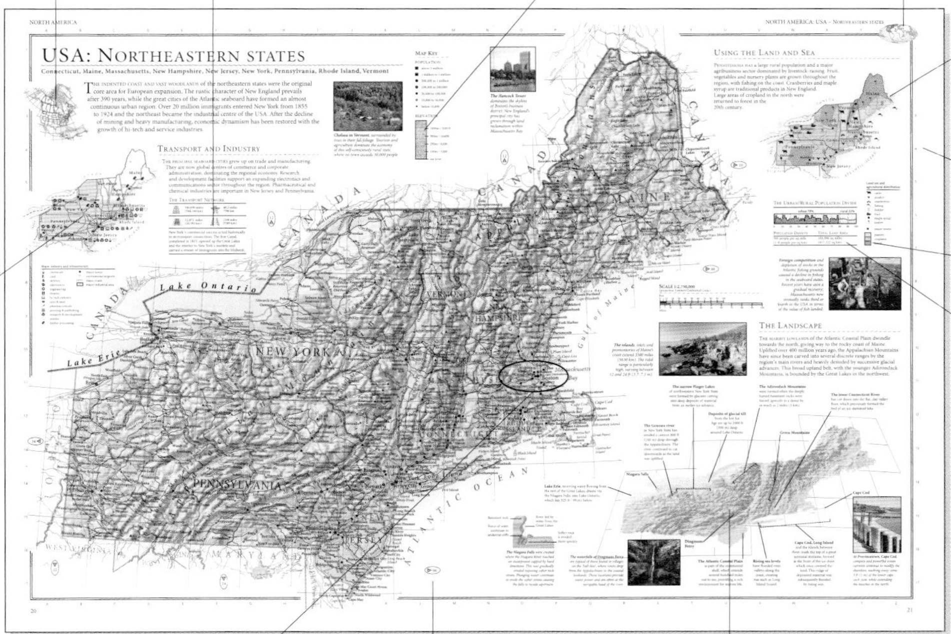

Land use map
This shows the different types of land use which characterize the region, as well as indicating the principal agricultural activities.

Grid reference
The framing grid provides a location reference for each place listed in the Index.

Map keys
Each supporting map has its own key.

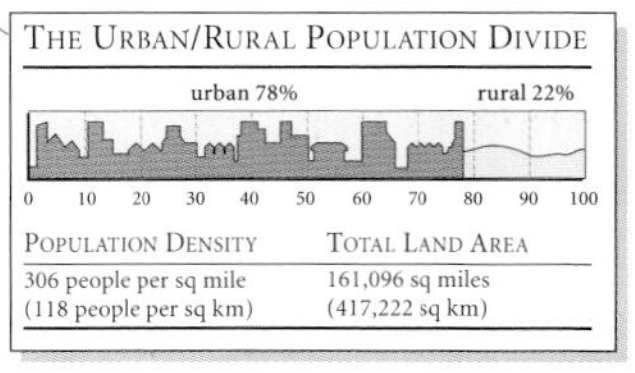

The Urban/Rural Population Divide
urban 78%
rural 22%
0 10 20 30 40 50 60 70 80 90 100
Population Density
306 people per sq mile (118 people per sq km)
Total Land Area
161,096 sq miles (417,222 sq km)

Urban/rural population divide
The proportion of people in the region who live in urban and rural areas, as well as the overall population density and land area are clearly shown in these simple graphics.

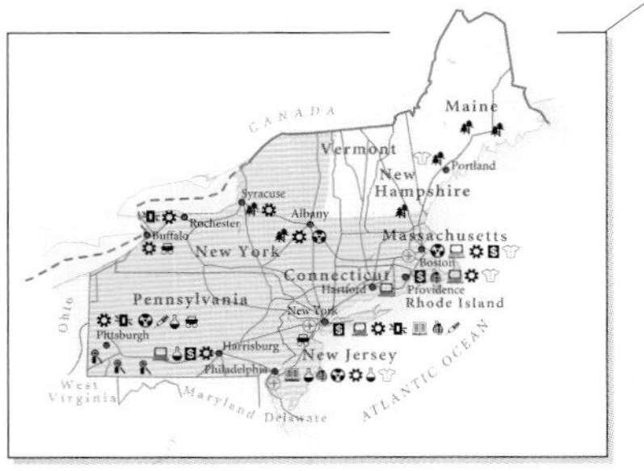

Transportation and industry map
The main industrial areas are mapped, and the most important industrial and economic activities of the region are shown.

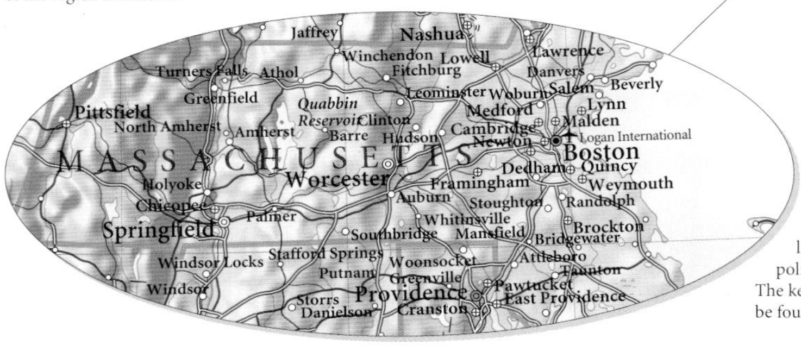

Continuation symbols
These symbols indicate where adjacent maps can be found.

Main regional map
A wealth of information is displayed on the main map, building up a rich portrait of the interaction between the physical landscape and the human and political geography of each region. The key to the regional maps can be found on page viii.

Landscape map
The computer-generated terrain model accurately portrays an oblique view of the region. Annotations highlight the most important geographic features of the region.

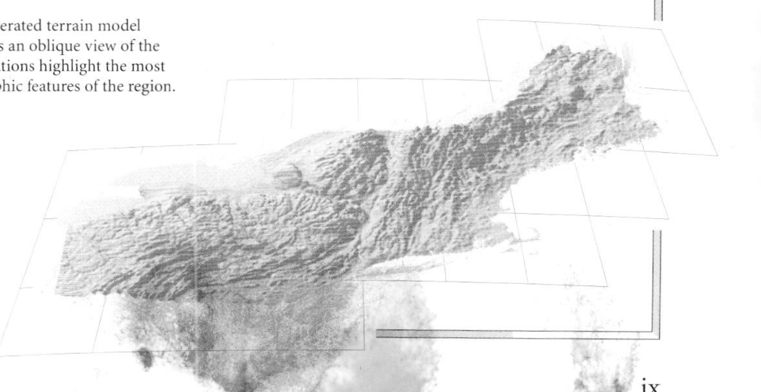

Jupiter

- **Diameter:** 88,846 miles (142,984 km)
- **Mass:** 1,900,000 million million million tons
- **Temperature:** -153°C (extremes not available)
- **Distance from Sun:** 483 million miles (778 million km)
- **Length of day:** 9.84 hours
- **Length of year:** 11.86 earth years
- **Surface gravity:** 1 kg = 2.53 kg

Mars

- **Diameter:** 4,217 miles (6,786 km)
- **Mass:** 642 million million million tons
- **Temperature:** -137 to 37°C
- **Distance from Sun:** 142 million miles (228 million km)
- **Length of day:** 24.623 hours
- **Length of year:** 1.88 earth years
- **Surface gravity:** 1 kg = 0.38 kg

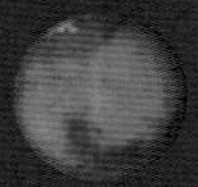

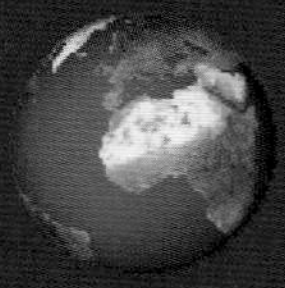

Earth

- **Diameter:** 7,926 miles (12,756 km)
- **Mass:** 5,976 million million million tons
- **Temperature:** -70 to 55°C
- **Distance from Sun:** 93 million miles (150 million km)
- **Length of day:** 23.92 hours
- **Length of year:** 365.25 earth days
- **Surface gravity:** 1 kg = 1 kg

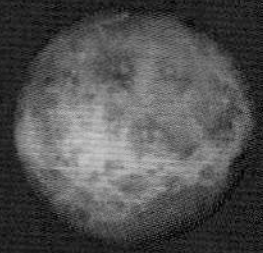

Venus

- **Diameter:** 7,520 miles (12,102 km)
- **Mass:** 4,870 million million million tons
- **Temperature:** 457°C (extremes not available)
- **Distance from Sun:** 67 million miles (108 million km)
- **Length of day:** 243.01 earth days
- **Length of year:** 224.7 earth days
- **Surface gravity:** 1 kg = 0.88 kg

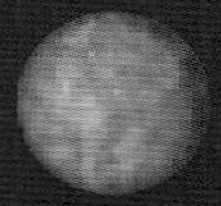

Mercury

- **Diameter:** 3,031 miles (4,878 km)
- **Mass:** 330 million million million tons
- **Temperature:** -173 to 427°C
- **Distance from Sun:** 36 million miles (58 million km)
- **Length of day:** 58.65 earth days
- **Length of year:** 87.97 earth days
- **Surface gravity:** 1 kg = 0.38 kg

The Solar System

Nine major planets, their satellites, and countless minor planets (asteroids) orbit the Sun to form the Solar System. The Sun, our nearest star, creates energy from nuclear reactions deep within its interior, providing all the light and heat which make life on Earth possible. The Earth is unique in the Solar System in that it supports life: its size, gravitational pull and distance from the Sun have all created the optimum conditions for the evolution of life. The planetary images seen here are composites derived from actual spacecraft images (not shown to scale).

The Sun

- **Diameter:** 864,948 miles (1,392,000 km)
- **Mass:** 1990 million million million million tons

The Sun was formed when a swirling cloud of dust and gas contracted, pulling matter into its center. When the temperature at the center rose to 1,000,000°C, nuclear fusion – the fusing of hydrogen into helium, creating energy – occurred, releasing a constant stream of heat and light.

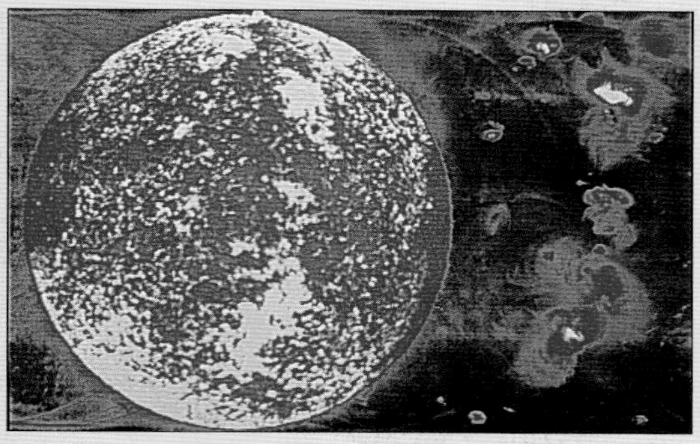

***Solar flares are sudden bursts** of energy from the Sun's surface. They can be 125,000 miles (200,000 km) long.*

The formation of the Solar System

The cloud of dust and gas thrown out by the Sun during its formation cooled to form the Solar System. The smaller planets nearest the Sun are formed of minerals and metals. The outer planets were formed at lower temperatures, and consist of swirling clouds of gases.

The Milankovitch Cycle

The amount of radiation from the Sun which reaches the Earth is affected by variations in the Earth's orbit and the tilt of the Earth's axis, as well as by "wobbles" in the axis. These variations cause three separate cycles, corresponding with the durations of recent ice ages.

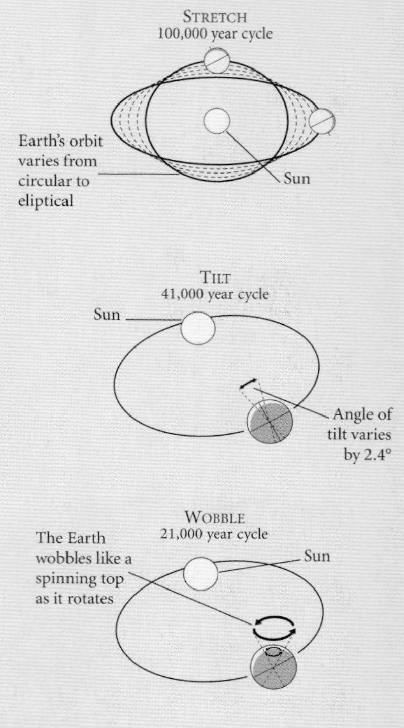

Stretch
100,000 year cycle
Earth's orbit varies from circular to eliptical
Sun
Tilt
41,000 year cycle
Sun
Angle of tilt varies by 2.4°
Wobble
21,000 year cycle
The Earth wobbles like a spinning top as it rotates
Sun

SATURN

- **Diameter:** 74,974 miles (120,660 km)
- **Mass:** 570,000 million million million tons
- **Temperature:** -185°C (extremes not available)
- **Distance from Sun:** 887 million miles (1,427 million km)
- **Length of day:** 10.23 hours
- **Length of year:** 29.46 earth years
- **Surface gravity:** 1 kg = 1.07 kg

URANUS

- **Diameter:** 31,763 miles (51,118 km)
- **Mass:** 86,800 million million million tons
- **Temperature:** -214°C (extremes not available)
- **Distance from Sun:** 1,783 million miles (2,870 million km)
- **Length of day:** 17.9 hours
- **Length of year:** 84.01 earth years
- **Surface gravity:** 1 kg = 0.92 kg

SPACE DEBRIS

MILLIONS OF OBJECTS, remnants of planetary formation, circle the Sun in a zone lying between Mars and Jupiter: the asteroid belt. Fragments of asteroids break off to form meteoroids, which can reach the Earth's surface. Comets, composed of ice and dust, originated outside our Solar System. Their elliptical orbit brings them close to the Sun and into the inner Solar System.

***Meteor Crater in Arizona** is 4200 ft (1300 m) wide and 660 ft (200 m) deep. It was formed over 10,000 years ago.*

METEOROIDS

Meteoroids are fragments of asteroids which hurtle through space at great velocity. Although millions of meteoroids enter the Earth's atmosphere, the vast majority burn up on entry, and fall to the Earth as a meteor or shooting star. Large meteoroids traveling at speeds of 155,000 mph (250,000 kmph) can sometimes withstand the atmosphere and hit the Earth's surface with tremendous force, creating large craters on impact.

POSSIBLE AND ACTUAL METEORITE CRATERS

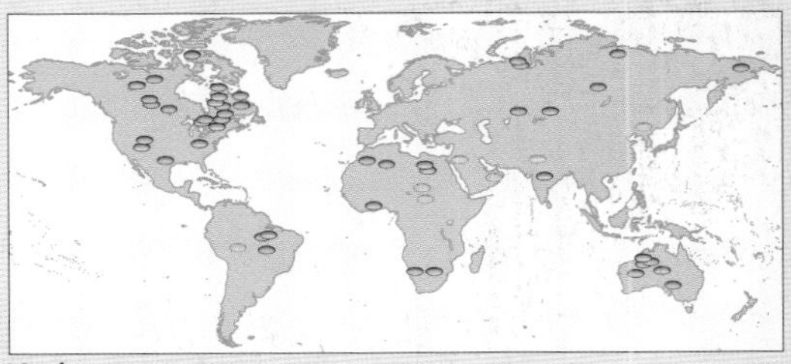

Map key
Possible impact craters
Meteorite impact craters

***The orbit of Halley's Comet** brings it close to the Earth every 76 years. It last visited in 1986.*

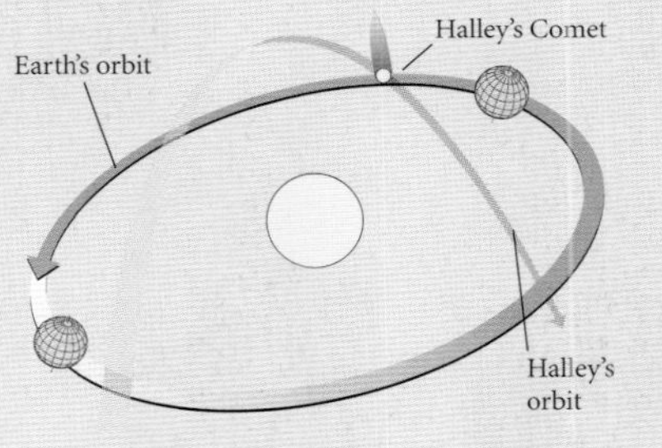

ORBIT OF HALLEY'S COMET AROUND THE SUN

NEPTUNE

- **Diameter:** 30,775 miles (49,528 km)
- **Mass:** 102,000 million million million tons
- **Temperature:** -225°C (extremes not available)
- **Distance from Sun:** 2794 million miles (4497 million km)
- **Length of day:** 19.2 hours
- **Length of year:** 164.79 earth years
- **Surface gravity:** 1 kg = 1.18 kg

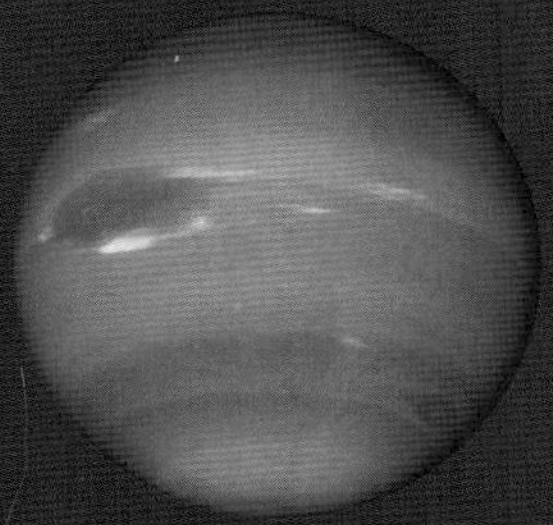

PLUTO

- **Diameter:** 1,429 miles (2,300 km)
- **Mass:** 13 million million million tons
- **Temperature:** -236°C (extremes not available)
- **Distance from Sun:** 3,666 million miles (5,900 million km)
- **Length of day:** 6.39 hours
- **Length of year:** 248.54 earth years
- **Surface gravity:** 1 kg = 0.30 kg

THE EARTH'S ATMOSPHERE

DURING THE EARLY STAGES of the Earth's formation, ash, lava, carbon dioxide, and water vapor were discharged onto the surface of the planet by constant volcanic eruptions. The water formed the oceans, while carbon dioxide entered the atmosphere or was dissolved in the oceans. Clouds, formed of water droplets, reflected some of the Sun's radiation back into space. The Earth's temperature stabilized and early life forms began to emerge, converting carbon dioxide into life-giving oxygen.

__It is thought__ that the gases that make up the Earth's atmosphere originated deep within the interior, and were released many millions of years ago during intense volcanic actvity, similar to this eruption at Mount St. Helens.

ORDER AND RELATIVE DISTANCE FROM THE SUN OF PLANETS

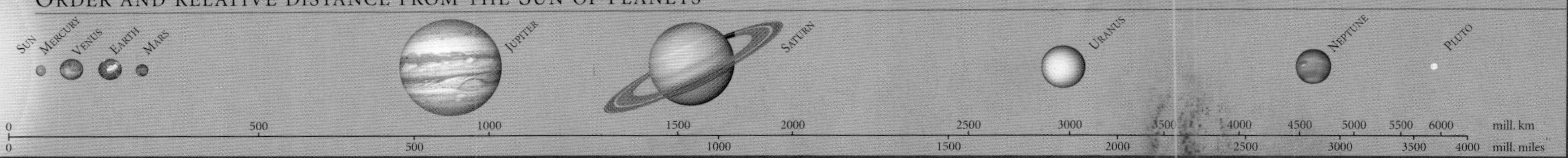

The Physical World

The Earth's surface is constantly being transformed: it is uplifted, folded and faulted by tectonic forces; weathered and eroded by wind, water, and ice. Sometimes change is dramatic, the spectacular results of earthquakes or floods. More often it is a slow process lasting millions of years. A physical map of the world represents a snapshot of the ever-evolving architecture of the Earth. This terrain map shows the whole surface of the Earth, both above and below the sea.

The World in Section

These cross-sections around the Earth, one in the northern hemisphere; one straddling the Equator, reveal the limited areas of land above sea level in comparison with the extent of the sea floor. The greater erosive effects of weathering by wind and water limit the upward elevation of land above sea level, while the deep oceans retain their dramatic mountain and trench profiles.

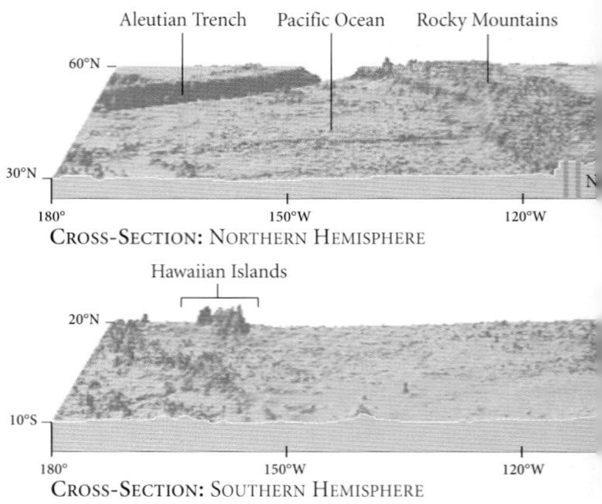

Map Key

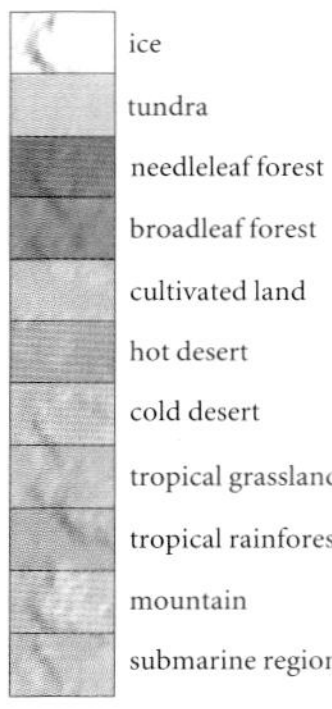

Scale 1:60,000,000
(projection: Wagner VII)

Km 0 250 500 1,000 1,500 2,000
Miles 0 250 500 1,000 1,500 2,000

Northern Hemisphere

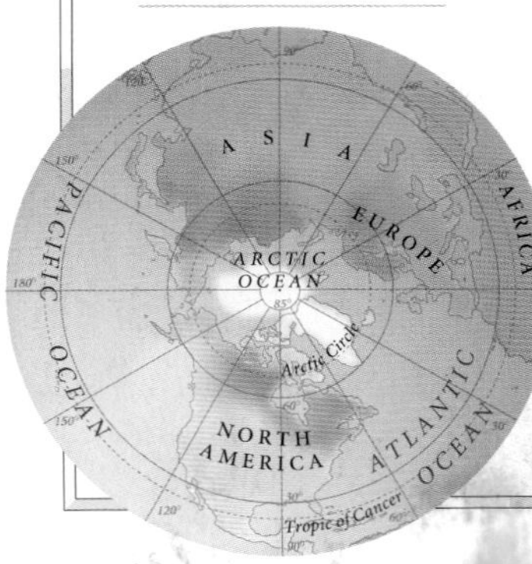

Most of the land on Earth is concentrated in the northern hemisphere, although Europe and North America are the only continents which lie wholly in the north.

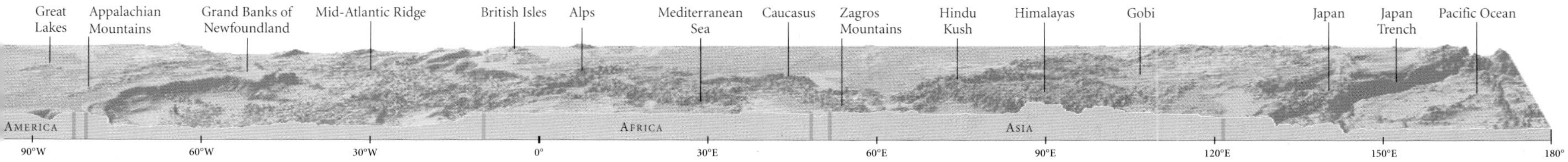

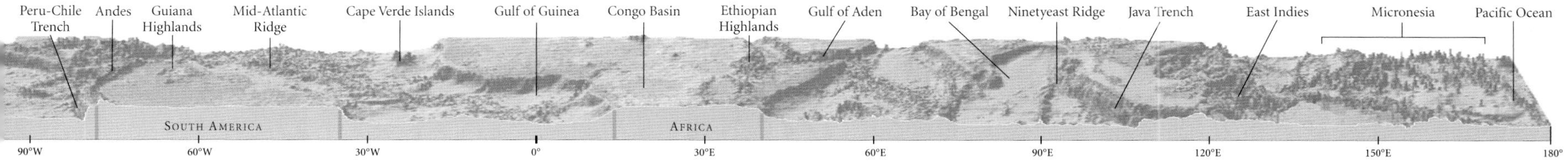

Physical Factfile

- **Diameter of Earth at Equator:** 7,927 miles (12,756 km)
- **Equatorial circumference of Earth:** 24,901 miles (40,075 km)
- **Diameter from Pole to Pole:** 7,900 miles (12,714 km)
- **Polar circumference of Earth:** 24,860 miles (40,008 km)
- **Mass:** 5,988 million million million tons (tonnes)

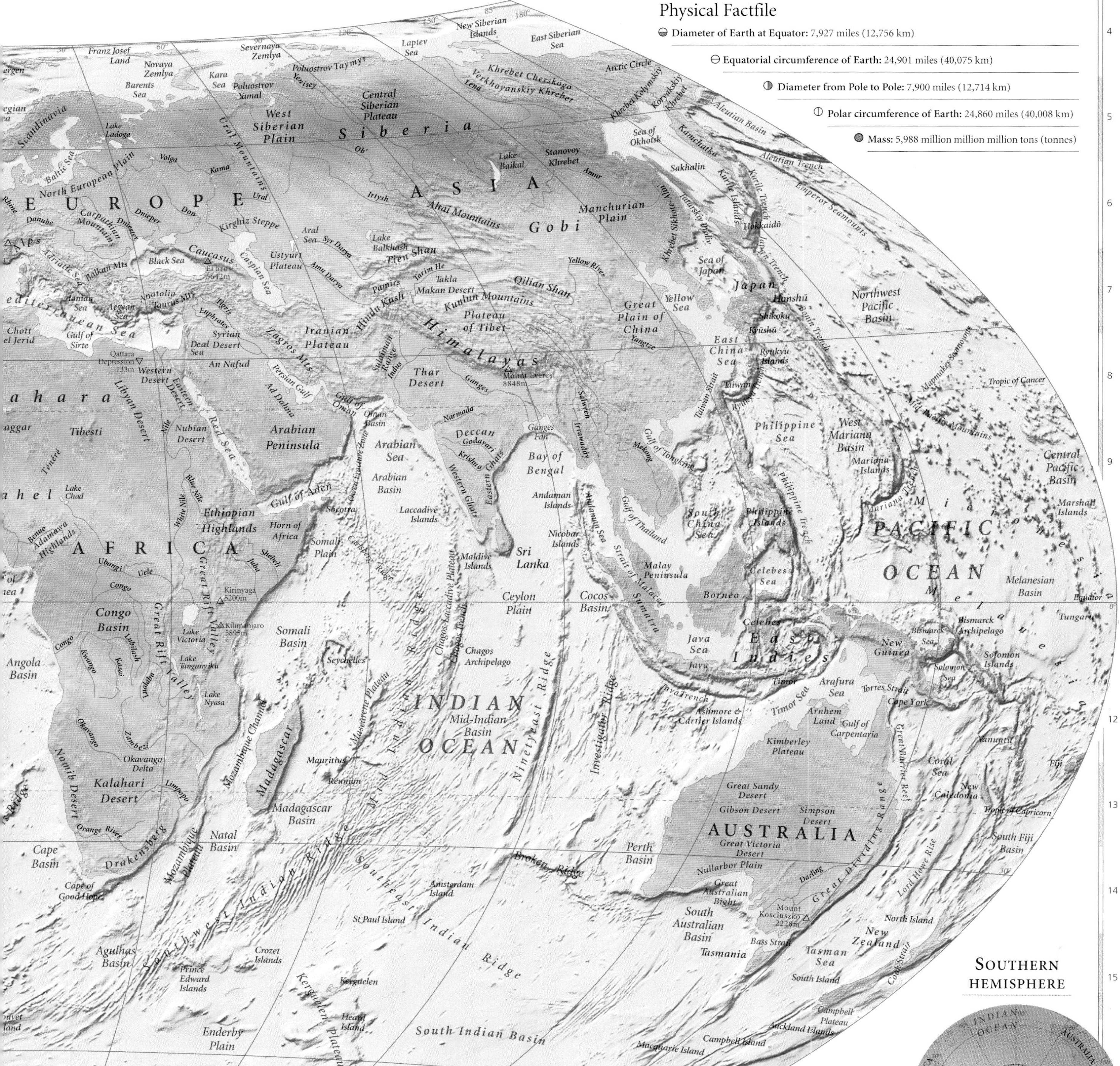

Oceans dominate the southern hemisphere. Australia and Antarctica are the only continental landmasses which lie entirely in the south.

Southern Hemisphere

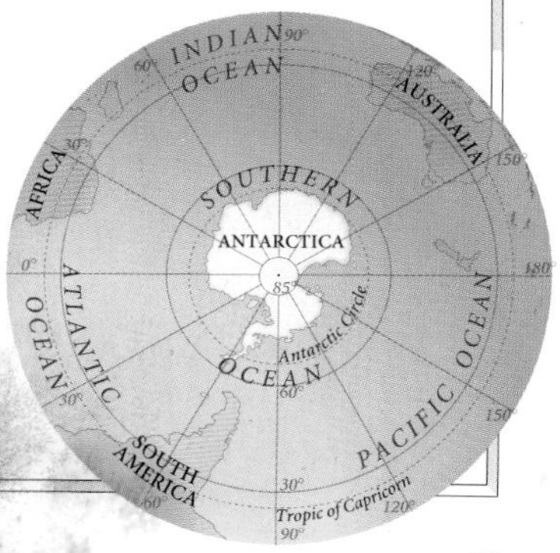

A B C D E F G H I J K L M

Structure of the Earth

The Earth as it is today is just the latest phase in a constant process of evolution which has occurred over the past 4.5 billion years. The Earth's continents are neither fixed nor stable; over the course of the Earth's history, propelled by currents rising from the intense heat at its center, the great plates on which they lie have moved, collided, joined together, and separated. These processes continue to mold and transform the surface of the Earth, causing earthquakes and volcanic eruptions and creating oceans, mountain ranges, deep ocean trenches, and island chains.

Inside the Earth

The Earth's hot inner core is made up of solid iron, while the outer core is composed of liquid iron and nickel. The mantle nearest the core is viscous, whereas the rocky upper mantle is fairly rigid. The crust is the rocky outer shell of the Earth. Together, the upper mantle and the crust form the lithosphere.

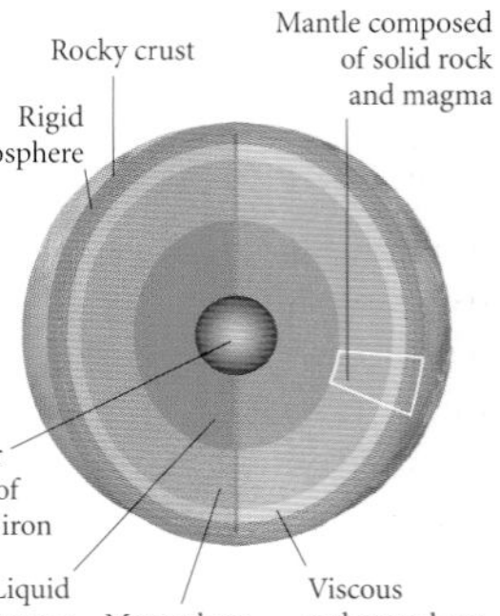

The Dynamic Earth

The Earth's crust is made up of eight major (and several minor) rigid continental and oceanic tectonic plates, which fit closely together. The positions of the plates are not static. They are constantly moving relative to one another. The type of movement between plates affects the way in which they alter the structure of the Earth. The oldest parts of the plates, known as shields, are the most stable parts of the Earth and little tectonic activity occurs here.

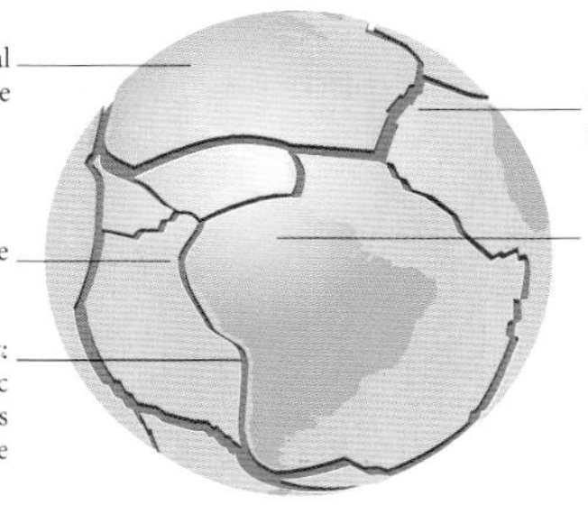

Convection Currents

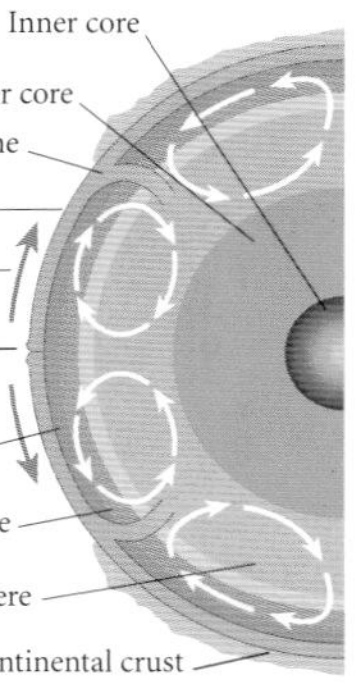

Deep within the Earth, at its inner core, temperatures may exceed 8,100°F (4,500°C). This heat warms rocks in the mesosphere which rise through the partially molten mantle, displacing cooler rocks just below the solid crust, which sink, and are warmed again by the heat of the mantle. This process is continuous, creating convection currents which form the moving force beneath the Earth's crust.

Plate Boundaries

The boundaries between the plates are the areas where most tectonic activity takes place. Three types of movement occur at plate boundaries: the plates can either move toward each other, move apart, or slide past each other. The effect this has on the Earth's structure depends on whether the margin is between two continental plates, two oceanic plates, or an oceanic and continental plate.

***The Mid-Atlantic Ridge** rises above sea level in Iceland, producing geysers and volcanoes.*

Mid-Ocean Ridges

Mid-ocean ridges are formed when two adjacent oceanic plates pull apart, allowing magma to force its way up to the surface, which then cools to form solid rock. Vast amounts of volcanic material are discharged at these mid-ocean ridges which can reach heights of 10,000 ft (3,000 m).

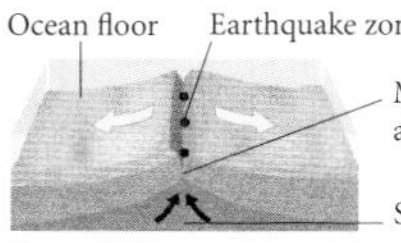

Formation of a mid-ocean ridge

***Mount Pinatubo** is an active volcano, lying on the Pacific "Ring of Fire."*

Ocean Plates Meeting

Oceanic crust is denser and thinner than continental crust; on average it is 3 miles (5 km) thick, while continental crust averages 18–24 miles (30–40 km). When oceanic plates of similar density meet, the crust is contorted as one plate overrides the other, forming deep sea trenches and volcanic island arcs above sea level.

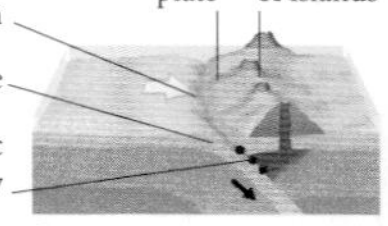

Ocean plates meeting to form an island arc

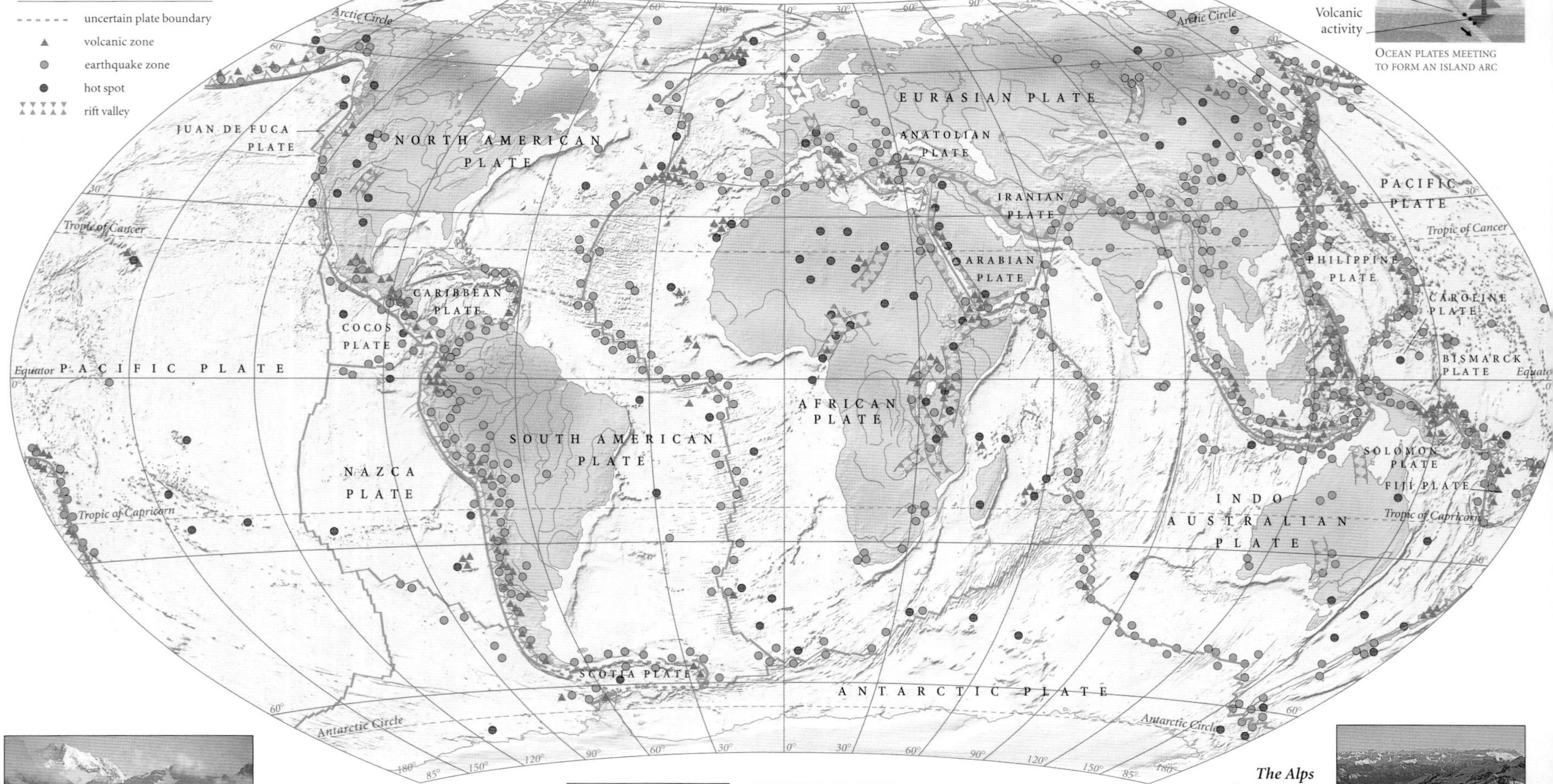

***The Andean mountain** chain is the typical result of the impact of a diving plate.*

Diving Plates

When an oceanic and a continental plate meet, the denser oceanic plate is driven underneath the continental plate, which is crumpled by the collision to form mountain ranges. As the ocean plate plunges downward, it heats up, and molten rock (magma) is forced up to the surface.

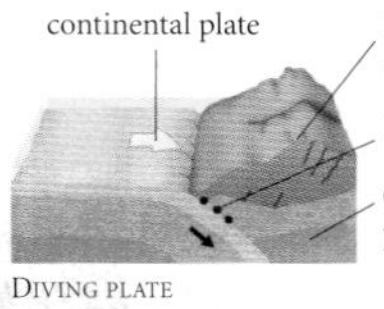

Diving plate

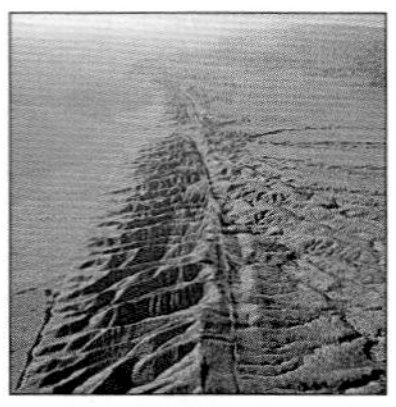

***The deep fracture** caused by the sliding plates of the San Andreas Fault can be clearly seen in parts of California.*

Sliding Plates

When two plates slide past each other, friction is caused along the fault line which divides them. The plates do not move smoothly, and the uneven movement causes earthquakes.

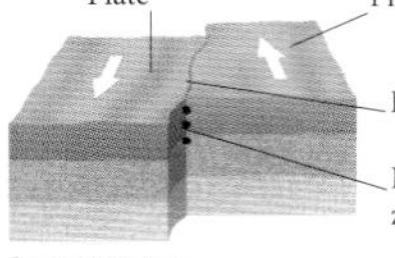

Sliding plates

***The Alps** were formed when the African plate collided with the Eurasian Plate, about 65 million years ago.*

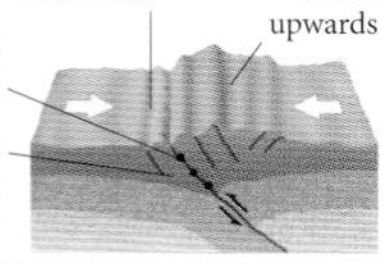

Continental plates colliding to form a mountain range

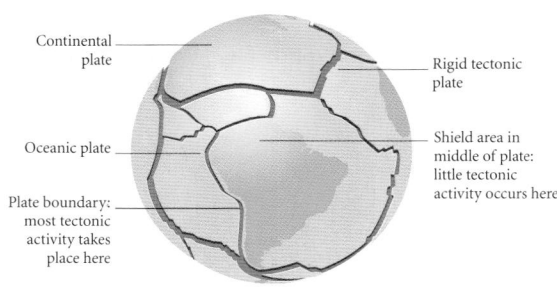

Colliding Plates

When two continental plates collide, great mountain chains are thrust upward as the crust buckles and folds under the force of the impact.

A B C D E F G H I J K L M

CONTINENTAL DRIFT

ALTHOUGH THE PLATES which make up the Earth's crust move only a few inches in a year, over the millions of years of the Earth's history, its continents have moved many thousands of miles, to create new continents, oceans, and mountain chains.

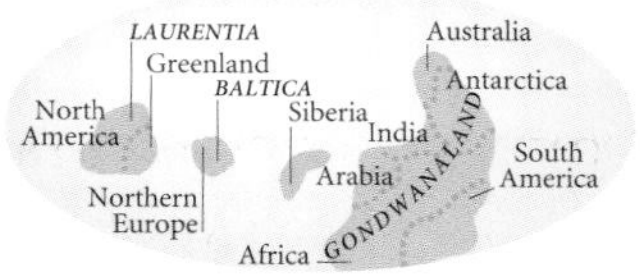

1: CAMBRIAN PERIOD

570–510 million years ago. *Most continents are in tropical latitudes. The supercontinent of Gondwanaland reaches the South Pole.*

2: DEVONIAN PERIOD

408–362 million years ago. *The continents of Gondwanaland and Laurentia are drifting northward.*

3: CARBONIFEROUS PERIOD

362–290 million years ago. *The Earth is dominated by three continents; Laurentia, Angaraland, and Gondwanaland.*

4: TRIASSIC PERIOD

245–208 million years ago. *All three major continents have joined to form the supercontinent of Pangea.*

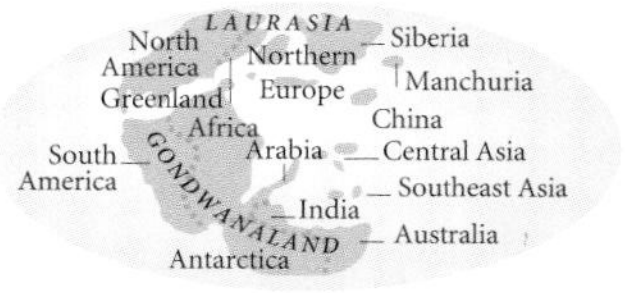

5: JURASSIC PERIOD

208–145 million years ago. *The supercontinent of Pangea begins to break up, causing an overall rise in sea levels.*

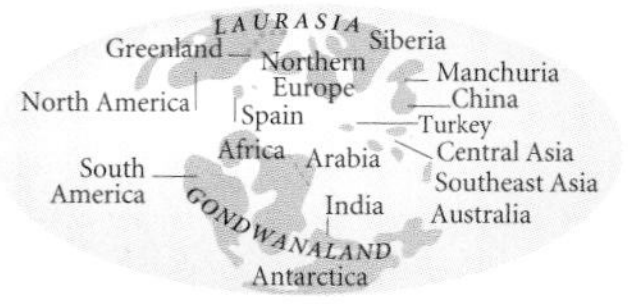

6: CRETACEOUS PERIOD

145–65 million years ago. *Warm, shallow seas cover much of the land: sea levels are about 80 ft (25 m) above present levels.*

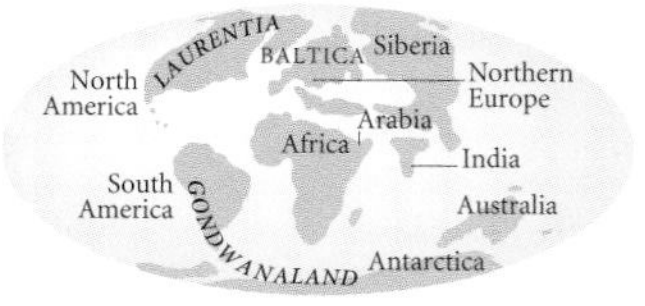

7: TERTIARY PERIOD

65–2 million years ago. *Although the world's geography is becoming more recognizable, major events such as the creation of the Himalayan mountain chain, are still to occur during this period.*

CONTINENTAL SHIELDS

THE CENTERS OF THE EARTH'S CONTINENTS, known as shields, were established between 2500 and 500 million years ago; some contain rocks over three billion years old. They were formed by a series of turbulent events: plate movements, earthquakes, and volcanic eruptions. Since the Pre-Cambrian period, over 570 million years ago, they have experienced little tectonic activity, and today, these flat, low-lying slabs of solidified molten rock form the stable centers of the continents. They are bounded or covered by successive belts of younger sedimentary rock.

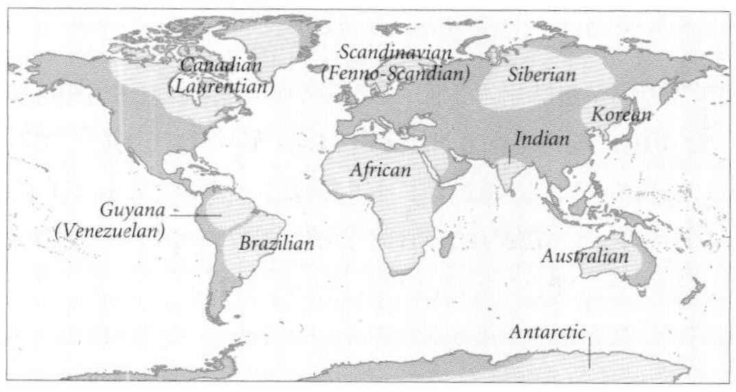

CREATION OF THE HIMALAYAS

BETWEEN 10 AND 20 MILLION YEARS AGO, the Indian subcontinent, part of the ancient continent of Gondwanaland, collided with the continent of Asia. The Indo-Australian Plate continued to move northward, displacing continental crust and uplifting the Himalayas, the world's highest mountain chain.

MOVEMENTS OF INDIA

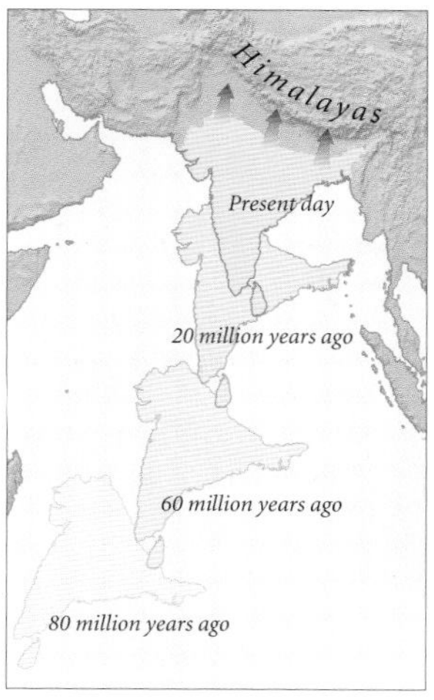

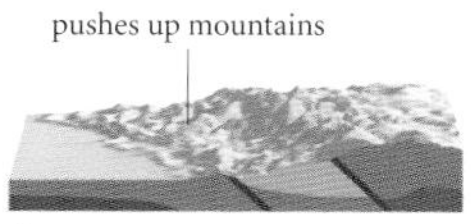

CROSS-SECTION THROUGH THE HIMALAYAS

The Himalayas *were uplifted when the Indian subcontinent collided with Asia.*

THE HAWAIIAN ISLAND CHAIN

A HOT SPOT lying deep beneath the Pacific Ocean pushes a plume of magma from the Earth's mantle up through the Pacific Plate to form volcanic islands. While the hot spot remains stationary, the plate on which the islands sit is moving slowly. A long chain of islands has been created as the plate passes over the hot spot.

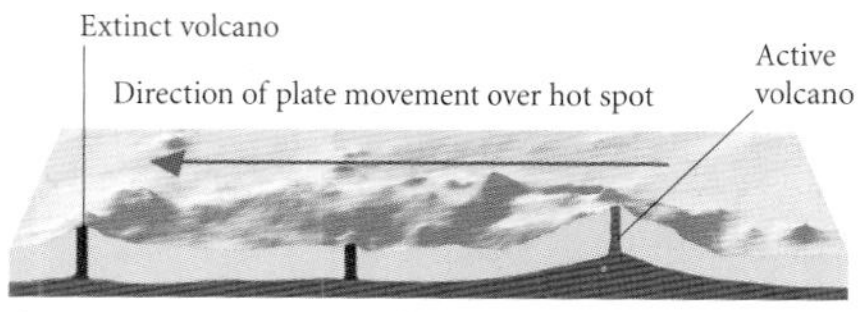

CROSS-SECTION THROUGH THE HAWAIIAN ISLANDS

EVOLUTION OF THE HAWAIIAN ISLANDS

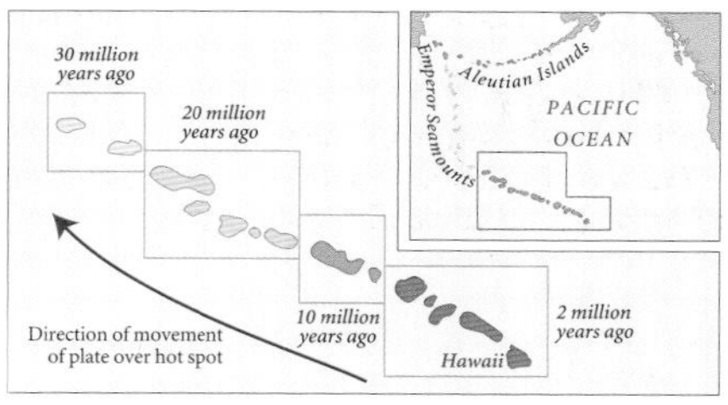

THE EARTH'S GEOLOGY

THE EARTH'S ROCKS are created in a continual cycle. Exposed rocks are weathered and eroded by wind, water and chemicals and deposited as sediments. If they pass into the Earth's crust they will be transformed by high temperatures and pressures into metamorphic rocks or they will melt and solidify as igneous rocks.

Gneiss *formations in Norway's Jotunheimen Mountains.*

GNEISS

1 Gneiss is a metamorphic rock made at great depth during the formation of mountain chains, when intense heat and pressure transform sedimentary or igneous rocks.

Basalt *columns at Giant's Causeway, Northern Ireland, UK.*

BASALT

2 Basalt is an igneous rock, formed when small quantities of magma lying close to the Earth's surface cool rapidly.

LIMESTONE

3 Limestone is a sedimentary rock, which is formed mainly from the calcite skeletons of marine animals which have been compressed into rock.

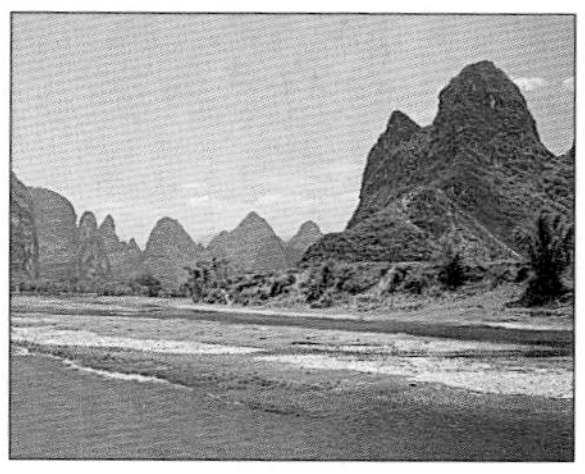

Limestone hills*, Guilin, China.*

SANDSTONE

8 Sandstones are sedimentary rocks formed mainly in deserts, beaches, and deltas. Desert sandstones are formed of grains of quartz which have been well rounded by wind erosion.

Rock stacks *of desert sandstone, at Bryce Canyon National Park, Utah.*

THE WORLD'S MAJOR GEOLOGICAL REGIONS

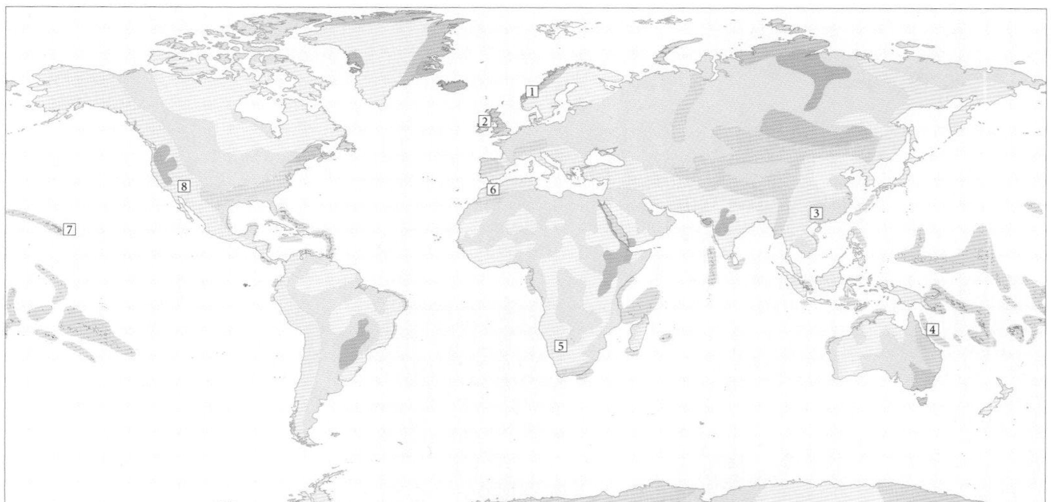

Geological Regions
- continental shield
- sedimentary cover
- coral formation
- igneous rock types

Mountain Ranges
- Alpine (new)
- Hercynian (old)
- Caledonian (ancient)

CORAL

4 Coral reefs are formed from the skeletons of millions of individual corals.

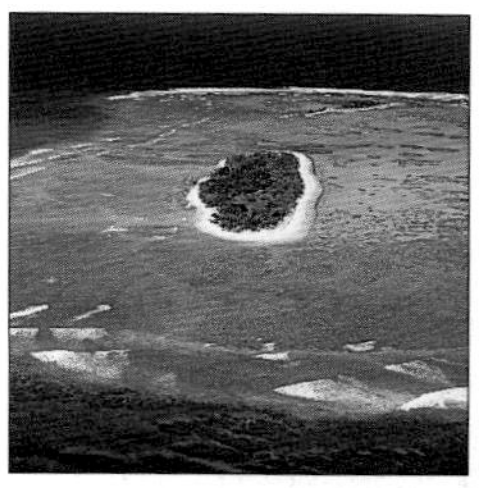

Great Barrier Reef*, Australia.*

Extrusive igneous rocks *are formed during volcanic eruptions, as here in Hawaii.*

ANDESITE

7 Andesite is an extrusive igneous rock formed from magma which has solidified on the Earth's crust after a volcanic eruption.

SCHIST

6 Schist is a metamorphic rock formed during mountain building, when temperature and pressure are comparatively high. Both mudstones and shales reform into schist under these conditions.

Schist formations *in the Atlas Mountains, northwestern Africa.*

GRANITE

5 Granite is an intrusive igneous rock formed from magma which has solidified deep within the Earth's crust. The magma cools slowly, producing a coarse-grained rock.

Namibia's *Namaqualand Plateau is formed of granite.*

Shaping the Landscape

THE BASIC MATERIAL OF THE EARTH'S SURFACE is solid rock: valleys, deserts, soil, and sand are all evidence of the powerful agents of weathering, erosion, and deposition which constantly shape and transform the Earth's landscapes. Water, either flowing continually in rivers or seas, or frozen and compacted into solid sheets of ice, has the most clearly visible impact on the Earth's surface. But wind can transport fragments of rock over huge distances and strip away protective layers of vegetation, exposing rock surfaces to the impact of extreme heat and cold.

Water

LESS THAN 2% of the world's water is on the land, but it is the most powerful agent of landscape change. Water, as rainfall, groundwater, and rivers, can transform landscapes through both erosion and deposition. Eroded material carried by rivers forms the world's most fertile soils.

Waterfalls such as the Iguaçu Falls *on the border between Argentina and southern Brazil, erode the underlying rock, causing the falls to retreat.*

Coastal water

THE WORLD'S COASTLINES are constantly changing; every day, tides deposit, sift and sort sand and gravel on the shoreline. Over longer periods, powerful wave action erodes cliffs and headlands and carves out bays.

A low, wide sandy beach *on South Africa's Cape Peninsula is continually re-shaped by the action of the Atlantic waves.*

The sheer chalk cliffs *at Seven Sisters in southern England are constantly under attack from waves.*

Groundwater

IN REGIONS where there are porous rocks such as chalk, water is stored underground in large quantities; these reservoirs of water are known as aquifers. Rain percolates through topsoil into the underlying bedrock, creating an underground store of water. The limit of the saturated zone is called the water table.

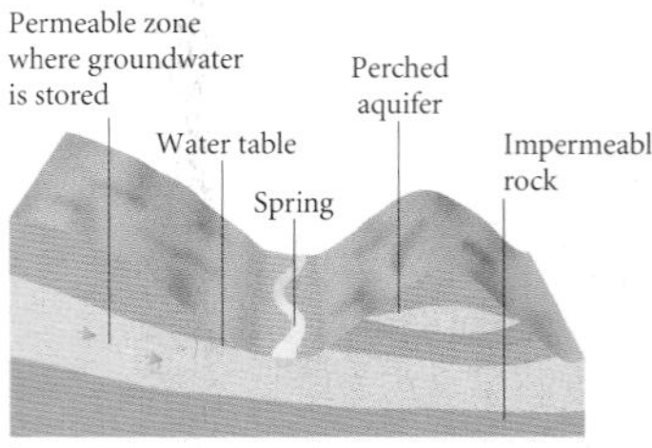

STORAGE OF GROUNDWATER IN AN AQUIFER

World river systems

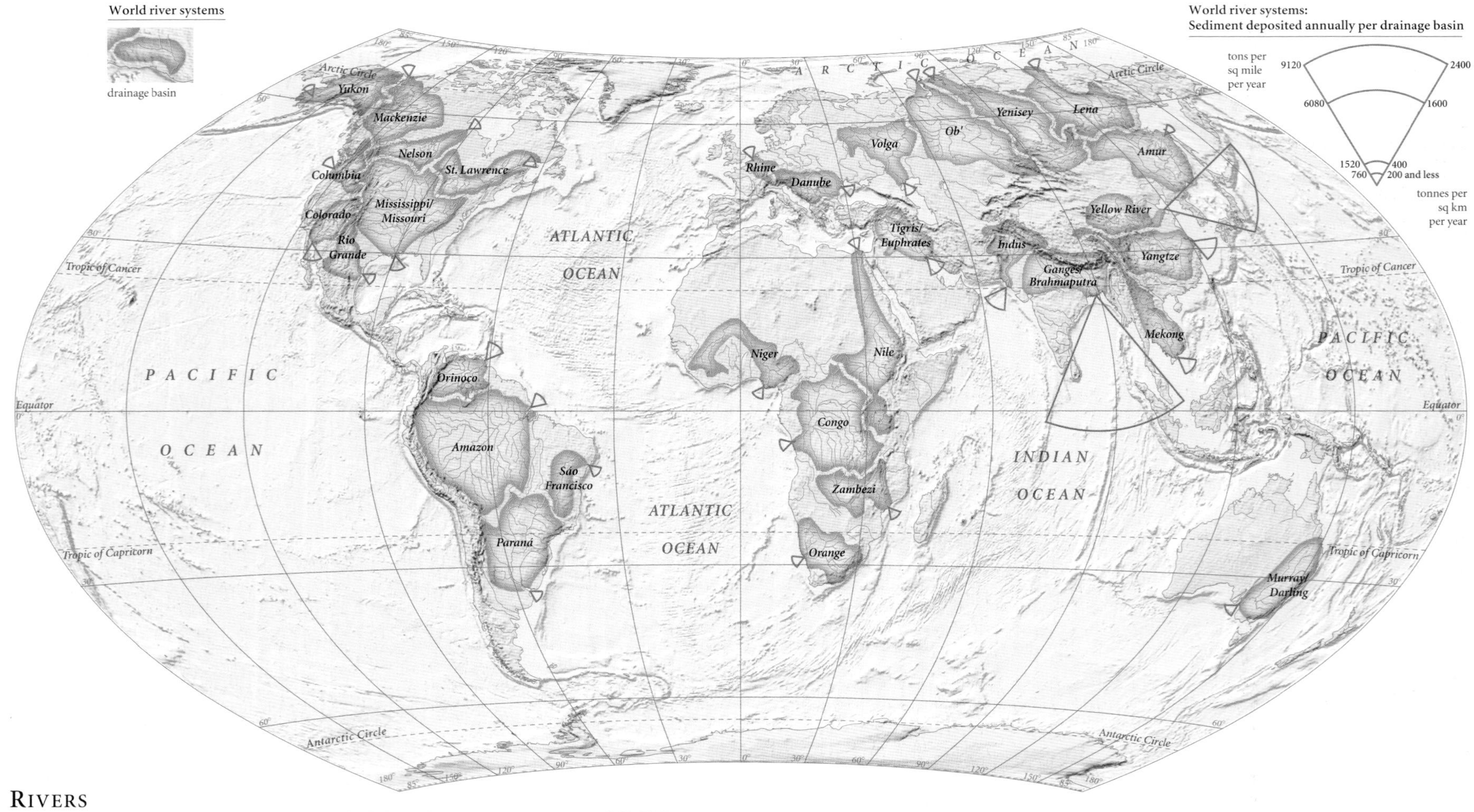

Rivers

RIVERS ERODE THE LAND by grinding and dissolving rocks and stones. Most erosion occurs in the river's upper course as it flows through highland areas. Rock fragments are moved along the river bed by fast-flowing water and deposited in areas where the river slows down, such as flat plains, or where the river enters seas or lakes.

River valleys

Over long periods of time rivers erode uplands to form characteristic V-shaped valleys with smooth sides.

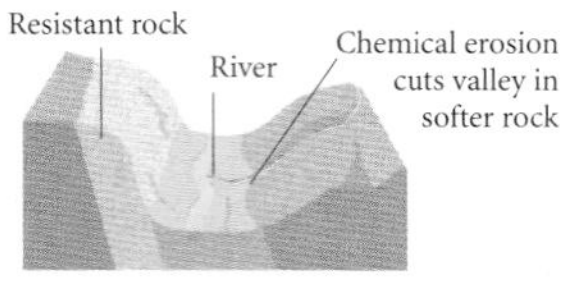

RIVER VALLEY EROSION

Deltas

When a river deposits its load of silt and sediment (alluvium) on entering the sea, it may form a delta. As this material accumulates, it chokes the mouth of the river, forcing it to create new channels to reach the sea.

The Nile *forms a broad delta as it flows into the Mediterranean.*

Drainage basins

The drainage basin is the area of land drained by a major trunk river and its smaller branch rivers or tributaries. Drainage basins are separated from one another by natural boundaries known as watersheds.

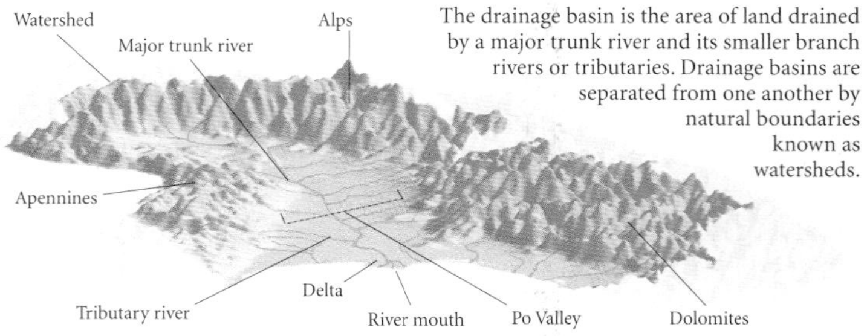

The drainage basin *of the Po River, northern Italy.*

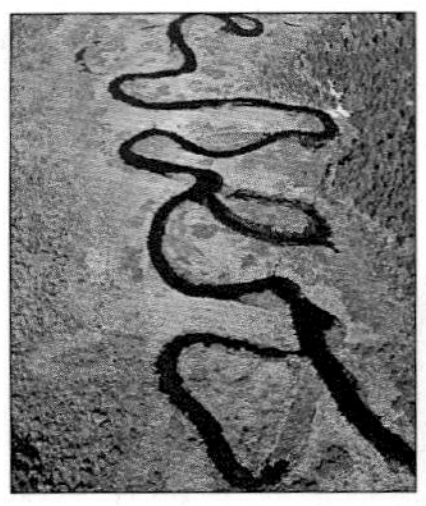

The Mississippi River *forms meanders as it flows across the southern US.*

Meanders

In their lower courses, rivers flow slowly. As they flow across the lowlands, they form looping bends called meanders.

The meanders *of Utah's San Juan River have become deeply incised.*

Mud is *deposited by China's Yellow River in its lower course.*

Deposition

When rivers have deposited large quantities of fertile alluvium, they are forced to find new channels through the alluvium deposits, creating braided river systems.

Landslides

Heavy rain and associated flooding on slopes can loosen underlying rocks, which crumble, causing the top layers of rock and soil to slip.

A huge landslide *in the Swiss Alps has left massive piles of rocks and pebbles called scree.*

A deep gully *in the French Alps caused by the scouring of upper layers of turf.*

Gullies

In areas where soil is thin, rainwater is not effectively absorbed, and may flow overland. The water courses downhill in channels, or gullies, and may lead to rapid erosion of soil.

ICE

DURING ITS LONG HISTORY, the Earth has experienced a number of glacial episodes when temperatures were considerably lower than today. During the last Ice Age, 18,000 years ago, ice covered an area three times larger than it does today. Over these periods, the ice has left a remarkable legacy of transformed landscapes.

GLACIERS

GLACIERS ARE FORMED by the compaction of snow into "rivers" of ice. As they move over the landscape, glaciers pick up and carry a load of rocks and boulders which erode the landscape they pass over, and are eventually deposited at the end of the glacier.

***A massive glacier** advancing down a valley in southern Argentina.*

GLACIAL VALLEYS

GLACIERS CAN ERODE much more powerfully than rivers. They form steep-sided, flat-bottomed valleys with a typical U-shaped profile. Valleys created by tributary glaciers, whose floors have not been eroded to the same depth as the main glacial valley floor, are called hanging valleys.

***The U-shaped profile** and piles of morainic debris are characteristic of a valley once filled by a glacier.*

***A series of hanging valleys** high up in the Chilean Andes.*

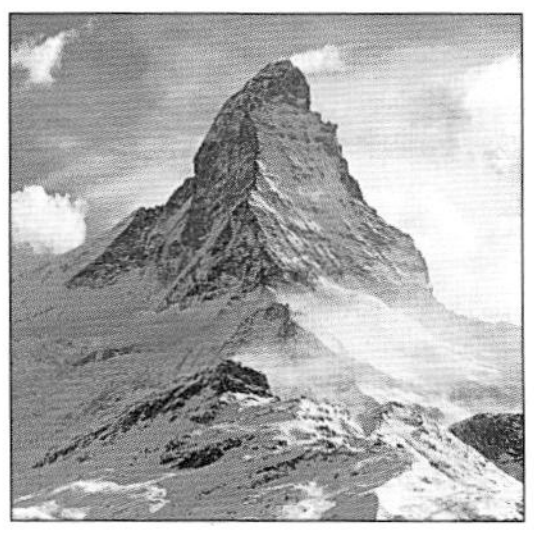

***The profile** of the Matterhorn has been formed by three cirques lying "back-to-back."*

CIRQUES

Cirques are basin-shaped hollows which mark the head of a glaciated valley. Where neighboring cirques meet, they are divided by sharp rock ridges called arêtes. It is these arêtes which give the Matterhorn its characteristic profile.

FJORDS

Fjords are ancient glacial valleys flooded by the sea following the end of a period of glaciation. Beneath the water, the valley floor can be 4,000 ft (1,300 m) deep.

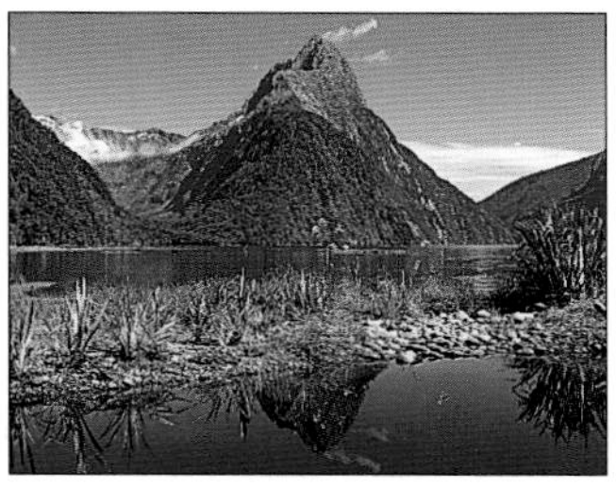

***A fjord** fills a former glacial valley in southern New Zealand.*

PAST AND PRESENT WORLD ICE-COVER AND GLACIAL FEATURES

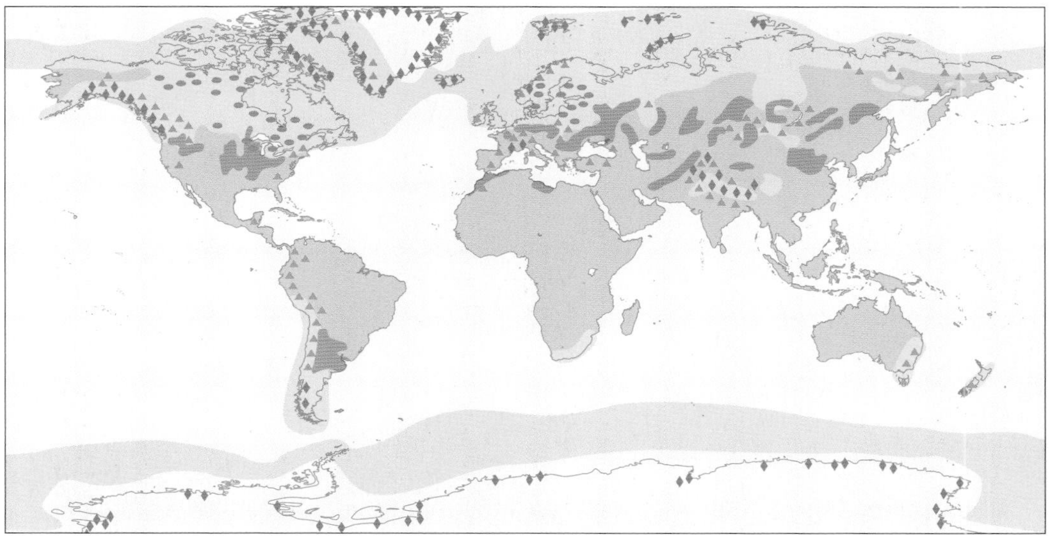

Past and present world ice cover and glacial features

- extent of last Ice Age
- loess deposits
- post-glacial feature
- glacial feature
- present day ice cover
- glacial field

POST-GLACIAL FEATURES

WHEN A GLACIAL EPISODE ENDS, the retreating ice leaves many features. These include depositional ridges called moraines, which may be eroded into low hills known as drumlins; sinuous ridges called eskers; kames, which are rounded hummocks; depressions known as kettle holes; and windblown loess deposits.

POST-GLACIAL LANDSCAPE FEATURES

ICE SHATTERING

Water drips into fissures in rocks and freezes, expanding as it does so. The pressure weakens the rock, causing it to crack, and eventually to shatter into polygonal patterns.

***Irregular polygons** show through the sedge-grass tundra in the Yukon, Canada.*

PERIGLACIATION

Periglacial areas occur near to the edge of ice sheets. A layer of frozen ground lying just beneath the surface of the land is known as permafrost. When the surface melts in the summer, the water is unable to drain into the frozen ground, and so "creeps" downhill, a process known as solifluction.

WIND

STRONG WINDS can transport rock fragments great distances, especially where there is little vegetation to protect the rock. In desert areas, wind picks up loose, unprotected sand particles, carrying them over great distances. This powerfully abrasive debris is blasted at the surface by the wind, eroding the landscape into dramatic shapes.

PREVAILING WINDS AND DUST TRAJECTORIES

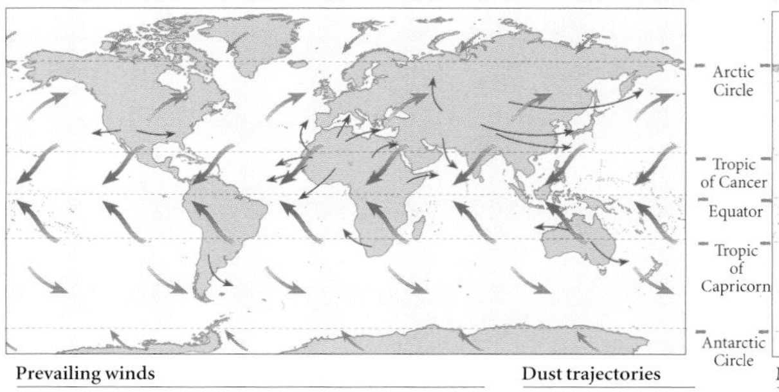

Prevailing winds: northeast trade, southeast trade; westerly, westerly; polar easterly, polar easterly

Dust trajectories: trajectory of aeolian dust

DEPOSITION

THE ROCKY, STONY FLOORS of the world's deserts are swept and scoured by strong winds. The smaller, finer particles of sand are shaped into surface ripples, dunes, or sand mountains, which rise to a height of 650 ft (200 m). Dunes usually form single lines, running perpendicular to the direction of the prevailing wind. These long, straight ridges can extend for over 100 miles (160 km).

***Barchan dunes** in the Arabian Desert.*

***Complex dune system** in the Sahara.*

DUNES

Dunes are shaped by wind direction and sand supply. Where sand supply is limited, crescent-shaped barchan dunes are formed.

TYPES OF DUNE

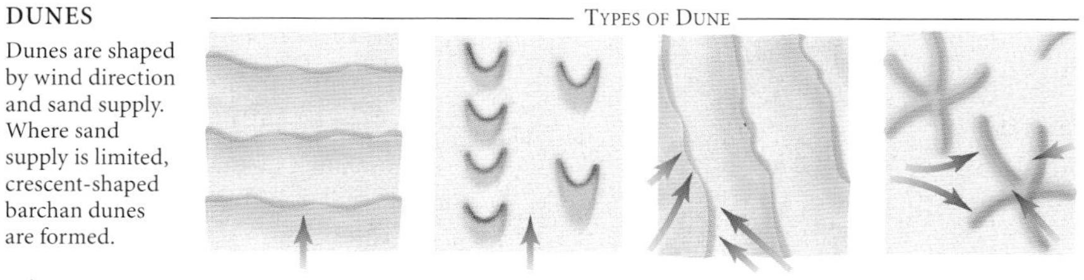

TEMPERATURE

HOT AND COLD DESERTS

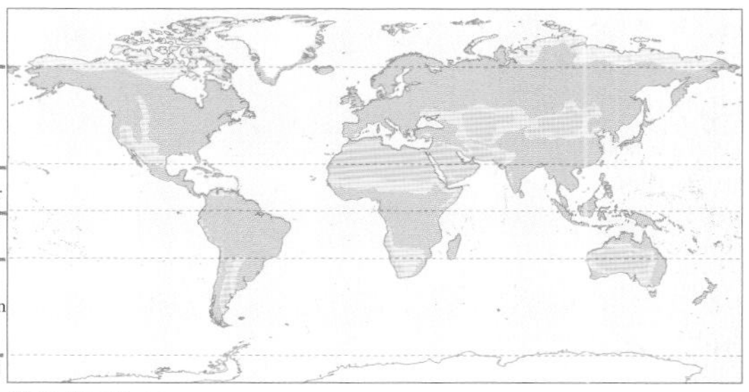

Main desert types: hot arid; semiarid; cold polar

MOST OF THE WORLD'S deserts are in the tropics. The cold deserts which occur elsewhere are arid because they are a long way from the rain-giving sea. Rock in deserts is exposed because of lack of vegetation and is susceptible to changes in temperature; extremes of heat and cold can cause both cracks and fissures to appear in the rock.

HEAT

FIERCE SUN can heat the surface of rock, causing it to expand more rapidly than the cooler, underlying layers. This creates tensions which force the rock to crack or break up. In arid regions, the evaporation of water from rock surfaces dissolves certain minerals within the water, causing salt crystals to form in small openings in the rock. The hard crystals force the openings to widen into cracks and fissures.

***The cracked and parched floor** of Death Valley, California. This is one of the hottest deserts on Earth.*

DESERT ABRASION

Abrasion creates a wide range of desert landforms from faceted pebbles and wind ripples in the sand, to large-scale features such as yardangs (low, streamlined ridges), and scoured desert pavements.

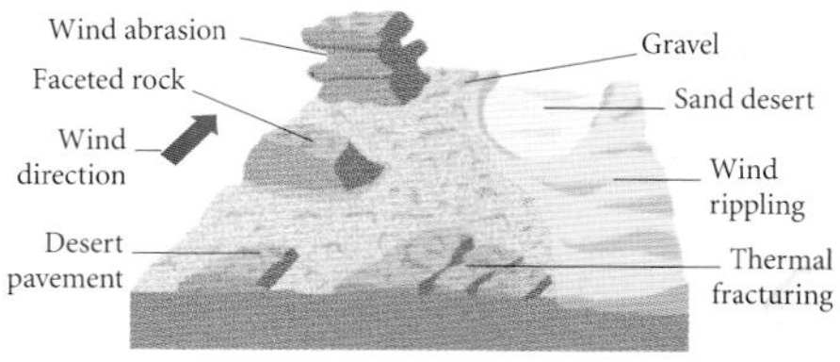

FEATURES OF A DESERT SURFACE

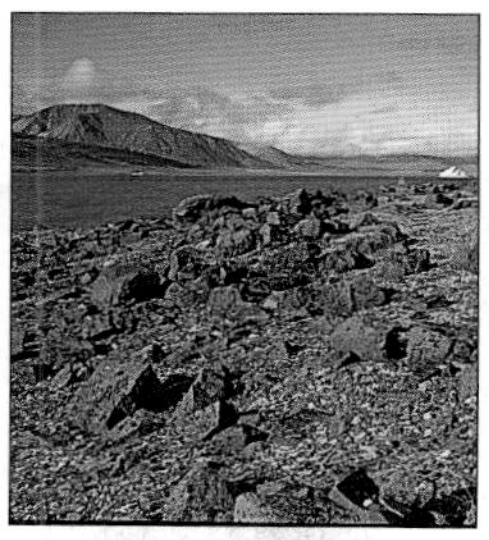

***This dry valley at Ellesmere Island** in the Canadian Arctic is an example of a cold desert. The cracked floor and scoured slopes are features also found in hot deserts.*

The World's Oceans

Two-thirds of the Earth's surface is covered by the oceans. The landscape of the ocean floor, like the surface of the land, has been shaped by movements of the Earth's crust over millions of years to form volcanic mountain ranges, deep trenches, basins, and plateaus. Ocean currents constantly redistribute warm and cold water around the world. A major warm current, such as El Niño in the Pacific Ocean, can increase surface temperature by up to 46°F (8°C), causing changes in weather patterns which can lead to both droughts and flooding.

The great oceans

There are five oceans on Earth: the Pacific, Atlantic, Indian, and Southern oceans, and the much smaller Arctic Ocean. These five ocean basins are relatively young, having evolved within the last 80 million years. One of the most recent plate collisions, between the Eurasian and African plates, created the present-day arrangement of continents and oceans.

***The Indian Ocean** accounts for approximately 20% of the total area of the world's oceans.*

Sea level

If the influence of tides, winds, currents, and variations in gravity were ignored, the surface of the Earth's oceans would closely follow the topography of the ocean floor, with an underwater ridge 3,000 ft (915 m) high producing a rise of up to 3 ft (1 m) in the level of the surface water.

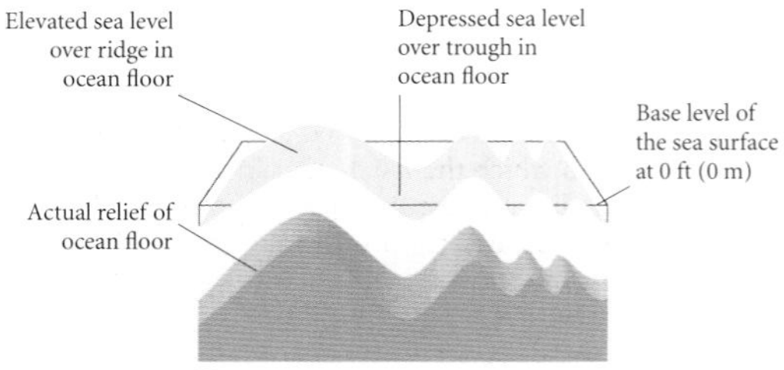

How surface waters reflect the relief of the ocean floor

***The low relief** of many small Pacific islands such as these atolls at Huahine in French Polynesia makes them vulnerable to changes in sea level.*

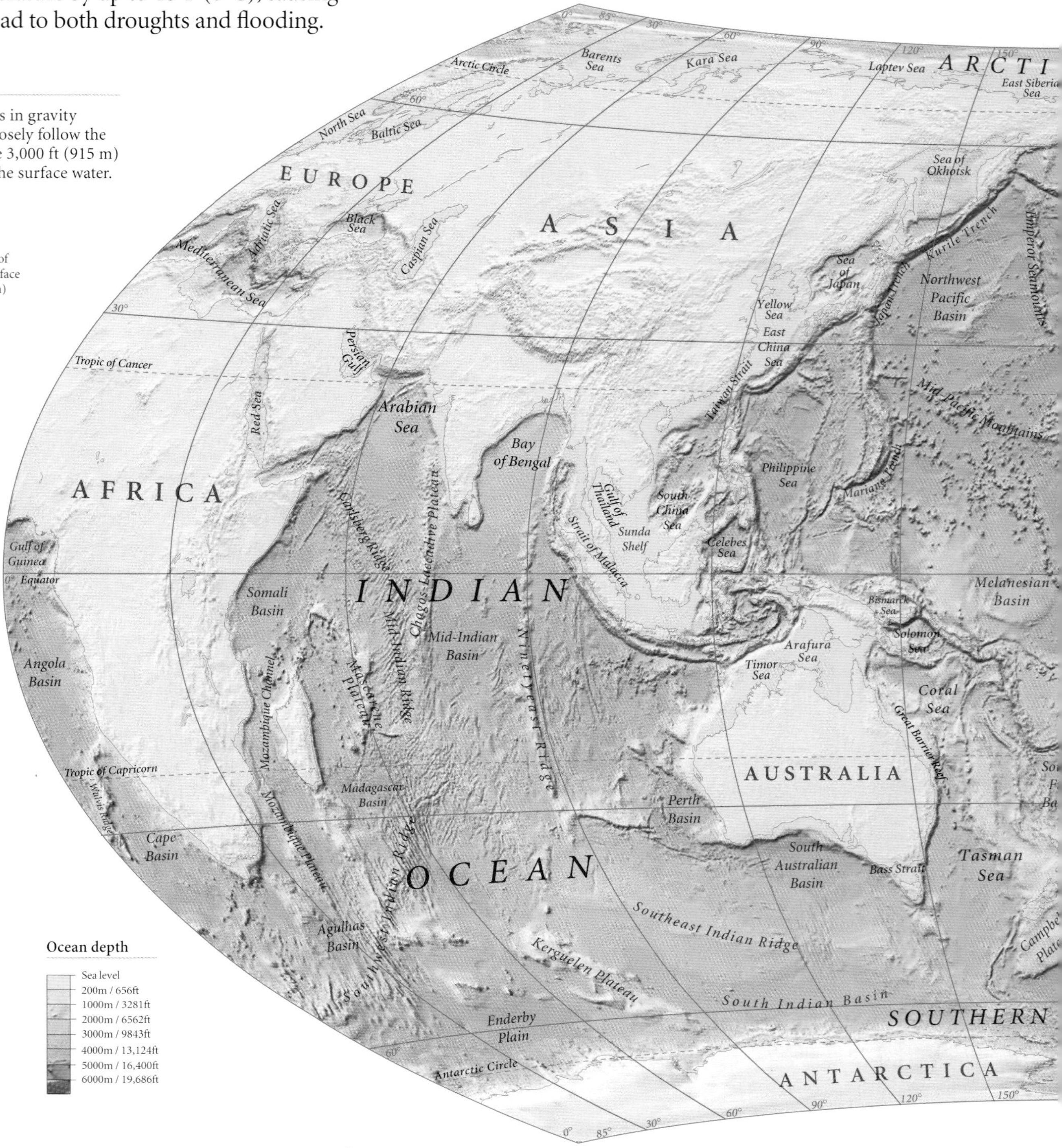

Ocean structure

The continental shelf is a shallow, flat seabed surrounding the Earth's continents. It extends to the continental slope, which falls to the ocean floor. Here, the flat abyssal plains are interrupted by vast, underwater mountain ranges, the mid-ocean ridges, and ocean trenches which plunge to depths of 35,828 ft (10,920 m).

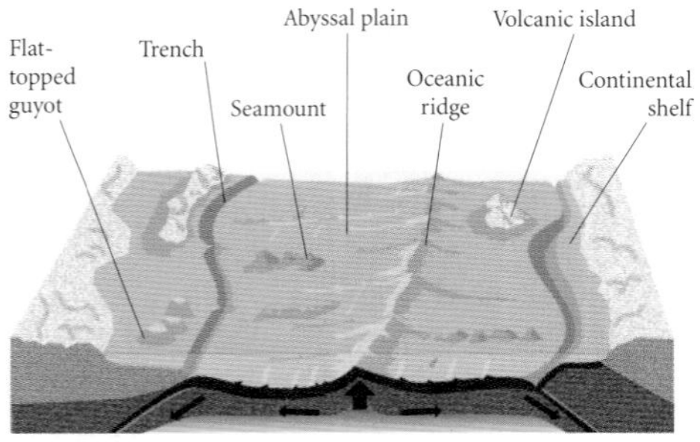

Typical sea-floor features

Black smokers

These vents in the ocean floor disgorge hot, sulfur-rich water from deep in the Earth's crust. Despite the great depths, a variety of lifeforms have adapted to the chemical-rich environment which surrounds black smokers.

***A black smoker** in the Atlantic Ocean.*

***Surtsey, near Iceland**, is a volcanic island lying directly over the Mid-Atlantic Ridge. It was formed in the 1960s following intense volcanic activity nearby.*

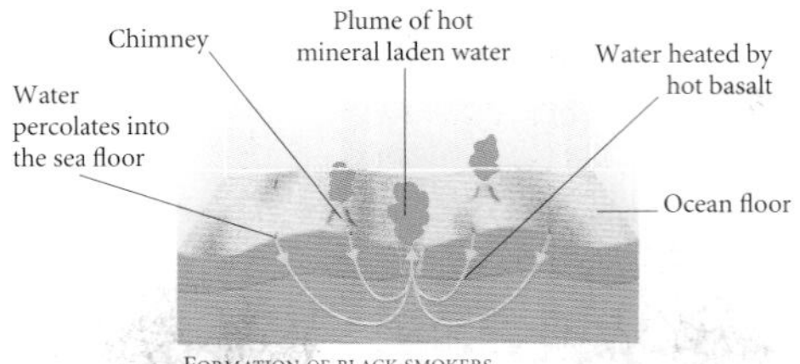

Formation of black smokers

Ocean floors

Mid-ocean ridges are formed by lava which erupts beneath the sea and cools to form solid rock. This process mirrors the creation of volcanoes from cooled lava on the land. The ages of sea floor rocks increase in parallel bands outward from central ocean ridges.

Ages of the ocean floor

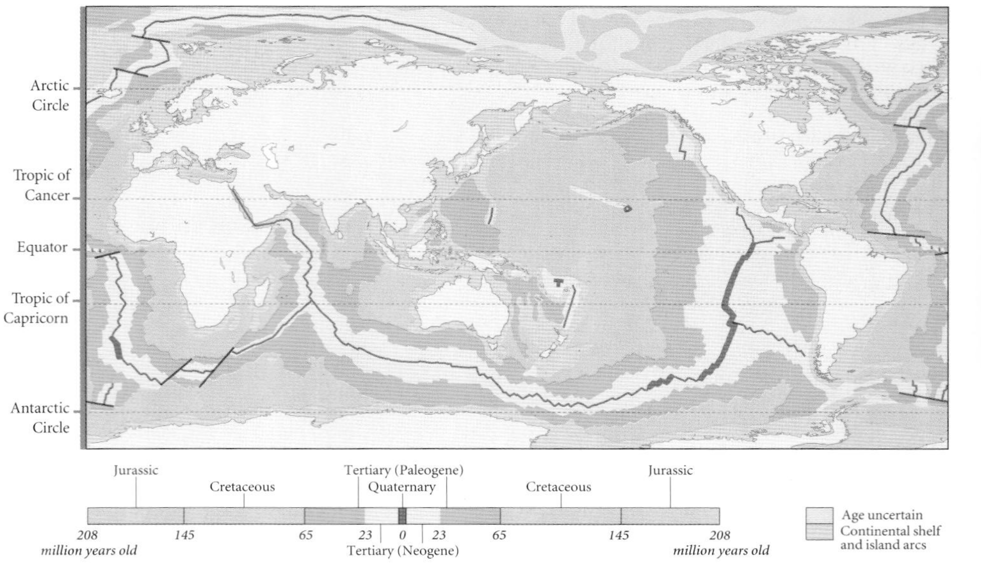

N O P Q R S T U V W X Y Z

***Currents in the Southern Ocean** are driven by some of the world's fiercest winds, including the Roaring Forties, Furious Fifties, and Shrieking Sixties.*

***The Pacific Ocean** is the world's largest and deepest ocean, covering over one-third of the surface of the Earth.*

***The Atlantic Ocean** was formed when the landmasses of the eastern and western hemispheres began to drift apart 180 million years ago.*

DEPOSITION OF SEDIMENT

STORMS, EARTHQUAKES, and volcanic activity trigger underwater currents known as turbidity currents which scour sand and gravel from the continental shelf, creating underwater canyons. These strong currents pick up material deposited at river mouths and deltas, and carry it across the continental shelf and through the underwater canyons, where it is eventually laid down on the ocean floor in the form of fans.

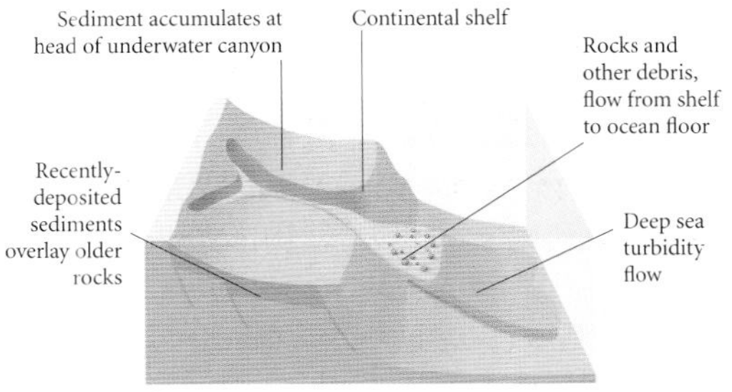

HOW SEDIMENT IS DEPOSITED ON THE OCEAN FLOOR

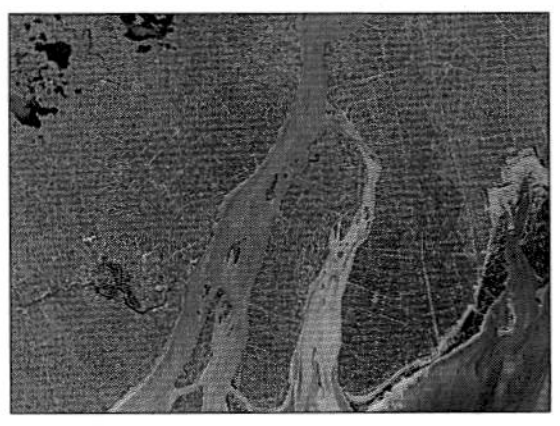

***Satellite image** of the Yangtze (Chang Jiang) Delta, in which the land appears red. The river deposits immense quantities of silt into the East China Sea, much of which will eventually reach the deep ocean floor.*

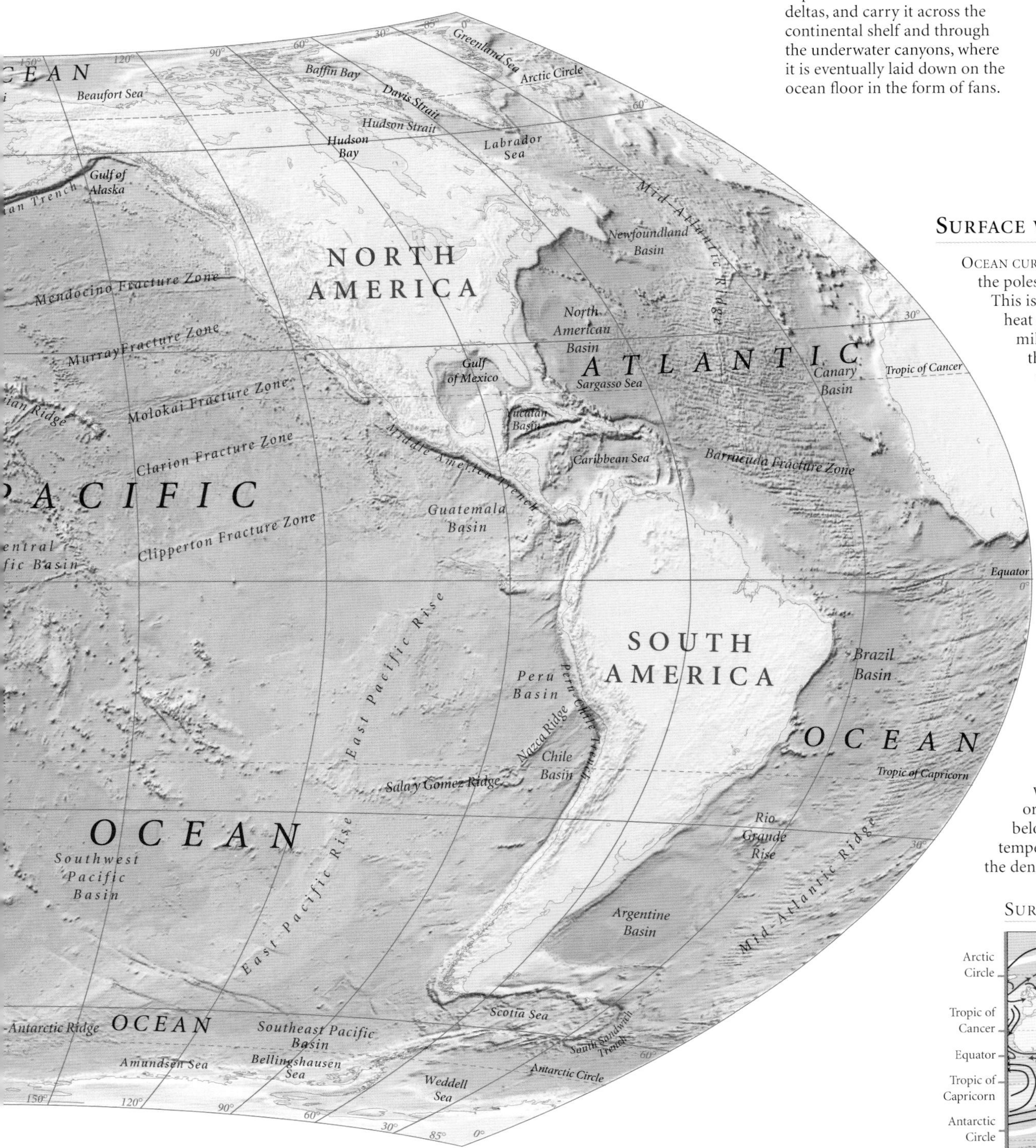

SURFACE WATER

OCEAN CURRENTS move warm water away from the Equator toward the poles, while cold water is, in turn, moved towards the Equator. This is the main way in which the Earth distributes surface heat and is a major climatic control. Approximately 4,000 million years ago, the Earth was dominated by oceans and there was no land to interrupt the flow of the currents, which would have flowed as straight lines, simply influenced by the Earth's rotation.

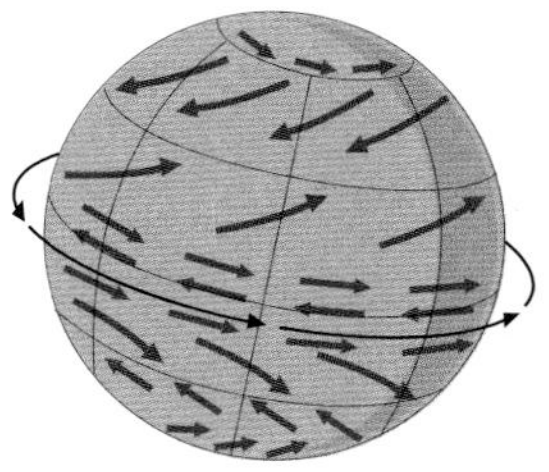

***Idealized globe** showing the movement of water around a landless Earth.*

OCEAN CURRENTS

SURFACE CURRENTS are driven by the prevailing winds and by the spinning motion of the Earth, which drives the currents into circulating whirlpools, or gyres. Deep sea currents, over 330 ft (100 m) below the surface, are driven by differences in water temperature and salinity, which have an impact on the density of deep water and on its movement.

SURFACE TEMPERATURE AND CURRENTS

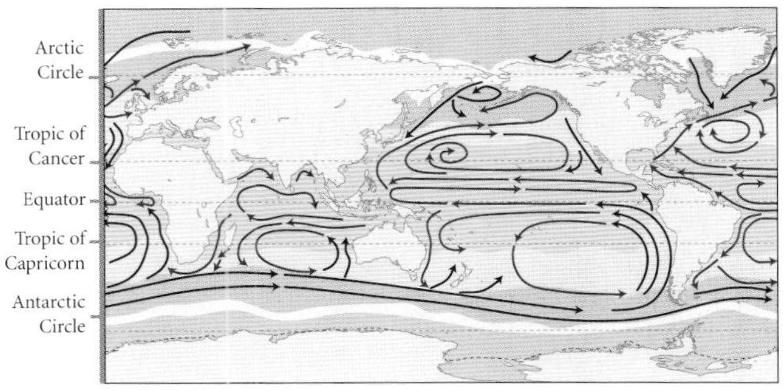

Surface temperature and currents

- Ice-shelf (below 32°F / 0°C)
- Sea-ice* (average) below 28°F / -2°C
- Sea-water 28–32°F / -2–0°C
- 32–50°F / 0–10°C
- 50–68°F / 10–20°C
- 68–86°F / 20–30°C
- warm current
- cold current

* Sea-water freezes at 28.4°F / -1.9°C

TIDES AND WAVES

TIDES ARE CREATED by the pull of the Sun and Moon's gravity on the surface of the oceans. The levels of high and low tides are influenced by the position of the Moon in relation to the Earth and Sun. Waves are formed by wind blowing over the surface of the water.

TIDAL RANGE AND WAVE ENVIRONMENTS

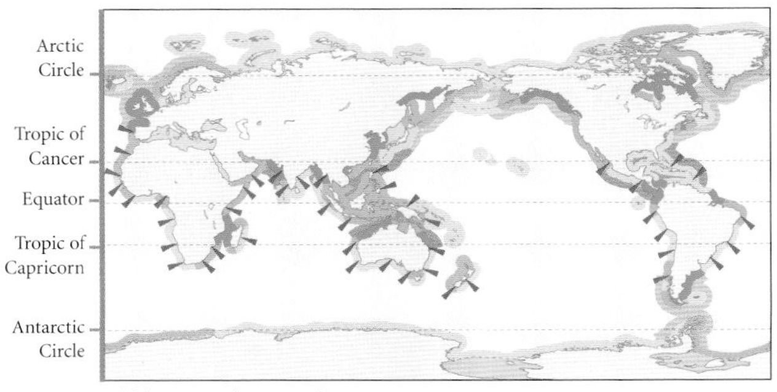

Tidal range and wave environments

- less than 7ft / 2m
- 7–13ft / 2–4m
- greater than 13ft / 4m
- east coast swell
- west coast swell
- tropical cyclone storm wave
- ice-shelf

HIGH AND LOW TIDES

The highest tides occur when the Earth, the Moon and the Sun are aligned *(below left)*. The lowest tides are experienced when the Sun and Moon align at right angles to one another *(below right)*.

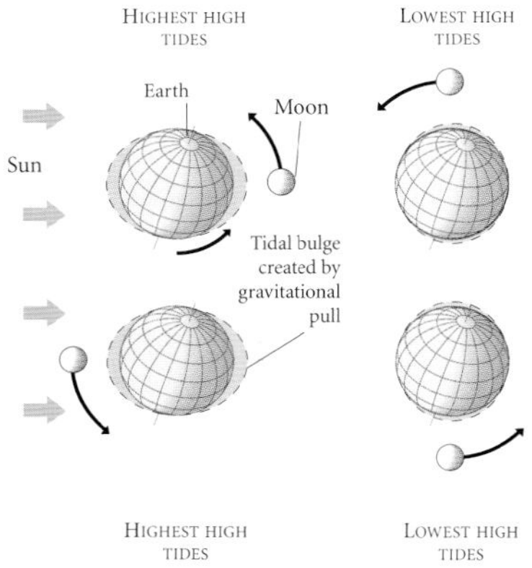

DEEP SEA TEMPERATURE AND CURRENTS

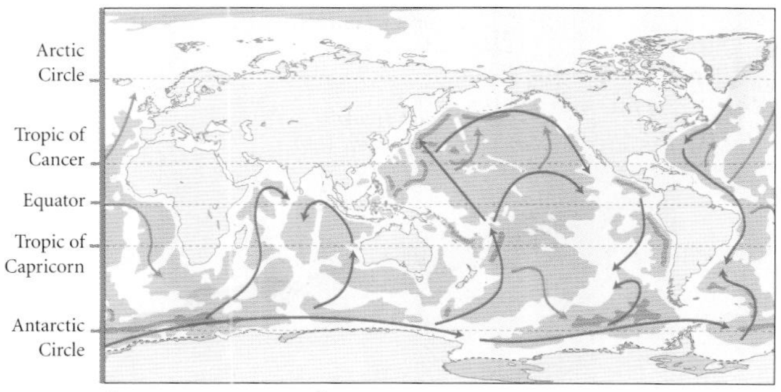

Deep sea temperature and currents

- Ice-shelf (below 32°F/ 0°C)
- Sea-water 28–32°F /-2–0°C (below 16,400ft/ 5000m)
- Sea-water 32–41° F/0–5°C (below 13,120ft/4000m)
- Primary currents
- Secondary currents

N O P Q R S T U V W X Y Z

THE GLOBAL CLIMATE

THE EARTH'S CLIMATIC TYPES CONSIST of stable patterns of weather conditions averaged out over a long period of time. Different climates are categorized according to particular combinations of temperature and humidity. By contrast, weather consists of short-term fluctuations in wind, temperature, and humidity conditions. Different climates are determined by latitude, altitude, the prevailing wind, and circulation of ocean currents. Longer-term changes in climate, such as global warming or the onset of ice ages, are punctuated by shorter-term events which comprise the day-to-day weather of a region, such as frontal depressions, hurricanes, and blizzards.

THE ATMOSPHERE, WIND, AND WEATHER

THE EARTH'S ATMOSPHERE has been compared to a giant ocean of air which surrounds the planet. Its circulation patterns are similar to the currents in the oceans and are influenced by three factors; the Earth's orbit around the Sun and rotation about its axis, and variations in the amount of heat radiation received from the Sun. If both heat and moisture were not redistributed between the Equator and the poles, large areas of the Earth would be uninhabitable.

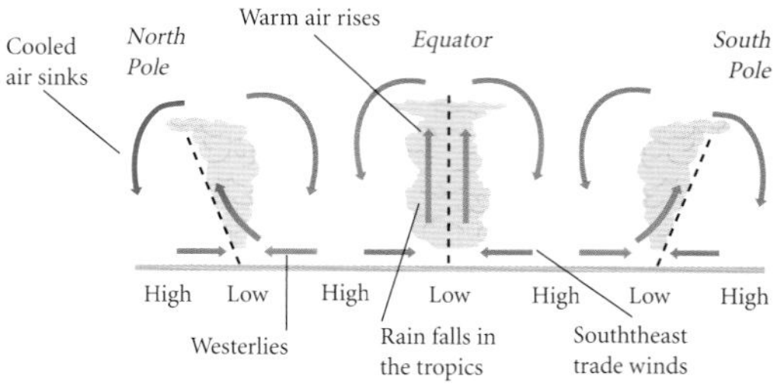

Heavy fogs, as here in southern England, form as moisture-laden air passes over cold ground.

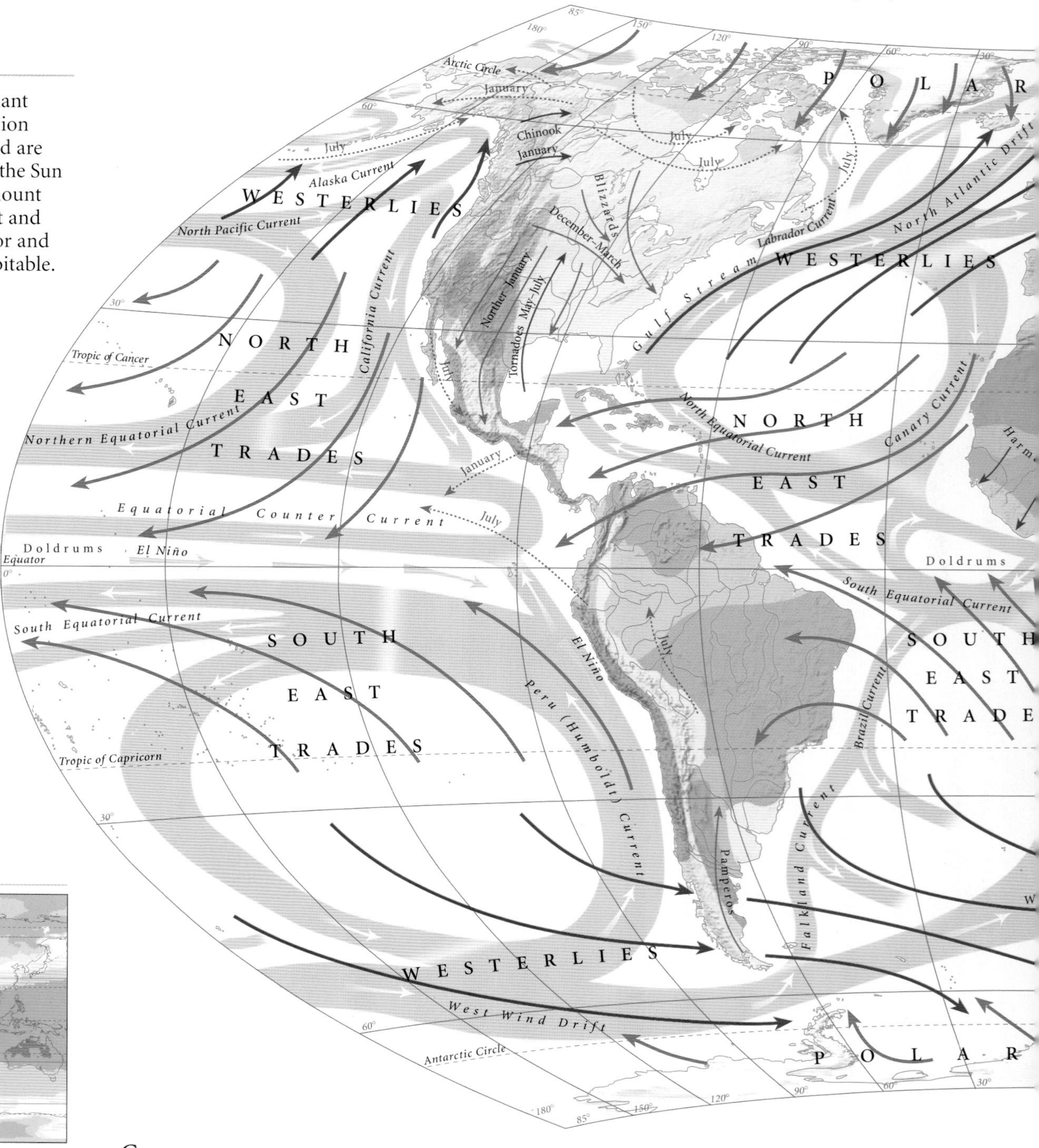

TEMPERATURE

THE WORLD CAN BE DIVIDED into three major climatic zones, stretching like large belts across the latitudes: the tropics which are warm; the cold polar regions and the temperate zones which lie between them. Temperatures across the Earth range from above 86°F (30°C) in the deserts to as low as -70°F (-55°C) at the poles. Temperature is also controlled by altitude; because air becomes cooler and less dense the higher it gets, mountainous regions are typically colder than those areas which are at, or close to, sea level.

AVERAGE JANUARY TEMPERATURES

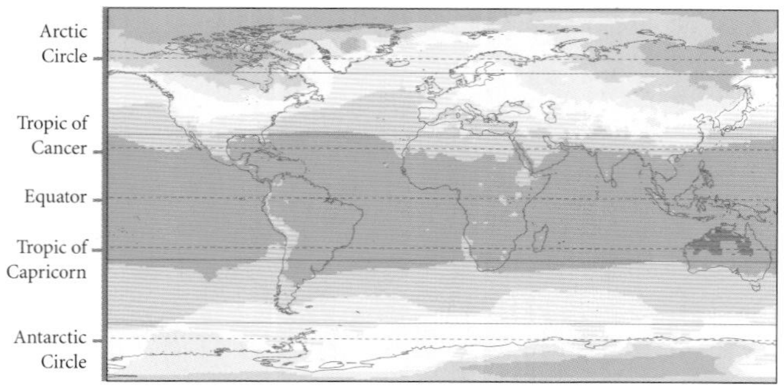

AVERAGE JULY TEMPERATURES

below - -22°F (30°C)	14 to 32°F (-10 to 0°C)	68 to 86°F (20 to 30°C)
-22 to -4°F (-30 to -20°C)	32 to 50°F (0 to 10°C)	86°F (above 30°C)
-4 to 14°F (-20 to - 10°C)	50 to 68°F (10 to 20°C)	

GLOBAL AIR CIRCULATION

AIR DOES NOT SIMPLY FLOW FROM THE EQUATOR TO THE POLES, it circulates in giant cells known as Hadley and Ferrel cells. As air warms it expands, becoming less dense and rising; this creates areas of low pressure. As the air rises it cools and condenses, causing heavy rainfall over the tropics and slight snowfall over the poles. This cool air then sinks, forming high pressure belts. At surface level in the tropics these sinking currents are deflected poleward as the westerlies and toward the Equator as the trade winds. At the poles they become the polar easterlies.

The Antarctic pack ice expands its area by almost seven times during the winter as temperatures drop and surrounding seas freeze.

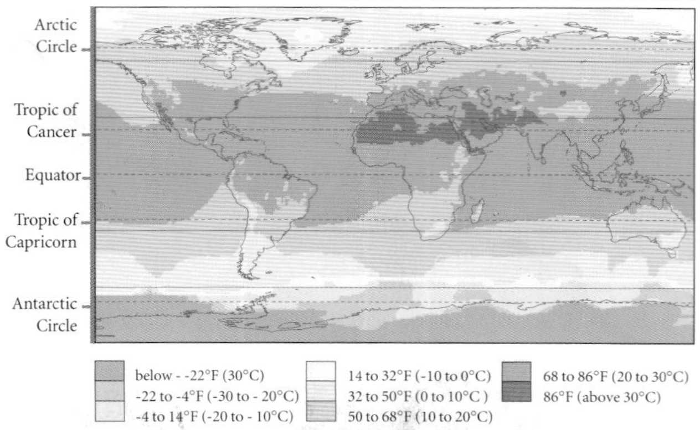

CLIMATIC CHANGE

THE EARTH IS CURRENTLY IN A WARM PHASE between ice ages. Warmer temperatures result in higher sea levels as more of the polar ice caps melt. Most of the world's population lives near coasts, so any changes which might cause sea levels to rise, could have a potentially disastrous impact.

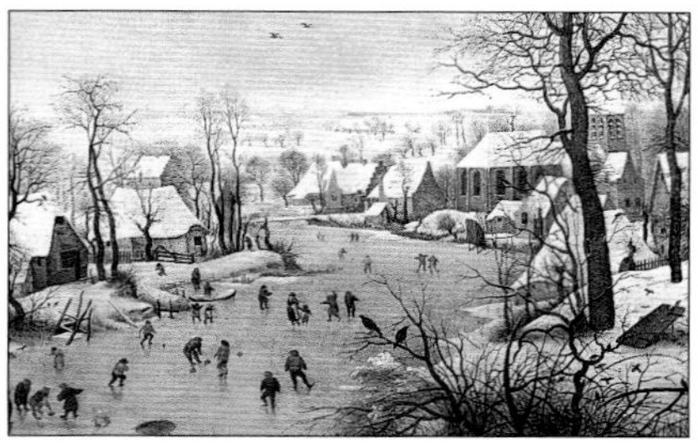

This ice fair, painted by Pieter Brueghel the Younger in the 17th century, shows the Little Ice Age which peaked around 300 years ago.

THE GREENHOUSE EFFECT

Gases such as carbon dioxide are known as "greenhouse gases" because they allow shortwave solar radiation to enter the Earth's atmosphere, but help to stop longwave radiation from escaping. This traps heat, raising the Earth's temperature. An excess of these gases, such as that which results from the burning of fossil fuels, helps trap more heat and can lead to global warming.

Incoming shortwave solar radiation

Deflected longwave radiation emitted by the Earth heats the atmosphere

Deflected shortwave solar radiation

Greenhouse gases prevent the escape of longwave radiation

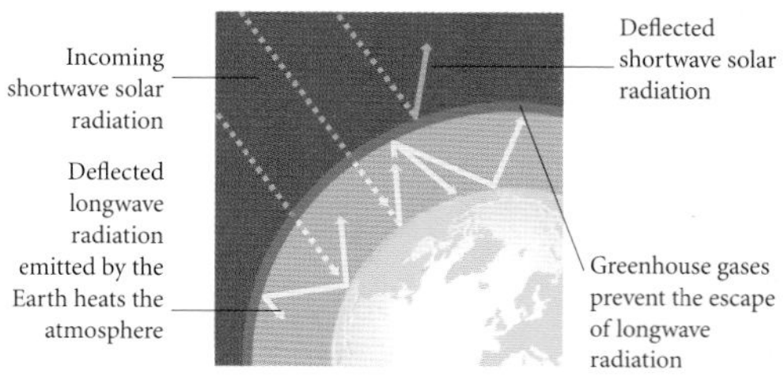

***The islands** of the Caribbean, Mexico's Gulf coast and the southeastern US are often hit by hurricanes formed far out in the Atlantic.*

OCEANIC WATER CIRCULATION

IN GENERAL, OCEAN CURRENTS parallel the movement of winds across the Earth's surface. Incoming solar energy is greatest at the Equator and least at the poles. So, water in the oceans heats up most at the Equator and flows poleward, cooling as it moves north or south toward the Arctic or Antarctic. The flow is eventually reversed and cold water currents move back toward the Equator. These ocean currents act as a vast system for moving heat from the Equator toward the poles and are a major influence on the distribution of the Earth's climates.

***In marginal climatic zones** years of drought can completely dry out the land and transform grassland to desert.*

TILT AND ROTATION

The tilt and rotation of the Earth during its annual orbit largely control the distribution of heat and moisture across its surface, which correspondingly controls its large-scale weather patterns. As the Earth annually rotates around the Sun, half its surface is receiving maximum radiation, creating summer and winter seasons. The angle of the Earth means that on average the tropics receive two and a half times as much heat from the Sun each day as the poles.

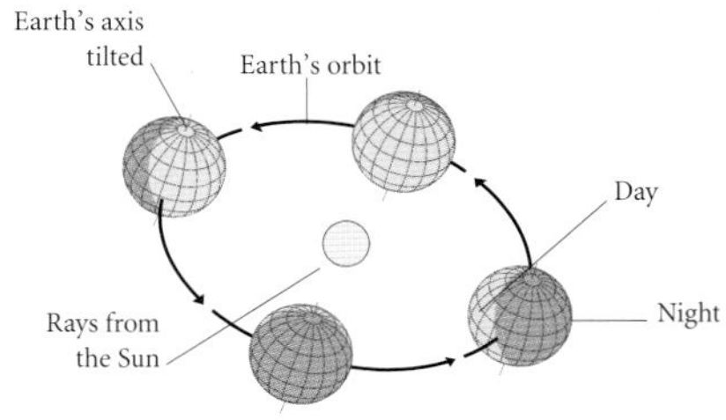

***The wide range** of environments found in the Andes is strongly related to their altitude, which modifies climatic influences. While the peaks are snow-capped, many protected interior valleys are semitropical.*

MAP KEY

Climate zones		Ocean currents	Prevailing winds	Local winds
ice cap	mediterranean	warm	warm	warm
subarctic	semiarid	cold	cold	cold
tundra	arid			seasonal*
continental	hot humid			
temperate	humid equatorial			
warm temperate	tropical			

* (seasonal winds which can either be warm or cold)

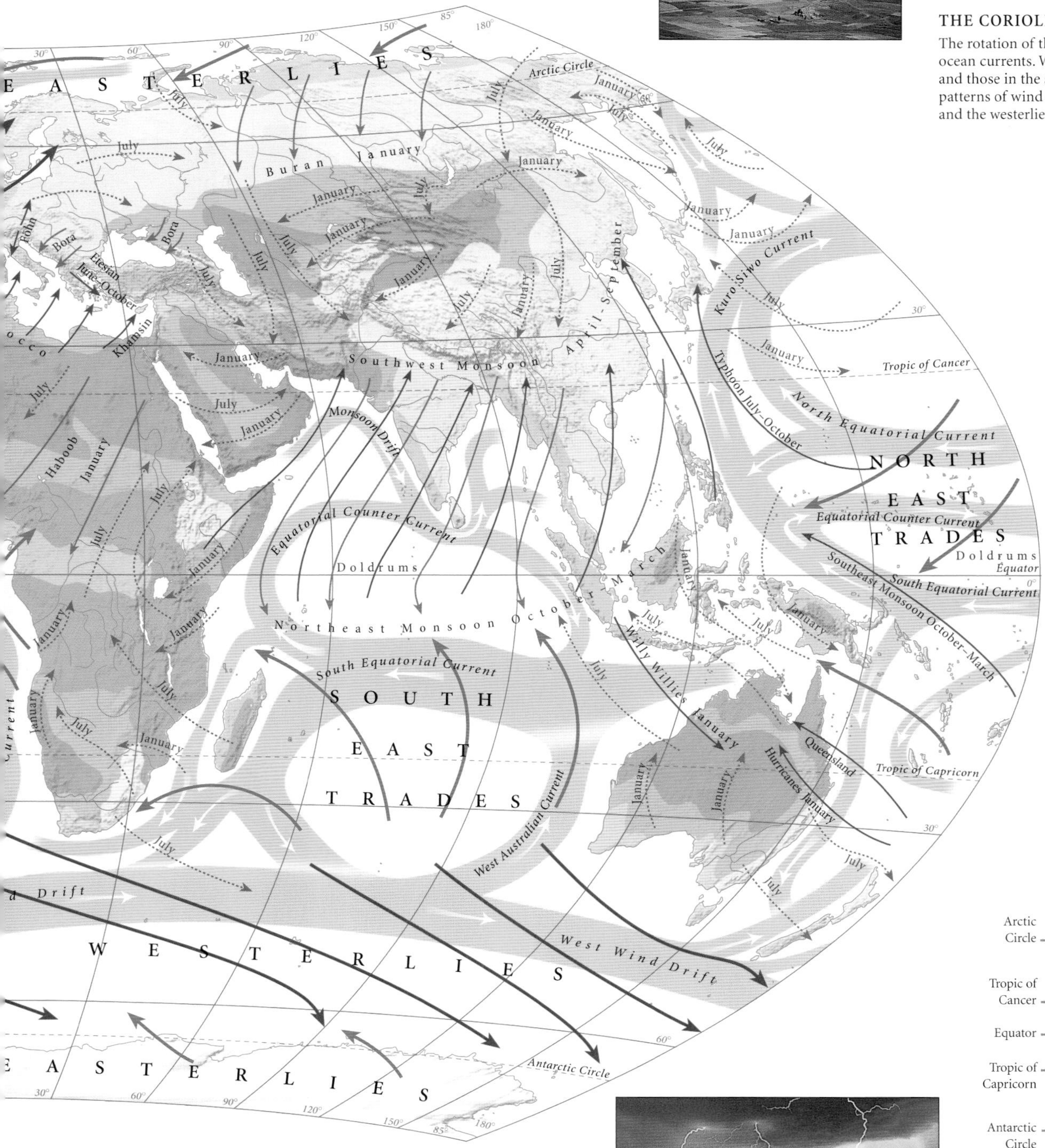

THE CORIOLIS EFFECT

The rotation of the Earth influences atmospheric circulation by deflecting winds and ocean currents. Winds blowing in the northern hemisphere are deflected to the right and those in the southern hemisphere are deflected to the left, creating large-scale patterns of wind circulation, such as the northeast and southeast trade winds and the westerlies. This effect is greatest at the poles and least at the Equator.

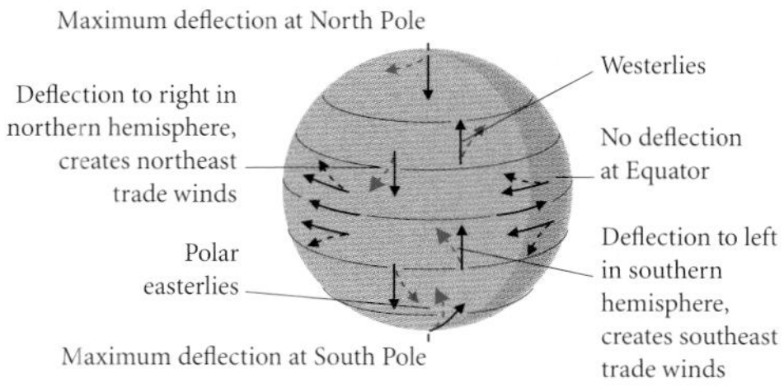

PRECIPITATION

WHEN WARM AIR EXPANDS, it rises and cools, and the water vapor it carries condenses to form clouds. Heavy, regular rainfall is characteristic of the equatorial region, while the poles are cold and receive only slight snowfall. Tropical regions have marked dry and rainy seasons, while in the temperate regions rainfall is relatively unpredictable.

***Monsoon rains**, which affect southern Asia from May to September, are caused by sea winds blowing across the warm land.*

***Heavy tropical rainstorms** occur frequently in Papua New Guinea, often causing soil erosion and landslides in cultivated areas.*

AVERAGE JANUARY RAINFALL

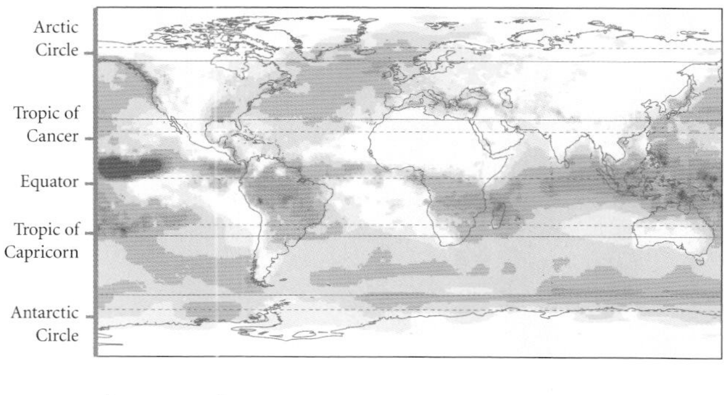

AVERAGE JULY RAINFALL

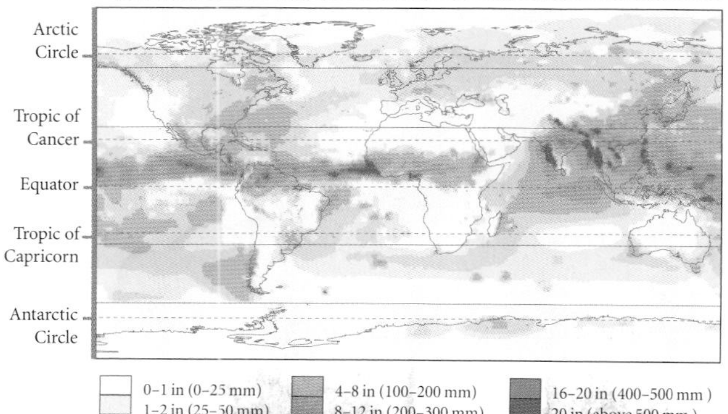

0–1 in (0–25 mm)
1–2 in (25–50 mm)
2–4 in (50–100 mm)
4–8 in (100–200 mm)
8–12 in (200–300 mm)
12–16 in (300–400 mm)
16–20 in (400–500 mm)
20 in (above 500 mm)

***The intensity of some blizzards** in Canada and the northern US can give rise to snowdrifts as high as 10 ft (3 m).*

***The Atacama Desert in Chile** is one of the driest places on Earth, with an average rainfall of less than 2 inches (50 mm) per year.*

***Violent thunderstorms** occur along advancing cold fronts, when cold, dry air masses meet warm, moist air, which rises rapidly, its moisture condensing into thunderclouds. Rain and hail become electrically charged, causing lightning.*

THE RAINSHADOW EFFECT

When moist air is forced to rise by mountains, it cools and the water vapor falls as precipitation, either as rain or snow. Only the dry, cold air continues over the mountains, leaving inland areas with little or no rain. This is called the rainshadow effect and is one reason for the existence of the Mojave Desert in California, which lies east of the Coast Ranges.

THE RAINSHADOW EFFECT

Life on Earth

A unique combination of an oxygen-rich atmosphere and plentiful water is the key to life on Earth. Apart from the polar ice caps, there are few areas which have not been colonized by animals or plants over the course of the Earth's history. Plants process sunlight to provide them with their energy, and ultimately all the Earth's animals rely on plants for survival. Because of this reliance, plants are known as primary producers, and the availability of nutrients and temperature of an area is defined as its primary productivity, which affects the quantity and type of animals which are able to live there. This index is affected by climatic factors – cold and aridity restrict the quantity of life, whereas warmth and regular rainfall allow a greater diversity of species.

Biogeographical Regions

The Earth can be divided into a series of biogeographical regions, or biomes, ecological communities where certain species of plant and animal coexist within particular climatic conditions. Within these broad classifications, other factors including soil richness, altitude, and human activities such as urbanization, intensive agriculture, and deforestation, affect the local distribution of living species within each biome.

POLAR REGIONS

A layer of permanent ice at the Earth's poles covers both seas and land. Very little plant and animal life can exist in these harsh regions.

TUNDRA

A desolate region, with long, dark freezing winters and short, cold summers. With virtually no soil and large areas of permanently frozen ground known as permafrost, the tundra is largely treeless, though it is briefly clothed by small flowering plants in the summer months.

NEEDLELEAF FORESTS

With milder summers than the tundra and less wind, these areas are able to support large forests of coniferous trees.

BROADLEAF FORESTS

Much of the northern hemisphere was once covered by deciduous forests, which occurred in areas with marked seasonal variations. Most deciduous forests have been cleared for human settlement.

TEMPERATE RAIN FORESTS

In warmer wetter areas, such as southern China, temperate deciduous forests are replaced by evergreen forest.

DESERTS

Deserts are areas with negligible rainfall. Most hot deserts lie within the tropics; cold deserts are dry because of their distance from the moisture-providing sea.

MEDITERRANEAN

Hot, dry summers and short winters typify these areas, which were once covered by evergreen shrubs and woodland, but have now been cleared by humans for agriculture.

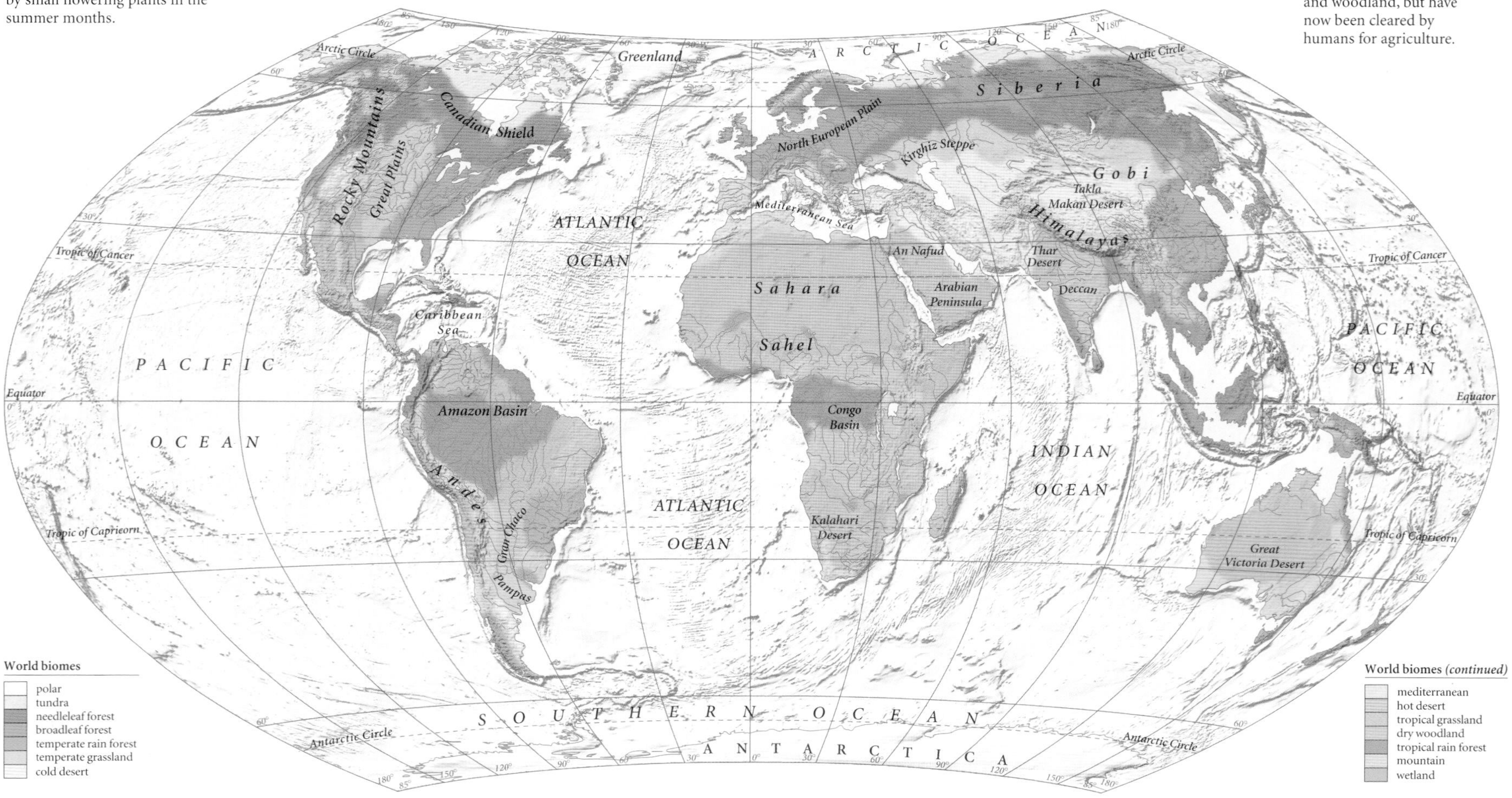

TROPICAL AND TEMPERATE GRASSLANDS

The major grassland areas are found in the centers of the larger continental landmasses. In Africa's tropical savannah regions, seasonal rainfall alternates with drought. Temperate grasslands, also known as *steppes* and *prairies* are found in the northern hemisphere, and in South America, where they are known as the *pampas*.

DRY WOODLANDS

Trees and shrubs, adapted to dry conditions, grow widely spaced from one another, interspersed by savannah grasslands.

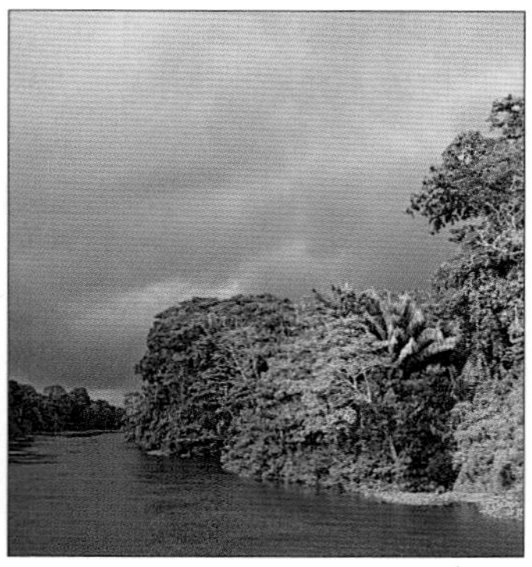

TROPICAL RAIN FORESTS

Characterized by year-round warmth and high rainfall, tropical rain forests contain the highest diversity of plant and animal species on Earth.

MOUNTAINS

Though the lower slopes of mountains may be thickly forested, only ground-hugging shrubs and other vegetation will grow above the tree line which varies according to both altitude and latitude.

WETLANDS

Rarely lying above sea level, wetlands are marshes, swamps and tidal flats. Some, with their moist, fertile soils, are rich feeding grounds for fish and breeding grounds for birds. Others have little soil structure and are too acidic to support much plant and animal life.

Biodiversity

The number of plant and animal species, and the range of genetic diversity within the populations of each species, make up the Earth's biodiversity. The plants and animals which are endemic to a region – that is, those which are found nowhere else in the world – are also important in determining levels of biodiversity. Human settlement and intervention have encroached on many areas of the world once rich in endemic plant and animal species. Increasing international efforts are being made to monitor and conserve the biodiversity of the Earth's remaining wild places.

Animal adaptation

The degree of an animal's adaptability to different climates and conditions is extremely important in ensuring its success as a species. Many animals, particularly the largest mammals, are becoming restricted to ever-smaller regions as human development and modern agricultural practices reduce their natural habitats. In contrast, humans have been responsible – both deliberately and accidentally – for the spread of some of the world's most successful species. Many of these introduced species are now more numerous than the indigenous animal populations.

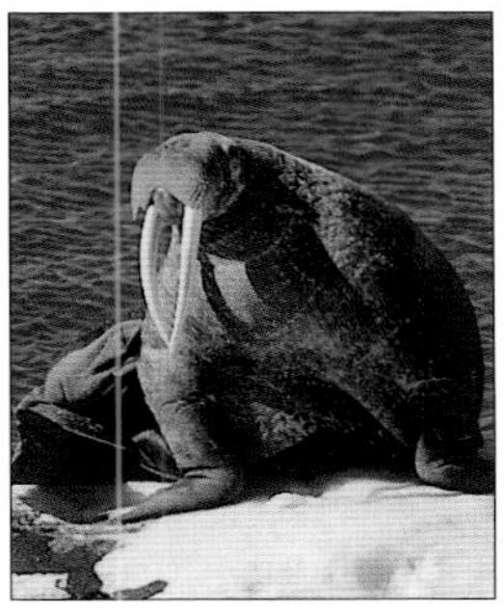

POLAR ANIMALS

The frozen wastes of the polar regions are able to support only a small range of species which derive their nutritional requirements from the sea. Animals such as the walrus *(left)* have developed insulating fat, stocky limbs, and double-layered coats to enable them to survive in the freezing conditions.

DESERT ANIMALS

Many animals which live in the extreme heat and aridity of the deserts are able to survive for days and even months with very little food or water. Their bodies are adapted to lose heat quickly and to store fat and water. The Gila monster *(above)* stores fat in its tail.

AMAZON RAINFOREST

The vast Amazon Basin is home to the world's greatest variety of animal species. Animals are adapted to live at many different levels from the treetops to the tangled undergrowth which lies beneath the canopy. The sloth *(below)* hangs upside down in the branches. Its fur grows from its stomach to its back to enable water to run off quickly.

Diversity of animal species

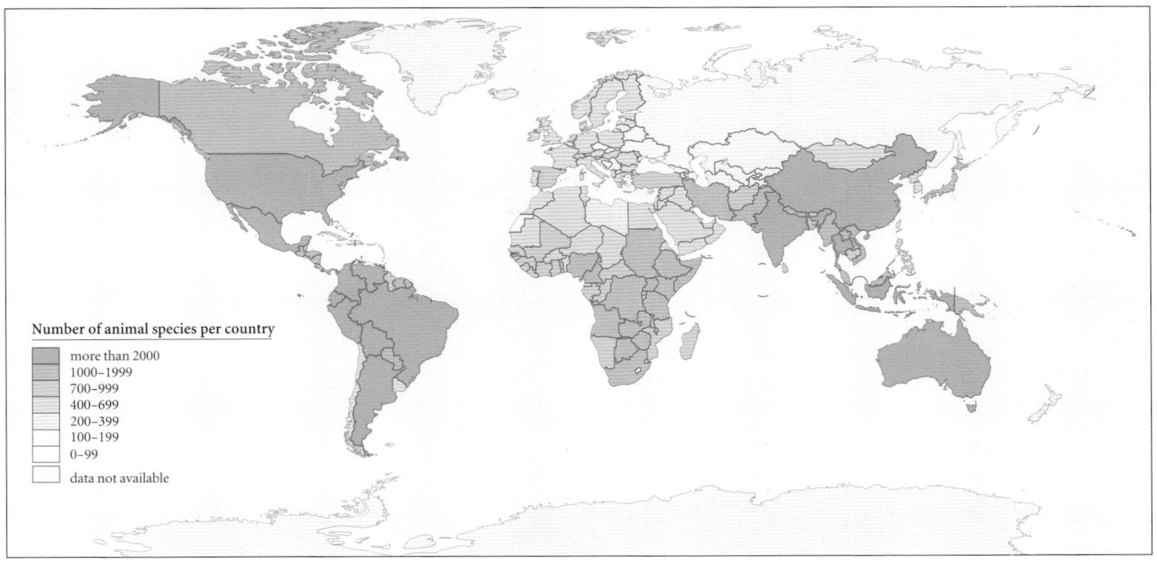

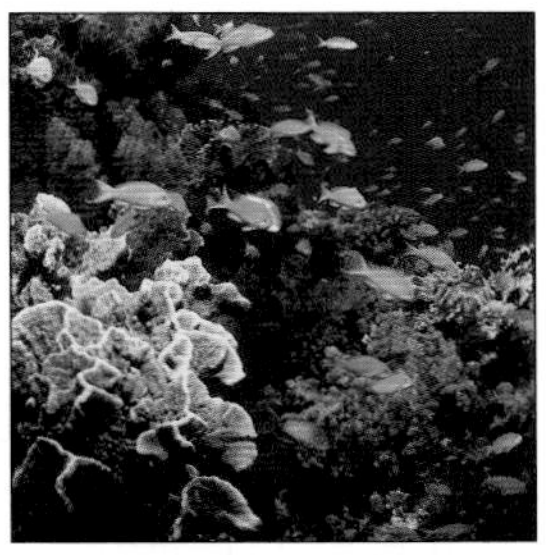

MARINE BIODIVERSITY

The oceans support a huge variety of different species, from the world's largest mammals like whales and dolphins down to the tiniest plankton. The greatest diversities occur in the warmer seas of continental shelves, where plants are easily able to photosynthesize, and around coral reefs, where complex ecosystems are found. On the ocean floor, nematodes can exist at a depth of more than 10,000 ft (3,000 m) below sea level.

HIGH ALTITUDES

Few animals exist in the rarefied atmosphere of the highest mountains. However, birds of prey such as eagles and vultures *(above)*, with their superb eyesight can soar as high as 23,000 ft (7,000 m) to scan for prey below.

URBAN ANIMALS

The growth of cities has reduced the amount of habitat available to many species. A number of animals are now moving closer into urban areas to scavenge from the detritus of the modern city *(left)*. Rodents, particularly rats and mice, have existed in cities for thousands of years, and many insects, especially moths, quickly develop new coloring to provide them with camouflage.

ENDEMIC SPECIES

Isolated areas such as Australia and the island of Madagascar, have the greatest range of endemic species. In Australia, these include marsupials such as the kangaroo *(below)*, which carry their young in pouches on their bodies. Destruction of habitat, pollution, hunting, and predators introduced by humans, are threatening this unique biodiversity.

Plant adaptation

Environmental conditions, particularly climate, soil type, and the extent of competition with other organisms, influence the development of plants into a number of distinctive forms. Similar conditions in quite different parts of the world create similar adaptations in the plants, which may then be modified by other, local, factors specific to the region.

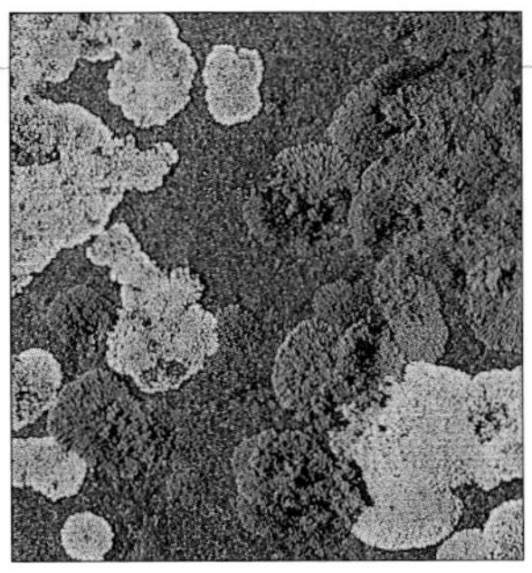

COLD CONDITIONS

In areas where temperatures rarely rise above freezing, plants such as lichens *(left)* and mosses grow densely, close to the ground.

RAIN FORESTS

Most of the world's largest and oldest plants are found in rain forests; warmth and heavy rainfall provide ideal conditions for vast plants like the world's largest flower, the rafflesia *(left)*.

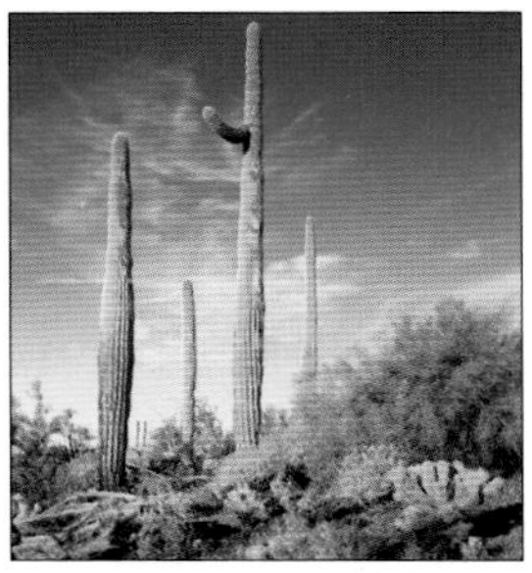

HOT, DRY CONDITIONS

Arid conditions lead to the development of plants whose surface area has been reduced to a minimum to reduce water loss. In cacti *(above)*, which can survive without water for months, leaves are minimal or not present at all.

ANCIENT PLANTS

Some of the world's most primitive plants still exist today, including algae, cycads, and many ferns *(above)*, reflecting the success with which they have adapted to changing conditions.

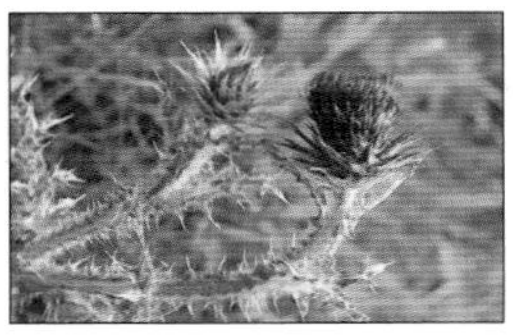

RESISTING PREDATORS

A great variety of plants have developed devices including spines *(above)*, poisons, stinging hairs, and an unpleasant taste or smell to deter animal predators.

Diversity of plant species

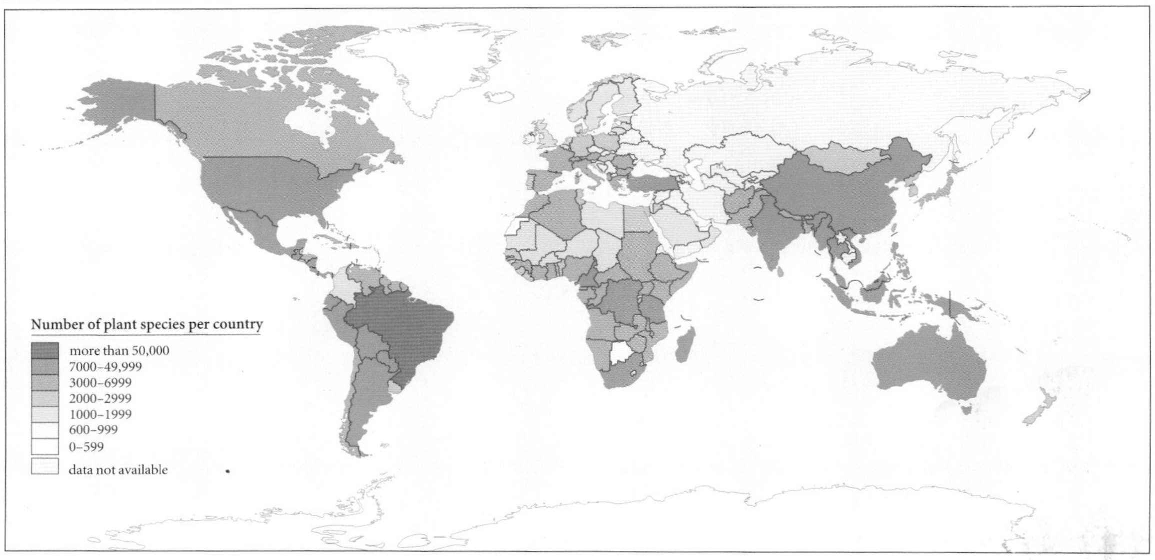

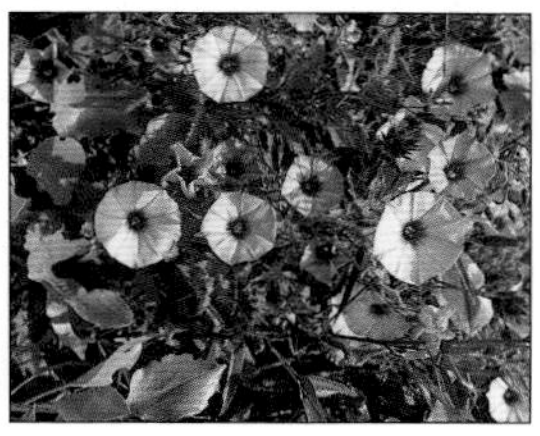

WEEDS

Weeds such as bindweed *(above)* are fast-growing, easily dispersed, and tolerant of a number of different environments, enabling them to quickly colonize suitable habitats. They are among the most adaptable of all plants.

POPULATION AND SETTLEMENT

THE EARTH'S POPULATION IS PROJECTED to rise from its current level of about 5.5 billion to reach some 10 billion by 2025. The global distribution of this rapidly growing population is very uneven, and is dictated by climate, terrain, and natural and economic resources. The great majority of the Earth's people live in coastal zones, and along river valleys. Deserts cover over 20% of the Earth's surface, but support less than 5% of the world's population. It is estimated that over half of the world's population live in cities – most of them in Asia – as a result of mass migration from rural areas in search of jobs. Many of these people live in the so-called "megacities," some with populations as great as 40 million.

PATTERNS OF SETTLEMENT

THE PAST 200 YEARS have seen the most radical shift in world population patterns in recorded history.

NOMADIC LIFE

ALL THE WORLD'S PEOPLES were hunter-gatherers 10,000 years ago. Today nomads, who live by following available food resources, account for less than 0.0001% of the world's population. They are mainly pastoral herders, moving their livestock from place to place in search of grazing land.

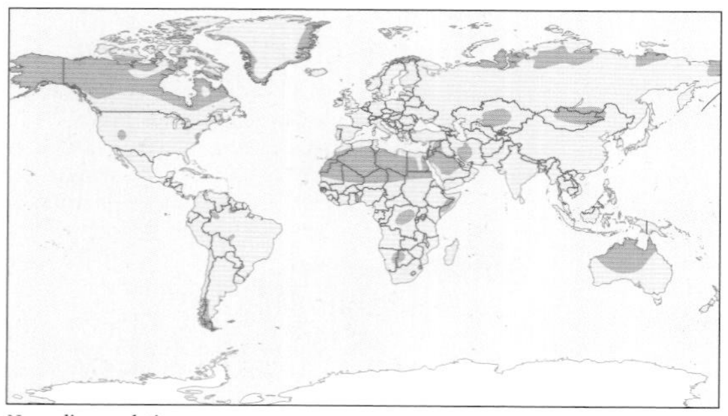

Nomadic population

▨ Nomadic population area

THE GROWTH OF CITIES

IN 1900 there were only 14 cities in the world with populations of more than a million, mostly in the northern hemisphere. Today, as more and more people in the developing world migrate to towns and cities, there are 29 cities whose population exceeds 5 million, and around 200 "million-cities."

MILLION-CITIES IN 1900

Million-cities in 1900

• Cities over 1 million population

MILLION-CITIES IN 1995

Million-cities in 1995

• Cities over 1 million population

NORTH AMERICA

THE EASTERN AND WESTERN SEABOARDS of the US, with huge expanses of interconnected cities, towns, and suburbs, are vast, densely-populated megalopolises. Central America and the Caribbean also have high population densities. Yet, away from the coasts and in the wildernesses of northern Canada the land is very sparsely settled.

Vancouver on Canada's west coast, grew up as a port city. In recent years it has attracted many Asian immigrants, particularly from the Pacific Rim.

North America's central plains, the continent's agricultural heartland, are thinly populated and highly productive.

EUROPE

WITH ITS TEMPERATE CLIMATE, and rich mineral and natural resources, Europe is generally very densely settled. The continent acts as a magnet for economic migrants from the developing world, and immigration is now widely restricted. Birthrates in Europe are generally low, and in some countries, such as Germany, the populations have stabilized at zero growth, with a fast-growing elderly population.

Many European cities, like Siena, once reflected the "ideal" size for human settlements. Modern technological advances have enabled them to grow far beyond the original walls.

Within the densely-populated Netherlands the reclamation of coastal wetlands is vital to provide much-needed land for agriculture and settlement.

Population density (inhabitants per sq mile)

- More than 520
- 260–519
- 130–259
- 55–129
- 28–54
- 15–27
- 1–15
- Less than 1

NORTH AMERICA

Population 9% World land area 17%

EUROPE

Population 14% World land area 7.1%

AFRICA

Population 12% World land area 20.2%

SOUTH AMERICA

Population 5.5% World land area 11.8%

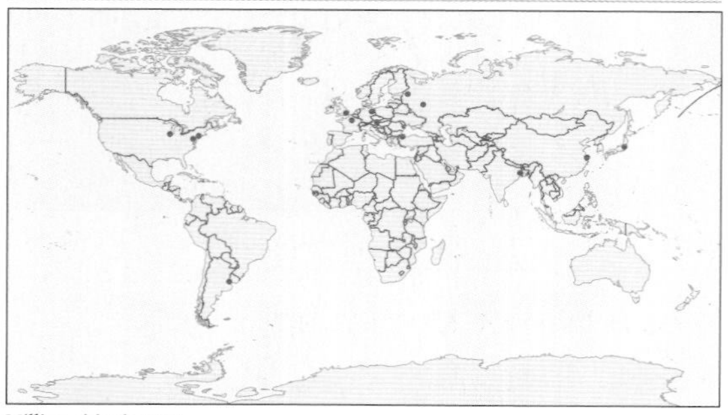

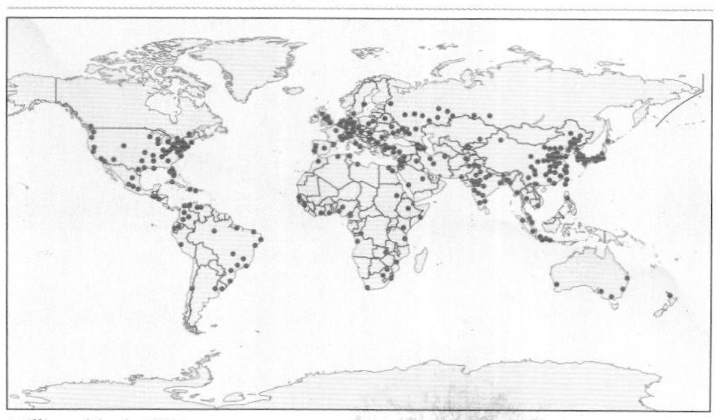

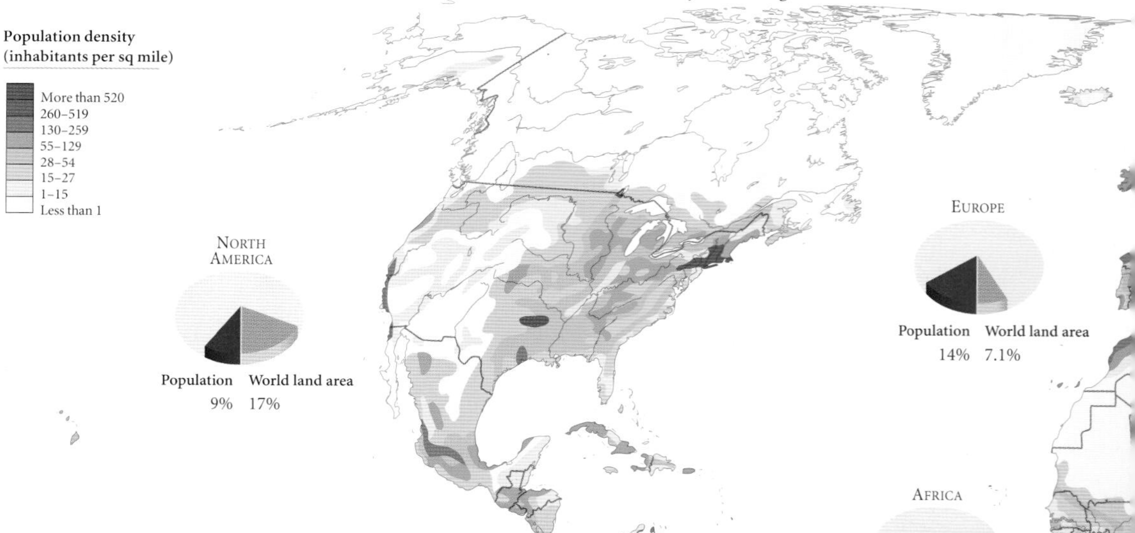

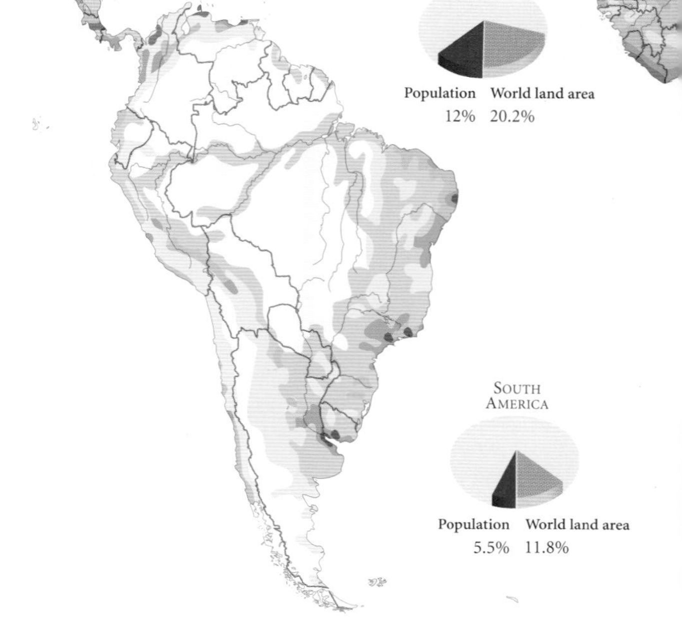

SOUTH AMERICA

MOST SETTLEMENT IN SOUTH AMERICA is clustered in a narrow belt in coastal zones and in the northern Andes. During the 20th century, cities such as São Paulo and Buenos Aires grew enormously, acting as powerful economic magnets to the rural population. Shantytowns have grown up on the outskirts of many major cities to house these immigrants, often lacking basic amenities.

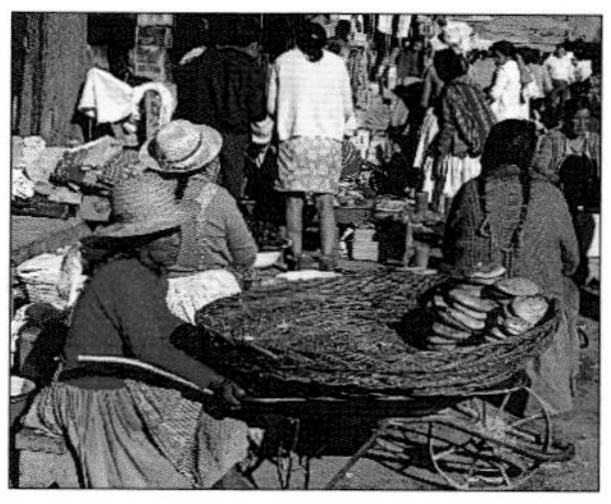

Many people in western South America live at high altitudes in the Andes, both in cities and in villages such as this one in Bolivia.

Venezuela is the most highly urbanized country in South America, with more than 90% of the population living in cities such as Caracas.

AFRICA

THE ARID CLIMATE of much of Africa means that settlement of the continent is sparse, focusing in coastal areas and fertile regions such as the Nile Valley. Africa still has a high proportion of nomadic agriculturalists, although many are now becoming settled, and the population is predominantly rural.

Cities such as Nairobi (above), Cairo and Johannesburg have grown rapidly in recent years, although only Cairo has a significant population on a global scale.

Traditional lifestyles and homes persist across much of Africa, which has a higher proportion of rural or village-based population than any other continent.

ASIA

MOST ASIAN SETTLEMENT originally centered around the great river valleys such as the Indus, the Ganges, and the Yangtze. Today, almost 60% of the world's population lives in Asia, many in burgeoning cities – particularly in the economically-buoyant Pacific Rim countries. Even rural population densities are high in many countries; practices such as terracing in Southeast Asia making the most of the available land.

Many of China's cities are now vast urban areas with populations of more than 5 million people.

This stilt village in Bangladesh is built to resist the regular flooding. Pressure on land, even in rural areas, forces many people to live in marginal areas.

POPULATION STRUCTURES

POPULATION PYRAMIDS are an effective means of showing the age structures of different countries, and highlighting changing trends in population growth and decline. The typical pyramid for a country with a growing, youthful population, is broad-based *(left)*, reflecting a high birthrate and a far larger number of young rather than elderly people. In contrast, countries with populations whose numbers are stabilizing have a more balanced distribution of people in each age band, and may even have lower numbers of people in the youngest age ranges, indicating both a high life expectancy, and that the population is now barely replacing itself *(right)*. The Russian Federation *(center)* still bears the scars of World War II, reflected in the dramatically lower numbers of men than women in the 60–80+ age range.

YOUTHFUL POPULATION
(INDIA)
MALES / FEMALES
Population in millions

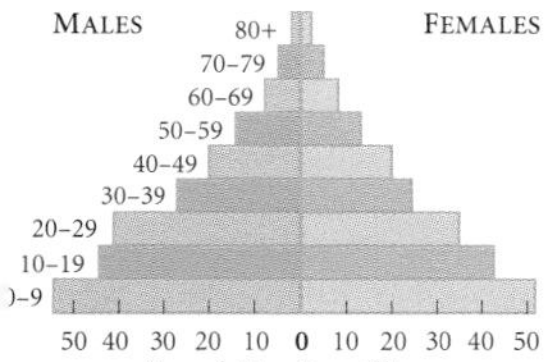

DISTORTED POPULATION
(RUSSIAN FEDERATION)
MALES / FEMALES
Population in millions

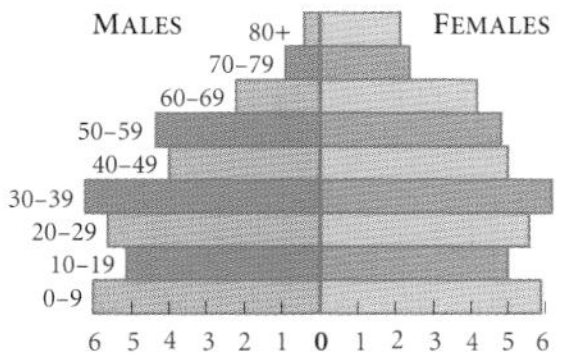

AGING POPULATION
(UNITED STATES OF AMERICA)
MALES / FEMALES
Population in millions

ASIA
Population World land area
59% 29.1%

AUSTRALASIA & OCEANIA
Population World land area
0.5% 5.9%

ANTARCTICA
Population World land area
0% 8.9%

AUSTRALASIA & OCEANIA

THIS IS THE WORLD's most sparsely settled region. The peoples of Australia and New Zealand live mainly in the coastal cities, with only scattered settlements in the arid interior. The Pacific islands can only support limited populations because of their remoteness and lack of resources.

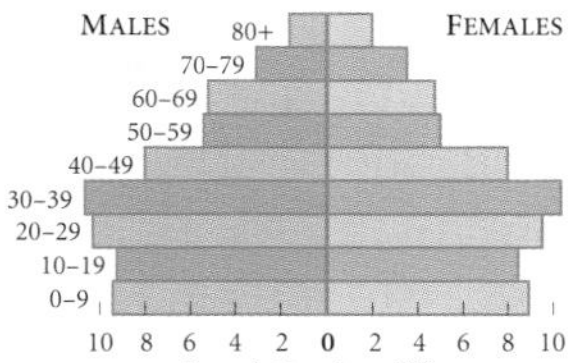

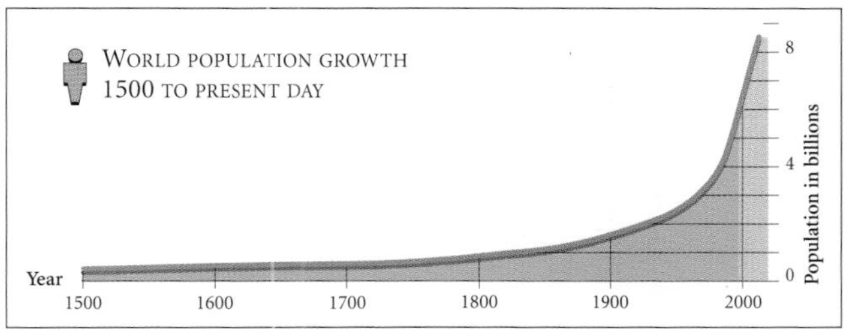

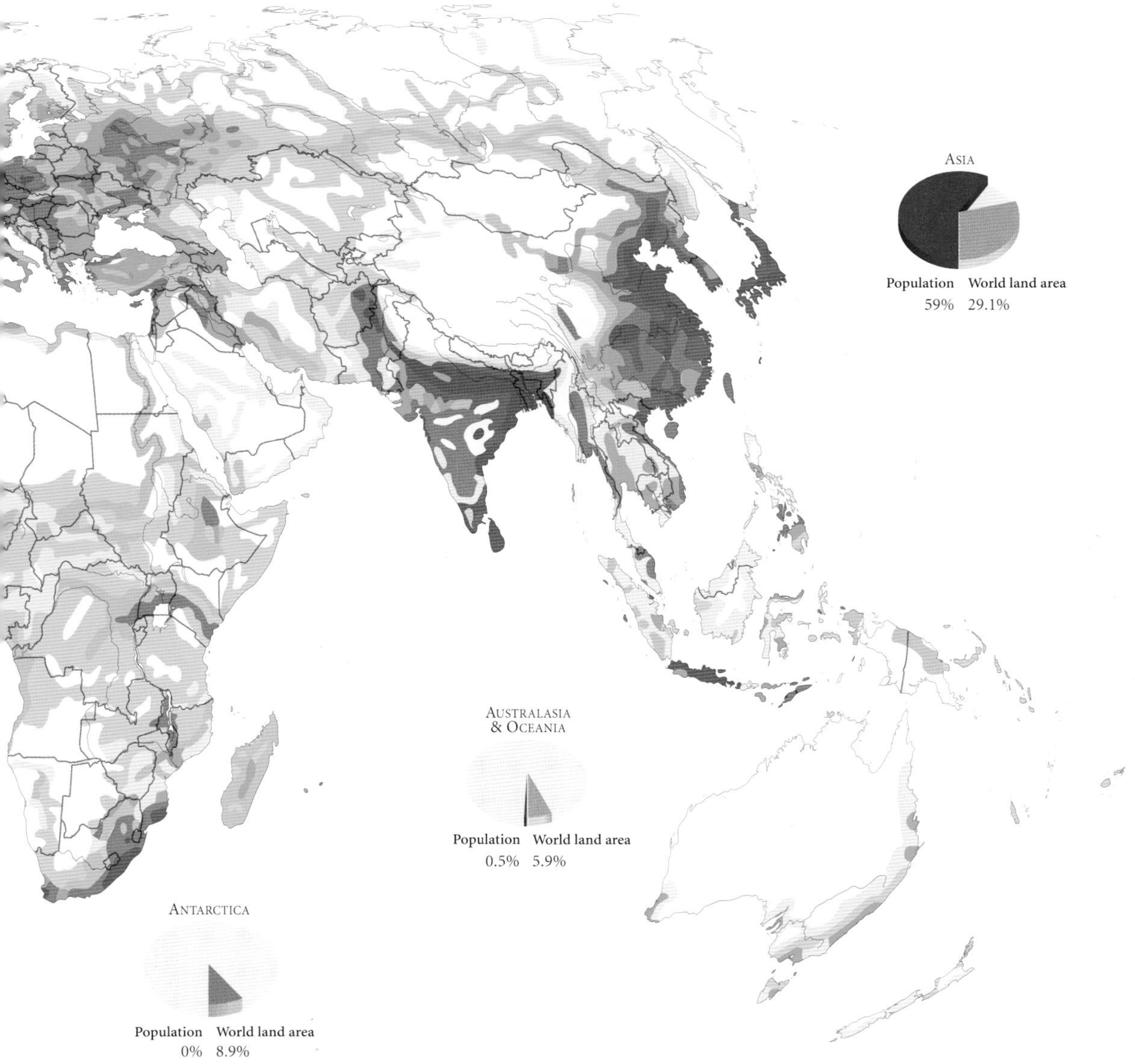

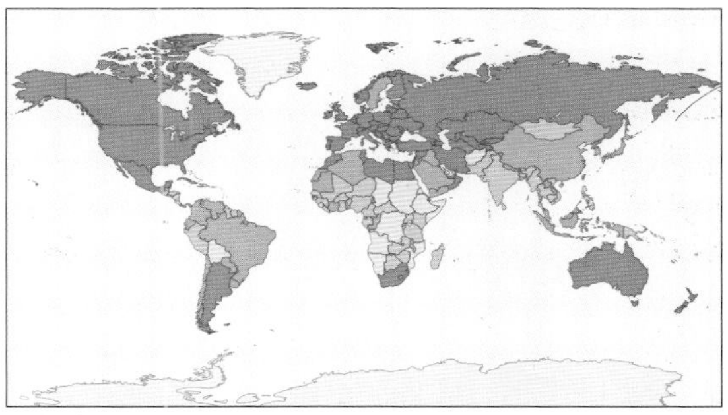

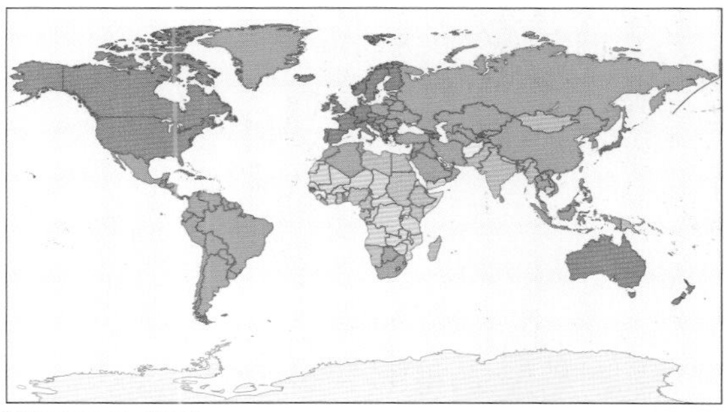

Brisbane, on Australia's Gold Coast is the most rapidly expanding city in the country. The great majority of Australia's population lives in cities near the coasts.

The remote highlands of Papua New Guinea are home to a wide variety of peoples, many of whom still subsist by traditional hunting and gathering.

AVERAGE WORLD BIRTHRATES

BIRTHRATES ARE MUCH HIGHER in Africa, Asia, and South America than in Europe and North America. Increased affluence and easy access to contraception are both factors which can lead to a significant decline in a country's birthrate.

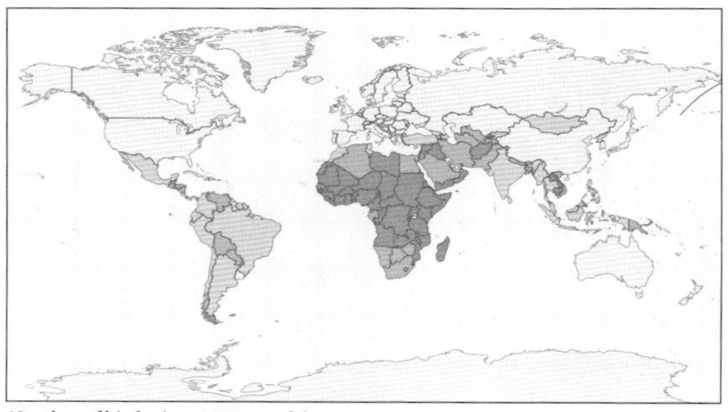

Number of births (per 1,000 people)
- above 40
- 30–39
- 20–29
- below 20
- data not available

POPULATION GROWTH

IMPROVEMENTS IN FOOD SUPPLY and advances in medicine have both played a major role in the remarkable growth in global population, which has increased five-fold over the last 150 years. Food supplies have risen with the mechanization of agriculture and improvements in crop yields. Better nutrition, together with higher standards of public health and sanitation, have led to increased longevity and higher birthrates.

WORLD POPULATION GROWTH
1500 TO PRESENT DAY
Year 1500 1600 1700 1800 1900 2000
Population in billions

WORLD NUTRITION

TWO-THIRDS OF THE WORLD's food supply is consumed by the industrialized nations, many of which have a daily calorific intake far higher than is necessary for their populations to maintain a healthy body weight. In contrast, in the developing world, about 800 million people do not have enough food to meet their basic nutritional needs.

Daily calorie intake per capita
- above 3,000
- 2,500–2,999
- 2,000–2,499
- below 2,000
- data not available

WORLD LIFE EXPECTANCY

IMPROVED PUBLIC HEALTH and living standards have greatly increased life expectancy in the developed world, where people can now expect to live twice as long as they did 100 years ago. In many of the world's poorest nations, inadequate nutrition and disease, means that the average life expectancy still does not exceed 45 years.

Life expectancy at birth
- above 75 years
- 65–74 years
- 55–64 years
- 45–54 years
- below 44 years
- data not available

WORLD INFANT MORTALITY

IN PARTS OF THE DEVELOPING WORLD infant mortality rates are still high; access to medical services such as immunization, adequate nutrition, and the promotion of breast-feeding have been important in combating infant mortality.

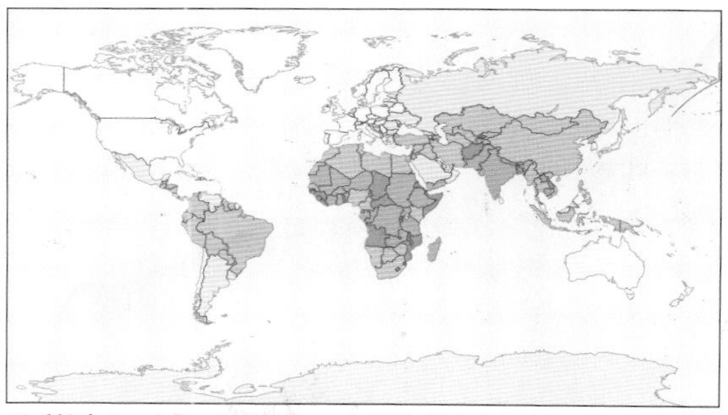

World infant mortality rates (deaths per 1,000 live births)
- above 125
- 75–124
- 35–74
- 15–43
- below 15
- data not available

The Economic System

THE WEALTHY COUNTRIES OF THE DEVELOPED WORLD, with their aggressive, market-led economies and their access to productive new technologies and international markets, dominate the world economic system. At the other extreme, many of the countries of the developing world are locked in a cycle of national debt, rising populations, and unemployment. The state-managed economies of the former communist bloc began to be dismantled during the 1990s, and China is emerging as a major economic power following decades of isolation.

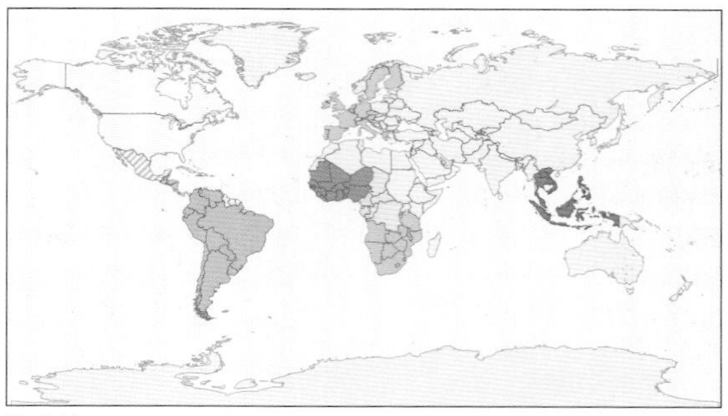

Trade blocs

EU / CACM — NAFTA / SADC — ASEAN / ECOWAS — LAIA / CEEAC

Trade Blocs

INTERNATIONAL TRADE BLOCS are formed when groups of countries, often already enjoying close military and political ties, join together to offer mutually preferential terms of trade for both imports and exports. Increasingly, global trade is dominated by three main blocs: the EU, NAFTA, and ASEAN. They are supplanting older trade blocs such as the Commonwealth, a legacy of colonialism.

International Trade Flows

WORLD TRADE acts as a stimulus to national economies, encouraging growth. Over the last three decades, as heavy industries have declined, services – banking, insurance, tourism, airlines, and shipping – have taken an increasingly large share of world trade. Manufactured articles now account for nearly two-thirds of world trade; raw materials and food make up less than a quarter of the total.

SHIPPING
Ships carry 80% of international cargo, and extensive container ports, where cargo is stored, are vital links in the international transportation network.

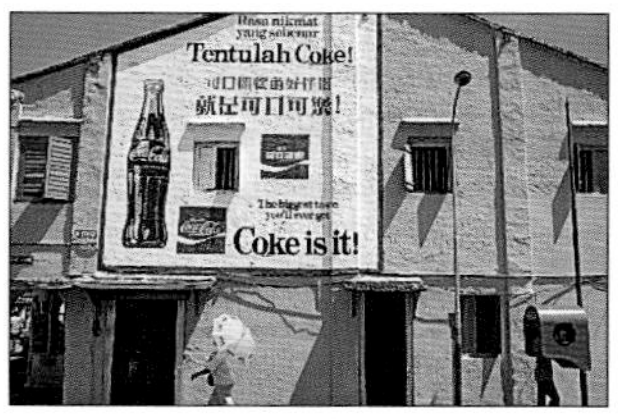

MULTINATIONALS
Multinational companies are increasingly penetrating inaccessible markets. The reach of many American commodities is now global.

PRIMARY PRODUCTS
Many countries, particularly in the Caribbean and Africa, are still reliant on primary products such as rubber and coffee, which makes them vulnerable to fluctuating prices.

SERVICE INDUSTRIES
Service industries such as banking, tourism and insurance were the fastest-growing industrial sector in the last half of the 20th century. Lloyds of London is the center of the world insurance market.

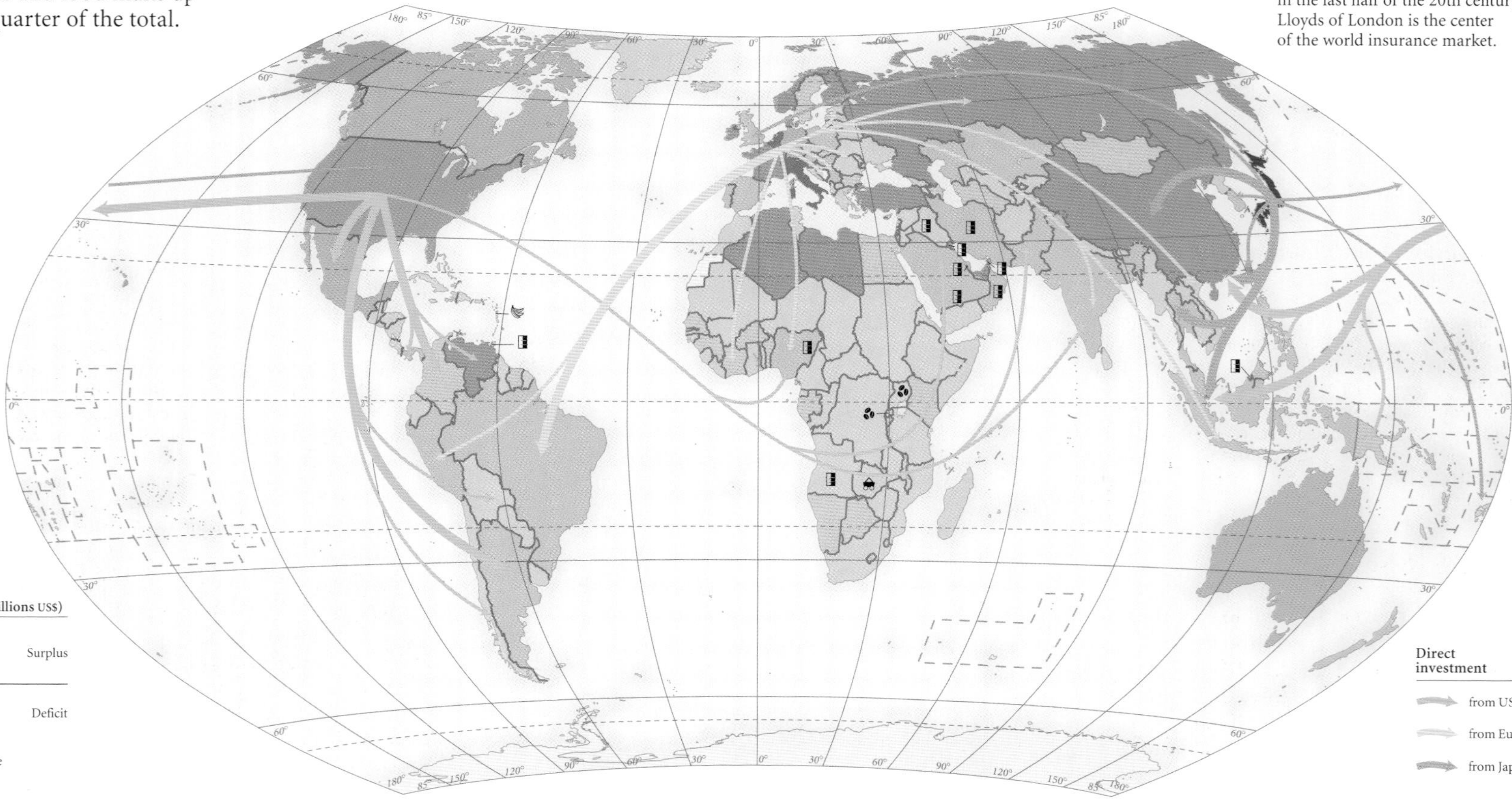

World Money Markets

THE FINANCIAL WORLD has traditionally been dominated by three major centers – Tokyo, New York and London, which house the headquarters of stock exchanges, multinational corporations and international banks. Their geographic location means that, at any one time in a 24-hour day, one major market is open for trading in shares, currencies, and commodities. Since the late 1980s, technological advances have enabled transactions between financial centers to occur at ever-greater speed, and new markets have sprung up throughout the world.

Major Money Markets

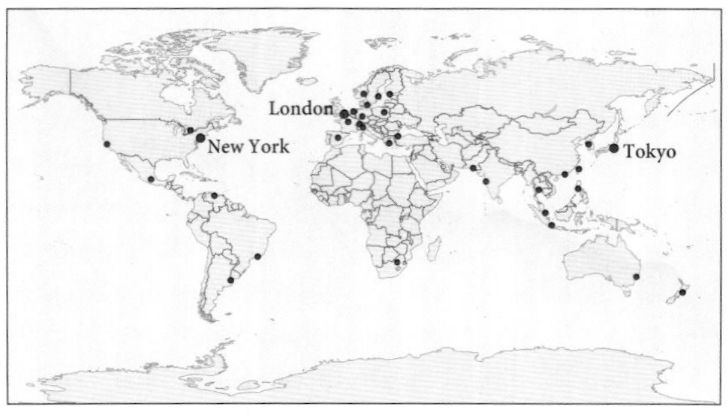

Location of major stock markets
● Major stock markets

The Tokyo Stock Market crashed in 1990, leading to a slow-down in the growth of the world's most powerful economy, and a refocusing on economic policy away from export-led growth and toward the domestic market.

New Stock Markets

NEW STOCK MARKETS are now opening in many parts of the world, where economies have recently emerged from state controls. In Moscow and Beijing, and several countries in eastern Europe, newly-opened stock exchanges reflect the transition to market-driven economies.

Dealers at the Calcutta Stock Market. *The Indian economy has been opened up to foreign investment and many multinationals now have bases there.*

The Developing World

INTERNATIONAL TRADE in capital and currency is dominated by the rich nations of the northern hemisphere. In parts of Africa and Asia, where exports of any sort are extremely limited, home-produced commodities are simply sold in local markets.

Markets have thrived *in communist Vietnam since the introduction of a liberal economic policy.*

World Wealth Disparity

A global assessment of Gross Domestic Product (GDP) by nation reveals great disparities. The developed world, with only a quarter of the world's population, has 80% of the world's manufacturing income. Civil war, conflict, and political instability further undermine the economic self-sufficiency of many of the world's poorest nations.

***Cities such as Detroit** have been badly hit by the decline in heavy industry.*

Urban Decay

Although the US still dominates the global economy, it faces deficits in both the federal budget and the balance of trade. Vast discrepancies in personal wealth, high levels of unemployment, and the dismantling of welfare provisions throughout the 1980s have led to severe deprivation in several of the inner cities of North America's industrial heartland.

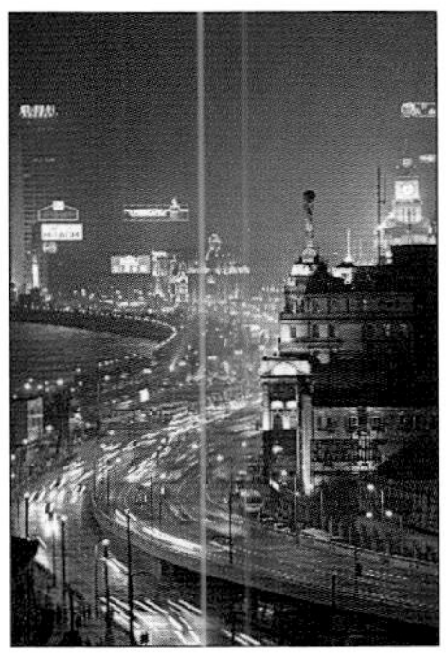

Booming Cities

Since the 1980s the Chinese government has set up special industrial zones, such as Shanghai, where foreign investment is encouraged through tax incentives. Migrants from rural China pour into these regions in search of work, creating "boomtown" economies.

***Foreign investment** has encouraged new infrastructure development in cities like Shanghai.*

Urban Sprawl

Cities are expanding all over the developing world, attracting economic migrants in search of work and opportunities. In cities such as Rio de Janeiro, housing has not kept pace with the population explosion, and squalid shanty towns *(favelas)* rub shoulders with middle-class housing.

***The favelas of Rio de Janeiro** sprawl over the hills surrounding the city.*

Comparative World Wealth

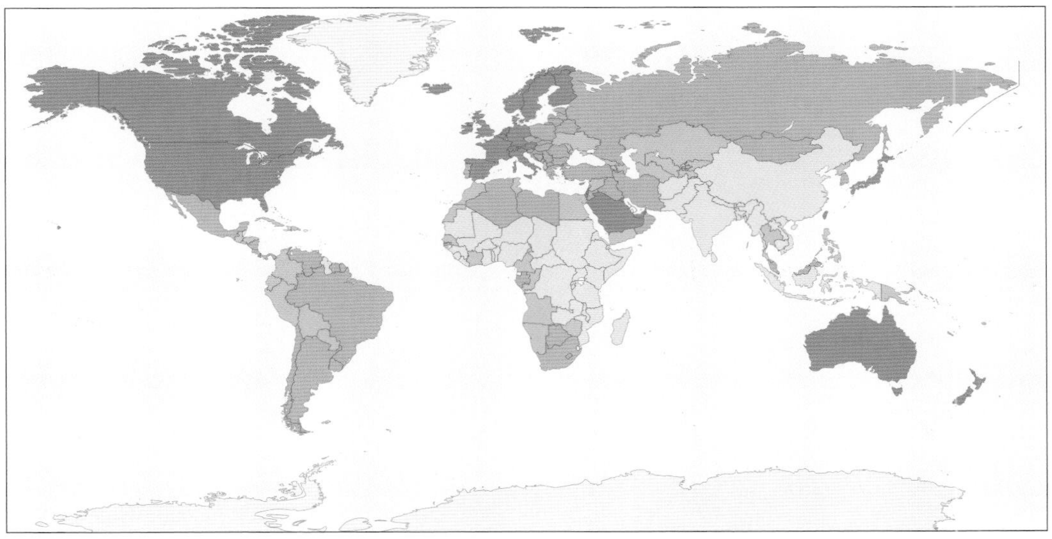

World economies
- high income
- upper-middle income
- lower-middle income
- low income
- data unavailable

Economic "Tigers"

The economic "tigers" of the Pacific Rim – Taiwan, Singapore, and South Korea – have grown faster than Europe and the US over the last decade. Their export- and service-led economies have benefited from stable government, low labor costs, and foreign investment.

***Hong Kong**, with its fine natural harbor, is one of the most important ports in Asia.*

Agricultural Economies

In parts of the developing world, people survive by subsistence farming – only growing enough food for themselves and their families. With no surplus product, they are unable to exchange goods for currency, the only means of escaping the poverty trap. In other countries, farmers have been encouraged to concentrate on growing a single crop for the export market. This reliance on cash crops leaves farmers vulnerable to crop failure and to changes in the market price of the crop.

***The Ugandan uplands** are fertile, but poor infrastructure hampers the export of cash crops.*

***A shopping arcade** in Paris displays a great profusion of luxury goods.*

The Affluent West

The capital cities of many countries in the developed world are showcases for consumer goods, reflecting the increasing importance of the service sector, and particularly the retail sector, in the world economy. The idea of shopping as a leisure activity is unique to the western world. Luxury goods and services attract visitors, who in turn generate tourist revenue.

Tourism

In 1995, there were 567 million tourists worldwide. Tourism is now the world's biggest single industry, employing 127 million people, though frequently in low-paid unskilled jobs. While tourists are increasingly exploring inaccessible and less-developed regions of the world, the benefits of the industry are not always felt at a local level. There are also worries about the environmental impact of tourism, as the world's last wildernesses increasingly become tourist attractions.

***Botswana's Okavango Delta** is an area rich in wildlife. Tourists go on safaris to the region, but the impact of tourism is controlled.*

Tourist Arrivals

Tourist arrivals
- over 20 million / 10–20 million
- 5–10 million / 2.5–5 million
- 1–2.5 million / 700,000–999,000
- under 700,000 / data unavailable

Money Flows

Foreign investment in the developing world during the 1970s led to a global financial crisis in the 1980s, when many countries were unable to meet their debt repayments. The International Monetary Fund (IMF) was forced to reschedule the debts and, in some cases, write them off completely. Within the developing world, austerity programs have been initiated to cope with the debt, leading in turn to high unemployment and galloping inflation. In many parts of Africa, stricken economies are now dependent on international aid.

***In rural Southeast Asia**, babies are given medical checks by UNICEF as part of a global aid program sponsored by the UN.*

International Debt: Donors and Receivers

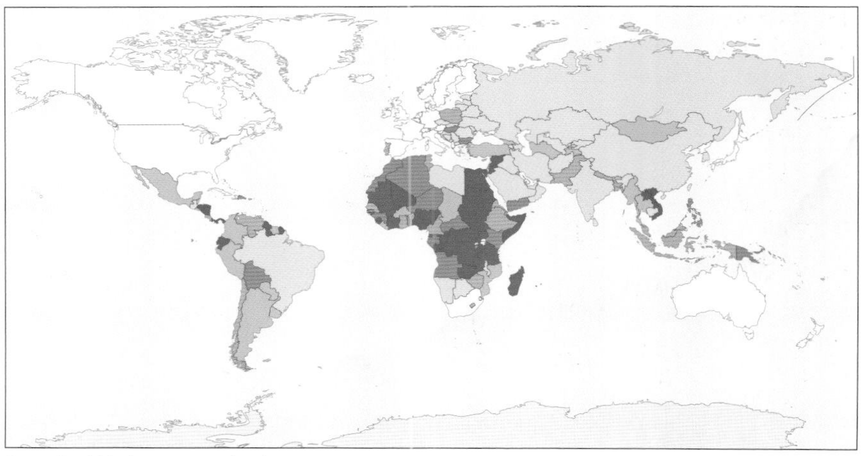

International debt (as percentage of GNP)
- over 100% / 70–90%
- 50–69% / 30–49%
- below 30 / negligible
- data unavailable

The Political World

There are 193 independent countries in the world today. With the exception of Antarctica, where territorial claims have been deferred by international treaty, every land area of the Earth's surface either belongs to, or is claimed by, one country or another. The largest country in the world is the Russian Federation, the smallest is Vatican City. Some 60 overseas dependent territories remain, administered variously by France, Australia, Denmark, New Zealand, Norway, Portugal, the UK, the US, and the Netherlands.

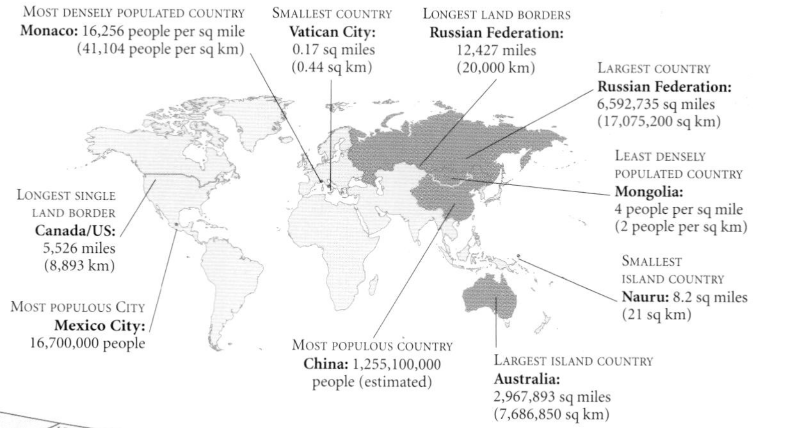

International Borders

The map shows three main types of boundary between states. Full borders represent internationally agreed and recognized territorial boundaries. Undefined borders exist where no fixed boundary between states has been demarcated; the boundaries indicated in this way show approximate areas of sovereignty. A disputed border is indicated where a *de facto* territorial boundary exists, which is not agreed or is subject to arbitration.

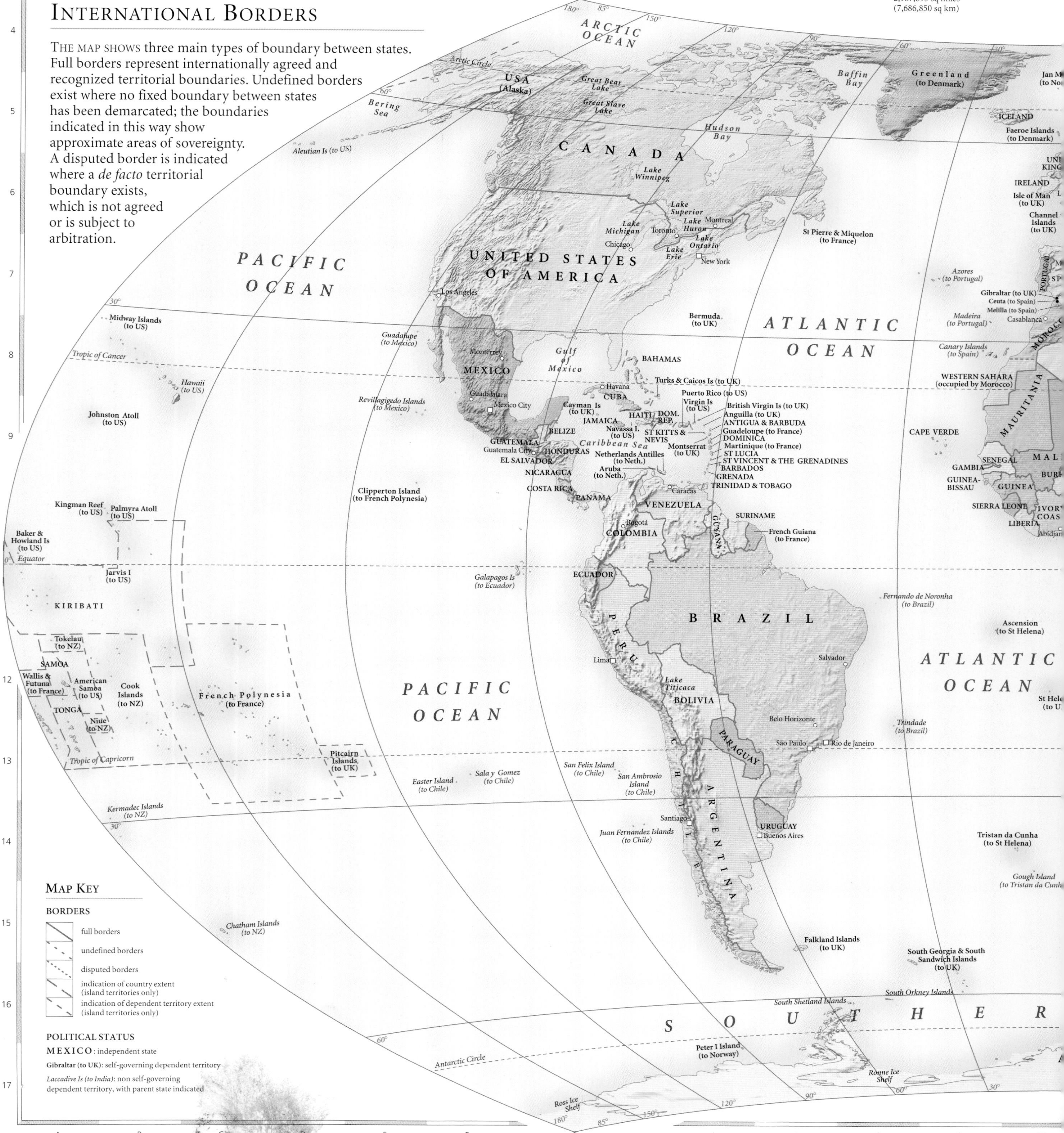

N O P Q R S T U V W X Y Z

The World in 1914

The early years of the 20th century saw the mainly European colonial empires reaching their greatest extents by 1914. Two world wars inaugurated their disintegration, but even in 1950 there were only 82 independent countries. Since then, over 100 have gained their independence, culminating in the breakup of the Soviet Union and former Yugoslavia in the early 1990s.

Percentage of Earth's Land Surface Controlled by Colonial Empires in 1914

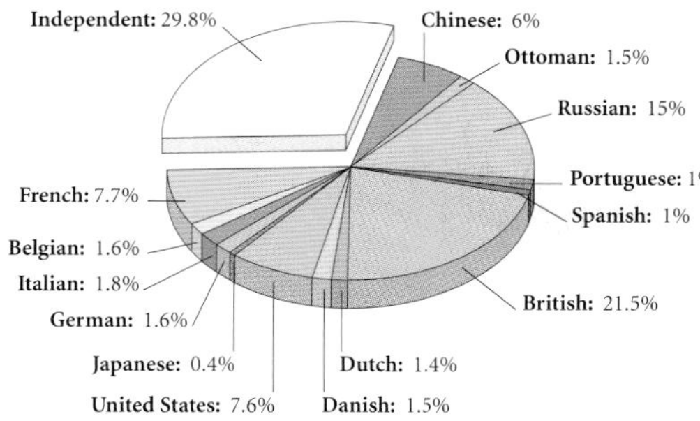

Colonial Empires in 1914

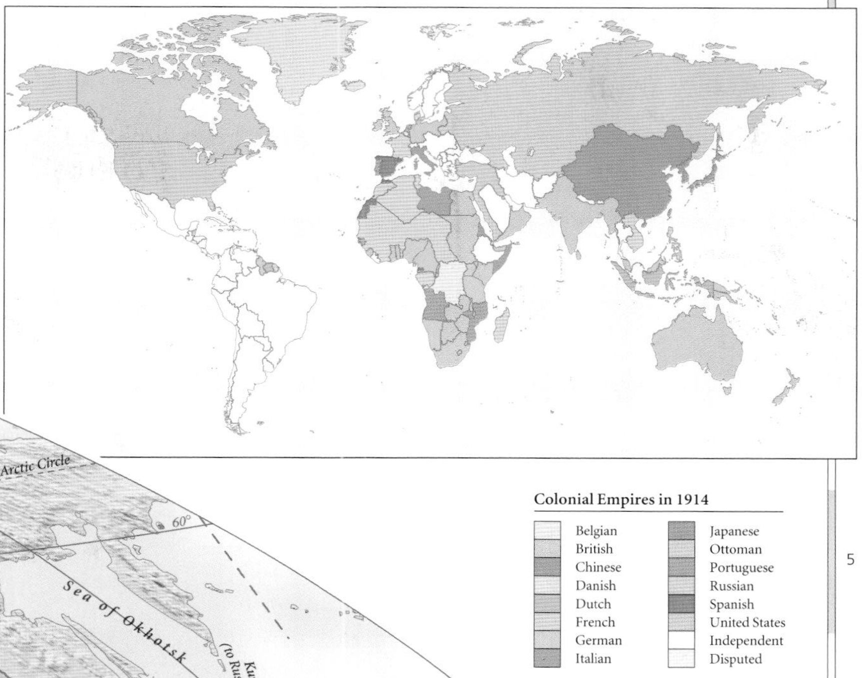

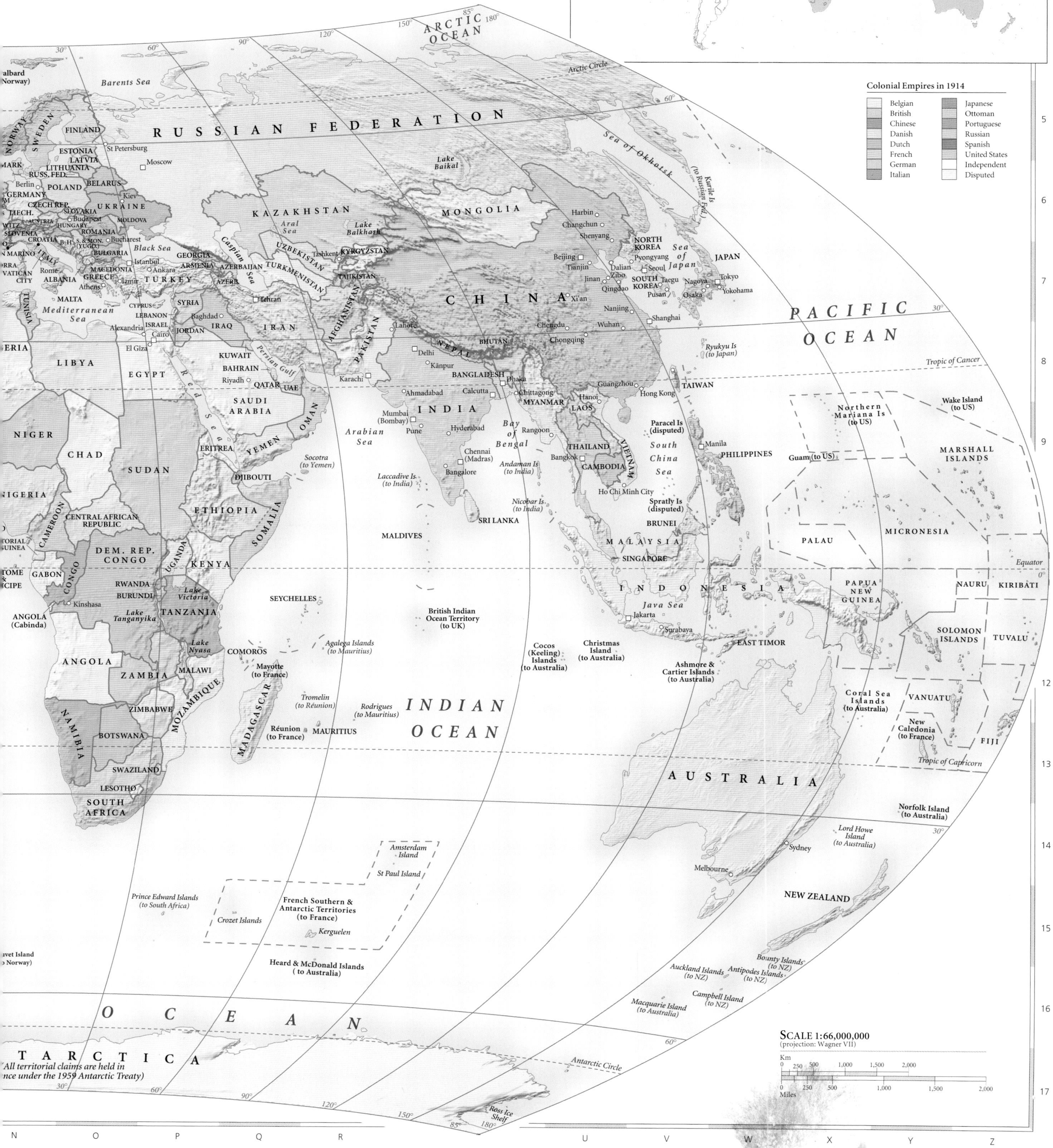

N O P Q R U V W X Y Z

States and Boundaries

There are over 190 sovereign states in the world today; in 1950 there were only 82. Over the last half-century national self-determination has been a driving force for many states with a history of colonialism and oppression. As more borders are added to the world map, the number of international border disputes increases.

In many cases, where the impetus toward independence has been religious or ethnic, disputes with minority groups have also caused violent internal conflict. While many newly-formed states have moved peacefully toward independence, successfully establishing government by multi-party democracy, dictatorship by military regime or individual despot is often the result of the internal power-struggles which characterize the early stages in the lives of new nations.

The Nature of Politics

Democracy is a broad term: it can range from the ideal of multiparty elections and fair representation to, in countries such as Singapore and Indonesia, a thin disguise for single-party rule. In despotic regimes, on the other hand, a single, often personal authority has total power; institutions such as parliament and the military are mere instruments of the dictator.

The stars and stripes *of the US flag are a potent symbol of the country's status as a federal democracy.*

The Changing World Map

Decolonization

In 1950, large areas of the world remained under the control of a handful of European countries (*page xxviii*). The process of decolonization had begun in Asia, where, following World WarII, much of southern and southeastern Asia sought and achieved self-determination. In the 1960s, a host of African states achieved independence, so that by 1965, most of the larger tracts of the European overseas empires had been substantially eroded. The final major stage in decolonization came with the breakup of the Soviet Union and the Eastern bloc after 1990. The process continues today as the last toeholds of European colonialism, often tiny island nations, press increasingly for independence.

Icons of communism*, including statues of former leaders such as Lenin and Stalin, were destroyed when the Soviet bloc was dismantled in 1989, creating several new nations.*

Iran *is one of the world's true theocracies; Islam has an impact on every aspect of political life.*

North Korea is *an independent communist republic. Power is concentrated in the hands of Kim Jong Il.*

New nations 1945–1965

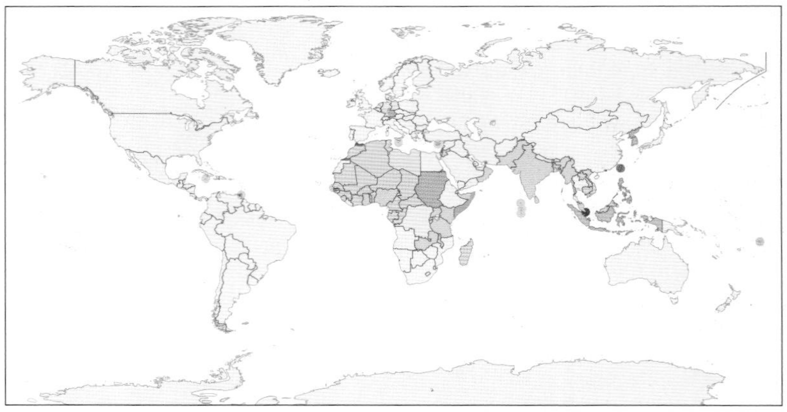

New nations 1965–1996

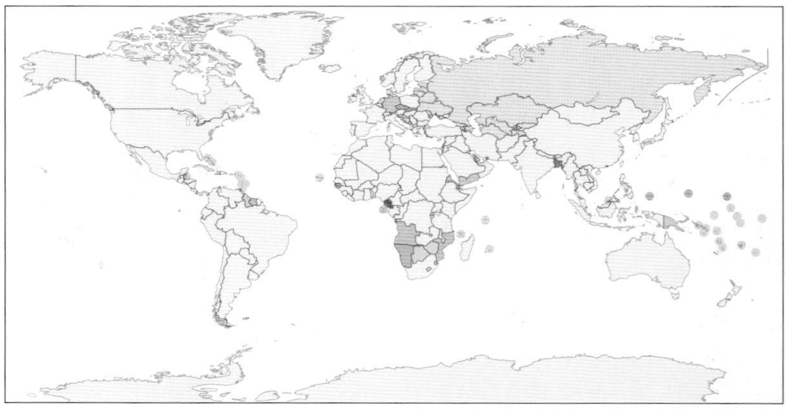

Administration at the time of independence

- Australia
- Aust/NZ/UK
- Belgium
- China
- Czechoslovakia
- Egypt/UK
- Ethiopia
- France
- France/UK
- Italy
- Japan
- Malaysia
- Netherlands
- New Zealand
- Pakistan
- Portugal
- South Africa
- Spain
- UK
- Unified country
- USA
- USSR
- Yugoslavia

Saddam Hussein, *former autocratic leader of Iraq, promoted an extreme personality cult for over 20 years. He was ousted by a US-led coalition in 2003.*

South Africa *became a democracy in 1994, when elections ended over a century of white minority rule.*

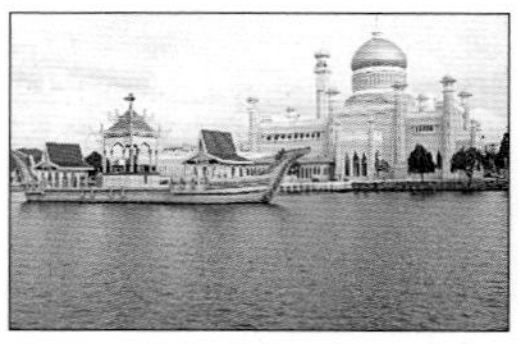

In Brunei *the Sultan has ruled by decree since 1962; power is closely tied to the royal family. The Sultan's brothers are responsible for finance and foreign affairs.*

Types of government

- Multiparty democracy for more than 10 yrs
- Multiparty/transitional democracy within last 10 yrs
- Single-party government
- Military regime
- Theocracy
- Absolute monarchy
- Current civil unrest

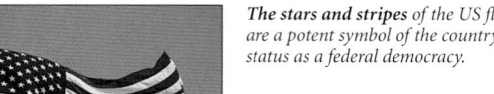

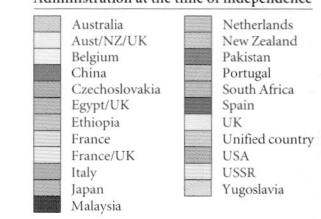

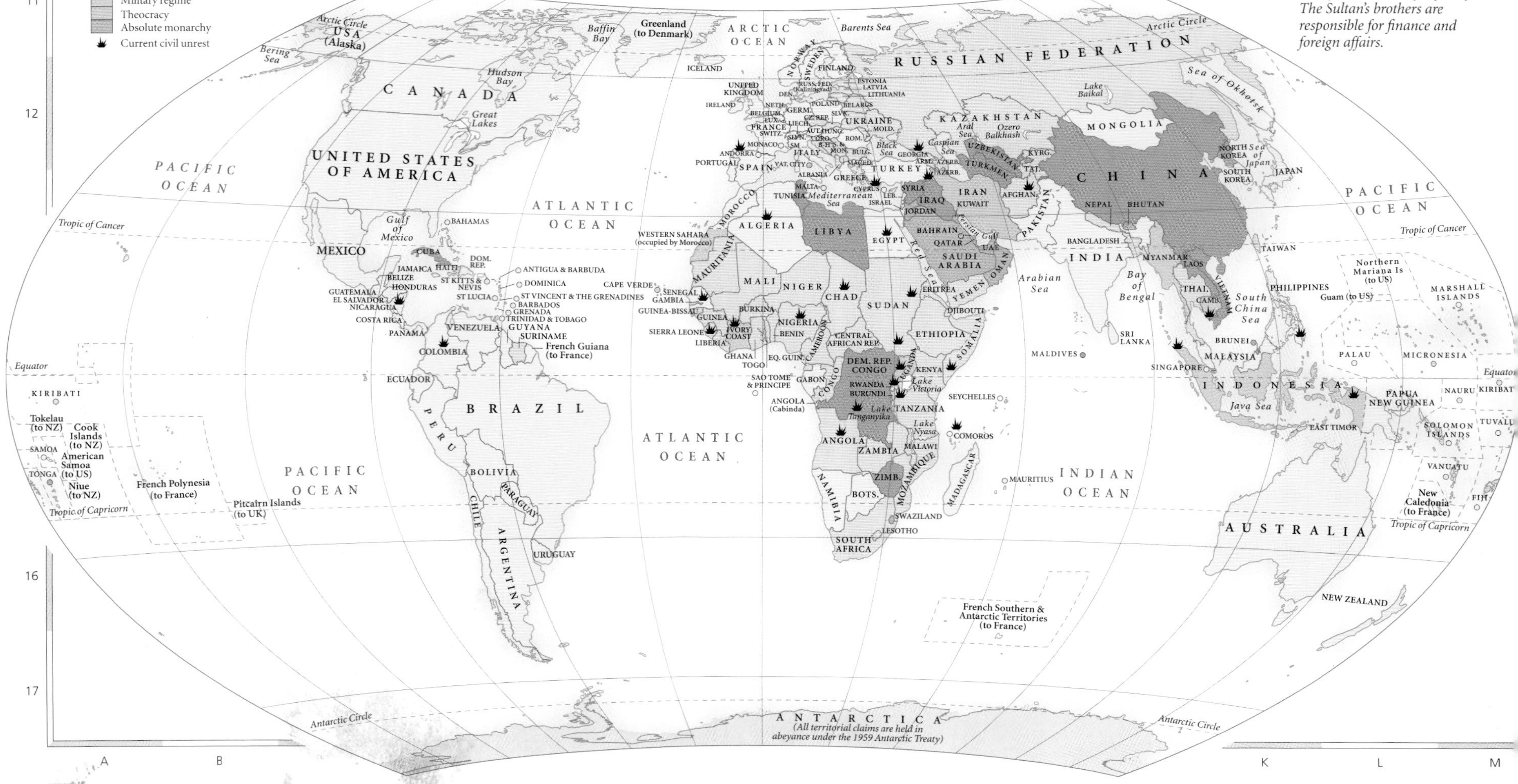

Lines on the Map

The determination of international boundaries can use a variety of criteria. Many of the borders between older states follow physical boundaries; some mirror religious and ethnic differences; others are the legacy of complex histories of conflict and colonialism, while others have been imposed by international agreements or arbitration.

Enclaves

The shifting political map over the course of history has frequently led to anomalous situations. Parts of national territories may become isolated by territorial agreement, forming an enclave. The West German part of the city of Berlin, which until 1989 lay several hundred miles within East German territory, was a famous example.

Since the independence of Lithuania and Belarus, the peoples of the Russian enclave of Kaliningrad have become physically isolated.

Post-colonial borders

When the European colonial empires in Africa were dismantled during the second half of the 20th century, the outlines of the new African states mirrored colonial boundaries. These boundaries had been drawn up by colonial administrators, often based on inadequate geographical knowledge. Such arbitrary boundaries were imposed on people of different languages, racial groups, religions, and customs. This confused legacy often led to civil and international war.

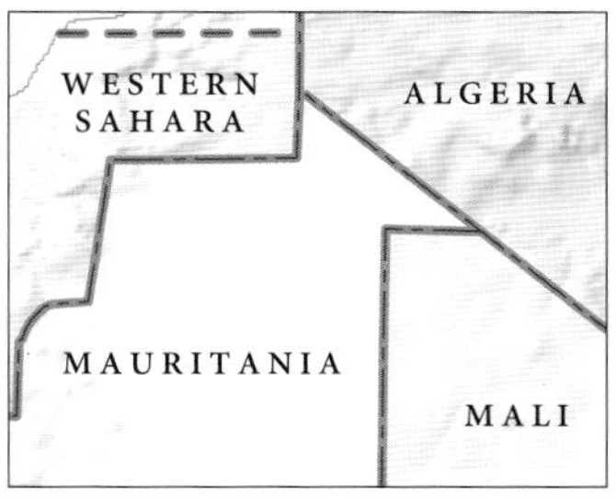

Antarctica

When Antarctic exploration began a century ago, seven nations, Australia, Argentina, Britain, Chile, France, New Zealand, and Norway, laid claim to the new territory. In 1961 the Antarctic Treaty, signed by 39 nations, agreed to hold all territorial claims in abeyance.

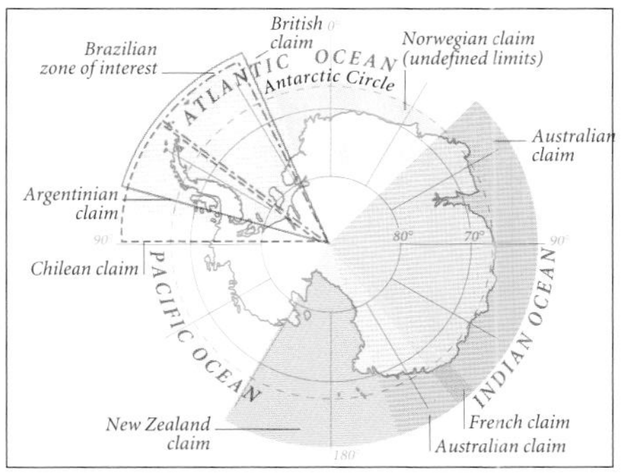

Geometric borders

Straight lines and lines of longitude and latitude have occasionally been used to determine international boundaries; and indeed the world's longest international boundary, between Canada and the USA follows the 49th Parallel for over one-third of its course. Many Canadian, American and Australian internal administrative boundaries are similarly determined using a geometric solution.

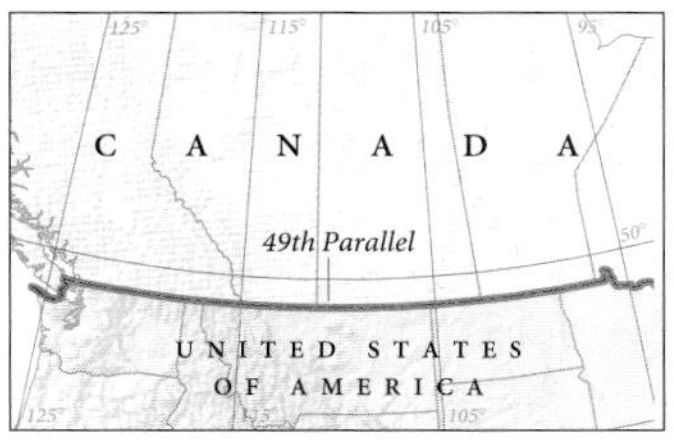

Different farming techniques in Canada and the US clearly mark the course of the international boundary in this satellite map.

World boundaries

Dates from which current boundaries have existed

- 1990–1993
- 1966–1989
- 1946–1965
- 1915–1945
- 1850–1914
- 1800–1849
- Pre-1800

The conflict that has plagued many African countries since independence has caused millions of people to become refugees.

Physical borders

Many of the world's countries are divided by physical borders: lakes, rivers, mountains. The demarcation of such boundaries can, however, lead to disputes. Control of waterways, water supplies, and fisheries are frequent causes of international friction.

Lake borders

Countries which lie next to lakes usually fix their borders in the middle of the lake. Unusually the Lake Nyasa border between Malawi and Tanzania runs along Tanzania's shore.

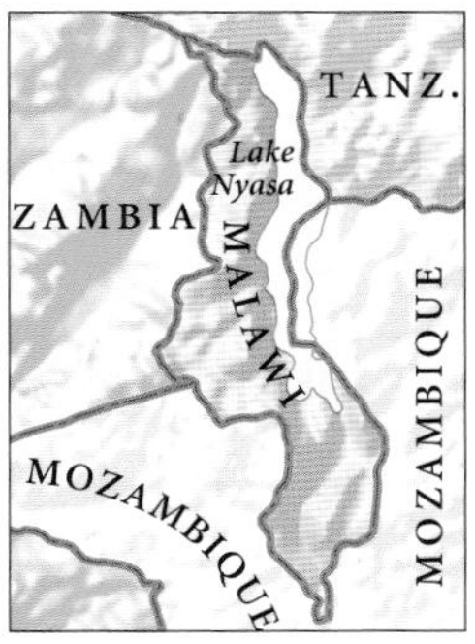

Complicated agreements between colonial powers led to the awkward division of Lake Nyasa.

River borders

Rivers alone account for one-sixth of the world's borders. Many great rivers form boundaries between a number of countries. Changes in a river's course and interruptions of its natural flow can lead to disputes, particularly in areas where water is scarce. The center of the river's course is the nominal boundary line.

The Danube forms all or part of the border between nine European nations.

Mountain borders

Mountain ranges form natural barriers and are the basis for many major borders, particularly in Europe and Asia. The watershed is the conventional boundary demarcation line, but its accurate determination is often problematic.

The Pyrenees form a natural mountain border between France and Spain.

Shifting boundaries – Poland

Borders between countries can change dramatically over time. The nations of eastern Europe have been particularly affected by changing boundaries. Poland is an example of a country whose boundaries have changed so significantly that it has literally moved around Europe. At the start of the 16th century, Poland was the largest nation in Europe. Between 1772 and 1795, it was absorbed into Prussia, Austria, and Russia, and it effectively ceased to exist. After World War I, Poland became an independent country once more, but its borders changed again after World War II following invasions by both Soviet Russia and Nazi Germany.

In 1634, Poland was the largest nation in Europe, its eastern boundary reaching toward Moscow.

From 1772–1795, Poland was gradually partitioned between Austria, Russia, and Prussia. Its eastern boundary receded by over 100 miles (160 km).

Following World War I, Poland was reinstated as an independent state, but it was less than half the size it had been in 1634.

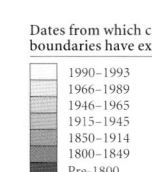

After World War II, the Baltic Sea border was extended westward, but much of the eastern territory was annexed by Russia.

International disputes

There are more than 60 disputed borders or territories in the world today. Although many of these disputes can be settled by peaceful negotiation, some areas have become a focus for international conflict. Ethnic tensions have been a major source of territorial disagreement throughout history, as has the ownership of, and access to, valuable natural resources. The turmoil of the postcolonial era in many parts of Africa is partly a result of the 19th century "carve-up" of the continent, which created potential for conflict by drawing often arbitrary lines through linguistic and cultural areas.

Jammu and Kashmir

Disputes over Jammu and Kashmir have caused three serious wars between India and Pakistan since 1947. Pakistan wishes to annex the largely Muslim territory, while India refuses to cede any territory or to hold a referendum, and also lays claim to the entire territory. Most international maps show the "line of control" agreed in 1972 as the *de facto* border. In addition, both Pakistan and India have territorial disputes with neighboring China. The situation is further complicated by a Kashmiri independence movement, active since the late 1980s.

***Indian army troops** maintain their positions in the mountainous terrain of northern Kashmir.*

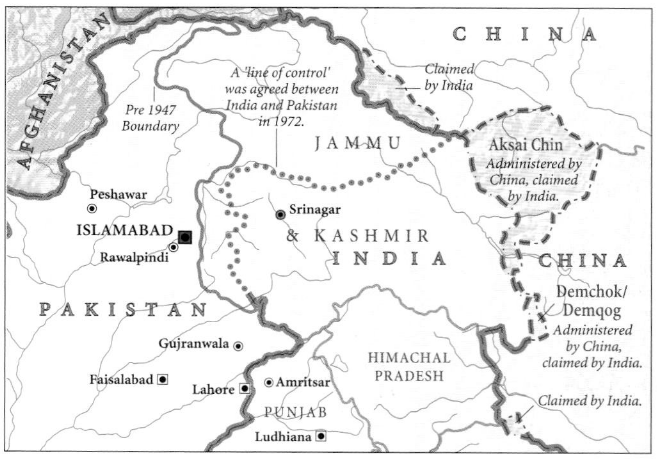

North and South Korea

Since 1953, the *de facto* border between North and South Korea has been a ceasefire line which straddles the 38th Parallel and is designated as a demilitarized zone. Both countries have heavy fortifications and troop concentrations behind this zone.

***Heavy fortifications** on the border between North and South Korea.*

***The so-called 'green line'** divides Cyprus into Greek and Turkish sectors.*

Cyprus

Cyprus was partitioned in 1974, following an invasion by Turkish troops. The south is now the Greek Cypriot Republic of Cyprus, while the self-proclaimed Turkish Republic of Northern Cyprus is recognized only by Turkey.

The Falkland Islands

The British Dependent Territory of the Falkland Islands was invaded by Argentina in 1982, sparking a full-scale war with the UK. In 1995, the UK and Argentina reached an agreement on the exploitation of oil reserves around the islands.

***British** warships in Falkland Sound during the 1982 war with Argentina.*

Former Yugoslavia

Following the disintegration in 1991 of the communist state of Yugoslavia, the breakaway states of Croatia and Bosnia-Herzegovina came into conflict with the "parent" state (consisting of Serbia and Montenegro). Warfare focused on ethnic and territorial ambitions in Bosnia. The tenuous Dayton Accord of 1995 sought to recognize the post-1990 borders, whilst providing for ethnic partition and required international peace-keeping troops to maintain the terms of the peace.

***Most claimant** states have small military garrisons on the Spratly Islands.*

The Spratly Islands

The site of potential oil and natural gas reserves, the Spratly Islands in the South China Sea have been claimed by China, Vietnam, Taiwan, Malaysia, and the Philippines since the Japanese gave up a wartime claim in 1951.

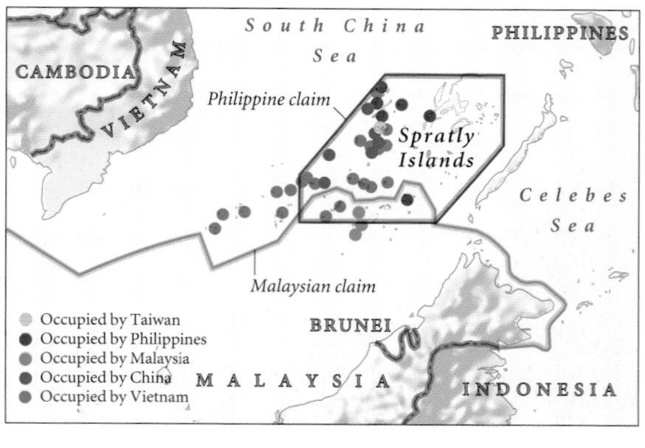

Israel

Israel was created in 1948 following the 1947 UN Resolution (147) on Palestine. Until 1979 Israel had no borders, only ceasefire lines from a series of wars in 1948, 1967 and 1973. Treaties with Egypt in 1979 and Jordan in 1994 led to these borders being defined and agreed. Negotiations over Israeli settlements in disputed territories such as the West Bank, and the issue of self-government for the Palestinians, continue.

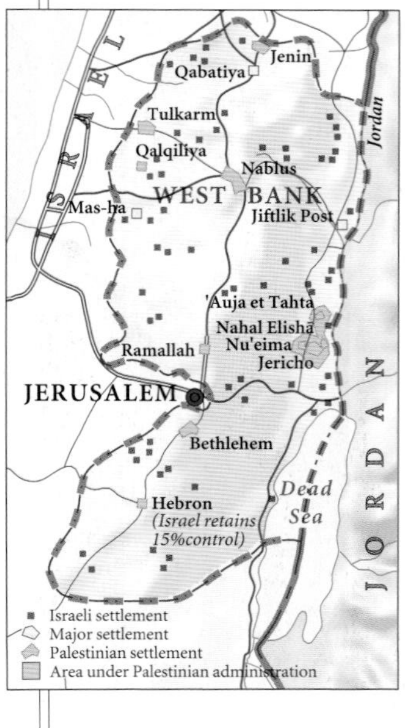

***Barbed-wire fences** surround a settlement in the Golan Heights.*

ATLAS OF THE WORLD

THE MAPS IN THIS ATLAS ARE ARRANGED CONTINENT BY CONTINENT, STARTING FROM THE INTERNATIONAL DATE LINE, AND MOVING EASTWARD. THE MAPS PROVIDE A UNIQUE VIEW OF TODAY'S WORLD, COMBINING TRADITIONAL CARTOGRAPHIC TECHNIQUES WITH THE LATEST REMOTE-SENSED AND DIGITAL TECHNOLOGY.

A B C D E F G H I J K L M
1 2 3 4 5 6 7 8 9 10 11 12 13 14 15 16 17
ARCTIC OCEAN
North Pole
EURASIAN PLATE
NORTH AMERICAN PLATE
Franz Josef Land
East Siberian Sea
Sea of Okhotsk
Khrebet Cherskogo
Khrebet Kolymskiy
Kamchatka
Koryakskoye Nagor'ye
Komandorskaya Basin
Kuril Trench
Northwest Pacific Basin
Anadyrskiy Zaliv
Chukchi Sea
Cape Prince of Wales
St Lawrence Island
Bering Strait
Seward Peninsula
Norton Sound
Aleutian Basin
Bering Sea
Bowers Ridge
Nunivak Island
Attu
Aleutian Islands
Aleutian Trench
Kuskokwim Bay
Kuskokwim
Bristol Bay
Aleutian Range
Alaska Peninsula
Kodiak Island
Point Barrow
Brooks Range
Colville
Koyukuk
Yukon
Mount McKinley (Denali) 6194m
Alaska Range
Kenai Mountains
Tanana
Porcupine
Mackenzie Bay
Beaufort Sea
Peel
Mackenzie Mountains
Arctic Red River
Mount Logan 6050m
Gulf of Alaska
PACIFIC PLATE
Patton Seamount
Cowie Seamount
Gilbert Seamount
Dickins Seamount
Queen Charlotte Islands
Alexander Archipelago
Skeena
Coast Mountains
Morton Seamount
Union Seamount
Cobb Seamount
Vancouver Island
Cascadia Basin
Astoria Fan
JUAN DE FUCA PLATE
Gorda Ridges
Delgada Fan
Mendocino Fracture Zone
Pioneer Fracture Zone
Murray Fracture Zone
Moonless Mountains
Molokai Fracture Zone
Tropic of Cancer
PACIFIC OCEAN
Clarion Fracture Zone
Clipperton Fracture Zone
Equator
Mathematicians Seamounts
Revillagigedo Islands
Clipperton Seamounts
Clipperton Island
Islas Alijos
Cabo San Lucas
Lower California
Gulf of California
East Pacific Rise
COCOS PLATE
Orozco Fracture Zone
Siqueiros Fracture Zone
Tehuantepec Ridge
Albatross Plateau
Guatemala Basin
Berlanga Rise
Colón Ridge
Cocos Ridge
Middle America Trench
Golfo de Tehuantepec
Golfo de Fonseca
Sierra Madre del Sur
Popocatépetl
Citlaltépetl 5700m
Lago de Chapala
Río Grande de Santiago
Sierra Madre Occidental
Sierra Madre Oriental
Río Yaqui
Sierra Grande
Rio Grande
Pecos
Sonoran Desert
Gila
Humphreys Peak 3851m
Baldy Peak 3476m
Colorado Plateau
Painted Desert
Grand Canyon
Lake Mead
Mojave Desert
Lake Powell
Death Valley
Mount Whitney 4418m
Mount Elbert 4399m
Sierra Nevada
San Joaquin
Coast Ranges
Monterey Bay
San Francisco Bay
Great Basin
Great Salt Lake
Harney Basin
Columbia Plateau
Columbia
Snake
Mount Rainier 4392m
Mount St Helens
Cascade Range
Yellowstone
Bighorn
Powder
Cheyenne
North Platte
South Platte
Platte
Arkansas
Kansas
Canadian
Red River
Missouri
Niobrara
Black Hills
Lake Oahe
Rocky Mountains
Great Plains
NORTH AMERICA
Clark Fork
Fraser
Peace
Athabasca
Hay
North Saskatchewan
South Saskatchewan
Assiniboine
Souris
Great Slave Lake
Great Bear Lake
Mackenzie
Coppermine
Coronation Gulf
Queen Maud Gulf
Arctic Circle
Dubawnt Lake
Thelon
Back
Kazan
Garry Lake
Baker Lake
Lake Athabasca
Wollaston Lake
Reindeer Lake
Churchill
Nelson
Lake Winnipeg
Lake Manitoba
Lake of the Woods
Winnipeg
Canadian Shield
Severn
Winisk
Attawapiskat
Albany
Moose
James Bay
Lac Mistassini
La Grande Rivière
Hudson Bay
Belcher Islands
Roes Welcome Sound
Southampton Island
Coats Island
Mansel Island
Péninsule d'Ungava
Arnaud
Ungava Bay
Rivière aux Feuilles
Rivière aux Mélèzes
George
Labrador Sea
Foxe Basin
Foxe Channel
Hudson Strait
Frobisher Bay
Amadjuak Lake
Nettilling Lake
Cumberland Sound
Baffin Island
Baffin Bay
Davis Strait
Greenland
Greenland Sea
Norwegian Sea
Iceland
Nordøstrundingen
Kap Morris Jesup
King Frederik VIII Land
King Christian X Land
Denmark Strait
Ellesmere Island
Queen Elizabeth Islands
Parry Islands
Jones Sound
Lancaster Sound
Viscount Melville Sound
Prince of Wales Island
McClure Strait
Banks Island
Amundsen Gulf
Victoria Island
McClintock Channel
Boothia Peninsula
Gulf of Boothia
Red River
Lake Nipigon
Lake Superior
Great Lakes
Lake Michigan
Lake Huron
Ontario Peninsula
Lake St Clair
Lake Erie
Lake Ontario
Niagara Falls
Ottawa
St Lawrence
Saguenay
Laurentian Mountains
Hudson
Connecticut
Long Island
Delaware Bay
Chesapeake Bay
Cape Hatteras
Cape Lookout
Allegheny Mountains
Appalachian Mountains
Blue Ridge
Roanoke
Mount Mitchell 2037m
Cumberland Plateau
Tennessee
Ohio
Illinois
Des Moines
Missouri
Wisconsin
Minnesota
Mississippi
Arkansas
Alabama
Chattahoochee
Savannah
Mississippi Delta
Mississippi Fan
Galveston Bay
Sigsbee Escarpment
Gulf of Mexico
Mexico Basin
Apalachee Bay
Tampa Bay
Lake Okeechobee
The Everglades
Cape Canaveral
Blake Plateau
Blake-Bahama Ridge
Straits of Florida
Great Bahama Bank
Bahamas
Cuba
Campeche Bank
Yucatan Channel
Yucatan Peninsula
Yucatan Basin
Bay of Campeche
Cayman Trench
Jamaica
NORTH AMERICAN PLATE
CARIBBEAN PLATE
Gulf of Honduras
Nicaraguan Rise
La Mosquitia
Lake Nicaragua
Mosquito Gulf
Colombian Basin
Gulf of Darién
Isthmus of Panama
Gulf of Panama
Peninsula de Azuero
Panama Basin
NAZCA PLATE
Caribbean Sea

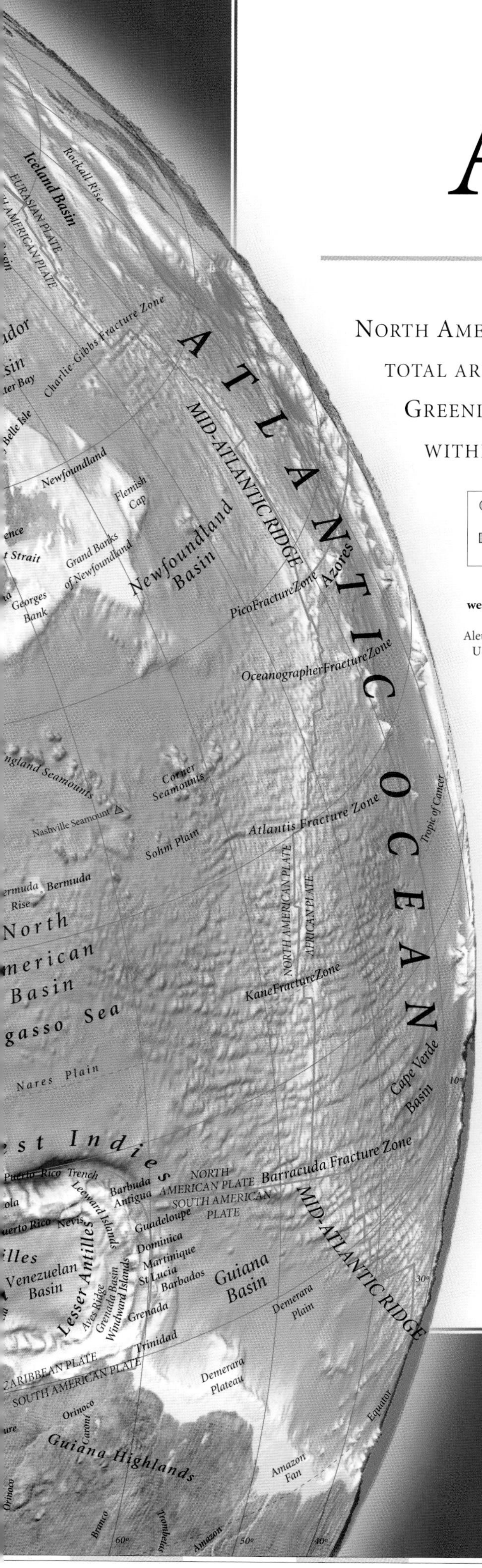
Iceland Basin
Rockall Rise
EURASIAN PLATE
NORTH AMERICAN PLATE
Charlie-Gibbs Fracture Zone
ATLANTIC OCEAN
MID-ATLANTIC RIDGE
Belle Isle
Newfoundland
Flemish Cap
Grand Banks of Newfoundland
Newfoundland Basin
Georges Bank
Azores
Pico Fracture Zone
Oceanographer Fracture Zone
Corner Seamounts
Nashville Seamount
Sohm Plain
Atlantis Fracture Zone
Tropic of Cancer
NORTH AMERICAN PLATE
AFRICAN PLATE
Bermuda Rise
Bermuda
North American Basin
Sargasso Sea
Kane Fracture Zone
Nares Plain
Cape Verde Basin
West Indies
Puerto Rico Trench
Barbuda
Antigua
NORTH AMERICAN PLATE
SOUTH AMERICAN PLATE
Barracuda Fracture Zone
Leeward Islands
Guadeloupe
Dominica
Martinique
St Lucia
Barbados
Lesser Antilles
Venezuelan Basin
Aves Ridge
Grenada Basin
Windward Islands
Grenada
Guiana Basin
Demerara Plain
MID-ATLANTIC RIDGE
Trinidad
CARIBBEAN PLATE
SOUTH AMERICAN PLATE
Demerara Plateau
Orinoco
Caroni
Guiana Highlands
Equator
Amazon Fan
Branco
Trombetas
Amazon

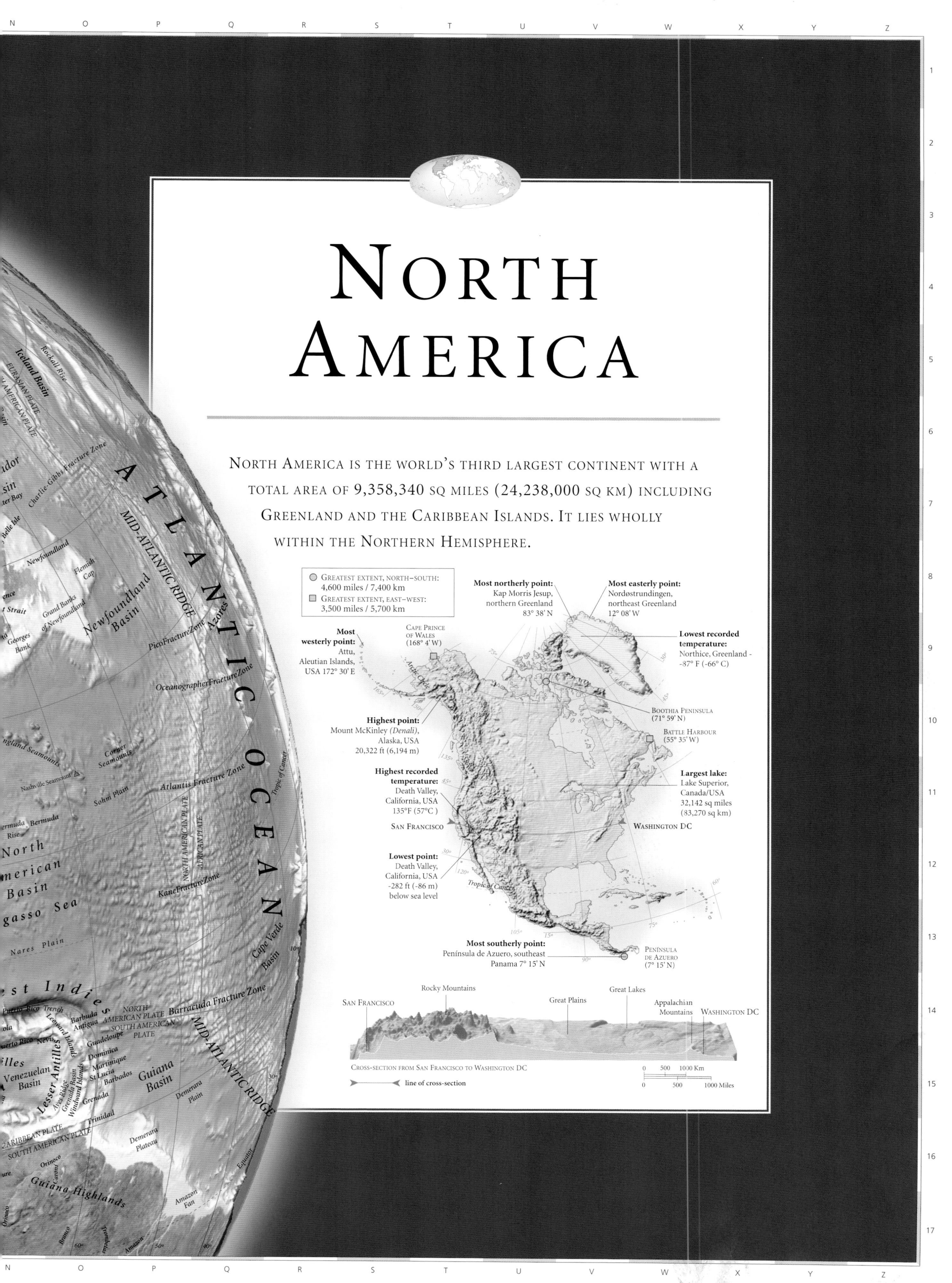

NORTH AMERICA

NORTH AMERICA IS THE WORLD'S THIRD LARGEST CONTINENT WITH A TOTAL AREA OF 9,358,340 SQ MILES (24,238,000 SQ KM) INCLUDING GREENLAND AND THE CARIBBEAN ISLANDS. IT LIES WHOLLY WITHIN THE NORTHERN HEMISPHERE.

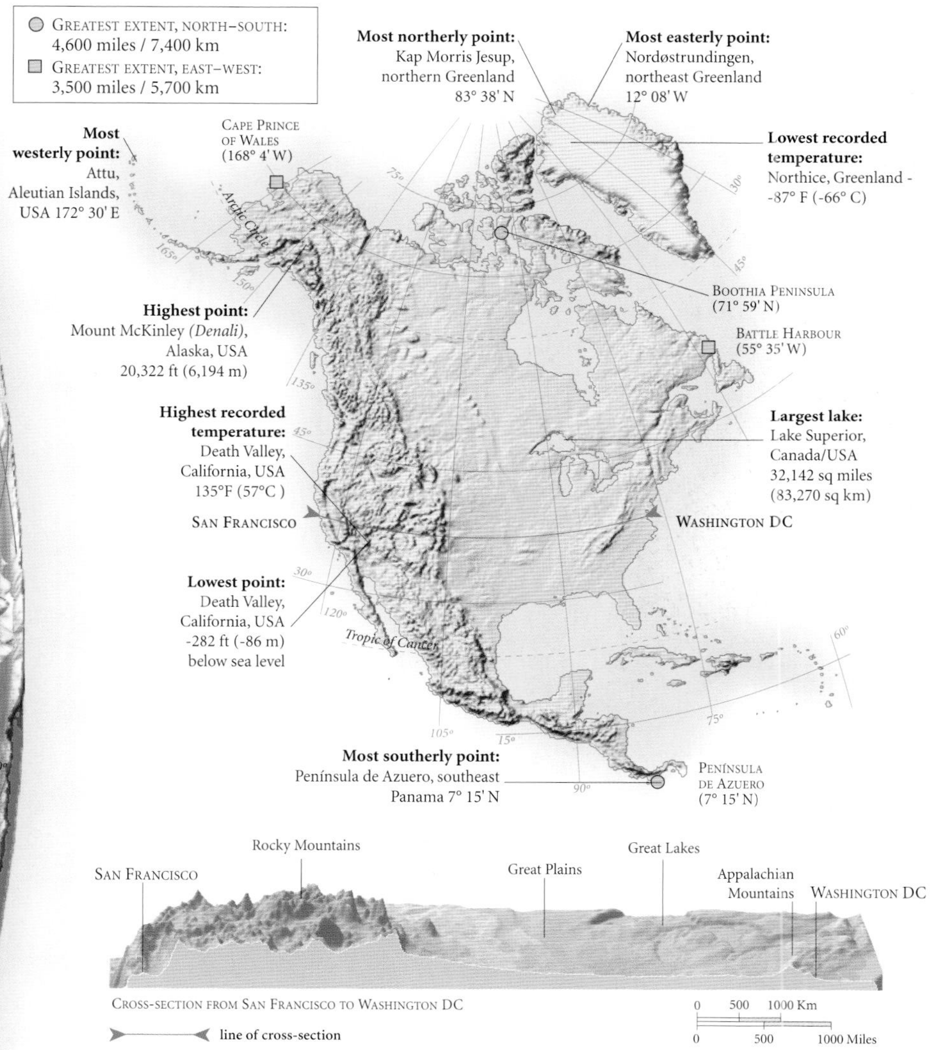
GREATEST EXTENT, NORTH–SOUTH: 4,600 miles / 7,400 km
GREATEST EXTENT, EAST–WEST: 3,500 miles / 5,700 km
Most northerly point: Kap Morris Jesup, northern Greenland 83° 38' N
Most easterly point: Nordøstrundingen, northeast Greenland 12° 08' W
Most westerly point: Attu, Aleutian Islands, USA 172° 30' E
CAPE PRINCE OF WALES (168° 4' W)
Lowest recorded temperature: Northice, Greenland - -87° F (-66° C)
BOOTHIA PENINSULA (71° 59' N)
BATTLE HARBOUR (55° 35' W)
Highest point: Mount McKinley (Denali), Alaska, USA 20,322 ft (6,194 m)
Highest recorded temperature: Death Valley, California, USA 135°F (57°C)
Largest lake: Lake Superior, Canada/USA 32,142 sq miles (83,270 sq km)
SAN FRANCISCO
WASHINGTON DC
Lowest point: Death Valley, California, USA -282 ft (-86 m) below sea level
Arctic Circle
Tropic of Cancer
Most southerly point: Península de Azuero, southeast Panama 7° 15' N
PENÍNSULA DE AZUERO (7° 15' N)
San Francisco
Rocky Mountains
Great Plains
Great Lakes
Appalachian Mountains
Washington DC
CROSS-SECTION FROM SAN FRANCISCO TO WASHINGTON DC
0 500 1000 Km
0 500 1000 Miles
line of cross-section

PHYSICAL NORTH AMERICA

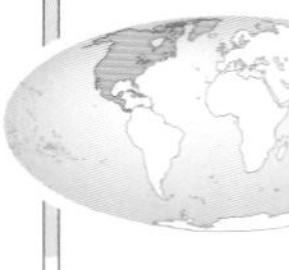

THE NORTH AMERICAN CONTINENT can be divided into a number of major structural areas: the Western Cordillera, the Canadian Shield, the Great Plains, and Central Lowlands, and the Appalachians. Other smaller regions include the Gulf Atlantic Coastal Plain which borders the southern coast of North America from the southern Appalachians to the Great Plains. This area includes the expanding Mississippi Delta. A chain of volcanic islands, running in an arc around the margin of the Caribbean Plate, lie to the east of the Gulf of Mexico.

THE CANADIAN SHIELD

SPANNING NORTHERN CANADA and Greenland, this geologically stable plain forms the heart of the continent, containing rocks more than two billion years old. A long history of weathering and repeated glaciation has scoured the region, leaving flat plains, gentle hummocks, numerous small basins and lakes, and the bays and islands of the Arctic.

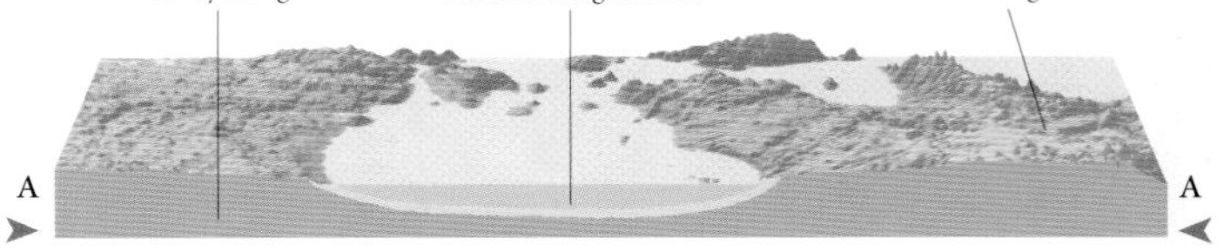

Section across the Canadian Shield showing where the ice sheet has depressed the underlying rock and formed bays and islands.

THE WESTERN CORDILLERA

ABOUT 80 MILLION YEARS ago the Pacific and North American plates collided, uplifting the Western Cordillera. This consists of the Aleutian, Coast, Cascade and Sierra Nevada mountains, and the inland Rocky Mountains. These run parallel from the Arctic to Mexico.

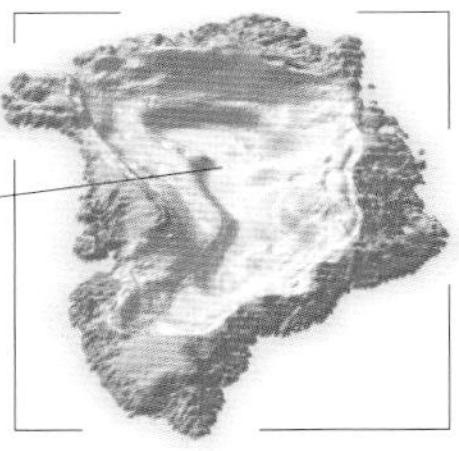

***This computer-generated** view shows the ice-covered island of Greenland without its ice cap.*

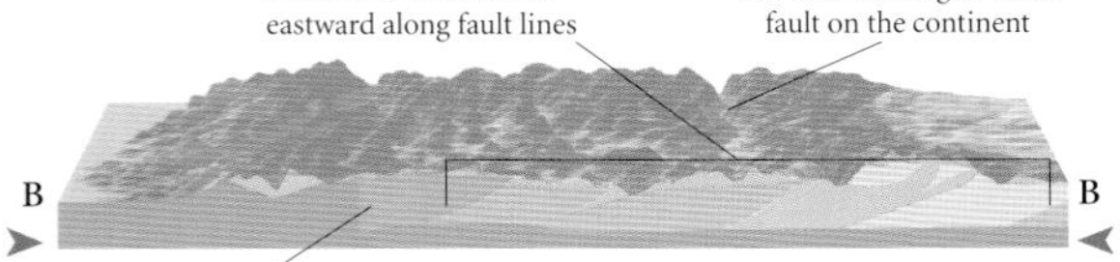

***Cross-section** through the Western Cordillera showing direction of mountain building.* ⟶

MAP KEY

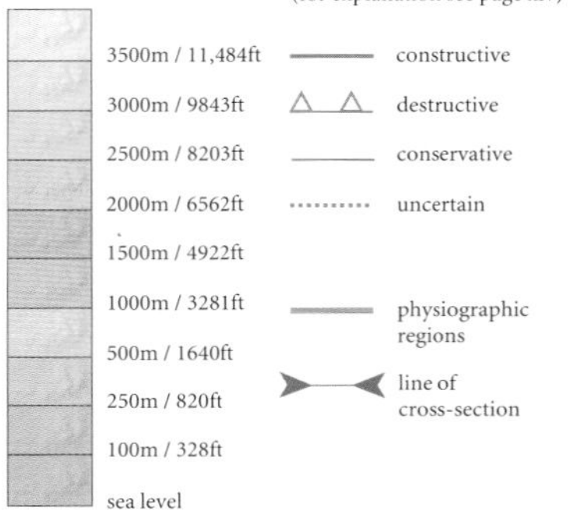

SCALE 1:38,000,000
(projection: Lambert Azimuthal Equal Area)

Km 0 100 200 400 600 800 1000
0 50 100 200 300 400 500 600 700 800 900 1000 Miles

THE APPALACHIANS

THE APPALACHIAN MOUNTAINS, uplifted about 400 million years ago, are some of the oldest in the world. They have been lowered and rounded by erosion and now slope gently toward the Atlantic across a broad coastal plain.

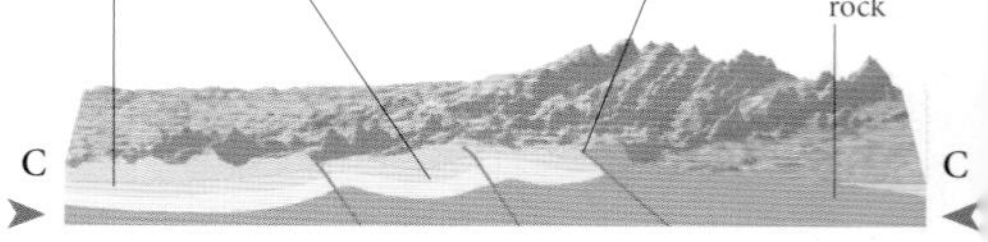

***Cross-section** through the Appalachians showing the numerous folds, which have subsequently been weathered to create a rounded relief.*

THE GREAT PLAINS & CENTRAL LOWLANDS

DEPOSITS LEFT by retreating glaciers and rivers have made this vast flat area very fertile. In the north this is the result of glaciation, with deposits up to one mile (1.7 km) thick, covering the basement rock. To the south and west, the massive Missouri/Mississippi river system has for centuries deposited silt across the plains, creating broad, flat floodplains and deltas.

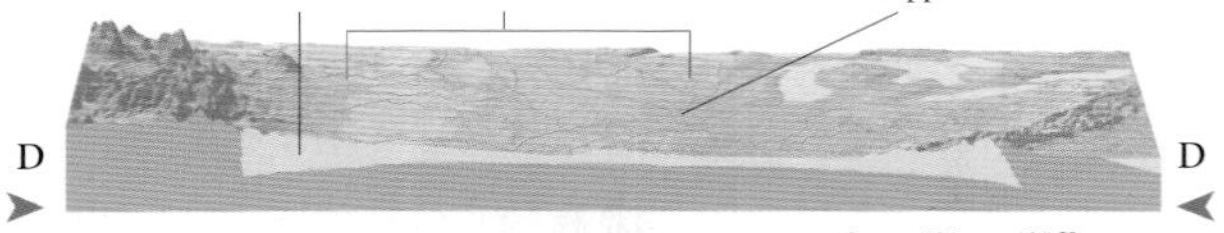

***Section** across the Great Plains and Central Lowlands showing river systems and structure.*

"Tornado alley" in the Mississippi Valley suffers frequent tornadoes.

CLIMATE

NORTH AMERICA'S climate includes extremes ranging from freezing Arctic conditions in Alaska and Greenland, to desert in the southwest, and tropical conditions in southeastern Florida, the Caribbean, and Central America. Central and southern regions are prone to severe storms including tornadoes and hurricanes.

Climate

- ice cap
- tundra
- subarctic
- cool continental
- warm humid
- semiarid
- arid
- humid equatorial
- tropical
- daily hours of sunshine, January
- daily hours of sunshine, July
- direction of hurricanes
- tornado zones

Much of the southwest is semi-desert; receiving less than 12 inches (300 mm) of rainfall a year.

TEMPERATURE

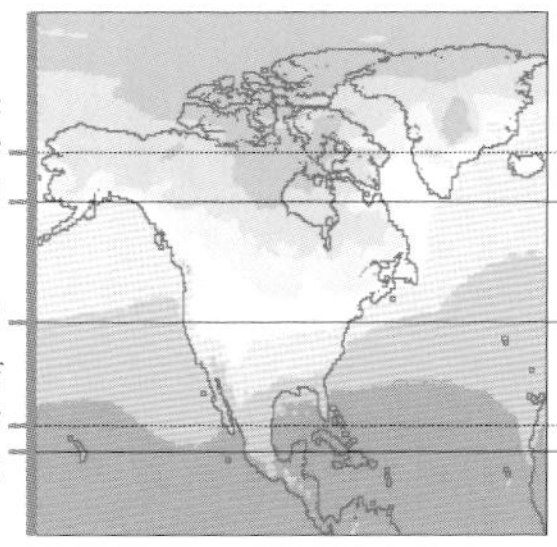

Average January temperature

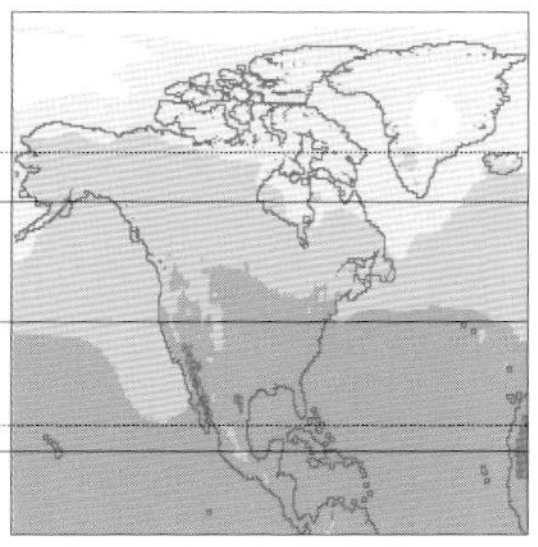

Average July temperature

Temperature

- below -30°C (-22°F)
- -30 to -20°C (-22 to -4°F)
- -20 to -10°C (-4 to 14°F)
- -10 to 0°C (14 to 32°F)
- 0 to 10°C (32 to 50° F)
- 10 to 20°C (50 to 68°F)
- 20 to 30°C (68 to 86°F)
- above 30°C (86° F)

RAINFALL

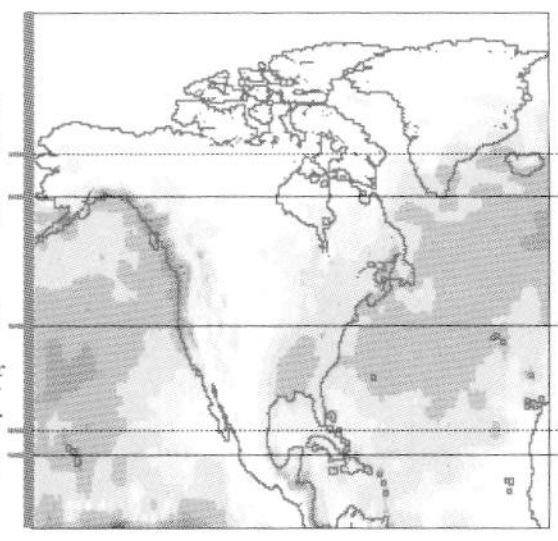

Average January rainfall

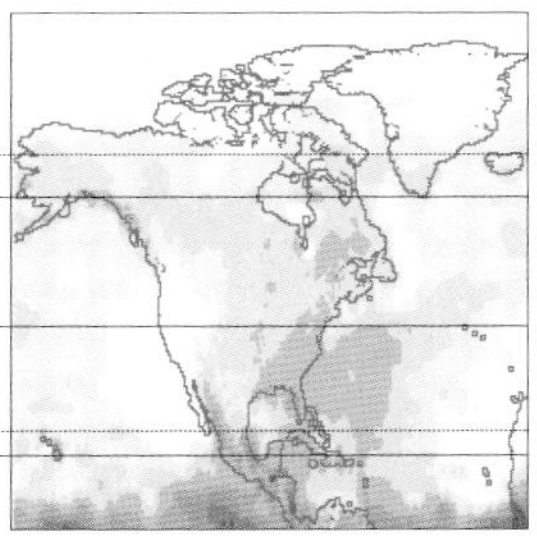

Average July rainfall

Rainfall

- 0–25 mm (0–1 in)
- 25–50 mm (1–2 in)
- 50–100 mm (2–4 in)
- 100–200 mm (4–8 in)
- 200–300 mm (8–12 in)
- 300–400 mm (12–16 in)
- 400–500 mm (16–20 in)
- more than 500 mm (20 in)

The lush, green mountains of the Lesser Antilles receive annual rainfalls of up to 360 inches (9,000 mm).

SHAPING THE CONTINENT

GLACIAL PROCESSES affect much of northern Canada, Greenland and the Western Cordillera. Along the western coast of North America, Central America, and the Caribbean, underlying plates moving together lead to earthquakes and volcanic eruptions. The vast river systems, fed by mountain streams, constantly erode and deposit material along their paths.

VOLCANIC ACTIVITY

1 Mount St. Helens volcano *(right)* in the Cascade Range erupted violently in May 1980, killing 57 people and leveling large areas of forest. The lateral blast filled a valley with debris for 15 miles (25 km).

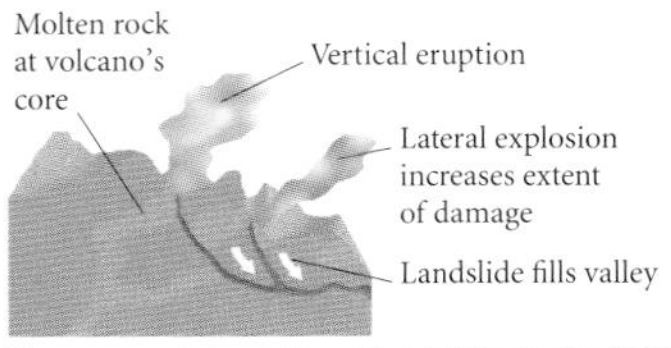

VOLCANIC ACTIVITY: ERUPTION OF MOUNT ST. HELENS

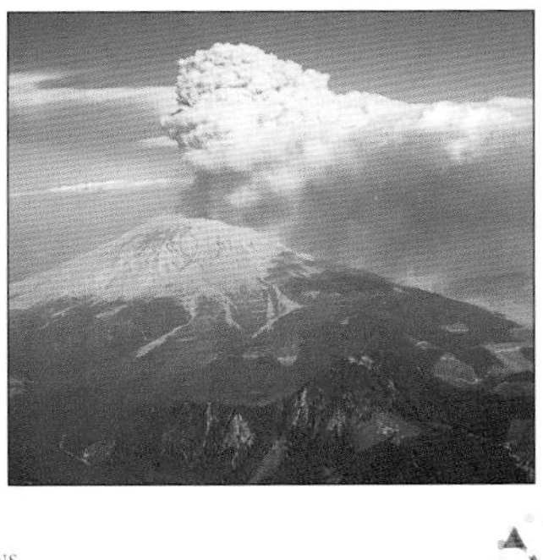

PERIGLACIATION

2 The ground in the far north is nearly always frozen: the surface thaws only in summer. This freeze-thaw process produces features such as pingos *(left)*; formed by the freezing of groundwater. With each successive winter ice accumulates producing a mound with a core of ice.

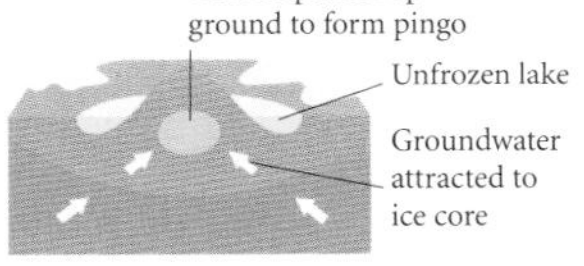

PERIGLACIATION: FORMATION OF A PINGO IN THE MACKENZIE DELTA

POST-GLACIAL LAKES

3 A chain of lakes from Great Bear Lake to the Great Lakes *(above)* was created as the ice retreated northward. Glaciers scoured hollows in the softer lowland rock. Glacial deposits at the lip of the hollows, and ridges of harder rock, trapped water to form lakes.

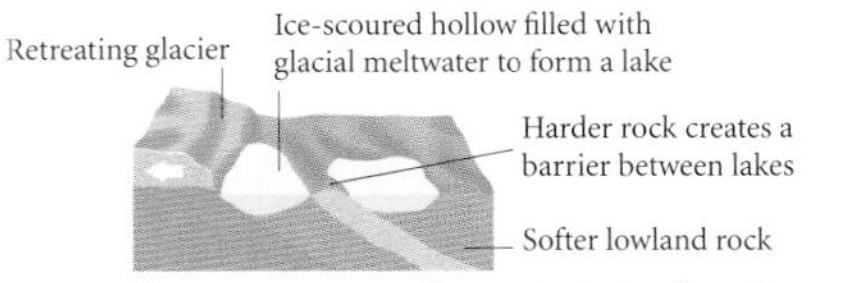

POST-GLACIAL LAKES: FORMATION OF THE GREAT LAKES

THE EVOLVING LANDSCAPE

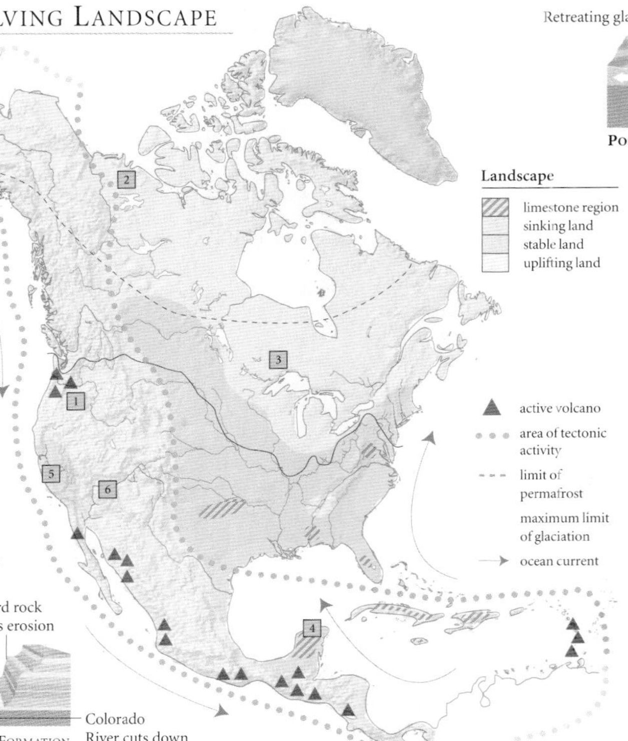

Landscape

- limestone region
- sinking land
- stable land
- uplifting land
- active volcano
- area of tectonic activity
- limit of permafrost
- maximum limit of glaciation
- ocean current

SEISMIC ACTIVITY

5 The San Andreas Fault *(above)* places much of the North America's west coast under constant threat from earthquakes. It is caused by the Pacific Plate grinding past the North American Plate at a faster rate, though in the same direction.

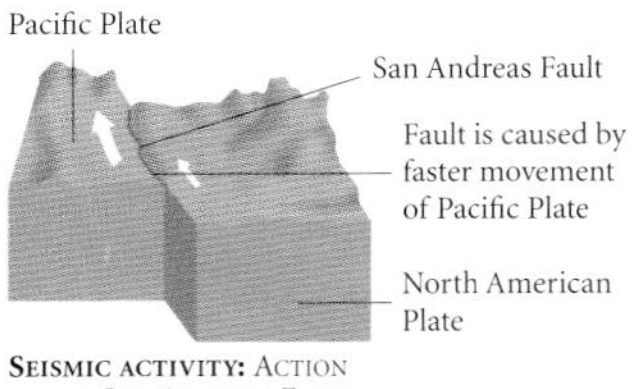

SEISMIC ACTIVITY: ACTION OF THE SAN ANDREAS FAULT

RIVER EROSION

6 The Grand Canyon *(above)* in the Colorado Plateau was created by the downward erosion of the Colorado River, combined with the gradual uplift of the plateau, over the past 30 million years. The contours of the canyon formed as the softer rock layers eroded into gentle slopes, and the hard rock layers into cliffs. The depth varies from 3,855–6,560 ft (1,175–2,000 m).

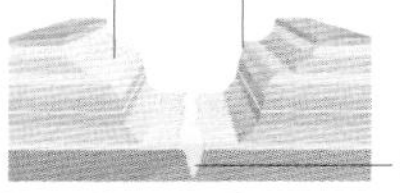

RIVER EROSION: FORMATION OF THE GRAND CANYON

WEATHERING

4 The Yucatan Peninsula is a vast, flat limestone plateau in southern Mexico. Weathering action from both rainwater and underground streams has enlarged fractures in the rock to form caves and hollows, called sinkholes *(above)*.

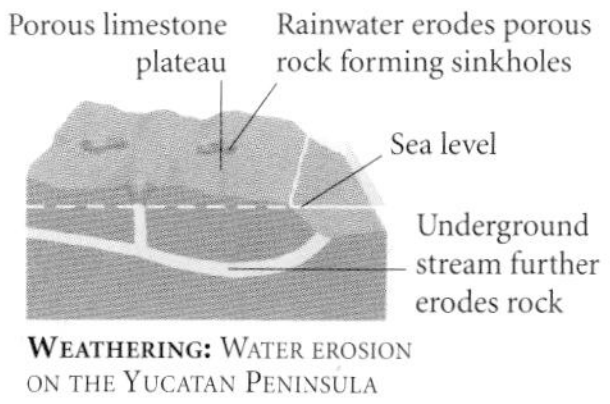

WEATHERING: WATER EROSION ON THE YUCATAN PENINSULA

Political North America

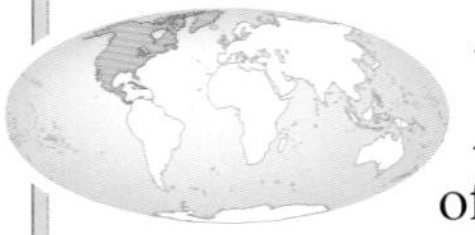

Democracy is well established in some parts of the continent but is a recent phenomenon in others. The economically dominant nations of Canada and the US have a long democratic tradition but elsewhere, notably in the countries of Central America, political turmoil has been more common. In Nicaragua and Haiti, harsh dictatorships have only recently been superseded by democratically-elected governments. North America's largest countries, Canada, Mexico, and the US have federal state systems, sharing political power between national and state governments. The US has intervened militarily on several occasions in Central America and the Caribbean to protect its strategic interests.

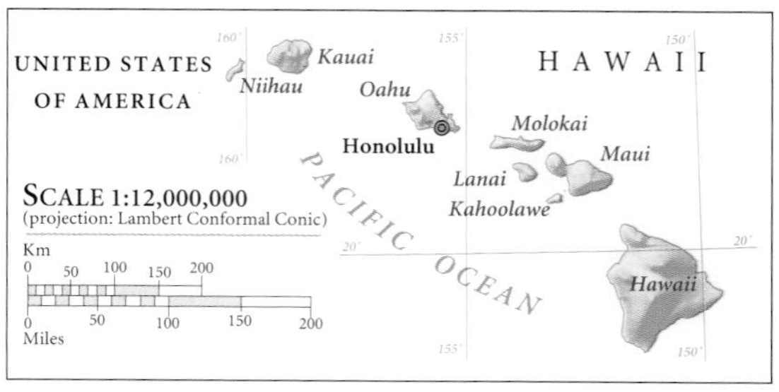

Transportation

In the 19th century, railroads opened up the North American continent. Air transportation is now more common for long distance passenger travel, although railroads are still extensively used for bulk freight transportation. Waterways like the Mississippi River are important for the transportation of bulk materials, and the Panama Canal is a vital link between the Pacific and Atlantic Oceans. In the 20th century, road transportation increased massively, with the introduction of cheap, mass-produced motor cars and extensive highway construction.

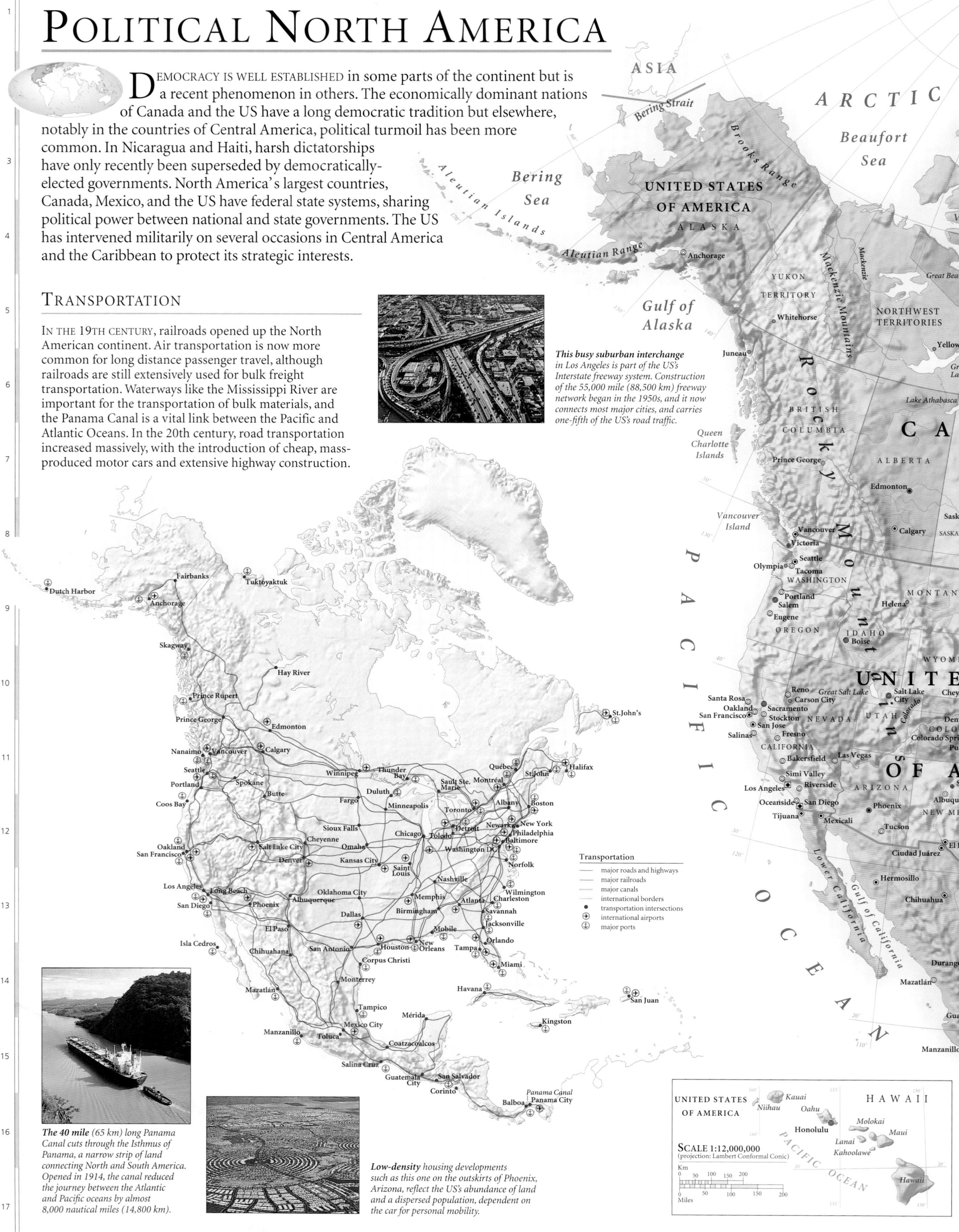

This busy suburban interchange *in Los Angeles is part of the US's Interstate freeway system. Construction of the 55,000 mile (88,500 km) freeway network began in the 1950s, and it now connects most major cities, and carries one-fifth of the US's road traffic.*

The 40 mile *(65 km) long Panama Canal cuts through the Isthmus of Panama, a narrow strip of land connecting North and South America. Opened in 1914, the canal reduced the journey between the Atlantic and Pacific oceans by almost 8,000 nautical miles (14,800 km).*

Low-density *housing developments such as this one on the outskirts of Phoenix, Arizona, reflect the US's abundance of land and a dispersed population, dependent on the car for personal mobility.*

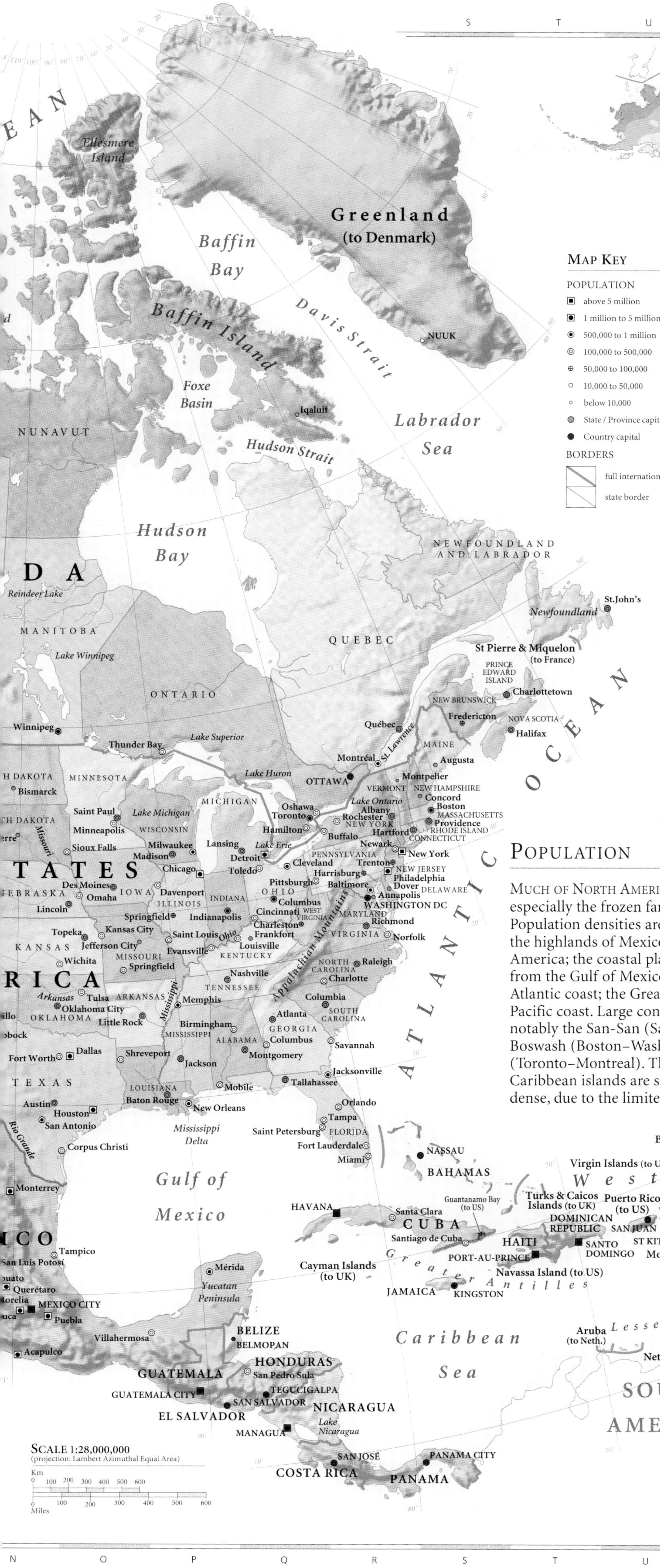

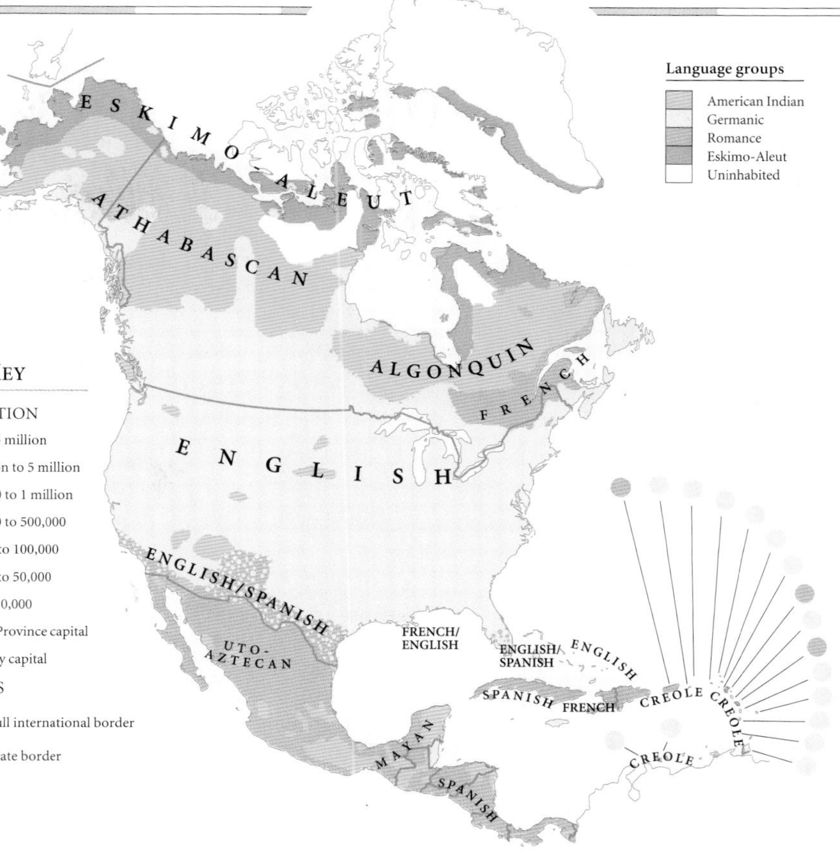

Land in northern Canada has been set aside for Inuit reserves, allowing the Inuit and other Native American groups to maintain their traditional practices and culture.

LANGUAGES

THE THREE MAJOR official languages of North America are of European origin, brought by settlers in the 16th century. In Canada, French and English are spoken; in the US, English is the main language, with large Spanish-speaking areas in the southwest; Mexicans are Spanish-speaking; while the Caribbean islands use French, English and Spanish as well as the hybrid Creole patois. In isolated areas, languages of the indigenous peoples still exist, such as Inuit in the far north of the continent.

POPULATION

MUCH OF NORTH AMERICA is almost empty, especially the frozen far north. Population densities are highest in the highlands of Mexico and Central America; the coastal plain stretching from the Gulf of Mexico along the Atlantic coast; the Great Lakes area; and the Pacific coast. Large conurbations have developed, notably the San-San (San Francisco–San Diego), Boswash (Boston–Washington), and Main Street (Toronto–Montreal). The populations of the Caribbean islands are small, but settlement is dense, due to the limited amount of land available.

Mexico City is one of the world's largest and highest cities. Fresh water supplies are dwindling, while air pollution regularly creates thick smog.

North American Resources

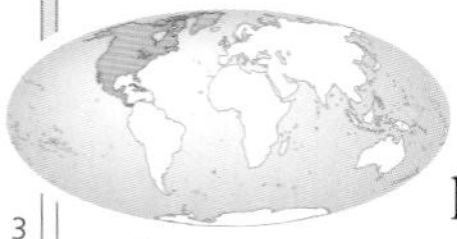

The two northern countries of Canada and the US are richly endowed with natural resources that have helped to fuel economic development. The US is the world's largest economy, although today it is facing stiff competition from the Far East. Mexico has relied on oil revenues but there are hopes that the North American Free Trade Agreement (NAFTA), will encourage trade growth with Canada and the US. The poorer countries of Central America and the Caribbean depend largely on cash crops and tourism.

Standard of Living

The US and Canada have one of the highest overall standards of living in the world. However, many people still live in poverty, especially in urban ghettos and some rural areas. Central America and the Caribbean are markedly poorer than their wealthier northern neighbors. Haiti is the poorest country in the western hemisphere.

Industry

The modern, industrialized economies of the US and Canada contrast sharply with those of Mexico, Central America, and the Caribbean. Manufacturing is especially important in the US; vehicle production is concentrated around the Great Lakes, while electronic and hi-tech industries are increasingly found in the western and southern states. Mexico depends on oil exports and assembly work, taking advantage of cheap labor. Many Central American and Caribbean countries rely heavily on agricultural exports.

After its purchase from Russia in 1867, Alaska's frozen lands were largely ignored by the US. Oil reserves similar in magnitude to those in eastern Texas were discovered in Prudhoe Bay, Alaska in 1968. Freezing temperatures and a fragile environment hamper oil extraction.

Fish such as cod, flounder, and plaice are caught in the Grand Banks, off the Newfoundland coast, and processed in many North Atlantic coastal settlements.

South of San Francisco, "Silicon Valley" is both a national and international center for hi-tech industries, electronic industries, and research institutions.

Multinational companies rely on cheap labor and tax benefits to assemble vehicles in Mexican factories.

The health of the Wall Street stock market in New York is the standard measure of the state of the world's economy.

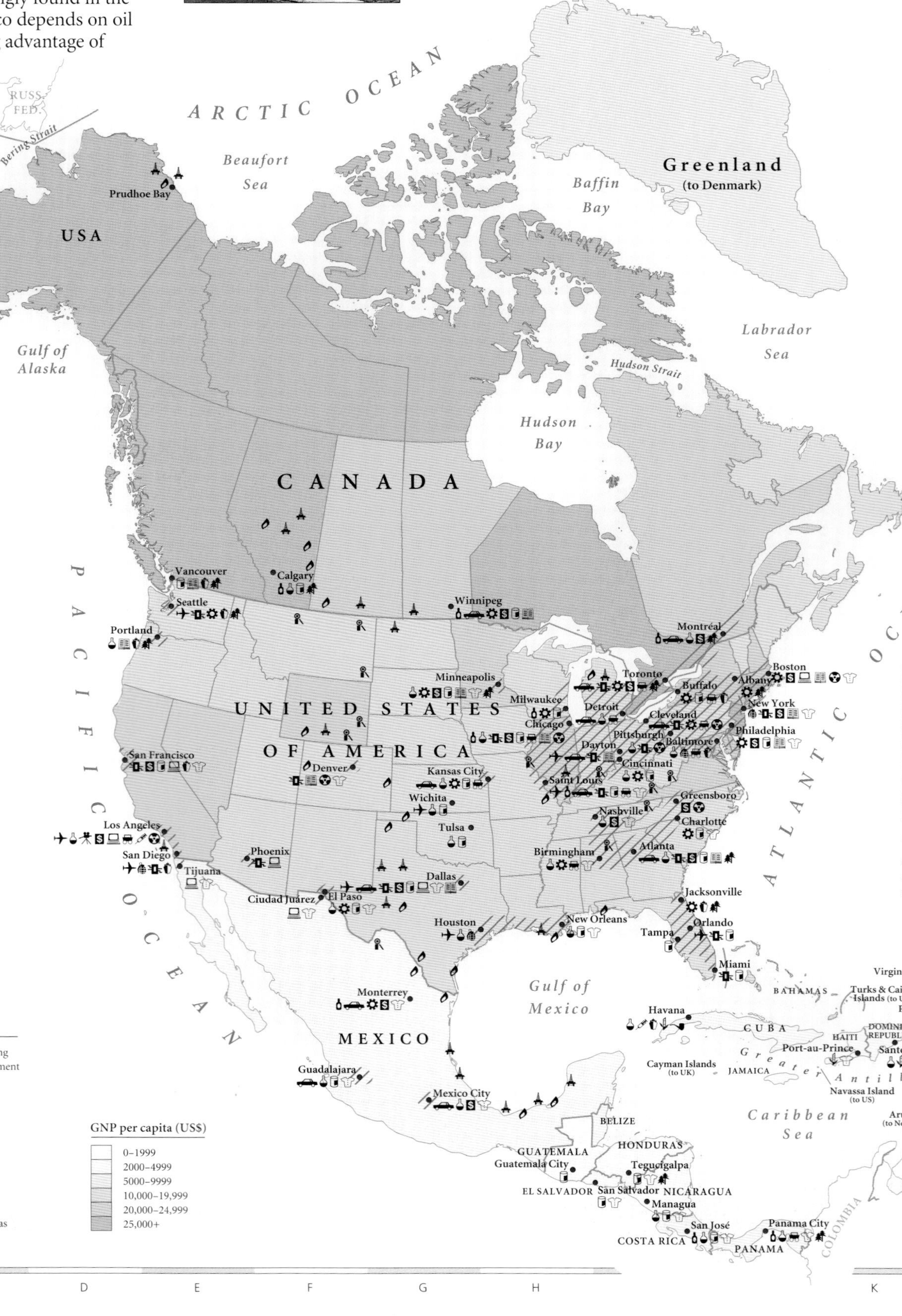

N O P Q R S T U V W X Y Z

Environmental Issues

Many fragile environments are under threat throughout the region. In Haiti, all the primary rain forest has been destroyed, while air pollution from factories and cars in Mexico City is among the worst in the world. Elsewhere, industry and mining pose threats, particularly in the delicate arctic environment of Alaska where oil spills have polluted coastlines and decimated fish stocks.

***Wild bison** graze in Yellowstone National Park, the world's first national park. Designated in 1872, geothermal springs and boiling mud are among its natural spectacles, making it a major tourist attraction.*

Mineral Resources

Fossil fuels are exploited in considerable quantities throughout the continent. Coal mining in the Appalachians is declining but vast open pits exist further west in Wyoming. Oil and natural gas are found in Alaska, Texas, the Gulf of Mexico, and the Canadian West. Canada has large quantities of nickel, while Jamaica has considerable deposits of bauxite, and Mexico has large reserves of silver.

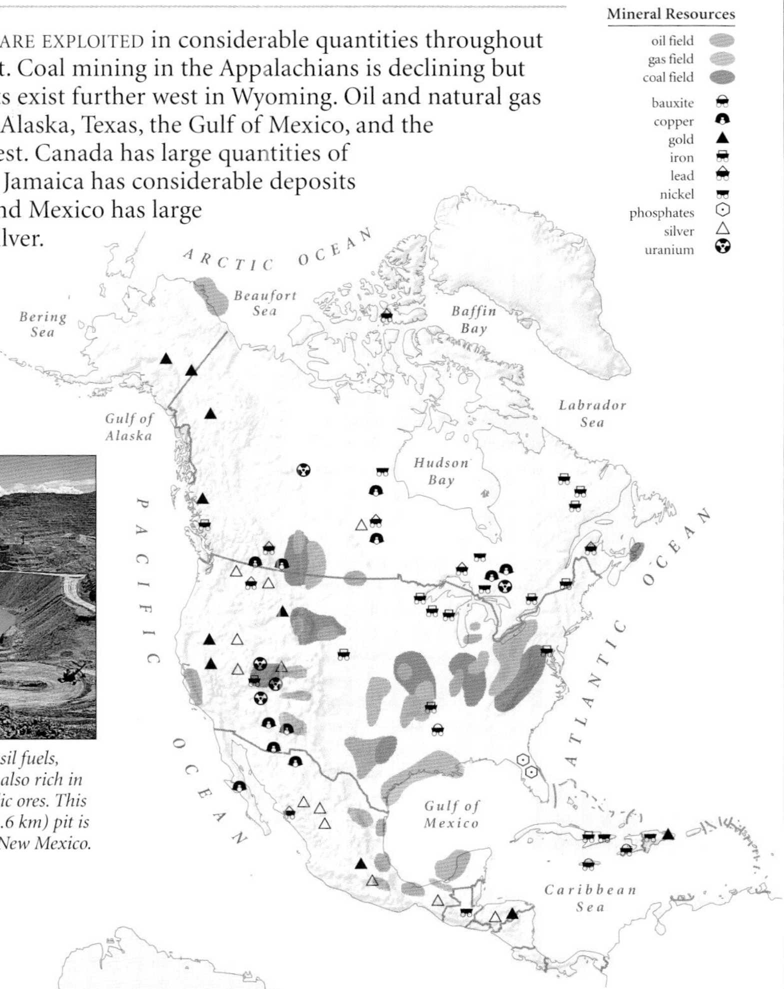

***In addition** to fossil fuels, North America is also rich in exploitable metallic ores. This vast, mile-deep (1.6 km) pit is a copper mine in New Mexico.*

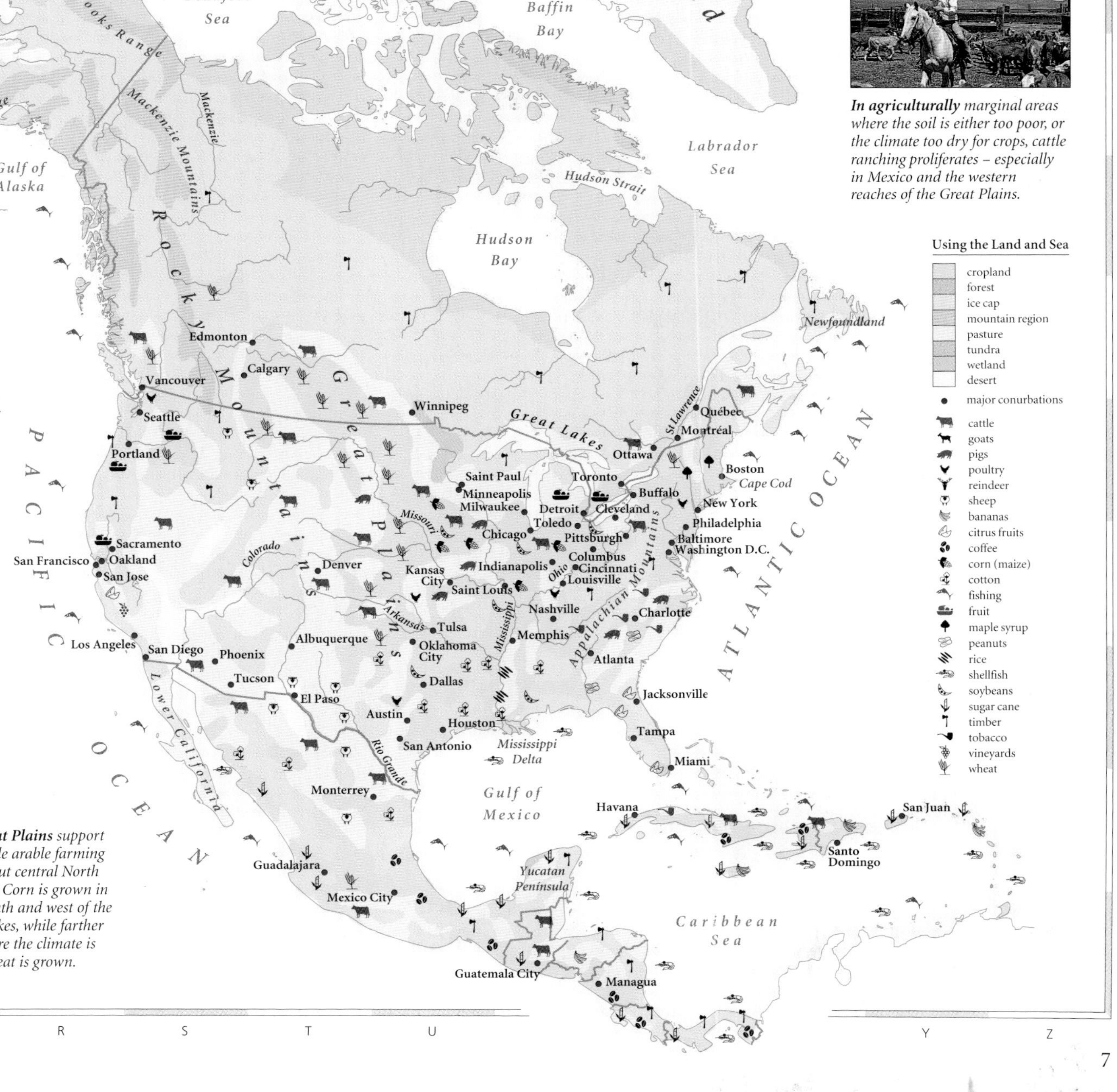

***In agriculturally** marginal areas where the soil is either too poor, or the climate too dry for crops, cattle ranching proliferates – especially in Mexico and the western reaches of the Great Plains.*

Using the Land and Sea

Abundant land and fertile soils stretch from the Canadian prairies to Texas creating North America's agricultural heartland. Cereals and cattle ranching form the basis of the farming economy, with corn and soybeans also important. Fruit and vegetables are grown in California using irrigation, while Florida is a leading producer of citrus fruits. Caribbean and Central American countries depend on cash crops such as bananas, coffee, and sugar cane, often grown on large plantations. This reliance on a single crop can leave these countries vulnerable to fluctuating world crop prices.

***Sugar cane is Cuba's** main agricultural crop, and is grown and processed throughout the Caribbean. Fermented sugar is used to make rum.*

***The Great Plains** support large-scale arable farming throughout central North America. Corn is grown in a belt south and west of the Great Lakes, while farther west where the climate is drier, wheat is grown.*

N O P Q R S T U Y Z

Canada: Western Provinces

Alberta, British Columbia, Manitoba, Saskatchewan, Yukon Territory

The mountains of the west coast, incorporating British Columbia and the Yukon Territory, descend into the vast, flat prairies of Alberta, Saskatchewan, and Manitoba. The empty lands and fertile soils of the prairie provinces attracted migrants, and the descendants of early European immigrants still make up a large proportion of the population. The mechanization of agriculture has reduced the need for labor, and rural population densities remain low. The majority of the people live within 100 miles (160 km) of the southern Canada–US border, and in British Columbia, one of the leading Canadian provinces in terms of economic wealth. The Yukon Territory, in the far north, remains a relatively unspoiled wilderness, containing large, untapped mineral reserves. This province has a significant population of Native Americans people, many of whom maintain a traditional lifestyle.

Using the Land and Sea

Wheat farming is the economic mainstay of Alberta, Manitoba, and Saskatchewan, which contain 82% of farmland in Canada. Cattle are also raised on the prairies. Forestry and fishing are the most prominent resource-based industries in British Columbia. Despite the mountainous terrain, fruit and specialized grains can be grown in the Okanagan and Fraser valleys.

Land use and agricultural distribution

- cattle
- cereals
- fishing
- fruit
- timber
- major towns
- pasture
- cropland
- forest
- wetland
- barren
- tundra

Large, highly-mechanized and often very specialized farms, requiring huge investment but little labor, characterize modern farming in the prairies.

The Urban/Rural Population Divide

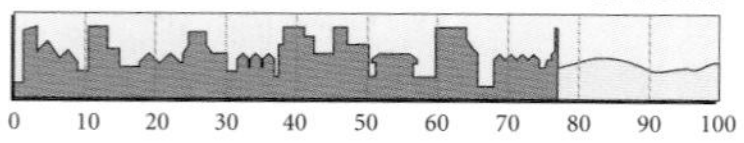

Population Density	Total Land Area
7 people per sq mile (3 people per sq km)	1,224,449 sq miles (3,172,150 sq km)

Transportation & Industry

The western provinces contain a wealth of mineral resources. Alberta holds the bulk of Canada's fossil fuels; the other provinces contain reserves of metallic ores, such as zinc, lead, and silver. Isolation from markets has slowed the development of manufacturing, restricting it to the large cities like Vancouver, Winnipeg, and Calgary. Hydroelectric power is widely exploited, although there is increasing concern about potential ecological damage.

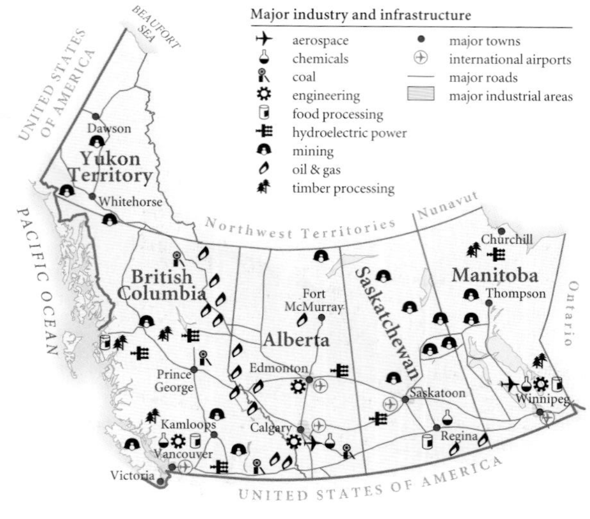

Transportation Network

Roads	82,438 miles (135,145 km)
Railways	6,459 miles (10,401 km)
Waterways	10,811 miles (17,410 km)
Air	None

The transportation network of the western provinces is dominated by east–west routes that weave through mountain passes and spread across the plains. Access to some northern areas is restricted to air travel.

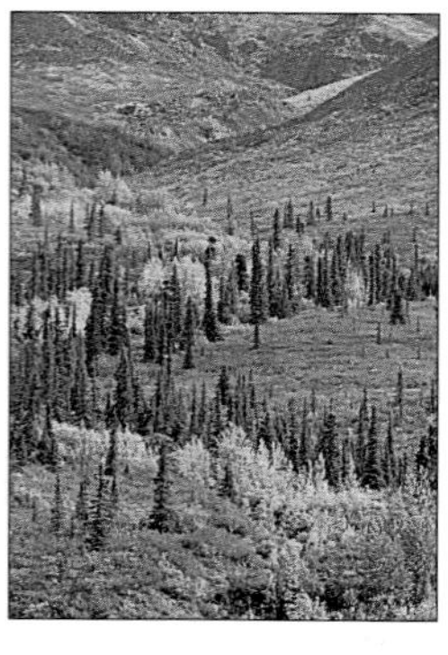

***Much of the Yukon Territory** is uninhabited tundra. Industry is based on the extraction of mineral resources, and to a lesser extent, on the scattered forests of the south.*

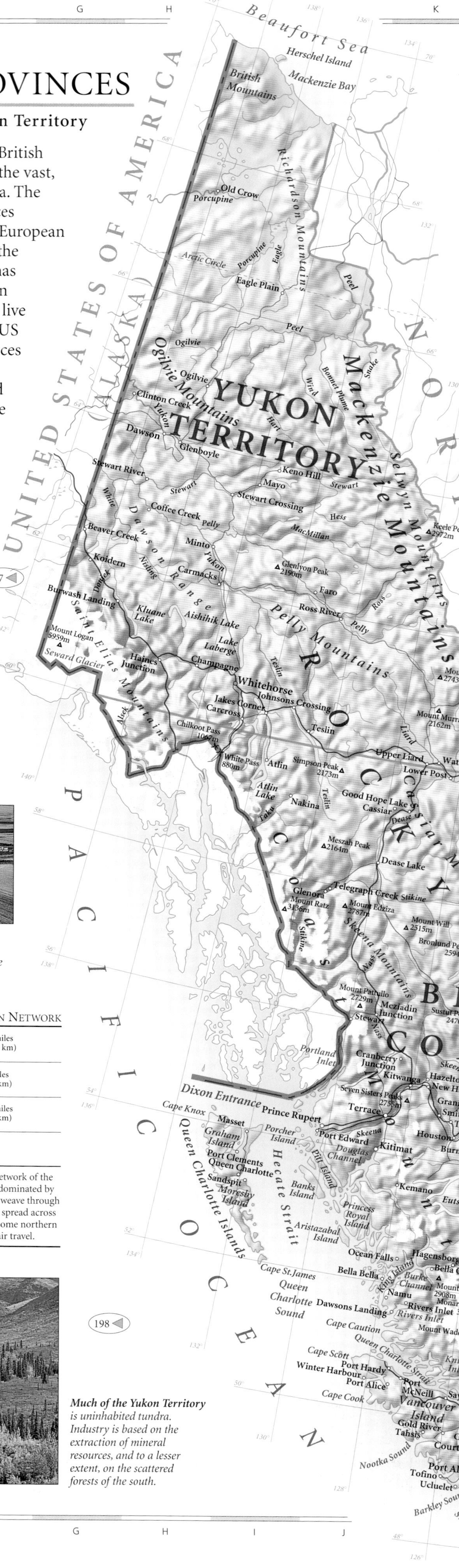

17

198

***The Fraser River valley** is a major area of settlement in British Columbia. Railraods cross the Rocky Mountains via this valley.*

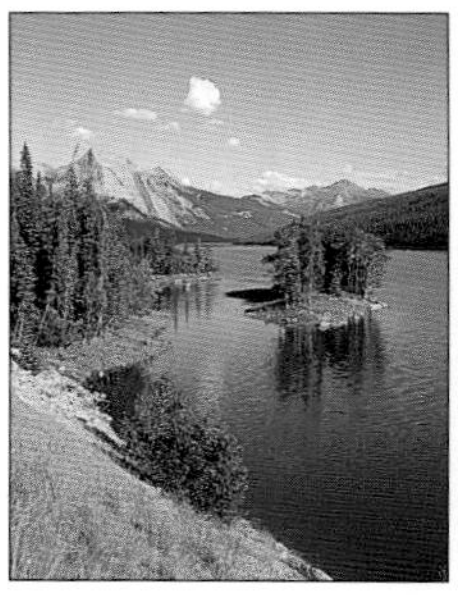

***Established in 1907**, Jasper National Park lies in the heart of the Rocky Mountains. It is noted for its spectacular alpine scenery and contains part of the large Columbia Icefield.*

THE LANDSCAPE

THE MASSIVE ROCKY MOUNTAINS form a continental divide between rivers flowing eastward and westward. The interior plains lie east of the mountains, stretching from the Arctic Circle south into the US. Covered with glacial deposits from the last Ice Age, these are interspersed with hilly regions and long, steep escarpments.

MAP KEY

POPULATION

- 500,000 to 1 million
- 100,000 to 500,000
- 50,000 to 100,000
- 10,000 to 50,000
- below 10,000

ELEVATION

- 6000m / 19,686ft
- 4000m / 13,124ft
- 3000m / 9843ft
- 2000m / 6562ft
- 1000m / 3281ft
- 500m / 1640ft
- 250m / 820ft
- 100m / 328ft
- sea level

SCALE 1:7,500,000
(projection: Lambert Conformal Conic)

Km 0 25 50 100 150 200 250
Miles 0 25 50 100 150 200 250

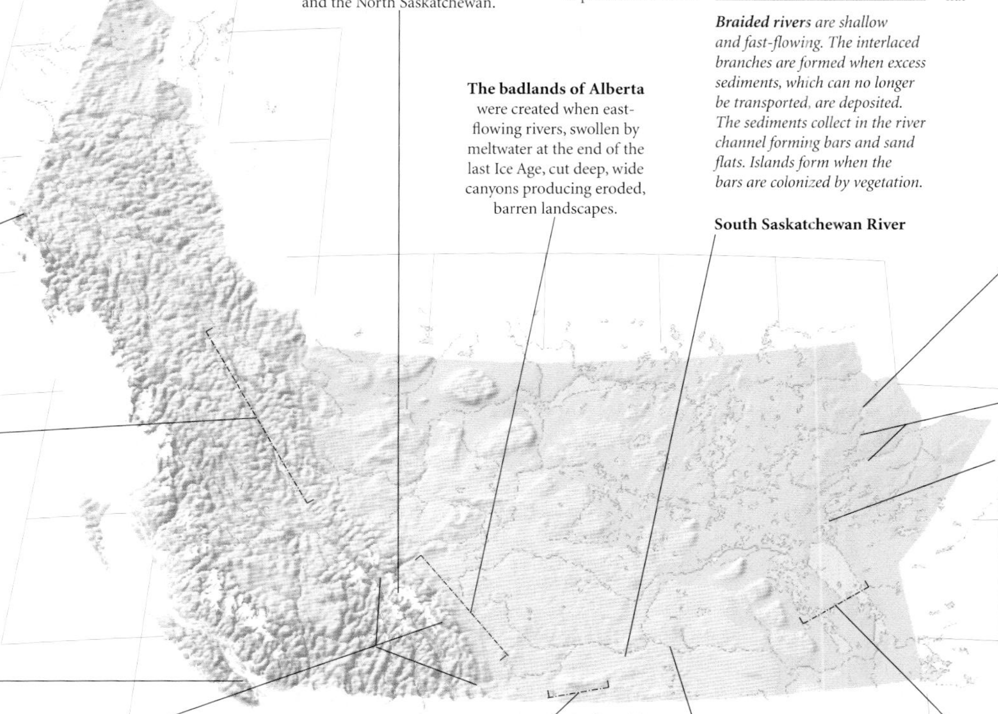

Mount Logan rises 19,551 ft (5,959 m). It is the highest peak in Canada.

The Rocky Mountain Trench is the longest linear fault in the world. It has formed a straight, flat-bottomed valley between 2–9 miles (4–15 km) wide, and up to 3,280 ft (1,000 m) deep.

Hundreds of islands dot the fjord-indented coast of British Columbia; the largest is Vancouver Island.

Three major passes cut through the Rocky Mountains: Yellowhead, Kicking Horse, and Crowsnest. They are all used as transportation routes through the mountains.

The Columbia Icefield in the Rocky Mountains is the source of two major rivers, the Athabasca and the North Saskatchewan.

The badlands of Alberta were created when east-flowing rivers, swollen by meltwater at the end of the last Ice Age, cut deep, wide canyons producing eroded, barren landscapes.

The Cypress Hills rise to 4,806 ft (1,465 m) above the surrounding plain. Having escaped the last glaciation they contain unique plant and animal life. The silvery lupine, bunchberry, and lodgepole pine all grow in the cool, moist climate of the hills.

South Saskatchewan River

The Alberta and Saskatchewan plains bear strong testament to past glaciations. The Assiniboine, Saskatchewan and Qu'Appelle Rivers occupy flat-bottomed, steep-sided valleys eroded during the last Ice Age by glacial meltwater.

***Braided rivers** are shallow and fast-flowing. The interlaced branches are formed when excess sediments, which can no longer be transported, are deposited. The sediments collect in the river channel forming bars and sand flats. Islands form when the bars are colonized by vegetation.*

***Across the tundra** of northern Manitoba, widespread permafrost inhibits water from permeating the soil. This causes rivers like the Churchill to flow in many channels, which can be frozen for up to six months during the winter.*

The Nelson and Churchill Rivers drain northward across the Canadian Shield to Hudson Bay. The shield covers three-fifths of Saskatchewan.

Setting Lake

***Ancient granite outcrops**, part of the Canadian Shield, rise above the surface of Setting Lake, which was initially formed by meltwater from the last Ice Age.*

The lowlands of Manitoba are a basin that once held the vast post-glacial Lake Agassiz, remnants of which include Lake Winnipeg, Lake Winnipegosis, and Lake Manitoba.

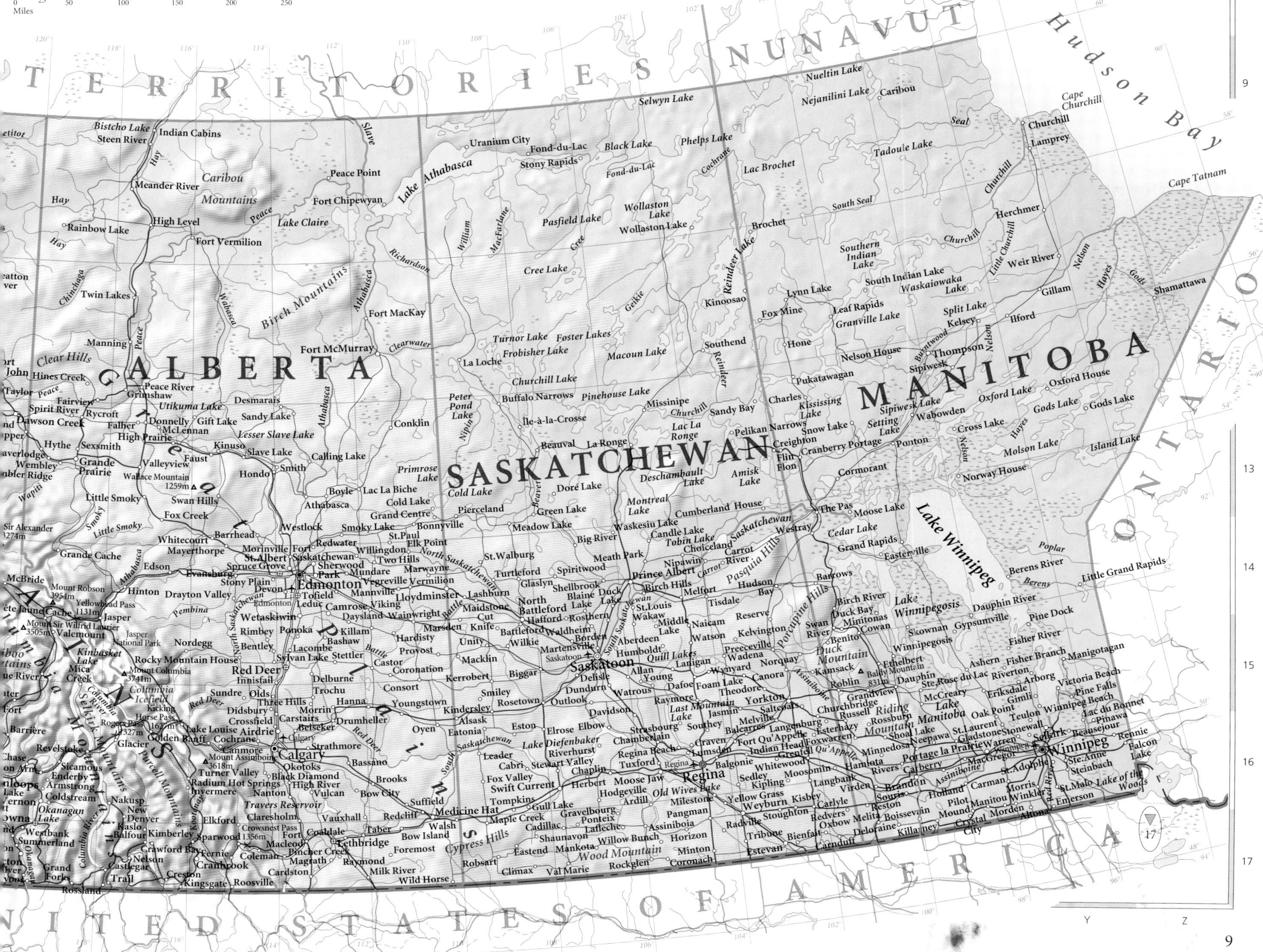

CANADA: EASTERN PROVINCES

New Brunswick, Newfoundland & Labrador, Nova Scotia, Ontario, Prince Edward Island, Quebec, *St. Pierre & Miquelon* (to France)

COLONIZED BY BOTH THE ENGLISH AND THE FRENCH during the 16th century, Canada's eastern provinces are still marked by their dual influences. They contain the last fragment of once-sizeable French territories, the islands of St. Pierre and Miquelon. French remains Canada's second official language and Quebec's first language. The population of the eastern provinces is highly concentrated in the south, especially along the border with the US. A recent decline in fishing in the Atlantic provinces has encouraged a steady flow of westerly migration to more properous regions. The north, around Hudson Bay, remains snow-covered for most of the year and the indigenous Inuit people make up the bulk of its sparse population.

Rocher Percé, is 290 ft (88 m) high. Lying off the southeastern coast of Quebec, it is a sanctuary for sea birds.

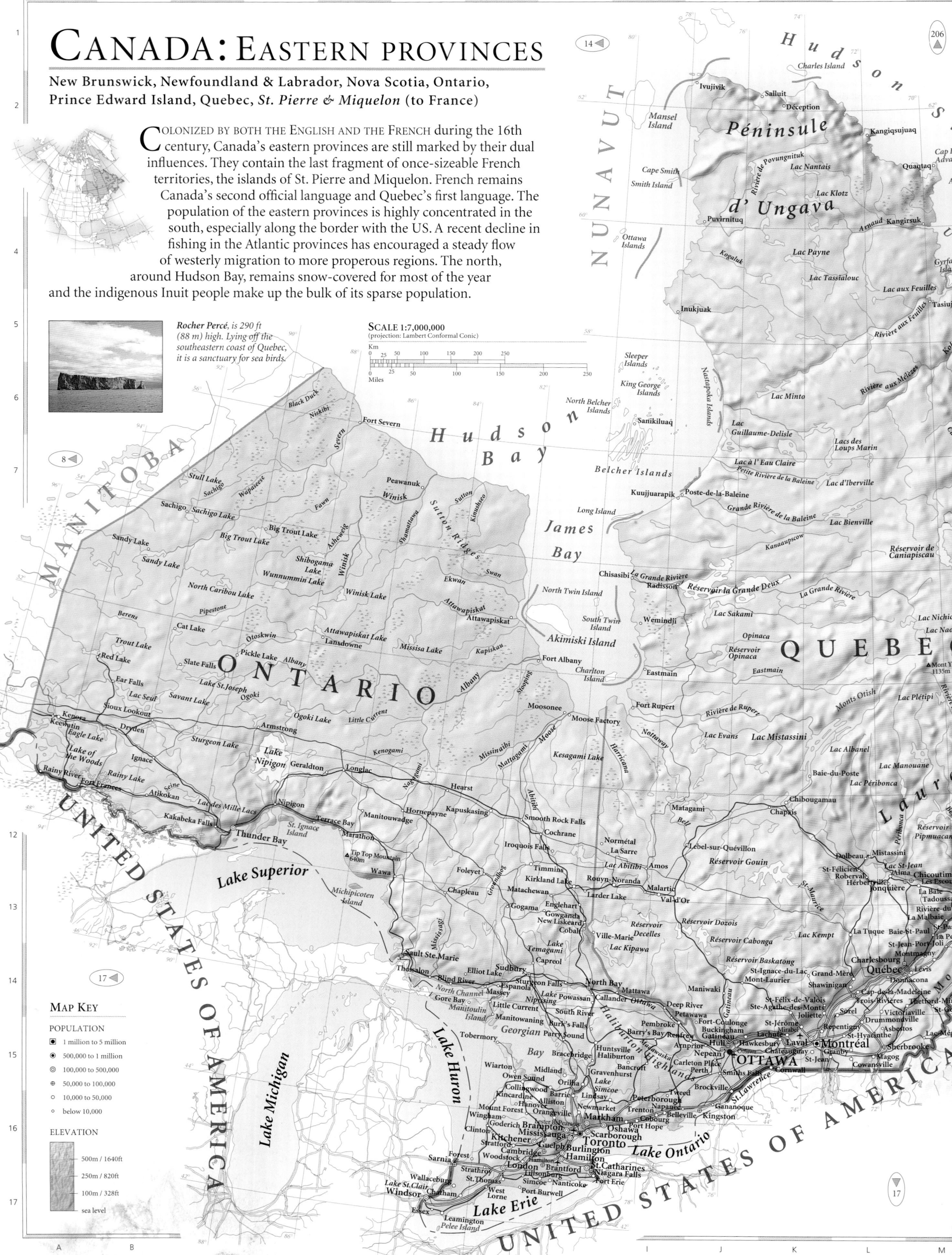

MAP KEY

POPULATION
- 1 million to 5 million
- 500,000 to 1 million
- 100,000 to 500,000
- 50,000 to 100,000
- 10,000 to 50,000
- below 10,000

ELEVATION
- 500m / 1640ft
- 250m / 820ft
- 100m / 328ft
- sea level

The Landscape

Much of eastern Canada is part of the Canadian Shield. Glaciers have scoured the land leaving deposits that have dammed and diverted streams, to create a rocky landscape strewn with lakes and swamps. Much of the ground is subject to permafrost, which further impedes drainage. The uplands in the far east are the most northerly extension of the Appalachian mountain chain.

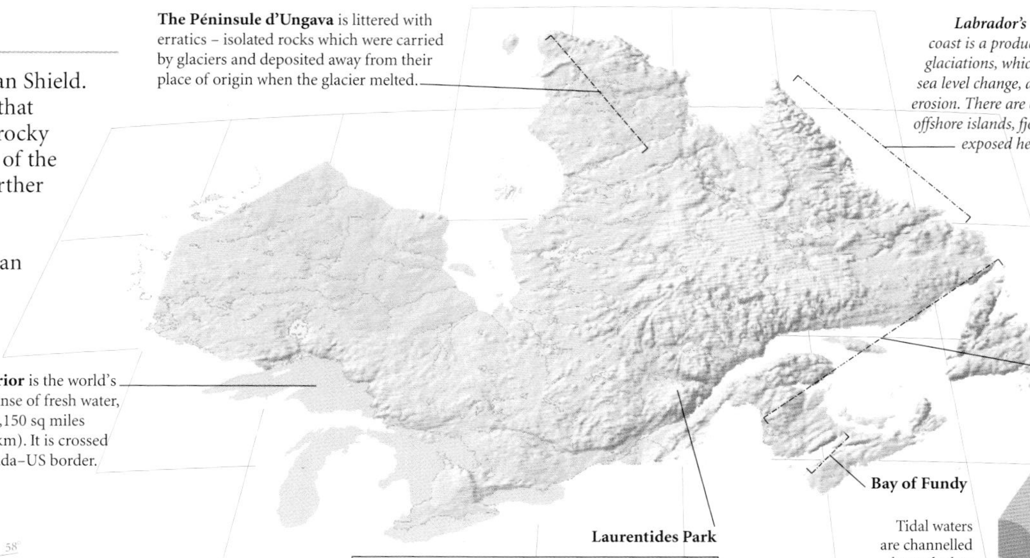

The Péninsule d'Ungava is littered with erratics – isolated rocks which were carried by glaciers and deposited away from their place of origin when the glacier melted.

Lake Superior is the world's largest expanse of fresh water, covering 32,150 sq miles (83,270 sq km). It is crossed by the Canada–US border.

The eroded highlands of New Brunswick, Nova Scotia and Newfoundland are part of the Appalachian mountain chain, formed over 400 million years ago.

***Labrador's** indented coast is a product of past glaciations, which caused sea level change, and wave erosion. There are countless offshore islands, fjords, and exposed headlands.*

The forested Laurentides Park incorporates part of the Laurentian Mountains. Within its boundaries are over 1,600 lakes.

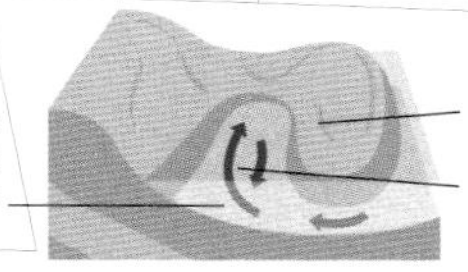

***At the Bay of Fundy**, incoming waves are funneled down the long, narrow, steep-sided bay. These topographical features cause fast-flowing tides which can rise 70 ft (21 m).*

***The tides** at the Bay of Fundy are among the highest in the world. At low tide the tree-topped rocks have been likened to flowerpots.*

Transportation & Industry

Both Quebec and Ontario have a diversified manufacturing sector located in the south. Across the rest of the region, industry is largely based around local resources, which accounts for the large number of fish and timber processing plants and mines. Many of the fast-flowing rivers are also gradually being harnessed for hydroelectric power.

Major industry and infrastructure
- aerospace
- vehicle manufacture
- chemicals
- fish processing
- food processing
- hi-tech industry
- hydroelectric power
- mining
- timber processing
- capital cities
- major towns
- international airports
- major roads
- major industrial areas

Transportation Network

84,522 miles (136,325 km)	
1,858 miles (2,998 km)	
12,774 miles (20,602 km)	
376 miles (606 km)	

The majority of Canada's large ports lie in the east. Since the 1960s the region's rail network has been steadily reduced; Newfoundland recently lost its last remaining line, the Long-Cross Island line.

***Fish processing** is a major industry in the Atlantic provinces. Fogo Island, off Newfoundland, has barely a thousand inhabitants but it is able to sustain a number of cod canneries.*

Using the Land and Sea

With thin soils restricting farming to the south, the forests that grow in vast unbroken tracts across eastern Canada provide an important source of revenue. Coastal communities rely heavily on the rich fishing grounds of the Atlantic Ocean, although foreign competition and overfishing have resulted in strict policies to conserve stocks.

The Urban/Rural Population Divide

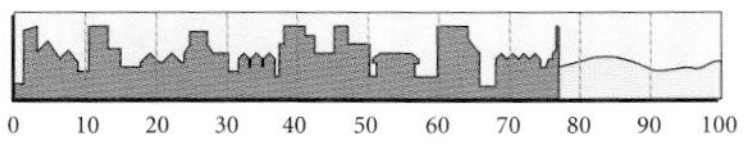

Population Density	Total Land Area
17 people per sq mile (6 people per sq km)	1,061,600 sq miles (2,750,260 sq km)

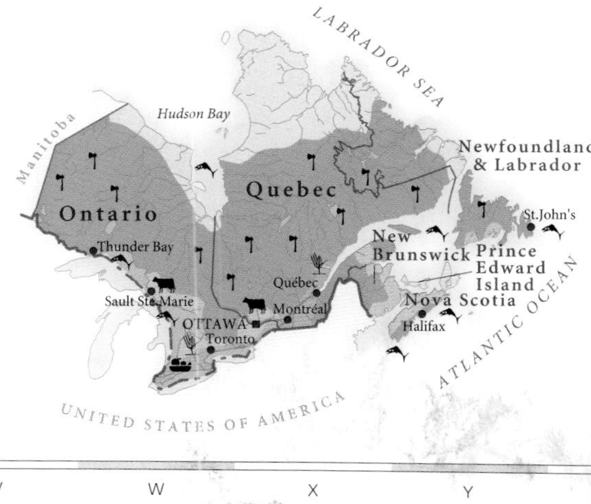

Land use and agricultural distribution
- cattle
- cereals
- fishing
- fruit
- timber
- capital cities
- major towns
- pasture
- cropland
- forest
- tundra

***Prince Edward Island** is the only Atlantic province with notable agricultural land. The island is Canada's leading producer of potatoes.*

66

Southeastern Canada

Southern Ontario, Southern Quebec

The southern parts of Quebec and Ontario form the economic heart of Canada. The two provinces are divided by their language and culture; in Quebec, French is the main language, whereas English is spoken in Ontario. Separatist sentiment in Quebec has led to a provincial referendum on the question of a sovereignty association with Canada. The region contains Canada's capital, Ottawa and its two largest cities: Toronto, the center of commerce and Montréal, the cultural and administrative heart of French Canada.

***The port at Montréal** is situated on the St. Lawrence Seaway. A network of 16 locks allows sea-going vessels access to routes once plied by fur-trappers and early settlers.*

***Niagara Falls** lies on the border between Canada and the US. It comprises a system of two falls: American Falls, in New York, is separated from Horseshoe Falls, in Ontario, by Goat Island. Horseshoe Falls, seen here, plunges 184 ft (56 m) and is 2,500 ft (762 m) wide.*

Transportation & Industry

The cities of southern Quebec and Ontario, and their hinterlands, form the heart of Canadian manufacturing industry. Toronto is Canada's leading financial center, and Ontario's motor and aerospace industries have developed around the city. A major center for nickel mining lies to the north of Toronto. Most of Quebec's industry is located in Montréal, the oldest port in North America. Chemicals, paper manufacture, and the construction of transportation equipment are leading industrial activities.

Transportation Network

The opening of the St. Lawrence Seaway in 1959 finally allowed ocean-going ships (up to 24,000 tons (tonnes)) access to the interior of Canada, creating a vital trading route.

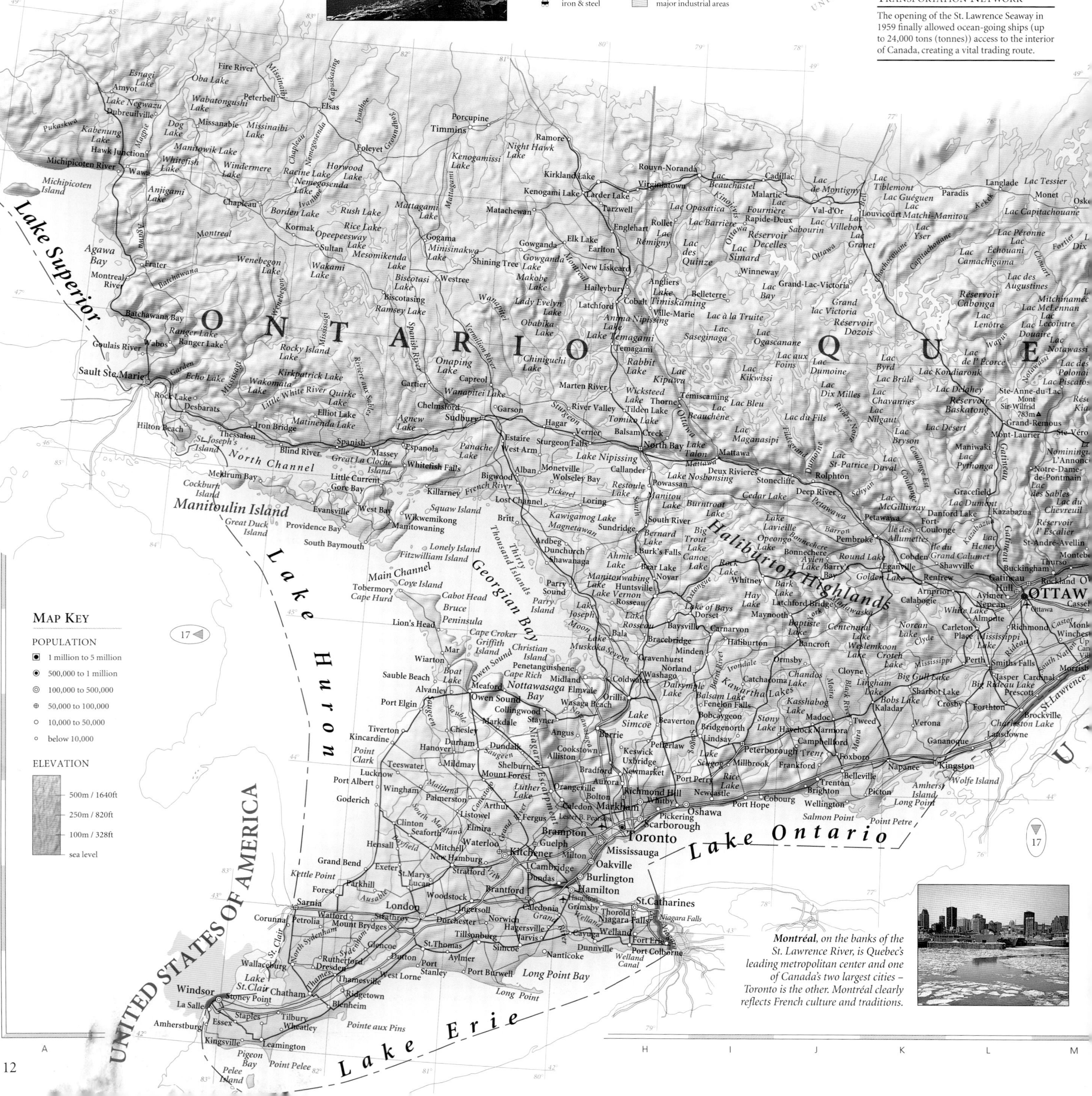

***Montréal**, on the banks of the St. Lawrence River, is Quebec's leading metropolitan center and one of Canada's two largest cities – Toronto is the other. Montréal clearly reflects French culture and traditions.*

N O P Q Y W X Y

USING THE LAND AND SEA

THE PRODUCTIVE NIAGARA "FRUIT BELT" on the shores of Lake Erie and Lake Ontario is a major farming region, although available farmland is being challenged by urban expansion. Quebec is Canada's leading producer of maple syrup and dairy products. In the north, farmland gives way to extensive areas of forest, partly used for commercial logging. Fishing occurs in Atlantic waters and in the Great Lakes.

Land use and agricultural distribution

- cattle
- fish
- cereals
- fruit
- maple syrup
- timber
- tobacco
- capital cities
- major towns
- pasture
- cropland
- forest

Pumpkins are just one of the crops grown in the Niagara "fruit belt." The mild climate, moderated by the lakes, allows the cultivation of a wide range of fruit and vegetables, including cherries, apples, peaches, grapes, and asparagus. Fruit and vegetable growing is confined to southern Canada, due to the colder climate and short growing season of the northern regions.

THE URBAN/RURAL POPULATION DIVIDE

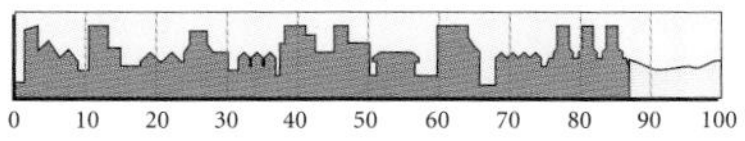

POPULATION DENSITY	TOTAL LAND AREA
64 people per sq mile (25 people per sq km)	214,230 sq miles (555,000 sq km)

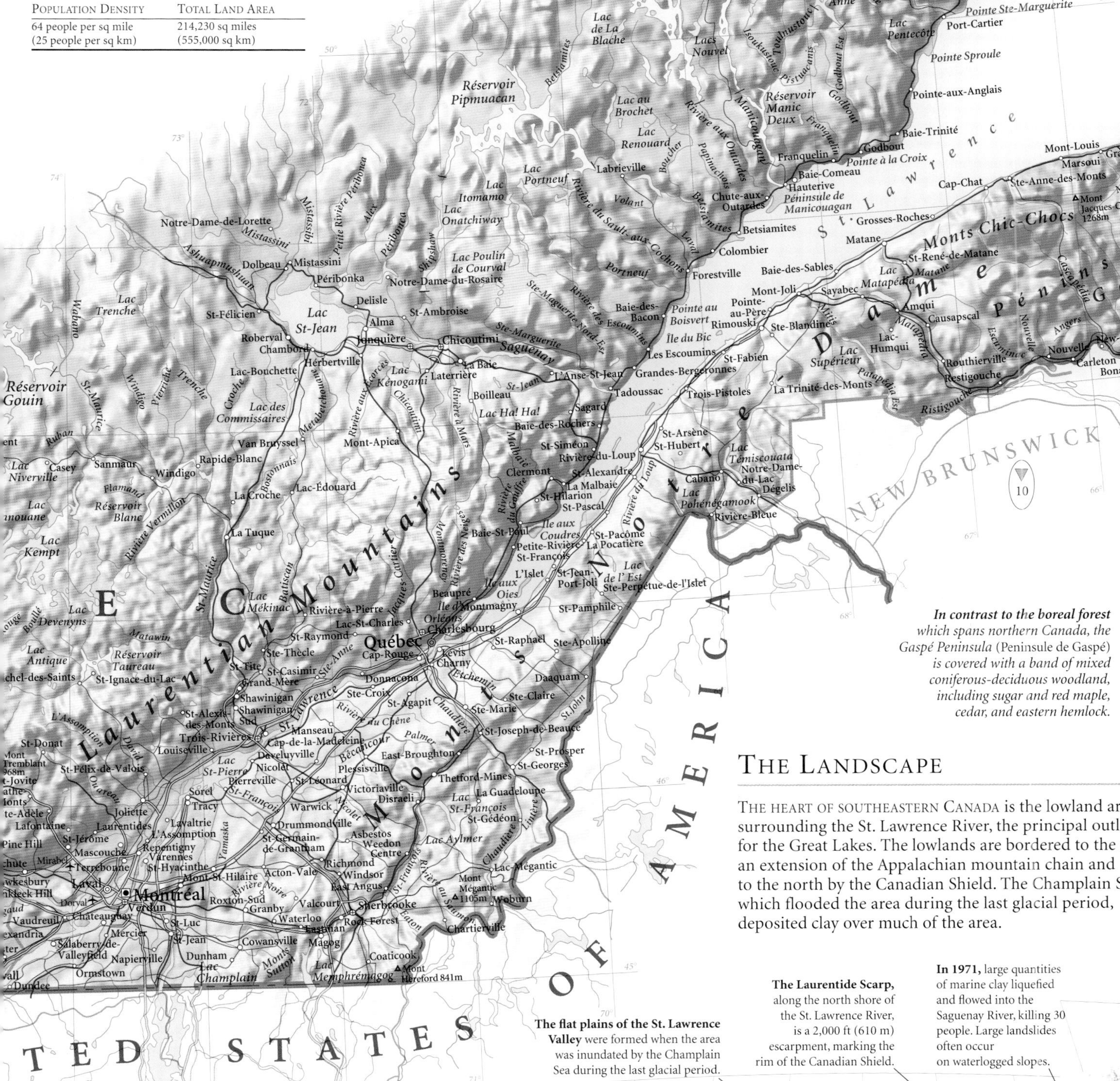

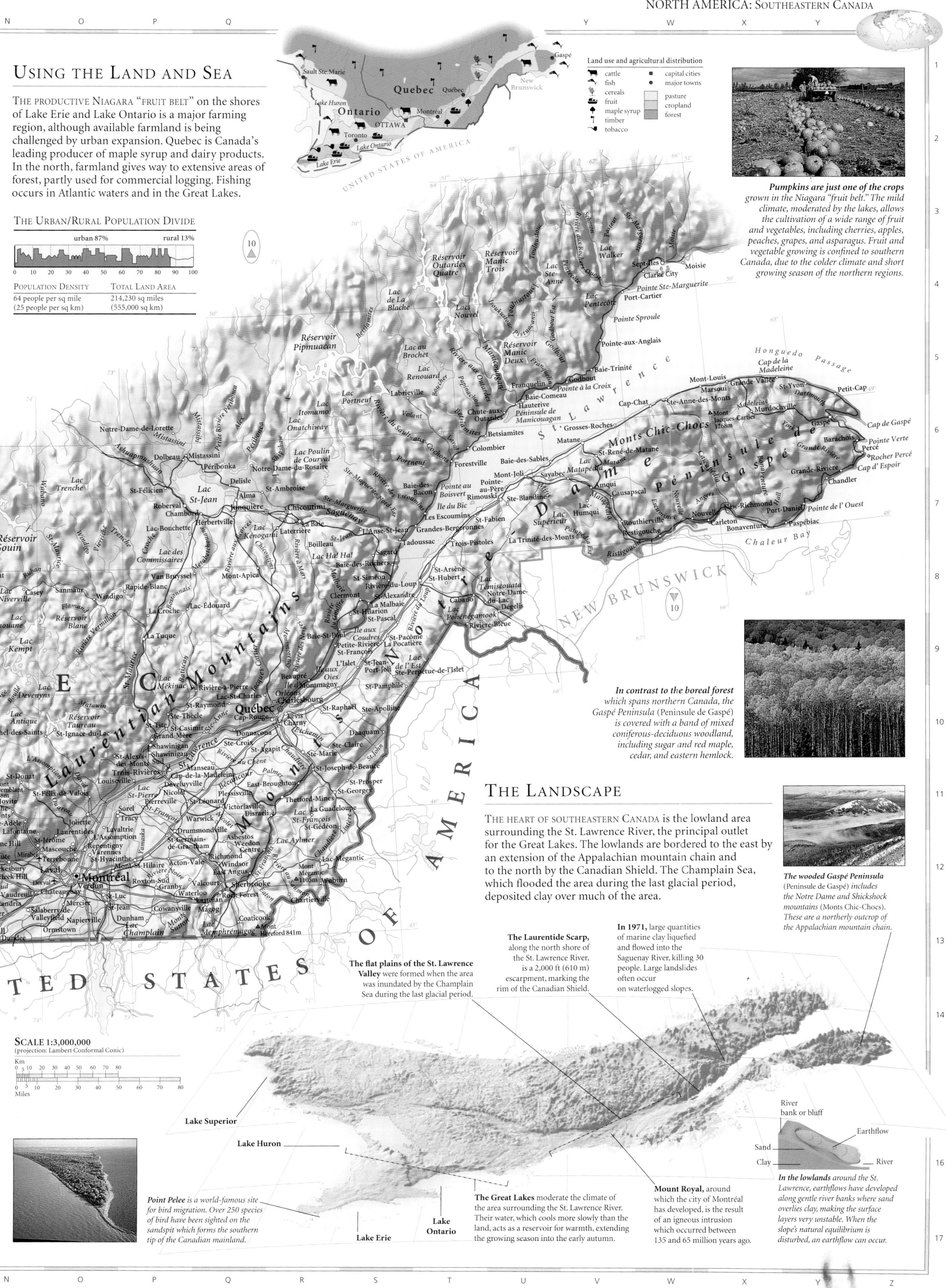

In contrast to the boreal forest which spans northern Canada, the Gaspé Peninsula (Peninsule de Gaspé) *is covered with a band of mixed coniferous-deciduous woodland, including sugar and red maple, cedar, and eastern hemlock.*

THE LANDSCAPE

THE HEART OF SOUTHEASTERN CANADA is the lowland area surrounding the St. Lawrence River, the principal outlet for the Great Lakes. The lowlands are bordered to the east by an extension of the Appalachian mountain chain and to the north by the Canadian Shield. The Champlain Sea, which flooded the area during the last glacial period, deposited clay over much of the area.

The wooded Gaspé Peninsula *(Peninsule de Gaspé) includes the Notre Dame and Shickshock mountains (Monts Chic-Chocs). These are a northerly outcrop of the Appalachian mountain chain.*

The flat plains of the St. Lawrence Valley were formed when the area was inundated by the Champlain Sea during the last glacial period.

The Laurentide Scarp, along the north shore of the St. Lawrence River, is a 2,000 ft (610 m) escarpment, marking the rim of the Canadian Shield.

In 1971, large quantities of marine clay liquefied and flowed into the Saguenay River, killing 30 people. Large landslides often occur on waterlogged slopes.

The Great Lakes moderate the climate of the area surrounding the St. Lawrence River. Their water, which cools more slowly than the land, acts as a reservoir for warmth, extending the growing season into the early autumn.

Mount Royal, around which the city of Montréal has developed, is the result of an igneous intrusion which occurred between 135 and 65 million years ago.

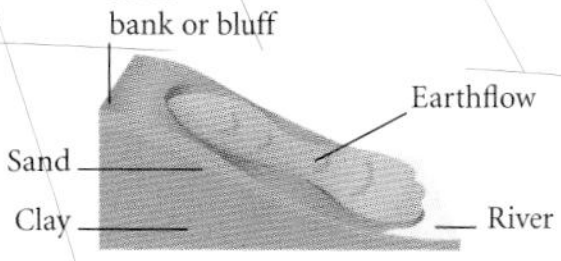

In the lowlands *around the St. Lawrence, earthflows have developed along gentle river banks where sand overlies clay, making the surface layers very unstable. When the slope's natural equilibrium is disturbed, an earthflow can occur.*

Point Pelee *is a world-famous site for bird migration. Over 250 species of bird have been sighted on the sandspit which forms the southern tip of the Canadian mainland.*

N O P Q R S T U V W X Y Z

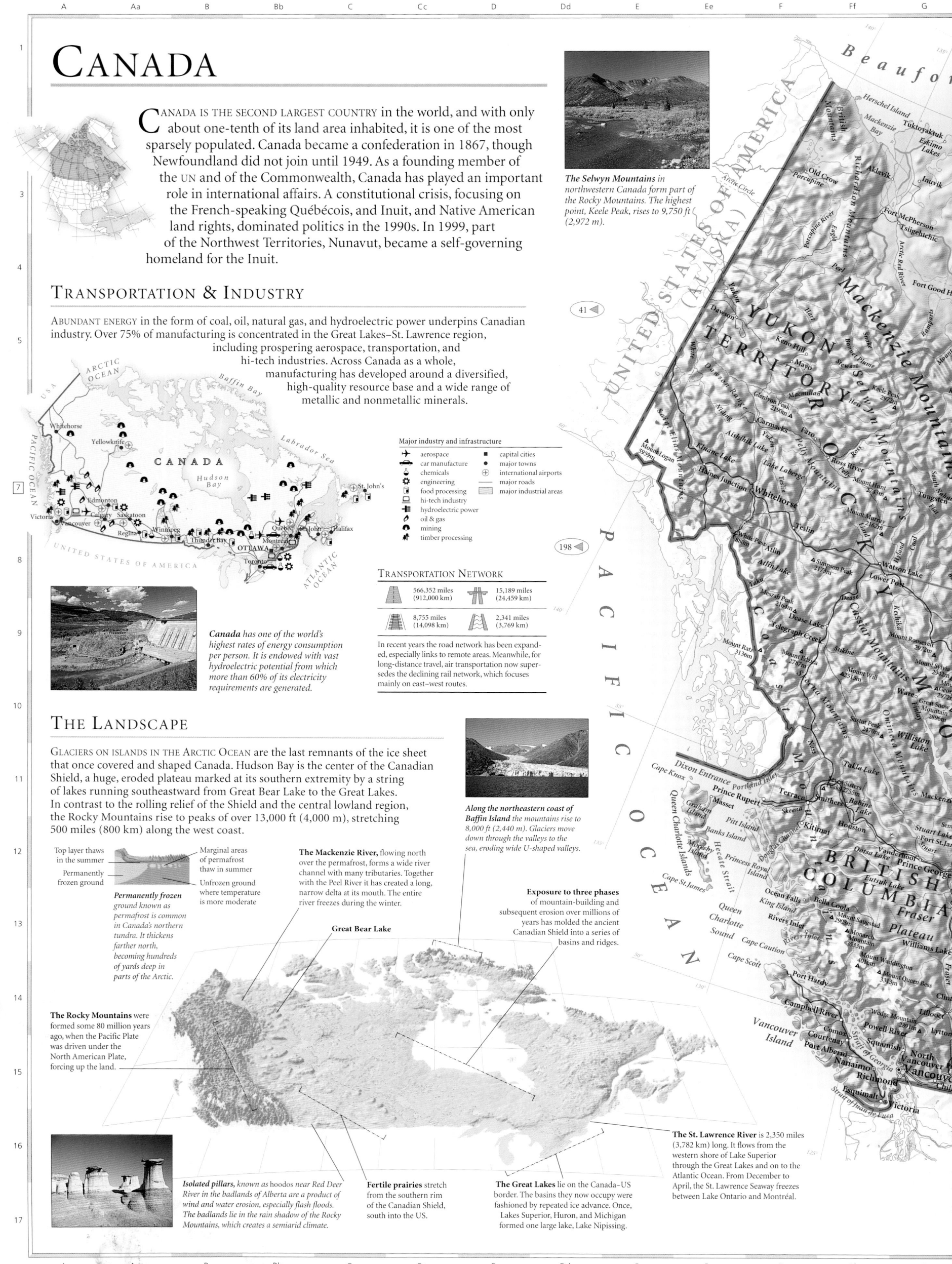

CANADA

CANADA IS THE SECOND LARGEST COUNTRY in the world, and with only about one-tenth of its land area inhabited, it is one of the most sparsely populated. Canada became a confederation in 1867, though Newfoundland did not join until 1949. As a founding member of the UN and of the Commonwealth, Canada has played an important role in international affairs. A constitutional crisis, focusing on the French-speaking Québécois, and Inuit, and Native American land rights, dominated politics in the 1990s. In 1999, part of the Northwest Territories, Nunavut, became a self-governing homeland for the Inuit.

The Selwyn Mountains in northwestern Canada form part of the Rocky Mountains. The highest point, Keele Peak, rises to 9,750 ft (2,972 m).

TRANSPORTATION & INDUSTRY

ABUNDANT ENERGY in the form of coal, oil, natural gas, and hydroelectric power underpins Canadian industry. Over 75% of manufacturing is concentrated in the Great Lakes–St. Lawrence region, including prospering aerospace, transportation, and hi-tech industries. Across Canada as a whole, manufacturing has developed around a diversified, high-quality resource base and a wide range of metallic and nonmetallic minerals.

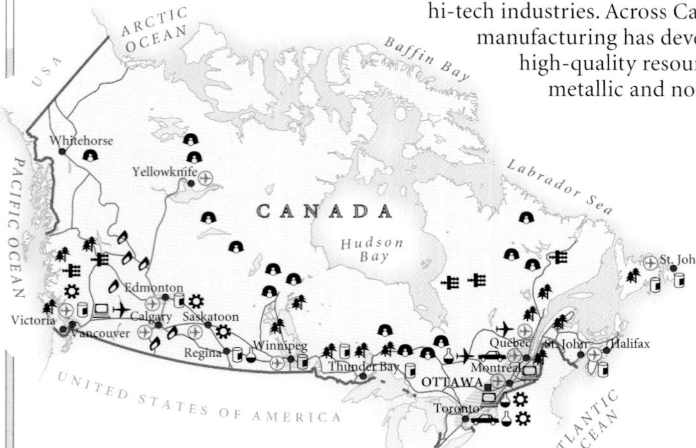

Major industry and infrastructure

- aerospace
- car manufacture
- chemicals
- engineering
- food processing
- hi-tech industry
- hydroelectric power
- oil & gas
- mining
- timber processing
- capital cities
- major towns
- international airports
- major roads
- major industrial areas

Canada has one of the world's highest rates of energy consumption per person. It is endowed with vast hydroelectric potential from which more than 60% of its electricity requirements are generated.

TRANSPORTATION NETWORK

566,352 miles (912,000 km)	15,189 miles (24,459 km)
8,755 miles (14,098 km)	2,341 miles (3,769 km)

In recent years the road network has been expanded, especially links to remote areas. Meanwhile, for long-distance travel, air transportation now supersedes the declining rail network, which focuses mainly on east–west routes.

THE LANDSCAPE

GLACIERS ON ISLANDS IN THE ARCTIC OCEAN are the last remnants of the ice sheet that once covered and shaped Canada. Hudson Bay is the center of the Canadian Shield, a huge, eroded plateau marked at its southern extremity by a string of lakes running southeastward from Great Bear Lake to the Great Lakes. In contrast to the rolling relief of the Shield and the central lowland region, the Rocky Mountains rise to peaks of over 13,000 ft (4,000 m), stretching 500 miles (800 km) along the west coast.

Along the northeastern coast of Baffin Island the mountains rise to 8,000 ft (2,440 m). Glaciers move down through the valleys to the sea, eroding wide U-shaped valleys.

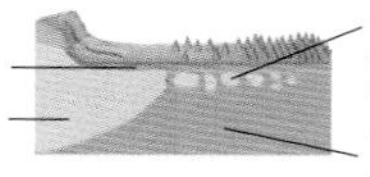

***Permanently frozen** ground known as permafrost is common in Canada's northern tundra. It thickens farther north, becoming hundreds of yards deep in parts of the Arctic.*

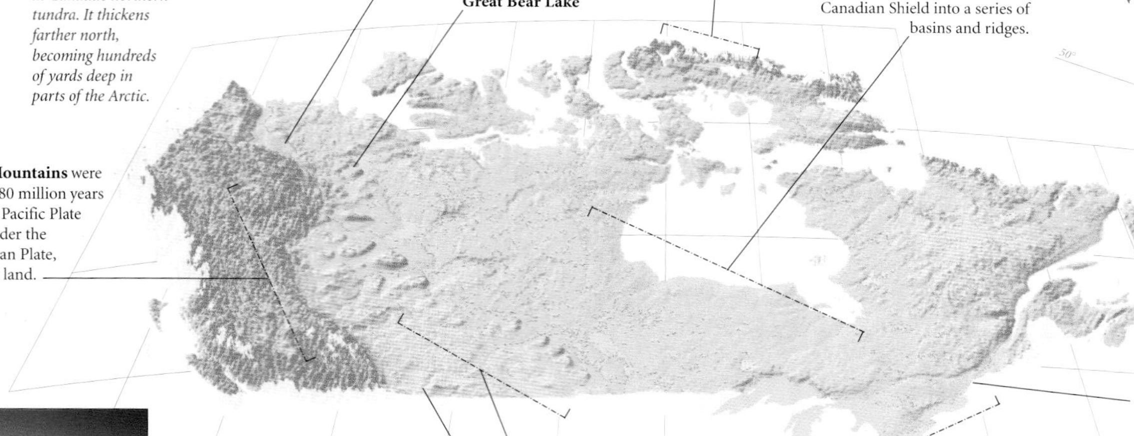

The Mackenzie River, flowing north over the permafrost, forms a wide river channel with many tributaries. Together with the Peel River it has created a long, narrow delta at its mouth. The entire river freezes during the winter.

Great Bear Lake

Exposure to three phases of mountain-building and subsequent erosion over millions of years has molded the ancient Canadian Shield into a series of basins and ridges.

The Rocky Mountains were formed some 80 million years ago, when the Pacific Plate was driven under the North American Plate, forcing up the land.

The St. Lawrence River is 2,350 miles (3,782 km) long. It flows from the western shore of Lake Superior through the Great Lakes and on to the Atlantic Ocean. From December to April, the St. Lawrence Seaway freezes between Lake Ontario and Montréal.

***Isolated pillars,** known as hoodoos near Red Deer River in the badlands of Alberta are a product of wind and water erosion, especially flash floods. The badlands lie in the rain shadow of the Rocky Mountains, which creates a semiarid climate.*

Fertile prairies stretch from the southern rim of the Canadian Shield, south into the US.

The Great Lakes lie on the Canada–US border. The basins they now occupy were fashioned by repeated ice advance. Once, Lakes Superior, Huron, and Michigan formed one large lake, Lake Nipissing.

Viscount Melville Sound
Banks Island
Sachs Harbour
Cape Kellett
Prince Albert Peninsula
Prince of Wales Strait
Amundsen Gulf
Cape Bathurst
Cape Parry
Cape Lambton
Cape Wollaston
Holman
Franklin Bay
Cape Lyon
Paulatuk
Prince Albert Sound
Wollaston Peninsula
Victoria Island
Dolphin & Union Strait
Passage Point
Peel Point
Stefansson Island
Hadley Bay
McClintock Channel
Zeta Lake
Prince of Wales Island
Peel Sound
Somerset Island
Prince Regent Inlet
Franklin Strait
Boothia Peninsula
Gulf of Boothia
Gateshead Island
Larsen Sound
Brodeur Peninsula
Admiralty Inlet
Borden Peninsula
Baffin
Cape Henry Kater
Gifford
Igloolik
Jens Munk Island
Rowley Island
Baird Peninsula
Cape Englefield
Melville Peninsula
Hall Beach
Cape Chapman
Prince Charles Island
Air Force Island
Nettilling Lake
Koukdjuak
Talovoak
Pelly Bay
Simpson Peninsula
Committee Bay
Wales Island
Foxe Basin
Bowman Bay
King William Island
Gjoa Haven
Rae Strait
Chantrey Inlet
Cambridge Bay
Jenny Lind Island
Queen Maud Gulf
Adelaide Peninsula
Kent Peninsula
Bowes Point
Coronation Gulf
Cape Krusenstern
Kugluktuk
Bluenose Lake
Bathurst Inlet
Ellice
Hayes
Repulse Bay
Vansittart Island
Cape Dorchester
Foxe Peninsula
Foxe Channel
Cape Dorset
Salisbury Island
NUNAVUT
Wager Bay
Roes Welcome Sound
Southampton Island
Coral Harbour
Nottingham Island
Evans Strait
Ivujivik
Hood
Burnside
Coppermine
Takijuq Lake
Back
Garry Lake
Great Bear Lake
Echo Bay
Deline
Tulita
Hottah Lake
Aberdeen Lake
Quoich
Baker Lake
Chesterfield Inlet
Cape Kendall
Cape Low
Fisher Strait
Coats Island
Mansel Island
Rankin Inlet
NORTHWEST TERRITORIES
Wrigley
Lac La Martre
Wha Ti
Aylmer Lake
Clinton-Colden Lake
Thelon
Hanbury
Dubawnt Lake
Yathkyed Lake
Whale Cove
Willowlake
Edzo
Yellowknife
Reliance
Lutselk'e
Snowdrift
Nonacho Lake
Kazan
Eskimo Point
Arviat
Ottawa Islands
Fort Simpson
Horn
Fort Providence
Great Slave Lake
Fort Resolution
Taltson
Dubawnt
Tha-Anne
Thlewiaza
Hudson Bay
Hay River
Pine Point
Trout
Thoa
Wholdaia Lake
Kasba Lake
Nueltin Lake
Nejanilini Lake
Petitot
Bistcho Lake
Steen River
Fort Smith
Caribou Mountains
Slave
Uranium City
Selwyn Lake
Seal
Cape Churchill
Churchill
Fort Nelson
Fontas
Peace
Fort Chipewyan
Lake Athabasca
Black Lake
Phelps Lake
Lac Brochet
Tadoule Lake
High Level
Fort Vermilion
Lake Claire
William
MacFarlane
Pasfield Lake
Cree
Wollaston Lake
South Seal
Cape Tatnam
Chinchaga
Clear Hills
Birch Mountains
Cree Lake
Geikie
Reindeer Lake
Southern Indian Lake
Fort Severn
Fort St. John
Manning
SASKATCHEWAN
Lynn Lake
Waskaiowaka Lake
Gillam
Nelson
Hayes
Gods
Severn
Winisk
Shamattawa
ALBERTA
Grimshaw
Fairview
Peace River
Wabasca
Athabasca
Clearwater
Fort McMurray
Turner Lake
La Loche
Frobisher Lake
Foster Lakes
Macoun Lake
Leaf Rapids
Granville Lake
Split Lake
Thompson
Fawn
Dawson Creek
Smoky
Desmarais
Utikuma Lake
Churchill Lake
Pinehouse Lake
Reindeer
Burntwood
Grande Prairie
Wapiti
High Prairie
Lesser Slave Lake
Peter Pond Lake
Buffalo Narrows
Missinipe
Churchill
Sipiwesk Lake
Gods Lake
Sachigo
Big Trout Lake
Valleyview
Slave Lake
Wallace Mountain 1259m
Primrose Lake
Beaver
La Ronge
Lac La Ronge
Kississing Lake
Wabowden
Oxford Lake
Sachigo Lake
Winisk Lake
Attawapiskat
Swan Hills
Athabasca
Cold Lake
Deschambault Lake
Creighton
Flin Flon
Molson Lake
Island Lake
Grande Cache
Whitecourt
Barrhead
Westlock
Grand Centre
Meadow Lake
Montreal Lake
Amisk Lake
MANITOBA
The Pas
Cedar Lake
Grand Rapids
Lake Winnipeg
Poplar
Sandy Lake
North Caribou Lake
Attawapiskat Lake
Edson
Mount Robson 3954m
Hinton
St. Albert
Spruce Grove
Stony Plain
Edmonton
Morinville
St. Paul
Fort Saskatchewan
North Saskatchewan
Tobin Lake
Saskatchewan
St. Walburg
Pipestone
ONTARIO
Drayton Valley
Pembina
Devon
Leduc
Vegreville
Vermilion
Lloydminster
Prince Albert
Nipawin
Pasquia Hills
Hudson Bay
Tisdale
Lake Winnipegosis
Berens
Mount Sir Wilfrid Laurier 3505m
Rocky Mountain House
Camrose
Wetaskiwin
Wainwright
North Battleford
Melfort
Swan River
Gypsumville
Trout Lake
Lake St. Joseph
Ogoki
Armstrong
Kinbasket Lake
Mount Columbia 3747m
North Saskatchewan
Ponoka
Lacombe
Stettler
Battle
Battleford
Unity
Martensville
Humboldt
Porcupine Hills
Duck Mountain
Lake Nipigon
Red Deer
Sylvan Lake
Innisfail
Saskatoon
Lanigan
Quill Lakes
Canora
Baldy Mountain 831m
Lake Manitoba
Eriksdale
Red Lake
Ear Falls
Lac Seul
Sioux Lookout
Didsbury
Kicking Horse Pass 1627m
Olds
Drumheller
Airdrie
Rosetown
Outlook
Kindersley
Watrous
Wynyard
Kamsack
Yorkton
Melville
Dauphin
Gimli
Golden
Banff
Canmore
Mount Assiniboine 3618m
Calgary
Strathmore
Oyen
Last Mountain Lake
Esterhazy
Riding Mountain
Selkirk
Pinawa
Beausejour
Kenora
Dryden
Nipigon
Invermere
Okotoks
High River
South Saskatchewan
Lake Diefenbaker
Fort Qu'Appelle
Indian Head
Qu'Appelle
Neepawa
Minnedosa
Stonewall
Winnipeg
Eagle Lake
Lac des Milles Lacs
Salmon Arm
Kamloops
Okanagan Lake
Kelowna
Penticton
Claresholm
Crowsnest Pass 1356m
Travers Reservoir
Redcliff
Medicine Hat
Swift Current
Lumsden
Regina
Moosomin
Virden
Portage la Prairie
Assiniboine
Steinbach
Red River
Seine
Rainy Lake
Atikokan
Thunder Bay
Kimberley
Fort Macleod
Lethbridge
Taber
Coaldale
Maple Creek
Moose Jaw
Old Wives Lake
Weyburn
Carlyle
Brandon
Carman
Winkler
Killarney
Morden
Altona
Fort Frances
Lake of the Woods
Rainy River
Nelson
Castlegar
Cranbrook
Pincher Creek
Raymond
Cardston
Milk River
Cypress Hills
Assiniboia
Val Marie
Wood Mountain
Rockglen
Estevan
Melita
Lake
UNITED STATES OF AMERICA
SCALE 1:9,250,000
Projection: Lambert Azimuthal Equal Area
50 100 150 200 250 300 350
50 100 150 200 250 300 350
206
17
H Hh I Ii J Jj K Kk L Ll M Mm

***The Sonoran Desert** in southwestern Arizona stretches into Mexico and merges to the northwest with California's Mojave Desert. Much of the southwest is very arid, especially the "rain-starved" areas between the Coast Ranges and the Rocky Mountains.*

THE UNITED STATES OF AMERICA

CONTERMINOUS US (FOR ALASKA AND HAWAII SEE PAGES 40-41)

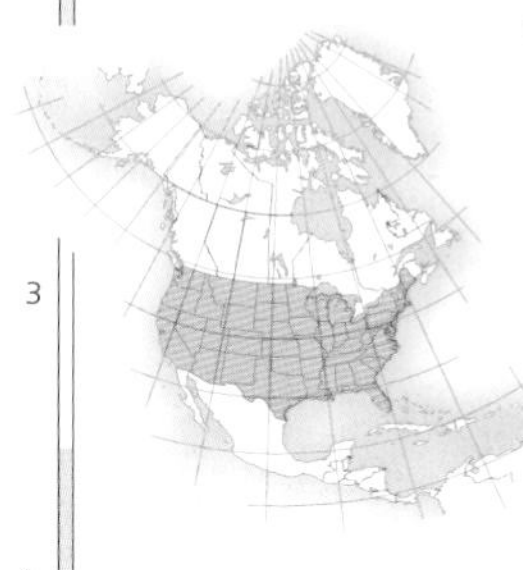

T HE US'S PROGRESSION FROM FRONTIER TERRITORY to economic and political superpower has taken less than 200 years. The 48 conterminous states, along with the outlying states of Alaska and Hawaii, are part of a federal union, held together by the guiding principles of the US Constitution, which embodies the ideals of democracy and liberty for all. Abundant fertile land and a rich resource-base fueled and sustained US economic development. With the spread of agriculture and the growth of trade and industry came the need for a larger workforce, which was supplied by millions of immigrants, many seeking an escape from poverty and political or religious persecution. Immigration continues today, particularly from Central America and Asia.

Mount Rainier is a dormant volcano in the Cascade Range, Washington. This 14,090 ft (4,392 m) peak is flanked by the most extensive glacier outside Alaska.

TRANSPORTATION & INDUSTRY

THE US HAS BEEN THE INDUSTRIAL POWERHOUSE of the world since the Second World War, pioneering mass-production and the consumer lifestyle. Initially, heavy engineering and manufacturing in the northeast led the economy. Today, heavy industry has declined and the US economy is driven by service and financial industries, with the most important being defense, hi-tech, and electronics.

Washington D.C. was established as the nation's capital in 1790. It is home to the seat of national government, on Capitol Hill, as well as the President's official residence, the White House.

198 ◀

Major industry and infrastructure

aerospace	research & development
car manufacture	textiles
chemicals	tourism
coal	■ capital cities
electronics	● major towns
engineering	✈ international airports
food processing	major roads
hi-tech industry	major industrial areas
oil & gas	

TRANSPORTATION NETWORK

3,875,040 miles (6,240,000 km)		52,388 miles (84,361 km)
148,308 miles (235,238 km)		25,467 miles (41,009 km)

Transportation in the US is dominated by the car which, with the extensive Interstate Highway system, allows great personal mobility. Today, internal air flights between major cities provide the most rapid cross-country travel.

198 ◀

THE LANDSCAPE

THE HIGH, RUGGED MOUNTAIN RANGES of the west are about 80 million years old, geologically young compared to the old, eroded, Appalachian mountain chain, which dates from when North America and Europe were joined together as part of the supercontinent Pangaea, 400 million years ago. In contrast, the Great Plains and Mississippi Basin have a low relief and fertile soils.

Devils Tower, in Wyoming is a 1,280 ft (390 m) intrusion of basalt rock, which cooled to form octagonal pillars. In 1906 it became the first US National Monument.

Missouri River — Ohio River
Mississippi River — Mississippi Delta

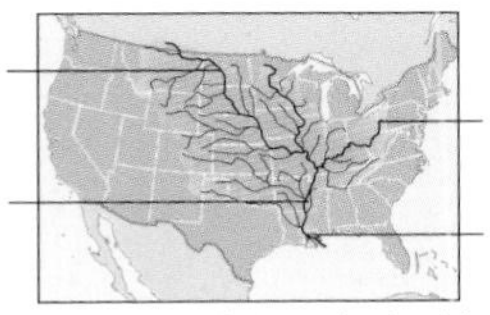

The massive drainage basin of the Mississippi covers 1,250,000 sq miles (3,200,000 sq km). It includes all areas drained by the Mississippi and its chief tributaries, the Missouri and Ohio Rivers, and drains the entire region from the Appalachians to the Rockies.

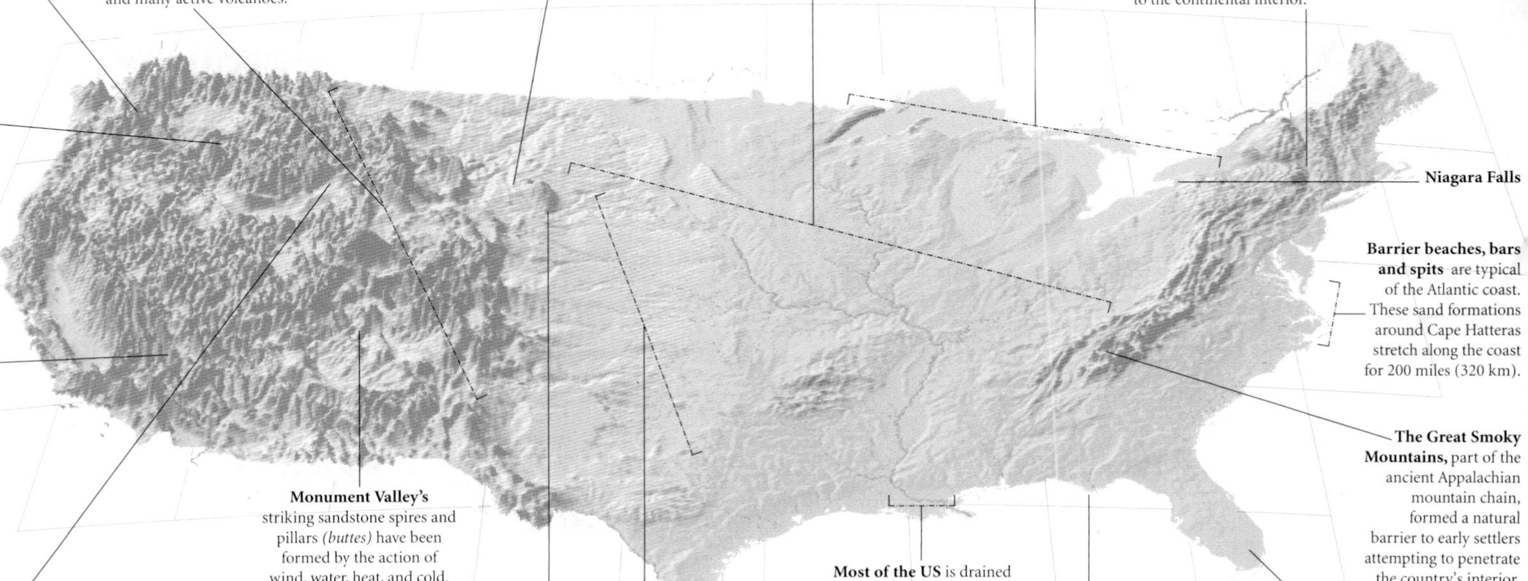

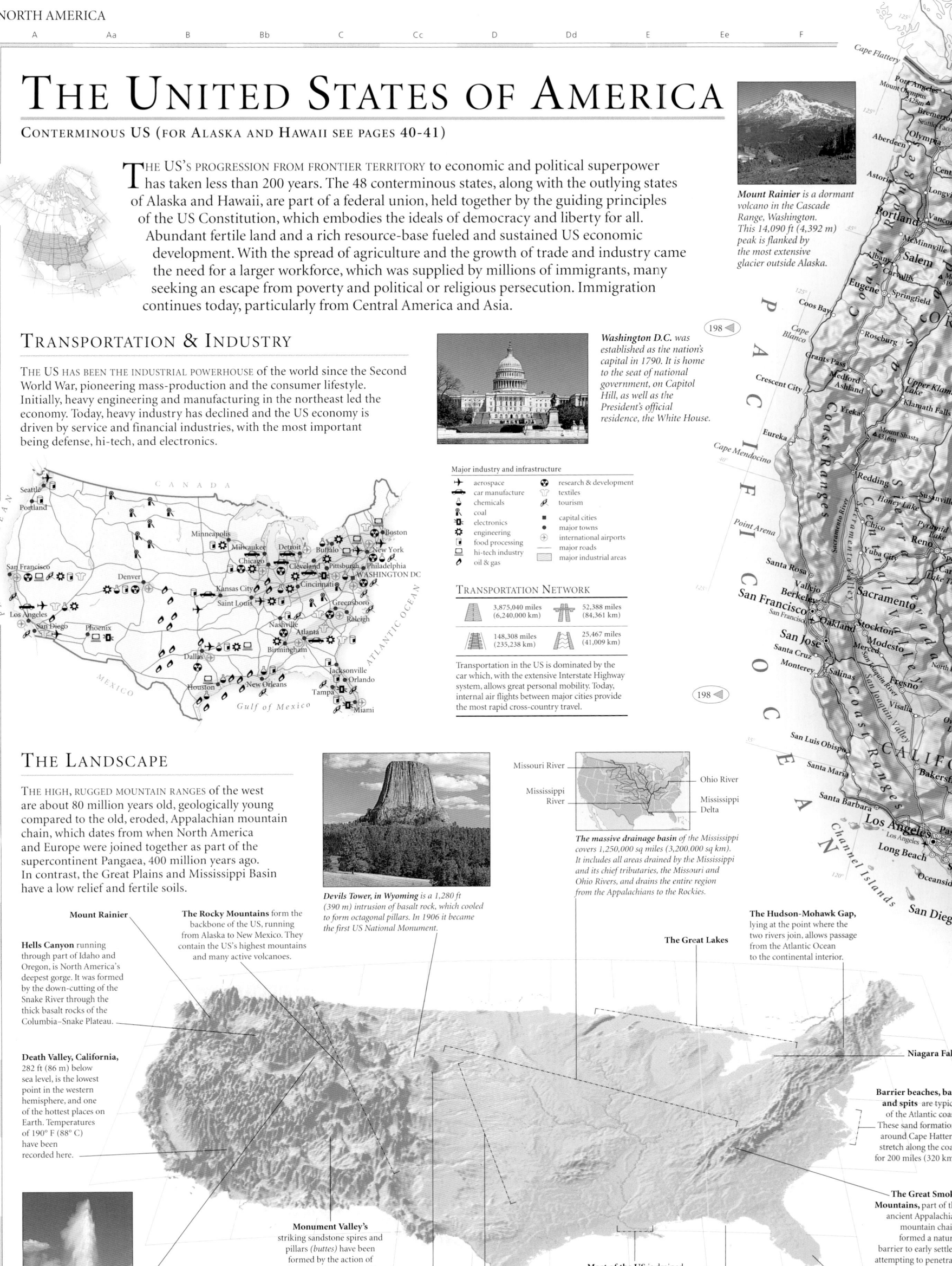

Mount Rainier

Hells Canyon running through part of Idaho and Oregon, is North America's deepest gorge. It was formed by the down-cutting of the Snake River through the thick basalt rocks of the Columbia–Snake Plateau.

The Rocky Mountains form the backbone of the US, running from Alaska to New Mexico. They contain the US's highest mountains and many active volcanoes.

The Hudson-Mohawk Gap, lying at the point where the two rivers join, allows passage from the Atlantic Ocean to the continental interior.

The Great Lakes

Death Valley, California, 282 ft (86 m) below sea level, is the lowest point in the western hemisphere, and one of the hottest places on Earth. Temperatures of 190° F (88° C) have been recorded here.

Niagara Falls

Barrier beaches, bars and spits are typical of the Atlantic coast. These sand formations around Cape Hatteras stretch along the coast for 200 miles (320 km).

The Great Smoky Mountains, part of the ancient Appalachian mountain chain, formed a natural barrier to early settlers attempting to penetrate the country's interior.

Monument Valley's striking sandstone spires and pillars (buttes) have been formed by the action of wind, water, heat, and cold.

Volcanically heated water erupts every 40-80 minutes from Old Faithful geyser in Yellowstone National Park, Wyoming. The 170 ft (50 m) column of water and steam persists for 4 minutes.

The deep gullies of South Dakota's badlands are created by periodic, torrential rainfall, which erodes the soft soils and rocks. Their form has been greatly affected by changes in land use.

Great Plains

Most of the US is drained by the great Mississippi River system. At its mouth, where levées are breached, floodwaters are carried to the swamps through a series of channels. This region is known as the bayou.

The US Gulf Coast is seriously affected by hurricane erosion which reshapes its beaches and sandbanks.

The Everglades are a vast area of sawgrass swamp covering 4,000 sq miles (10,300 sq km) of southern Florida.

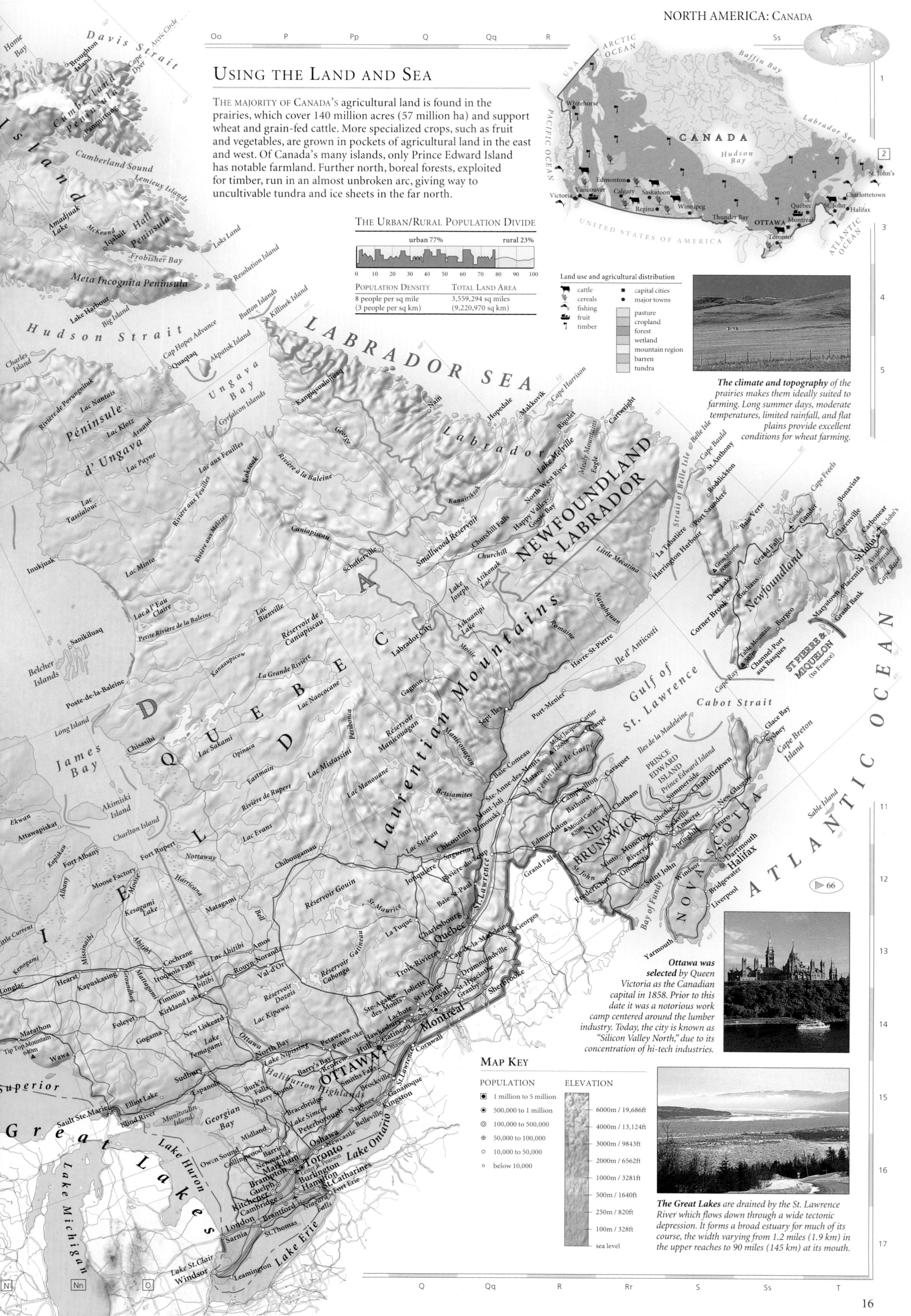

USING THE LAND AND SEA

THE MAJORITY OF CANADA'S agricultural land is found in the prairies, which cover 140 million acres (57 million ha) and support wheat and grain-fed cattle. More specialized crops, such as fruit and vegetables, are grown in pockets of agricultural land in the east and west. Of Canada's many islands, only Prince Edward Island has notable farmland. Further north, boreal forests, exploited for timber, run in an almost unbroken arc, giving way to uncultivable tundra and ice sheets in the far north.

THE URBAN/RURAL POPULATION DIVIDE

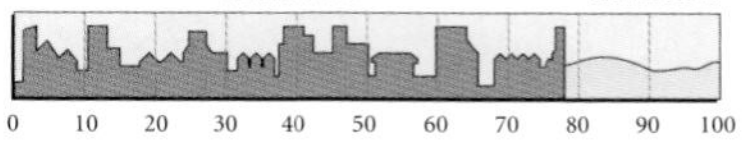

POPULATION DENSITY	TOTAL LAND AREA
8 people per sq mile (3 people per sq km)	3,559,294 sq miles (9,220,970 sq km)

Land use and agricultural distribution

- cattle
- cereals
- fishing
- fruit
- timber
- capital cities
- major towns
- pasture
- cropland
- forest
- wetland
- mountain region
- barren
- tundra

The climate and topography of the prairies makes them ideally suited to farming. Long summer days, moderate temperatures, limited rainfall, and flat plains provide excellent conditions for wheat farming.

***Ottawa was selected** by Queen Victoria as the Canadian capital in 1858. Prior to this date it was a notorious work camp centered around the lumber industry. Today, the city is known as "Silicon Valley North," due to its concentration of hi-tech industries.*

MAP KEY

POPULATION

- 1 million to 5 million
- 500,000 to 1 million
- 100,000 to 500,000
- 50,000 to 100,000
- 10,000 to 50,000
- below 10,000

ELEVATION

- 6000m / 19,686ft
- 4000m / 13,124ft
- 3000m / 9843ft
- 2000m / 6562ft
- 1000m / 3281ft
- 500m / 1640ft
- 250m / 820ft
- 100m / 328ft
- sea level

***The Great Lakes** are drained by the St. Lawrence River which flows down through a wide tectonic depression. It forms a broad estuary for much of its course, the width varying from 1.2 miles (1.9 km) in the upper reaches to 90 miles (145 km) at its mouth.*

The clear waters of Niagara Falls cascade 190 ft (58 m) into the gorge below. It is one of America's most famous spectacles and a leading tourist attraction. The falls are slowly receding and the gorge may one day stretch from Lake Ontario to Lake Erie.

Fakahatchee Strand is part of the extensive subtropical swamps in the Florida Everglades. The swamps support a wide variety of animal life, including many rare birds, fish, alligators, and crocodiles.

Using the Land and Sea

OVER HALF OF THE US is used for agriculture, typified by the large cereal grain farms and cattle ranches of the Great Plains and Midwest prairie regions. Although wheat and corn are still primary crops, a diverse range of fruits and vegetables are grown in the fertile areas, particularly near the east and west coasts. Despite the abundance of cultivable land, inadequate soil management has resulted in a third of the topsoil being lost through wind and water erosion.

The Urban/Rural Population Divide

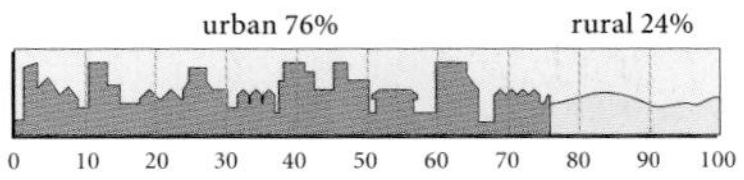

Population Density	Total Land Area
76 people per sq mile (29 people per sq km)	3,538,307 sq miles (9,166,600 sq km)

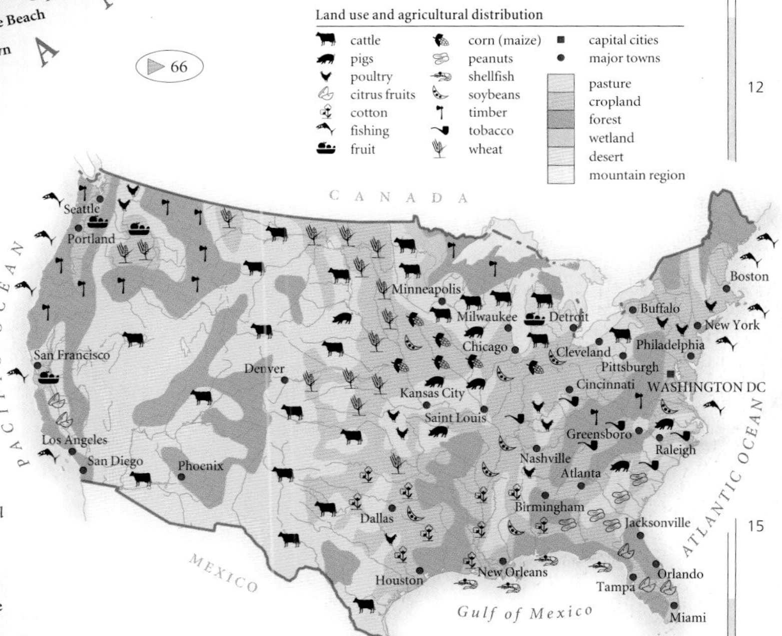

Farming on the Great Plains and in the Midwest is characterized by large-scale, mechanized wheat farms.

USA: Northeastern States

Connecticut, Maine, Massachusetts, New Hampshire, New Jersey, New York, Pennsylvania, Rhode Island, Vermont

The indented coast and vast woodlands of the northeastern states were the original core area for European expansion. The rustic character of New England prevails after nearly four centuries, while the great cities of the Atlantic seaboard have formed an almost continuous urban region. Over 20 million immigrants entered New York from 1855 to 1924 and the northeast became the industrial center of the US. After the decline of mining and heavy manufacturing, economic dynamism has been restored with the growth of hi-tech and service industries.

Chelsea in Vermont, surrounded by trees in their fall foliage. Tourism and agriculture dominate the economy of this self-consciously rural state, where no town exceeds 30,000 people.

Map Key

POPULATION

- above 5 million
- 1 million to 5 million
- 500,000 to 1 million
- 100,000 to 500,000
- 50,000 to 100,000
- 10,000 to 50,000
- below 10,000

ELEVATION

- 1000m / 3281ft
- 500m / 1640ft
- 250m / 820ft
- 100m / 328ft
- sea level

Transportation & Industry

The principal seaboard cities grew up on trade and manufacturing. They are now global centers of commerce and corporate administration, dominating the regional economy. Research and development facilities support an expanding electronics and communications sector throughout the region. Pharmaceutical and chemical industries are important in New Jersey and Pennsylvania.

Major industry and infrastructure

- chemicals
- coal
- defense
- electronics
- engineering
- finance
- hi-tech industry
- iron & steel
- pharmaceuticals
- printing & publishing
- research & development
- textiles
- timber processing
- major towns
- international airports
- major roads
- major industrial area

Transportation Network

340,090 miles (544,144 km)	4813 miles 7700 km
12,872 miles (20,592 km)	2108 miles (3389 km)

New York's commercial success is tied historically to its transportation connections. The Erie Canal, completed in 1825, opened up the Great Lakes and the interior to New York's markets and carried a stream of immigrants into the Midwest.

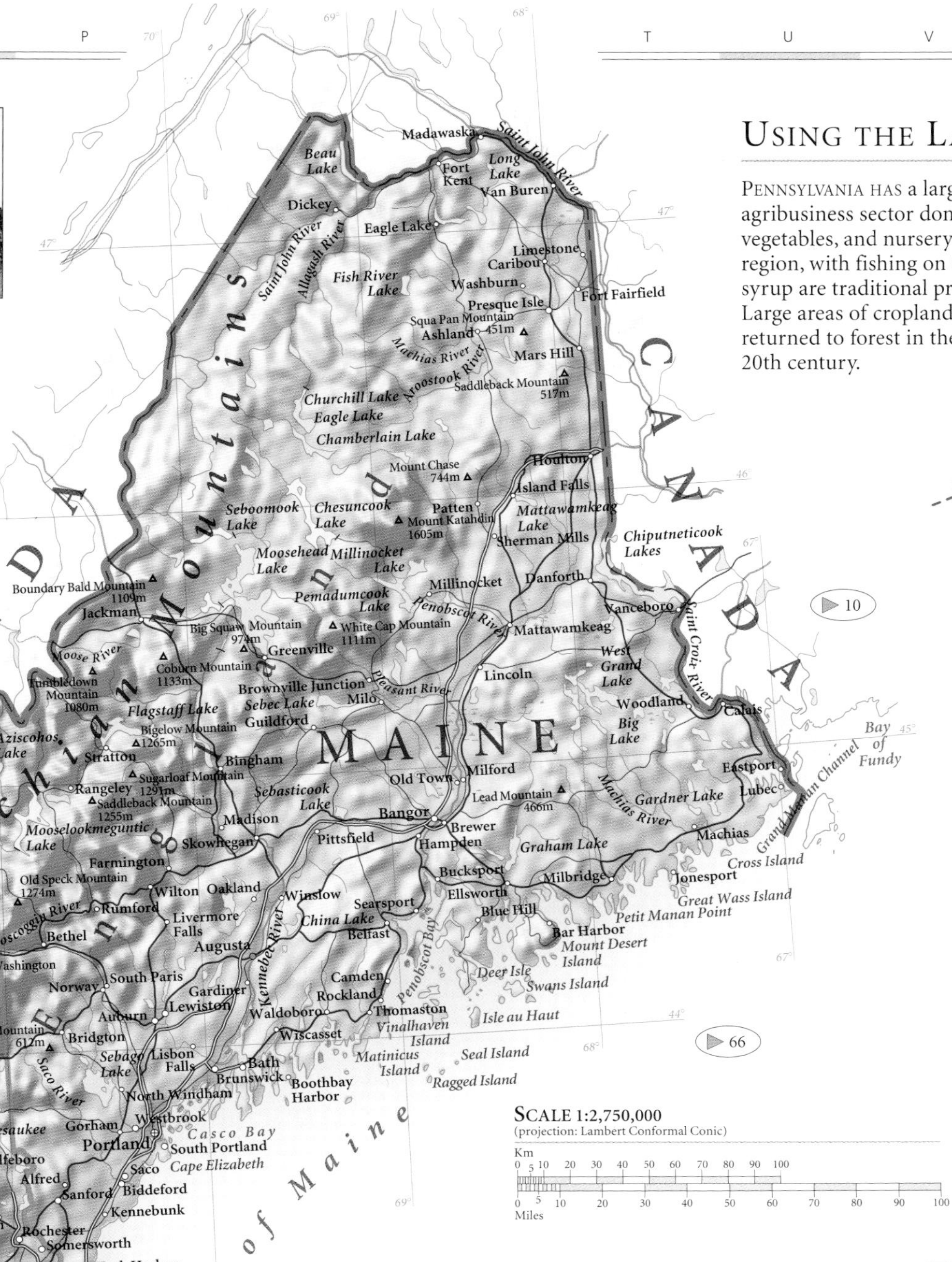

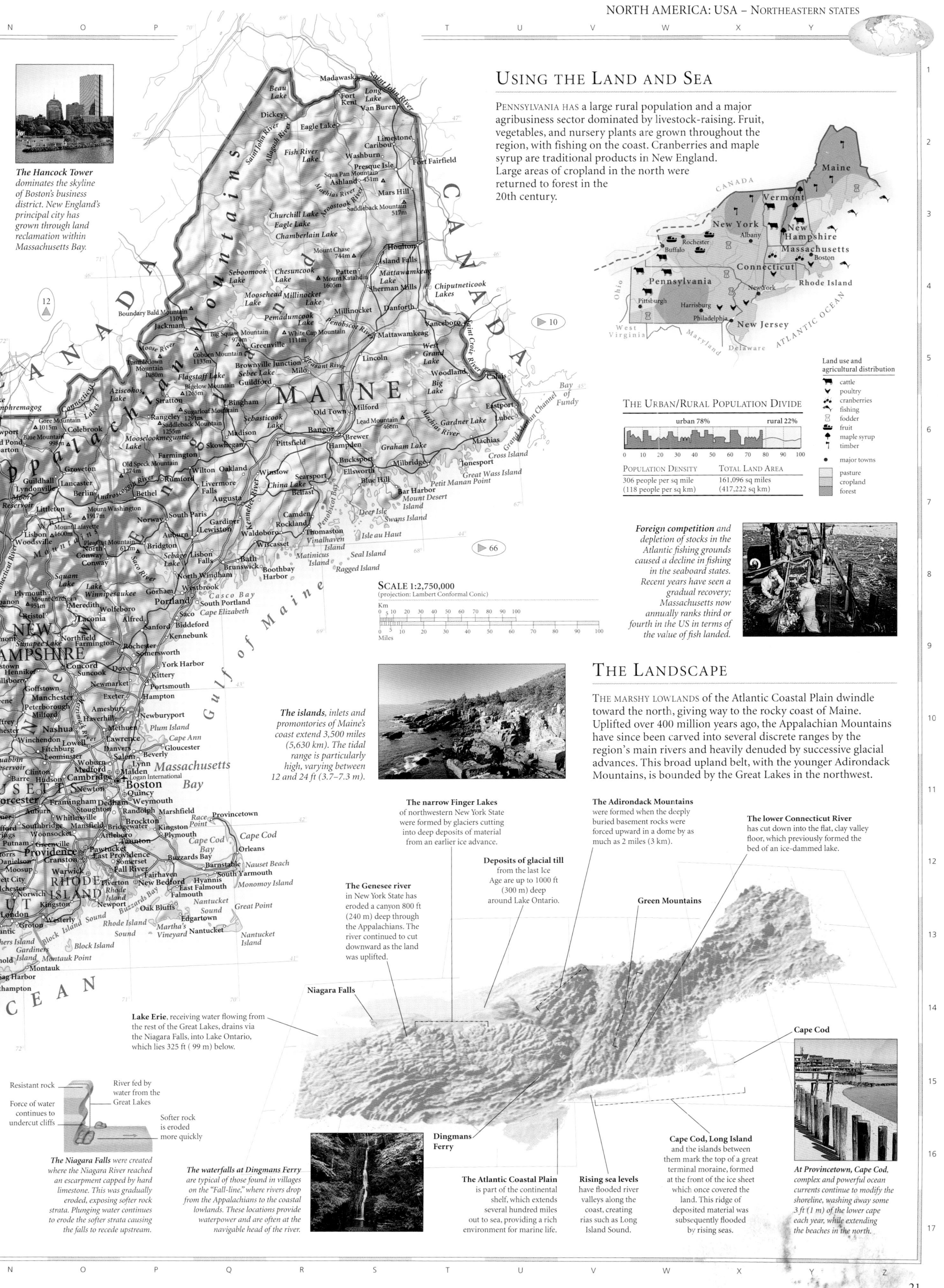

The Hancock Tower dominates the skyline of Boston's business district. New England's principal city has grown through land reclamation within Massachusetts Bay.

USING THE LAND AND SEA

PENNSYLVANIA HAS a large rural population and a major agribusiness sector dominated by livestock-raising. Fruit, vegetables, and nursery plants are grown throughout the region, with fishing on the coast. Cranberries and maple syrup are traditional products in New England. Large areas of cropland in the north were returned to forest in the 20th century.

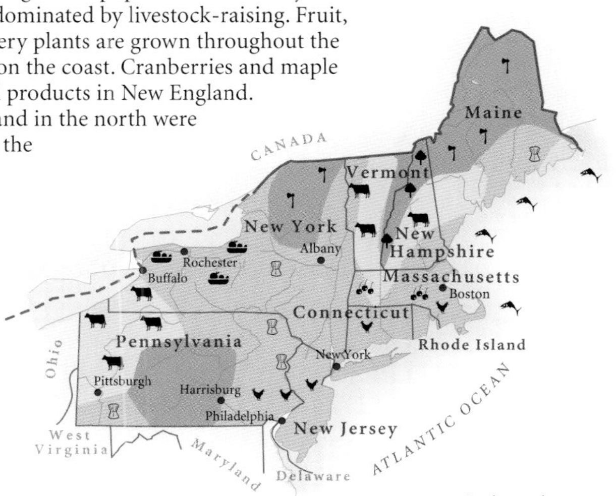

THE URBAN/RURAL POPULATION DIVIDE

urban 78% rural 22%

0 10 20 30 40 50 60 70 80 90 100

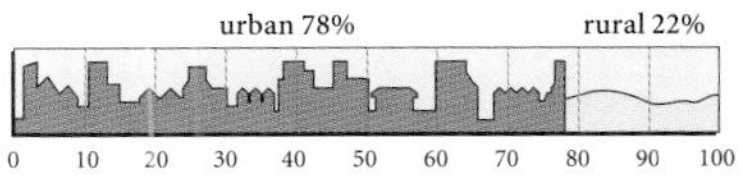

POPULATION DENSITY TOTAL LAND AREA

306 people per sq mile 161,096 sq miles
(118 people per sq km) (417,222 sq km)

Land use and agricultural distribution

- cattle
- poultry
- cranberries
- fishing
- fodder
- fruit
- maple syrup
- timber
- major towns
- pasture
- cropland
- forest

Foreign competition and depletion of stocks in the Atlantic fishing grounds caused a decline in fishing in the seaboard states. Recent years have seen a gradual recovery; Massachusetts now annually ranks third or fourth in the US in terms of the value of fish landed.

The islands, inlets and promontories of Maine's coast extend 3,500 miles (5,630 km). The tidal range is particularly high, varying between 12 and 24 ft (3.7–7.3 m).

SCALE 1:2,750,000
(projection: Lambert Conformal Conic)

Km
0 5 10 20 30 40 50 60 70 80 90 100

Miles
0 5 10 20 30 40 50 60 70 80 90 100

THE LANDSCAPE

THE MARSHY LOWLANDS of the Atlantic Coastal Plain dwindle toward the north, giving way to the rocky coast of Maine. Uplifted over 400 million years ago, the Appalachian Mountains have since been carved into several discrete ranges by the region's main rivers and heavily denuded by successive glacial advances. This broad upland belt, with the younger Adirondack Mountains, is bounded by the Great Lakes in the northwest.

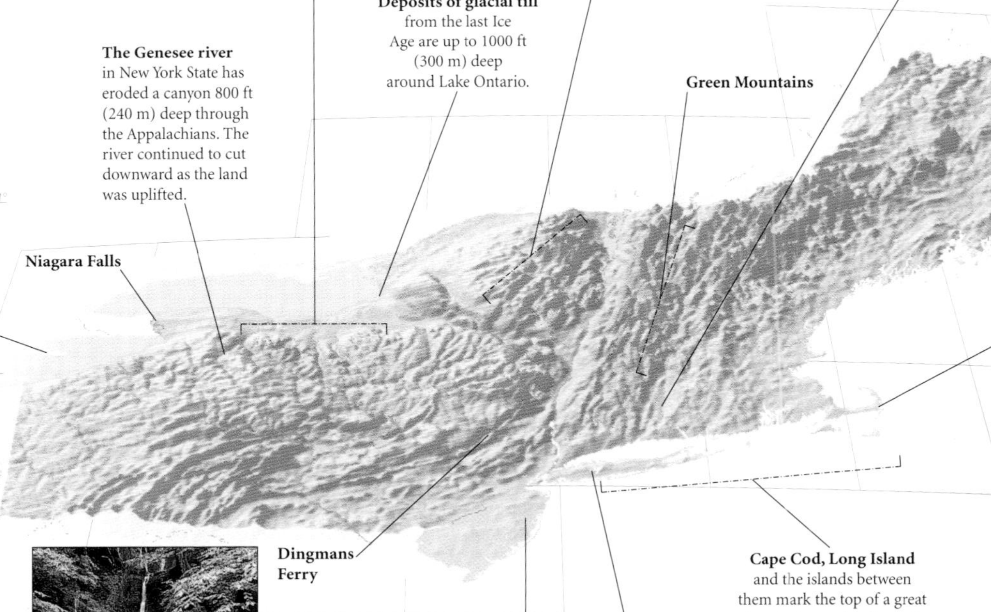

The narrow Finger Lakes of northwestern New York State were formed by glaciers cutting into deep deposits of material from an earlier ice advance.

The Adirondack Mountains were formed when the deeply buried basement rocks were forced upward in a dome by as much as 2 miles (3 km).

The lower Connecticut River has cut down into the flat, clay valley floor, which previously formed the bed of an ice-dammed lake.

Deposits of glacial till from the last Ice Age are up to 1000 ft (300 m) deep around Lake Ontario.

Green Mountains

The Genesee river in New York State has eroded a canyon 800 ft (240 m) deep through the Appalachians. The river continued to cut downward as the land was uplifted.

Niagara Falls

Cape Cod

Lake Erie, receiving water flowing from the rest of the Great Lakes, drains via the Niagara Falls, into Lake Ontario, which lies 325 ft (99 m) below.

Resistant rock

River fed by water from the Great Lakes

Force of water continues to undercut cliffs

Softer rock is eroded more quickly

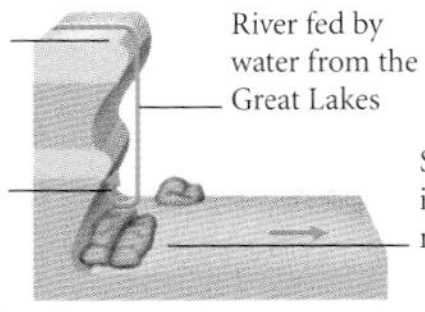

The Niagara Falls were created where the Niagara River reached an escarpment capped by hard limestone. This was gradually eroded, exposing softer rock strata. Plunging water continues to erode the softer strata causing the falls to recede upstream.

The waterfalls at Dingmans Ferry are typical of those found in villages on the "Fall-line," where rivers drop from the Appalachians to the coastal lowlands. These locations provide waterpower and are often at the navigable head of the river.

Dingmans Ferry

The Atlantic Coastal Plain is part of the continental shelf, which extends several hundred miles out to sea, providing a rich environment for marine life.

Rising sea levels have flooded river valleys along the coast, creating rias such as Long Island Sound.

Cape Cod, Long Island and the islands between them mark the top of a great terminal moraine, formed at the front of the ice sheet which once covered the land. This ridge of deposited material was subsequently flooded by rising seas.

At Provincetown, Cape Cod, complex and powerful ocean currents continue to modify the shoreline, washing away some 3 ft (1 m) of the lower cape each year, while extending the beaches in the north.

USA: Mid-Eastern States

Delaware, District of Columbia, Kentucky, Maryland, North Carolina, South Carolina, Tennessee, Virginia, West Virginia

KEY EVENTS IN AMERICAN HISTORY took place in this diverse region, which became the front line between the North and the South during the Civil War of the 1860s. Strong regional contrasts exist between the fertile coastal plains, the isolated upcountry of the Appalachian Mountains, and the cotton-growing areas of the Mississippi lowlands to the west. While coal mining, a traditional industry in the Appalachians, has declined in recent years leaving much rural poverty, service industries elsewhere have increased, especially in Washington D.c, the nation's capital.

Map Key

POPULATION
- 500,000 to 1 million
- 100,000 to 500,000
- 50,000 to 100,000
- 10,000 to 50,000
- below 10,000

ELEVATION
- 6000m / 19,686ft
- 4000m / 13,124ft
- 3000m / 9843ft
- 2000m / 6562ft
- 1000m / 3281ft
- 500m / 1640ft
- 250m / 820ft
- 100m / 328ft
- sea level

SCALE 1:3,000,000
(projection: Lambert Conformal Conic)

Km 0 5 10 20 30 40 50 60 70 80
Miles 0 5 10 20 30 40 50 60 70 80

The Bluegrass region of Kentucky centers on the town of Lexington. This exceptionally fertile rolling plain is well known for its thoroughbred horse-breeding ranches.

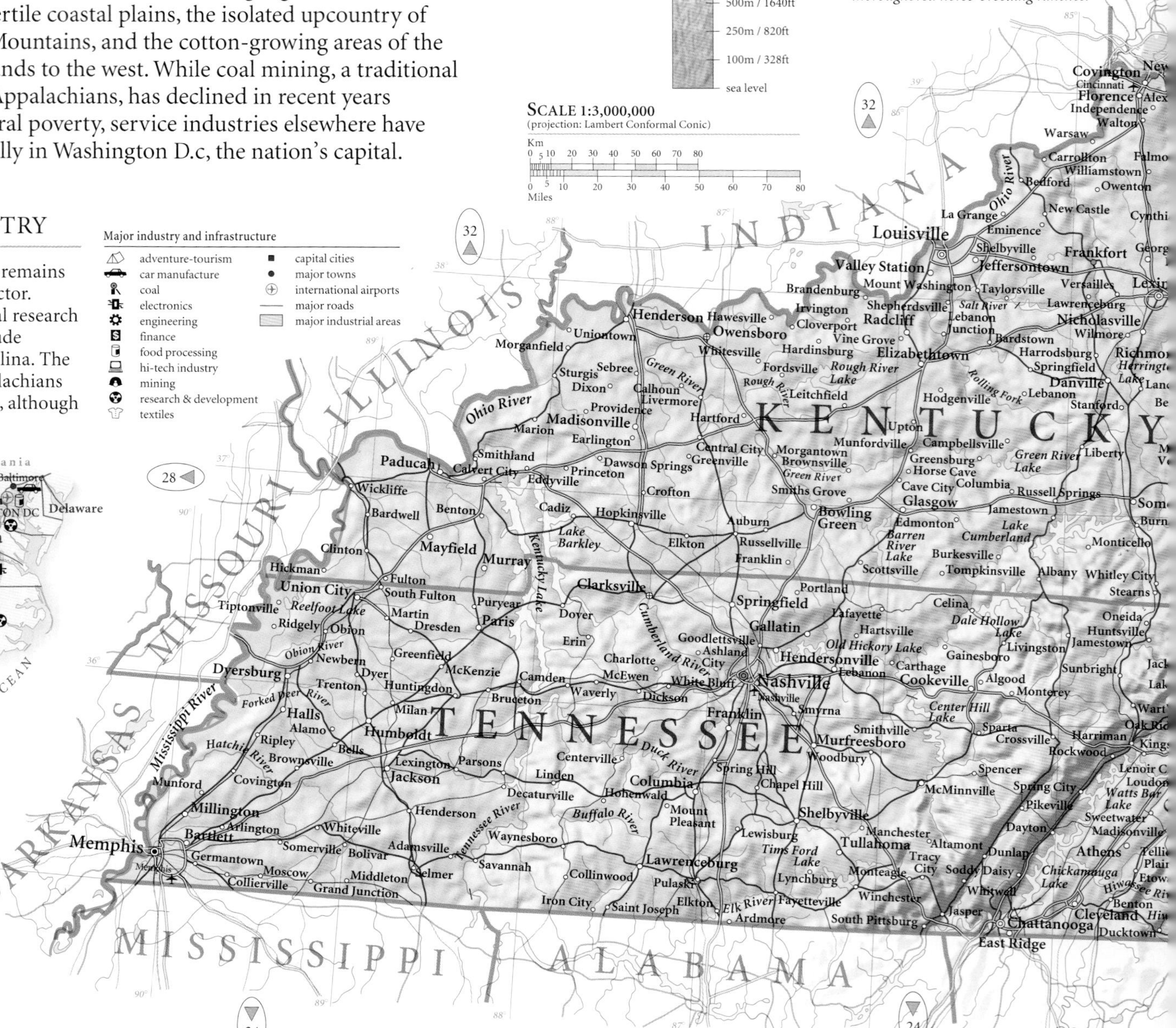

Transportation & Industry

IN THE URBANIZED NORTHEAST, manufacturing remains important, alongside a burgeoning service sector. North Carolina is a major center for industrial research and development. Traditional industries include Tennessee whiskey and textiles in South Carolina. The decline of open-cast coal mining in the Appalachians has been hastened by environmental controls, although adventure-tourism is a flourishing new industry.

Major industry and infrastructure
- adventure-tourism
- car manufacture
- coal
- electronics
- engineering
- finance
- food processing
- hi-tech industry
- mining
- research & development
- textiles
- capital cities
- major towns
- international airports
- major roads
- major industrial areas

Transportation Network

452,218 miles (723,548 km)	5,737 miles (8,267 km)
18,336 miles (29,503 km)	4,404 miles (7,081 km)

Tennessee's rivers are part of an important inland bulk-transportation network. Memphis connects with New Orleans in the south, and with cities as distant as Minneapolis, Sioux City, Chicago, and Pittsburgh, via the Mississippi and its tributaries.

The Landscape

THE EASTERN TRIBUTARIES OF THE MISSISSIPPI drain the interior lowlands. The Cumberland Plateau and the parallel ranges of the Appalachians have been successively uplifted and eroded over time, with the eastern side reduced to a series of foothills known as the Piedmont. The broad coastal plain gradually falls away into salt marshes, lagoons, and offshore bars, broken by flooded estuaries along the shores of the Atlantic.

Farmland on the eastern shores of Chesapeake Bay is sustained by artificial drainage. The area also provides refuge for a variety of waterfowl.

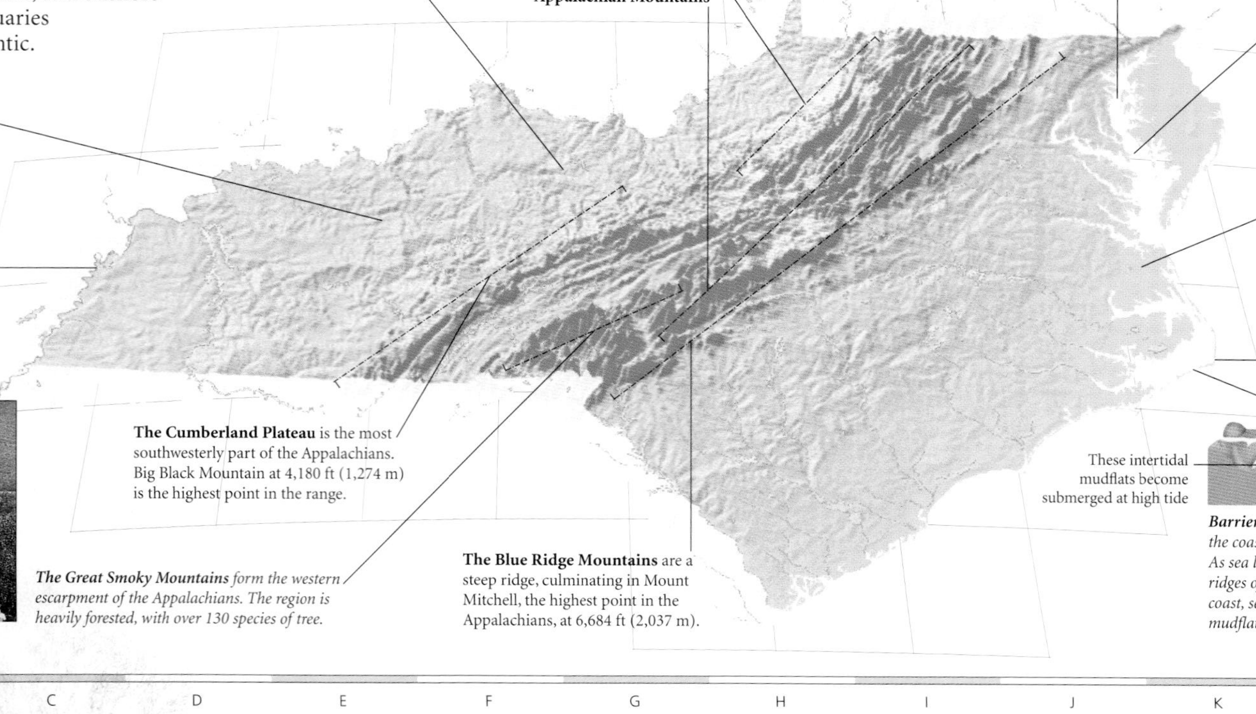

Natural Bridge in eastern Kentucky is an arch 78 ft (26 m) long and 65 ft (20 m) high. It has been shaped from resistant sandstone by gradual weathering processes, which removed the softer rock lying underneath.

The Allegheny Mountains form the northwestern edge of the Appalachian mountain chain. Continuous folding has formed rich seams of bituminous coal.

The many inlets of Chesapeake Bay are the flooded tributaries of the main river valley, which have been inundated by rising sea levels.

Salt marshes such as Great Dismal Swamp, develop where the coast is sheltered. Vast areas of such marshland have been reclaimed for farmland and settlement.

Cape Hatteras is the easternmost point of an offshore barrier island; a wave-deposited sandbar which has become permanent, establishing its own vegetation.

The Mammoth Cave is part of an extensive cave system in the limestone region of southwestern Kentucky. It stretches for over 300 miles (485 km) on five different levels and contains three rivers and three lakes.

The Mississippi River and its tributary the Ohio River form the western border of the region.

The Cumberland Plateau is the most southwesterly part of the Appalachians. Big Black Mountain at 4,180 ft (1,274 m) is the highest point in the range.

The Blue Ridge Mountains are a steep ridge, culminating in Mount Mitchell, the highest point in the Appalachians, at 6,684 ft (2,037 m).

The Great Smoky Mountains form the western escarpment of the Appalachians. The region is heavily forested, with over 130 species of tree.

Barrier islands

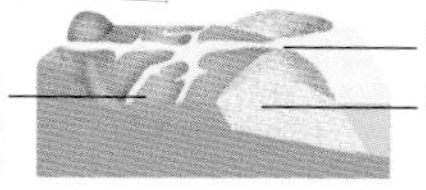

Barrier islands are common along the coasts of North and South Carolina. As sea levels rise, wave action builds up ridges of sand and pebbles parallel to the coast, separated by lagoons or intertidal mudflats, which are flooded at high tide.

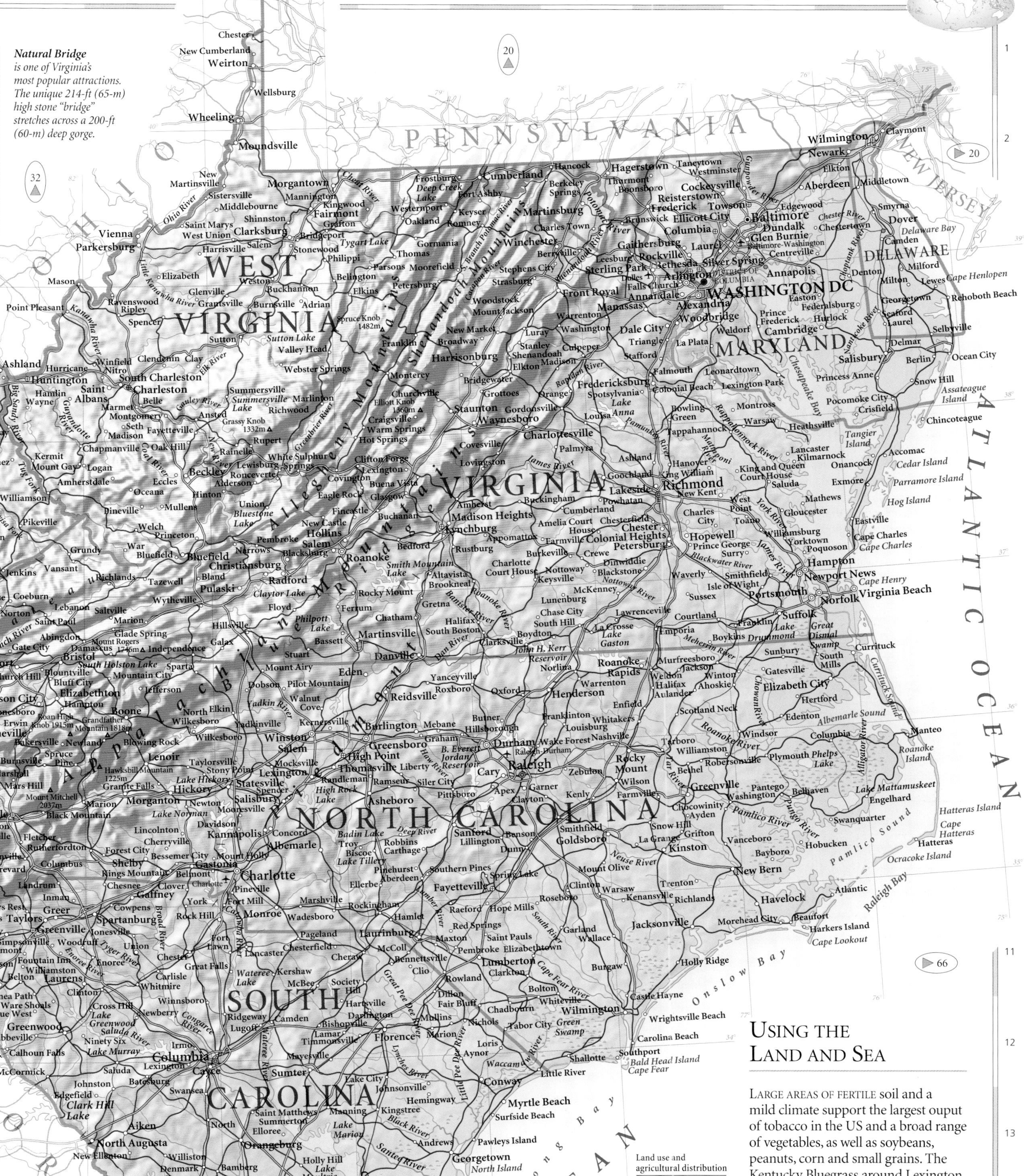

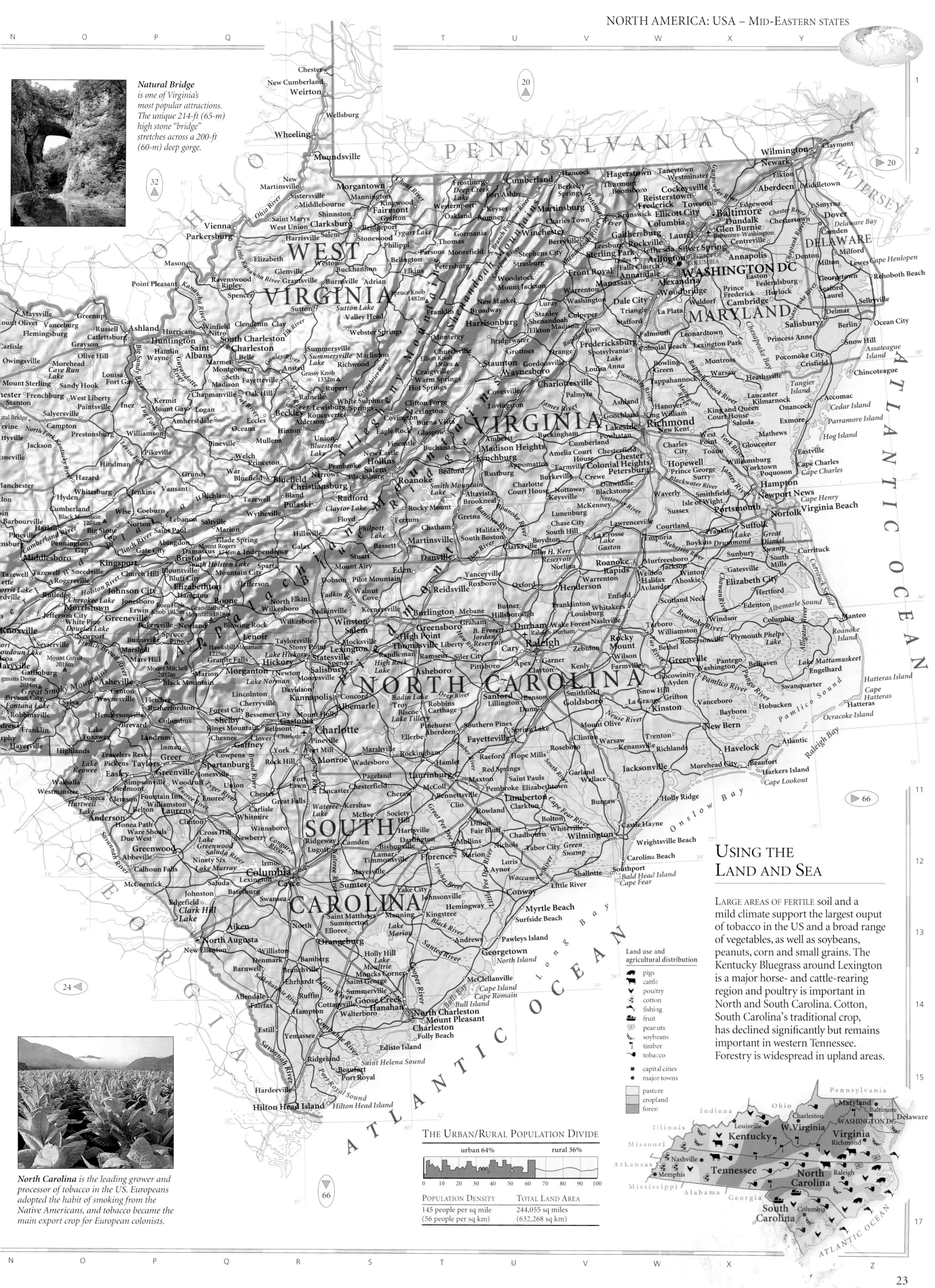

Natural Bridge
is one of Virginia's
most popular attractions.
The unique 214-ft (65-m)
high stone "bridge"
stretches across a 200-ft
(60-m) deep gorge.

North Carolina is the leading grower and
processor of tobacco in the US. Europeans
adopted the habit of smoking from the
Native Americans, and tobacco became the
main export crop for European colonists.

USING THE LAND AND SEA

LARGE AREAS OF FERTILE soil and a
mild climate support the largest ouput
of tobacco in the US and a broad range
of vegetables, as well as soybeans,
peanuts, corn and small grains. The
Kentucky Bluegrass around Lexington
is a major horse- and cattle-rearing
region and poultry is important in
North and South Carolina. Cotton,
South Carolina's traditional crop,
has declined significantly but remains
important in western Tennessee.
Forestry is widespread in upland areas.

**Land use and
agricultural distribution**

- pigs
- cattle
- poultry
- cotton
- fishing
- fruit
- peanuts
- soybeans
- timber
- tobacco

- ■ capital cities
- ● major towns

- pasture
- cropland
- forest

THE URBAN/RURAL POPULATION DIVIDE

urban 64%	rural 36%

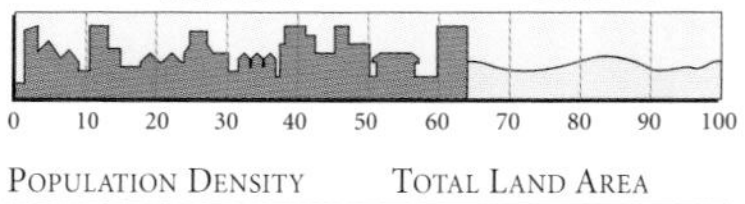

POPULATION DENSITY	TOTAL LAND AREA
145 people per sq mile	244,055 sq miles
(56 people per sq km)	(632,268 sq km)

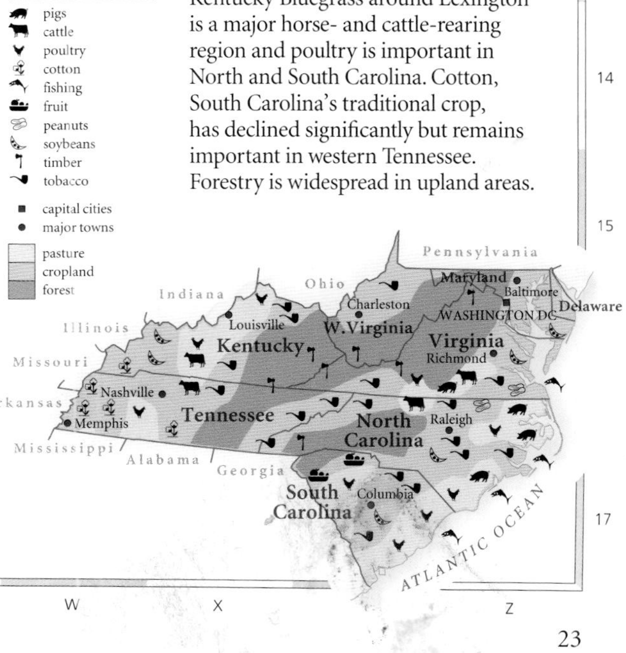

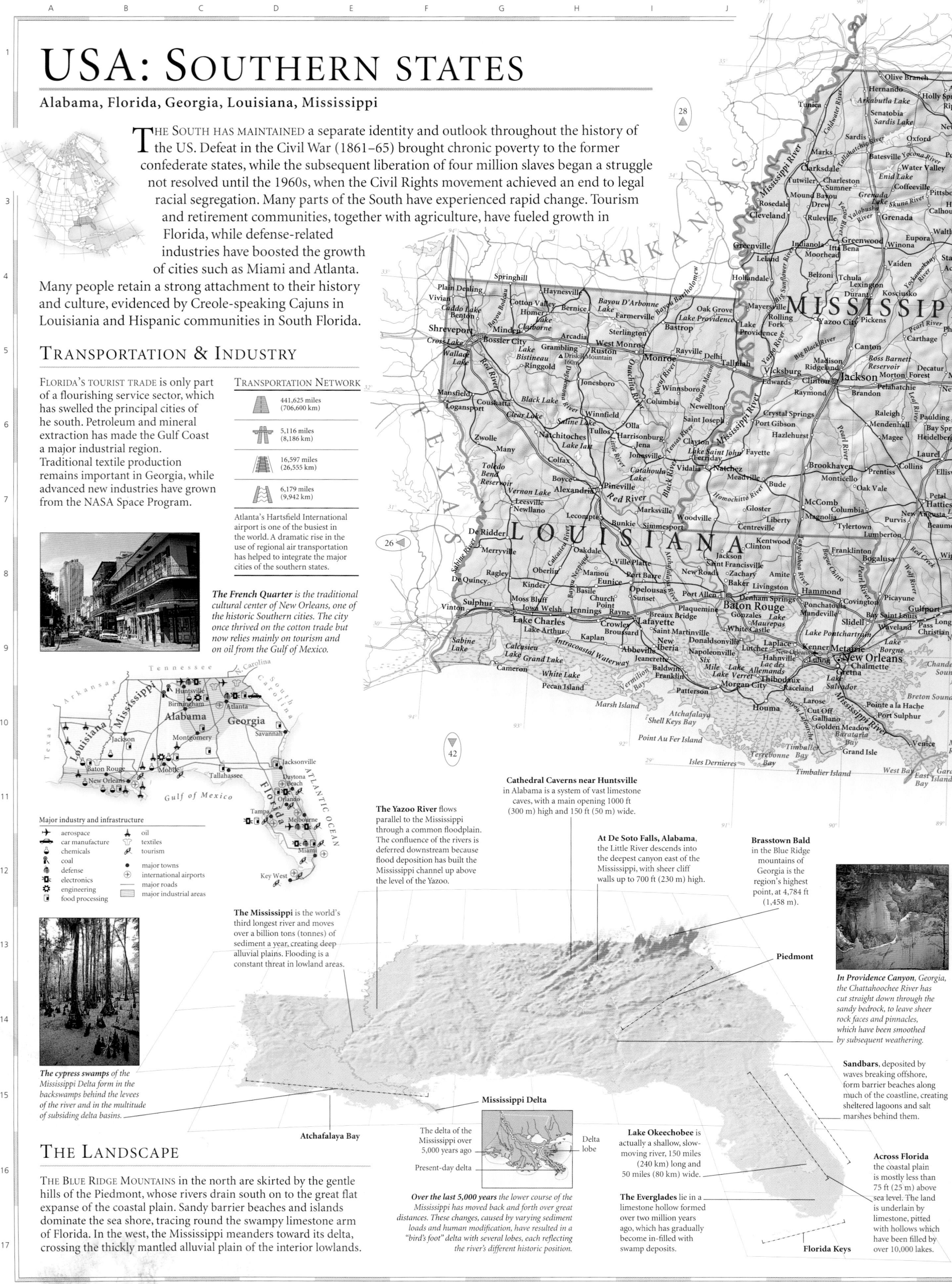

USA: Southern states

Alabama, Florida, Georgia, Louisiana, Mississippi

The South has maintained a separate identity and outlook throughout the history of the US. Defeat in the Civil War (1861–65) brought chronic poverty to the former confederate states, while the subsequent liberation of four million slaves began a struggle not resolved until the 1960s, when the Civil Rights movement achieved an end to legal racial segregation. Many parts of the South have experienced rapid change. Tourism and retirement communities, together with agriculture, have fueled growth in Florida, while defense-related industries have boosted the growth of cities such as Miami and Atlanta. Many people retain a strong attachment to their history and culture, evidenced by Creole-speaking Cajuns in Louisiana and Hispanic communities in South Florida.

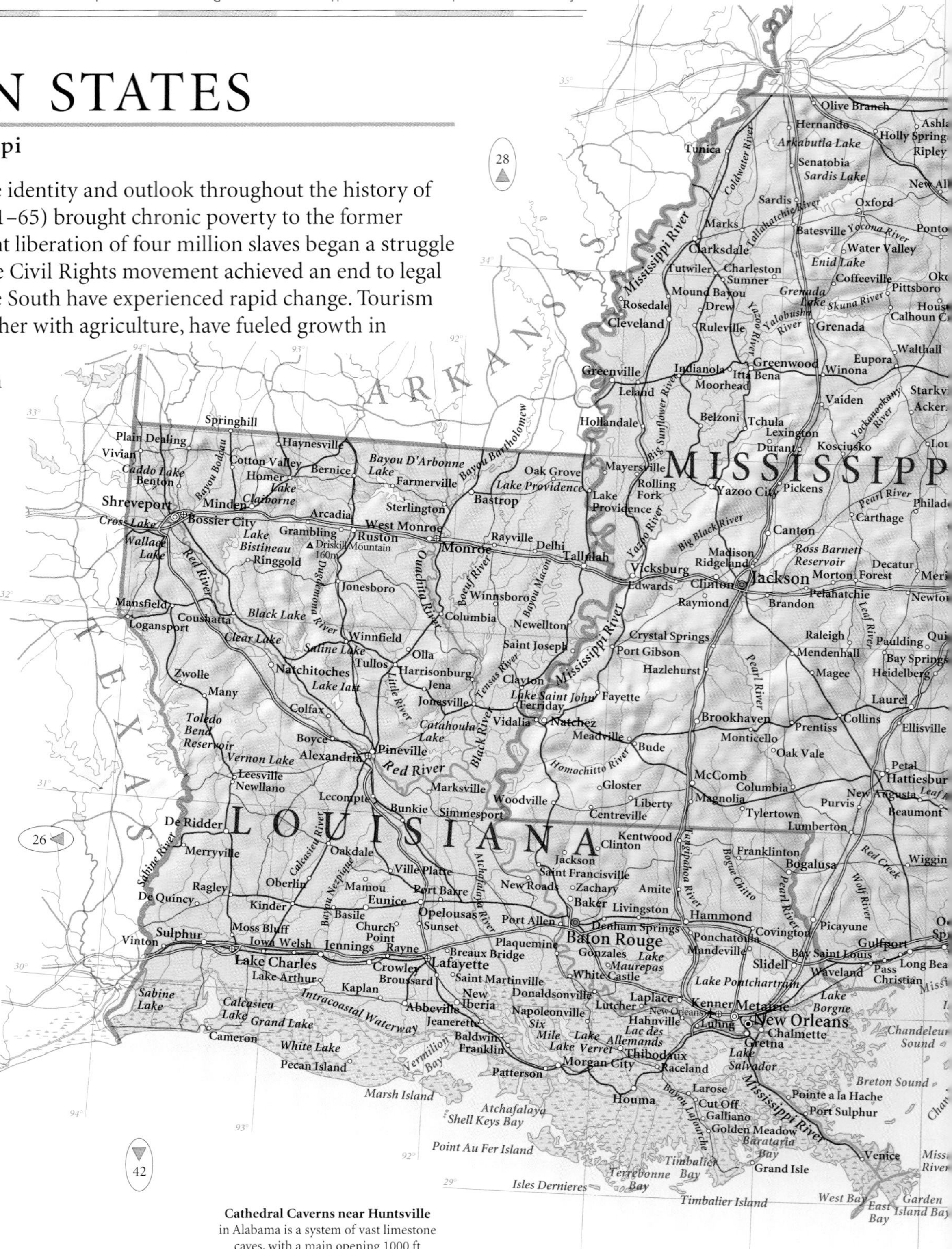

Transportation & Industry

Florida's tourist trade is only part of a flourishing service sector, which has swelled the principal cities of he south. Petroleum and mineral extraction has made the Gulf Coast a major industrial region. Traditional textile production remains important in Georgia, while advanced new industries have grown from the NASA Space Program.

Transportation Network

441,625 miles (706,600 km)
5,116 miles (8,186 km)
16,597 miles (26,555 km)
6,179 miles (9,942 km)

Atlanta's Hartsfield International airport is one of the busiest in the world. A dramatic rise in the use of regional air transportation has helped to integrate the major cities of the southern states.

The French Quarter is the traditional cultural center of New Orleans, one of the historic Southern cities. The city once thrived on the cotton trade but now relies mainly on tourism and on oil from the Gulf of Mexico.

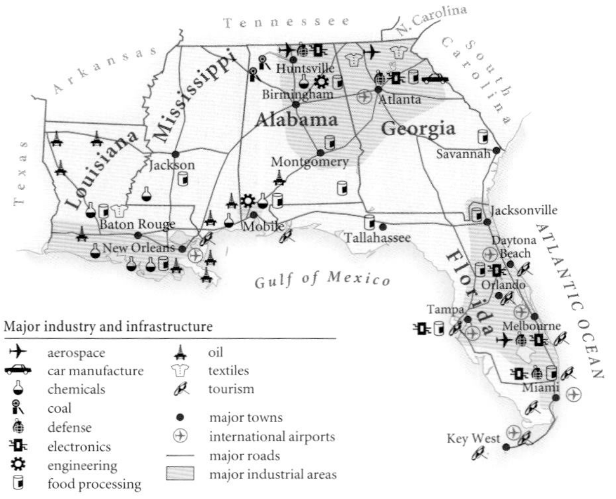

The cypress swamps of the Mississippi Delta form in the backswamps behind the levees of the river and in the multitude of subsiding delta basins.

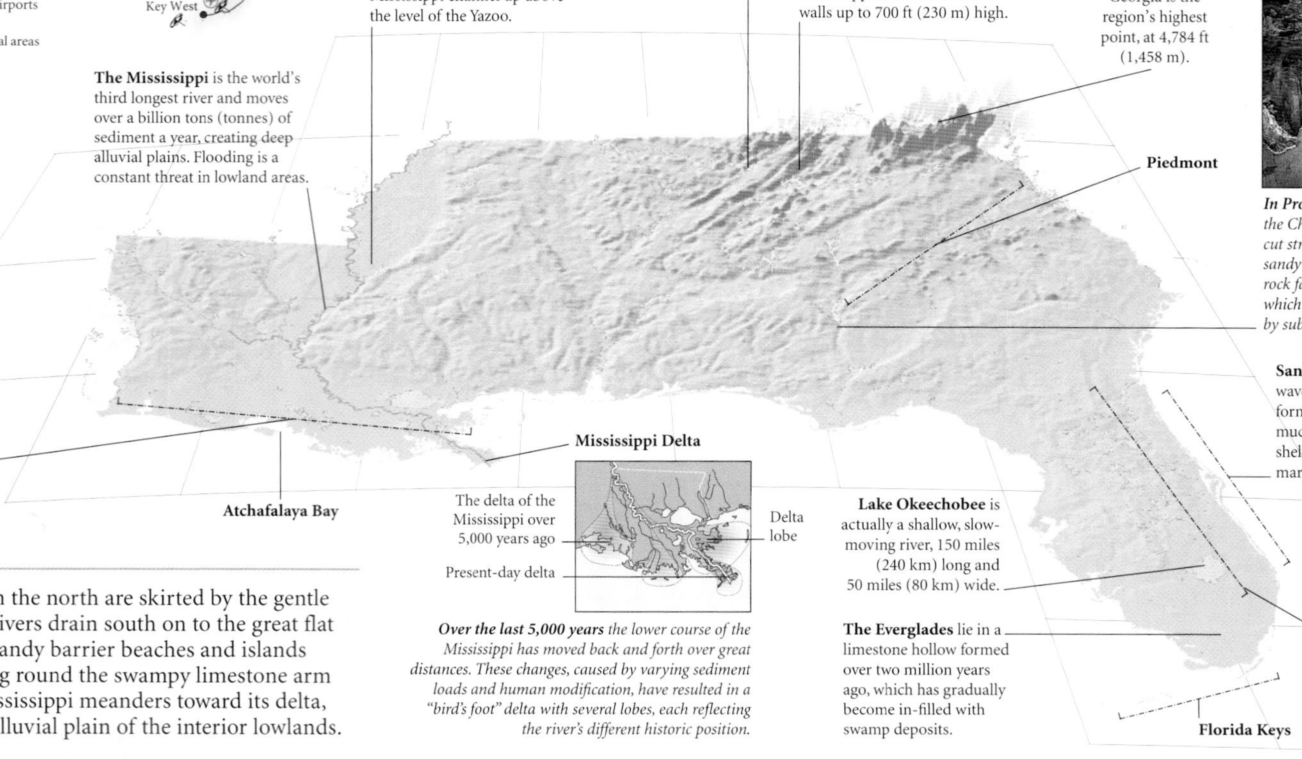

In Providence Canyon, Georgia, the Chattahoochee River has cut straight down through the sandy bedrock, to leave sheer rock faces and pinnacles, which have been smoothed by subsequent weathering.

Over the last 5,000 years the lower course of the Mississippi has moved back and forth over great distances. These changes, caused by varying sediment loads and human modification, have resulted in a "bird's foot" delta with several lobes, each reflecting the river's different historic position.

The Landscape

The Blue Ridge Mountains in the north are skirted by the gentle hills of the Piedmont, whose rivers drain south on to the great flat expanse of the coastal plain. Sandy barrier beaches and islands dominate the sea shore, tracing round the swampy limestone arm of Florida. In the west, the Mississippi meanders toward its delta, crossing the thickly mantled alluvial plain of the interior lowlands.

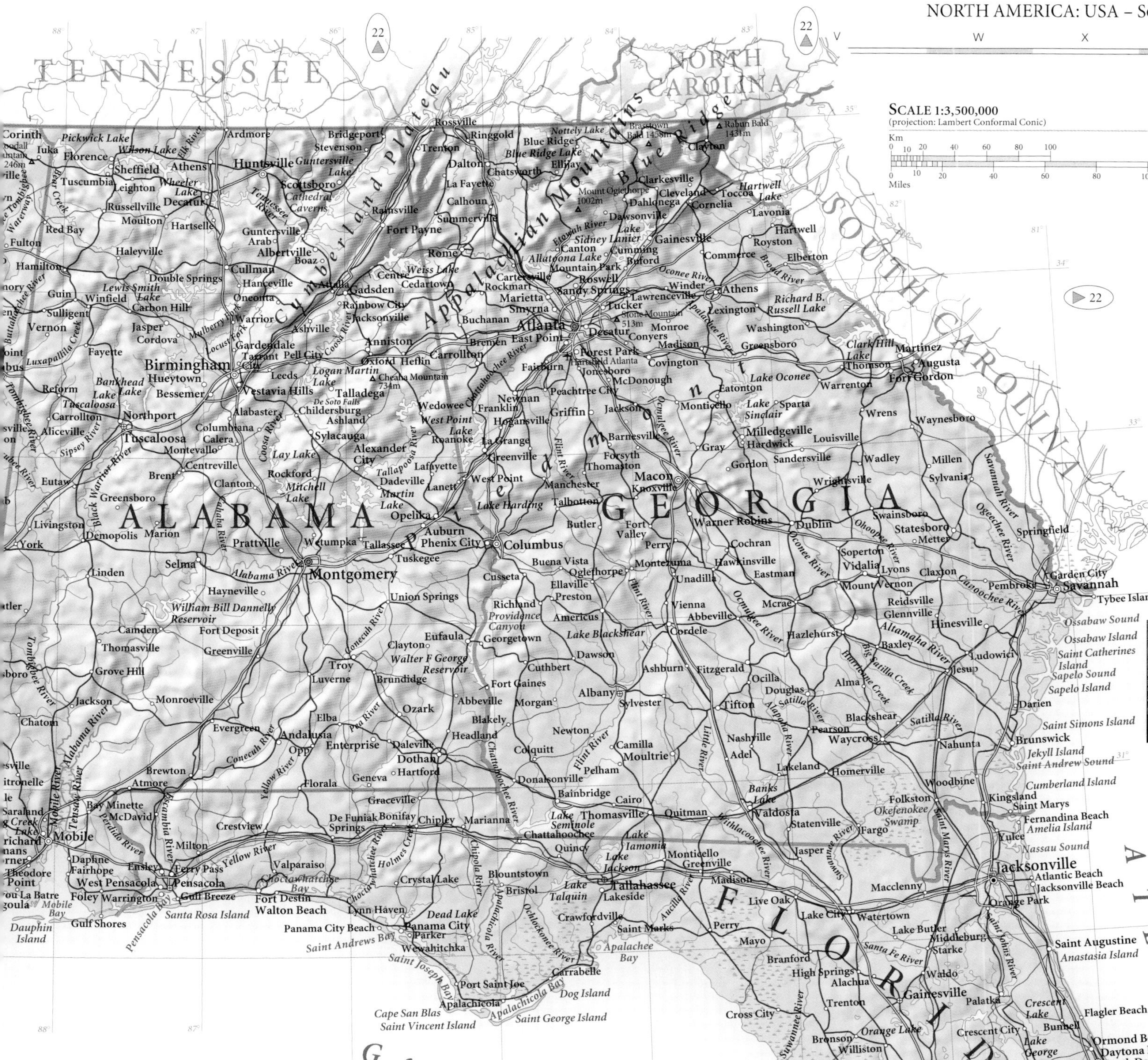

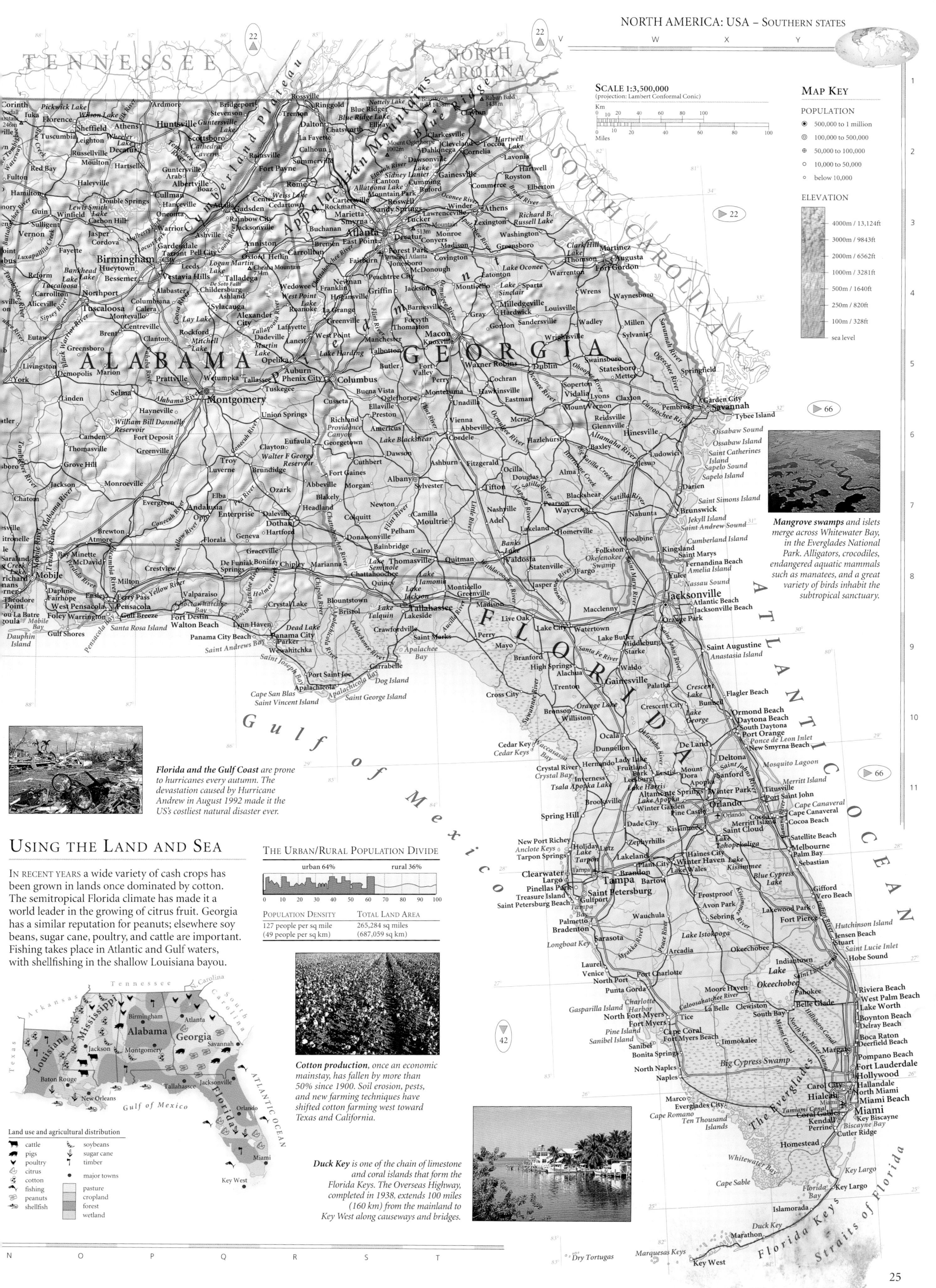

SCALE 1:3,500,000
(projection: Lambert Conformal Conic)

MAP KEY

POPULATION
- 500,000 to 1 million
- 100,000 to 500,000
- 50,000 to 100,000
- 10,000 to 50,000
- below 10,000

ELEVATION
- 4000m / 13,124ft
- 3000m / 9843ft
- 2000m / 6562ft
- 1000m / 3281ft
- 500m / 1640ft
- 250m / 820ft
- 100m / 328ft
- sea level

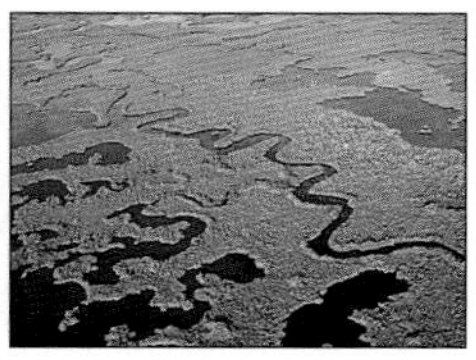

Mangrove swamps and islets merge across Whitewater Bay, in the Everglades National Park. Alligators, crocodiles, endangered aquatic mammals such as manatees, and a great variety of birds inhabit the subtropical sanctuary.

***Florida and the Gulf Coast** are prone to hurricanes every autumn. The devastation caused by Hurricane Andrew in August 1992 made it the US's costliest natural disaster ever.*

USING THE LAND AND SEA

IN RECENT YEARS a wide variety of cash crops has been grown in lands once dominated by cotton. The semitropical Florida climate has made it a world leader in the growing of citrus fruit. Georgia has a similar reputation for peanuts; elsewhere soy beans, sugar cane, poultry, and cattle are important. Fishing takes place in Atlantic and Gulf waters, with shellfishing in the shallow Louisiana bayou.

THE URBAN/RURAL POPULATION DIVIDE

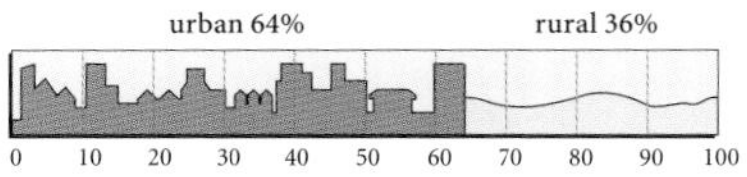

POPULATION DENSITY	TOTAL LAND AREA
127 people per sq mile (49 people per sq km)	265,284 sq miles (687,059 sq km)

***Cotton production**, once an economic mainstay, has fallen by more than 50% since 1900. Soil erosion, pests, and new farming techniques have shifted cotton farming west toward Texas and California.*

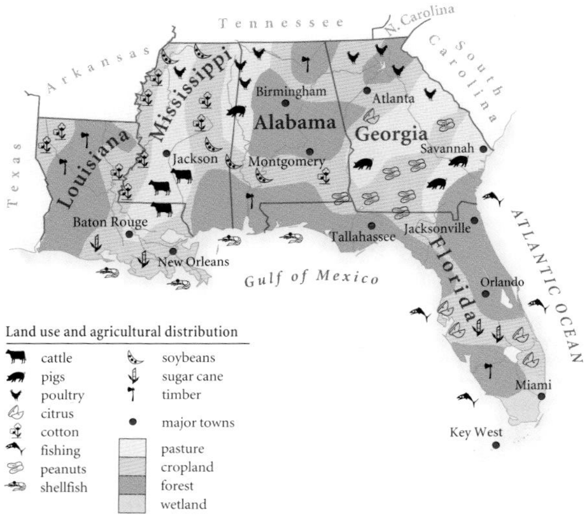

***Duck Key** is one of the chain of limestone and coral islands that form the Florida Keys. The Overseas Highway, completed in 1938, extends 100 miles (160 km) from the mainland to Key West along causeways and bridges.*

USA: Texas

First explored by Spaniards moving north from Mexico in search of gold, Texas was controlled by Spain and then by Mexico, before becoming an independent republic in 1836, and joining the Union of States in 1845. During the 19th century, many migrants who came to Texas raised cattle on the abundant land; in the 20th century, they were joined by prospectors attracted by the promise of oil riches. Today, although natural resources, especially oil, still form the basis of its wealth, the diversified Texan economy includes thriving hi-tech and financial industries. The major urban centers, home to 80% of the population, lie in the south and east, and include Houston, the "oil-city," and Dallas Fort Worth. Hispanic influences remain strong, especially in southern and western Texas.

***Dallas was founded** in 1841 as a prairie trading post and its development was stimulated by the arrival of railroads. Cotton and then oil funded the town's early growth. Today, the modern, high-rise skyline of Dallas reflects the city's position as a leading center of banking, insurance, and the petroleum industry in the southwest.*

Using the Land

Cotton production and livestock-raising, particularly cattle, dominate farming, although crop failures and the demands of local markets have led to some diversification. Following the introduction of modern farming techniques, cotton production spread out from the east to the plains of western Texas. Cattle ranches are widespread, while sheep and goats are raised on the dry Edwards Plateau.

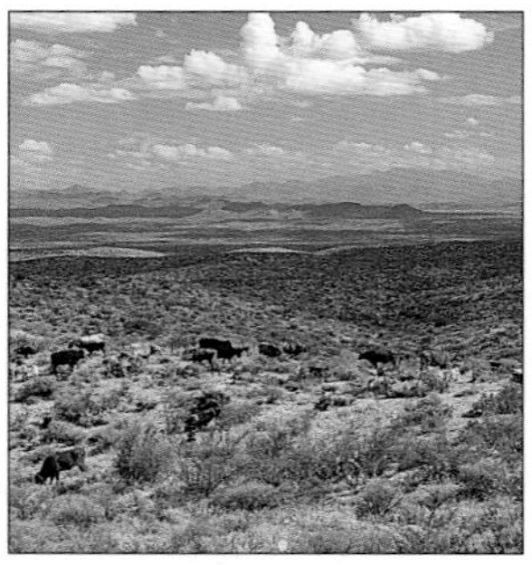

***The huge cattle ranches of Texas** developed during the 19th century when land was plentiful and could be acquired cheaply. Today, more cattle and sheep are raised in Texas than in any other state.*

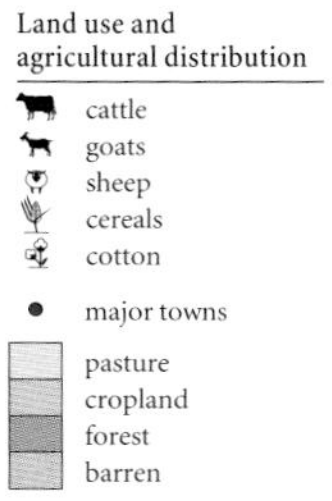

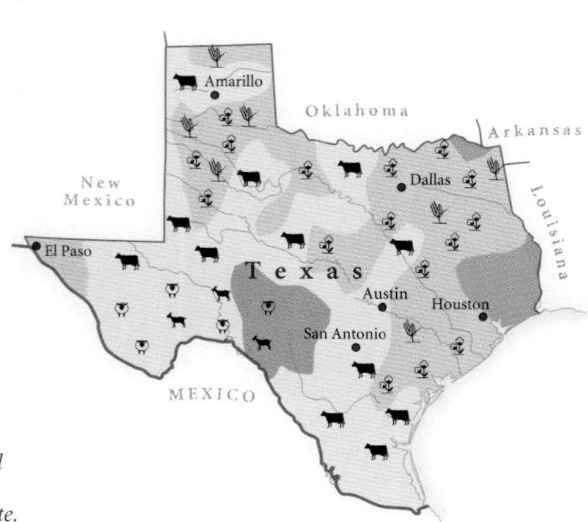

The Urban/Rural Population Divide

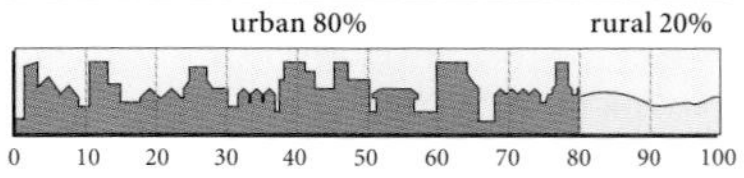

Population Density	Total Land Area
73 people per sq mile (28 people per sq km)	267,338 sq miles (692,402 sq km)

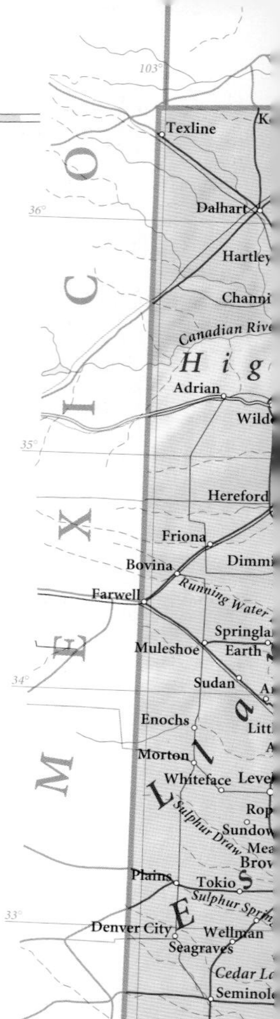

38◀

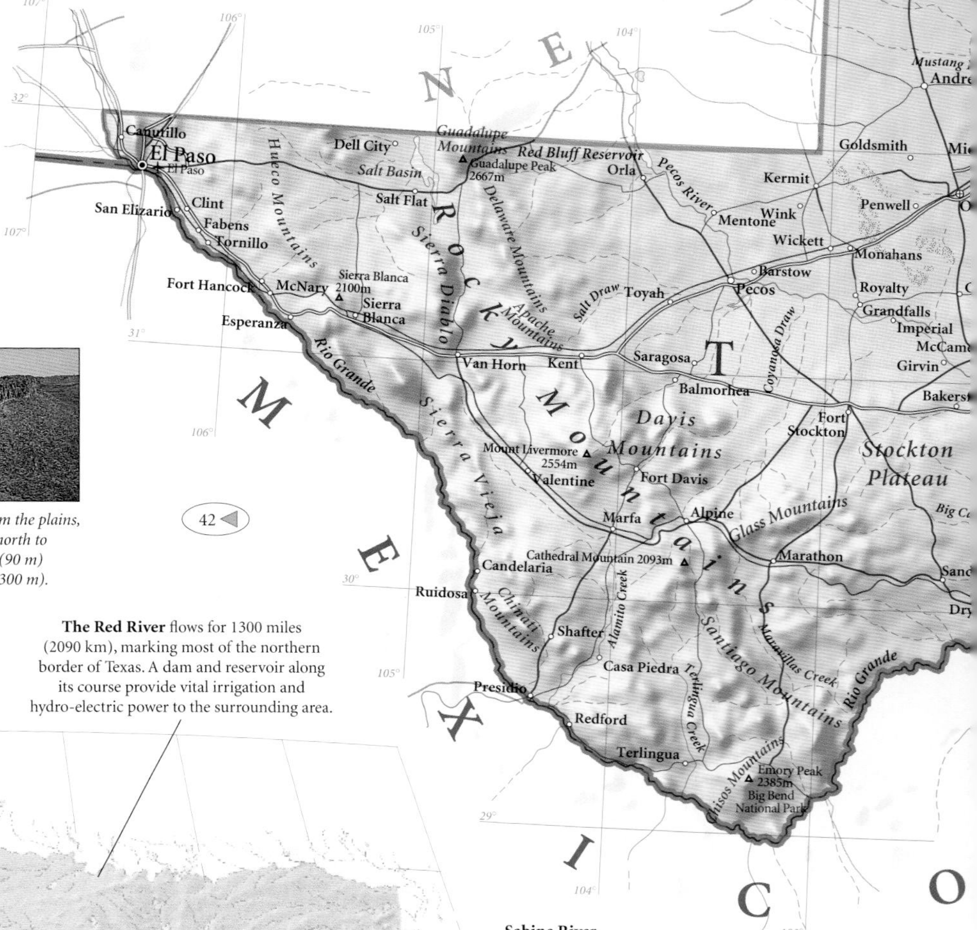

42◀

The Landscape

Texas is made up of a series of massive steps descending from the mountains and high plains of the west and northwest to the coastal lowlands in the southeast. Many of the state's borders are delineated by water. The Rio Grande flows from the Rocky Mountains to the Gulf of Mexico, marking the border with Mexico.

***Cap Rock Escarpment** juts out from the plains, running 200 miles (320 km) from north to south. Its height varies from 300 ft (90 m) rising to sheer cliffs up to 1,000 ft (300 m).*

The Llano Estacado or Staked Plain in northern Texas is known for its harsh environment. In the north, freezing winds carrying ice and snow sweep down from the Rocky Mountains. To the south, sandstorms frequently blow up, scouring anything in their paths. Flash floods, in the wide, flat riverbeds that remain dry for most of the year, are another hazard.

The Guadalupe Mountains lie in the southern Rocky Mountains. They incorporate Guadalupe Peak, the highest in Texas, rising 8,749 ft (2,667 m).

The Rio Grande flows from the Rocky Mountains through semi-arid land, supporting sparse vegetation. The river actually shrinks along its course, losing more water through evaporation and seepage than it gains from its tributaries and rainfall.

Big Bend National Park

The Red River flows for 1300 miles (2090 km), marking most of the northern border of Texas. A dam and reservoir along its course provide vital irrigation and hydro-electric power to the surrounding area.

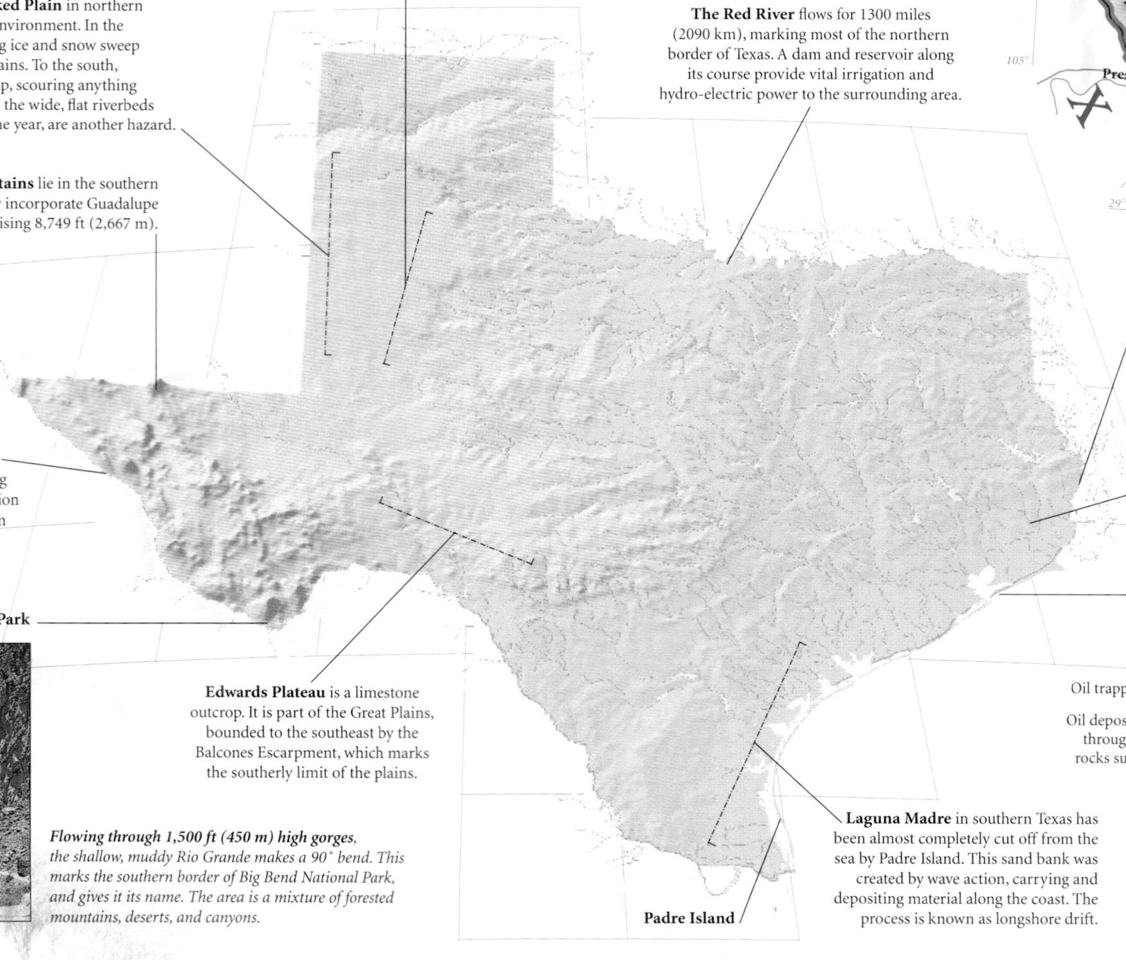

Sabine River

Extensive forests of pine and cypress grow in the eastern corner of the coastal lowlands where the average rainfall is 45 inches (1145 mm) a year. This is higher than the rest of the state and over twice the average in the west.

In the coastal lowlands of southeastern Texas the Earth's crust is warping, causing the land to subside and allowing the sea to invade. Around Galveston, the rate of downward tilting is 6 inches (15 cm) per year. Erosion of the coast is also exacerbated by hurricanes.

***Flowing through 1,500 ft (450 m) high gorges,** the shallow, muddy Rio Grande makes a 90° bend. This marks the southern border of Big Bend National Park, and gives it its name. The area is a mixture of forested mountains, deserts, and canyons.*

Edwards Plateau is a limestone outcrop. It is part of the Great Plains, bounded to the southeast by the Balcones Escarpment, which marks the southerly limit of the plains.

Padre Island

Laguna Madre in southern Texas has been almost completely cut off from the sea by Padre Island. This sand bank was created by wave action, carrying and depositing material along the coast. The process is known as longshore drift.

Oil deposits

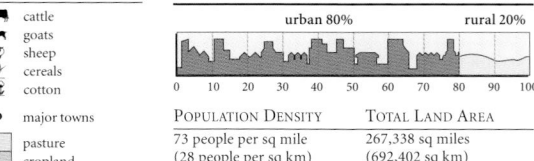

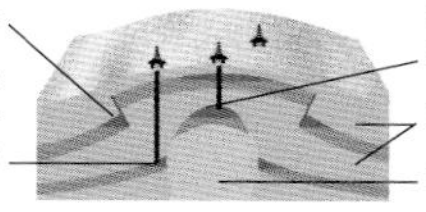

***Oil deposits** are found beneath much of Texas. They collect as oil migrates upward through porous layers of rock until it is trapped, either by a cap of rock above a salt dome, or by a fault line which exposes impermeable rock through which the oil cannot rise.*

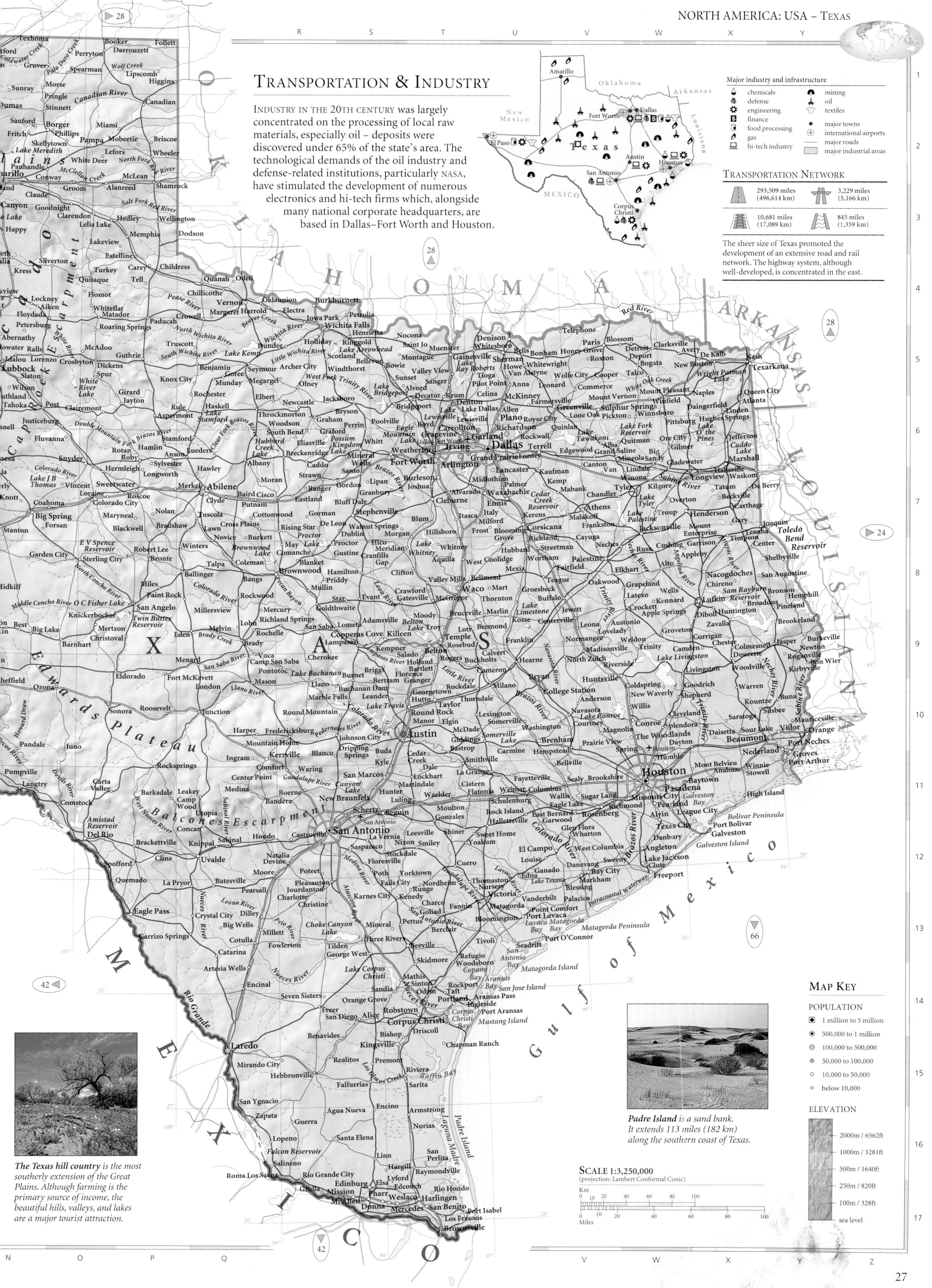

TRANSPORTATION & INDUSTRY

INDUSTRY IN THE 20TH CENTURY was largely concentrated on the processing of local raw materials, especially oil – deposits were discovered under 65% of the state's area. The technological demands of the oil industry and defense-related institutions, particularly NASA, have stimulated the development of numerous electronics and hi-tech firms which, alongside many national corporate headquarters, are based in Dallas–Fort Worth and Houston.

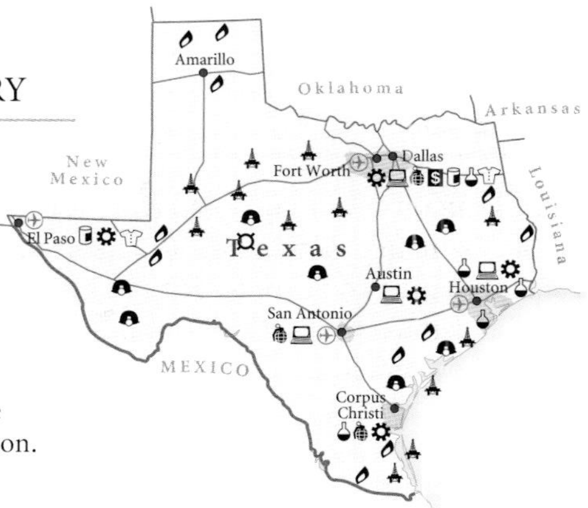

Major industry and infrastructure

- chemicals
- defense
- engineering
- finance
- food processing
- gas
- hi-tech industry
- mining
- oil
- textiles
- major towns
- international airports
- major roads
- major industrial areas

TRANSPORTATION NETWORK

293,509 miles (496,614 km)	3,229 miles (5,166 km)
10,681 miles (17,089 km)	845 miles (1,359 km)

The sheer size of Texas promoted the development of an extensive road and rail network. The highway system, although well-developed, is concentrated in the east.

The Texas hill country is the most southerly extension of the Great Plains. Although farming is the primary source of income, the beautiful hills, valleys, and lakes are a major tourist attraction.

***Padre Island** is a sand bank. It extends 113 miles (182 km) along the southern coast of Texas.*

SCALE 1:3,250,000
(projection: Lambert Conformal Conic)

MAP KEY

POPULATION

- 1 million to 5 million
- 500,000 to 1 million
- 100,000 to 500,000
- 50,000 to 100,000
- 10,000 to 50,000
- below 10,000

ELEVATION

- 2000m / 6562ft
- 1000m / 3281ft
- 500m / 1640ft
- 250m / 820ft
- 100m / 328ft
- sea level

USA: SOUTH MIDWESTERN STATES

Arkansas, Kansas, Missouri, Oklahoma

THE EXPANSION OF THE US focused on this region in the mid-19th century. Settlers spread from the confluence of the Missouri and Mississippi Rivers up onto the Great Plains. This treeless expanse, which early explorers had called the Great American Desert was turned into one of the world's richest agricultural regions. But periodic droughts, coupled with overintensive farming, led to the "dustbowl" soil erosion crisis of the 1930s, the abandonment of many farms, and a mass exodus to the west coast. The land has since recovered, although the mechanization of agriculture has led to a decline in the rural population. In recent years, suburban residential development has spread rapidly across the wooded Ozark Plateau in the east of the region.

TRANSPORTATION & INDUSTRY

THE PROCESSING OF AGRICULTURAL PRODUCTS, such as brewing and meatpacking, has been traditionally important in these states. In Kansas and Oklahoma, diversified manufacturing now supplements income from fossil fuels; Wichita has become a world center for aeronautical engineering, an industry which also employs many people in neighboring Missouri.

Major industry and infrastructure

- aerospace
- engineering
- finance
- food processing
- gas
- mining
- oil
- vehicle manufacture
- major towns
- international airports
- major roads
- major industrial areas

Agricultural produce from the plains is moved by barges along the Mississippi. The river now carries a far greater tonnage of freight than any other waterway system in the US.

TRANSPORTATION NETWORK

380,307 miles (608,491 km)	4068 miles (6508 km)
16,185 miles (25,896 km)	1994 miles (3208 km)

The Arkansas River and its tributaries allow access to over half of the US's navigable inland waterways. A system of locks and dams along the river provides Tulsa, in Oklahom, with a navigable water route to the Gulf of Mexico.

MAP KEY

POPULATION

- 100,000 to 500,000
- 50,000 to 100,000
- 10,000 to 50,000
- below 10,000

ELEVATION

- 1000m / 3281ft
- 500m / 1640ft
- 250m / 820ft
- 100m / 328ft
- sea level

THE LANDSCAPE

MOST OF THE REGION consists of high, treeless plains, which gradually descend east from the Rocky Mountains. Drainage follows this slope, with rivers flowing toward the alluvial lowlands of the Mississippi in the southeast. Between the plains and the lowlands lie various ranges of wooded hills, including the deeply incised Ozark Plateau.

The Mississippi, North America's longest river, is joined by the Missouri, its main tributary, on a flood plain which spreads south to the Gulf of Mexico.

The Ozark Plateau is a wooded, hilly region of rivers and narrow, winding lakes. The Lake of the Ozarks was created by the damming of the Osage River in 1930.

Collapsed limestone caverns led to the formation of Big Basin in Kansas; a depression 100 ft (33 m) deep and 1 mile (1.6 km) wide.

Flint Hills is the region's easternmost major escarpment. Steep, grassy uplands are interspersed with rocky, wooded ravines and outcrops of limestone and chert.

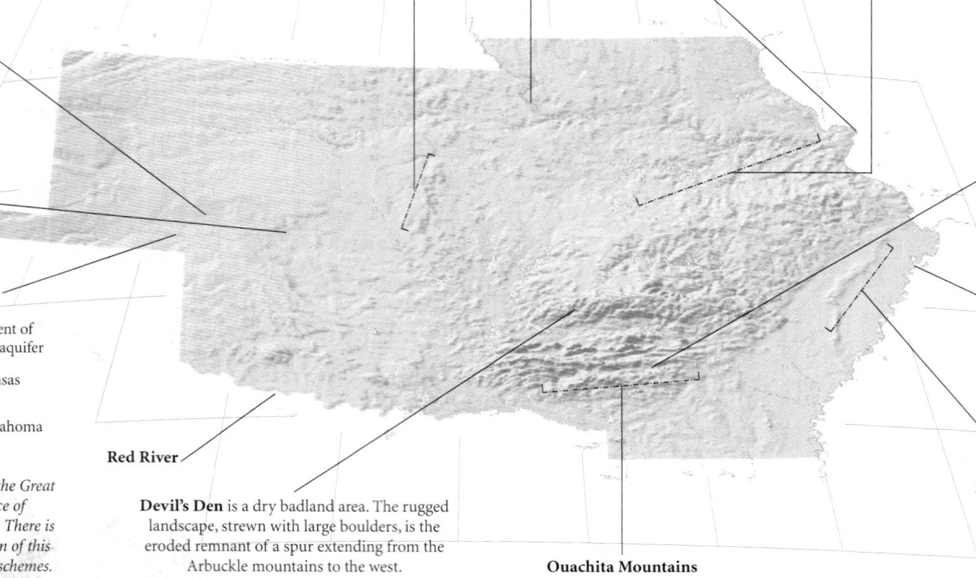

The Great Salt Plains of northern Oklahoma cover 45 sq miles (116 sq km). The arid, white flats were left by the gradual evaporation of an ancient salt lake.

Lake Ouachita, in Arkansas is one of a number of irregularly-shaped lakes found among the ridges of the Ouachita Mountains.

Underground water reserves

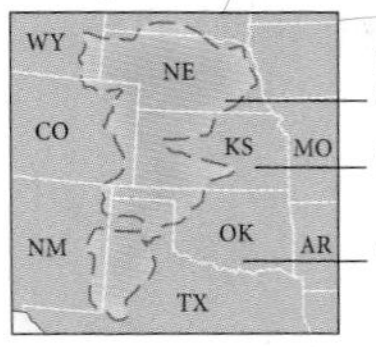

The Ogallala Aquifer, beneath the Great Plains, is the largest known source of underground water in the world. There is concern about the rapid depletion of this finite water supply by irrigation schemes.

Red River

Devil's Den is a dry badland area. The rugged landscape, strewn with large boulders, is the eroded remnant of a spur extending from the Arbuckle mountains to the west.

Ouachita Mountains

Mississippi River

Crowleys Ridge is a long, sandy ridge, rising from the Mississippi floodplain. It was formed over thousands of years by the deposition of sand blown eastward from the Great Plains.

SCALE 1:3,000,000
(projection: Lambert Conformal Conic)

The landscape of northeast Kansas is interlaced by rivers which have cut broad wooded valleys through the gentle hills. All the rivers in Kansas form part of the massive Missouri/Mississippi drainage basin.

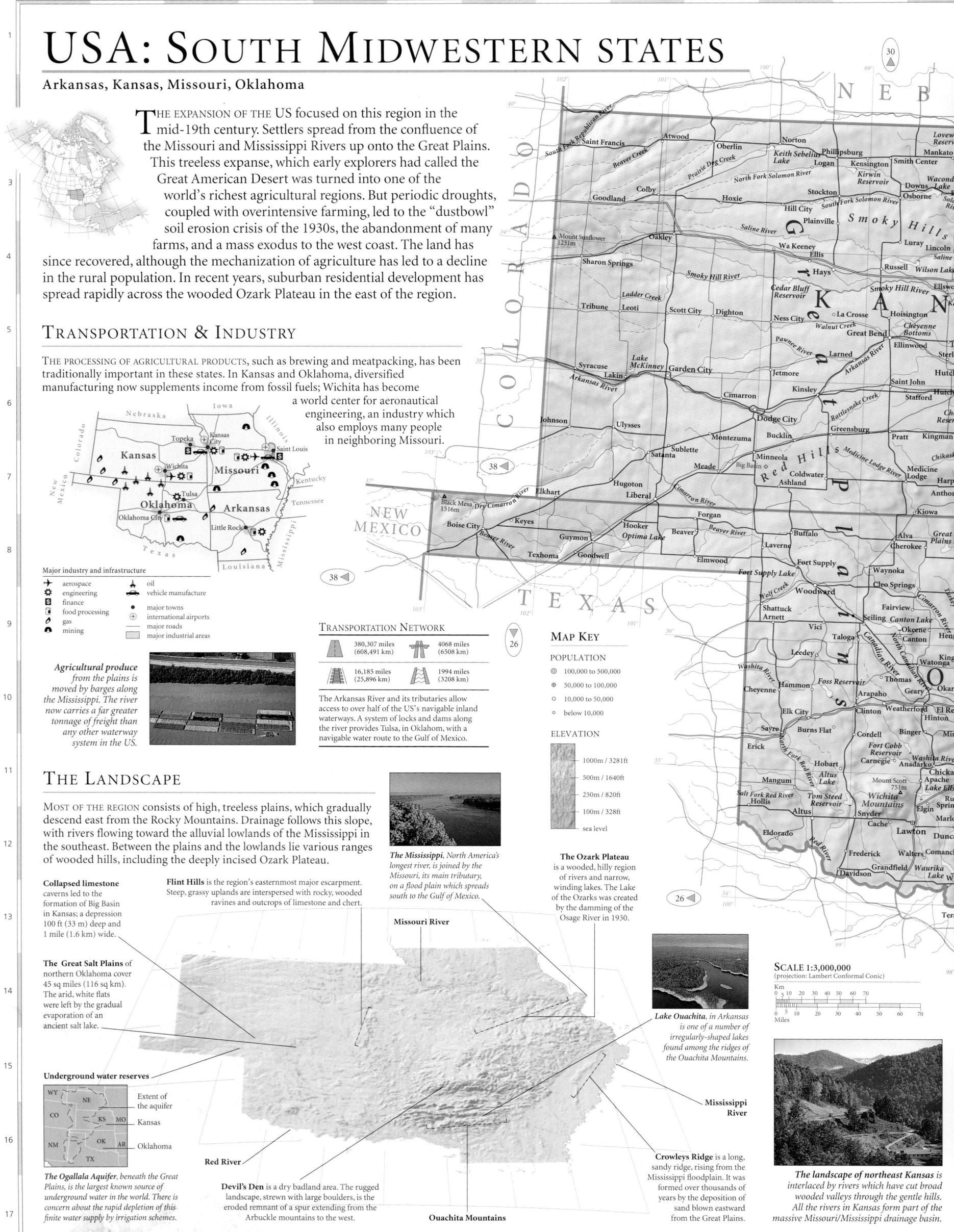

Gateway Arch, in Saint Louis, Missouri, is 634 ft (192 m) high. The huge steel arch symbolizes the city's historic role as the "Gateway to the West".

USING THE LAND

THE PROBLEMS of a harsh continental climate, with severe winters and hot, dry summers, are partially offset by the rich soils of the plains. Kansas is a major cereal crop producer, ranking first in US production of wheat and sorghum. Rainfall increases toward the east, favoring the cultivation of soybeans, cotton, and rice, with corn concentrated in Missouri. Huge herds of cattle are raised in Oklahoma, Kansas, and Missouri.

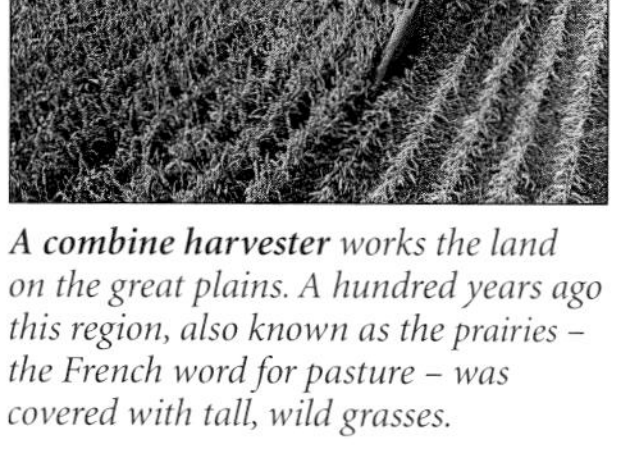

***A combine harvester** works the land on the great plains. A hundred years ago this region, also known as the prairies – the French word for pasture – was covered with tall, wild grasses.*

THE URBAN/RURAL POPULATION DIVIDE

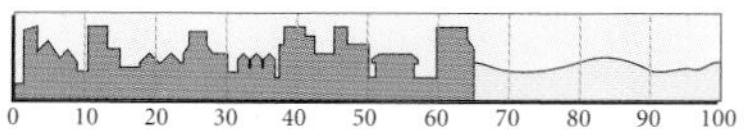

POPULATION DENSITY	TOTAL LAND AREA
50 people per sq mile (19 people per sq km)	274,900 sq miles (712,177 sq km)

USA: Upper Plains States

Iowa, Minnesota, Nebraska, North Dakota, South Dakota

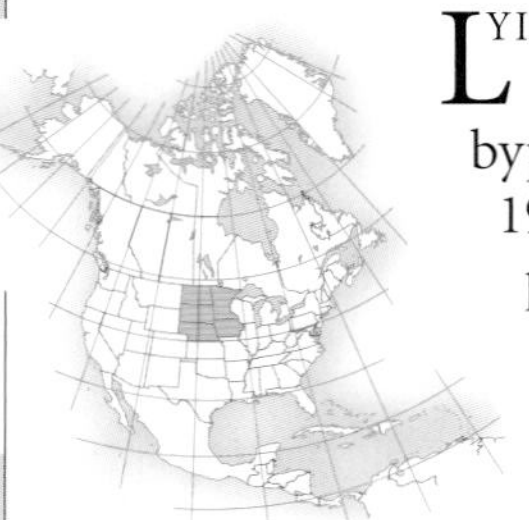

LYING AT THE VERY HEART of the North American continent, much of this region was acquired from France as part of the Louisiana Purchase in 1803. The area was largely bypassed by the early waves of westward migrants. When Europeans did settle, during the 19th century, they displaced the Native Americans who lived on the plains. The settlers planted arable crops and raised cattle on the immensely fertile prairie land, founding an agrarian tradition which flourishes today. Most of this region remains rural; of the five states, only in Minnesota has there been significant diversification away from agriculture and resource-based industries into the hi-tech and service sectors.

Using the Land

THE POPULAR IMAGE of these states as agricultural is entirely justified; prairies stretch uninterrupted across most of the area. Croplands fall into two regions: the wheat belt of the plains, and the corn belt of the central US. Cash crops, such as soybeans, are grown to supplement incomes. Livestock, particularly pigs and cattle, are raised throughout this region.

The Urban/Rural Population Divide

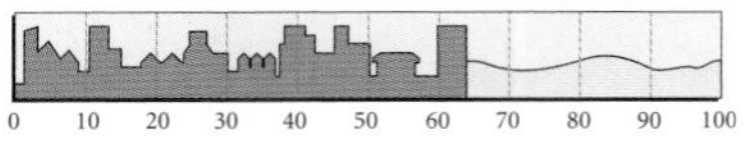

Population Density	Total Land Area
29 people per sq mile (11 people per sq km)	365,287 sq miles (946,056 sq km)

Dark, fertile prairie soils in the southeast provide Minnesota's most productive farmland. Hot, humid summers create a long growing season for corn cultivation.

Land use and agricultural distribution
- cattle
- pigs
- corn (maize)
- soybeans
- wheat
- major towns
- pasture
- cropland
- forest
- wetland

Transportation & Industry

FOOD PROCESSING and the production of farm machinery are supported by the large agricultural sector. Mineral exploitation is also an important activity: gold is mined in the ore-rich Black Hills of South Dakota, and both North Dakota and Nebraska are emerging as major petroleum producers.

Transportation Network

504,522 miles (807,235 km)	3,422 miles (5,475 km)
16,940 miles (27,104 km)	683 miles (1,098 km)

Nebraska's central location has made it an important transportation artery for east–west traffic. Minnesota's road network radiates out from the hub of the twin cities, Minneapolis–Saint Paul.

Water erosion along the Little Missouri River has carried away sedimentary deposits, creating rugged landscapes known as badlands.

Major industry and infrastructure
- coal
- engineering
- electronics
- finance
- food processing
- oil & gas
- mining
- major towns
- international airports
- major roads
- major industrial areas

The Landscape

THESE STATES STRADDLE the Great Plains and the lowlands of the central US, with Minnesota lying in a transition zone between the eastern forests and the prairies. The region was shaped by repeated ice advances and retreats, leaving a flat relief, broken only by the numerous lakes and broad river networks that drain the prairies.

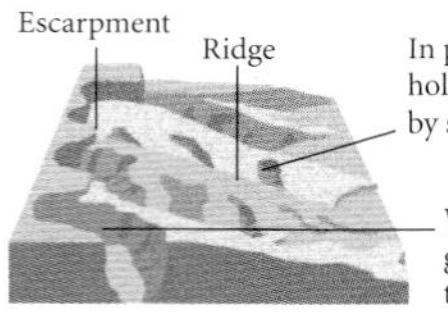

Badlands are formed by stormwater run-off. This flows down the impermeable strata of the escarpment and saturates the permeable strata, leading to mudslides and the formation of gullies.

The Minnesota landscape contains many post-glacial features, including its numerous lakes, boulder-strewn hills, and mineral-rich deposits.

In the badlands of North and South Dakota, horizontal layers of sandstone have been eroded by rivers, leaving a landscape of narrow gullies, sharp crests and pinnacles.

South Dakota Badlands

Chimney Rock is a remnant of an ancient land surface, eroded by the North Platte River. The tip of its spire stands 500 ft (150 m) above the plain.

North Dakota Badlands

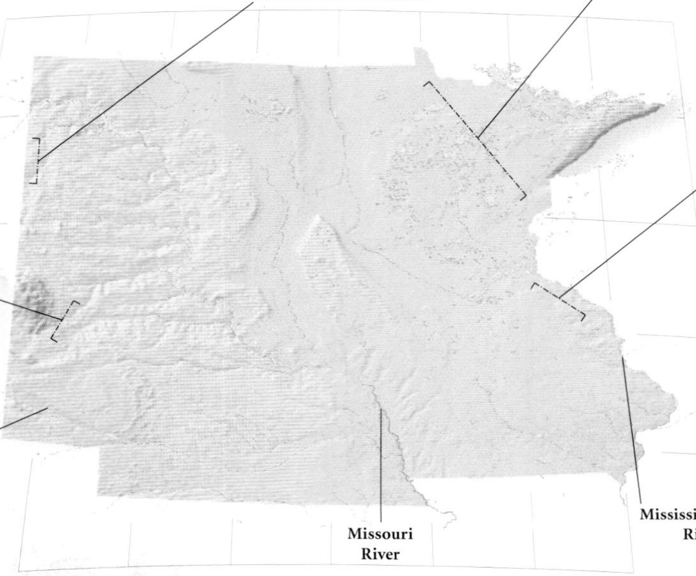

Although it escaped the last glaciation, the limestone bedrock of southeastern Minnesota has been eroded by surface and subterranean streams, leaving a network of underground caverns and steep-sided valleys.

Missouri River

Mississippi River

In northeastern Iowa, the Mississippi and its tributaries have deeply incised the underlying bedrock creating a hilly terrain, with bluffs standing 300 ft (90 m) above the valley.

34

Along the shores of Lake Superior in Minnesota, the average number of frost-free days can be as few as 90, and frosts may occur in any month of the year.

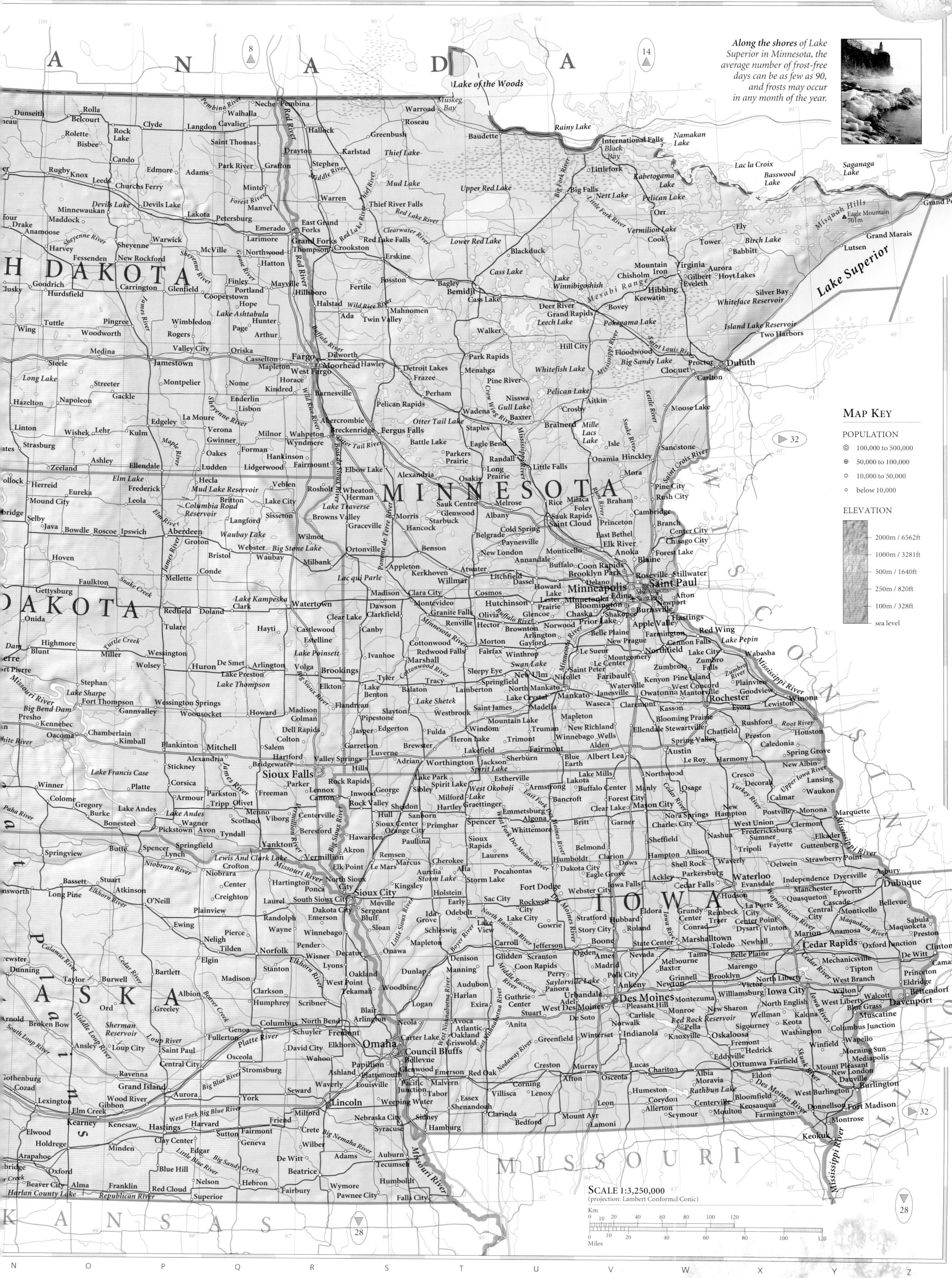

USA: Great Lakes states

Illinois, Indiana, Michigan, Ohio, Wisconsin

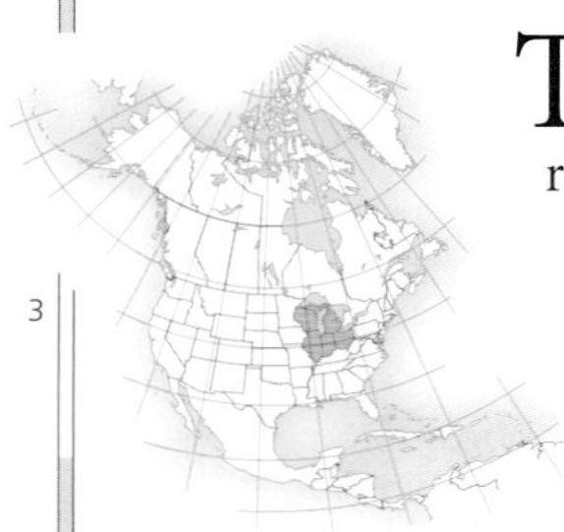

The states bordering the Great Lakes developed rapidly in the second half of the 19th century as a result of improvements in communications: railroads to the west and waterways to the south and east. Fertile land and good links with growing eastern seaboard cities encouraged the development of agriculture and food processing. Migrants from Europe and other parts of the US flooded into the region and for much of the 20th century the region's economy boomed. However, in recent years heavy industry has declined, earning the region the unwanted label the "Rustbelt."

Transportation & Industry

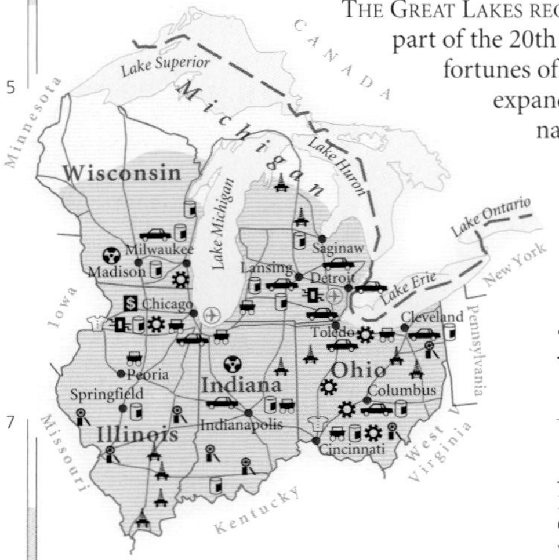

Major industry and infrastructure

- car manufacture
- coal
- electronics
- engineering
- finance
- food processing
- iron & steel
- oil
- research & development
- textiles
- major towns
- international airports
- major roads
- major industrial areas

The Great Lakes region is the center of the US car industry. Since the early part of the 20th century, its prosperity has been closely linked to the fortunes of automobile manufacturing. Iron and steel production has expanded to meet demand from this industry. In the 1970s, nationwide recession, cheaper foreign competition in the automobile sector, pollution in and around the Great Lakes, and the collapse of the meatpacking industry, centered on Chicago, forced these states to diversify their industrial base. New industries have emerged, notably electronics, service, and finance industries.

Transportation Network

540,682 miles (865,091 km)	6,550 miles (10,480 km)
24,928 miles (39,884 km)	2,330 miles (3,748 km)

Few areas of the US have a comparable system. Chicago is a principal transportation terminus with a dense network of roads, railroads, and Interstate freeways that radiates out from the city.

*Ever since **Ransom Olds** and Henry Ford started mass-producing automobiles in Detroit early in the 20th century, the city's name has become synonymous with the American automotive industry.*

The Landscape

Much of this region shows the impact of glaciation which lasted until about 10,000 years ago, and extended as far south as Illinois and Ohio. Although the relief of the region slopes toward the Great Lakes, because the ice sheets blocked northerly drainage, most of the rivers today flow southward, forming part of the massive Mississippi/Missouri drainage basin.

***The dunes** near Sleeping Bear Point rise 400 ft (120 m) from the banks of Lake Michigan. They are constantly being resculpted by wind action.*

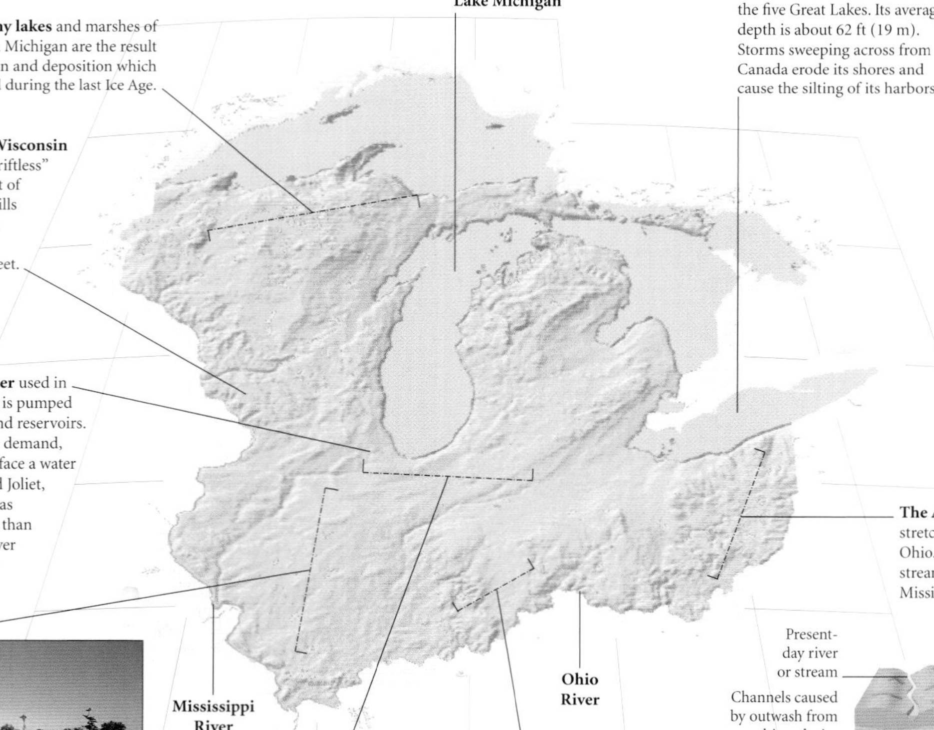

Lake Michigan

The many lakes and marshes of Wisconsin and Michigan are the result of glacial erosion and deposition which occurred during the last Ice Age.

Lake Erie is the shallowest of the five Great Lakes. Its average depth is about 62 ft (19 m). Storms sweeping across from Canada erode its shores and cause the silting of its harbors.

Southwestern Wisconsin is known as a "driftless" area. Unlike most of the region, low hills protected it from erosion by the advancing ice sheet.

Most of the water used in northern Illinois is pumped from underground reservoirs. Due to increased demand, many areas now face a water shortage. Around Joliet, the water table was lowered by more than 700 ft (210 m) over the last century.

The Appalachian plateau stretches eastward from Ohio. It is dissected by streams flowing west into the Mississippi and Ohio Rivers.

Illinois plains

The plains of Illinois are characteristic of drift landscapes, scoured and flattened by glacial erosion and covered with fertile glacial deposits.

Mississippi River

Ohio River

Relict landforms from the last glaciation, such as shallow basins and ridges, cover all but the south of this region. Ridges, known as moraines, up to 300 ft (100 m) high, lie to the south of Lake Michigan.

Unlike the level prairie to the north, southern Indiana is relatively rugged. Limestone in the hills has been dissolved by water, producing features such as sinkholes and underground caves.

Glacial till

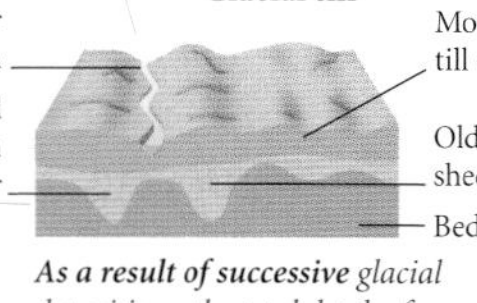

***As a result of successive** glacial depositions, the total depth of till along the former southern margin of the Laurentide ice sheet can exceed 1,300 ft (400 m).*

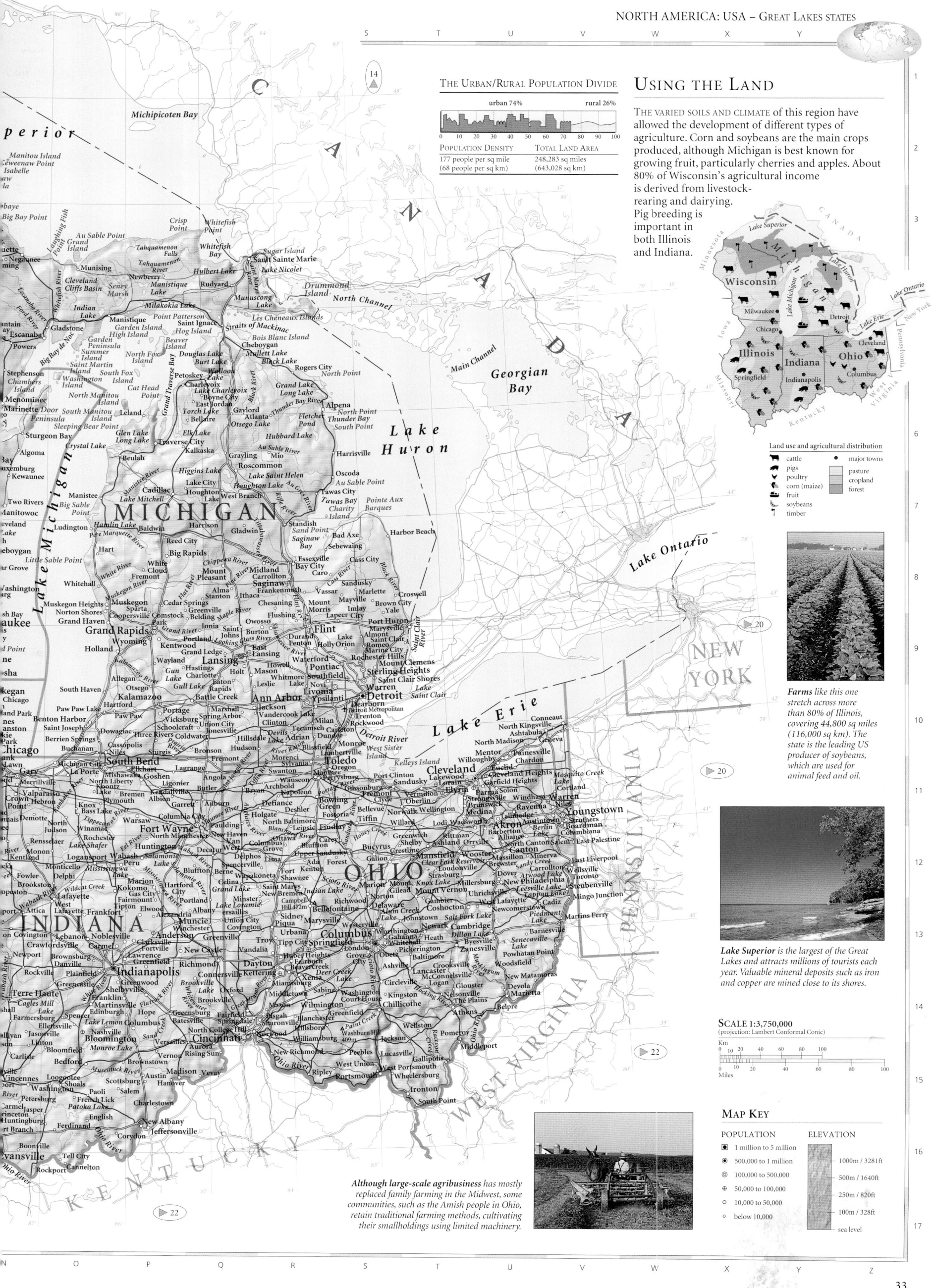

The Urban/Rural Population Divide

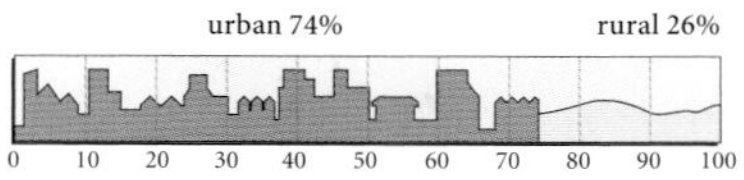

Population Density	Total Land Area
177 people per sq mile (68 people per sq km)	248,283 sq miles (643,028 sq km)

Using the Land

The varied soils and climate of this region have allowed the development of different types of agriculture. Corn and soybeans are the main crops produced, although Michigan is best known for growing fruit, particularly cherries and apples. About 80% of Wisconsin's agricultural income is derived from livestock-rearing and dairying. Pig breeding is important in both Illinois and Indiana.

***Farms** like this one stretch across more than 80% of Illinois, covering 44,800 sq miles (116,000 sq km). The state is the leading US producer of soybeans, which are used for animal feed and oil.*

***Lake Superior** is the largest of the Great Lakes and attracts millions of tourists each year. Valuable mineral deposits such as iron and copper are mined close to its shores.*

SCALE 1:3,750,000
(projection: Lambert Conformal Conic)

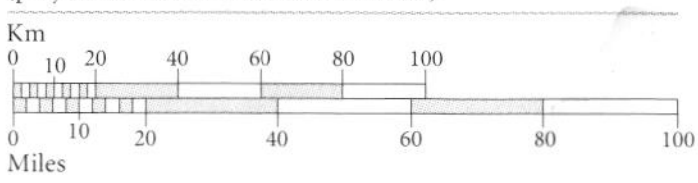

***Although large-scale agribusiness** has mostly replaced family farming in the Midwest, some communities, such as the Amish people in Ohio, retain traditional farming methods, cultivating their smallholdings using limited machinery.*

Map Key

Population	Elevation
1 million to 5 million	1000m / 3281ft
500,000 to 1 million	500m / 1640ft
100,000 to 500,000	250m / 820ft
50,000 to 100,000	100m / 328ft
10,000 to 50,000	sea level
below 10,000	

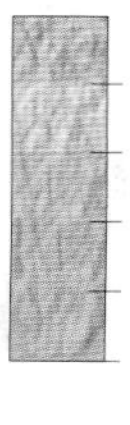

USA: NORTH MOUNTAIN STATES

Idaho, Montana, Oregon, Washington, Wyoming

THE REMOTENESS OF THE NORTHWESTERN STATES, coupled with the rugged landscape, ensured that this was one of the last areas settled by Europeans in the 19th century. Fur-trappers and gold-prospectors followed the Snake River westward as it wound its way through the Rocky Mountains. The states of the northwest have pioneered many conservationist policies, with the first US National Park opened at Yellowstone in 1872. More recently, the Cascades and Rocky Mountains have become havens for adventure tourism. The mountains still serve to isolate the western seaboard from the rest of the continent. This isolation has encouraged West Coast cities to expand their trade links with countries of the Pacific Rim.

The Snake River has cut down into the basalt of the Columbia Basin to form Hells Canyon, the deepest in the US, with cliffs up to 7,900 ft (2,408 m) high.

MAP KEY

POPULATION
- ⦿ 500,000 to 1 million
- ⊚ 100,000 to 500,000
- ⊕ 50,000 to 100,000
- ○ 10,000 to 50,000
- ∘ below 10,000

ELEVATION
- 4000m / 13,124ft
- 3000m / 9843ft
- 2000m / 6562ft
- 1000m / 3281ft
- 500m / 1640ft
- 250m / 820ft
- 100m / 328ft
- sea level

Fine-textured, volcanic soils in the hilly Palouse region of eastern Washington are susceptible to erosion.

USING THE LAND

WHEAT FARMING IN THE EAST gives way to cattle ranching as rainfall decreases. Irrigated farming in the Snake River valley produces large yields of potatoes and other vegetables. Dairying and fruit-growing take place in the wet western lowlands between the mountain ranges.

THE URBAN/RURAL POPULATION DIVIDE

urban 70% rural 30%

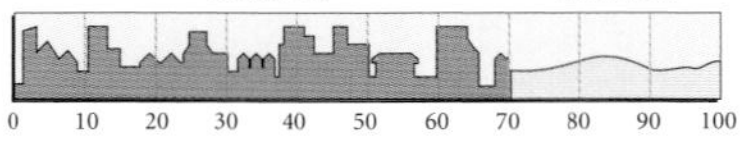

POPULATION DENSITY	TOTAL LAND AREA
23 people per sq mile	493,782 sq miles
(9 people per sq km)	(1,278,846 sq km)

SCALE 1:3,750,000
(projection: Lambert Conformal Conic)

Km 10 20 40 60 80 100

Miles 10 20 40 60 80 100

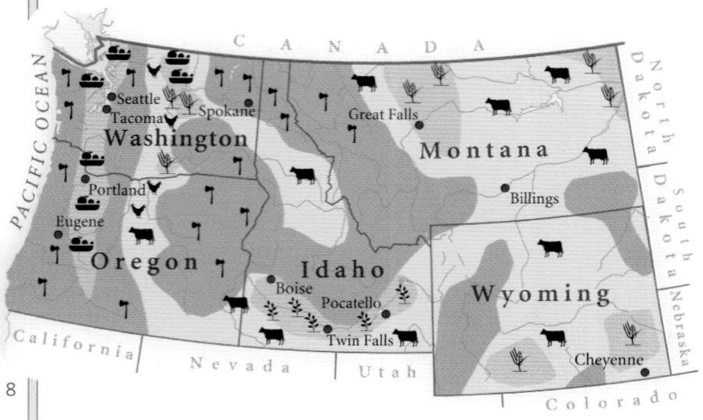

Land use and agricultural distribution
- cattle
- poultry
- cereals
- fruit
- potatoes
- timber
- major towns
- pasture
- cropland
- forest

198 ◄

TRANSPORTATION & INDUSTRY

MINERALS AND TIMBER are extremely important in this region. Uranium, precious metals, copper, and coal are all mined, the latter in vast open-cast pits in Wyoming; oil and natural gas are extracted further north. Manufacturing, notably related to the aerospace and electronics industries, is important in western cities.

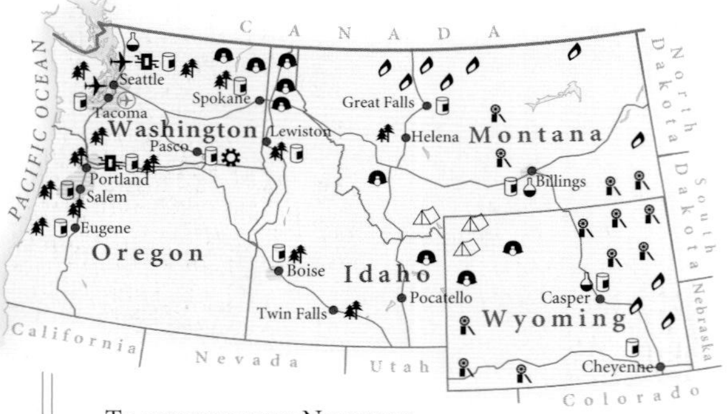

TRANSPORTATION NETWORK

- 347,857 miles (556,571 km)
- 4,200 miles (6,720 km)
- 12,354 miles (19,766 km)
- 1,108 miles (1,782 km)

Major industry and infrastructure
- adventure tourism
- aerospace
- coal
- chemicals
- electronics
- food processing
- mining
- oil & gas
- timber processing
- major towns
- international airports
- major roads
- major industrial areas

The Union Pacific Railroad has been in service across Wyoming since 1867. The route through the Rocky Mountains is now shared with the Interstate 80, a major east–west highway.

Seattle lies in one of Puget Sound's many inlets. The city receives oil and other resources from Alaska, and benefits from expanding trade across the Pacific.

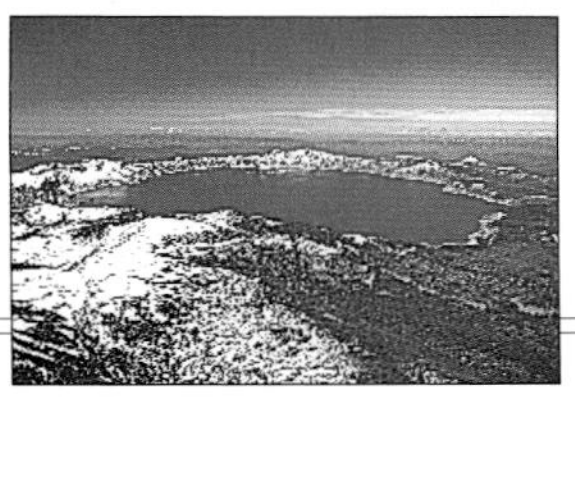

Crater Lake, Oregon, is 6 miles (10 km) wide and 1,800 ft (600 m) deep. It marks the site of a volcanic cone, which collapsed after an eruption within the last 7,000 years.

THE LANDSCAPE

THE ROCKY MOUNTAINS are flanked by lower parallel ranges, which spread onto the Great Plains in the east and surmount the broad lava plateau which extends westward. The Cascade Range divides the Columbia Basin from the coastlands, where the low areas around Puget Sound are broken by the steep, volcanic Olympic Mountains and the wooded hills of the Coast Ranges.

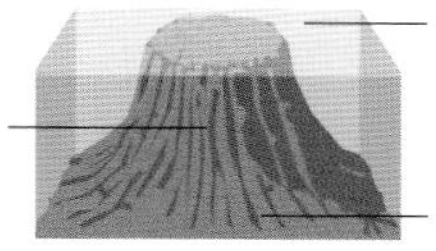

***Devil's Tower in Wyoming** is an igneous intrusion, formed below the Earth's surface. Molten rock intruded through cracks in the overlying strata and cooled. Over time, the softer rock layers have been eroded away, leaving only the tower standing.*

Glacial valleys on the seaward side of the Olympic Mountains receive about 142 inches (3,600 mm) of rain per year, supporting the only true rain forest of the northern hemisphere.

The Cascades are glacially scoured volcanic mountains, the highest of which is Mount Rainier, a dormant volcano at 14,409 ft (4,392 m).

Mount St. Helens erupted in 1980, killing 57 people and devastating a huge area.

Grand Coulee and the lesser *coulées* (ravines) were cut by cataclysmic floods, from the release of an ice-dammed lake, at the end of the last ice age.

The Continental Divide, or watershed, crosses the Lewis Range. From here, rivers flow east to Hudson Bay, south to the Gulf of Mexico and west to the Pacific Ocean.

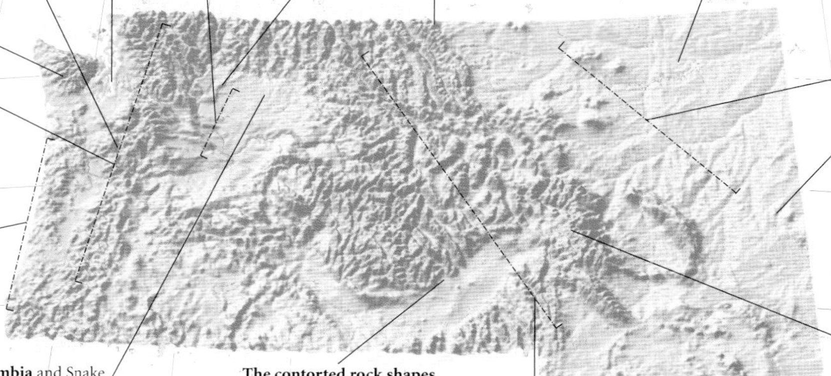

The plateaus of the Columbia and Snake Rivers represent one of the world's largest accumulations of lava. Over 5 million years ago, successive flows of molten basalt buried the existing land surface by up to 450 ft (150 m).

The contorted rock shapes at "Craters of the Moon" National Monument in Idaho were left 2,000 years ago by the sporadic upwelling of viscous lava from fissures in the basalt plateau.

***Piney Buttes** are the remnants of an older, higher land surface gradually weathered and eroded into isolated outcrops with flat tops and steep sides.*

***Water from the hot springs** in Yellowstone National Park deposits minerals as it cools in rock pools. Long periods of deposition have created these rock terraces.*

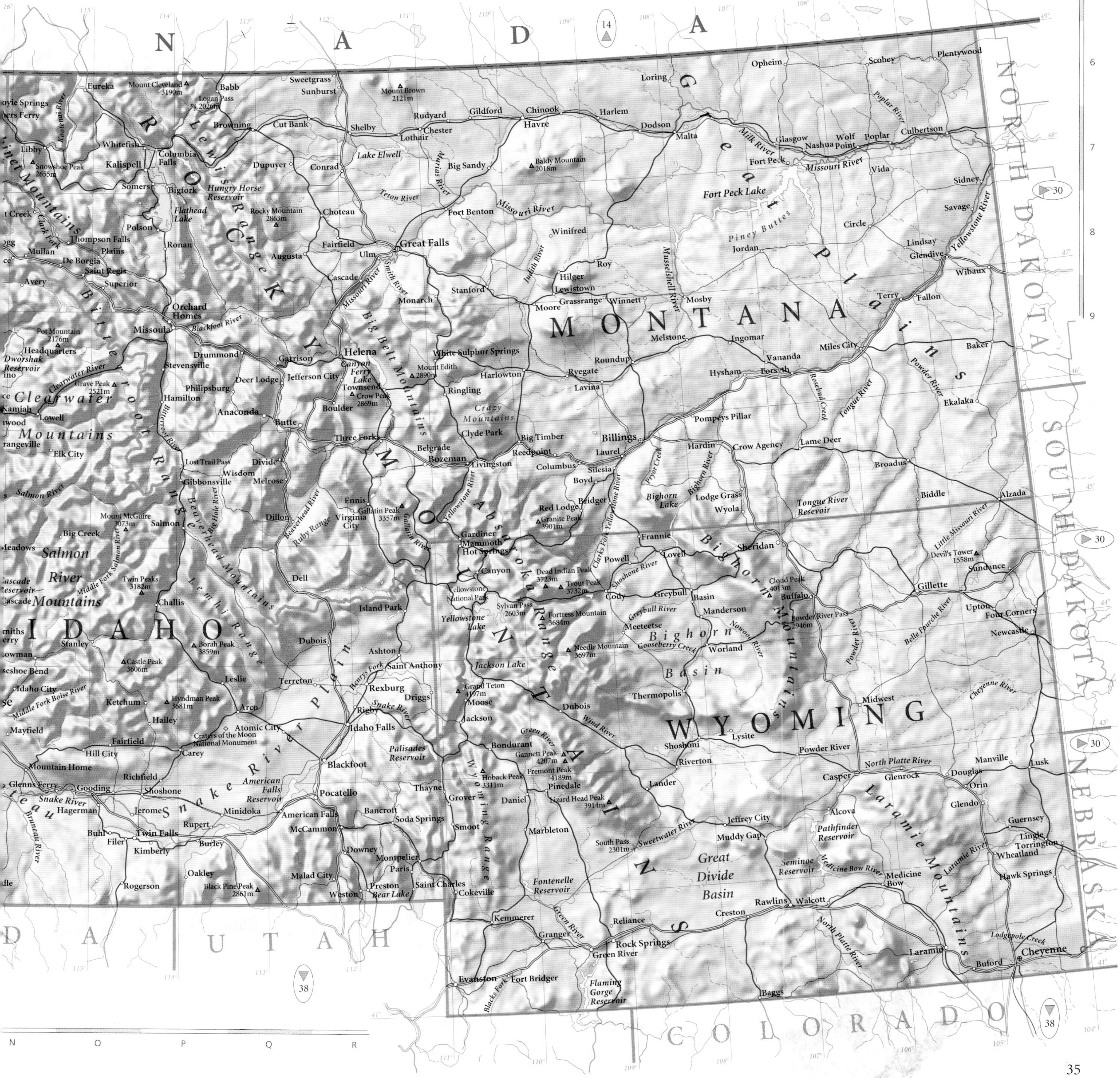

USA: California & Nevada

The Gold Rush of 1849 attracted the first major wave of European settlers to the West Coast. The pleasant climate, beautiful scenery and dynamic economy continue to attract immigrants – despite the ever-present danger of earthquakes – and California has become the US's most populous state. The overwhelmingly urban population is concentrated in the vast conurbations of Los Angeles, San Francisco, and San Diego; new immigrants include people from South Korea, the Philippines, Vietnam, and Mexico. Nevada's arid lands were initially exploited for minerals; in recent years, revenue from mining has been superseded by income from the tourist and gambling centers of Las Vegas and Reno.

Map Key

Population

- 1 million to 5 million
- 500,000 to 1 million
- 100,000 to 500,000
- 50,000 to 100,000
- 10,000 to 50,000
- below 10,000

Elevation

- 4000m / 13,124ft
- 3000m / 9843ft
- 2000m / 6562ft
- 1000m / 3281ft
- 500m / 1640ft
- 250m / 820ft
- 100m / 328ft
- sea level

Scale 1:3,000,000
(projection: Lambert Conformal Conic)

Km 0 5 10 20 30 40 50 60 70 80
Miles 0 5 10 20 30 40 50 60 70 80

Transportation & Industry

Nevada's rich mineral reserves ushered in a period of mining wealth which has now been replaced by revenue generated from gambling. California supports a broad set of activities including defense-related industries and research and development facilities. "Silicon Valley," near San Francisco, is a world leading center for microelectronics, while tourism and the Los Angeles film industry also generate large incomes.

Gambling was legalized in Nevada in 1931. Las Vegas has since become the center of this multimillion dollar industry.

Major industry and infrastructure

- aerospace
- car manufacture
- defense
- movie industry
- finance
- food processing
- gambling
- hi-tech industry
- mining
- pharmaceuticals
- research & development
- textiles
- tourism
- major towns
- international airports
- major roads
- major industrial areas

Transportation Network

- 211,459 miles (338,334 km)
- 2,944 miles (4,710 km)
- 7,872 miles (12,595 km)
- 190 miles (306 km)

In California, the motor vehicle is a vital part of daily life, and an extensive freeway system runs throughout the state, which has a greater *per capita* car ownership than anywhere else in the world.

The Landscape

The broad Central Valley divides California's coastal mountains from the Sierra Nevada. The San Andreas Fault, running beneath much of the state, is the site of frequent earth tremors and sometimes more serious earthquakes. East of the Sierra Nevada, the landscape is characterized by the basin and range topography with stony deserts and many salt lakes.

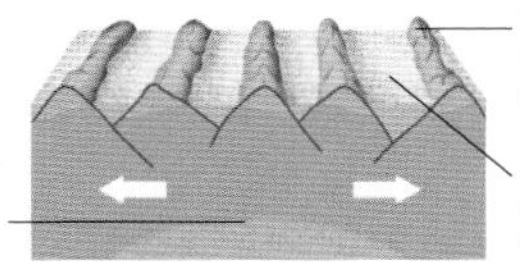

***Molten rock** (magma) welling up to form a dome in the Earth's interior, causes the brittle surface rocks to stretch and crack. Some areas were uplifted to form mountains (ranges), while others sunk to form flat valleys (basins).*

***The General Sherman** sequoia tree in Sequoia National Park is 3000 years old and at 275 ft (84 m) is one of the largest living things on earth.*

Most of California's agriculture is confined to the fertile and extensively irrigated Central Valley, running between the Coast Ranges and the Sierra Nevada. It incorporates the San Joaquin and Sacramento valleys.

The dramatic granitic rock formations of Half Dome and El Capitan, and the verdant coniferous forests, attract millions of visitors annually to Yosemite National Park in the Sierra Nevada.

The Great Basin dominates most of Nevada's topography containing large open basins, punctuated by eroded features such as *buttes* and *mesas*. River flow tends to be seasonal, dependent upon spring showers and winter snow melt.

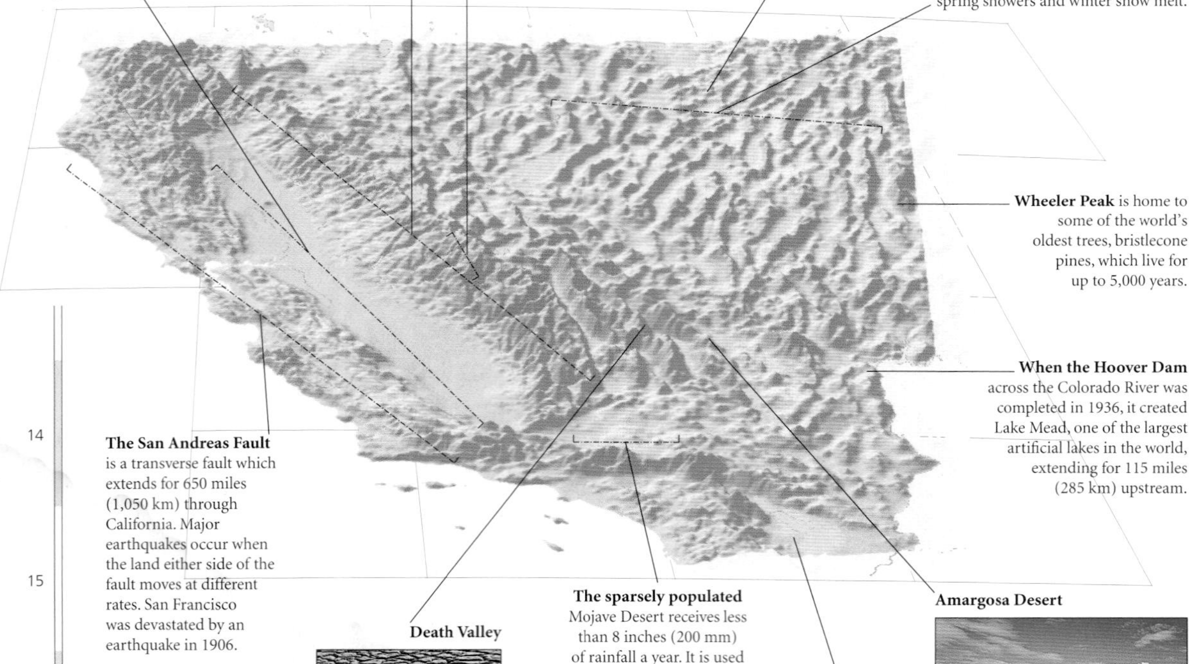

Sierra Nevada

Wheeler Peak is home to some of the world's oldest trees, bristlecone pines, which live for up to 5,000 years.

When the Hoover Dam across the Colorado River was completed in 1936, it created Lake Mead, one of the largest artificial lakes in the world, extending for 115 miles (285 km) upstream.

The San Andreas Fault is a transverse fault which extends for 650 miles (1,050 km) through California. Major earthquakes occur when the land either side of the fault moves at different rates. San Francisco was devastated by an earthquake in 1906.

Death Valley

***Named by migrating settlers** in 1849, Death Valley is the driest, hottest place in North America, as well as being the lowest point on land in the western hemisphere, at 282 ft (86 m) below sea level.*

The sparsely populated Mojave Desert receives less than 8 inches (200 mm) of rainfall a year. It is used extensively for testing weapons and other military purposes.

The Salton Sea was created accidentally between 1905 and 1907 when an irrigation channel from the Colorado River broke out of its banks and formed this salty 300 sq mile (777 sq km), landlocked lake.

Amargosa Desert

***The Sierra Nevada** create a "rainshadow," preventing rain from reaching much of Nevada. Pacific air masses, passing over the mountains, are stripped of their moisture.*

Using the Land

California is the leading agricultural producer in the US, although low rainfall makes irrigation essential. The long growing season and abundant sunshine allow many crops to be grown in the fertile Central Valley including grapes, citrus fruits, vegetables, and cotton. Almost 17 million acres (6.8 million hectares) of California's forests are used commercially. Nevada's arid climate and poor soil are largely unsuitable for agriculture; 85% of its land is state owned and large areas are used for underground testing of nuclear weapons.

Land use and agricultural distribution

- cattle
- citrus fruits
- fruit
- irrigation
- timber
- vineyards
- major towns
- pasture
- cropland
- forest
- desert

***Without considerable** irrigation, this fertile valley at Palm Springs would still be part of the Sonoran Desert. California's farmers account for about 80% of the state's total water usage.*

The Urban/Rural Population Divide

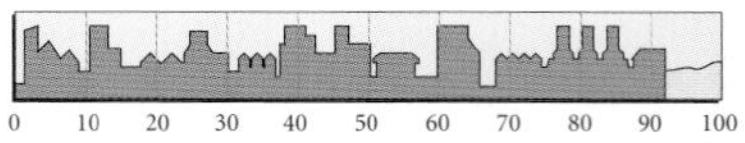

Population Density	Total Land Area
126 people per sq mile (49 people per sq km)	269,233 sq miles (697,286 sq km)

198

The towering granite cliff of El Capitan typifies the Yosemite Valley, which is often choked with tourists during the summer months.

USA: South Mountain States

Arizona, Colorado, New Mexico, Utah

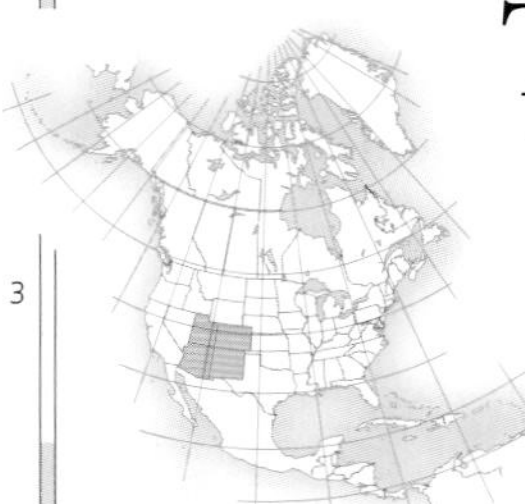

This arid region, characterized by expansive plateaus and spectacular canyons is home to several distinct peoples. The ruins of cliff dwellings built a thousand years ago by the Anasazi people still exist today, and native Americans own one-third of the land in Arizona. Spanish and Mexican conquest and settlement left a Hispanic presence which is strongest in New Mexico. The Mormons, who came to the Great Salt Lake seeking religious freedom in 1847, were among the earliest Anglo-American settlers and now make up over 70% of Utah's population. The region's mineral wealth drove rapid development in the 20th century, yet the constraints of a fragile environment, including widespread water shortages, may limit prospects for growth.

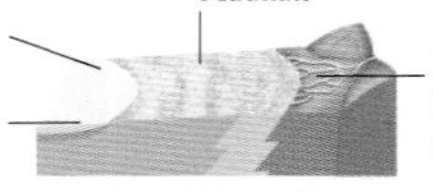

The Great Salt Lake is an ephemeral lake; it can remain dry for extended periods, leaving a pan of evaporated mineral salts in its center.

The Landscape

The arid, rocky expanse of the Colorado Plateau is dissected by immense canyons of the Colorado River. Desert lies to the north and south and branches of the Rocky Mountains run east and west. The Great Salt Lake and Desert lie within the Great Basin, a barren region of parallel mountain ranges that extends into Arizona.

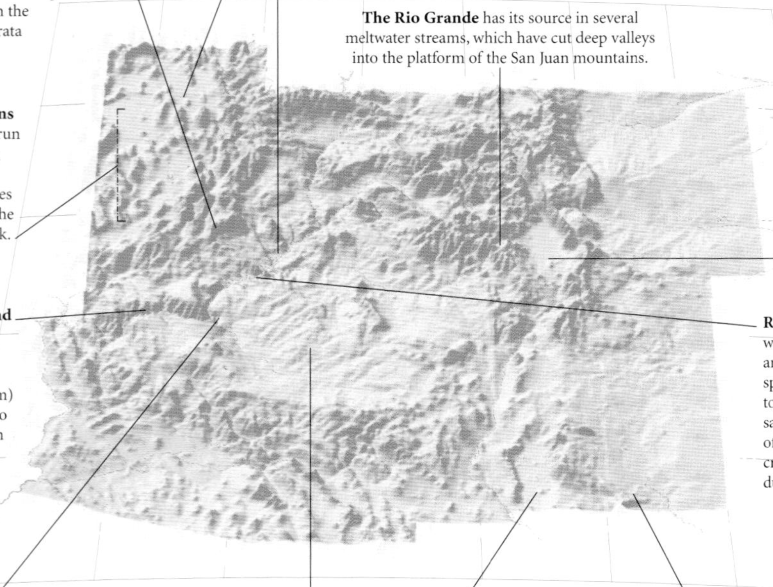

Over 13 million years of weathering has created thousands of spires and pinnacles from the alternating rock strata of Bryce Canyon.

Lake Powell

The Rio Grande has its source in several meltwater streams, which have cut deep valleys into the platform of the San Juan mountains.

The parallel basins and ridges, which run north–south along the Great Basin, reflect a major series of block-faults in the underlying bedrock.

Sand dunes, 600 ft (180 m) high, have been deposited in San Luis Valley, by winds funneled through the San Juan and Sangre de Cristo mountains in the Rockies.

Parts of the Grand Canyon, which cuts through the Colorado Plateau, are 16 miles (25 km) wide. The Colorado River has cut down 6262 ft (2000 m), exposing rock strata more than 2 billion years old.

Rainbow Bridge is the world's largest natural arch. The 309 ft (94 m) span probably began to grow when the sandstone spur of a meandering creek was breached during a flash flood.

The striking colour effects seen in the Painted Desert come from minerals such as gypsum and haematite, combined with ambient heat and dust.

Shifting gypsum sands produce a constantly changing land surface, overwhelming plants and any other obstacles in Tularosa Valley.

Petrified Forest

In the arid landscape of Petrified Forest National Park in Arizona, the grain of prehistoric trees has been preserved as a fossil imprint in the rocks. The bog-preserved trees were gradually turned to stone by seeping mineral-rich water.

Carlsbad Caverns

The intricate stalactites of Carlsbad Caverns have grown with the seepage of calcium-rich water over the last 100,000 years. The huge caves are home to around 100,000 Mexican freetail bats.

Transportation & Industry

New industries have helped reduce the region's dependence on the extraction of minerals and fossil fuels. Precision manufacture has grown rapidly, particularly in Arizona and Colorado. Salt Lake City and Denver are well-established financial centers and New Mexico, the main US producer of uranium, is a prominent region for nuclear research. Colorado is the most important US center for winter sports.

Transportation Network

232,434 miles (373,986 km)	4,059 miles (6,515 km)
8,627 miles (13,881 km)	none

The Colorado Rockies are crossed by 32 mountain passes, some as high as 12,183 ft (3,713 m). The Eisenhower Tunnel west of Denver carries Interstate Highway 70 straight through the Continental Divide.

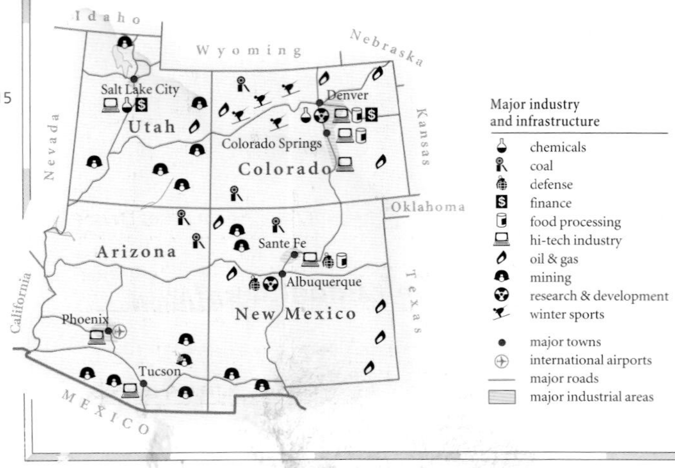

Glen Canyon Dam on the Colorado river was completed in 1964. it provides hydroelectric power and irrigation water as part of a long-term federal project to harness the river.

***The flat tablelands** (mesas), and the isolated pinnacles (buttes) which rise from the floor of Monument Valley are the resistant remnants of an earlier land surface, gradually cut back by erosion under arid conditions.*

The Bonneville Salt Flats are in the Great Salt Lake. Sodium chloride (salt), magnesium, and other minerals are commercially extracted from these flats.

SCALE 1:3,500,000
(projection: Lambert Conformal Conic)
Km 0 10 20 40 60 80 100
Miles 0 10 20 40 60 80 100

MAP KEY

POPULATION
- 500,000 to 1 million
- 100,000 to 500,000
- 50,000 to 100,000
- 10,000 to 50,000
- below 10,000

ELEVATION
- 4000m / 13124ft
- 3000m / 9843ft
- 2000m / 6562ft
- 1000m / 3281ft
- 500m / 1640ft
- 250m / 820ft
- 100m / 328ft
- sea level

A glacially-eroded valley in Rocky Mountain National Park, Colorado. There are 1,500 peaks exceeding 10,000 ft (3,000 m) within the state, six times the number of major mountains found in the Swiss Alps.

USING THE LAND

LIVESTOCK, PARTICULARLY cattle-ranching, is the main source of agricultural income. The region has a long growing season and areas of rich soil, but depends heavily on water for irrigation. Crops include corn and wheat in eastern areas, and chili peppers, fruit, and cotton aided by additional irrigation.

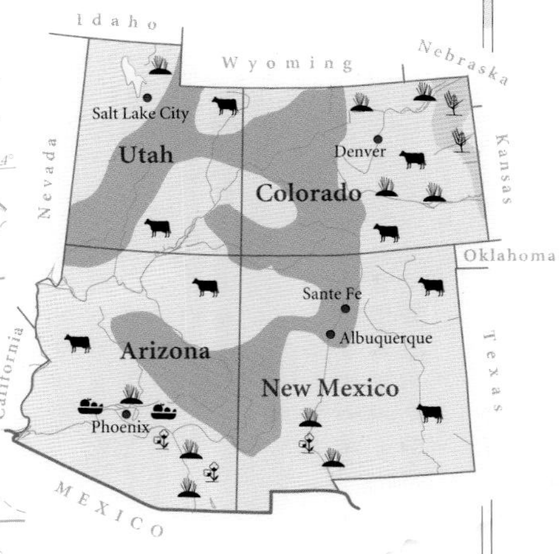

Land use and agricultural distribution
- cattle
- cereals
- cotton
- fruit
- irrigation
- major towns
- pasture
- cropland
- forest
- desert

Cattle-ranching was introduced to New Mexico via Texas in the 19th century, and has become the principal agricultural land use across this region.

THE URBAN/RURAL POPULATION DIVIDE

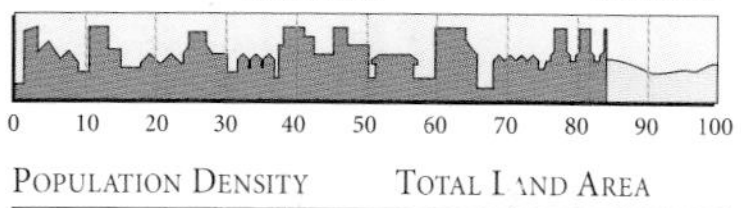

POPULATION DENSITY	TOTAL LAND AREA
11 people per sq mile (29 people per sq km)	424,738 sq miles (1,100,028 sq km)

USA: Hawaii

The 122 islands of the Hawaiian archipelago – which are part of Polynesia – are the peaks of the world's largest volcanoes. They rise approximately 6 miles (9.7 km) from the floor of the Pacific Ocean. The largest, the island of Hawaii, remains highly active. Hawaii became the US's 50th state in 1959. A tradition of receiving immigrant workers is reflected in the islands' ethnic diversity, with peoples drawn from around the rim of the Pacific. Only 2% of the current population are native Polynesians.

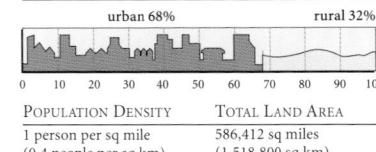

***The island of Molokai** is formed from volcanic rock. Mature sand dunes cover the rocks in coastal areas.*

Transportation & Industry

Tourism dominates the economy, with over half of the population employed in services. The naval base at Pearl Harbor is also a major source of employment. Industry is concentrated on the island of Oahu and relies mostly on imported materials, while agricultural produce is processed locally.

Transportation Network

4,102 miles (6,600 km)	43 miles (69 km)
none	none

Hawaii relies on ocean-surface transportation. Honolulu is the main focus of this network, bringing foreign trade and the markets of mainland US to Hawaii's outer islands.

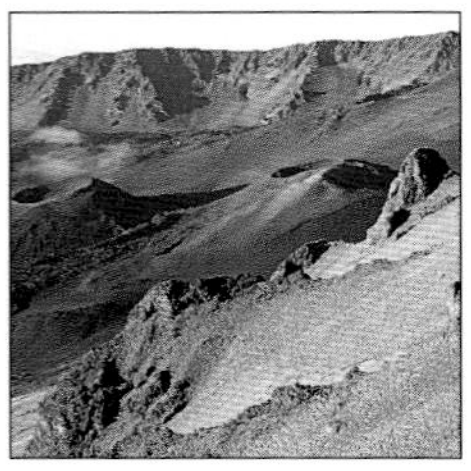

***Haleakala's extinct volcanic** crater is the world's largest. The giant caldera, containing many secondary cones, is 2,000 ft (600 m) deep and 20 miles (32 km) in circumference.*

Major industry and infrastructure

- food processing
- military base
- textiles
- tourism
- major towns
- international airports
- major roads
- major industrial areas

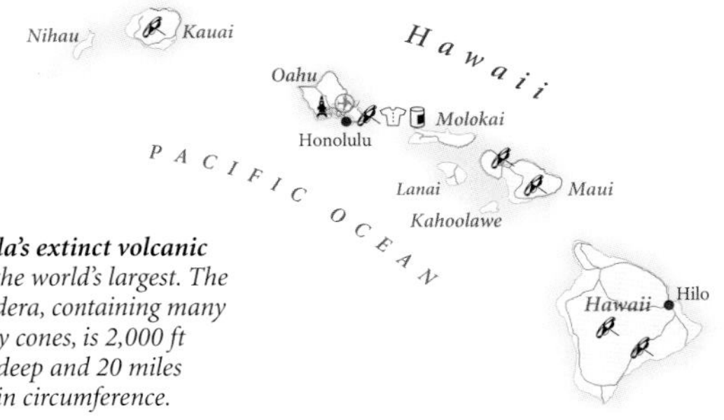

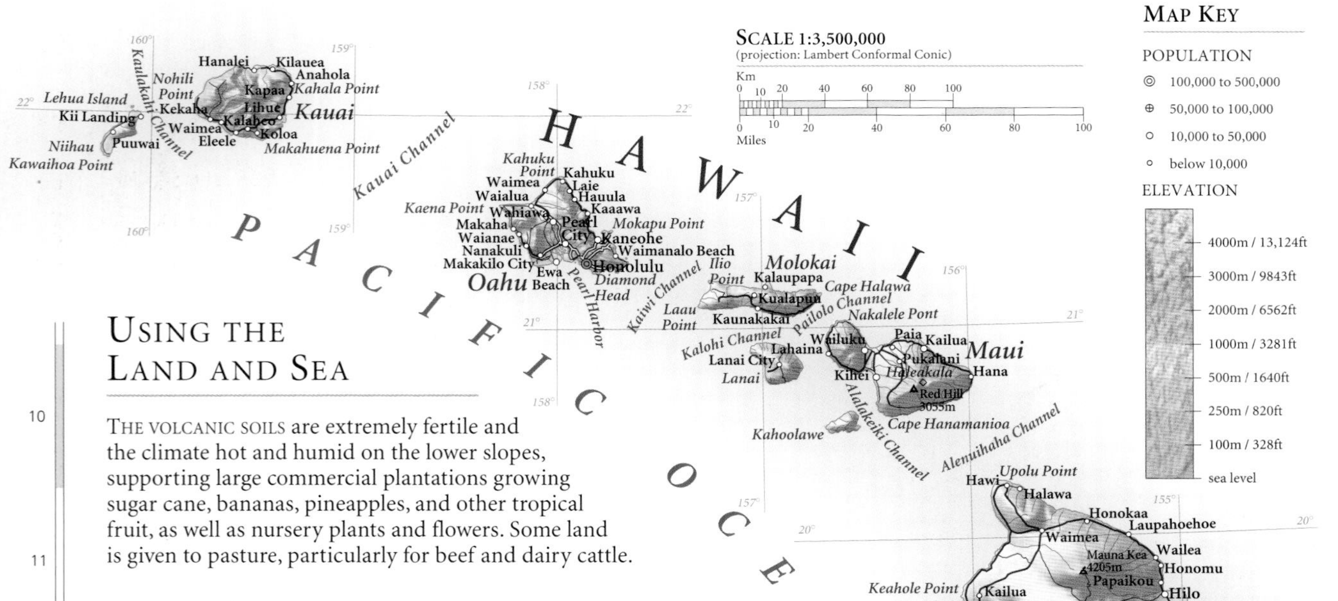

Scale 1:3,500,000
(projection: Lambert Conformal Conic)

Map Key

Population

- 100,000 to 500,000
- 50,000 to 100,000
- 10,000 to 50,000
- below 10,000

Elevation

- 4000m / 13,124ft
- 3000m / 9843ft
- 2000m / 6562ft
- 1000m / 3281ft
- 500m / 1640ft
- 250m / 820ft
- 100m / 328ft
- sea level

Using the Land and Sea

The volcanic soils are extremely fertile and the climate hot and humid on the lower slopes, supporting large commercial plantations growing sugar cane, bananas, pineapples, and other tropical fruit, as well as nursery plants and flowers. Some land is given to pasture, particularly for beef and dairy cattle.

Land use and agricultural distribution

- cattle
- fishing
- fruit
- sugar cane
- major towns
- pasture
- cropland
- forest
- mountain region

***The island of Kauai** is one of the wettest places in the world, receiving some 450 inches (11,500 mm) of rain a year.*

The Urban/Rural Population Divide

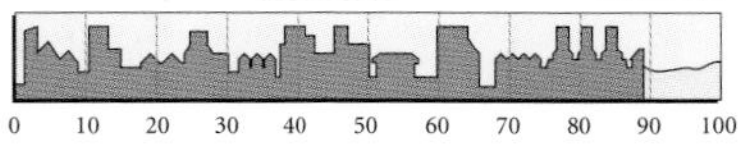

Population Density	Total Land Area
183 people per sq mile (71 people per sq km)	6,423 sq miles (16,636 sq km)

Using the Land and Sea

The ice-free coastline of Alaska provides access to salmon fisheries and more than 5.5 million acres (2.2 million ha) of forest. Most of Alaska is uncultivable, and around 90% of food is imported. Barley, hay, and hothouse products are grown around Anchorage, where dairy farming is also concentrated.

The Urban/Rural Population Divide

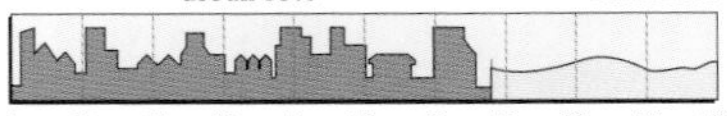

Population Density	Total Land Area
1 person per sq mile (0.4 people per sq km)	586,412 sq miles (1,518,800 sq km)

***A raft of timber** from the Tongass forest is hauled by a tug, bound for the pulp mills of the Alaskan coast between Juneau and Ketchikan.*

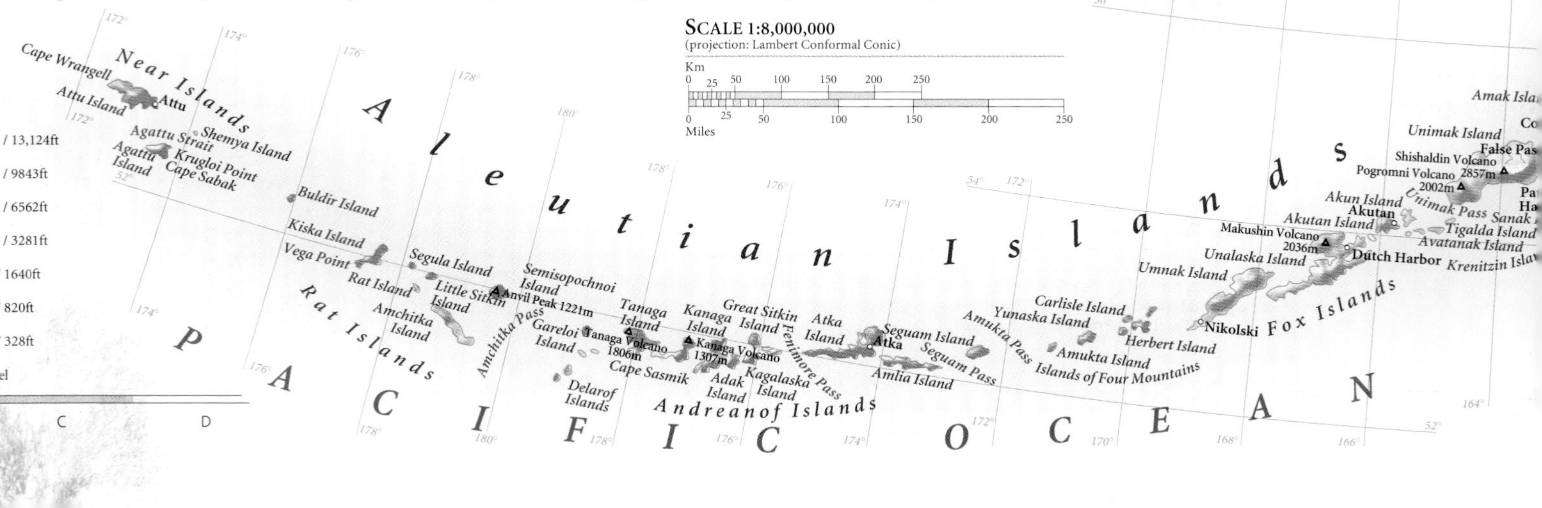

Scale 1:8,000,000
(projection: Lambert Conformal Conic)

Map Key

Population

- 100,000 to 500,000
- 50,000 to 100,000
- 10,000 to 50,000
- below 10,000

Elevation

- 4000m / 13,124ft
- 3000m / 9843ft
- 2000m / 6562ft
- 1000m / 3281ft
- 500m / 1640ft
- 250m / 820ft
- 100m / 328ft
- sea level

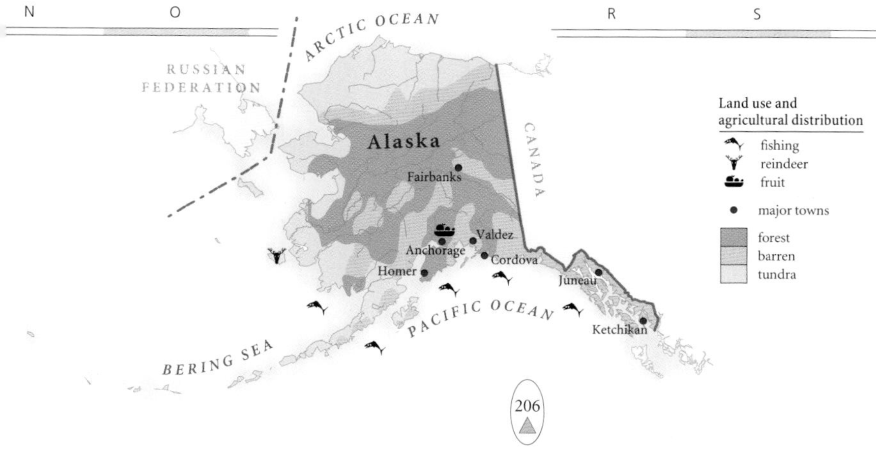
ARCTIC OCEAN
RUSSIAN FEDERATION
Alaska
Fairbanks
Anchorage
Valdez
Cordova
Homer
Juneau
Ketchikan
CANADA
PACIFIC OCEAN
BERING SEA
Land use and agricultural distribution
fishing
reindeer
fruit
major towns
forest
barren
tundra

USA: Alaska

Just over half a million people live in Alaska, a wilderness of ice, forest, mountains, and plains, purchased from Russia in 1867 and twice the size of Texas. The discovery of large oil reserves has brought prosperity to the US's "last frontier," while advancing the need to preserve natural habitats and the traditional livelihoods of indigenous peoples, such as the Aleuts and Inupiaq.

The Landscape

The mountains of the Pacific coast culminate in the heavily glaciated Alaska Range and extend west, to the Alaska Peninsula and the great volcanic arc of the Aleutian Islands. The interior plains are drained by the Yukon River and bounded by the bare, jagged peaks of the Brooks Range to the north.

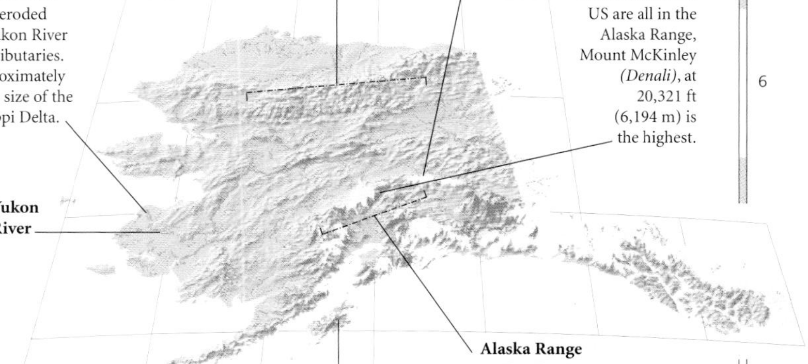
The Yukon Delta is a fan of alluvial material eroded by the Yukon River and its tributaries. It is approximately twice the size of the Mississippi Delta.
Brooks Range
West Fork Glacier
The ten highest mountains in the US are all in the Alaska Range, Mount McKinley (*Denali*), at 20,321 ft (6,194 m) is the highest.
Yukon River
Alaska Range
The arc of the Aleutian Islands marks the boundary between the Eurasian and Pacific tectonic plates.
Fjords are found along the coast where valleys, deeply excavated by large glaciers, were inundated by rising seas.

By August, the Alaska Range is covered with autumnal tundra vegetation.

West Fork Glacier

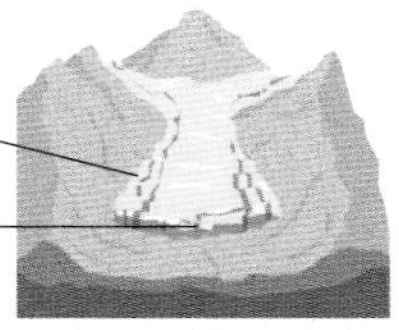
The surging ice mass shears along the glacier margin
Deep crevasses divide the front of the surging glacier into large ice blocks

***Surging glaciers** make rapid and dramatic advances, normally after periods of snow accumulation. West Fork Glacier in the Susitna River Basin traveled 2.5 miles (4 km) in 1987.*

ARCTIC OCEAN
BEAUFORT SEA
Barrow
Point Barrow
Wainwright
Prudhoe Bay
Deadhorse
Kaktovik
Demarcation Point
Brooks Range
Endicott Mountains
Philip Smith Mountains
Baird Mountains
Arctic Village
Yukon Flats
ALASKA
Fort Yukon
Circle
Fairbanks
North Pole
Delta Junction
Tok
Alaska Range
Mount McKinley (Denali) 6194m
Denali
Talkeetna
Wasilla
Palmer
Anchorage
Valdez
Cordova
Chugach Mountains
Wrangell Mountains
Saint Elias Mountains
Yakutat
Kenai Peninsula
Seward
Homer
Kodiak Island
Kodiak
Gulf of Alaska
Bristol Bay
Alaska Peninsula
Aleutian Range
Kuskokwim Mountains
Yukon River
Haines
Skagway
Juneau
Sitka
Petersburg
Wrangell
Ketchikan
Alexander Archipelago
Dixon Entrance
Coast Mountains
CANADA
206
14
199
199

Transportation & Industry

Large areas of Alaska are undeveloped, and much of the existing infrastructure is a legacy of Cold War military investment. Mineral ores, including gold, have been mined for over a century, but the oil business now dominates the economy. Processing industries such as paper-pulp mills supply Japan and other markets on the Pacific Rim.

Transportation Network

(road)	13,524 miles (21,760 km)	(motorway)	49 miles (78 km)
(rail)	482 miles (772 km)	(waterway)	none

Nearly 80 million gallons of oil are pumped through the Trans-Alaska Pipeline every day. The oil takes six days to travel the 789 miles (1,262 km) from Prudhoe Bay to Valdez.

Major industry and infrastructure
fish processing
gold mining
oil
timber processing
major towns
international airports
major roads
ARCTIC OCEAN
RUSSIAN FEDERATION
Prudhoe Bay
Alaska
Nome
Fairbanks
Trans-Alaska Pipeline
Anchorage
Valdez
Cordova
Homer
Juneau
Ketchikan
CANADA
PACIFIC OCEAN
BERING SEA

***The Trans-Alaska Pipeline** has carried crude oil from Prudhoe Bay since 1977. The oilfield is the US's largest and is estimated to be equal in size to the biggest oilfields of the Persian Gulf.*

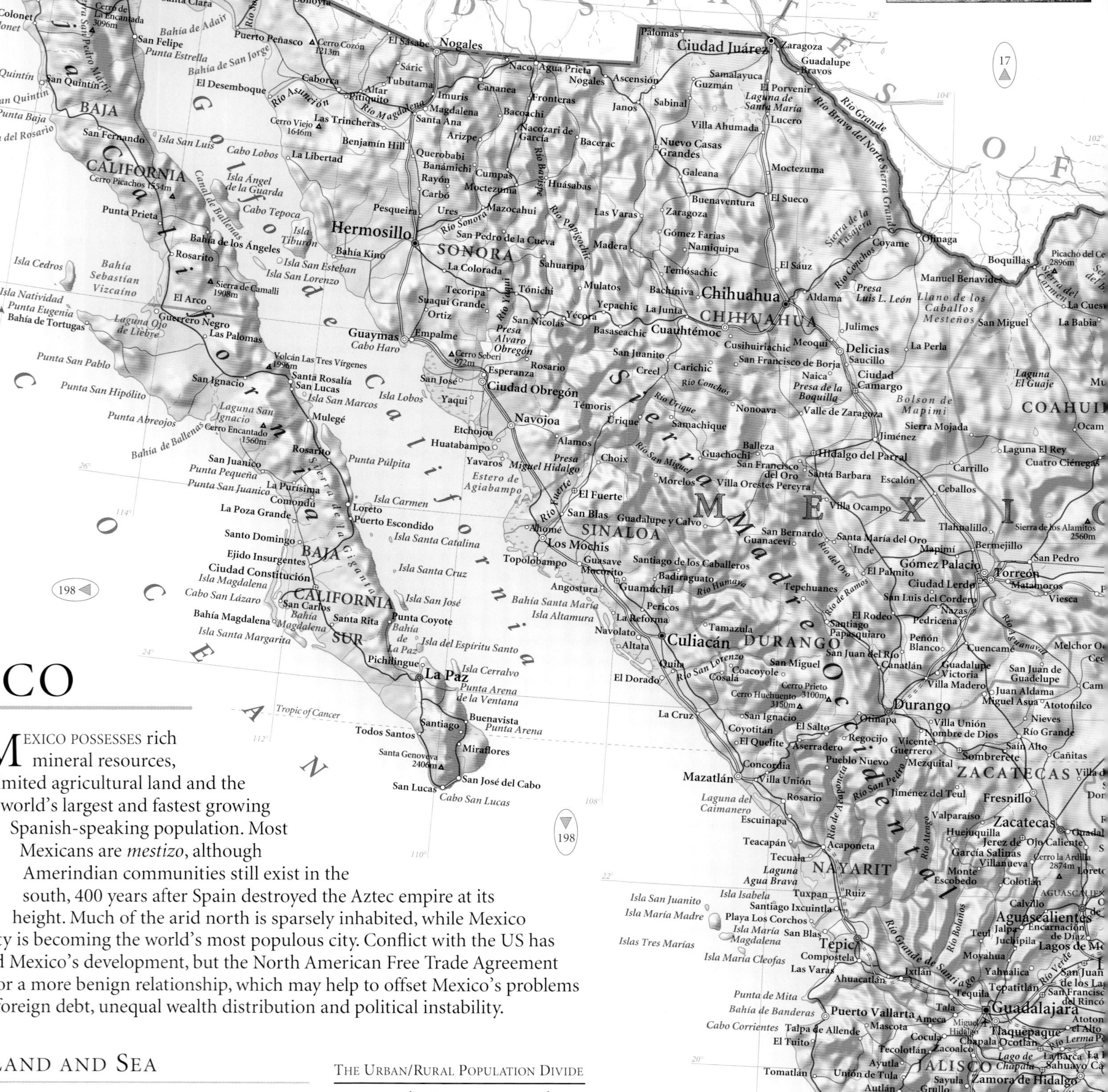

The rugged, desert landscape of the Sierra Madre del Sur is a product of complex tectonic processes, where the fold mountains in western North America, running north–south, meet the Caribbean mountain arc which runs east–west.

Wave action *has cut steep cliffs into the igneous rocks of Isla Cedros, off the Pacific coast of Baja California. The island is home to sea lions, reptiles, and deer.*

MEXICO

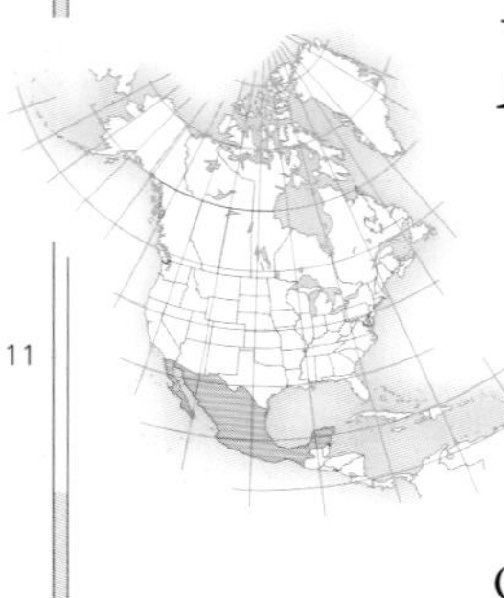

MEXICO POSSESSES rich mineral resources, limited agricultural land and the world's largest and fastest growing Spanish-speaking population. Most Mexicans are *mestizo*, although Amerindian communities still exist in the south, 400 years after Spain destroyed the Aztec empire at its height. Much of the arid north is sparsely inhabited, while Mexico City is becoming the world's most populous city. Conflict with the US has long overshadowed Mexico's development, but the North American Free Trade Agreement offers the chance for a more benign relationship, which may help to offset Mexico's problems of hyperinflation, foreign debt, unequal wealth distribution and political instability.

Using the Land and Sea

CORN OCCUPIES much of the cultivated area. Commercial plantations of coffee, sugar, vanilla, and cotton are found along the Gulf coastal plain and in irrigated parts of the arid north, which is otherwise used for extensive ranching. Fishing is important, particularly shellfish for export. A soaring population has created the need for grain imports since 1980.

The Urban/Rural Population Divide

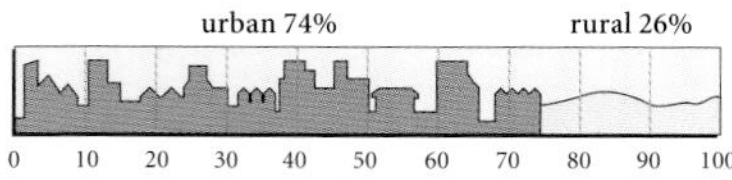

Population Density	Total Land Area
130 people per sq mile	755,865 sq miles
(50 people per sq km)	(1,958,200 sq km)

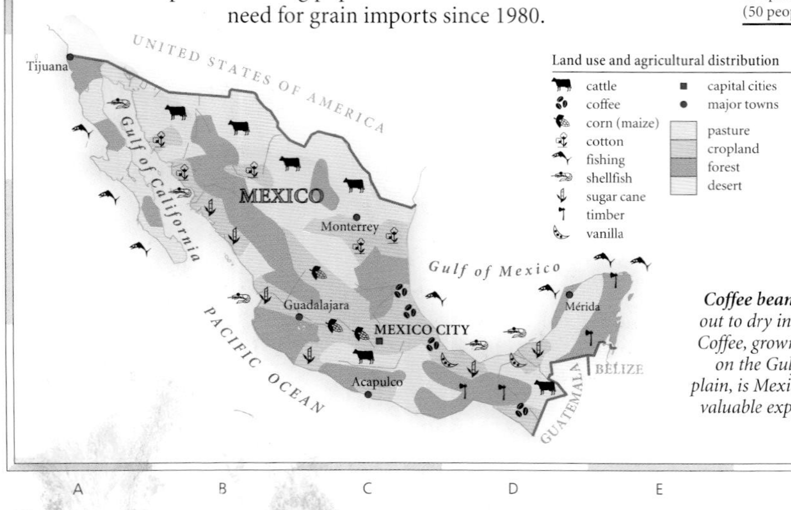

Coffee beans *spread out to dry in the sun. Coffee, grown mainly on the Gulf coastal plain, is Mexico's most valuable export crop.*

Mexico: Administrative Regions

① DISTRITO FEDERAL

Map Key

POPULATION
- ▣ above 5 million
- ◼ 1 million to 5 million
- ◉ 500,000 to 1 million
- ◎ 100,000 to 500,000
- ⊕ 50,000 to 100,000
- ○ 10,000 to 50,000
- ○ below 10,000

ELEVATION
- 4000m / 13,124ft
- 3000m / 9843ft
- 2000m / 6562ft
- 1000m / 3281ft
- 500m / 1640ft
- 250m / 820ft
- 100m / 328ft
- sea level

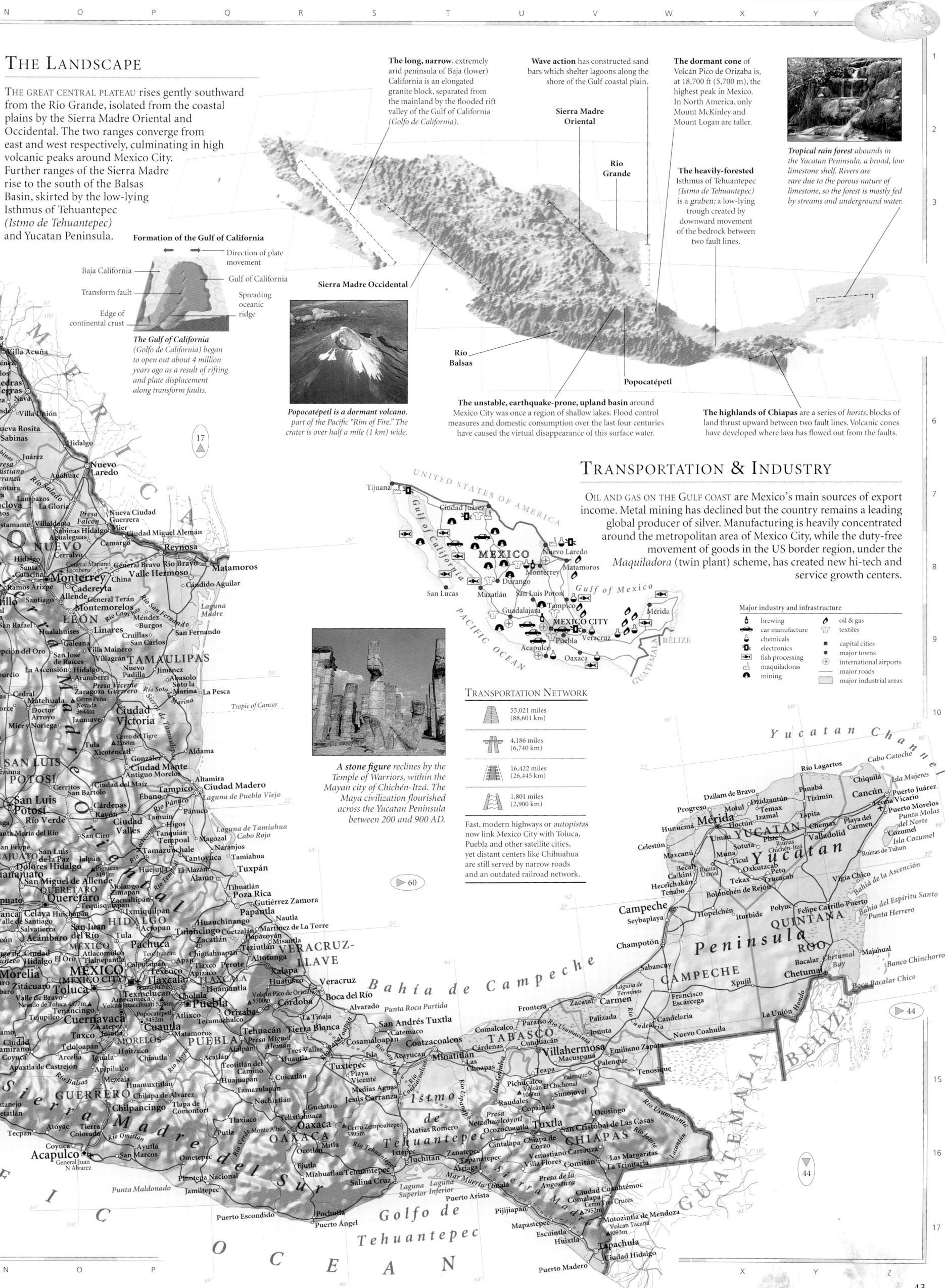

N O P Q R S T U V W X Y

THE LANDSCAPE

THE GREAT CENTRAL PLATEAU rises gently southward from the Rio Grande, isolated from the coastal plains by the Sierra Madre Oriental and Occidental. The two ranges converge from east and west respectively, culminating in high volcanic peaks around Mexico City. Further ranges of the Sierra Madre rise to the south of the Balsas Basin, skirted by the low-lying Isthmus of Tehuantepec *(Istmo de Tehuantepec)* and Yucatan Peninsula.

The long, narrow, extremely arid peninsula of Baja (lower) California is an elongated granite block, separated from the mainland by the flooded rift valley of the Gulf of California *(Golfo de California).*

Wave action has constructed sand bars which shelter lagoons along the shore of the Gulf coastal plain.

The dormant cone of Volcán Pico de Orizaba is, at 18,700 ft (5,700 m), the highest peak in Mexico. In North America, only Mount McKinley and Mount Logan are taller.

***Tropical rain forest** abounds in the Yucatan Peninsula, a broad, low limestone shelf. Rivers are rare due to the porous nature of limestone, so the forest is mostly fed by streams and underground water.*

The heavily-forested Isthmus of Tehuantepec *(Istmo de Tehuantepec)* is a *graben;* a low-lying trough created by downward movement of the bedrock between two fault lines.

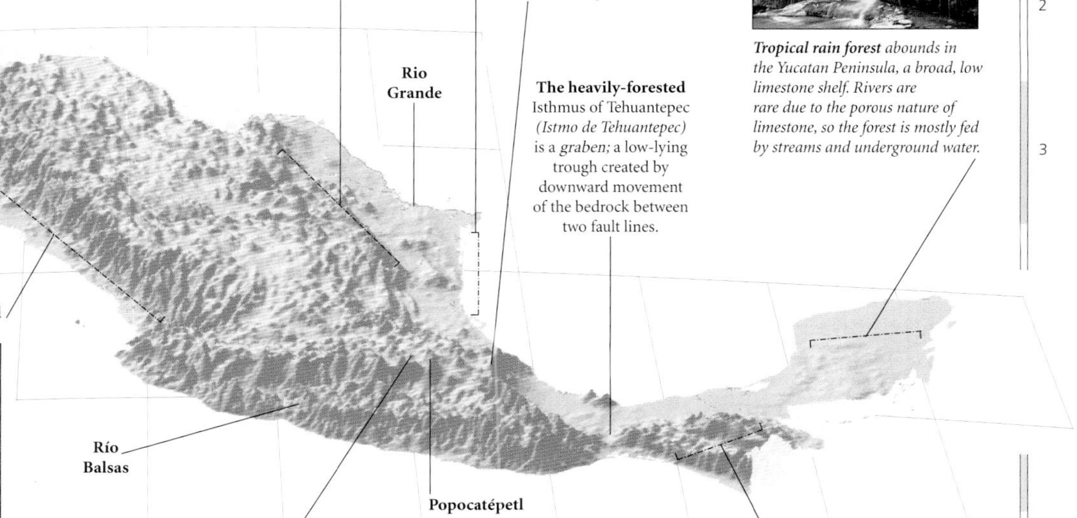

The unstable, earthquake-prone, upland basin around Mexico City was once a region of shallow lakes. Flood control measures and domestic consumption over the last four centuries have caused the virtual disappearance of this surface water.

The highlands of Chiapas are a series of *horsts*, blocks of land thrust upward between two fault lines. Volcanic cones have developed where lava has flowed out from the faults.

Formation of the Gulf of California

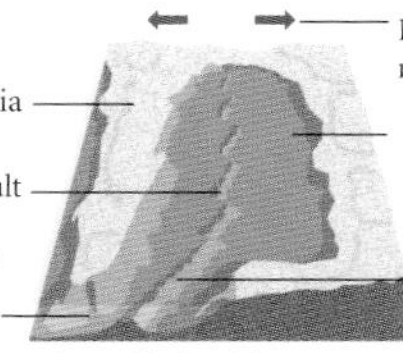

***The Gulf of California** (Golfo de California) began to open out about 4 million years ago as a result of rifting and plate displacement along transform faults.*

***Popocatépetl is a dormant volcano,** part of the Pacific "Rim of Fire." The crater is over half a mile (1 km) wide.*

TRANSPORTATION & INDUSTRY

OIL AND GAS ON THE GULF COAST are Mexico's main sources of export income. Metal mining has declined but the country remains a leading global producer of silver. Manufacturing is heavily concentrated around the metropolitan area of Mexico City, while the duty-free movement of goods in the US border region, under the *Maquiladora* (twin plant) scheme, has created new hi-tech and service growth centers.

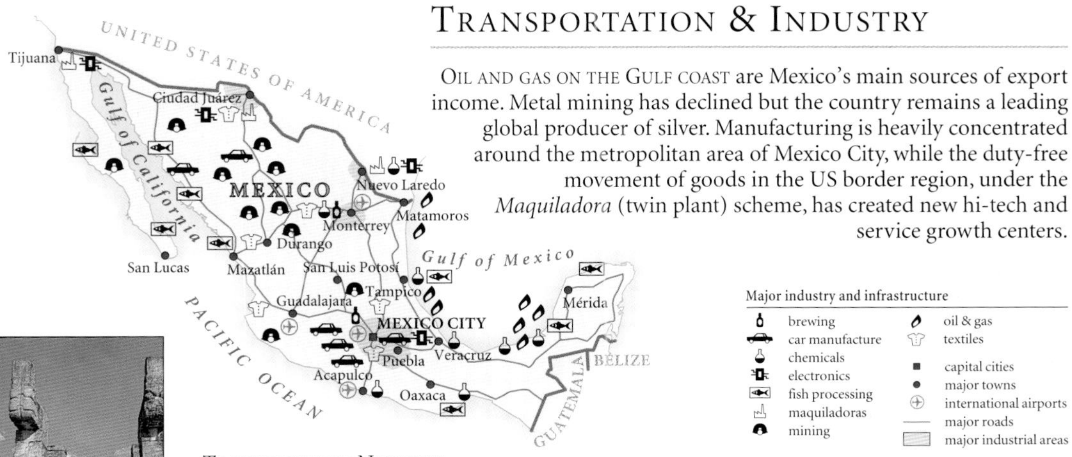

***A stone figure** reclines by the Temple of Warriors, within the Mayan city of Chichén-Itzá. The Maya civilization flourished across the Yucatan Peninsula between 200 and 900 AD.*

TRANSPORTATION NETWORK

(roads)	55,021 miles (88,601 km)
(highways)	4,186 miles (6,740 km)
(railroads)	16,422 miles (26,445 km)
(waterways)	1,801 miles (2,900 km)

Fast, modern highways or *autopistas* now link Mexico City with Toluca, Puebla and other satellite cities, yet distant centers like Chihuahua are still served by narrow roads and an outdated railroad network.

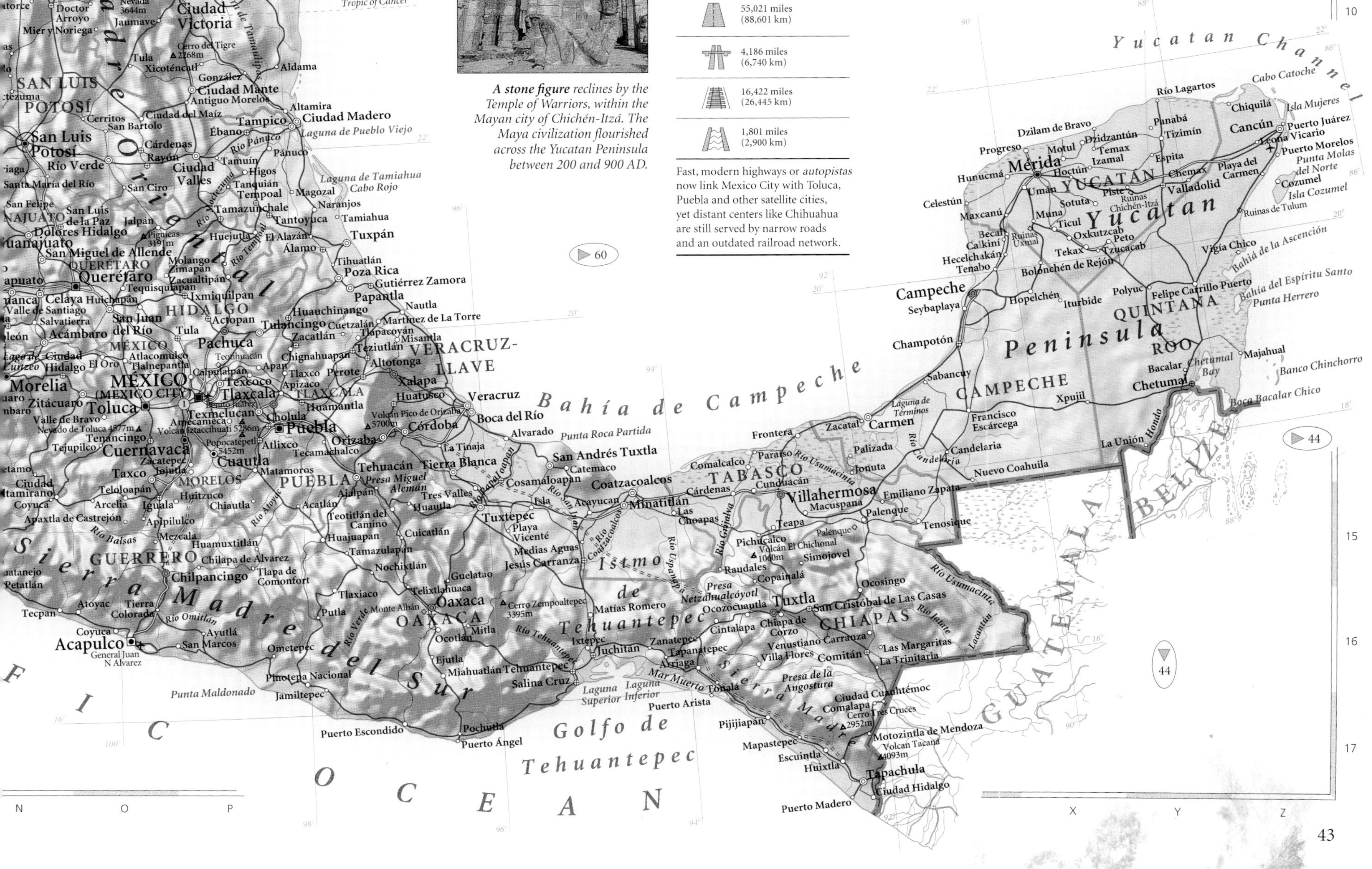

17
60
44
44

N O P X Y Z

Guatemala: Administrative Regions

1. Retalhuleu
2. Quezaltenango
3. Totonicapán
4. Sololá
5. Suchitepéquez
6. Escuintla
7. Chimaltenango
8. Sacatepéquez
9. Guatemala
10. El Progreso
11. Jalapa
12. Santa Rosa
13. Jutiapa
14. Chiquimula
15. Zacapa

Lighthouse Reef *is one of a series of coral reefs lying off the coast of Belize in the shallow waters of the Caribbean.*

El Salvador: Administrative Regions

1. Ahuachapán
2. Santa Ana
3. Sonsonate
4. Chalatenango
5. La Libertad
6. San Salvador
7. Cuscatlán
8. Cabañas
9. La Paz
10. San Vicente
11. Usulután
12. San Miguel
13. Morazán
14. La Unión

Scale 1:4,000,000
(projection: Lambert Conformal Conic)
Km 0 10 20 40 60 80 100 120
Miles 0 10 20 40 60 80 100 120

Central America

Belize, Costa Rica, El Salvador, Guatemala, Honduras, Nicaragua, Panama

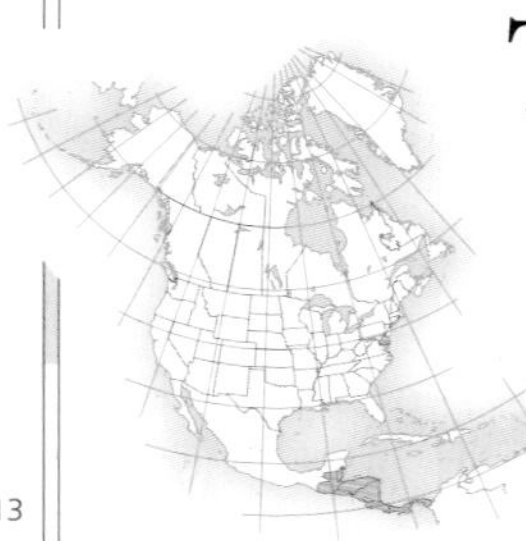

The natural beauty of tropical Central America belies the civil strife which has long plagued this region. The imprint of Spanish colonization prevails in the official language and Catholic religion of the people, who are mostly of mixed heritage. Indigenous Maya peoples remain most numerous in Guatemala. The US has frequently intervened in Central America, purchasing from Panama the right to build the canal in 1903, and sponsoring guerrilla activity in Nicaragua during the 1980s. Initiatives for a common market with Mexico offer hope of overcoming foreign economic dependency and attaining the relative prosperity enjoyed by Costa Rica. However, gaping disparities of wealth and land ownership remain fundamental obstacles to peace and stability.

Using the Land and Sea

About half of all agricultural produce is exported. Five commodities dominate commercial farming: bananas, grown on the humid coastal lowlands of the Caribbean; coffee; cotton; sugar, and beef on the Pacific side of the isthmus. Corn is the main subsistence crop and many varieties are grown, supplemented by beans, squash, and sorghum. Large areas of tropical rain forest are commercially exploited, causing concern about deforestation.

The Urban/Rural Population Divide

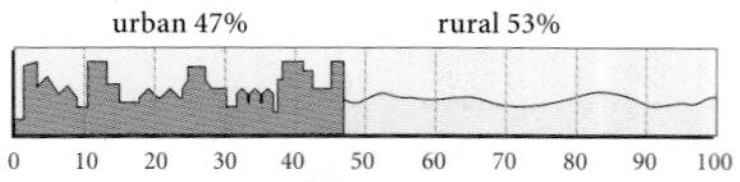

Population Density
178 people per sq mile
(69 people per sq km)

Total Land Area
196,721 sq miles
(509,640 sq km)

Land use and agricultural distribution
- cattle
- bananas
- coffee
- cotton
- corn (maize)
- shellfish
- sugar cane
- timber
- capital cities
- major towns
- pasture
- cropland
- forest

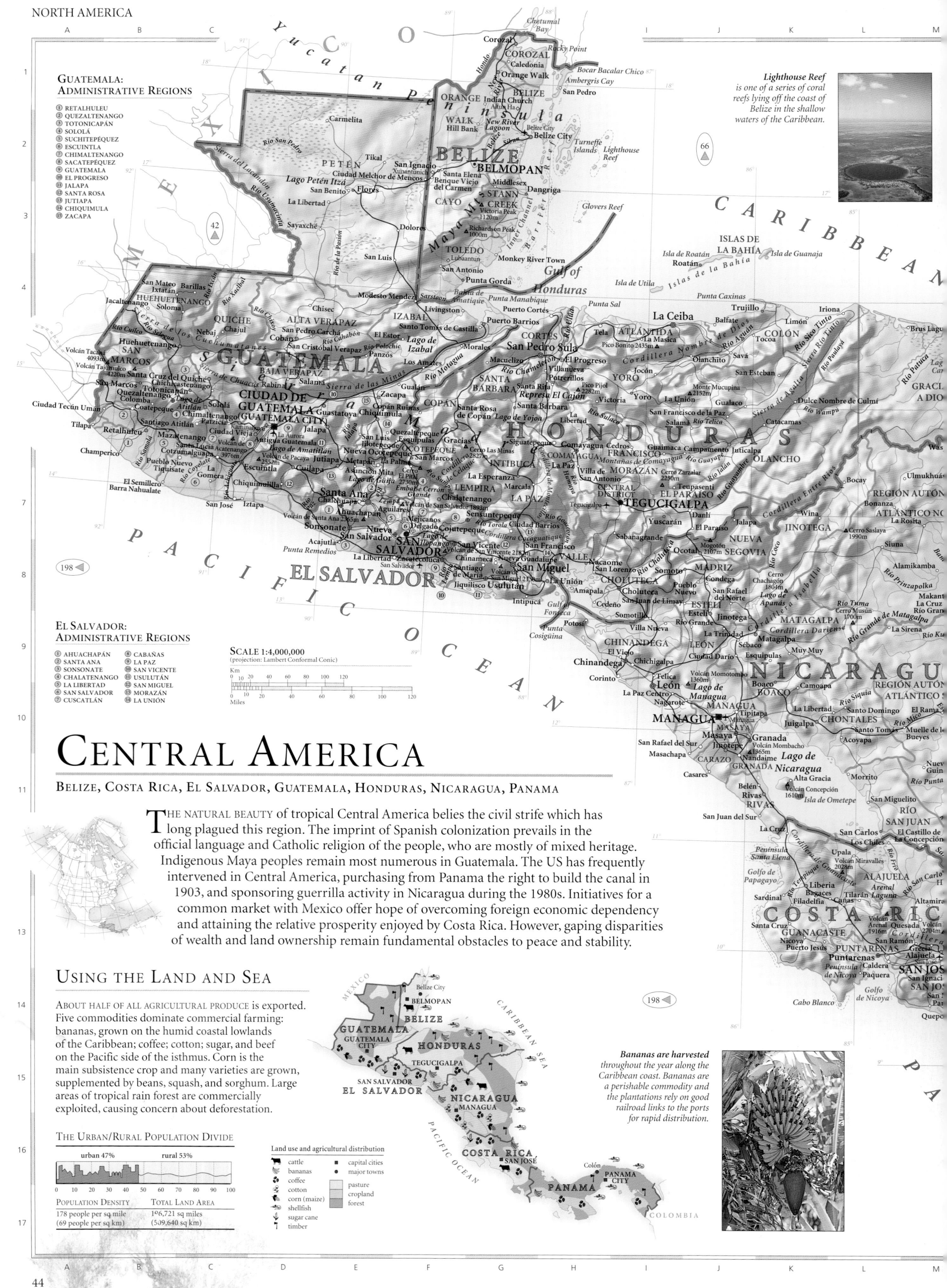

Bananas are harvested *throughout the year along the Caribbean coast. Bananas are a perishable commodity and the plantations rely on good railroad links to the ports for rapid distribution.*

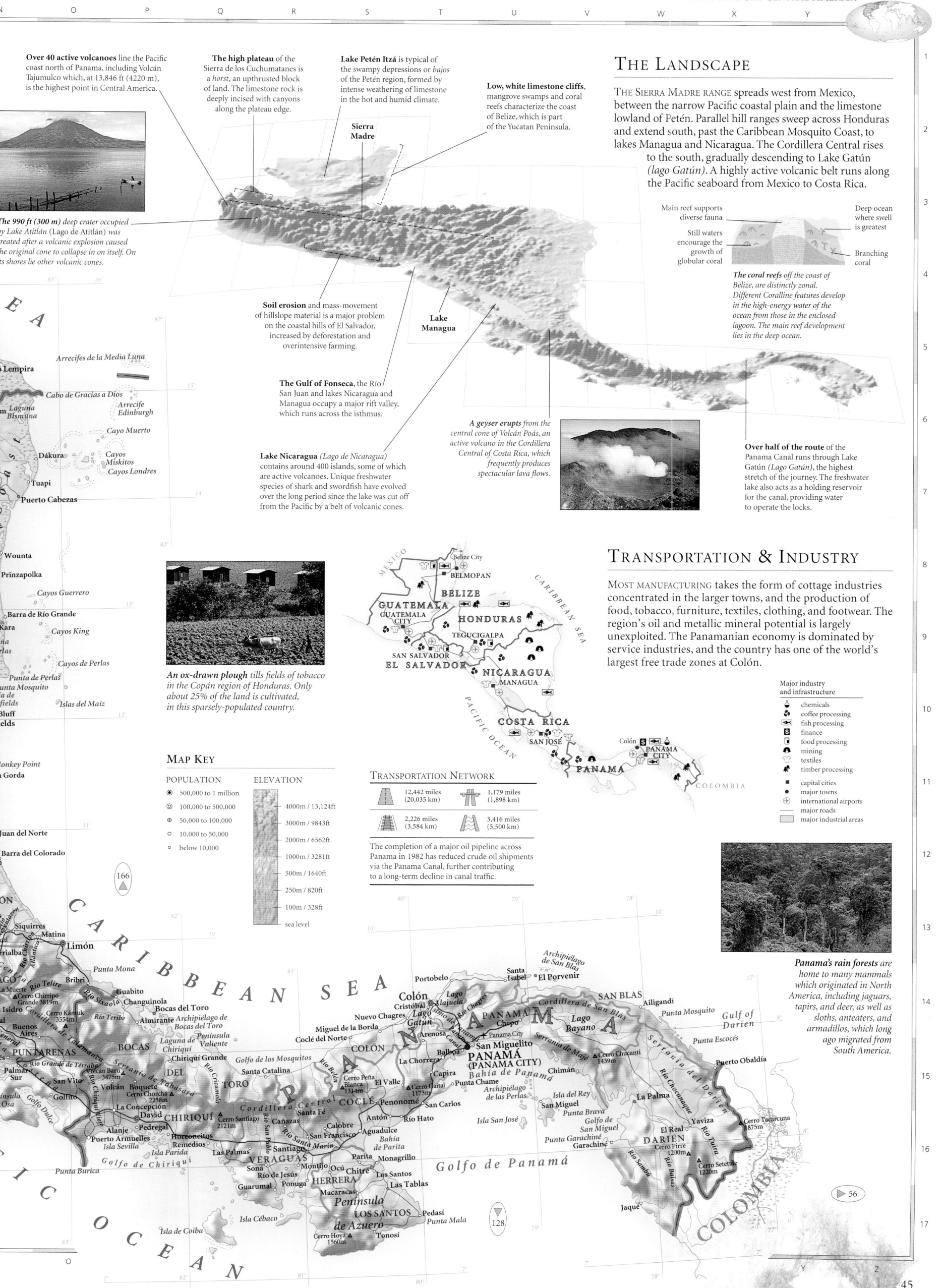

THE LANDSCAPE

THE SIERRA MADRE RANGE spreads west from Mexico, between the narrow Pacific coastal plain and the limestone lowland of Petén. Parallel hill ranges sweep across Honduras and extend south, past the Caribbean Mosquito Coast, to lakes Managua and Nicaragua. The Cordillera Central rises to the south, gradually descending to Lake Gatún *(lago Gatún)*. A highly active volcanic belt runs along the Pacific seaboard from Mexico to Costa Rica.

***The 990 ft (300 m)** deep crater occupied by Lake Atitlán (Lago de Atitlán) was created after a volcanic explosion caused the original cone to collapse in on itself. On its shores lie other volcanic cones.*

Over 40 active volcanoes line the Pacific coast north of Panama, including Volcán Tajumulco which, at 13,846 ft (4220 m), is the highest point in Central America.

The high plateau of the Sierra de los Cuchumatanes is a *horst*, an upthrusted block of land. The limestone rock is deeply incised with canyons along the plateau edge.

Lake Petén Itzá is typical of the swampy depressions or *bajos* of the Petén region, formed by intense weathering of limestone in the hot and humid climate.

Low, white limestone cliffs, mangrove swamps and coral reefs characterize the coast of Belize, which is part of the Yucatan Peninsula.

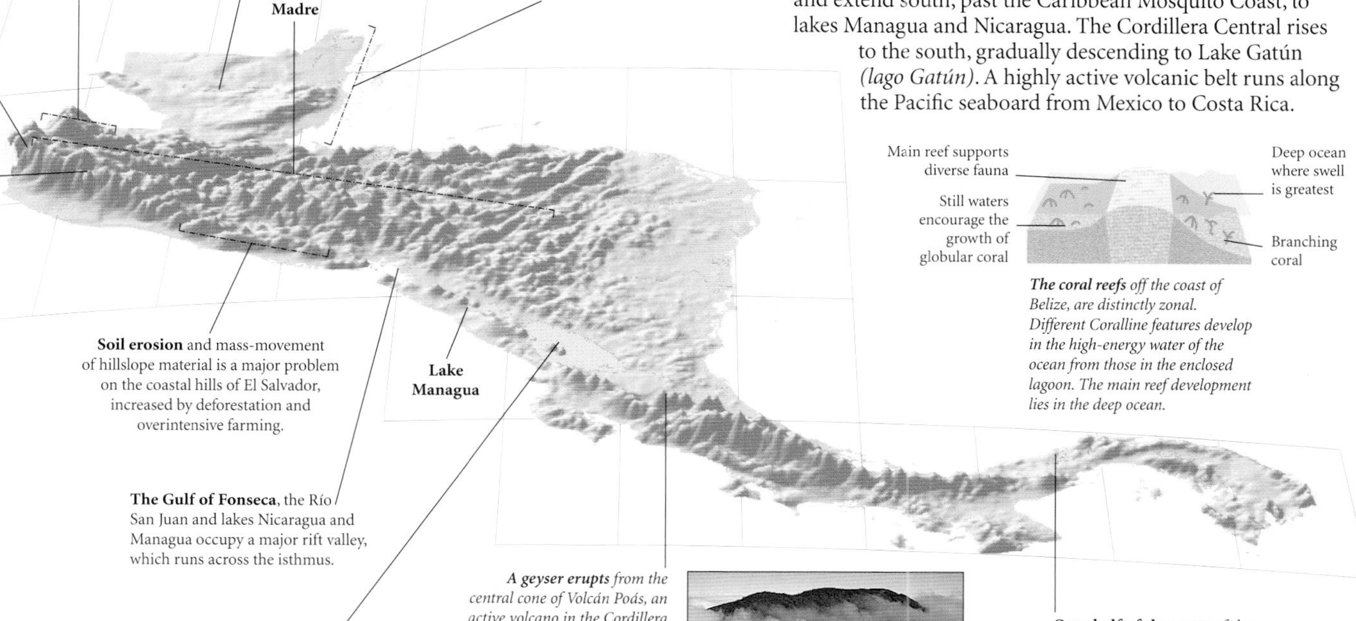

Soil erosion and mass-movement of hillslope material is a major problem on the coastal hills of El Salvador, increased by deforestation and overintensive farming.

The Gulf of Fonseca, the Río San Juan and lakes Nicaragua and Managua occupy a major rift valley, which runs across the isthmus.

Lake Nicaragua *(Lago de Nicaragua)* contains around 400 islands, some of which are active volcanoes. Unique freshwater species of shark and swordfish have evolved over the long period since the lake was cut off from the Pacific by a belt of volcanic cones.

***A geyser erupts** from the central cone of Volcán Poás, an active volcano in the Cordillera Central of Costa Rica, which frequently produces spectacular lava flows.*

Over half of the route of the Panama Canal runs through Lake Gatún *(Lago Gatún)*, the highest stretch of the journey. The freshwater lake also acts as a holding reservoir for the canal, providing water to operate the locks.

Main reef supports diverse fauna

Still waters encourage the growth of globular coral

Deep ocean where swell is greatest

Branching coral

***The coral reefs** off the coast of Belize, are distinctly zonal. Different Coralline features develop in the high-energy water of the ocean from those in the enclosed lagoon. The main reef development lies in the deep ocean.*

***An ox-drawn plough** tills fields of tobacco in the Copán region of Honduras. Only about 25% of the land is cultivated, in this sparsely-populated country.*

TRANSPORTATION & INDUSTRY

MOST MANUFACTURING takes the form of cottage industries concentrated in the larger towns, and the production of food, tobacco, furniture, textiles, clothing, and footwear. The region's oil and metallic mineral potential is largely unexploited. The Panamanian economy is dominated by service industries, and the country has one of the world's largest free trade zones at Colón.

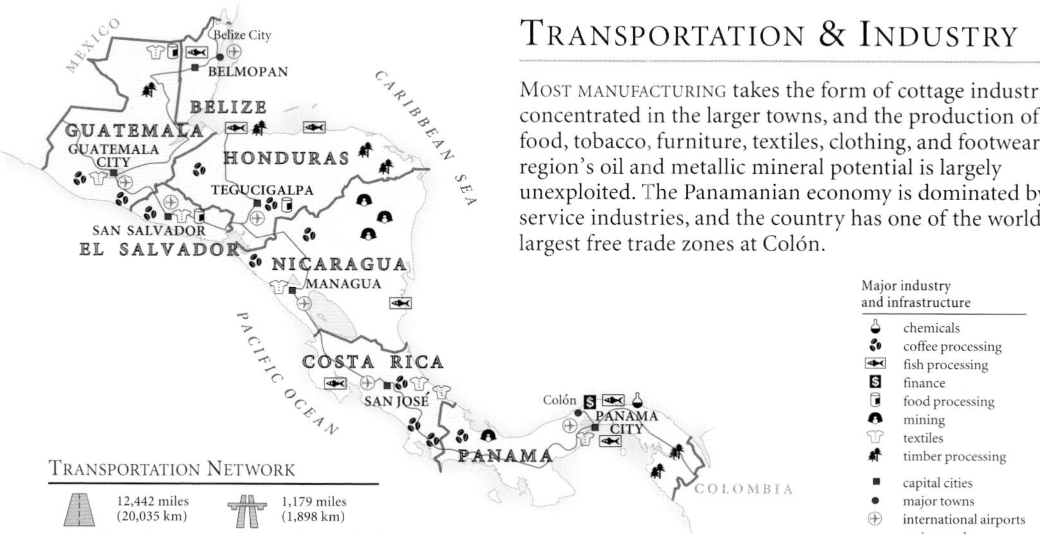

TRANSPORTATION NETWORK

12,442 miles (20,035 km)		1,179 miles (1,898 km)	
2,226 miles (3,584 km)		3,416 miles (5,500 km)	

The completion of a major oil pipeline across Panama in 1982 has reduced crude oil shipments via the Panama Canal, further contributing to a long-term decline in canal traffic.

MAP KEY

POPULATION	ELEVATION
500,000 to 1 million	4000m / 13,124ft
100,000 to 500,000	3000m / 9843ft
50,000 to 100,000	2000m / 6562ft
10,000 to 50,000	1000m / 3281ft
below 10,000	500m / 1640ft
	250m / 820ft
	100m / 328ft
	sea level

***Panama's rain forests** are home to many mammals which originated in North America, including jaguars, tapirs, and deer, as well as sloths, anteaters, and armadillos, which long ago migrated from South America.*

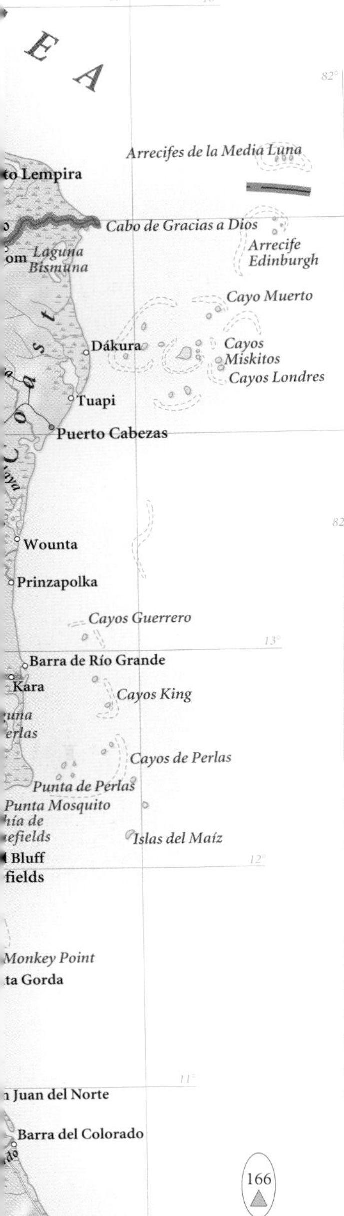

166
128
56

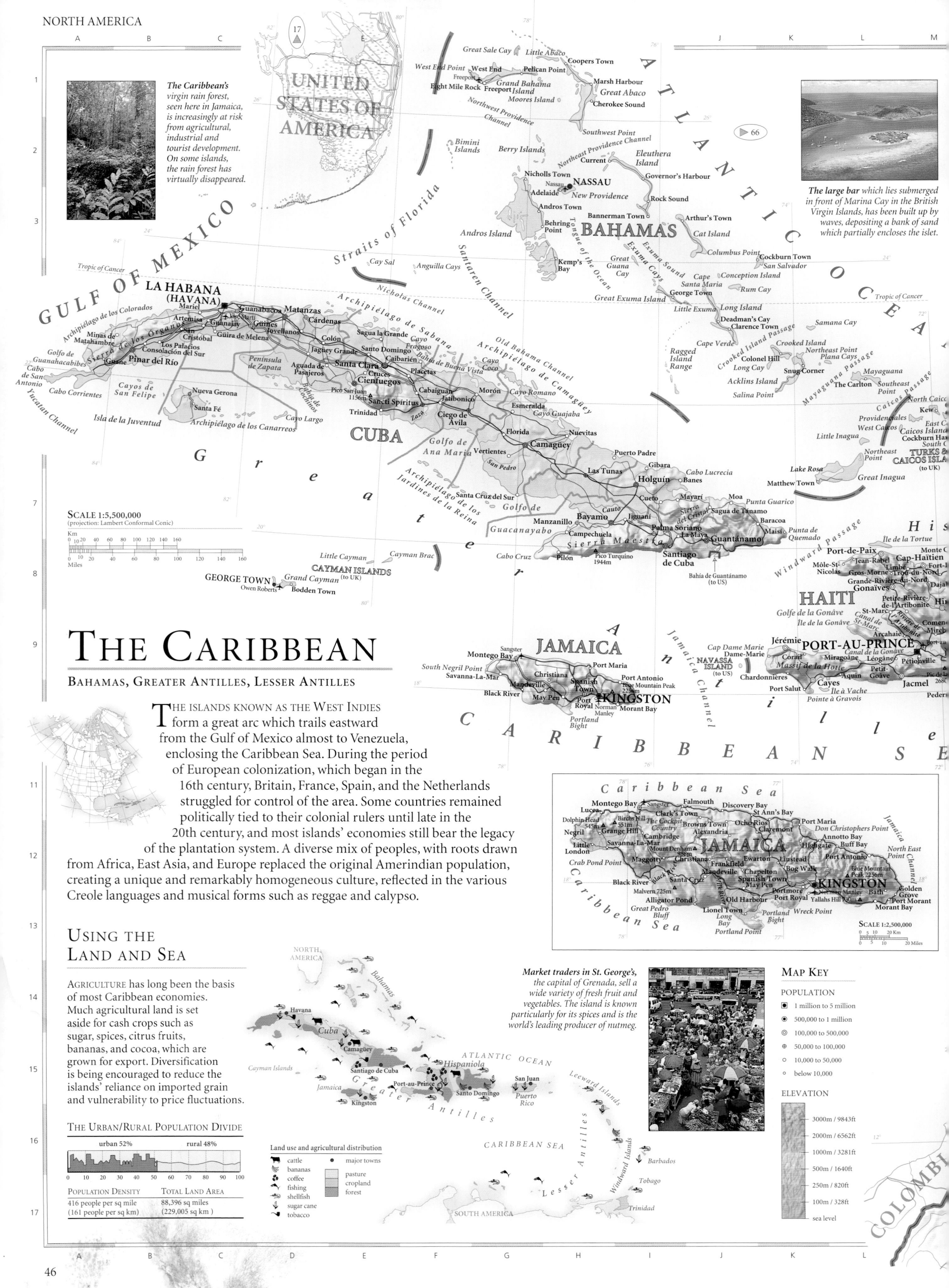

The Caribbean's virgin rain forest, seen here in Jamaica, is increasingly at risk from agricultural, industrial and tourist development. On some islands, the rain forest has virtually disappeared.

The large bar which lies submerged in front of Marina Cay in the British Virgin Islands, has been built up by waves, depositing a bank of sand which partially encloses the islet.

The Caribbean

Bahamas, Greater Antilles, Lesser Antilles

The islands known as the West Indies form a great arc which trails eastward from the Gulf of Mexico almost to Venezuela, enclosing the Caribbean Sea. During the period of European colonization, which began in the 16th century, Britain, France, Spain, and the Netherlands struggled for control of the area. Some countries remained politically tied to their colonial rulers until late in the 20th century, and most islands' economies still bear the legacy of the plantation system. A diverse mix of peoples, with roots drawn from Africa, East Asia, and Europe replaced the original Amerindian population, creating a unique and remarkably homogeneous culture, reflected in the various Creole languages and musical forms such as reggae and calypso.

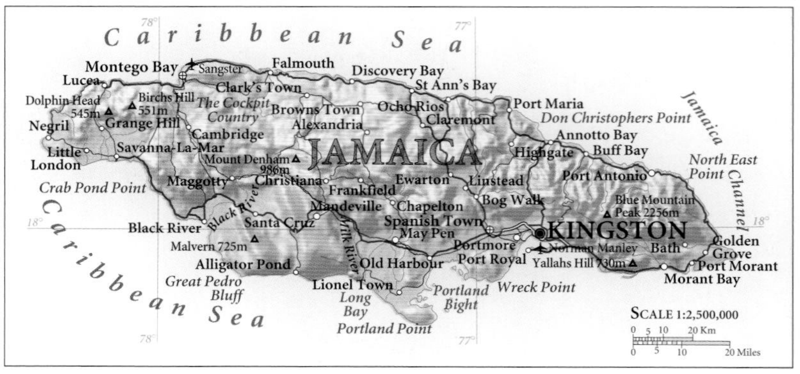

Using the Land and Sea

Agriculture has long been the basis of most Caribbean economies. Much agricultural land is set aside for cash crops such as sugar, spices, citrus fruits, bananas, and cocoa, which are grown for export. Diversification is being encouraged to reduce the islands' reliance on imported grain and vulnerability to price fluctuations.

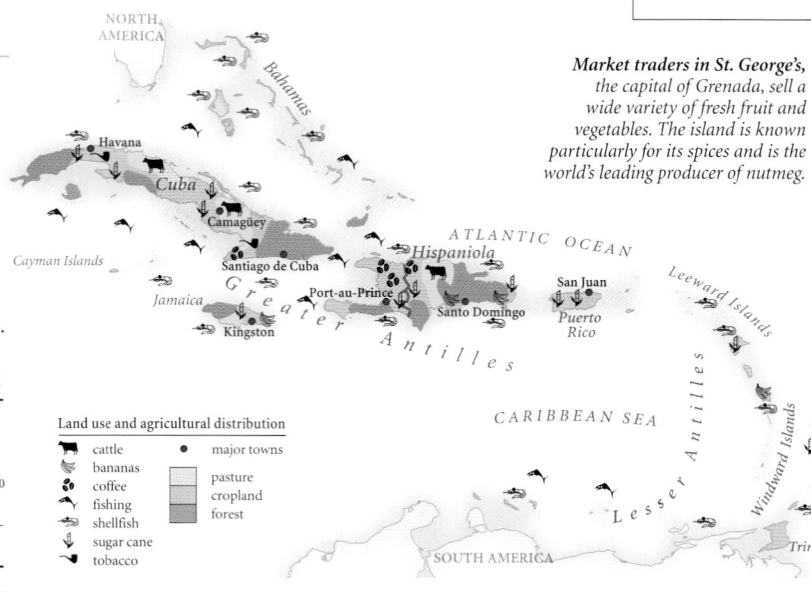

Market traders in St. George's, the capital of Grenada, sell a wide variety of fresh fruit and vegetables. The island is known particularly for its spices and is the world's leading producer of nutmeg.

The Urban/Rural Population Divide

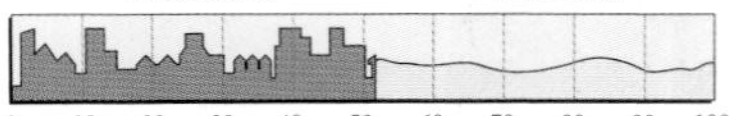

Population Density	Total Land Area
416 people per sq mile (161 people per sq km)	88,396 sq miles (229,005 sq km)

Map Key

Population

- 1 million to 5 million
- 500,000 to 1 million
- 100,000 to 500,000
- 50,000 to 100,000
- 10,000 to 50,000
- below 10,000

Elevation

- 3000m / 9843ft
- 2000m / 6562ft
- 1000m / 3281ft
- 500m / 1640ft
- 250m / 820ft
- 100m / 328ft
- sea level

TRANSPORTATION & INDUSTRY

CARIBBEAN INDUSTRY remains, with few exceptions, agricultural, and export-led, or service-based, supporting the flourishing tourist industry. However, several countries including Jamaica, Barbados, Trinidad and Tobago, and Puerto Rico have developed important mineral industries, and Cuba is attempting to diversify its economy by importing capital goods to start up new manufacturing businesses.

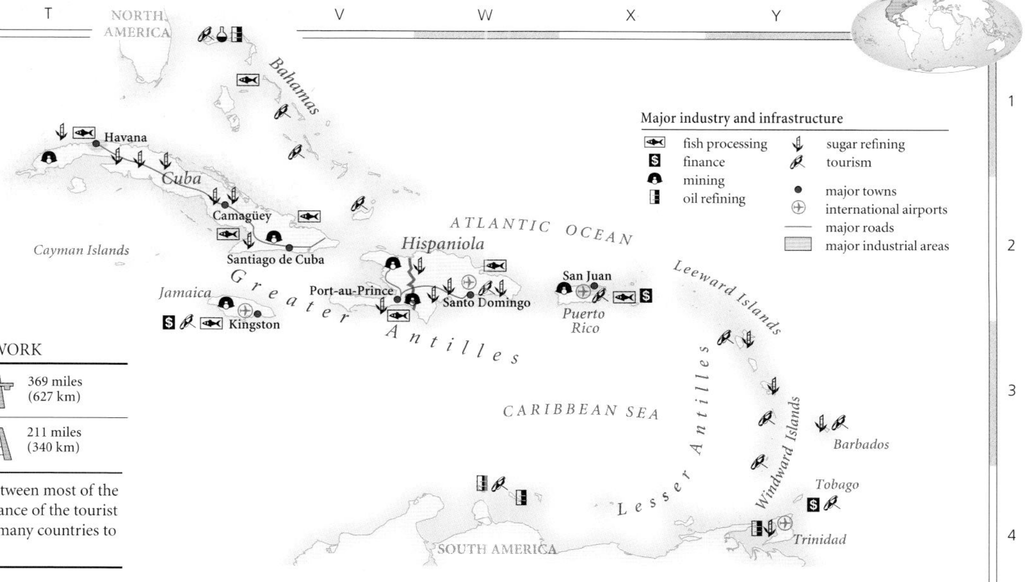

Cruise ships, such as this one moored at Castries in St. Lucia, have become a popular way for tourists to travel round the Caribbean islands, stopping off at several islands for sightseeing and shopping.

This rock stack on the coast of St. Martin in the Leeward Islands has been created by wave action which undercut the cliffs, forming an arch. Continued wave action weakened the arch, which eventually collapsed leaving a single tower of rock.

Major industry and infrastructure

- fish processing
- finance
- mining
- oil refining
- sugar refining
- tourism
- major towns
- international airports
- major roads
- major industrial areas

TRANSPORTATION NETWORK

21,197 miles (34,133 km)	369 miles (627 km)
9,100 miles (14,654 km)	211 miles (340 km)

Air links are well-developed between most of the Caribbean islands. The importance of the tourist trade has recently encouraged many countries to upgrade their paved roads.

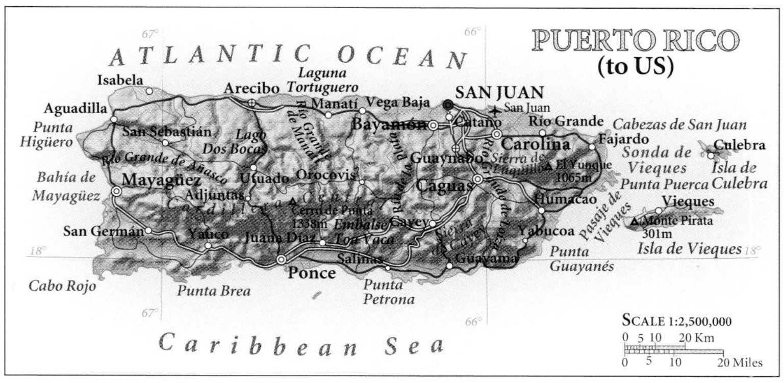

The Pitons in St. Lucia are two volcanic domes; the tallest is 2,620 ft (798 m) high. Their steep slopes are covered in thick forest.

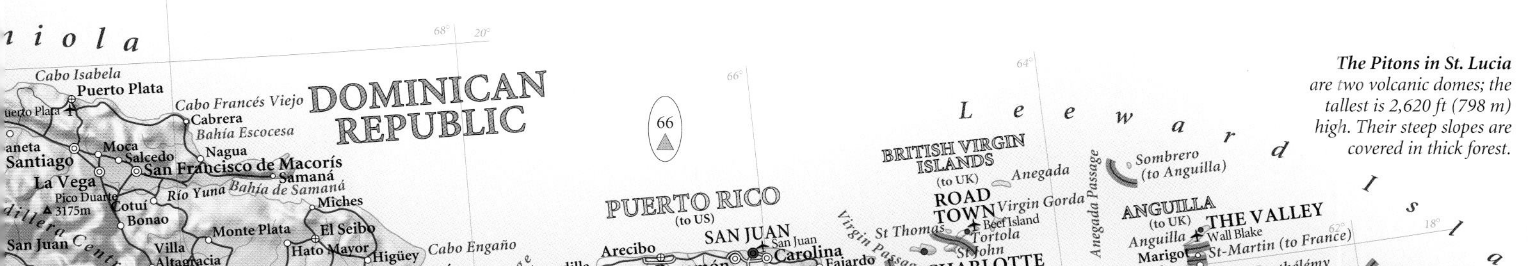

SOUTH AMERICA

REACHING FROM THE HUMID TROPICS DOWN INTO THE COLD SOUTH ATLANTIC, SOUTH AMERICA HAS AN AREA OF 6,886,000 SQ MILES (17,835,000 SQ KM). THERE ARE 12 SEPARATE COUNTRIES, WITH THE LARGEST, BRAZIL, COVERING ALMOST HALF THE CONTINENT.

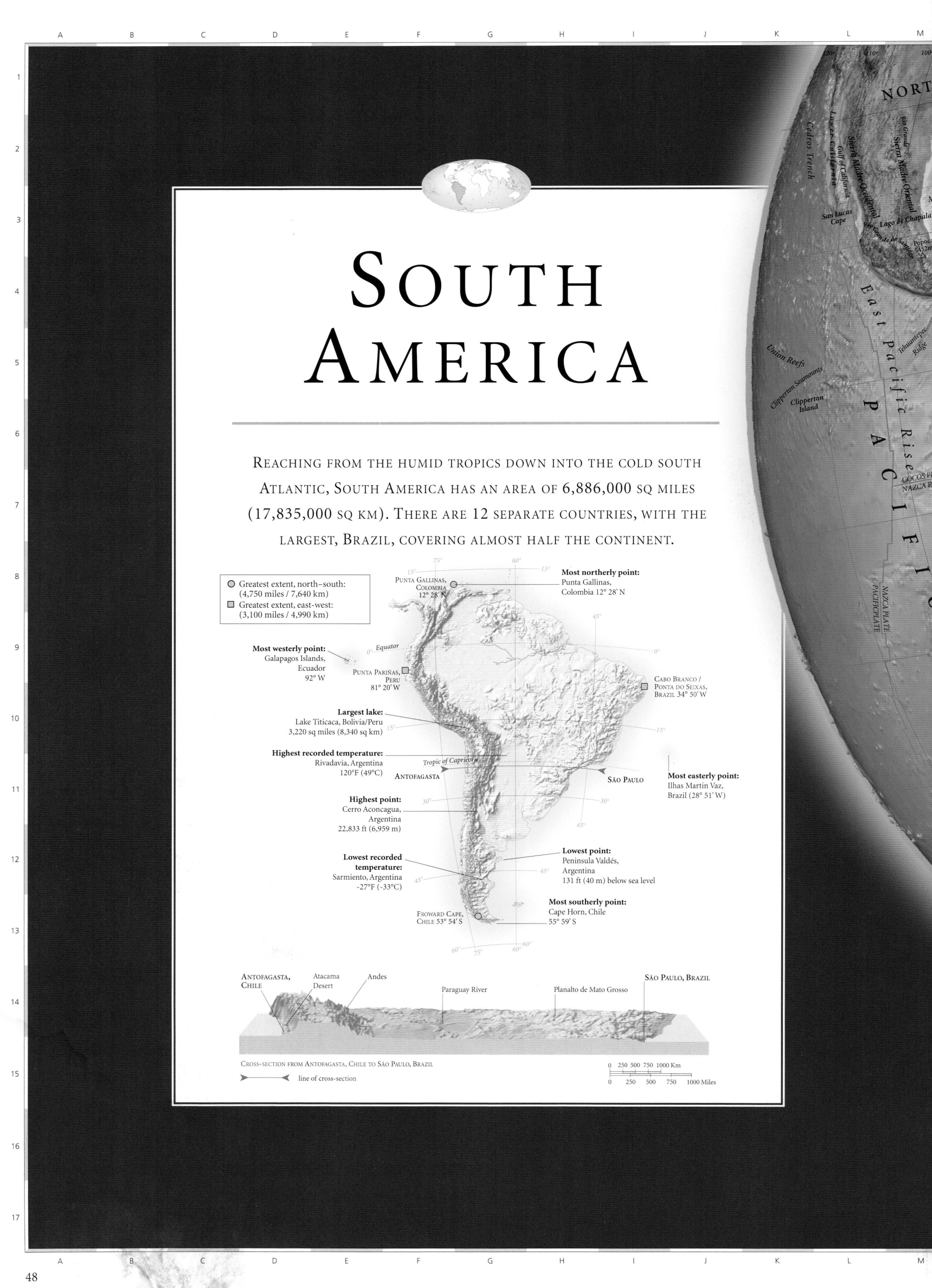

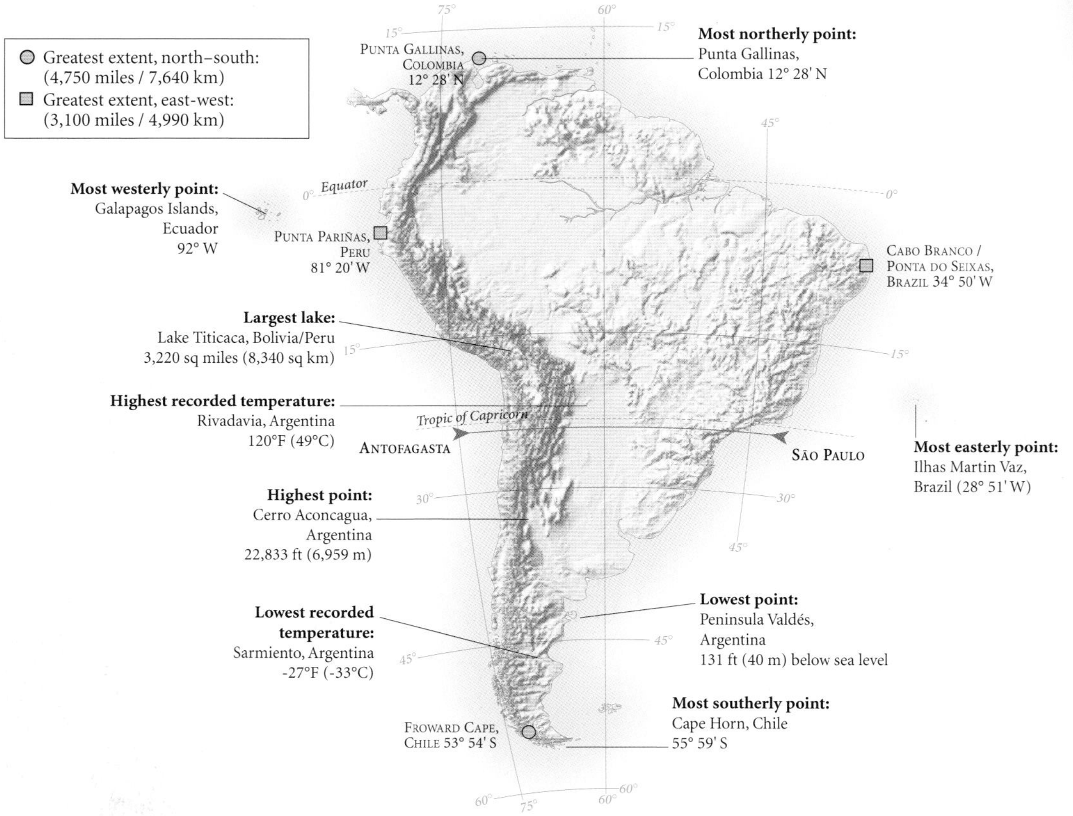

CROSS-SECTION FROM ANTOFAGASTA, CHILE TO SÃO PAULO, BRAZIL

line of cross-section

0 250 500 750 1000 Km
0 250 500 750 1000 Miles

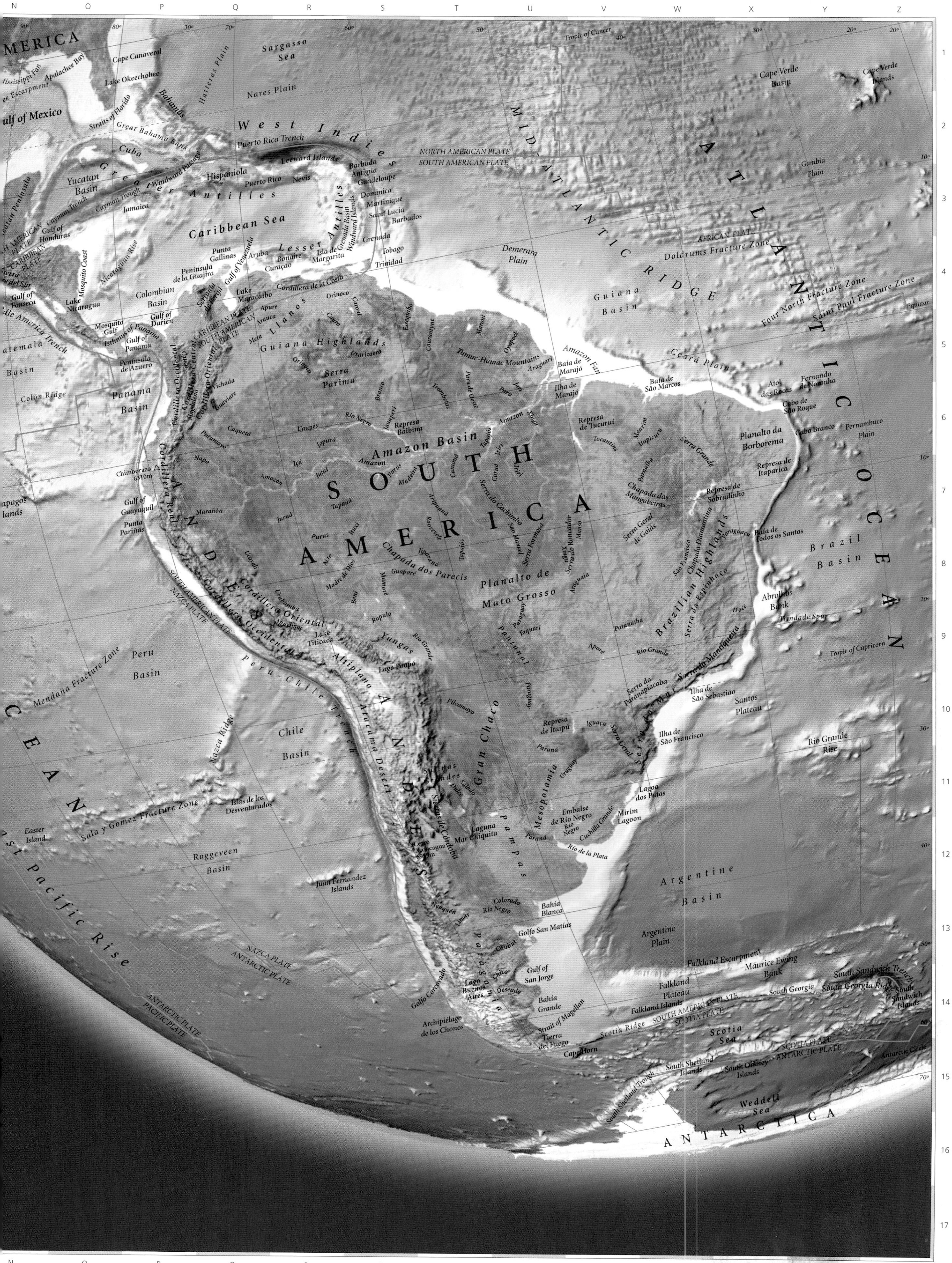

SOUTH AMERICA
ATLANTIC OCEAN
MID-ATLANTIC RIDGE
West Indies
Greater Antilles
Lesser Antilles
Caribbean Sea
Gulf of Mexico
Sargasso Sea
Nares Plain
Hatteras Plain
Cape Canaveral
Lake Okeechobee
Apalachee Bay
Straits of Florida
Great Bahama Bank
Bahamas
Cuba
Yucatan Basin
Cayman Trench
Cayman Trough
Jamaica
Windward Passage
Hispaniola
Puerto Rico
Puerto Rico Trench
Leeward Islands
Nevis
Barbuda
Antigua
Guadeloupe
Dominica
Martinique
Saint Lucia
Barbados
Grenada Basin
Isla de Margarita
Windward Islands
Grenada
Tobago
Trinidad
Aruba
Bonaire
Curaçao
Punta Gallinas
Península de la Guajira
Gulf of Venezuela
Gulf of Honduras
Mosquito Coast
Nicaraguan Rise
Lake Nicaragua
Gulf of Fonseca
Colombian Basin
Lake Maracaibo
Cordillera de la Costa
Orinoco
Gulf of Darién
Isthmus of Panama
Mosquito Gulf
Gulf of Panama
Península de Azuero
Panama Basin
Colón Ridge
Middle America Trench
CARIBBEAN PLATE
SOUTH AMERICAN PLATE
NORTH AMERICAN PLATE
AFRICAN PLATE
Llanos
Apure
Arauca
Meta
Guiana Highlands
Serra Parima
Uraricoera
Tumuc-Humac Mountains
Essequibo
Courantyne
Maroni
Oyapock
Demerara Plain
Guiana Basin
Dolorums Fracture Zone
Four North Fracture Zone
Saint Paul Fracture Zone
Equator
Cape Verde Basin
Cape Verde Islands
Gambia Plain
Tropic of Cancer
Amazon Fan
Ceará Plain
Baía de Marajó
Ilha de Marajó
Baía de São Marcos
Atol das Rocas
Fernando de Noronha
Cabo de São Roque
Cabo Branco
Pernambuco Plain
Planalto da Borborema
Represa de Itaparica
Represa de Sobradinho
Baía de Todos os Santos
Brazil Basin
Abrolhos Bank
Vitória-Trindade Spur
Tropic of Capricorn
Amazon Basin
Amazon
Rio Negro
Represa Balbina
Japurá
Içá
Putumayo
Caquetá
Napo
Juruá
Purus
Madeira
Tapajós
Xingu
Tocantins
Represa de Tucuruí
Araguaia
Serra do Cachimbo
Serra Formosa
Serra do Roncador
Chapada dos Parecis
Planalto de Mato Grosso
Chapada das Mangabeiras
Serra Geral de Goiás
Serra Grande
Chapada Diamantina
Brazilian Highlands
Serra do Espinhaço
Serra da Mantiqueira
Serra do Mar
São Francisco
Paranaíba
Rio Grande
Pantanal
Paraguay
Paraná
Represa de Itaipu
Iguaçu
Uruguay
Mesopotamia
Gran Chaco
Pilcomayo
Ilha de São Sebastião
Santos Plateau
Ilha de São Francisco
Rio Grande Rise
Lagoa dos Patos
Mirim Lagoon
Embalse de Río Negro
Cuchilla Grande
Río de la Plata
Pampas
Laguna Mar Chiquita
Sierra de Córdoba
Argentine Basin
Argentine Plain
Bahía Blanca
Colorado
Río Negro
Golfo San Matías
Chubut
Gulf of San Jorge
Patagonia
Bahía Grande
Falkland Escarpment
Maurice Ewing Bank
Falkland Plateau
Falkland Islands
South Georgia
South Georgia Ridge
South Sandwich Trench
South Sandwich Islands
Scotia Ridge
Scotia Sea
SCOTIA PLATE
ANTARCTIC PLATE
Antarctic Circle
Strait of Magellan
Tierra del Fuego
Cape Horn
South Shetland Islands
South Shetland Trough
South Orkney Islands
Weddell Sea
ANTARCTICA
ANDES
Cordillera Occidental
Cordillera Central
Cordillera Oriental
Chimborazo 6310m
Gulf of Guayaquil
Punta Pariñas
Marañón
Ucayali
Lake Titicaca
Lago Poopó
Altiplano
Yungas
Atacama Desert
Cerro Aconcagua 6959m
Lago Buenos Aires
Golfo Corcovado
Archipiélago de los Chonos
Peru Basin
Peru-Chile Trench
Mendaña Fracture Zone
Nazca Ridge
Chile Basin
Islas de los Desventurados
Sala y Gomez Fracture Zone
Easter Island
Roggeveen Basin
Juan Fernández Islands
East Pacific Rise
NAZCA PLATE
PACIFIC PLATE

A B C D E F G H I J K L M

Physical South America

THREE MAJOR PHYSIOGRAPHIC REGIONS characterize South America. The oldest, the ancient Brazilian Shield and the smaller Guyana and Patagonian shields, form the stable core of the continent. Stretching along the entire west coast are the younger Andean fold mountains with many summits rising to 20,000 ft (6,100 m). These two diverse regions are separated by a number of sedimentary basins carrying South America's large river systems to the sea. These include the massive Amazon Basin and the basin of the Gran Chaco.

The Amazon Basin and Guyana Shield

THE RIVER AMAZON occupies a large depression in the Earth's crust, formed by the uplift of the Andes. It is covered by thick volcanic deposits and layers of alluvium – these have been laid down by the Amazon's many tributaries. To the north is the smaller Guyana Shield.

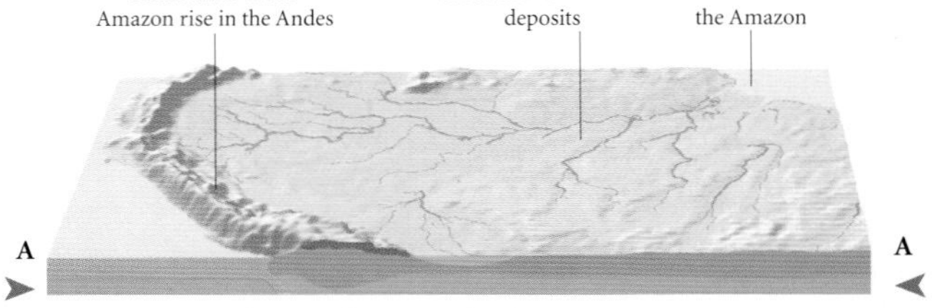

Section across northern South America showing Amazon Basin and its drainage pattern.

0 500 1000 Km
0 500 1000 Miles

SCALE 1:27,500,000
(projection: Lambert Azimuthal Equal Area)

Km 0 100 200 400 600 800
Miles 0 100 200 400 600 800

The Andean Uplands

THE ANDEAN UPLANDS run along the west coast of South America. They are being uplifted as the Nazca Plate is subducted beneath the South American Plate. They contain some of the world's largest volcanoes, such as Cotopaxi, and Lake Titicaca which occupies a dormant site. The far south has many large ice-sheets and a fragmented coastline.

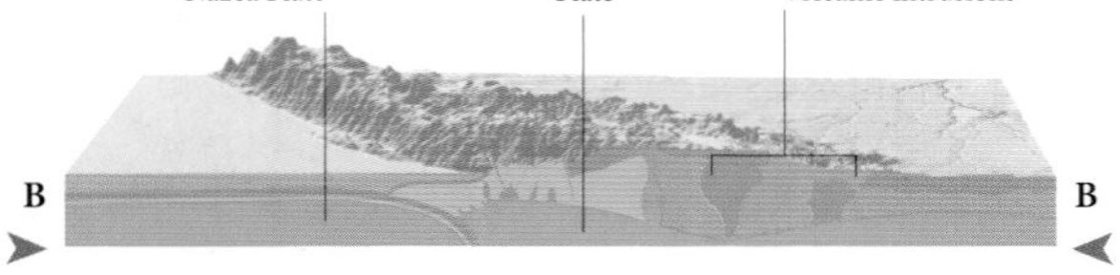

Cross-section through the Andes showing the subduction of the Nazca Plate beneath the South American Plate.

0 200 400 Km
0 200 400 Miles

Map Key

ELEVATION

6000m / 19,686ft
4000m / 13,124ft
3000m / 9843ft
2000m / 6562ft
1500m / 4922ft
1000m / 3281ft
500m / 1640ft
250m / 820ft
100m / 328ft
sea level

PLATE MARGINS
(for explanation see page xiv)

constructive
destructive
conservative
uncertain

physiographic regions

line of cross-section

The Brazilian Shield and Gran Chaco

THE IMMENSE BRAZILIAN SHIELD underlies more than one-third of South America. It is pitted with numerous volcanic intrusions, and a large basaltic plateau exists between the Paraná River and the Atlantic Ocean. The flat Gran Chaco lies to the west of the shield, covered by sedimentary deposits eroded from the Andes, and transported by South America's mighty rivers.

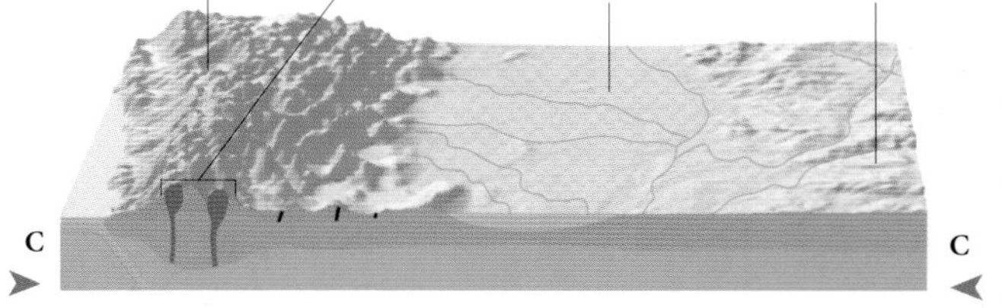

Section across central South America showing the flat basin of the Gran Chaco and the ancient Brazilian Shield.

0 200 400 Km
0 200 400 Miles

A B C D E I J K L M

N O P Q R S T U V W X Y Z

Mild winters and cool summers typify the extensive Pampas grasslands of Argentina.

Climate

The climate of South America is influenced by three principal factors: the seasonal shift of high pressure air masses over the tropics, cold ocean currents along the western coast, affecting temperature and precipitation, and the mountain barrier produced by by the Andes, which creates a rain shadow over much of the south.

Climate
- tundra
- cool continental
- warm humid
- semiarid
- arid
- humid equatorial
- tropical
- daily hours of sunshine, January
- daily hours of sunshine, July
- → cold wind

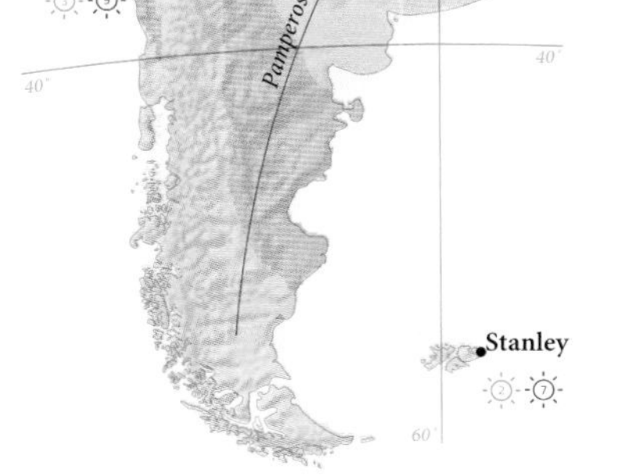

Chile's hyperarid Atacama Desert is renowned as one of the driest places on Earth.

Temperature

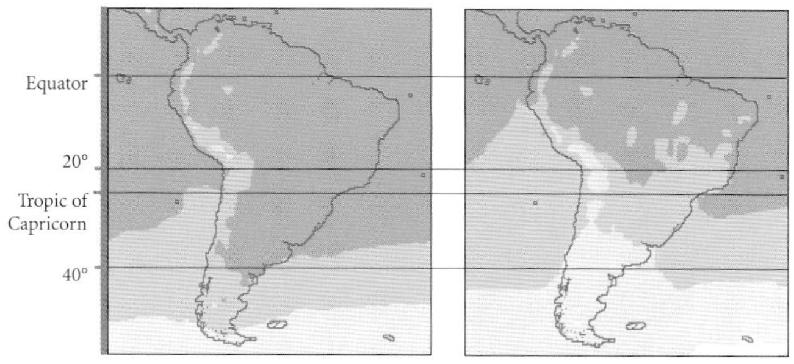

Average January temperature

Average July temperature

Temperature
- below -22°F (-30°C)
- -22 to -4°F (-30 to -20°C)
- -4 to 14°F (-20 to -10°C)
- 14 to 32°F (-10 to 0°C)
- 32 to 50°F (0 to 10°C)
- 50°F (10 to 20°C)
- 68 to 86°F (20 to 30°C)
- above 86°F (30°C)

Rainfall

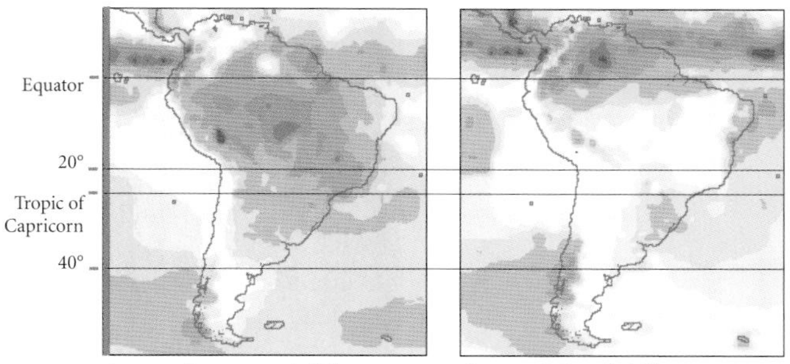

Average January rainfall

Average July rainfall

Rainfall
- 0–1 in (0–25 mm)
- 1–2 in (25–50 mm)
- 2–4 in (50–100 mm)
- 4–8 in (100–200 mm)
- 8–12 in (200–300 mm)
- 12–16 in (300–400 mm)
- 16–20 in (400–500 mm)
- more than 20 in (500 mm)

Tropical conditions are found across over half of South America. When both rainfall and temperatures are high, hot humid rain forests prevail.

Shaping the Continent

South America's active tectonic belt has been extensively folded over millions of years; landslides are still frequent in the mountains. The large river systems that erode the mountains flow across resistant shield areas, depositing sediment. Present-day glaciation affects the distinctive landscape of the far south.

Chemical Weathering

1 Table mountains *(left)* are the eroded remnants of an ancient upland. As water percolates along cracks in these high, flat-topped mountains it forms intricate cave systems. Chemical weathering also isolates large blocks which then collapse, accumulating as rockfalls at the foot of scarp slopes.

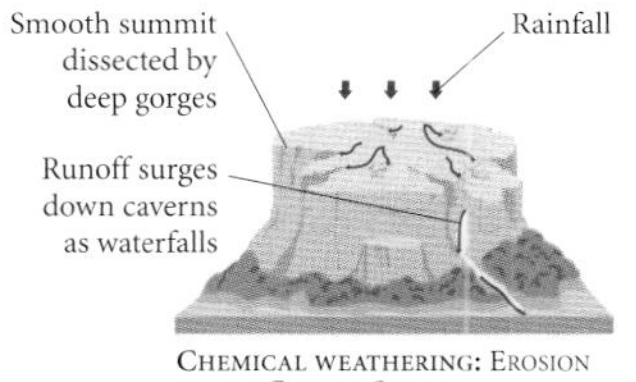

Chemical weathering: Erosion of the Guyana Shield

River Systems

2 Along the Amazon *(above)* there is a great variation in rates of erosion. As the headwaters of the Amazon flow down from the Andes, they erode and transport vast quantities of sediment, and are known as whitewaters. Across the shield areas erosion rates are very low. These rivers, carrying rotting vegetation, are called blackwaters.

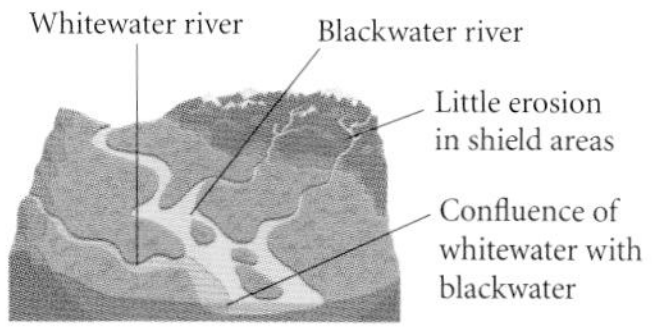

River systems: Suspended sediments in the Amazon

Mass Movement

6 Debris slides are common in the highlands of South America *(left)*. They occur where soil on a slope is saturated by rainwater and therefore less stable. The actual slides are often triggered by earthquakes.

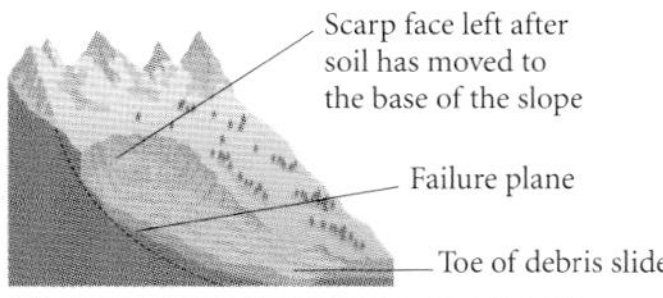

Mass movement: A section of a debris slide

The Evolving Landscape

Landscape
- uplifting land
- stable land
- sinking land
- glacier
- ocean current
- aluvial fan
- inselberg
- river

Folding

5 Folding occurs beneath the surface under high temperatures and pressures. Rocks become sufficiently malleable to flow and not fracture as tectonic plates collide. In the Valley of the Moon in Chile *(above)*, anticlines (or upfolds) and synclines (or troughs) have been exploited by erosion.

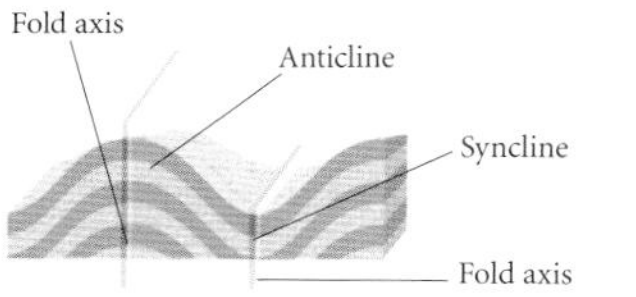

Folding: Synclines and anticlines

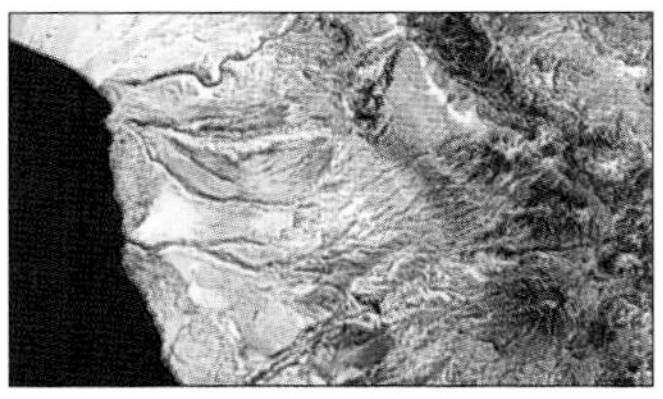

Deposition

4 Large alluvial fans are found extensively across South America *(above)*. Confined mountain rivers, carrying large quantities of eroded material, emerge from a mountain gorge onto the plains, where they deposit their load in huge fans.

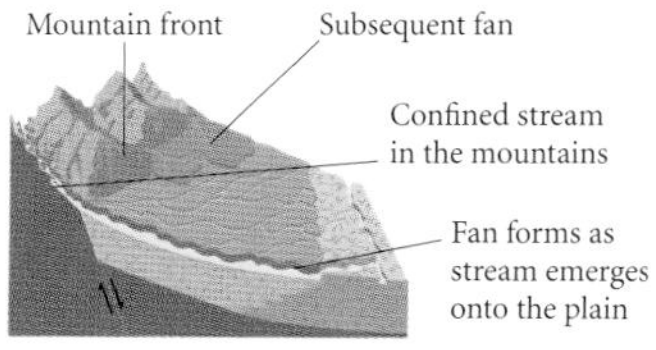

Deposition: Formation of an alluvial fan

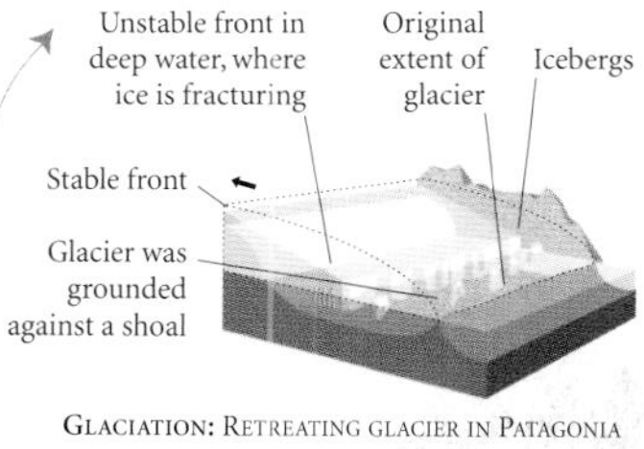

Glaciation: Retreating glacier in Patagonia

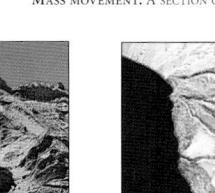

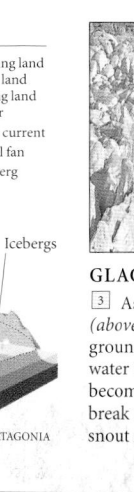

Glaciation

3 As fjord glaciers in Patagonia *(above)* retreat, they become grounded on shoals. In deeper water the base of the glacier becomes unstable, and icebergs break off (calve) until the glacier snout grounds once more.

N O P Q R S V W X Y Z

Political South America

Modern South America's political boundaries have their origins in the territorial endeavors of explorers during the 16th century, who claimed almost the entire continent for Portugal and Spain. The Portuguese land in the east later evolved into the federal state of Brazil, while the Spanish vice-royalties eventually emerged as separate independent nation-states in the early 19th century. South America's growing population has become increasingly urbanized, with the growth of coastal cities into large conurbations like Rio de Janeiro and Buenos Aires. In Brazil, Argentina, Chile and Uruguay, a succession of military dictatorships has given way to fragile, but strengthening, democracies.

***Europe retains** a small foothold in South America. Kourou in French Guiana was the site chosen by the European Space Agency to launch the Ariane rocket. As a result of its status as a French overseas department, French Guiana is actually part of the European Union.*

SCALE 1:21,500,000
(projection: Lambert Azimuthal Equal Area)

Km: 0 50 100 200 300 400 500 600 700 800
Miles: 0 50 100 200 300 400 500 600 700 800

Transportation

Most major road and rail routes are confined to the coastal regions by the forbidding natural barriers of the Andes Mountains and the Amazon Basin. Few major cross-continental routes exist, although Buenos Aires serves as a transportation center for the main rail links to La Paz and Valparaíso, while the construction of the Trans-Amazon and Pan-American Highways have made direct road travel possible from Recife to Lima and from Puerto Montt up the coast into central America. A new waterway project is proposed to transform the River Paraguay into a major shipping route, although it involves considerable wetland destruction.

***South America's** most extensive rail network is centered on the Argentinian capital, Buenos Aires. The construction of new rail lines ouward from this important port, allowed the colonization of the Pampas lands for agriculture.*

Languages

Prior to European exploration in the 16th century, a diverse range of indigenous languages were spoken across the continent. With the arrival of Iberian settlers, Spanish became the dominant language, with Portuguese spoken in Brazil, and Native American languages such as Quechua and Guaraní, becoming concentrated in the continental interior. Today this pattern persists, although successive European colonization has led to Dutch being spoken in Suriname, English in Guyana, and French in French Guiana, while in large urban areas, Japanese and Chinese are increasingly common.

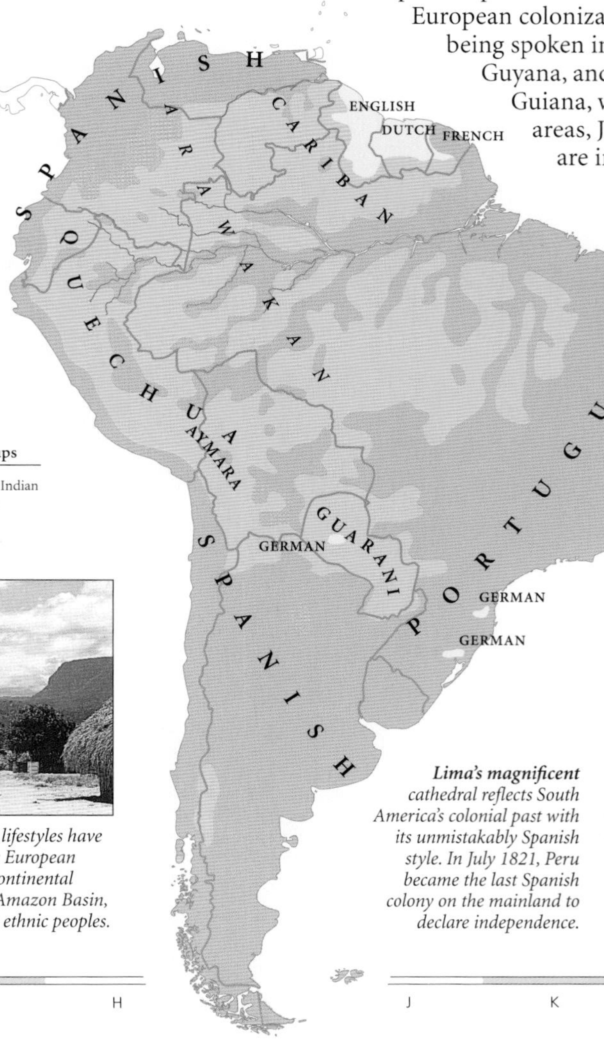

***Chile's main port, Valparaíso,** is a vital national shipping center, in addition to playing a key role in the growing trade with Pacific nations. The country's awkward, elongated shape means that sea transportation is frequently used for internal travel and communications in Chile.*

***Indigenous South American** lifestyles have not been totally submerged by European cultures and languages. The continental interior, and particularly the Amazon Basin, is still home to many different ethnic peoples.*

***Lima's magnificent** cathedral reflects South America's colonial past with its unmistakably Spanish style. In July 1821, Peru became the last Spanish colony on the mainland to declare independence.*

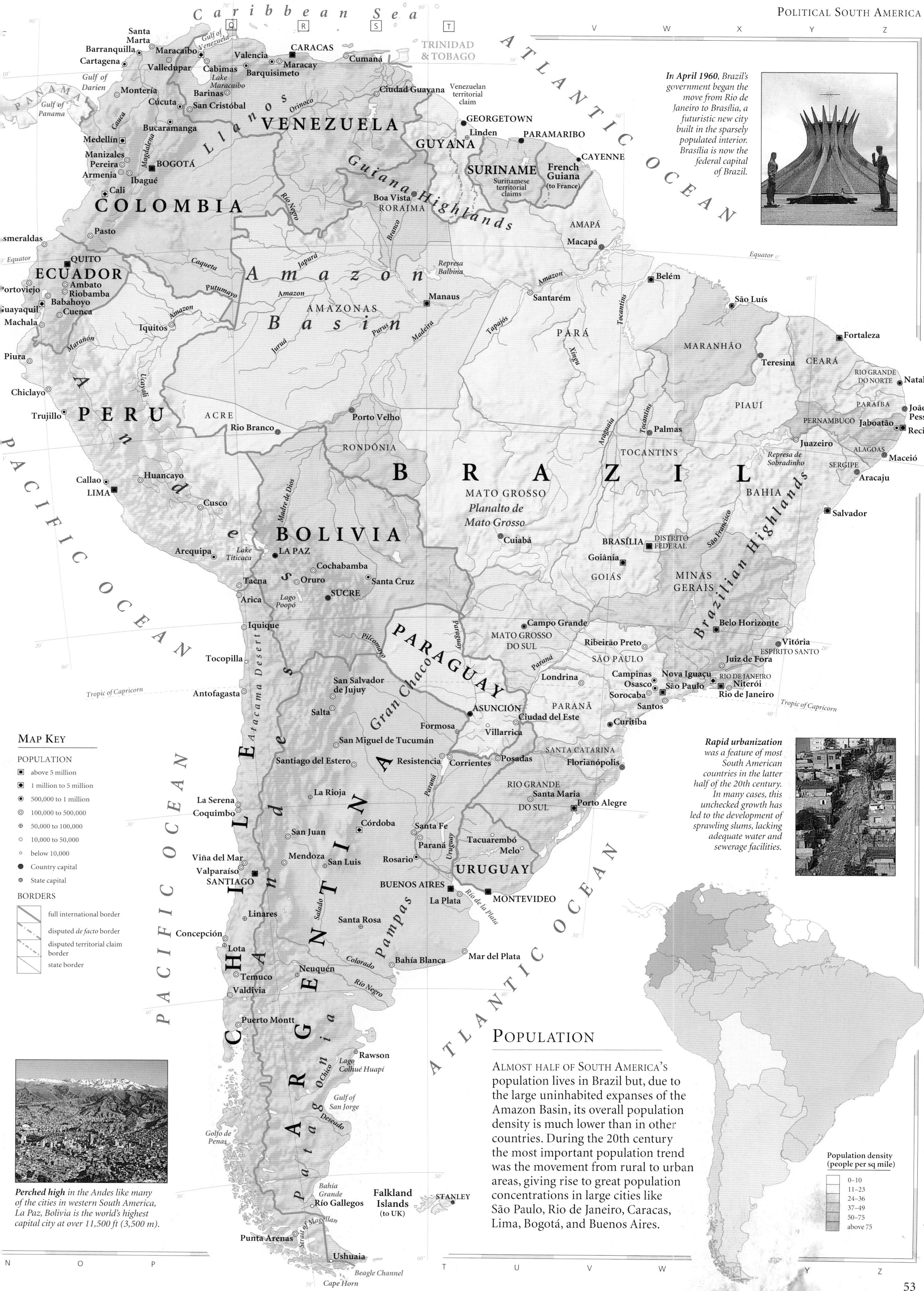

In April 1960, Brazil's government began the move from Rio de Janeiro to Brasília, a futuristic new city built in the sparsely populated interior. Brasília is now the federal capital of Brazil.

Rapid urbanization *was a feature of most South American countries in the latter half of the 20th century. In many cases, this unchecked growth has led to the development of sprawling slums, lacking adequate water and sewerage facilities.*

Perched high *in the Andes like many of the cities in western South America, La Paz, Bolivia is the world's highest capital city at over 11,500 ft (3,500 m).*

Population

Almost half of South America's population lives in Brazil but, due to the large uninhabited expanses of the Amazon Basin, its overall population density is much lower than in other countries. During the 20th century the most important population trend was the movement from rural to urban areas, giving rise to great population concentrations in large cities like São Paulo, Rio de Janeiro, Caracas, Lima, Bogotá, and Buenos Aires.

South American Resources

Agriculture still provides the largest single form of employment in South America, although rural unemployment and poverty continue to drive people toward the huge coastal cities in search of jobs and opportunities. Mineral and fuel resources, although substantial, are distributed unevenly; few countries have both fossil fuels and minerals. To break industrial dependence on raw materials, boost manufacturing, and improve infrastructure, governments borrowed heavily from the World Bank in the 1960s and 1970s. This led to the accumulation of massive debts which are unlikely ever to be repaid. Today, Brazil dominates the continent's economic output, followed by Argentina. Recently, the less-developed western side of South America has benefited due to its geographical position; for example Chile is increasingly exporting raw materials to Japan.

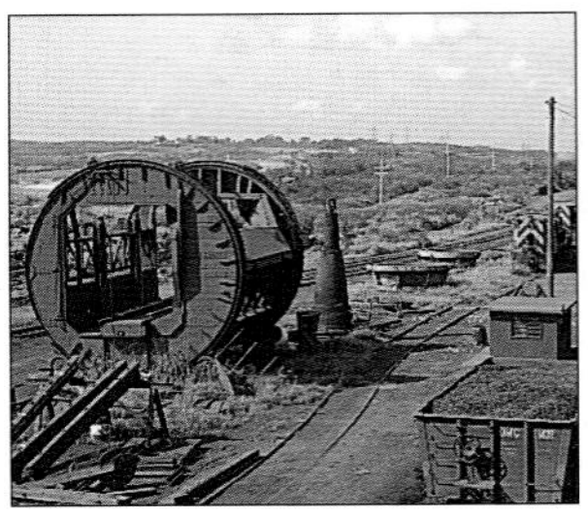

***Ciudad Guayana** is a planned industrial complex in eastern Venezuela, built as an iron and steel centre to exploit the nearby iron ore reserves.*

***The cold Peru Current** flows north from the Antarctic along the Pacific coast of Peru, providing rich nutrients for one of the world's largest fishing grounds. Overexploitation has severely reduced Peru's anchovy catch.*

Standard of Living

Wealth disparities throughout the continent create a wide gulf between affluent landowners and the chronically poor in inner-city slums. The illicit production of cocaine, and the hugely influential drug barons who control its distribution, contribute to the violent disorder and corruption which affect northwestern South America, de-stabilizing local governments and economies.

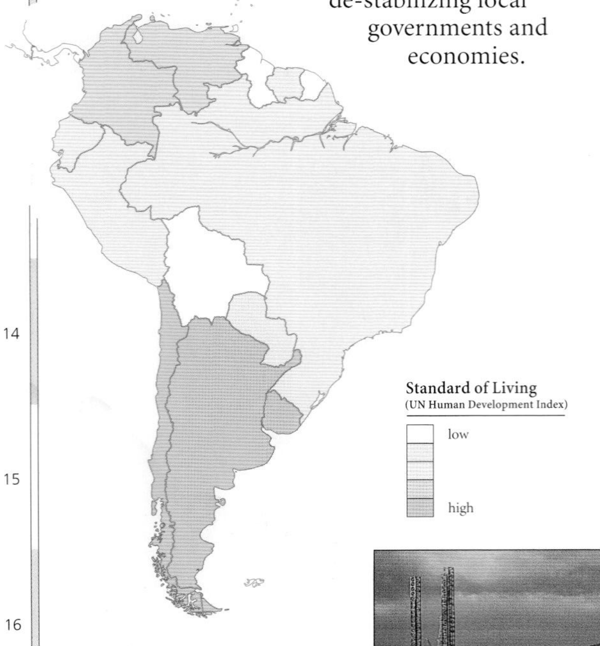

***Both Argentina and Chile** are now exploring the southernmost tip of the continent in search of oil. Here in Punta Arenas, a drilling rig is being prepared for exploratory drilling in the Strait of Magellan.*

Industry

Argentina and Brazil are South America's most industrialized countries and São Paulo is the continent's leading industrial center. Long-term government investment in Brazilian industry has encouraged a diverse industrial base; engineering, steel production, food processing, textile manufacture, and chemicals predominate. The illegal production of cocaine is economically significant in the Andean countries of Colombia and Bolivia. In Venezuela, the oil-dominated economy has left the country vulnerable to world oil price fluctuations. Food processing and mineral exploitation are common throughout the less industrially developed parts of the continent, including Bolivia, Chile, Ecuador, and Peru.

Environmental Issues

The Amazon Basin is one of the last great wilderness areas left on Earth. The tropical rain forests which grow there are a valuable genetic resource, containing innumerable unique plants and animals. The forests are increasingly under threat from new and expanding settlements and "slash and burn" farming techniques, which clear land for the raising of beef cattle, causing land degradation and soil erosion.

***Clouds of smoke billow** from the burning Amazon rain forest. Over 25,000 sq miles (60,000 sq km) of virgin rain forest are being cleared annually, destroying an ancient, irreplaceable, natural resource and biodiverse habitat.*

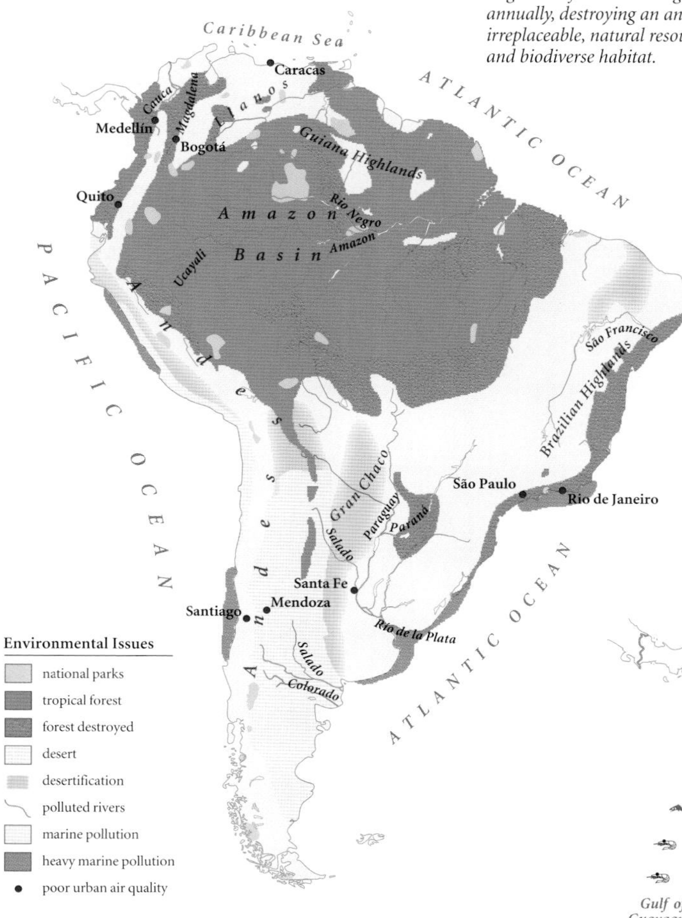

Mineral Resources

Over a quarter of the world's known copper reserves are found at the Chuquicamata mine in northern Chile, and other metallic minerals such as tin are found along the length of the Andes. The discovery of oil and gas at Venezuela's Lake Maracaibo in 1917 turned the country into one of the world's leading oil producers. In contrast, South America is virtually devoid of coal, the only significant deposit being on the peninsula of Guajira in Colombia.

***Copper is Chile's** largest export, most of which is mined at Chuquicamata. Along the length of the Andes, metallic minerals like copper and tin are found in abundance, formed by the excessive pressures and heat involved in mountain-building.*

Using the Land and Sea

Many foods now common worldwide originated in South America. These include the potato, tomato, squash, and cassava. Today, large herds of beef cattle roam the temperate grasslands of the Pampas, supporting an extensive meatpacking trade in Argentina, Uruguay and Paraguay. Corn (maize) is grown as a staple crop across the continent and coffee is grown as a cash crop in Brazil and Colombia. Coca plants grown in Bolivia, Peru, and Colombia provide most of the world's cocaine. Fish and shellfish are caught off the western coast, especially anchovies off Peru, shrimps off Ecuador and pilchards off Chile.

***South America**, and Brazil in particular, now leads the world in coffee production, mainly growing Coffea Arabica in large plantations. Coffee beans are harvested, roasted, and brewed to produce the world's second most popular drink, after tea.*

***The Pampas region** of southeast South America is characterized by extensive, flat plains, and populated by cattle and ranchers (gauchos). Argentina is a major world producer of beef, much of which is exported to the US for use in hamburgers.*

***High in the Andes**, hardy alpacas graze on the barren land. Alpacas are thought to have been domesticated by the Incas, whose nobility wore robes made from their wool. Today, they are still reared and prized for their soft, warm fleeces.*

Northern South America

Colombia, Guyana, Suriname, Venezuela, ***French Guiana*** **(to France)**

Flowers grown in Colombia are exported all over the world, and include fine carnations and roses. Here, workers are cutting roses which have been grown in plastic greenhouses.

Fringed by the Pacific and Atlantic oceans and the Caribbean Sea, South America's northern region has a rich range of natural resources, some exploited for centuries by colonial powers including the Spanish, French, Dutch, and British, others still to be fully explored. The prospects for further economic development in Colombia, Guyana and Suriname are blighted by drug-related violence and political instability. Venezuela, despite huge incomes from its oil reserves, remains less developed in other industrial sectors.

French Guiana is an overseas *département* of France, now seeking greater autonomy. Most of the major population centers, such as Bogotá, have grown up in the temperate conditions of the high Andes or, like Caracas, at strategic points along the Caribbean coast.

Map Key

Population
- 1 million to 5 million
- 500,000 to 1 million
- 100,000 to 500,000
- 50,000 to 100,000
- 10,000 to 50,000
- below 10,000

Elevation
- 4000m / 13,124ft
- 3000m / 9843ft
- 2000m / 6562ft
- 1000m / 3281ft
- 500m / 1640ft
- 250m / 820ft
- 100m / 328ft
- sea level

Large open squares like the Plaza de Bolivar in Bogotá are characteristic of many cities founded by the Spanish.

Scattered farms and villages have grown up on the gentle slopes of this Colombian river valley, utilizing the fertile soils for farming.

Scale 1:6,500,000
(projection: Lambert Azimuthal Equal Area)

Km 0 25 50 100 150 200
Miles 0 25 50 100 150 200

The River Orinoco flows from its source in the southern Guiana Highlands to form a broad delta on Venezuela's Atlantic coast. One of its distributary channels opens into a wide bay called the Serpent's Mouth.

TRANSPORTATION & INDUSTRY

MANY MINERAL RESOURCES are mined in Colombia, including fuels, gold, and precious and semiprecious stones. Revenues from coffee and exports of illegal narcotics are crucial to the economy. Venezuela's major economic activity is the oil industry around Lake Maracaibo (*Lago de Maracaibo*). Sugar and bauxite are exported from Guyana and Suriname.

TRANSPORTATION NETWORK

🛣️	29,185 miles (46,996 km)
🛤️	1,795 miles (2,890 km)
🚉	1,729 miles (2,785 km)
〰️	17,947 miles (28,900 km)

Rivers are an important means of transportation in Colombia; many are extensively navigable. The Pan-American Highway runs through Colombia. In Venezuela, much infrastructure investment is linked to the oil industry.

Major industry and infrastructure
- chemicals
- finance
- food processing
- iron & steel
- narcotics
- mining
- oil
- oil refining
- pharmaceuticals
- textiles
- timber processing
- ■ capital cities
- ● major towns
- ✈ international airports
- — major roads
- major industrial areas

Vast oil reserves around Lake Maracaibo (*Lago de Maracaibo*) *form the focus of Venezuelan industry. Incomes from oil are used to invest in other industries and in the development of infrastructure.*

USING THE LAND

THE ANDEAN BASINS support cereals and potatoes. Livestock graze at higher altitudes and on the drier tropical grasslands known as the *llanos*; hardy goats are reared in scrubland areas. Grown at higher elevations, coffee is an important cash crop, as is cotton, sugar cane, bananas, citrus fruits, cocoa, and rice, farmed on the Caribbean lowlands. Coca is the most widely-grown narcotic plant, with heroin poppies grown in Colombia and marijuana in lowland areas throughout the region.

Land use and agricultural distribution
- cattle
- goats
- bananas
- cereals
- coffee
- cotton
- sugar cane
- ■ capital cities
- ● major towns
- pasture
- cropland
- forest
- wetlands
- mountain region

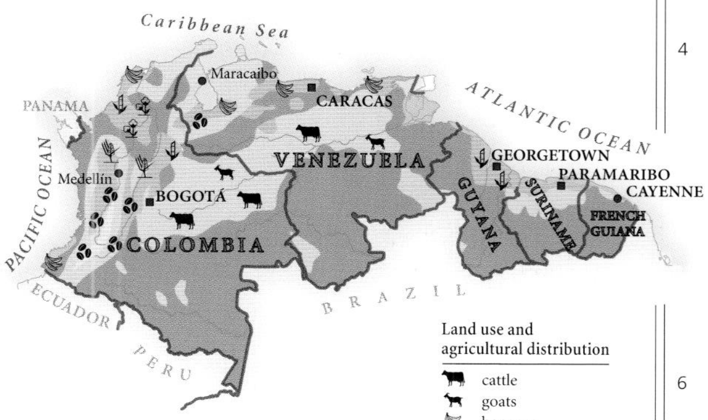

THE URBAN/RURAL POPULATION DIVIDE

urban 80% rural 20%

0 10 20 30 40 50 60 70 80 90 100

POPULATION DENSITY	TOTAL LAND AREA
56 people per sq mile (22 people per sq km)	1,111,317 sq miles (2,879,060 sq km)

The Sierra Nevada de Santa Marta is a granite massif which rises sharply from the Caribbean lowlands to snow-covered peaks, the tallest of which is 18,947 ft (5,775 m) high.

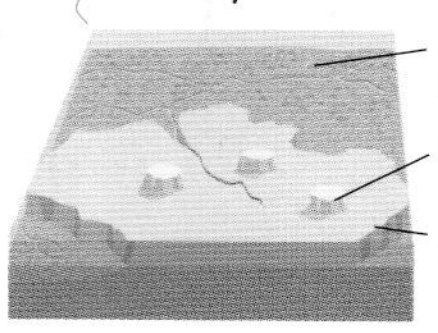

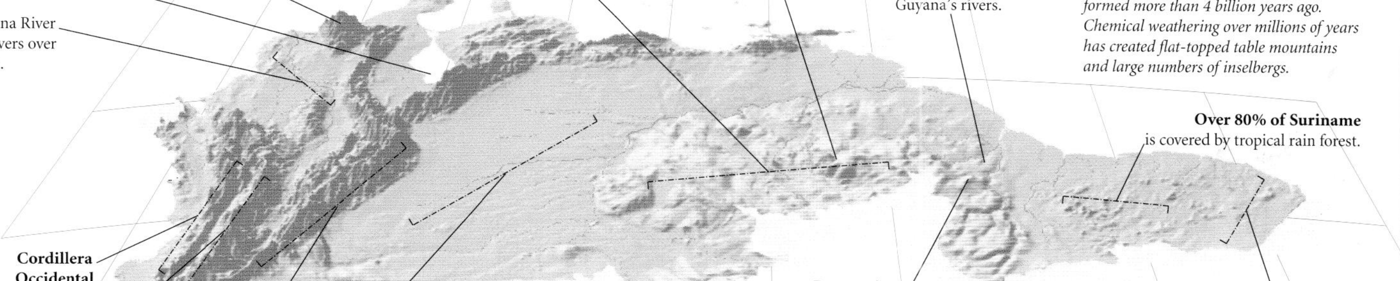

Lake Maracaibo (*Lago de Maracaibo*) is not a true lake but a shallow inlet of the Caribbean Sea. It is the main source of Venezuela's oil.

The drainage basin of the Magdalena River and the Cauca, its main tributary, covers over 20% of Colombia's total surface area.

In the Guiana Highlands, Venezuela's most remote region, the ancient crystalline rocks contain deposits of iron ore, gold, and diamonds.

Angel Falls (*Salto Ángel*), at 3,212 ft (979 m), is the world's highest waterfall.

Igneous intrusions into the crystalline plateau which forms most of central Guyana have led to the formation of the many rapids that characterize Guyana's rivers.

Guyana Shield
- Alluvial plains
- Inselbergs
- Table mountains

The Guyana Shield is one of the oldest land surfaces in the world – probably formed more than 4 billion years ago. Chemical weathering over millions of years has created flat-topped table mountains and large numbers of inselbergs.

Over 80% of Suriname is covered by tropical rain forest.

THE LANDSCAPE

AT ITS NORTHERNMOST REACHES, in western Colombia and Venezuela, the great Andean mountain chain splits into three distinct ranges: the Cordillera Oriental, Cordillera Central, and Cordillera Occidental, intercut by a complex series of lesser ranges and basins. The relief becomes lower toward the coast and the interior plains of the northern Amazon Basin, rising again into the tropical hills of the Guiana Highlands.

Cordillera Occidental

Cordillera Central

Cordillera Oriental

Colombia's eastern lowlands are known locally as *llanos,* meaning grasslands.

Potaru river

The Potaru River descends 741 ft (226 m) over a sandstone ledge at the Kaieteur Falls in Guyana.

Most of the land in French Guiana is low-lying; here, the rocks of the Guiana Highlands have been eroded by rivers flowing toward the sea.

Map labels

Caribbean Sea
PANAMA
Maracaibo · Valencia · CARACAS · Cumaná
VENEZUELA · Ciudad Guayana
Medellín · GEORGETOWN · PARAMARIBO · Cayenne
BOGOTÁ · GUYANA · SURINAME · FRENCH GUIANA
COLOMBIA
PACIFIC OCEAN · ATLANTIC OCEAN
ECUADOR · PERU · BRAZIL

N S E A
Isla Blanquilla
▶ 66
Isla de Margarita · Islas Los Testigos
Isla de Margarita · Juangriego · La Asunción
Boca de Pozo · Pampatar
NUEVA ESPARTA · Punta de Piedras · Puerto de Hierro
Cumaná · SUCRE · Carúpano · Río Caribe
Araya · Cariaco · Casanay · Irapa · Güiria
La Cruz · Guanta · Cumanacoa · Gulf of Paria
Barcelona · Cerro Tataracual 1145m
Puerto Píritu · Onoto · Quiriquire · The Serpent's Mouth
Aragua de Maturín · Carito · Punta Baja
Maturín
San Joaquín · San Mateo · Anaco · Caño Mánamo
Santa Rosa de Mata · Aguasay · Pedernales
La Horqueta · Temblador
MONAGAS
El Tigre · San José de Guanipa · Tucupita
San Tomé · Barrancas · DELTA AMACURO
ANZOÁTEGUI
Ciudad Guayana
Ciudad Bolívar · Soledad · Río Orinoco · Guayabones · Curiapo
Moitaco · Borbón · El Rao · Upata · Waini Point
Mapire · Ciudad Piar · El Palmar · Waini
BOLÍVAR · Embalse de Guri · Arakaka · Port Kaituma
La Paragua · Guasipati · Matthews Ridge · Charity
El Manteco · El Callao · Tumeremo · Spring Garden
Cerro Turagua 1838m · El Dorado · Kuracki · Essequibo Islands
El Casabe · Caño Negro · Aurora · GEORGETOWN
Canaima · Cuyuni River · Bartica · Georgetown
Cerro Venamo 1563m · New Amsterdam
Auyan Tebuy 2950m · Enachu Landing · Peters Mine · Rose Hall
Cerro Guaiquinima 2100m · Kamarang · Rockstone · Corriverton
Carapo · Uruyén · Imbaimadai · Wineperu · Nieuw Nickerie
Salto Ángel · Issano · Linden · Friendship
Santa María de Erebato · GUYANA · NICKERIE
Caruana de Montaña · Mount Roraima 2810m · Mazaruni River · Wageningen
Santa Elena de Uairén · Ayanganna Mountain 2042m · Ituni · CORONIE
Uonán · Potaru River · Mahdia · Berbice River
Pakaraima Mountains · Kaieteur Falls · Orealla · Wasjabo · Apoera
(Venezuela claims all of Guyana west of Essequibo river) · Glendor Mountains · Kaaimanston
Sarariña · Kurupukari · Kabalebo River
Catisimina · SURINAME
Rupununi River · SIPALIWINI
Lethem · Kanuku Mountains · Lucie River
Sierra Parima · Saurwaunawa · Jacobs Ladder Falls
Boca Mavaca · New River · Wilhelmina Gebergte
Horqueta Minas · Kuyuwini Landing · Juliana Top 1230m
Río Orinoco · Johi Village · Apetina
Sierra de Unturán · Acaraí Mountains · Tapanahoni River
Sierra Tapirapecó · (Claimed by Suriname) · Appikalo
Equator · (Claimed by Suriname) · Tumuc-Humac Mountains
BRAZIL

PARAMARIBO · Mana · Iracoubo · Sinnamary
SARAMACCA · WANICA · COMMEWIJNE
Groningen · Totness · Albina · St-Laurent-du-Maroni
Lelydorp · Onverwacht · Kourou
Nieuw Amsterdam · Paranam · St-Jean
Donderkamp · Kwakoegron · Herminadorp · CAYENNE
Brownsweg · Brokopondo · Citron · Cayenne · Rémire
Pokigron · Grand-Santi · Délices · Matoury
Hendrik Top 957m · Pokeeti · St-Elie · Régina
Tafelberg 1026m · Djoemoe · Boti-Pasi · Roura
FRENCH GUIANA (to France)
W.J. van Blommesteinmeer · Maripasoula · Saül
Alimimuni Piek 728m · Pédima · Sommet Tabulaire
Massif du Mitaraka 690m · Mont Saint-Marcel 635m · Camopi
Trois Sauts · L'Oyapok Fleuve · Baie de L'Oyapok
Îles du Salut · Île du Diable · Centre Spatial Guyanais
Pointe Béhague · Ouanary · St-Georges

TRINIDAD & TOBAGO

▼ 60

Western South America

Bolivia, Ecuador, Peru

The three states of Western South America share a similar geography and recent history. Dominated by the Inca empire until Spanish conquest in the 16th century, they achieved independence from Spain in the early 19th century. The precipitous terrain of the Andes presents severe difficulties for overland transportation and continues to be a barrier to national unity and stability. Although Ecuador is now a relatively stable democracy, the military is highly influential in Peru and Bolivia, while the drug trade and associated corruption discourages external aid and economic progress. Wealth and power are still largely concentrated in the hands of a small elite of families, who attained their position during the Spanish colonial period. Land rights and political recognition for the indigenous peoples are becoming increasingly important issues, particularly in Ecuador.

Ecuador's capital city, Quito, lies high in the Andes, nestling between snowcapped peaks. At 9,350 ft (2,850 m), Quito is the second highest capital in the world – La Paz in Bolivia is the highest.

Ecuadorean Administrative Regions

1. Carchi
2. Tungurahua
3. Bolívar
4. Chimborazo
5. Zamora Chinchipe

Map Key

Population

- above 5 million
- 1 million to 5 million
- 500,000 to 1 million
- 100,000 to 500,000
- 50,000 to 100,000
- 10,000 to 50,000
- below 10,000

Elevation

- 6000m / 19,686ft
- 4000m / 13,124ft
- 3000m / 9843ft
- 2000m / 6562ft
- 1000m / 3281ft
- 500m / 1640ft
- 250m / 820ft
- 100m / 328ft
- sea level

The Landscape

Bolivia, Peru, and Ecuador each possess a high Andean mountain region and an eastern region consisting of tropical lowlands and the Andean slope leading down to them. Toward the south of the region, the mountains widen to form the high plateau of the Altiplano. Peru and Ecuador also have fertile, lowland coastal plains. A wide variety of environments include *selva* (tropical rain forest), *montaña* (mountain forest), and grassland.

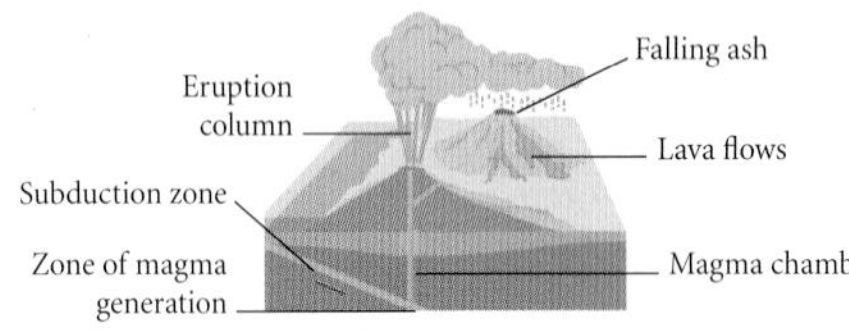

***There are many large** and active volcanoes in the Andes. Magma generated in the heart of the volcano erupts in a huge cloud of ash. Ash-fall deposits are common throughout the Andes and the rock produced is known as andesite. This is rapidly soaked by heavy rain, causing massive debris flows.*

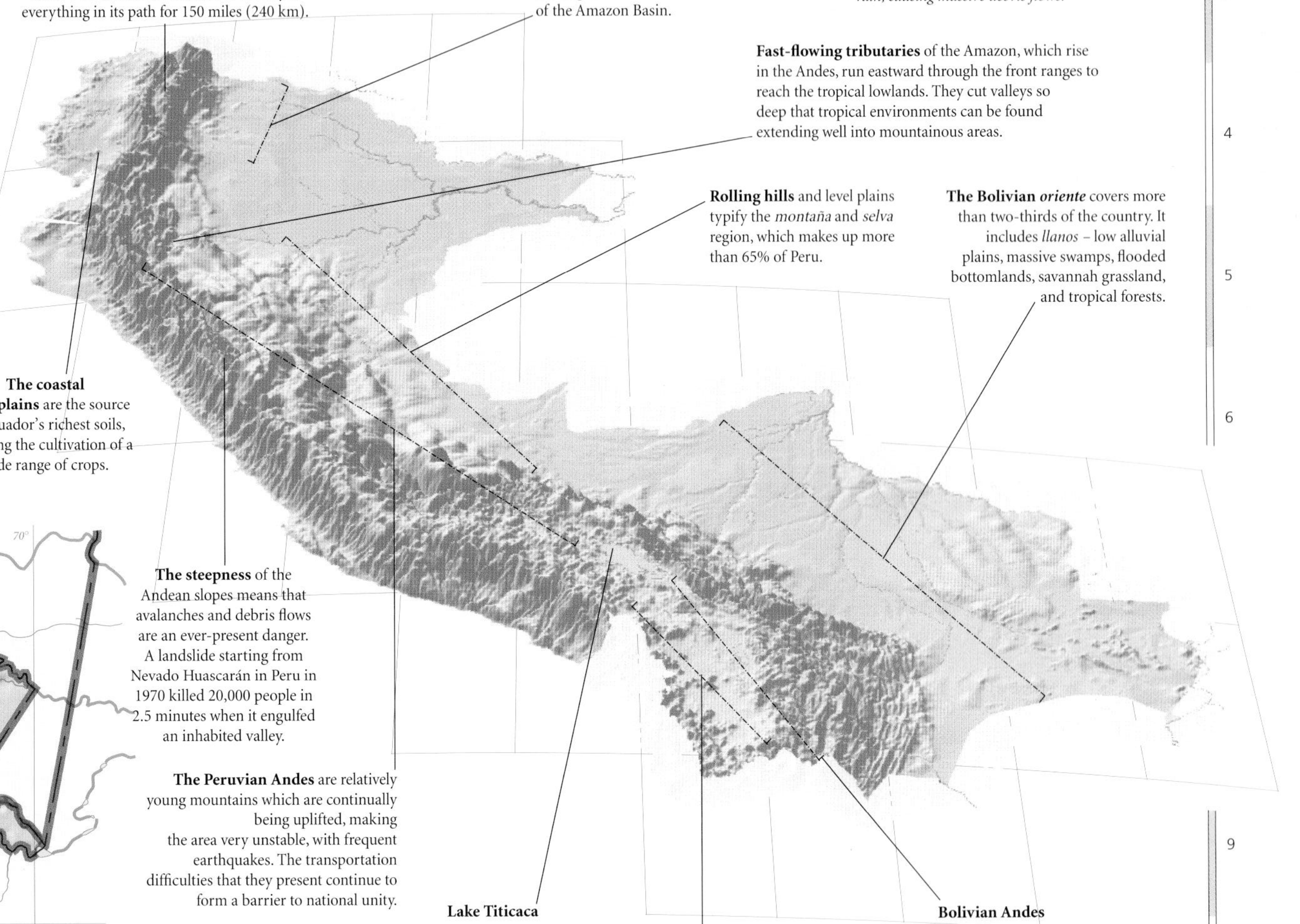

Cotopaxi is the world's highest active volcano, with a peak 19,347 ft (5,897 m) high. A massive eruption in 1877 caused a mudflow which destroyed everything in its path for 150 miles (240 km).

Much of eastern Ecuador is covered by the tropical rain forest of the Amazon Basin.

Fast-flowing tributaries of the Amazon, which rise in the Andes, run eastward through the front ranges to reach the tropical lowlands. They cut valleys so deep that tropical environments can be found extending well into mountainous areas.

Rolling hills and level plains typify the *montaña* and *selva* region, which makes up more than 65% of Peru.

The Bolivian *oriente* covers more than two-thirds of the country. It includes *llanos* – low alluvial plains, massive swamps, flooded bottomlands, savannah grassland, and tropical forests.

The coastal floodplains are the source of Ecuador's richest soils, enabling the cultivation of a wide range of crops.

The steepness of the Andean slopes means that avalanches and debris flows are an ever-present danger. A landslide starting from Nevado Huascarán in Peru in 1970 killed 20,000 people in 2.5 minutes when it engulfed an inhabited valley.

The Peruvian Andes are relatively young mountains which are continually being uplifted, making the area very unstable, with frequent earthquakes. The transportation difficulties that they present continue to form a barrier to national unity.

Lake Titicaca

***Lake Titicaca**, which forms part of the border between Peru and Bolivia, is the largest lake in South America and the highest significant body of water in the world at an altitude of 12,507 ft (3,812 m).*

The Altiplano is a flat, high plateau lying between the Cordillera Oriental and the Cordillera Occidental at a height of up to 12,500 ft (3,800 m). At its margins lie many spurs and alluvial fans.

Bolivian Andes

***Nevado de Illampu and Nevado de Ancohuma**, at 21,275 ft (6,485 m) and 21,490 ft (6,550 m) respectively, form Illampu, the highest mountain in the Bolivian Andes.*

Scale 1:7,750,000
(projection: Lambert Azimuthal Equal Area)

Km 0 25 50 100 150 200 250 300
0 25 50 100 150 200 250 300 Miles

***A colony of marine iguanas** basks on the rocks of Isla Fernandina in the Galapagos Islands. Charles Darwin's theory of evolution was inspired by the differences he found between the animal species on neighboring islands in the Galapagos.*

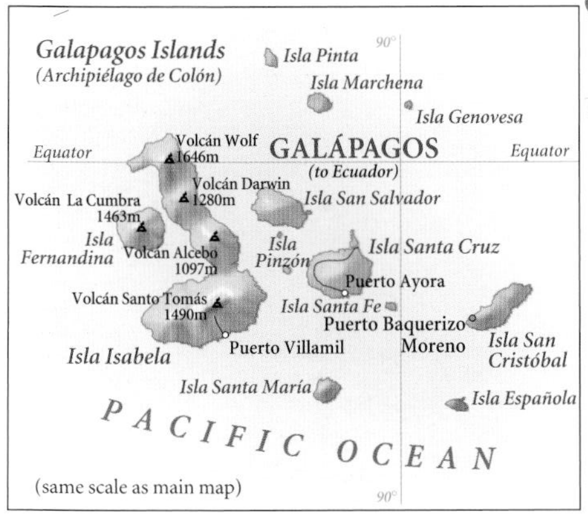

***The Galapagos Islands** are mainly composed of lava, with very little vegetation near to the coasts, although the wetter inland slopes are mantled with forest.*

***The ancient city of Machupicchu,** in the Peruvian Andes was built prior to the Inca period. Its impressive ruins reflect a culture which had developed a high degree of sophistication.*

Transportation & Industry

The mountain regions are rich in minerals including lead, copper, silver, gold, zinc, and tungsten, though high production and transportation costs have meant that they are expensive to extract and vulnerable to price collapses. Foreign debt remains a major burden, hampering industrial development. Manufacturing tends to be small-scale and concentrates on products for local needs, including textiles, food processing, and pharmaceuticals. Narcotics are an important, though illegal, export.

Major industry and infrastructure
- car manufacture
- chemicals
- engineering
- fish processing
- food processing
- iron & steel
- mining
- narcotics
- oil
- pharmaceuticals
- shipbuilding
- capital cities
- major towns
- international airports
- major roads
- major industrial areas

Transportation Network

50,274 miles (80,956 km)	1,860 miles (2,995 km)	3,940 miles (6,344 km)	14,966 miles (24,100 km)

A transcontinental highway is under construction to link Ilo, on Peru's Pacific coast, to Porto Esperança in Brazil, via Puerto Suárez in Bolivia. Establishing port facilities on the Pacific coast is crucial to landlocked Bolivia's further development.

***At Potosí in Bolivia,** silver has been mined for over 400 years.*

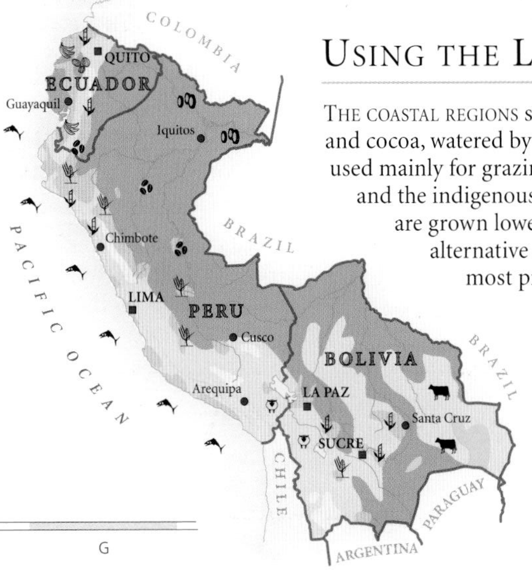

Land use and agricultural distribution
- cattle
- sheep
- bananas
- cereals
- cocoa
- coffee
- fishing
- rubber
- sugar cane
- capital cities
- major towns
- pasture
- cropland
- forest
- mountain region
- desert
- wetlands

Using the Land and Sea

The coastal regions support a variety of cash crops including rice, sugar cane, bananas, coffee, and cocoa, watered by rainfall or by irrigation schemes. The grasslands of the high *sierra* are used mainly for grazing a wide range of livestock; cattle and sheep are reared, along with pigs, and the indigenous llama and alpaca. Subsistence crops, especially potatoes and cereals, are grown lower down the mountain flanks. Despite government incentives to grow alternative crops, coca, used for cocaine, is the Bolivian and Peruvian *oriente's* most profitable commercial crop.

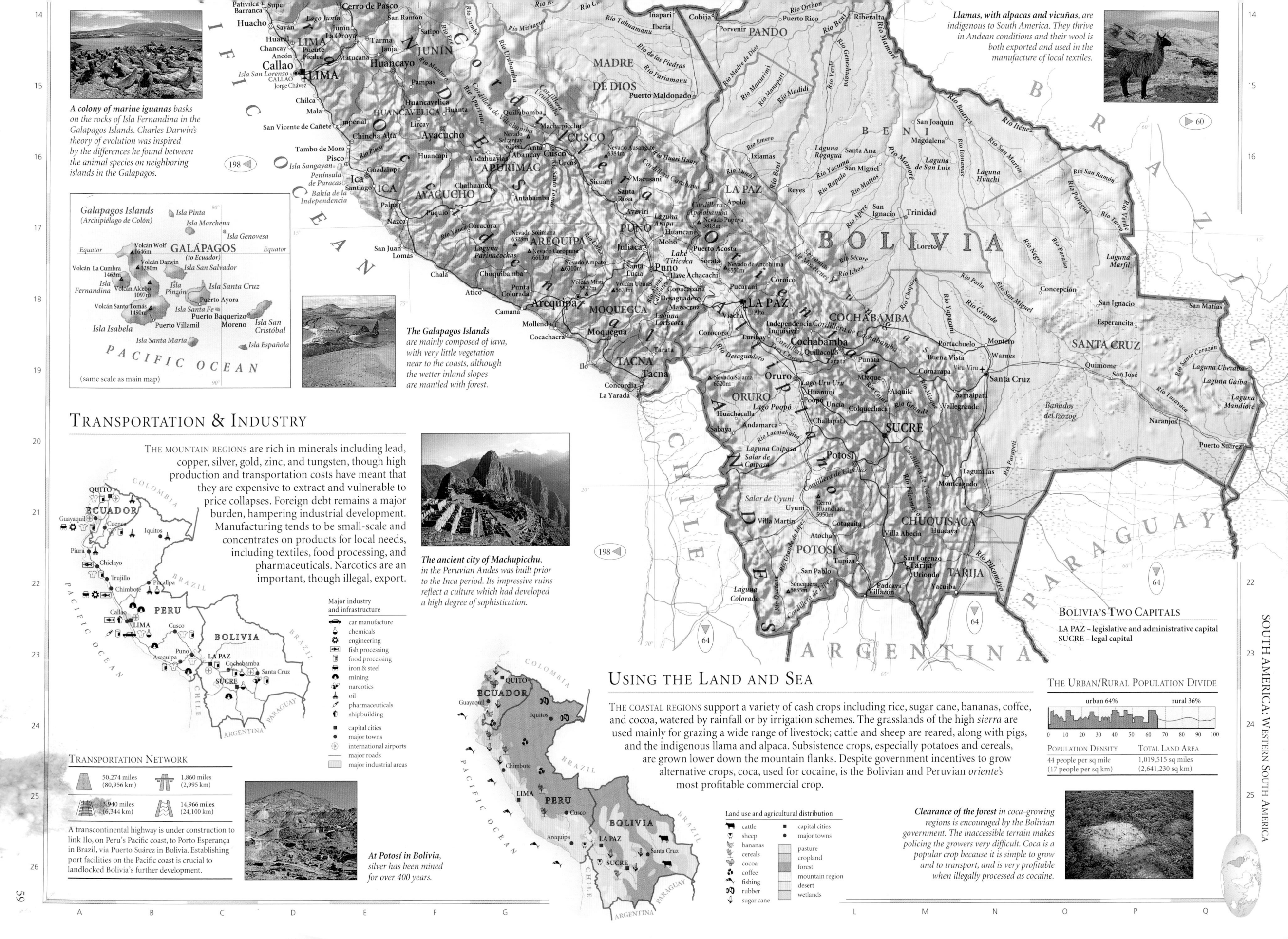

***Llamas, with alpacas and vicuñas,** are indigenous to South America. They thrive in Andean conditions and their wool is both exported and used in the manufacture of local textiles.*

Bolivia's Two Capitals

LA PAZ – legislative and administrative capital
SUCRE – legal capital

The Urban/Rural Population Divide

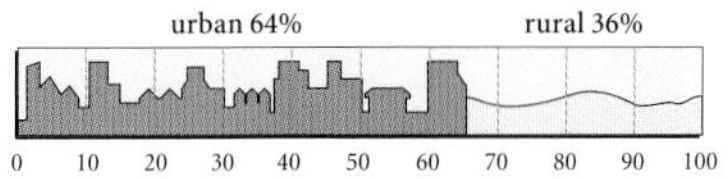

Population Density	Total Land Area
44 people per sq mile (17 people per sq km)	1,019,515 sq miles (2,641,230 sq km)

***Clearance of the forest** in coca-growing regions is encouraged by the Bolivian government. The inaccessible terrain makes policing the growers very difficult. Coca is a popular crop because it is simple to grow and to transport, and is very profitable when illegally processed as cocaine.*

BRAZIL

BRAZIL IS THE LARGEST COUNTRY in South America, with a population of over 165 million – greater than the combined total for the whole of the rest of the continent. The 26 states which make up the federal republic of Brazil are administered from the purpose-built capital, Brasília. Tropical rain forest, covering more than one-third of the country, contains rich natural resources, but great tracts are sacrificed to agriculture, industry and urban expansion on a daily basis. Most of Brazil's multiethnic population now live in cities, some of which are vast areas of urban sprawl; São Paulo is one of the world's biggest conurbations, with more than 17 million inhabitants. Although prosperity is a reality for some, many people still live in great poverty, and mounting foreign debts continue to damage Brazil's prospects of economic advancement.

USING THE LAND

BRAZIL HAS IMMENSE NATURAL RESOURCES, including minerals and hardwoods, many of which are found in the fragile rain forest. Brazil is the world's leading coffee grower and a major producer of livestock, sugar, and orange juice concentrate. Soybeans for animal feed, particularly for poultry feed, have become the country's most significant crop.

THE URBAN/RURAL POPULATION DIVIDE

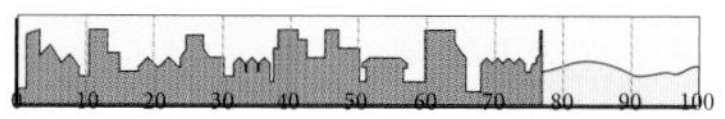

POPULATION DENSITY	TOTAL LAND AREA
50 people per sq mile (19 people per sq km)	3,286,472 sq miles (8,511,970 sq km)

The fecundity of parts of Brazil's rain forest results from exceptionally high levels of rainfall and the quantities of silt deposited by the Amazon River system.

THE LANDSCAPE

THE AMAZON BASIN, containing the largest area of tropical rain forest on Earth, covers nearly half of Brazil. It is bordered by two shield areas: in the south by the Brazilian Highlands, and in the north by the Guiana Highlands. The east coast is dominated by a great escarpment which runs for 1,600 miles (2,565 km).

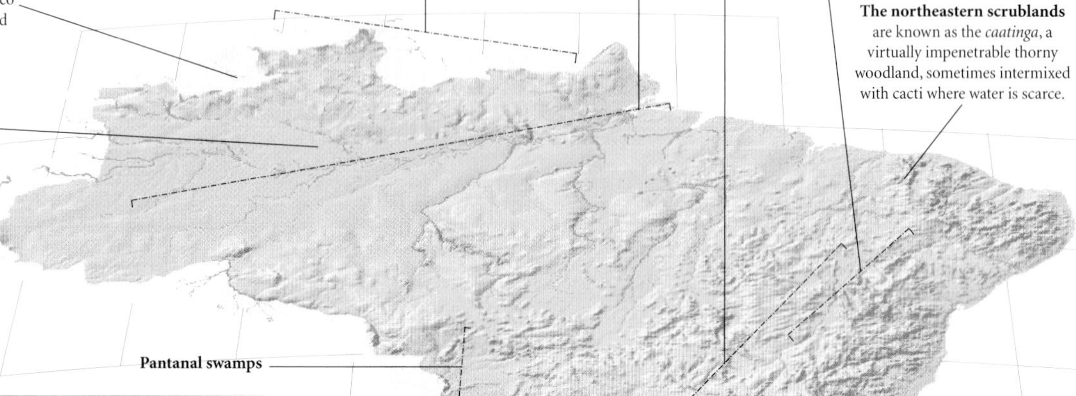

The Amazon Basin is the largest river basin in the world. The Amazon River and over a thousand tributaries drain an area of 2,375,000 sq miles (6,150,000 sq km) and carry one-fifth of the world's fresh water out to sea.

The ancient Brazilian Highlands have a varied topography. Their plateaus, hills, and deep valleys are bordered by highly-eroded mountains containing important mineral deposits. They are drained by three great river systems, the Amazon, the Paraguay–Paraná, and the São Francisco.

The São Francisco Basin has a climate unique in Brazil. Known as the "drought polygon," it has almost no rain during the dry season, leading to regular disastrous droughts.

The northeastern scrublands are known as the *caatinga*, a virtually impenetrable thorny woodland, sometimes intermixed with cacti where water is scarce.

Brazil's highest mountain is the Pico da Neblina which was only discovered in 1962. It is 9,888 ft (3,014 m) high.

The floodplains which border the Amazon River are made up of a variety of different features including shallow lakes and swamps, mangrove forests in the tidal delta area, and fertile levées on river banks and point bars.

The Pantanal region in the south of Brazil is an extension of the Gran Chaco plain. The swamps and marshes of this area are renowned for their beauty, and abundant and unique wildlife, including wildfowl and these caimans, a type of crocodile.

The Iguaçu River surges over the spectacular Iguaçu Falls (Saltos do Iguaçu) toward the Paraná River. Falls like these are increasingly under pressure from large-scale hydroelectric projects such as that at Itaipú.

The famous Sugar Loaf Mountain (*Pão de Açúcar*) which overlooks Rio de Janeiro is a fine example of a volcanic plug a domed core of solidified lava left after the slopes of the original volcano have eroded away.

Hillslope gullying

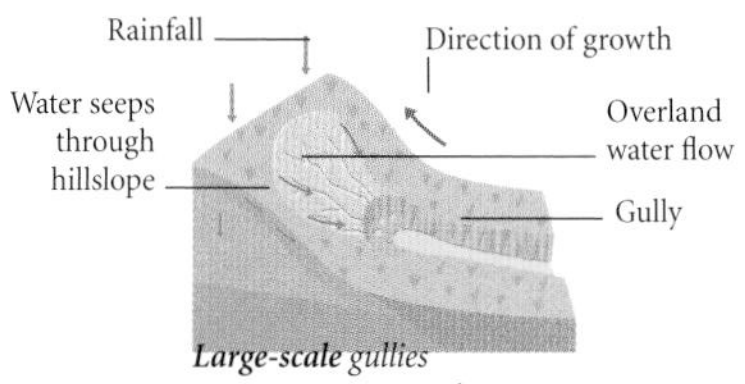

Large-scale gullies are common in Brazil, particularly on hillslopes from which vegetation has been removed. Gullies grow headwards (up the slope), aided by a combination of erosion through water seepage and rainwater runoff.

Deep natural harbors such as Baia de Guanabara were created where the steep slopes of the Serra da Mantiqueira plunge directly into the ocean.

MAP KEY

POPULATION	ELEVATION
above 5 million	3000m / 9843ft
1 million to 5 million	2000m / 6562ft
500,000 to 1 million	1000m / 3281ft
100,000 to 500,000	500m / 1640ft
50,000 to 100,000	250m / 820ft
10,000 to 50,000	100m / 328ft
below 10,000	sea level

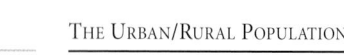

SCALE 1:12,750,000
(projection: Lambert Azimuthal Equal Area)

Km 0 25 50 100 150 200 250 300 350 400
Miles 0 25 50 100 150 200 250 300 350 400

TRANSPORTATION & INDUSTRY

BRAZILIAN INDUSTRY is diverse and well developed, in part as a result of past government incentives, including the prohibition of imports. Industries which have benefited include car manufacture, petrochemicals, and microelectronics. Textiles, clothing, and footwear are among Brazil's most successful exports. The country's services and tourism sectors are also expanding rapidly.

TRANSPORTATION NETWORK

	139,351 miles (224,397 km)
	3,105 miles (5,000 km)
	18,865 miles (30,379 km)
	31,050 miles (50,000 km)

Major industry and infrastructure

car manufacture	mining	capital cities
chemicals	oil	major towns
electronics	printing & publishing	international airports
finance	textiles	major roads
food processing	timber processing	major industrial areas
iron & steel	tourism	

An extensive new road network is being built to link Brazil's main centers. Investment is needed to update the antiquated railroad system. In São Paulo, the subway system is being extended to accommodate the expanding population.

***Brazil's urban population** has grown by over 6% per year since the mid-1970s – at current population levels a rate of nearly 6 million people annually. In Rio de Janeiro prosperous neighborhoods exist alongside over 450 shantytowns or favelas, some of which house as many as 250,000 people.*

***A gaucho** in traditional costume herds beef cattle on the grasslands of the Rio Grande do Sul in southern Brazil.*

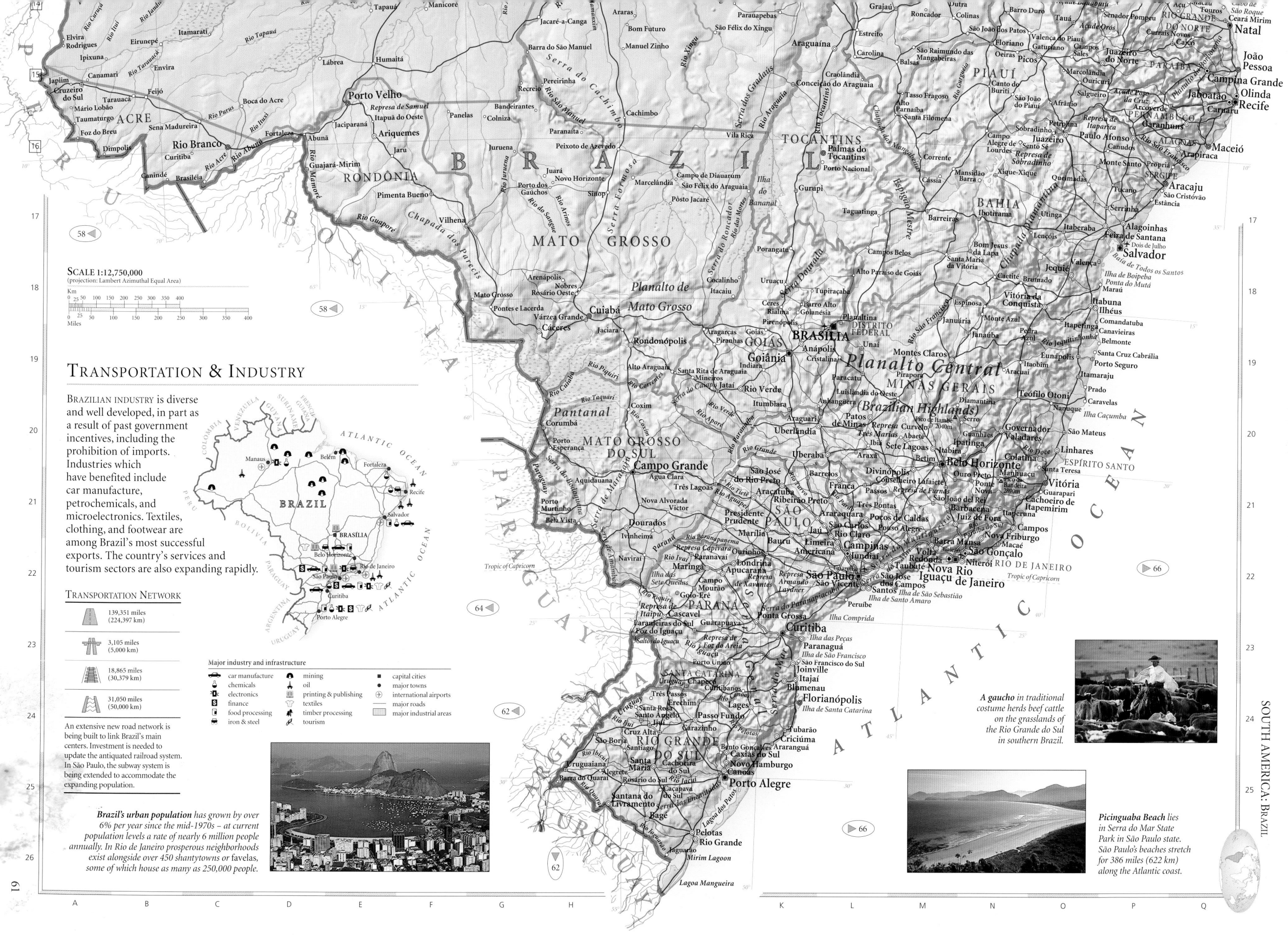

***Picinguaba Beach** lies in Serra do Mar State Park in São Paulo state. São Paulo's beaches stretch for 386 miles (622 km) along the Atlantic coast.*

EASTERN SOUTH AMERICA

URUGUAY, NORTHEAST ARGENTINA, SOUTHEAST BRAZIL

THE VAST CONURBATIONS of Rio de Janeiro, São Paulo, and Buenos Aires form the core of South America's highly-urbanized eastern region. São Paulo state, with almost 35 million inhabitants, is among the world's 20 most powerful economies, and São Paulo is the fastest growing city on the continent. Rio de Janeiro and Buenos Aires, transformed in the last hundred years from port cities to great metropolitan areas each with more than 10 million inhabitants, typify the unstructured growth and wealth disparities of South America's great cities. In Uruguay, over half of the population lives in the capital, Montevideo, which faces Buenos Aires across the Plate River (*Rio de la Plata*). Immigration from the countryside has created severe pressure on the urban infrastructure, particularly on available housing, leading to a profusion of crowded shanty settlements (*favelas or barrios*).

USING THE LAND

MOST OF URUGUAY and the Pampas of northern Argentina are devoted to the rearing of livestock, especially cattle and sheep, which are central to both countries' economies. Soybeans, first produced in Brazil's Rio Grande do Sul, are now more widely grown for large-scale export, as are cereals, sugar cane, and grapes. Subsistence crops, including potatoes, corn and sugar beets, are grown on the remaining arable land.

Land use and agricultural distribution

- cattle
- sheep
- cereals
- coffee
- fruit
- soybeans
- sugar cane
- capital cities
- major towns

- pasture
- cropland
- forest
- wetlands
- barren land

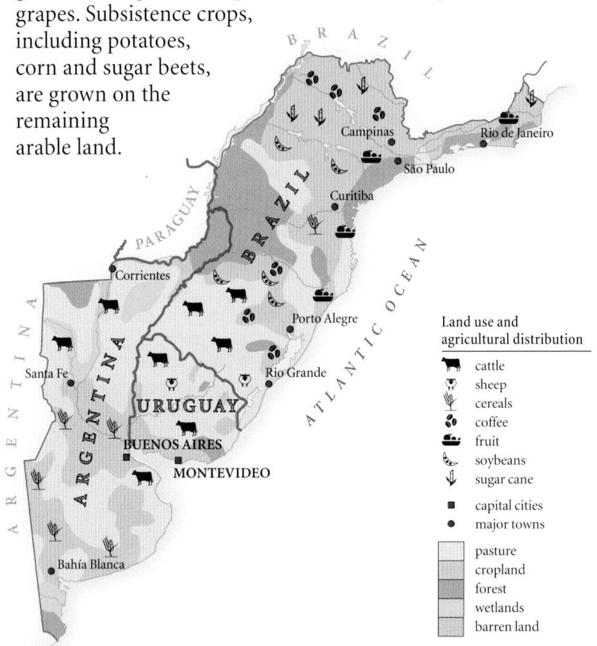

The rolling grasslands of Uruguay are ideally suited to the rearing of cattle, which are concentrated in great herds throughout the region.

TRANSPORTATION & INDUSTRY

SOUTHEAST BRAZIL IS HOME TO MUCH of the important motor and capital goods industry, largely based around São Paulo; iron and steel production is also concentrated in this region. Uruguay's economy continues to be based mainly on the export of livestock products including meat and leather goods. Buenos Aires is Argentina's chief port, and the region has a varied and sophisticated economic base including service-based industries such as finance and publishing, as well as primary processing.

Major industry and infrastructure

- car manufacture
- chemicals
- engineering
- finance
- food processing
- iron & steel
- meat processing
- printing & publishing
- shipbuilding
- textiles
- timber processing
- capital cities
- major towns
- international airports
- major roads
- major industrial areas

MAP KEY

POPULATION
- above 5 million
- 1 million to 5 million
- 500,000 to 1 million
- 100,000 to 500,000
- 50,000 to 100,000
- 10,000 to 50,000
- below 10,000

ELEVATION
- 2000m / 6562ft
- 1000m / 3281ft
- 500m / 1640ft
- 250m / 820ft
- 100m / 328ft
- sea level

SCALE 1: 6,250,000
(projection: Lambert Azimuthal Equal Area)

Soybeans are harvested, pressed, and processed into soycake, which is used as animal feed. The cake is fed mainly to chickens on large-scale factory farms, and the growth in soy production has been an important factor in the expansion of the Brazilian poultry trade.

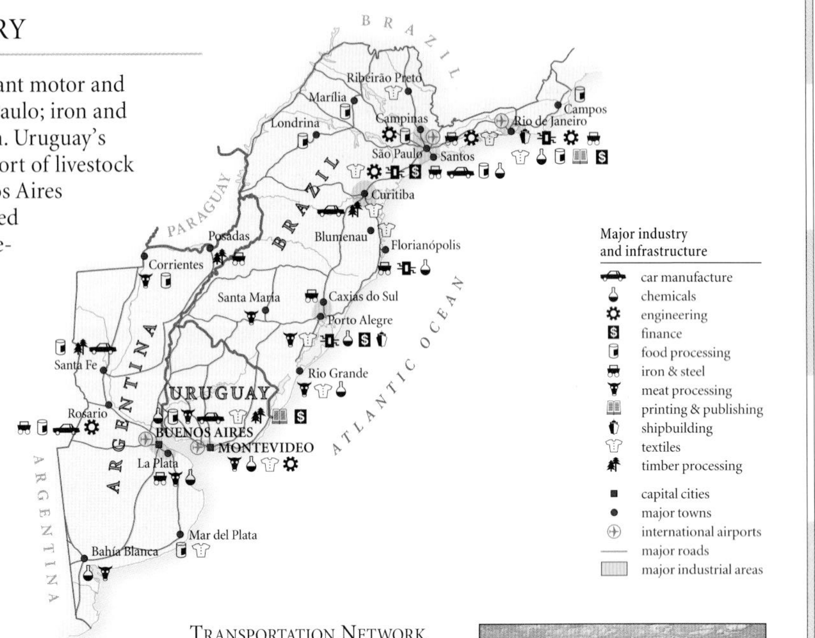

TRANSPORTATION NETWORK

Throughout the region, road networks need to be expanded to cope with urban development. Plans are underway to build a bridge over the Plate River (*Rio de la Plata*) to link Colonia and Buenos Aires.

The Itaipú dam on the Paraná River is one of the largest hydroelectric projects in the world, jointly financed by Brazil and Paraguay.

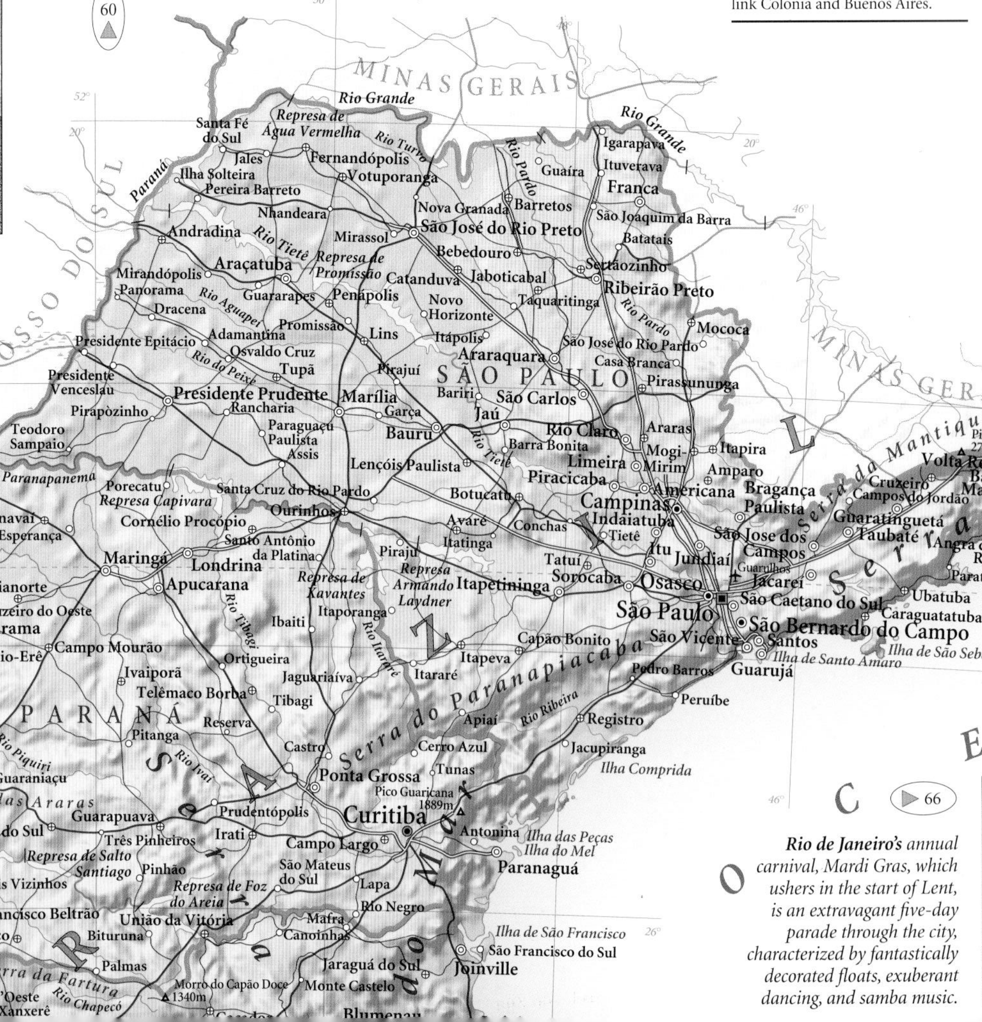

Rio de Janeiro's annual carnival, Mardi Gras, which ushers in the start of Lent, is an extravagant five-day parade through the city, characterized by fantastically decorated floats, exuberant dancing, and samba music.

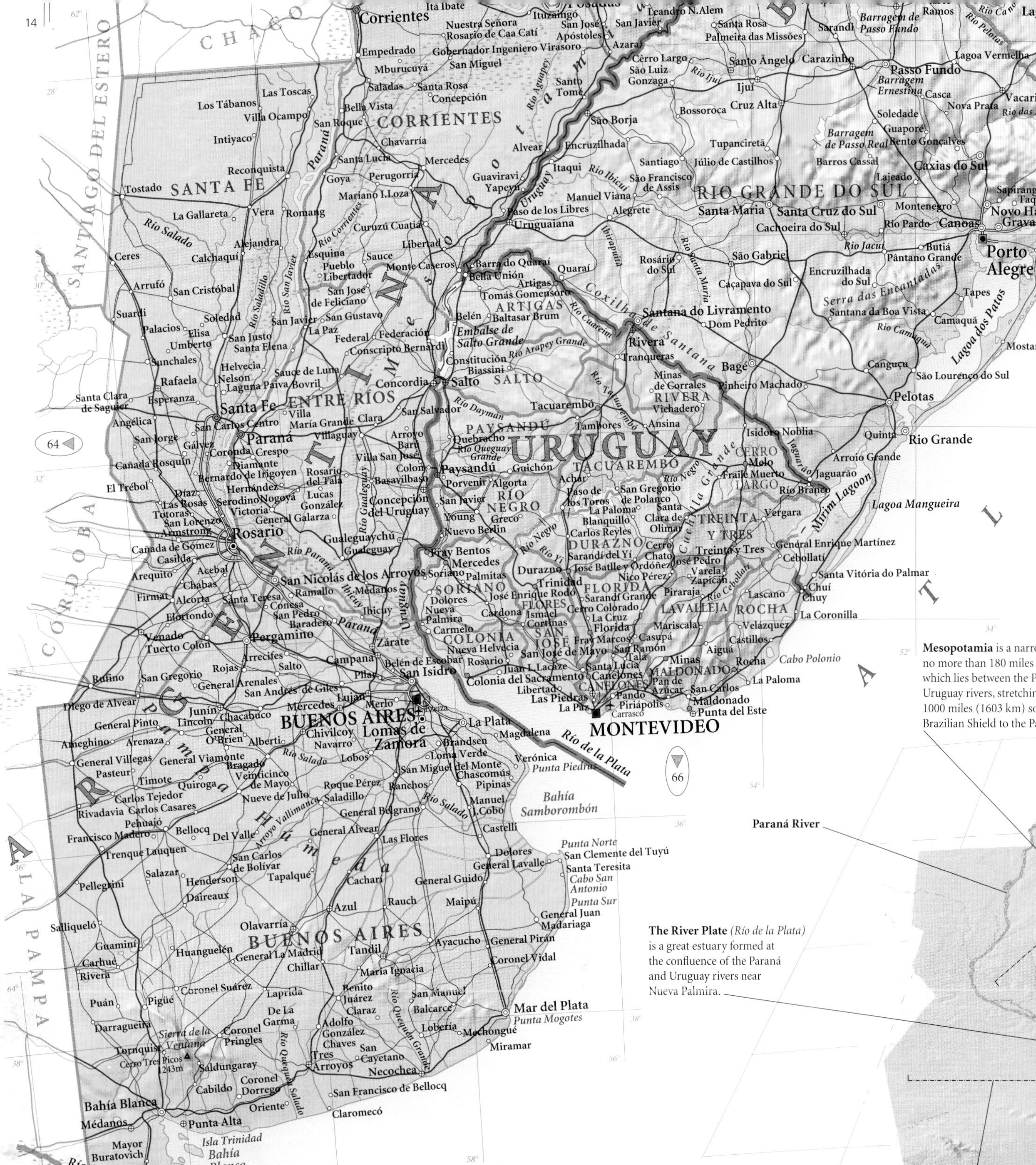

The Landscape

The southern reaches of the Brazilian Highlands follow the Atlantic coast to form low, rolling hills in the northeast of Uruguay. Much of South America's mid-eastern region and all of Uruguay has a gentle relief with land rarely rising above 300 ft (100 m). Argentina's northeast comprises two main regions: a long, narrow lowland known as Mesopotamia; and part of the Pampas grasslands.

***In 1900, Buenos Aires** was a modest port city with a population of less than 1 million. Today, more than 14 million people live in the city and its environs.*

***Tall lines** of palm trees edge the savannah landscape of Mesopotamia in northeastern Argentina.*

Tracing the edge of São Paulo state, the Paraná River drains the Brazilian Highlands, finally reaching the sea at the Plate River (*Río de la Plata*). Along with the Paraguay River, it is at the center of a controversial scheme to turn the largely unnavigable route into a great shipping canal.

In winter, polar air masses and the cyclonic storms associated with them, can bring heavy rain, frosts, and even snow, as far north as São Paulo.

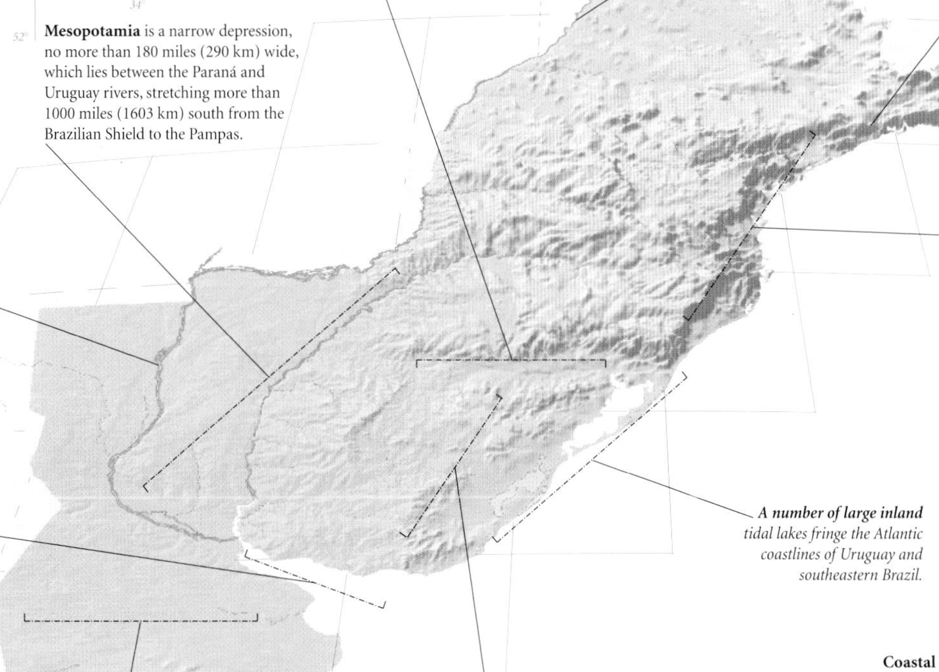

The state of Rio Grande do Sul contains some of Brazil's most fertile soils. The weathered rocks produce *terra rossa*, a reddish-purple soil renowned for the rich coffee it produces.

Mesopotamia is a narrow depression, no more than 180 miles (290 km) wide, which lies between the Paraná and Uruguay rivers, stretching more than 1000 miles (1603 km) south from the Brazilian Shield to the Pampas.

The Serra do Mar runs along the Atlantic coast toward Porto Alegre. South of this, the land slopes away to become lower and more level in Uruguay.

Paraná River

The River Plate (*Río de la Plata*) is a great estuary formed at the confluence of the Paraná and Uruguay rivers near Nueva Palmira.

***A number of large inland** tidal lakes fringe the Atlantic coastlines of Uruguay and southeastern Brazil.*

Coastal lagoons

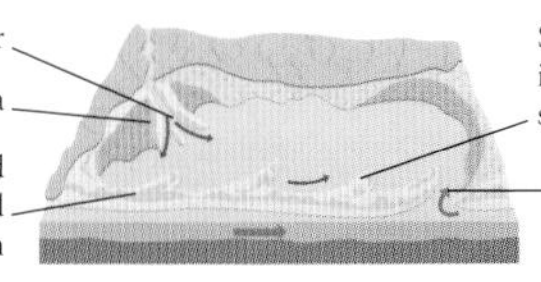

***The Atlantic coast of Uruguay** and southern Brazil has many large lagoons. Long-term lagoons are formed when sea levels change; 6,000 years ago, the sea level near Buenos Aires was 6.5 ft (2 m) higher than it is today. More temporary lagoons are enclosed by spits and sandbars, created by the drifting of sand and sediment in parallel with the shoreline.*

***Montevideo** became the capital of Uruguay following independence in 1828. The focus for Uruguayan industry and trade, it is also a popular destination for tourists from other South American countries.*

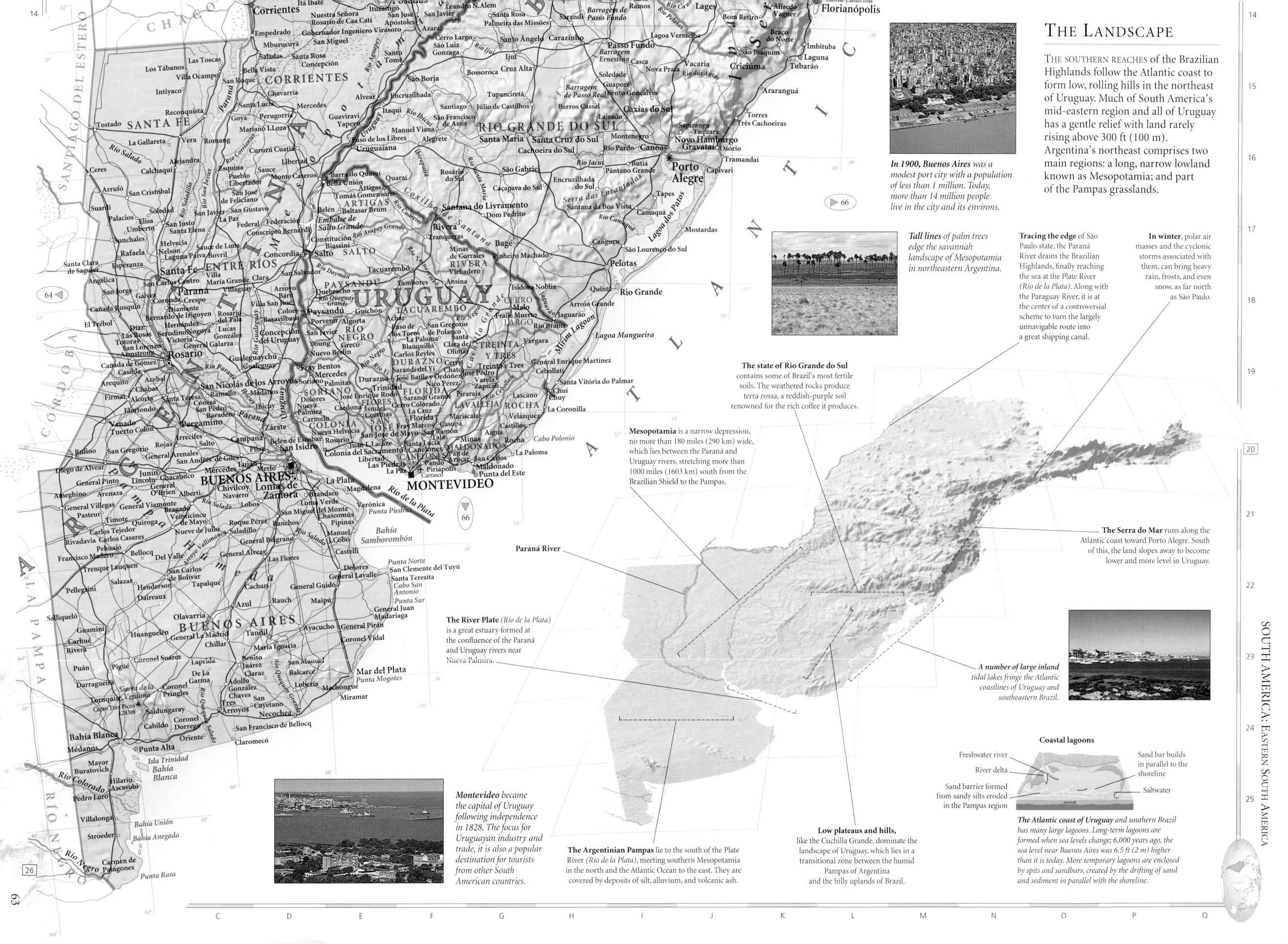

The Argentinian Pampas lie to the south of the Plate River (*Río de la Plata*), meeting southern Mesopotamia in the north and the Atlantic Ocean to the east. They are covered by deposits of silt, alluvium, and volcanic ash.

Low plateaus and hills, like the Cuchilla Grande, dominate the landscape of Uruguay, which lies in a transitional zone between the humid Pampas of Argentina and the hilly uplands of Brazil.

SOUTHERN SOUTH AMERICA

ARGENTINA, CHILE, PARAGUAY

SOUTH AMERICA'S CONE-SHAPED SOUTHERN REGION is shared by Argentina and Chile, two overwhelmingly urbanized nations whose populations live mainly in or around the capital cities, Buenos Aires and Santiago. The people are largely *mestizo* or of European origin; in the early 20th century Argentina absorbed waves of new European immigrants, many from Italy and Germany. Paraguay is far less urbanized than its neighbors, with a homogeneous population of mixed Spanish and Guaraní origin, who retain their Indian roots through the Guaraní language. Though most Paraguayans live in the southeast, near Asunción, the indigenous Indians live in the sparsely populated Gran Chaco. The Gran Chaco is also home to some of Argentina's minority indigenous peoples, who otherwise live mainly in Andean regions. Chile's estimated 800,000 Mapauche Indians live almost exclusively in the south.

TRANSPORTATION & INDUSTRY

FOOD PROCESSING AND AGRICULTURAL EXPORTS remain a fundamental part of Argentina's economy. The growth of manufacturing is regularly hampered by hyper-inflation and massive foreign debts. The world's most important copper-producer and one of the top ten gold producers, Chile also has a thriving wine and grape industry. Most Paraguayan exports involve primary processing, although domestic goods are produced for home markets.

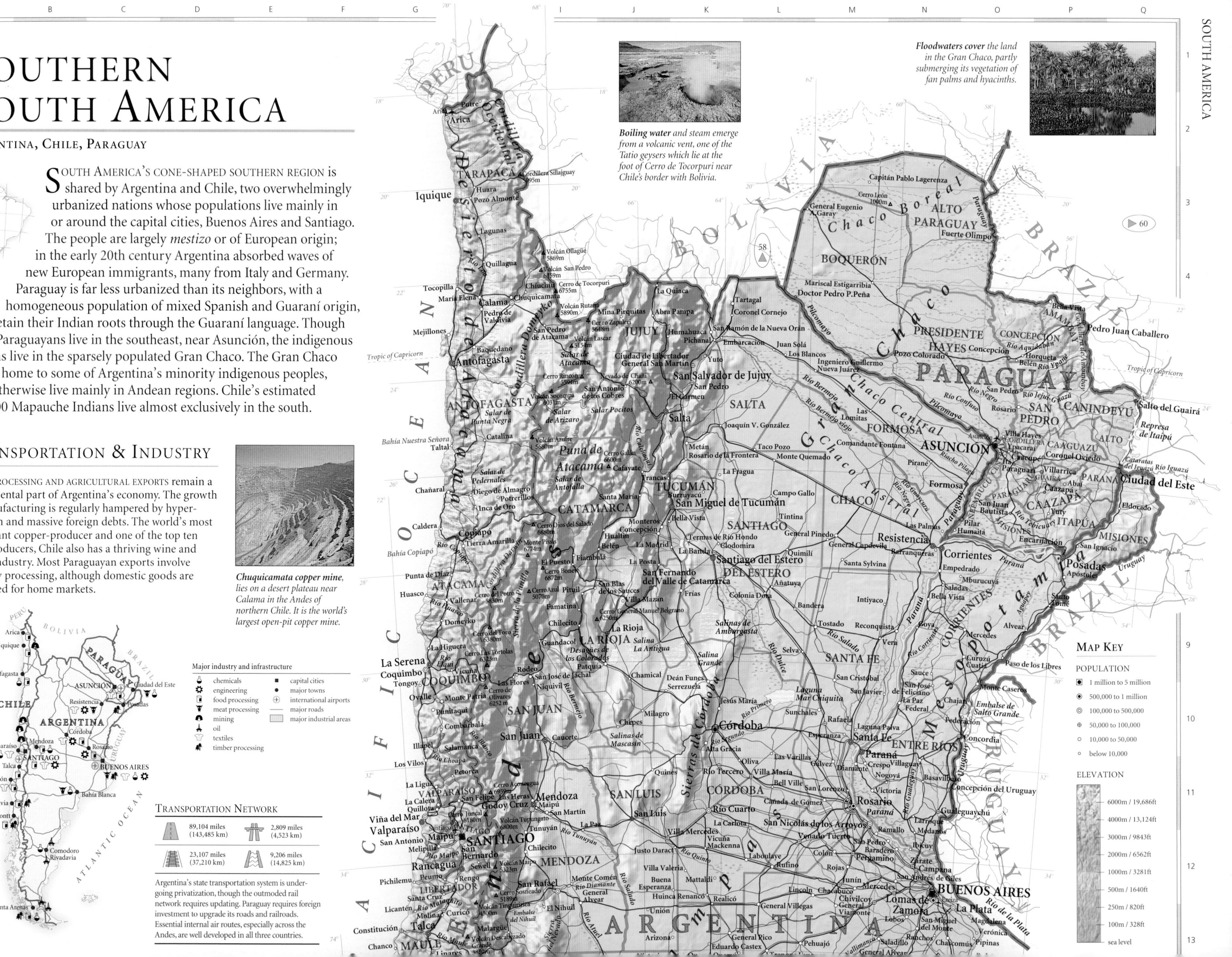

***Chuquicamata copper mine**, lies on a desert plateau near Calama in the Andes of northern Chile. It is the world's largest open-pit copper mine.*

Major industry and infrastructure

- chemicals
- engineering
- food processing
- meat processing
- mining
- oil
- textiles
- timber processing
- capital cities
- major towns
- international airports
- major roads
- major industrial areas

TRANSPORTATION NETWORK

89,104 miles (143,485 km)	2,809 miles (4,523 km)
23,107 miles (37,210 km)	9,206 miles (14,825 km)

Argentina's state transportation system is undergoing privatization, though the outmoded rail network requires updating. Paraguay requires foreign investment to upgrade its roads and railroads. Essential internal air routes, especially across the Andes, are well developed in all three countries.

***Boiling water** and steam emerge from a volcanic vent, one of the Tatio geysers which lie at the foot of Cerro de Tocorpuri near Chile's border with Bolivia.*

***Floodwaters cover** the land in the Gran Chaco, partly submerging its vegetation of fan palms and hyacinths.*

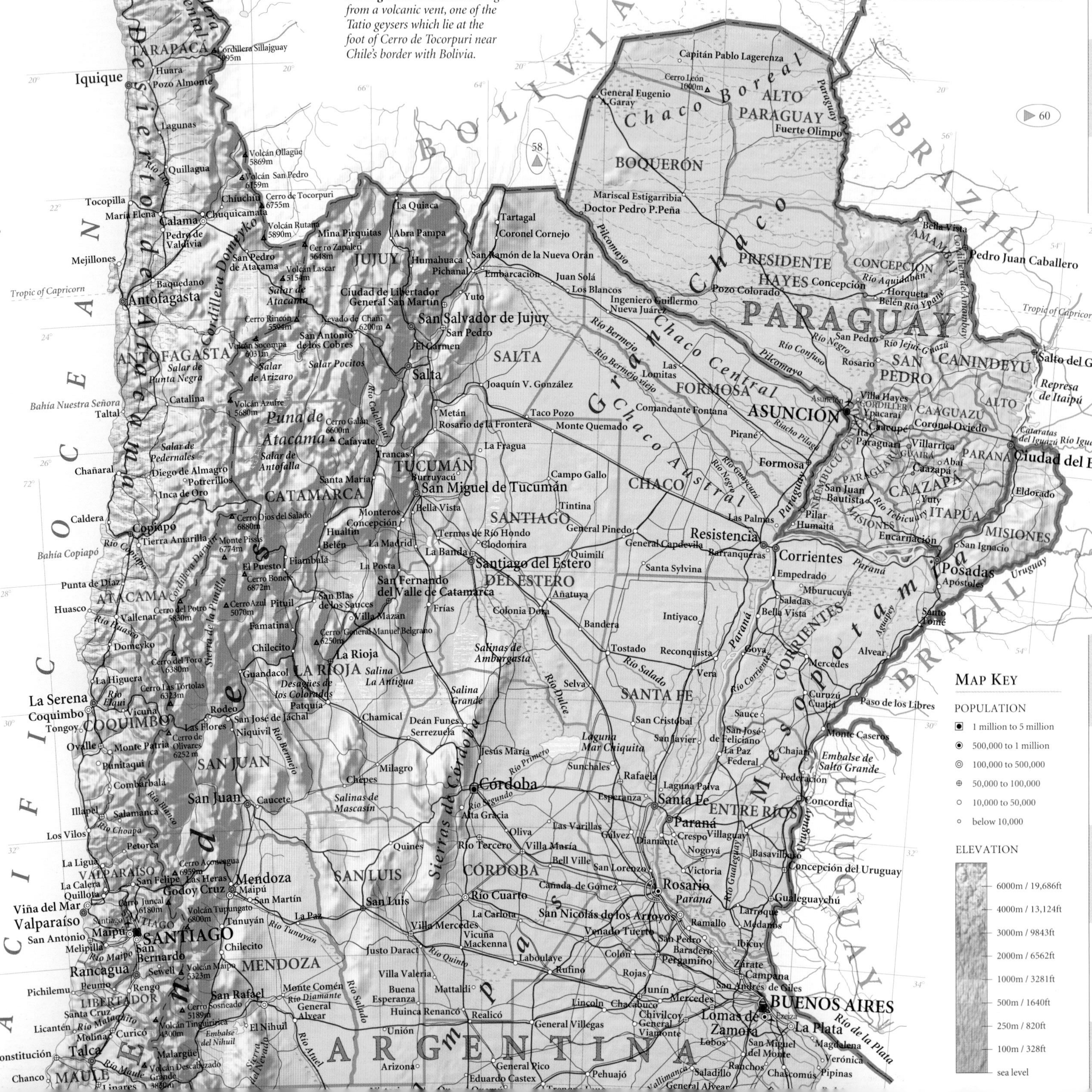

▶ 60
58 ▲

The Landscape

The Andes run from north to south, forming a precipitous natural border between Chile and Argentina. East of the Andes are the scrublands of the Gran Chaco and the plains of the Pampas, which extend northward toward Paraguay. In the far southwest, Chile's indented Pacific coastline has many features typical of areas which have been affected by glaciation.

The Atacama Desert (Desierto de Atacama) *in Chile is one of the driest places on Earth where some areas have never recorded any rain. It contains a number of salt lakes.*

Landlocked Paraguay relies on its river system for access to the sea and to produce hydroelectric power. The most important river system is the Paraguay–Paraná which provides links into neighboring countries including Brazil, Uruguay, and Argentina.

The Gran Chaco combines poor drainage, extremely hot temperatures and thorn-infested scrub to make it one of South America's most inhospitable regions.

Most of the highest mountains in Chile's northern Andes are volcanoes like Volcán Lascar and Volcán Rutana.

Cerro Aconcagua in the central Andes is the tallest mountain in the whole chain, rising to 22,834 ft (6,959 m).

Alluvial deposits from the many rivers in central Chile have created rich soils, ideal for a wide range of agriculture.

The Pampas derive their name from an Indian word meaning flat surface. The dry western region is largely desert, whereas the east is well-watered, supporting temperate grasses.

Patagonia divides into two zones, with the Andes in the west, and the lower main plateau, extending east toward the Atlantic. It is a desolate area with climatic extremes; dark lava fields scattered with light bunchgrass give a "leopard skin" effect to the landscape.

The Patagonian ice sheet is the world's third largest ice field, covering 6,560 sq miles (17,000 sq km). Patagonia also contains many typical features from past glaciations. These include glacial lakes, U-shaped valleys, fjords, and deep-cut channels.

Cape Horn is the most southerly point of South America. The severity of the "Roaring Forties" winds makes the Horn one of the world's most treacherous shipping regions.

The Andean mountain system, *which forms Argentina's western border, was created by folding and faulting, following the convergence of the Nazca and South American tectonic plates.*

Argentinian Pampas

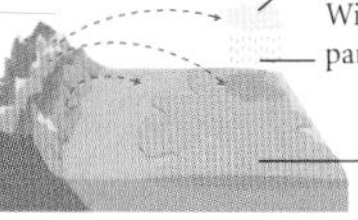

A thick, fertile layer *of loess lies in the basin underlying the Argentinian Pampas. It has been laid down following successive periods of glaciation. The minute loess particles are transported as dust and deposited by a downward air motion, or following rainfall.*

Great blocks of ice *break away from the jagged blue peaks of these ice mountains to form icebergs off the coast of Patagonia, Argentina's most southerly region.*

Using the Land and Sea

The rich plains of the Pampas support massive herds of cattle, producing meat, milk, and hides essential to the domestic and export markets of both Argentina and Paraguay. Wheat and fruit are Argentina's other major agricultural products. A wide range of soft fruits, citrus fruits, and more specialized crops such as walnuts, and grapes for wine and the table, are grown in Chile's fertile Central Valley, while the landscape to the south is dominated by forestry, mainly growing commercial radiata pine. Paraguay is self-sufficient in wheat and other staples. Cotton, coffee, tobacco, and oil sources such as soybeans, are the major export crops.

The Urban/Rural Population Divide

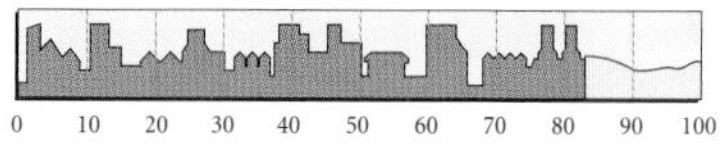

Population Density	Total Land Area
37 people per sq mile (14 people per sq km)	1,498,757 sq miles (3,882,790 sq km)

Scale 1:8,750,000
(projection: Lambert Azimuthal Equal Area)
Km 0 25 50 100 150 200
Miles 0 25 50 100 150 200

Charred tree stumps *surround a cattle enclosure on the island of Tierra del Fuego in southern Argentina. Forest clearance to provide grazing land for cattle is of major environmental concern.*

The Atlantic Ocean

The Atlantic is the youngest of the world's oceans, formed about 180 million years ago when the landmasses of the eastern and western hemispheres separated. Its underwater topography is dominated by the Mid-Atlantic Ridge, a huge mountain system running north to south along the center of the ocean. Although most of the ridge's peaks lie below the sea, some emerge as volcanic islands, like Iceland and the Azores. The Atlantic contains a wealth of resources, including substantial oil and gas reserves and rich fishing grounds. Until the 1950s, the north Atlantic was the world's busiest shipping route; cheaper air transportation and alternative routes have shifted patterns of world trade.

Surtsey near Iceland, lies on the Mid-Atlantic Ridge. The island was formed in 1963 following a volcanic eruption caused by sea-floor spreading.

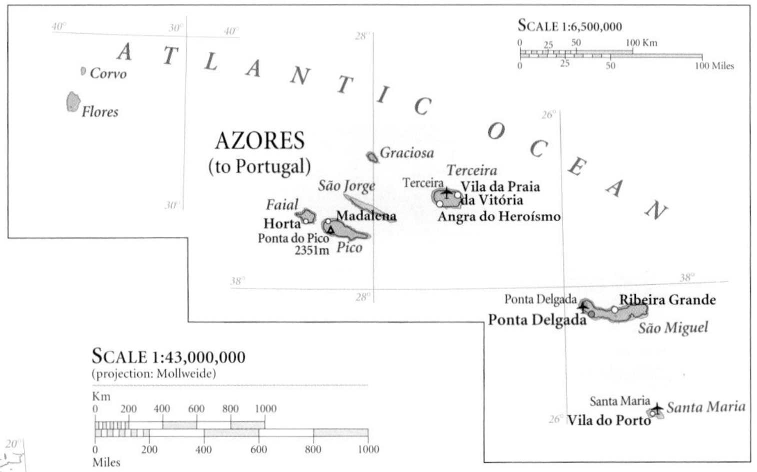

Resources

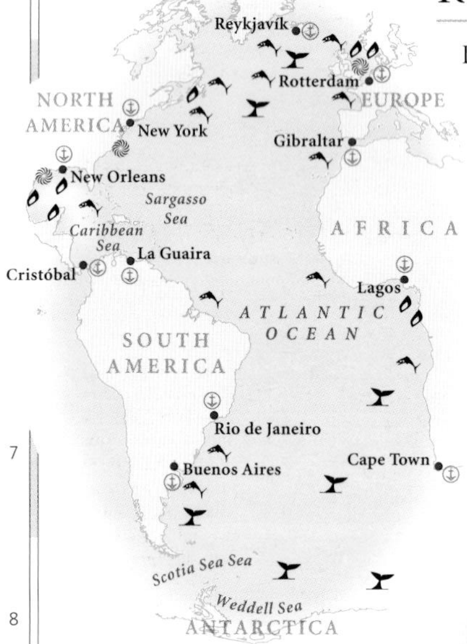

Development of the oil and gas reserves in the Atlantic began in the 1940s around the Gulf of Mexico. Since then other areas have been exploited, including the North Sea, the west coast of Africa and the area east of Newfoundland and Nova Scotia. There is also extensive mining of sand, gravel, and shell deposits by the US and UK. For centuries, the north Atlantic's fishing grounds have been utilized more heavily than other oceans, leading to a serious decline in many fish stocks.

Fishing in the seas around northwestern Europe dates back over 1,500 years. The high nutrient content of the seas makes them ideal breeding grounds for many species of fish.

On January 5 1993, the oil tanker Braer ran aground in the Shetland Islands, spilling 83,660 tons (85,000 tonnes) of light crude oil into the ocean, devastating the local marine ecosystem.

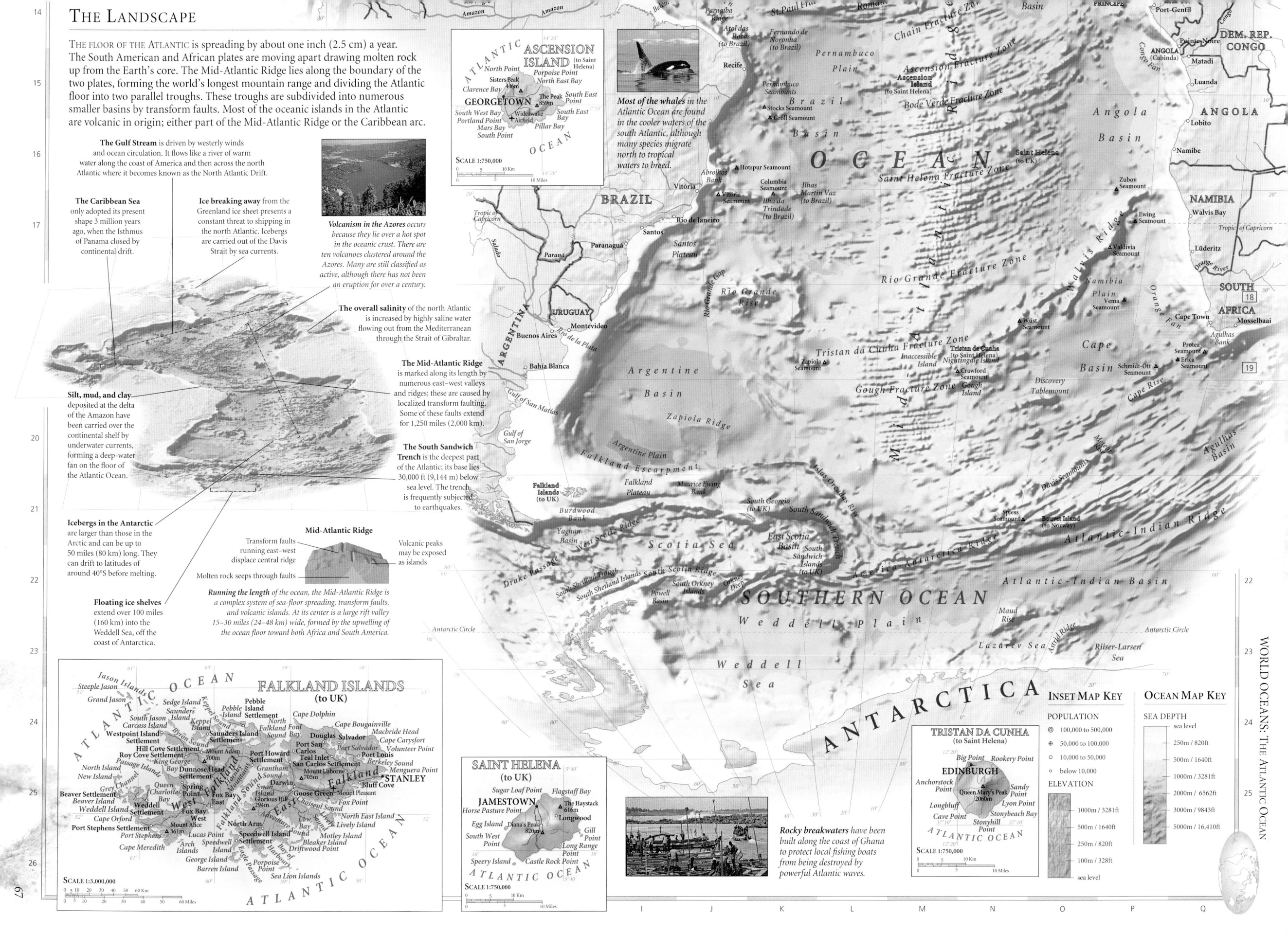

THE LANDSCAPE

THE FLOOR OF THE ATLANTIC is spreading by about one inch (2.5 cm) a year. The South American and African plates are moving apart drawing molten rock up from the Earth's core. The Mid-Atlantic Ridge lies along the boundary of the two plates, forming the world's longest mountain range and dividing the Atlantic floor into two parallel troughs. These troughs are subdivided into numerous smaller basins by transform faults. Most of the oceanic islands in the Atlantic are volcanic in origin; either part of the Mid-Atlantic Ridge or the Caribbean arc.

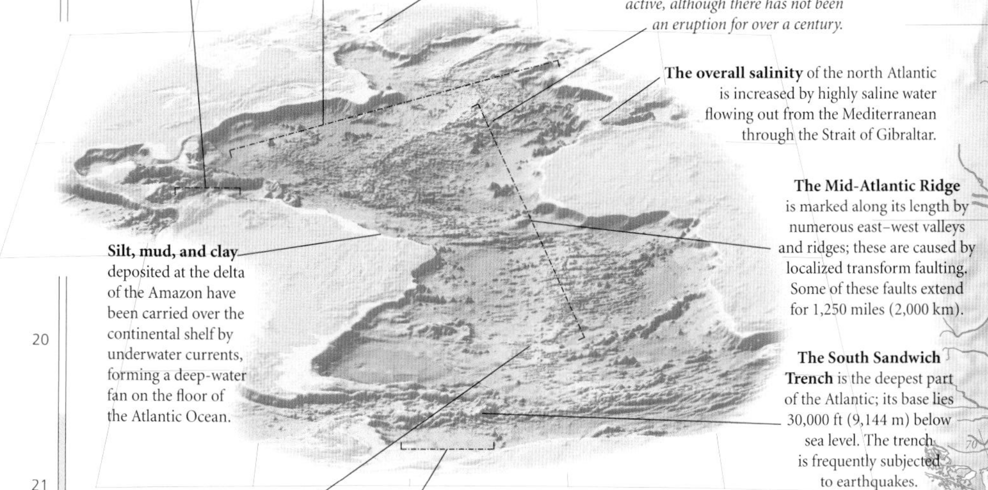

The Gulf Stream is driven by westerly winds and ocean circulation. It flows like a river of warm water along the coast of America and then across the north Atlantic where it becomes known as the North Atlantic Drift.

The Caribbean Sea only adopted its present shape 3 million years ago, when the Isthmus of Panama closed by continental drift.

Ice breaking away from the Greenland ice sheet presents a constant threat to shipping in the north Atlantic. Icebergs are carried out of the Davis Strait by sea currents.

Volcanism in the Azores *occurs because they lie over a hot spot in the oceanic crust. There are ten volcanoes clustered around the Azores. Many are still classified as active, although there has not been an eruption for over a century.*

The overall salinity of the north Atlantic is increased by highly saline water flowing out from the Mediterranean through the Strait of Gibraltar.

The Mid-Atlantic Ridge is marked along its length by numerous east–west valleys and ridges; these are caused by localized transform faulting. Some of these faults extend for 1,250 miles (2,000 km).

Silt, mud, and clay deposited at the delta of the Amazon have been carried over the continental shelf by underwater currents, forming a deep-water fan on the floor of the Atlantic Ocean.

The South Sandwich Trench is the deepest part of the Atlantic; its base lies 30,000 ft (9,144 m) below sea level. The trench is frequently subjected to earthquakes.

Icebergs in the Antarctic are larger than those in the Arctic and can be up to 50 miles (80 km) long. They can drift to latitudes of around 40°S before melting.

Floating ice shelves extend over 100 miles (160 km) into the Weddell Sea, off the coast of Antarctica.

Mid-Atlantic Ridge

Running the length *of the ocean, the Mid-Atlantic Ridge is a complex system of sea-floor spreading, transform faults, and volcanic islands. At its center is a large rift valley 15–30 miles (24–48 km) wide, formed by the upwelling of the ocean floor toward both Africa and South America.*

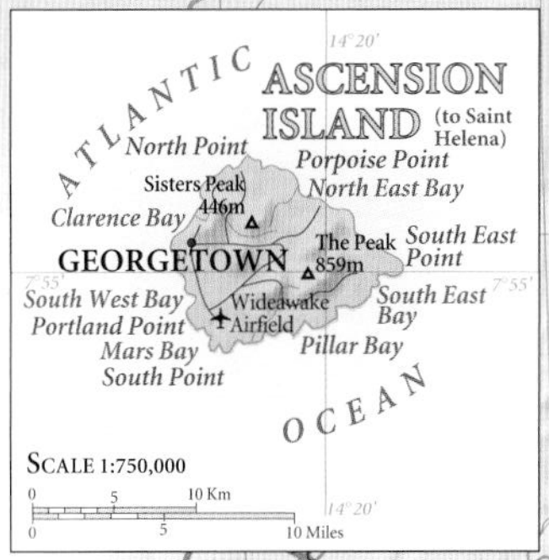

Most of the whales *in the Atlantic Ocean are found in the cooler waters of the south Atlantic, although many species migrate north to tropical waters to breed.*

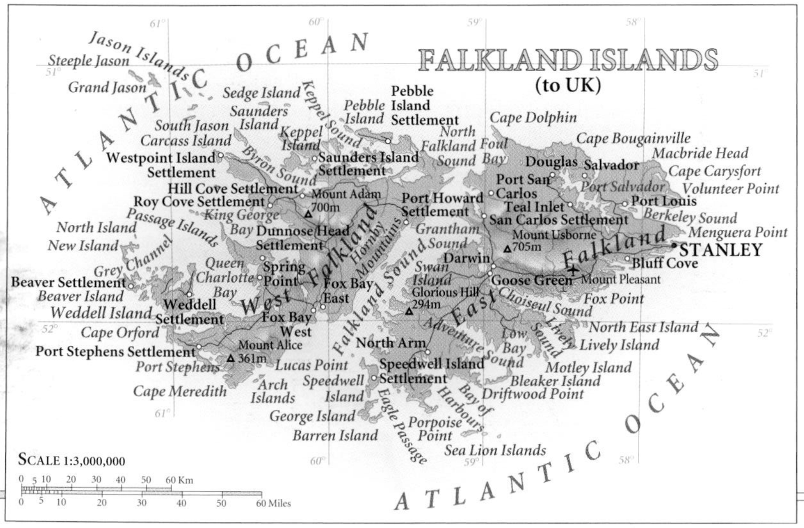

Rocky breakwaters *have been built along the coast of Ghana to protect local fishing boats from being destroyed by powerful Atlantic waves.*

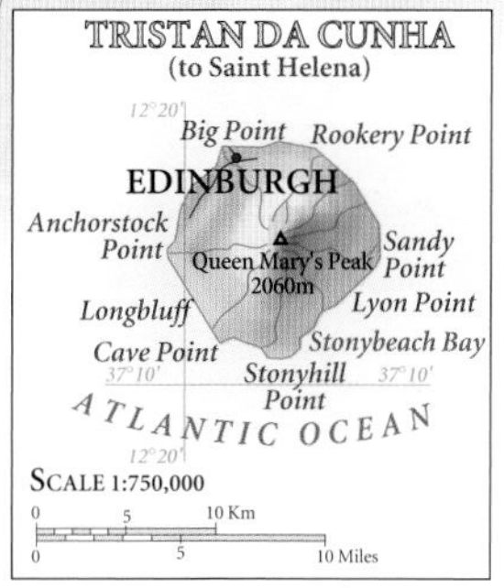

INSET MAP KEY

POPULATION
- ◎ 100,000 to 500,000
- ⊕ 50,000 to 100,000
- ○ 10,000 to 50,000
- ○ below 10,000

ELEVATION
- 1000m / 3281ft
- 500m / 1640ft
- 250m / 820ft
- 100m / 328ft
- sea level

OCEAN MAP KEY

SEA DEPTH
- sea level
- 250m / 820ft
- 500m / 1640ft
- 1000m / 3281ft
- 2000m / 6562ft
- 3000m / 9843ft
- 5000m / 16,410ft

AFRICA

THE WORLD'S SECOND LARGEST CONTINENT, AFRICA COVERS AN AREA OF 11,712,434 SQ MILES (30,335,000 SQ KM). IT HAS 53 SEPARATE COUNTRIES, INCLUDING MADAGASCAR IN THE INDIAN OCEAN – THE HIGHEST NUMBER OF ANY CONTINENT.

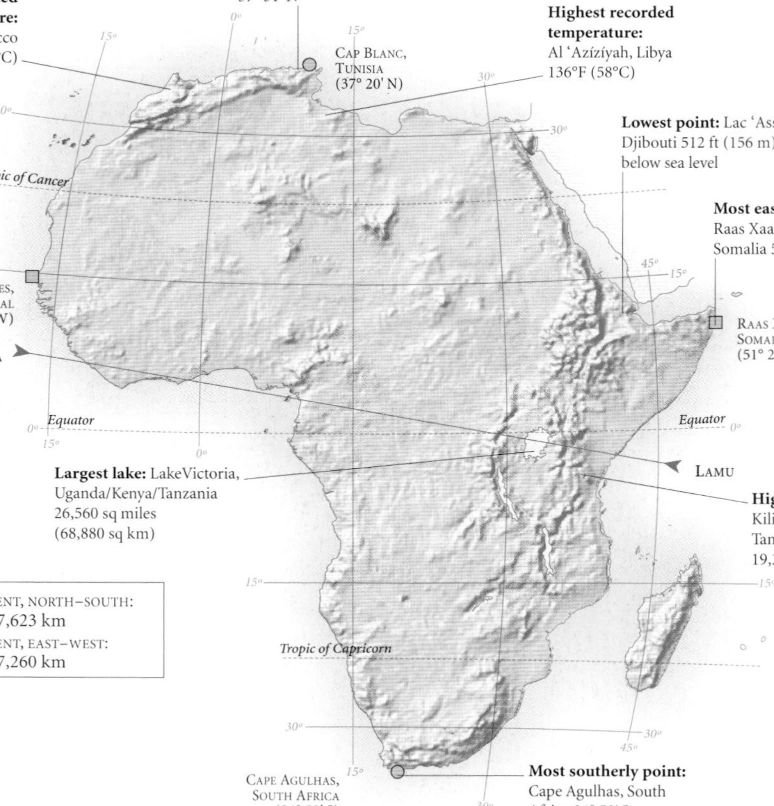

Greatest extent, north–south: 4,737 miles / 7,623 km
Greatest extent, east–west: 4,511 miles / 7,260 km

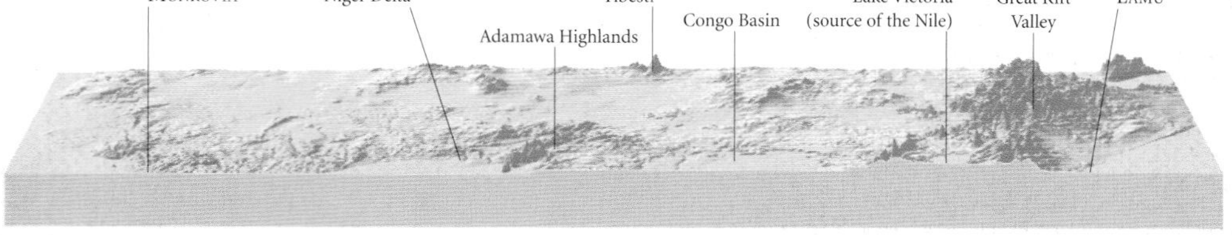

Cross-section from Monrovia, Liberia to Lamu, Kenya

line of cross-section

0 500 1000 1500 Km
0 500 1000 1500 Miles

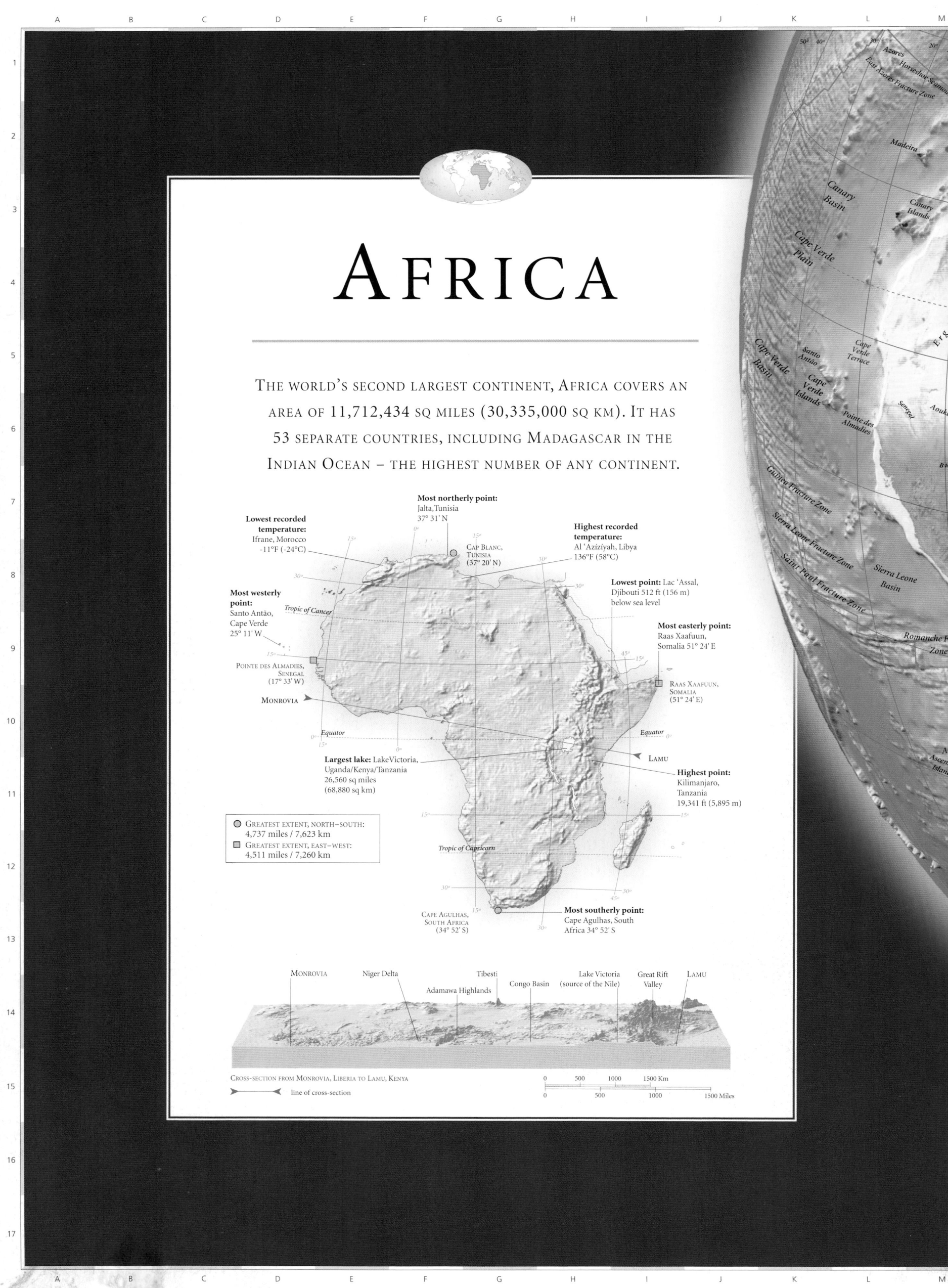

N O P Q R S T U V W X Y Z
1 2 3 4 5 6 7 8 9 10 11 12 13 14 15 16 17
Iberian Peninsula
E U R O P E
Corsica
Sardinia
Balearic Islands
Adriatic Sea
Gulf of Taranto
Tyrrhenian Sea
Sicily
Mount Etna 3340m
Sierra Nevada
M e d i t e r r a n e a n S e a
Jalta
Cap Blanc
EURASIAN PLATE
AFRICAN PLATE
Malta
Mejerda
Ionian Sea
Ionian Basin
ANATOLIAN PLATE
AFRICAN PLATE
Aegean Sea
Peloponnese
Sea of Crete
Crete
Hellenic Trough
Lake Tuz
A n a t o l i a
Taurus Mountains
Gulf of Antalya
Cyprus
Lake Van
Lake Urmia
Caspian Sea
Elburz Mountains
Iranian Plateau
A S I A
Zagros Mountains
IRANIAN PLATE
ARABIAN PLATE
Tigris
Euphrates
Kārūn
Mand
Nahr al Khābūr
Saharan Atlas
Atlas Mountains
Grand Erg Occidental
Chott el Jerid
Gulf of Sirte
Al Jabal al Akhḑar
Grand Erg Oriental
Qattara Depression
Nile Fan
Suez Canal
Sinai
Jordan
Dead Sea
Syrian Desert
Wādī al Ubayyiḑ
Wādī al Khirr
An Nafūd
Persian Gulf
Gulf of Oman
Tropic of Cancer
Arabian Sea
Murray Ridge
Az Zāhirah
Wahibah Sands
Plateau du Tademaït
Oued Saoura
Great Sand Sea
Western Desert
Eastern Desert
Nile
Wādī al Jizl
Arabian Peninsula
S A H A R A
Erg Chech
Tassili-n-Ajjer
Idhān Murzuq
Libyan Desert
Ahaggar
Oued Tafassâsset
Tanezrouft
Lake Nasser
Nubian Desert
Red Sea
Wādī Bīshah
Wādī Tathlīth
Asir
Ar Rub' al Khālī
East Sheba Ridge
Owen Fracture Zone
Adrar des Ifôghas
Ténéré du Tafassâsset
Tibesti
Massif de l'Aïr
Grand Erg de Bilma
Ténéré
Ouadi Haouach
Ouadi Howa
Wadi al Milk
Wadi Muqaddam
Barka
Atbara
Gash
Tekezē
ARABIAN PLATE
AFRICAN PLATE
Gulf of Aden
Alula-Fartak Trench
Socotra
Raas Xaafuun
Vallée de l'Azaouagh
S a h e l
Niger
Lake Chad
Blue Nile
White Nile
Rahad
Lake Tana
Abuye Meda 3000m
Lac Assal
Horn of Africa
Komadugu Gana
Hadejia
Chari
Black Volta
Jos Plateau
Gongola
Logone
Bahr Kameur
Massif des Bongo
Sudd
Baro
Ethiopian Highlands
Fafen Shet'
Wabē Gestro
Mendebo
Ogaden
Chain Ridge
Lake Volta
Ouémé
Shebshi Mountains
Katsina Ala
Donga
Bangoran
Gilo
A F R I C A
Kangen
Genale
Dawa
Somali Basin
Equator
Niger
Niger Delta
Adamawa Highlands
Cameroon Mountain 4070m
Kotto
Yei
White Nile
Lotagipi Swamp
Dudinga Hills
Lake Turkana (Lake Rudolf)
Huri Hills
Jubba
Shebeli
Somali Plain
Gulf of Guinea
Niger Fan
Isla de Bioco
Guinea Basin
Príncipe
São Tomé
Lobaye
Vele
Itimbiri
Aruwimi
Kibali
Nepoko
Lake Albert
Cherangany Hills
Kirinyaga 5200m
INDIAN OCEAN
Seychelles
Ubangi
Zadié
Congo
Congo Basin
Lake Edward
Kagera
Lake Victoria
Grumeti
Western Rift Valley
Great Rift Valley
Kilimanjaro 5895m
Ogooué
Maiko
Lomami
Busira
Ulindi
Lake Kivu
Pemba Channel
Pemba
Zanzibar
Zanzibar Channel
Providence Atoll
Amirante Trench
Chain Fracture Zone
Congo Canyon
Congo Fan
Loge
Cuango
Kwilu
Kasai
Lulua
Lukuga
Lake Tanganyika
Gombe
Lake Rukwa
Lake Mweru
Mitumba Range
Luvua
Luapula
Lubilandji
Kilombero
Mbarangandu
Ruvuma
Tanjona Bobaomby
Comoro Islands
Comoro Basin
Angola Basin
Lucala
Cuanza
Kabompo
Muchinga Escarpment
Lake Nyasa
Lugenda
Lúrio
Ligonha
Saint Helena
Catumbela
Bié Plateau
Cacuso
Cunene
Cubango
Cuando
Lake Kariba
Zambezi
Lake Cabora Bassa
Luenha
Sabi
Mozambique Channel
Sambao
Madagascar
Tsiribihina
Mangoky
Mascarene Plain
Wilshaw Ridge
Tropic of Capricorn
AFRICAN PLATE
SOUTH AMERICAN PLATE
Mid-Atlantic Ridge
ATLANTIC OCEAN
Walvis Ridge
Omatako
Chobe
Kafue Flats
Okavango Delta
Ntwetwe Pan
Eiseb
Ghanzi
Kalahari Desert
Khomas Hochland
Nosop
Auob
Molopo
Lundi
Limpopo
Olifants
Crocodile
Tugela
Madagascar Basin
Tanjona Vohimena
Madagascar Plateau
Natal Basin
Namib Desert
Groot Karasberge
Kuruman
Orange River
Orange Fan
Harts
Vaal
Orange River
Riet
Drakensberg
Doring
Breede
Great Karoo
Natal Valley
Mozambique Plateau
Discovery II Fracture Zone
Southwest Indian Ridge
Indomed Fracture Zone
Tristan da Cunha
Cape of Good Hope
Cape Agulhas
Gough Island
Cape Basin
Agulhas Plateau
Cape Rise
Agulhas Basin
Du Toit Fracture Zone
Prince Edward Fracture Zone
Prince Edward Islands
Crozet Islands
Crozet Plateau
AFRICAN PLATE
ANTARCTICA PLATE
Atlantic-Indian Ridge

Physical Africa

The structure of Africa was dramatically influenced by the break up of the supercontinent Gondwanaland about 160 million years ago and, more recently, rifting and hot spot activity. Today, much of Africa is remote from active plate boundaries and comprises a series of extensive plateaus and deep basins, which influence the drainage patterns of major rivers. The relief rises to the east, where volcanic uplands and vast lakes mark the Great Rift Valley. In the far north and south sedimentary rocks have been folded to form the Atlas Mountains and the Great Karoo.

Northern Africa

Northern Africa comprises a system of basins and plateaus. The Tibesti and Ahaggar are volcanic uplands, whose uplift has been matched by subsidence within large surrounding basins. Many of the basins have been infilled with sand and gravel, creating the vast Saharan lands. The Atlas Mountains in the north were formed by convergence of the African and Eurasian plates.

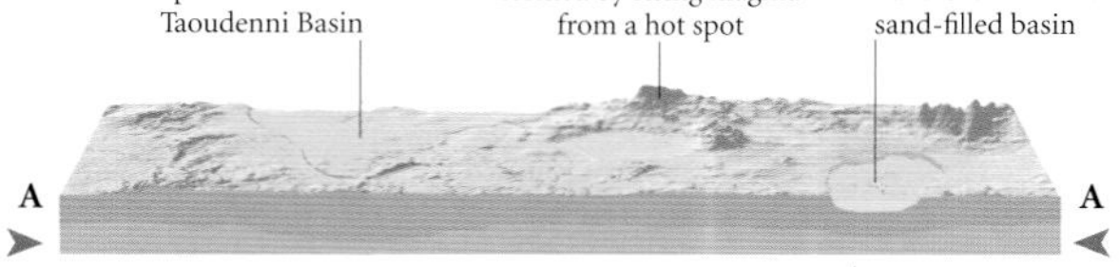

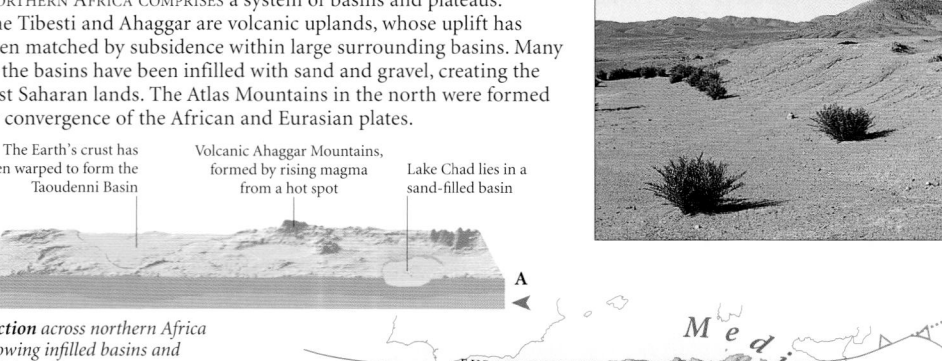

***Section** across northern Africa showing infilled basins and uplifted plateaus.*

East Africa

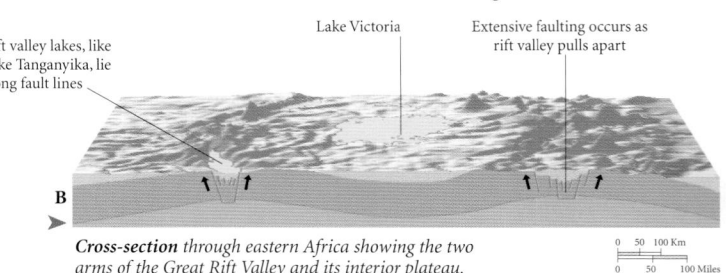

The Great Rift Valley is the most striking feature of this region, running for 4,475 miles (7,200 km) from Lake Nyasa to the Red Sea. North of Lake Nyasa it splits into two arms and encloses an interior plateau which contains Lake Victoria. A number of elongated lakes and volcanoes lie along the fault lines. To the west lies the Congo Basin, a vast, shallow depression, which rises to form an almost circular rim of highlands.

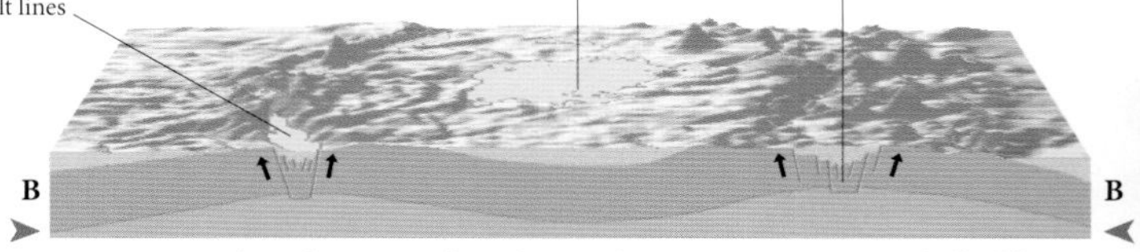

***Cross-section** through eastern Africa showing the two arms of the Great Rift Valley and its interior plateau.*

Scale 1:36,000,000
(projection: Lambert Azimuthal Equal Area)

Km 0 100 200 400 600 800
Miles 0 100 200 400 600 800

Map Key

Elevation

- 5000m / 16,405ft
- 4000m / 13,124ft
- 3000m / 9843ft
- 2000m / 6562ft
- 1000m / 3281ft
- 500m / 1640ft
- 250m / 820ft
- 100m / 328ft
- sea level
- below sea level

Plate margins (for explanation see page xiv)

- constructive
- destructive
- conservative
- uncertain
- line of cross-section

Southern Africa

The Great Escarpment marks the southern boundary of Africa's basement rock and includes the Drakensberg range. It was uplifted when Gondwanaland fragmented about 160 million years ago and it has gradually been eroded back from the coast. To the north, the relief drops steadily, forming the Kalahari Basin. In the far south are the fold mountains of the Great Karoo.

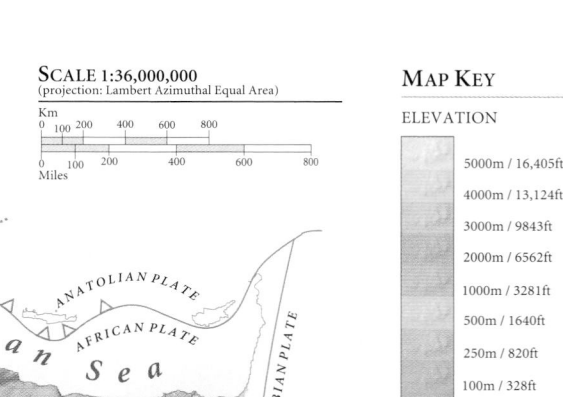

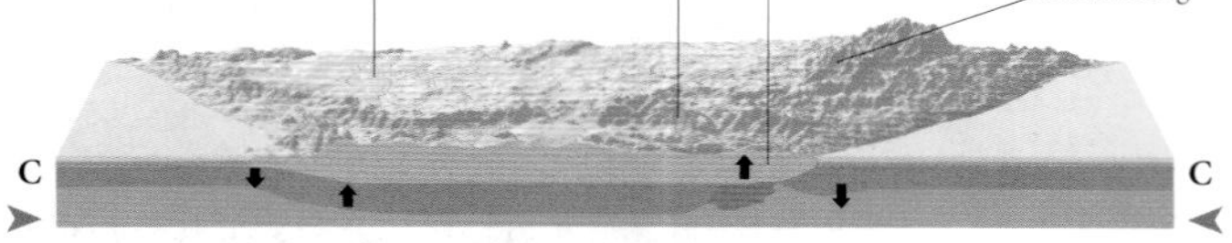

***Cross-section** through southern Africa showing the boundary of the Great Escarpment.*

0 100 200 Km
0 100 200 Miles

CLIMATE

THE CLIMATES OF AFRICA range from mediterranean to arid, dry savannah and humid equatorial. In East Africa, where snow settles at the summit of volcanoes such as Kilimanjaro, climate is also modified by altitude. The winds of the Sahara export millions of tonnes of dust a year both northward and eastward.

Savannah grasslands run in a belt across Africa; limited rainfall inhibits tree growth.

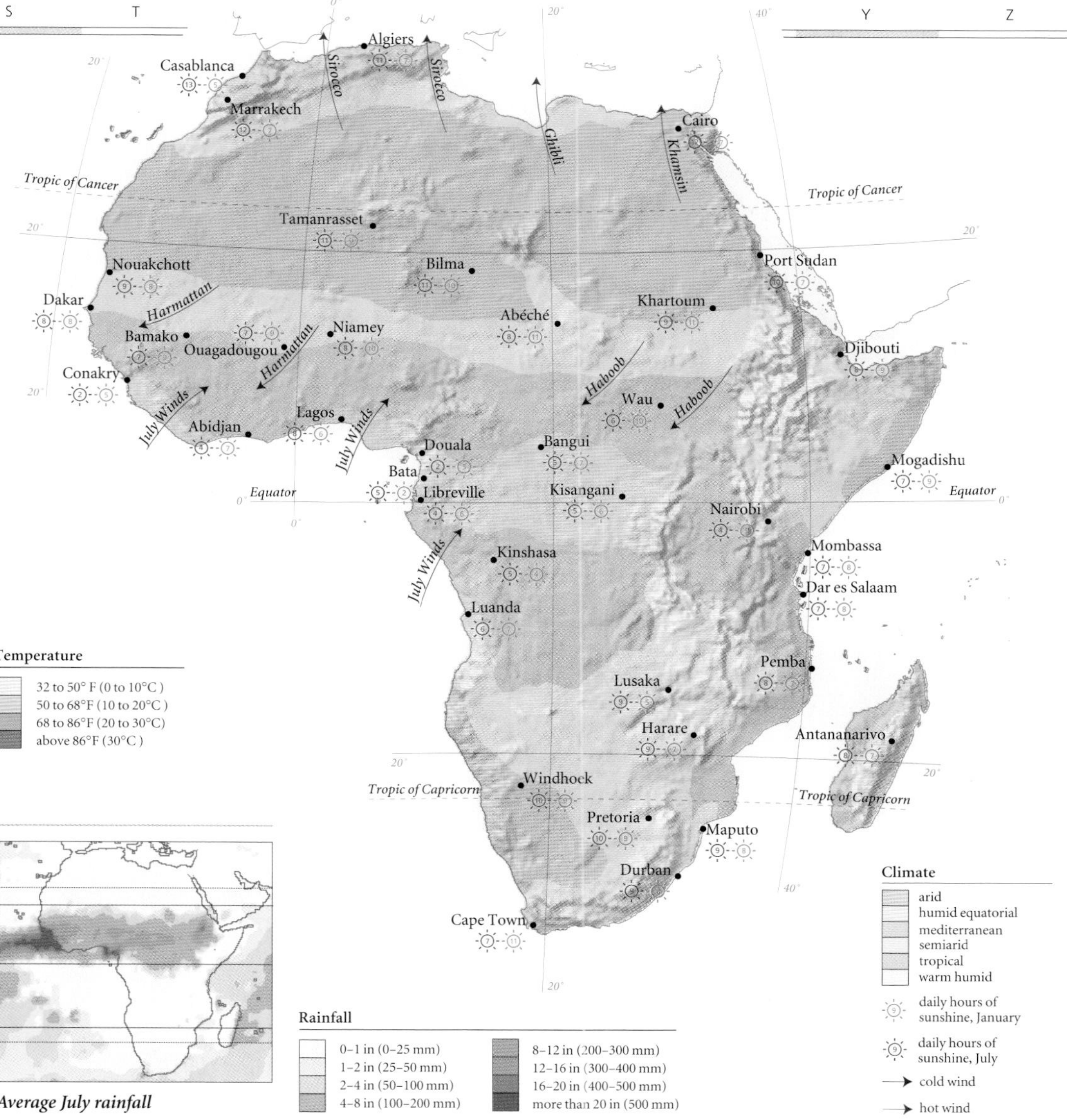

TEMPERATURE

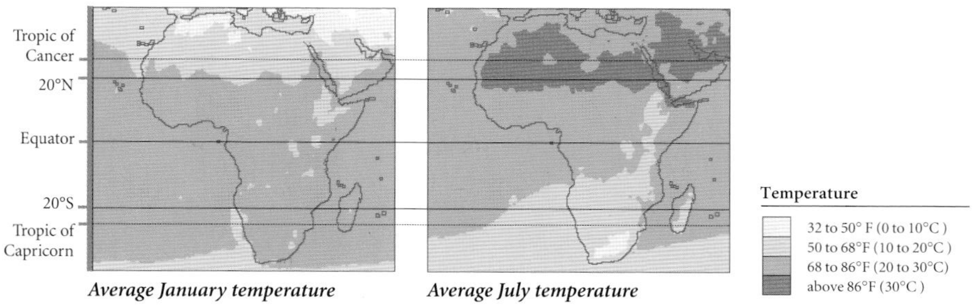

Average January temperature

Average July temperature

Temperature

	32 to 50° F (0 to 10°C)
	50 to 68°F (10 to 20°C)
	68 to 86°F (20 to 30°C)
	above 86°F (30°C)

RAINFALL

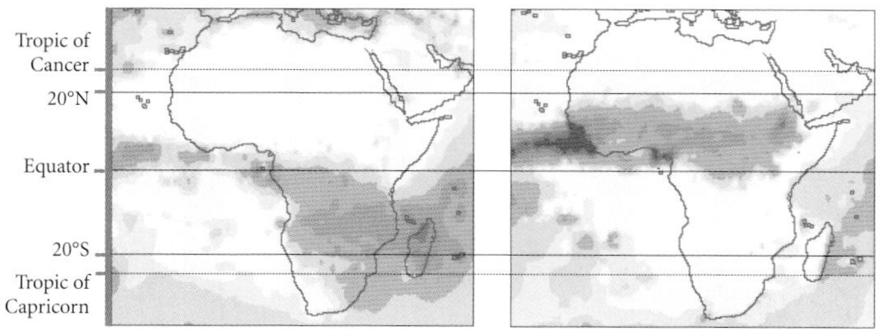

Average January rainfall

Average July rainfall

The hot, equatorial basin of the Congo River receives over 48 inches (1,200 mm) of rainfall per year.

Rainfall

0–1 in (0–25 mm)	8–12 in (200–300 mm)
1–2 in (25–50 mm)	12–16 in (300–400 mm)
2–4 in (50–100 mm)	16–20 in (400–500 mm)
4–8 in (100–200 mm)	more than 20 in (500 mm)

Climate

	arid
	humid equatorial
	mediterranean
	semiarid
	tropical
	warm humid
☀	daily hours of sunshine, January
☀	daily hours of sunshine, July
→	cold wind
→	hot wind

SHAPING THE CONTINENT

AFRICAN LANDSCAPES are shaped by the intensity of climatic extremes and by tectonic action. High aridity, wind action, and infrequent but heavy rainstorms, lead to the migration of sand dunes and dramatic flash flooding across much of the north and west. In the wetter areas, high precipitation increases the rate of weathering. To the east, the rift system has created a volcanic and lake environment and allowed rivers to erode weaknesses left in the crustal structure by faults.

GROUNDWATER

1 Oases are found in desert areas such as the Sahara (*left*). Groundwater migrates through permeable rock strata, confined between two impermeable layers. Oases form either when the permeable rocks come near to the surface, or at a fault line, when water is able to seep up to the surface through the crushed rocks at the fault.

Rainwater feeds the aquifer
Water migrates up through fault
Aquifer exposed near the surface
Groundwater trapped between impermeable strata

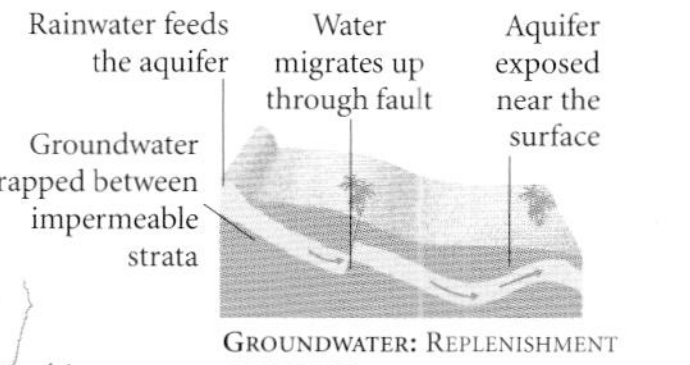

GROUNDWATER: REPLENISHMENT OF AN OASIS

RIVER SYSTEMS

2 The Zambezi River (*above*) drops 360 ft (110 m) over the Victoria Falls into a zigzag gorge. The river has eroded the gorge along lines of weakness in the bedrock, created by fault lines running in two directions.

Old site of Victoria Falls
River plunges over falls
Fault and joint lines running in two directions
Zig-zag gorge of the Zambezi

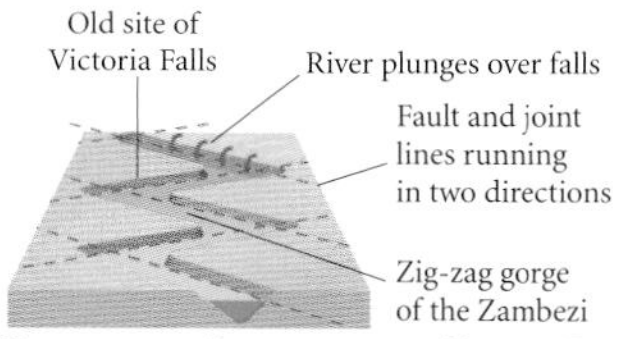

RIVER SYSTEMS: RETREATING OF THE VICTORIA FALLS

THE EVOLVING LANDSCAPE

Landscape

	sinking land
	stable land
	uplifting land
▽▽▽	escarpment
→	ocean current
—	rift
▲	active volcano
⌂	inselberg
	oasis
～	river
～	wadi
～	waterfall

WEATHERING

Exfoliated layers
External stresses act on the surface of the inselberg
Joints or cracks caused by expansion and contraction

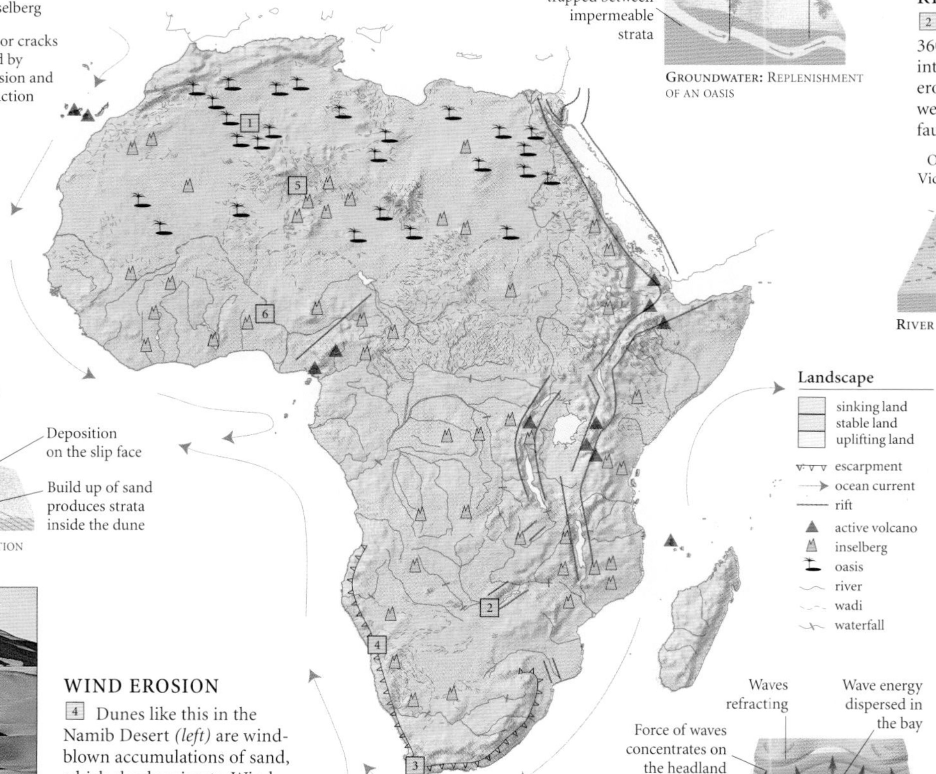

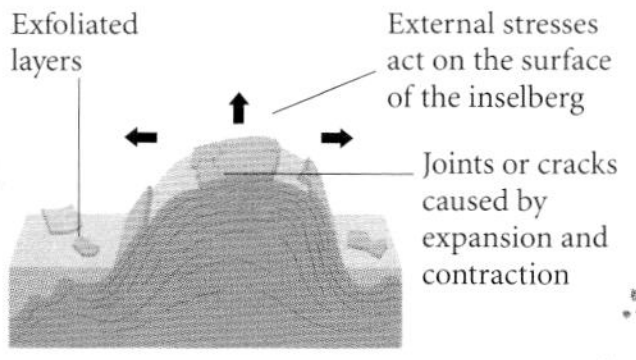

WEATHERING: FORMATION OF AN INSELBERG

6 Inselbergs (*above*), found extensively across West Africa, are exposed remnants of an extensive upland area. Erosion of the surrounding uplands leaves a resistant rock outcrop. Its spheroidal shape is the result of "onion-skin" weathering – the exfoliating of layers – due to repeated expansion and contraction.

EPHEMERAL CHANNELS

5 Wadis (*above*) drain much of northern Africa. These drybed courses are flooded only after infrequent, but intense, storms in the uplands cause water to surge along their channels.

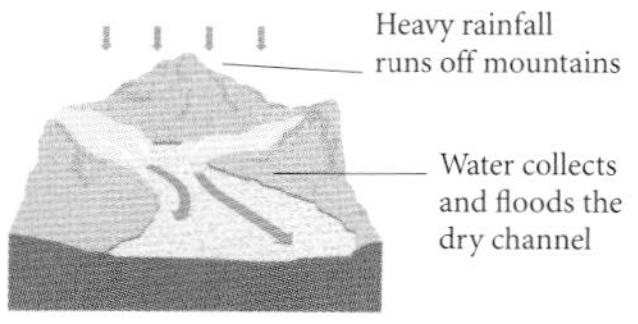

Heavy rainfall runs off mountains
Water collects and floods the dry channel

EPHEMERAL CHANNELS: FLASH FLOODING OF A WADI

WIND EROSION

Sand is gradually blown up the back slope
Deposition on the slip face
Build up of sand produces strata inside the dune

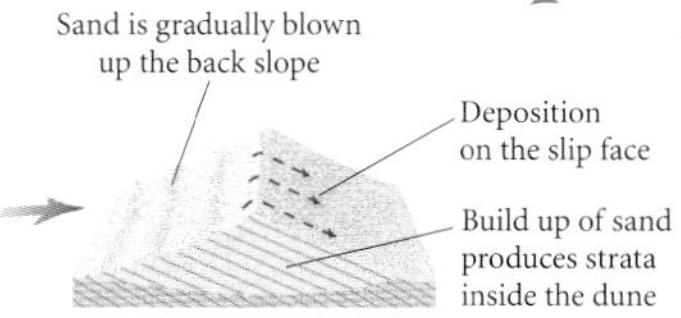

WIND EROSION: MIGRATION OF A DUNE

4 Dunes like this in the Namib Desert (*left*) are wind-blown accumulations of sand, which slowly migrate. Wind action moves sand up the shallow back slope; when the sand reaches the crest of the dune it is deposited on the slip face.

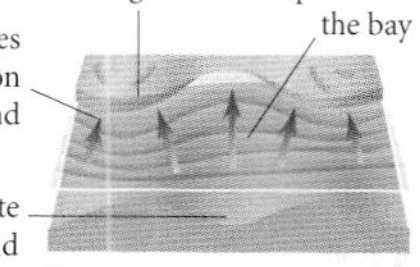

COASTAL PROCESSES

3 Houtbaai (*above*), in southern Africa, is constantly being modified by wave action. As waves approach the indented coastline, they reach the shallow water of the headland, slowing down and reducing in length. This causes them to bend or refract, concentrating their erosive force at the headlands.

Waves refracting
Wave energy dispersed in the bay
Force of waves concentrates on the headland
The sea bed is deeper opposite the bay than at the headland

COASTAL PROCESSES: EROSION OF A BAY

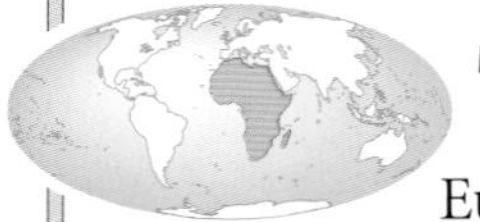

Political Africa

The political map of modern Africa only emerged following the end of the Second World War. Over the next half-century, all of the countries formerly controlled by European powers gained independence from their colonial rulers – only Liberia and Ethiopia were never colonized. The postcolonial era has not been an easy period for many countries, but there have been moves toward multiparty democracy in much of West Africa, and in Zambia, Tanzania, and Kenya. In South Africa, democratic elections replaced the internationally-condemned apartheid system only in 1994. Other countries have still to find political stability; corruption in government, and ethnic tensions are serious problems. National infrastructures, based on the colonial transportation systems built to exploit Africa's resources, are often inappropriate for independent economic development.

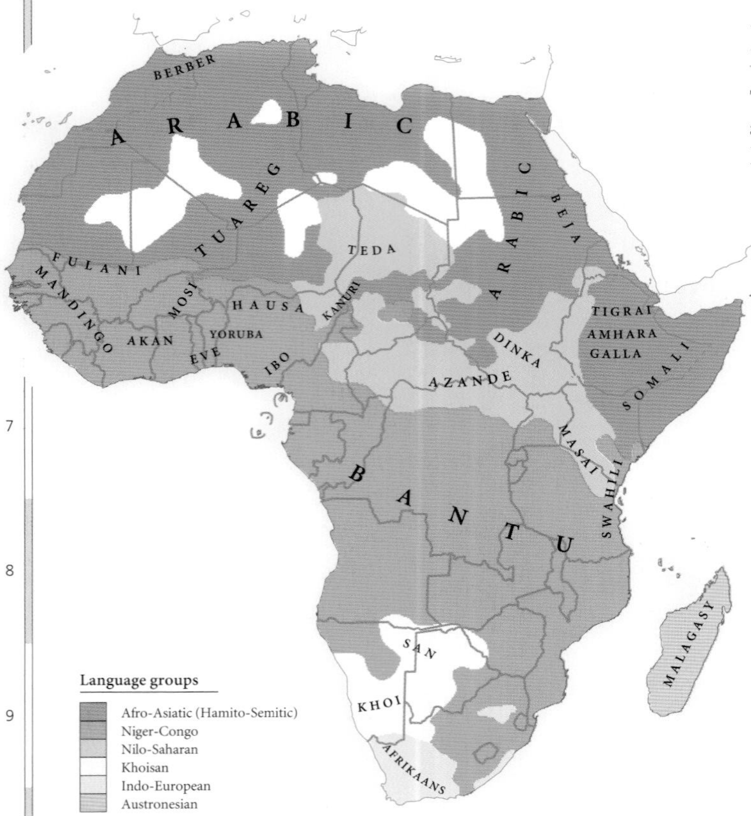

Languages

Three major world languages act as *lingua francas* across the African continent: Arabic in North Africa; English in southern and eastern Africa and Nigeria; and French in Central and West Africa, and in Madagascar. A huge number of African languages are spoken as well – over 2,000 have been recorded, with more than 400 in Nigeria alone – reflecting the continuing importance of traditional cultures and values. In the north of the continent, the extensive use of Arabic reflects Middle Eastern influences while Bantu is widely-spoken across much of southern Africa.

Official African languages

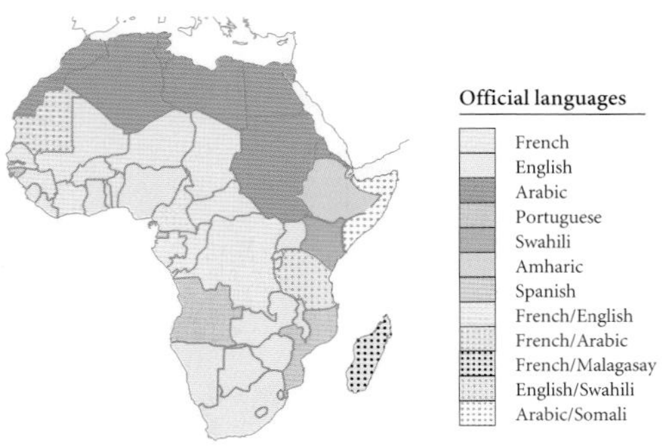

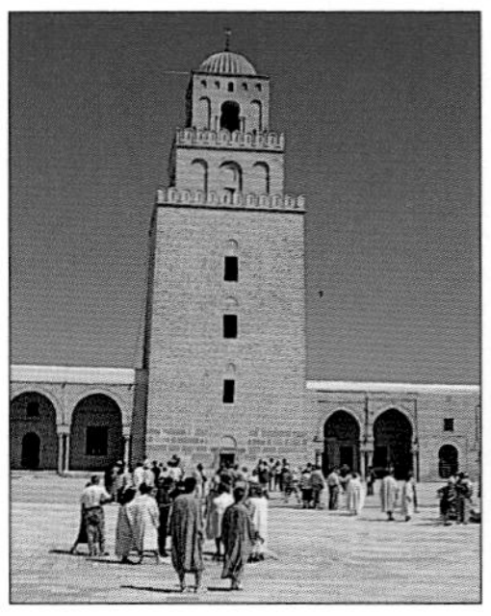

Islamic influences are evident throughout North Africa. The Great Mosque at Kairouan, Tunisia, is Africa's holiest Islamic place.

In northeastern Nigeria, *people speak Kanuri – a dialect of the Saharan language group.*

Transportation

African railroads were built to aid the exploitation of natural resources, and most offer passage only from the interior to the coastal cities, leaving large parts of the continent untouched – five landlocked countries have no railroads at all. The Congo, Nile, and Niger River networks offer limited access to land within the continental interior, but have a number of waterfalls and cataracts which prevent navigation from the sea. Many roads were developed in the 1960s and 1970s, but economic difficulties are making the maintenance and expansion of the networks difficult.

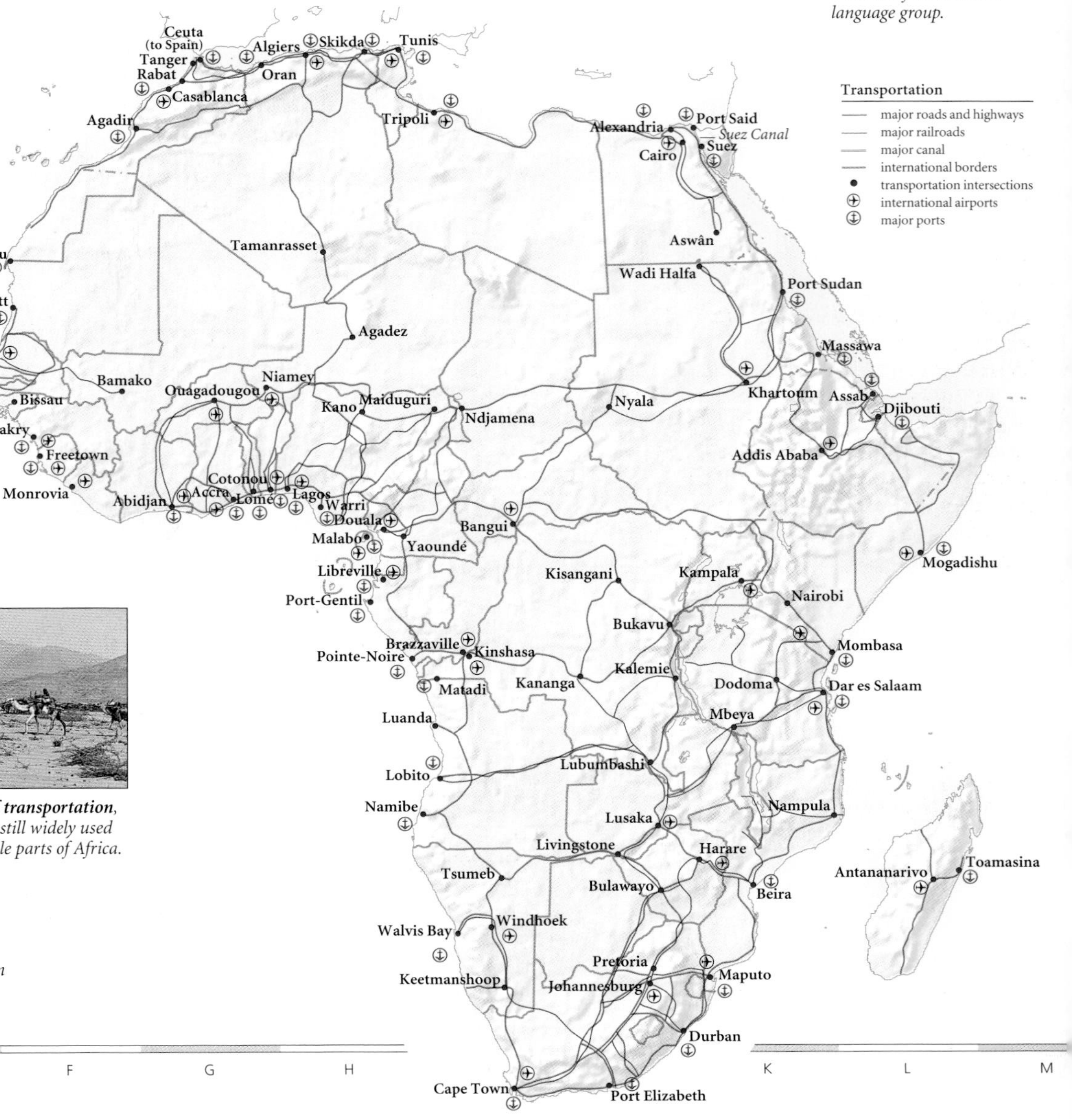

South Africa *has the largest concentration of railroads in Africa. Over 20,000 miles (32,000 km) of routes have been built since 1870.*

Traditional means of transportation, *such as the camel, are still widely used across the less accessible parts of Africa.*

The Congo River, *though not suitable for river transportation along its entire length, forms a vital link for people and goods in its navigable inland reaches.*

POPULATION

AFRICA HAS A rapidly-growing population of nearly 700 million people, yet over 75% of the continent remains sparsely populated. Most Africans still pursue a traditional rural lifestyle, though urbanization is increasing as people move to the cities in search of employment. The greatest population densities occur where water is more readily available, such as in the Nile Valley, the coasts of North and West Africa, along the Niger, the eastern African highlands, and in South Africa.

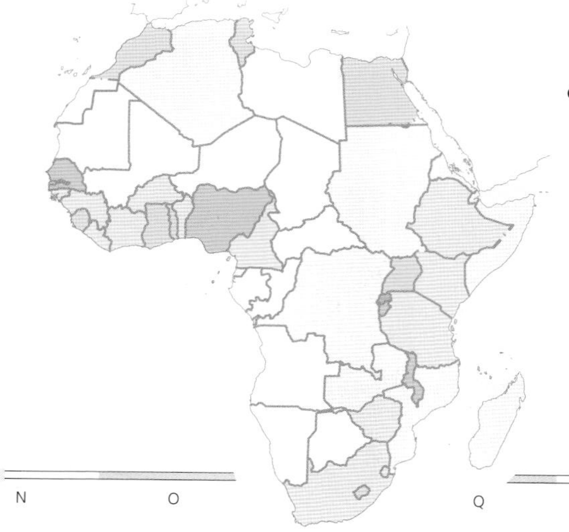

Population density (people per sq mile)

- below 130
- 130–259
- 260–379
- 380–519
- 520–780
- above 780

***A thin layer of smog** blankets the dusty streets of Cairo, Africa's most populous city and home to over six million people. In the 1990s Cairo grew at a rate of about 1,500 people per day.*

***Thriving street markets** in Gambia's capital, Banjul, trade a variety of locally-grown produce. Africa's population is still predominantly rural.*

A B C D E F G H I J K L M

African Resources

The economies of most African countries are dominated by subsistence and cash crop agriculture, with limited industrialization. Manufacturing is largely confined to South Africa. Many countries depend on a single resource, such as copper or gold, or a cash crop, such as coffee, for export income, which can leave them vulnerable to fluctuations in world commodity prices. In order to diversify their economies and develop a wider industrial base, investment from overseas is being actively sought by many African governments.

Industry

Many African industries concentrate on the extraction and processing of raw materials. These include the oil industry, food processing, mining, and textile production. South Africa accounts for over half of the continent's industrial output with much of the remainder coming from the countries along the northern coast. Over 60% of Africa's workforce is employed in agriculture.

***The unspoiled natural splendor** of wildlife reserves, like the Serengeti National Park in Tanzania, attract tourists to Africa from around the globe. The tourist industry in Kenya and Tanzania is particularly well developed, where it accounts for almost 10% of GNP.*

Standard of Living

Since the 1960s most countries in Africa have seen significant improvements in life expectancy, healthcare and education. However, 18 of the 20 most deprived countries in the world are African, and the continent as a whole lies well behind the rest of the world in terms of meeting many basic human needs.

Standard of Living
(UN Human Development Index)
high
low

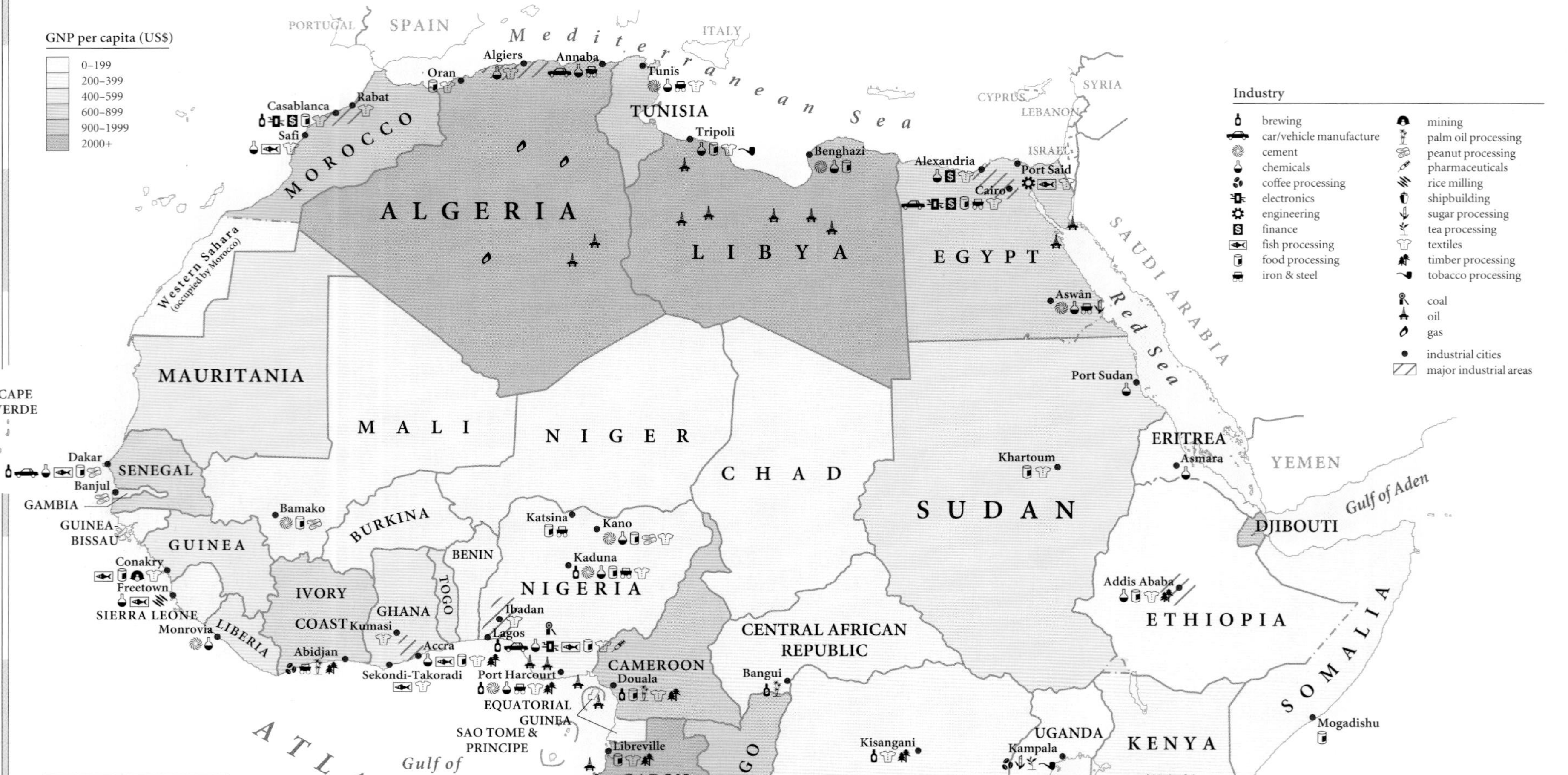

***The discovery of oil** in the swampy Niger Delta during the 1960s made Nigeria one of Africa's richer nations. As world oil prices fell in the 1980s, the Nigerian economy faltered.*

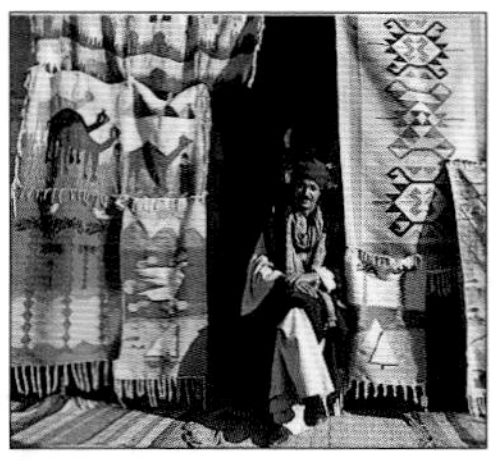

***Exotic rugs** and brightly-colored textiles are sold in a street market along the banks of the Nile River in Luxor, Egypt.*

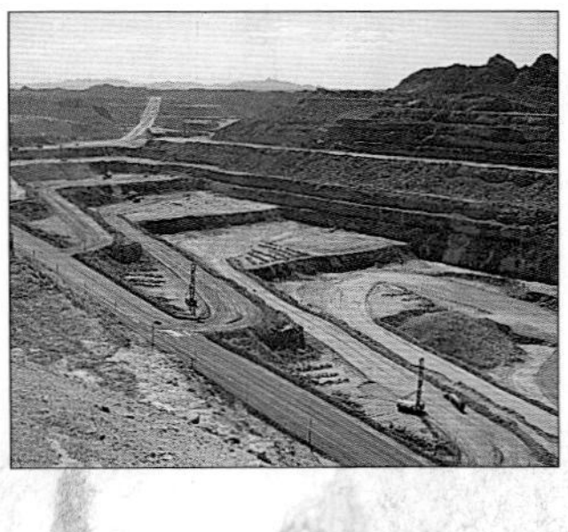

***The Rössing uranium** mines in Namibia are the largest in the world. Africa and the US produce over half the world's uranium ore, used to fuel nuclear power plants. Elsewhere, South Africa and Niger also mine uranium on a large scale.*

A B C D E K L M

Environmental Issues

One of Africa's most serious environmental problems occurs in marginal areas such as the Sahel where scrub and forest clearance, often for cooking fuel, combined with overgrazing, are causing desertification. Game reserves in southern and eastern Africa have helped to preserve many endangered animals, although the needs of growing populations have led to conflict over land use, and poaching is a serious problem.

Environmental Issues

- national parks
- tropical forest
- forest destroyed
- desert
- desertification
- polluted rivers
- radioactive contamination
- marine pollution
- heavy marine pollution
- poor urban air quality

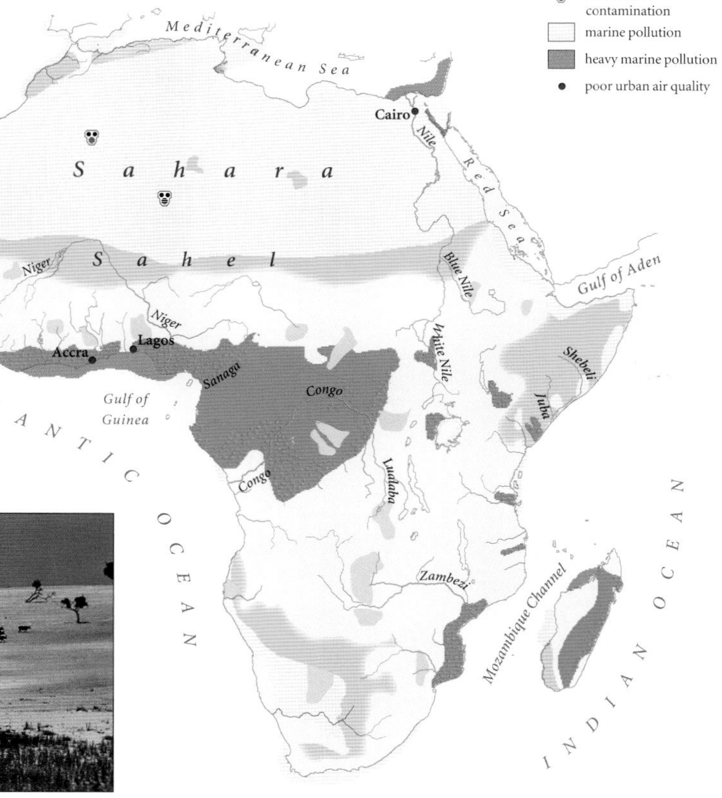

***The Sahel's** delicate natural equilibrium is easily destroyed by the clearing of vegetation, drought, and overgrazing. This causes the Sahara to advance south, engulfing the savannah grasslands.*

Mineral Resources

Africa's ancient plateaus contain some of the world's most substantial reserves of precious stones and metals. About 30% of the world's gold is mined in South Africa; Zambia has great copper deposits; and diamonds are mined in Botswana, Dem. Rep. Congo, and South Africa. Oil has brought great economic benefits to Algeria, Libya, and Nigeria.

Mineral Resources

- oil field
- gas field
- coal field
- bauxite
- copper
- diamonds
- gold
- iron
- phosphates
- tin
- uranium

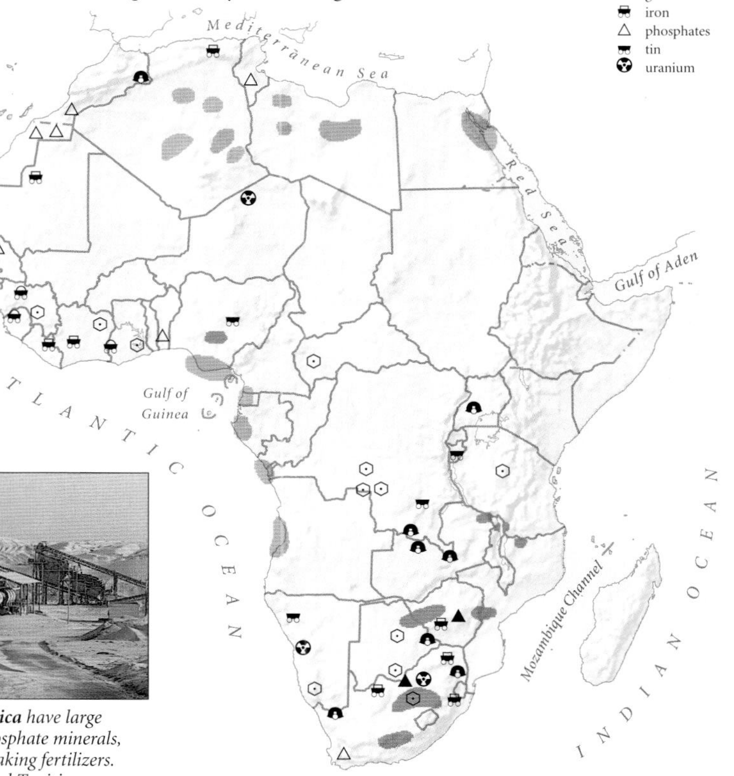

***North and West Africa** have large deposits of white phosphate minerals, which are used in making fertilizers. Morocco, Senegal, and Tunisia are the continent's leading producers.*

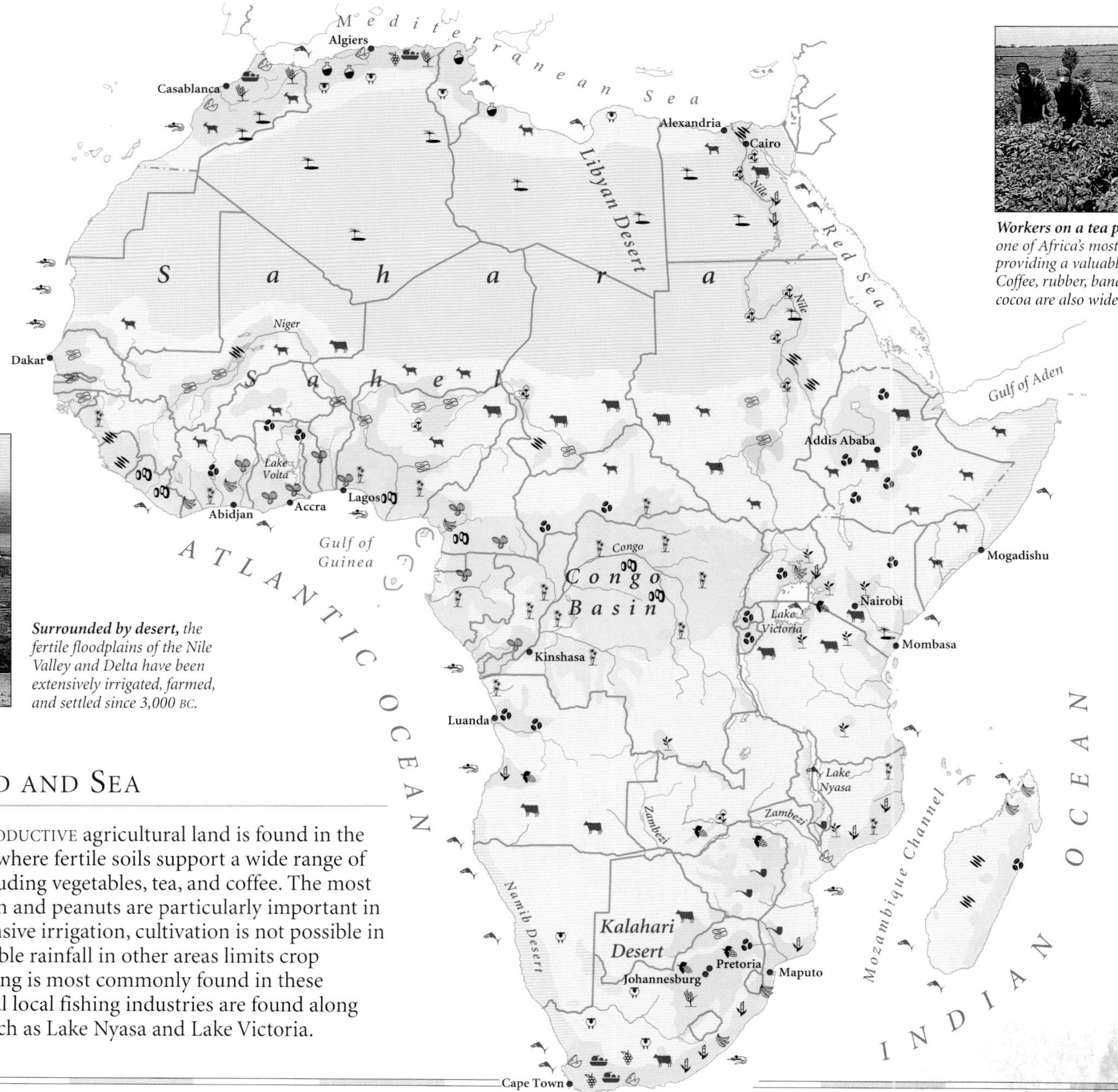

***Workers on a tea plantation** gather one of Africa's most important cash crops, providing a valuable source of income. Coffee, rubber, bananas, cotton, and cocoa are also widely grown as cash crops.*

***Surrounded by desert,** the fertile floodplains of the Nile Valley and Delta have been extensively irrigated, farmed, and settled since 3,000 BC.*

Using the Land and Sea

Some of Africa's most productive agricultural land is found in the eastern volcanic uplands, where fertile soils support a wide range of valuable export crops including vegetables, tea, and coffee. The most widely-grown grain is corn and peanuts are particularly important in West Africa. Without intensive irrigation, cultivation is not possible in desert regions and unreliable rainfall in other areas limits crop production. Pastoral herding is most commonly found in these marginal lands. Substantial local fishing industries are found along coasts and in vast lakes such as Lake Nyasa and Lake Victoria.

Using the Land and Sea

- cropland
- desert
- forest
- pasture
- wetland
- major conurbations
- cattle
- goats
- cereals
- sheep
- bananas
- corn (maize)
- citrus fruits
- cocoa
- cotton
- coffee
- dates
- fishing
- fruit
- oil palms
- olives
- peanuts
- rice
- rubber
- shellfish
- sugar cane
- tea
- tobacco
- vineyards
- wheat

North Africa

Algeria, Egypt, Libya, Morocco, Tunisia, Western Sahara

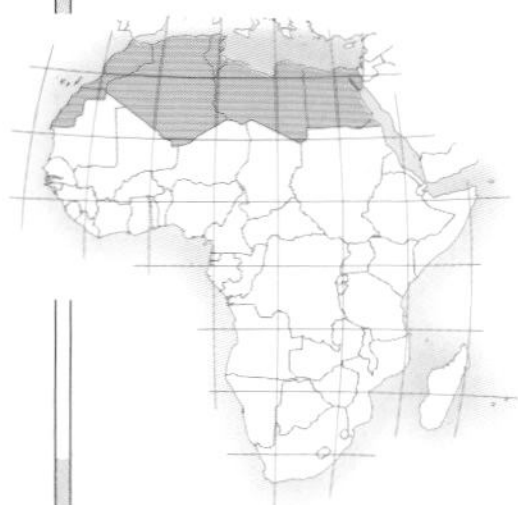

Fringed by the Mediterranean along the northern coast and by the arid Sahara in the south, North Africa reflects the influence of many invaders, both European and, most importantly, Arab, giving the region an almost universal Islamic flavor and a common Arabic language. The countries lying to the west of Egypt are often referred to as the Maghreb, an Arabic term for "west." Today, Morocco and Tunisia exploit their culture and landscape for tourism, while rich oil and gas deposits aid development in Libya and Algeria, despite political turmoil. Egypt, with its fertile, Nile-watered agricultural land and varied industrial base, is the most populous nation.

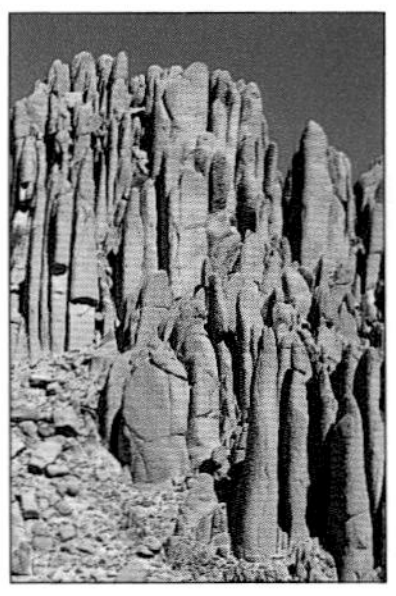

***These rock piles** in Algeria's Ahaggar Mountains are the result of weathering caused by extremes of temperature. Great cracks or joints appear in the rocks, which are then worn and smoothed by the wind.*

The Landscape

The Atlas Mountains, which extend across much of Morocco, northern Algeria, and Tunisia, are part of the fold mountain system which also runs through much of southern Europe. They recede to the south and east, becoming a steppe landscape before meeting the Sahara desert which covers more than 90% of the region. The sediments of the Sahara overlie an ancient plateau of crystalline rock, some of which is more than four billion years old.

Map Key

Population
- above 5 million
- 1 million to 5 million
- 500,000 to 1 million
- 100,000 to 500,000
- 50,000 to 100,000
- 10,000 to 50,000
- below 10,000

Elevation
- 4000m / 13,124ft
- 3000m / 9843ft
- 2000m / 6562ft
- 1000m / 3281ft
- 500m / 1640ft
- 250m / 820ft
- 100m / 328ft
- sea level

Scale 1:11,000,000
(projection: Lambert Azimuthal Equal Area)

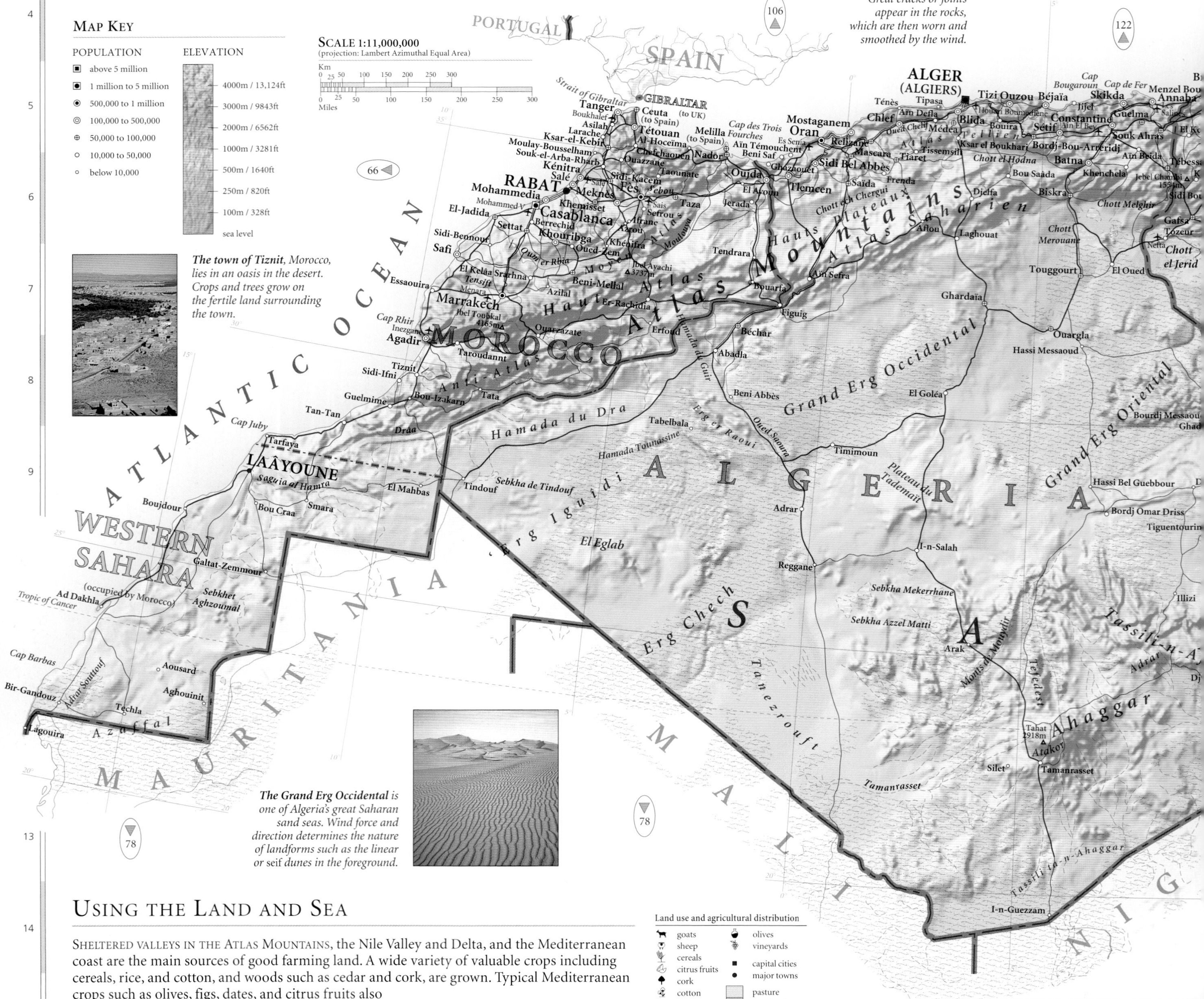

***The town of Tiznit**, Morocco, lies in an oasis in the desert. Crops and trees grow on the fertile land surrounding the town.*

***The Grand Erg Occidental** is one of Algeria's great Saharan sand seas. Wind force and direction determines the nature of landforms such as the linear or seif dunes in the foreground.*

Using the Land and Sea

Sheltered valleys in the Atlas Mountains, the Nile Valley and Delta, and the Mediterranean coast are the main sources of good farming land. A wide variety of valuable crops including cereals, rice, and cotton, and woods such as cedar and cork, are grown. Typical Mediterranean crops such as olives, figs, dates, and citrus fruits also thrive in these areas. The Nile Valley is particularly fertile, and most of Egypt's population lives close to the river. Elsewhere, irrigation is essential to improve crop yields on the desert margins.

Land use and agricultural distribution
- goats
- sheep
- cereals
- citrus fruits
- cork
- cotton
- dates
- fishing
- olives
- vineyards
- capital cities
- major towns
- pasture
- cropland
- forest
- desert

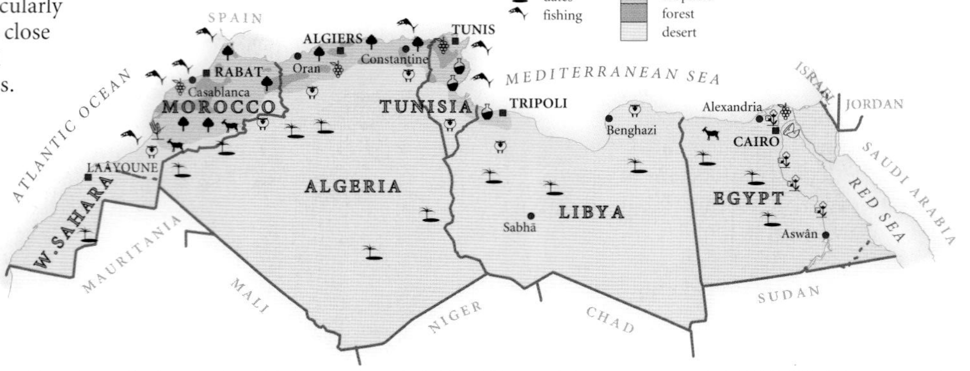

The Urban/Rural Population Divide

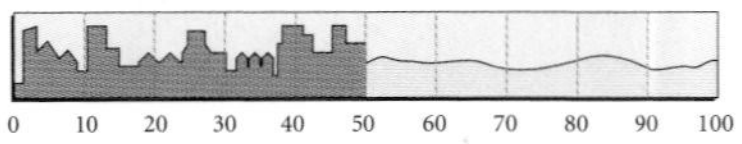

Population Density	Total Land Area
62 people per sq mile	2,215,020 sq miles
(24 people per sq km)	(5,738,394 sq km)

***Many North African nomads,** such as the Bedouin, maintain a traditional pastoral lifestyle on the desert fringes, moving their herds of sheep, goats, and camels from place to place – crossing country borders in order to find sufficient grazing land.*

N O P Q R S T U V W X Y

***The Atlas Mountains** run from Morocco to Tunisia, covering more than 1,200 miles (1,931 km). The northern Tell Atlas (Atlas Tellien) are well watered, with forested slopes; the drier southern High Atlas (Haut Atlas) (left) have the highest peaks, such as Jbel Toubkal, 13,665 ft (4,165 m) high.*

The spectacular sand seas of the Grand Ergs Occidental and Oriental in Algeria are only one of the varied landscapes of the Sahara. *Hammadas*, boulder-strewn rock plateaus, and *reg*, or desert pavements, plains strewn with gravel and small pebbles, are other important landforms.

Despite its outward aridity, the Sahara has several underground aquifers. Libya has built an underground pipeline, the Great Man-made River Project, to enable fuller exploitation of this valuable resource.

Split from the rest of Egypt by the Suez Canal, the Sinai Peninsula is partially desert, dissected by countless *wadis*.

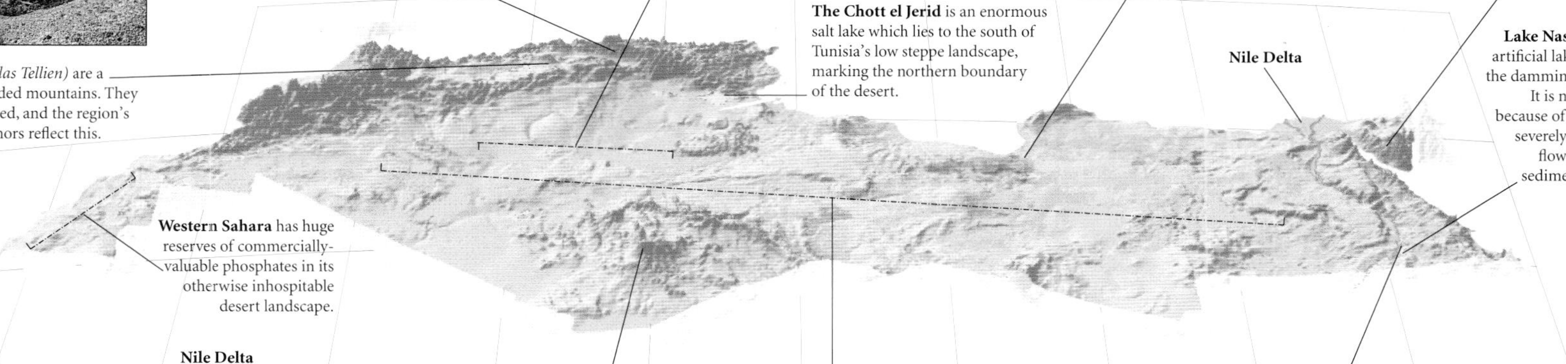

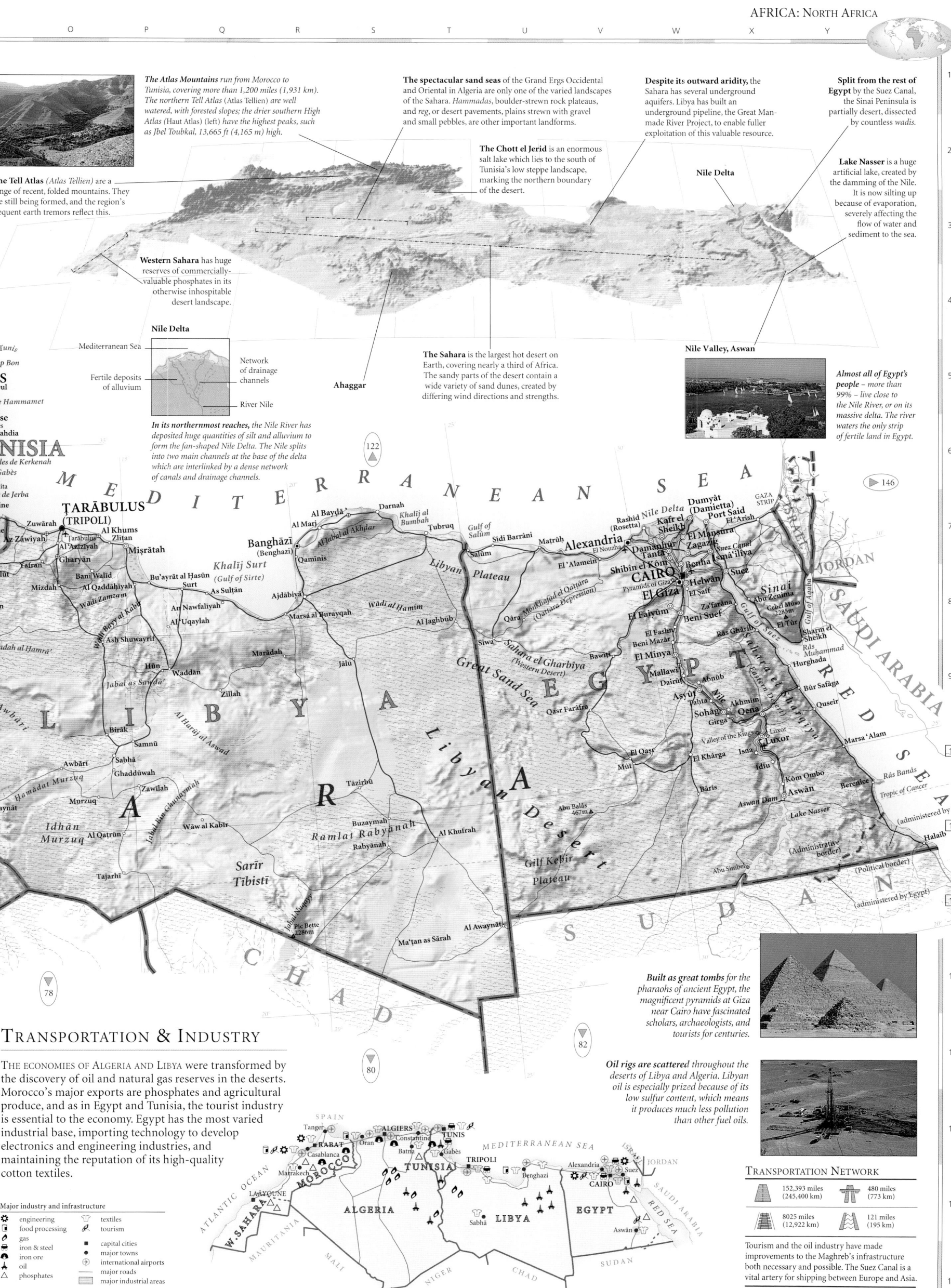

The Tell Atlas *(Atlas Tellien)* are a range of recent, folded mountains. They are still being formed, and the region's frequent earth tremors reflect this.

The Chott el Jerid is an enormous salt lake which lies to the south of Tunisia's low steppe landscape, marking the northern boundary of the desert.

Nile Delta

Lake Nasser is a huge artificial lake, created by the damming of the Nile. It is now silting up because of evaporation, severely affecting the flow of water and sediment to the sea.

Western Sahara has huge reserves of commercially-valuable phosphates in its otherwise inhospitable desert landscape.

Ahaggar

The Sahara is the largest hot desert on Earth, covering nearly a third of Africa. The sandy parts of the desert contain a wide variety of sand dunes, created by differing wind directions and strengths.

Nile Valley, Aswan

Nile Delta

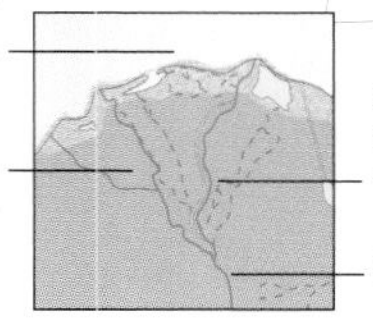

***In its northernmost reaches,** the Nile River has deposited huge quantities of silt and alluvium to form the fan-shaped Nile Delta. The Nile splits into two main channels at the base of the delta which are interlinked by a dense network of canals and drainage channels.*

***Almost all of Egypt's people** – more than 99% – live close to the Nile River, or on its massive delta. The river waters the only strip of fertile land in Egypt.*

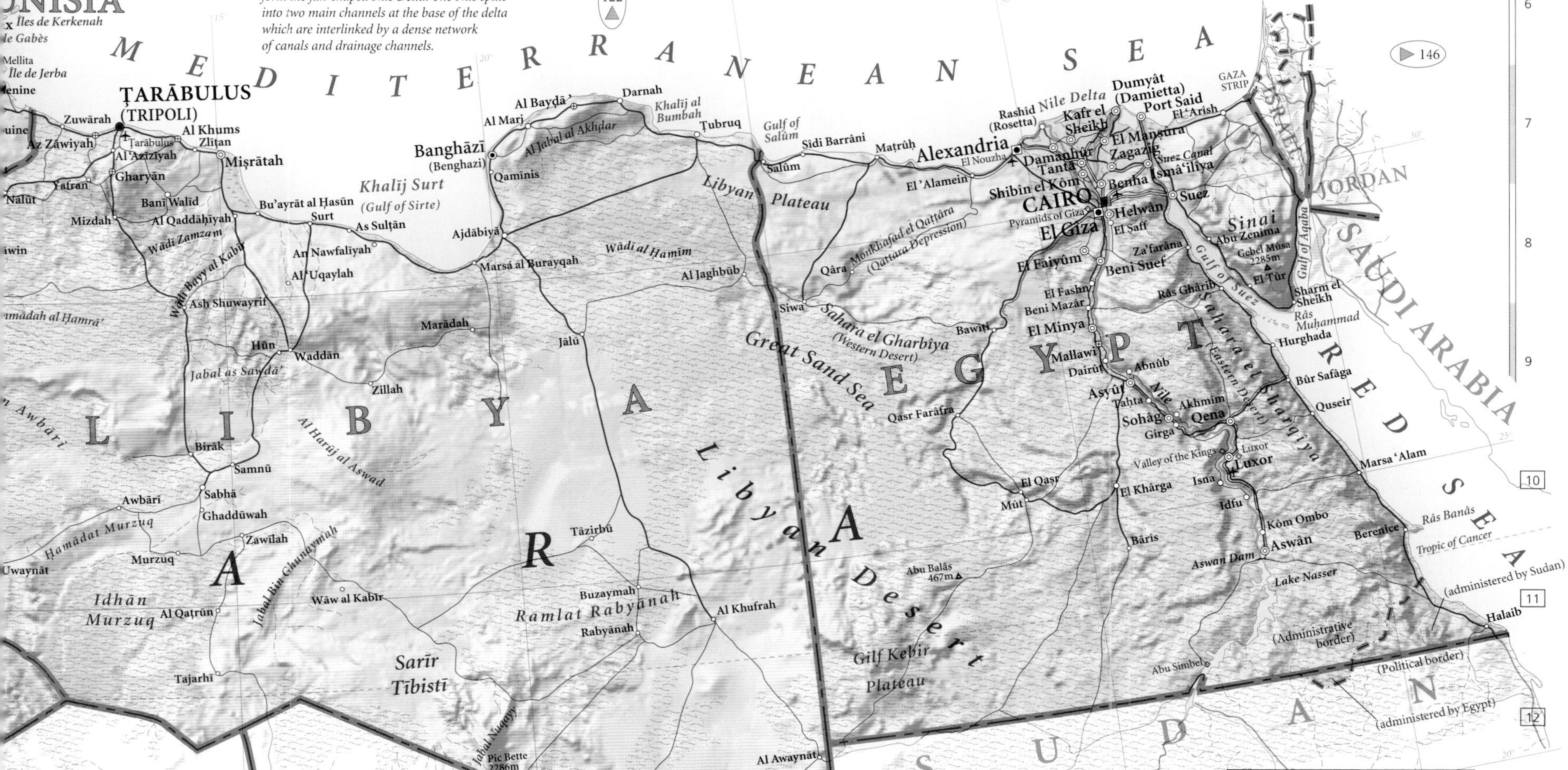

122
146
10
11
12
78
80
82

***Built as great tombs** for the pharaohs of ancient Egypt, the magnificent pyramids at Giza near Cairo have fascinated scholars, archaeologists, and tourists for centuries.*

Transportation & Industry

The economies of Algeria and Libya were transformed by the discovery of oil and natural gas reserves in the deserts. Morocco's major exports are phosphates and agricultural produce, and as in Egypt and Tunisia, the tourist industry is essential to the economy. Egypt has the most varied industrial base, importing technology to develop electronics and engineering industries, and maintaining the reputation of its high-quality cotton textiles.

***Oil rigs are scattered** throughout the deserts of Libya and Algeria. Libyan oil is especially prized because of its low sulfur content, which means it produces much less pollution than other fuel oils.*

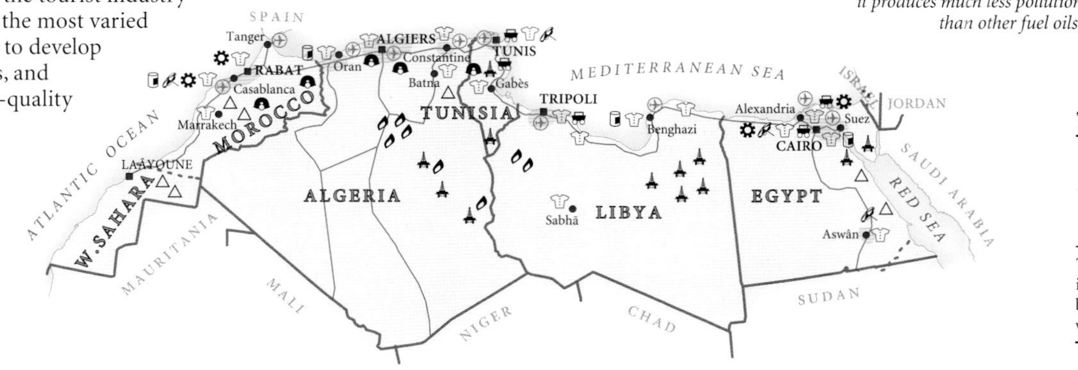

Major industry and infrastructure

- engineering
- food processing
- gas
- iron & steel
- iron ore
- oil
- phosphates
- textiles
- tourism
- capital cities
- major towns
- international airports
- major roads
- major industrial areas

Transportation Network

152,393 miles (245,400 km)	480 miles (773 km)
8025 miles (12,922 km)	121 miles (195 km)

Tourism and the oil industry have made improvements to the Maghreb's infrastructure both necessary and possible. The Suez Canal is a vital artery for shipping between Europe and Asia.

N O P Q R S T U V W X Y Z

WEST AFRICA

BENIN, BURKINA, CAPE VERDE, GAMBIA, GHANA, GUINEA, GUINEA-BISSAU, IVORY COAST, LIBERIA, MALI, MAURITANIA, NIGER, NIGERIA, SENEGAL, SIERRA LEONE, TOGO

WEST AFRICA IS AN IMMENSELY DIVERSE REGION, encompassing the desert landscapes and mainly Muslim populations of the southern Saharan countries, and the tropical rain forests of the more humid south, with a great variety of local languages and cultures. The rich natural resources and accessibility of the area were quickly exploited by Europeans; most of the Africans taken by slave traders came from this region, causing serious depopulation. The very different influences of West Africa's leading colonial powers, Britain and France, remain today, reflected in the languages and institutions of the countries they once governed.

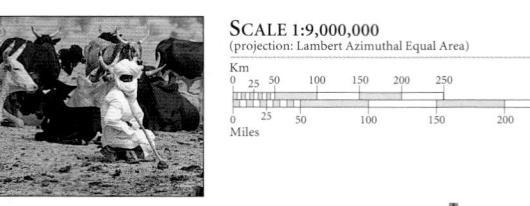

The dry scrub of the Sahel is only suitable for grazing herd animals like these cattle in Mali.

TRANSPORTATION & INDUSTRY

ABUNDANT NATURAL RESOURCES including oil and metallic minerals are found in much of West Africa, although investment is required for their further exploitation. Nigeria experienced an oil boom during the 1970s but subsequent growth has been sporadic. Most industry in other countries has a primary basis, including mining, logging, and food processing.

TRANSPORTATION NETWORK

163,769 miles (263,719 km)		1,554 miles (2,502 km)	
6,819 miles (10,980 km)		9,470 miles (15,250 km)	

The road and rail systems are most developed near the coasts. Some of the landlocked countries remain disadvantaged by the difficulty of access to ports, and their poor road networks.

Major industry and infrastructure
- chemicals
- cotton spinning
- food processing
- mining
- oil
- palm oil processing
- peanut processing
- textiles
- vehicle manufacture
- capital cities
- major towns
- international airports
- major roads
- major industrial areas

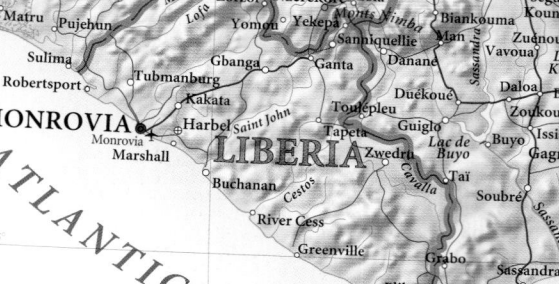

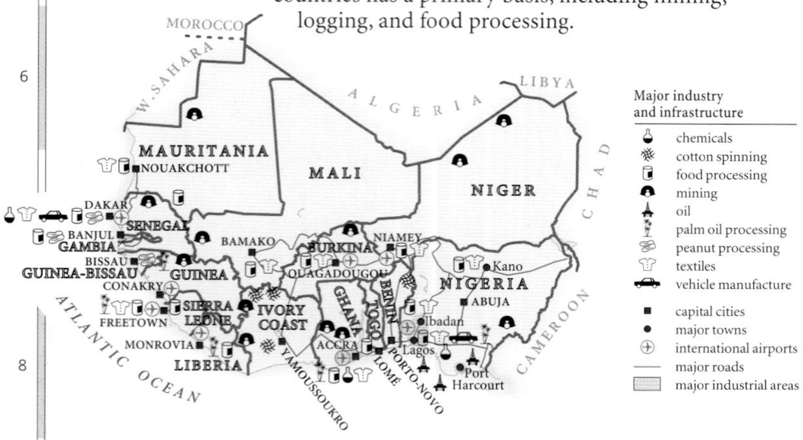

MAP KEY

POPULATION
- 1 million to 5 million
- 500,000 to 1 million
- 100,000 to 500,000
- 50,000 to 100,000
- 10,000 to 50,000
- below 10,000

ELEVATION
- 2000m / 6562ft
- 1000m / 3281ft
- 500m / 1640ft
- 250m / 820ft
- 100m / 328ft
- sea level

CAPE VERDE

Santo Antão, Pombas, Ilhas de Barlavento, Mindelo, São Vicente, Ribeira Brava, São Nicolau, Amílcar Cabral, Pedra Lume, Sal, Boa Vista, João Barrosa

ATLANTIC OCEAN

Tarrafal, Maio, Fogo, Maio, São Filipe, Santiago, PRAIA, Ilhas de Sotavento

(same scale as main map)

The southern regions of West Africa still contain great swaths of tropical rain forest, including some of the world's most prized hardwood trees, such as mahogany and iroko.

USING THE LAND AND SEA

THE HUMID SOUTHERN REGIONS are most suitable for cultivation; in these areas, cash crops such as coffee, cotton, cocoa, and rubber are grown in large quantities. Peanuts are grown throughout West Africa. In the north, advancing desertification has made the Sahel increasingly uncultivable, and pastoral farming is more common. Great herds of sheep, cattle, and goats are grazed on the savannah grasses. Fishing is important in coastal and delta areas.

Land use and agricultural distribution
- goats
- sheep
- cocoa
- coffee
- cotton
- oil palms
- peanuts
- rubber
- shellfish
- capital cities
- major towns
- pasture
- cropland
- forest
- desert

The Gambia, mainland Africa's smallest country, produces great quantities of peanuts. Winnowing is used to separate the nuts from their stalks.

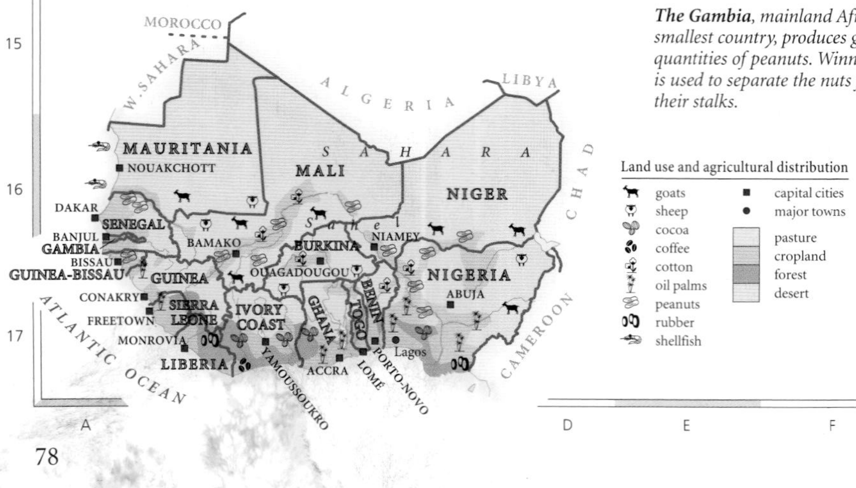

THE URBAN/RURAL POPULATION DIVIDE

urban 36% rural 64%

0 10 20 30 40 50 60 70 80 90 100

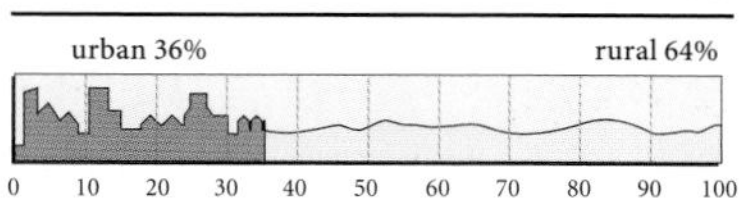

POPULATION DENSITY
98 people per sq mile
(38 people per sq km)

TOTAL LAND AREA
2,337,137 sq miles
(6,054,760 sq km)

SCALE 1:9,000,000
(projection: Lambert Azimuthal Equal Area)

Km
0 25 50 100 150 200 250
Miles

N O P Q R S T U V W X Y

Inselbergs are isoloated hills, formed where the surrounding plain has eroded away, leaving only a remnant of the original plateau. They are found across the Sahel and may include even more resistant outcrops.

Two types of coastline characterize West Africa. Swampy, muddy coasts, colonized by mangroves occur on river deltas and where ocean currents are weak, like the coast of Senegal. Sandy beaches, with barrier ridges and lagoons, form where currents are stronger.

The dry grasslands of the Sahel border the southern reaches of the Sahara. Overgrazing, drought, and the cutting down of trees for firewood, means that much of the Sahel is turning irrevocably to desert.

***The Niger River** flows for 2,600 miles (4,181 km) from Fouta Djallon, on the plateau of Guinea, via southern Mali, where it supports rich fish stocks, on through the desert, and finally through Nigeria to the Gulf of Guinea.*

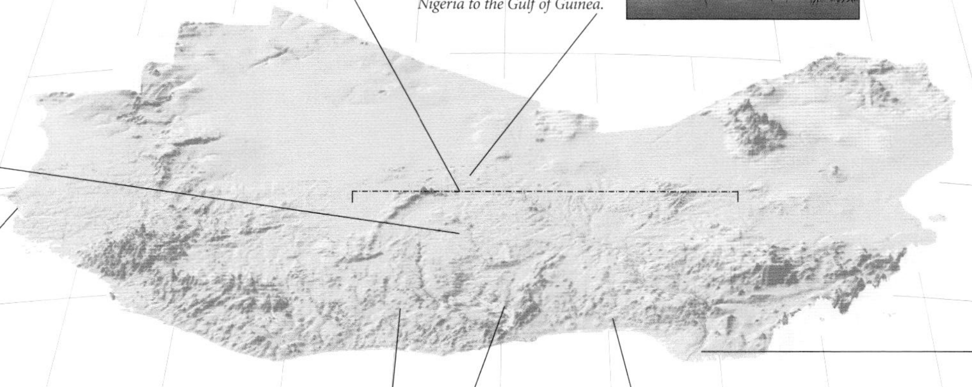

The Landscape

There are two major topographical areas in West Africa: the northern deserts are part of the Saharan region which stretches across the whole continent; the grasslands of the Sahel and the southern Guinea coast are part of Africa's central plateau. The landscape is generally low, rarely rising above 1,500 ft (457 m) and consists mainly of plains, broken by an occasional high plateau or mountain range.

As it nears the Gulf of Guinea, the Niger forks into many strands. When the river floods, alluvium is deposited over a wide area. This creates fertile soils, able to support both crops and livestock.

Virgin rainforest which once covered much of the West African coast, has been drastically reduced by logging and agricultural land clearance.

Lake Volta is an artificial lake, created by the damming of the Volta River. It links the drier northern areas with the coast and is intended to provide fresh water for drinking, fisheries, and irrigation.

Barrier beaches

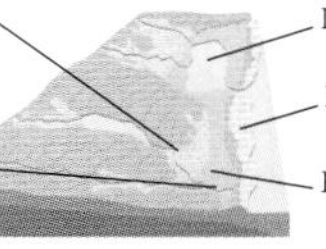

***Along much of the West** African coast, barrier beaches have built up and dammed river mouths, forming fluvial and estuarine plains.*

CENTRAL AFRICA

CAMEROON, CENTRAL AFRICAN REPUBLIC, CHAD, CONGO, DEM. REP. CONGO, EQUATORIAL GUINEA, GABON, SAO TOME & PRINCIPE

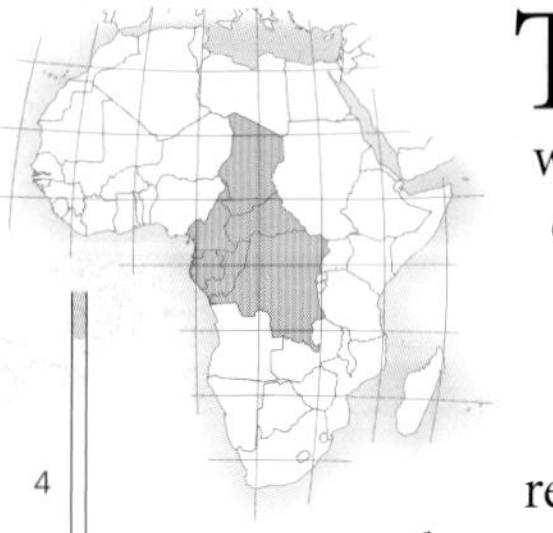

THE GREAT RAIN FOREST BASIN of the Congo River embraces most of remote Central Africa. The interior was largely unknown to Europeans until late in the 19th century, when its tribal kingdoms were split – principally between France and Belgium – with Sao Tome and Principe the lone Portuguese territory, and Equatorial Guinea controlled by Spain. Open democracy and regional economic integration are important goals for these nations – several of which have only recently emerged from restrictive regimes – and investment is needed to improve transportation infrastructures. Many of the small, but fast-growing and increasingly urban population, speak French, the regional *lingua franca*, along with several hundred Pygmy, Bantu, and Sudanic dialects.

THE LANDSCAPE

LAKE CHAD LIES in a desert basin bounded by the volcanic Tibesti Mountains in the north, plateaus in the east and, in the south, the broad watershed of the Congo Basin. The vast circular depression of the Congo is isolated from the coastal plain by the granite Massif du Chaillu. To the northwest, the volcanoes and fold mountains of the Cameroon Ridge *(Dorsale Camerounaise)* extend as islands into the Gulf of Guinea. The high fold mountains fringing the east of the Congo Basin fall steeply to the lakes of the Great Rift Valley.

A plug of resistant lava, *at the southwestern end of the Cameroon Ridge* (Dorsale Camerounaise), *is all that remains of an eroded volcano.*

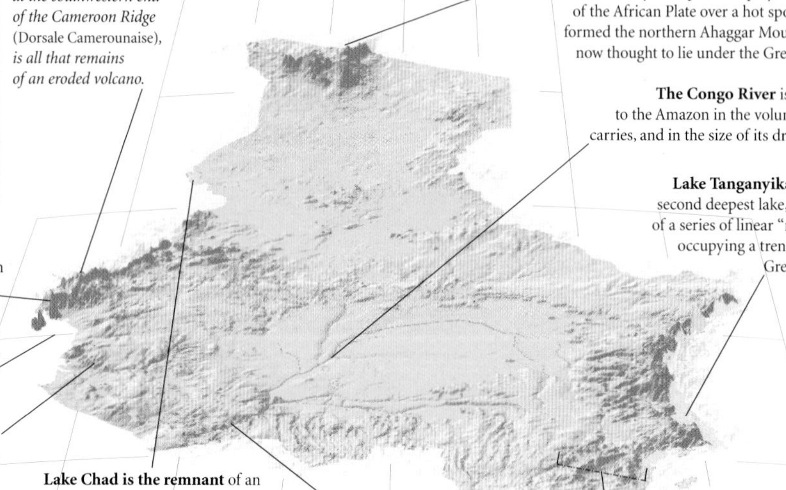

The volcanic massif of Cameroon Mountain occupies an area which remains volcanically active.

Lake Chad is the remnant of an inland sea, which once occupied much of the surrounding basin. A series of droughts since the 1970s has reduced the area of this shallow freshwater lake to about 1,000 sq miles (2,599 sq km).

The lake-like expansion of the Congo River at Stanley Pool is the lowest point of the interior basin, although the river still descends more than 1,000 ft (300 m) to reach the sea.

The Tibesti Mountains are the highest in the Sahara. They were pushed up by the movement of the African Plate over a hot spot, which first formed the northern Ahaggar Mountains and is now thought to lie under the Great Rift Valley.

The Congo River is second only to the Amazon in the volume of water it carries, and in the size of its drainage basin.

Lake Tanganyika, the world's second deepest lake, is the largest of a series of linear "ribbon" lakes occupying a trench within the Great Rift Valley.

Rich mineral deposits in the "Copper Belt" of Dem. Rep. Congo were formed under intense heat and pressure when the ancient African Shield was uplifted to form the region's mountains.

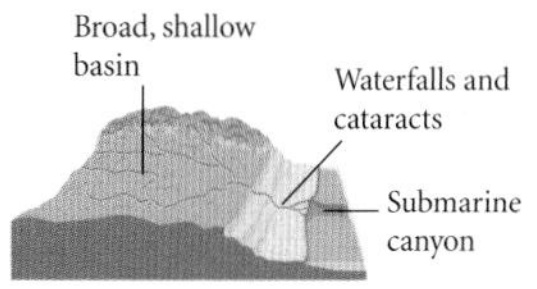

The Congo River *flows sluggishly through the rain forest of the interior basin. Toward the coast, the river drops steeply in a series of waterfalls and cataracts. At this point, the erosional power of the river becomes so great that it has formed a deep submarine canyon offshore.*

Virgin tropical rain forest *covers the Ruwenzori range on the borders of Dem. Rep. Congo and Uganda.*

The vast sandflats *surrounding Lake Chad were once covered by water. Changing climatic patterns caused the lake to shrink, and desert now covers much of its previous area.*

TRANSPORTATION & INDUSTRY

LARGE RESERVES OF VALUABLE MINERALS are found in Central Africa: copper, cobalt, zinc, and tin are mined in Dem. Rep. Congo and Cameroon; diamonds in the Central African Republic, and manganese in Gabon. Congo, Cameroon, Gabon, and Dem. Rep. Congo have oil deposits and oil has also been recently discovered in Chad. Goods such as palm oil and rubber are processed for export.

The ancient rocks *of Dem. Rep. Congo hold immense and varied mineral reserves. This open pit copper mine is at Kolwezi in the far south.*

Major industry and infrastructure
- brewing
- chemicals
- cobalt
- copper
- diamonds
- food processing
- manganese
- oil
- palm oil processing
- textiles
- tin
- capital cities
- major towns
- international airports
- major roads
- major industrial areas

TRANSPORTATION NETWORK

124,349 miles (200,240 km)	342 miles (550 km)
3,830 miles (6,167 km)	15,261 miles (24,575 km)

The Trans-Gabon railroad, which began operating in 1987, has opened up new sources of timber and manganese. Elsewhere, much investment is needed to update and improve road, rail, and water transportation.

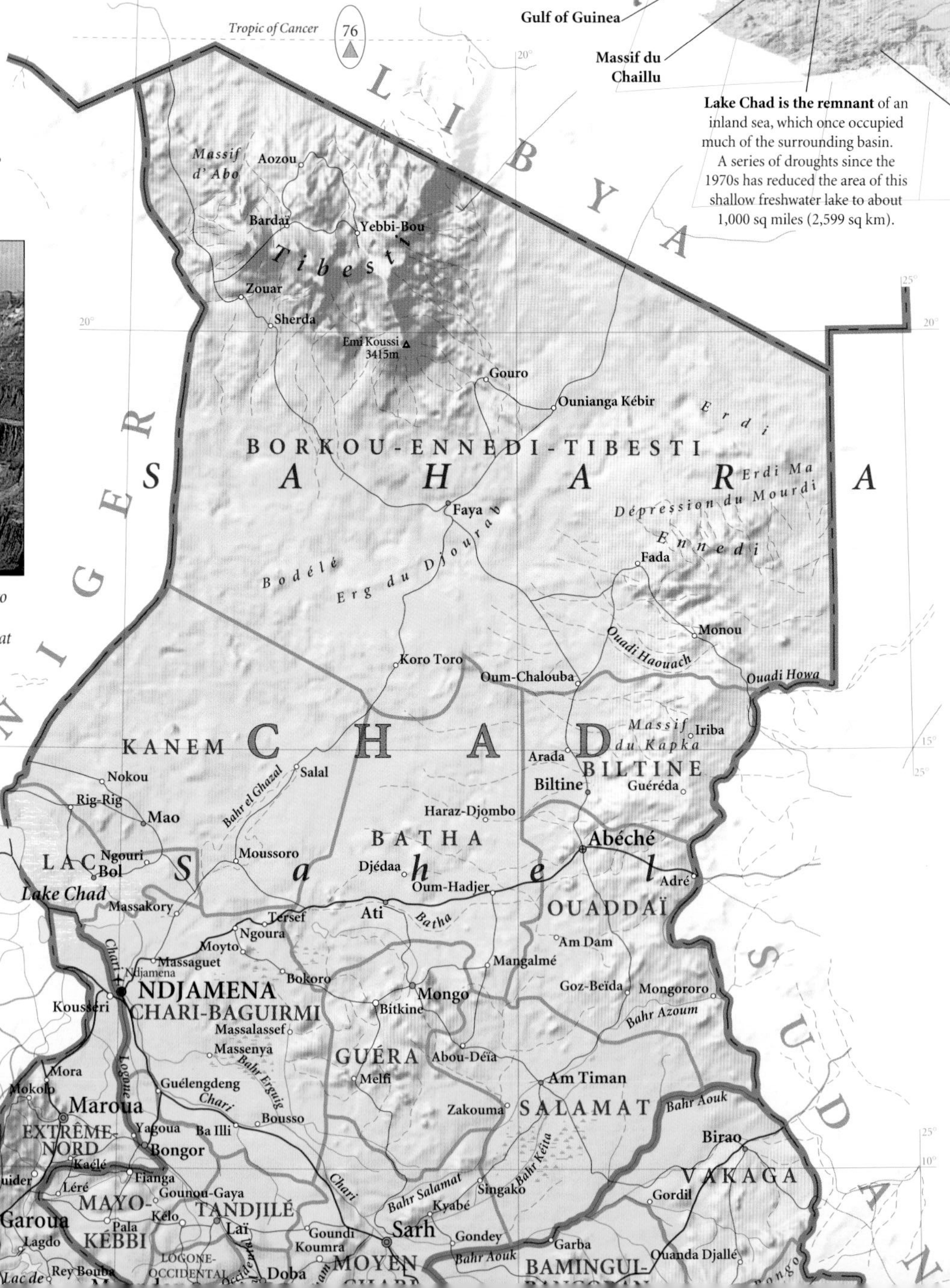

MAP KEY

POPULATION
- 1 million to 5 million
- 500,000 to 1 million
- 100,000 to 500,000
- 50,000 to 100,000
- 10,000 to 50,000
- below 10,000

ELEVATION
- 4000m / 13,124ft
- 3000m / 9843ft
- 2000m / 6562ft
- 1000m / 3281ft
- 500m / 1640ft
- 250m / 820ft
- 100m / 328ft
- sea level

SCALE 1:9,500,000
(projection: Lambert Azimuthal Equal Area)

Km 0 25 50 100 150 200 250
Miles 0 25 50 100 150 200 250

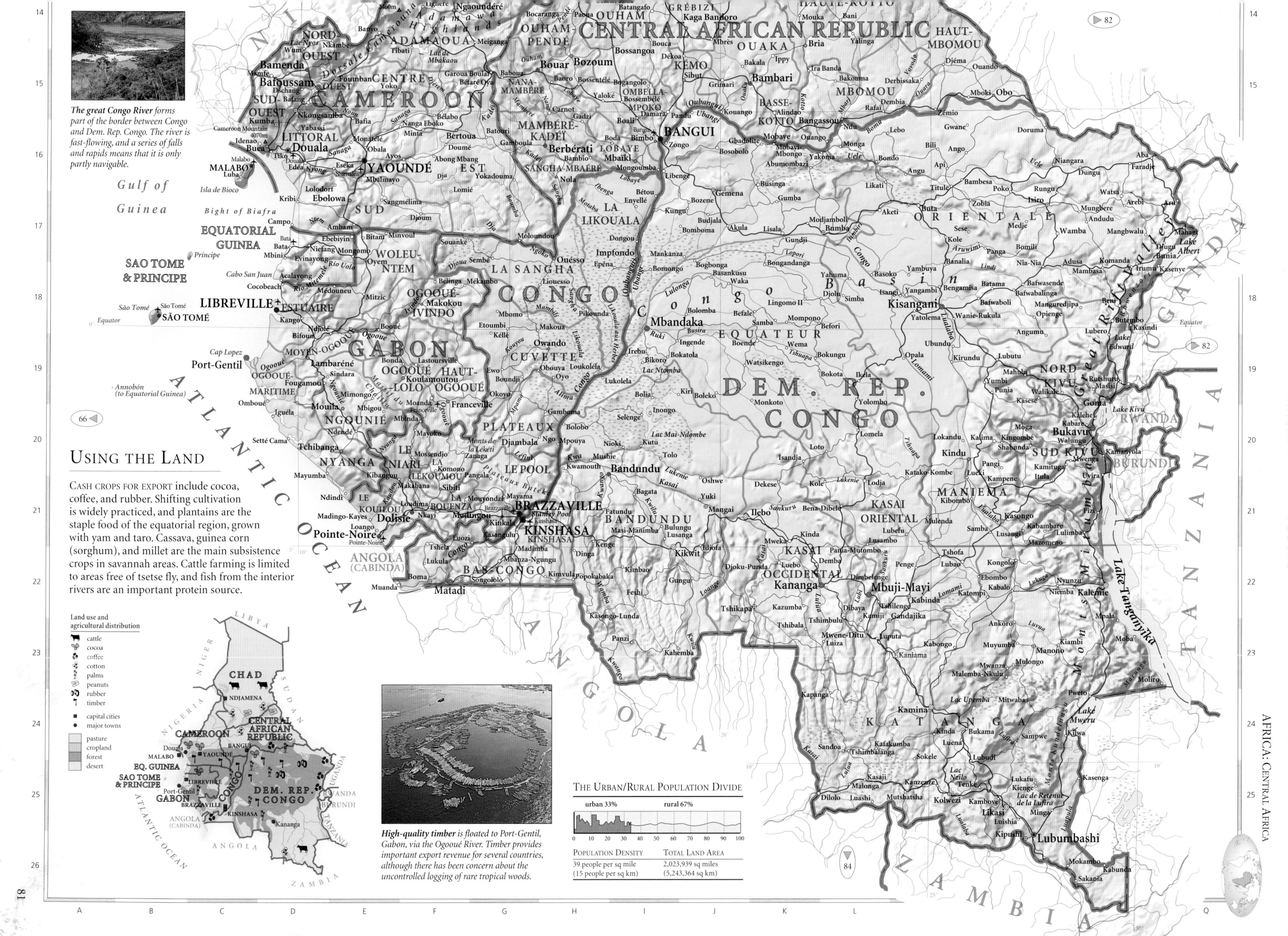

The great Congo River forms part of the border between Congo and Dem. Rep. Congo. The river is fast-flowing, and a series of falls and rapids means that it is only partly navigable.

Using the Land

Cash crops for export include cocoa, coffee, and rubber. Shifting cultivation is widely practiced, and plantains are the staple food of the equatorial region, grown with yam and taro. Cassava, guinea corn (sorghum), and millet are the main subsistence crops in savannah areas. Cattle farming is limited to areas free of tsetse fly, and fish from the interior rivers are an important protein source.

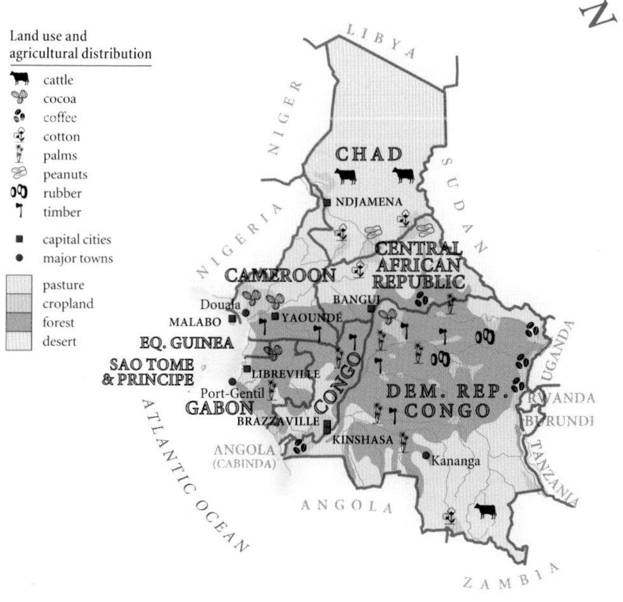

***High-quality timber** is floated to Port-Gentil, Gabon, via the Ogooué River. Timber provides important export revenue for several countries, although there has been concern about the uncontrolled logging of rare tropical woods.*

The Urban/Rural Population Divide

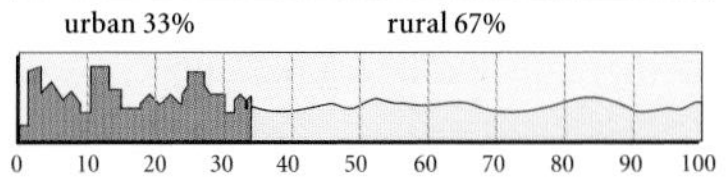

Population Density	Total Land Area
39 people per sq mile (15 people per sq km)	2,023,939 sq miles (5,243,364 sq km)

East Africa

Burundi, Djibouti, Eritrea, Ethiopia, Kenya, Rwanda, Somalia, Sudan, Tanzania, Uganda

The countries of East Africa divide into two distinct cultural regions. Sudan and the "Horn" nations have been influenced by the Middle East; Ethiopia was the home of one of the earliest Christian civilizations, and Sudan reflects both Muslim and Christian influences. The southern countries share a closer cultural affinity with other sub-Saharan nations. Some of Africa's most densely populated countries lie in this region, and the needs of a growing number of people have put pressure on marginal lands and fragile environments. Although most East African economies remain strongly agricultural, Kenya has developed a varied industrial base.

The Landscape

East Africa's most significant landscape feature is the Great Rift Valley, which formed during the most recent phase of continental movement when the rigid basement rocks cracked and buckled. Great blocks of land were raised and lowered, creating huge flat-bottomed valleys and steep escarpments, sometimes covered by volcanic extrusions in highland areas.

This dome at Gonder, in Ethiopia, is a volcanic intrusion, formed when molten rock pushed up the surface of the Earth and then solidified, leaving an outcrop of igneous rock.

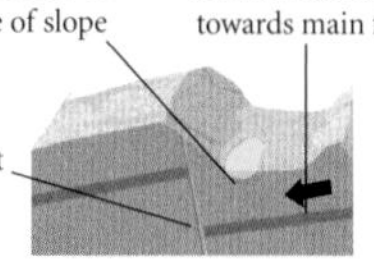

***The eastern arm** of the Great Rift Valley is gradually being pulled apart; however the forces on one side are greater than the other causing the land to slope. This affects regional drainage which migrates down the slope.*

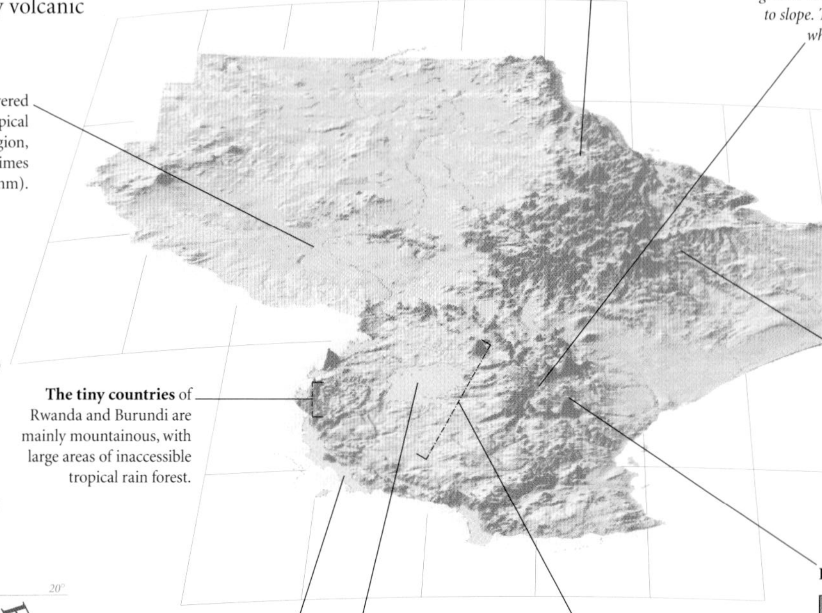

Much of northern Sudan is covered by desert. However, in the tropical wetlands of the southern Sudd region, annual rainfall can sometimes exceed 40 inches (1,000 mm).

The tiny countries of Rwanda and Burundi are mainly mountainous, with large areas of inaccessible tropical rain forest.

Lava flows on uplifted areas either side of the eastern branch of the Great Rift Valley gave the Ethiopian Highlands – a series of high, wide plateaus – their distinctive rounded appearance and fertile soils.

Lake Tanganyika lies 8,202 ft (2,500 m) above sea level. It has a depth of nearly 4,700 ft (1,435 m). The lake traces the valley floor for some 400 miles (644 km) of the western arm of the Great Rift Valley.

Lake Victoria occupies a vast basin between the two arms of the Great Rift Valley. It is the world's second largest lake in terms of surface area, extending 26,560 sq miles (68,880 sq km). The lake contains numerous islands and coral reefs.

A vast plateau lies between the eastern and western rift valleys in Kenya, Uganda, and western Tanzania. It has been leveled by long periods of erosion to form a peneplain, but is dotted with inselbergs – outcrops of more resistant rocks.

Kilimanjaro

***An extinct volcano,** Kilimanjaro is Africa's highest mountain, rising 19,340 ft (5,895 m). It is one of the few places in Africa where snow settles, allowing glacier ice to form.*

***The Kassala region** in eastern Sudan is watered by the Atbara River, an important tributary of the Nile. Most of the population is engaged in agriculture, growing cotton and cereals.*

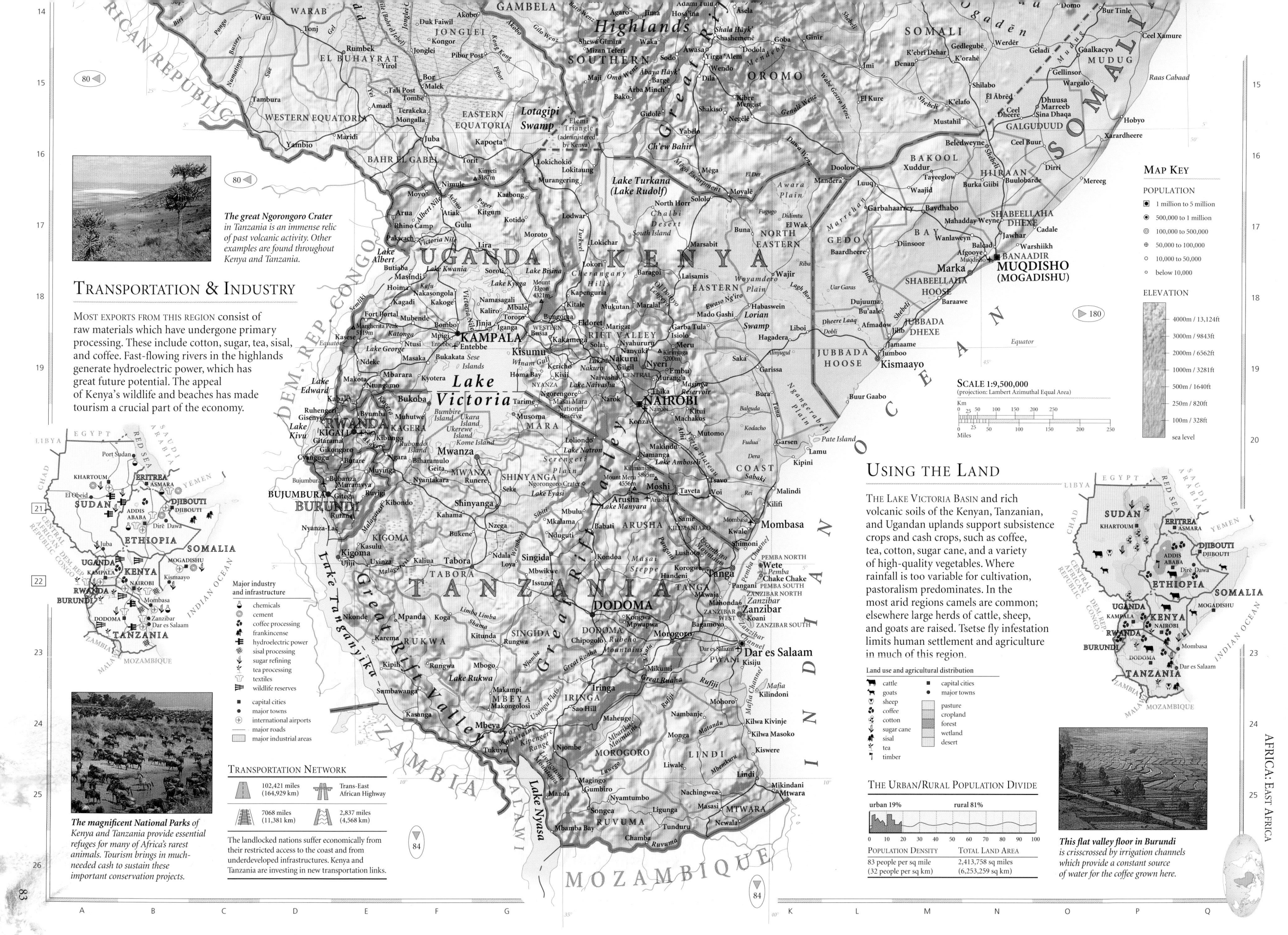

Map Key

POPULATION

- 1 million to 5 million
- 500,000 to 1 million
- 100,000 to 500,000
- 50,000 to 100,000
- 10,000 to 50,000
- below 10,000

ELEVATION

- 4000m / 13,124ft
- 3000m / 9843ft
- 2000m / 6562ft
- 1000m / 3281ft
- 500m / 1640ft
- 250m / 820ft
- 100m / 328ft
- sea level

SCALE 1:9,500,000
(projection: Lambert Azimuthal Equal Area)

80 ◀ 180 ▶ 84 ▼

The great Ngorongoro Crater in Tanzania is an immense relic of past volcanic activity. Other examples are found throughout Kenya and Tanzania.

Transportation & Industry

Most exports from this region consist of raw materials which have undergone primary processing. These include cotton, sugar, tea, sisal, and coffee. Fast-flowing rivers in the highlands generate hydroelectric power, which has great future potential. The appeal of Kenya's wildlife and beaches has made tourism a crucial part of the economy.

Major industry and infrastructure

- chemicals
- cement
- coffee processing
- frankincense
- hydroelectric power
- sisal processing
- sugar refining
- tea processing
- textiles
- wildlife reserves
- capital cities
- major towns
- international airports
- major roads
- major industrial areas

The magnificent National Parks of Kenya and Tanzania provide essential refuges for many of Africa's rarest animals. Tourism brings in much-needed cash to sustain these important conservation projects.

Transportation Network

102,421 miles (164,929 km)	Trans-East African Highway
7068 miles (11,381 km)	2,837 miles (4,568 km)

The landlocked nations suffer economically from their restricted access to the coast and from underdeveloped infrastructures. Kenya and Tanzania are investing in new transportation links.

Using the Land

The Lake Victoria Basin and rich volcanic soils of the Kenyan, Tanzanian, and Ugandan uplands support subsistence crops and cash crops, such as coffee, tea, cotton, sugar cane, and a variety of high-quality vegetables. Where rainfall is too variable for cultivation, pastoralism predominates. In the most arid regions camels are common; elsewhere large herds of cattle, sheep, and goats are raised. Tsetse fly infestation limits human settlement and agriculture in much of this region.

Land use and agricultural distribution

- cattle
- goats
- sheep
- coffee
- cotton
- sugar cane
- sisal
- tea
- timber
- capital cities
- major towns
- pasture
- cropland
- forest
- wetland
- desert

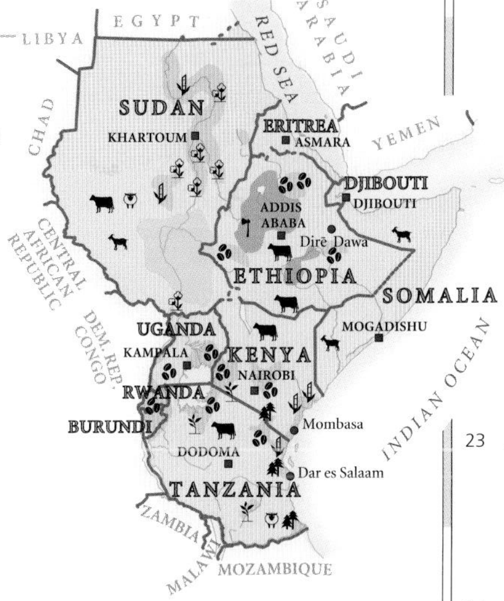

The Urban/Rural Population Divide

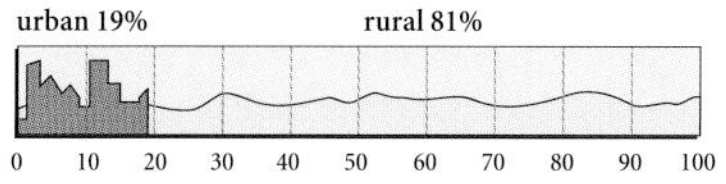

Population Density	Total Land Area
83 people per sq mile (32 people per sq km)	2,413,758 sq miles (6,253,259 sq km)

This flat valley floor in Burundi is crisscrossed by irrigation channels which provide a constant source of water for the coffee grown here.

Southern Africa

Angola, Botswana, Lesotho, Malawi, Mozambique, Namibia, South Africa, Swaziland, Zambia, Zimbabwe

Africa's vast southern plateau has been a contested homeland for disparate peoples for many centuries. The European incursion began with the slave trade and quickened in the 19th century, when the discovery of enormous mineral wealth secured South Africa's regional economic dominance. The struggle against white minority rule led to strife in Namibia, Zimbabwe, and the former Portuguese territories of Angola and Mozambique. South Africa's notorious apartheid laws, which denied basic human rights to more than 75% of the people, led to the state being internationally ostracized until 1994, when the first fully democratic elections inaugurated a new era of racial justice.

Transportation & Industry

South Africa, the world's largest exporter of gold, has a varied economy which generates about 75% of the region's income and draws migrant labor from neighboring states. Angola exports petroleum; Botswana and Namibia rely on diamond mining; and Zambia is seeking to diversify its economy to compensate for declining copper reserves.

Almost all new mining ventures in Zimbabwe are now subject to government control. This mine at Bindura in northeastern Zimbabwe produces nickel, one of the country's top three minerals in terms of economic value.

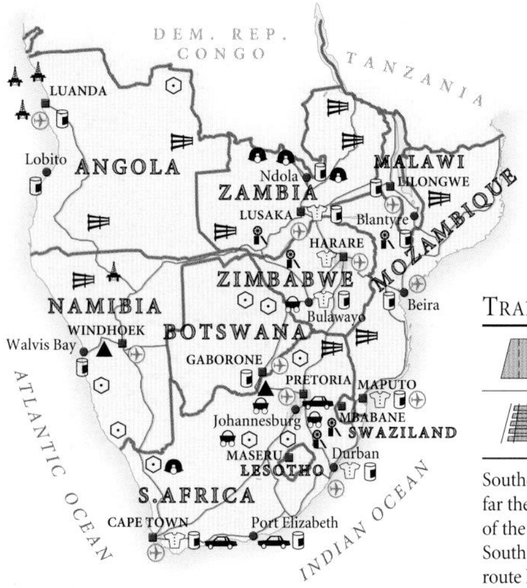

Major industry and infrastructure

car manufacture	gold	capital cities
coal	oil	major towns
copper	textiles	international airports
diamonds	uranium	major roads
food processing	wildlife reserves	major industrial areas

Transportation Network

84,213 miles (135,609 km)	746 miles (1,202 km)
23,208 miles (37,372 km)	3,815 miles (6,144 km)

Southern Africa's Cape-gauge rail network is by far the largest in the continent. About two-thirds of the 20,000 mile (32,000 km) system lies within South Africa. Lines such as the Harare–Bulawayo route have become corridors for industrial growth.

The Landscape

Most of southern Africa rests on a concave plateau comprising the Kalahari basin and a mountainous fringe, skirted by a coastal plain which widens out in Mozambique. The plateau extends north, toward the Planalto de Bié in Angola, the Congo Basin and the lake-filled troughs of the Great Rift Valley. The eastern region is drained by the Zambezi and Limpopo Rivers, and the Orange is the major western river.

Thousands of years of evaporating water have produced the Etosha Pan, one of the largest salt flats in the world. Lake and river sediments in the area indicate that the region was once less arid.

***Finger Rock, near Khorixas, Namibia** is a remnant of a former land surface, which has been denuded by erosion over the last 5 million years. These occasional stacks of partially weathered rocks interrupt the plains of the dry southern interior.*

***Following a series of droughts,** this baobab tree in Zimbabwe now stands alone in a field once filled by sugar cane. The thick trunk and small leaves of the baobab help it to conserve water, enabling it to survive even in drought conditions.*

At Victoria Falls, the Zambezi River has cut a spectacular gorge taking advantage of large joints in the basalt, which were first formed as the lava cooled and contracted.

The Okavango/Cubango River flows from the Planalto de Bié to the swamplands of the Okavango Delta, one of the world's largest inland deltas, where it divides into countless distributary channels, feeding out into the desert.

*The **fast-flowing** Zambezi River cuts a deep, wide channel as it flows along the Zimbabwe/Zambia border.*

Lake Nyasa occupies one of the deep troughs of the Great Rift Valley, where the land has been displaced downward by as much as 3,000 ft (920 m).

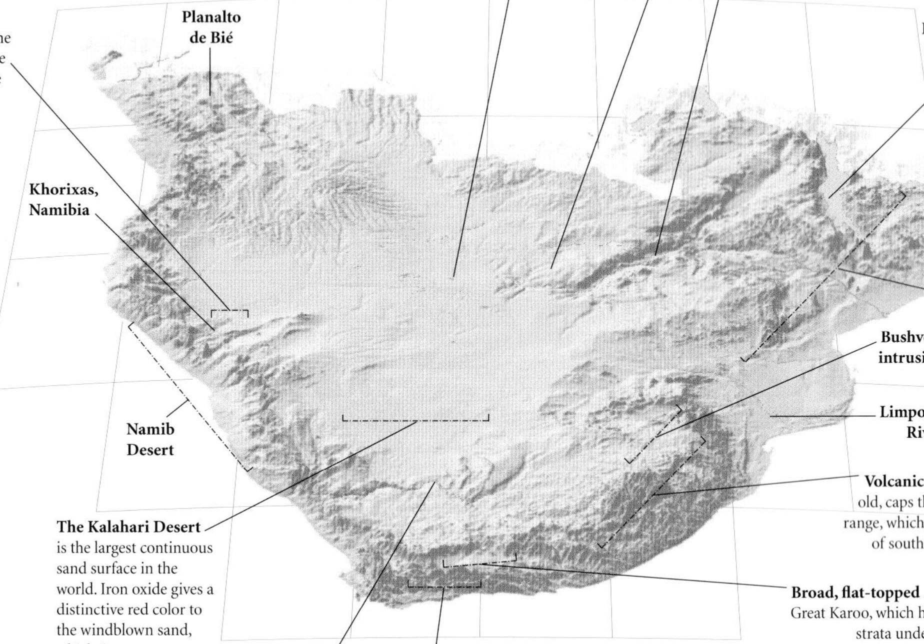

Volcanic lava, over 250 million years old, caps the peaks of the Drakensberg range, which lie on the mountainous rim of southern Africa's interior plateau.

Broad, flat-topped mountains characterize the Great Karoo, which have been cut from level rock strata under extremely arid conditions.

The Kalahari Desert is the largest continuous sand surface in the world. Iron oxide gives a distinctive red color to the windblown sand, which, in eastern areas covers the bedrock by over 200 ft (60 m).

The Orange River, one of the longest in Africa, rises in Lesotho and is the only major river in the south which flows westward, rather than to the east coast.

The mountains of the Little Karoo are composed of sedimentary rocks which have been substantially folded and faulted.

Bushveld intrusion

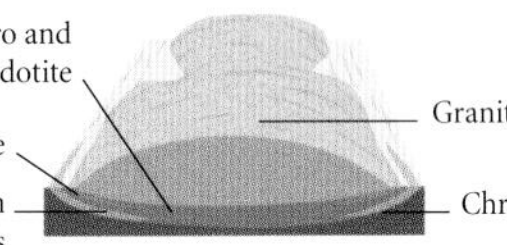

***The Bushveld intrusion** lies on South Africa's high "veld." Molten magma intruded into the Earth's crust creating a saucer-shaped feature, more than 180 miles (300 km) across, containing regular layers of precious minerals, overlain by a dome of granite.*

Scale 1:9,500,000
(projection: Lambert Azimuthal Equal Area)

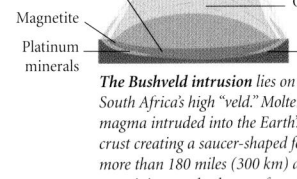

South Africa's Three Capitals

PRETORIA – administrative capital
CAPE TOWN – legislative capital
BLOEMFONTEIN – judicial capital

Map Key

POPULATION
- 1 million to 5 million
- 500,000 to 1 million
- 100,000 to 500,000
- 50,000 to 100,000
- 10,000 to 50,000
- below 10,000

ELEVATION
- 3000m / 9843ft
- 2000m / 6562ft
- 1000m / 3281ft
- 500m / 1640ft
- 250m / 820ft
- 100m / 328ft
- sea level

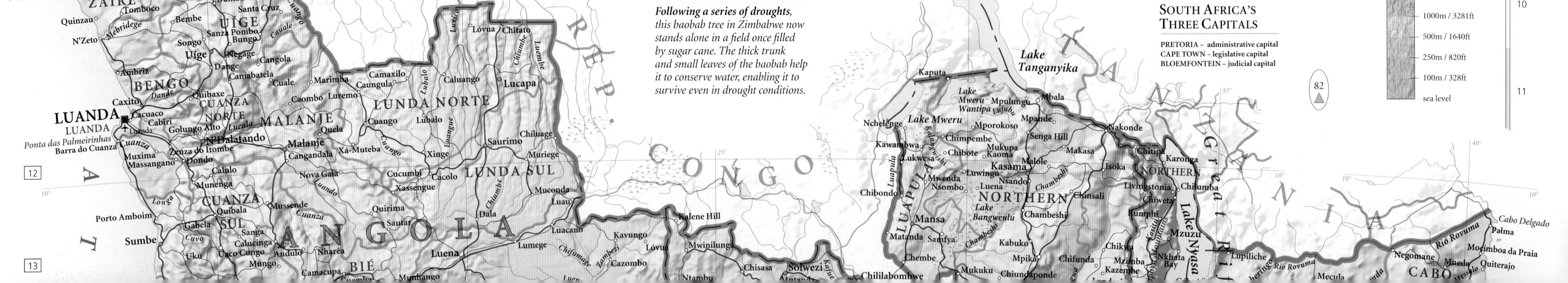

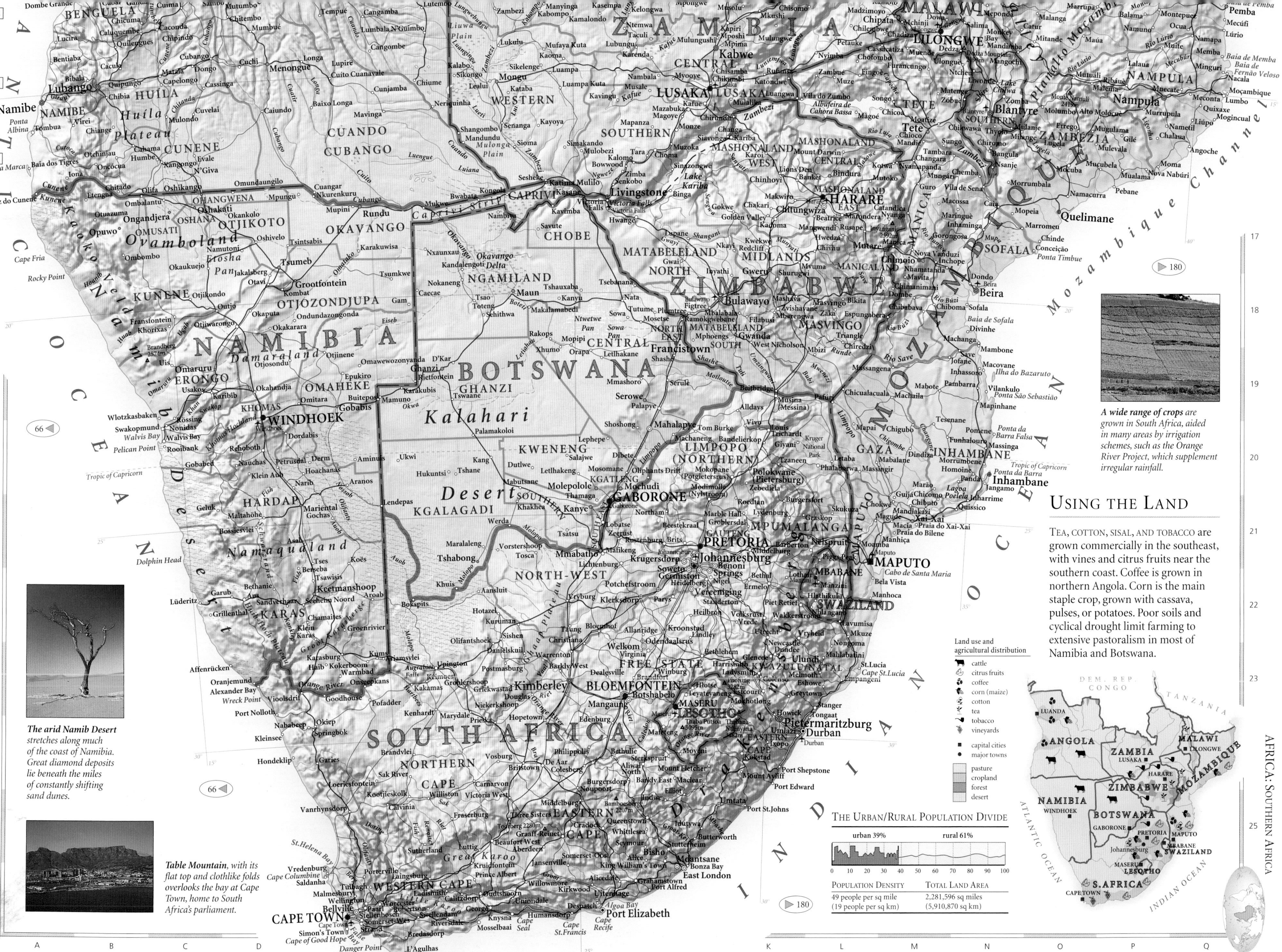

A wide range of crops are grown in South Africa, aided in many areas by irrigation schemes, such as the Orange River Project, which supplement irregular rainfall.

Using the Land

Tea, cotton, sisal, and tobacco are grown commercially in the southeast, with vines and citrus fruits near the southern coast. Coffee is grown in northern Angola. Corn is the main staple crop, grown with cassava, pulses, or potatoes. Poor soils and cyclical drought limit farming to extensive pastoralism in most of Namibia and Botswana.

Land use and agricultural distribution
- cattle
- citrus fruits
- coffee
- corn (maize)
- cotton
- tea
- tobacco
- vineyards
- capital cities
- major towns
- pasture
- cropland
- forest
- desert

The Urban/Rural Population Divide

urban 39% | rural 61%

0 10 20 30 40 50 60 70 80 90 100

Population Density	Total Land Area
49 people per sq mile	2,281,596 sq miles
(19 people per sq km)	(5,910,870 sq km)

The arid Namib Desert stretches along much of the coast of Namibia. Great diamond deposits lie beneath the miles of constantly shifting sand dunes.

Table Mountain, with its flat top and clothlike folds overlooks the bay at Cape Town, home to South Africa's parliament.

66 ◀
▶ 180

ARCTIC OCEAN
North Pole
Ellesmere Island
Laptey Sea
Severnaya Zemlya
Ostrov Rudol'fa
Franz Josef Land
Poluostrov Taymyr
Kara Sea
Mys Flissingskiy
King Frederik VIII Land
Greenland
NORTH AMERICAN PLATE
EURASIAN PLATE
Spitsbergen
Greenland Sea
King Christian X Land
Barents Sea
Novaya Zemlya
Poluostrov Yamal
Baydaratskaya Guba
Gulf of Ob
Yenisey
Bjørnøya
Barents Trough
North Cape
Nordkinn
Kara Strait
Murmansk Rise
Tromsøflaket
Fugløya Bank
Ostrov Kolguyev
Poluostrov Kanin
Pechora
Ob'
West Siberian Plain
Jan Mayen Fracture Zone
Jan Mayen
Kolbeinsey Ridge
Arctic Circle
Denmark Strait
Iceland Plateau
Jan Mayen Ridge
Norwegian Sea
Norwegian Basin
Vesterålen
Inarijärvi
Kola Peninsula
Ozero Imandra
Bjartangar
Iceland
Vatnajokull
Reykjanes Ridge
Voring Plateau
Lofoten
Kebnekaise 2117m
Torneälven
Luleälven
Kemijoki
Tuloma
White Sea
Timanskiy Kryazh
Mezen'
Gora Narodnaya 1895m
Vychegda
Ural Mountains
ASIA
Faeroe-Iceland Ridge
Traena Bank
Kölen
Umeälven
Oulujoki
Onega Bay
Ozero Vygozero
Northern Dvina
Iceland Basin
Faeroe Islands
Bill Baileys Bank
Faeroe-Shetland Trough
Galdhøpiggen 2469m
Scandinavia
Ljungan
Ljusnan
Gulf of Bothnia
Lake Ladoga
Lake Onega
Onega
Vaga
Svir
Ozero Beloye
Sukhona
Yug
Kama
Chusovaya
Tobol
Hatton Ridge
Shetland Islands
Viking Bank
Glåma
Åland
Gulf of Finland
Rybinsk Reservoir
Votkinsk Reservoir
Vyatka
Outer Hebrides
Orkney Islands
Norwegian Trench
Vänern
Lake Peipus
Msta
Lake Ilmen
Gor'kiy Reservoir
Kuybyshev Reservoir
Rockall Rise
Ben Nevis 1343m
Grampian Mountains
Jutland Bank
Skagerrak
Kattegat
Vättern
Gotland
Gulf of Riga
Lake Pskov
Moskva
Oka
Sura
Belaya
Ural
Feni Ridge
Rockall Trough
North Channel
North Sea
Great Fisher Bank
Jylland
Sjælland
Baltic Sea
Western Dvina
North European Plain
Volga Upland
Volga
Samara
ATLANTIC OCEAN
British Isles
Ireland
Irish Sea
Pennines
Dogger Bank
Neman
Shannon
Snowdon 1085m
Trent
Britain
Frisian Islands
Dnieper
Berezina
Khoper
Central Russian Upland
Don
Porcupine Plain
Celtic Sea
St. George's Channel
Severn
The Fens
Elbe
Oder
Warta
Vistula
Bug
Pripet Marshes
Desna
Seym
Celtic Shelf
Bristol Channel
Thames
Strait of Dover
Harz
EUROPE
Dnieper Lowlands
Donets
Kirghiz Steppe
Land's End
English Channel
Channel Islands
Ardennes
Rhine
Kiev Reservoir
Kremenchuk Reservoir
Tsimlyansk Reservoir
Volga
Seine
Marne
Moselle
Dniester
Podil's'ka Vysochina
Pivdennyy Buh
Dnieper
Don
Manych
Yergeni
Loire
Vienne
Cher
Vosges
Black Forest
Danube
Lake Constance
Carpathian Mountains
Tisza
Siret
Prut
Black Sea Lowland
Sea of Azov
Kuban'
Charcot Seamounts
Biscay Plain
Bay of Biscay
Massif Central
Saône
Lake Geneva
Alps
Mont Blanc 4807m
Bakony
Lake Balaton
Great Hungarian Plain
Mureş
Transylvanian Alps
Crimea
Kerch Strait
Azores-Biscay Rise
Theta Gap
Galicia Bank
Garonne
Dordogne
Lot
Cévennes
Rhône
Lake Garda
Po
Drava
Sava
Tisza
Black Sea
Miño
Cordillera Cantabrica
Iberian Peninsula
Aragón
Pyrenees
Aneto 3404m
Gulf of Lion
Ligurian Sea
Adriatic Sea
Apennines
Dinaric Alps
Drina
Danube
Balkan Mountains
Iberian Plain
Douro
Duero
Sistema Ibérico
Ebro
Tiber
Corno Grande 2912m
Lake Scutari
Maritsa
Rhodope Mountains
Bosporus
EURASIAN PLATE
ANATOLIAN PLATE
Sistema Central
Corsica
Strait of Bonifacio
Adriatic Basin
Lake Ohrid
Lake Prespa
Sea of Marmara
Tagus
Cabo da Roca
Guadiana
Júcar
Gulf of Valencia
Tyrrhenian Sea
Gulf of Taranto
Strait of Otranto
Pindus Mountains
Aegean Sea
Anatolia
Lake Tuz
Tagus Plain
Sierra Morena
Guadalquivir
Segura
Balearic Islands
Algerian Basin
Sardinia
Tyrrhenian Basin
Strait of Messina
Gorringe Ridge
Cape Saint Vincent
Punta de Tarifa
Sistemas Beticos
Sierra Nevada
Mediterranean Sea
Horseshoe Seamounts
Ampere Seamount
Strait of Gibraltar
Alboran Sea
Oued Chelif
EURASIAN PLATE
AFRICAN PLATE
Mount Etna 3340m
Strait of Sicily
Sicily
Ionian Sea
Peloponnese
Mirtoan Sea
Taurus Mountains
Gulf of Antalya
Karpathian Strait
Rhodes Basin
Seine Plain
Seine Seamount
Rif
Sebou
Tell Atlas
Malta
Ionian Basin
Sea of Crete
Crete
Kasos Strait
Gavdos
Cyprus
Cyprus Basin
Madeira
Oum er Rbia
Middle Atlas
Moulouya
Atlas Mountains
Mediterranean Ridge
Agadir Canyon
Dacia Seamount
High Atlas
Saharan Atlas
Chott el Jerid
Levantine Basin
Nile Fan
Canary Islands
Gulf of Sirte
Suez Canal
Nile
Grand Erg Occidental
Grand Erg Oriental
Qattara Depression -133m
Western Desert
Libyan Desert
AFRICA
SAHARA
'Erg Iguidi
Erg Chech

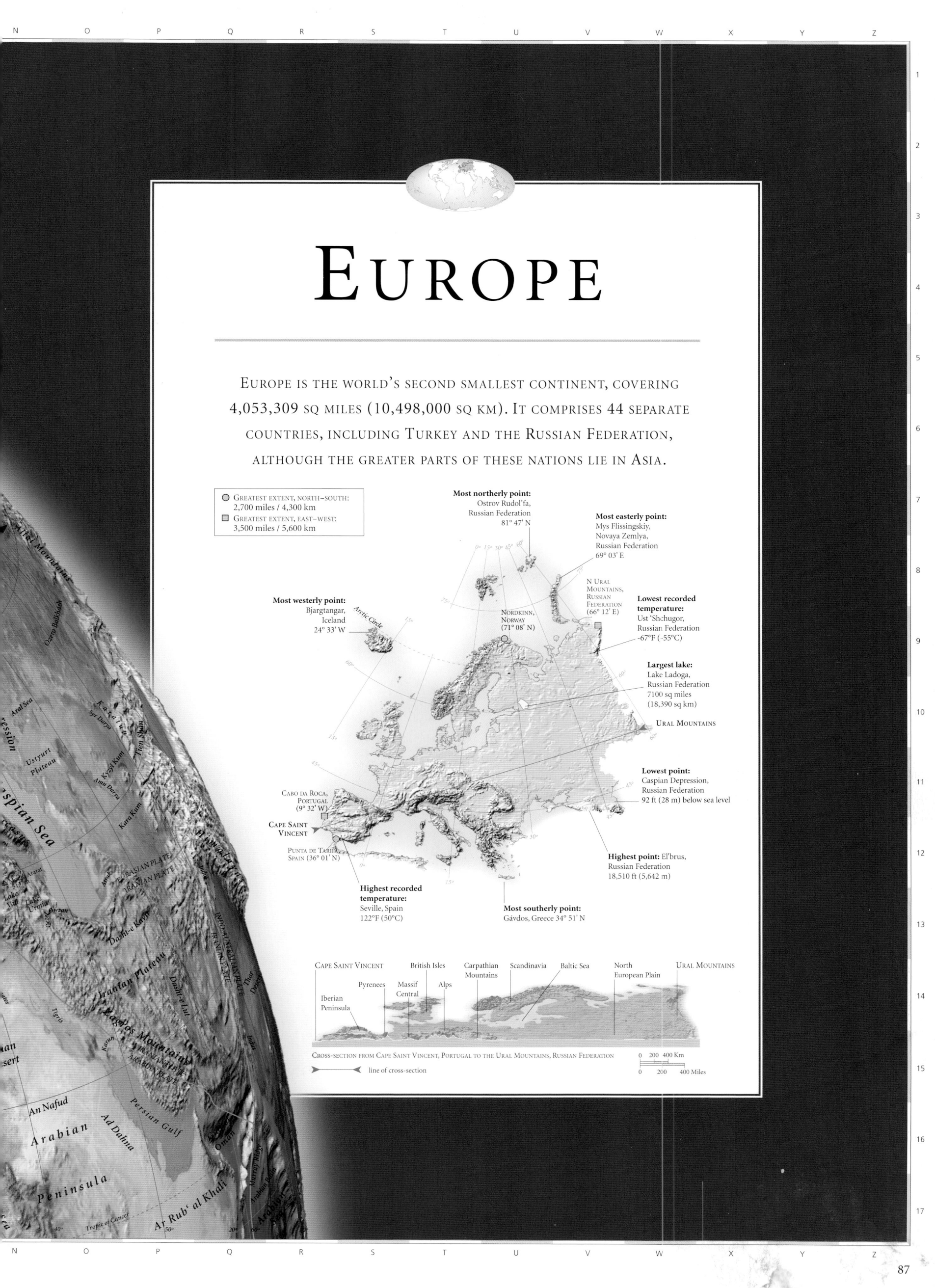

EUROPE

EUROPE IS THE WORLD'S SECOND SMALLEST CONTINENT, COVERING 4,053,309 SQ MILES (10,498,000 SQ KM). IT COMPRISES 44 SEPARATE COUNTRIES, INCLUDING TURKEY AND THE RUSSIAN FEDERATION, ALTHOUGH THE GREATER PARTS OF THESE NATIONS LIE IN ASIA.

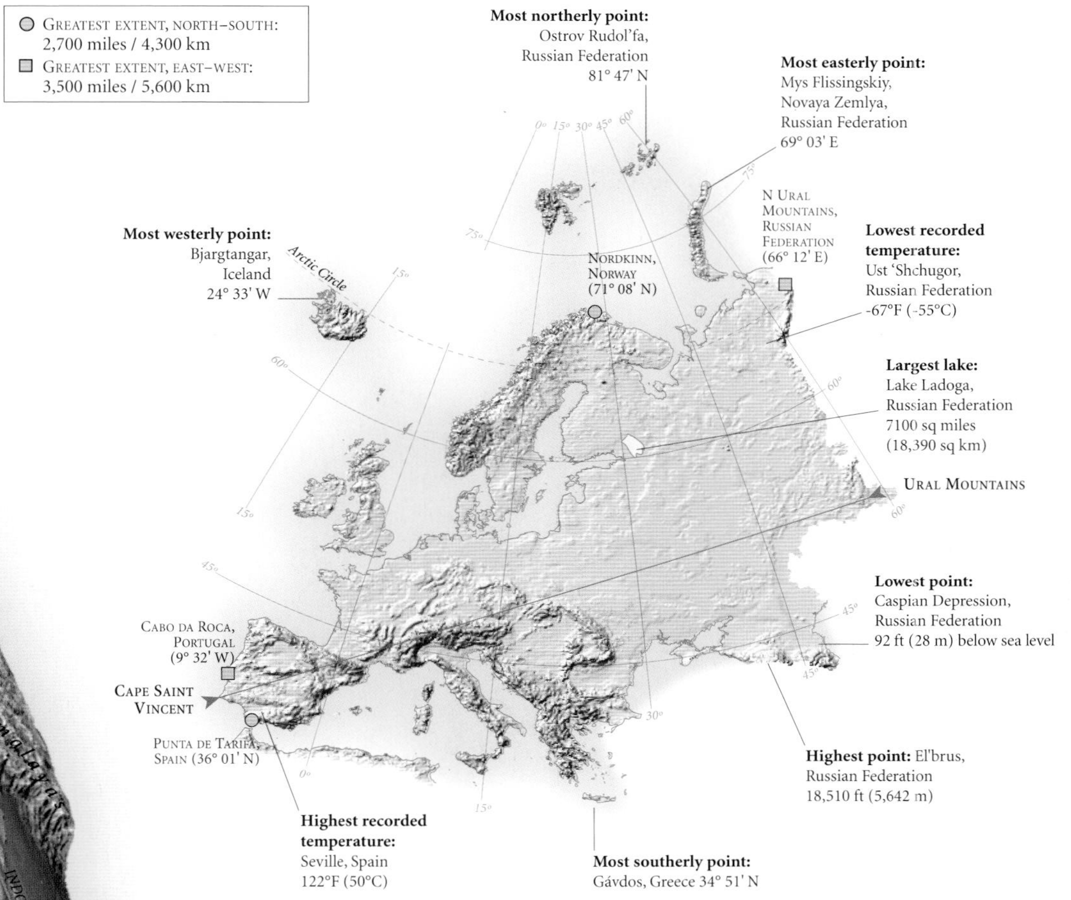

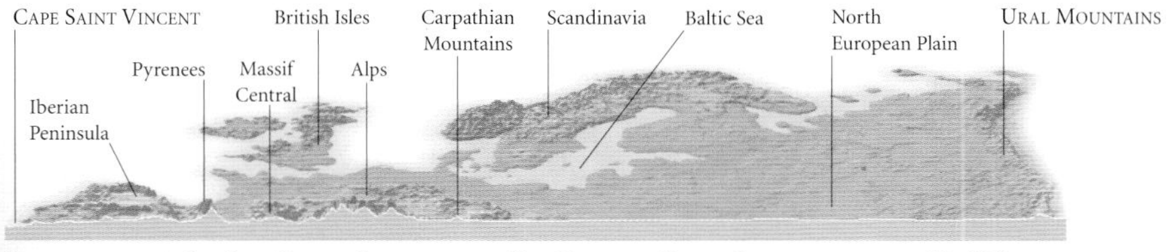

CROSS-SECTION FROM CAPE SAINT VINCENT, PORTUGAL TO THE URAL MOUNTAINS, RUSSIAN FEDERATION

line of cross-section

PHYSICAL EUROPE

THE PHYSICAL DIVERSITY of Europe belies its relatively small size. To the northwest and south it is enclosed by mountains. The older, rounded Atlantic Highlands of Scandinavia and the British Isles lie to the north and the younger, rugged peaks of the Alpine Uplands to the south. In between lies the North European Plain, stretching 2,485 miles (4,000 km) from The Fens in England to the Ural Mountains in Russia. South of the plain lies a series of gently folded sedimentary rocks separated by ancient plateaus, known as massifs.

THE NORTH EUROPEAN PLAIN

RISING LESS THAN 1,000 ft (300 m)above sea level, the North European Plain strongly reflects past glaciation. Ridges of both coarse moraine and finer, wind-blown deposits have accumulated over much of the region. The ice sheet also diverted a number of river channels from their original courses.

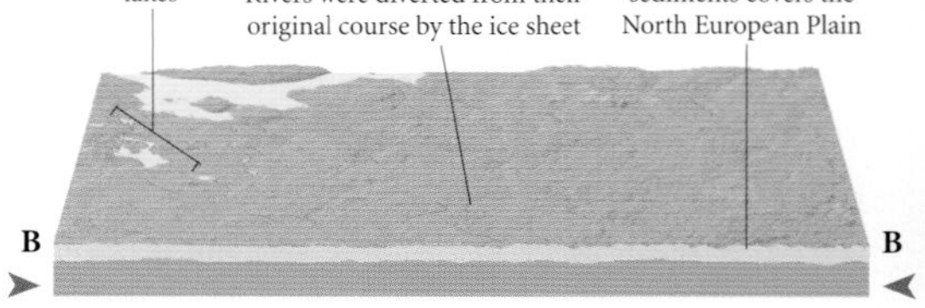

Section across the North European Plain showing its low relief and drainage.

THE ATLANTIC HIGHLANDS

THE ATLANTIC HIGHLANDS were formed by compression against the Scandinavian Shield during the Caledonian mountain-building period over 500 million years ago. The highlands were once part of a continuous mountain chain, now divided by the North Sea and a submerged rift valley.

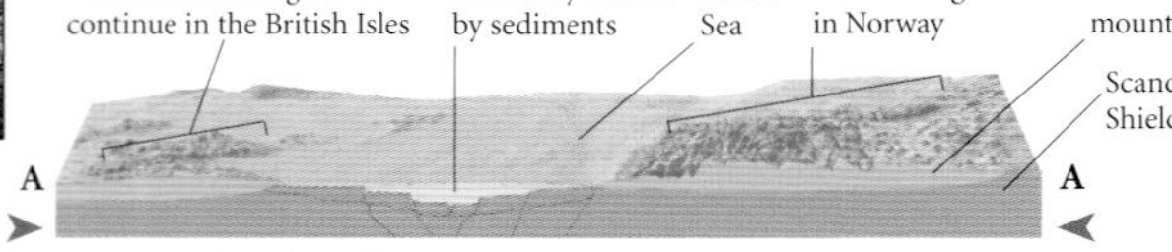

Cross-section *through northeastern Europe showing the continuous mountain chain and rift valley system.*

SCALE 1:23,000,000
(projection: Lambert Azimuthal Equal Area)

Km: 0 100 200 400 600
Miles: 0 50 100 200 300 400 500 600

MAP KEY

ELEVATION

PLATE MARGINS
(for explanation see page xiv)

- constructive
- destructive
- conservative
- uncertain
- physiographic regions
- line of cross-section

THE PLATEAUS AND LOWLANDS

THE UPLIFTED PLATEAUS or massifs of southern central Europe are the result of long-term erosion, later followed by uplift. They are the source areas of many of the rivers which drain Europe's lowlands. In some of the higher reaches, fractures have enabled igneous rocks from deep in the Earth to reach the surface.

THE ALPINE UPLANDS

THE COLLISION OF the African and European continents, which began about 65 million years ago, folded and then uplifted a series of mountain ranges running across southern Europe and into Asia. Two major lines of folding can be traced: one includes the Pyrenees, the Alps, and the Carpathian Mountains; the other incorporates the Apennines and the Dinaric Alps.

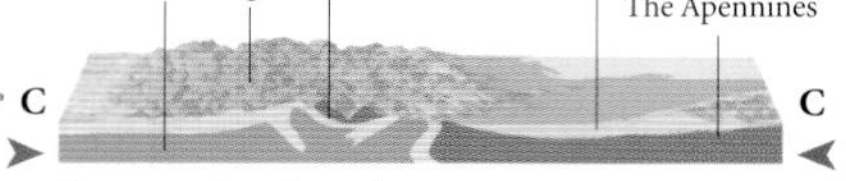

Cross-section *through the Alps showing folding and faulting caused by plate tectonics.*

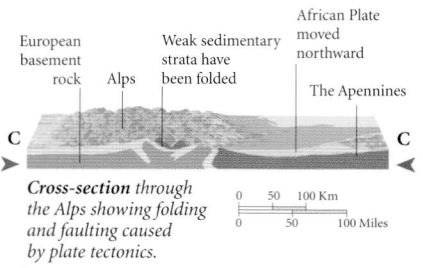

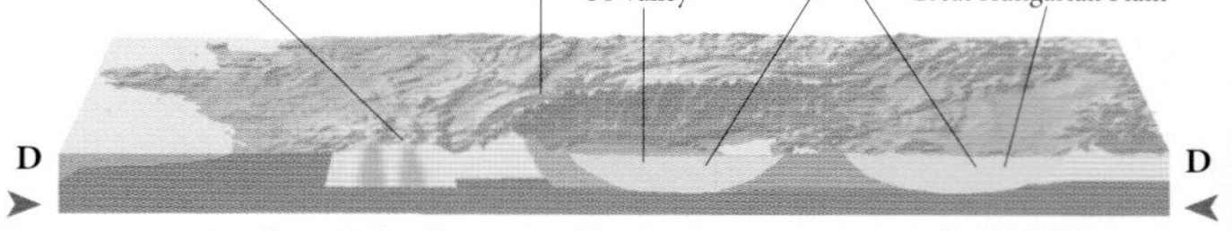

Cross-section *through the plateaus and lowlands showing the lower elevation of the ancient massifs.*

Climate

***Frost grips** northern and eastern Europe during the long cold winters. Lakes and rivers frequently freeze.*

Europe experiences few extremes in either rainfall or temperature, with the exception of the far north and south. Along the west coast, the warm currents of the North Atlantic Drift moderate temperatures. Although east–west air movement is relatively unimpeded by relief, the Alpine Uplands halt the progress of north–south air masses, protecting most of the Mediterranean from cold, north winds.

Climate
- tundra
- subarctic
- cool continental
- warm humid
- mediterranean
- semiarid
- daily hours of sunshine, January
- daily hours of sunshine, July
- cold wind
- hot wind

Temperature

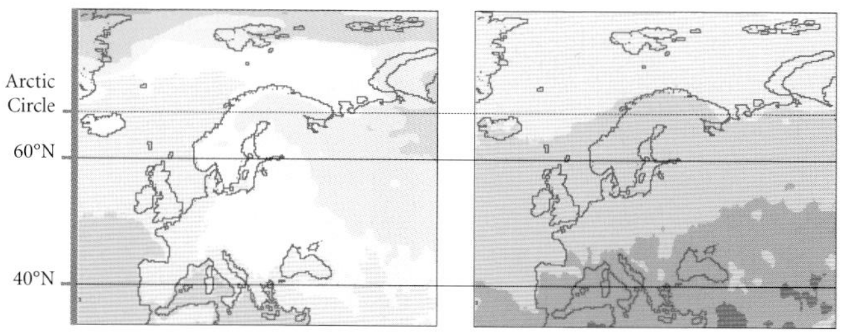

Average January temperature *Average July temperature*

Temperature
- below -22°F (-30°C)
- -22 to -4°F (-30 to -20°C)
- -4 to 14°F (-20 to -10°C)
- 14 to 32°F (-10 to 0°C)
- 32 to 50° F (0 to 10°C)
- 50 to 60°F (10 to 20°C)
- 68 to 86°F (20 to 30°C)
- above 86°F (30°C)

***Mild temperatures** and frequent rainfall contribute to the fertile farming land found over much of northwestern Europe.*

Rainfall

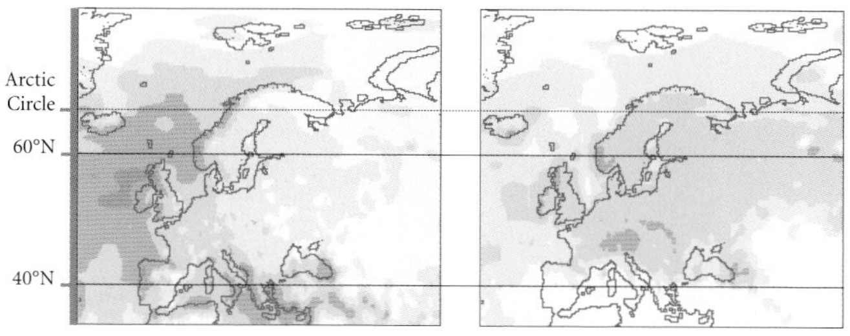

Average January rainfall *Average July rainfall*

Rainfall
- 0–1 in (0–25 mm)
- 1–2 in (25–50 mm)
- 2–4 in (50–100 mm)
- 4–8 in (100–200 mm)
- 8–12 in (200–300 mm)
- 12–16 in (300–400 mm)
- 16–20 in (400–500 mm)
- more than 20 in (500 mm)

***Dusty Sirocco winds** from Africa help create the semiarid scrubland common across the Mediterranean coastlands of southern Europe.*

Shaping the Continent

Successive Ice Ages have left many relict landforms across Europe. Present glaciers continue to carve peaks and valleys in the northern Atlantic Highlands and Alpine Uplands. Tectonic activity, both past and present, has shaped southern Europe and Iceland. Active volcanoes and earthquakes still occur in Italy and Greece. Europe's extensive coastline, particularly in the northwest, is constantly modified by wave action and fluvial deposits.

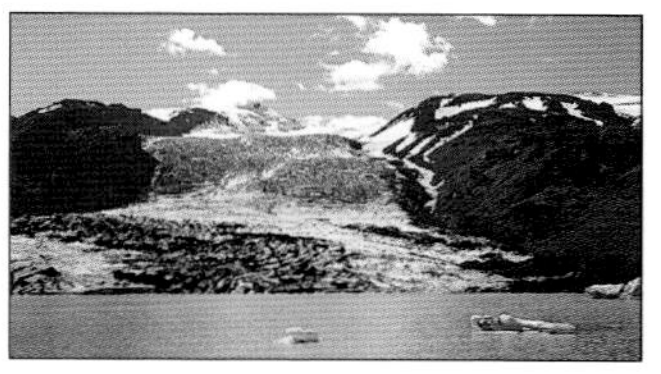

Glaciation

1 Valley glaciers, such as this one *(left)* in Iceland, form in hollows at the top of valleys and flow downward, drawn by gravity. Their growth is dynamic; new snowfall constantly accumulates at the head of the glacier, while the snout melts, depositing material eroded and carried by the glacier.

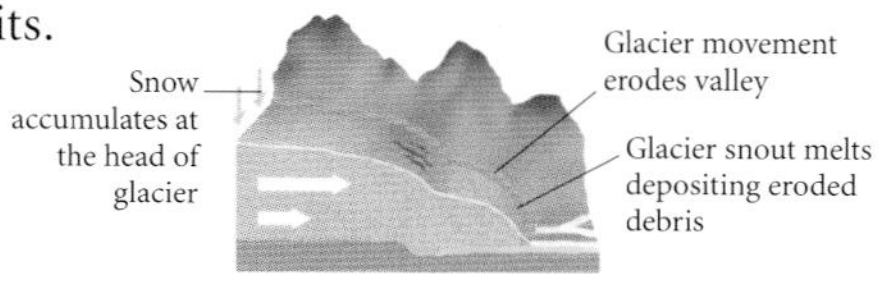

Glaciation: Development of a glacier

River Systems

2 Rivers are continuously transporting eroded material toward the sea. Slow-moving, low-gradient rivers, like this one in western Russia *(above)*, deposit their alluvium load, infilling valleys creating a floodplain. Subsequent climatic and tectonic fluctuations may erode the floodplain to form terraces.

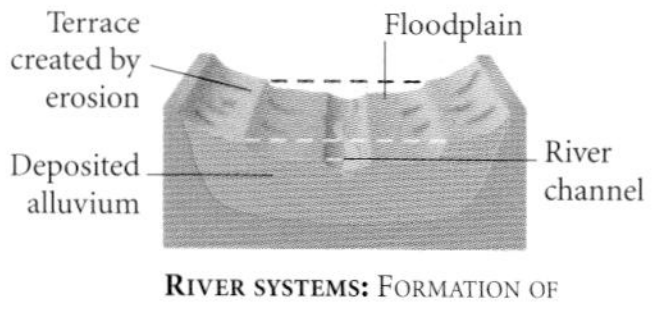

River systems: Formation of a floodplain and terraces

Coastal Processes

5 Spits are narrow bands of sand or shingle, formed by longshore drift; a process whereby waves carry material along the beach. They usually form where the coastline changes direction, and their growth is then halted by an opposing river current, as at Spurn Head, in the British Isles *(left)*. Coastal features such as these are constantly being created and destroyed.

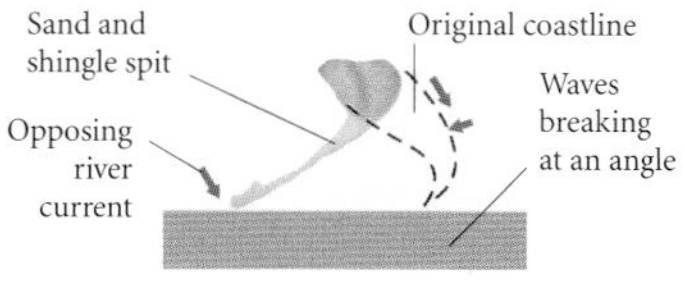

Coastal processes: Formation of a spit

The Evolving Landscape

Landscape
- uplifting land
- stable land
- sinking land
- limestone region
- glacier
- active volcano
- ocean current
- area of tectonic activity
- maximum limit of glaciation

Erosion and Weathering

4 Much of Europe was once subjected to folding and faulting, exposing hard and soft rock layers. Subsequent erosion and weathering has worn away the softer strata, leaving up-ended layers of hard rock as in the French Pyrenees *(above)*.

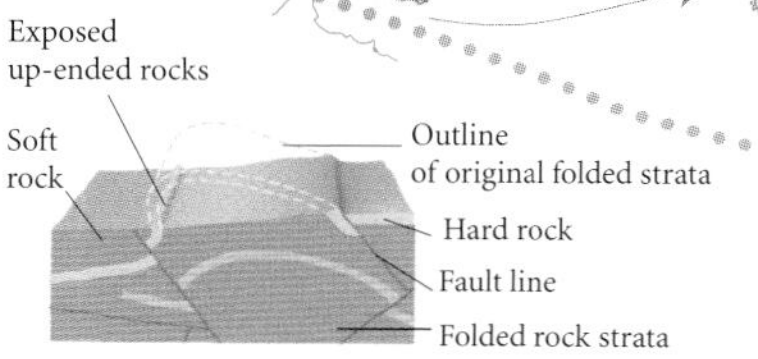

Erosion and weathering: Modification of a fold

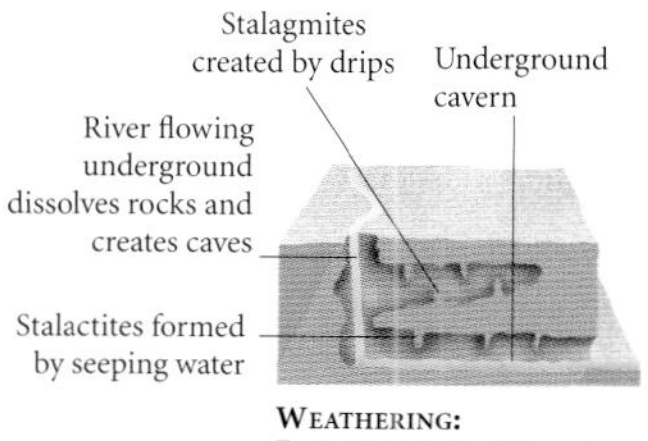

Weathering: Formation of a cave

Weathering

3 As surface water filters through permeable limestone, the rock dissolves to form underground caves, like Postojna in the Karst region of Slovenia *(above)*. Stalactites grow downward as lime-enriched water seeps from roof fractures; stalagmites grow upward where drips splash down.

Political Europe

THE POLITICAL BOUNDARIES OF EUROPE have changed many times, especially during the 20th century in the aftermath of two world wars, the breakup of the empires of Austria-Hungary, Nazi Germany and, toward the end of the century, the collapse of communism in eastern Europe. The fragmentation of Yugoslavia has again altered the political map of Europe, highlighting a trend toward nationalism and devolution. In contrast, economic federalism is growing. In 1958, the formation of the European Economic Community (now the European Union or EU) started a move toward economic and political union.

***The Brandenburg Gate in Berlin** is a potent symbol of German reunification. From 1961, the road beneath it ended in a wall, built to stop the flow of refugees to the West. It was opened again in 1989 when the wall was destroyed and East and West Germany were reunited.*

Population

EUROPE IS A DENSELY POPULATED, urbanized continent; in Belgium over 90% of people live in urban areas. The highest population densities are found in an area stretching east from southern Britain and northern France, into Germany. The northern fringes are only sparsely populated.

Population density (people per sq mile)

- below 130
- 130–259
- 260–379
- 380–519
- 520–780
- above 780

***Demand for space** in densely populated European cities like London has led to the development of high-rise offices and urban sprawl.*

***Traditional lifestyles** still persist in many remote and rural parts of Europe, especially in the south, east, and in the far north.*

Map Key

POPULATION

- above 5 million
- 1 million to 5 million
- 500,000 to 1 million
- 100,000 to 500,000
- 50,000 to 100,000
- 10,000 to 50,000
- Country capital

BORDERS

- full international border

SCALE 1:15,500,000
(projection: Lambert Azimuthal Equal Area)

Km 0 50 100 200 300 400 500 600 700 800 900 1000

Miles 0 50 100 200 300 400 500 600 700

***Overcoming** natural barriers, the Brenner Autobahn, one of the main routes across the Alps, links Innsbruck in Austria with Verona in Italy.*

TRANSPORTATION

DESPITE ITS FRAGMENTED GEOGRAPHY and many natural frontiers, communications in Europe are well developed. Extensive highway links allow rapid road transportation. High-speed rail connections like France's TGV *(Train à Grande Vitesse)*, and the Channel Tunnel have improved rail travel. Outdated communication infrastructures in parts of eastern Europe, and insufficient transportation links across the Alps, however, remain weak parts of the network.

LANGUAGES

THERE ARE THREE MAIN EUROPEAN language groups: Germanic languages predominate in central and northern Europe; Romance languages in western and Mediterranean Europe and Romania; while Slavic languages are spoken in eastern Europe and the Russian Federation. Isolated pockets of local languages, such as Basque and Gaelic, persist and frequently provide a focus for national identity.

***The architecture** of the Grand Place lies at the heart of Brussels – home city to one of the EU headquarters.*

EUROPEAN RESOURCES

EUROPE'S LARGE TRACTS OF FERTILE, accessible land, combined with its generally temperate climate, have allowed a greater percentage of land to be used for agricultural purposes than in any other continent. Extensive coal and iron ore deposits were used to create steel and manufacturing industries during the 19th and 20th centuries. Today, although natural resources have been widely exploited, and heavy industry is of declining importance, the growth of hi-tech and service industries has enabled Europe to maintain its wealth.

STANDARD OF LIVING

LIVING STANDARDS IN WESTERN EUROPE are among the highest in the world, although there is a growing sector of homeless, jobless people. Eastern Europeans have lower overall standards of living – a legacy of stagnated economies.

INDUSTRY

EUROPE'S WEALTH WAS GENERATED by the rise of industry and colonial exploitation during the 19th century. The mining of abundant natural resources made Europe the industrial center of the world. Adaptation has been essential in the changing world economy, and a move to service-based industries has been widespread except in eastern Europe, where heavy industry still dominates.

***Countries like Hungary** are still struggling to modernize inefficient factories left over from extensive, centrally-planned industrialization during the communist era.*

***Frankfurt am Main** is an example of a modern service-based city. The skyline is dominated by headquarters from the worlds of banking and commerce.*

***Other power sources** are becoming more attractive as fossil fuels run out; 16% of Europe's electricity is now provided by hydroelectric power.*

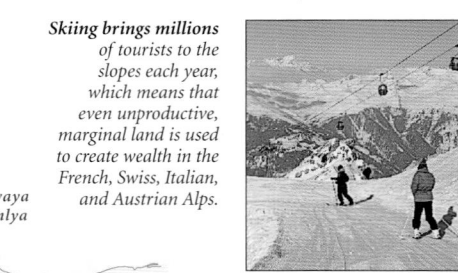

***Skiing brings millions** of tourists to the slopes each year, which means that even unproductive, marginal land is used to create wealth in the French, Swiss, Italian, and Austrian Alps.*

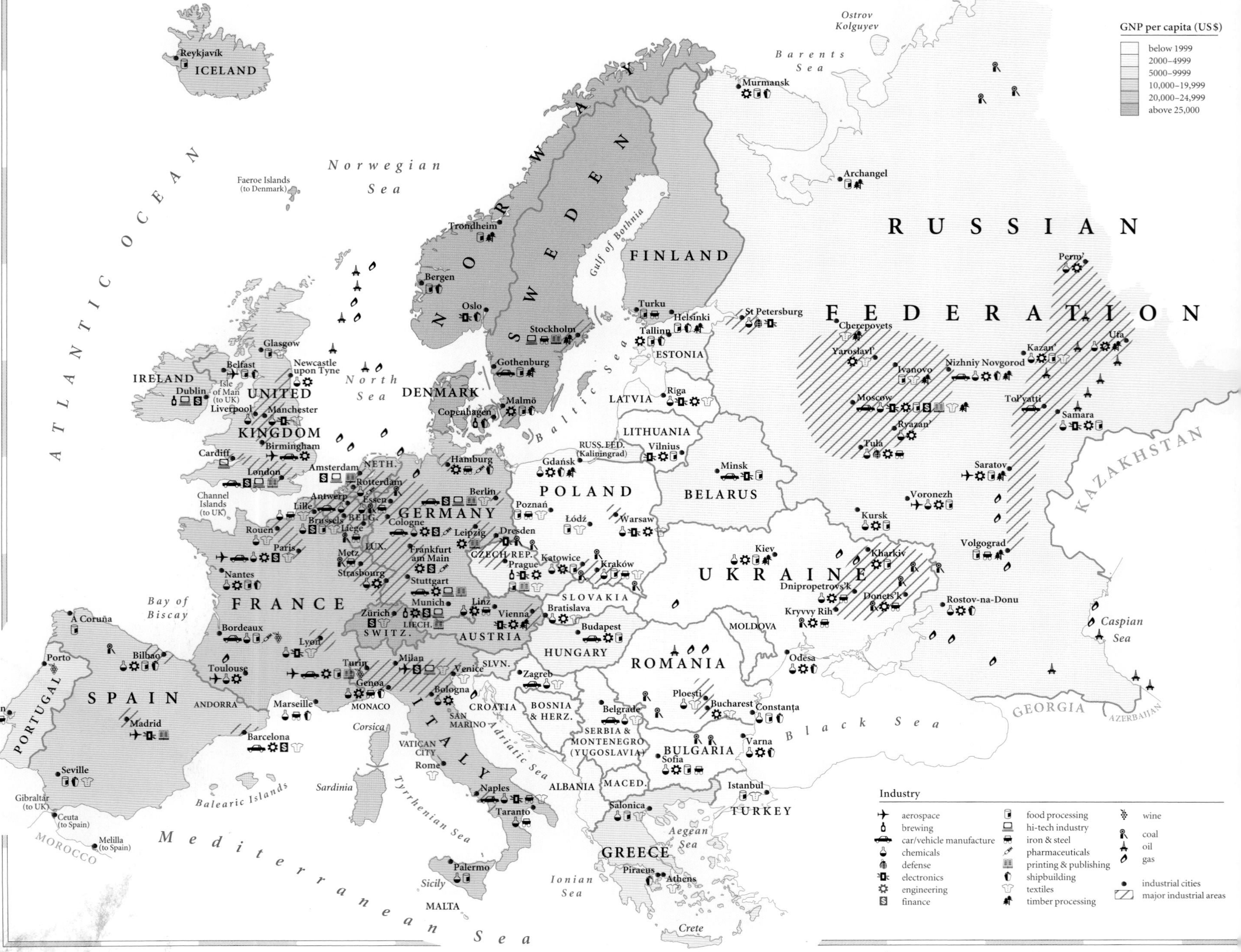

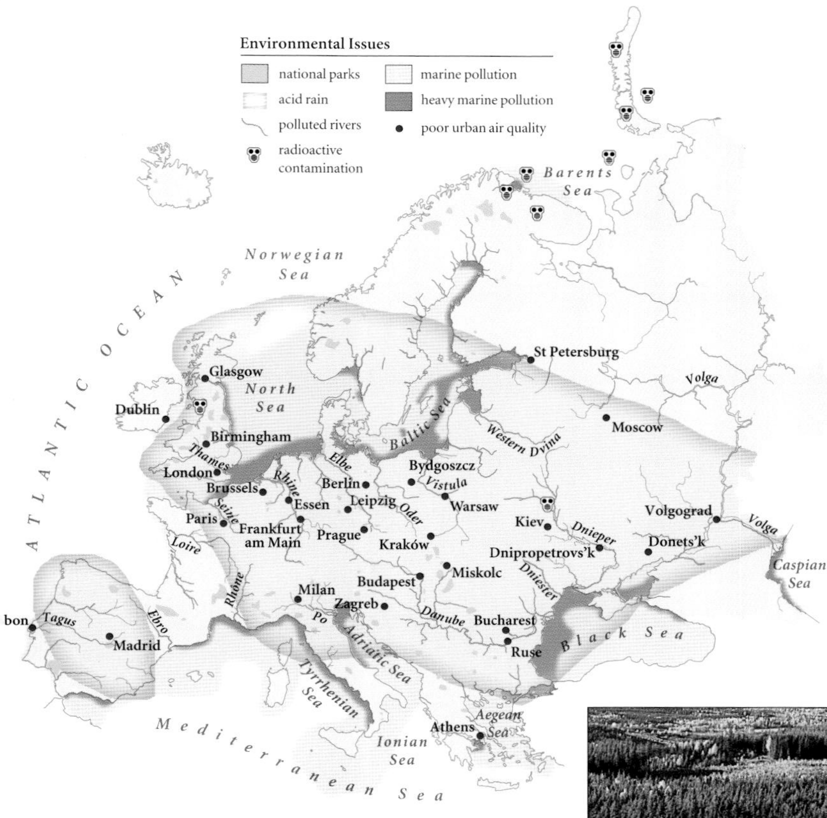

Environmental Issues

- national parks
- acid rain
- polluted rivers
- radioactive contamination
- marine pollution
- heavy marine pollution
- poor urban air quality

MINERAL RESOURCES

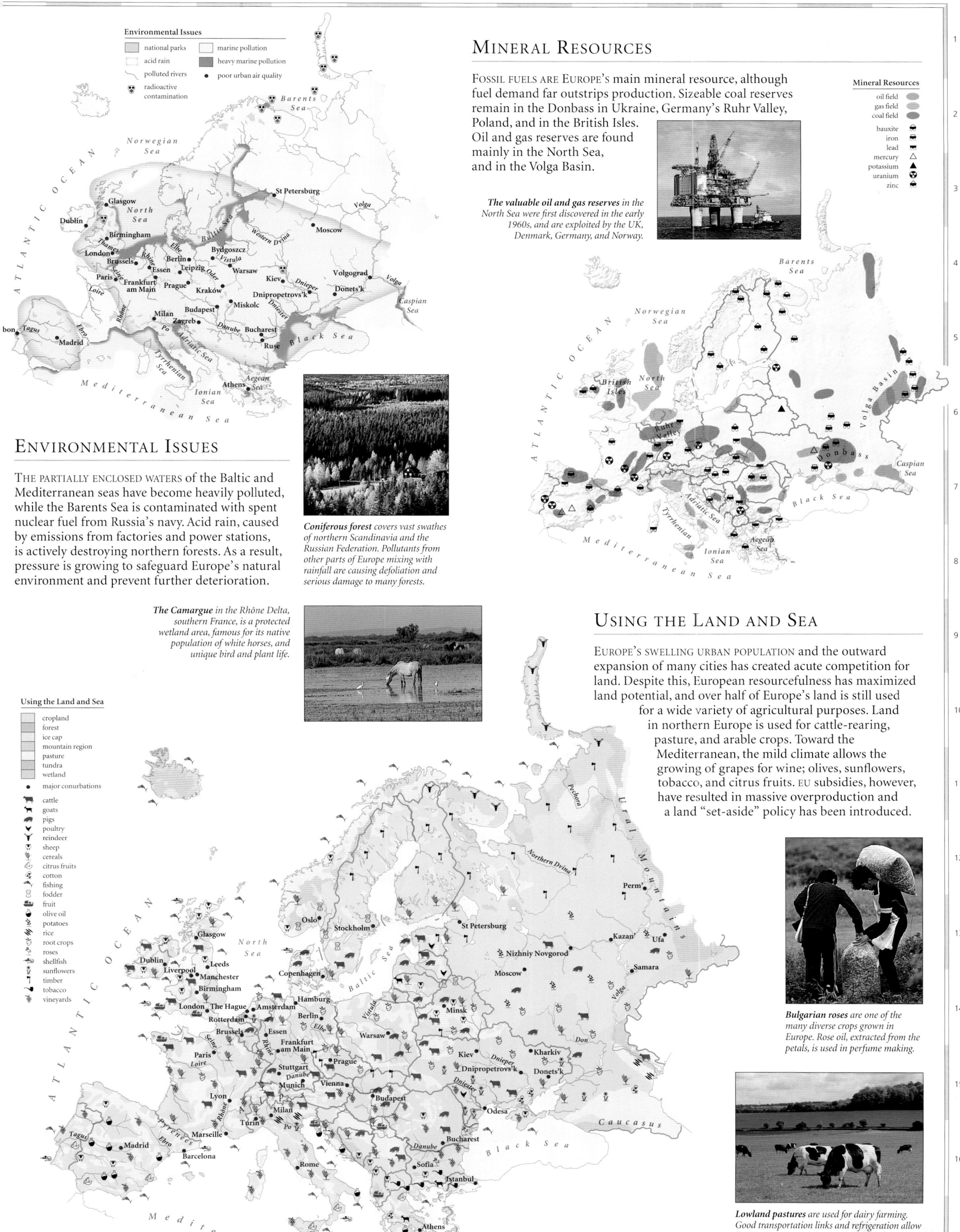

FOSSIL FUELS ARE EUROPE'S main mineral resource, although fuel demand far outstrips production. Sizeable coal reserves remain in the Donbass in Ukraine, Germany's Ruhr Valley, Poland, and in the British Isles. Oil and gas reserves are found mainly in the North Sea, and in the Volga Basin.

Mineral Resources
- oil field
- gas field
- coal field
- bauxite
- iron
- lead
- mercury
- potassium
- uranium
- zinc

The valuable oil and gas reserves in the North Sea were first discovered in the early 1960s, and are exploited by the UK, Denmark, Germany, and Norway.

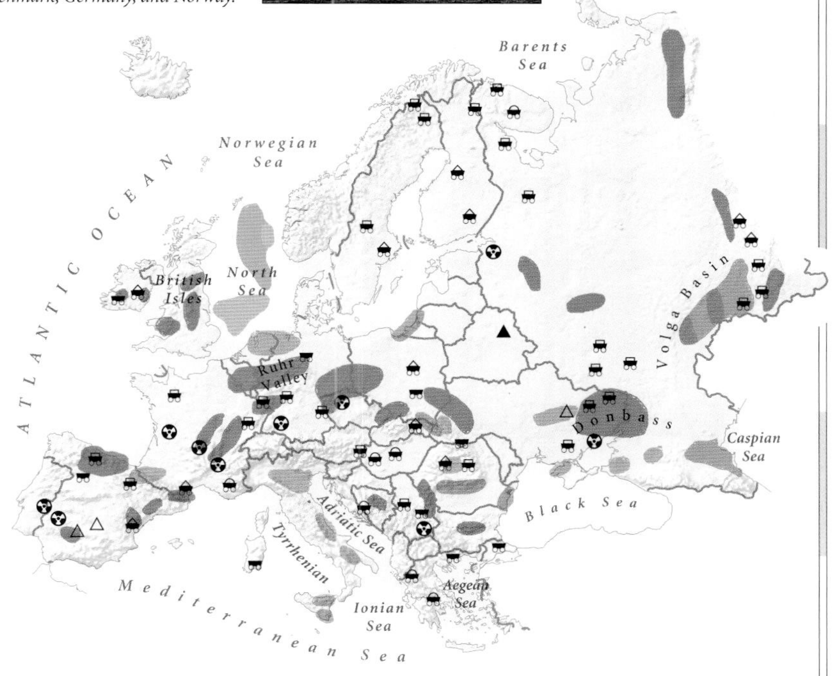

ENVIRONMENTAL ISSUES

THE PARTIALLY ENCLOSED WATERS of the Baltic and Mediterranean seas have become heavily polluted, while the Barents Sea is contaminated with spent nuclear fuel from Russia's navy. Acid rain, caused by emissions from factories and power stations, is actively destroying northern forests. As a result, pressure is growing to safeguard Europe's natural environment and prevent further deterioration.

Coniferous forest covers vast swathes of northern Scandinavia and the Russian Federation. Pollutants from other parts of Europe mixing with rainfall are causing defoliation and serious damage to many forests.

The Camargue in the Rhône Delta, southern France, is a protected wetland area, famous for its native population of white horses, and unique bird and plant life.

USING THE LAND AND SEA

EUROPE'S SWELLING URBAN POPULATION and the outward expansion of many cities has created acute competition for land. Despite this, European resourcefulness has maximized land potential, and over half of Europe's land is still used for a wide variety of agricultural purposes. Land in northern Europe is used for cattle-rearing, pasture, and arable crops. Toward the Mediterranean, the mild climate allows the growing of grapes for wine; olives, sunflowers, tobacco, and citrus fruits. EU subsidies, however, have resulted in massive overproduction and a land "set-aside" policy has been introduced.

Using the Land and Sea
- cropland
- forest
- ice cap
- mountain region
- pasture
- tundra
- wetland
- major conurbations
- cattle
- goats
- pigs
- poultry
- reindeer
- sheep
- cereals
- citrus fruits
- cotton
- fishing
- fodder
- fruit
- olive oil
- potatoes
- rice
- root crops
- roses
- shellfish
- sunflowers
- timber
- tobacco
- vineyards

Bulgarian roses are one of the many diverse crops grown in Europe. Rose oil, extracted from the petals, is used in perfume making.

Lowland pastures are used for dairy farming. Good transportation links and refrigeration allow fresh milk to be distributed throughout Europe.

Scandinavia, Finland & Iceland

Denmark, Norway, Sweden, Finland, Iceland

Jutting into the Arctic Circle, this northern swath of Europe has some of the continent's harshest environments, but benefits from great reserves of oil, gas, and natural evergreen forests. While most early settlers came from the south, migrants to Finland came from the east, giving it a distinct language and culture. Since the late 19th century, the Scandinavian states have developed strong egalitarian traditions. Today, their welfare benefits systems are among the most extensive in the world, and standards of living are high. The Lapps, or Sami, maintain their traditional lifestyle in the northern regions of Norway, Sweden, and Finland.

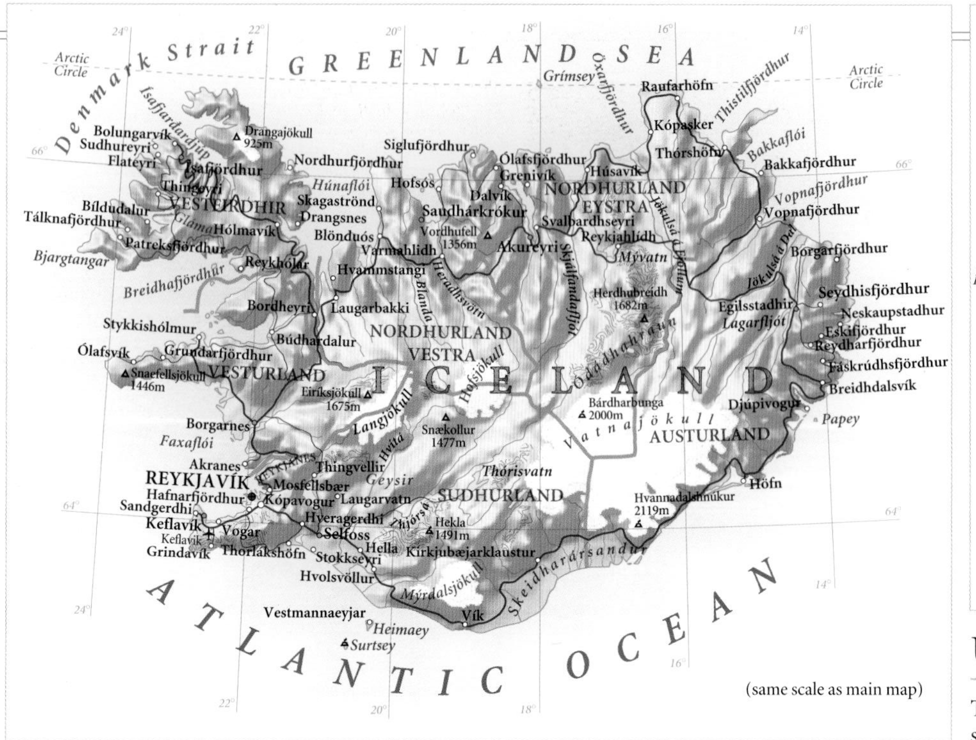

(same scale as main map)

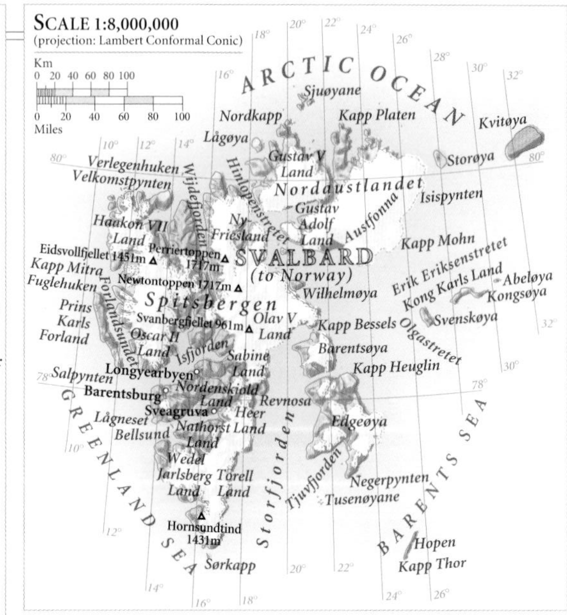

Using the Land and Sea

The cold climate, short growing season, poorly developed soil, steep slopes, and exposure to high winds across northern regions means that most agriculture is concentrated, with the population, in the south. Most of Finland and much of Norway and Sweden are covered by dense forests of pine, spruce and birch, which supply the timber industries.

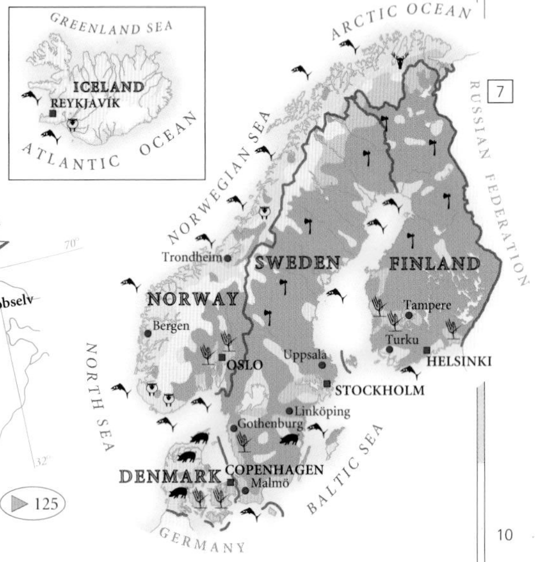

The Urban/Rural Population Divide

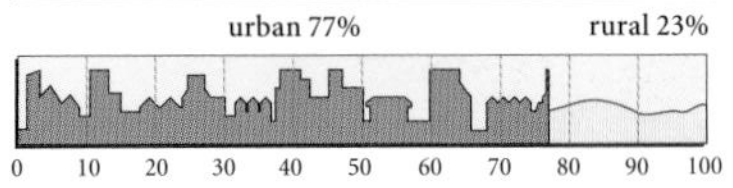

Population Density	Total Land Area
51 people per sq mile (20 people per sq km)	473,970 sq miles (1,227,610 sq km)

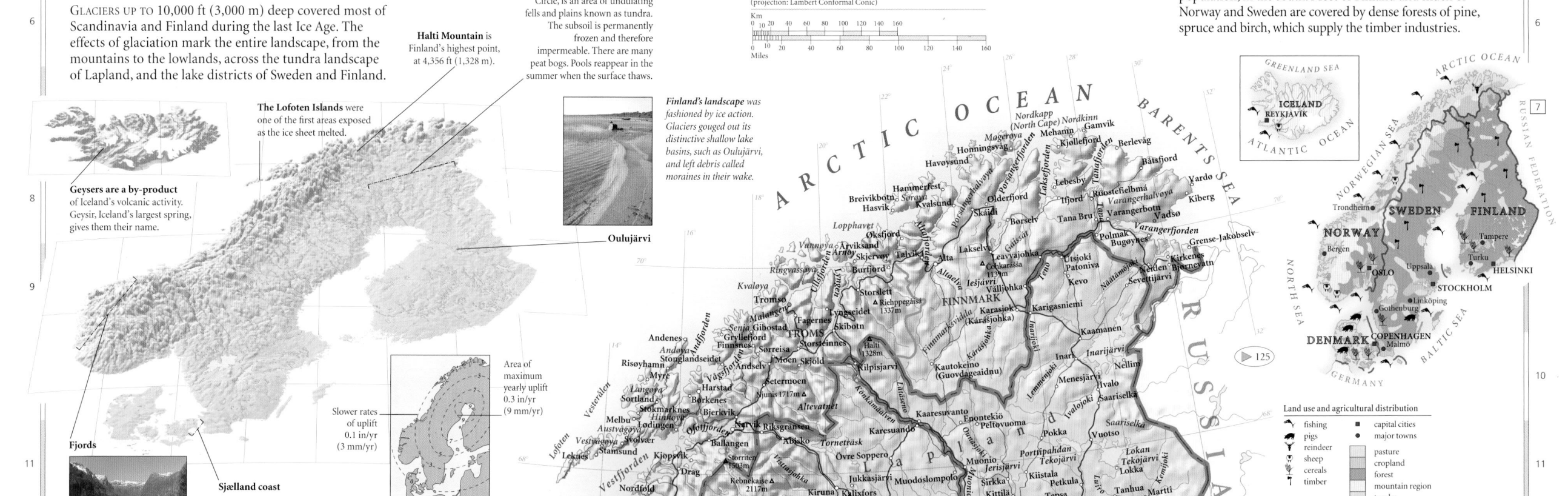

The Landscape

Glaciers up to 10,000 ft (3,000 m) deep covered most of Scandinavia and Finland during the last Ice Age. The effects of glaciation mark the entire landscape, from the mountains to the lowlands, across the tundra landscape of Lapland, and the lake districts of Sweden and Finland.

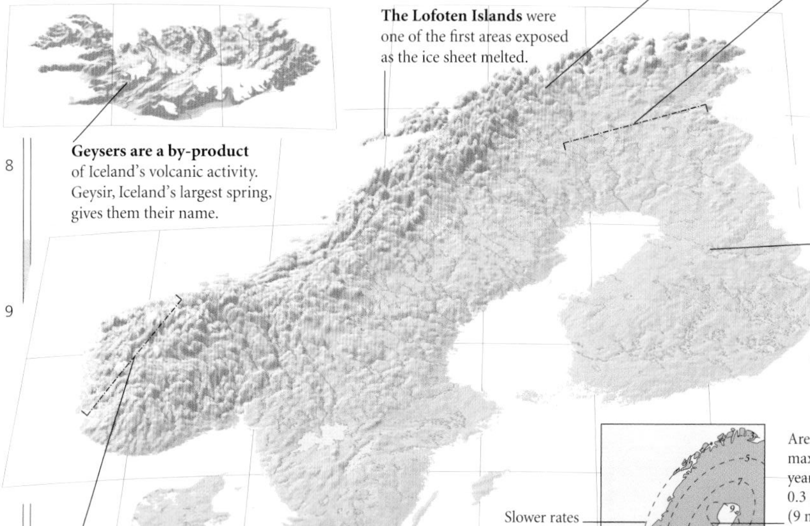

Halti Mountain is Finland's highest point, at 4,356 ft (1,328 m).

Lapland, north of the Arctic Circle, is an area of undulating fells and plains known as tundra. The subsoil is permanently frozen and therefore impermeable. There are many peat bogs. Pools reappear in the summer when the surface thaws.

The Lofoten Islands were one of the first areas exposed as the ice sheet melted.

Geysers are a by-product of Iceland's volcanic activity. Geysir, Iceland's largest spring, gives them their name.

Oulujärvi

Finland's landscape was fashioned by ice action. Glaciers gouged out its distinctive shallow lake basins, such as Oulujärvi, and left debris called moraines in their wake.

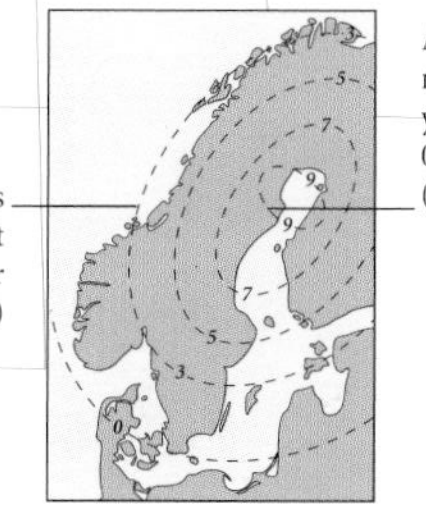

***Scandinavia** is still recovering from the last Ice Age, when ice depressed the land by 2,000 ft (600 m). This gradual uplift is known as isostatic rebound.*

Fjords

***The fjords** on the western coast of Norway were once gentle river valleys. Their deep floors and steep sides were carved out by glaciers during the last Ice Age, and they were later flooded by the sea.*

Sjælland coast

***On the coast of Sjælland,** these cliffs have been eroded by the sea, exposing layers of chalk and limestone.*

Scale 1:5,000,000
(projection: Lambert Conformal Conic)

▶ 125

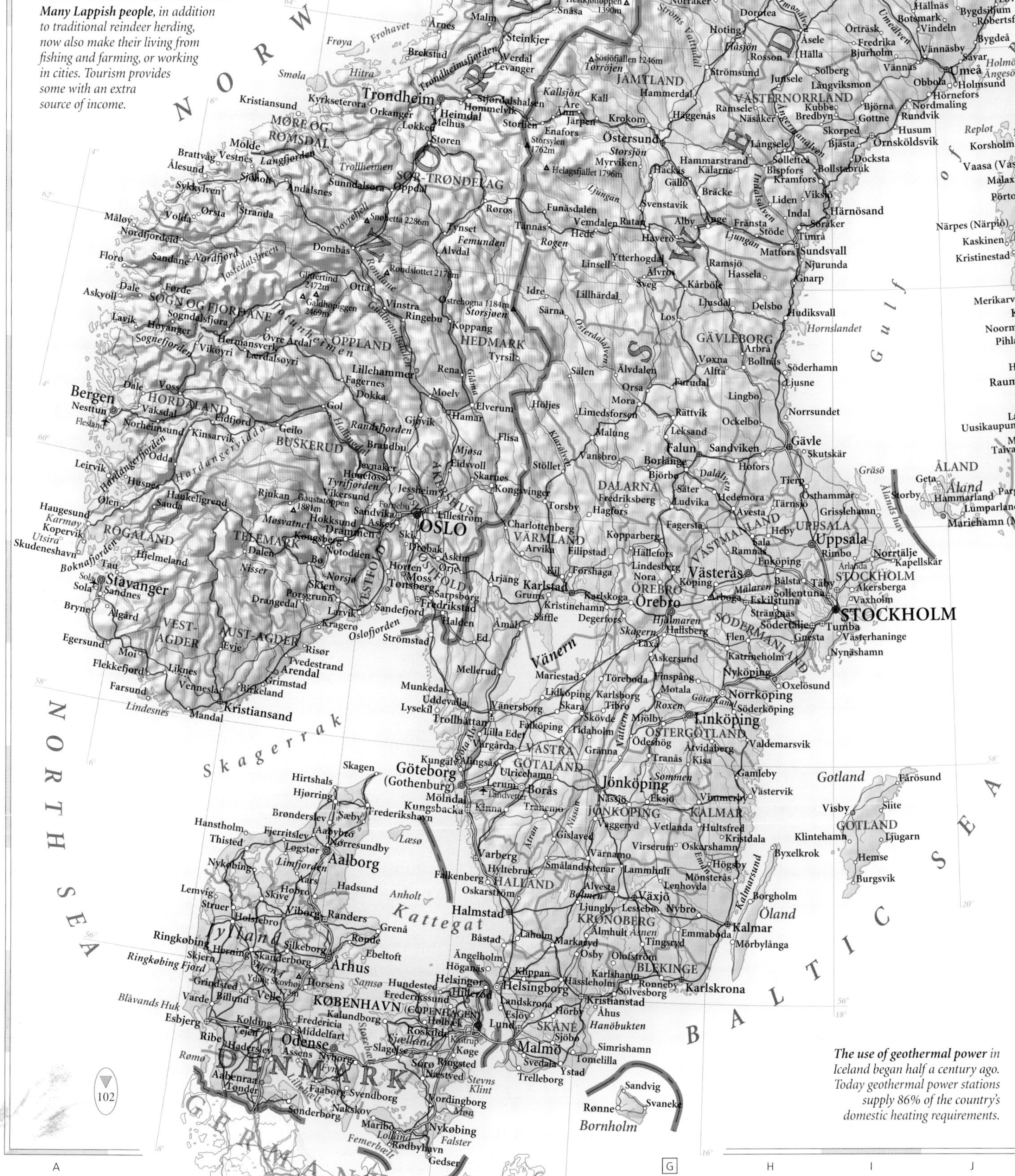

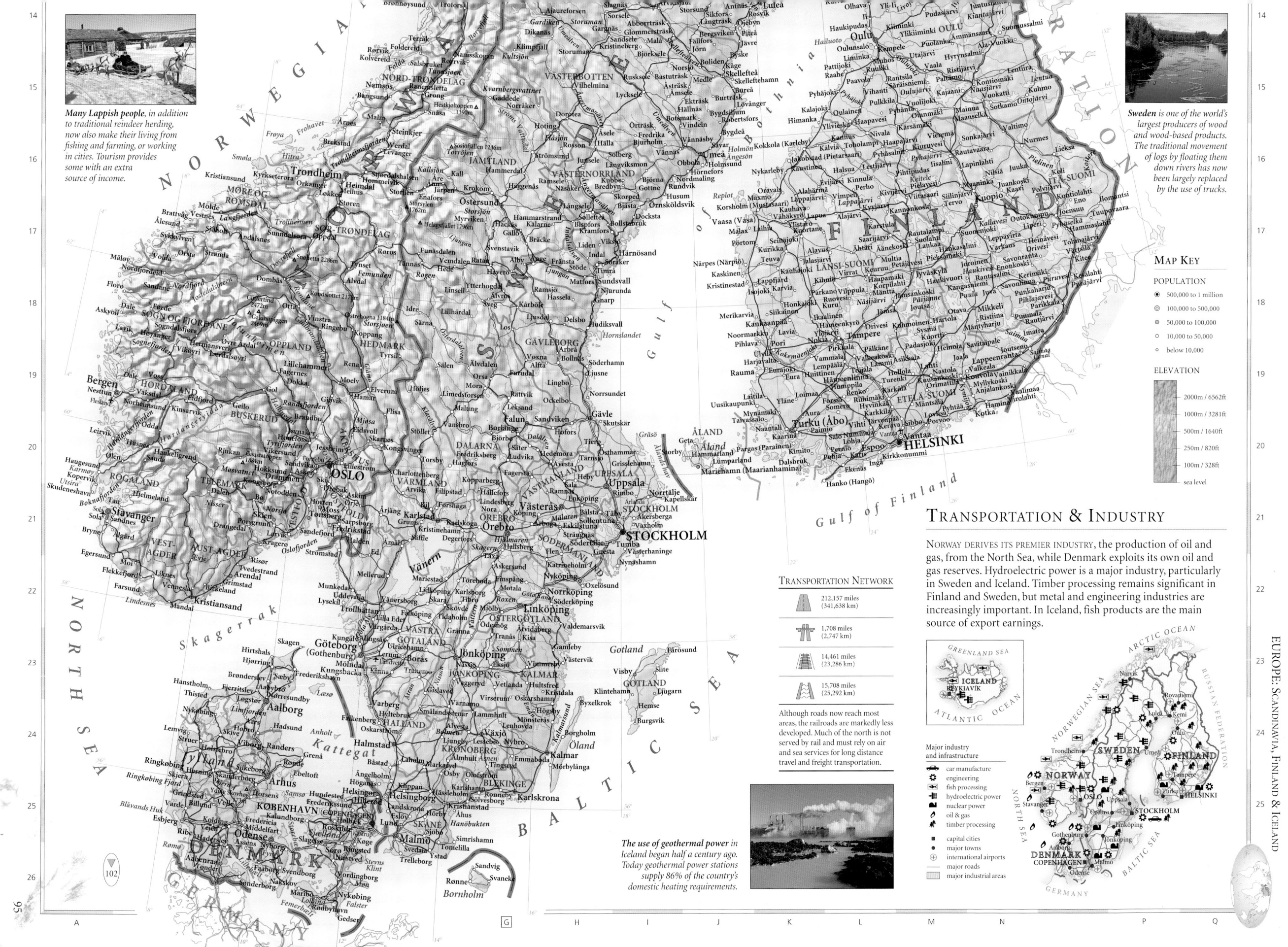

Sweden is one of the world's largest producers of wood and wood-based products. The traditional movement of logs by floating them down rivers has now been largely replaced by the use of trucks.

MAP KEY

POPULATION

- ◉ 500,000 to 1 million
- ◎ 100,000 to 500,000
- ⊕ 50,000 to 100,000
- ○ 10,000 to 50,000
- ○ below 10,000

ELEVATION

2000m / 6562ft
1000m / 3281ft
500m / 1640ft
250m / 820ft
100m / 328ft
sea level

Transportation & Industry

Norway derives its premier industry, the production of oil and gas, from the North Sea, while Denmark exploits its own oil and gas reserves. Hydroelectric power is a major industry, particularly in Sweden and Iceland. Timber processing remains significant in Finland and Sweden, but metal and engineering industries are increasingly important. In Iceland, fish products are the main source of export earnings.

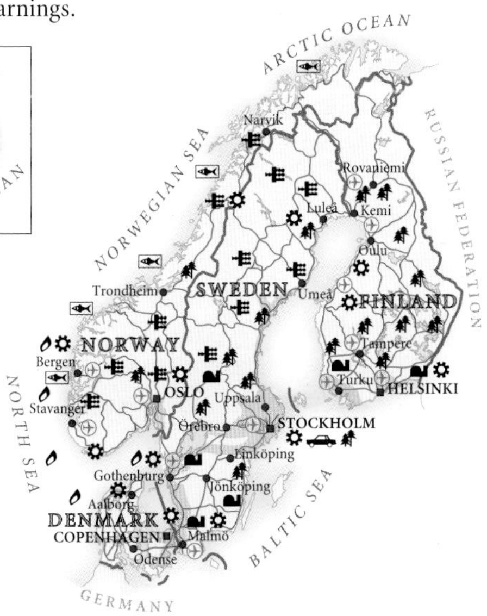

Major industry and infrastructure

- car manufacture
- engineering
- fish processing
- hydroelectric power
- nuclear power
- oil & gas
- timber processing
- capital cities
- major towns
- international airports
- major roads
- major industrial areas

Transportation Network

212,157 miles (341,638 km)	
1,708 miles (2,747 km)	
14,461 miles (23,286 km)	
15,708 miles (25,292 km)	

Although roads now reach most areas, the railroads are markedly less developed. Much of the north is not served by rail and must rely on air and sea services for long distance travel and freight transportation.

The use of geothermal power in Iceland began half a century ago. Today geothermal power stations supply 86% of the country's domestic heating requirements.

Many Lappish people, in addition to traditional reindeer herding, now also make their living from fishing and farming, or working in cities. Tourism provides some with an extra source of income.

Southern Scandinavia

Southern Norway, Southern Sweden, Denmark

SCANDINAVIA'S ECONOMIC AND POLITICAL HUB is the more habitable and accessible southern region. Many of the area's major cities are on the southern coasts, including Oslo and Stockholm, the capitals of Norway and Sweden. In Denmark, most of the population and the capital, Copenhagen, are located on its many islands. A cultural unity links the three Scandinavian countries. Their main languages, Danish, Swedish, and Norwegian, are mutually intelligible, and they all retain their monarchies, although the parliaments have legislative control.

Using the Land

AGRICULTURE IN SOUTHERN SCANDINAVIA is highly mechanized although farms are small. Denmark is the most intensively farmed country and its western pastureland is used mainly for pig farming. Cereal crops including wheat, barley, and oats, predominate in eastern Denmark and in the far south of Sweden. Southern Norway, and Sweden have large tracts of forest which are exploited for logging.

The Urban/Rural Population Divide

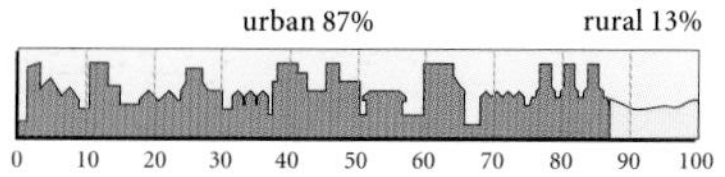

Population Density	Total Land Area
152 people per sq mile (61 people per sq km)	173,487 sq miles (456,564 sq km)

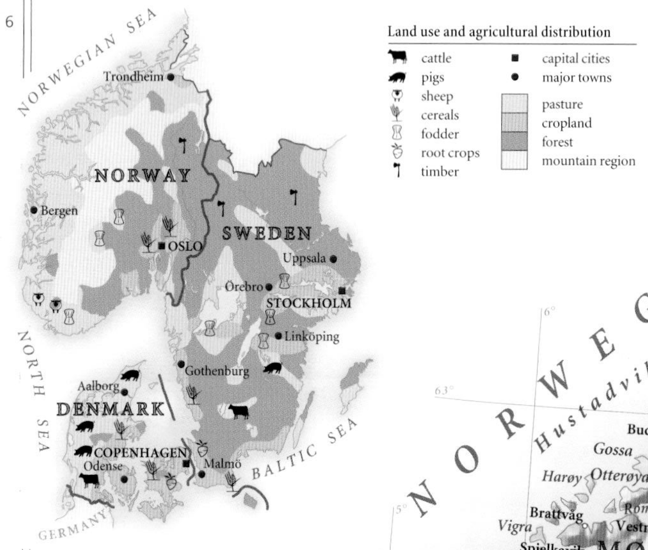

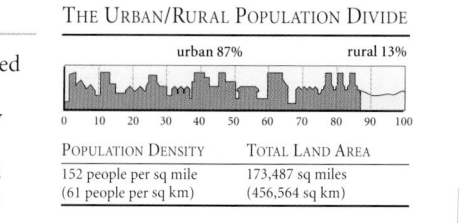

The Landscape

SOUTHERN SCANDINAVIA, with the exception of Norway, has a flatter terrain than the rest of the region. Denmark and southern Sweden are both extensions of the North European Plain. In this area, because of glacial deposition rather than erosion, the soils are deeper and more fertile.

In the past, glaciers such as this one in Olden, Norway, were much larger. Today, many are retreating to yield the spectacular glacial scenery.

Limestone pillars eroded by the sea dot the coast of Gotland and surrounding islands.

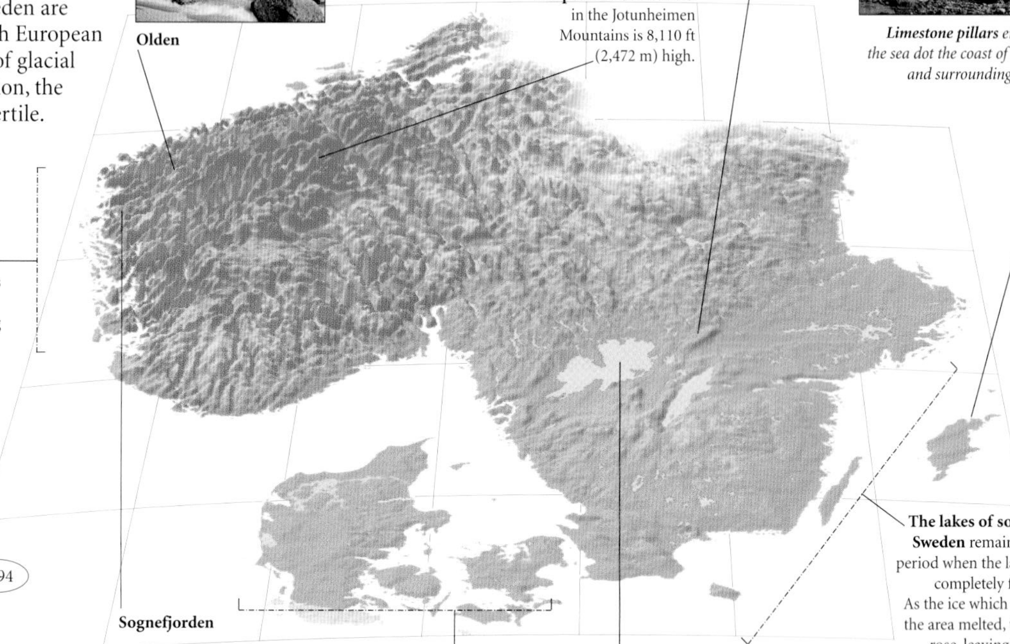

Distinctive low ridges, called eskers, are found across southern Sweden. They are formed from sand and gravel deposits left by retreating glaciers.

The peak of Glittertind in the Jotunheimen Mountains is 8,110 ft (2,472 m) high.

Acid rain, caused by industrial pollution carried north from elsewhere in Europe, harms plant and animal life in Scandinavian forests and lakes. The region's surface rocks lack lime to neutralize the acid, so making the problem more serious.

The lakes of southern Sweden remain from a period when the land was completely flooded. As the ice which covered the area melted, the land rose, leaving lakes in shallow, ice-scoured depressions. Sweden has over 90,000 lakes.

Vänern in Sweden is the largest lake in Scandinavia. It covers an area of 2,080 sq miles (5,390 sq km).

Denmark's flat and fertile soils are formed on glacial deposits between 100–160 ft (30–50 m) deep.

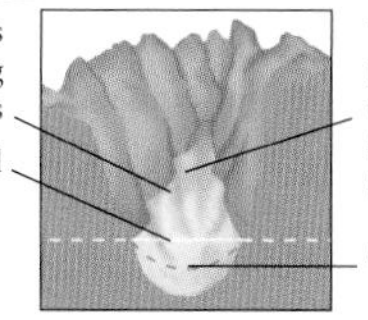

Sognefjorden is the deepest of Norway's many fjords. It drops to 4,291 ft (1,308 m) below sea level.

In Norway winters are longer and colder inland than in coastal areas, where the warm current of the North Atlantic Drift moderates the climate.

Scale 1:2,900,000
(projection: Lambert Conformal Conic)

Km 0 5 10 20 30 40 50 60 70 80 90 100
Miles 0 5 10 20 30 40 50 60 70 80 90 100

Map Key

POPULATION
- 500,000 to 1 million
- 100,000 to 500,000
- 50,000 to 100,000
- 10,000 to 50,000
- below 10,000

ELEVATION
- 2000m / 6562ft
- 1000m / 3281ft
- 500m / 1640ft
- 250m / 820ft
- 100m / 328ft
- sea level

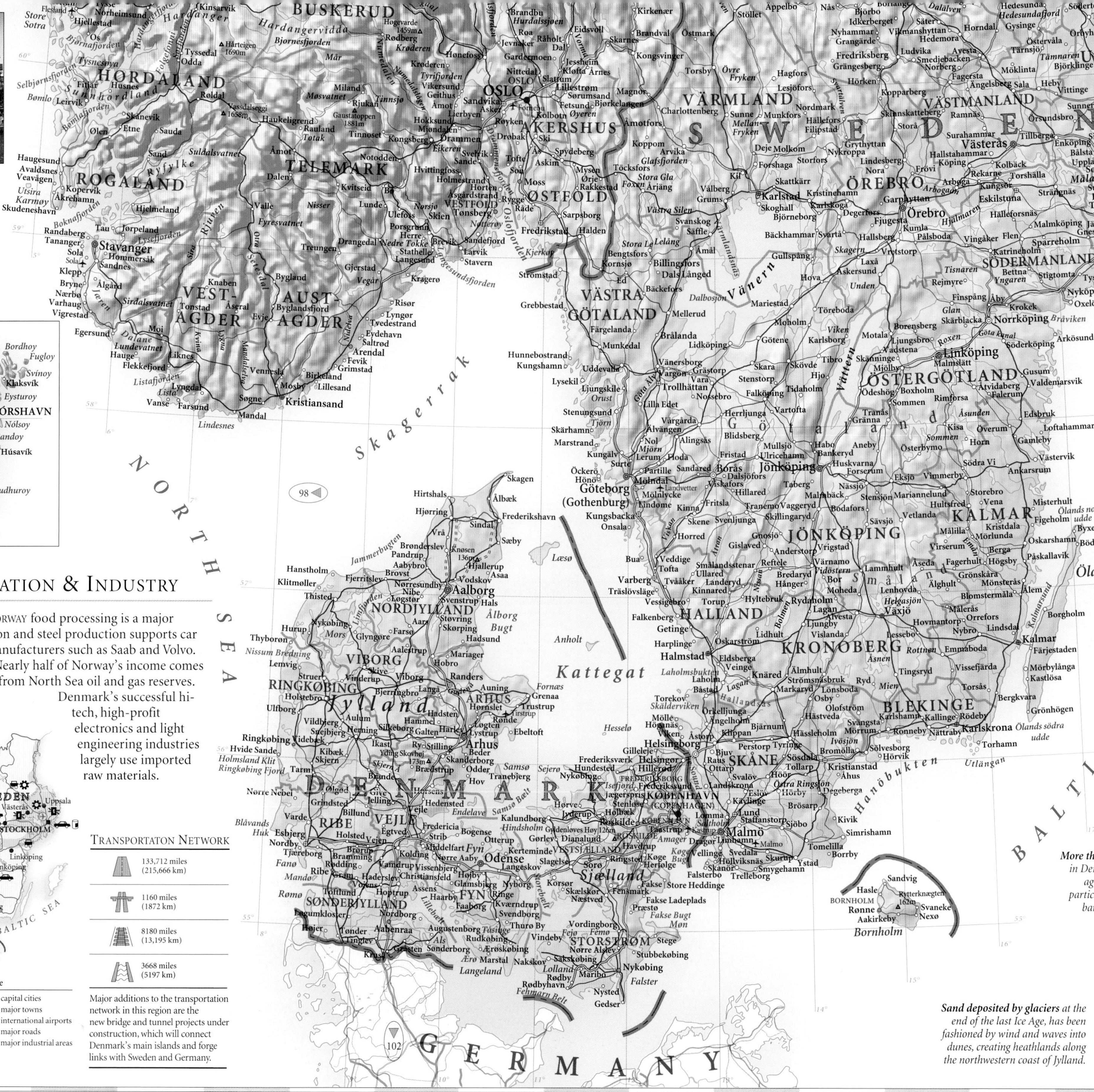

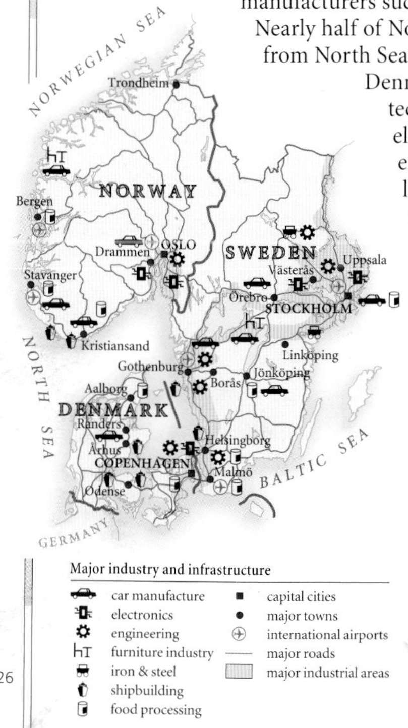

More than half the land in Denmark is used for agriculture. Grains, particularly wheat and barley, are the main crops cultivated.

Sand deposited by glaciers at the end of the last Ice Age, has been fashioned by wind and waves into dunes, creating heathlands along the northwestern coast of Jylland.

TRANSPORTATION & INDUSTRY

In DENMARK AND NORWAY food processing is a major industry. Swedish iron and steel production supports car manufacturers such as Saab and Volvo. Nearly half of Norway's income comes from North Sea oil and gas reserves. Denmark's successful hi-tech, high-profit electronics and light engineering industries largely use imported raw materials.

TRANSPORTATION NETWORK

133,712 miles (215,666 km)	
1160 miles (1872 km)	
8180 miles (13,195 km)	
3668 miles (5197 km)	

Major additions to the transportation network in this region are the new bridge and tunnel projects under construction, which will connect Denmark's main islands and forge links with Sweden and Germany.

Shipbuilding in Gothenburg has declined in recent years as manufacturers in other sectors have come to the fore. One of these is the car firm, Volvo, a major employer in Gothenburg.

Major industry and infrastructure

- capital cities
- major towns
- international airports
- major roads
- major industrial areas

- car manufacture
- electronics
- engineering
- furniture industry
- iron & steel
- shipbuilding
- food processing

FAEROE ISLANDS (to Denmark)

(same scale as main map)

The British Isles

United Kingdom, Ireland

The British Isles have for centuries played a central role in European and world history. England, Wales, Scotland, and Northern Ireland together form the United Kingdom (UK), while the southern portion of Ireland is an independent country, self-governing since 1921. Although England has tended to be the politically and economically dominant partner in the UK, the Scots, Welsh and Irish maintain independent cultures, distinct national identities and languages. Southeastern England is the most densely populated part of this crowded region, with over nine million people living in and around the London area.

***The valley of Glen Coe** in the Scottish Highlands is a U-shaped valley, typical of the north and west of the British Isles, where glaciers shaped much of the landscape.*

Transportation and Industry

The British Isles' industrial base was founded primarily on coal, iron and textiles, based largely in the north. Today, the most productive sectors include hi-tech industries clustered mainly in southeastern England, chemicals, finance and the service sector, particularly tourism.

Major industry and infrastructure: car manufacture; chemicals; engineering; hi-tech industry; iron & steel; tourism; capital cities; major towns; international airports; major roads; major industrial areas

Transportation Network

288,330 miles (464,300 km)	2,046 miles (3,295 km)
11,874 miles (19,121 km)	3,806 miles (6,129 km)

The UK's congested roads have become a major focus of environmental concern in recent years. No longer an island, the UK was finally linked to continental Europe by the Channel Tunnel in 1994.

***Clew Bay** in western Ireland, is characteristic of the heavily indented west coast, where deep wide-mouthed bays separate the mountains of Mayo, Donegal, and Kerry as they thrust out into the Atlantic Ocean.*

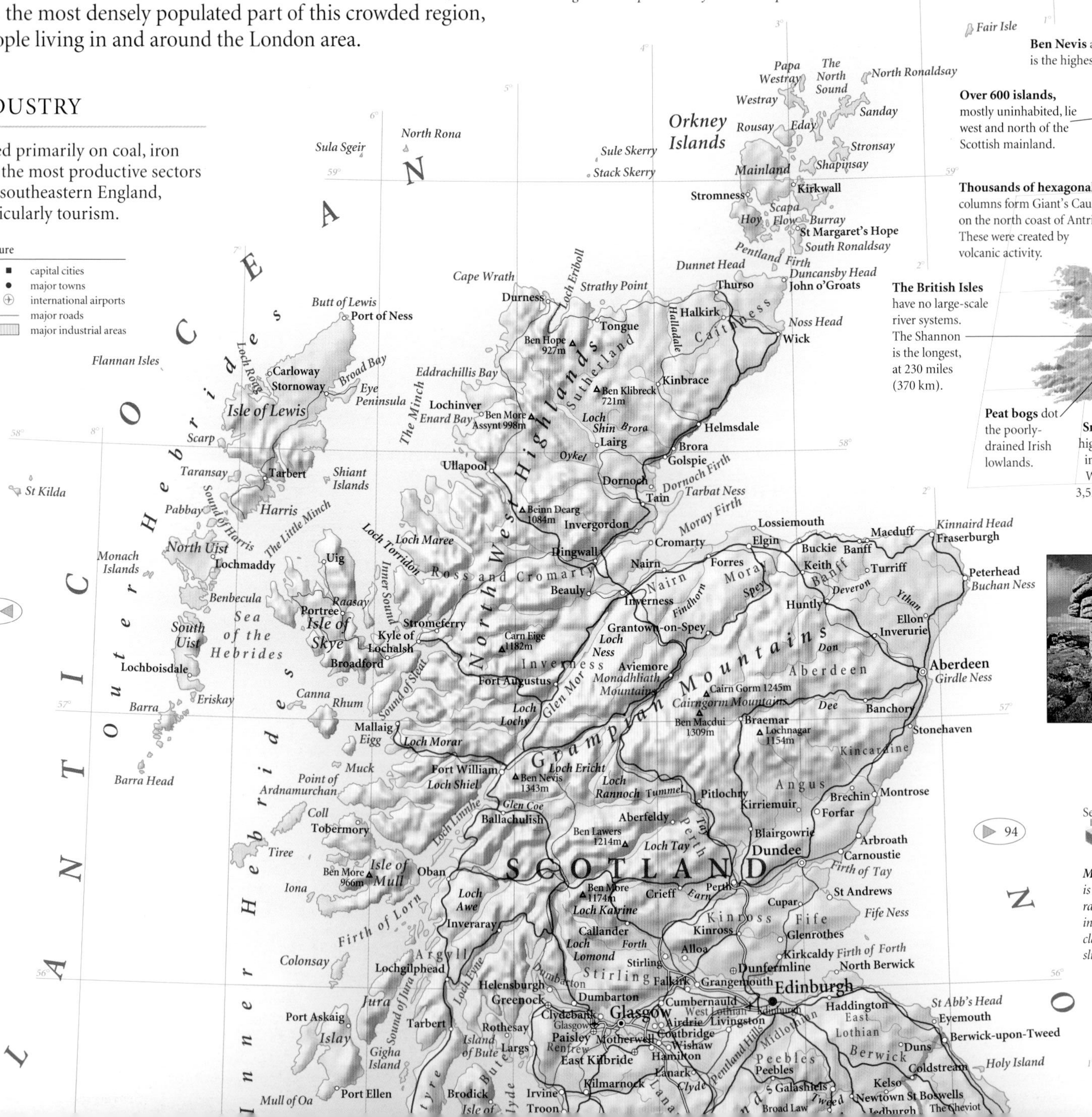

66

94

The Landscape

Rugged uplands dominate the landscape of Scotland, Wales, and northern England. All the peaks in the British Isles over 4,000 ft (1,219 m) lie in highland Scotland. Lowland England rises into several ranges of rolling hills, including the older Mendips, and the Cotswolds and the Chilterns, which were formed at the same time as the Alps in southern Europe.

The lowlands of Scotland, drained by the Tay, Forth, and Clyde Rivers, are centred on a rift valley. The region contains valuable coal reserves.

Ben Nevis at 4,409 ft (1,343 m) is the highest peak in the UK.

Over 600 islands, mostly uninhabited, lie west and north of the Scottish mainland.

Thousands of hexagonal basalt columns form Giant's Causeway on the north coast of Antrim. These were created by volcanic activity.

The British Isles have no large-scale river systems. The Shannon is the longest, at 230 miles (370 km).

Peat bogs dot the poorly-drained Irish lowlands.

Snowdon is the highest mountain in England and Wales reaching 3,556 ft (1,085 m).

The Pennines, sometimes called "the backbone of England," are formed of limestones and grits.

***Ullswater in the Lake District** fills a deep valley formed by glacial erosion.*

The Fens are a low-lying area reclaimed from the sea.

The Cotswold Hills are characterized by a series of limestone ridges overlooking clay vales.

***Dartmoor,** studded with tors, is an exposed part of a vast granite dome, formed when molten rock intruded into the Earth's crust.*

Durdle Door

***Coastal erosion** around the British Isles forms striking features such as this limestone arch, Durdle Door in Dorset.*

Black Ven, Lyme Regis

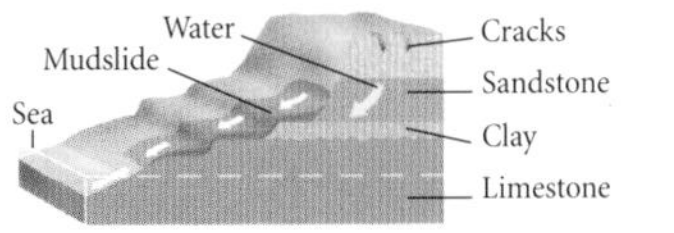

***Much of the south coast** is subject to landslides. Following rain, porous sandstones feed water into the underlying, less permeable clays which then crumble and slide into the sea.*

Map Key

Population	Elevation
above 5 million	1000m / 3281ft
1 million to 5 million	500m / 1640ft
500,000 to 1 million	250m / 820ft
100,000 to 500,000	100m / 328ft
50,000 to 100,000	sea level
10,000 to 50,000	
below 10,000	

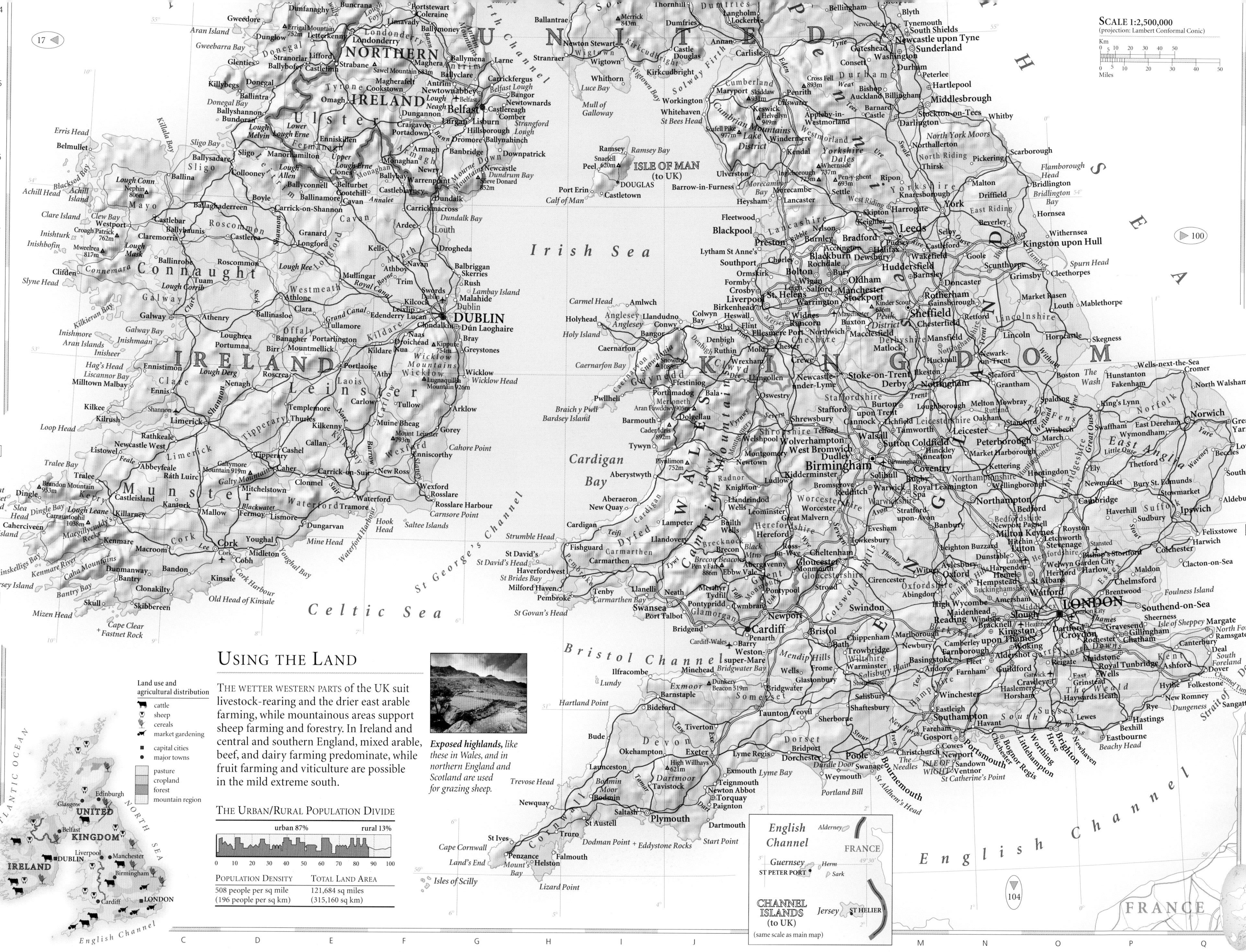

USING THE LAND

THE WETTER WESTERN PARTS of the UK suit livestock-rearing and the drier east arable farming, while mountainous areas support sheep farming and forestry. In Ireland and central and southern England, mixed arable, beef, and dairy farming predominate, while fruit farming and viticulture are possible in the mild extreme south.

Exposed highlands, *like these in Wales, and in northern England and Scotland are used for grazing sheep.*

THE URBAN/RURAL POPULATION DIVIDE

POPULATION DENSITY	TOTAL LAND AREA
508 people per sq mile (196 people per sq km)	121,684 sq miles (315,160 sq km)

THE LOW COUNTRIES

BELGIUM, LUXEMBOURG, NETHERLANDS

O NE OF NORTHWESTERN EUROPE'S strategic crossroads, the Low Countries are united by a common history in which they have often been a battleground in European wars. For over a thousand years they were ruled by foreign powers. Even after they achieved independence, the three countries maintained close links, later forming the world's first totally free labor and goods market, the Benelux Economic Union, which became the core of the European Community (now the European Union or EU). These states have remained at the forefront of wider European cooperation; Brussels, The Hague, and Luxembourg are hosts to major institutions of the EU.

THE LANDSCAPE

THE MAIN GEOGRAPHICAL REGIONS of the Netherlands are the northern glacial heathlands, the low-lying lands of the Rhine and Maas/Meuse, the reclaimed polders, and the dune coast and islands. Belgium includes part of the Ardennes, together with the coalfields on its northern flanks, and the fertile Flanders Plain.

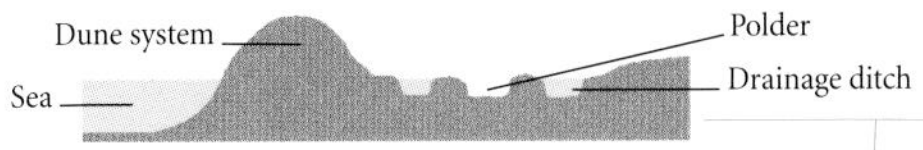

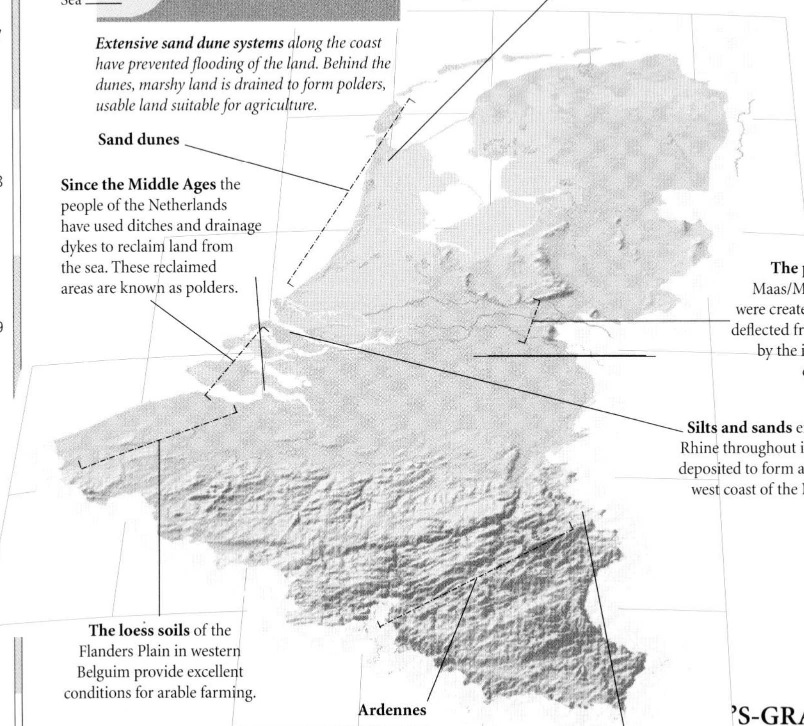

Since the Middle Ages the people of the Netherlands have used ditches and drainage dykes to reclaim land from the sea. These reclaimed areas are known as polders.

Extensive sand and dune systems along the coast have prevented flooding of the land. Behind the dunes, marshy land is drained to form polders, usable land suitable for agriculture.

Sand dunes

Polder
Drainage ditch
Dune system
Sea

The loess soils of the Flanders Plain in western Belgium provide excellent conditions for arable farming.

Uplifted and folded 220 million years ago, the Ardennes have since been reduced to relatively level plateaus, then sharply incised by rivers such as the Maas/Meuse.

Schoorl

Heathlands, like these at Schoorl, are found along the coast of the Netherlands. Much of the coast was breached by the sea in the 5th century, creating its distinctive inlets and islands.

One-third of the Netherlands lies below sea level and flooding is a constant threat. Barrages have been built across the mouths of many rivers to contain floodwaters.

The parallel valleys of the Maas/Meuse and Rhine Rivers were created when the Rhine was deflected from its previous course by the ice sheet which formed during the last Ice Age.

Silts and sands eroded by the Rhine throughout its course are deposited to form a delta on the west coast of the Netherlands.

Ardennes

Hautes Fagnes is the highest part of Belgium. The bogs and streams in this upland region result from high rainfall and low temperatures.

TRANSPORTATION & INDUSTRY

IN THE WESTERN NETHERLANDS, a massive, sprawling industrialized zone encompasses many new hi-tech and service industries. Belgium's central region has emerged as the country's light manufacturing and services center. Luxembourg city is home to more than 160 banks and the European headquarters of many international companies.

TRANSPORTATION NETWORK

280,630 miles (451,900 km)		2,536 miles (4,083 km)	
4,037 miles (6,501 km)		4,366 miles (7,031 km)	

The Low Countries hold a key position on the North Sea, containing Europe's two largest ports, Rotterdam and Antwerp, which are connected to a comprehensive system of inland waterways.

Major industry and infrastructure

aerospace
finance
engineering
hi-tech industry
pharmaceuticals
textiles

capital cities
major towns
international airports
major roads
major industrial areas

▲ 102

The Dutch city *of Rotterdam lies within one of the most densely populated and highly industrialized regions in the world, known as "Randstad Holland."*

NETHERLANDS' TWO CAPITALS

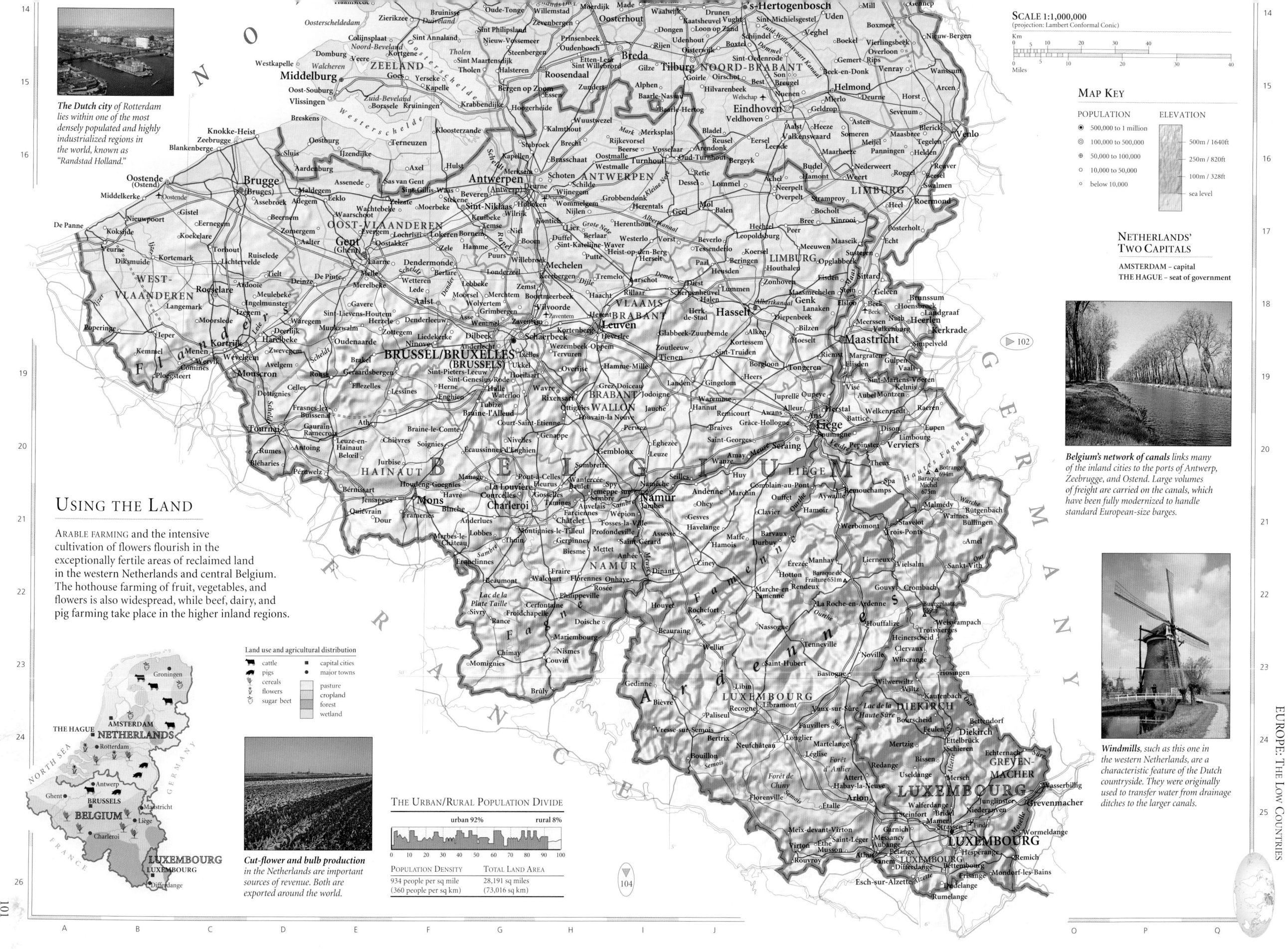

AMSTERDAM – capital
THE HAGUE – seat of government

Belgium's network of canals *links many of the inland cities to the ports of Antwerp, Zeebrugge, and Ostend. Large volumes of freight are carried on the canals, which have been fully modernized to handle standard European-size barges.*

Windmills, *such as this one in the western Netherlands, are a characteristic feature of the Dutch countryside. They were originally used to transfer water from drainage ditches to the larger canals.*

USING THE LAND

ARABLE FARMING and the intensive cultivation of flowers flourish in the exceptionally fertile areas of reclaimed land in the western Netherlands and central Belgium. The hothouse farming of fruit, vegetables, and flowers is also widespread, while beef, dairy, and pig farming take place in the higher inland regions.

Cut-flower and bulb production *in the Netherlands are important sources of revenue. Both are exported around the world.*

THE URBAN/RURAL POPULATION DIVIDE

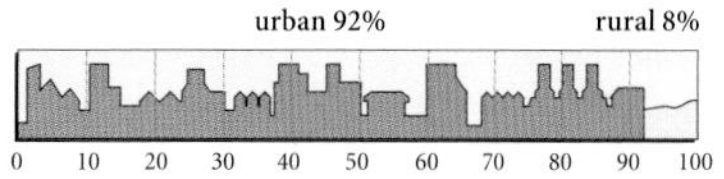

POPULATION DENSITY	TOTAL LAND AREA
934 people per sq mile (360 people per sq km)	28,191 sq miles (73,016 sq km)

Germany

Despite the devastation of its industry and infrastructure during the Second World War and its separation from eastern Germany during the Cold War, West Germany made a rapid recovery in the following generation to become Europe's most formidable economic power. When the Berlin Wall was dismantled in 1989, the two halves of Germany were politically united for the first time in 40 years. Complete social and economic unity remain a longer term goal, as East German industry and society adapt to a free market. Germany has been a key player in the creation of the European Union (EU) and in moves toward a single European currency.

Using the Land

Germany has a large, efficient agricultural sector, and produces more than three-quarters of its own food. The major crops grown are cereals and sugar beet on the more fertile soils, and root crops, rye, oats, and fodder on the poorer soils of the northern plains and central uplands. Southern Germany is also a principal producer of high quality wines. Vineyards cover the slopes surrounding the Rhine and its tributaries.

The Urban/Rural Population Divide

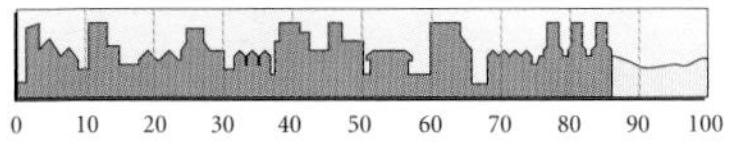

Population Density	Total Land Area
598 people per sq mile (231 people per sq km)	13,804 sq miles (356,910 sq km)

The Moselle River flows through the Rhine State Uplands (Rheinisches Schiefergebirge). *During a period of uplift, preexisting river meanders were deeply incised, to form its present dramatic contours.*

***The heathlands** of northern Germany are covered by glacial deposits of sandy outwash soil which makes them largely infertile. They support only sheep and solitary trees.*

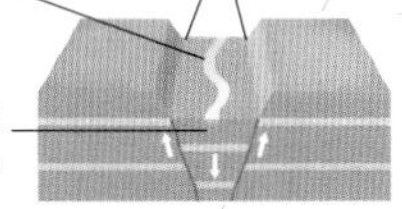

***Part of the floor** of the Rhine Rift Valley was let down between two parallel faults in the Earth's crust.*

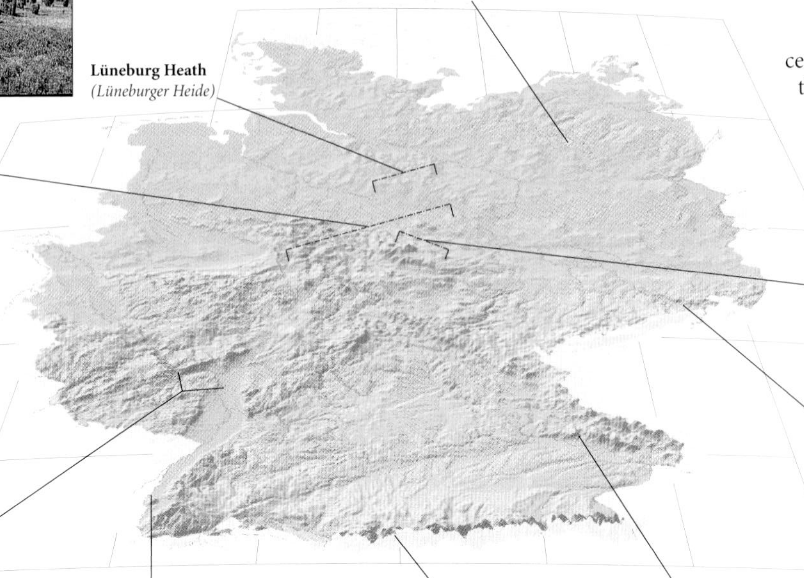

Müritz lake covers 45 sq miles (117 sq km), but is only 1,08 ft (33 m) deep. It lies in a shallow valley formed by meltwater flowing out from a retreating ice sheet. These valleys are known as *Urstromtäler.*

Lüneburg Heath (*Lüneburger Heide*)

Much of the landscape of northern Germany has been shaped by glaciation. During the last Ice Age, the ice sheet advanced as far the northern slopes of the central uplands.

Rhine Rift Valley

The Rhine is Germany's principal waterway and one of Europe's longest rivers, flowing 820 miles (1,320 km).

Zugspitze, the highest peak in Germany at 9,719 ft (2,962 m), was formed during the Alpine mountain-building period, 30 million years ago.

The Danube rises in the Black Forest (*Schwarzwald*) and flows east, across a wide valley, on its course to the Black Sea.

The Harz Mountains were formed 300 million years ago. They are block-faulted mountains, formed when a section of the Earth's crust was thrust up between two faults.

Elbe River

***The Elbe flows** in wide meanders across the north German plain to the North Sea. At its mouth it is 10 miles (16 km) wide.*

The Landscape

The plains of northern Germany, the volcanic plateaus and mountains of the central uplands, and the Bavarian Alps are the three principal geographic regions in Germany. North to south the land rises steadily from barely 300 ft (90 m) in the plains to 6,500 ft (2,000 m) in the Bavarian Alps, which are a small but distinct region in the far south.

Scale 1:2,250,000
(projection: Lambert Conformal Conic)

Map Key

POPULATION

- 1 million to 5 million
- 500,000 to 1 million
- 100,000 to 500,000
- 50,000 to 100,000
- 10,000 to 50,000
- below 10,000

ELEVATION

- 2000m / 6562ft
- 1000m / 3281ft
- 500m / 1640ft
- 250m / 820ft
- 100m / 328ft
- sea level

Transportation Network

- 393,093 miles (633,000 km)
- 6949 miles (11,190 km)
- 23,877 miles (38,450 km)
- 4,595 miles (7,400 km)

Germany has a complex network of inland waterways. The Rhine and Danube are at the center of a vast canal system which links central and eastern Europe to the north.

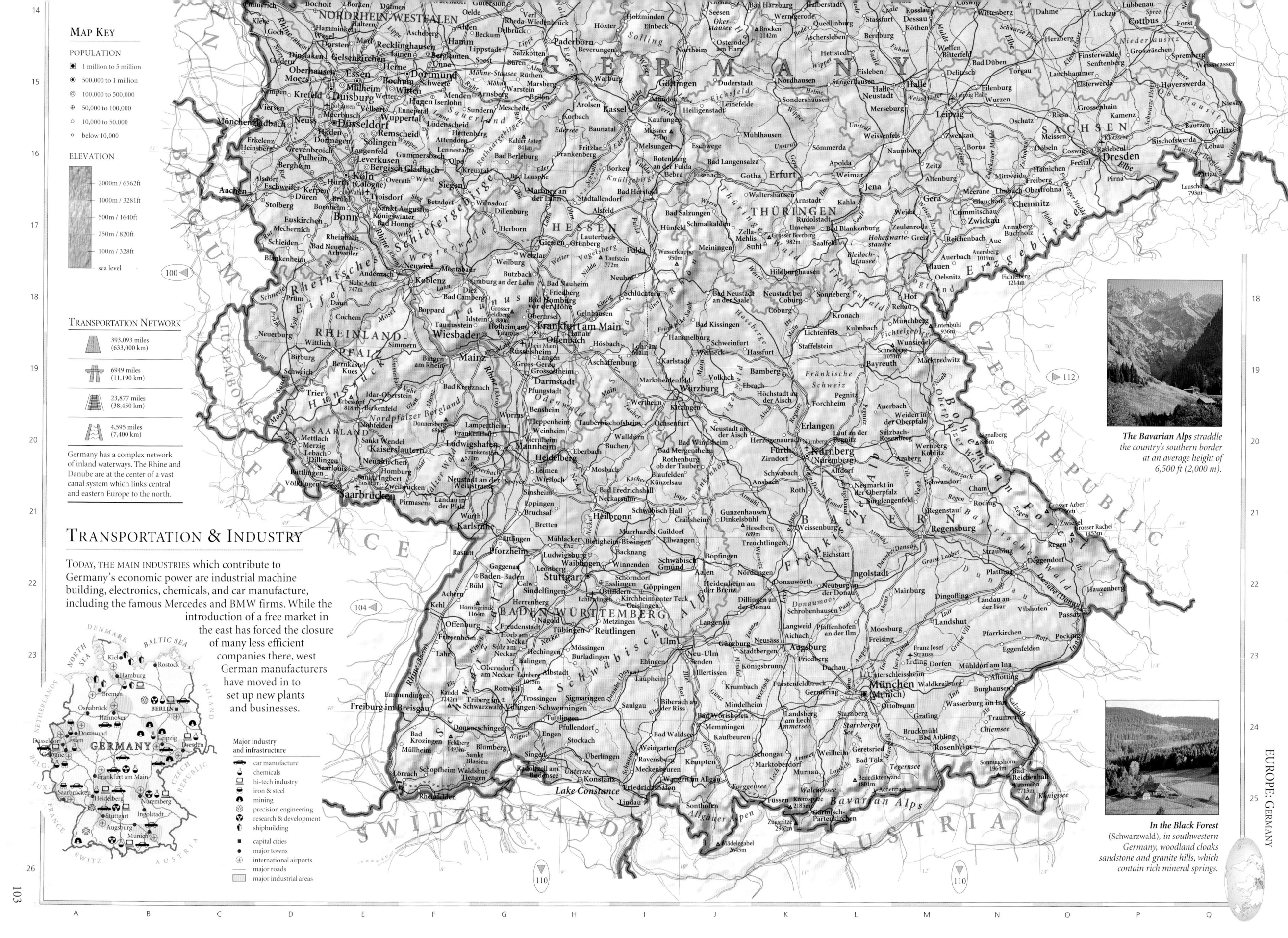

The Bavarian Alps straddle the country's southern border at an average height of 6,500 ft (2,000 m).

In the Black Forest (Schwarzwald), *in southwestern Germany, woodland cloaks sandstone and granite hills, which contain rich mineral springs.*

Transportation & Industry

TODAY, THE MAIN INDUSTRIES which contribute to Germany's economic power are industrial machine building, electronics, chemicals, and car manufacture, including the famous Mercedes and BMW firms. While the introduction of a free market in the east has forced the closure of many less efficient companies there, west German manufacturers have moved in to set up new plants and businesses.

Major industry and infrastructure

- car manufacture
- chemicals
- hi-tech industry
- iron & steel
- mining
- precision engineering
- research & development
- shipbuilding
- capital cities
- major towns
- international airports
- major roads
- major industrial areas

France

France, Monaco

Europe's second largest nation and the founder of modern Republican government, France is a major center of culture and fashion, and a leading producer of both agricultural and industrial goods. It has played a leading role in European events for centuries, and remains a key player in the push toward European unity. The Paris Basin is the most highly populated area; Île de France is home to over nine million people. Large parts of France remain thinly populated, particularly the mountainous Massif Central, Pyrenees, and southern Alps.

The chalk cliffs of Normandy (Normandie) and southeastern England form part of a single geological region, now divided in two by the English Channel.

66

106

The Landscape

France's landscape was fashioned by two phases of mountain-building. The northwestern peninsula, the Massif Central, and the Vosges date from 220 million years ago. The complex folds of the Alps and Pyrenees, the gently-folded Jura, and the low-lying sedimentary areas of the Paris, Garonne, and Rhône basins started to form 65 million years ago.

The coast of Brittany *(Bretagne)* is highly indented where deep valleys in the northwestern peninsula were drowned by the sea.

The Paris Basin consists of a layered sequence of sedimentary rocks. Fertile soils over much of the area make good agricultural land.

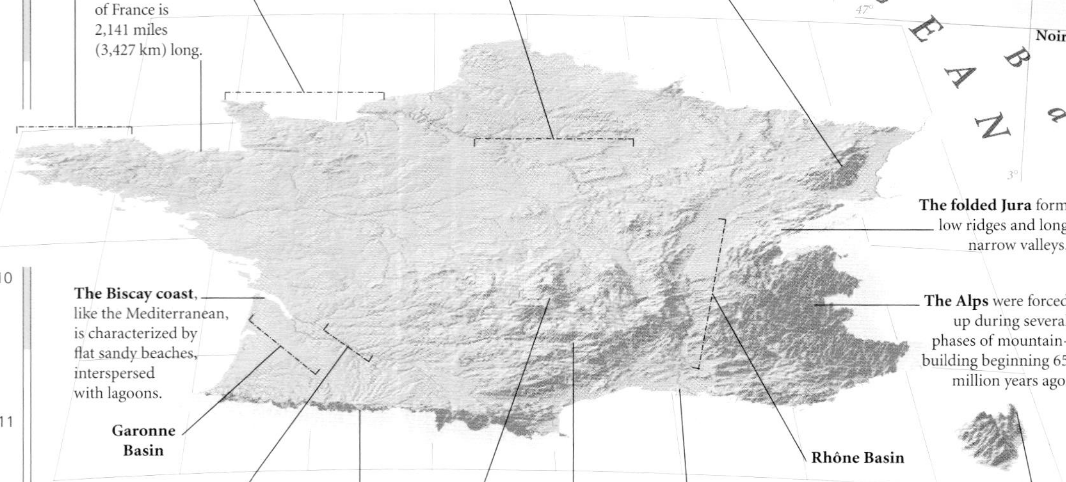

The Normandy *(Normandie)* coastline is characterized by high chalk cliffs.

The coastline of France is 2,141 miles (3,427 km) long.

The gently rounded summits of the Vosges are over 200 million years old.

The folded Jura form low ridges and long narrow valleys.

The Biscay coast, like the Mediterranean, is characterized by flat sandy beaches, interspersed with lagoons.

The Alps were forced up during several phases of mountain-building beginning 65 million years ago.

Garonne Basin

Rhône Basin

The Dordogne region contains spectacular examples of limestone scenery including caves and gorges.

The Pyrenees form a natural border between France and Spain.

The ancient Massif Central, disturbed by the formation of the Alps, was subject to volcanism that only ceased during the last 10,000 years.

Corsica's northeastern peninsula has dramatic cliffs of folded limestone.

Rhône Delta

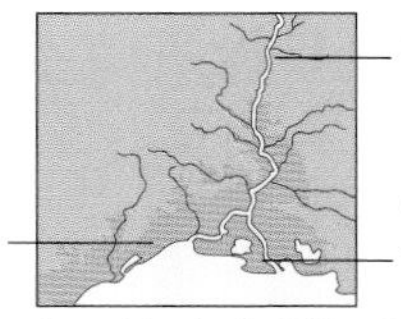

Deposition in the Rhône Delta is wave-dominated. Sea currents carry river sediments extending the delta plain westwards.

The volcanic landscape of the Auvergne where the cones of its extinct volcanoes have worn away to leave "plugs" of lava.

Transportation & Industry

Today the main French growth industries are hi-tech, including microelectronics, telecommunications, and aerospace. Other important sectors are the nuclear industry, only rivalled in scale by that of the USA, car manufacture, dominated by the giants Renault and Peugeot and a highly diversified tourist industry.

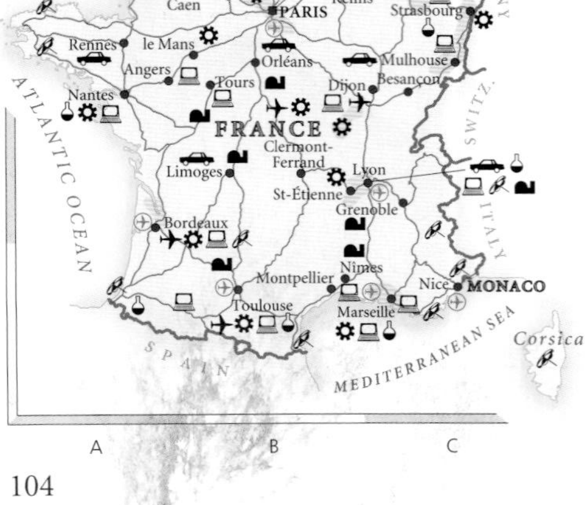

Major industry and infrastructure
- aerospace industry
- car manufacture
- chemicals
- engineering
- hi-tech industry
- nuclear power
- tourism
- capital cities
- major towns
- international airports
- major roads
- major industrial areas

Transportation Network

599,017 miles (964,600 km)	5,900 miles (9,500 km)
19,761 miles (31,821 km)	5,279 miles (8,500 km)

The French TGV (*Train à Grande Vitesse*) leads the world in high-speed train technology, and provides a service which is faster, door-to-door, than air travel.

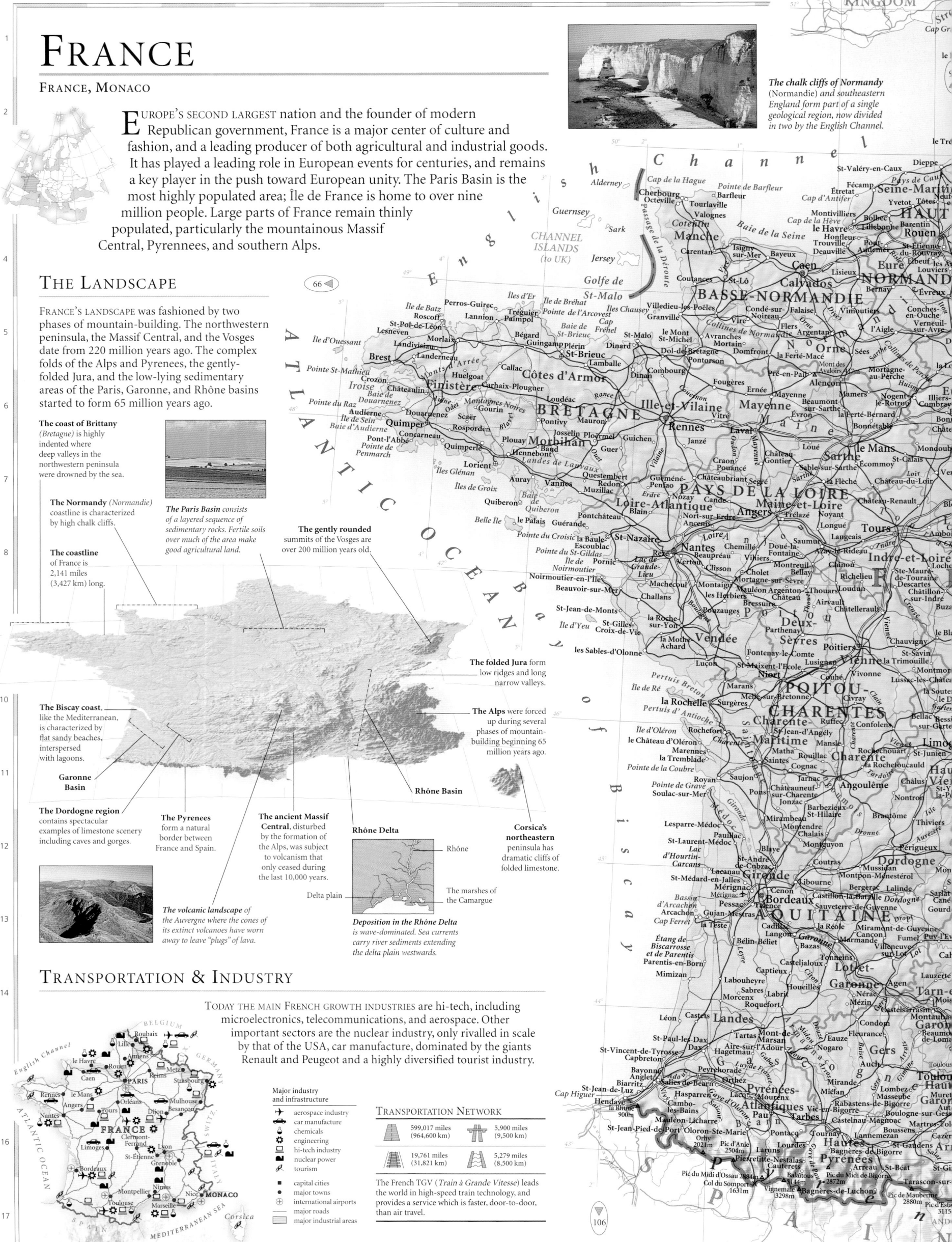

SCALE 1:2,750,000
(projection: Lambert Conformal Conic)

MAP KEY

POPULATION
- above 5 million
- 1 million to 5 million
- 500,000 to 1 million
- 100,000 to 500,000
- 50,000 to 100,000
- 10,000 to 50,000
- below 10,000

ELEVATION
- 4000m / 13,124ft
- 3000m / 9843ft
- 2000m / 6562ft
- 1000m / 3281ft
- 500m / 1640ft
- 250m / 820ft
- 100m / 328ft
- sea level

100
102
110
108

USING THE LAND

FRANCE IS WESTERN EUROPE'S leading agricultural producer, and benefits from high levels of EU subsidy. The variation in climate and soils across the country provides great potential for agriculture and forestry, reflected in the range of products cultivated, including cereals, olives, herbs, and grapes for its famous wines.

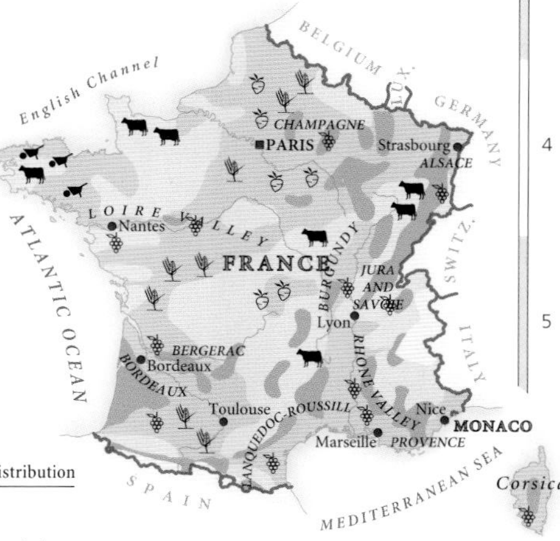

The Romans first introduced winemaking to France when they occupied the region. Traditional vineyards can be found all over France, producing many of the world's classic wines.

THE URBAN/RURAL POPULATION DIVIDE

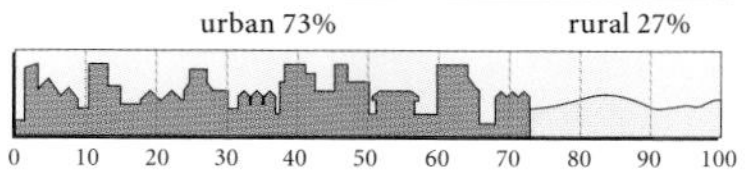

POPULATION DENSITY	TOTAL LAND AREA
276 people per sq mile (106 people per sq km)	212,930 sq mile (551,500 sq km)

The rugged hills and cliffs of Corsica were uplifted when the African and Eurasian plates collided. Frost action during the Ice Age created their present form.

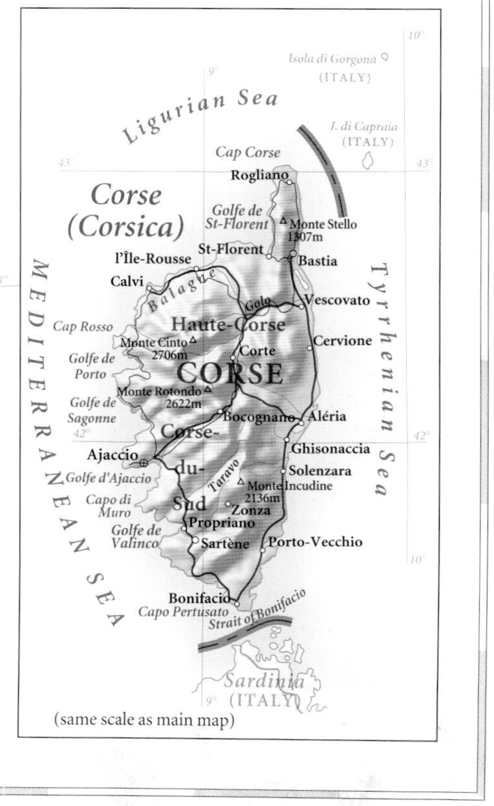

(same scale as main map)

In the sunny climate of southern France olives, vines, peppers, garlic, and lavender now grow in place of the forests that once covered much of the area.

The Iberian Peninsula

Andorra, Gibraltar, Portugal, Spain *(Azores, Canary Islands, Madeira on p.66)*

The Iberian peninsula is separated from the rest of Europe by the Pyrenees, and at its most southerly point is only 5 miles (8 km) from North Africa. The location of Iberia has been central to its diverse history. The Greeks, Carthaginians, Romans, Visigoths, and most recently the Moors, invaded Iberia at various times. For much of the 20th century, both Spain and Portugal were governed by right-wing dictators. Since the establishment of democratic governments in the mid-1970s, modernization has been rapid and both countries are now among the most popular of European holiday destinations.

Using the Land

The principal crops grown in Iberia are cereals, especially wheat and barley. Both countries are major wine producers, most notably of Rioja, sherry, and port. Sheep are kept throughout the region, and citrus fruits thrive on the Mediterranean coast. The successful forest industry in Iberia produces two-thirds of the world's cork.

The steep, terraced slopes *of the Douro Valley in northern Portugal, are used to cultivate vines. The grapes harvested produce Portugal's famous port wine.*

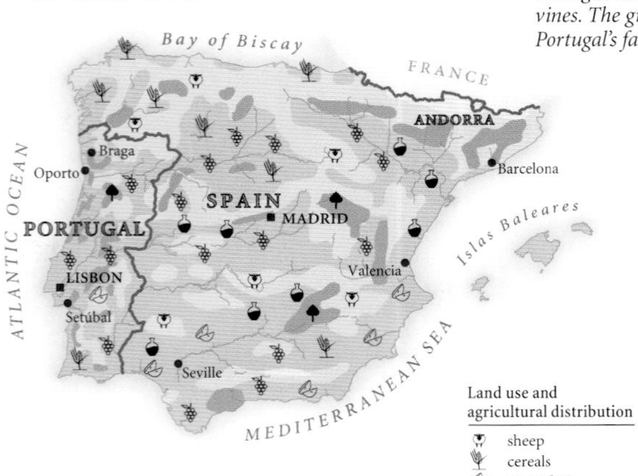

The Urban/Rural Population Divide

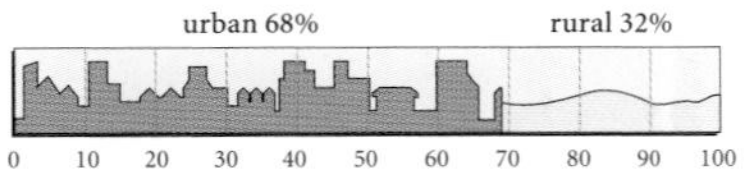

Population Density	Total Land Area
215 people per sq mile (83 people per sq km)	230,569 sq miles (597,170 sq km)

Transportation & Industry

Since the 1970s, the economies of Spain and Portugal have expanded and diversified. In both countries, tourism has outstripped agriculture in economic importance. Spain's resource base is varied, including coal, iron, and the world's largest reserves of mercury. Portugal is a leading producer of tungsten ore.

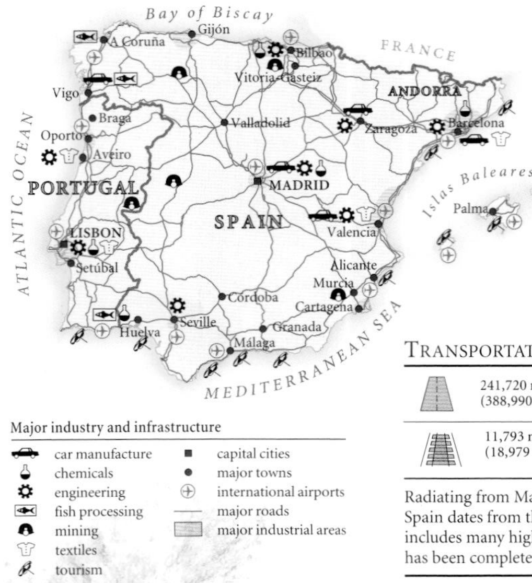

Transportation Network

241,720 miles (388,990 km)	1,552 miles (2,529 km)
11,793 miles (18,979 km)	1,159 miles (1,865 km)

Radiating from Madrid, the road network in Spain dates from the 18th century, but now includes many highways. Portugal's road system has been completely modernized in recent years.

The eroded cliffs *of the Algarve in southern Portugal were carved by Atlantic waves. The numerous rocky bays and beaches, and the region's pleasant climate, have made it a popular tourist destination.*

66
76

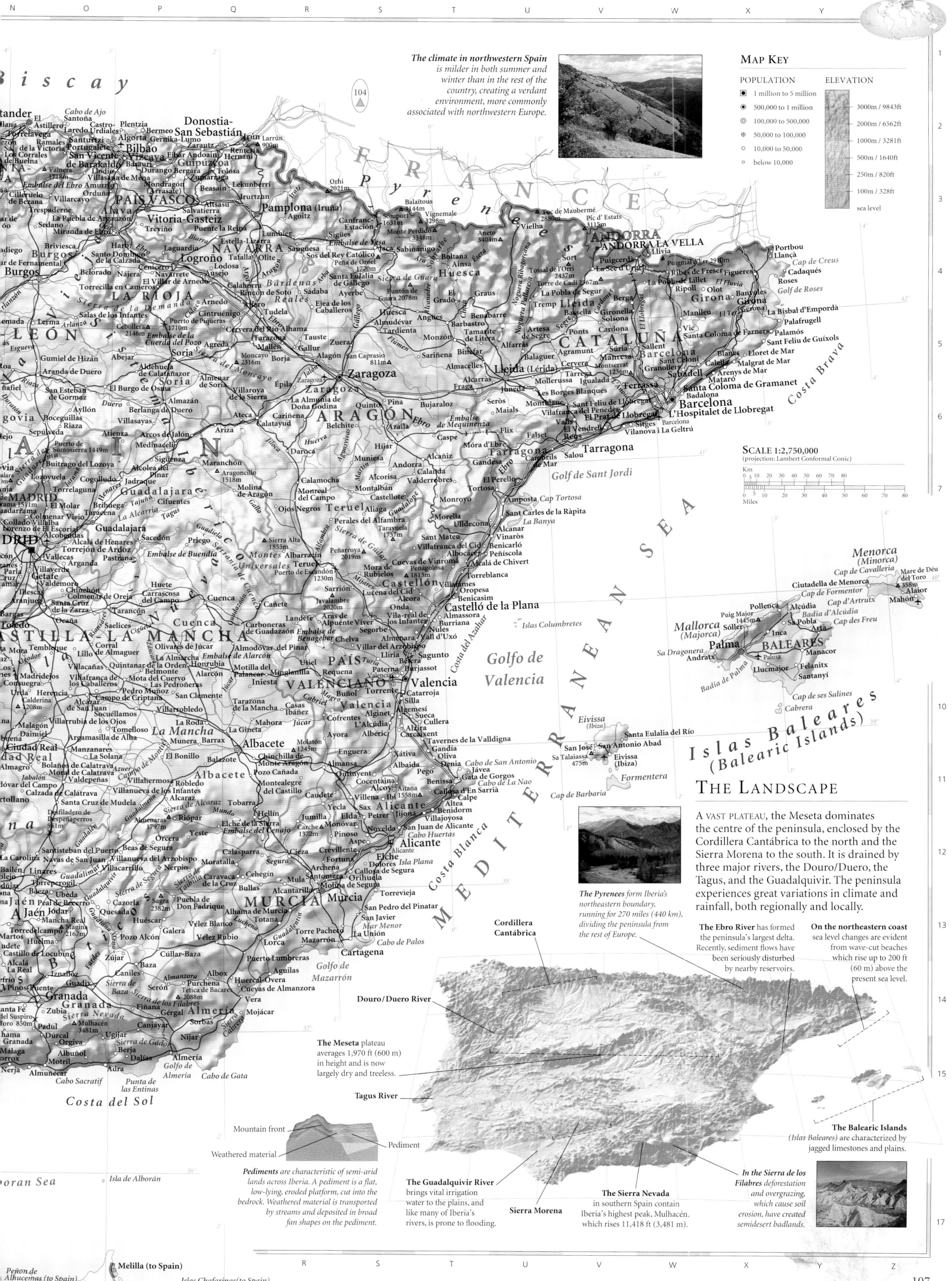

The climate in northwestern Spain is milder in both summer and winter than in the rest of the country, creating a verdant environment, more commonly associated with northwestern Europe.

MAP KEY

POPULATION

- 1 million to 5 million
- 500,000 to 1 million
- 100,000 to 500,000
- 50,000 to 100,000
- 10,000 to 50,000
- below 10,000

ELEVATION

- 3000m / 9843ft
- 2000m / 6562ft
- 1000m / 3281ft
- 500m / 1640ft
- 250m / 820ft
- 100m / 328ft
- sea level

SCALE 1:2,750,000
(projection: Lambert Conformal Conic)

Km 0 5 10 20 30 40 50 60 70 80
Miles 0 5 10 20 30 40 50 60 70 80

THE LANDSCAPE

A VAST PLATEAU, the Meseta dominates the centre of the peninsula, enclosed by the Cordillera Cantábrica to the north and the Sierra Morena to the south. It is drained by three major rivers, the Douro/Duero, the Tagus, and the Guadalquivir. The peninsula experiences great variations in climate and rainfall, both regionally and locally.

The Pyrenees form Iberia's northeastern boundary, running for 270 miles (440 km), dividing the peninsula from the rest of Europe.

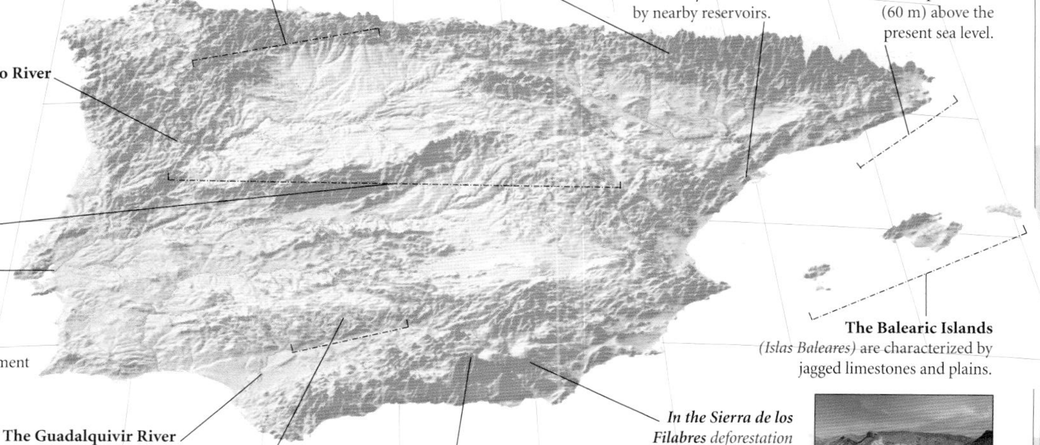

The Ebro River has formed the peninsula's largest delta. Recently, sediment flows have been seriously disturbed by nearby reservoirs.

On the northeastern coast sea level changes are evident from wave-cut beaches which rise up to 200 ft (60 m) above the present sea level.

The Meseta plateau averages 1,970 ft (600 m) in height and is now largely dry and treeless.

The Balearic Islands (*Islas Baleares*) are characterized by jagged limestones and plains.

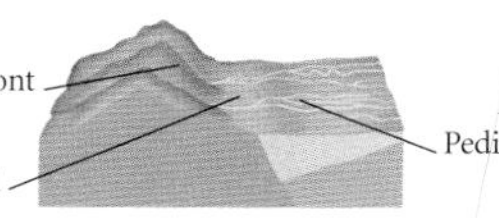

Pediments *are characteristic of semi-arid lands across Iberia. A pediment is a flat, low-lying, eroded platform, cut into the bedrock. Weathered material is transported by streams and deposited in broad fan shapes on the pediment.*

The Guadalquivir River brings vital irrigation water to the plains, and like many of Iberia's rivers, is prone to flooding.

The Sierra Nevada in southern Spain contain Iberia's highest peak, Mulhacén, which rises 11,418 ft (3,481 m).

In the Sierra de los Filabres deforestation and overgrazing, which cause soil erosion, have created semidesert badlands.

The Italian Peninsula

Italy, San Marino, Vatican City

The Italian peninsula is a land of great contrasts. Until unification in 1861, Italy was a collection of independent states, whose competitiveness during the Renaissance resulted in the architectural and artistic magnificence of cities such as Rome, Florence, and Venice. The majority of Italy's population and economic activity is concentrated in the north, centered on the sophisticated industrial city of Milan. Southern Italy, the *Mezzogiorno*, has a harsh terrain, and remains far less developed than the north. Attempts to attract industry and investment in the south are frequently deterred by the entrenched network of organized crime and corruption.

The Landscape

The mainly mountainous and hilly Italian peninsula took its present form following a collision between the African and Eurasian tectonic plates. The Alps in the northwest rise to a high point of 15,772 ft (4,807 m) at Mont Blanc *(Monte Bianco)* on the French border, while the Apennines *(Appennino)* form a rugged backbone, running along the entire length of the country.

The island of Sardinia is an ancient land mass; an uplifted section of very old igneous rocks. Its rugged mountainous regions provide pasture for sheep and goats, while its valleys support some agriculture.

Costa Smeralda

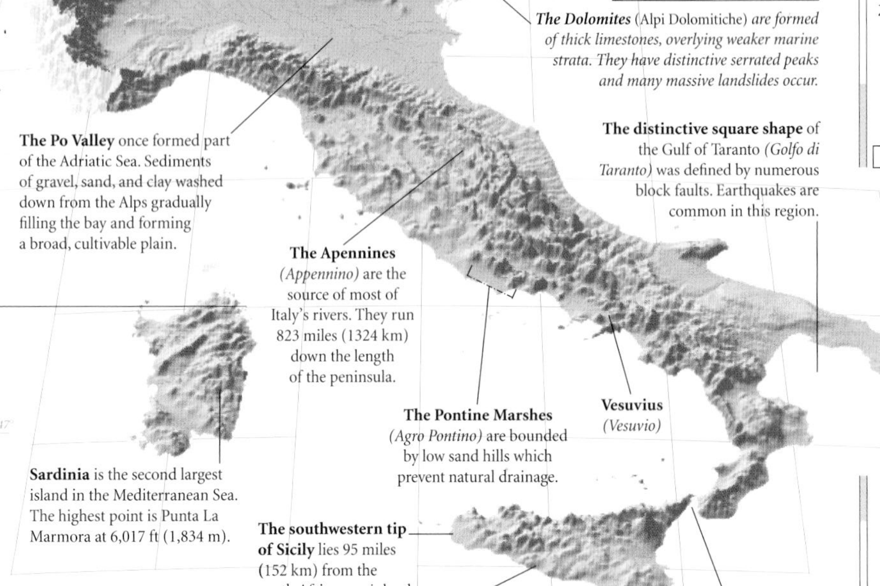

Mont Blanc *(Monte Bianco)*

***The Dolomites** (Alpi Dolomitiche) are formed of thick limestones, overlying weaker marine strata. They have distinctive serrated peaks and many massive landslides occur.*

The distinctive square shape of the Gulf of Taranto *(Golfo di Taranto)* was defined by numerous block faults. Earthquakes are common in this region.

The Po Valley once formed part of the Adriatic Sea. Sediments of gravel, sand, and clay washed down from the Alps gradually filling the bay and forming a broad, cultivable plain.

The Apennines *(Appennino)* are the source of most of Italy's rivers. They run 823 miles (1324 km) down the length of the peninsula.

The Pontine Marshes *(Agro Pontino)* are bounded by low sand hills which prevent natural drainage.

Vesuvius *(Vesuvio)*

Sardinia is the second largest island in the Mediterranean Sea. The highest point is Punta La Marmora at 6,017 ft (1,834 m).

The southwestern tip of Sicily lies 95 miles (152 km) from the north African mainland and is part of the same geological region.

Sicily is the largest island in the Mediterranean at 9,926 sq miles (25,708 sq km).

The Strait of Messina *(Stretto di Messina)* is between 2 and 12 miles (3–19 km) wide, and is a rich fishing ground.

Vesuvius *(Vesuvio)*

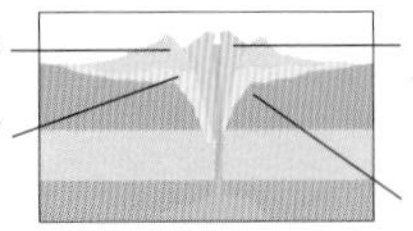

***There have been four volcanoes** on the site of Vesuvius since volcanic activity began here more than 10,000 years ago.*

Using the Land

Italy produces 95% of its own food. The best farming land is in the Po Valley in northern Italy, where soft wheat and rice are grown. Irrigation is essential to agriculture in much of the south. Italy is a major producer and exporter of citrus fruits, olives, tomatoes, and wine.

The Urban/Rural Population Divide

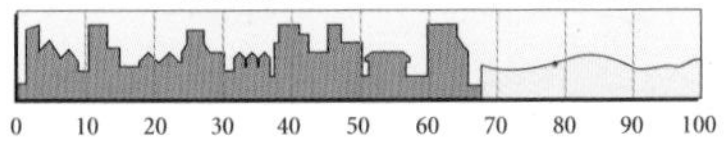

Population Density	Total Land Area
492 people per sq mile (190 people per sq km)	116,320 sq miles (301,270 sq km)

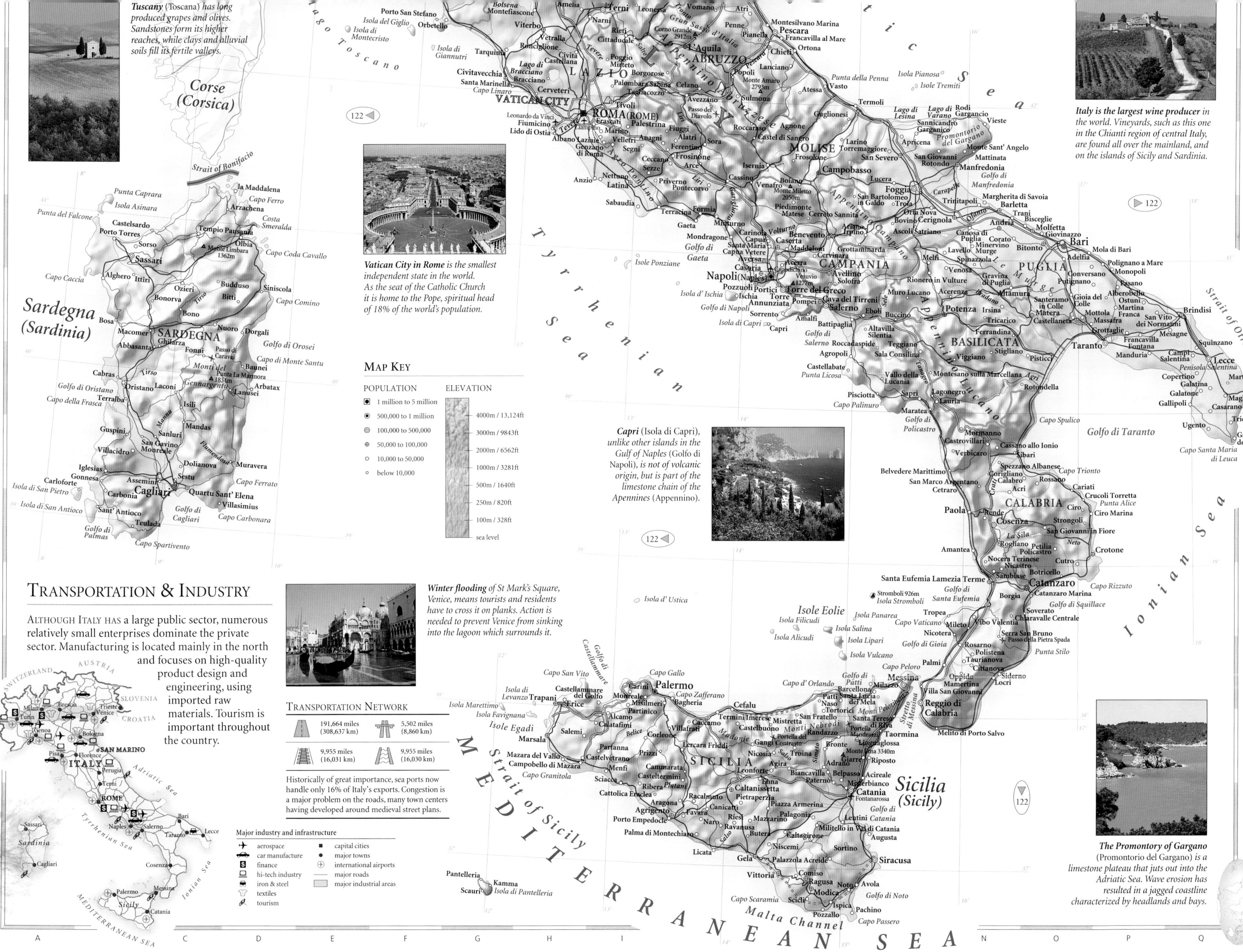

Tuscany (Toscana) *has long produced grapes and olives. Sandstones form its higher reaches, while clays and alluvial soils fill its fertile valleys.*

Italy is the largest wine producer *in the world. Vineyards, such as this one in the Chianti region of central Italy, are found all over the mainland, and on the islands of Sicily and Sardinia.*

Vatican City in Rome *is the smallest independent state in the world. As the seat of the Catholic Church it is home to the Pope, spiritual head of 18% of the world's population.*

Capri (Isola di Capri), *unlike other islands in the Gulf of Naples* (Golfo di Napoli), *is not of volcanic origin, but is part of the limestone chain of the Apennines* (Appennino).

Map Key

Population

- 1 million to 5 million
- 500,000 to 1 million
- 100,000 to 500,000
- 50,000 to 100,000
- 10,000 to 50,000
- below 10,000

Elevation

- 4000m / 13,124ft
- 3000m / 9843ft
- 2000m / 6562ft
- 1000m / 3281ft
- 500m / 1640ft
- 250m / 820ft
- 100m / 328ft
- sea level

Winter flooding *of St Mark's Square, Venice, means tourists and residents have to cross it on planks. Action is needed to prevent Venice from sinking into the lagoon which surrounds it.*

The Promontory of Gargano (Promontorio del Gargano) *is a limestone plateau that juts out into the Adriatic Sea. Wave erosion has resulted in a jagged coastline characterized by headlands and bays.*

Transportation & Industry

Although Italy has a large public sector, numerous relatively small enterprises dominate the private sector. Manufacturing is located mainly in the north and focuses on high-quality product design and engineering, using imported raw materials. Tourism is important throughout the country.

Major industry and infrastructure

- aerospace
- car manufacture
- finance
- hi-tech industry
- iron & steel
- textiles
- tourism
- capital cities
- major towns
- international airports
- major roads
- major industrial areas

Transportation Network

191,664 miles (308,637 km)	5,502 miles (8,860 km)
9,955 miles (16,031 km)	9,955 miles (16,030 km)

Historically of great importance, sea ports now handle only 16% of Italy's exports. Congestion is a major problem on the roads, many town centers having developed around medieval street plans.

THE ALPINE STATES

AUSTRIA, LIECHTENSTEIN, SLOVENIA, SWITZERLAND

THE ALPINE COUNTRIES of Austria, Switzerland, Liechtenstein, and Slovenia form a narrow strip across western Europe's geographical core, lying on the main north–south trading routes across the Alps. Switzerland, politically neutral since 1815, is an important international meeting place and houses one of the headquarters of the United Nations, although not itself a member. Austria, once at the heart of the great Habsburg Empire has been a fully independent nation since 1955, and maintains a deserved reputation as an international center of culture. Slovenia declared independence from the former Yugoslavia in 1991 and despite initial economic hardship, is now starting to achieve the prosperity enjoyed by its Alpine neighbors.

USING THE LAND

THE ALPINE REGION'S mountainous terrain discourages cultivation over much of the land area. The primary agricultural activity is the raising of dairy and beef cattle on the pasture land of the lower mountain slopes. Austria is self-supporting in grains, and crops such as wheat, barley, and grapes are grown on the east Austrian lowlands. Woodlands are more prevalent in the eastern Alps; both Austria and Slovenia have large tracts of forest.

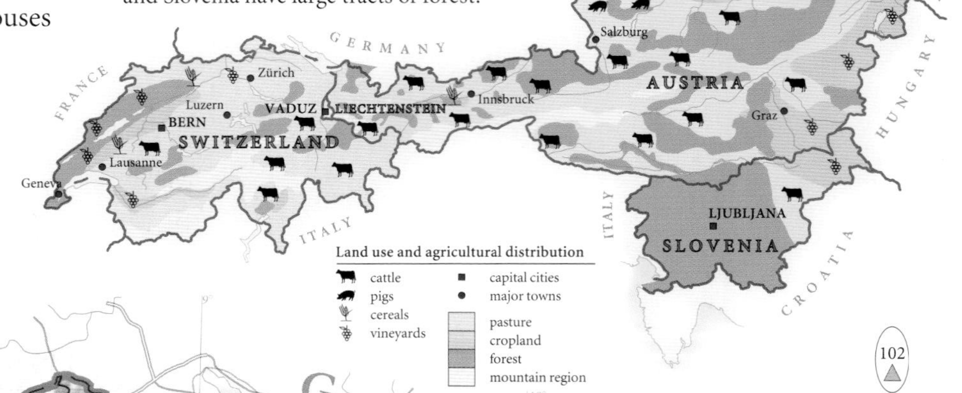

The Matterhorn, on the Swiss-Italian border, is one of the highest mountains in the Alps, at 14,692 ft (4,478 m). The term "horn" refers to its distinctive peak, formed by three glaciers eroding hollows, known as cirques, in each of its sides.

THE LANDSCAPE

THE ALPS OCCUPY THREE-FIFTHS OF SWITZERLAND, most of southern Austria and the northwest of Slovenia. They were formed by the collision of the African and Eurasian tectonic plates, which began 65 million years ago. Their complex geology is reflected in the differing heights and rock types of the various ranges. The Rhine flows along Liechtenstein's border with Switzerland, creating a broad floodplain in the north and west of Liechtenstein. In the far northeast and east are a number of lowland regions, including the Vienna Basin, Burgenland, and the plain of the Danube. Slovenia's major rivers flow across the lower eastern regions; in the west, the rivers flow underground through the limestone Karst region.

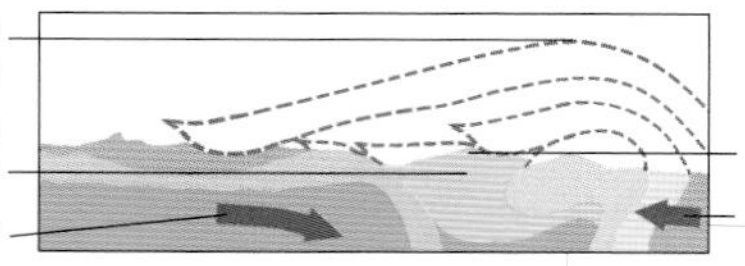

***The convergence of the African and Eurasian plates** compressed and folded huge masses of rock strata. As the plates continued to move together, the folded strata were overturned, creating complex nappes. Much of the rock strata has since been eroded, resulting in the current topography of the Alps.*

***Constricted as it cuts through** ridges in the Alps, the Danube meanders across the lowlands, where uplift combined with river erosion has deepened meanders.*

The Vienna Basin lies mainly below 390 ft (120 m). It gradually subsided and filled with sediment as the Alps were uplifted.

Neusiedler See straddles the border of Austria and Hungary; the area around it provides some of the best wine-growing land in Austria.

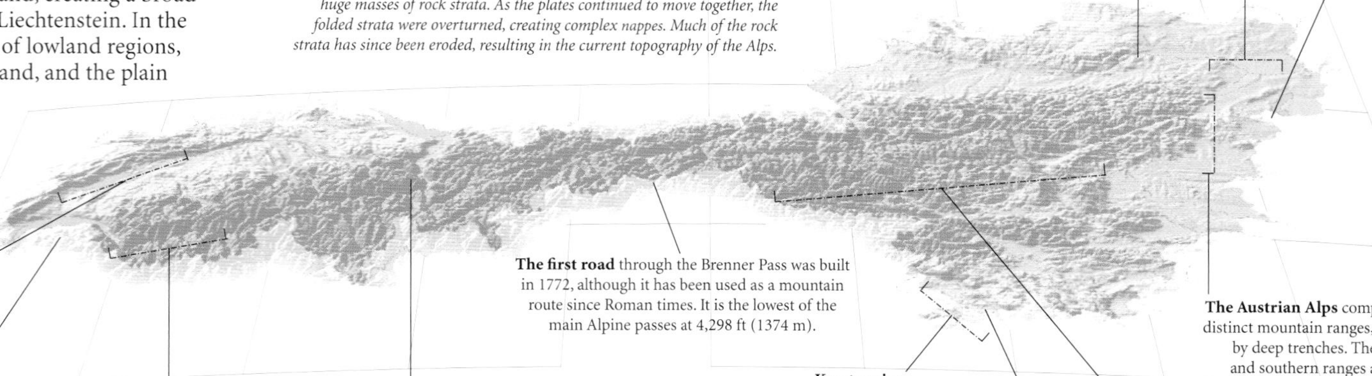

The mountains of the Jura form a natural border between Switzerland and France. Their marine limestones date from over 200 million years ago. When the Alps were formed the Jura were folded into a series of parallel ridges and troughs.

Tectonic activity has resulted in dramatic changes in land height over very short distances. Lake Geneva, lying at 1,221 ft (372 m) is only 43 miles (70 km) away from the 15,772 ft (4,807 m) peak of Mont Blanc, on the France–Italy border.

The Bernese Alps *(Berner Alpen)* contain the Aletsch, which at 15 miles (24 km) is the longest Alpine glacier.

The Rhine, like other major Alpine rivers, follows a broad, flat trough between the mountains. Along part of its course, the Rhine forms the boundary between Switzerland and Liechtenstein.

The first road through the Brenner Pass was built in 1772, although it has been used as a mountain route since Roman times. It is the lowest of the main Alpine passes at 4,298 ft (1374 m).

Karst region

***The deep, blue lakes** of the Karst region are part of a drainage network which runs largely underground through this limestone area.*

The limestone cave system at Postojna extends for more than 10 miles (16 km) and includes caverns reaching 125 ft (40 m) in height and width.

The Austrian Alps comprise three distinct mountain ranges, separated by deep trenches. The northern and southern ranges are rugged limestones, while the Tauern range is formed of crystalline rocks.

The Tauern range in the central Austrian Alps contains the highest mountain in Austria, the towering Grossglockner, rising 12,461 ft (3,798 m).

THE URBAN/RURAL POPULATION DIVIDE

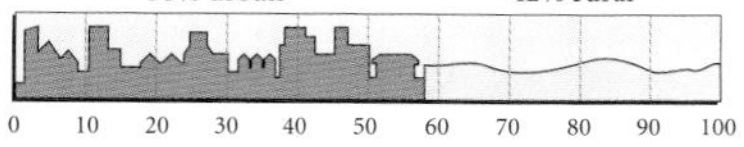

POPULATION DENSITY	TOTAL LAND AREA
310 people per sq mile (120 people per sq km)	56,135 sq miles (145,390 sq km)

In this mountainous region, the flatter, more accessible areas are often used for both cattle grazing and recreation.

These converging glaciers are marked by dark lines of moraine. This eroded material is carried by glaciers, and deposited as the ice melts.

SCALE 1:1,750,000
(projection: Lambert Conformal Conic)

Km 0 5 10 20 30 40 50 60
Miles 0 5 10 20 30 40 50 60

MAP KEY

POPULATION
- 1 million to 5 million
- 500,000 to 1 million
- 100,000 to 500,000
- 50,000 to 100,000
- 10,000 to 50,000
- below 10,000

ELEVATION
- 4000m / 13,124ft
- 3000m / 9843ft
- 2000m / 6562ft
- 1000m / 3281ft
- 500m / 1640ft
- 250m / 820ft
- 100m / 328ft
- sea level

***The Austrian Tirol** contains some of the most spectacular Alpine scenery. Snow cover is a permanent feature in the highest reaches.*

TRANSPORTATION & INDUSTRY

ALL FOUR NATIONS concentrate on high-quality manufacturing and services. Austrian iron and steel production is complemented by construction industries; and Slovenia, traditionally the industrial powerhouse of the western Balkans has increasingly diversified industries. Liechtenstein and Switzerland, lacking raw materials, produce pharmaceuticals and precision instruments, such as watches, and act as international banking centers. The spectacular scenery of the region encourages tourism all year round.

TRANSPORTATION NETWORK

119,805 miles (192,923 km)	2044 miles (3292 km)
6227 miles (10,028 km)	984 miles (1584 km)

Tunnels and passes through the Alps are an important feature of this region. The NEAT project, providing two new high-speed rail links between Basel and Milan, was given approval in 1992.

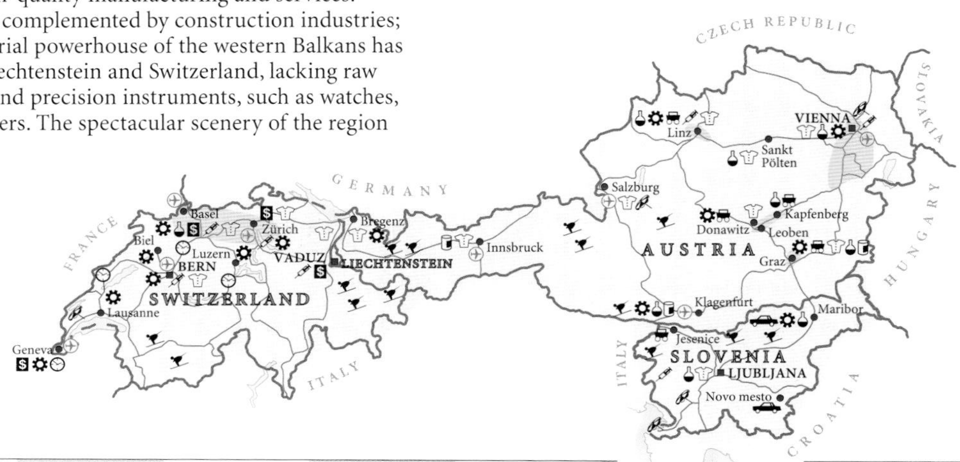

Major industry and infrastructure
- car manufacture
- chemicals
- engineering
- finance
- food processing
- iron & steel
- pharmaceuticals
- textiles
- tourism
- watch making
- winter sports
- capital cities
- major towns
- international airports
- major roads
- major industrial areas

***The Schönbrunn Palace** in Vienna was the summer residence of the Habsburg monarchy. Today, it is a major tourist attraction.*

CENTRAL EUROPE

CZECH REPUBLIC, HUNGARY, POLAND, SLOVAKIA

WHEN SLOVAKIA AND THE CZECH REPUBLIC became separate countries in 1993, they joined Hungary and Poland in a new role as independent nation states, following centuries of shifting boundaries and imperial strife. This turbulent history bequeathed the region a rich cultural heritage, shared through the works of its many great writers and composers, and celebrated in the vibrant historic capitals of Prague, Budapest, and Warsaw. Having shaken off Soviet domination in 1989, these states are facing up to the challenge of winning commercial investment to modernize outmoded industry, while bearing the severe environmental impact from forty years of large-scale industrialization.

TRANSPORTATION & INDUSTRY

HEAVY INDUSTRY HAS DOMINATED POSTWAR LIFE in Central Europe. Poland has large coal reserves, having inherited the Silesian coalfield from Germany after the Second World War, allowing the export of large quantities of coal, along with other minerals. Hungary specializes in consumer goods and services, while Slovakia's industrial base is still relatively small. The Czech Republic's traditional glassworks and breweries bring some stability to its precarious Soviet-built manufacturing sector.

Major industry and infrastructure

- car manufacture
- chemicals
- engineering
- food processing
- mining
- shipbuilding
- tourism
- capital cities
- major towns
- international airports
- major roads
- major industrial areas

TRANSPORTATION NETWORK

213,997 miles (344,600 km)	817 miles (1,315 km)
27,479 miles (44,249 km)	3,784 miles (6,094 km)

The huge growth of tourism and business has prompted major investment in the transportation infrastructure, with new roadbuilding schemes within and between the main cities of the region.

Budapest, the capital of Hungary, straddles the Danube. It comprises the historic towns of Buda, on the west bank, and Pest, which contains the Parliament Building, seen here on the far bank.

THE LANDSCAPE

THE FORESTED Carpathian Mountains, uplifted with the Alps, lie southeast of the older Bohemian massif, which contains the Sudeten and Krušné Hory (*Erzgebirge*) ranges. They divide the fertile plains of the Danube to the south and the Vistula (*Wisła*), which flows north across vast expanses of glacial deposits into the Baltic Sea.

The Berounka River cuts through the precipitous wooded landscape of the Bohemian massif, banked by a broad floodplain.

Krušné Hory (*Erzgebirge*)

Hot mineral springs occur where geothermally heated water wells up through faults and fractures in the rocks of the Sudeten Mountains.

Pomerania is a sandy coastal region of glacially-formed lakes stretching west from the Vistula (*Wisła*).

Longshore currents moving east along the Baltic coast have built a 40 mile (65 km) spit composed of material from the Vistula (*Wisła*) River.

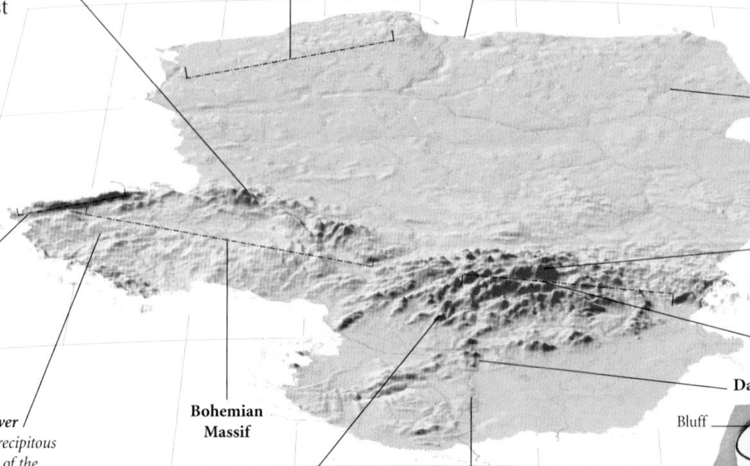

The Biebrza River has left meanders and oxbow lakes as it flows across low-lying ground.

Gerlachovský štít, in the Tatra Mountains, is Slovakia's highest mountain, at 8,711 ft (2,655 m).

Carpathian Mountains

Danube River

Slip-off slope

Bluff

Direction of flow

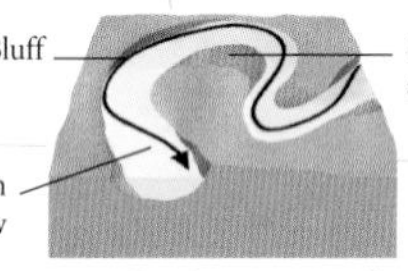

Meanders form as rivers flow across plains at a low gradient. A steep cliff or bluff, forms on the outside curve, and a gentler slip-off slope on the inside bend.

The Great Hungarian Plain formed by the floodplain of the Danube is a mixture of steppe and cultivated land, covering nearly half of Hungary's total area.

Bohemian Massif

The Slovak Ore Mountains (*Slovenské Rudohorie*) are noted for their mineral resources, including high-grade iron ore.

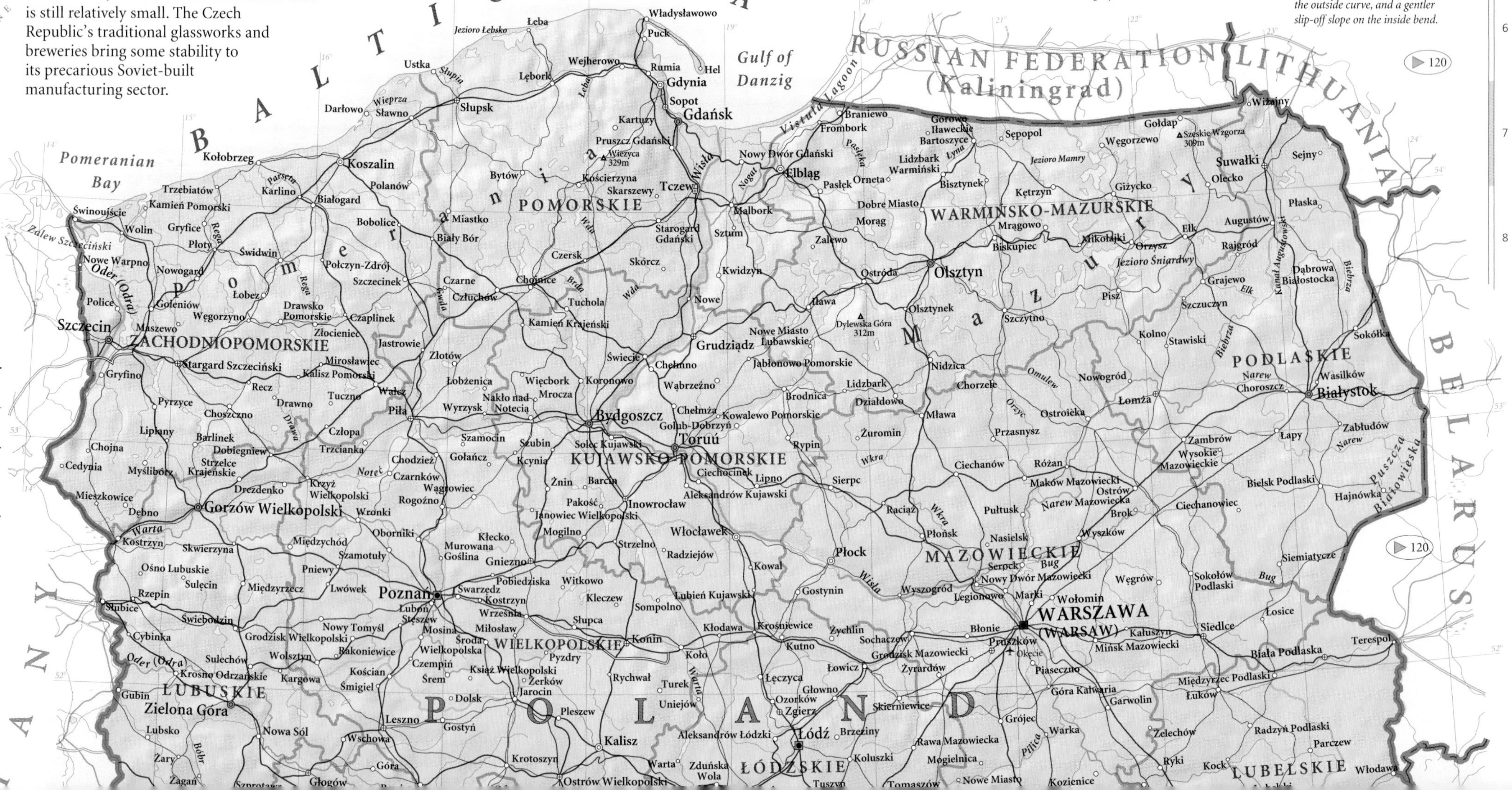

Map Key

POPULATION
- 1 million to 5 million
- 500,000 to 1 million
- 100,000 to 500,000
- 50,000 to 100,000
- 10,000 to 50,000
- below 10,000

ELEVATION
- 2000m / 6562ft
- 1000m / 3281ft
- 500m / 1640ft
- 250m / 820ft
- 100m / 328ft
- sea level

SCALE 1:2,500,000
(projection: Lambert Conformal Conic)

Using the Land

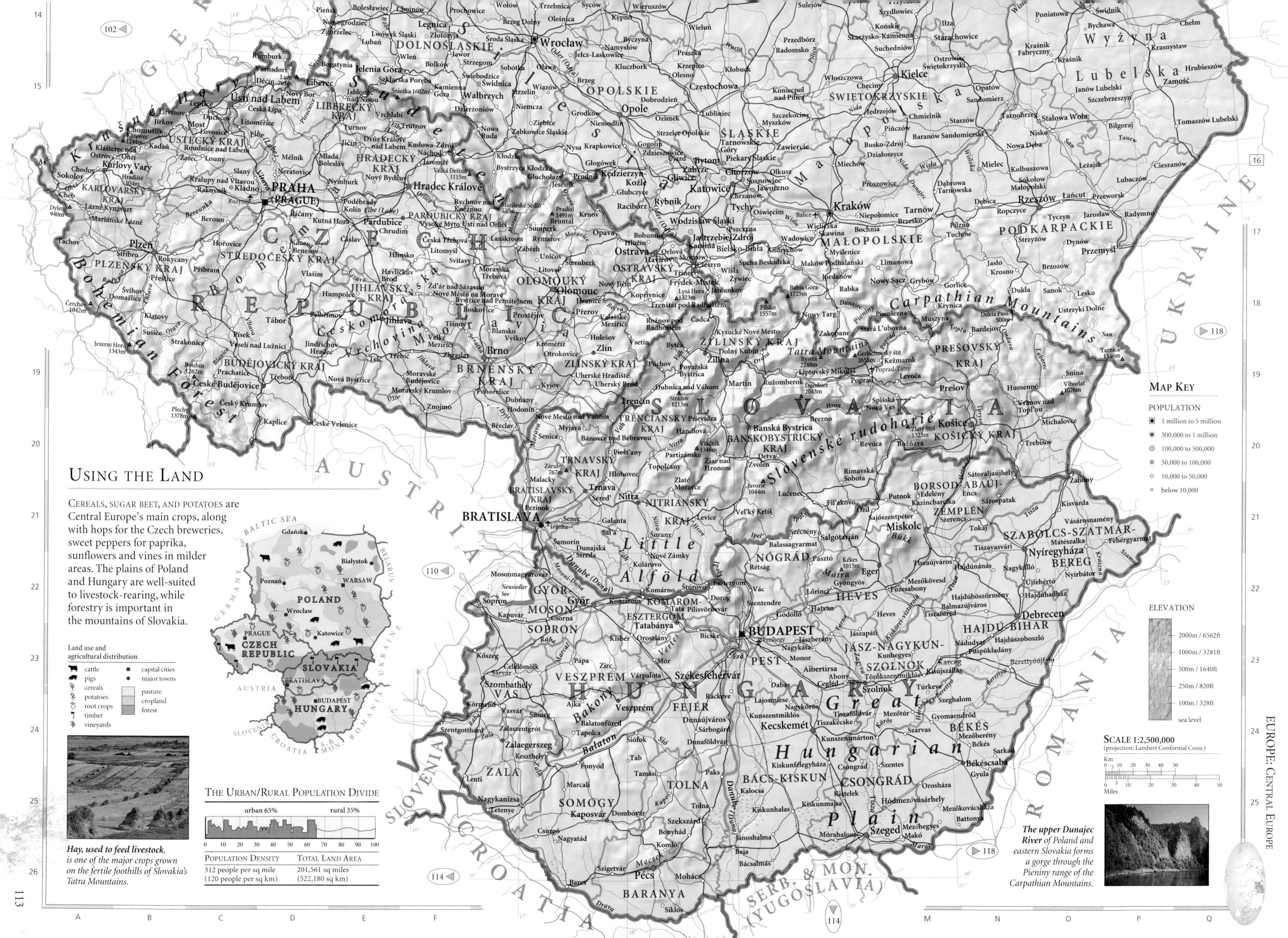

Cereals, sugar beet, and potatoes are Central Europe's main crops, along with hops for the Czech breweries, sweet peppers for paprika, sunflowers and vines in milder areas. The plains of Poland and Hungary are well-suited to livestock-rearing, while forestry is important in the mountains of Slovakia.

Hay, used to feed livestock, *is one of the major crops grown on the fertile foothills of Slovakia's Tatra Mountains.*

The Urban/Rural Population Divide

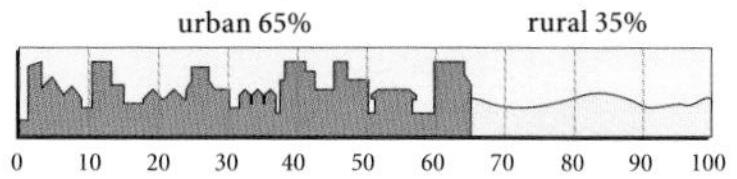

Population Density	Total Land Area
312 people per sq mile (120 people per sq km)	201,561 sq miles (522,180 sq km)

The upper Dunajec River *of Poland and eastern Slovakia forms a gorge through the Pieniny range of the Carpathian Mountains.*

Southeast Europe

Albania, Bosnia & Herzegovina, Croatia, Macedonia, Serbia & Montenegro (Yugoslavia)

For 46 years the federation of Yugoslavia held together the most diverse ethnic region in Europe, along the picturesque mountain hinterland of the Dalmatian coast. Economic collapse resulted in internal tensions. In the early 1990s, civil war broke out in both Croatia and Bosnia as the ethnic populations struggled to establish their own exclusive territories. Peace was only restored by the UN after NATO launched air strikes in 1995. In the province of Kosovo, attempts to gain autonomy from Yugoslavia in 1998 were crushed by the Serbian government. The slaughter of ethnic Albanians in Kosovo provoked the West to launch NATO air strikes yet again in the region, and Yugoslav forces withdrew. The flood of refugees from Kosovo has severely strained Albania.

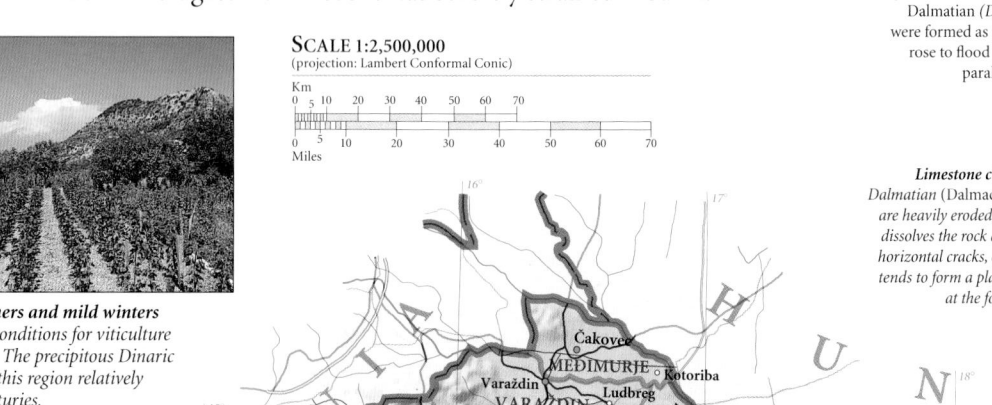

Hot, dry summers and mild winters *offer excellent conditions for viticulture in Montenegro. The precipitous Dinaric Alps have kept this region relatively isolated for centuries.*

Scale 1:2,500,000
(projection: Lambert Conformal Conic)
Km 0 5 10 20 30 40 50 60 70
Miles 0 5 10 20 30 40 50 60 70

The Landscape

The Tisza, Sava, and Drava Rivers drain the broad northern lowland, meeting the Danube after it crosses the Hungarian border. In the west, the Dinaric Alps divide the Adriatic Sea from the interior. Mainland valleys and elongated islands run parallel to the steep Dalmatian *(Dalmacija)* coastline, following alternating bands of resistant limestone.

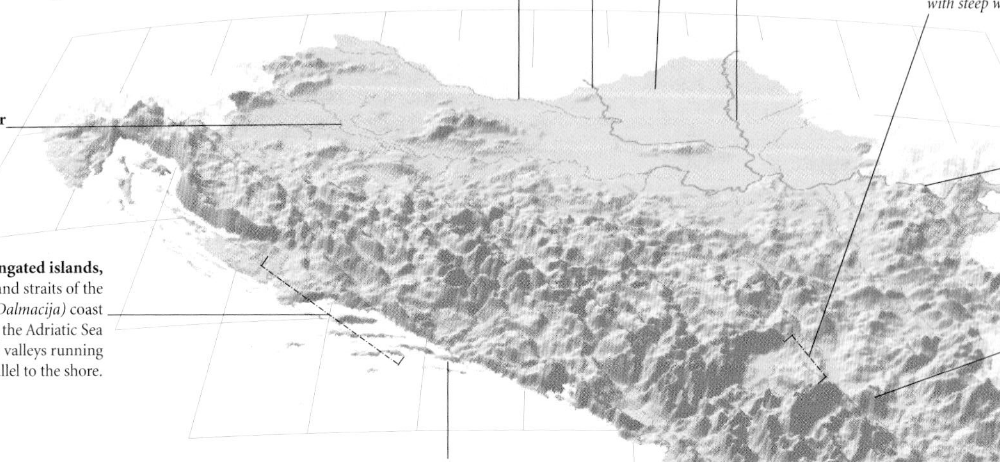

At least 70% of the fresh water in the Western Balkans drains eastward into the Black Sea, mostly via the Danube *(Dunav)*.

The river floodplains of the Pannonian Basin are flanked by terraces of gravel and wind-blown glacial deposits known as loess.

Poljes in the Kosovo region

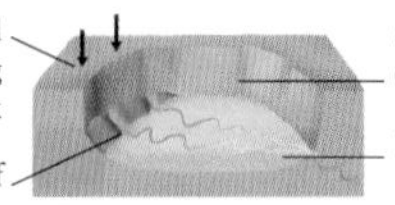

Rain and underground water *dissolve limestone along massive vertical joints (cracks). This creates poljes: depressions several miles across with steep walls and broad, flat floors.*

At Iron Gate *(derdap)*, on the border with Romania, the Danube narrows and cuts through foothills of the Balkan and Carpathian mountains, forming the deepest gorge in Europe.

The elongated islands, promontories and straits of the Dalmatian *(Dalmacija)* coast were formed as the Adriatic Sea rose to flood valleys running parallel to the shore.

A major earthquake at Skopje, Macedonia, in 1963 killed 1,000 people. The whole region lies on an active crustal plate margin.

Limestone cliffs *along the Dalmatian* (Dalmacija) *shoreline are heavily eroded, as salt water dissolves the rock along existing horizontal cracks, or joints. This tends to form a platform of rock at the foot of the cliff.*

A series of river valleys breaking through the Dinaric Alps from the lowlands of western Albania, give access to the interior.

Lake Ohrid *borders Albania and Macedonia. Ohrid is the deepest lake in the Western Balkans, reaching depths of 938 ft (286 m).*

110 ◀
112
▶ 118
122

The historic center *of Mostar in southern Bosnia, with its famous 16th-century Turkish bridge, was destroyed by shelling during 1993. The town was formerly the capital of Herzegovina.*

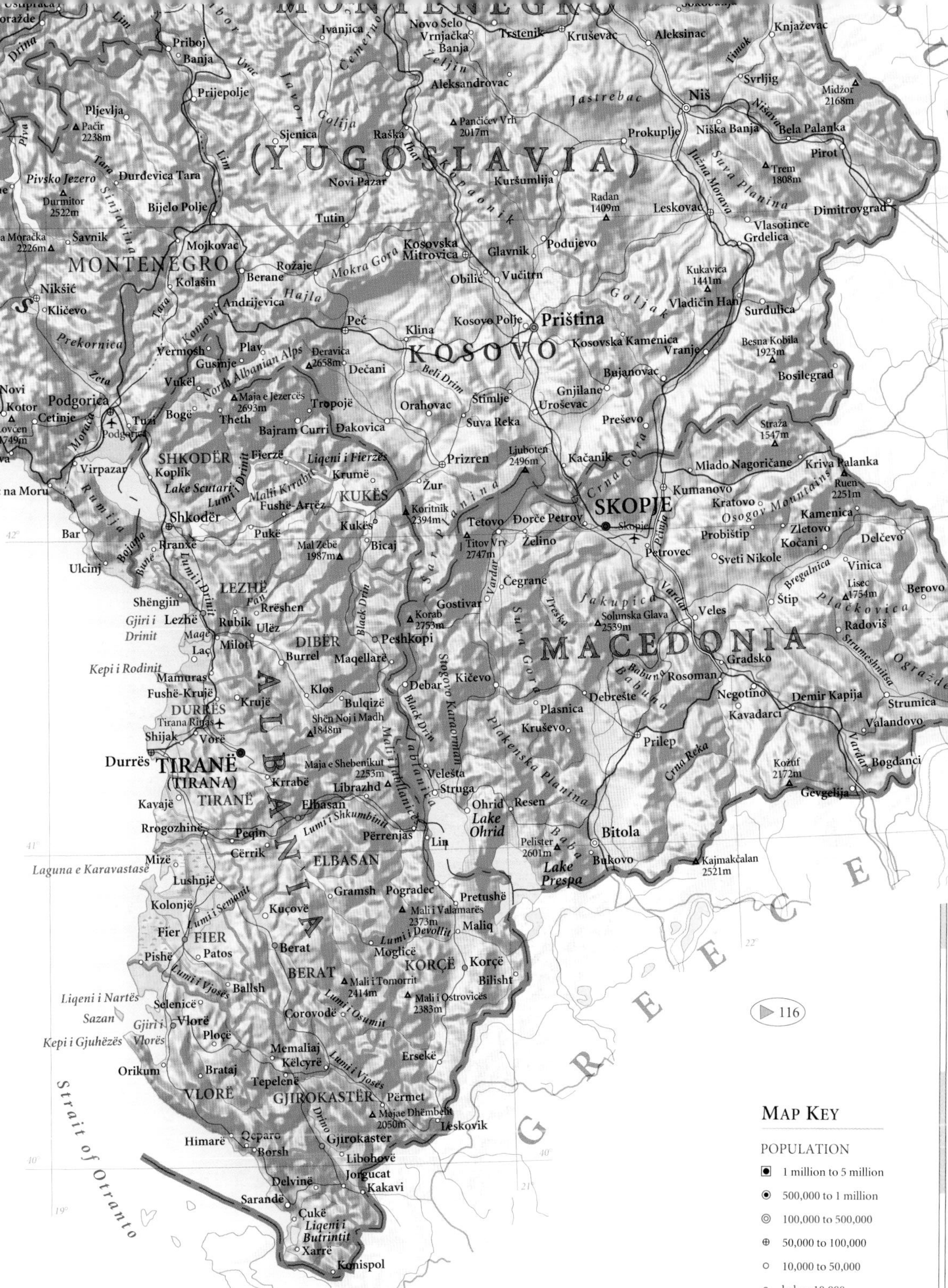

116

Map Key

POPULATION

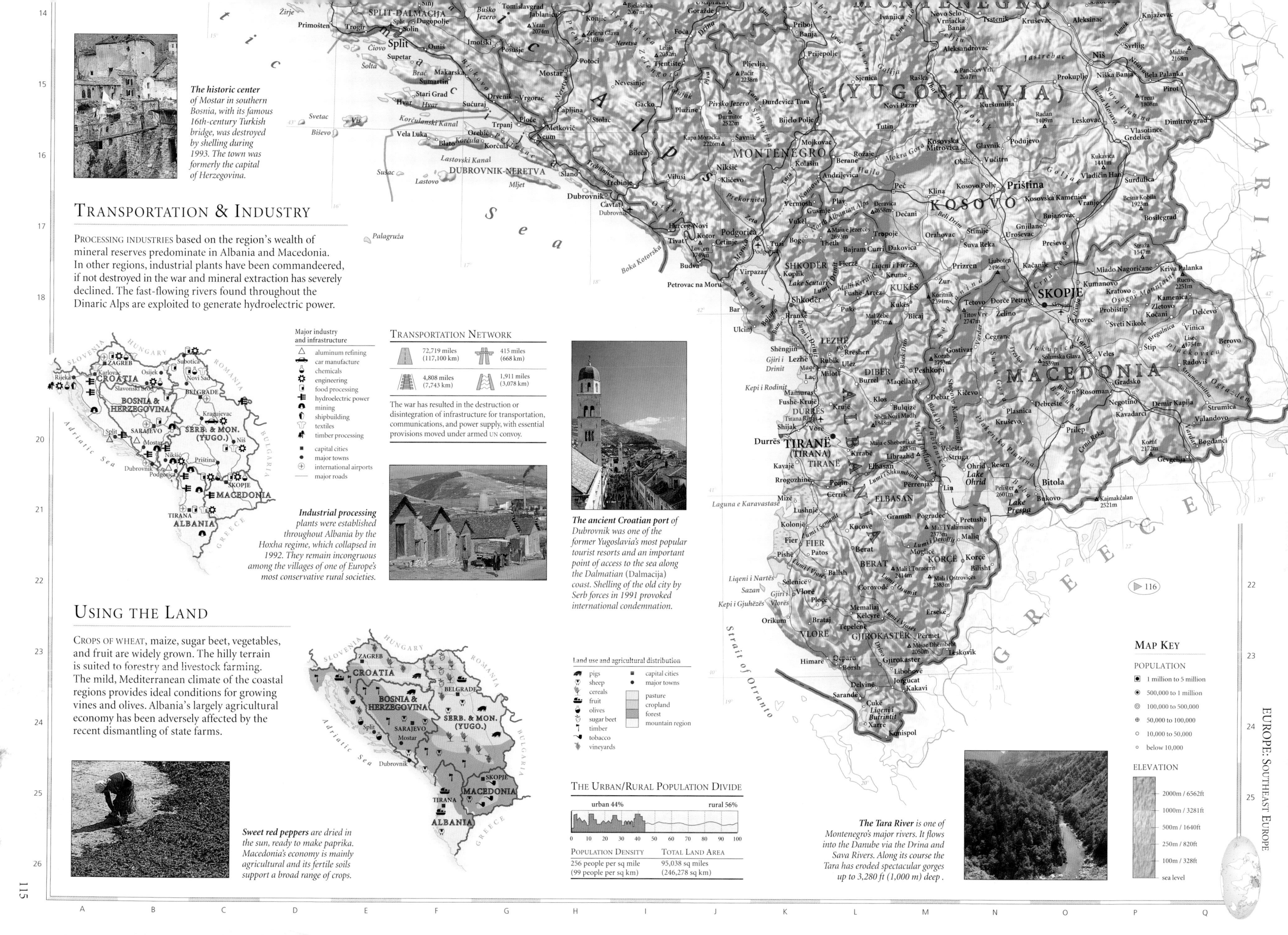

- 1 million to 5 million
- 500,000 to 1 million
- 100,000 to 500,000
- 50,000 to 100,000
- 10,000 to 50,000
- below 10,000

ELEVATION

- 2000m / 6562ft
- 1000m / 3281ft
- 500m / 1640ft
- 250m / 820ft
- 100m / 328ft
- sea level

Transportation & Industry

Processing industries based on the region's wealth of mineral reserves predominate in Albania and Macedonia. In other regions, industrial plants have been commandeered, if not destroyed in the war and mineral extraction has severely declined. The fast-flowing rivers found throughout the Dinaric Alps are exploited to generate hydroelectric power.

Major industry and infrastructure

- aluminum refining
- car manufacture
- chemicals
- engineering
- food processing
- hydroelectric power
- mining
- shipbuilding
- textiles
- timber processing
- capital cities
- major towns
- international airports
- major roads

Transportation Network

72,719 miles (117,100 km)	415 miles (668 km)
4,808 miles (7,743 km)	1,911 miles (3,078 km)

The war has resulted in the destruction or disintegration of infrastructure for transportation, communications, and power supply, with essential provisions moved under armed UN convoy.

Industrial processing *plants were established throughout Albania by the Hoxha regime, which collapsed in 1992. They remain incongruous among the villages of one of Europe's most conservative rural societies.*

The ancient Croatian port *of Dubrovnik was one of the former Yugoslavia's most popular tourist resorts and an important point of access to the sea along the Dalmatian* (Dalmacija) *coast. Shelling of the old city by Serb forces in 1991 provoked international condemnation.*

Using the Land

Crops of wheat, maize, sugar beet, vegetables, and fruit are widely grown. The hilly terrain is suited to forestry and livestock farming. The mild, Mediterranean climate of the coastal regions provides ideal conditions for growing vines and olives. Albania's largely agricultural economy has been adversely affected by the recent dismantling of state farms.

Land use and agricultural distribution

- pigs
- sheep
- cereals
- fruit
- olives
- sugar beet
- timber
- tobacco
- vineyards
- capital cities
- major towns
- pasture
- cropland
- forest
- mountain region

Sweet red peppers *are dried in the sun, ready to make paprika. Macedonia's economy is mainly agricultural and its fertile soils support a broad range of crops.*

The Urban/Rural Population Divide

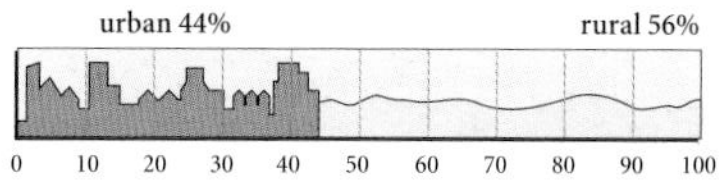

Population Density	Total Land Area
256 people per sq mile (99 people per sq km)	95,038 sq miles (246,278 sq km)

The Tara River *is one of Montenegro's major rivers. It flows into the Danube via the Drina and Sava Rivers. Along its course the Tara has eroded spectacular gorges up to 3,280 ft (1,000 m) deep.*

BULGARIA & GREECE

Including EUROPEAN TURKEY

GREECE IS RENOWNED as the original hearth of Western civilization. The rugged terrain and numerous islands have profoundly affected its development, creating a strong agricultural and maritime tradition. In the past 50 years, this formerly rural society has rapidly urbanized, with more than half the population now living in the capital, Athens, and in the northern city of Salonica. Bulgaria, dominated for centuries by the Ottoman Turks, became part of the eastern bloc after the Second World War, only slowly emerging from Soviet influence in 1989. Moves toward democracy have led to some political instability and Bulgaria has been slow to align its economy with the rest of Europe.

TRANSPORTATION & INDUSTRY

SOVIET INVESTMENT introduced heavy industry into Bulgaria, and the processing of agricultural produce, such as tobacco, is important throughout the country. Both countries have substantial shipyards and Greece has one of the world's largest merchant fleets. Many small craft workshops, producing textiles and processed foods, are clustered around Greek cities. The service and construction sectors have profited from the successful tourist industry.

Major industry and infrastructure
- chemicals
- engineering
- food processing
- shipbuilding
- textiles
- tourism
- capital cities
- major towns
- international airports
- major roads
- major industrial areas

TRANSPORTATION NETWORK

- 103,930 miles (167,630 km)
- 345 miles (557 km)
- 4,346 miles (6,995 km)
- 294 miles (474 km)

Bulgaria's railroads require investment to revive an outdated infrastructure. In Greece, despite a developing road network, ferry-boats remain the most effective form of transportation in many areas.

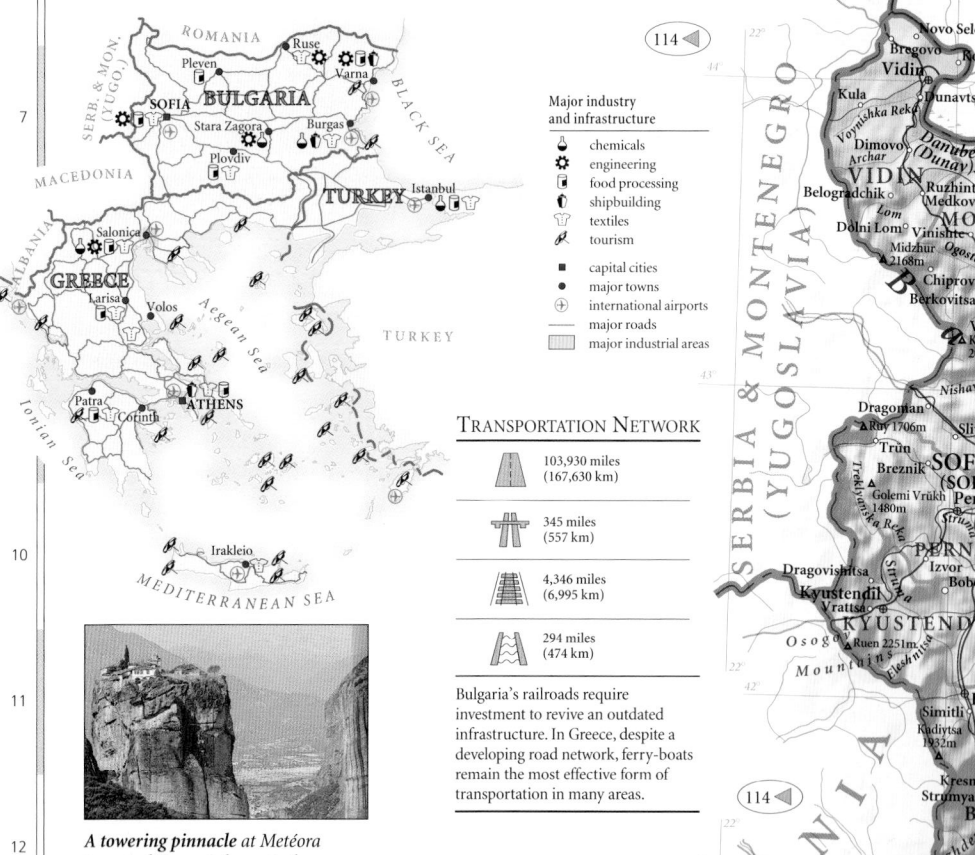

***A towering pinnacle** at Metéora in central Greece is home to the monastery of Roussanou. The 24 rock towers which dominate the plain of Thessaly* (Thessalía) *are remnants of an old plateau. Long-term weathering along fissures in the rock has worn away the rest of the plateau.*

THE LANDSCAPE

BULGARIA'S BALKAN MOUNTAINS divide the Danubian Plain *(Dunavska Ravnina)* and Maritsa Basin, meeting the Black Sea in the east along sandy beaches. The steep Rhodope Mountains form a natural barrier with Greece, while the younger Pindus form a rugged central spine which descends into the Aegean Sea to give a vast archipelago of over 2000 islands, the largest of which is Crete.

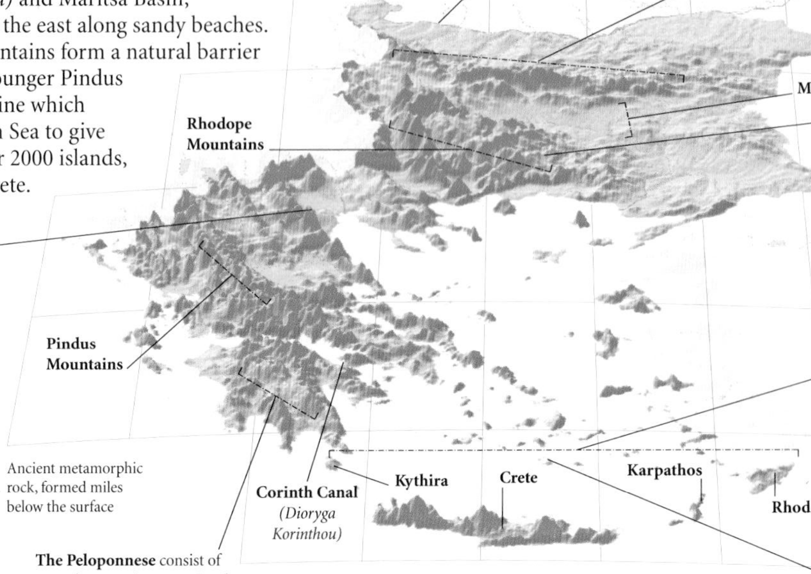

The Danube, Europe's second longest river, forms most of Bulgaria's northern border. The Danubian Plain *(Dunavska Ravnina)*, extending from the southern bank, is extremely fertile.

Mount Olympus is the mythical home of the Greek Gods and, at 9,570 ft (2,917 m), is the highest mountain in Greece.

Mount Olympus is a composite of rocks formed by two major tectonic events. First the older metamorphic rocks were thrust over the limestones, then two million years ago regional warping and subsequent erosion, reexposed the limestone.

The Peloponnese consist of several mountainous peninsulas, linked to the mainland by the Isthmus of Corinth. The Corinth Canal *(Dioryga Korinthou)*, built in 1893, cuts through the isthmus, linking the Aegean and Ionian Seas.

The islands of Crete, Kythira, Karpathos, and Rhodes are part of an arc which bends southeastward from the Peloponnese, forming the southern boundary of the Aegean.

*The **Arda river** cuts through the Rhodope mountains in rugged, rocky gorges.*

***Layers of black volcanic ash** still cover the island of Thira. This volcano last erupted 3,500 years ago, but still shows signs of volcanic activity.*

114
118

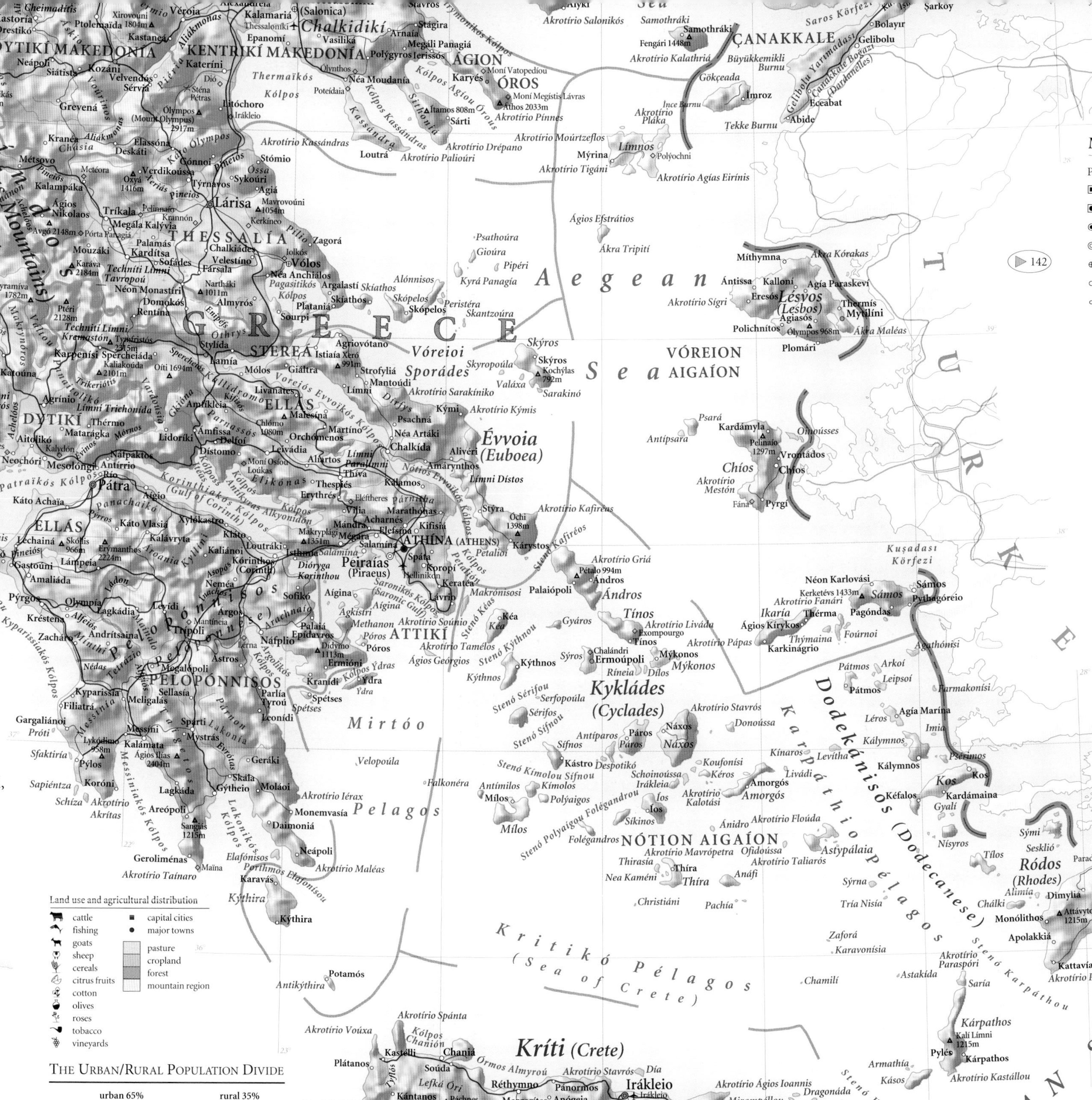

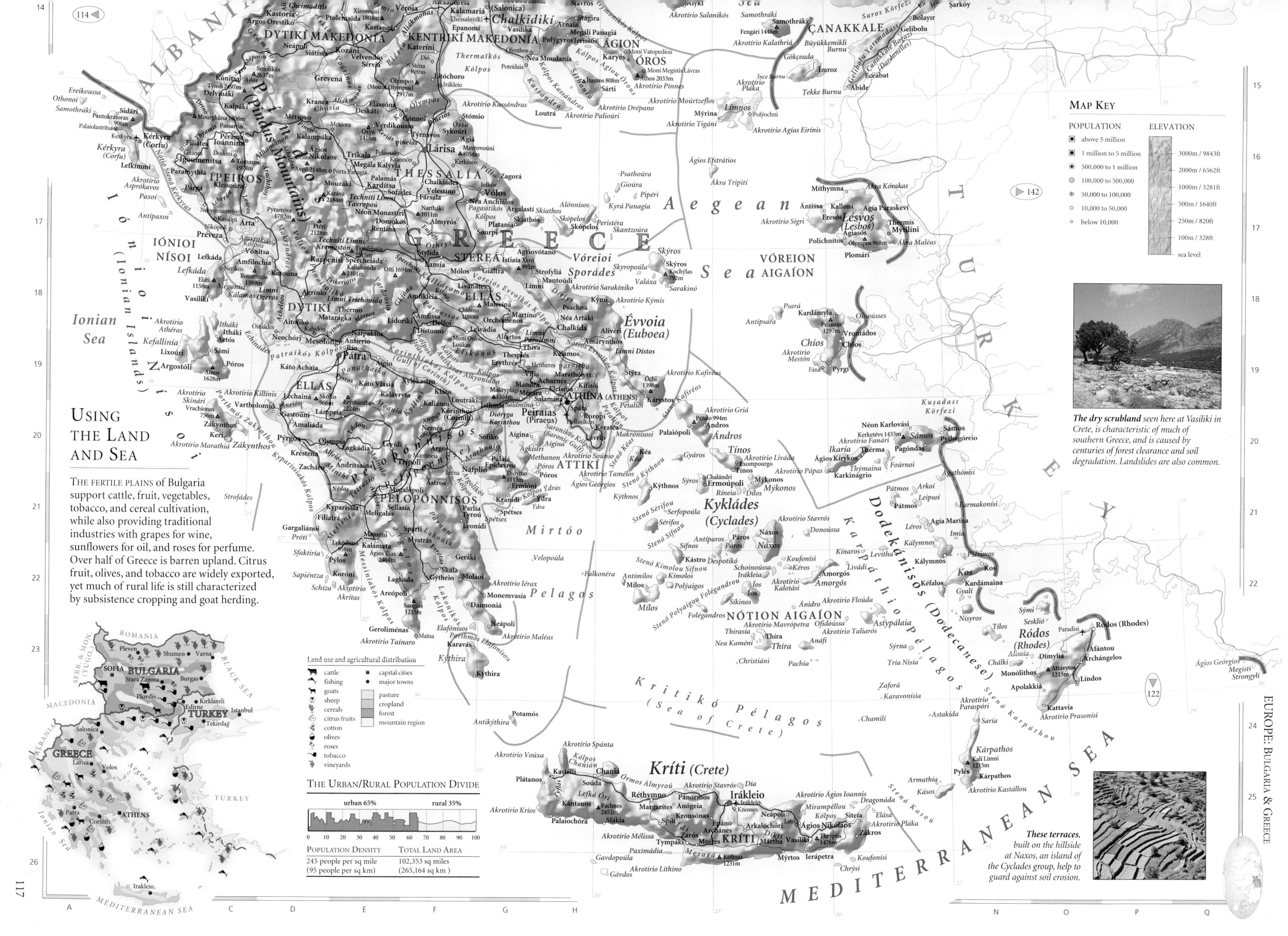

114
142
122

Map Key

POPULATION
- above 5 million
- 1 million to 5 million
- 500,000 to 1 million
- 100,000 to 500,000
- 50,000 to 100,000
- 10,000 to 50,000
- below 10,000

ELEVATION
- 3000m / 9843ft
- 2000m / 6562ft
- 1000m / 3281ft
- 500m / 1640ft
- 250m / 820ft
- 100m / 328ft
- sea level

The dry scrubland seen here at Vasiliki in Crete, is characteristic of much of southern Greece, and is caused by centuries of forest clearance and soil degradation. Landslides are also common.

Using the Land and Sea

The fertile plains of Bulgaria support cattle, fruit, vegetables, tobacco, and cereal cultivation, while also providing traditional industries with grapes for wine, sunflowers for oil, and roses for perfume. Over half of Greece is barren upland. Citrus fruit, olives, and tobacco are widely exported, yet much of rural life is still characterized by subsistence cropping and goat herding.

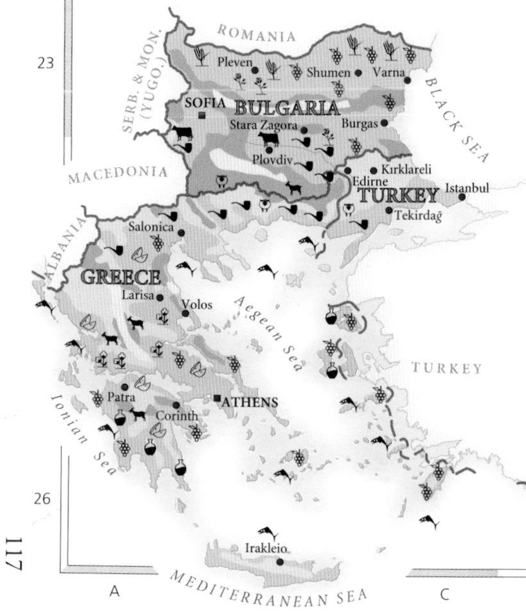

Land use and agricultural distribution

- cattle
- fishing
- goats
- sheep
- cereals
- citrus fruits
- cotton
- olives
- roses
- tobacco
- vineyards
- capital cities
- major towns
- pasture
- cropland
- forest
- mountain region

The Urban/Rural Population Divide

urban 65% — rural 35%

Population Density	Total Land Area
245 people per sq mile (95 people per sq km)	102,353 sq miles (265,164 sq km)

These terraces, built on the hillside at Naxos, an island of the Cyclades group, help to guard against soil erosion.

Romania, Moldova & Ukraine

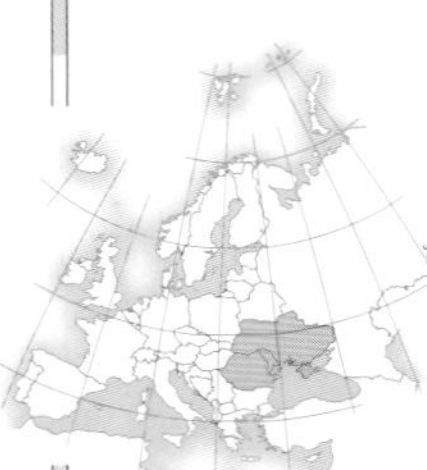

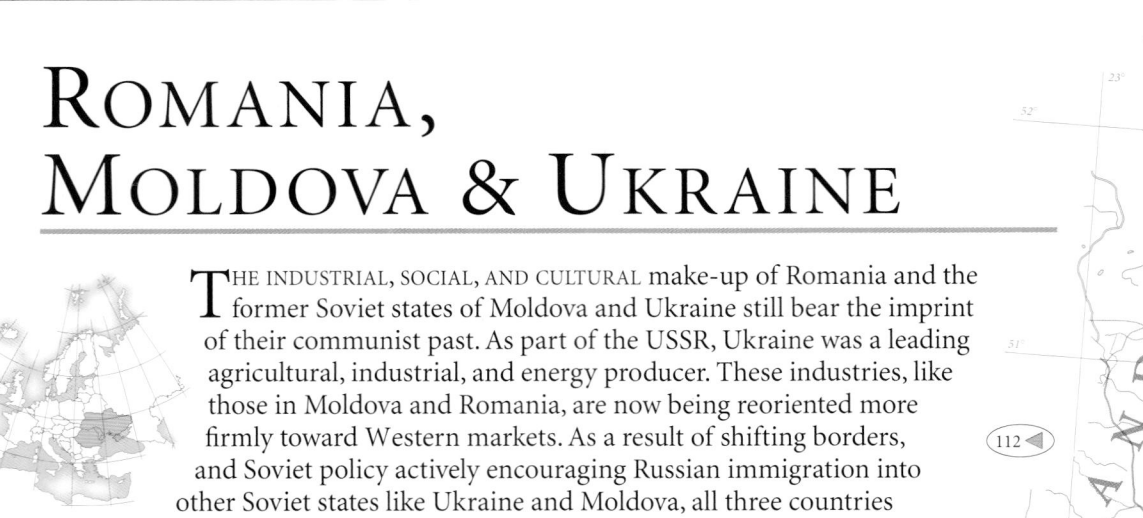

The industrial, social, and cultural make-up of Romania and the former Soviet states of Moldova and Ukraine still bear the imprint of their communist past. As part of the USSR, Ukraine was a leading agricultural, industrial, and energy producer. These industries, like those in Moldova and Romania, are now being reoriented more firmly toward Western markets. As a result of shifting borders, and Soviet policy actively encouraging Russian immigration into other Soviet states like Ukraine and Moldova, all three countries now contain large numbers of foreign nationals. Moldovans and Romanians are still close in terms of language and culture, although Moldova is striving to remain an independent nation.

Using the Land

The fertile black soils of Ukraine, often called "the breadbasket of Europe," have enabled the cultivation of a variety of cereals and vegetables, which are widely exported. Romania and Moldova also grow cereals, sunflowers, and vegetables, and are noted for the quality of their wines.

The fertile lands and tolerant climate of Moldova are ideally suited to growing grapes for wine.

112

112

Land use and agricultural distribution
- cattle
- pigs
- poultry
- sheep
- cereals
- cotton
- sugar beet
- sunflowers
- vineyards
- capital cities
- major towns
- pasture
- cropland
- forest
- wetland

The Urban/Rural Population Divide

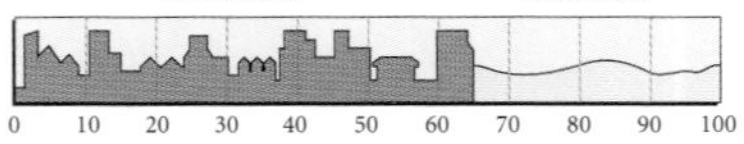

Population Density	Total Land Area
232 people per sq mile (89 people per sq km)	334,947 sq miles (867,740 sq km)

Glacial lakes are found throughout the Transylvanian Alps (Carpații Meridionali), although the mountains no longer have any permanent snow cover.

Transportation & Industry

Heavy industry using local raw materials characterizes much of this region. The industrial heartland of Ukraine, specializing in metal and machine-building industries, is based around its vast mineral reserves in the Donbass region. In Moldova, food processing draws on produce from its agricultural sector. Romanian industry relies both on local raw materials and imported iron, steel, and oil.

114

Major industry and infrastructure
- car manufacture
- chemicals
- coal
- engineering
- food processing
- mining
- oil & gas
- textiles
- tourism
- capital cities
- major towns
- international airports
- major roads
- major industrial areas

Transportation Network

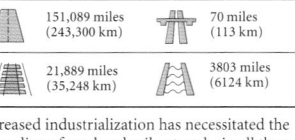

151,089 miles (243,300 km)	70 miles (113 km)
21,889 miles (35,248 km)	3803 miles (6124 km)

Increased industrialization has necessitated the upgrading of road and rail networks in all three countries. Modernization has tended to focus only on major cities and industrial areas.

116

During the 1960s and 1970s, many industries, like this carbon factory, developed using the mineral resources on the flanks of the Transylvanian Alps (Carpații Meridionali).

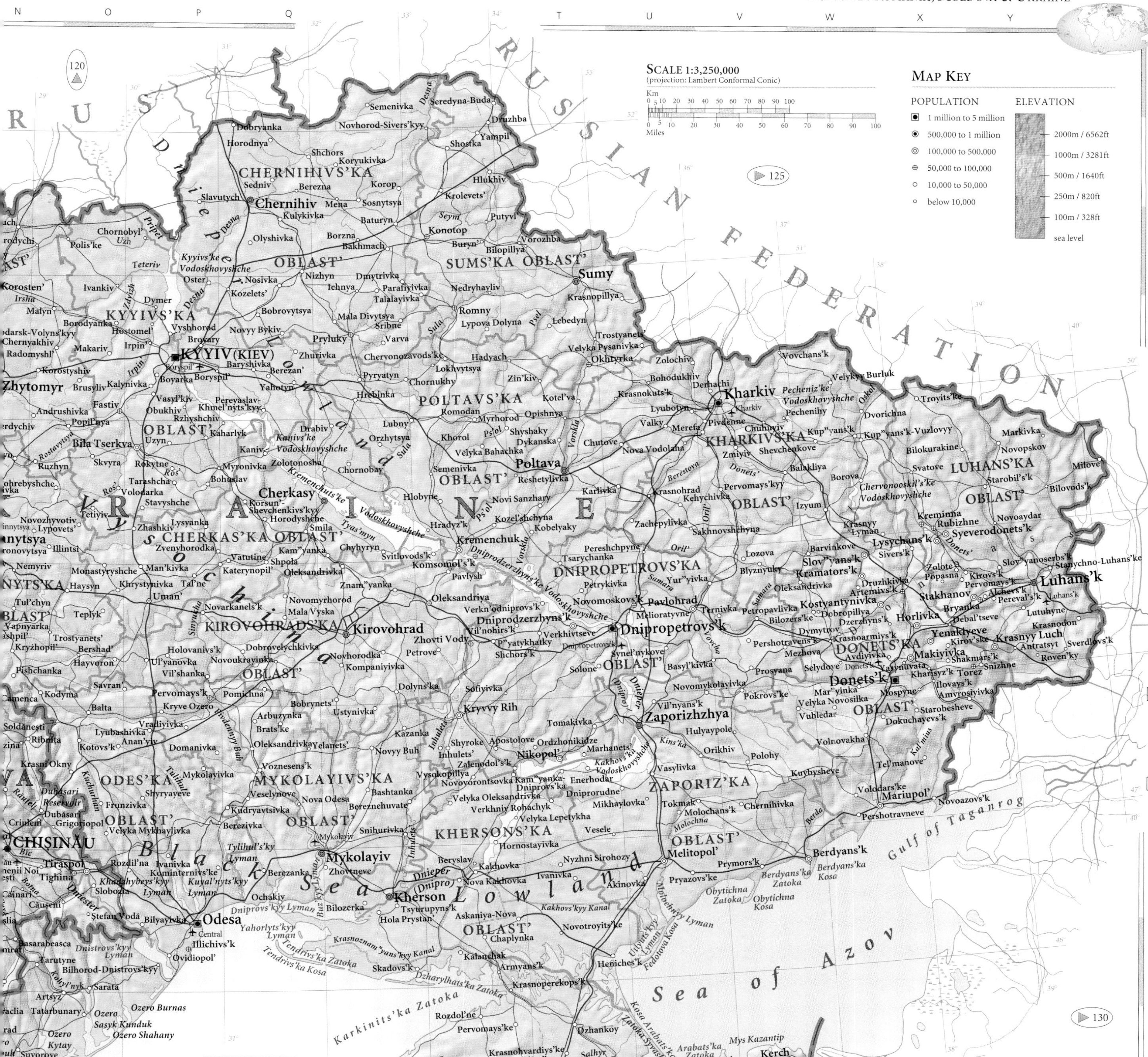

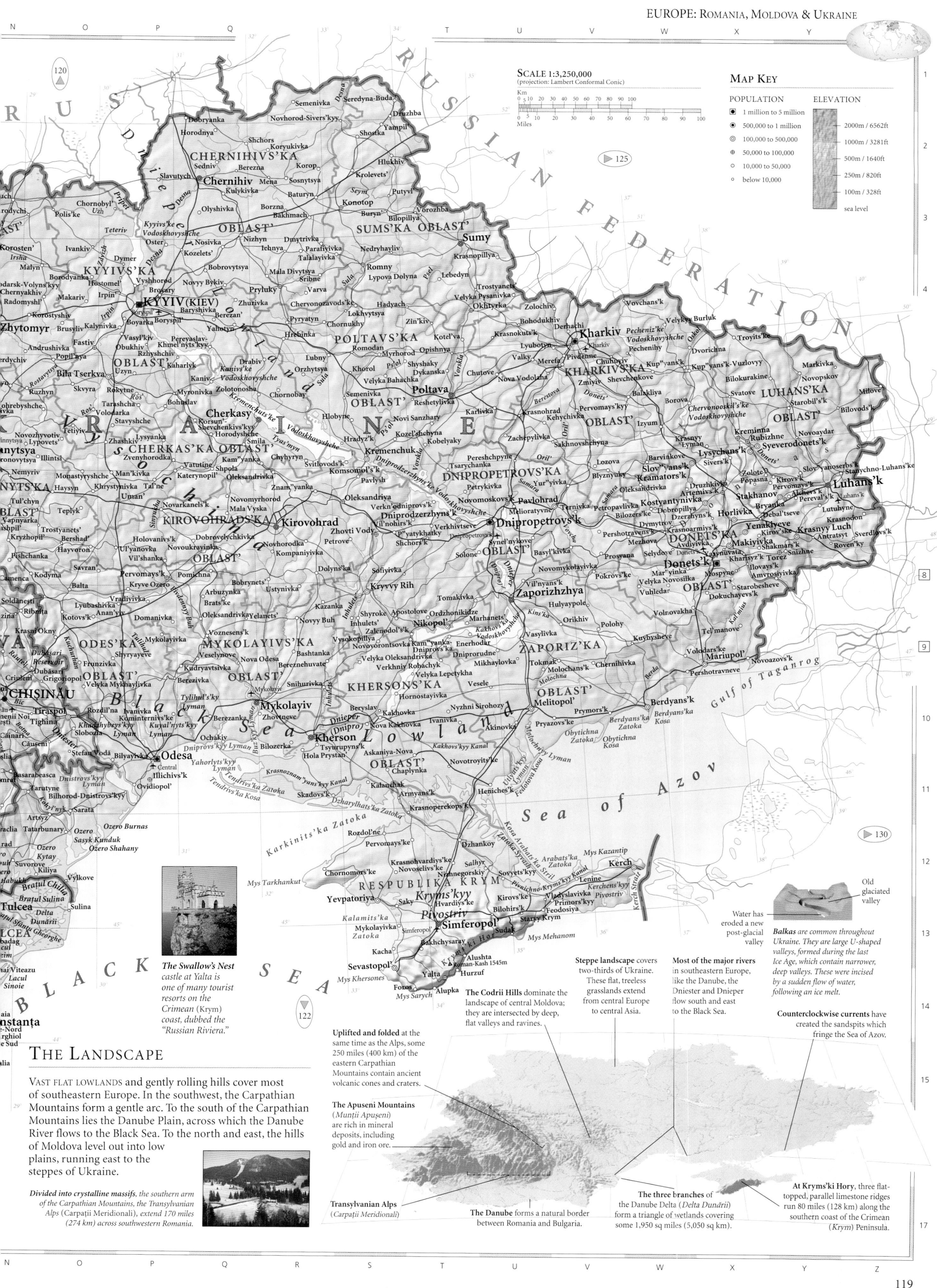

The Swallow's Nest castle at Yalta is one of many tourist resorts on the Crimean (Krym) *coast, dubbed the "Russian Riviera."*

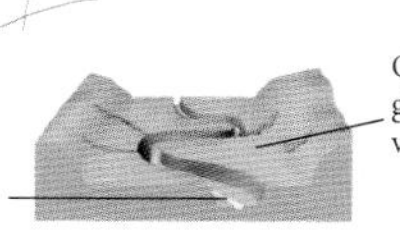

Balkas *are common throughout Ukraine. They are large U-shaped valleys, formed during the last Ice Age, which contain narrower, deep valleys. These were incised by a sudden flow of water, following an ice melt.*

The Landscape

VAST FLAT LOWLANDS and gently rolling hills cover most of southeastern Europe. In the southwest, the Carpathian Mountains form a gentle arc. To the south of the Carpathian Mountains lies the Danube Plain, across which the Danube River flows to the Black Sea. To the north and east, the hills of Moldova level out into low plains, running east to the steppes of Ukraine.

Divided into crystalline massifs, *the southern arm of the Carpathian Mountains, the Transylvanian Alps* (Carpații Meridionali), *extend 170 miles (274 km) across southwestern Romania.*

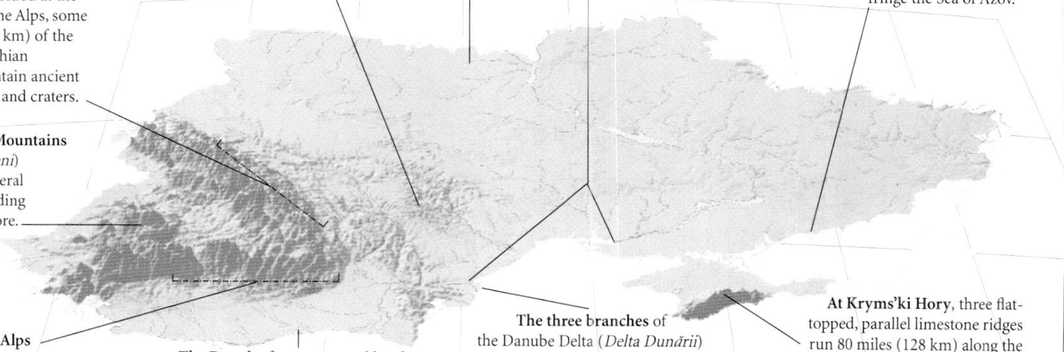

THE BALTIC STATES & BELARUS

BELARUS, ESTONIA, LATVIA, LITHUANIA, Kaliningrad

OCCUPYING EUROPE'S main corridor to Russia, the four distinct cultures of Estonia, Latvia, Lithuania, and Belarus share a history of struggle for nationhood against the interests of more powerful neighbors. As the first republics to declare their independence from the Soviet Union in 1990–91, the Baltic states of Estonia, Latvia, and Lithuania have sought an economic role in the EU, while reaffirming their European cultural roots through the church and a strong musical tradition. Meanwhile, Belarus has shown economic and political allegiance to Russia by joining the Commonwealth of Independent States.

The seaport of Rīga is Latvia's capital and the center of economic and cultural life. With a 34% Russian minority in Latvia, language and the right to national citizenship are key issues.

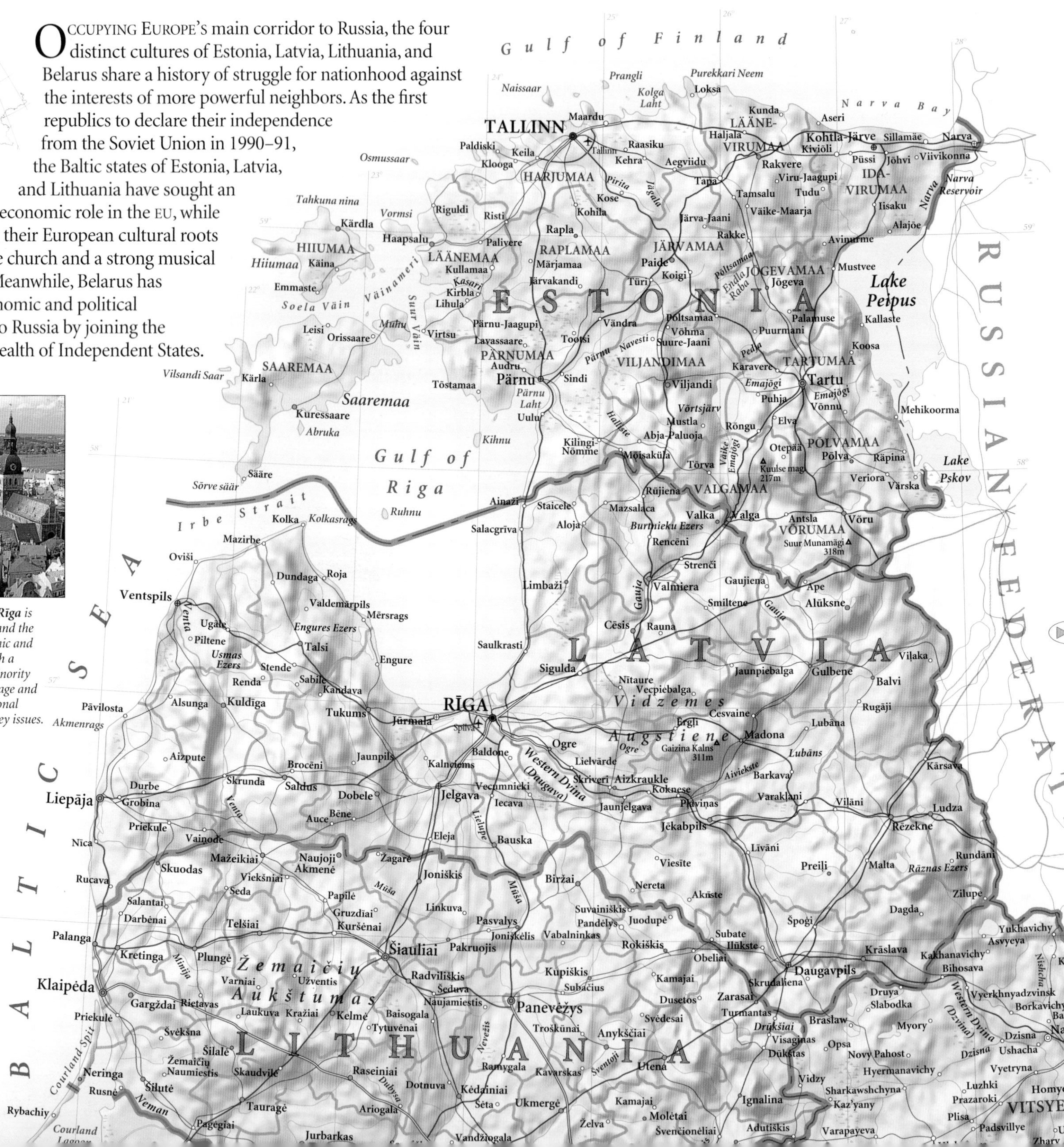

USING THE LAND

ACROSS THE FOUR NATIONS cattle and pig farming are widespread, together with diverse arable crops, including flax for making linen, potatoes used to produce vodka, cereals, and other vegetables. Almost a third of the land is forested; demand for timber has increased the importance of forest management.

THE URBAN/RURAL POPULATION DIVIDE

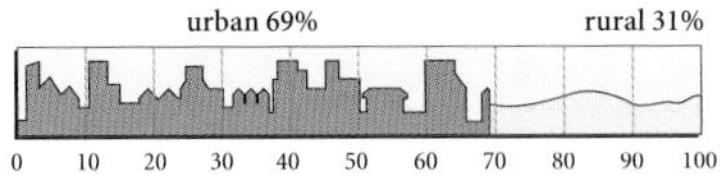

POPULATION DENSITY	TOTAL LAND AREA
122 people per sq mile (47 people per sq km)	145,006 sq miles (375,656 sq km)

A pine forest in northern Belarus. *Conifers in the north give way to hardwood forest farther south. Timber mills are supplied with logs floated along the country's many navigable waterways.*

***The Western Dvina River** provides hydro-electric power and, during the summer months, access to the Baltic Sea. The lower course of the river freezes from December to April.*

MAP KEY

POPULATION
- 1 million to 5 million
- 500,000 to 1 million
- 100,000 to 500,000
- 50,000 to 100,000
- 10,000 to 50,000
- below 10,000

ELEVATION
- 250m / 820ft
- 100m / 328ft
- sea level

THE LANDSCAPE

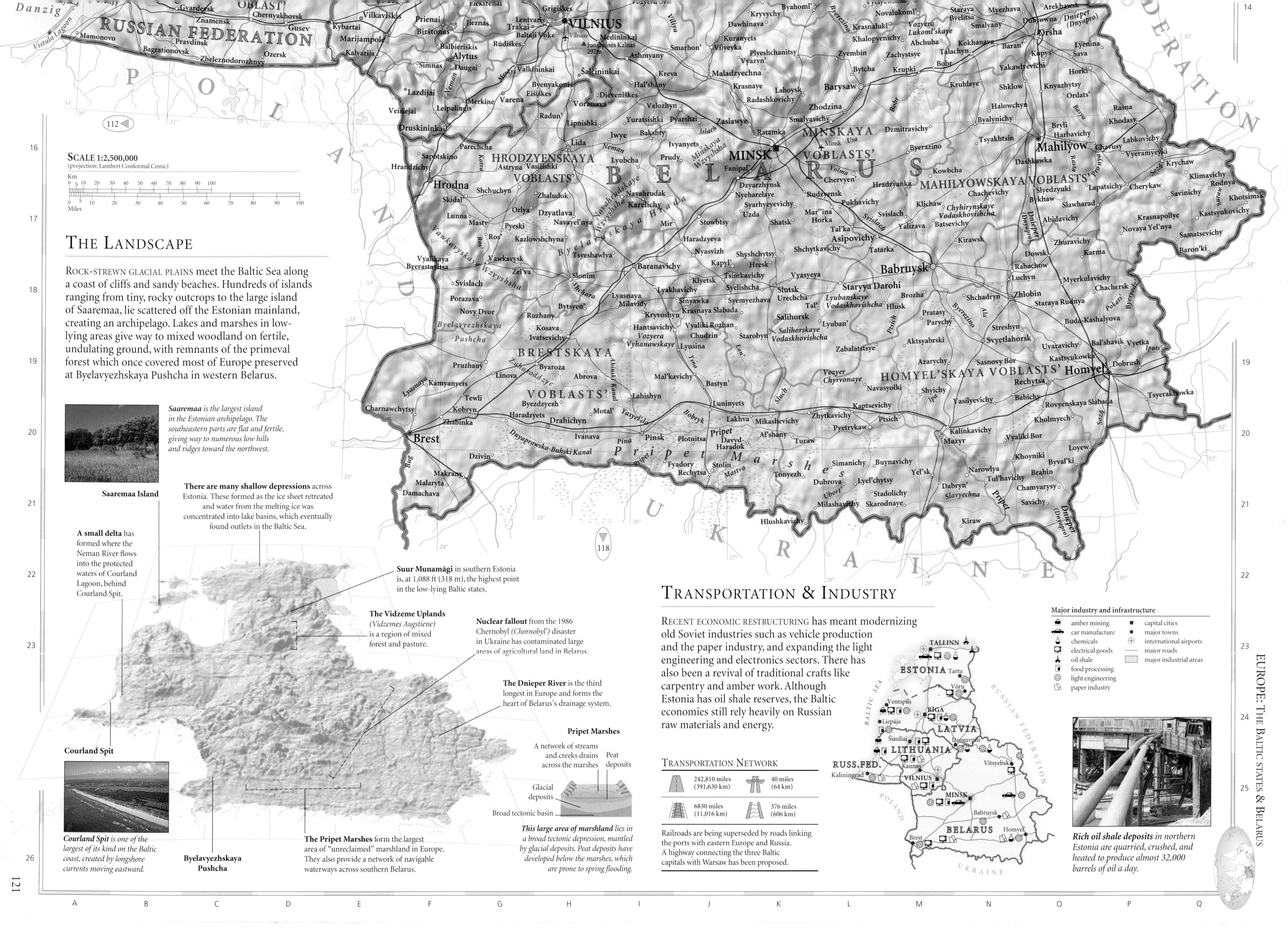

ROCK-STREWN GLACIAL PLAINS meet the Baltic Sea along a coast of cliffs and sandy beaches. Hundreds of islands ranging from tiny, rocky outcrops to the large island of Saaremaa, lie scattered off the Estonian mainland, creating an archipelago. Lakes and marshes in low-lying areas give way to mixed woodland on fertile, undulating ground, with remnants of the primeval forest which once covered most of Europe preserved at Byelavyezhskaya Pushcha in western Belarus.

SCALE 1:2,500,000
(projection: Lambert Conformal Conic)

Saaremaa is the largest island in the Estonian archipelago. The southeastern parts are flat and fertile, giving way to numerous low hills and ridges toward the northwest.

Saaremaa Island

A small delta has formed where the Neman River flows into the protected waters of Courland Lagoon, behind Courland Spit.

There are many shallow depressions across Estonia. These formed as the ice sheet retreated and water from the melting ice was concentrated into lake basins, which eventually found outlets in the Baltic Sea.

Suur Munamägi in southern Estonia is, at 1,088 ft (318 m), the highest point in the low-lying Baltic states.

The Vidzeme Uplands (*Vidzemes Augstiene*) is a region of mixed forest and pasture.

Nuclear fallout from the 1986 Chernobyl (*Chornobyl*) disaster in Ukraine has contaminated large areas of agricultural land in Belarus.

The Dnieper River is the third longest in Europe and forms the heart of Belarus's drainage system.

Pripet Marshes

A network of streams and creeks drains across the marshes

Peat deposits

Glacial deposits

Broad tectonic basin

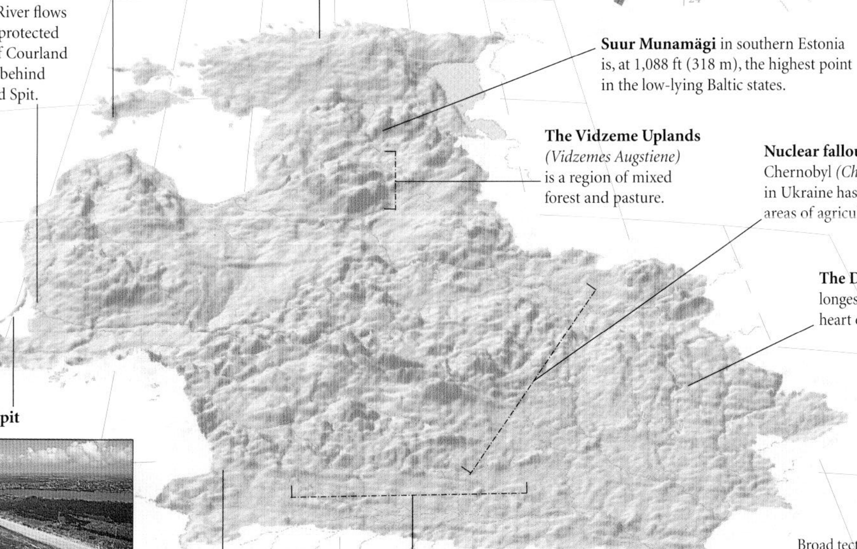

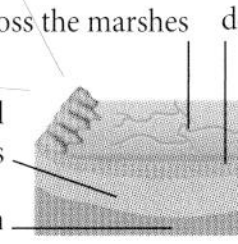

This large area of marshland lies in a broad tectonic depression, mantled by glacial deposits. Peat deposits have developed below the marshes, which are prone to spring flooding.

The Pripet Marshes form the largest area of "unreclaimed" marshland in Europe. They also provide a network of navigable waterways across southern Belarus.

Byelavyezhskaya Pushcha

Courland Spit is one of the largest of its kind on the Baltic coast, created by longshore currents moving eastward.

Courland Spit

TRANSPORTATION & INDUSTRY

RECENT ECONOMIC RESTRUCTURING has meant modernizing old Soviet industries such as vehicle production and the paper industry, and expanding the light engineering and electronics sectors. There has also been a revival of traditional crafts like carpentry and amber work. Although Estonia has oil shale reserves, the Baltic economies still rely heavily on Russian raw materials and energy.

TRANSPORTATION NETWORK

242,810 miles (391,650 km)		40 miles (64 km)	
6830 miles (11,016 km)		376 miles (606 km)	

Railroads have been superseded by roads linking the ports with eastern Europe and Russia. A highway connecting the three Baltic capitals with Warsaw has been proposed.

Major industry and infrastructure

- capital cities
- major towns
- international airports
- major roads
- major industrial areas

amber mining
car manufacture
chemicals
electrical goods
oil shale
food processing
light engineering
paper industry

Rich oil shale deposits in northern Estonia are quarried, crushed, and heated to produce almost 32,000 barrels of oil a day.

112

118

The Mediterranean

The Mediterranean Sea stretches over 2,500 miles (4,000 km) east to west, separating Europe from Africa. At its westernmost point it is connected to the Atlantic Ocean through the Strait of Gibraltar. In the east, the Suez Canal, opened in 1869, gives passage to the Indian Ocean. In the northeast, linked by the Sea of Marmara, lies the Black Sea. The Mediterranean is bordered by 28 states and territories, and more than 100 million people live on its shores and islands. Throughout history, the Mediterranean has been a focal area for many great empires and civilizations, reflected in the variety of cultures found on its shores. Since the 1960s, development along the southern coast of Europe has expanded rapidly to accommodate increasing numbers of tourists and to enable the exploitation of oil and gas reserves. This has resulted in rising levels of pollution, threatening the future of the sea.

Using the Land and Sea

A quarter of the fish species found in the Mediterranean are economically important. Sardines are the main catch in northern and western regions and aquaculture, including oyster farming, is becoming increasingly important in the eastern Mediterranean. Olives, citrus fruit, cork trees, and vines thrive in the Mediterranean climate, enjoying hot, dry summers and mild, wet winters. Italy and Spain are world leaders in commercial olive production.

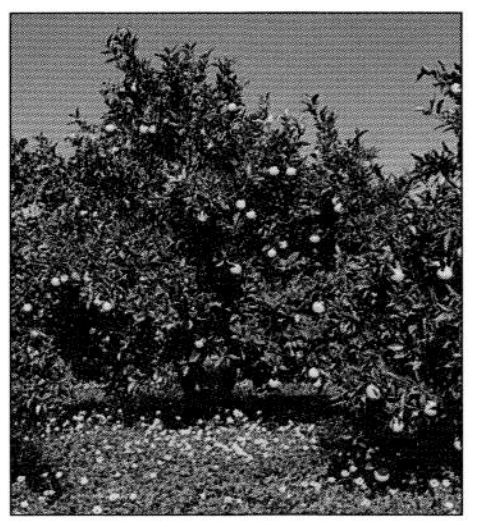

***The growing of citrus fruit** such as lemons, limes, oranges, and grapefruit is common along the coasts surrounding the Mediterranean.*

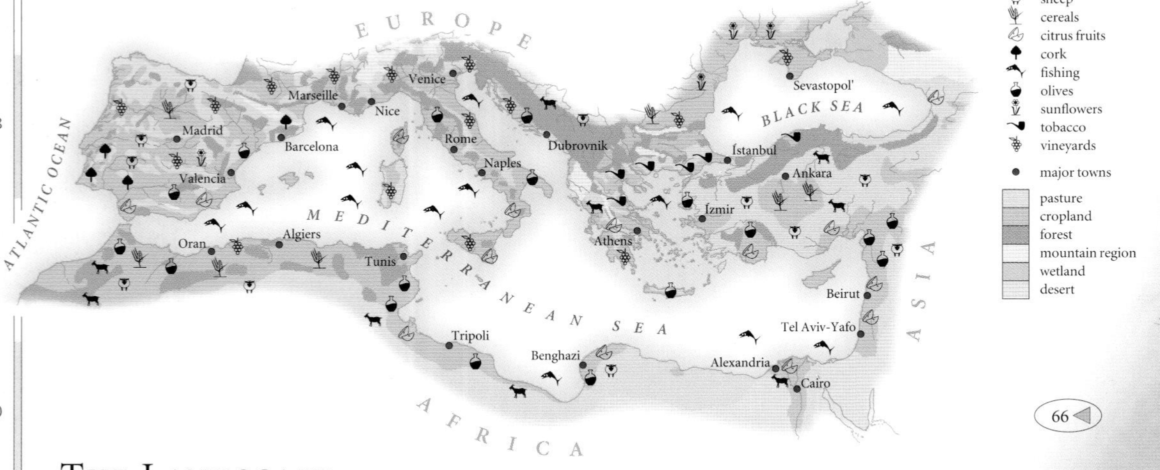

The Landscape

The Mediterranean Sea is almost totally landlocked, joined to the Atlantic Ocean through the Strait of Gibraltar, which is only 8 miles (13 km) wide. Lying on an active plate margin, sea floor movements have formed a variety of basins, troughs, and ridges. A submarine ridge running from Tunisia to the island of Sicily divides the Mediterranean into two distinct basins. The western basin is characterized by broad, smooth abyssal (or ocean) plains. In contrast, the eastern basin is dominated by a large ridge system, running east to west.

The narrow Strait of Gibraltar inhibits water exchange between the Mediterranean Sea and the Atlantic Ocean, producing a high degree of salinity and a low tidal range within the Mediterranean. The lack of tides has encouraged the build-up of pollutants in many semienclosed bays.

***The Dalmatian** (Dalmacija) **coast** has many long, elongated islands running parallel to the mainland. These resulted when rising sea levels drowned valleys running parallel with the coast.*

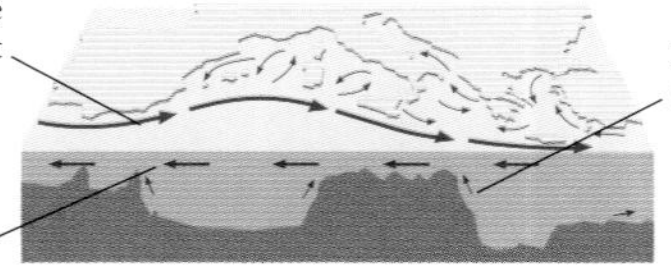

***Because the Mediterranean** is almost enclosed by land, its circulation is quite different to the oceans. There is one major current which flows in from the Atlantic and moves east. Currents flowing back to the Atlantic are denser and flow below the main current.*

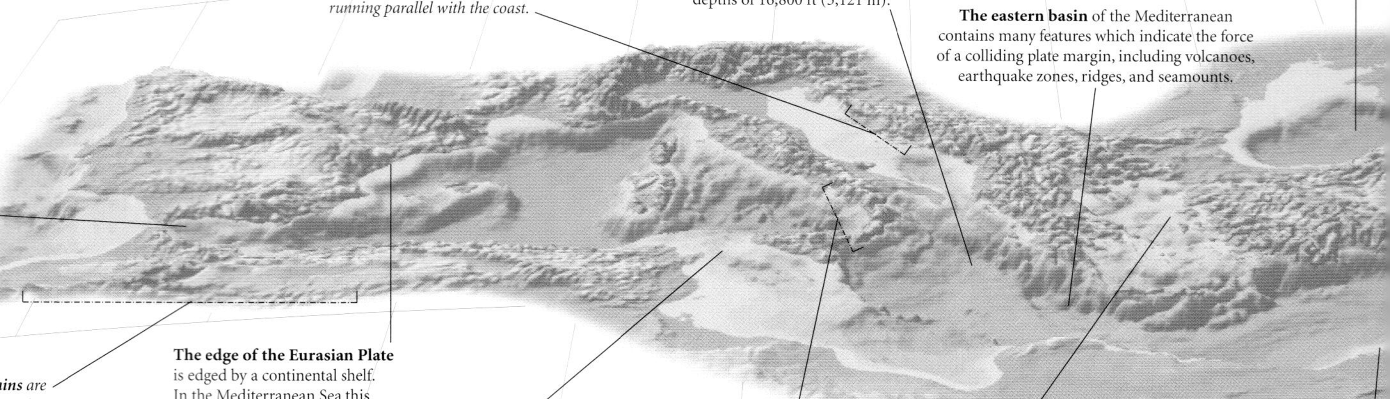

The Ionian Basin is the deepest in the Mediterranean, reaching depths of 16,800 ft (5,121 m).

Industrial pollution flowing from the Dnieper and Danube Rivers has destroyed a large proportion of the fish population that used to inhabit the upper layers of the Black Sea.

The eastern basin of the Mediterranean contains many features which indicate the force of a colliding plate margin, including volcanoes, earthquake zones, ridges, and seamounts.

The edge of the Eurasian Plate is edged by a continental shelf. In the Mediterranean Sea this is widest at the Ebro Fan where it extends 60 miles (96 km).

Beneath the Strait of Sicily lies a submarine ridge which rises to 1,200 ft (360 m) below sea level. It divides the eastern and western basins of the Mediterranean.

An arc of active submarine, island and mainland volcanoes, including Etna and Vesuvius, lie in and around southern Italy. The area is also susceptible to earthquakes and landslides.

The shallow basin of the Aegean contains numerous small islands, many of volcanic origin.

Nutrient flows into the eastern Mediterranean, and sediment flows to the Nile Delta have been severely lowered by the building of the Aswan Dam across the Nile in Eygpt. This is causing the delta to shrink.

***The Atlas Mountains** are a range of fold mountains that lie in Morocco and Algeria. They run parallel to the Mediterranean, forming a topographical and climatic divide between the Mediterranean coast and the western Sahara.*

Transportation & Industry

The opening of the Suez Canal in 1869 made the Mediterranean a key shipping route to Asia. Oil and gas reserves, although comparatively small on a world scale, are being explored and exploited off the coasts of Libya, Greece, Italy, Spain, and Tunisia. The Mediterranean's greatest natural resources are its miles of beaches and warm sea. Over half the world's income from tourism is generated in the Mediterranean.

***Benidorm** is one of the most popular resorts on Spain's Costa Blanca. Many of the Mediterranean's coastal resorts have grown up since the 1950s, expanding from small fishing villages to large resorts catering almost exclusively for tourists.*

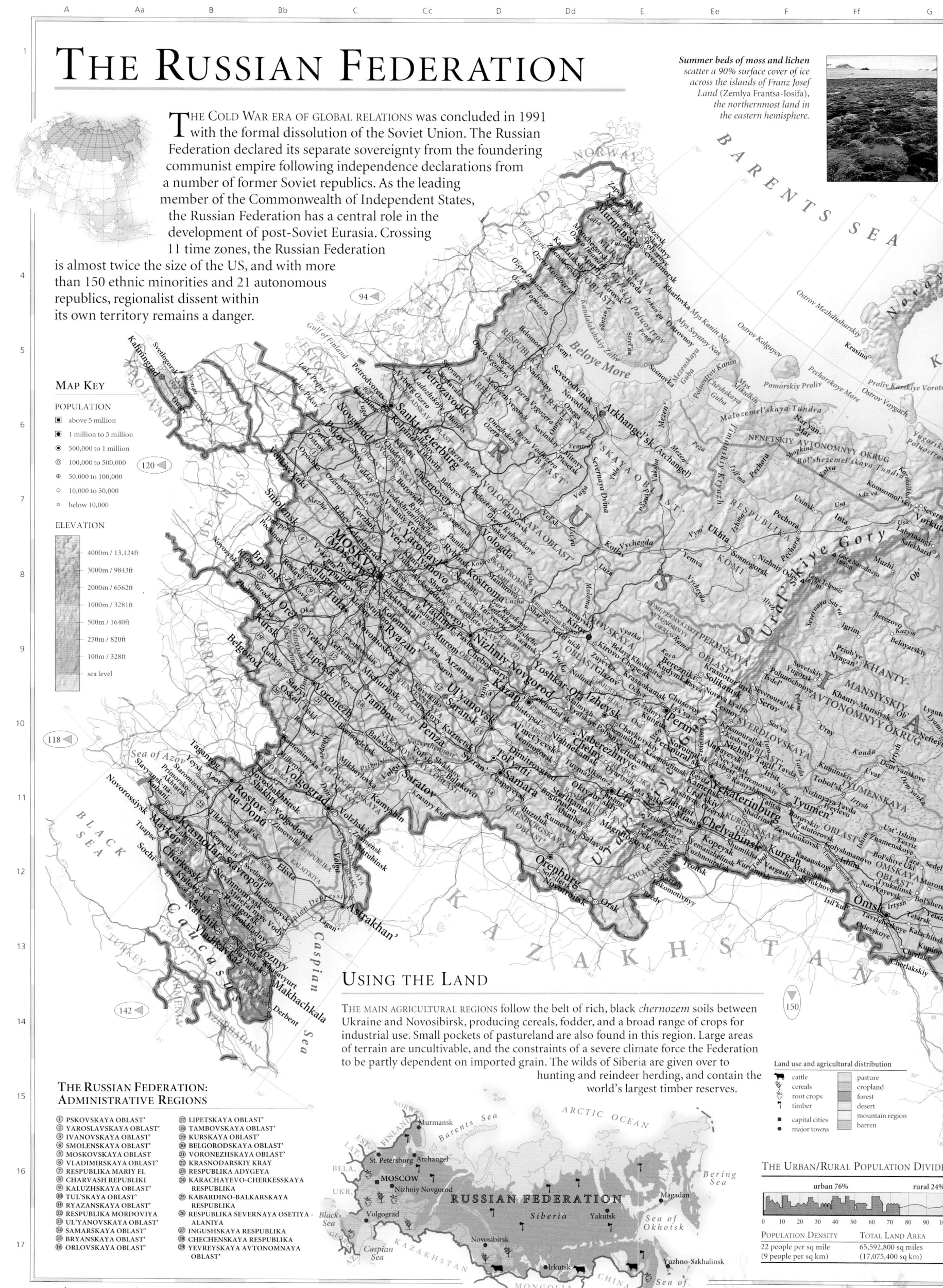

The Russian Federation

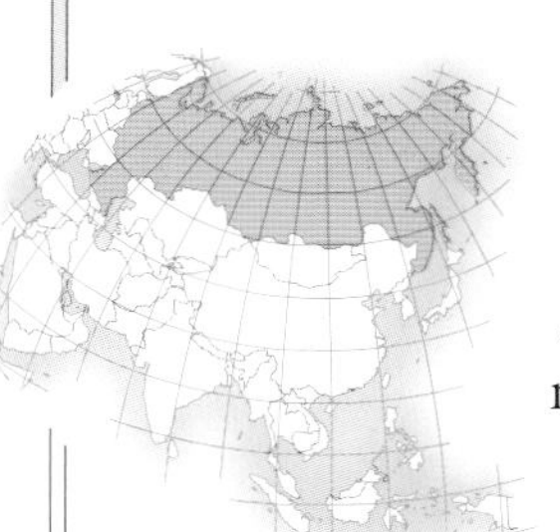

The Cold War era of global relations was concluded in 1991 with the formal dissolution of the Soviet Union. The Russian Federation declared its separate sovereignty from the foundering communist empire following independence declarations from a number of former Soviet republics. As the leading member of the Commonwealth of Independent States, the Russian Federation has a central role in the development of post-Soviet Eurasia. Crossing 11 time zones, the Russian Federation is almost twice the size of the US, and with more than 150 ethnic minorities and 21 autonomous republics, regionalist dissent within its own territory remains a danger.

Summer beds of moss and lichen scatter a 90% surface cover of ice across the islands of Franz Josef Land (Zemlya Frantsa-Iosifa), the northernmost land in the eastern hemisphere.

Map Key

POPULATION

- ■ above 5 million
- ■ 1 million to 5 million
- ● 500,000 to 1 million
- ◎ 100,000 to 500,000
- ⊕ 50,000 to 100,000
- ○ 10,000 to 50,000
- ○ below 10,000

ELEVATION

- 4000m / 13,124ft
- 3000m / 9843ft
- 2000m / 6562ft
- 1000m / 3281ft
- 500m / 1640ft
- 250m / 820ft
- 100m / 328ft
- sea level

94 ◄ 120 ◄ 118 ◄ 142 ◄ 150 ▼

The Russian Federation: Administrative Regions

1. PSKOVSKAYA OBLAST'
2. YAROSLAVSKAYA OBLAST'
3. IVANOVSKAYA OBLAST'
4. SMOLENSKAYA OBLAST'
5. MOSKOVSKAYA OBLAST
6. VLADIMIRSKAYA OBLAST'
7. RESPUBLIKA MARIY EL
8. CHARVASH REPUBLIKI
9. KALUZHSKAYA OBLAST'
10. TUL'SKAYA OBLAST'
11. RYAZANSKAYA OBLAST'
12. RESPUBLIKA MORDOVIYA
13. UL'YANOVSKAYA OBLAST'
14. SAMARSKAYA OBLAST'
15. BRYANSKAYA OBLAST'
16. ORLOVSKAYA OBLAST'
17. LIPETSKAYA OBLAST'
18. TAMBOVSKAYA OBLAST'
19. KURSKAYA OBLAST'
20. BELGORODSKAYA OBLAST'
21. VORONEZHSKAYA OBLAST'
22. KRASNODARSKIY KRAY
23. RESPUBLIKA ADYGEYA
24. KARACHAYEVO-CHERKESSKAYA RESPUBLIKA
25. KABARDINO-BALKARSKAYA RESPUBLIKA
26. RESPUBLIKA SEVERNAYA OSETIYA - ALANIYA
27. INGUSHSKAYA RESPUBLIKA
28. CHECHENSKAYA RESPUBLIKA
29. YEVREYSKAYA AVTONOMNAYA OBLAST'

Using the Land

The main agricultural regions follow the belt of rich, black *chernozem* soils between Ukraine and Novosibirsk, producing cereals, fodder, and a broad range of crops for industrial use. Small pockets of pastureland are also found in this region. Large areas of terrain are uncultivable, and the constraints of a severe climate force the Federation to be partly dependent on imported grain. The wilds of Siberia are given over to hunting and reindeer herding, and contain the world's largest timber reserves.

Land use and agricultural distribution

cattle	pasture
cereals	cropland
root crops	forest
timber	desert
capital cities	mountain region
major towns	barren

The Urban/Rural Population Divide

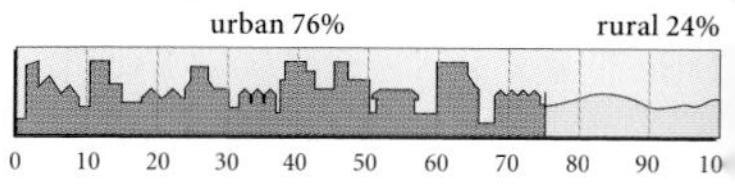

Population Density	Total Land Area
22 people per sq mile (9 people per sq km)	65,592,800 sq miles (17,075,400 sq km)

N Nn O Oo P Pp Q Qq R Rr S Ss

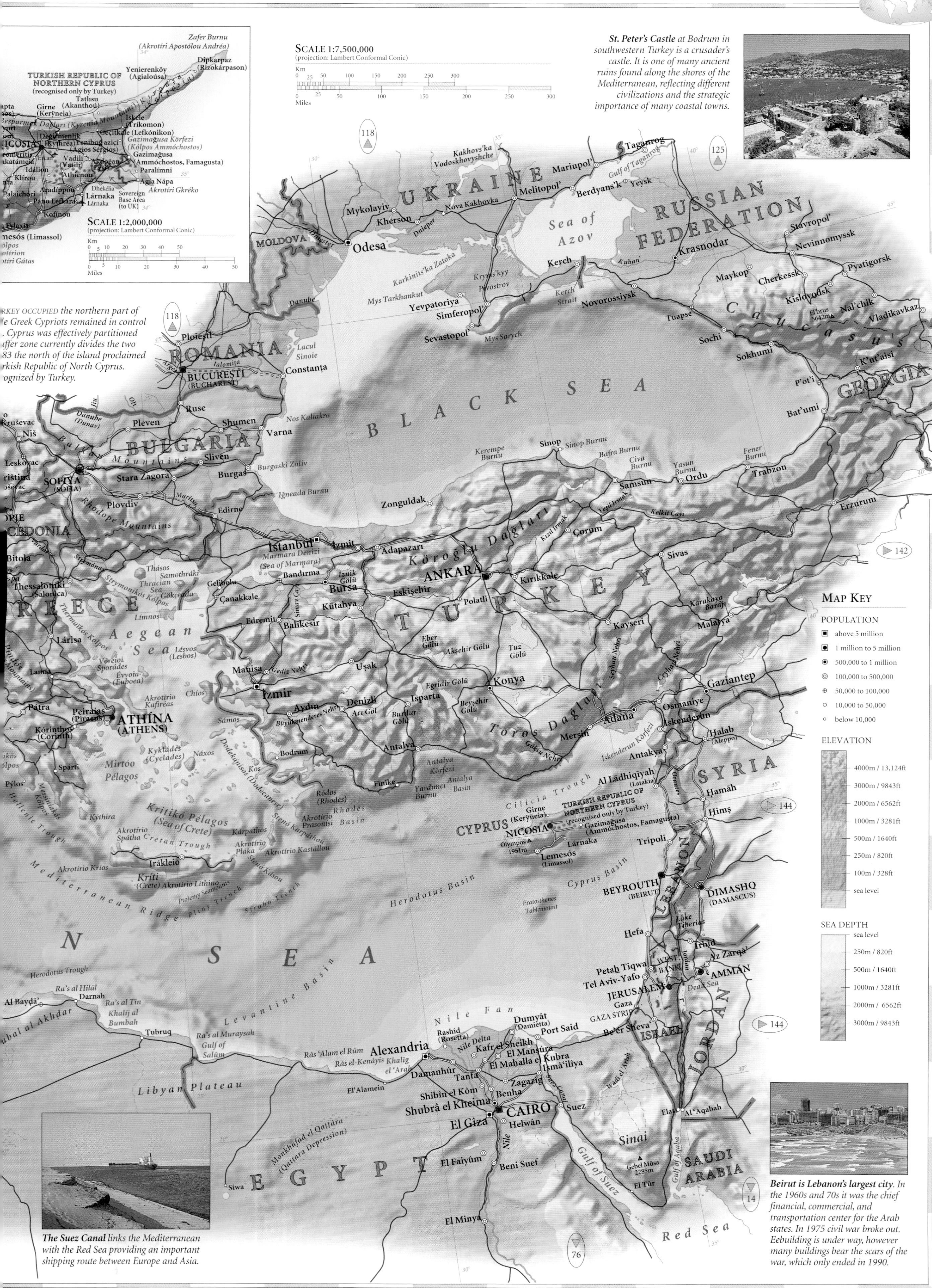

...rkey occupied the northern part of ...e Greek Cypriots remained in control ... Cyprus was effectively partitioned ...uffer zone currently divides the two ...83 the north of the island proclaimed ...rkish Republic of North Cyprus. ...ognized by Turkey.

St. Peter's Castle at Bodrum in southwestern Turkey is a crusader's castle. It is one of many ancient ruins found along the shores of the Mediterranean, reflecting different civilizations and the strategic importance of many coastal towns.

The Suez Canal links the Mediterranean with the Red Sea providing an important shipping route between Europe and Asia.

Beirut is Lebanon's largest city. In the 1960s and 70s it was the chief financial, commercial, and transportation center for the Arab states. In 1975 civil war broke out. Eebuilding is under way, however many buildings bear the scars of the war, which only ended in 1990.

N Nn O Oo P Pp Q Qq R Rr S Ss T

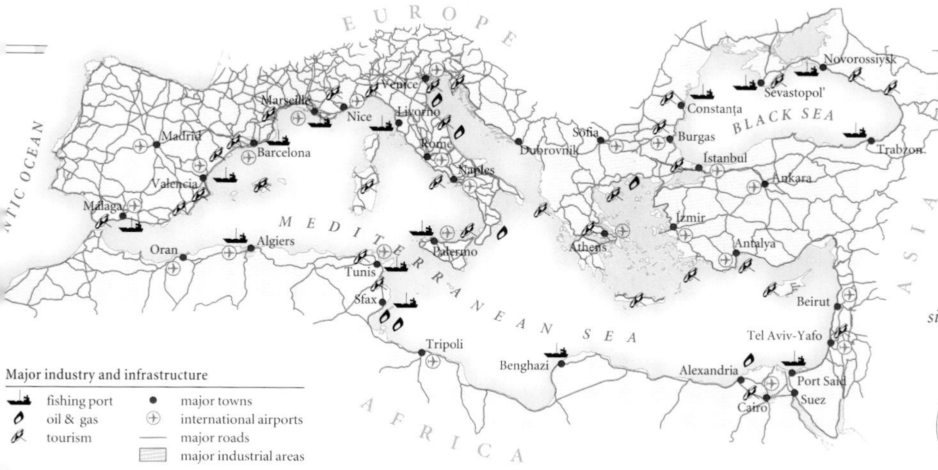

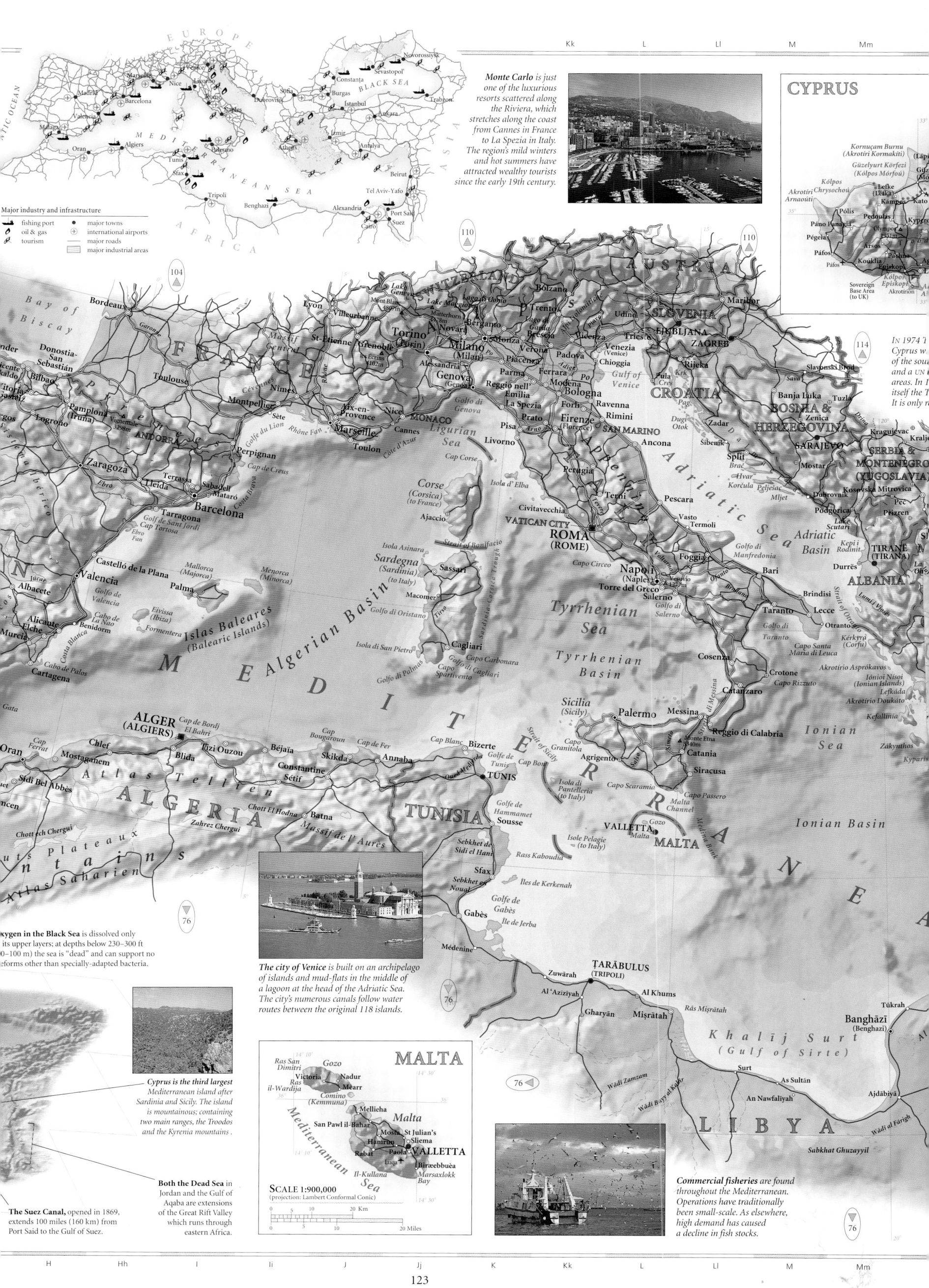

Monte Carlo is just one of the luxurious resorts scattered along the Riviera, which stretches along the coast from Cannes in France to La Spezia in Italy. The region's mild winters and hot summers have attracted wealthy tourists since the early 19th century.

CYPRUS

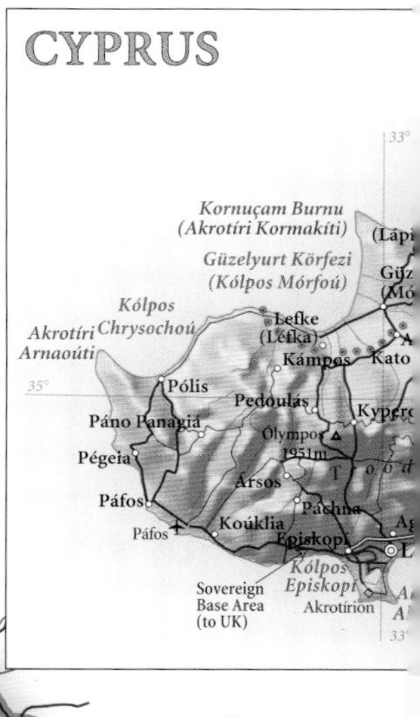

IN 1974 T...
Cyprus w...
of the sou...
and a UN...
areas. In I...
itself the T...
It is only re...

Major industry and infrastructure
- fishing port
- oil & gas
- tourism
- major towns
- international airports
- major roads
- major industrial areas

...xygen in the **Black Sea** is dissolved only ...its upper layers; at depths below 230–300 ft (0–100 m) the sea is "dead" and can support no ...forms other than specially-adapted bacteria.

The city of Venice is built on an archipelago of islands and mud-flats in the middle of a lagoon at the head of the Adriatic Sea. The city's numerous canals follow water routes between the original 118 islands.

Cyprus is the third largest Mediterranean island after Sardinia and Sicily. The island is mountainous; containing two main ranges, the Troodos and the Kyrenia mountains.

Both the Dead Sea in Jordan and the Gulf of Aqaba are extensions of the Great Rift Valley which runs through eastern Africa.

The Suez Canal, opened in 1869, extends 100 miles (160 km) from Port Said to the Gulf of Suez.

MALTA

Ras San Dimitri
Gozo
Victoria Nadur Mearr
Ras il-Wardija
Comino (Kemmuna)
Mellieha
Malta
San Pawl il-Bahar
Mosta St Julian's
Hamrun Sliema
Rabat Paola VALLETTA
Luqa
Birżebbuġa
Il-Kullana
Marsaxlokk Bay

Mediterranean Sea

SCALE 1:900,000
(projection: Lambert Conformal Conic)

0 10 20 Km
0 5 10 20 Miles

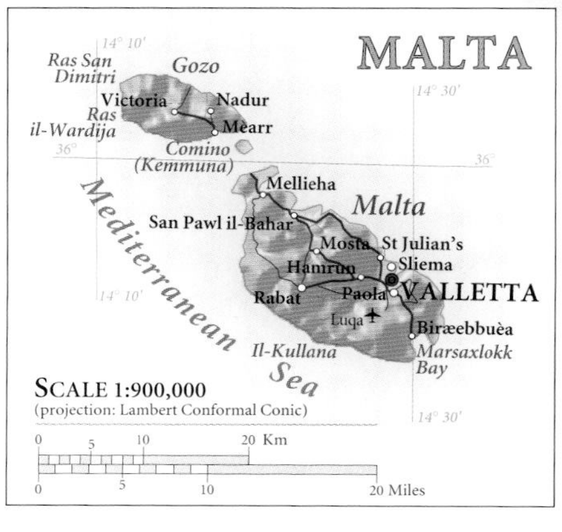

Commercial fisheries are found throughout the Mediterranean. Operations have traditionally been small-scale. As elsewhere, high demand has caused a decline in fish stocks.

A fishing trawler *lies at anchor in the icy waters of Karaginskiy Zaliv, at the northern end of the Kamchatka Peninsula* (Poluostrov Kamchatka) *in eastern Siberia. The Russian Federation's fishing fleet is the largest in the world and operates worldwide.*

The shores of Lake Baikal (Ozero Baykal) *are a mixture of forest and the grassy steppe seen here. The lake freezes to a depth of 33 ft (10 m) in winter.*

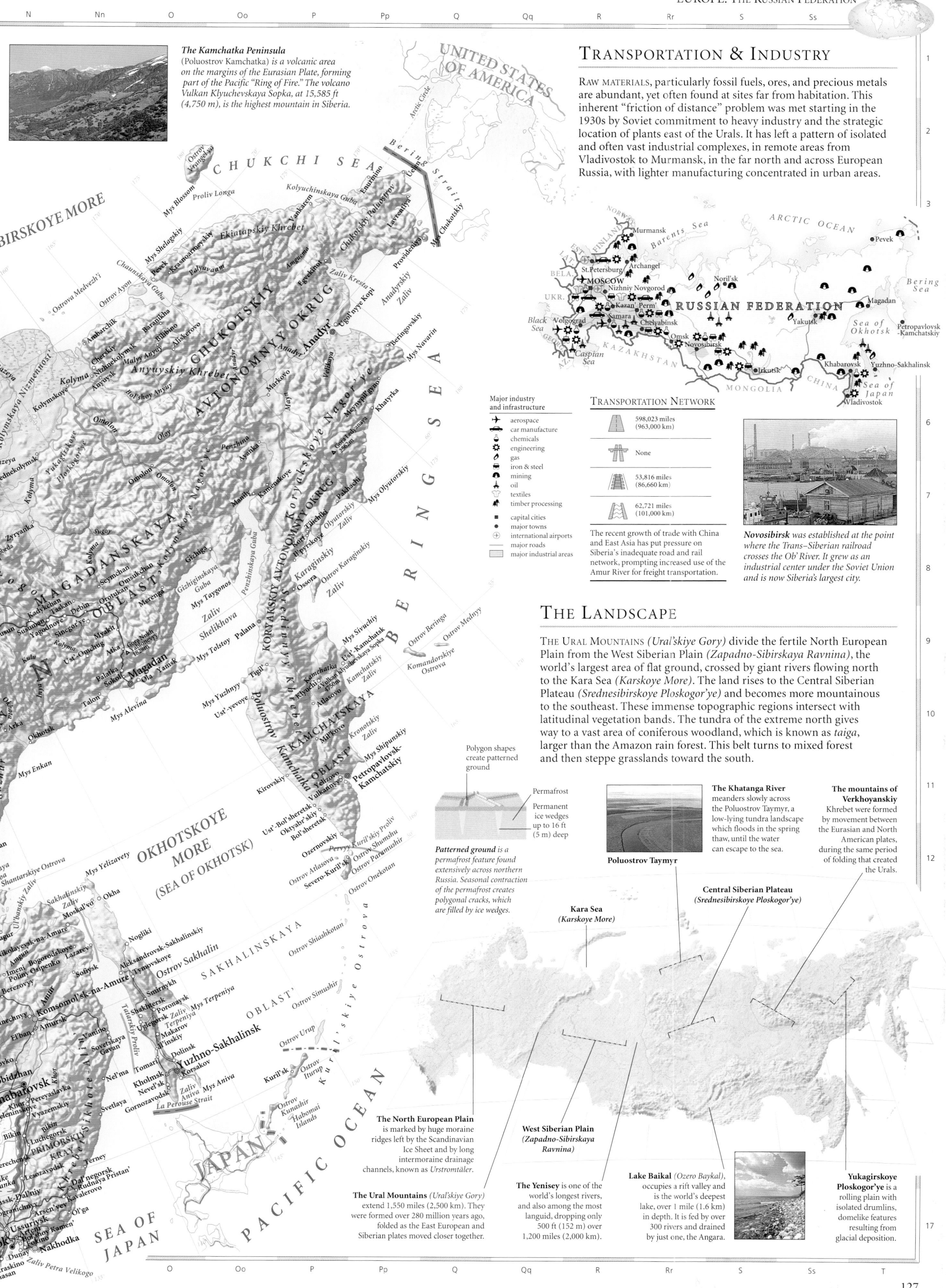

The Kamchatka Peninsula *(Poluostrov Kamchatka) is a volcanic area on the margins of the Eurasian Plate, forming part of the Pacific "Ring of Fire." The volcano Vulkan Klyuchevskaya Sopka, at 15,585 ft (4,750 m), is the highest mountain in Siberia.*

TRANSPORTATION & INDUSTRY

RAW MATERIALS, particularly fossil fuels, ores, and precious metals are abundant, yet often found at sites far from habitation. This inherent "friction of distance" problem was met starting in the 1930s by Soviet commitment to heavy industry and the strategic location of plants east of the Urals. It has left a pattern of isolated and often vast industrial complexes, in remote areas from Vladivostok to Murmansk, in the far north and across European Russia, with lighter manufacturing concentrated in urban areas.

Major industry and infrastructure
- aerospace
- car manufacture
- chemicals
- engineering
- gas
- iron & steel
- mining
- oil
- textiles
- timber processing
- capital cities
- major towns
- international airports
- major roads
- major industrial areas

TRANSPORTATION NETWORK

	598,023 miles (963,000 km)
	None
	53,816 miles (86,660 km)
	62,721 miles (101,000 km)

The recent growth of trade with China and East Asia has put pressure on Siberia's inadequate road and rail network, prompting increased use of the Amur River for freight transportation.

Novosibirsk *was established at the point where the Trans-Siberian railroad crosses the Ob' River. It grew as an industrial center under the Soviet Union and is now Siberia's largest city.*

THE LANDSCAPE

THE URAL MOUNTAINS *(Ural'skiye Gory)* divide the fertile North European Plain from the West Siberian Plain *(Zapadno-Sibirskaya Ravnina)*, the world's largest area of flat ground, crossed by giant rivers flowing north to the Kara Sea *(Karskoye More)*. The land rises to the Central Siberian Plateau *(Srednesibirskoye Ploskogor'ye)* and becomes more mountainous to the southeast. These immense topographic regions intersect with latitudinal vegetation bands. The tundra of the extreme north gives way to a vast area of coniferous woodland, which is known as *taiga*, larger than the Amazon rain forest. This belt turns to mixed forest and then steppe grasslands toward the south.

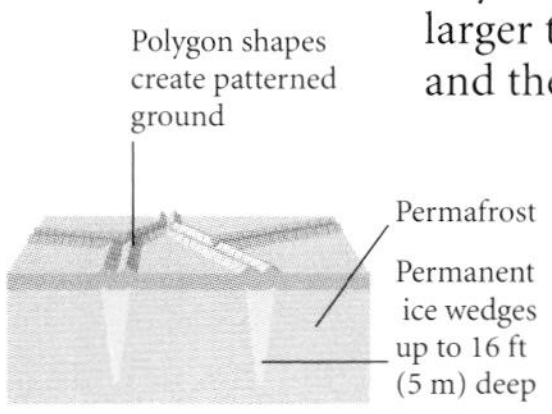

Patterned ground *is a permafrost feature found extensively across northern Russia. Seasonal contraction of the permafrost creates polygonal cracks, which are filled by ice wedges.*

The Khatanga River meanders slowly across the Poluostrov Taymyr, a low-lying tundra landscape which floods in the spring thaw, until the water can escape to the sea.

The mountains of Verkhoyanskiy Khrebet were formed by movement between the Eurasian and North American plates, during the same period of folding that created the Urals.

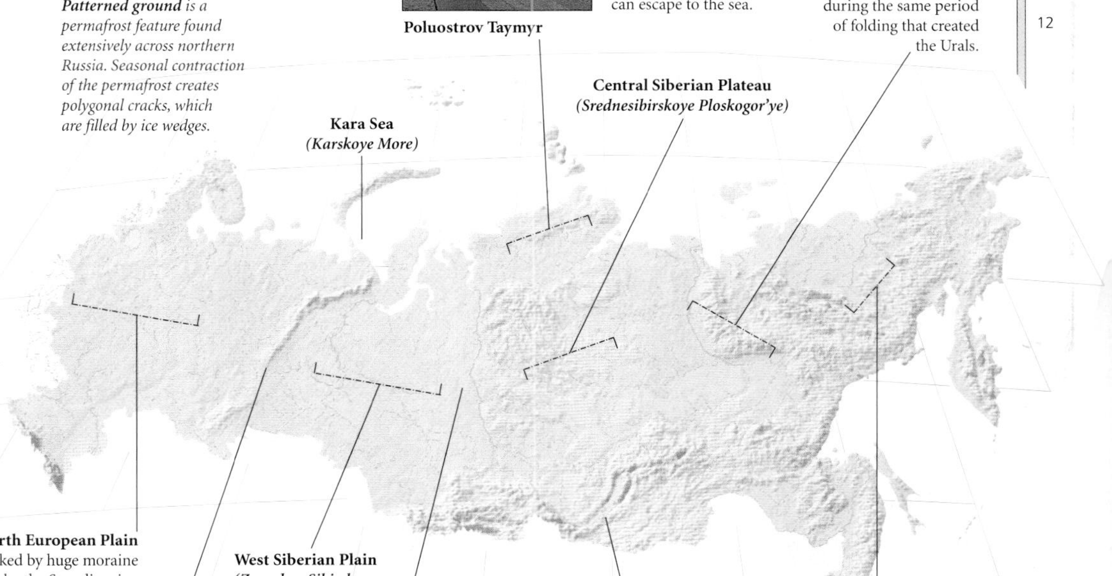

The North European Plain is marked by huge moraine ridges left by the Scandinavian Ice Sheet and by long intermoraine drainage channels, known as *Urstromtäler*.

The Ural Mountains *(Ural'skiye Gory)* extend 1,550 miles (2,500 km). They were formed over 280 million years ago, folded as the East European and Siberian plates moved closer together.

West Siberian Plain ***(Zapadno-Sibirskaya Ravnina)***

The Yenisey is one of the world's longest rivers, and also among the most languid, dropping only 500 ft (152 m) over 1,200 miles (2,000 km).

Lake Baikal *(Ozero Baykal)*, occupies a rift valley and is the world's deepest lake, over 1 mile (1.6 km) in depth. It is fed by over 300 rivers and drained by just one, the Angara.

Yukagirskoye Ploskogor'ye is a rolling plain with isolated drumlins, domelike features resulting from glacial deposition.

NORTHERN EUROPEAN RUSSIA

Reaching into the Arctic Circle, this region of lakeland, forest, and tundra is historically bound to Europe by St. Petersburg, the old imperial capital of Tsarist Russia and home to a third of the region's population. Communist rule from Moscow left the north politically marginalized, contributing to the present problems of outmoded industry, poor infrastructure, and serious environmental neglect. However, with borders embracing Finland, Norway, the Baltic, and the northern sea route to the Atlantic, the region's success in foreign trade is now of prime importance to the Russian economy.

St. Peter and Paul Fortress is the oldest building in St. Petersburg, founded by Peter the Great in 1703 as a modern, European capital for Russia.

THE LANDSCAPE

The ancient bedrock of the Scandinavian Shield lies exposed across the glacially scoured Khibiny Mountains of the Kola Peninsula *(Kol'skiy Poluostrov)*, becoming mantled with till toward the North European Plain. The Valdai Hills *(Valdayskaya Vozvyshennost')* form an important watershed for the plain's rivers, while thick forest veils a complicated topography of moraines, lakes, and ground disturbed by frost action. The Ural Mountains *(Ural'skiye Gory)* form a border with Asia in the east.

The Kola Peninsula (Kol'skiy Poluostrov) is part of the Scandinavian Shield, an area of ancient bedrock underlying Scandinavia. Rocks in excess of 2,500 million years old are exposed across the peninsula.

94 ◀

The Khibiny Mountains were formed by volcanic intrusions into the Scandinavian Shield, over 570 million years ago.

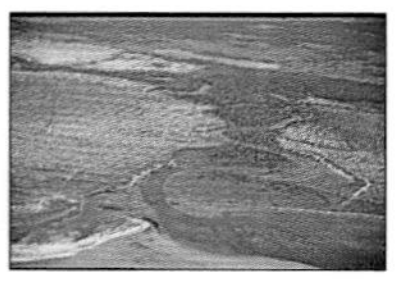

Kola Peninsula *(Kol'skiy Poluostrov)*

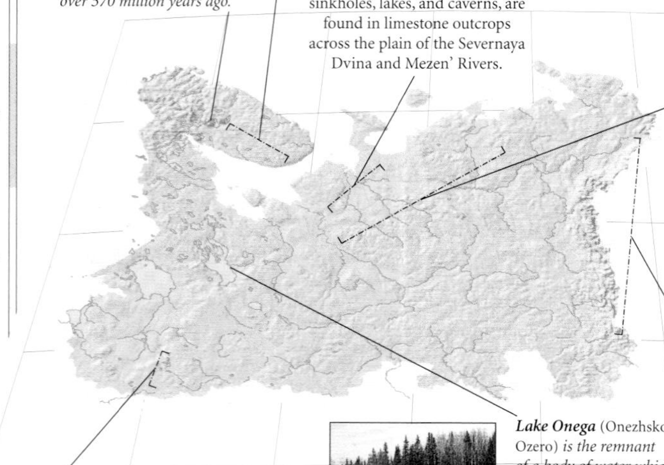

Karst features, including sinkholes, lakes, and caverns, are found in limestone outcrops across the plain of the Severnaya Dvina and Mezen' Rivers.

The low-lying plains of the Pechora, Mezen', and Severnaya Dvina Rivers were flooded by the sea while the land was still isostatically depressed following the last Ice Age, a process which has hidden the landforms created by glacial deposition.

Retreating glacier
Meltwater channels
Terminal moraine

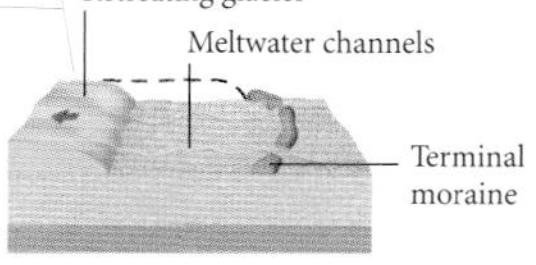

Terminal moraines are crescent-shaped ridges of glacial deposits, widely found in central Russia. Detritus is carried by the glacier and deposited at its terminus (snout) as it melts, marking the limit of the ice advance.

Lake Onega (Onezhskoye Ozero) is the remnant of a body of water which, 12,000 years ago, connected the White Sea (Beloye More) with the Gulf of Finland and the Baltic Sea.

Ural Mountains *(Ural'skiye Gory)*

Two of Europe's biggest rivers, the Volga and Western Dvina, rise in the swampy uplands of the Valdai Hills *(Valdayskaya Vozvyshennost')*.

USING THE LAND AND SEA

The cold climate confines agriculture mainly to southern and western provinces, where dairy farming predominates and arable land is given over to fodder crops as well as flax, potatoes, oats, and rye. Areas beyond the northern margins of cultivation are used for forestry, hunting, herding, and fishing, with some vegetables grown in hothouses around urban areas.

120 ◀

Land use and agricultural distribution
- cattle
- fishing
- reindeer
- timber
- fodder
- major towns
- pasture
- cropland
- forest
- mountain region
- wetland
- tundra
- barren
- ice

RUSSIAN FEDERATION

THE URBAN/RURAL POPULATION DIVIDE

urban 74%	rural 26%

0 10 20 30 40 50 60 70 80 90 100

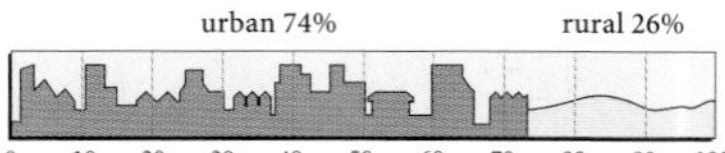

POPULATION DENSITY
26 people per sq mile
10 people per sq km

TOTAL LAND AREA
829,398 sq miles
(2,148,700 sq km)

Many rapids are found along the 175 mile (280 km) course of the Suna River.

120 ▽

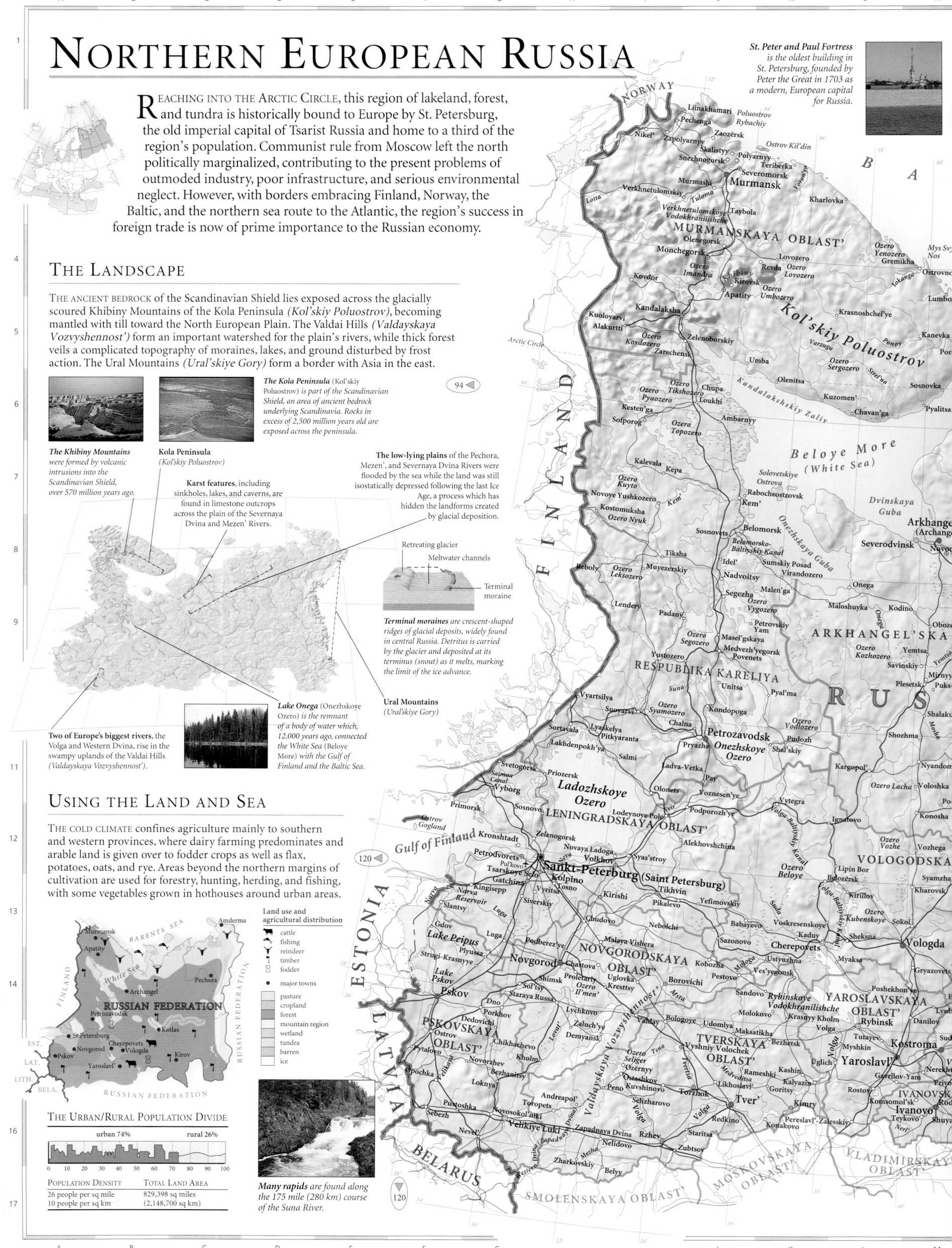

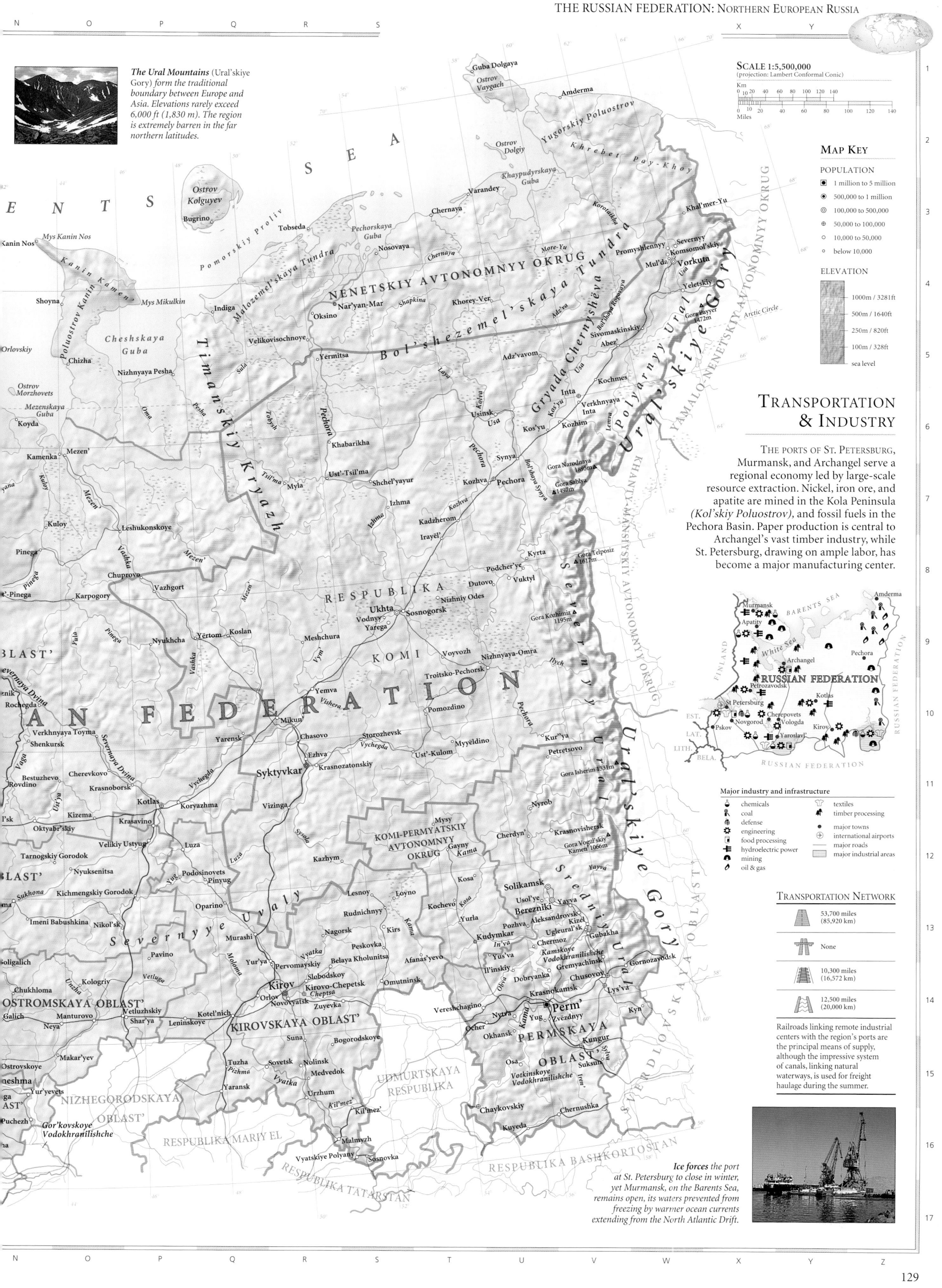

The Ural Mountains (Ural'skiye Gory) *form the traditional boundary between Europe and Asia. Elevations rarely exceed 6,000 ft (1,830 m). The region is extremely barren in the far northern latitudes.*

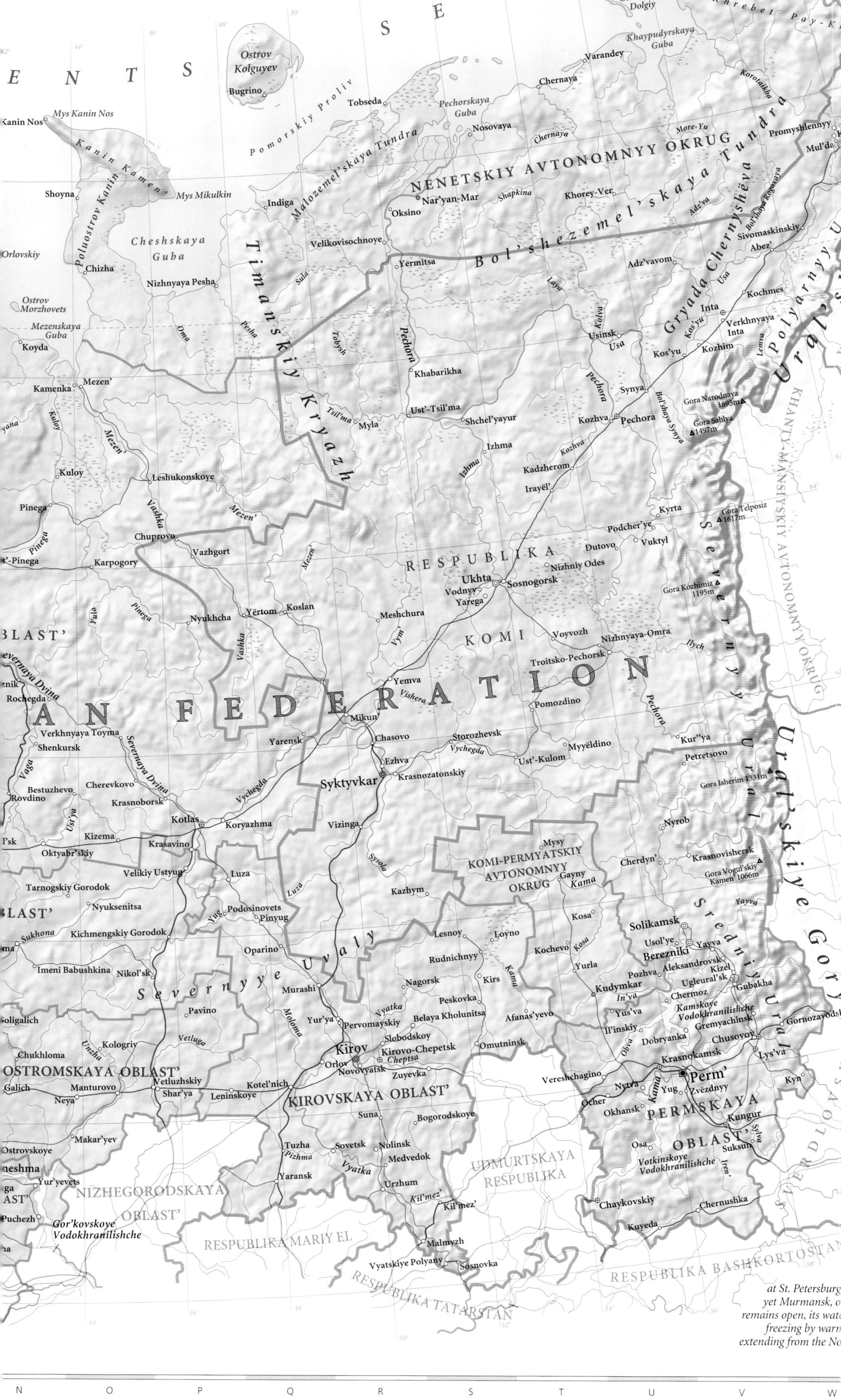

SCALE 1:5,500,000
(projection: Lambert Conformal Conic)

Km 0 10 20 40 60 80 100 120 140
Miles 0 10 20 40 60 80 100 120 140

MAP KEY

POPULATION

- 1 million to 5 million
- 500,000 to 1 million
- 100,000 to 500,000
- 50,000 to 100,000
- 10,000 to 50,000
- below 10,000

ELEVATION

- 1000m / 3281ft
- 500m / 1640ft
- 250m / 820ft
- 100m / 328ft
- sea level

TRANSPORTATION & INDUSTRY

THE PORTS OF ST. PETERSBURG, Murmansk, and Archangel serve a regional economy led by large-scale resource extraction. Nickel, iron ore, and apatite are mined in the Kola Peninsula *(Kol'skiy Poluostrov)*, and fossil fuels in the Pechora Basin. Paper production is central to Archangel's vast timber industry, while St. Petersburg, drawing on ample labor, has become a major manufacturing center.

Major industry and infrastructure

- chemicals
- coal
- defense
- engineering
- food processing
- hydroelectric power
- mining
- oil & gas
- textiles
- timber processing
- major towns
- international airports
- major roads
- major industrial areas

TRANSPORTATION NETWORK

Roads	53,700 miles (85,920 km)
Motorways	None
Railways	10,300 miles (16,572 km)
Waterways	12,500 miles (20,000 km)

Railroads linking remote industrial centers with the region's ports are the principal means of supply, although the impressive system of canals, linking natural waterways, is used for freight haulage during the summer.

***Ice forces** the port at St. Petersburg to close in winter, yet Murmansk, on the Barents Sea, remains open, its waters prevented from freezing by warmer ocean currents extending from the North Atlantic Drift.*

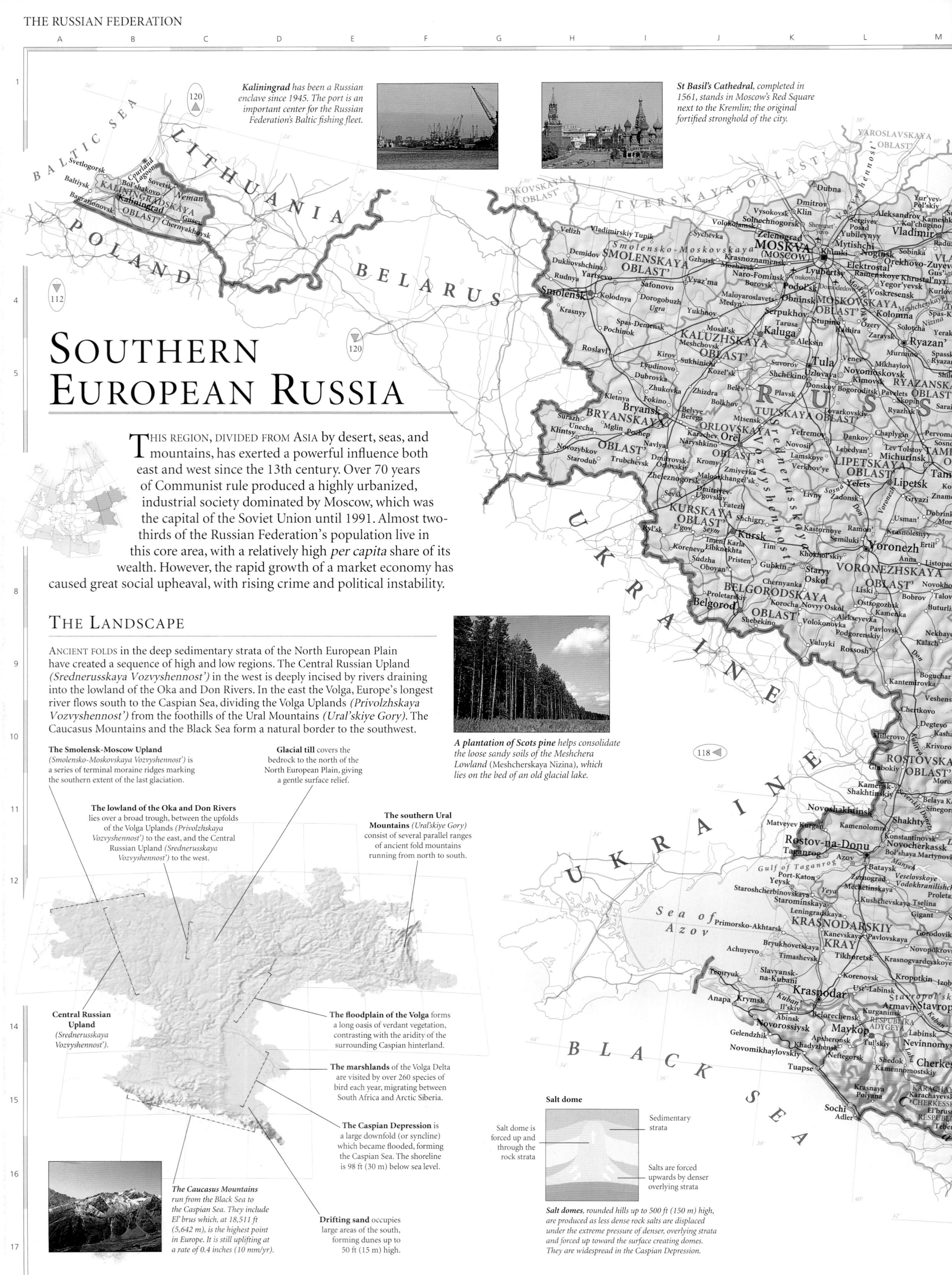

Kaliningrad *has been a Russian enclave since 1945. The port is an important center for the Russian Federation's Baltic fishing fleet.*

St Basil's Cathedral, *completed in 1561, stands in Moscow's Red Square next to the Kremlin; the original fortified stronghold of the city.*

SOUTHERN EUROPEAN RUSSIA

THIS REGION, DIVIDED FROM ASIA by desert, seas, and mountains, has exerted a powerful influence both east and west since the 13th century. Over 70 years of Communist rule produced a highly urbanized, industrial society dominated by Moscow, which was the capital of the Soviet Union until 1991. Almost two-thirds of the Russian Federation's population live in this core area, with a relatively high *per capita* share of its wealth. However, the rapid growth of a market economy has caused great social upheaval, with rising crime and political instability.

THE LANDSCAPE

ANCIENT FOLDS in the deep sedimentary strata of the North European Plain have created a sequence of high and low regions. The Central Russian Upland *(Srednerusskaya Vozvyshennost')* in the west is deeply incised by rivers draining into the lowland of the Oka and Don Rivers. In the east the Volga, Europe's longest river flows south to the Caspian Sea, dividing the Volga Uplands *(Privolzhskaya Vozvyshennost')* from the foothills of the Ural Mountains *(Ural'skiye Gory)*. The Caucasus Mountains and the Black Sea form a natural border to the southwest.

***A plantation of Scots pine** helps consolidate the loose sandy soils of the Meshchera Lowland* (Meshcherskaya Nizina), *which lies on the bed of an old glacial lake.*

The Smolensk-Moscow Upland *(Smolensko-Moskovskaya Vozvyshennost')* is a series of terminal moraine ridges marking the southern extent of the last glaciation.

Glacial till covers the bedrock to the north of the North European Plain, giving a gentle surface relief.

The lowland of the Oka and Don Rivers lies over a broad trough, between the upfolds of the Volga Uplands *(Privolzhskaya Vozvyshennost')* to the east, and the Central Russian Upland *(Srednerusskaya Vozvyshennost')* to the west.

The southern Ural Mountains *(Ural'skiye Gory)* consist of several parallel ranges of ancient fold mountains running from north to south.

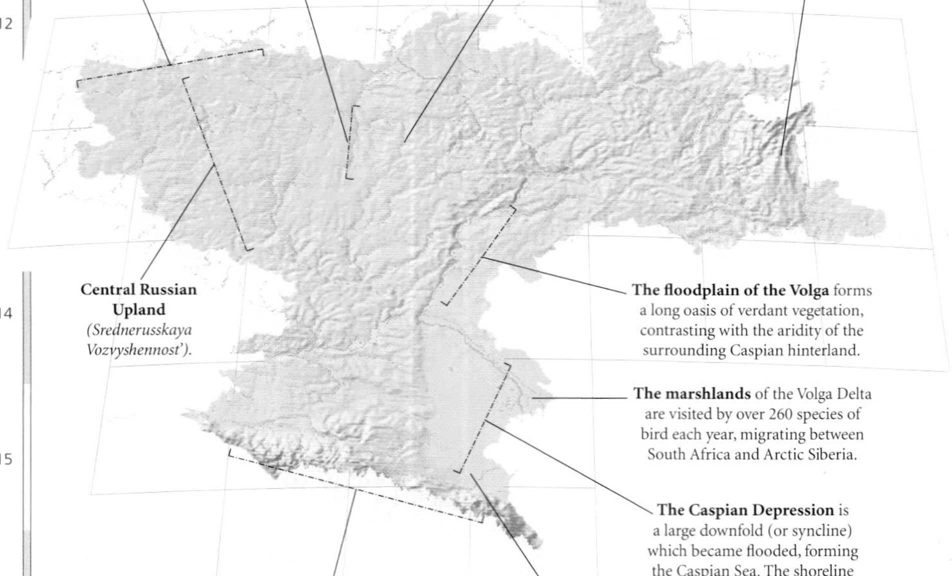

Central Russian Upland *(Srednerusskaya Vozvyshennost').*

The floodplain of the Volga forms a long oasis of verdant vegetation, contrasting with the aridity of the surrounding Caspian hinterland.

The marshlands of the Volga Delta are visited by over 260 species of bird each year, migrating between South Africa and Arctic Siberia.

The Caspian Depression is a large downfold (or syncline) which became flooded, forming the Caspian Sea. The shoreline is 98 ft (30 m) below sea level.

***The Caucasus Mountains** run from the Black Sea to the Caspian Sea. They include El'brus which, at 18,511 ft (5,642 m), is the highest point in Europe. It is still uplifting at a rate of 0.4 inches (10 mm/yr).*

Drifting sand occupies large areas of the south, forming dunes up to 50 ft (15 m) high.

Salt dome

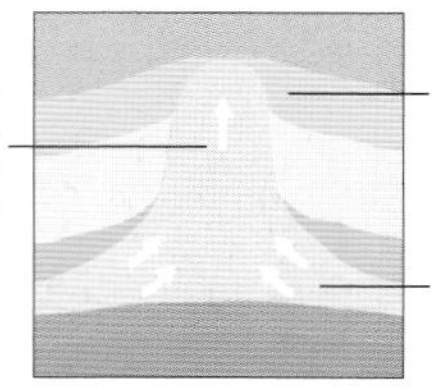

***Salt domes**, rounded hills up to 500 ft (150 m) high, are produced as less dense rock salts are displaced under the extreme pressure of denser, overlying strata and forced up toward the surface creating domes. They are widespread in the Caspian Depression.*

120 112 120 118

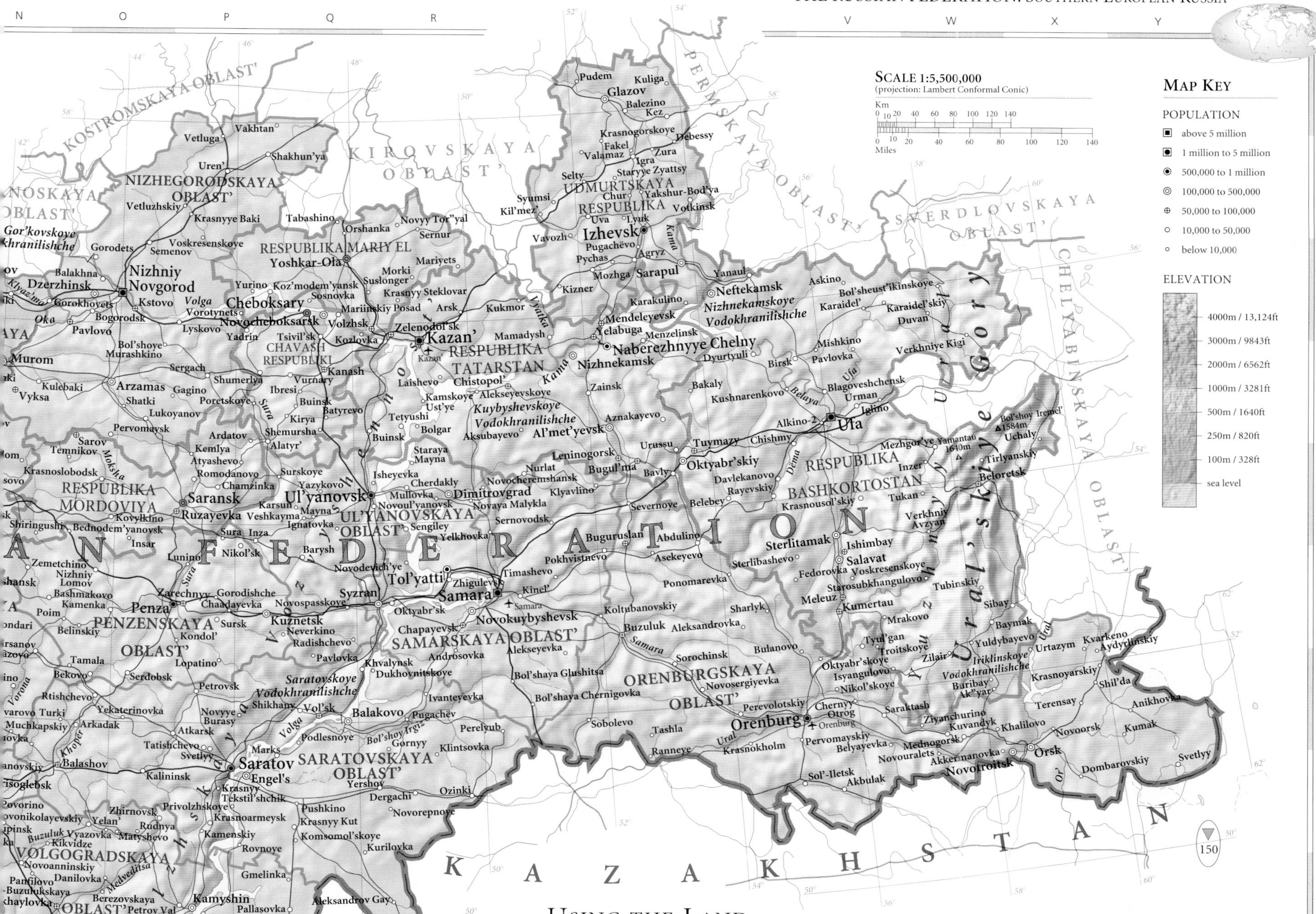

USING THE LAND

IN THE COLD, HUMID NORTH and in the southern Urals *(Ural'skiye Gory)*, small grains, potatoes and flax are commonly rotated with legumes which support livestock farming. The rich chernozem (or black earth) areas support diverse crops such as sugar beet, hemp, sunflowers, millet and vegetables. Further south, aridity restricts husbandry to extensive grazing, with intensive fruit and rice cultivation along the oasis of the Volga.

THE URBAN/RURAL POPULATION DIVIDE

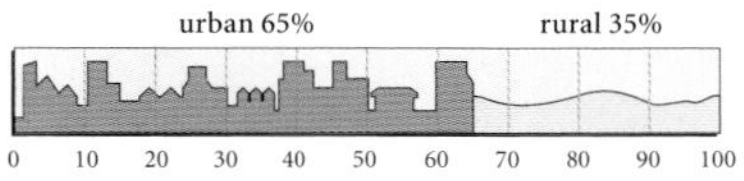

POPULATION DENSITY	TOTAL LAND AREA
119 people per sq mile (46 people per sq km)	705,916 sq miles (1,828,800 sq km)

Land use and agricultural distribution

- sheep
- flax
- potatoes
- rice
- sunflowers
- sugar beet
- timber
- capital cities
- major towns
- pasture
- cropland
- forest
- wetland
- mountain region
- tundra

TRANSPORTATION & INDUSTRY

MANUFACTURING is largely based around Moscow and the Volga region, which became a major industrial area during the Second World War. Both Moscow and Nizhniy Novgorod are centers of skilled labor for light manufacturing and engineering. Most of Russia's main chemical plants are located along the Volga, and one of the world's largest car factories was recently opened in Tol'yatti. Processing and machine construction plants use oil, gas, and hydroelectric power from the Volga Basin and metallic minerals from the Urals *(Ural'skiye Gory)* and Kursk.

***Industrial plants** are massed along the Volga. Environmental stress from decades of unbridled industrial development has prompted widespread concern about pollution levels.*

TRANSPORTATION NETWORK

250,000 miles (402,000 km)	None
28,000 miles (44,800 km)	16,300 miles (26,080 km)

Seventy private and national flag airlines have been created from the reorganization of the state airline Aeroflot, which maintained the world's largest fleet of aircraft during the Soviet era.

Major industry and infrastructure

- aerospace
- car manufacture
- chemicals
- defense
- electronics
- engineering
- gas
- mining
- oil
- textiles
- capital cities
- major towns
- international airports
- major roads
- major industrial areas

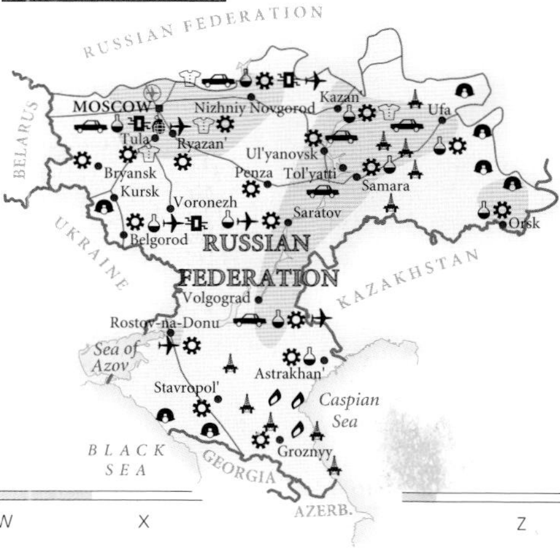

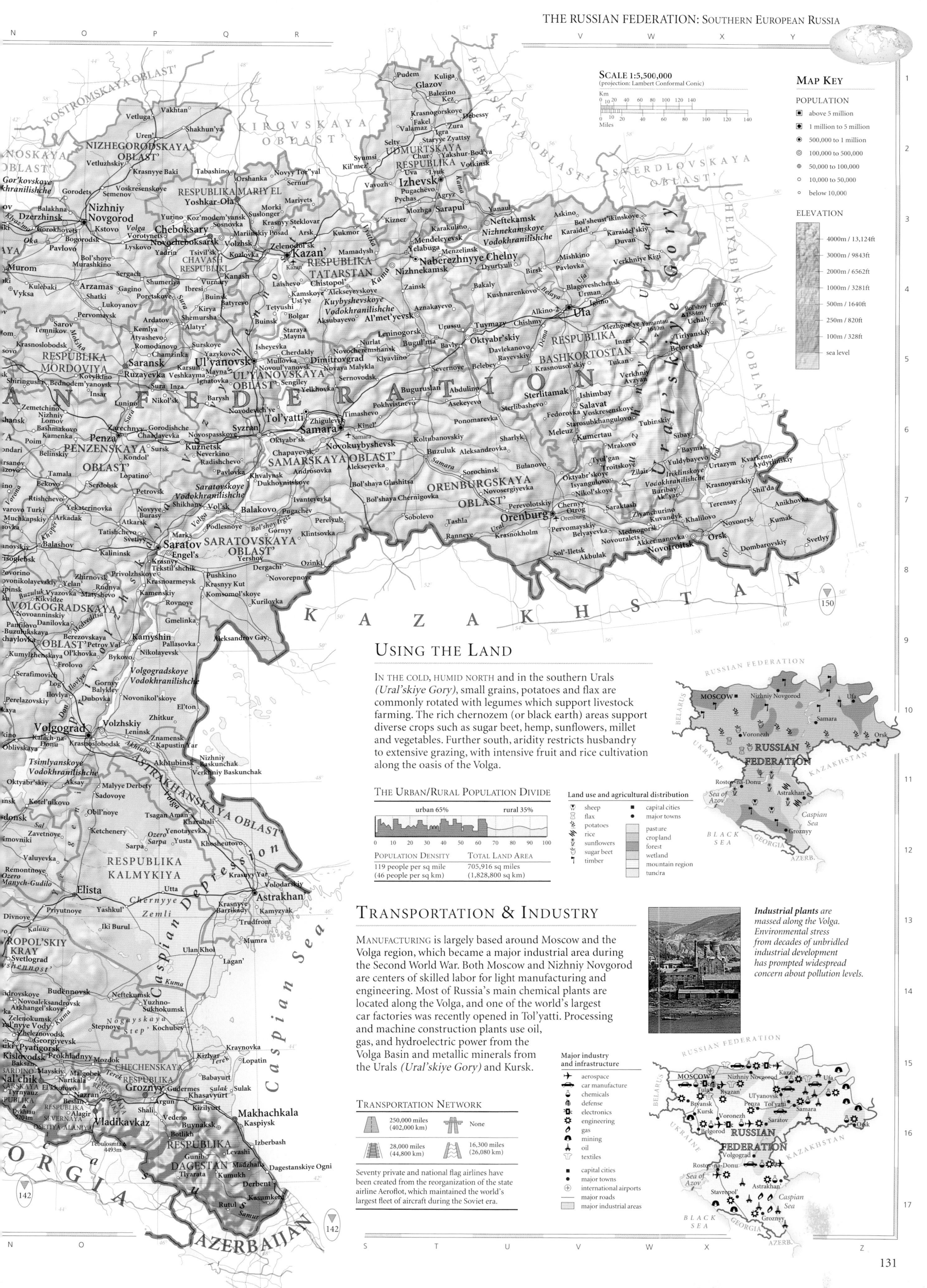

ASIA

ASIA, THE WORLD'S LARGEST CONTINENT, COVERS 16,838,365 SQ MILES (43,608,000 SQ KM). IT COMPRISES 49 SEPARATE COUNTRIES, INCLUDING 97% OF TURKEY AND 72% OF THE RUSSIAN FEDERATION. ALMOST 60% OF THE WORLD'S POPULATION LIVES IN ASIA.

○ GREATEST EXTENT NORTH–SOUTH:
(4,000 miles / 6,440 km)
□ GREATEST EXTENT EAST–WEST:
(6,000 miles / 9,650 km)

Most northerly point:
Mys Articesku,
Russian Federation
81° 12' N

Most easterly point:
Mys Dezhneva,
Russian Federation
169° 40' W

Largest lake:
Caspian Sea
(143,205 sq miles)
(371,000 sq km)

MYS DEZHNEVA,
RUSSIAN FEDERATION
169° 40' W

Lowest recorded temperature:
Verkhoyansk,
Russian Federation
-90°F (-68°C)

MYS CHELYUSKIN,
RUSSIAN FEDERATION
77° 44' N

Most westerly point:
Bozca Adası,
Turkey 26° 2' E

Arctic Circle

BABA BUR-NU,
TURKEY
26° 4' E

KAGOSHIMA

Tropic of Cancer

Highest point:
Mount Everest,
China/Nepal
29,029 ft (8,848 m)

HODEIDA

Highest recorded temperature:
Tirat Tsvi, Israel
129°F (54°C)

Equator

Lowest point:
Dead Sea,
Israel/Jordan
1,286 ft (392 m)
below sea level

TANJONG PIAI
MALAYSIA
1° 16' N

Most southerly point:
Pulau Pamana, Indonesia 11' S

Zagros
Mountains

Gobi

Manchurian Plain

KAGOSHIMA,
JAPAN

HODEIDA,
YEMEN

The Gulf

Plateau of Tibet

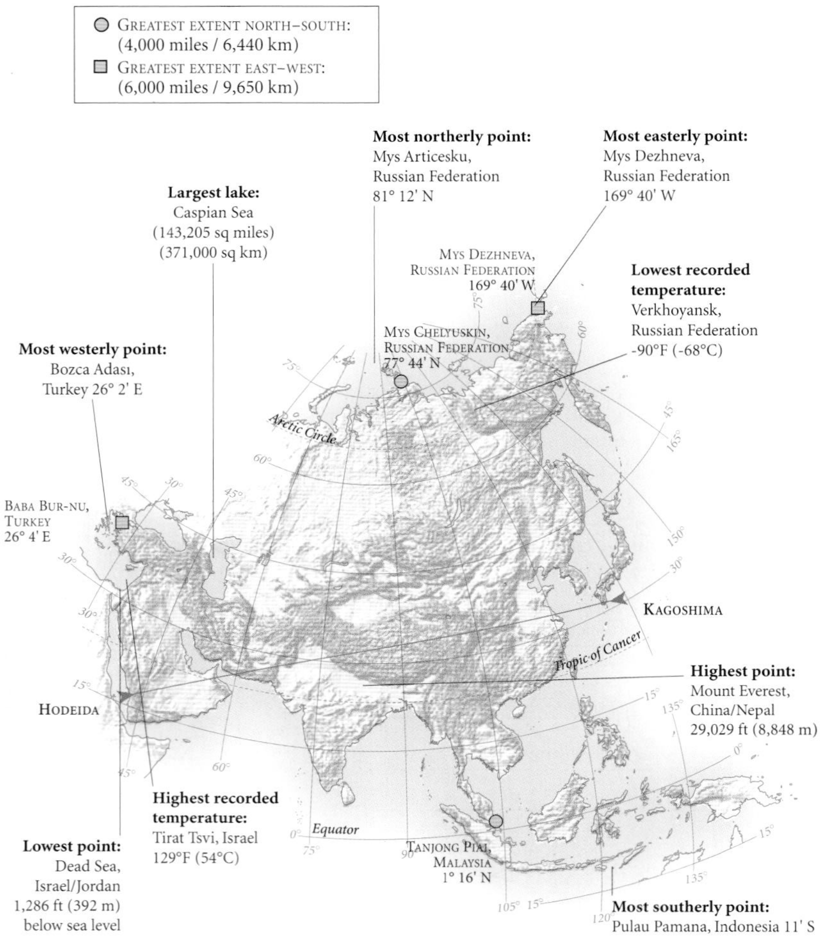

CROSS-SECTION FROM HODEIDA, YEMEN TO KAGOSHIMA, JAPAN

◄ line of cross-section

| 0 | 500 | 1000 | 1500 Km |

| 0 | 500 | 1000 | 1500 Miles |

Sahara

Mediterranean Sea

Dead Sea

Syrian
Desert

Cyprus

Eastern Desert

Nile

Lake
Nasser

An
Nafud

AFRICAN PLATE

ARABIAN PLATE

White Nile

Arabian
Peninsula

Ar Rub' al
(Empty Qu

Red Sea

Gulf of Aden

Ethiopian
Highlands

Horn of
Africa

A F R I C A

Great Rift Valley

Fafen Shet

Shebeli

Juba

Lake
Chad

Lake
Victoria

Lake
Tanganyika

Somali
Basin

Chain Ridge

I N

Lake
Nyasa

Amirante
Islands

Seychelles

Aldabra
Group

Comoro
Islands

Farquhar
Group

Agalega
Islands

Mascarene

Mozambique Channel

Madagascar

Madagascar
Plain

Ile Tromelin

Réunion

Madagascar
Plateau

Madagascar
Basin

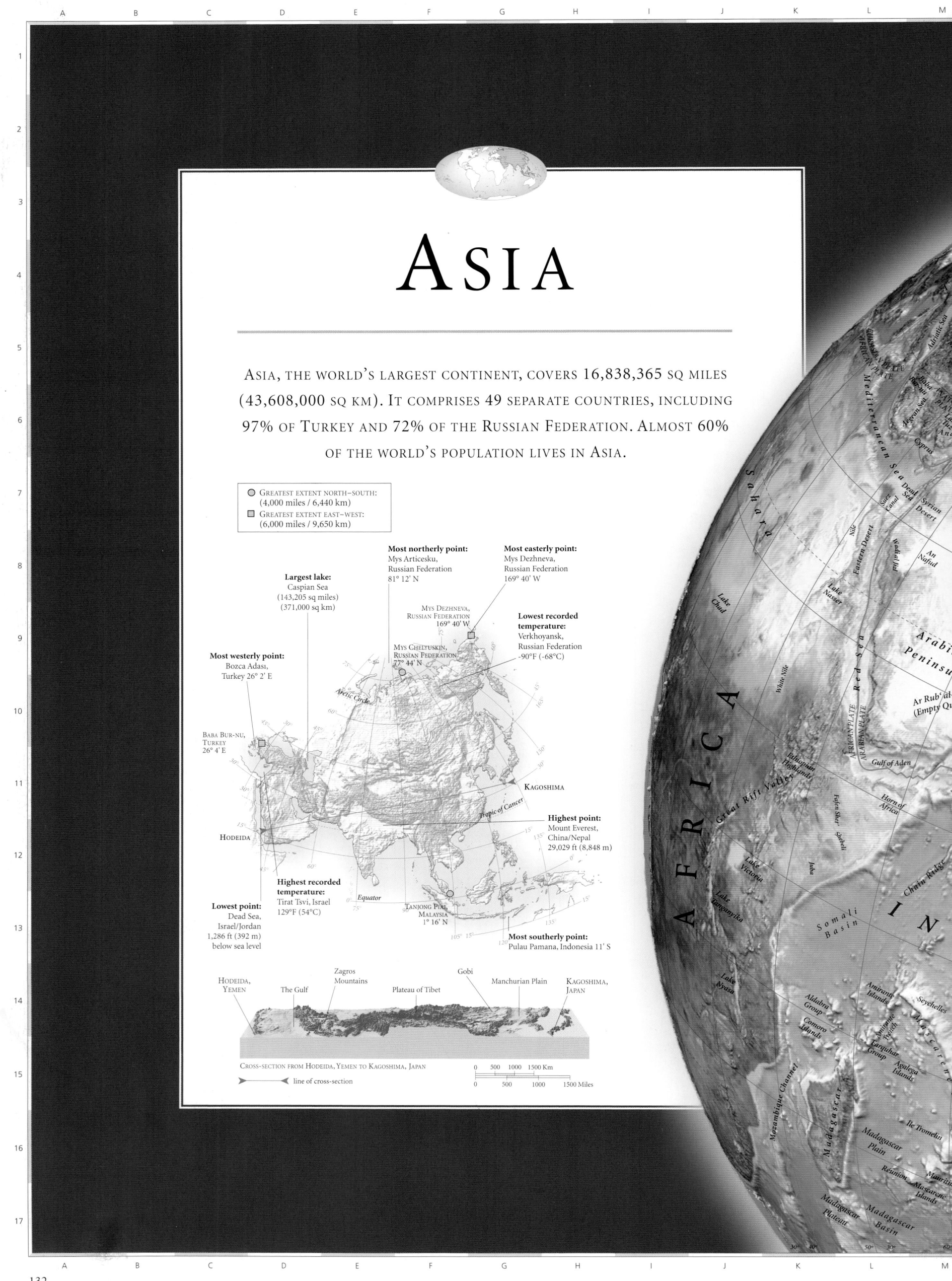

N O P Q R S T U V W X Y Z
1 2 3 4 5 6 7 8 9 10 11 12 13 14 15 16 17
ARCTIC OCEAN
North Pole
NORTH AMERICAN PLATE
EURASIAN PLATE
Norwegian Sea
Scandinavia
North Sea
Gulf of Bothnia
Barents Sea
North Cape
Franz Josef Land
Novaya Zemlya
Kola Peninsula
White Sea
Baltic Sea
Gulf of Finland
Lake Ladoga
Lake Onega
Kara Sea
Severnaya Zemlya
Mys Chelyuskin
Laptev Sea
New Siberian Islands
East Siberian Sea
Long Strait
Bering Strait
Chukot Range
Bering Sea
Poluostrov Taymyr
Poluostrov Yamal
North European Plain
Central Russian Upland
EUROPE
Ural Mountains
West Siberian Plain
Putorana Mountains
North Siberian Lowland
Central Siberian Plateau
Siberia
Verkhoyanskiy Khrebet
Khrebet Cherskogo
Kolyma Range
Koryak Range
Kamchatka
Aleutian Basin
Sea of Okhotsk
Stanovoy Khrebet
Zeya Reservoir
Yablonovyy Khrebet
Lake Baikal
Sayanskiy Khrebet
Uvs Nuur
Hövsgöl Nuur
Hyargas Nuur
Sea of Azov
Caspian Depression
Caucasus
Caspian Sea
Ustyurt Plateau
Aral Sea
Kirghiz Steppe
Lake Balkhash
Lake Zaysan
Ozero Alakol'
Turan Lowland
Kara Kum
Elburz Mountains
EURASIAN PLATE
IRANIAN PLATE
Great Salt Desert
ASIA
Altai Mountains
Tien Shan
Ozero Issyk-Kul'
Dzungaria
Plateau of Mongolia
Gobi
Hulun Nur
Great Khingan Range
Manchurian Plain
Lake Khanka
Hokkaido
Sea of Japan
Japan
Honshu
Shikoku
Kyushu
Japan Trench
Kurile Islands
Kurile Trench
Zagros Mountains
Iranian Plateau
Kuh-e Fuladi 5143m
Kuh-e-Baba
Hindu Kush
Pamirs
Karakoram Range
K2 8611m
Tarim Basin
Takla Makan Desert
Lop Nur
Kunlun Mountains
Altun Shan
Nan Shan
Qilian Shan
Plateau of Tibet
Qinghai Hu
Ordos Desert
Bo Hai
Korea Bay
Yellow Sea
Cheju-do
Korea Strait
Great Plain of China
Taihang Shan
Wutai Shan
Xiqing Shan
Bayan Har Shan
Rigestan
Strait of Hormuz
Hamun Jaz Murian
Central Makran Range
Gulf of Oman
Sulaiman Range
Punjab Plains
Thar Desert
Himalayas
Annapurna 8091m
Mount Everest 8848m
Nam Co
Siling Co
Tangra Yumco
Dogai Coring
ARABIAN PLATE
INDO-AUSTRALIAN PLATE
Gulf of Kachchh
Vindhya Range
Satpura Range
Ajanta Range
Gulf of Khambhat
Khasi Hills
Patkai Range
Dongting Hu
Tai Hu
Hong Hu
East China Sea
Ryukyu Islands
Shikoku Basin
Taiwan Strait
Taiwan
Tropic of Cancer
Arabian Sea
Arabian Basin
Deccan
Western Ghats
Eastern Ghats
Mouths of the Ganges
Arakan Yoma
Bay of Bengal
Hainan Strait
Gulf of Tongking
Hainan
Luzon Strait
Philippine Sea
PHILIPPINE PLATE
Malabar Coast
Coromandel Coast
Laccadive Islands
Cape Comorin
Gulf of Mannar
Sri Lanka
Gulf of Martaban
Andaman Islands
Andaman Sea
Gulf of Thailand
Tônlé Sap
South China Sea
Luzon
Mindoro
Panay
Negros
Philippines
Philippine Basin
Philippine Trench
Kyushu-Palau Ridge
PACIFIC OCEAN
Maldives
INDIAN OCEAN
Isthmus of Kra
Nicobar Islands
Mouths of the Mekong
South China Basin
Palawan
Sulu Sea
Mindanao
Palau
Celebes Sea
Chagos-Laccadive Plateau
Ceylon Plain
Ninetyeast Ridge
Malay Peninsula
Strait of Malacca
Danau Toba
Anambas Islands
Natuna Islands
Sunda Shelf
Gunung Kinabalu 4094m
Chagos Bank
Chagos Trench
Nikitin Seamount
Tanjong Piai
Greater Sunda Islands
Borneo
Makassar Strait
Celebes
Moluccas
Halmahera
Moluccas Sea
New Guinea Trench
Sumatra
Gunung Kerinci 3806m
Pulau Bangka
Mid-Indian Basin
Cocos Basin
Mentawai Ridge
Selat Sunda
East Indies
Java Sea
Buru
Seram
Banda Sea
New Guinea
Java
Bali
Flores Sea
Lesser Sunda Islands
Flores
Sumba
Timor
Timor Trough
Arafura Sea
Torres Strait
Sunda Trough
Java Trench
Investigator Ridge
Cocos Islands
Christmas Island
AUSTRALIA
Equator

Asian Resources

ALTHOUGH AGRICULTURE REMAINS THE ECONOMIC MAINSTAY of most Asian countries, the number of people employed in agriculture has steadily declined, as new industries have been developed during the past 30 years. China, Indonesia, Malaysia, Thailand, and Turkey have all experienced far-reaching structural change in their economies, while the breakup of the Soviet Union has created a new economic challenge in the Central Asian republics. The countries of the Persian Gulf illustrate the rapid transformation from rural nomadism to modern, urban society which oil wealth has brought to parts of the continent. Asia's most economically dynamic countries, Japan, Singapore, South Korea, and Taiwan, fringe the Pacific Ocean and are known as the Pacific Rim. In contrast, other Southeast Asian countries like Laos and Cambodia remain both economically and industrially underdeveloped.

Standard of Living

DESPITE JAPAN'S HIGH STANDARDS OF LIVING, and Southwest Asia's oil-derived wealth, immense disparities exist across the continent. Afghanistan remains one of the world's most underdeveloped nations, as do the mountain states of Nepal and Bhutan. Further rapid population growth is exacerbating poverty and overcrowding in many parts of India and Bangladesh.

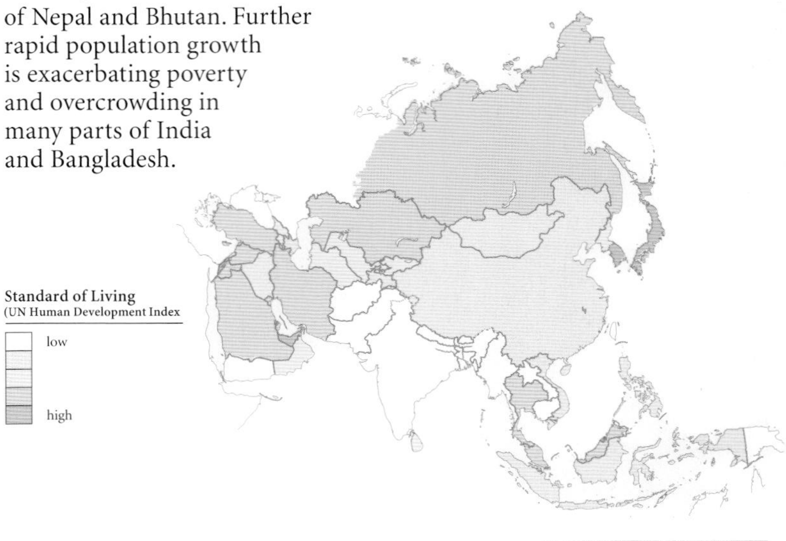

Industry

JAPANESE INDUSTRY LEADS THE CONTINENT in both productivity and efficiency; electronics, hi-tech industries, car manufacture and shipbuilding are important. In recent years, the so-called economic "tigers" of the Pacific Rim such as Taiwan and South Korea are now challenging Japan's economic dominance. Heavy industries such as engineering, chemicals, and steel typify the industrial complexes along the corridor created by the Trans-Siberian Railway, the Fergana Valley in Central Asia, and also much of the huge industrial plain of east China. The discovery of oil in the Persian Gulf has brought immense wealth to countries that previously relied on subsistence agriculture on marginal desert land.

On a small island at the southern tip of the Malay Peninsula lies Singapore, one of the Pacific Rim's most vibrant economic centers. Multinational banking and finance form the core of the city's wealth.

Iron and steel, engineering, and shipbuilding typify the heavy industry found in eastern China's industrial cities, especially the nation's leading manufacturing center, Shanghai.

Traditional industries are still crucial to many rural economies across Asia. Here, on the Vietnamese coast, salt has been extracted from seawater by evaporation and is being loaded into a van to take to market.

ENVIRONMENTAL ISSUES

THE TRANSFORMATION OF UZBEKISTAN by the former Soviet Union into the world's second largest producer of cotton led to the diversion of several major rivers for irrigation. Starved of this water, the Aral Sea diminished in volume by over 50% in 30 years, irreversibly altering the ecology of the area. Heavy industries in eastern China have polluted coastal waters, rivers, and urban air, while in Myanmar, Malaysia, and Indonesia, ancient hardwood rain forests are felled faster than they can regenerate.

***The long-term environmental** impact of the Gulf War (1991) is still uncertain. As Iraqi troops left Kuwait, equipment was abandoned to rust and thousands of oil wells were set alight, pouring crude oil into the Persian Gulf.*

***Although Siberia** remains a quintessentially frozen, inhospitable wasteland, vast untapped mineral reserves – especially the oil and gas of the West Siberian Plain – have lured industrial development to the area since the 1950s and 1960s.*

MINERAL RESOURCES

AT LEAST 60% OF THE WORLD'S known oil and gas deposits are found in Asia; notably the vast oil fields of the Persian Gulf, and the less-exploited oil and gas fields of the Ob' Basin in west Siberia. Immense coal reserves in Siberia and China have been utilized to support large steel industries. Southeast Asia has some of the world's largest deposits of tin, found in a belt running down the Malay Peninsula to Indonesia.

USING THE LAND AND SEA

VAST AREAS OF ASIA REMAIN UNCULTIVATED as a result of unsuitable climatic and soil conditions. In favorable areas such as river deltas, farming is intensive. Rice is the staple crop of most Asian countries, grown in paddy fields on waterlogged alluvial plains and terraced hillsides, and often irrigated for higher yields. Across the black earth region of the Eurasian steppe in southern Siberia and Kazakhstan, wheat farming is the dominant activity. Cash crops, like tea in Sri Lanka and dates in the Arabian Peninsula, are grown for export, and provide valuable income. The sovereignty of the rich fishing grounds in the South China Sea is disputed by China, Malaysia, Taiwan, the Philippines, and Vietnam, because of potential oil reserves.

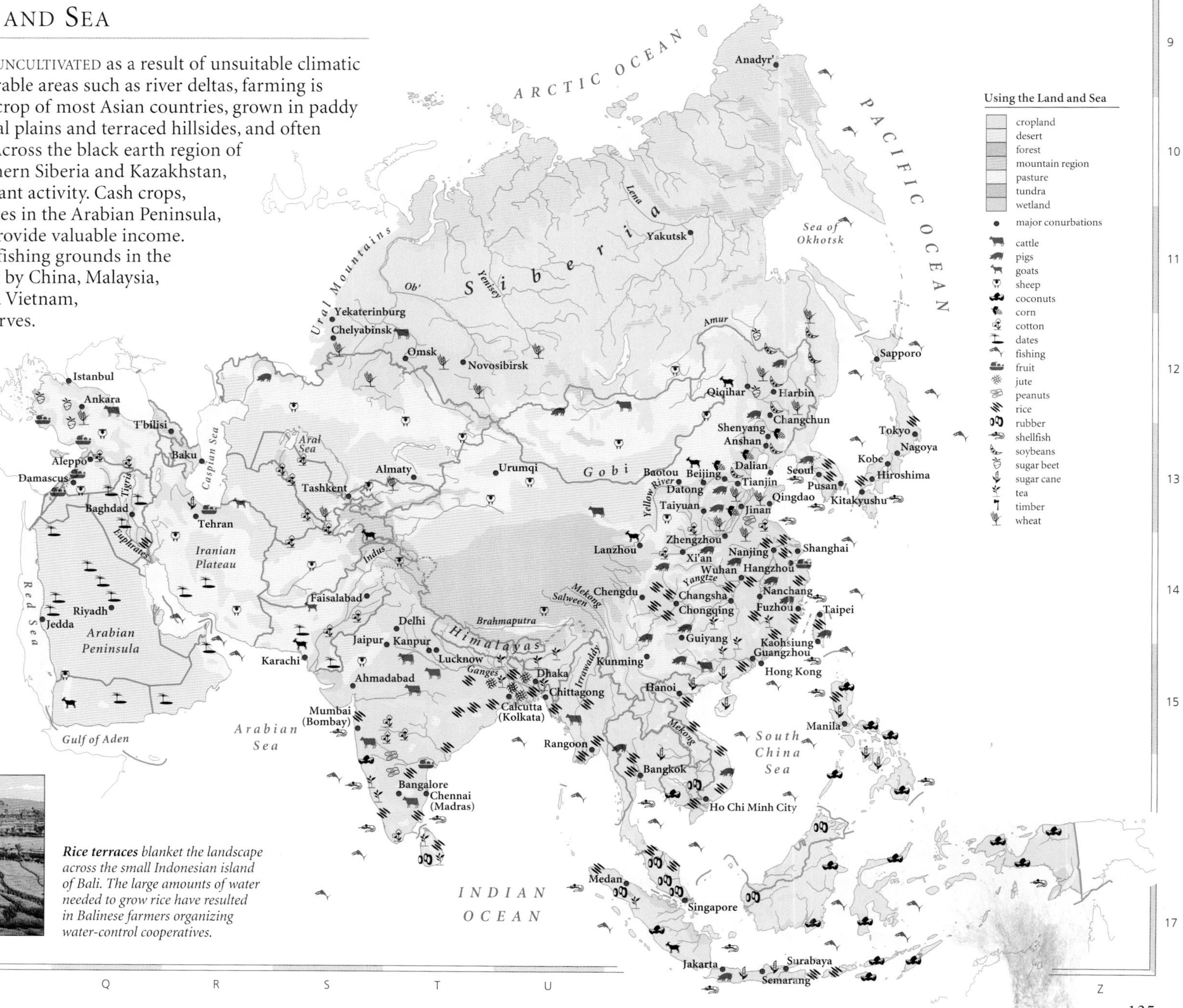

***Date palms** have been cultivated in oases throughout the Arabian Peninsula since antiquity. In addition to the fruit, palms are used for timber, fuel, rope, and for making vinegar, syrup, and a liquor known as arrack.*

***Rice terraces** blanket the landscape across the small Indonesian island of Bali. The large amounts of water needed to grow rice have resulted in Balinese farmers organizing water-control cooperatives.*

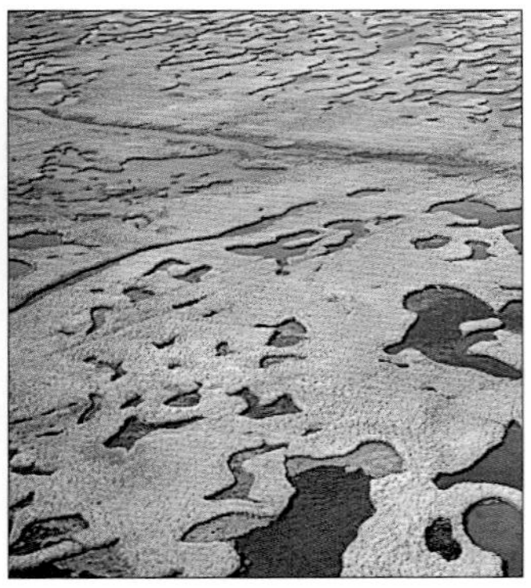

Siberian Plateau and Plain

The West Siberian Plain is one of the largest in the world, and contains a vast system of marshes. The whole area is covered by glacial deposits, underlain by the Angara Shield, a remnant of the ancient continent of Laurasia. The flat relief of the region and thick surface deposits result in poor drainage; this, combined with the freezing and thawing of the extensive permafrost layer leads to the formation of the vast swamps which cover the area. Many of the north-flowing rivers are also frozen for up to half the year.

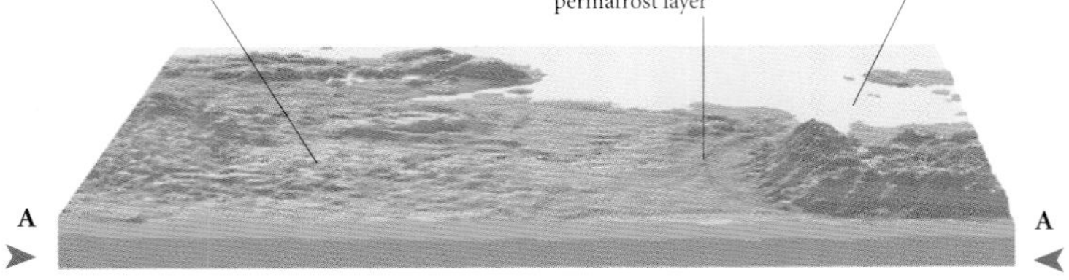

***Section** across Siberia showing the Central Siberian Plateau and its drainage.*

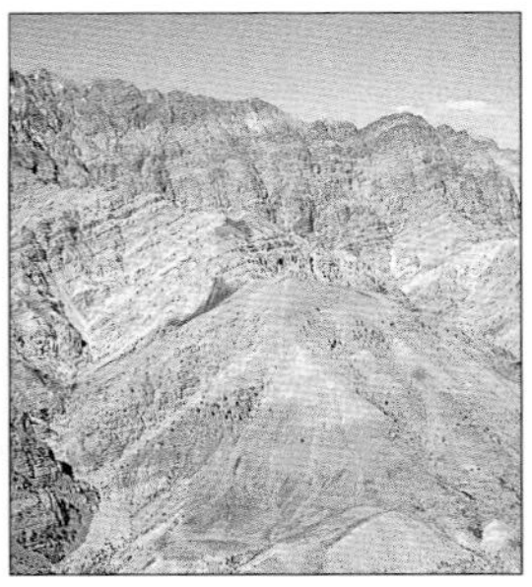

The Arabian Shield and Iranian Plateau

Approximately five million years ago, rifting of the continental crust split the Arabian Plate from the African Plate and flooded the Red Sea. As this rift spread, the Arabian Plate collided with the Eurasian Plate, transforming part of the Tethys seabed into the Zagros Mountains which run northwest-southeast across western Iran.

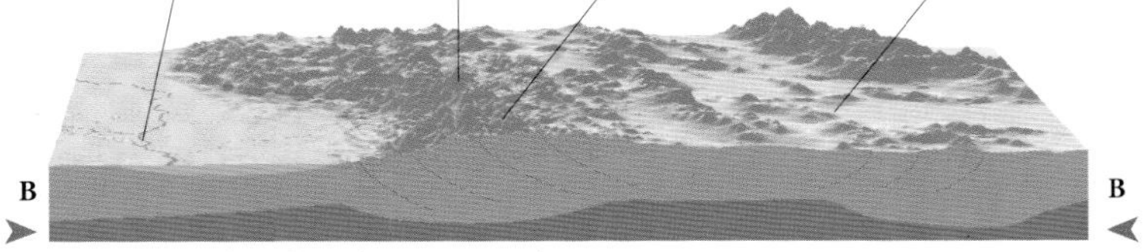

***Cross-section** through southwestern Asia, showing the Mesopotamian Depression, the folded Zagros Mountains, and the Iranian Plateau.*

The Turan Basin and Kazakh Uplands

The Turan Basin and Kazakh Uplands are a complex mixture of mountain foothills, an arid limestone plateau, and deserts including the Kyzl Kum and Kara Kum. In the center of the Turan Lowland – an area of inland drainage – is the desiccated Aral Sea, reduced to a fraction of its former size because of the diversion of its flow into irrigation channels. The only rivers with sufficient water to cross this arid region are the Syr Dayra and Amu Dayra.

The Indian Shield and Himalayan System

The large shield area beneath the Indian subcontinent is between 2.5 and 3.5 billion years old. As the floor of the southern Indian Ocean spread, it pushed the Indian Shield north. This was eventually driven beneath the Plateau of Tibet. This process closed up the ancient Tethys Sea and uplifted the world's highest mountain chain, the Himalayas. Much of the uplifted rock strata was from the seabed of the Tethys Sea, partly accounting for the weakness of the rocks and the high levels of erosion found in the Himalayas.

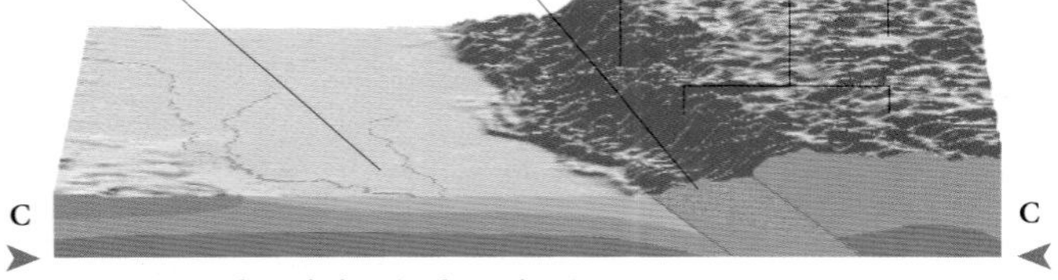

***Cross-section** through the Himalayas showing thrust faulting of the rock strata.*

Central Asian Plateaus and Basins

The Plateau of Tibet lies north of the Himalayas and covers 965,250 sq miles (2,500,000 sq km); its average elevation is 16,500 ft (5,000 m). The region is noted for its extreme aridity. In the south, the Himalayan mountain belt blocks moisture-bearing winds. The pressure from the Indo-Australian Plate against the plateau is causing both uplift and, when combined with the downward force caused by weight of the plateau, extension east and west of the of the more malleable underlying crust. The brittle upper rock layers are extensively faulted.

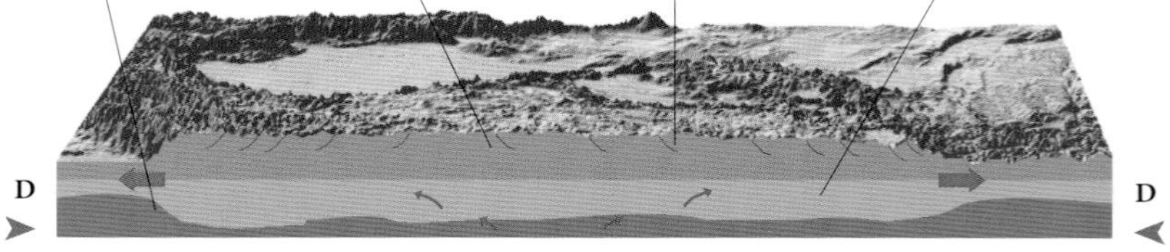

***Cross-section** across the Plateau of Tibet showing uplift and crustal extension caused by the collision of the Indo-Australian and Eurasian plates.*

PHYSICAL ASIA

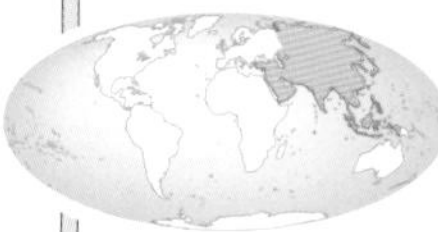

THE STRUCTURE OF ASIA can be divided into two distinct regions. The landscape of northern Asia consists of old mountain chains, shields, plateaus, and basins, like the Ural Mountains in the west and the Central Siberian Plateau to the east. To the south of this region, are a series of plateaux and basins, including the vast Plateau of Tibet and the Tarim Basin. In contrast, the landscapes of southern Asia are much younger, formed by tectonic activity beginning about 65 million years ago, leading to an almost continuous mountain chain running from Europe, across much of Asia, and culminating in the mighty Himalayan mountain belt, formed when the Indo-Australian Plate collided with the Eurasian Plate. They are still being uplifted today. North of the mountains lies a belt of deserts, including the Gobi and the Takla Makan. In the far south, tectonic activity has formed narrow island arcs, extending over 4,000 miles (7,000 km). To the west lies the Arabian Shield, once part of the African Plate. As it was rifted apart from Africa, the Arabian Plate collided with the Eurasian Plate, uplifting the Zagros Mountains.

SHAPING THE LANDSCAPE

IN THE NORTH, melting of extensive permafrost leads to typical periglacial features such as thermokarst. In the arid areas wind action transports sand creating extensive dune systems. An active tectonic margin in the south causes continued uplift, and volcanic and seismic activity, but also high rates of weathering and erosion. Across the continent, huge rivers erode and transport vast quantities of sediment depositing it on the plains or forming large deltas.

PERIGLACIATION

[1] Permafrost is widespread across northern Siberia. When ground ice, which makes up a large proportion of the soil layer, melts, it contracts and extensive ground subsidence occurs. Over time this process leads to depressions in the landscape and the gradual movement of soil down slopes. Eventually the accumulation of water in the depressions leads to thermokarstic lakes (left).

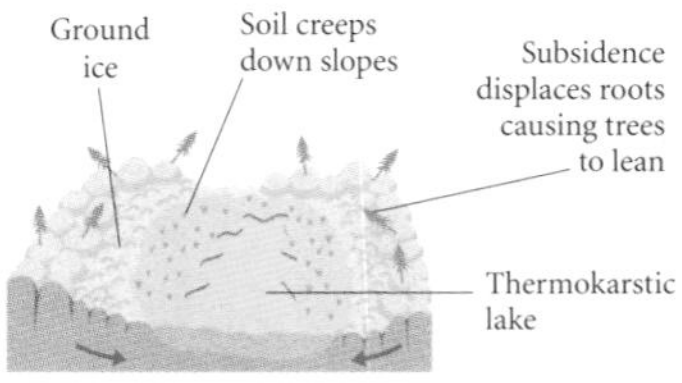

PERIGLACIATION: FORMATION OF THERMOKARST

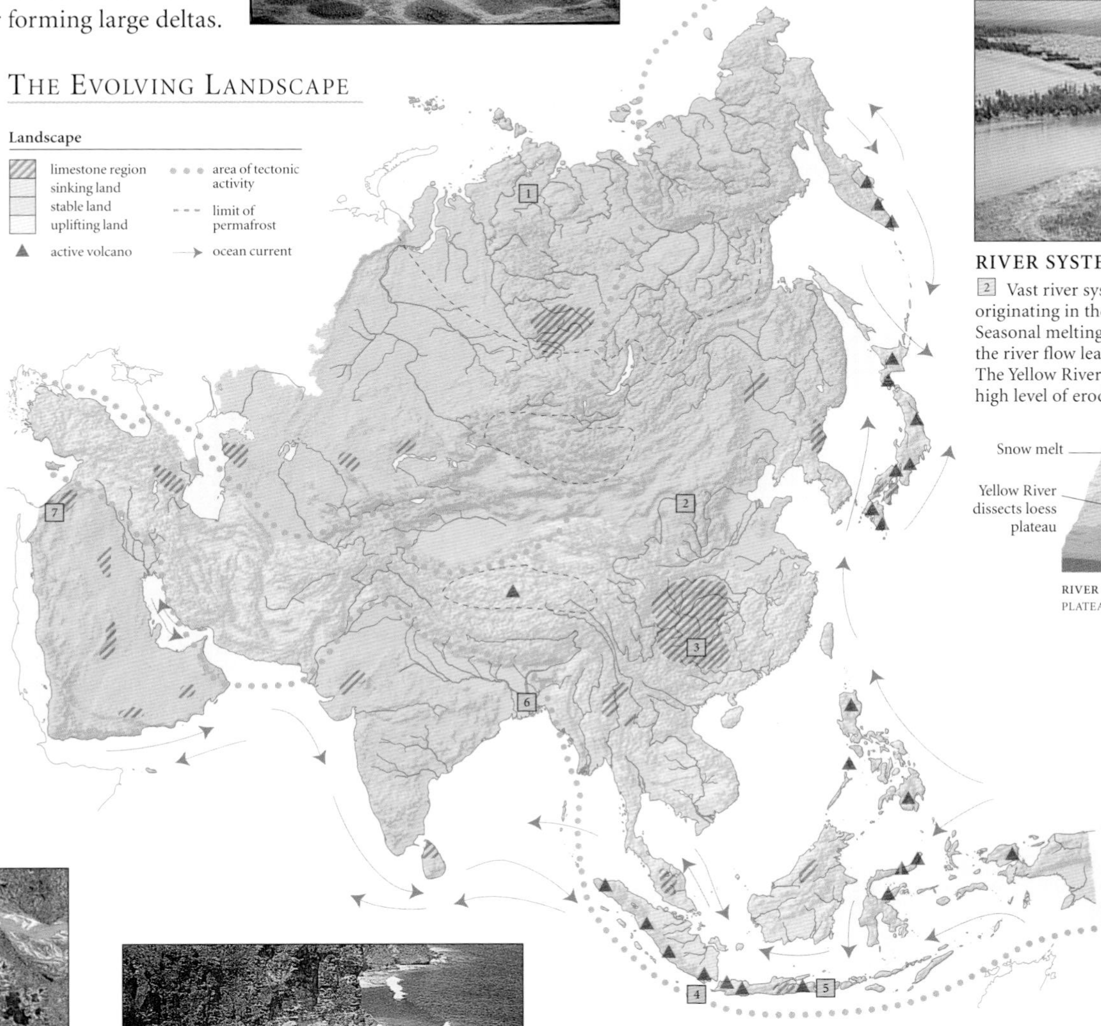

RIVER SYSTEMS

[2] Vast river systems flow across Asia, many originating in the Himalayas and the Plateau of Tibet. Seasonal melting of snow and monsoon rains swell the river flow leading to flooding and erosion. The Yellow River (above) gets its color from the high level of eroded material from the loess plateau.

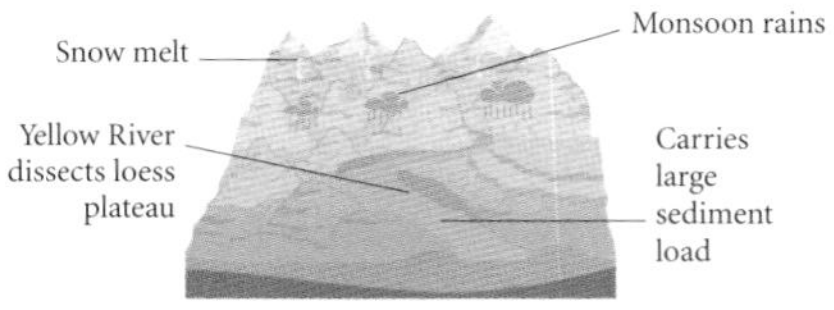

RIVER SYSTEMS: EROSION OF THE LOESS PLATEAU BY THE YELLOW RIVER

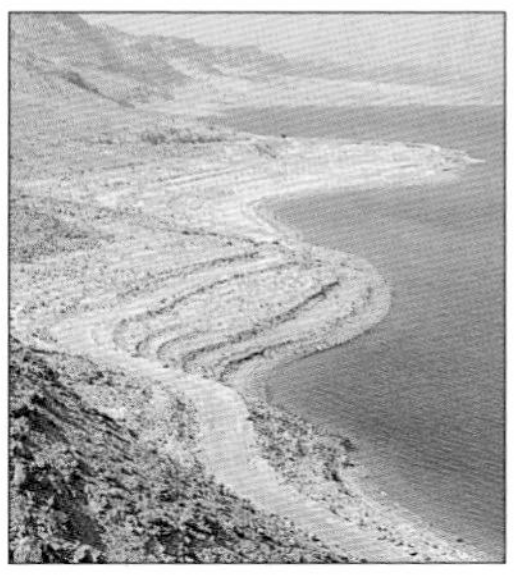

THE EVOLVING LANDSCAPE

Landscape

- limestone region
- sinking land
- stable land
- uplifting land
- ● ● ● area of tectonic activity
- – – – limit of permafrost
- ▲ active volcano
- → ocean current

TECTONIC ACTIVITY

[7] The Dead Sea (above) lies in a pull-apart basin. The sliding of the African Plate against the Arabian Plate, at unequal rates, led to the sinking of blocks of crust. This depression has been filled by the waters of the Dead Sea and Lake Tiberias (Sea of Galilee). The plates continue to move causing intermittent earthquakes.

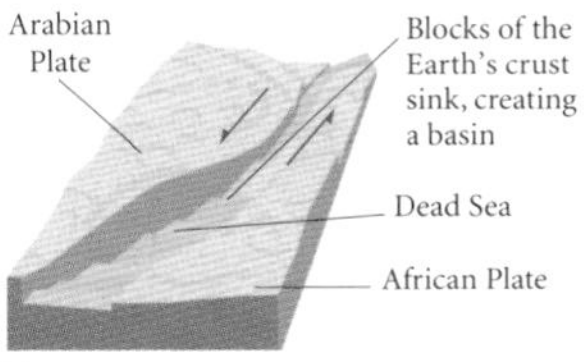

Arabian Plate

Blocks of the Earth's crust sink, creating a basin

Dead Sea

African Plate

TECTONIC ACTIVITY: THE FORMATION OF A PULL-APART BASIN

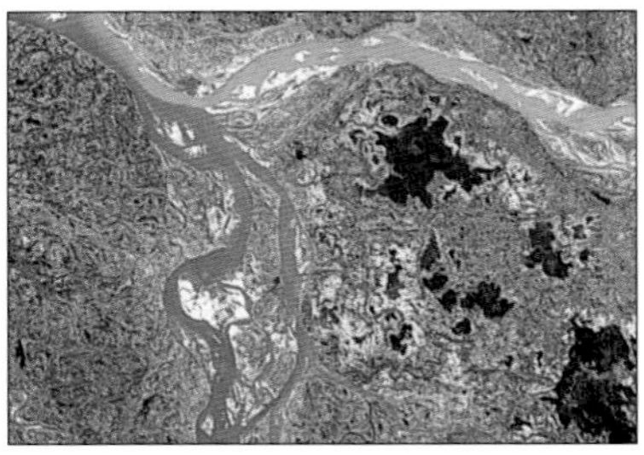

SEDIMENTATION

[6] The Ganges/Brahmaputra is a tide-dominated delta (above). The two rivers transport huge quantities of mountain sediment, which is deposited on the delta plain. This debris is then redistributed by tidal currents, to form extensions to the bars, beach ridges, and deltaic deposits.

Distributary channels

Ganges/Brahmaputra River

Delta plain

Redistributed sediment

Sea level at high tide

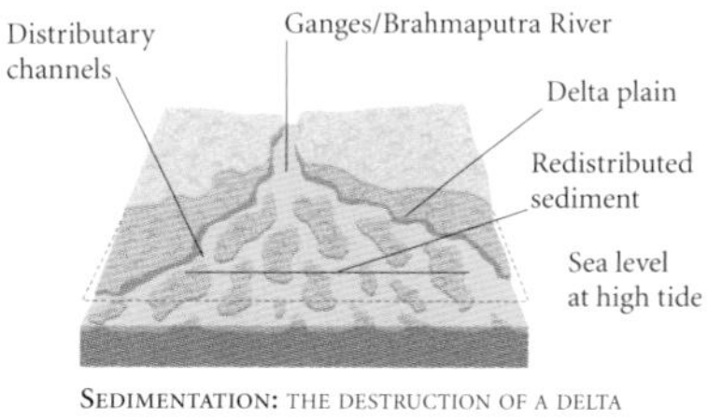

SEDIMENTATION: THE DESTRUCTION OF A DELTA

COASTAL EROSION

[5] The erosion of cliffs along the coast of Indonesia (above) and Thailand occurs when waves and currents undermine the base leading to collapse of material. The surf then gradually erodes this material away, exposing the cliff to further undercutting. This process eventually creates shore platforms.

Undercutting by sea waves

Collapsed debris is eventually transported away by the surf

Shore platform showing how far cliffs have been eroded back

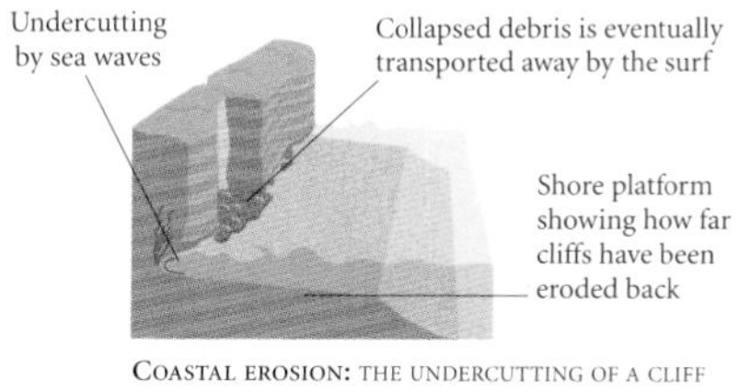

COASTAL EROSION: THE UNDERCUTTING OF A CLIFF

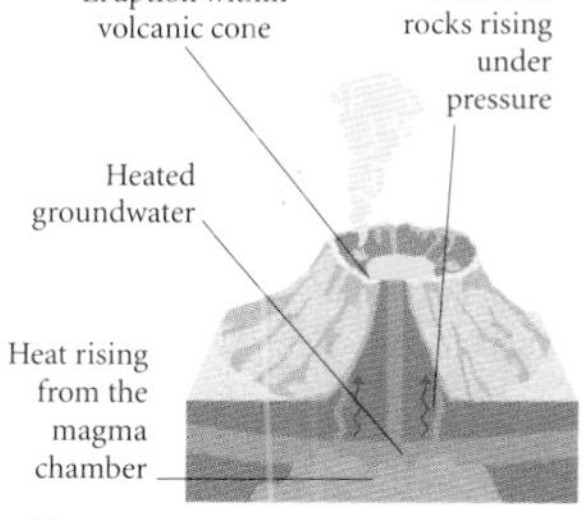

VOLCANIC ACTIVITY

[4] Volcanic eruptions occur frequently across Southeast Asia's island arcs (above). Low-level eruptions occur when groundwater, superheated by underlying magma, becomes pressurized, forcing hot fluid and rocks up through cracks in the volcanic cone. This is known as a phreatic eruption.

Eruption within volcanic cone

Fluid and rocks rising under pressure

Heated groundwater

Heat rising from the magma chamber

VOLCANIC ACTIVITY: A PHREATIC ERUPTION

CHEMICAL WEATHERING

[3] Tower karsts are widespread across south China (above) and Vietnam. It is thought the karstic towers were formed under a soil cover, where small depressions in the limestone bedrock began to be weathered by soil water acids, eventually creating larger hollows. This process continued over millions of years, deepening the hollows and leaving steep-sided limestone hills.

Limestone hills

Old soil cover

Hollow being eroded by soil water acidity

Eroded hollow

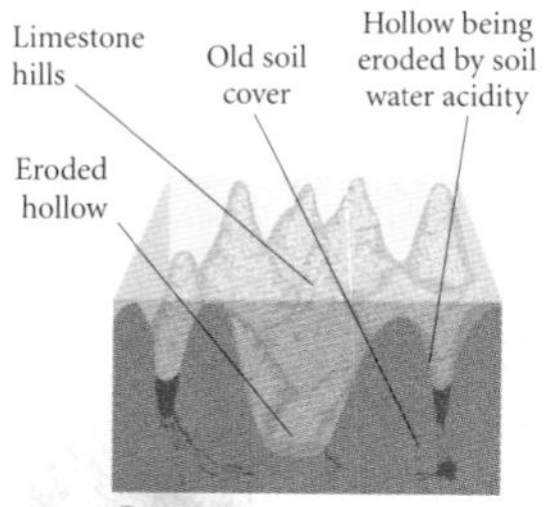

CHEMICAL WEATHERING: FORMATION OF TOWER KARST

Political Asia

Asia is the world's largest continent, encompassing many different and discrete realms, from the desert Arab lands of the southwest to the subtropical archipelago of Indonesia; from the vast barren wastes of Siberia to the fertile river valleys of China and South Asia, seats of some of the world's most ancient civilizations. The collapse of the Soviet Union has fragmented the north of the continent into the Siberian portion of the Russian Federation, and the new republics of Central Asia. Strong religious traditions heavily influence the politics of South and Southwest Asia. Hindu and Muslim rivalries threaten to upset the political equilibrium in South Asia where India – in terms of population – remains the world's largest democracy. Communist China is the last great world empire; a population giant, but still relatively closed to the western world, while on its doorstep, the economically progressive and dynamic Pacific Rim countries, led by Japan, continue to assert their worldwide economic force.

Population

Some of the world's most populous and least populous regions are in Asia. The plains of eastern China, the Ganges River in India, Japan, and the Indonesian island of Java, all have very high population densities; by contrast parts of Siberia and the Plateau of Tibet are virtually uninhabited. China has the world's greatest population – 20% of the globe's total – while India, with the second largest, is likely to overtake China within 20 years.

Calcutta's 12 million inhabitants bustle through a maze of crowded, narrow streets. Population densities in India's largest city reach almost 85,000 per sq mile (33,000 per sq km).

Population density (people per sq mile)

- below 25
- 26–124
- 125–259
- 260–649
- 650–10,400
- above 10,400

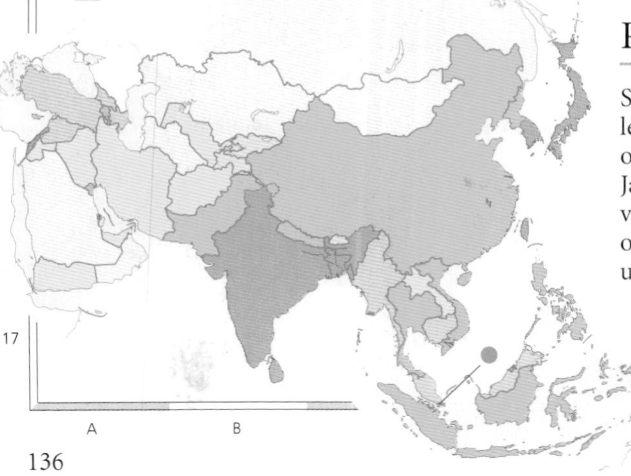

LANGUAGES

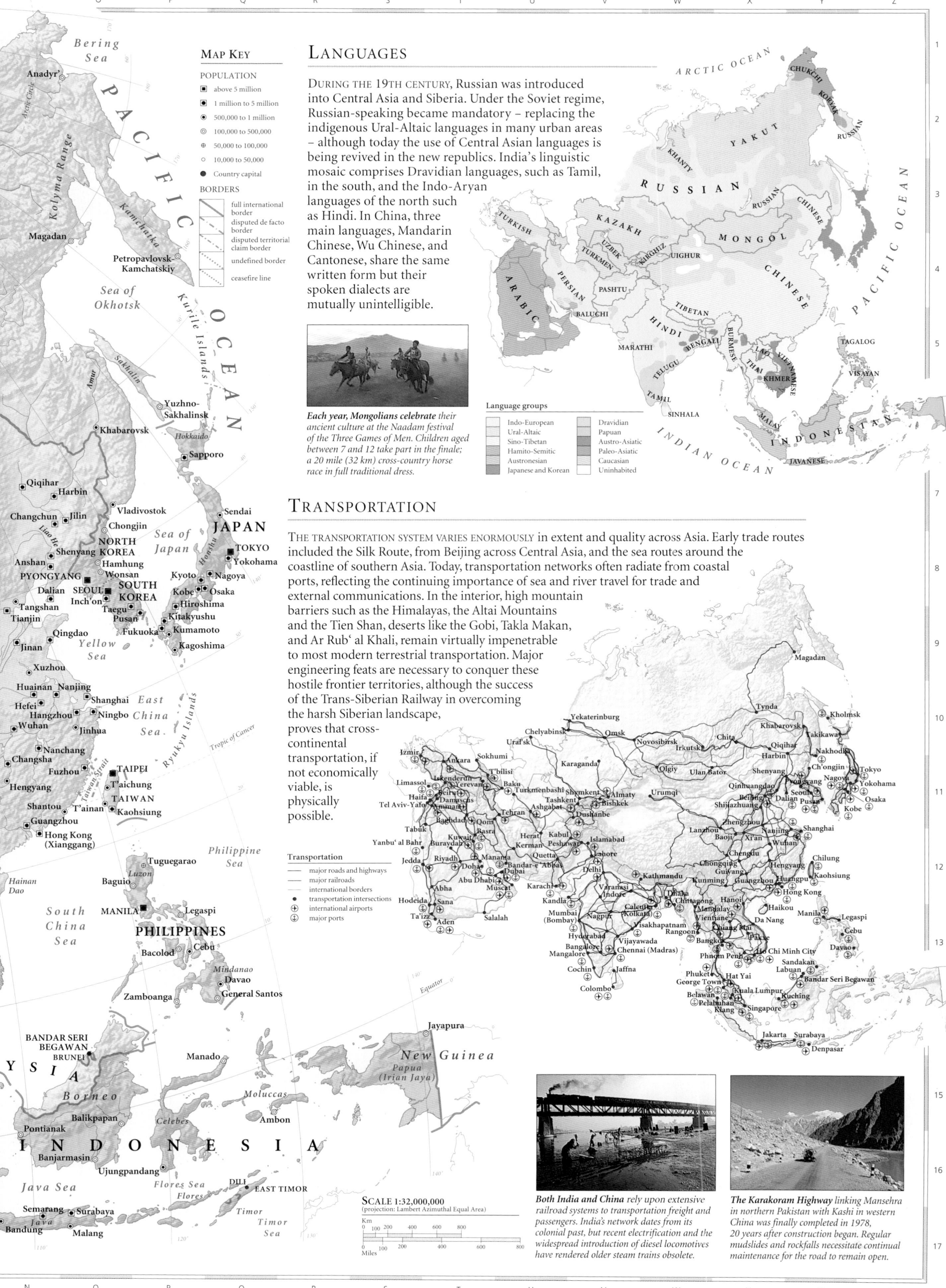

DURING THE 19TH CENTURY, Russian was introduced into Central Asia and Siberia. Under the Soviet regime, Russian-speaking became mandatory – replacing the indigenous Ural-Altaic languages in many urban areas – although today the use of Central Asian languages is being revived in the new republics. India's linguistic mosaic comprises Dravidian languages, such as Tamil, in the south, and the Indo-Aryan languages of the north such as Hindi. In China, three main languages, Mandarin Chinese, Wu Chinese, and Cantonese, share the same written form but their spoken dialects are mutually unintelligible.

Each year, Mongolians celebrate their ancient culture at the Naadam festival of the Three Games of Men. Children aged between 7 and 12 take part in the finale; a 20 mile (32 km) cross-country horse race in full traditional dress.

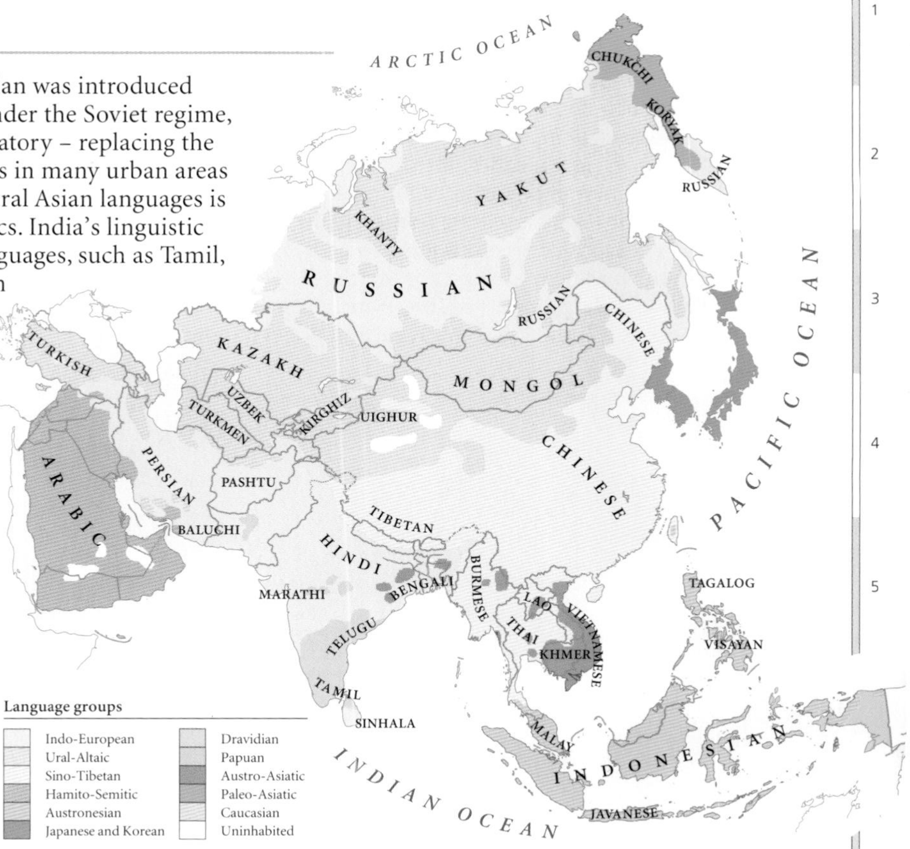

TRANSPORTATION

THE TRANSPORTATION SYSTEM VARIES ENORMOUSLY in extent and quality across Asia. Early trade routes included the Silk Route, from Beijing across Central Asia, and the sea routes around the coastline of southern Asia. Today, transportation networks often radiate from coastal ports, reflecting the continuing importance of sea and river travel for trade and external communications. In the interior, high mountain barriers such as the Himalayas, the Altai Mountains and the Tien Shan, deserts like the Gobi, Takla Makan, and Ar Rub' al Khali, remain virtually impenetrable to most modern terrestrial transportation. Major engineering feats are necessary to conquer these hostile frontier territories, although the success of the Trans-Siberian Railway in overcoming the harsh Siberian landscape, proves that cross-continental transportation, if not economically viable, is physically possible.

***Both India and China** rely upon extensive railroad systems to transportation freight and passengers. India's network dates from its colonial past, but recent electrification and the widespread introduction of diesel locomotives have rendered older steam trains obsolete.*

***The Karakoram Highway** linking Mansehra in northern Pakistan with Kashi in western China was finally completed in 1978, 20 years after construction began. Regular mudslides and rockfalls necessitate continual maintenance for the road to remain open.*

SCALE 1:32,000,000
(projection: Lambert Azimuthal Equal Area)

U Uu V Vv W Ww X Xx Y Yy Z Zz

Climate

The climate of Asia exhibits marked differences from region to region, with freezing polar conditions in the north, hot and cold deserts in central regions and subtropical conditions throughout the south. Much of this variation can be attributed to enormous mountain barriers and internal depressions found across the continent. Monsoon winds, which reverse semiannually, cause alternate wet and dry seasons across southern Asia. These air masses moving north from the ocean are stripped of their moisture over the Himalayas causing arid conditions across the Plateau of Tibet. Both the south and east are susceptible to tropical cyclones or typhoons.

Treeless, frozen plains, *with permanently frozen soil layers characterize much of Siberia. Even during the summer only the top 2–3 ft (1 m) of soil thaws.*

Tundra-like marshes *are found alongside vast sand dunes in the Takla Makan Desert in China. In the spring, windstorms of hurricane-force can send dust as high as 13,000 ft (4,000 m) in the air.*

The Gobi Desert *experiences major extremes in climate, with winter temperatures sometimes falling below -40°C (-40°F) and summer temperatures exceeding 45°C (113°F).*

Climate
- tundra
- subarctic
- cool continental
- warm humid
- mediterranean
- semiarid
- arid
- humid equatorial
- tropical
- daily hours of sunshine, January
- daily hours of sunshine, July
- cyclone
- typhoon
- cold/dry monsoon
- warm/wet monsoon
- cold wind

Temperature

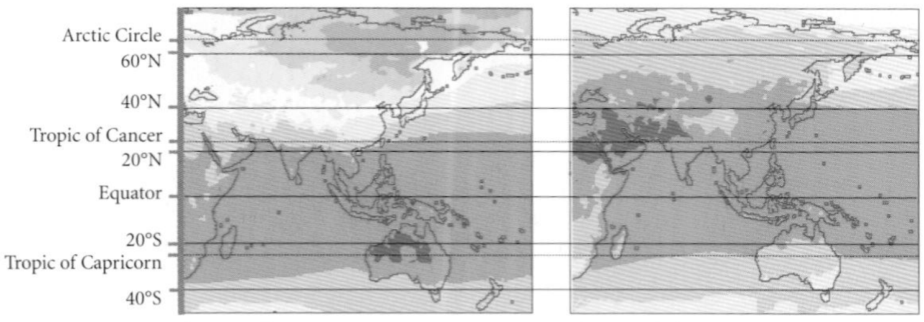

Average January temperature *Average July temperature*

Temperature
- below -22°F (-30°C)
- -22 to -4°F (-30 to -20°C)
- -4 to 14°F (-20 to -10°C)
- 14 to 32°F (-10 to 0°C)
- 32 to 50° F (0 to 10°C)
- 50°F (10 to 20°C)
- 68 to 86°F (20 to 30°C)
- above 86 °F (30°C)

Tropical cyclones *occur principally during late summer and early autumn. The intense winds and heavy rainfall can devastate entire villages.*

Through India, *the southwest monsoon, which brings heavy rainfall from May to September, accounts for 80% of annual precipitation.*

Rainfall

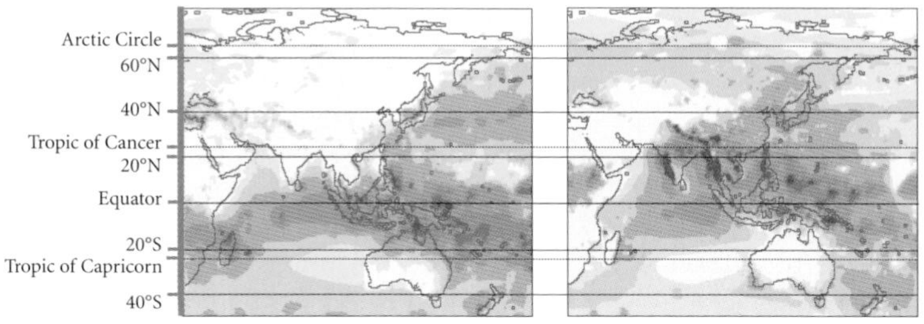

Average January rainfall *Average July rainfall*

Rainfall
- 0–1 in (0–25 mm)
- 1–2 in (25–50 mm)
- 2–4 in (50–100 mm)
- 4–8 in (100–200 mm)
- 8–12 in (200–300 mm)
- 12–16 in (300–400 mm)
- 16–20 in (400–500 mm)
- more than 20 in (500 mm)

U Uu V Vv W Ww X Xx Y Yy Z Zz

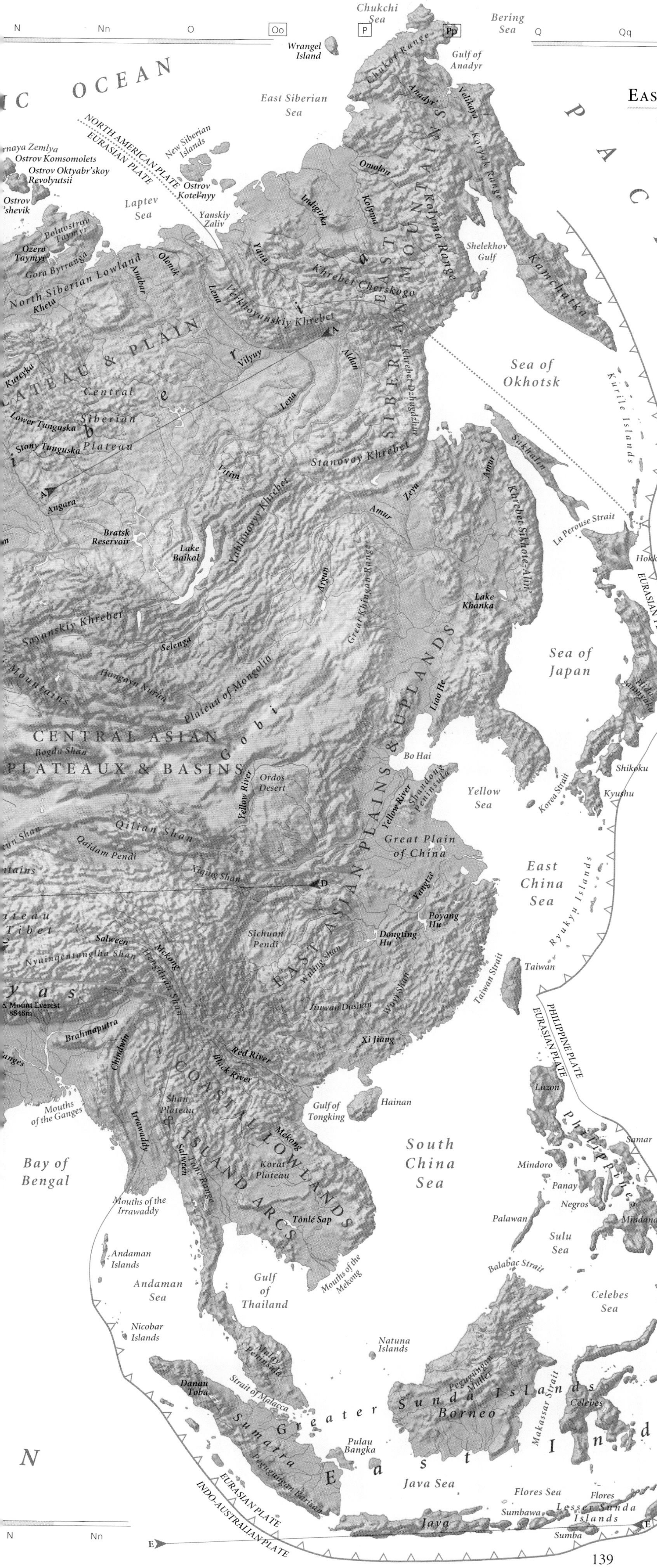

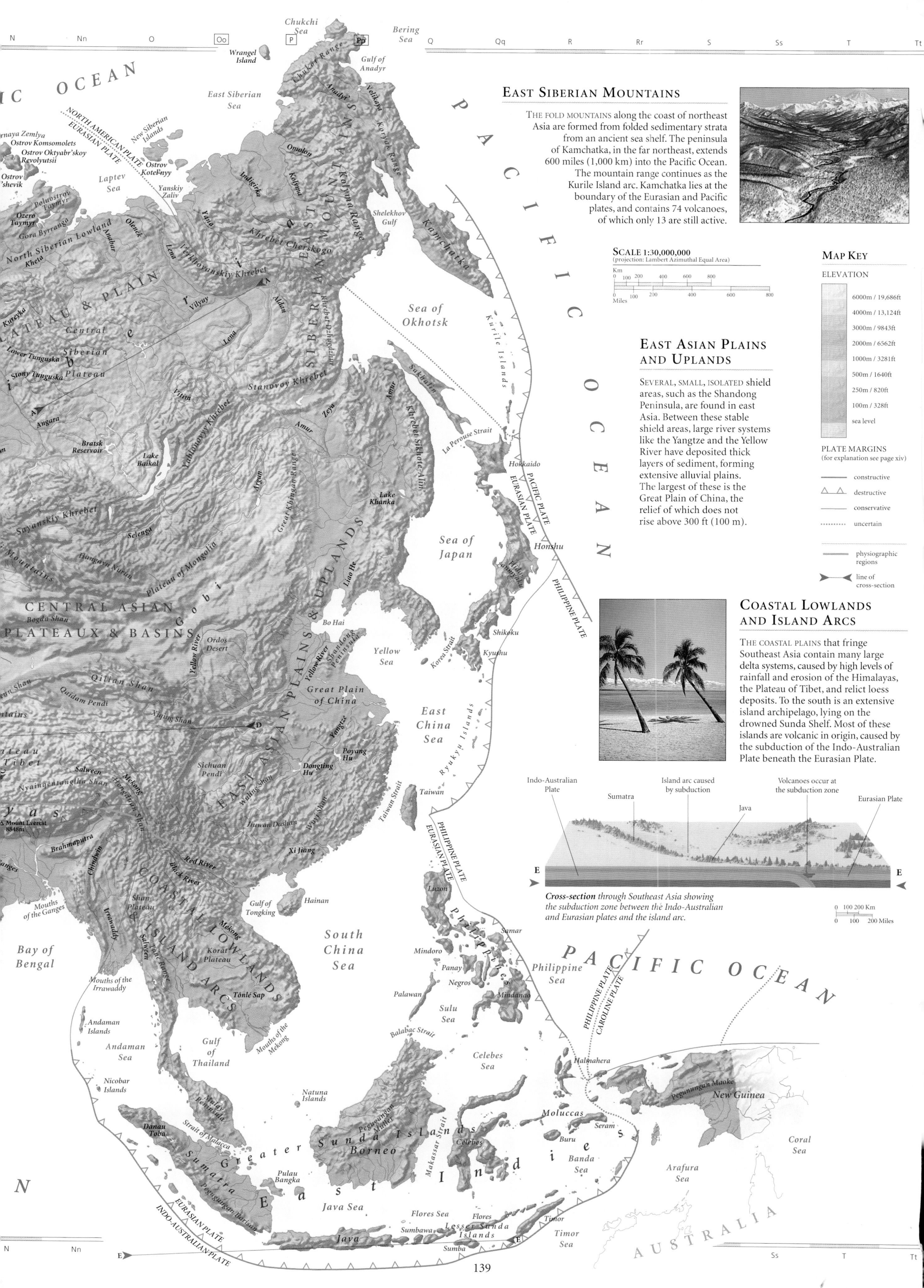

East Siberian Mountains

The fold mountains along the coast of northeast Asia are formed from folded sedimentary strata from an ancient sea shelf. The peninsula of Kamchatka, in the far northeast, extends 600 miles (1,000 km) into the Pacific Ocean. The mountain range continues as the Kurile Island arc. Kamchatka lies at the boundary of the Eurasian and Pacific plates, and contains 74 volcanoes, of which only 13 are still active.

Scale 1:30,000,000
(projection: Lambert Azimuthal Equal Area)

Km 0 100 200 400 600 800
Miles 0 100 200 400 600 800

Map Key

ELEVATION

- 6000m / 19,686ft
- 4000m / 13,124ft
- 3000m / 9843ft
- 2000m / 6562ft
- 1000m / 3281ft
- 500m / 1640ft
- 250m / 820ft
- 100m / 328ft
- sea level

PLATE MARGINS
(for explanation see page xiv)

- constructive
- destructive
- conservative
- uncertain
- physiographic regions
- line of cross-section

East Asian Plains and Uplands

Several, small, isolated shield areas, such as the Shandong Peninsula, are found in east Asia. Between these stable shield areas, large river systems like the Yangtze and the Yellow River have deposited thick layers of sediment, forming extensive alluvial plains. The largest of these is the Great Plain of China, the relief of which does not rise above 300 ft (100 m).

Coastal Lowlands and Island Arcs

The coastal plains that fringe Southeast Asia contain many large delta systems, caused by high levels of rainfall and erosion of the Himalayas, the Plateau of Tibet, and relict loess deposits. To the south is an extensive island archipelago, lying on the drowned Sunda Shelf. Most of these islands are volcanic in origin, caused by the subduction of the Indo-Australian Plate beneath the Eurasian Plate.

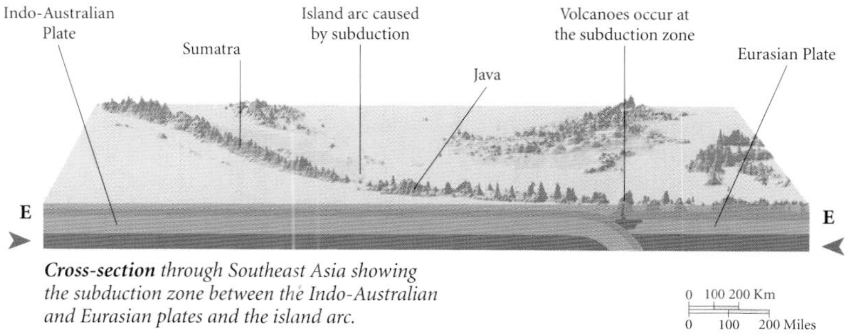

***Cross-section** through Southeast Asia showing the subduction zone between the Indo-Australian and Eurasian plates and the island arc.*

TURKEY & THE CAUCASUS

ARMENIA, AZERBAIJAN, GEORGIA, TURKEY

THIS REGION OCCUPIES THE FRAGMENTED JUNCTION between Europe, Asia, and the Russian Federation. Sunni Islam provides a common identity for the secular state of Turkey, which the revered leader Kemal Atatürk established from the remnants of the Ottoman Empire after the First World War. Turkey has a broad resource base and expanding trade links with Europe, but the east is relatively undeveloped and strife between the state and a large Kurdish minority has yet to be resolved. Georgia is similarly challenged by ethnic separatism, while the Christian state of Armenia and the mainly Muslim and oil-rich Azerbaijan are locked in conflict over the territory of Nagornyy Karabakh.

TRANSPORTATION & INDUSTRY

TURKEY LEADS THE REGION'S well-diversified economy. Petrochemicals, textiles, engineering, and food processing are the main industries. Azerbaijan is able to export oil, while the other states rely heavily on hydro-electric power and imported fuel. Georgia produces precision machinery. War and earthquake damage have devastated Armenia's infrastructure.

***Azerbaijan** has substantial oil reserves, located in and around the Caspian Sea. They were some of the earliest oilfields in the world to be exploited.*

Major industry and infrastructure

- carpet weaving
- cement
- chemicals
- coal
- engineering
- food processing
- oil
- textiles
- tourism
- vehicle manufacture
- capital cities
- major towns
- international airports
- major roads
- major industrial areas

TRANSPORTATION NETWORK

	76,289 miles (122,849 km)
	7,74 miles (1,246 km)
	9,047 miles (14,569 km)
	745 miles (1,200 km)

Physical and political barriers have severely limited communications between Armenia, Georgia and Azerbaijan. Turkey has a relatively well-developed transportation network.

USING THE LAND AND SEA

TURKEY IS LARGELY SELF-SUFFICIENT in food. The irrigated Black Sea coastlands have the world's highest yields of hazelnuts. Tobacco, cotton, sultanas, tea, and figs are the region's main cash crops and a great range of fruit and vegetables are grown. Wine grapes are among the labor-intensive crops which allow full use of limited agricultural land in the Caucasus. Sturgeon fishing is particularly important in Azerbaijan.

Land use and agricultural distribution

- cattle
- goats
- cotton
- fishing
- fruit
- hazelnuts
- olives
- sugar beet
- tobacco
- vineyards
- capital cities
- major towns
- pasture
- cropland
- forest

THE URBAN/RURAL POPULATION DIVIDE

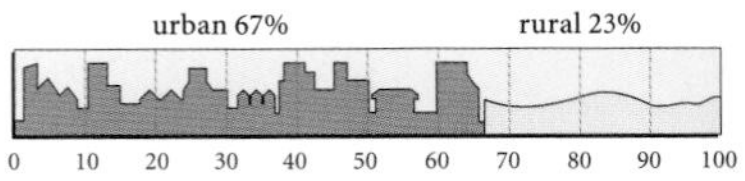

POPULATION DENSITY	TOTAL LAND AREA
218 people per sq mile (84 people per sq km)	368,912 sq miles (955,730 sq km)

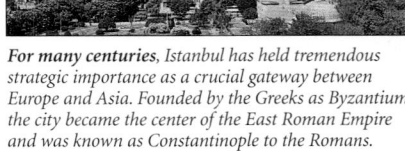

***For many centuries**, Istanbul has held tremendous strategic importance as a crucial gateway between Europe and Asia. Founded by the Greeks as Byzantium, the city became the center of the East Roman Empire and was known as Constantinople to the Romans. From the 15th century onward the city became the center of the great Ottoman Empire.*

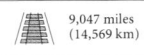

THE LANDSCAPE

THE DEEPLY ERODED HILLS and salty basins of the Anatolian Plateau are bordered by several mountain ranges along the Black Sea coast, and the limestone Taurus Mountains (*Toros Dağlari*) in the south. A lowland trough divides the Caucasus and the Lesser Caucasus, which form a formidable barrier of peaks in the north.

Limestone weathering in the Anatolian Plateau

Eroded gully — High plateau
Remnant landforms
Layers of tephra

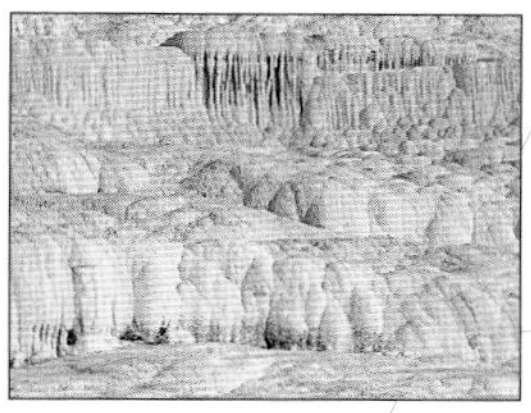

In central Turkey, rainwater has chemically weathered away numerous layers of limestone, leaving isolated outcrops and pinnacles and deep eroded gullies.

The Caucasus are fold mountains, which formed around the same time as the Taurus Mountains (*Toros Dağlari*) around 65 million years ago and have since been modified by volcanic erruptions.

The white rock terraces at Pamukkale in western Turkey were formed when underground water, heated by volcanic activity, dissolved minerals in the rocks. When the water reached the surface and evaporated the minerals were left behind in these extraordinary formations.

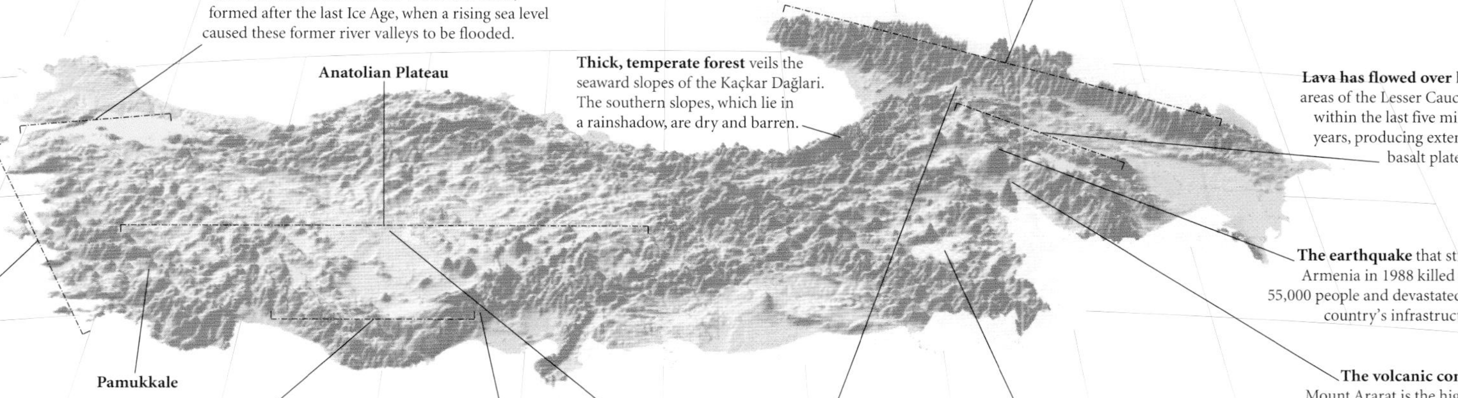

The straits of the Bosporus and the Dardanelles, respectively linking the Black and Mediterranean seas with the Sea of Marmara, formed after the last Ice Age, when a rising sea level caused these former river valleys to be flooded.

Anatolian Plateau

Thick, temperate forest veils the seaward slopes of the Kaçkar Dağlari. The southern slopes, which lie in a rainshadow, are dry and barren.

Lava has flowed over large areas of the Lesser Caucasus within the last five million years, producing extensive basalt plateaus.

The earthquake that struck Armenia in 1988 killed over 55,000 people and devastated the country's infrastructure.

Long, parallel mountain ranges run from east to west into the Aegean Sea, which has risen since the last Ice Age to form a drowned coastline of numerous islands and extended inlets.

Pamukkale

The volcanic cone of Mount Ararat is the highest peak in Turkey, with an altitude of 16,853 ft (5,137 m).

MAP KEY

POPULATION

- ■ above 5 million
- ■ 1 million to 5 million
- ◉ 500,000 to 1 million
- ◎ 100,000 to 500,000
- ⊕ 50,000 to 100,000
- ○ 10,000 to 50,000
- ○ below 10,000

ELEVATION

- 4000m / 13,124ft
- 3000m / 9843ft
- 2000m / 6562ft
- 1000m / 3281ft
- 500m / 1640ft
- 250m / 820ft
- 100m / 328ft
- sea level

The folded peaks of the Taurus Mountains (*Toros Dağlari*) were formed 60–65 million years ago, at the same time as the Alps. The rock is mainly limestone, with deep caves, gorges, and underground rivers.

The Cilician Gates (*Gülek Boğazi*), a major pass through the Taurus Mountains (*Toros Dağlari*), is the point where streams flow from the interior plateau onto the lowland of Adana.

Many of the rivers crossing the Anatolian Plateau never reach the sea, but drain into salt marshes and shallow salt lakes such as Lake Tuz (*Tuz Gölü*), where much of the water is lost to evaporation.

The granite massif near Suram divides the lowlands of Georgia from the oil-rich basin of Azerbaijan's Kura River, which has built a large delta into the Caspian Sea.

The shallow, saline Lake Van (*Van Gölü*) is the largest lake in Turkey. Dry terraces mark a previous shoreline 181 ft (55 m) above the present water level.

Since the 6th century BC, the pinnacles and caves of east-central Anatolia have been utilized as dwellings. Many are still inhabited today.

SCALE 1:4,000,000
(projection: Lambert Conformal Conic)

Km
0 10 20 40 60 80 100 120

Miles
0 20 40 60 80 100 120

The fisheries of Azerbaijan are noted for their hauls of sturgeon, and the Caspian Sea accounts for 80% of the world's total catch. Sturgeon roe is used to make internationally-famed caviar.

Traditional steam baths are found throughout the region, and are used for socializing as well as for bathing.

The Near East

Iraq, Israel, Jordan, Lebanon, Syria

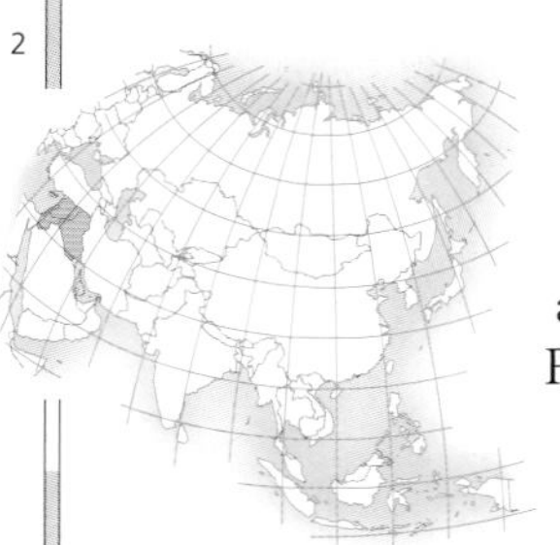

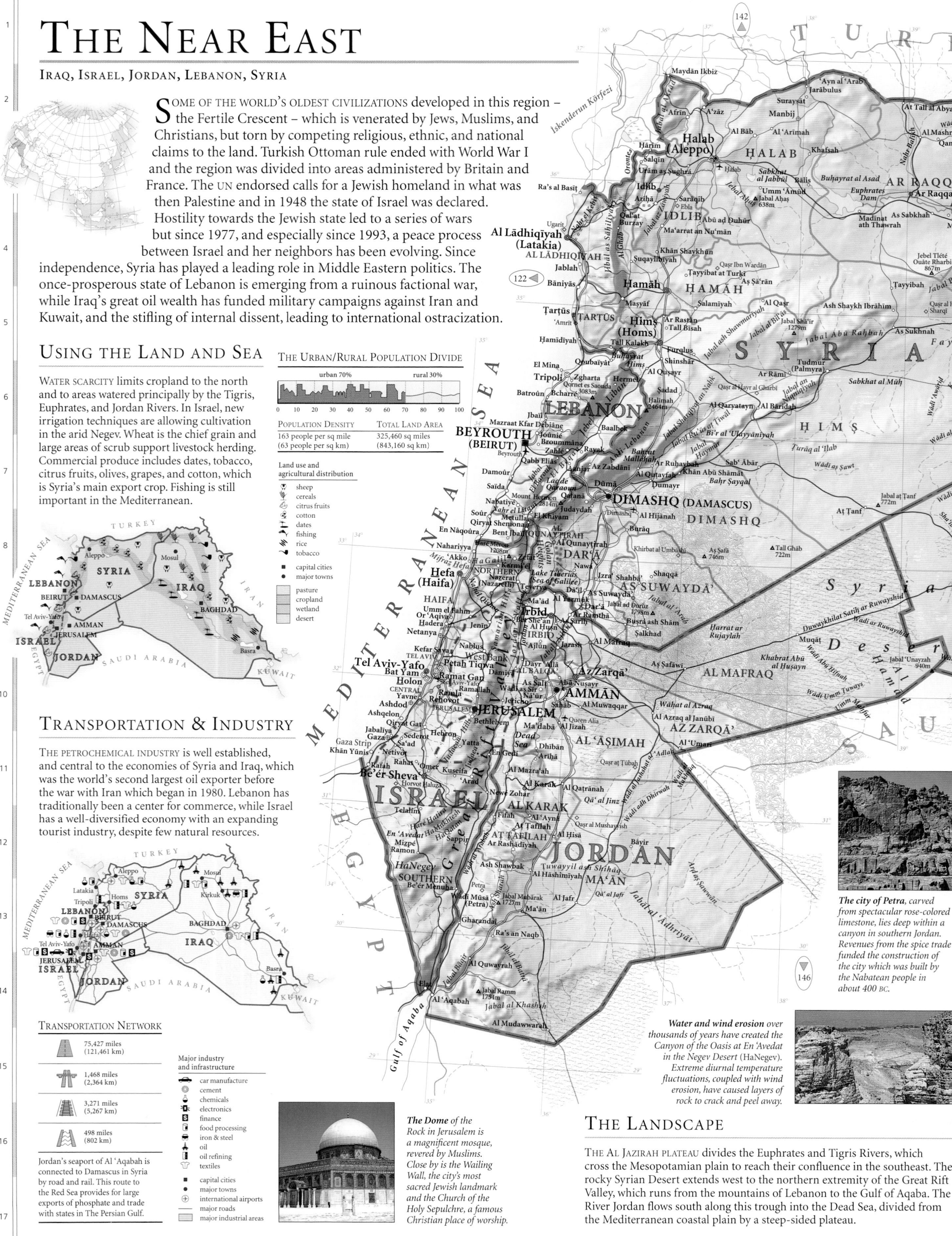

Some of the world's oldest civilizations developed in this region – the Fertile Crescent – which is venerated by Jews, Muslims, and Christians, but torn by competing religious, ethnic, and national claims to the land. Turkish Ottoman rule ended with World War I and the region was divided into areas administered by Britain and France. The UN endorsed calls for a Jewish homeland in what was then Palestine and in 1948 the state of Israel was declared. Hostility towards the Jewish state led to a series of wars but since 1977, and especially since 1993, a peace process between Israel and her neighbors has been evolving. Since independence, Syria has played a leading role in Middle Eastern politics. The once-prosperous state of Lebanon is emerging from a ruinous factional war, while Iraq's great oil wealth has funded military campaigns against Iran and Kuwait, and the stifling of internal dissent, leading to international ostracization.

Using the Land and Sea

Water scarcity limits cropland to the north and to areas watered principally by the Tigris, Euphrates, and Jordan Rivers. In Israel, new irrigation techniques are allowing cultivation in the arid Negev. Wheat is the chief grain and large areas of scrub support livestock herding. Commercial produce includes dates, tobacco, citrus fruits, olives, grapes, and cotton, which is Syria's main export crop. Fishing is still important in the Mediterranean.

The Urban/Rural Population Divide

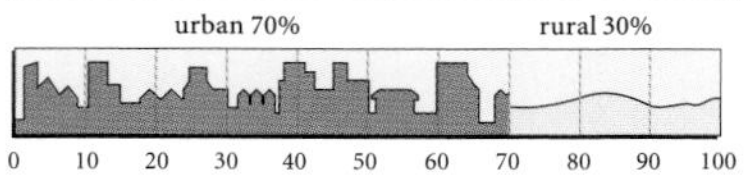

Population Density	Total Land Area
163 people per sq mile (63 people per sq km)	325,460 sq miles (843,160 sq km)

Land use and agricultural distribution
- sheep
- cereals
- citrus fruits
- cotton
- dates
- fishing
- rice
- tobacco
- capital cities
- major towns
- pasture
- cropland
- wetland
- desert

Transportation & Industry

The petrochemical industry is well established, and central to the economies of Syria and Iraq, which was the world's second largest oil exporter before the war with Iran which began in 1980. Lebanon has traditionally been a center for commerce, while Israel has a well-diversified economy with an expanding tourist industry, despite few natural resources.

Transportation Network

75,427 miles (121,461 km)	
1,468 miles (2,364 km)	
3,271 miles (5,267 km)	
498 miles (802 km)	

Jordan's seaport of Al 'Aqabah is connected to Damascus in Syria by road and rail. This route to the Red Sea provides for large exports of phosphate and trade with states in The Persian Gulf.

Major industry and infrastructure
- car manufacture
- cement
- chemicals
- electronics
- finance
- food processing
- iron & steel
- oil
- oil refining
- textiles
- capital cities
- major towns
- international airports
- major roads
- major industrial areas

The Dome of the Rock in Jerusalem is a magnificent mosque, revered by Muslims. Close by is the Wailing Wall, the city's most sacred Jewish landmark and the Church of the Holy Sepulchre, a famous Christian place of worship.

***The city of Petra**, carved from spectacular rose-colored limestone, lies deep within a canyon in southern Jordan. Revenues from the spice trade funded the construction of the city which was built by the Nabatean people in about 400 BC.*

***Water and wind erosion** over thousands of years have created the Canyon of the Oasis at En 'Avedat in the Negev Desert (HaNegev). Extreme diurnal temperature fluctuations, coupled with wind erosion, have caused layers of rock to crack and peel away.*

The Landscape

The Al Jazirah plateau divides the Euphrates and Tigris Rivers, which cross the Mesopotamian plain to reach their confluence in the southeast. The rocky Syrian Desert extends west to the northern extremity of the Great Rift Valley, which runs from the mountains of Lebanon to the Gulf of Aqaba. The River Jordan flows south along this trough into the Dead Sea, divided from the Mediterranean coastal plain by a steep-sided plateau.

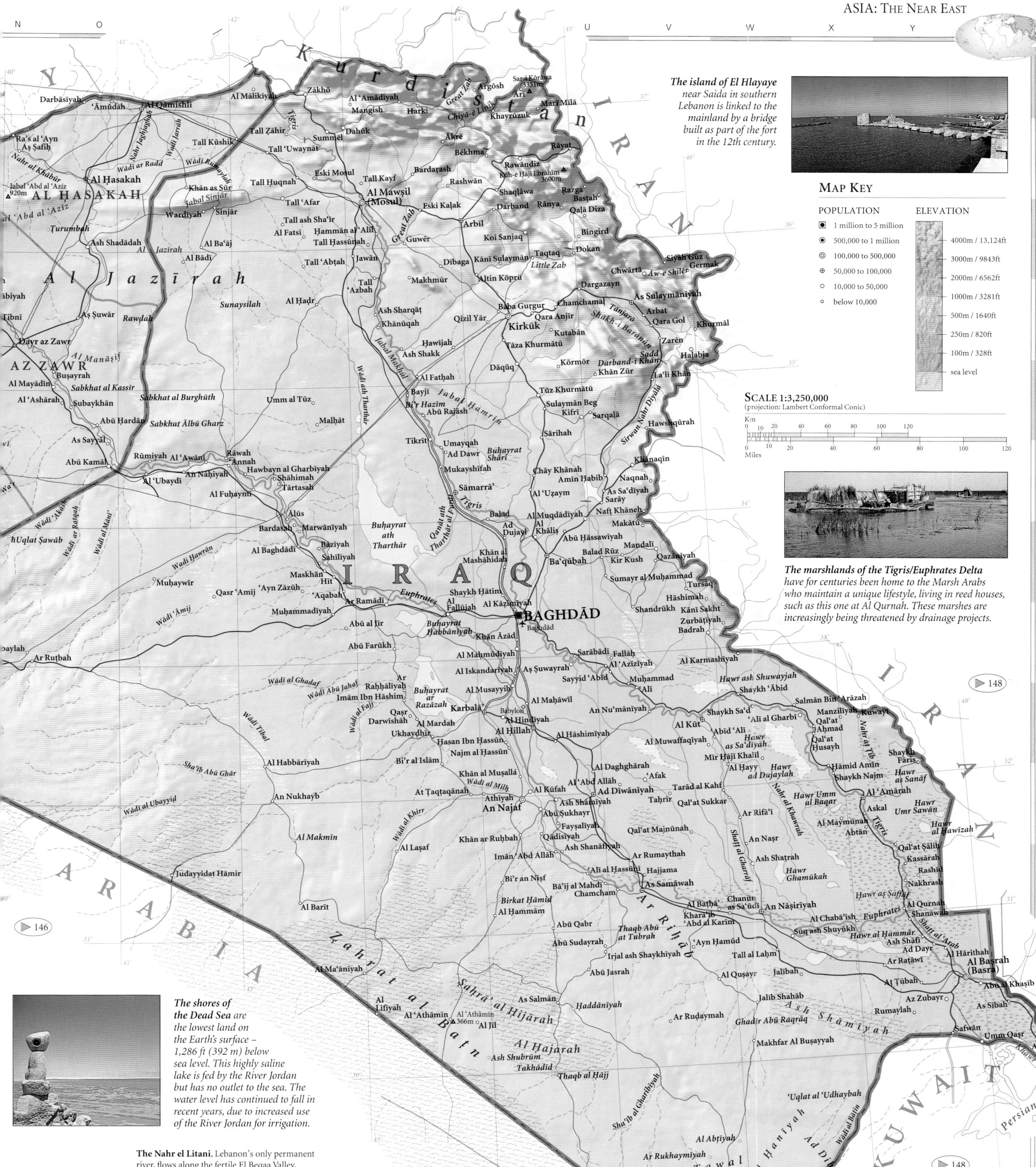

146
148
148

The island of El Hlayaye near Saida in southern Lebanon is linked to the mainland by a bridge built as part of the fort in the 12th century.

MAP KEY

POPULATION

- 1 million to 5 million
- 500,000 to 1 million
- 100,000 to 500,000
- 50,000 to 100,000
- 10,000 to 50,000
- below 10,000

ELEVATION

- 4000m / 13,124ft
- 3000m / 9843ft
- 2000m / 6562ft
- 1000m / 3281ft
- 500m / 1640ft
- 250m / 820ft
- 100m / 328ft
- sea level

SCALE 1:3,250,000
(projection: Lambert Conformal Conic)

The marshlands of the Tigris/Euphrates Delta have for centuries been home to the Marsh Arabs who maintain a unique lifestyle, living in reed houses, such as this one at Al Qurnah. These marshes are increasingly being threatened by drainage projects.

The shores of the Dead Sea *are the lowest land on the Earth's surface – 1,286 ft (392 m) below sea level. This highly saline lake is fed by the River Jordan but has no outlet to the sea. The water level has continued to fall in recent years, due to increased use of the River Jordan for irrigation.*

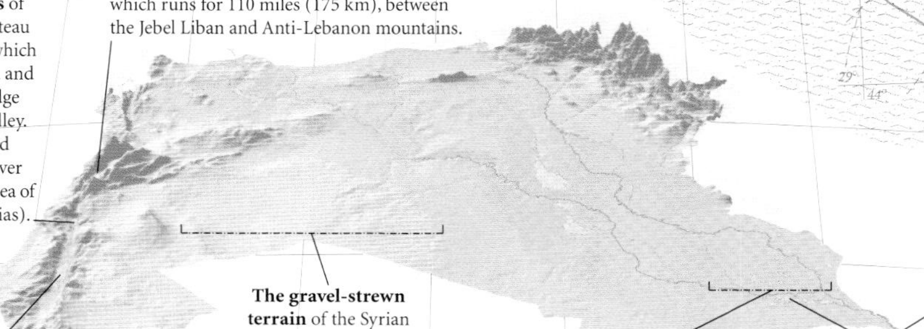

Ancient eruptions of lava formed the plateau of Jabal ad Duruz which is deeply weathered and eroded along the edge of the Great Rift Valley. The lava impounded the waters of the River Jordan to form the Sea of Galilee (Lake Tiberias).

The Nahr el Litani, Lebanon's only permanent river, flows along the fertile El Beqaa Valley, which runs for 110 miles (175 km), between the Jebel Liban and Anti-Lebanon mountains.

Dead Sea

The gravel-strewn terrain of the Syrian Desert is interrupted by *wadis* – river valleys which remain dry for most of the year.

Iraq Marshlands

Great quantities of sediment, deposited by the Tigris and Euphrates Rivers, have infilled the head of the Persian Gulf, shifting the coastline south by more than 150 miles (250 km) in the last 5,000 years.

Extensive marshlands surround the lake of Hawr al Hammar, which is 70 miles (110 km) long.

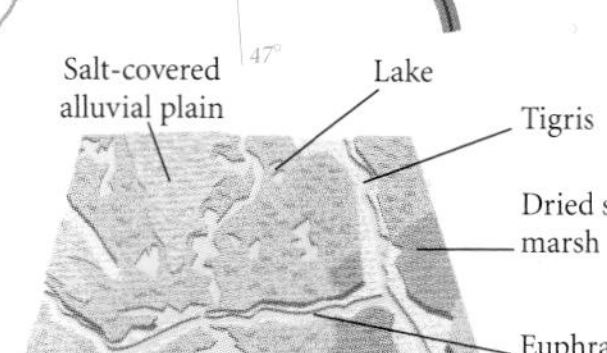

The floodplains of southern Iraq *are crossed by the Tigris and Euphrates rivers. Salt marshes and alluvial plains crusted with salt cover much of the area. The many small lakes are filled with brackish water and the marshes are colonized by reeds.*

A B C D E F G H I J K L M

The Arabian Peninsula

Bahrain, Kuwait, Oman, Qatar, Saudi Arabia, United Arab Emirates (UAE), Yemen

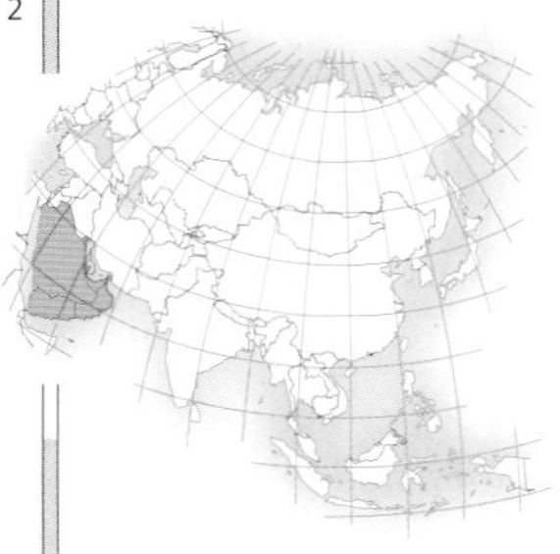

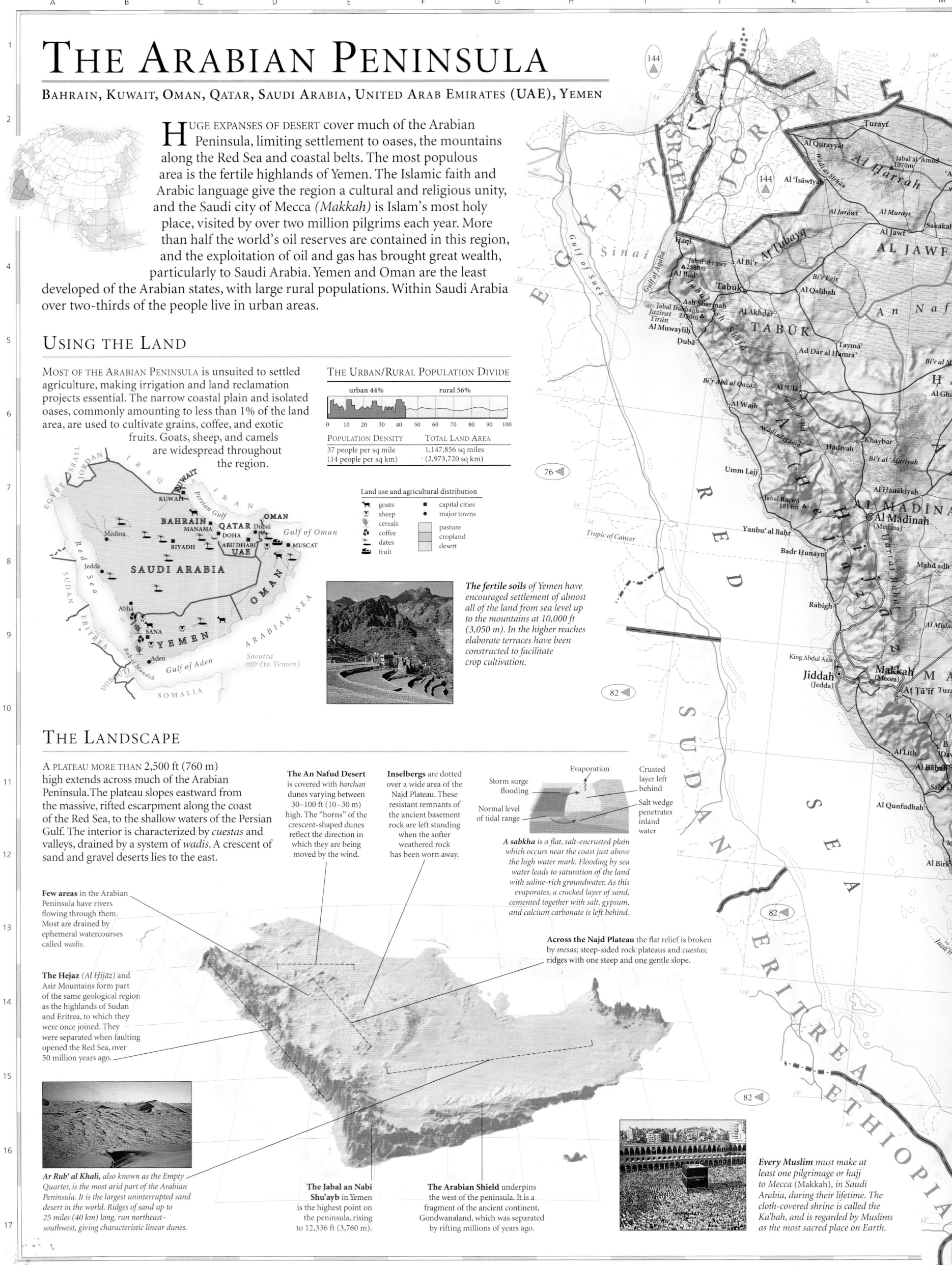

Huge expanses of desert cover much of the Arabian Peninsula, limiting settlement to oases, the mountains along the Red Sea and coastal belts. The most populous area is the fertile highlands of Yemen. The Islamic faith and Arabic language give the region a cultural and religious unity, and the Saudi city of Mecca *(Makkah)* is Islam's most holy place, visited by over two million pilgrims each year. More than half the world's oil reserves are contained in this region, and the exploitation of oil and gas has brought great wealth, particularly to Saudi Arabia. Yemen and Oman are the least developed of the Arabian states, with large rural populations. Within Saudi Arabia over two-thirds of the people live in urban areas.

Using the Land

Most of the Arabian Peninsula is unsuited to settled agriculture, making irrigation and land reclamation projects essential. The narrow coastal plain and isolated oases, commonly amounting to less than 1% of the land area, are used to cultivate grains, coffee, and exotic fruits. Goats, sheep, and camels are widespread throughout the region.

The Urban/Rural Population Divide

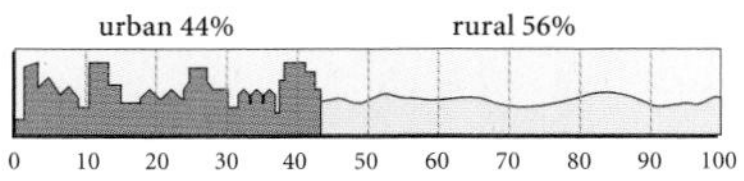

Population Density	Total Land Area
37 people per sq mile (14 people per sq km)	1,147,856 sq miles (2,973,720 sq km)

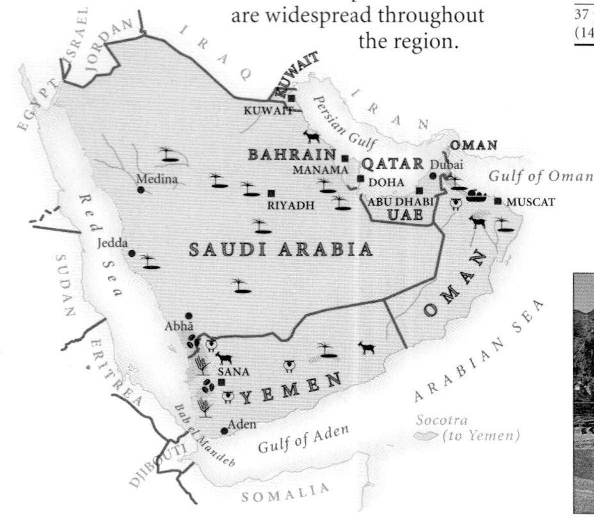

Land use and agricultural distribution

- goats
- sheep
- cereals
- coffee
- dates
- fruit
- capital cities
- major towns
- pasture
- cropland
- desert

***The fertile soils** of Yemen have encouraged settlement of almost all of the land from sea level up to the mountains at 10,000 ft (3,050 m). In the higher reaches elaborate terraces have been constructed to facilitate crop cultivation.*

The Landscape

A plateau more than 2,500 ft (760 m) high extends across much of the Arabian Peninsula. The plateau slopes eastward from the massive, rifted escarpment along the coast of the Red Sea, to the shallow waters of the Persian Gulf. The interior is characterized by *cuestas* and valleys, drained by a system of *wadis*. A crescent of sand and gravel deserts lies to the east.

The An Nafud Desert is covered with *barchan* dunes varying between 30–100 ft (10–30 m) high. The "horns" of the crescent-shaped dunes reflect the direction in which they are being moved by the wind.

Inselbergs are dotted over a wide area of the Najd Plateau. These resistant remnants of the ancient basement rock are left standing when the softer weathered rock has been worn away.

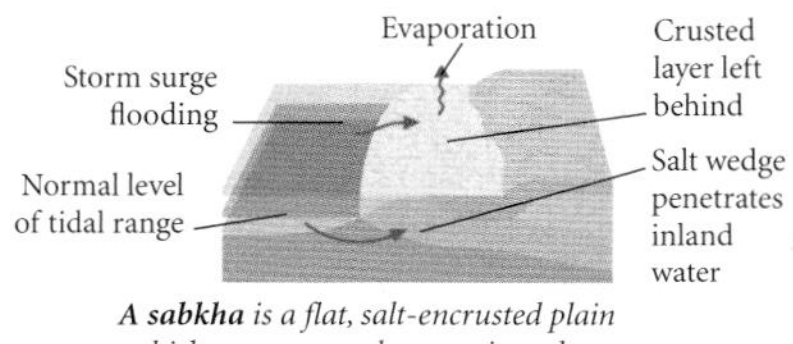

***A sabkha** is a flat, salt-encrusted plain which occurs near the coast just above the high water mark. Flooding by sea water leads to saturation of the land with saline-rich groundwater. As this evaporates, a cracked layer of sand, cemented together with salt, gypsum, and calcium carbonate is left behind.*

Few areas in the Arabian Peninsula have rivers flowing through them. Most are drained by ephemeral watercourses called *wadis.*

Across the Najd Plateau the flat relief is broken by *mesas;* steep-sided rock plateaus and *cuestas;* ridges with one steep and one gentle slope.

The Hejaz *(Al Ḩijāz)* and Asir Mountains form part of the same geological region as the highlands of Sudan and Eritrea, to which they were once joined. They were separated when faulting opened the Red Sea, over 50 million years ago.

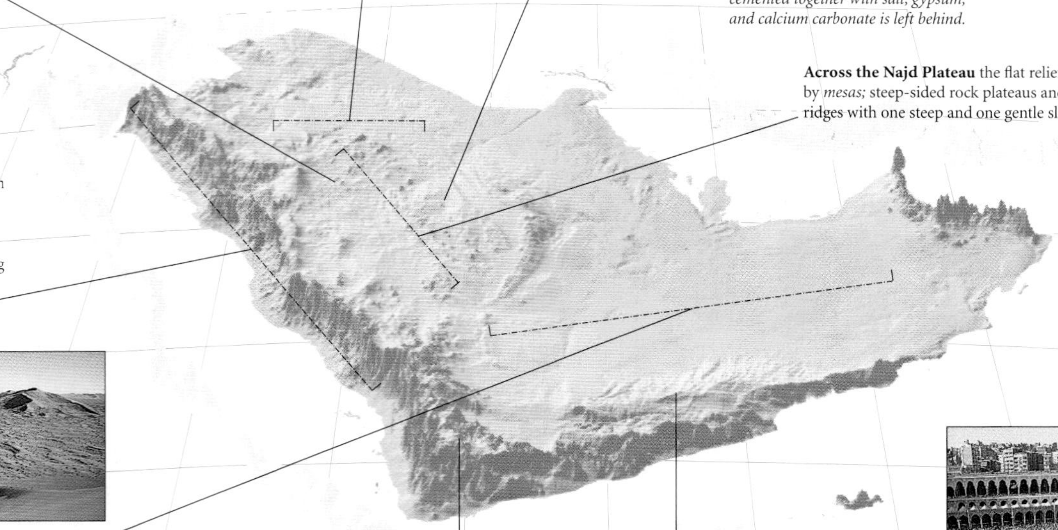

***Ar Rub' al Khali,** also known as the Empty Quarter, is the most arid part of the Arabian Peninsula. It is the largest uninterrupted sand desert in the world. Ridges of sand up to 25 miles (40 km) long, run northeast–southwest, giving characteristic linear dunes.*

The Jabal an Nabi Shu'ayb in Yemen is the highest point on the peninsula, rising to 12,336 ft (3,760 m).

The Arabian Shield underpins the west of the peninsula. It is a fragment of the ancient continent, Gondwanaland, which was separated by rifting millions of years ago.

***Every Muslim** must make at least one pilgrimage or hajj to Mecca (Makkah), in Saudi Arabia, during their lifetime. The cloth-covered shrine is called the Ka'bah, and is regarded by Muslims as the most sacred place on Earth.*

A B C D E F G H I J K L

Saudi Arabia contains the world's largest oil reserves, lying mainly along the Persian Gulf coast. Each day the region produces 8.3 million barrels of oil. Here, in the desert, excess oil is being burnt off.

TRANSPORTATION & INDUSTRY

THE EXTRACTION AND REFINING OF OIL AND GAS are the major industrial activities in the Arabian Peninsula. The region also has an active construction sector, with many Arab cities reflecting the wealth generated by the oil industry. The service sector is dominated by financial and technical institutions, which, like the construction sector, mainly serve the oil industry. Traditional handicrafts such as carpet-weaving are found in rural areas.

TRANSPORTATION NETWORK

65,239 miles (105,054 km)	2,071 miles (3,333 km)
864 miles (1,392 km)	none

Internal surface transportation is poorly developed across the peninsula. Along the coast, commercial routes have developed, but connections between bordering states rely on major airports.

Major industry and infrastructure

cement	capital cities
chemicals	major towns
iron & steel	international airports
oil	major roads
oil refining	major industrial areas
food processing	

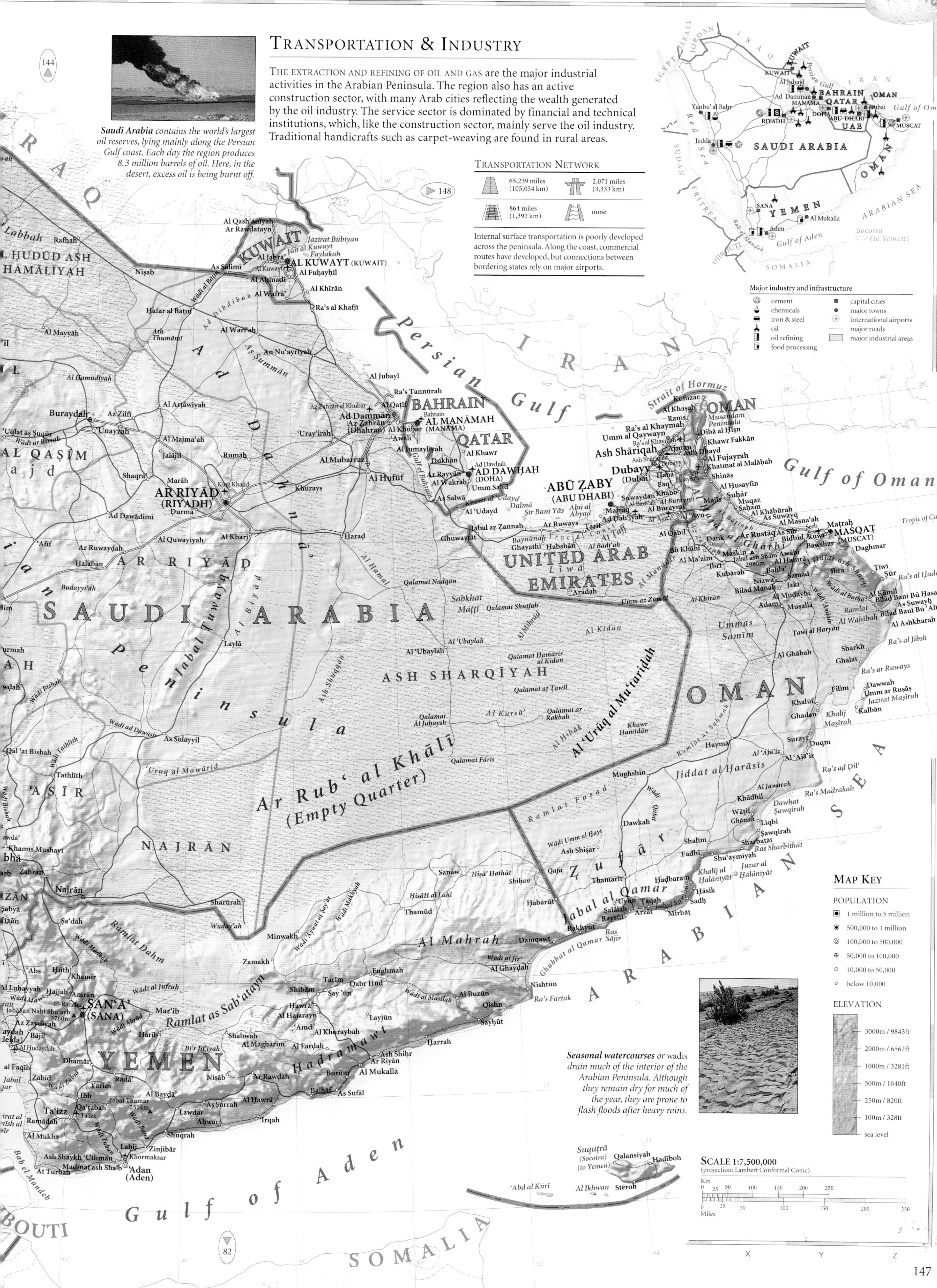

Seasonal watercourses or wadis drain much of the interior of the Arabian Peninsula. Although they remain dry for much of the year, they are prone to flash floods after heavy rains.

MAP KEY

POPULATION

- 1 million to 5 million
- 500,000 to 1 million
- 100,000 to 500,000
- 50,000 to 100,000
- 10,000 to 50,000
- below 10,000

ELEVATION

- 3000m / 9843ft
- 2000m / 6562ft
- 1000m / 3281ft
- 500m / 1640ft
- 250m / 820ft
- 100m / 328ft
- sea level

SCALE 1:7,500,000
(projection: Lambert Conformal Conic)

IRAN & THE GULF STATES

BAHRAIN, IRAN, KUWAIT, QATAR, UNITED ARAB EMIRATES (UAE)

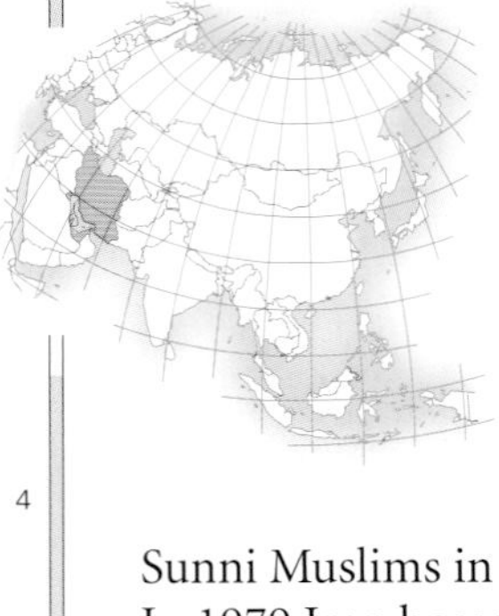

THE DISCOVERY OF OIL in the Persian Gulf in the 1930s brought great wealth to the surrounding states. The revenue was largely used to modernize industry and infrastructure, initiating great social change in these formerly agrarian countries. Today, over 80% of the people in the Gulf states live in urban areas, and foreign nationals make up a sizeable proportion of the population in Kuwait, Qatar, and the United Arab Emirates. The importance of control of the oil reserves has led to a number of territorial disputes, including most recently the Iran–Iraq War and the Gulf War. Islam is practiced almost exclusively throughout the region and two distinct strands are found; Sunni Muslims in Qatar, Kuwait, and UAE, and Shi'a Muslims in Iran and Bahrain. In 1979 Iran became the world's largest theocracy.

THE LANDSCAPE

THE LAND RISES STEEPLY from the fragmented coastal lowlands bordering the Persian Gulf, to reach Iran's interior plateau, bounded by heavily-eroded mountain chains. An unstable plate boundary runs northwest to southeast across Iran causing frequent earthquakes. On the sandy west coast of the Persian Gulf, the relief is generally flat, with patches of salt marsh. Bahrain consists of two groups of islands, which are mostly small and rocky.

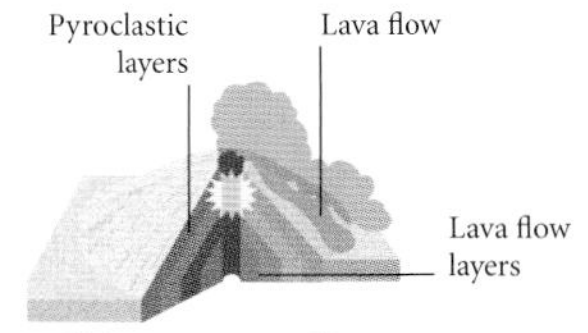

Pyroclastic layers • Lava flow

Lava flow layers

Qolleh-ye Damavand in the Elburz Mountains is a composite volcano. It comprises layers of lava and pyroclasts fragmentary rocks which accumulate on the slopes of the volcano after being ejected into the air.

Marine sediments from deep beneath the ancient Tethys Sea have been uplifted to form the Elburz Mountains, which stretch along the shores of the Caspian Sea, northern Iran.

Lava and ash from previous volcanic activity covers a 200-mile (320-km) stretch from the border with Azerbaijan to the Caspian Sea.

Iran's two mountain chains, the Zagros and Elburz, were uplifted at the same time as the Alps in Europe, when the African Plate collided with the Eurasian Plate.

Caspian Sea

Qolleh-ye Damavand

Dominated by a vast, semi-arid interior plateau, most of Iran lies above 1,640 ft (500 m). The region is poorly drained with many of its basins remaining dry for months at a time.

The fierce Shamal wind affects much of this region. Every summer it blows dust south from the flood plains of the Tigris and Euphrates, reducing visibility to such an extent that Kuwait International Airport is frequently forced to close.

The oilfields of The Gulf are formed from marine shale deposits lying in sedimentary basins at the margins of the Zagros Mountains.

Autumn winds blowing across The Gulf can reach speeds of up to 95 mph (150 kmph) causing severe storms, squalls, and waterspouts.

The Dasht-e Lut

Prolific springs tapping artesian water make cultivation possible across the north of Bahrain's main island. This provides a sharp contrast to the sandy plains in the south and west.

Numerous islands lie along the southern coast of the Persian Gulf. Some of these are salt domes, created when less dense salts were displaced and forced up to the surface by denser, overlying strata.

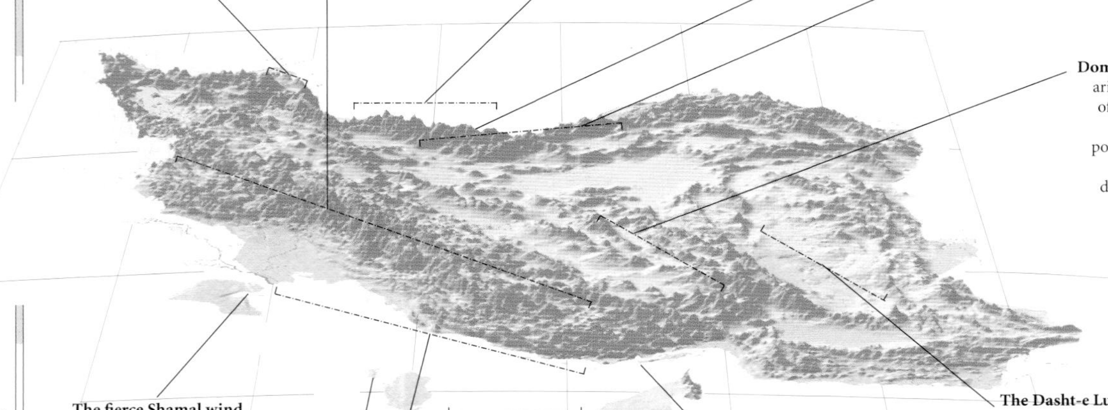

The Dasht-e Lut covers a large portion of eastern Iran with its dry, wind-eroded plain of scattered sandstone pillars and salty depressions. During the summer, temperatures soar, making it one of the world's hottest, driest places.

USING THE LAND AND SEA

ALONG THE COAST of the Caspian Sea, desalinated water allows fruits and vegetables to be produced, although water shortages and desert soils still limit farming. Sheep are the most important livestock raised in Iran and commercial forests cover the northwest of the country. Shrimp stocks were decimated by pollution during the Gulf War, but fishing remains important for domestic and export markets.

All of the Gulf states have commercial fishing fleets. Before the discovery of oil, fishing was the region's leading industry.

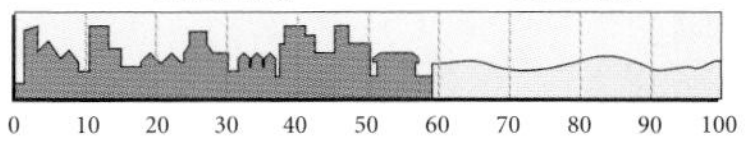

The Kuwait Towers in the centre of Kuwait are symbols of the vast wealth oil has brought to the country. Before 1960, the city had only one main street and was surrounded by a mud wall.

Land use and agricultural distribution

- goats
- sheep
- cereals
- citrus fruits
- cotton
- dates
- fishing
- timber

■ capital cities
• major towns

pasture
cropland
forest
desert
wetland

THE URBAN/RURAL POPULATION DIVIDE

urban 59% rural 41%

0 10 20 30 40 50 60 70 80 90 100

POPULATION DENSITY TOTAL LAND AREA
118 people per sq mile 642,883 sq miles
(46 people per sq km) (1,665,500 sq km)

N O P Q R S T U V W X Y

Many volcanoes lie in Iran's 1,200 mile (1930 km) volcanic belt, including the country's highest peak, the now-extinct Qolleh-ye Damavand at 18,600 ft (5,671 m).

152

Extensive oil and gas exploitation in the Gulf region has allowed the economic transformation of the Gulf states. Kuwait and the United Arab Emirates today have the highest per capita incomes in the world.

TRANSPORTATION & INDUSTRY

BOTH ONSHORE AND OFFSHORE oil reserves are exploited throughout the region. Kuwait not only extracts but also refines 80% of its oil. Bahrain has diversified its economy to become the main commercial and financial center in the Persian Gulf. Iran produces a wide range of products: textile mills are widespread and carpet weaving is an important export industry.

Major industry and infrastructure

carpet manufacture	capital city
chemicals	major towns
finance	international airports
food processing	major roads
oil	major industrial areas
oil refining	
textiles	

TRANSPORTATION NETWORK

50,340 miles (81,063 km)	466 miles (750 km)
3723 miles (5995 km)	81 miles (130 km)

Major towns and neighboring countries are linked by adequate road networks, although rural areas are less well served. Bahrain is linked to the mainland by a 15 mile (25 km) long causeway.

MAP KEY

POPULATION
- above 5 million
- 1 million to 5 million
- 500,000 to 1 million
- 100,000 to 500,000
- 50,000 to 100,000
- 10,000 to 50,000
- below 10,000

ELEVATION
- 4000m / 13,124ft
- 3000m / 9843ft
- 2000m / 6562ft
- 1000m / 3281ft
- 500m / 1640ft
- 250m / 820ft
- 100m / 328ft
- sea level

SCALE 1:5,500,000

(projection: Lambert Conformal Conic)

V W X Y Z

KAZAKHSTAN

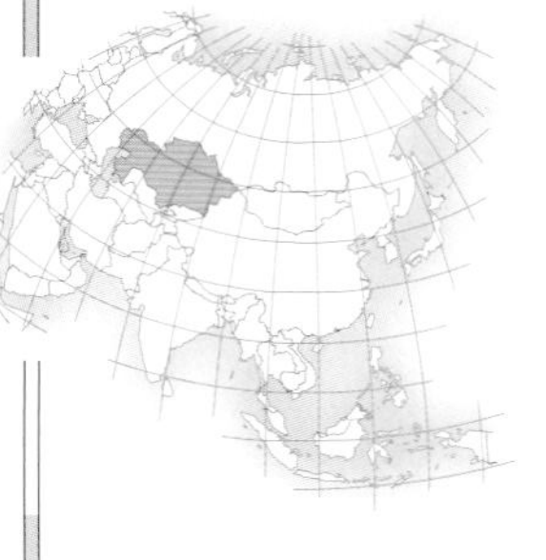

ABUNDANT NATURAL RESOURCES lie in the immense steppe grasslands, deserts, and central plateau of the former Soviet republic of Kazakhstan. An intensive program of industrial and agricultural development to exploit these resources during the Soviet era resulted in catastrophic industrial pollution, including fallout from nuclear testing and the shrinkage of the Aral Sea. Since independence, the government has encouraged foreign investment and liberalized the economy to promote growth. The adoption of Kazakh as the national language is intended to encourage a new sense of national identity in a state where living conditions for the majority remain harsh, both in cramped urban centers and impoverished rural areas.

TRANSPORTATION & INDUSTRY

THE SINGLE MOST IMPORTANT INDUSTRY in Kazakhstan is mining, based around extensive oil deposits near the Caspian Sea, the world's largest chromium mine, and vast reserves of iron ore. Recent foreign investment has helped to develop industries including food processing and steel manufacture, and to expand the exploitation of mineral resources. The Russian space program is still based at Baykonur, near Zhezkazgan in central Kazakhstan.

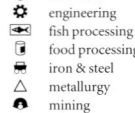

Major industry and infrastructure

⚗ chemicals	■ capital cities
✿ engineering	● major towns
🐟 fish processing	⊕ international airports
🍴 food processing	— major roads
△ iron & steel	major industrial areas
△ metallurgy	
⛏ mining	
⚓ oil	

TRANSPORTATION NETWORK

 87,561 miles (141,000 km)

 none

 8,483 miles (13,660 km)

 none

Industrial areas in the north and east are well-connected to Russia. Air and rail links with Germany and China have been established through foreign investment. Better access to Baltic ports is being sought.

An open-cast coal mine in Kazakhstan. Foreign investment is being actively sought by the Kazakh government in order to fully exploit the potential of the country's rich mineral reserves.

MAP KEY

POPULATION

◉	1 million to 5 million
◉	500,000 to 1 million
◉	100,000 to 500,000
⊕	50,000 to 100,000
○	10,000 to 50,000
∘	below 10,000

ELEVATION

- 4000m / 13,124ft
- 3000m / 9843ft
- 2000m / 6562ft
- 1000m / 3281ft
- 500m / 1640ft
- 250m / 820ft
- 100m / 328ft
- sea level

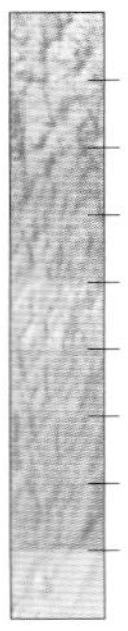

USING THE LAND AND SEA

THE REARING OF LARGE HERDS of sheep and goats on the steppe grasslands forms the core of Kazakh agriculture. Arable cultivation and cotton-growing in pasture and desert areas was encouraged during the Soviet era, but relative yields are low. The heavy use of fertilizers and the diversion of natural water sources for irrigation has degraded much of the land.

THE URBAN/RURAL POPULATION DIVIDE

urban 60% rural 40%

| 0 | 10 | 20 | 30 | 40 | 50 | 60 | 70 | 80 | 90 | 100 |

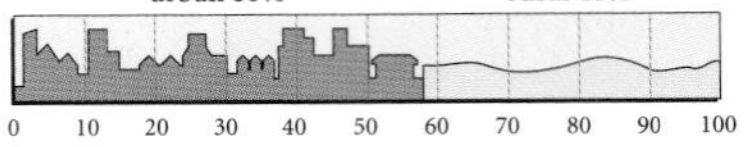

POPULATION DENSITY	TOTAL LAND AREA
16 people per sq mile (6 people per sq km)	1,048,878 sq miles (2,717,300 sq km)

Land use and agricultural distribution

🐄	cattle
🐐	goats
🐑	sheep
❀	cotton
🐟	fishing
🌾	wheat
■	capital cities
●	major towns
	pasture
	cropland
	forest
	mountain region
	desert

The nomadic peoples who moved their herds around the steppe grasslands are now largely settled, although echoes of their traditional lifestyle, in particular their superb riding skills, remain.

SCALE 1:6,250,000
(projection: Lambert Conformal Conic)

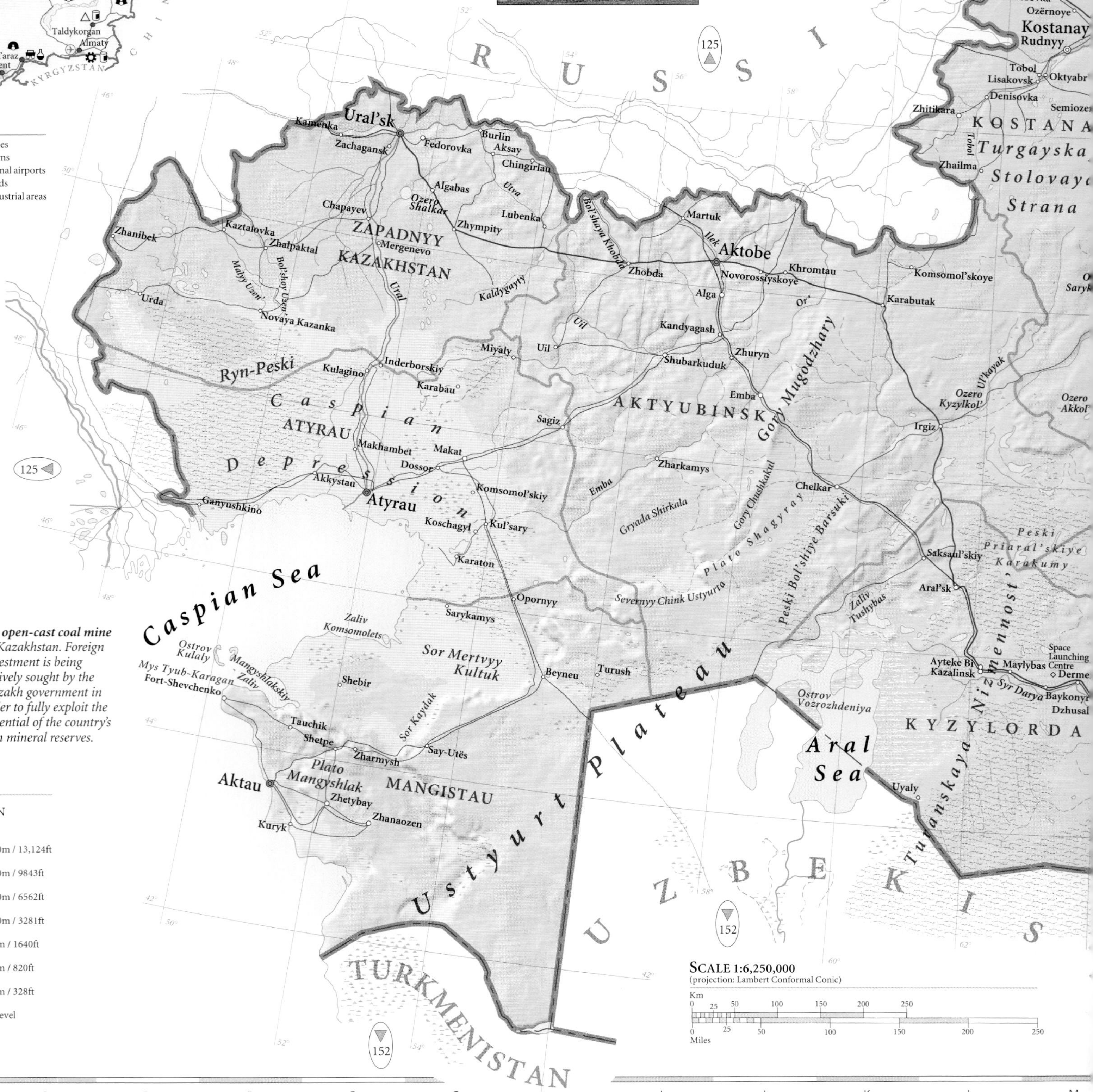

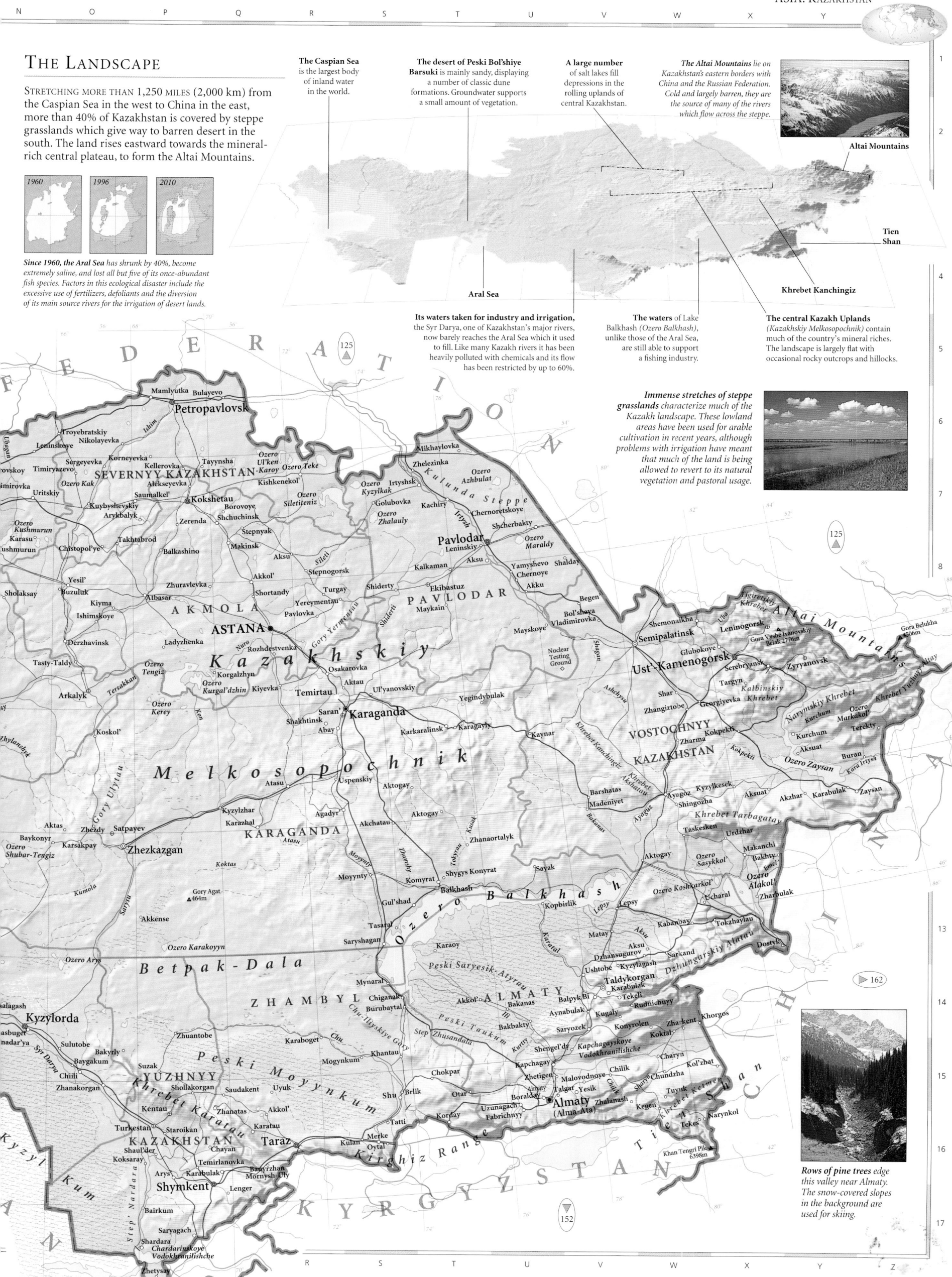

THE LANDSCAPE

STRETCHING MORE THAN 1,250 MILES (2,000 km) from the Caspian Sea in the west to China in the east, more than 40% of Kazakhstan is covered by steppe grasslands which give way to barren desert in the south. The land rises eastward towards the mineral-rich central plateau, to form the Altai Mountains.

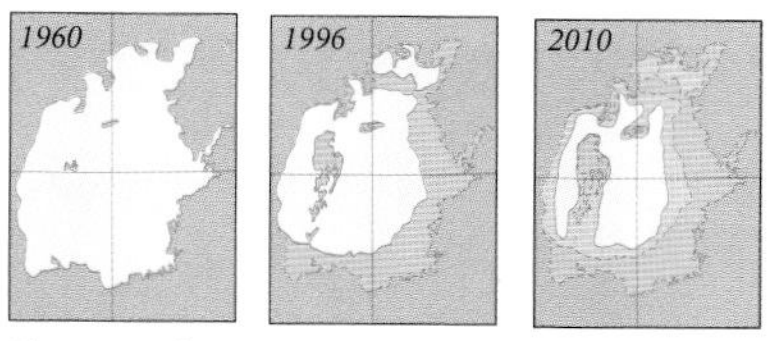

Since 1960, the Aral Sea has shrunk by 40%, become extremely saline, and lost all but five of its once-abundant fish species. Factors in this ecological disaster include the excessive use of fertilizers, defoliants and the diversion of its main source rivers for the irrigation of desert lands.

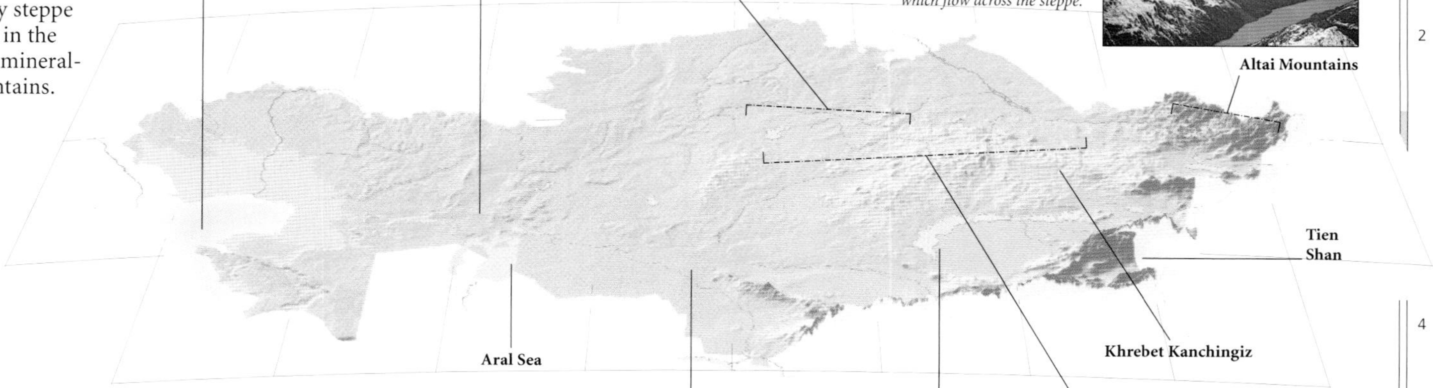

The Caspian Sea is the largest body of inland water in the world.

The desert of Peski Bol'shiye Barsuki is mainly sandy, displaying a number of classic dune formations. Groundwater supports a small amount of vegetation.

A large number of salt lakes fill depressions in the rolling uplands of central Kazakhstan.

Its waters taken for industry and irrigation, the Syr Darya, one of Kazakhstan's major rivers, now barely reaches the Aral Sea which it used to fill. Like many Kazakh rivers it has been heavily polluted with chemicals and its flow has been restricted by up to 60%.

The waters of Lake Balkhash *(Ozero Balkhash)*, unlike those of the Aral Sea, are still able to support a fishing industry.

The central Kazakh Uplands *(Kazakhskiy Melkosopochnik)* contain much of the country's mineral riches. The landscape is largely flat with occasional rocky outcrops and hillocks.

***The Altai Mountains** lie on Kazakhstan's eastern borders with China and the Russian Federation. Cold and largely barren, they are the source of many of the rivers which flow across the steppe.*

***Immense stretches of steppe grasslands** characterize much of the Kazakh landscape. These lowland areas have been used for arable cultivation in recent years, although problems with irrigation have meant that much of the land is being allowed to revert to its natural vegetation and pastoral usage.*

***Rows of pine trees** edge this valley near Almaty. The snow-covered slopes in the background are used for skiing.*

Central Asia

Kyrgyzstan, Tajikistan, Turkmenistan, Uzbekistan

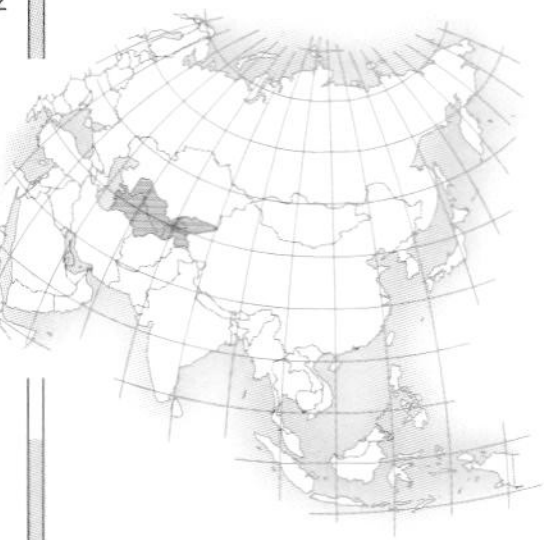

The four republics that declared independence in 1991 were created in the early years of the Soviet Union, promoting ethnic divisions in a region whose common focus, since the 8th century, has been Islam. Traditional rural, nomadic ways of life have survived the Soviet era, while the benefits of modern industry and grand irrigation schemes have resulted in severe pollution in the delicate, arid environment of the steppe, particularly in Uzbekistan. Many ethnic minority groups are scattered among the four republics, with isolated communities in the mountains of Kyrgyzstan. The current Islamic revival has brought hope of greater regional unity, in spite of religious factionalism which, in 1992, plunged Tajikistan into civil war.

The southern shoreline *of the Aral Sea has retreated over 30 miles (48 km) since 1960. A major cause is the diversion of water from the Amu Darya River for irrigation via the Kara Kum Canal* (Garagumskiy Kanal).

Map Key

POPULATION
- 1 million to 5 million
- 500,000 to 1 million
- 100,000 to 500,000
- 50,000 to 100,000
- 10,000 to 50,000
- below 10,000

ELEVATION
- 6000m / 19,686ft
- 4000m / 13,124ft
- 3000m / 9843ft
- 2000m / 6562ft
- 1000m / 3281ft
- 500m / 1640ft
- 250m / 820ft
- 100m / 328ft
- sea level

The desert of the Kara Kum (Garagumy) *occupies over 70% of Turkmenistan; its wind-scoured surface of dune ridges and depressions severely limits human settlement.*

Transportation & Industry

Fossil fuels are extracted and processed in all four states, with scope for further exploitation. Agriculture provides raw materials for many industries, including food and textiles processing, and the manufacture of leather goods, clothing, and carpets. Farm machinery is also produced.

Transportation Network

85,574 miles (137,800 km)	None
4,184 miles (6,738 km)	1,180 miles (1,900 km)

The Kara Kum Canal *(Garagumskiy Kanal)* runs for 870 miles (1,400 km) from the Amu Darya River to the Caspian Sea. The canal is principally used for irrigation but is navigable for 280 miles (450 km).

Major industry and infrastructure
- carpet weaving
- chemicals
- engineering
- food processing
- oil & gas
- textiles
- capital cities
- major towns
- international airports
- major roads
- major industrial areas

THE LANDSCAPE

THE GREAT TIEN SHAN and Pamir Ranges meet in a succession of high mountain chains. These mountains encircle the fertile Fergana Valley and reach west into the desert of the Kyzyl Kum, dividing the Syr Darya and Amu Darya Rivers. Sandy steppeland extends to the shores of the Caspian Sea, with the desert of the Kara Kum (Garagumy) in the south. The Amu Darya drains into the Aral Sea in the north.

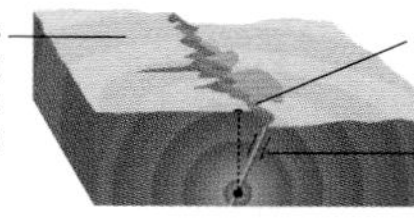

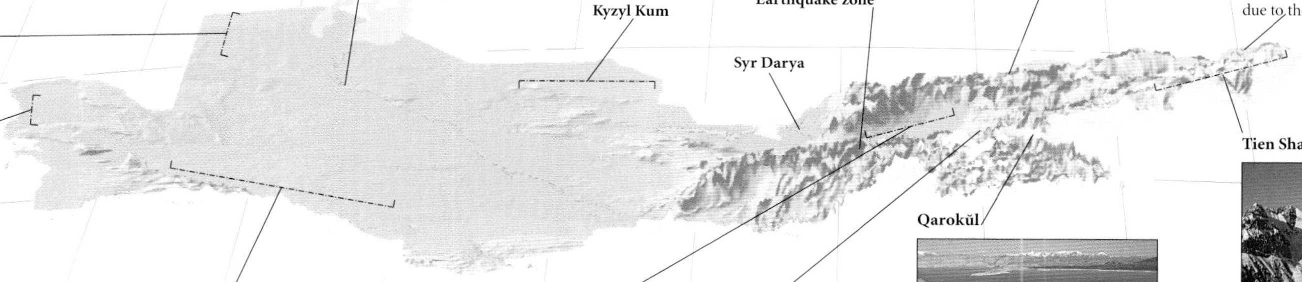

Salt marshes fill many of the depressions in the Ustyurt Plateau, a barren, rocky tableland about 650 ft (200 m) above sea level.

Some of the world's largest deposits of marine salts are found in Zaliv Kara-Bogaz-Gol. This shallow, saline gulf has an average depth of only 33 ft (10 m), and a very high evaporation rate, producing the salty deposits.

The Kara Kum (Garagumy) is one of the world's largest expanses of sand. Wind action has created a terrain of shifting, crescent-shaped sand dunes known as barchans.

The Amu Darya is the only river in Central Asia with a sufficient volume of water to cross the desert of the Kara Kum (Garagumy) from the Pamirs to the Aral Sea, where it forms a delta largely vegetated by scrub grasses.

A series of major rock faults has created the Fergana Valley, a deep depression surrounded by high mountains. Water from the Syr Darya River and from underground sources supports intensive agriculture, despite minimal rainfall.

Shock waves travel through ground — Epicentre — Fault

In the heavily-fractured and faulted mountain region, earthquakes are common, caused by the sudden release of tension along active fault lines.

Kyzyl Kum

Earthquake zone

Syr Darya

Naryn River

Mount Communism (Qullai Kommunizm), in the northern Pamirs, was so named for being the highest point in the former Soviet Union, rising to 24,590 ft (7,495 m).

Qarokŭl

Nestling high in the Pamir range, and fed by glacial meltwater, Qarokŭl is the largest of the lakes in this region.

Bare mountains provide a stark background to the croplands along the Naryn River in Kyrgyzstan. Irrigation is essential for cultivation in this dry region.

Ozero Issyk-Kul' lies at an altitude of 5,193 ft (1,584 m). The lake remains ice-free throughout the year, due to the slight salinity of the water.

Tien Shan

The Tien Shan extend from China in the east, reaching heights over 24,400 ft (7,439 m) and branching into many parallel ranges in the west.

SCALE 1:4,250,000
(projection: Lambert Conformal Conic)

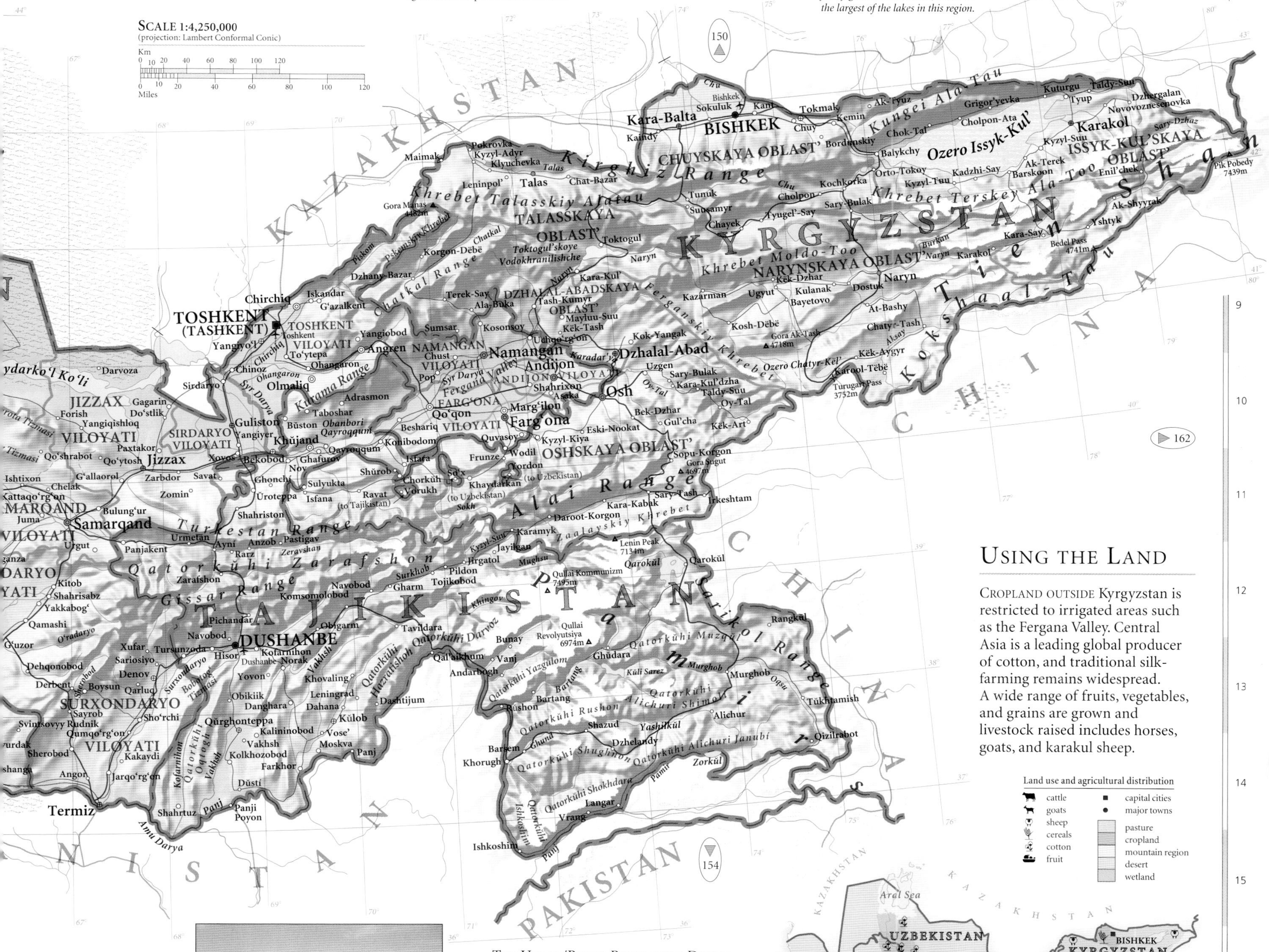

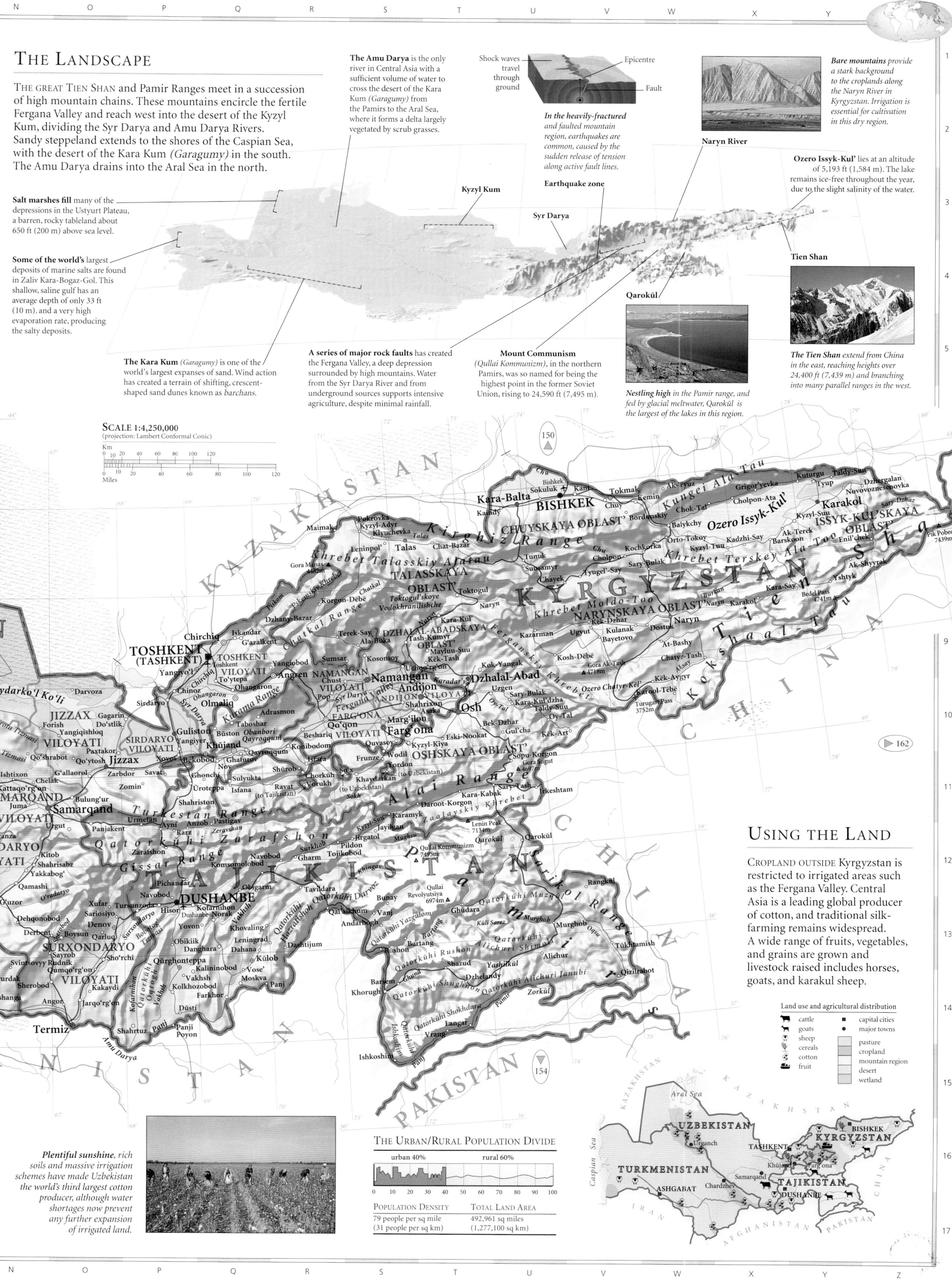

USING THE LAND

CROPLAND OUTSIDE Kyrgyzstan is restricted to irrigated areas such as the Fergana Valley. Central Asia is a leading global producer of cotton, and traditional silk-farming remains widespread. A wide range of fruits, vegetables, and grains are grown and livestock raised includes horses, goats, and karakul sheep.

Land use and agricultural distribution

cattle | capital cities
goats | major towns
sheep | pasture
cereals | cropland
cotton | mountain region
fruit | desert
| wetland

Plentiful sunshine, rich soils and massive irrigation schemes have made Uzbekistan the world's third largest cotton producer, although water shortages now prevent any further expansion of irrigated land.

THE URBAN/RURAL POPULATION DIVIDE

urban 40% rural 60%

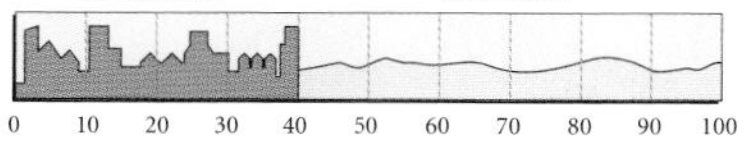

POPULATION DENSITY
79 people per sq mile
(31 people per sq km)

TOTAL LAND AREA
492,961 sq miles
(1,277,100 sq km)

AFGHANISTAN & PAKISTAN

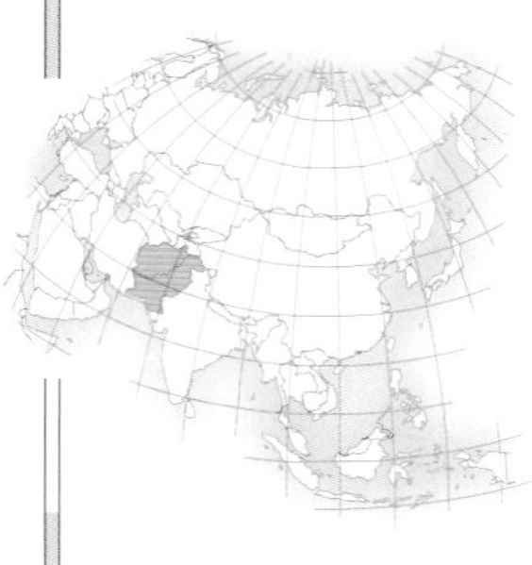

PAKISTAN WAS CREATED by the partition of British India in 1947, becoming the western arm of a new Islamic state for Indian Muslims; the eastern sector, in Bengal, seceded to become the separate country of Bangladesh in 1971. Over half of Pakistan's 147 million people live in the Punjab, at the fertile head of the great Indus Basin. The river sustains a national economy based on irrigated agriculture, including cotton for the vital textiles industry. Afghanistan, a mountainous, landlocked country, with an ancient and independent culture, has been wracked by war since 1979. Factional strife escalated into an international conflict in late 2001, as US-led troops ousted the miltant and fundamentally Islamist *taliban* regime as part of their war on terrorism.

The town of Bamian lies high in the Hindu Kush west of Kabul. Between the 2nd and 5th centuries two huge statues of Buddha were carved into the nearby rock, the largest of which stood 125ft (38m) high. The statues were destroyed by the taliban regime in March 2001.

TRANSPORTATION & INDUSTRY

PAKISTAN IS HIGHLY dependent on the cotton textiles industry, although diversified manufacture is expanding around cities such as Karachi and Lahore. Afghanistan's limited industry is based mainly on the processing of agricultural raw materials and includes traditional crafts such as carpet weaving.

Major industry and infrastructure

- carpet weaving
- chemicals
- engineering
- finance
- food processing
- iron & steel
- oil & gas
- textiles
- capital cities
- major towns
- international airports
- major roads
- major industrial areas

TRANSPORTATION NETWORK

- 141,340 miles (227,600 km)
- 211 miles (340 km)
- 4,852 miles (7,814 km)
- 745 miles (1,200 km)

The Karakoram Highway was completed after 20 years of construction in 1978. It breaches the Himalayan mountain barrier providing a commercial motor route linking lowland Pakistan and China.

The Karakoram Highway is one of the highest major roads in the world. It took over 24,000 workers almost 20 years to complete.

THE LANDSCAPE

AFGHANISTAN'S TOPOGRAPHY is dominated by the mountains of the Hindu Kush, which spread south and west into numerous mountain spurs. The dry plateau of southwestern Afghanistan extends into Pakistan and the hills which overlook the great Indus Basin. In northern Pakistan the Hindu Kush, Himalayan and Karakoram ranges meet to form one of the world's highest mountain regions.

The arid Hindu Kush makes much of Afghanistan uninhabitable, with over 50% of the land lying above 6,500 ft (2,000 m).

Frequent earthquakes mean that mountain-building processes are continuing in this region, as the Indo-Australian Plate drifts northward, colliding with the Eurasian Plate.

Mountain chains running southwest from the Hindu Kush into Pakistan form a barrier to the humid winds which blow from the Indian Ocean, creating arid conditions across southern Afghanistan.

The Indus Basin is part of the Indus-Ganges lowland, a vast depression which has been filled with layers of sediment over the last 50 million years. These deposits are estimated to be over 16,400 ft (5,000 m) deep.

The Indus Delta is prone to heavy flooding and high levels of salinity. It remains a largely uncultivated wilderness area.

The Hunza River rises in the northern Karakoram Range, running for 120 miles (193 km) before joining the Gilgit River.

Hunza River

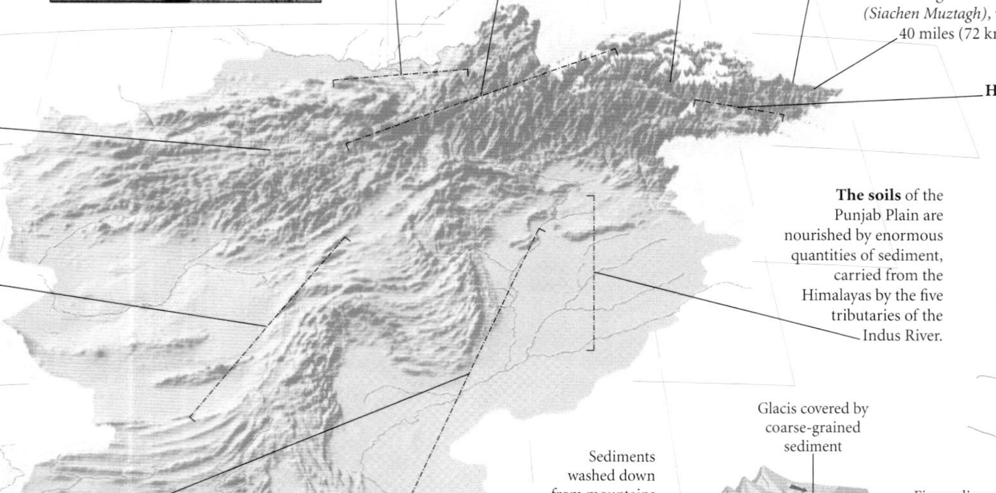

The plains and foothills which extend from the northern slopes of the Hindu Kush are part of the great grassy steppe lands of Central Asia.

Hindu Kush

K2 (Mount Godwin Austen), in the Karakoram Range, is the second highest mountain in the world, at an altitude of 28,251 ft (8,611 m).

Some of the largest glaciers outside the polar regions are found in the Karakoram Range, including Siachen Glacier (Siachen Muztagh), which is 40 miles (72 km) long.

Himalayas

The soils of the Punjab Plain are nourished by enormous quantities of sediment, carried from the Himalayas by the five tributaries of the Indus River.

Sediments washed down from mountains accumulate on glacis slopes

Glacis covered by coarse-grained sediment

Fine sediments deposited on salt flats are removed by wind erosion.

Bedrock

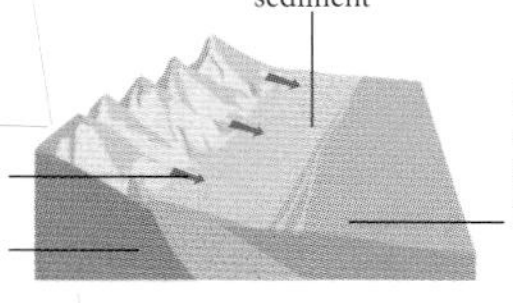

Glacis are gentle, debris-covered slopes which lead into saltflats or deserts. They typically occur at the base of mountains in arid regions such as Afghanistan.

SCALE 1:4,500,000
(projection: Lambert Conformal Conic)

Km
0 10 20 40 60 80 100 120 140 160 180 200

0 10 20 40 60 80 100 120 140 160 180 200
Miles

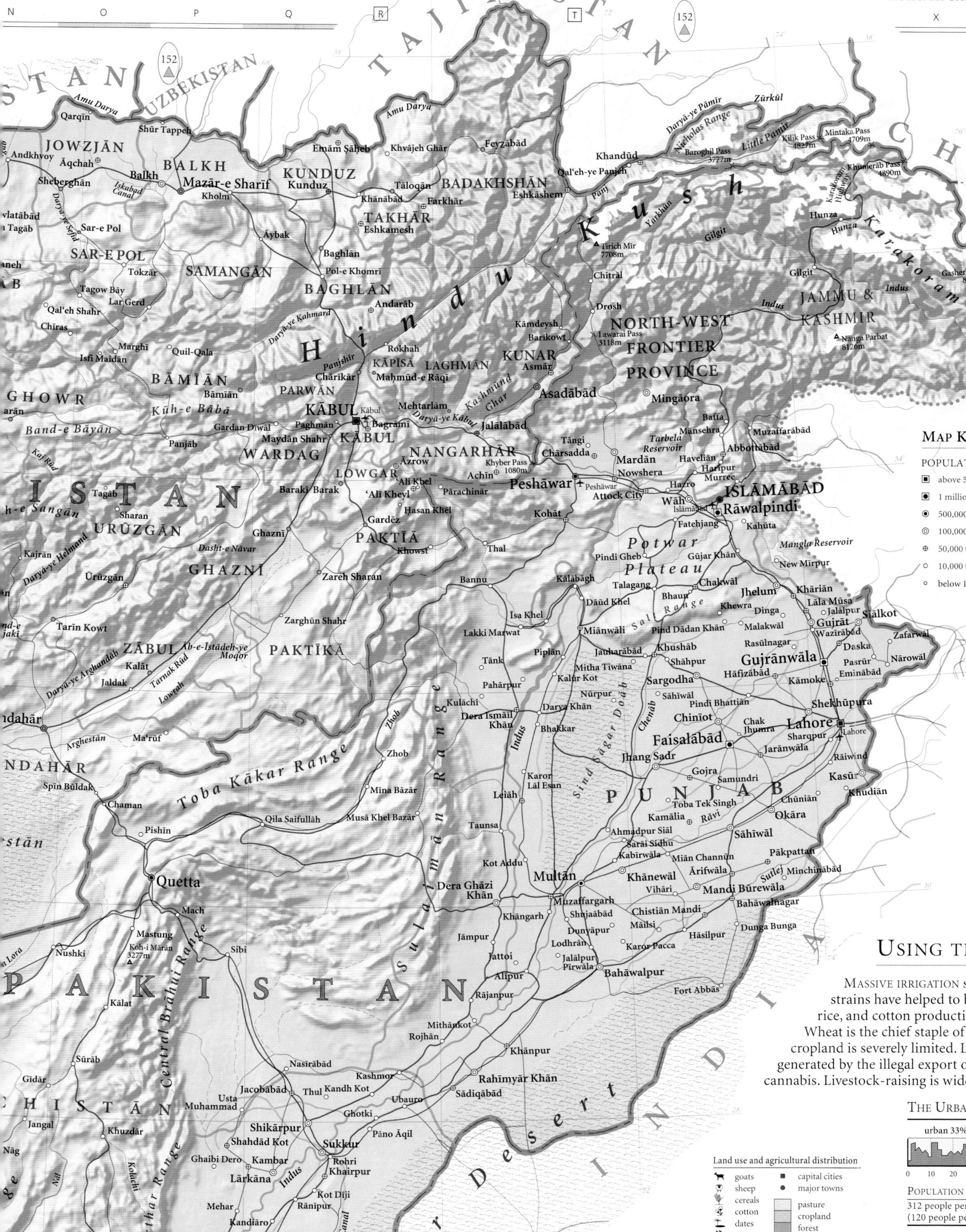

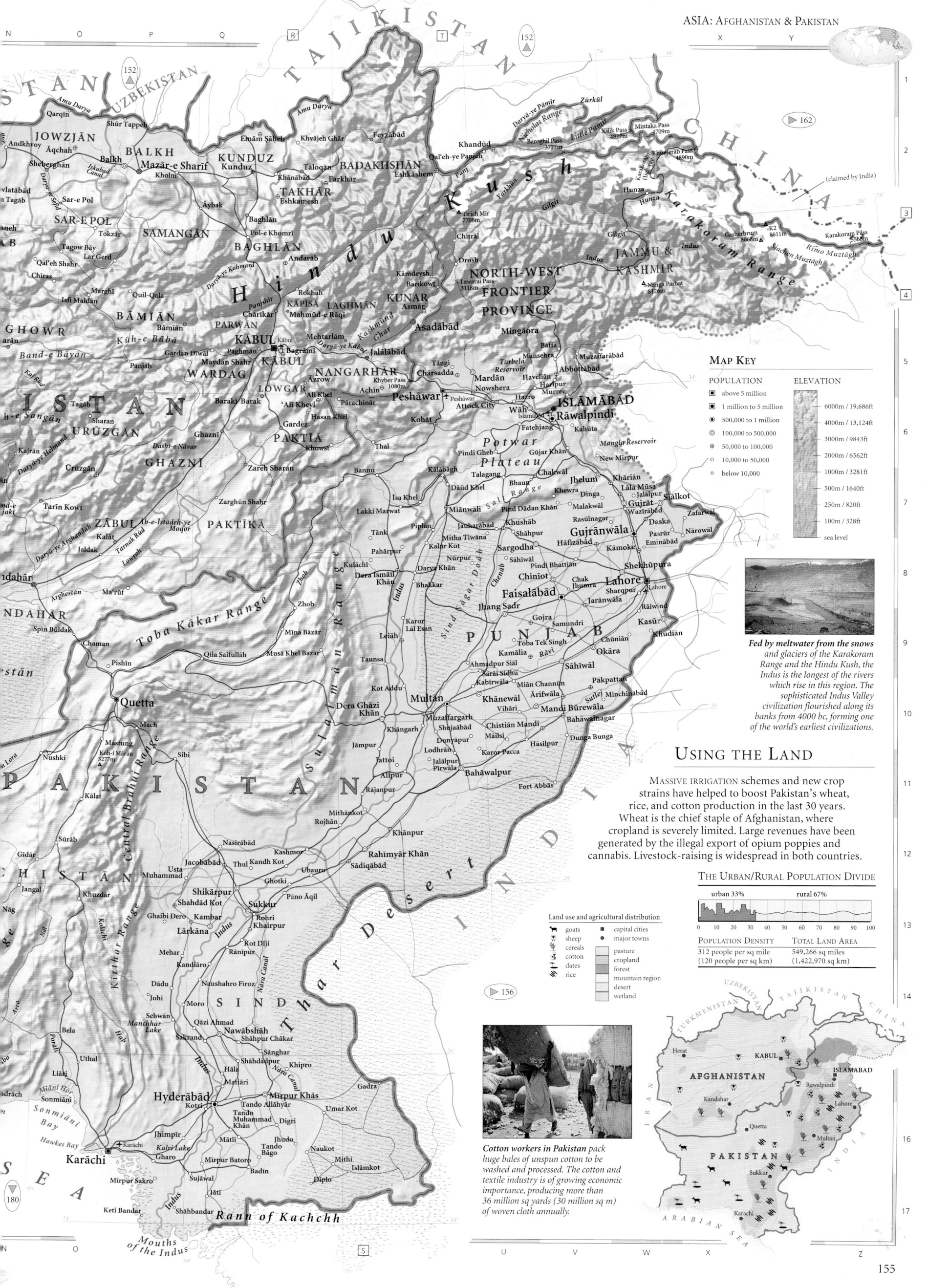

MAP KEY

POPULATION

- above 5 million
- 1 million to 5 million
- 500,000 to 1 million
- 100,000 to 500,000
- 50,000 to 100,000
- 10,000 to 50,000
- below 10,000

ELEVATION

- 6000m / 19,686ft
- 4000m / 13,124ft
- 3000m / 9843ft
- 2000m / 6562ft
- 1000m / 3281ft
- 500m / 1640ft
- 250m / 820ft
- 100m / 328ft
- sea level

Fed by meltwater from the snows and glaciers of the Karakoram Range and the Hindu Kush, the Indus is the longest of the rivers which rise in this region. The sophisticated Indus Valley civilization flourished along its banks from 4000 bc, forming one of the world's earliest civilizations.

USING THE LAND

MASSIVE IRRIGATION schemes and new crop strains have helped to boost Pakistan's wheat, rice, and cotton production in the last 30 years. Wheat is the chief staple of Afghanistan, where cropland is severely limited. Large revenues have been generated by the illegal export of opium poppies and cannabis. Livestock-raising is widespread in both countries.

THE URBAN/RURAL POPULATION DIVIDE

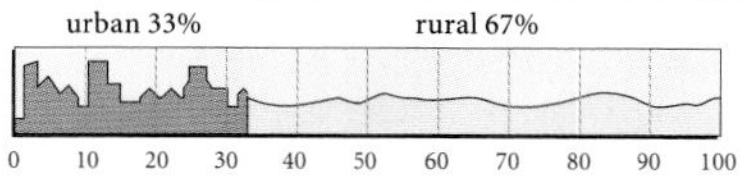

POPULATION DENSITY	TOTAL LAND AREA
312 people per sq mile (120 people per sq km)	549,266 sq miles (1,422,970 sq km)

Cotton workers in Pakistan pack huge bales of unspun cotton to be washed and processed. The cotton and textile industry is of growing economic importance, producing more than 36 million sq yards (30 million sq m) of woven cloth annually.

Land use and agricultural distribution

- goats
- sheep
- cereals
- cotton
- dates
- rice
- capital cities
- major towns
- pasture
- cropland
- forest
- mountain region
- desert
- wetland

SOUTH ASIA

BANGLADESH, BHUTAN, INDIA, MALDIVES, NEPAL, PAKISTAN, SRI LANKA

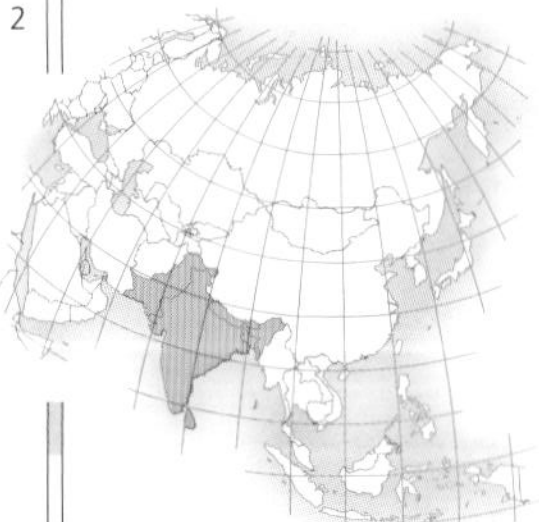

MORE THAN ONE-FIFTH of the world's population lives in the south Asian subcontinent. Great cultural diversity has come from a long succession of foreign invaders, including Hindu Aryans, Islamic Moguls, and the British, whose empire incorporated the princely states of the Maharajas and extended to the borders of Nepal and Bhutan in the Himalayas. Half a century after independence, India is the world's largest democracy, and at the current rate of growth, may overtake China as the world's most populous country within the next century. There are points of tension in the region over claims for independence by the Sikhs in the Indian Punjab and the Tamil separatists in Sri Lanka, and the long-standing dispute with Pakistan over Jammu and Kashmir in the north.

The towering Karakoram and Hindu Kush ranges, formed at the same time as the Himalayas, dominate Pakistan's northern borders. K2 on the border of northern Pakistan is the second highest mountain on Earth, at 28,251 ft (8,611 m).

THE LANDSCAPE

SOUTH ASIA is effectively isolated from the rest of Asia by desert along the western flank of Pakistan, and a continuous wall of mountains, dominated by the Himalayas, to the north and east. The great basins of the Indus and Ganges separate this mountain fringe from the rolling plateau of the Indian peninsula, which is bordered by a line of coastal hills, the Eastern and Western Ghats.

The Indus Valley near Skardu in northern Pakistan has been partially infilled by great quantities of eroded sediment. Most of this is carried from the region's bare slopes by swollen rivers during the spring thaw and mass movement activity.

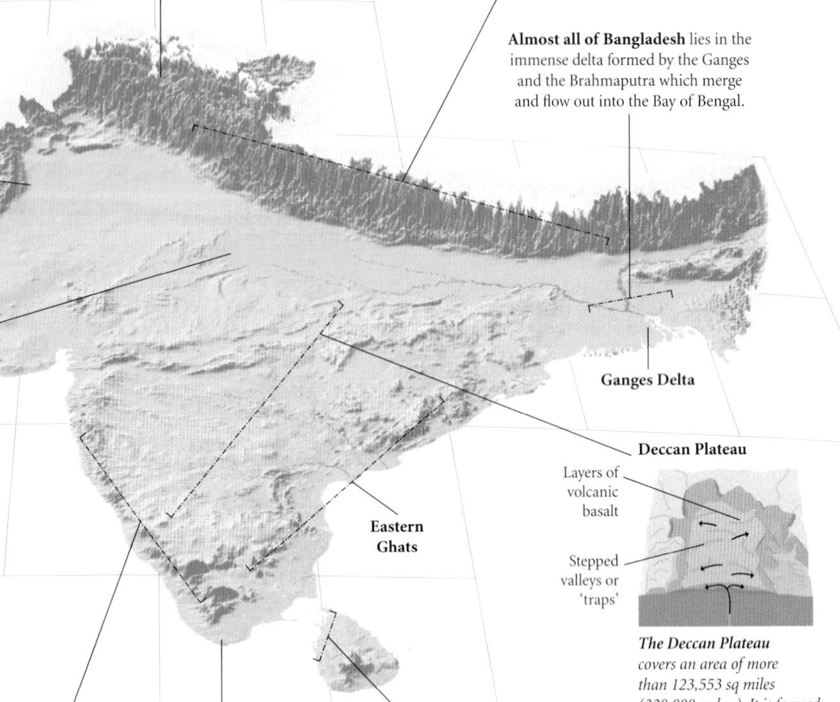

The Himalayas are the highest and most extensive mountain system in the world. They were formed when the Indo-Australian Plate collided with the Eurasian Plate about 40 million years ago, thrusting up huge masses of land and creating a "ripple" effect, which formed lesser mountain ranges in Tibet and Southeast Asia. Mount Everest is the world's tallest mountain at 29,028 ft (8,848 m).

Almost all of Bangladesh lies in the immense delta formed by the Ganges and the Brahmaputra which merge and flow out into the Bay of Bengal.

The Indus River flows more than 1,970 miles (3,180 km) from southwestern Tibet to its mouth on the Arabian Sea. It has an estimated catchment area of 450,000 sq miles (1,165,500 sq km).

The coast of western Pakistan is a staircase of folded rock strata caused by successive periods of rapid uplift.

Rivers flowing from the Himalayas into a broad depression in northern India have formed marshes around Bharatpur. They are now a sanctuary for numerous bird species.

The Deccan Plateau covers an area of more than 123,553 sq miles (320,000 sq km). It is formed of deep layers of volcanic basalt, reaching thicknesses of more than 9,800 ft (3,000 m) toward the coast. Distinctive stepped valleys cut in the basalt plateau by rivers are known as "traps."

The Western Ghats are formed by a fault scarp which runs unbroken for more than 930 miles (1,500 km). They reach their highest point at the southern Cardamon Hills.

Trivandrum in southern India normally receives the first of the monsoon rains, which are essential to south Asian agriculture and moderate the extreme summer heat. The monsoon then moves northward over a period of about two months.

Coastal deposition has formed many typical features along the western coast of Sri Lanka. These include spits and bars, sometimes enclosing lagoons.

MAP KEY

POPULATION
- above 5 million
- 1 million to 5 million
- 500,000 to 1 million
- 100,000 to 500,000
- 50,000 to 100,000
- 10,000 to 50,000
- below 10,000

ELEVATION
- 6000m / 19,686ft
- 4000m / 13,124ft
- 3000m / 9843ft
- 2000m / 6562ft
- 1000m / 3281ft
- 500m / 1640ft
- 250m / 820ft
- 100m / 328ft
- sea level

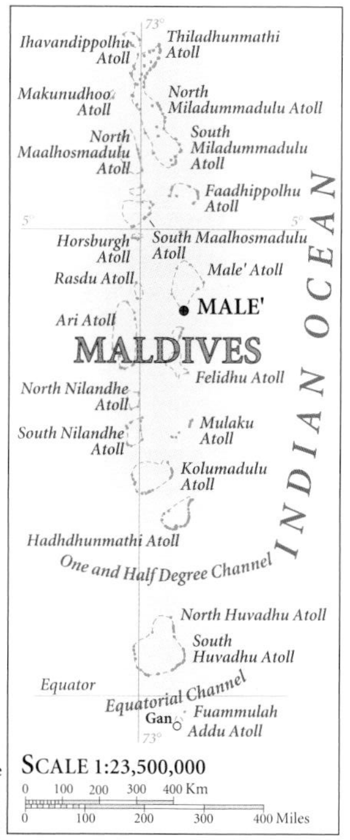

TRANSPORTATION & INDUSTRY

MOST INDUSTRIAL WORKERS across South Asia are involved in small-scale production serving local markets. Large-scale industry remains concentrated around great cities such as Calcutta and Mumbai (Bombay). India has a broad industrial base and manufacturing growth has accelerated under a recently liberalized economy. Textiles and clothing, leather, and jewelry are among South Asia's leading exports.

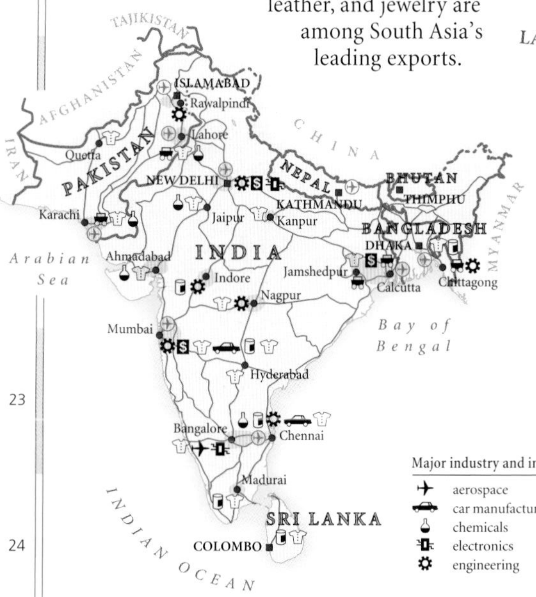

Major industry and infrastructure

aerospace	finance	capital cities	
car manufacture	food processing	major towns	
chemicals	iron & steel	international airports	
electronics	textiles	major roads	
engineering		major industrial areas	

TRANSPORTATION NETWORK

335,154 miles (539,701 km)	21,015 miles (33,840 km)
44,166 miles (71,120 km)	17,225 miles (27,738 km)

India's railroad network, established under British colonial rule, is the sixth most extensive in the world and continues to play a unique role in integrating the country's disparate regions.

***Religion and commerce** sit side by side in the Nepalese capital, Kathmandu. Nepal is a Hindu state and these small, highly decorated shrines are commonplace. As in India, cows are venerated, and allowed free rein throughout the city.*

USING THE LAND AND SEA

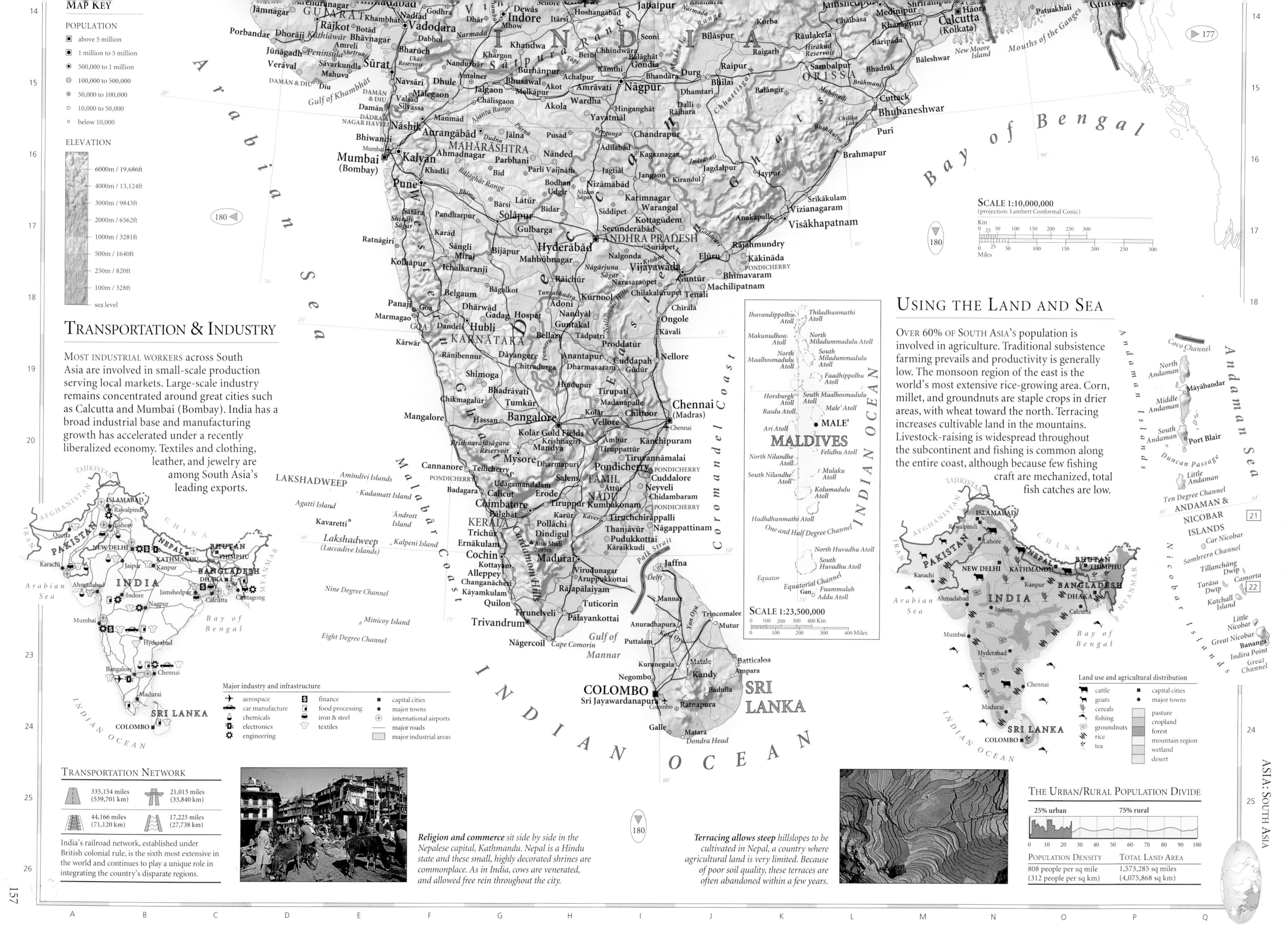

OVER 60% OF SOUTH ASIA'S population is involved in agriculture. Traditional subsistence farming prevails and productivity is generally low. The monsoon region of the east is the world's most extensive rice-growing area. Corn, millet, and groundnuts are staple crops in drier areas, with wheat toward the north. Terracing increases cultivable land in the mountains. Livestock-raising is widespread throughout the subcontinent and fishing is common along the entire coast, although because few fishing craft are mechanized, total fish catches are low.

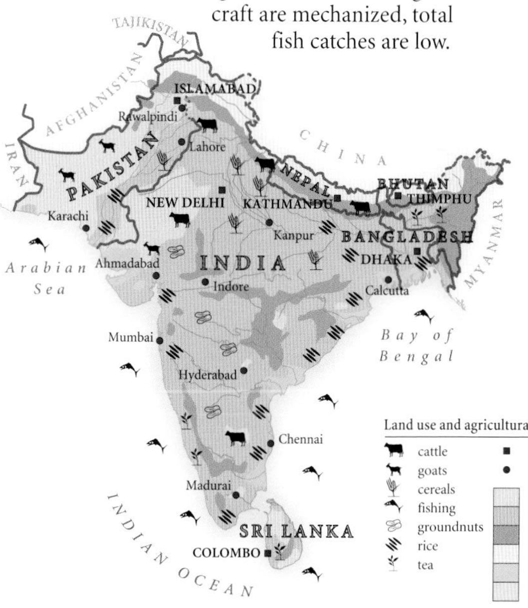

Land use and agricultural distribution

cattle	capital cities	pasture
goats	major towns	cropland
cereals		forest
fishing		mountain region
groundnuts		wetland
rice		desert
tea		

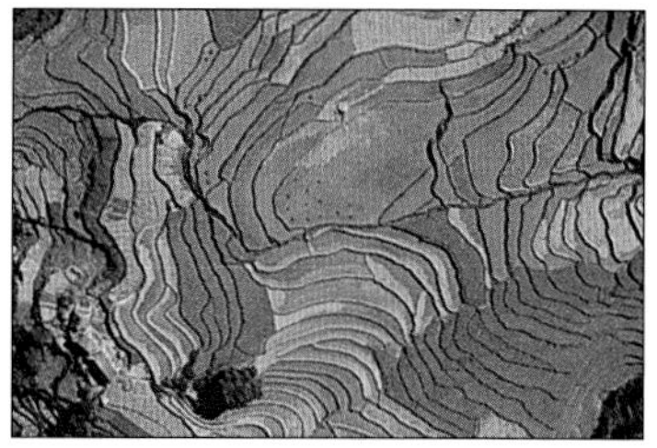

***Terracing allows steep** hillslopes to be cultivated in Nepal, a country where agricultural land is very limited. Because of poor soil quality, these terraces are often abandoned within a few years.*

THE URBAN/RURAL POPULATION DIVIDE

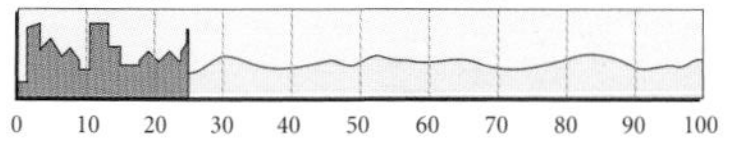

POPULATION DENSITY	TOTAL LAND AREA
808 people per sq mile (312 people per sq km)	1,573,285 sq miles (4,075,868 sq km)

Northern India & the Himalayan States

Bangladesh, Bhutan, Nepal, Arunachal Pradesh, Assam, Bihar, Chandigarh, Delhi, Haryana, Himachal Pradesh, Jammu & Kashmir, Manipur, Meghalaya, Mizoram, Nagaland, Punjab, Rajasthan, Sikkim, Tripura, Uttar Pradesh, West Bengal

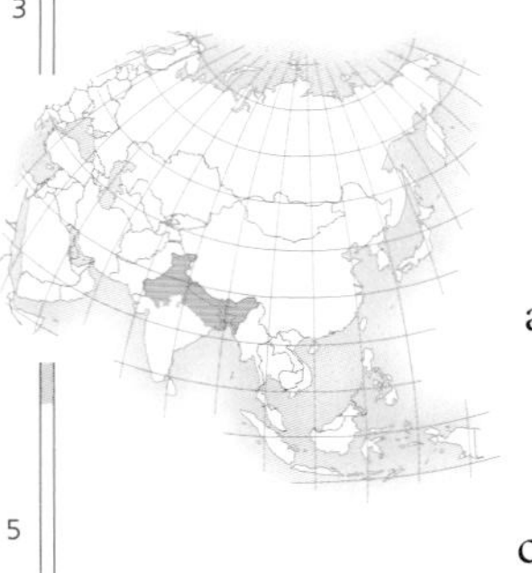

The Ganges and Brahmaputra river basins and the massive mountain barrier of the Himalayas define this region's landscape and have served to reinforce potent cultural and religious differences among its people. Hinduism pervades most aspects of national life and is a growing political force within India, a secular country which also encompasses the center of Sikhism at Amritsar and the world's largest Muslim minority. Nepal is a crowded mountain state, which faces severe ecological problems from deforestation, while the tiny Himalayan Buddhist kingdom of Bhutan is emerging from long-term isolation, to welcome selected visitors. The Muslim state of Bangladesh, formerly East Pakistan, is one of the world's most densely populated countries and one of the poorest, with more than 120 million people living largely on the massive Ganges/Brahmaputra Delta. Many Bangladeshis live under threat of repeated, catastrophic floods.

The Golden Temple in Amritsar, the most sacred shrine of the Sikh religion, was the scene of violent clashes between Sikh separatists and government forces in 1984.

Map Key

POPULATION
- 1 million to 5 million
- 500,000 to 1 million
- 100,000 to 500,000
- 50,000 to 100,000
- 10,000 to 50,000
- below 10,000

ELEVATION
- 6000m / 19,686ft
- 4000m / 13,124ft
- 3000m / 9843ft
- 2000m / 6562ft
- 1000m / 3281ft
- 500m / 1640ft
- 250m / 820ft
- 100m / 328ft
- sea level

Transportation & Industry

Textiles, engineering, chemicals, and electronics are leading industries in north India. The plateau of Chota Nagpur provides ore for iron and steel production in the major industrial region northeast of Calcutta. Bangladesh processes jute and Nepal has a small manufacturing sector based on agricultural produce, while Bhutan's limited industry is concentrated in the southern lowland area.

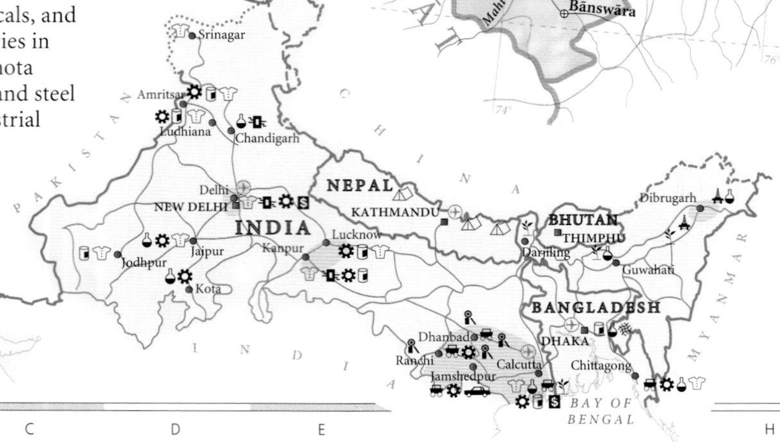

Major industry and infrastructure
- adventure tourism
- car manufacture
- chemicals
- coal
- electronics
- engineering
- finance
- food processing
- iron & steel
- jute processing
- oil
- tea processing
- textiles
- capital cities
- major towns
- international airports
- major roads
- major industrial areas

Transportation Network

Over 60% of Bangladesh's internal trade is carried by boat. The country has a very disjointed land transportation network, with no bridges over the Brahmaputra and few road crossings on the Ganges River.

The Landscape

Most of the region is drained by the Ganges River, which meets the Brahmaputra in Bangladesh to form an immense delta before flowing into the Bay of Bengal. The Himalayas extend eastward over 1,500 miles (2,400 km), from the parallel ranges running through Jammu and Kashmir. The Thar Desert occupies the southwest.

The Indian Punjab lies mainly to the west of the Ganges watershed and its rivers flow into the Indus. Control of this water resource has been a source of great friction with neighboring Pakistan.

The border between India and Pakistan runs through the Thar Desert, an area of sandy *seif* dunes 50–100 ft (15–30 m) in height. Fossils found in the desert indicate that the dunes, stabilized by vegetation, have been in their current position for about 3,000 years.

Sambhar Salt Lake in Rajasthan is India's largest lake. Unlike most of the Himalayan lakes which are glacial in origin – formed in ice-scoured basins or as the result of depositional damming – it is an ephemeral salt lake filled periodically by flash flooding.

The Pir Panjal Range in southwestern Kashmir rises to elevations of 12,500 ft (3,810 m). Despite the freezing conditions, settlements and extensive pastures are found above the tree line.

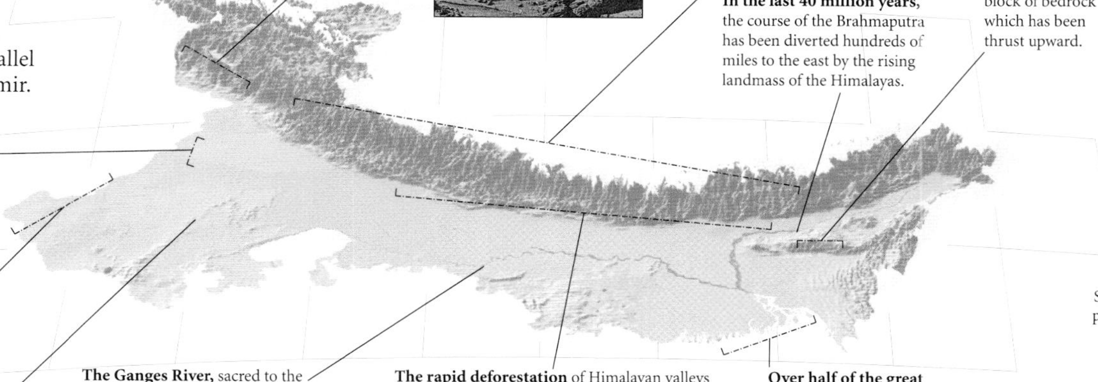

The northern ranges of the Himalayas contain the highest mountains in the world, with average heights of more than 23,000 ft (7,000 m) and many peaks higher than 26,000 ft (8,000 m).

In the last 40 million years, the course of the Brahmaputra has been diverted hundreds of miles to the east by the rising landmass of the Himalayas.

The Khasi Hills are an example of a *horst*, a fractured block of bedrock which has been thrust upward.

The Ganges River, sacred to the Hindu people, drains a vast lowland area at the base of the Himalayas. The northern plains are covered by sandy deposits, broken by mud-banks formed when the river floods.

The rapid deforestation of Himalayan valleys has led to acute soil erosion and increased rates of rainwater runoff, both cited as possible causes of the worsening floods downstream in the Ganges/Brahmaputra Delta, although natural rates are high and may be the real cause.

Over half of the great Ganges/Brahmaputra Delta floods each year during the monsoon as rivers, swollen by meltwater from the Himalayas and by excess rainwater, break their banks and fertilize the land with nutrient-rich sediment.

The summit of Machhapuchhre rises to 22,942 ft (6,993 m). It is also known as the "Fish's Tail" because of its distinctive peak.

Debris slides in the middle Himalayas

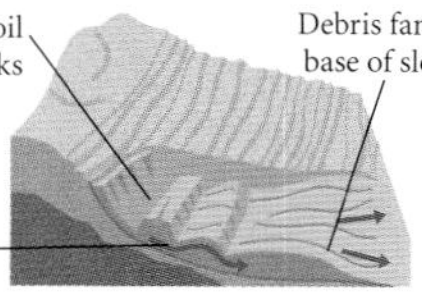

Soil loss in the middle Himalayas has largely been attributed to debris slides, where large blocks of soil are mobilized by saturation along a slide plane. Once mobile, the soil slides down the slope, gaining speed and thinning to form a fan at the base of the slope.

Using the Land

Grain production dominates land use. Rice is most widely grown in the east. Irrigation and new crop strains have dramatically increased yields in the Punjab, a major wheat-producing area. River floodplains are intensively farmed and livestock-herding is widespread, particularly in Bhutan. Regional crops include jute in Bangladesh, tea in Assam, cardamom in Sikkim, and saffron in Kashmir.

Land use and agricultural distribution

cattle		capital cities	
goats		major towns	
sheep		pasture	
cereals		cropland	
jute		forest	
rice		mountain region	
tea		wetland	
		desert	

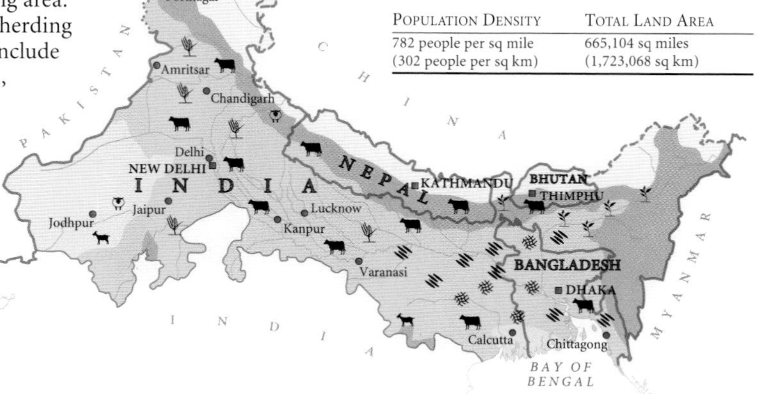

The Urban/Rural Population Divide

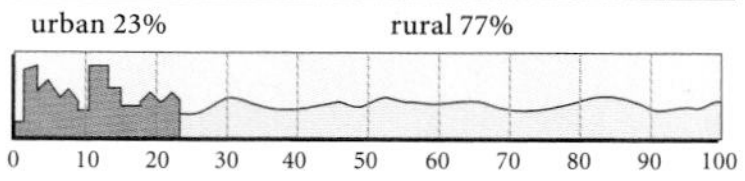

Population Density	Total Land Area
782 people per sq mile (302 people per sq km)	665,104 sq miles (1,723,068 sq km)

An adverse climate, steep slopes, and poor soils limit crop cultivation in Bhutan, which is a largely agrarian economy. Rice, corn, and wheat are the main staples, although orchards are being established as the soil and climate suit this type of farming.

Flooded streets in Dhaka, Bangladesh are a testament to the region's vulnerability to flooding. In 1988 alone, 75% of the country was flooded, leaving thousands of people dead and over 25 million homeless.

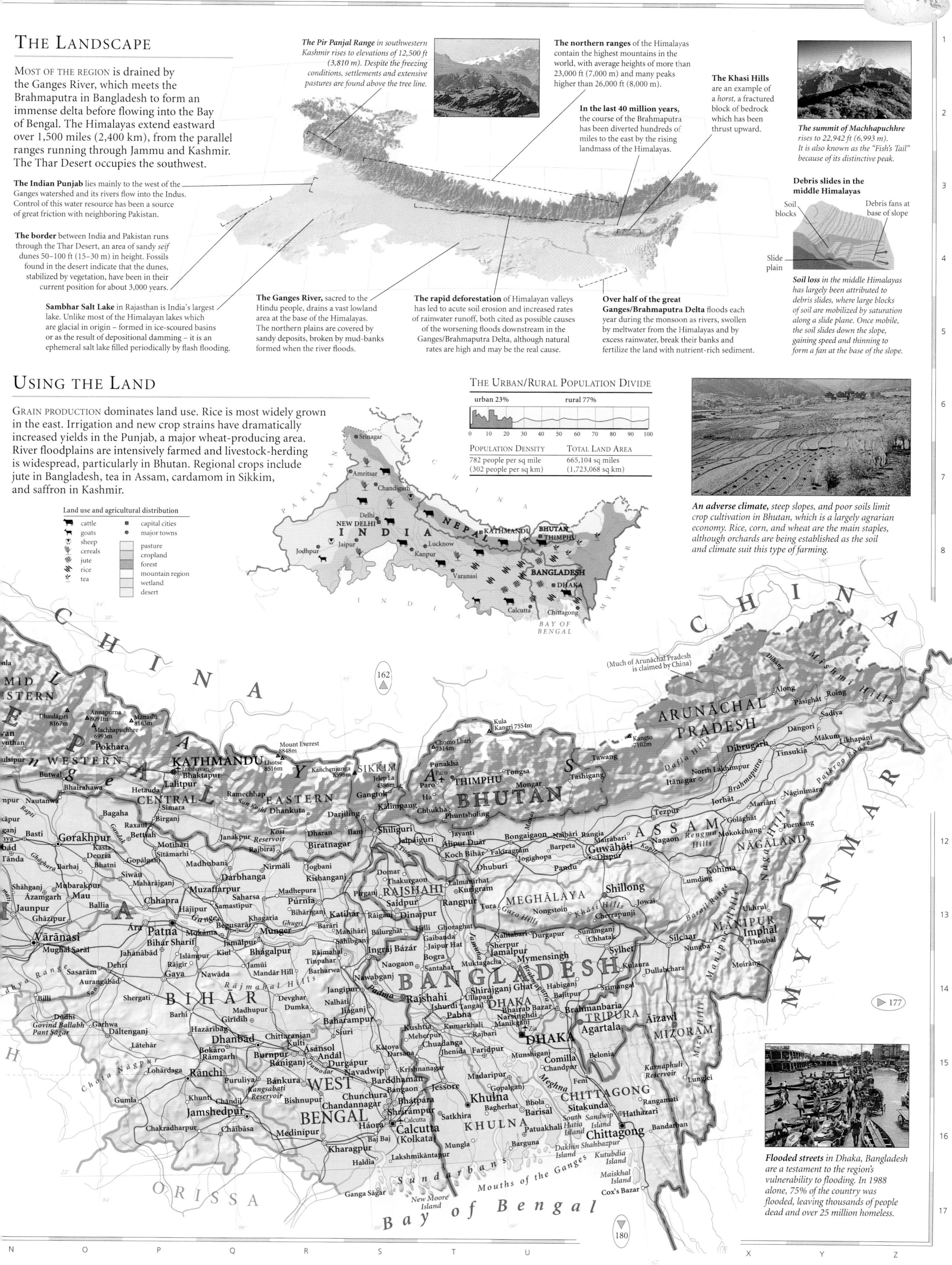

Southern India & Sri Lanka

Sri Lanka, Andhra Pradesh, Dadra & Nagar Haveli, Daman & Diu, Goa, Gujarat, Karnataka, Kerala, Lakshadweep, Madhya Pradesh, Maharashtra, Orissa, Pondicherry, Tamil Nadu

The unique and highly independent southern states reflect the diverse and decentralized nature of India, which has fourteen official languages. The southern half of the peninsula lay beyond the reach of early invaders from the north and retained the distinct and ancient culture of Dravidian peoples such as the Tamils, whose language is spoken in preference to Hindi throughout southern India. The interior plateau of southern India is less densely populated than the coastal lowlands, where the European colonial imprint is strongest. Urban and industrial growth is accelerating, but southern India's vast population remains predominantly rural. The island of Sri Lanka has two distinct cultural groups; the mainly Buddhist Sinhalese majority, and the Tamil minority whose struggle for a homeland in the northeast has led to prolonged civil war.

Using the Land and Sea

Rice is the main staple in the east, in Sri Lanka and along the humid Malabar Coast. Peanuts are grown on the Deccan Plateau, with wheat, corn, and chickpeas, toward the north. Sri Lanka is a leading exporter of tea, coconuts and rubber. Cotton plantations supply local mills around Nagpur and Mumbai (Bombay). Fishing supports many communities in Kerala and the Laccadive Islands.

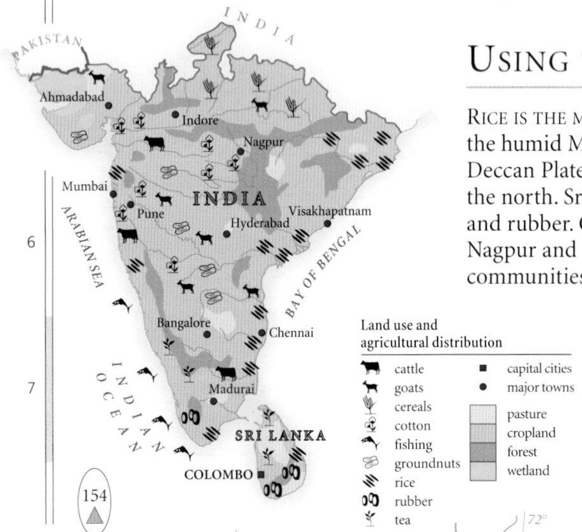

The Urban/Rural Population Divide

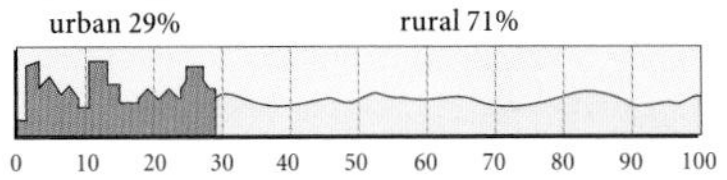

Population Density	Total Land Area
715 people per sq mile (276 people per sq km)	698,295 sq miles (1,809,054 sq km)

Commercial plantations, growing tea, (seen here), cardamom, coffee, coconuts, and rubber, occupy about half the agricultural land in Kerala, necessitating food imports for local consumption.

The Landscape

The undulating Deccan Plateau underlies most of southern India; it slopes gently down toward the east and is largely enclosed by the Ghats coastal hill ranges. The Western Ghats run continuously along the Arabian Sea coast, while the Eastern Ghats are interrupted by rivers which follow the slope of the plateau and flow across broad lowlands into the Bay of Bengal. The plateaus and basins of Sri Lanka's central highlands are surrounded by a broad plain.

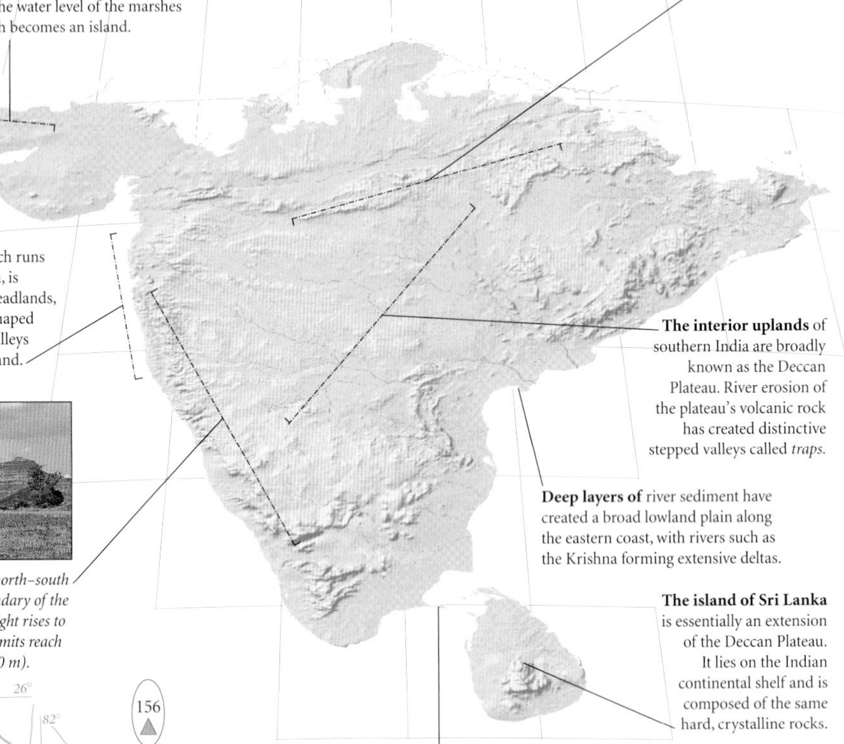

Along the northern boundary of the Deccan Plateau, old basement rocks are interspersed with younger sedimentary strata. This creates spectacular scarplands, cut by numerous waterfalls along the softer sedimentary strata.

The Rann of Kachchh tidal marshes encircle the low-lying Kachchh Peninsula. For several months during the rainy season the water level of the marshes rises and Kachchh becomes an island.

The Konkan coast, which runs between Daman and Goa, is characterized by rocky headlands, and bays with crescent-shaped beaches. Flooded river valleys known as *rias* extend inland.

The interior uplands of southern India are broadly known as the Deccan Plateau. River erosion of the plateau's volcanic rock has created distinctive stepped valleys called *traps*.

Deep layers of river sediment have created a broad lowland plain along the eastern coast, with rivers such as the Krishna forming extensive deltas.

The island of Sri Lanka is essentially an extension of the Deccan Plateau. It lies on the Indian continental shelf and is composed of the same hard, crystalline rocks.

The Western Ghats run north–south marking the western boundary of the Deccan Plateau. Their height rises to the south where their summits reach altitudes of 8,000 ft (2,500 m).

Adam's Bridge

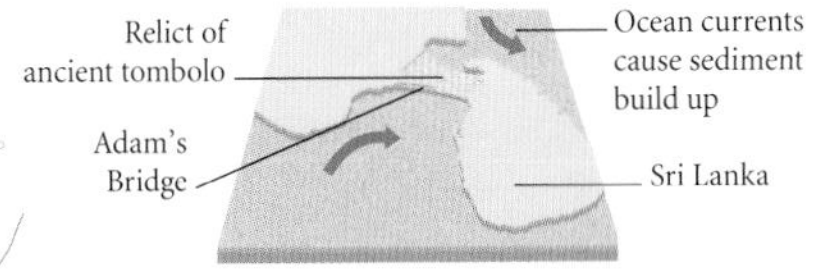

Adam's Bridge (Rama's Bridge) is a chain of sandy shoals lying about 4 ft (1.2 m) under the sea between India and Sri Lanka. They once formed the world's longest tombolo, or land bridge, before the sea level began to rise several thousand years ago.

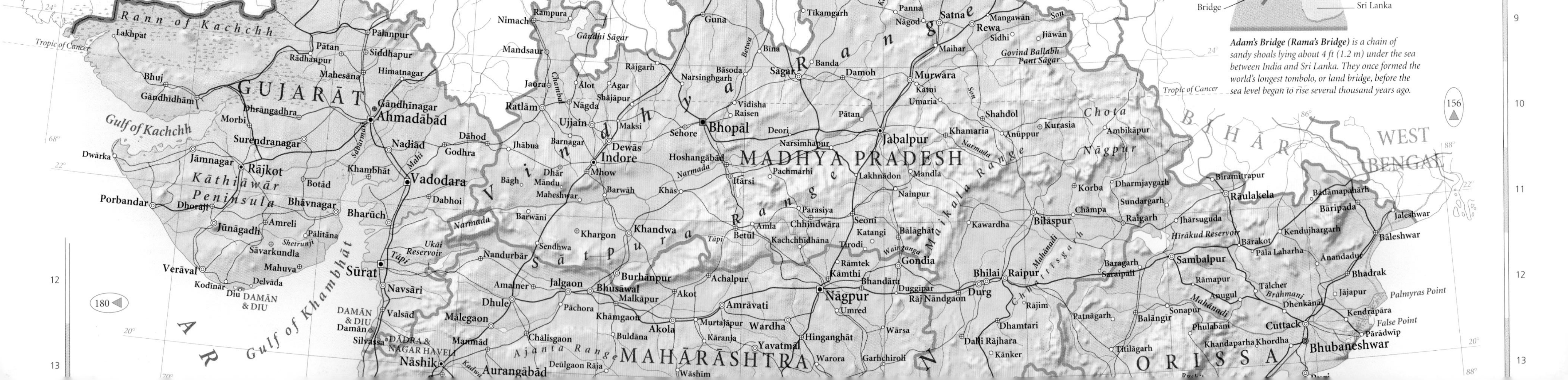

Map Key

POPULATION
- above 5 million
- 1 million to 5 million
- 500,000 to 1 million
- 100,000 to 500,000
- 50,000 to 100,000
- 10,000 to 50,000
- below 10,000

ELEVATION
- 2000m / 6562ft
- 1000m / 3281ft
- 500m / 1640ft
- 250m / 820ft
- 100m / 328ft
- sea level

Sea pencils *thrive on the coral reefs around the coast of the Laccadive Islands and Sri Lanka. The reefs support an amazing diversity of marine life, but are increasingly under threat from growing coastal populations.*

Local fisheries around Sri Lanka *afford great potential for exploitation, but development has been hampered by technological constraints. Most fishermen live on the coastal fringes and operate on a small scale.*

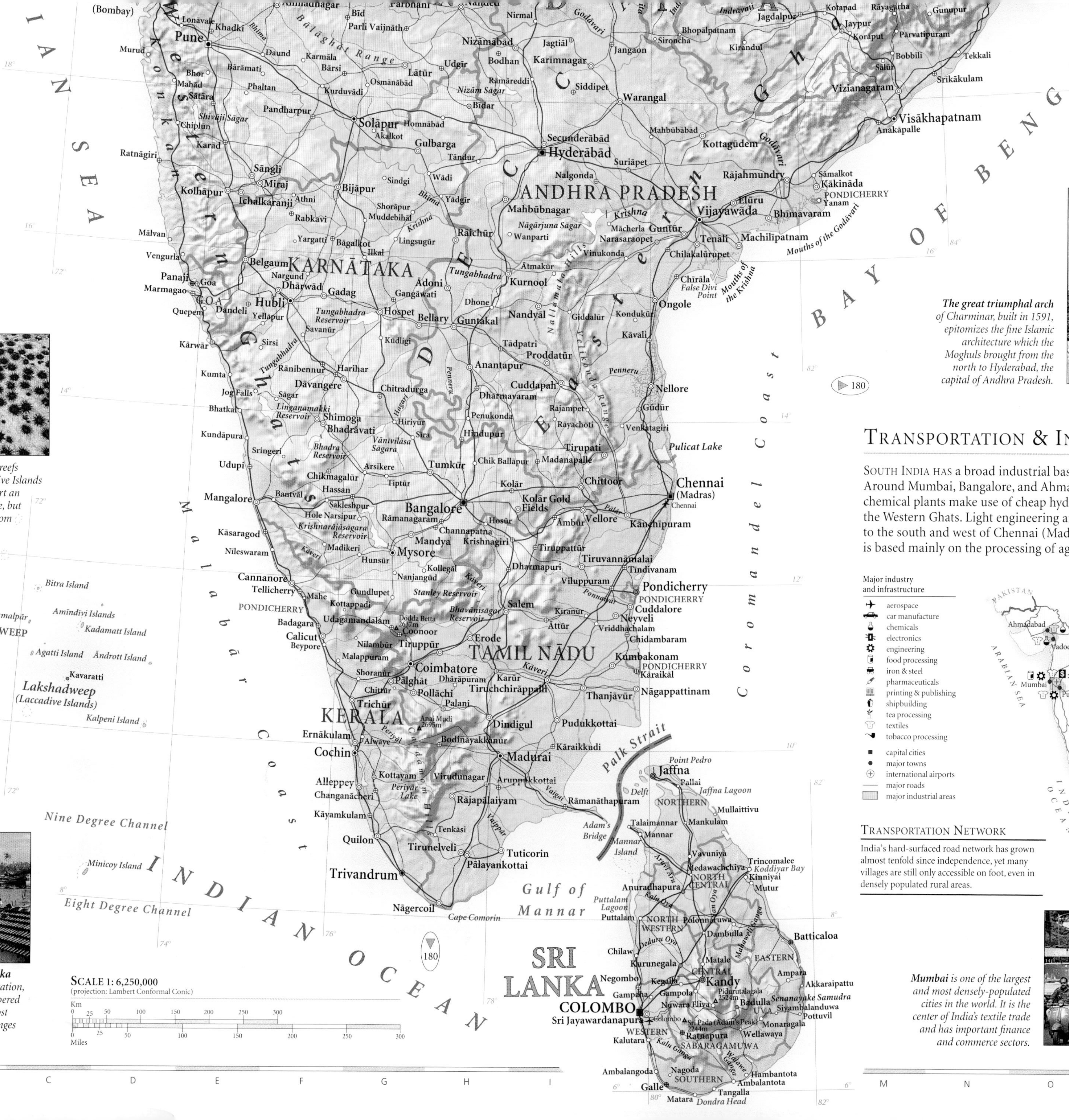

180

***The great triumphal arch** of Charminar, built in 1591, epitomizes the fine Islamic architecture which the Moghuls brought from the north to Hyderabad, the capital of Andhra Pradesh.*

Transportation & Industry

South India has a broad industrial base, with three leading regions. Around Mumbai, Bangalore, and Ahmadabad, cotton mills and chemical plants make use of cheap hydroelectric power generated in the Western Ghats. Light engineering and textiles are well established to the south and west of Chennai (Madras). Sri Lanka's industry is based mainly on the processing of agricultural products.

Major industry and infrastructure
- aerospace
- car manufacture
- chemicals
- electronics
- engineering
- food processing
- iron & steel
- pharmaceuticals
- printing & publishing
- shipbuilding
- tea processing
- textiles
- tobacco processing
- capital cities
- major towns
- international airports
- major roads
- major industrial areas

Transportation Network

India's hard-surfaced road network has grown almost tenfold since independence, yet many villages are still only accessible on foot, even in densely populated rural areas.

***Mumbai** is one of the largest and most densely-populated cities in the world. It is the center of India's textile trade and has important finance and commerce sectors.*

Mainland East Asia

China, Mongolia, North Korea, South Korea, Taiwan

China, the world's most populous nation, has an unbroken cultural history, longer than that of any other country, and is rapidly emerging as a leading world power. When Mao Zedong established Communist rule in 1949, China had become a backward feudal empire, stricken by civil war and over a century of European and Japanese incursions. The closed regime withstood the traumas of rapid industrialization, communal farming, and the brutal purges of the Cultural Revolution. Since the 1980s has introduced economic reforms, led by expanded foreign trade. China's population is heavily concentrated in the east and, despite accelerating urban growth, remains predominantly rural. One cultural group, the Han, make up over 90% of the people, while five "Autonomous Regions" have been established in the south and west for the main ethnic minorities.

***Gansu province,** through which the ancient Silk Route passes on its way to the west, is characterized by extensive loess deposits which are terraced and used for crop cultivation.*

Transportation & Industry

Large-scale industrial growth has always been a priority of the Communist government. Metals and machine production, chemicals, and engineering are among the leading industries, concentrated in the major cities of the east coast. Textiles and clothing manufacture, the main consumer goods sector, is relatively well dispersed, with a few significant centers such as Shanghai, Beijing, and Hong Kong.

Transportation Network

734,473 miles (1,182,727 km)	1,182 miles (1,904 km)
41,798 miles (67,308 km)	70,495 miles (113,519 km)

Steam trains use China's abundant coal and are still the main form of passenger and goods transportation. The railroad network is now struggling to meet an ever-growing demand.

156

***Coal is China's** most abundant mineral resource. This mine at Fuxin in Liaoning province is used to provide coal for a nearby power station.*

The Landscape

The East Asian landmass is arranged in three distinct levels, the highest of which is the Plateau of Tibet in the southwest. The arid uplands of northwestern China form a barren middle step. The main rivers flow eastward from these two platforms to the East China and South China sea coasts, across a broad region of alluvial lowlands and low hills.

***Paektu-san,** at 9,023 ft (2,750 m), is North Korea's highest peak; an extinct volcanic cone now filled by a crater lake.*

***Because of its very small grain-size,** loess has been easily transported and deposited by winds which scour the plains, and in northern China, deposits of loess can be up to 3,000 ft (1,000 m) thick. Loess-based soils are very fertile, but clearing land for agriculture quickly destabilizes the soil and allows it to be eroded.*

***The Plateau of Tibet** occupies about a quarter of China's total area. The Yangtze, Mekong, Indus, and Brahmaputra Rivers all originate in the south and east of the plateau.*

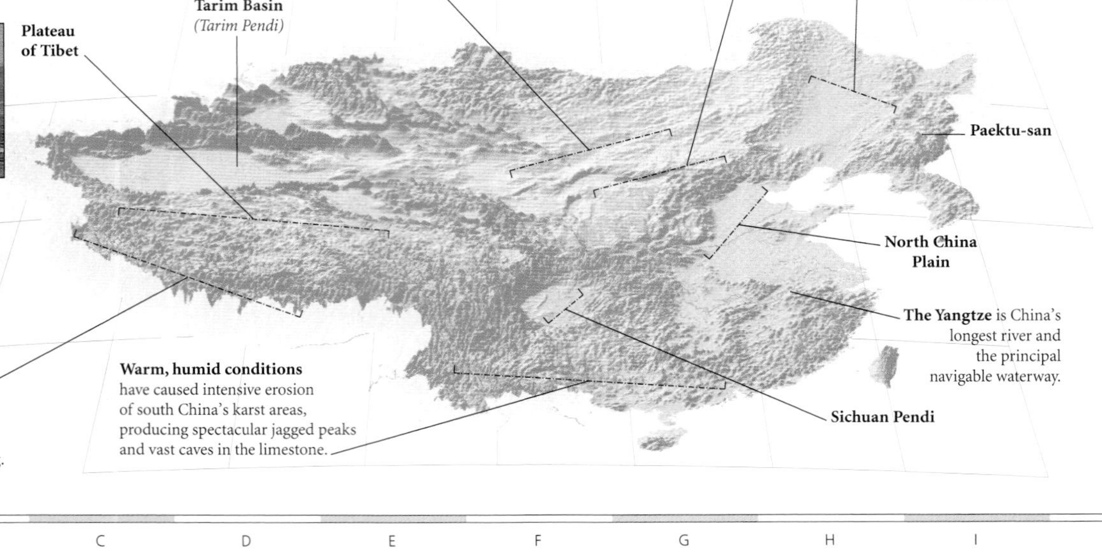

The Gobi Desert extends across the Nei Mongol Gaoyuan; a vast saucer-shaped upland surrounded by a rim of higher mountains.

The loess plateau of northern China is the world's greatest expanse of loess, a loose soil made up of wind-blown material. The plateau has been heavily eroded by tributaries of the Yellow River.

Shifting sand dunes are found in the arid west of the northeast China Plain, while the eastern part of this great expanse is wet and swampy.

The Yangtze is China's longest river and the principal navigable waterway.

The Himalayas extend along the southwestern edge of the Plateau of Tibet, forming a continuous mountain barrier over 1,500 miles (2,500 km) long.

Warm, humid conditions have caused intensive erosion of south China's karst areas, producing spectacular jagged peaks and vast caves in the limestone.

***Although it is over 20 years** since his death, the legacy of Chairman Mao Zedong, architect of the Great Proletariat Cultural Revolution, is still very much in evidence across China's landscape. In 1959 Mao launched a 20-year period of industrialization and socioeconomic realignment, rejecting western ideals and social codes.*

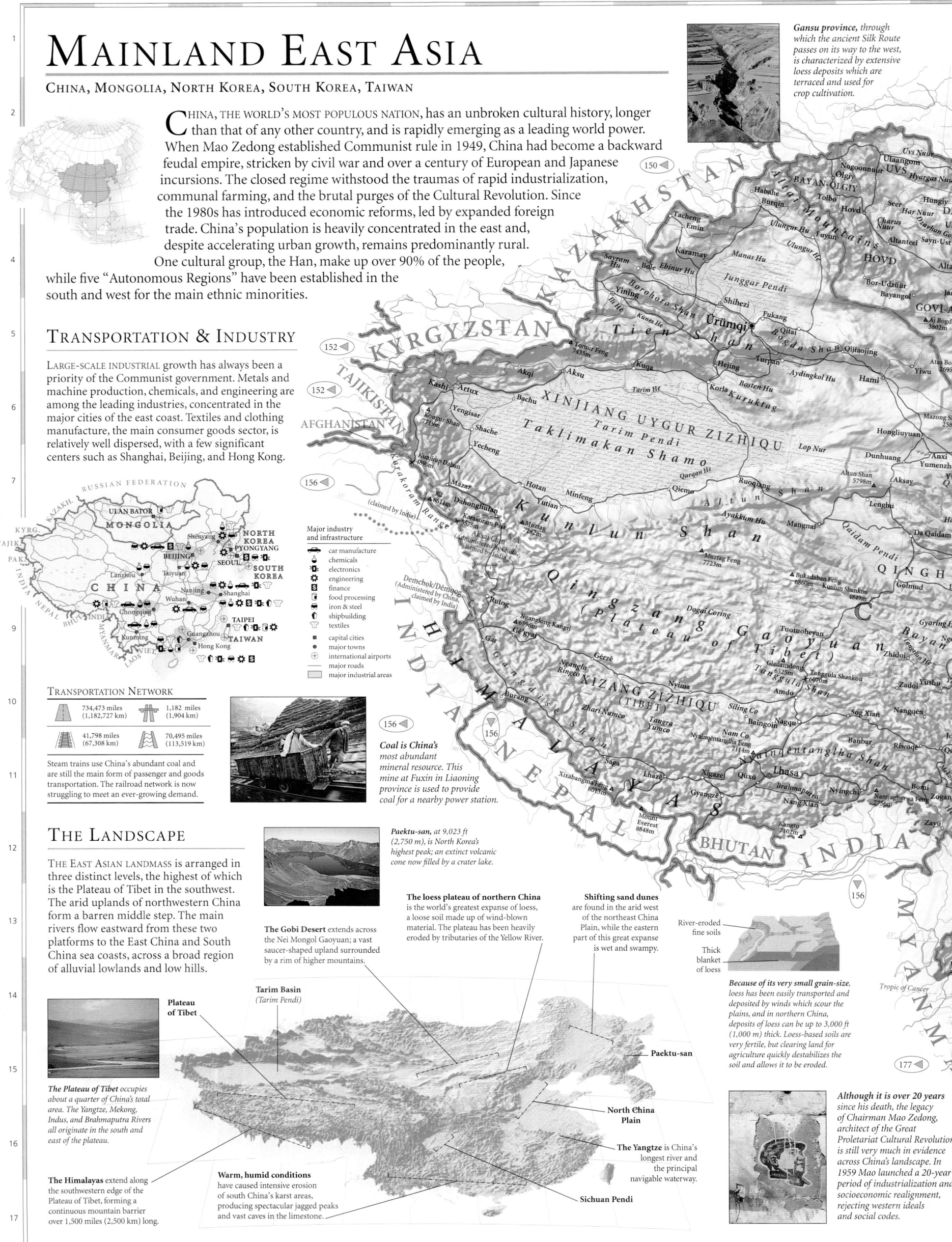

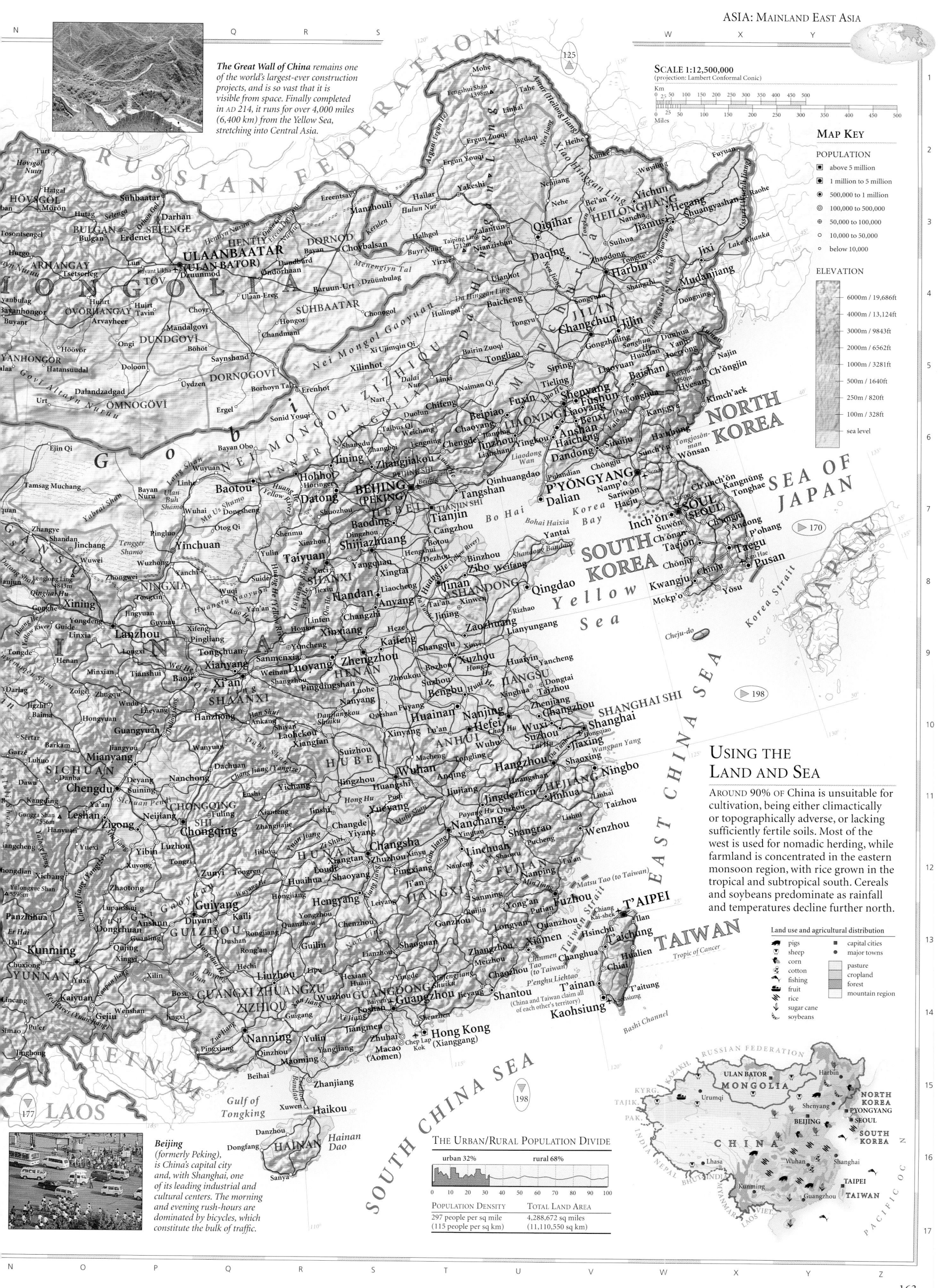

The Great Wall of China remains one of the world's largest-ever construction projects, and is so vast that it is visible from space. Finally completed in AD 214, it runs for over 4,000 miles (6,400 km) from the Yellow Sea, stretching into Central Asia.

SCALE 1:12,500,000
(projection: Lambert Conformal Conic)

MAP KEY

POPULATION
- above 5 million
- 1 million to 5 million
- 500,000 to 1 million
- 100,000 to 500,000
- 50,000 to 100,000
- 10,000 to 50,000
- below 10,000

ELEVATION
- 6000m / 19,686ft
- 4000m / 13,124ft
- 3000m / 9843ft
- 2000m / 6562ft
- 1000m / 3281ft
- 500m / 1640ft
- 250m / 820ft
- 100m / 328ft
- sea level

USING THE LAND AND SEA

AROUND 90% OF China is unsuitable for cultivation, being either climactically or topographically adverse, or lacking sufficiently fertile soils. Most of the west is used for nomadic herding, while farmland is concentrated in the eastern monsoon region, with rice grown in the tropical and subtropical south. Cereals and soybeans predominate as rainfall and temperatures decline further north.

Land use and agricultural distribution
- pigs
- sheep
- corn
- cotton
- fishing
- fruit
- rice
- sugar cane
- soybeans
- capital cities
- major towns
- pasture
- cropland
- forest
- mountain region

Beijing (formerly Peking), is China's capital city and, with Shanghai, one of its leading industrial and cultural centers. The morning and evening rush-hours are dominated by bicycles, which constitute the bulk of traffic.

THE URBAN/RURAL POPULATION DIVIDE
urban 32% rural 68%

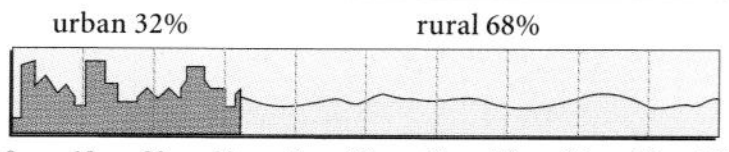

POPULATION DENSITY	TOTAL LAND AREA
297 people per sq mile	4,288,672 sq miles
(115 people per sq km)	(11,110,550 sq km)

WESTERN CHINA

Gansu, Ningxia, Qinghai, Tibet, Xinjiang

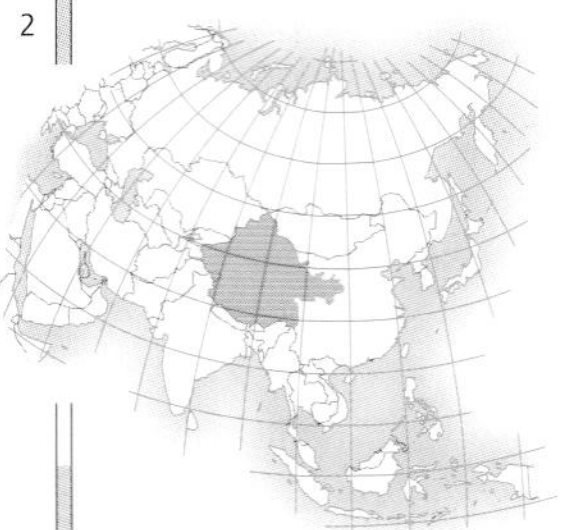

The PLATEAUS AND BASINS of China's dry, desolate western domain are sparsely populated and largely undeveloped, although they have rich mineral reserves; they also form a critical buffer zone for China, in a geographically important and culturally sensitive part of the Asian continent. Across most of the west, the Han Chinese are outnumbered by a range of cultural groups, including the Uygur, the largest group of the various seminomadic Muslim peoples from Central Asia. The remote, inhospitable Plateau of Tibet is the world's coldest and highest plateau. It has been occupied by the Chinese since 1950. Tibet is one of western China's five "Autonomous Regions," but its reclusive Buddhist culture has been systematically undermined by the Chinese government.

MAP KEY

POPULATION

- ■ 1 million to 5 million
- ◉ 500,000 to 1 million
- ⊙ 100,000 to 500,000
- ⊕ 50,000 to 100,000
- ○ 10,000 to 50,000
- ○ below 10,000

ELEVATION

- 6000m / 19,686ft
- 4000m / 13,124ft
- 3000m / 9843ft
- 2000m / 6562ft
- 1000m / 3281ft
- 500m / 1640ft
- 250m / 820ft
- 100m / 328ft
- sea level

SCALE 1:7,000,000
(projection: Lambert Conformal Conic)

The Lhasa He is one of the many rivers that drain the vast Plateau of Tibet. From its source in the Nyainqêntanglha Shan range and fed by the spring meltwater, it eventually joins the upper Brahmaputra 40 miles (65 km) southwest of Lhasa.

USING THE LAND

AGRICULTURE IS CONSTRAINED by the cold, dry climate and lack of fertile soils in the region, although irrigation and glasshouse farming are increasing agricultural potential. Large quantities of fruit, like melons and grapes, are grown at the oases of Hami and Turpan in Xinjiang, and new irrigation schemes have greatly increased cotton and wheat production in the Tarim Basin *(Tarim Pendi)*. Most of the great area of Tibet and Qinghai is devoted to pastoralism. Sheep are the principal livestock.

Land use and agricultural distribution

- goats
- sheep
- cereals
- cotton
- grapes
- melons
- oases
- major towns
- pasture
- cropland
- forest
- mountain region
- desert

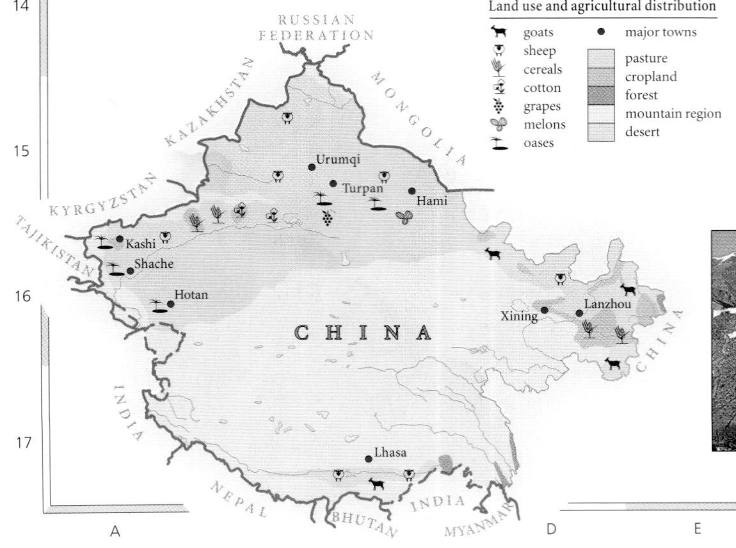

The Potala Palace, in Tibet's capital, Lhasa, was the former residence of the Dalai Lama, Tibetan Buddhism's spiritual leader. Tibet remains only sparsely populated; forming over 20% of China's landmass, it supports fewer than 1% of its population.

THE LANDSCAPE

THE HIMALAYAS MARK the southwestern edge of the Plateau of Tibet, an extreme mountain wilderness which occupies nearly a quarter of China's total area. A large structural depression, the Qaidam Pendi, lies at its northeastern edge. The Kunlun mountain chain isolates the plateau from the desert to the north, where the Tien Shan range forms a spur between the Tarim Basin *(Tarim Pendi)* and Dzungarian Basin *(Junggar Pendi)*.

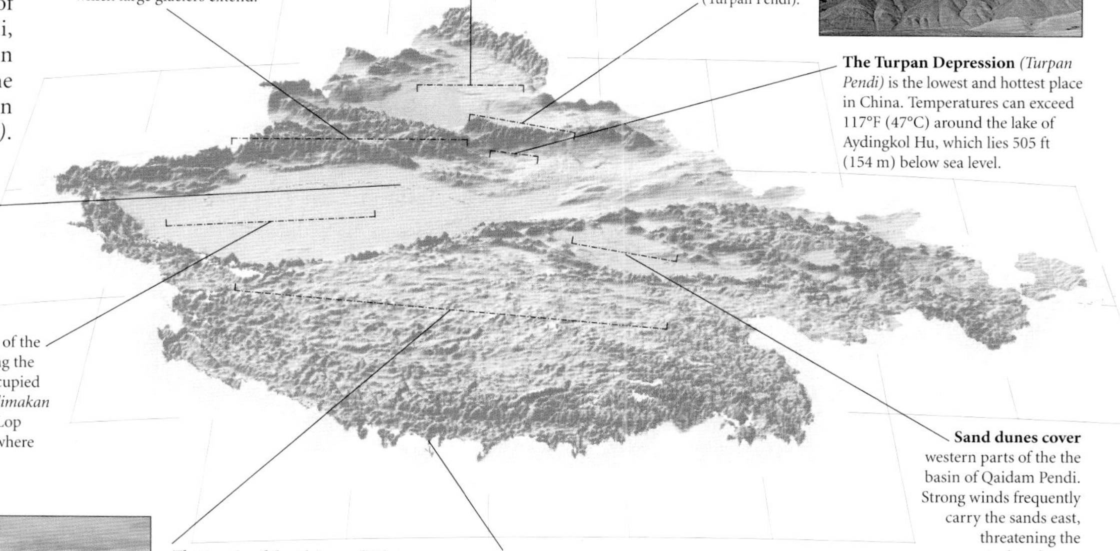

The Bogda Shan, an eastward arm of the Tien Shan range, rise high above the Turpan Depression (Turpan Pendi).

The terrain of the Plateau of Tibet consists of mountain peaks and open plateaus, dotted with brackish lakes. These are probably remnants of the Tethys Sea, which covered the area before it was uplifted following the collision of the Indo-Australian and Eurasian plates.

Tarim Basin *(Tarim Pendi)*

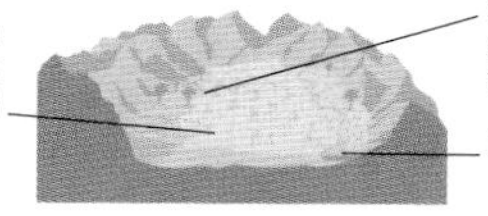

The Tarim Basin (Tarim Pendi) *has no permanent rivers. Rainfall from the surrounding Plateau of Tibet and Tien Shan ranges drains into the basin's sand and gravel floor.*

From its source, *high in eastern Qinghai, the Yellow River starts on a 3,395 mile (5,464 km) journey to the Yellow Sea.*

TRANSPORTATION & INDUSTRY

OIL EXTRACTION AT Yumen and in the Dzungarian and Qaidam basins has led to the growth of the petrochemical industry and a range of heavy manufacturing plants in the cities of Lanzhou and Urumqi. Tibet, and most of Xinjiang, have little industry beyond traditional handicrafts, especially textiles at Hotan and Kashi, located along the ancient Silk Route. Nuclear and space-research testing are carried out at Lop Nur in Xinjiang.

TRANSPORTATION NETWORK

The construction of roads connecting Lhasa in Tibet with Sichuan, Qinghai, and Xinjiang was achieved in the 1950s, in spite of the extreme physical conditions of the Plateau of Tibet.

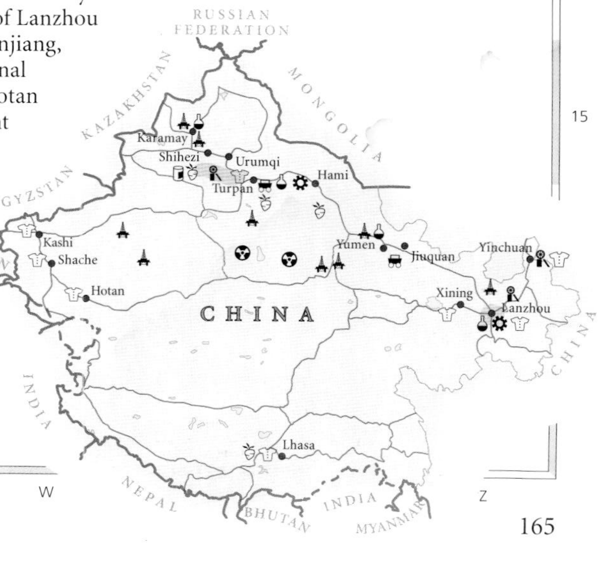

Major industry and infrastructure
- agribusiness
- chemicals
- coal
- engineering
- food processing
- iron & steel
- nuclear testing
- oil
- textiles
- major towns
- major roads
- major industrial areas

Eastern China

Taiwan, Anhui, Beijing, Fujian, Guangdong, Guangxi, Guizhou, Hainan, Hebei, Henan, Hubei, Hunan, Jiangsu, Jiangxi, Shaanxi, Shandong, Shanghai, Shanxi, Sichuan, Tianjin, Yunnan, Zhejiang

North of the Qin Ling range in Shaanxi province, is an agriculturally fertile region covered with fine, wind-blown deposits and known as the loess plateau. The loose sediments are vulnerable to water erosion.

The east is China's heartland. Massive industrial development since 1949 has transformed much of the densely populated rural landscape, in a region still prone to flooding and drought. Over 20 cities have populations of over a million, including the giant metropolis of Shanghai and the capital Beijing, which has been China's cultural and political center since the 13th century. The ethnically diverse southwest and the oil-rich interior provinces of Sichuan and Shaanxi have largely missed out on the remarkable economic growth occurring in designated free-trade areas along the coasts of the South and East China seas. The republic of Taiwan was established in 1949 by Chinese nationalists ousted from the mainland by the victorious Communist forces. Taiwan now has one of the strongest economies in the world but its sovereignty is not recognized by China. Hong Kong provides a major international trade link for China; a 99-year "lease" period of British control was concluded in 1997.

Using the Land and Sea

This is a region of intensive cultivation. Wheat, millet, sorghum, and cotton are the main crops of the Yellow River basin. South from Sichuan, rice becomes the principal crop, grown with wheat, corn, and cotton along the Yangtze River. Tea is produced in the hills and sugar cane along the coast of the southeast, where flat land is limited. Pigs and poultry are raised in great numbers.

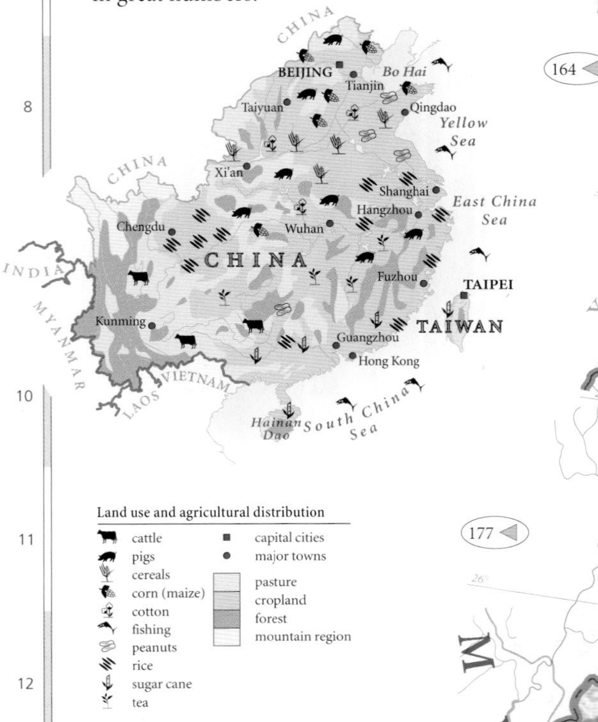

On the hills above the North China Plain, slopes are terraced to utilize the rich loess soils of the Taihang Shan range.

The former Portuguese territory of Macao, with its colonial architecture, bars and casinos, reverted to Chinese rule in 1999.

Map Key

Population

- above 5 million
- 1 million to 5 million
- 500,000 to 1 million
- 100,000 to 500,000
- 50,000 to 100,000
- 10,000 to 50,000
- below 10,000

Elevation

- 6000m / 19,686ft
- 4000m / 13,124ft
- 3000m / 9843ft
- 2000m / 6562ft
- 1000m / 3281ft
- 500m / 1640ft
- 250m / 820ft
- 100m / 328ft
- sea level

Scale 1:7,750,000
(projection: Lambert Conformal Conic)

Km 0 25 50 100 150 200 250 300
Miles 0 25 50 100 150 200 250 300

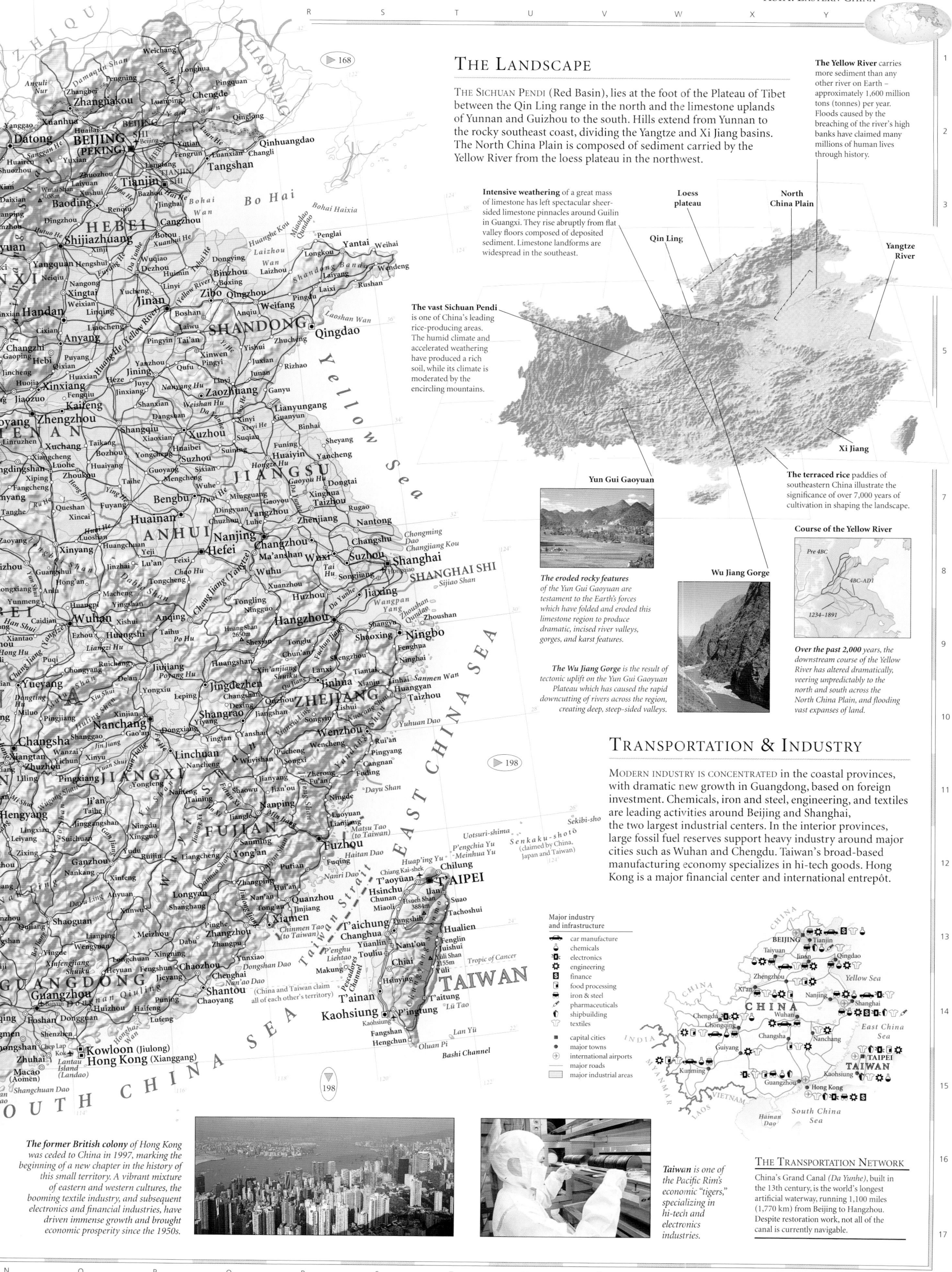

THE LANDSCAPE

THE SICHUAN PENDI (Red Basin), lies at the foot of the Plateau of Tibet between the Qin Ling range in the north and the limestone uplands of Yunnan and Guizhou to the south. Hills extend from Yunnan to the rocky southeast coast, dividing the Yangtze and Xi Jiang basins. The North China Plain is composed of sediment carried by the Yellow River from the loess plateau in the northwest.

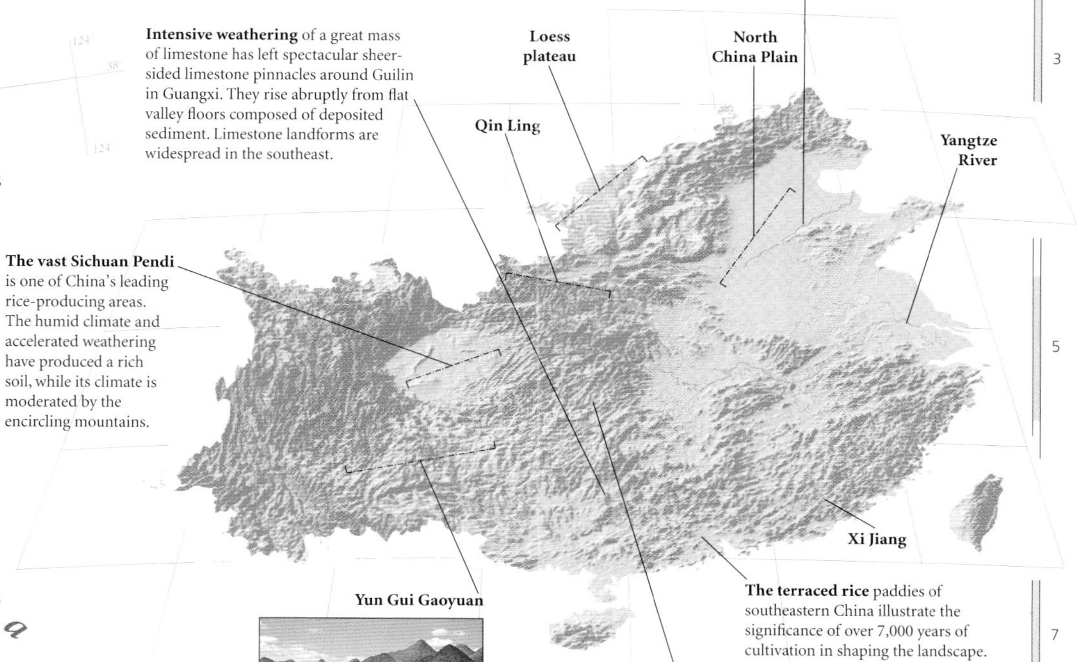

The Yellow River carries more sediment than any other river on Earth – approximately 1,600 million tons (tonnes) per year. Floods caused by the breaching of the river's high banks have claimed many millions of human lives through history.

Intensive weathering of a great mass of limestone has left spectacular sheer-sided limestone pinnacles around Guilin in Guangxi. They rise abruptly from flat valley floors composed of deposited sediment. Limestone landforms are widespread in the southeast.

The vast Sichuan Pendi is one of China's leading rice-producing areas. The humid climate and accelerated weathering have produced a rich soil, while its climate is moderated by the encircling mountains.

The terraced rice paddies of southeastern China illustrate the significance of over 7,000 years of cultivation in shaping the landscape.

***The eroded rocky features** of the Yun Gui Gaoyuan are testament to the Earth's forces which have folded and eroded this limestone region to produce dramatic, incised river valleys, gorges, and karst features.*

***The Wu Jiang Gorge** is the result of tectonic uplift on the Yun Gui Gaoyuan Plateau which has caused the rapid downcutting of rivers across the region, creating deep, steep-sided valleys.*

Course of the Yellow River

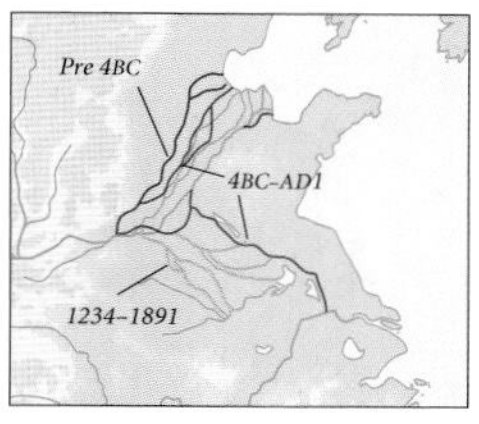

***Over the past 2,000** years, the downstream course of the Yellow River has altered dramatically, veering unpredictably to the north and south across the North China Plain, and flooding vast expanses of land.*

TRANSPORTATION & INDUSTRY

MODERN INDUSTRY IS CONCENTRATED in the coastal provinces, with dramatic new growth in Guangdong, based on foreign investment. Chemicals, iron and steel, engineering, and textiles are leading activities around Beijing and Shanghai, the two largest industrial centers. In the interior provinces, large fossil fuel reserves support heavy industry around major cities such as Wuhan and Chengdu. Taiwan's broad-based manufacturing economy specializes in hi-tech goods. Hong Kong is a major financial center and international entrepôt.

***The former British colony** of Hong Kong was ceded to China in 1997, marking the beginning of a new chapter in the history of this small territory. A vibrant mixture of eastern and western cultures, the booming textile industry, and subsequent electronics and financial industries, have driven immense growth and brought economic prosperity since the 1950s.*

***Taiwan** is one of the Pacific Rim's economic "tigers," specializing in hi-tech and electronics industries.*

THE TRANSPORTATION NETWORK

China's Grand Canal *(Da Yunhe)*, built in the 13th century, is the world's longest artificial waterway, running 1,100 miles (1,770 km) from Beijing to Hangzhou. Despite restoration work, not all of the canal is currently navigable.

NORTHEASTERN CHINA, MONGOLIA & KOREA

MONGOLIA, NORTH KOREA, SOUTH KOREA, Heilongjiang, Inner Mongolia, Jilin, Liaoning

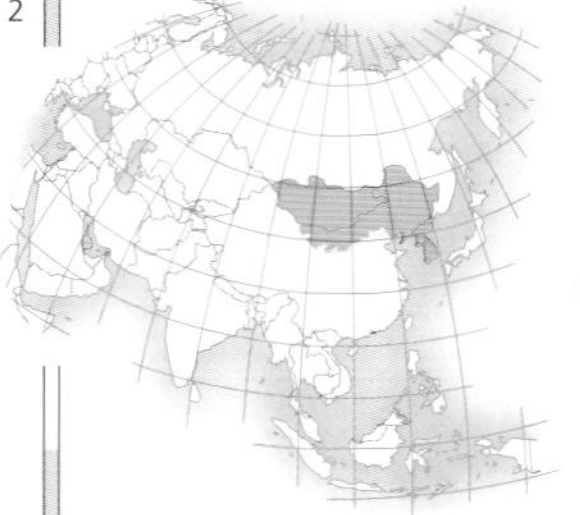

THIS NORTHERLY REGION has been a domain of shifting borders and competing colonial powers for centuries. Mongolia was the heartland of Chinghiz Khan's vast Mongol empire in the 13th century, while northeastern China was home to the Manchus, China's last ruling dynasty (1644–1911). The mineral and forest wealth of the northeast helped make this China's principal region of heavy industry, although the outdated state factories now face decline. South Korea's state-led market economy has grown dramatically and Seoul is now one of the world's largest cities. The austere communist regime of North Korea has isolated itself from the expanding markets of the Pacific Rim and faces continuing economic stagnation.

The Eurasian steppe stretches from the mouth of the Danube in Europe, to Mongolia. In Mongolia, nomadic people have lived in felt huts called yurts or gers, for thousands of years.

MAP KEY

POPULATION

- above 5 million
- 1 million to 5 million
- 500,000 to 1 million
- 100,000 to 500,000
- 50,000 to 100,000
- 10,000 to 50,000
- below 10,000

ELEVATION

- 4000m / 13,124ft
- 3000m / 9843ft
- 2000m / 6562ft
- 1000m / 3281ft
- 500m / 1640ft
- 250m / 820ft
- 100m / 328ft
- sea level

SCALE 1:7,000,000
(projection: Lambert Conformal Conic)

Km 0 25 50 100 150 200
Miles 0 25 50 100 150 200

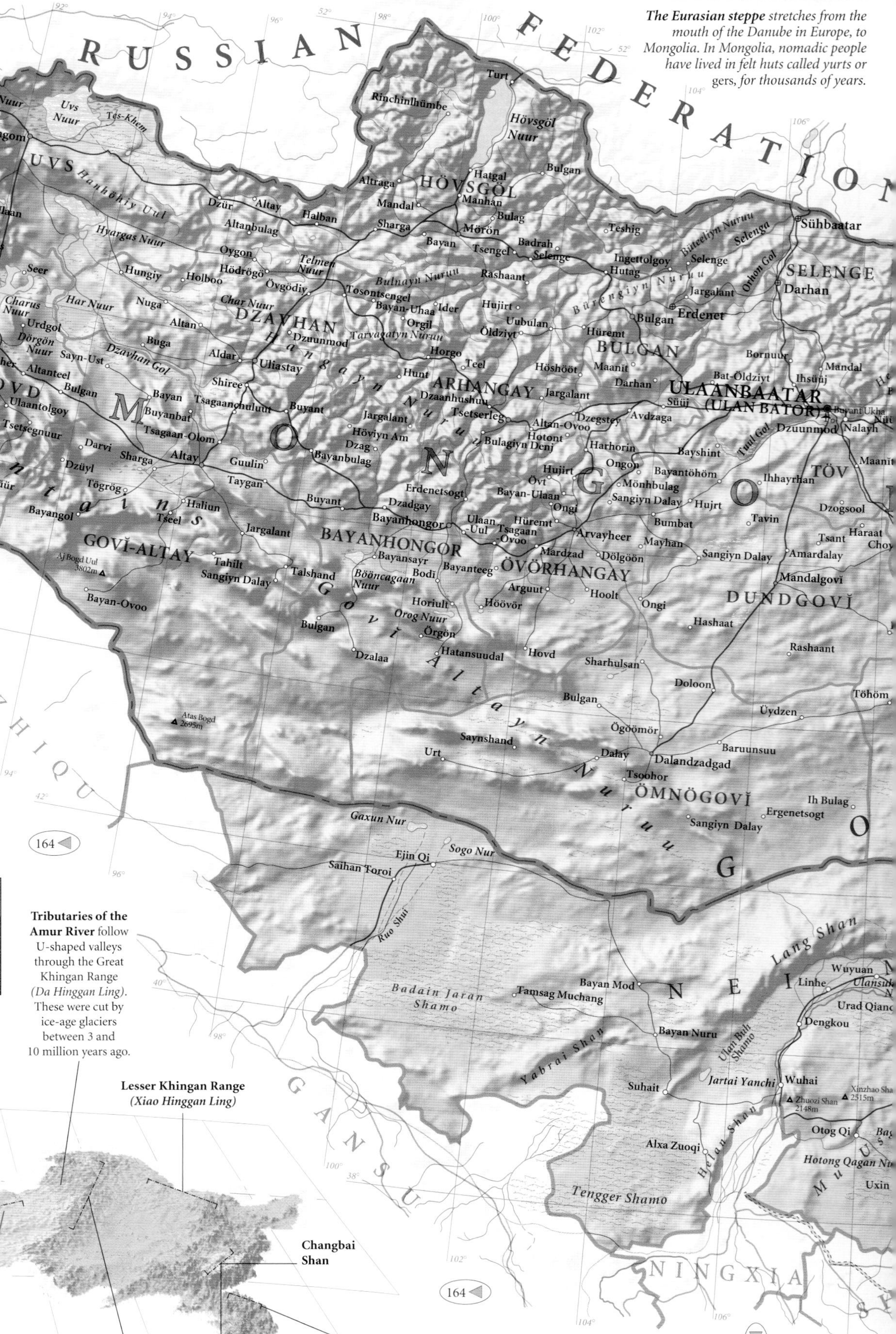

THE LANDSCAPE

THE GREAT NORTH CHINA PLAIN is largely enclosed by mountain ranges including the Great and Lesser Khingan Ranges *(Da Hinggan Ling* and *Xiao Hinggan Ling)* in the north, and the Changbai Shan, which extend south into the rugged peninsula of Korea. The broad steppeland plateau of Nei Mongol Gaoyuan borders the southeastern edge of the great cold desert of the Gobi which extends west across the southern reaches of Mongolia. In northwest Mongolia the Altai Mountains and various lesser ranges are interspersed with lakeland basins.

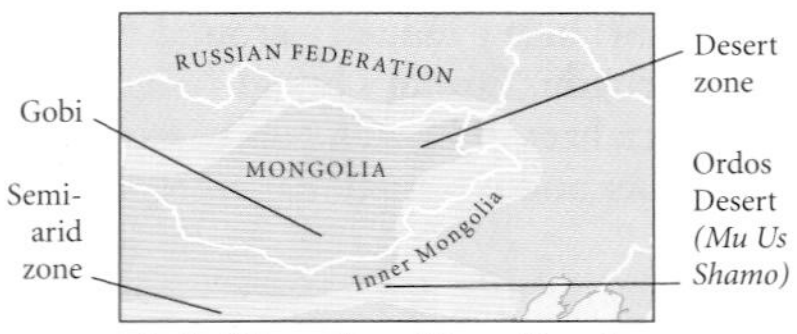

Much of Mongolia and Inner Mongolia is a vast desert area. To the south and east, a semiarid region extends into China proper.

The Gobi Desert stretches from Central Asia, through Mongolia and into China. Bare rock surfaces, rather than sand dunes, typify the cold desert landscape of the Gobi.

Tributaries of the Amur River follow U-shaped valleys through the Great Khingan Range *(Da Hinggan Ling)*. These were cut by ice-age glaciers between 3 and 10 million years ago.

Lesser Khingan Range *(Xiao Hinggan Ling)*

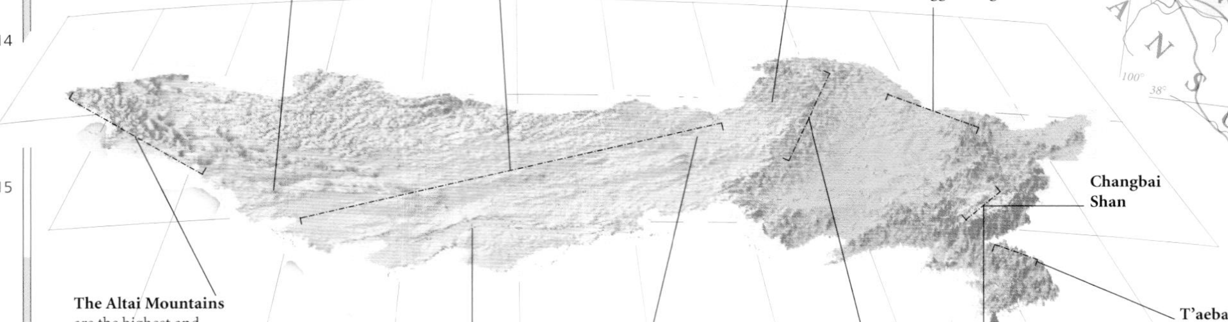

Changbai Shan

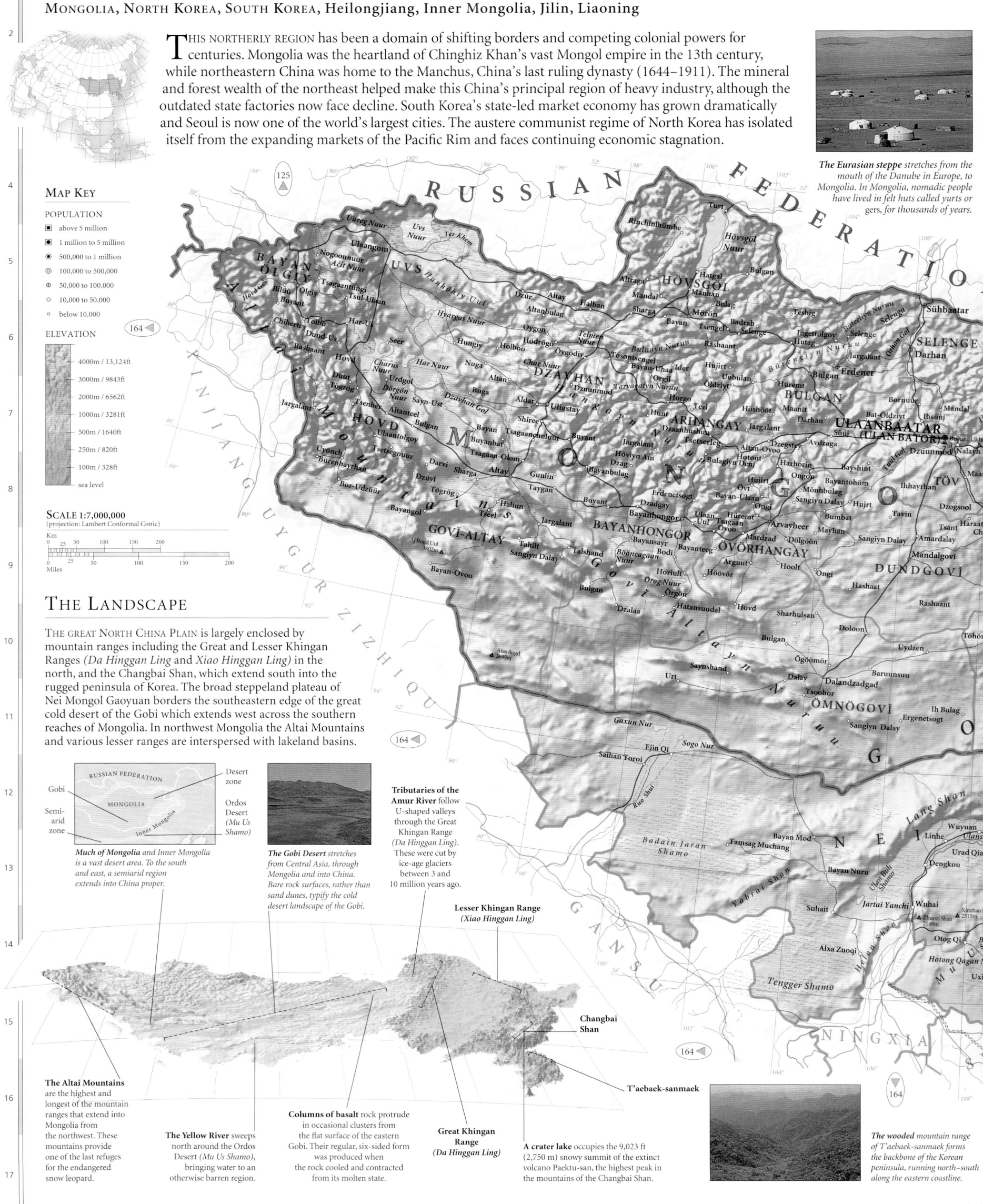

T'aebaek-sanmaek

The Altai Mountains are the highest and longest of the mountain ranges that extend into Mongolia from the northwest. These mountains provide one of the last refuges for the endangered snow leopard.

The Yellow River sweeps north around the Ordos Desert *(Mu Us Shamo)*, bringing water to an otherwise barren region.

Columns of basalt rock protrude in occasional clusters from the flat surface of the eastern Gobi. Their regular, six-sided form was produced when the rock cooled and contracted from its molten state.

Great Khingan Range *(Da Hinggan Ling)*

A crater lake occupies the 9,023 ft (2,750 m) snowy summit of the extinct volcano Paektu-san, the highest peak in the mountains of the Changbai Shan.

The wooded mountain range of T'aebaek-sanmaek forms the backbone of the Korean peninsula, running north–south along the eastern coastline.

N O P Q R S T U V W X Y

TRANSPORTATION & INDUSTRY

NORTH KOREA'S CENTRALLY-PLANNED ECONOMY is strongly oriented toward heavy industry, while South Korea has a broad manufacturing base which includes textiles, steel, electronics, and one of the world's largest shipbuilding industries. Mongolia and Inner Mongolia's great mineral resource potential is largely undeveloped. The heavy industrial region around Shenyang produces iron, steel, chemicals, and cement on a massive scale.

Ulan Bator, *the Mongolian capital bears many of the hallmarks of Soviet-style central planning, the result of economic and industrial assistance from the Soviet Union following Mongolian independence in 1921.*

TRANSPORTATION NETWORK

Liaoning has China's most comprehensive railroad network, the legacy of the Japanese occupation of Manchuria in the 20th century. The railroads are used primarily for freight transportation.

While North Korea has remained politically and economically isolated from the rest of the world, South Korea has enjoyed immense economic growth. It has benefited considerably from US economic aid in the aftermath of the Korean war of 1950–1953.

USING THE LAND AND SEA

MONGOLIA AND INNER MONGOLIA rely heavily on livestock farming, with only about 1% of the land area cultivated. Northeastern China produces wheat, corn, soybeans, and sugar beet. The cool climate limits the range of crops and large upland areas of the northeast remain forested. Rice is the staple food of North and South Korea. The latter has become a leading ocean-fishing nation.

N O P Q R S T U V

JAPAN

IN THE YEARS SINCE THE END of the Second World War, Japan has become the world's most dynamic industrial nation. The country comprises a string of over 4,000 islands which lie in a great northeast to southwest arc in the northwest Pacific. Four major islands: Hokkaido, Honshu, Shikoku, and Kyushu are home to the great majority of Japan's population of 125.9 million people, although the mountainous terrain of the central region means that most cities are situated on the coast. A densely populated industrial belt stretches along much of Honshu's southern coast, including Japan's crowded capital, Tokyo. Alongside its spectacular economic growth and the increasing westernization of its cities, Japan still maintains a highly individual culture, reflected in its traditional food, formal behavioral codes, unique Shinto religion, and a deep reverence for the emperor.

TRANSPORTATION & INDUSTRY

JAPAN IS THE WORLD'S second largest market economy, outranked only by the US. Technological development, particularly of computers, electronic goods, cars, and motorcycles is second to none. Japanese industry invests in its workforce and in long-term research and development to maintain the high standard of its products and a reputation for innovation. Japanese businesses are now global both in their manufacturing bases and in the distribution of goods.

Major industry and infrastructure
- brewing
- car manufacture
- chemicals
- hi-tech industry
- engineering
- finance
- iron & steel
- research & development
- shipbuilding
- textiles
- winter sports
- ■ capital cities
- □ major towns
- ⊕ international airports
- major roads
- major industrial areas

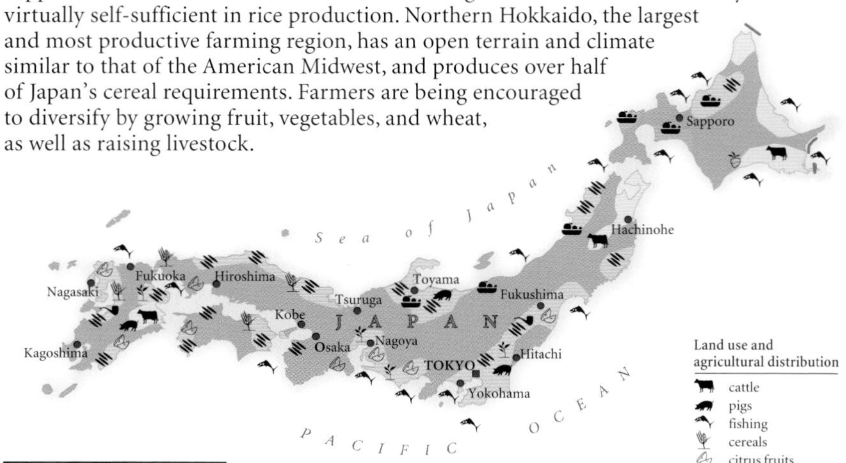

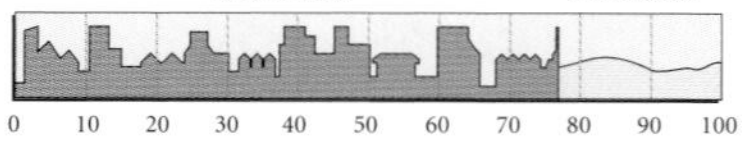

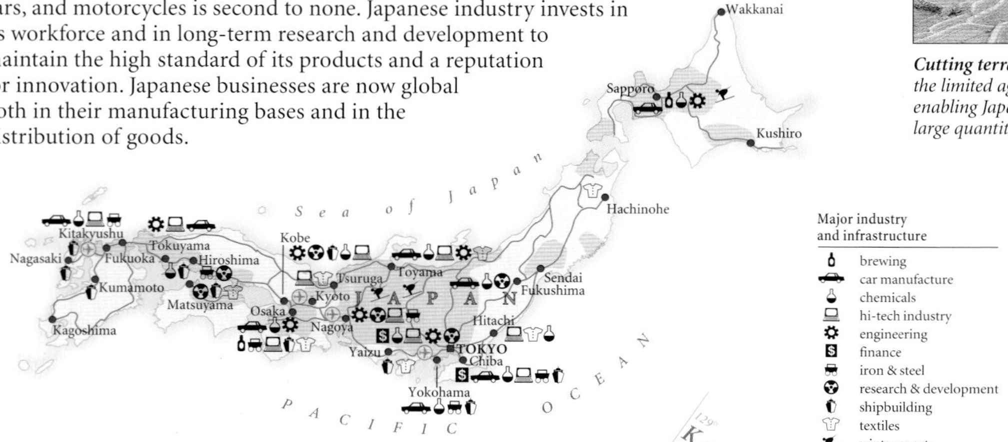

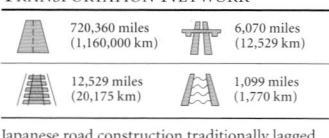

TRANSPORTATION NETWORK

720,360 miles (1,160,000 km)	6,070 miles (12,529 km)
12,529 miles (20,175 km)	1,099 miles (1,770 km)

Japanese road construction traditionally lagged behind that of its extensive and technologically advanced railroad network. The road network's relative lack of development has led to severe urban congestion, although expressways have now been built in some cities.

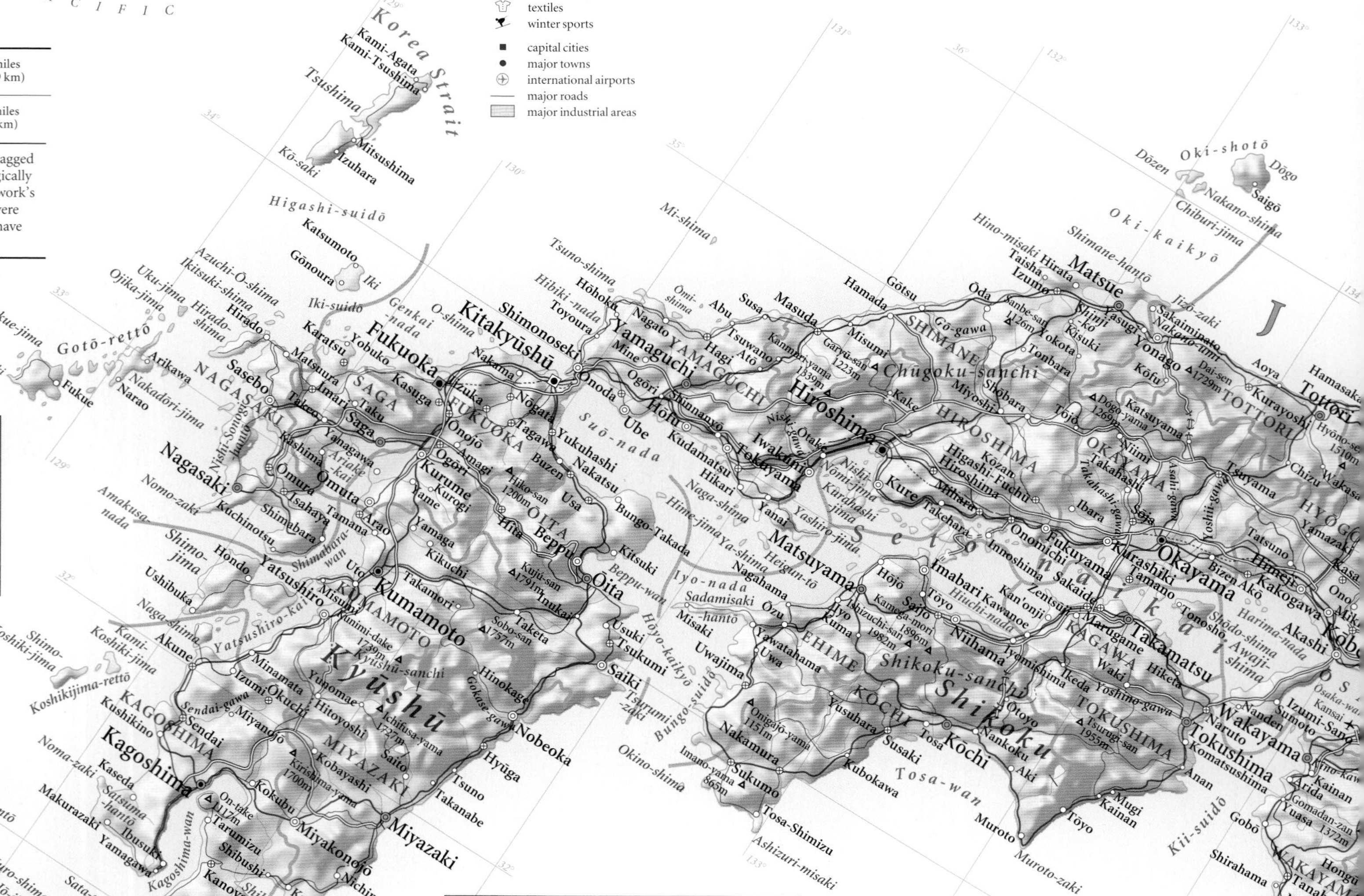

Known in the west as the "bullet train," the Shinkansen is the second-fastest train in the world. It speeds past the snowcapped peak of Mount Fuji between the cities of Tokyo and Osaka.

USING THE LAND AND SEA

ALTHOUGH ONLY ABOUT 11% OF JAPAN is suitable for cultivation, substantial government support, a favorable climate and intensive farming methods enable the country to be virtually self-sufficient in rice production. Northern Hokkaido, the largest and most productive farming region, has an open terrain and climate similar to that of the American Midwest, and produces over half of Japan's cereal requirements. Farmers are being encouraged to diversify by growing fruit, vegetables, and wheat, as well as raising livestock.

Land use and agricultural distribution
- cattle
- pigs
- fishing
- cereals
- citrus fruits
- fruit
- herbs
- rice
- root crops
- tobacco
- ■ capital cities
- □ major towns
- pasture
- cropland
- forest

THE URBAN/RURAL POPULATION DIVIDE

urban 78% rural 22%

0 10 20 30 40 50 60 70 80 90 100

POPULATION DENSITY	TOTAL LAND AREA
863 people per sq mile (333 people per sq km)	145,869 sq miles (377,800 sq km)

Cutting terraces maximizes the limited agricultural land, enabling Japan to produce large quantities of rice.

The Kobe earthquake in January 1995 highlighted Japan's vulnerability to earthquakes, despite technological advances. It shattered much of the infrastructure of this important port. More than 5,000 people died as buildings and overhead highways collapsed and fires broke out.

A number of new volcanoes emerged in Japan during the 20th century. They exist alongside older cones like this one in Aso-Kuju National Park on Kyushu, now dormant and grass-covered.

The Landscape

The islands of Japan lie on the Pacific "Ring of Fire," and form a series of clearly defined arcs. The largely mountainous landscape was formed very recently in geological terms. Volcanic eruptions and earthquakes continue to reshape the terrain and shake the country's complex infrastructure. There is no single continuous mountain range; the mountains divide into many small land blocks separated by lowlands and dissected by numerous river valleys.

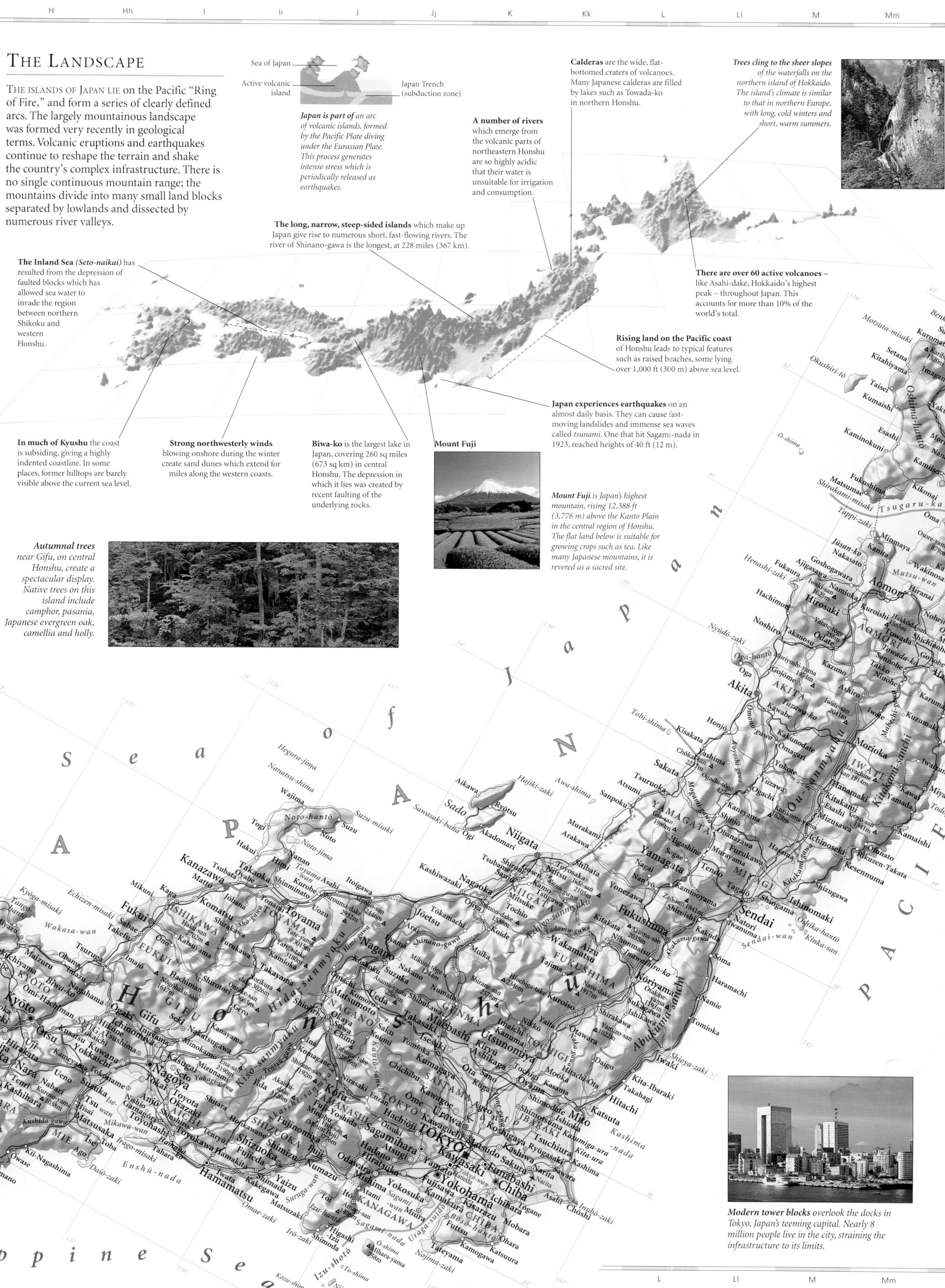

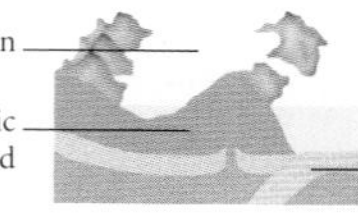

***Japan is part of** an arc of volcanic islands, formed by the Pacific Plate diving under the Eurasian Plate. This process generates intense stress which is periodically released as earthquakes.*

Calderas are the wide, flat-bottomed craters of volcanoes. Many Japanese calderas are filled by lakes such as Towada-ko in northern Honshu.

***Trees cling to the sheer slopes** of the waterfalls on the northern island of Hokkaido. The island's climate is similar to that in northern Europe, with long, cold winters and short, warm summers.*

A number of rivers which emerge from the volcanic parts of northeastern Honshu are so highly acidic that their water is unsuitable for irrigation and consumption.

The long, narrow, steep-sided islands which make up Japan give rise to numerous short, fast-flowing rivers. The river of Shinano-gawa is the longest, at 228 miles (367 km).

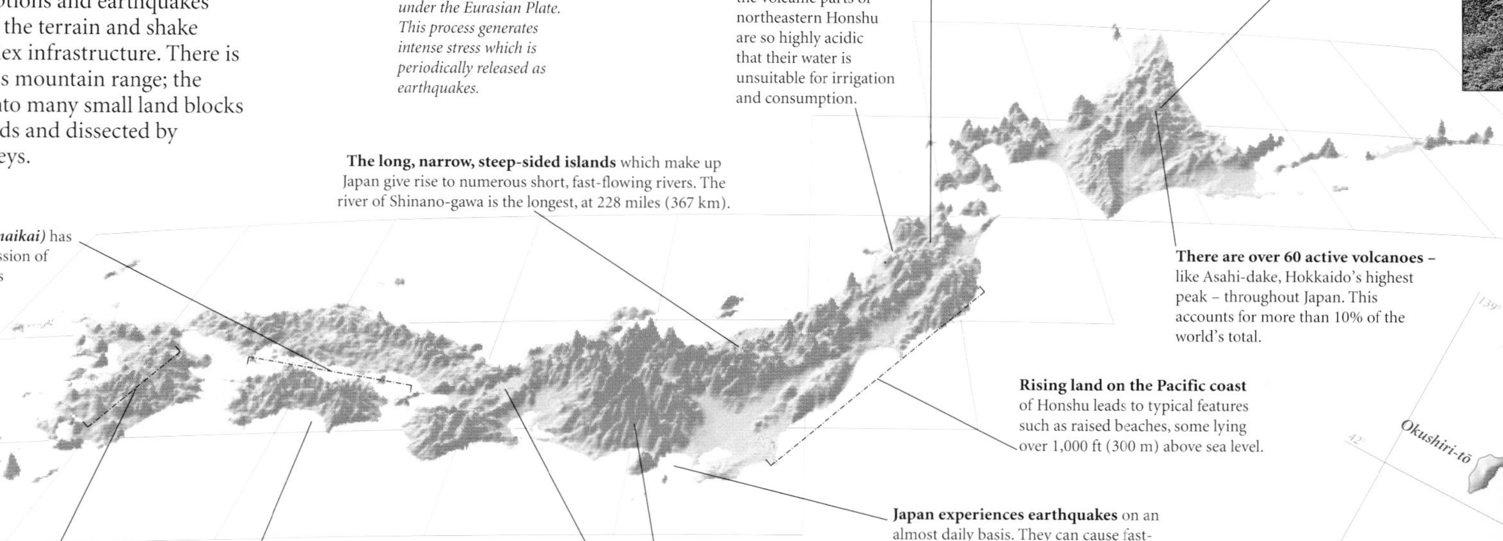

The Inland Sea ***(Seto-naikai)*** has resulted from the depression of faulted blocks which has allowed sea water to invade the region between northern Shikoku and western Honshu.

There are over 60 active volcanoes – like Asahi-dake, Hokkaido's highest peak – throughout Japan. This accounts for more than 10% of the world's total.

Rising land on the Pacific coast of Honshu leads to typical features such as raised beaches, some lying over 1,000 ft (300 m) above sea level.

Japan experiences earthquakes on an almost daily basis. They can cause fast-moving landslides and immense sea waves called *tsunami*. One that hit Sagami-nada in 1923, reached heights of 40 ft (12 m).

In much of Kyushu the coast is subsiding, giving a highly indented coastline. In some places, former hilltops are barely visible above the current sea level.

Strong northwesterly winds blowing onshore during the winter create sand dunes which extend for miles along the western coasts.

Biwa-ko is the largest lake in Japan, covering 260 sq miles (673 sq km) in central Honshu. The depression in which it lies was created by recent faulting of the underlying rocks.

Mount Fuji

***Mount Fuji** is Japan's highest mountain, rising 12,388 ft (3,776 m) above the Kanto Plain in the central region of Honshu. The flat land below is suitable for growing crops such as tea. Like many Japanese mountains, it is revered as a sacred site.*

***Autumnal trees** near Gifu, on central Honshu, create a spectacular display. Native trees on this island include camphor, pasania, Japanese evergreen oak, camellia and holly.*

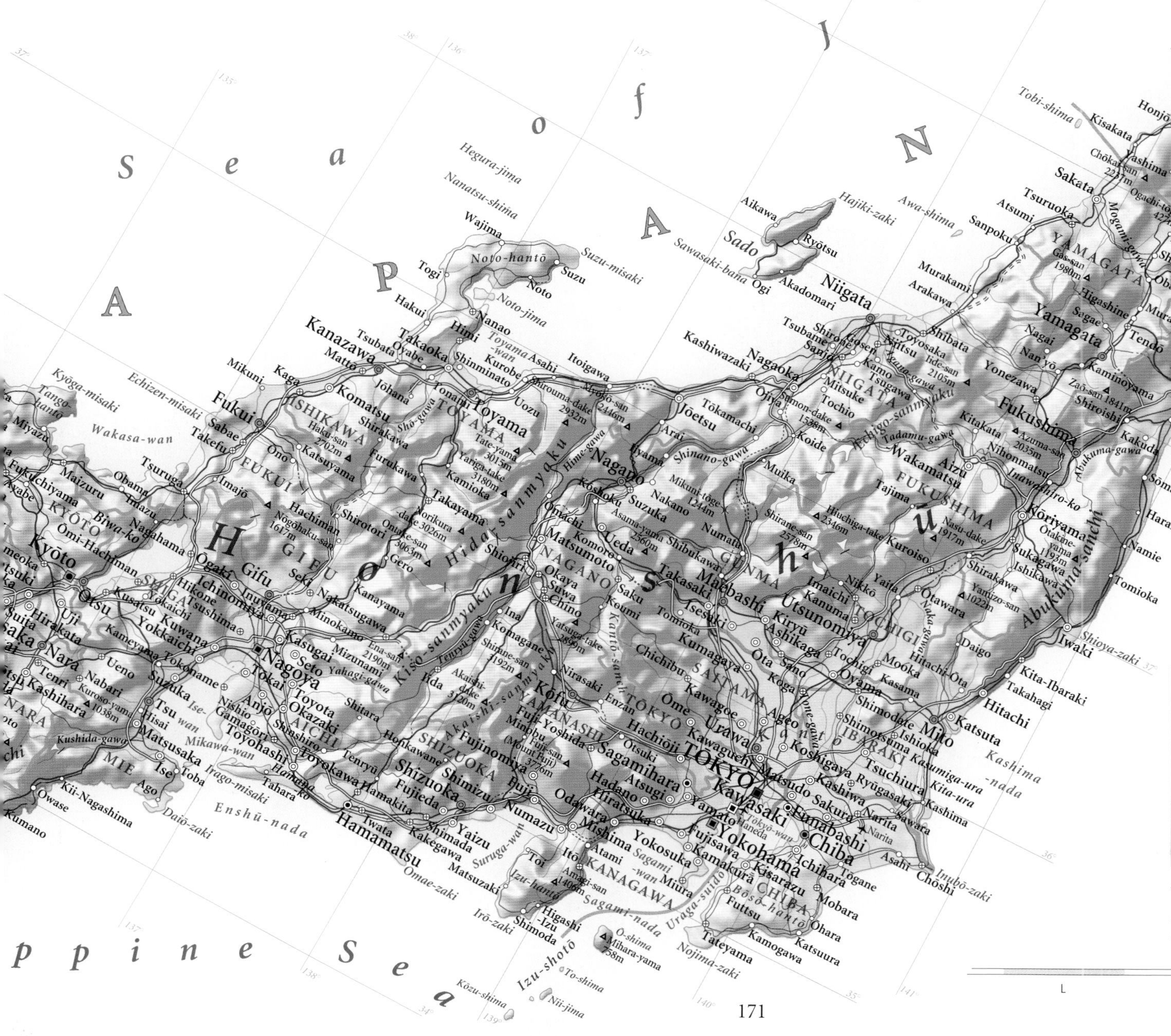

***Modern tower blocks** overlook the docks in Tokyo, Japan's teeming capital. Nearly 8 million people live in the city, straining the infrastructure to its limits.*

***Malaysia** exports a greater tonnage of tropical timber than anywhere else in the world. Much of it comes from Sarawak in Borneo. Although in principle logging is only allowed on a sustainable basis, environmentalists fear that the rainforest in Sarawak will have disappeared by the early 21st century.*

***This tiny island** near Kota Kinabalu, in Sabah, eastern Malaysia, is a part of a designated national park. Thickly forested, it is surrounded by broad, sandy beaches and shallow inland seas.*

Map Key

Population
- above 5 million
- 1 million to 5 million
- 500,000 to 1 million
- 100,000 to 500,000
- 50,000 to 100,000
- 10,000 to 50,000
- below 10,000

Elevation
- 4000m / 13,124ft
- 3000m / 9843ft
- 2000m / 6562ft
- 1000m / 3281ft
- 500m / 1640ft
- 250m / 820ft
- 100m / 328ft
- sea level

Scale 1:6,250,000
(projection: Mercator)

180

***Throughout Southeast Asia,** where agricultural land is at a premium, terraces are cut into the slopes to maximize the area available for cultivation. These terraces on the Indonesian island of Bali are used to support rice paddies.*

180

Maritime Southeast Asia

Brunei, East Timor, Indonesia, Malaysia, Singapore

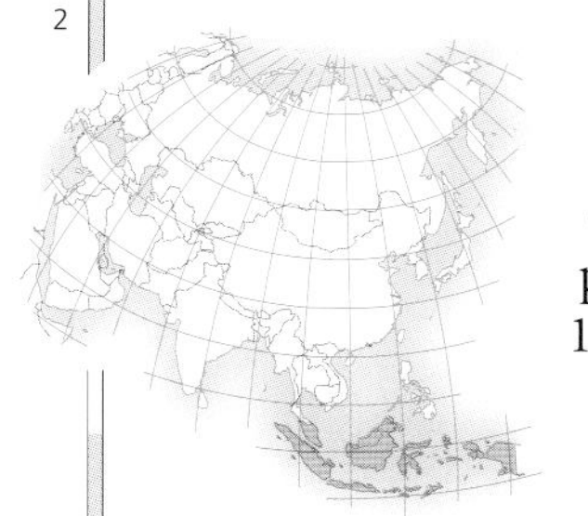

The intricate arc of islands which runs from peninsular Malaysia east to Irian Jaya in western New Guinea sustains a huge variety of peoples, languages, and cultures. Indonesia is by far the largest country in the region, and 87% of its huge, predominantly Muslim, population is crowded onto Java, the most habitable of Indonesia's 13,677 islands. Malaysia, split between the mainland and the east Malaysian states of Sabah and Sarawak on Borneo, has a diverse population, as well as a fast-growing economy, although the pace of its development is still far outstripped by that of Singapore. This small island nation is the financial and commercial capital of Southeast Asia, and an Asian "tiger" economy. The Sultanate of Brunei in northern Borneo, one of the world's last princely states, also has an extremely high standard of living, based on its oil revenues.

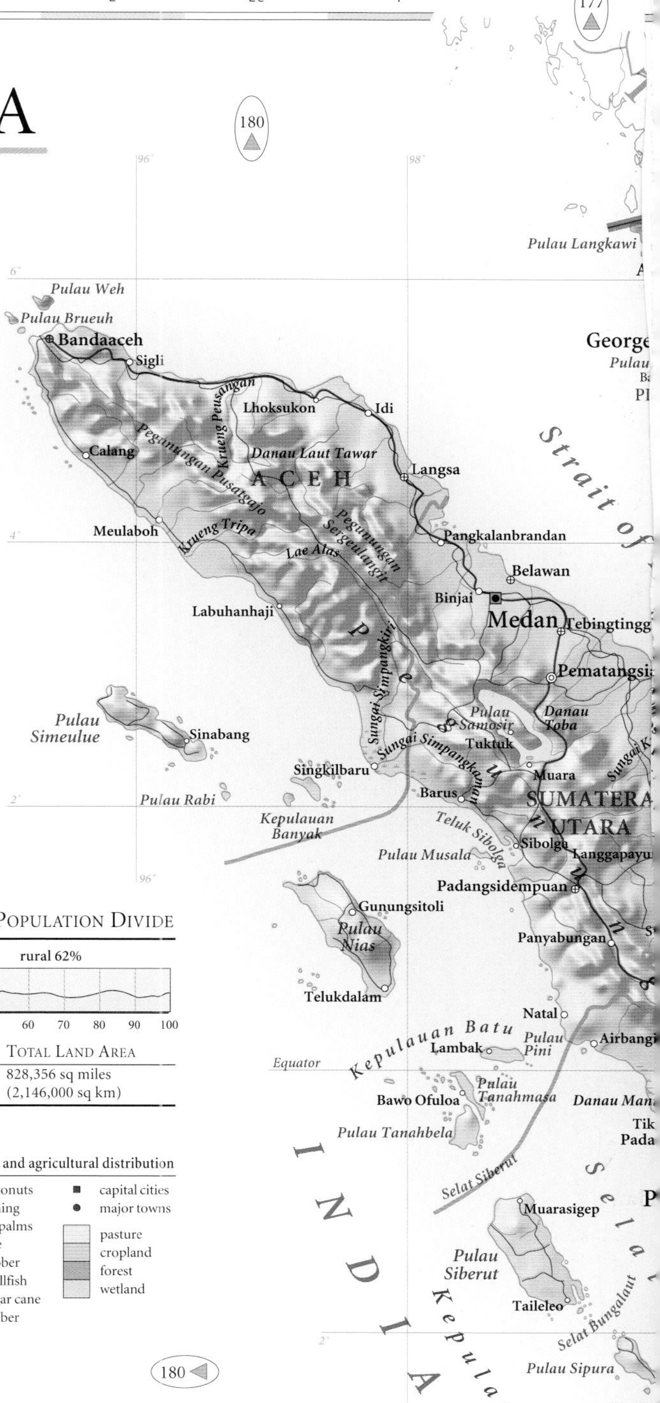

177

180

Using the Land and Sea

Rice is the most important arable crop in Indonesia and Malaysia, and both countries manage to meet almost all of their domestic demand. Malaysian rubber accounts for 25% of world production and is the main cash crop, grown on plantations and small farms, along with oil palms and copra. Timber is exported from both Malaysia and Indonesia. Modern agricultural techniques enable Singapore to produce fruit and vegetables despite a shortage of suitable land.

***Spiral cuts** in the bark of this rubber palm show where it has been tapped. Sophisticated "cloning" techniques mean that trees which produce consistently high quantities of rubber can be easily reproduced.*

The Urban/Rural Population Divide

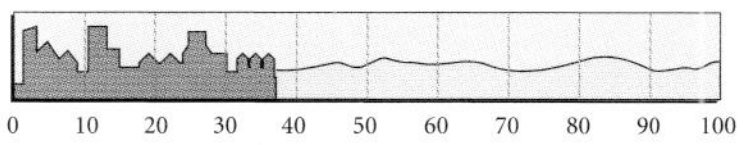

Population Density	Total Land Area
262 people per sq mile (101 people per sq km)	828,356 sq miles (2,146,000 sq km)

180

The Landscape

From Sumatra in the west, the volcanic islands of Indonesia run for nearly 3,100 miles (5,000 km). The Sunda Shelf, an extension of the Eurasian Plate, lies between Java, Bali, Sumatra, Lombok, and Borneo. Their volcanic mountains rise from a base below the sea and they were once joined together by dry land, which has since been submerged by rising sea levels.

The river of Sungai Mahakam cuts through the central highlands of Borneo, the third largest island in the world, with a total area of 290,000 sq miles (757,050 sq km). Although mountainous, Borneo is one of the most stable of the Indonesian islands, with little volcanic activity.

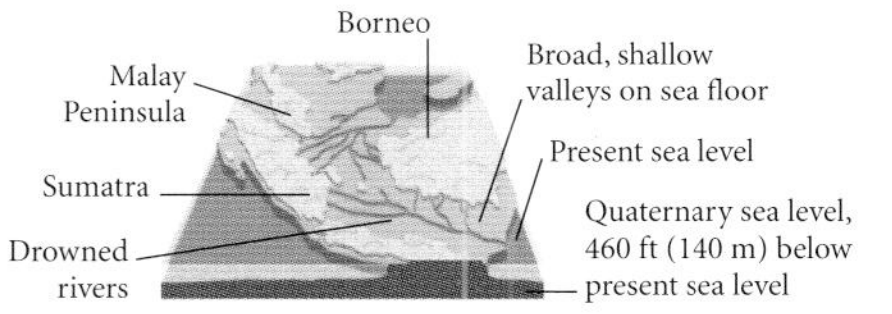

***The Sunda Shelf** underlies this whole region. It is one of the largest submarine shelves in the world, covering an area of 714,285 sq miles (1,850,000 sq km). During the early Quaternary period, when the sea levels were lower, the shelf was exposed.*

Malay Peninsula has a rugged east coast, but the west coast, fronting the Strait of Malacca, has many sheltered beaches and bays. The two coasts are divided by the Banjaran Titiwangsa, which run the length of the peninsula.

Gunung Kinabalu is the highest peak in Malaysia, rising 13,455 ft (4,101 m).

The four-pronged island of Celebes is the product of complex tectonic activity which ruptured and then reattached small fragments of the Earth's crust to form the island's many peninsulas.

Papua (Irian Jaya) contains some of the most dense and least explored tropical rain forests in the world, inhabited by many rare species of plants and animals.

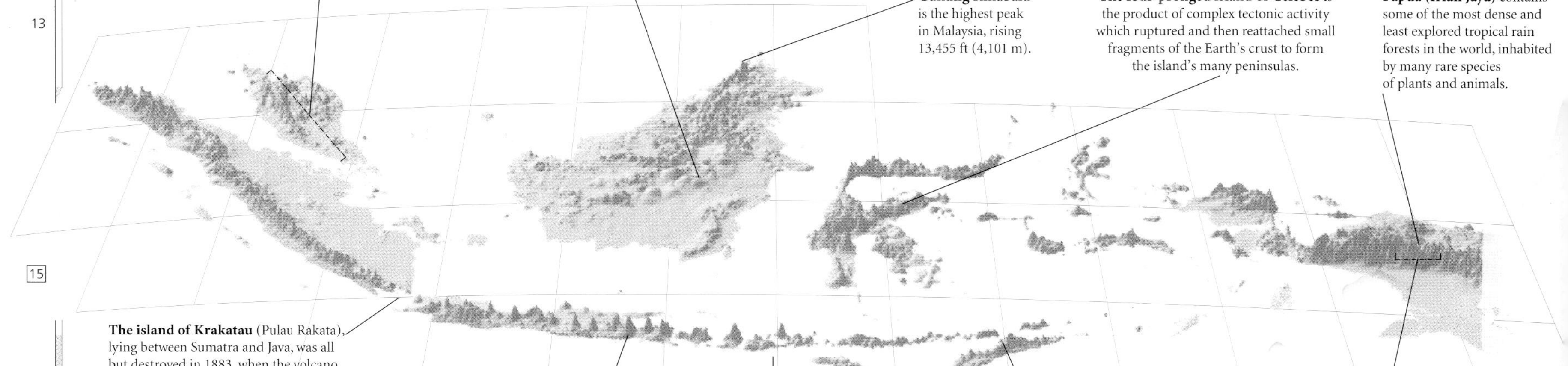

The island of Krakatau (Pulau Rakata), lying between Sumatra and Java, was all but destroyed in 1883, when the volcano erupted. The release of gas and dust into the atmosphere disrupted cloud cover and global weather patterns for several years.

Gunung Semeru

The volcano of Gunung Semeru in eastern Java lies on the Pacific "Rim of Fire." It is part of the ancient Tennegger volcano and remains highly active.

Indonesia has more than 220 volcanoes, most of which are still active. They are strung out along the island arc from Sumatra through the Lesser Sunda Islands, into the Moluccas and Celebes.

Coral islands such as Timor in eastern Indonesia show evidence of very recent and dramatic movements of the Earth's plates. Reefs in Timor have risen by as much as 4,000 ft (1,300 m) in the last million years.

The Pegunungan Jayawijaya range in central papua (Irian Jaya) contains the world's highest range of limestone mountains, some with peaks more than 16,400 ft (5,000 m) high. Heavy rainfall and high temperatures, which promote rapid weathering, have led to the creation of large underground caves and river systems such as the river of Sungai Baliem.

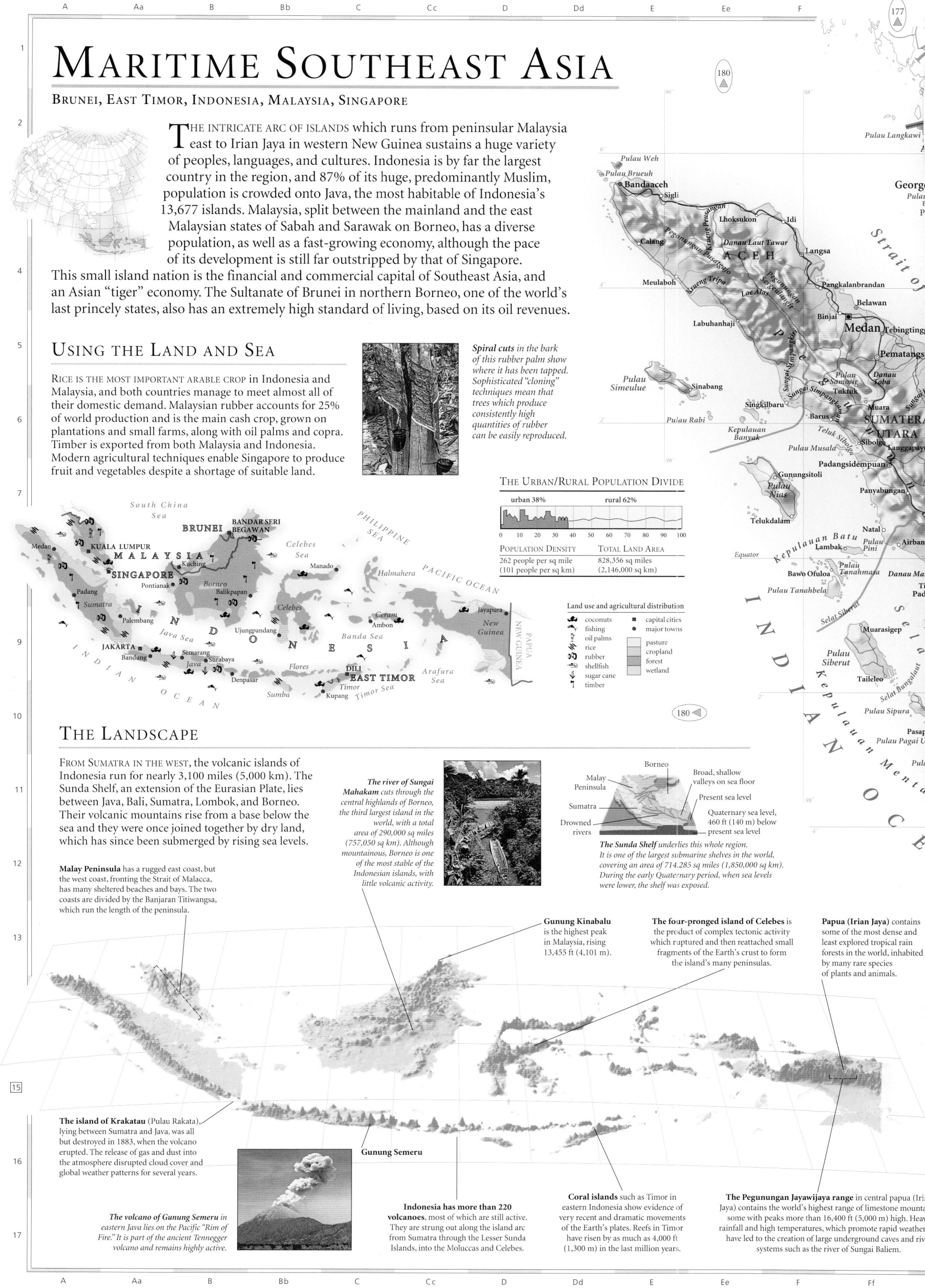

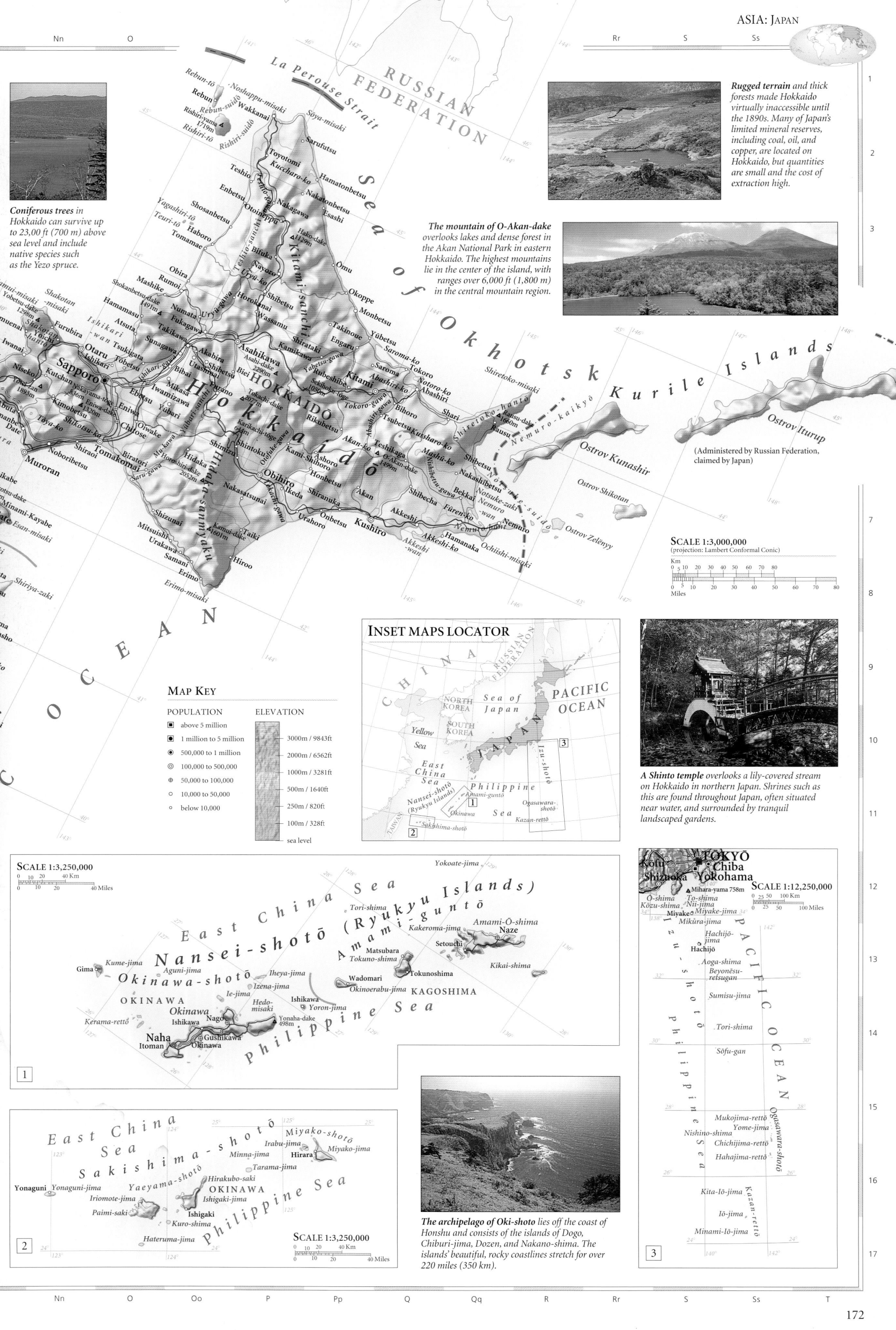

***Coniferous trees** in Hokkaido can survive up to 23,00 ft (700 m) above sea level and include native species such as the Yezo spruce.*

***Rugged terrain** and thick forests made Hokkaido virtually inaccessible until the 1890s. Many of Japan's limited mineral reserves, including coal, oil, and copper, are located on Hokkaido, but quantities are small and the cost of extraction high.*

***The mountain of O-Akan-dake** overlooks lakes and dense forest in the Akan National Park in eastern Hokkaido. The highest mountains lie in the center of the island, with ranges over 6,000 ft (1,800 m) in the central mountain region.*

SCALE 1:3,000,000
(projection: Lambert Conformal Conic)

Km 0 5 10 20 30 40 50 60 70 80
Miles 0 5 10 20 30 40 50 60 70 80

MAP KEY

POPULATION	ELEVATION
above 5 million	3000m / 9843ft
1 million to 5 million	2000m / 6562ft
500,000 to 1 million	1000m / 3281ft
100,000 to 500,000	500m / 1640ft
50,000 to 100,000	250m / 820ft
10,000 to 50,000	100m / 328ft
below 10,000	sea level

INSET MAPS LOCATOR

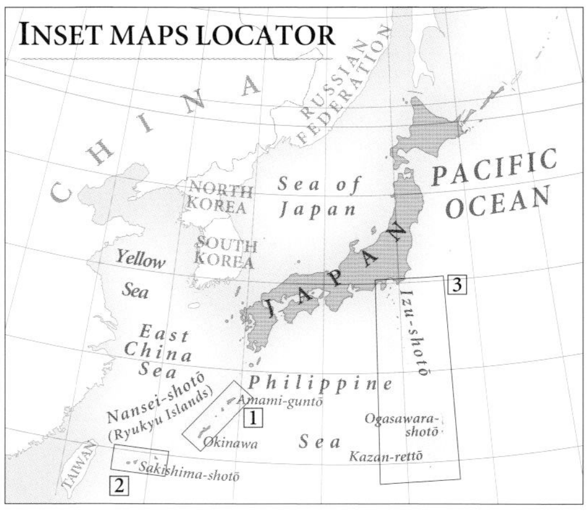

***A Shinto temple** overlooks a lily-covered stream on Hokkaido in northern Japan. Shrines such as this are found throughout Japan, often situated near water, and surrounded by tranquil landscaped gardens.*

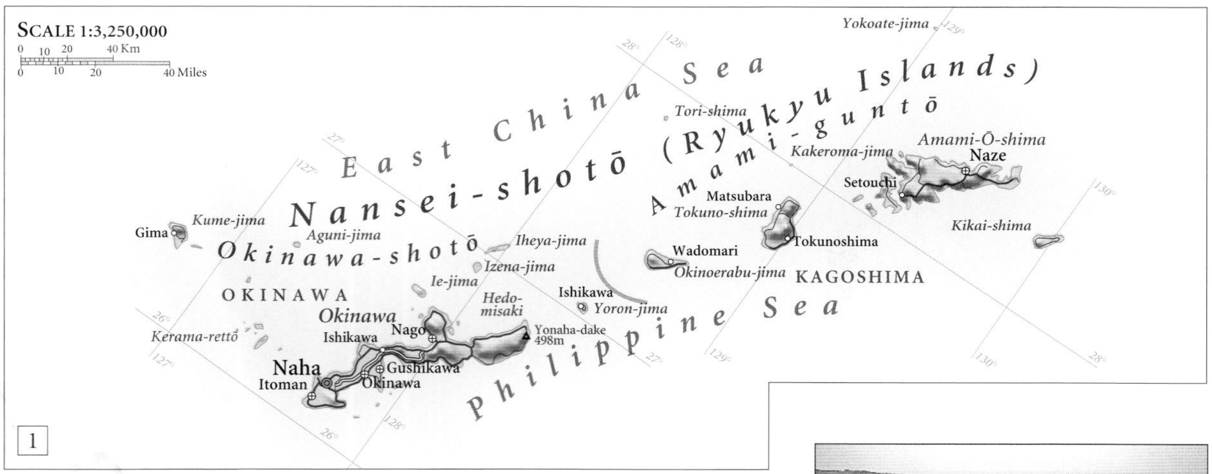

***The archipelago of Oki-shoto** lies off the coast of Honshu and consists of the islands of Dogo, Chiburi-jima, Dozen, and Nakano-shima. The islands' beautiful, rocky coastlines stretch for over 220 miles (350 km).*

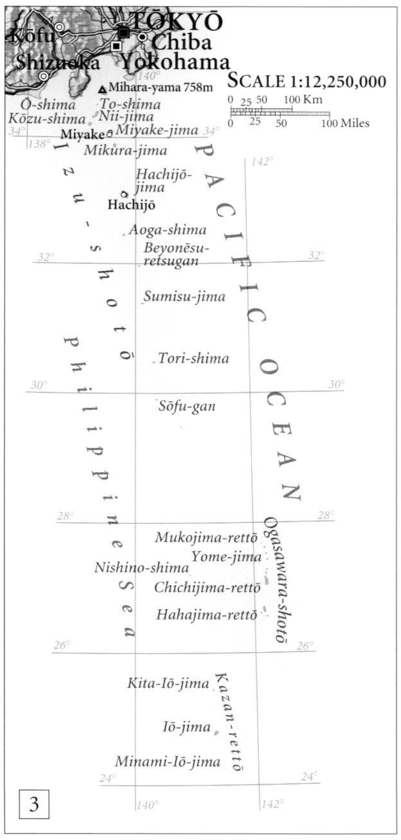

Nn O Oo P Pp Q Qq R Rr S Ss T

Mainland Southeast Asia & the Philippines

Cambodia, Laos, Myanmar, Philippines, Thailand, Vietnam

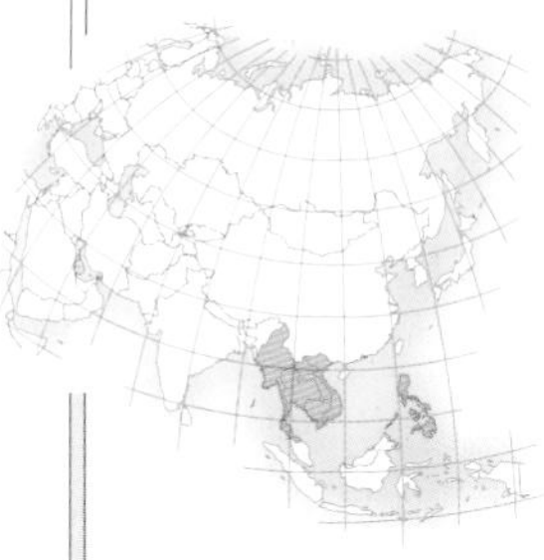

Thickly forested mountains, intercut by the broad valleys of five great rivers characterize the landscape of Southeast Asia's mainland countries. Agriculture remains the main activity for much of the population, which is concentrated in the river floodplains and deltas. Linked ethnic and cultural roots give the region a distinct identity. Most people on the mainland are Theravada Buddhists, and the Philippines is the only predominantly Christian country in Southeast Asia. Foreign intervention began in the 16th century with the opening of the spice trade; Cambodia, Laos, and Vietnam were French colonies until the end of the Second World War, Myanmar was under British control; and the Philippines was controlled by Spain and the US in the 20th century. Only Thailand was never colonized. Today, Thailand and the Philippines are poised to play a leading role in the economic development of the Pacific Rim, and Laos and Vietnam have begun to mend the devastation of the Vietnam War, and to develop their economies. With continuing political instability and a shattered infrastructure, Cambodia faces an uncertain future, while Myanmar is seeking investment and the ending of its 38-year isolation from the world community.

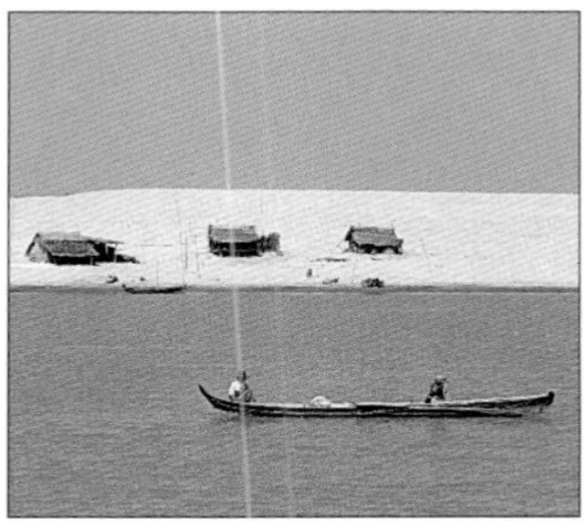

***The Irrawaddy River** is Myanmar's vital central artery, watering the rice paddies and providing a rich source of fish, as well as an important transportation link, particularly for local traffic.*

156

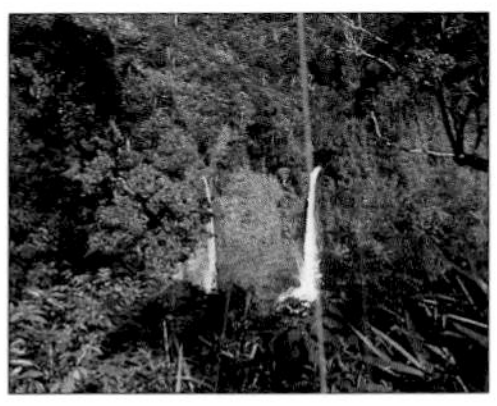

***Commercial logging** – still widespread in Myanmar – has now been stopped in Thailand because of overexploitation of the tropical rain forest.*

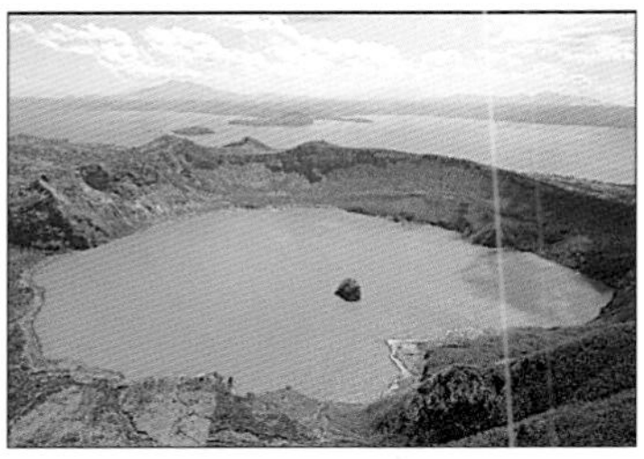

***Lake Taal** on the Philippine island of Luzon lies within the crater of an immense volcano which erupted twice in the 20th century, first in 1911 and again in 1965, causing the deaths of more than 3,200 people.*

The Landscape

A series of mountain ranges runs north–south through the mainland, formed as the result of the collision between the Eurasian Plate and the Indian subcontinent, which created the Himalayas. They are interspersed by the valleys of a number of great rivers. On their passage to the sea these rivers have deposited sediment, forming huge, fertile floodplains and deltas. The Philippines' 7,000 islands are mountainous and volcanic, with narrow coastal plains.

The Irrawaddy River runs virtually north–south, draining the plains of northern Myanmar. The Irrawaddy Delta is the country's main rice-growing area.

Hkakabo Razi is the highest point in mainland Southeast Asia. It rises 19,300 ft (5,885 m) at the border between China and Myanmar.

Mountains dominate the Laotian landscape with more than 90% of the land lying more than 600 ft (180 m) above sea level. The mountains of the Chaine Annamitique form the country's eastern border.

The Red River Delta in northern Vietnam is fringed to the north by steep-sided, round-topped limestone hills, typical of karst scenery.

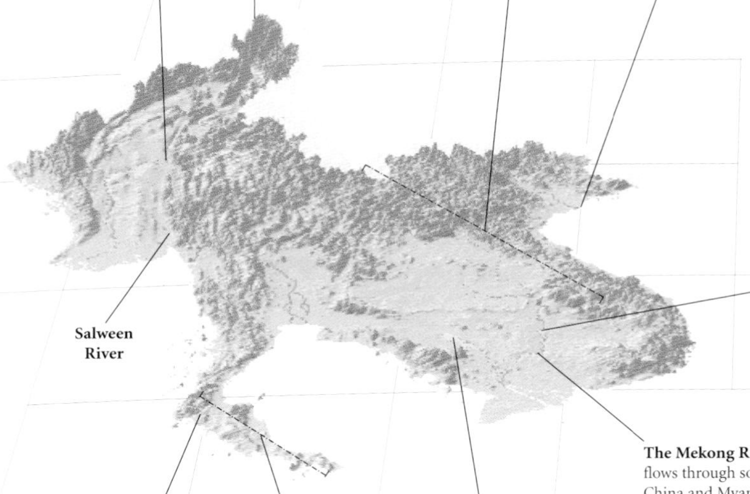

***The fast-flowing waters** of the Mekong River cascade over this waterfall in Champasak province in Laos. The force of the water erodes rocks at the base of the fall.*

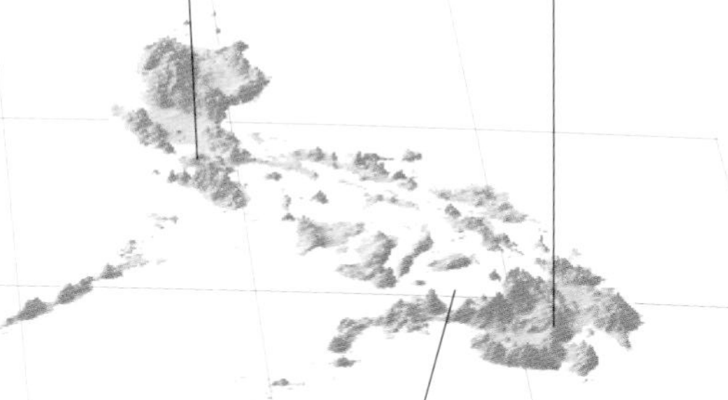

Mindanao has five mountain ranges, many of which have large numbers of active volcanoes. Lying just west of the Philippine Trench, which forms the boundary between the colliding Philippine and Eurasian plates, the entire island chain is subject to earthquakes and volcanic activity.

Salween River

Malay Peninsula

Thailand

Tonle Sap, a freshwater lake, drains into the Mekong Delta via the Mekong River. It is the largest lake in Southeast Asia.

The Mekong River flows through southern China and Myanmar, then for much of its length forms the border between Laos and Thailand, flowing through Cambodia before terminating in a vast delta on the southern Vietnamese coast.

The coastline of the Isthmus of Kra

***The east and west coasts** of the Isthmus of Kra differ greatly. The tectonically uplifting west coast is exposed to the harsh south-westerly monsoon and is heavily eroded. On the east coast, longshore currents produce depositional features such as spits and lagoons.*

Bohol

***Bohol in the southern Philippines** is famous for its so-called "chocolate hills". There are more than 1,000 of these regular mounds on the island. The hills are limestone in origin, the smoothed remains of an earlier cycle of erosion. Their brown appearance in the dry season gives the hills their name.*

***The coast of the Isthmus of Kra,** in southeast Thailand has many small, precipitous islands like these, formed by chemical erosion on limestone, which is weathered along vertical cracks. The humidity of the climate in Southeast Asia increases the rate of weathering.*

U Uu V Vv W Ww X Xx Y Yy Z

TRANSPORTATION & INDUSTRY

SINGAPORE HAS A THRIVING ECONOMY based on international trade and finance. Annual trade through the port is among the highest of any port in the world. Indonesia still depends on natural resources, particularly wood, petroleum, and gas, although the economy is rapidly diversifying, with manufactured exports including garments, consumer electronics, and footwear; a high-profile aircraft industry has developed at Bandung. In Malaysia, although oil, gas, and timber remain important resource-based industries, it has a fast-growing and varied manufacturing sector.

Major industry and infrastructure

- aerospace
- copra processing
- chemicals
- electronics
- engineering
- finance
- food processing
- iron & steel
- oil
- ship building
- timber processing
- textiles
- capital cities
- major towns
- international airports
- major roads
- major industrial areas

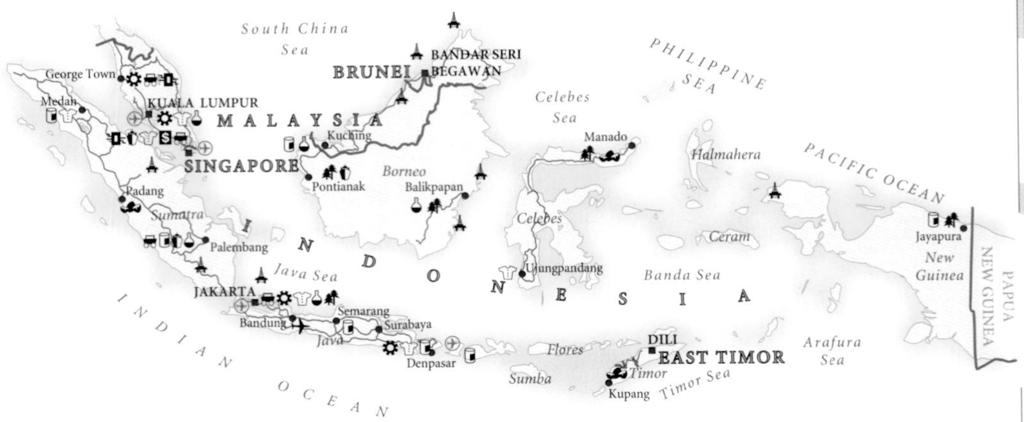

Ranks of gleaming skyscrapers, new highways and infrastructure construction reflect the investment which is pouring into Southeast Asian cities like the Malaysian capital, Kuala Lumpur. Traditional housing and markets still exist amidst the new developments. Many of the city's inhabitants subsist at a level far removed from the prosperity implied by its outward modernity.

TRANSPORTATION NETWORK

160,350 miles (258,213 km)
188 miles (302 km)
5,482 miles (8,828 km)
15,523 miles (32,903km)

Singapore's subway system, completed in 1991, is among the most efficient in the world. Malaysia has several fast, modern highways and most roads are paved. Indonesia's many islands make improvement of the shipping infrastructure a priority.

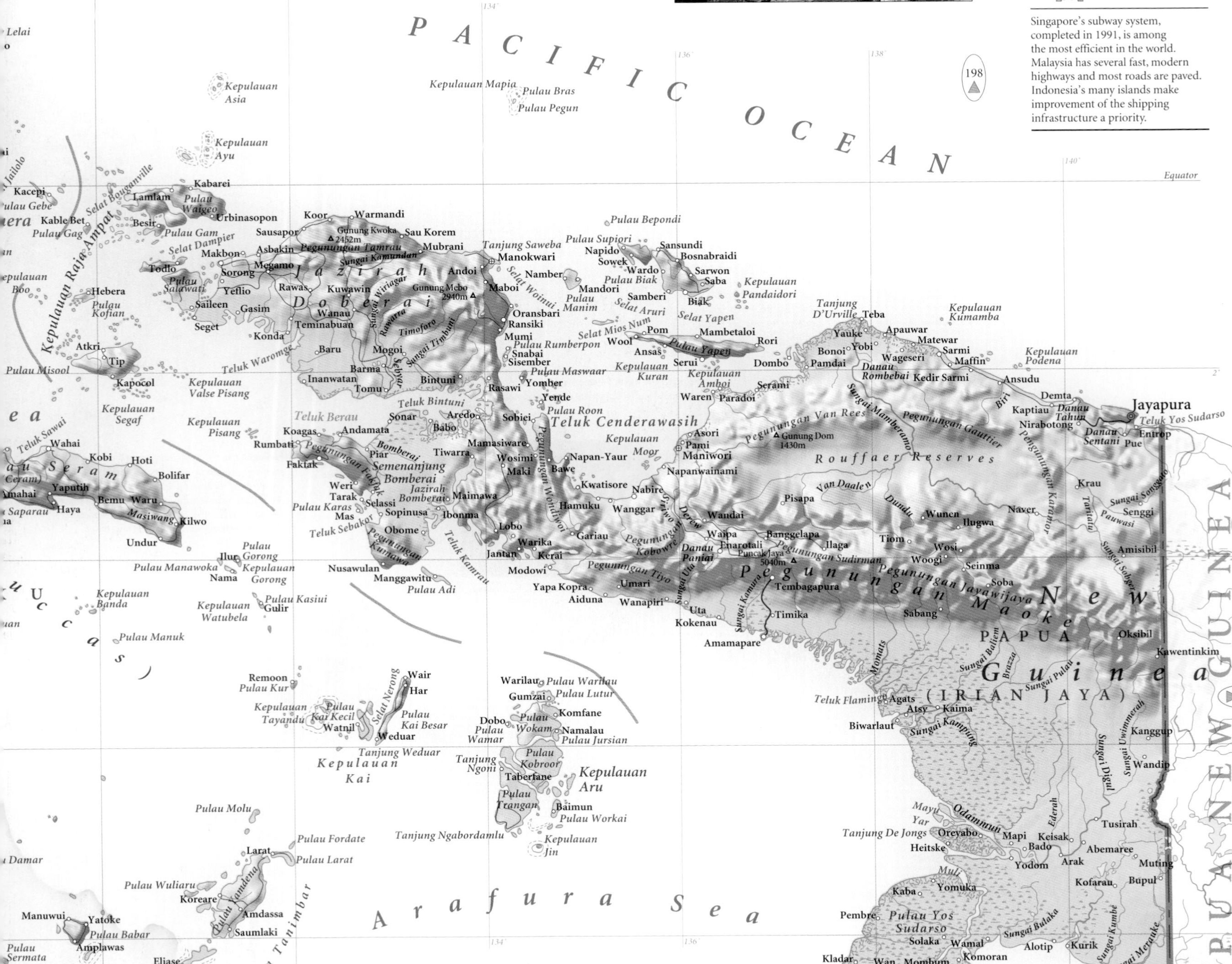

Although Indonesia is now a mainly Muslim country, relics of other civilizations are found throughout its many islands. These scattered columns are the ruins of a Hindu settlement which flourished on Java more than a thousand years ago.

U Uu V Vv W Ww X Xx Y Yy

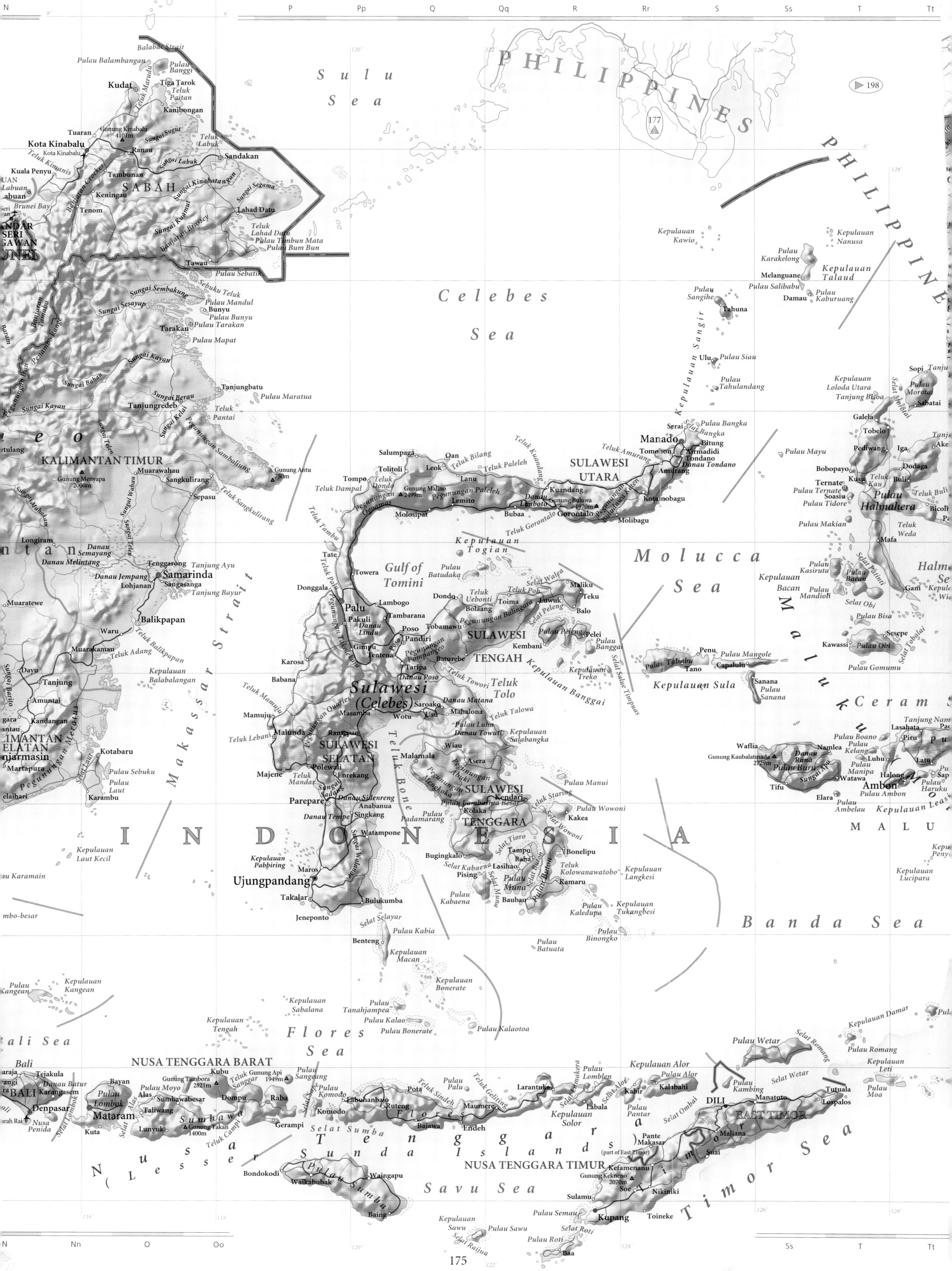

PHILIPPINES
Sulu Sea
Celebes Sea
Molucca Sea
Gulf of Tomini
Makassar Strait
Banda Sea
Flores Sea
Savu Sea
Timor Sea
Bali Sea
INDONESIA
Sulawesi (Celebes)
SULAWESI UTARA
SULAWESI TENGAH
SULAWESI SELATAN
SULAWESI TENGGARA
SABAH
KALIMANTAN TIMUR
NUSA TENGGARA BARAT
NUSA TENGGARA TIMUR
EAST TIMOR
Nusa Tenggara (Lesser Sunda Islands)
Maluku
Kota Kinabalu
Kudat
Sandakan
Lahad Datu
Tawau
Tarakan
Tanjungredeb
Samarinda
Balikpapan
Manado
Gorontalo
Palu
Poso
Kendari
Ujungpandang
Parepare
Ternate
Ambon
Mataram
Denpasar
Kupang
DILI
Gunung Kinabalu 4101m
Gunung Tambora 2821m
Gunung Kaubalatmada 2729m
Gunung Malino 2499m
Pulau Halmahera
Ceram
Pulau Buru
Pulau Sumba
Pulau Lombok
Flores
Sumbawa
Timor
Kepulauan Sula
Kepulauan Banggai
Kepulauan Talaud
Kepulauan Sangir
Pulau Muna
Pulau Buton
Pulau Wetar
Kepulauan Alor
198
177

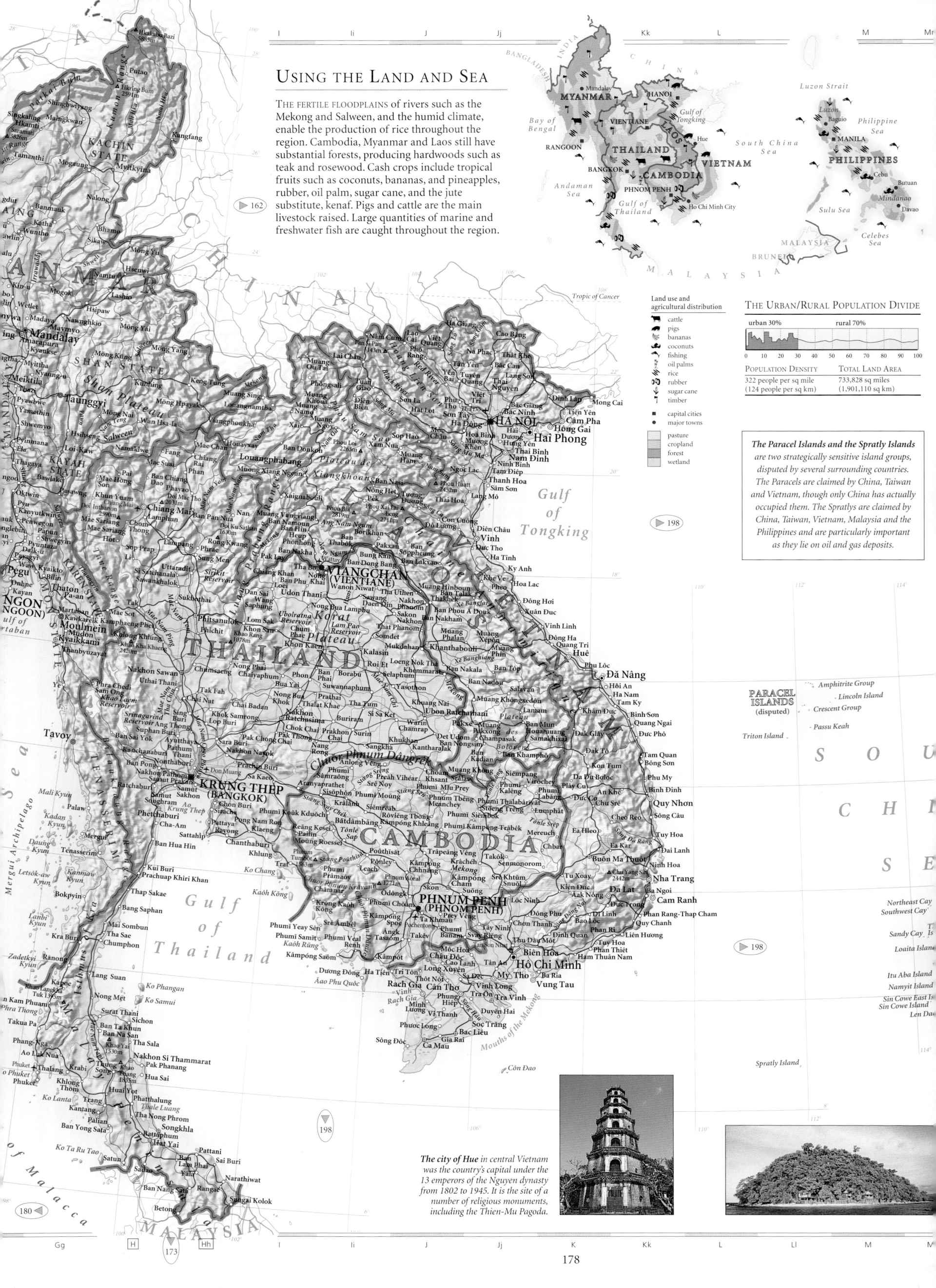

Using the Land and Sea

The fertile floodplains of rivers such as the Mekong and Salween, and the humid climate, enable the production of rice throughout the region. Cambodia, Myanmar and Laos still have substantial forests, producing hardwoods such as teak and rosewood. Cash crops include tropical fruits such as coconuts, bananas, and pineapples, rubber, oil palm, sugar cane, and the jute substitute, kenaf. Pigs and cattle are the main livestock raised. Large quantities of marine and freshwater fish are caught throughout the region.

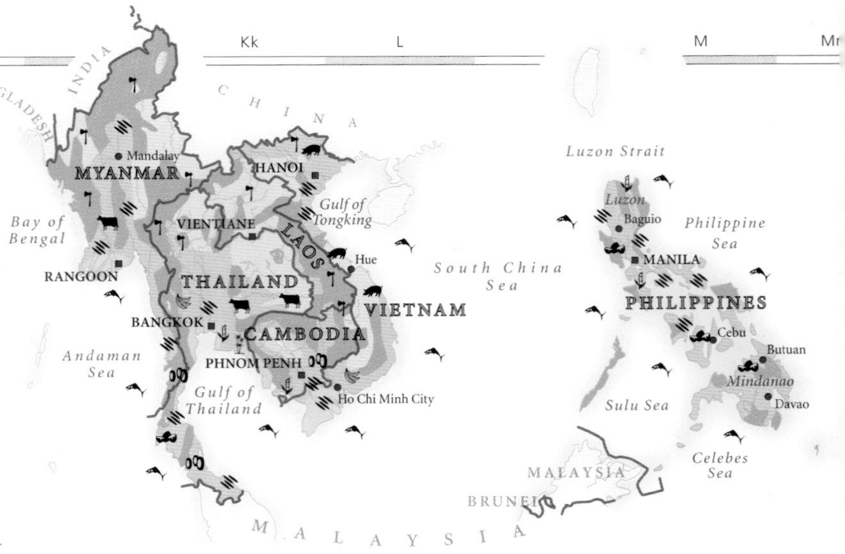

The Urban/Rural Population Divide

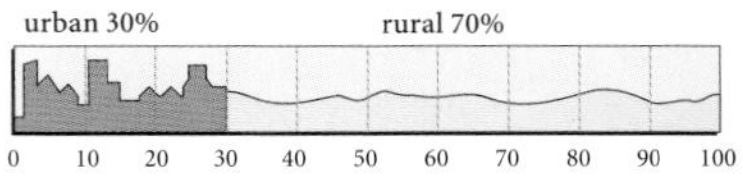

Population Density	Total Land Area
322 people per sq mile (124 people per sq km)	733,828 sq miles (1,901,110 sq km)

The Paracel Islands and the Spratly Islands *are two strategically sensitive island groups, disputed by several surrounding countries. The Paracels are claimed by China, Taiwan and Vietnam, though only China has actually occupied them. The Spratlys are claimed by China, Taiwan, Vietnam, Malaysia and the Philippines and are particularly important as they lie on oil and gas deposits.*

The city of Hue *in central Vietnam was the country's capital under the 13 emperors of the Nguyen dynasty from 1802 to 1945. It is the site of a number of religious monuments, including the Thien-Mu Pagoda.*

TRANSPORTATION & INDUSTRY

INDUSTRIAL MANUFACTURING has become increasingly important in Thailand, Vietnam, and the Philippines in recent years. The assembling of component-based electrical and electronic goods is becoming more common throughout this region, with foreign companies benefiting from low labor costs and the upgrading of technology. The economies of Myanmar and Cambodia are still based on agricultural produce and the processing of raw materials. Tin is the region's most important metal, and nickel, copper, and chromite are also mined, although the quantities produced are not significant on a global scale. Thailand's successful tourist industry is the country's highest earner of foreign exchange.

TRANSPORTATION NETWORK

131,566 miles (211,845 km)	267 miles (430 km)
7,785 miles (12,536 km)	28,393 miles (45,722 km)

Transportation development has concentrated on the building of road networks. Water and sea transportation remain important, although air links have improved, particularly in Thailand and the Philippines.

Major industry and infrastructure

chemicals	oil & gas	capital cities
electronics	mining	major towns
engineering	shipbuilding	international airports
finance	textiles	major roads
food processing	timber processing	major industrial areas
iron & steel		

Opium poppies are destroyed under army supervision in Thailand. This action is part of a government-sponsored initiative to reduce the trade in drugs such as heroin, which is derived from these plants. Drug trafficking is a major problem throughout the region; the area is known as the "Golden Triangle," and Laos is the third-largest producer of opium poppies in the world.

***The terracing of land** to restrict soil erosion and create flat surfaces for agriculture is a common practice throughout Southeast Asia, particularly where land is scarce. These terraces are on Luzon in the Philippines.*

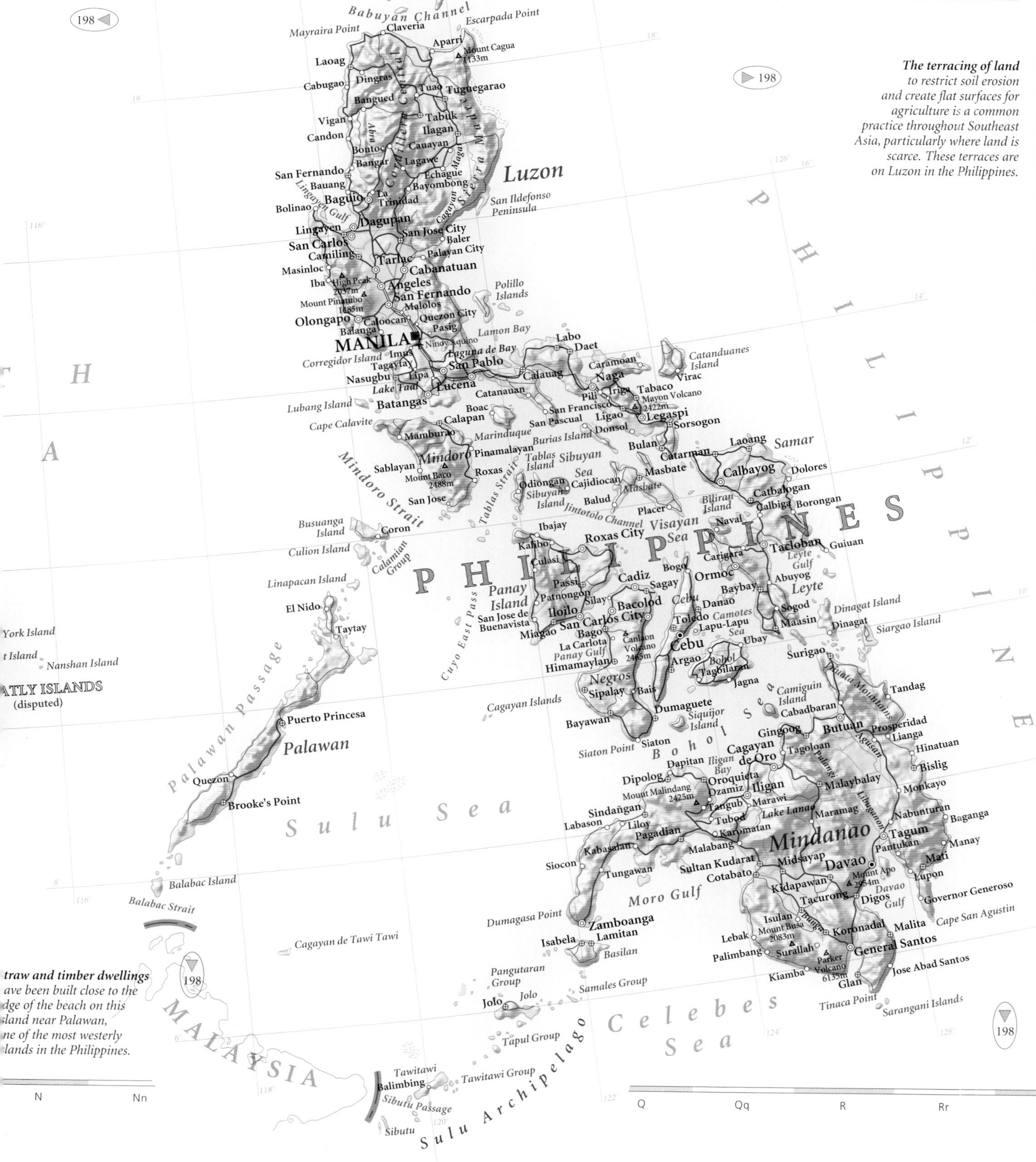

Straw and timber dwellings have been built close to the edge of the beach on this island near Palawan, one of the most westerly islands in the Philippines.

SCALE 1:7,750,000
(projection: Lambert Conformal Conic)
Km 0 25 50 100 150 200
Miles 0 25 50 100 150 200

MAP KEY

POPULATION
- above 5 million
- 1 million to 5 million
- 500,000 to 1 million
- 100,000 to 500,000
- 50,000 to 100,000
- 10,000 to 50,000
- below 10,000

ELEVATION
- 4000m / 13,124ft
- 3000m / 9843ft
- 2000m / 6562ft
- 1000m / 3281ft
- 500m / 1640ft
- 250m / 820ft
- 100m / 328ft
- sea level

198 ◀ ▶ 198 ▶ 198 ▼ 198 ▼ 198

THE INDIAN OCEAN

DESPITE BEING THE SMALLEST of the three major oceans, the evolution of the Indian Ocean was the most complex. The ocean basin was formed during the breakup of the supercontinent Gondwanaland, when the Indian subcontinent moved northeast, Africa moved west and Australia separated from Antarctica. Like the Pacific Ocean, the warm waters of the Indian Ocean are punctuated by coral atolls and islands. About one-fifth of the world's population – over a billion people – live on its shores. Those people living along the northern coasts are constantly threatened by flooding and typhoons caused by the monsoon winds.

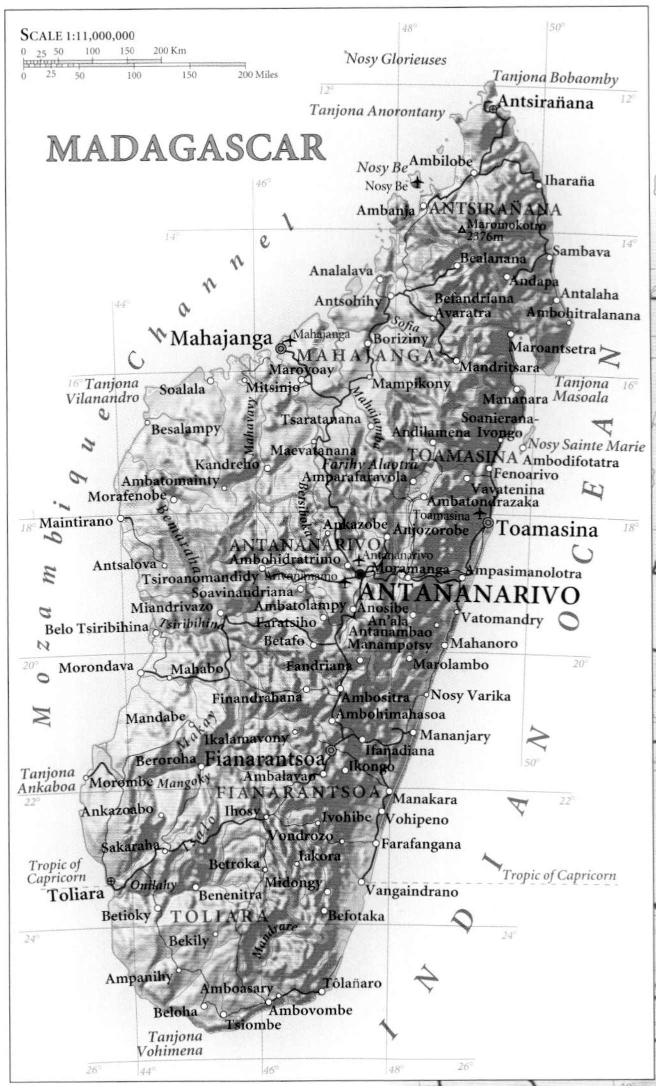

THE LANDSCAPE

THE INDIAN OCEAN BEGAN FORMING about 150 million years ago, but in its present form it is relatively young, only about 36 million years old. Along the three subterranean mountain chains of its mid-ocean ridge the seafloor is still spreading. The Indian Ocean has fewer trenches than other oceans and only a narrow continental shelf around most of its surrounding land.

Sediments come from Ganges/Brahmaputra river system

Submarine canyons transport sediment to fan – some of these are more than 1,500 miles (2,500 km) long

Sri Lanka

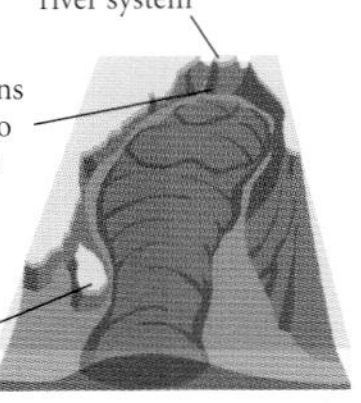

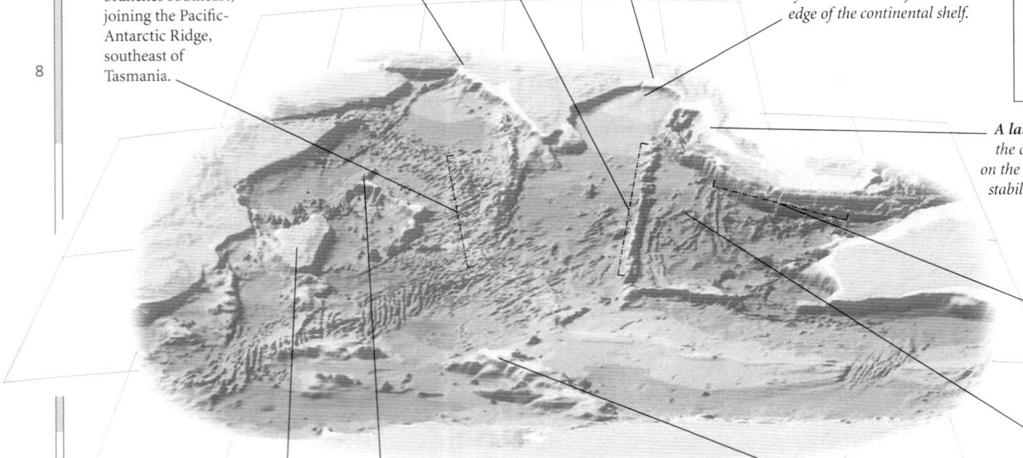

The mid-oceanic ridge runs from the Arabian Sea. It diverges east of Madagascar. One arm runs southwest to join the Mid-Atlantic Ridge, the other branches southeast, joining the Pacific-Antarctic Ridge, southeast of Tasmania.

The Ninetyeast Ridge takes its name from the line of longitude it follows. It is the world's longest and straightest under-sea ridge.

Indus River

Two of the world's largest rivers flow into the Indian Ocean; the Indus and the Ganges/Brahmaputra. Both have deposited enormous fans of sediment.

The Ganges Fan is one of the world's largest submarine accumulations of sediment, extending far beyond Sri Lanka. It is fed by the Ganges/Brahmaputra River system, whose sediment is carried through a network of underwater canyons at the edge of the continental shelf.

A large proportion of the coast of Thailand, on the Isthmus of Kra, is stabilized by mangrove thickets. They act as an important breeding ground for wildlife.

The Java Trench is the world's longest, it runs 1,600 miles (2,570 km) from the southwest of Java, but is only 50 miles (80 km) wide.

The relief of Madagascar rises from a low-lying coastal strip in the east, to the central plateau. The plateau is also a major watershed separating Madagascar's three main river basins.

The central group of the Seychelles are mountainous, granite islands. They have a narrow coastal belt and lush, tropical vegetation cloaks the highlands.

The Kerguelen Islands in the Southern Ocean were created by a hot spot in the Earth's crust. The islands were formed in succession as the Antarctic Plate moved slowly over the hot spot.

The circulation in the northern Indian Ocean is controlled by the monsoon winds. Biannually these winds reverse their pattern, causing a reversal in the surface currents and alternative high and low pressure conditions over Asia and Australia.

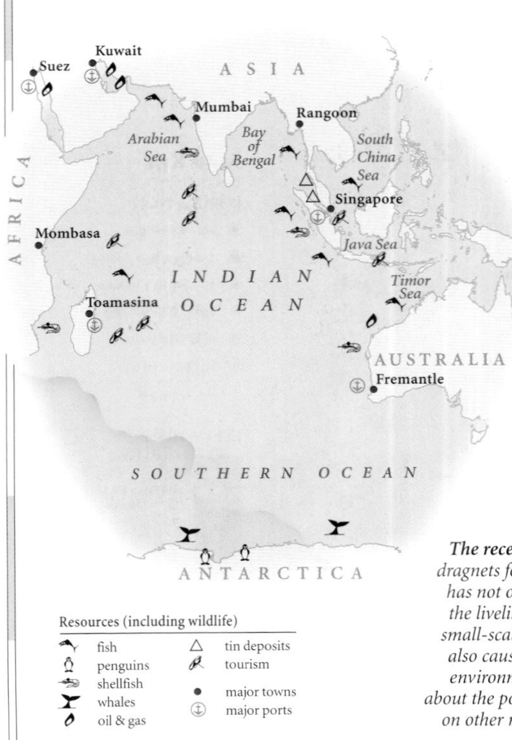

RESOURCES

MANY OF THE SMALL ISLANDS in the Indian Ocean rely exclusively on tuna-fishing and tourism to maintain their economies. Most fisheries are artisanal, although large-scale tuna-fishing does take place in the Seychelles, Mauritius and the western Indian Ocean. Nonliving resources include oil in the Persian Gulf, pearls in the Red Sea, and tin from deposits off the shores of Myanmar, Thailand, and Indonesia.

Resources (including wildlife)

fish	△ tin deposits
penguins	● tourism
shellfish	● major towns
whales	● major ports
oil & gas	

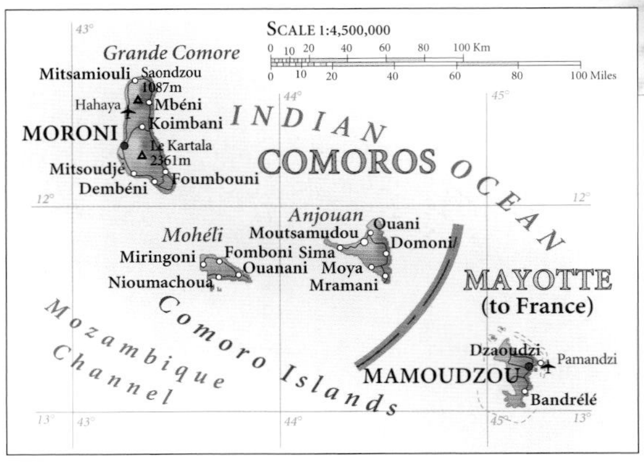

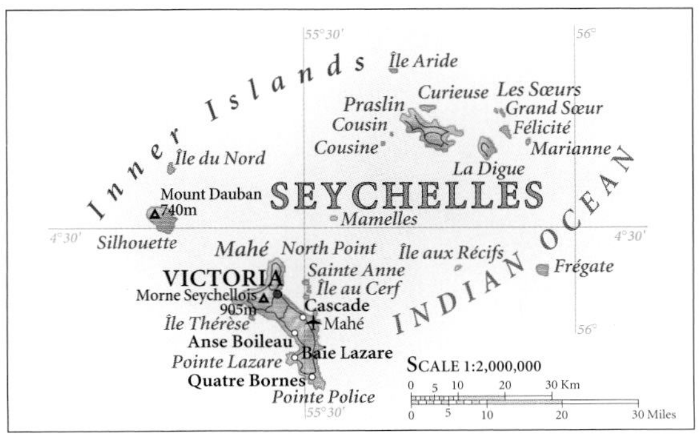

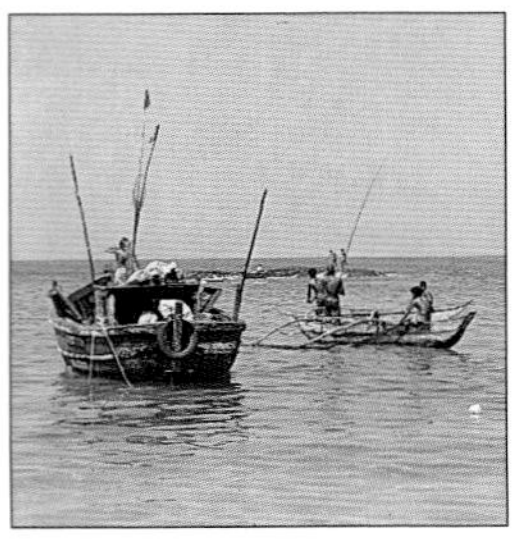

The recent use of large dragnets for tuna-fishing has not only threatened the livelihoods of many small-scale fisheries, but also caused widespread environmental concern about the potential impact on other marine species.

SCALE 1:11,000,000

MADAGASCAR

SCALE 1:4,500,000

COMOROS

MAYOTTE (to France)

SEYCHELLES

SCALE 1:2,000,000

Coral reefs support an enormous diversity of animal and plant life. Many species of tiny tropical fish, like these squirrel fish, live and feed around the profusion of reefs and atolls in the Indian Ocean.

The steeper eastern side of Madagascar is drained by numerous short, fast-flowing rivers. In contrast, larger, more languid rivers flow across the west. Both erode huge quantities of Madagascar's reddish soil.

There are over 1,300 small coral islands in the Maldives, but only about 200 are inhabited. They are based around an ancient submerged volcanic mountain range and all the islands are low-lying, none rising more than 6 ft (1.8 m) above sea level.

The island of Mauritius is volcanic in origin. Its central plateau is bounded by mountains which may once have formed the rim of a volcanic crater.

AUSTRALASIA AND OCEANIA

AUSTRALASIA AND OCEANIA, COVERING A LAND AREA OF 3,285,048 SQ MILES (8,508,238 SQ KM), TAKES IN 14 COUNTRIES INCLUDING THE CONTINENT OF AUSTRALIA, NEW ZEALAND, PAPUA NEW GUINEA, AND MANY ISLAND GROUPS SCATTERED ACROSS THE PACIFIC OCEAN.

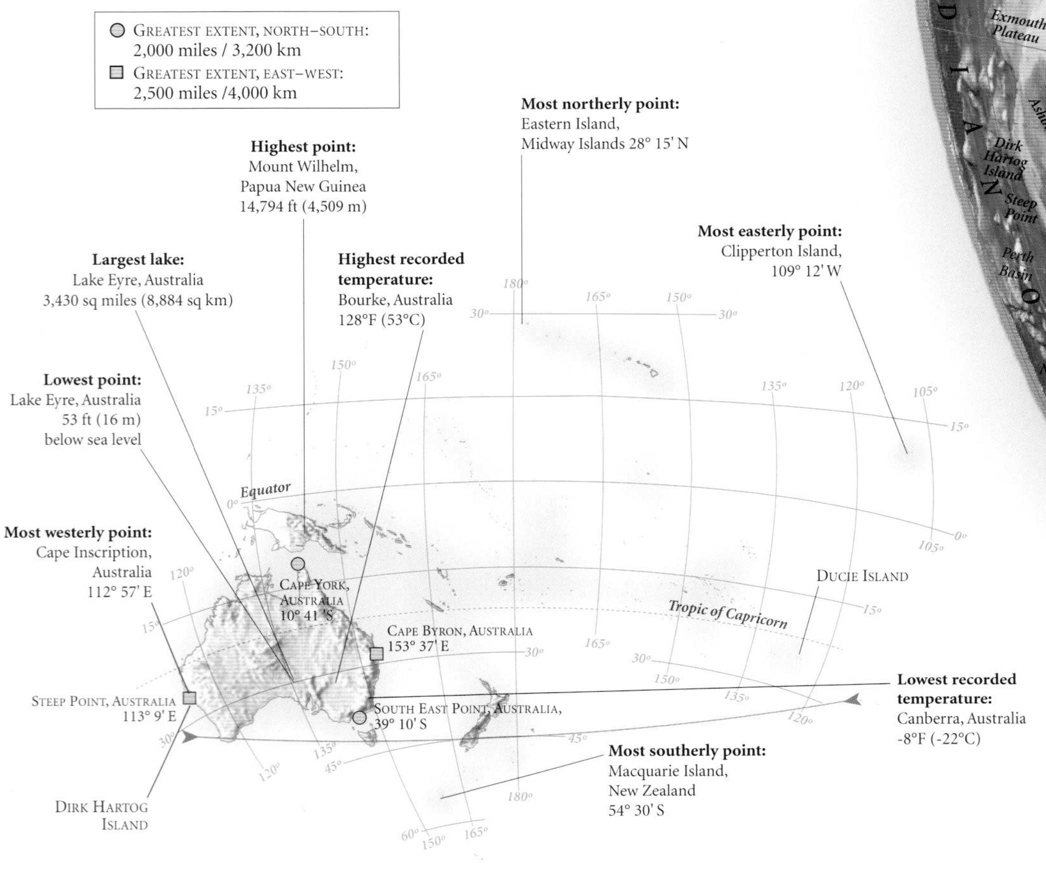

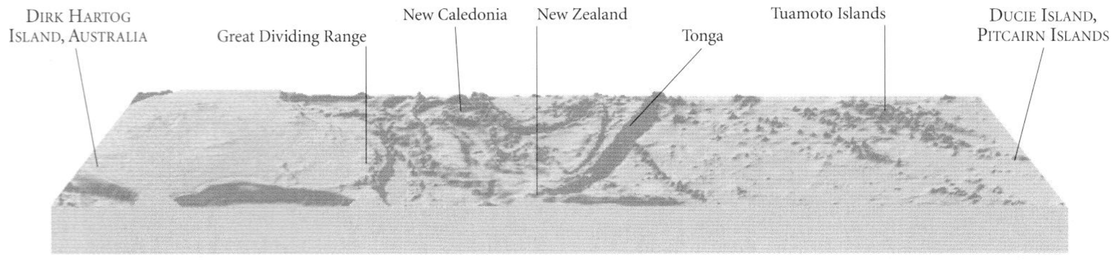

Cross-section from Dirk Hartog Island, Australia to Ducie Island, Pitcairn Islands

line of cross-section

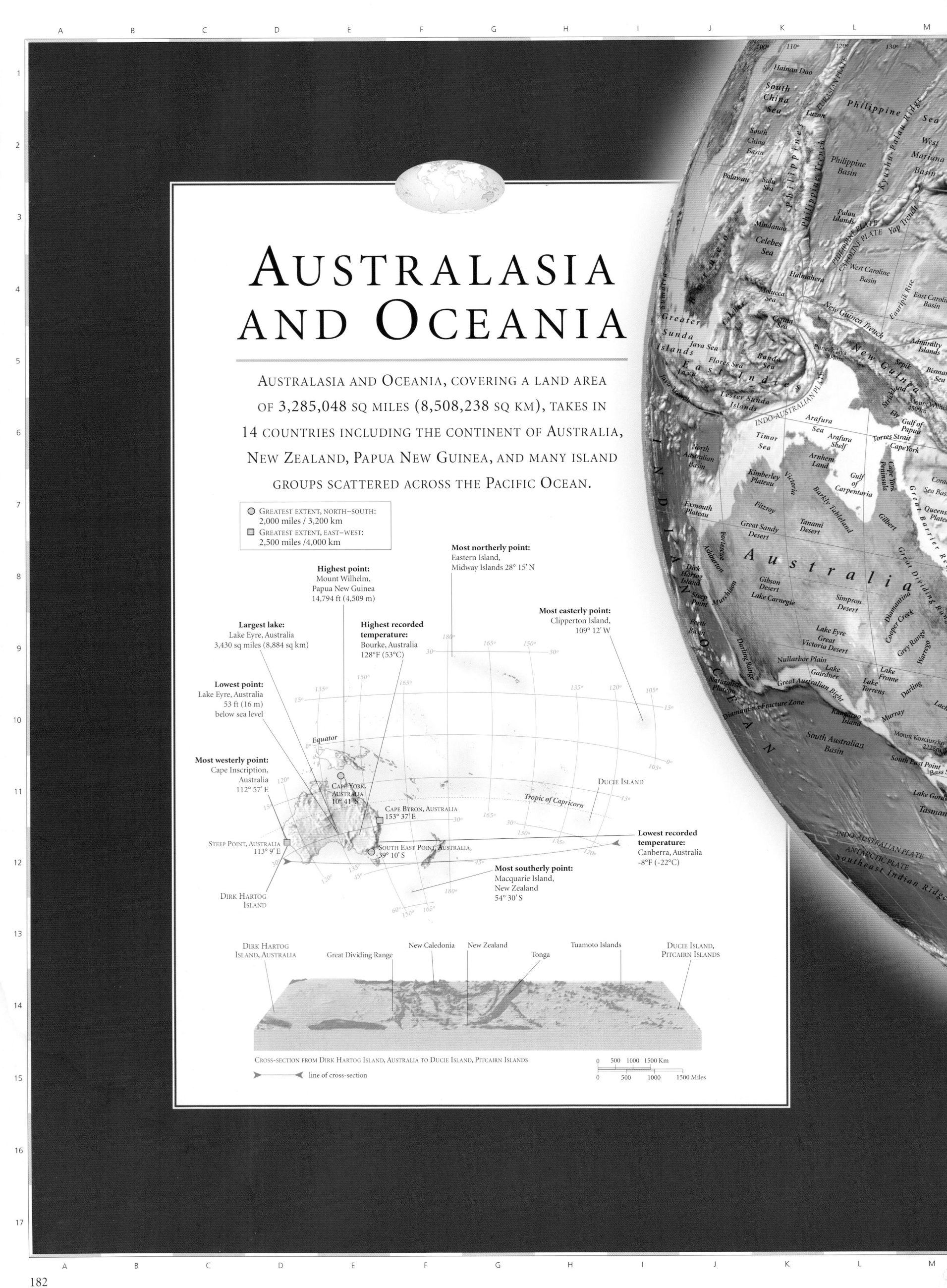

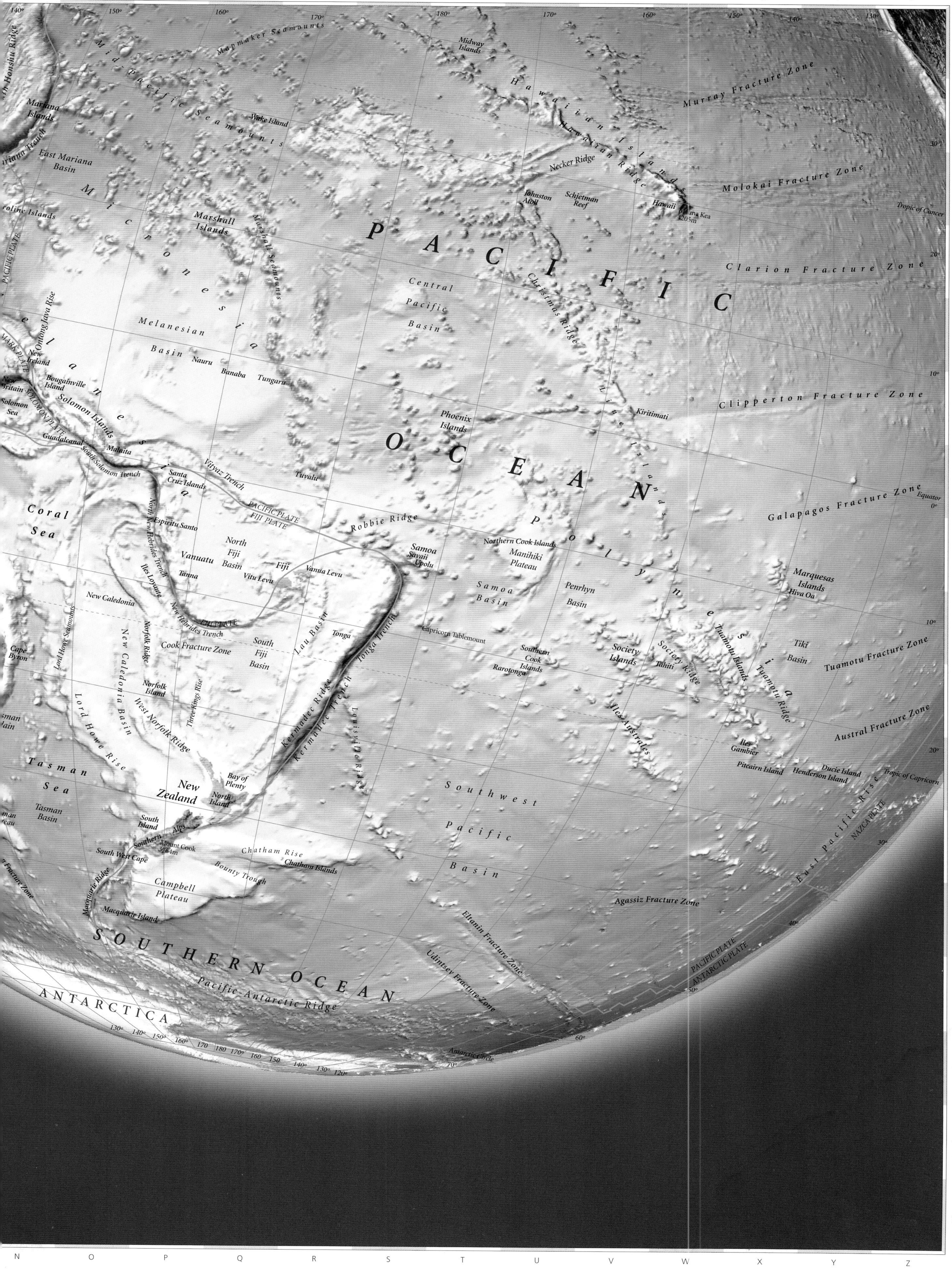
N O P Q R S T U V W X Y Z
1 2 3 4 5 6 7 8 9 10 11 12 13 14 15 16 17
PACIFIC OCEAN
SOUTHERN OCEAN
ANTARCTICA
Mapmaker Seamounts
Mid-Pacific Seamounts
Midway Islands
Hawaiian Islands
Hawaiian Ridge
Murray Fracture Zone
Molokai Fracture Zone
Tropic of Cancer
Necker Ridge
Johnston Atoll
Schjetman Reef
Hawaii
Mauna Kea 4205m
Wake Island
Mariana Islands
Mariana Trench
East Mariana Basin
Caroline Islands
Micronesia
Marshall Islands
Marshall Seamounts
PACIFIC PLATE
Central Pacific Basin
Christmas Ridge
Clarion Fracture Zone
Ontong Java Rise
Melanesian Basin
Melanesia
Nauru
Banaba
Tungaru
New Ireland
New Britain
Bougainville Island
Solomon Sea
Solomon Islands
SOLOMON PLATE
Guadalcanal
Malaita
South Solomon Trench
Vityaz Trench
Santa Cruz Islands
Tuvalu
Phoenix Islands
Kiritimati
Line Islands
Clipperton Fracture Zone
Galapagos Fracture Zone
Equator
Coral Sea
North New Hebrides Trench
Espiritu Santo
PACIFIC PLATE
FIJI PLATE
Robbie Ridge
North Fiji Basin
Vanuatu
Tanna
Fiji
Vitu Levu
Vanua Levu
Samoa
Savaii
Upolu
Northern Cook Islands
Manihiki Plateau
Samoa Basin
Penrhyn Basin
Polynesia
Marquesas Islands
Hiva Oa
New Caledonia
Iles Loyaute
New Hebrides Trench
Lord Howe Seamounts
Cape Byron
Norfolk Ridge
New Caledonia Basin
Cook Fracture Zone
South Fiji Basin
Lau Basin
Tonga
Tonga Trench
Capricorn Tablemount
Southern Cook Islands
Rarotonga
Society Islands
Tahiti
Society Ridge
Tuamotu Islands
Tuamotu Ridge
Tiki Basin
Tuamotu Fracture Zone
Norfolk Island
Three Kings Rise
West Norfolk Ridge
Lord Howe Rise
Kermadec Ridge
Kermadec Trench
Louisville Ridge
Iles Australes
Iles Gambier
Austral Fracture Zone
Pitcairn Island
Henderson Island
Ducie Island
Tropic of Capricorn
Tasman Sea
Tasman Basin
New Zealand
Bay of Plenty
North Island
South Island
Southern Alps
Mount Cook 3764m
South West Cape
Southwest Pacific Basin
East Pacific Rise
NAZCA PLATE
Chatham Rise
Chatham Islands
Bounty Trough
Campbell Plateau
Macquarie Ridge
Macquarie Island
Agassiz Fracture Zone
Eltanin Fracture Zone
Udintsev Fracture Zone
PACIFIC PLATE
ANTARCTIC PLATE
Pacific-Antarctic Ridge
Antarctic Circle

Political Australasia and Oceania

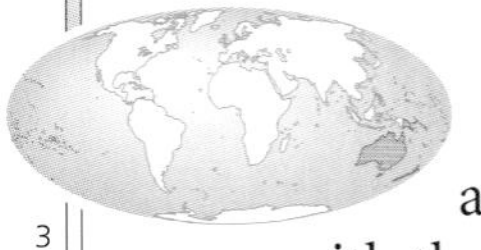

Vast expanses of ocean separate this geographically fragmented realm, characterized more by each country's isolation than by any political unity. Australia's and New Zealand's traditional ties with the United Kingdom, as members of the Commonwealth, are now being called into question as Australasian and Oceanian nations are increasingly looking to forge new relationships with neighboring Asian countries like Japan. External influences have featured strongly in the politics of the Pacific Islands; the various territories of Micronesia were largely under US control until the late 1980s, and France, New Zealand, the US, and the UK still have territories under colonial rule in Polynesia. Nuclear weapons-testing by Western superpowers was widespread during the Cold War period, but has now been discontinued.

Western Australia's mineral wealth *has transformed its state capital, Perth, into one of Australia's major cities. Perth is one of the world's most isolated cities – over 2,500 miles (4,000 km) from the population centers of the eastern seaboard.*

Population

Density of settlement in the region is generally low. Australia is one of the least densely populated countries on Earth with over 80% of its population living within 25 miles (40 km) of the coast – mostly in the southeast of the country. New Zealand, and the island groups of Melanesia, Micronesia, and Polynesia, are much more densely populated, although many of the smaller islands remain uninhabited.

The myriad of small coral islands *that are scattered across the Pacific Ocean are often uninhabited, as they offer little shelter from the weather, often no fresh water, and only limited food supplies.*

The planes *of the Australian Royal Flying Doctor Service are able to cover large expanses of barren land quickly, bringing medical treatment to the most inaccessible and far-flung places.*

Languages

English is spoken throughout Australia and New Zealand. In Australia, English has been superimposed on a mosaic of Aboriginal languages. In New Zealand, the indigenous language, Maori, is the official language besides Polynesian. In Papua New Guinea, Melanesian Pidgin has become a *lingua franca* alongside several hundred indigenous languages. Across the region, the indigenous languages can be grouped into(1) the Aboriginal languages of Australia, (2) the Papuan languages spoken mostly inland in Papua New Guinea, and (3) the widely dispersed Austronesian, which includes coastal languages of Papua New Guinea, New Zealand Maori and languages of Oceania.

Aboriginal languages and cultures are preserved in the central and northern regions of Australia. Ever since the arrival of European settlers, Australia's indigenous peoples have been marginalized. Recently, both their culture and land rights have been increasingly recognized.

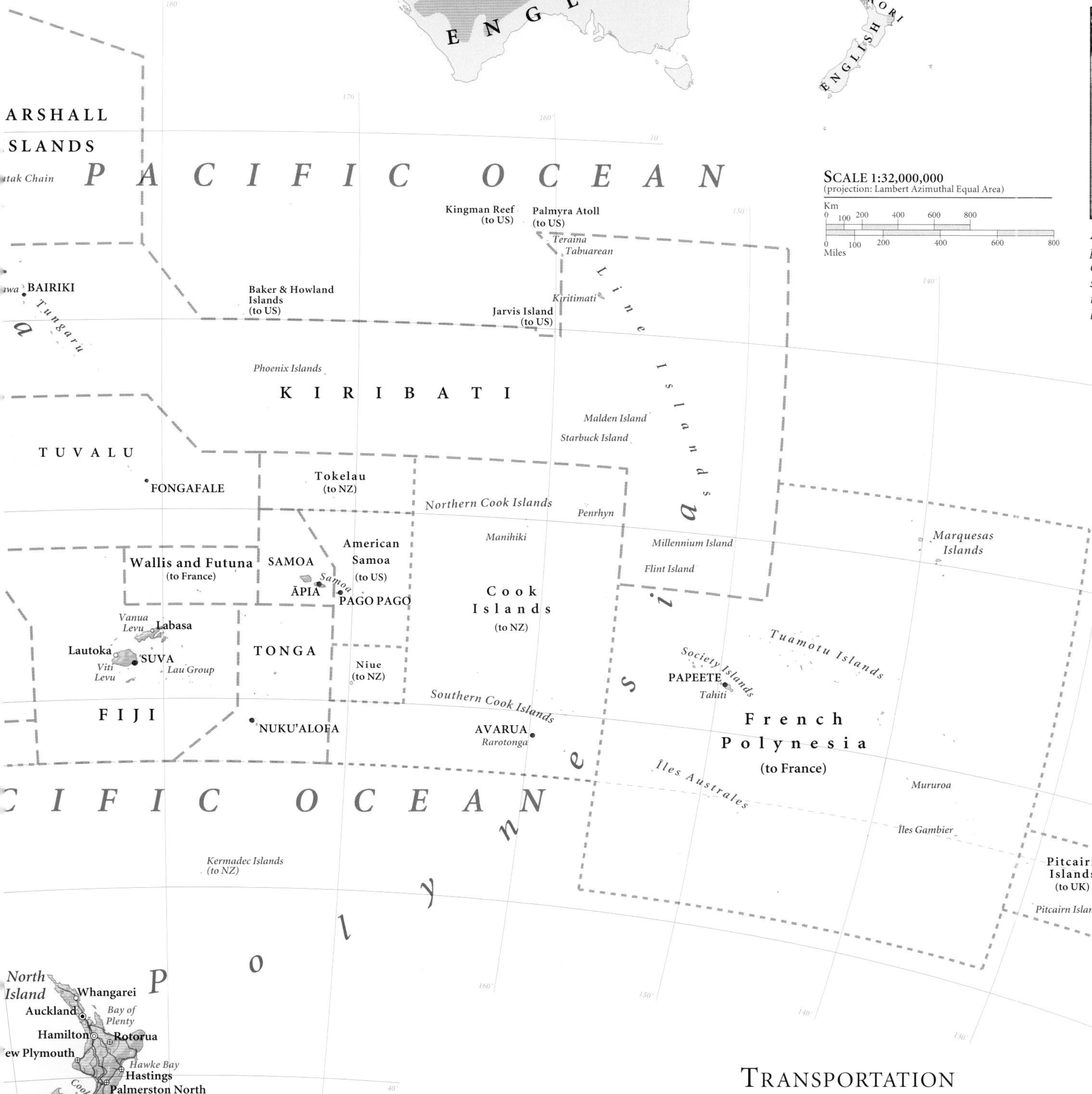

Scale 1:32,000,000
(projection: Lambert Azimuthal Equal Area)

Km 0 100 200 400 600 800
Miles 0 100 200 400 600 800

Map Key

POPULATION
- above 5 million
- 1 million to 5 million
- 500,000 to 1 million
- 100,000 to 500,000
- 50,000 to 100,000
- 10,000 to 50,000
- below 10,000
- Country capital
- State capital

BORDERS
- full international border
- indication of maritime country extent
- indication of maritime dependent territory extent
- state border

COMMUNICATIONS
- major roads
- major railways

Outrigger canoes *have been used for centuries throughout the Pacific islands, especially in Micronesia. Hunting and fishing expeditions traditionally required several nights spent at sea, and stronger canoes were built for this purpose.*

Transportation

While sea travel remains of paramount importance throughout the continent, well-developed regional and international air travel has reduced the region's global isolation. Internal air travel is particularly important in Australia, where distances are great and road systems are poorly developed or in some areas nonexistent. Australia's railroad system is highly concentrated in the east and southeast, and still operates on three different gauges; a legacy of its piecemeal, colonial development.

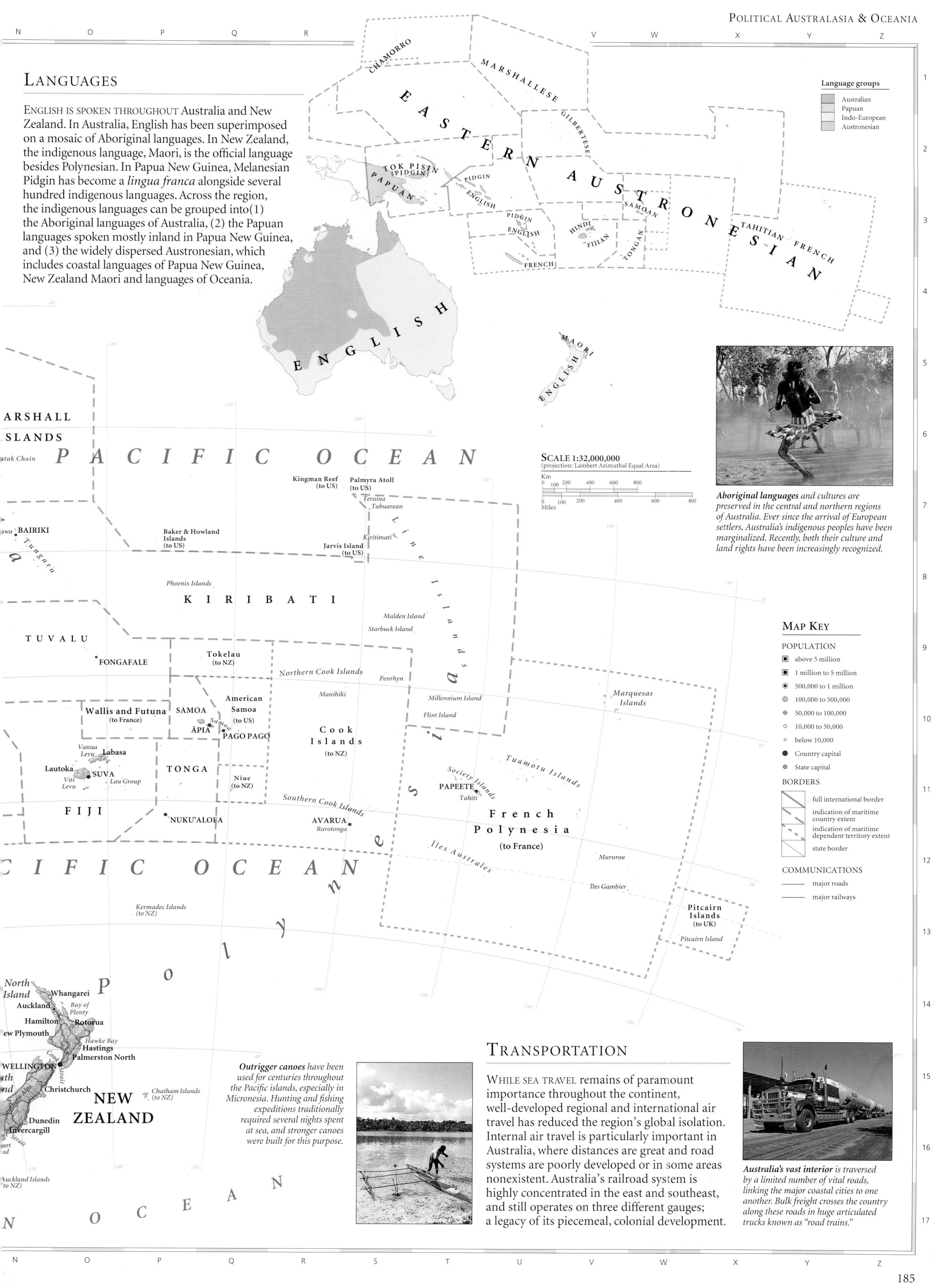

Australia's vast interior *is traversed by a limited number of vital roads, linking the major coastal cities to one another. Bulk freight crosses the country along these roads in huge articulated trucks known as "road trains."*

Australasian and Oceanian Resources

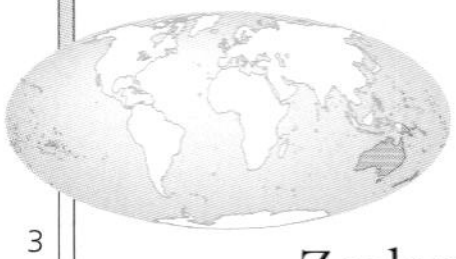

NATURAL RESOURCES ARE OF MAJOR ECONOMIC IMPORTANCE throughout Australasia and Oceania. Australia in particular is a major world exporter of raw materials such as coal, iron ore, and bauxite, while New Zealand's agricultural economy is dominated by sheep-raising. Trade with western Europe has declined significantly in the last 20 years, and the Pacific Rim countries of Southeast Asia are now the main trading partners, as well as a source of new settlers to the region. Australasia and Oceania's greatest resources are its climate and environment; tourism increasingly provides a vital source of income for the whole continent.

***The largely unpolluted** waters of the Pacific Ocean support rich and varied marine life, much of which is farmed commercially. Here, oysters are gathered for market off the coast of New Zealand's South Island.*

***Huge flocks of sheep** are a common sight in New Zealand, where they outnumber people by 20 to 1. New Zealand is one of the world's largest exporters of wool and frozen lamb.*

Standard of Living

IN MARKED CONTRAST TO ITS NEIGHBOR, Australia, with one of the world's highest life expectancies and standards of living, Papua New Guinea is one of the world's least developed countries. In addition, high population growth and urbanization rates throughout the Pacific islands contribute to overcrowding. In Australia and New Zealand, the Aboriginal and Maori people have been isolated, although recently their traditional land ownership rights have begun to be legally recognized in an effort to ease their social and economic isolation, and to improve living standards.

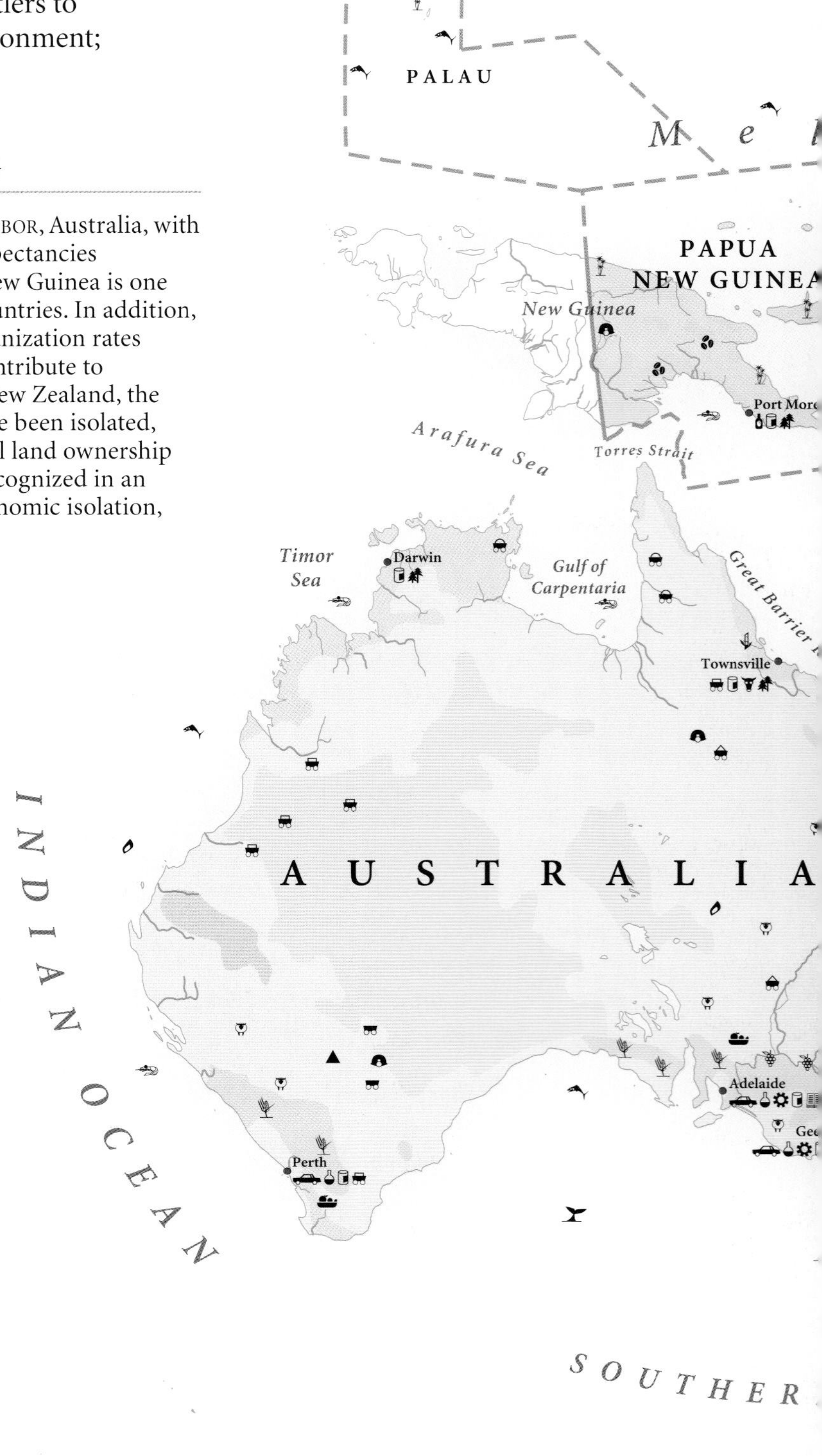

Environmental Issues

THE PROSPECT OF RISING SEA LEVELS poses a threat to many low-lying islands in the Pacific. The testing of nuclear weapons, once common throughout the region, was finally discontinued in 1996. Australia's ecological balance has been irreversibly altered by the introduction of alien species. Although it has the world's largest underground water reserve, the Great Artesian Basin, the availability of fresh water in Australia remains critical. Periodic droughts combined with overgrazing lead to desertification and increase the risk of devastating bush fires, and occasional flash floods.

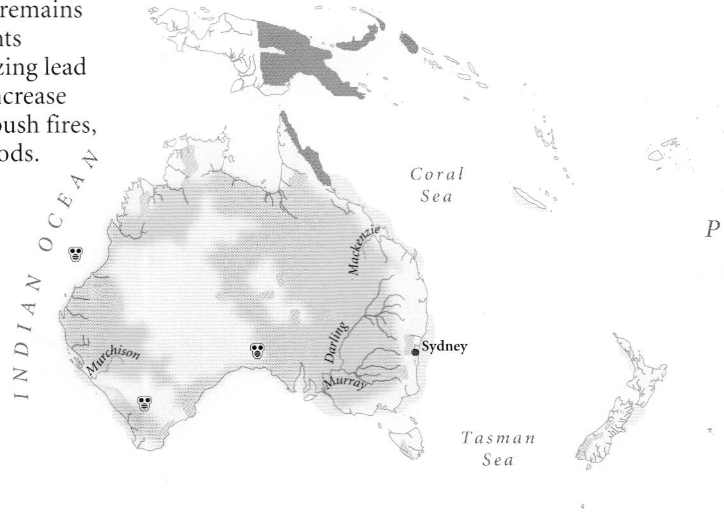

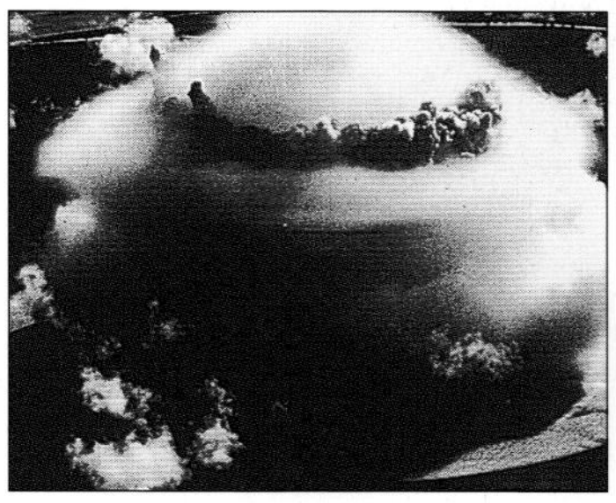

***In 1946 Bikini Atoll**, in the Marshall Islands, was chosen as the site for Operation Crossroads – investigating the effects of atomic bombs upon naval vessels. Further nuclear tests continued until the early 1990s. The long-term environmental effects are unknown.*

The massive Ok Tedi copper mine *was opened in 1988. It is situated in the midst of remote tropical jungle in Papua New Guinea.*

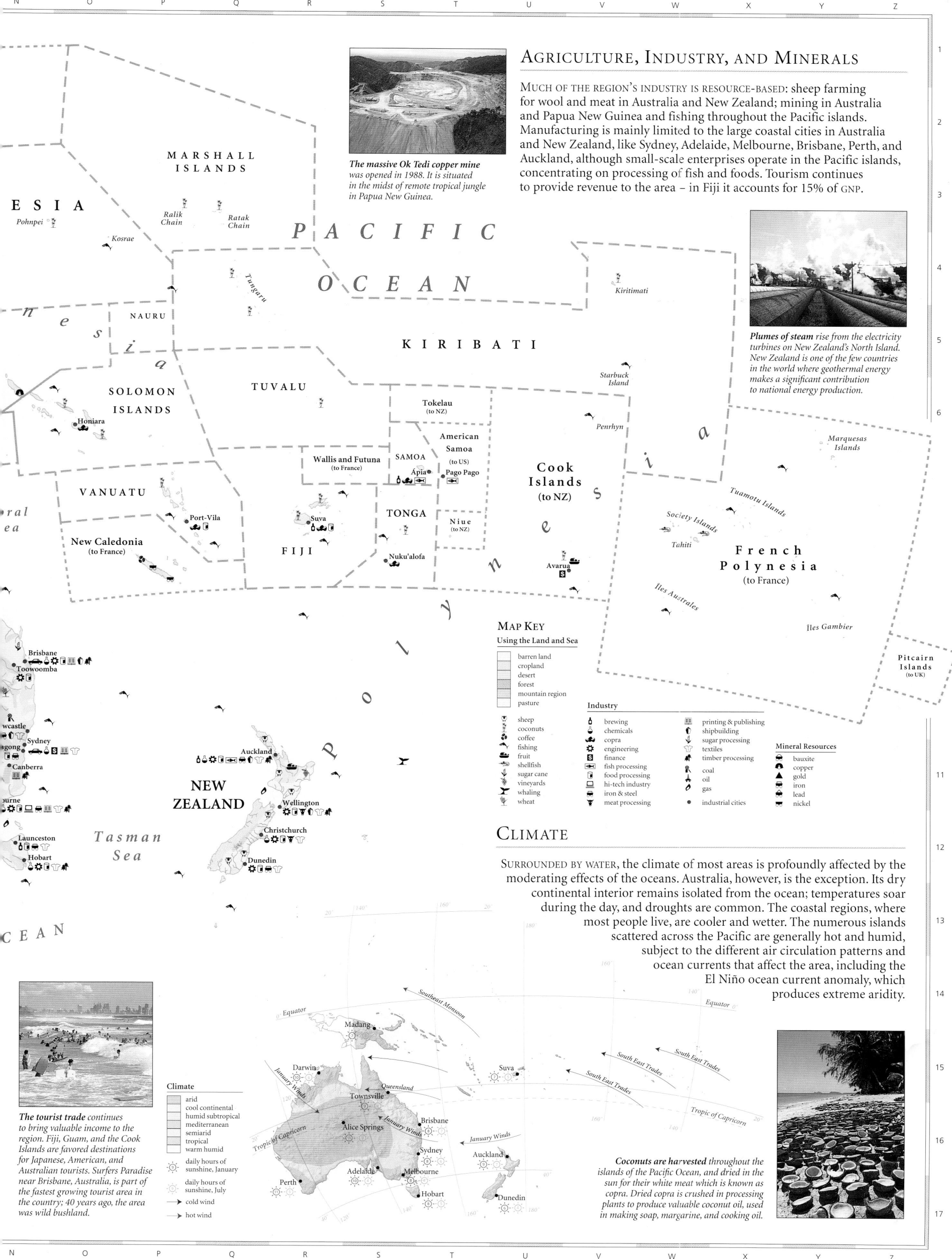

AGRICULTURE, INDUSTRY, AND MINERALS

MUCH OF THE REGION'S INDUSTRY IS RESOURCE-BASED: sheep farming for wool and meat in Australia and New Zealand; mining in Australia and Papua New Guinea and fishing throughout the Pacific islands. Manufacturing is mainly limited to the large coastal cities in Australia and New Zealand, like Sydney, Adelaide, Melbourne, Brisbane, Perth, and Auckland, although small-scale enterprises operate in the Pacific islands, concentrating on processing of fish and foods. Tourism continues to provide revenue to the area – in Fiji it accounts for 15% of GNP.

***Plumes of steam** rise from the electricity turbines on New Zealand's North Island. New Zealand is one of the few countries in the world where geothermal energy makes a significant contribution to national energy production.*

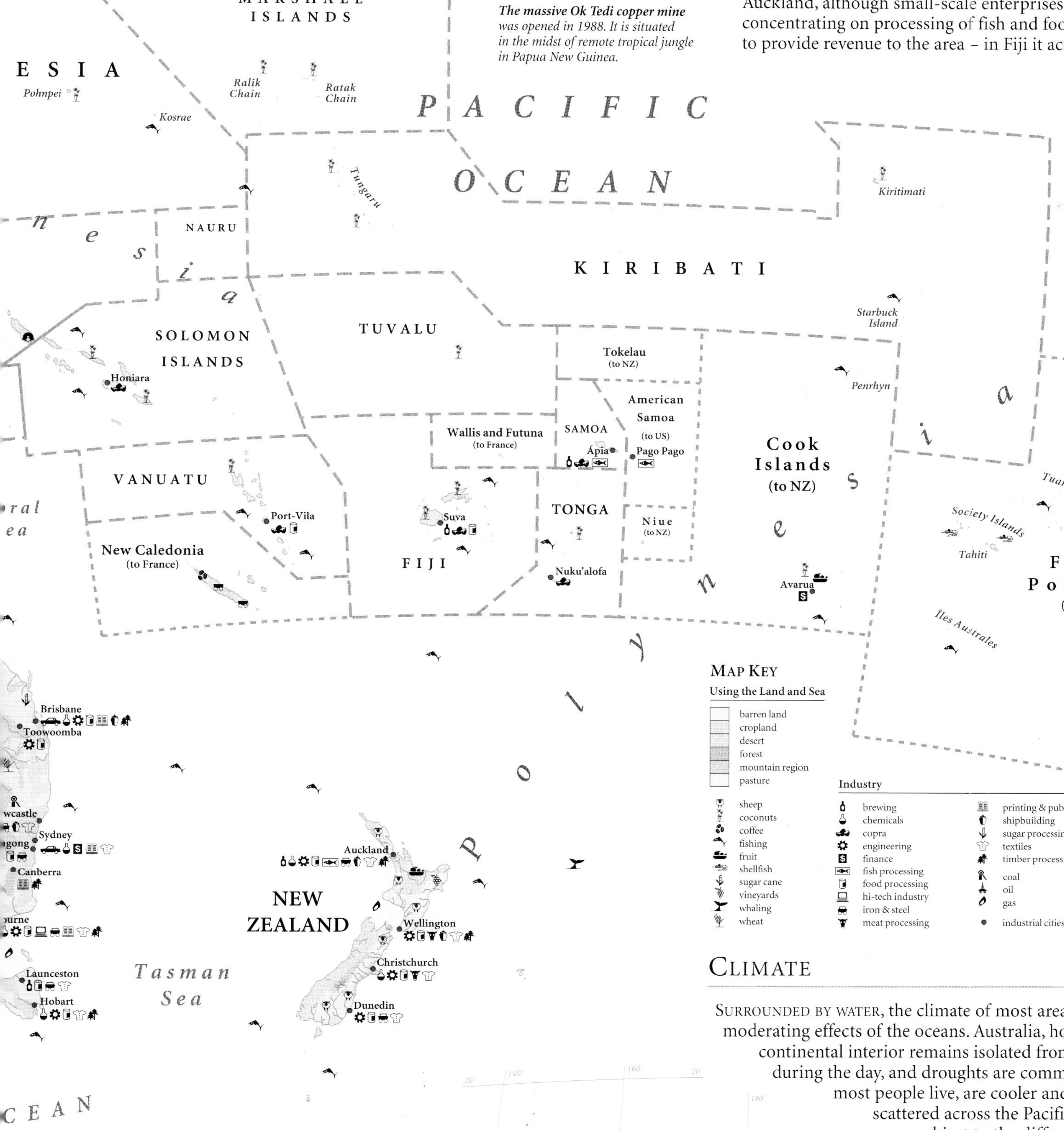

CLIMATE

SURROUNDED BY WATER, the climate of most areas is profoundly affected by the moderating effects of the oceans. Australia, however, is the exception. Its dry continental interior remains isolated from the ocean; temperatures soar during the day, and droughts are common. The coastal regions, where most people live, are cooler and wetter. The numerous islands scattered across the Pacific are generally hot and humid, subject to the different air circulation patterns and ocean currents that affect the area, including the El Niño ocean current anomaly, which produces extreme aridity.

***The tourist trade** continues to bring valuable income to the region. Fiji, Guam, and the Cook Islands are favored destinations for Japanese, American, and Australian tourists. Surfers Paradise near Brisbane, Australia, is part of the fastest growing tourist area in the country; 40 years ago, the area was wild bushland.*

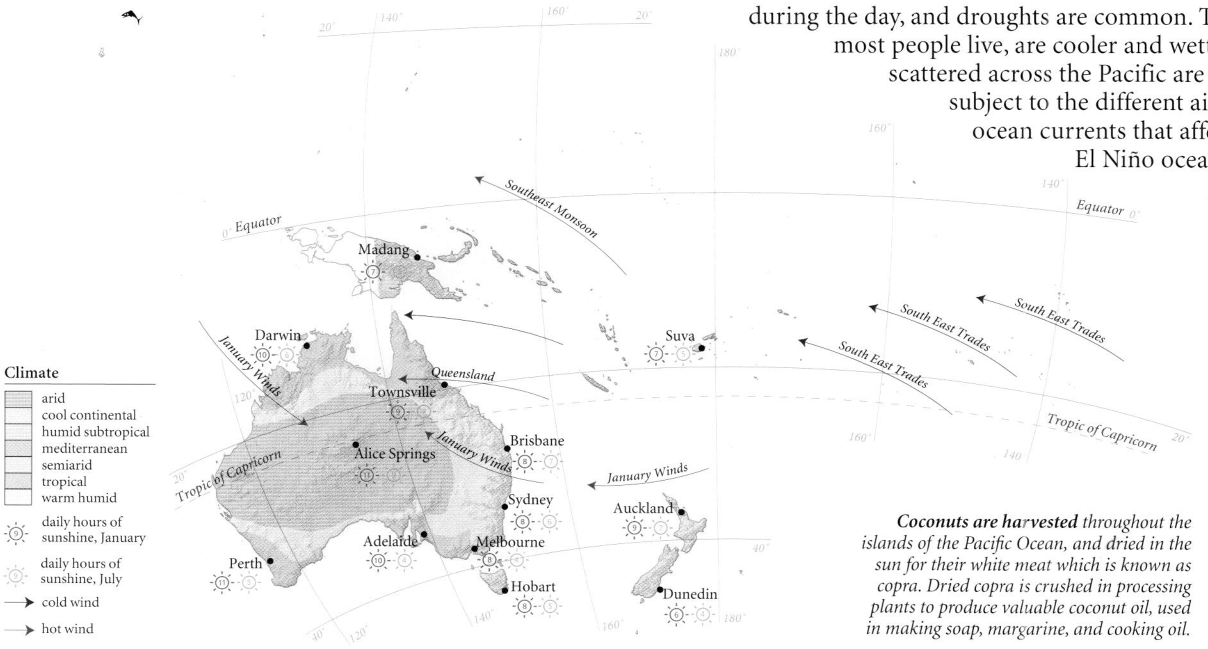

***Coconuts are harvested** throughout the islands of the Pacific Ocean, and dried in the sun for their white meat which is known as copra. Dried copra is crushed in processing plants to produce valuable coconut oil, used in making soap, margarine, and cooking oil.*

AUSTRALIA

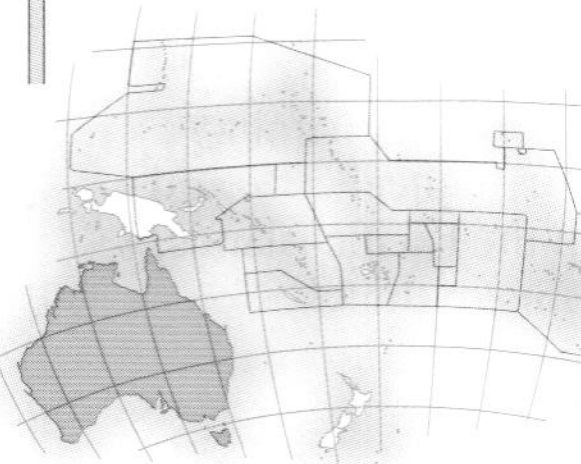

AUSTRALIA IS THE WORLD's smallest continent, a stable landmass lying between the Indian and Pacific oceans. Previously home to its aboriginal peoples only, since the end of the 18th century immigration has transformed the face of the country. Initially settlers came mainly from western Europe, particularly the UK, and for years Australia remained wedded to its British colonial past. More recent immigrants have come from eastern Europe, and from Asian countries such as Japan, South Korea, and Indonesia. Australia is now forging strong trading links with these "Pacific Rim" countries and its economic future seems to lie with Asia and the Americas, rather than Europe, its traditional partner.

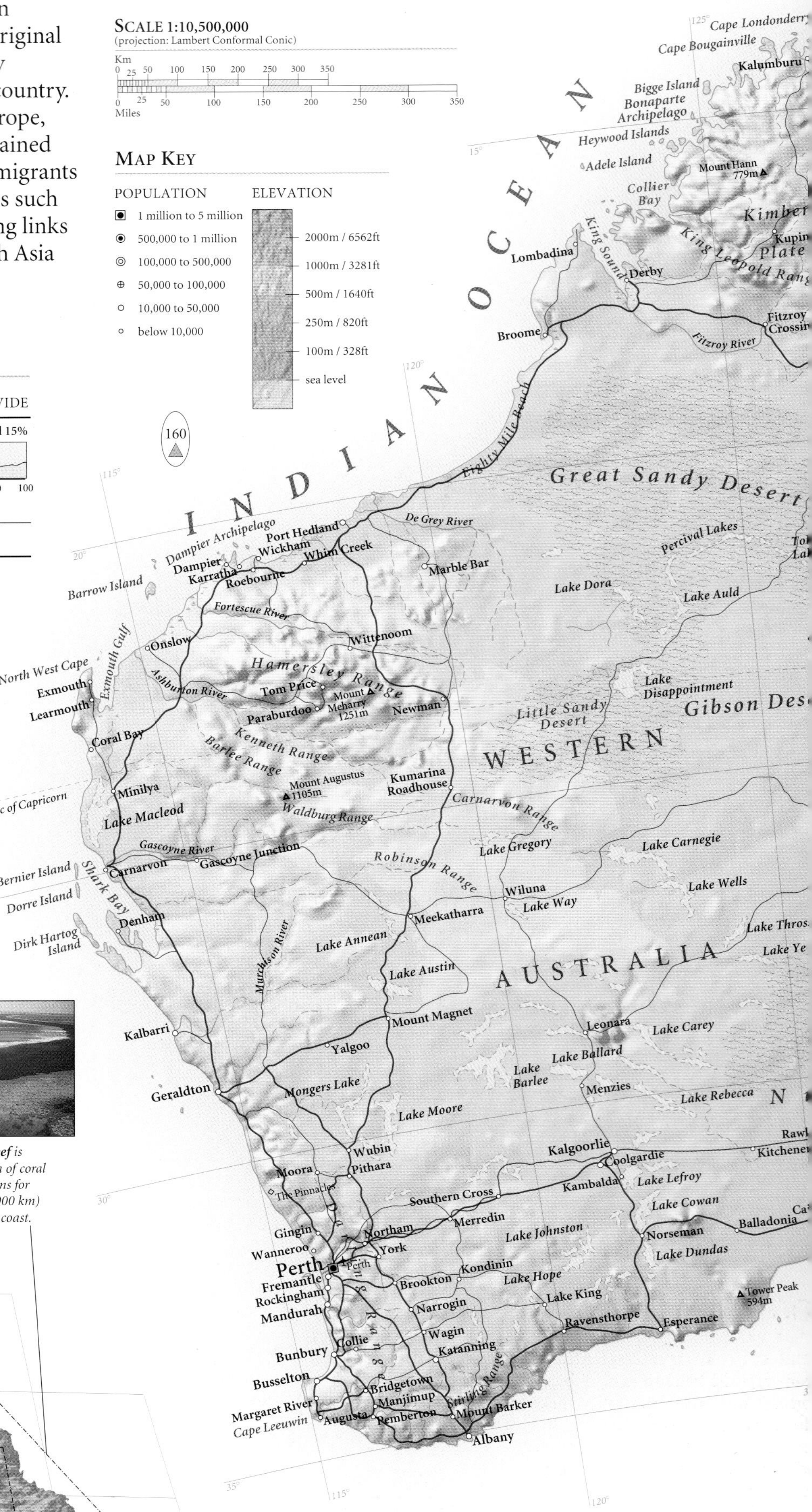

USING THE LAND

OVER 165 MILLION SHEEP are dispersed in vast herds around the country, contributing to a major export industry. Cattle-ranching is important, particularly in the west. Wheat, and grapes for Australia's wine industry, are grown mainly in the south. Much of the country is desert, unsuitable for agriculture unless irrigation is used.

THE URBAN/RURAL POPULATION DIVIDE

urban 85%		rural 15%

0 10 20 30 40 50 60 70 80 90 100

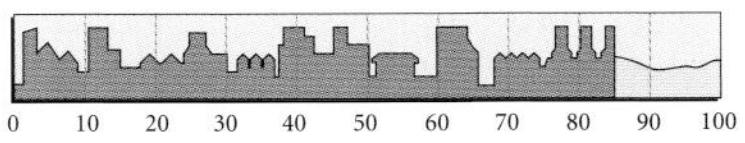

POPULATION DENSITY | TOTAL LAND AREA
6 people per sq mile | 2,967,893 sq miles
(2 people per sq km) | (7,686,850 sq km)

Land use and agricultural distribution

cattle — capital cities
sheep • major towns
cereals — pasture
sugar cane — cropland
timber — forest
vineyards — desert
— mountain region

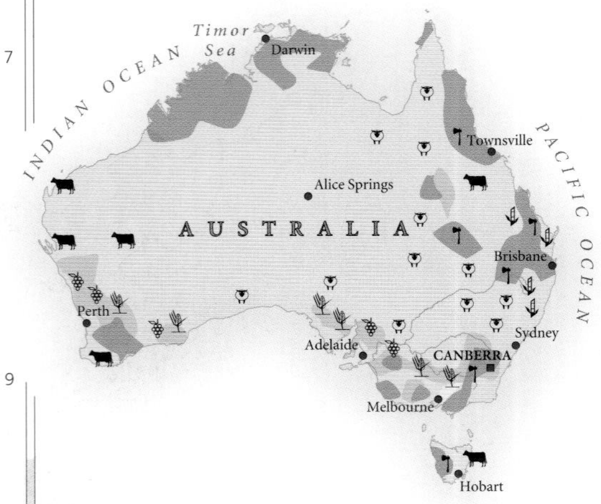

Lines of ripening vines stretch for miles in Barossa Valley, a major wine-growing region near Adelaide.

THE LANDSCAPE

AUSTRALIA CONSISTS OF MANY ERODED PLATEAUS, lying firmly in the middle of the Indo-Australian Plate. It is the world's flattest continent, and the driest, after Antarctica. The coasts tend to be more hilly and fertile, especially in the east. The mountains of the Great Dividing Range form a natural barrier between the eastern coastal areas and the flat, dry plains and desert regions of the Australian "outback."

The Great Barrier Reef is the world's largest area of coral islands and reefs. It runs for about 1,240 miles (2,000 km) along the Queensland coast.

The Pinnacles are a series of rugged sandstone pillars. Their strange shapes have been formed by water and wind erosion.

The ancient Kimberley Plateau is the source of some of Australia's richest mineral deposits, including diamonds.

Arnhem Land

Uluru (Ayers Rock)

The tropical rainforest of the Cape York Peninsula contains more than 600 different varieties of tree.

Great Artesian Basin

More than half of Australia rests on a uniform shield over 600 million years old. It is one of the Earth's original geological plates.

The Nullarbor Plain is a low-lying limestone plateau which is so flat that the Trans-Australian Railway runs through it in a straight line for more than 300 miles (483 km).

The Simpson Desert has a number of large salt pans, created by the evaporation of past rivers and now sourced by seasonal rains. Some are crusted with gypsum, but most are covered by common salt crystals.

The Lake Eyre basin, lying 51 ft (16 m) below sea level, is one of the largest inland drainage systems in the world, covering an area of more than 500,000 sq miles (1,300,000 sq km).

Australian Alps

Tasmania has the same geological structure as the Australian Alps. During the last period of glaciation, 18,000 years ago, sea levels were some 300 ft (100 m) lower and it was joined to the mainland.

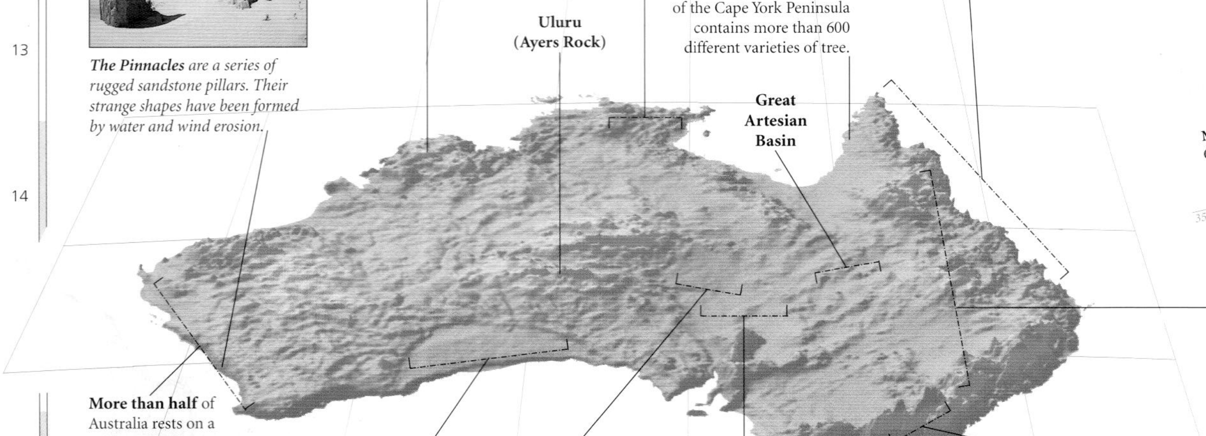

The Great Dividing Range forms a watershed between east- and west-flowing rivers. Erosion has created deep valleys, gorges, and waterfalls where rivers tumble over escarpments on their way to the sea.

Great Artesian Basin

Rainwater replenishes aquifer
Lake Eyre
Aquifers from which artesian water is obtained
Underground water movements

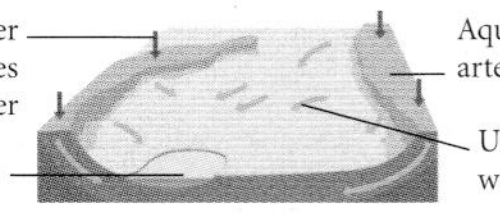

The Great Artesian Basin underlies nearly 20% of the total area of Australia, providing a valuable store of underground water, essential to Australian agriculture. The ephemeral rivers which drain the northern part of the basin have highly braided courses and, in consequence, the area is known as "channel country."

Uluru (Ayers Rock), the world's largest free-standing rock, is a massive outcrop of red sandstone in Australia's desert center. Wind and sandstorms have ground the rock into the smooth curves seen here. Uluru is revered as a sacred site by many aboriginal peoples.

SCALE 1:10,500,000
(projection: Lambert Conformal Conic)

Km
0 25 50 100 150 200 250 300 350
Miles
0 25 50 100 150 200 250 300 350

MAP KEY

POPULATION
▣ 1 million to 5 million
◉ 500,000 to 1 million
◉ 100,000 to 500,000
⊕ 50,000 to 100,000
○ 10,000 to 50,000
○ below 10,000

ELEVATION
2000m / 6562ft
1000m / 3281ft
500m / 1640ft
250m / 820ft
100m / 328ft
sea level

Map labels

INDIAN OCEAN
PACIFIC OCEAN
Timor Sea
Darwin
Alice Springs
AUSTRALIA
Townsville
Brisbane
Perth
Adelaide
Sydney
CANBERRA
Melbourne
Hobart

Cape Londonderry
Cape Bougainville
Bigge Island
Bonaparte Archipelago
Kalumburu
Heywood Islands
Adele Island
Mount Hann 779m
Kimber...
Collier Bay
Lombadina
King Leopold Rang...
Plate...
Derby
Broome
Fitzroy Cross...
Fitzroy River
Eighty Mile Beach
Great Sandy Desert
Dampier Archipelago
Dampier
Karratha
Port Hedland
Wickham
Whim Creek
De Grey River
Percival Lakes
Lake Dora
Lake Auld
Barrow Island
Roebourne
Marble Bar
Fortescue River
Onslow
Wittenoom
Lake Disappointment
North West Cape
Hamersley Range
Little Sandy Desert
Gibson Des...
Exmouth
Tom Price
Mount Meharry 1251m
Newman
WESTERN
Learmouth
Paraburdoo
Coral Bay
Kenneth Range
Kumarina Roadhouse
Carnarvon Range
Lake Carnegie
Minilya
Barlee Range
Mount Augustus 1105m
Waldburg Range
Lake Gregory
Tropic of Capricorn
Lake Macleod
Gascoyne River
Robinson Range
Wiluna
Lake Way
Lake Wells
Carnarvon
Gascoyne Junction
AUSTRALIA
Bernier Island
Meekatharra
Lake Annean
Lake Thros...
Dorre Island
Denham
Lake Ye...
Dirk Hartog Island
Murchison River
Lake Austin
Kalbarri
Mount Magnet
Leonora
Lake Carey
Yalgoo
Lake Ballard
Menzies
Lake Rebecca
Geraldton
Mongers Lake
Lake Barlee
N...
Lake Moore
Kalgoorlie
Rawl...
Wubin
Coolgardie
Kitchener...
Moora
Pithara
Southern Cross
Lake Lefroy
Kambalda
The Pinnacles
Merredin
Lake Johnston
Lake Cowan
Gingin
Northam
Norseman
Balladonia
Wanneroo
York
Lake Hope
Lake Dundas
Perth
Brookton
Kondinin
Lower Peak 594m
Fremantle
Rockingham
Mandurah
Narrogin
Lake King
Ravensthorpe
Esperance
Jollie
Wagin
Bunbury
Katanning
Busselton
Bridgetown
Manjimup
Margaret River
Augusta
Pemberton
Mount Barker
Cape Leeuwin
Albany

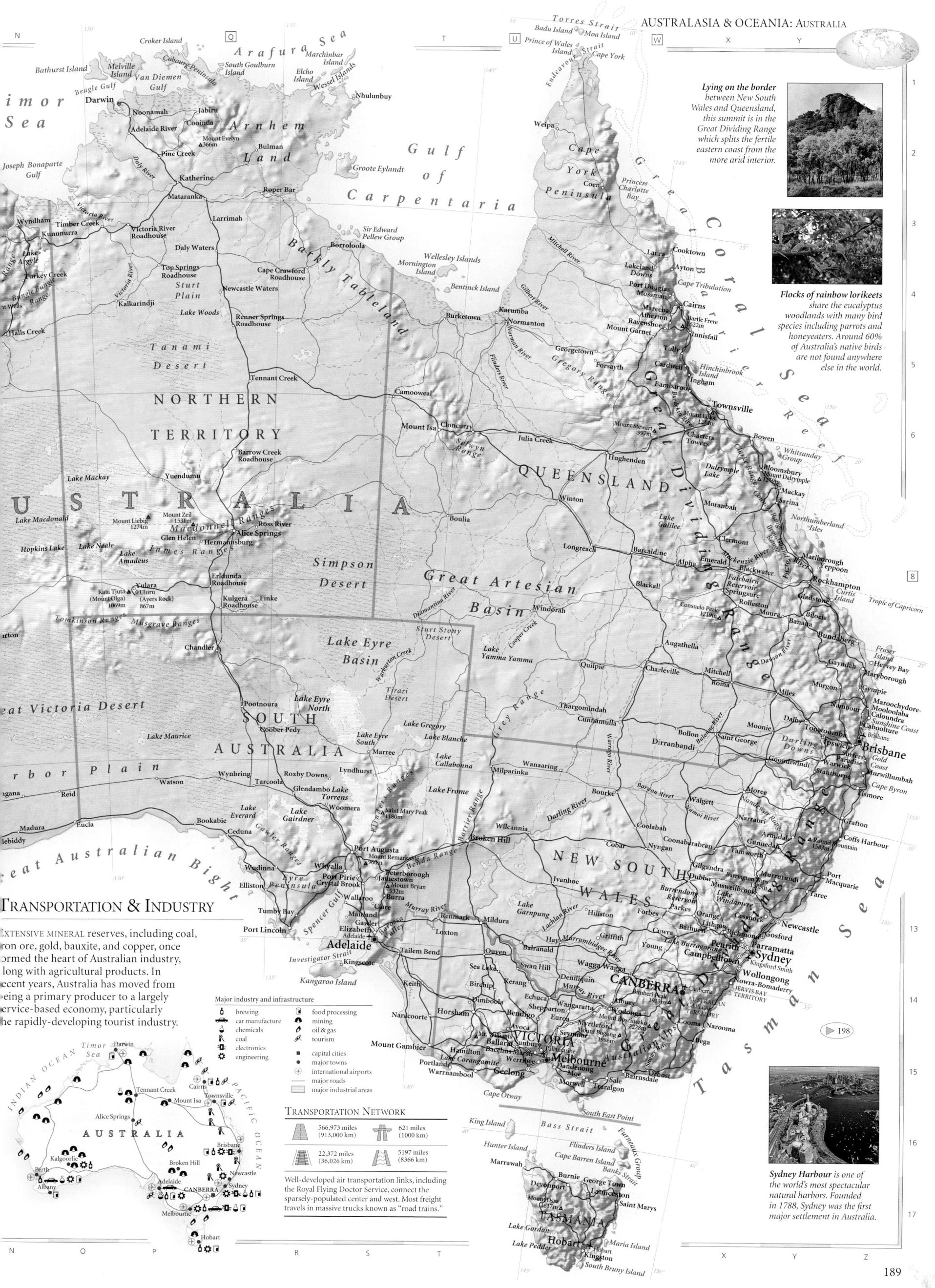

Lying on the border between New South Wales and Queensland, this summit is in the Great Dividing Range which splits the fertile eastern coast from the more arid interior.

Flocks of rainbow lorikeets share the eucalyptus woodlands with many bird species including parrots and honeyeaters. Around 60% of Australia's native birds are not found anywhere else in the world.

Transportation & Industry

Extensive mineral reserves, including coal, iron ore, gold, bauxite, and copper, once formed the heart of Australian industry, along with agricultural products. In recent years, Australia has moved from being a primary producer to a largely service-based economy, particularly the rapidly-developing tourist industry.

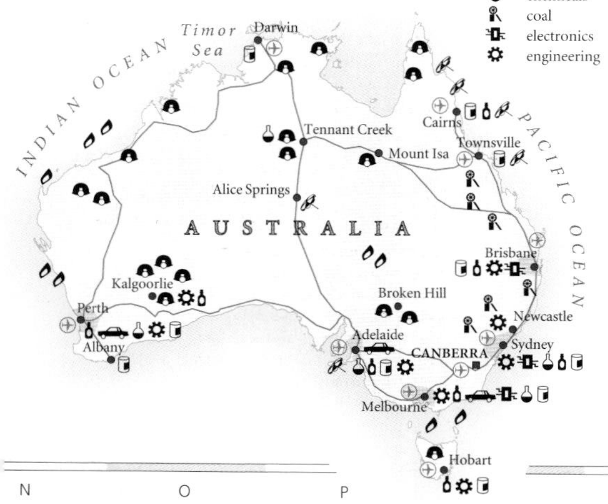

Transportation Network

566,973 miles (913,000 km)	621 miles (1000 km)
22,372 miles (36,026 km)	5197 miles (8366 km)

Well-developed air transportation links, including the Royal Flying Doctor Service, connect the sparsely-populated center and west. Most freight travels in massive trucks known as "road trains."

198

Sydney Harbour is one of the world's most spectacular natural harbors. Founded in 1788, Sydney was the first major settlement in Australia.

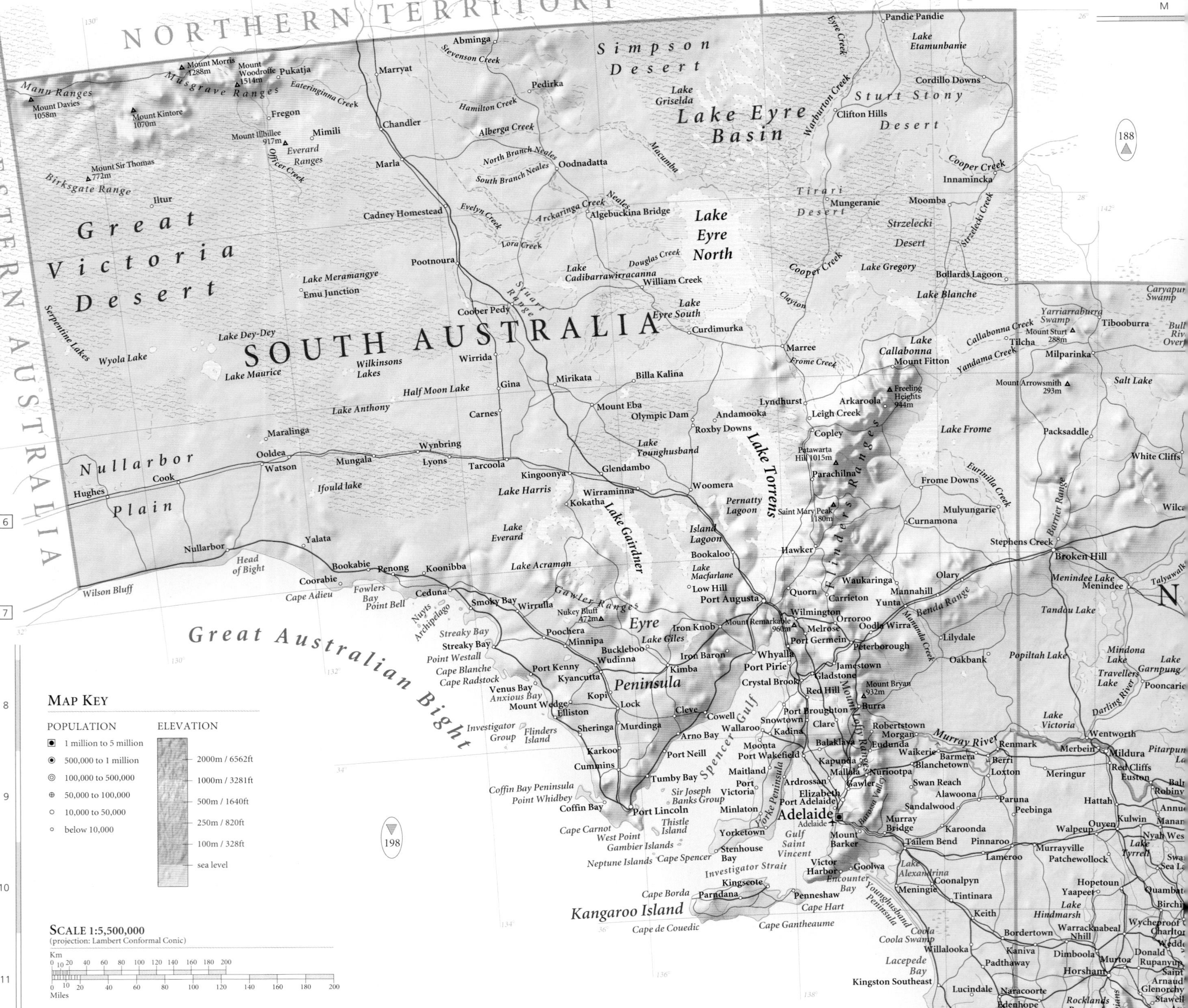

Map Key

POPULATION
- 1 million to 5 million
- 500,000 to 1 million
- 100,000 to 500,000
- 50,000 to 100,000
- 10,000 to 50,000
- below 10,000

ELEVATION
- 2000m / 6562ft
- 1000m / 3281ft
- 500m / 1640ft
- 250m / 820ft
- 100m / 328ft
- sea level

SCALE 1:5,500,000
(projection: Lambert Conformal Conic)

Km 0 10 20 40 60 80 100 120 140 160 180 200
Miles 0 10 20 40 60 80 100 120 140 160 180 200

Southeast Australia

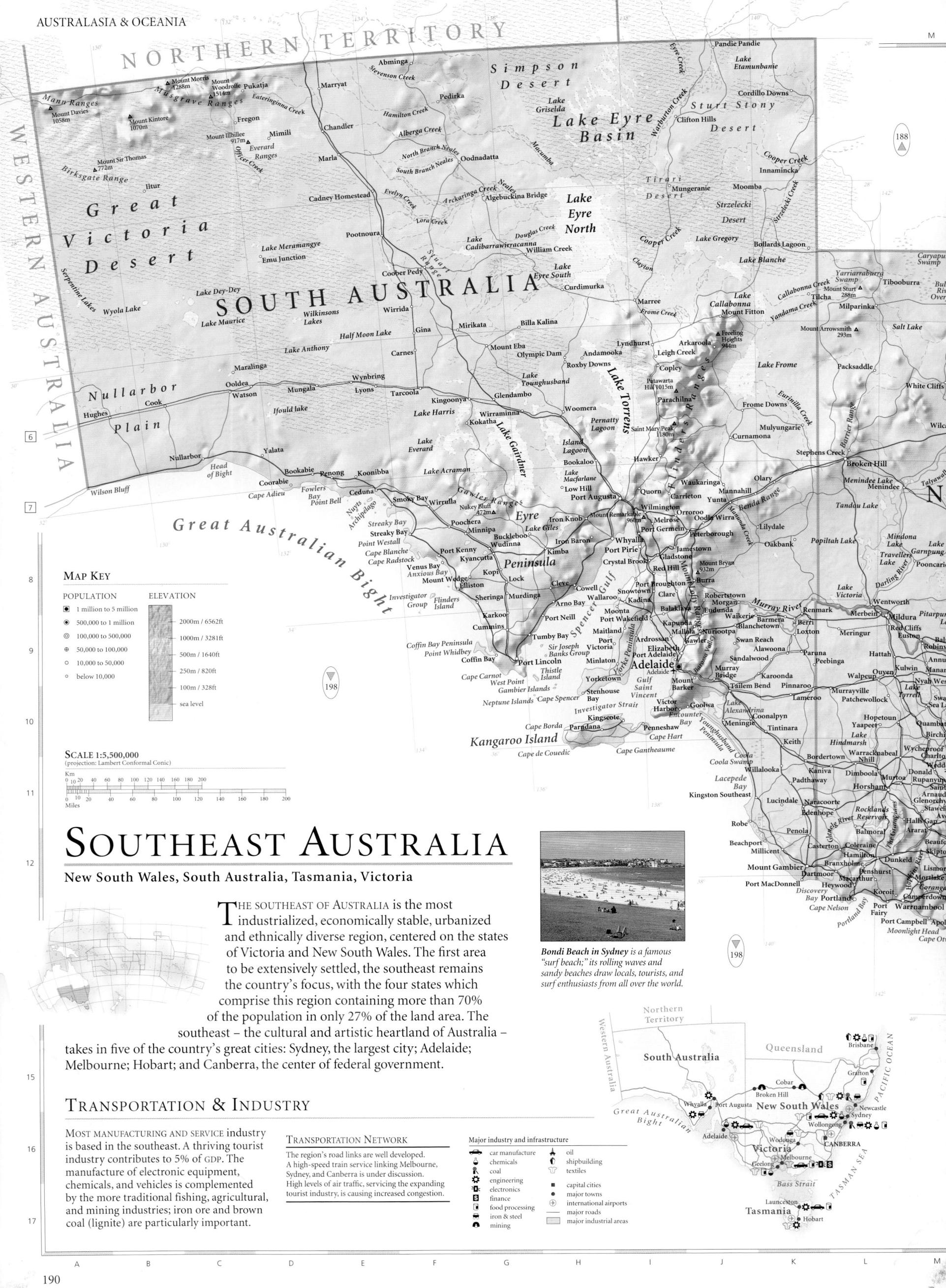

New South Wales, South Australia, Tasmania, Victoria

THE SOUTHEAST OF AUSTRALIA is the most industrialized, economically stable, urbanized and ethnically diverse region, centered on the states of Victoria and New South Wales. The first area to be extensively settled, the southeast remains the country's focus, with the four states which comprise this region containing more than 70% of the population in only 27% of the land area. The southeast – the cultural and artistic heartland of Australia – takes in five of the country's great cities: Sydney, the largest city; Adelaide; Melbourne; Hobart; and Canberra, the center of federal government.

Bondi Beach in Sydney *is a famous "surf beach;" its rolling waves and sandy beaches draw locals, tourists, and surf enthusiasts from all over the world.*

Transportation & Industry

MOST MANUFACTURING AND SERVICE industry is based in the southeast. A thriving tourist industry contributes to 5% of GDP. The manufacture of electronic equipment, chemicals, and vehicles is complemented by the more traditional fishing, agricultural, and mining industries; iron ore and brown coal (lignite) are particularly important.

Transportation Network

The region's road links are well developed. A high-speed train service linking Melbourne, Sydney, and Canberra is under discussion. High levels of air traffic, servicing the expanding tourist industry, is causing increased congestion.

Major industry and infrastructure
- car manufacture
- chemicals
- coal
- engineering
- electronics
- finance
- food processing
- iron & steel
- mining
- oil
- shipbuilding
- textiles
- capital cities
- major towns
- international airports
- major roads
- major industrial areas

USING THE LAND AND SEA

THE WESTERN FLANKS of the Great Dividing Range and the northern deserts of South Australia support massive herds of sheep and cattle, while more intensive stockrearing occurs near the cities. Sugar cane is the most important industrial crop, and cereal grains including wheat, corn, barley, and sorghum are also grown. Grapes, citrus, and orchard fruits are among the wide range of fruit and vegetables cultivated in this region. Tasmania's forestry and fishing contributes to over one-third of the state's exports.

The fertile Darling Downs, known as the "breadbasket of Australia," support a wide range of crops including cereals, sugar cane, and fruit.

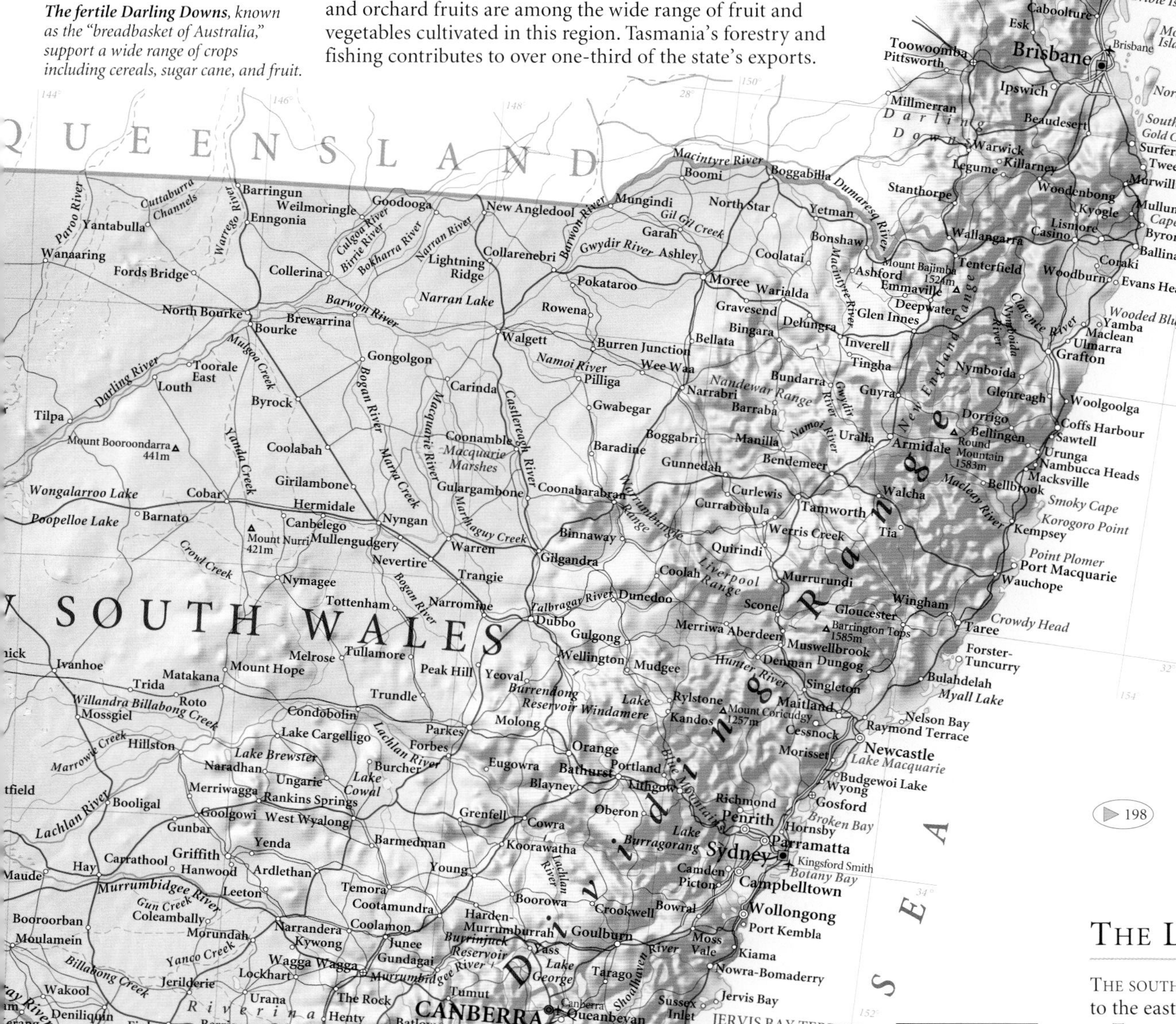

The Murray River has its source in the eastern uplands of the Great Dividing Range. Fed by melting snow, it runs for 1,609 miles (2,589 km), and has sufficient volume to reach the ocean southeast of Adelaide despite a minimal gradient for most of its lower reaches.

THE URBAN/RURAL POPULATION DIVIDE

89% urban | 11% rural

0 10 20 30 40 50 60 70 80 90 100

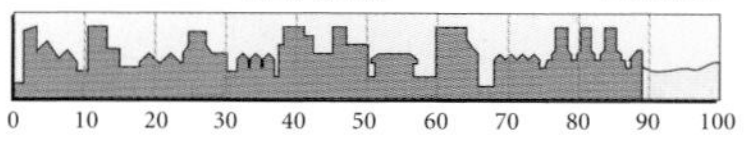

POPULATION DENSITY	TOTAL LAND AREA
16 people per sq mile (6 people per sq km)	778,022 sq miles (2,015,600 sq km)

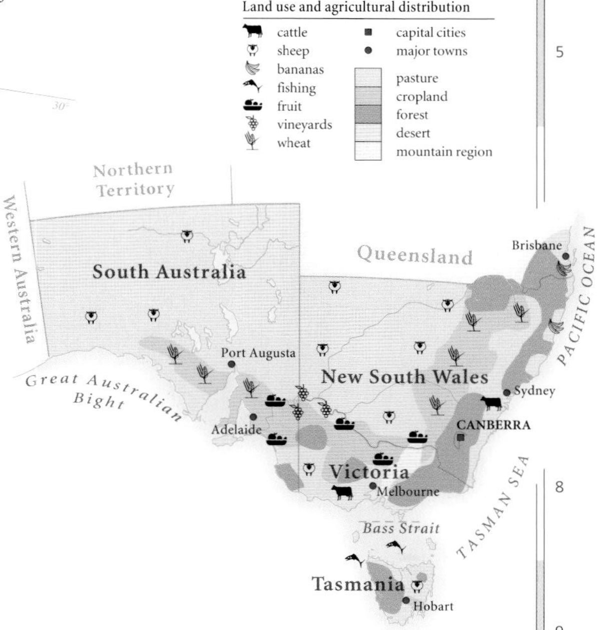

Land use and agricultural distribution

- cattle
- sheep
- bananas
- fishing
- fruit
- vineyards
- wheat
- capital cities
- major towns
- pasture
- cropland
- forest
- desert
- mountain region

THE LANDSCAPE

THE SOUTHERN HALF of the Great Dividing Range runs parallel to the eastern coast of Victoria and New South Wales as far as Tasmania, which, though divided from the mainland is part of the same mountain chain. South Australia comprises the Australian Shield and half of the dry, flat Nullarbor Plain. The Murray/Darling River Basin is the only major river system.

The Musgrave and Everard ranges form bare, rounded hills made up of ancient granite and gneiss.

Lake Eyre is the largest of southern Australia's dry lakes. Lying -51 ft (-16 m) below sea level, it has flooded only three times in the last century.

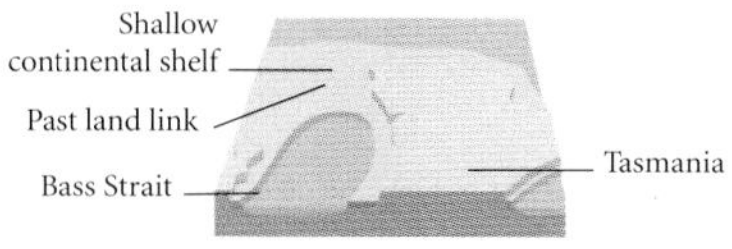

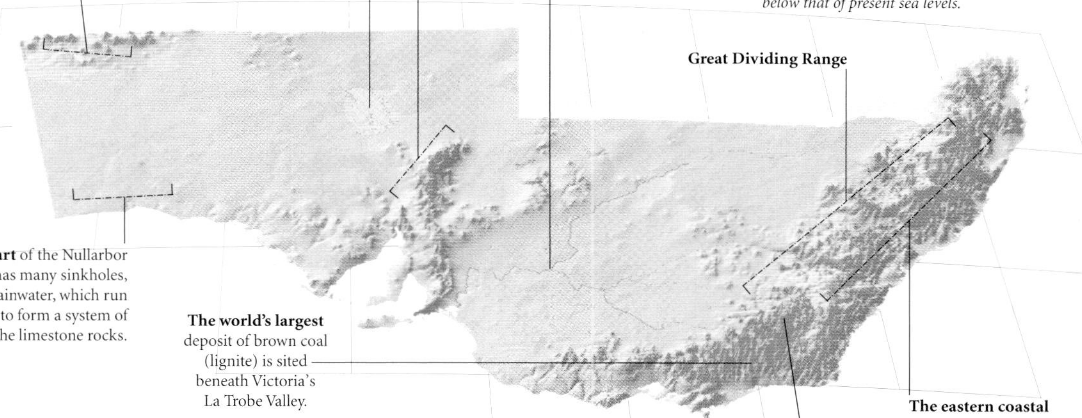

The heavily folded Flinders Range is part of an arc of sedimentary rocks reaching northward from Kangaroo Island.

The Murray/Darling is Australia's longest river at 1,703 miles (2,739 km).

Shallow continental shelf
Past land link
Bass Strait
Tasmania

Tasmania is part of Australia's eastern highlands, separated from the mainland by 155 miles (250 km) of the Bass Strait. In the recent geological past, dry land links between Tasmania and Victoria would have been possible during periods of world-wide glaciation, when the sea level was more than 1,80 ft (55 m) below that of present sea levels.

Great Dividing Range

The eastern part of the Nullarbor Plain has many sinkholes, eroded by rainwater, which run underground to form a system of long caves in the limestone rocks.

The world's largest deposit of brown coal (lignite) is sited beneath Victoria's La Trobe Valley.

The glaciated central plateau of Tasmania has many lakes, including Lake St. Clair. a piedmont lake more than 700 ft (200 m) deep.

Though temperate rain forest grows in the wettest parts of Tasmania, extreme variations in the levels of rainfall over the island mean that some drier areas may experience forest fires.

Mount Kosciuszko, the highest point in the Snowy Mountains, is the tallest mountain in Australia at 7,316 ft (2,228 m).

The eastern coastal plains of New South Wales rise into a series of plateaus known as the tableland.

New Zealand

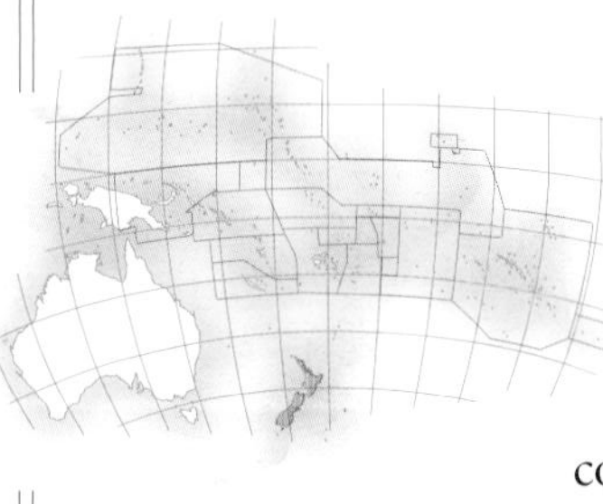

Lying 1,500 miles east-southeast of Australia, New Zealand was originally settled by the Maori people of Polynesia. It was visited by Europeans for the first time only as recently as the 1770s. The islands' rugged topography means that most settlement has concentrated in coastal areas. People of European origin make up more than 85% of the population of 3.7 million, following immigration which began in the 1920s. Many recent settlers have come from Asia, including India and China, and a number of the Pacific islands. The Maori now make up a minority of less than half a million. Their ancient claims to at least half of national territory, however, are gaining increasing legal credence.

The Landscape

New Zealand comprises two large islands and many scattered smaller islands. On South Island the Alpine Fault marks the boundary between the Pacific and Indo-Australian plates. Tectonic activity has strongly influenced the formation of the Southern Alps, snowcapped mountains with several peaks over 9,800 ft (3,000 m). North Island has a lower and less extensive mountain region, containing forested hills, a central volcanic plateau, and downlands.

Mountain-building in the Southern Alps

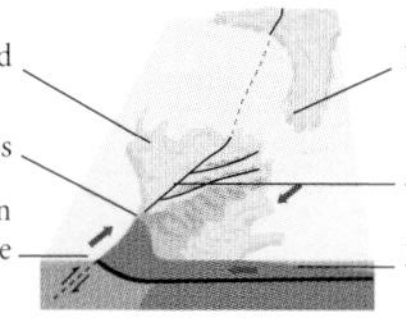

The Southern Alps have been formed by "slip" faulting. The Indo-Australian and Pacific plates run in opposite directions along the Alpine Fault. Although they slide past each other, they are also being thrust over one another, causing the continental crust of the Pacific Plate to be uplifted to form the Alps.

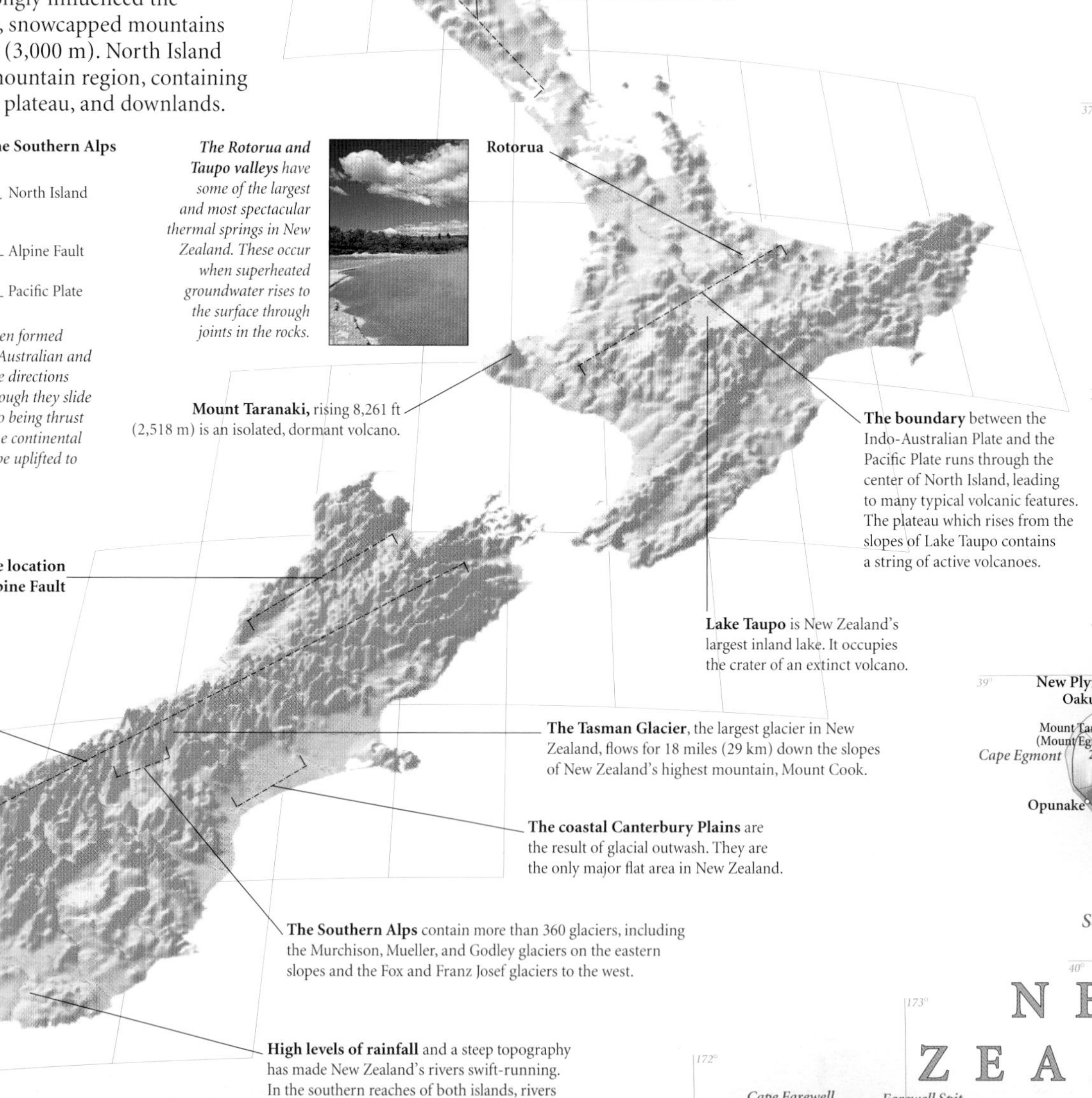

***The Northland region** is characterized by many coastal inlets. These are lined by mangrove swamps, signaling the change to a subtropical climate in the far north of the island.*

***The Rotorua and Taupo valleys** have some of the largest and most spectacular thermal springs in New Zealand. These occur when superheated groundwater rises to the surface through joints in the rocks.*

Mount Taranaki, rising 8,261 ft (2,518 m) is an isolated, dormant volcano.

The boundary between the Indo-Australian Plate and the Pacific Plate runs through the center of North Island, leading to many typical volcanic features. The plateau which rises from the slopes of Lake Taupo contains a string of active volcanoes.

Lake Taupo is New Zealand's largest inland lake. It occupies the crater of an extinct volcano.

The Southern Alps run for more than 300 miles, (483 km) forming the backbone of South Island. They were uplifted following the collision of the Pacific and Indo-Australian plates.

Fiordland, in the far south west, contains a large number of flooded glacial valleys.

The Tasman Glacier, the largest glacier in New Zealand, flows for 18 miles (29 km) down the slopes of New Zealand's highest mountain, Mount Cook.

The coastal Canterbury Plains are the result of glacial outwash. They are the only major flat area in New Zealand.

The Southern Alps contain more than 360 glaciers, including the Murchison, Mueller, and Godley glaciers on the eastern slopes and the Fox and Franz Josef glaciers to the west.

High levels of rainfall and a steep topography has made New Zealand's rivers swift-running. In the southern reaches of both islands, rivers such as the Mokoreta form broad, braided streams.

***Clouds of steam** rise from White Island, an active, offshore volcano lying in the Bay of Plenty, off the northern coast of North Island.*

Scale 1:2,750,000
(projection: Lambert Conformal Conic)

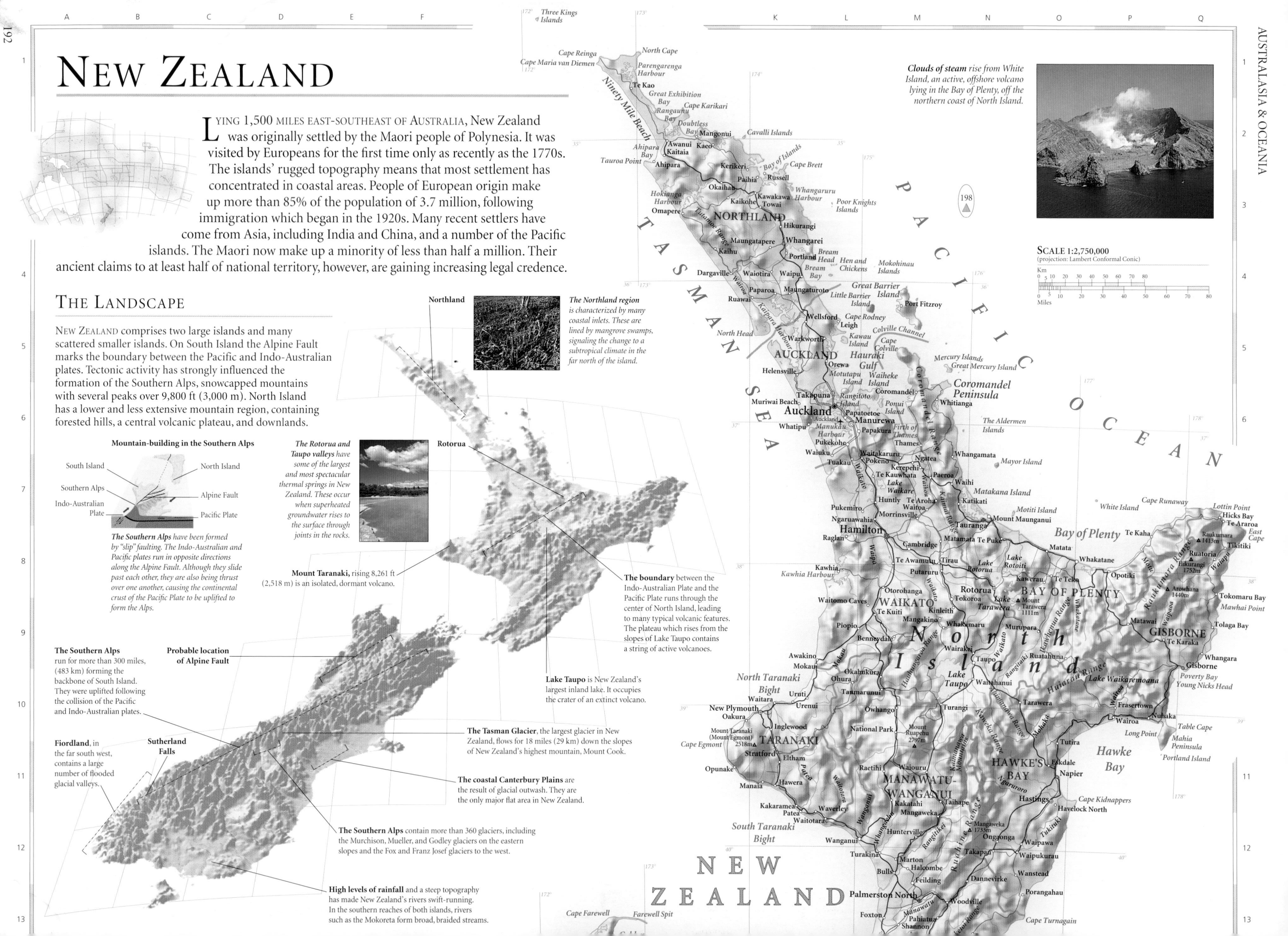

TRANSPORTATION & INDUSTRY

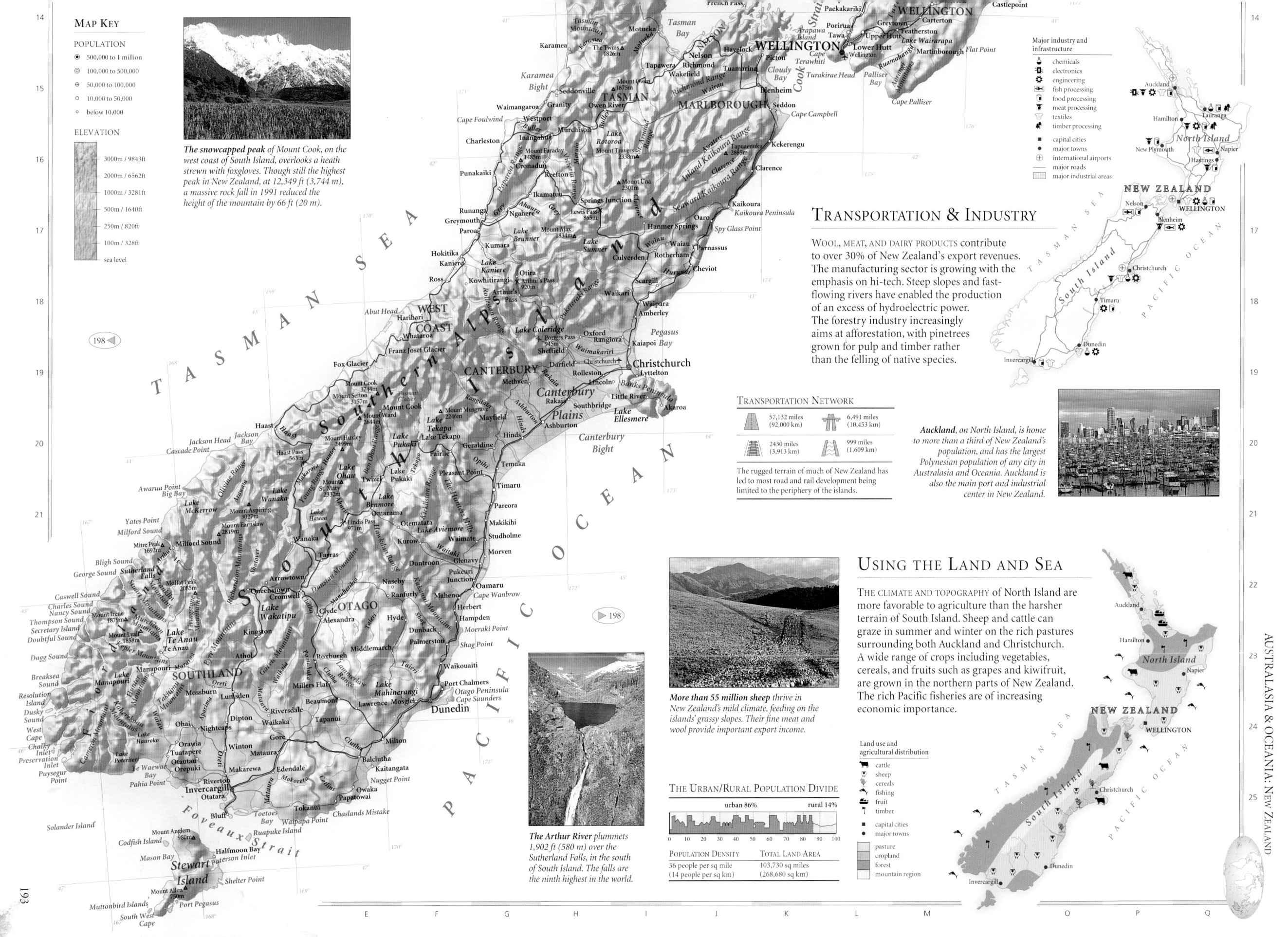

WOOL, MEAT, AND DAIRY PRODUCTS contribute to over 30% of New Zealand's export revenues. The manufacturing sector is growing with the emphasis on hi-tech. Steep slopes and fast-flowing rivers have enabled the production of an excess of hydroelectric power. The forestry industry increasingly aims at afforestation, with pinetrees grown for pulp and timber rather than the felling of native species.

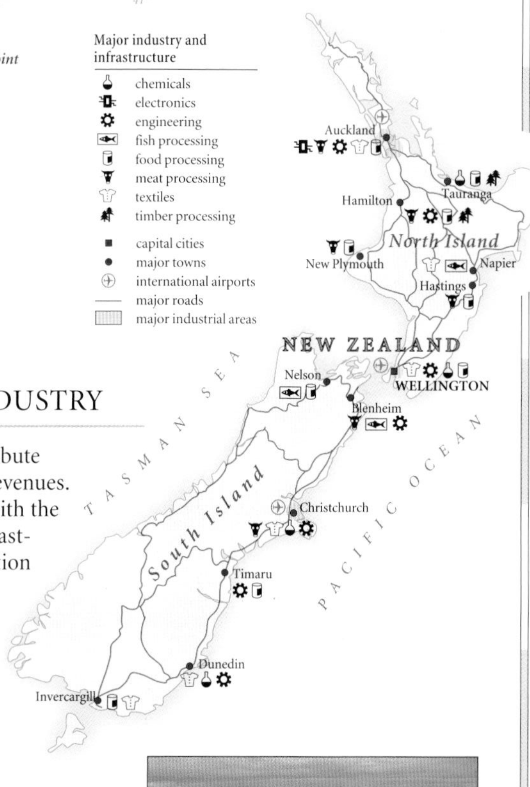

Auckland, on North Island, is home to more than a third of New Zealand's population, and has the largest Polynesian population of any city in Australasia and Oceania. Auckland is also the main port and industrial center in New Zealand.

TRANSPORTATION NETWORK

57,132 miles (92,000 km)		6,491 miles (10,453 km)	
2430 miles (3,913 km)		999 miles (1,609 km)	

The rugged terrain of much of New Zealand has led to most road and rail development being limited to the periphery of the islands.

Major industry and infrastructure
- chemicals
- electronics
- engineering
- fish processing
- food processing
- meat processing
- textiles
- timber processing
- capital cities
- major towns
- international airports
- major roads
- major industrial areas

USING THE LAND AND SEA

THE CLIMATE AND TOPOGRAPHY of North Island are more favorable to agriculture than the harsher terrain of South Island. Sheep and cattle can graze in summer and winter on the rich pastures surrounding both Auckland and Christchurch. A wide range of crops including vegetables, cereals, and fruits such as grapes and kiwifruit, are grown in the northern parts of New Zealand. The rich Pacific fisheries are of increasing economic importance.

Land use and agricultural distribution
- cattle
- sheep
- cereals
- fishing
- fruit
- timber
- capital cities
- major towns
- pasture
- cropland
- forest
- mountain region

More than 55 million sheep thrive in New Zealand's mild climate, feeding on the islands' grassy slopes. Their fine meat and wool provide important export income.

The Arthur River plummets 1,902 ft (580 m) over the Sutherland Falls, in the south of South Island. The falls are the ninth highest in the world.

THE URBAN/RURAL POPULATION DIVIDE

urban 86% rural 14%

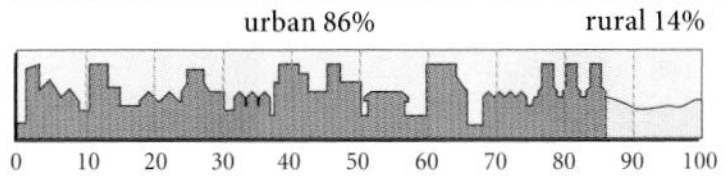

POPULATION DENSITY	TOTAL LAND AREA
36 people per sq mile (14 people per sq km)	103,730 sq miles (268,680 sq km)

The snowcapped peak of Mount Cook, on the west coast of South Island, overlooks a heath strewn with foxgloves. Though still the highest peak in New Zealand, at 12,349 ft (3,744 m), a massive rock fall in 1991 reduced the height of the mountain by 66 ft (20 m).

MAP KEY

POPULATION
- ● 500,000 to 1 million
- ◉ 100,000 to 500,000
- ⊕ 50,000 to 100,000
- ○ 10,000 to 50,000
- ○ below 10,000

ELEVATION
- 3000m / 9843ft
- 2000m / 6562ft
- 1000m / 3281ft
- 500m / 1640ft
- 250m / 820ft
- 100m / 328ft
- sea level

PAPUA NEW GUINEA & THE SOLOMON ISLANDS

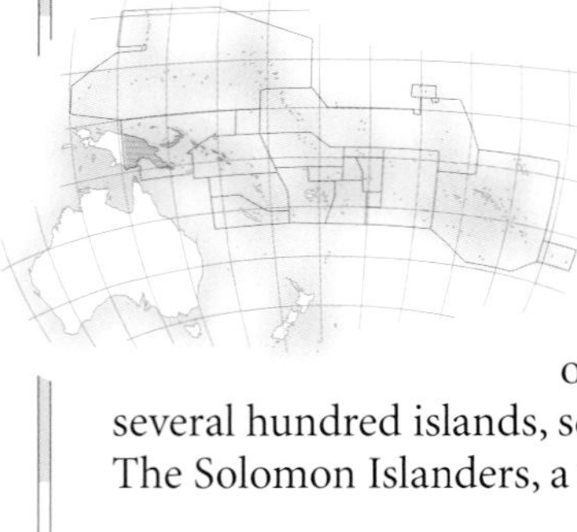

CUT OFF BY INACCESSIBLE, largely mountainous terrain, the peoples of Papua New Guinea have maintained a remarkable diversity of language and culture. There are over 750 separate languages, and yet more distinct tribes. Much of the country remains isolated, with many of the indigenous inhabitants of the interior living as hunter-gatherers. To the east of Papua New Guinea, the Solomons form an archipelago of several hundred islands, scattered over an area of 252,897 sq miles (655,000 sq km). The Solomon Islanders, a mainly Melanesian people, live on the six largest islands.

USING THE LAND AND SEA

MOST AGRICULTURE IN Papua New Guinea is at a subsistence level, with more than two-thirds of the land used for rough grazing, particularly for pigs. The tropical rain forest is a rich timber resource. The Solomon Islanders rely heavily on coconuts for export revenue and fishing, mainly for tuna, is a staple industry.

Over 70% of Papua New Guinea is covered by dense, tropical rain forest, sustained by high levels of rainfall. Uncontrolled logging in the formerly inaccessible rain forest has led to species loss and soil erosion on steep slopes.

Land use and agricultural distribution
- bananas
- cocoa
- coconuts
- fishing
- oil palms
- rubber
- timber
- capital cities
- major towns
- cropland
- forest
- wetland

THE URBAN/RURAL POPULATION DIVIDE

urban 16% rural 84%

0 10 20 30 40 50 60 70 80 90 100

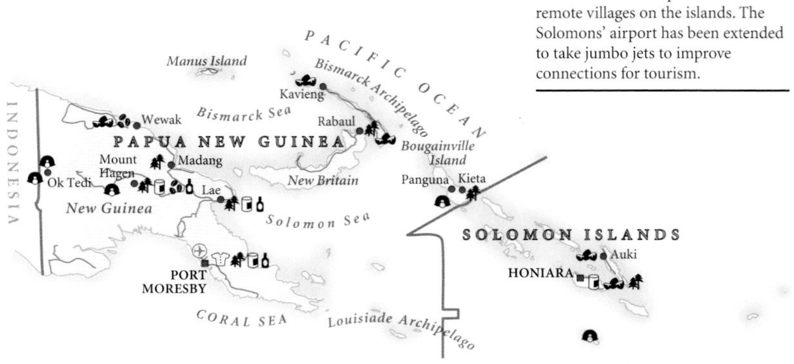

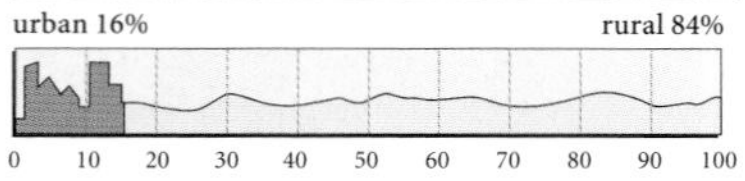

POPULATION DENSITY | TOTAL LAND AREA
17 people per sq mile | 290,210 sq miles
(7 people per sq km) | (751,840 sq km)

MAP KEY

POPULATION
- ◉ 100,000 to 500,000
- ⊕ 50,000 to 100,000
- ○ 10,000 to 50,000
- ○ below 10,000

ELEVATION
- 4000m / 13,124ft
- 3000m / 9843ft
- 2000m / 6562ft
- 1000m / 3281ft
- 500m / 1640ft
- 250m / 820ft
- 100m / 328ft
- sea level

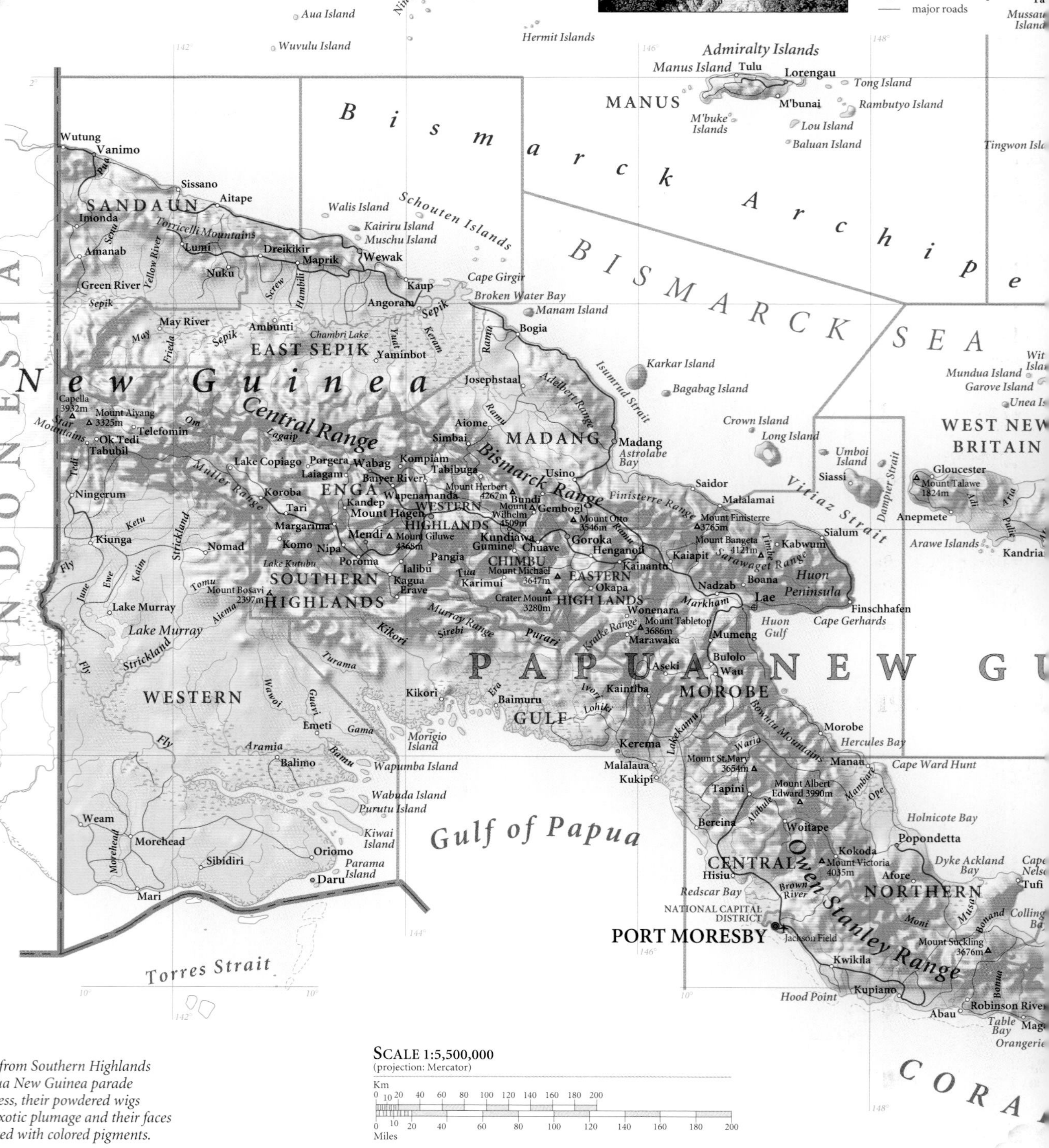

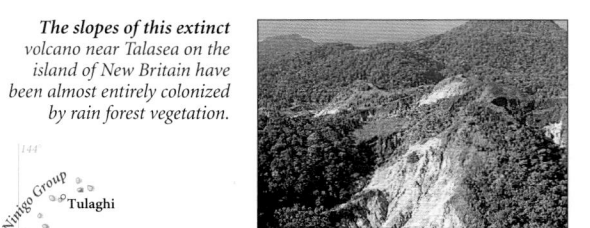

Huli tribesmen from Southern Highlands Province in Papua New Guinea parade in ceremonial dress, their powdered wigs decorated with exotic plumage and their faces and bodies painted with colored pigments.

TRANSPORTATION & INDUSTRY

PAPUA NEW GUINEA has substantial mineral resources including the world's largest copper reserves at Panguna on Bougainville Island; gold, and potential oil and natural gas. Political instability on Bougainville and an undeveloped infrastructure deters the investment necessary for exploitation of these reserves. The Solomon Islanders rely mainly on copra and timber with some production of palm oil and cocoa. Traditional crafts are made for the tourist market and for export.

TRANSPORTATION NETWORK

- 460 miles (740 km)
- None
- None
- 6,794 miles (10,940 km)

Much of Papua New Guinea and the Solomons is inaccessible by road. A network of airstrips serves even remote villages on the islands. The Solomons' airport has been extended to take jumbo jets to improve connections for tourism.

The slopes of this extinct volcano near Talasea on the island of New Britain have been almost entirely colonized by rain forest vegetation.

Major industry and infrastructure
- beverages
- coffee processing
- copra processing
- food processing
- mining
- textiles
- timber processing
- ■ capital cities
- ⊕ major towns
- ✛ international airports
- — major roads

SCALE 1:5,500,000
(projection: Mercator)

Km
0 10 20 40 60 80 100 120 140 160 180 200

0 10 20 40 60 80 100 120 140 160 180 200
Miles

N O P Q R S T U V W X Y

THE LANDSCAPE

THE PLATE MARGIN between the Pacific and Indo-Australian plates runs through the mainland of Papua New Guinea, which is dominated by steep and forested mountain ranges. The 600 or so outer islands are mainly high, volcanic islands, fringed by coral reefs. The Solomons comprise six large volcanic islands which form two parallel chains, and several hundred small islands and atolls.

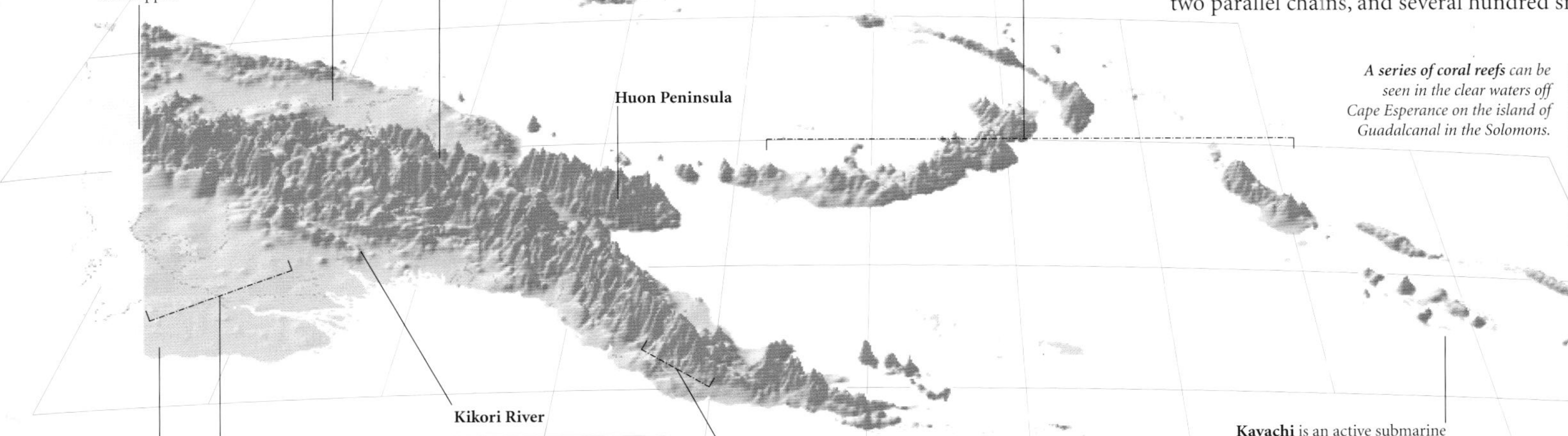

The Sepik River drains the lowlands north of the Central Range, flowing eastward into the Bismarck Sea.

The Bismarck Range is precipitous, rugged and covered in dense vegetation, rising to 14,793 ft (4,509 m) at Mount Wilhelm in central Papua New Guinea.

Most of Papua New Guinea's outlying islands, including New Britain, Bougainville Island, and New Ireland, are precipitous and of volcanic origin.

The Star Mountains include some of the most remote terrain on Earth. The area is rich in gold and copper.

A series of coral reefs can be seen in the clear waters off Cape Esperance on the island of Guadalcanal in the Solomons.

Southern Papua New Guinea is part of the Indo-Australian Plate. New Guinea only became separated physically from Australia about 8,000 years ago following the flooding of the Torres Strait.

The lowland plains in the south and north of the main island are swampy, and contain some fertile alluvial soils. This contrasts with the mountainous islands in the rest of Papua New Guinea where soils are generally thin and nutrients are retained in the existing vegetation.

Papua New Guinea's rivers, though fairly short, carry extremely high sediment loads, largely due to soil erosion. This is caused by a combination of very steep slopes and heavy rainfall, and is made worse by forest clearance, particularly "slash and burn" techniques and road or mine operations.

The Owen Stanley Range contains several of Papua New Guinea's highest peaks, the greatest of which is Mount Victoria at 13,200 ft (4,035 m).

Kavachi is an active submarine volcano near New Georgia, which erupts every few years.

The Louisiade Archipelago contains 10 volcanic islands and numerous coral islets. Tagula Island is the largest of the islands, containing the archipelago's highest peak at 2,645 ft (806 m).

Huon Peninsula

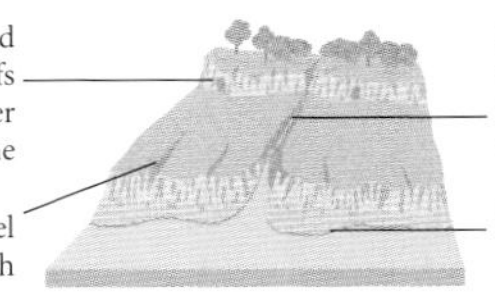

***Uplift of the land** in tectonically active regions can lead to former coastlines being lifted beyond the reach of the sea. New cliffs and caves are formed at a lower level, and rivers cut down through the lower land to reach sea level once more.*

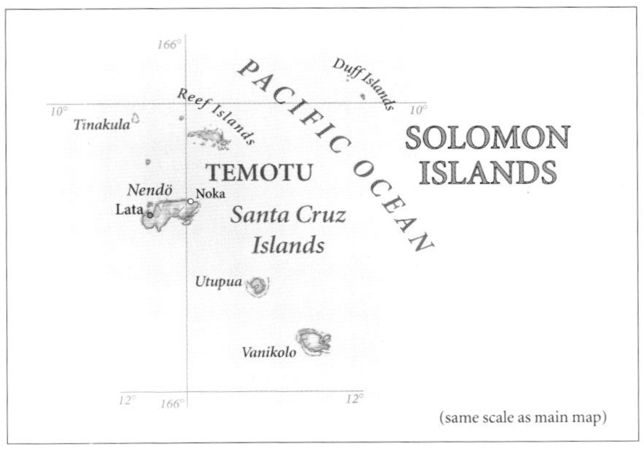

***Lying close to the banks** of the Sepik River in northern Papua New Guinea, this building is known as the Spirit House. It is constructed from leaves and twigs, ornately woven and trimmed into geometric patterns. The house is decorated with a mask and topped by a carved statue.*

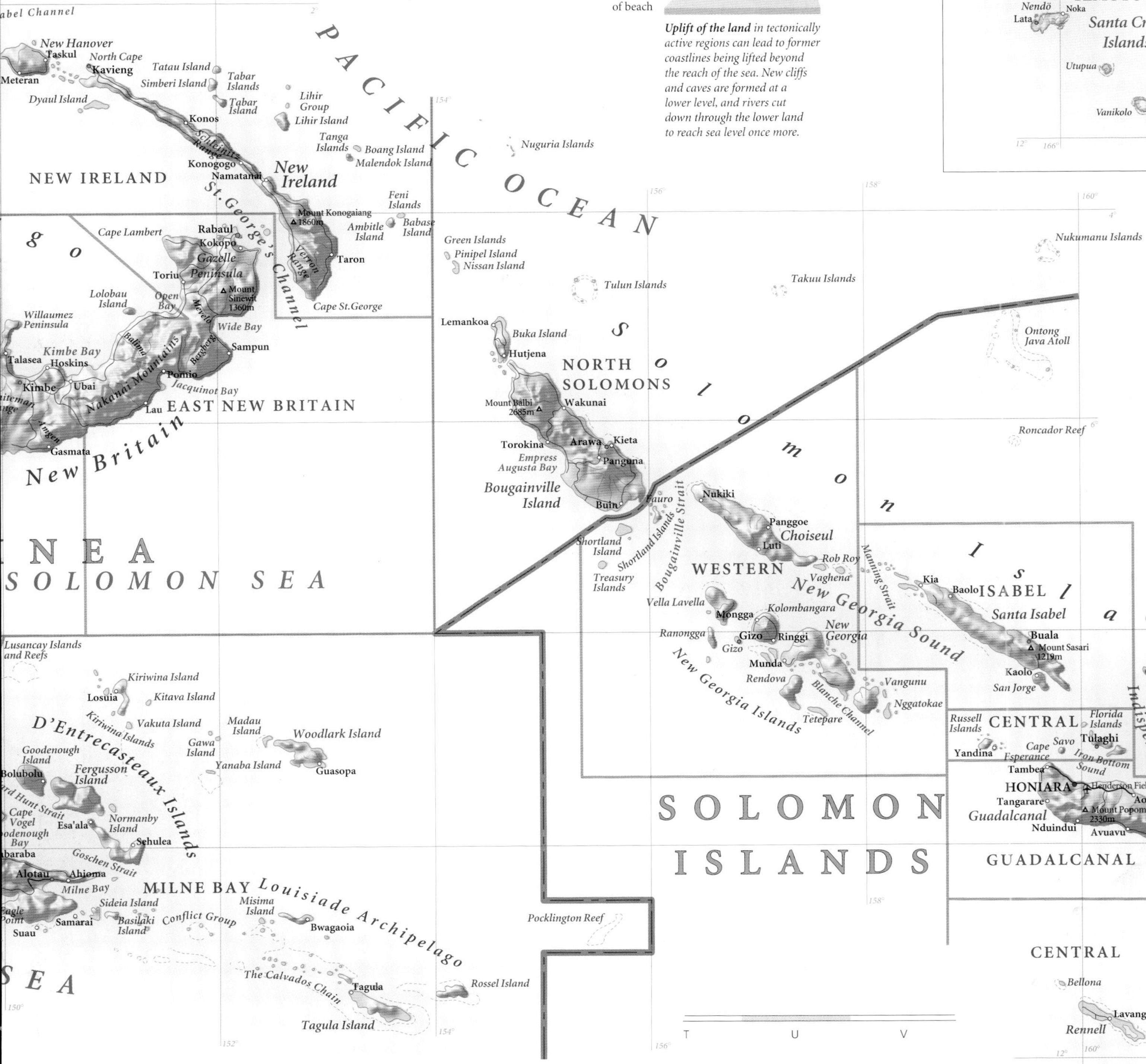

T U V

Pacific Ocean

The Pacific is the world's largest and deepest ocean. It is nearly twice the area of the Atlantic and contains almost three times as much water. The ocean is dotted with islands and surrounded by some of the world's most populous states; over half the world's population lives on its shores. The Pacific is bordered by active plate margins known as the "Ring of Fire," causing earthquakes and tsunamis, and creating volcanic islands and subterranean mountain chains. The largest underwater mountains break the surface as island arcs. The fisheries of the Pacific are some of the most productive in the world and provide a vital resource for many of the Pacific islands. Since the Second World War there has been a shift in trading patterns, with a considerable growth in trade between the US and the countries of the Pacific Rim.

Inset Map Key

POPULATION
- below 10,000

ELEVATION
1000m / 3281ft
500m / 1640ft
250m / 820ft
100m / 328ft
sea level

Ocean Map Key

SEA DEPTH
sea level
250m / 820ft
500m / 1640ft
1000m / 3281ft
2000m / 6562ft
3000m / 9843ft
5000m / 16,410ft

Scale 1:50,000,000
(projection: Mollweide)
Km 0 200 400 600 800 1000
Miles 0 200 400 600 800

American Samoa and Samoa

American Samoa and Samoa are part of the island archipelago of Polynesia. The two most populous islands are Tutuila in American Samoa and Upolu in Samoa. Although the economies of both these states remain predominantly resource-based, both are expanding their light manufacturing sectors, and the US administration is the primary employer in American Samoa. Tuna fishing is particularly important: 25% of all tuna consumed in the US is processed and canned in Pago Pago.

Japan is one of the major trading nations within the Pacific, importing iron and steel from Australia, and grain from the US. The major exports from the 'Pacific Rim' are electronics, precision equipment, and motor cars.

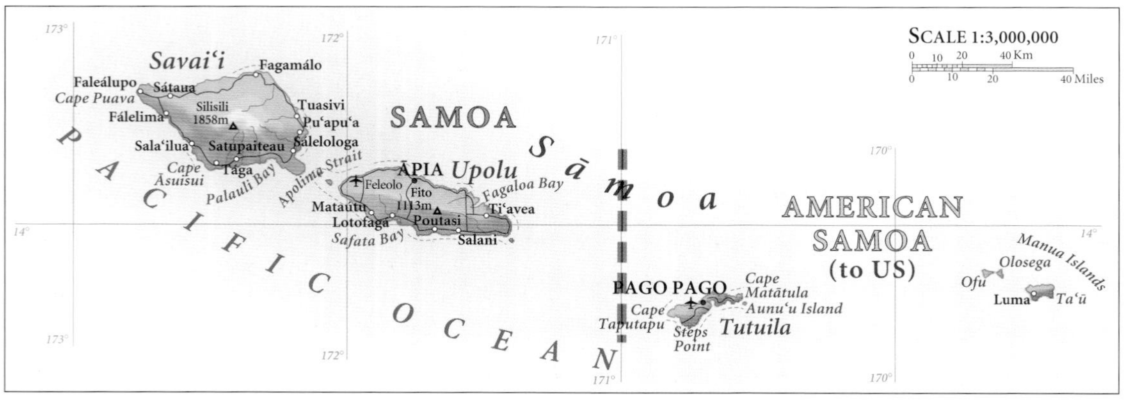

Many of the buildings in Samoa reflect the country's colonial past. Once a colony of New Zealand, Samoa is now an independent state; American Samoa remains an unincorporated territory of the United States.

The Ring of Fire

The active plate margins surrounding the Pacific have created numerous land and island volcanoes along its border. The actual basin of the Pacific is made up of a number of separate tectonic plates which move away from each other, colliding with other plates. When they collide, the oceanic plates, being thinner, are forced beneath the thicker continental plates, forming deep ocean trenches and high ridges. These collision zones are known as subduction zones and are characterized by intense seismic and volcanic activity.

Resources

Many of the small islands in the Pacific rely heavily on marine resources to provide valuable export incomes. These fisheries tend to be small-scale and are forced to compete with the large commerical fleets from Japan and the Russian Federation. Although many metallic mineral deposits have been discovered in the Pacific, few are exploited. The major areas of oil and gas extraction are off the coast of Vietnam, along the Kamchatka Peninsula and off the coast of Alaska. The numerous reefs which fringe the islands of the Pacific are harvested for corals.

Farms such as this black pearl oyster farm in Tahiti are widespread throughout the Pacific. The culturing or farming of marine organisms, such as mollusks and crustaceans, has been practiced for hundreds of years.

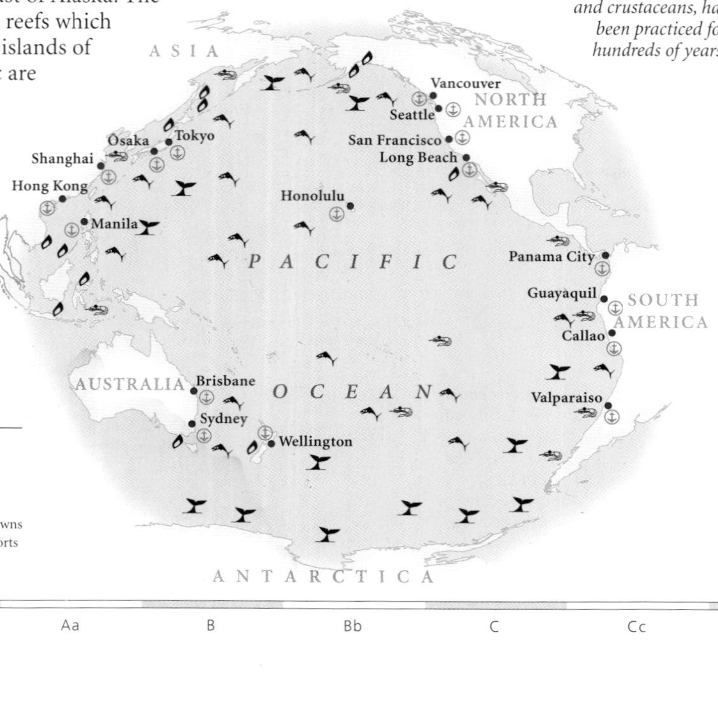

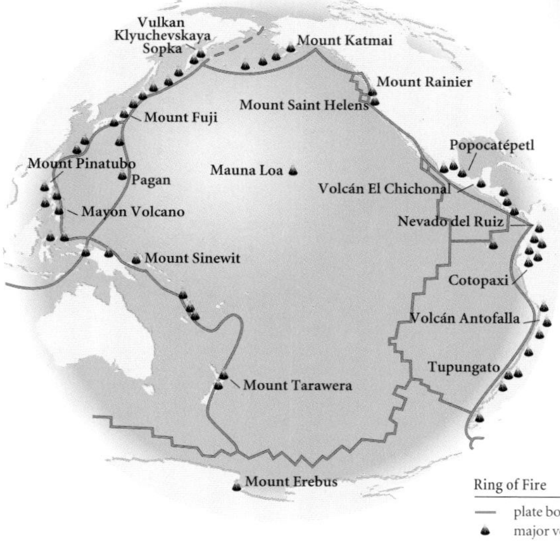

Mayon Volcano in the Philippines is one of many active volcanoes on the Pacific "Ring of Fire." It is noted for its perfect conical shape; the base of the cone is 80 miles (130 km) in circumference.

The Hawaiian volcanoes lie in the center of a plate, not on a plate margin, and are known as intraplate volcanoes. They are associated with hot spots, whereby a plume of hot molten rock rises to the surface as the plate moves over it.

MELANESIA

FIJI, VANUATU, *New Caledonia* (to France)

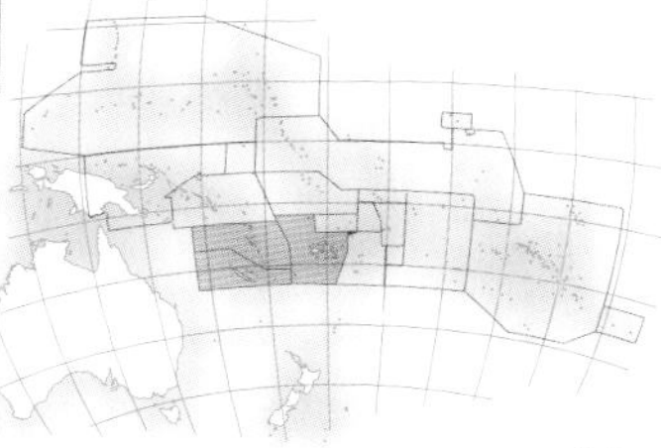

THREE MAIN ISLAND groups make up the area of southern Melanesia in the southwestern Pacific: the independent countries of Fiji and Vanuatu and the French overseas territory of New Caledonia. The major Melanesian island group, the Solomon Islands, lies to the east of Papua New Guinea (pages 194–95). Most of the larger islands are volcanic in origin; the smaller ones are mainly coral atolls and are largely uninhabited. The economy in all three island groups is increasingly driven by tourism, not necessarily to the benefit of other economic activities.

NEW CALEDONIA (to France)

NEW CALEDONIA, a French overseas territory known as Kanaky by its indigenous peoples, comprises a large main island, 260 miles (418 km) long, and many smaller islands and atolls. Socioeconomic inequality, unemployment, and the issue of independence have caused tension between the Kanaks and the French-speaking expatriate population. This resulted in a long history of political violence, although the Nouméa accord, signed in 1998, allowed for greater autonomy. New Caledonia produces 25% of the world's nickel, and improved incomes from tourism and agriculture have benefited the economy.

On New Caledonia's main island, relatively high interior plateaus descend to coastal plains. Nickel is the most important mineral resource, but the hills also harbor metallic deposits including chrome, cobalt, iron, gold, silver, and copper.

MAP KEY

POPULATION
- ⊕ 50,000 to 100,000
- ○ 10,000 to 50,000
- ○ below 10,000

ELEVATION
- 1000m / 3281ft
- 500m / 1640ft
- 250m / 820ft
- 100m / 328ft
- sea level

VANUATU

A STRING OF MOUNTAINOUS VOLCANIC ISLANDS covering more than 4,706 sq miles (12,190 sq km) of the south Pacific, Vanuatu achieved independence from France and the UK in 1980. The majority of the population relies on subsistence fishing and agriculture. Once-important copra and cocoa exports are declining as a result of cost-effective substitutes from elsewhere, and alternatives are being explored. There is further resource potential in the forests and fishing grounds, and beef and arable farming are of growing importance. Tourism, accounting for 40% of GDP, is the fastest-growing sector of the economy, and further expansion is planned.

On one of Vanuatu's many islands, simple beach houses stand at the water's edge, surrounded by coconut palms and other tropical vegetation. The unspoiled beaches and tranquillity of its islands are drawing ever-larger numbers of tourists to Vanuatu.

FIJI

FIJI IS A VOLCANIC ARCHIPELAGO in the southwestern Pacific consisting of two large islands and 880 smaller islets, and covering a total area of 7,054 sq miles (18,270 sq km). The majority of the population lives on the two largest islands. The people are split fairly evenly between Indo-Fijians, who arrived when Fiji was still a British colony, and the indigenous Fijians who have, since 1987, controlled the government. Sugar and copra are the most important crops in a diversified agricultural base and forestry is becoming increasingly important. A relatively varied economy has potential for mineral and hydroelectric exploitation, while Fiji's climate and location on the main Pacific air routes are an impetus to tourism.

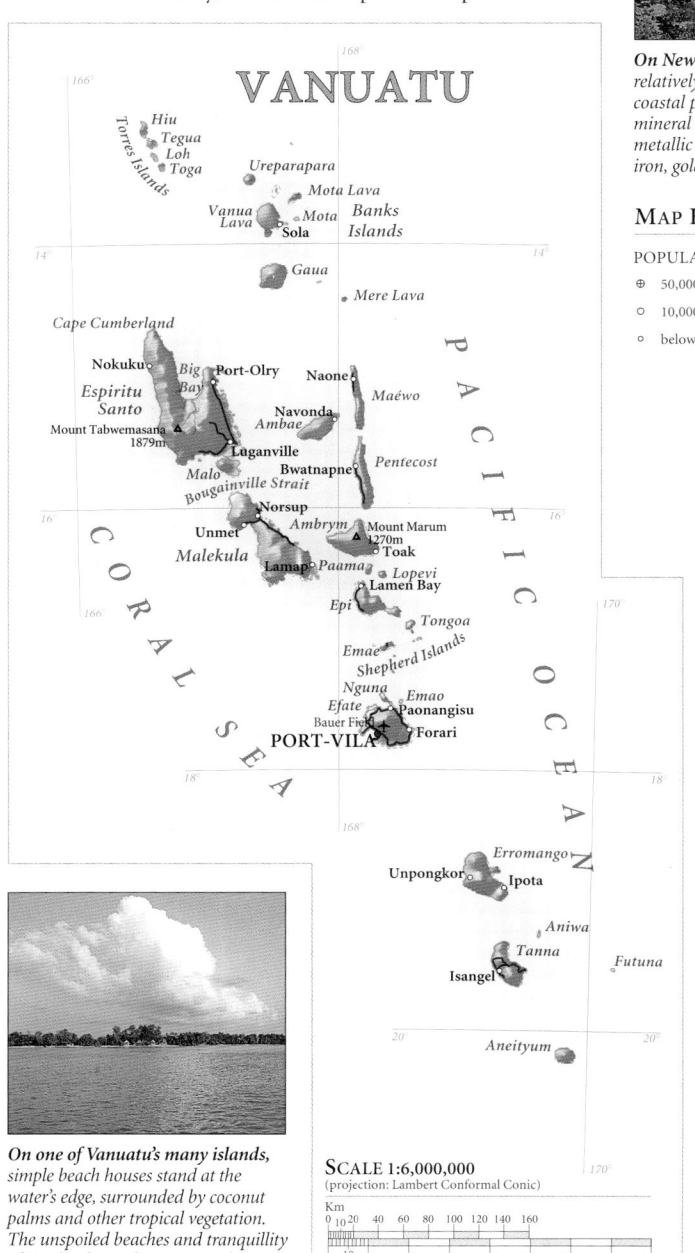

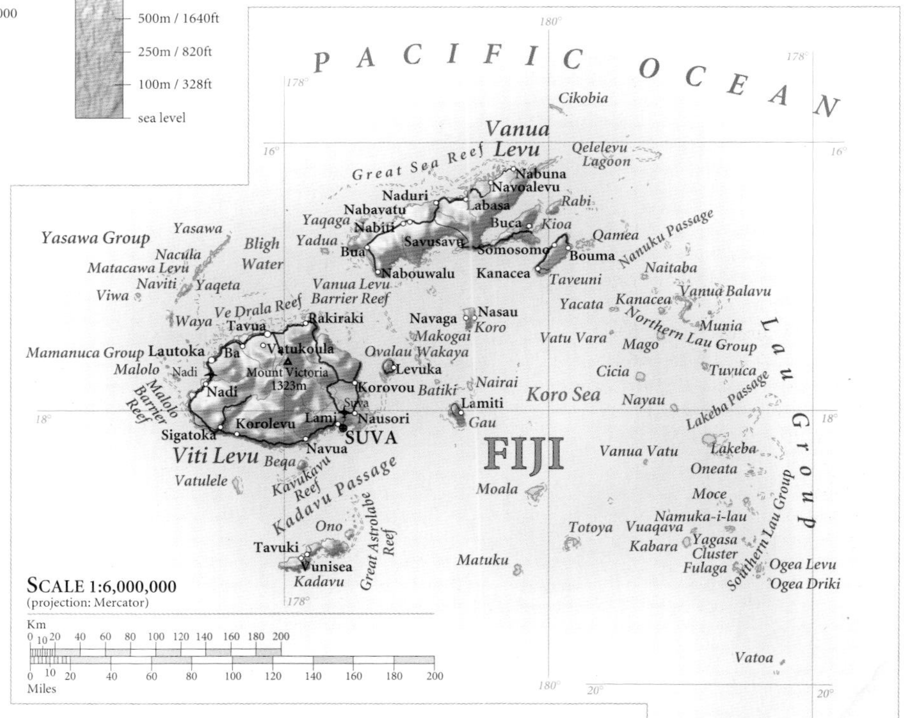

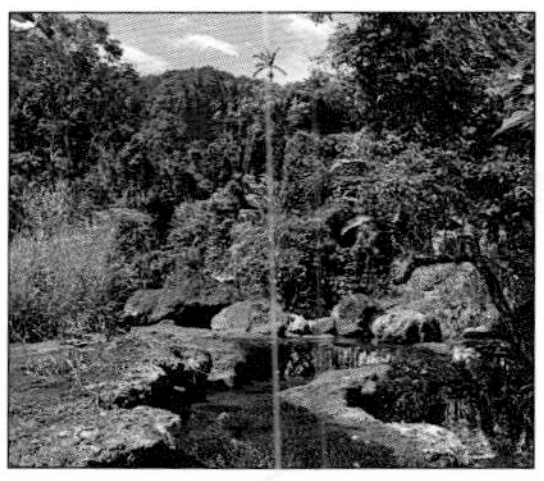

***Abaca Eco-tourist Park** near Lautoka on the island of Viti Levu in western Fiji is one of a number of projects aimed at combining tourism with awareness about the environment. The government and people of Fiji are keen to protect the unique ecology of the islands and prevent further damage to the coral reefs. Until the recent ending of nuclear testing in the Pacific by Western nations, Fiji lay downwind of some of the main testing sites.*

Micronesia

Marshall Islands, Micronesia, Nauru, Palau,
Guam, Northern Mariana Islands, Wake Island

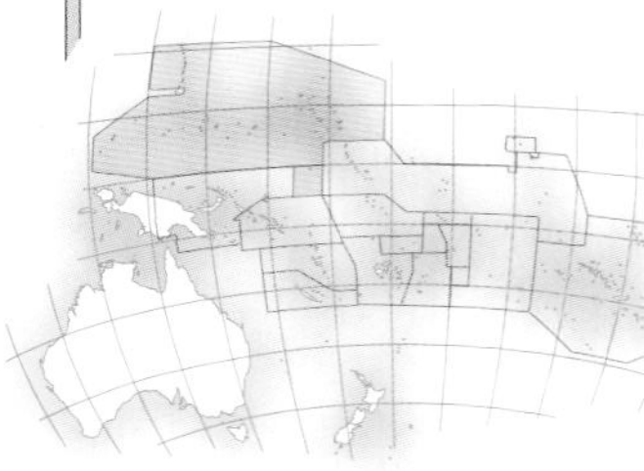

The Micronesian islands lie in the western reaches of the Pacific Ocean and are all part of the same volcanic zone. The Federated States of Micronesia is the largest group, with more than 600 atolls and forested volcanic islands in an area of more than 1,120 sq miles (2,900 sq km). Micronesia is a mixture of former colonies, overseas territories, and dependencies. Most of the region still relies on aid and subsidies to sustain economies limited by resources, isolation, and an emigrating population, drawn to New Zealand and Australia by the attractions of a western lifestyle.

Palau

Palau is an archipelago of over 200 islands, only eight of which are inhabited. It was the last remaining UN trust territory in the Pacific, controlled by the US until 1994, when it became independent. The economy operates on a subsistence level, with coconuts and cassava the principal crops. Fishing licenses and tourism provide foreign currency.

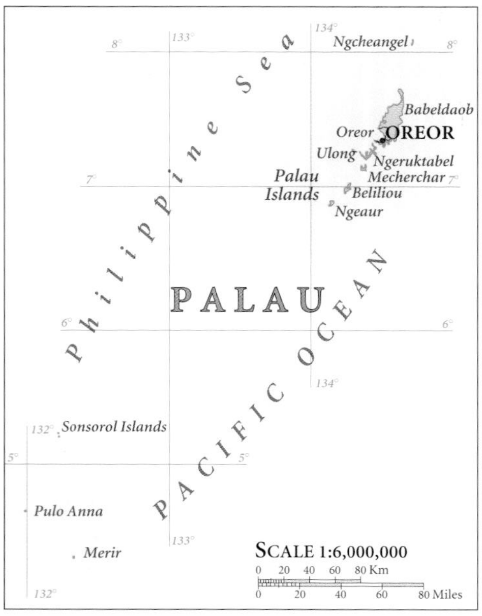

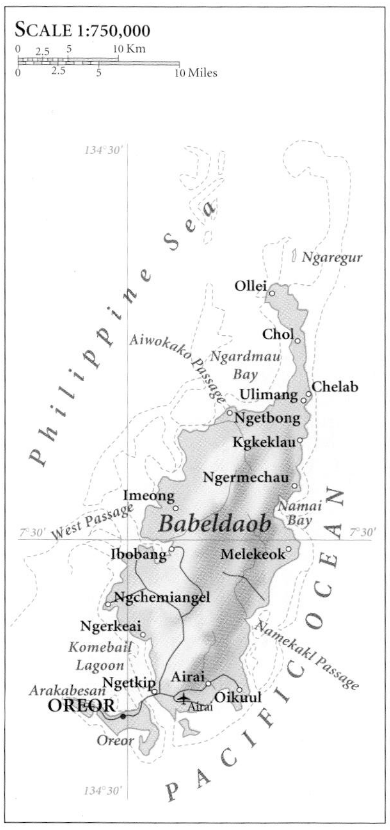

Northern Mariana Islands (to US)

A US commonwealth territory, the Northern Marianas comprise the whole of the Mariana archipelago except for Guam. The islands retain their close links with the US and continue to receive American aid. Tourism, though bringing in much-needed revenue, has speeded the decline of the traditional subsistence economy. Most of the population lives on Saipan.

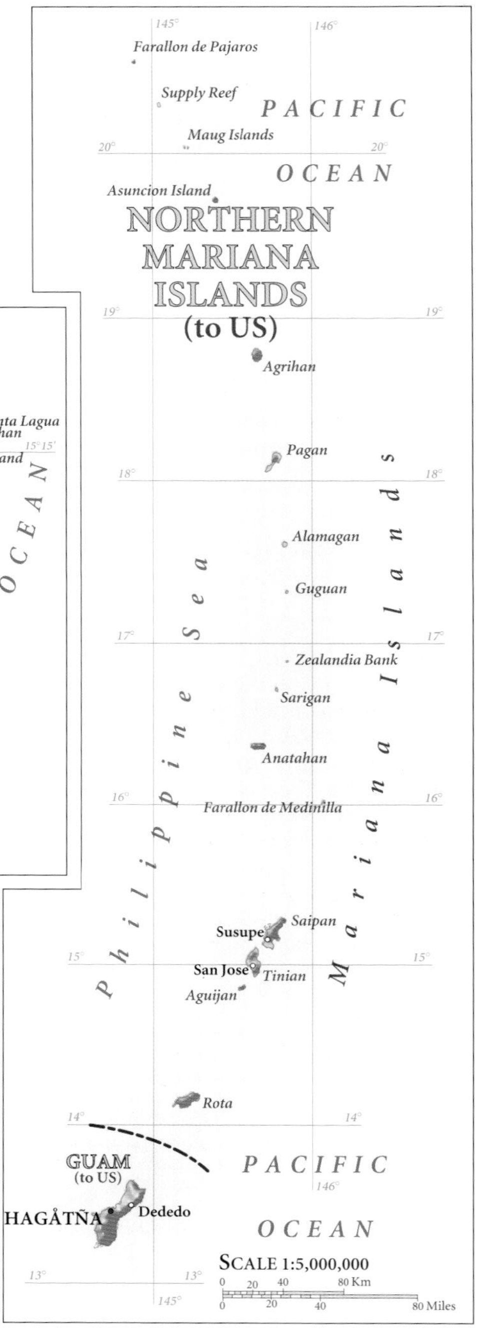

***The Palau Islands** have numerous hidden lakes and lagoons. These sustain their own ecosystems which have developed in isolation. This has produced adaptations in the animals and plants that are often unique to each lake.*

Guam (to US)

Lying at the southern end of the Mariana Islands, Guam is an important US military base and tourist destination. Social and political life is dominated by the indigenous Chamorro, who make up just under half the population, although the increasing prevalence of western culture threatens Guam's traditional social stability.

***The tranquillity** of these coastal lagoons, at Inarajan in southern Guam, belies the fact that the island lies in a region where typhoons are common.*

Micronesia

A mixture of high volcanic islands and low-lying coral atolls, the Federated States of Micronesia include all the Caroline Islands except Palau. Pohnpei, Kosrae, Chuuk, and Yap are the four main island cluster states, each of which has its own language, with English remaining the official language. Nearly half the population is concentrated on Pohnpei, the largest island. Independent since 1986, the islands continue to receive considerable aid from the US which supplements an economy based primarily on fishing and copra processing.

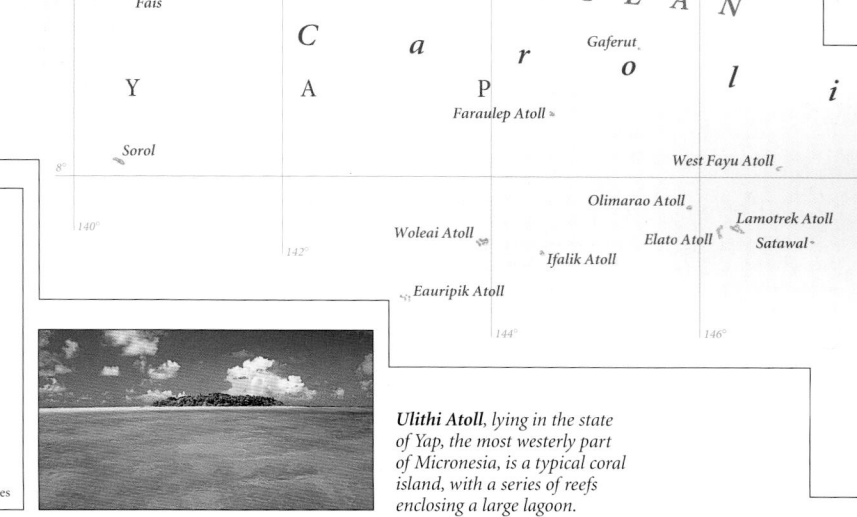

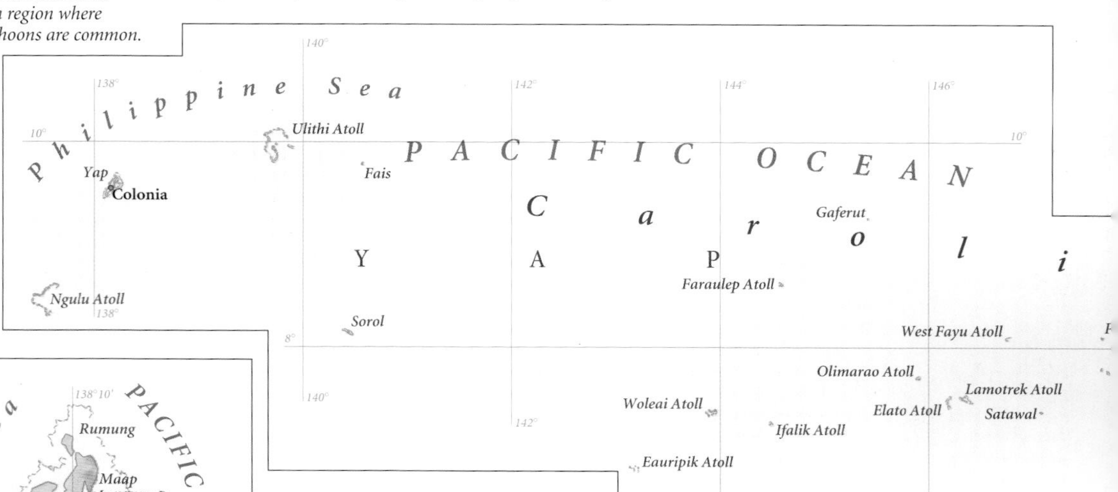

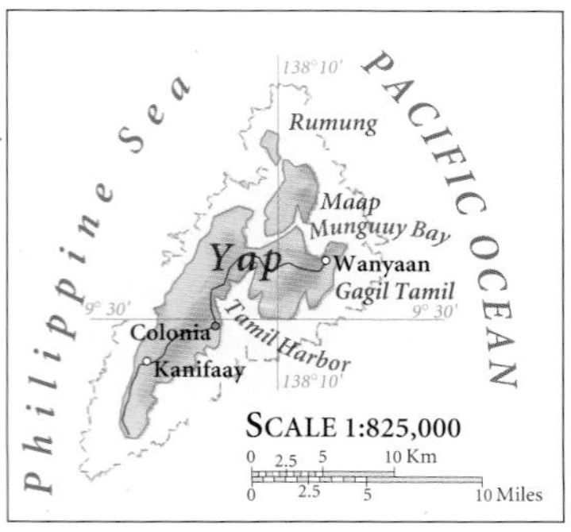

***Ulithi Atoll**, lying in the state of Yap, the most westerly part of Micronesia, is a typical coral island, with a series of reefs enclosing a large lagoon.*

MARSHALL ISLANDS

A GROUP OF 34 WIDELY-SCATTERED ATOLLS in the central Pacific Ocean, the Marshall Islands include some of the largest atolls in the world, formed from low coral islands with sandy beaches and enclosing vast lagoons. Formerly under US protection as part of the UN Trust Territory of the Pacific Islands, and including the former US nuclear testing sites of Bikini Atoll and Enewetak Atoll, the Marshall Islands became self-governing in 1979. The economy is reliant on US aid and on the rent paid by the US for its missile base on Kwajalein Atoll.

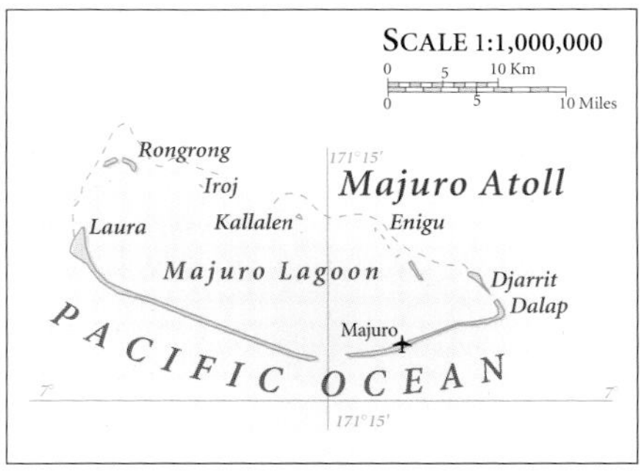

***Majuro Atoll** is the Marshall Islands' capital and commercial center. Almost half the population live on the narrow islands, often in overcrowded conditions.*

NAURU

A FORMER BRITISH COLONY, the tiny island of Nauru, with an area of only 8.2 sq miles (21.2 sq km), has been exploited for its substantial phosphate deposits by the UK, Australia, and New Zealand. Since independence in 1968, the phosphate industry has made its citizens some of the wealthiest in the world, and scars from the vast mining operation pit the island's landscape. Phosphate reserves are now virtually exhausted and investment overseas will in future form the bulk of Nauru's income.

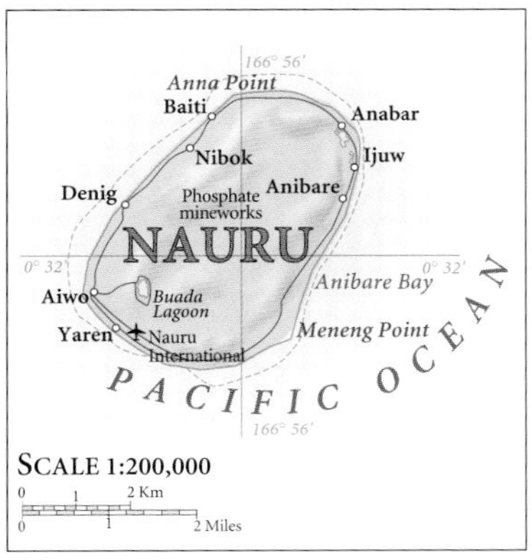

***A series of coral pinnacles** stand exposed in the shallow water off the coast of Nauru. Much of the island has an extraordinary "unar" landscape, created by years of phosphate extraction.*

WAKE ISLAND (to US)

AN UNINCORPORATED TERRITORY of the US with a tiny population, Wake Island remains strategically important to US forces, and has been used as a base in several conflicts. Formed by the rim of an extinct underwater volcano, it is now used as an emergency airstrip for trans-Pacific flights, and as a stopover for cargo planes.

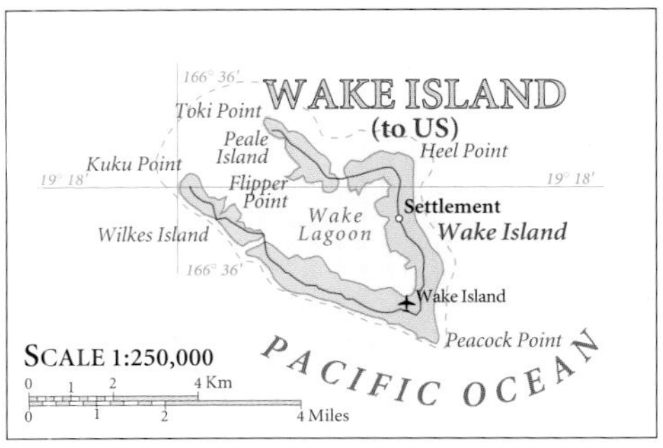

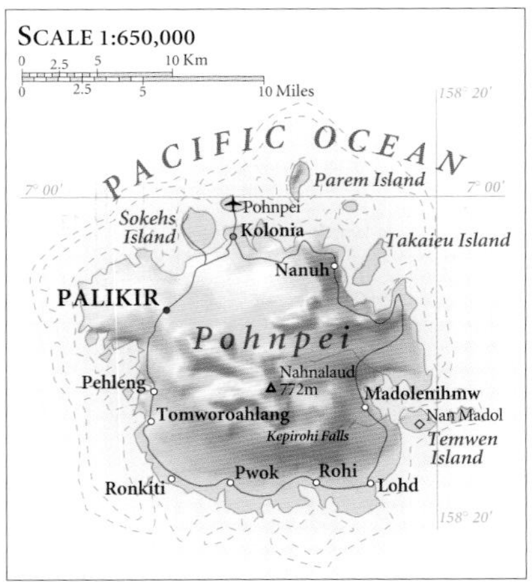

***Canoes, built following tradition,** are still important in Micronesia, and are used for transportation and for fishing. This large canoe, on Satawal, in the state of Yap, needs nearly 20 people to return it to the boathouse.*

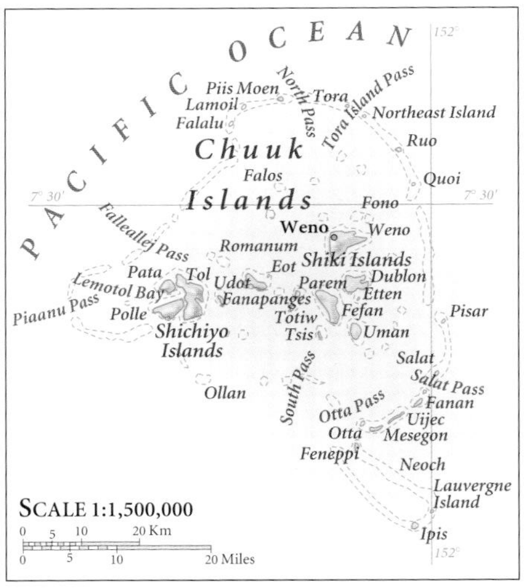

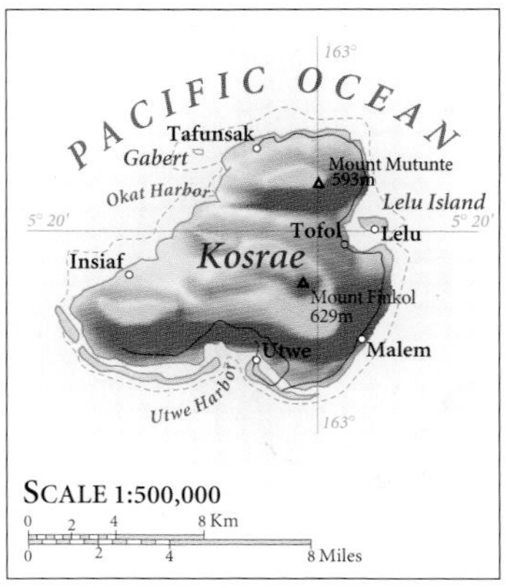

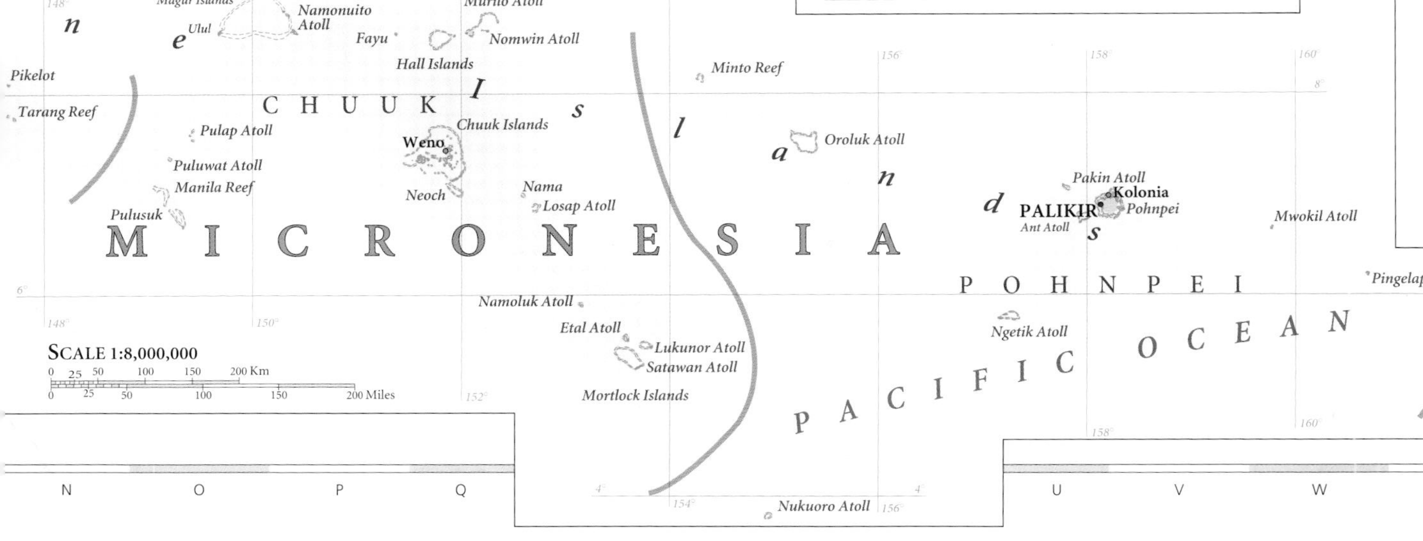

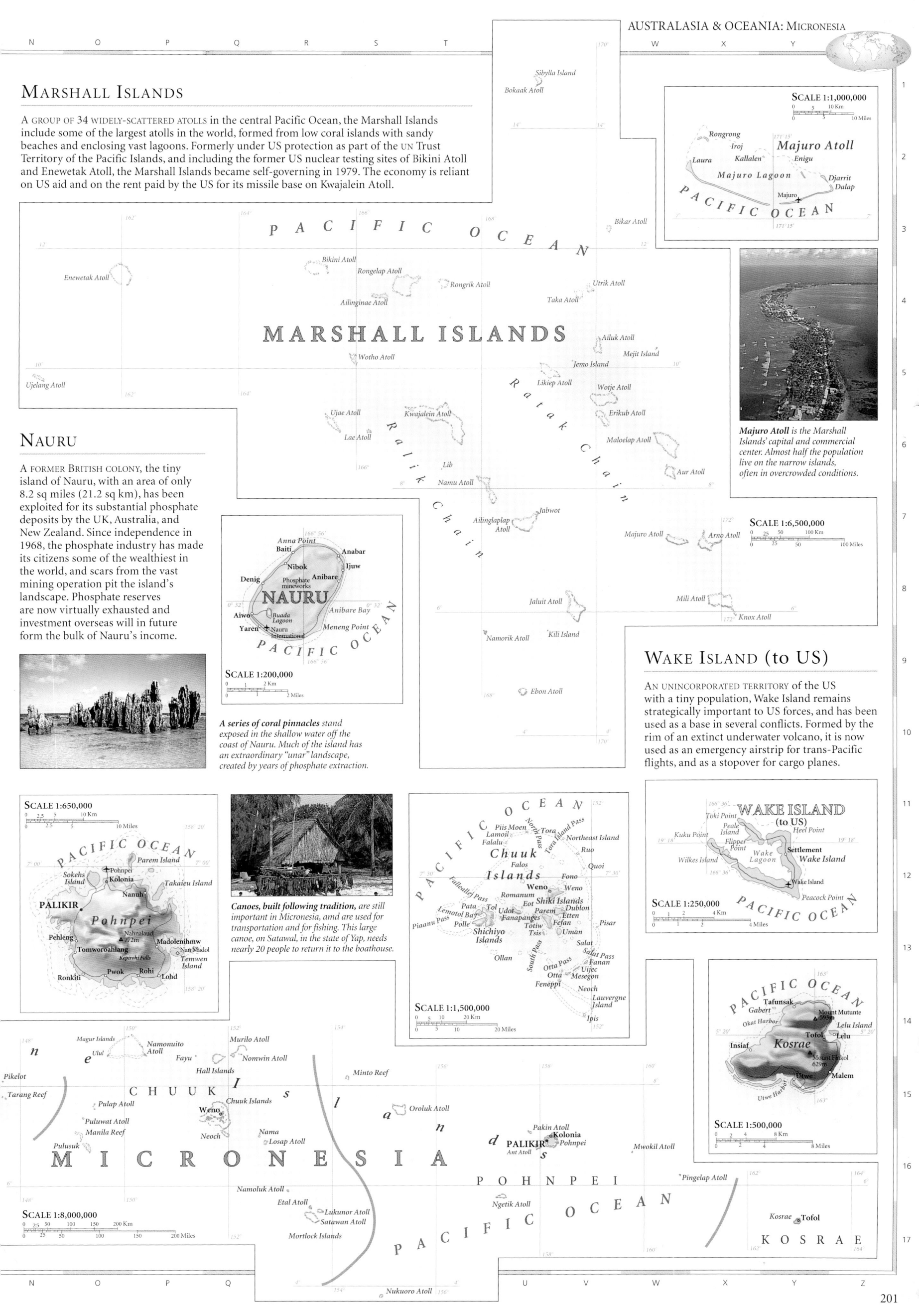

THE LANDSCAPE

ALTHOUGH IT IS STILL THE LARGEST OCEAN, the basin of the Pacific has been gradually decreasing in size due to the movement of the Indo-Australian Plate. The oldest parts are about 135 million years old. The eastern border of the Pacific is characterized by a continuous mountain chain running the length of the North and South American continents. The eastern basin has a low, uninterrupted relief, at depths averaging 15,000 ft (4570 m). In contrast, the western Pacific is scattered with island arcs and bounded by a series of deep ocean trenches. An almost continuous chain of volcanoes surrounds the ocean and an active mid-ocean ridge runs northeast–southwest.

Micronesia consists of numerous small, oceanic islands in the western Pacific. The Micronesian islands are all oceanic in origin, rising directly up from the ocean floor.

The Emperor Seamounts were formed over 40 million years ago. Like other islands and seamounts of the same era, they trend in a north–south direction. Younger chains run northwest–southeast.

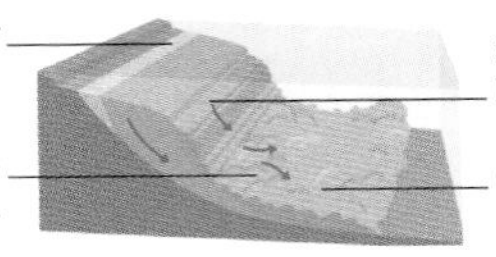

***Turbidity currents** are sinking masses of sediment-laden water. Their erosive force creates deep, narrow submarine canyons along the continental shelf to the ocean floor, where the sediments are deposited.*

The Mariana Trench marks a subduction zone between the Pacific Plate and the Philippine Plate. It is the world's deepest trench, reaching depths of 36,201 ft (11,034 m).

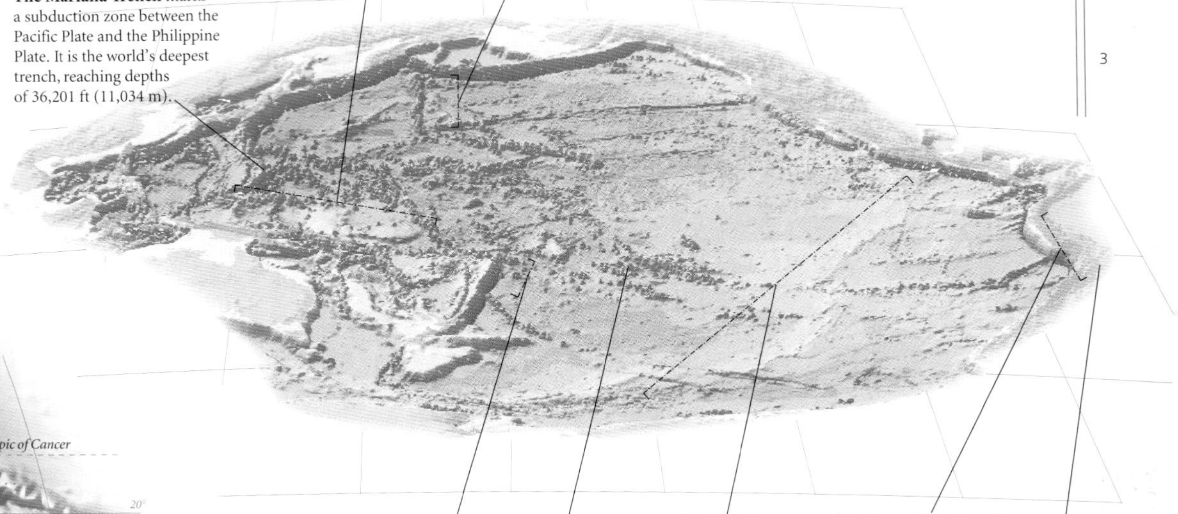

The Tonga Trench lies north of New Zealand's North Island. The trench reaches average depths of 34,448 ft (10,500 m), which is more than twice the average depth of the ocean.

The Pacific mid-ocean ridge is spreading at a rate of 6.5 inches (15 cm) a year. The northeastern part is no longer apparent, having merged with the strike-slip fault systems of North America.

The Peru–Chile Trench is the longest trench in the Pacific, extending 3,660 miles (5,900 km), and following the line of the Andes mountain range down the west coast of South America.

Bora-Bora

Bora-Bora's twin mountain peaks are the remnants of an ancient volcano, now surrounded by a large lagoon, fringed with coral.

Northern Chile

***The powerful erosive capacity** of Pacific waves can be seen along this stretch of coastline in northern Chile. Wave erosion has cut back the bedrock, exposing numerous rock layers.*

TONGA

THE KINGDOM OF TONGA lies in the southwest Pacific, about 2,000 miles (3,000 km) off the east coast of Australia. It comprises 169 islands of which only 36 are permanently inhabited. The majority of the population live on the largest island, Tongatapu. There are only three sizeable towns and the main commercial center is the capital Nuku'alofa. Tonga's economy is based mainly on agriculture; coconuts, bananas, and vanilla are grown as cash crops for export. Although there is some light manufacturing, growing land shortages have forced increased migration to New Zealand and Australia.

***The islands of Tonga** fall into two belts; those in the east are low, coral islands, while those in the west are high and volcanic. Four of the islands still contain active volcanoes. The mountainous, western islands are covered with verdant tropical vegetation.*

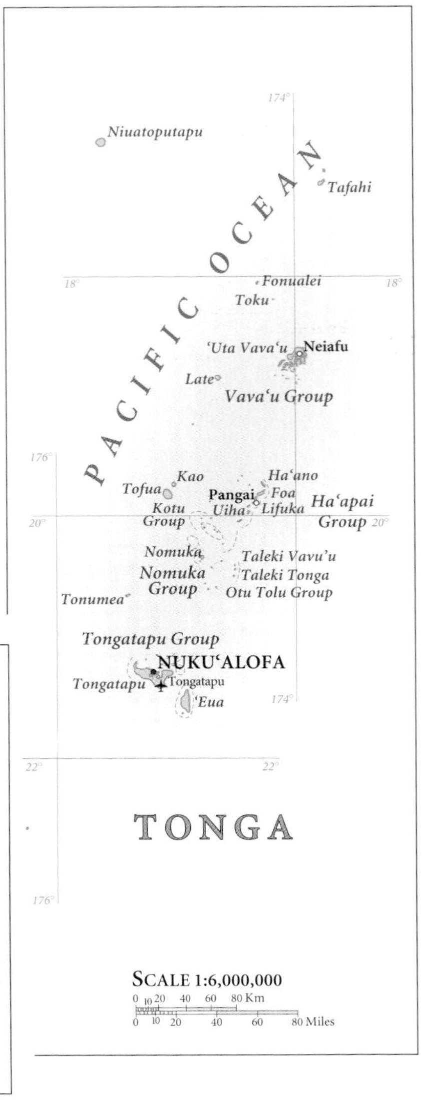

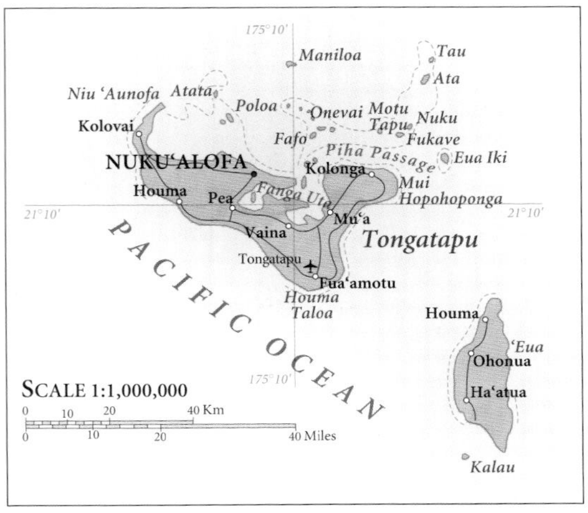

***Coral reefs and atolls** are found throughout the warm waters of the south Pacific. Reefs build up from the skeletons of millions of coral polyps – tiny sea creatures that cling to the reef and secrete calcium carbonate around their bodies, forming a hard protective skeleton.*

Wave action *has eroded this shoreline near Port Campbell in southeastern Australia leaving isolated pinnacles of rock cut off from the main coastline. They are known as the "Twelve Apostles."*

Polynesia

Kiribati, Tuvalu, *Cook Islands, Easter Island, French Polynesia, Niue, Pitcairn Islands, Tokelau, Wallis & Futuna*

The numerous island groups of Polynesia lie to the east of Australia, scattered over a vast area in the south Pacific. The islands are a mixture of low-lying coral atolls, some of which enclose lagoons, and the tips of great underwater volcanoes. The populations on the islands are small, and most people are of Polynesian origin, as are the Maori of New Zealand. Local economies remain simple, relying mainly on subsistence crops, mineral deposits, many now exhausted, fishing, and tourism.

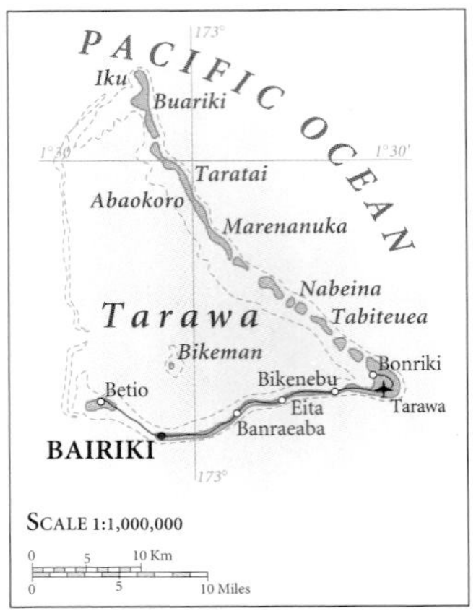

With the exception of Banaba all the islands in Kiribati's three groups are low-lying, coral atolls. This aerial view shows the sparsely vegetated islands, intercut by many small lagoons.

Kiribati

A former British colony, Kiribati became independent in 1979. Banaba's phosphate deposits ran out in 1980, following decades of exploitation by the British. Economic development remains slow and most agriculture is at a subsistence level, though coconuts provide export income, and underwater agriculture is being developed.

Tuvalu

A chain of nine coral atolls, 360 miles (579 km) long with a land area of just over 9 sq miles (23 sq km), Tuvalu is one of the world's smallest and most isolated states. As the Ellice Islands, Tuvalu was linked to the Gilbert Islands (now part of Kiribati) as a British colony until independence in 1978. Politically and socially conservative, Tuvaluans live by fishing and subsistence farming.

***Funafuti Atoll** contains more than 40% of Tuvalu's people, giving it an extremely high population density.*

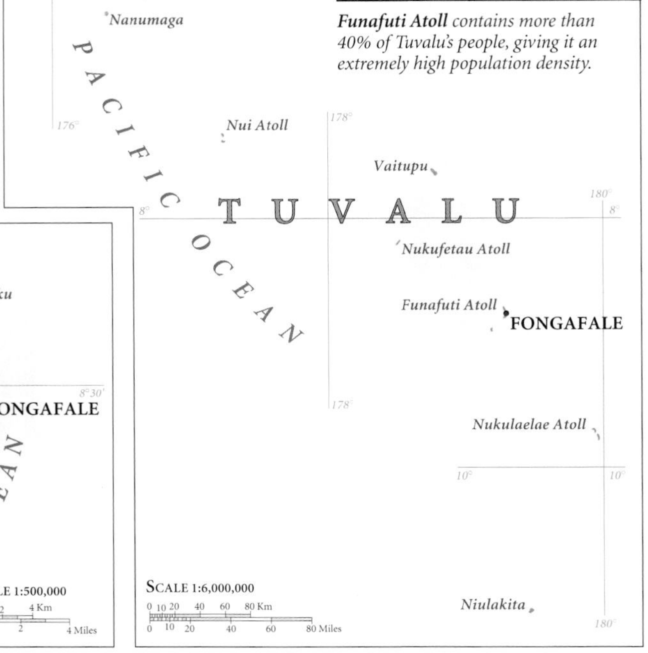

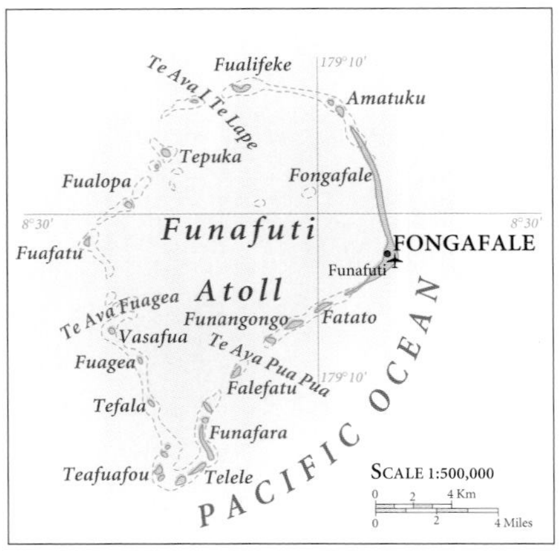

Tokelau (to New Zealand)

A low-lying coral atoll, Tokelau is a dependent territory of New Zealand with few natural resources. Although a 1990 cyclone destroyed crops and infrastructure, a tuna cannery and the sale of fishing licenses have raised revenue and a catamaran link between the islands has increased their tourism potential. Tokelau's small size and economic weakness makes independence from New Zealand unlikely.

***Fishermen cast their nets** to catch small fish in the shallow waters off Atafu Atoll, the most westerly island in Tokelau.*

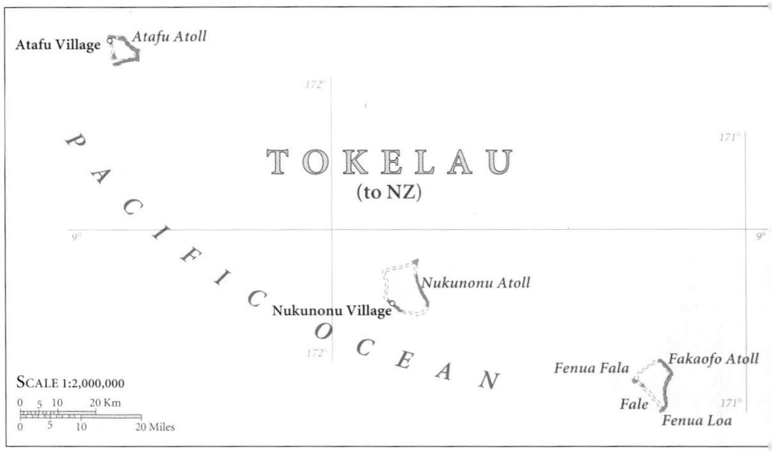

Wallis & Futuna (to France)

In contrast to other French overseas territories in the south Pacific, the inhabitants of Wallis and Futuna have shown little desire for greater autonomy. A subsistence economy produces a variety of tropical crops, while foreign currency remittances come from expatriates and from the sale of licenses to Japanese and Korean fishing fleets.

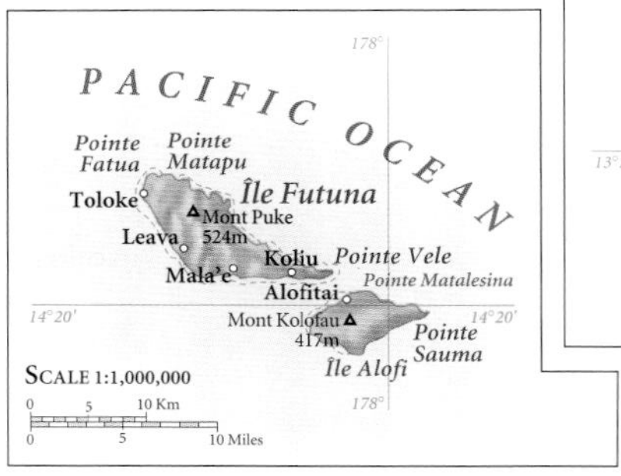

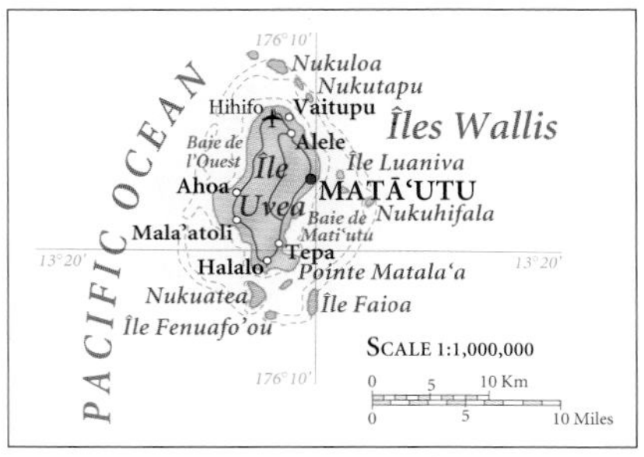

Cook Islands (to New Zealand)

A mixture of coral atolls and volcanic peaks, the Cook Islands achieved self-government in 1965 but exist in free association with New Zealand. A diverse economy includes pearl and giant clam farming, and an ostrich farm, plus tourism and banking. A 1991 friendship treaty with France provides for French surveillance of territorial waters.

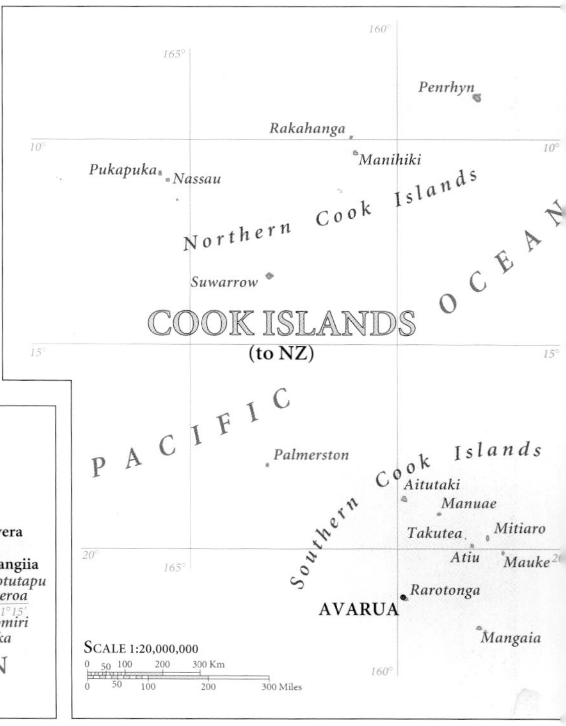

Niue (to New Zealand)

Niue, the world's largest coral island, is self-governing but exists in free association with New Zealand. Tropical fruits are grown for local consumption; tourism and the sale of postage stamps provide foreign currency. The lack of local job prospects has led more than 10,000 Niueans to emigrate to New Zealand, which has now invested heavily in Niue's economy in the hope of reversing this trend.

***Palm trees fringe** the white sands of a beach on Aitutaki in the Southern Cook Islands, where tourism is of increasing economic importance.*

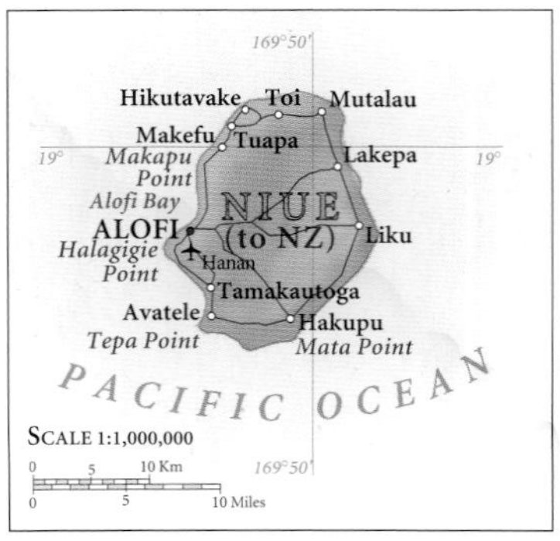

***Waves have cut back** the original coastline, exposing a sandy beach, near Mutalau in the northeast corner of Niue.*

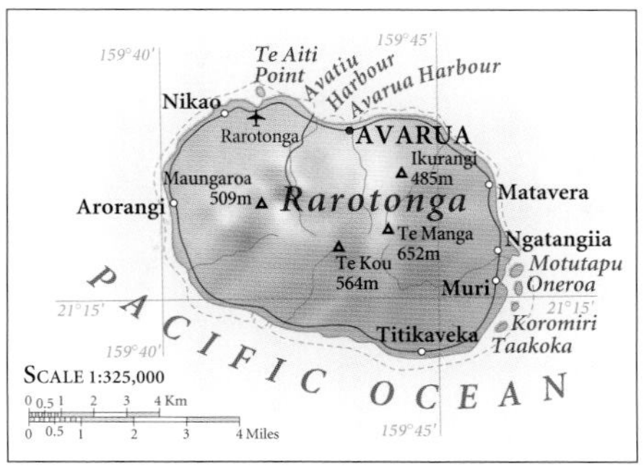

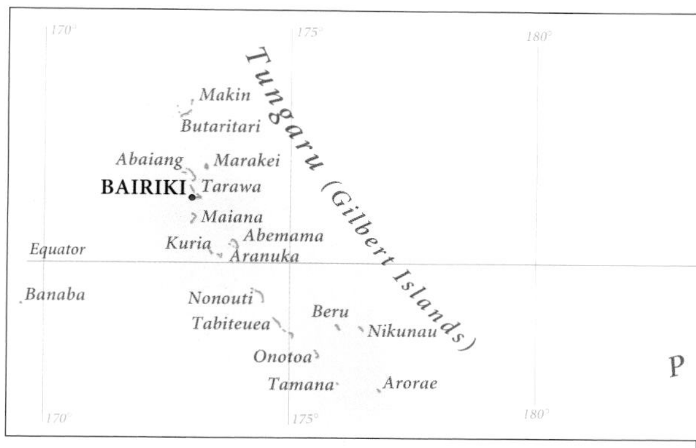

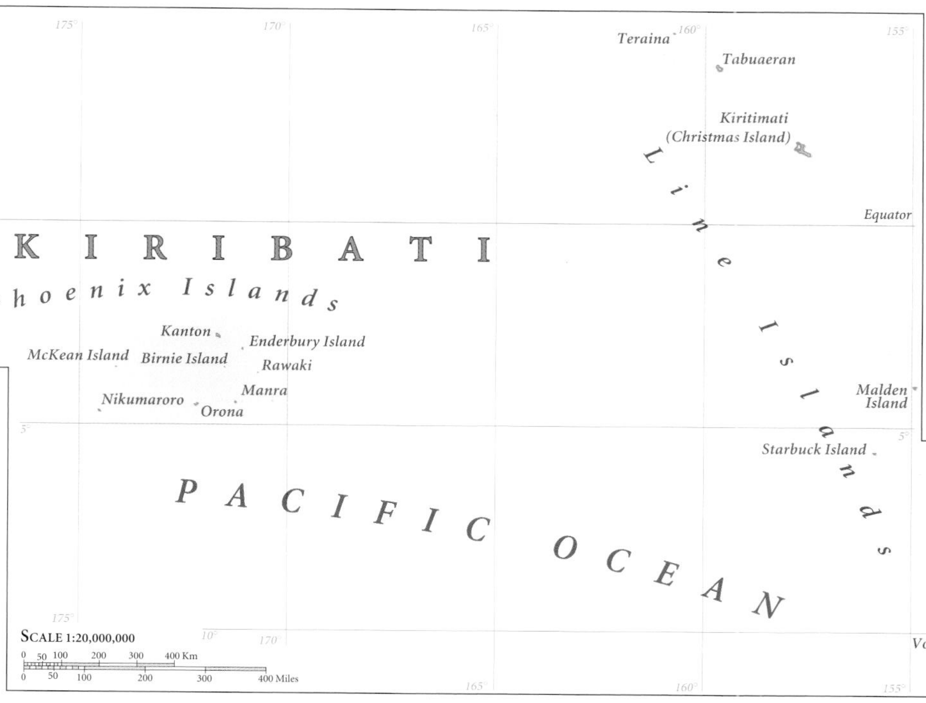

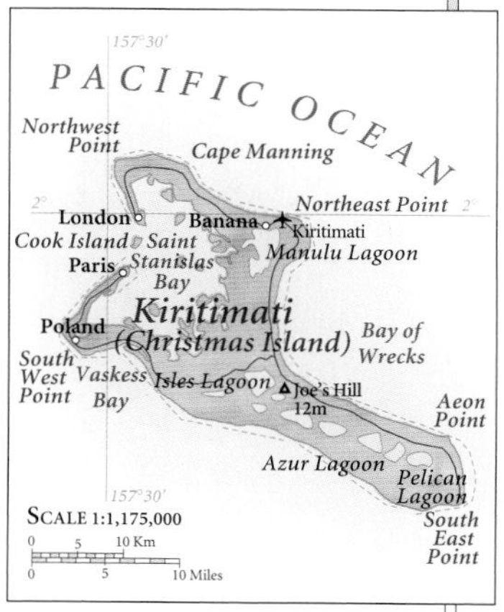

FRENCH POLYNESIA (to France)

THE 130 ISLANDS OF FRENCH POLYNESIA cover 4 million sq miles (10.5 million sq km). Nearly 75% of the people live on Tahiti. The use of Mururoa as a nuclear testing site by the French military transformed the economy, creating many jobs. The end of testing led to calls from the Polynesian majority for greater autonomy from France, the rebuilding of indigenous trade, and a reduction in tourism to stop the erosion of the islands' traditional culture.

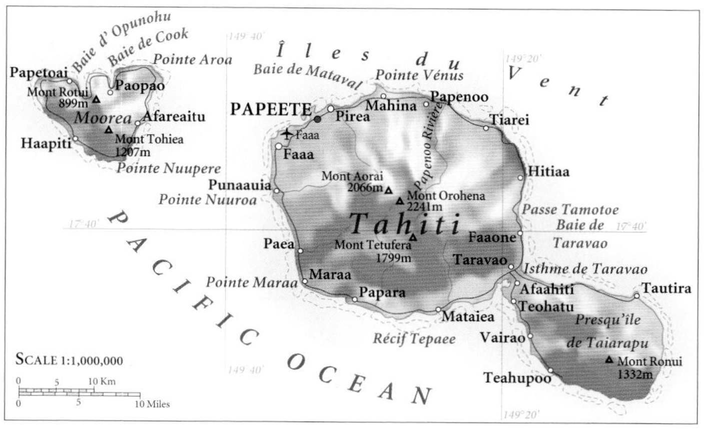

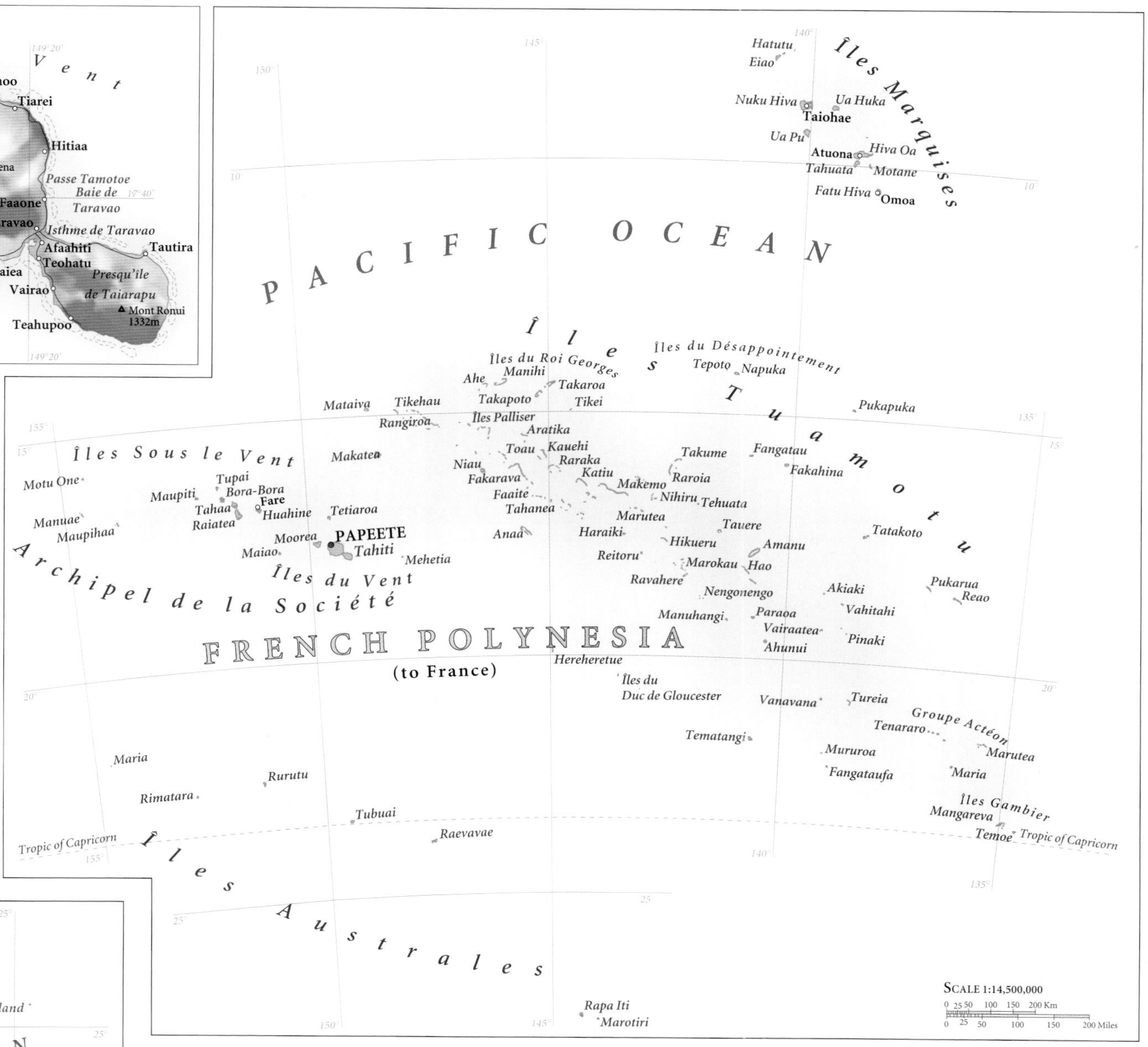

The traditional Tahitian welcome for visitors, who are greeted by parties of canoes, has become a major tourist attraction.

PITCAIRN ISLANDS (to UK)

BRITAIN'S MOST ISOLATED DEPENDENCY, Pitcairn Island was first populated by mutineers from the HMS *Bounty* in 1790. Emigration is further depleting the already limited gene pool of the island's inhabitants, with associated social and health problems. Barter, fishing, and subsistence farming form the basis of the economy although postage stamp sales provide foreign currency earnings, and offshore mineral exploitation may boost the economy in future.

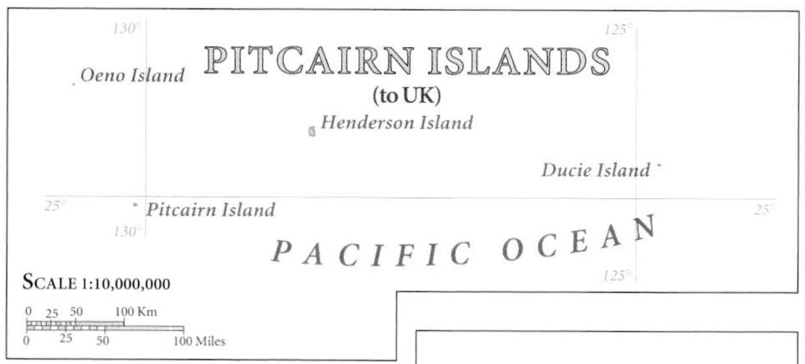

***The Pitcairn Islanders** rely on regular airdrops from New Zealand and periodic visits by supply vessels to provide them with basic commodities.*

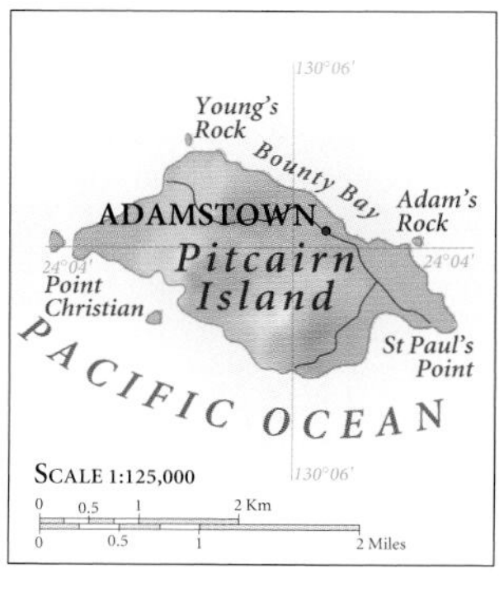

EASTER ISLAND (to Chile)

ONE OF THE MOST EASTERLY ISLANDS in Polynesia, Easter Island *(Isla de Pascua)* – also known as Rapa Nui, is part of Chile. The mainly Polynesian inhabitants support themselves by farming, which is mainly of a subsistence nature, and includes cattle rearing and crops such as sugar cane, bananas, corn, gourds, and potatoes. In recent years, tourism has become the most important source of income and the island sustains a small commercial airport.

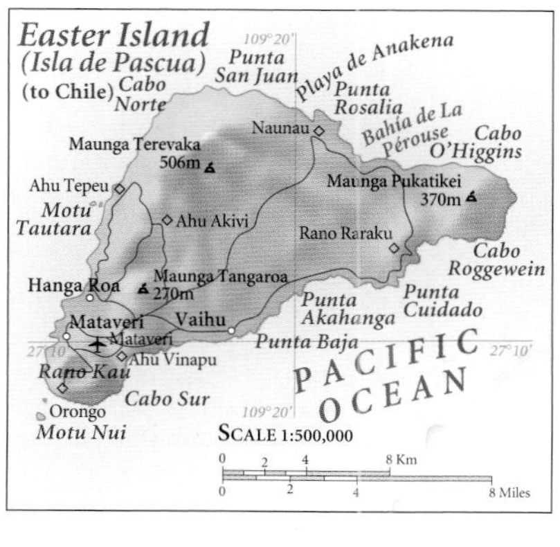

***The Naunau**, a series of huge stone statues overlook Playa de Anakena, on Easter Island. Carved from a soft volcanic rock, they were erected between 400 and 900 years ago.*

ANTARCTICA

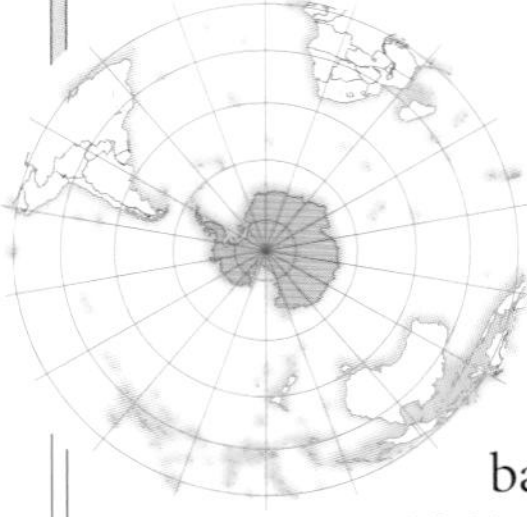

THE ICE-COVERED CONTINENT of Antarctica, which is the Earth's most southerly region, has drawn explorers and entrepreneurs seeking challenge and riches in its wintry lands for over 200 years. The extreme climate has deterred any large-scale settlement of the continent, and though commercial hunters built outposts in the past, habitation is now limited to scientific bases. The Antarctic Treaty, which came into force in 1961, provides for international governance and scientific cooperation in place of potential territorial conflict.

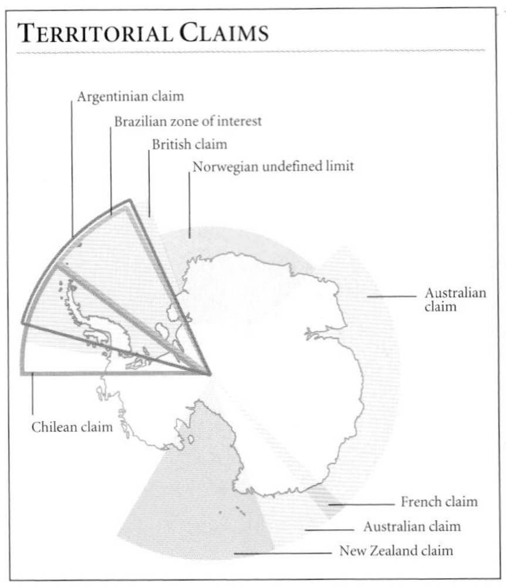

RESOURCES

MANY ORE MINERALS, including iron and gold, are found in the Antarctic, and there are also coal reserves in the Transantarctic Mountains. The severe conditions and environmental importance of the region mean that exploitation of potential mineral resources is both uneconomic and undesirable. The unique wildlife and landscape draw a small number of tourists annually.

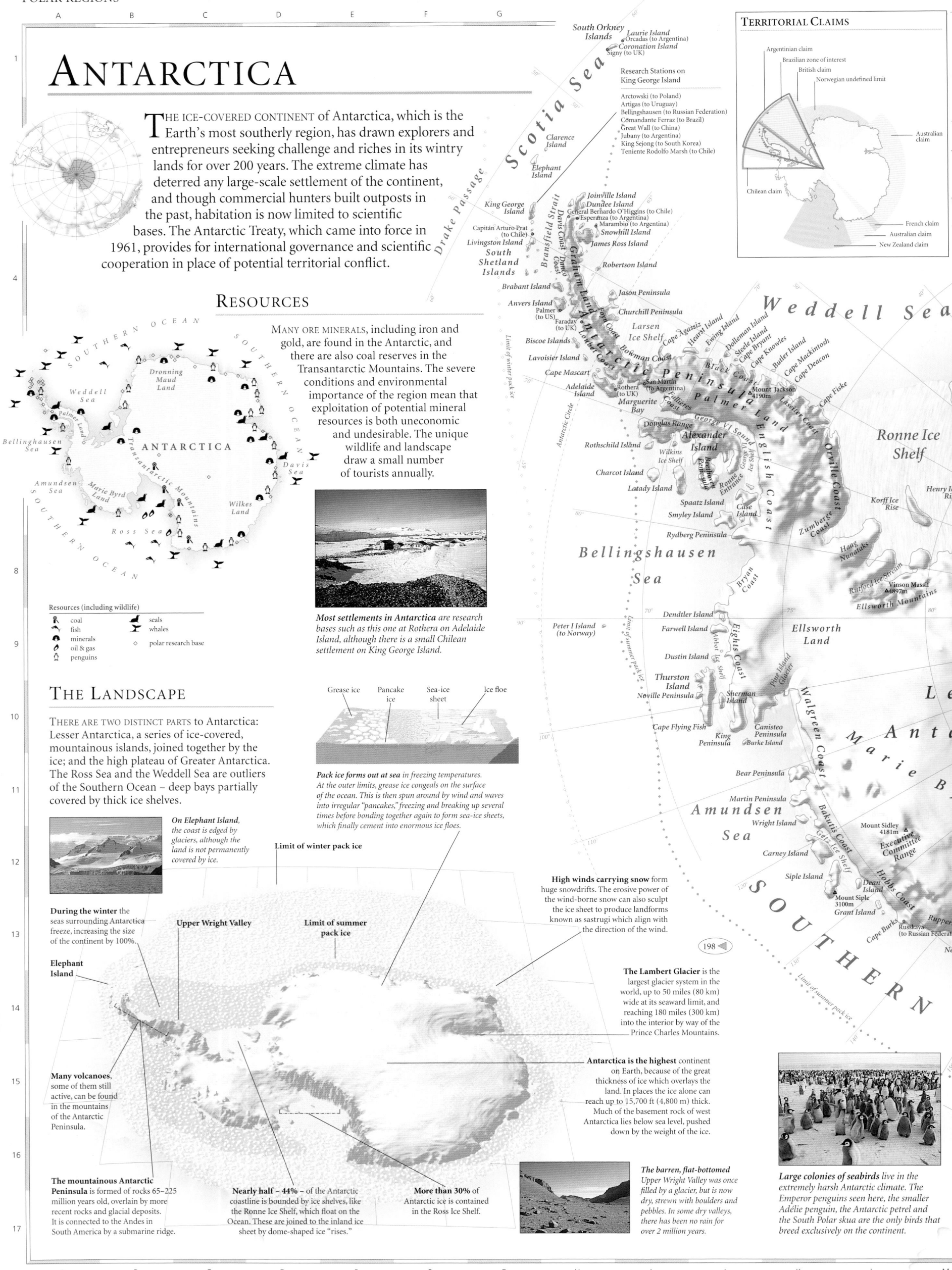

Most settlements in Antarctica are research bases such as this one at Rothera on Adelaide Island, although there is a small Chilean settlement on King George Island.

THE LANDSCAPE

THERE ARE TWO DISTINCT PARTS to Antarctica: Lesser Antarctica, a series of ice-covered, mountainous islands, joined together by the ice; and the high plateau of Greater Antarctica. The Ross Sea and the Weddell Sea are outliers of the Southern Ocean – deep bays partially covered by thick ice shelves.

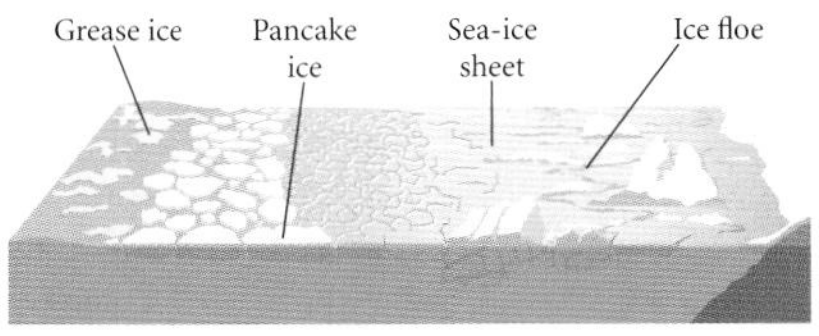

Pack ice forms out at sea *in freezing temperatures. At the outer limits, grease ice congeals on the surface of the ocean. This is then spun around by wind and waves into irregular "pancakes," freezing and breaking up several times before bonding together again to form sea-ice sheets, which finally cement into enormous ice floes.*

On Elephant Island, *the coast is edged by glaciers, although the land is not permanently covered by ice.*

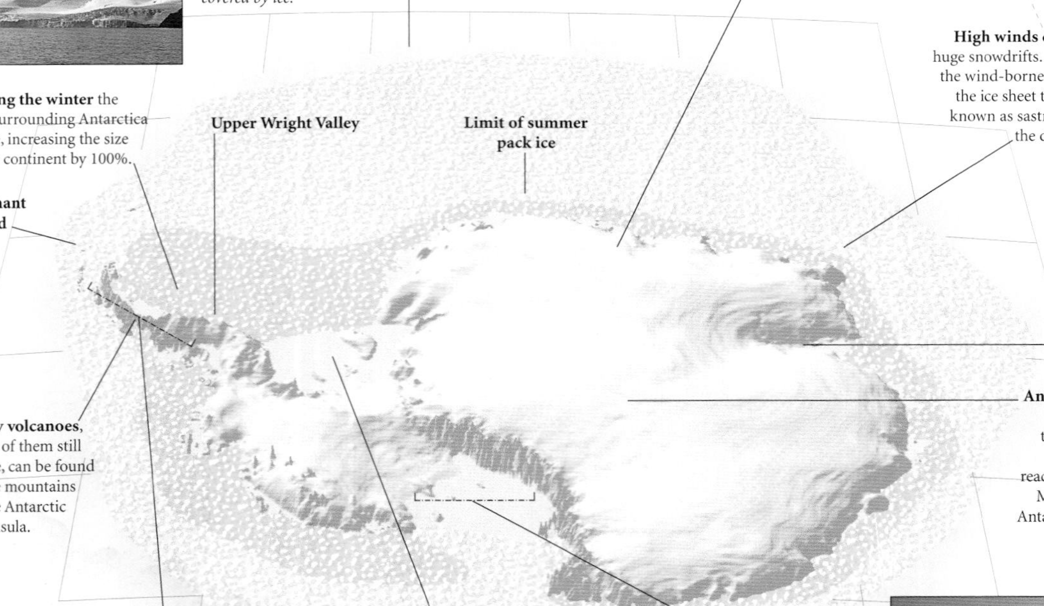

During the winter the seas surrounding Antarctica freeze, increasing the size of the continent by 100%.

High winds carrying snow form huge snowdrifts. The erosive power of the wind-borne snow can also sculpt the ice sheet to produce landforms known as sastrugi which align with the direction of the wind.

The Lambert Glacier is the largest glacier system in the world, up to 50 miles (80 km) wide at its seaward limit, and reaching 180 miles (300 km) into the interior by way of the Prince Charles Mountains.

Antarctica is the highest continent on Earth, because of the great thickness of ice which overlays the land. In places the ice alone can reach up to 15,700 ft (4,800 m) thick. Much of the basement rock of west Antarctica lies below sea level, pushed down by the weight of the ice.

Many volcanoes, some of them still active, can be found in the mountains of the Antarctic Peninsula.

The mountainous Antarctic Peninsula is formed of rocks 65–225 million years old, overlain by more recent rocks and glacial deposits. It is connected to the Andes in South America by a submarine ridge.

Nearly half – 44% – of the Antarctic coastline is bounded by ice shelves, like the Ronne Ice Shelf, which float on the Ocean. These are joined to the inland ice sheet by dome-shaped ice "rises."

More than 30% of Antarctic ice is contained in the Ross Ice Shelf.

***The barren, flat-bottomed** Upper Wright Valley was once filled by a glacier, but is now dry, strewn with boulders and pebbles. In some dry valleys, there has been no rain for over 2 million years.*

***Large colonies of seabirds** live in the extremely harsh Antarctic climate. The Emperor penguins seen here, the smaller Adélie penguin, the Antarctic petrel and the South Polar skua are the only birds that breed exclusively on the continent.*

***The sun sets** over the Antarctic Peninsula for more than six months during the winter. However, there are more hours of sunshine during the brief Antarctic summer than most equatorial countries experience in a whole year.*

***Immense, flat-topped icebergs** are formed when blocks of ice break away from the main ice sheet. Though the exposed area is enormous, the volume of ice concealed beneath the water may be many times greater.*

THE ARCTIC

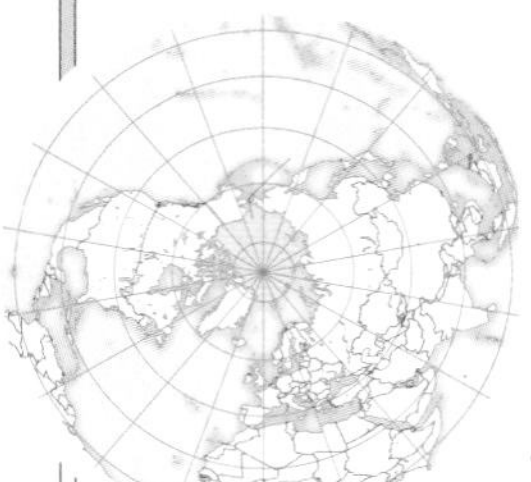

THREE CONTINENTS, ASIA, NORTH AMERICA, AND EUROPE, reach into the Arctic Circle at their northernmost limits, almost entirely encircling the Arctic Ocean. Despite the region's extraordinarily harsh climate, it has been inhabited for thousands of years by peoples such as the European Lapps, the Russian Nenet, and the North American Inuit, who draw a living from fishing, herding, and hunting. More recently, particularly in the Russian Arctic, opportunities to exploit oil and other mineral reserves have encouraged immigration. Pollution of the Arctic's unique ecology and damage to the traditional lifestyles of many native peoples have been the unfortunate results of this activity, and international cooperation is needed to safeguard the future of the region.

MAP KEY

POPULATION

- above 5 million
- 1 million to 5 million
- 500,000 to 1 million
- 100,000 to 500,000
- 50,000 to 100,000
- 10,000 to 50,000
- below 10,000

SEA DEPTH

- sea level
- 250m / 820ft
- 500m / 1640ft
- 1000m / 3281ft
- 2000m / 6562ft
- 3000m / 9843ft

SCALE 1:21,000,000
(projection: Lambert Azimuthal Equal Area)

Km 0 100 200 300 400 500 600

Miles 0 100 200 300 400 500 600

***Windblown snow** etches deep patterns in the ice sheet known as sastrugi. They align with the direction of the wind*

RESOURCES

LARGE QUANTITIES of coal, oil, and natural gas are to be found in the basins of the Arctic Ocean, and in northern Canada, Alaska and the Russian Federation. The cost and difficulty of extraction and, more recently, awareness of damage to the environment, have limited exploitation to coastal regions. The unfrozen waters have stocks of fish including cod, flounder, and haddock. Quotas have now been put in place to restrict the number of fish caught annually. Reindeer are herded in large numbers by many of the native Arctic peoples. Most grain and vegetables are imported from elsewhere.

***Icebreakers** are ships with specially strengthened hulls, designed to break a path through the ice. They are used to keep important routes open during the winter, when falling temperatures cause much of the Arctic Ocean to freeze over.*

THE LANDSCAPE

THE ARCTIC OCEAN comprises two large ocean basins divided by three submarine ridges, the greatest of which, the Lomonosov Ridge, is a huge underwater mountain range which has an average height of more than 10,000 ft (3,000 m). The lands which encircle the Arctic Ocean are underlain by great shield areas of ancient rocks, which were heavily glaciated during the last Ice Age.

***Icebergs** are constantly broken up and reshaped by wind and the oceans. This flat-topped iceberg has been undercut, leaving a craggy ice cliff.*

A complex and ancient mountain system, extending from the Queen Elizabeth Islands to eastern Greenland was formed more than 245 million years ago.

The Canadian Shield underlies almost all of the Canadian Arctic. It is a very stable plateau of ancient rock, now covered by glacial lakes and sediment, which supports tundra vegetation.

The Arctic Ocean is the world's smallest ocean with a total area of 5,440,000 sq miles (15,100,000 sq km).

At a latitude of more than 75° N, the Arctic Ocean is almost permanently covered by pack-ice, though high winds and the movement of the seas may cause the ice to crack and break up.

In the more southerly reaches of the Arctic, like Siberia, much of the land is covered by permafrost. In the summer, higher temperatures warm the frozen ground, causing a number of typical phenomena. These include solifluction, the fast downhill movement of top soil layers; freeze/thaw activity, which patterns the ground into regular polygonal shapes, and the formation of large domes with a frozen ice core, known as pingos.

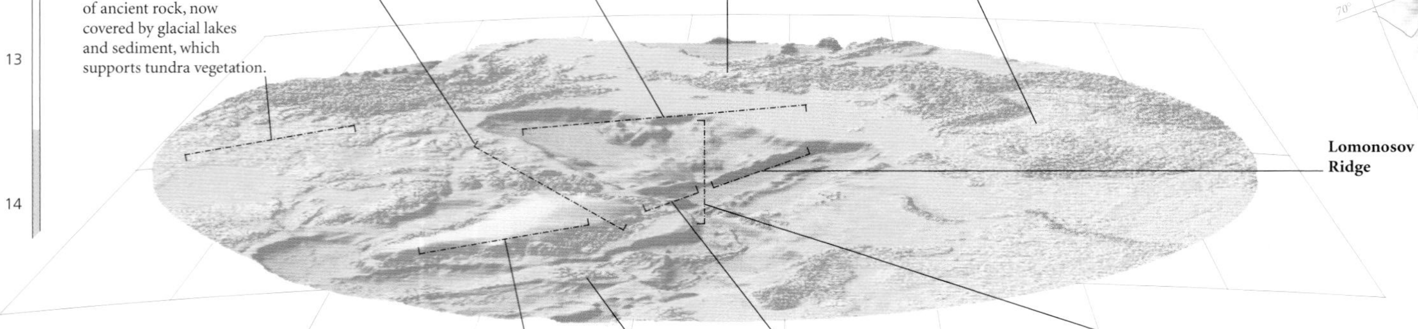

***Much of Greenland** is covered by a massive ice sheet more than 650,000 sq miles (1,683,400 sq km) in extent. The weight of the ice has depressed the central land area to form a basin lying more than 1,000 ft (300 m) below sea level. Only at the edges of the island is bare rock visible.*

Iceland has five major glaciers, sustained by heavy snowfall. Parts of the ice cap cover active volcanoes, such as Bárdharbunga, which periodically erupt causing the melted ice to form a great lake at the glacier margins.

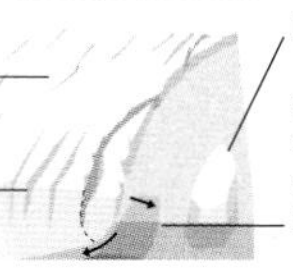

At the boundary of the Arctic ice shelves, sea water flows under the ice causing melting and forming crevasses on the surface. This eventually weakens blocks of ice which break away as icebergs. This process is known as calving.

198
14
14
66

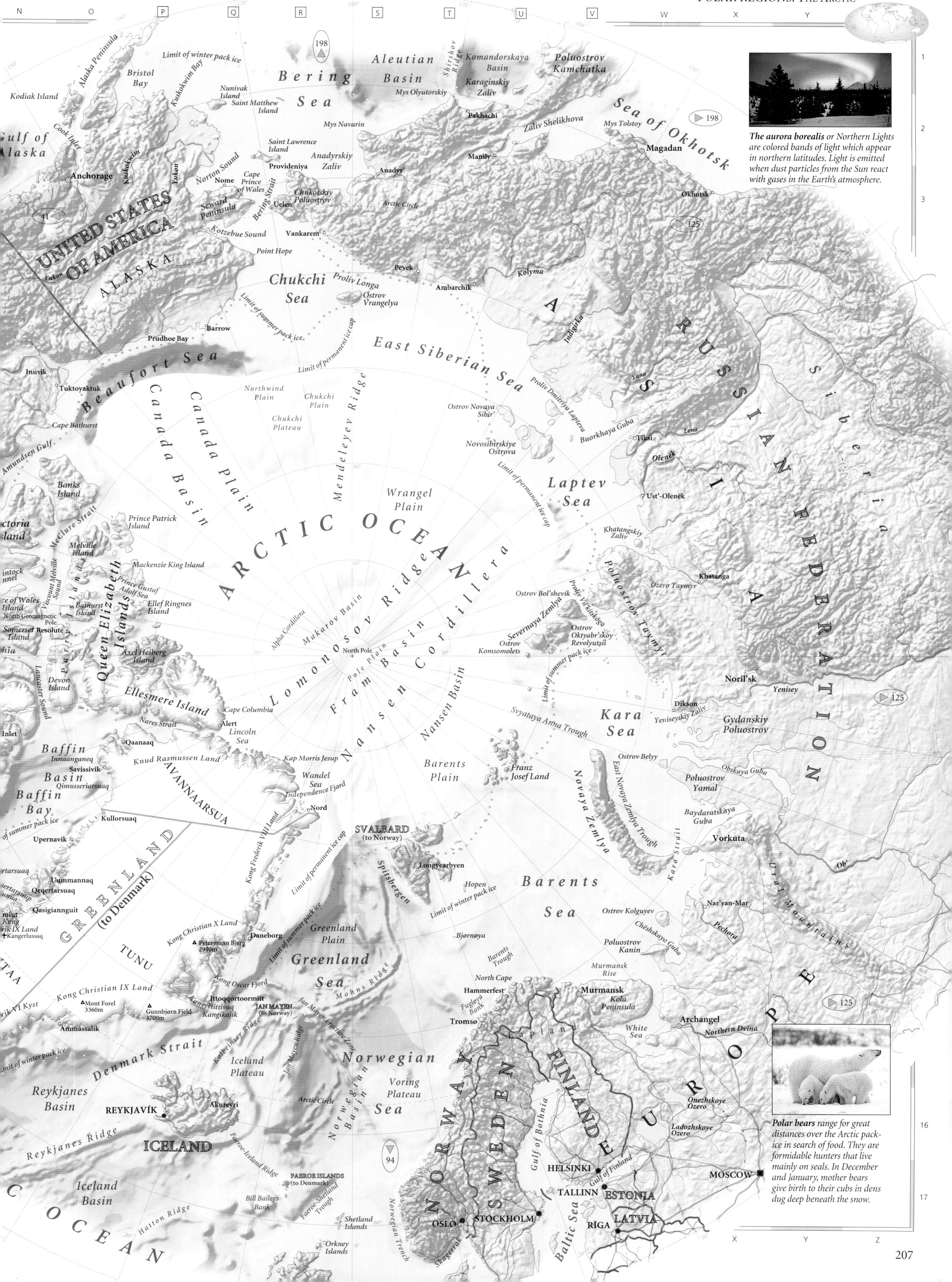

***The aurora borealis** or Northern Lights are colored bands of light which appear in northern latitudes. Light is emitted when dust particles from the Sun react with gases in the Earth's atmosphere.*

***Polar bears** range for great distances over the Arctic pack-ice in search of food. They are formidable hunters that live mainly on seals. In December and January, mother bears give birth to their cubs in dens dug deep beneath the snow.*

GEOGRAPHICAL COMPARISONS

Largest Countries

Russian Federation	6,592,735 sq miles	(17,075,200 sq km)
Canada	3,851,788 sq miles	(9,976,140 sq km)
USA	3,717,792 sq miles	(9,629,091 sq km)
China	3,705,386 sq miles	(9,596,960 sq km)
Brazil	3,286,470 sq miles	(8,511,965 sq km)
Australia	2,967,893 sq miles	(7,686,850 sq km)
India	1,269,339 sq miles	(3,287,590 sq km)
Argentina	1,068,296 sq miles	(2,766,890 sq km)
Kazakhstan	1,049,150 sq miles	(2,717,300 sq km)
Sudan	967,493 sq miles	(2,505,810 sq km)

Smallest Countries

Vatican City	0.17 sq miles	(0.44 sq km)
Monaco	0.75 sq miles	(1.95 sq km)
Nauru	8.2 sq miles	(21.2 sq km)
Tuvalu	10 sq miles	(26 sq km)
San Marino	24 sq miles	(61 sq km)
Liechtenstein	62 sq miles	(160 sq km)
Marshall Islands	70 sq miles	(181 sq km)
St. Kitts & Nevis	101 sq miles	(261 sq km)
Maldives	116 sq miles	(300 sq km)
Malta	122 sq miles	(316 sq km)

Largest Islands

(to the nearest 1000 - or 100,000 for the largest)

Greenland	849,400 sq miles	(2,200,000 sq km)
New Guinea	312,000 sq miles	(808,000 sq km)
Borneo	292,222 sq miles	(757,050 sq km)
Madagascar	229,300 sq miles	(594,000 sq km)
Sumatra	202,300 sq miles	(524,000 sq km)
Baffin Island	183,800 sq miles	(476,000 sq km)
Honshu	88,800 sq miles	(230,000 sq km)
Britain	88,700 sq miles	(229,800 sq km)
Victoria Island	81,900 sq miles	(212,000 sq km)
Ellesmere Island	75,700 sq miles	(196,000 sq km)

Richest Countries

(GNP per capita, in US$)

Luxembourg	45,360
Switzerland	44,350
Japan	40,940
Liechtenstein	40,000
Norway	34,510
Denmark	32,100
Singapore	30,550
Germany	28,870
Austria	28,110
USA	28,020

Poorest Countries

(GNP per capita, in US$)

Mozambique	80
Somalia	100
Ethiopia	100
Eritrea	100
Congo, Dem. Rep.	130
Chad	160
Tanzania	170
Burundi	170
Malawi	180
Rwanda	190
Sierra Leone	200
Niger	200

Most Populous Countries

China	1,255,100,000
India	935,700,000
USA	263,300,000
Indonesia	197,600,000
Brazil	165,800,000
Russian Federation	147,000,000
Pakistan	140,500,000
Japan	125,100,000
Bangladesh	120,400,000
Nigeria	111,700,000

Least Populous Countries

Vatican City	1000
Tuvalu	9000
Nauru	10,000
Palau	16,200
San Marino	24,000
Liechtenstein	30,630
Monaco	31,000
St. Kitts & Nevis	44,000
Marshall Islands	52,000
Andorra	64,000
Dominica	71,000
Seychelles	73,000

Most Densely Populated Countries

Monaco	41,104 people per sq mile	(16,256 per sq km)
Singapore	16,400 people per sq mile	(6332 per sq km)
Malta	3213 people per sq mile	(1241 per sq km)
Vatican City	3084 people per sq mile	(1191 per sq km)
Bahrain	2724 people per sq mile	(1052 per sq km)
Maldives	2590 people per sq mile	(1000 per sq km)
Bangladesh	2525 people per sq mile	(975 per sq km)
Mauritius	1671 people per sq mile	(645 per sq km)
Barbados	1614 people per sq mile	(623 per sq km)
Taiwan	1598 people per sq mile	(617 per sq km)

Most Sparsely Populated Countries

Mongolia	4 people per sq mile	(2 per sq km)
Namibia	6 people per sq mile	(2 per sq km)
Australia	7 people per sq mile	(3 per sq km)
Mauritania	7 people per sq mile	(3 per sq km)
Suriname	7 people per sq mile	(3 per sq km)
Botswana	7 people per sq mile	(3 per sq km)
Iceland	7 people per sq mile	(3 per sq km)
Canada	8 people per sq mile	(3 per sq km)
Libya	8 people per sq mile	(3 per sq km)
Guyana	9 people per sq mile	(4 per sq km)

Most Widely Spoken Languages

1. Chinese (Mandarin)	6. Arabic
2. English	7. Bengali
3. Hindi	8. Portuguese
4. Spanish	9. Malay-Indonesian
5. Russian	10. French

Countries With The Most Land Borders

14: China *(Afghanistan, Bhutan, India, Kazakhstan, Kyrgyzstan, Laos, Mongolia, Myanmar, Nepal, North Korea, Pakistan, Russian Federation, Tajikistan, Vietnam)*

14: Russian Federation *(Azerbaijan, Belarus, China, Estonia, Finland, Georgia, Kazakhstan, Latvia, Lithuania, Mongolia, North Korea, Norway, Poland, Ukraine)*

10: Brazil *(Argentina, Bolivia, Colombia, French Guiana, Guyana, Paraguay, Peru, Suriname, Uruguay, Venezuela)*

9: Congo, Dem. Rep. *(Angola, Burundi, Central African Republic, Congo, Rwanda, Sudan, Tanzania, Uganda, Zambia)*

9: Germany *(Austria, Belgium, Czech Republic, Denmark, France, Luxembourg, Netherlands, Poland, Switzerland)*

9: Sudan *(Central African Republic, Chad, Congo, Dem. Rep., Egypt, Eritrea, Ethiopia, Kenya, Libya, Uganda)*

8: Austria *(Czech Republic, Germany, Hungary, Italy, Liechtenstein, Slovakia, Slovenia, Switzerland)*

8: France *(Andorra, Belgium, Germany, Italy, Luxembourg, Monaco, Spain, Switzerland)*

8: Tanzania *(Burundi, Congo, Dem. Rep., Kenya, Malawi, Mozambique, Rwanda, Uganda, Zambia)*

8: Turkey *(Armenia, Azerbaijan, Bulgaria, Georgia, Greece, Iran, Iraq, Syria)*

8: Zambia *(Angola, Botswana, Congo, Dem. Rep., Malawi, Mozambique, Namibia, Tanzania, Zimbabwe)*

Longest Rivers

Nile (NE Africa)	4160 miles	(6695 km)
Amazon (South America)	4049 miles	(6516 km)
Yangtze (China)	3915 miles	(6299 km)
Mississippi/Missouri (USA)	3710 miles	(5969 km)
Ob'-Irtysh (Russian Federation)	3461 miles	(5570 km)
Yellow River (China)	3395 miles	(5464 km)
Congo (Central Africa)	2900 miles	(4667 km)
Mekong (Southeast Asia)	2749 miles	(4425 km)
Lena (Russian Federation)	2734 miles	(4400 km)
Mackenzie (Canada)	2640 miles	(4250 km)
Yenisey (Russian Federation)	2541 miles	(4090km)

Highest Mountains

(HEIGHT ABOVE SEA LEVEL)

Everest	29,030 ft	(8848 m)
K2	28,253 ft	(8611 m)
Kanchenjunga I	28,210 ft	(8598 m)
Makalu I	27,767 ft	(8463 m)
Cho Oyu	26,907 ft	(8201 m)
Dhaulagiri I	26,796 ft	(8167 m)
Manaslu I	26,783 ft	(8163 m)
Nanga Parbat I	26,661 ft	(8126 m)
Annapurna I	26,547 ft	(8091 m)
Gasherbrum I	26,471 ft	(8068 m)

Largest Bodies of Inland Water

(WITH AREA AND DEPTH)

Caspian Sea	143,243 sq miles (371,000 sq km)	3215 ft (980 m)
Lake Superior	31,151 sq miles (83,270 sq km)	1289 ft (393 m)
Lake Victoria	26,828 sq miles (69,484 sq km)	328 ft (100 m)
Lake Huron	23,436 sq miles (60,700 sq km)	751 ft (229 m)
Lake Michigan	22,402 sq miles (58,020 sq km)	922 ft (281 m)
Lake Tanganyika	12,703 sq miles (32,900 sq km)	4700 ft (1435 m)
Great Bear Lake	12,274 sq miles (31,790 sq km)	1047 ft (319 m)
Lake Baikal	11,776 sq miles (30,500 sq km)	5712 ft (1741 m)
Great Slave Lake	10,981 sq miles (28,440 sq km)	459 ft (140 m)
Lake Erie	9,915 sq miles (25,680 sq km)	197 ft (60 m)

Deepest Ocean Features

Challenger Deep, Marianas Trench (Pacific)	36,201 ft	(11,034 m)
Vityaz III Depth, Tonga Trench (Pacific)	35,704 ft	(10,882 m)
Vityaz Depth, Kurile-Kamchatka Trench (Pacific)	34,588 ft	(10,542 m)
Cape Johnson Deep, Philippine Trench (Pacific)	34,441 ft	(10,497 m)
Kermadec Trench (Pacific)	32,964 ft	(10,047 m)
Ramapo Deep, Japan Trench (Pacific)	32,758 ft	(9984 m)
Milwaukee Deep, Puerto Rico Trench (Atlantic)	30,185 ft	(9200 m)
Argo Deep, Torres Trench (Pacific)	30,070 ft	(9165 m)
Meteor Depth, South Sandwich Trench (Atlantic)	30,000 ft	(9144 m)
Planet Deep, New Britain Trench (Pacific)	29,988 ft	(9140 m)

Greatest Waterfalls

(MEAN FLOW OF WATER)

Boyoma (Congo, Dem. Rep.)	600,400 cu. ft/sec	(17,000 cu.m/sec)
Khône (Laos/Cambodia)	410,000 cu. ft/sec	(11,600 cu.m/sec)
Niagara (USA/Canada)	195,000 cu. ft/sec	(5500 cu.m/sec)
Grande (Uruguay)	160,000 cu. ft/sec	(4500 cu.m/sec)
Paulo Afonso (Brazil)	100,000 cu. ft/sec	(2800 cu.m/sec)
Urubupunga (Brazil)	97,000 cu. ft/sec	(2750 cu.m/sec)
Iguaçu (Argentina/Brazil)	62,000 cu. ft/sec	(1700 cu.m/sec)
Maribondo (Brazil)	53,000 cu. ft/sec	(1500 cu.m/sec)
Victoria (Zimbabwe)	39,000 cu. ft/sec	(1100 cu.m/sec)
Kabalega (Uganda)	42,000 cu. ft/sec	(1200 cu.m/sec)
Churchill (Canada)	35,000 cu. ft/sec	(1000 cu.m/sec)
Cauvery (India)	33,000 cu. ft/sec	(900 cu.m/sec)

Highest Waterfalls

Angel (Venezuela)	3212 ft	(979 m)
Tugela (South Africa)	3110 ft	(948 m)
Utigard (Norway)	2625 ft	(800 m)
Mongefossen (Norway)	2539 ft	(774 m)
Mtarazi (Zimbabwe)	2500 ft	(762 m)
Yosemite (USA)	2425 ft	(739 m)
Ostre Mardola Foss (Norway)	2156 ft	(657 m)
Tyssestrengane (Norway)	2119 ft	(646 m)
***Cuquenan** (Venezuela)	2001 ft	(610 m)
Sutherland (New Zealand)	1903 ft	(580 m)
***Kjellfossen** (Norway)	1841 ft	(561 m)

** indicates that the total height is a single leap*

Largest Deserts

Sahara	3,450,000 sq miles	(9,065,000 sq km)
Gobi	500,000 sq miles	(1,295,000 sq km)
Ar Rub al Khali	289,600 sq miles	(750,000 sq km)
Great Victorian	249,800 sq miles	(647,000 sq km)
Sonoran	120,000 sq miles	(311,000 sq km)
Kalahari	120,000 sq miles	(310,800 sq km)
Kara Kum	115,800 sq miles	(300,000 sq km)
Takla Makan	100,400 sq miles	(260,000 sq km)
Namib	52,100 sq miles	(135,000 sq km)
Thar	33,670 sq miles	(130,000 sq km)

NB – Most of Antarctica is a polar desert, with only 50 mm of precipitation annually

Hottest Inhabited Places

Djibouti (Djibouti)	86° F	(30 °C)
Timbouctou (Mali)	84.7° F	(29.3 °C)
Tirunelveli (India)		
Tuticorin (India)		
Nellore (India)	84.5° F	(29.2 °C)
Santa Marta (Colombia)		
Aden (Yemen)	84° F	(28.9 °C)
Madurai (India)		
Niamey (Niger)		
Hodeida (Yemen)	83.8° F	(28.8 °C)
Ouagadougou (Burkina)		
Thanjavur (India)		
Tiruchchirappalli (India)		

Driest Inhabited Places

Aswân (Egypt)	0.02 in	(0.5 mm)
Luxor (Egypt)	0.03 in	(0.7 mm)
Arica (Chile)	0.04 in	(1.1 mm)
Ica (Peru)	0.1 in	(2.3 mm)
Antofagasta (Chile)	0.2 in	(4.9 mm)
El Minya (Egypt)	0.2 in	(5.1 mm)
Asyût (Egypt)	0.2 in	(5.2 mm)
Callao (Peru)	0.5 in	(12.0 mm)
Trujillo (Peru)	0.55 in	(14.0 mm)
El Faiyûm (Egypt)	0.8 in	(19.0 mm)

Wettest Inhabited Places

Buenaventura (Colombia)	265 in	(6743 mm)
Monrovia (Liberia)	202 in	(5131 mm)
Pago Pago (American Samoa)	196 in	(4990 mm)
Moulmein (Myanmar)	191 in	(4852 mm)
Lae (Papua New Guinea)	183 in	(4645 mm)
Baguio (Luzon Island, Philippines)	180 in	(4573 mm)
Sylhet (Bangladesh)	176 in	(4457 mm)
Padang (Sumatra, Indonesia)	166 in	(4225 mm)
Bogor (Java, Indonesia)	166 in	(4225 mm)
Conakry (Guinea)	171 in	(4341 mm)

The Time Zones

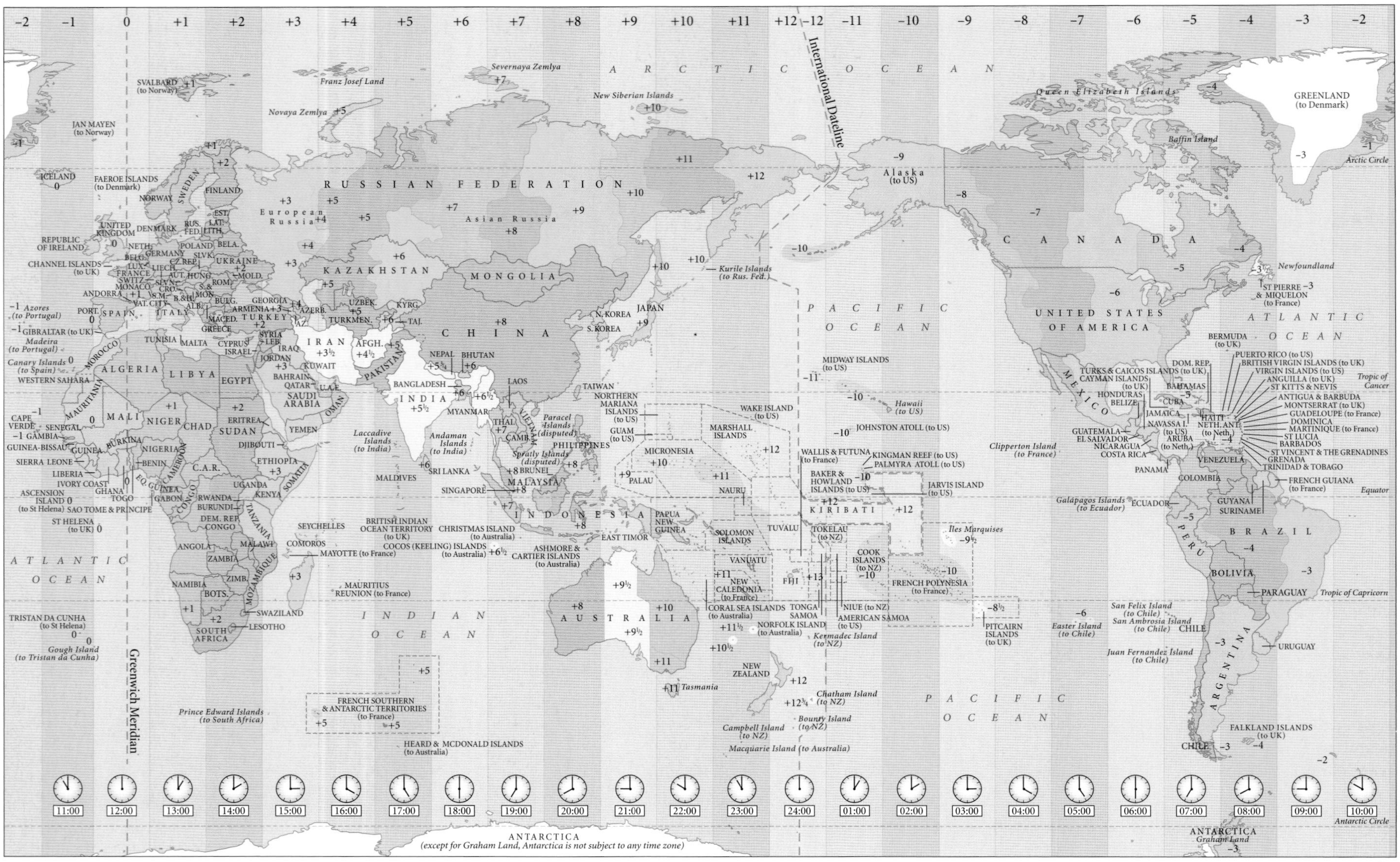

The numbers at the top of the map indicate the number of hours each time zone is ahead or behind Greenwich Mean Time (GMT). The clocks and 24-hour times given at the bottom of the map show the time in each time zone when it is 12:00 hours noon GMT.

Time Zones

The present system of international timekeeping divides the world into 24 time zones by means of 24 standard meridians of longitude, each 15° apart. Time is measured in each zone as so many hours ahead or behind the time at the Greenwich Meridian (GMT). Countries, or parts of countries, falling in the vicinity of each zone, adopt its time as shown on the map above. Therefore, using the map, when it is 12:00 noon GMT, it will be 2:00 pm in Zambia; similarly, when it is 4:30 pm. GMT, it will be 11:30 am in Peru.

Greenwich Mean Time (GMT)

Greenwich Mean Time (or Universal Time, as it is more correctly called) has been the internationally accepted basis for calculating solar time – measured in relation to the Earth's rotation around the Sun – since 1884. Greenwich Mean Time is specifically the solar time at the site of the former Royal Observatory in the London Borough of Greenwich, United Kingdom. The Greenwich Meridian is an imaginary line around the world that runs through the North and South poles. It corresponds to 0° of longitude, which lies on this site at Greenwich. Time is measured around the world in relation to the official time along the Meridian.

Standard Time

Standard time is the official time, designated by law, in any specific country or region. Standard time was initiated in 1884, after it became apparent that the practice of keeping various systems of local time was causing confusion – particularly in the USA and Canada, where several railroad routes passed through scores of areas which calculated local time by different rules. The standard time of a particular region is calculated in reference to the longitudinal time zone in which it falls. In practice, these zones do not always match their longitudinal position; in some places the area of the zone has been altered in shape for the convenience of inhabitants, as can be seen in the map. For example, while Greenland occupies three time zones, the majority of the territory uses a standard time of -3 hours GMT. Similarly China, which spans five time zones, is standardized at +8 hours GMT.

The International Dateline

The International Dateline is an imaginary line that extends from pole to pole, and roughly corresponds to a line of 180° longitude for much of its length. This line is the arbitrary marker between calendar days. By moving from east to west across the line, a traveller will need to set their calendar back one day, while those travelling in the opposite direction will need to add a day. This is to compensate for the use of standard time around the world, which is based on the time at noon along the Greenwich Meridian, approximately halfway around the world. Wide deviations from 180° longitude occur through the Bering Strait – to avoid dividing Siberia into two separate calendar days – and in the Pacific Ocean – to allow certain Pacific islands the same calendar day as New Zealand. Changes were made to the International Dateline in 1995 that made Millennium Island (formerly Caroline Island) in Kiribati the first land area to witness the beginning of the year 2000.

Daylight Saving Time

Also known as summer time, daylight saving is a system of advancing clocks in order to extend the waking day during periods of later daylight hours. This normally means advancing clocks by one hour in early spring, and reverting back to standard time in early autumn. The system of daylight saving is used throughout much of Europe, the USA, Australia, and many other countries worldwide, although there are no standardized dates for the changeover to summer time due to the differences in hours of daylight at different latitudes. Daylight saving was first introduced in certain countries during the First World War, to decrease the need for artificial light and heat – the system stayed in place after the war, as it proved practical. During the Second World War, some countries went so far as to keep their clocks an hour ahead of standard time continuously, and the UK temporarily introduced 'double summer time', which advanced clocks two hours ahead of standard time during the summer months.

COUNTRIES OF THE WORLD

THERE ARE CURRENTLY 193 independent countries in the world – more than at any previous time – and 59 dependencies. Antarctica is the only land area on Earth that is not officially part of, and does not belong to, any single country.

In 1950, the world comprised 82 countries. In the decades following, many more states came into being as they achieved independence from their former colonial rulers. Most recent additions were caused by the breakup of the former Soviet Union in 1991, and the former Yugoslavia in 1992, which swelled the ranks of independent states. In 2002 East Timor became the latest country to gain independence.

COUNTRY FACTFILE KEY

Formation Date of independence / date current borders were established
Population Total population / population density – based on total *land* area / percentage of urban-based population
Languages An asterisk (*) denotes the official language(s)
Calorie consumption Average number of calories consumed daily per person

AFGHANISTAN
Central Asia

Official name Islamic State of Afghanistan
Formation 1919 / 1919
Capital Kabul
Population 23.4 million / 93 people per sq mile (36 people per sq km) / 22%
Total area 251,770 sq miles (652,090 sq km)
Languages Persian*, Pashtu*, Dari, Uzbek, Turkmen
Religions Sunni Muslim 84%, Shi'a Muslim 15%, other 1%
Ethnic mix Pashto 38%, Tajik 25%, Hazara 19%, Uzbek 6%, other 12%
Government Islamic regime
Currency Afghani = 100 puls
Literacy rate 31%
Calorie consumption 1523 kilocalories

ALBANIA
Southeast Europe

Official name Republic of Albania
Formation 1912 / 1921
Capital Tiranë
Population 3.1 million/279 people per sq mile (108 people per sq km) / 42%
Total area 11,100 sq miles (28,748 sq km)
Languages Albanian*, Greek, Macedonian
Religions Muslim 70%, Greek Orthodox 20%, Roman Catholic 10%
Ethnic mix Albanian 86%, Greek 12%, other (including Macedonian) 2%
Government Multiparty republic
Currency Lek = 100 qindars
Literacy rate 84.7%
Calorie consumption 2,864 kilocalories

ALGERIA
North Africa

Official name People's Democratic Republic of Algeria
Formation 1962 / 1962
Capital Algiers
Population 30.8 million / 33 people per sq mile (13 people per sq km) / 60%
Total area 919,590 sq miles (2,381,740 sq km)
Languages Arabic, Tamazight, French
Religions Muslim 99%, Christian and Jewish 1%
Ethnic mix Arab 75%, Berber 24%, European 1%
Government Multiparty republic
Currency Algerian dinar = 100 centimes
Literacy rate 67.8%
Calorie consumption 2,944 kilocalories

ANDORRA
Southwest Europe

Official name Principality of Andorra
Formation 1278 / 1278
Capital Andorra la Vella
Population 66,800 / 370 people per sq mile (143 people per sq km) / 63%
Total area 181 sq miles (468 sq km)
Languages Catalan, Spanish, French, Portuguese
Religions Roman Catholic 94%, other 6%
Ethnic mix Spanish 46%, Andorrian 28%, other 18%, French 8%
Government Parliamentary democracy
Currency Euro (French franc and Spanish peseta until 2002)
Literacy rate 99%
Calorie consumption not available

ANGOLA
Southern Africa

Official name Republic of Angola
Formation 1975 / 1975
Capital Luanda
Population 13.5 million /28 people per sq mile (11 people per sq km) / 34%
Total area 481,351 sq miles (1,246,700 sq km)
Languages Portuguese*, Umbundu, Kimbundu, Kongo
Religions Roman Catholic 50%, traditional beliefs 28%, Protestant 20%, other 2%
Ethnic mix Ovimbundu 37%, other 25%, Kimbundu 25%, Bakongo 13%
Government Presidential regime
Currency Readjusted kwanza = 100 lwei
Literacy rate 40%
Calorie consumption 1,903 kilocalories

ANTIGUA & BARBUDA
West Indies

Official name Antigua and Barbuda
Formation 1981 /1981
Capital St. John's
Population 66,400 / 389 people per sq mile (150 people per sq km) / 37%
Total area 171 sq miles (442 sq km)
Languages English, English patois
Religions Anglican 45%, other Protestant 42%, Roman Catholic 10%, Rastafarian 1%, other 2%
Ethnic mix Black African 95%,other 5%
Government Parliamentary democracy
Currency Eastern Caribbean dollar = 100 cents
Literacy rate 95%
Calorie consumption 2,396 kilocalories

ARGENTINA
South America

Official name Republic of Argentina
Formation 1816 / 1816
Capital Buenos Aires
Population 37.5 million / 35 people per sq mile (14 people per sq km) / 90%
Total area 1,068,296 sq miles (2,766,890 sq km)
Languages Spanish*, Italian, English German, French, Indian languages
Religions Roman Catholic 90%, Jewish 2%, Protestant 2%,other 6%
Ethnic mix Indo European 85%,Mestizo 14%, Amerindian 1%
Government Presidential democracy
Currency Peso = 100 centavos
Literacy rate 96.8%
Calorie consumption 3,181 kilocalories

ARMENIA
Southwest Asia

Official name Republic of Armenia
Formation 1991 / 1991
Capital Yerevan
Population 3.8 million/330 people per sq mile (128 peopleper sq km) / 70%
Total area 11,506 sq miles (29,800 sq km)
Languages Armenian*, Azerbaijani, Russian, Kurdish
Religions The Armenian Apostolic Church 94%, other Christian and Muslim 6%
Ethnic mix Armenian 93%, Azeri 3%, Russian 2%,other 2%
Government Multiparty republic
Currency Dram = 100 louma
Literacy rate 98.4%
Calorie consumption 1,944 kilocalories

AUSTRALIA
Australasia & Oceania

Official name Commonwealth of Australia
Formation 1901 / 1901
Capital Canberra
Population 19.3 million / 7 people per sq mile (3 people per sq km) / 85%
Total area 2,967,893 sq miles (7,686,893 sq km)
Languages English*, Vietnamese, Greek, Arabic, Italian, Aboriginal languages
Religions Christian 64%, other 34%
Ethnic mix European 95%, Asian 4%, Aboriginal and other 1%
Government Parliamentary democracy
Currency Australian dollar = 100 cents
Literacy rate 99%
Calorie consumption 3,176 kilocalories

AUSTRIA
Central Europe

Official name Republic of Austria
Formation 1918 / 1919
Capital Vienna
Population 8.1 million / 250 people per sq mile (97 people per sq km) / 65%
Total area 32,378 sq miles (83,858 sq km)
Languages German*, Croatian, Slovene, Hungarian (Magyar)
Religions Roman Catholic 78%, non-religious 9%, Protestant 5%, other 8%
Ethnic mix German 93%, other (including Hungarian, Slovene, Croat) 7%
Government Parliamentary democracy
Currency Euro (Austrian schilling until 2002)
Literacy rate 99%
Calorie consumption 3,757 kilocalories

AZERBAIJAN
Southwest Asia

Official name Republic of Azerbaijan
Formation 1991 / 1991
Capital Baku
Population 8.1 million / 242 people per sq mile (94 people per sq km) / 57%
Total area 33,436 sq miles (86,600 sq km)
Languages Azerbaijani*, Russian, Armenian,other
Religions Shi'a ithna Muslims 61%, Sunni Muslims 26%, Armenian and Russian Orthodox 11%, other 2%
Ethnic mix Azeri 90%, Russian 3%, Daghestani 3%, Armenian 2%,other 2%
Government Multiparty republic
Currency Manat = 100 gopik
Literacy rate 96%
Calorie consumption 2,468 kilocalories

BAHAMAS
West Indies

Official name Commonwealth of the Bahamas
Formation 1973 / 1973
Capital Nassau
Population 308,000 / 57 people per sq mile (22 people per sq km) / 89%
Total area 5,382 sq miles (13,940 sq km)
Languages English*, English Creole, French Creole
Religions Baptist 32%, Anglican 20%, Roman Catholic 19%, Church of God 6%, Methodist 6%, other 17%
Ethnic mix Black African 85%, Other 15%
Government Parliamentary democracy
Currency Bahamian dollar = 100 cents
Literacy rate 95.7%
Calorie consumption 2,443 kilocalories

BAHRAIN
Southwest Asia

Official name State of Bahrain
Formation 1971 / 1971
Capital Manama
Population 652,000 /2,724 people per sq mile (1,052 people per sq km) / 97%
Total area 239 sq miles (620 sq km)
Languages Arabic*, English, Urdu
Religions Muslim (mainly Shi'a) 99%, other 1%
Ethnic mix Bahraini 70%, Iranian, Indian, Pakistani 24%, other Arab 4%, European 2%
Government Constitutional monarchy
Currency Bahraini dinar = 1,000 fils
Literacy rate 87.6%
Calorie consumption not available

BANGLADESH
South Asia

Official name People's Republic of Bangladesh
Formation 1971 / 1971
Capital Dhaka
Population 140.4 million /2,525 people per sq mile (975 people per sq km) / 25%
Total area 55,598 sq miles (144,000 sq km)
Languages Bengali*, Urdu, Chakma, Marma (Magh), Garo, Khasi, Santhali, Tripuri, Mro
Religions Muslim (mainly Sunni) 87%, Hindu 12%, other 1%
Ethnic mix Bengali 98%, other 2%
Government Parliamentary democracy
Currency Taka = 100 paisa
Literacy rate 41.4%
Calorie consumption 2,103 kilocalories

BARBADOS
West Indies

Official name Barbados
Formation 1966 / 1966
Capital Bridgetown
Population 268,000 /1,614 people per sq mile (623 people per sq km) / 50%
Total area 166 sq miles(430 sq km)
Languages English*, Bajan (Barbadian English)
Religions Anglican 40%, other 24%, non-religious 17%, Pentecostal 8%, Methodist 7%, Roman Catholic 4%
Ethnic mix Black African 90%, other 10%
Government Parliamentary democracy
Currency Barbados dollar = 100 cents
Literacy rate 98%
Calorie consumption 3,022 kilocalories

BELARUS
Eastern Europe

Official name Republic of Belarus
Formation 1991 / 1991
Capital Minsk
Population 10.1 million / 126 people per sq mile (49 people per sq km) / 71%
Total area 80,154 sq miles(207,600 sq km)
Languages Belorussian*, Russian
Religions Russian Orthodox 60%, other (including Muslim, Jews and Protestant) 32% Roman Catholic 8%
Ethnic mix Belorussian 78%, Russian 13%, Polish 4%, Ukrainian 3%, other 2%
Government Presidential regime
Currency Belorussian rouble = 100 kopeks
Literacy rate 99%
Calorie consumption 2,902 kilocalories

BELGIUM
Northwest Europe

Official name Kingdom of Belgium
Formation 1830 / 1919
Capital Brussels
Population 10.3 million / 874 people per sq mile (338 people per sq km) / 97%
Total area 11,780 sq miles 30,510 sq km)
Languages Dutch*, French*, German, Flemish
Religions Roman Catholic 88%, Muslim 2%, other 10%
Ethnic mix Fleming 58%, Walloon 33%, Italian 2%, Moroccan 1%, other 6%
Government Parliamentary democracy
Currency Euro = 100 cents
Literacy rate 99%
Calorie consumption 3,701 kilocalories

BELIZE
Central America

Official name Belize
Formation 1981 / 1981
Capital Belmopan
Population 200,000 /23 people per sq mile (9 people per sq km) / 54%
Total area 8,867 sq miles (22,966 sq km)
Languages English*, English Creole, Spanish, Mayan, Garifuna (Carib)
Religions Roman Catholic 62%, Anglican 12%, Mennonite 4%, Methodist 6%, other 16%
Ethnic mix Mestizo 44%, Creole 30%, Maya 11%, Garifuna 7%, Asian Indian 4%, other 4%
Government Parliamentary democracy
Currency Belizean dollar = 100 cents
Literacy rate 93.2%
Calorie consumption 2,888 kilocalories

BENIN
West Africa

Official name Republic of Benin
Formation 1960 / 1960
Capital Porto-Novo
Population 6.4 million / 147 people per sq mile (57 people per sq km) / 42%
Total area 43,483 sq miles (112,620 sq km)
Languages French*, Fon, Bariba, Yoruba, Adja, Houeda, Somba
Religions Indigenous beliefs 70%, Muslim 15%, Christian 15%
Ethnic mix Fon 47%, Baraba 10%, Adja 12%, other 31%
Government Presidential democracy
Currency CFA franc = 100 centimes
Literacy rate 40.3%
Calorie consumption 2,558 kilocalories

BHUTAN
Southeast Asia

Official name Kingdom of Bhutan
Formation 1656 / 1865
Capital Thimpu
Population 2.1 million /116 people per sq mile (45 people per sq km) / 7%
Total area 18,147 sq miles (47,000 sq km)
Languages Dzongkha*, Nepali, Assamese
Religions Mahayana Buddhist 70%, Hindu 24%, other 6%
Ethnic mix Bhote 50%, Nepalese 25%, other 25%
Government Monarchy
Currency Ngultrum = 100 chetrum
Literacy rate 47.3%
Calorie consumption not available

BOLIVIA
South America

Official name Republic of Bolivia
Formation 1825 / 1938
Capital Sucre (judicial)/La Paz (administrative)
Population 8.5 million / 20 people per sq mile (8 people per sq km) / 63%
Total area 424,162 sq miles (1,098,580 sq km)
Languages Spanish*, Aymara*, Quechua*
Religions Roman Catholic 93%, other 7%
Ethnic mix Quechua 37%, Aymara 32%, mixed 13%, European 10%,other 8%
Government Presidential democracy
Currency Boliviano = 100 centavos
Literacy rate 85.6%
Calorie consumption 2,218 kilocalories

BOSNIA & HERZEGOVINA
Southeast Europe

Official name Bosnia and Herzegovina
Formation 1992 / 1992
Capital Sarajevo
Population 4.1 million /208 people per sq mile (80 people per sq km) / 43%
Total area 19,741 sq miles (51,129 sq km)
Languages Serbo-Croat*
Religions Muslim (mainly Sunni) 40%, Serbian Orthodox 31%, Roman Catholic 15%, Protestant 4%, other 10%
Ethnic mix Bosniak 44%, Serb 31%, Croat 17%, other 8%
Government Multiparty republic
Currency Marka = 100 pfenniga
Literacy rate 93%
Calorie consumption 2,661 kilocalories

BOTSWANA
Southern Africa

Official name Republic of Botswana
Formation 1966 / 1966
Capital Gaborone
Population 1.6 million / 7 people per sq mile (3 people per sq km) / 50%
Total area 231,803 sq miles (600,370 sq km)
Languages English*, Tswana, Shona, San, Khoikhoi, Ndebele
Religions Traditional beliefs 50%, Christian (mainly Protestant) 30%, other (including Muslim) 20%
Ethnic mix Tswana 98% other 2%
Government Presidential democracy
Currency Pula = 100 thebe
Literacy rate 77.2%
Calorie consumption 2,255 kilocalories

BRAZIL
South America

Official name Federative Republic of Brazil
Formation 1822 / 1828
Capital Brasilia
Population 172.6 million / 53 people per sq mile (20 people per sq km) / 81%
Total area 3,286,470 sq miles (8,511,965 sq km)
Languages Portuguese*, German, Italian, Spanish, Polish, Japanese
Religions Roman Catholic 74%, Protestant 15%, Atheist 7%, other 4%
Ethnic mix Black 53%, Mixed 40%, White 6%, other 1%
Government Presidential democracy
Currency Real = 100 centavos
Literacy rate 85.2%
Calorie consumption 2,985 kilocalories

BRUNEI
Southeast Asia

Official name Sultanate of Brunei
Formation 1984 / 1984
Capital Bandar Seri Begawan
Population 335,000 / 150 people per sq mile (58 people per sq km) / 72%
Total area 2,228 sq miles (5,770 sq km)
Languages Malay*, English, Chinese
Religions Muslim 66%, Buddhist 14%, Christian 10%, other 10%
Ethnic mix Malay 67%, Chinese 16%, Indigenous 6%, other 11%
Government Monarchy
Currency Brunei dollar = 100 cents
Literacy rate 91.5%
Calorie consumption 2,832 kilocalories

BULGARIA
Southeast Europe

Official name Republic of Bulgaria
Formation 1908 / 1947
Capital Sofia
Population 7.9 million / 184 people per sq mile (71 people per sq km) / 70%
Total area 42,822 sq miles (110,910 sq km)
Languages Bulgarian*, Turkish, Macedonian, Romany
Religions Bulgarian Orthodox 84%, Muslim 13%, Jewish 1%, Roman Catholic 1%, other 1%
Ethnic mix Bulgarian 85%, Turkish 9%, Macedonian 3%, Romany 3%
Government Multiparty republic
Currency Lev = 100 stoninki
Literacy rate 98.4%
Calorie consumption 2,467 kilocalories

BURKINA
West Africa

Official name Burkina Faso
Formation 1960 / 1960
Capital Ouagadougou
Population 11.9 million / 112 people per sq mile (43 people per sq km) / 19%
Total area 105,869 sq miles (274,200 sq km)
Languages French*, Mossi, Fulani, Tuareg, Dyula, Songhai
Religions Traditional beliefs 55%, Muslim 35%, Roman Catholic 9%, other Christian 1%
Ethnic mix Mossi 50%, other 50%
Government Multiparty republic
Currency CFA franc = 100 centimes
Literacy rate 23.9%
Calorie consumption 2,293 kilocalories

BURUNDI
Central Africa

Official name Republic of Burundi
Formation 1962 / 1962
Capital Bujumbura
Population 6.5 million / 605 people per sq mile (234 people per sq km) / 9%
Total area 10,745 sq miles(27,830 sq km)
Languages Kirundi*, French*, Kiswahili
Religions Christian 60%, Traditional beliefs 39%, Muslim 1%
Ethnic mix Hutu 85%, Tutsi 14%, Twa 1%
Government Transitional regime
Currency Burundi franc = 100 centimes
Literacy rate 48.3%
Calorie consumption 1,605 kilocalories

CAMBODIA
Southeast Asia

Official name Kingdom of Cambodia
Formation 1953 / 1953
Capital Phnom Penh
Population 13.4 million / 192 people per sq mile (74 people per sq km) / 16%
Total area 69,900 sq miles (181,040 sq km)
Languages Khmer*, French, Chinese, Vietnamese, Cham
Religions Buddhist 93%, Muslim 6%, Christian 1%
Ethnic mix Khmer 90%,Vietnamese 4%, Chinese 1%, other 5%
Government Constitutional monarchy
Currency Riel = 100 sen
Literacy rate 37.4%
Calorie consumption 2,070 kilocalories

CAMEROON
Central Africa

Official name Republic of Cameroon
Formation 1960 / 1961
Capital Yaoundé
Population 15.2 million / 83 people per sq mile (32 people per sq km) / 49%
Total area 183,567 sq miles (475,440 sq km)
Languages English*, French*, Bamileke, Fang, Fulani
Religions Traditional beliefs 25%, Christian 53%, Muslim 22%
Ethnic mix Cameroon highlanders 31%, Bantu 19%, Kirdi 11%, other 39%
Government Presidential democracy
Currency CFA franc = 100 centimes
Literacy rate 75.9%
Calorie consumption 2,255 kilocalories

CANADA
North America

Official name Canada
Formation 1867 / 1949
Capital Ottawa
Population 31 million /8 people per sq mile (3 people per sq km) / 77%
Total area 3,851,788 sq miles (9,976,140 sq km)
Languages English*, French*, Chinese, Italian, German, Ukranian, Inuktitut
Religions Roman Catholic 47%, Protestant 41%, non-religious 12%
Ethnic mix British origin 44%, French origin 25%, Other European 20%, other 11%
Government Parlimentary democracy
Currency Canadian dollar = 100 cents
Literacy rate 99%
Calorie consumption 3,174 kilocalories

CAPE VERDE
Atlantic Ocean

Official name Republic of Cape Verde
Formation 1975 / 1975
Capital Praia
Population 437,000/ 281 people per sq mile (108 people per sq km) / 62%
Total area 1,557 sq miles (4,033 sq km)
Languages Portuguese*, Portuguese Creole,
Religions Roman Catholic 97%, Protestant (Church of Nazarene) 1%, other 2%
Ethnic mix Mestico 60%, African 30%, other 10%
Government Multiparty republic
Currency Cape Verde escudo = 100 centavos
Literacy rate 74.2%
Calorie consumption 3,278 kilocalories

CENTRAL AFRICAN REPUBLIC
Central Africa

Official name Central African Republic
Formation 1960 / 1960
Capital Bangui
Population 3.8 million / 16 people per sq mile (6 people per sq km) / 41%
Total area 240,534 sq miles (622,984 sq km)
Languages French*, Sango, Banda, Gbaya
Religions Traditional beliefs 60%, Christian 35%, Muslim 5%
Ethnic mix Baya 34%, Banda 27%, Mandjia 21%, Sara 10%, other 8%
Government Multiparty republic
Currency CFA franc = 100 centimes
Literacy rate 46.7%
Calorie consumption 1,946 kilocalories

CHAD
Central Africa

Official name Republic of Chad
Formation 1960 / 1960
Capital N'Djamena
Population 8.1 million / 16 people per sq mile (6 people per sq km) / 24%
Total area 495,752 sq miles (1,284,000 sq km)
Languages French, Arabic, Sara, Maba
Religions Muslim 50%, Traditional beliefs 43%, Christian 7%
Ethnic mix Nomads (Tuareg and Toubou) 38%, Sara 30, Arab 15%, Other 17%
Government Presidential democracy
Currency CFA franc = 100 centimes
Literacy rate 42.6%
Calorie consumption 2,046 kilocalories

CHILE
South America

Official name Republic of Chile
Formation 1818 / 1883
Capital Santiago
Population 15.4 million / 53 people per sq mile (20 people per sq km) / 86%
Total area 292,258 sq miles (756,950 sq km)
Languages Spanish*, Amerindian languages
Religions Roman Catholic 80%, other and non-religious 20%
Ethnic mix Mixed and European 90%, Amerindian 10%
Government Multiparty republic
Currency Chilean peso = 100 centavos
Literacy rate 95.7%
Calorie consumption 2,882 kilocalories

CHINA
East Asia

Official name People's Republic of China
Formation 960 / 1999
Capital Beijing
Population 1.29 billion / 348 people per sq mile (134 people per sq km) / 32%
Total area 3,705,386 sq miles (9,596,960 sq km)
Languages Mandarin*, Wu, Cantonese, Hsiang, Min, Hakka, Kan
Religions Non-religious 59%, Traditional beliefs 20%, other 21%
Ethnic mix Han 93%, other 7%
Government One-party state
Currency Yuan (Renminbi) = 10 jiao
Literacy rate 84.2%
Calorie consumption 3,029 kilocalories

COLOMBIA
South America

Official name Republic of Columbia
Formation 1819 / 1903
Capital Bogotá
Population 42.8 million /97 people per sq mile (38 people per sq km) / 74%
Total area 439,733 sq miles (1,138,910 sq km)
Languages Spanish*, Amerindian languages, English Creole
Religions Roman Catholic 95%, other 5%
Ethnic mix Mestizo 58%, White 20%, mixed 14%, other 8%
Government Presidential democracy
Currency Colombian peso = 100 centavos
Literacy rate 91.8%
Calorie consumption 2,597 kilocalories

COMOROS
Indian Ocean

Official name Federal Islamic Republic of the Comoros
Formation 1975 / 1975
Capital Moroni
Population 727,000 / 868 people per sq mile (335 people per sq km) / 33%
Total area 838 sq miles (2,170 sq km)
Languages Arabic*, French*, Comoran
Religions Muslim (mainly Sunni) 98%, Roman Catholic 1%, other 1%
Ethnic mix Comorian 97%, other 3%
Government Presidential democracy
Currency Comoros franc = 100 centimes
Literacy rate 59.6%
Calorie consumption 1,753 kilocalories

CONGO
Central Africa

Official name Republic of the Congo
Formation 1960 / 1960
Capital Brazzaville
Population 3.1 million / 23 people per sq mile (9 people per sq km) / 63%
Total area 132,046 sq miles (342,000 sq km)
Languages French*, Kongo, Teke, Lingala
Religions Traditional beliefs 50%, Roman Catholic 25%, Protestant 23%, Muslim 2%
Ethnic mix Bakongo 48%, Sangha 20%, Teke 17%, Mbochi 12%, other 3%
Government Presidential democracy
Currency CFA franc = 100 centimes
Literacy rate 80.7%
Calorie consumption 2,223 kilocalories

CONGO, DEM. REP.
Central Africa

Official name Democratic Republic of the Congo
Formation 1960 / 1960
Capital Kinshasa
Population 52.5 million / 58 people per sq mile (22 people per sq km) / 30%
Total area 905,563 sq miles (2,345,410 sq km)
Languages French*, Kiswahili, Tshiluba, Kikongo, Lingala
Religions Traditional beliefs 50%, Roman Catholic 37%, Protestant 13%
Ethnic mix Bantu and Hamitic 45%, other 55%
Government Military-based regime
Currency franc = 100 centimes
Literacy rate 61.4%
Calorie consumption 1,514 kilocalories

COSTA RICA
Central America

Official name Republic of Costa Rica
Formation 1838 / 1838
Capital San José
Population 4.1 million / 208 people per sq mile (80 people per sq km) 52%
Total area 19,730 sq miles (51,100 sq km)
Languages Spanish*, English Creole, Bribri, Cabecar
Religions Roman Catholic 76%, other (including Protestant) 24%
Ethnic mix Mesitzo and European 96%, Black 2%, Indian 1%, Chinese 1%
Government Presidential democracy
Currency Costa Rican colón = 100 centimes
Literacy rate 95.6%
Calorie consumption 2,783 kilocalories

CROATIA
Southeast Europe

Official name Republic of Croatia
Formation 1991 / 1991
Capital Zagreb
Population 4.7 million / 215 people per sq mile (83 peopleper sq km) / 58%
Total area 21,831 sq miles (56,542 sq km)
Languages Croatian*, Serbian, Hungarian (Magyar), Slovenian
Religions Roman Catholic 76%, Orthodox 11%, Muslim 1%, other 12%
Ethnic mix Croat 78%, Serb 12%, Yugoslav 2%, other 8%
Government Parliamentary democracy
Currency Kuna = 100 lipa
Literacy rate 98.3%
Calorie consumption 2,843 kilocalories

CUBA
West Indies

Official name Republic of Cuba
Formation 1902 / 1902
Capital Havana
Population 11.2 million / 262 people per sq mile (101 people per sq km) / 75%
Total area 42,803 sq miles (110,860 sq km)
Languages Spanish*, English, French, Chinese
Religions Non-religious 49%, Roman Catholic 40%, Atheist 6%, Protestant 1%, other 4%
Ethnic mix White 66%, European-African 22%, Black 12%
Government One-party state
Currency Cuban peso = 100 centavos
Literacy rate 96.7%
Calorie consumption 2,564 kilocalories

CYPRUS
Southeast Europe

Official name Republic of Cyprus
Formation 1960 / 1960
Capital Nicosia
Population 790,000 / 221 people per sq mile (85 people per sq km) / 57%
Total area 3,571 sq miles (9,250 sq km)
Languages Greek*, Turkish, English
Religions Greek Orthodox 73%, Muslim 23%, other 4%
Ethnic mix Greek 77%, Turkish 18%, other (mainly British) 5%
Government Presidential democracy
Currency Cyprus pound/Turkish lira
Literacy rate 97.1%
Calorie consumption 3,259 kilocalories

CZECH REPUBLIC
Central Europe

Official name Czech Republic
Formation 1993 / 1993
Capital Prague
Population 10.3 million / 338 people per sq mile (131 people per sq km) / 75%
Total area 30,450 sq miles (78,866 sq km)
Languages Czech*, Slovak, Romany, Hungarian (Magyar)
Religions Roman Catholic 39%, Atheist 38%, Protestant 3%, Hussites 2%, other 18%
Ethnic mix Czech 81%, Moravian 13%, Slovak 6%
Government Parliamentary democracy
Currency Czech koruna = 100 halura
Literacy rate 99%
Calorie consumption 3,104 kilocalories

DENMARK
Northern Europe

Official name Kingdom of Denmark
Formation AD 950 / 1944
Capital Copenhagen (Koebenhavn)
Population 5.3 million / 319 people per sq mile (123 people per sq km) / 85%
Total area 16,639 sq miles (43,094 sq km)
Languages Danish*, Faeroese, Inuit
Religions Evangelical Lutheran 89%, Roman Catholic 1%, other 10%
Ethnic mix Danish 96%, Faeroe and Inuit 1%, other (including Scandinavian) 3%
Government Parliamentary democracy
Currency Danish krone = 100 ore
Literacy rate 99%
Calorie consumption 3,396 kilocalories

DJIBOUTI
East Africa

Official name Republic of Djibouti
Formation 1977 / 1977
Capital Djibouti
Population 644,000 / 76 people per sq mile (29 people per sq km) / 83%
Total area 8,490 sq miles (22,000 sq km)
Languages French*, Arabic*, Somali, Afar
Religions Muslim 94%, Christian 6%
Ethnic mix Issa 60%, Afar 35%, other 5%
Government Presidential democracy
Currency Djibouti franc = 100 centimes
Literacy rate 64.6%
Calorie consumption 2,050 kilocalories

DOMINICA
West Indies

Official name Commonwealth of Dominica
Formation 1978 / 1978
Capital Roseau
Population 73,000 / 251 people per sq mile (97 people per sq km) / 71%
Total area 291 sq miles (754 sq km)
Languages English*, French Creole, Carib, Cocoy
Religions Roman Catholic 77%, Protestant 15%, other 8%
Ethnic mix Black 91%, Mixed 6%, Indian 2%, other 1%
Government Parliamentary democracy
Currency East Caribbean dollar = 100 cents
Literacy rate 94%
Calorie consumption 2,994 kilocalories

DOMINICAN REPUBLIC
West Indies

Official name Dominican Republic
Formation 1865 / 1865
Capital Santo Domingo
Population 8.5 million / 452 people per sq mile (174 people per sq km) / 65%
Total area 18,815 sq miles (48,730 sq km)
Languages Spanish*, French Creole
Religions Roman Catholic 92%, other and non-religious 8%
Ethnic mix Mixed 75%, White 15%, Black 10%
Government Presidential democracy
Currency Dominican Republic peso = 100 centavos
Literacy rate 83.6%
Calorie consumption 2,325 kilocalories

EAST TIMOR
Southeast Asia

Official name East Timor
Formation 2002 / 2002
Capital Dili
Population 737,811 /196 people per sq mile (49 per sq km) / 8%
Total area 3,756 sq miles (14, 874 sq km)
Languages Tetum (Portuguese/ Austronesian), Bahasa Indonesia, Portuguese
Religions Roman Catholic 93%, other 7%
Ethnic mix Various Papuan groups 78%, Indonesian 20%, Chinese 2%
Government Multiparty republic
Currency US dollar
Literacy rate 41 %
Calorie consumption not available

ECUADOR
South America

Official name Republic of Ecuador
Formation 1830 / 1941
Capital Quito
Population 12.9 million / 118 people per sq mile (45 people per sq km) / 65%
Total area 109,483 sq miles (283,560 sq km)
Languages Spanish*, Quechua*, other Amerindian languages
Religions Roman Catholic 93%, Protestant, Jewish and other 7%
Ethnic mix Mestizo (Euro-Indian) 55%, Indian 25%, Black 10%, White 10%
Government Presidential democracy
Currency US dollar
Literacy rate 91.3%
Calorie consumption 2,693 kilocalories

EGYPT
North Africa

Official name Arab Republic of Egypt
Formation 1936 / 1982
Capital Cairo
Population 69.1 million / 179 people per sq mile (69 people per sq km) / 45%
Total area 386,660 sq miles (1,001,450 sq km)
Languages Arabic*, French, English, Berber
Religions Muslim (mainly Sunni) 94%, Coptic Christian and other 6%
Ethnic mix Eastern Hamitic 90%, other (Nubian, Armenian,Greek) 10%
Government Presidential democracy
Currency Egyptian pound = 100 piastres
Literacy rate 55.4%
Calorie consumption 3,346 kilocalories

EL SALVADOR
Central America

Official name Republic of El Salvador
Formation 1841 / 1841
Capital San Salvador
Population 6.4 million / 788 people per sq mile (304 people per sq km) / 47%
Total area 8,124 sq miles (21,040 sq km)
Languages Spanish*, Nahua
Religions Roman Catholic 80%, Evangelical 18%, other 2%
Ethnic mix Mestizo (Euro-Indian) 94%, Indian 5%, White 1%
Government Presidential democracy
Currency Salvadorean colón = 100 centavos
Literacy rate 78.8%
Calorie consumption 2,503 kilocalories

EQUATORIAL GUINEA
Central Africa

Official name Republic of Equatorial Guinea
Formation 1968 / 1968
Capital Malabo
Population 470,000 / 43 people per sq mile (17 people per sq km) / 48%
Total area 10,830 sq miles (28,051 sq km)
Languages Spanish*, Fang, Bubi
Religions Roman Catholic 90%, other 10%
Ethnic mix Fang 85%, Bubi 4%, other 11%
Government Presidential regime
Currency CFA franc = 100 centimes
Literacy rate 83.2%
Calorie consumption not available

ERITREA
East Africa

Official name State of Eritrea
Formation 1993 / 2002
Capital Asmara
Population 3.8 million / 81 people per sq mile (31 people per sq km) / 19%
Total area 46,842 sq miles (121,320 sq km)
Languages Tigrinya*, Arabic*, English, Tigre, Afar, Bilen, Kunama, Nara, Saho, Hadareb
Religions Coptic Christian 45%, Muslim 45%, other 10%
Ethnic mix Tigray and Kunama 40%, Tigray 50%, Afar 4%, Saho 3%, other 4%
Government Transitional regime
Currency Nafka = 100 cents
Literacy rate 55.7%
Calorie consumption 1,665 kilocalories

Estonia
Northeast Europe

Official name Republic of Estonia
Formation 1991 / 1991
Capital Tallinn
Population 1.4 million / 80 people per sq mile (31 people per sq km) / 69%
Total area 17,462 sq miles (45,226 sq km)
Languages Estonian*, Russian
Religions Evangelical Lutheran 56%, Russian Orthodox 25%, Other 19%
Ethnic mix Estonian 62%, Russian 30%, other 8%
Government Parliamentary democracy
Currency Kroon = 100 cents
Literacy rate 99%
Calorie consumption 3 376 kilocalories

Ethiopia
East Africa

Official name Federal Democratic Republic of Ethiopia
Formation 1896 / 2002
Capital Addis Ababa
Population 64.5 million / 148 people per sq mile (57 people per sq km) / 18%
Total area 435,184 sq miles (1,127,127 sq km)
Languages Amharic*, Tigrinya, Galla
Religions Muslim 40%, Ethopian Orthodox 40%, traditional beliefs 15%, other 5%,
Ethnic mix Oromo 40%, Amhara 25%, Sidamo 9%, Somali 6%, Berta 6%, other 14%
Government Multiparty republic
Currency Ethopian birr = 100 cents
Literacy rate 38.4%
Calorie consumption 2,023 kilocalories

Fiji
Australasia & Oceania

Official name Republic of the Fiji Islands
Formation 1970 / 1970
Capital Suva
Population 823,000 / 117 people per sq mile (45 people per sq km) / 49%
Total area 7,054 sq miles (18,270 sq km)
Languages Fijian*, English*, Hindi, Urdu, Tamil, Telegu
Religions Hindu 38%, Methodist 37%, Roman Catholic 9%, Muslim 8%, other 8%
Ethnic mix Melanesian 48%, Indian 46%, other 6%
Government Multiparty republic
Currency Fiji dollar = 100 cents
Literacy rate 92.9%
Calorie consumption 2,861 kilocalories

Finland
Northern Europe

Official name Republic of Finland
Formation 1917 /1947
Capital Helsinki
Population 5.2 million / 40 people per sq mile (15 people per sq km) / 67%
Total area 130,127 sq miles (337,030 sq km)
Languages Finnish*, Swedish, Sami
Religions Evangelical Lutheran 89%, Finnish Orthodox 1%, Roman Catholic 1%, other 9%
Ethnic mix Finnish 93%, other (including Sami) 7%
Government Paliamentary democracy
Currency Euro (Markka until 2002)
Literacy rate 99%
Calorie consumption 3,227 kilocalories

France
Western Europe

Official name French Republic
Formation 987 / 1919
Capital Paris
Population 59.5 million / 282 people per sq mile (109 people per sq km) / 76%
Total area 211,208 sq miles (547,030 sq km)
Languages French*, Provenial, German, Breton, Catalan, Basque
Religions Roman Catholic 88%, Muslim 8%, Protestant 2%, other 2%
Ethnic mix French 90%, North African 6%, German 2%, other 2%
Government Multiparty republic
Currency Euro = 100 cents
Literacy rate 99%
Calorie consumption 3,591 kilocalories

Gabon
Central Africa

Official name Gabonese Republic
Formation 1960 / 1960
Capital Libreville
Population 1.3 million / 13 people per sq mile (5 people per sq km) / 81%
Total area 103,346 sq miles (267,667 sq km)
Languages French*, Fang, Punu, Sira, Nzebi, Mpongwe
Religions Christian 55%, Traditional beliefs 40%, Muslim 1%, other 4%
Ethnic mix Fang 35%, other Bantu 29%, Eshira 25%, other 11%
Government Multiparty republic
Currency CFA franc = 100 centimes
Literacy rate 70.8%
Calorie consumption 2,564 kilocalories

Gambia
West Africa

Official name Republic of The Gambia
Formation 1965 / 1965
Capital Banjul
Population 1.34 million / 307 people per sq mile (119 people per sq km) / 33%
Total area 4,363 sq miles (11,300 sq km)
Languages English*, Mandinka, Fulani, Wolof, Jola, Soninke
Religions Sunni Muslim 90%, Christian 9%, Indigenous beliefs 1%
Ethnic mix Mandinka 42%, Fulani 18%, Wolof 16%, Jola 10%, Serahuli 9%, other 5%
Government Multiparty republic
Currency Dalasi = 100 butut
Literacy rate 36.6%
Calorie consumption 2,474 kilocalories

Georgia
Southwest Asia

Official name Georgia
Formation 1991 / 1991
Capital Tbilisi
Population 5.2 million /193 people per sq mile (75 people per sq km) /61%
Total area 26,911 sq miles (69,700 sq km)
Languages Georgian, Russian
Religions Georgian Orthodox 65%, Muslim 11%, Russian Orthodox 10%, Amenian Orthodox 8%, Unknown 6%
Ethnic mix Georgian 70%, Armenian 8%, Russian 6%, Azeri 6%, Ossetian 3%, other 7%
Government Presidential democracy
Currency Lari = 100 tetri
Literacy rate 99%
Calorie consumption 2,412 kilocalories

Germany
Northern Europe

Official name Federal Republic of Germany
Formation 1871 / 1990
Capital Berlin
Population 82 million / 595 people per sq mile (230 people per sq km) / 88%
Total area 137,846 sq miles (357,021 sq km)
Languages German*, Turkish
Religions Protestant 34%, Roman Catholic 33%, Muslim 3%, other 30%
Ethnic mix German 92%, other 8%
Government Parliamentary democracy
Currency Euro = 100 cents
Literacy rate 99%
Calorie consumption 3,451 kilocalories

Ghana
West Africa

Official name Republic of Ghana
Formation 1957 / 1957
Capital Accra
Population 19.7 million / 214 people per sq mile (83 people per sq km) / 38%
Total area 92,100 sq miles (238,540 sq km)
Languages English*, Twi, Fanti, Ewe, Ga, Adangbe, Gurma, Dagomba
Religions Christian 43%, Traditional beliefs 38%, Muslim 11%, other 8%
Ethnic mix Ashanti and Fanti 52%, Moshi-Dagomba 16%, Ewe 12%, Ga 8%, other 12%
Government Presidential democracy
Currency Cedi = 100 pesewas
Literacy rate 71.5%
Calorie consumption 2,699 kilocalories

Greece
Southeast Europe

Official name Hellenic Republic
Formation 1829 / 1947
Capital Athens
Population 10.6 million / 208 people per sq mile (80 people per sq km) / 60%
Total area 50,942 sq miles (131,940 sq km)
Languages Greek*, Turkish, Macedonian, Albanian
Religions Greek Orthodox 98%, Muslim 1%, other 1%
Ethnic mix Greek 98%, other 2%
Government Presidential democracy
Currency Euro = 100 cents
Literacy rate 97.3%
Calorie consumption 3,705 kilocalories

Grenada
West Indies

Official name Grenada
Formation 1974 / 1974
Capital St. George's
Population 98,000 / 747 people per sq mile (288 people per sq km) / 38%
Total area 131 sq miles (340 sq km)
Languages English*, English Creole
Religions Roman Catholic 68%, Anglican 17%, other 15%
Ethnic mix Black 82%, Mulatto 13%, Indian 3%, other 2%
Government Parliamentary democracy
Currency East Caribbean dollar = 100 cents
Literacy rate 96%
Calorie consumption 2,764 kilocalorie

Guatemala
Central America

Official name Republic of Guatemala
Formation 1838 / 1838
Capital Guatemala City
Population 11.7 million / 278 people per sq mile (107 people per sq km) / 40%
Total area 42,042 sq miles (108,890 sq km)
Languages Spanish*, Quiché, Mam, others
Religions Roman Catholic 65%, Protestant 33%, other 2%
Ethnic mix Amerindian 60%, Mestizo (Euro-Indian) 30%, other 10%
Government Presidential democracy
Currency Quetzal = 100 centavos
Literacy rate 68.8%
Calorie consumption 2,171 kilocalories

Guinea
West Africa

Official name Republic of Guinea
Formation 1958 / 1958
Capital Conakry
Population 8.3 million / 87 people per sq mile (34 people per sq km) / 33%
Total area 94,925 sq miles (245,857 sq km)
Languages French, Fulani, Malinke, Soussou
Religions Muslim 65%, Traditional beliefs 33%, Christian 2%,
Ethnic mix Fila (Fulani) 30%, Malinke 30%, Soussou 15%, Kissi 10%, other tribes 15%
Government Multiparty republic
Currency Guinea franc = 100 centimes
Literacy rate 41.1%
Calorie consumption 2,353 kilocalories

Guinea-Bissau
West Africa

Official name Republic of Guinea-Bissau
Formation 1974 / 1974
Capital Bissau
Population 1.2 million / 86 people per sq mile (33 people per sq km) / 24%
Total area 13,946 sq miles (36,120 sq km)
Languages Portuguese Creole, Fulani Balante, Malinke, Portuguese*
Religions Indigenous beliefs 52%, Muslim 40%, Christian 8%
Ethnic mix Balante 25%, Madinka 12%, Fila 20%, Mandyako 11%, other 32%
Government Presidential democracy
Currency CFA france = 100 centimes
Literacy rate 38.8%
Calorie consumption 2,333 kilocalories

Guyana
South America

Official name Cooperative Republic of Guyana
Formation 1966 / 1966
Capital Georgetown
Population 763,000 / 9 people per sq mile (4 people per sq km) / 38%
Total area 83,000 sq miles (214,970 sq km)
Languages English*, English Creole, Hindi, Tamil, Amerindian languages
Religions Christian 57%, Hindu 33%, Muslim 9%, other 1%
Ethnic mix East Indian 52%, Black African 38%, other 10%
Government Presidential democracy
Currency Guyana dollar = 100 cents
Literacy rate 98.5%
Calorie consumption 2,582 kilocalories

Haiti
West Indies

Official name Republic of Haiti
Formation 1804/ 1844
Capital Port-au-Prince
Population 8.3 million / 775 people per sq mile (299 people per sq km) / 36%
Total area 10,714 sq miles (27,750 sq km)
Languages French*, French Creole*, English
Religions Roman Catholic 80%, Protestant 16%, non-religious 1%, other 3%
Ethnic mix Black African 95%, Mulatto and European 5%
Government Multiparty republic
Currency Gourde = 100 centimes
Literacy rate 49.8%
Calorie consumption 2,056 kilocalories

Honduras
Central America

Official name Republic of Honduras
Formation 1838 / 1838
Capital Tegucigalpa
Population 6.6 million / 153 people per sq mile (59 people per sq km) / 53%
Total area 43,278 sq miles (112,090 sq km)
Languages Spanish*, Black Carib, English Creole
Religions Roman Catholic 97%, Protestant minority 3%
Ethnic mix Mestizo (Euro-Indian) 90%, Black African 5%, Amerindian 4%,White 1%
Government Presidential democracy
Currency Lempira = 100 centavos
Literacy rate 74.6%
Calorie consumption 2,395 kilocalories

Hungary
Central Europe

Official name Republic of Hungary
Formation 1918 / 1947
Capital Budapest
Population 9.9 million / 276 people per sq mile (106 people per sq km) / 64%
Total area 35,919 sq miles (93,030 sq km)
Languages Hungarian (Magyar)*, German, Slovak
Religions Roman Catholic 64%, Calvinist 20%, non-religious 7%, Lutheran 4%, other 5%
Ethnic mix Hungarian (Magyar) 90%, German 2%, Romany 1%, Slovak 1%, other 6%
Government Parliamentary democracy
Currency Forint = 100 filler
Literacy rate 99%
Calorie consumption 3,458 kilocalories

Iceland
Northwest Europe

Official name Republic of Iceland
Formation 1944 / 1944
Capital Reykjavik
Population 281,000 / 7 people per sq mile (3 people per sq km) / 93%
Total area 39,768 sq miles (103,000 sq km)
Languages Icelandic*, English, other
Religions Evangelical Lutheran 93%, non-religious 6%, other Christian 1%
Ethnic mix Icelandic (Norwegian-Celtic descent) 94%, Danish 1%, other 5%
Government Parliamentary democracy
Currency Icelandic króna = 100 aurar
Literacy rate 99%
Calorie consumption 3,342 kilocalories

India
South Asia

Official name Republic of India
Formation 1947 / 1947
Capital New Delhi
Population 1.03 billion / 790 people per sq mile (305 people per sq km) / 28%
Total area 1,269,339 sq miles (3,287,590 sq km)
Languages Hindi*, English*, Urdu, Bengali, Marathi, Telugu, Tamil, Kannada, other
Religions Hindu 83%, Muslim 11%, Christian 2%, Sikh 2%, other 2%
Ethnic mix Indo-Aryan 72%, Dravidian 25%, Mongoloid and other 3%
Government Parliamentary democracy
Currency Indian rupee = 100 paisa
Literacy rate 57.2%
Calorie consumption 2,428 kilocalories

Indonesia
Southeast Asia

Official name Republic of Indonesia
Formation 1949 / 1999
Capital Jakarta
Population 214 million / 289 people per sq mile (111 people per sq km) / 41%
Total area 741,096 sq miles (1,919,440 sq km)
Languages Bahasa Indonesia*, 250 (est.) languages or dialects
Religions Muslim 87%, Christian 9%, Hindu 2%, Buddhist 1%, other 1%
Ethnic mix Javanese 45%, Sundanese 14%, Coastal Malays 8%, Madurese 8%, other 25%
Government Multiparty republic
Currency Rupiah = 100 sen
Literacy rate 86.9%
Calorie consumption 2,902 kilocalories

Iran
Southwest Asia

Official name Islamic Republic of Iran
Formation 1502 / 1990
Capital Tehran
Population 71.4 million / 112 people per sq mile (43 people per sq km) / 62%
Total area 636,406 sq miles (1,648,293 sq km)
Languages Farsi (Persian)*, Azeri, Gilaki, Baluchi, Mazanderani, Kurdish, Arabic
Religions Shi'a Muslim 95%, Sunni Muslim 4%, other 1%
Ethnic mix Persian 50%, Azeri 24%, Lur and Bakhtiari 8%, Kurd 8%, other 10%
Government Islamic theocracy
Currency Iranian rial = 100 dinars
Literacy rate 76.8%
Calorie consumption 2,913 kilocalories

Iraq
Southwest Asia

Official name Republic of Iraq
Formation 1932 / 1990
Capital Baghdad
Population 23.6 million / 140 people per sq mile (54 people per sq km) / 77%
Total area 168,753 sq miles (437,072 sq km)
Languages Arabic*, Kurdish, Armenian, Assyrian, Turkic languages
Religions Shi'a ithna Muslim 62%, Sunni Muslim 33%, other 5%
Ethnic mix Arab 79%, Kurdish 16%, Persian 3%, Turkman 2%
Government One-party republic
Currency Iraqi dinar = 1,000 fils
Literacy rate 55.9%
Calorie consumption 2,197 kilocalories

Ireland
Northwest Europe

Official name Ireland
Formation 1922 / 1922
Capital Dublin
Population 3.8 million / 140 people per sq mile (54 people per sq km) / 59%
Total area 27,135 sq miles (70,280 sq km)
Languages English*, Irish Gaelic*
Religions Roman Catholic 88%, Anglican 3%, other and non-religious 9%,
Ethnic mix Irish 95%, other 5%
Government Parliamentary democracy
Currency Euro = 100 cents
Literacy rate 99%
Calorie consumption 3,613 kilocalories

Israel
Southwest Asia

Official name State of Israel
Formation 1948 / 1994
Capital Jerusalem
Population 6.2 million / 773 people per sq mile (305 people per sq km) / 91%
Total area 8,019 sq miles (20,770 sq km)
Languages Hebrew*, Arabic, Yiddish, German, Russian, Polish, Romanian, Persian
Religions Jewish 82%, Muslim (mainly Sunni) 14%, other (including Druze) 4%
Ethnic mix Jewish 82%, other (mostly Arab) 18%
Government Parliamentary democracy
Currency Shekel = 100 agorat
Literacy rate 96%
Calorie consumption 3,562 kilocalories

Italy
Southern Europe

Official name Italian Republic
Formation 1861 / 1947
Capital Rome
Population 57.5 million / 494 people per sq mile (191 people per sq km) / 67%
Total area 116,305 sq miles (301,230 sq km)
Languages Italian*, German, French, Rhaeto-Romanic, Sardinian
Religions Roman Catholic 83%, other and non-religious 17%
Ethnic mix Italian 94%, Sardinian 2%, other 4%
Government Parliamentary democracy
Currency Euro
Literacy rate 98.4%
Calorie consumption 3,661 kilocalories

Ivory Coast
West Africa

Official name Republic of Côte d'Ivoire
Formation 1960 / 1960
Capital Yamoussoukro
Population 16.3 million / 131 people per sq mile (51 people per sq km) / 46%
Total area 124,502 sq miles (322,460 sq km)
Languages French*, Akan, Kru, Voltaic
Religions Traditional beliefs 23%, Muslim 25%, Roman Catholic 23%, Protestant 6%, other 23%
Ethnic mix Baoule 23%, Bete 18%, Senufo 15% Agni-Ashanti 14%, Mandinka 11%, other 19%
Government Multiparty republic
Currency CFA franc = 100 centimes
Literacy rate 47.1%
Calorie consumption 2,590 kilocalories

Jamaica
West Indies

Official name Jamaica
Formation 1962 / 1962
Capital Kingston
Population 2.6 million / 613 people per sq mile (237 people per sq km) / 56%
Total area 4,243 sq miles (10,990 sq km)
Languages English*, English Creole, other
Religions Christian 55%, other and non-religious 45%
Ethnic mix Black African 75%, Mulatto 13%, European and Chinese 11%, Indian 1%
Government Parliamentary democracy
Currency Jamaican dollar = 100 cents
Literacy rate 86.8%
Calorie consumption 2,693 kilocalories

Japan
East Asia

Official name Japan
Formation 1590 / 1972
Capital Tokyo
Population 127.3 million / 873 people per sq mile (337 people per sq km) / 79%
Total area 145,882 sq miles (377,835 sq km)
Languages Japanese, Korean, Chinese
Religions Shinto and Buddhist 76%, Buddhist 16%, other (including Christian) 8%
Ethnic mix Japanese 99%, other (mainly Korean) 1%
Government Parliamentary democracy
Currency Yen = 100 sen
Literacy rate 99%
Calorie consumption 2,762 kilocalories

JORDAN
Southwest Asia

Official name Hashemite Kingdom of Jordan
Formation 1946 / 1967
Capital Amman
Population 5.1 million / 143 people per sq mile (55 people per sq km) / 74%
Total area 35,637 sq miles (92,300 sq km)
Languages Arabic*, other
Religions Muslim (mainly Sunni) 92%, other (mostly Christian) 8%
Ethnic mix Arab 98% (Palestinian 40%), Armenian 1%, Circassian 1%
Government Constitutional monarchy
Currency Jordanian dinar = 1,000 fils
Literacy rate 89.2%
Calorie consumption 2,749 kilocalories

KAZAKHSTAN
Central Asia

Official name Republic of Kazakhstan
Formation 1991 / 1991
Capital Astana
Population 16.1 million / 15 people per sq mile (6 people per sq km) / 56%
Total area 1,049,150 sq miles (2,717,300 sq km)
Languages Kazakh*, Russian, German, Uighur, Korean
Religions Muslim (mainly Sunni) 50%, Russian Orthodox 13%, other 37%
Ethnic mix Kazakh 53%, Russian 30%, Ukranian 4%, German 2%, Tartar 2%, other 9%
Government Presidential democracy
Currency Tenge = 100 tein
Literacy rate 99%
Calorie consumption 2,991 kilocalories

KENYA
East Africa

Official name Republic of Kenya
Formation 1963 / 1963
Capital Nairobi
Population 31.3 million / 139 people per sq mile (54 people per sq km) / 33%
Total area 224,961 sq miles (582,650 sq km)
Languages Kiswahili*, English, Kikuyu, Luo, Kamba
Religions Christian 60%, Traditional beliefs 25%, Muslim 6%, other 9%
Ethnic mix Kikuyu 21%, Luhya 14%, Luo 13%, Kamba 11%, Kalenjin 11%, other 30%
Government Presidential democracy
Currency Kenya shilling = 100 cents
Literacy rate 82.4%
Calorie consumption 1,965 kilocalories

KIRIBATI
Australasia & Oceania

Official name Republic of Kiribati
Formation 1979 / 1979
Capital Bairiki (Tarawa Atoll)
Population 92,000 / 332 people per sq mile (128 people per sq km) / 36%
Total area 277 sq miles (717 sq km)
Languages English*, Micronesian dialect
Religions Roman Catholic 53%, Kiribati Protestant Church 39%, other 8%
Ethnic mix Micronesian 96%, other 4%
Government Non-party democracy
Currency Australian dollar = 100 cents
Literacy rate 98%
Calorie consumption 2,957 kilocalories

KUWAIT
Southwest Asia

Official name State of Kuwait
Formation 1961 / 1961
Capital Kuwait City
Population 2 million / 291 people per sq mile (112 people per sq km) / 98%
Total area 6880 sq miles (17,820 sq km)
Languages Arabic*, English, other
Religions Muslim (mainly Sunni) 85%, Christian, Hindu and other 15%
Ethnic mix Kuwaiti 45%, other Arab 35%, South Asian 9%, Iranian 4%, other 7%
Government Constitutional monarchy
Currency Kuwaiti dinar = 1,000 fils
Literacy rate 82.6%
Calorie consumption 3,132 kilocalories

KYRGYZSTAN
Central Asia

Official name Kyrgyz Republic
Formation 1991 / 1991
Capital Bishkek
Population 5 million / 65 people per sq mile (25 people per sq km) / 33%
Total area 76,641 sq miles (198,500 sq km)
Languages Kyrgyz*, Russian*, Uzbek
Religions Muslim (mainly Sunni) 70%, other (mostly Russian Orthodox) 30%
Ethnic mix Kyrgyz 57%, Russian 19%, Uzbek 13%,Tartar 2%, Ukranian 2%, other 7%
Government Presidential democracy
Currency Som = 100 teen
Literacy rate 97%
Calorie consumption 2,871 kilocalories

LAOS
Southeast Asia

Official name Lao People's Democratic Republic
Formation 1953 / 1953
Capital Vientiane
Population 5.4 million / 59 people per sq mile (23 people per sq km) / 24%
Total area 91,428 sq miles (236,800 sq km)
Languages Lao*, Mon-Khmer, Chinese, Yao, Vietnamese, French
Religions Buddhist 85%, other (including Animist) 15%
Ethnic mix Lao Loum 66%, Lao Theung 30%, Lao Soung 2%, other 2%
Government One-party republic
Currency New kip = 100 cents
Literacy rate 48.7%
Calorie consumption 2,266 kilocalories

LATVIA
Northeast Europe

Official name Republic of Latvia
Formation 1991 / 1991
Capital Riga
Population 2.4 million / 96 people per sq mile (37 people per sq km) / 69%
Total area 24,938 sq miles (64,589 sq km)
Languages Latvian*, Russian
Religions Lutheran 55%, Roman Catholic 24%, Russian Orthodox 9%, other 12%
Ethnic mix Latvian 57%, Russian 32%, Belarussian 4%, Ukranian 3%, other 4%
Government Presidential democracy
Currency Lat = 100 santimi
Literacy rate 99%
Calorie consumption 2,855 kilocalories

LEBANON
Southwest Asia

Official name Republic of Lebanon
Formation 1941 / 1941
Capital Beirut
Population 3.6 million / 897 people per sq mile (346 people per sq km) / 90%
Total area 4,015 sq miles (10,400 sq km)
Languages Arabic*, French, Armenian, Assyrian
Religions Muslim 70%, Christian 30%
Ethnic mix Arab 94%, Armenian 4%, other 2%
Government Multiparty republic
Currency Lebanese pound = 100 piastres
Literacy rate 86%
Calorie consumption 3,155 kilocalories

LESOTHO
Southern Africa

Official name Kingdom of Lesotho
Formation 1966 / 1966
Capital Maseru
Population 2.1 million / 179 people per sq mile (69 people per sq km) / 28%
Total area 11,720 sq miles (30,355 sq km)
Languages English*, Sesotho*, Zulu
Religions Traditional beliefs 10% Christian 90%,
Ethnic mix Sotho 97%, European and Asian 3%
Government Constitutional monarchy
Currency Loti = 100 lisente
Literacy rate 83.3%
Calorie consumption 2,300 kilocalories

LIBERIA
West Africa

Official name Republic of Liberia
Formation 1847 / 1847
Capital Monrovia
Population 3.1 million / 72 people per sq mile (28 people per sq km) / 45%
Total area 43,000 sq miles (111,370 sq km)
Languages English*, Kpelle, Vai, Bassa, Kru, Grebo, Kissi, Gola, Loma
Religions Christian 68%, Traditional beliefs 18%, Muslim 14%
Ethnic mix Indigenous tribes (16 main groups) 95%, Americo-Liberians 5%
Government Multiparty republic
Currency Liberian dollar = 100 cents
Literacy rate 54%
Calorie consumption 2,076 kilocalories

LIBYA
North Africa

Official name Great Socialist People's Libyan Arab Jamahariyah
Formation 1951 / 1951
Capital Tripoli
Population 5.4 million / 8 people per sq mile (3 people per sq km) 88%
Total area 679,358 sq miles (1,759,540 sq km)
Languages Arabic*, Tuareg
Religions Muslim (mainly Sunni) 97%, other 3%
Ethnic mix Arab and Berber 95%, other 5%
Government One-party state
Currency Libyan dinar = 1,000 dirhams
Literacy rate 80.1%
Calorie consumption 3,305 kilocalories

LIECHTENSTEIN
Central Europe

Official name Principality of Liechtenstein
Formation 1719 / 1719
Capital Vaduz
Population 32,200/ 521 people per sq mile (201 people per sq km) / 21%
Total area 62 sq miles (160 sq km)
Languages German*, Alemannish dialect, Italian
Religions Roman Catholic 81%, Protestant 7%, other 12%
Ethnic mix Liectensteiner 63%, Swiss 15%, German 9%, other 13%
Government Parliamentary democracy
Currency Swiss franc = 100 centimes
Literacy rate 99%
Calorie consumption not available

LITHUANIA
Northeast Europe

Official name Republic of Lithuania
Formation 1991 / 1991
Capital Vilnius
Population 3.7 million / 147 people per sq mile (57 people per sq km) / 68%
Total area 25,174 sq miles (65,200 sq km)
Languages Lithuanian*, Russian
Religions Roman Catholic 83%, Protestant 5%, other 12%
Ethnic mix Lithuanian 80%, Russian 9%, Polish 7%, Belarussian 2%, other 2%
Government Parliamentary democracy
Currency Litas = 100 centas
Literacy rate 99%
Calorie consumption 3,040 kilocalories

LUXEMBOURG
Northwest Europe

Official name Grand Duchy of Luxembourg
Formation 1867 / 1867
Capital Luxembourg
Population 442,000/ 433 people per sq mile (171 people per sq km) / 92%
Total area 998 sq miles (2,586 sq km)
Languages French*, German*, Luxembourgish*, Portuguese, Italian, other
Religions Roman Catholic 97%, other 3%
Ethnic mix Luxembourger 73%, Foreign residents 27%
Government Parliamentary democracy
Currency Euro (Luxembourg and Belgian Franc until 2002)
Literacy rate 99%
Calorie consumption 3,701 kilocalories

MACEDONIA
Southeast Europe

Official name Former Yugoslav Republic of Macedonia
Formation 1991 / 1991
Capital Skopje
Population 2 million / 204 people per sq mile (79 people per sq km) / 62%
Total area 9,781 sq miles (25,333 sq km)
Languages Macedonian, Albania, Serbo-Croat (no official language)
Religions Christian 74%, Muslim 26%
Ethnic mix Macedonian 67%, Albanian 23%, Turkish 4%, Serb 2%, other 4%
Government Multiparty republic
Currency Macedonian denar =100 deni
Literacy rate 94%
Calorie consumption 3,006 kilocalories

MADAGASCAR
Indian Ocean

Official name Republic of Madagascar
Formation 1960 / 1960
Capital Antananarivo
Population 16.4 million / 72 people per sq mile (28 people per sq km) / 30%
Total area 226,656 sq miles (587,040 sq km)
Languages French*, Malagasy*
Religions Traditional beliefs 52%, Christian 41%, Muslim 7%
Ethnic mix Merina 26%, Betsilio 12%, Betsimisaraka 15%, other 47%
Government Presidential democracy
Currency Malagasy franc = 100 centimes
Literacy rate 66.5%
Calorie consumption 2,007 kilocalories

MALAWI
Southern Africa

Official name Republic of Malawi
Formation 1964 / 1964
Capital Lilongwe
Population 11.6 million / 254 people per sq mile (98 people per sq km) / 25%
Total area 45,745 sq miles (118,480 sq km)
Languages English*, Chewa*, Lomwe, Yao, Ngoni
Religions Protestant 55%, Roman Catholic 20%, Muslim 20%, other 5%
Ethnic mix Bantu 99%, other 1%
Government Presidential democracy
Currency Malawi kwacha = 100 tambala
Literacy rate 60.1%
Calorie consumption 2,181 kilocalories

MALAYSIA
Southeast Asia

Official name Federation of Malaysia
Formation 1963 / 1965
Capital Kuala Lumpur
Population 22.6 million / 178 people per sq mile (69 people per sq km) / 57%
Total area 127,316 sq miles (329,750 sq km)
Languages Malay*, Chinese*, English, Bahasa Malaysia, Tamil
Religions Muslim 53%, Buddhist 19%, Chinese faiths 12%, other 16%
Ethnic mix Malay 48%, Chinese 29%, Indigenous tribes 12%, other 11%
Government Presidential democracy
Currency Ringgit = 100 cents
Literacy rate 87.5%
Calorie consumption 2,919 kilocalories

MALDIVES
Indian Ocean

Official name Republic of Maldives
Formation 1965 / 1965
Capital Malé
Population 300,000 / 2,590 people per sq mile (1000 people per sq km) / 26%
Total area 116 sq miles (300 sq km)
Languages Dhivehi (Maldivian)*, Sinhala, Tamil
Religions Sunni Muslim 100%
Ethnic mix Mixed Arab, Sinhalese, Malay 100%
Government Non-party democracy
Currency Rufiyaa (Maldivian rupee)= 100 laari
Literacy rate 96.4%
Calorie consumption 2,592 kilocalories

MALI
West Africa

Official name Republic of Mali
Formation 1960 / 1960
Capital Bamako
Population 11.7 million / 24 people per sq mile (9 people per sq km) / 30%
Total area 478,764 sq miles (1,240,000 sq km)
Languages French*, Bambara, Fulani, Senufo, Soninké
Religions Muslim (mainly Sunni) 80%, Traditional beliefs 18%, other 2%
Ethnic mix Bambara 32%, Fula 14%, Senufu 12%, Soninka 9%, other 33%
Government Multiparty republic
Currency CFA franc = 100 centimes
Literacy rate 41.4%
Calorie consumption 2,403 kilocalories

MALTA
Southern Europe

Official name Republic of Malta
Formation 1964 / 1964
Capital Valletta
Population 392,000 / 3,213 people per sq mile (1,241 people per sq km) / 91%
Total area 122 sq miles (316 sq km)
Languages Maltese*, English
Religions Roman Catholic 98%, other and non-religious 2%
Ethnic mix Maltese (mixed Arab, Sicilian, Norman, Spanish, Italian, English) 96%, other 4%
Government Parliamentary democracy
Currency Maltese lira = 100 cents
Literacy rate 92.1%
Calorie consumption 3,543 kilocalories

MARSHALL ISLANDS
Australasia & Oceania

Official name Republic of the Marshall Islands
Formation 1986 / 1986
Capital Majuro
Population 68,100 / 973 people per sq mile (376 people per sq km) / 69%
Total area 70 sq miles (181 sq km)
Languages Marshallese*, English*, Japanese, German
Religions Protestant 90%, Roman Catholic 8%, other 2%
Ethnic mix Micronesian 97%, other 3%
Government Parliamentary democracy
Currency US dollar = 100 cents
Literacy rate 91%
Calorie consumption not available

MAURITANIA
West Africa

Official name Islamic Republic of Mauritania
Formation 1960 / 1960
Capital Nouakchott
Population 2.7 million / 7 people per sq mile (3 people per sq km) / 58%
Total area 397,953 sq miles (1,030,700 sq km)
Languages French*, Hassaniyah Arabic, Wolof
Religions Muslim (Sunni) 100%
Ethnic mix Maure 81%, Wolof 7%, Tukolor 5%, Soninka 3%, other 4%
Government Multiparty republic
Currency Ouguiya = 5 khoums
Literacy rate 42.3%
Calorie consumption 2,638 kilocalories

MAURITIUS
Indian Ocean

Official name Mauritius
Formation 1968 / 1968
Capital Port Louis
Population 1.2 million / 1,671 people per sq mile (645 people per sq km) / 41%
Total area 718 sq miles (1,860 sq km)
Languages English*, French, French Creole, Hindi, Urdu, Tamil, Chinese
Religions Hindu 52%, Roman Catholic 26%, Muslim 17%, other 5%
Ethnic mix Indo-Mauritian 68%, Creole 27%, Sino Mauritian 3%, Franco-Mauritian 2%
Government Parliamentary democracy
Currency Mauritian rupee = 100 cents
Literacy rate 84.6%
Calorie consumption 2,985 kilocalories

MEXICO
North America

Official name United States of Mexico
Formation 1836 / 1848
Capital Mexico City
Population 100.4 million / 132 people per sq mile (51 people per sq km) / 74%
Total area 761,602 sq miles (1,972,550 sq km)
Languages Spanish*, Nahuatl, Mayan, Zapotec, Mixtec, Otomi, Totonac, Tzotzil, Tzeltal
Religions Roman Catholic 95%, Protestant 1%, other 4%
Ethnic mix Mestizo 55%, Amerindian 20%, European 16%, other 9%
Government Presidential democracy
Currency Mexican peso = 100 centavos
Literacy rate 91.3%
Calorie consumption 3,165 kilocalories

MICRONESIA
Australasia & Oceania

Official name Federated States of Micronesia
Formation 1986 / 1986
Capital Palikir (Pohnpei island)
Population 133,000 / 490 people per sq mile (189 people per sq km) / 28%
Total area 271 sq miles (702 sq km)
Languages English, Trukese, Pohnpeian, Mortlockese, Losrean
Religions Roman Catholic 50%, Protestant 48%, other 2%
Ethnic mix Micronesian 100%
Government Non-party democracy
Currency US dollar = 100 cents
Literacy rate 89%
Calorie consumption not available

MOLDOVA
Southeast Europe

Official name Republic of Moldova
Formation 1991 / 1991
Capital Chisinau
Population 4.3 million / 329 people per sq mile (127 people per sq km) / 46%
Total area 13,067 sq miles (33,843 sq km)
Languages Moldovan*, Romanian, Russian
Religions Eastern Orthodox 98%, Jewish 2%
Ethnic mix Moldovan 65%, Ukranian 14%, Russian 13%, Gagauzi 4%, other 4%
Government Parliamentary democracy
Currency Moldovan leu = 100 bani
Literacy rate 99%
Calorie consumption 2,764 kilocalories

MONACO
Southern Europe

Official name Principality of Monaco
Formation 1861 / 1861
Capital Monaco
Population 31,700 / 42,104 people per sq mile (16,256 people per sq km) / 100%
Total area 0.75 sq miles (1.95 sq km)
Languages French*, Italian, Monégasque, English
Religions Roman Catholic, 89%, Protestant 6%, other 5%
Ethnic mix French 47%, Monégasque 17%, Italian 16%,other 20%
Government Constitutional monarchy
Currency Euro (French franc until 2002)
Literacy rate 99%
Calorie consumption not available

MONGOLIA
EastAsia

Official name Mongolia
Formation 1924 / 1924
Capital Ulan Bator
Population 2.6 million / 4 people per sq mile (2 people per sq km) / 64%
Total area 604,247 sq miles (1,565,000 sq km)
Languages Khalkha Mongolian*, Kazakh, Chinese, Russian
Religions Tibetan Buddhist 96%, Muslim 4%
Ethnic mix Mongol 90%, Kazakh 4%, Chinese 2%, Russian 2%, other 2%
Government Multiparty republic
Currency Tugrik (togrog) = 100 möngös
Literacy rate 99%
Calorie consumption 1,981 kilocalories

Morocco
North Africa

Official name Kingdom of Morocco
Formation 1956 / 1956
Capital Rabat
Population 30.4 million / 176 people per sq mile (68 people per sq km) / 56%
Total area 172,316 sq miles (446,300 sq km)
Languages Arabic, Berber (Shluh, Tamazight, Riffian), French, Spanish
Religions Muslim 99%, other 1%
Ethnic mix Arab 70%, Berber 29%, European 1%
Government Constititional monarchy
Currency Moroccan dirham = 100 centimes
Literacy rate 48.9%
Calorie consumption 2,964 kilocalories

Mozambique
Southern Africa

Official name Republic of Mozambique
Formation 1975 / 1975
Capital Maputo
Population 18.6 million / 60 people per sq mile (23 people per sq km) / 40%
Total area 309,494 sq miles (801,590 sq km)
Languages Portuguese*, Makua, Tsonga, Sena, Lomwe
Religions Traditional beliefs 60%, Christian 30%, Muslim 10%
Ethnic mix Makua Lomwe 47%, Tsonga 23%, Malawi 12%, Shona 11%, Yao 4%, other 3%
Government Multiparty republic
Currency Metical = 100 centavos
Literacy rate 44%
Calorie consumption 1,927 kilocalories

Myanmar
Southeast Asia

Official name Union of Myanmar
Formation 1948 / 1948
Capital Rangoon (Yangoon)
Population 48.4 million / 185 people per sq mile (71 people per sq km) / 28%
Total area 261,969 sq miles (678,500 sq km)
Languages Burmese*, Karen, Shan, Chin, Kachin, Mon, Palaung, Wa
Religions Buddhist 87%, Christian 6%, Muslim 4%, Hindu 1%, other 2%
Ethnic mix Burman (Bamah) 68%, Shan 9%, Karen 6%, Rakhine 4%, other 13%
Government Military-based regime
Currency Kyat = 100 pyas
Literacy rate 84.7%
Calorie consumption 2,842 kilocalories

Namibia
Southern Africa

Official name Republic of Namibia
Formation 1990 / 1994
Capital Windhoek
Population 1.8 million / 6 people per sq mile (2 people per sq km) / 31%
Total area 318,694 sq miles (825,418 sq km)
Languages English*, Ovambo, Kavango, Bergdama, German, Afrikaans
Religions Christian 90%, other 10%
Ethnic mix Ovambo 50%, other tribes 16%, Kavango 9%, Herero 8%, Damara 8%, other 9%
Government Parliamentary democracy
Currency Namibian dollar = 100 cents
Literacy rate 82%
Calorie consumption 2,649 kilocalories

Nauru
Australasia & Oceania

Official name Republic of Nauru
Formation 1968 / 1968
Capital No official capital
Population 11,800 / 1,455 people per sq mile (562 people per sq km) / 100%
Total area 8 sq miles (21 sq km)
Languages Nauruan*, English, Kiribati, Chinese, Tuvaluan
Religions Nauruan Congregational Church 60%, Roman Catholic 35, other 5%
Ethnic mix Nauruan 62%, other Pacific islanders 25%, Chinese 8%, European 5%
Government Non-party democracy
Currency Australian dollar = 100 cents
Literacy rate 99%
Calorie consumption not available

Nepal
South Asia

Official name Kingdom of Nepal
Formation 1769 / 1769
Capital Kathmandu
Population 23.6 million / 434 people per sq mile (168 people per sq km) / 12%
Total area 54,363 sq miles (140,800 sq km)
Languages Nepali*, Maithili, Bhojpuri
Religions Hindu 90%, Buddhist 5%, Muslim 3%, other 2%
Ethnic mix Nepalese 52%, Maithili 11%, Tibeto-Burmese 10%, Bhojpuri 8%, other 19%
Government Constitutional monarchy
Currency Nepalese rupee = 100 paisa
Literacy rate 41.5%
Calorie consumption 2,436 kilocalories

Netherlands
Northwest Europe

Official name Kingdom of the Netherlands
Formation 1648 / 1839
Capital Amsterdam, The Hague
Population 16.2 million / 1,010 people per sq mile (390 people per sq km) / 89%
Total area 16,033 sq miles(41,526 sq km)
Languages Dutch*, Frisian
Religions Roman Catholic 36%, Protestant 27%, Muslim 3%,other 34%
Ethnic mix Dutch 82%, other 18%
Government Parliamentary democracy
Currency Euro = 100 cents
Literacy rate 99%
Calorie consumption 3,294 kilocalories

New Zealand
Australasia & Oceania

Official name Dominion of New Zealand
Formation 1947 / 1947
Capital Wellington
Population 3.8 million /37 people per sq mile (14 people per sq km) / 86%
Total area 103,737 sq miles(268,680 sqkm)
Languages English*, Maori
Religions Methodist 24%, Presbyterian 18%, Roman Catholic 15%, other/non-religious 43%
Ethnic mix European 77%, Maori 12%, Pacific Islanders 5%, other 6%
Government Parliamentary democracy
Currency New Zealand dollar = 100 cents
Literacy rate 99%
Calorie consumption 3152 kilocalories

Nicaragua
Central America

Official name Republic of Nicaragua
Formation 1838 / 1838
Capital Managua
Population 5.2 million /104 people per sq mile (40 people per sq km) / 65%
Total area 49,998 sq miles (129,494 sq km)
Languages Spanish*, English Creole, Miskito
Religions Roman Catholic 80%, Protestant Evangelicals 17%, Zambos 3%
Ethnic mix Mestizo 69%, White 14%, Black 8%, Amerindian 5%, Zambos 4%
Government Presidential democracy
Currency Córdoba oro = 100 pence
Literacy rate 68.6%
Calorie consumption 2,227 kilocalories

Niger
West Africa

Official name Republic of Niger
Formation 1960 / 1960
Capital Niamey
Population 11.2 million / 23 people per sq mile (9 people per sq km) / 21%
Total area 489,189 sq miles (1,267,000 sq km)
Languages French*, Hausa,Djerma, Fulani, Tuareg, Teda
Religions Muslim 85%, Traditional beliefs 14%, other 1%
Ethnic mix Hausa 54%, Djerma and Songhai 21%, Fulani 10%, Tuareg 9%, other 6%
Government Multiparty republic
Currency CFA franc = 100 centimes
Literacy rate 15.9%
Calorie consumption 2,089 kilocalories

Nigeria
West Africa

Official name Federal Republic of Nigeria
Formation 1960 / 1961
Capital Abuja
Population 116.9 million / 328 people per sq mile (127 people per sq km) / 44%
Total area 356,667 sq miles (923,768 sq km)
Languages English*, Hausa, Yoruba, Ibo
Religions Muslim 50%, Christian 40%, Traditional beliefs 10%
Ethnic mix Hausa 21%, Yoruba 21%, Ibo 18%, Fulani 11%, other 29%
Government Multiparty republic
Currency Naira = 100 kobo
Literacy rate 63.9%
Calorie consumption 2,850 kilocalories

North Korea
East Asia

Official name Democratic People's Republic of Korea
Formation 1948 / 1953
Capital Pyongyang
Population 22.4 million / 481 people per sq mile (186 people per sq km) / 60%
Total area 46,540 sq miles (120,540 sq km)
Languages Korean*, Chinese
Religions Atheist 100%
Ethnic mix Korean 100%
Government One-party republic
Currency N Korean won = 100 chon
Literacy rate 95%
Calorie consumption 2,185 kilocalories

Norway
Northern Europe

Official name Kingdom of Norway
Formation 1905 / 1905
Capital Oslo
Population 4.5 million / 36 people per sq mile (14 people per sq km) / 76%
Total area 125,181 sq miles (324,220 sq km)
Languages Norwegian* (Bokmal and Nynorsk), Lappish, Finnish
Religions Evangelical Lutheran 89%, Roman Catholic 1%, other and non-religious 10%
Ethnic mix Norwegian 93%, Sami 1%, other 6%
Government Parliamentary democracy
Currency Norwegian krone = 100 ore
Literacy rate 99%
Calorie consumption 3,414 kilocalories

Oman
Southwest Asia

Official name Sultanate of Oman
Formation 1951 / 1951
Capital Muscat
Population 2.6 million / 32 people per sq mile (12 people per sq km) / 84%
Total area 82,031 sq miles (212,460 sq km)
Languages Arabic*, Baluchi
Religions Ibadi Muslim 75%, other Muslim and Hindu 25%
Ethnic mix Arab 88%, Baluch 4%, Persian 3%, Indian and Pakistani 3%, African 2%
Government Monarchy
Currency Omani rial = 1,000 baizas
Literacy rate 71.8%
Calorie consumption not available

Pakistan
South Asia

Official name Islamic Republic of Pakistan
Formation 1947 / 1971
Capital Islamabad
Population 145 million / 467 people per sq mile (180 people per sq km) / 37%
Total area 310,401 sq miles (803,940 sq km)
Languages Urdu*, Punjabi, Sindhi, Pashtu, Baluchi
Religions Sunni Muslim 77%, Shi'a Muslim 20%, Hindu 2%, Christian 1%
Ethnic mix Punjabi 50%, Sindhi 15%, Pashto 15%, Mohajir 8%, other 12%
Government Military-based regime
Currency Pakistani rupee = 100 paisa
Literacy rate 46.1%
Calorie consumption 2,452 kilocalories

Palau
Australasia & Oceania

Official name Republic of Palau
Formation 1994 / 1994
Capital Koror
Population 19,100 / 108 people per sq mile (42 people per sq km) / 70%
Total area 177 sq miles (458 sq km)
Languages Palauan, English, Japanese, Angaur, Tobi, Sonsorolese (no official language)
Religions Christian 66%, Modekngei 34%
Ethnic mix Micronesian 87%, Filipino 8%, Chinese 5%
Government Non-party democracy
Currency US dollar = 100 cents
Literacy rate 92%
Calorie consumption not available

Panama
Central America

Official name Republic of Panama
Formation 1903 / 1903
Capital Panama City
Population 2.9 million / 96 people per sq mile (37 people per sq km) / 56%
Total area 30,193 sq miles (78,200 sq km)
Languages Spanish*, English Creole, Amerindian languages, Chibchan
Religions Roman Catholic 86%, Protestant 6%, other 8%
Ethnic mix Mestizo 60%, White 14%, Black 12%, Amerindian 8%, Asian 4%, other 2%
Government Presidential democracy
Currency Balboa = 100 centesimos
Literacy rate 91.9%
Calorie consumption 2,488 kilocalories

Papua New Guinea
Australasia & Oceania

Official name Independent State of Papua New Guinea
Formation 1975 / 1975
Capital Port Moresby
Population 5.2 million / 29 people per sq mile (11 people per sq km) / 17%
Total area 178,703 sq miles (462,840 sq km)
Languages English, Pidgin English*, Papuan*, Motu, 750 (est.) native languages
Religions Protestant 60%, Roman Catholic 37%, other 3%
Ethnic mix Melanesian and mixed 100%
Government Multiparty republic
Currency Kina = 100 toea
Literacy rate 63.9%
Calorie consumption 2,175 kilocalories

Paraguay
South America

Official name Republic of Paraguay
Formation 1811 / 1938
Capital Asunción
Population 5.6 million / 36 people per sq mile (14 people per sq km) / 56%
Total area 157,046 sq miles (406,750 sq km)
Languages Spanish*, Guaraní*, other
Religions Roman Catholic 96%, Protestant (including Mennonite) 4%
Ethnic mix Mestizo (Euro-Indian) 90%, Amerindian 2%, other 8%
Government Presidential democracy
Currency Guaraní = 100 centimos
Literacy rate 93.3%
Calorie consumption 2,533 kilocalories

Peru
South America

Official name Republic of Peru
Formation 1824 / 1941
Capital Lima
Population 26.1 million / 53 people per sq mile (20 people per sq km) / 73%
Total area 496,223 sq miles (1,285,220 sq km)
Languages Spanish*, Quechua*, Aymará*, other Indian languages
Religions Roman Catholic 95%, other 5%
Ethnic mix Amerindian 54%, Mestizo 32%, White 12%, other 2%
Government Presidential democracy
Currency New sol = 100 centimos
Literacy rate 89.9%
Calorie consumption 2,624 kilocalories

Philippines
Southwest Asia

Official name Republic of the Philippines
Formation 1946 / 1946
Capital Manila
Population 77.1 million / 666 people per sq mile (257 people per sq km) / 59%
Total area 115,830 sq miles (300,000 sq km)
Languages Filipino*, English*, Cebuano
Religions Roman Catholic 83%, Protestant 9%, Muslim 5%, other 3%
Ethnic mix Filipino 50%, Indonesian and Polynesian 30%, other 20%
Government Presidential democracy
Currency Peso = 100 centavos
Literacy rate 95.3%
Calorie consumption 2,379 kilocalories

Poland
Northern Europe

Official name Republic of Poland
Formation 1918 / 1945
Capital Warsaw
Population 38.6 million / 320 people per sq mile (123 people per sq km) / 66%
Total area 120,728 sq miles (312,685 sq km)
Languages Polish*, German, other
Religions Roman Catholic 93%, Eastern Orthodox 2%, other and non-religious 5%
Ethnic mix Polish 98%, German 1%, other 1%
Government Parliamentary democracy
Currency Zloty = 100 groszy
Literacy rate 99%
Calorie consumption 3,376 kilocalories

Portugal
Southwest Europe

Official name Republic of Portugal
Formation 1139 / 1640
Capital Lisbon
Population 10 million / 280 people per sq mile (108 people per sq km) / 64%
Total area 35,672 sq miles (92,391 sq km)
Languages Portuguese*
Religions Roman Catholic 97%, Protestant 1%, other 2%
Ethnic mix Portuguese 98%, African and other 2%
Government Parliamentary democracy
Currency Euro (Portuguese escudo until 2002)
Literacy rate 92.3%
Calorie consumption 3,716 kilocalories

Qatar
Southwest Asia

Official name State of Qatar
Formation 1971 / 1971
Capital Doha
Population 575,000 / 130 people per sq mile (50 people per sq km) / 93%
Total area 4,416 sq miles (11,437 sq km)
Languages Arabic*, Farsi (Persian), Urdu, Hindi, English
Religions Muslim (mainly Sunni) 95%, other 5%
Ethnic mix Arab 40%, Pakistani 18%, Indian 18%, Iranian 10%, other 14%
Government Monarchy
Currency Qatar riyal = 100 dirhams
Literacy rate 81.2%
Calorie consumption not available

Romania
Southeast Europe

Official name Romania
Formation 1878 / 1947
Capital Bucharest
Population 21.7 million / 237 people per sq mile (91 people per sq km) / 56%
Total area 91,699 sq miles (237,500 sq km)
Languages Romanian*, Hungarian, German, Romany
Religions Romanian Orthodox 87%, Roman Catholic 5%, other 8%
Ethnic mix Romanian 89%, Magyar 9%, Romany 1%, other 1%
Government Multiparty republic
Currency Romanian Leu = 100 bani
Literacy rate 98.1%
Calorie consumption 3,274 kilocalories

Russian Federation
Europe / Asia

Official name Russian Federation
Formation 1991 / 1991
Capital Moscow
Population 144.7 million / 22 people per sq mile (8 people per sq km) / 78%
Total area 6,592,735 sq miles (17,075,200 sq km)
Languages Russian*, Tatar, Ukrainian
Religions Russian Orthodox 75%, other 25%
Ethnic mix Russian 82%, Tatar 4%, Ukranian 3%, Chavash 1%, other 10%
Government Presidential democracy
Currency Rouble = 100 kopeks
Literacy rate 99%
Calorie consumption 2,917 kilocalories

Rwanda
Central Africa

Official name Republic of Rwanda
Formation 1962 / 1962
Capital Kigali
Population 7.9 million / 777 people per sq mile (300 people per sq km) / 6%
Total area 10,169 sq miles (26,338 sq km)
Languages French*, Kinyarwanda*, Kiswahili, English
Religions Roman Catholic 65%, Traditional beliefs 25%, Protestant 9%, Muslim 1%
Ethnic mix Hutu 90%, Tutsi 9%, other (including Twa) 1%
Government Transitional regime
Currency Rwanda franc = 100 centimes
Literacy rate 66.8%
Calorie consumption 2,2077 kilocalories

Saint Kitts & Nevis
West Indies

Official name Federation of Saint Christopher and Nevis
Formation 1983 / 1983
Capital Basseterre
Population 41,000 / 407 people per sq mile (157 people per sq km) / 34%
Total area 101 sq miles (261 sq km)
Languages English*, English Creole
Religions Anglican 33%,Methodist 29%, Moravian 9%, Roman Catholic 7%, other 22%
Ethnic mix Black 94%, Mixed 3%, Other and Amerindian 2%, other 1%
Government Parliamentary democracy
Currency Eastern Caribbean dollar = 100 cents
Literacy rate 90%
Calorie consumption 2,685 kilocalories

Saint Lucia
West Indies

Official name Saint Lucia
Formation 1979 / 1979
Capital Castries
Population 156,300 / 653 people per sq mile (252 people per sq km) / 38%
Total area 239 sq miles (620 sq km)
Languages English*, French Creole, Hindi, Urdu
Religions Roman Catholic 90%, other 10%
Ethnic mix Black 90%, Mulatto 6%, Asian 3%, White 1%
Government Parliamentary democracy
Currency Eastern Caribbean dollar = 100 cents
Literacy rate 82%
Calorie consumption 2,838 kilocalories

Saint Vincent & the Grenadines *West Indies*

Official name Saint Vincent and the Grenadines
Formation 1979 / 1979
Capital Kingston
Population 115,500 / 769 people per sq mile (297 people per sq km) / 55%
Total area 150 sq miles (389 sq km)
Languages English*, English Creole
Religions Anglican 42%, Methodist 20%, Roman Catholic 19%, other 19%
Ethnic mix Black 66%, Mulatto 19%, Asian 6%, White 4%, other 5%
Government Parliamentary democracy
Currency Eastern Caribbean dollar = 100 cents
Literacy rate 82%
Calorie consumption 2,579 kilocalories

SAMOA
Australasia & Oceania

Official name Independent State of Samoa
Formation 1962 / 1962
Capital Apia
Population 159,000/ 144 people per sq mile (56 people per sq km) /22%
Total area 1,104 sq miles (2,860 sq km)
Languages Samoan*, English*
Religions Christian 99%, other 1%
Ethnic mix Polynesian 90%, Euronesian 9%, other 1%
Government Parliamentary democracy
Currency Tala = 100 sene
Literacy rate 80.2%
Calorie consumption not available

SAN MARINO
Southern Europe

Official name Republic of San Marino
Formation 1631 / 1631
Capital San Marino
Population 26,900 / 1,138 people per sq mile (440 people per sq km) / 94%
Total area 24 sq miles (61 sq km)
Languages Italian*, other
Religions Roman Catholic 93%, other and non-religious 7%
Ethnic mix Sammarinese 80%, Italian 19%, other 1%
Government Parliamentary democracy
Currency Euro = 100 cents
Literacy rate 99%
Calorie consumption not available

SAO TOME & PRINCIPE
West Africa

Official name Democratic Republic of São Tomé and Príncipe
Formation 1975 / 1975
Capital São Tomé
Population 159,900 / 414 people per sq mile (160 people per sq km) / 47%
Total area 386 sq miles (1,001 sq km)
Languages Portuguese*, Portuguese Creole
Religions Roman Catholic 84%, other Christian 16%
Ethnic mix Black 90%, Portuguese and Creole 10%
Government Multiparty republic
Currency Dobra = 100 centimos
Literacy rate 75%
Calorie consumption 2,390 kilocalories

SAUDI ARABIA
Southwest Asia

Official name Kingdom of Saudi Arabia
Formation 1932 / 1932
Capital Riyadh
Population 21 million / 28 people per sq mile (11 people per sq km) / 86%
Total area 756,981 sq miles (1,960,582 sq km)
Languages Arabic*, other
Religions Sunni Muslim 85%, Shi'a Muslim 15%
Ethnic mix Arab 90%, Afro-Asian 10%
Government Monarchy
Currency Saudi riyal = 100 malalah
Literacy rate 77%
Calorie consumption 2,875 kilocalories

SENEGAL
West Africa

Official name Republic of Senegal
Formation 1960 / 1960
Capital Dakar
Population 9.7 million / 128 people per sq mile (49 people per sq km) / 47%
Total area 75,749 sq miles (196,190 sq km)
Languages French*, Wolof, Fulani, Serer, Diola, Malinke, Soninke, Arabic
Religions Sunni Muslim 90%, Christian (mainly Roman Catholic) 5%, Traditional beliefs 5%
Ethnic mix Wolof 44%, Serer 15%, Fula 12%, Diola 5%, Malinke 4%, other 20%
Government Presidential democracy
Currency CFA franc = 100 centimes
Literacy rate 37.4%
Calorie consumption 2,257 kilocalories

SERBIA & MONTENEGRO (YUGOSLAVIA) *Europe*

Official name Union of Serbia and Montenegro
Formation 1992 / 1992
Capital Belgrade
Population 10.5 million / 266 people per sq mile (103 people per sq km) / 52%
Total area 39,449 sq miles (102,173 sq km)
Languages Serbo-Croat*, Albanian, Hungarian
Religions Eastern Orthodox 65, Muslim 19%, Roman Catholic 4%, other 12%
Ethnic mix Serb 62%, Albanian 17%, Montenegrin 5%, other 16%
Government Multiparty republic
Currency Dinar (Euro widely used in Montenegro)
Literacy rate 93.3%
Calorie consumption 2,570 kilocalories

SEYCHELLES
Indian Ocean

Official name Republic of the Seychelles
Formation 1976 / 1976
Capital Victoria
Population 79,300/ 451 people per sq mile (174 people per sq km) / 64%
Total area 176 sq miles (455 sq km)
Languages French Creole (Seselwa)*, English, French
Religions Roman Catholic 90%, Anglican 8%, other 2%
Ethnic mix Creole 89%, Indian 5%, Chinese 2%, other 4%
Government Multiparty republic
Currency Seychelles rupee = 100 cents
Literacy rate 84%
Calorie consumption 2,432 kilocalories

SIERRA LEONE
West Africa

Official name Republic of Sierra Leone
Formation 1961 / 1961
Capital Freetown
Population 4.6 million / 166 people per sq mile (64 people per sq km) / 37%
Total area 27,699 sq miles (71,740 sq km)
Languages English*, Mende, Temne, Krio
Religions Traditional beliefs 30%, Muslim 30%, Christian 10%, other 30%
Ethnic mix Mende 35%, Temne 32%, Limba 8%, Kuranko 4%, other 21%
Government Multiparty republic
Currency Leone = 100 cents
Literacy rate 36.3%
Calorie consumption 1,863 kilocalories

SINGAPORE
Southeast Asia

Official name Republic of Singapore
Formation 1965 / 1965
Capital Singapore
Population 4.1 million / 16,400 people per sq mile (6,332 people per sq km) / 100%
Total area 250 sq miles (648 sq km)
Languages Malay*, English, Mandarin*, Tamil
Religions Buddhist 55%, Taoism 22%, Muslim 16%, Hindu, Christian, Sikh 7%
Ethnic mix Chinese 77%, Malay 14%, Indian 8%, other 1%
Government Parliamentary democracy
Currency Singapore dollar = 100 cents
Literacy rate 92.4%
Calorie consumption not available

SLOVAKIA
Central Europe

Official name Slovak Republic
Formation 1993 / 1993
Capital Bratislava
Population 5.4 million / 286 people per sq mile (111 people per sq km) / 57%
Total area 18,859 sq miles (48,845 sq km)
Languages Slovak*, Hungarian (Magyar), Romany, Czech, other
Religions Roman Catholic 60%, Atheist 10%, Protestant 8%, Orthodox 4%, other 18%
Ethnic mix Slovak 85%, Magyar 11%, Romany 1%, Czech 1%, other 2%
Government Parliamentary democracy
Currency Koruna = 100 halierov
Literacy rate 99%
Calorie consumption 3,133 kilocalories

SLOVENIA
Central Europe

Official name Republic of Slovenia
Formation 1991 / 1991
Capital Ljubljana
Population 2 million / 256 people per sq mile (99 people per sq km) / 50%
Total area 7820 sq miles (20,253 sq km)
Languages Slovene*, Serbo-Croat
Religions Roman Catholic 96%, Muslim 1%, other 3%
Ethnic mix Slovene 88%, Croat 3%, Serb 2%, Muslim 1%, other 6%
Government Parliamentary democracy
Currency Tolar = 100 stotins
Literacy rate 99%
Calorie consumption 3,168 kilocalories

SOLOMON ISLANDS
Australasia & Oceania

Official name Solomon Islands
Formation 1978 / 1978
Capital Honiara
Population 463,000 / 42 people per sq mile (16 people per sq km) / 20%
Total area 10,985 sq miles (28,450 sq km)
Languages English*, Pidgin English, 87 (est.) native languages
Religions Anglican 34%, Roman Catholic 19%, South Seas Evangelical Church 17%, Methodist 11%, other 19%
Ethnic mix Melanesian 94%, other 6%
Government Parliamentary democracy
Currency Solomon Islands dollar = 100 cents
Literacy rate 62%
Calorie consumption 2,277 kilocalories

SOMALIA
East Africa

Official name Somali Democratic Republic
Formation 1960 / 1960
Capital Mogadishu
Population 9.2 million / 37 people per sq mile (14 people per sq km) / 28%
Total area 246,199 sq miles (637,657 sq km)
Languages Arabic*, Somali*, English, Italian
Religions Sunni Muslim 98%, other 2%
Ethnic mix Somali 85%, other 15%
Government Transitional regime
Currency Somali shilling = 100 cents
Literacy rate 24.1%
Calorie consumption 1,628 kilocalories

SOUTH AFRICA
Southern Africa

Official name Republic of South Africa
Formation 1934 / 1994
Capital Pretoria (administrative)
Population 43.8 million / 93 people per sq mile (36 people per sq km) / 55%
Total area 471,008 sq miles (1,219,912 sq km)
Languages Afrikaans, English, 9 other African languages
Religions Black Independent 17%, Duthc reformed 11%, Roman Catholic 8%, other 66%
Ethnic mix Zulu 23%, other Black 38%, White 16%, Mixed 10%, other 13%
Government Parliamentary democracy
Currency Rand = 100 cents
Literacy rate 85.3%
Calorie consumption 2,886 kilocalories

SOUTH KOREA
East Asia

Official name Republic of Korea
Formation 1948 / 1953
Capital Seoul
Population 47.1 million / 1,239 people per sq mile (478 people per sq km) / 82%
Total area 38,023 sq miles (98,480 sq km)
Languages Korean*, Chinese
Religions Mahayana Buddhist 47%, Protestant 38%, Roman Catholic 11%, Confucian 3%, other 1%
Ethnic mix Korean 100%
Government Presidential democracy
Currency Korean won = 100 chon
Literacy rate 97.8%
Calorie consumption 3,093 kilocalories

SPAIN
Southeast Europe

Official name Kingdom of Spain
Formation 1492 / 1713
Capital Madrid
Population 39.9 million / 205 people per sq mile (79 people per sq km) / 78%
Total area 194,896 sq miles (504,782 sq km)
Languages Castilian Spanish*, Catalan*, Galician*, Basque*, other
Religions Roman Catholic 96%, other 4%
Ethnic mix Castilian Spanish 72%, Catalan 17%, Galician 6%, other 5%
Government Parliamentary democracy
Currency Euro = 100 cents
Literacy rate 97.7%
Calorie consumption 3,352 kilocalories

SRI LANKA
South Asia

Official name Democratic Socialist Republic of Sri Lanka
Formation 1948 / 1948
Capital Colombo
Population 19.1 million / 754 people per sq mile (291 people per sq km) / 24%
Total area 25,332 sq miles (65,610 sq km)
Languages Sinhalese, Tamil, English
Religions Buddhist 69%, Hindu 15%, Christian 8%, Muslim 8%
Ethnic mix Sinhalese 74%, Tamil 18%, Moor 7%, other 1%
Government Presidential democracy
Currency Sri Lanka rupee = 100 cents
Literacy rate 91.7%
Calorie consumption 2,405 kilocalories

SUDAN
East Africa

Official name Republic of the Sudan
Formation 1956 / 1956
Capital Khartoum
Population 31.8 million / 33 people per sq mile (13 people per sq km) / 36%
Total area 967,493 sq miles (2,505,810 sq km)
Languages Arabic*, Dinka, Nuer, Zande, Nubian, Beja, Bari, Fur, Shilluk, Lotuko
Religions Muslim (mainly Sunni) 70%, Traditional beliefs 20%, other 10%
Ethnic mix Arab 40%, Tribal 30%, Dinka and Beja 7%, other 23%
Government Presidential regime
Currency Sudanese pound or dinar = 100 piastres
Literacy rate 58%
Calorie consumption 2,348 kilocalories

SURINAME
South America

Official name Republic of Suriname
Formation 1975 / 1975
Capital Paramaribo
Population 419,000 / 7 people per sq mile (3 people per sq km) / 74%
Total area 63,039 sq miles (163,270 sq km)
Languages Dutch*, Sranan, Saramaccan, Javavese, Sarnami Hindi, Chinese
Religions Christian 48%, Hindu 27%, Muslim 20%, other 5%
Ethnic mix South Asian 34%, Creole 34%, Javanese 18%, Black 9%, other 5%
Government Parliamentary democracy
Currency Suriname guilder = 100 cents
Literacy rate 94.2%
Calorie consumption 2,652 kilocalories

SWAZILAND
Southern Africa

Official name Kingdom of Swaziland
Formation 1968 / 1968
Capital Mbabane
Population 938,000 / 140 people per sq mile (54 people per sq km) 26%
Total area 6,704 sq miles (17,363 sq km)
Languages Siswati*, English*, Zulu, Tsonga
Religions Christian 60%, Traditional beliefs 40%
Ethnic mix Swazi 97%, other 3%
Government Constitutional monarchy
Currency Lilangeni = 100 cents
Literacy rate 79.6%
Calorie consumption 2,620 kilocalories

SWEDEN
Northern Europe

Official name Kingdom of Sweden
Formation 1523 / 1905
Capital Stockholm
Population 8.8 million / 51 people per sq mile (20 people per sq km) / 83%
Total area 173,731 sq miles (449,964 sq km)
Languages Swedish*, Finnish, Sami
Religions Evangelical Lutheran 89%, Roman Catholic 2%, other 9%
Ethnic mix Swedish 91%, Finnish and Sami 3%, other European 6%
Government Parliamentary democracy
Currency Swedish krona = 100 ore
Literacy rate 99%
Calorie consumption 3,109 kilocalories

SWITZERLAND
Central Europe

Official name Swiss Confederation
Formation 1291 / 1857
Capital Bern
Population 7.2 million / 469 people per sq mile (174 people per sq km) / 68%
Total area 15,942 sq miles (41,290 sq km)
Languages German*, French*, Italian*, Romansch*, Swiss German
Religions Roman Catholic 46%, Protestant 40%, other 14%
Ethnic mix German 65%, French 18%, Italian 10%, Romansh 1%, other 6%
Government Parliamentary democracy
Currency Swiss franc = 100 centimes
Literacy rate 99%
Calorie consumption 3,293 kilocalories

SYRIA
Southwest Asia

Official name Syrian Arab Republic
Formation 1941 / 1967
Capital Damascus
Population 16.6 million / 232 people per sq mile (90 people per sq km) / 55%
Total area 71,498 sq miles (185,180 sq km)
Languages Arabic*, French, Kurdish, Armenian, Circassian, Aramaic
Religions Sunni Muslim 74%, other Muslim 16%, Christian 10%
Ethnic mix Arab 89%, Kurdish 6%, Armenian, Turkmen, Circassian 2%, other 3%
Government One-party republic
Currency Syrian pound = 100 piastres
Literacy rate 74.5%
Calorie consumption 3,038 kilocalories

TAIWAN
East Asia

Official name Republic of China (Taiwan)
Formation 1949 / 1949
Capital Taipei
Population 22.2 million / 1,598 people per sq mile (617 people per sq km) / 69%
Total area 13,892 sq miles (35,980 sq km)
Languages Mandarin Chinese*, Amoy Chinese, Hakka Chinese
Religions Buddhist, Confucian and Taoist 93%, Christian 5%, other 2%
Ethnic mix Indigenous Chinese 84%, Mainland Chinese 14%, Aborigine 2%
Government Multiparty republic
Currency Taiwan dollar = 100 cents
Literacy rate 94%
Calorie consumption not available

TAJIKISTAN
Central Asia

Official name Republic of Tajikistan
Formation 1991 / 1991
Capital Dushanbe
Population 6.1 million / 110 people per sq mile (43 people per sq km) / 28%
Total area 55,251 sq miles (143,100 sq km)
Languages Tajik*, Uzbek, Russian
Religions Sunni Muslim 80%, Shi'a Muslim 5%, other 15%
Ethnic mix Tajik 62%, Uzbek 24%, Russian 8%, Tatar 1%, Kyrgyz 1%, other 4%
Government Multiparty republic
Currency Somoni
Literacy rate 99%
Calorie consumption 1720 kilocalories

TANZANIA
East Africa

Official name United Republic of Tanzania
Formation 1964 / 1964
Capital Dodoma
Population 36 million / 99 people per sq mile (38 people per sq km) / 33%
Total area 364,898 sq miles (945,087 sq km)
Languages English*, Swahili*, Sukuma, Chagga, Nyamwezi, Hehe, Makonde
Religions Muslim 33%, Christian 33%, Traditional beliefs 30%, other 4%
Ethnic mix Native African (120 ethnic Bantu groups) 99%, European and Asian 1%
Government Presidential democracy
Currency Tanzanian shilling = 100 cents
Literacy rate 75.8%
Calorie consumption 1,906 kilocalories

THAILAND
Southeastern Asia

Official name Kingdom of Thailand
Formation 1238 / 1907
Capital Bangkok
Population 63.6 million / 322 people per sq mile (124 people per sq km) / 22%
Total area 197,254 sq miles (510,890 sq km)
Languages Thai*, Chinese, Malay, Khmer, Mon, Karen, Miao
Religions Buddhist 95%, Muslim 3%, Christian 1%, other 1%
Ethnic mix Thai 83%, Chinese 12%, Malay 3%, Khmer and other 2%
Government Parliamentary democracy
Currency Baht = 100 stangs
Literacy rate 95.5%
Calorie consumption 2,506 kilocalories

TOGO
Western Africa

Official name Republic of Togo
Formation 1960 / 1960
Capital Lomé
Population 4.7 million / 214 people per sq mile (83 people per sq km) / 33%
Total area 21,925 sq miles (56,785 sq km)
Languages French*, Ewe, Kabye, Gurma
Religions Traditional beliefs 50%, Christian 35%, Muslim 15%
Ethnic mix Ewe 46%, other African 53%, European 1%
Government Presidential regime
Currency CFA franc = 100 centimes
Literacy rate 57.3%
Calorie consumption 2,329 kilocalories

TONGA
Australasia & Oceania

Official name Kingdom of Tonga
Formation 1970 / 1970
Capital Nuku'alofa
Population 102,200 / 354 people per sq mile (137 people per sq km) / 43%
Total area 289 sq miles (748 sq km)
Languages Tongan*, English
Religions Free Wesleyan 64%, Roman Catholic 15%, Other 21%
Ethnic mix Polynesian 99%, other Pacific groups and European 1%
Government Monarchy
Currency Pa'anga (Tongan dollar) = 100 seniti
Literacy rate 98.5%
Calorie consumption not available

TRINIDAD & TOBAGO
West Indies

Official name Republic of Trinidad and Tobago
Formation 1962 / 1962
Capital Port-of-Spain
Population 1.3 million / 657 people per sq mile (254 people per sq km) / 74%
Total area 1980 sq miles (5,128 sq km)
Languages English*, English Creole, Hindi. French, Spanish
Religions Christian 61%, Hindu 24%, other and non-religious 15%
Ethnic mix Asian 40%, Black 40%, Mixed 19%, White and Chinese 1%
Government Parliamentary democracy
Currency Trinidad and Tobago dollar = 100 cents
Literacy rate 93.8%
Calorie consumption 2,777 kilocalories

TUNISIA
North Africa

Official name Republic of Tunisia
Formation 1956 / 1956
Capital Tunis
Population 9.6 million / 152 people per sq mile (59 people per sq km) / 68%
Total area 63,170 sq miles (163,610 sq km)
Languages Arabic*, French
Religions Muslim (mainly Sunni) 98%, Christian 1%, Jewish 1%
Ethnic mix Arab and Berber 98%, European 1%, other 1%
Government Presidential democracy
Currency Tunisian dinar = 1,000 millimes
Literacy rate 71%
Calorie consumption 3,299 kilocalories

TURKEY
Asia / Europe

Official name Republic of Turkey
Formation 1923 / 1939
Capital Ankara
Population 67.6 million / 224 people per sq mile (87 people per sq km) / 75%
Total area 301,382 sq miles (780,580 sq km)
Languages Turkish*, Kurdish, Arabic, Circassian, Armenian, Greek, Georgian
Religions Muslim (mainly Sunni) 99%, other 1%
Ethnic mix Turkish 70%, Kurdish 20%, Arab 2%, other 8%
Government Parliamentary democracy
Currency Turkish lira = 100 krural
Literacy rate 85.1%
Calorie consumption 3,416 kilocalories

TURKMENISTAN
Central Asia

Official name Turkmenistan
Formation 1991 / 1991
Capital Ashgabat
Population 4.8 million / 25 people per sq mile (10 people per sq km) / 45%
Total area 188,455 sq miles (488,100 sq km)
Languages Turkmen*, Uzbek, Russian
Religions Sunni Muslim 87%, Eastern Orthodox 11%, other 2%
Ethnic mix Turkmen 73%, Russian 10%, Uzbek 9%, Kazakh 2%, Tatar 1%,other 5%
Government One-party state
Currency Manat = 100 tenge
Literacy rate 98%
Calorie consumption 2,675 kilocalories

TUVALU
Australasia & Oceania

Official name Tuvalu
Formation 1978 / 1978
Capital Fongafale, on Funafuti Atoll
Population 10,800 / 1,076 people per sq mile (415 people per sq km) / 45%
Total area 10 sq miles (26 sq km)
Languages English, Tuvaluan, Kiribati, other (no official language)
Religions Church of Tuvalu 97%, Seventh-day Adventist 1%, Baha'i 1%,other 1%
Ethnic mix Polynesian 96%, other 4%
Government Non-party democracy
Currency Australian dollar and Tuvaluan dollar = 100 cents
Literacy rate 95%
Calorie consumption not available

UGANDA
East Africa

Official name Republic of Uganda
Formation 1962 / 1962
Capital Kampala
Population 24 million / 263 people per sq mile (102 people per sq km) / 14%
Total area 91,135 sq miles (236,040 sq km)
Languages English*, Luganda, Nkole, Chiga, Lango, Acholi, Teso
Religions Roman Catholic 38%, Protestant 33%, Traditional beliefs 13%, Muslim (mainly Sunni) 5%, other 11%
Ethnic mix Bantu Tribes 50%, other 50%
Government Non-party democracy
Currency New Uganda shilling = 100 cents
Literacy rate 67.1%
Calorie consumption 2,359 kilocalories

UKRAINE
Eastern Europe

Official name Ukraine
Formation 1991 / 1991
Capital Kiev
Population 48.4 million / 208 people per sq mile (80 people per sq km) / 68%
Total area 223,089 sq miles (603,700 sq km)
Languages Ukrainian*, Russian, Tartar
Religions Christian (mainly Ukrainian Orthodox) 95%, Jewish 1%, other 4%
Ethnic mix Ukrainian 73%, Russian 22%, Jewish 1%, other 4%
Government Presidential democracy
Currency Hryvnia = 100 kopiykas
Literacy rate 99%
Calorie consumption 2,871 kilocalories

UNITED ARAB EMIRATES
Southwest Asia

Official name United Arab Emirates
Formation 1971 / 1972
Capital Abu Dhabi
Population 2.7 million / 84 people per sq mile (33 people per sq km) / 86%
Total area 32,000 sq miles (82,880 sq km)
Languages Arabic*, Farsi, English, Indian and Pakistani languages
Religions Muslim (mainly Sunni) 96%, Christian, Hindu and other 4%
Ethnic mix Asian 60%, Emirian 25%, other Arab 12%, European 3%
Government Monarchy
Currency UAE dirham = 100 fils
Literacy rate 75.6%
Calorie consumption 3,192 kilocalories

UNITED KINGDOM
Northwest Europe

Official name United Kingdom of Great Britain and Northern Ireland
Formation 1707 / 1922
Capital London
Population 59.5 million / 629 people per sq mile (243 people per sq km) / 90%
Total area 94,525 sq miles (244,820 sq km)
Languages English*, Welsh, Scottish, Gaelic
Religions Anglican 47%, Presbyterian 4%, Roman Catholic 9% , other 40%
Ethnic mix English 80%, Scottish 9%, Northern Irish 3%, Welsh 3%, other 5%
Government Parliamentary democracy
Currency Pound sterling = 100 pence
Literacy rate 99%
Calorie consumption 3,334 kilocalories

UNITED STATES
North America

Official name United States of America
Formation 1776 / 1959
Capital Washington DC
Population 281.4 million /76 people per sq mile (29 people per sq km) / 77%
Total area 3,717,792 sq miles (9,629,091 sq km)
Languages English*, Spanish, Italian, German, French, Polish, Chinese, Greek
Religions Protestant 61%, Roman Catholic 25%, Jewish 2%, other 12%
Ethnic mix White (including Hispanic) 81%, Native American 2%, Asia 4%, Black American/African 13%
Government Presidential democracy
Currency US dollar = 100 cents
Literacy rate 99%
Calorie consumption 3,772 kilocalories

URUGUAY
South America

Official name Eastern Republic of Uruguay
Formation 1828 / 1828
Capital Montevideo
Population 3.4 million /50 people per sq mile (19 people per sq km) / 91%
Total area 68,039 sq miles (176,220 sqkm)
Languages Spanish*, other
Religions Roman Catholic 66%, non-religious 30%, Jewish 2%, Protestant 2%
Ethnic mix White 90%, other 10%
Government Presidential democracy
Currency Uruguayan peso = 100 centimes
Literacy rate 97.8%
Calorie consumption 2,879 kilocalories

UZBEKISTAN
Central Asia

Official name Republic of Uzbekistan
Formation 1991 / 1991
Capital Tashkent
Population 25.3 million / 146 people per sq mile (57 people per sq km) / 37%
Total area 172,741 sq miles (447,400 sq km)
Languages Uzbek*, Russian
Religions Sunni Muslim 88%, Eastern Orthodox 9%, other 3%
Ethnic mix Uzbek 71%, Russian 8%, Tajik 5%, Kazakh 4%, other 12%
Government Presidential democracy
Currency Som = 100 teen
Literacy rate 88.9%
Calorie consumption 2,317 kilocalories

VANUATU
Australasia & Oceania

Official name Republic of Vanuatu
Formation 1980 / 1980
Capital Port Vila
Population 200,000 / 42 people per sq mile (16 people per sq km) / 20%
Total area 4,710 sq miles (12,200 sq km)
Languages Bislama*, English*, French*
Religions Presbyterian 37%, Anglican 15%, Roman Catholic 15%, Indigenous beliefs 8%, Seventh-day Adventist 6%, other 19%
Ethnic mix Melanesian 94%, Polynesian 3%, other 3%
Government Parliamentary democracy
Currency Vatu = 100 centimes
Literacy rate 64%
Calorie consumption 2,587 kilocalories

VATICAN CITY
Southern Europe

Official name State of the Vatican City
Formation 1929 / 1929
Capital Not applicable
Population 524 /3,082 people per sq mile (1,191 people per sq km) / 100%
Total area 0.17 sq miles (0.44 sq km)
Languages Italian*, Latin*, other
Religions Roman Catholic 100%
Ethnic mix Italian 90%, Swiss 10% (including the Swiss Guard, which is responsible for papal security)
Government Papal state
Currency Euro (Lira until 2002)
Literacy rate 99%
Calorie consumption not available

VENEZUELA
South America

Official name Bolivarian Republic of Venezuela
Formation 1830 / 1830
Capital Caracas
Population 24.6 million /70 people per sq mile (27 people per sq km) / 87%
Total area 352,143 sq miles (912,050 sq km)
Languages Spanish*, Amerindian languages
Religions Roman Catholic 89%, Protestant and other 11%
Ethnic mix Mestizo 69%, White 20%, Black 9%, Amerindian 2%
Government Presidential democracy
Currency Bolivar = 100 centimos
Literacy rate 92.6%
Calorie consumption 2,256 kilocalories

VIETNAM
Southeast Asia

Official name Socialist Republic of Vietnam
Formation 1976 / 1976
Capital Hanoi
Population 79.2 million / 622 people per sq mile (240 people per sq km) / 20%
Total area 127,243 sq miles (329,560 sq km)
Languages Vietnamese*, Chinese, Thai, Khmer, Muong, Nung, Miao, Yao
Religions Buddhist 55%, Christian 7%, other and non-religious 38%
Ethnic mix Vietnamese 88%, Chinese 4%, Thai 2%, other 6%
Government One-party republic
Currency Đông = 10 hao = 100 xu
Literacy rate 93.4%
Calorie consumption 2,583 kilocalories

YEMEN
Southwest Asia

Official name Republic of Yemen
Formation 1990 / 1990
Capital Sana
Population 19.1 million / 94 people per sq mile (36 people per sq km) / 25%
Total area 203,849 sq miles (527,970 sq km)
Languages Arabic*, Hindi, Tamil, Urdu
Religions Shi'a Muslim 42%, Sunni Muslim 55%, Christian, Hindu and Jewish 3%
Ethnic mix Arab 95%, Afro-Arab 3%, Indian, Somali and European 2%
Government Multiparty republic
Currency Yemeni Rial
Literacy rate 46.3%
Calorie consumption 2,038 kilocalories

ZAMBIA
Southern Africa

Official name Republic of Zambia
Formation 1964 / 1964
Capital Lusaka
Population 10.6 million / 36 people per sq mile (14 people per sq km) / 45%
Total area 290,584 sq miles (752,612 sq km)
Languages English*, Bemba, Nyanja, Tonga, Kaonde, Lunda, Luvale, Lozi
Religions Christian 63%, Indigenous beliefs 36%, other 1%
Ethnic mix Bemba 34%, European 1%, other African 65%
Government Presidential democracy
Currency Zambian kwacha = 100 ngwee
Literacy rate 78.1%
Calorie consumption 1,912 kilocalories

ZIMBABWE
Southern Africa

Official name Republic of Zimbabwe
Formation 1980 / 1980
Capital Harare
Population 12.9 million / 86 people per sq mile (33 people per sq km) / 35%
Total area 150,803 sq miles (390,580 sq km)
Languages English*, Shona, Ndebele
Religions Syncretic (Christian and traditional beliefs) 50%, Christian 25%, Traditional beliefs 24%, other 1%
Ethnic mix Shona 71%, Ndebele 16%, other African 11%, Asian 1%, White 1%
Government Presidential regime
Currency Zimbabwe dollar = 100 cents
Literacy rate 88.7%
Calorie consumption 2,117 kilocalories

GEOGRAPHICAL NAMES

THE FOLLOWING GLOSSARY lists all geographical terms occurring on the maps and in main-entry names in the Index-Gazetteer. These terms may precede, follow or be run together with the proper element of the name; where they precede it the term is reversed for indexing purposes – thus Poluostrov Yamal is indexed as Yamal, Poluostrov.

KEY
Geographical term *Language*, Term

A
Å *Danish, Norwegian*, River
Āb *Persian*, River
Adrar *Berber*, Mountains
Agía, Ágios *Greek*, Saint
Air *Indonesian*, River
Ákra *Greek*, Cape, point
Alpen *German*, Alps
Alt- *German*, Old
Altiplanicie *Spanish*, Plateau
Älve(en) *Swedish*, River
-ån *Swedish*, River
Anse *French*, Bay
'Aqabat *Arabic*, Pass
Archipiélago *Spanish*, Archipelago
Arcipelago *Italian*, Archipelago
Arquipélago *Portuguese*, Archipelago
Arrecife(s) *Spanish*, Reef(s)
Aru *Tamil*, River
Augstiene *Latvian*, Upland
Aukštuma *Lithuanian*, Upland
Aust- *Norwegian*, Eastern
Avtonomnyy Okrug *Russian*, Autonomous district
Āw *Kurdish*, River
'Ayn *Arabic*, Spring, well
'Ayoûn *Arabic*, Wells

B
Baelt *Danish*, Strait
Bahía *Spanish*, Bay
Baḩr *Arabic*, River
Baía *Portuguese*, Bay
Baie *French*, Bay
Bañado *Spanish*, Marshy land
Bandao *Chinese*, Peninsula
Banjaran *Malay*, Mountain range
Barajı *Turkish*, Dam
Barragem *Portuguese*, Reservoir
Bassin *French*, Basin
Batang *Malay*, Stream
Beinn, Ben *Gaelic*, Mountain
-berg *Afrikaans, Norwegian*, Mountain
Besar *Indonesian, Malay*, Big
Birkat, Birket *Arabic*, Lake, well, cistern
Boğazi *Turkish*, Lake
Boka *Serbo-Croatian*, Bay
Bol'sh-aya, -iye, -oy, -oye *Russian*, Big
Botigh(i) *Uzbek*, Depression basin
-bre(en) *Norwegian*, Glacier
Bredning *Danish*, Bay
Bucht *German*, Bay
Bugt(en) *Danish*, Bay
Buḩayrat *Arabic*, Lake, reservoir
Buḩeiret *Arabic*, Lake
Bukit *Malay*, Mountain
-bukta *Norwegian*, Bay
bukten *Swedish*, Bay
Bulag *Mongolian*, Spring
Bulak *Uighur*, Spring
Burnu *Turkish*, Cape, point
Buuraha *Somali*, Mountains

C
Cabo *Portuguese*, Cape
Caka *Tibetan*, Salt lake
Canal *Spanish*, Channel
Cap *French*, Cape
Capo *Italian*, Cape, headland
Cascada *Portuguese*, Waterfall
Cayo(s) *Spanish*, Islet(s), rock(s)
Cerro *Spanish*, Mountain
Chaîne *French*, Mountain range
Chapada *Portuguese*, Hills, upland
Chau *Cantonese*, Island
Chāy *Turkish*, River
Chhâk *Cambodian*, Bay
Chhu *Tibetan*, River
-chŏsuji *Korean*, Reservoir
Chott *Arabic*, Depression, salt lake
Chŭli *Uzbek*, Grassland, steppe
Ch'ün-tao *Chinese*, Island group
Chuŏr Phnum *Cambodian*, Mountains
Ciudad *Spanish*, City, town
Co *Tibetan*, Lake
Colline(s) *French*, Hill(s)
Cordillera *Spanish*, Mountain range
Costa *Spanish*, Coast
Côte *French*, Coast
Coxilha *Portuguese*, Mountains
Cuchilla *Spanish*, Mountains

D
Daban *Mongolian, Uighur*, Pass
Daği *Azerbaijani, Turkish*, Mountain
Dağlari *Azerbaijani, Turkish*, Mountains
-dake *Japanese*, Peak
-dal(en) *Norwegian*, Valley
Danau *Indonesian*, Lake
Dao *Chinese*, Island
Đao *Vietnamese*, Island
Daryā *Persian*, River
Daryācheh *Persian*, Lake
Dasht *Persian*, Desert, plain
Dawḩat *Arabic*, Bay
Denizi *Turkish*, Sea
Dere *Turkish*, Stream
Desierto *Spanish*, Desert
Dili *Azerbaijani*, Spit
-do *Korean*, Island
Dooxo *Somali*, Valley
Düzü *Azerbaijani*, Steppe
-dwīp *Bengali*, Island

E
-eilanden *Dutch*, Islands
Embalse *Spanish*, Reservoir
Ensenada *Spanish*, Bay
Erg *Arabic*, Dunes
Estany *Catalan*, Lake
Estero *Spanish*, Inlet
Estrecho *Spanish*, Strait
Étang *French*, Lagoon, lake
-ey *Icelandic*, Island
Ezero *Bulgarian, Macedonian*, Lake
Ezers *Latvian*, Lake

F
Feng *Chinese*, Peak
Fjord *Danish*, Fjord
-fjord(en) *Danish, Norwegian, Swedish*, fjord
-fjørdhur *Faeroese*, Fjord
Fleuve *French*, River
Fliegu *Maltese*, Channel
-fljór *Icelandic*, River
-flói *Icelandic*, Bay
Forêt *French*, Forest

G
-gan *Japanese*, Rock
-gang *Korean*, River
Ganga *Hindi, Nepali, Sinhala*, River
Gaoyuan *Chinese*, Plateau
Garagumy *Turkmen*, Sands
-gawa *Japanese*, River
Gebel *Arabic*, Mountain
-gebirge *German*, Mountain range
Ghadīr *Arabic*, Well
Ghubbat *Arabic*, Bay
Gjiri *Albanian*, Bay
Gol *Mongolian*, River
Golfe *French*, Gulf
Golfo *Italian, Spanish*, Gulf
Göl(ü) *Turkish*, Lake
Golyam, -a *Bulgarian*, Big
Gora *Russian, Serbo-Croatian*, Mountain
Góra *Polish*, Mountain
Gory *Russian*, Mountain
Gryada *Russian*, Ridge
Guba *Russian*, Bay
-gundo *Korean*, Island group
Gunung *Malay*, Mountain

H
Ḩadd *Arabic*, Spit
-haehyŏp *Korean*, Strait
Haff *German*, Lagoon
Hai *Chinese*, Bay, lake, sea
Haixia *Chinese*, Strait
Hamada *Arabic*, Plateau
Ḩammādat *Arabic*, Plateau
Hāmūn *Persian*, Lake
-hantō *Japanese*, Peninsula
Har, Haré *Hebrew*, Mountain
Ḩarrat *Arabic*, Lava-field
Hav(et) *Danish, Swedish*, Sea
Hawr *Arabic*, Lake
Hāyk' *Amharic*, Lake
He *Chinese*, River
-hegység *Hungarian*, Mountain range
Heide *German*, Heath, moorland
Helodrano *Malagasy*, Bay
Higashi- *Japanese*, East(ern)
Ḩişā' *Arabic*, Well
Hka *Burmese*, River
-ho *Korean*, Lake
Hô *Korean*, Reservoir
Ḩolot *Hebrew*, Dunes
Hora *Belorussian, Czech*, Mountain
Hrada *Belorussian*, Mountain, ridge
Hsi *Chinese*, River
Hu *Chinese*, Lake
Huk *Danish*, Point

I
Île(s) *French*, Island(s)
Ilha(s) *Portuguese*, Island(s)
Ilhéu(s) *Portuguese*, Islet(s)
Imeni *Russian*, In the name of
Inish- *Gaelic*, Island
Insel(n) *German*, Island(s)
Irmağı, Irmak *Turkish*, River
Isla(s) *Spanish*, Island(s)
Isola (Isole) *Italian*, Island(s)

J
Jabal *Arabic*, Mountain
Jāl *Arabic*, Ridge
-järv *Estonian*, Lake
-järvi *Finnish*, Lake
Jazā'ir *Arabic*, Islands
Jazīrat *Arabic*, Island
Jazīreh *Persian*, Island
Jebel *Arabic*, Mountain
Jezero *Serbo-Croatian*, Lake
Jezioro *Polish*, Lake
Jiang *Chinese*, River
-jima *Japanese*, Island
Jižní *Czech*, Southern
-jõgi *Estonian*, River
-joki *Finnish*, River
-jökull *Icelandic*, Glacier
Jūn *Arabic*, Bay
Juzur *Arabic*, Islands

K
Kaikyō *Japanese*, Strait
-kaise *Lappish*, Mountain
Kali *Nepali*, River
Kalnas *Lithuanian*, Mountain
Kalns *Latvian*, Mountain
Kang *Chinese*, Harbor
Kangri *Tibetan*, Mountain(s)
Kaôh *Cambodian*, Island
Kapp *Norwegian*, Cape
Káto *Greek*, Lower
Kavīr *Persian*, Desert
K'edi *Georgian*, Mountain range
Kediet *Arabic*, Mountain
Kepi *Albanian*, Cape, point
Kepulauan *Indonesian, Malay*, Island group
Khalig, Khalīj *Arabic*, Gulf
Khawr *Arabic*, Inlet
Khola *Nepali*, River
Khrebet *Russian*, Mountain range
Ko *Thai*, Island
-ko *Japanese*, Inlet, lake
Kólpos *Greek*, Bay
-kopf *German*, Peak
Körfäzi *Azerbaijani*, Bay
Körfezi *Turkish*, Bay
Kõrgustik *Estonian*, Upland
Kosa *Russian, Ukrainian*, Spit
Koshi *Nepali*, River
Kou *Chinese*, River-mouth
Kowtal *Persian*, Pass
Kray *Russian*, Region, territory
Kryazh *Russian*, Ridge
Kuduk *Uighur*, Well
Kūh(hā) *Persian*, Mountain(s)
-kul' *Russian*, Lake
Kŭl(i) *Tajik, Uzbek*, Lake
-kundo *Korean*, Island group
-kysten *Norwegian*, Coast
Kyun *Burmese*, Island

L
Laaq *Somali*, Watercourse
Lac *French*, Lake
Lacul *Romanian*, Lake
Lagh *Somali*, Stream
Lago *Italian, Portuguese, Spanish*, Lake
Lagoa *Portuguese*, Lagoon
Laguna *Italian, Spanish*, Lagoon, lake
Laht *Estonian*, Bay
Laut *Indonesian*, Bay
Lembalemba *Malagasy*, Plateau
Lerr *Armenian*, Mountain
Lerrnashght'a *Armenian*, Mountain range
Les *Czech*, Forest
Lich *Armenian*, Lake
Liehtao *Chinese*, Island group
Liqeni *Albanian*, Lake
Límni *Greek*, Lake
Ling *Chinese*, Mountain range
Llano *Spanish*, Plain, prairie
Lumi *Albanian*, River
Lyman *Ukrainian*, Estuary

M
Madīnat *Arabic*, City, town
Mae Nam *Thai*, River
-mägi *Estonian*, Hill
Maja *Albanian*, Mountain
Mal *Albanian*, Mountains
Mal-aya, -oye, -yy, *Russian*, Small
-man *Korean*, Bay
Mar *Spanish*, Lake
Marios *Lithuanian*, Lake
Massif *French*, Mountains
Meer *German*, Lake
-meer *Dutch*, Lake
Melkosopochnik *Russian*, Plain
-meri *Estonian*, Sea
Mifraẕ *Hebrew*, Bay
Minami- *Japanese*, South(ern)
-misaki *Japanese*, Cape, point
Monkhafad *Arabic*, Depression
Montagne(s) *French*, Mountain(s)
Montañas *Spanish*, Mountains
Mont(s) *French*, Mountain(s)
Monte *Italian, Portuguese*, Mountain
More *Russian*, Sea
Mörön *Mongolian*, River
Mys *Russian*, Cape, point

N
-nada *Japanese*, Open stretch of water
Nagor'ye *Russian*, Upland
Naḩal *Hebrew*, River
Nahr *Arabic*, River
Nam *Laotian*, River
Namakzār *Persian*, Salt desert
Né-a, -on, -os *Greek*, New
Nedre- *Norwegian*, Lower
-neem *Estonian*, Cape, point
Nehri *Turkish*, River
-nes *Norwegian*, Cape, point
Nevado *Spanish*, Mountain (snow-capped)
Nieder- *German*, Lower
Nishi- *Japanese*, West(ern)
-nísi *Greek*, Island
Nisoi *Greek*, Islands
Nizhn-eye, -iy, -iye, -yaya *Russian*, Lower
Nizmennost' *Russian*, Lowland, plain
Nord *Danish, French, German*, North
Norte *Portuguese, Spanish*, North
Nos *Bulgarian*, Point, spit
Nosy *Malagasy*, Island
Nov-a, -i, *Bulgarian, Serbo-Croatian*, New
Nov-aya, -o, -oye, -yy, -yye *Russian*, New
Now-a, -e, -y *Polish*, New
Nur *Mongolian*, Lake
Nuruu *Mongolian*, Mountains
Nuur *Mongolian*, Lake
Nyzovyna *Ukrainian*, Lowland, plain

O
-ø *Danish*, Island
Ober- *German*, Upper
Oblast' *Russian*, Province
Órmos *Greek*, Bay
Orol(i) *Uzbek*, Island
Øster- *Norwegian*, Eastern
Ostrov(a) *Russian*, Island(s)
Otok *Serbo-Croatian*, Island
Oued *Arabic*, Watercourse
-oy *Faeroese*, Island
-øy(a) *Norwegian*, Island
Oya *Sinhala*, River
Ozero *Russian, Ukrainian*, Lake

P
Passo *Italian*, Pass
Pegunungan *Indonesian, Malay*, Mountain range
Pélagos *Greek*, Sea
Pendi *Chinese*, Basin
Penisola *Italian*, Peninsula
Pertuis *French*, Strait
Peski *Russian*, Sands
Phanom *Thai*, Mountain
Phou *Laotian*, Mountain
Pi *Chinese*, Point
Pic *Catalan, French*, Peak
Pico *Portuguese, Spanish*, Peak
-piggen *Danish*, Peak
Pik *Russian*, Peak
Pivostriv *Ukrainian*, Peninsula
Planalto *Portuguese*, Plateau
Planina, Planini *Bulgarian, Macedonian, Serbo-Croatian*, Mountain range
Plato *Russian*, Plateau
Ploskogor'ye *Russian*, Upland
Poluostrov *Russian*, Peninsula
Ponta *Portuguese*, Point
Porthmós *Greek*, Strait
Pótamos *Greek*, River
Presa *Spanish*, Dam
Prokhod *Bulgarian*, Pass
Proliv *Russian*, Strait
Pulau *Indonesian, Malay*, Island
Pulu *Malay*, Island
Punta *Spanish*, Point
Pushcha *Belarussian*, Forest
Puszcza *Polish*, Forest

Q
Qā' *Arabic*, Depression
Qalamat *Arabic*, Well
Qatorkŭh(i) *Tajik*, Mountain
Qiuling *Chinese*, Hills
Qolleh *Persian*, Mountain
Qu *Tibetan*, Stream
Quan *Chinese*, Well
Qulla(i) *Tajik*, Peak
Qundao *Chinese*, Island group

R
Raas *Somali*, Cape
-rags *Latvian*, Cape
Ramlat *Arabic*, Sands
Ra's *Arabic*, Cape, headland, point
Ravnina *Bulgarian, Russian*, Plain
Récif *French*, Reef
Recife *Portuguese*, Reef
Reka *Bulgarian*, River
Represa (Rep.) *Portuguese, Spanish*, Reservoir
Reshteh *Persian*, Mountain range
Respublika *Russian*, Republic, first-order administrative division
Respublika(si) *Uzbek*, Republic, first-order administrative division
-retsugan *Japanese*, Chain of rocks
-rettō *Japanese*, Island chain
Riacho *Spanish*, Stream
Riban' *Malagasy*, Mountains
Rio *Portuguese*, River
Río *Spanish*, River
Riu *Catalan*, River
Rivier *Dutch*, River
Rivière *French*, River
Rowd *Pashtu*, River
Rt *Serbo-Croatian*, Point
Rūd *Persian*, River
Rūdkhāneh *Persian*, River
Rudohorie *Slovak*, Mountains
Ruisseau *French*, Stream

S
-saar *Estonian*, Island
-saari *Finnish*, Island
Sabkhat *Arabic*, Salt marsh
Sāgar(a) *Hindi*, Lake, reservoir
Şaḩrā' *Arabic*, Desert
Saint, Sainte *French*, Saint
Salar *Spanish*, Salt-pan
Salto *Portuguese, Spanish*, Waterfall
Samudra *Sinhala*, Reservoir
-san *Japanese, Korean*, Mountain
-sanchi *Japanese*, Mountains
-sandur *Icelandic*, Beach
Sankt *German, Swedish*, Saint
-sanmaek *Korean*, Mountain range
-sanmyaku *Japanese*, Mountain range
San, Santa, Santo *Italian, Portuguese, Spanish*, Saint
São *Portuguese*, Saint
Sarīr *Arabic*, Desert
Sebkha, Sebkhet *Arabic*, Depression, salt marsh
Sedlo *Czech*, Pass
See *German*, Lake
Selat *Indonesian*, Strait
Selatan *Indonesian*, Southern
-selkä *Finnish*, Lake, ridge
Selseleh *Persian*, Mountain range
Serra *Portuguese*, Mountain
Serranía *Spanish*, Mountain
-seto *Japanese*, Channel, strait
Sever-naya, -noye, -nyy, -o *Russian*, Northern
Sha'īb *Arabic*, Watercourse
Shākh *Kurdish*, Mountain
Shamo *Chinese*, Desert
Shan *Chinese*, Mountain(s)
Shankou *Chinese*, Pass
Shanmo *Chinese*, Mountain range
Shaţţ *Arabic*, Distributary
Shet' *Amharic*, River
Shi *Chinese*, Municipality
-shima *Japanese*, Island
Shiqqat *Arabic*, Depression
-shotō *Japanese*, Group of islands
Shuiku *Chinese*, Reservoir
Shūrkhog(i) *Uzbek*, Salt marsh
Sierra *Spanish*, Mountains
Sint *Dutch*, Saint
-sjø(en) *Norwegian*, Lake
-sjön *Swedish*, Lake
Solonchak *Russian*, Salt lake
Solonchakovyye Vpadiny *Russian*, Salt basin, wetlands
Son *Vietnamese*, Mountain
Sông *Vietnamese*, River
Sør- *Norwegian*, Southern
-spitze *German*, Peak
Star-á, -é *Czech*, Old
Star-aya, -oye, -yy, -yye *Russian*, Old
Stenó *Greek*, Strait
Step' *Russian*, Steppe
Štít *Slovak*, Peak
Stœng *Cambodian*, River
Stolovaya Strana *Russian*, Plateau
Stredné *Slovak*, Middle
Střední *Czech*, Middle
Stretto *Italian*, Strait
Su Anbari *Azerbaijani*, Reservoir
-suidō *Japanese*, Channel, strait
Sund *Swedish*, Sound, strait
Sungai *Indonesian, Malay*, River
Suu *Turkish*, River

T
Tal *Mongolian*, Plain
Tandavan' *Malagasy*, Mountain range
Tangorombohitr' *Malagasy*, Mountain massif
Tanjung *Indonesian, Malay*, Cape, point
Tao *Chinese*, Island
Ţaraq *Arabic*, Hills
Tassili *Berber*, Mountain, plateau
Tau *Russian*, Mountain(s)
Taungdan *Burmese*, Mountain range
Techníti Límni *Greek*, Reservoir
Tekojärvi *Finnish*, Reservoir
Teluk *Indonesian, Malay*, Bay
Tengah *Indonesian*, Middle
Terara *Amharic*, Mountain
Timur *Indonesian*, Eastern
-tind(an) *Norwegian*, Peak
Tizma(si) *Uzbek*, Mountain range, ridge
-tō *Japanese*, Island
Tog *Somali*, Valley
-tōge *Japanese*, Pass
Togh(i) *Uzbek*, Mountain
Tônlé *Cambodian*, Lake
Top *Dutch*, Peak
-tunturi *Finnish*, Mountain
Ţurāq *Arabic*, Hills
Tur'at *Arabic*, Channel

U
Udde(n) *Swedish*, Cape, point
'Uqlat *Arabic*, Well
Utara *Indonesian*, Northern
Uul *Mongolian*, Mountains

V
Väin *Estonian*, Strait
Vallée *French*, Valley
-vatn *Icelandic*, Lake
-vatnet *Norwegian*, Lake
Velayat *Turkmen*, Province
-vesi *Finnish*, Lake
Vestre- *Norwegian*, Western
-vidda *Norwegian*, Plateau
-vík *Icelandic*, Bay
-viken *Swedish*, Bay, inlet
Vinh *Vietnamese*, Bay
Víztárloló *Hungarian*, Reservoir
Vodaskhovishcha *Belarussian*, Reservoir
Vodokhranilishche (Vdkhr.) *Russian*, Reservoir
Vodoskhovyshche (Vdskh.) *Ukrainian*, Reservoir
Volcán *Spanish*, Volcano
Vostochn-o, yy *Russian*, Eastern
Vozvyshennost' *Russian*, Upland, plateau
Vozyera *Belarussian*, Lake
Vpadina *Russian*, Depression
Vrchovina *Czech*, Mountains
Vrha *Macedonian*, Peak
Vychodné *Slovak*, Eastern
Vysochyna *Ukrainian*, Upland
Vysočina *Czech*, Upland

W
Waadi *Somali*, Watercourse
Wādī *Arabic* Watercourse
Wāḩat, Wâhat *Arabic*, Oasis
Wald *German*, Forest
Wan *Chinese*, Bay
Way *Indonesian*, River
Webi *Somali*, River
Wenz *Amharic*, River
Wiloyat(i) *Uzbek*, Province
Wyżyna *Polish*, Upland
Wzgórza *Polish*, Upland
Wzvyshsha *Belarussian*, Upland

X
Xé *Laotian*, River
Xi *Chinese*, Stream

Y
-yama *Japanese*, Mountain
Yanchi *Chinese*, Salt lake
Yang *Chinese*, Bay
Yanhu *Chinese*, Salt lake
Yarımadası *Azerbaijani, Turkish*, Peninsula
Yaylası *Turkish*, Plateau
Yazovir *Bulgarian*, Reservoir
Yoma *Burmese*, Mountains
Ytre- *Norwegian*, Outer
Yü *Chinese*, Island
Yunhe *Chinese*, Canal
Yuzhn-o, -yy *Russian*, Southern

Z
-zaki *Japanese*, Cape, point
Zaliv *Bulgarian, Russian*, Bay
-zan *Japanese*, Mountain
Zangbo *Tibetan*, River
Zapadn-aya, -o, -yy *Russian*, Western
Západné *Slovak*, Western
Západní *Czech*, Western
Zatoka *Polish, Ukrainian*, Bay
-zee *Dutch*, Sea
Zemlya *Russian*, Earth, land
Zizhiqu *Chinese*, Autonomous region

INDEX

GLOSSARY OF ABBREVIATIONS

This glossary provides a comprehensive guide to the abbreviations used in this Atlas, and in the Index.

A
abbrev. abbreviated
AD Anno Domini
Afr. Afrikaans
Alb. Albanian
Amh. Amharic
anc. ancient
approx. approximately
Ar. Arabic
Arm. Armenian
ASEAN Association of South East Asian Nations
ASSR Autonomous Soviet Socialist Republic
Aust. Australian
Az. Azerbaijani
Azerb. Azerbaijan

B
Basq. Basque
BC before Christ
Bel. Belorussian
Ben. Bengali
Ber. Berber
B-H Bosnia-Herzegovina
bn billion (one thousand million)
BP British Petroleum
Bret. Breton
Brit. British
Bul. Bulgarian
Bur. Burmese

C
C central
C. Cape
°C degrees Centigrade
CACM Central America Common Market
Cam. Cambodian
Cant. Cantonese
CAR Central African Republic
Cast. Castilian
Cat. Catalan
CEEAC Central America Common Market
Chin. Chinese
CIS Commonwealth of Independent States
cm centimetre(s)
Cro. Croat
Cz. Czech
Czech Rep. Czech Republic

D
Dan. Danish
Div. Divehi
Dom. Rep. Dominican Republic
Dut. Dutch

E
E east
EC *see* EU
EEC *see* EU
ECOWAS Economic Community of West African States
ECU European Currency Unit
EMS European Monetary System
Eng. English
est estimated
Est. Estonian
EU European Union (previously European Community [EC], European Economic Community [EEC])

F
°F degrees Fahrenheit
Faer. Faeroese
Fij. Fijian
Fin. Finnish
Fr. French
Fris. Frisian
ft foot/feet
FYROM Former Yugoslav Republic of Macedonia

G
g gram(s)
Gael. Gaelic
Gal. Galician
GDP Gross Domestic Product (the total value of goods and services produced by a country excluding income from foreign countries)
Geor. Georgian
Ger. German
Gk Greek
GNP Gross National Product (the total value of goods and services produced by a country)

H
Heb. Hebrew
HEP hydro-electric power
Hind. Hindi
hist. historical
Hung. Hungarian

I
I. Island
Icel. Icelandic
in inch(es)
In. Inuit (Eskimo)
Ind. Indonesian
Intl International
Ir. Irish
Is Islands
It. Italian

J
Jap. Japanese

K
Kaz. Kazakh
kg kilogram(s)
Kir. Kirghiz
km kilometre(s)
km² square kilometre (singular)
Kor. Korean
Kurd. Kurdish

L
L. Lake
LAIA Latin American Integration Association
Lao. Laotian
Lapp. Lappish
Lat. Latin
Latv. Latvian
Liech. Liechtenstein
Lith. Lithuanian
Lux. Luxembourg

M
m million/metre(s)
Mac. Macedonian
Maced. Macedonia
Mal. Malay
Malg. Malagasy
Malt. Maltese
mi. mile(s)
Mong. Mongolian
Mt. Mountain
Mts Mountains

N
N north
NAFTA North American Free Trade Agreement
Nep. Nepali
Neth. Netherlands
Nic. Nicaraguan
Nor. Norwegian
NZ New Zealand

P
Pash. Pashtu
PNG Papua New Guinea
Pol. Polish
Poly. Polynesian
Port. Portuguese
prev. previously

R
Rep. Republic
Res. Reservoir
Rmsch Romansch
Rom. Romanian
Rus. Russian
Russ. Fed. Russian Federation

S
S south
SADC Southern Africa Development Community
SCr. Serbian, Croatian
Sinh. Sinhala
Slvk Slovak
Slvn. Slovene
Som. Somali
Sp. Spanish
St., St Saint
Strs Straits
Swa. Swahili
Swe. Swedish
Switz. Switzerland

T
Taj. Tajik
Th. Thai
Thai. Thailand
Tib. Tibetan
Turk. Turkish
Turkm. Turkmenistan

U
UAE United Arab Emirates
Uigh. Uighur
UK United Kingdom
Ukr. Ukrainian
UN United Nations
Urd. Urdu
US/USA United States of America
USSR Union of Soviet Socialist Republics
Uzb. Uzbek

V
var. variant
Vdkhr. Vodokhranilishche (Russian for reservoir)
Vdskh. Vodoskhovyshche (Ukrainian for reservoir)
Vtn. Vietnamese

W
W west
Wel. Welsh

Y
Yugo. Yugoslavia

THIS INDEX LISTS all the placenames and features shown on the regional and continental maps in this Atlas. Placenames are referenced to the largest scale map on which they appear. The policy followed throughout the Atlas is to use the local spelling or local name at regional level; commonly-used English language names may occasionally be added (in parentheses) where this is an aid to identification e.g. Firenze (Florence). English names, where they exist, have been used for all international features e.g. oceans and country names; they are also used on the continental maps and in the introductory World Today section; these are then fully cross-referenced to the local names found on the regional maps. The index also contains commonly-found alternative names and variant spellings, which are also fully cross-referenced.

All main entry names are those of settlements unless otherwise indicated by the use of italicized definitions or representative symbols, which are keyed at the foot of each page.

1

25 de Mayo *see* Veinticinco de Mayo
143 *Y13* **26 Bakı Komissarı** ***Rus.*** Imeni 26 Bakinskikh Komissarov. SE Azerbaijan *39.18N 49.13E*
26 Baku Komissarlary Adyndaky *see* Imeni 26 Bakinskikh Komissarov
8 *M16* **100 Mile House** ***var.*** Hundred Mile House. British Columbia, SW Canada *51.39N 121.19W*

A

Aa *see* Gauja
97 *G24* **Aabenraa** ***var.*** Åbenrå, ***Ger.*** Apenrade. Sønderjylland, SW Denmark *55.03N 9.25E*
97 *G20* **Aabybro** ***var.*** Åbybro. Nordjylland, N Denmark *57.09N 9.45E*
103 *C16* **Aachen** ***Dut.*** Aken, ***Fr.*** Aix-la-Chapelle; ***anc.*** Aquae Grani, Aquisgranum. Nordrhein-Westfalen, W Germany *50.47N 6.06E*
Aaiún *see* Laâyoune
97 *M24* **Aakirkeby** ***var.*** Åkirkeby. Bornholm, E Denmark *55.04N 14.55E*
97 *G20* **Aalborg** ***var.*** Ålborg, Ålborg-Nørresundby; ***anc.*** Alburgum. Nordjylland, N Denmark *57.03N 9.55E*
Aalborg Bugt *see* Ålborg Bugt
103 *J21* **Aalen** Baden-Württemberg, S Germany *48.49N 10.06E*
97 *G21* **Aalestrup** ***var.*** Ålestrup. Viborg, NW Denmark *56.42N 9.31E*
100 *I11* **Aalsmeer** Noord-Holland, C Netherlands *52.16N 4.43E*
101 *F18* **Aalst** ***Fr.*** Alost. Oost-Vlaanderen, C Belgium *50.57N 4.03E*
101 *K18* **Aalst** Noord-Brabant, S Netherlands *51.46N 5.07E*
100 *O12* **Aalten** Gelderland, E Netherlands *51.55N 6.34E*
101 *D17* **Aalter** Oost-Vlaanderen, NW Belgium *51.04N 3.28E*
Aanaar *see* Inari
Aanaarjävri *see* Inarijärvi
95 *M17* **Äänekoski** Länsi-Suomi, W Finland *62.33N 25.44E*
144 *H7* **Aanjar** ***var.*** 'Anjar. C Lebanon *33.45N 35.56E*
85 *G21* **Aansluit** Northern Cape, N South Africa *26.41S 22.24E*
Aar *see* Aare
110 *F7* **Aarau** Aargau, N Switzerland *47.22N 8.00E*
110 *D8* **Aarberg** Bern, W Switzerland *47.02N 7.15E*
101 *D16* **Aardenburg** Zeeland, SW Netherlands *51.16N 3.27E*
110 *D8* **Aare** ***var.*** Aar. ≈ W Switzerland
110 *F7* **Aargau** ***Fr.*** Argovie. ◈ *canton* N Switzerland
Aarhus *see* Århus
Aarlen *see* Arlon
97 *G21* **Aars** ***var.*** Års. Nordjylland, N Denmark *56.49N 9.31E*
101 *I17* **Aarschot** Vlaams Brabant, C Belgium *50.58N 4.49E*
Aassi, Nahr el *see* Orontes
Aat *see* Ath
166 *G7* **Aba** ***prev.*** Ngawa. Sichuan, C China *32.51N 101.46E*
79 *V17* **Aba** Abia, S Nigeria *5.06N 7.22E*
81 *P16* **Aba** Orientale, NE Dem. Rep. Congo *3.52N 30.13E*
146 *J6* **Abā al Qazāz, Bi'r** *well* NW Saudi Arabia *26.37N 36.50E*
Abā as Su'ūd *see* Najrān
61 *G14* **Abacaxis, Rio** ≈ NW Brazil
Abaco Island *see* Great Abaco/Little Abaco
Abaco Island *see* Great Abaco, N Bahamas
148 *K10* **Ābādān** Khūzestān, SW Iran *30.24N 48.18E*
149 *O10* **Ābādeh** Fārs, C Iran *31.10N 52.39E*
76 *H8* **Abadla** W Algeria *31.04N 2.39W*
61 *M20* **Abaeté** Minas Gerais, SE Brazil *19.10S 45.24W*
169 *Q10* **Abag Qi** ***var.*** Xin Hot. Nei Mongol Zizhiqu, N China *43.58N 114.59E*
64 *P7* **Abaí** Caazapá, S Paraguay *25.58S 55.54W*
203 *O2* **Abaiang** ***var.*** Apia; ***prev.*** Charlotte Island. *atoll* Tungaru, W Kiribati
Abaj *see* Abay
79 *U15* **Abaji** Federal Capital District, C Nigeria *8.35N 6.54E*
39 *O7* **Abajo Peak** ▲ Utah, W USA *37.51N 109.28W*
79 *V16* **Abakaliki** Ebonyi, SE Nigeria *6.18N 8.07E*
126 *Hh15* **Abakan** Respublika Khakasiya, S Russian Federation *53.43N 91.25E*
126 *Hh15* **Abakan** ≈ S Russian Federation
79 *S11* **Abala** Tillabéri, SW Niger *14.55N 3.27E*
79 *U11* **Abalak** Tahoua, C Niger *15.28N 6.18E*
121 *N14* **Abalyanka** ***Rus.*** Obolyanka. ≈ N Belarus
126 *Ii14* **Aban** Krasnoyarskiy Kray, S Russian Federation *56.41N 96.04E*
149 *P9* **Āb Anbār-e Kān Sorkh** Yazd, C Iran *31.22N 53.37E*
59 *G16* **Abancay** Apurímac, SE Peru *13.37S 72.52W*
202 *H2* **Abaokoro** *atoll* Tungaru, W Kiribati
Abariringa *see* Kanton
149 *P10* **Abarkū** Yazd, C Iran
172 *Qq5* **Abashiri** ***var.*** Abasiri. Hokkaidō, NE Japan *44.00N 144.15E*
172 *Q6* **Abashiri-gawa** ≈ Hokkaidō, NE Japan
172 *Q5* **Abashiri-ko** ◎ Hokkaidō, NE Japan
Abasiri *see* Abashiri
43 *P10* **Abasolo** Tamaulipas, C Mexico *24.02N 98.18W*
194 *L16* **Abau** Central, S PNG *10.09S 148.40E*
151 *R10* **Abay** ***var.*** Abaj. Karaganda, C Kazakhstan *49.34N 72.54E*
83 *I15* **Ābaya Hāyk'** ***Eng.*** Lake Margherita, ***It.*** Abbaia. ◎ SW Ethiopia
Ābay Wenz *see* Blue Nile
126 *Hh15* **Abaza** Respublika Khakasiya, S Russian Federation *52.40N 89.58E*
Abbaia *see* Ābaya Hāyk'
149 *Q13* **Āb Bārīk** Fārs, S Iran
109 *C18* **Abbasanta** Sardegna, Italy, C Mediterranean Sea *40.08N 8.49E*
Abbatis Villa *see* Abbeville
32 *M3* **Abbaye, Point** *headland* Michigan, N USA *46.58N 88.08W*
Abbazia *see* Opatija
Abbé, Lake *see* Abhe, Lake
105 *N2* **Abbeville** ***anc.*** Abbatis Villa. Somme, N France *50.06N 1.50E*
25 *R7* **Abbeville** Alabama, S USA *31.34N 85.16W*
25 *U6* **Abbeville** Georgia, SE USA *31.58N 83.18W*
24 *I9* **Abbeville** Louisiana, S USA *29.58N 92.08W*
23 *P12* **Abbeville** South Carolina, SE USA *34.10N 82.22W*
99 *B20* **Abbeyfeale** ***Ir.*** Mainistir na Féile. SW Ireland *52.24N 9.21W*
108 *D8* **Abbiategrasso** Lombardia, NW Italy *45.24N 9.04E*
95 *I14* **Abborrträsk** Norrbotten, N Sweden *65.24N 19.33E*
204 *J9* **Abbot Ice Shelf** *ice shelf* Antarctica
8 *M17* **Abbotsford** British Columbia, SW Canada *49.01N 122.18W*
32 *K6* **Abbotsford** Wisconsin, N USA *44.57N 90.19W*
155 *U5* **Abbottābād** North-West Frontier Province, NW Pakistan *34.08N 73.10E*
121 *M14* **Abchuha** ***Rus.*** Obchuga. Minskaya Voblasts', NW Belarus *54.30N 29.23E*
100 *I10* **Abcoude** Utrecht, C Netherlands *52.16N 4.58E*
145 *N2* **'Abd al 'Azīz, Jabal** ▲▲ NE Syria
147 *U17* **'Abd al Kūrī** *island* SE Yemen
145 *Z13* **'Abd Allāh, Khawr** *bay* Iraq/Kuwait
131 *U6* **Abdulino** Orenburgskaya Oblast', W Russian Federation *53.37N 53.39E*
80 *J10* **Abéché** ***var.*** Abécher, Abeshr. Ouaddaï, SE Chad *13.49N 20.49E*
Abécher *see* Abéché
149 *S8* **Āb-e Garm va Sard** Khorāsān, E Iran
79 *R8* **Abeïbara** Kidal, NE Mali *19.07N 1.52E*
107 *P5* **Abejar** Castilla-León, N Spain *41.48N 2.46W*
56 *E9* **Abejorral** Antioquia, W Colombia *5.52N 75.34W*
Abela *see* Ávila
Abellinum *see* Avellino
94 *Q2* **Abeløya** *island* Kong Karls Land, E Svalbard
82 *I13* **Ābeltī** Oromo, C Ethiopia *8.09N 37.31E*
203 *O2* **Abemama** ***var.*** Apamama; ***prev.*** Roger Simpson Island. *atoll* Tungaru, W Kiribati
176 *Yy14* **Abemaree** ***var.*** Abemarre. Papua, E Indonesia *7.03S 140.10E*
79 *O16* **Abengourou** E Ivory Coast *6.42N 3.27W*
Åbenrå *see* Aabenraa
103 *L22* **Abens** ≈ SE Germany
79 *S16* **Abeokuta** Ogun, SW Nigeria *7.07N 3.21E*
99 *I20* **Aberaeron** SW Wales, UK *52.15N 4.15W*
Aberbrothock *see* Arbroath
Abercorn *see* Mbala
31 *R6* **Abercrombie** North Dakota, N USA *46.25N 96.42W*
191 *T7* **Aberdeen** New South Wales, SE Australia *32.09S 150.55E*
9 *T15* **Aberdeen** Saskatchewan, S Canada *52.15N 106.19W*
85 *H25* **Aberdeen** Eastern Cape, S South Africa *32.30S 24.00E*
98 *L9* **Aberdeen** ***anc.*** Devana. NE Scotland, UK *57.10N 2.04W*
23 *X2* **Aberdeen** Maryland, NE USA *39.28N 76.09W*
25 *N3* **Aberdeen** Mississippi, S USA *33.49N 88.32W*
23 *T10* **Aberdeen** North Carolina, SE USA *35.07N 79.25W*
31 *P8* **Aberdeen** South Dakota, N USA *45.27N 98.29W*
34 *F8* **Aberdeen** Washington, NW USA *46.57N 123.48W*
98 *K9* **Aberdeen** *cultural region* NE Scotland, UK
15 *K6* **Aberdeen Lake** ◎ Nunavut, NE Canada
98 *J10* **Aberfeldy** C Scotland, UK *56.38N 3.48W*
99 *K21* **Abergavenny** ***anc.*** Gobannium. SE Wales, UK *51.50N 3.00W*
Abergwaun *see* Fishguard
Abermarre *see* Abemaree
27 *N5* **Abernathy** Texas, SW USA *33.49N 101.50W*
Abersee *see* Wolfgangsee
Abertawe *see* Swansea
Aberteifi *see* Cardigan
34 *I15* **Abert, Lake** ◎ Oregon, NW USA
99 *I20* **Aberystwyth** W Wales, UK *52.25N 4.04W*
Abeshr *see* Abéché
108 *F10* **Abetone** Toscana, C Italy *44.09N 10.42E*
129 *V5* **Abez'** Respublika Komi, NW Russian Federation *66.32N 61.41E*
148 *M5* **Āb Garm** Qazvin, N Iran
147 *N12* **Abhā** 'Asīr, SW Saudi Arabia *18.16N 42.31E*
148 *M5* **Abhar** Zanjān, NW Iran *36.07N 49.19E*
Abhé Bad/Ābhē Bid Hāyk' *see* Abhe, Lake
82 *K12* **Abhe, Lake** ***var.*** Lake Abbé, ***Amh.*** Ābhē Bid Hāyk', ***Som.*** Abhé Bad. ◎ Djibouti/Ethiopia
79 *V17* **Abia** ◈ *state* SE Nigeria
145 *V9* **'Abīd 'Alī** E Iraq *32.20N 45.58E*
121 *O17* **Abidavichy** ***Rus.*** Obidovichi. Mahilyowskaya Voblasts', E Belarus *53.21N 30.24E*
117 *L15* **Abide** Çanakkale, NW Turkey *40.04N 26.13E*
79 *N17* **Abidjan** S Ivory Coast *5.19N 4.01W*
Āb-i-Istāda *see* Īstādeh-ye Moqor, Āb-e-
29 *N4* **Abilene** Kansas, C USA *38.55N 97.12W*
27 *Q7* **Abilene** Texas, SW USA *32.27N 99.43W*
Abindonia *see* Abingdon
99 *M21* **Abingdon** ***anc.*** Abindonia. S England, UK *51.40N 1.16W*
32 *K12* **Abingdon** Illinois, N USA *40.48N 90.24W*
23 *P8* **Abingdon** Virginia, NE USA *36.42N 81.58W*
Abingdon *see* Pinta, Isla
20 *J15* **Abington** Pennsylvania, NE USA *40.06N 75.05W*
130 *K14* **Abinsk** Krasnodarskiy Kray, SW Russian Federation *44.51N 38.12E*
39 *R9* **Abiquiu Reservoir** ⊠ New Mexico, SW USA
94 *I10* **Abisko** Norrbotten, N Sweden *68.21N 18.49E*
10 *G12* **Abitibi** ≈ Ontario, S Canada
10 *H12* **Abitibi, Lac** ◎ Ontario/Quebec, S Canada
82 *J10* **Ābīy Ādī** Tigray, N Ethiopia *13.40N 38.57E*
120 *H6* **Abja-Paluoja** Viljandimaa, S Estonia *58.07N 25.19E*
143 *Q8* **Abkhazia** ◈ *autonomous republic* NW Georgia
190 *F1* **Abminga** South Australia *26.07S 134.49E*
77 *W9* **Abnûb** C Egypt *27.18N 31.09E*
Åbo *see* Turku
158 *G9* **Abohar** Punjab, N India *30.10N 74.12E*
79 *O17* **Aboisso** SE Ivory Coast *5.27N 3.06W*
80 *H5* **Abo, Massif d'** ▲▲ NW Chad
79 *R16* **Abomey** S Benin *7.14N 2.00E*
81 *F16* **Abong Mbang** Est, SE Cameroon *3.58N 13.10E*
113 *L23* **Abony** Pest, C Hungary *47.10N 20.00E*
80 *J11* **Abou-Déïa** Salamat, SE Chad *11.30N 19.18E*
Aboudouhour *see* Abū aḑ Ḑuhūr
Abou Kémal *see* Abū Kamāl
Abou Simbel *see* Abu Simbel
143 *T12* **Abovyan** C Armenia *40.16N 44.33E*
179 *P8* **Abra** ≈ Luzon, N Philippines
147 *P15* **Abrād, Wādī** *seasonal river* W Yemen
Abraham Bay *see* The Carlton
106 *G10* **Abrantes** ***var.*** Abrántes. Santarém, C Portugal *39.28N 8.12W*
64 *J4* **Abra Pampa** Jujuy, N Argentina *22.46S 65.40W*
Abrashlare *see* Brezovo
56 *G7* **Abrego** Norte de Santander, N Colombia *8.07N 73.15W*
Abrene *see* Pytalovo
42 *C7* **Abreojos, Punta** *headland* W Mexico *26.43N 113.36W*
67 *J16* **Abrolhos Bank** *undersea feature* W Atlantic Ocean
121 *H19* **Abrova** ***Rus.*** Obrovo. Brestskaya Voblasts', SW Belarus *52.30N 25.31E*
118 *G11* **Abrud** ***Ger.*** Gross-Schlatten, ***Hung.*** Abrudbánya. Alba, SW Romania *46.15N 23.07E*
Abrudbánya *see* Abrud
120 *E6* **Abruka** *island* SW Estonia
109 *J15* **Abruzzese, Appennino** ▲▲ C Italy
109 *J14* **Abruzzo** ◈ *region* C Italy
147 *N14* **'Abs** ***var.*** Sūq 'Abs. W Yemen *16.42N 42.55E*
35 *T12* **Absaroka Range** ▲▲ Montana/Wyoming, NW USA
143 *Z11* **Abşeron Yarımadası** ***Rus.*** Apsheronskiy Poluostrov. *peninsula* E Azerbaijan
149 *N6* **Āb Shīrīn** Eşfahān, C Iran
145 *X10* **Abtān** SE Iraq *31.37N 47.06E*
111 *R6* **Abtenau** Salzburg, NW Austria *47.33N 13.21E*
170 *Dd12* **Abu** Yamaguchi, Honshū, SW Japan *34.30N 131.26E*
158 *E14* **Ābu** Rājasthān, N India *24.40N 72.49E*
144 *I4* **Abū aḑ Ḑuhūr** ***Fr.*** Aboudouhour. Idlib, NW Syria *35.30N 37.00E*
149 *P17* **Abū al Abyaḑ** *island* C UAE
144 *K10* **Abū al Ḩuşayn, Khabrat** ◎ N Jordan
145 *R8* **Abū al Jīr** C Iraq *33.16N 42.55E*
145 *Y12* **Abū al Khaşīb** ***var.*** Abul Khasib. SE Iraq *30.26N 48.00E*
145 *U12* **Abū at Tubrah, Thaqb** *well* S Iraq *30.54N 45.02E*
77 *V11* **Abu Balâs** ▲ SW Egypt *24.28N 27.36E*
Abu Dhabi *see* Abū Ẓaby
145 *R8* **Abū Farūkh** C Iraq *33.06N 43.18E*
82 *C12* **Abu Gabra** Southern Darfur, W Sudan *11.01N 26.49E*
145 *P10* **Abū Ghār, Sha'īb** *dry watercourse* S Iraq
82 *G7* **Abu Hamed** River Nile, N Sudan *19.31N 33.19E*
145 *O5* **Abū Ḩardān** ***var.*** Hajîne. Dayr az Zawr, E Syria *34.45N 40.49E*
145 *T7* **Abū Ḩassawīyah** E Iraq *33.52N 44.47E*
144 *K10* **Abū Ḩifnah, Wādī** *dry watercourse* N Jordan
79 *V15* **Abuja** ● (Nigeria) Federal Capital District, C Nigeria *9.04N 7.28E*
145 *R9* **Abū Jahaf, Wādī** *dry watercourse* C Iraq
58 *F12* **Abujao, Río** ≈ E Peru
145 *U12* **Abū Jasrah** S Iraq *30.43N 44.50E*
145 *O6* **Abū Kamāl** ***Fr.*** Abou Kémal. Dayr az Zawr, E Syria *34.28N 40.55E*
175 *Q11* **Abuki, Pegunungan** ▲▲ Sulawesi, C Indonesia
171 *Ll14* **Abukuma-gawa** ≈ Honshū, C Japan
171 *Ll15* **Abukuma-sanchi** ▲▲ Honshū, C Japan
Abula *see* Ávila
Abul Khasib *see* Abū al Khaşīb
81 *K16* **Abumombazi** ***var.*** Abumonbazi. Equateur, N Dem. Rep. Congo *3.43N 22.06E*
Abumonbazi *see* Abumombazi
61 *D15* **Abunã** Rondônia, W Brazil *9.40S 65.19W*
58 *K13* **Abunã, Rio** ***var.*** Río Abuná. ≈ Bolivia/Brazil
144 *G10* **Abū Nuşayr** ***var.*** Abu Nuseir. Al 'Āşimah, W Jordan *32.03N 35.58E*
Abu Nuseir *see* Abū Nuşayr
145 *T12* **Abū Qabr** S Iraq *31.03N 44.34E*
144 *K5* **Abū Raḩbah, Jabal** ▲▲ C Syria
145 *S5* **Abū Rajāsh** N Iraq *34.47N 43.36E*
145 *W13* **Abū Raqrāq, Ghadīr** *well* S Iraq *30.15N 45.57E*
158 *E14* **Ābu Road** Rājasthān, N India *24.28N 72.46E*
82 *I6* **Abu Shagara, Ras** *headland* NE Sudan *18.04N 38.31E*
77 *W12* **Abu Simbel** ***var.*** Abou Simbel, Abū Sunbul. *ancient monument* S Egypt *22.25N 31.37E*
145 *U12* **Abū Sudayrah** S Iraq *30.55N 44.58E*
145 *T10* **Abū Şukhayr** S Iraq *31.54N 44.27E*
Abū Sunbul *see* Abu Simbel
172 *Nn6* **Abuta** Hokkaidō, NE Japan *42.34N 140.44E*

◆ Country
● Country Capital
◇ Dependent Territory
○ Dependent Territory Capital
◈ Administrative Region
✈ International Airport
▲ Mountain
▲▲ Mountain Range
⛰ Volcano
≈ River
◎ Lake
⊠ Reservoir

193 E18 **Abut Head** headland South Island, NZ 43.06S 170.16E
82 E9 **Abu 'Urug** Northern Kordofan, C Sudan 15.52N 30.25E
82 K12 **Ābuyē Mēda** ▲ C Ethiopia 10.23N 39.46E
179 R13 **Abuyog** Leyte, C Philippines 10.45N 124.58E
82 D11 **Abu Zabad** Western Kordofan, C Sudan 12.21N 29.16E
Abū Ẓabī see Abū Ẓaby
149 P16 **Abū Ẓaby** var. Abū Ẓabī, Eng. Abu Dhabi. ● (UAE) Abū Ẓaby, C UAE 24.30N 54.20E
77 X8 **Abu Zenima** E Egypt 29.01N 33.08E
97 N17 **Åby** Östergötland, S Sweden 58.40N 16.19E
Abyaḍ, Al Baḥr al see White Nile
Ābybro see Aabybro
82 D13 **Abyei** Western Kordofan, S Sudan 9.34N 28.28E
Abyla see Ávila
Abymes see les Abymes
Abyssinia see Ethiopia
Açâba see Assaba
56 F11 **Acacías** Meta, C Colombia 3.58N 73.46W
60 L13 **Açailândia** Maranhão, E Brazil 4.51S 47.25W
Acaill see Achill Island
44 E8 **Acajutla** Sonsonate, W El Salvador 13.35N 89.48W
81 D17 **Acalayong** SW Equatorial Guinea 1.05N 9.34E
43 N13 **Acámbaro** Guanajuato, C Mexico 20.01N 100.45W
56 C6 **Acandí** Chocó, NW Colombia 8.28N 77.18W
106 H4 **A Cañiza** var. La Cañiza. Galicia, NW Spain 42.13N 8.16W
42 J11 **Acaponeta** Nayarit, C Mexico 22.30N 105.21W
42 J11 **Acaponeta, Río de** ≈ C Mexico
43 O16 **Acapulco** var. Acapulco de Juárez. Guerrero, S Mexico 16.51N 99.53W
Acapulco de Juárez see Acapulco
57 T13 **Acarai Mountains** Sp. Serra Acaraí. ▲ Brazil/Guyana
Acaraí, Serra see Acarai Mountains
60 O13 **Acaraú** Ceará, NE Brazil 4.35S 37.37W
56 J6 **Acarigua** Portuguesa, N Venezuela 9.34N 69.12W
44 C6 **Acatenango, Volcán de** ▲ S Guatemala 14.30N 90.52W
43 Q15 **Acatlán** var. Acatlán de Osorio. Puebla, S Mexico 18.12N 98.01W
Acatlán de Osorio see Acatlán
43 S15 **Acayucan** var. Acayucán. Veracruz-Llave, E Mexico 17.58N 94.58W
Accho see 'Akko
23 Y5 **Accomac** Virginia, NE USA 37.43N 75.39W
79 Q17 **Accra** ● (Ghana) SE Ghana 5.33N 0.15W
99 L17 **Accrington** NW England, UK 53.46N 2.21W
63 B19 **Acebal** Santa Fe, C Argentina 33.13S 60.49W
173 Ee4 **Aceh** off. Daerah Istimewa Aceh, var. Acheen, Achin, Atchin, Atjeh. ◆ autonomous district NW Indonesia
109 M18 **Acerenza** Basilicata, S Italy 40.46N 15.51E
109 K17 **Acerra** anc. Acerrae. Campania, S Italy 40.55N 14.22E
Acerrae see Acerra
Ach'asar Lerr see Achkasar
59 J17 **Achacachi** La Paz, W Bolivia 16.04S 68.39W
56 K7 **Achaguas** Apure, C Venezuela 7.46N 68.13W
160 H12 **Achalpur** prev. Elichpur, Ellichpur. Mahārāshtra, C India 21.19N 77.30E
63 F18 **Achar** Tacuarembó, C Uruguay 32.26S 56.10W
117 H19 **Acharnés** var. Aharnes; prev. Akharnaí. Attikí, C Greece 38.09N 23.58E
Acheen see Aceh
101 K16 **Achel** Limburg, NE Belgium 51.15N 5.31E
117 D16 **Achelóos** var. Akhelóös, Aspropótamos; anc. Achelous. ≈ W Greece
Achelous see Achelóos
169 W8 **Acheng** Heilongjiang, NE China 45.31N 126.55E
111 N6 **Achenkirch** Tirol, W Austria 47.31N 11.42E
103 L24 **Achenpass** pass Austria/Germany 47.35N 11.39E
111 N7 **Achensee** ◎ W Austria
103 F22 **Achern** Baden-Württemberg, SW Germany 48.37N 8.04E
117 C16 **Acherón** ≈ W Greece
79 W11 **Achétinamou** ≈ S Niger
158 J12 **Achhnera** Uttar Pradesh, N India 27.10N 77.45E
44 C7 **Achiguate, Río** ≈ S Guatemala
99 A16 **Achill Head** Ir. Ceann Acla. headland W Ireland 53.58N 10.14W
99 A16 **Achill Island** Ir. Acaill. island W Ireland
102 H11 **Achim** Niedersachsen, NW Germany 53.01N 9.01E
155 S5 **Achīn** Nangarhār, E Afghanistan 34.04N 70.40E
Achin see Aceh
126 Hh14 **Achinsk** Krasnoyarskiy Kray, S Russian Federation 56.21N 90.25E
168 E5 **Achit Nuur** ◎ NW Mongolia
143 T11 **Achkasar** Arm. Ach'asar Lerr. ▲ Armenia/Georgia 41.09N 43.55E
130 K13 **Achuyevo** Krasnodarskiy Kray, SW Russian Federation 46.00N 38.01E
83 F16 **Achwa** var. Aswa. ≈ N Uganda
142 E15 **Acıgöl** salt lake SW Turkey
109 L24 **Acireale** Sicilia, Italy, C Mediterranean Sea 37.36N 15.10E
Aciris see Agri
27 N7 **Ackerly** Texas, SW USA 32.31N 101.43W
24 M4 **Ackerman** Mississippi, S USA 33.18N 89.10W
31 W13 **Ackley** Iowa, C USA 42.33N 93.03W
46 J5 **Acklins Island** island SE Bahamas
Acla, Ceann see Achill Head
64 H11 **Aconcagua, Cerro** ▲ W Argentina 32.36S 69.53W
Açores/Açores, Arquipélago dos/Açores, Ilhas dos see Azores
106 G2 **A Coruña** Cast. La Coruña. ◆ province Galicia, NW Spain
106 H2 **A Coruña** Cast. La Coruña, Eng. Corunna; anc. Caronium. Galicia, NW Spain 43.22N 8.24W
44 L10 **Acoyapa** Chontales, S Nicaragua 12.01N 85.08W
108 H13 **Acquapendente** Lazio, C Italy 42.44N 11.52E
108 J13 **Acquasanta Terme** Marche, C Italy 42.46N 13.24E
108 I13 **Acquasparta** Lazio, C Italy 42.41N 12.31E
108 C9 **Acqui Terme** Piemonte, NW Italy 44.40N 8.28E
Acrae see Palazzola Acreide
190 F7 **Acraman, Lake** salt lake South Australia
61 A15 **Acre** off. Estado do Acre. ◆ state W Brazil
Acre see 'Akko
61 C16 **Acre, Rio** ≈ W Brazil
109 N20 **Acri** Calabria, SW Italy 39.30N 16.22E
Acte see Ágion Óros
203 Y12 **Actéon, Groupe** island group Îles Tuamotu, SE French Polynesia
13 P12 **Acton-Vale** Quebec, SE Canada 45.39N 72.31W
43 P13 **Actopan** var. Actopán. Hidalgo, C Mexico 20.16N 98.57W
61 P14 **Açu** var. Assu. Rio Grande do Norte, E Brazil 5.33S 36.55W
Acunum Acusio see Montélimar
79 Q17 **Ada** SE Ghana 5.46N 0.37E
31 R5 **Ada** Minnesota, N USA 47.18N 96.31W
33 R12 **Ada** Ohio, N USA 40.46N 83.49W
29 O12 **Ada** Oklahoma, C USA 34.48N 96.38W
114 L8 **Ada** Serbia, N Serbia and Montenegro (Yugoslavia) 45.48N 20.08E
Ada Bazar see Adapazarı
42 D3 **Adair, Bahía de** bay NW Mexico
106 M7 **Adaja** ≈ N Spain
40 H17 **Adak Island** island Aleutian Islands, Alaska, USA
Adalia see Antalya
Adalia, Gulf of see Antalya Körfezi
147 X9 **Adam** N Oman 22.22N 57.30E
Adama see Nazrēt
62 I8 **Adamantina** São Paulo, S Brazil 21.40S 51.04W
81 E14 **Adamaoua** Eng. Adamawa. ◆ province N Cameroon
70 F11 **Adamaoua, Massif d'** Eng. Adamawa Highlands. plateau NW Cameroon
79 Y14 **Adamawa** ◆ state E Nigeria
Adamawa see Adamaoua
Adamawa Highlands see Adamaoua, Massif d'
108 F6 **Adamello** ▲ N Italy 46.09N 10.33E
83 J14 **Ādamī Tulu** Oromo, C Ethiopia 7.52N 38.39E
65 M23 **Adam, Mount** var. Monte Independencia. ▲ West Falkland, Falkland Islands 51.36S 60.00W
31 R16 **Adams** Nebraska, C USA 40.25N 96.30W
20 H8 **Adams** New York, NE USA 43.48N 75.57W
31 Q3 **Adams** North Dakota, N USA 48.23N 98.01W
161 I23 **Adam's Bridge** chain of shoals NW Sri Lanka
34 H10 **Adams, Mount** ▲ Washington, NW USA 46.12N 121.29W
Adam's Peak see Sri Pada
203 R16 **Adam's Rock** island Pitcairn Island, Pitcairn Islands
203 P16 **Adamstown** O (Pitcairn Islands) Pitcairn Island, Pitcairn Islands 25.04S 130.04W
22 G10 **Adamsville** Tennessee, S USA 35.14N 88.23W
27 S9 **Adamsville** Texas, SW USA 31.15N 98.09W
147 O17 **'Adan** Eng. Aden. SW Yemen 12.51N 45.04E
142 K16 **Adana** var. Seyhan. Adana, S Turkey 37.00N 35.19E
142 K16 **Adana** var. Seyhan. ◆ province S Turkey
Adâncata see Horlivka
175 Nn10 **Adang, Teluk** bay Borneo, C Indonesia
142 F11 **Adapazarı** prev. Ada Bazar. Sakarya, NW Turkey 40.48N 30.24E
82 H8 **Adarama** River Nile, NE Sudan 17.04N 34.57E
205 Q16 **Adare, Cape** headland Antarctica 71.24S 170.27E
108 E6 **Adda** anc. Addua. ≈ N Italy
82 A13 **Adda** ≈ W Sudan
149 Q17 **Ad Dab'īyah** Abū Ẓaby, C UAE 24.16N 54.07E
149 O18 **Ad Ḍafrah** desert S UAE
147 Q6 **Ad Dahnā'** desert E Saudi Arabia
76 A11 **Ad Dakhla** var. Dakhla. SW Western Sahara 23.46N 15.56W
Ad Dalanj see Dilling
Ad Damar see Ed Damer
Ad Damazīn see Ed Damazin
Ad Dāmir see Ed Damer
181 N2 **Ad Dammām** desert NE Saudi Arabia
147 R6 **Ad Dammān** var. Dammām. Ash Sharqīyah, NE Saudi Arabia 26.23N 50.04E
Ad Dāmūr see Damoûr
146 K5 **Ad Dār al Ḥamrā'** Tabūk, NW Saudi Arabia 27.21N 37.45E
146 M13 **Ad Darb** Jīzān, SW Saudi Arabia 17.45N 42.15E
147 O8 **Ad Dawādimī** Ar Riyāḍ, C Saudi Arabia 24.31N 44.21E
149 N16 **Ad Dawḥah** Eng. Doha. ● (Qatar) C Qatar 25.15N 51.36E
149 N16 **Ad Dawḥah** Eng. Doha. ✕ C Qatar 25.11N 51.37E
145 S6 **Ad Dawr** N Iraq 34.30N 43.49E
145 Y12 **Ad Dayr** var. Dayr, Shahbān. E Iraq 30.45N 47.36E
Addi Arkay see Ādī Ārk'ay
145 X15 **Ad Dibdibah** physical region Iraq/Kuwait
Ad Diffah see Libyan Plateau
Addis Ababa see Ādīs Ābeba
Addison see Webster Springs
145 U10 **Ad Dīwānīyah** var. Diwaniyah. C Iraq 32.00N 44.57E
Addua see Adda
157 K22 **Addu Atoll** atoll S Maldives
Ad Dujail see Ad Dujayl
145 T7 **Ad Dujayl** var. Ad Dujail. N Iraq 33.49N 44.16E
Ad Duwaym/Ad Duwēm see Ed Dueim
101 D16 **Adegem** Oost-Vlaanderen, NW Belgium 51.12N 3.31E
25 U7 **Adel** Georgia, SE USA 31.08N 83.25W
31 U14 **Adel** Iowa, C USA 41.36N 94.01W
190 I9 **Adelaide** state capital South Australia 34.55S 138.36E
46 H2 **Adelaide** New Providence, N Bahamas 24.59N 77.30W
190 I9 **Adelaide** ✕ South Australia 34.55S 138.31E
204 H6 **Adelaide Island** island Antarctica
15 K4 **Adelaide Peninsula** peninsula Nunavut, N Canada
189 P2 **Adelaide River** Northern Territory, N Australia 13.12S 131.06E
78 M10 **'Adel Bagrou** Hodh ech Chargui, SE Mauritania 15.33N 7.04W
194 I11 **Adelbert Range** ▲ N PNG
188 K3 **Adele Island** island Western Australia
109 O17 **Adelfia** Puglia, SE Italy 41.01N 16.52E
205 V16 **Adélie Coast** physical region Antarctica
205 V14 **Adélie, Terre** physical region Antarctica
Adelnau see Odolanów
Adelsberg see Postojna
Aden see 'Adan
147 Q17 **Aden, Gulf of** gulf SW Arabian Sea
79 V10 **Aderbissinat** Agadez, C Niger 15.30N 7.57E
Adhaim see Al 'Uẓaym
149 R16 **Adh Dhayd** var. Al Dhaid. Ash Shāriqah, NE UAE 25.19N 55.51E
146 M4 **'Adhfā'** spring/well NW Saudi Arabia 29.15N 41.24E
144 I13 **'Ādhriyāt, Jabāl al** ▲ S Jordan
194 L12 **Adi** ≈ New Britain, C PNG
82 I10 **Ādī Ārk'ay** var. Addi Arkay. Amhara, N Ethiopia 13.18N 37.56E
190 C7 **Adieu, Cape** headland South Australia 32.01S 132.12E
108 H8 **Adige** Ger. Etsch. ≈ N Italy
82 J10 **Ādīgrat** Tigray, N Ethiopia 14.17N 39.27E
160 I13 **Ādilābād** var. Ādilābād. Andhra Pradesh, C India 19.40N 78.31E
37 P2 **Adin** California, W USA 41.10N 120.57W
176 Vv12 **Adi, Pulau** island E Indonesia
20 K8 **Adirondack Mountains** ▲ New York, NE USA
82 J13 **Ādīs Ābeba** Eng. Addis Ababa. ● (Ethiopia) Ādīs Ābeba, C Ethiopia 8.59N 38.43E
82 J13 **Ādīs Ābeba** ✕ Ādīs Ābeba, C Ethiopia 8.58N 38.53E
82 I11 **Ādīs Zemen** Amhara, N Ethiopia 12.00N 37.43E
Adi Ugri see Mendefera
143 N15 **Adıyaman** Adıyaman, SE Turkey 37.46N 38.15E
143 N15 **Adıyaman** ◆ province S Turkey
118 L11 **Adjud** Vrancea, E Romania 46.06N 27.11E
47 T6 **Adjuntas** C Puerto Rico 18.10N 66.44W
Adjuntas, Presa de las see Vicente Guerrero, Presa
Ādkup see Erikub Atoll
130 L15 **Adler** Krasnodarskiy Kray, SW Russian Federation 43.25N 39.58E
Adler see Orlice
110 G7 **Adliswil** Zürich, NW Switzerland 47.20N 8.30E
15 L1 **Admiralty Inlet** fjord Baffin Island, Nunavut, NE Canada
34 G7 **Admiralty Inlet** inlet Washington, NW USA
41 X13 **Admiralty Island** island Alexander Archipelago, Alaska, USA
194 K8 **Admiralty Islands** island group N PNG
142 B14 **Adnan Menderes** ✕ (İzmir) İzmir, W Turkey 38.16N 27.09E
39 V6 **Adobe Creek Reservoir** ⊠ Colorado, C USA
79 T16 **Ado-Ekiti** Ekiti, SW Nigeria 7.42N 5.13E
Adola see Kibre Mengist
63 C23 **Adolfo González Chaues** Buenos Aires, E Argentina
161 H17 **Ādoni** Andhra Pradesh, C India 15.37N 77.16E
104 K15 **Adour** anc. Aturus. ≈ SW France
Adowa see Ādwa
107 O15 **Adra** Andalucía, S Spain 36.45N 3.01W
109 L24 **Adrano** Sicilia, Italy, C Mediterranean Sea 37.39N 14.49E
76 I9 **Adrar** C Algeria 27.55N 0.12W
78 K7 **Adrar** ◆ region C Mauritania
76 L11 **Adrar** ▲ SE Algeria
76 A12 **Adrar Souttouf** ▲ SW Western Sahara
Adrasman see Adrasmon
153 Q10 **Adrasmon** Rus. Adrasman. NW Tajikistan 40.38N 69.56E
80 K10 **Adré** Ouaddaï, E Chad 13.39N 22.09E
108 H9 **Adria** anc. Atria, Hadria, Hatria. Veneto, NE Italy 45.03N 12.04E
33 R10 **Adrian** Michigan, N USA 41.54N 84.02W
31 S11 **Adrian** Minnesota, N USA 43.38N 95.55W
29 R5 **Adrian** Missouri, C USA 38.24N 94.21W
26 M2 **Adrian** Texas, SW USA 35.16N 102.39W
23 S4 **Adrian** West Virginia, NE USA 38.53N 80.14W
Adrianople/Adrianopolis see Edirne
123 Mm8 **Adriatic Basin** undersea feature Adriatic Sea, N Mediterranean Sea
Adriatico, Mare see Adriatic Sea
108 L13 **Adriatic Sea** Alb. Deti Adriatik, It. Mare Adriatico, SCr. Jadransko More, Slvn. Jadransko Morje. sea N Mediterranean Sea
Adriatik, Deti see Adriatic Sea
Adua see Ādwa
Aduana del Sásabe see El Sásabe
81 O17 **Adusa** Orientale, NE Dem. Rep. Congo 1.25N 28.04E
120 J13 **Adutiškis** Švenčionys, E Lithuania 55.09N 26.34E
29 Y7 **Advance** Missouri, C USA 37.06N 89.54W
67 D25 **Adventure Sound** bay East Falkland, Falkland Islands
82 J10 **Ādwa** var. Adowa, It. Adua. Tigray, N Ethiopia 14.08N 38.51E
126 M8 **Adycha** ≈ NE Russian Federation
130 L14 **Adygeya, Respublika** ◆ autonomous republic SW Russian Federation
152 C11 **Adzhikui** Turkm. Ajyguyy. Balkanskiy Velayat, W Turkmenistan 39.46N 53.57E
79 N17 **Adzopé** SE Ivory Coast 6.07N 3.54W
129 U4 **Adz'va** ≈ NW Russian Federation
129 U5 **Adz'vavom** Respublika Komi, NW Russian Federation 66.35N 59.13E
Ædua see Autun
117 K19 **Aegean Islands** island group Greece/Turkey
Aegean North see Vóreion Aigaíon
117 I17 **Aegean Sea** Gk. Aigaíon Pélagos, Aigaío Pélagos, Turk. Ege Denizi. sea NE Mediterranean Sea
Aegean South see Nótion Aigaíon
120 H3 **Aegviidu** Ger. Charlottenhof. Harjumaa, NW Estonia 59.16N 25.37E
Aegyptus see Egypt
Aelana see Al 'Aqabah
Aelok see Ailuk Atoll
Aelōninae see Ailinginae Atoll
Aelōnļaplap see Ailinglaplap Atoll
Æmilia see Emilia-Romagna
Æmilianum see Millau
Aemona see Ljubljana
Aenaria see Ischia
Aeolian Islands see Eolie, Isole
203 Z3 **Aeon Point** headland Kiritimati, NE Kiribati 1.46N 157.10W
97 G24 **Ærø** Ger. Arrö. island C Denmark
97 H24 **Ærøskøbing** Fyn, C Denmark 54.52N 10.24E
Æsernia see Isernia
106 G3 **A Estrada** Galicia, NW Spain 42.40N 8.28W
117 C18 **Aetós** Itháki, Iónioi Nísoi, Greece, C Mediterranean Sea 38.21N 20.40E
203 Q8 **Afaahiti** Tahiti, W French Polynesia 17.43S 149.18W
145 U10 **'Afak** C Iraq 32.04N 45.16E
Afanasjevo see Afanas'yevo
129 T14 **Afanas'yevo** var. Afanasjevo. Kirovskaya Oblast', NW Russian Federation 58.55N 53.13E
Afándou see Afántou
117 O23 **Afántou** var. Afándou. Ródos, Dodekánisos, Greece, Aegean Sea 36.16N 28.10E
Afar Depression see Danakil Desert
82 K11 **Afar** ◆ region NE Ethiopia
203 O7 **Afareaitu** Moorea, W French Polynesia 17.33S 149.46W
146 L7 **'Afariyah, Bi'r al** well NW Saudi Arabia 25.28N 39.21E
Afars et des Issas, Territoire Français des see Djibouti
85 D22 **Affenrücken** Karas, SW Namibia 28.05S 15.49E
Afghānestān, Dowlat-e Eslāmī-ye see Afghanistan
154 M6 **Afghanistan** off. Islamic State of Afghanistan, Per. Dowlat-e Eslāmī-ye Afghānestān; prev. Republic of Afghanistan. ◆ Islamic state C Asia
Afgoi see Afgooye
83 N17 **Afgooye** It. Afgoi. Shabeellaha Hoose, S Somalia 2.09N 45.07E
147 N8 **'Afīf** Ar Riyāḍ, C Saudi Arabia 23.57N 42.57E
79 U17 **Afikpo** Ebonyi, SE Nigeria 5.52N 7.58E
Afiun Karahissar see Afyon
96 H7 **Åfjord** Sør-Trøndelag, C Norway 63.57N 10.12E
111 V6 **Aflenz Kurort** Steiermark, E Austria 47.33N 15.14E
76 J6 **Aflou** N Algeria 34.09N 2.06E
83 L18 **Afmadow** Jubbada Hoose, S Somalia 0.24N 42.03E
41 Q14 **Afognak Island** island Alaska, USA
106 J2 **A Fonsagrada** Galicia, NW Spain 43.09N 7.03W
194 L15 **Afore** Northern, S PNG 9.01S 148.22E
61 O15 **Afrânio** Pernambuco, E Brazil 8.31S 40.54W
68-69 **Africa** continent
70 L11 **Africa, Horn of** physical region Ethiopia/Somalia
180 K11 **Africana Seamount** undersea feature SW Indian Ocean 37.10S 29.10E
88 A14 **African Plate** tectonic feature
144 I2 **'Afrīn** Ḥalab, N Syria 36.31N 36.51E
142 M15 **Afşin** Kahramanmaraş, C Turkey 38.13N 36.54E
100 J7 **Afsluitdijk** dam N Netherlands 53.00N 5.10E
31 U15 **Afton** Iowa, C USA 41.01N 94.12W
31 W9 **Afton** Minnesota, N USA 44.54N 92.46W
29 R8 **Afton** Oklahoma, C USA 36.41N 94.57W
142 F14 **Afyon** prev. Afyonkarahisar. Afyon, W Turkey 38.46N 30.31E
142 F14 **Afyon** var. Afiun Karahissar, Afyonkarahisar. ◆ province W Turkey
Afyonkarahisar see Afyon
Agadès see Agadez
79 V10 **Agadez** prev. Agadès. Agadez, C Niger 16.57N 7.56E
79 W8 **Agadez** ◆ department N Niger
76 E8 **Agadir** SW Morocco 30.30N 9.36W
66 M9 **Agadir Canyon** undersea feature SE Atlantic Ocean
151 R12 **Agadyr'** Zhezkazgan, C Kazakhstan 48.15N 72.54E
181 O7 **Agalega Islands** island group N Mauritius
44 K6 **Agalta, Sierra de** ▲ E Honduras
126 Gg10 **Agan** ≈ C Russian Federation
Agana/Agaña see Hagåtña
196 B15 **Agana Bay** bay NW Guam
196 C16 **Agana Field** ✕ (Agana) C Guam 13.28N 144.48E
171 Kk13 **Agano-gawa** ≈ Honshū, C Japan
196 B17 **Aga Point** headland S Guam
160 G9 **Agar** Madhya Pradesh, C India 23.43N 76.01E
83 I14 **Āgaro** Oromo, C Ethiopia 7.52N 36.36E
159 V15 **Agartala** Tripura, NE India 23.49N 91.15E
204 I5 **Agassiz, Cape** headland Antarctica 68.28S 62.58W
183 V13 **Agassiz Fracture Zone** tectonic feature S Pacific Ocean
196 B16 **Agat** W Guam 13.20N 144.38E
196 B16 **Agat Bay** bay W Guam
151 P13 **Agat, Gory** hill C Kazakhstan 46.55N 69.13E
Agatha see Agde
117 M20 **Agathónisi** island Dodekánisos, Greece, Aegean Sea
176 Y13 **Agats** Papua, E Indonesia 5.33S 138.07E
161 C21 **Agatti Island** island Lakshadweep, India, N Indian Ocean
40 D16 **Agattu Island** island Aleutian Islands, Alaska, USA
40 D16 **Agattu Strait** strait Aleutian Islands, Alaska, USA
12 B8 **Agawa** ≈ Ontario, S Canada
12 B8 **Agawa Bay** lake bay Ontario, S Canada
79 N17 **Agboville** SE Ivory Coast 5.56N 4.13W
143 V12 **Ağdam** Rus. Agdam. SW Azerbaijan 40.04N 46.00E
105 P16 **Agde** anc. Agatha. Hérault, S France 43.19N 3.28E
105 P16 **Agde, Cap d'** headland S France 43.17N 3.30E
Agedabia see Ajdābiyā
104 L14 **Agen** anc. Aginnum. Lot-et-Garonne, SW France 44.12N 0.37E
Agendicum see Sens
171 K16 **Ageo** Saitama, Honshū, S Japan 35.58N 139.36E
111 R5 **Ager** ≈ N Austria
Agere Hiywet see Hāgere Hiywet
110 G8 **Ägerisee** ◎ W Switzerland
148 M10 **Āghā Jārī** Khūzestān, SW Iran 30.48N 49.45E
41 P15 **Aghiyuk Island** island Alaska, USA
76 B12 **Aghouinit** SE Western Sahara 22.14N 13.10W
Aghri Dagh see Büyükağrı Dağı
76 B10 **Aghzoumal, Sebkhet** var. Sebjet Agsumal. salt lake E Western Sahara
117 F15 **Agiá** var. Ayiá. Thessalía, C Greece 39.43N 22.45E
42 G7 **Agiabampo, Estero de** estuary NW Mexico
124 Nn4 **Agía Fýlaxis** var. Ayia Phyla. S Cyprus 34.43N 33.02E
Agialoúsa see Yenierenköy
117 M21 **Agía Marína** Léros, Dodekánisos, Greece, Aegean Sea 37.09N 26.51E
124 Oo3 **Agía Nápa** var. Ayia Napa. E Cyprus 34.59N 34.00E
117 L16 **Agía Paraskeví** Lésvos, E Greece 39.13N 26.19E
117 J15 **Agías Eirínis, Akrotírio** headland Límnos, E Greece 39.47N 25.21E
117 L17 **Agiasós** var. Ayiásos, Ayiássos. Lésvos, E Greece 39.04N 26.22E
Aginnum see Agen
126 K16 **Aginskiy Buryatskiy Avtonomnyy Okrug** ◆ autonomous district S Russian Federation
126 Kk16 **Aginskoye** Aginskiy Buryatskiy Avtonomnyy Okrug, S Russian Federation 51.10N 114.31E
117 I14 **Ágion Óros** Eng. Mount Athos. ◆ monastic republic NE Greece
117 H14 **Ágion Óros** var. Akte, Aktí; anc. Acte. peninsula NE Greece
116 D13 **Ágios Achílleios** religious building Dytikí Makedonía, N Greece 40.46N 21.04E
117 J16 **Ágios Efstrátios** var. Áyios Evstrátios, Hagios Evstrátios. island E Greece
117 H20 **Ágios Geórgios** island Kykládes, Greece, Aegean Sea
117 Q23 **Ágios Geórgios** island SE Greece
117 E21 **Ágios Ilías** ▲ S Greece 36.57N 22.19E
117 K25 **Ágios Ioannis, Akrotírio** headland Kríti, Greece, E Mediterranean Sea 35.19N 25.46E
117 L20 **Ágios Kírykos** var. Áyios Kírikos. Ikaría, Dodekánisos, Greece, Aegean Sea 37.04N 26.16E
117 D16 **Ágios Nikolaos** Thessalía, C Greece 39.33N 21.21E
117 K25 **Ágios Nikólaos** var. Áyios Nikólaos. Kríti, Greece, E Mediterranean Sea 35.12N 25.43E
Ágios Sérgios see Yeniboğaziçi
117 H14 **Ágiou Órous, Kólpos** gulf N Greece
109 K24 **Agira** anc. Agyrium. Sicilia, Italy, C Mediterranean Sea 37.39N 14.31E
117 G20 **Agkístri** island S Greece
116 G12 **Agkistro** var. Angistro. ▲ NE Greece 41.21N 23.29E
105 O17 **Agly** ≈ S France
Agnetheln see Agnita
12 E10 **Agnew Lake** ◎ Ontario, S Canada
79 O16 **Agnibilékrou** E Ivory Coast 7.10N 3.10W
118 I11 **Agnita** Ger. Agnetheln, Hung. Szentágota. Sibiu, SW Romania 45.59N 24.39E
109 K15 **Agnone** Molise, C Italy 41.49N 14.21E
171 Hh17 **Ago** Mie, Honshū, SW Japan 34.18N 136.50E
108 C8 **Agogna** ≈ N Italy
Agoitz see Aoiz-Agoitz
79 P17 **Agona Swedru** var. Swedru. SE Ghana 5.31N 0.42W
Agordat see Akurdet
105 N15 **Agout** ≈ S France
158 J12 **Āgra** Uttar Pradesh, N India 27.09N 78.00E
Agra and Oudh, United Provinces of see Uttar Pradesh
Agram see Zagreb
107 U5 **Agramunt** Cataluña, NE Spain 41.48N 1.07E
107 Q5 **Agreda** Castilla-León, N Spain 41.51N 1.55W
143 S13 **Ağrı** var. Karaköse; prev. Karakılısse. Ağrı, NE Turkey 39.43N 43.04E
143 S13 **Ağrı** ◆ province NE Turkey
109 N19 **Agri** anc. Aciris. ≈ S Italy
Agri Dagi see Büyükağrı Dağı
109 J24 **Agrigento** Gk. Akragas; prev. Girgenti. Sicilia, Italy, C Mediterranean Sea 37.19N 13.33E
196 K4 **Agrihan** island N Northern Mariana Islands
117 D18 **Agrínio** prev. Agrinion. Dytikí Ellás, W Greece 38.37N 21.25E
Agrinion see Agrínio
117 G17 **Agriovótano** Évvoia, C Greece 39.00N 23.18E
109 L18 **Agropoli** Campania, S Italy 40.21N 14.58E
131 T3 **Agryz** Udmurtskaya Respublika, NW Russian Federation 56.27N 52.58E
143 U11 **Ağstafa** Rus. Akstafa. NW Azerbaijan 41.06N 45.28E
Agsumal, Sebjet see Aghzoumal, Sebkhet
42 J11 **Agua Brava, Laguna** lagoon W Mexico
56 F7 **Aguachica** Cesar, N Colombia 8.16N 73.35W
61 J20 **Água Clara** Mato Grosso do Sul, SW Brazil 20.21S 52.58W
46 D5 **Aguada de Pasajeros** Cienfuegos, C Cuba 22.22N 80.50W
56 J5 **Aguada Grande** Lara, N Venezuela 10.34N 69.30W
47 S5 **Aguadilla** W Puerto Rico 18.24N 67.09W
45 S16 **Aguadulce** Coclé, S Panama 8.16N 80.31W
106 L14 **Aguadulce** Andalucía, S Spain 37.15N 4.58W
43 O8 **Agualeguas** Nuevo León, NE Mexico 26.17N 99.30W
42 L9 **Aguanaval, Río** ≈ C Mexico
44 J5 **Aguán, Río** ≈ N Honduras
27 R16 **Agua Nueva** Texas, SW USA 26.57N 98.34W
62 J8 **Aguapeí, Rio** ≈ S Brazil
63 E14 **Aguapey, Río** ≈ NE Argentina
42 G3 **Agua Prieta** Sonora, NW Mexico 31.16N 109.33W
106 G5 **A Guardia** var. Laguardia, La Guardia. Galicia, NW Spain 41.54N 8.52W
58 E6 **Aguarico, Río** ≈ Ecuador/Peru
57 O6 **Aguasay** Monagas, NE Venezuela 9.25N 63.43W
42 M12 **Aguascalientes** Aguascalientes, C Mexico 21.53N 102.17W
42 L12 **Aguascalientes** ◆ state C Mexico
118 **Aguas Calientes, Río** ≈ S Peru
107 R7 **Aguasvivas** ≈ NE Spain
62 J7 **Água Vermelha, Represa de** ⊠ S Brazil
58 E12 **Aguaytía** Ucayali, C Peru 9.04S 75.32W
106 I5 **A Gudiña** var. La Gudiña. Galicia, NW Spain 42.04N 7.07W
106 G7 **Águeda** Aveiro, N Portugal 40.34N 8.28W
106 J8 **Águeda** ≈ Portugal/Spain
79 Q8 **Aguelhok** Kidal, NE Mali 19.18N 0.50E
79 V12 **Aguié** Maradi, S Niger 13.28N 7.43E
196 K8 **Aguijan** island S Northern Mariana Islands
106 M14 **Aguilar** var. Aguilar de la Frontera. Andalucía, S Spain 37.31N 4.40W
106 M3 **Aguilar de Campóo** Castilla-León, N Spain 42.46N 4.15W
Aguilar de la Frontera see Aguilar
44 F7 **Aguilares** San Salvador, C El Salvador 13.56N 89.09W
107 Q14 **Águilas** Murcia, SE Spain 37.24N 1.36W
42 L15 **Aguililla** Michoacán de Ocampo, SW Mexico 18.43N 102.45W
Agulhas see L'Agulhas
180 J11 **Agulhas Bank** undersea feature SW Indian Ocean
180 K11 **Agulhas Basin** undersea feature SW Indian Ocean
85 F26 **Agulhas, Cape** Afr. Kaap Agulhas. headland SW South Africa 34.51S 19.59E
Agulhas, Kaap see Agulhas, Cape
62 O9 **Agulhas Negras, Pico das** ▲ SE Brazil 22.21S 44.39W
180 K11 **Agulhas Plateau** undersea feature SW Indian Ocean
172 Oo14 **Aguni-jima** island Nansei-shotō, SW Japan
Agurain see Salvatierra
179 Rr15 **Agusan** ≈ Mindanao, S Philippines
56 G5 **Agustín Codazzi** var. Codazzi. Cesar, N Colombia 10.01N 73.15W
Agyrium see Agira
76 L12 **Ahaggar** high plateau region SE Algeria
Ahal Welayaty see Akhalskiy Velayat
148 K2 **Ahar** Āzarbāyjān-e Khāvarī, NW Iran 38.25N 47.07E
Aharnes see Acharnés
144 J3 **Aḥaṣ, Jabal** ▲ NW Syria
144 J3 **Aḥaṣ, Jebal** ▲ W Syria
193 G16 **Ahaura** ≈ South Island, NZ
102 E13 **Ahaus** Nordrhein-Westfalen, NW Germany 52.04N 7.01E
203 U9 **Ahe** atoll Îles Tuamotu, C French Polynesia
192 N10 **Ahimanawa Range** ▲ North Island, NZ
121 I19 **Ahinski Kanal** Rus. Oginskiy Kanal. canal SW Belarus
195 N16 **Ahioma** SE PNG 10.18S 150.33E
192 I2 **Ahipara** Northland, North Island, NZ 35.11S 173.07E
192 I2 **Ahipara Bay** bay SE Tasman Sea
41 N13 **Ahklun Mountains** ▲ Alaska, USA
143 R14 **Ahlat** Bitlis, E Turkey 38.45N 42.30E
103 F14 **Ahlen** Nordrhein-Westfalen, W Germany 51.46N 7.52E
160 D10 **Ahmadābād** var. Ahmedabad. Gujarāt, W India 23.03N 72.40E
149 R10 **Ahmadābād** Kermān, C Iran 35.51N 59.36E
Ahmadī see Al Aḥmadī
Ahmad Khel see Ḥasan Khēl
161 F14 **Ahmadnagar** var. Ahmednagar. Mahārāshtra, W India 19.07N 74.48E
155 T9 **Ahmadpur Siāl** Punjab, E Pakistan 30.40N 71.47E
79 N5 **Aḥmar, 'Erg el** desert N Mali
82 K13 **Ahmar Mountains** ▲ C Ethiopia
Ahmedabad see Ahmadābād
Ahmednagar see Ahmadnagar
116 N12 **Ahmetbey** Kırklareli, NW Turkey 41.26N 27.35E
12 H12 **Ahmic Lake** ◎ Ontario, S Canada
202 G12 **Ahoa** Île Uvea, E Wallis and Futuna 13.16S 176.12W
42 G8 **Ahomé** Sinaloa, C Mexico 25.55N 109.10W
23 X8 **Ahoskie** North Carolina, SE USA 36.17N 76.59W
103 D17 **Ahr** ≈ W Germany
149 N12 **Ahram** var. Ahrom. Būshehr, S Iran 28.52N 51.18E
102 J9 **Ahrensburg** Schleswig-Holstein, N Germany 53.40N 10.13E
Ahrom see Ahram
95 L17 **Ähtäri** Länsi-Suomi, W Finland 62.31N 24.14E
42 K12 **Ahuacatlán** Nayarit, C Mexico 21.04N 104.32W
44 E7 **Ahuachapán** Ahuachapán, W El Salvador 13.55N 89.49W
44 A9 **Ahuachapán** ◆ department W El Salvador
203 V16 **Ahu Akivi** var. Siete Moai. ancient monument Easter Island, Chile, E Pacific Ocean
203 W11 **Ahunui** atoll Îles Tuamotu, C French Polynesia
193 E20 **Ahuriri** ≈ South Island, NZ
97 L22 **Åhus** Skåne, S Sweden 55.55N 14.18E
Ahu Tahira see Ahu Vinapu
203 V16 **Ahu Tepeu** ancient monument Easter Island, Chile, E Pacific Ocean
203 V17 **Ahu Vinapu** var. Ahu Tahira. ancient monument Easter Island, Chile, E Pacific Ocean
148 L9 **Ahvāz** var. Ahwāz; prev. Nāsiri. Khūzestān, SW Iran 31.19N 48.37E
Ahvenanmaa see Åland
147 Q16 **Aḥwar** SW Yemen 13.34N 46.41E
Ahwāz see Ahvāz
Aibak see Āybak
103 K22 **Aichach** Bayern, SE Germany 48.26N 11.06E
171 I16 **Aichi** off. Aichi-ken, var. Aiti. ◆ prefecture Honshū, SW Japan
Aïdin see Aydın
176 Ww12 **Aiduna** Papua, E Indonesia 4.20S 135.15E
Aidussina see Ajdovščina
194 F13 **Aiema** ≈ W PNG
Aifir, Clochán an see Giant's Causeway
Aigaíon Pélagos/Aigaío Pélagos see Aegean Sea
111 S3 **Aigen im Mülkreis** Oberösterreich, N Austria 48.39N 13.57E
117 G20 **Aígina** var. Aíyina, Egina. Aígina, C Greece 37.45N 23.25E
117 G20 **Aígina** island S Greece
117 E18 **Aígio** var. Egio; prev. Aíyion. Dytikí Ellás, S Greece 38.15N 22.04E
110 C10 **Aigle** Vaud, SW Switzerland 46.19N 6.58E
105 P14 **Aigoual, Mont** ▲ S France 44.09N 3.34E
181 O16 **Aigrettes, Pointe des** headland W Réunion 21.01S 55.13E
63 G19 **Aiguá** var. Aigua. Maldonado, S Uruguay 34.13S 54.46W
105 S13 **Aigues** ≈ SE France
105 N10 **Aigurande** Indre, C France 46.26N 1.49E
Ai-hun see Heihe
171 K11 **Aikawa** Niigata, Sado, C Japan 38.04N 138.15E
23 Q13 **Aiken** South Carolina, SE USA 33.33N 81.43W
27 N4 **Aiken** Texas, SW USA 34.06N 101.31W
166 F13 **Ailao Shan** ▲ SW China
45 W14 **Ailigandí** San Blas, NE Panama 9.13N 78.04W
201 R4 **Ailinginae Atoll** var. Aelōninae. atoll Ralik Chain, SW Marshall Islands
201 T7 **Ailinglaplap Atoll** var. Aelōnļaplap. atoll Ralik Chain, S Marshall Islands
Aillionn, Loch see Allen, Lough
98 H13 **Ailsa Craig** island SW Scotland, UK
201 V5 **Ailuk Atoll** var. Aelok. atoll Ratak Chain, NE Marshall Islands
126 Mm12 **Aim** Khabarovskiy Kray, E Russian Federation 58.45N 134.08E
105 R11 **Ain** ◆ department E France
105 S10 **Ain** ≈ E France
120 G7 **Ainaži** Est. Heinaste, Ger. Hainasch. Limbaži, N Latvia 57.51N 24.24E
76 L6 **Aïn Beida** NE Algeria 35.52N 7.25E
78 K4 **'Aïn Ben Tili** Tiris Zemmour, N Mauritania 25.58N 9.30W
76 J5 **Aïn Defla** var. Aïn Eddefla. N Algeria 36.16N 1.58E
Aïn Eddefla see Aïn Defla
76 L5 **Aïn El Bey** ✕ (Constantine) NE Algeria 36.15N 6.36E
117 C19 **Aínos** ▲ Kefallinía, Iónioi Nísoi, Greece, C Mediterranean Sea 38.08N 20.39E
107 T4 **Ainsa** Aragón, NE Spain 42.25N 0.07E
76 I7 **Aïn Sefra** NW Algeria 32.45N 0.32W
31 N13 **Ainsworth** Nebraska, C USA 42.33N 99.51W
Aintab see Gaziantep
76 H5 **Aïn Témouchent** N Algeria 35.18N 1.09W
194 H11 **Aiome** Madang, N PNG 5.04S 144.43E
Aïoun el Atrous/Aïoun el Atroûss see 'Ayoûn el 'Atroûs
56 E11 **Aipe** Huila, C Colombia 3.15N 75.16W
58 D9 **Aipena, Río** ≈ N Peru
59 L19 **Aiquile** Cochabamba, C Bolivia 18.10S 65.10W

◆ Country ● Country Capital ◇ Dependent Territory O Dependent Territory Capital ◆ Administrative Region ✕ International Airport ▲ Mountain ▲ Mountain Range ▲ Volcano ≈ River ◎ Lake ⊠ Reservoir

Aïr see Aïr, Massif de l'
196 E10 **Airai** Babeldaob, C Palau
196 E10 **Airai** ✈ (Oreor) Babeldaob, N Palau 7.22N 134.34E
173 Ff8 **Airbangis** Sumatera, NW Indonesia 0.12N 99.22E
9 Q16 **Airdrie** Alberta, SW Canada 51.20N 114.00W
98 I12 **Airdrie** S Scotland, UK 55.52N 3.58W
Air du Azbine see Aïr, Massif de l'
99 M17 **Aire** ≈ N England, UK
104 K15 **Aire-sur-l'Adour** Landes, SW France 43.43N 0.16W
105 O1 **Aire-sur-la-Lys** Pas-de-Calais, N France 50.39N 2.24E
16 N2 **Air Force Island** island Baffin Island, Nunavut, NE Canada
174 L11 **Airhitam, Teluk** bay Borneo, C Indonesia
175 Rr7 **Airmadidi** Sulawesi, N Indonesia 1.25N 124.58E
79 V8 **Aïr, Massif de l'** var. Aïr, Air du Azbine, Asben. ▲▲ NC Niger
110 G10 **Airolo** Ticino, S Switzerland 46.32N 8.38E
104 K9 **Airvault** Deux-Sèvres, W France 46.51N 0.07W
103 K19 **Aisch** ≈ S Germany
65 G20 **Aisén** off. Región Aisén del General Carlos Ibañez del Campo, var. Aysen. ◈ region S Chile
8 H7 **Aishihik Lake** ◎ Yukon Territory, W Canada
105 P3 **Aisne** ◈ department N France
105 R4 **Aisne** ≈ NE France
111 T4 **Aist** ≈ N Austria
116 K13 **Aisými** Anatolikí Makedonía kai Thráki, NE Greece 41.00N 25.55E
107 S11 **Aitana** ▲ E Spain 38.39N 0.15W
194 F9 **Aitape** var. Eitape. Sandaun, NW PNG 3.07S 142.22E
Aiti see Aichi
31 V6 **Aitkin** Minnesota, N USA 46.31N 93.42W
117 D18 **Aitolikó** var. Etoliko; prev. Aitolikón. Dytikí Ellás, C Greece 38.25N 21.21E
Aitolikón see Aitolikó
202 L15 **Aitutaki** island S Cook Islands
118 H11 **Aiud** Ger. Strassburg, Hung. Nagyenyed; prev. Engeten. Alba, SW Romania 46.16N 23.42E
120 I9 **Aiviekste** ≈ C Latvia
201 Q8 **Aiwo** SW Nauru 0.32S 166.54E
196 E8 **Aiwokako Passage** passage Babeldaob, N Palau
Aix see Aix-en-Provence
105 S15 **Aix-en-Provence** var. Aix; anc. Aquae Sextiae. Bouches-du-Rhône, SE France 43.31N 5.27E
Aix-la-Chapelle see Aachen
105 T11 **Aix-les-Bains** Savoie, E France 45.40N 5.55E
194 E11 **Aiyang, Mount** ▲ NW PNG 5.03S 141.15E
Aíyina see Aígina
Aíyion see Aígio
159 W15 **Āīzawl** Mizoram, NE India 23.40N 92.45E
120 H9 **Aizkraukle** Aizkraukle, S Latvia 56.39N 25.07E
120 C9 **Aizpute** Liepāja, W Latvia 56.43N 21.32E
171 L14 **Aizu-Wakamatsu** var. Aizuwakamatu. Fukushima, Honshū, C Japan 37.27N 139.55E
Aizuwakamatu see Aizu-Wakamatsu
105 X15 **Ajaccio** Corse, France, C Mediterranean Sea 41.54N 8.43E
105 X15 **Ajaccio, Golfe d'** gulf Corse, France, C Mediterranean Sea
43 Q15 **Ajalpán** Puebla, S Mexico 18.25N 97.19W
160 F13 **Ajanta Range** ▲▲ C India
143 R10 **Ajaria** ◈ autonomous republic SW Georgia
Ajastan see Armenia
95 G14 **Ajaureforsen** Västerbotten, N Sweden 65.31N 15.43E
193 H17 **Ajax, Mount** ▲ South Island, NZ 42.34S 172.06E
168 F9 **Aj Bogd Uul** ▲ SW Mongolia 44.49N 95.01E
77 R8 **Ajdābiyā** var. Agedabia, Ajdābiyah. NE Libya 30.46N 20.13E
Ajdābiyah see Ajdābiyā
111 S12 **Ajdovščina** Ger. Haidenschaft, It. Aidussina. W Slovenia 45.52N 13.55E
171 Mm8 **Ajigasawa** Aomori, Honshū, C Japan 40.45N 140.11E
Ajjinena see El Geneina
113 H23 **Ajka** Veszprém, W Hungary 47.07N 17.31E
144 G9 **'Ajlūn** Irbid, N Jordan 32.19N 35.45E
144 H9 **'Ajlūn, Jabal** ▲▲ W Jordan
149 R15 **'Ajmān** var. Ajman, 'Ujmān. 'Ajmān, NE UAE 25.36N 55.42E
158 G12 **Ajmer** var. Ajmere. Rājasthān, N India 26.28N 74.40E
38 J15 **Ajo** Arizona, SW USA 32.22N 112.51W
107 N2 **Ajo, Cabo de** headland N Spain 43.31N 3.36W
38 J16 **Ajo Range** ▲▲ Arizona, SW USA
Ajyguyy see Adzhikui
Akaba see Al 'Aqabah
172 P5 **Akabira** Hokkaidō, NE Japan 43.31N 142.03E
171 K12 **Akadomari** Niigata, Sado, C Japan 37.54N 138.24E
83 E20 **Akagera** var. Kagera. ≈ Rwanda/Tanzania see also Kagera
203 W16 **Akahanga, Punta** headland Easter Island, Chile, E Pacific Ocean
171 Ii16 **Akaishi-dake** ▲ Honshū, S Japan 35.26N 138.09E
171 J16 **Akaishi-sanmyaku** ▲▲ Honshū, S Japan
82 J13 **Āk'ak'i** Oromo, C Ethiopia 8.50N 38.51E
161 G15 **Akalkot** Mahārāshtra, W India 17.36N 76.10E
Akamagaseki see Shimonoseki
172 Q7 **Akan** Hokkaidō, NE Japan 43.09N 144.08E
172 Q6 **Akan-ko** ◎ Hokkaidō, NE Japan
Akanthoú see Tatlısu
193 I19 **Akaroa** Canterbury, South Island, NZ 43.48S 172.58E
82 E6 **Akasha** Northern, N Sudan 21.03N 30.45E
170 G14 **Akashi** var. Akasi. Hyōgo, Honshū, SW Japan 34.37N 134.59E
145 N7 **'Akāsh, Wādī** var. Wādī 'Ukash. dry watercourse W Iraq
Akasi see Akashi
94 K11 **Äkäsjokisuu** Lappi, N Finland 67.28N 23.44E
143 S11 **Akbaba Dağı** ▲ Armenia/Turkey 41.04N 43.28E
142 B15 **Akbük Limanı** bay W Turkey
131 V8 **Akbulak** Orenburgskaya Oblast', W Russian Federation 51.01N 55.35E
143 O11 **Akçaabat** Trabzon, NE Turkey 41.00N 39.36E
143 N15 **Akçadağ** Malatya, C Turkey 38.21N 37.58E
142 G11 **Akçakoca** Bolu, NW Turkey 41.04N 31.07E
Akchakaya, Vpadina see Akdzhakaya, Vpadina
78 H7 **Akchâr** desert W Mauritania
151 S12 **Akchatau** Kaz. Aqshataū. Zhezkazgan, C Kazakhstan 47.58N 74.01E
142 L13 **Akdağlar** ▲▲ C Turkey
142 E17 **Ak Dağları** ▲▲ SW Turkey
142 K13 **Akdağmadeni** Yozgat, C Turkey 39.39N 35.48E
152 G8 **Akdepe** prev. Ak-Tepe, Leninsk, Turkm. Lenin. Dashkhovuzskiy Velayat, N Turkmenistan 42.10N 59.17E
Ak-Dere see Byala
124 O3 **Akdoğan** Gk. Lýsi. C Cyprus 35.06N 33.42E
126 Hh16 **Ak-Dovurak** Respublika Tyva, S Russian Federation 51.09N 90.36E
152 F9 **Akdzhakaya, Vpadina** var. Vpadina Akchakaya. depression N Turkmenistan
175 Tt7 **Akelamo** Pulau Halmahera, E Indonesia 1.27N 128.39E
Aken see Aachen
Akermanceaster see Bath
97 P15 **Åkersberga** Stockholm, C Sweden 59.28N 18.19E
97 H15 **Akershus** ◈ county S Norway
81 L16 **Aketi** Orientale, N Dem. Rep. Congo 2.46N 23.42E
Akgyr Erezi see Gryada Akkyr
152 E12 **Akhalskiy Velayat** Turkm. Ahal Welayaty. ◈ province C Turkmenistan
143 S10 **Akhalts'ikhe** SW Georgia 41.38N 43.03E
Akhangaran see Ohangaron
Akharnaí see Acharnés
77 R7 **Akhḑar, Al Jabal al** hill range NE Libya
Akhelóös see Achelóos
41 Q15 **Akhiok** Kodiak Island, Alaska, USA 56.57N 154.12W
142 C13 **Akhisar** Manisa, W Turkey 38.54N 27.49E
77 X10 **Akhmîm** anc. Panopolis. C Egypt 26.24N 31.50E
158 H6 **Akhnūr** Jammu and Kashmir, NW India 32.57N 74.43E
131 P11 **Akhtuba** ≈ SW Russian Federation
131 P11 **Akhtubinsk** Astrakhanskaya Oblast', SW Russian Federation 48.16N 46.13E
Akhtyrka see Okhtyrka
170 F15 **Aki** Kōchi, Shikoku, SW Japan 33.30N 133.54E
41 N12 **Akiachak** Alaska, USA 60.54N 161.25W
41 N12 **Akiak** Alaska, USA 60.54N 161.12W
203 X11 **Akiaki** atoll Îles Tuamotu, E French Polynesia
10 H9 **Akimiski Island** island Nunavut, C Canada
142 K17 **Akıncı Burnu** headland S Turkey 36.21N 35.47E
Akıncılar see Selçuk
119 U10 **Akinovka** Zaporiz'ka Oblast', S Ukraine
Åkirkeby see Aakirkeby
171 M10 **Akita** Akita, Honshū, C Japan 39.44N 140.06E
171 M10 **Akita** off. Akita-ken. ◈ prefecture Honshū, C Japan
78 H8 **Akjoujt** prev. Fort-Repoux. Inchiri, W Mauritania 19.42N 14.28W
94 H11 **Akka** ▲ N Sweden 67.33N 17.27E
94 H11 **Akkajaure** ◎ N Sweden
Akkala see Oqqal'a
161 L25 **Akkaraipattu** Eastern Province, E Sri Lanka 7.13N 81.51E
151 P13 **Akkense** Zhezkazgan, C Kazakhstan 46.39N 68.06E
Akkerman see Bilhorod-Dnistrovs'kyy
131 W8 **Akkermanovka** Orenburgskaya Oblast', W Russian Federation 51.11N 58.03E
172 Qq7 **Akkeshi** Hokkaidō, NE Japan 43.03N 144.48E
172 Qq7 **Akkeshi-ko** ◎ Hokkaidō, NE Japan
172 Qq8 **Akkeshi-wan** bay NW Pacific Ocean
144 F8 **'Akko** Eng. Acre, Fr. Saint-Jean-d'Acre; Bibl. Accho, Ptolemaïs. Northern, N Israel 32.55N 35.04E
151 Q8 **Akkol'** Kaz. Aqköl; prev. Alekseyevka, Kaz. Alekseevka. Akmola, C Kazakhstan 51.58N 70.58E
151 T14 **Akkol'** Kaz. Aqköl. Almaty, SE Kazakhstan 45.01N 75.38E
151 Q16 **Akkol'** Kaz. Aqköl. Zhambyl, S Kazakhstan 43.25N 70.46E
150 M11 **Akkol', Ozero** prev. Ozero Zhaman-Akkol'. ◎ C Kazakhstan
100 L6 **Akkrum** Friesland, N Netherlands 53.01N 5.52E
151 U8 **Akku** prev. Lebyazh'ye. Pavlodar, NE Kazakhstan 51.29N 77.48E
150 F12 **Akkystau** Kaz. Aqqystaū. Atyrau, SW Kazakhstan 47.13N 51.01E
14 Ff3 **Aklavik** Northwest Territories, NW Canada 68.15N 135.01W
120 B9 **Akmenrags** headland W Latvia 56.49N 21.03E
164 E9 **Akmeqit** Xinjiang Uygur Zizhiqu, NW China 37.10N 76.59E
152 J14 **Akmeydan** Maryyskiy Velayat, C Turkmenistan 37.50N 62.08E
Akmola see Astana
151 P9 **Akmola** off. Akmolinskaya Oblast', Kaz. Aqmola Oblysy; prev. Tselinogradskaya Oblast. ◈ province C Kazakhstan
Akmolinsk see Astana
Akmolinskaya Oblast' see Akmola
Aknavásár see Târgu Ocna
120 I11 **Aknīste** Jēkabpils, S Latvia 56.09N 25.43E
170 G14 **Akō** Hyōgo, Honshū, SW Japan 34.44N 134.22E
83 G14 **Akobo** Jonglei, SE Sudan 7.49N 33.04E
83 G14 **Akobo** var. Ākobowenz. ≈ Ethiopia/Sudan
Ākobowenz see Akobo
160 H12 **Akola** Mahārāshtra, C India 20.44N 77.00E
Akordat see Akurdet
79 Q16 **Akosombo Dam** dam SE Ghana 6.23N 0.06E
160 H12 **Akot** Mahārāshtra, C India 20.45N 77.00E
79 N16 **Akoupé** SE Ivory Coast 6.19N 3.54W
10 M3 **Akpatok Island** island Nunavut, E Canada
164 G7 **Akqi** Xinjiang Uygur Zizhiqu, NW China 40.51N 78.20E
144 I2 **Akrād, Jabal al** ▲▲ N Syria
Akragas see Agrigento
94 H3 **Akranes** Vesturland, W Iceland 64.19N 22.01W
145 S2 **Ākrē** Ar. 'Aqrah. N Iraq 36.46N 43.52E
97 C16 **Åkrehamn** Rogaland, S Norway 59.15N 5.12E
79 V9 **Akrérèb** Agadez, C Niger 17.45N 9.01E
117 D22 **Akrítas, Akrotírio** headland S Greece 36.43N 21.52E
39 V3 **Akron** Colorado, C USA 40.09N 103.12W
31 R12 **Akron** Iowa, C USA 42.49N 96.33W
33 U12 **Akron** Ohio, N USA 41.04N 81.31W
Akrotiri see Akrotírion
Akrotiri Bay see Akrotírion, Kólpos
124 N4 **Akrotírion** var. Akrotiri. UK air base S Cyprus 34.36N 32.57E
124 Nn4 **Akrotírion, Kólpos** var. Akrotiri Bay. bay S Cyprus
123 Mm4 **Akrotiri Sovereign Base Area** UK military installation S Cyprus 34.34N 32.58E
164 F11 **Aksai Chin** Chin. Aksayqin. disputed region China/India
Aksaj see Aksay
142 I15 **Aksaray** Aksaray, C Turkey 38.23N 33.50E
142 I15 **Aksaray** ◈ province C Turkey
165 P8 **Aksay** var. Aksay Kazakzu Zizhixian. Gansu, N China 39.25N 94.09E
150 G8 **Aksay** var. Aksaj, Kaz. Aqsay. Zapadnyy Kazakhstan, NW Kazakhstan 51.10N 53.03E
131 O11 **Aksay** Volgogradskaya Oblast', SW Russian Federation 47.59N 43.54E
153 W10 **Aksay** var. Toxkan He. ≈ China/Kyrgyzstan
Aksay Kazakzu Zizhixian see Aksay
Aksayqin see Aksai Chin
164 G11 **Aksayqin Hu** ◎ NW China
142 G14 **Akşehir** Konya, W Turkey 38.22N 31.24E
142 G14 **Akşehir Gölü** ◎ C Turkey
142 G16 **Akseki** Antalya, SW Turkey 37.03N 31.46E
126 L15 **Aksenovo-Zilovskoye** Chitinskaya Oblast', S Russian Federation 53.01N 117.26E
126 Kk16 **Aksha** Chitinskaya Oblast', S Russian Federation 50.16N 113.22E
151 V11 **Akshatau, Khrebet** ▲▲ E Kazakhstan
153 Y8 **Ak-Shyyrak** Issyk-Kul'skaya Oblast', E Kyrgyzstan 41.46N 78.34E
Akstafa see Ağstafa
164 H7 **Aksu** Xinjiang Uygur Zizhiqu, NW China 41.16N 80.15E
151 R8 **Aksu** Kaz. Aqsū. Akmola, N Kazakhstan 52.31N 72.00E
151 T8 **Aksu** var. Jermak, Kaz. Ermak; prev. Yermak. Pavlodar, NE Kazakhstan 52.03N 76.55E
151 W13 **Aksu** Kaz. Aqsū. Almaty, SE Kazakhstan 45.31N 79.28E
151 V13 **Aksu** Kaz. Aqsū. ≈ SE Kazakhstan
151 X11 **Aksuat** Kaz. Aqsūat. Vostochnyy Kazakhstan, E Kazakhstan 47.46N 82.49E
151 Y11 **Aksuat** Kaz. Aqsūat. Vostochnyy Kazakhstan, SE Kazakhstan 48.16N 83.39E
131 S4 **Aksubayevo** Respublika Tatarstan, W Russian Federation 54.52N 50.50E
164 H7 **Aksu He** Rus. Sary-Dzhaz. ≈ China/Kyrgyzstan see also Sary-Dzhaz
82 J10 **Āksum** Tigray, N Ethiopia 14.06N 38.42E
151 O12 **Aktas** Kaz. Aqtas. Zhezkazgan, C Kazakhstan 48.03N 66.21E
Aktash see Oqtosh
153 V9 **Ak-Tash, Gora** ▲ C Kyrgyzstan 40.53N 74.39E
151 R10 **Aktau** Kaz. Aqtaū. Karaganda, C Kazakhstan 50.13N 73.06E
150 E11 **Aktau** Kaz. Aqtaū; prev. Shevchenko. Mangistau, W Kazakhstan 43.37N 51.13E
Aktau, Khrebet see Oqtogh, SW Tajikistan
Aktau, Khrebet see Oqtov Tizmasi, C Uzbekistan
Akte see Ágion Óros
Ak-Tepe see Akdepe
153 X7 **Ak-Terek** Issyk-Kul'skaya Oblast', E Kyrgyzstan 42.14N 77.46E
Aktí see Ágion Óros
164 E8 **Akto** Xinjiang Uygur Zizhiqu, NW China 39.07N 75.43E
150 I10 **Aktobe** Kaz. Aqtöbe, prev. Aktyubinsk. Aktyubinsk, NW Kazakhstan 50.18N 57.09E
151 V12 **Aktogay** Kaz. Aqtoghay. Vostochnyy Kazakhstan, E Kazakhstan 46.56N 79.40E
151 T12 **Aktogay** Kaz. Aqtoghay. Zhezkazgan, C Kazakhstan 47.46N 74.06E
121 M18 **Aktsyabrski** Rus. Oktyabr'skiy; prev. Karpilovka. Homyel'skaya Voblasts', SE Belarus 52.37N 28.52E
Aktyubinsk see Aktobe
150 H11 **Aktyubinsk** off. Aktyubinskaya Oblast', Kaz. Aqtöbe Oblysy. ◈ province W Kazakhstan
153 W7 **Ak-Tyuz** var. Aktyuz. Chuyskaya Oblast', N Kyrgyzstan 42.50N 76.05E
81 J17 **Akula** Equateur, NW Dem. Rep. Congo 2.21N 20.13E
170 Bb15 **Akune** Kagoshima, Kyūshū, SW Japan 31.59N 130.11E
40 L16 **Akun Island** island Aleutian Islands, Alaska, USA
82 J9 **Akurdet** var. Agordat, Akordat. C Eritrea 15.33N 38.01E
79 T16 **Akure** Ondo, SW Nigeria 7.18N 5.12E
94 J2 **Akureyri** Nordhurland Eystra, N Iceland 65.40N 18.06W
40 L17 **Akutan** Akutan Island, Alaska, USA 54.08N 165.47W
40 K17 **Akutan Island** island Aleutian Islands, Alaska, USA
79 V17 **Akwa Ibom** ◈ state SE Nigeria
Akyab see Sittwe
131 W7 **Ak"yar** Respublika Bashkortostan, W Russian Federation 51.51N 58.13E
151 Y11 **Akzhar** Kaz. Aqzhar. Vostochnyy Kazakhstan, E Kazakhstan 47.36N 83.37E
96 F13 **Ål** Buskerud, S Norway 60.37N 8.33E
121 N18 **Ala** Rus. Ola. ≈ SE Belarus
22 H11 **Alabama** off. State of Alabama; also known as Camellia State, Heart of Dixie, The Cotton State, Yellowhammer State. ◈ state S USA
25 P6 **Alabama River** ≈ Alabama, S USA
25 P4 **Alabaster** Alabama, S USA 33.14N 86.49W
145 U10 **Al 'Abd Allāh** var. Al Abdullah. S Iraq 32.06N 45.08E
Al Abdullah see Al 'Abd Allāh
145 W14 **Al Abṭīyah** well S Iraq 29.27N 45.56E
153 S9 **Ala-Buka** Dzhalal-Abadskaya Oblast', W Kyrgyzstan 41.22N 71.27E
194 K15 **Alabule** ≈ C PNG
142 J12 **Alaca** Çorum, N Turkey 40.10N 34.52E
142 K10 **Alaçam** Samsun, N Turkey 41.35N 35.37E
Alacant see Alicante
25 V9 **Alachua** Florida, SE USA 29.48N 82.29W
143 S13 **Aladağlar** ▲▲ W Turkey
142 K15 **Ala Dağları** ▲▲ C Turkey
131 O16 **Alagir** Respublika Severnaya Osetiya, SW Russian Federation 43.02N 44.10E
108 B6 **Alagna Valsesia** Valle d'Aosta, NW Italy 45.51N 7.50E
105 P12 **Alagnon** ≈ C France
61 P16 **Alagoas** off. Estado de Alagoas. ◈ state E Brazil
61 P17 **Alagoinhas** Bahia, E Brazil 12.09S 38.21W
107 R5 **Alagón** Aragón, NE Spain 41.46N 1.07W
106 J9 **Alagón** ≈ W Spain
95 K16 **Alahärmä** Länsi-Suomi, W Finland 63.15N 22.49E
al Ahdar see Al Akhḑar
148 K12 **Al Aḩmadī** var. Ahmadi. E Kuwait 29.02N 48.01E
Al Ain see Al 'Ayn
107 Z8 **Alaior** prev. Alayor. Menorca, Spain, W Mediterranean Sea 39.55N 4.07E
153 T11 **Alai Range** Rus. Alayskiy Khrebet. ▲▲ Kyrgyzstan/Tajikistan
Alais see Alès
147 X11 **Al 'Ajā'iz** E Oman 19.33N 57.12E
147 X11 **Al 'Ajā'iz** oasis SE Oman 19.40N 57.13E
95 L16 **Alajärvi** Länsi-Suomi, W Finland 63.00N 23.50E
120 K4 **Alajõe** Ida-Virumaa, NE Estonia 59.00N 27.26E
44 M13 **Alajuela** Alajuela, C Costa Rica 10.00N 84.12W
44 L12 **Alajuela** off. Provincia de Alajuela. ◈ province N Costa Rica
45 T14 **Alajuela, Lago** ◎ C Panama
40 M11 **Alakanuk** Alaska, USA 62.41N 164.37W
146 K5 **Al Akhḑar** var. al Ahdar. Tabūk, NW Saudi Arabia 28.04N 37.13E
Alaköl see Alakol', Ozero
151 X13 **Alakol', Ozero** Kaz. Alaköl. ◎ SE Kazakhstan
128 I5 **Alakurtti** Murmanskaya Oblast', NW Russian Federation 66.57N 30.27E
40 F10 **Alalakeiki Channel** channel Hawaii, USA, C Pacific Ocean
Al 'Alamayn see El 'Alamein
145 R1 **Al 'Amādīyah** N Iraq 37.09N 43.27E
196 K5 **Alamagan** island C Northern Mariana Islands
145 X10 **Al 'Amārah** var. Amara. E Iraq 31.51N 47.10E
82 J11 **Ālamat'ā** Tigray, N Ethiopia 12.22N 39.32E
39 R11 **Alameda** New Mexico, SW USA 35.09N 106.37W
124 Pp15 **'Alam el Rûm, Râs** headland N Egypt 31.21N 27.23E
Alamícamba see Alamikamba
44 M8 **Alamikamba** var. Alamícamba. Región Autónoma Atlántico Norte, NE Nicaragua 13.29N 84.17W
26 K11 **Alamito Creek** ≈ Texas, SW USA
42 M8 **Alamitos, Sierra de los** ▲ NE Mexico 26.15N 102.14W
37 X9 **Alamo** Nevada, W USA 37.21N 115.07W
22 F9 **Alamo** Tennessee, S USA 35.46N 89.07W
43 Q12 **Álamo** Veracruz-Llave, C Mexico 20.55N 97.40W
39 S14 **Alamogordo** New Mexico, SW USA 32.52N 105.57W
38 J12 **Alamo Lake** ⊠ Arizona, SW USA
42 H7 **Alamos** Sonora, NW Mexico 26.59N 108.53W
39 S7 **Alamosa** Colorado, C USA 37.25N 105.51W
95 J20 **Åland** var. Aland Islands, Fin. Ahvenanmaa. ◈ province SW Finland
95 J19 **Åland** Fin. Ahvenanmaa. island SW Finland
90 K9 **Åland** var. Aland Islands, Fin. Ahvenanmaa. island group SW Finland
Aland Islands see Åland
Aland Sea see Ålands Hav
97 Q14 **Ålands Hav** var. Aland Sea. strait Baltic Sea/Gulf of Bothnia
45 P16 **Alanje** Chiriquí, SW Panama 8.22N 82.36W
27 O2 **Alanreed** Texas, SW USA 35.12N 100.45W
142 G17 **Alanya** Antalya, S Turkey 36.31N 32.01E
25 U7 **Alapaha River** ≈ Florida/Georgia, SE USA
125 Ee11 **Alapayevsk** Sverdlovskaya Oblast', C Russian Federation 57.48N 61.50E
Alappuzha see Alleppey
144 F14 **Al 'Aqabah** var. Akaba, Aqaba, 'Aqaba; anc. Aelana, Elath. Ma'ān, SW Jordan 29.32N 35.00E
Al 'Arabīyah as Su'ūdīyah see Saudi Arabia
al Araïch see Larache
107 Q10 **Alarcón** Castilla-La Mancha, C Spain 39.33N 2.04W
107 Q9 **Alarcón, Embalse de** ⊠ C Spain
144 J2 **Al 'Arīmah** Fr. Arime. Ḩalab, N Syria 36.27N 37.41E
Al 'Arīsh see El 'Arîsh
147 P6 **Al Arṭāwīyah** Ar Riyāḑ, N Saudi Arabia 26.33N 45.19E
175 O16 **Alas** Sumbawa, S Indonesia 8.27S 117.04E
Alasca, Golfo de see Alaska, Gulf of
142 D14 **Alaşehir** Manisa, W Turkey 38.19N 28.30E
145 N5 **Al 'Ashārah** var. Ashara. Dayr az Zawr, E Syria 34.51N 40.36E
144 H10 **Al 'Āşimah** prev. Muḩāfaẓat 'Ammān. ◈ governorate NW Jordan
Al Ashkhara see Al Ashkharah
147 Z9 **Al Ashkharah** var. Al Ashkhara. NE Oman 21.46N 59.30E
41 P8 **Alaska** off. State of Alaska; also known as Land of the Midnight Sun, The Last Frontier, Seward's Folly; prev. Russian America. ◈ state NW USA
41 T13 **Alaska, Gulf of** var. Golfo de Alasca. gulf Canada/USA
41 O15 **Alaska Peninsula** peninsula Alaska, USA
41 Q11 **Alaska Range** ▲▲ Alaska, USA
173 Ee4 **Alas, Lae** ≈ Sumatera, NW Indonesia
Al-Asnam see Chlef
175 O16 **Alas, Selat** strait Nusa Tenggara, C Indonesia
108 B10 **Alassio** Liguria, NW Italy 44.01N 8.12E
Alat see Olot
143 Y12 **Älät** Rus. Alyat; prev. Alyaty-Pristan'. SE Azerbaijan 39.57N 49.24E
145 S13 **Al 'Athāmīn** S Iraq 30.27N 43.40E
41 P7 **Alatna River** ≈ Alaska, USA
109 J15 **Alatri** Lazio, C Italy 41.43N 13.21E
Alattio see Alta
131 P5 **Alatyr'** Chavash Respubliki, W Russian Federation 54.50N 46.28E
58 C7 **Alausí** Chimborazo, C Ecuador 2.07S 78.44W
107 O3 **Álava** Basq. Araba. ◈ province País Vasco, N Spain
143 T11 **Alaverdi** N Armenia 41.06N 44.37E
Alavo see Alavus
95 N14 **Ala-Vuokki** Oulu, E Finland 64.46N 29.29E
95 K17 **Alavus** Swe. Alavo. Länsi-Suomi, W Finland 62.33N 23.37E
Al 'Awābī see Awābī
145 P6 **Al 'Awānī** W Iraq 34.28N 41.43E
77 U12 **Al Awaynāt** SE Libya 21.46N 24.51E
Al Awaynāt see Al 'Uwaynāt
190 K9 **Alawoona** South Australia 34.45S 140.28E
Alaykel'/Alay-Kuu see Kēk-Art
149 R17 **Al 'Ayn** var. Al Ain. Abū Ẓaby, E UAE 24.13N 55.44E
149 R17 **Al 'Ayn** var. Al Ain. ✈ Abū Ẓaby, E UAE 24.16N 55.31E
144 G12 **Al 'Aynā** Al Karak, W Jordan 30.59N 35.43E
Alayor see Alaior
Alayskiy Khrebet see Alai Range
127 N7 **Alazeya** ≈ NE Russian Federation
145 U8 **Al 'Azīzīyah** var. Aziziya. E Iraq 32.54N 45.05E
123 L14 **Al 'Azīzīyah** NW Libya 32.31N 13.01E
144 I10 **Al Azraq al Janūbī** Az Zarqā', N Jordan 31.49N 36.48E
108 B9 **Alba** anc. Alba Pompeia. Piemonte, NW Italy 44.40N 8.01E
27 V6 **Alba** Texas, SW USA 32.47N 95.37W
118 G11 **Alba** ◈ county W Romania
145 P3 **Al Ba'āj** N Iraq 36.02N 41.43E
144 J2 **Al Bāb** Ḩalab, N Syria 36.24N 37.31E
118 G10 **Albac** Hung. Fehérvölgy; prev. Álbák. Alba, SW Romania 46.25N 22.58E
107 Q11 **Albacete** Castilla-La Mancha, C Spain 39.00N 1.52W
107 P11 **Albacete** ◈ province Castilla-La Mancha, C Spain
146 I4 **Al Bad'** Tabūk, NW Saudi Arabia 28.28N 35.00E
106 L7 **Alba de Tormes** Castilla-León, N Spain 40.49N 5.30W
145 P3 **Al Bādī** N Iraq 35.57N 41.37E
147 V8 **Al Badī'ah** ✈ (Abū Ẓaby) Abū Ẓaby, C UAE 24.27N 54.39E
149 P17 **Al Badī'ah** var. Al Bedei'ah. spring/well C UAE 23.44N 53.50E
145 Q7 **Al Baghdādī** var. Khān al Baghdādī. SW Iraq 33.19N 44.22E
Al Bāha see Al Bāḩah
146 M11 **Al Bāḩah** var. Al Bāha. Al Bāḩah, SW Saudi Arabia 20.00N 41.29E
146 M11 **Al Bāḩah** off. Minṭaqat al Bāḩah. ◈ province W Saudi Arabia
Al Baḩrayn see Bahrain
107 S11 **Albaida** País Valenciano, E Spain 38.51N 0.31W
118 H11 **Alba Iulia** Ger. Weissenburg, Hung. Gyulafehérvár; prev. Bălgrad, Karlsburg, Károly-Fehérvár. Alba, W Romania 46.06N 23.33E
Álbák see Albac
144 G10 **Al Balqā'** off. Muḩāfaẓat al Balqā', var. Balqā'. ◈ governorate NW Jordan
12 F11 **Alban** Ontario, S Canada 46.07N 80.37W
105 O15 **Alban** Tarn, S France 43.52N 2.30E
10 K11 **Albanel, Lac** ◎ Quebec, SE Canada
115 L20 **Albania** off. Republic of Albania, Alb. Republika e Shqipërisë, Shqipëria; prev. People's Socialist Republic of Albania. ◆ republic SE Europe
Albania see Aubagne
109 H15 **Albano Laziale** Lazio, C Italy 41.43N 12.40E
188 J14 **Albany** Western Australia 35.03S 117.54E
25 S7 **Albany** Georgia, SE USA 31.34N 84.09W
33 P13 **Albany** Indiana, N USA 40.18N 85.14W
22 L8 **Albany** Kentucky, S USA 36.41N 85.07W
31 U7 **Albany** Minnesota, N USA 45.39N 94.33W
29 R2 **Albany** Missouri, C USA 40.15N 94.15W
20 L10 **Albany** state capital New York, NE USA 42.39N 73.45W
34 G12 **Albany** Oregon, NW USA 44.38N 123.06W
27 Q6 **Albany** Texas, SW USA 32.43N 99.18W
10 F10 **Albany** ≈ Ontario, S Canada
Alba Pompeia see Alba
Alba Regia see Székesfehérvár
144 J6 **Al Bāridah** var. Bāridah. Ḩimş, C Syria 34.15N 37.39E
145 Q11 **Al Barīt** S Iraq 31.16N 42.28E
107 R8 **Albarracín** Aragón, NE Spain 40.24N 1.25W
145 Y12 **Al Başrah** Eng. Basra; hist. Busra, Bussora. SE Iraq 30.30N 47.49E
145 V11 **Al Baṭḩā'** SE Iraq 31.06N 45.49E
147 X8 **Al Bāṭinah** var. Batinah. coastal region N Oman
(0) H16 **Albatross Plateau** undersea feature E Pacific Ocean
Al Batrūn see Batroûn
124 Nn14 **Al Bayḑā'** var. Beida. NE Libya 32.46N 21.43E
147 P16 **Al Bayḑā'** var. Al Beida. SW Yemen 13.58N 45.38E
Al Bedei'ah see Al Badī'ah
Al Beida see Al Bayḑā'
23 S10 **Albemarle** var. Albermarle. North Carolina, SE USA 35.21N 80.12W
Albemarle Island see Isabela, Isla
23 N8 **Albemarle Sound** inlet W Atlantic Ocean
108 B10 **Albenga** Liguria, NW Italy 44.04N 8.13E
106 L8 **Alberche** ≈ C Spain
105 O17 **Albères, Chaîne des** var. les Albères, Montes Albères. ▲▲ France/Spain
Albères, Montes see Albères, Chaîne des
190 F2 **Alberga Creek** seasonal river South Australia
106 G7 **Albergaria-a-Velha** Aveiro, N Portugal 40.42N 8.28W
107 S10 **Alberic** País Valenciano, E Spain 39.07N 0.31W
Albermarle see Albemarle
109 P18 **Alberobello** Puglia, SE Italy 40.47N 17.14E
110 J7 **Alberschwende** Vorarlberg, W Austria 47.28N 9.49E
105 O3 **Albert** Somme, N France 50.00N 2.37E
9 O12 **Alberta** ◈ province SW Canada
194 K14 **Albert Edward, Mount** ▲ S PNG 8.23S 147.23E
Albert Edward Nyanza see Edward, Lake
63 C20 **Alberti** Buenos Aires, E Argentina 35.03S 60.15W
113 K23 **Albertirsa** Pest, C Hungary 47.15N 19.36E
101 I16 **Albertkanaal** canal N Belgium
81 P17 **Albert, Lake** var. Albert Nyanza, Lac Mobutu Sese Seko. ◎ Uganda/Dem. Rep. Congo
31 V11 **Albert Lea** Minnesota, N USA 43.39N 93.22W
83 F16 **Albert Nile** ≈ NW Uganda
Albert Nyanza see Albert, Lake
105 T11 **Albertville** Savoie, E France 45.41N 6.24E
25 Q2 **Albertville** Alabama, S USA 34.16N 86.12W
Albertville see Kalemie
105 N15 **Albi** anc. Albiga. Tarn, S France 43.55N 2.09E
31 W15 **Albia** Iowa, C USA 41.01N 92.48W
Albiga see Albi
57 X9 **Albina** Marowijne, NE Suriname 5.31N 54.04W
85 A15 **Albina, Ponta** headland SW Angola 15.52S 11.45E
32 M16 **Albion** Illinois, N USA 38.22N 88.03W
33 P11 **Albion** Indiana, N USA 41.22N 85.23W
31 P14 **Albion** Nebraska, C USA 41.41N 98.00W
20 E9 **Albion** New York, NE USA 43.13N 78.09W
20 B12 **Albion** Pennsylvania, NE USA 41.52N 80.18W
Al Biqā' see El Beqaa
146 J4 **Al Bi'r** var. Bi'r Ibn Hirmās. Tabūk, NW Saudi Arabia 28.52N 36.16E
146 M12 **Al Birk** Makkah, SW Saudi Arabia 18.12N 41.36E
147 Q9 **Al Biyāḑ** desert C Saudi Arabia
100 H13 **Alblasserdam** Zuid-Holland, SW Netherlands 51.52N 4.40E
107 T8 **Albocácer** var. Albocasser. País Valenciano, E Spain 40.21N 0.01E
Albocasser see Albocácer
97 H19 **Ålbæk** Nordjylland, N Denmark 57.33N 10.24E
Albona see Labin
107 O17 **Alborán, Isla de** island S Spain
Alborán, Mar de see Alboran Sea
107 N17 **Alboran Sea** Sp. Mar de Alborán. sea SW Mediterranean Sea
Ålborg see Aalborg
97 H21 **Ålborg Bugt** var. Aalborg Bugt. bay N Denmark
Ålborg-Nørresundby see Aalborg
149 O5 **Alborz, Reshteh-ye Kūhhā-ye** Eng. Elburz Mountains. ▲▲ N Iran
107 Q14 **Albox** Andalucía, S Spain 37.22N 2.08W
103 H23 **Albstadt** Baden-Württemberg, SW Germany 48.13N 9.01E
106 G14 **Albufeira** Beja, S Portugal 37.04N 8.15W
145 P5 **Ālbū Gharz, Sabkhat** ◎ W Iraq
107 O15 **Albuñol** Andalucía, S Spain 36.48N 3.10W
39 Q11 **Albuquerque** New Mexico, SW USA 35.04N 106.37W
147 W8 **Al Buraymī** var. Buraimi. N Oman 24.16N 55.48E
149 R17 **Al Buraymī** var. Buraimi. spring/well Oman/UAE 24.27N 55.33E
Al Burayqah see Marsá al Burayqah
Alburgum see Aalborg
106 I10 **Alburquerque** Extremadura, W Spain 39.12N 7.00W
189 V14 **Albury** New South Wales, SE Australia 36.03S 146.52E
147 T14 **Al Buzūn** SE Yemen 15.40N 50.53E
95 G17 **Alby** Västernorrland, C Sweden 62.30N 15.25E
Albyn, Glen see Mor, Glen
106 G12 **Alcácer do Sal** Setúbal, W Portugal 38.21N 8.29W
Alcalá de Chisvert see Alcalá de Chivert
107 T8 **Alcalá de Chivert** var. Alcalá de Chisvert. País Valenciano, E Spain 40.19N 0.13E
106 K14 **Alcalá de Guadaira** Andalucía, S Spain 37.19N 5.49W
107 O8 **Alcalá de Henares** Ar. Alkal'a; anc. Complutum. Madrid, C Spain 40.28N 3.22W
106 K16 **Alcalá de los Gazules** Andalucía, S Spain 36.28N 5.43W
107 N14 **Alcalá La Real** Andalucía, S Spain 37.28N 3.55W
109 I23 **Alcamo** Sicilia, Italy, C Mediterranean Sea 37.58N 12.58E
107 T4 **Alcanadre** ≈ NE Spain
107 T8 **Alcanar** Cataluña, NE Spain 40.33N 0.28E
106 J5 **Alcañices** Castilla-León, N Spain 41.40N 6.21W
107 T7 **Alcañiz** Aragón, NE Spain 41.03N 0.09W
106 I9 **Alcántara** Extremadura, W Spain 39.42N 6.54W
106 J9 **Alcántara, Embalse de** ⊠ W Spain
107 R13 **Alcantarilla** Murcia, SE Spain 37.58N 1.12W
107 P11 **Alcaraz** Castilla-La Mancha, C Spain 38.40N 2.28W
107 P12 **Alcaraz, Sierra de** ▲▲ C Spain
106 I12 **Alcarrache** ≈ SW Spain
107 T6 **Alcarràs** Cataluña, NE Spain 41.34N 0.31E
107 N14 **Alcaudete** Andalucía, S Spain 37.34N 4.04W
Alcázar see Ksar-el-Kebir
107 O10 **Alcázar de San Juan** anc. Alce. Castilla-La Mancha, C Spain 39.24N 3.12W
Alcazarquivir see Ksar-el-Kebir
Alce see Alcázar de San Juan
59 B17 **Alcebo, Volcán** ⛰ Galapagos Islands, Ecuador, E Pacific Ocean 0.25S 91.06W
145 X12 **Al Chabā'ish** var. Al Kaba'ish. SE Iraq 30.58N 47.01E
119 Y7 **Alchevs'k** prev. Kommunarsk, Voroshilovsk. Luhans'ka Oblast', E Ukraine 48.29N 38.52E
Alcira see Alzira
23 N9 **Alcoa** Tennessee, S USA 35.47N 83.58W
106 F9 **Alcobaça** Leiria, C Portugal 39.31N 8.58W
107 N8 **Alcobendas** Madrid, C Spain 40.31N 3.37W
Alcoi see Alcoy
107 P7 **Alcolea del Pinar** Castilla-La Mancha, C Spain 41.01N 2.28W
106 I11 **Alconchel** Extremadura, W Spain 38.31N 7.04W
107 S9 **Alcora** País Valenciano, E Spain 40.04N 0.13W
107 N8 **Alcorcón** Madrid, C Spain 40.20N 3.52W
107 S7 **Alcorisa** Aragón, NE Spain 40.52N 0.22W
63 B19 **Alcorta** Santa Fe, C Argentina 33.31S 61.07W
106 H14 **Alcoutim** Faro, S Portugal 37.28N 7.28W
35 W15 **Alcova** Wyoming, C USA 42.33N 106.40W
107 S11 **Alcoy** var. Alcoi. País Valenciano, E Spain 38.42N 0.28W
107 Y9 **Alcúdia, Badia d'** bay Mallorca, Spain, W Mediterranean Sea
180 M7 **Aldabra Group** island group SW Seychelles
145 U10 **Al Daghghārah** C Iraq 32.10N 44.57E
42 J5 **Aldama** Chihuahua, N Mexico 28.49N 105.52W
43 P11 **Aldama** Tamaulipas, C Mexico 22.55N 98.03W
126 Ll12 **Aldan** Respublika Sakha (Yakutiya), NE Russian Federation 58.31N 125.15E
126 Mm12 **Aldan** ≈ NE Russian Federation
168 G7 **Aldar** Dzavhan, W Mongolia 47.43N 96.36E

◆ Country
● Country Capital
◇ Dependent Territory
○ Dependent Territory Capital
◈ Administrative Region
✈ International Airport
▲ Mountain
▲▲ Mountain Range
⛰ Volcano
≈ River
◎ Lake
⊠ Reservoir

al Dar al Baida see Rabat
99 Q20 Aldeburgh E England, UK 52.12N 1.35E
107 P5 Aldehuela de Calatañazor Castilla-León, N Spain 41.42N 2.46W
Aldeia Nova see Aldeia Nova de São Bento
106 H13 Aldeia Nova de São Bento var. Aldeia Nova. Beja, S Portugal 37.55N 7.24W
31 V11 Alden Minnesota, N USA 43.40N 93.34W
192 N6 Aldermen Islands, The island group N NZ
99 L25 Alderney island Channel Islands
99 N22 Aldershot S England, UK 51.15N 0.46W
23 R6 Alderson West Virginia, NE USA 37.43N 80.38W
Al Dhaid see Adh Dhayd
32 J11 Aledo Illinois, N USA 41.12N 90.45W
78 H9 Aleg Brakna, SW Mauritania 17.03N 13.52W
66 Q10 Alegranza island Islas Canarias, Spain, NE Atlantic Ocean
39 P12 Alegres Mountain ▲ New Mexico, SW USA 34.09N 108.11W
63 F15 Alegrete Rio Grande do Sul, S Brazil 29.46S 55.46W
63 C16 Alejandra Santa Fe, C Argentina 29.54S 59.49W
200 Oo12 Alejandro Selkirk, Isla island Islas Juan Fernández, Chile, E Pacific Ocean
128 I12 Alekhovshchina Leningradskaya Oblast', NW Russian Federation 60.22N 33.57E
41 O13 Aleknagik Alaska, USA 59.16N 158.37W
Aleksandriya see Oleksandriya
Aleksandropol' see Gyumri
130 L3 Aleksandrov Vladimirskaya Oblast', W Russian Federation 56.24N 38.42E
115 N14 Aleksandrovac Serbia, C Serbia and Montenegro (Yugoslavia) 43.28N 21.05E
131 R9 Aleksandrov Gay Saratovskaya Oblast', W Russian Federation 50.08N 48.34E
131 U6 Aleksandrovka Orenburgskaya Oblast', W Russian Federation 52.47N 54.14E
Aleksandrovka see Oleksandrivka
116 J8 Aleksandrovo Lovech, N Bulgaria 43.16N 24.53E
129 V13 Aleksandrovsk Permskaya Oblast', NW Russian Federation 59.12N 57.27E
Aleksandrovsk see Zaporizhzhya
131 N14 Aleksandrovskoye Stavropol'skiy Kray, SW Russian Federation 44.43N 42.56E
127 O14 Aleksandrovsk-Sakhalinskiy Ostrov Sakhalin, Sakhalinskaya Oblast', SE Russian Federation 50.55N 142.12E
112 J10 Aleksandrów Kujawski Kujawsko-pomorskie, C Poland 52.51N 18.42E
112 K12 Aleksandrów Łódzki Łódzkie, C Poland 51.48N 19.18E
Alekseevka see Terekty
130 L9 Alekseyevka Belgorodskaya Oblast', W Russian Federation 50.35N 38.41E
151 P7 Alekseyevka Kaz. Alekseevka. Akmola, N Kazakhstan 53.31N 69.30E
Alekseyevka see Terekty
131 S7 Alekseyevka Samarskaya Oblast', W Russian Federation 52.37N 51.20E
Alekseyevka see Akkol'
126 Jj13 Alekseyevsk Irkutskaya Oblast', C Russian Federation 57.46N 108.07E
131 R4 Alekseyevskoye Respublika Tatarstan, W Russian Federation 55.18N 50.11E
130 K5 Aleksin Tul'skaya Oblast', W Russian Federation 54.30N 37.07E
115 O14 Aleksinac Serbia, SE Serbia and Montenegro (Yugoslavia) 43.33N 21.43E
202 G11 Alele Île Uvea, E Wallis and Futuna 13.13S 176.09W
97 N20 Ålem Kalmar, S Sweden 56.57N 16.25E
104 L6 Alençon Orne, N France 48.25N 0.04E
60 I12 Alenquer Pará, NE Brazil 1.58S 54.45W
40 G10 Alenuihaha Channel channel Hawaii, USA, C Pacific Ocean
Alep/Aleppo see Ḥalab
105 Y15 Aléria Corse, France, C Mediterranean Sea 42.06N 9.29E
207 Q11 Alert Ellesmere Island, Nunavut, N Canada 82.28N 62.13W
105 Q14 Alès prev. Alais. Gard, S France 44.07N 4.04E
118 G9 Aleşd Hung. Élesd. Bihor, SW Romania 47.03N 22.22E
108 C9 Alessandria Fr. Alexandrie. Piemonte, N Italy 44.54N 8.37E
Ålestrup see Aalestrup
96 D9 Ålesund Møre og Romsdal, S Norway 62.28N 6.11E
110 E10 Aletschhorn ▲ SW Switzerland 46.33N 8.01E
207 S1 Aleutian Basin undersea feature Bering Sea
40 H17 Aleutian Islands island group Alaska, USA
41 P14 Aleutian Range ▲ Alaska, USA
(0) B5 Aleutian Trench undersea feature S Bering Sea
127 O10 Alevina, Mys headland E Russian Federation 58.52N 151.21E
13 Q6 Alex ↝ Quebec, SE Canada
30 J3 Alexander North Dakota, N USA 47.48N 103.38W
41 W14 Alexander Archipelago island group Alaska, USA
Alexanderbaai see Alexander Bay
85 D23 Alexander Bay Afr. Alexanderbaai. Northern Cape, W South Africa 28.35S 16.30E
25 Q5 Alexander City Alabama, S USA 32.56N 85.57W
204 J6 Alexander Island island Antarctica
Alexander Range see Kirghiz Range
191 O12 Alexandra Victoria, SE Australia 37.12S 145.43E
193 D22 Alexandra Otago, South Island, NZ 45.15S 169.24E
117 F14 Alexándreia var. Alexándria. Kentrikí Makedonía, N Greece 40.38N 22.27E
Alexandretta see İskenderun
Alexandretta, Gulf of see İskenderun Körfezi
13 N13 Alexandria Ontario, SE Canada 45.19N 74.37W
124 Q15 Alexandria Ar. Al Iskandarīyah. N Egypt 31.07N 29.51E
46 J12 Alexandria C Jamaica 18.18N 77.21W
118 J15 Alexandria Teleorman, S Romania 43.58N 25.18E
33 P13 Alexandria Indiana, N USA 40.15N 85.40W
22 M4 Alexandria Kentucky, S USA 38.56N 84.21W
24 H7 Alexandria Louisiana, S USA 31.18N 92.27W
31 T7 Alexandria Minnesota, N USA 45.54N 95.22W
31 Q11 Alexandria South Dakota, N USA 43.39N 97.46W
23 W4 Alexandria Virginia, NE USA 38.48N 77.03W
Alexándria see Alexándreia
20 I7 Alexandria Bay New York, NE USA 44.20N 75.54W
Alexandrie see Alessandria
190 J10 Alexandrina, Lake ◎ South Australia
116 K13 Alexandroúpoli var. Alexandroúpolis, Turk. Dedeagaç, Dedeagach. Anatolikí Makedonía kai Thráki, NE Greece 40.51N 25.52E
Alexandroúpolis see Alexandroúpoli
8 L15 Alexis Creek British Columbia, SW Canada 52.06N 123.25W
126 Gg15 Aleysk Altayskiy Kray, S Russian Federation 52.32N 82.46E
8 L15 Alexis Creek British Columbia, SW Canada 52.06N 123.25W
126 Gg15 Aleysk Altayskiy Kray, S Russian Federation 52.32N 82.46E
145 S8 Al Fallūjah var. Falluja. C Iraq 33.21N 43.46E
107 R8 Alfambra ↝ E Spain
Al Faqa see Faq'
147 R15 Al Farḍah C Yemen 14.51N 48.33E
107 Q4 Alfaro La Rioja, N Spain 42.09N 1.46W
107 U5 Alfarràs Cataluña, NE Spain 41.49N 0.34E
Al Fāshir see El Fasher
Al Fashn see El Fashn
116 M7 Alfatar Silistra, NE Bulgaria 43.56N 27.17E
145 S5 Al Fatḥah C Iraq 35.06N 43.34E
145 Q3 Al Fatsī N Iraq 36.04N 42.39E
145 Z13 Al Fāw var. Fao. SE Iraq 29.55N 48.25E
Al Fayyūm see El Faiyûm
117 D20 Alfeiós prev. Alfiós, anc. Alpheius, Alpheus. ↝ S Greece
102 I13 Alfeld Niedersachsen, C Germany 51.58N 9.49E
Alfiós see Alfeiós
Alföld see Great Hungarian Plain
96 C11 Ålfotbreen glacier S Norway
21 P9 Alfred Maine, NE USA 43.28N 70.43W
20 F11 Alfred New York, NE USA 42.15N 77.47W
63 K14 Alfredo Vagner Santa Catarina, S Brazil 27.40S 49.22W
96 M12 Alfta Gävleborg, C Sweden 61.19N 16.04E
146 K12 Al Fuḥayḥīl var. Fahaheel. SE Kuwait 29.01N 48.04E
145 Q6 Al Fuḥaymī C Iraq 34.17N 42.09E
149 S16 Al Fujayrah Eng. Fujairah. Al Fujayrah, NE UAE 25.09N 56.18E
149 S16 Al Fujayrah Eng. Fujairah. ✈ Al Fujayrah, NE UAE 25.04N 56.12E
Al Furāt see Euphrates
150 I10 Alga Kaz. Algha. Aktyubinsk, NW Kazakhstan 49.55N 57.19E
150 G9 Algabas Zapadnyy Kazakhstan, NW Kazakhstan 50.45N 52.07E
97 C17 Ålgård Rogaland, S Norway 58.45N 5.52E
106 G14 Algarve cultural region S Portugal
190 G3 Algebuckina Bridge South Australia 28.03S 135.48E
106 K16 Algeciras Andalucía, SW Spain 36.07N 5.27W
107 S10 Algemesí País Valenciano, E Spain 39.10N 0.27W
Al-Genain see El Geneina
123 I11 Alger var. Algiers, El Djazaïr, Al Jazair. ● (Algeria) N Algeria 36.47N 2.58E
76 H9 Algeria off. Democratic and Popular Republic of Algeria. ◆ republic N Africa
123 J9 Algerian Basin var. Balearic Plain undersea feature W Mediterranean Sea
Algha see Alga
144 I4 Al Ghāb ◎ NW Syria
147 X10 Al Ghābah var. Ghaba. C Oman 21.21N 57.13E
147 U14 Al Ghayḍah E Yemen 16.15N 52.13E
146 M6 Al Ghazālah Ḥā'il, NW Saudi Arabia 26.55N 41.23E
109 B17 Alghero Sardegna, Italy, C Mediterranean Sea 40.34N 8.19E
97 M20 Älghult Kronoberg, S Sweden 57.00N 15.34E
Al Ghurdaqah see Hurghada
Algiers see Alger
107 S10 Alginet País Valenciano, E Spain 39.13N 0.28W
85 I26 Algoa Bay bay S South Africa
106 L15 Algodonales Andalucía, S Spain 36.54N 5.24W
107 N9 Algodor ↝ C Spain
Al Golea see El Goléa
33 N6 Algoma Wisconsin, N USA 44.41N 87.24W
31 U12 Algona Iowa, C USA 43.04N 94.13W
22 L8 Algood Tennessee, S USA 36.12N 85.27W
107 O2 Algorta País Vasco, N Spain 43.20N 3.00W
63 E18 Algorta Río Negro, W Uruguay 32.21S 57.12W
Al Haba see Haba
145 Q10 Al Habbārīyah S Iraq 32.16N 42.12E
Al Hadhar see Al Ḥaḍr
145 Q4 Al Ḥaḍr var. Al Hadhar; anc. Hatra. NW Iraq 35.33N 42.43E
145 T13 Al Ḥajarah desert S Iraq
147 W8 Al Ḥajar al Gharbī ▲ N Oman
147 Y8 Al Ḥajar ash Sharqī ▲ NE Oman
147 R15 Al Hajarayn C Yemen 15.29N 48.24E
144 L10 Al Ḥamād desert Jordan/Saudi Arabia
Al Hamad see Syrian Desert
77 N9 Al Ḥamādah al Ḥamrā' var. Al Ḥamrā'. desert NW Libya
107 N15 Alhama de Granada Andalucía, S Spain 37.00N 3.58W
107 R13 Alhama de Murcia Murcia, SE Spain 37.51N 1.25W
37 T15 Alhambra California, W USA 34.07N 118.06W
145 T12 Al Ḥammām S Iraq 31.09N 44.04E
147 X8 Al Ḥamrā' NE Oman 23.07N 57.22E
Al Ḥamrā' see Al Ḥamādah al Ḥamrā'
147 O6 Al Ḥamūdīyah spring/well N Saudi Arabia 27.05N 44.24E
146 M7 Al Ḥanākīyah Al Madīnah, W Saudi Arabia 24.54N 40.31E
145 W14 Al Ḥanīyah escarpment Iraq/Saudi Arabia
145 Y12 Al Hārithah SE Iraq 30.43N 47.43E
146 L3 Al Ḥarrah desert NW Saudi Arabia
77 Q10 Al Harūj al Aswad desert C Libya
Al Hasaifin see Al Ḥusayfīn
145 N2 Al Ḥasakah var. Al Hasijah, El Haseke, Fr. Hassetché. Al Ḥasakah, NE Syria 36.22N 40.43E
145 O2 Al Ḥasakah off. Muḥāfaẓat al Ḥasakah, var. Al Hasakah, Āl Hasakah, Hasaka, Hassakeh. ◈ governorate NE Syria
145 T9 Al Hāshimīyah C Iraq 32.24N 44.39E
144 G13 Al Hāshimīyah Ma'ān, S Jordan 30.31N 35.46E
Al Hasijah see Al Ḥasakah
106 M15 Alhaurín el Grande Andalucía, S Spain 36.39N 4.40W
147 Q16 Al Ḥawrā S Yemen 13.54N 47.36E
145 V10 Al Ḥayy var. Kut al Hai, Kūt al Ḥayy. E Iraq 32.10N 46.03E
147 U11 Al Ḥibāk desert E Saudi Arabia
144 H8 Al Hījānah var. Hejanah, Hijanah. Dimashq, W Syria 33.23N 36.34E
146 K7 Al Ḥijāz Eng. Hejaz. physical region NW Saudi Arabia
Al Hilbeh see 'Ulayyānīyah, Bi'r al
145 T9 Al Ḥillah var. Hilla. C Iraq 32.28N 44.28E
145 T9 Al Hindīyah var. Hindiya. C Iraq 32.31N 44.13E
144 G12 Al Ḥisā Aṭ Ṭafīlah, W Jordan 30.49N 35.58E
76 G5 Al-Hoceïma var. al Hoceima, Al-Hoceima, Alhucemas; prev. Villa Sanjurjo. N Morocco 35.13N 3.55W
Alhucemas see Al-Hoceïma
107 N17 Alhucemas, Peñon de island group S Spain
147 N15 Al Ḥudaydah Eng. Hodeida. W Yemen 15.00N 42.50E
147 N15 Al Ḥudaydah Eng. Hodeida. ✈ W Yemen 14.45N 43.01E
146 M4 Al Ḥudūd ash Shamālīyah var. Minṭaqat al Ḥudūd ash Shamālīyah, Eng. Northern Border Region. ◈ province N Saudi Arabia
147 S7 Al Hufūf var. Hofuf. Ash Sharqīyah, NE Saudi Arabia 25.21N 49.33E
al-Hurma see Al Khurmah
147 X7 Al Ḥusayfīn var. Al Hasaifin. N Oman 24.33N 56.33E
144 G9 Al Ḥuṣn var. Husn. Irbid, N Jordan 32.28N 35.52E
145 U9 'Alī E Iraq 32.43N 45.21E
106 L10 Alia Extremadura, W Spain 39.25N 5.12W
149 N7 'Alīābād Yazd, C Iran 36.55N 54.33E
'Alīābad see Qā'emshahr
107 S7 Aliaga Aragón, NE Spain 40.40N 0.42W
142 B13 Aliağa İzmir, W Turkey 38.49N 26.58E
Aliákmon see Aliákmonas
117 F14 Aliákmonas prev. Aliákmon, anc. Haliacmon. ↝ N Greece
145 W9 'Alī al Gharbī E Iraq 32.28N 46.42E
145 U11 'Alī al Ḥassūnī S Iraq 31.25N 44.50E
117 G18 Alíartos Stereá Ellás, C Greece 38.22N 23.06E
143 Y12 Äli-Bayramlı Rus. Ali-Bayramly. SE Azerbaijan 39.57N 48.54E
Ali-Bayramly see Äli-Bayramlı
116 P12 Alibey Barajı ⊠ NW Turkey
79 S13 Alibori ↝ N Benin
114 M10 Alibunar Serbia, NE Serbia and Montenegro (Yugoslavia) 45.06N 20.59E
107 S12 Alicante Cat. Alacant; Lat. Lucentum. País Valenciano, SE Spain 38.21N 0.28W
107 S12 Alicante ◈ province País Valenciano, SE Spain
107 S12 Alicante ✈ Murcia, E Spain 38.21N 0.28W
85 I25 Alice Eastern Cape, S South Africa 32.49S 26.49E
27 S14 Alice Texas, SW USA 27.45N 98.04W
85 I25 Alicedale Eastern Cape, S South Africa 33.19S 26.04E
67 B25 Alice, Mount hill West Falkland, Falkland Islands
109 P20 Alice, Punta headland S Italy 39.24N 17.09E
189 Q7 Alice Springs Northern Territory, C Australia 23.42S 133.52E
25 N4 Aliceville Alabama, S USA 33.07N 88.09W
153 U13 Alichur SE Tajikistan 37.49N 73.45E
153 U14 Alichuri Janubí, Qatorkŭhi Rus. Yuzhno-Alichurskiy Khrebet. ▲ SE Tajikistan
153 U13 Alichuri Shimolí, Qatorkŭhi Rus. Severo-Alichurskiy Khrebet. ▲ SE Tajikistan
109 K22 Alicudi, Isola island Isole Eolie, S Italy
158 J11 Aligarh Uttar Pradesh, N India 27.54N 78.04E
148 M7 Alīgūdarz Lorestān, W Iran 33.27N 49.33E
(0) F12 Alijos, Islas island group California, SW USA
155 R6 'Alī Kbel Pash. 'Alī Khēl. Paktīkā, E Afghanistan 33.55N 69.49E
Ali Khel see 'Alī Kheyl, Paktīā, Afghanistan
'Alī Khēl see 'Alī Kbel, Paktīkā, Afghanistan
155 R6 'Alī Kheyl var. Ali Khel, Jajı. Paktīā, SE Afghanistan 33.55N 69.46E
147 V17 Al Ikhwān island group SE Yemen
Aliki see Alykí
81 H19 Alima ↝ C Congo
Al Imārāt al 'Arabīyah al Muttaḥidah see United Arab Emirates
194 M12 Alimbit ↝ New Britain, C PNG
117 N23 Alimia island Dodekánisos, Greece, Aegean Sea
57 V12 Alimimuni Piek ▲ S Suriname 2.25N 55.46W
81 K15 Alindao Basse-Kotto, S Central African Republic 4.58N 21.16E
97 J18 Alingsås Västra Götaland, S Sweden 57.55N 12.30E
83 K18 Alinjugul spring/well E Kenya 0.03S 40.31E
155 S11 Alīpur Punjab, E Pakistan 29.22N 70.58E
159 T12 Alīpur Duār West Bengal, NE India 26.28N 89.25E
20 B14 Aliquippa Pennsylvania, NE USA 40.36N 80.15W
82 L12 'Ali Sabieh var. 'Alī Sabīḥ. S Djibouti 11.07N 42.44E
'Alī Sabīḥ see 'Ali Sabieh
146 K3 Al 'Isāwīyah Al Jawf, NW Saudi Arabia 30.41N 37.58E
106 J10 Aliseda Extremadura, W Spain 39.25N 6.42W
145 T8 Al Iskandarīyah C Iraq 32.52N 44.22E
Al Iskandarīyah see Alexandria
127 Oo5 Aliskerovo Chukotskiy Avtonomnyy Okrug, NE Russian Federation 67.40N 167.37E
116 H13 Alistráti Kentrikí Makedonía, NE Greece 41.03N 23.58E
41 P15 Alitak Bay bay Kodiak Island, Alaska, USA
Al Ittiḥād see Madīnat ash Sha'b
117 H18 Alivéri var. Alivérion. Évvoia, C Greece 38.25N 24.02E
Alivérion see Alivéri
Aliwal-Noord see Aliwal North
85 I24 Aliwal North Afr. Aliwal-Noord. Eastern Cape, SE South Africa 30.39S 26.43E
124 Nn15 Al Jabal al Akhḍar ▲ NE Libya
144 H13 Al Jafr Ma'ān, S Jordan 30.18N 36.13E
77 T8 Al Jaghbūb NE Libya 29.45N 24.31E
148 K11 Al Jahrā' var. Al Jahrah, Jahra. C Kuwait 29.17N 47.36E
Al Jahrah see Al Jahrā'
Al Jamāhīrīyah al 'Arabīyah al Lībīyah ash Sha'bīyah al Ishtirākī see Libya
146 K3 Al Jarāwī spring/well NW Saudi Arabia 30.12N 38.48E
147 X11 Al Jawārah oasis SE Oman 18.59N 57.16E
146 L3 Al Jawf var. Jauf. Al Jawf, NW Saudi Arabia 29.51N 39.49E
146 L4 Al Jawf off. Minṭaqat al Jawf. ◈ province N Saudi Arabia
Al Jawlān see Golan Heights
Al Jazair see Alger
145 N4 Al Jazīrah physical region Iraq/Syria
106 F14 Aljezur Faro, S Portugal 37.18N 8.49W
145 S13 Al Jil S Iraq 30.28N 43.57E
144 G11 Al Jīzah var. Jiza. Al 'Āṣimah, N Jordan 31.42N 35.57E
Al Jīzah see El Gîza
Al Jubail see Al Jubayl
147 S6 Al Jubayl var. Al Jubail. Ash Sharqīyah, NE Saudi Arabia 27.00N 49.36E
147 T10 Al Juḥaysh, Qalamat well SE Saudi Arabia 20.35N 51.00E
149 N15 Al Jumaylīyah N Qatar 25.37N 51.04E
Al Junaynah see El Geneina
106 G13 Aljustrel Beja, S Portugal 37.52N 8.10W
Al Kaba'ish see Al Chabā'ish
Al-Kadhimain see Al Kāẓimīyah
Al Kāf see El Kef
Alkal'a see Alcalá de Henares
37 W4 Alkali Flat salt flat Nevada, W USA
37 Q1 Alkali Lake ◎ Nevada, W USA
147 Z9 Al Kāmil NE Oman 22.15N 59.12E
144 G11 Al Karak var. El Kerak, Karak, Kerak; anc. Kir Moab, Kir of Moab. Al Karak, W Jordan 31.10N 35.42E
144 G12 Al Karak off. Muḥāfaẓat al Karak. ◈ governorate W Jordan
145 W8 Al Karmashīyah E Iraq 32.57N 46.10E
Al-Kashaniya see Al Qash'ānīyah
Al-Kasr al-Kebir see Ksar-el-Kebir
145 T8 Al Kāẓimīyah var. Al-Kadhimain, Kadhimain. C Iraq 33.22N 44.19E
101 J18 Alken Limburg, NE Belgium 50.52N 5.19E
147 X8 Al Khābūrah var. Khabura. N Oman 23.56N 57.06E
Al Khalīl see Hebron
145 T7 Al Khāliṣ C Iraq 33.51N 44.33E
Al Khaluf see Khalūf
Al Khārijah see El Khârga
147 Q8 Al Kharj Ar Riyāḍ, C Saudi Arabia 24.12N 47.12E
147 W6 Al Khaṣab var. Khasab. N Oman 26.10N 56.18E
Al Khaur see Al Khawr
149 N15 Al Khawr var. Al Khaur, Al Khor. N Qatar 25.40N 51.33E
148 K12 Al Khīrān var. Al Khiran. SE Kuwait 28.34N 48.21E
147 W9 Al Khīrān spring/well NW Oman 22.31N 55.42E
Al Khiyām see El Khiyam
Al-Khobar see Al Khubar
Al Khor see Al Khawr
147 S6 Al Khubar var. Al-Khobar. Ash Sharqīyah, NE Saudi Arabia 26.15N 50.10E
77 T11 Al Khufrah SE Libya 24.10N 23.19E
123 L14 Al Khums var. Homs, Khoms, Khums. NW Libya 32.39N 14.16E
147 R15 Al Khuraybah C Yemen 15.05N 48.16E
146 M9 Al Khurmah var. al-Hurma. Makkah, W Saudi Arabia 21.58N 42.00E
147 V9 Al Kidan desert NE Saudi Arabia
131 V4 Alkino-2 Respublika Bashkortostan, W Russian Federation 54.30N 55.40E
100 H9 Alkmaar Noord-Holland, NW Netherlands 52.37N 4.45E
145 T10 Al Kūfah var. Kufa. S Iraq 32.01N 44.25E
147 T10 Al Kursū' desert E Saudi Arabia
145 V9 Al Kūt var. Kūt al 'Amārah, Kut al Imara. E Iraq 32.30N 45.51E
Al-Kuwait see Al Kuwayt
Al Kuwayr see Guwēr
148 K11 Al Kuwayt var. Al-Kuwait, Eng. Kuwait, Kuwait City; prev. Qurein. ● (Kuwait) E Kuwait 29.23N 48.00E
148 K11 Al Kuwayt ✈ C Kuwait 29.13N 47.57E
117 G19 Alkyonídon, Kólpos gulf C Greece
147 N4 Al Labbah physical region N Saudi Arabia
144 G4 Al Lādhiqīyah Eng. Latakia, Fr. Lattaquié; anc. Laodicea, Laodicea ad Mare. Al Lādhiqīyah, W Syria 35.31N 35.46E
144 H4 Al Lādhiqīyah off. Muḥāfaẓat al Lādhiqīyah, var. Al Lathqiyah, Latakia, Lattakia. ◈ governorate W Syria
21 R2 Allagash River ↝ Maine, NE USA
158 M13 Allahābād Uttar Pradesh, N India 25.27N 81.49E
149 S3 Allāh Dāgh, Reshteh-ye ▲ NE Iran
41 Q8 Allakaket Alaska, USA 66.34N 152.39W
126 Mm11 Allakh-Yun' ↝ NE Russian Federation
9 T15 Allan Saskatchewan, S Canada 51.50N 105.59W
177 Ff6 Allanmyo Magwe, C Myanmar 19.25N 95.13E
85 I22 Allanridge Free State, C South Africa 27.43S 26.42E
106 H4 Allariz Galicia, NW Spain 42.10N 7.48W
145 R11 Al Laṣaf var. Al Lussuf. S Iraq 31.38N 43.16E
Al Lathqiyah see Al Lādhiqīyah
25 S2 Allatoona Lake ⊠ Georgia, SE USA
85 J19 Alldays :Limpopo NE South Africa 22.39S 29.04E
Alle see Łyna
33 P10 Allegan Michigan, N USA 42.31N 85.51W
19 Qq8 Allegheny Mountains ▲ NE USA
20 E12 Allegheny Plateau ▲ New York/Pennsylvania, NE USA
20 D11 Allegheny Reservoir ⊠ New York/Pennsylvania, NE USA
20 E12 Allegheny River ↝ New York/Pennsylvania, NE USA
24 K9 Allemands, Lac des ◎ Louisiana, S USA
27 U6 Allen Texas, SW USA 33.06N 96.40W
23 R14 Allendale South Carolina, SE USA 33.01N 81.19W
43 N6 Allende Coahuila de Zaragoza, NE Mexico 28.22N 100.47W
43 O9 Allende Nuevo León, NE Mexico 25.19N 100.01W
99 D16 Allen, Lough Ir. Loch Aillionn. ◎ NW Ireland
193 B26 Allen, Mount ▲ Stewart Island, Southland, SW NZ 47.05S 167.49E
111 V2 Allensteig Niederösterreich, N Austria 48.40N 15.24E
Allenstein see Olsztyn
20 I14 Allentown Pennsylvania, NE USA 40.37N 75.30W
161 G23 Alleppey var. Alappuzha; prev. Alleppi. Kerala, SW India 9.30N 76.22E
Alleppi see Alleppey
102 J12 Aller ↝ NW Germany
31 V16 Allerton Iowa, C USA 40.42N 93.22W
101 K19 Alleur Liège, E Belgium 50.40N 5.33E
103 J25 Allgäuer Alpen ▲ Austria/Germany
30 J13 Alliance Nebraska, C USA 42.05N 102.52W
33 U12 Alliance Ohio, N USA 40.55N 81.06W
105 O10 Allier ◈ department N France
145 R13 Al Līfīyah S Iraq 30.25N 43.03E
46 J13 Alligator Pond C Jamaica 17.52N 77.34W
23 Y9 Alligator River ↝ North Carolina, SE USA
31 W12 Allison Iowa, C USA 42.45N 92.48W
12 G14 Alliston Ontario, S Canada 44.09N 79.51W
146 L11 Al Līth Makkah, SW Saudi Arabia 21.00N 41.00E
Al Liwā' see Līwā
98 J12 Alloa C Scotland, UK 56.07N 3.49W
105 U14 Allos Alpes-de-Haute-Provence, SE France 44.16N 6.37E
110 D6 Allschwil Basel-Land, NW Switzerland 47.34N 7.32E
Al Lubnān see Lebanon
147 N14 Al Luḥayyah W Yemen 15.43N 42.45E
12 K12 Allumettes, Île des island Quebec, SE Canada
Al Lussuf see Al Laṣaf
111 S5 Alm ↝ N Austria
13 Q7 Alma Quebec, SE Canada 48.33N 71.43W
29 S10 Alma Arkansas, C USA 35.28N 94.13W
25 V7 Alma Georgia, SE USA 31.32N 82.27W
29 P4 Alma Kansas, C USA 39.01N 96.17W
33 Q8 Alma Michigan, N USA 43.22N 84.39W
31 O17 Alma Nebraska, C USA 40.06N 99.21W
32 I7 Alma Wisconsin, N USA 44.21N 91.54W
145 R12 Al Ma'ānīyah S Iraq 30.45N 42.57E
Alma-Ata see Almaty
Alma-Atinskaya Oblast' see Almaty
Almacelles see Almacelles
107 T5 Almacelles var. Almacellas. Cataluña, NE Spain 41.43N 0.25E
106 F11 Almada Setúbal, W Portugal 38.40N 9.09W
106 L11 Almadén Castilla-La Mancha, C Spain 38.46N 4.49W
68 L6 Almadies, Pointe des headland W Senegal 14.43N 17.31W
146 L7 Al Madīnah Eng. Medina. Al Madīnah, W Saudi Arabia 24.25N 39.29E
146 L7 Al Madīnah off. Minṭaqat al Madīnah. ◈ province W Saudi Arabia
144 H9 Al Mafraq var. Mafraq. Al Mafraq, N Jordan 32.19N 36.12E
144 J10 Al Mafraq off. Muḥāfaẓat al Mafraq. ◈ governorate NW Jordan
147 R15 Al Maghārīm C Yemen 15.00N 47.49E
107 N11 Almagro Castilla-La Mancha, C Spain 38.54N 3.43W
Al Maḥallah al Kubrá see El Maḥalla el Kubra
145 T9 Al Maḥāwīl var. Khān al Maḥāwīl. C Iraq 32.39N 44.28E
Al Mahdīyah see Mahdia
145 T8 Al Maḥmūdīyah var. Mahmudiya. C Iraq 33.04N 44.22E
147 T14 Al Mahrah ▲ E Yemen
147 P7 Al Majma'ah Ar Riyāḍ, C Saudi Arabia 25.55N 45.18E
145 Q11 Al Makmin well S Iraq 31.38N 42.10E
145 Q1 Al Mālikīyah var. Malkiye. Al Ḥasakah, N Syria 37.12N 42.13E
Almalyk see Olmaliq
Al Mamlakah al Urdunīyah al Hāshimīyah see Jordan
Al Mamlakah see Morocco
149 Q18 Al Manādir var. Al Manadir. desert Oman/UAE
148 L15 Al Manāmah Eng. Manama. ● (Bahrain) N Bahrain 26.13N 50.33E
145 O5 Al Manāṣif ▲ E Syria
37 O4 Almanor, Lake ⊠ California, W USA
107 R11 Almansa Castilla-La Mancha, C Spain 38.52N 1.06W
Al Manṣūrah see El Manṣûra
106 L3 Almanza Castilla-León, N Spain 42.40N 5.01W
106 L8 Almanzor ▲ W Spain 40.13N 5.18W
107 P14 Almanzora ↝ SE Spain
145 S9 Al Mardah C Iraq 32.35N 43.30E
Al-Mariyya see Almería
77 R7 Al Marj var. Barka, It. Barce. NE Libya 32.30N 20.54E
144 L2 Al Mashrafah Ar Raqqah, N Syria 36.25N 39.07E
147 X8 Al Maṣna'ah var. Al Muṣana'a. NE Oman 23.45N 57.37E
107 T9 Almassora País Valenciano, E Spain 39.55N 0.02W
Almatinskaya Oblast' see Almaty
151 U15 Almaty var. Alma-Ata. Almaty, SE Kazakhstan 43.19N 76.55E
151 S14 Almaty off. Almatinskaya Oblast', Kaz. Almaty Oblysy; prev. Alma-Atinskaya Oblast'. ◈ province SE Kazakhstan
151 U15 Almaty ✈ Almaty, SE Kazakhstan 43.15N 76.57E
Almaty Oblysy see Almaty
al-Mawailih see Al Muwayliḥ
145 R3 Al Mawṣil Eng. Mosul. N Iraq 36.21N 43.07E
145 N5 Al Mayādīn var. Mayadin, Fr. Meyadine. Dayr az Zawr, E Syria 35.00N 40.31E
145 X10 Al Maymūnah var. Maimuna. SE Iraq 31.43N 46.55E
147 N5 Al Mayyāh Ḥā'il, N Saudi Arabia 27.56N 42.53E
Al Ma'zam see Al Ma'zim
107 P6 Almazán Castilla-León, N Spain 41.28N 2.31W
147 W8 Al Ma'zim var. Al Ma'zam. NW Oman 23.22N 56.16E
126 Kk11 Almaznyy Respublika Sakha (Yakutiya), NE Russian Federation 62.19N 114.14E
Al Mazra' see Al Mazra'ah
144 G11 Al Mazra'ah var. Al Mazra', Mazra'a. Al Karak, W Jordan 31.17N 35.31E
103 G15 Alme ↝ W Germany
106 I7 Almeida Guarda, N Portugal 40.43N 6.52W
106 G10 Almeirim Santarém, C Portugal 39.12N 8.37W
100 O10 Almelo Overijssel, E Netherlands 52.22N 6.42E
107 S9 Almenara País Valenciano, E Spain 39.46N 0.13W
107 P12 Almenaras ▲ S Spain 38.31N 2.27W
107 P5 Almenar de Soria Castilla-León, N Spain 41.40N 2.12W
106 J6 Almendra, Embalse de ⊠ Castilla-León, NW Spain
106 J11 Almendralejo Extremadura, W Spain 38.40N 6.25W
100 J10 Almere var. Almere-stad. Flevoland, C Netherlands 52.22N 5.12E
100 J10 Almere-Buiten Flevoland, C Netherlands 52.24N 5.15E
100 J10 Almere-Haven Flevoland, C Netherlands 52.19N 5.13E
Almere-stad see Almere
107 P15 Almería Ar. Al-Mariyya; anc. Unci, Lat. Portus Magnus. Andalucía, S Spain 36.49N 2.25W
107 P14 Almería ◈ province Andalucía, S Spain
107 P15 Almería, Golfo de gulf S Spain
131 S5 Al'met'yevsk Respublika Tatarstan, W Russian Federation 54.52N 52.19E
97 L21 Älmhult Kronoberg, S Sweden 56.31N 14.10E
147 U9 Al Miḥrāḍ desert NE Saudi Arabia
Al Mīnā' see El Mina
106 L17 Almina, Punta headland Ceuta, Spain, N Africa 35.54N 5.16W
Al Minyā see El Minya
Al Miqdādīyah see Al Muqdādīyah
45 P14 Almirante Bocas del Toro, NW Panama 9.16N 82.24W
Almirós see Almyrós
146 M9 Al Mislaḥ spring/well W Saudi Arabia 22.46N 40.47E
Almissa see Omiš
106 G13 Almodôvar var. Almodóvar. Beja, S Portugal 37.31N 8.03W
106 M11 Almodóvar del Campo Castilla-La Mancha, C Spain 38.43N 4.10W
107 Q9 Almodóvar del Pinar Castilla-La Mancha, C Spain 39.43N 1.55W
33 S9 Almont Michigan, N USA 42.53N 83.02W
12 L13 Almonte Ontario, SE Canada 45.13N 76.12W
106 J14 Almonte Andalucía, S Spain 37.16N 6.31W
106 K9 Almonte ↝ W Spain
158 K9 Almora Uttar Pradesh, N India 29.36N 79.40E
106 M8 Almorox Castilla-La Mancha, C Spain 40.13N 4.22W
147 S7 Al Mubarraz Ash Sharqīyah, E Saudi Arabia 25.28N 49.34E
Al Muḍaibī see Al Muḍaybī
144 G15 Al Mudawwarah Ma'ān, SW Jordan 29.20N 36.00E
147 Y9 Al Muḍaybī var. Al Muḍaibī. NE Oman 22.34N 58.07E
Almudébar see Almudévar
107 S5 Almudévar var. Almudébar. Aragón, NE Spain 42.03N 0.34W
147 S15 Al Mukallā var. Mukalla. SE Yemen 14.36N 49.07E
147 N16 Al Mukhā Eng. Mocha. SW Yemen 13.18N 43.16E
107 N15 Almuñécar Andalucía, S Spain 36.43N 3.40W
145 U7 Al Muqdādīyah var. Al Miqdādīyah. C Iraq 33.58N 44.58E
146 L3 Al Murayr spring/well NW Saudi Arabia 30.06N 39.54E
142 M12 Almus Tokat, N Turkey 40.22N 36.54E
Al Muṣana'a see Al Maṣna'ah
145 T9 Al Musayyib var. Musaiyib. C Iraq 32.46N 44.19E
145 V9 Al Muwaffaqīyah S Iraq 32.19N 45.22E
144 H10 Al Muwaqqar var. El Muwaqqar. Al 'Āṣimah, W Jordan 31.49N 36.06E
146 J5 Al Muwayliḥ var. al-Mawailih. Tabūk, NW Saudi Arabia 27.39N 35.33E
117 F17 Almyrós var. Almirós. Thessalía, C Greece 39.10N 22.45E
117 I24 Almyroú, Órmos bay Kriti, Greece, E Mediterranean Sea
Al Nūwfalīyah see An Nawfalīyah
98 L13 Alnwick N England, UK 55.26N 1.44W
Al Obayyid see El Obeid
Al Odaid see Al 'Udayd
202 B16 Alofi O (Niue) W Niue 19.01S 169.55W
202 A16 Alofi Bay bay W Niue, C Pacific Ocean
202 E13 Alofi, Île island S Wallis and Futuna
202 E13 Alofitai Île Alofi, W Wallis and Futuna 14.21S 178.03W
Aloha State see Hawaii
120 G7 Aloja Limbaži, N Latvia 57.47N 24.53E
159 X10 Along Arunāchel Pradesh, NE India 28.15N 94.56E
117 H16 Alónnisos island Vóreioi Sporádes, Greece, Aegean Sea
106 M15 Álora Andalucía, S Spain 36.49N 4.43W
175 Rr15 Alor, Kepulauan island group E Indonesia
175 Rr16 Alor, Pulau prev. Ombai. island Kepulauan Alor, E Indonesia
175 R16 Alor, Selat strait Flores Sea/Savu Sea
173 G2 Alor Setar var. Alor Star, Alur Setar. Kedah, Peninsular Malaysia 6.06N 100.22E
Alost see Aalst
160 F9 Ālot Madhya Pradesh, C India 23.58N 75.40E
195 N16 Alotau Milne Bay, SE PNG 10.18S 150.39E
176 Yy15 Alotip Papua, E Indonesia 8.07S 140.06E
Al Oued see El Oued
37 R12 Alpaugh California, W USA 35.52N 119.29W
Alpen see Alps
33 R6 Alpena Michigan, N USA 45.04N 83.27W
Alpes see Alps
105 S14 Alpes-de-Haute-Provence ◈ department SE France
105 U14 Alpes-Maritimes ◈ department SE France
189 W8 Alpha Queensland, E Australia 23.40S 146.38E
207 R9 Alpha Cordillera var. Alpha Ridge. undersea feature Arctic Ocean
Alpha Ridge see Alpha Cordillera
Alpheius see Alfeiós
101 I15 Alphen Noord-Brabant, S Netherlands 51.29N 4.57E
100 H11 Alphen aan den Rijn var. Alphen. Zuid-Holland, C Netherlands 52.07N 4.40E
Alpheus see Alfeiós
Alpi see Alps
106 G10 Alpiarça Santarém, C Portugal 39.15N 8.34W
26 K10 Alpine Texas, SW USA 30.22N 103.40W

◆ Country ● Country Capital ◇ Dependent Territory ○ Dependent Territory Capital ◈ Administrative Region ✈ International Airport ▲ Mountain ▲ Mountain Range ⛰ Volcano ↝ River ◎ Lake ⊠ Reservoir

110 F8 **Alpnach** Unterwalden, W Switzerland 46.56N 8.17E
110 D11 **Alps** Fr. Alpes, Ger. Alpen, It. Alpi. ▲▲ C Europe
147 W8 **Al Qābil** var. Qabil. N Oman 23.55N 55.49E
Al Qaḍārif see Gedaref
77 P8 **Al Qaddāḥīyah** N Libya 31.21N 15.16E
Al Qāhirah see Cairo
146 K4 **Al Qalībah** Tabūk, NW Saudi Arabia 28.28N 37.40E
145 O1 **Al Qāmishlī** var. Kamishli, Qamishly. Al Ḥasakah, NE Syria 37.00N 41.00E
144 I6 **Al Qaryatayn** var. Qaryatayn, Fr. Qariateïne. Ḥimṣ, C Syria 34.13N 37.13E
148 K11 **Al Qash'ānīyah** var. Al-Kashaniya. NE Kuwait 29.59N 47.42E
147 N7 **Al Qaṣīm** off. Minṭaqat Qaṣīm, Qassim. ◈ province C Saudi Arabia
144 J5 **Al Qaṣr** Ḥimṣ, C Syria 35.06N 37.39E
Al Qaṣr see El Qaṣr
Al Qaṣrayn see Kasserine
147 S6 **Al Qaṭīf** Ash Sharqīyah, NE Saudi Arabia 26.27N 50.01E
144 G11 **Al Qaṭrānah** var. El Qatrani, Qatrana. Al Karak, W Jordan 31.13N 36.03E
77 P11 **Al Qaṭrūn** SW Libya 24.57N 14.40E
Al Qayrawān see Kairouan
Al-Qsar al-Kbir see Ksar-el-Kebir
Al Qubayyāt see Qoubaïyât
Al Quds/Al Quds ash Sharīf see Jerusalem
144 G8 **Al Qunayṭirah** var. El Kuneitra, El Quneitra, Kuneitra, Qunaytra. Al Qunayṭirah, SW Syria 33.07N 35.49E
144 G8 **Al Qunayṭirah** off. Muḥāfaẓat al Qunayṭirah, var. El Q'unayṭirah, Qunaytirah, Fr. Kuneitra. ◈ governorate SW Syria
146 M11 **Al Qunfudhah** Makkah, SW Saudi Arabia 19.19N 41.02E
146 K2 **Al Qurayyāt** Al Jawf, NW Saudi Arabia 31.24N 37.25E
145 Y11 **Al Qurnah** var. Kurna. SE Iraq 31.01N 47.27E
145 V12 **Al Quṣayr** S Iraq 30.36N 45.52E
144 I6 **Al Quṣayr** var. El Quseir, Quṣayr, Fr. Kousseir. Ḥimṣ, W Syria 34.36N 36.36E
Al Quṣayr see Quseir
144 H7 **Al Quṭayfah** var. Quṭayfah, Qutayfe, Quteife, Fr. Kouteifé. Dimashq, W Syria 33.44N 36.33E
147 P8 **Al Quwayīyah** Ar Riyāḍ, C Saudi Arabia 24.06N 45.18E
Al Quwayr see Guwēr
144 F14 **Al Quwayrah** var. El Quweira. Ma'ān, SW Jordan 29.49N 35.19E
Al Rayyan see Ar Rayyān
Al Ruweis see Ar Ruways
97 G24 **Als** Ger. Alsen. island SW Denmark
105 U5 **Alsace** Ger. Elsass; anc. Alsatia. ◈ region NE France
9 R16 **Alsask** Saskatchewan, S Canada 51.24N 109.55W
Alsasua see Altsasu
Alsatia see Alsace
103 C16 **Alsdorf** Nordrhein-Westfalen, W Germany 50.52N 6.09E
8 G8 **Alsek** ≈ Canada/USA
Alsen see Als
103 F19 **Alsenz** ≈ W Germany
103 H17 **Alsfeld** Hessen, C Germany 50.45N 9.14E
121 K20 **Al'shany** Rus. Ol'shany. Brestskaya Voblasts', SW Belarus 52.04N 27.19E
Alsókubin see Dolný Kubín
120 C9 **Alsunga** Kuldīga, W Latvia 56.59N 21.31E
Alt see Olt
94 K9 **Alta** Fin. Alattio. Finnmark, N Norway 69.58N 23.16E
31 T12 **Alta** Iowa, C USA 42.40N 95.17W
110 I7 **Altach** Vorarlberg, W Austria 47.22N 9.39E
94 K9 **Altaelva** ≈ N Norway
94 J8 **Altafjorden** fjord NE Norwegian Sea
64 K10 **Alta Gracia** Córdoba, C Argentina 31.42S 64.25W
44 K11 **Alta Gracia** Rivas, SW Nicaragua 11.33N 85.35W
56 H4 **Altagracia** Zulia, NW Venezuela 10.43N 71.30W
56 M5 **Altagracia de Orituco** Guárico, N Venezuela 9.49N 66.22W
Altai see Altai Mountains
133 T7 **Altai Mountains** var. Altai, Chin. Altay Shan, Rus. Altay. ▲▲ Asia/Europe
25 V6 **Altamaha River** ≈ Georgia, SE USA
60 J13 **Altamira** Pará, NE Brazil 3.13S 52.15W
56 D12 **Altamira** Huila, S Colombia 2.02N 75.51W
44 M13 **Altamira** Alajuela, N Costa Rica 10.25N 84.21W
43 Q11 **Altamira** Tamaulipas, C Mexico 22.24N 97.57W
32 L15 **Altamont** Illinois, N USA 39.03N 88.45W
29 Q7 **Altamont** Kansas, C USA 37.11N 95.18W
34 H16 **Altamont** Oregon, NW USA 42.12N 121.44W
22 K10 **Altamont** Tennessee, S USA 35.25N 85.42W
25 X11 **Altamonte Springs** Florida, SE USA 28.39N 81.22W
109 O17 **Altamura** anc. Lupatia. Puglia, SE Italy 40.50N 16.33E
42 H9 **Altamura, Isla** island C Mexico
168 G7 **Altan** Dzavhan, W Mongolia 48.05N 95.48E
168 G6 **Altanbulag** Dzavhan, N Mongolia 49.16N 96.22E
Altan Emel see Xin Barag Youqi
168 J8 **Altan-Ovoo** Arhangay, C Mongolia 47.24N 101.51E
168 E7 **Altanteel** Hovd, W Mongolia 47.05N 92.57E
42 F3 **Altar** Sonora, NW Mexico 30.44N 111.49W
42 D2 **Altar, Desierto de** var. Sonoran Desert. desert Mexico/USA see also Sonoran Desert
107 Q8 **Alta, Sierra** ▲ N Spain 40.29N 1.36W
42 H9 **Altata** Sinaloa, C Mexico 24.39N 107.55W
44 D4 **Alta Verapaz** off. Departamento de Alta Verapaz. ◈ department C Guatemala
109 L18 **Altavilla Silentia** Campania, S Italy 40.32N 15.06E
23 T7 **Altavista** Virginia, NE USA 37.06N 79.17W
164 L2 **Altay** Xinjiang Uygur Zizhiqu, NW China 47.51N 88.06E
168 G5 **Altay** Dzavhan, N Mongolia 49.40N 96.21E
168 G8 **Altay** Govĭ-Altay, W Mongolia 46.23N 96.16E
Altay see Altai Mountains
126 H16 **Altay, Respublika** var. Gornyy Altay; prev. Gorno-Altayskaya Respublika. ◈ autonomous republic S Russian Federation
Altay Shan see Altai Mountains
125 G15 **Altayskiy Kray** ◈ territory S Russian Federation
Altbetsche see Bečej
103 L20 **Altdorf** Bayern, SE Germany 49.23N 11.22E
110 G8 **Altdorf** var. Altorf. Uri, C Switzerland 46.52N 8.37E
107 T11 **Altea** País Valenciano, E Spain 38.37N 0.03W
102 L10 **Alte Elde** ≈ N Germany
103 M16 **Altenburg** Thüringen, E Germany 50.58N 12.27E
Altenburg see București, Romania
Altenburg see Baia de Criș, Romania
102 P12 **Alte Oder** ≈ NE Germany
106 H10 **Alter do Chão** Portalegre, C Portugal 39.12N 7.40W
94 I10 **Altevatnet** ◎ N Norway
29 V12 **Altheimer** Arkansas, C USA 34.19N 91.51W
111 T9 **Althofen** Kärnten, S Austria 46.52N 14.27E
116 H7 **Altimir** Vratsa, NW Bulgaria 43.33N 23.48E
142 K11 **Altınkaya Barajı** ▣ N Turkey
145 S3 **Altin Köprü** var. Altun Kupri. N Iraq 35.45N 44.08E
142 E13 **Altıntaş** Kütahya, W Turkey 39.04N 30.07E
59 K18 **Altiplano** physical region W South America
Altkanischa see Kanjiža
105 U7 **Altkirch** Haut-Rhin, NE France 47.37N 7.14E
Altlublau see Stará L'ubovňa
102 L12 **Altmark** cultural region N Germany
Altmoldowa see Moldova Veche
27 W8 **Alto** Texas, SW USA 31.39N 95.04W
106 H11 **Alto Alentejo** physical region S Portugal
61 I19 **Alto Araguaia** Mato Grosso, C Brazil 17.19S 53.10W
60 L12 **Alto Bonito** Pará, NE Brazil 1.48S 46.18W
85 O15 **Alto Molócuè** Zambézia, NE Mozambique 15.41S 37.42E
32 K15 **Alton** Illinois, N USA 38.53N 90.10W
29 W8 **Alton** Missouri, C USA 36.41N 91.24W
9 X17 **Altona** Manitoba, S Canada 49.12N 97.38W
20 E14 **Altoona** Pennsylvania, NE USA 40.31N 78.22W
32 J6 **Altoona** Wisconsin, N USA 44.49N 91.22W
64 N3 **Alto Paraguay** off. Departamento del Alto Paraguay. ◈ department N Paraguay
61 L17 **Alto Paraíso de Goiás** Goiás, S Brazil 14.04S 47.15W
64 P6 **Alto Paraná** off. Departamento del Alto Paraná. ◈ department E Paraguay
Alto Paraná see Paraná
61 L15 **Alto Parnaíba** Maranhão, E Brazil 9.07S 45.55W
58 H13 **Alto Purús, Río** ≈ E Peru
Altorf see Altdorf
65 H19 **Alto Río Senguer** var. Alto Río Senguerr. Chubut, S Argentina 45.03S 70.48W
43 Q13 **Altotonga** Veracruz-Llave, E Mexico 19.43N 97.12W
103 N23 **Altötting** Bayern, SE Germany 48.12N 12.37E
Altpasua see Stara Pazova
168 I5 **Altraga** Hövsgöl, N Mongolia 50.08N 98.54E
Alt-Schwanenburg see Gulbene
107 P3 **Altsasu** Cast. Alsasua. Navarra, N Spain 42.54N 2.10W
Altsohl see Zvolen
110 I7 **Altstätten** Sankt Gallen, NE Switzerland 47.22N 9.33E
44 G1 **Altun Ha** ruins Belize, N Belize 17.46N 88.20W
Altun Kupri see Altin Köprü
164 D8 **Altun Shan** ▲ C China 39.19N 93.37E
164 L9 **Altun Shan** var. Altyn Tagh. ▲▲ NW China
37 P2 **Alturas** California, W USA 41.28N 120.32W
28 K12 **Altus** Oklahoma, C USA 34.38N 99.19W
28 K11 **Altus Lake** ▣ Oklahoma, C USA
Altvater see Praděd
Altyn Tagh see Altun Shan
Alu see Shortland Island
al-'Ubaila see Al 'Ubaylah
145 O6 **Al 'Ubaydī** W Iraq 34.22N 41.15E
147 T9 **Al 'Ubaylah** var. al-'Ubaila. Ash Sharqīyah, E Saudi Arabia 22.01N 50.57E
147 T9 **Al 'Ubaylah** spring/well E Saudi Arabia 22.02N 50.56E
Al Ubayyiḍ see El Obeid
147 T7 **Al 'Udayd** var. Al Odaid. Abū Ẓaby, W UAE 24.34N 51.27E
120 J8 **Alūksne** Ger. Marienburg. Alūksne, NE Latvia 57.26N 27.02E
146 K6 **Al 'Ulā** Al Madīnah, NW Saudi Arabia 26.39N 37.55E
181 N4 **Alula-Fartak Trench** var. Illaue Fartak Trench. undersea feature W Indian Ocean
144 I11 **Al 'Umarī** 'Ammān, E Jordan 37.30N 31.30E
33 S13 **Alum Creek Lake** ▣ Ohio, N USA
65 H15 **Aluminé** Neuquén, C Argentina 39.15S 71.00W
97 O14 **Alunda** Uppsala, C Sweden 60.04N 18.04E
119 T14 **Alupka** Respublika Krym, S Ukraine 44.24N 34.01E
77 P8 **Al 'Uqaylah** N Libya 30.13N 16.10E
Al Uqṣur see Luxor
Al Urdunn see Jordan
173 G6 **Alur Panal** bay Sumatera, W Indonesia
147 V10 **Al 'Urūq al Mu'tariḍah** salt lake SE Saudi Arabia
145 Q7 **Ālūs** C Iraq 34.04N 42.27E
119 T13 **Alushta** Respublika Krym, S Ukraine 44.40N 34.24E
77 N11 **Al 'Uwaynāt** var. Al Awaynāt. SW Libya 25.47N 10.34E
145 T6 **Al 'Uẓaym** var. Adhaim. E Iraq 34.12N 44.31E
28 L8 **Alva** Oklahoma, C USA 36.48N 98.40W
106 H8 **Alva** ≈ N Portugal
97 J18 **Älvängen** Västra Götaland, S Sweden 57.55N 12.09E
12 F14 **Alvanley** Ontario, S Canada 44.33N 81.05W
43 S14 **Alvarado** Veracruz-Llave, E Mexico 18.46N 95.45W
27 T7 **Alvarado** Texas, SW USA 32.24N 97.12W
60 D13 **Alvarães** Amazonas, NW Brazil 3.13S 64.53W
42 G6 **Alvaro Obregón, Presa** ▣ W Mexico
96 H10 **Alvdal** Hedmark, S Norway 62.07N 10.39E
96 K12 **Älvdalen** Dalarna, C Sweden 61.13N 14.04E
63 E15 **Alvear** Corrientes, NE Argentina 29.03S 56.30W
106 F10 **Alverca do Ribatejo** Lisboa, C Portugal 38.55N 9.01W
97 L20 **Alvesta** Kronoberg, S Sweden 56.52N 14.34E
96 D13 **Ålvik** Hordaland, S Norway 60.26N 6.27E
27 W12 **Alvin** Texas, SW USA 29.25N 95.14W
96 O13 **Älvkarleby** Uppsala, C Sweden 60.34N 17.30E
27 S5 **Alvord** Texas, SW USA 33.22N 97.39W
95 G18 **Älvros** Jämtland, C Sweden 62.04N 14.30E
94 J13 **Älvsbyn** Norrbotten, N Sweden 65.41N 21.00E
148 K12 **Al Wafrā'** SE Kuwait 28.37N 47.56E
146 J6 **Al Wajh** Tabūk, NW Saudi Arabia 26.15N 36.29E
149 N16 **Al Wakrah** var. Wakra. C Qatar 25.09N 51.36E
144 M8 **al Walaj, Sha'īb** dry watercourse W Iraq
158 I11 **Alwar** Rājasthān, N India 27.31N 76.34E
147 Q5 **Al Wari'ah** Ash Sharqīyah, N Saudi Arabia 27.54N 47.22E
161 G22 **Alwaye** Kerala, SW India 10.06N 76.22E
168 K14 **Alxa Zuoqi** var. Ehen Hudag. Nei Mongol Zizhiqu, N China 38.49N 105.40E
Al Yaman see Yemen
144 G9 **Al Yarmūk** Irbid, N Jordan 32.41N 35.55E
Alyat/Alyaty-Pristan' see Älät
117 I14 **Alykí** var. Aliki. Thásos, N Greece 40.36N 24.45E
121 F14 **Alytus** Pol. Olita. Alytus, S Lithuania 54.24N 24.02E
103 N23 **Alz** ≈ SE Germany
35 Y11 **Alzada** Montana, NW USA 45.00N 104.24W
126 Ii14 **Alzamay** Irkutskaya Oblast', S Russian Federation 55.33N 98.36E
101 M25 **Alzette** ≈ S Luxembourg
107 S10 **Alzira** var. Alcira ; anc. Saetabicula, Suero. País Valenciano, E Spain 39.10N 0.27W
Al Zubair see Az Zubayr
189 O8 **Amadeus, Lake** seasonal lake Northern Territory, C Australia
83 E15 **Amadi** Western Equatoria, SW Sudan 5.31N 30.19E
16 Nn3 **Amadjuak Lake** ◎ Baffin Island, Nunavut, N Canada
97 J23 **Amager** island E Denmark
170 Cc13 **Amagi** Fukuoka, Kyūshū, SW Japan 33.24N 130.37E
171 J17 **Amagi-san** ▲ Honshū, S Japan 34.51N 138.57E
175 Tt11 **Amahai** var. Masohi. Pulau Seram, E Indonesia 3.19S 128.55E
40 M16 **Amak Island** island Alaska, USA
170 Bb14 **Amakusa-nada** gulf Kyūshū, SW Japan
97 J16 **Åmål** Västra Götaland, S Sweden 59.04N 12.40E
56 E8 **Amalfi** Antioquia, N Colombia 6.54N 75.04W
109 L18 **Amalfi** Campania, S Italy 40.37N 14.35E
117 D19 **Amaliáda** var. Amaliás. Dytikí Ellás, S Greece 37.48N 21.21E
Amaliás see Amaliáda
160 F12 **Amalner** Mahārāshtra, C India 21.03N 75.04E
176 X12 **Amamapare** Papua, E Indonesia 4.51S 136.43E
61 H21 **Amambaí, Serra de** var. Cordillera de Amambay, Serra de Amambay. ▲▲ Brazil/Paraguay see also Amambay, Cordillera de
64 P4 **Amambay** off. Departamento del Amambay. ◈ department E Paraguay
64 P5 **Amambay, Cordillera de** var. Serra de Amambaí, Serra de Amambay. ▲▲ Brazil/Paraguay see also Amambaí, Serra de
Amambay, Serra de see Amambaí, Serra de/Amambay, Cordillera de
172 Q13 **Amami-guntō** island group SW Japan
172 Qq13 **Amami-Ō-shima** island S Japan
194 E10 **Amanab** Sandaun, NW PNG 3.34S 141.10E
108 J13 **Amandola** Marche, C Italy 42.58N 13.22E
109 N21 **Amantea** Calabria, SW Italy 39.06N 16.05E
203 W10 **Amanu** island Îles Tuamotu, C French Polynesia
60 J10 **Amapá** Amapá, NE Brazil 02.00N 50.50W
60 J11 **Amapá** off. Estado de Amapá; prev. Território de Amapá. ◈ state NE Brazil
44 H8 **Amapala** Valle, S Honduras 13.18N 87.37W
Amara see Al 'Amārah
106 H6 **Amarante** Porto, N Portugal 41.16N 8.04W
177 G5 **Amarapura** Mandalay, C Myanmar 21.54N 96.01E
168 L9 **Amardalay** Dundgovĭ, C Mongolia 46.09N 106.24E
106 I12 **Amareleja** Beja, S Portugal 38.12N 7.13W
37 V11 **Amargosa Range** ▲▲ California, W USA
27 N2 **Amarillo** Texas, SW USA 35.13N 101.49W
Amarinthos see Amárynthos
109 K15 **Amaro, Monte** ▲ C Italy 42.03N 14.06E
117 H18 **Amárynthos** var. Amarinthos. Évvoia, C Greece 38.24N 23.53E
Amasia see Amasya
142 K12 **Amasya** anc. Amasia. Amasya, N Turkey 40.40N 35.49E
142 K11 **Amasya** ◈ province N Turkey
44 F4 **Amatique, Bahía de** bay Gulf of Honduras, W Caribbean Sea
44 D6 **Amatitlán, Lago de** ◎ S Guatemala
109 J14 **Amatrice** Lazio, C Italy 42.38N 13.19E
202 C8 **Amatuku** atoll C Tuvalu
101 J20 **Amay** Liège, E Belgium 50.33N 5.19E
50 F7 **Amazon** Sp. Amazonas. ≈ Brazil/Peru
61 C14 **Amazonas** off. Estado do Amazonas. ◈ state N Brazil
56 G15 **Amazonas** off. Comisaria del Amazonas. ◈ province SE Colombia
58 C10 **Amazonas** off. Departamento de Amazonas. ◈ department N Peru
56 M12 **Amazonas** off. Territorio Amazonas. ◈ federal territory S Venezuela
Amazonas see Amazon
50 F7 **Amazon Basin** basin N South America
49 V5 **Amazon Fan** undersea feature W Atlantic Ocean
60 K11 **Amazon, Mouths of the** delta NE Brazil
197 C12 **Ambae** var. Aoba, Omba. island C Vanuatu
158 I9 **Ambāla** Haryāna, NW India 30.22N 76.49E
161 J26 **Ambalangoda** Southern Province, SW Sri Lanka 6.13N 80.03E
161 K26 **Ambalantota** Southern Province, S Sri Lanka 6.07N 81.01E
180 I6 **Ambalavao** Fianarantsoa, C Madagascar 21.49S 46.55E
56 E10 **Ambalema** Tolima, C Colombia 4.49N 74.48W
81 E17 **Ambam** Sud, S Cameroon 2.22N 11.16E
180 J2 **Ambanja** Antsirañana, N Madagascar 13.40S 48.27E
127 O5 **Ambarchik** Respublika Sakha (Yakutiya), NE Russian Federation 69.33N 162.08E
64 K9 **Ambargasta, Salinas de** salt lake C Argentina
128 J6 **Ambarnyy** Respublika Kareliya, NW Russian Federation 65.53N 33.44E
58 C7 **Ambato** Tungurahua, C Ecuador 1.18S 78.39W
180 I5 **Ambatolampy** Antananarivo, C Madagascar 19.21S 47.27E
180 H4 **Ambatomainty** Mahajanga, W Madagascar 17.40S 45.39E
180 J4 **Ambatondrazaka** Toamasina, C Madagascar 17.49S 48.28E
175 Ss12 **Ambelau, Pulau** see Ambelau, Pulau
103 L20 **Amberg** var. Amberg in der Oberpfalz. Bayern, SE Germany 49.27N 11.51E
Amberg in der Oberpfalz see Amberg
44 H1 **Ambergris Cay** island NE Belize
105 S11 **Ambérieu-en-Bugey** Ain, E France 45.57N 5.21E
193 I18 **Amberley** Canterbury, South Island, NZ 43.09S 172.43E
105 P11 **Ambert** Puy-de-Dôme, C France 45.34N 3.42E
Ambianum see Amiens
78 J11 **Ambidédi** Kayes, SW Mali 14.37N 11.49W
160 M10 **Ambikāpur** Madhya Pradesh, C India 23.09N 83.12E
180 J2 **Ambilobe** Antsirañana, N Madagascar 13.10S 49.03E
195 Q10 **Ambitle Island** island Feni Islands, NE PNG
41 O7 **Ambler** Alaska, USA 67.05N 157.51W
Amblève see Amel
Ambo see Hāgere Hiywet
180 I8 **Amboasary** Toliara, S Madagascar 25.01S 46.22E
180 J4 **Ambodifotatra** var. Ambodifototra. Toamasina, E Madagascar 16.58S 49.51E
Amboenten see Ambunten
180 I5 **Ambohidratrimo** Antananarivo, C Madagascar 18.48S 47.25E
180 I6 **Ambohimahasoa** Fianarantsoa, SE Madagascar 21.07S 47.13E
180 K3 **Ambohitralanana** Antsirañana, NE Madagascar 15.13S 50.28E
176 X10 **Amboi, Kepulauan** island group E Indonesia
Amboina see Ambon
104 M8 **Amboise** Indre-et-Loire, C France 47.25N 1.00E
175 T11 **Ambon** prev. Amboina, Amboyna. Pulau Ambon, E Indonesia 3.40S 128.10E
175 T12 **Ambon, Pulau** island E Indonesia
83 I20 **Amboseli, Lake** ◎ Kenya/Tanzania
180 I6 **Ambositra** Fianarantsoa, SE Madagascar 20.31S 47.15E
180 I8 **Ambovombe** Toliara, S Madagascar 25.10S 46.06E
37 W14 **Amboy** California, W USA 34.33N 115.44W
32 L11 **Amboy** Illinois, N USA 41.42N 89.19W
Amboyna see Ambon
Ambracia see Árta
20 B14 **Ambridge** Pennsylvania, NE USA 40.33N 80.11W
Ambrim see Ambrym
84 A11 **Ambriz** Bengo, NW Angola 7.55S 13.11E
Ambrizete see N'Zeto
197 C13 **Ambrym** var. Ambrim. island C Vanuatu
174 Mm14 **Ambunten** prev. Amboenten. Pulau Madura, E Indonesia 6.55S 113.45E
194 G10 **Ambunti** East Sepik, NW PNG 4.06S 142.49E
161 I20 **Āmbūr** Tamil Nādu, SE India 12.48N 78.43E
40 E17 **Amchitka Island** island Aleutian Islands, Alaska, USA
40 F17 **Amchitka Pass** strait Aleutian Islands, Alaska, USA
147 R15 **'Amd** C Yemen 15.09N 47.58E
80 J10 **Am Dam** Ouaddaï, E Chad 12.46N 20.28E
176 Uu15 **Amdassa** Pulau Yamdena, E Indonesia 7.40S 131.24E
129 U1 **Amderma** Nenetskiy Avtonomnyy Okrug, NW Russian Federation 69.45N 61.36E
165 N14 **Amdo** Xizang Zizhiqu, W China 32.15N 91.43E
42 K13 **Ameca** Jalisco, SW Mexico 20.31N 104.02W
43 P14 **Amecameca** var. Amecameca de Juárez. México, C Mexico 19.07N 98.45W
Amecameca de Juárez see Amecameca
63 A20 **Ameghino** Buenos Aires, E Argentina 34.51S 62.28W
101 M21 **Amel** Fr. Amblève. Liège, E Belgium 50.20N 6.13E
100 K4 **Ameland** Fris. It Amelân. island Waddeneilanden, N Netherlands
Amelân, It see Ameland
109 H14 **Amelia** Umbria, C Italy 42.33N 12.26E
23 V6 **Amelia Court House** Virginia, NE USA 37.19N 77.57W
25 W8 **Amelia Island** island Florida, SE USA
20 L12 **Amenia** New York, NE USA 41.51N 73.31W
America see United States of America
67 M21 **America-Antarctica Ridge** undersea feature S Atlantic Ocean
America in Miniature see Maryland
62 L9 **Americana** São Paulo, S Brazil 22.43S 47.19W
35 Q15 **American Falls** Idaho, NW USA 42.47N 112.51W
35 Q15 **American Falls Reservoir** ▣ Idaho, NW USA
38 L3 **American Fork** Utah, W USA 40.24N 111.47W
198 D8 **American Samoa** ◇ US unincorporated territory W Polynesia
25 S6 **Americus** Georgia, SE USA 32.04N 84.13W
100 K12 **Amerongen** Utrecht, C Netherlands 52.00N 5.30E
100 K11 **Amersfoort** Utrecht, C Netherlands 52.09N 5.22E
99 N21 **Amersham** SE England, UK 51.39N 0.37W
32 I5 **Amery** Wisconsin, N USA 45.18N 92.20W
205 W6 **Amery Ice Shelf** ice shelf Antarctica
31 V13 **Ames** Iowa, C USA 42.01N 93.37W
21 P10 **Amesbury** Massachusetts, NE USA 42.51N 70.55W
Amestratus see Mistretta
117 F18 **Amfíkleia** var. Amfíklia. Stereá Ellás, C Greece 38.37N 22.34E
Amfíklia see Amfíkleia
117 D17 **Amfilochía** var. Amfilokhía. Dytikí Ellás, C Greece 38.52N 21.09E
Amfilokhía see Amfilochía
116 H13 **Amfípoli** anc. Amphipolis. site of ancient city Kentrikí Makedonía, NE Greece 40.49N 23.51E
117 F18 **Ámfissa** Stereá Ellás, C Greece 38.31N 22.22E
126 M11 **Amga** Respublika Sakha (Yakutiya), NE Russian Federation 60.55N 131.45E
126 M11 **Amga** ≈ NE Russian Federation
Amgalang see Xin Barag Zuoqi
195 N12 **Amgen** ≈ New Britain, C PNG
127 P4 **Amguema** ≈ NE Russian Federation
127 Nn14 **Amgun'** ≈ SE Russian Federation
82 J12 **Amhara** ◈ region N Ethiopia
11 P15 **Amherst** Nova Scotia, SE Canada 45.49N 64.13W
20 M11 **Amherst** Massachusetts, NE USA 42.22N 72.31W
20 D10 **Amherst** New York, NE USA 42.57N 78.47W
26 M4 **Amherst** Texas, SW USA 33.59N 102.24W
23 U6 **Amherst** Virginia, NE USA 37.35N 79.03W
Amherst see Kyaikkami
12 C18 **Amherstburg** Ontario, S Canada 42.05N 83.06W
23 Q6 **Amherstdale** West Virginia, NE USA 37.46N 81.46W
12 K15 **Amherst Island** island Ontario, SE Canada
Amida see Diyarbakır
30 J6 **Amidon** North Dakota, N USA 46.26N 103.18W
105 O3 **Amiens** anc. Ambianum, Samarobriva. Somme, N France 49.54N 2.18E
145 P8 **'Āmij, Wādī** var. Wadi 'Amīq. dry watercourse W Iraq
142 L17 **Amik Ovası** ◎ S Turkey
78 E9 **Amilcar Cabral** ✈ Sal, NE Cape Verde 16.45N 22.56E
Amilḥayt, Wādī see Umm al Ḥayt, Wādī
Amíndaion/Amindeo see Amýntaio
161 C21 **Amīndīvi Islands** island group Lakshadweep, India, N Indian Ocean
145 U6 **Amīn Ḥabīb** E Iraq 34.17N 45.10E
85 E20 **Aminuis** Omaheke, E Namibia 23.37S 19.21E
'Amīq, Wadi see 'Āmij, Wādī
148 J7 **Amīrābād** Īlām, NW Iran 33.19N 46.16E
Amirante Bank see Amirante Ridge
181 N6 **Amirante Basin** undersea feature W Indian Ocean
181 N6 **Amirante Islands** var. Amirantes Group. island group C Seychelles
181 N7 **Amirante Ridge** var. Amirante Bank. undersea feature W Indian Ocean
Amirantes Group see Amirante Islands
181 N7 **Amirante Trench** undersea feature W Indian Ocean
176 Z12 **Amisibil** Papua, E Indonesia 3.59S 140.35E
9 U13 **Amisk Lake** ◎ Saskatchewan, C Canada
Amistad, Presa de la see Amistad Reservoir
27 O12 **Amistad Reservoir** var. Presa de la Amistad. ▣ Mexico/USA
Amisus see Samsun
24 K8 **Amite** var. Amite City. Louisiana, S USA 30.40N 90.30W
Amite City see Amite
29 T12 **Amity** Arkansas, C USA 34.15N 93.27W
160 H11 **Amla** prev. Amulla. Madhya Pradesh, C India 21.57N 78.06E
40 I17 **Amlia Island** island Aleutian Islands, Alaska, USA
99 I18 **Amlwch** NW Wales, UK 53.25N 4.22W
Ammaia see Portalegre
144 H10 **'Ammān** var. Amman; anc. Philadelphia, Bibl. Rabbah Ammon, Rabbath Ammon. ● (Jordan) Al 'Āṣmiah, NW Jordan 31.57N 35.55E
'Ammān see Al 'Āṣimah
95 N14 **Ämmänsaari** Oulu, E Finland 64.51N 28.58E
94 H13 **Ammarnäs** Västerbotten, N Sweden 65.58N 16.10E
207 O15 **Ammassalik** var. Angmagssalik. Tunu, S Greenland 65.51N 37.30W
103 K24 **Ammer** ≈ SE Germany
103 K24 **Ammersee** ◎ SE Germany
100 J13 **Ammerzoden** Gelderland, C Netherlands 51.46N 5.07E
Ammóchostos see Gazimağusa
Ammóchostos, Kólpos see Gazimağusa Körfezi
Amnok-kang see Yalu
Amoea see Portalegre
Amoentai see Amuntai
Amoerang see Amurang
149 O4 **Āmol** var. Amul. Māzandarān, N Iran 36.30N 52.24E
117 K21 **Amorgós** Amorgós, Kykládes, Greece, Aegean Sea 36.49N 25.54E
117 K22 **Amorgós** island Kykládes, Greece, Aegean Sea
25 N3 **Amory** Mississippi, S USA 33.58N 88.29W
10 I13 **Amos** Quebec, SE Canada 48.34N 78.07W
97 G15 **Åmot** Buskerud, S Norway 59.52N 9.55E
97 E15 **Åmot** Telemark, S Norway 59.34N 7.59E
97 J15 **Åmotfors** Värmland, C Sweden 59.46N 12.24E
78 L10 **Amourj** Hodh ech Chargui, SE Mauritania 16.04N 7.12W
Amoy see Xiamen
180 H7 **Ampanihy** Toliara, SW Madagascar 24.40S 44.45E
161 L25 **Ampara** var. Amparai. Eastern Province, E Sri Lanka 7.16N 81.40E
180 J4 **Amparafaravola** Toamasina, E Madagascar 17.33S 48.13E
Amparai see Ampara
62 M9 **Amparo** São Paulo, S Brazil 22.40S 46.49W
180 J5 **Ampasimanolotra** Toamasina, E Madagascar 18.49S 49.04E
59 H17 **Ampato, Nevado** ▲ S Peru 15.52S 71.51W
103 L23 **Amper** ≈ SE Germany
66 M9 **Ampère Seamount** undersea feature E Atlantic Ocean 35.05N 13.00W
Amphipolis see Amfípoli
178 M10 **Amphitrite Group** island group N Paracel Islands
176 U15 **Amplawas** var. Emplawas. Pulau Babar, E Indonesia 8.01S 129.42E
107 U7 **Amposta** Cataluña, NE Spain 40.43N 0.34E
13 V7 **Amqui** Quebec, SE Canada 48.28N 67.27W
147 O14 **'Amrān** W Yemen 15.39N 43.59E
Amraoti see Amrāvati
160 H12 **Amrāvati** prev. Amraoti. Mahārāshtra, C India 20.55N 77.45E
160 C11 **Amreli** Gujarāt, W India 21.36N 71.19E
110 H6 **Amriswil** Thurgau, NE Switzerland 47.33N 9.18E
144 H5 **'Amrīt** ruins Tarṭūs, W Syria 34.48N 35.54E
158 H7 **Amritsar** Punjab, N India 31.38N 74.54E
158 J10 **Amroha** Uttar Pradesh, N India 28.54N 78.28E
102 G7 **Amrum** island NW Germany
95 I15 **Åmsele** Västerbotten, N Sweden 64.31N 19.24E
100 I10 **Amstelveen** Noord-Holland, C Netherlands 52.18N 4.49E
100 I10 **Amsterdam** ● (Netherlands) Noord-Holland, C Netherlands 52.22N 4.54E
20 K10 **Amsterdam** New York, NE USA 42.56N 74.11W
181 Q11 **Amsterdam Fracture Zone** tectonic feature S Indian Ocean
181 R11 **Amsterdam Island** island NE French Southern and Antarctic Territories
111 U4 **Amstetten** Niederösterreich, N Austria 48.07N 14.52E
80 J11 **Am Timan** Salamat, SE Chad 11.01N 20.16E
152 L12 **Amu-Buxoro Kanali** var. Aral-Bukhorskiy Kanal. canal C Uzbekistan
145 O1 **'Āmūdah** var. Amude. Al Ḥasakah, N Syria 37.06N 40.56E
152 M14 **Amu-Dar'ya** Lebapskiy Velayat, NE Turkmenistan 37.58N 65.14E
153 O15 **Amu Darya** Rus. Amudar'ya, Taj. Dar"yoi Amu, Turkm. Amyderya, Uzb. Amudaryo; anc. Oxus. ≈ C Asia
Amudar'ya/Amudaryo/Amu, Dar"yoi see Amu Darya
Amude see 'Āmūdah
146 L3 **'Amūd, Jabal al** ▲ NW Saudi Arabia 30.59N 39.17E
40 J17 **Amukta Island** island Aleutian Islands, Alaska, USA
40 I17 **Amukta Pass** strait Aleutian Islands, Alaska, USA
Amul see Āmol
Amulla see Amla
Amundsen Basin see Fram Basin
205 X3 **Amundsen Bay** bay Antarctica
205 P10 **Amundsen Coast** physical region Antarctica
15 H2 **Amundsen Gulf** gulf Northwest Territories, N Canada
199 Ll16 **Amundsen Plain** undersea feature S Pacific Ocean
205 Q9 **Amundsen-Scott** US research station Antarctica 89.59S 10.00E
204 J11 **Amundsen Sea** sea S Pacific Ocean
96 M12 **Amungen** ◎ C Sweden
175 N10 **Amuntai** prev. Amoentai. Borneo, C Indonesia 2.24S 115.13E
133 W6 **Amur** Chin. Heilong Jiang. ≈ China/Russian Federation
175 Rr7 **Amurang** prev. Amoerang. Sulawesi, C Indonesia 1.12N 124.37E
175 Rr7 **Amurang, Teluk** bay Sulawesi, C Indonesia
107 O3 **Amurrio** País Vasco, N Spain 43.03N 3.00W
127 Nn15 **Amursk** Khabarovskiy Kray, SE Russian Federation 50.13N 136.34E
126 M14 **Amurskaya Oblast'** ◈ province SE Russian Federation
82 G7 **'Amur, Wadi** ≈ NE Sudan
117 C17 **Amvrakikós Kólpos** gulf W Greece
Amvrosiyevka see Amvrosiyivka
119 X8 **Amvrosiyivka** Rus. Amvrosiyevka. Donets'ka Oblast', SE Ukraine 47.46N 38.31E
Amyderya see Amu Darya
116 E13 **Amýntaio** var. Amindeo; prev. Amíndaion. Dytikí Makedonía, N Greece 40.42N 21.42E
12 B6 **Amyot** Ontario, S Canada 48.28N 84.58W
203 U10 **Anaa** atoll Îles Tuamotu, C French Polynesia
Anabanoea see Anabanua
175 Pp12 **Anabanua** prev. Anabanoea. Sulawesi, C Indonesia 3.58S 120.07E
201 R8 **Anabar** NE Nauru 0.30S 166.56E
126 K7 **Anabar** ≈ NE Russian Federation
An Abhainn Mhór see Blackwater
57 O6 **Anaco** Anzoátegui, NE Venezuela 9.30N 64.28W
35 Q10 **Anaconda** Montana, NW USA 46.09N 112.55W
34 H7 **Anacortes** Washington, NW USA 48.30N 122.36W
28 M11 **Anadarko** Oklahoma, C USA 35.04N 98.14W
116 N12 **Ana Dere** ≈ NW Turkey
106 G8 **Anadia** Aveiro, N Portugal 40.25N 8.27W
Anadolu Dağları see Doğu Karadeniz Dağları
127 Pp5 **Anadyr'** Chukotskiy Avtonomnyy Okrug, NE Russian Federation 64.40N 177.22E
127 P5 **Anadyr'** ≈ NE Russian Federation
Anadyr, Gulf of see Anadyrskiy Zaliv
133 X4 **Anadyrskiy Khrebet** var. Chukot Range. ▲▲ NE Russian Federation
127 Q4 **Anadyrskiy Zaliv** Eng. Gulf of Anadyr. gulf NE Russian Federation
117 K22 **Anáfi** anc. Anaphe. island Kykládes, Greece, Aegean Sea
109 J15 **Anagni** Lazio, C Italy 41.43N 13.12E
'Ānah see 'Annah
37 T15 **Anaheim** California, W USA 33.50N 117.54W
8 L15 **Anahim Lake** British Columbia, SW Canada 52.26N 125.13W
40 B8 **Anahola** Kauai, Hawaii, USA, C Pacific Ocean 22.09N 159.19W
27 X11 **Anahuac** Texas, SW USA 29.46N 94.40W
43 O7 **Anáhuac** Nuevo León, NE Mexico 27.13N 100.09W
161 G22 **Anai Mudi** ▲ S India 10.16N 77.08E
Anaiza see 'Unayzah
161 M15 **Anakāpalle** Andhra Pradesh, E India 17.42N 83.06E
203 W15 **Anakena, Playa de** beach Easter Island, Chile, E Pacific Ocean
41 Q7 **Anaktuvuk Pass** Alaska, USA 68.08N 151.44W
41 Q6 **Anaktuvuk River** ≈ Alaska, USA
180 J3 **Analalava** Mahajanga, NW Madagascar 14.37S 47.46E
46 F6 **Ana Maria, Golfo de** gulf C Cuba
Anambas Islands see Anambas, Kepulauan
174 Ii5 **Anambas, Kepulauan** var. Anambas Islands island group W Indonesia
79 U17 **Anambra** ◈ state SE Nigeria
31 N4 **Anamoose** North Dakota, N USA 47.50N 100.14W
31 Y13 **Anamosa** Iowa, C USA 42.06N 91.17W
142 H17 **Anamur** İçel, S Turkey 36.06N 32.49E
142 H17 **Anamur Burnu** headland S Turkey 36.03N 32.49E
170 Ff16 **Anan** Tokushima, Shikoku, SW Japan 33.54N 134.40E
160 O12 **Ānandadur** Orissa, E India 21.13N 86.08E

◆ Country
● Country Capital
◇ Dependent Territory
○ Dependent Territory Capital
◈ Administrative Region
✈ International Airport
▲ Mountain
▲▲ Mountain Range
Volcano
≈ River
◎ Lake
▣ Reservoir

161 H18 **Anantapur** Andhra Pradesh, S India 14.40N 77.36E
158 H5 **Anantnāg** *var.* Islamabad. Jammu and Kashmir, NW India 33.43N 75.10E
Ananyev *see* Anan'yiv
119 O9 **Anan'yiv** *Rus.* Ananyev. Odes'ka Oblast', SW Ukraine 47.43N 29.51E
130 J14 **Anapa** Krasnodarskiy Kray, SW Russian Federation 44.55N 37.20E
Anaphe *see* Anáfi
61 K18 **Anápolis** Goiás, C Brazil 16.19S 48.58W
149 R10 **Anār** Kermān, C Iran 30.48N 55.17E
Anár *see* Inari
149 P7 **Anārak** Eşfahān, C Iran 33.21N 53.43E
Anar Dara *see* Anār Darreh
154 J7 **Anār Darreh** *var.* Anar Dara. Farāh, W Afghanistan 32.45N 61.37E
Anárjohka *see* Inarijoki
25 X9 **Anastasia Island** *island* Florida, SE USA
196 K7 **Anatahan** *island* C Northern Mariana Islands
132 M6 **Anatolia** *plateau* C Turkey
88 F14 **Anatolian Plate** *tectonic feature* Asia/Europe
116 H13 **Anatolikí Makedonía kai Thráki** *Eng.* Macedonia East and Thrace. ⬖ *region* NE Greece
Anatom *see* Aneityum
64 L8 **Añatuya** Santiago del Estero, N Argentina 28.27S 62.52W
An Baile Meánach *see* Ballymena
An Bhearú *see* Barrow
An Bhóinn *see* Boyne
An Blascaod Mór *see* Great Blasket Island
An Cabhán *see* Cavan
An Caisleán Nua *see* Newcastle
An Caisleán Riabhach *see* Castlereagh, Northern Ireland, UK
An Caisleán Riabhach *see* Castlerea, Ireland
58 C13 **Ancash** *off.* Departamento de Ancash. ⬖ *department* W Peru
An Cathair *see* Caher
104 J8 **Ancenis** Loire-Atlantique, NW France 47.22N 1.10W
An Chanáil Ríoga *see* Royal Canal
An Cheacha *see* Caha Mountains
41 R11 **Anchorage** Alaska, USA 61.12N 149.52W
41 R12 **Anchorage** ✕ Alaska, USA 61.08N 150.00W
41 Q13 **Anchor Point** Alaska, USA 59.46N 151.49W
An Chorr Chríochach *see* Cookstown
67 M24 **Anchorstack Point** *headland* W Tristan da Cunha 37.07S 12.21W
An Clár *see* Clare
An Clochán *see* Clifden
An Clochán Liath *see* Dunglow
25 U12 **Anclote Keys** *island group* Florida, SE USA
An Cóbh *see* Cobh
59 J17 **Ancohuma, Nevado de** ▲ W Bolivia 15.51S 68.33W
An Comar *see* Comber
59 D14 **Ancón** Lima, W Peru 11.47S 77.09W
108 J12 **Ancona** Marche, C Italy 43.37N 13.30E
Ancuabe *see* Ancuabi
84 Q13 **Ancuabi** *var.* Ancuabe. Cabo Delgado, NE Mozambique 12.57S 39.54E
65 F17 **Ancud** *prev.* San Carlos de Ancud. Los Lagos, S Chile 41.52S 73.49W
65 G17 **Ancud, Golfo de** *gulf* S Chile
Ancyra *see* Ankara
169 V8 **Anda** Heilongjiang, NE China 46.22N 125.15E
59 G16 **Andahuaylas** Apurímac, S Peru 13.38S 73.20W
An Daingean *see* Dingle
159 R15 **Andāl** West Bengal, NE India 23.34N 87.13E
96 E9 **Åndalsnes** Møre og Romsdal, S Norway 62.33N 7.42E
106 K13 **Andalucía** *Eng.* Andalusia. ⬖ *autonomous community* S Spain
25 P7 **Andalusia** Alabama, S USA 31.18N 86.29W
Andalusia *see* Andalucía
157 Q21 **Andaman and Nicobar Islands** *var.* Andamans and Nicobars. ⬖ *union territory* India, NE Indian Ocean
181 T4 **Andaman Basin** *undersea feature* NE Indian Ocean
157 P19 **Andaman Islands** *island group* India, NE Indian Ocean
181 T4 **Andaman Sea** *sea* NE Indian Ocean
59 K19 **Andamarca** Oruro, C Bolivia 18.50S 67.24W
176 V10 **Andamata** Papua, E Indonesia 2.40S 132.30E
190 H5 **Andamooka** South Australia 30.26S 137.12E
147 Y9 **'Andām, Wādī** *seasonal river* NE Oman
180 J3 **Andapa** Antsirañana, NE Madagascar 14.39S 49.40E
155 R4 **Andarāb** *var.* Banow. Baghlān, NE Afghanistan 35.36N 69.18E
Andarbag *see* Andarbogh
153 S13 **Andarbogh** *Rus.* Andarbag, Anderbak. S Tajikistan 37.51N 71.45E
111 Z5 **Andau** Burgenland, E Austria 47.46N 17.03E
110 I10 **Andeer** Graubünden, S Switzerland 46.36N 9.24E
94 H9 **Andenes** Nordland, C Norway 69.18N 16.06E
101 J20 **Andenne** Namur, SE Belgium 50.28N 5.06E
79 S11 **Andéramboukane** Gao, E Mali 15.24N 3.03E
Anderbak *see* Andarbogh
101 G18 **Anderlecht** Brussels, C Belgium 50.50N 4.18E
101 G21 **Anderlues** Hainaut, S Belgium 50.24N 4.16E
110 G9 **Andermatt** Uri, C Switzerland 46.39N 8.36E
103 E17 **Andernach** *anc.* Antunnacum. Rheinland-Pfalz, SW Germany 50.25N 7.25E
196 D15 **Andersen Air Force Base** *air base* NE Guam 13.34N 144.55E
41 R9 **Anderson** Alaska, USA 64.20N 149.11W
37 N4 **Anderson** California, W USA 40.26N 122.21W
33 P13 **Anderson** Indiana, N USA 40.06N 85.40W
29 R8 **Anderson** Missouri, C USA 36.39N 94.26W
23 P11 **Anderson** South Carolina, SE USA 34.30N 82.39W
27 V10 **Anderson** Texas, SW USA 30.29N 96.00W
15 Gg3 **Anderson** ≈ Northwest Territories, NW Canada
97 K20 **Anderstorp** Jönköping, S Sweden 57.16N 13.46E
56 D9 **Andes** Antioquia, W Colombia 5.40N 75.55W
49 P7 **Andes** ▲▲ W South America
31 P12 **Andes, Lake** ◎ South Dakota, N USA
94 H9 **Andfjorden** *fjord* E Norwegian Sea
161 H16 **Andhra Pradesh** ⬖ *state* E India
100 J8 **Andijk** Noord-Holland, NW Netherlands 52.38N 5.00E
153 S10 **Andijon** *Rus.* Andizhan. Andijon Viloyati, E Uzbekistan 40.46N 72.19E
153 S10 **Andijon Viloyati** *Rus.* Andizhanskaya Oblast'. ⬖ *province* E Uzbekistan
Andikíthira *see* Antikýthira
180 J4 **Andilamena** Toamasina, C Madagascar 17.00S 48.35E
148 L8 **Andīmeshk** *var.* Andimishk; *prev.* Salehābād. Khūzestān, SW Iran 32.28N 48.21E
Andimishk *see* Andīmeshk
Andipáros *see* Antíparos
Andipaxi *see* Antípaxoi
Andípsara *see* Antípsara
142 L16 **Andırın** Kahramanmaraş, S Turkey 37.33N 36.18E
164 J8 **Andirlangar** Xinjiang Uygur Zizhiqu, NW China 37.38N 83.40E
Andírrion *see* Antírrio
Ándissa *see* Ántissa
Andizhan *see* Andijon
Andizhanskaya Oblast' *see* Andijon Viloyati
155 N2 **Andkhvoy** Fāryāb, N Afghanistan 36.55N 65.07E
107 Q2 **Andoain** País Vasco, N Spain 43.13N 2.01W
176 W9 **Andoi** Papua, E Indonesia 0.53S 133.59E
169 Y15 **Andong** *Jap.* Antō. E South Korea 36.34N 128.43E
111 R4 **Andorf** Oberösterreich, N Austria 48.22N 13.33E
107 S7 **Andorra** Aragón, NE Spain 40.58N 0.27W
107 V4 **Andorra** *off.* Principality of Andorra, *Cat.* Valls d'Andorra, *Fr.* Vallée d'Andorre. ◆ *monarchy* SW Europe
Andorra *see* Andorra la Vella
107 V4 **Andorra la Vella** *var.* Andorra, *Fr.* Andorre la Vielle, *Sp.* Andorra la Vieja. ● (Andorra) C Andorra 42.30N 1.30E
Andorra la Vieja *see* Andorra la Vella
Andorra, Valls d'/Andorre, Vallée d' *see* Andorra
Andorre la Vielle *see* Andorra la Vella
99 M22 **Andover** S England, UK 51.13N 1.28W
29 N6 **Andover** Kansas, C USA 37.42N 97.08W
94 G10 **Andøya** *island* C Norway
62 I8 **Andradina** São Paulo, S Brazil 20.54S 51.25W
41 N10 **Andreafsky River** ≈ Alaska, USA
40 H17 **Andreanof Islands** *island group* Aleutian Islands, Alaska, USA
128 H16 **Andreapol'** Tverskaya Oblast', W Russian Federation 56.38N 32.17E
Andreas, Cape *see* Zafer Burnu
Andreevka *see* Kabanbay
23 N10 **Andrews** North Carolina, SE USA 35.19N 84.01W
23 T13 **Andrews** South Carolina, SE USA 33.27N 79.33W
26 M7 **Andrews** Texas, SW USA 32.19N 102.33W
181 N5 **Andrew Tablemount** *var.* Gora Andryu. *undersea feature* W Indian Ocean 6.45N 50.30E
Andreyevka *see* Kabanbay
109 N17 **Andria** Puglia, SE Italy 41.13N 16.16E
115 K16 **Andrijevica** Montenegro, SW Serbia and Montenegro (Yugoslavia) 42.45N 19.45E
117 E20 **Andrítsaina** Pelopónnisos, S Greece 37.29N 21.52E
An Droichead Nua *see* Newbridge
Andropov *see* Rybinsk
117 J19 **Ándros** Ándros, Kykládes, Greece, Aegean Sea 37.49N 24.55E
117 J20 **Ándros** *island* Kykládes, Greece, Aegean Sea
21 O7 **Androscoggin River** ≈ Maine/New Hampshire, NE USA
46 F3 **Andros Island** *island* NW Bahamas
131 R7 **Androsovka** Samarskaya Oblast', W Russian Federation 52.41N 49.34E
46 G3 **Andros Town** Andros Island, NW Bahamas 24.40N 77.47W
161 D21 **Āndrott Island** *island* Lakshadweep, India, N Indian Ocean
119 N5 **Andrushivka** Zhytomyrs'ka Oblast', N Ukraine 50.01N 29.02E
113 K17 **Andrychów** Małopolskie, S Poland 49.51N 19.23E
Andryu, Gora *see* Andrew Tablemount
94 I10 **Andselv** Troms, N Norway 69.05N 18.30E
81 O17 **Andudu** Orientale, NE Dem. Rep. Congo 2.25N 28.39E
107 N13 **Andújar** *anc.* Illiturgis. Andalucía, SW Spain 38.01N 4.03W
84 C12 **Andulo** Bié, W Angola 11.28S 16.43E
105 Q14 **Anduze** Gard, S France 44.03N 3.59E
An Earagail *see* Errigal Mountain
97 L19 **Aneby** Jönköping, S Sweden 57.49N 14.45E
Anécho *see* Aného
79 Q9 **Anéfis** Kidal, NE Mali 18.05N 0.38E
47 U8 **Anegada** *island* NE British Virgin Islands
63 B25 **Anegada, Bahía** *bay* E Argentina
47 U9 **Anegada Passage** *passage* Anguilla/British Virgin Islands
79 R17 **Aného** *var.* Anécho; *prev.* Petit-Popo. S Togo 6.13N 1.36E
197 D17 **Aneityum** *var.* Anatom; *prev.* Kéamu. *island* S Vanuatu
119 N10 **Anenii Noi** *Rus.* Novyye Aneny. C Moldova 46.52N 29.10E
194 L12 **Anepmete** New Britain, E PNG 5.47S 148.37E
107 U4 **Aneto** ▲ NE Spain 42.36N 0.37E
Änew *see* Annau
Änewetak *see* Enewetak Atoll
79 Y8 **Aney** Agadez, NE Niger 19.22N 13.00E
An Fheoir *see* Nore
126 Ii13 **Angara** ≈ C Russian Federation
126 J15 **Angarsk** Irkutskaya Oblast', S Russian Federation 52.31N 103.55E
95 G17 **Ånge** Västernorrland, C Sweden 62.31N 15.40E
Angel *see* Úhlava
42 D4 **Ángel de la Guarda, Isla** *island* NW Mexico
179 P10 **Angeles** *off.* Angeles City. Luzon, N Philippines 15.16N 120.37E
Angeles City *see* Angeles
Angel Falls *see* Ángel, Salto
97 J22 **Ängelholm** Skåne, S Sweden 56.14N 12.52E
63 A17 **Angélica** Santa Fe, C Argentina 31.33S 61.33W
27 W8 **Angelina River** ≈ Texas, SW USA
57 Q9 **Ángel, Salto** *Eng.* Angel Falls. *waterfall* E Venezuela 5.52N 62.19W
97 M15 **Ängelsberg** Västmanland, C Sweden 59.57N 16.01E
37 P8 **Angels Camp** California, W USA 38.03N 120.31W
111 W7 **Anger** Steiermark, SE Austria 47.16N 15.41E
Angerapp *see* Ozersk
Angerburg *see* Węgorzewo
95 H15 **Ångermanälven** ≈ N Sweden
102 P11 **Angermünde** Brandenburg, NE Germany 53.01N 13.59E
104 K7 **Angers** *anc.* Juliomagus. Maine-et-Loire, NW France 47.30N 0.33W
13 W7 **Angers** ≈ Quebec, SE Canada
95 J16 **Ängesön** *island* N Sweden
Angistro *see* Ágkistro
116 H13 **Angítis** ≈ NE Greece
178 J14 **Ângk Tasaôm** *prev.* Angtassom. Takêv, S Cambodia 10.59N 104.39E
193 C25 **Anglem, Mount** ▲ Stewart Island, Southland, SW NZ 46.44S 167.56E
99 I18 **Anglesey** *cultural region* NW Wales, UK
99 I18 **Anglesey** *island* NW Wales, UK
104 I15 **Anglet** Pyrénées-Atlantiques, SW France 43.28N 1.30W
27 W12 **Angleton** Texas, SW USA 29.10N 95.25W
Anglia *see* England
12 H9 **Angliers** Quebec, SE Canada 47.33N 79.17W
Anglo-Egyptian Sudan *see* Sudan
Angmagssalik *see* Ammassalik
178 Ii8 **Ang Nam Ngum** ◎ C Laos
81 N16 **Ango** Orientale, N Dem. Rep. Congo 4.02N 25.49E
85 Q15 **Angoche** Nampula, E Mozambique 16.12S 39.55E
65 G14 **Angol** Araucanía, C Chile 37.48S 72.40W
33 Q11 **Angola** Indiana, N USA 41.37N 85.00W
84 A9 **Angola** *off.* Republic of Angola; *prev.* People's Republic of Angola, Portuguese West Africa. ◆ *republic* SW Africa
67 P15 **Angola Basin** *undersea feature* E Atlantic Ocean
41 X13 **Angoon** Admiralty Island, Alaska, USA 57.33N 134.30W
153 O14 **Angor** Surkhondaryo Viloyati, S Uzbekistan 37.30N 67.06E
Angora *see* Ankara
194 H10 **Angoram** East Sepik, NW PNG 4.01S 144.03E
42 H8 **Angostura** Sinaloa, C Mexico 25.18N 108.10W
Angostura *see* Ciudad Bolívar
43 U17 **Angostura, Presa de la** ▣ SE Mexico
30 J11 **Angostura Reservoir** ▣ South Dakota, N USA
104 L11 **Angoulême** *anc.* Iculisma. Charente, W France 45.39N 0.10E
104 K11 **Angoumois** *cultural region* W France
66 O2 **Angra do Heroísmo** Terceira, Azores, Portugal, NE Atlantic Ocean 38.40N 27.13W
62 O10 **Angra dos Reis** Rio de Janeiro, SE Brazil 22.58S 44.16W
Angra Pequena *see* Lüderitz
153 Q10 **Angren** Toshkent Viloyati, E Uzbekistan 41.04N 70.17E
Angtassom *see* Ângk Tasaôm
178 Hh11 **Ang Thong** *var.* Angthong. Ang Thong, C Thailand 14.34N 100.25E
81 M16 **Angu** Orientale, N Dem. Rep. Congo 3.38N 24.14E
107 S5 **Angües** Aragón, NE Spain 42.07N 0.10W
47 U9 **Anguilla** ◇ *UK dependent territory* E West Indies
47 V9 **Anguilla** *island* E West Indies
46 F4 **Anguilla Cays** *islets* SW Bahamas
Angul *see* Anugul
167 N1 **Anguli Nur** ◎ E China
81 O18 **Angumu** Orientale, E Dem. Rep. Congo 0.10S 27.42E
12 G14 **Angus** Ontario, S Canada 44.19N 79.52W
98 J10 **Angus** *cultural region* E Scotland, UK
61 K19 **Anhangüera** Goiás, S Brazil 18.12S 48.19W
101 I21 **Anhée** Namur, S Belgium 50.18N 4.52E
97 I21 **Anholt** *island* C Denmark
166 M11 **Anhua** *prev.* Dongping. Hunan, S China 28.25N 111.10E
167 P8 **Anhui** *var.* Anhui Sheng, Anhwei, Wan. ⬖ *province* E China
Anhui Sheng/Anhwei *see* Anhui
41 O11 **Aniak** Alaska, USA 61.34N 159.31W
41 O12 **Aniak River** ≈ Alaska, USA
An Iarmhí *see* Westmeath
201 R8 **Anibare** E Nauru 0.31S 166.56E
201 R8 **Anibare Bay** *bay* E Nauru, W Pacific Ocean
Anicium *see* le Puy
117 K22 **Ánidro** *island* Kykládes, Greece, Aegean Sea
79 R15 **Anié** C Togo 7.48N 1.12E
79 Q15 **Anié** ≈ C Togo
104 J16 **Anie, Pic d'** ▲ SW France 42.56N 0.44W
131 Y7 **Anikhovka** Orenburgskaya Oblast', W Russian Federation 51.27N 60.17E
12 G9 **Anima Nipissing Lake** ◎ Ontario, S Canada
39 O16 **Animas** New Mexico, SW USA 31.55N 108.49W
39 P16 **Animas Peak** ▲ New Mexico, SW USA 31.34N 108.46W
39 P16 **Animas Valley** *valley* New Mexico, SW USA
118 F13 **Anina** *Ger.* Steierdorf, *Hung.* Stájerlakanina; *prev.* Ştaierdorf-Anina, Steierdorf-Anina, Steyerlak-Anina. Caraş-Severin, SW Romania 45.04N 21.51E
31 U14 **Anita** Iowa, C USA 41.27N 94.45W
127 Oo16 **Aniva, Mys** *headland* Ostrov Sakhalin, SE Russian Federation 46.02N 143.25E
127 Oo16 **Aniva, Zaliv** *bay* SE Russian Federation
197 E16 **Aniwa** *island* S Vanuatu
95 M19 **Anjalankoski** Etelä-Suomi, S Finland 60.39N 26.54E
'Anjar *see* Aanjar
Anjiangying *see* Luanping
12 B8 **Anjigami Lake** ◎ Ontario, S Canada
171 Hh16 **Anjō** *var.* Anzyô. Aichi, Honshū, SW Japan 34.58N 137.07E
104 J8 **Anjou** *cultural region* NW France
180 I13 **Anjouan** *var.* Nzwani, Johanna Island. *island* SE Comoros
180 J4 **Anjozorobe** Antananarivo, C Madagascar 18.22S 47.52E
169 W13 **Anju** W North Korea 39.36N 125.44E
100 M5 **Anjum** *Fris.* Eanjum. Friesland, N Netherlands 53.22N 6.09E
180 G6 **Ankaboa, Tanjona** *headland* W Madagascar 21.57S 43.16E
166 L7 **Ankang** *prev.* Xing'an. Shaanxi, C China 32.45N 109.00E
142 I12 **Ankara** *prev.* Angora, *anc.* Ancyra. ● (Turkey) Ankara, C Turkey 39.55N 32.49E
142 H12 **Ankara** ⬖ *province* C Turkey
97 N19 **Ankarsrum** Kalmar, S Sweden 57.40N 16.19E
180 H6 **Ankazoabo** Toliara, SW Madagascar 22.18S 44.30E
180 I4 **Ankazobe** Antananarivo, C Madagascar 18.19S 47.07E
31 V14 **Ankeny** Iowa, C USA 41.43N 93.37W
178 Kk11 **An Khê** Gia Lai, C Vietnam 13.57N 108.39E
102 O9 **Anklam** Mecklenburg-Vorpommern, NE Germany 53.51N 13.42E
82 K13 **Ānkober** Amhara, N Ethiopia 9.36N 39.44E
79 O17 **Ankobra** ≈ S Ghana
81 N22 **Ankoro** Katanga, SE Dem. Rep. Congo 6.45S 26.58E
101 L24 **Anlier, Forêt d'** *forest* SE Belgium
166 I13 **Anlong** Guizhou, S China 25.05N 105.29E
An Longfort *see* Longford
178 Ii11 **Ânlong Vêng** Siĕmréab, NW Cambodia 14.16N 104.07E
An Lorgain *see* Lurgan
167 N8 **Anlu** Hubei, C China 31.15N 113.41E
An Mhí *see* Meath
An Mhuir Cheilteach *see* Celtic Sea
An Muileann gCearr *see* Mullingar
95 F16 **Ånn** Jämtland, C Sweden 63.19N 12.34E
130 M8 **Anna** Voronezhskaya Oblast', W Russian Federation 51.31N 40.23E
32 L17 **Anna** Illinois, N USA 37.27N 89.15W
27 U5 **Anna** Texas, SW USA 33.21N 96.33W
76 L5 **Annaba** *prev.* Bône. NE Algeria 36.55N 7.46E
An Nabatīyah at Taḥtā *see* Nabatîyé
103 N17 **Annaberg-Buchholz** Sachsen, E Germany 50.34N 13.01E
111 T9 **Annabichl** ✕ (Klagenfurt) Kärnten, S Austria 46.39N 14.21E
146 M5 **An Nafūd** *desert* NW Saudi Arabia
145 P6 **'Annah** *var.* 'Ānah. NW Iraq 33.27N 43.19E
145 P6 **An Nāḩiyah** W Iraq 34.24N 41.33E
145 T10 **An Najaf** *var.* Najaf. S Iraq 31.58N 44.19E
23 V5 **Anna, Lake** ▣ Virginia, NE USA
99 F16 **Annalee** ≈ N Ireland
178 Jj9 **Annamitique, Chaîne** ▲▲ C Laos
99 J14 **Annan** S Scotland, UK 55.00N 3.19W
31 U8 **Annandale** Minnesota, N USA 45.15N 94.07W
23 W4 **Annandale** Virginia, NE USA 38.48N 77.10W
201 Q7 **Anna Point** *headland* N Nauru 0.30S 166.55E
23 X3 **Annapolis** *state capital* Maryland, NE USA 38.58N 76.29W
196 A10 **Anna, Pulo** *island* S Palau
159 O10 **Annapurna** ▲ C Nepal 28.30N 83.49E
An Nāqūrah *see* En Nâqoûra
33 R10 **Ann Arbor** Michigan, N USA 42.16N 83.45W
An Nás *see* Naas
145 W12 **An Nāşirīyah** *var.* Nasiriya. SE Iraq 31.04N 46.16E
145 W11 **An Naşr** E Iraq 31.34N 46.08E
152 F13 **Annau** *Turkm.* Änew. Akhalskiy Velayat, C Turkmenistan 37.51N 58.22E
123 Mm16 **An Nawfalīyah** *var.* Al Nūwfalīyah. N Libya 30.46N 17.48E
21 P10 **Ann, Cape** *headland* Massachusetts, NE USA 42.39N 70.35W
188 I10 **Annean, Lake** ◎ Western Australia
Anneciacum *see* Annecy
105 T11 **Annecy** *anc.* Anneciacum. Haute-Savoie, E France 45.53N 6.09E
105 T11 **Annecy, Lac d'** ◎ E France
105 T10 **Annemasse** Haute-Savoie, E France 46.10N 6.13E
41 Z14 **Annette Island** *island* Alexander Archipelago, Alaska, USA
An Nhon *see* Binh Đinh
An Nīl al Abyaḑ *see* White Nile
An Nīl al Azraq *see* Blue Nile
25 Q3 **Anniston** Alabama, S USA 33.39N 85.49W
81 A19 **Annobón** *island* W Equatorial Guinea
105 R12 **Annonay** Ardèche, E France 45.15N 4.40E
46 K12 **Annotto Bay** C Jamaica 18.16N 76.45W
147 R5 **An Nu'ayrīyah** *var.* Narıya. Ash Sharqīyah, NE Saudi Arabia 27.30N 48.30E
190 M9 **Annuello** Victoria, SE Australia 34.54S 142.50E
145 Q10 **An Nukhayb** S Iraq 32.01N 42.15E
145 U9 **An Nu'mānīyah** E Iraq 32.34N 45.22E
Áno Arkhánai *see* Epáno Archánes
117 J25 **Anógeia** *var.* Anogia, Anóyia. Kríti, Greece, E Mediterranean Sea 35.17N 24.55E
Anogia *see* Anógeia
31 V8 **Anoka** Minnesota, N USA 45.15N 93.26W
An Ómaigh *see* Omagh
180 I1 **Anorontany, Tanjona** *headland* N Madagascar
180 J5 **Anosibe An'Ala** Toamasina, E Madagascar 19.24S 48.10E
Anóyia *see* Anógeia
An Pointe *see* Warrenpoint
167 P9 **Anqing** Anhui, E China 30.31N 116.58E
167 Q5 **Anqiu** Shandong, E China 36.25N 119.10E
An Ráth *see* Ráth Luirc
An Ribhéar *see* Kenmare River
An Ros *see* Rush
101 K19 **Ans** Liège, E Belgium 50.39N 5.31E
Anşāb *see* Nişāb
176 Ww10 **Ansas** Papua, E Indonesia 1.44S 135.52E
103 J20 **Ansbach** Bayern, SE Germany 49.15N 10.34E
An Sciobairín *see* Skibbereen
An Scoil *see* Skull
An Seancheann *see* Old Head of Kinsale
47 Y5 **Anse-Bertrand** Grande Terre, N Guadeloupe 16.28N 61.30W
180 H17 **Anse Boileau** Mahé, NE Seychelles 4.43S 55.28E
47 S11 **Anse La Raye** NW Saint Lucia 13.57N 61.01W
56 D9 **Anserma** Caldas, W Colombia 5.15N 75.46W
111 T4 **Ansfelden** Oberösterreich, N Austria 48.12N 14.17E
169 U12 **Anshan** Liaoning, NE China 41.06N 122.55E
166 J12 **Anshun** Guizhou, S China 26.15N 105.58E
63 F17 **Ansina** Tacuarembó, C Uruguay 31.58S 55.28W
31 O15 **Ansley** Nebraska, C USA 41.16N 99.22W
27 P6 **Anson** Texas, SW USA 32.45N 99.54W
79 Q10 **Ansongo** Gao, E Mali 15.39N 0.33E
An Srath Bán *see* Strabane
23 R5 **Ansted** West Virginia, NE USA 38.08N 81.06W
176 Yy10 **Ansudu** Papua, E Indonesia 2.09S 139.19E
59 G15 **Anta** Cusco, S Peru 13.31S 72.12W
59 G16 **Antabamba** Apurímac, C Peru 14.26S 72.51W
Antafalva *see* Kovačica
142 L17 **Antakya** *anc.* Antioch, Antiochia. Hatay, S Turkey 36.12N 36.10E
180 K3 **Antalaha** Antsirañana, NE Madagascar 14.52S 50.16E
142 F17 **Antalya** *prev.* Adalia, *anc.* Attaleia, *Bibl.* Attalia. Antalya, SW Turkey 36.52N 30.42E
142 F17 **Antalya** ⬖ *province* SW Turkey
142 F16 **Antalya** ✕ Antalya, SW Turkey 36.53N 30.45E
124 Qq11 **Antalya Basin** *undersea feature* E Mediterranean Sea
Antalya, Gulf of *see* Antalya Körfezi
142 F16 **Antalya Körfezi** *var.* Gulf of Adalia, *Eng.* Gulf of Antalya. *gulf* SW Turkey
180 J5 **Antanambao Manampotsy** Toamasina, E Madagascar 19.30S 48.36E
180 I5 **Antananarivo** *prev.* Tananarive. ● (Madagascar) Antananarivo, C Madagascar 18.52S 47.30E
180 I4 **Antananarivo** ⬖ *province* C Madagascar
180 J5 **Antananarivo** ✕ Antananarivo, C Madagascar 18.52S 47.30E
An tAonach *see* Nenagh
204-205 **Antarctica** *continent*
204 I5 **Antarctic Peninsula** *peninsula* Antarctica
63 J15 **Antas, Rio das** ≈ S Brazil
201 U16 **Ant Atoll** *atoll* Caroline Islands, E Micronesia
An Teampall Mór *see* Templemore
Antep *see* Gaziantep
106 M15 **Antequera** *anc.* Anticaria, Antiquaria. Andalucía, S Spain 37.01N 4.34W
Antequera *see* Oaxaca
39 S5 **Antero Reservoir** ▣ Colorado, C USA
28 M7 **Anthony** Kansas, C USA 37.09N 98.01W
39 R16 **Anthony** New Mexico, SW USA 32.00N 106.36W
190 D5 **Anthony, Lake** *salt lake* South Australia
76 E8 **Anti-Atlas** ▲▲ SW Morocco
105 U15 **Antibes** *anc.* Antipolis. Alpes-Maritimes, SE France 43.34N 7.07E
105 U15 **Antibes, Cap d'** *headland* SE France 43.33N 7.08E
Anticaria *see* Antequera
11 Q11 **Anticosti, Île d'** *Eng.* Anticosti Island. *island* Quebec, E Canada
Anticosti Island *see* Anticosti, Île d'
104 K3 **Antifer, Cap d'** *headland* N France 49.43N 0.10E
32 L6 **Antigo** Wisconsin, N USA 45.10N 89.10W
11 Q15 **Antigonish** Nova Scotia, SE Canada 45.39N 62.00W
66 P11 **Antigua** Fuerteventura, Islas Canarias, NE Atlantic Ocean
47 X10 **Antigua** *island* S Antigua and Barbuda, Leeward Islands
Antigua *see* Antigua Guatemala
47 W9 **Antigua and Barbuda** ◆ *commonwealth republic* E West Indies
44 C6 **Antigua Guatemala** *var.* Antigua. Sacatepéquez, SW Guatemala 14.33N 90.39W
43 P11 **Antiguo Morelos** *var.* Antiguo-Morelos. Tamaulipas, C Mexico 22.34N 99.06W
117 F19 **Antíkyras, Kólpos** *gulf* C Greece
117 G24 **Antikýthira** *var.* Andikíthira. *island* S Greece
144 I7 **Anti-Lebanon** *var.* Jebel esh Sharqi, *Ar.* Al Jabal ash Sharqī, *Fr.* Anti-Liban. ▲▲ Lebanon/Syria
Anti-Liban *see* Anti-Lebanon
117 I22 **Antímilos** *island* Kykládes, Greece, Aegean Sea
38 L6 **Antimony** Utah, W USA 38.07N 112.00W
An tInbhear Mór *see* Arklow
32 M10 **Antioch** Illinois, N USA 42.28N 88.06W
Antioch *see* Antakya
104 I10 **Antioche, Pertuis d'** *inlet* W France
Antiochia *see* Antakya
56 D8 **Antioquia** Antioquia, C Colombia 6.24N 75.52W
56 E8 **Antioquia** *off.* Departamento de Antioquia. ⬖ *province* C Colombia
117 J21 **Antíparos** *var.* Andipáros. *island* Kykládes, Greece, Aegean Sea
117 B17 **Antípaxoi** *var.* Andipaxi. *island* Iónioi Nísoi, Greece, C Mediterranean Sea
126 H7 **Antipayuta** Yamalo-Nenetskiy Avtonomnyy Okrug, N Russian Federation 69.08N 76.43E
199 J14 **Antipodes Islands** *island group* S NZ
Antipolis *see* Antibes
117 J18 **Antípsara** *var.* Andípsara. *island* E Greece
Antiquaria *see* Antequera
13 N10 **Antique, Lac** ◎ Quebec, SE Canada
117 E18 **Antírrio** *var.* Andírrion. Dytikí Ellás, C Greece 38.20N 21.46E
117 K16 **Ántissa** *var.* Ándissa. Lésvos, E Greece 39.15N 25.59E
An tIúr *see* Newry
Antivari *see* Bar
58 C6 **Antizana** ▲ N Ecuador 0.29S 78.08W
29 Q13 **Antlers** Oklahoma, C USA 34.13N 95.37W
95 J14 **Antnäs** Norrbotten, N Sweden 65.32N 21.53E
Antō *see* Andong
64 G5 **Antofagasta** Antofagasta, N Chile 23.40S 70.22W
64 G6 **Antofagasta** *off.* Región de Antofagasta. ⬖ *region* N Chile
64 I7 **Antofalla, Salar de** *salt lake* NW Argentina
101 D20 **Antoing** Hainaut, SW Belgium 50.34N 3.26E
26 M5 **Anton** Texas, SW USA 33.48N 102.09W
45 S16 **Antón** Coclé, C Panama 8.22N 80.15W
39 T11 **Anton Chico** New Mexico, SW USA 35.12N 105.09W
62 K12 **Antonina** Paraná, S Brazil 25.28S 48.43W
105 O5 **Antony** Hauts-de-Seine, N France 48.45N 2.16E
Antratsit *see* Antratsyt
119 Y8 **Antratsyt** *Rus.* Antratsit. Luhans'ka Oblast', E Ukraine 48.07N 39.04E
99 G15 **Antrim** *Ir.* Aontroim. NE Northern Ireland, UK 54.43N 6.13W
99 G14 **Antrim** *Ir.* Aontroim. *cultural region* NE Northern Ireland, UK
99 G14 **Antrim Mountains** ▲▲ NE Northern Ireland, UK
180 H5 **Antsalova** Mahajanga, W Madagascar 18.40S 44.37E
Antserana *see* Antsirañana
An tSionainn *see* Shannon
180 J2 **Antsirañana** *var.* Antserana; *prev.* Antsirane, Diégo-Suarez. Antsirañana, N Madagascar 12.19S 49.16E
180 J2 **Antsirañana** ⬖ *province* N Madagascar
Antsirane *see* Antsirañana
An tSiúir *see* Suir
120 I7 **Antsla** *Ger.* Anzen. Võrumaa, SE Estonia 57.49N 26.34E
An tSláine *see* Slaney
180 J3 **Antsohihy** Mahajanga, NW Madagascar 14.49S 47.58E
65 G14 **Antuco, Volcán** ▲ C Chile 37.29S 71.25W
175 P7 **Antu, Gunung** ▲ Borneo, N Indonesia 0.57N 118.51E
An Tullach *see* Tullow
An-tung *see* Dandong
Antunnacum *see* Andernach
Antwerp *see* Antwerpen
101 G16 **Antwerpen** *Eng.* Antwerp, *Fr.* Anvers. Antwerpen, N Belgium 51.13N 4.25E
101 H16 **Antwerpen** *Eng.* Antwerp. ⬖ *province* N Belgium
An Uaimh *see* Navan
160 N12 **Anugul** *var.* Angul. Orissa, E India 20.51N 84.59E
158 F9 **Anūpgarh** Rājasthān, NW India 29.10N 73.13E
160 K10 **Anūppur** Madhya Pradesh, C India 23.06N 81.45E
161 K24 **Anuradhapura** North Central Province, C Sri Lanka 8.19N 80.25E
Anvers *see* Antwerpen
204 G4 **Anvers Island** *island* Antarctica
41 N11 **Anvik** Alaska, USA 62.39N 160.12W
41 N10 **Anvik River** ≈ Alaska, USA
40 F17 **Anvil Peak** ▲ Semisopochnoi Island, Alaska, USA 51.59N 179.36E
165 P7 **Anxi** Gansu, N China 40.31N 95.45E
190 F8 **Anxious Bay** *bay* South Australia
167 O5 **Anyang** Henan, C China 36.10N 114.18E
165 S11 **A'nyêmaqên Shan** ▲▲ C China
120 H12 **Anykščiai** Anykščiai, E Lithuania 55.30N 25.34E
167 P13 **Anyuan** Jiangxi, S China 25.10N 115.25E
127 O6 **Anyuysk** Chukotskiy Avtonomnyy Okrug, NE Russian Federation 68.22N 161.33E
127 Oo5 **Anyuyskiy Khrebet** ▲▲ NE Russian Federation
56 D8 **Anza** Antioquia, C Colombia 6.18N 75.54W
Anzen *see* Antsla
126 H13 **Anzhero-Sudzhensk** Kemerovskaya Oblast', S Russian Federation 56.00N 85.42E
109 I16 **Anzio** Lazio, C Italy 41.27N 12.37E
57 O6 **Anzoátegui** *off.* Estado Anzoátegui. ⬖ *state* NE Venezuela
153 P12 **Anzob** W Tajikistan 39.24N 68.55E
Anzyô *see* Anjō
Aoba *see* Ambae
172 Ss13 **Aoga-shima** *island* Izu-shotō, SE Japan
169 T12 **Aohan Qi** Nei Mongol Zizhiqu, N China 42.12N 119.57E
Aoiz *see* Aoiz-Agoitz
107 R3 **Aoiz-Agoitz** *var.* Agoitz, Aoiz. Navarra, N Spain 42.47N 1.23W
195 X16 **Aola** *var.* Tenaghau. Guadalcanal, C Solomon Islands 9.32S 160.28E
178 Gg15 **Ao Luk Nua** Krabi, SW Thailand 8.21N 98.43E
Aomen *see* Macao
172 N8 **Aomori** Aomori, Honshū, C Japan 40.49N 140.43E
171 Mm9 **Aomori** *off.* Aomori-ken. ⬖ *prefecture* Honshū, C Japan
Aontroim *see* Antrim
117 C15 **Aóos** *var.* Vijosa, Vijosë, *Alb.* Lumi i Vjosës,. ≈ Albania/Greece *see also* Vjosës, Lumi i
203 Q7 **Aorai, Mont** ⛰ Tahiti, W French Polynesia 17.36S 149.28W
Aoraki *see* Cook, Mount
178 Ii13 **Aôral, Phnum** *prev.* Phnom Aural. ▲ W Cambodia 12.01N 104.10E
Aorangi *see* Cook, Mount
193 L15 **Aorangi Mountains** ▲▲ North Island, NZ
192 H13 **Aorere** ≈ South Island, NZ
108 A7 **Aosta** *anc.* Augusta Praetoria. Valle d'Aosta, NW Italy 45.43N 7.19E
79 O11 **Aougoundou, Lac** ◎ S Mali
78 K9 **Aoukâr** *var.* Aouker. *plateau* C Mauritania
80 J13 **Aouk, Bahr** ≈ Central African Republic/Chad
Aouker *see* Aoukâr
76 B11 **Aousard** SE Western Sahara 22.42N 14.22W
170 G12 **Aoya** Tottori, Honshū, SW Japan 35.31N 134.01E
80 H5 **Aozou** Borkou-Ennedi-Tibesti, N Chad 22.00N 17.11E
28 M11 **Apache** Oklahoma, C USA 34.57N 98.21W
38 L14 **Apache Junction** Arizona, SW USA 33.25N 111.33W
26 J9 **Apache Mountains** ▲▲ Texas, SW USA
38 M16 **Apache Peak** ▲ Arizona, SW USA 31.50N 110.25W
118 H10 **Apahida** Cluj, NW Romania 46.49N 23.45E
25 T9 **Apalachee Bay** *bay* Florida, SE USA
25 T3 **Apalachee River** ≈ Georgia, SE USA
25 S10 **Apalachicola** Florida, SE USA 29.43N 84.58W
25 S10 **Apalachicola Bay** *bay* Florida, SE USA
25 R9 **Apalachicola River** ≈ Florida, SE USA
Apam *see* Apan
Apamama *see* Abemama
43 P14 **Apan** *var.* Apam. Hidalgo, C Mexico 19.41N 98.24W
44 J8 **Apanás, Lago de** ◎ NW Nicaragua
56 H14 **Apaporis, Río** ≈ Brazil/Colombia
193 C23 **Aparima** ≈ South Island, NZ
179 P7 **Aparri** Luzon, N Philippines 18.16N 121.42E
114 J9 **Apatin** Serbia, NW Serbia and Montenegro (Yugoslavia) 45.40N 19.01E
128 J4 **Apatity** Murmanskaya Oblast', NW Russian Federation 67.33N 33.26E
57 X9 **Apatou** NW French Guiana 5.07N 54.20W
42 M14 **Apatzingán** *var.* Apatzingán de la Constitución. Michoacán de Ocampo, SW Mexico 19.04N 102.19W
176 Y9 **Apauwar** Papua, E Indonesia 1.36S 138.10E
Apaxtla *see* Apaxtla de Castrejón
43 O15 **Apaxtla de Castrejón** *var.* Apaxtla. Guerrero, S Mexico 18.06N 99.55W
120 J7 **Ape** Alūksne, NE Latvia 57.32N 26.42E
100 L11 **Apeldoorn** Gelderland, E Netherlands 52.13N 5.57E
Apennines *see* Appennino
Apenrade *see* Aabenraa
59 L17 **Apere, Río** ≈ C Bolivia

◆ Country
● Country Capital
◇ Dependent Territory
○ Dependent Territory Capital
⬖ Administrative Region
✕ International Airport
▲ Mountain
▲▲ Mountain Range
⛰ Volcano
≈ River
◎ Lake
▣ Reservoir

57 W11 **Apetina** Sipaliwini, SE Suriname 3.30N 55.03W
23 U9 **Apex** North Carolina, SE USA 35.43N 78.51W
81 M16 **Api** Orientale, N Dem. Rep. Congo 3.42N 25.22E
158 M9 **Api** ▲ NW Nepal 30.07N 80.57E
Apia *see* Abaiang
198 Bb8 **Āpia** ● (Samoa) Upolu, SE Samoa 13.49S 171.46W
62 K11 **Apiaí** São Paulo, S Brazil 24.28S 48.51W
175 P16 **Api, Gunung** ▲ Pulau Sangeang, S Indonesia 8.09S 119.03E
195 Y16 **Apio** Maramasike Island, N Solomon Islands 9.36S 161.25E
43 O15 **Apipilulco** Guerrero, S Mexico 18.10N 99.40W
43 P14 **Apizaco** Tlaxcala, S Mexico 19.24N 98.10W
106 I4 **A Pobla de Trives** *Cast.* Puebla de Trives. Galicia, NW Spain 42.21N 7.16W
57 U9 **Apoera** Sipaliwini, NW Suriname 5.10N 57.08W
117 O23 **Apolakkiá** Ródos, Dodekánisos, Greece, Aegean Sea 36.02N 27.48E
103 L16 **Apolda** Thüringen, C Germany 51.01N 11.31E
198 B8 **Apolima Strait** *strait* C Pacific Ocean
190 M13 **Apollo Bay** Victoria, SE Australia 38.40S 143.44E
Apollonia *see* Sozopol
59 J16 **Apolo** La Paz, W Bolivia 14.40S 68.33W
59 J16 **Apolobamba, Cordillera** ▲▲ Bolivia/Peru
179 Rr16 **Apo, Mount** ⛰ Mindanao, S Philippines 6.54N 125.16E
25 W11 **Apopka** Florida, SE USA 28.40N 81.30W
25 W11 **Apopka, Lake** ◎ Florida, SE USA
61 J19 **Aporé, Rio** ∽ SW Brazil
32 K2 **Apostle Islands** *island group* Wisconsin, N USA
Apostolas Andreas, Cape *see* Zafer Burnu
63 F14 **Apóstoles** Misiones, NE Argentina 27.54S 55.45W
Apostolou Andréa, Akrotíri *see* Zafer Burnu
119 S9 **Apostolove** *Rus.* Apostolovo. Dnipropetrovs'ka Oblast', E Ukraine 47.40N 33.45E
Apostolovo *see* Apostolove
19 Qq9 **Appalachian Mountains** ▲▲ E USA
97 K14 **Äppelbo** Dalarna, C Sweden 60.30N 14.00E
100 N7 **Appelscha** *Fris.* Appelskea. Friesland, N Netherlands 52.57N 6.19E
Appelskea *see* Appelscha
108 G11 **Appennino** *Eng.* Apennines. ▲▲ Italy/San Marino
109 L17 **Appennino Campano** ▲▲ C Italy
110 I7 **Appenzell** Appenzell, NW Switzerland 47.19N 9.25E
110 H7 **Appenzell** ⬗ *canton* NE Switzerland
57 V12 **Appikalo** Sipaliwini, S Suriname 2.07N 56.16W
100 O5 **Appingedam** Groningen, NE Netherlands 53.18N 6.52E
27 X8 **Appleby** Texas, SW USA 31.43N 94.36W
99 L15 **Appleby-in-Westmorland** NW England, UK 54.34N 2.26W
32 K10 **Apple River** ∽ Illinois, N USA
32 I5 **Apple River** ∽ Wisconsin, N USA
27 W9 **Apple Springs** Texas, SW USA 31.13N 94.57W
31 S8 **Appleton** Minnesota, N USA 45.12N 96.01W
32 M7 **Appleton** Wisconsin, N USA 44.16N 88.24W
29 S5 **Appleton City** Missouri, C USA 38.11N 94.01W
37 U14 **Apple Valley** California, W USA 34.30N 117.11W
31 V9 **Apple Valley** Minnesota, N USA 44.43N 93.13W
23 U6 **Appomattox** Virginia, NE USA 37.21N 78.49W
196 B16 **Apra Harbour** *harbor* W Guam
196 B16 **Apra Heights** W Guam
108 F6 **Aprica, Passo dell'** *pass* N Italy 46.10N 10.08E
109 M15 **Apricena** *anc.* Hadria Picena. Puglia, SE Italy 41.46N 15.27E
130 L14 **Apsheronsk** Krasnodarskiy Kray, SW Russian Federation 44.27N 39.45E
Apsheronskiy Poluostrov *see* Abşeron Yarımadası
105 S15 **Apt** *anc.* Apta Julia. Vaucluse, SE France 43.54N 5.24E
Apta Julia *see* Apt
40 H12 **Apua Point** *headland* Hawaii, USA, C Pacific Ocean 19.15N 155.13W
62 I10 **Apucarana** Paraná, S Brazil 23.34S 51.28W
Apulia *see* Puglia
56 K8 **Apure** *off.* Estado Apure. ⬗ *state* C Venezuela
56 J7 **Apure, Río** ∽ W Venezuela
59 F16 **Apurímac** *off.* Departamento de Apurímac. ⬗ *department* C Peru
59 F15 **Apurímac, Río** ∽ S Peru
118 G10 **Apuseni, Munţii** ▲▲ W Romania
Aqaba/'Aqaba *see* Al 'Aqabah
144 F15 **Aqaba, Gulf of** *var.* Gulf of Elat, *Ar.* Khalīj al 'Aqabah; *anc.* Sinus Aelaniticus. *gulf* NE Red Sea
145 R7 **'Aqabah** C Iraq 33.33N 42.55E
'Aqabah, Khalīj al *see* Aqaba, Gulf of
155 O2 **Āqchah** *var.* Āqcheh. Jowzjān, N Afghanistan 36.59N 66.07E
Āqcheh *see* Āqchah
Aqköl *see* Akkol'
Aqmola *see* Astana
Aqmola Oblysy *see* Akmola
164 L10 **Aqqikkol Hu** ◎ NW China
Aqqystaū *see* Akkystau
'Aqrah *see* Ākrē
Aqsay *see* Aksay
Aqshataū *see* Akchatau
Aqsū *see* Aksu
Aqsūat *see* Aksuat
Aqtas *see* Aktas
Aqtaū *see* Aktau
Aqtöbe/Aqtöbe Oblysy *see* Aktobe
Aqtoghay *see* Aktogay
Aquae Augustae *see* Dax
Aquae Calidae *see* Bath
Aquae Flaviae *see* Chaves
Aquae Grani *see* Aachen
Aquae Panoniae *see* Baden
Aquae Sextiae *see* Aix-en-Provence
Aquae Solis *see* Bath
Aquae Tarbelicae *see* Dax
38 J11 **Aquarius Mountains** ▲▲ Arizona, SW USA
64 O5 **Aquidabán, Río** ∽ E Paraguay
61 H20 **Aquidauana** Mato Grosso do Sul, S Brazil 20.27S 55.45W
42 L15 **Aquila** Michoacán de Ocampo, S Mexico 18.36N 103.32W
Aquila/Aquila degli Abruzzi *see* L'Aquila
27 T8 **Aquilla** Texas, SW USA 31.51N 97.13W
46 L9 **Aquin** S Haiti 18.16N 73.24W
Aquisgranum *see* Aachen
104 J13 **Aquitaine** ⬗ *region* SW France
Aqzhar *see* Akzhar
159 P13 **Āra** *prev.* Arrah. Bihār, N India 25.34N 84.40E
107 S4 **Ara** ∽ NE Spain
25 P2 **Arab** Alabama, S USA 34.19N 86.30W
Araba *see* Álava
144 G12 **'Arabah, Wādī al** *Heb.* Ha'Arava. *dry watercourse* Israel/Jordan
119 U12 **Arabats'ka Strilka, Kosa** *spit* S Ukraine
119 U12 **Arabats'ka Zatoka** *gulf* S Ukraine
'Arab, Baḩr al *see* Arab, Bahr el
82 C12 **Arab, Bahr el** *var.* Baḩr al 'Arab. ∽ S Sudan
58 E7 **Arabela, Río** ∽ N Peru
181 O4 **Arabian Basin** *undersea feature* N Arabian Sea
Arabian Desert *see* Sahara el Sharqîya
147 N9 **Arabian Peninsula** *peninsula* SW Asia
87 P15 **Arabian Plate** *tectonic feature* Africa/Asia/Europe
147 W14 **Arabian Sea** *sea* NW Indian Ocean
Arabicus, Sinus *see* Red Sea
'Arabī, Khalīj al *see* The Gulf
Arabistan *see* Khūzestān
'Arabīyah as Su'ūdīyah, Al Mamlakah al *see* Saudi Arabia
'Arabīyah Jumhūrīyah, Mişr al *see* Egypt
144 I9 **'Arab, Jabal al** ▲▲ S Syria
124 Pp14 **'Arab, Khalīg el** *Eng.* Arabs Gulf. *gulf* N Egypt
Arab Republic of Egypt *see* Egypt
Arabs Gulf *see* 'Arab, Khalīg el
145 Y12 **'Arab, Shaṭṭ al** *Eng.* Shatt al Arab, *Per.* Arvand Rūd. ∽ Iran/Iraq
142 I11 **Araç** Kastamonu, N Turkey 41.13N 33.19E
61 P16 **Aracaju** *state capital* Sergipe, E Brazil 10.45S 37.07W
56 F5 **Aracataca** Magdalena, N Colombia 10.36N 74.13W
60 P13 **Aracati** Ceará, E Brazil 4.31S 37.45W
62 J8 **Araçatuba** São Paulo, S Brazil 21.12S 50.24W
106 J13 **Aracena** Andalucía, S Spain 37.54N 6.33W
117 F20 **Árachnaío** ▲▲ S Greece
117 D16 **Árachthos** *var.* Arta; *prev.* Árakhthos, *anc.* Arachthus. ∽ W Greece
Arachthus *see* Árachthos
61 N19 **Araçuai** Minas Gerais, SE Brazil 16.52S 42.03W
142 I11 **Araç Çayı** ∽ N Turkey
144 F11 **'Arad** Southern, S Israel 31.16N 35.09E
118 F11 **Arad** Arad, W Romania 46.12N 21.20E
118 F11 **Arad** ⬗ *county* W Romania
80 J9 **Arada** Biltine, NE Chad 15.00N 20.38E
149 P18 **'Arādah** Abū Ẓaby, S UAE 22.57N 53.24E
Aradhippou *see* Aradíppou
124 O3 **Aradíppou** *var.* Aradhippou. SE Cyprus 34.57N 33.37E
182 K6 **Arafura Sea** *Ind.* Laut Arafuru. *sea* W Pacific Ocean
182 L6 **Arafura Shelf** *undersea feature* C Arafura Sea
Arafuru, Laut *see* Arafura Sea
61 J18 **Aragarças** Goiás, C Brazil 15.55S 52.12W
Aragats, Gora *see* Aragats Lerr
143 T12 **Aragats Lerr** *Rus.* Gora Aragats. ▲ W Armenia 40.31N 44.06E
34 E14 **Arago, Cape** *headland* Oregon, NW USA 43.17N 124.25W
107 R6 **Aragón** ⬗ *autonomous community* E Spain
107 Q4 **Aragón** ∽ NE Spain
109 I24 **Aragona** Sicilia, Italy, C Mediterranean Sea 37.25N 13.37E
107 Q7 **Aragoncillo** ▲ C Spain 40.59N 2.01W
56 L5 **Aragua** *off.* Estado Aragua. ⬗ *state* N Venezuela
57 N6 **Aragua de Barcelona** Anzoátegui, NE Venezuela 9.30N 64.45W
57 O5 **Aragua de Maturín** Monagas, NE Venezuela 9.58N 63.30W
61 K15 **Araguaia, Río** *var.* Araguaya. ∽ C Brazil
61 K19 **Araguari** Minas Gerais, SE Brazil 18.37S 48.13W
60 J11 **Araguari, Rio** ∽ SW Brazil
Araguaya *see* Araguaia, Río
106 K14 **Arahal** Andalucía, S Spain 37.15N 5.33W
171 Jj13 **Arai** Niigata, Honshū, C Japan 36.58N 138.14E
Árainn *see* Inishmore
Árainn Mhór *see* Aran Island
Ara Jovis *see* Aranjuez
76 J11 **Arak** C Algeria 25.17N 3.45E
176 Yy15 **Arak** Papua, E Indonesia 7.14S 139.40E
148 M7 **Arāk** *prev.* Sultānābād. Markazī, W Iran 34.07N 49.39E
196 D10 **Arakabesan** *island* Palau Islands, N Palau
57 S7 **Arakaka** NW Guyana 7.37N 59.58W
177 Ff6 **Arakan State** *var.* Rakhine State. ⬗ *state* W Myanmar
177 Ff5 **Arakan Yoma** ▲▲ W Myanmar
171 Kk12 **Arakawa** Niigata, Honshū, C Japan 38.06N 139.25E
Árakhthos *see* Árachthos
Araks/Arak's *see* Aras
164 H7 **Aral** Xinjiang Uygur Zizhiqu, NW China 40.40N 81.19E
Aral *see* Aral'sk, Kazakhstan
Aral *see* Vose', Tajikistan
Aral-Bukhorskiy Kanal *see* Amu-Buxoro Kanali
143 T12 **Aralık** Iğdır, E Turkey 39.54N 44.28E
152 H5 **Aral Sea** *Kaz.* Aral Tengizi, *Rus.* Aral'skoye More, *Uzb.* Orol Dengizi. *inland sea* Kazakhstan/Uzbekistan
150 L13 **Aral'sk** *Kaz.* Aral. Kzylorda, SW Kazakhstan 46.48N 61.40E
Aral'skoye More/Aral Tengizi *see* Aral Sea
43 O10 **Aramberri** Nuevo León, NE Mexico 24.05N 99.52W
194 F14 **Aramia** ∽ SW PNG
149 N6 **Ārān** *var.* Golārā. Eşfahān, C Iran 34.03N 51.30E
107 N5 **Aranda de Duero** Castilla-León, N Spain 41.40N 3.40W
114 M12 **Aranđelovac** *prev.* Arandjelovac. Serbia, C Serbia and Montenegro (Yugoslavia) 44.18N 20.32E
Arandjelovac *see* Aranđelovac
99 J19 **Aran Fawddwy** ▲ NW Wales, UK 52.48N 3.42W
99 C14 **Aran Island** *Ir.* Árainn Mhór. *island* NW Ireland
99 A18 **Aran Islands** *island group* W Ireland
107 N9 **Aranjuez** *anc.* Ara Jovis. Madrid, C Spain 40.01N 3.37W
85 E20 **Aranos** Hardap, SE Namibia 24.11S 19.07E
27 U14 **Aransas Bay** *inlet* Texas, SW USA
27 T14 **Aransas Pass** Texas, SW USA 27.54N 97.09W
203 O3 **Aranuka** *prev.* Nanouki. *atoll* Tungaru, W Kiribati
178 I11 **Aranyaprathet** Prachin Buri, S Thailand 13.42N 102.32E
Aranyosasztal *see* Zlatý Stôl
Aranyosgyéres *see* Câmpia Turzii
Aranyosmarót *see* Zlaté Moravce
170 Cc14 **Arao** Kumamoto, Kyūshū, SW Japan 33.16N 130.25E
79 O8 **Araouane** Tombouctou, N Mali 18.58N 3.39W
28 L10 **Arapaho** Oklahoma, C USA 35.34N 98.57W
31 N16 **Arapahoe** Nebraska, C USA 40.18N 99.54W
59 I16 **Arapa, Laguna** ◎ SE Peru
193 K14 **Arapawa Island** *island* C NZ
63 E17 **Arapey Grande, Río** ∽ N Uruguay
61 P16 **Arapiraca** Alagoas, E Brazil 9.45S 36.40W
146 M3 **'Ar'ar** Al Ḩudūd ash Shamālīyah, NW Saudi Arabia 31.00N 41.00E
56 G15 **Araracuara** Caquetá, S Colombia 0.36S 72.24W
63 K15 **Araranguá** Santa Catarina, S Brazil 28.55S 49.30W
62 L8 **Araraquara** São Paulo, S Brazil 21.46S 48.07W
61 O13 **Araras** Ceará, E Brazil 4.08S 40.30W
60 I14 **Araras** Pará, N Brazil 6.03S 54.34W
62 L9 **Araras** São Paulo, S Brazil 22.21S 47.21W
62 H11 **Araras, Serra das** ▲▲ S Brazil
143 U12 **Ararat** S Armenia 39.49N 44.45E
190 M12 **Ararat** Victoria, SE Australia 37.18S 142.57E
Ararat, Mount *see* Büyükağrı Dağı
146 M3 **'Ar'ar, Wādī** *dry watercourse* Iraq/Saudi Arabia
133 N7 **Aras** *Arm.* Arak's, *Az.* Araz Nehri, *Per.* Rūd-e Aras, *Rus.* Araks; *prev.* Araxes. ∽ SW Asia
107 R9 **Aras de Alpuente** País Valenciano, E Spain 39.55N 1.09W
143 S13 **Aras Güneyi Dağları** ▲▲ NE Turkey
Aras, Rūd-e *see* Aras
203 U9 **Aratika** *atoll* Îles Tuamotu, C French Polynesia
Aratürük *see* Yiwu
56 I8 **Arauca** Arauca, NE Colombia 7.03N 70.46W
56 I8 **Arauca** *off.* Intendencia de Arauca. ⬗ *province* NE Colombia
65 G15 **Araucanía** *off.* Región de la Araucanía. ⬗ *region* C Chile
56 L7 **Arauca, Río** ∽ Colombia/Venezuela
65 F14 **Arauco** Bío Bío, C Chile 37.16S 73.15W
65 F14 **Arauco, Golfo de** *gulf* S Chile
56 H8 **Arauquita** Arauca, C Colombia 7.01N 71.20W
Arausio *see* Orange
158 F13 **Arāvali Range** ▲▲ N India
195 S12 **Arawa** Bougainville Island, NE PNG 6.13S 155.37E
193 C20 **Arawata** ∽ South Island, NZ
194 L12 **Arawe Islands** *island group* E PNG
61 L20 **Araxá** Minas Gerais, SE Brazil 19.37S 46.49W
Araxes *see* Aras
57 O5 **Araya** Sucre, N Venezuela 10.34N 64.15W
107 R4 **Arba** ∽ N Spain
83 I15 **Ārba Minch'** Southern, S Ethiopia 6.02N 37.34E
145 U4 **Arbat** NE Iraq 35.26N 45.34E
109 D19 **Arbatax** Sardegna, Italy, C Mediterranean Sea 39.57N 9.42E
Arbe *see* Rab
Arbela *see* Arbīl
145 S3 **Arbīl** *var.* Erbil, Irbīl, *Kurd.* Hawlêr; *anc.* Arbela. N Iraq 36.12N 44.01E
97 M16 **Arboga** Västmanland, C Sweden 59.24N 15.49E
97 M16 **Arbogaån** ∽ C Sweden
105 S9 **Arbois** Jura, E France 46.54N 5.45E
56 D6 **Arboletes** Antioquia, NW Colombia 8.52N 76.25W
9 X15 **Arborg** Manitoba, S Canada 50.52N 97.20W
96 N12 **Arbrå** Gävleborg, C Sweden 61.27N 16.21E
98 K10 **Arbroath** *anc.* Aberbrothock. E Scotland, UK 56.34N 2.34W
37 N6 **Arbuckle** California, W USA 39.00N 122.05W
29 N12 **Arbuckle Mountains** ▲▲ Oklahoma, C USA
Arbuzinka *see* Arbyzynka
119 Q8 **Arbyzynka** *Rus.* Arbuzinka. Mykolayivs'ka Oblast', S Ukraine 47.54N 31.19E
105 U12 **Arc** ∽ E France
104 J13 **Arcachon** Gironde, SW France 44.40N 1.10W
104 J13 **Arcachon, Bassin d'** *inlet* SW France
20 E10 **Arcade** New York, NE USA 42.32N 78.19W
25 W14 **Arcadia** Florida, SE USA 27.13N 81.51W
24 H5 **Arcadia** Louisiana, S USA 32.33N 92.55W
32 J7 **Arcadia** Wisconsin, N USA 44.15N 91.30W
Arcae Remorum *see* Châlons-en-Champagne
46 L9 **Arcahaie** C Haiti 18.46N 72.32W
36 K3 **Arcata** California, W USA 40.51N 124.06W
37 U6 **Arc Dome** ▲ Nevada, W USA 38.52N 117.20W
109 J16 **Arce** Lazio, C Italy 41.35N 13.34E
43 O15 **Arcelia** Guerrero, S Mexico 18.19N 100.16W
101 M15 **Arcen** Limburg, SE Netherlands 51.28N 6.10E
Archangel *see* Arkhangel'sk
Archangel Bay *see* Chëshskaya Guba
117 O23 **Archángelos** *var.* Arhangelos, Arkhángelos. Ródos, Dodekánisos, Greece, Aegean Sea 36.13N 28.07E
116 F7 **Archar** ∽ NW Bulgaria
33 R11 **Archbold** Ohio, N USA 41.31N 84.18W
107 R12 **Archena** Murcia, SE Spain 38.07N 1.16W
27 R5 **Archer City** Texas, SW USA 33.36N 98.37W
106 M14 **Archidona** Andalucía, S Spain 37.06N 4.22W
67 B25 **Arch Islands** *island group* SW Falkland Islands
108 G13 **Arcidosso** Toscana, C Italy 42.52N 11.30E
105 Q5 **Arcis-sur-Aube** Aube, N France 48.32N 4.09E
190 F3 **Arckaringa Creek** *seasonal river* South Australia
108 G7 **Arco** Trentino-Alto Adige, N Italy 45.53N 10.51E
35 Q14 **Arco** Idaho, NW USA 43.38N 113.18W
32 M14 **Arcola** Illinois, N USA 39.39N 88.19W
107 P6 **Arcos de Jalón** Castilla-León, N Spain 41.12N 2.13W
106 K15 **Arcos de la Frontera** Andalucía, S Spain 36.45N 5.49W
106 G5 **Arcos de Valdevez** Viana do Castelo, N Portugal 41.51N 8.25W
61 P15 **Arcoverde** Pernambuco, E Brazil 08.23S 37.00W
104 H5 **Arcovest, Pointe de l'** *headland* NW France 48.49N 2.58W
Arctic-Mid Oceanic Ridge *see* Nansen Cordillera
207 R8 **Arctic Ocean** *ocean*
14 G4 **Arctic Red River** ∽ Northwest Territories/Yukon Territory, NW Canada
Arctic Red River *see* Tsiigehtchic
41 S6 **Arctic Village** Alaska, USA 68.07N 145.32W
204 H1 **Arctowski** *Polish research station* South Shetland Islands, Antarctica 61.57S 58.23W
116 I12 **Arda** *var.* Ardhas, *Gk.* Ardas. ∽ Bulgaria/Greece *see also* Ardas
148 L2 **Ardabīl** *var.* Ardebil. Ardabīl, NW Iran 38.15N 48.18E
148 L2 **Ardabīl** *off.* Ostān-e Ardabīl. ⬗ *province* NW Iran
143 R11 **Ardahan** Ardahan, NE Turkey 41.07N 42.40E
143 S11 **Ardahan** ⬗ *province* NE Turkey
149 P8 **Ardakān** Yazd, C Iran 32.20N 54.02E
96 E12 **Årdalstangen** Sogn og Fjordane, S Norway 61.13N 7.43E
143 R11 **Ardanuç** Artvin, NE Turkey 41.07N 42.04E
116 L12 **Ardas** *var.* Ardhas, *Bul.* Arda. ∽ Bulgaria/Greece *see also* Arda
144 I13 **Arḑ aş Şawwān** *var.* Ardh es Suwwān. *plain* S Jordan
131 P5 **Ardatov** Respublika Mordoviya, W Russian Federation 54.49N 46.13E
12 G12 **Ardbeg** Ontario, S Canada 45.38N 80.05W
Ardeal *see* Transylvania
Ardebil *see* Ardabīl
105 Q13 **Ardèche** ⬗ *department* E France
105 Q13 **Ardèche** ∽ C France
99 F17 **Ardee** *Ir.* Baile Átha Fhirdhia. NE Ireland 53.52N 6.33W
105 Q3 **Ardennes** ⬗ *department* NE France
101 J23 **Ardennes** *physical region* Belgium/France
143 Q11 **Ardeşen** Rize, NE Turkey 41.12N 41.02E
149 O7 **Ardestān** *var.* Ardistan. Eşfahān, C Iran 33.29N 52.16E
110 J9 **Ardez** Graubünden, SE Switzerland 46.47N 10.09E
Ardhas *see* Arda/Ardas
Ardh es Suwwān *see* Arḑ aş Şawwān
106 I12 **Ardila, Ribeira de** *Sp.* Ardilla. ∽ Portugal/Spain *see also* Ardilla
9 T17 **Ardill** Saskatchewan, S Canada 49.56N 105.49W
106 I12 **Ardilla** *Port.* Ribeira de Ardila. ∽ Portugal/Spain *see also* Ardila, Ribeira de
42 M11 **Ardilla, Cerro la** ▲ C Mexico 22.15N 102.33W
116 J12 **Ardino** Kŭrdzhali, S Bulgaria 41.38N 25.22E
Ardistan *see* Ardestān
191 P9 **Ardlethan** New South Wales, SE Australia 34.24S 146.52E
Ard Mhacha *see* Armagh
25 P1 **Ardmore** Alabama, S USA 34.59N 86.51W
29 N13 **Ardmore** Oklahoma, C USA 34.10N 97.08W
22 J10 **Ardmore** Tennessee, S USA 35.00N 86.48W
98 G10 **Ardnamurchan, Point of** *headland* N Scotland, UK 56.42N 6.15W
101 C17 **Ardooie** West-Vlaanderen, W Belgium 50.59N 3.10E
190 I9 **Ardrossan** South Australia 34.27S 137.54E
118 H9 **Ardusat** *Hung.* Erdőszáda. Maramureş, N Romania 47.36N 23.25E
95 F16 **Åre** Jämtland, C Sweden 63.25N 13.04E
81 P16 **Arebi** Orientale, NE Dem. Rep. Congo 2.46N 29.34E
47 T5 **Arecibo** C Puerto Rico 18.28N 66.43W
176 W10 **Aredo** Papua, E Indonesia 2.27S 133.59E
61 P14 **Areia Branca** Rio Grande do Norte, E Brazil 4.53S 37.03W
121 O14 **Arekhawsk** *Rus.* Orekhovsk. Vitsyebskaya Voblasts', N Belarus 54.42N 30.30E
Arel *see* Arlon
Arelas/Arelate *see* Arles
Arenal, Embalse de *see* Arenal Laguna
44 L12 **Arenal Laguna** *var.* Embalse de Arenal. ◎ NW Costa Rica
44 L13 **Arenal, Volcán** ⛰ NW Costa Rica 10.21N 84.42W
36 K6 **Arena, Point** *headland* California, W USA 38.57N 123.44W
61 H17 **Arenápolis** Mato Grosso, W Brazil 14.25S 56.52W
42 G10 **Arena, Punta** *headland* W Mexico 23.28N 109.24W
106 L8 **Arenas de San Pedro** Castilla-León, N Spain 40.12N 5.04W
65 I24 **Arenas, Punta de** *headland* S Argentina 53.10S 68.15W
63 B20 **Arenaza** Buenos Aires, E Argentina 34.55S 61.45W
97 F17 **Arendal** Aust-Agder, S Norway 58.27N 8.45E
101 J16 **Arendonk** Antwerpen, N Belgium 51.18N 5.06E
45 T15 **Arenosa** Panamá, N Panama 9.02N 79.57W
Arensburg *see* Kuressaare
107 W5 **Arenys de Mar** Cataluña, NE Spain 41.34N 2.33E
108 C9 **Arenzano** Liguria, NW Italy 44.25N 8.43E
117 F22 **Areópoli** *prev.* Areópolis. Pelopónnisos, S Greece 36.39N 22.24E
Areópolis *see* Areópoli
59 H18 **Arequipa** Arequipa, SE Peru 16.24S 71.33W
59 G17 **Arequipa** *off.* Departamento de Arequipa. ⬗ *department* SW Peru
63 B19 **Arequito** Santa Fe, C Argentina 33.09S 61.28W
106 M7 **Arévalo** Castilla-León, N Spain 41.04N 4.43W
108 H12 **Arezzo** *anc.* Arretium. Toscana, C Italy 43.28N 11.49E
107 Q4 **Arga** ∽ N Spain
Argaeus *see* Erciyes Dağı
117 G17 **Argalastí** Thessalía, C Greece 39.13N 23.14E
107 O10 **Argamasilla de Alba** Castilla-La Mancha, C Spain 39.07N 3.04W
164 L8 **Argan** Xinjiang Uygur Zizhiqu, NW China 40.09N 88.16E
107 O8 **Arganda** Madrid, C Spain 40.19N 3.25W
106 H8 **Arganil** Coimbra, N Portugal 40.13N 8.03W
179 Qq14 **Argao** Cebu, C Philippines 9.52N 123.33E
159 V15 **Argartala** Tripura, NE India
126 K9 **Arga-Sala** ∽ NE Russian Federation
105 P17 **Argelès-sur-Mer** Pyrénées-Orientales, S France 42.33N 3.01E
105 T15 **Argens** ∽ SE France
108 H9 **Argenta** Emilia-Romagna, N Italy 44.37N 11.49E
104 K5 **Argentan** Orne, N France 48.45N 0.01W
105 N12 **Argentat** Corrèze, C France 45.06N 1.57E
108 A9 **Argentera** Piemonte, NE Italy 44.25N 6.57E
105 N5 **Argenteuil** Val-d'Oise, N France 48.57N 2.13E
64 K13 **Argentina** *off.* Republic of Argentina. ◆ *republic* S South America
Argentina Basin *see* Argentine Basin
Argentine Abyssal Plain *see* Argentine Plain
67 I19 **Argentine Basin** *var.* Argentina Basin. *undersea feature* SW Atlantic Ocean
67 I20 **Argentine Plain** *var.* Argentine Abyssal Plain. *undersea feature* SW Atlantic Ocean
Argentine Rise *see* Falkland Plateau
65 H22 **Argentino, Lago** ◎ S Argentina
104 K8 **Argenton-Château** Deux-Sèvres, W France 46.59N 0.22W
104 M9 **Argenton-sur-Creuse** Indre, C France 46.34N 1.32E
Argentoratum *see* Strasbourg
118 I12 **Argeş** ⬗ *county* S Romania
118 K14 **Argeş** ∽ S Romania
155 O8 **Arghandāb, Daryā-ye** ∽ SE Afghanistan
Arghastān *see* Arghestān
155 O8 **Arghestān** *Pash.* Arghastān. ∽ SE Afghanistan
Argirocastro *see* Gjirokastër
82 E7 **Argo** Northern, N Sudan 19.31N 30.25E
181 P7 **Argo Fracture Zone** *tectonic feature* C Indian Ocean
117 F20 **Argolikós Kólpos** *gulf* S Greece
105 R4 **Argonne** *physical region* NE France
174 Mm15 **Argopuro, Gunung** ▲ Jawa, S Indonesia 7.57S 113.22E
117 F20 **Árgos** Pelopónnisos, S Greece 37.38N 22.42E
145 S1 **Argōsh** N Iraq 37.07N 44.13E
117 D14 **Árgos Orestikó** Dytikí Makedonía, N Greece 40.27N 21.15E
117 B19 **Argostóli** *var.* Argostólion. Kefallinía, Iónioi Nísoi, Greece, C Mediterranean Sea 38.10N 20.29E
Argostólion *see* Argostóli
Argovie *see* Aargau
37 O14 **Arguello, Point** *headland* California, W USA 34.34N 120.39W
131 P16 **Argun** Chechenskaya Respublika, SW Russian Federation 43.16N 45.53E
163 T2 **Argun** *Chin.* Ergun He, *Rus.* Argun'. ∽ China/Russian Federation
79 T12 **Argungu** Kebbi, NW Nigeria 12.45N 4.24E
168 J9 **Arguut** Övörhangay, C Mongolia 45.27N 102.25E
189 N3 **Argyle, Lake** *salt lake* Western Australia
98 G12 **Argyll** *cultural region* W Scotland, UK
Argyrokastron *see* Gjirokastër
168 I7 **Arhangay** ⬗ *province* C Mongolia
Arhangelos *see* Archángelos
97 P14 **Arholma** Stockholm, C Sweden 59.51N 19.01E
97 G22 **Århus** *var.* Aarhus. Århus, C Denmark 56.09N 10.10E
97 G22 **Århus** ⬗ *county* C Denmark
145 T1 **Ārī** E Iraq 37.07N 44.34E
194 M12 **Aria** ∽ New Britain, E PNG
Aria *see* Herāt
170 C13 **Ariake-kai** *bay* NE East China Sea
85 F22 **Ariamsvlei** Karas, SE Namibia 28.07S 19.49E
109 L17 **Ariano Irpino** Campania, S Italy 41.08N 15.00E
56 F11 **Ariari, Río** ∽ C Colombia
157 K19 **Ari Atoll** *atoll* C Maldives
79 P11 **Aribinda** N Burkina 14.12N 0.50W
64 G2 **Arica** *hist.* San Marcos de Arica. Tarapacá, N Chile 18.30S 70.18W
56 H16 **Arica** Amazonas, S Colombia 2.09S 71.48W
64 G2 **Arica** ✕ Tarapacá, N Chile 18.30S 70.19W
170 G16 **Arida** Wakayama, Honshū, SW Japan 34.05N 135.07E
116 E13 **Aridaía** *var.* Aridea, Aridhaía. Dytikí Makedonía, N Greece 40.58N 22.04E
Aridea *see* Aridaía
180 I15 **Aride, Île** *island* Inner Islands, NE Seychelles
Aridhaía *see* Aridaía
105 N17 **Ariège** ⬗ *department* S France
104 M16 **Ariège** *var.* la Riege. ∽ Andorra/France
118 H11 **Arieş** ∽ W Romania
155 U10 **Ārifwāla** Punjab, E Pakistan 30.14N 73.04E
Ariguaní *see* El Difícil
144 G11 **Arīḩā** Al Karak, W Jordan 31.25N 35.46E
144 I3 **Arīḩā** *var.* Arīhā. Idlib, W Syria 35.49N 36.36E
Arīḩā *see* Jericho
39 W4 **Arikaree River** ∽ Colorado/Nebraska, C USA
170 Bb12 **Arikawa** Nagasaki, Nakadōri-jima, SW Japan 32.58N 129.06E
114 L13 **Arilje** Serbia, W Serbia and Montenegro (Yugoslavia) 43.45N 20.06E
47 U14 **Arima** Trinidad, Trinidad and Tobago 10.38N 61.16W
Arime *see* Al 'Arīmah
Ariminum *see* Rimini
61 H16 **Arinos, Rio** ∽ W Brazil
42 M14 **Ario de Rosales** *var.* Ario de Rosáles. Michoacán de Ocampo, SW Mexico 19.12N 101.43W
120 F12 **Ariogala** Raseiniai, C Lithuania 55.16N 23.30E
49 T7 **Aripuanã** ∽ W Brazil
61 E15 **Ariquemes** Rondônia, W Brazil 9.55S 63.06W
124 Rr15 **'Arīsh, Wādī el** ∽ NE Egypt
56 K6 **Arismendi** Barinas, C Venezuela 8.28N 68.22W
8 J14 **Aristazabal Island** *island* SW Canada
62 F13 **Aristóbulo del Valle** Misiones, NE Argentina 27.09S 54.54W
180 I5 **Arivonimamo** ✕ (Antananarivo) Antananarivo, C Madagascar 19.00S 47.11E
Arixang *see* Wenquan
107 Q6 **Ariza** Aragón, NE Spain 41.19N 2.03W
64 I6 **Arizaro, Salar de** *salt lake* NW Argentina
64 K13 **Arizona** San Luis, C Argentina 35.43S 65.16W
38 J12 **Arizona** *off.* State of Arizona; *also known as* Copper State, Grand Canyon State. ⬗ *state* SW USA
42 G4 **Arizpe** Sonora, NW Mexico 30.19N 110.11W
97 J16 **Årjäng** Värmland, C Sweden 59.24N 12.09E
149 P8 **Arjenān** Yazd, C Iran 32.19N 53.48E
94 I13 **Arjeplog** Norrbotten, N Sweden 66.04N 18.00E
56 E5 **Arjona** Bolívar, N Colombia 10.13N 75.22W
107 N13 **Arjona** Andalucía, S Spain 37.55N 4.04W
127 N11 **Arka** Khabarovskiy Kray, E Russian Federation 60.04N 142.17E
24 L2 **Arkabutla Lake** ⊠ Mississippi, S USA
131 O7 **Arkadak** Saratovskaya Oblast', W Russian Federation 51.55N 43.29E
29 T13 **Arkadelphia** Arkansas, C USA 34.07N 93.03W
117 J25 **Arkalohori** *prev.* Arkalokhórion. Kríti, Greece, E Mediterranean Sea 35.09N 25.15E
Arkalokhórion *see* Arkalohori
151 O10 **Arkalyk** *Kaz.* Arqalyq. Kostanay, N Kazakhstan 50.15N 66.52E
29 U10 **Arkansas** *off.* State of Arkansas; *also known as* The Land of Opportunity. ⬗ *state* S USA
29 W14 **Arkansas City** Arkansas, C USA 33.36N 91.12W
29 O7 **Arkansas City** Kansas, C USA 37.03N 97.02W
18 Kk10 **Arkansas River** ∽ C USA
190 J5 **Arkaroola** South Australia 30.21S 139.20E
Arkhángelos *see* Archángelos
128 L8 **Arkhangel'sk** *Eng.* Archangel. Arkhangel'skaya Oblast', NW Russian Federation 64.31N 40.40E
128 L9 **Arkhangel'skaya Oblast'** ⬗ *province* NW Russian Federation
131 O14 **Arkhangel'skoye** Stavropol'skiy Kray, SW Russian Federation 44.37N 44.03E
127 N16 **Arkhara** Amurskaya Oblast', S Russian Federation 49.20N 130.04E
99 G19 **Arklow** *Ir.* An tInbhear Mór. SE Ireland 52.48N 6.09W
117 M20 **Arkoí** *island* Dodekánisos, Greece, Aegean Sea
29 R11 **Arkoma** Oklahoma, C USA 35.19N 94.27W
102 O7 **Arkona, Kap** *headland* NE Germany 54.40N 13.24E
97 N17 **Arkösund** Östergötland, S Sweden 58.28N 16.55E
126 H4 **Arkticheskogo Instituta, Ostrova** *island* N Russian Federation
97 O15 **Arlanda** ✕ (Stockholm) Stockholm, C Sweden 59.40N 17.58E
152 C11 **Arlan, Gora** ▲ W Turkmenistan 39.39N 54.28E
107 O5 **Arlanza** ∽ N Spain
107 N5 **Arlanzón** ∽ N Spain
105 R15 **Arles** *var.* Arles-sur-Rhône; *anc.* Arelas, Arelate. Bouches-du-Rhône, SE France 43.40N 4.37E
Arles-sur-Rhône *see* Arles
105 O17 **Arles-sur-Tech** Pyrénées-Orientales, S France 42.27N 2.37E
31 U9 **Arlington** Minnesota, N USA 44.36N 94.04W
31 R15 **Arlington** Nebraska, C USA 41.27N 96.21W
34 J11 **Arlington** Oregon, NW USA 45.43N 120.10W
31 R10 **Arlington** South Dakota, N USA 44.21N 97.07W
22 E10 **Arlington** Tennessee, S USA 35.17N 89.40W
27 T6 **Arlington** Texas, SW USA 32.43N 97.04W
23 W4 **Arlington** Virginia, NE USA 38.54N 77.09W
34 H7 **Arlington** Washington, NW USA 48.12N 122.07W
32 M10 **Arlington Heights** Illinois, N USA 42.08N 88.03W
79 U8 **Arlit** Agadez, C Niger 18.54N 7.25E
101 L24 **Arlon** *Dut.* Aarlen, *Ger.* Arel; *Lat.* Orolaunum. Luxembourg, SE Belgium 49.40N 5.49E
29 R7 **Arma** Kansas, C USA 37.32N 94.42W
99 F16 **Armagh** *Ir.* Ard Mhacha. S Northern Ireland, UK 54.15N 6.33W
99 F16 **Armagh** *cultural region* S Northern Ireland, UK
104 K15 **Armagnac** *cultural region* S France
105 Q7 **Armançon** ∽ C France
62 K10 **Armando Laydner, Represa** ⊠ S Brazil
117 M24 **Armathía** *island* SE Greece
130 M14 **Armavir** Krasnodarskiy Kray, SW Russian Federation 44.59N 41.07E
143 T12 **Armavir** *prev.* Hoktemberyan, *Rus.* Oktemberyan. SW Armenia 40.09N 43.58E
56 E10 **Armenia** Quindío, W Colombia 4.31N 75.40W
143 T12 **Armenia** *off.* Republic of Armenia, *var.* Ajastan, *Arm.* Hayastani Hanrapetut'yun; *prev.* Armenian Soviet Socialist Republic. ◆ *republic* SW Asia
Armenierstadt *see* Gherla
105 O1 **Armentières** Nord, N France 50.40N 2.52E
42 K14 **Armería** Colima, SW Mexico 18.55N 103.55W
191 T5 **Armidale** New South Wales, SE Australia 30.31S 151.40E
31 P11 **Armour** South Dakota, N USA 43.19N 98.21W
63 B18 **Armstrong** Santa Fe, C Argentina 32.46S 61.39W
9 N16 **Armstrong** British Columbia, SW Canada 50.27N 119.13W
10 D11 **Armstrong** Ontario, S Canada 50.19N 89.01W
31 U11 **Armstrong** Iowa, C USA 43.24N 94.28W
27 S16 **Armstrong** Texas, SW USA 26.55N 97.47W
119 S11 **Armyans'k** *Rus.* Armyansk. Respublika Krym, S Ukraine 46.05N 33.43E
117 H14 **Arnaía** *var.* Arnea. Kentrikí Makedonía, N Greece 40.30N 23.36E
123 Mm3 **Arnaoúti, Akrotíri** *var.* Arnaoútis, Cape Arnaouti. *headland* W Cyprus 35.06N 32.16E
Arnaouti, Cape/Arnaoútis *see* Arnaoúti, Akrotíri
10 L4 **Arnaud** ∽ Quebec, E Canada
105 Q8 **Arnay-le-Duc** Côte d'Or, C France 47.08N 4.27E
Arnea *see* Arnaía
107 Q4 **Arnedo** La Rioja, N Spain 42.13N 2.04W
97 I14 **Årnes** Akershus, S Norway 60.07N 11.28E
95 E15 **Årnes** Sør-Trøndelag, S Norway 63.58N 10.12E
28 K9 **Arnett** Oklahoma, C USA 36.07N 99.46W
100 L12 **Arnhem** Gelderland, SE Netherlands 51.58N 5.54E
189 Q2 **Arnhem Land** *physical region* Northern Territory, N Australia
108 F11 **Arno** ∽ C Italy
Arno *see* Arno Atoll
201 W7 **Arno Atoll** *var.* Arņo. *atoll* Ratak Chain, NE Marshall Islands
190 H8 **Arno Bay** South Australia 33.55S 136.31E
37 Q8 **Arnold** California, W USA 38.15N 120.19W
29 X5 **Arnold** Missouri, C USA 38.25N 90.22W
31 N15 **Arnold** Nebraska, C USA 41.25N 100.11W
111 R10 **Arnoldstein** *Slvn.* Pod Klošter. Kärnten, S Austria 46.34N 13.43E
105 N9 **Arnon** ∽ C France
47 P14 **Arnos Vale** ✕ (Kingstown) Saint Vincent, SE Saint Vincent and the Grenadines 13.08N 61.13W

◆ Country ● Country Capital ◇ Dependent Territory ○ Dependent Territory Capital ⬗ Administrative Region ✕ International Airport ▲ Mountain ▲▲ Mountain Range ⛰ Volcano ∽ River ◎ Lake ⊠ Reservoir

94 I8 **Arnøy** *island* N Norway
12 L12 **Arnprior** Ontario, SE Canada *45.31N 76.11W*
103 G15 **Arnsberg** Nordrhein-Westfalen, W Germany *51.24N 8.04E*
103 K16 **Arnstadt** Thüringen, C Germany *50.49N 10.57E*
Arnswalde *see* Choszczno
56 K5 **Aroa** Yaracuy, N Venezuela *10.25N 68.54W*
85 E21 **Aroab** Karas, SE Namibia *26.47S 19.37E*
117 E19 **Ároania** ▲ S Greece
203 O6 **Aroa, Pointe** *headland* Moorea, W French Polynesia *17.27S 149.45W*
Aroe Islands *see* Aru, Kepulauan
103 H15 **Arolsen** Niedersachsen, C Germany *51.23N 9.00E*
108 C7 **Arona** Piemonte, NE Italy *45.45N 8.33E*
21 R3 **Aroostook River** ≈ Canada/USA
Arop Island *see* Long Island
40 M12 **Aropuk Lake** ◎ Alaska, USA
203 P4 **Arorae** *atoll* Tungaru, W Kiribati
202 G16 **Arorangi** Rarotonga, S Cook Islands *21.13S 159.49W*
110 I9 **Arosa** Graubünden, S Switzerland *46.48N 9.42E*
106 F4 **Arousa, Ría de** *estuary* E Atlantic Ocean
176 Uu16 **Aro Usu, Tanjung** *headland* Pulau Selaru, SE Indonesia *8.19S 130.45E*
192 P8 **Arowhana** ▲ North Island, NZ *38.07S 177.52E*
143 V12 **Arp'a** *Az.* Arpaçay. ≈ Armenia/Azerbaijan
143 S11 **Arpaçay** Kars, NE Turkey *40.51N 43.19E*
Arpaçay *see* Arp'a
Arqalyq *see* Arkalyk
155 N14 **Arra** ≈ SW Pakistan
Arrabona *see* Győr
Arrah *see* Āra
Ar Rahad *see* Er Rahad
145 R9 **Ar Raḥḥālīyah** C Iraq *32.53N 43.21E*
62 Q10 **Arraial do Cabo** Rio de Janeiro, SE Brazil *22.57S 42.00W*
106 H11 **Arraiolos** Évora, S Portugal *38.43N 7.58W*
145 R8 **Ar Ramādī** *var.* Ramadi, Rumadiya. SW Iraq *33.27N 43.19E*
144 J6 **Ar Rāmī** Ḥimṣ, C Syria *34.32N 37.54E*
Ar Rams *see* Rams
144 H9 **Ar Ramthā** *var.* Ramtha. Irbid, N Jordan *32.34N 36.00E*
98 H13 **Arran, Isle of** *island* SW Scotland, UK
144 L3 **Ar Raqqah** *var.* Rakka; *anc.* Nicephorium. Ar Raqqah, N Syria *35.57N 39.03E*
144 L3 **Ar Raqqah** *off.* Muḥāfaẓat al Raqqah, *var.* Raqqah, *Fr.* Rakka. ◈ *governorate* N Syria
105 O2 **Arras** *anc.* Nemetocenna. Pas-de-Calais, N France *50.16N 2.46E*
Arrasate *see* Mondragón
144 G12 **Ar Rashādīyah** Aṭ Ṭafīlah, W Jordan *30.42N 35.37E*
144 I5 **Ar Rastān** *var.* Rastâne. Ḥimṣ, W Syria *34.57N 36.43E*
145 X12 **Ar Raṭāwī** E Iraq *30.37N 47.12E*
104 L15 **Arrats** ≈ S France
147 N10 **Ar Rawḍah** Makkah, S Saudi Arabia *21.19N 42.48E*
147 Q15 **Ar Rawḍah** S Yemen *14.26N 47.13E*
148 K11 **Ar Rawḍatayn** *var.* Raudhatain. N Kuwait *29.52N 47.42E*
149 N16 **Ar Rayyān** *var.* Al Rayyan. C Qatar *25.18N 51.24E*
104 L17 **Arreau** Hautes-Pyrénées, S France *42.55N 0.21E*
66 Q11 **Arrecife** *var.* Arrecife de Lanzarote, Puerto Arrecife. Lanzarote, Islas Canarias, NE Atlantic Ocean *28.57N 13.33W*
Arrecife de Lanzarote *see* Arrecife
45 P6 **Arrecife Edinburgh** *reef* NE Nicaragua
63 C19 **Arrecifes** Buenos Aires, E Argentina *34.06S 60.09W*
104 F6 **Arrée, Monts d'** ▲▲ NW France
Ar Refā'ī *see* Ar Rifā'ī
Arretium *see* Arezzo
Arriaca *see* Guadalajara
111 S9 **Arriach** Kärnten, S Austria *46.43N 13.52E*
43 T16 **Arriaga** Chiapas, SE Mexico *16.13N 93.54W*
43 N12 **Arriaga** San Luis Potosí, C Mexico *21.55N 101.22W*
145 W10 **Ar Rifā'ī** *var.* Ar Refā'ī. SE Iraq *31.46N 46.07E*
145 U11 **Ar Riḥāb** *salt flat* S Iraq
106 L2 **Arriondas** Asturias, N Spain *43.22N 5.10W*
147 Q7 **Ar Riyāḍ** *Eng.* Riyadh. ● (Saudi Arabia) Ar Riyāḍ, C Saudi Arabia *24.49N 46.49E*
147 O8 **Ar Riyāḍ** *off.* Minṭaqat ar Riyāḍ. ◈ *province* C Saudi Arabia
147 S15 **Ar Riyān** S Yemen *14.43N 49.18E*
Arrö *see* Ærø
63 H18 **Arroio Grande** Rio Grande do Sul, S Brazil *32.15S 53.02W*
104 K15 **Arros** ≈ S France
105 Q9 **Arroux** ≈ C France
27 R5 **Arrowhead, Lake** ⊠ Texas, SW USA
190 L5 **Arrowsmith, Mount** *hill* New South Wales, SE Australia *30.07S 141.37E*
193 D21 **Arrowtown** Otago, South Island, NZ *44.57S 168.51E*
63 D17 **Arroyo Barú** Entre Ríos, E Argentina *31.52S 58.25W*
106 J10 **Arroyo de la Luz** Extremadura, W Spain *39.28N 6.36W*
65 J16 **Arroyo de la Ventana** Río Negro, SE Argentina *41.41S 66.03W*
37 P13 **Arroyo Grande** California, W USA *35.07N 120.35W*
Ar Ru'ays *see* Ar Ruways
147 R11 **Ar Rub' al Khālī** *Eng.* Empty Quarter, Great Sandy Desert. *desert* SW Asia
145 V13 **Ar Rudaymah** S Iraq *30.19N 45.25E*
63 A16 **Arrufó** Santa Fe, C Argentina *30.15S 61.45W*
144 I7 **Ar Ruḥaybah** *var.* Ruhaybeh, *Fr.* Rouhaïbé. Dimashq, W Syria *33.45N 36.40E*
145 V15 **Ar Rukhaymīyah** *well* S Iraq *29.22N 45.43E*
145 U11 **Ar Rumaythah** *var.* Rumaitha. S Iraq *31.31N 45.15E*
147 X8 **Ar Rustāq** *var.* Rostak, Rustaq. N Oman *23.34N 57.25E*
145 N8 **Ar Ruṭbah** *var.* Rutba. SW Iraq *33.03N 40.16E*
146 M3 **Ar Rūthīyah** *spring/well* NW Saudi Arabia *31.18N 41.23E*
ar-Ruwaida *see* Ar Ruwayḍah
147 O8 **Ar Ruwayḍah** *var.* ar-Ruwaida. Jīzān, C Saudi Arabia *23.48N 44.44E*
149 N15 **Ar Ruways** *var.* Al Ruweis, Ar Ru'ays, Ruwais. N Qatar *26.07N 51.13E*
149 O17 **Ar Ruways** *var.* Ar Ru'ays, Ruwaisc. Abū Ẓaby, W UAE *24.09N 52.57E*
Års *see* Aars
Arsanias *see* Murat Nehri
127 Nn18 **Arsen'yev** Primorskiy Kray, SE Russian Federation *44.09N 133.28E*
161 G19 **Arsikere** Karnātaka, W India *13.18N 76.15E*
131 R3 **Arsk** Respublika Tatarstan, W Russian Federation *56.07N 49.54E*
96 N10 **Årskogen** Gävleborg, C Sweden *62.07N 17.19E*
124 N3 **Ársos** C Cyprus *34.51N 32.46E*
96 N13 **Årsunda** Gävleborg, C Sweden *60.31N 16.45E*
Arta *see* Árachthos
117 C17 **Árta** *anc.* Ambracia. Ípeiros, W Greece *39.07N 20.59E*
143 T12 **Artashat** S Armenia *39.57N 44.34E*
42 M15 **Arteaga** Michoacán de Ocampo, SW Mexico *18.20N 102.18W*
127 Nn18 **Artem** Primorskiy Kray, SE Russian Federation *43.24N 132.20E*
46 C4 **Artemisa** La Habana, W Cuba *22.49N 82.46W*
119 W7 **Artemivs'k** Donets'ka Oblast', E Ukraine *48.35N 37.58E*
126 I14 **Artemovsk** Krasnoyarskiy Kray, S Russian Federation *54.22N 93.24E*
126 Kk13 **Artemovskiy** Irkutskaya Oblast', C Russian Federation *58.15N 114.51E*
125 Ee13 **Artemovskiy** Sverdlovskaya Oblast', C Russian Federation *57.22N 61.55E*
107 U5 **Artesa de Segre** Cataluña, NE Spain *41.54N 1.03E*
39 U14 **Artesia** New Mexico, SW USA *32.50N 104.24W*
27 Q14 **Artesia Wells** Texas, SW USA *28.13N 99.18W*
110 G8 **Arth** Schwyz, C Switzerland *47.05N 8.39E*
12 F15 **Arthur** Ontario, S Canada *43.49N 80.31W*
32 M14 **Arthur** Illinois, N USA *39.42N 88.28W*
30 L14 **Arthur** Nebraska, C USA *41.32N 101.42W*
31 Q5 **Arthur** North Dakota, N USA *47.03N 97.12W*
193 B21 **Arthur** ≈ South Island, NZ
20 B13 **Arthur, Lake** ⊠ Pennsylvania, NE USA
191 N15 **Arthur River** ≈ Tasmania, SE Australia
193 G18 **Arthur's Pass** Canterbury, South Island, NZ *42.59S 171.33E*
193 G17 **Arthur's Pass** *pass* South Island, NZ *42.57S 171.33E*
46 I3 **Arthur's Town** Cat Island, C Bahamas *24.34N 75.39W*
46 M9 **Artibonite, Rivière de l'** ≈ C Haiti
63 E16 **Artigas** *prev.* San Eugenio, San Eugenio del Cuareim. Artigas, N Uruguay *30.25S 56.28W*
63 E16 **Artigas** ◈ *department* N Uruguay
204 H1 **Artigas** *Uruguayan research station* Antarctica *61.57S 58.23W*
143 T11 **Art'ik** W Armenia *40.38N 43.57E*
197 G4 **Art, Île** *island* Îles Belep, W New Caledonia
105 O2 **Artois** *cultural region* N France
142 L12 **Artova** Tokat, N Turkey *40.06N 36.18E*
107 Y9 **Artrutx, Cap d'** *var.* Cabo Dartuch. *headland* Menorca, Spain, W Mediterranean Sea *39.55N 3.49E*
Artsiz *see* Artsyz
119 N11 **Artsyz** *Rus.* Artsiz. Odes'ka Oblast', SW Ukraine *45.58N 29.25E*
164 E7 **Artux** Xinjiang Uygur Zizhiqu, NW China *39.45N 76.09E*
143 R11 **Artvin** Artvin, NE Turkey *41.12N 41.48E*
143 R11 **Artvin** ◈ *province* NE Turkey
152 G14 **Artyk** Akhalskiy Velayat, C Turkmenistan *37.32N 59.16E*
81 Q16 **Aru** Orientale, NE Dem. Rep. Congo *2.52N 30.49E*
106 I4 **A Rúa** *var.* La Rúa. Galicia, NW Spain *42.22N 7.12W*
83 E17 **Arua** NW Uganda *3.01N 30.55E*
Aruângua *see* Luangwa
47 O15 **Aruba** *var.* Oruba. ◇ *Dutch autonomous region* S West Indies
49 Q4 **Aruba** *island* Aruba, Lesser Antilles
Aru Islands *see* Aru, Kepulauan
176 Ww14 **Aru, Kepulauan** *Eng.* Aru Islands; *prev.* Aroe Islands. *island group* E Indonesia
159 W10 **Arunāchal Pradesh** *prev.* North East Frontier Agency, North East Frontier Agency of Assam. ◈ *state* NE India
169 U7 **Arun Qi** Nei Mongol Zizhiqu, N China *48.10N 123.28E*
161 H23 **Aruppukkottai** Tamil Nādu, SE India *9.31N 78.03E*
176 Ww9 **Aruri, Selat** *strait* Papua, E Indonesia
83 I20 **Arusha** Arusha, N Tanzania *3.22S 36.40E*
83 I21 **Arusha** ◈ *region* E Tanzania
83 I20 **Arusha** ✕ Arusha, N Tanzania *3.26S 37.07E*
56 C9 **Arusí, Punta** *headland* NW Colombia *5.36N 77.30W*
174 Ll10 **Arut, Sungai** ≈ Borneo, C Indonesia
161 J23 **Aruvi Aru** ≈ NW Sri Lanka
81 M17 **Aruwimi** *var.* Ituri (upper course). ≈ NE Dem. Rep. Congo
Árva *see* Orava
39 T4 **Arvada** Colorado, C USA *39.48N 105.06W*
Arvand Rūd *see* 'Arab, Shaṭṭ al
168 J8 **Arvayheer** Övörhangay, C Mongolia *46.13N 102.47E*
15 L8 **Arviat** *prev.* Eskimo Point. Nunavut, C Canada *61.10N 94.15W*
95 I14 **Arvidsjaur** Norrbotten, N Sweden *65.34N 19.12E*
97 J15 **Arvika** Värmland, C Sweden *59.40N 12.37E*
94 J8 **Årviksand** Troms, N Norway *70.10N 20.30E*
37 S13 **Arvin** California, W USA *35.12N 118.52W*
151 P7 **Arykbalyk** *Kaz.* Aryqbalyq. Severnyy Kazakhstan, N Kazakhstan *53.00N 68.11E*
Aryqbalyq *see* Arykbalyk
151 P17 **Arys'** *Kaz.* Arys. Yuzhnyy Kazakhstan, S Kazakhstan *42.25N 68.49E*
Arys *see* Arys'
Arys *see* Orzysz
Arys Köli *see* Arys, Ozero
151 O14 **Arys, Ozero** *Kaz.* Arys Köli. ◎ C Kazakhstan
109 D16 **Arzachena** Sardegna, Italy, C Mediterranean Sea *41.05N 9.21E*
131 O4 **Arzamas** Nizhegorodskaya Oblast', W Russian Federation *55.25N 43.51E*
147 V13 **Arzāt** S Oman *17.03N 54.19E*
106 H3 **Arzúa** Galicia, NW Spain *42.55N 8.10W*
113 A16 **Aš** *Ger.* Asch. Karlovarský Kraj, W Czech Republic *50.12N 12.12E*
97 H15 **Ås** Akershus, S Norway *59.39N 10.48E*
Aså *see* Asaa
97 H20 **Asaa** *var.* Aså. Nordjylland, N Denmark *57.07N 10.24E*
85 E21 **Asab** Karas, S Namibia *25.28S 17.58E*
79 U16 **Asaba** Delta, S Nigeria *6.10N 6.44E*
155 S4 **Asadābād** *var.* Asadābād; *prev.* Chaghasarāy. Kunar, E Afghanistan *34.52N 71.09E*
144 K3 **Asad, Buḥayrat al** ◎ N Syria
65 H20 **Asador, Pampa del** *plain* S Argentina
171 Kk17 **Asahi** Chiba, Honshū, S Japan *36.08N 140.37E*
171 J13 **Asahi** Toyama, Honshū, SW Japan *36.56N 137.34E*
172 Pp5 **Asahi-dake** ▲ Hokkaidō, N Japan *43.42N 142.50E*
170 Ff13 **Asahi-gawa** ≈ Honshū, SW Japan
172 P5 **Asahikawa** Hokkaidō, N Japan *43.46N 142.22E*
153 S10 **Asaka** *Rus.* Assake; *prev.* Leninsk. Andijon Viloyati, E Uzbekistan *40.39N 72.16E*
79 P17 **Asamankese** SE Ghana *5.46N 0.41W*
171 Jj15 **Asama-yama** ▲ Honshū, S Japan *36.25N 138.34E*
196 B15 **Asan** W Guam *13.28N 144.43E*
196 B15 **Asan Point** *headland* W Guam
159 R15 **Āsānsol** West Bengal, NE India *23.40N 86.58E*
82 K12 **Āsayita** Afar, NE Ethiopia *11.35N 41.23E*
176 V9 **Asbakin** Papua, E Indonesia *0.45S 131.40E*
Asben *see* Aïr, Massif de l'
125 Ee11 **Asbest** Sverdlovskaya Oblast', C Russian Federation *57.12N 61.18E*
13 Q12 **Asbestos** Quebec, SE Canada *45.46N 71.55W*
31 Y13 **Asbury** Iowa, C USA *42.30N 90.45W*
20 K15 **Asbury Park** New Jersey, NE USA *40.13N 74.00W*
43 Z12 **Ascensión, Bahía de la** *bay* NW Caribbean Sea
42 I3 **Ascensión** Chihuahua, N Mexico *31.07N 107.58W*
67 M14 **Ascension Fracture Zone** *tectonic feature* C Atlantic Ocean
67 G14 **Ascension Island** ◇ *dependency of St. Helena* C Atlantic Ocean
67 N16 **Ascension Island** *island* C Atlantic Ocean
Asch *see* Aš
111 S3 **Aschach an der Donau** Oberösterreich, N Austria *48.22N 14.00E*
103 H18 **Aschaffenburg** Bayern, SW Germany *49.58N 9.09E*
103 F14 **Ascheberg** Nordrhein-Westfalen, W Germany *51.46N 7.36E*
103 L14 **Aschersleben** Sachsen-Anhalt, C Germany *51.46N 11.28E*
108 G12 **Asciano** Toscana, C Italy *43.15N 11.32E*
108 J13 **Ascoli Piceno** *anc.* Asculum Picenum. Marche, C Italy *42.51N 13.34E*
109 M17 **Ascoli Satriano** *anc.* Asculub, Ausculum Apulum. Puglia, SE Italy *41.13N 15.31E*
110 G11 **Ascona** Ticino, S Switzerland *46.10N 8.45E*
Asculub *see* Ascoli Satriano
Asculum Picenum *see* Ascoli Piceno
82 L11 **Aseb** *var.* Assab, *Amh.* Āseb. SE Eritrea *13.03N 42.36E*
97 M20 **Åseda** Kronoberg, S Sweden *57.10N 15.19E*
131 T6 **Asekeyevo** Orenburgskaya Oblast', W Russian Federation *53.36N 52.53E*
194 J13 **Aseki** Morobe, C PNG *7.18S 156.16E*
83 J14 **Āsela** *var.* Asella, Aselle, Asselle. Oromo, C Ethiopia *7.55N 39.08E*
95 H15 **Åsele** Västerbotten, N Sweden *64.10N 17.19E*
Asella/Aselle *see* Āsela
96 K12 **Åsen** Dalarna, C Sweden *61.18N 13.49E*
116 J11 **Asenovgrad** *prev.* Stanimaka. Plovdiv, C Bulgaria *42.01N 24.54E*
175 Q11 **Asera** Sulawesi, C Indonesia *3.24S 121.42E*
97 E17 **Åseral** Vest-Agder, S Norway *58.37N 7.27E*
120 J3 **Aseri** *var.* Asserien, *Ger.* Asserin. Ida-Virumaa, NE Estonia *59.28N 26.50E*
42 J10 **Aserradero** Durango, W Mexico
97 H16 **Åsgårdstrand** Vestfold, S Norway *59.19N 10.28E*
125 E11 **Asha** Chelyabinskaya Oblast', C Russian Federation *55.01N 57.11E*
Ashara *see* Al 'Ashārah
25 T6 **Ashburn** Georgia, SE USA *31.42N 83.39W*
193 G19 **Ashburton** Canterbury, South Island, NZ *43.55S 171.46E*
193 G19 **Ashburton** ≈ South Island, NZ
188 H8 **Ashburton River** ≈ Western Australia
151 V10 **Ashchysu** ≈ E Kazakhstan
8 M16 **Ashcroft** British Columbia, SW Canada *50.40N 121.16W*
144 E10 **Ashdod** *anc.* Azotos, *Lat.* Azotus. Central, W Israel *31.48N 34.37E*
29 S14 **Ashdown** Arkansas, C USA *33.40N 94.07W*
23 T9 **Asheboro** North Carolina, SE USA *35.42N 79.48W*
9 X15 **Ashern** Manitoba, S Canada *51.10N 98.22W*
23 P10 **Asheville** North Carolina, SE USA *35.36N 82.33W*
10 E8 **Asheweig** ≈ Ontario, C Canada
29 V9 **Ash Flat** Arkansas, C USA *36.13N 91.36W*
191 T4 **Ashford** New South Wales, SE Australia *29.18S 151.09E*
99 P22 **Ashford** SE England, UK *51.09N 0.52E*
38 K11 **Ash Fork** Arizona, SW USA *35.12N 112.31W*
152 F13 **Ashgabat** *prev.* Ashkhabad, Poltoratsk. ● (Turkmenistan) Akhalskiy Velayat, C Turkmenistan *37.58N 58.22E*
152 F13 **Ashgabat** ✕ Akhalskiy Velayat, C Turkmenistan *38.06N 58.10E*
29 T7 **Ash Grove** Missouri, C USA *37.19N 93.35W*
171 K15 **Ashikaga** *var.* Asikaga. Tochigi, Honshū, S Japan *36.19N 139.26E*
171 Mm10 **Ashiro** Iwate, Honshū, C Japan *40.04N 141.00E*
170 E16 **Ashizuri-misaki** *headland* Shikoku, SW Japan *32.43N 132.59E*
Ashkelon *see* Ashqelon
Ashkhabad *see* Ashgabat
25 Q4 **Ashland** Alabama, S USA *33.16N 85.50W*
28 K7 **Ashland** Kansas, C USA *37.11N 99.46W*
23 P5 **Ashland** Kentucky, S USA *38.28N 82.39W*
21 S2 **Ashland** Maine, NE USA *46.36N 68.24W*
24 M1 **Ashland** Mississippi, S USA *34.51N 89.10W*
29 U4 **Ashland** Missouri, C USA *38.46N 92.15W*
31 S15 **Ashland** Nebraska, C USA *41.01N 96.21W*
33 T12 **Ashland** Ohio, N USA *40.52N 82.19W*
34 G15 **Ashland** Oregon, NW USA *42.11N 122.42W*
23 W6 **Ashland** Virginia, NE USA *37.45N 77.28W*
32 K3 **Ashland** Wisconsin, N USA *46.34N 90.54W*
22 I8 **Ashland City** Tennessee, S USA *36.16N 87.03W*
191 S4 **Ashley** New South Wales, SE Australia *29.21S 149.49E*
31 O7 **Ashley** North Dakota, N USA *46.00N 99.22W*
181 W7 **Ashmore and Cartier Islands** ◇ *Australian external territory* E Indian Ocean
121 I14 **Ashmyany** *Rus.* Oshmyany. Hrodzyenskaya Voblasts', W Belarus *54.24N 25.57E*
20 K12 **Ashokan Reservoir** ⊠ New York, NE USA
172 Pp6 **Ashoro** Hokkaidō, NE Japan *43.16N 143.33E*
144 E10 **Ashqelon** *var.* Ashkelon. Southern, C Israel *31.40N 34.34E*
Ashraf *see* Behshahr
145 O3 **Ash Shadādah** *var.* Ash Shaddādah, Jisr ash Shadadi, Shaddādī, Shedadi, Tell Shedadi. Al Ḥasakah, NE Syria *36.00N 40.42E*
Ash Shaddādah *see* Ash Shadādah
145 Y12 **Ash Shāfī** E Iraq *30.49N 47.30E*
145 R4 **Ash Shakk** *var.* Shaykh. C Iraq *35.15N 43.27E*
Ash Sham/Ash Shām *see* Dimashq
145 T10 **Ash Shāmīyah** *var.* Shamiya. C Iraq *31.55N 44.37E*
145 Y13 **Ash Shāmīyah** *var.* Al Bādiyah al Janūbīyah. *desert* S Iraq
145 T11 **Ash Shanāfīyah** *var.* Ash Shināfīyah. S Iraq *31.34N 44.38E*
144 G13 **Ash Sharāh** *var.* Esh Sharā. ▲▲ W Jordan
149 R16 **Ash Shāriqah** *Eng.* Sharjah. Ash Shāriqah, NE UAE *25.22N 55.28E*
149 R16 **Ash Shāriqah** *var.* Sharjah. ✕ Ash Shāriqah, NE UAE *25.19N 55.37E*
146 I4 **Ash Sharmah** *var.* Šarma. Tabūk, NW Saudi Arabia *28.01N 35.16E*
145 R4 **Ash Sharqāṭ** NW Iraq *35.30N 43.15E*
147 S10 **Ash Sharqīyah** *off.* Al Minṭaqah ash Sharqīyah, *Eng.* Eastern Region. ◈ *province* E Saudi Arabia
145 W11 **Ash Shaṭrah** *var.* Shatra. SE Iraq *31.25N 46.10E*
144 G13 **Ash Shawbak** Ma'ān, W Jordan *30.31N 35.34E*
144 L5 **Ash Shaykh Ibrāhīm** Ḥimṣ, C Syria *35.03N 38.50E*
147 O17 **Ash Shaykh 'Uthmān** SW Yemen *12.53N 45.00E*
147 S15 **Ash Shiḥr** SE Yemen *14.45N 49.24E*
Ash Shināfīyah *see* Ash Shanāfīyah
147 V12 **Ash Shiṣar** *var.* Shisur. SW Oman *18.13N 53.34E*
145 S13 **Ash Shubrūm** *well* S Iraq *30.09N 43.59E*
147 R10 **Ash Shuqqān** *desert* E Saudi Arabia
77 O9 **Ash Shuwayrif** *var.* Ash Shwayrif. N Libya *29.54N 14.16E*
Ash Shwayrif *see* Ash Shuwayrif
33 U10 **Ashtabula** Ohio, N USA *41.54N 80.46W*
31 Q5 **Ashtabula, Lake** ⊠ North Dakota, N USA
143 T12 **Ashtarak** W Armenia *40.18N 44.22E*
148 M6 **Āshtīān** *var.* Āshtiyān. Markazī, W Iran *34.24N 49.55E*
Āshtiyān *see* Āshtīān
35 R13 **Ashton** Idaho, NW USA *44.04N 111.27W*
11 O10 **Ashuanipi Lake** ◎ Newfoundland and Labrador, E Canada
13 P6 **Ashuapmushuan** ≈ Quebec, SE Canada
25 Q3 **Ashville** Alabama, S USA *33.50N 86.15W*
33 S14 **Ashville** Ohio, N USA *39.43N 82.57W*
32 K3 **Ashwabay, Mount** *hill* Wisconsin, N USA *46.49N 90.57W*
176 Uu7 **Asia, Kepulauan** *island group* E Indonesia
160 N13 **Āsika** Orissa, E India *19.37N 84.40E*
Asikaga *see* Ashikaga
95 M18 **Asikkala** *var.* Vääksy. Etelä-Suomi, S Finland *61.09N 25.36E*
76 G5 **Asilah** N Morocco *35.18N 6.04W*
'Aṣī, Nahr al *see* Orontes
109 B16 **Asinara, Isola** *island* W Italy
126 H13 **Asino** Tomskaya Oblast', C Russian Federation *56.56N 86.02E*
121 O14 **Asintorf** *Rus.* Osintorf. Vitsyebskaya Voblasts', N Belarus *54.43N 30.35E*
121 L17 **Asipovichy** *Rus.* Osipovichi. Mahilyowskaya Voblasts', C Belarus *53.18N 28.40E*
147 N12 **'Asīr** *off.* Minṭaqat 'Asīr. ◈ *province* SW Saudi Arabia
146 M11 **'Asīr** *Eng.* Asir. ▲▲ SW Saudi Arabia
145 X10 **Askal** E Iraq *31.45N 47.07E*
143 P13 **Aşkale** Erzurum, NE Turkey *39.56N 40.39E*
119 T11 **Askaniya-Nova** Khersons'ka Oblast', S Ukraine *46.27N 33.54E*
97 H15 **Asker** Akershus, S Norway *59.49N 10.29E*
97 L17 **Askersund** Örebro, C Sweden *58.55N 14.55E*
Askī Kalak *see* Eski Kaļak
97 I15 **Askim** Østfold, S Norway *59.34N 11.10E*
131 V3 **Askino** Respublika Bashkortostan, W Russian Federation *56.07N 56.39E*
117 D14 **Áskio** ▲▲ N Greece
158 L9 **Askot** Uttar Pradesh, N India *29.43N 80.19E*
96 C12 **Askvoll** Sogn og Fjordane, S Norway *61.21N 5.04E*
142 A13 **Aslan Burnu** *headland* W Turkey *38.44N 26.43E*
142 L16 **Aslantaş Barajı** ⊠ S Turkey
155 S4 **Asmār** *var.* Bar Kunar. Kunar, E Afghanistan *34.58N 71.28E*
82 I9 **Asmara** *Amh.* Āsmera. ● (Eritrea) C Eritrea *15.15N 38.57E*
Āsmera *see* Asmara
97 L21 **Åsnen** ◎ S Sweden
117 F19 **Asopós** ≈ S Greece
176 X10 **Asori** Papua, E Indonesia *2.37S 136.06E*
82 G12 **Āsosa** Benishangul, W Ethiopia *10.06N 34.27E*
34 M10 **Asotin** Washington, NW USA *46.18N 117.03W*
Aspadana *see* Eşfahān
Aspang *see* Aspang Markt
111 X6 **Aspang Markt** *var.* Aspang. Niederösterreich, E Austria *47.34N 16.07E*
107 S12 **Aspe** País Valenciano, E Spain *38.21N 0.43W*
39 R5 **Aspen** Colorado, C USA *39.12N 106.49W*
27 P6 **Aspermont** Texas, SW USA *33.07N 100.13W*
Asphaltites, Lacus *see* Dead Sea
Aspinwall *see* Colón
193 C20 **Aspiring, Mount** ▲ South Island, NZ *44.21S 168.47E*
117 B16 **Asprókavos, Akrotírio** *headland* Kérkyra, Iónioi Nísoi, Greece, C Mediterranean Sea *39.22N 20.07E*
Aspropótamos *see* Achelóos
Assab *see* Āseb
78 J10 **Assaba** *var.* Açâba. ◈ *region* S Mauritania
144 L4 **As Sabkhah** *var.* Sabkha. Ar Raqqah, NE Syria *35.30N 35.54E*
145 U6 **As Sa'dīyah** E Iraq *34.11N 45.09E*
Assad, Lake *see* Asad, Buḥayrat al
144 I8 **Aş Şafā** ▲ S Syria *33.03N 37.07E*
144 I10 **Aş Şafāwī** Al Mafraq, N Jordan *32.12N 32.30E*
Aş Şaff *see* El Şaff
145 N2 **Aş Şafīḥ** Al Ḥasakah, N Syria *36.42N 40.12E*
Aş Şaḥrā' al Gharbīyah *see* Sahara el Gharbîya
Aş Şaḥrā' ash Sharqīyah *see* Sahara el Sharqîya
Assake *see* Asaka
As Salamīyah *see* Salamīyah
147 Q4 **As Sālimī** *var.* Salemy. SW Kuwait *29.07N 46.41E*
69 W7 **'Assal, Lac** ◎ C Djibouti
As Sallūm *see* Salûm
145 T13 **As Salmān** S Iraq *30.28N 44.34E*
144 G10 **As Salṭ** *var.* Salt. Al Balqā', NW Jordan *32.03N 35.43E*
148 M16 **As Salwā** *var.* Salwa, Salwah. S Qatar *24.43N 50.52E*
159 V12 **Assam** ◈ *state* NE India
Assamaka *see* Assamakka
79 T8 **Assamakka** *var.* Assamaka. Agadez, NW Niger *19.24N 5.52E*
145 U11 **As Samāwah** *var.* Samawa. S Iraq *31.17N 45.05E*
As Saqia al Hamra *see* Saguia al Hamra
144 J4 **Aş Şā'rān** Ḥamāh, C Syria *35.15N 37.28E*
144 G9 **Aş Şarīḥ** Irbid, N Jordan *32.31N 35.54E*
23 Z5 **Assateague Island** *island* Maryland, NE USA
145 O6 **As Sayyāl** *var.* Sayyāl. Dayr az Zawr, E Syria *34.37N 40.52E*
101 G18 **Asse** Vlaams Brabant, C Belgium *50.55N 4.12E*
101 D16 **Assebroek** West-Vlaanderen, NW Belgium *51.12N 3.16E*
Asselle *see* Āsela
109 C20 **Assemini** Sardegna, Italy, C Mediterranean Sea *39.16N 8.58E*
100 N7 **Assen** Drenthe, NE Netherlands *53.00N 6.34E*
101 E16 **Assenede** Oost-Vlaanderen, NW Belgium *51.15N 3.43E*
97 G24 **Assens** Fyn, C Denmark *55.16N 9.54E*
Asserien/Asserin *see* Aseri
101 I21 **Assesse** Namur, SE Belgium *50.22N 5.01E*
147 Y8 **As Sīb** *var.* Seeb. NE Oman *23.40N 58.03E*
145 Z13 **As Sībah** *var.* Sibah. SE Iraq *30.13N 47.24E*
9 T17 **Assiniboia** Saskatchewan, S Canada *49.39N 105.58W*
9 V15 **Assiniboine** ≈ Manitoba, S Canada
9 P16 **Assiniboine, Mount** ▲ Alberta/British Columbia, SW Canada *50.54N 115.43W*
Assiout *see* Asyût
62 J9 **Assis** São Paulo, S Brazil *22.37S 50.25W*
108 I13 **Assisi** Umbria, C Italy *43.04N 12.36E*
Assiut *see* Asyût
Assling *see* Jesenice
Assouan *see* Aswân
Assu *see* Açu
Assuan *see* Aswân
148 K12 **Aş Şubayḥīyah** *var.* Subiyah. S Kuwait *28.55N 47.57E*
147 R16 **As Sufāl** S Yemen *14.06N 48.42E*
144 L5 **As Sukhnah** *var.* Sukhne, *Fr.* Soukhné. Ḥimṣ, C Syria *34.55N 38.52E*
145 U4 **As Sulaymānīyah** *var.* Sulaimaniya, *Kurd.* Slēmānī. NE Iraq *35.31N 45.27E*
147 P11 **As Sulayyil** Ar Riyāḍ, S Saudi Arabia *20.28N 45.33E*
123 M16 **As Sulṭān** N Libya *31.01N 17.21E*
147 Q5 **Aş Şummān** *desert* N Saudi Arabia
147 Q16 **Aş Şurrah** SW Yemen *13.56N 46.23E*
145 N4 **Aş Şuwār** *var.* Şuwār. Dayr az Zawr, E Syria *35.31N 40.37E*
144 H9 **As Suwaydā'** *var.* El Suweida, Es Suweida, Suweida, *Fr.* Soueida. As Suwaydā', SW Syria *32.43N 36.33E*
144 H9 **As Suwaydā'** *off.* Muḥāfaẓat as Suwaydā', *var.* As Suwaydā, Suwaydá, Suweida, *Fr.* Soueida. ◈ *governorate* S Syria
147 Z9 **As Suwayḥ** NE Oman *22.07N 59.42E*
147 X8 **As Suwayq** *var.* Suwaik. N Oman *23.51N 57.20E*
145 T8 **Aş Şuwayrah** *var.* Suwaira. E Iraq *32.57N 44.46E*
As Suways *see* Suez
Asta Colonia *see* Asti
Astacus *see* İzmit
117 M23 **Astakída** *island* SE Greece
151 Q9 **Astana** *prev.* Akmola, Akmolinsk, Tselinograd, Aqmola. ● (Kazakhstan) Akmola, N Kazakhstan *51.12N 71.25E*
148 M3 **Āstāneh** Gīlān, NW Iran *37.16N 49.58E*
Asta Pompeia *see* Asti
143 Y14 **Astara** S Azerbaijan *38.28N 48.51E*
Astarabad *see* Gorgān
101 L15 **Asten** Noord-Brabant, SE Netherlands *51.24N 5.45E*
Asterābād *see* Gorgān
108 C8 **Asti** *anc.* Asta Colonia, Asta Pompeia, Hasta Colonia, Hasta Pompeia. Piemonte, NW Italy *44.54N 8.10E*
Astigi *see* Ecija
Astipálaia *see* Astypálaia
154 L16 **Astola Island** *island* SW Pakistan
158 H4 **Astor** Jammu and Kashmir, NW India *35.21N 74.52E*
106 K4 **Astorga** *anc.* Asturica Augusta. Castilla-León, N Spain *42.27N 6.04W*
34 F10 **Astoria** Oregon, NW USA *46.12N 123.49W*
(0) F8 **Astoria Fan** *undersea feature* E Pacific Ocean
97 J22 **Åstorp** Skåne, S Sweden *56.09N 12.57E*
Astrabad *see* Gorgān
131 Q13 **Astrakhan'** Astrakhanskaya Oblast', SW Russian Federation *46.20N 48.00E*
Astrakhan-Bazar *see* Cälilabad
131 Q11 **Astrakhanskaya Oblast'** ◈ *province* SW Russian Federation
95 J15 **Åsträsk** Västerbotten, N Sweden *64.38N 20.00E*
Astrida *see* Butare
67 O22 **Astrid Ridge** *undersea feature* S Atlantic Ocean
194 J11 **Astrolabe Bay** *inlet* N PNG
197 I4 **Astrolabe, Récifs de l'** *reef* C New Caledonia
124 Nn3 **Astromerítis** N Cyprus *35.09N 33.02E*
117 F20 **Ástros** Pelopónnisos, S Greece *37.24N 22.43E*
121 G16 **Astryna** *Rus.* Ostryna. Hrodzyenskaya Voblasts', W Belarus *53.44N 24.33E*
106 J2 **Asturias** ◈ *autonomous community* NW Spain
Asturias *see* Oviedo
Asturica Augusta *see* Astorga
117 L22 **Astypálaia** *var.* Astipálaia, *It.* Stampalia. *island* Kykládes, Greece, Aegean Sea
198 Aa8 **Āsuisui, Cape** *headland* Savai'i, W Samoa *13.43S 172.28W*
205 S2 **Asuka** *Japanese research station* Antarctica *71.49S 23.52E*
64 O6 **Asunción** ● (Paraguay) Central, S Paraguay *25.16S 57.36W*
64 O6 **Asunción** ✕ Central, S Paraguay *25.15S 57.40W*
196 K3 **Asuncion Island** *island* N Northern Mariana Islands
44 E6 **Asunción Mita** Jutiapa, SE Guatemala *14.19N 89.42W*
Asunción Nochixtlán *see* Nochixtlán
42 E3 **Asunción, Río** ≈ NW Mexico
97 M18 **Åsunden** ◎ S Sweden
120 K11 **Asvyeya** *Rus.* Osveya. Vitsyebskaya Voblasts', N Belarus *56.00N 28.05E*
Aswa *see* Achwa
77 X11 **Aswân** *var.* Assouan, Assuan; *anc.* Syene. SE Egypt *24.03N 32.58E*
77 X11 **Aswân High Dam** *dam* SE Egypt *23.54N 32.51E*
77 W9 **Asyût** *var.* Assiout, Assiut, Siut; *anc.* Lycopolis. C Egypt *27.05N 31.10E*
200 R15 **Ata** *island* Tongatapu Group, SW Tonga
64 G8 **Atacama** *off.* Región de Atacama. ◈ *region* C Chile
Atacama Desert *see* Atacama, Desierto de
64 H4 **Atacama, Desierto de** *Eng.* Atacama Desert. *desert* N Chile
64 I6 **Atacama, Puna de** ▲▲ NW Argentina
64 I5 **Atacama, Salar de** *salt lake* N Chile
56 E11 **Ataco** Tolima, C Colombia *3.33N 75.25W*
202 H8 **Atafu Atoll** *island* NW Tokelau
202 H8 **Atafu Village** Atafu Atoll, NW Tokelau *8.40S 172.40W*
76 K12 **Atakor** ▲▲ SE Algeria
79 R14 **Atakora, Chaîne de l'** *var.* Atakora Mountains. ▲▲ N Benin
Atakora Mountains *see* Atakora, Chaîne de l'
79 R16 **Atakpamé** C Togo *7.31N 1.07E*
152 F11 **Atakui** Akhalskiy Velayat, C Turkmenistan *40.04N 58.03E*
60 B13 **Atalaia do Norte** Amazonas, N Brazil *4.22S 70.10W*
171 J17 **Atami** Shizuoka, Honshū, S Japan *35.04N 139.03E*
78 I7 **Aṭâr** Adrar, W Mauritania *20.30N 13.03W*
168 G10 **Atas Bogd** ▲ SW Mongolia *43.17N 96.47E*
37 P12 **Atascadero** California, W USA *35.28N 120.40W*
27 S13 **Atascosa River** ≈ Texas, SW USA
151 R11 **Atasu** Zhezkazgan, C Kazakhstan *48.42N 71.37E*
151 R12 **Atasu** ≈ C Kazakhstan
200 Qq15 **Atata** *island* Tongatapu Group, S Tonga
142 H10 **Atatürk** ✕ (İstanbul) İstanbul, NW Turkey *40.58N 28.50E*
143 N16 **Atatürk Barajı** ⊠ S Turkey
Atax *see* Aude
82 G8 **Atbara** *var.* 'Aṭbārah. River Nile, NE Sudan *17.42N 34.00E*
82 H8 **Atbara** *var.* Nahr 'Aṭbarah. ≈ Eritrea/Sudan
'Aṭbārah/'Aṭbarah, Nahr *see* Atbara
151 P9 **Atbasar** Akmola, N Kazakhstan *51.49N 68.18E*
At-Bashi *see* At-Bashy
153 W9 **At-Bashy** *var.* At-Bashi. Narynskaya Oblast', C Kyrgyzstan *41.07N 75.48E*
24 I10 **Atchafalaya Bay** *bay* Louisiana, S USA
24 I8 **Atchafalaya River** ≈ Louisiana, S USA
Atchin *see* Aceh
29 Q3 **Atchison** Kansas, C USA *39.31N 95.07W*
79 P16 **Atebubu** C Ghana *7.47N 1.00W*
107 Q6 **Ateca** Aragón, NE Spain *41.19N 1.49W*
42 K11 **Atengo, Río** ≈ C Mexico
Aternum *see* Pescara
109 K15 **Atessa** Abruzzo, C Italy *42.03N 14.25E*
Ateste *see* Este
101 E19 **Ath** *var.* Aat. Hainaut, SW Belgium *50.37N 3.46E*
9 Q13 **Athabasca** Alberta, SW Canada *54.43N 113.15W*
9 Q12 **Athabasca** *var.* Athabaska. ≈ Alberta, SW Canada
9 R10 **Athabasca, Lake** ◎ Alberta/Saskatchewan, SW Canada
Athabaska *see* Athabasca
117 C16 **Athamánon** ▲▲ C Greece
99 F17 **Athboy** *Ir.* Baile Átha Buí. E Ireland *53.37N 6.54W*
Athenae *see* Athína
99 C18 **Athenry** *Ir.* Baile Átha an Rí. W Ireland *53.19N 8.49W*
25 P2 **Athens** Alabama, S USA *34.48N 86.58W*
25 T3 **Athens** Georgia, SE USA *33.57N 83.24W*
33 T14 **Athens** Ohio, N USA *39.19N 82.06W*
22 M10 **Athens** Tennessee, S USA *35.26N 84.35W*
27 V7 **Athens** Texas, SW USA *32.12N 95.51W*
Athens *see* Athína
117 B18 **Athéras, Akrotírio** *headland* Kefallinía, Iónioi Nísoi, Greece, C Mediterranean Sea *38.20N 20.24E*
189 W4 **Atherton** Queensland, NE Australia *17.18S 145.29E*
83 I19 **Athi** ≈ S Kenya
124 O3 **Athíenou** SE Cyprus *35.01N 33.31E*
117 H19 **Athína** *Eng.* Athens; *prev.* Athínai, *anc.* Athenae. ● (Greece) Attikí, C Greece *37.58N 23.44E*
Athínai *see* Athína
145 S10 **Athīyah** C Iraq *32.01N 44.04E*
99 D18 **Athlone** *Ir.* Baile Átha Luain. C Ireland *53.25N 7.55W*
161 F16 **Athni** Karnātaka, W India *16.43N 75.04E*
193 C23 **Athol** Southland, South Island, NZ *45.30S 168.35E*
21 N11 **Athol** Massachusetts, NE USA *42.35N 72.11W*
117 I15 **Áthos** ▲ NE Greece *40.10N 24.21E*
Athos, Mount *see* Ágion Óros
Ath Thawrah *see* Madīnat ath Thawrah
147 P5 **Ath Thumāmī** *spring/well* N Saudi Arabia *27.56N 45.06E*
101 L25 **Athus** Luxembourg, SE Belgium *49.34N 5.49E*
99 E19 **Athy** *Ir.* Baile Átha Í. C Ireland *52.58N 6.58W*
80 I10 **Ati** Batha, C Chad *13.10N 18.19E*
83 F16 **Atiak** NW Uganda *3.13N 32.04E*
59 G17 **Atico** Arequipa, SW Peru *16.13S 73.13W*
107 O6 **Atienza** Castilla-La Mancha, C Spain *41.12N 2.52W*
41 Q6 **Atigun Pass** *pass* Alaska, USA *68.01N 149.36W*

◆ Country ● Country Capital ◇ Dependent Territory ○ Dependent Territory Capital ◈ Administrative Region ✕ International Airport ▲ Mountain ▲▲ Mountain Range ⛰ Volcano ≈ River ◎ Lake ⊠ Reservoir

10 B12 **Atikokan** Ontario, S Canada *48.45N 91.37W*
11 O9 **Atikonak Lac** ◎ Newfoundland and Labrador, E Canada
44 C6 **Atitlán, Lago de** ◎ W Guatemala
202 L16 **Atiu** *island* S Cook Islands
Atjeh *see* Aceh
127 O9 **Atka** Magadanskaya Oblast', E Russian Federation *60.45N 151.34E*
40 H17 **Atka** Atka Island, Alaska, USA *52.12N 174.13W*
40 H17 **Atka Island** *island* Aleutian Islands, Alaska, USA
131 O7 **Atkarsk** Saratovskaya Oblast', W Russian Federation *52.15N 43.48E*
29 U11 **Atkins** Arkansas, C USA *35.15N 92.56W*
31 O13 **Atkinson** Nebraska, C USA *42.31N 98.57W*
176 U10 **Atkri** Papua, E Indonesia *1.45S 130.04E*
43 O13 **Atlacomulco** *var.* Atlacomulco de Fabela. México, C Mexico *19.48N 99.52W*
Atlacomulco de Fabela *see* Atlacomulco
25 S3 **Atlanta** *state capital* Georgia, SE USA *33.45N 84.22W*
33 R6 **Atlanta** Michigan, N USA *45.01N 84.07W*
27 X6 **Atlanta** Texas, SW USA *33.06N 94.09W*
31 T15 **Atlantic** Iowa, C USA *41.24N 95.00W*
23 Y10 **Atlantic** North Carolina, SE USA *34.52N 76.20W*
25 W8 **Atlantic Beach** Florida, SE USA *30.19N 81.24W*
20 J17 **Atlantic City** New Jersey, NE USA *39.22N 74.27W*
180 L14 **Atlantic-Indian Basin** *undersea feature* SW Indian Ocean
180 K13 **Atlantic-Indian Ridge** *undersea feature* SW Indian Ocean
56 E4 **Atlántico** *off.* Departamento del Atlántico. ◈ *province* NW Colombia
66-67 **Atlantic Ocean** *ocean*
44 K7 **Atlántico Norte, Región Autónoma** *prev.* Zelaya Norte. ◈ *autonomous region* NE Nicaragua
44 L10 **Atlántico Sur, Región Autónoma** *prev.* Zelaya Sur. ◈ *autonomous region* SE Nicaragua
44 I5 **Atlántida** ◈ *department* N Honduras
79 Y15 **Atlantika Mountains** ▲▲ E Nigeria
66 J10 **Atlantis Fracture Zone** *tectonic feature* NW Atlantic Ocean
76 H7 **Atlas Mountains** ▲▲ NW Africa
127 Pp13 **Atlasova, Ostrov** *island* SE Russian Federation
127 Pp10 **Atlasovo** Kamchatskaya Oblast', E Russian Federation *55.42N 159.34E*
123 H13 **Atlas Saharien** *var.* Saharan Atlas. ▲▲ Algeria/Morocco
Atlas, Tell *see* Atlas Tellien
123 Gg10 **Atlas Tellien** *Eng.* Tell Atlas. ▲▲ N Algeria
8 I9 **Atlin** British Columbia, W Canada *59.31N 133.40W*
8 I9 **Atlin Lake** ◎ British Columbia, W Canada
43 P14 **Atlixco** Puebla, S Mexico *18.55N 98.25W*
96 B11 **Atløyna** *island* S Norway
161 I17 **Ātmakūr** Andhra Pradesh, C India *15.52N 78.42E*
25 O8 **Atmore** Alabama, S USA *31.01N 87.29W*
103 J20 **Atmühl** ≈ S Germany
96 H11 **Atna** ≈ S Norway
170 E12 **Atō** Yamaguchi, Honshū, SW Japan *34.24N 131.42E*
59 L21 **Atocha** Potosí, S Bolivia *20.55S 66.13W*
29 P12 **Atoka** Oklahoma, C USA *34.23N 96.07W*
29 O12 **Atoka Lake** *var.* Atoka Reservoir. ⊠ Oklahoma, C USA
Atoka Reservoir *see* Atoka Lake
35 Q14 **Atomic City** Idaho, NW USA *43.26N 112.48W*
42 L10 **Atotonilco** Zacatecas, C Mexico *24.12N 102.46W*
42 M13 **Atotonilco el Alto** *var.* Atotonilco. Jalisco, SW Mexico *20.32N 102.27W*
79 N7 **Atouila, 'Erg** *desert* N Mali
43 N16 **Atoyac** *var.* Atoyac de Alvarez. Guerrero, S Mexico *17.10N 100.27W*
Atoyac de Alvarez *see* Atoyac
43 P15 **Atoyac, Río** ≈ S Mexico
41 O5 **Atqasuk** Alaska, USA *70.28N 157.24W*
152 C13 **Atrak** *Per.* Rūd-e Atrak, *Rus.* Atrek, *Turkm.* Etrek. ≈ Iran/Turkmenistan
Atrak, Rūd-e *see* Atrak
97 J20 **Ätran** ≈ S Sweden
56 C7 **Atrato, Río** ≈ NW Colombia
Atrek *see* Atrak
109 K14 **Atri** Abruzzo, C Italy *42.34N 13.58E*
Atria *see* Adria
171 Jj16 **Atsugi** *var.* Atugi. Kanagawa, Honshū, S Japan *35.27N 139.21E*
171 L12 **Atsumi** Yamagata, Honshū, C Japan *38.38N 139.36E*
172 Oo4 **Atsuta** Hokkaidō, NE Japan *43.28N 141.24E*
176 Y13 **Atsy** Papua, E Indonesia *5.40S 138.19E*
149 Q17 **Aṭ Ṭaff** *desert* C UAE
144 G12 **Aṭ Ṭafilah** *var.* Et Tafila, Tafila. Aṭ Ṭafilah, W Jordan *30.52N 35.36E*
144 G12 **Aṭ Ṭafilah** *off.* Muḥāfaẓat aṭ Ṭafilah. ◈ *governorate* W Jordan
146 L10 **Aṭ Ṭā'if** Makkah, W Saudi Arabia *21.49N 40.49E*
Attaleia/Attalia *see* Antalya
25 Q3 **Attalla** Alabama, S USA *34.01N 86.05W*
144 L2 **At Tall al Abyaḍ** *var.* Tall al Abyaḍ, Tell Abyad, *Fr.* Tell Abiad. Ar Raqqah, N Syria *36.36N 34.00E*
144 L7 **At Tanf** Ḥimṣ, S Syria *33.29N 38.39E*
Attapu *see* Samakhixai
145 S10 **At Ṭaqṭaqānah** C Iraq *32.03N 43.54E*
117 O23 **Attávytos** ▲ Ródos, Dodekánisos, Greece, Aegean Sea *36.10N 27.50E*
145 V15 **At Tawal** *desert* Iraq/Saudi Arabia
10 G9 **Attawapiskat** Ontario, C Canada *52.55N 82.25W*
10 F9 **Attawapiskat** ≈ Ontario, S Canada
10 D9 **Attawapiskat Lake** ◎ Ontario, C Canada
At Taybé *see* Ṭayyibah
103 F16 **Attendorn** Nordrhein-Westfalen, W Germany *51.07N 7.54E*
111 R5 **Attersee** Salzburg, NW Austria *47.55N 13.31E*
111 R5 **Attersee** ◎ N Austria
101 L24 **Attert** Luxembourg, SE Belgium *49.45N 5.47E*
144 M4 **At Tibnī** *var.* Tibnī. Dayr az Zawr, NE Syria *35.30N 39.48E*
33 N13 **Attica** Indiana, N USA *40.17N 87.15W*
20 E10 **Attica** New York, NE USA *42.51N 78.13W*
Attica *see* Attikí
11 N7 **Attikamagen Lake** ◎ Newfoundland and Labrador, E Canada
117 H20 **Attikí** *Eng.* Attica. ◈ *region* C Greece
21 O12 **Attleboro** Massachusetts, NE USA *41.55N 71.15W*
111 R5 **Attnang** Oberösterreich, N Austria *48.01N 13.43E*
155 U6 **Attock City** Punjab, E Pakistan *33.52N 72.19E*
Attopeu *see* Samakhixai
27 X8 **Attoyac River** ≈ Texas, SW USA
40 D16 **Attu** Attu Island, Alaska, USA *52.53N 173.18E*
145 Y12 **Aṭ Ṭūbah** E Iraq *30.29N 47.28E*
146 K4 **Aṭ Ṭubayq** *plain* Jordan/Saudi Arabia
40 C16 **Attu Island** *island* Aleutian Islands, Alaska, USA
Aṭ Ṭūr *see* El Ṭûr
161 I21 **Āttūr** Tamil Nādu, SE India *11.34N 78.39E*
147 N17 **At Turbah** SW Yemen *12.42N 43.31E*
64 I12 **Atuel, Río** ≈ C Argentina
Atugi *see* Atsugi
203 X7 **Atuona** Hiva Oa, NE French Polynesia *9.46S 139.03W*
Aturus *see* Adour
97 M18 **Åtvidaberg** Östergötland, S Sweden *58.12N 16.00E*
37 P9 **Atwater** California, W USA *37.19N 120.33W*
31 T8 **Atwater** Minnesota, N USA *45.08N 94.48W*
28 I2 **Atwood** Kansas, C USA *39.48N 101.02W*
33 U12 **Atwood Lake** ⊠ Ohio, N USA
131 P5 **Atyashevo** Respublika Mordoviya, W Russian Federation *54.36N 46.04E*
150 F12 **Atyrau** *prev.* Gur'yev. Atyrau, W Kazakhstan *47.07N 51.55E*
150 E11 **Atyrau** *off.* Atyrauskaya Oblast', *var. Kaz.* Atyraū Oblysy; *prev.* Gur'yevskaya Oblast'. ◈ *province* W Kazakhstan
Atyraū Oblysy/Atyrauskaya Oblast' *see* Atyrau
110 J7 **Au** Vorarlberg, NW Austria *47.19N 10.01E*
194 G8 **Aua Island** *island* NW PNG
105 S16 **Aubagne** *anc.* Albania. Bouches-du-Rhône, SE France *43.16N 5.34E*
101 L25 **Aubange** Luxembourg, SE Belgium *49.34N 5.48E*
105 Q6 **Aube** ◈ *department* N France
105 R6 **Aube** ≈ N France
101 L19 **Aubel** Liège, E Belgium *50.45N 5.49E*
105 Q13 **Aubenas** Ardèche, E France *44.37N 4.24E*
105 O8 **Aubigny-sur-Nère** Cher, C France *47.30N 2.27E*
105 O13 **Aubin** Aveyron, S France *44.30N 2.18E*
105 O13 **Aubrac, Monts d'** ▲▲ S France
38 J10 **Aubrey Cliffs** *cliff* Arizona, SW USA
25 R5 **Auburn** Alabama, S USA *32.37N 85.30W*
37 P6 **Auburn** California, W USA *38.53N 121.03W*
32 K14 **Auburn** Illinois, N USA *39.35N 89.45W*
33 Q11 **Auburn** Indiana, N USA *41.22N 85.03W*
22 J7 **Auburn** Kentucky, S USA *36.52N 86.42W*
21 P8 **Auburn** Maine, NE USA *44.05N 70.15W*
21 N11 **Auburn** Massachusetts, NE USA *42.11N 71.47W*
31 S16 **Auburn** Nebraska, C USA *40.23N 95.50W*
20 H10 **Auburn** New York, NE USA *42.55N 76.31W*
34 H8 **Auburn** Washington, NW USA *47.18N 122.13W*
105 N11 **Aubusson** Creuse, C France *45.58N 2.10E*
120 E10 **Auce** *Ger.* Autz. Dobele, SW Latvia *56.28N 22.54E*
104 L15 **Auch** *Lat.* Augusta Auscorum, Elimberrum. Gers, S France *43.39N 0.37E*
79 U16 **Auchi** Edo, S Nigeria *7.01N 6.17E*
25 T9 **Aucilla River** ≈ Florida/Georgia, SE USA
192 L6 **Auckland** Auckland, North Island, NZ *36.53S 174.46E*
192 K5 **Auckland** *off.* Auckland Region. ◈ *region* North Island, NZ
192 L6 **Auckland** ✈ Auckland, North Island, NZ *37.01S 174.49E*
199 Ii15 **Auckland Islands** *island group* S NZ
105 O16 **Aude** ◈ *department* S France
105 N16 **Aude** *anc.* Atax. ≈ S France
Audenarde *see* Oudenaarde
Audern *see* Audru
104 E6 **Audierne** Finistère, NW France *48.01N 4.30W*
104 E6 **Audierne, Baie d'** *bay* NW France
105 U7 **Audincourt** Doubs, E France *47.28N 6.49E*
120 G5 **Audru** *Ger.* Audern. Pärnumaa, SW Estonia *58.25N 24.21E*
31 T14 **Audubon** Iowa, C USA *41.44N 94.56W*
103 N17 **Aue** Sachsen, E Germany *50.34N 12.42E*
102 H12 **Aue** ≈ NW Germany
102 L9 **Auerbach** Bayern, SE Germany *49.41N 11.41E*
103 M17 **Auerbach** Sachsen, E Germany *50.30N 12.24E*
110 I10 **Auererrhein** ≈ SW Switzerland
103 N17 **Auersberg** ▲ E Germany
189 W9 **Augathella** Queensland, E Australia *25.54S 146.38E*
33 Q12 **Auglaize River** ≈ Ohio, N USA
85 F22 **Augrabies Falls** *waterfall* W South Africa *28.37S 20.24E*
33 R7 **Au Gres River** ≈ Michigan, N USA
Augsbourg *see* Augsburg
103 K22 **Augsburg** *Fr.* Augsbourg; *anc.* Augusta Vindelicorum. Bayern, S Germany *48.22N 10.54E*
188 I14 **Augusta** Western Australia *34.18S 115.10E*
109 L25 **Augusta** *It.* Agosta. Sicilia, Italy, C Mediterranean Sea *37.19N 15.13E*
29 W11 **Augusta** Arkansas, C USA *35.16N 91.22W*
25 V3 **Augusta** Georgia, SE USA *33.29N 81.58W*
29 O6 **Augusta** Kansas, C USA *37.40N 96.59W*
21 Q7 **Augusta** *state capital* Maine, NE USA *44.19N 69.44W*
35 Q8 **Augusta** Montana, NW USA *47.28N 112.23W*
Augusta *see* London
Augusta Auscorum *see* Auch
Augusta Emerita *see* Mérida
Augusta Praetoria *see* Aosta
Augusta Suessionum *see* Soissons
Augusta Trajana *see* Stara Zagora
Augusta Treverorum *see* Trier
Augusta Vangionum *see* Worms
Augusta Vindelicorum *see* Augsburg
97 G24 **Augustenborg** *Ger.* Augustenburg. Sønderjylland, SW Denmark *54.57N 9.52E*
Augustenburg *see* Augustenborg
41 Q13 **Augustine Island** *island* Alaska, USA
12 L9 **Augustines, Lac des** ◎ Quebec, SE Canada
Augustobona Tricassium *see* Troyes
Augustodunum *see* Autun
Augustodurum *see* Bayeux
Augustoritum Lemovicensium *see* Limoges
112 O8 **Augustów** *Rus.* Avgustov. Podlaskie, NE Poland *53.51N 22.58E*
Augustow Canal *see* Augustowski, Kanał
112 O8 **Augustowski, Kanał** *Eng.* Augustow Canal, *Rus.* Avgustovskiy Kanal. *canal* NE Poland
188 I9 **Augustus, Mount** ▲ Western Australia *24.42S 117.42E*
195 X15 **Auki** Malaita, N Solomon Islands *8.48S 160.45E*
23 W8 **Aulander** North Carolina, SE USA *36.15N 77.16W*
188 L7 **Auld, Lake** *salt lake* Western Australia
Aulie Ata/Auliye-Ata *see* Taraz
108 E10 **Aulla** Toscana, C Italy *44.15N 10.00E*
104 F6 **Aulne** ≈ NW France
Aulong *see* Ulong
39 T3 **Ault** Colorado, C USA *40.34N 104.43W*
97 F22 **Aulum** *var.* Avlum. Ringkøbing, C Denmark *56.16N 8.48E*
105 N3 **Aumale** Seine-Maritime, N France *49.45N 1.43E*
Auminzatau, Gory *see* Ovminzatovo Tog'lari
79 T14 **Auna** Niger, W Nigeria *10.13N 4.43E*
97 H21 **Auning** Århus, C Denmark *56.25N 10.22E*
198 Cc9 **Aunu'u Island** *island* W American Samoa
85 E20 **Auob** *var.* Oup. ≈ Namibia/South Africa
95 K19 **Aura** Länsi-Suomi, W Finland *60.37N 22.34E*
111 R5 **Aurach** ≈ N Austria
Aural, Phnom *see* Aôral, Phnum
159 O14 **Aurangābād** Bihār, N India *24.48N 84.22E*
160 F13 **Aurangābād** Mahārāshtra, C India *19.52N 75.22E*
201 V7 **Aur Atoll** *atoll* E Marshall Islands
104 G7 **Auray** Morbihan, NW France *47.40N 2.58W*
96 G13 **Aurdal** Oppland, S Norway *60.51N 9.25E*
96 F8 **Aure** Møre og Romsdal, S Norway *63.16N 8.31E*
31 T12 **Aurelia** Iowa, C USA *42.42N 95.26W*
Aurelia Aquensis *see* Baden-Baden
Aurelianum *see* Orléans
123 J12 **Aurès, Massif de l'** ▲▲ NE Algeria
102 F10 **Aurich** Niedersachsen, NW Germany *53.28N 7.28E*
105 O13 **Aurillac** Cantal, C France *44.55N 2.25E*
Aurine, Alpi *see* Zillertaler Alpen
Aurium *see* Ourense
12 H15 **Aurora** Ontario, S Canada *44.00N 79.26W*
57 S8 **Aurora** NW Guyana *6.46N 59.45W*
39 T4 **Aurora** Colorado, C USA *39.42N 104.51W*
32 M11 **Aurora** Illinois, N USA *41.45N 88.19W*
33 Q15 **Aurora** Indiana, N USA *39.01N 84.55W*
31 W4 **Aurora** Minnesota, N USA *47.31N 92.14W*
29 S8 **Aurora** Missouri, C USA *36.58N 93.43W*
31 P16 **Aurora** Nebraska, C USA *40.52N 98.00W*
38 J5 **Aurora** Utah, W USA *38.55N 111.55W*
Aurora *see* Maéwo, Vanuatu
Aurora *see* San Francisco, Philippines
96 F10 **Aursjøen** ◎ S Norway
96 I9 **Aursunden** ◎ S Norway
85 D21 **Aus** Karas, SW Namibia *26.37S 16.18E*
Ausa *see* Vic
12 E16 **Ausable** ≈ Ontario, S Canada
33 O3 **Au Sable Point** *headland* Michigan, N USA *46.40N 86.08W*
33 S7 **Au Sable Point** *headland* Michigan, N USA *44.19N 83.20W*
33 R6 **Au Sable River** ≈ Michigan, N USA
59 H16 **Ausangate, Nevado** ▲ C Peru *13.46S 71.13W*
Auschwitz *see* Oświęcim
Ausculum Apulum *see* Ascoli Satriano
107 Q4 **Ausejo** La Rioja, N Spain *42.21N 2.10W*
Aussig *see* Ústí nad Labem
97 F17 **Aust-Agder** ◈ *county* S Norway
94 P2 **Austfonna** *glacier* NE Svalbard
33 P15 **Austin** Indiana, N USA *38.45N 85.48W*
31 W11 **Austin** Minnesota, N USA *43.40N 92.58W*
37 U5 **Austin** Nevada, W USA *39.28N 117.04W*
27 S10 **Austin** *state capital* Texas, S USA *30.16N 97.44W*
188 J10 **Austin, Lake** *salt lake* Western Australia
33 V11 **Austintown** Ohio, N USA *41.06N 80.45W*
27 V9 **Austonio** Texas, SW USA *31.09N 95.39W*
Australes, Archipel des *see* Australes, Îles
Australes et Antarctiques Françaises, Terres *see* French Southern and Antarctic Territories
203 T14 **Australes, Îles** *var.* Archipel des Australes, Îles Tubuai, Tubuai Islands, *Eng.* Austral Islands. *island group* SW French Polynesia
183 Y11 **Austral Fracture Zone** *tectonic feature* S Pacific Ocean
189 O7 **Australia** *off.* Commonwealth of Australia. ◆ *commonwealth republic*
182 M8 **Australia** *continent*
191 Q12 **Australian Alps** ▲▲ SE Australia
191 R11 **Australian Capital Territory** *prev.* Federal Capital Territory. ◈ *territory* SE Australia
Australie, Bassin Nord de l' *see* North Australian Basin
Austral Islands *see* Australes, Îles
Austrava *see* Ostrov
111 T6 **Austria** *off.* Republic of Austria, *Ger.* Österreich. ◆ *republic* C Europe
94 K3 **Austurland** ◈ *region* SE Iceland
94 G10 **Austvågøya** *island* C Norway
60 G13 **Autazes** Amazonas, N Brazil *3.37S 59.07W*
104 M16 **Auterive** Haute-Garonne, S France *43.22N 1.28E*
Autesiodorum *see* Auxerre
105 N2 **Authie** ≈ N France
Autissiodorum *see* Auxerre
42 K14 **Autlán** *var.* Autlán de Navarro. Jalisco, SW Mexico *19.46N 104.22W*
Autlán de Navarro *see* Autlán
Autricum *see* Chartres
105 Q9 **Autun** *anc.* Ædua, Augustodunum. Saône-et-Loire, C France *46.57N 4.18E*
Autz *see* Auce
101 H20 **Auvelais** Namur, S Belgium *50.27N 4.37E*
105 P11 **Auvergne** ◈ *region* C France
104 M12 **Auvézère** ≈ W France
105 P7 **Auxerre** *anc.* Autesiodorum, Autissiodorum. Yonne, C France *47.48N 3.34E*
105 N2 **Auxi-le-Château** Pas-de-Calais, N France *50.14N 2.06E*
105 S8 **Auxonne** Côte d'Or, C France *47.12N 5.22E*
57 P9 **Auyan Tebuy** ▲ SE Venezuela *5.48N 62.27W*
105 O10 **Auzances** Creuse, C France *46.01N 2.29E*
29 U8 **Ava** Missouri, C USA *36.57N 92.39W*
148 M5 **Āvaj** Qazvīn, N Iran
97 C15 **Avaldsnes** Rogaland, S Norway *59.21N 5.16E*
105 Q8 **Avallon** Yonne, C France *47.30N 3.54E*
104 K6 **Avaloirs, Mont des** ▲ NW France *48.27N 0.11W*
37 S16 **Avalon** Santa Catalina Island, California, W USA *33.20N 118.19W*
20 J17 **Avalon** New Jersey, NE USA *39.04N 74.42W*
11 V13 **Avalon Peninsula** *peninsula* Newfoundland and Labrador, E Canada
207 Q11 **Avannaarsua** ◈ *province* N Greenland
62 K10 **Avaré** São Paulo, S Brazil *23.06S 48.57W*
Avaricum *see* Bourges
202 H16 **Avarua** ○ (Cook Islands) Rarotonga, S Cook Islands *21.12S 159.46W*
202 H16 **Avarua Harbour** *harbor* Rarotonga, S Cook Islands
Avasfelsőfalu *see* Negrești-Oaș
40 L17 **Avatanak Island** *island* Aleutian Islands, Alaska, USA
202 B16 **Avatele** S Niue *19.06S 169.55E*
202 H16 **Avatiu** Rarotonga, S Cook Islands *21.12S 159.46W*
202 H15 **Avatiu Harbour** *harbor* Rarotonga, S Cook Islands
Avdeyevka *see* Avdiyivka
116 J13 **Ávdira** Anatolikí Makedonía kai Thráki, NE Greece *40.58N 24.58E*
119 X8 **Avdiyivka** *Rus.* Avdeyevka. Donets'ka Oblast', SE Ukraine *48.05N 37.45E*
168 K7 **Avdzaga** C Mongolia *47.43N 103.30E*
106 G6 **Ave** ≈ N Portugal
106 G7 **Aveiro** *anc.* Talabriga. Aveiro, W Portugal *40.37N 8.40W*
106 G7 **Aveiro** ◈ *district* N Portugal
Avela *see* Ávila
101 D18 **Avelgem** West-Vlaanderen, W Belgium *50.46N 3.25E*
63 D20 **Avellaneda** Buenos Aires, E Argentina *34.43S 58.23W*
109 L17 **Avellino** *anc.* Abellinum. Campania, S Italy *40.54N 14.46E*
37 Q12 **Avenal** California, W USA *36.00N 120.07W*
Avenio *see* Avignon
96 E8 **Averøya** *island* S Norway
109 K17 **Aversa** Campania, S Italy *40.58N 14.13E*
35 N9 **Avery** Idaho, NW USA *47.14N 115.48W*
27 W5 **Avery** Texas, SW USA *33.33N 94.46W*
Aves, Islas de *see* Las Aves, Islas
Avesnes *see* Avesnes-sur-Helpe
105 Q2 **Avesnes-sur-Helpe** *var.* Avesnes. Nord, N France *50.07N 3.57E*
66 G12 **Aves Ridge** *undersea feature* SE Caribbean Sea
97 M14 **Avesta** Dalarna, C Sweden *60.09N 16.10E*
105 O14 **Aveyron** ◈ *department* S France
105 N14 **Aveyron** ≈ S France
109 J15 **Avezzano** Abruzzo, C Italy *42.01N 13.25E*
117 D16 **Avgó** ▲ C Greece *39.31N 21.24E*
Avgustov *see* Augustów
Avgustovskiy Kanal *see* Augustowski, Kanał
98 J9 **Aviemore** N Scotland, UK *57.06N 4.01W*
193 F21 **Aviemore, Lake** ◎ South Island, NZ
105 R15 **Avignon** *anc.* Avenio. Vaucluse, SE France *43.57N 4.49E*
106 M7 **Ávila** *var.* Avila; *anc.* Abela, Abula, Abyla, Avela. Castilla-León, C Spain *40.39N 4.42W*
106 L8 **Ávila** ◈ *province* Castilla-León, C Spain
106 K2 **Avilés** Asturias, NW Spain *43.33N 5.55W*
120 J4 **Avinurme** *Ger.* Awwinorm. Ida-Virumaa, NE Estonia *58.58N 26.52E*
106 H10 **Avis** Portalegre, C Portugal *39.03N 7.52W*
Avlum *see* Aulum
190 M11 **Avoca** Victoria, SE Australia *37.09S 143.34E*
31 T14 **Avoca** Iowa, C USA *41.27N 95.20W*
190 M11 **Avoca River** ≈ Victoria, SE Australia
109 L25 **Avola** Sicilia, Italy, C Mediterranean Sea *36.54N 15.07E*
20 F10 **Avon** New York, NE USA *42.53N 77.41W*
31 P12 **Avon** South Dakota, N USA *43.00N 98.03W*
99 M23 **Avon** ≈ S England, UK
99 L20 **Avon** ≈ C England, UK
38 K13 **Avondale** Arizona, SW USA *33.25N 112.20W*
25 X13 **Avon Park** Florida, SE USA *27.36N 81.30W*
104 J5 **Avranches** Manche, N France *48.42N 1.21W*
105 O3 **Avre** ≈ N France
195 X16 **Avuavu** *var.* Kolotambu. Guadalcanal, C Solomon Islands *9.52S 160.25E*
Avveel *see* Ivalo, Finland
Avveel *see* Ivalojoki, Finland
Avvil *see* Ivalo
79 O17 **Awaaso** *var.* Awaso. SW Ghana *6.10N 2.18W*
147 X8 **Awābī** *var.* Al 'Awābī. NE Oman *23.19N 57.34E*
170 G15 **Awaji-shima** *island* SW Japan
192 L9 **Awakino** Waikato, North Island, NZ *38.40S 174.37E*
148 M15 **'Awālī** C Bahrain *26.06N 50.33E*
101 K19 **Awans** Liège, E Belgium *50.39N 5.30E*
192 I2 **Awanui** Northland, North Island, NZ *35.01S 173.16E*
154 M14 **Awārān** Baluchistān, SW Pakistan *26.31N 65.10E*
83 K16 **Awara Plain** *plain* NE Kenya
82 M13 **Āwarē** Somali, E Ethiopia *8.12N 44.09E*
144 M6 **'Awāriḍ, Wādī** *dry watercourse* E Syria
193 B20 **Awarua Point** *headland* South Island, NZ *44.15S 168.03E*
83 J14 **Āwasa** Southern, S Ethiopia *6.54N 38.26E*
82 K13 **Āwash** Afar, NE Ethiopia *8.59N 40.15E*
82 K12 **Āwash** *var.* Hawash. ≈ C Ethiopia
171 Kk11 **Awa-shima** *island* C Japan
Awaso *see* Awaaso
164 H7 **Awat** Xinjiang Uygur Zizhiqu, NW China *40.36N 80.22E*
193 J15 **Awatere** ≈ South Island, NZ
77 O10 **Awbārī** SW Libya *26.34N 12.46E*
77 N9 **Awbārī, Idhān** *var.* Edeyen d'Oubari. *desert* Algeria/Libya
82 C13 **Aweil** Northern Bahr el Ghazal, SW Sudan *8.44N 27.25E*
98 H11 **Awe, Loch** ◎ W Scotland, UK
79 U16 **Awka** Anambra, SW Nigeria *6.12N 7.04E*
41 O6 **Awuna River** ≈ Alaska, USA
Awwinorm *see* Avinurme
Ax *see* Dax
Axarfjördhur *see* Öxarfjördhur
105 N17 **Axat** Aude, S France *42.46N 2.13E*
101 F16 **Axel** Zeeland, SW Netherlands *51.16N 3.55E*
207 P9 **Axel Heiberg Island** *var.* Axel Heiburg. *island* Nunavut, N Canada
Axel Heiburg *see* Axel Heiberg Island
79 O17 **Axim** S Ghana *4.52N 2.13W*
116 F13 **Axiós** *var.* Vardar. ≈ Greece/FYR Macedonia *see also* Vardar
105 N17 **Ax-les-Thermes** Ariège, S France *42.43N 1.49E*
171 Gg14 **Ayabe** Kyōto, Honshū, SW Japan *35.16N 135.15E*
122 F13 **Ayachi, Jbel** ▲ C Morocco *32.30N 5.00W*
63 D22 **Ayacucho** Buenos Aires, E Argentina *37.09S 58.30W*
59 F15 **Ayacucho** Ayacucho, S Peru *13.10S 74.15W*
59 E16 **Ayacucho** *off.* Departamento de Ayacucho. ◈ *department* SW Peru
151 W11 **Ayagoz** *var.* Ayaguz, *Kaz.* Ayaköz; *prev.* Sergiopol. Vostochnyy Kazakhstan, E Kazakhstan *47.54N 80.25E*
151 V12 **Ayagoz** *var.* Ayaguz, *Kaz.* Ayaköz. ≈ E Kazakhstan
Ayaguz *see* Ayagoz
Ayakagytma *see* Oyoqog'itma
Ayakkuduk *see* Oyoqquduq
164 L10 **Ayakkum Hu** ◎ NW China
Ayaköz *see* Ayagoz
106 H14 **Ayamonte** Andalucía, S Spain *37.13N 7.24W*
127 N12 **Ayan** Khabarovskiy Kray, E Russian Federation *56.27N 138.09E*
142 J10 **Ayancık** Sinop, N Turkey *41.55N 34.34E*
57 S9 **Ayanganna Mountain** ▲ C Guyana *5.21N 59.54W*
79 U16 **Ayangba** Kogi, C Nigeria *7.36N 7.10E*
127 P6 **Ayanka** Koryakskiy Avtonomnyy Okrug, E Russian Federation *63.42N 167.31E*
56 E7 **Ayapel** Córdoba, NW Colombia *8.17N 75.13W*
142 H12 **Ayaş** Ankara, N Turkey *40.01N 32.21E*
59 I16 **Ayaviri** Puno, S Peru *14.52S 70.34W*
155 P3 **Āybak** *var.* Aibak, Haibak; *prev.* Samangān. Samangān, NE Afghanistan *36.16N 68.04E*
153 N10 **Aydarko'l Ko'li** *Rus.* Ozero Aydarkul'. ◎ C Uzbekistan
Aydarkul', Ozero *see* Aydarko'l Ko'li
23 W10 **Ayden** North Carolina, SE USA *35.28N 77.25W*
142 C15 **Aydın** *var.* Aïdin; *anc.* Tralles. Aydın, SW Turkey *37.51N 27.51E*
142 C15 **Aydın** *var.* Aïdin. ◈ *province* SW Turkey
142 I17 **Aydıncık** İçel, S Turkey *36.10N 33.16E*
142 C15 **Aydın Dağları** ▲▲ W Turkey
164 L6 **Aydingkol Hu** ◎ NW China
131 X7 **Aydyrlinskiy** Orenburgskaya Oblast', W Russian Federation *52.03N 59.54E*
107 S4 **Ayerbe** Aragón, NE Spain *42.16N 0.40W*
Ayers Rock *see* Uluru
Ayeyarwady *see* Irrawaddy
Ayia Napa *see* Agía Nápa
Ayia Phyla *see* Agía Fýlaxis
Ayiásos/Ayiássos *see* Agiasós
Áyios Evstrátios *see* Ágios Efstrátios
Áyios Kírikos *see* Ágios Kírykos
Áyios Nikólaos *see* Ágios Nikólaos
Ayios Seryios *see* Yeniboğaziçi
82 I11 **Āykel** Amhara, N Ethiopia *12.33N 37.01E*
126 K10 **Aykhal** Respublika Sakha (Yakutiya), NE Russian Federation *66.07N 110.25E*
12 J12 **Aylen Lake** ◎ Ontario, SE Canada
99 N21 **Aylesbury** SE England, UK *51.49N 0.49W*
107 O6 **Ayllón** Castilla-León, N Spain *41.25N 3.22W*
12 F17 **Aylmer** Ontario, S Canada *42.46N 80.57W*
12 L12 **Aylmer** Quebec, SE Canada *45.22N 75.51W*
13 R12 **Aylmer, Lac** ◎ Quebec, SE Canada
15 J6 **Aylmer Lake** ◎ Northwest Territories, NW Canada
151 V14 **Aynabulak** Almaty, SE Kazakhstan *44.37N 77.58E*
144 K2 **'Ayn al 'Arab** Ḥalab, N Syria *36.55N 38.21E*
Aynayn *see* 'Aynīn
145 V12 **'Ayn Ḥamūd** S Iraq *30.51N 45.37E*
153 P12 **Ayní** *prev. Rus.* Varzimanor Ayni. W Tajikistan *39.24N 68.30E*
146 M10 **'Aynīn** *var.* Aynayn. *spring/well* SW Saudi Arabia *20.52N 41.41E*
23 U12 **Aynor** South Carolina, SE USA *33.59N 79.11W*
145 Q7 **'Ayn Zāzūh** C Iraq *33.29N 42.34E*
159 N12 **Ayodhya** Uttar Pradesh, N India *26.46N 82.12E*
127 O5 **Ayon, Ostrov** *island* NE Russian Federation
107 R11 **Ayora** País Valenciano, E Spain *39.04N 1.04W*
79 Q11 **Ayorou** Tillabéri, W Niger *14.44N 0.54E*
81 E16 **Ayos** Centre, S Cameroon *3.52N 12.31E*
78 L5 **'Ayoûn 'Abd el Mâlek** *well* N Mauritania *24.51N 7.38W*
78 K10 **'Ayoûn el 'Atroûs** *var.* Aïoun el Atrous, Aïoun el Atroûss. Hodh el Gharbi, SE Mauritania *16.37N 9.36W*
98 I13 **Ayr** W Scotland, UK *55.28N 4.37W*
98 I13 **Ayr** ≈ W Scotland, UK
98 I13 **Ayrshire** *cultural region* SW Scotland, UK
Aysen *see* Aisén
82 L12 **Āysha** Somali, E Ethiopia *10.36N 42.31E*
150 L14 **Ayteke Bi** *Kaz.* Zhangaqazaly *prev.* Novokazalinsk. Kyzylorda, SW Kazakhstan *45.52N 62.09E*
152 K8 **Aytim** Navoiy Viloyati, N Uzbekistan *42.15N 63.25E*
189 W4 **Ayton** Queensland, NE Australia *15.54S 145.19E*
116 M9 **Aytos** Burgas, E Bulgaria *42.43N 27.13E*
176 Uu7 **Ayu, Kepulauan** *island group* E Indonesia
A Yun Pa *see* Cheo Reo
175 O8 **Ayu, Tanjung** *headland* Borneo, N Indonesia *0.25N 117.34E*
42 K13 **Ayutla** Jalisco, C Mexico *20.07N 104.18W*
43 P16 **Ayutlá** *var.* Ayutla de los Libres. Guerrero, S Mexico *16.56N 99.22W*
Ayutla de los Libres *see* Ayutlá
178 H11 **Ayutthaya** *var.* Phra Nakhon Si Ayutthaya. Phra Nakhon Si Ayutthaya, C Thailand *14.19N 100.34E*
142 B13 **Ayvalık** Balıkesir, W Turkey *39.18N 26.42E*
101 L20 **Aywaille** Liège, E Belgium *50.28N 5.40E*
147 R13 **'Aywat aş Şay'ar, Wādī** *seasonal river* N Yemen
Azaffal *see* Azeffâl
107 T9 **Azahar, Costa del** *coastal region* E Spain
107 S6 **Azaila** Aragón, NE Spain *41.16N 0.30W*
106 F10 **Azambuja** Lisboa, C Portugal *39.04N 8.52W*
159 N13 **Āzamgarh** Uttar Pradesh, N India *26.03N 83.10E*
79 O9 **Azaouâd** *desert* C Mali
79 S10 **Azaouagh, Vallée de l'** *var.* Azaouak. ≈ W Niger
Azaouak *see* Azaouagh, Vallée de l'
63 F14 **Azara** Misiones, NE Argentina *28.03S 55.42W*
148 K3 **Āzarān** Āzarbāyjān-e Khāvarī, N Iran *37.34N 47.10E*
Azärbaycan/Azärbaycan Respublikası *see* Azerbaijan
Āzarbāyjān-e Bākhtarī *see* Āzarbāyjān-e Gharbī
148 I4 **Āzarbāyjān-e Gharbī** *off.* Ostān-e Āzarbāyjān-e Gharbī *Eng.* West Azerbaijan *prev.* Āzarbāyjān-e Bākhtarī. ◈ *province* NW Iran
Āzarbāyjān-e Khāvarī *see* Āzarbāyjān-e Sharqī
148 J3 **Āzarbāyjān-e Sharqī** *off.* Ostān-e Āzarbāyjān-e Sharqī, *Eng.* East Azerbaijan; *prev.* Āzarbāyjān-e Khāvarī. ◈ *province* NW Iran
79 W13 **Azare** Bauchi, N Nigeria *11.41N 10.09E*
121 M19 **Azarychy** *Rus.* Ozarichi. Homyel'skaya Voblasts', SE Belarus *52.31N 29.19E*
104 L8 **Azay-le-Rideau** Indre-et-Loire, C France *47.16N 0.25E*
144 I2 **A'zāz** Ḥalab, NW Syria *36.34N 37.03E*
78 H7 **Azeffâl** *var.* Azaffal. *desert* Mauritania/Western Sahara
143 V12 **Azerbaijan** *off.* Azerbaijani Republic, *Az.* Azärbaycan, Azärbaycan Respublikası; *prev.* Azerbaijan SSR. ◆ *republic* SE Asia
151 T7 **Azhbulat, Ozero** ◎ NE Kazakhstan
76 F7 **Azilal** C Morocco *31.58N 6.53W*
Azimabad *see* Patna
21 O6 **Aziscohos Lake** ⊠ Maine, NE USA
Azizbekov *see* Vayk'
Azizie *see* Telish
Aziziya *see* Al 'Azīzīyah
131 T4 **Aznakayevo** Respublika Tatarstan, W Russian Federation *54.55N 53.15E*
58 C8 **Azogues** Cañar, S Ecuador *2.41S 78.54W*
66 N2 **Azores** *var.* Açores, Ilhas dos Açores, *Port.* Arquipélago dos Açores. *island group* Portugal, NE Atlantic Ocean
66 L8 **Azores-Biscay Rise** *undersea feature* E Atlantic Ocean
Azotos/Azotus *see* Ashdod
80 K11 **Azoum, Bahr** *seasonal river* SE Chad
130 L12 **Azov** Rostovskaya Oblast', SW Russian Federation *47.06N 39.26E*
130 J13 **Azov, Sea of** *Rus.* Azovskoye More, *Ukr.* Azovs'ke More. *sea* NE Black Sea
Azovs'ke More/Azovskoye More *see* Azov, Sea of
144 I10 **Azraq, Wāḥat al** *oasis* N Jordan *31.51N 36.51E*
Āzro *see* Āzrow
76 G6 **Azrou** C Morocco *33.30N 5.12W*
155 R5 **Āzrow** *var.* Āzro. Lowgar, E Afghanistan *34.10N 69.39E*
39 P8 **Aztec** New Mexico, SW USA *36.49N 107.59W*
38 M13 **Aztec Peak** ▲ Arizona, SW USA *33.48N 110.54W*
47 N9 **Azua** *var.* Azua de Compostela. S Dominican Republic *18.25N 70.44W*
Azua de Compostela *see* Azua
106 K12 **Azuaga** Extremadura, W Spain *38.16N 5.40W*
58 B8 **Azuay** ◈ *province* W Ecuador
170 Bb11 **Azuchi-Ō-shima** *island* SW Japan
107 O11 **Azuer** ≈ C Spain
45 S17 **Azuero, Península de** *peninsula* S Panama
64 I6 **Azufre, Volcán** *var.* Volcán Lastarria. ▲ N Chile *25.16S 68.35W*
118 J12 **Azuga** Prahova, SE Romania *45.27N 25.34E*
63 C22 **Azul** Buenos Aires, E Argentina *36.46S 59.49W*
64 I8 **Azul, Cerro** ▲ NW Argentina *28.28S 68.43W*
58 E12 **Azul, Cordillera** ▲▲ C Peru
171 Ll14 **Azuma-san** ▲ Honshū, C Japan *37.44N 140.05E*
105 V15 **Azur, Côte d'** *coastal region* SE France
203 Z3 **Azur Lagoon** ◎ Kiritimati, E Kiribati
'Azza *see* Gaza
Az Zāb al Kabīr *see* Great Zab
144 H7 **Az Zabdānī** *var.* Zabadani. Dimashq, W Syria *33.45N 36.07E*
147 W8 **Az Zāhirah** *desert* NW Oman
147 S6 **Az Ẓahrān** *Eng.* Dhahran. Ash Sharqīyah, NE Saudi Arabia *26.18N 50.01E*
147 R6 **Az Ẓahrān al Khubar** *var.* Dhahran Al Khobar. ✈ Ash Sharqīyah, NE Saudi Arabia *26.28N 49.42E*
Az Zaqāziq *see* Zagazig
144 H10 **Az Zarqā'** *var.* Zarqa. Az Zarqā', NW Jordan *32.04N 36.06E*
144 I11 **Az Zarqā'** *off.* Muḥāfaẓat az Zarqā', *var.* Zarqa. ◈ *governorate* N Jordan
77 O7 **Az Zāwiyah** *var.* Zawia. NW Libya *32.45N 12.43E*
147 N15 **Az Zaydīyah** W Yemen *15.19N 43.03E*
76 I11 **Azzel Matti, Sebkha** *var.* Sebkra Azz el Matti. *salt flat* C Algeria
147 P6 **Az Zilfī** Ar Riyāḍ, N Saudi Arabia *26.16N 44.48E*
145 Y13 **Az Zubayr** *var.* Al Zubair. SE Iraq *30.24N 47.45E*

◆ Country ● Country Capital ◇ Dependent Territory ○ Dependent Territory Capital ◈ Administrative Region ✈ International Airport ▲ Mountain ▲▲ Mountain Range Volcano ≈ River ◎ Lake ⊠ Reservoir

Az Zuqur see Jabal Zuuqar, Jazīrat

B

197 H14 **Ba** prev. Mba. Viti Levu, W Fiji 17.34S 177.40E
Ba see Đa Răng
175 R18 **Baa** Pulau Rote, C Indonesia 10.43S 123.06E
197 G5 **Baaba, Île** island Îles Belep, W New Caledonia
144 H7 **Baalbek** var. Ba'labakk; anc. Heliopolis. E Lebanon 34.00N 36.15E
110 G8 **Baar** Zug, N Switzerland 47.12N 8.31E
83 L17 **Baardheere** var. Bardere, It. Bardera. Gedo, SW Somalia 2.13N 42.19E
82 Q12 **Baargaal** Bari, NE Somalia 11.12N 51.04E
101 I15 **Baarle-Hertog** Antwerpen, N Belgium 51.26N 4.56E
101 I15 **Baarle-Nassau** Noord-Brabant, S Netherlands 51.27N 4.56E
100 J11 **Baarn** Utrecht, C Netherlands 52.13N 5.16E
116 D13 **Baba** var. Buševa, Gk. Varnoús. ▲▲ FYR Macedonia/Greece
78 H10 **Bababé** Brakna, W Mauritania 16.22N 13.57W
142 G10 **Baba Burnu** headland NW Turkey 41.18N 31.24E
119 N13 **Babadag** Tulcea, SE Romania 44.53N 28.46E
143 X10 **Babadağ Dağı** ▲ NE Azerbaijan 41.02N 48.04E
Babadayhan see Babadaykhan
152 H14 **Babadaykhan** Turkm. Babadayhan; prev. Kirovsk. Akhalskiy Velayat, C Turkmenistan 37.39N 60.17E
152 G14 **Babadurmaz** Akhalskiy Velayat, C Turkmenistan 37.39N 59.03E
116 M12 **Babaeski** Kırklareli, NW Turkey 41.26N 27.06E
145 T4 **Bāba Gurgur** N Iraq 35.34N 44.18E
58 B7 **Babahoyo** prev. Bodegas. Los Ríos, C Ecuador 1.49S 79.33W
155 P5 **Bābā, Kūh-e** ▲▲ C Afghanistan
175 P10 **Babana** Sulawesi, C Indonesia 2.03S 119.13E
176 U16 **Babar, Kepulauan** island group E Indonesia
176 U15 **Babar, Pulau** island Kepulauan Babar, E Indonesia
158 G4 **Bābāsar Pass** pass India/Pakistan
195 Q10 **Babase Island** island Feni Islands, NE PNG
152 C9 **Babashy** ▲▲ W Turkmenistan
174 Ll15 **Babat** Jawa, S Indonesia 7.07S 112.07E
174 I10 **Babat** Sumatera, W Indonesia 2.45S 104.01E
Babatag, Khrebet see Botogot', Tizmasi
83 H21 **Babati** Arusha, NE Tanzania 4.12S 35.45E
128 J13 **Babayevo** Vologodskaya Oblast', NW Russian Federation 59.22N 35.51E
131 Q15 **Babayurt** Respublika Dagestan, SW Russian Federation 43.38N 46.49E
35 P6 **Babb** Montana, NW USA 48.51N 113.26W
31 X4 **Babbitt** Minnesota, N USA 47.42N 91.56W
196 E9 **Babeldaob** var. Babeldaop, Babelthuap. island N Palau
Babeldaop see Babeldaob
147 N17 **Bab el Mandeb** strait Gulf of Aden/Red Sea
Babelthuap see Babeldaob
113 K17 **Babia Góra** var. Babia Hora. ▲ Poland/Slovakia 49.33N 19.32E
Babia Hora see Babia Góra
Babian Jiang see Black River
Babichi see Babichy
121 N19 **Babichy** Rus. Babichi. Homyel'skaya Voblasts', SE Belarus 52.17N 30.00E
114 I10 **Babina Greda** Vukovar-Srijem, E Croatia 45.09N 18.33E
8 K13 **Babine Lake** ⊚ British Columbia, SW Canada
176 Vv10 **Babo** Papua, E Indonesia 2.29S 133.30E
149 O4 **Bābol** var. Babul, Balfrush, Barfrush; prev. Barfurush. Māzandarān, N Iran 36.34N 52.39E
149 O4 **Bābolsar** var. Babulsar; prev. Meshed-i-Sar. Māzandarān, N Iran 36.42N 52.37E
38 L16 **Baboquivari Peak** ▲ Arizona, SW USA 31.46N 111.36W
81 G15 **Baboua** Nana-Mambéré, W Central African Republic 5.46N 14.47E
121 M17 **Babruysk** Rus. Bobruysk. Mahilyowskaya Voblasts', E Belarus 53.07N 29.13E
Babu see Hexian
Babul see Bābol
Babulsar see Bābolsar
115 O19 **Babuna** ≈ C FYR Macedonia
115 O19 **Babuna** ▲▲ C FYR Macedonia
154 K7 **Bābūs, Dasht-e** Pash. Bebas, Dasht-i. ▲▲ W Afghanistan
126 Jj16 **Babushkin** Respublika Buryatiya, S Russian Federation 51.35N 105.49E
179 P7 **Babuyan Channel** channel N Philippines
179 Pp7 **Babuyan Island** island N Philippines
145 T9 **Babylon** site of ancient city C Iraq 32.33N 44.25E
114 J9 **Bač** Ger. Batsch. Serbia, NW Serbia and Montenegro (Yugoslavia) 45.24N 19.17E
60 M13 **Bacabal** Maranhão, E Brazil 4.15S 44.45W
43 Y14 **Bacalar** Quintana Roo, SE Mexico 18.38N 88.17W
43 Y14 **Bacalar Chico, Boca** strait SE Mexico
175 Ss8 **Bacan, Kepulauan** island group E Indonesia
175 T8 **Bacan, Pulau** prev. Batjan. island Maluku, E Indonesia
118 L10 **Bacău** Hung. Bákó. Bacău, NE Romania 46.36N 26.55E
118 K11 **Bacău** ◈ county E Romania
Băc Bô, Vịnh see Tongking, Gulf of
178 Jj5 **Bắc Can** Băc Thai, N Vietnam 22.07N 105.50E
105 T5 **Baccarat** Meurthe-et-Moselle, NE France 48.27N 6.46E
191 N12 **Bacchus Marsh** Victoria, SE Australia 37.46S 144.27E
42 H4 **Bacerac** Sonora, NW Mexico 30.27N 108.55W
118 L10 **Băceşti** Vaslui, E Romania 46.49N 27.13E
178 Jj6 **Băc Giang** Ha Băc, N Vietnam 21.17N 106.12E
56 I5 **Bachaquero** Zulia, NW Venezuela 9.57N 71.09W
Bacher see Pohorje
120 M13 **Bacheykava** Rus. Bocheykovo. Vitsyebskaya Voblasts', N Belarus 55.01N 29.09E
42 I5 **Bachíniva** Chihuahua, N Mexico 28.41N 107.13W
164 G8 **Bachu** Xinjiang Uygur Zizhiqu, NW China 39.46N 78.30E
15 J6 **Back** ≈ Nunavut, N Canada
114 K10 **Bačka Palanka** prev. Palanka. Serbia, NW Serbia and Montenegro (Yugoslavia) 44.22N 20.57E
114 K8 **Bačka Topola** Hung. Topolya; prev. Hung. Bácstopolya. Serbia, N Serbia and Montenegro (Yugoslavia) 45.48N 19.39E
97 J17 **Bäckefors** Västra Götaland, S Sweden 58.49N 12.07E
Bäckermühle Schulzenmühle see Żywiec
97 L16 **Bäckhammar** Värmland, C Sweden 59.09N 14.13E
114 K9 **Bački Petrovac** Hung. Petrőcz; prev. Petrovac, Petrovácz. Serbia, NW Serbia and Montenegro (Yugoslavia) 45.22N 19.34E
103 I21 **Backnang** Baden-Württemberg, SW Germany 48.46N 9.25E
178 J15 **Bac Liêu** var. Vinh Loi. Minh Hai, S Vietnam 9.19N 105.42E
178 Jj6 **Băc Ninh** Ha Băc, N Vietnam 21.10N 106.04E
42 G4 **Bacoachi** Sonora, NW Mexico 30.37N 109.57W
179 Q13 **Bacolod** off. Bacolod City. Negros, C Philippines 10.43N 122.58E
179 P12 **Baco, Mount** ▲ Mindoro, N Philippines 12.50N 121.08E
113 K25 **Bácsalmás** Bács-Kiskun, S Hungary 46.09N 19.17E
Bácsjózseffalva see Žednik
113 J24 **Bács-Kiskun** off. Bács-Kiskun Megye. ◈ county S Hungary
Bácsszenttamás see Srbobran
Bácstopolya see Bačka Topola
Bactra see Balkh
161 F21 **Badagara** Kerala, SW India 11.24N 75.45E
103 M24 **Bad Aibling** Bayern, SE Germany 47.52N 12.00E
168 I13 **Badain Jaran Shamo** desert N China
106 I11 **Badajoz** anc. Pax Augusta. Extremadura, W Spain 38.52N 6.58W
106 J11 **Badajoz** ◈ province Extremadura, W Spain
155 S2 **Badakhshān** ◈ province NE Afghanistan
107 W6 **Badalona** anc. Baetulo. Cataluña, E Spain 41.27N 2.15E
160 O11 **Bādāmapāhārh** Orissa, E India 22.04N 86.06E
158 K8 **Badarīnāth** ▲ N India 30.43N 79.28E
174 Jj8 **Badas, Kepulauan** island group W Indonesia
111 S6 **Bad Aussee** Salzburg, E Austria 47.35N 13.44E
33 S8 **Bad Axe** Michigan, N USA 43.48N 83.00W
103 G16 **Bad Berleburg** Nordrhein-Westfalen, W Germany 51.03N 8.24E
103 L17 **Bad Blankenburg** Thüringen, C Germany 50.43N 11.19E
Bad Borseck see Borsec
103 G18 **Bad Camberg** Hessen, W Germany 50.18N 8.15E
102 L8 **Bad Doberan** Mecklenburg-Vorpommern, N Germany 54.06N 11.55E
103 N14 **Bad Düben** Sachsen, E Germany 51.35N 12.34E
111 X4 **Baden** var. Baden bei Wien; anc. Aquae Panoniae, Thermae Pannonicae. Niederösterreich, NE Austria 48.01N 16.13E
110 F9 **Baden** Aargau, N Switzerland 47.28N 8.19E
103 G21 **Baden-Baden** anc. Aurelia Aquensis. Baden-Württemberg, SW Germany 48.46N 8.13E
Baden bei Wien see Baden
103 G22 **Baden-Württemberg** Fr. Bade-Wurtemberg. ◈ state SW Germany
114 A10 **Baderna** Istra, NW Croatia 45.12N 13.45E
Bade-Wurtemberg see Baden-Württemberg
103 H20 **Bad Fredrichshall** Baden-Württemberg, S Germany 49.13N 9.15E
102 P11 **Bad Freienwalde** Brandenburg, NE Germany 52.46N 14.03E
111 Q8 **Badgastein** var. Gastein. Salzburg, NW Austria 47.07N 13.09E
Badger State see Wisconsin
154 L4 **Bādghīs** ◈ province NW Afghanistan
111 T5 **Bad Hall** Oberösterreich, N Austria 48.03N 14.13E
103 J14 **Bad Harzburg** Niedersachsen, C Germany 51.52N 10.34E
103 I16 **Bad Hersfeld** Hessen, C Germany 50.52N 9.41E
100 I10 **Badhoevedorp** Noord-Holland, C Netherlands 52.21N 4.46E
111 Q8 **Bad Hofgastein** Salzburg, NW Austria 47.10N 13.07E
Bad Homburg see Bad Homburg vor der Höhe
103 G18 **Bad Homburg vor der Höhe** var. Bad Homburg. Hessen, W Germany 50.13N 8.37E
103 E17 **Bad Honnef** Nordrhein-Westfalen, W Germany 50.39N 7.13E
155 Q17 **Badīn** Sind, SE Pakistan 24.40N 68.49E
23 S10 **Badin Lake** ⊠ North Carolina, SE USA
42 I8 **Badiraguato** Sinaloa, C Mexico 25.26N 107.33W
111 R6 **Bad Ischl** Oberösterreich, N Austria 47.43N 13.35E
Badjawa see Bajawa
103 J18 **Bad Kissingen** Bayern, SE Germany 50.12N 10.04E
Bad Königswart see Lázně Kynžvart
103 F19 **Bad Kreuznach** Rheinland-Pfalz, SW Germany 49.49N 7.52E
103 F24 **Bad Krozingen** Baden-Württemberg, SW Germany 47.55N 7.43E
103 G16 **Bad Laasphe** Nordrhein-Westfalen, W Germany 50.57N 8.24E
30 J6 **Badlands** physical region North Dakota, N USA
103 K16 **Bad Langensalza** Thüringen, C Germany 51.05N 10.40E
111 T3 **Bad Leonfelden** Oberösterreich, N Austria 48.31N 14.17E
103 I20 **Bad Mergentheim** Baden-Württemberg, SW Germany 49.30N 9.46E
103 H17 **Bad Nauheim** Hessen, W Germany 50.22N 8.45E
103 E17 **Bad Neuenahr-Arhweiler** Rheinland-Pfalz, W Germany 50.33N 7.07E
Bad Neustadt see Bad Neustadt an der Saale
103 J18 **Bad Neustadt an der Saale** var. Bad Neustadt. Berlin, C Germany 50.21N 10.13E
Badnur see Betūl
176 Yy15 **Badō** Papua, E Indonesia 7.06S 139.33E
102 H13 **Bad Oeynhausen** Nordrhein-Westfalen, NW Germany 52.12N 8.48E
102 J9 **Bad Oldesloe** Schleswig-Holstein, N Germany 53.49N 10.22E
79 Q16 **Badou** C Togo 7.37N 0.37E
Bad Polzin see Połczyn-Zdrój
102 H13 **Bad Pyrmont** Niedersachsen, C Germany 51.58N 9.16E
111 X9 **Bad Radkersburg** Steiermark, SE Austria 46.40N 16.02E
145 Y10 **Badrah** E Iraq 33.06N 45.58E
168 J6 **Badrah** Hövsgöl, N Mongolia 49.33N 101.58E
103 N24 **Bad Reichenhall** Bayern, SE Germany 47.43N 12.52E
146 K8 **Badr Ḩunayn** Al Madīnah, W Saudi Arabia 23.46N 38.45E
30 M10 **Bad River** ≈ South Dakota, N USA
32 K4 **Bad River** ≈ Wisconsin, N USA
102 H13 **Bad Salzuflen** Nordrhein-Westfalen, NW Germany 52.04N 8.45E
103 J16 **Bad Salzungen** Thüringen, C Germany 50.48N 10.15E
111 V8 **Bad Sankt Leonhard im Lavanttal** Kärnten, S Austria 46.55N 14.51E
102 K9 **Bad Schwartau** Schleswig-Holstein, N Germany 53.55N 10.42E
103 L24 **Bad Tölz** Bayern, SE Germany 47.44N 11.34E
189 U1 **Badu Island** island Queensland, NE Australia
161 K25 **Badulla** Uva Province, C Sri Lanka 6.58N 81.03E
111 X5 **Bad Vöslau** Niederösterreich, NE Austria 47.58N 16.12E
103 I24 **Bad Waldsee** Baden-Württemberg, S Germany 47.54N 9.44E
37 U11 **Badwater Basin** depression California, W USA
103 J20 **Bad Windsheim** Bayern, C Germany 49.30N 10.25E
103 J23 **Bad Wörishofen** Bayern, S Germany 48.00N 10.36E
102 G10 **Bad Zwischenahn** Niedersachsen, NW Germany 53.10N 8.01E
106 M13 **Baena** Andalucía, S Spain 37.37N 4.22W
Baeterrae/Baeterrae Septimanorum see Béziers
Baetic Cordillera/Baetic Mountains see Béticos, Sistemas
Baetulo see Badalona
59 K18 **Baeza** Napo, NE Ecuador 0.30S 77.52W
107 N13 **Baeza** Andalucía, S Spain 38.00N 3.28W
81 D15 **Bafang** Ouest, W Cameroon 5.10N 10.10E
78 H12 **Bafatá** C Guinea-Bissau 12.09N 14.37W
155 U5 **Baffa** North-West Frontier Province, NW Pakistan 34.28N 73.14E
207 O11 **Baffin Basin** undersea feature N Labrador Sea
207 N12 **Baffin Bay** bay Canada/Greenland
27 T15 **Baffin Bay** inlet Texas, SW USA
206 M12 **Baffin Island** island Nunavut, NE Canada
81 E15 **Bafia** Centre, C Cameroon 4.49N 11.13E
79 R14 **Bafilo** NE Togo 9.22N 1.19E
78 J12 **Bafing** ≈ W Africa
78 J12 **Bafoulabé** Kayes, W Mali 13.43N 10.49W
81 D15 **Bafoussam** Ouest, W Cameroon 5.31N 10.25E
149 R9 **Bāfq** Yazd, C Iran 31.34N 55.21E
142 L10 **Bafra** Samsun, N Turkey 41.34N 35.55E
142 L10 **Bafra Burnu** headland N Turkey 41.42N 36.02E
149 S12 **Bāft** Kermān, S Iran 29.12N 56.36E
81 N18 **Bafwabalinga** Orientale, NE Dem. Rep. Congo 0.52N 26.55E
81 N18 **Bafwaboli** Orientale, NE Dem. Rep. Congo 0.42N 26.06E
81 N17 **Bafwasende** Orientale, NE Dem. Rep. Congo 1.00N 27.09E
194 J11 **Bagabag Island** island N PNG
44 K13 **Bagaces** Guanacaste, NW Costa Rica 10.29N 85.13W
159 O12 **Bagaha** Bihār, N India 27.07N 84.04E
161 F16 **Bāgalkot** Karnātaka, W India 16.10N 75.42E
83 J22 **Bagamoyo** Pwani, E Tanzania 6.25S 38.55E
174 Gg4 **Bagan Datuk** var. Bagan Datok. Perak, Peninsular Malaysia 3.58N 100.46E
179 Rr15 **Baganga** Mindanao, S Philippines 7.31N 126.34E
174 Gg6 **Bagansiapiapi** var. Pasirpangarayan. Sumatera, W Indonesia 2.09N 100.50E
Bagaria see Bagheria
79 T11 **Bagaroua** Tahoua, W Niger 14.34N 4.24E
81 I20 **Bagata** Bandundu, W Dem. Rep. Congo 3.46S 17.57E
Bagdad see Baghdād
126 Kk15 **Bagdarin** Respublika Buryatiya, S Russian Federation 54.27N 113.34E
63 G17 **Bagé** Rio Grande do Sul, S Brazil 31.22S 54.06W
Bagenalstown see Muine Bheag
Bagerhat see Bagherhat
105 P16 **Bages et de Sigean, Étang de** ⊚ S France
35 W17 **Baggs** Wyoming, C USA 41.02N 107.39W
160 F11 **Bāgh** Madhya Pradesh, C India 22.22N 74.49E
145 T8 **Baghdād** var. Bagdad, Eng. Baghdad. ● (Iraq) C Iraq 33.19N 44.25E
145 T8 **Baghdād** ✖ C Iraq 33.19N 44.25E
159 T16 **Bagherhat** var. Bagerhat. Khulna, S Bangladesh 22.40N 89.48E
109 J23 **Bagheria** var. Bagaria. Sicilia, Italy, C Mediterranean Sea 38.04N 13.31E
149 S10 **Bāghīn** Kermān, C Iran 30.50N 57.00E
155 Q3 **Baghlān** Baghlān, NE Afghanistan 36.10N 68.43E
155 Q3 **Baghlān** var. Bāghlān. ◈ province NE Afghanistan
154 M7 **Bāghrān** Helmand, S Afghanistan 32.55N 64.57E
31 T4 **Bagley** Minnesota, N USA 47.31N 95.24W
108 H10 **Bagnacavallo** Emilia-Romagna, C Italy 44.00N 12.59E
104 K16 **Bagnères-de-Bigorre** Hautes-Pyrénées, S France 43.04N 0.09E
104 L17 **Bagnères-de-Luchon** Hautes-Pyrénées, S France 42.46N 0.34E
108 F11 **Bagni di Lucca** Toscana, C Italy 44.01N 10.38E
108 H11 **Bagno di Romagna** Emilia-Romagna, C Italy 43.51N 11.57E
105 R14 **Bagnols-sur-Cèze** Gard, S France 44.10N 4.37E
168 M14 **Bag Nur** ⊚ N China
179 Q13 **Bago** off. Bago City. Negros, C Philippines 10.30N 122.49E
Bago see Pegu
78 M13 **Bagoé** ≈ Ivory Coast/Mali
Bagrāmē see Bagrāmī
155 R5 **Bagrāmī** var. Bagrāmē. Kābul, E Afghanistan 34.28N 69.16E
121 B14 **Bagrationovsk** Ger. Preussisch Eylau. Kaliningradskaya Oblast', W Russian Federation 54.24N 20.39E
Bagrax see Bohu
Bagrax Hu see Bosten Hu
58 C10 **Bagua** Amazonas, NE Peru 5.34S 78.24W
179 P9 **Baguio** off. Baguio City. Luzon, N Philippines 16.25N 120.36E
79 V9 **Bagzane, Monts** ▲ N Niger 17.48N 8.43E
Bāḩah, Minṭaqat al see Al Bāḩah
Bahama Islands see Bahamas
46 H3 **Bahamas** off. Commonwealth of the Bahamas. ◆ commonwealth republic N West Indies
(0) L13 **Bahamas** var. Bahama Islands. island group N West Indies
159 S15 **Baharampur** prev. Berhampore. West Bengal, NE India 24.03N 88.16E
175 Nn6 **Bahau, Sungai** ≈ Borneo, N Indonesia
155 U10 **Bahāwalnagar** Punjab, E Pakistan 30.00N 73.03E
155 T11 **Bahāwalpur** Punjab, E Pakistan 29.24N 71.39E
142 L16 **Bahçe** Osmaniye, S Turkey 37.11N 36.32E
166 J8 **Ba He** ≈ C China
Bäherden see Bakharden
61 N16 **Bahia** off. Estado da Bahia. ◈ state E Brazil
63 B24 **Bahía Blanca** Buenos Aires, E Argentina 38.43S 62.19W
42 L15 **Bahía Bufadero** Michoacán de Ocampo, SW Mexico
65 J19 **Bahía Bustamante** Chubut, SE Argentina 45.06S 66.30W
42 D5 **Bahía de los Ángeles** Baja California, NW Mexico
42 C6 **Bahía de Tortugas** Baja California Sur, W Mexico 27.42N 114.54W
44 J4 **Bahía, Islas de la** Eng. Bay Islands. island group N Honduras
42 E5 **Bahía Kino** Sonora, NW Mexico 28.48N 111.55W
42 E9 **Bahía Magdalena** var. Puerto Magdalena. Baja California Sur, W Mexico 24.34N 112.07W
56 C8 **Bahía Solano** var. Ciudad Mutis, Solano. Chocó, W Colombia 6.13N 77.27W
82 I11 **Bahir Dar** var. Bahr Dar, Bahrdar Giyorgis. Amhara, N Ethiopia 11.33N 37.22E
147 X8 **Bahlā'** var. Bahlah, Bahlat. NW Oman 22.55N 57.16E
Bāhla see Bālān
Bahlah/Bahlat see Bahlā'
158 M11 **Bahraich** Uttar Pradesh, N India 27.34N 81.36E
149 M14 **Bahrain** off. State of Bahrain, Dawlat al Bahrayn, Ar. Al Baḩrayn; prev. Bahrein, anc. Tylos or Tyros. ◆ monarchy SW Asia
148 M14 **Bahrain** ✖ C Bahrain 26.15N 50.39E
148 M15 **Bahrain, Gulf of** gulf Persian Gulf, NW Arabian Sea
144 I7 **Baḩrat Mallāḩah** ⊚ W Syria
Bahrayn, Dawlat al see Bahrain
Bahr Dar/Bahrdar Giyorgis see Bahir Dar
Bahrein see Bahrain
83 E16 **Bahr el Gabel** ◈ state S Sudan
82 E13 **Bahr ez Zaref** ≈ C Sudan
69 R8 **Bahr Kameur** ≈ N Central African Republic
Bahr Tabariya, Sea of see Tiberias, Lake
149 W15 **Bāhū Kalāt** Sīstān va Balūchestān, SE Iran 25.42N 61.28E
120 N13 **Bahushewsk** Rus. Bogushëvsk. Vitsyebskaya Voblasts', NE Belarus 54.51N 30.13E
Bai see Tagow Bāy
118 G13 **Baia de Aramă** Mehedinți, SW Romania 45.00N 22.43E
118 G11 **Baia de Criş** Ger. Altenburg, Hung. Körösbánya. Hunedoara, SW Romania 46.10N 22.40E
85 A16 **Baia dos Tigres** Namibe, SW Angola 16.36S 11.44E
84 A13 **Baia Farta** Benguela, W Angola 12.38S 13.12E
118 H9 **Baia Mare** Ger. Frauenbach, Hung. Nagybánya; prev. Neustadt. Maramureş, NW Romania 47.39N 23.35E
118 H8 **Baia Sprie** Ger. Mittelstadt, Hung. Felsőbánya. Maramureş, NW Romania 47.40N 23.42E
80 G13 **Baïbokoum** Logone-Oriental, SW Chad 7.46N 15.43E
166 F12 **Baicao Ling** ▲ SW China
169 U9 **Baicheng** var. Pai-ch'eng; prev. T'aon-an. Jilin, NE China 45.31N 122.50E
164 I6 **Baicheng** var. Bay. Xinjiang Uygur Zizhiqu, NW China 41.49N 81.45E
118 J13 **Băicoi** Prahova, SE Romania 45.01N 25.52E
Baidoa see Baydhabo
13 U6 **Baie-Comeau** Quebec, SE Canada 49.12N 68.10W
13 T7 **Baie-des-Bacon** Quebec, SE Canada 48.31N 69.17W
13 S8 **Baie-des-Rochers** Quebec, SE Canada 47.57N 69.50W
13 U6 **Baie-des-Sables** Quebec, SE Canada 48.41N 67.55W
10 K11 **Baie-du-Poste** Quebec, SE Canada 50.19N 73.49W
180 H17 **Baie Lazare** Mahé, NE Seychelles 4.45S 55.28E
47 Y5 **Baie-Mahault** Basse Terre, C Guadeloupe 16.17N 61.34W
13 R9 **Baie-St-Paul** Quebec, SE Canada 47.27N 70.30W
13 V5 **Baie-Trinité** Quebec, SE Canada 49.25N 67.19W
11 T11 **Baie Verte** Newfoundland and Labrador, SE Canada 49.58N 56.06W
169 X11 **Baihe** prev. Erdaobaihe. Jilin, NE China 42.24N 128.09E
Baiguan see Shangyu
145 U11 **Ba'ij al Mahdī** S Iraq 31.21N 44.57E
Baiji see Bayjī
Baikal, Lake see Baykal, Ozero
Bailādila see Kirandul
Baile an Chaistil see Ballycastle
Baile an Róba see Ballinrobe
Baile an tSratha see Ballintra
Baile Átha an Rí see Athenry
Baile Átha Buí see Athboy
Baile Átha Cliath see Dublin
Baile Átha Fhirdhia see Ardee
Baile Átha Í see Athy
Baile Átha Luain see Athlone
Baile Átha Troim see Trim
Baile Brigín see Balbriggan
Baile Easa Dara see Ballysadare
118 I13 **Băile Govora** Vâlcea, SW Romania 45.00N 24.08E
118 F13 **Băile Herculane** Ger. Herkulesbad, Hung. Herkulesfürdő. Caraş-Severin, SW Romania 44.50N 22.23E
Baile Locha Riach see Loughrea
Baile Mhistéala see Mitchelstown
Baile Monaidh see Ballymoney
107 N12 **Bailén** Andalucía, S Spain 38.06N 3.46W
Baile na hInse see Ballynahinch
Baile na Lorgan see Castleblayney
Baile na Mainistreach see Newtownabbey
Baile Nua na hArda see Newtownards
118 I12 **Băile Olăneşti** Vâlcea, SW Romania 45.16N 24.13E
118 H14 **Băileşti** Dolj, SW Romania 44.01N 23.20E
Bailingmiao see Darhan Muminggan Lianheqi
60 K11 **Bailique, Ilha** island NE Brazil
105 O1 **Bailleul** Nord, N France 50.43N 2.43E
80 H12 **Ba Illi** Chari-Baguirmi, SW Chad 10.31N 16.28E
165 V12 **Bailong Jiang** ≈ C China
84 C13 **Bailundo** Port. Vila Teixeira da Silva. Huambo, C Angola 12.12S 15.52E
165 T13 **Baima** var. Sêraitang. Qinghai, C China 32.55N 100.44E
176 W14 **Baimun** Pulau Workai, E Indonesia 6.41S 134.40E
194 H14 **Baimuru** Gulf, S PNG 7.31S 144.44E
164 M16 **Bainang** Xizang Zizhiqu, W China 28.57N 89.31E
25 S8 **Bainbridge** Georgia, SE USA 30.54N 84.33W
175 Pp17 **Baing** Pulau Sumba, SE Indonesia 10.09S 120.34E
164 M14 **Baingoin** Xizang Zizhiqu, W China 31.25N 90.01E
106 G2 **Baio Grande** Galicia, NW Spain 43.08N 8.58W
106 G4 **Baiona** Galicia, NW Spain 42.06N 8.49W
169 V7 **Baiquan** Heilongjiang, NE China 47.37N 126.04E
Bā'ir see Bāyir
164 I11 **Bairab Co** ⊚ W China
27 Q7 **Baird** Texas, SW USA 32.23N 99.23W
41 N7 **Baird Mountains** ▲▲ Alaska, USA
15 Mm2 **Baird Peninsula** peninsula Baffin Island, Nunavut, NE Canada
Baireuth see Bayreuth
202 H3 **Bairiki** ● (Kiribati) Tarawa, NW Kiribati 1.19N 173.01E
169 S11 **Bairin Youqi** var. Daban. Nei Mongol Zizhiqu, N China 43.33N 118.40E
169 S10 **Bairin Zuoqi** var. Lindong. Nei Mongol Zizhiqu, N China 43.59N 119.24E
151 P17 **Bairkum** Kaz. Bayyrqum. Yuzhnyy Kazakhstan, S Kazakhstan 41.57N 68.05E
191 P12 **Bairnsdale** Victoria, SE Australia 37.51S 147.37E
179 Q14 **Bais** Negros, S Philippines 9.36N 123.07E
104 L15 **Baïse** var. Baise. ≈ S France
169 W11 **Baishan** prev. Hunjiang. Jilin, NE China 41.57N 126.31E
120 F12 **Baisogala** Radviliškis, C Lithuania 55.38N 23.44E
201 Q7 **Baiti** N Nauru 0.30S 166.55E
106 G13 **Baixo Alentejo** physical region S Portugal
66 P5 **Baixo, Ilhéu de** island Madeira, Portugal, NE Atlantic Ocean
85 E15 **Baixo Longa** Cuando Cubango, SE Angola 15.39S 18.39E
165 V10 **Baiyin** Gansu, C China 36.33N 104.11E
166 E8 **Baiyü** Sichuan, C China 30.37N 97.15E
167 N14 **Baiyun** ✖ (Guangzhou) Guangdong, S China 23.12N 113.19E
166 K4 **Baiyu Shan** ▲▲ C China
113 J25 **Baja** Bács-Kiskun, S Hungary 46.12N 18.56E
42 C4 **Baja California** ◈ state NW Mexico
42 C4 **Baja California** Eng. Lower California. peninsula NW Mexico
42 E9 **Baja California Sur** ◈ state W Mexico
Bājah see Béja
Bajan see Bayan
203 V16 **Baja, Punta** headland Easter Island, Chile, E Pacific Ocean 27.10S 109.21W
42 B4 **Baja, Punta** headland NW Mexico 29.57N 115.48W
57 R5 **Baja, Punta** headland NE Venezuela
44 D5 **Baja Verapaz** off. Departamento de Baja Verapaz. ◈ department C Guatemala
175 Q16 **Bajawa** prev. Badjawa. Flores, S Indonesia 8.46S 120.58E
159 S16 **Baj Baj** prev. Budge-Budge. West Bengal, E India 22.28N 88.10E
147 N15 **Bājil** W Yemen 15.05N 43.16E
191 U4 **Bajimba, Mount** ▲ New South Wales, SE Australia 29.19S 152.04E
114 K13 **Bajina Bašta** Serbia, W Serbia and Montenegro (Yugoslavia) 43.58N 19.33E
159 U14 **Bajitpur** Dhaka, E Bangladesh 24.12N 90.57E
114 K8 **Bajmok** Serbia, NW Serbia and Montenegro (Yugoslavia) 45.59N 19.25E
Bajo Boquete see Boquete
115 L17 **Bajram Curri** Kukës, N Albania 42.22N 20.06E
81 J14 **Bakala** Ouaka, C Central African Republic 6.03N 20.31E
131 T4 **Bakaly** Respublika Bashkortostan, W Russian Federation 55.10N 53.46E
Bakan see Shimonoseki
151 U14 **Bakanas** Kaz. Baqanas. Almaty, SE Kazakhstan 44.50N 76.13E
151 V12 **Bakanas** Kaz. Baqanas. ≈ E Kazakhstan
151 U14 **Bakbakty** Kaz. Baqbaqty. Almaty, SE Kazakhstan 44.36N 76.41E
126 Gg13 **Bakchar** Tomskaya Oblast', C Russian Federation 56.58N 81.59E
78 I11 **Bakel** E Senegal 13.43N 13.40W
37 W13 **Baker** California, W USA 35.15N 116.04W
24 J8 **Baker** Louisiana, S USA 30.35N 91.10W
35 Y9 **Baker** Montana, NW USA 46.22N 104.16W
34 L12 **Baker** Oregon, NW USA 44.46N 117.49W
199 Jj8 **Baker and Howland Islands** ◇ US unincorporated territory W Polynesia
38 L12 **Baker Butte** ▲ Arizona, SW USA 34.24N 111.22W
41 X15 **Baker Island** island Alexander Archipelago, Alaska, USA
15 Kk6 **Baker Lake** Nunavut, N Canada 64.19N 96.10W
15 Kk6 **Baker Lake** ⊚ Nunavut, N Canada
34 H6 **Baker, Mount** ▲ Washington, NW USA 48.46N 121.48W
37 R13 **Bakersfield** California, W USA 35.22N 119.01W
26 M9 **Bakersfield** Texas, SW USA 30.54N 102.21W
23 P9 **Bakersville** North Carolina, SE USA 36.03N 82.10W
Bakhābī see Bū Khābī
152 E12 **Bakharden** Turkm. Bäherden; prev. Bakherden. Akhalskiy Velayat, C Turkmenistan 38.30N 57.18E
152 F12 **Bakhardok** Turkm. Bokurdak. Akhalskiy Velayat, C Turkmenistan 38.51N 58.34E
149 U5 **Bākharz, Kuhhā-ye** ▲▲ NE Iran
158 D13 **Bākhāsar** Rājasthān, NW India 24.43N 71.09E
Bakhchisaray see Bakhchysaray
119 T13 **Bakhchysaray** Rus. Bakhchisaray. Respublika Krym, S Ukraine 44.43N 33.53E
Bakherden see Bakharden
119 R3 **Bakhmach** Chernihivs'ka Oblast', N Ukraine 51.10N 32.48E
126 Hh11 **Bakhta** Krasnoyarskiy Kray, C Russian Federation 62.25N 88.56E
148 K6 **Bākhtarān** prev. Kermānshāh, Qahremānshahr. Kermānshāh, W Iran 34.19N 47.04E
Bākhtarān see Kermānshāh
149 Q11 **Bakhtegān, Daryācheh-ye** ⊚ C Iran
151 X12 **Bakhty** Vostochnyy Kazakhstan, E Kazakhstan 46.41N 82.45E
143 Z11 **Bakı** Eng. Baku. ● (Azerbaijan) E Azerbaijan 40.23N 49.51E
143 Z11 **Bakı** ✖ E Azerbaijan 40.26N 49.55E
142 C13 **Bakır Çayı** ≈ W Turkey
94 L1 **Bakkafjörður** Austurland, NE Iceland 66.01N 14.49W
94 L1 **Bakkaflói** sea area W Norwegian Sea
83 I15 **Bako** Southern, S Ethiopia 5.45N 36.39E
78 L15 **Bako** NW Ivory Coast 9.06N 7.34W
Bákó see Bacău
113 H23 **Bakony** Eng. Bakony Mountains, Ger. Bakonywald. ▲▲ W Hungary
Bakony Mountains/Bakonywald see Bakony
83 M16 **Bakool** off. Gobolka Bakool. ◈ region W Somalia
81 L15 **Bakouma** Mbomou, SE Central African Republic 5.42N 22.43E
131 N15 **Baksan** Kabardino-Balkarskaya Respublika, SW Russian Federation 43.43N 43.31E
121 I16 **Bakshty** Hrodzyenskaya Voblasts', W Belarus 53.56N 26.13E
Baku see Bakı
204 K12 **Bakutis Coast** physical region Antarctica
Bakwanga see Mbuji-Mayi
151 O15 **Bakyrly** Yuzhnyy Kazakhstan, S Kazakhstan 44.30N 67.41E
12 H13 **Bala** Ontario, S Canada 45.01N 79.37W
99 J19 **Bala** NW Wales, UK 52.54N 3.31W
142 I13 **Bala** Ankara, C Turkey 39.34N 33.07E
179 O16 **Balabac Island** island W Philippines
Balabac, Selat see Balabac Strait
175 O1 **Balabac Strait** var. Selat Balabac. strait Malaysia/Philippines
Ba'labakk see Baalbek
175 O10 **Balabalangan, Kepulauan** island group N Indonesia
197 H14 **Balabio, Île** island Province Nord, W New Caledonia
118 I14 **Balaci** Teleorman, S Romania 44.21N 24.55E
145 S7 **Balad** N Iraq 34.00N 44.07E
127 N14 **Baladek** Khabarovskiy Kray, SE Russian Federation 53.45N 133.22E
145 U7 **Balad Rūz** E Iraq 33.42N 45.04E
126 J15 **Balagansk** Irkutskaya Oblast', S Russian Federation 54.02N 102.48E
160 J11 **Bālāghāt** Madhya Pradesh, C India 21.48N 80.16E
161 F14 **Bālāghāt Range** ▲▲ W India
105 X14 **Balagne** physical region Corse, France, C Mediterranean Sea
107 U5 **Balaguer** Cataluña, NE Spain 41.48N 0.48E
107 S3 **Balaïtous** var. Pic de Balaitous, Pic de Balaïtous. ▲ France/Spain 42.51N 0.17W
Balaitous, Pic de see Balaïtous
131 O3 **Balakhna** Nizhegorodskaya Oblast', W Russian Federation 56.26N 43.43E
126 I14 **Balakhta** Krasnoyarskiy Kray, S Russian Federation 55.22N 91.24E
190 I9 **Balaklava** South Australia 34.10S 138.22E
Balakleya see Balakliya
119 V6 **Balakliya** Rus. Balakleya. Kharkivs'ka Oblast', E Ukraine 49.26N 36.51E
131 Q7 **Balakovo** Saratovskaya Oblast', W Russian Federation 52.03N 47.47E
85 P14 **Balama** Cabo Delgado, N Mozambique 13.18S 38.39E
175 Nn1 **Balambangan, Pulau** island East Malaysia
154 L3 **Bālā Morghāb** Laghmān, NW Afghanistan 35.37N 63.21E
158 E11 **Bālān** prev. Bāhla. Rājasthān, NW India 27.45N 71.31E
118 J10 **Bălan** Hung. Balánbánya. Harghita, C Romania 46.39N 25.45E
Balánbánya see Bălan
179 P10 **Balanga** Luzon, N Philippines 14.40N 120.32E
160 M12 **Balāngīr** prev. Bolangir. Orissa, E India 20.46N 83.31E
131 N8 **Balashov** Saratovskaya Oblast', W Russian Federation 51.31N 43.14E
Balasore see Bāleshwar
113 K21 **Balassagyarmat** Nógrád, N Hungary 48.04N 19.16E
31 S10 **Balaton** Minnesota, N USA 44.13N 95.52W
113 H24 **Balaton** var. Lake Balaton, Ger. Plattensee. ⊚ W Hungary
113 I23 **Balatonfüred** var. Füred. Veszprém, W Hungary 46.56N 17.51E
Balaton, Lake see Balaton
118 I11 **Bălăuşeri** Ger. Bladenmarkt, Hung. Balavásár. Mureş, C Romania 46.24N 24.41E
Balavásár see Bălăuşeri
107 Q11 **Balazote** Castilla-La Mancha, C Spain 38.54N 2.09W
Balázsfalva see Blaj
121 F14 **Balbieriškis** Prienai, S Lithuania 54.29N 23.52E
195 S12 **Balbi, Mount** ▲ Bougainville Island, NE PNG 5.51S 154.58E
60 F11 **Balbina, Represa** ⊠ NW Brazil
45 T15 **Balboa** Panamá, C Panama 8.55N 79.36W
99 G17 **Balbriggan** Ir. Baile Brigín. E Ireland 53.37N 6.10W
Balbunar see Kubrat
83 N17 **Balcad** Shabeellaha Dhexe, C Somalia 2.19N 45.19E
63 D23 **Balcarce** Buenos Aires, E Argentina 37.51S 58.16W
9 U16 **Balcarres** Saskatchewan, S Canada 50.49N 103.31W
116 O8 **Balchik** Dobrich, NE Bulgaria 43.25N 28.11E
193 E24 **Balclutha** Otago, South Island, NZ 46.15S 169.44E
27 Q12 **Balcones Escarpment** escarpment Texas, SW USA
20 F14 **Bald Eagle Creek** ≈ Pennsylvania, NE USA
Baldenburg see Biały Bór
23 V12 **Bald Head Island** island North Carolina, SE USA
29 W10 **Bald Knob** Arkansas, C USA 35.18N 91.34W
32 K17 **Bald Knob** hill Illinois, N USA 37.33N 89.21W
Baldohn see Baldone

◆ Country
● Country Capital
◇ Dependent Territory
○ Dependent Territory Capital
◈ Administrative Region
✖ International Airport
▲ Mountain
▲▲ Mountain Range
Ѫ Volcano
≈ River
⊚ Lake
⊠ Reservoir

120 G9 Baldone Ger. Baldohn. Rīga, W Latvia 56.46N 24.18E
24 I9 Baldwin Louisiana, S USA 29.50N 91.32W
33 P7 Baldwin Michigan, N USA 43.54N 85.49W
29 Q4 Baldwin City Kansas, C USA 38.43N 95.12W
41 N8 Baldwin Peninsula headland Alaska, USA 66.45N 162.19W
20 H9 Baldwinsville New York, NE USA 43.09N 76.19W
25 N2 Baldwyn Mississippi, S USA 34.30N 88.38W
9 W15 Baldy Mountain ▲ Manitoba, S Canada 51.29N 100.46W
35 T7 Baldy Mountain ▲ Montana, NW USA 48.09N 109.39W
39 O13 Baldy Peak ▲ Arizona, SW USA 33.56N 109.37W
Bâle see Basel
107 X9 Baleares ◆ autonomous community E Spain
107 X11 Baleares, Islas Eng. Balearic Islands. island group Spain, W Mediterranean Sea
Baleares Major see Mallorca
Balearic Islands see Baleares, Islas
Balearic Plain see Algerian Basin
Balearis Minor see Menorca
174 M6 Baleh, Batang ~ East Malaysia
10 J8 Baleine, Grande Rivière de la ~ Quebec, E Canada
10 K7 Baleine, Petite Rivière de la ~ Quebec, SE Canada
11 N6 Baleine, Rivière à la ~ Quebec, E Canada
101 J16 Balen Antwerpen, N Belgium 51.11N 5.12E
179 P9 Baler Luzon, N Philippines 15.47N 121.30E
160 P11 Bāleshwar prev. Balasore. Orissa, E India 21.31N 86.58E
126 L16 Baley Chitinskaya Oblast', S Russian Federation 51.30N 116.16E
79 S12 Baléyara Tillabéri, W Niger 13.48N 2.57E
131 T1 Balezino Udmurtskaya Respublika, NW Russian Federation 57.57N 53.03E
44 J4 Balfate Colón, N Honduras 15.47N 86.24W
9 O17 Balfour British Columbia, SW Canada 49.39N 116.57W
31 N3 Balfour North Dakota, N USA 47.55N 100.34W
Balfrush see Bābol
126 I16 Balgazyn Respublika Tyva, S Russian Federation 50.53N 95.12E
9 U16 Balgonie Saskatchewan, S Canada 50.30N 104.12W
Bălgrad see Alba Iulia
83 J19 Balguda spring/well S Kenya 1.28S 39.50E
164 K6 Balguntay Xinjiang Uygur Zizhiqu, NW China 42.51N 86.19E
147 R16 Balḩāf S Yemen 14.02N 48.15E
158 F13 Bāli Rājasthān, N India 25.17N 73.16E
175 N15 Bali ◆ province S Indonesia
175 N16 Bali island C Indonesia
113 K16 Balice ✕ (Kraków) Małopolskie, S Poland 49.57N 19.49E
176 Yy13 Baliem, Sungai ~ Papua, E Indonesia
142 C12 Balıkesir Balıkesir, W Turkey 39.38N 27.52E
142 C12 Balıkesir ◆ province NW Turkey
144 L3 Balīkh, Nahr ~ N Syria
175 O9 Balikpapan Borneo, C Indonesia 1.15S 116.49E
175 O9 Balikpapan, Teluk bay Borneo, C Indonesia
Bali, Laut see Bali Sea
195 O11 Balima ~ New Britain, C PNG
179 P17 Balimbing Tawitawi, SW Philippines 5.10N 120.00E
194 G14 Balimo Western, SW PNG 8.01S 142.52E
Bâlinc see Balinţ
175 Qq9 Balingara, Pegunungan ▲ Sulawesi, N Indonesia
103 H23 Balingen Baden-Württemberg, SW Germany 48.16N 8.51E
118 F11 Balinţ Hung. Bálinc. Timiş, W Romania 45.52N 21.54E
179 Pp6 Balintang Channel channel N Philippines
144 K3 Bālis Ḩalab, N Syria 36.01N 38.03E
175 N15 Bali Sea Ind. Laut Bali. sea C Indonesia
175 N16 Bali, Selat strait C Indonesia
100 K7 Balk Friesland, N Netherlands 52.54N 5.34E
124 O7 Balkan Mountains Bul./SCr. Stara Planina. ▲▲ Bulgaria/Serbia and Montenegro (Yugoslavia)
152 B9 Balkanskiy Velayat Turkm. Balkan Welaýaty. ◆ province W Turkmenistan
Balkan Welayaty see Balkanskiy Velayat
151 P8 Balkashino Akmola, N Kazakhstan 52.32N 68.43E
155 O2 Balkh anc. Bactra. Balkh, N Afghanistan 36.46N 66.54E
155 P2 Balkh ◆ province N Afghanistan
151 T13 Balkhash Kaz. Balqash. Zhezkazgan, SE Kazakhstan 46.52N 74.54E
Balkhash, Lake see Balkhash, Ozero
151 T13 Balkhash, Ozero Eng. Lake Balkhash, Kaz. Balqash. ◎ SE Kazakhstan
Balla Balla see Mbalabala
98 H10 Ballachulish N Scotland, UK 56.40N 5.10W
188 M12 Balladonia Western Australia 32.21S 123.31E
99 C16 Ballaghaderreen Ir. Bealach an Doirín. C Ireland 53.51N 8.29W
94 H10 Ballangen Nordland, NW Norway 68.18N 16.48E
99 H14 Ballantrae W Scotland, UK 55.04N 5.00W
191 N12 Ballarat Victoria, SE Australia 37.36S 143.51E
188 K11 Ballard, Lake salt lake Western Australia
Ballari see Bellary
78 L11 Ballé Koulikoro, W Mali 15.18N 8.31W
42 D7 Ballenas, Bahía de bay W Mexico
42 D5 Ballenas, Canal de channel NW Mexico
205 R17 Balleny Islands island group Antarctica
42 J7 Balleza var. San Pablo Balleza. Chihuahua, N Mexico 26.55N 106.21W
116 M13 Ballı Tekirdağ, NW Turkey 40.48N 27.03E
159 O13 Ballia Uttar Pradesh, N India 25.45N 84.09E
191 V4 Ballina New South Wales, SE Australia 28.49S 153.33E
99 C16 Ballina Ir. Béal an Átha. W Ireland 54.07N 9.09W
99 D16 Ballinamore Ir. Béal an Átha Móir. NW Ireland 54.03N 7.46W
99 D18 Ballinasloe Ir. Béal Átha na Sluaighe. W Ireland 53.19N 8.13W
27 P8 Ballinger Texas, SW USA 31.44N 99.57W
99 C17 Ballinrobe Ir. Baile an Róba. W Ireland 53.37N 9.14W
99 A21 Ballinskelligs Bay Ir. Bá na Scealg. inlet SW Ireland
99 D15 Ballintra Ir. Baile an tSratha. NW Ireland 54.34N 8.07W
105 T7 Ballon d'Alsace ▲ NE France 47.50N 6.54E
Ballon de Guebwiller see Grand Ballon
115 K21 Ballsh var. Ballshi. Fier, SW Albania 40.35N 19.45E
Ballshi see Ballsh
100 K4 Ballum Friesland, N Netherlands 53.27N 5.40E
99 F16 Ballybay Ir. Béal Átha Beithe. N Ireland 54.07N 6.54W
99 E14 Ballybofey Ir. Bealach Féich. NW Ireland 54.48N 7.46W
99 G14 Ballycastle Ir. Baile an Chaistil. N Northern Ireland, UK 55.12N 6.13W
99 G15 Ballyclare Ir. Bealach Cláir. E Northern Ireland, UK 54.45N 6.00W
99 E16 Ballyconnell Ir. Béal Átha Conaill. N Ireland 54.07N 7.34W
99 C17 Ballyhaunis Ir. Beál Átha hAmhnais. W Ireland 53.45N 8.45W
99 G14 Ballymena Ir. An Baile Meánach. NE Northern Ireland, UK 54.52N 6.16W
99 F14 Ballymoney Ir. Baile Monaidh. NE Northern Ireland, UK 55.10N 6.30W
99 G15 Ballynahinch Ir. Baile na hInse. SE Northern Ireland, UK 54.24N 5.54W
99 D16 Ballysadare Ir. Baile Easa Dara. NW Ireland 54.13N 8.30W
99 D15 Ballyshannon Ir. Béal Átha Seanaidh. NW Ireland 54.30N 8.10W
65 H19 Balmaceda Aisén, S Chile 45.54S 71.47W
65 G23 Balmaceda, Cerro ▲ S Chile 51.27S 73.26W
113 N22 Balmazújváros Hajdú-Bihar, E Hungary 47.36N 21.18E
110 E10 Balmhorn ▲ SW Switzerland 46.27N 7.41E
190 L12 Balmoral Victoria, SE Australia 37.16S 141.38E
26 K9 Balmorhea Texas, SW USA 30.58N 103.44W
Balneario Claromecó see Claromecó
175 R9 Balo Sulawesi, N Indonesia 0.58S 123.19E
Balochistān see Baluchistān
84 B13 Balombo Port. Norton de Matos, Vila Norton de Matos. Benguela, W Angola 12.21S 14.46E
84 B13 Balombo ~ W Angola
189 X10 Balonne River ~ Queensland, E Australia
158 E13 Bālotra Rājasthān, N India 25.51N 72.18E
151 V14 Balpyk Bi prev. Kirovskiy Kaz. Kīrov. Almaty, SE Kazakhstan 44.52N 78.10E
Balqā'/Balqā', Muḩāfaẓat al see Al Balqā'
Balqash see Balkhash/Balkhash, Ozero
158 M12 Balrāmpur Uttar Pradesh, N India 27.25N 82.10E
190 M9 Balranald New South Wales, SE Australia 34.39S 143.33E
118 H14 Balş Olt, S Romania 44.19N 24.06E
12 H11 Balsam Creek Ontario, S Canada 46.26N 79.10W
32 I5 Balsam Lake Wisconsin, N USA 45.27N 92.28W
12 I14 Balsam Lake ◎ Ontario, SE Canada
61 M14 Balsas Maranhão, E Brazil 07.30S 46.00W
42 M15 Balsas, Río var. Río Mexcala. ~ S Mexico
45 W16 Balsas, Río ~ SE Panama
121 O18 Bal'shavik Rus. Bol'shevik. Homyel'skaya Voblasts', SE Belarus 52.34N 30.49E
97 O15 Bålsta Uppsala, C Sweden 59.33N 17.35E
110 E7 Balsthal Solothurn, NW Switzerland 47.20N 7.50E
119 O8 Balta Odes'ka Oblast', SW Ukraine 47.58N 29.39E
121 H14 Baltaji Voke Vilnius, SE Lithuania 54.35N 25.13E
107 N5 Baltanás Castilla-León, N Spain 41.56N 4.12W
63 E16 Baltasar Brum Artigas, N Uruguay 30.43S 57.19W
118 M9 Bălţi Rus. Bel'tsy. N Moldova 47.45N 27.57E
Baltic Port see Paldiski
120 B10 Baltic Sea Ger. Ostee, Rus. Baltiskoye More. sea N Europe
23 X3 Baltimore Maryland, NE USA 39.17N 76.36W
33 T13 Baltimore Ohio, N USA 39.48N 82.33W
23 X3 Baltimore-Washington ✕ Maryland, E USA 39.10N 76.40W
Baltischport/Baltiski see Paldiski
Baltiskoye More see Baltic Sea
121 A14 Baltiysk Ger. Pillau. Kaliningradskaya Oblast', W Russian Federation 54.39N 19.54E
Baltkrievija see Belarus
194 K9 Baluan Island island N PNG
Balūchestān va Sīstān see Sīstān va Balūchestān
154 M12 Baluchistān var. Balochistān, Beluchistan. ◆ province SW Pakistan
179 Q12 Balud Masbate, N Philippines 12.03N 123.12E
174 Mm6 Balui, Batang ~ East Malaysia
159 S13 Bālurghat West Bengal, NE India 25.14N 88.43E
120 J8 Balvi Balvi, NE Latvia 57.07N 27.14E
194 H12 Balyer River Western Highlands, C PNG
153 W7 Balykchy Kir. Ysyk-Köl; prev. Issyk-Kul', Rybach'ye. Issyk-Kul'skaya Oblast', NE Kyrgyzstan 42.28N 76.08E
58 B7 Balzar Guayas, W Ecuador 1.25S 79.54W
110 I8 Balzers S Liechtenstein 47.04N 9.31E
149 T12 Bam Kermān, SE Iran 29.08N 58.27E
79 Y13 Bama Borno, NE Nigeria 11.28N 13.46E
78 L12 Bamako ● (Mali) Capital District, SW Mali 12.39N 8.01W
79 P10 Bamba Gao, C Mali 17.03N 1.19W
44 M8 Bambana, Río ~ NE Nicaragua
81 J15 Bambari Ouaka, C Central African Republic 5.45N 20.37E
189 W5 Bambaroo Queensland, NE Australia 19.00S 146.16E
103 K19 Bamberg Bayern, SE Germany 49.54N 10.52E
23 R14 Bamberg South Carolina, SE USA 33.18N 81.02W
81 M16 Bambesa Orientale, N Dem. Rep. Congo 3.25N 25.43E
78 G11 Bambey W Senegal 14.43N 16.26W
81 H16 Bambio Sangha-Mbaéré, SW Central African Republic 3.57N 16.54E
85 I24 Bamboesberge ▲ S South Africa 31.24S 26.10E
81 D14 Bamenda Nord-Ouest, W Cameroon 5.55N 10.09E
8 K17 Bamfield Vancouver Island, British Columbia, SW Canada 48.48N 125.05W
152 E12 Bami Turkm. Bamy. Akhalskiy Velayat, C Turkmenistan 38.42N 56.47E
155 P4 Bāmīān var. Bāmiān. Bāmīān, NE Afghanistan 34.50N 67.51E
155 O4 Bāmīān ◆ province C Afghanistan
81 J14 Bamingui Bamingui-Bangoran, C Central African Republic 7.38N 20.06E
80 J13 Bamingui ~ N Central African Republic
80 J13 Bamingui-Bangoran ◆ prefecture N Central African Republic
149 V13 Bampūr Sīstān va Balūchestān, SE Iran 27.13N 60.28E
194 G14 Bamu ~ SW PNG
Bamy see Bami
Bán see Bánovce nad Bebravou
83 N17 Banaadir off. Gobolka Banaadir. ◆ region S Somalia
203 N3 Banaba var. Ocean Island. island Tungaru, W Kiribati
61 O14 Banabuiú, Açude ⊠ NE Brazil
59 O19 Bañados del Izozog salt lake SE Bolivia
99 D18 Banagher Ir. Beannchar. C Ireland 53.12N 7.56W
81 M17 Banalia Orientale, N Dem. Rep. Congo 1.39N 25.19E
78 L12 Banamba Koulikoro, W Mali 13.33N 7.25W
42 G4 Banámichi Sonora, NW Mexico 30.01N 110.13W
189 Y9 Banana Queensland, E Australia 24.33S 150.07E
203 Z2 Banana prev. Main Camp. Kiritimati, E Kiribati 02.00N 157.25W
61 K16 Bananal, Ilha do island C Brazil
25 Y12 Banana River lagoon Florida, SE USA
157 Q22 Bananga Andaman and Nicobar Islands, India, NE Indian Ocean 6.57N 93.54E
Banaras see Vārānasi
116 N13 Banarlı Tekirdağ, NW Turkey 41.04N 27.21E
158 H12 Banās ~ N India
77 Z11 Banâs, Râs headland E Egypt 23.55N 35.47E
114 N10 Banatski Karlovac Serbia, NE Serbia and Montenegro (Yugoslavia) 45.03N 21.02E
147 P16 Banā, Wādī dry watercourse SW Yemen
142 E14 Banaz Uşak, W Turkey 38.46N 29.46E
142 E14 Banaz Çayı ~ W Turkey
165 P14 Banbar Xizang Zizhiqu, W China 31.01N 94.43E
99 G15 Banbridge Ir. Droichead na Banna. SE Northern Ireland, UK 54.21N 6.16W
Ban Bua Yai see Bua Yai
99 M21 Banbury S England, UK 52.04N 1.19W
178 H7 Ban Chiang Dao Chiang Mai, NW Thailand 19.22N 98.59E
98 K9 Banchory NE Scotland, UK 57.04N 2.30W
12 J13 Bancroft Ontario, SE Canada 45.04N 77.49W
35 R15 Bancroft Idaho, NW USA 42.43N 111.54W
31 U11 Bancroft Iowa, C USA 43.17N 94.13W
160 I9 Banda Madhya Pradesh, C India 24.04N 78.57E
158 L13 Bānda Uttar Pradesh, N India 25.28N 80.19E
173 E3 Bandaaceh var. Banda Atjeh; prev. Koetaradja, Kutaradja, Kutaraja. Sumatera, W Indonesia 5.30N 95.19E
Banda Atjeh see Bandaaceh
176 U12 Banda, Kepulauan island group E Indonesia
Banda, Laut see Banda Sea
79 N17 Bandama var. Bandama Fleuve. ~ S Ivory Coast
79 N15 Bandama Blanc ~ C Ivory Coast
Bandama Fleuve see Bandama
Bandar 'Abbās see Bandar-e 'Abbās
159 W16 Bandarban Chittagong, SE Bangladesh 22.13N 92.13E
82 Q13 Bandarbeyla var. Bender Beila, Bender Beyla. Bari, NE Somalia 9.28N 50.48E
149 R14 Bandar-e 'Abbās var. Bandar 'Abbās; prev. Gombroon. Hormozgān, S Iran 27.10N 56.10E
148 M3 Bandar-e Anzalī Gīlān, NW Iran 37.25N 49.28E
149 N12 Bandar-e Būshehr var. Būshehr, Eng. Bushire. Būshehr, S Iran 28.58N 50.49E
148 M11 Bandar-e Gonāveh var. Ganāveh; prev. Gonāveh. Būshehr, SW Iran 29.33N 50.39E
149 R14 Bandar-e Khamīr Hormozgān, S Iran 26.59N 55.30E
149 Q14 Bandar-e Langeh var. Bandar-e Lengeh, Lingeh. Hormozgān, S Iran 26.34N 54.52E
Bandar-e Lengeh see Bandar-e Langeh
148 L10 Bandar-e Māhshahr var. Māh-Shahr; prev. Bandar-e Ma'shūr. Khūzestān, SW Iran 30.33N 49.10E
Bandar-e Ma'shūr see Bandar-e Māhshahr
149 O14 Bandar-e Nakhīlū Hormozgān, S Iran
Bandar-e Shāh see Bandar-e Torkaman
149 P4 Bandar-e Torkaman var. Bandar-e Torkeman, Bandar-e Torkman; prev. Bandar-e Shāh. Golestān, N Iran 36.55N 54.04E
Bandar-e Torkeman/Bandar-e Torkman see Bandar-e Torkaman
Bandar Kassim see Boosaaso
174 Ii13 Bandarlampung prev. Tanjungkarang, Teloekbetoeng, Telukbetung. Sumatera, W Indonesia 5.28N 105.16E
Bandar Maharani see Muar
Bandar Masulipatnam see Machilīpatnam
Bandar Penggaram see Batu Pahat
175 N3 Bandar Seri Begawan prev. Brunei Town. ● (Brunei) N Brunei 4.55N 114.58E
174 Mm3 Bandar Seri Begawan ✕ N Brunei 4.55N 114.58E
175 Ss13 Banda Sea var. Laut Banda. sea E Indonesia
106 H5 Bande Galicia, NW Spain 42.01N 7.58W
61 G15 Bandeirantes Mato Grosso, W Brazil 9.04S 57.53W
61 N20 Bandeira, Pico da ▲ SE Brazil 20.25S 41.45W
85 K19 Bandelierkop Limpopo, NE South Africa 23.21S 29.46E
64 L8 Bandera Santiago del Estero, N Argentina 28.52S 62.15W
27 Q11 Bandera Texas, SW USA 29.43N 99.07W
42 J13 Banderas, Bahía de bay W Mexico
79 O11 Bandiagara Mopti, C Mali 14.22N 3.42W
158 I12 Bāndīkūi Rājasthān, N India 27.07N 76.34E
142 C11 Bandırma var. Penderma. Balıkesir, NW Turkey 40.21N 27.58E
Bandjarmasin see Banjarmasin
Bandoeng see Bandung
99 C21 Bandon Ir. Droicheadna Bandan. SW Ireland 51.43N 8.43W
34 E14 Bandon Oregon, NW USA 43.07N 124.24W
178 J8 Ban Dong Bang Nong Khai, E Thailand 18.00N 104.08E
178 I6 Ban Donkon Oudômxai, N Laos 20.20N 101.37E
180 J14 Bandrélé SE Mayotte
81 H20 Bandundu prev. Banningville. Bandundu, W Dem. Rep. Congo 3.18S 17.24E
81 I21 Bandundu off. Région de Bandundu. ◆ region W Dem. Rep. Congo
174 Jj14 Bandung prev. Bandoeng. Jawa, C Indonesia 6.47S 107.28E
118 L15 Băneasa Constanţa, SW Romania 44.03N 27.42E
148 J4 Bāneh Kordestān, N Iran 35.58N 45.54E
46 I7 Banes Holguín, E Cuba 20.58N 75.43W
9 P16 Banff Alberta, SW Canada 51.10N 115.34W
98 K8 Banff NE Scotland, UK 57.39N 2.33W
98 K8 Banff cultural region NE Scotland, UK
Bánffyhunyad see Huedin
79 N14 Banfora SW Burkina 10.36N 4.45W
161 H19 Bangalore Karnātaka, S India 12.58N 77.34E
159 S16 Bangaon West Bengal, NE India 23.01N 88.49E
179 P9 Bangar Luzon, N Philippines 16.51N 120.25E
81 L15 Bangassou Mbomou, SE Central African Republic 4.51N 22.55E
194 K12 Bangeta, Mount ▲ C PNG 6.11S 147.02E
175 Qq10 Banggai, Kepulauan island group C Indonesia
175 R9 Banggai, Pulau island Kepulauan Banggai, N Indonesia
176 X11 Banggelapa Papua, E Indonesia 3.47S 136.53E
Banggi see Banggi, Pulau
175 O1 Banggi, Pulau var. Banggi. island East Malaysia
124 N15 Banghāzī Eng. Bengazi, Benghazi, It. Bengasi. NE Libya 32.07N 20.04E
Bang Hieng see Xé Banghiang
174 K8 Bangkai, Tanjung var. Bankai. headland Borneo, N Indonesia 0.21N 108.53E
174 M14 Bangkalan Pulau Madura, C Indonesia 7.05S 112.43E
175 S6 Bangka, Pulau island C Indonesia
174 J10 Bangka, Pulau island W Indonesia
174 Ii10 Bangka, Selat strait Sumatera, W Indonesia
175 Rr6 Bangka, Selat var. Selat Likupang. strait Sulawesi, N Indonesia
174 Gg8 Bangkinang Sumatera, W Indonesia 0.21N 100.56E
174 H10 Bangko Sumatera, W Indonesia 2.05S 102.15E
Bangkok see Krung Thep
Bangkok, Bight of see Krung Thep, Ao
159 T14 Bangladesh off. People's Republic of Bangladesh; prev. East Pakistan. ◆ republic S Asia
178 Kk13 Ba Ngoi Khanh Hoa, S Vietnam 11.55N 109.07E
158 K5 Bangong Co var. Pangong Tso. ◎ China/India see also Pangong Tso
99 G15 Bangor Ir. Beannchar. E Northern Ireland, UK 54.40N 5.40W
99 I18 Bangor NW Wales, UK 53.13N 4.07W
21 R6 Bangor Maine, NE USA 44.48N 68.46W
20 I14 Bangor Pennsylvania, NE USA 40.52N 75.12W
69 R8 Bangoran ~ S Central African Republic
Bang Phra see Trat
Bang Pla Soi see Chon Buri
27 Q8 Bangs Texas, SW USA 31.43N 99.07W
178 H13 Bang Saphan var. Bang Saphan Yai. Prachuap Khiri Khan, SW Thailand 11.10N 99.27E
Bang Saphan Yai see Bang Saphan
38 I8 Bangs, Mount ▲ Arizona, SW USA 36.47N 113.51W
95 E15 Bangsund Nord-Trøndelag, C Norway 64.22N 11.22E
179 P8 Bangued Luzon, N Philippines 17.36N 120.40E
81 I15 Bangui ● (Central African Republic) Ombella-Mpoko, SW Central African Republic 4.21N 18.31E
81 I15 Bangui ✕ Ombella-Mpoko, SW Central African Republic 4.19N 18.34E
85 N16 Bangula Southern, S Malawi 16.38S 35.04E
Bangwaketse see Southern
84 K12 Bangweulu, Lake var. Lake Bengweulu. ◎ N Zambia
Banhā see Benha
Ban Hat Yai see Hat Yai
178 I8 Ban Hin Heup Viangchan, C Laos 18.37N 102.19E
Ban Houayxay/Ban Houei Sai see Houayxay
178 H12 Ban Hua Hin var. Hua Hin. Prachuap Khiri Khan, SW Thailand 12.29N 99.55E
81 L14 Bani Haute-Kotto, E Central African Republic 7.06N 22.51E
79 N12 Bani ~ S Mali
47 O9 Baní S Dominican Republic 18.14N 70.18W
Banias see Bāniyās
79 S11 Bani Bangou Tillabéri, SW Niger 15.04N 2.40E
78 M12 Banifing var. Ngorolaka. ~ Burkina/Mali
79 R13 Banikoara N Benin 11.18N 2.25E
Banī Mazār see Beni Mazâr
116 K8 Baniski Lom ~ N Bulgaria
23 U7 Banister River ~ Virginia, NE USA
Banī Suwayf see Beni Suef
77 O8 Banī Walīd NW Libya 31.46N 13.58E
144 H5 Bāniyās var. Banias, Baniyas, Paneas. Ţarţūs, W Syria 35.12N 35.57E
115 K14 Banja Serbia, W Serbia and Montenegro (Yugoslavia) 43.33N 19.35E
Banjak, Kepulauan see Banyak, Kepulauan
114 J12 Banja Koviljača Serbia, W Serbia and Montenegro (Yugoslavia) 44.31N 19.11E
114 G11 Banja Luka Republika Srpska, NW Bosnia and Herzegovina 44.46N 17.10E
175 N11 Banjarmasin prev. Bandjarmasin. Borneo, C Indonesia 3.22S 114.33E
Banjoewangi see Banyuwangi
78 F11 Banjul prev. Bathurst. ● (Gambia) W Gambia 13.25N 16.43W
78 F11 Banjul ✕ W Gambia 13.18N 16.39W
Banjuwangi see Banyuwangi
Bank see Bankä
143 Y13 Bankä Rus. Bank. SE Azerbaijan 39.25N 49.13E
178 Jj11 Ban Kadian var. Ban Kadiene. Champasak, S Laos 14.25N 105.42E
Ban Kadiene see Ban Kadian
Bankai see Bangkai, Tanjung
178 Gg15 Ban Kam Phuam Phangnga, SW Thailand 9.16N 98.24E
Ban Kantang see Kantang
79 O11 Bankass Mopti, S Mali 14.05N 3.30W
97 L19 Bankeryd Jönköping, S Sweden 57.51N 14.07E
85 K16 Banket Mashonaland West, N Zimbabwe 17.25S 30.25E
178 Jj11 Ban Khamphô Attapu, S Laos 14.35N 106.18E
25 O4 Bankhead Lake ⊠ Alabama, S USA
79 Q11 Bankilaré Tillabéri, SW Niger 14.34N 0.41E
Banks, Îles see Banks Islands
8 I14 Banks Island island British Columbia, SW Canada
15 Hh1 Banks Island island Banks Island, Northwest Territories, NW Canada
197 C10 Banks Islands Fr. Îles Banks. island group N Vanuatu
25 U8 Banks Lake ◎ Georgia, SE USA
34 K8 Banks Lake ⊠ Washington, NW USA
193 I19 Banks Peninsula peninsula South Island, NZ
191 Q15 Banks Strait strait SW Tasman Sea
Ban Kui Nua see Kui Buri
159 R16 Bānkura West Bengal, NE India 23.13N 87.04E
178 J8 Ban Lakxao var. Lak Sao. Bolikhamxai, C Laos 18.10N 104.58E
178 H17 Ban Lam Phai Songkhla, SW Thailand 6.43N 100.57E
Ban Mae Sot see Mae Sot
Ban Mae Suai see Mae Suai
Ban Mak Khaeng see Udon Thani
177 G3 Banmauk Sagaing, N Myanmar 24.25N 95.54E
Banmo see Bhamo
178 Jj10 Ban Mun-Houamuang S Laos 15.11N 106.44E
99 F14 Bann var. Lower Bann, Upper Bann. ~ N Northern Ireland, UK
178 Jj10 Ban Nadou Salavan, S Laos 15.51N 105.37E
178 J10 Ban Nakala Savannakhét, S Laos 16.14N 105.09E
178 I8 Ban Nakha Viangchan, C Laos 18.13N 102.29E
178 Jj9 Ban Nakham Khammouan, S Laos 17.10N 105.25E
178 I8 Ban Namoun Xaignabouli, N Laos 18.40N 101.34E
178 Hh17 Ban Nang Sata Yala, SW Thailand 6.15N 101.13E
178 Gg15 Ban Na San Surat Thani, SW Thailand 8.52N 99.21E
178 Ii7 Ban Nasi Xiangkhoang, N Laos 19.37N 103.33E
46 I3 Bannerman Town Eleuthera Island, C Bahamas 24.38N 76.09W
37 V15 Banning California, W USA 33.55N 116.52W
Banningville see Bandundu
178 Jj11 Ban Nongsim Champasak, S Laos 14.45N 106.00E
155 S7 Bannu prev. Edwardesabad. North-West Frontier Province, NW Pakistan 32.00N 70.36E
Bañolas see Banyoles
58 C7 Baños Tungurahua, C Ecuador 1.20S 78.24W
Bánovce see Bánovce nad Bebravou
113 I19 Bánovce nad Bebravou var. Bánovce, Hung. Bán. Trenčiansky Kraj, W Slovakia 48.43N 18.15E
114 I12 Banovići Federacija Bosna I Hercegovina, E Bosnia and Herzegovina 44.25N 18.31E
Banow see Andarāb
Ban Pak Phanang see Pak Phanang
178 Hh7 Ban Pan Nua Lampang, NW Thailand 18.51N 99.57E
178 I10 Ban Phai Khon Kaen, E Thailand 16.00N 102.42E
178 Jj9 Ban Phou A Douk Khammouan, C Laos 17.12N 106.07E
178 I8 Ban Phu Uthai Thani, W Thailand
178 H11 Ban Pong Ratchaburi, W Thailand 13.49N 99.52E
202 I3 Banraeaba Tarawa, W Kiribati 1.19N 173.01E
178 Gg11 Ban Sai Yok Kanchanaburi, W Thailand 14.24N 98.54E
Ban Sattahip/Ban Sattahipp see Sattahip
Ban Sichon see Sichon
Ban Si Racha see Si Racha
113 J19 Banská Bystrica Ger. Neusohl, Hung. Besztercebánya. Banskobystrický Kraj, C Slovakia 48.45N 19.08E
113 K20 Banskobystrický Kraj ◆ region C Slovakia
178 J8 Ban Sôppheung Bolikhamxai, C Laos 18.33N 104.18E
Ban Sop Prap see Sop Prap
158 G15 Bānswāra Rājasthān, N India 23.31N 74.28E
178 Gg15 Ban Ta Khun Surat Thani, SW Thailand 8.53N 98.52E
Ban Takua Pa see Takua Pa
178 Jj9 Ban Talak Khammouan, C Laos 17.33N 105.40E
79 R15 Bantè W Benin 8.21N 1.55E
178 Ii8 Ban Thabôk Bolikhamxai, C Laos 18.21N 103.12E
178 Jj10 Ban Tôp Savannakhét, S Laos 16.07N 106.07E
99 B21 Bantry Ir. Beanntraí. SW Ireland 51.40N 9.27W
99 A21 Bantry Bay Ir. Bá Bheanntraí. bay SW Ireland
174 L15 Bantul prev. Bantoel. Jawa, C Indonesia 7.55S 110.21E
161 F19 Bantvāl var. Bantwāl. Karnātaka, E India 12.57N 75.04E
Bantwāl see Bantvāl
116 N9 Banya Burgas, E Bulgaria 42.46N 27.49E
173 Ee6 Banyak, Kepulauan prev. Kepulauan Banjak. island group NW Indonesia
107 U8 Banya, La headland E Spain 40.34N 0.37E
81 E14 Banyo Adamaoua, NW Cameroon 6.46N 11.49E
107 X4 Banyoles var. Bañolas. Cataluña, NE Spain 42.07N 2.46E
178 H16 Ban Yong Sata Trang, SW Thailand 7.09N 99.42E
174 Mm16 Banyuwangi var. Banjuwangi; prev. Banjoewangi. Jawa, S Indonesia 8.12S 114.22E
205 X14 Banzare Coast physical region Antarctica
181 Q14 Banzare Seamounts undersea feature S Indian Ocean
Banzart see Bizerte
Baochang see Taibus Qi
167 O3 Baoding var. Pao-ting; prev. Tsingyuan. Hebei, E China 38.52N 115.28E
Baoebaoe see Baubau
Baoi, Oileán see Dursey Island
166 J6 Baoji var. Pao-chi, Paoki. Shaanxi, C China 34.22N 107.16E
195 V14 Baolo Santa Isabel, N Solomon Islands 7.41S 158.47E
178 K13 Bao Lôc Lâm Đông, S Vietnam 11.33N 107.48E
169 Z7 Baoqing Heilongjiang, NE China 46.15N 132.12E
Baoqing see Shaoyang
81 H15 Baoro Nana-Mambéré, W Central African Republic 5.40N 16.00E
166 E12 Baoshan var. Pao-shan. Yunnan, SW China 25.04N 99.07E
169 N13 Baotou var. Pao-t'ou, Paotow. Nei Mongol Zizhiqu, N China 40.37N 109.58E
78 L14 Baoulé ~ S Mali
78 K12 Baoulé ~ W Mali
105 O2 Bapaume Pas-de-Calais, N France 50.06N 2.50E
12 J13 Baptiste Lake ◎ Ontario, SE Canada
Baqanas see Bakanas
Baqbaqty see Bakbakty
165 P14 Baqên var. Dartang. Xizang Zizhiqu, W China 31.50N 94.08E
144 F14 Bāqir, Jabal ▲ S Jordan
145 T7 Ba'qūbah var. Qubba. C Iraq 33.45N 44.40E
64 H5 Baquedano Antofagasta, N Chile 23.19S 69.49W
118 M6 Bar Vinnyts'ka Oblast', C Ukraine 49.04N 27.39E
115 J18 Bar It. Antivari. Montenegro, SW Serbia and Montenegro (Yugoslavia) 42.02N 19.09E
82 E10 Bara Northern Kordofan, C Sudan 13.42N 30.21E
83 M18 Baraawe It. Brava. Shabeellaha Hoose, S Somalia 1.09N 43.59E
158 M12 Bāra Banki Uttar Pradesh, N India 26.55N 81.10E
125 G13 Barabinsk Novosibirskaya Oblast', C Russian Federation 55.19N 78.01E
32 L8 Baraboo Wisconsin, N USA 43.27N 89.45W
32 K8 Baraboo Range hill range Wisconsin, N USA
Baracaldo see San Vicente de Barakaldo
13 Y6 Barachois Quebec, SE Canada 48.37N 64.14W
46 J7 Baracoa Guantánamo, E Cuba 20.19N 74.31W
63 C19 Baradero Buenos Aires, E Argentina 33.47S 59.29W
191 R6 Baradine New South Wales, SE Australia 30.55S 149.03E
Baraf Daja Islands see Damar, Kepulauan
160 M12 Baragarh Orissa, E India 21.20N 83.36E
83 I17 Baragoi Rift Valley, W Kenya 1.39N 36.46E
47 N9 Barahona SW Dominican Republic 18.13N 71.07W
159 W13 Barail Range ▲▲ NE India
82 I9 Baraka var. Barka, Ar. Khawr Barakah. seasonal river Eritrea/Sudan
82 G10 Barakat Gezira, C Sudan 14.18N 33.31E
Barakī see Barakī Barak
155 Q6 Barakī Barak var. Barakī, Baraki Rajan. Lowgar, E Afghanistan 33.58N 68.58E
Baraki Rajan see Barakī Barak
160 N11 Bārākot Orissa, E India 21.35N 85.00E
Baram see Baram, Batang
57 S7 Barama River ~ N Guyana
161 E14 Bārāmati Mahārāshtra, W India 18.12N 74.39E
174 Mm4 Baram, Batang var. Baram, Barram. ~ East Malaysia
158 H5 Bārāmūla Jammu and Kashmir, NW India 34.15N 74.24E
121 N14 Baran' Vitsyebskaya Voblasts', NE Belarus 54.28N 30.18E
158 I14 Bārān Rājasthān, N India 25.07N 76.31E
145 U4 Barānān, Shākh-i ▲ E Iraq
121 I17 Baranavichy Pol. Baranowicze, Rus. Baranovichi. Brestskaya Voblasts', SW Belarus 53.07N 26.01E
127 Oo5 Baranikha Chukotskiy Avtonomnyy Okrug, NE Russian Federation 68.29N 168.13E
118 M4 Baranivka Zhytomyrs'ka Oblast', N Ukraine 50.16N 27.40E
41 W14 Baranof Island island Alexander Archipelago, Alaska, USA
Baranovichi/Baranowicze see Baranavichy
113 N15 Baranów Sandomierski Podkarpackie, SE Poland 50.28N 21.31E
113 I26 Baranya off. Baranya Megye. ◆ county S Hungary
159 R13 Barauli Bihār, NE India 25.31N 87.22E
24 L10 Barataria Bay bay Louisiana, S USA
Barat Daya, Kepulauan see Damar, Kepulauan
120 L12 Baravukha Rus. Borovukha. Vitsyebskaya Voblasts', N Belarus 55.36N 28.33E
56 E11 Baraya Huila, C Colombia 3.10N 75.04W
61 M21 Barbacena Minas Gerais, SE Brazil 21.13S 43.46W
56 B13 Barbacoas Nariño, SW Colombia 1.37N 78.07W
56 L6 Barbacoas Aragua, N Venezuela 9.28N 66.58W
47 Z13 Barbados ◆ commonwealth republic SE West Indies
49 S3 Barbados island Barbados
107 U11 Barbaria, Cap de var. Cabo de Berberia. headland Formentera, E Spain 38.39N 1.24E
116 N13 Barbaros Tekirdağ, NW Turkey 40.55N 27.28E
76 A11 Barbas, Cap headland S Western Sahara 22.14N 16.45W
107 T5 Barbastro Aragón, NE Spain 42.01N 0.07E
106 K16 Barbate ~ SW Spain
106 K16 Barbate de Franco Andalucía, S Spain 36.11N 5.55W
85 K21 Barberton Mpumalanga, NE South Africa 25.45S 31.01E
33 U12 Barberton Ohio, N USA 41.02N 81.37W
104 K12 Barbezieux-St-Hilaire Charente, W France 45.28N 0.09W
56 G9 Barbosa Boyaca, C Colombia 5.57N 73.37W
23 N7 Barbourville Kentucky, S USA 36.52N 83.53W
47 W9 Barbuda island N Antigua and Barbuda
189 W8 Barcaldine Queensland, E Australia 23.33S 145.20E
Barcarozsnyó see Râşnov
106 I11 Barcarrota Extremadura, W Spain 38.31N 6.51W
Barcău see Berettyó
Barce see Al Marj

◆ Country
● Country Capital
◇ Dependent Territory
○ Dependent Territory Capital
◆ Administrative Region
✕ International Airport
▲ Mountain
▲▲ Mountain Range
Volcano
~ River
◎ Lake
⊠ Reservoir

109 L23 **Barcellona** var. Barcellona Pozzo di Gotto. Sicilia, Italy, C Mediterranean Sea 38.09N 15.15E
Barcellona Pozzo di Gotto see Barcellona
107 W6 **Barcelona** anc. Barcino, Barcinona. Cataluña, E Spain 41.25N 2.10E
57 N5 **Barcelona** Anzoátegui, NE Venezuela 10.07N 64.43W
107 S5 **Barcelona** ◆ province Cataluña, NE Spain
107 W6 **Barcelona** ✕ Cataluña, E Spain 41.25N 2.10E
105 U14 **Barcelonnette** Alpes-de-Haute-Provence, SE France 44.24N 6.37E
60 E12 **Barcelos** Amazonas, N Brazil 0.58S 62.58W
106 G5 **Barcelos** Braga, N Portugal 41.31N 8.37W
112 I10 **Barcin** Ger. Bartschin. Kujawski-pomorskie, C Poland 52.51N 17.55E
Barcino/Barcinona see Barcelona
Barcoo see Cooper Creek
113 H26 **Barcs** Somogy, SW Hungary 45.57N 17.26E
143 W11 **Bärdä** Rus. Barda. C Azerbaijan 40.25N 47.07E
80 H5 **Bardaï** Borkou-Ennedi-Tibesti, N Chad 21.21N 16.55E
145 R2 **Bardaraṣh** N Iraq 36.32N 43.36E
145 Q7 **Bardasah** SW Iraq 34.02N 42.28E
159 S16 **Barddhamān** West Bengal, NE India 23.10N 88.03E
113 N18 **Bardejov** Ger. Bartfeld, Hung. Bártfa. Prešovský Kraj, E Slovakia 49.17N 21.18E
107 R4 **Bárdenas Reales** physical region N Spain
Bardera/Bardere see Baardheere
Bardesīr see Bardsīr
94 K3 **Bárdharbunga** ▲ C Iceland 64.39N 17.30W
Bardhë, Drini i see Beli Drim
108 E9 **Bardi** Emilia-Romagna, C Italy 44.39N 9.44E
108 A8 **Bardonecchia** Piemonte, W Italy 45.04N 6.40E
99 H19 **Bardsey Island** island NW Wales, UK
149 S11 **Bardsīr** var. Bardesīr, Mashīz. Kermān, C Iran 29.58N 56.29E
22 L6 **Bardstown** Kentucky, S USA 37.48N 85.28W
Barduli see Barletta
22 G7 **Bardwell** Kentucky, S USA 36.52N 89.01W
158 K11 **Bareilly** var. Bareli. Uttar Pradesh, N India 28.19N 79.24E
Bareli see Bareilly
100 H13 **Barendrecht** Zuid-Holland, SW Netherlands 51.52N 4.31E
104 M3 **Barentin** Seine-Maritime, N France 49.33N 0.57E
94 N3 **Barentsburg** Spitsbergen, W Svalbard 78.01N 14.19E
Barentsevo More/Barents Havet see Barents Sea
94 O3 **Barentsøya** island E Svalbard
207 T11 **Barents Plain** undersea feature N Barents Sea
129 P3 **Barents Sea** Nor. Barents Havet, Rus. Barentsevo More. sea Arctic Ocean
207 U14 **Barents Trough** undersea feature SW Barents Sea
82 I9 **Barentu** W Eritrea 15.08N 37.35E
104 J3 **Barfleur** Manche, N France 49.41N 1.18W
104 J3 **Barfleur, Pointe de** headland N France 49.46N 1.09W
Barfrush/Barfurush see Bābol
164 H14 **Barga** Xizang Zizhiqu, W China 30.51N 81.19E
107 N9 **Bargas** Castilla-La Mancha, C Spain 39.56N 4.00W
83 I15 **Bargē** Southern, S Ethiopia 6.11N 37.04E
108 A9 **Barge** Piemonte, NE Italy 44.49N 7.21E
159 U16 **Barguna** Khulna, S Bangladesh 22.09N 90.07E
Bärgușad see Vorotan
126 K15 **Barguzin** Respublika Buryatiya, S Russian Federation 53.37N 109.47E
159 O13 **Barhaj** Uttar Pradesh, N India 26.16N 83.43E
191 N10 **Barham** New South Wales, SE Australia 35.39S 144.09E
158 J12 **Barhan** Uttar Pradesh, N India 27.21N 78.10E
21 S7 **Bar Harbor** Mount Desert Island, Maine, NE USA 44.23N 68.14W
159 R14 **Barharwa** Bihār, NE India 24.52N 87.46E
159 P15 **Barhi** Bihār, N India 24.19N 85.25E
109 O17 **Bari** var. Bari delle Puglie; anc. Barium. Puglia, SE Italy 41.06N 16.52E
82 P12 **Bari** off. Gobolka Bari. ◆ region NE Somalia
167 K14 **Ba Ria** Ba Ria-Vung Tau, S Vietnam 10.30N 107.10E
Bāridah see Al Bāridah
Bari delle Puglie see Bari
Barikot see Barīkowṭ
155 T4 **Barīkowṭ** var. Barikot. Kunar, NE Afghanistan 35.18N 71.36E
44 C4 **Barillas** var. Santa Cruz Barillas. Huehuetenango, NW Guatemala 15.49N 91.19W
56 J6 **Barinas** Barinas, W Venezuela 8.36N 70.15W
56 I7 **Barinas** off. Estado Barinas; prev. Zamora. ◆ state C Venezuela
56 I6 **Barinitas** Barinas, NW Venezuela 8.47N 70.26W
160 P11 **Bāripada** Orissa, E India 21.58N 86.45E
62 K9 **Bariri** São Paulo, S Brazil 22.04S 48.46W
77 W11 **Bârîs** S Egypt 24.28N 30.39E
158 G14 **Bari Sādri** Rājasthān, N India 24.25N 74.28E
159 U16 **Barisal** Khulna, S Bangladesh 22.40N 90.19E
173 G7 **Barisan, Pegunungan** ▲▲ Sumatera, W Indonesia
175 N10 **Barito, Sungai** ∽ Borneo, C Indonesia
Barium see Bari
Barka see Baraka
Barka see Al Marj
166 H8 **Barkam** Sichuan, C China 31.56N 102.22E
120 J9 **Barkava** Madona, C Latvia 56.43N 26.34E
8 M15 **Barkerville** British Columbia, SW Canada 53.06N 121.34W
12 J12 **Bark Lake** ◎ Ontario, SE Canada
22 H7 **Barkley, Lake** ⊠ Kentucky/Tennessee, S USA
8 K17 **Barkley Sound** inlet British Columbia, W Canada
85 J24 **Barkly East** Afr. Barkly-Oos. Eastern Cape, SE South Africa 30.58S 27.34E
Barkly-Oos see Barkly East
189 S4 **Barkly Tableland** plateau Northern Territory/Queensland, N Australia
Barkly-Wes see Barkly West
85 H22 **Barkly West** Afr. Barkly-Wes. Northern Cape, N South Africa 28.31S 24.31E
165 O5 **Barkol** var. Barkol Kazak Zizhixian. Xinjiang Uygur Zizhiqu, NW China 43.37N 93.01E
165 O5 **Barkol Hu** ◎ NW China
Barkol Kazak Zizhixian see Barkol
32 J3 **Bark Point** headland Wisconsin, N USA 46.53N 91.11W
27 P11 **Barksdale** Texas, SW USA 29.43N 100.03W
Bar Kunar see Asmār
118 L11 **Bârlad** prev. Bîrlad. Vaslui, E Romania 46.12N 27.39E
118 M11 **Bârlad** prev. Bîrlad. ∽ E Romania
78 D9 **Barlavento, Ilhas de** var. Windward Islands. island group N Cape Verde
105 R5 **Bar-le-Duc** var. Bar-sur-Ornain. Meuse, NE France 48.46N 5.10E
188 K11 **Barlee, Lake** ◎ Western Australia
188 H8 **Barlee Range** ▲▲ Western Australia
109 N16 **Barletta** anc. Barduli. Puglia, SE Italy 41.19N 16.16E
112 E10 **Barlinek** Ger. Berlinchen. Zachodniopomorskie, NW Poland 53.00N 15.11E
29 S11 **Barling** Arkansas, C USA 35.19N 94.18W
176 Vv10 **Barma** Papua, E Indonesia 1.55S 132.57E
191 Q9 **Barmedman** New South Wales, SE Australia 34.09S 147.21E
Barmen-Elberfeld see Wuppertal
158 D12 **Bārmer** Rājasthān, NW India 25.46N 71.24E
190 K9 **Barmera** South Australia 34.14S 140.26E
99 I19 **Barmouth** NW Wales, UK 52.44N 4.03W
160 F10 **Barnagar** Madhya Pradesh, C India 23.01N 75.28E
158 H9 **Barnāla** Punjab, NW India 30.19N 75.33E
99 L15 **Barnard Castle** N England, UK 54.34N 1.55W
191 O6 **Barnato** New South Wales, SE Australia 31.39S 145.01E
126 H14 **Barnaul** Altayskiy Kray, C Russian Federation 53.21N 83.45E
111 V8 **Bärnbach** Steiermark, SE Austria 47.05N 15.07E
20 K16 **Barnegat** New Jersey, NE USA 39.43N 74.12W
25 S4 **Barnesville** Georgia, SE USA 33.03N 84.09W
31 R6 **Barnesville** Minnesota, N USA 46.39N 96.25W
33 U13 **Barnesville** Ohio, N USA 39.59N 81.10W
100 K11 **Barneveld** var. Barnveld. Gelderland, C Netherlands 52.10N 5.34E
27 O9 **Barnhart** Texas, SW USA 31.07N 101.09W
29 P8 **Barnsdall** Oklahoma, C USA 36.33N 96.09W
99 M17 **Barnsley** N England, UK 53.34N 1.28W
21 Q12 **Barnstable** Massachusetts, NE USA 41.42N 70.16W
99 I23 **Barnstaple** SW England, UK 51.04N 4.04W
Barnveld see Barneveld
23 Q14 **Barnwell** South Carolina, SE USA 33.14N 81.21W
69 U8 **Baro** var. Baro Wenz. ∽ Ethiopia/Sudan
79 U15 **Baro** Niger, C Nigeria 8.35N 6.28E
Baro see Baro Wenz
Baroda see Vadodara
155 U2 **Baroghil Pass** var. Kowtal-e Barowghīl. pass Afghanistan/Pakistan 36.54N 73.22E
121 Q17 **Baron'ki** Rus. Boron'ki. Mahilyowskaya Voblasts', E Belarus 53.07N 32.09E
190 J9 **Barossa Valley** valley South Australia
Baroui see Salisbury
83 H14 **Baro Wenz** var. Baro, Nahr Barū. ∽ Ethiopia/Sudan
159 U12 **Barpeta** Assam, NE India 26.19N 91.05E
33 S7 **Barques, Pointe Aux** headland Michigan, N USA 44.04N 82.57W
56 J5 **Barquisimeto** Lara, NW Venezuela 10.03N 69.18W
61 N16 **Barra** Bahia, E Brazil 11.06S 43.15W
98 E9 **Barra** island NW Scotland, UK
191 T5 **Barraba** New South Wales, SE Australia 30.24S 150.37E
62 L9 **Barra Bonita** São Paulo, S Brazil 22.30S 48.34W
66 J12 **Barracuda Fracture Zone** var. Fifteen Twenty Fracture Zone. tectonic feature SW Atlantic Ocean
66 G11 **Barracuda Ridge** undersea feature N Atlantic Ocean
45 N12 **Barra del Colorado** Limón, NE Costa Rica 10.44N 83.35W
45 N9 **Barra de Río Grande** Región Autónoma Atlántico Sur, E Nicaragua 12.56N 83.30W
84 A11 **Barra do Cuanza** Luanda, NW Angola 9.12S 13.08E
62 O9 **Barra do Piraí** Rio de Janeiro, SE Brazil 22.30S 43.47W
63 D16 **Barra do Quaraí** Rio Grande do Sul, SE Brazil 31.03S 58.10W
61 G14 **Barra do São Manuel** Pará, N Brazil 7.12S 58.03W
85 N19 **Barra Falsa, Ponta da** headland S Mozambique 22.57S 35.36E
98 E10 **Barra Head** headland NW Scotland, UK 56.46N 7.37W
Barram see Baram, Batang
62 O9 **Barra Mansa** Rio de Janeiro, SE Brazil 22.25S 44.03W
59 D14 **Barranca** Lima, W Peru 10.46S 77.46W
56 F8 **Barrancabermeja** Santander, N Colombia 7.00N 73.51W
56 H4 **Barrancas** La Guajira, N Colombia 10.58N 72.46W
56 J6 **Barrancas** Barinas, NW Venezuela 8.46N 70.07W
57 Q6 **Barrancas** Monagas, NE Venezuela 8.45N 62.12W
56 F6 **Barranco de Loba** Bolívar, N Colombia 8.55N 74.07W
106 I12 **Barrancos** Beja, S Portugal 38.07N 6.58W
64 N7 **Barranqueras** Chaco, N Argentina 27.31S 58.53W
56 F4 **Barranquilla** Atlántico, N Colombia 10.58N 74.48W
85 N20 **Barra, Ponta da** headland S Mozambique 23.46S 35.33E
107 P11 **Barrax** Castilla-La Mancha, C Spain 39.04N 2.12W
21 N11 **Barre** Massachusetts, NE USA 42.24N 72.06W
20 M7 **Barre** Vermont, NE USA 44.09N 72.25W
61 M17 **Barreiras** Bahia, E Brazil 12.09S 44.58W
106 F11 **Barreiro** Setúbal, W Portugal 38.40N 9.04W
67 C26 **Barren Island** island S Falkland Islands
22 K7 **Barren River Lake** ⊠ Kentucky, S USA
62 L7 **Barretos** São Paulo, S Brazil 20.33S 48.33W
9 P14 **Barrhead** Alberta, SW Canada 54.08N 114.28W
12 G14 **Barrie** Ontario, S Canada 44.24N 79.39W
9 N16 **Barrière** British Columbia, SW Canada 51.10N 120.06W
12 H8 **Barrière, Lac** ◎ Quebec, SE Canada
190 L6 **Barrier Range** hill range New South Wales, SE Australia
44 G3 **Barrier Reef** reef E Belize
196 C16 **Barrigada** C Guam 13.27N 144.48E
Barrington Island see Santa Fe, Isla
191 T7 **Barrington Tops** ▲ New South Wales, SE Australia 32.06S 151.18E
191 O4 **Barringun** New South Wales, SE Australia 29.02S 145.45E
61 K18 **Barro Alto** Goiás, S Brazil 15.07S 48.56W
61 N14 **Barro Duro** Piauí, NE Brazil 5.49S 42.30W
32 I5 **Barron** Wisconsin, N USA 45.24N 91.49W
12 J12 **Barron** ∽ Ontario, SE Canada
63 H15 **Barros Cassal** Rio Grande do Sul, S Brazil 29.12S 52.33W
47 P14 **Barrouallie** Saint Vincent, W Saint Vincent and the Grenadines 13.13N 61.16W
41 O4 **Barrow** Alaska, USA 71.17N 156.47W
99 E20 **Barrow** Ir. An Bhearú. ∽ SE Ireland
189 Q6 **Barrow Creek Roadhouse** Northern Territory, N Australia 21.30S 133.52E
99 J16 **Barrow-in-Furness** NW England, UK 54.07N 3.13W
188 G7 **Barrow Island** island Western Australia
41 O4 **Barrow, Point** headland Alaska, USA 71.23N 156.28W
9 V14 **Barrows** Manitoba, S Canada 52.49N 101.36W
99 J22 **Barry** S Wales, UK 51.24N 3.18W
12 J12 **Barry's Bay** Ontario, SE Canada 45.28N 77.40W
150 K14 **Barsakel'mes, Ostrov** island SW Kazakhstan
Baršć Łužyca see Forst
153 S14 **Barsem** S Tajikistan 37.36N 71.43E
151 V11 **Barshatas** Vostochnyy Kazakhstan, E Kazakhstan 48.04N 78.38E
161 F14 **Bārsi** Mahārāshtra, W India 18.13N 75.42E
102 I13 **Barsinghausen** Niedersachsen, C Germany 53.19N 9.30E
153 X8 **Barskoon** Issyk-Kul'skaya Oblast', E Kyrgyzstan 42.07N 77.34E
102 F10 **Barssel** Niedersachsen, NW Germany 53.10N 7.46E
37 U14 **Barstow** California, W USA 34.52N 117.00W
26 L8 **Barstow** Texas, SW USA 31.27N 103.23W
105 R6 **Bar-sur-Aube** Aube, NE France 48.13N 4.43E
Bar-sur-Ornain see Bar-le-Duc
105 Q6 **Bar-sur-Seine** Aube, N France 48.06N 4.22E
153 Q13 **Bartang** S Tajikistan 38.06N 71.48E
153 T13 **Bartang** ∽ SE Tajikistan
Bartenstein see Bartoszyce
Bártfa/Bartfeld see Bardejov
102 N7 **Barth** Mecklenburg-Vorpommern, NE Germany 54.21N 12.43E
29 W13 **Bartholomew, Bayou** ∽ Arkansas/Louisiana, S USA
57 T8 **Bartica** N Guyana 6.24N 58.36W
142 H10 **Bartın** Bartın, NW Turkey 41.37N 32.19E
142 H10 **Bartın** ◆ province NW Turkey
189 W4 **Bartle Frere** ▲ Queensland, E Australia 17.15S 145.43E
29 P8 **Bartlesville** Oklahoma, C USA 36.45N 95.58W
31 P14 **Bartlett** Nebraska, C USA 41.51N 98.32W
22 E10 **Bartlett** Tennessee, S USA 35.12N 89.52W
27 T9 **Bartlett** Texas, SW USA 30.47N 97.25W
38 L13 **Bartlett Reservoir** ⊠ Arizona, SW USA
21 N6 **Barton** Vermont, NE USA 44.44N 72.09W
112 L7 **Bartoszyce** Ger. Bartenstein. Warmińsko-Mazurskie, NE Poland, 54.16N 20.49E
25 W12 **Bartow** Florida, SE USA 27.54N 81.50W
Bartschin see Barcin
176 V10 **Baru** Papua, E Indonesia 1.44S 132.16E
173 G6 **Barumun, Sungai** ∽ Sumatera, W Indonesia
Barū, Nahr see Baro Wenz
174 M16 **Barung, Nusa** island S Indonesia
173 Ff6 **Barus** Sumatera, NW Indonesia 2.08N 98.15E
168 L10 **Baruunsuu** Ömnögovĭ, S Mongolia 43.46N 105.28E
169 P8 **Baruun-Urt** Sühbaatar, E Mongolia 46.39N 113.17E
45 P15 **Barú, Volcán** var. Volcán de Chiriquí. Ѫ W Panama 8.49N 82.32W
101 K21 **Barvaux** Luxembourg, SE Belgium 50.21N 5.30E
44 M13 **Barva, Volcán** Ѫ NW Costa Rica 10.07N 84.08W
119 W6 **Barvinkove** Kharkivs'ka Oblast', E Ukraine 48.54N 37.03E
160 G11 **Barwāh** Madhya Pradesh, C India 22.17N 76.01E
Bärwalde Neumark see Mieszkowice
160 F11 **Barwāni** Madhya Pradesh, C India 22.01N 74.55E
191 P5 **Barwon River** ∽ New South Wales, SE Australia
121 L15 **Barysaw** Rus. Borisov. Minskaya Voblasts', NE Belarus 54.14N 28.30E
131 Q6 **Barysh** Ul'yanovskaya Oblast', W Russian Federation 53.32N 47.06E
119 Q4 **Baryshivka** Kyyivs'ka Oblast', N Ukraine 50.21N 31.21E
81 J17 **Basankusu** Equateur, NW Dem. Rep. Congo 1.12N 19.49E
119 N11 **Basarabeasca** Rus. Bessarabka. SE Moldova 46.22N 28.56E
118 M14 **Basarabi** Constanța, SW Romania 44.07N 28.27E
42 H6 **Basaseachic** Chihuahua, NW Mexico 28.18N 108.13W
107 O2 **Basauri** País Vasco, N Spain 43.13N 2.54W
63 D18 **Basavilbaso** Entre Ríos, E Argentina 32.23S 58.48W
81 F21 **Bas-Congo** off. Région du Bas-Congo; prev. Bas-Zaire. ◆ region SW Dem. Rep. Congo
110 E6 **Basel** Eng. Basle, Fr. Bâle. Basel-Stadt, NW Switzerland 47.33N 7.36E
110 E7 **Basel** Eng. Basle, Fr. Bâle. ◆ canton NW Switzerland
149 T14 **Bashākerd, Kūhhā-ye** ▲▲ SE Iran
9 Q15 **Bashaw** Alberta, SW Canada 52.40N 112.53W
152 K16 **Bashbedeng** Maryyskiy Velayat, S Turkmenistan 35.44N 63.07E
167 T15 **Bashi Channel** Chin. Pa-shih Hai-hsia. channel Philippines/Taiwan
Bashkiria see Bashkortostan, Respublika
125 Dd12 **Bashkortostan, Respublika** prev. Bashkiria. ◆ autonomous republic W Russian Federation
131 N6 **Bashmakovo** Penzenskaya Oblast', W Russian Federation 53.13N 43.00E
152 J10 **Bashsakarba** Lebapskiy Velayat, NE Turkmenistan 40.25N 62.16E
119 R9 **Bashtanka** Mykolayivs'ka Oblast', S Ukraine 47.24N 32.27E
195 O17 **Basilaki Island** island SE PNG
24 H8 **Basile** Louisiana, S USA 30.29N 92.36W
109 M18 **Basilicata** ◆ region S Italy
35 V13 **Basin** Wyoming, C USA 44.22N 108.02W
99 N22 **Basingstoke** S England, UK 51.16N 1.08W
149 U8 **Bāsīrān** Khorāsān, E Iran 31.57N 59.07E
114 B10 **Baška** It. Bescanuova. Primorje-Gorski Kotar, NW Croatia 44.58N 14.46E
143 T15 **Başkale** Van, SE Turkey 38.03N 44.01E
12 L10 **Baskatong, Réservoir** ⊠ Quebec, SE Canada
143 O14 **Baskil** Elâzığ, E Turkey 38.35N 38.52E
Basle see Basel
160 H9 **Bāsoda** Madhya Pradesh, C India 23.54N 77.58E
81 L17 **Basoko** Orientale, N Dem. Rep. Congo 1.13N 23.25E
Basque Country, The see País Vasco
Basra see Al Başrah
105 U5 **Bas-Rhin** ◆ department NE France
Bassam see Grand-Bassam
9 Q16 **Bassano** Alberta, SW Canada 50.48N 112.28W
108 H7 **Bassano del Grappa** Veneto, NE Italy 45.45N 11.45E
79 Q15 **Bassar** var. Bassari. NW Togo 9.15N 0.46E
Bassari see Bassar
180 L9 **Bassas da India** island group W Madagascar
110 D7 **Bassecourt** Jura, W Switzerland 47.20N 7.16E
177 Ff8 **Bassein** var. Pathein. Irrawaddy, SW Myanmar 16.46N 94.45E
81 J15 **Basse-Kotto** ◆ prefecture S Central African Republic
107 V5 **Bassella** Cataluña, NE Spain 42.01N 1.16E
104 J5 **Basse-Normandie** Eng. Lower Normandy. ◆ region N France
47 Q11 **Basse-Pointe** N Martinique 14.52N 61.07W
78 H12 **Basse Santa Su** E Gambia 13.18N 14.10W
Basse-Saxe see Niedersachsen
47 X6 **Basse-Terre** ○ (Guadeloupe) Basse Terre, SW Guadeloupe 16.07N 61.40W
47 X6 **Basse Terre** island W Guadeloupe
47 V10 **Basseterre** ● (Saint Kitts and Nevis) Saint Kitts, Saint Kitts and Nevis 17.15N 62.45W
31 O13 **Bassett** Nebraska, C USA 42.34N 99.32W
23 S7 **Bassett** Virginia, NE USA 36.45N 79.59W
39 N15 **Bassett Peak** ▲ Arizona, SW USA 32.30N 110.16W
78 M10 **Bassikounou** Hodh ech Chargui, SE Mauritania 15.55N 5.58W
79 R15 **Bassila** W Benin 9.01N 1.46E
Bass, Îlots de see Marotiri
33 O11 **Bass Lake** Indiana, N USA 41.12N 86.35W
191 O14 **Bass Strait** strait SE Australia
102 H11 **Bassum** Niedersachsen, NW Germany 52.51N 8.43E
31 X3 **Basswood Lake** ◎ Canada/USA
97 J21 **Båstad** Skåne, S Sweden 56.25N 12.49E
145 U2 **Basṭah** E Iraq 36.20N 45.14E
159 N12 **Basti** Uttar Pradesh, N India 26.48N 82.43E
105 X14 **Bastia** Corse, France, C Mediterranean Sea 42.42N 9.27E
101 L23 **Bastogne** Luxembourg, SE Belgium 50.00N 5.43E
24 I5 **Bastrop** Louisiana, S USA 32.46N 91.54W
27 T11 **Bastrop** Texas, SW USA 30.06N 97.19W
95 J15 **Bastuträsk** Västerbotten, N Sweden 64.46N 20.05E
121 J19 **Bastyn'** Rus. Bostyn'. Brestskaya Voblasts', SW Belarus 52.23N 26.46E
Basuo see Dongfang
Basutoland see Lesotho
121 O15 **Basya** ∽ E Belarus
119 V8 **Basyl'kivka** Dnipropetrovs'ka Oblast', E Ukraine 48.12N 36.00E
81 D17 **Bata** NW Equatorial Guinea 1.50N 9.47E
81 D17 **Bata** ✕ S Equatorial Guinea 1.55N 9.48E
Batae Coritanorum see Leicester
126 M8 **Batagay** Respublika Sakha (Yakutiya), NE Russian Federation 67.36N 134.44E
126 Ll8 **Batagay-Alyta** Respublika Sakha (Yakutiya), NE Russian Federation 67.48N 130.15E
114 L10 **Batajnica** Serbia, N Serbia and Montenegro (Yugoslavia) 44.55N 20.17E
142 H15 **Bataklık Gölü** ◎ S Turkey
116 H11 **Batak, Yazovir** ⊠ SW Bulgaria
158 H7 **Batāla** Punjab, N India 31.50N 75.10E
106 F9 **Batalha** Leiria, C Portugal 39.40N 8.49W
81 N17 **Batama** Orientale, NE Dem. Rep. Congo 0.54N 26.25E
126 Ll10 **Batamay** Respublika Sakha (Yakutiya), NE Russian Federation 63.28N 129.33E
174 I7 **Batam, Pulau** island Kepulauan Riau, W Indonesia
166 F9 **Batang** Sichuan, C China 30.04N 99.10E
174 Kk14 **Batang** Jawa, C Indonesia 6.55S 109.42E
81 I14 **Batangafo** Ouham, NW Central African Republic 7.19N 18.22E
179 P11 **Batangas** off. Batangas City. Luzon, N Philippines 13.47N 121.02E
Bătania see Battonya
179 Pp6 **Batan Islands** island group N Philippines
62 L8 **Batatais** São Paulo, S Brazil 20.54S 47.37W
20 E10 **Batavia** New York, NE USA 43.00N 78.11W
Batavia see Jakarta
181 T9 **Batavia Seamount** undersea feature E Indian Ocean 27.42S 100.36E
130 L12 **Bataysk** Rostovskaya Oblast', SW Russian Federation 47.10N 39.46E
12 B9 **Batchawana** ∽ Ontario, S Canada
12 B9 **Batchawana Bay** Ontario, S Canada 46.55N 84.36W
178 Ii12 **Bătdâmbâng** prev. Battambang. Bătdâmbâng, NW Cambodia 13.06N 103.13E
81 G20 **Batéké, Plateaux** plateau S Congo
191 S11 **Batemans Bay** New South Wales, SE Australia 35.45S 150.09E
23 Q13 **Batesburg** South Carolina, SE USA 33.54N 81.33W
30 K12 **Batesland** South Dakota, N USA 43.05N 102.07W
29 V10 **Batesville** Arkansas, C USA 35.47N 91.37W
33 Q14 **Batesville** Indiana, N USA 39.18N 85.13W
24 L2 **Batesville** Mississippi, S USA 34.18N 89.56W
27 Q13 **Batesville** Texas, SW USA 28.56N 99.38W
46 L13 **Bath** E Jamaica 17.56N 76.20W
99 L22 **Bath** hist. Akermanceaster, anc. Aquae Calidae, Aquae Solis. SW England, UK 51.22N 2.22W
21 Q8 **Bath** Maine, NE USA 43.54N 69.49W
20 F11 **Bath** New York, NE USA 42.20N 77.16W
Bath see Berkeley Springs
80 I10 **Batha** off. Préfecture du Batha. ◆ prefecture C Chad
80 I10 **Batha** seasonal river C Chad
147 Y8 **Baṭḥā', Wādī al** dry watercourse NE Oman
158 H9 **Bathinda** Punjab, NW India 30.13N 74.54E
100 M11 **Bathmen** Overijssel, E Netherlands 52.15N 6.16E
47 Z14 **Bathsheba** E Barbados 13.12N 59.31W
191 R8 **Bathurst** New South Wales, SE Australia 33.32S 149.34E
11 O13 **Bathurst** New Brunswick, SE Canada 47.37N 65.40W
Bathurst see Banjul
15 Gg2 **Bathurst, Cape** headland Northwest Territories, NW Canada 70.33N 128.00W
206 L8 **Bathurst Inlet** Nunavut, N Canada 66.23N 107.00W
15 J4 **Bathurst Inlet** inlet Nunavut, N Canada
189 N1 **Bathurst Island** island Northern Territory, N Australia
207 O9 **Bathurst Island** island Parry Islands, Nunavut, N Canada
79 O14 **Batié** SW Burkina 9.53N 2.57W
197 J14 **Batiki** prev. Mbatiki. island C Fiji
Batinah see Al Bāṭinah
147 Y9 **Bāṭin, Wādī al** dry watercourse SW Asia
13 P9 **Batiscan** ∽ Quebec, SE Canada
142 F16 **Batı Toroslar** ▲▲ SW Turkey
Batjan see Bacan, Pulau
Batlle y Ordóñez see José Batlle y Ordóñez
191 Q10 **Batlow** New South Wales, SE Australia 35.32S 148.09E
143 Q15 **Batman** var. Îluh. Batman, SE Turkey 37.52N 41.06E
143 Q15 **Batman** ◆ province SE Turkey
76 L6 **Batna** NE Algeria 35.34N 6.10E
Batoe see Batu, Kepulauan
168 K7 **Bat-Öldziyt** Töv, C Mongolia 48.10N 104.49E
24 J8 **Baton Rouge** state capital Louisiana, S USA 30.28N 91.09W
81 G15 **Batouri** Est, E Cameroon 4.26N 14.24E
144 G14 **Batrā', Jibāl al** ▲▲ S Jordan
144 G6 **Batroûn** var. Al Batrūn. N Lebanon 34.15N 35.42E
Batsch see Bač
Batsevichi see Batsevichy
121 M17 **Batsevichy** Rus. Batsevichi. Mahilyowskaya Voblasts', E Belarus 53.24N 29.13E
94 M7 **Båtsfjord** Finnmark, N Norway 70.37N 29.42E
Battambang see Bătdâmbâng
205 X3 **Batterbee, Cape** headland Antarctica
161 L24 **Batticaloa** Eastern Province, E Sri Lanka 7.43N 81.43E
101 L19 **Battice** Liège, E Belgium 50.39N 5.50E
109 L18 **Battipaglia** Campania, S Italy 40.36N 14.58E
9 R15 **Battle** ∽ Alberta/Saskatchewan, SW Canada
Battle Born State see Nevada
33 Q10 **Battle Creek** Michigan, N USA 42.19N 85.10W
29 T7 **Battlefield** Missouri, C USA 37.07N 93.22W
9 S15 **Battleford** Saskatchewan, S Canada 52.45N 108.19W
31 S6 **Battle Lake** Minnesota, N USA 46.16N 95.42W
37 U3 **Battle Mountain** Nevada, W USA 40.37N 116.55W
113 M25 **Battonya** Rom. Bătania. Békés, SE Hungary 46.16N 21.00E
175 Qq14 **Batuata, Pulau** island C Indonesia
175 Q8 **Batudaka, Pulau** island N Indonesia
173 F8 **Batu, Kepulauan** prev. Batoe. island group W Indonesia
143 Q10 **Bat'umi** W Georgia 41.39N 41.37E
174 H6 **Batu Pahat** prev. Bandar Penggaram. Johor, Peninsular Malaysia 1.51N 102.55E
175 Q10 **Baturebe** Sulawesi, N Indonesia 1.43S 121.43E
126 H13 **Baturino** Tomskaya Oblast', C Russian Federation 57.46N 85.08E
119 R3 **Baturyn** Chernihivs'ka Oblast', N Ukraine 51.20N 32.54E
144 F10 **Bat Yam** Tel Aviv, C Israel 32.01N 34.45E
131 Q4 **Batyrevo** Chuvashskaya Respublika, W Russian Federation 55.04N 47.34E
Batys Qazaqstan Oblysy see Zapadnyy Kazakhstan
104 F5 **Batz, Île de** island NW France
174 L7 **Bau** Sarawak, East Malaysia 1.25N 110.10E
179 P9 **Bauang** Luzon, N Philippines 16.33N 120.19E
175 Qq13 **Baubau** var. Baoebaoe. Pulau Buton, C Indonesia 5.30S 122.37E
79 W14 **Bauchi** Bauchi, NE Nigeria 10.18N 9.46E
79 W14 **Bauchi** ◆ state C Nigeria
104 H7 **Baud** Morbihan, NW France 47.52N 2.59W
31 T2 **Baudette** Minnesota, N USA 48.42N 94.36W
200 Nn10 **Bauer Basin** undersea feature E Pacific Ocean
197 C14 **Bauer Field** var. Port Vila. ✕ (Port-Vila) Éfaté, C Vanuatu 17.42S 168.21E
11 T9 **Bauld, Cape** headland Newfoundland and Labrador, E Canada 51.35N 55.22W
105 T8 **Baume-les-Dames** Doubs, E France 47.22N 6.20E
195 X15 **Baunani** Malaita, N Solomon Islands 9.06S 160.52E
103 I15 **Baunatal** Hessen, C Germany 51.15N 9.25E
109 D18 **Baunei** Sardegna, Italy, C Mediterranean Sea 40.04N 9.36E
59 M15 **Baures, Río** ∽ N Bolivia
62 K9 **Bauru** São Paulo, S Brazil 22.19S 49.07W
Baushar see Bawshar
120 G10 **Bauska** Ger. Bauske. Bauska, S Latvia 56.24N 24.11E
Bauske see Bauska
103 Q15 **Bautzen** Lus. Budyšin. Sachsen, E Germany 51.10N 14.28E
151 Q16 **Bauyrzhan Momysh-Uly** Kaz. Baūyrzhan Momyshuly; prev. Burnoye. Zhambyl, S Kazakhstan 42.36N 70.46E
Bauzanum see Bolzano
Bavaria see Bayern
111 N7 **Bavarian Alps** Ger. Bayrische Alpen. ▲▲ Austria/Germany
Bavière see Bayern
42 H4 **Bavispe, Río** ∽ NW Mexico
131 T5 **Bavly** Respublika Tatarstan, W Russian Federation 54.20N 53.21E
174 Kk10 **Bawal, Pulau** island N Indonesia
174 Mm10 **Bawan** Borneo, C Indonesia 1.36S 113.55E
191 O12 **Baw Baw, Mount** ▲ Victoria, SE Australia 37.49S 146.16E
176 W11 **Bawe** Papua, E Indonesia 2.56S 134.39E
174 M13 **Bawean, Pulau** island S Indonesia
174 L15 **Bawen** Jawa, S Indonesia 7.13S 110.25E
77 V9 **Bawīṭī** N Egypt 28.18N 28.52E
79 Q13 **Bawku** N Ghana 11.00N 0.12W
178 Gg7 **Bawlakè** Kayah State, C Myanmar 19.10N 97.19E
173 Ff8 **Bawo Ofuloa** Pulau Tanahmasa, W Indonesia 0.10S 98.24E
147 Y8 **Bawshar** var. Baushar. NE Oman 23.26N 58.19E
Ba Xian see Bazhou
164 M8 **Baxkorgan** Xinjiang Uygur Zizhiqu, W China 39.05N 90.00E
25 V6 **Baxley** Georgia, SE USA 31.46N 82.21W
165 R15 **Baxoi** Xizang Zizhiqu, W China 30.01N 96.53E
31 W14 **Baxter** Iowa, C USA 41.49N 93.09W
31 U6 **Baxter** Minnesota, N USA 46.21N 94.18W
29 R8 **Baxter Springs** Kansas, C USA 37.01N 94.45W
83 M17 **Bay** off. Gobolka Bay. ◆ region SW Somalia
Bay see Baicheng
46 H7 **Bayamo** Granma, E Cuba 20.21N 76.38W
47 U5 **Bayamón** E Puerto Rico 18.24N 66.09W
169 W8 **Bayan** Heilongjiang, NE China 46.04N 127.24E
175 Nn16 **Bayan** prev. Bajan. Pulau Lombok, C Indonesia 8.16S 116.28E
168 I6 **Bayan** Arhangay, C Mongolia 49.36N 99.36E
169 P7 **Bayan** Dornod, E Mongolia 47.56N 112.58E
169 N9 **Bayan** Dornogovĭ, SE Mongolia 46.15N 110.16E
168 F7 **Bayan** Govĭ-Altay, W Mongolia 47.05N 95.13E
169 O8 **Bayan** Hentiy, C Mongolia 47.13N 110.57E
158 I12 **Bayāna** Rājasthān, N India 26.55N 77.18E
155 N5 **Bāyān, Band-e** ▲▲ C Afghanistan
168 H8 **Bayanbulag** Bayanhongor, C Mongolia 46.46N 98.07E
169 N7 **Bayanbulag** Hentiy, C Mongolia 47.54N 109.51E
164 J5 **Bayanbulak** Xinjiang Uygur Zizhiqu, W China 43.04N 84.04E
126 Jj15 **Bayanday** Ust'-Ordynskiy Buryatskiy Avtonomnyy Okrug, S Russian Federation 53.01N 105.24E
Bayan Gol see Dengkou
168 F8 **Bayangol** Govĭ-Altay, SW Mongolia 45.33N 94.22E
165 R12 **Bayan Har Shan** var. Bayan Khar. ▲▲ C China
168 I8 **Bayanhongor** Bayanhongor, C Mongolia 46.07N 100.42E
168 H9 **Bayanhongor** ◆ province C Mongolia
Bayan Khar see Bayan Har Shan
173 G3 **Bayan Lepas** ✕ (George Town) Pinang, Peninsular Malaysia 5.18N 100.15E
168 K13 **Bayan Mod** Nei Mongol Zizhiqu, N China 40.45N 104.29E
168 K13 **Bayan Nuru** Nei Mongol Zizhiqu, N China 40.09N 104.48E
169 N12 **Bayan Obo** Nei Mongol Zizhiqu, N China 41.45N 109.58E
45 V15 **Bayano, Lago** ◎ E Panama
168 C5 **Bayan-Ölgiy** ◆ province NW Mongolia
168 F8 **Bayan-Ovoo** Govĭ-Altay, SW Mongolia 44.39N 94.45E
168 H9 **Bayansayr** Bayanhongor, C Mongolia 45.36N 99.27E
165 Q9 **Bayan Shan** ▲ C China 37.36N 96.23E
168 J9 **Bayanteeg** Övörhangay, C Mongolia 45.39N 101.30E
168 L8 **Bayantöhöm** Töv, C Mongolia 46.57N 105.09E
168 H6 **Bayan-Uhaa** Dzavhan, C Mongolia 48.41N 98.46E
168 J8 **Bayan-Ulaan** Övörhangay, C Mongolia 46.38N 102.30E
Bayan Ul Hot see Xi Ujimqin Qi
30 J14 **Bayard** Nebraska, C USA 41.45N 103.19W
39 P15 **Bayard** New Mexico, SW USA 32.45N 108.07W
105 T13 **Bayard, Col** pass SE France 44.37N 6.04E
169 O8 **Bayasgalant** Sühbaatar, E Mongolia 46.55N 112.11E
142 J12 **Bayat** Çorum, N Turkey 40.34N 34.07E
179 Q14 **Bayawan** Negros, C Philippines 9.22N 122.50E
149 R10 **Bayāz** Kermān, C Iran 30.40N 55.28E
179 R13 **Baybay** Leyte, C Philippines 10.41N 124.49E
23 X10 **Bayboro** North Carolina, SE USA 35.06N 76.46W
143 P12 **Bayburt** Bayburt, NE Turkey 40.15N 40.16E
143 P12 **Bayburt** ◆ province NE Turkey
33 R8 **Bay City** Michigan, N USA 43.34N 83.52W
27 V12 **Bay City** Texas, SW USA 28.59N 96.00W
125 G7 **Baydaratskaya Guba** var. Baydarata Bay. bay N Russian Federation
83 M16 **Baydhabo** var. Baydhowa, Isha Baydhabo, It. Baidoa. Bay, SW Somalia 3.07N 43.39E
Baydhowa see Baydhabo
103 N21 **Bayerischer Wald** ▲▲ SE Germany
103 K21 **Bayern** Eng. Bavaria, Fr. Bavière. ◆ state SE Germany
153 V9 **Bayetovo** Narynskaya Oblast', C Kyrgyzstan 41.14N 74.55E
104 K4 **Bayeux** anc. Augustodurum. Calvados, N France 49.16N 0.42W
12 E15 **Bayfield** ∽ Ontario, S Canada
151 O15 **Baygakum** Kaz. Bäygequm. Kzylorda, S Kazakhstan 44.15N 66.34E
Bäygequm see Baygakum
142 C14 **Bayındır** İzmir, SW Turkey 38.14N 27.37E
144 H12 **Bāyir** var. Bā'ir. Ma'ān, S Jordan 30.46N 36.40E
Bay Islands see Bahía, Islas de la
145 R5 **Bayjī** var. Baiji. N Iraq 34.55N 43.28E
Baykadam see Saudakent
126 K15 **Baykal, Ozero** Eng. Lake Baikal. ◎ S Russian Federation
126 Jj16 **Baykal'sk** Irkutskaya Oblast', S Russian Federation 51.30N 104.03E
143 R15 **Baykan** Siirt, SE Turkey 38.07N 41.43E
126 Ii12 **Baykit** Evenkiyskiy Avtonomnyy Okrug, C Russian Federation 61.37N 96.23E
Baykonur see Baykonyr
150 M14 **Baykonyr** var. Baykonur. Kaz. Baygongyr; prev. Leninsk. Kyzylorda, S Kazakhstan 45.38N 63.20E

◆ Country ● Country Capital ◇ Dependent Territory ○ Dependent Territory Capital ◆ Administrative Region ✕ International Airport ▲ Mountain ▲▲ Mountain Range Ѫ Volcano ∽ River ◎ Lake ⊠ Reservoir

151 N12 **Baykonyr** var. Baykonur. Zhezkazgan, C Kazakhstan 47.50N 66.05E
164 E7 **Baykurt** Xinjiang Uygur Zizhiqu, W China 39.55N 75.33E
158 I9 **Bay, Lac** ◎ Quebec, SE Canada
179 Pp11 **Bay, Laguna de** ◎ Luzon, N Philippines
131 W6 **Baymak** Respublika Bashkortostan, W Russian Federation 52.34N 58.20E
25 O8 **Bay Minette** Alabama, S USA 30.52N 87.46W
149 O17 **Baynūnah** desert W UAE
192 O8 **Bay of Plenty** off. Bay of Plenty Region. ◐ region North Island, NZ
203 Z3 **Bay of Wrecks** bay Kiritimati, E Kiribati
179 P9 **Bayombong** Luzon, N Philippines 16.29N 121.08E
104 I15 **Bayonne** anc. Lapurdum. Pyrénées-Atlantiques, SW France 43.30N 1.28W
24 H4 **Bayou D'Arbonne Lake** ⊠ Louisiana, S USA
25 N9 **Bayou La Batre** Alabama, S USA 30.24N 88.15W
Bayou State see Mississippi
Bayqadam see Saudakent
Bayqongyr see Baykonyr
Bayram-Ali see Bayramaly
152 J14 **Bayramaly** prev. Bayram-Ali. Maryyskiy Velayat, S Turkmenistan 37.33N 62.08E
103 L19 **Bayreuth** var. Baireuth. Bayern, SE Germany 49.57N 11.34E
Bayrische Alpen see Bavarian Alps
Bayrūt see Beyrouth
24 L9 **Bay Saint Louis** Mississippi, S USA 30.18N 89.19W
Baysān see Bet She'an
168 L8 **Bayshint** Töv, C Mongolia 47.22N 105.04E
12 H13 **Bays, Lake of** ◎ Ontario, S Canada
24 M6 **Bay Springs** Mississippi, S USA 31.58N 89.17W
Bay State see Massachusetts
Baysun see Boysun
12 H13 **Baysville** Ontario, S Canada 45.10N 79.03W
147 N15 **Bayt al Faqīh** W Yemen 14.30N 43.20E
164 M4 **Baytik Shan** ▲▲ China/Mongolia
Bayt Laḥm see Bethlehem
27 W11 **Baytown** Texas, SW USA 29.44N 94.58W
175 O9 **Bayur, Tanjung** headland Borneo, N Indonesia 0.43S 117.32E
123 Ll16 **Bayy al Kabīr, Wādī** dry watercourse NW Libya
Bayyrqum see Bairkum
107 P14 **Baza** Andalucía, S Spain 37.30N 2.45W
143 X10 **Bazardüzü Dağı** Rus. Gora Bazardyuzyu. ▲ N Azerbaijan 41.13N 47.50E
Bazardyuzyu, Gora see Bazardüzü Dağı
Bazargic see Dobrich
85 N18 **Bazaruto, Ilha do** island SE Mozambique
104 K14 **Bazas** Gironde, SW France 44.27N 0.11W
107 O14 **Baza, Sierra de** ▲▲ S Spain
166 J8 **Bazhong** Sichuan, C China 31.55N 106.44E
167 P3 **Bazhou** prev. Baxian, Ba Xian. Hebei, E China 39.04N 116.24E
12 M9 **Bazin** ≈ Quebec, SE Canada
Bazin see Pezinok
145 Q7 **Bāzīyah** C Iraq 33.49N 42.41E
144 H6 **Bcharré** var. Bcharreh, Bsharrī, Bsherri. NE Lebanon 34.16N 36.01E
Bcharreh see Bcharré
30 J5 **Beach** North Dakota, N USA 46.55N 104.00W
190 K12 **Beachport** South Australia 37.29S 140.03E
99 O23 **Beachy Head** headland SE England, UK 50.44N 0.16E
20 K13 **Beacon** New York, NE USA 41.30N 73.54W
65 J25 **Beagle Channel** channel Argentina/Chile
189 O1 **Beagle Gulf** gulf Northern Territory, N Australia
Bealach an Doirín see Ballaghaderreen
Bealach Cláir see Ballyclare
Bealach Féich see Ballybofey
180 J3 **Bealanana** Mahajanga, NE Madagascar 14.33S 48.43E
Béal an Átha see Ballina
Béal an Átha Móir see Ballinamore
Béal an Mhuirhead see Belmullet
Béal Átha Beithe see Ballybay
Béal Átha Conaill see Ballyconnell
Beál Átha hAmhnais see Ballyhaunis
Béal Átha na Sluaighe see Ballinasloe
Béal Átha Seanaidh see Ballyshannon
Bealdovuopmi see Peltovuoma
Béal Feirste see Belfast
Béal Tairbirt see Belturbet
Beanna Boirche see Mourne Mountains
Beannchar see Banagher, Ireland
Beannchar see Bangor, Northern Ireland, UK
Beanntraí see Bantry
25 N2 **Bear Creek** ≈ Alabama/Mississippi, S USA
32 J13 **Bear Creek** ≈ Illinois, N USA
29 U13 **Bearden** Arkansas, C USA 33.43N 92.37W
205 Q10 **Beardmore Glacier** glacier Antarctica
32 K13 **Beardstown** Illinois, N USA 40.01N 90.25W
30 L14 **Bear Hill** ▲ Nebraska, C USA 41.24N 101.49W
Bear Island see Bjørnøya
12 H12 **Bear Lake** Ontario, S Canada 45.28N 79.31W
38 M1 **Bear Lake** ◎ Idaho/Utah, NW USA
41 U11 **Bear, Mount** ▲ Alaska, USA 61.16N 141.09W
104 J16 **Béarn** cultural region SW France
204 J11 **Bear Peninsula** peninsula Antarctica
158 I7 **Beās** ≈ India/Pakistan
107 P3 **Beasain** País Vasco, N Spain 43.03N 2.10W
107 O12 **Beas de Segura** Andalucía, S Spain 38.16N 2.53W
47 N10 **Beata, Cabo** headland SW Dominican Republic 17.34N 71.25W
47 N10 **Beata, Isla** island SW Dominican Republic
66 F11 **Beata Ridge** undersea feature N Caribbean Sea
31 R17 **Beatrice** Nebraska, C USA 40.14N 96.43W
85 L16 **Beatrice** Mashonaland East, NE Zimbabwe 18.13S 30.52E
9 N11 **Beatton** ≈ British Columbia, W Canada
9 N11 **Beatton River** British Columbia, W Canada 57.35N 121.10W
37 V10 **Beatty** Nevada, W USA 36.53N 116.44W
23 N6 **Beattyville** Kentucky, S USA 37.34N 83.39W
181 X16 **Beau Bassin** W Mauritius 20.13S 57.27E
105 R15 **Beaucaire** Gard, S France 43.49N 4.37E
12 I8 **Beauchastel, Lac** ◎ Quebec, SE Canada
12 I10 **Beauchêne, Lac** ◎ Quebec, SE Canada
191 V3 **Beaudesert** Queensland, E Australia 28.00S 152.27E
190 M12 **Beaufort** Victoria, SE Australia 37.27S 143.24E
23 X11 **Beaufort** North Carolina, SE USA 34.45N 76.50W
23 R15 **Beaufort** South Carolina, SE USA 32.25N 80.40W
40 M11 **Beaufort Sea** sea Arctic Ocean
Beaufort-Wes see Beaufort West
85 G25 **Beaufort West** Afr. Beaufort-Wes. Western Cape, SW South Africa 32.21S 22.34E
105 N7 **Beaugency** Loiret, C France 47.46N 1.38E
21 R1 **Beau Lake** ⊠ Maine, NE USA
98 I8 **Beauly** N Scotland, UK 57.28N 4.28W
101 G21 **Beaumont** Hainaut, S Belgium 50.12N 4.13E
193 E23 **Beaumont** Otago, South Island, NZ 45.48S 169.32E
24 M7 **Beaumont** Mississippi, S USA 31.10N 88.55W
27 X10 **Beaumont** Texas, SW USA 30.05N 94.06W
104 M15 **Beaumont-de-Lomagne** Tarn-et-Garonne, S France 43.54N 1.00E
104 L6 **Beaumont-sur-Sarthe** Sarthe, NW France 48.15N 0.07E
105 R8 **Beaune** Côte d'Or, C France 47.01N 4.49E
13 R9 **Beaupré** Quebec, SE Canada 47.03N 70.52W
104 J8 **Beaupréau** Maine-et-Loire, NW France 47.13N 0.57W
101 I22 **Beauraing** Namur, SE Belgium 50.07N 4.57E
105 R12 **Beaurepaire** Isère, E France 45.20N 5.03E
9 Y16 **Beausejour** Manitoba, S Canada 50.04N 96.30W
105 N4 **Beauvais** anc. Bellovacum, Caesaromagus. Oise, N France 49.27N 2.04E
9 S13 **Beauval** Saskatchewan, C Canada 55.10N 107.37W
104 I9 **Beauvoir-sur-Mer** Vendée, NW France 46.54N 2.03W
41 R8 **Beaver** Alaska, USA 66.22N 147.31W
28 J8 **Beaver** Oklahoma, C USA 36.49N 100.31W
20 B14 **Beaver** Pennsylvania, NE USA 40.39N 80.19W
38 K6 **Beaver** Utah, W USA 38.16N 112.38W
8 L9 **Beaver** ≈ British Columbia/Yukon Territory, W Canada
9 S13 **Beaver** ≈ Saskatchewan, C Canada
31 N17 **Beaver City** Nebraska, C USA 40.08N 99.49W
8 G6 **Beaver Creek** Yukon Territory, W Canada 62.19N 140.45W
33 R14 **Beavercreek** Ohio, N USA 39.42N 83.58W
41 S8 **Beaver Creek** ≈ Alaska, USA
28 H3 **Beaver Creek** ≈ Kansas/Nebraska, C USA
30 J5 **Beaver Creek** ≈ Montana/North Dakota, N USA
31 Q14 **Beaver Creek** ≈ Nebraska, C USA
27 Q4 **Beaver Creek** ≈ Texas, SW USA
32 M8 **Beaver Dam** Wisconsin, N USA 43.28N 88.49W
32 M8 **Beaver Dam Lake** ◎ Wisconsin, N USA
20 B14 **Beaver Falls** Pennsylvania, NE USA 40.45N 80.20W
35 P12 **Beaverhead Mountains** ▲▲ Idaho/Montana, NW USA
35 Q12 **Beaverhead River** ≈ Montana, NW USA
67 A25 **Beaver Island** island W Falkland Islands
33 P5 **Beaver Island** island Michigan, N USA
29 S9 **Beaver Lake** ⊠ Arkansas, C USA
9 N13 **Beaverlodge** Alberta, W Canada 55.10N 119.28W
20 I8 **Beaver River** ≈ New York, NE USA
28 J8 **Beaver River** ≈ Oklahoma, C USA
20 B13 **Beaver River** ≈ Pennsylvania, NE USA
67 A25 **Beaver Settlement** Beaver Island, W Falkland Islands 51.30S 61.15W
Beaver State see Oregon
12 H14 **Beaverton** Ontario, S Canada 44.24N 79.07W
34 G11 **Beaverton** Oregon, NW USA 45.29N 122.48W
158 G12 **Beāwar** Rājasthān, N India 26.07N 74.21E
Bebas, Dasht-i see Bābūs, Dasht-e
62 L8 **Bebedouro** São Paulo, S Brazil 20.58S 48.28W
103 I16 **Bebra** Hessen, C Germany 50.59N 9.46E
43 W12 **Becal** Campeche, SE Mexico 19.49N 90.28W
13 Q11 **Bécancour** ≈ Quebec, SE Canada
99 Q19 **Beccles** E England, UK 52.27N 1.32E
114 L9 **Bečej** Ger. Altbetsche, Hung. Óbecse, Rácz-Becse; prev. Magyar-Becse, Stari Bečej. Serbia, N Serbia and Montenegro (Yugoslavia) 45.36N 20.02E
106 I3 **Becerréa** Galicia, NW Spain 42.51N 7.10W
76 H7 **Béchar** prev. Colomb-Béchar. W Algeria 31.38N 2.10W
41 O14 **Becharof Lake** ◎ Alaska, USA
118 H15 **Bechet** var. Bechetu. Dolj, SW Romania 43.45N 23.57E
Bechetu see Bechet
23 R6 **Beckley** West Virginia, NE USA 37.46N 81.11W
103 G14 **Beckum** Nordrhein-Westfalen, W Germany 51.45N 8.03E
27 X7 **Beckville** Texas, SW USA 32.14N 94.27W
37 X4 **Becky Peak** ▲ Nevada, W USA 39.59N 114.33W
118 I9 **Beclean** Hung. Bethlen; prev. Betlen. Bistriţa-Năsăud, N Romania 47.10N 24.10E
Bécs see Wien
113 H18 **Bečva** Ger. Betschau, Pol. Beczwa. ≈ E Czech Republic
Beczwa see Bečva
105 P15 **Bédarieux** Hérault, S France 43.37N 3.10E
122 Dd12 **Beddouza, Cap** headland W Morocco 32.35N 9.16W
82 I13 **Bedelē** Oromo, C Ethiopia 8.25N 36.21E
153 Y8 **Bedel Pass** Rus. Pereval Bedel. pass China/Kyrgyzstan 41.22N 78.19E
Bedel, Pereval see Bedel Pass
97 H22 **Beder** Århus, C Denmark 56.03N 10.13E
99 N20 **Bedford** E England, UK 52.07N 0.28W
33 O15 **Bedford** Indiana, N USA 38.51N 86.29W
31 U16 **Bedford** Iowa, C USA 40.40N 94.43W
22 L4 **Bedford** Kentucky, S USA 38.34N 85.18W
20 D15 **Bedford** Pennsylvania, NE USA 40.00N 78.29W
23 T6 **Bedford** Virginia, NE USA 37.19N 79.31W
99 N20 **Bedfordshire** cultural region E England, UK
131 N5 **Bednodem'yanovsk** Penzenskaya Oblast', W Russian Federation 53.55N 43.14E
100 N5 **Bedum** Groningen, NE Netherlands 53.18N 6.36E
29 V11 **Beebe** Arkansas, C USA 35.04N 91.52W
47 T9 **Beef Island** ✕ (Road Town) Tortola, E British Virgin Islands 18.25N 64.31W
Beehive State see Utah
101 L18 **Beek** Limburg, SE Netherlands 50.55N 5.46E
101 L18 **Beek** ✕ (Maastricht) Limburg, SE Netherlands 50.55N 5.47E
101 K14 **Beek-en-Donk** Noord-Brabant, S Netherlands 51.31N 5.37E
144 F13 **Be'er Menuḥa** var. Be'ér Menukha. Southern, S Israel 30.21N 35.09E
Be'er Menukha see Be'ér Menuḥa
101 D16 **Beernem** West-Vlaanderen, NW Belgium 51.09N 3.18E
101 I16 **Beerse** Antwerpen, N Belgium 51.20N 4.52E
Beersheba see Be'ér Sheva'
144 E11 **Be'ér Sheva'** var. Beersheba, Ar. Bir es Saba. Southern, S Israel 31.15N 34.46E
100 J13 **Beesd** Gelderland, C Netherlands 51.52N 5.12E
101 M16 **Beesel** Limburg, SE Netherlands 51.16N 6.01E
85 J21 **Beestekraal** North-West, N South Africa 25.21S 27.40E
204 J7 **Beethoven Peninsula** peninsula Alexander Island, Antarctica
Beetstersweach see Beetsterzwaag
100 M6 **Beetsterzwaag** Fris. Beetstersweach. Friesland, N Netherlands 53.03N 6.04E
27 S13 **Beeville** Texas, SW USA 28.25N 97.46W
81 J18 **Befale** Equateur, NW Dem. Rep. Congo 0.25N 20.48E
Befandriana see Befandriana Avaratra
180 J3 **Befandriana Avaratra** var. Befandriana, Befandriana Nord. Mahajanga, NW Madagascar 15.13S 48.33E
Befandriana Nord see Befandriana Avaratra
81 K18 **Befori** Equateur, N Dem. Rep. Congo 0.09N 22.18E
180 I7 **Befotaka** Fianarantsoa, S Madagascar 23.49S 47.00E
191 R11 **Bega** New South Wales, SE Australia 36.43S 149.49E
104 G5 **Bégard** Côtes d'Armor, NW France 48.37N 3.18W
114 M9 **Begejski Kanal** canal NE Serbia and Montenegro (Yugoslavia)
151 V9 **Begen'** Vostochnyy Kazakhstan, E Kazakhstan 51.11N 79.03E
96 G13 **Begna** ≈ S Norway
Begoml' see Byahoml'
Begovat see Bekobod
159 Q13 **Begusarāi** Bihār, NE India 25.25N 86.07E
149 R9 **Behābād** Yazd, C Iran 32.22N 59.49E
Behagle see Laï
57 Z10 **Béhague, Pointe** headland E French Guiana 4.37N 51.52W
Behar see Bihar
148 M10 **Behbahān** var. Behbehān. Khūzestān, SW Iran 30.37N 50.07E
Behbehān see Behbahān
46 G3 **Behring Point** Andros Island, W Bahamas 24.28N 77.44W
149 P4 **Behshahr** prev. Ashraf. Māzandarān, N Iran 36.42N 53.36E
169 V6 **Bei'an** Heilongjiang, NE China 48.16N 126.28E
Beibunar see Sredishte
Beibu Wan see Tongking, Gulf of
Beida see Al Bayḍā'
82 H13 **Beigi** Oromo, C Ethiopia 9.13N 34.48E
166 L16 **Beihai** Guangxi Zhuangzu Zizhiqu, S China 21.28N 109.10E
165 Q10 **Bei Hulsan Hu** ◎ C China
167 N13 **Bei Jiang** ≈ S China
167 O2 **Beijing** var. Pei-ching, Eng. Peking; prev. Pei-p'ing. country/municipality capital (China) Beijing Shi, E China 39.58N 116.22E
167 P2 **Beijing** ✕ Beijing Shi, E China 39.54N 116.22E
Beijing see Beijing Shi
167 O2 **Beijing Shi** var. Beijing, Jing, Pei-ching, Eng. Peking; prev. Pei-p'ing. ◐ municipality E China
78 G8 **Beïla** Trarza, W Mauritania 18.07N 15.55W
100 N7 **Beilen** Drenthe, NE Netherlands 52.52N 6.27E
166 L15 **Beiliu** Guangxi Zhuangzu Zizhiqu, S China 22.43N 110.21E
165 O12 **Beilu He** ≈ W China
Beilul see Beylul
98 H8 **Beinn Dearg** ▲ N Scotland, UK 57.47N 4.52W
Beinn MacDuibh see Ben Macdui
166 I12 **Beipan Jiang** ≈ S China
169 T12 **Beipiao** Liaoning, NE China 41.46N 120.51E
85 N17 **Beira** Sofala, C Mozambique 19.45S 34.55E
85 N17 **Beira** ✕ Sofala, C Mozambique 19.39S 35.05E
106 I7 **Beira Alta** former province N Portugal
106 H9 **Beira Baixa** former province C Portugal
106 G8 **Beira Litoral** former province N Portugal
Beirut see Beyrouth
Beisān see Bet She'an
9 Q16 **Beiseker** Alberta, SW Canada 51.20N 113.34W
85 K19 **Beitbridge** Matabeleland South, S Zimbabwe 22.10S 30.02E
118 G10 **Beiuş** Hung. Belényes. Bihor, NW Romania 46.40N 22.18E
169 U12 **Beizhen** Liaoning, NE China 41.34N 121.51E
106 H12 **Beja** anc. Pax Julia. Beja, SE Portugal 38.01N 7.52W
106 G13 **Beja** ◐ district S Portugal
76 M5 **Béja** var. Bājah. N Tunisia 36.45N 9.04E
123 Ii11 **Béjaïa** var. Bejaïa, Fr. Bougie; anc. Saldae. NE Algeria 36.45N 5.02E
106 K8 **Béjar** Castilla-León, N Spain 40.24N 5.45W
Bejraburi see Phetchaburi
Bekaa Valley see El Beqaa
Bekabad see Bekobod
Békás see Bicaz
174 J14 **Bekasi** Jawa, C Indonesia 6.13S 106.59E
Bek-Budi see Qarshi
152 A8 **Bekdash** Balkanskiy Velayat, NW Turkmenistan 41.33N 52.33E
153 T10 **Bek-Dzhar** Oshskaya Oblast', SW Kyrgyzstan 40.22N 73.08E
113 N24 **Békés** Rom. Bichiş. Békés, SE Hungary 46.47N 21.07E
113 M24 **Békés** off. Békés Megye. ◐ county SE Hungary
113 M24 **Békéscsaba** Rom. Bichiş-Ciaba. Békés, SE Hungary 46.40N 21.04E
145 S2 **Bēkhma** E Iraq 36.40N 44.15E
180 H7 **Bekily** Toliara, S Madagascar 24.12S 45.19E
172 Qq7 **Bekkai** Hokkaidō, NE Japan 43.23N 145.07E
153 Q11 **Bekobod** Rus. Bekabad; prev. Begovat. Toshkent Viloyati, E Uzbekistan 40.17N 69.10E
131 O7 **Bekovo** Penzenskaya Oblast', W Russian Federation 52.27N 43.41E
Bél see Beliu
158 M13 **Bela** Uttar Pradesh, N India 25.55N 82.00E
155 N15 **Bela** Baluchistān, SW Pakistan 26.12N 66.22E
81 F15 **Bélabo** Est, C Cameroon 4.54N 13.10E
114 N10 **Bela Crkva** Ger. Weisskirchen, Hung. Fehértemplom. Serbia, W Serbia and Montenegro (Yugoslavia) 44.55N 21.28E
181 Y16 **Bel Air** var. Rivière Sèche. E Mauritius
106 L12 **Belalcázar** Andalucía, S Spain 38.33N 5.07W
115 P15 **Bela Palanka** Serbia, SE Serbia and Montenegro (Yugoslavia) 43.13N 22.19E
121 H16 **Belarus** off. Republic of Belarus, var. Belorussia, Latv. Baltkrievija; prev. Belorussian SSR, Rus. Belorusskaya SSR. ◆ republic E Europe
Belau see Palau
61 H21 **Bela Vista** Mato Grosso do Sul, SW Brazil 22.04S 56.25W
85 L21 **Bela Vista** Maputo, S Mozambique 26.19S 32.40E
173 Ff4 **Belawan** Sumatera, W Indonesia 3.44N 98.39E
Běla Woda see Weisswasser
131 U4 **Belaya** ≈ W Russian Federation
127 N7 **Belaya Gora** Respublika Sakha (Yakutiya), NE Russian Federation 68.25N 146.12E
130 M11 **Belaya Kalitva** Rostovskaya Oblast', SW Russian Federation 48.09N 40.43E
129 R14 **Belaya Kholunitsa** Kirovskaya Oblast', NW Russian Federation 58.54N 50.52E
Belaya Tserkov' see Bila Tserkva
79 V11 **Belbédji** Zinder, S Niger 14.35N 8.00E
112 K13 **Bełchatów** var. Belchatow. Łodzkie, C Poland 51.22N 19.19E
Belcher, Îles see Belcher Islands
10 H7 **Belcher Islands** Fr. Îles Belcher. island group Nunavut, SE Canada
107 S6 **Belchite** Aragón, NE Spain 41.18N 0.45W
31 O2 **Belcourt** North Dakota, N USA 48.50N 99.44W
33 P9 **Belding** Michigan, N USA 43.06N 85.13W
131 U5 **Belebey** Respublika Bashkortostan, W Russian Federation 54.04N 54.13E
83 N16 **Beledweyne** var. Belet Huen, It. Belet Uen. Hiiraan, C Somalia 4.39N 45.12E
152 B10 **Belek** Balkanskiy Velayat, W Turkmenistan 39.57N 53.51E
60 L12 **Belém** var. Pará. state capital Pará, N Brazil 1.27S 48.28W
67 I14 **Belém Ridge** undersea feature C Atlantic Ocean
39 R12 **Belen** New Mexico, SW USA 34.37N 106.46W
64 I7 **Belén** Catamarca, NW Argentina 27.40S 67.01W
56 G9 **Belén** Boyacá, C Colombia 5.59N 72.55W
44 J11 **Belén** Rivas, SW Nicaragua 11.30N 85.55W
64 O5 **Belén** Concepción, C Paraguay 23.25S 57.13W
63 D16 **Belén** Salto, N Uruguay 30.46S 57.46W
63 D20 **Belén de Escobar** Buenos Aires, E Argentina 34.21S 58.46W
116 J7 **Belene** Pleven, N Bulgaria 43.39N 25.09E
116 J7 **Belene, Ostrov** island N Bulgaria
45 R15 **Belén, Río** ≈ C Panama
Belényes see Beiuş
197 G4 **Belep, Îles** island group W New Caledonia
106 H3 **Belesar, Embalse de** ⊠ NW Spain
Belet Huen/Belet Uen see Beledweyne
130 J5 **Belëv** Tul'skaya Oblast', W Russian Federation 53.48N 36.07E
99 G15 **Belfast** Ir. Béal Feirste. ◐ E Northern Ireland, UK 54.34N 5.55W
21 R7 **Belfast** Maine, NE USA 44.25N 69.02W
99 G15 **Belfast** ✕ E Northern Ireland, UK 54.37N 6.11W
99 G15 **Belfast Lough** Ir. Loch Lao inlet E Northern Ireland, UK
30 K5 **Belfield** North Dakota, N USA 46.53N 103.12W
105 U7 **Belfort** Territoire-de-Belfort, E France 47.37N 6.52E
Belgard see Białogard
161 E17 **Belgaum** Karnātaka, W India 15.52N 74.30E
Belgian Congo see Congo (Democratic Republic of)
205 T3 **Belgica Mountains** ▲ Antarctica
België/Belgique see Belgium
101 F20 **Belgium** off. Kingdom of Belgium, Dut. België, Fr. Belgique. ◆ monarchy NW Europe
130 J8 **Belgorod** Belgorodskaya Oblast', W Russian Federation 50.37N 36.37E
Belgorod-Dnestrovskiy see Bilhorod-Dnistrovs'kyy
130 J8 **Belgorodskaya Oblast'** ◐ province W Russian Federation
Belgrad see Beograd
31 T8 **Belgrade** Minnesota, N USA 45.27N 94.59W
35 S11 **Belgrade** Montana, NW USA 45.46N 111.10W
Belgrade see Beograd
205 N5 **Belgrano II** Argentinian research station Antarctica 77.50S 35.25W
Belgrano, Cabo see Meredith, Cape
23 X9 **Belhaven** North Carolina, SE USA 35.36N 76.50W
109 J23 **Belice** anc. Hypsas. ≈ Sicilia, Italy, C Mediterranean Sea
Belice see Belize/Belize City
115 M16 **Beli Drim** Alb. Drini i Bardhë. ≈ Albania/Serbia and Montenegro (Yugoslavia)
Beligrad see Berat
196 C8 **Beliliou** prev. Peleliu. island S Palau
116 L8 **Beli Lom, Yazovir** ⊠ NE Bulgaria
114 I8 **Beli Manastir** Hung. Pélmonostor; prev. Monostor. Osijek-Baranja, NE Croatia 45.46N 16.38E
104 J13 **Bélin-Béliet** Gironde, SW France 44.30N 0.48W
81 F17 **Bélinga** Ogooué-Ivindo, NE Gabon 1.05N 13.12E
23 S4 **Belington** West Virginia, NE USA 39.01N 79.57W
131 O6 **Belinskiy** Penzenskaya Oblast', W Russian Federation 52.58N 43.25E
174 Ii9 **Belinyu** Pulau Bangka, W Indonesia 1.34S 105.45E
174 Jj11 **Belitung, Pulau** island W Indonesia
118 F10 **Beliu** Hung. Bel. Arad, W Romania 46.31N 21.57E
116 I9 **Beli Vit** ≈ NW Bulgaria
44 G2 **Belize** Sp. Belice; prev. British Honduras, Colony of Belize. ◆ commonwealth republic Central America
44 F2 **Belize** Sp. Belice. ◐ district NE Belize
44 G2 **Belize** ≈ Belize/Guatemala
Belize see Belize City
44 G2 **Belize City** var. Belize, Sp. Belice. Belize, NE Belize 17.29N 88.10W
44 G2 **Belize City** ✕ Belize, NE Belize 17.31N 88.15W
Beljak see Villach
41 N16 **Belkofski** Alaska, USA 55.06N 162.03W
126 L4 **Bel'kovskiy, Ostrov** island Novosibirskiye Ostrova, NE Russian Federation
12 J8 **Bell** ≈ Quebec, SE Canada
8 J15 **Bella Bella** British Columbia, SW Canada 52.04N 128.07W
104 M10 **Bellac** Haute-Vienne, C France 46.07N 1.04E
8 K15 **Bella Coola** British Columbia, SW Canada 52.22N 126.46W
108 D6 **Bellagio** Lombardia, N Italy 45.58N 9.15E
33 P6 **Bellaire** Michigan, N USA 44.58N 85.12W
108 D6 **Bellano** Lombardia, N Italy 46.06N 9.21E
161 G17 **Bellary** var. Ballari. Karnātaka, S India 15.10N 76.54E
191 S5 **Bellata** New South Wales, SE Australia 29.58S 149.49E
63 D16 **Bella Unión** Artigas, N Uruguay 30.18S 57.34W
63 C14 **Bella Vista** Corrientes, NE Argentina 28.34S 58.58W
64 J7 **Bella Vista** Tucumán, N Argentina 27.04S 65.19W
64 P4 **Bella Vista** Amambay, C Paraguay 22.12S 56.30W
58 B10 **Bellavista** Cajamarca, N Peru 5.43S 78.46W
58 D11 **Bellavista** San Martín, N Peru 7.02S 76.36W
191 U6 **Bellbrook** New South Wales, SE Australia 30.48S 152.32E
29 V5 **Belle** Missouri, C USA 38.17N 91.43W
23 Q5 **Belle** West Virginia, NE USA 38.13N 81.32W
33 R13 **Bellefontaine** Ohio, N USA 40.21N 83.45W
20 F14 **Bellefonte** Pennsylvania, NE USA 40.54N 77.43W
30 J9 **Belle Fourche** South Dakota, N USA 44.40N 103.49W
30 J9 **Belle Fourche Reservoir** ⊠ South Dakota, N USA
30 K9 **Belle Fourche River** ≈ South Dakota/Wyoming, N USA
105 S10 **Bellegarde-sur-Valserine** Ain, E France 46.06N 5.49E
25 Y14 **Belle Glade** Florida, SE USA 26.40N 80.40W
104 G8 **Belle Île** island NW France
11 T9 **Belle Isle** island Belle Isle, Newfoundland and Labrador, E Canada
11 S10 **Belle Isle, Strait of** strait Newfoundland and Labrador, E Canada
Bellenz see Bellinzona
31 W14 **Belle Plaine** Iowa, C USA 41.54N 92.16W
31 V9 **Belle Plaine** Minnesota, N USA 44.39N 93.47W
12 I9 **Belleterre** Quebec, SE Canada 47.24N 78.40W
12 J15 **Belleville** Ontario, SE Canada 44.10N 77.22W
105 R10 **Belleville** Rhône, E France 46.09N 4.42E
32 K15 **Belleville** Illinois, N USA 38.31N 89.58W
29 N3 **Belleville** Kansas, C USA 39.46N 97.37W
31 Z13 **Bellevue** Iowa, C USA 42.15N 90.25W
31 S15 **Bellevue** Nebraska, C USA 41.08N 95.53W
33 S11 **Bellevue** Ohio, N USA 41.16N 82.50W
27 S5 **Bellevue** Texas, SW USA 33.38N 98.00W
34 H8 **Bellevue** Washington, NW USA 47.36N 122.12W
57 Y11 **Bellevue de l'Inini, Montagnes** ▲▲ S French Guiana
105 S11 **Belley** Ain, E France 45.46N 5.40E
Bellin see Kangirsuk
191 V6 **Bellingen** New South Wales, SE Australia 30.27S 152.53E
99 L14 **Bellingham** N England, UK 55.09N 2.16W
34 H6 **Bellingham** Washington, NW USA 48.45N 122.29W
Belling Hausen Mulde see Southeast Pacific Basin
204 H2 **Bellingshausen** Russian research station South Shetland Islands, Antarctica 61.57S 58.23W
Bellingshausen see Motu One
Bellingshausen Abyssal Plain see Bellingshausen Plain
200 N16 **Bellingshausen Plain** var. Bellingshausen Abyssal Plain. undersea feature SE Pacific Ocean
204 I8 **Bellingshausen Sea** sea Antarctica
100 P6 **Bellingwolde** Groningen, NE Netherlands 53.07N 7.10E
110 H11 **Bellinzona** Ger. Bellenz. Ticino, S Switzerland 46.12N 9.01E
27 T8 **Bellmead** Texas, SW USA 31.36N 97.02W
56 E8 **Bello** Antioquia, W Colombia 6.19N 75.34W
63 B21 **Bellocq** Buenos Aires, E Argentina 35.55S 61.31W
Bello Horizonte see Belo Horizonte
195 W17 **Bellona** var. Mungiki. island S Solomon Islands
Bellovacum see Beauvais
190 D7 **Bell, Point** headland South Australia 32.13S 133.08E
22 F9 **Bells** Tennessee, S USA 35.42N 89.05W
27 U5 **Bells** Texas, SW USA 33.36N 96.24W
94 N3 **Bellsund** inlet SW Svalbard
108 H6 **Belluno** Veneto, NE Italy 46.07N 12.06E
64 L11 **Bell Ville** Córdoba, C Argentina 32.42S 62.42W
85 E26 **Bellville** Western Cape, SW South Africa 33.49S 18.43E
27 U11 **Bellville** Texas, SW USA 29.57N 96.15W
106 L12 **Belmez** Andalucía, S Spain 38.16N 5.12W
31 V12 **Belmond** Iowa, C USA 42.51N 93.36W
20 E11 **Belmont** New York, NE USA 42.13N 78.01W
23 R10 **Belmont** North Carolina, SE USA 35.13N 81.01W
61 O18 **Belmonte** Bahia, E Brazil 15.52S 38.54W
106 I8 **Belmonte** Castelo Branco, C Portugal 40.21N 7.19W
107 P10 **Belmonte** Castilla-La Mancha, C Spain 39.34N 2.43W
44 G2 **Belmopan** ● (Belize) Cayo, C Belize 17.13N 88.48W
99 B16 **Belmullet** Ir. Béal an Mhuirhead. W Ireland 54.13N 9.58W
126 Mm15 **Belogorsk** Amurskaya Oblast', SE Russian Federation 50.53N 128.24E
Belogorsk see Bilohirs'k
116 F7 **Belogradchik** Vidin, NW Bulgaria 43.37N 22.42E
180 H8 **Beloha** Toliara, S Madagascar 25.09S 45.04E
61 M20 **Belo Horizonte** prev. Bello Horizonte. state capital Minas Gerais, SE Brazil 19.54S 43.54W
28 M3 **Beloit** Kansas, C USA 39.27N 98.06W
32 L9 **Beloit** Wisconsin, N USA 42.31N 89.01W
Belokorovichi see Bilokorovychi
126 H15 **Belokurikha** Altayskiy Kray, S Russian Federation 51.57N 84.56E
128 J8 **Belomorsk** Respublika Kareliya, NW Russian Federation 64.30N 34.43E
128 J8 **Belomorsko-Baltiyskiy Kanal** Eng. White Sea-Baltic Canal, White Sea Canal. canal NW Russian Federation
159 V15 **Belonia** Tripura, NE India 23.15N 91.25E
Belopol'ye see Bilopillya
107 O4 **Belorado** Castilla-León, N Spain 42.25N 3.10W
130 L14 **Belorechensk** Krasnodarskiy Kray, SW Russian Federation 44.46N 39.53E
131 W5 **Beloretsk** Respublika Bashkortostan, W Russian Federation 53.56N 58.26E
Belorussia/Belorussian SSR see Belarus
Belorusskaya Gryada see Byelaruskaya Hrada
Belorusskaya SSR see Belarus
Beloshchel'ye see Nar'yan-Mar
116 N8 **Beloslav** Varna, E Bulgaria 43.13N 27.42E
Belostok see Białystok
180 H5 **Belo Tsiribihina** var. Belo-sur-Tsiribihina. Toliara, W Madagascar 19.40S 44.30E
Belovár see Bjelovar
Belovezhskaya Pushcha see Białowieska, Puszcza/Byelavyezhskaya Pushcha
116 H10 **Belovo** Pazardzhik, C Bulgaria 42.12N 24.02E
126 H14 **Belovo** Kemerovskaya Oblast', S Russian Federation 54.25N 86.13E
Belovodsk see Bilovods'k
125 Ff9 **Beloyarskiy** Khanty-Mansiyskiy Avtonomnyy Okrug, N Russian Federation 63.40N 66.31E
128 K7 **Beloye More** Eng. White Sea. sea NW Russian Federation
128 K13 **Beloye, Ozero** ◎ NW Russian Federation
116 J10 **Belozem** Plovdiv, C Bulgaria 42.11N 25.00E
128 K13 **Belozërsk** Vologodskaya Oblast', NW Russian Federation 59.58N 37.49E
101 E20 **Belœil** Hainaut, SW Belgium 50.33N 3.45E
110 D8 **Belp** Bern, W Switzerland 46.54N 7.31E
110 D8 **Belp** ✕ (Bern) Bern, C Switzerland 46.55N 7.29E
109 L24 **Belpasso** Sicilia, Italy, C Mediterranean Sea 37.34N 14.58E
33 U14 **Belpre** Ohio, N USA 39.14N 81.34W
100 M8 **Belterwijde** ◎ N Netherlands
29 R4 **Belton** Missouri, C USA 38.48N 94.31W
23 P11 **Belton** South Carolina, SE USA 34.31N 82.29W
27 T9 **Belton** Texas, SW USA 31.03N 97.27W
27 S9 **Belton Lake** ⊠ Texas, SW USA
Bel'tsy see Bălţi
99 E16 **Belturbet** Ir. Béal Tairbirt. N Ireland 54.06N 7.25W
Beluchistan see Baluchistān
151 Z9 **Belukha, Gora** ▲ Kazakhstan/Russian Federation 49.42N 86.33E
109 M20 **Belvedere Marittimo** Calabria, SW Italy 39.37N 15.52E
32 L10 **Belvidere** Illinois, N USA 42.15N 88.50W
20 J14 **Belvidere** New Jersey, NE USA 40.49N 75.03W
Bely see Belyy
131 V8 **Belyayevka** Orenburgskaya Oblast', W Russian Federation 51.25N 56.26E
Belynichi see Byalynichy
128 H17 **Belyy** var. Bely, Beyj. Tverskaya Oblast', W Russian Federation 55.51N 32.57E
130 I6 **Belyye Berega** Bryanskaya Oblast', W Russian Federation 53.11N 34.42E
126 H5 **Belyy, Ostrov** island N Russian Federation
126 H12 **Belyy Yar** Tomskaya Oblast', C Russian Federation 58.26N 84.57E
102 N13 **Belzig** Brandenburg, NE Germany 52.09N 12.37E
24 K4 **Belzoni** Mississippi, S USA 33.10N 90.29W
180 H4 **Bemaraha** var. Plateau du Bemaraha. ▲▲ W Madagascar
84 B10 **Bembe** Uíge, NW Angola 7.01S 14.18E
79 S14 **Bembèrèkè** var. Bimbéréké. N Benin 10.10N 2.40E
106 K12 **Bembézar** ≈ SW Spain
106 J3 **Bembibre** Castilla-León, N Spain 42.37N 6.25W
31 T4 **Bemidji** Minnesota, N USA 47.27N 94.53W
100 L12 **Bemmel** Gelderland, SE Netherlands 51.52N 5.54E
176 U11 **Bemu** Pulau Seram, E Indonesia 3.21S 129.58E
Benāb see Bonāb
107 T5 **Benabarre** var. Benavarn. Aragón, NE Spain 42.06N 0.28E
Benaco see Garda, Lago di
81 L20 **Bena-Dibele** Kasai Oriental, C Dem. Rep. Congo 4.01S 22.50E
107 R9 **Benageber, Embalse de** ⊠ E Spain
191 O11 **Benalla** Victoria, SE Australia 36.33S 146.00E
106 M14 **Benamejí** Andalucía, S Spain 37.16N 4.33W
Benares see Vārānasi
Benavarn see Benabarre

◆ Country ● Country Capital ◇ Dependent Territory ○ Dependent Territory Capital ◐ Administrative Region ✕ International Airport ▲ Mountain ▲▲ Mountain Range Volcano ≈ River ◎ Lake ⊠ Reservoir

106 F10 **Benavente** Santarém, C Portugal 38.58N 8.49W
106 K5 **Benavente** Castilla-León, N Spain 42.00N 5.40W
27 S15 **Benavides** Texas, SW USA 27.36N 98.24W
98 F8 **Benbecula** *island* NW Scotland, UK
Bencovazzo *see* Benkovac
34 H13 **Bend** Oregon, NW USA 44.03N 121.18W
190 K7 **Benda Range** ▲ South Australia
191 T6 **Bendemeer** New South Wales, SE Australia 30.54S 151.12E
Bender *see* Tighina
Bender Beila/Bender Beyla *see* Bandarbeyla
Bender Cassim/Bender Qaasim *see* Boosaaso
Bendery *see* Tighina
191 N11 **Bendigo** Victoria, SE Australia 36.46S 144.18E
120 E10 **Bēne** Dobele, SW Latvia 56.30N 23.04E
100 K13 **Beneden-Leeuwen** Gelderland, C Netherlands 51.52N 5.32E
103 L24 **Benediktenwand** ▲ S Germany 47.39N 11.28E
Benemérita de San Cristóbal *see* San Cristóbal
79 N12 **Bénéna** Ségou, S Mali 13.04N 4.20W
Bénoué *see* Benue
180 I7 **Benenitra** Toliara, S Madagascar 23.25S 45.06E
Beneschau *see* Benešov
Beneški Zaliv *see* Venice, Gulf of
113 D17 **Benešov** *Ger.* Beneschau. Středočeský Kraj, W Czech Republic 49.48N 14.40E
126 Ll3 **Benetta, Ostrov** *island* Novosibirskiye Ostrova, NE Russian Federation
109 L17 **Benevento** *anc.* Beneventum, Malventum. Campania, S Italy 41.07N 14.45E
Beneventum *see* Benevento
181 S3 **Bengal, Bay of** *bay* N Indian Ocean
81 M17 **Bengamisa** Orientale, N Dem. Rep. Congo 0.58N 25.10E
Bengasi *see* Banghāzī
174 Ll15 **Bengawan, Sungai** ∾ Jawa, S Indonesia
Bengazi *see* Banghāzī
167 P7 **Bengbu** *var.* Peng-pu. Anhui, E China 32.57N 117.17E
34 L9 **Benge** Washington, NW USA 46.55N 118.01W
Benghazi *see* Banghāzī
174 H7 **Bengkalis** Pulau Bengkalis, W Indonesia 1.29N 102.07E
174 H6 **Bengkalis, Pulau** *island* W Indonesia
174 Kk7 **Bengkayang** Borneo, C Indonesia 0.45N 109.28E
Bengkoelen/Bengkoeloe *see* Bengkulu
174 H12 **Bengkulu** *prev.* Bengkoeloe, Benkoelen, Benkulen. Sumatera, W Indonesia 3.46S 102.16E
174 H11 **Bengkulu** *off.* Propinsi Bengkulu; *prev.* Bengkoelen, Benkoelen, Benkulen. ◆ *province* W Indonesia
84 A11 **Bengo** ◆ *province* W Angola
97 J16 **Bengtsfors** Västra Götaland, S Sweden 59.03N 12.13E
85 B13 **Benguela** *var.* Benguella. Benguela, W Angola 12.34S 13.30E
85 A14 **Benguela** ◆ *province* W Angola
Benguella *see* Benguela
Bengweulu, Lake *see* Bangweulu, Lake
124 Qq15 **Benha** *var.* Banhā. N Egypt 30.22N 31.16E
198 G6 **Benham Seamount** *undersea feature* W Philippine Sea 15.48N 124.15E
98 H6 **Ben Hope** ▲ N Scotland, UK 58.25N 4.36W
81 P18 **Beni** Nord Kivu, NE Dem. Rep. Congo 0.31N 29.29E
59 L15 **Beni** *var.* El Beni. ◆ *department* N Bolivia
76 H8 **Beni Abbès** W Algeria 30.07N 2.09W
107 T8 **Benicarló** País Valenciano, E Spain 40.25N 0.25E
107 T9 **Benicasim** País Valenciano, E Spain 40.03N 0.03E
107 T12 **Benidorm** País Valenciano, SE Spain 38.33N 0.09W
77 W9 **Beni Mazâr** *var.* Banī Mazār. C Egypt 28.24N 30.38E
122 F12 **Beni-Mellal** C Morocco 32.20N 6.21W
79 R14 **Benin** *off.* Republic of Benin; *prev.* Dahomey. ◆ *republic* W Africa
79 S17 **Benin, Bight of** *gulf* W Africa
79 U16 **Benin City** Edo, SW Nigeria 6.22N 5.39E
59 K16 **Beni, Río** ∾ N Bolivia
123 Gg11 **Beni Saf** *var.* Beni-Saf. NW Algeria 35.16N 1.33W
82 H12 **Benishangul** ◆ *region* W Ethiopia
107 T11 **Benissa** País Valenciano, E Spain 38.43N 0.03E
124 Qq17 **Beni Suef** *var.* Banī Suwayf. N Egypt 29.09N 31.03E
9 V15 **Benito** Manitoba, S Canada 51.57N 101.24W
Benito *see* Uolo, Río
63 C23 **Benito Juárez** Buenos Aires, E Argentina 37.43S 59.48W
43 P14 **Benito Juaréz Internacional** ✈ (México) México, S Mexico 19.24N 99.02W
27 P5 **Benjamin** Texas, SW USA 33.34N 99.47W
60 B13 **Benjamin Constant** Amazonas, N Brazil 4.22S 70.01W
42 F4 **Benjamín Hill** Sonora, NW Mexico 30.13N 111.07W
65 F19 **Benjamín, Isla** *island* Archipiélago de los Chonos, S Chile
172 N5 **Benkei-misaki** *headland* Hokkaidō, NE Japan 42.49N 140.10E
30 L17 **Benkelman** Nebraska, C USA 40.04N 101.30W
98 I7 **Ben Klibreck** ▲ N Scotland, UK 58.15N 4.23W
Benkoelen *see* Bengkulu
114 D13 **Benkovac** *It.* Bencovazzo. Zadar, SW Croatia 44.02N 15.36E
Benkulen *see* Bengkulu
98 I11 **Ben Lawers** ▲ C Scotland, UK 56.33N 4.13W
98 J9 **Ben Macdui** *var.* Beinn MacDuibh. ▲ C Scotland, UK 57.02N 3.42W
98 G11 **Ben More** ▲ W Scotland, UK 56.26N 6.00W
98 I11 **Ben More** ▲ C Scotland, UK 56.22N 4.31W
98 H7 **Ben More Assynt** ▲ N Scotland, UK 58.09N 4.51W
193 E20 **Benmore, Lake** ◎ South Island, NZ
100 L12 **Bennekom** Gelderland, SE Netherlands 52.00N 5.40E
23 T11 **Bennettsville** South Carolina, SE USA 34.37N 79.41W
98 H10 **Ben Nevis** ▲ N Scotland, UK 56.46N 5.00W
192 M9 **Benneydale** Waikato, North Island, NZ 38.31S 175.22E
Bennichab *see* Bennichchâb
78 H8 **Bennichchâb** *var.* Bennichab. Inchiri, W Mauritania 19.25N 15.21W
20 L10 **Bennington** Vermont, NE USA 42.51N 73.09W
193 E20 **Ben Ohau Range** ▲ South Island, NZ
85 J21 **Benoni** Gauteng, NE South Africa 26.04S 28.18E
180 J2 **Be, Nosy** *var.* Nossi-Bé. *island* NW Madagascar
44 F2 **Benque Viejo del Carmen** Cayo, W Belize 17.04N 89.08W
103 G19 **Bensheim** Hessen, W Germany 49.40N 8.37E
39 N16 **Benson** Arizona, SW USA 31.55N 110.16W
31 S8 **Benson** Minnesota, N USA 45.19N 95.36W
23 U10 **Benson** North Carolina, SE USA 35.22N 78.33W
175 Pp14 **Benteng** Pulau Selayar, C Indonesia 6.07S 120.28E
85 A14 **Bentiaba** Namibe, SW Angola 14.18S 12.27E
189 T4 **Bentinck Island** *island* Wellesley Islands, Queensland, N Australia
82 E13 **Bentiu** Wahda, S Sudan 9.13N 29.49E
144 G8 **Bent Jbaïl** *var.* Bint Jubayl. S Lebanon 33.07N 35.25E
9 Q15 **Bentley** Alberta, SW Canada 52.27N 114.02W
63 I15 **Bento Gonçalves** Rio Grande do Sul, S Brazil 29.06S 51.29W
29 U12 **Benton** Arkansas, C USA 34.33N 92.35W
32 L16 **Benton** Illinois, N USA 38.00N 88.55W
22 H7 **Benton** Kentucky, S USA 36.51N 88.21W
24 G5 **Benton** Louisiana, S USA 32.41N 93.44W
29 Y7 **Benton** Missouri, C USA 37.05N 89.34W
22 M10 **Benton** Tennessee, S USA 35.10N 84.39W
33 O10 **Benton Harbor** Michigan, N USA 42.07N 86.27W
29 S9 **Bentonville** Arkansas, C USA 36.22N 94.12W
79 V16 **Benue** ◆ *state* SE Nigeria
80 F13 **Benue** *Fr.* Bénoué. ∾ Cameroon/Nigeria
174 Hh6 **Benut** Johor, Peninsular Malaysia 1.37N 103.15E
169 V12 **Benxi** *prev.* Pen-ch'i, Penhsihu, Penki. Liaoning, NE China 41.11N 123.46E
Benyakoni *see* Byenyakoni
114 K10 **Beočin** Serbia, N Serbia and Montenegro (Yugoslavia) 45.13N 19.43E
Beodericsworth *see* Bury St Edmunds
114 M11 **Beograd** *Eng.* Belgrade, *Ger.* Belgrad; *anc.* Singidunum. ● (Serbia and Montenegro (Yugoslavia)) Serbia, N Serbia and Montenegro (Yugoslavia) 44.48N 20.27E
114 L11 **Beograd** *Eng.* Belgrade. ✈ Serbia, N Serbia and Montenegro (Yugoslavia) 44.45N 20.21E
78 M16 **Béoumi** C Ivory Coast 7.40N 5.34W
37 V3 **Beowawe** Nevada, W USA 40.33N 116.31W
176 Ww8 **Bepondi, Pulau** *see* Bepondi, Pulau
170 D13 **Beppu** Ōita, Kyūshū, SW Japan 33.16N 131.28E
170 Dd14 **Beppu-wan** *bay* SW Japan
187 Y15 **Beqa** *prev.* Mbengga. *island* W Fiji
Beqa Barrier Reef *see* Kavukavu Reef
47 Y14 **Bequia** *island* C Saint Vincent and the Grenadines
115 L16 **Berane** *prev.* Ivangrad. Montenegro, SW Serbia and Montenegro (Yugoslavia) 42.51N 19.51E
115 L21 **Berat** *var.* Berati, *SCr.* Beligrad. Berat, C Albania 40.42N 19.57E
115 L21 **Berat** ◆ *district* C Albania
Berătău *see* Berettyó
Berati *see* Berat
Beraun *see* Berounka, Czech Republic
Beraun *see* Beroun, Czech Republic
175 O6 **Berau, Sungai** ∾ Borneo, N Indonesia
176 V10 **Berau, Teluk** *var.* MacCluer Gulf. *bay* Papua, E Indonesia
82 G8 **Berber** River Nile, NE Sudan 18.01N 34.00E
82 N12 **Berbera** Woqooyi Galbeed, NW Somalia 10.24N 45.01E
81 H16 **Berbérati** Mambéré-Kadéï, SW Central African Republic 4.13N 15.49E
Berberia, Cabo de *see* Barbaria, Cap de
57 T9 **Berbice River** ∾ NE Guyana
Berchid *see* Berrechid
105 N2 **Berck-Plage** Pas-de-Calais, N France 50.24N 1.34E
27 T13 **Berclair** Texas, SW USA 28.33N 97.32W
119 W10 **Berda** ∾ SE Ukraine
Berdichev *see* Berdychiv
126 Ll11 **Berdigestyakh** Respublika Sakha (Yakutiya), NE Russian Federation 62.02N 127.03E
126 H14 **Berdsk** Novosibirskaya Oblast', C Russian Federation 54.42N 82.56E
119 W10 **Berdyans'k** *Rus.* Berdyansk; *prev.* Osipenko. Zaporiz'ka Oblast', SE Ukraine 46.46N 36.48E
119 W10 **Berdyans'ka Kosa** *spit* SE Ukraine
119 V10 **Berdyans'ka Zatoka** *gulf* S Ukraine
119 N5 **Berdychiv** *Rus.* Berdichev. Zhytomyrs'ka Oblast', N Ukraine 49.52N 28.39E
22 M6 **Berea** Kentucky, S USA 37.34N 84.18W
Beregovo/Beregszász *see* Berehove
118 G8 **Berehove** *Cz.* Berehovo, *Hung.* Beregszász, *Rus.* Beregovo. Zakarpats'ka Oblast', W Ukraine 48.13N 22.39E
Berehovo *see* Berehove
194 J15 **Bereina** Central, S PNG 8.33S 146.25E
47 O12 **Berekua** S Dominica 15.14N 61.19W
79 O16 **Berekum** W Ghana 7.27N 2.34W
77 Y11 **Berenice** *var.* Mînâ Baranîs. SE Egypt 23.58N 35.29E
15 L14 **Berens** ∾ Manitoba/Ontario, C Canada
9 X14 **Berens River** Manitoba, C Canada 52.22N 97.00W
31 R12 **Beresford** South Dakota, N USA 43.02N 96.45W
118 J4 **Berestechko** Volyns'ka Oblast', NW Ukraine 50.21N 25.06E
118 M11 **Bereşti** Galaţi, E Romania 46.04N 27.54E
119 U6 **Berestova** ∾ E Ukraine
Beretău *see* Berettyó
113 N23 **Berettyó** *Rom.* Barcău; *prev.* Berătău, Beretău. ∾ Hungary/Romania
113 N23 **Berettyóújfalu** Hajdú-Bihar, E Hungary 47.15N 21.33E
Berëza/Bereza Kartuska *see* Byaroza
119 Q4 **Berezan'** Kyyivs'ka Oblast', N Ukraine 50.18N 31.30E
119 Q10 **Berezanka** Mykolayivs'ka Oblast', S Ukraine 46.51N 31.24E
118 J6 **Berezhany** *Pol.* Brzeżany. Ternopil's'ka Oblast', W Ukraine 49.29N 25.00E
Berezina *see* Byerezino
Berezino *see* Byerazino
119 P10 **Berezivka** *Rus.* Berezovka. Odes'ka Oblast', SW Ukraine 47.12N 30.55E
119 Q2 **Berezna** Chernihivs'ka Oblast', NE Ukraine 51.35N 31.50E
118 L3 **Berezne** Rivnens'ka Oblast', NW Ukraine 51.00N 26.46E
119 R9 **Bereznehuvate** Mykolayivs'ka Oblast', S Ukraine 47.18N 32.52E
129 N10 **Bereznik** Arkhangel'skaya Oblast', NW Russian Federation 62.50N 42.40E
129 U13 **Berezniki** Permskaya Oblast', NW Russian Federation 59.25N 56.49E
Berezovka *see* Berezivka
125 Ff9 **Berezovo** Khanty-Mansiyskiy Avtonomnyy Okrug, N Russian Federation 63.48N 64.38E
131 O9 **Berezovskaya** Volgogradskaya Oblast', SW Russian Federation 50.17N 43.58E
126 H14 **Berezovskiy** Kemerovskaya Oblast', S Russian Federation 55.40N 86.06E
127 N14 **Berezovyy** Khabarovskiy Kray, E Russian Federation 51.42N 135.39E
85 E25 **Berg** ∾ W South Africa
Berg *see* Berg bei Rohrbach
107 V4 **Berga** Cataluña, NE Spain 42.06N 1.40E
97 N20 **Berga** Kalmar, S Sweden 57.13N 16.03E
142 B13 **Bergama** İzmir, W Turkey 39.07N 27.10E
108 E7 **Bergamo** *anc.* Bergomum. Lombardia, N Italy 45.42N 9.40E
107 P3 **Bergara** País Vasco, N Spain 43.05N 2.25W
111 S3 **Berg bei Rohrbach** *var.* Berg. Oberösterreich, N Austria 48.34N 14.02E
195 O11 **Bergberg** ∾ New Britain, C Papau New Guinea
102 O6 **Bergen** Mecklenburg-Vorpommern, NE Germany 54.25N 13.24E
103 I11 **Bergen** Niedersachsen, NW Germany 52.49N 9.57E
100 H8 **Bergen** Noord-Holland, NW Netherlands 52.40N 4.42E
96 C13 **Bergen** Hordaland, S Norway 60.24N 5.19E
Bergen *see* Mons
57 W9 **Berg en Dal** Brokopondo, C Suriname 5.15N 55.20W
101 G15 **Bergen op Zoom** Noord-Brabant, S Netherlands 51.30N 4.18E
104 L13 **Bergerac** Dordogne, SW France 44.51N 0.30E
101 J16 **Bergeyk** Noord-Brabant, S Netherlands 51.19N 5.21E
103 D16 **Bergheim** Nordrhein-Westfalen, W Germany 50.57N 6.39E
57 X10 **Bergi** Sipaliwini, E Suriname 4.36N 54.24W
103 E16 **Bergisch Gladbach** Nordrhein-Westfalen, W Germany 50.59N 7.07E
103 F14 **Bergkamen** Nordrhein-Westfalen, W Germany 51.36N 7.39E
97 N21 **Bergkvara** Kalmar, S Sweden 56.22N 16.04E
Bergomum *see* Bergamo
100 K13 **Bergse Maas** ∾ S Netherlands
97 P15 **Bergshamra** Stockholm, C Sweden 59.37N 18.40E
96 N10 **Bergsjö** Gävleborg, C Sweden 62.00N 17.10E
95 J14 **Bergsviken** Norrbotten, N Sweden 65.16N 21.24E
100 L6 **Bergum** *Fris.* Burgum. Friesland, N Netherlands 53.12N 5.58E
Bergumer Meer ◎ N Netherlands
100 M6
96 N12 **Bergviken** ◎ C Sweden
174 I9 **Berhala, Selat** *strait* Sumatera, W Indonesia
Berhampore *see* Baharampur
127 Q9 **Beringa, Ostrov** *island* E Russian Federation
101 J17 **Beringen** Limburg, NE Belgium 51.04N 5.13E
41 T12 **Bering Glacier** *glacier* Alaska, USA
Beringov Proliv *see* Bering Strait
127 Q5 **Beringovskiy** Chukotskiy Avtonomnyy Okrug, NE Russian Federation 63.04N 179.09E
199 K2 **Bering Sea** *sea* N Pacific Ocean
40 L9 **Bering Strait** *Rus.* Beringov Proliv. *strait* Bering Sea/ Chukchi Sea
Berislav *see* Beryslav
107 O15 **Berja** Andalucía, S Spain 36.51N 2.55W
96 H9 **Berkåk** Sør-Trøndelag, S Norway 62.50N 10.01E
100 N11 **Berkel** ∾ Germany/Netherlands
37 N8 **Berkeley** California, W USA 37.52N 122.16W
67 E24 **Berkeley Sound** *sound* NE Falkland Islands
23 V2 **Berkeley Springs** *var.* Bath. West Virginia, NE USA 39.36N 78.12W
205 N6 **Berkner Island** *island* Antarctica
116 G8 **Berkovitsa** Montana, NW Bulgaria 43.16N 23.07E
99 M22 **Berkshire** *cultural region* S England, UK
101 H17 **Berlaar** Antwerpen, N Belgium 51.08N 4.39E
Berlanga *see* Berlanga de Duero
107 P6 **Berlanga de Duero** *var.* Berlanga. Castilla-León, N Spain 41.28N 2.51W
(0) I16 **Berlanga Rise** *undersea feature* E Pacific Ocean
101 F17 **Berlare** Oost-Vlaanderen, NW Belgium 51.01N 4.01E
106 E9 **Berlenga, Ilha da** *island* C Portugal
94 M7 **Berlevåg** Finnmark, N Norway 70.51N 29.04E
102 O12 **Berlin** ● (Germany) Berlin, NE Germany 52.31N 13.26E
23 Z4 **Berlin** Maryland, NE USA 38.19N 75.13W
21 O7 **Berlin** New Hampshire, NE USA 44.27N 71.13W
20 D16 **Berlin** Pennsylvania, NE USA 39.54N 78.57W
32 L7 **Berlin** Wisconsin, N USA 43.57N 88.59W
102 O12 **Berlin** ◆ *state* NE Germany
Berlinchen *see* Barlinek
33 U12 **Berlin Lake** ▣ Ohio, N USA
191 R11 **Bermagui** New South Wales, SE Australia 36.26S 150.01E
42 L8 **Bermejillo** Durango, C Mexico 25.55N 103.39W
64 M6 **Bermejo (viejo), Río** ∾ N Argentina
64 L5 **Bermejo, Río** ∾ N Argentina
64 I10 **Bermejo, Río** ∾ W Argentina
107 P2 **Bermeo** País Vasco, N Spain 43.25N 2.43W
106 K6 **Bermillo de Sayago** Castilla-León, N Spain 41.22N 6.07W
108 E6 **Bermina, Pizzo** *Rmsch.* Piz Bernina. ▲ Italy/Switzerland *see also* Bernina, Piz 46.22N 9.52E
66 A12 **Bermuda** *var.* Bermuda Islands, Bermudas; *prev.* Somers Islands. ◇ *UK crown colony* NW Atlantic Ocean
1 N11 **Bermuda** *var.* Great Bermuda, Long Island, Main Island. *island* Bermuda
Bermuda Islands *see* Bermuda
Bermuda-New England Seamount Arc *see* New England Seamounts
1 N11 **Bermuda Rise** *undersea feature* C Sargasso Sea
Bermudas *see* Bermuda
110 D8 **Bern** *Fr.* Berne. ● (Switzerland) Bern, W Switzerland 46.57N 7.25E
110 D9 **Bern** *Fr.* Berne. ◆ *canton* W Switzerland
39 R11 **Bernalillo** New Mexico, SW USA 35.18N 106.33W
12 H12 **Bernard Lake** ◎ Ontario, S Canada
63 B18 **Bernardo de Irigoyen** Santa Fe, NE Argentina 32.09S 61.06W
20 J14 **Bernardsville** New Jersey, NE USA 40.43N 74.34W
65 K14 **Bernasconi** La Pampa, C Argentina 37.55S 63.43W
102 O12 **Bernau** Brandenburg, NE Germany 52.40N 13.36E
104 L4 **Bernay** Eure, N France 49.04N 0.36E
103 L14 **Bernburg** Sachsen-Anhalt, C Germany 51.46N 11.45E
111 X5 **Berndorf** Niederösterreich, NE Austria 47.55N 16.10E
33 Q12 **Berne** Indiana, N USA 40.39N 84.57W
Berne *see* Bern
110 D10 **Berner Alpen** *var.* Berner Oberland, *Eng.* Bernese Oberland. ▲ SW Switzerland
Berner Oberland/Bernese Oberland *see* Berner Alpen
111 Y2 **Bernhardsthal** Niederösterreich, N Austria 48.40N 16.51E
24 H4 **Bernice** Louisiana, S USA 32.49N 92.39W
29 Y8 **Bernie** Missouri, C USA 36.40N 89.58W
188 G9 **Bernier Island** *island* Western Australia
Bernina Pass *see* Bernina, Passo del
110 J10 **Bernina, Passo del** *Eng.* Bernina Pass. *pass* SE Switzerland 46.23N 10.00E
110 J10 **Bernina, Piz** *It.* Pizzo Bermina. ▲ Italy/Switzerland *see also* Bermina, Pizzo 46.22N 9.55E
101 E20 **Bérnissart** Hainaut, SW Belgium 50.29N 3.37E
103 E18 **Bernkastel-Kues** Rheinland-Pfalz, W Germany 49.55N 7.04E
Beroea *see* Ḥalab
180 H6 **Beroroha** Toliara, SW Madagascar 21.40S 45.10E
Béroubouay *see* Gbéroubouè
113 C17 **Beroun** *Ger.* Beraun. Středočeský Kraj, W Czech Republic 49.58N 14.04E
113 C16 **Berounka** *Ger.* Beraun. ∾ W Czech Republic
115 Q18 **Berovo** E FYR Macedonia 41.45N 22.50E
76 F6 **Berrechid** *var.* Berchid. W Morocco 33.16N 7.32W
105 R15 **Berre, Étang de** ◎ SE France
105 S15 **Berre-l'Étang** Bouches-du-Rhône, SE France 43.28N 5.10E
190 K9 **Berri** South Australia 34.16S 140.35E
33 O10 **Berrien Springs** Michigan, N USA 41.57N 86.20W
191 O10 **Berrigan** New South Wales, SE Australia 35.41S 145.50E
105 N9 **Berry** *cultural region* C France
37 N7 **Berryessa, Lake** ◎ California, W USA
46 G2 **Berry Islands** *island group* N Bahamas
29 T9 **Berryville** Arkansas, C USA 36.21N 93.30W
23 V3 **Berryville** Virginia, NE USA 39.09N 77.58W
85 D21 **Berseba** Karas, S Namibia 26.00S 17.46E
119 O8 **Bershad'** Vinnyts'ka Oblast', C Ukraine 48.19N 29.28E
30 L3 **Berthold** North Dakota, N USA 48.16N 101.48W
39 T3 **Berthoud** Colorado, C USA 40.18N 105.04W
39 S4 **Berthoud Pass** *pass* Colorado, C USA 39.48N 105.46W
81 F15 **Bertoua** Est, E Cameroon 4.34N 13.42E
27 S10 **Bertram** Texas, SW USA 30.44N 98.03W
65 G22 **Bertrand, Cerro** ▲ S Argentina 50.00S 73.27W
101 J23 **Bertrix** Luxembourg, SE Belgium 49.52N 5.15E
203 P3 **Beru** *var.* Peru. *atoll* Tungaru, W Kiribati
Beruni *see* Beruniy
152 I9 **Beruniy** *var.* Biruni, *Rus.* Beruni. Qoraqalpog'iston Respublikasi, W Uzbekistan 41.48N 60.39E
60 F13 **Beruri** Amazonas, NW Brazil 3.44S 61.13W
20 H14 **Berwick** Pennsylvania, NE USA 41.03N 76.13W
98 K12 **Berwick** *cultural region* SE Scotland, UK
98 L12 **Berwick-upon-Tweed** N England, UK 55.46N 2.00W
119 S10 **Beryslav** *Rus.* Berislav. Khersons'ka Oblast', S Ukraine 46.51N 33.27E
Berytus *see* Beyrouth
180 H4 **Besalampy** Mahajanga, W Madagascar 16.43S 44.28E
105 T8 **Besançon** *anc.* Besontium, Vesontio. Doubs, E France 47.13N 6.01E
105 P10 **Besbre** ∾ C France
Bescanuova *see* Baška
Besdan *see* Bezdan
Besed' *see* Byesyedz'
153 R10 **Beshariq** *Rus.* Besharyk; *prev.* Kirovo. Farg'ona Viloyati, E Uzbekistan 40.26N 70.33E
Besharyk *see* Beshariq
152 L9 **Beshbuloq** *Rus.* Beshulak. Navoiy Viloyati, N Uzbekistan 41.55N 64.13E
Beshenkovichi *see* Byeshankovichy
152 M13 **Beshkent** Qashqadaryo Viloyati, S Uzbekistan 38.47N 65.42E
Beshulak *see* Beshbuloq
176 Uu8 **Besir** Papua, E Indonesia 0.25S 130.38E
114 L10 **Beška** Serbia, N Serbia and Montenegro (Yugoslavia) 45.09N 20.04E
Beskra *see* Biskra
131 O16 **Beslan** Respublika Severnaya Osetiya, SW Russian Federation 43.12N 44.33E
115 P16 **Besna Kobila** ▲ SE Serbia and Montenegro (Yugoslavia) 42.30N 22.16E
143 N16 **Besni** Adıyaman, S Turkey 37.42N 37.52E
Besontium *see* Besançon
124 Nn2 **Beşparmak Dağları** *Eng.* Kyrenia Mountains. ▲ N Cyprus
Bessarabka *see* Basarabeasca
94 O2 **Bessels, Kapp** *headland* C Svalbard 78.36N 21.43E
25 P4 **Bessemer** Alabama, S USA 33.24N 86.57W
32 K3 **Bessemer** Michigan, N USA 46.28N 90.03W
23 Q10 **Bessemer City** North Carolina, SE USA 35.16N 81.16W
104 M10 **Bessines-sur-Gartempe** Haute-Vienne, C France 46.06N 1.22E
101 K15 **Best** Noord-Brabant, S Netherlands 51.31N 5.24E
27 N9 **Best** Texas, SW USA 31.13N 101.34W
129 O11 **Bestuzhevo** Arkhangel'skaya Oblast', NW Russian Federation 61.36N 43.54E
126 M11 **Bestyakh** Respublika Sakha (Yakutiya), NE Russian Federation 61.25N 129.05E
Besztercze *see* Bistriţa
Beszterczebánya *see* Banská Bystrica
180 I5 **Betafo** Antananarivo, C Madagascar 19.49S 46.49E
106 H2 **Betanzos** Galicia, NW Spain 43.16N 8.16W
106 G2 **Betanzos, Ría de** *estuary* NW Spain
81 G15 **Bétaré Oya** Est, E Cameroon 5.34N 14.09E
107 S9 **Bétera** País Valenciano, E Spain 39.34N 0.28W
79 R15 **Bétérou** C Benin 9.13N 2.18E
85 K21 **Bethal** Mpumalanga, NE South Africa 26.27S 29.28E
32 K15 **Bethalto** Illinois, N USA 38.54N 90.02W
85 D21 **Bethanie** *var.* Bethanien, Bethany. Karas, S Namibia 26.26S 17.06E
Bethanien *see* Bethanie
29 S2 **Bethany** Missouri, C USA 40.15N 94.03W
29 N10 **Bethany** Oklahoma, C USA 35.31N 97.37W
Bethany *see* Bethanie
41 N12 **Bethel** Alaska, USA 60.47N 161.45W
21 P7 **Bethel** Maine, NE USA 44.24N 70.47W
23 W9 **Bethel** North Carolina, SE USA 35.46N 77.21W
20 B15 **Bethel Park** Pennsylvania, NE USA 40.21N 80.03W
23 W3 **Bethesda** Maryland, NE USA 38.58N 77.06W
85 J22 **Bethlehem** Free State, C South Africa 28.11S 28.16E
20 I14 **Bethlehem** Pennsylvania, NE USA 40.36N 75.22W
144 F10 **Bethlehem** *Ar.* Bayt Laḥm, *Heb.* Bet Leḥem. C West Bank 31.43N 35.12E
Bethlen *see* Beclean
85 I24 **Bethulie** Free State, C South Africa 30.29S 25.54E
105 O1 **Béthune** Pas-de-Calais, N France 50.31N 2.37E
104 M3 **Béthune** ∾ N France
106 M14 **Béticos, Sistemas** *var.* Sistema Penibético, *Eng.* Baetic Cordillera, Baetic Mountains. ▲ S Spain
56 I6 **Betijoque** Trujillo, NW Venezuela 9.27N 70.47W
61 M20 **Betim** Minas Gerais, SE Brazil 19.55S 44.10W
202 H3 **Betio** Tarawa, W Kiribati 1.21N 172.55E
180 H7 **Betioky** Toliara, S Madagascar 23.42S 44.22E
Bet Leḥem *see* Bethlehem
Betlen *see* Beclean
178 H17 **Betong** Yala, SW Thailand 5.47N 101.04E
81 I16 **Bétou** La Likouala, N Congo 3.07N 18.30E
151 P14 **Betpak-Dala** *Kaz.* Betpaqdala. *plateau* S Kazakhstan
Betpaqdala *see* Betpak-Dala
180 H7 **Betroka** Toliara, S Madagascar 23.15S 46.07E
Betschau *see* Bečva
144 G9 **Bet She'an** *Ar.* Baysān, Beisān; *anc.* Scythopolis. Northern, N Israel 32.29N 35.25E
13 T6 **Betsiamites** Quebec, SE Canada 48.55N 68.40W
13 T6 **Betsiamites** ∾ Quebec, SE Canada
180 I4 **Betsiboka** ∾ N Madagascar
101 M25 **Bettembourg** Luxembourg, S Luxembourg 49.31N 6.06E
101 M23 **Bettendorf** Diekirch, NE Luxembourg 49.52N 6.13E
31 Z14 **Bettendorf** Iowa, C USA 41.31N 90.31W
77 R13 **Bette, Pic** *var.* Bikkū Bittī, *It.* Picco Bette. ▲ S Libya 22.02N 19.07E
Bette, Picco *see* Bette, Pic
159 P12 **Bettiah** Bihār, N India 26.49N 84.30E
41 Q7 **Bettles** Alaska, USA 66.54N 151.40W
97 N17 **Bettna** Södermanland, C Sweden 58.52N 16.40E
160 H11 **Betūl** *prev.* Badnur. Madhya Pradesh, C India 21.55N 77.54E
160 H9 **Betwa** ∾ C India
103 F16 **Betzdorf** Rheinland-Pfalz, W Germany 50.47N 7.50E
84 C9 **Béu** Uíge, NW Angola 6.16S 15.28E
33 P6 **Beulah** Michigan, N USA 44.37N 86.04W
30 L5 **Beulah** North Dakota, N USA 47.16N 101.48W
100 M8 **Beulakerwijde** ◎ N Netherlands
100 L13 **Beuningen** Gelderland, SE Netherlands 51.52N 5.47E
Beuthen *see* Bytom
105 N7 **Beuvron** ∾ C France
101 F16 **Beveren** Oost-Vlaanderen, N Belgium 51.13N 4.15E
23 T9 **B.Everett Jordan Reservoir** *var.* Jordan Lake. ▣ North Carolina, SE USA
99 N17 **Beverley** E England, UK 53.51N 0.25W
Beverley *see* Beverly
101 J17 **Beverlo** Limburg, NE Belgium 51.06N 5.14E
21 P11 **Beverly** Massachusetts, NE USA 42.33N 70.49W
34 J9 **Beverly** *var.* Beverley. Washington, NW USA 46.50N 119.57W
37 S15 **Beverly Hills** California, W USA 34.02N 118.25W
103 I14 **Beverungen** Nordrhein-Westfalen, C Germany 51.39N 9.22E
100 H9 **Beverwijk** Noord-Holland, W Netherlands 52.28N 4.37E
110 C10 **Bex** Vaud, W Switzerland 46.15N 7.00E
99 P23 **Bexhill** *var.* Bexhill-on-Sea. SE England, UK 50.49N 0.28E
Bexhill-on-Sea *see* Bexhill
142 E17 **Bey Dağları** ▲ SW Turkey
Beyj *see* Belyy
142 E10 **Beykoz** İstanbul, NW Turkey 41.09N 29.06E
78 K15 **Beyla** Guinée-Forestière, SE Guinea 8.43N 8.41W
143 X12 **Beyläqan** *prev.* Zhdanov. SW Azerbaijan 39.43N 47.38E
82 L10 **Beylul** *var.* Beilul. SE Eritrea 13.10N 42.27E
150 H14 **Beyneu** *Kaz.* Beyneū. Mangistau, SW Kazakhstan 45.19N 55.11E
Beyneū *see* Beyneu
172 Ss14 **Beyonēsu-retsugan** *Eng.* Bayonnaise Rocks. *island group* SE Japan
142 G12 **Beypazarı** Ankara, NW Turkey 40.10N 31.55E
161 F21 **Beypore** Kerala, SW India 11.10N 75.49E
144 G7 **Beyrouth** *var.* Bayrūt, *Eng.* Beirut; *anc.* Berytus. ● (Lebanon) W Lebanon 33.54N 35.31E
144 G7 **Beyrouth** ✈ W Lebanon 33.52N 35.30E
142 G15 **Beyşehir** Konya, SW Turkey 37.39N 31.42E
142 G15 **Beyşehir Gölü** ◎ C Turkey
110 J7 **Bezau** Vorarlberg, NW Austria 47.24N 9.55E
114 J8 **Bezdan** *Ger.* Besdan, *Hung.* Bezdán. Serbia, NW Serbia and Montenegro (Yugoslavia) 45.51N 19.00E
Bezdezh *see* Byezdzyezh
128 G15 **Bezhanitsy** Pskovskaya Oblast', W Russian Federation 56.57N 29.53E
128 K15 **Bezhetsk** Tverskaya Oblast', W Russian Federation 57.47N 36.42E
105 P16 **Béziers** *anc.* Baeterrae, Baeterrae Septimanorum, Julia Beterrae. Hérault, S France 43.21N 3.13E
Bezmein *see* Byuzmeyin
Bezwada *see* Vijayawāda
160 P12 **Bhadrak** *var.* Bhadrakh. Orissa, E India 21.06N 86.31E
Bhadrakh *see* Bhadrak
161 F19 **Bhadra Reservoir** ▣ SW India
161 F18 **Bhadrāvati** Karnātaka, SW India 13.52N 75.43E
159 R14 **Bhāgalpur** Bihār, NE India 25.13N 86.58E
Bhairab *see* Bhairab Bazar
159 U14 **Bhairab Bazar** *var.* Bhairab. Dhaka, C Bangladesh 24.04N 91.00E
159 O11 **Bhairahawa** Western, S Nepal 27.31N 83.27E
155 S8 **Bhakkar** Punjab, E Pakistan 31.41N 71.04E
159 P11 **Bhaktapur** Central, C Nepal 27.47N 85.21E
178 Gg3 **Bhamo** *var.* Banmo. Kachin State, N Myanmar 24.15N 97.15E
Bhāmragad *see* Bhāmragarh
160 K13 **Bhāmragarh** *var.* Bhāmragad. Mahārāshtra, C India 19.28N 80.39E
160 J12 **Bhandāra** Mahārāshtra, C India 21.10N 79.40E
Bhārat *see* India
158 J12 **Bharatpur** *prev.* Bhurtpore. Rājasthān, N India 27.13N 77.28E
160 D11 **Bharūch** Gujarāt, W India 21.48N 72.54E
161 E18 **Bhatkal** Karnātaka, W India 13.59N 74.34E
159 O13 **Bhatni** *var.* Bhatni Junction. Uttar Pradesh, N India 26.22N 83.55E
Bhatni Junction *see* Bhatni
159 S16 **Bhātpāra** West Bengal, NE India 22.55N 88.30E
155 U7 **Bhaun** Punjab, E Pakistan 32.53N 72.45E
Bhaunagar *see* Bhāvnagar
160 M13 **Bhavānipātna** Orissa, E India 19.56N 83.09E
161 H21 **Bhavānisāgar Reservoir** ▣ S India
160 D11 **Bhāvnagar** *prev.* Bhaunagar. Gujarāt, W India 21.46N 72.13E
Bheanntraí, Bá *see* Bantry Bay
Bheara, Béal an *see* Gweebarra Bay
160 K12 **Bhilai** Madhya Pradesh, C India 21.13N 81.26E
158 G13 **Bhīlwāra** Rājasthān, N India 25.22N 74.39E
161 E14 **Bhīma** ∾ S India
161 K16 **Bhīmavaram** Andhra Pradesh, E India 16.34N 81.34E
160 I7 **Bhind** Madhya Pradesh, C India 26.33N 78.46E
158 E13 **Bhīnmāl** Rājasthān, N India 25.01N 72.22E
Bhir *see* Bīd
160 D13 **Bhiwandi** Mahārāshtra, W India 19.21N 73.07E
158 H10 **Bhiwāni** Haryāna, N India 28.49N 76.07E
158 L13 **Bhognīpur** Uttar Pradesh, N India 26.12N 79.48E
159 U16 **Bhola** Khulna, S Bangladesh 22.42N 90.43E
160 H10 **Bhopāl** Madhya Pradesh, C India 23.16N 77.24E
161 J14 **Bhopālpatnam** Madhya Pradesh, C India 18.51N 80.22E
161 E14 **Bhor** Mahārāshtra, W India 18.10N 73.55E
160 O12 **Bhubaneshwar** *prev.* Bhubaneswar, Bhuvaneshwar. Orissa, E India 20.16N 85.51E
Bhubaneswar *see* Bhubaneshwar
160 B9 **Bhuj** Gujarāt, W India 23.16N 69.40E
Bhuket *see* Phuket
Bhurtpore *see* Bharatpur
Bhusaval *see* Bhusāwal
160 G12 **Bhusāwal** *prev.* Bhusaval. Mahārāshtra, C India 21.01N 75.49E
159 T12 **Bhutan** *off.* Kingdom of Bhutan, *var.* Druk-yul. ◆ *monarchy* S Asia
Bhuvaneshwar *see* Bhubaneshwar
149 T15 **Bīābān, Kūh-e** ▲ S Iran
79 V18 **Biafra, Bight of** *var.* Bight of Bonny. *bay* W Africa
176 X9 **Biak** Papua, E Indonesia 1.10S 136.04E
176 Ww9 **Biak, Pulau** *island* E Indonesia
112 P12 **Biała Podlaska** Lubelskie, E Poland 52.03N 23.08E
112 F7 **Białogard** *Ger.* Belgard. Zachodniopomorskie, NW Poland 54.00N 15.58E
112 P10 **Białowieska, Puszcza** *Bel.* Byelavyezhskaya Pushcha, *Rus.* Belovezhskaya Pushcha. *physical region* Belarus/Poland *see also* Byelavyezhskaya Pushcha
112 G8 **Biały Bór** *Ger.* Baldenburg. Zachodniopomorskie, NW Poland 53.53N 16.49E
112 P9 **Białystok** *Rus.* Belostok, Bielostok. Podlaskie, NE Poland 53.08N 23.09E
109 L24 **Biancavilla** *prev.* Inessa. Sicilia, Italy, C Mediterranean Sea 37.37N 14.52E
Bianco, Monte *see* Blanc, Mont
78 L15 **Biankouma** W Ivory Coast 7.43N 7.37W
178 E7 **Bia, Phou** *var.* Pou Bia. ▲ C Laos 18.59N 103.09E
Bia, Pou *see* Bia, Phou
149 R5 **Bīārjmand** Semnān, N Iran 36.04N 55.49E
107 P4 **Biarra** ∾ NE Spain
104 I15 **Biarritz** Pyrénées-Atlantiques, SW France 43.24N 1.39W
110 H10 **Biasca** Ticino, S Switzerland 46.22N 8.59E
63 E17 **Biassini** Salto, N Uruguay 31.18S 57.05W
172 Oo5 **Bibai** Hokkaidō, NE Japan 43.22N 141.52E
85 B15 **Bibala** *Port.* Vila Arriaga. Namibe, SW Angola 14.45S 13.18E
106 I4 **Bibéi** ∾ NW Spain
Biberach *see* Biberach an der Riss
103 I23 **Biberach an der Riss** *var.* Biberach, *Ger.* Biberach an der Riß. Baden-Württemberg, S Germany 48.06N 9.46E
110 E7 **Biberist** Solothurn, NW Switzerland 47.10N 7.34E

◆ Country ● Country Capital ◇ Dependent Territory ○ Dependent Territory Capital ◆ Administrative Region ✈ International Airport ▲ Mountain ▲ Mountain Range ⛰ Volcano ∾ River ◎ Lake ▣ Reservoir

79 O16 **Bibiani** SW Ghana *6.28N 2.19W*
114 C13 **Bibinje** Zadar, SW Croatia *44.04N 15.17E*
Biblical Gebal *see* Jbaïl
118 I5 **Bibrka** *Pol.* Bóbrka, *Rus.* Bobrka. L'vivs'ka Oblast', NW Ukraine *49.39N 24.16E*
119 N10 **Bic** ≈ S Moldova
115 M18 **Bicaj** Kukës, NE Albania *42.00N 20.24E*
118 K10 **Bicaz** *Hung.* Békás. Neamţ, NE Romania *46.53N 26.04E*
191 Q16 **Bicheno** Tasmania, SE Australia *41.56S 148.15E*
Bichiş *see* Békés
Bichiş-Ciaba *see* Békéscsaba
Bichitra *see* Phichit
143 P8 **Bichvint'a** *Rus.* Pitsunda. NW Georgia *43.12N 40.21E*
13 T7 **Bic, Île du** *island* Quebec, SE Canada
34 J10 **Bickleton** Washington, NW USA *46.00N 120.16W*
38 L6 **Bicknell** Utah, W USA *38.20N 111.32W*
175 Tt7 **Bicoli** Pulau Halmahera, E Indonesia *0.34N 128.33E*
113 J22 **Bicske** Fejér, C Hungary *47.28N 18.38E*
161 F14 **Bīd** *prev.* Bhir. Mahārāshtra, W India *19.17N 75.22E*
79 U15 **Bida** Niger, C Nigeria *9.06N 6.02E*
161 H15 **Bīdar** Karnātaka, C India *17.55N 77.34E*
147 Y8 **Bidbid** NE Oman *23.25N 58.07E*
21 P9 **Biddeford** Maine, NE USA *43.28N 70.27W*
100 L9 **Biddinghuizen** Flevoland, C Netherlands *52.28N 5.41E*
35 X11 **Biddle** Montana, NW USA *45.04N 105.21W*
99 J23 **Bideford** SW England, UK *51.01N 4.12W*
84 D13 **Bié** ◈ *province* C Angola
37 O2 **Bieber** California, W USA *41.07N 121.09W*
110 O9 **Biebrza** ≈ NE Poland
172 P5 **Biei** Hokkaidō, NE Japan *43.33N 142.28E*
110 D8 **Biel** *Fr.* Bienne. Bern, W Switzerland *47.09N 7.16E*
102 G13 **Bielefeld** Nordrhein-Westfalen, NW Germany *52.01N 8.31E*
110 D8 **Bieler See** *Fr.* Lac de Bienne. ◎ W Switzerland
Bielitz/Bielitz-Biala *see* Bielsko-Biała
108 C7 **Biella** Piemonte, N Italy *45.33N 8.03E*
Bielostok *see* Białystok
113 J17 **Bielsko-Biała** *Ger.* Bielitz, Bielitz-Biala. Śląskie, S Poland *49.48N 19.01E*
112 P10 **Bielsk Podlaski** Białystok, E Poland *52.45N 23.11E*
Bien Bien *see* Điên Biên
Biên Đông *see* South China Sea
9 V17 **Bienfait** Saskatchewan, S Canada *49.06N 102.47W*
178 Jj14 **Biên Hoa** Đông Nai, S Vietnam *10.58N 106.49E*
Bienne *see* Biel
Bienne, Lac de *see* Bieler See
10 K8 **Bienville, Lac** ◎ Quebec, C Canada
84 D13 **Bié, Planalto do** *var.* Bié Plateau. *plateau* C Angola
Bié Plateau *see* Bié, Planalto do
110 B9 **Bière** Vaud, W Switzerland *46.32N 6.19E*
100 O4 **Bierum** Groningen, NE Netherlands *53.25N 6.51E*
100 I13 **Biesbos** *var.* Biesbosch. *wetland* S Netherlands
Biesbosch *see* Biesbos
101 H21 **Biesme** Namur, S Belgium *50.19N 4.43E*
103 H21 **Bietigheim-Bissingen** Baden-Württemberg, SW Germany *48.57N 9.07E*
101 I23 **Bièvre** Namur, SE Belgium *49.56N 5.01E*
81 D18 **Bifoun** Moyen-Ogooué, NW Gabon *0.15S 10.24E*
172 Pp3 **Bifuka** Hokkaidō, NE Japan *44.28N 142.20E*
142 C11 **Biga** Çanakkale, NW Turkey *40.13N 27.13E*
142 C13 **Bigadiç** Balıkesir, W Turkey *39.24N 28.07E*
28 J7 **Big Basin** *basin* Kansas, C USA
193 B20 **Big Bay** *bay* South Island, NZ
197 B12 **Big Bay** *bay* C Vanuatu
33 O5 **Big Bay de Noc** ◎ Michigan, N USA
33 N3 **Big Bay Point** *headland* Michigan, N USA *46.51N 87.40W*
35 R10 **Big Belt Mountains** ▲▲ Montana, NW USA
31 N10 **Big Bend Dam** *dam* South Dakota, N USA *44.03N 99.27W*
26 K12 **Big Bend National Park** *national park* Texas, S USA
24 K5 **Big Black River** ≈ Mississippi, S USA
29 O3 **Big Blue River** ≈ Kansas/Nebraska, C USA
26 M10 **Big Canyon** ≈ Texas, SW USA
35 N12 **Big Creek** Idaho, NW USA *45.05N 115.20W*
25 N8 **Big Creek Lake** ⊠ Alabama, S USA
25 X15 **Big Cypress Swamp** *wetland* Florida, SE USA
41 S9 **Big Delta** Alaska, USA *64.09N 145.50W*
32 K6 **Big Eau Pleine Reservoir** ⊠ Wisconsin, N USA
21 P5 **Bigelow Mountain** ▲ Maine, NE USA *45.09N 70.17W*
31 U3 **Big Falls** Minnesota, N USA *48.13N 93.48W*
35 P8 **Bigfork** Montana, NW USA *48.03N 114.04W*
31 U3 **Big Fork River** ≈ Minnesota, N USA
9 S15 **Biggar** Saskatchewan, S Canada *52.03N 107.58W*
188 L3 **Bigge Island** *island* Western Australia
37 O5 **Biggs** California, W USA *39.24N 121.44W*
34 I11 **Biggs** Oregon, NW USA *45.39N 120.49W*
12 K13 **Big Gull Lake** ◎ Ontario, SE Canada
39 P16 **Big Hachet Peak** ▲ New Mexico, SW USA *31.38N 108.24W*
35 P11 **Big Hole River** ≈ Montana, NW USA
35 V13 **Bighorn Basin** *basin* Wyoming, C USA
35 U11 **Bighorn Lake** ◎ Montana/Wyoming, N USA
35 W13 **Bighorn Mountains** ▲▲ Wyoming, C USA
38 J13 **Big Horn Peak** ▲ Arizona, SW USA *33.40N 113.01W*
35 V11 **Bighorn River** ≈ Montana/Wyoming, NW USA
16 O5 **Big Island** *island* Nunavut, NE Canada
41 O16 **Big Koniuji Island** *island* Shumagin Islands, Alaska, USA
27 N9 **Big Lake** Texas, SW USA *31.11N 101.27W*
21 T5 **Big Lake** ◎ Maine, NE USA
32 I3 **Big Manitou Falls** *waterfall* Wisconsin, N USA *46.32N 92.07W*
37 R2 **Big Mountain** ▲ Nevada, W USA *41.18N 119.03W*
110 G10 **Bignasco** Ticino, S Switzerland *46.21N 8.37E*
31 R16 **Big Nemaha River** ≈ Nebraska, C USA
78 G12 **Bignona** SW Senegal *12.49N 16.16W*
Bigorra *see* Tarbes
Bigosovo *see* Bihosava
37 S10 **Big Pine** California, W USA *37.09N 118.18W*
37 Q14 **Big Pine Mountain** ▲ California, W USA *34.41N 119.37W*
29 V6 **Big Piney Creek** ≈ Missouri, C USA
67 M24 **Big Point** *headland* N Tristan da Cunha
33 P8 **Big Rapids** Michigan, N USA *43.42N 85.28W*
32 K6 **Big Rib River** ≈ Wisconsin, N USA
12 L14 **Big Rideau Lake** ◎ Ontario, SE Canada
9 T14 **Big River** Saskatchewan, C Canada *53.48N 106.55W*
29 X5 **Big River** ≈ Missouri, C USA
33 N7 **Big Sable Point** *headland* Michigan, N USA *44.03N 86.30W*
35 S7 **Big Sandy** Montana, NW USA *48.08N 110.09W*
27 W6 **Big Sandy** Texas, SW USA *32.34N 95.06W*
39 V5 **Big Sandy Creek** ≈ Colorado, C USA
31 Q16 **Big Sandy Creek** ≈ Nebraska, C USA
31 V5 **Big Sandy Lake** ◎ Minnesota, N USA
38 J11 **Big Sandy River** ≈ Arizona, SW USA
23 P5 **Big Sandy River** ≈ S USA
25 V6 **Big Satilla Creek** ≈ Georgia, SE USA
31 R12 **Big Sioux River** ≈ Iowa/South Dakota, N USA
37 U7 **Big Smoky Valley** *valley* Nevada, W USA
27 N7 **Big Spring** Texas, SW USA *32.15N 101.30W*
21 Q5 **Big Squaw Mountain** ▲ Maine, NE USA *45.28N 69.42W*
23 O7 **Big Stone Gap** Virginia, NE USA *36.52N 82.45W*
31 Q8 **Big Stone Lake** ◎ Minnesota/South Dakota, N USA
24 K4 **Big Sunflower River** ≈ Mississippi, S USA
35 T11 **Big Timber** Montana, NW USA *45.50N 109.57W*
10 D8 **Big Trout Lake** Ontario, C Canada *53.40N 90.00W*
12 I12 **Big Trout Lake** ◎ Ontario, SE Canada
37 O2 **Big Valley Mountains** ▲▲ California, W USA
27 Q13 **Big Wells** Texas, SW USA *28.34N 99.34W*
12 F11 **Bigwood** Ontario, S Canada *46.03N 80.37W*
114 D11 **Bihać** Federacija Bosna I Hercegovina, NW Bosnia and Herzegovina *44.49N 15.53E*
159 P14 **Bihār** *prev.* Behar. ◈ *state* N India
Bihār *see* Bihār Sharīf
83 F20 **Biharamulo** Kagera, NW Tanzania *2.37S 31.19E*
159 R13 **Bihārīganj** Bihār, NE India *25.43N 86.58E*
159 P14 **Bihār Sharīf** *var.* Bihār. Bihār, N India *25.13N 85.31E*
118 F10 **Bihor** ◈ *county* NW Romania
172 Q6 **Bihoro** Hokkaidō, NE Japan *43.50N 144.05E*
120 K11 **Bihosava** *Rus.* Bigosovo. Vitsyebskaya Voblasts', NW Belarus *55.50N 27.45E*
Bijagos Archipelago *see* Bijagós, Arquipélago dos
78 G13 **Bijagós, Arquipélago dos** *var.* Bijagos Archipelago. *island group* W Guinea-Bissau
161 F16 **Bijāpur** Karnātaka, C India *16.49N 75.42E*
148 K5 **Bījār** Kordestān, W Iran *35.54N 47.36E*
114 J11 **Bijeljina** Republika Srpska, NE Bosnia and Herzegovina *44.46N 19.13E*
115 K15 **Bijelo Polje** Montenegro, SW Serbia and Montenegro (Yugoslavia) *43.03N 19.44E*
166 I11 **Bijie** Guizhou, S China *27.18N 105.15E*
158 J10 **Bijnor** Uttar Pradesh, N India *29.22N 78.09E*
158 F11 **Bīkāner** Rājasthān, NW India *28.01N 73.22E*
201 V3 **Bikar Atoll** *var.* Pikaar. *atoll* Ratak Chain, N Marshall Islands
202 H3 **Bikeman** *atoll* Tungaru, W Kiribati
203 I3 **Bikenebu** Tarawa, W Kiribati *1.22N 173.04E*
127 Nn16 **Bikin** Khabarovskiy Kray, SE Russian Federation *46.45N 134.06E*
127 Nn16 **Bikin** ≈ SE Russian Federation
201 R3 **Bikini Atoll** *var.* Pikinni. *atoll* Ralik Chain, NW Marshall Islands
85 L17 **Bikita** Masvingo, E Zimbabwe *20.04S 31.38E*
Bikkū Bittī *see* Bette, Pic
81 I19 **Bikoro** Equateur, W Dem. Rep. Congo *0.45S 18.09E*
147 Z9 **Bilād Banī Bū 'Alī** NE Oman *22.01N 59.18E*
147 Z9 **Bilād Banī Bū Ḩasan** NE Oman *22.09N 59.13E*
147 X9 **Bilād Manaḩ** *var.* Manaḩ. NE Oman *22.37N 57.27E*
79 Q12 **Bilanga** C Burkina *12.35N 0.08W*
175 Q7 **Bilang, Teluk** *bay* Sulawesi, N Indonesia
158 F12 **Bilāra** Rājasthān, N India *26.14N 73.48E*
158 K10 **Bilāri** Uttar Pradesh, N India *28.37N 78.48E*
144 J5 **Bil'ās, Jabal al** ▲▲ C Syria
158 I8 **Bilāspur** Himāchal Pradesh, N India *31.19N 76.46E*
160 L11 **Bilāspur** Madhya Pradesh, C India *22.06N 82.08E*
173 G6 **Bila, Sungai** ≈ Sumatera, W Indonesia
143 Y13 **Biläsuvar** *Rus.* Bilyasuvar; *prev.* Pushkino. SE Azerbaijan *39.26N 48.33E*
119 O5 **Bila Tserkva** *Rus.* Belaya Tserkov'. Kyyivs'ka Oblast', N Ukraine *49.48N 30.07E*
178 H11 **Bilauktaung Range** *var.* Thanintari Taungdan. ▲▲ Myanmar/Thailand
107 O2 **Bilbao** *Basq.* Bilbo. País Vasco, N Spain *43.15N 2.55W*
Bilbo *see* Bilbao
94 H2 **Bíldudalur** Vestfirdhir, NW Iceland *65.40N 23.35W*
115 I16 **Bileća** Republika Srpska, S Bosnia and Herzegovina *42.53N 18.27E*
142 E12 **Bilecik** Bilecik, NW Turkey *39.59N 29.54E*
142 F12 **Bilecik** ◈ *province* NW Turkey
118 E11 **Biled** *Ger.* Billed, *Hung.* Billéd. Timiş, W Romania *45.55N 20.55E*
113 O15 **Biłgoraj** Lubelskie, E Poland *50.32N 22.42E*
119 P11 **Bilhorod-Dnistrovs'kyy** *Rus.* Belgorod-Dnestrovskiy, *Rom.* Cetatea Albă; *prev.* Akkerman, *anc.* Tyras. Odes'ka Oblast', SW Ukraine *46.10N 30.18E*
81 M16 **Bili** Orientale, N Dem. Rep. Congo *4.07N 25.09E*
127 Oo5 **Bilibino** Chukotskiy Avtonomnyy Okrug, NE Russian Federation *67.56N 166.45E*
178 Gg8 **Bilin** Mon State, S Myanmar *17.13N 97.12E*
179 Qq12 **Biliran Island** *island* C Philippines
115 N21 **Bilisht** *var.* Bilishti. Korçë, SE Albania *40.36N 21.00E*
Bilishti *see* Bilisht
191 N10 **Billabong Creek** *var.* Moulamein Creek. *seasonal river* New South Wales, SE Australia
190 G4 **Billa Kalina** South Australia *29.57S 136.13E*
207 Q17 **Bill Baileys Bank** *undersea feature* N Atlantic Ocean *60.34N 10.15W*
Billed/Billéd *see* Biled
159 N14 **Billi** Uttar Pradesh, N India *24.30N 82.58E*
99 M15 **Billingham** N England, UK *54.36N 1.16W*
35 U11 **Billings** Montana, NW USA *45.47N 108.32W*
97 J16 **Billingsfors** Västra Götaland, S Sweden *58.57N 12.14E*
Bill of Cape Clear, The *see* Clear, Cape
30 L9 **Billsburg** South Dakota, N USA *44.22N 101.40W*
97 F23 **Billund** Ribe, W Denmark *55.43N 9.07E*
38 L11 **Bill Williams Mountain** ▲ Arizona, SW USA *35.12N 112.12W*
38 I12 **Bill Williams River** ≈ Arizona, SW USA
79 Y8 **Bilma** Agadez, NE Niger *18.22N 13.01E*
79 Y8 **Bilma, Grand Erg de** *desert* NE Niger
189 Y9 **Biloela** Queensland, E Australia *24.27S 150.31E*
114 G8 **Bilo Gora** ▲▲ N Croatia
119 U13 **Bilohirs'k** *Rus.* Belogorsk; *prev.* Karasubazar. Respublika Krym, S Ukraine *45.01N 34.35E*
118 M3 **Bilokorovychi** *Rus.* Belokorovichi. Zhytomyrs'ka Oblast', N Ukraine *51.07N 28.02E*
119 X5 **Bilokurakine** Luhans'ka Oblast', E Ukraine *49.32N 38.44E*
119 T3 **Bilopillya** *Rus.* Belopol'ye. Sums'ka Oblast', NE Ukraine *51.09N 34.16E*
119 Y6 **Bilovods'k** *Rus.* Belovodsk. Luhans'ka Oblast', E Ukraine *49.10N 39.34E*
24 M9 **Biloxi** Mississippi, S USA *30.24N 88.53W*
119 R10 **Bilozerka** Khersons'ka Oblast', S Ukraine *46.36N 32.23E*
119 W7 **Bilozers'ke** Donets'ka Oblast', E Ukraine *48.29N 37.03E*
100 J11 **Bilthoven** Utrecht, C Netherlands *52.07N 5.12E*
80 K9 **Biltine** Biltine, E Chad *14.30N 20.52E*
80 J9 **Biltine** *off.* Préfecture de Biltine. ◈ *prefecture* E Chad
168 D5 **Bilüü** Bayan-Ölgiy, W Mongolia *48.54N 89.40E*
Bilwi *see* Puerto Cabezas
Bilyasuvar *see* Biläsuvar
119 O11 **Bilyayivka** Odes'ka Oblast', SW Ukraine *46.28N 30.11E*
101 K18 **Bilzen** Limburg, NE Belgium *50.52N 5.31E*
Bimbéréké *see* Bembèrèkè
191 R10 **Bimberi Peak** ▲ New South Wales, SE Australia *35.42S 148.46E*
79 Q15 **Bimbila** E Ghana *8.54N 0.04E*
81 I15 **Bimbo** Ombella-Mpoko, SW Central African Republic *4.19N 18.27E*
46 F2 **Bimini Islands** *island group* W Bahamas
160 I9 **Bīna** Madhya Pradesh, C India *24.09N 78.10E*
149 T4 **Bīnālūd, Kūh-e** ▲▲ NE Iran
101 F20 **Binche** Hainaut, S Belgium *50.25N 4.10E*
Bindloe Island *see* Marchena, Isla
85 L16 **Bindura** Mashonaland Central, NE Zimbabwe *17.18S 31.13E*
107 T5 **Binefar** Aragón, NE Spain *41.51N 0.16E*
85 J16 **Binga** Matabeleland North, W Zimbabwe *17.42S 27.21E*
191 T5 **Bingara** New South Wales, SE Australia *29.54S 150.36E*
103 F18 **Bingen am Rhein** Rheinland-Pfalz, SW Germany *49.58N 7.54E*
28 M11 **Binger** Oklahoma, C USA *35.19N 98.19W*
Bingerau *see* Węgrów
Bin Ghalfān, Jazā'ir *see* Ḩalāniyāt, Juzur al
21 Q6 **Bingham** Maine, NE USA *45.01N 69.51W*
20 H11 **Binghamton** New York, NE USA *42.06N 75.55W*
Bin Ghanīmah, Jabal *see* Bin Ghunaymah, Jabal
77 P11 **Bin Ghunaymah, Jabal** *var.* Jabal Bin Ghanīmah. ▲ C Libya
145 U3 **Bingird** NE Iraq *36.03N 45.03E*
143 P14 **Bingöl** Bingöl, E Turkey *38.54N 40.28E*
143 P14 **Bingöl** ◈ *province* E Turkey
167 R6 **Binhai** *var.* Binhai Xian, Dongkan. Jiangsu, E China *34.03N 119.46E*
Binhai Xian *see* Binhai
178 Kk12 **Binh Đinh** *var.* An Nhon. Binh Đinh, C Vietnam *13.52N 109.07E*
178 Kk10 **Binh Sơn** *var.* Châu Ổ. Quang Ngai, C Vietnam *15.18N 108.45E*
Binimani *see* Bintimani
173 Ff5 **Binjai** Sumatera, W Indonesia *3.37N 98.30E*
191 R6 **Binnaway** New South Wales, SE Australia *31.34S 149.24E*
110 E6 **Binningen** Basel-Land, NW Switzerland *47.31N 7.34E*
175 R13 **Binongko, Pulau** *island* Kepulauan Tukangbesi, C Indonesia
174 Gg3 **Bintang, Banjaran** ▲▲ Peninsular Malaysia
174 I7 **Bintan, Pulau** *island* Kepulauan Riau, W Indonesia
78 J14 **Bintimani** *var.* Binimani. ▲ NE Sierra Leone *9.21N 11.09W*
Bint Jubayl *see* Bent Jbaïl
174 M5 **Bintulu** Sarawak, East Malaysia *3.12N 113.01E*
176 Vv10 **Bintuni** *prev.* Steenkool. Papua, E Indonesia *2.03S 133.45E*
176 Vv10 **Bintuni, Teluk** *bay* Papua, E Indonesia
169 W8 **Bin Xian** Heilongjiang, NE China *45.43N 127.24E*
166 K14 **Binyang** Guangxi Zhuangzu Zizhiqu, S China *23.15N 108.47E*
167 Q4 **Binzhou** Shandong, E China *37.22N 118.03E*
65 G14 **Bío Bío** *off.* Región del Bío Bío. ◈ *region* C Chile
65 G14 **Bío Bío, Río** ≈ C Chile
81 C16 **Bioco, Isla de** *var.* Bioko, *Eng.* Fernando Po, *Sp.* Fernando Póo; *prev.* Macías Nguema Biyogo. *island* NW Equatorial Guinea
114 D13 **Biograd na Moru** *It.* Zaravecchia. Zadar, SW Croatia *43.57N 15.27E*
Bioko *see* Bioco, Isla de
115 F14 **Biokovo** ▲▲ S Croatia
Biorra *see* Birr
Bipontium *see* Zweibrücken
149 W13 **Birag, Kūh-e** ▲▲ SE Iran
77 O10 **Birāk** *var.* Brak. C Libya *27.31N 14.16E*
145 S10 **Bi'r al Islām** C Iraq *32.15N 43.40E*
160 N11 **Biramitrapur** Orissa, E India *22.24N 84.42E*
145 T11 **Bi'r an Nişf** S Iraq *31.22N 44.07E*
80 L12 **Birao** Vakaga, NE Central African Republic *10.14N 22.49E*
164 M6 **Biratar Bulak** *well* NW China *42.00N 90.26E*
159 R12 **Biratnagar** Eastern, SE Nepal *26.28N 87.16E*
172 Oo6 **Biratori** Hokkaidō, NE Japan *42.35N 142.07E*
41 S8 **Birch Creek** Alaska, USA *66.17N 145.54W*
40 M11 **Birch Creek** ≈ Alaska, USA
9 T14 **Birch Hills** Saskatchewan, S Canada *52.58N 105.22W*
190 M10 **Birchip** Victoria, SE Australia *36.01S 142.55E*
31 X4 **Birch Lake** ◎ Minnesota, N USA
9 Q11 **Birch Mountains** ▲ Alberta, W Canada
9 V15 **Birch River** Manitoba, S Canada *52.22N 101.03W*
46 H12 **Birchs Hill** *hill* W Jamaica *18.22N 78.05W*
41 R11 **Birchwood** Alaska, USA *61.24N 149.28W*
196 I5 **Bird Island** *island* S Northern Mariana Islands
143 N16 **Birecik** Şanlıurfa, S Turkey *37.02N 38.01E*
158 M10 **Birendranagar** *var.* Surkhet. Mid Western, W Nepal *28.35N 81.36E*
Bir es Saba *see* Be'ér Sheva'
76 A12 **Bir-Gandouz** SW Western Sahara *21.35N 16.27W*
159 P12 **Birganj** Central, C Nepal *27.03N 84.53E*
83 B14 **Biri** ≈ W Sudan
Bi'r Ibn Hirmās *see* Al Bi'r
176 Yy10 **Biri, Sungai** ≈ Papua, E Indonesia
149 U8 **Bīrjand** Khorāsān, E Iran *32.54N 59.13E*
145 T11 **Birkat Ḩāmid** *well* S Iraq *31.16N 44.04E*
97 F18 **Birkeland** Aust-Agder, S Norway *58.18N 8.13E*
103 E19 **Birkenfeld** Rheinland-Pfalz, SW Germany *49.39N 7.09E*
99 K18 **Birkenhead** NW England, UK *53.24N 3.01W*
111 W7 **Birkfeld** Steiermark, SE Austria *47.21N 15.40E*
190 A2 **Birksgate Range** ▲▲ South Australia
Birlad *see* Bârlad
99 K20 **Birmingham** C England, UK *52.30N 1.49W*
25 P4 **Birmingham** Alabama, S USA *33.30N 86.47W*
99 M20 **Birmingham** ✈ C England, UK *52.27N 1.46W*
Bir Moghrein *see* Bîr Mogreïn
78 J4 **Bîr Mogreïn** *var.* Bir Moghrein; *prev.* Fort-Trinquet. Tiris Zemmour, N Mauritania *25.10N 11.34W*
203 S4 **Birnie Island** *atoll* Phoenix Islands, C Kiribati
Birni-Ngaouré *see* Birnin Gaouré
79 S12 **Birnin Gaouré** *var.* Birni-Ngaouré. Dosso, SW Niger *12.59N 3.02E*
79 S12 **Birnin Kebbi** Kebbi, NW Nigeria *12.28N 4.08E*
Birni-Nkonni *see* Birnin Konni
79 T12 **Birnin Konni** *var.* Birni-Nkonni. Tahoua, SW Niger *13.50N 5.14E*
79 W13 **Birnin Kudu** Jigawa, N Nigeria *11.28N 9.29E*
127 N16 **Birobidzhan** Yevreyskaya Avtonomnaya Oblast', SE Russian Federation *48.41N 132.55E*
99 D18 **Birr** *var.* Parsonstown, *Ir.* Biorra. C Ireland *53.06N 7.54W*
191 P4 **Birrie River** ≈ New South Wales/Queensland, SE Australia
110 D7 **Birse** ≈ NW Switzerland
Birsen *see* Biržai
110 E6 **Birsfelden** Basel-Land, NW Switzerland *47.33N 7.37E*
131 U4 **Birsk** Respublika Bashkortostan, W Russian Federation *55.24N 55.33E*
121 F14 **Birštonas** Prienai, C Lithuania *54.37N 24.00E*
165 P14 **Biru** Xinjiang Uygur Zizhiqu, W China *31.30N 93.55E*
Biruni *see* Beruniy
126 Ii14 **Biryusa** ≈ C Russian Federation
126 Ii14 **Biryusinsk** Irkutskaya Oblast', C Russian Federation *55.52N 97.48E*
120 G10 **Biržai** *Ger.* Birsen. Biržai, NE Lithuania *56.12N 24.47E*
123 Jj17 **Birżebbuġa** SE Malta *35.50N 14.32E*
Bisanthe *see* Tekirdağ
175 T9 **Bisa, Pulau** *island* Maluku, E Indonesia
39 N17 **Bisbee** Arizona, SW USA *31.27N 109.55W*
31 O2 **Bisbee** North Dakota, N USA *48.36N 99.21W*
Biscaia, Baía de *see* Biscay, Bay of
104 I13 **Biscarrosse et de Parentis, Étang de** ◎ SW France
106 M1 **Biscay, Bay of** *Sp.* Golfo de Vizcaya, *Port.* Baía de Biscaia. *bay* France/Spain
25 Z16 **Biscayne Bay** *bay* Florida, SE USA
66 M7 **Biscay Plain** *undersea feature* SE Bay of Biscay
109 N17 **Bisceglie** Puglia, SE Italy *41.13N 16.31E*
Bischofflack *see* Škofja Loka
Bischofsburg *see* Biskupiec
111 Q7 **Bischofshofen** Salzburg, NW Austria *47.25N 13.13E*
103 P15 **Bischofswerda** Sachsen, E Germany *51.07N 14.13E*
105 V5 **Bischwiller** Bas-Rhin, NE France *48.46N 7.52E*
23 T10 **Biscoe** North Carolina, SE USA *35.20N 79.46W*
204 G5 **Biscoe Islands** *island group* Antarctica
12 E9 **Biscotasi Lake** ◎ Ontario, S Canada
12 E9 **Biscotasing** Ontario, S Canada *47.16N 82.04W*
56 J6 **Biscucuy** Portuguesa, NW Venezuela *9.22N 69.58W*
116 K11 **Biser** Khaskovo, S Bulgaria *41.52N 25.58E*
115 D15 **Biševo** *It.* Busi. *island* SW Croatia
147 N12 **Bishah, Wādī** *dry watercourse* C Saudi Arabia
153 U7 **Bishkek** *var.* Pishpek; *prev.* Frunze. ● (Kyrgyzstan) Chuyskaya Oblast', N Kyrgyzstan *42.53N 74.46E*
153 U7 **Bishkek** ✈ Chuyskaya Oblast', N Kyrgyzstan *42.55N 74.37E*
159 R16 **Bishnupur** West Bengal, NE India *23.04N 87.19E*
85 J25 **Bisho** Eastern Cape, S South Africa *32.46S 27.21E*
37 S9 **Bishop** California, W USA *37.22N 118.24W*
27 S15 **Bishop** Texas, SW USA *27.36N 97.49W*
99 L15 **Bishop Auckland** N England, UK *54.40N 1.40W*
Bishop's Lynn *see* King's Lynn
99 O21 **Bishop's Stortford** E England, UK *51.45N 0.12E*
23 S12 **Bishopville** South Carolina, SE USA *34.13N 80.15W*
144 M5 **Bishri, Jabal** ▲▲ E Syria
169 U4 **Bishui** Heilongjiang, NE China *52.06N 123.42E*
83 G17 **Bisina, Lake** *prev.* Lake Salisbury. ◎ E Uganda
Biskara *see* Biskra
76 L6 **Biskra** *var.* Beskra, Biskara. NE Algeria *34.51N 5.44E*
112 M8 **Biskupiec** *Ger.* Bischofsburg. Warmińsko-Mazurskie, NE Poland *53.51N 20.56E*
179 Rr15 **Bislig** Mindanao, S Philippines *8.10N 126.18E*
29 X6 **Bismarck** Missouri, C USA *37.46N 90.37W*
30 M5 **Bismarck** *state capital* North Dakota, N USA *46.48N 100.46W*
194 K9 **Bismarck Archipelago** *island group* NE PNG
133 Z16 **Bismarck Plate** *tectonic feature* W Pacific Ocean
194 I12 **Bismarck Range** ▲▲ N PNG
194 J10 **Bismarck Sea** *sea* W Pacific Ocean
143 P15 **Bismil** Diyarbakır, SE Turkey *37.52N 40.37E*
45 N6 **Bismuna, Laguna** *lagoon* NE Nicaragua
Bisnulok *see* Phitsanulok
175 T6 **Bisoa, Tanjung** *headland* Pulau Halmahera, N Indonesia *2.15N 127.57E*
30 K7 **Bison** South Dakota, N USA *45.30N 102.25W*
95 H17 **Bispfors** Jämtland, C Sweden *63.00N 16.40E*
78 G13 **Bissau** ● (Guinea-Bissau) W Guinea-Bissau *11.52N 15.39W*
78 G13 **Bissau** ✈ W Guinea-Bissau *11.53N 15.41W*
101 M24 **Bissen** Luxembourg, C Luxembourg *49.46N 6.04E*
78 G12 **Bissorã** W Guinea-Bissau *12.16N 15.34W*
9 O10 **Bistcho Lake** ◎ Alberta, W Canada
24 G5 **Bistineau, Lake** ⊠ Louisiana, S USA
Bistrica *see* Ilirska Bistrica
118 I9 **Bistriţa** *Ger.* Bistritz, *Hung.* Beszterce; *prev.* Nösen. Bistriţa-Năsăud, N Romania *47.10N 24.30E*
118 K10 **Bistriţa** *Ger.* Bistritz. ≈ NE Romania
118 I9 **Bistriţa-Năsăud** ◈ *county* N Romania
Bistritz *see* Bistriţa
Bistritz ober Pernstein *see* Bystřice nad Pernštejnem
158 L11 **Biswān** Uttar Pradesh, N India *27.30N 81.00E*
112 M7 **Bisztynek** Warmińsko-Mazurskie, NE Poland *54.05N 20.53E*
81 E17 **Bitam** Woleu-Ntem, N Gabon *2.04N 11.30E*
103 D18 **Bitburg** Rheinland-Pfalz, SW Germany *49.57N 6.31E*
105 U4 **Bitche** Moselle, NE France *49.01N 7.27E*
80 I11 **Bitkine** Guéra, C Chad *11.58N 18.13E*
143 R15 **Bitlis** Bitlis, SE Turkey *38.22N 42.04E*
143 R14 **Bitlis** ◈ *province* E Turkey
Bitoeng *see* Bitung
115 N20 **Bitola** *Turk.* Monastir; *prev.* Bitolj. S FYR Macedonia *41.01N 21.21E*
Bitolj *see* Bitola
109 O17 **Bitonto** *anc.* Butuntum. Puglia, SE Italy *41.07N 16.40E*
79 Q13 **Bitou** *var.* Bittou. SE Burkina *11.19N 0.16W*
161 C20 **Bitra Island** *island* Lakshadweep, India, N Indian Ocean
103 M14 **Bitterfeld** Sachsen-Anhalt, E Germany *51.36N 12.18E*
34 O9 **Bitterroot Range** ▲▲ Idaho/Montana, NW USA
35 P10 **Bitterroot River** ≈ Montana, NW USA
109 D18 **Bitti** Sardegna, Italy, C Mediterranean Sea *40.30N 9.31E*
Bittou *see* Bitou
175 S7 **Bitung** *prev.* Bitoeng. Sulawesi, C Indonesia *1.28N 125.13E*
62 I12 **Bituruna** Paraná, S Brazil *26.11S 51.34W*
79 Y13 **Biu** Borno, E Nigeria *10.35N 12.13E*
Biumba *see* Byumba
171 H14 **Biwa-ko** ◎ Honshū, SW Japan
176 Y13 **Biwarlaut** Papua, E Indonesia *5.44S 138.14E*
29 P10 **Bixby** Oklahoma, C USA *35.56N 95.52W*
126 H15 **Biya** ≈ S Russian Federation
Biy-Khem *see* Bol'shoy Yenisey
126 H15 **Biysk** Altayskiy Kray, S Russian Federation *52.34N 85.09E*
170 Ff14 **Bizen** Okayama, Honshū, SW Japan *34.43N 134.10E*
Bizerta *see* Bizerte
123 K11 **Bizerte** *Ar.* Banzart, *Eng.* Bizerta. N Tunisia *37.18N 9.48E*
Bizkaia *see* Vizcaya
94 G2 **Bjargtangar** *headland* W Iceland *63.30N 24.28W*
Bjärnå *see* Perniö
97 K22 **Bjärnum** Skåne, S Sweden *56.15N 13.45E*
95 I16 **Bjästa** Västernorrland, C Sweden *63.12N 18.30E*
115 I14 **Bjelašnica** ▲ SE Bosnia and Herzegovina *43.13N 18.18E*
114 C10 **Bjelolasica** ▲ NW Croatia *45.13N 14.56E*
114 F8 **Bjelovar** *Hung.* Belovár. Bjelovar-Bilogora, N Croatia *45.54N 16.49E*
114 F8 **Bjelovar-Bilogora** *off.* Bjelovarsko-Bilogorska Županija. ◈ *province* NE Croatia
Bjelovarsko-Bilogorska Županija *see* Bjelovar-Bilogora
94 H10 **Bjerkvik** Nordland, C Norway *68.31N 16.08E*
97 G21 **Bjerringbro** Viborg, NW Denmark *56.22N 9.40E*
Bjeshkët e Namuna *see* North Albanian Alps
97 L14 **Björbo** Dalarna, C Sweden *60.28N 14.44E*
97 I15 **Bjørkelangen** Akershus, S Norway *59.52N 11.34E*
97 O14 **Björklinge** Uppsala, C Sweden *60.03N 17.33E*
95 I14 **Björksele** Västerbotten, N Sweden *64.58N 18.30E*
95 I16 **Björna** Västernorrland, C Sweden *63.34N 18.38E*
97 C14 **Bjørnafjorden** *fjord* S Norway
97 L16 **Björneborg** Värmland, C Sweden *59.13N 14.15E*
Björneborg *see* Pori
97 E14 **Bjornesfjorden** ◎ S Norway
94 M9 **Bjørnevatn** Finnmark, N Norway *69.29N 29.57E*
207 T13 **Bjørnøya** *Eng.* Bear Island. *island* N Norway
95 I15 **Bjurholm** Västerbotten, N Sweden *63.57N 19.16E*
97 J22 **Bjuv** Skåne, S Sweden *56.04N 12.57E*
78 M12 **Bla** Ségou, W Mali *12.58N 5.45W*
189 W8 **Blackall** Queensland, E Australia *24.25S 145.31E*
31 V2 **Black Bay** *lake bay* Minnesota, N USA
29 N9 **Black Bear Creek** ≈ Oklahoma, C USA
99 K17 **Blackburn** NW England, UK *53.45N 2.28W*
47 W10 **Blackburne** ✈ (Plymouth) E Montserrat *16.45N 62.09W*
41 T11 **Blackburn, Mount** ▲ Alaska, USA *61.43N 143.25W*
37 N5 **Black Butte Lake** ⊠ California, W USA
204 J5 **Black Coast** *physical region* Antarctica
9 Q16 **Black Diamond** Alberta, SW Canada *50.42N 114.09W*
20 K11 **Black Dome** ▲ New York, NE USA *42.16N 74.07W*
115 L18 **Black Drin** *Alb.* Lumi i Drinit të Zi, *SCr.* Crni Drim. ≈ Albania/FYR Macedonia
10 D6 **Black Duck** ≈ Ontario, C Canada
31 U4 **Blackduck** Minnesota, N USA *47.45N 94.33W*
35 R14 **Blackfoot** Idaho, NW USA *43.11N 112.20W*
35 P9 **Blackfoot River** ≈ Montana, NW USA
Black Forest *see* Schwarzwald
30 J10 **Blackhawk** South Dakota, N USA *44.09N 103.18W*
30 I10 **Black Hills** ▲▲ South Dakota/Wyoming, N USA
9 T10 **Black Lake** ◎ Saskatchewan, C Canada
33 Q5 **Black Lake** ◎ Michigan, N USA
20 I7 **Black Lake** ◎ New York, NE USA
24 G6 **Black Lake** ⊠ Louisiana, S USA
28 F7 **Black Mesa** ▲ Oklahoma, C USA *37.00N 103.07W*
23 P10 **Black Mountain** North Carolina, SE USA *35.37N 82.19W*
37 P13 **Black Mountain** ▲ California, W USA *35.22N 120.21W*
39 Q2 **Black Mountain** ▲ Colorado, C USA *40.47N 107.23W*
23 O7 **Black Mountain** ▲ Kentucky, E USA *36.54N 82.53W*
98 K1 **Black Mountains** ▲▲ SE Wales, UK
38 H10 **Black Mountains** ▲▲ Arizona, SW USA
35 Q16 **Black Pine Peak** ▲ Idaho, NW USA *42.07N 113.07W*
99 K17 **Blackpool** NW England, UK *53.49N 3.03W*
39 Q14 **Black Range** ▲▲ New Mexico, SW USA
46 I12 **Black River** W Jamaica *18.01N 77.52W*
12 J14 **Black River** ≈ Ontario, SE Canada
133 U12 **Black River** *Chin.* Babian Jiang, Lixian Jiang, *Fr.* Rivière Noire, *Vtn.* Sông Đa. ≈ China/Vietnam
46 I12 **Black River** ≈ W Jamaica
41 T7 **Black River** ≈ Alaska, USA
39 N13 **Black River** ≈ Arizona, SW USA
29 X7 **Black River** ≈ Arkansas/Missouri, C USA
24 I7 **Black River** ≈ Louisiana, S USA
33 S8 **Black River** ≈ Michigan, N USA
33 Q5 **Black River** ≈ Michigan, N USA
20 I8 **Black River** ≈ New York, NE USA
23 T13 **Black River** ≈ South Carolina, SE USA
32 J7 **Black River** ≈ Wisconsin, N USA
32 J7 **Black River Falls** Wisconsin, N USA *44.18N 90.51W*
37 R3 **Black Rock Desert** *desert* Nevada, W USA
Black Sand Desert *see* Garagumy
23 S7 **Blacksburg** Virginia, NE USA *37.16N 80.24W*
142 H10 **Black Sea** *var.* Euxine Sea, *Bul.* Cherno More, *Rom.* Marea Neagră, *Rus.* Chernoye More, *Turk.* Karadeniz, *Ukr.* Chorne More. *sea* Asia/Europe
119 Q10 **Black Sea Lowland** *Ukr.* Prychornomors'ka Nyzovyna. *depression* SE Europe
35 S17 **Blacks Fork** ≈ Wyoming, C USA
25 V7 **Blackshear** Georgia, SE USA *31.18N 82.14W*
25 S6 **Blackshear, Lake** ⊠ Georgia, SE USA
99 A16 **Blacksod Bay** *Ir.* Cuan an Fhóid Duibh. *inlet* W Ireland
23 V7 **Blackstone** Virginia, NE USA *37.04N 78.00W*
79 O14 **Black Volta** *var.* Borongo, Mouhoun, Moun Hou, *Fr.* Volta Noire. ≈ W Africa
25 O5 **Black Warrior River** ≈ Alabama, S USA
189 X8 **Blackwater** Queensland, E Australia *23.34S 148.51E*
99 D20 **Blackwater** *Ir.* An Abhainn Mhór. ≈ S Ireland
29 T4 **Blackwater River** ≈ Missouri, C USA
23 W7 **Blackwater River** ≈ Virginia, NE USA
Blackwater State *see* Nebraska
29 N8 **Blackwell** Oklahoma, C USA *36.48N 97.16W*
27 P7 **Blackwell** Texas, SW USA *32.05N 100.19W*
101 J15 **Bladel** Noord-Brabant, S Netherlands *51.22N 5.13E*
Bladenmarkt *see* Bălăuşeri
116 G11 **Blagoevgrad** *prev.* Gorna Dzhumaya. Blagoevgrad, SW Bulgaria *42.01N 23.04E*
116 G11 **Blagoevgrad** ◈ *province* SW Bulgaria
126 Gg14 **Blagoveshchenka** Altayskiy Kray, S Russian Federation *52.49N 79.54E*
126 M16 **Blagoveshchensk** Amurskaya Oblast', SE Russian Federation *50.19N 127.30E*
131 V4 **Blagoveshchensk** Respublika Bashkortostan, W Russian Federation *55.03N 56.01E*
104 I7 **Blain** Loire-Atlantique, NW France *47.26N 1.47W*
31 V8 **Blaine** Minnesota, N USA *45.09N 93.13W*
34 H6 **Blaine** Washington, NW USA *48.59N 122.45W*
9 T15 **Blaine Lake** Saskatchewan, S Canada *52.49N 106.48W*
31 S14 **Blair** Nebraska, C USA *41.32N 96.07W*
98 J10 **Blairgowrie** C Scotland, UK *56.18N 3.24W*
20 C15 **Blairsville** Pennsylvania, NE USA *40.25N 79.12W*
118 H11 **Blaj** *Ger.* Blasendorf, *Hung.* Balázsfalva. Alba, SW Romania *46.10N 23.56E*
66 F9 **Blake-Bahama Ridge** *undersea feature* W Atlantic Ocean
25 S7 **Blakely** Georgia, SE USA *31.22N 84.55W*
66 E10 **Blake Plateau** *var.* Blake Terrace. *undersea feature* W Atlantic Ocean
32 M1 **Blake Point** *headland* Michigan, N USA *48.11N 88.25W*
Blake Terrace *see* Blake Plateau
63 B24 **Blanca, Bahía** *bay* E Argentina
58 C12 **Blanca, Cordillera** ▲▲ W Peru
107 T12 **Blanca, Costa** *physical region* SE Spain

◆ Country ● Country Capital ◇ Dependent Territory ○ Dependent Territory Capital ◈ Administrative Region ✈ International Airport ▲ Mountain ▲▲ Mountain Range Volcano ≈ River ◎ Lake ⊠ Reservoir

39 *S7* **Blanca Peak** ▲ Colorado, C USA *37.34N 105.29W*
26 *I9* **Blanca, Sierra** ▲ Texas, SW USA *31.15N 105.26W*
123 *K11* **Blanc, Cap** *headland* N Tunisia *37.20N 9.41E*
Blanc, Cap *see* Nouâdhibou, Râs
33 *R12* **Blanchard River** 〜 Ohio, N USA
190 *E8* **Blanche, Cape** *headland* South Australia *33.03S 134.10E*
195 *U15* **Blanche Channel** *channel* NW Solomon Islands
190 *J4* **Blanche, Lake** ◎ South Australia
33 *R14* **Blanchester** Ohio, N USA *39.17N 83.59W*
190 *J9* **Blanchetown** South Australia *34.21S 139.36E*
47 *U13* **Blanchisseuse** Trinidad, Trinidad and Tobago *10.47N 61.18W*
105 *T11* **Blanc, Mont** *It.* Monte Bianco. ▲ France/Italy *45.45N 6.51E*
27 *R11* **Blanco** Texas, SW USA *30.06N 98.25W*
44 *K14* **Blanco, Cabo** *headland* NW Costa Rica *9.34N 85.06W*
34 *D14* **Blanco, Cape** *headland* Oregon, NW USA *42.49N 124.33W*
64 *H10* **Blanco, Río** 〜 W Argentina
58 *F10* **Blanco, Río** 〜 NE Peru
13 *O9* **Blanc, Réservoir** ▣ Quebec, SE Canada
23 *R7* **Bland** Virginia, NE USA *37.06N 81.07W*
94 *I2* **Blanda** 〜 N Iceland
39 *O7* **Blanding** Utah, W USA *37.37N 109.28W*
107 *X5* **Blanes** Cataluña, NE Spain *41.40N 2.48E*
105 *N3* **Blangy-sur-Bresle** Seine-Maritime, N France *49.55N 1.37E*
113 *C18* **Blanice** *Ger.* Blanitz. 〜 SE Czech Republic
Blanitz *see* Blanice
101 *C16* **Blankenberge** West-Vlaanderen, NW Belgium *51.19N 3.07E*
103 *D17* **Blankenheim** Nordrhein-Westfalen, W Germany *50.25N 6.41E*
27 *R8* **Blanket** Texas, SW USA *31.49N 98.47W*
57 *O3* **Blanquilla, Isla** *var.* La Blanquilla. *island* N Venezuela
Blanquilla, La *see* Blanquilla, Isla
63 *F18* **Blanquillo** Durazno, C Uruguay *32.52S 55.37W*
113 *G18* **Blansko** *Ger.* Blanz. Brněnský Kraj, SE Czech Republic *49.22N 16.39E*
85 *N15* **Blantyre** *var.* Blantyre-Limbe. Southern, S Malawi *15.45S 35.03E*
85 *N15* **Blantyre** ✖ Southern, S Malawi *15.34S 35.03E*
Blantyre-Limbe *see* Blantyre
Blanz *see* Blansko
100 *J10* **Blaricum** Noord-Holland, C Netherlands *52.16N 5.15E*
Blasendorf *see* Blaj
Blatnitsa *see* Durankulak
115 *F15* **Blato** *It.* Blatta. Dubrovnik-Neretva, S Croatia *42.57N 16.47E*
Blatta *see* Blato
110 *E10* **Blatten** Valais, SW Switzerland *46.22N 8.00E*
103 *J20* **Blaufelden** Baden-Württemberg, SW Germany *49.21N 10.01E*
97 *E23* **Blåvands Huk** *headland* W Denmark *55.33N 8.04E*
104 *G6* **Blavet** 〜 NW France
104 *J12* **Blaye** Gironde, SW France *45.07N 0.36W*
191 *R8* **Blayney** New South Wales, SE Australia *33.33S 149.13E*
67 *D25* **Bleaker Island** *island* SE Falkland Islands
111 *T10* **Bled** *Ger.* Veldes. NW Slovenia *46.23N 14.06E*
101 *D20* **Bléharies** Hainaut, SW Belgium *50.31N 3.25E*
111 *U9* **Bleiburg** *Slvn.* Pliberk. Kärnten, S Austria *46.36N 14.49E*
103 *L17* **Bleiloch-Stausee** ▣ C Germany
100 *H12* **Bleiswijk** Zuid-Holland, W Netherlands *52.01N 4.31E*
97 *L22* **Blekinge** ⬖ *county* S Sweden
12 *D17* **Blenheim** Ontario, S Canada *42.19N 81.58W*
193 *K15* **Blenheim** Marlborough, South Island, NZ *41.31S 174.00E*
101 *M15* **Blerick** Limburg, SE Netherlands *51.22N 6.10E*
Blesae *see* Blois
27 *V13* **Blessing** Texas, SW USA *28.52N 96.12W*
12 *I10* **Bleu, Lac** ◎ Quebec, SE Canada
Blibba *see* Blitta
123 *I11* **Blida** *var.* El Boulaida, El Boulaïda. N Algeria *36.32N 2.49E*
97 *P15* **Blidö** Stockholm, C Sweden *59.37N 18.55E*
97 *K18* **Blidsberg** Västra Götaland, S Sweden *57.55N 13.30E*
193 *A21* **Bligh Sound** *sound* South Island, NZ
197 *H13* **Bligh Water** *strait* NW Fiji
12 *D11* **Blind River** Ontario, S Canada *46.11N 82.55W*
33 *R11* **Blissfield** Michigan, N USA *41.49N 83.51W*
174 *Ll16* **Blitar** Jawa, C Indonesia *8.06S 112.12E*
79 *R15* **Blitta** *prev.* Blibba. C Togo *8.19N 0.58E*
21 *O13* **Block Island** *island* Rhode Island, NE USA
21 *O13* **Block Island Sound** *sound* Rhode Island, NE USA
100 *H10* **Bloemendaal** Noord-Holland, W Netherlands *52.23N 4.39E*
85 *H23* **Bloemfontein** *var.* Mangaung. ● (South Africa-judicial capital) Free State, C South Africa *29.07S 26.13E*
85 *I22* **Bloemhof** North-West, NW South Africa *27.38S 25.33E*
104 *M7* **Blois** *anc.* Blesae. Loir-et-Cher, C France *47.36N 1.19E*
100 *L8* **Blokzijl** Overijssel, N Netherlands *52.46N 5.58E*
97 *N20* **Blomstermåla** Kalmar, S Sweden *56.58N 16.19E*
94 *I2* **Blönduós** Nordhurland Vestra, N Iceland *65.39N 20.15W*
112 *L11* **Błonie** Mazowieckie, C Poland *52.13N 20.36E*
99 *C14* **Bloody Foreland** *Ir.* Cnoc Fola. *headland* NW Ireland *55.09N 8.18W*
33 *N15* **Bloomfield** Indiana, N USA *39.01N 86.58W*
31 *X16* **Bloomfield** Iowa, C USA *40.45N 92.24W*
29 *Y8* **Bloomfield** Missouri, C USA *36.53N 89.55W*
39 *P9* **Bloomfield** New Mexico, SW USA *36.42N 108.00W*
27 *U7* **Blooming Grove** Texas, SW USA *32.05N 96.43W*
31 *W10* **Blooming Prairie** Minnesota, N USA *43.52N 93.03W*
32 *L13* **Bloomington** Illinois, N USA *40.28N 88.59W*
33 *O15* **Bloomington** Indiana, N USA *39.10N 86.31W*
31 *V9* **Bloomington** Minnesota, N USA *44.50N 93.18W*
27 *U13* **Bloomington** Texas, SW USA *28.39N 96.53W*
20 *H14* **Bloomsburg** Pennsylvania, NE USA *40.58N 76.27W*
189 *X7* **Bloomsbury** Queensland, NE Australia *20.46S 148.34E*
174 *Ll14* **Blora** Jawa, C Indonesia *6.55S 111.28E*
20 *G12* **Blossburg** Pennsylvania, NE USA *41.38N 77.00W*
27 *V5* **Blossom** Texas, SW USA *33.39N 95.23W*
127 *Oo3* **Blossom, Mys** *headland* Ostrov Vrangelya, NE Russian Federation *70.49N 178.49E*
25 *R8* **Blountstown** Florida, SE USA *30.26N 85.03W*
23 *P8* **Blountville** Tennessee, S USA *36.31N 82.19W*
23 *Q9* **Blowing Rock** North Carolina, SE USA *36.15N 81.53W*
110 *J8* **Bludenz** Vorarlberg, W Austria *47.10N 9.49E*
38 *L6* **Blue Bell Knoll** ▲ Utah, W USA *38.11N 111.31W*
25 *Y12* **Blue Cypress Lake** ◎ Florida, SE USA
31 *U11* **Blue Earth** Minnesota, N USA *43.38N 94.06W*
23 *Q7* **Bluefield** Virginia, NE USA *37.15N 81.16W*
23 *R7* **Bluefield** West Virginia, NE USA *37.16N 81.13W*
45 *N10* **Bluefields** Región Autónoma Atlántico Sur, SE Nicaragua *12.01N 83.47W*
45 *N10* **Bluefields, Bahía de** *bay* W Caribbean Sea
31 *Z14* **Blue Grass** Iowa, C USA *41.30N 90.46W*
Bluegrass State *see* Kentucky
Blue Hen State *see* Delaware
21 *S7* **Blue Hill** Maine, NE USA *44.25N 68.36W*
31 *P16* **Blue Hill** Nebraska, C USA *40.19N 98.27W*
32 *J5* **Blue Hills** *hill range* Wisconsin, N USA
36 *L3* **Blue Lake** California, W USA *40.52N 124.00W*
Blue Law State *see* Connecticut
39 *Q6* **Blue Mesa Reservoir** ▣ Colorado, C USA
29 *S12* **Blue Mountain** ▲ Arkansas, C USA *34.42N 94.04W*
21 *O6* **Blue Mountain** ▲ New Hampshire, NE USA *44.48N 71.26W*
20 *K8* **Blue Mountain** ▲ New York, NE USA *43.52N 74.24W*
20 *H15* **Blue Mountain** *ridge* Pennsylvania, NE USA
46 *H10* **Blue Mountain Peak** ▲ E Jamaica *18.02N 76.34W*
191 *S8* **Blue Mountains** ▲▲ New South Wales, SE Australia
34 *L11* **Blue Mountains** ▲▲ Oregon/Washington, NW USA
82 *G12* **Blue Nile** ⬖ *state* E Sudan
82 *H12* **Blue Nile** *var.* Abai, Bahr el Azraq, *Amh.* Ābay Wenz, *Ar.* An Nīl al Azraq. 〜 Ethiopia/Sudan
15 *Hh4* **Bluenose Lake** ◎ Nunavut, NW Canada
29 *O3* **Blue Rapids** Kansas, C USA *39.39N 96.38W*
25 *S1* **Blue Ridge** Georgia, SE USA *34.51N 84.19W*
19 *Q10* **Blue Ridge** *var.* Blue Ridge Mountains. ▲▲ North Carolina/Virginia, E USA
25 *S1* **Blue Ridge Lake** ▣ Georgia, SE USA
Blue Ridge Mountains *see* Blue Ridge
9 *N15* **Blue River** British Columbia, SW Canada *52.03N 119.21W*
29 *O12* **Blue River** 〜 Oklahoma, C USA
29 *R4* **Blue Springs** Missouri, C USA *39.01N 94.16W*
23 *R6* **Bluestone Lake** ▣ West Virginia, NE USA
193 *C25* **Bluff** Southland, South Island, NZ *46.36S 168.22E*
39 *O8* **Bluff** Utah, W USA *37.15N 109.36W*
23 *P8* **Bluff City** Tennessee, S USA *36.28N 82.15W*
67 *E24* **Bluff Cove** East Falkland, Falkland Islands *51.45S 58.10W*
27 *S7* **Bluff Dale** Texas, SW USA *32.18N 98.01W*
191 *N15* **Bluff Hill Point** *headland* Tasmania, SE Australia *41.03S 144.35E*
33 *Q12* **Bluffton** Indiana, N USA *40.44N 85.10W*
33 *R12* **Bluffton** Ohio, N USA *40.54N 83.53W*
27 *T7* **Blum** Texas, SW USA *32.08N 97.24W*
103 *G24* **Blumberg** Baden-Württemberg, SW Germany *47.48N 8.31E*
62 *K13* **Blumenau** Santa Catarina, S Brazil *26.55S 49.07W*
31 *N9* **Blunt** South Dakota, N USA *44.30N 99.58E*
34 *H15* **Bly** Oregon, NW USA *42.22N 121.04W*
41 *R13* **Blying Sound** *sound* Alaska, USA
99 *M14* **Blyth** N England, UK *55.07N 1.30W*
37 *Y16* **Blythe** California, W USA *33.35N 114.36W*
29 *Y9* **Blytheville** Arkansas, C USA *35.55N 89.55W*
119 *V7* **Blyznyuky** Kharkivs'ka Oblast', E Ukraine *48.51N 36.32E*
78 *I15* **Bo** S Sierra Leone *7.58N 11.45W*
97 *G16* **Bø** Telemark, S Norway *59.24N 9.04E*
179 *Pp11* **Boac** Marinduque, N Philippines *13.26N 121.50E*
44 *K10* **Boaco** Boaco, S Nicaragua *12.27N 85.45W*
44 *J10* **Boaco** ⬖ *department* C Nicaragua
81 *I15* **Boali** Ombella-Mpoko, SW Central African Republic *4.52N 18.00E*
Boalsert *see* Bolsward
194 *K13* **Boana** Morobe, C PNG *6.30S 146.54E*
195 *Q10* **Boang Island** *island* Tanga Islands, NE PNG
33 *V12* **Boardman** Ohio, N USA *41.01N 80.39W*
34 *J11* **Boardman** Oregon, NW USA *45.50N 119.42W*
12 *F13* **Boat Lake** ◎ Ontario, S Canada
60 *F10* **Boa Vista** *state capital* Roraima, NW Brazil *2.51N 60.43W*
78 *D9* **Boa Vista** *island* Ilhas de Barlavento, E Cape Verde
25 *Q2* **Boaz** Alabama, S USA *34.12N 86.10W*
166 *L15* **Bobai** Guangxi Zhuangzu Zizhiqu, S China *22.09N 109.57E*
180 *J1* **Bobaomby, Tanjona** *Fr.* Cap d'Ambre. *headland* N Madagascar *11.58S 49.13E*
161 *M14* **Bobbili** Andhra Pradesh, E India *18.31N 83.28E*
108 *D9* **Bobbio** Emilia-Romagna, C Italy *44.48N 9.27E*
12 *I14* **Bobcaygeon** Ontario, SE Canada *44.31N 78.33W*
Bober *see* Bóbr
105 *O5* **Bobigny** Seine-St-Denis, N France *48.55N 2.27E*
79 *N13* **Bobo-Dioulasso** SW Burkina *11.12N 4.21W*
112 *G8* **Bobolice** *Ger.* Bublitz. Zachodniopomorskie, NW Poland *53.56N 16.37E*
175 *T7* **Bobopayo** Pulau Halmahera, E Indonesia *1.07N 127.26E*
116 *G10* **Bobovdol** Kyustendil, W Bulgaria *42.21N 22.58E*
121 *M15* **Bobr** Minskaya Voblasts', NW Belarus *54.20N 29.18E*
121 *M15* **Bobr** 〜 C Belarus
113 *E14* **Bóbr** *Eng.* Bobrawa, *Ger.* Bober. 〜 SW Poland
Bobrawa *see* Bóbr
Bobrik *see* Bobryk
Bobrinets *see* Bobrynets'
Bobrka/Bóbrka *see* Bibrka
130 *L8* **Bobrov** Voronezhskaya Oblast', W Russian Federation *51.10N 40.03E*
119 *Q4* **Bobrovytsya** Chernihivs'ka Oblast', N Ukraine *50.43N 31.24E*
Bobruysk *see* Babruysk
121 *J19* **Bobryk** *Rus.* Bobrik. 〜 SW Belarus
119 *Q8* **Bobrynets'** *Rus.* Bobrinets. Kirovohrads'ka Oblast', C Ukraine *48.01N 32.09E*
12 *K14* **Bobs Lake** ◎ Ontario, SE Canada
56 *I6* **Bobures** Zulia, NW Venezuela *9.15N 71.10W*
44 *H1* **Boca Bacalar Chico** *headland* N Belize *15.05N 82.12W*
114 *G11* **Bočac** Republika Srpska, NW Bosnia and Herzegovina *44.32N 17.09E*
43 *R14* **Boca del Río** Veracruz-Llave, S Mexico *19.07N 96.07W*
57 *O4* **Boca de Pozo** Nueva Esparta, NE Venezuela *11.01N 64.21W*
61 *C15* **Boca do Acre** Amazonas, N Brazil *8.45S 67.22W*
57 *N12* **Boca Mavaca** Amazonas, S Venezuela *2.30N 65.10W*
81 *G14* **Bocaranga** Ouham-Pendé, W Central African Republic *7.07N 15.40E*
25 *Z15* **Boca Raton** Florida, SE USA *26.22N 80.04W*
45 *P14* **Bocas del Toro** Bocas del Toro, NW Panama *9.21N 82.14W*
45 *P15* **Bocas del Toro** *off.* Provincia de Bocas del Toro. ⬖ *province* NW Panama
45 *P15* **Bocas del Toro, Archipiélago de** *island group* NW Panama
44 *L7* **Bocay** Jinotega, N Nicaragua *14.19N 85.07W*
107 *N6* **Boceguillas** Castilla-León, N Spain *41.23N 3.37W*
Bocheykovo *see* Bacheykava
113 *L17* **Bochnia** Małopolskie, SE Poland *49.58N 20.27E*
101 *K16* **Bocholt** Limburg, NE Belgium *51.10N 5.37E*
103 *D14* **Bocholt** Nordrhein-Westfalen, W Germany *51.49N 6.37E*
103 *E15* **Bochum** Nordrhein-Westfalen, W Germany *51.28N 7.13E*
105 *Y15* **Bocognano** Corse, France, C Mediterranean Sea *42.04N 9.03E*
56 *I6* **Boconó** Trujillo, NW Venezuela *9.12N 70.16W*
118 *F12* **Bocşa** *Ger.* Bokschen, *Hung.* Boksánbánya. Caraş-Severin, SW Romania *45.24N 21.46E*
81 *H15* **Boda** Lobaye, SW Central African Republic *4.17N 17.25E*
96 *L12* **Boda** Dalarna, C Sweden *61.00N 15.15E*
97 *O20* **Böda** Kalmar, S Sweden *57.16N 17.04E*
97 *L19* **Bodafors** Jönköping, S Sweden *57.30N 14.40E*
126 *Kk13* **Bodaybo** Irkutskaya Oblast', E Russian Federation *57.52N 114.04E*
24 *G5* **Bodcau, Bayou** *var.* Bodcau Creek. 〜 Louisiana, S USA
Bodcau Creek *see* Bodcau, Bayou
46 *D8* **Bodden Town** *var.* Boddentown. Grand Cayman, SW Cayman Islands *19.17N 81.10W*
103 *K14* **Bode** 〜 C Germany
36 *L7* **Bodega Head** *headland* California, W USA *38.16N 123.04W*
Bodegas *see* Babahoyo
100 *H11* **Bodegraven** Zuid-Holland, C Netherlands *52.04N 4.45E*
80 *H8* **Bodélé** *depression* W Chad
94 *J13* **Boden** Norrbotten, N Sweden *65.49N 21.43E*
Bodensee *see* Constance, Lake, C Europe
67 *M15* **Bode Verde Fracture Zone** *tectonic feature* E Atlantic Ocean
161 *H14* **Bodhan** Andhra Pradesh, C India *18.40N 77.51E*
168 *I9* **Bodĭ** Bayanhongor, C Mongolia *45.25N 100.33E*
161 *H22* **Bodināyakkanūr** Tamil Nādu, SE India *10.01N 77.18E*
110 *H10* **Bodio** Ticino, S Switzerland *46.23N 8.55E*
99 *I24* **Bodmin** SW England, UK *50.28N 4.43W*
99 *I24* **Bodmin Moor** *moorland* SW England, UK
94 *G12* **Bodø** Nordland, C Norway *67.16N 14.22E*
61 *H20* **Bodoquena, Serra da** ▲▲ SW Brazil
142 *B16* **Bodrum** Muğla, SW Turkey *37.03N 27.28E*
Bodzafordulő *see* Întorsura Buzăului
101 *L14* **Boekel** Noord-Brabant, SE Netherlands *51.35N 5.42E*
Boeloekoemba *see* Bulukumba
105 *Q11* **Boën** Loire, E France *45.45N 4.01E*
81 *K18* **Boende** Equateur, C Dem. Rep. Congo *0.12S 20.54E*
27 *R11* **Boerne** Texas, SW USA *29.47N 98.43W*
Boeroe *see* Buru, Pulau
Boetoeng *see* Buton, Pulau
24 *I5* **Boeuf River** 〜 Arkansas/Louisiana, S USA
78 *H14* **Boffa** Guinée-Maritime, W Guinea *10.12N 14.01W*
Bó Finne, Inis *see* Inishbofin
Boga *see* Bogë
177 *Ff9* **Bogale** Irrawaddy, SW Myanmar *16.16N 95.21E*
24 *L8* **Bogalusa** Louisiana, S USA *30.47N 89.51W*
79 *Q12* **Bogandé** C Burkina *13.01N 0.07W*
81 *I15* **Bogangolo** Ombella-Mpoko, C Central African Republic *5.36N 18.17E*
191 *Q7* **Bogan River** 〜 New South Wales, SE Australia
27 *W5* **Bogata** Texas, SW USA *33.28N 95.12W*
113 *D14* **Bogatynia** *Ger.* Reichenau. Dolnośląskie, SW Poland *50.52N 14.54E*
142 *K13* **Boğazlıyan** Yozgat, C Turkey *39.13N 35.16E*
81 *J17* **Bogbonga** Equateur, NW Dem. Rep. Congo *1.36N 19.24E*
164 *J14* **Bogcang Zangbo** 〜 W China
164 *L5* **Bogda Feng** ▲ NW China *43.51N 88.14E*
116 *I9* **Bogdan** ▲ C Bulgaria *42.37N 24.28E*
115 *Q20* **Bogdanci** SE FYR Macedonia *41.12N 22.34E*
164 *M5* **Bogda Shan** *var.* Po-ko-to Shan. ▲▲ NW China
115 *K17* **Bogë** *var.* Boga. Shkodër, N Albania *42.25N 19.38E*
Bogendorf *see* Łuków
97 *G23* **Bogense** Fyn, C Denmark *55.34N 10.06E*
191 *T3* **Boggabilla** New South Wales, SE Australia *28.37S 150.21E*
191 *S6* **Boggabri** New South Wales, SE Australia *30.44S 150.00E*
194 *I10* **Bogia** Madang, N PNG *4.12S 144.55E*
99 *N23* **Bognor Regis** SE England, UK *50.46N 0.40W*
179 *Qq13* **Bogo** Cebu, C Philippines *11.04N 123.59E*
Bogodukhov *see* Bohodukhiv
189 *V15* **Bogong, Mount** ▲ Victoria, SE Australia *36.43S 147.19E*
174 *J14* **Bogor** *Dut.* Buitenzorg. Jawa, C Indonesia *6.34S 106.45E*
130 *L5* **Bogoroditsk** Tul'skaya Oblast', W Russian Federation *53.46N 38.09E*
131 *O3* **Bogorodsk** Nizhegorodskaya Oblast', W Russian Federation *56.06N 43.29E*
Bogorodskoje *see* Bogorodskoye
127 *Nn14* **Bogorodskoye** Khabarovskiy Kray, SE Russian Federation *52.22N 140.33E*
129 *R15* **Bogorodskoye** *var.* Bogorodskoje. Kirovskaya Oblast', NW Russian Federation *57.50N 50.41E*
56 *F10* **Bogotá** *prev.* Santa Fe, Santa Fe de Bogotá. ● (Colombia) Cundinamarca, C Colombia *4.37N 74.04W*
159 *T14* **Bogra** Rajshahi, N Bangladesh *24.52N 89.28E*
Bogschan *see* Boldu
126 *Ii13* **Boguchany** Krasnoyarskiy Kray, C Russian Federation *58.20N 97.20E*
130 *M9* **Boguchar** Voronezhskaya Oblast', W Russian Federation *49.57N 40.34E*
78 *H10* **Bogué** Brakna, SW Mauritania *16.36N 14.15W*
24 *K8* **Bogue Chitto** 〜 Louisiana/Mississippi, S USA
Bogushëvsk *see* Bahushewsk
Boguslav *see* Bohuslav
46 *K12* **Bog Walk** C Jamaica *18.06N 77.01W*
167 *Q3* **Bo Hai** *var.* Gulf of Chihli. *gulf* NE China
167 *R3* **Bohai Haixia** *strait* NE China
167 *Q3* **Bohai Wan** *bay* NE China
113 *C17* **Bohemia** *Cz.* Čechy, *Ger.* Böhmen. *cultural and historical region* W Czech Republic
113 *B18* **Bohemian Forest** *Cz.* Ceský Les, Šumava, *Ger.* Böhmerwald. ▲▲ C Europe
Bohemian-Moravian Highlands *see* Českomoravská Vrchovina
79 *R16* **Bohicon** S Benin *7.08N 2.07E*
111 *S11* **Bohinjska Bistrica** *Ger.* Wocheiner Feistritz. NW Slovenia *46.16N 13.55E*
Bohkká *see* Pokka
Böhmen *see* Bohemia
Böhmerwald *see* Bohemian Forest
Böhmisch-Krumau *see* Český Krumlov
Böhmisch-Leipa *see* Česká Lípa
Böhmisch-Mährische Höhe *see* Českomoravská Vrchovina
Böhmisch-Trübau *see* Česká Třebová
119 *U5* **Bohodukhiv** *Rus.* Bogodukhov. Kharkivs'ka Oblast', E Ukraine *50.09N 35.31E*
179 *Qq14* **Bohol** *island* C Philippines
179 *Qq15* **Bohol Sea** *var.* Mindanao Sea. *sea* S Philippines
118 *I7* **Bohorodchany** Ivano-Frankivs'ka Oblast', W Ukraine *48.46N 24.31E*
168 *M9* **Böhöt** Dundgovĭ, C Mongolia *45.13N 108.12E*
164 *K6* **Bohu** *var.* Bagrax. Xinjiang Uygur Zizhiqu, NW China *42.00N 86.28E*
113 *I17* **Bohumín** *Ger.* Oderberg; *prev.* Neuoderberg, Nový Bohumín. Ostravský Kray, E Czech Republic *49.55N 18.19E*
119 *P6* **Bohuslav** *Rus.* Boguslav. Kyyivs'ka Oblast', N Ukraine *49.33N 30.53E*
60 *F11* **Boiaçu** Roraima, N Brazil *0.27S 61.46W*
109 *K16* **Boiano** Molise, C Italy *41.28N 14.28E*
13 *R8* **Boilleau** Quebec, SE Canada *48.06N 70.49W*
61 *O17* **Boipeba, Ilha de** *island* SE Brazil
106 *G3* **Boiro** Galicia, NW Spain *42.39N 8.53W*
33 *Q5* **Bois Blanc Island** *island* Michigan, N USA
31 *R7* **Bois de Sioux River** 〜 Minnesota, N USA
35 *N14* **Boise** *var.* Boise City. *state capital* Idaho, NW USA *43.38N 116.14W*
28 *G8* **Boise City** Oklahoma, C USA *36.43N 102.30W*
35 *N14* **Boise River, Middle Fork** 〜 Idaho, NW USA
Bois, Lac des *see* Woods, Lake of the
Bois-le-Duc *see* 's-Hertogenbosch
9 *W17* **Boissevain** Manitoba, S Canada *49.13N 100.01W*
13 *T7* **Boisvert, Pointe au** *headland* Quebec, SE Canada *48.34N 69.07W*
102 *K10* **Boizenburg** Mecklenburg-Vorpommern, N Germany *53.23N 10.43E*
Bojador *see* Boujdour
115 *K18* **Bojana** *Alb.* Bunë. 〜 Albania/Serbia and Montenegro (Yugoslavia) ***see also*** Bunë
149 *S3* **Bojnūrd** *var.* Bujnurd. Khorāsān, N Iran *37.30N 57.24E*
174 *Ll15* **Bojonegoro** *prev.* Bodjonegoro. Jawa, C Indonesia *7.06S 111.49E*
201 *T1* **Bokaak Atoll** *var.* Bokak, Taongi. *atoll* Ratak Chain, NE Marshall Islands
Bokak *see* Bokaak Atoll
152 *K8* **Bo'kantov Tog'lari** *Rus.* Gory Bukantau. ▲▲ N Uzbekistan
159 *Q15* **Bokāro** Bihār, N India *23.46N 85.55E*
81 *I18* **Bokatola** Equateur, NW Dem. Rep. Congo *0.37S 18.45E*
78 *H13* **Boké** Guinée-Maritime, W Guinea *10.55N 14.18W*
Bokhara *see* Buxoro
191 *Q4* **Bokharra River** 〜 New South Wales/Queensland, SE Australia
97 *C16* **Boknafjorden** *fjord* S Norway
80 *H11* **Bokoro** Chari-Baguirmi, W Chad *12.22N 17.03E*
81 *K19* **Bokota** Equateur, NW Dem. Rep. Congo *0.56S 22.20E*
178 *Gg13* **Bokpyin** Tenasserim, S Myanmar *11.16N 98.47E*
Boksánbánya/Bokschen *see* Bocşa
85 *F21* **Bokspits** Kgalagadi, SW Botswana *26.50S 20.41E*
81 *K18* **Bokungu** Equateur, C Dem. Rep. Congo *0.39S 22.13E*
Bokurdak *see* Bakhardok
80 *G10* **Bol** Lac, W Chad *13.27N 14.40E*
175 *Qq9* **Bolaang** Sulawesi, N Indonesia *0.58S 122.10E*
78 *G13* **Bolama** SW Guinea-Bissau *11.34N 15.32W*
Bolangir *see* Balāngīr
Bolanos *see* Bolanos, Mount, Guam
Bolaños *see* Bolaños de Calatrava, Spain
107 *N11* **Bolaños de Calatrava** *var.* Bolaños. Castilla-La Mancha, C Spain *38.55N 3.39W*
196 *B17* **Bolanos, Mount** *var.* Bolanos. ▲ S Guam *13.18N 144.41E*
42 *L12* **Bolaños, Río** 〜 C Mexico
117 *M14* **Bolayır** Çanakkale, NW Turkey *40.31N 26.46E*
104 *L3* **Bolbec** Seine-Maritime, N France *49.34N 0.31E*
118 *L13* **Boldu** *var.* Bogschan. Buzău, SE Romania *45.18N 27.15E*
152 *H8* **Boldumsaz** *prev.* Kalinin, Kalininsk, Porsy. Dashkhovuzskiy Velayat, N Turkmenistan *42.12N 59.33E*
164 *I4* **Bole** *var.* Bortala. Xinjiang Uygur Zizhiqu, NW China *44.52N 82.06E*
79 *O15* **Bole** NW Ghana *9.01N 2.28W*
81 *J19* **Boleko** Equateur, W Dem. Rep. Congo *1.27S 19.52E*
113 *E14* **Bolesławiec** *Ger.* Bunzlau. Dolnośląskie, SW Poland *51.16N 15.34E*
131 *R4* **Bolgar** *prev.* Kuybyshev. Respublika Tatarstan, W Russian Federation *54.58N 49.03E*
79 *P14* **Bolgatanga** N Ghana *10.45N 0.52W*
Bolgrad *see* Bolhrad
119 *N12* **Bolhrad** *Rus.* Bolgrad. Odes'ka Oblast', SW Ukraine *45.42N 28.34E*
169 *Y8* **Boli** Heilongjiang, NE China *45.45N 130.32E*
81 *I19* **Bolia** Bandundu, W Dem. Rep. Congo *1.34S 18.24E*
95 *J14* **Boliden** Västerbotten, N Sweden *64.52N 20.19E*
176 *Uu11* **Bolifar** Pulau Seram, E Indonesia *3.08S 130.34E*
179 *Oo9* **Bolinao** Luzon, N Philippines *16.22N 119.52E*
29 *T6* **Bolivar** Missouri, C USA *37.36N 93.24W*
22 *F10* **Bolivar** Tennessee, S USA *35.15N 88.59W*
56 *C12* **Bolívar** Cauca, SW Colombia *1.49N 76.58W*
56 *F7* **Bolívar** *off.* Departmento de Bolívar. ⬖ *province* N Colombia
58 *A13* **Bolívar** ⬖ *province* C Ecuador
57 *N9* **Bolívar** *off.* Estado Bolívar. ⬖ *state* SE Venezuela
27 *X12* **Bolivar Peninsula** *headland* Texas, SW USA *29.26N 94.41W*
56 *I6* **Bolívar, Pico** ▲ W Venezuela *8.33N 71.05W*
59 *K17* **Bolivia** *off.* Republic of Bolivia. ◆ *republic* W South America
114 *O13* **Boljevac** Serbia, E Serbia and Montenegro (Yugoslavia) *43.50N 21.57E*
Bolkenhain *see* Bolków
130 *J5* **Bolkhov** Orlovskaya Oblast', W Russian Federation *53.28N 36.00E*
113 *F14* **Bolków** *Ger.* Bolkenhain. Dolnośląskie, SW Poland *50.55N 15.49E*
190 *K3* **Bollards Lagoon** South Australia *28.58S 140.52E*
105 *R14* **Bollène** Vaucluse, SE France *44.16N 4.45E*
96 *N12* **Bollnäs** Gävleborg, C Sweden *61.18N 16.27E*
189 *W10* **Bollon** Queensland, C Australia *28.07S 147.28E*
199 *Jj14* **Bollons Tablemount** *undersea feature* S Pacific Ocean *49.40S 176.10W*
95 *H17* **Bollstabruk** Västernorrland, C Sweden *63.00N 17.41E*
Bolluilos de Par del Condado *see* Bollulos Par del Condado
106 *J14* **Bollulos Par del Condado** *var.* Bolluilos de Par del Condado. Andalucía, S Spain *37.19N 6.31W*
97 *K21* **Bolmen** ◎ S Sweden
143 *T10* **Bolnisi** S Georgia *41.28N 44.34E*
81 *H19* **Bolobo** Bandundu, W Dem. Rep. Congo *2.10S 16.16E*
108 *G10* **Bologna** Emilia-Romagna, N Italy *44.30N 11.19E*
128 *I15* **Bologoye** Tverskaya Oblast', W Russian Federation *57.54N 34.04E*
81 *J18* **Bolomba** Equateur, NW Dem. Rep. Congo *0.24N 19.10E*
43 *X13* **Bolónchén de Rejón** *var.* Bolonchén de Rejón. Campeche, SE Mexico *20.00N 89.34W*
126 *H14* **Bolotnoye** Novosibirskaya Oblast', C Russian Federation *55.39N 84.19E*
116 *J13* **Boloústra, Akrotírio** *headland* NE Greece *40.56N 24.58E*
178 *Jj10* **Bolovens, Plateau des** *plateau* S Laos
108 *H13* **Bolsena** Lazio, C Italy *42.39N 11.59E*
109 *G14* **Bolsena, Lago di** ◎ C Italy
130 *B3* **Bol'shakovo** *Ger.* Kreuzingen; *prev.* Gross-Skaisgirren. Kaliningradskaya Oblast', W Russian Federation *54.53N 21.38E*
126 *J6* **Bol'shaya Balakhnya** 〜 N Russian Federation
Bol'shaya Berëstovitsa *see* Vyalikaya Byerastavitsa
131 *S7* **Bol'shaya Chernigovka** Samarskaya Oblast', W Russian Federation *52.07N 50.49E*
131 *S7* **Bol'shaya Glushitsa** Samarskaya Oblast', W Russian Federation *52.22N 50.29E*
150 *H9* **Bol'shaya Khobda** *Kaz.* Ülkenqobda. 〜 Kazakhstan/Russian Federation
126 *Jj8* **Bol'shaya Kuonamka** 〜 NE Russian Federation
130 *M12* **Bol'shaya Martynovka** Rostovskaya Oblast', SW Russian Federation *47.19N 41.40E*
126 *I13* **Bol'shaya Murta** Krasnoyarskiy Kray, C Russian Federation *56.51N 93.10E*
129 *V4* **Bol'shaya Rogovaya** 〜 NW Russian Federation
129 *U7* **Bol'shaya Synya** 〜 NW Russian Federation
151 *V9* **Bol'shaya Vladimirovka** Vostochnyy Kazakhstan, E Kazakhstan *50.52N 79.28E*
125 *G13* **Bol'sherech'ye** Omskaya Oblast', C Russian Federation *56.03N 74.37E*
127 *Pp12* **Bol'sheretsk** Kamchatskaya Oblast', E Russian Federation *52.20N 156.24E*
131 *W3* **Bol'sheust'ikinskoye** Respublika Bashkortostan, W Russian Federation *56.00N 58.13E*
Bol'shevik *see* Bal'shavik
126 *Ii3* **Bol'shevik, Ostrov** *island* Severnaya Zemlya, N Russian Federation
129 *U4* **Bol'shezemel'skaya Tundra** *physical region* NW Russian Federation
150 *J13* **Bol'shiye Barsuki, Peski** *desert* SW Kazakhstan
125 *Ff12* **Bol'shiye Uki** Omskaya Oblast', C Russian Federation *56.57N 72.26E*
127 *O6* **Bol'shoy Anyuy** 〜 NE Russian Federation
126 *K6* **Bol'shoy Begichev, Ostrov** *island* NE Russian Federation
127 *N17* **Bol'shoye Kamen'** Primorskiy Kray, SE Russian Federation *43.06N 132.21E*
131 *O4* **Bol'shoye Murashkino** Nizhegorodskaya Oblast', W Russian Federation *55.46N 44.48E*
131 *W4* **Bol'shoy Iremel'** ▲ W Russian Federation *54.31N 58.47E*
131 *R7* **Bol'shoy Irgiz** 〜 W Russian Federation
126 *M5* **Bol'shoy Lyakhovskiy, Ostrov** *island* NE Russian Federation
126 *Ll13* **Bol'shoy Nimnyr** Respublika Sakha (Yakutiya), NE Russian Federation *57.55N 125.34E*
Bol'shoy Rozhan *see* Vyaliki Rozhan
150 *E10* **Bol'shoy Uzen'** *Kaz.* Ülkenözen. 〜 Kazakhstan/Russian Federation
126 *Ii15* **Bol'shoy Yenisey** *var.* Biy-Khem. 〜 S Russian Federation
42 *K6* **Bolson de Mapimi** ▲▲ NW Mexico
100 *K6* **Bolsward** *Fris.* Boalsert. Friesland, N Netherlands *53.04N 5.31E*
107 *T4* **Boltaña** Aragón, NE Spain *42.28N 0.02E*
12 *G15* **Bolton** Ontario, S Canada *43.52N 79.45W*
99 *K17* **Bolton** *prev.* Bolton-le-Moors. NW England, UK *53.34N 2.25W*
23 *V12* **Bolton** North Carolina, SE USA *34.22N 78.26W*
Bolton-le-Moors *see* Bolton
142 *G11* **Bolu** Bolu, NW Turkey *40.45N 31.37E*
142 *G11* **Bolu** ⬖ *province* NW Turkey
195 *N15* **Bolubolu** Goodenough Island, S PNG *9.22S 150.22E*
94 *H1* **Bolungarvík** Vestfirdhir, NW Iceland *66.09N 23.16W*
165 *O10* **Boluntay** Qinghai, W China *36.30N 92.10E*
142 *F14* **Bolvadin** Afyon, W Turkey *38.43N 31.01E*
116 *M10* **Bolyarovo** *prev.* Pashkeni. Yambol, E Bulgaria *42.09N 26.49E*
108 *G6* **Bolzano** *Ger.* Bozen; *anc.* Bauzanum. Trentino-Alto Adige, N Italy *46.30N 11.22E*
81 *F22* **Boma** Bas-Congo, W Dem. Rep. Congo *5.42S 13.05E*
191 *R12* **Bombala** New South Wales, SE Australia *36.54S 149.15E*
106 *F10* **Bombarral** Leiria, C Portugal *39.15N 9.09W*
Bombay *see* Mumbai
176 *Vv11* **Bomberai** 〜 Papua, E Indonesia
176 *Vv11* **Bomberai, Jazirah** *peninsula* Papua, E Indonesia
176 *Vv11* **Bomberai, Semenanjung** *headland* Papua, E Indonesia *3.01S 133.25E*
83 *F18* **Bombo** S Uganda *0.38N 32.31E*
81 *I17* **Bomboma** Equateur, NW Dem. Rep. Congo *2.22N 19.03E*
61 *I14* **Bom Futuro** Pará, N Brazil *6.27S 54.44W*
165 *Q15* **Bomi** *var.* Bowo, Zhamo. Xizang Zizhiqu, W China *29.43N 96.12E*
81 *N17* **Bomili** Orientale, NE Dem. Rep. Congo *1.45N 27.01E*
61 *N17* **Bom Jesus da Lapa** Bahia, E Brazil *13.16S 43.22W*
62 *Q8* **Bom Jesus do Itabapoana** Rio de Janeiro, SE Brazil *21.07S 41.43W*
97 *C15* **Bømlafjorden** *fjord* S Norway
97 *B15* **Bømlo** *island* S Norway
126 *M14* **Bomnak** Amurskaya Oblast', SE Russian Federation *54.43N 128.50E*
81 *I17* **Bomongo** Equateur, NW Dem. Rep. Congo *1.22N 18.21E*
63 *K14* **Bom Retiro** Santa Catarina, S Brazil *27.52S 49.33W*
81 *L15* **Bomu** *var.* Mbomou, Mbomu, M'Bomu. 〜 Central African Republic/Dem. Rep. Congo
148 *J3* **Bonāb** *var.* Benāb, Bunab. Āẕarbāyjān-e Khāvarī, N Iran *37.24N 45.59E*
47 *Q16* **Bonaire** *island* E Netherlands Antilles
41 *U11* **Bona, Mount** ▲ Alaska, USA *61.22N 141.45W*
194 *M16* **Bonando** 〜 SE Papau New Guinea
191 *Q12* **Bonang** Victoria, SE Australia *37.13S 148.43E*
44 *L7* **Bonanza** Región Autónoma Atlántico Norte, NE Nicaragua *13.58N 84.37W*
39 *O4* **Bonanza** Utah, W USA *40.01N 109.12W*
47 *O9* **Bonao** C Dominican Republic *18.55N 70.25W*
188 *L3* **Bonaparte Archipelago** *island group* Western Australia
34 *K6* **Bonaparte, Mount** ▲ Washington, NW USA *48.47N 119.07W*
41 *N11* **Bonasila Dome** ▲ Alaska, USA *62.24N 160.28W*
94 *H11* **Bonåsjøen** Nordland, C Norway *67.35N 15.39E*
47 *T15* **Bonasse** Trinidad, Trinidad and Tobago *10.02N 61.48W*
13 *X7* **Bonaventure** Quebec, SE Canada *48.03N 65.30W*
13 *X7* **Bonaventure** 〜 Quebec, SE Canada
11 *V11* **Bonavista** Newfoundland and Labrador, SE Canada *48.36N 53.07W*
11 *U11* **Bonavista Bay** *inlet* NW Atlantic Ocean
123 *Kk11* **Bon, Cap** *headland* N Tunisia *37.05N 11.04E*
81 *E19* **Bonda** Ogooué-Lolo, C Gabon *0.50S 12.28E*
131 *N6* **Bondari** Tambovskaya Oblast', W Russian Federation *52.58N 42.02E*
108 *G9* **Bondeno** Emilia-Romagna, C Italy *44.53N 11.24E*
32 *L4* **Bond Falls Flowage** ◎ Michigan, N USA
81 *L16* **Bondo** Orientale, N Dem. Rep. Congo *3.51N 23.41E*
175 *P17* **Bondokodi** Pulau Sumba, S Indonesia *9.36S 119.01E*
79 *O15* **Bondoukou** E Ivory Coast *8.03N 2.45W*
Bondoukui/Bondoukuy *see* Boundoukui
174 *Mm15* **Bondowoso** Jawa, C Indonesia *7.54S 113.49E*
35 *S14* **Bondurant** Wyoming, C USA *43.14N 110.26W*
Bone *see* Watampone, Indonesia
Bône *see* Annaba, Algeria
32 *I5* **Bone Lake** ◎ Wisconsin, N USA
175 *R12* **Bonelipu** Pulau Buton, C Indonesia *4.42S 123.09E*
175 *Q14* **Bonerate, Kepulauan** *var.* Macan. *island group* C Indonesia
175 *Pp15* **Bonerate, Pulau** *island* Kepulauan Bonerate, C Indonesia
31 *O12* **Bonesteel** South Dakota, N USA *43.01N 98.55W*
64 *I8* **Bonete, Cerro** ▲ N Argentina *27.58S 68.22W*
175 *Pp11* **Bone, Teluk** *bay* Sulawesi, C Indonesia
110 *D6* **Bonfol** Jura, NW Switzerland *47.28N 7.08E*
159 *U12* **Bongaigaon** Assam, NE India *26.30N 90.30E*
81 *K17* **Bongandanga** Equateur, NW Dem. Rep. Congo *1.30N 21.03E*
80 *L13* **Bongo, Massif des** *var.* Chaîne des Mongos. ▲▲ NE Central African Republic
80 *G12* **Bongor** Mayo-Kébbi, SW Chad *10.18N 15.19E*
79 *N16* **Bongouanou** E Ivory Coast *6.39N 4.12W*
178 *Kk11* **Bông Sơn** *var.* Hoai Nhơn. Binh Đinh, C Vietnam *14.28N 109.00E*

◆ Country
● Country Capital
◇ Dependent Territory
○ Dependent Territory Capital
⬖ Administrative Region
✖ International Airport
▲ Mountain
▲▲ Mountain Range
Volcano
〜 River
◎ Lake
▣ Reservoir

27 U5 **Bonham** Texas, SW USA 33.34N 96.10W
Bonhard see Bonyhád
105 U6 **Bonhomme, Col du** pass NE France 48.10N 7.07E
105 Y16 **Bonifacio** Corse, France, C Mediterranean Sea 41.23N 9.09E
Bonifacio, Bocche de/Bonifacio, Bouches de see Bonifacio, Strait of
105 Y16 **Bonifacio, Strait of** Fr. Bouches de Bonifacio, It. Bocche de Bonifacio. strait C Mediterranean Sea
25 Q8 **Bonifay** Florida, SE USA 30.49N 85.42W
Bonin Islands see Ogasawara-shotō
199 H6 **Bonin Trench** undersea feature NW Pacific Ocean
25 W15 **Bonita Springs** Florida, SE USA 26.19N 81.48W
44 I5 **Bonito, Pico** ▲ N Honduras 15.33N 86.55W
103 E17 **Bonn** Nordrhein-Westfalen, W Germany 50.43N 7.06E
12 J12 **Bonnechere** Ontario, SE Canada 45.39N 77.36W
12 J12 **Bonnechere** ≈ Ontario, SE Canada
35 N7 **Bonners Ferry** Idaho, NW USA 48.41N 116.19W
29 R4 **Bonner Springs** Kansas, C USA 39.03N 94.52W
104 L6 **Bonnétable** Sarthe, NW France 48.09N 0.24E
29 X6 **Bonne Terre** Missouri, C USA 37.55N 90.33W
8 J5 **Bonnet Plume** ≈ Yukon Territory, NW Canada
104 M6 **Bonneval** Eure-et-Loir, C France 48.12N 1.23E
105 T10 **Bonneville** Haute-Savoie, E France 46.04N 6.25E
38 J3 **Bonneville Salt Flats** salt flat Utah, W USA
79 U18 **Bonny** Rivers, S Nigeria 4.25N 7.13E
Bonny, Bight of see Biafra, Bight of
39 W4 **Bonny Reservoir** ▣ Colorado, C USA
9 R14 **Bonnyville** Alberta, SW Canada 54.16N 110.46W
109 C18 **Bono** Sardegna, Italy, C Mediterranean Sea 40.24N 9.01E
176 Xx10 **Bonoi** Papua, E Indonesia 1.46S 137.45E
Bononia see Vidin, Bulgaria
Bononia see Boulogne-sur-Mer, France
109 B18 **Bonorva** Sardegna, Italy, C Mediterranean Sea 40.27N 8.46E
32 M15 **Bonpas Creek** ≈ Illinois, N USA
202 I3 **Bonriki** Tarawa, W Kiribati 1.22N 173.09E
191 T4 **Bonshaw** New South Wales, SE Australia 29.06S 151.15E
78 I16 **Bonthe** SW Sierra Leone 7.26N 12.32W
179 P8 **Bontoc** Luzon, N Philippines 17.04N 120.58E
194 M16 **Bonua** ≈ S PNG
27 Y9 **Bon Wier** Texas, SW USA 30.43N 93.40W
113 J25 **Bonyhád** Ger. Bonhard. Tolna, S Hungary 46.17N 18.31E
Bonzabaai see Bonza Bay
85 J25 **Bonza Bay** Afr. Bonzabaai. Eastern Cape, S South Africa 32.58S 27.58E
190 D7 **Bookabie** South Australia 31.49S 132.41E
190 H6 **Bookaloo** South Australia 31.56S 137.21E
39 P5 **Book Cliffs** cliff Colorado/Utah, W USA
175 Tt9 **Boo, Kepulauan** island group E Indonesia
27 P1 **Booker** Texas, SW USA 36.27N 100.32W
78 K15 **Boola** Guinée-Forestière, SE Guinea 8.22N 8.40W
191 O8 **Booligal** New South Wales, SE Australia 33.56S 144.54E
101 G17 **Boom** Antwerpen, N Belgium 51.05N 4.24E
45 N6 **Boom** var. Boon. Región Autónoma Atlántico Norte, NE Nicaragua 14.52N 83.36W
191 S3 **Boomi** New South Wales, SE Australia 28.43S 149.35E
Boon see Boom
31 V13 **Boone** Iowa, C USA 42.04N 93.52W
23 Q8 **Boone** North Carolina, SE USA 36.13N 81.40W
29 S11 **Booneville** Arkansas, C USA 35.08N 93.55W
23 N6 **Booneville** Kentucky, S USA 37.27N 83.41W
25 N2 **Booneville** Mississippi, S USA 34.39N 88.34W
23 V3 **Boonsboro** Maryland, NE USA 39.30N 77.39W
168 H9 **Böön Tsagaan Nuur** ◎ S Mongolia
36 L6 **Boonville** California, W USA 38.58N 123.21W
33 N16 **Boonville** Indiana, N USA 38.03N 87.16W
29 U4 **Boonville** Missouri, C USA 38.58N 92.44W
20 I9 **Boonville** New York, NE USA 43.28N 75.17W
82 M12 **Boorama** Woqooyi Galbeed, NW Somalia 9.58N 43.15E
191 O6 **Booroondarra, Mount** hill New South Wales, SE Australia 31.07S 145.20E
191 N9 **Booroorban** New South Wales, SE Australia 34.55S 144.45E
191 R9 **Boorowa** New South Wales, SE Australia 34.26S 148.42E
101 H17 **Boortmeerbeek** Vlaams Brabant, C Belgium 50.58N 4.27E
82 P11 **Boosaaso** var. Bandar Kassim, Bender Qaasim, Bosaso, It. Bender Cassim. Bari, N Somalia 11.26N 49.37E
21 Q8 **Boothbay Harbor** Maine, NE USA 43.52N 69.35W
Boothia Felix see Boothia Peninsula
15 Kk2 **Boothia, Gulf of** gulf Nunavut, NE Canada
15 K2 **Boothia Peninsula** prev. Boothia Felix. peninsula Nunavut, NE Canada
81 E18 **Booué** Ogooué-Ivindo, NE Gabon 0.03S 11.58E
103 J21 **Bopfingen** Baden-Württemberg, S Germany 48.51N 10.21E
103 F18 **Boppard** Rheinland-Pfalz, W Germany 50.13N 7.35E
64 M4 **Boquerón** off. Departamento de Boquerón. ❖ department W Paraguay
45 P15 **Boquete** var. Bajo Boquete. Chiriquí, W Panama 8.45N 82.26W
42 J6 **Boquilla, Presa de la** ▣ N Mexico
42 L5 **Boquillas** var. Boquillas del Carmen. Coahuila de Zaragoza, NE Mexico 29.10N 102.55W
Boquillas del Carmen see Boquillas
126 I11 **Bor** Krasnoyarskiy Kray, C Russian Federation 61.28N 90.09E
83 F15 **Bor** Jonglei, S Sudan 6.12N 31.33E
97 L20 **Bor** Jönköping, S Sweden 57.04N 14.10E
142 J15 **Bor** Niğde, S Turkey 37.48N 34.30E
114 P12 **Bor** Serbia, E Serbia and Montenegro (Yugoslavia) 44.05N 22.06E
203 S10 **Bora-Bora** island Îles Sous le Vent, W French Polynesia
178 Ii10 **Borabu** Maha Sarakham, E Thailand 16.01N 103.06E
35 P13 **Borah Peak** ▲ Idaho, NW USA 44.21N 113.53W
151 U16 **Boralday** prev. Burunday. Almaty, SE Kazakhstan 43.21N 76.48E
97 J19 **Borås** Västra Götaland, S Sweden 57.43N 12.55E
149 N11 **Borāzjān** var. Borazjān. Būshehr, S Iran 29.19N 51.12E
Borazjān see Borāzjān
60 G13 **Borba** Amazonas, N Brazil 4.39S 59.34W
106 H11 **Borba** Évora, S Portugal 38.48N 7.28W
Borbetomagus see Worms
57 O7 **Borbón** Bolívar, E Venezuela 7.55N 64.03W
61 Q15 **Borborema, Planalto da** plateau NE Brazil
118 M14 **Borcea, Braţul** ≈ S Romania
Borchalo see Marneuli
205 R15 **Borchgrevink Coast** physical region Antarctica
143 Q11 **Borçka** Artvin, NE Turkey 41.24N 41.37E
100 N11 **Borculo** Gelderland, E Netherlands 52.07N 6.31E
190 G10 **Borda, Cape** headland South Australia 35.45S 136.34E
104 K13 **Bordeaux** anc. Burdigala. Gironde, SW France 44.49N 0.33W
9 T15 **Borden** Saskatchewan, S Canada 52.23N 107.10W
12 D8 **Borden Lake** ◎ Ontario, S Canada
15 L1 **Borden Peninsula** peninsula Baffin Island, Nunavut, NE Canada
190 K11 **Bordertown** South Australia 36.21S 140.48E
94 H2 **Bordheyri** Vestfirdhir, NW Iceland 65.12N 21.09W
97 B18 **Bordhoy** Dan. Bordø Island Faeroe Islands 62.17N 6.30W
108 B11 **Bordighera** Liguria, NW Italy 43.48N 7.40E
76 K5 **Bordj-Bou-Arreridj** var. Bordj Bou Arreridj, Bordj Bou Arréridj. N Algeria 36.04N 4.45E
123 I10 **Bordj El Bahri, Cap de** headland N Algeria 36.52N 3.13E
76 L10 **Bordj Omar Driss** E Algeria 28.09N 6.52E
149 N13 **Bord Khūn** Hormozgān, S Iran
153 V7 **Bordunskiy** Chuyskaya Oblast', N Kyrgyzstan 42.37N 75.31E
97 M17 **Borensberg** Östergötland, S Sweden 58.33N 15.15E
Borgå see Porvoo
94 L2 **Borgarfjördhur** Austurland, NE Iceland 65.32N 13.46W
94 H3 **Borgarnes** Vesturland, W Iceland 64.33N 21.54W
95 G14 **Børgefjell** ▲▲ C Norway
100 O7 **Borger** Drenthe, NE Netherlands 52.54N 6.48E
27 N2 **Borger** Texas, SW USA 35.40N 101.24W
97 N20 **Borgholm** Kalmar, S Sweden 56.50N 16.40E
109 N22 **Borgia** Calabria, SW Italy 38.48N 16.28E
101 J18 **Borgloon** Limburg, NE Belgium 50.48N 5.21E
205 P2 **Borg Massif** ▲▲ Antarctica
24 L9 **Borgne, Lake** ◎ Louisiana, S USA
108 C7 **Borgomanero** Piemonte, NE Italy 45.42N 8.33E
108 G10 **Borgo Panigale** ✈ (Bologna) Emilia-Romagna, N Italy 44.33N 11.16E
109 J15 **Borgorose** Lazio, C Italy 42.10N 13.15E
108 A9 **Borgo San Dalmazzo** Piemonte, N Italy 44.19N 7.28E
108 G11 **Borgo San Lorenzo** Toscana, C Italy 43.58N 11.22E
108 C7 **Borgosesia** Piemonte, NE Italy 45.41N 8.21E
108 E9 **Borgo Val di Taro** Emilia-Romagna, C Italy 44.29N 9.48E
108 G6 **Borgo Valsugana** Trentino-Alto Adige, N Italy 46.04N 11.31E
169 O11 **Borhoyn Tal** Dornogovĭ, SE Mongolia 43.43N 111.53E
178 Ii8 **Borikhan** var. Borikhane. Bolikhamxai, C Laos 18.36N 103.43E
Borikhane see Borikhan
Borislav see Boryslav
131 N8 **Borisoglebsk** Voronezhskaya Oblast', W Russian Federation 51.23N 42.00E
Borisov see Barysaw
Borisovgrad see Pŭrvomay
Borispol' see Boryspil'
180 I3 **Boriziny** Mahajanga, NW Madagascar 15.31S 47.40E
107 Q5 **Borja** Aragón, NE Spain 41.49N 1.31W
Borjas Blancas see Les Borges Blanques
143 S10 **Borjomi** Rus. Borzhomi. C Georgia 41.50N 43.24E
120 L12 **Borkavichy** Rus. Borkovichi. Vitsyebskaya Voblasts', N Belarus 55.40N 28.18E
103 H16 **Borken** Hessen, C Germany 51.01N 9.16E
103 E14 **Borken** Nordrhein-Westfalen, W Germany 51.51N 6.51E
94 H10 **Borkenes** Troms, N Norway 68.46N 16.10E
80 H7 **Borkou-Ennedi-Tibesti** off. Préfecture du Borkou-Ennedi-Tibesti. ❖ prefecture N Chad
Borkovichi see Borkavichy
102 E9 **Borkum** island NW Germany
83 K17 **Bor, Lagh** var. Lak Bor. dry watercourse NE Kenya
Bor, Lak see Bor, Lagh
97 M14 **Borlänge** Dalarna, C Sweden 60.28N 15.25E
108 C9 **Bormida** ≈ NW Italy
108 F6 **Bormio** Lombardia, N Italy 46.27N 10.24E
103 M16 **Borna** Sachsen, E Germany 51.07N 12.30E
100 O10 **Borne** Overijssel, E Netherlands 52.18N 6.45E
101 F17 **Bornem** Antwerpen, N Belgium 51.06N 4.13E
174 M6 **Borneo** island Brunei/Indonesia/Malaysia
103 E16 **Bornheim** Nordrhein-Westfalen, W Germany 50.46N 6.58E
97 L24 **Bornholm** ❖ county E Denmark
97 L24 **Bornholm** island E Denmark
79 Y13 **Borno** ❖ state NE Nigeria
106 K15 **Bornos** Andalucía, S Spain 36.49N 5.42W
168 L7 **Bornuur** Töv, C Mongolia 48.28N 106.15E
119 O4 **Borodyanka** Kyyivs'ka Oblast', N Ukraine 50.40N 29.54E
126 M10 **Borogontsy** Respublika Sakha (Yakutiya), NE Russian Federation 62.42N 131.01E
164 I5 **Borohoro Shan** ▲▲ NW China
79 O13 **Boromo** SW Burkina 11.46N 2.54W
37 T13 **Boron** California, W USA 35.00N 117.42W
179 R12 **Borongan** Samar, C Philippines 11.26N 125.30E
Borongo see Black Volta
Boron'ki see Baron'ki
Borosjenő see Ineu
Borossebes see Sebiş
78 L15 **Borotou** NW Ivory Coast 8.46N 7.30W
119 W6 **Borova** Kharkivs'ka Oblast', E Ukraine 49.22N 37.39E
116 H8 **Borovan** Vratsa, NW Bulgaria 43.25N 23.45E
128 I14 **Borovichi** Novgorodskaya Oblast', W Russian Federation 58.23N 33.56E
Borovlje see Ferlach
114 J9 **Borovo** Vukovar-Srijem, NE Croatia 45.22N 18.57E
151 Q7 **Borovoye** Kaz. Būrabay. Akmola, N Kazakhstan 53.07N 70.19E
130 K4 **Borovsk** Kaluzhskaya Oblast', W Russian Federation 55.12N 36.22E
125 F12 **Borovskiy** Tyumenskaya Oblast', C Russian Federation 57.04N 65.37E
151 N7 **Borovskoy** Kostanay, N Kazakhstan 53.49N 64.12E
Borovukha see Baravukha
97 L23 **Borrby** Skåne, S Sweden 55.27N 14.10E
189 R3 **Borroloola** Northern Territory, N Australia 16.09S 136.18E
118 F9 **Borş** Bihor, NW Romania 47.06N 21.47E
118 I9 **Borşa** Hung. Borsa. Maramureş, N Romania 47.40N 24.37E
118 J10 **Borsec** Ger. Bad Borseck, Hung. Borszék. Harghita, C Romania 46.57N 25.32E
94 K8 **Børselv** Finnmark, N Norway 70.18N 25.35E
115 L23 **Borsh** var. Borshi. Vlorë, S Albania 40.04N 19.51E
Borshchev see Borshchiv
118 K7 **Borshchiv** Pol. Borszczów, Rus. Borshchev. Ternopil's'ka Oblast', W Ukraine 48.48N 26.00E
Borshi see Borsh
113 L20 **Borsod-Abaúj-Zemplén** off. Borsod-Abaúj-Zemplén Megye. ❖ county NE Hungary
101 E15 **Borssele** Zeeland, SW Netherlands 51.26N 3.45E
Borszczów see Borshchiv
Borszék see Borsec
Bortala see Bole
105 O12 **Bort-les-Orgues** Corrèze, C France 45.28N 2.31E
Bor u České Lípy see Nový Bor
168 E8 **Bor-Udzüür** Hovd, W Mongolia 45.46N 92.13E
149 N9 **Borūjen** Chahār Maḩall va Bakhtīārī, C Iran 32.00N 51.08E
148 L7 **Borūjerd** var. Burujird. Lorestān, W Iran 33.55N 48.45E
118 H6 **Boryslav** Pol. Borysław, Rus. Borislav. L'vivs'ka Oblast', NW Ukraine 49.18N 23.28E
Borysław see Boryslav
119 P4 **Boryspil'** Rus. Borispol'. Kyyivs'ka Oblast', N Ukraine 50.20N 30.58E
119 P4 **Boryspil'** Rus. Borispol'. ✈ (Kyyiv) Kyyivs'ka Oblast', N Ukraine 50.21N 30.46E
Borzhomi see Borjomi
119 R3 **Borzna** Chernihivs'ka Oblast', NE Ukraine 51.15N 32.25E
126 L16 **Borzya** Chitinskaya Oblast', S Russian Federation 50.18N 116.24E
109 B18 **Bosa** Sardegna, Italy, C Mediterranean Sea 40.18N 8.28E
114 F10 **Bosanska Dubica** var. Kozarska Dubica. Republika Srpska, NW Bosnia and Herzegovina 45.09N 16.47E
114 G10 **Bosanska Gradiška** var. Gradiška. Republika Srpska, N Bosnia and Herzegovina 45.09N 17.14E
114 F10 **Bosanska Kostajnica** var. Srpska Kostajnica. Republika Srpska, NW Bosnia and Herzegovina 45.12N 16.33E
114 E11 **Bosanska Krupa** var. Krupa, Krupa na Uni. Federacija Bosna I Hercegovina, NW Bosnia and Herzegovina 44.52N 16.09E
114 H10 **Bosanski Brod** var. Srpski Brod. Republika Srpska, N Bosnia and Herzegovina 45.07N 17.59E
114 E10 **Bosanski Novi** var. Novi Grad. Republika Srpska, NW Bosnia and Herzegovina 45.03N 16.22E
114 E11 **Bosanski Petrovac** var. Petrovac. Federacija Bosna I Hercegovina, NW Bosnia and Herzegovina 44.34N 16.21E
114 N12 **Bosanski Petrovac** Serbia, E Serbia and Montenegro (Yugoslavia) 44.22N 21.25E
114 I10 **Bosanski Šamac** var. Šamac. Republika Srpska, N Bosnia and Herzegovina 45.03N 18.27E
114 E12 **Bosansko Grahovo** var. Grahovo, Hrvatsko Grahovo. Federacija Bosna I Hercegovina, W Bosnia and Herzegovina 44.10N 16.22E
Bosaso see Boosaaso
194 G13 **Bosavi, Mount** ⛰ W PNG 6.33S 142.50E
166 J14 **Bose** Guangxi Zhuangzu Zizhiqu, S China 23.55N 106.31E
167 Q5 **Boshan** Shandong, E China 36.31N 117.46E
115 P16 **Bosilegrad** prev. Bosiljgrad. Serbia, SE Serbia and Montenegro (Yugoslavia) 42.30N 22.30E
Bosiljgrad see Bosilegrad
Bösing see Pezinok
100 H12 **Boskoop** Zuid-Holland, C Netherlands 52.04N 4.40E
113 G18 **Boskovice** Ger. Boskowitz. Brněnský Kraj, SE Czech Republic 49.30N 16.39E
Boskowitz see Boskovice
114 I10 **Bosna** ≈ N Bosnia and Herzegovina
176 X9 **Bosnabraidi** Papua, E Indonesia 0.49S 136.00E
115 G14 **Bosna I Hercegovina, Federacija** ❖ republic Bosnia and Herzegovina
114 H12 **Bosnia and Herzegovina** off. Republic of Bosnia and Herzegovina. ◆ republic SE Europe
81 J16 **Bosobolo** Equateur, NW Dem. Rep. Congo 4.10N 19.55E
171 K17 **Bōsō-hantō** peninsula Honshū, S Japan
Bosora see Buşrá ash Shām
Bosphorus/Bosporus see İstanbul Boğazı
Bosporus Cimmerius see Kerch Strait
Bosporus Thracius see İstanbul Boğazı
Bosra see Buşrá ash Shām
81 H14 **Bossangoa** Ouham, C Central African Republic 6.31N 17.24E
Bossé Bangou see Bossey Bangou
81 I15 **Bossembélé** Ombella-Mpoko, C Central African Republic 5.13N 17.39E
81 H15 **Bossentélé** Ouham-Pendé, W Central African Republic 5.36N 16.37E
79 R12 **Bossey Bangou** var. Bossé Bangou. Tillabéri, SW Niger 13.22N 1.18E
24 G5 **Bossier City** Louisiana, S USA 32.31N 93.43W
85 D20 **Bossiesvlei** Hardap, S Namibia 25.01S 16.45E
79 Y11 **Bosso** Diffa, SE Niger 13.42N 13.18E
63 F15 **Bossoroca** Rio Grande do Sul, S Brazil 28.45S 54.54W
164 J10 **Bostan** Xinjiang Uygur Zizhiqu, W China 41.19N 83.15E
148 K3 **Bostānābād** Āžarbāyjān-e Khāvarī, N Iran 37.52N 46.51E
164 K6 **Bosten Hu** var. Bagrax Hu. ◎ NW China
99 O18 **Boston** prev. St.Botolph's Town. E England, UK 52.58N 0.01W
21 O11 **Boston** state capital Massachusetts, NE USA 42.21N 71.03W
152 I9 **Bo'ston** Rus. Bustan. Qoraqalpog'iston Respublikasi, W Uzbekistan 41.49N 60.51E
8 M17 **Boston Bar** British Columbia, SW Canada 49.54N 121.22W
29 T10 **Boston Mountains** ▲▲ Arkansas, C USA
13 P8 **Bostonnais** ≈ Quebec, SE Canada
Bostyn' see Bastyn'
114 J10 **Bosut** ≈ E Croatia
160 C11 **Botād** Gujarāt, W India 22.12N 71.43E
191 T9 **Botany Bay** inlet New South Wales, SE Australia
85 G18 **Boteti** var. Botletle. ≈ N Botswana
116 J9 **Botev** ▲ C Bulgaria 42.45N 24.57E
116 H9 **Botevgrad** prev. Orkhaniye. Sofiya, W Bulgaria 42.55N 23.46E
95 J16 **Bothnia, Gulf of** Fin. Pohjanlahti, Swe. Bottniska Viken. gulf N Baltic Sea
191 P17 **Bothwell** Tasmania, SE Australia 42.24S 147.01E
106 H5 **Boticas** Vila Real, N Portugal 41.40N 7.40W
57 W10 **Boti-Pasi** Sipaliwini, C Suriname 4.08N 55.27W
Botletle see Boteti
131 P16 **Botlikh** Chechenskaya Respublika, SW Russian Federation 42.39N 46.12E
119 N10 **Botna** ≈ E Moldova
153 P13 **Botogot', Tizmasi** Rus. Khrebet Babatag. ▲▲ Tajikistan/Uzbekistan
118 I9 **Botoşani** Hung. Botosány. Botoşani, NE Romania 47.43N 26.40E
118 K8 **Botoşani** ❖ county NE Romania
Botosány see Botoşani
167 P4 **Botou** prev. Bozhen. Hebei, E China 38.09N 116.37E
101 M20 **Botrange** ▲ E Belgium 50.30N 6.03E
109 O21 **Botricello** Calabria, SW Italy 38.56N 16.51E
85 I23 **Botshabelo** Free State, C South Africa 29.15S 26.51E
95 J15 **Botsmark** Västerbotten, N Sweden 64.15N 20.15E
85 G19 **Botswana** off. Republic of Botswana. ◆ republic S Africa
31 N2 **Bottineau** North Dakota, N USA 48.49N 100.28W
Bottniska Viken see Bothnia, Gulf of
62 L9 **Botucatu** São Paulo, S Brazil 22.52S 48.30W
78 M16 **Bouaflé** C Ivory Coast 6.58N 5.45W
79 N16 **Bouaké** var. Bwake. C Ivory Coast 7.39N 5.01W
81 G14 **Bouar** Nana-Mambéré, W Central African Republic 5.58N 15.38E
76 H7 **Bouarfa** NE Morocco 32.33N 1.54W
113 B19 **Boubín** ▲ SW Czech Republic 49.00N 13.51E
81 I14 **Bouca** Ouham, W Central African Republic 6.57N 18.18E
13 T5 **Boucher** ≈ Quebec, SE Canada
105 R15 **Bouches-du-Rhône** ❖ department SE France
76 C9 **Bou Craa** var. Bu Craa. NW Western Sahara 26.31N 12.52W
79 O9 **Boû Djébéha** oasis C Mali 18.39N 3.45W
110 C8 **Boudry** Neuchâtel, W Switzerland 46.57N 6.46E
188 L2 **Bougainville, Cape** headland Western Australia 13.53S 126.01E
67 E24 **Bougainville, Cape** headland East Falkland, Falkland Islands 51.18S 58.28W
Bougainville, Détroit de see Bougainville Strait, Vanuatu
195 S13 **Bougainville Island** island NE PNG
195 T13 **Bougainville Strait** strait N Solomon Islands
197 B12 **Bougainville Strait** Fr. Détroit de Bougainville. strait C Vanuatu
176 U8 **Bouganville, Selat** strait Papua, E Indonesia
123 J11 **Bougaroun, Cap** headland NE Algeria 37.07N 6.18E
79 R8 **Boughessa** Kidal, NE Mali 20.05N 2.13E
Bougie see Béjaïa
78 L13 **Bougouni** Sikasso, SW Mali 11.22N 7.24W
101 J24 **Bouillon** Luxembourg, SE Belgium 49.46N 5.04E
76 K5 **Bouira** var. Bouïra. N Algeria 36.22N 3.55E
76 D8 **Bou-Izakarn** SW Morocco 29.12N 9.43W
76 B9 **Boujdour** var. Bojador. W Western Sahara 26.06N 14.28W
76 G5 **Boukhalef** ✈ (Tanger) N Morocco 35.45N 5.53W
Boukombé see Boukoumbé
79 R14 **Boukoumbé** var. Boukombé. C Benin 10.13N 1.09E
78 G6 **Boû Lanouâr** Dakhlet Nouâdhibou, W Mauritania 21.16N 16.28W
39 T4 **Boulder** Colorado, C USA 40.01N 105.18W
35 R10 **Boulder** Montana, NW USA 46.14N 112.07W
37 X12 **Boulder City** Nevada, W USA 35.58N 114.49W
189 T7 **Boulia** Queensland, C Australia 23.02S 139.58E
13 N10 **Boullé** ≈ Quebec, SE Canada
104 J9 **Boulogne** ≈ NW France
Boulogne see Boulogne-sur-Mer
104 L16 **Boulogne-sur-Gesse** Haute-Garonne, S France 43.18N 0.39E
105 N1 **Boulogne-sur-Mer** var. Boulogne; anc. Bononia, Gesoriacum, Gessoriacum. Pas-de-Calais, N France 50.43N 1.36E
197 I7 **Bouloupari** Province Sud, S New Caledonia 21.54S 166.04E
79 Q12 **Boulsa** C Burkina 12.40N 0.28W
79 W11 **Boultoum** Zinder, C Niger 14.43N 10.22E
197 K13 **Bouma** Taveuni, N Fiji 16.49S 179.50W
81 G16 **Boumba** ≈ SE Cameroon
78 J9 **Boûmdeïd** var. Boumdeït. Assaba, S Mauritania 17.25N 11.21W
Boumdeït see Boûmdeïd
117 C17 **Boumistós** ▲ W Greece 38.48N 20.59E
79 O15 **Bouna** NE Ivory Coast 9.16N 3.00W
21 P4 **Boundary Bald Mountain** ▲ Maine, NE USA 45.45N 70.10W
37 S8 **Boundary Peak** ▲ Nevada, W USA 37.50N 118.21W
78 M14 **Boundiali** N Ivory Coast 9.31N 6.28W
81 G19 **Boundji** Cuvette, C Congo 1.04S 15.18E
79 O13 **Boundoukui** var. Bondoukui, Bondoukuy. W Burkina 11.51N 3.47W
38 L2 **Bountiful** Utah, W USA 40.53N 111.52W
Bounty Basin see Bounty Trough
203 Q16 **Bounty Bay** bay Pitcairn Island, C Pacific Ocean
199 Jj14 **Bounty Islands** island group S NZ
183 Q13 **Bounty Trough** var. Bounty Basin. undersea feature S Pacific Ocean
197 I6 **Bourail** Province Sud, C New Caledonia 21.35S 165.29E
29 V5 **Bourbeuse River** ≈ Missouri, C USA
105 Q9 **Bourbon-Lancy** Saône-et-Loire, C France 46.39N 3.48E
33 N11 **Bourbonnais** Illinois, N USA 41.08N 87.52W
105 O10 **Bourbonnais** cultural region C France
105 S7 **Bourbonne-les-Bains** Haute-Marne, N France 48.00N 5.43E
Bourbon Vendée see la Roche-sur-Yon
76 M8 **Bourdj Messaouda** E Algeria 30.18N 9.19E
79 Q10 **Bourem** Gao, C Mali 16.56N 0.21W
Bourg see Bourg-en-Bresse
105 N11 **Bourganeuf** Creuse, C France 45.57N 1.47E
Bourgas see Burgas
Bourge-en-Bresse see Bourg-en-Bresse
105 S10 **Bourg-en-Bresse** var. Bourg, Bourge-en-Bresse. Ain, E France 46.12N 5.13E
105 O8 **Bourges** anc. Avaricum. Cher, C France 47.06N 2.24E
105 T11 **Bourget, Lac du** ◎ E France
105 P8 **Bourgogne** Eng. Burgundy. ❖ region E France
105 S11 **Bourgoin-Jallieu** Isère, E France 45.34N 5.16E
105 R14 **Bourg-St-Andéol** Ardèche, E France 44.24N 4.36E
105 U11 **Bourg-St-Maurice** Savoie, E France 45.37N 6.49E
110 C11 **Bourg St.Pierre** Valais, SW Switzerland 45.54N 7.10E
78 H8 **Boû Rjeimât** well W Mauritania 19.06N 15.16W
191 P5 **Bourke** New South Wales, SE Australia 30.07S 145.57E
99 M24 **Bournemouth** S England, UK 50.43N 1.54W
101 M23 **Bourscheid** Diekirch, NE Luxembourg 49.55N 6.04E
76 K6 **Bou Saâda** var. Bou Saada. N Algeria 35.13N 4.09E
38 I13 **Bouse Wash** ≈ Arizona, SW USA
105 N10 **Boussac** Creuse, C France 46.20N 2.12E
104 M16 **Boussens** Haute-Garonne, S France 43.10N 0.58E
80 H12 **Bousso** prev. Fort-Bretonnet. Chari-Baguirmi, S Chad 10.31N 16.45E
78 H9 **Boutilimit** Trarza, SW Mauritania 17.33N 14.42W
67 D21 **Bouvet Island** ◇ Norwegian dependency S Atlantic Ocean
79 U11 **Bouza** Tahoua, SW Niger 14.25N 6.09E
111 R10 **Bovec** Ger. Flitsch, It. Plezzo. NW Slovenia 46.21N 13.33E
100 J8 **Bovenkarspel** Noord-Holland, NW Netherlands 52.33N 5.03E
31 V5 **Bovey** Minnesota, N USA 47.18N 93.25W
34 M9 **Bovill** Idaho, NW USA 46.50N 116.24W
26 L4 **Bovina** Texas, SW USA 34.30N 102.52W
109 M17 **Bovino** Puglia, SE Italy 41.14N 15.19E
63 C17 **Bovril** Entre Ríos, E Argentina 31.24S 59.25W
30 L2 **Bowbells** North Dakota, N USA 48.48N 102.15W
9 Q16 **Bow City** Alberta, SW Canada 50.27N 112.16W
31 O8 **Bowdle** South Dakota, N USA 45.27N 99.39W
189 X6 **Bowen** Queensland, NE Australia 20.00S 148.10E
198 B4 **Bowers Ridge** undersea feature S Bering Sea
15 Jj4 **Bowes Point** headland Nunavut, N Canada 67.46N 101.51W
27 S5 **Bowie** Texas, SW USA 33.33N 97.51W
9 R17 **Bow Island** Alberta, SW Canada 49.52N 111.24W
Bowkān see Būkān
22 J7 **Bowling Green** Kentucky, S USA 36.59N 86.26W
29 V3 **Bowling Green** Missouri, C USA 39.20N 91.12W
33 R11 **Bowling Green** Ohio, N USA 41.22N 83.40W
23 W5 **Bowling Green** Virginia, NE USA 38.01N 77.20W
30 J6 **Bowman** North Dakota, N USA 46.10N 103.25W
16 N3 **Bowman Bay** bay NW Atlantic Ocean
204 I5 **Bowman Coast** physical region Antarctica
30 J7 **Bowman-Haley Lake** ▣ North Dakota, N USA
205 Z11 **Bowman Island** island Antarctica
Bowo see Bomi
191 S9 **Bowral** New South Wales, SE Australia 34.29S 150.28E
194 K14 **Bowutu Mountains** ▲▲ C PNG
85 I16 **Bowwood** Southern, S Zambia 17.09S 26.16E
30 I12 **Box Butte Reservoir** ▣ Nebraska, C USA
30 J10 **Box Elder** South Dakota, N USA 44.06N 103.04W
97 M18 **Boxholm** Östergötland, S Sweden 58.12N 15.04E
Bo Xian/Boxian see Bozhou
167 Q4 **Boxing** Shandong, E China 37.06N 118.05E
101 L14 **Boxmeer** Noord-Brabant, SE Netherlands 51.39N 5.57E
101 J14 **Boxtel** Noord-Brabant, S Netherlands 51.36N 5.19E
142 J10 **Boyabat** Sinop, N Turkey 41.27N 34.45E
56 F9 **Boyacá** off. Departamento de Boyacá. ❖ province C Colombia
119 O4 **Boyarka** Kyyivs'ka Oblast', N Ukraine 50.19N 30.19E
24 H7 **Boyce** Louisiana, S USA 31.23N 92.40W
35 U11 **Boyd** Montana, NW USA 45.27N 109.03W
27 S6 **Boyd** Texas, SW USA 33.01N 97.33W
23 V8 **Boydton** Virginia, NE USA 36.40N 78.24W
Boyer Ahmadī va Kohkīlūyeh see Kohkīlūyeh va Būyer Aḩmadī
31 T13 **Boyer River** ≈ Iowa, C USA
23 W8 **Boykins** Virginia, NE USA 36.35N 77.11W
9 Q13 **Boyle** Alberta, SW Canada 54.38N 112.45W
99 D16 **Boyle** Ir. Mainistirna Búille. C Ireland 53.58N 8.18W
99 F17 **Boyne** Ir. An Bhóinn. ≈ E Ireland
33 Q5 **Boyne City** Michigan, N USA 45.13N 85.00W
25 Z14 **Boynton Beach** Florida, SE USA 26.31N 80.04W
153 O13 **Boysun** Rus. Baysun. Surkhondaryo Viloyati, S Uzbekistan 38.13N 67.07E
Bozau see Întorsura Buzăului
142 B12 **Bozcaada** island Çanakkale, NW Turkey
142 C14 **Boz Dağları** ▲▲ W Turkey
35 S11 **Bozeman** Montana, NW USA 45.40N 111.02W
Bozen see Bolzano
81 J16 **Bozene** Equateur, NW Dem. Rep. Congo 2.55N 19.15E
167 P7 **Bozhou** var. Boxian, Bo Xian. Anhui, E China 33.49N 115.49E
142 H16 **Bozkır** Konya, S Turkey 37.10N 32.15E
142 K13 **Bozok Yaylası** plateau C Turkey
81 H14 **Bozoum** Ouham-Pendé, W Central African Republic 6.17N 16.26E
143 N16 **Bozova** Sanlıurfa, S Turkey 37.22N 38.33E
Bozrah see Buşrá ash Shām
142 E12 **Bozüyük** Bilecik, NW Turkey 39.55N 30.01E
108 B9 **Bra** Piemonte, NW Italy 44.42N 7.51E
204 G4 **Brabant Island** island Antarctica
101 I20 **Brabant Wallon** ❖ province C Belgium
115 F15 **Brač** var. Brach, It. Brazza; anc. Brattia. island S Croatia
Bracara Augusta see Braga
109 H15 **Bracciano** Lazio, C Italy 42.04N 12.12E
109 H14 **Bracciano, Lago di** ◎ C Italy
12 H13 **Bracebridge** Ontario, S Canada 45.01N 79.19W
Brach see Brač
95 G17 **Bräcke** Jämtland, C Sweden 62.42N 15.30E
27 P12 **Brackettville** Texas, SW USA 29.18N 100.25W
99 N22 **Bracknell** S England, UK 51.25N 0.46W
63 K14 **Braço do Norte** Santa Catarina, S Brazil 28.16S 49.11W
118 G11 **Brad** Hung. Brád. Hunedoara, SW Romania 45.52N 23.00E
109 N18 **Bradano** ≈ S Italy
25 V13 **Bradenton** Florida, SE USA 27.30N 82.34W
12 H14 **Bradford** Ontario, S Canada 44.09N 79.34W
99 L17 **Bradford** N England, UK 53.48N 1.45W
29 W10 **Bradford** Arkansas, C USA 35.25N 91.27W
20 D12 **Bradford** Pennsylvania, NE USA 41.57N 78.38W
29 T15 **Bradley** Arkansas, C USA 33.06N 93.39W
27 P7 **Bradshaw** Texas, SW USA 32.06N 99.52W
27 Q9 **Brady** Texas, SW USA 31.07N 99.22W
27 Q9 **Brady Creek** ≈ Texas, SW USA
98 J10 **Braemar** NE Scotland, UK 57.12N 2.52W
118 K8 **Brăeşti** Botoşani, NW Romania 47.50N 26.26E
106 G5 **Braga** anc. Bracara Augusta. Braga, NW Portugal 41.31N 8.25W
106 G5 **Braga** ❖ district N Portugal
118 J15 **Bragadiru** Teleorman, S Romania 43.43N 25.32E
63 C20 **Bragado** Buenos Aires, E Argentina 35.10S 60.28W
106 J5 **Bragança** Eng. Braganza; anc. Julio Briga. Bragança, NE Portugal 41.46N 6.46W
106 I5 **Bragança** ❖ district N Portugal
62 N9 **Bragança Paulista** São Paulo, S Brazil 22.55S 46.30W
Braganza see Bragança
Bragin see Brahin
31 V7 **Braham** Minnesota, N USA 45.43N 93.10W
Brahe see Brda
Brahestad see Raahe
121 O20 **Brahin** Rus. Bragin. Homyel'skaya Voblasts', SE Belarus 51.46N 30.16E
159 U15 **Brahmanbaria** Chittagong, E Bangladesh 23.58N 91.04E
160 O12 **Brāhmani** ≈ E India
160 N13 **Brahmapur** Orissa, E India 19.21N 84.51E
133 S10 **Brahmaputra** var. Padma, Tsangpo, Ben. Jamuna, Chin. Yarlung Zangbo Jiang, Ind. Bramaputra, Dihang, Siang. ≈ S Asia
99 H19 **Braich y Pwll** headland NW Wales, UK 52.47N 4.46W
191 R10 **Braidwood** New South Wales, SE Australia 35.26S 149.48E
32 M11 **Braidwood** Illinois, N USA 41.16N 88.12W
118 M13 **Brăila** Brăila, E Romania 45.17N 27.57E
118 L13 **Brăila** ❖ county SE Romania
101 G19 **Braine-l'Alleud** Brabant Wallon, C Belgium 50.40N 4.22E
101 F19 **Braine-le-Comte** Hainaut, SW Belgium 50.37N 4.07E
31 U6 **Brainerd** Minnesota, N USA 46.22N 94.10W
101 J19 **Braives** Liège, E Belgium 50.37N 5.09E
85 H23 **Brak** ≈ C South Africa
Brak see Birāk
101 E18 **Brakel** Oost-Vlaanderen, SW Belgium 50.50N 3.48E
100 J13 **Brakel** Gelderland, C Netherlands 51.49N 5.05E
78 H9 **Brakna** ❖ region S Mauritania
97 J17 **Brålanda** Västra Götaland, S Sweden 58.32N 12.18E
Bramaputra see Brahmaputra
97 F23 **Bramming** Ribe, W Denmark 55.28N 8.42E
12 G15 **Brampton** Ontario, S Canada 43.42N 79.46W
102 F12 **Bramsche** Niedersachsen, NW Germany 52.25N 7.58E
118 J12 **Bran** Ger. Törzburg, Hung. Törcsvár. Braşov, S Romania 45.31N 25.23E
31 W8 **Branch** Minnesota, N USA 45.29N 92.57W
23 R14 **Branchville** South Carolina, SE USA 33.15N 80.49W
49 Y6 **Branco, Cabo** headland E Brazil 7.07S 34.45W
60 F11 **Branco, Rio** ≈ N Brazil
110 J8 **Brand** Vorarlberg, W Austria 47.07N 9.45E
85 B18 **Brandberg** ▲ NW Namibia 21.20S 14.22E
97 H14 **Brandbu** Oppland, S Norway 60.24N 10.30E
97 F22 **Brande** Ringkøbing, W Denmark 55.57N 9.07E
Brandebourg see Brandenburg
102 M12 **Brandenburg** var. Brandenburg an der Havel. Brandenburg, NE Germany 52.25N 12.34E
22 K5 **Brandenburg** Kentucky, S USA 37.58N 86.11W
102 N12 **Brandenburg** off. Freie und Hansestadt Hamburg, Fr. Brandebourg. ❖ state NE Germany
Brandenburg an der Havel see Brandenburg

◆ Country
● Country Capital
◇ Dependent Territory
○ Dependent Territory Capital
❖ Administrative Region
✈ International Airport
▲ Mountain
▲▲ Mountain Range
⛰ Volcano
≈ River
◎ Lake
▣ Reservoir

85 *I23* **Brandfort** Free State, C South Africa *28.42S 26.28E*
9 *W16* **Brandon** Manitoba, S Canada *49.49N 99.57W*
25 *V12* **Brandon** Florida, SE USA *27.56N 82.17W*
24 *L6* **Brandon** Mississippi, S USA *32.16N 90.01W*
99 *A20* **Brandon Mountain** *Ir.* Cnoc Bréanainn. ▲ SW Ireland *52.13N 10.16W*
Brandsen *see* Coronel Brandsen
97 *I14* **Brandval** Hedmark, S Norway *60.18N 12.01E*
85 *F24* **Brandvlei** Northern Cape, W South Africa *30.19S 20.31E*
25 *U9* **Branford** Florida, SE USA *29.57N 82.54W*
112 *K7* **Braniewo** *Ger.* Braunsberg. Warmińsko-Mazurskie, NE Poland *54.24N 19.49E*
204 *H3* **Bransfield Strait** *strait* Antarctica
39 *U8* **Branson** Colorado, C USA *37.01N 103.52W*
29 *T8* **Branson** Missouri, C USA *36.38N 93.13W*
12 *G16* **Brantford** Ontario, S Canada *43.04N 80.21W*
104 *L12* **Brantôme** Dordogne, SW France *45.21N 0.37E*
190 *L12* **Branxholme** Victoria, SE Australia *37.51S 141.48E*
Brasil *see* Brazil
61 *C16* **Brasiléia** Acre, W Brazil *10.58S 48.45W*
61 *K18* **Brasília** ● (Brazil) Distrito Federal, C Brazil *15.45S 47.57W*
Braslav *see* Braslaw
120 *J12* **Braslaw** *Pol.* Brasław, *Rus.* Braslav. Vitsyebskaya Voblasts', N Belarus *55.37N 27.01E*
118 *J12* **Braşov** *Ger.* Kronstadt, *Hung.* Brassó; *prev.* Oraşul Stalin. Braşov, C Romania *45.40N 25.34E*
118 *I12* **Braşov** ◈ *county* C Romania
176 *W7* **Bras, Pulau** *island* Kepulauan Mapia, E Indonesia
79 *U18* **Brass** Bayelsa, S Nigeria *4.19N 6.21E*
101 *H16* **Brasschaat** *var.* Brasschaet. Antwerpen, N Belgium *51.16N 4.30E*
Brasschaet *see* Brasschaat
175 *O4* **Brassey, Banjaran** *var.* Brassey Range. ▲▲ East Malaysia
Brassey Range *see* Brassey, Banjaran
Brassó *see* Braşov
25 *T1* **Brasstown Bald** ▲ Georgia, SE USA *34.52N 83.48W*
115 *K22* **Brataj** Vlorë, SW Albania *40.18N 19.37E*
116 *J10* **Bratan** *var.* Morozov. ▲ C Bulgaria *42.31N 25.08E*
113 *F21* **Bratislava** *Ger.* Pressburg, *Hung.* Pozsony. ● (Slovakia) Bratislavský Kraj, W Slovakia *48.10N 17.10E*
113 *H21* **Bratislavský Kraj** ◈ *region* W Slovakia
116 *H10* **Bratiya** ▲ C Bulgaria *42.36N 24.08E*
126 *J14* **Bratsk** Irkutskaya Oblast', C Russian Federation *56.19N 101.49E*
119 *Q8* **Brats'ke** Mykolayivs'ka Oblast', S Ukraine *47.52N 31.34E*
126 *J14* **Bratskoye Vodokhranilishche** *Eng.* Bratsk Reservoir. ⊠ S Russian Federation
Bratsk Reservoir *see* Bratskoye Vodokhranilishche
Brattia *see* Brač
96 *D9* **Brattvåg** Møre og Romsdal, S Norway *62.36N 6.21E*
114 *K12* **Bratunac** Republika Srpska, E Bosnia and Herzegovina *44.10N 19.21E*
116 *J10* **Bratya Daskalovi** *prev.* Grozdovo. Stara Zagora, C Bulgaria *42.13N 25.21E*
111 *U2* **Braunau** ≈ N Austria
Braunau *see* Braunau am Inn
111 *Q4* **Braunau am Inn** *var.* Braunau. Oberösterreich, N Austria *48.16N 13.03E*
Braunsberg *see* Braniewo
102 *J13* **Braunschweig** *Eng./Fr.* Brunswick. Niedersachsen, N Germany *52.16N 10.31E*
Brava *see* Baraawe
107 *Y6* **Brava, Costa** *coastal region* NE Spain
45 *V16* **Brava, Punta** *headland* E Panama *8.21N 78.22W*
97 *N17* **Bråviken** *inlet* S Sweden
58 *B10* **Bravo, Cerro** ▲ N Peru *5.33S 79.10W*
Bravo del Norte, Río/Bravo, Río *see* Grande, Rio
37 *X17* **Brawley** California, W USA *32.58N 115.31W*
99 *G18* **Bray** *Ir.* Bré. E Ireland *53.12N 6.06W*
61 *G16* **Brazil** *off.* Federative Republic of Brazil, *Port.* Repùblica Federativa do Brasil, *Sp.* Brasil; *prev.* United States of Brazil. ◆ *federal republic* South America
67 *K15* **Brazil Basin** *var.* Brazilian Basin, Brazil'skaya Kotlovina. *undersea feature* W Atlantic Ocean
Brazilian Basin *see* Brazil Basin
Brazilian Highlands *see* Central, Planalto
Brazil'skaya Kotlovina *see* Brazil Basin
27 *U10* **Brazos River** ≈ Texas, SW USA
176 *Yy13* **Brazza** ≈ Papua, E Indonesia
Brazza *see* Brač
81 *G21* **Brazzaville** ● (Congo) Capital District, S Congo *4.13S 15.13E*
81 *G21* **Brazzaville** ✈ Le Pool, S Congo *4.15S 15.15E*
114 *J11* **Brčko** Republika Srpska, NE Bosnia and Herzegovina *44.52N 18.49E*
112 *H8* **Brda** *Ger.* Brahe. ≈ N Poland
Bré *see* Bray
193 *A23* **Breaksea Sound** *sound* South Island, NZ
192 *L4* **Bream Bay** *bay* North Island, NZ
192 *L4* **Bream Head** *headland* North Island, NZ *35.51S 174.35E*
Bréanainn, Cnoc *see* Brandon Mountain
47 *S6* **Brea, Punta** *headland* W Puerto Rico *17.56N 66.55W*
24 *I9* **Breaux Bridge** Louisiana, S USA *30.16N 91.54W*
118 *J13* **Breaza** Prahova, SE Romania *45.06N 25.44E*
174 *K14* **Brebes** Jawa, C Indonesia *6.54S 109.00E*
98 *K10* **Brechin** E Scotland, UK *56.44N 2.38W*
101 *H15* **Brecht** Antwerpen, N Belgium *51.21N 4.32E*
39 *S4* **Breckenridge** Colorado, C USA *39.28N 106.02W*
31 *R6* **Breckenridge** Minnesota, N USA *46.15N 96.35W*
27 *R6* **Breckenridge** Texas, SW USA *32.45N 98.54W*
99 *J21* **Brecknock** *cultural region* SE Wales, UK
65 *G25* **Brecknock, Península** *headland* S Chile *54.39S 71.48W*
113 *G19* **Břeclav** *Ger.* Lundenburg. Brněnský Kraj, SE Czech Republic *49.04N 16.51E*
99 *J21* **Brecon** E Wales, UK *51.57N 3.26W*
99 *J21* **Brecon Beacons** ▲▲ S Wales, UK
101 *I14* **Breda** Noord-Brabant, S Netherlands *51.34N 4.46E*
97 *K20* **Bredaryd** Jönköping, S Sweden *57.10N 13.45E*
85 *F26* **Bredasdorp** Western Cape, SW South Africa *34.28S 20.03E*
95 *H16* **Bredbyn** Västernorrland, N Sweden *63.28N 18.04E*
125 *E13* **Bredy** Chelyabinskaya Oblast', C Russian Federation *52.23N 60.24E*
101 *K17* **Bree** Limburg, NE Belgium *51.07N 5.36E*
69 *T15* **Breede** ≈ S South Africa
100 *I7* **Breezand** Noord-Holland, NW Netherlands *52.52N 4.47E*
115 *P18* **Bregalnica** ≈ E FYR Macedonia
110 *I6* **Bregenz** *anc.* Brigantium. Vorarlberg, W Austria *47.31N 9.44E*
110 *J7* **Bregenzer Wald** ▲▲ W Austria
116 *F6* **Bregovo** Vidin, NW Bulgaria *44.07N 22.40E*
104 *H5* **Bréhat, Île de** *island* NW France
94 *H2* **Breidhafjördhur** *bay* W Iceland
94 *L3* **Breidhdalsvík** Austurland, E Iceland *64.48N 14.02W*
110 *H9* **Breil** *Ger.* Brigels. Graubünden, S Switzerland *46.46N 9.04E*
94 *J8* **Breivikbotn** Finnmark, N Norway *70.36N 22.19E*
96 *I9* **Brekken** Sør-Trøndelag, S Norway *62.39N 11.49E*
96 *G7* **Brekstad** Sør-Trøndelag, S Norway *63.42N 9.40E*
96 *B10* **Bremangerlandet** *island* S Norway
Brême *see* Bremen
102 *H11* **Bremen** *Fr.* Brême. Bremen, NW Germany *53.05N 8.48E*
25 *R3* **Bremen** Georgia, SE USA *33.43N 85.09W*
33 *O11* **Bremen** Indiana, N USA *41.24N 86.07W*
102 *H10* **Bremen** *off.* Freie Hansestadt Bremen, *Fr.* Brême. ◈ *state* N Germany
102 *G9* **Bremerhaven** Bremen, NW Germany *53.33N 8.34E*
Bremersdorp *see* Manzini
34 *G8* **Bremerton** Washington, NW USA *47.34N 122.37W*
102 *H10* **Bremervörde** Niedersachsen, NW Germany *53.29N 9.06E*
27 *U9* **Bremond** Texas, SW USA *31.10N 96.40W*
27 *U10* **Brenham** Texas, SW USA *30.10N 96.24W*
110 *M8* **Brenner** Tirol, W Austria *47.10N 11.51E*
Brenner, Col du/Brennero, Passo del *see* Brenner Pass
110 *M8* **Brenner Pass** *var.* Brenner Sattel, *Fr.* Col du Brenner, *Ger.* Brennerpass, *It.* Passo del Brennero. *pass* Austria/Italy *47.00N 11.29E*
Brenner Sattel *see* Brenner Pass
110 *G10* **Brenno** ≈ SW Switzerland
108 *F7* **Breno** Lombardia, N Italy *45.58N 10.18E*
25 *O5* **Brent** Alabama, S USA *32.54N 87.10W*
108 *H7* **Brenta** ≈ NE Italy
99 *P21* **Brentwood** E England, UK *51.38N 0.21E*
20 *L14* **Brentwood** Long Island, New York, NE USA *40.46N 73.12W*
108 *F7* **Brescia** *anc.* Brixia. Lombardia, N Italy *45.33N 10.13E*
101 *D15* **Breskens** Zeeland, SW Netherlands *51.24N 3.33E*
Breslau *see* Dolnośląskie
108 *H5* **Bressanone** *Ger.* Brixen. Trentino-Alto Adige, N Italy *46.43N 11.41E*
98 *M2* **Bressay** *island* NE Scotland, UK
104 *K9* **Bressuire** Deux-Sèvres, W France *46.50N 0.29W*
121 *F20* **Brest** *Pol.* Brześć nad Bugiem, *Rus.* Brest-Litovsk; *prev.* Brześć Litewski. Brestskaya Voblasts', SW Belarus *52.06N 23.42E*
104 *F5* **Brest** Finistère, NW France *48.24N 4.30W*
Brest-Litovsk *see* Brest
114 *A10* **Brestova** Istra, NW Croatia *45.09N 14.13E*
Brestskaya Oblast' *see* Brestskaya Voblasts'
121 *G19* **Brestskaya Voblasts'** *prev. Rus.* Brestskaya Oblast'. ◈ *province* SW Belarus
104 *G6* **Bretagne** *Eng.* Brittany; *Lat.* Britannia Minor. ◈ *region* NW France
118 *G12* **Bretea-Română** *Hung.* Oláhbrettye; *prev.* Bretea-Romînă. Hunedoara, W Romania *45.39N 23.00E*
Bretea-Romînă *see* Bretea-Română
105 *O3* **Breteuil** Oise, N France *49.37N 2.18E*
104 *I10* **Breton, Pertuis** *inlet* W France
24 *L10* **Breton Sound** *sound* Louisiana, S USA
192 *K2* **Brett, Cape** *headland* North Island, NZ *35.11S 174.21E*
103 *G21* **Bretten** Baden-Württemberg, SW Germany *49.01N 8.42E*
101 *K15* **Breugel** Noord-Brabant, S Netherlands *51.30N 5.30E*
108 *B6* **Breuil-Cervinia** *It.* Cervinia. Valle d'Aosta, NW Italy *45.57N 7.37E*
100 *I11* **Breukelen** Utrecht, C Netherlands *52.11N 5.01E*
23 *P10* **Brevard** North Carolina, SE USA *35.13N 82.43W*
40 *L9* **Brevig Mission** Alaska, USA *65.19N 166.29W*
97 *G16* **Brevik** Telemark, S Norway *59.03N 9.40E*
191 *P5* **Brewarrina** New South Wales, SE Australia *30.01S 146.50E*
21 *R6* **Brewer** Maine, NE USA *44.46N 68.44W*
31 *T11* **Brewster** Minnesota, N USA *43.43N 95.28W*
31 *N14* **Brewster** Nebraska, C USA *41.54N 99.52W*
33 *U12* **Brewster** Ohio, N USA *40.42N 81.36W*
191 *O8* **Brewster, Lake** ◎ New South Wales, SE Australia
25 *P7* **Brewton** Alabama, S USA *31.06N 87.04W*
Brezhnev *see* Naberezhnyye Chelny
111 *W12* **Brežice** *Ger.* Rann. E Slovenia *45.54N 15.35E*
116 *G9* **Breznik** Pernik, W Bulgaria *42.45N 22.54E*
113 *K19* **Brezno** *Ger.* Bries, Briesen, *Hung.* Breznóbánya; *prev.* Brezno nad Hronom. Banskobystrický Kraj, C Slovakia *48.49N 19.40E*
Breznóbánya/Brezno nad Hronom *see* Brezno
118 *I12* **Brezoi** Vâlcea, SW Romania *45.18N 24.15E*
116 *J10* **Brezovo** *prev.* Abrashlare. Plovdiv, C Bulgaria *42.19N 25.05E*
81 *K14* **Bria** Haute-Kotto, C Central African Republic *6.30N 22.00E*
105 *U13* **Briançon** *anc.* Brigantio. Hautes-Alpes, SE France *44.55N 6.37E*
38 *K7* **Brian Head** ▲ Utah, W USA *37.40N 112.49W*
105 *O7* **Briare** Loiret, C France *47.35N 2.46E*
191 *V2* **Bribie Island** *island* Queensland, E Australia
45 *O14* **Bribrí** Limón, E Costa Rica *9.37N 82.51W*
118 *L8* **Briceni** *var.* Brinceni, *Rus.* Brichany. N Moldova *48.21N 27.02E*
Bricgstow *see* Bristol
Brichany *see* Briceni
101 *M24* **Bridel** Luxembourg, C Luxembourg *49.40N 6.03E*
99 *J22* **Bridgend** S Wales, UK *51.30N 3.37W*
12 *I14* **Bridgenorth** Ontario, SE Canada *44.21N 78.22W*
25 *Q1* **Bridgeport** Alabama, S USA *34.57N 85.42W*
37 *R8* **Bridgeport** California, W USA *38.14N 119.13W*
20 *L13* **Bridgeport** Connecticut, NE USA *41.10N 73.12W*
33 *N15* **Bridgeport** Illinois, N USA *38.42N 87.45W*
30 *J14* **Bridgeport** Nebraska, C USA *41.37N 103.07W*
27 *S6* **Bridgeport** Texas, SW USA *33.12N 97.45W*
23 *S3* **Bridgeport** West Virginia, NE USA *39.17N 80.15W*
27 *S5* **Bridgeport, Lake** ⊠ Texas, SW USA
35 *U11* **Bridger** Montana, NW USA *45.16N 108.55W*
20 *I17* **Bridgeton** New Jersey, NE USA *39.24N 75.10W*
188 *J14* **Bridgetown** Western Australia *34.01S 116.07E*
47 *Y14* **Bridgetown** ● (Barbados) SW Barbados *13.05N 59.36W*
191 *P17* **Bridgewater** Tasmania, SE Australia *42.47S 147.15E*
11 *P16* **Bridgewater** Nova Scotia, SE Canada *44.19N 64.30W*
21 *P12* **Bridgewater** Massachusetts, NE USA *41.59N 70.58W*
31 *Q11* **Bridgewater** South Dakota, N USA *43.33N 97.30W*
23 *U5* **Bridgewater** Virginia, NE USA *38.22N 78.58W*
21 *P8* **Bridgton** Maine, NE USA *44.04N 70.43W*
99 *K23* **Bridgwater** SW England, UK *51.08N 3.00W*
99 *K22* **Bridgwater Bay** *bay* SW England, UK
99 *O16* **Bridlington** E England, UK *54.04N 0.12W*
99 *O16* **Bridlington Bay** *bay* E England, UK
191 *P15* **Bridport** Tasmania, SE Australia *41.03S 147.26E*
99 *K24* **Bridport** S England, UK *50.43N 2.43W*
105 *O5* **Brie** *cultural region* N France
Brieg *see* Brzeg
Briel *see* Brielle
100 *G12* **Brielle** *var.* Briel, Bril, *Eng.* The Brill. Zuid-Holland, SW Netherlands *51.54N 4.10E*
110 *E9* **Brienz** Bern, C Switzerland *46.45N 8.00E*
110 *E9* **Brienzer See** ◎ SW Switzerland
Bries/Briesen *see* Brezno
Brietzig *see* Brzesko
105 *S4* **Briey** Meurthe-et-Moselle, NE France *49.15N 5.57E*
110 *E10* **Brig** *Fr.* Brigue, *It.* Briga. Valais, SW Switzerland *46.19N 8.00E*
Briga *see* Brig
103 *G24* **Brigach** ≈ S Germany
20 *K17* **Brigantine** New Jersey, NE USA *39.23N 74.21W*
Brigantio *see* Briançon
Brigantium *see* Bregenz
Brigels *see* Breil
27 *S9* **Briggs** Texas, SW USA *30.52N 97.55W*
38 *L1* **Brigham City** Utah, W USA *41.30N 112.00W*
12 *J15* **Brighton** Ontario, SE Canada *44.01N 77.44W*
99 *O23* **Brighton** SE England, UK *50.49N 0.10W*
39 *T4* **Brighton** Colorado, C USA *39.58N 104.46W*
32 *K15* **Brighton** Illinois, N USA *39.01N 90.09W*
105 *T16* **Brignoles** Var, W France *43.25N 6.03E*
Brigue *see* Brig
107 *O7* **Brihuega** Castilla-La Mancha, C Spain *40.45N 2.52W*
114 *A10* **Brijuni** *It.* Brioni. *island group* NW Croatia
78 *G12* **Brikama** W Gambia *13.13N 16.37W*
Bril *see* Brielle
Brill, The *see* Brielle
103 *G15* **Brilon** Nordrhein-Westfalen, W Germany *51.24N 8.34E*
Brinceni *see* Briceni
109 *Q18* **Brindisi** *anc.* Brundisium, Brundusium. Puglia, SE Italy *40.39N 17.55E*
29 *W11* **Brinkley** Arkansas, C USA *34.53N 91.11W*
Brioni *see* Brijuni
105 *P12* **Brioude** *anc.* Brivas. Haute-Loire, C France *45.18N 3.22E*
Briovera *see* St-Lô
191 *U2* **Brisbane** *state capital* Queensland, E Australia *27.30S 153.00E*
191 *V2* **Brisbane** ✈ Queensland, E Australia *27.30S 153.00E*
27 *P2* **Briscoe** Texas, SW USA *35.34N 100.17W*
108 *H10* **Brisighella** Emilia-Romagna, C Italy *44.12N 11.45E*
110 *G11* **Brissago** Ticino, S Switzerland *46.07N 8.40E*
99 *K22* **Bristol** *anc.* Bricgstow. SW England, UK *51.27N 2.34W*
20 *M12* **Bristol** Connecticut, NE USA *41.40N 72.56W*
25 *R9* **Bristol** Florida, SE USA *30.25N 84.58W*
21 *N9* **Bristol** New Hampshire, NE USA *43.34N 71.42W*
31 *Q8* **Bristol** South Dakota, N USA *45.18N 97.45W*
23 *P8* **Bristol** Tennessee, S USA *36.36N 82.11W*
20 *M8* **Bristol** Vermont, NE USA *44.07N 73.00W*
41 *N14* **Bristol Bay** *bay* Alaska, USA
99 *I22* **Bristol Channel** *inlet* England/Wales, UK
37 *W14* **Bristol Lake** ◎ California, W USA
29 *P10* **Bristow** Oklahoma, C USA *35.49N 96.23W*
88 *C10* **Britain** *var.* Great Britain. *island* UK
Britannia Minor *see* Bretagne
8 *L12* **British Columbia** *Fr.* Colombie-Britannique. ◈ *province* SW Canada
British Guiana *see* Guyana
British Honduras *see* Belize
181 *Q7* **British Indian Ocean Territory** ◇ *UK dependent territory* C Indian Ocean
88 *B9* **British Isles** *island group* NW Europe
8 *I1* **British Mountains** ▲▲ Yukon Territory, NW Canada
British North Borneo *see* Sabah
British Solomon Islands Protectorate *see* Solomon Islands
47 *S8* **British Virgin Islands** *var.* Virgin Islands. ◇ *UK dependent territory* E West Indies
85 *J21* **Brits** North-West, N South Africa *25.39S 27.46E*
85 *H24* **Britstown** Northern Cape, W South Africa *30.36S 23.30E*
12 *F12* **Britt** Ontario, S Canada *45.46N 80.34W*
31 *V12* **Britt** Iowa, C USA *43.06N 93.48W*
Brittany *see* Bretagne
31 *Q7* **Britton** South Dakota, N USA *45.47N 97.45W*
Briva Curretia *see* Brive-la-Gaillarde
Briva Isarae *see* Pontoise
Brivas *see* Brioude
Brive *see* Brive-la-Gaillarde
104 *M12* **Brive-la-Gaillarde** *prev.* Brive, *anc.* Briva Curretia. Corrèze, C France *45.09N 1.31E*
107 *O4* **Briviesca** Castilla-León, N Spain *42.33N 3.19W*
Brixen *see* Bressanone
Brixia *see* Brescia
151 *S15* **Brlik** *prev.* Novotroickoje, Novotroitskoye. Zhambyl, SE Kazakhstan *43.39N 73.45E*
113 *G19* **Brněnský Kraj** ◈ *region* SE Czech Republic
113 *G18* **Brno** *Ger.* Brünn. Brněnský Kraj, SE Czech Republic *49.10N 16.35E*
98 *G7* **Broad Bay** *bay* NW Scotland, UK
27 *X8* **Broaddus** Texas, SW USA *31.18N 94.16W*
191 *O12* **Broadford** Victoria, SE Australia *37.07S 145.04E*
98 *G9* **Broadford** N Scotland, UK *57.14N 5.54W*
98 *J13* **Broad Law** ▲ S Scotland, UK *55.30N 3.22W*
25 *U3* **Broad River** ≈ Georgia, SE USA
23 *N8* **Broad River** ≈ North Carolina/South Carolina, SE USA
189 *Y8* **Broadsound Range** ▲▲ Queensland, E Australia
35 *X11* **Broadus** Montana, NW USA *45.28N 105.22W*
23 *U4* **Broadway** Virginia, NE USA *38.36N 78.48W*
120 *E9* **Brocēni** Saldus, SW Latvia *56.41N 22.31E*
9 *U11* **Brochet** Manitoba, C Canada *57.55N 101.40W*
9 *U10* **Brochet, Lac** ◎ Manitoba, C Canada
13 *S5* **Brochet, Lac au** ◎ Quebec, SE Canada
103 *K14* **Brocken** ▲ C Germany *51.48N 10.38E*
21 *O12* **Brockton** Massachusetts, NE USA *42.04N 71.01W*
12 *L14* **Brockville** Ontario, SE Canada *44.36N 75.42W*
20 *D13* **Brockway** Pennsylvania, NE USA *41.14N 78.45W*
Brod/Bród *see* Slavonski Brod
15 *Kk1* **Brodeur Peninsula** *peninsula* Baffin Island, Nunavut, NE Canada
98 *H13* **Brodick** W Scotland, UK *55.34N 5.09W*
Brod na Savi *see* Slavonski Brod
112 *K9* **Brodnica** *Ger.* Buddenbrock. Kujawski-pomorskie, C Poland *53.15N 19.22E*
114 *G10* **Brod-Posavina** *off.* Brodsko-Posavska Županija. ◈ *province* NE Croatia
118 *J5* **Brody** L'vivs'ka Oblast', NW Ukraine *50.04N 25.07E*
97 *G22* **Brædstrup** Vejle, C Denmark *55.58N 9.37E*
100 *I10* **Broek-in-Waterland** Noord-Holland, C Netherlands *52.27N 4.58E*
34 *L13* **Brogan** Oregon, NW USA *44.15N 117.34W*
112 *N10* **Brok** Mazowieckie, C Poland *52.42N 21.53E*
29 *P9* **Broken Arrow** Oklahoma, C USA *36.03N 95.47W*
191 *T9* **Broken Bay** *bay* New South Wales, SE Australia
31 *N15* **Broken Bow** Nebraska, C USA *41.24N 99.38W*
29 *R13* **Broken Bow** Oklahoma, C USA *34.01N 94.44W*
29 *R12* **Broken Bow Lake** ⊠ Oklahoma, C USA
190 *L6* **Broken Hill** New South Wales, SE Australia *31.58S 141.27E*
181 *S10* **Broken Ridge** *undersea feature* S Indian Ocean
194 *H10* **Broken Water Bay** *bay* W Bismarck Sea
57 *W10* **Brokopondo** Brokopondo, NE Suriname *05.04N 55.00W*
57 *W10* **Brokopondo** ◈ *district* C Suriname
Bromberg *see* Bydgoszcz
97 *L22* **Bromölla** Skåne, S Sweden *56.04N 14.28E*
99 *L20* **Bromsgrove** W England, UK *52.19N 2.03W*
97 *G20* **Brønderslev** Nordjylland, N Denmark *57.16N 9.58E*
108 *D8* **Broni** Lombardia, N Italy *45.04N 9.18E*
8 *K11* **Bronlund Peak** ▲ British Columbia, W Canada *57.27N 126.43W*
95 *F14* **Brønnøysund** Nordland, C Norway *65.28N 12.13E*
25 *V10* **Bronson** Florida, SE USA *29.25N 82.38W*
33 *Q11* **Bronson** Michigan, N USA *41.52N 85.11W*
27 *X8* **Bronson** Texas, SW USA *31.20N 94.00W*
109 *L24* **Bronte** Sicilia, Italy, C Mediterranean Sea *37.46N 14.49E*
27 *P8* **Bronte** Texas, SW USA *31.53N 100.17W*
27 *Y9* **Brookeland** Texas, SW USA *31.05N 93.57W*
179 *O15* **Brooke's Point** Palawan, W Philippines *8.54N 117.54E*
29 *T3* **Brookfield** Missouri, C USA *39.46N 93.04W*
24 *K7* **Brookhaven** Mississippi, S USA *31.34N 90.26W*
34 *E16* **Brookings** Oregon, NW USA *42.03N 124.16W*
31 *R10* **Brookings** South Dakota, N USA *44.15N 96.46W*
31 *W14* **Brooklyn** Iowa, C USA *41.43N 92.27W*
31 *U8* **Brooklyn Park** Minnesota, N USA *45.06N 93.18W*
23 *U7* **Brookneal** Virginia, NE USA *37.03N 78.56W*
9 *R16* **Brooks** Alberta, SW Canada *50.34N 111.54W*
27 *V11* **Brookshire** Texas, SW USA *29.47N 95.57W*
40 *L8* **Brooks Mountain** ▲ Alaska, USA *65.31N 167.24W*
40 *M11* **Brooks Range** ▲▲ Alaska, USA
33 *O12* **Brookston** Indiana, N USA *40.34N 86.53W*
25 *V11* **Brooksville** Florida, SE USA *28.33N 82.23W*
25 *N4* **Brooksville** Mississippi, S USA *33.13N 88.34W*
188 *J13* **Brookton** Western Australia *32.24S 117.04E*
33 *Q14* **Brookville** Indiana, N USA *39.25N 85.00W*
20 *D13* **Brookville** Pennsylvania, NE USA *41.07N 79.05W*
33 *Q14* **Brookville Lake** ⊠ Indiana, N USA
188 *K5* **Broome** Western Australia *17.58S 122.15E*
39 *S4* **Broomfield** Colorado, C USA *39.55N 105.05W*
Broos *see* Orăştie
98 *J7* **Brora** N Scotland, UK *57.58N 4.00W*
98 *I7* **Brora** ≈ N Scotland, UK
97 *F23* **Brørup** Ribe, W Denmark *55.28N 9.01E*
97 *L23* **Brösarp** Skåne, S Sweden *55.43N 14.10E*
118 *J9* **Broşteni** Suceava, NE Romania *47.13N 25.43E*
104 *M6* **Brou** Eure-et-Loir, C France *48.12N 1.10E*
Broucsella *see* Brussel/Bruxelles
Broughton Bay *see* Tongjosŏn-man
16 *O1* **Broughton Island** Nunavut, NE Canada *67.34N 63.55W*
144 *G7* **Broummâna** C Lebanon *33.53N 35.39E*
24 *I9* **Broussard** Louisiana, S USA *30.09N 91.57W*
100 *E13* **Brouwersdam** *dam* SW Netherlands *51.46N 3.51E*
100 *E13* **Brouwershaven** Zeeland, SW Netherlands *51.44N 3.50E*
119 *P4* **Brovary** Kyyivs'ka Oblast', N Ukraine *50.30N 30.43E*
97 *G20* **Brovst** Nordjylland, N Denmark *57.06N 9.31E*
33 *S8* **Brown City** Michigan, N USA *43.12N 82.50W*
26 *M6* **Brownfield** Texas, SW USA *33.10N 102.16W*
35 *Q7* **Browning** Montana, NW USA *48.33N 113.00W*
35 *R6* **Brown, Mount** ▲ Montana, NW USA *48.52N 111.08W*
194 *K15* **Brown River** ≈ S PNG
(0) *M9* **Browns Bank** *undersea feature* NW Atlantic Ocean
33 *O14* **Brownsburg** Indiana, N USA *39.50N 86.24W*
20 *J16* **Browns Mills** New Jersey, NE USA *39.58N 74.33W*
46 *J12* **Browns Town** C Jamaica *18.28N 77.22W*
33 *P15* **Brownstown** Indiana, N USA *38.52N 86.02W*
31 *R8* **Browns Valley** Minnesota, N USA *45.36N 96.49W*
22 *K7* **Brownsville** Kentucky, S USA *37.09N 86.13W*
22 *F9* **Brownsville** Tennessee, S USA *35.34N 89.15W*
27 *T17* **Brownsville** Texas, SW USA *25.55N 97.28W*
57 *W10* **Brownsweg** Brokopondo, C Suriname
31 *U9* **Brownton** Minnesota, N USA *44.43N 94.21W*
21 *R5* **Brownville Junction** Maine, NE USA *45.20N 69.04W*
27 *R8* **Brownwood** Texas, SW USA *31.41N 98.59W*
27 *R8* **Brownwood Lake** ⊠ Texas, SW USA
106 *I9* **Brozas** Extremadura, W Spain *39.37N 6.48W*
121 *M18* **Brozha** Mahilyowskaya Voblasts', E Belarus *52.57N 29.07E*
105 *O2* **Bruay-en-Artois** Pas-de-Calais, N France *50.31N 2.30E*
105 *P2* **Bruay-sur-l'Escaut** Nord, N France *50.24N 3.33E*
12 *F13* **Bruce Peninsula** *peninsula* Ontario, S Canada
22 *H9* **Bruceton** Tennessee, S USA *36.02N 88.14W*
27 *T9* **Bruceville** Texas, SW USA *31.17N 97.15W*
103 *G21* **Bruchsal** Baden-Württemberg, SW Germany *49.07N 8.34E*
111 *Q7* **Bruck** Salzburg, NW Austria *47.18N 12.51E*
Bruck *see* Bruck an der Mur
111 *Y4* **Bruck an der Leitha** Niederösterreich, NE Austria *48.02N 16.47E*
111 *V7* **Bruck an der Mur** *var.* Bruck. Steiermark, C Austria *47.26N 15.13E*
103 *M24* **Bruckmühl** Bayern, SE Germany *47.52N 11.54E*
173 *Dd3* **Brueuh, Pulau** *island* NW Indonesia
Bruges *see* Brugge
110 *F6* **Brugg** Aargau, NW Switzerland *47.28N 8.13E*
101 *C16* **Brugge** *Fr.* Bruges. West-Vlaanderen, NW Belgium *51.13N 3.13E*
111 *R9* **Bruggen** Kärnten, S Austria *46.46N 13.13E*
103 *E16* **Brühl** Nordrhein-Westfalen, W Germany *50.49N 6.54E*
101 *F14* **Bruinisse** Zeeland, SW Netherlands *51.40N 4.04E*
174 *L5* **Bruit, Pulau** *island* East Malaysia
12 *K10* **Brûlé, Lac** ◎ Quebec, SE Canada
32 *M4* **Brule River** ≈ Michigan/Wisconsin, N USA
101 *H23* **Brûly** Namur, S Belgium *49.55N 4.31E*
61 *N17* **Brumado** Bahia, E Brazil *14.13S 41.37W*
100 *M11* **Brummen** Gelderland, E Netherlands *52.04N 6.10E*
96 *H13* **Brumunddal** Hedmark, S Norway *60.52N 10.55E*
25 *Q6* **Brundidge** Alabama, S USA *31.43N 85.49W*
Brundisium/Brundusium *see* Brindisi
35 *N15* **Bruneau River** ≈ Idaho, NW USA
Bruneck *see* Brunico
174 *Mm4* **Brunei** *off.* Sultanate of Brunei, *Mal.* Negara Brunei Darussalam. ◆ *monarchy* SE Asia
175 *N3* **Brunei Bay** *var.* Teluk Brunei. *bay* N Brunei
Brunei, Teluk *see* Brunei Bay
Brunei Town *see* Bandar Seri Begawan
108 *H5* **Brunico** *Ger.* Bruneck. Trentino-Alto Adige, N Italy *46.49N 11.57E*
Brünn *see* Brno
193 *G17* **Brunner, Lake** ◎ South Island, NZ
101 *M18* **Brunssum** Limburg, SE Netherlands *50.57N 5.58E*
25 *W7* **Brunswick** Georgia, SE USA *31.09N 81.30W*
21 *Q8* **Brunswick** Maine, NE USA *43.54N 69.58W*
23 *V3* **Brunswick** Maryland, NE USA *39.18N 77.37W*
29 *T3* **Brunswick** Missouri, C USA *39.25N 93.07W*
33 *T11* **Brunswick** Ohio, N USA *41.14N 81.50W*
Brunswick *see* Braunschweig
65 *H24* **Brunswick, Península** *headland* S Chile *53.30S 71.27W*
113 *H17* **Bruntál** *Ger.* Freudenthal. Ostravský Kraj, E Czech Republic *50.00N 17.27E*
205 *N3* **Brunt Ice Shelf** *ice shelf* Antarctica
Brusa *see* Bursa
39 *U3* **Brush** Colorado, C USA *40.15N 103.37W*
44 *M5* **Brus Laguna** Gracias a Dios, E Honduras *15.46N 84.31W*
62 *K13* **Brusque** Santa Catarina, S Brazil *27.07S 48.54W*
Brussa *see* Bursa
101 *E18* **Brussel** *var.* Brussels, *Fr.* Bruxelles, *Ger.* Brüssel; *anc.* Broucsella. ● (Belgium) Brussels, C Belgium *see also* Bruxelles *50.52N 4.21E*
Brüssel/Brussels *see* Brussel/Bruxelles
119 *O5* **Brusyliv** Zhytomyrs'ka Oblast', N Ukraine *50.16N 29.31E*
191 *Q12* **Bruthen** Victoria, SE Australia *37.43S 147.49E*
Bruttium *see* Calabria
Brüx *see* Most
101 *E18* **Bruxelles** *var.* Brussels, *Dut.* Brussel, *Ger.* Brüssel; *anc.* Broucsella. ● (Belgium) Brussels, C Belgium *see also* Brussel *50.52N 4.21E*
56 *J7* **Bruzual** Apure, W Venezuela *7.59N 69.18W*
33 *Q11* **Bryan** Ohio, N USA *41.28N 84.33W*
27 *U10* **Bryan** Texas, SW USA *30.40N 96.22W*
204 *J4* **Bryan Coast** *physical region* Antarctica
126 *I13* **Bryanka** Krasnoyarskiy Kray, C Russian Federation *59.01N 93.13E*
119 *Y7* **Bryanka** Luhans'ka Oblast', E Ukraine *48.30N 38.45E*
190 *J8* **Bryan, Mount** ▲ South Australia *33.25S 138.59E*
130 *I6* **Bryansk** Bryanskaya Oblast', W Russian Federation *53.15N 34.06E*
130 *H6* **Bryanskaya Oblast'** ◈ *province* W Russian Federation
204 *J5* **Bryant, Cape** *headland* Antarctica
29 *U8* **Bryant Creek** ≈ Missouri, C USA
38 *K8* **Bryce Canyon** *canyon* Utah, W USA
121 *O15* **Bryli** *Rus.* Bryli. Mahilyowskaya Voblasts', E Belarus *53.55N 30.31E*
97 *C17* **Bryne** Rogaland, S Norway *58.43N 5.37E*
27 *R6* **Bryson** Texas, SW USA *33.09N 98.23W*
23 *N10* **Bryson City** North Carolina, SE USA *35.33N 83.39W*
12 *K11* **Bryson, Lac** ◎ Quebec, SE Canada
130 *K13* **Bryukhovetskaya** Krasnodarskiy Kray, SW Russian Federation *45.49N 38.01E*
113 *H15* **Brzeg** *Ger.* Brieg; *anc.* Civitas Altae Ripae. Opolskie, S Poland *50.52N 17.27E*
113 *G14* **Brzeg Dolny** *Ger.* Dyhernfurth. Dolnośląskie, SW Poland *51.15N 16.42E*
Brześć Litewski/Brześć nad Bugiem *see* Brest
113 *L17* **Brzesko** *Ger.* Brietzig. Małopolskie, S Poland *49.57N 20.35E*
Brzeżany *see* Berezhany
112 *K12* **Brzeziny** Łódzkie, C Poland *51.48N 19.42E*
Brzostowica Wielka *see* Vyalikaya Byerastavitsa
113 *O17* **Brzozów** Podkarpackie, SE Poland *49.38N 22.00E*
Bsharrī/Bsherri *see* Bcharré
197 *I13* **Bua** Vanua Levu, N Fiji *16.48S 178.36E*
97 *J20* **Bua** Halland, S Sweden *57.13N 12.07E*
84 *M13* **Bua** ≈ C Malawi
Bua *see* Čiovo
83 *L18* **Bu'aale** *It.* Buale. Jubbada Dhexe, SW Somalia *0.52N 42.37E*
201 *Q8* **Buada Lagoon** *lagoon* Nauru, C Pacific Ocean
195 *W14* **Buala** Santa Isabel, E Solomon Islands *8.06S 159.31E*
Buale *see* Bu'aale
202 *H1* **Buariki** *atoll* Tungaru, W Kiribati
178 *I10* **Bua Yai** *var.* Ban Bua Yai. Nakhon Ratchasima, E Thailand *15.34N 102.25E*
77 *P8* **Bu'ayrāt al Ḩasūn** *var.* Buwayrāt al Hasūn. C Libya *31.22N 15.41E*
78 *H13* **Buba** S Guinea-Bissau *11.36N 14.55W*
175 *Qq7* **Bubaa** Sulawesi, N Indonesia *0.32N 122.27E*
83 *D20* **Bubanza** NW Burundi *3.04S 29.22E*
85 *K18* **Bubi** *prev.* Bubye. ≈ S Zimbabwe
148 *L11* **Būbīyan, Jazīrat** *island* E Kuwait
Bublitz *see* Bobolice
Bubye *see* Bubi
197 *J13* **Buca** *prev.* Mbutha. Vanua Levu, N Fiji *16.39S 179.51E*
142 *F16* **Bucak** Burdur, SW Turkey *37.26N 30.32E*
56 *G8* **Bucaramanga** Santander, N Colombia *7.07N 73.10W*
109 *M18* **Buccino** Campania, S Italy *40.37N 15.25E*
118 *K9* **Bucecea** Botoşani, NE Romania *47.43N 26.24E*
118 *J6* **Buchach** *Pol.* Buczacz. Ternopil's'ka Oblast', W Ukraine *49.04N 25.22E*
191 *Q12* **Buchan** Victoria, SE Australia *37.26S 148.11E*
78 *J17* **Buchanan** *prev.* Grand Bassa. SW Liberia *5.52N 10.03W*
25 *R3* **Buchanan** Georgia, SE USA *33.48N 85.11W*
33 *O11* **Buchanan** Michigan, N USA *41.49N 86.21W*
23 *T6* **Buchanan** Virginia, NE USA *37.31N 79.40W*
27 *R10* **Buchanan Dam** Texas, SW USA *30.42N 98.24W*
27 *R10* **Buchanan, Lake** ⊠ Texas, SW USA
98 *L8* **Buchan Ness** *headland* NE Scotland, UK *57.28N 1.46W*
11 *T12* **Buchans** Newfoundland and Labrador, SE Canada *48.49N 56.44W*
Bucharest *see* Bucureşti
103 *H20* **Buchen** Baden-Württemberg, SW Germany *49.31N 9.18E*
102 *I10* **Buchholz in der Nordheide** Niedersachsen, NW Germany *53.19N 9.52E*
110 *F7* **Buchs** Aargau, N Switzerland *47.24N 8.03E*
110 *I8* **Buchs** Sankt Gallen, NE Switzerland *47.10N 9.26E*
102 *H13* **Bückeburg** Niedersachsen, NW Germany *52.16N 9.03E*
38 *K14* **Buckeye** Arizona, SW USA *33.22N 112.34W*
Buckeye State *see* Ohio
23 *S4* **Buckhannon** West Virginia, NE USA *38.59N 80.13W*
27 *T9* **Buckholts** Texas, SW USA *30.52N 97.07W*
98 *K8* **Buckie** NE Scotland, UK *57.39N 2.55W*
12 *M12* **Buckingham** Quebec, SE Canada *45.34N 75.25W*
23 *U6* **Buckingham** Virginia, NE USA *37.33N 78.33W*
99 *N21* **Buckinghamshire** *cultural region* SE England, UK
41 *N8* **Buckland** Alaska, USA *65.58N 161.07W*
190 *G7* **Buckleboo** South Australia *32.55S 136.11E*
28 *K7* **Bucklin** Kansas, C USA *37.33N 99.37W*
29 *T3* **Bucklin** Missouri, C USA *39.46N 92.53W*
38 *I12* **Buckskin Mountains** ▲▲ Arizona, SW USA
21 *R7* **Bucksport** Maine, NE USA *44.34N 68.46W*
84 *A9* **Buco Zau** Cabinda, NW Angola *4.47S 12.32E*
Bu Craa *see* Bou Craa
118 *K14* **Bucureşti** *Eng.* Bucharest, *Ger.* Bukarest; *prev.* Altenburg, *anc.* Cetatea Damboviţei. ● (Romania) Bucureşti, S Romania *44.27N 26.06E*
33 *S12* **Bucyrus** Ohio, N USA *40.48N 82.58W*
Buczacz *see* Buchach

◆ Country
● Country Capital
◇ Dependent Territory
○ Dependent Territory Capital
◈ Administrative Region
✈ International Airport
▲ Mountain
▲▲ Mountain Range
Volcano
≈ River
◎ Lake
⊠ Reservoir

96 E9 **Bud** Møre og Romsdal, S Norway 62.55N 6.55E
27 S11 **Buda** Texas, SW USA 30.05N 97.50W
121 O18 **Buda-Kashalyova** *Rus.* Buda-Koshelëvo. Homyel'skaya Voblasts', SE Belarus 52.43N 30.34E
Buda-Koshelëvo *see* Buda-Kashalyova
177 G4 **Budalin** Sagaing, C Myanmar 22.24N 95.07E
113 J22 **Budapest** *off.* Budapest Főváros, *SCr.* Budimpešta. ● (Hungary) Pest, N Hungary 47.30N 19.03E
158 K11 **Budaun** Uttar Pradesh, N India 28.01N 79.07E
147 O9 **Budayyi'ah** *oasis* C Saudi Arabia 23.04N 43.29E
205 Y12 **Budd Coast** *physical region* Antarctica
Buddenbrock *see* Brodnica
109 C17 **Budduso** Sardegna, Italy, C Mediterranean Sea 40.37N 9.19E
99 I23 **Bude** SW England, UK 50.49N 4.33W
24 J7 **Bude** Mississippi, S USA 31.27N 90.51W
113 C18 **Budějovický Kraj** ◈ *region* S Czech Republic
101 K16 **Budel** Noord-Brabant, SE Netherlands 51.16N 5.34E
102 I8 **Büdelsdorf** Schleswig-Holstein, N Germany 54.20N 9.40E
131 O14 **Budënnovsk** Stavropol'skiy Kray, SW Russian Federation 44.46N 44.07E
118 K14 **Budeşti** Călăraşi, SE Romania 44.13N 26.31E
Budgewoi *see* Budgewoi Lake
191 T8 **Budgewoi Lake** *var.* Budgewoi. New South Wales, SE Australia 33.13S 151.34E
94 I2 **Búdhardalur** Vesturland, W Iceland 65.07N 21.45W
Budimpešta *see* Budapest
81 J16 **Budjala** Equateur, NW Dem. Rep. Congo 2.39N 19.42E
108 G10 **Budrio** Emilia-Romagna, C Italy 44.33N 11.34E
Budslav *see* Budslaw
121 K14 **Budslaw** *Rus.* Budslav. Minskaya Voblasts', N Belarus 54.46N 27.26E
Budua *see* Budva
174 Ll5 **Budu, Tanjung** *headland* East Malaysia 2.51N 111.42E
115 J17 **Budva** *It.* Budua. Montenegro, SW Serbia and Montenegro (Yugoslavia) 42.17N 18.49E
Budweis *see* České Budějovice
Budyšin *see* Bautzen
81 D16 **Buea** Sud-Ouest, SW Cameroon 4.09N 9.13E
105 S13 **Buëch** ≈ SE France
20 J17 **Buena** New Jersey, NE USA 39.30N 74.55W
64 K12 **Buena Esperanza** San Luis, C Argentina 34.45S 65.15W
56 C11 **Buenaventura** Valle del Cauca, W Colombia 3.54N 77.01W
42 I4 **Buenaventura** Chihuahua, N Mexico 29.52N 107.25W
59 M18 **Buena Vista** Santa Cruz, C Bolivia 17.27S 63.40W
42 G10 **Buenavista** Baja California Sur, W Mexico 23.39N 109.40W
39 S5 **Buena Vista** Colorado, C USA 38.50N 106.07W
25 S5 **Buena Vista** Georgia, SE USA 32.19N 84.31W
23 T6 **Buena Vista** Virginia, NE USA 37.43N 79.21W
46 F5 **Buena Vista, Bahia de** *bay* N Cuba
37 R13 **Buena Vista Lake Bed** ◎ California, W USA
107 P8 **Buendía, Embalse de** ▣ C Spain
65 F16 **Bueno, Río** ≈ S Chile
64 N12 **Buenos Aires** *hist.* Santa Maria del Buen Aire. ● (Argentina) Buenos Aires, E Argentina 34.40S 58.30W
45 O15 **Buenos Aires** Puntarenas, SE Costa Rica 9.09N 83.15W
63 C20 **Buenos Aires** *off.* Provincia de Buenos Aires. ◈ *province* E Argentina
65 H19 **Buenos Aires, Lago** *var.* Lago General Carrera. ◎ Argentina/Chile
56 C13 **Buesaco** Nariño, SW Colombia 1.22N 77.07W
31 U8 **Buffalo** Minnesota, N USA 45.10N 93.49W
28 T6 **Buffalo** Missouri, C USA 37.38N 93.05W
20 D10 **Buffalo** New York, NE USA 42.53N 78.52W
29 K8 **Buffalo** Oklahoma, C USA 36.50N 99.37W
30 J7 **Buffalo** South Dakota, N USA 45.35N 103.32W
27 V8 **Buffalo** Texas, SW USA 31.25N 96.04W
35 W12 **Buffalo** Wyoming, C USA 44.21N 106.40W
31 U11 **Buffalo Center** Iowa, C USA 43.23N 93.57W
26 M3 **Buffalo Lake** ▣ Texas, SW USA
32 K7 **Buffalo Lake** ▣ Wisconsin, N USA
9 S12 **Buffalo Narrows** Saskatchewan, C Canada 55.52N 108.28W
29 U9 **Buffalo River** ≈ Arkansas, C USA
31 R5 **Buffalo River** ≈ Minnesota, N USA
22 I10 **Buffalo River** ≈ Tennessee, S USA
32 J6 **Buffalo River** ≈ Wisconsin, N USA
46 L12 **Buff Bay** E Jamaica 18.18N 76.40W
25 T3 **Buford** Georgia, SE USA 34.07N 84.00W
30 J3 **Buford** North Dakota, N USA 48.00N 103.58W
35 Y17 **Buford** Wyoming, C USA 41.05N 105.17W
118 J14 **Buftea** Bucureşti, S Romania 44.34N 25.57E
86 I9 **Bug** *Bel.* Zakhodni Buh, *Eng.* Western Bug, *Rus.* Zapadnyy Bug, *Ukr.* Zakhidnyy Buh. ≈ E Europe
56 D11 **Buga** Valle del Cauca, W Colombia 3.52N 76.16W
168 F7 **Buga** Dzavhan, W Mongolia 47.42N 94.53E
105 O17 **Bugarach, Pic du** ▲ S France 42.52N 2.23E
152 B12 **Bugdayly** Balkanskiy Velayat, W Turkmenistan 38.42N 54.14E
Buggs Island Lake *see* John H.Kerr Reservoir
Bughotu *see* Santa Isabel
175 Q12 **Bugingkalo** Sulawesi, C Indonesia 4.49S 121.42E
66 P6 **Bugio** *island* Madeira, Portugal, NE Atlantic Ocean
94 M8 **Bugøynes** Finnmark, N Norway 69.57N 29.34E
129 Q3 **Bugrino** Nenetskiy Avtonomnyy Okrug, NW Russian Federation 68.48N 49.12E
131 T5 **Bugul'ma** Respublika Tatarstan, W Russian Federation 54.31N 52.45E
Bügür *see* Luntai
131 T6 **Buguruslan** Orenburgskaya Oblast', W Russian Federation 53.37N 52.30E
165 R9 **Buh He** ≈ C China
35 O15 **Buhl** Idaho, NW USA 42.36N 114.45W
103 F22 **Bühl** Baden-Württemberg, SW Germany 48.42N 8.07E
118 K10 **Buhuşi** Bacău, E Romania 46.34N 26.55E
Buie d'Istria *see* Buje
99 J20 **Builth Wells** E Wales, UK 52.07N 3.27W
195 S13 **Buin** Bougainville Island, NE PNG 6.50S 155.42E
110 J9 **Buin, Piz** ▲ Austria/Switzerland 46.51N 10.07E
131 Q4 **Buinsk** Chuvashskaya Respublika, W Russian Federation 55.09N 47.00E
131 Q4 **Buinsk** Respublika Tatarstan, W Russian Federation 54.58N 48.16E
169 R8 **Buir Nur** *Mong.* Buyr Nuur. ◎ China/Mongolia *see also* Buyr Nuur
100 M5 **Buitenpost** *Fris.* Bûtenpost. Friesland, N Netherlands 53.15N 6.09E
Buitenzorg *see* Bogor
85 F19 **Buitepos** Omaheke, E Namibia 22.17S 19.59E
107 N7 **Buitrago del Lozoya** Madrid, C Spain 41.00N 3.38W
Buj *see* Buy
106 M13 **Bujalance** Andalucía, S Spain 37.54N 4.22W
115 O17 **Bujanovac** Serbia, SE Serbia and Montenegro (Yugoslavia) 42.29N 21.43E
107 S6 **Bujaraloz** Aragón, NE Spain 41.28N 0.10W
114 A9 **Buje** *It.* Buie d'Istria. Istra, NW Croatia 45.23N 13.40E
Bujnurd *see* Bojnūrd
83 D21 **Bujumbura** *prev.* Usumbura. ● (Burundi) W Burundi 3.25S 29.23E
83 D20 **Bujumbura** ✕ W Burundi 3.21S 29.19E
126 L15 **Bukachacha** Chitinskaya Oblast', S Russian Federation 52.49N 116.39E
165 N11 **Bukadaban Feng** ▲ C China 36.09N 90.52E
195 R11 **Buka Island** *island* NE PNG
83 F18 **Bukakata** S Uganda 0.18S 31.57E
81 N24 **Bukama** Katanga, SE Dem. Rep. Congo 9.13S 25.52E
148 J4 **Būkān** *var.* Bowkān. Āẕarbāyjān-e Bākhtarī, NW Iran 36.31N 46.14E
Bukantau, Gory *see* Bo'kantov Tog'lari
Bukarest *see* Bucureşti
81 O19 **Bukavu** *prev.* Costermansville. Sud Kivu, E Dem. Rep. Congo 2.18S 28.49E
83 F21 **Bukene** Tabora, NW Tanzania 4.15S 32.51E
147 W8 **Bū Khābī** *var.* Bakhābī. NW Oman 23.28N 56.06E
Bukhara *see* Buxoro
Bukharskaya Oblast' *see* Buxoro Viloyati
174 I12 **Bukitkemuning** Sumatera, W Indonesia 4.43S 104.27E
173 G8 **Bukittinggi** *prev.* Fort de Kock. Sumatera, W Indonesia 0.18S 100.19E
113 L21 **Bükk** ▲▲ NE Hungary
83 F19 **Bukoba** Kagera, NW Tanzania 1.19S 31.49E
115 N20 **Bukovo** S FYR Macedonia 40.59N 21.20E
110 G6 **Bülach** Zürich, NW Switzerland 47.31N 8.30E
Būlaevo *see* Bulayevo
168 I6 **Bulag** Hövsgöl, N Mongolia 49.51N 100.41E
168 M7 **Bulag** Töv, C Mongolia 48.09N 108.33E
168 I8 **Bulagiyn Denj** Arhangay, C Mongolia 47.14N 100.56E
191 U7 **Bulahdelah** New South Wales, SE Australia 32.24S 152.13E
176 Yy15 **Bulaka, Sungai** ≈ Papua, E Indonesia
179 Qq12 **Bulan** Luzon, N Philippines 12.40N 123.55E
143 N11 **Bulancak** Giresun, N Turkey 40.57N 38.13E
158 J10 **Bulandshahr** Uttar Pradesh, N India 28.30N 77.49E
143 R14 **Bulanık** Muş, E Turkey 39.04N 42.16E
131 V7 **Bulanovo** Orenburgskaya Oblast', W Russian Federation 52.27N 55.08E
85 J17 **Bulawayo** *var.* Buluwayo. Matabeleland North, SW Zimbabwe 20.08S 28.36E
85 J17 **Bulawayo** ✕ Matabeleland North, SW Zimbabwe 20.00S 28.36E
151 Q6 **Bulayevo** *Kaz.* Būlaevo. Severnyy Kazakhstan, N Kazakhstan 54.55N 70.28E
142 D15 **Buldan** Denizli, SW Turkey 38.03N 28.49E
160 G12 **Buldāna** Mahārāshtra, C India 20.31N 76.18E
40 E16 **Buldir Island** *island* Aleutian Islands, Alaska, USA
Buldur *see* Burdur
168 H9 **Bulgan** Bayanhongor, C Mongolia 44.48N 98.39E
168 K6 **Bulgan** Bulgan, N Mongolia 50.31N 101.30E
168 F7 **Bulgan** Hovd, W Mongolia 46.57N 93.40E
168 J5 **Bulgan** Hövsgöl, N Mongolia 50.30N 101.28E
168 J10 **Bulgan** Ömnögovĭ, S Mongolia 44.07N 103.28E
168 J7 **Bulgan** ◈ *province* N Mongolia
116 H10 **Bulgaria** *off.* Republic of Bulgaria, *Bul.* Bŭlgariya; *prev.* People's Republic of Bulgaria. ◆ *republic* SE Europe
Bŭlgariya *see* Bulgaria
116 L9 **Bŭlgarka** ▲ E Bulgaria 42.43N 26.19E
175 T7 **Buli** Pulau Halmahera, E Indonesia 0.56N 128.17E
175 Tt7 **Buli, Teluk** *bay* Pulau Halmahera, E Indonesia
166 J13 **Buliu He** ≈ S China
Bullange *see* Büllingen
106 M11 **Bullaque** ≈ C Spain
107 Q13 **Bullas** Murcia, SE Spain 38.01N 1.40W
82 M12 **Bullaxaar** Woqooyi Galbeed, NW Somalia 10.28N 44.15E
110 C9 **Bulle** Fribourg, SW Switzerland 46.37N 7.04E
193 G15 **Buller** ≈ South Island, NZ
191 P12 **Buller, Mount** ▲ Victoria, SE Australia 37.10S 146.31E
38 H11 **Bullhead City** Arizona, SW USA 35.07N 114.32W
101 N21 **Büllingen** *Fr.* Bullange. Liège, E Belgium 50.23N 6.15E
Bullion State *see* Missouri
23 T14 **Bull Island** *island* South Carolina, SE USA
190 M4 **Bulloo River Overflow** *wetland* New South Wales, SE Australia
192 M12 **Bulls** Manawatu-Wanganui, North Island, NZ 40.10S 175.22E
23 T14 **Bulls Bay** *bay* South Carolina, SE USA
29 U9 **Bull Shoals Lake** ▣ Arkansas/Missouri, C USA
189 Q2 **Bulman** Northern Territory, N Australia 13.39S 134.21E
168 I6 **Bulnayn Nuruu** ▲▲ N Mongolia
194 J13 **Bulolo** Morobe, C PNG 7.11S 146.34E
175 Qq7 **Bulowa, Gunung** ▲ Sulawesi, N Indonesia 0.33N 123.39E
Bulqiza *see* Bulqizë
115 L19 **Bulqizë** *var.* Bulqiza. Dibër, C Albania 41.30N 20.16E
Bulsar *see* Valsād
175 R7 **Buludawa Keten, Pegunungan** ▲▲ Sulawesi, N Indonesia
175 Pp13 **Bulukumba** *prev.* Boeloekoemba. Sulawesi, C Indonesia 5.34S 120.13E
153 O11 **Bulung'ur** *Rus.* Bulungur; *prev.* Krasnogvardeysk. Samarqand Viloyati, C Uzbekistan 39.46N 67.18E
81 I21 **Bulungu** Bandundu, SW Dem. Rep. Congo 4.34S 18.33E
Bulungur *see* Bulung'ur
Buluwayo *see* Bulawayo
81 K17 **Bumba** Equateur, N Dem. Rep. Congo 2.14N 22.25E
124 O15 **Bumbah, Khalīj al** *gulf* N Libya
168 K8 **Bumbat** Övörhangay, C Mongolia 46.30N 104.08E
83 F19 **Bumbire Island** *island* N Tanzania
175 Oo4 **Bum Bun, Pulau** *island* East Malaysia
83 J17 **Buna** North Eastern, NE Kenya 2.40N 39.34E
27 Y10 **Buna** Texas, SW USA 30.25N 94.00W
Bunab *see* Bonāb
Bunai *see* M'bunai
153 S13 **Bunay** S Tajikistan 38.29N 71.41E
188 I13 **Bunbury** Western Australia 33.24S 115.43E
99 E14 **Buncrana** *Ir.* Bun Cranncha. NW Ireland 55.07N 7.27W
Bun Cranncha *see* Buncrana
189 Z9 **Bundaberg** Queensland, E Australia 24.49S 152.16E
191 T5 **Bundarra** New South Wales, SE Australia 30.12S 151.06E
102 G13 **Bünde** Nordrhein-Westfalen, NW Germany 52.12N 8.34E
158 H13 **Būndi** Rājasthān, N India 25.28N 75.42E
194 I12 **Bundi** Madang, N PNG 5.40S 145.10E
Bun Dobhráin *see* Bundoran
99 D15 **Bundoran** *Ir.* Bun Dobhráin. NW Ireland 54.28N 8.16W
115 K18 **Bunë** *SCr.* Bojana. ≈ Albania/Serbia and Montenegro (Yugoslavia) *see also* Bojana
179 R16 **Bunga** ≈ Mindanao, S Philippines
173 Ff10 **Bungalaut, Selat** *strait* W Indonesia
178 Ii8 **Bung Kan** Nong Khai, E Thailand 18.19N 103.39E
189 N4 **Bungle Bungle Range** ▲▲ Western Australia
84 C10 **Bungo** Uíge, NW Angola 7.30S 15.24E
83 G18 **Bungoma** Western, W Kenya 0.34N 34.34E
170 Dd15 **Bungo-suidō** *strait* SW Japan
170 Dd13 **Bungo-Takada** Ōita, Kyūshū, SW Japan 33.36N 131.28E
102 K8 **Bungsberg** *hill* N Germany 54.12N 10.45E
Bungur *see* Bunyu
81 P17 **Bunia** Orientale, NE Dem. Rep. Congo 1.33N 30.16E
37 U6 **Bunker Hill** ▲ Nevada, W USA 39.16N 117.06W
24 I7 **Bunkie** Louisiana, S USA 30.58N 92.12W
25 X10 **Bunnell** Florida, SE USA 29.28N 81.15W
107 S10 **Buñol** País Valenciano, E Spain 39.25N 0.46W
100 K11 **Bunschoten** Utrecht, C Netherlands 52.15N 5.22E
142 K14 **Bünyan** Kayseri, C Turkey 38.51N 35.49E
175 Oo5 **Bunyu** *var.* Bungur. Borneo, N Indonesia 3.33N 117.50E
175 Oo5 **Bunyu, Pulau** *island* N Indonesia
Bunzlau *see* Bolesławiec
Buoddobohki *see* Patoniva
126 Ll6 **Buorkhaya Guba** *bay* N Russian Federation
176 Z15 **Bupul** Papua, E Indonesia 7.24S 140.57E
83 K19 **Bura** Coast, SE Kenya 1.06S 40.01E
82 P12 **Buraan** Sanaag, N Somalia 10.03N 49.08E
Būrabay *see* Borovoye
Buraida *see* Buraydah
Buraimi *see* Al Buraymī
151 Y11 **Buran** Vostochnyy Kazakhstan, E Kazakhstan 48.00N 85.09E
164 G15 **Burang** Xizang Zizhiqu, W China 30.28N 81.13E
Burao *see* Burco
144 H8 **Burāq** Dar'ā, S Syria 33.10N 36.28E
147 O6 **Buraydah** *var.* Buraida. Al Qaşīm, N Saudi Arabia 26.50N 44.00E
37 S15 **Burbank** California, W USA 34.10N 118.19W
33 N11 **Burbank** Illinois, N USA 41.45N 87.48W
191 Q8 **Burcher** New South Wales, SE Australia 33.29S 147.16E
82 N13 **Burco** *var.* Burao, Bur'o. Togdheer, NW Somalia 9.29N 45.30E
152 L13 **Burdalyk** Lebapskiy Velayat, E Turkmenistan 38.31N 64.21E
189 W6 **Burdekin River** ≈ Queensland, NE Australia
29 O7 **Burden** Kansas, C USA 37.18N 96.45W
Burdigala *see* Bordeaux
142 E15 **Burdur** *var.* Buldur. Burdur, SW Turkey 37.43N 30.16E
142 E15 **Burdur** *var.* Buldur. ◈ *province* SW Turkey
142 E15 **Burdur Gölü** *salt lake* SW Turkey
67 H21 **Burdwood Bank** *undersea feature* SW Atlantic Ocean
82 I12 **Burē** Amhara, N Ethiopia 10.43N 37.09E
82 H13 **Burē** Oromo, C Ethiopia 8.13N 35.09E
95 J15 **Bureå** Västerbotten, N Sweden 64.36N 21.15E
103 G14 **Büren** Nordrhein-Westfalen, W Germany 51.34N 8.34E
168 K6 **Bürengiyn Nuruu** ▲▲ N Mongolia
168 E8 **Bürenhayrhan** Hovd, W Mongolia 46.04N 91.34E
Būrewāla *see* Mandi Būrewāla
127 N17 **Bureya** ≈ SE Russian Federation
94 J9 **Burfjord** Troms, N Norway 69.55N 21.54E
102 L13 **Burg** *var.* Burg an der Ihle, Burg bei Magdeburg. Sachsen-Anhalt, C Germany 52.16N 11.51E
Burg an der Ihle *see* Burg
116 N10 **Burgas** *var.* Bourgas. Burgas, E Bulgaria 42.31N 27.30E
116 N9 **Burgas** ✕ Burgas, E Bulgaria 42.35N 27.33E
116 M10 **Burgas** ◈ *province* E Bulgaria
116 N10 **Burgaski Zaliv** *gulf* E Bulgaria
116 M10 **Burgasko Ezero** *lagoon* E Bulgaria
23 V11 **Burgaw** North Carolina, SE USA 34.33N 77.54W
Burg bei Magdeburg *see* Burg
110 E8 **Burgdorf** Bern, NW Switzerland 47.03N 7.37E
111 Y7 **Burgenland** *off.* Land Burgenland. ◈ *state* SE Austria
11 S13 **Burgeo** Newfoundland and Labrador, SE Canada 47.42N 57.29W
85 I24 **Burgersdorp** Eastern Cape, SE South Africa 31.00S 26.20E
85 K20 **Burgersfort** Mpumalanga, NE South Africa 24.39S 30.18E
103 N23 **Burghausen** Bayern, SE Germany 48.10N 12.48E
145 O5 **Burghūth, Sabkhat al** ◎ E Syria
103 M20 **Burglengenfeld** Bayern, SE Germany 49.11N 12.01E
43 P9 **Burgos** Tamaulipas, C Mexico 24.55N 98.46W
107 N4 **Burgos** Castilla-León, N Spain 42.21N 3.40W
107 N4 **Burgos** ◈ *province* Castilla-León, N Spain
Burgstadlberg *see* Hradiště
97 P20 **Burgsvik** Gotland, SE Sweden 57.01N 18.18E
Burgum *see* Bergum
Burgundy *see* Bourgogne
165 Q11 **Burhan Budai Shan** ▲▲ C China
142 B12 **Burhaniye** Balıkesir, W Turkey 39.28N 26.58E
160 G12 **Burhānpur** Madhya Pradesh, C India 21.18N 76.13E
179 Q11 **Burias Island** *island* C Philippines
131 W7 **Buribay** Respublika Bashkortostan, W Russian Federation 51.57N 58.11E
45 O17 **Burica, Punta** *headland* Costa Rica/Panama 8.02N 82.53W
178 Ii10 **Buriram** *var.* Buri Ram, Puriramya. Buri Ram, E Thailand 15.01N 103.06E
107 S10 **Burjassot** País Valenciano, E Spain 39.33N 0.25W
83 N16 **Burka Giibi** Hiiraan, C Somalia 3.52N 45.07E
153 X8 **Burkan** ≈ E Kyrgyzstan
27 R4 **Burkburnett** Texas, SW USA 34.06N 98.34W
31 O12 **Burke** South Dakota, N USA 43.09N 99.18W
8 K15 **Burke Channel** *channel* British Columbia, W Canada
204 J10 **Burke Island** *island* Antarctica
22 L7 **Burkesville** Kentucky, S USA 36.47N 85.22W
189 T4 **Burketown** Queensland, NE Australia 17.48S 139.28E
27 Q8 **Burkett** Texas, SW USA 32.01N 99.17W
27 Y9 **Burkeville** Texas, SW USA 30.58N 93.41W
23 V7 **Burkeville** Virginia, NE USA 37.11N 78.12W
79 O12 **Burkina** *off.* Burkina Faso; *prev.* Upper Volta. ◆ *republic* W Africa
Burkina Faso *see* Burkina
204 L13 **Burks, Cape** *headland* Antarctica
12 H12 **Burk's Falls** Ontario, S Canada 45.38N 79.25W
103 H23 **Burladingen** Baden-Württemberg, S Germany 48.18N 9.05E
27 T7 **Burleson** Texas, SW USA 32.32N 97.19W
35 P15 **Burley** Idaho, NW USA 42.32N 113.47W
150 G8 **Burlin** Zapadnyy Kazakhstan, NW Kazakhstan 51.25N 52.42E
12 G16 **Burlington** Ontario, S Canada 43.21N 79.45W
39 W4 **Burlington** Colorado, C USA 39.16N 102.16W
31 Y15 **Burlington** Iowa, C USA 40.48N 91.05W
29 P5 **Burlington** Kansas, C USA 38.11N 95.44W
23 T9 **Burlington** North Carolina, SE USA 36.06N 79.26W
30 M3 **Burlington** North Dakota, N USA 48.16N 101.25W
20 L7 **Burlington** Vermont, NE USA 44.28N 73.13W
32 M9 **Burlington** Wisconsin, N USA 42.38N 88.12W
29 Q1 **Burlington Junction** Missouri, C USA 40.27N 95.04W
Burma *see* Myanmar
8 L17 **Burnaby** British Columbia, SW Canada 49.16N 122.58W
119 O12 **Burnas, Ozero** ◎ SW Ukraine
27 S10 **Burnet** Texas, SW USA 30.45N 98.13W
37 O3 **Burney** California, W USA 40.52N 121.42W
191 O16 **Burnie** Tasmania, SE Australia 41.06S 145.52E
99 L17 **Burnley** NW England, UK 53.48N 2.13W
Burnoye *see* Bauyrzhan Momysh-Uly
159 R15 **Burnpur** West Bengal, NE India 23.39N 86.55E
34 K14 **Burns** Oregon, NW USA 43.35N 119.03W
28 K11 **Burns Flat** Oklahoma, C USA 35.21N 99.10W
22 M7 **Burnside** Kentucky, S USA 36.55N 84.34W
15 Ii5 **Burnside** ≈ Nunavut, NW Canada
34 L15 **Burns Junction** Oregon, NW USA 42.46N 117.51W
8 L13 **Burns Lake** British Columbia, SW Canada 54.13N 125.45W
31 V9 **Burnsville** Minnesota, N USA 44.49N 93.14W
23 P9 **Burnsville** North Carolina, SE USA 35.55N 82.18W
23 R4 **Burnsville** West Virginia, NE USA 38.50N 80.39W
12 I13 **Burnt River** ≈ Ontario, SE Canada
12 I11 **Burntroot Lake** ◎ Ontario, SE Canada
9 W12 **Burntwood** ≈ Manitoba, C Canada
Bur'o *see* Burco
164 L2 **Burqin** Xinjiang Uygur Zizhiqu, NW China 47.42N 86.49E
190 J8 **Burra** South Australia 33.41S 138.54E
191 S9 **Burragorang, Lake** ▣ New South Wales, SE Australia
98 K5 **Burray** *island* NE Scotland, UK
115 L19 **Burrel** *var.* Burreli. Dibër, C Albania 41.36N 20.00E
Burreli *see* Burrel
191 R8 **Burrendong Reservoir** ▣ New South Wales, SE Australia
191 R5 **Burren Junction** New South Wales, SE Australia 30.06S 149.01E
107 T9 **Burriana** País Valenciano, E Spain 39.54N 0.04W
191 R10 **Burrinjuck Reservoir** ▣ New South Wales, SE Australia
38 J12 **Burro Creek** ≈ Arizona, SW USA
42 M5 **Burro, Serranías del** ▲▲ NW Mexico
64 K7 **Burruyacú** Tucumán, N Argentina 26.28S 64.30W
142 E12 **Bursa** *var.* Brussa; *prev.* Brusa, *anc.* Prusa. Bursa, NW Turkey 40.12N 29.04E
142 D12 **Bursa** *var.* Brusa, Brussa. ◈ *province* NW Turkey
77 Y9 **Bûr Safâga** *var.* Būr Safājah. E Egypt 26.41N 33.58E
Būr Safājah *see* Bûr Safâga
Būr Sa'īd *see* Port Said
83 O14 **Bur Tinle** Mudug, C Somalia 7.50N 48.01E
33 Q5 **Burt Lake** ◎ Michigan, N USA
Burtnieks *see* Burtnieku Ezers
120 H7 **Burtnieku Ezers** *var.* Burtnieks. ◎ N Latvia
33 Q9 **Burton** Michigan, N USA 43.00N 84.16W
Burton on Trent *see* Burton upon Trent
99 M19 **Burton upon Trent** *var.* Burton on Trent, Burton-upon-Trent. C England, UK 52.48N 1.36W
95 J15 **Burträsk** Västerbotten, N Sweden 64.31N 20.40E
151 S14 **Burubaytal** *prev.* Burylbaytal. Zhambyl, SE Kazakhstan 45.01N 73.58E
Burujird *see* Borūjerd
Burultokay *see* Fuhai
147 R15 **Burūm** SE Yemen 14.22N 48.53E
Burunday *see* Boralday
83 D21 **Burundi** *off.* Republic of Burundi; *prev.* Kingdom of Burundi, Urundi. ◆ *republic* C Africa
175 S11 **Buru, Pulau** *prev.* Boeroe. *island* E Indonesia
79 T17 **Burutu** Delta, S Nigeria 5.18N 5.32E
8 G7 **Burwash Landing** Yukon Territory, W Canada 61.26N 139.12W
31 O14 **Burwell** Nebraska, C USA 41.46N 99.04W
99 L17 **Bury** NW England, UK 53.36N 2.16W
126 K15 **Buryatiya, Respublika** *prev.* Buryatskaya ASSR. ◈ *autonomous republic* S Russian Federation
Buryatskaya ASSR *see* Buryatiya, Respublika
Burylbaytal *see* Burubaytal
119 S3 **Buryn'** Sums'ka Oblast', NE Ukraine 51.12N 33.49E
99 P20 **Bury St Edmunds** *hist.* Beodericsworth. E England, UK 52.15N 0.43E
116 G8 **Bŭrziya** ≈ NW Bulgaria
108 D9 **Busalla** Liguria, NW Italy 44.35N 8.55E
179 R17 **Busa, Mount** ▲ Mindanao, S Philippines 6.19N 124.29E
Busan *see* Pusan
145 N5 **Buşayrah** Dayr az Zawr, E Syria 35.03N 40.28E
Buševa *see* Baba
149 N12 **Būshehr** *off.* Ostān-e Būshehr. ◈ *province* SW Iran
Būshehr/Bushire *see* Bandar-e Būshehr
27 N2 **Bushland** Texas, SW USA 35.11N 102.04W
32 J12 **Bushnell** Illinois, N USA 40.33N 90.30W
Busi *see* Biševo
83 G18 **Busia** SE Uganda 1.20N 34.48E
Busiasch *see* Buziaş
81 K16 **Businga** Equateur, NW Dem. Rep. Congo 3.19N 20.52E
81 J18 **Busira** ≈ NW Dem. Rep. Congo
118 I5 **Bus'k** *Rus.* Busk. L'vivs'ka Oblast', W Ukraine 49.59N 24.34E
97 E14 **Buskerud** ◈ *county* S Norway
115 F14 **Buško Jezero** ▣ SW Bosnia and Herzegovina
113 M15 **Busko-Zdrój** Świętokrzyskie, C Poland 50.28N 20.43E
Busra *see* Al Başrah, Iraq
Buşrá *see* Buşrá ash Shām, Syria
144 H9 **Buşrá ash Shām** *var.* Bosora, Bosra, Bozrah, Buşrá. Dar'ā, S Syria 32.31N 36.31E
188 I13 **Busselton** Western Australia 33.43S 115.15E
83 C14 **Busseri** ≈ W Sudan
108 E9 **Busseto** Emilia-Romagna, C Italy 45.00N 10.06E
108 A8 **Bussoleno** Piemonte, NE Italy 45.11N 7.07E
Bussora *see* Al Başrah
100 J10 **Bussum** Noord-Holland, C Netherlands 52.16N 5.10E
43 N7 **Bustamante** Nuevo León, NE Mexico 26.29N 100.30W
65 I23 **Bustamante, Punta** *headland* S Argentina 51.34S 68.58W
Bustan *see* Bo'ston
118 J12 **Buşteni** Prahova, SE Romania 45.23N 25.31E
108 D7 **Busto Arsizio** Lombardia, N Italy 45.37N 8.49E
153 Q10 **Bŭston** *Rus.* Buston. NW Tajikistan 40.31N 69.21E
179 P12 **Busuanga Island** *island* Calamian Group, W Philippines
102 H8 **Büsum** Schleswig-Holstein, N Germany 54.08N 8.52E
81 M16 **Buta** Orientale, N Dem. Rep. Congo 2.50N 24.41E
83 E20 **Butare** *prev.* Astrida. S Rwanda 2.39S 29.44E
203 O2 **Butaritari** *atoll* Tungaru, W Kiribati
Butawal *see* Butwal
98 H13 **Bute** *cultural region* SW Scotland, UK
168 K6 **Büteeliyn Nuruu** ▲▲ N Mongolia
8 L16 **Bute Inlet** *fjord* British Columbia, W Canada
98 H12 **Bute, Island of** *island* SW Scotland, UK
81 P18 **Butembo** Nord Kivu, NE Dem. Rep. Congo 0.09N 29.16E
Bûtenpost *see* Buitenpost
109 K25 **Butera** Sicilia, Italy, C Mediterranean Sea 37.12N 14.12E
101 M20 **Bütgenbach** Liège, E Belgium 50.25N 6.12E
Butha Qi *see* Zalantun
177 F5 **Buthidaung** Arakan State, W Myanmar 20.52N 92.32E
63 I16 **Butiá** Rio Grande do Sul, S Brazil 30.09S 51.55W
83 F17 **Butiaba** NW Uganda 1.48N 31.21E
25 N6 **Butler** Alabama, S USA 32.05N 88.13W
25 S5 **Butler** Georgia, SE USA 32.33N 84.14W
33 Q11 **Butler** Indiana, N USA 41.25N 84.52W
29 R5 **Butler** Missouri, C USA 38.15N 94.19W
20 B14 **Butler** Pennsylvania, NE USA 40.51N 79.52W
204 K5 **Butler Island** *island* Antarctica
23 U8 **Butner** North Carolina, SE USA 36.07N 78.45W
175 Qq13 **Buton, Pulau** *var.* Pulau Butung; *prev.* Boetoeng. *island* C Indonesia
175 Qq13 **Buton, Selat** *strait* C Indonesia
Bütow *see* Bytów
115 L23 **Butrintit, Liqeni i** ◎ S Albania
25 N3 **Buttahatchee River** ≈ Alabama/Mississippi, S USA
35 Q10 **Butte** Montana, NW USA 46.01N 112.33W
31 O12 **Butte** Nebraska, C USA 42.54N 98.51W
173 G3 **Butterworth** Pinang, Peninsular Malaysia 5.24N 100.22E
85 J25 **Butterworth** *var.* Gcuwa. Eastern Cape, SE South Africa 32.19S 28.09E
11 O3 **Button Islands** *island group* Nunavut, NE Canada
37 R13 **Buttonwillow** California, W USA 35.24N 119.26W
179 R14 **Butuan** *off.* Butuan City. Mindanao, S Philippines 8.56N 125.32E
Butung, Pulau *see* Buton, Pulau
Butuntum *see* Bitonto
130 M8 **Buturlinovka** Voronezhskaya Oblast', W Russian Federation 50.48N 40.33E
159 O11 **Butwal** *var.* Butawal. Western, C Nepal 27.41N 83.28E
103 G17 **Butzbach** Hessen, W Germany 50.26N 8.40E
102 L9 **Bützow** Mecklenburg-Vorpommern, N Germany 53.49N 11.58E
82 N13 **Buuhoodle** Togdheer, N Somalia 8.18N 46.15E
83 N16 **Buulobarde** *var.* Buulo Berde. Hiiraan, C Somalia Africa 3.52N 45.36E
Buulo Berde *see* Buulobarde
82 P12 **Buuraha Cal Miskaat** ▲▲ NE Somalia
83 L19 **Buur Gaabo** Jubbada Hoose, S Somalia 1.14S 41.48E
101 M22 **Buurgplaatz** ▲ N Luxembourg 50.09N 6.02E
Buwayrāt al Hasūn *see* Bu'ayrāt al Ḩasūn
152 L11 **Buxoro** *var.* Bokhara, *Rus.* Bukhara. Buxoro Viloyati, C Uzbekistan 39.50N 64.22E
152 J11 **Buxoro Viloyati** *Rus.* Bukharskaya Oblast'. ◈ *province* C Uzbekistan
102 I10 **Buxtehude** Niedersachsen, NW Germany 53.28N 9.42E
99 L18 **Buxton** C England, UK 53.18N 1.52W
128 M14 **Buy** *var.* Buj. Kostromskaya Oblast', NW Russian Federation 58.27N 41.31E
168 G7 **Buyanbat** Govĭ-Altay, W Mongolia 47.00N 95.57E
168 H8 **Buyant** Bayanhongor, C Mongolia 46.07N 98.45E
168 D6 **Buyant** Bayan-Ölgiy, W Mongolia 48.31N 89.36E
168 H7 **Buyant** Dzavhan, C Mongolia 47.14N 97.14E
169 N9 **Buyant** Hentiy, C Mongolia 46.15N 110.50E
169 N10 **Buyant-Uhaa** Dornogovĭ, SE Mongolia 44.52N 110.12E
168 M7 **Buyant Ukha** ✕ (Ulaanbaatar) Töv, N Mongolia
131 Q16 **Buynaksk** Respublika Dagestan, SW Russian Federation 42.52N 47.03E
121 L20 **Buynavichy** *Rus.* Buynovichi. Homyel'skaya Voblasts', SE Belarus 51.53N 28.31E
Buynovichi *see* Buynavichy
78 L16 **Buyo** SW Ivory Coast 6.23N 7.04W
78 L16 **Buyo, Lac de** ▣ W Ivory Coast
169 R7 **Buyr Nuur** *var.* Buir Nur. ◎ China /Mongolia *see also* Buir Nur
143 T13 **Büyükağrı Dağı** *var.* Aghri Dagh, Agri Dagi, Koh I Noh, Masis, *Eng.* Great Ararat, Mount Ararat. ▲ E Turkey 39.43N 44.19E
143 R15 **Büyük Çayı** ≈ NE Turkey
116 O13 **Büyük Çekmece** İstanbul, NW Turkey 41.02N 28.36E
116 N12 **Büyükkarıştıran** Kırklareli, NW Turkey 41.17N 27.33E
117 L14 **Büyükkemikli Burnu** *headland* NW Turkey 40.19N 26.14E
142 E15 **Büyükmenderes Nehri** ≈ SW Turkey
Büyükzap Suyu *see* Great Zab
104 M9 **Buzançais** Indre, C France 46.53N 1.25E
118 K13 **Buzău** Buzău, SE Romania 45.08N 26.51E
118 K13 **Buzău** ◈ *county* SE Romania
118 L12 **Buzău** ≈ E Romania
77 S11 **Buzaymah** *var.* Bzīmah. SE Libya 24.53N 22.01E
170 D13 **Buzen** Fukuoka, Kyūshū, SW Japan 33.30N 131.26E
118 F12 **Buziaş** *Ger.* Busiasch, *Hung.* Buziásfürdő; *prev.* Buziás. Timiş, W Romania 45.38N 21.37E
Buziásfürdő *see* Buziaş
85 M18 **Búzi, Rio** ≈ C Mozambique
119 Q10 **Buz'kyy Lyman** *bay* S Ukraine
Büzmeyin *see* Byuzmeyin
151 O8 **Buzuluk** Akmola, C Kazakhstan 51.52N 66.09E
131 T6 **Buzuluk** Orenburgskaya Oblast', W Russian Federation 52.47N 52.15E
131 N8 **Buzuluk** ≈ SW Russian Federation
21 P12 **Buzzards Bay** Massachusetts, NE USA 41.45N 70.37W
21 P13 **Buzzards Bay** *bay* Massachusetts, NE USA
85 G16 **Bwabata** Caprivi, NE Namibia 17.52S 22.39E
195 P17 **Bwagaoia** Misima Island, SE PNG 10.39S 152.48E
Bwake *see* Bouaké
197 C12 **Bwatnapne** Pentecost, C Vanuatu 15.42S 168.07E
121 K14 **Byahoml'** *Rus.* Begoml'. Vitsyebskaya Voblasts', N Belarus 54.44N 28.03E
116 J8 **Byala** Ruse, N Bulgaria 43.32N 27.51E
116 N9 **Byala** *prev.* Ak-Dere. Varna, E Bulgaria 42.52N 27.53E
Byala Reka *see* Erydropótamos
116 H8 **Byala Slatina** Vratsa, NW Bulgaria 43.28N 23.57E
121 N15 **Byalynichy** *Rus.* Belynichi. Mahilyowskaya Voblasts', E Belarus 53.58N 29.44E
121 G19 **Byaroza** *Pol.* Bereza Kartuska, *Rus.* Berëza. Brestskaya Voblasts', SW Belarus 52.33N 24.58E
Bybles *see* Jbaïl
113 O14 **Bychawa** Lubelskie, SE Poland 51.06N 22.34E
Bychikha *see* Bychykha
120 N11 **Bychykha** *Rus.* Bychikha. Vitsyebskaya Voblasts', NE Belarus 55.40N 29.58E
113 I14 **Byczyna** *Ger.* Pitschen. Opolskie, S Poland 51.06N 18.13E
112 I10 **Bydgoszcz** *Ger.* Bromberg. Kujawski-pomorskie, C Poland 53.16N 18.00E
121 I17 **Byelaruskaya Hrada** *Rus.* Belorusskaya Gryada. *ridge* N Belarus
121 G18 **Byelavyezhskaya Pushcha** *Pol.* Puszcza Białowieska, *Rus.* Belovezhskaya Pushcha. *forest* Belarus/Poland *see also* Białowieska, Puszcza
121 H15 **Byenyakoni** *Rus.* Benyakoni. Hrodzyenskaya Voblasts', W Belarus 54.15N 25.22E
121 M16 **Byerazino** *Rus.* Berezino. Minskaya Voblasts', C Belarus 53.49N 28.58E
120 L13 **Byerazino** *Rus.* Berezino. Vitsyebskaya Voblasts', N Belarus 54.54N 28.12E
121 L14 **Byerezino** *Rus.* Berezina. ≈ C Belarus
120 M13 **Byeshankovichy** *Rus.* Beshenkovichi. Vitsyebskaya Voblasts', N Belarus 55.03N 29.28E
33 U13 **Byesville** Ohio, N USA 39.58N 81.32W
121 P18 **Byesyedz'** *Rus.* Besed'. ≈ SE Belarus
121 H19 **Byezdzyezh** *Rus.* Bezdezh. Brestskaya Voblasts', SW Belarus 52.18N 25.16E
95 J15 **Bygdeå** Västerbotten, N Sweden 64.03N 20.49E
96 F12 **Bygdin** ◎ S Norway
95 J15 **Bygdsiljum** Västerbotten, N Sweden 64.20N 20.31E
97 E17 **Bygland** Aust-Agder, S Norway 58.46N 7.50E
97 E17 **Byglandsfjord** Aust-Agder, S Norway 58.42N 7.51E
121 N16 **Bykhaw** *Rus.* Bykhov. Mahilyowskaya Voblasts', E Belarus 53.31N 30.15E

◆ Country
● Country Capital
◇ Dependent Territory
○ Dependent Territory Capital
◈ Administrative Region
✕ International Airport
▲ Mountain
▲▲ Mountain Range
Volcano
≈ River
◎ Lake
▣ Reservoir

Bykhov see Bykhaw
131 P9 **Bykovo** Volgogradskaya Oblast', SW Russian Federation 49.52N 45.24E
126 L6 **Bykovskiy** Respublika Sakha (Yakutiya), NE Russian Federation 71.57N 129.07E
205 R12 **Byrd Glacier** glacier Antarctica
12 K10 **Byrd, Lac** ⊚ Quebec, SE Canada
191 P5 **Byrock** New South Wales, SE Australia 30.40S 146.24E
32 L10 **Byron** Illinois, N USA 42.06N 89.15W
191 V4 **Byron Bay** New South Wales, SE Australia 28.39S 153.34E
191 V4 **Byron, Cape** headland New South Wales, E Australia 28.37S 153.40E
65 F21 **Byron, Isla** island S Chile
Byron Island see Nikunau
67 B24 **Byron Sound** sound NW Falkland Islands
126 J5 **Byrranga, Gora** ▲▲ N Russian Federation
95 J14 **Byske** Västerbotten, N Sweden 64.58N 21.10E
113 K18 **Bystrá** ▲ N Slovakia 49.10N 19.49E
113 F18 **Bystřice nad Pernštejnem** Ger. Bistritz ober Pernstein. Jihlavský Kraj, C Czech Republic 49.30N 16.16E
Bystrovka see Kemin
113 G16 **Bystrzyca Kłodzka** Ger. Habelschwerdt. Wałbrzych, SW Poland 50.19N 16.39E
113 I18 **Bytča** Žilinský Kraj, N Slovakia 49.15N 18.31E
121 L15 **Bytcha** Rus. Bytcha. Minskaya Voblasts', NE Belarus 54.19N 28.24E
Byteń/Byten' see Bytsyen'
113 J16 **Bytom** Ger. Beuthen. Śląskie, S Poland 50.21N 18.51E
112 H7 **Bytów** Ger. Bütow. Pomorskie, N Poland 54.09N 17.30E
121 H18 **Bytsyen'** Pol. Byteń, Rus. Byten'. Brestskaya Voblasts', SW Belarus 52.53N 25.32E
83 E19 **Byumba** var. Biumba. N Rwanda 1.37S 30.05E
152 F13 **Byuzmeyin** Turkm. Büzmeyin; prev. Bezmein. Akhalskiy Velayat, C Turkmenistan 38.07N 57.52E
121 O20 **Byval'ki** Homyel'skaya Voblasts', SE Belarus 51.51N 30.37E
97 O20 **Byxelkrok** Kalmar, S Sweden 57.18N 17.01E
Byzantium see İstanbul
Bzīmah see Buzaymah

C

64 O6 **Caacupé** Cordillera, S Paraguay 25.22S 57.04W
64 P6 **Caaguazú** off. Departamento de Caaguazú. ◆ department C Paraguay
84 C13 **Caála** var. Kaala, Robert Williams, Port. Vila Robert Williams. Huambo, C Angola 12.51S 15.33E
64 P7 **Caazapá** Caazapá, S Paraguay 26.09S 56.21W
64 P7 **Caazapá** off. Departamento de Caazapá. ◆ department SE Paraguay
83 P15 **Cabaad, Raas** headland C Somalia 6.13N 49.01E
179 R14 **Cabadbaran** Mindanao, S Philippines 9.07N 125.34E
57 N10 **Cabadisocaña** Amazonas, S Venezuela 4.28N 64.45W
46 F5 **Cabaiguán** Sancti Spíritus, C Cuba 22.04N 79.31W
Caballeria, Cabo see Cavalleria, Cap de
39 Q14 **Caballo Reservoir** ⊠ New Mexico, SW USA
42 L6 **Caballos Mesteños, Llano de los** plain N Mexico
106 L2 **Cabañaquinta** Asturias, N Spain 43.10N 5.37W
44 B9 **Cabañas** ◆ department E El Salvador
179 P10 **Cabanatuan** off. Cabanatuan City. Luzon, N Philippines 15.27N 120.57E
13 T8 **Cabano** Quebec, SE Canada 47.40N 68.55W
106 L11 **Cabeza del Buey** Extremadura, W Spain 38.43N 5.13W
47 V5 **Cabezas de San Juan** headland E Puerto Rico 18.23N 65.37W
107 N2 **Cabezón de la Sal** Cantabria, N Spain 43.19N 4.13W
Cabhán see Cavan
63 B23 **Cabildo** Buenos Aires, E Argentina 38.28S 61.49W
Cabillonum see Chalon-sur-Saône
56 H5 **Cabimas** Zulia, NW Venezuela 10.25N 71.27W
84 A9 **Cabinda** var. Kabinda. Cabinda, NW Angola 5.34S 12.12E
84 A9 **Cabinda** var. Kabinda. ◆ province NW Angola
35 N7 **Cabinet Mountains** ▲▲ Idaho/Montana, NW USA
84 B11 **Cabiri** Bengo, NW Angola 8.50S 13.42E
65 J20 **Cabo Blanco** Santa Cruz, SE Argentina 47.13S 65.43W
84 P13 **Cabo Delgado** off. Província de Capo Delgado. ◆ province NE Mozambique
12 L9 **Cabonga, Réservoir** ⊠ Quebec, SE Canada
29 V7 **Cabool** Missouri, C USA 37.07N 92.06W
191 V2 **Caboolture** Queensland, E Australia 27.05S 152.56E
Cabora Bassa, Lake see Cahora Bassa, Albufeira de
42 F3 **Caborca** Sonora, NW Mexico 30.44N 112.06W
Cabo San Lucas see San Lucas
29 V11 **Cabot** Arkansas, C USA 34.58N 92.01W
12 F12 **Cabot Head** headland Ontario, S Canada 45.13N 81.17W
16 Ss10 **Cabot Strait** strait E Canada
Cabo Verde, Ilhas do see Cape Verde
106 M14 **Cabra** Andalucía, S Spain 37.28N 4.28W
109 B19 **Cabras** Sardegna, Italy, C Mediterranean Sea 39.55N 8.30E
196 A15 **Cabras Island** island W Guam
47 O8 **Cabrera** N Dominican Republic 19.34N 69.55W
107 X10 **Cabrera** anc. Capraria. island Islas Baleares, Spain, W Mediterranean Sea
106 J4 **Cabrera** ∽ NW Spain
107 Q15 **Cabrera, Sierra** ▲▲ S Spain
9 S16 **Cabri** Saskatchewan, S Canada 50.37N 108.28W
107 R10 **Cabriel** ∽ E Spain
56 M7 **Cabruta** Guárico, C Venezuela 7.39N 66.19W
179 Oo8 **Cabugao** Luzon, N Philippines 17.55N 120.29E
56 G10 **Cabuyaro** Meta, C Colombia 4.16N 72.47W
62 I13 **Caçador** Santa Catarina, S Brazil 26.47S 51.00W
44 G8 **Cacaguatique, Cordillera** var. Cordillera. ▲▲ NE El Salvador
114 L13 **Čačak** Serbia, C Serbia and Montenegro (Yugoslavia) 43.52N 20.23E
57 Y10 **Cacao** NE French Guiana 4.37N 52.28W
63 H16 **Caçapava do Sul** Rio Grande do Sul, S Brazil 30.28S 53.28W
23 U3 **Cacapon River** ∽ West Virginia, NE USA
109 J23 **Caccamo** Sicilia, Italy, C Mediterranean Sea 37.55N 13.40E
109 A17 **Caccia, Capo** headland Sardegna, Italy, C Mediterranean Sea 40.34N 8.09E
61 G18 **Cáceres** Mato Grosso, W Brazil 16.04S 57.40W
106 J10 **Cáceres** Ar. Qazris. Extremadura, W Spain 39.28N 6.22W
106 J9 **Cáceres** ◆ province Extremadura, W Spain
Cachacrou see Scotts Head Village
63 C21 **Cacharí** Buenos Aires, E Argentina 36.24S 59.31W
28 L12 **Cache** Oklahoma, C USA 34.37N 98.37W
8 M16 **Cache Creek** British Columbia, SW Canada 50.49N 121.19W
37 N6 **Cache Creek** ∽ California, W USA
39 S3 **Cache La Poudre River** ∽ Colorado, C USA
Cacheo see Cacheu
29 W11 **Cache River** ∽ Arkansas, C USA
32 L17 **Cache River** ∽ Illinois, N USA
78 G12 **Cacheu** var. Cacheo. W Guinea-Bissau 12.12N 16.10W
61 I15 **Cachimbo** Pará, NE Brazil 9.21S 54.58W
61 H15 **Cachimbo, Serra do** ▲▲ C Brazil
84 D13 **Cachingues** Bié, C Angola 13.05S 16.48E
56 G7 **Cáchira** Norte de Santander, N Colombia 7.46N 73.03W
63 H16 **Cachoeira do Sul** Rio Grande do Sul, S Brazil 29.58S 52.54W
61 O20 **Cachoeiro de Itapemirim** Espírito Santo, SE Brazil 20.51S 41.07W
84 E12 **Cacolo** Lunda Sul, NE Angola 10.09S 19.17E
85 C14 **Caconda** Huíla, C Angola 13.43S 15.03E
84 A9 **Cacongo** Cabinda, NW Angola 5.16S 12.10E
37 U9 **Cactus Peak** ▲ Nevada, W USA 37.42N 116.51W
84 A11 **Cacuaco** Luanda, NW Angola 8.49S 13.24E
85 B14 **Cacula** Huíla, SW Angola 14.31S 14.07E
69 R12 **Caculuvar** ∽ SW Angola
61 O19 **Caçumba, Ilha** island SE Brazil
57 N10 **Cacuri** Amazonas, S Venezuela
83 N17 **Cadale** Shabeellaha Dhexe, E Somalia 2.48N 46.19E
107 X4 **Cadaqués** Cataluña, NE Spain 42.16N 3.16E
113 J18 **Čadca** Hung. Csaca. Žilinský Kraj, N Slovakia 49.27N 18.46E
29 P13 **Caddo** Oklahoma, C USA 34.07N 96.15W
27 R6 **Caddo** Texas, SW USA 32.42N 98.40W
27 X6 **Caddo Lake** ⊠ Louisiana/Texas, SW USA
29 S12 **Caddo Mountains** ▲▲ Arkansas, C USA
43 O8 **Cadereyta** Nuevo León, NE Mexico 25.35N 99.54W
99 J19 **Cader Idris** ▲ NW Wales, United Kingdom 52.43N 3.57W
190 F3 **Cadibarrawirracanna, Lake** salt lake South Australia
12 I7 **Cadillac** Quebec, SE Canada 48.12N 78.23W
9 T17 **Cadillac** Saskatchewan, S Canada 49.43N 107.41W
104 K13 **Cadillac** Gironde, SW France 44.37N 0.16W
33 P7 **Cadillac** Michigan, N USA 44.16N 85.22W
107 V4 **Cadí, Torre de** ▲ NE Spain 42.16N 1.38E
179 Q13 **Cadiz** off. Cadiz City. Negros, C Philippines 10.58N 123.18E
22 H7 **Cadiz** Kentucky, S USA 36.53N 87.49W
33 U13 **Cadiz** Ohio, N USA 40.16N 81.00W
106 J15 **Cádiz** anc. Gades, Gadier, Gadir, Gadire. Andalucía, SW Spain 36.31N 6.18W
106 K15 **Cádiz** ◆ province Andalucía, SW Spain
106 I15 **Cadiz, Bahía de** bay SW Spain
106 H15 **Cádiz, Golfo de** Eng. Gulf of Cadiz. gulf Portugal/Spain
Cadiz, Gulf of see Cádiz, Golfo de
37 X14 **Cadiz Lake** ⊚ California, W USA
190 E2 **Cadney Homestead** South Australia 27.52S 134.03E
Cadurcum see Cahors
85 F17 **Caecae** Ngamiland, NW Botswana 19.52S 21.04E
104 K4 **Caen** Calvados, N France 49.10N 0.19W
Caene/Caenepolis see Qena
Caerdydd see Cardiff
Caer Glou see Gloucester
Caer Gybi see Holyhead
Caerleon see Chester
Caer Luel see Carlisle
99 I18 **Caernarfon** var. Caernarvon, Carnarvon. NW Wales, UK 53.07N 4.16W
99 H18 **Caernarfon Bay** bay NW Wales, UK
99 I19 **Caernarvon** cultural region NW Wales, UK
Caernarvon see Caernarfon
Caesaraugusta see Zaragoza
Caesarea Mazaca see Kayseri
Caesarobriga see Talavera de la Reina
Caesarodunum see Tours
Caesaromagus see Beauvais
Caesena see Cesena
61 N17 **Caetité** Bahia, E Brazil 14.04S 42.28W
64 J6 **Cafayate** Salta, N Argentina 26.02S 66.00W
179 Pp9 **Cagayan** ∽ Luzon, N Philippines
179 R15 **Cagayan de Oro** off. Cagayan de Oro City. Mindanao, S Philippines 8.28N 124.38E
179 Oo17 **Cagayan de Tawi Tawi** island S Philippines
179 Pp14 **Cagayan Islands** island group C Philippines
33 O14 **Cagles Mill Lake** ⊠ Indiana, N USA
108 I12 **Cagli** Marche, C Italy 43.33N 12.39E
109 C20 **Cagliari** anc. Caralis. Sardegna, Italy, C Mediterranean Sea 39.15N 9.06E
109 C20 **Cagliari, Golfo di** gulf Sardegna, Italy, C Mediterranean Sea
105 U15 **Cagnes-sur-Mer** Alpes-Maritimes, SE France 43.40N 7.09E
56 L5 **Cagua** Aragua, N Venezuela 10.09N 67.27W
179 Pp8 **Cagua, Mount** ▲ Luzon, N Philippines 18.10N 122.03E
56 F13 **Caguán, Río** ∽ SW Colombia
47 U6 **Caguas** E Puerto Rico 18.13N 66.02W
25 P5 **Cahaba River** ∽ Alabama, S USA
44 E5 **Cahabón, Río** ∽ C Guatemala
85 B15 **Cahama** Cunene, SW Angola 16.16S 14.19E
99 B21 **Caha Mountains** Ir. An Cheacha. ▲▲ SW Ireland
99 D20 **Caher** Ir. An Cathair. S Ireland 52.21N 7.58W
99 A21 **Cahersiveen** Ir. Cathair Saidhbhín. SW Ireland 51.56N 10.12W
32 K15 **Cahokia** Illinois, N USA 38.34N 90.11W
85 L15 **Cahora Bassa, Albufeira de** var. Lake Cabora Bassa. ⊠ NW Mozambique
99 G20 **Cahore Point** Ir. Rinn Chathóir. headland SE Ireland 52.33N 6.11W
104 M14 **Cahors** anc. Cadurcum. Lot, S France 44.26N 1.27E
58 D9 **Cahuapanas, Río** ∽ N Peru
118 M12 **Cahul** Rus. Kagul. S Moldova 45.52N 28.13E
Cahul, Lacul see Kahul, Ozero
85 N16 **Caia** Sofala, C Mozambique 17.51S 35.22E
61 J19 **Caiapó, Serra do** ▲▲ C Brazil
46 F5 **Caibarién** Villa Clara, C Cuba 22.31N 79.28W
57 O5 **Caicara** Monagas, NE Venezuela 9.49N 63.37W
56 L5 **Caicara del Orinoco** Bolívar, C Venezuela 7.38N 66.10W
61 P14 **Caicó** Rio Grande do Norte, E Brazil 6.25S 37.04W
46 M6 **Caicos Islands** island group W Turks and Caicos Islands
46 L5 **Caicos Passage** strait Bahamas/Turks and Caicos Islands
167 O9 **Caidian** prev. Hanyang. Hubei, C China 30.33N 114.03E
Caiffa see Ḥefa
188 M12 **Caiguna** Western Australia 32.14S 125.33E
Caillí, Ceann see Hag's Head
42 J11 **Caimanero, Laguna del** var. Laguna del Camaronero. lagoon E Pacific Ocean
119 N10 **Căinari** Rus. Kaynary. C Moldova 46.43N 29.00E
59 L19 **Caine, Río** ∽ C Bolivia
Caiphas see Ḥefa
205 N4 **Caird Coast** physical region Antarctica
98 J9 **Cairn Gorm** ▲ C Scotland, UK 57.07N 3.38W
98 J9 **Cairngorm Mountains** ▲▲ C Scotland, UK
41 P12 **Cairn Mountain** ▲ Alaska, USA 61.07N 155.23W
189 W4 **Cairns** Queensland, NE Australia 16.51S 145.43E
124 Qq16 **Cairo** Ar. Al Qāhirah, var. El Qâhira. ● (Egypt) N Egypt 30.01N 31.18E
25 T8 **Cairo** Georgia, SE USA 30.52N 84.12W
32 L17 **Cairo** Illinois, N USA 37.00N 89.10W
77 V8 **Cairo** ✈ C Egypt 30.06N 31.36E
Caiseal see Cashel
Caisleán an Bharraigh see Castlebar
Caisleán na Finne see Castlefinn
98 J6 **Caithness** cultural region N Scotland, UK
85 D15 **Caiundo** Cuando Cubango, S Angola 15.41S 17.28E
58 C11 **Cajamarca** prev. Caxamarca. Cajamarca, NW Peru 7.09S 78.31W
58 B11 **Cajamarca** off. Departamento de Cajamarca. ◆ department N Peru
105 N14 **Cajarc** Lot, S France 44.28N 1.51E
179 Q12 **Cajidiocan** Sibuyan Island, C Philippines 12.20N 122.39E
44 G6 **Cajón, Represa El** ⊠ NW Honduras
60 N12 **Caju, Ilha do** island NE Brazil
Cakaubalavu Reef see Kavukavu Reef
165 R10 **Caka Yanhu** ⊚ C China
114 E7 **Čakovec** Ger. Csakathurn, Hung. Csáktornya; prev. Ger. Tschakathurn. Medimurje, N Croatia 46.24N 16.29E
79 V17 **Calabar** Cross River, S Nigeria 4.55N 8.25E
12 K13 **Calabogie** Ontario, SE Canada 45.18N 76.43W
56 L6 **Calabozo** Guárico, C Venezuela 8.53N 67.28W
109 N20 **Calabria** anc. Bruttium. ◆ region SW Italy
106 M16 **Calaburra, Punta de** headland S Spain 36.30N 4.38W
118 G14 **Calafat** Dolj, SW Romania 43.55N 23.01E
Calafate see El Calafate
107 Q4 **Calahorra** La Rioja, N Spain 42.19N 1.58W
105 N1 **Calais** Pas-de-Calais, N France 51.00N 1.53E
21 T5 **Calais** Maine, NE USA 45.09N 67.15W
Calais, Pas de see Dover, Strait of
Calalen see Kallalen
64 H4 **Calama** Antofagasta, N Chile 22.25S 68.54W
Calamianes see Calamian Group
179 P13 **Calamian Group** var. Calamianes. island group W Philippines
107 R7 **Calamocha** Aragón, NE Spain 40.54N 1.18W
31 N14 **Calamus River** ∽ Nebraska, C USA
118 G12 **Călan** Ger. Kalan, Hung. Pusztakalán. Hunedoara, SW Romania 45.45N 22.59E
107 S7 **Calanda** Aragón, NE Spain 40.55N 0.15W
173 E4 **Calang** Sumatera, W Indonesia 4.37N 95.37E
179 P11 **Calapan** Mindoro, N Philippines 13.23N 121.08E
Călăras see Călărași
118 M9 **Călărași** var. Călăras, Rus. Kalarash. C Moldova 47.19N 28.13E
118 L14 **Călărași** Călărași, SE Romania 44.18N 26.52E
118 K14 **Călărași** ◆ county SE Romania
56 E10 **Calarca** Quindío, W Colombia 4.31N 75.37W
107 Q12 **Calasparra** Murcia, SE Spain 38.13N 1.40W
109 I23 **Calatafimi** Sicilia, Italy, C Mediterranean Sea 37.54N 12.52E
107 Q6 **Calatayud** Aragón, NE Spain 41.21N 1.39W
179 Pp11 **Calauag** Luzon, N Philippines 13.57N 122.18E
37 P8 **Calaveras River** ∽ California, W USA
179 Oo11 **Calavite, Cape** headland Mindoro, N Philippines 13.25N 120.16E
179 Qq12 **Calbayog** off. Calbayog City. Samar, C Philippines 12.07N 124.35E
179 R12 **Calbiga** Samar, C Philippines 11.37N 125.00E
24 G9 **Calcasieu Lake** ⊚ Louisiana, S USA
24 H8 **Calcasieu River** ∽ Louisiana, S USA
58 B6 **Calceta** Manabí, W Ecuador 0.51S 80.09W
63 B16 **Calchaquí** Santa Fe, C Argentina 29.55S 60.13W
64 J6 **Calchaquí, Río** ∽ NW Argentina
60 J10 **Calçoene** Amapá, NE Brazil 2.29N 51.01W
159 S16 **Calcutta** var. Kolkata. West Bengal, NE India 22.30N 88.19E
159 S16 **Calcutta** ✈ West Bengal, N India 22.30N 88.19E
56 E9 **Caldas** off. Departamento de Caldas. ◆ province W Colombia
106 F10 **Caldas da Rainha** Leiria, W Portugal 39.24N 9.07W
106 G3 **Caldas de Reis** var. Caldas de Reyes. Galicia, NW Spain 42.36N 8.39W
Caldas de Reyes see Caldas de Reis
60 F13 **Caldeirão** Amazonas, NW Brazil 3.18S 60.22W
64 G7 **Caldera** Atacama, N Chile 27.04S 70.48W
44 L14 **Caldera** Puntarenas, W Costa Rica 9.55N 84.42W
107 N10 **Calderina** ▲ C Spain 39.18N 3.49W
143 T13 **Çaldıran** Van, E Turkey 39.10N 43.52E
34 M14 **Caldwell** Idaho, NW USA 43.39N 116.41W
29 N8 **Caldwell** Kansas, C USA 37.01N 97.36W
12 G15 **Caledon** Ontario, S Canada 43.51N 79.58W
85 I23 **Caledon** var. Mohokare. ∽ Lesotho/South Africa
44 G1 **Caledonia** Corozal, N Belize 18.13N 88.27W
12 G16 **Caledonia** Ontario, S Canada 43.04N 79.57W
31 X11 **Caledonia** Minnesota, N USA 43.37N 91.30W
107 X5 **Calella** var. Calella de la Costa. Cataluña, NE Spain 41.37N 2.40E
Calella de la Costa see Calella
25 P4 **Calera** Alabama, S USA 33.06N 86.45W
65 I19 **Caleta Olivia** Santa Cruz, SE Argentina 46.21S 67.37W
37 X17 **Calexico** California, W USA 32.39N 115.28W
99 H16 **Calf of Man** island SW Isle of Man
9 Q16 **Calgary** Alberta, SW Canada 51.04N 114.04W
9 Q16 **Calgary** ✈ Alberta, SW Canada 51.15N 114.03W
39 U5 **Calhan** Colorado, C USA 39.00N 104.18W
66 O5 **Calheta** Madeira, Portugal, NE Atlantic Ocean 32.42N 17.12W
25 R2 **Calhoun** Georgia, SE USA 34.30N 84.57W
22 I6 **Calhoun** Kentucky, S USA 37.32N 87.10W
24 M3 **Calhoun City** Mississippi, S USA 33.51N 89.18W
23 P12 **Calhoun Falls** South Carolina, SE USA 34.05N 82.36W
56 D11 **Cali** Valle del Cauca, W Colombia 3.24N 76.30W
29 V9 **Calico Rock** Arkansas, C USA 36.07N 92.08W
161 F21 **Calicut** var. Kozhikode. Kerala, SW India 11.17N 75.49E
37 Y9 **Caliente** Nevada, W USA 37.37N 114.30W
29 U5 **California** Missouri, C USA 38.38N 92.33W
20 B15 **California** Pennsylvania, NE USA 40.02N 79.52W
37 Q12 **California** off. State of California; also known as El Dorado, The Golden State. ◆ state W USA
37 P11 **California Aqueduct** aqueduct California, W USA
37 T13 **California City** California, W USA 35.06N 117.55W
42 F6 **California, Golfo de** Eng. Gulf of California; prev. Sea of Cortez. gulf W Mexico
California, Gulf of see California, Golfo de
143 Y13 **Cälilabad** Rus. Dzhalilabad; prev. Astrakhan-Bazar. S Azerbaijan 39.15N 48.30E
118 I12 **Călimănești** Vâlcea, SW Romania 45.13N 24.19E
118 J9 **Călimani, Munții** ▲▲ N Romania
Calinisc see Cupcina
37 X17 **Calipatria** California, W USA 33.07N 115.30W
Calisia see Kalisz
36 M7 **Calistoga** California, W USA 38.34N 122.37W
85 G25 **Calitzdorp** Western Cape, SW South Africa 33.31S 21.40E
43 W12 **Calkiní** Campeche, E Mexico 20.21N 90.03W
190 K4 **Callabonna Creek** var. Tilcha Creek. seasonal river New South Wales/South Australia
190 J4 **Callabonna, Lake** ⊚ South Australia
104 G5 **Callac** Côtes d'Armor, NW France 48.28N 3.22W
37 U5 **Callaghan, Mount** ▲ Nevada, W USA 39.38N 116.57W
Callain see Callan
99 E19 **Callan** Ir. Callain. S Ireland 52.33N 7.22W
12 H11 **Callander** Ontario, S Canada 46.12N 79.20W
98 I11 **Callander** C Scotland, UK 56.14N 4.16W
100 H7 **Callantsoog** Noord-Holland, NW Netherlands 52.51N 4.41E
59 D14 **Callao** Callao, W Peru 12.03S 77.09W
59 D15 **Callao** off. Departamento del Callao. ◆ constitutional province W Peru
58 F11 **Callaria, Río** ∽ E Peru
Callatis see Mangalia
9 Q13 **Calling Lake** Alberta, W Canada 55.12N 113.07W
Callosa de Ensarriá see Callosa d'En Sarrià
107 T11 **Callosa d'En Sarrià** var. Callosa de Ensarriá. País Valenciano, E Spain 38.40N 0.07W
107 S12 **Callosa de Segura** País Valenciano, E Spain 38.07N 0.52W
31 X11 **Calmar** Iowa, C USA 43.10N 91.51W
Calmar see Kalmar
45 R16 **Calobre** Veraguas, C Panama 8.18N 80.49W
179 P10 **Caloocan** municipality Luzon, N Philippines 14.37N 120.58E
25 X14 **Caloosahatchee River** ∽ Florida, SE USA
191 V2 **Caloundra** Queensland, E Australia 26.48S 153.07E
107 T11 **Calpe** País Valenciano, E Spain 38.39N 0.03E
43 P14 **Calpulalpan** Tlaxcala, S Mexico 19.36N 98.30W
109 K25 **Caltagirone** Sicilia, Italy, C Mediterranean Sea 37.13N 14.31E
109 J24 **Caltanissetta** Sicilia, Italy, C Mediterranean Sea 37.30N 14.00E
84 E11 **Caluango** Lunda Norte, NE Angola 8.16S 19.36E
84 C12 **Calucinga** Bié, W Angola 11.18S 16.10E
84 B12 **Calulo** Cuanza Sul, NW Angola 9.58S 14.56E
85 B14 **Caluquembe** Huíla, W Angola 13.46S 14.40E
82 Q11 **Caluula** Bari, NE Somalia 11.55N 50.51E
104 K4 **Calvados** ◆ department N France
195 P17 **Calvados Chain, The** island group SE PNG
27 U9 **Calvert** Texas, SW USA 30.58N 96.40W
22 H7 **Calvert City** Kentucky, S USA 37.01N 88.21W
105 X14 **Calvi** Corse, France, C Mediterranean Sea 42.34N 8.44E
42 L12 **Calvillo** Aguascalientes, C Mexico 21.51N 102.42W
85 F24 **Calvinia** Northern Cape, W South Africa 31.26S 19.45E
106 K8 **Calvitero** ▲ W Spain 40.16N 5.48W
103 G22 **Calw** Baden-Württemberg, SW Germany 48.43N 8.43E
Calydon see Kalydón
107 N11 **Calzada de Calatrava** Castilla-La Mancha, C Spain 38.42N 3.46W
Cama see Kama
84 C11 **Camabatela** Cuanza Norte, NW Angola 8.13S 15.22E
66 Q5 **Camacha** Porto Santo, Madeira, Portugal, NE Atlantic Ocean 32.40N 16.52W
12 L8 **Camachigama, Lac** ⊚ Quebec, SE Canada
42 M9 **Camacho** Zacatecas, C Mexico 24.23N 102.20W
84 D13 **Camacupa** var. General Machado, Port. Vila General Machado. Bié, C Angola 11.59S 17.30E
56 L7 **Camaguán** Guárico, C Venezuela 8.05N 67.34W
46 G6 **Camagüey** prev. Puerto Príncipe. Camagüey, C Cuba 21.24N 77.54W
46 G5 **Camagüey, Archipiélago de** island group C Cuba
42 D5 **Camalli, Sierra de** ▲ NW Mexico 28.21N 113.26W
59 G18 **Camana** var. Camaná. Arequipa, SW Peru 16.37S 72.42W
31 Z14 **Camanche** Iowa, C USA 41.47N 90.15W
37 P8 **Camanche Reservoir** ⊠ California, W USA
63 I16 **Camaquã** Rio Grande do Sul, S Brazil 30.49S 51.46W
63 H16 **Camaquã, Rio** ∽ S Brazil
66 P6 **Câmara de Lobos** Madeira, Portugal, NE Atlantic Ocean 32.37N 16.58W
105 U16 **Camarat, Cap** headland SE France 43.12N 6.42E
43 O8 **Camargo** Tamaulipas, C Mexico 26.16N 98.49W
105 R15 **Camargue** physical region SE France
106 F2 **Camariñas** Galicia, NW Spain 43.07N 9.10W
Camaronero, Laguna del see Caimanero, Laguna del
65 J18 **Camarones** Chaco, S Argentina 44.48S 65.42W
65 J18 **Camarones, Bahía** bay S Argentina
106 J14 **Camas** Andalucía, S Spain 37.24N 6.01W
178 J15 **Ca Mau** prev. Quan Long. Minh Hai, S Vietnam 9.11N 105.09E
84 E11 **Camaxilo** Lunda Norte, NE Angola 8.19S 18.52E
106 G3 **Cambados** Galicia, NW Spain 42.31N 8.49W
Cambay, Gulf of see Khambhāt, Gulf of
Camberia see Chambéry
99 N22 **Camberley** SE England, UK 51.21N 0.45W
178 Ii12 **Cambodia** off. Kingdom of Cambodia, var. Democratic Kampuchea, Roat Kampuchea, Cam. Kampuchea; prev. People's Democratic Republic of Kampuchea. ◆ republic SE Asia
104 I16 **Cambo-les-Bains** Pyrénées-Atlantiques, SW France 43.22N 1.24W
105 P2 **Cambrai** Flem. Kambryk; prev. Cambray, anc. Cameracum. Nord, N France 50.10N 3.13E
Cambray see Cambrai
106 H2 **Cambre** Galicia, NW Spain 43.18N 8.21W
37 O12 **Cambria** California, W USA 35.33N 121.04W
99 J20 **Cambrian Mountains** ▲▲ C Wales, UK
12 G16 **Cambridge** Ontario, S Canada 43.22N 80.16W
46 I12 **Cambridge** W Jamaica 18.19N 77.54W
192 M8 **Cambridge** Waikato, North Island, NZ 37.53S 175.28E
99 O20 **Cambridge** Lat. Cantabrigia. E England, UK 52.12N 0.07E
34 M12 **Cambridge** Idaho, NW USA 44.34N 116.42W
32 K11 **Cambridge** Illinois, N USA 41.18N 90.11W
23 Y4 **Cambridge** Maryland, NE USA 38.33N 76.04W
21 O11 **Cambridge** Massachusetts, NE USA 42.21N 71.05W
31 V7 **Cambridge** Minnesota, N USA 45.34N 93.13W
31 N16 **Cambridge** Nebraska, C USA 40.18N 100.10W
33 U13 **Cambridge** Ohio, NE USA 40.00N 81.34W
15 J3 **Cambridge Bay** Victoria Island, Nunavut, NW Canada 68.55N 105.08W
99 O20 **Cambridgeshire** cultural region E England, UK
107 U6 **Cambrils de Mar** Cataluña, NE Spain 41.06N 1.02E
Cambundi-Catembo see Nova Gaia
143 N11 **Çam Burnu** headland N Turkey 41.07N 37.48E
191 S9 **Camden** New South Wales, SE Australia 34.04S 150.40E
25 O6 **Camden** Alabama, S USA 31.59N 87.17W
29 U14 **Camden** Arkansas, C USA 33.34N 92.49W
23 Y3 **Camden** Delaware, NE USA 39.06N 75.30W
21 R7 **Camden** Maine, NE USA 44.12N 69.04W
20 I16 **Camden** New Jersey, NE USA 39.55N 75.07W
20 I9 **Camden** New York, NE USA 43.21N 75.45W
23 R12 **Camden** South Carolina, SE USA 34.15N 80.36W
22 H8 **Camden** Tennessee, S USA 36.03N 88.06W
27 X9 **Camden** Texas, SW USA 30.55N 94.43W
41 S5 **Camden Bay** bay S Beaufort Sea
29 U6 **Camdenton** Missouri, C USA 38.01N 92.44W
Camellia State see Alabama
20 M7 **Camels Hump** ▲ Vermont, NE USA 44.18N 72.50W
119 N8 **Camenca** Rus. Kamenka. N Moldova 48.01N 28.43E
Cameracum see Cambrai
24 G9 **Cameron** Louisiana, S USA 29.48N 93.19W
27 T9 **Cameron** Texas, SW USA 30.51N 96.58W
32 J5 **Cameron** Wisconsin, N USA 45.25N 91.42W
8 M12 **Cameron** ∽ British Columbia, W Canada
193 A24 **Cameron Mountains** ▲▲ South Island, NZ
81 D15 **Cameroon** off. Republic of Cameroon, Fr. Cameroun. ◆ republic W Africa
81 D15 **Cameroon Mountain** ▲ SW Cameroon 4.12N 9.00E
Cameroon Ridge see Camerounaise, Dorsale
Cameroun see Cameroon
81 E14 **Camerounaise, Dorsale** Eng. Cameroon Ridge. ridge NW Cameroon
179 R14 **Camiguin Island** island S Philippines
179 P10 **Camiling** Luzon, N Philippines 15.41N 120.22E
25 T7 **Camilla** Georgia, SE USA 31.13N 84.12W
106 G5 **Caminha** Viana do Castelo, N Portugal 41.52N 8.49W
37 P7 **Camino** California, W USA 38.43N 120.39W
142 B15 **Çamiçi Gölü** ⊚ SW Turkey
109 J24 **Cammarata** Sicilia, Italy, C Mediterranean Sea 37.36N 13.39E
44 K10 **Camoapa** Boaco, S Nicaragua 12.24N 85.32W
60 O13 **Camocim** Ceará, E Brazil 2.55S 40.49W
108 D10 **Camogli** Liguria, NW Italy 44.21N 9.10E
189 S5 **Camooweal** Queensland, C Australia 19.57S 138.14E
57 Y11 **Camopi** E French Guiana 3.12N 52.19W
157 Q22 **Camorta** island Nicobar Islands, India, NE Indian Ocean
179 R13 **Camotes Sea** sea C Philippines
44 I6 **Campamento** Olancho, C Honduras 14.33N 86.37W
63 D19 **Campana** Buenos Aires, E Argentina 34.06S 59.04W
65 F21 **Campana, Isla** island S Chile
106 K11 **Campanario** Extremadura, W Spain 38.52N 5.36W
109 L17 **Campania** Eng. Champagne. ◆ region S Italy
29 Y8 **Campbell** Missouri, C USA 36.29N 90.04W
193 K15 **Campbell, Cape** headland South Island, NZ 41.44S 174.16E
12 J14 **Campbellford** Ontario, SE Canada 44.18N 77.48W
33 R13 **Campbell Hill** hill Ohio, N USA 40.22N 83.43W
199 J14 **Campbell Island** island S NZ
183 P13 **Campbell Plateau** undersea feature SW Pacific Ocean
8 K17 **Campbell River** Vancouver Island, British Columbia, SW Canada 49.58N 125.18W
22 L6 **Campbellsville** Kentucky, S USA 37.20N 85.20W
11 O13 **Campbellton** New Brunswick, SE Canada 48.00N 66.41W
191 P16 **Campbell Town** Tasmania, SE Australia 41.57S 147.30E
191 S9 **Campbelltown** New South Wales, SE Australia 34.04S 150.46E
98 G13 **Campbeltown** W Scotland, UK 55.25N 5.37W
43 W13 **Campeche** Campeche, SE Mexico 19.46N 90.28W
43 W14 **Campeche** ◆ state SE Mexico
43 T14 **Campeche, Bahía de** Eng. Bay of Campeche. bay E Mexico
Campeche, Banco de see Campeche Bank
66 C11 **Campeche Bank** Sp. Banco de Campeche, Sonda de Campeche. undersea feature S Gulf of Mexico
Campeche, Bay of see Campeche, Bahía de
Campeche, Sonda de see Campeche Bank
46 H7 **Campechuela** Granma, E Cuba 20.11N 77.14W
190 M13 **Camperdown** Victoria, SE Australia 38.16S 143.10E
178 K6 **Câm Pha** Quang Ninh, N Vietnam 21.04N 107.20E
118 H10 **Câmpia Turzii** Ger. Jerischmarkt, Hung. Aranyosgyéres; prev. Cîmpia Turzii, Ghiriş, Gyéres. Cluj, NW Romania 46.33N 23.53E
106 K12 **Campillo de Llerena** Extremadura, W Spain 38.30N 5.48W
106 L15 **Campillos** Andalucía, S Spain 37.04N 4.51W
118 J13 **Câmpina** prev. Cîmpina. Prahova, SE Romania 45.08N 25.44E
61 Q15 **Campina Grande** Paraíba, E Brazil 7.15S 35.49W
62 L9 **Campinas** São Paulo, S Brazil 22.54S 47.06W
40 L10 **Camp Kulowiye** Saint Lawrence Island, Alaska, USA 63.15N 168.45W
81 D17 **Campo** var. Kampo. Sud, SW Cameroon 2.22N 9.49E
Campo see Ntem
61 N15 **Campo Alegre de Lourdes** Bahia, E Brazil 9.28S 43.01W
109 L16 **Campobasso** Molise, C Italy 41.34N 14.40E
109 H24 **Campobello di Mazara** Sicilia, Italy, C Mediterranean Sea 37.37N 12.45E
Campo Criptana see Campo de Criptana
107 O10 **Campo de Criptana** var. Campo Criptana. Castilla-La Mancha, C Spain 39.25N 3.07W
61 I16 **Campo de Diauarum** var. Pôsto Diuarum. Mato Grosso, W Brazil 11.08S 53.16W
56 E5 **Campo de la Cruz** Atlántico, N Colombia 10.22N 74.52W
107 P11 **Campo de Montiel** physical region C Spain
Campo dos Goitacazes see Campos
62 H12 **Campo Erê** Santa Catarina, S Brazil 26.24S 53.04W
64 L7 **Campo Gallo** Santiago del Estero, N Argentina 26.36S 62.50W
61 I20 **Campo Grande** state capital Mato Grosso do Sul, SW Brazil 20.24S 54.34W
62 K12 **Campo Largo** Paraná, S Brazil 25.27S 49.29W
60 N13 **Campo Maior** Piauí, E Brazil 4.49S 42.12W
106 I10 **Campo Maior** Portalegre, C Portugal 39.01N 7.04W
62 H10 **Campo Mourão** Paraná, S Brazil 24.01S 52.24W
62 Q9 **Campos** var. Campo dos Goitacazes. Rio de Janeiro, SE Brazil 21.46S 41.21W
61 L17 **Campos Belos** Goiás, S Brazil 13.11S 46.46W
62 N9 **Campos do Jordão** São Paulo, S Brazil 22.45S 45.36W
62 I13 **Campos Novos** Santa Catarina, S Brazil 27.22S 51.11W
61 O14 **Campos Sales** Ceará, E Brazil 7.01S 40.21W
27 Q9 **Camp San Saba** Texas, SW USA 30.57N 99.16W
23 N6 **Campton** Kentucky, S USA 37.43N 83.28W

◆ Country ● Country Capital ◇ Dependent Territory ○ Dependent Territory Capital ◈ Administrative Region ✈ International Airport ▲ Mountain ▲▲ Mountain Range ⛰ Volcano ∽ River ⊚ Lake ⊠ Reservoir

118 I13 **Câmpulung** prev. Câmpulung-Muşcel, Cîmpulung. Argeş, S Romania 45.16N 25.03E
118 J9 **Câmpulung Moldovenesc** var. Cîmpulung Moldovenesc, Ger. Kimpolung, Hung. Hosszúmezjő. Suceava, NE Romania 47.31N 25.34E
Câmpulung-Muşcel see Câmpulung
Campus Stellae see Santiago
38 L12 **Camp Verde** Arizona, SW USA 34.33N 111.52W
27 P11 **Camp Wood** Texas, SW USA 29.40N 100.00W
178 Kk13 **Cam Ranh** Khanh Hoa, S Vietnam 11.54N 109.13E
9 Q15 **Camrose** Alberta, SW Canada 53.01N 112.48W
Camulodunum see Colchester
142 B12 **Çan** Çanakkale, NW Turkey 40.01N 26.59E
20 L12 **Canaan** Connecticut, NE USA 42.00N 73.17W
15 Kk13 **Canada** ◆ commonwealth republic N North America
207 P6 **Canada Basin** undersea feature Arctic Ocean
63 B18 **Cañada de Gómez** Santa Fe, C Argentina 32.49S 61.22W
207 P6 **Canada Plain** undersea feature Arctic Ocean
63 A18 **Cañada Rosquín** Santa Fe, C Argentina 32.04S 61.35W
27 P1 **Canadian** Texas, SW USA 35.54N 100.22W
18 Kk11 **Canadian River** 〰 SW USA
15 K12 **Canadian Shield** physical region Canada
65 I18 **Cañadón Grande, Sierra** ⛰ S Argentina
57 P9 **Canaima** Bolívar, SE Venezuela 9.40N 72.33W
142 B11 **Çanakkale** var. Dardanelli; prev. Chanak, Kale Sultanie. Çanakkale, W Turkey 40.09N 26.25E
142 B12 **Çanakkale** ⬖ province NW Turkey
142 B11 **Çanakkale Boğazı** Eng. Dardanelles. strait NW Turkey
197 I6 **Canala** Province Nord, C New Caledonia 21.31S 165.57E
61 A15 **Canamari** Amazonas, W Brazil 7.37S 72.33W
20 G10 **Canandaigua** New York, NE USA 42.52N 77.14W
20 F10 **Canandaigua Lake** ◎ New York, NE USA
42 G3 **Cananea** Sonora, NW Mexico 30.58N 110.19W
58 B8 **Cañar** ⬖ province C Ecuador
66 N10 **Canarias, Islas** Eng. Canary Islands. ⬖ autonomous community Spain, NE Atlantic Ocean
Canaries Basin see Canary Basin
46 C6 **Canarreos, Archipiélago de los** island group W Cuba
68 K3 **Canary Basin** var. Canaries Basin, Monaco Basin. undersea feature E Atlantic Ocean
Canary Islands see Canarias, Islas
44 L13 **Cañas** Guanacaste, NW Costa Rica 10.25N 85.07W
20 I10 **Canastota** New York, NE USA 43.04N 75.45W
42 K9 **Canatlán** Durango, C Mexico 24.33N 104.45W
106 J9 **Cañaveral** Extremadura, W Spain 39.46N 6.24W
25 Y11 **Canaveral, Cape** headland Florida, SE USA 28.27N 80.31W
61 O18 **Canavieiras** Bahia, E Brazil 15.43S 38.58W
45 R16 **Cañazas** Veraguas, W Panama 8.19N 81.09W
108 H6 **Canazei** Trentino-Alto Adige, N Italy 46.29N 11.50E
191 P6 **Canbelego** New South Wales, SE Australia 31.36S 146.20E
191 R10 **Canberra** ● (Australia) Australian Capital Territory, SE Australia 35.21S 149.08E
191 R10 **Canberra** ✈ Australian Capital Territory, SE Australia 35.19S 149.12E
37 P2 **Canby** California, W USA 41.27N 120.51W
31 S9 **Canby** Minnesota, N USA 44.42N 96.17W
105 N2 **Canche** 〰 N France
104 L13 **Cancon** Lot-et-Garonne, SW France 44.33N 0.37E
43 Z11 **Cancún** Quintana Roo, SE Mexico 21.05N 86.48W
106 K2 **Candás** Asturias, N Spain 43.35N 5.45W
104 J7 **Cande** Maine-et-Loire, NW France 47.33N 1.03W
43 W14 **Candelaria** Campeche, SE Mexico 18.10N 91.00W
26 J11 **Candelaria** Texas, SW USA 30.05N 104.40W
43 W15 **Candelaria, Río** 〰 Guatemala/Mexico
106 L8 **Candeleda** Castilla-León, N Spain 40.10N 5.13W
Candia see Irákleio
43 P8 **Cándido Aguilar** Tamaulipas, C Mexico 25.30N 97.57W
41 N8 **Candle** Alaska, USA 65.54N 161.55W
9 T14 **Candle Lake** Saskatchewan, C Canada 53.43N 105.09W
20 L13 **Candlewood, Lake** ▣ Connecticut, NE USA
31 O3 **Cando** North Dakota, N USA 48.29N 99.12W
179 P8 **Candon** Luzon, N Philippines 17.15N 120.25E
Canea see Chaniá
47 O12 **Canefield** ✈ (Roseau) SW Dominica 15.20N 61.24W
63 F20 **Canelones** prev. Guadalupe. Canelones, S Uruguay 34.31S 56.16W
63 E20 **Canelones** ⬖ department S Uruguay
Canendiyú see Canindeyú
65 F14 **Cañete** Bío Bío, C Chile 37.48S 73.21W
107 Q9 **Cañete** Castilla-La Mancha, C Spain 40.03N 1.39W
Cañete see San Vicente de Cañete
29 P8 **Caney** Kansas, C USA 37.00N 95.56W
29 P8 **Caney River** 〰 Kansas/Oklahoma, C USA
107 S3 **Canfranc-Estación** Aragón, NE Spain 42.42N 0.31W
85 E14 **Cangamba** Port. Vila de Aljustrel. Moxico, E Angola 13.39S 19.57E
84 C12 **Cangandala** Malanje, NW Angola 9.46S 16.27E
106 G4 **Cangas** Galicia, NW Spain 42.16N 8.46W
106 J2 **Cangas del Narcea** Asturias, N Spain 43.10N 6.31W
106 L2 **Cangas de Onís** Asturias, N Spain 43.21N 5.07W
167 S11 **Cangnan** prev. Lingxi. Zhejiang, SE China 27.29N 120.23E
84 C10 **Cangola** Uíge, NW Angola 7.54S 15.57E
85 E14 **Cangombe** Moxico, E Angola 14.27S 20.05E
65 H21 **Cangrejo, Cerro** ▲ S Argentina 49.19S 72.18W
63 H17 **Canguçu** Rio Grande do Sul, S Brazil 31.25S 52.37W
167 P3 **Cangzhou** Hebei, E China 38.19N 116.54E
10 M7 **Caniapiscau** 〰 Quebec, E Canada
10 M8 **Caniapiscau, Réservoir de** ▣ Quebec, C Canada
109 J24 **Canicattì** Sicilia, Italy, C Mediterranean Sea 37.22N 13.51E
142 L11 **Canik Dağları** ⛰ N Turkey
107 P14 **Caniles** Andalucía, S Spain 37.24N 2.41W
61 B16 **Canindé** Acre, W Brazil 10.55S 69.45W
64 P6 **Canindeyú** var. Canendiyú, Canindiyú. ⬖ department E Paraguay
Canindiyú see Canindeyú
204 J10 **Canisteo Peninsula** peninsula Antarctica
20 F11 **Canisteo River** 〰 New York, NE USA
42 M10 **Cañitas** var. Cañitas de Felipe Pescador. Zacatecas, C Mexico 23.35N 102.39W
Cañitas de Felipe Pescador see Cañitas
107 P15 **Canjáyar** Andalucía, S Spain 37.00N 2.45W
142 I12 **Çankırı** var. Chankiri; anc. Gangra, Germanicopolis. Çankın, N Turkey 40.36N 33.35E
142 I11 **Çankırı** var. Chankiri. ⬖ province N Turkey
179 Qq13 **Canlaon Volcano** 🌋 Negros, C Philippines 10.24N 123.05E
9 P16 **Canmore** Alberta, SW Canada 51.07N 115.18W
98 F9 **Canna** island NW Scotland, UK
161 F20 **Cannanore** var. Kananur, Kannur. Kerala, SW India 11.52N 75.22E
33 O17 **Cannelton** Indiana, N USA 37.54N 86.44W
105 U15 **Cannes** Alpes-Maritimes, SE France 43.33N 6.58E
41 R5 **Canning River** 〰 Alaska, USA
108 C6 **Cannobio** Piemonte, NE Italy 46.04N 8.39E
99 L19 **Cannock** C England, UK 52.40N 2.03W
30 M6 **Cannonball River** 〰 North Dakota, N USA
31 W9 **Cannon Falls** Minnesota, N USA 44.30N 92.54W
20 I11 **Cannonsville Reservoir** ▣ New York, NE USA
191 R12 **Cann River** Victoria, SE Australia 37.34S 149.11E
63 I16 **Canoas** Rio Grande do Sul, S Brazil 29.42S 51.07W
63 I14 **Canoas, Rio** 〰 S Brazil
12 I12 **Canoe Lake** ◎ Ontario, SE Canada
62 J12 **Canoinhas** Santa Catarina, S Brazil 26.12S 50.24W
39 T6 **Canon City** Colorado, C USA 38.25N 105.14W
57 P8 **Caño Negro** Bolívar, SE Venezuela
181 X15 **Canonniers Point** headland N Mauritius
25 W6 **Canoochee River** 〰 Georgia, SE USA
9 V15 **Canora** Saskatchewan, S Canada 51.37N 102.28W
47 Y14 **Canouan** island S Saint Vincent and the Grenadines
11 R15 **Canso** Nova Scotia, SE Canada 45.20N 61.00W
106 M3 **Cantabria** ⬖ autonomous community N Spain
106 K3 **Cantábrica, Cordillera** ⛰ N Spain
Cantabrigia see Cambridge
105 O12 **Cantal** ⬖ department C France
107 N6 **Cantalejo** Castilla-León, N Spain 41.15N 3.57W
105 O12 **Cantal, Monts du** ⛰ C France
106 G8 **Cantanhede** Coimbra, C Portugal 40.21N 8.37W
Cantaño see Cataño
57 O6 **Cantaura** Anzoátegui, NE Venezuela 9.18N 64.21W
118 M11 **Cantemir** Rus. Kantemir. S Moldova 46.17N 28.12E
99 Q22 **Canterbury** hist. Cantwaraburh, anc. Durovernum, Lat. Cantuaria. SE England, UK 51.16N 1.04E
193 F19 **Canterbury** off. Canterbury Region. ⬖ region South Island, NZ
193 H20 **Canterbury Bight** bight South Island, NZ
193 H19 **Canterbury Plains** plain South Island, NZ
178 Jj15 **Cân Thơ** Cân Thơ, S Vietnam 10.03N 105.46E
106 K13 **Cantillana** Andalucía, S Spain 37.34N 5.48W
61 N15 **Canto do Buriti** Piauí, NE Brazil 8.07S 43.00W
25 S2 **Canton** Georgia, SE USA 34.14N 84.29W
32 K12 **Canton** Illinois, N USA 40.33N 90.02W
24 L5 **Canton** Mississippi, S USA 32.36N 90.02W
29 V2 **Canton** Missouri, C USA 40.07N 91.31W
20 J7 **Canton** New York, NE USA 44.36N 75.10W
23 O10 **Canton** North Carolina, SE USA 35.31N 82.50W
33 U12 **Canton** Ohio, N USA 40.48N 81.22W
28 L9 **Canton** Oklahoma, C USA 36.03N 98.35W
20 G12 **Canton** Pennsylvania, NE USA 41.38N 76.49W
31 R11 **Canton** South Dakota, N USA 43.19N 96.33W
27 V7 **Canton** Texas, SW USA 32.34N 95.50W
Canton see Guangzhou
Canton Island see Kanton
28 L9 **Canton Lake** ▣ Oklahoma, C USA
108 D7 **Cantù** Lombardia, N Italy 45.43N 9.07E
Cantuaria/Cantwaraburh see Canterbury
41 R10 **Cantwell** Alaska, USA 63.23N 148.57W
61 O16 **Canudos** Bahia, E Brazil 9.51S 39.07W
49 T7 **Canumã, Rio** 〰 N Brazil
Canusium see Puglia, Canosa di
26 G7 **Canutillo** Texas, SW USA 31.53N 106.34W
27 N3 **Canyon** Texas, SW USA 34.58N 101.55W
35 S12 **Canyon** Wyoming, C USA 44.44N 110.30W
34 K13 **Canyon City** Oregon, NW USA 44.22N 118.58W
35 R10 **Canyon Ferry Lake** ◎ Montana, NW USA
27 S11 **Canyon Lake** ▣ Texas, SW USA
178 Jj5 **Cao Băng** var. Caobang. Cao Băng, N Vietnam 22.40N 106.16E
166 J12 **Caodu He** 〰 S China
178 J14 **Cao Lanh** Đông Thap, S Vietnam 10.35N 105.25E
84 C11 **Caombo** Malanje, NW Angola 8.42S 16.33E
Caorach, Cuan na g see Sheep Haven
Caozhou see Heze
175 S10 **Capalulu** Pulau Mangole, E Indonesia 1.51S 125.53E
56 K8 **Capanaparo, Río** 〰 Colomiba/Venezuela
60 L12 **Capanema** Pará, NE Brazil 1.07S 47.07W
62 L10 **Capão Bonito** São Paulo, S Brazil 24.01S 48.22W
62 I13 **Capão Doce, Morro do** ▲ S Brazil 26.37S 51.28W
56 I4 **Capatárida** Falcón, N Venezuela 11.10N 70.38W
104 I15 **Capbreton** Landes, SW France 43.40N 1.25W
Cap-Breton, Île du see Cape Breton Island
13 W6 **Cap-Chat** Quebec, SE Canada 49.04N 66.43W
13 P11 **Cap-de-la-Madeleine** Quebec, SE Canada 46.22N 72.31W
105 N13 **Capdenac** Aveyron, S France 44.35N 2.06E
191 Q15 **Cape Barren Island** island Furneaux Group, Tasmania, SE Australia
67 O18 **Cape Basin** undersea feature S Atlantic Ocean
11 R14 **Cape Breton Island** Fr. Île du Cap-Breton. island Nova Scotia, SE Canada
25 Y11 **Cape Canaveral** Florida, SE USA 28.24N 80.36W
23 Y6 **Cape Charles** Virginia, NE USA 37.16N 76.01W
79 P17 **Cape Coast** prev. Cape Coast Castle. S Ghana 5.10N 1.13W
Cape Coast Castle see Cape Coast
21 Q12 **Cape Cod Bay** bay Massachusetts, NE USA
25 W15 **Cape Coral** Florida, SE USA 26.33N 81.57W
189 R4 **Cape Crawford Roadhouse** Northern Territory, N Australia 16.39S 135.44E
16 N4 **Cape Dorset** Baffin Island, Nunavut, NE Canada 64.12N 76.31W
23 N8 **Cape Fear River** 〰 North Carolina, SE USA
29 Y7 **Cape Girardeau** Missouri, C USA 37.17N 89.31W
23 T14 **Cape Island** island South Carolina, SE USA
194 E11 **Capella** ▲ NW PNG 5.00S 141.09E
100 H12 **Capelle aan den IJssel** Zuid-Holland, SW Netherlands 51.55N 4.36E
85 C15 **Capelongo** Huíla, C Angola 14.45S 15.02E
20 J17 **Cape May** New Jersey, NE USA 38.54N 74.54W
20 J17 **Cape May Court House** New Jersey, NE USA 39.03N 74.46W
Cape Palmas see Harper
15 H2 **Cape Parry** Northwest Territories, N Canada 70.10N 124.33W
67 P19 **Cape Rise** undersea feature SW Indian Ocean
Cape Saint Jacques see Vung Tau
Capesterre see Capesterre-Belle-Eau
47 Y6 **Capesterre-Belle-Eau** var. Capesterre. Basse Terre, S Guadeloupe 16.03N 61.33W
85 D26 **Cape Town** var. Ekapa, Afr. Kaapstad, Kapstad. ● (South Africa-legislative capital) Western Cape, SW South Africa 33.55S 18.28E
85 E26 **Cape Town** ✈ Western Cape, SW South Africa 31.51S 21.06E
78 D9 **Cape Verde** off. Republic of Cape Verde, Port. Cabo Verde, Ilhas do Cabo Verde. ◆ republic E Atlantic Ocean
66 L11 **Cape Verde Basin** undersea feature E Atlantic Ocean
68 K5 **Cape Verde Islands** island group E Atlantic Ocean
66 L10 **Cape Verde Plain** undersea feature E Atlantic Ocean
Cape Verde Plateau/Cape Verde Rise see Cape Verde Terrace
66 L11 **Cape Verde Terrace** var. Cape Verde Plateau, Cape Verde Rise. undersea feature E Atlantic Ocean
189 V2 **Cape York Peninsula** peninsula Queensland, N Australia
46 M8 **Cap-Haïtien** var. Le Cap. N Haiti 19.43N 72.12W
45 T15 **Capira** Panamá, C Panama 8.45N 79.52W
12 K8 **Capitachouane** 〰 Quebec, SE Canada
12 L8 **Capitachouane, Lac** ◎ Quebec, SE Canada
39 T13 **Capitan** New Mexico, SW USA 33.33N 105.34W
204 G3 **Capitán Arturo Prat** Chilean research station South Shetland Islands, Antarctica 62.24S 59.42W
39 S13 **Capitan Mountains** ⛰ New Mexico, SW USA
64 M3 **Capitán Pablo Lagerenza** var. Mayor Pablo Lagerenza. Chaco, N Paraguay 19.55S 60.46W
39 T13 **Capitan Peak** ▲ New Mexico, SW USA 33.35N 105.15W
196 H5 **Capitol Hill** Saipan, S Northern Mariana Islands
62 I9 **Capivara, Represa** ▣ S Brazil
63 J16 **Capivari** Rio Grande do Sul, S Brazil 30.08S 50.32W
115 H15 **Čapljina** Federacija Bosna I Hercegovina, S Bosnia and Herzegovina 43.07N 17.42E
85 M15 **Capoche** var. Kapoche. 〰 Mozambique/Zambia
Capo Delgado, Província de see Cabo Delgado
109 K17 **Capodichino** ✈ (Napoli) Campania, S Italy 40.53N 14.15E
Capodistria see Koper
108 E12 **Capraia, Isola** island Archipelago Toscano, C Italy
109 B16 **Caprara, Punta** var. Punta dello Scorno. headland Isola Asinara, W Italy 41.07N 8.19E
Capraria, Isola di to Capraia, Isola see Cabrera
12 F10 **Capreol** Ontario, S Canada 46.43N 80.55W
109 K18 **Capri** Campania, S Italy 40.33N 14.14E
183 S9 **Capricorn Tablemount** undersea feature W Pacific Ocean 18.34S 172.12W
109 J18 **Capri, Isola di** island S Italy
85 G16 **Caprivi** ⬖ district NE Namibia
Caprivi Concession see Caprivi Strip
85 F16 **Caprivi Strip** Ger. Caprivizipfel; prev. Caprivi Concession. cultural region NE Namibia
Caprivizipfel see Caprivi Strip
27 O5 **Cap Rock Escarpment** cliffs Texas, SW USA
13 R10 **Cap-Rouge** Quebec, SE Canada 46.45N 71.18W
Cap Saint-Jacques see Vung Tau
40 F12 **Captain Cook** Hawaii, USA, C Pacific Ocean 19.30N 155.55W
191 R10 **Captains Flat** New South Wales, SE Australia 35.37S 149.28E
104 K14 **Captieux** Gironde, SW France 44.16N 0.15W
109 K17 **Capua** Campania, S Italy 41.06N 14.13E
56 F14 **Caquetá** off. Departamanto del Caquetá. ⬖ province S Colombia
56 E13 **Caquetá, Río** var. Rio Japurá, Yapurá. 〰 Brazil/Colombia see also Japurá, Rio
CAR see Central African Republic
Cara see Kara
59 I16 **Carabaya, Cordillera** ⛰ E Peru
56 K5 **Carabobo** off. Estado Carabobo. ⬖ state N Venezuela
118 I14 **Caracal** Olt, S Romania 44.07N 24.18E
60 F10 **Caracaraí** Rondônia, W Brazil 1.46N 61.10W
56 L5 **Caracas** ● (Venezuela) Distrito Federal, N Venezuela 10.28N 66.53W
56 I5 **Carache** Trujillo, N Venezuela 9.40N 70.15W
62 N10 **Caraguatatuba** São Paulo, S Brazil 23.37S 45.24W
50 I7 **Carajás, Serra dos** ⛰ N Brazil
Caralis see Cagliari
56 E9 **Caramanta** Antioquia, W Colombia 5.36N 75.37W
179 Q11 **Caramoan** Catanduanes Island, N Philippines 13.47N 123.49E
Caramurat see Mihail Kogălniceanu
118 F12 **Caransebeş** Ger. Karansebesch, Hung. Karánsebes. Caraş-Severin, SW Romania 45.23N 22.13E
Carapella see Carapelle
109 M16 **Carapelle** var. Carapella. 〰 SE Italy
57 O9 **Carapo** Bolívar, SE Venezuela
11 P13 **Caraquet** New Brunswick, SE Canada 47.48N 64.58W
Caras see Caraz
118 F12 **Caraşova** Hung. Krassóvár. Caraş-Severin, SW Romania 45.10N 21.51E
118 F12 **Caraş-Severin** ⬖ county SW Romania
44 M5 **Caratasca, Laguna de** lagoon NE Honduras
60 C13 **Carauari** Amazonas, NW Brazil 4.55S 66.57W
Caravaca see Caravaca de la Cruz
107 Q12 **Caravaca de la Cruz** var. Caravaca. Murcia, SE Spain 38.06N 1.51W
108 E7 **Caravaggio** Lombardia, N Italy 45.31N 9.39E
109 C18 **Caravai, Passo di** pass Sardegna, Italy, C Mediterranean Sea 40.06N 9.19E
61 O19 **Caravelas** Bahia, E Brazil 17.45S 39.15W
58 C12 **Caraz** var. Caras. Ancash, W Peru 9.01S 77.48W
63 H14 **Carazinho** Rio Grande do Sul, S Brazil 28.16S 52.46W
44 J11 **Carazo** ⬖ department SW Nicaragua
Carballiño see O Carballiño
106 G2 **Carballo** Galicia, NW Spain 43.12N 8.42W
9 W16 **Carberry** Manitoba, S Canada 49.52N 99.19W
42 F4 **Carbó** Sonora, NW Mexico 29.40N 110.54W
109 C20 **Carbonara, Capo** headland Sardegna, Italy, C Mediterranean Sea 39.06N 9.31E
39 Q5 **Carbondale** Colorado, C USA 39.24N 107.12W
32 L17 **Carbondale** Illinois, N USA 37.43N 89.13W
29 Q4 **Carbondale** Kansas, C USA 38.49N 95.41W
20 I13 **Carbondale** Pennsylvania, NE USA 41.34N 75.30W
11 V12 **Carbonear** Newfoundland and Labrador, SE Canada 47.45N 53.16W
107 Q9 **Carboneras de Guadazaón** var. Carboneras de Guadazón. Castilla-La Mancha, C Spain 39.54N 1.49W
Carboneras de Guadazón see Carboneras de Guadazaón
25 O3 **Carbon Hill** Alabama, S USA 33.53N 87.31W
109 B20 **Carbonia** var. Carbonia Centro. Sardegna, Italy, C Mediterranean Sea 39.10N 8.31E
Carbonia Centro see Carbonia
107 S10 **Carcaixent** País Valenciano, E Spain 39.07N 0.28W
Carcaso see Carcassonne
67 B24 **Carcass Island** island NW Falkland Islands
105 O16 **Carcassonne** anc. Carcaso. Aude, S France 43.13N 2.21E
107 R12 **Carche** ▲ S Spain 38.24N 1.11W
58 A13 **Carchi** ⬖ province N Ecuador
8 I8 **Carcross** Yukon Territory, W Canada 60.10N 134.40W
Cardamomes, Chaîne des see Krâvanh, Chuŏr Phnum
161 G22 **Cardamom Hills** ⛰ SW India
Cardamom Mountains see Krâvanh, Chuŏr Phnum
106 M12 **Cardeña** Andalucía, S Spain 38.16N 4.19W
46 D4 **Cárdenas** Matanzas, W Cuba 23.01N 81.12W
43 O11 **Cárdenas** San Luis Potosí, C Mexico 22.03N 99.30W
43 U15 **Cárdenas** Tabasco, SE Mexico 18.00N 93.21W
65 H21 **Cardiel, Lago** ◎ S Argentina
99 K22 **Cardiff** Wel. Caerdydd. ◐ S Wales, UK 51.30N 3.13W
99 J22 **Cardiff-Wales** ✈ S Wales, UK 51.24N 3.22W
99 I21 **Cardigan** Wel. Aberteifi. SW Wales, UK 52.06N 4.40W
99 I20 **Cardigan** cultural region W Wales, UK
99 I20 **Cardigan Bay** bay W Wales, UK
21 N8 **Cardigan, Mount** ▲ New Hampshire, NE USA 43.39N 71.52W
12 M13 **Cardinal** Ontario, SE Canada 44.48N 75.22W
107 V5 **Cardona** Cataluña, NE Spain 41.55N 1.40E
63 E19 **Cardona** Soriano, SW Uruguay 33.52S 57.18W
107 V4 **Cardoner** 〰 NE Spain
9 Q17 **Cardston** Alberta, SW Canada 49.13N 113.19W
189 W5 **Cardwell** Queensland, NE Australia 18.24S 146.06E
118 G8 **Carei** Ger. Gross-Karol, Karol, Hung. Nagykároly; prev. Careii-Mari. Satu Mare, NW Romania 47.40N 22.27E
Careii-Mari see Carei
60 F13 **Careiro** Amazonas, NW Brazil 3.39S 60.22W
104 J4 **Carentan** Manche, N France 49.18N 1.15W
106 M2 **Cares** 〰 N Spain
35 P14 **Carey** Idaho, NW USA 43.17N 113.58W
33 S12 **Carey** Ohio, N USA 40.57N 83.22W
27 P4 **Carey** Texas, SW USA 34.28N 100.18W
188 L11 **Carey, Lake** ◎ Western Australia
181 O8 **Cargados Carajos Bank** undersea feature C Indian Ocean
104 G6 **Carhaix-Plouguer** Finistère, NW France 48.16N 3.34W
63 A22 **Carhué** Buenos Aires, E Argentina 37.10S 62.45W
57 O5 **Cariaco** Sucre, NE Venezuela 10.28N 63.33W
109 O20 **Cariati** Calabria, SW Italy 39.30N 16.57E
2 H17 **Caribbean Plate** tectonic feature
46 I11 **Caribbean Sea** sea W Atlantic Ocean
9 N15 **Cariboo Mountains** ⛰ British Columbia, SW Canada
9 W9 **Caribou** Manitoba, C Canada 59.27N 97.43W
21 S2 **Caribou** Maine, NE USA 46.51N 68.00W
9 P10 **Caribou Mountains** ⛰ Alberta, SW Canada
Caribrod see Dimitrovgrad
42 I6 **Carichic** Chihuahua, N Mexico 27.57N 107.01W
179 Qq13 **Carigara** Leyte, C Philippines 11.15N 124.43E
105 R3 **Carignan** Ardennes, N France 49.38N 5.08E
191 Q5 **Carinda** New South Wales, SE Australia 30.26S 147.45E
107 R6 **Cariñena** Aragón, NE Spain 41.19N 1.13W
109 I23 **Carini** Sicilia, Italy, C Mediterranean Sea 38.06N 13.09E
109 K17 **Carinola** Campania, S Italy 41.14N 14.03E
Carinthi see Kärnten
57 O5 **Caripe** Monagas, NE Venezuela 10.06N 63.30W
57 P5 **Caripito** Monagas, NE Venezuela 10.03N 63.05W
13 W7 **Carleton** Quebec, SE Canada 48.07N 66.07W
33 S10 **Carleton** Michigan, N USA 42.03N 83.23W
11 O14 **Carleton, Mount** ▲ New Brunswick, SE Canada 47.10N 66.54W
12 L13 **Carleton Place** Ontario, SE Canada 45.09N 76.07W
37 V3 **Carlin** Nevada, W USA 40.40N 116.09W
32 K14 **Carlinville** Illinois, N USA 39.16N 89.52W
99 K14 **Carlisle** anc. Caer Luel, Luguvallium, Luguvallum. NW England, UK 54.54N 2.55W
29 V11 **Carlisle** Arkansas, C USA 34.46N 91.45W
33 N15 **Carlisle** Indiana, N USA 38.57N 87.23W
31 V14 **Carlisle** Iowa, C USA 41.30N 93.29W
23 N5 **Carlisle** Kentucky, S USA 38.19N 83.59W
20 F15 **Carlisle** Pennsylvania, NE USA 40.10N 77.10W
23 Q11 **Carlisle** South Carolina, SE USA 34.35N 81.27W
40 J17 **Carlisle Island** island Aleutian Islands, Alaska, USA
29 R7 **Carl Junction** Missouri, C USA 37.10N 94.34W
109 A20 **Carloforte** Sardegna, Italy, C Mediterranean Sea 39.10N 8.17E
Carlopago see Karlobag
63 B21 **Carlos Casares** Buenos Aires, E Argentina 35.39S 61.28W
63 E18 **Carlos Reyles** Durazno, C Uruguay 33.04S 56.28W
63 A21 **Carlos Tejedor** Buenos Aires, E Argentina 35.23S 62.31W
99 F19 **Carlow** Ir. Ceatharlach. SE Ireland 52.49N 6.55W
99 F19 **Carlow** Ir. Cheatharlach. cultural region SE Ireland
98 F7 **Carloway** NW Scotland, UK 58.16N 6.48W
Carlsbad see Karlovy Vary
37 U17 **Carlsbad** California, W USA 33.09N 117.21W
39 U15 **Carlsbad** New Mexico, SW USA 32.24N 104.14W
133 N13 **Carlsberg Ridge** undersea feature S Arabian Sea
Carlsruhe see Karlsruhe
31 W6 **Carlton** Minnesota, N USA 46.39N 92.25W
9 V17 **Carlyle** Saskatchewan, S Canada 49.39N 102.18W
32 L15 **Carlyle** Illinois, N USA 38.36N 89.22W
32 L15 **Carlyle Lake** ▣ Illinois, N USA
8 H7 **Carmacks** Yukon Territory, W Canada 62.04N 136.21W
108 B9 **Carmagnola** Piemonte, NW Italy 44.50N 7.43E
9 X16 **Carman** Manitoba, S Canada 49.31N 97.58W
Carmana/Carmania see Kermān
99 I21 **Carmarthen** SW Wales, UK 51.52N 4.19W
99 I21 **Carmarthen** cultural region SW Wales, UK
99 I22 **Carmarthen Bay** inlet SW Wales, UK
105 N14 **Carmaux** Tarn, S France 44.03N 2.09E
37 N11 **Carmel** California, W USA 36.32N 121.54W
33 O13 **Carmel** Indiana, N USA 39.58N 86.07W
20 L13 **Carmel** New York, NE USA 41.25N 73.40W
99 H18 **Carmel Head** headland NW Wales, UK 53.24N 4.35W
44 E2 **Carmelita** Petén, N Guatemala 17.33N 90.10W
63 D19 **Carmelo** Colonia, SW Uruguay 34.00S 58.20W
43 V14 **Carmen** var. Ciudad del Carmen. Campeche, SE Mexico 18.37N 91.49W
63 A25 **Carmen de Patagones** Buenos Aires, E Argentina 40.45S 63.00W
42 F8 **Carmen, Isla** island W Mexico
42 M5 **Carmen, Sierra del** ⛰ NW Mexico
32 M16 **Carmi** Illinois, N USA 38.05N 88.09W
37 O7 **Carmichael** California, W USA 38.36N 121.21W
Carmiel see Karmi'él
27 U11 **Carmine** Texas, SW USA 30.07N 96.40W
106 K14 **Carmona** Andalucía, S Spain 37.28N 5.37W
Carmona see Uíge
Carnaro see Kvarner
12 I13 **Carnarvon** Ontario, SE Canada 45.03N 78.41W
85 G24 **Carnarvon** Northern Cape, W South Africa 30.58S 22.07E
Carnarvon see Caernarfon
188 K9 **Carnarvon Range** ⛰ Western Australia
188 G9 **Carnarvon** Western Australia 24.57S 113.37E
Carn Domhnach see Carndonagh
98 E13 **Carndonagh** Ir. Carn Domhnach. NW Ireland 55.15N 7.15W
9 V17 **Carnduff** Saskatchewan, S Canada 49.10N 101.49W
28 L11 **Carnegie** Oklahoma, C USA 35.06N 98.36W
188 L9 **Carnegie, Lake** salt lake Western Australia
200 Oo8 **Carnegie Ridge** undersea feature E Pacific Ocean
98 H9 **Carn Eige** ▲ N Scotland, UK 57.18N 5.04W
190 F5 **Carnes** South Australia 30.12S 134.31E
204 J12 **Carney Island** island Antarctica
20 H16 **Carneys Point** New Jersey, NE USA 39.38N 75.29W
Carniche, Alpi see Karnische Alpen
157 Q21 **Car Nicobar** island Nicobar Islands, India, NE Indian Ocean
81 H15 **Carnot** Mambéré-Kadéï, W Central African Republic 4.58N 15.55E
190 F10 **Carnot, Cape** headland South Australia 34.57S 135.39E
98 K11 **Carnoustie** E Scotland, UK 56.29N 2.42W
99 F20 **Carnsore Point** Ir. Ceann an Chairn. headland SE Ireland 52.10N 6.22W
15 Gg4 **Carnwath** 〰 Northwest Territories, NW Canada
33 R8 **Caro** Michigan, N USA 43.29N 83.24W
25 Z15 **Carol City** Florida, SE USA 25.56N 80.15W
61 L14 **Carolina** Maranhão, E Brazil 7.19S 47.25W
47 U5 **Carolina** E Puerto Rico 18.22N 65.57W
23 V12 **Carolina Beach** North Carolina, SE USA 34.02N 77.53W
Caroline Island see Millennium Island
201 N15 **Caroline Islands** island group C Micronesia
133 Z14 **Caroline Plate** tectonic feature
199 H7 **Caroline Ridge** undersea feature E Philippine Sea
Carolopois see Châlons-en-Champagne
47 V14 **Caroni Arena Dam** ▣ Trinidad, Trinidad and Tobago
Caronie, Monti see Nebrodi, Monti
57 P7 **Caroní, Río** 〰 E Venezuela
47 U14 **Caroni River** 〰 Trinidad, Trinidad and Tobago
Caronium see A Coruña
56 J5 **Carora** Lara, N Venezuela 10.09N 70.06W
88 F12 **Carpathian Mountains** var. Carpathians, Cz./Pol. Karpaty, Ger. Karpaten. ⛰ E Europe
Carpathians see Carpathian Mountains
Carpathos/Carpathus see Kárpathos
118 H12 **Carpaţii Meridionali** var. Alpi Transilvaniei, Carpaţii Sudici, Eng. South Carpathians, Transylvanian Alps, Ger. Südkarpaten, Transsylvanische Alpen, Hung. Déli-Kárpátok, Erdélyi-Havasok. ⛰ C Romania
Carpaţii Sudici see Carpaţii Meridionali
182 L7 **Carpentaria, Gulf of** gulf N Australia
Carpentoracte see Carpentras
105 R14 **Carpentras** anc. Carpentoracte. Vaucluse, SE France 44.03N 5.03E
108 F9 **Carpi** Emilia-Romagna, N Italy 44.46N 10.52E
118 E11 **Cărpiniş** Hung. Gyertyámos. Timiş, W Romania 45.46N 20.51E
37 R14 **Carpinteria** California, W USA 34.24N 119.30W
25 S9 **Carrabelle** Florida, SE USA 29.51N 84.39W
Carraig Aonair see Fastnet Rock
Carraig Fhearghais see Carrickfergus
Carraig Mhachaire Rois see Carrickmacross
Carraig na Siúire see Carrick-on-Suir
Carrantual see Carrauntoohil
108 E10 **Carrara** Toscana, C Italy 44.04N 10.07E
63 F20 **Carrasco** ✈ (Montevideo) Canelones, S Uruguay 34.51S 56.00W
107 P9 **Carrascosa del Campo** Castilla-La Mancha, C Spain 40.01N 2.34W
56 H4 **Carrasquero** Zulia, NW Venezuela 11.00N 72.01W
191 O9 **Carrathool** New South Wales, SE Australia 34.25S 145.30E
Carrauntohil see Carrauntoohil
99 B21 **Carrauntoohil** Ir. Carrantual, Carrauntohil, Corrán Tuathail. ▲ SW Ireland 51.59N 9.45W
47 Y15 **Carriacou** island N Grenada
99 G15 **Carrickfergus** Ir. Carraig Fhearghais. NE Northern Ireland, UK 54.43N 5.49W
99 F16 **Carrickmacross** Ir. Carraig Mhachaire Rois. N Ireland 53.58N 6.43W
99 D16 **Carrick-on-Shannon** Ir. Cora Droma Rúisc. NW Ireland 53.37N 8.04W
99 E20 **Carrick-on-Suir** Ir. Carraig na Siúire. S Ireland 52.21N 7.25W
190 I7 **Carrieton** South Australia 32.27S 138.33E
42 L7 **Carrillo** Chihuahua, N Mexico 25.53N 103.54W
31 O4 **Carrington** North Dakota, N USA 47.27N 99.07W
106 M4 **Carrión** 〰 N Spain
106 M4 **Carrión de los Condes** Castilla-León, N Spain 42.19N 4.37W
27 P13 **Carrizo Springs** Texas, SW USA 28.31N 99.51W
39 S13 **Carrizozo** New Mexico, SW USA 33.38N 105.52W
31 T13 **Carroll** Iowa, C USA 42.04N 94.52W
25 N4 **Carrollton** Alabama, S USA 33.13N 88.05W
25 R3 **Carrollton** Georgia, SE USA 33.33N 85.04W
32 K14 **Carrollton** Illinois, N USA 39.18N 90.24W
22 L4 **Carrollton** Kentucky, S USA 38.40N 85.10W
33 R8 **Carrollton** Michigan, N USA 43.27N 83.55W
29 T3 **Carrollton** Missouri, C USA 39.21N 93.30W
33 U12 **Carrollton** Ohio, N USA 40.34N 81.05W
27 T6 **Carrollton** Texas, SW USA 32.57N 96.53W
9 U14 **Carrot** 〰 Saskatchewan, S Canada
9 U14 **Carrot River** Saskatchewan, C Canada 53.18N 103.31W
20 J7 **Carry Falls Reservoir** ▣ New York, NE USA
142 L11 **Çarşamba** Samsun, N Turkey 41.13N 36.43E
30 L6 **Carson** North Dakota, N USA 46.21N 101.33W
37 Q6 **Carson City** state capital Nevada, W USA 39.10N 119.46W
37 R6 **Carson River** 〰 Nevada, W USA
37 S5 **Carson Sink** salt flat Nevada, W USA
9 Q16 **Carstairs** Alberta, SW Canada 51.34N 114.01W
Carstensz, Puntjak see Jaya, Puncak

◆ Country ● Country Capital ◇ Dependent Territory ○ Dependent Territory Capital ⬖ Administrative Region ✈ International Airport ▲ Mountain ⛰ Mountain Range 🌋 Volcano 〰 River ◎ Lake ▣ Reservoir

56 E5 **Cartagena** *var.* Cartagena de los Indes. Bolívar, NW Colombia 10.24N 75.33W
107 R13 **Cartagena** *anc.* Carthago Nova. Murcia, SE Spain 37.36N 0.58W
Cartagena de los Indes *see* Cartagena
56 D10 **Cartago** Valle del Cauca, W Colombia 4.45N 75.55W
45 N14 **Cartago** Cartago, C Costa Rica 9.49N 83.53W
44 M14 **Cartago** *off.* Provincia de Cartago. ◈ *province* C Costa Rica
27 O11 **Carta Valley** Texas, SW USA 29.46N 100.37W
106 F10 **Cartaxo** Santarém, C Portugal 39.10N 8.46W
106 I14 **Cartaya** Andalucía, S Spain 37.16N 7.09W
Carteret Islands *see* Tulun Islands
31 S15 **Carter Lake** Iowa, C USA 41.17N 95.55W
25 S3 **Cartersville** Georgia, SE USA 34.10N 84.48W
193 M14 **Carterton** Wellington, North Island, NZ 41.01S 175.32E
32 J13 **Carthage** Illinois, N USA 40.25N 91.09W
24 L5 **Carthage** Mississippi, S USA 32.43N 89.31W
29 R7 **Carthage** Missouri, C USA 37.10N 94.18W
20 I8 **Carthage** New York, NE USA 43.58N 75.36W
23 T10 **Carthage** North Carolina, SE USA 35.19N 79.24W
22 K8 **Carthage** Tennessee, S USA 36.16N 85.57W
27 X7 **Carthage** Texas, SW USA 32.09N 94.20W
76 M5 **Carthage** ✈ (Tunis) N Tunisia 36.51N 10.12E
Carthago Nova *see* Cartagena
12 E10 **Cartier** Ontario, S Canada 46.40N 81.31W
56 E13 **Cartagena de Chaira** Caquetá, S Colombia 1.19N 74.52W
11 S8 **Cartwright** Newfoundland and Labrador, E Canada 53.40N 57.00W
57 P9 **Caruana de Montaña** Bolívar, SE Venezuela 5.16N 63.12W
61 Q15 **Caruaru** Pernambuco, E Brazil 8.15S 35.55W
57 P5 **Carúpano** Sucre, NE Venezuela 10.39N 63.13W
Carusbur *see* Cherbourg
60 M12 **Carutapera** Maranhão, E Brazil 1.12S 45.57W
29 Y9 **Caruthersville** Missouri, C USA 36.07N 89.38W
105 O1 **Carvin** Pas-de-Calais, N France 50.31N 3.00E
60 E12 **Carvoeiro** Amazonas, NW Brazil 1.24S 61.59W
106 E10 **Carvoeiro, Cabo** *headland* C Portugal 39.19N 9.27W
23 U9 **Cary** North Carolina, SE USA 35.47N 78.46W
190 M3 **Caryapundy Swamp** *wetland* New South Wales/Queensland, SE Australia
67 E24 **Carysfort, Cape** *headland* East Falkland, Falkland Islands 51.25S 57.49W
76 F6 **Casablanca** *Ar.* Dar-el-Beida. NW Morocco 33.39N 7.30W
62 M8 **Casa Branca** São Paulo, S Brazil 21.47S 47.05W
38 L14 **Casa Grande** Arizona, SW USA 32.52N 111.45W
108 C8 **Casale Monferrato** Piemonte, NW Italy 45.07N 8.28E
108 E8 **Casalpusterlengo** Lombardia, N Italy 45.10N 9.37E
56 H10 **Casanare** *off.* Intendencia de Casanare. ◈ *province* C Colombia
57 P5 **Casanay** Sucre, NE Venezuela 10.30N 63.25W
26 K11 **Casa Piedra** Texas, SW USA 29.43N 104.03W
109 Q19 **Casarano** Puglia, SE Italy 40.01N 18.10E
44 J11 **Casares** Carazo, W Nicaragua 11.37N 86.19W
107 R10 **Casas Ibáñez** Castilla-La Mancha, C Spain 39.16N 1.28W
63 I14 **Casca** Rio Grande do Sul, S Brazil 28.39S 51.55W
180 I17 **Cascade** Mahé, NE Seychelles 4.39S 55.28E
35 N13 **Cascade** Idaho, NW USA 44.31N 116.02W
31 Y13 **Cascade** Iowa, C USA 42.18N 91.00W
35 R9 **Cascade** Montana, NW USA 47.15N 111.46W
193 B20 **Cascade Point** *headland* South Island, NZ 44.00S 168.23E
34 G13 **Cascade Range** ▲▲ Oregon/Washington, NW USA
35 N12 **Cascade Reservoir** ⊠ Idaho, NW USA
(0) E8 **Cascadia Basin** *undersea feature* NE Pacific Ocean
106 E11 **Cascais** Lisboa, C Portugal 38.40N 9.25W
13 W7 **Cascapédia** ≈ Quebec, SE Canada
61 I22 **Cascavel** Ceará, E Brazil 4.10S 38.15W
62 G11 **Cascavel** Paraná, S Brazil 24.55S 53.28W
108 I13 **Cascia** Umbria, C Italy 42.45N 13.01E
108 F11 **Cascina** Toscana, C Italy 43.40N 10.33E
21 Q8 **Casco Bay** *bay* Maine, NE USA
204 J7 **Case Island** *island* Antarctica
108 B8 **Caselle** ✈ (Torino) Piemonte, NW Italy 45.06N 7.41E
109 K17 **Caserta** Campania, S Italy 41.04N 14.19E
13 N8 **Casey** Quebec, SE Canada 47.50N 74.09W
32 M14 **Casey** Illinois, N USA 39.18N 87.59W
205 Y12 **Casey** *Australian research station* Antarctica 65.58S 111.04E
205 W3 **Casey Bay** *bay* Antarctica
82 Q11 **Caseyr, Raas** *headland* NE Somalia 11.51N 51.16E
99 D20 **Cashel** *Ir.* Caiseal. S Ireland 52.31N 7.52W
56 G6 **Casigua** Zulia, W Venezuela 8.46N 72.30W
63 B19 **Casilda** Santa Fe, C Argentina 33.04S 61.10W
Casim *see* General Toshevo
191 V4 **Casino** New South Wales, SE Australia 28.49S 153.01E
Casinum *see* Cassino
113 E17 **Čáslav** *Ger.* Tschaslau. Střední Čechy, C Czech Republic 49.54N 15.22E
58 C13 **Casma** Ancash, C Peru 9.27S 78.21W
178 J7 **Ca, Sông** ≈ N Vietnam
109 K17 **Casoria** Campania, S Italy 40.54N 14.28E
107 T6 **Caspe** Aragón, NE Spain 41.13N 0.03W
35 X15 **Casper** Wyoming, C USA 42.48N 106.22W
86 M10 **Caspian Depression** *Kaz.* Kaspiy Mangy Oypaty, *Rus.* Prikaspiyskaya Nizmennost'. *depression* Kazakhstan/Russian Federation
138 Kk9 **Caspian Sea** *Az.* Xäzär Dänizi, *Kaz.* Kaspiy Tengizi, *Per.* Baḩr-e Khazar, Daryā-ye Khazar, *Rus.* Kaspiyskoye More. *inland sea* Asia/Europe
85 L14 **Cassacatiza** Tete, NW Mozambique 14.20S 32.24E
Cassai *see* Kasai
84 F13 **Cassamba** Moxico, E Angola 13.07S 20.22E
109 N20 **Cassano allo Ionio** Calabria, SE Italy 39.46N 16.16E
33 S8 **Cass City** Michigan, N USA 43.36N 83.10W
Cassel *see* Kassel
12 M13 **Casselman** Ontario, SE Canada 45.19N 75.04W
31 R5 **Casselton** North Dakota, N USA 46.53N 97.10W
61 M16 **Cássia** *var.* Santa Rita de Cassia. Bahia, E Brazil 11.03S 44.16W
8 J9 **Cassiar** British Columbia, W Canada 59.16N 129.45W
8 K10 **Cassiar Mountains** ▲▲ British Columbia, W Canada
85 C15 **Cassinga** Huíla, SW Angola 15.06S 16.05E
109 J16 **Cassino** *prev.* San Germano; *anc.* Casinum. Lazio, C Italy 41.28N 13.49E
31 T4 **Cass Lake** Minnesota, N USA 47.22N 94.36W
31 T4 **Cass Lake** ◎ Minnesota, N USA
33 P10 **Cassopolis** Michigan, N USA 41.56N 86.00W
33 S8 **Cass River** ≈ Michigan, N USA
29 S8 **Cassville** Missouri, C USA 36.40N 93.52W
Castamoni *see* Kastamonu
60 L12 **Castanhal** Pará, NE Brazil 1.16S 47.55W
106 G8 **Castanheira de Pêra** Leiria, C Portugal 40.01N 8.12W
43 N7 **Castaños** Coahuila de Zaragoza, NE Mexico 26.48N 101.25W
110 I10 **Castasegna** Graubünden, SE Switzerland 46.21N 9.30E
108 D8 **Casteggio** Lombardia, N Italy 45.01N 9.10E
109 K23 **Castelbuono** Sicilia, Italy, C Mediterranean Sea 37.55N 14.04E
109 K15 **Castel di Sangro** Abruzzo, C Italy 41.46N 14.03E
108 H7 **Castelfranco Veneto** Veneto, NE Italy 45.40N 11.55E
104 K14 **Casteljaloux** Lot-et-Garonne, SW France 44.19N 0.03E
109 L18 **Castellabate** *var.* Santa Maria di Castellabate. Campania, S Italy 40.16N 14.57E
109 I23 **Castellammare del Golfo** Sicilia, Italy, C Mediterranean Sea 38.01N 12.52E
109 H22 **Castellammare, Golfo di** *gulf* Sicilia, Italy, C Mediterranean Sea
105 U15 **Castellane** Alpes-de-Haute-Provence, SE France 43.49N 6.34E
109 O18 **Castellaneta** Puglia, SE Italy 40.37N 16.57E
108 E9 **Castel l'Arquato** Emilia-Romagna, C Italy 44.52N 9.51E
63 E21 **Castelli** Buenos Aires, E Argentina 36.07S 57.46W
107 T9 **Castelló de la Plana** *var.* Castellón. País Valenciano, E Spain 39.58N 0.03W
107 S8 **Castellón** ◈ *province* País Valenciano, E Spain
Castellón *see* Castelló de la Plana
107 S7 **Castellote** Aragón, NE Spain 40.46N 0.18W
105 N16 **Castelnaudary** Aude, S France 43.18N 1.57E
104 L16 **Castelnau-Magnoac** Hautes-Pyrénées, S France 43.18N 0.30E
108 F10 **Castelnovo ne' Monti** Emilia-Romagna, C Italy 44.26N 10.24E
Castelnuovo *see* Herceg-Novi
106 H9 **Castelo Branco** Castelo Branco, C Portugal 39.49N 7.30W
106 H8 **Castelo Branco** ◈ *district* C Portugal
106 I10 **Castelo de Vide** Portalegre, C Portugal 39.25N 7.27W
106 G9 **Castelo do Bode, Barragem do** ⊠ C Portugal
108 G10 **Castel San Pietro Terme** Emilia-Romagna, C Italy 44.22N 11.34E
109 B17 **Castelsardo** Sardegna, Italy, C Mediterranean Sea 40.54N 8.42E
104 M14 **Castelsarrasin** Tarn-et-Garonne, S France 44.01N 1.06E
109 I24 **Casteltermini** Sicilia, Italy, C Mediterranean Sea 37.33N 13.37E
109 H24 **Castelvetrano** Sicilia, Italy, C Mediterranean Sea 37.40N 12.46E
190 L12 **Casterton** Victoria, SE Australia 37.37S 141.22E
104 J15 **Castets** Landes, SW France 43.55N 1.08W
108 H12 **Castiglione del Lago** Umbria, C Italy 43.07N 12.02E
108 F13 **Castiglione della Pescaia** Toscana, C Italy 42.46N 10.53E
108 F8 **Castiglione delle Stiviere** Lombardia, N Italy 45.24N 10.31E
106 M9 **Castilla-La Mancha** ◈ *autonomous community* NE Spain
106 L5 **Castilla-León** *var.* Castillia y Leon. ◈ *autonomous community* NW Spain
107 N10 **Castilla Nueva** *cultural region* C Spain
107 N6 **Castilla Vieja** *cultural region* N Spain
Castillia y Leon *see* Castilla-León
Castillo de Locubim *see* Castillo de Locubín
107 N14 **Castillo de Locubín** *var.* Castillo de Locubim. Andalucía, S Spain 37.31N 3.55W
104 K13 **Castillon-la-Bataille** Gironde, SW France 44.51N 0.01W
65 I19 **Castillo, Pampa del** *plain* S Argentina
63 G19 **Castillos** Rocha, SE Uruguay 34.12S 53.52W
99 B16 **Castlebar** *Ir.* Caisleán an Bharraigh. W Ireland 53.52N 9.16W
99 F16 **Castleblayney** *Ir.* Baile na Lorgan. N Ireland 54.07N 6.43W
47 O11 **Castle Bruce** E Dominica 15.25N 61.15W
38 M5 **Castle Dale** Utah, W USA 39.10N 111.02W
38 I14 **Castle Dome Peak** ▲ Arizona, SW USA 33.04N 114.08W
99 J14 **Castle Douglas** S Scotland, UK 54.56N 3.55W
99 E14 **Castlefinn** *Ir.* Caisleán na Finne. NW Ireland 54.48N 7.36W
99 M17 **Castleford** N England, UK 53.43N 1.21W
9 O17 **Castlegar** British Columbia, SW Canada 49.18N 117.48W
66 B12 **Castle Harbour** *inlet* Bermuda, NW Atlantic Ocean
23 V12 **Castle Hayne** North Carolina, SE USA 34.23N 78.07W
99 B20 **Castleisland** *Ir.* Oileán Ciarral. SW Ireland 52.12N 9.30W
191 N12 **Castlemaine** Victoria, SE Australia 37.06S 144.13E
39 R5 **Castle Peak** ▲ Colorado, C USA 39.00N 106.51W
35 O13 **Castle Peak** ▲ Idaho, NW USA 44.02N 114.42W
192 N13 **Castlepoint** Wellington, North Island, NZ 40.54S 176.13E
99 D17 **Castlerea** *Ir.* An Caisleán Riabhach. W Ireland 53.45N 8.31W
99 G15 **Castlereagh** *Ir.* An Caisleán Riabhach. N Northern Ireland, UK 54.33N 5.53W
191 R6 **Castlereagh River** ≈ New South Wales, SE Australia
39 T5 **Castle Rock** Colorado, C USA 39.22N 104.51W
32 K7 **Castle Rock Lake** ⊠ Wisconsin, N USA
67 G25 **Castle Rock Point** *headland* S Saint Helena 16.01S 5.45W
99 I16 **Castletown** SE Isle of Man 54.04N 4.39W
31 R9 **Castlewood** South Dakota, N USA 44.43N 97.01W
9 R15 **Castor** Alberta, SW Canada 52.13N 111.54W
12 M13 **Castor** ≈ Ontario, SE Canada
29 X7 **Castor River** ≈ Missouri, C USA
Castra Albiensium *see* Castres
Castra Regina *see* Regensburg
105 N15 **Castres** *anc.* Castra Albiensium. Tarn, S France 43.36N 2.15E
100 H9 **Castricum** Noord-Holland, W Netherlands 52.33N 4.40E
47 S11 **Castries** ● (Saint Lucia) N Saint Lucia 14.01N 60.59W
62 J11 **Castro** Paraná, S Brazil 24.45S 50.58W
65 F17 **Castro** Los Lagos, W Chile 42.27S 73.48W
106 H7 **Castro Daire** Viseu, N Portugal 40.54N 7.55W
106 M13 **Castro del Río** Andalucía, S Spain 37.40N 4.28W
Castrogiovanni *see* Enna
106 H14 **Castro Marim** Faro, S Portugal 37.13N 7.25W
106 J2 **Castropol** Asturias, N Spain 43.30N 7.01W
107 O2 **Castro-Urdiales** *var.* Castro Urdiales. Cantabria, N Spain 43.22N 3.10W
106 G13 **Castro Verde** Beja, S Portugal 37.42N 8.04W
109 N19 **Castrovillari** Calabria, SW Italy 39.48N 16.12E
37 N10 **Castroville** California, W USA 36.46N 121.46W
27 R12 **Castroville** Texas, SW USA 29.21N 98.52W
106 K11 **Castuera** Extremadura, W Spain 38.43N 5.33W
63 F19 **Casupá** Florida, S Uruguay 34.04S 55.39W
193 A22 **Caswell Sound** *sound* South Island, NZ
143 Q13 **Çat** Erzurum, NE Turkey 39.40N 41.03E
44 K6 **Catacamas** Olancho, C Honduras 14.50N 85.54W
58 A10 **Catacaos** Piura, NW Peru 5.22S 80.40W
24 I7 **Catahoula Lake** ◎ Louisiana, S USA
143 S15 **Çatak** Van, SE Turkey 38.01N 43.04E
143 S15 **Çatak Çayi** ≈ SE Turkey
116 O12 **Çatalca** İstanbul, NW Turkey 41.09N 28.28E
116 O12 **Çatalca Yarımadası** *physical region* NW Turkey
64 H6 **Catalina** Antofagasta, N Chile 25.19S 69.37W
Catalonia *see* Cataluña
107 U5 **Cataluña** *Cat.* Catalunya; *Eng.* Catalonia. ◈ *autonomous community* N Spain
Catalunya *see* Cataluña
64 I7 **Catamarca** *off.* Provincia de Catamarca. ◈ *province* NW Argentina
Catamarca *see* San Fernando del Valle de Catamarca
179 Pp11 **Catanauan** Luzon, N Philippines 13.36N 122.19E
85 M16 **Catandica** Manica, C Mozambique 18.04S 33.10E
179 Qq11 **Catanduanes Island** *island* N Philippines
62 K8 **Catanduva** São Paulo, S Brazil 21.06S 48.57W
109 L24 **Catania** Sicilia, Italy, C Mediterranean Sea 37.31N 15.04E
109 M24 **Catania, Golfo di** *gulf* Sicilia, Italy, C Mediterranean Sea
47 U5 **Cataño** *var.* Cantaño. E Puerto Rico 18.26N 66.06W
109 O21 **Catanzaro** Calabria, SW Italy 38.53N 16.36E
109 O22 **Catanzaro Marina** *var.* Marina di Catanzaro. Calabria, S Italy 38.48N 16.33E
27 Q14 **Catarina** Texas, SW USA 28.19N 99.36W
179 Qq12 **Catarman** Samar, C Philippines 12.29N 124.34E
107 S10 **Catarroja** País Valenciano, E Spain 39.24N 0.24W
23 R11 **Catawba River** ≈ North Carolina/South Carolina, SE USA
179 R12 **Catbalogan** Samar, C Philippines 11.49N 124.55E
12 I14 **Catchacoma** Ontario, SE Canada 44.43N 78.19W
43 S15 **Catemaco** Veracruz-Llave, SE Mexico 18.28N 95.10W
Cathair na Mart *see* Westport
Cathair Saidhbhín *see* Cahersiveen
33 P5 **Cat Head Point** *headland* Michigan, N USA 45.11N 85.37W
25 Q2 **Cathedral Caverns** *cave* Alabama, S USA 34.36N 86.11W
37 V16 **Cathedral City** California, W USA 33.45N 116.27W
26 K10 **Cathedral Mountain** ▲ Texas, SW USA 30.10N 103.39W
34 G10 **Cathlamet** Washington, NW USA 46.12N 123.24W
78 G13 **Catió** S Guinea-Bissau 11.17N 15.16W
57 O10 **Catisimiña** Bolívar, SE Venezuela 4.07N 63.40W
46 J3 **Cat Island** *island* C Bahamas
10 B9 **Cat Lake** Ontario, S Canada 51.47N 91.52W
23 P5 **Catlettsburg** Kentucky, S USA 38.24N 82.37W
193 D24 **Catlins** ≈ South Island, NZ
37 R1 **Catnip Mountain** ▲ Nevada, W USA 41.53N 119.19W
43 Z11 **Catoche, Cabo** *headland* SE Mexico 21.36N 87.04W
29 P9 **Catoosa** Oklahoma, C USA 36.11N 95.45W
43 N10 **Catorce** San Luis Potosí, C Mexico 23.42N 100.49W
65 I14 **Catriel** Río Negro, C Argentina 37.54S 67.52W
64 K13 **Catriló** La Pampa, C Argentina 36.24S 63.25W
60 F11 **Catrimani** Roraima, N Brazil 0.24N 61.30W
60 E10 **Catrimani, Rio** ≈ N Brazil
20 K11 **Catskill** New York, NE USA 42.13N 73.52W
20 K11 **Catskill Creek** ≈ New York, NE USA
20 J11 **Catskill Mountains** ▲▲ New York, NE USA
20 D11 **Cattaraugus Creek** ≈ New York, NE USA
Cattaro *see* Kotor
Cattaro, Bocche di *see* Kotorska, Boka
109 I24 **Cattolica Eraclea** Sicilia, Italy, C Mediterranean Sea 37.27N 13.24E
85 B14 **Catumbela** ≈ W Angola
85 N14 **Catur** Niassa, N Mozambique 13.50S 35.43E
84 C10 **Cauale** ≈ NE Angola
179 Pp9 **Cauayan** Luzon, N Philippines 16.55N 121.46E
56 C12 **Cauca** *off.* Departamento del Cauca. ◈ *province* SW Colombia
49 P5 **Cauca** ≈ SE Venezuela
60 P13 **Caucaia** Ceará, E Brazil 3.43S 38.45W
56 E7 **Cauca, Río** ≈ N Colombia
56 E7 **Caucasia** Antioquia, NW Colombia 7.58N 75.13W
143 Q8 **Caucasus** *Rus.* Kavkaz. ▲▲ Georgia/Russian Federation
64 I10 **Caucete** San Juan, W Argentina 31.38S 68.16W
107 R11 **Caudete** Castilla-La Mancha, C Spain 38.42N 1.00W
105 P2 **Caudry** Nord, N France 50.07N 3.24E
84 D11 **Caungula** Lunda Norte, NE Angola 8.22S 18.37E
64 G13 **Cauquenes** Maule, C Chile 35.58S 72.22W
57 N8 **Caura, Río** ≈ C Venezuela
13 V7 **Causapscal** Quebec, SE Canada 48.22N 67.13W
119 N10 **Căuşeni** *Rus.* Kaushany. E Moldova 46.37N 29.21E
104 M14 **Caussade** Tarn-et-Garonne, S France 44.10N 1.31E
104 K17 **Cauterets** Hautes-Pyrénées, S France 42.53N 0.08W
8 J15 **Caution, Cape** *headland* British Columbia, SW Canada 51.10N 127.43W
46 H7 **Cauto** ≈ E Cuba
Cauvery *see* Kāveri
104 L3 **Caux, Pays de** *physical region* N France
109 L18 **Cava dei Tirreni** Campania, S Italy 40.42N 14.42E
106 G6 **Cávado** ≈ N Portugal
Cavaia *see* Kavajë
105 R15 **Cavaillon** Vaucluse, SE France 43.51N 5.01E
105 U16 **Cavalaire-sur-Mer** Var, SE France 43.10N 6.31E
108 G6 **Cavalese** *Ger.* Gablös. Trentino-Alto Adige, N Italy 46.18N 11.29E
31 Q2 **Cavalier** North Dakota, N USA 48.47N 97.37W
78 L17 **Cavalla** *var.* Cavally, Cavally Fleuve. ≈ Ivory Coast/Liberia
107 Y8 **Cavalleria, Cap de** *var.* Cabo Caballeria. *headland* Menorca, Spain, W Mediterranean Sea 40.04N 4.06E
192 K2 **Cavalli Islands** *island group* N NZ
Cavally/Cavally Fleuve *see* Cavalla
99 E16 **Cavan** *Ir.* Cabhán. N Ireland 54.00N 7.21W
99 E16 **Cavan** *Ir.* An Cabhán. *cultural region* N Ireland
108 H8 **Cavarzere** Veneto, NE Italy 45.07N 12.04E
29 W9 **Cave City** Arkansas, C USA 35.56N 91.33W
22 K7 **Cave City** Kentucky, S USA 37.08N 85.57W
67 M25 **Cave Point** *headland* S Tristan da Cunha
23 N5 **Cave Run Lake** ⊠ Kentucky, S USA
60 K11 **Caviana de Fora, Ilha** *var.* Ilha Caviana. *island* N Brazil
Caviana, Ilha *see* Caviana de Fora, Ilha
115 I16 **Cavtat** *It.* Ragusavecchia. Dubrovnik-Neretva, SE Croatia 42.36N 18.13E
Cawnpore *see* Kānpur
Caxamarca *see* Cajamarca
60 A13 **Caxias** Amazonas, W Brazil 4.27S 71.27W
60 N13 **Caxias** Maranhão, E Brazil 4.52S 43.19W
63 I15 **Caxias do Sul** Rio Grande do Sul, S Brazil 29.13S 51.10W
44 J4 **Caxinas, Punta** *headland* N Honduras 16.01N 86.02W
84 B11 **Caxito** Bengo, NW Angola 8.34S 13.37E
142 F14 **Çay** Afyon, W Turkey 38.34N 31.01E
42 L15 **Cayacal, Punta** *var.* Punta Mongrove. *headland* S Mexico 17.55N 102.09W
58 C6 **Cayambe** Pichincha, N Ecuador 0.01N 78.10W
58 C6 **Cayambe** ▲ N Ecuador 0.00N 77.58W
23 R12 **Cayce** South Carolina, SE USA 33.58N 81.04W
57 Y10 **Cayenne** ○ (French Guiana) NE French Guiana 4.55N 52.18W
57 Y10 **Cayenne** ✈ NE French Guiana 4.55N 52.18W
46 K10 **Cayes** *var.* Les Cayes. SW Haiti 18.10N 73.48W
47 U6 **Cayey** C Puerto Rico 18.06N 66.09W
47 U6 **Cayey, Sierra de** ▲▲ E Puerto Rico
105 N14 **Caylus** Tarn-et-Garonne, S France 44.13N 1.42E
46 E8 **Cayman Brac** *island* E Cayman Islands
46 D8 **Cayman Islands** ◇ *UK dependent territory* W West Indies
66 D11 **Cayman Trench** *undersea feature* NW Caribbean Sea
49 O3 **Cayman Trough** *undersea feature* NW Caribbean Sea
82 O13 **Caynabo** Togdheer, N Somalia 8.55N 46.28E
44 F3 **Cayo** ◈ *district* SW Belize
Cayo *see* San Ignacio
45 N9 **Cayos Guerrero** *reef* E Nicaragua
45 O9 **Cayos King** *reef* E Nicaragua
46 E4 **Cay Sal** *islet* SW Bahamas
12 G16 **Cayuga** Ontario, S Canada 42.57N 79.49W
27 V8 **Cayuga** Texas, SW USA 31.55N 95.57W
20 G10 **Cayuga Lake** ◎ New York, NE USA
106 K13 **Cazalla de la Sierra** Andalucía, S Spain 37.56N 5.46W
118 L14 **Căzănești** Ialomița, SE Romania 44.36N 27.02E
104 M16 **Cazères** Haute-Garonne, S France 43.15N 1.11E
114 E10 **Cazin** Federacija Bosna I Hercegovina, NW Bosnia and Herzegovina 44.58N 15.58E
84 G13 **Cazombo** Moxico, E Angola 11.53S 22.52E
107 O13 **Cazorla** Andalucía, S Spain 37.55N 3.00W
Cazza *see* Sušac
106 L4 **Cea** ≈ NW Spain
Ceadâr-Lunga *see* Ciadîr-Lunga
Ceanannas *see* Kells
Ceann Toirc *see* Kanturk
60 O13 **Ceará** *off.* Estado do Ceará. ◈ *state* C Brazil
Ceará *see* Fortaleza
Ceara Abyssal Plain *see* Ceará Plain
61 Q14 **Ceará Mirim** Rio Grande do Norte, E Brazil 5.30S 35.50W
66 J13 **Ceará Plain** *var.* Ceara Abyssal Plain. *undersea feature* W Atlantic Ocean
66 I13 **Ceará Ridge** *undersea feature* C Atlantic Ocean
Ceatharlach *see* Carlow
45 Q17 **Cébaco, Isla** *island* SW Panama
42 K7 **Ceballos** Durango, C Mexico 26.33N 104.07W
63 G19 **Cebollatí** Rocha, E Uruguay 33.15S 53.49W
63 G19 **Cebollatí, Río** ≈ E Uruguay
107 P5 **Cebollera** ▲ N Spain 42.01N 2.40W
106 M8 **Cebreros** Castilla-León, N Spain 40.27N 4.28W
179 Qq14 **Cebu** *off.* Cebu City. Cebu, C Philippines 10.16N 123.45E
179 Qq13 **Cebu** *island* C Philippines
109 J16 **Ceccano** Lazio, C Italy 41.34N 13.19E
Čechy *see* Bohemia
108 F12 **Cecina** Toscana, C Italy 43.18N 10.31E
28 K4 **Cedar Bluff Reservoir** ⊠ Kansas, C USA
32 M8 **Cedarburg** Wisconsin, N USA 43.18N 87.58W
38 J7 **Cedar City** Utah, W USA 37.40N 113.03W
27 T11 **Cedar Creek** Texas, SW USA 30.04N 97.30W
30 L7 **Cedar Creek** ≈ North Dakota, N USA
27 U7 **Cedar Creek Reservoir** ⊠ Texas, SW USA
31 W13 **Cedar Falls** Iowa, C USA 42.31N 92.27W
33 N8 **Cedar Grove** Wisconsin, N USA 43.31N 87.48W
23 Y6 **Cedar Island** *island* Virginia, NE USA
25 U11 **Cedar Key** Cedar Keys, Florida, SE USA 29.08N 83.01W
25 U11 **Cedar Keys** *island group* Florida, SE USA
9 V14 **Cedar Lake** ◎ Manitoba, C Canada
12 I11 **Cedar Lake** ◎ Ontario, SE Canada
26 M6 **Cedar Lake** ◎ Texas, SW USA
31 X13 **Cedar Rapids** Iowa, C USA 41.58N 91.39W
31 X14 **Cedar River** ≈ Iowa/Minnesota, C USA
31 O14 **Cedar River** ≈ Nebraska, C USA
33 P8 **Cedar Springs** Michigan, N USA 43.13N 85.33W
25 R3 **Cedartown** Georgia, SE USA 34.00N 85.16W
29 O7 **Cedar Vale** Kansas, C USA 37.06N 96.30W
37 Q2 **Cedarville** California, W USA 41.30N 120.10W
106 H1 **Cedeira** Galicia, NW Spain 43.40N 8.03W
44 H8 **Cedeño** Choluteca, S Honduras 13.10N 87.25W
43 N10 **Cedral** San Luis Potosí, C Mexico 23.47N 100.40W
44 I6 **Cedros** Francisco Morazán, C Honduras 14.38N 87.09W
42 M9 **Cedros** Zacatecas, C Mexico 24.39N 101.47W
42 B5 **Cedros, Isla** *island* W Mexico
199 Mm6 **Cedros Trench** *undersea feature* E Pacific Ocean
190 E7 **Ceduna** South Australia 32.09S 133.43E
112 D10 **Cedynia** *Ger.* Zehden. Zachodniopomorskie, W Poland 52.54N 14.15E
82 P12 **Ceelaayo** Sanaag, N Somalia 11.18N 49.20E
83 O16 **Ceel Buur** *It.* El Bur; Galguduud, C Somalia 4.36N 46.33E
83 N15 **Ceel Dheere** *var.* Ceel Dher, *It.* El Dere. Galguduud, C Somalia 5.18N 46.07E
Ceel Dher *see* Ceel Dheere
83 P14 **Ceel Xamure** Mudug, E Somalia 7.15N 48.55E
82 O12 **Ceerigaabo** *var.* Erigabo, Erigavo. Sanaag, N Somalia 10.34N 47.22E
109 J23 **Cefalu** *anc.* Cephaloedium. Sicilia, Italy, C Mediterranean Sea 38.01N 14.01E
107 N6 **Cega** ≈ N Spain
113 K23 **Cegléd** *prev.* Czegléd. Pest, C Hungary 47.08N 19.45E
115 N18 **Čegrane** W FYR Macedonia 41.50N 20.59E
107 Q13 **Cehegín** Murcia, SE Spain 38.04N 1.48W
142 K12 **Çekerek** Yozgat, N Turkey 40.04N 35.30E
109 J15 **Celano** Abruzzo, C Italy 42.06N 13.33E
106 H4 **Celanova** Galicia, NW Spain 42.09N 7.58W
44 F6 **Celaque, Cordillera de** ▲▲ W Honduras
43 N13 **Celaya** Guanajuato, C Mexico 20.31N 100.48W
Celebes *see* Sulawesi
198 Ff8 **Celebes Basin** *undersea feature* SE South China Sea
175 Qq4 **Celebes Sea** *Ind.* Laut Sulawesi. *sea* Indonesia/Philippines
43 W12 **Celestún** Yucatán, E Mexico 20.49N 90.22W
33 Q12 **Celina** Ohio, N USA 40.33N 84.34W
22 L8 **Celina** Tennessee, S USA 36.30N 85.30W
27 U5 **Celina** Texas, SW USA 33.19N 96.46W
114 G11 **Čelinac Donji** Republika Srpska, N Bosnia and Herzegovina 44.43N 17.19E
111 V10 **Celje** *Ger.* Cilli. C Slovenia 46.16N 15.14E
113 G23 **Celldömölk** Vas, W Hungary 47.16N 17.10E
102 J12 **Celle** *var.* Zelle. Niedersachsen, N Germany 52.37N 10.04E
101 D19 **Celles** Hainaut, SW Belgium 50.42N 3.25E
106 I7 **Celorico da Beira** Guarda, N Portugal 40.37N 7.24W
Celovec *see* Klagenfurt
66 M7 **Celtic Sea** *Ir.* An Mhuir Cheilteach. *sea* SW British Isles
66 N7 **Celtic Shelf** *undersea feature* E Atlantic Ocean
116 L13 **Çeltik Gölu** ◎ NW Turkey
115 M14 **Čemerno** ▲ C Serbia and Montenegro (Yugoslavia)
175 Oo16 **Cempi, Teluk** *bay* Nusa Tenggara, S Indonesia
107 Q12 **Cenajo, Embalse del** ⊠ S Spain
176 Ww10 **Cenderawasih, Teluk** *var.* Teluk Irian, Teluk Sarera. *bay* W Pacific Ocean
107 P4 **Cenicero** La Rioja, N Spain 42.28N 2.37W
108 E9 **Ceno** ≈ NW Italy
104 K13 **Cenon** Gironde, SW France 44.51N 0.33W
12 K13 **Centennial Lake** ◎ Ontario, SE Canada
Centennial State *see* Colorado
39 S7 **Center** Colorado, C USA 37.45N 106.06W
31 Q13 **Center** Nebraska, C USA 42.33N 97.51W
30 M5 **Center** North Dakota, N USA 47.07N 101.18W
27 X8 **Center** Texas, SW USA 31.48N 94.10W
31 W8 **Center City** Minnesota, N USA 45.22N 92.48W
38 L5 **Centerfield** Utah, W USA 39.07N 111.49W
22 K9 **Center Hill Lake** ⊠ Tennessee, S USA
31 X13 **Center Point** Iowa, C USA 42.11N 91.47W
27 R11 **Center Point** Texas, SW USA 29.56N 99.01W
31 W16 **Centerville** Iowa, C USA 40.42N 92.49W
29 W7 **Centerville** Missouri, C USA 37.27N 91.01W
31 R12 **Centerville** South Dakota, N USA 43.07N 96.57W
22 I9 **Centerville** Tennessee, S USA 35.43N 87.27W
27 V9 **Centerville** Texas, SW USA 31.15N 95.58W
42 M5 **Centinela, Picacho del** ▲ NE Mexico 29.07N 102.40W
108 G9 **Cento** Emilia-Romagna, N Italy 44.43N 11.16E
Centrafricaine, République *see* Central African Republic
41 S8 **Central** Alaska, USA 65.34N 144.48W
39 P15 **Central** New Mexico, SW USA 32.46N 108.09W
85 H18 **Central** ◈ *district* E Botswana
144 E10 **Central** ◈ *district* C Israel
83 I19 **Central** ◈ *province* C Kenya
84 M13 **Central** ◈ *region* C Malawi
159 P12 **Central** ◈ *zone* C Nepal
194 J15 **Central** ◈ *province* S PNG
65 I21 **Central** ◈ *department* C Paraguay
195 W15 **Central** *off.* Central Province. ◈ *province* S Solomon Islands
85 J14 **Central** ◈ *province* C Zambia
119 P11 **Central** ✈ (Odesa) Odes'ka Oblast', SW Ukraine 46.26N 30.41E
Central *see* Centre
81 H14 **Central African Republic** *var.* République Centrafricaine, *abbrev.* CAR; *prev.* Ubangi-Shari, Oubangui-Chari, Territoire de l'Oubangui-Chari. ◆ *republic* C Africa
198 G6 **Central Basin Trough** *undersea feature* W Pacific Ocean
Central Borneo *see* Kalimantan Tengah
155 P12 **Central Brāhui Range** ▲▲ W Pakistan
Central Celebes *see* Sulawesi Tengah
31 Y13 **Central City** Iowa, C USA 42.12N 91.31W
22 I6 **Central City** Kentucky, S USA 37.17N 87.07W
31 P15 **Central City** Nebraska, C USA 41.04N 97.59W
50 D6 **Central, Cordillera** ▲▲ W Bolivia
56 D11 **Central, Cordillera** ▲▲ W Colombia
44 M13 **Central, Cordillera** ▲▲ C Costa Rica
47 N9 **Central, Cordillera** ▲▲ C Dominican Republic
45 R16 **Central, Cordillera** ▲▲ C Panama
179 P8 **Central, Cordillera** ▲▲ Luzon, N Philippines
47 S6 **Central, Cordillera** ▲▲ Puerto Rico
44 H7 **Central District** *var.* Tegucigalpa. ◈ *district* C Honduras
32 L15 **Centralia** Illinois, N USA 38.31N 89.07W
29 U4 **Centralia** Missouri, C USA 39.12N 92.08W
34 G9 **Centralia** Washington, NW USA 46.43N 122.57W
Central Indian Ridge *see* Mid-Indian Ridge
Central Java *see* Jawa Tengah
Central Kalimantan *see* Kalimantan Tengah
154 L14 **Central Makrān Range** ▲▲ W Pakistan
199 J8 **Central Pacific Basin** *undersea feature* C Pacific Ocean
61 M19 **Central, Planalto** *var.* Brazilian Highlands. ▲▲ E Brazil
34 F15 **Central Point** Oregon, NW USA 42.22N 122.55W
161 K25 **Central Province** ◈ *province* C Sri Lanka
Central Provinces and Berar *see* Madhya Pradesh
194 G11 **Central Range** ▲▲ NW PNG
Central Russian Upland *see* Srednerusskaya Vozvyshennost'
Central Siberian Plateau/Central Siberian Uplands *see* Srednesibirskoye Ploskogor'ye
106 K8 **Central, Sistema** ▲▲ C Spain
Central Sulawesi *see* Sulawesi Tengah
37 N3 **Central Valley** California, W USA 40.39N 122.21W
37 P8 **Central Valley** *valley* California, W USA
25 Q3 **Centre** Alabama, S USA 34.09N 85.40W
81 E15 **Centre** *Eng.* Central. ◈ *province* C Cameroon
104 M8 **Centre** ◈ *region* N France
181 Y16 **Centre de Flacq** E Mauritius 20.12S 57.43E
57 Y9 **Centre Spatial Guyanais** *space station* N French Guiana 5.11N 52.44W
25 O5 **Centreville** Alabama, S USA 32.58N 87.08W
23 X3 **Centreville** Maryland, NE USA 39.02N 76.04W
24 J7 **Centreville** Mississippi, S USA 31.05N 91.04W
Centum Cellae *see* Civitavecchia
166 M14 **Cenxi** Guangxi Zhuangzu Zizhiqu, S China 22.58N 111.00E
Ceos *see* Kéa
Cephaloedium *see* Cefalu
114 I9 **Čepin** *Hung.* Csepén. Osijek-Baranja, E Croatia 45.32N 18.33E
174 Ll15 **Cepu** *prev.* Tjepoe, Tjepu. Jawa, C Indonesia 7.07S 111.34E
Ceram *see* Seram, Pulau
175 T10 **Ceram Sea** *Ind.* Laut Seram. *sea* E Indonesia
198 G9 **Ceram Trough** *undersea feature* W Pacific Ocean
Cerasus *see* Giresun
38 I10 **Cerbat Mountains** ▲▲ Arizona, SW USA
105 P17 **Cerbère, Cap** *headland* S France 42.28N 3.15E

◆ Country
● Country Capital
◇ Dependent Territory
○ Dependent Territory Capital
◈ Administrative Region
✈ International Airport
▲ Mountain
▲▲ Mountain Range
Volcano
≈ River
◎ Lake
⊠ Reservoir

106 *F13* **Cercal do Alentejo** Setúbal, S Portugal *37.48N 8.40W*
113 *A18* **Čerchov** ***Ger.*** Czerkow. ▲ W Czech Republic *49.24N 12.47E*
105 *O13* **Cère** ≈ C France
63 *A16* **Ceres** Santa Fe, C Argentina *29.55S 61.55W*
61 *K18* **Ceres** Goiás, C Brazil *15.21S 49.34W*
Ceresio *see* Lugano, Lago di
105 *O17* **Céret** Pyrénées-Orientales, S France *42.30N 2.43E*
56 *E6* **Cereté** Córdoba, NW Colombia *8.51N 75.48W*
180 *I17* **Cerf, Île au** *island* Inner Islands, NE Seychelles
101 *G22* **Cerfontaine** Namur, S Belgium *50.08N 4.25E*
Cergy-Pontoise *see* Pontoise
109 *N16* **Cerignola** Puglia, SE Italy *41.16N 15.52E*
Cerigo *see* Kýthira
105 *O9* **Cérilly** Allier, C France *46.38N 2.51E*
142 *I11* **Çerkeş** Çankın, N Turkey *40.51N 32.52E*
142 *D10* **Çerkezköy** Tekirdağ, NW Turkey *41.18N 27.58E*
111 *T12* **Cerknica** ***Ger.*** Zirknitz. SW Slovenia *45.48N 14.21E*
111 *S11* **Cerkno** W Slovenia *46.07N 13.58E*
118 *F10* **Cermei** ***Hung.*** Csermő. Arad, W Romania *46.33N 21.50E*
143 *O15* **Çermik** Dıyarbakır, SE Turkey *38.09N 39.27E*
114 *I10* **Cerna** Vukovar-Srijem, E Croatia *45.10N 18.36E*
Cernăuţi *see* Chernivtsi
118 *M14* **Cernavodă** Constanţa, SW Romania *44.19N 28.01E*
105 *U7* **Cernay** Haut-Rhin, NE France *47.49N 7.10E*
Černice *see* Schwarzach
43 *O8* **Cerralvo** Nuevo León, NE Mexico *26.01N 99.37W*
42 *G9* **Cerralvo, Isla** *island* W Mexico
109 *L16* **Cerreto Sannita** Campania, S Italy *41.17N 14.39E*
115 *L20* **Cërrik** ***var.*** Cerriku. Elbasan, C Albania *41.01N 19.55E*
Cerriku *see* Cërrik
43 *O11* **Cerritos** San Luis Potosí, C Mexico *22.25N 100.16W*
62 *K11* **Cerro Azul** Paraná, S Brazil *24.48S 49.13W*
63 *F18* **Cerro Chato** Treinta y Tres, E Uruguay *33.08S 55.07W*
63 *F19* **Cerro Colorado** Florida, S Uruguay *33.52S 55.33W*
58 *E13* **Cerro de Pasco** Pasco, C Peru *10.43S 76.15W*
63 *G18* **Cerro Largo** ◈ *department* NE Uruguay
63 *G14* **Cêrro Largo** Rio Grande do Sul, S Brazil *28.10S 54.43W*
44 *E7* **Cerrón Grande, Embalse** ⊠ N El Salvador
65 *I14* **Cerros Colorados, Embalse** ⊛ W Argentina
107 *V5* **Cervera** Cataluña, NE Spain *41.40N 1.16E*
106 *M3* **Cervera del Pisuerga** Castilla-León, N Spain *42.51N 4.30W*
107 *Q5* **Cervera del Río Alhama** La Rioja, N Spain *42.01N 1.58W*
109 *H15* **Cerveteri** Lazio, C Italy *42.00N 12.06E*
108 *H10* **Cervia** Emilia-Romagna, N Italy *44.14N 12.22E*
108 *J7* **Cervignano del Friuli** Friuli-Venezia Giulia, NE Italy *45.49N 13.18E*
109 *L17* **Cervinara** Campania, S Italy *41.01N 14.36E*
Cervinia *see* Breuil-Cervinia
108 *B6* **Cervino, Monte** ***var.*** Matterhorn. ▲ Italy/Switzerland ***see also*** Matterhorn *46.00N 7.39E*
105 *Y14* **Cervione** Corse, France, C Mediterranean Sea *42.22N 9.28E*
106 *I1* **Cervo** Galicia, NW Spain *43.39N 7.25W*
56 *F5* **Cesar** ***off.*** Departamento del Cesar. ◈ *province* N Colombia
108 *H10* **Cesena** ***anc.*** Caesena. Emilia-Romagna, N Italy *44.09N 12.13E*
108 *I10* **Cesenatico** Emilia-Romagna, N Italy *44.12N 12.24E*
120 *H8* **Cēsis** ***Ger.*** Wenden. Cēsis, C Latvia *57.19N 25.17E*
113 *D15* **Česká Lípa** ***Ger.*** Böhmisch-Leipa. Liberecký Kraj, N Czech Republic *50.40N 14.32E*
Česká Republika *see* Czech Republic
113 *F17* **Česká Třebová** ***Ger.*** Böhmisch-Trübau. Pardubický Kraj, C Czech Republic *49.54N 16.27E*
113 *D19* **České Budějovice** ***Ger.*** Budweis. Budějovický Kraj, S Czech Republic *48.58N 14.28E*
113 *D19* **České Velenice** Budějovický Kraj, S Czech Republic *48.49N 14.57E*
113 *E18* **Českomoravská Vrchovina** ***var.*** Českomoravská Vysočina, ***Eng.*** Bohemian-Moravian Highlands, ***Ger.*** Böhmisch-Mährische Höhe. ▲▲ S Czech Republic
Českomoravská Vysočina *see* Českomoravská Vrchovina
113 *C19* **Český Krumlov** ***var.*** Böhmisch-Krumau, ***Ger.*** Krummau. Budějovický Kraj, S Czech Republic *48.48N 14.18E*
Ceský Les *see* Bohemian Forest
114 *F8* **Česma** ≈ N Croatia
142 *A14* **Çeşme** İzmir, W Turkey *38.19N 26.19E*
Cess *see* Cestos
191 *T8* **Cessnock** New South Wales, SE Australia *32.51S 151.21E*
78 *K17* **Cestos** ***var.*** Cess. ≈ S Liberia
120 *I9* **Cesvaine** Madona, E Latvia *56.58N 26.15E*
118 *G14* **Cetate** Dolj, SW Romania *44.06N 23.03E*
Cetatea Albă *see* Bilhorod-Dnistrovs'kyy
115 *J17* **Cetinje** ***It.*** Cettigne. Montenegro, SW Serbia and Montenegro (Yugoslavia) *42.23N 18.55E*
109 *N20* **Cetraro** Calabria, S Italy *39.30N 15.59E*
Cette *see* Sète
196 *A17* **Cetti Bay** *bay* SW Guam
Cettigne *see* Cetinje
106 *L17* **Ceuta** ***var.*** Sebta. Ceuta, Spain, N Africa *35.52N 5.19W*
90 *C15* **Ceuta** *enclave* Spain, N Africa
108 *B9* **Ceva** Piemonte, NE Italy *44.24N 8.01E*
105 *P14* **Cévennes** ▲▲ S France
110 *G10* **Cevio** Ticino, S Switzerland *46.18N 8.36E*
142 *K16* **Ceyhan** Adana, S Turkey *37.01N 35.48E*
142 *K17* **Ceyhan Nehri** ≈ S Turkey
143 *P17* **Ceylanpınar** Şanlıurfa, SE Turkey *36.53N 40.01E*
Ceylon *see* Sri Lanka
181 *R6* **Ceylon Plain** *undersea feature* N Indian Ocean
Ceyre to the Caribs *see* Marie-Galante
105 *Q14* **Cèze** ≈ S France
152 *H15* **Chaacha** ***Turkm.*** Chäche. Akhalskiy Velayat, S Turkmenistan *36.49N 60.33E*
131 *P6* **Chaadayevka** Penzenskaya Oblast', W Russian Federation *53.07N 45.55E*
178 *H12* **Cha-Am** Phetchaburi, SW Thailand *12.48N 99.58E*
149 *W15* **Chābahār** ***var.*** Chāh Bahār, Chahbar. Sīstān va Balūchestān, SE Iran *25.21N 60.38E*
63 *B19* **Chabas** Santa Fe, C Argentina *33.16S 61.22W*
105 *T10* **Chablais** *physical region* E France
63 *B20* **Chacabuco** Buenos Aires, E Argentina *34.38S 60.31W*
44 *K8* **Chachagón, Cerro** ▲ N Nicaragua *13.18N 85.39W*
58 *C10* **Chachapoyas** Amazonas, NW Peru *6.13S 77.54W*
Chäche *see* Chaacha
121 *O18* **Chachersk** ***Rus.*** Chechersk. Homyel'skaya Voblasts', SE Belarus *52.54N 30.54E*
121 *N16* **Chachevichy** ***Rus.*** Chechevichi. Mahilyowskaya Voblasts', E Belarus *53.31N 29.49E*
63 *B14* **Chaco** ***off.*** Provincia de Chaco. ◈ *province* NE Argentina
Chaco *see* Gran Chaco
64 *M6* **Chaco Austral** *physical region* N Argentina
64 *M3* **Chaco Boreal** *physical region* N Paraguay
64 *M6* **Chaco Central** *physical region* N Argentina
41 *Y15* **Chacon, Cape** *headland* Prince of Wales Island, Alaska, USA *54.41N 132.00W*
80 *H9* **Chad** ***off.*** Republic of Chad, ***Fr.*** Tchad. ◆ *republic* C Africa
126 *Hh16* **Chadan** Respublika Tyva, S Russian Federation *51.16N 91.25E*
23 *U12* **Chadbourn** North Carolina, SE USA *34.19N 78.49W*
85 *L14* **Chadiza** Eastern, E Zambia *14.04S 32.27E*
69 *Q7* **Chad, Lake** ***Fr.*** Lac Tchad. ⊛ C Africa
126 *J13* **Chadobets** ≈ C Russian Federation
30 *J12* **Chadron** Nebraska, C USA *42.48N 102.57W*
Chadyr-Lunga *see* Ciadîr-Lunga
169 *W14* **Chaeryŏng** SW North Korea *38.22N 125.35E*
107 *P17* **Chafarinas, Islas** *island group* S Spain
29 *Y7* **Chaffee** Missouri, C USA *37.10N 89.39W*
154 *L12* **Chāgai Hills** ***var.*** Chāh Gay. ▲▲ Afghanistan/Pakistan
126 *M12* **Chagda** Respublika Sakha (Yakutiya), NE Russian Federation *58.43N 130.38E*
Chaghasarāy *see* Asadābād
155 *N5* **Chaghcharān** ***var.*** Chakhcharan, Cheghcheran, Qala Āhangarān. Ghowr, C Afghanistan *34.28N 65.18E*
105 *R9* **Chagny** Saône-et-Loire, C France *46.54N 4.45E*
181 *Q7* **Chagos Archipelago** ***var.*** Oil Islands. *island group* British Indian Ocean Territory
133 *O15* **Chagos Bank** *undersea feature* C Indian Ocean
133 *O14* **Chagos-Laccadive Plateau** *undersea feature* N Indian Ocean
181 *Q7* **Chagos Trench** *undersea feature* N Indian Ocean
45 *T14* **Chagres, Río** ≈ C Panama
47 *U14* **Chaguanas** Trinidad, Trinidad and Tobago *10.29N 61.24W*
56 *M6* **Chaguaramas** Guárico, N Venezuela *9.21N 66.15W*
152 *C9* **Chagyl** Balkanskiy Velayat, NW Turkmenistan *40.48N 55.21E*
Chahārmahāl and Bakhtiyāri *see* Chahār Maḩall va Bakhtīārī
148 *M9* **Chahār Maḩall va Bakhtīārī** ***off.*** Ostān-e Chahār Maḩall va Bakhtīārī, ***var.*** Chahārmahāl and Bakhtiyāri. ◈ *province* SW Iran
Chāh Bahār/Chahbar *see* Chābahār
149 *V13* **Chāh Derāz** Sīstān va Balūchestān, SE Iran
Chāh Gay *see* Chāgai Hills
178 *Hh10* **Chai Badan** Lop Buri, C Thailand *15.07N 101.03E*
159 *Q16* **Chāībāsa** Bihār, N India *22.34N 85.48E*
81 *E19* **Chaillu, Massif du** ▲▲ C Gabon
178 *Hh10* **Chai Nat** ***var.*** Chainat, Jainat, Jayanath. Chai Nat, C Thailand *15.12N 100.12E*
67 *M14* **Chain Fracture Zone** *tectonic feature* E Atlantic Ocean
181 *N5* **Chain Ridge** *undersea feature* W Indian Ocean
Chairn, Ceann an *see* Carnsore Point
164 *L5* **Chaiwopu** Xinjiang Uygur Zizhiqu, W China *43.31N 87.55E*
178 *I10* **Chaiyaphum** ***var.*** Jayabum. Chaiyaphum, C Thailand *15.49N 102.03E*
64 *N10* **Chajarí** Entre Ríos, E Argentina *30.45S 57.57W*
44 *C5* **Chajul** Quiché, W Guatemala *15.28N 91.02W*
85 *K16* **Chakari** Mashonaland West, N Zimbabwe *18.04S 29.49E*
154 *J9* **Chakhānsūr** Nīmrūz, SW Afghanistan *31.11N 62.06E*
Chakhānsūr *see* Nīmrūz
Chakhcharan *see* Chaghcharān
155 *V8* **Chak Jhumra** ***var.*** Jhumra. Punjab, E Pakistan *31.33N 73.13E*
152 *I16* **Chaknakdysonga** Akhalskiy Velayat, S Turkmenistan *35.39N 61.24E*
159 *P16* **Chakradharpur** Bihār, N India *22.37N 85.28E*
158 *J8* **Chakrāta** Uttar Pradesh, N India *30.42N 77.52E*
155 *U7* **Chakwāl** Punjab, NE Pakistan *32.56N 72.49E*
59 *F17* **Chala** Arequipa, SW Peru *15.52S 74.13W*
104 *K12* **Chalais** Charente, W France *45.16N 0.02E*
110 *D10* **Chalais** Valais, SW Switzerland *46.18N 7.37E*
117 *J20* **Chalándri** ***var.*** Halandri; ***prev.*** Khalándrion. *prehistoric site* Sýros, Kykládes, Greece, Aegean Sea *37.28N 24.56E*
196 *H6* **Chalan Kanoa** Saipan, S Northern Mariana Islands *15.07S 145.43E*
196 *C16* **Chalan Pago** C Guam
Chalap Dalam/Chalap Dalan *see* Chehel Abdālān, Kūh-e
44 *F7* **Chalatenango** Chalatenango, N El Salvador *14.03N 88.54W*
44 *A9* **Chalatenango** ◈ *department* NW El Salvador
85 *P15* **Chalaua** Nampula, NE Mozambique *16.04S 39.08E*
83 *I16* **Chalbi Desert** *desert* N Kenya
44 *D7* **Chalchuapa** Santa Ana, W El Salvador *13.58N 89.39W*
Chalcidice *see* Chalkidikí
Chalcis *see* Chalkída
105 *N6* **Châlette-sur-Loing** Loiret, C France *48.01N 2.45E*
13 *X8* **Chaleur Bay** ***Fr.*** Baie des Chaleurs. *bay* New Brunswick/Quebec, E Canada
Chaleurs, Baie des *see* Chaleur Bay
59 *G16* **Chalhuanca** Apurímac, S Peru *14.21S 73.16W*
160 *F12* **Chālisgaon** Mahārāshtra, C India *20.28N 75.10E*
117 *N23* **Chálki** *island* Dodekánisos, Greece, Aegean Sea
117 *F16* **Chalkiádes** Thessalía, C Greece *39.24N 22.25E*
117 *H18* **Chalkída** ***var.*** Halkida; ***prev.*** Khalkís, ***anc.*** Chalcis. Evvoia, E Greece *38.27N 23.37E*
117 *G14* **Chalkidikí** ***var.*** Khalkidhikí; ***anc.*** Chalcidice. *peninsula* NE Greece
193 *A24* **Chalky Inlet** *inlet* South Island, NZ
41 *S7* **Chalkyitsik** Alaska, USA *66.39N 143.43W*
104 *I9* **Challans** Vendée, NW France *46.51N 1.52W*
59 *K19* **Challapata** Oruro, SW Bolivia *19.02S 66.46W*
199 *H7* **Challenger Deep** *undersea feature* W Pacific Ocean
200 *Nn12* **Challenger Fracture Zone** *tectonic feature* SE Pacific Ocean
199 *Ii13* **Challenger Plateau** *undersea feature* E Tasman Sea
35 *P13* **Challis** Idaho, NW USA *44.31N 114.14W*
24 *L9* **Chalmette** Louisiana, S USA *29.56N 89.57W*
128 *J11* **Chalna** Respublika Kareliya, NW Russian Federation *61.53N 33.59E*
105 *Q5* **Châlons-en-Champagne** ***prev.*** Châlons-sur-Marne, ***hist.*** Arcae Remorum, ***anc.*** Carolopois. Marne, NE France *48.58N 4.22E*
Châlons-sur-Marne *see* Châlons-en-Champagne
105 *R9* **Chalon-sur-Saône** ***anc.*** Cabillonum. Saône-et-Loire, C France *46.46N 4.51E*
Chaltel, Cerro *see* Fitzroy, Monte
149 *N4* **Chālūs** Māzandarān, N Iran *36.40N 51.25E*
104 *M11* **Châlus** Haute-Vienne, C France *45.38N 1.00E*
103 *N20* **Cham** Bayern, SE Germany *49.13N 12.40E*
110 *F7* **Cham** Zug, N Switzerland *47.10N 8.28E*
39 *R8* **Chama** New Mexico, SW USA *36.54N 106.34W*
Cha Mai *see* Thung Song
85 *E22* **Chamaites** Karas, S Namibia *27.13S 17.55E*
155 *O9* **Chaman** Baluchistān, SW Pakistan *30.55N 66.27E*
39 *R9* **Chama, Rio** ≈ New Mexico, SW USA
158 *I6* **Chamba** Himāchal Pradesh, N India *32.33N 76.10E*
83 *I25* **Chamba** Ruvuma, S Tanzania *11.33S 37.01E*
156 *H12* **Chambal** ≈ C India
9 *U16* **Chamberlain** Saskatchewan, S Canada *50.49N 105.29W*
31 *O11* **Chamberlain** South Dakota, N USA *43.48N 99.19W*
21 *R3* **Chamberlain Lake** ⊛ Maine, NE USA
41 *S5* **Chamberlin, Mount** ▲ Alaska, USA *69.16N 144.54W*
39 *O11* **Chambers** Arizona, SW USA *35.11N 109.25W*
20 *F16* **Chambersburg** Pennsylvania, NE USA *39.54N 77.39W*
33 *N5* **Chambers Island** *island* Wisconsin, N USA
105 *T11* **Chambéry** ***anc.*** Camberia. Savoie, E France *45.34N 5.55E*
84 *L12* **Chambeshi** Northern, NE Zambia *10.55S 31.07E*
84 *L12* **Chambeshi** ≈ NE Zambia
76 *M6* **Chambi, Jebel** ***var.*** Jabal ash Sha'nabī. ▲ W Tunisia *35.16N 8.39E*
13 *Q7* **Chambord** Quebec, SE Canada *48.25N 72.02W*
194 *G10* **Chambri Lake** ⊛ W PNG
145 *U11* **Chamcham** S Iraq *31.17N 45.05E*
145 *T4* **Chamchamāl** N Iraq *35.31N 44.49E*
42 *J14* **Chamela** Jalisco, SW Mexico *19.33N 105.04W*
44 *G5* **Chamelecón, Río** ≈ NW Honduras
64 *J9* **Chamical** La Rioja, C Argentina *30.21S 66.19W*
117 *L23* **Chamilí** *island* Kykládes, Greece, Aegean Sea
178 *Ii13* **Châmnar** Kaôh Kông, SW Cambodia *11.45N 103.32E*
158 *K9* **Chamoli** Uttar Pradesh, N India *30.22N 79.19E*
105 *U11* **Chamonix-Mont-Blanc** Haute-Savoie, E France *45.55N 6.52E*
160 *L11* **Chāmpa** Madhya Pradesh, C India *22.01N 82.42E*
8 *H8* **Champagne** Yukon Territory, W Canada *60.48N 136.22W*
105 *Q5* **Champagne** *cultural region* N France
Champagne *see* Campania
105 *Q5* **Champagne-Ardenne** ◈ *region* N France
105 *S9* **Champagnole** Jura, E France *46.43N 5.55E*
32 *M13* **Champaign** Illinois, N USA *40.07N 88.14W*
178 *Jj11* **Champasak** Champasak, S Laos *14.50N 105.51E*
105 *U6* **Champ de Feu** ▲ NE France *48.24N 7.15E*
11 *O7* **Champdoré, Lac** ⊛ Quebec, NE Canada
44 *B6* **Champerico** Retalhuleu, SW Guatemala *14.18N 91.54W*
110 *C11* **Champéry** Valais, SW Switzerland *46.12N 6.52E*
20 *L6* **Champlain** New York, NE USA *44.58N 73.25W*
20 *L9* **Champlain Canal** *canal* New York, NE USA
13 *P13* **Champlain, Lac** ⊛ Quebec, SE Canada
20 *L7* **Champlain, Lake** ⊛ Canada/USA
105 *S7* **Champlitte** Haute-Saône, E France *47.36N 5.31E*
43 *W13* **Champotón** Campeche, SE Mexico *19.18N 90.43W*
106 *G10* **Chamusca** Santarém, C Portugal *39.21N 8.28W*
121 *O20* **Chamyarysy** ***Rus.*** Chemerisy. Homyel'skaya Voblasts', SE Belarus *51.42N 30.26E*
131 *P5* **Chamzinka** Respublika Mordoviya, W Russian Federation *54.22N 45.22E*
Chanáil Mhór, An *see* Grand Canal
Chanak *see* Çanakkale
64 *G7* **Chañaral** Atacama, N Chile *26.19S 70.34W*
106 *H13* **Chança, Rio** ***var.*** Chanza. ≈ Portugal/Spain
59 *D14* **Chancay** Lima, W Peru *11.33S 77.16W*
Chan-chiang/Chanchiang *see* Zhanjiang
64 *G13* **Chanco** Maule, Chile *35.43S 72.35W*
41 *R7* **Chandalar** Alaska, USA *67.30N 148.29W*
41 *R6* **Chandalar River** ≈ Alaska, USA
158 *L10* **Chandan Chauki** Uttar Pradesh, N India *28.31N 80.43E*
159 *S16* **Chandannagar** ***prev.*** Chandernagore. West Bengal, E India *22.52N 88.21E*
158 *K10* **Chandausi** Uttar Pradesh, N India *28.27N 78.43E*
24 *M10* **Chandeleur Islands** *island group* Louisiana, S USA
24 *M9* **Chandeleur Sound** *sound* N Gulf of Mexico
158 *I8* **Chandīgarh** Punjab, N India *30.41N 76.51E*
159 *Q16* **Chāndil** Bihār, NE India *22.58N 86.04E*
190 *D2* **Chandler** South Australia *26.59S 133.22E*
13 *Y7* **Chandler** Quebec, SE Canada *48.21N 64.40W*
38 *L14* **Chandler** Arizona, SW USA *33.18N 111.50W*
29 *O10* **Chandler** Oklahoma, C USA *35.42N 96.52W*
27 *V7* **Chandler** Texas, SW USA *32.18N 95.28W*
41 *Q6* **Chandler River** ≈ Alaska, USA
58 *H13* **Chandles, Río** ≈ E Peru
169 *N9* **Chandmanĭ** Dornogovĭ, SE Mongolia *45.36N 110.30E*
12 *J13* **Chandos Lake** ⊛ Ontario, SE Canada
159 *U15* **Chandpur** Chittagong, C Bangladesh *23.13N 90.43E*
160 *I13* **Chandrapur** Mahārāshtra, C India *19.58N 79.21E*
85 *J15* **Changa** Southern, S Zambia *16.24S 28.27E*
Changan *see* Xi'an, Shaanxi, China
Chang'an *see* Rong'an, Guangxi Zhuangzu Zizhiqu, China
161 *G23* **Changanācheri** Kerala, SW India *9.27N 76.34E*
85 *M19* **Changane** ≈ S Mozambique
85 *M16* **Changara** Tete, NW Mozambique *16.54S 33.15E*
169 *X11* **Changbai** ***var.*** Changbai Chaoxianzu Zizhixian. Jilin, NE China *41.25N 128.08E*
Changbai Chaoxianzu Zizhixian *see* Changbai
169 *X11* **Changbai Shan** ▲▲ NE China
169 *V10* **Changchun** ***var.*** Ch'angch'un, Ch'ang-ch'un; ***prev.*** Hsinking. Jilin, NE China *43.52N 125.18E*
166 *M10* **Changde** Hunan, S China *29.04N 111.42E*
167 *S13* **Changhua** ***Jap.*** Shōka. C Taiwan *24.06N 120.31E*
174 *I7* **Changi** ✈ (Singapore) E Singapore *1.22N 103.58E*
164 *L5* **Changji** Xinjiang Uygur Zizhiqu, NW China *44.02N 87.12E*
163 *O13* **Chang Jiang** ***var.*** Yangtze Kiang, ***Eng.*** Yangtze. ≈ C China
166 *L17* **Changjiang** ***prev.*** Shiliu. Hainan, S China *19.16N 109.09E*
167 *S8* **Changjiang Kou** *delta* E China
178 *I13* **Chang, Ko** *island* S Thailand
167 *Q2* **Changli** Hebei, E China *39.43N 119.13E*
169 *V10* **Changling** Jilin, NE China *44.15N 124.03E*
167 *N11* **Changsha** ***var.*** Ch'angsha, Ch'ang-sha. Hunan, S China *28.10N 113.00E*
167 *Q10* **Changshan** Zhejiang, SE China *28.54N 118.26E*
169 *V14* **Changshan Qundao** *island group* NE China
167 *S8* **Changshu** ***var.*** Ch'ang-shu. Jiangsu, E China *31.36N 120.42E*
169 *V11* **Changtu** Liaoning, NE China *42.49N 123.58E*
45 *P14* **Changuinola** Bocas del Toro, NW Panama *9.25N 82.31W*
165 *N9* **Changweiliang** Qinghai, W China *38.24N 92.07E*
166 *K6* **Changwu** Shaanxi, C China *35.12N 107.45E*
169 *U13* **Changxing Dao** *island* N China
166 *M9* **Changyang** Hubei, C China *30.45N 111.13E*
169 *W14* **Changyŏn** SW North Korea *38.19N 125.14E*
167 *N5* **Changzhi** Shanxi, C China *36.09N 113.01E*
167 *R8* **Changzhou** Jiangsu, E China *31.53N 119.50E*
117 *H24* **Chaniá** ***var.*** Hania, Khaniá, ***Eng.*** Canea; ***anc.*** Cydonia. Kríti, Greece, E Mediterranean Sea *35.31N 24.01E*
64 *J5* **Chañi, Nevado de** ▲ NW Argentina *24.09S 65.44W*
117 *H24* **Chanión, Kólpos** *gulf* Kríti, Greece, E Mediterranean Sea
Chankiri *see* Çankırı
32 *M11* **Channahon** Illinois, N USA *41.25N 88.13W*
161 *H20* **Channapatna** Karnātaka, E India *12.43N 77.13E*
99 *K26* **Channel Islands** ***Fr.*** Îles Normandes. *island group* S English Channel
37 *R16* **Channel Islands** *island group* California, W USA
11 *S13* **Channel-Port aux Basques** Newfoundland and Labrador, SE Canada *47.35N 59.02W*
Channel, The *see* English Channel
99 *Q23* **Channel Tunnel** *tunnel* France/UK
26 *M2* **Channing** Texas, SW USA *35.40N 102.19W*
Chantabun/Chantaburi *see* Chanthaburi
106 *H3* **Chantada** Galicia, NW Spain *42.36N 7.46W*
178 *I12* **Chanthaburi** ***var.*** Chantabun, Chantaburi. Chantaburi, S Thailand *12.34N 102.07E*
105 *O4* **Chantilly** Oise, N France *49.12N 2.28E*
15 *Kk4* **Chantrey Inlet** *inlet* Nunavut, N Canada
145 *V12* **Chanūn as Sa'ūdī** S Iraq *31.04N 46.00E*
29 *Q6* **Chanute** Kansas, C USA *37.40N 95.27W*
125 *G13* **Chany, Ozero** ⊛ C Russian Federation
Chanza *see* Chança, Rio
Ch'ao-an/Chaochow *see* Chaozhou
167 *P8* **Chao Hu** ⊛ E China
178 *Hh11* **Chao Phraya, Mae Nam** ≈ C Thailand
169 *T8* **Chaor He** ≈ NE China
Chaouèn *see* Chefchaouen
167 *P14* **Chaoyang** Guangdong, S China *23.16N 116.30E*
169 *T12* **Chaoyang** Liaoning, NE China *41.33N 120.28E*
Chaoyang *see* Huinan, Jilin, China
Chaoyang *see* Jiayin, Heilongjiang, China
167 *Q14* **Chaozhou** ***var.*** Chaoan, Chao'an, Ch'ao-an; ***prev.*** Chaochow. Guangdong, SE China *23.39N 116.34E*
60 *N13* **Chapadinha** Maranhão, E Brazil *3.45S 43.22W*
10 *K12* **Chapais** Quebec, SE Canada *49.46N 74.54W*
42 *L13* **Chapala** Jalisco, SW Mexico *20.17N 103.13W*
42 *L13* **Chapala, Lago de** ⊛ C Mexico
152 *F13* **Chapan, Gora** ▲ C Turkmenistan *37.48N 58.03E*
59 *M18* **Chapare, Río** ≈ C Bolivia
56 *E11* **Chaparral** Tolima, C Colombia *3.44N 75.33W*
126 *Kk12* **Chapayevo** Respublika Sakha (Yakutiya), NE Russian Federation *60.03N 117.19E*
150 *F9* **Chapayev** Zapadnyy Kazakhstan, NW Kazakhstan *50.13N 51.05E*
131 *R6* **Chapayevsk** Samarskaya Oblast', W Russian Federation *52.57N 49.41E*
62 *H13* **Chapecó** Santa Catarina, S Brazil *27.06S 52.39W*
62 *I13* **Chapecó, Rio** ≈ S Brazil
22 *J9* **Chapel Hill** Tennessee, S USA *35.38N 86.40W*
46 *J12* **Chapelton** C Jamaica *18.04N 77.16W*
12 *C8* **Chapleau** Ontario, SE Canada *47.49N 83.24W*
12 *D7* **Chapleau** ≈ Ontario, S Canada
9 *T16* **Chaplin** Saskatchewan, S Canada *50.27N 106.37W*
130 *M6* **Chaplygin** Lipetskaya Oblast', W Russian Federation *53.13N 39.58E*
119 *S11* **Chaplynka** Khersons'ka Oblast', S Ukraine *46.20N 33.34E*
15 *L3* **Chapman, Cape** *headland* Nunavut, NE Canada *69.15N 89.09W*
27 *T15* **Chapman Ranch** Texas, SW USA *27.32N 97.25W*
Chapman's *see* Okwa
23 *P5* **Chapmanville** West Virginia, NE USA *37.58N 82.01W*
30 *K15* **Chappell** Nebraska, C USA *41.05N 102.28W*
Chapra *see* Chhapra
58 *D9* **Chapuli, Río** ≈ N Peru
78 *I6* **Châr** *well* N Mauritania *21.31N 12.55W*
126 *Kk13* **Chara** Chitinskaya Oblast', S Russian Federation *56.57N 118.05E*
126 *Kk13* **Chara** ≈ C Russian Federation
56 *G8* **Charala** Santander, C Colombia *6.16N 73.09W*
43 *N10* **Charcas** San Luis Potosí, C Mexico *23.09N 101.04W*
27 *T13* **Charco** Texas, SW USA *28.42N 97.35E*
204 *H7* **Charcot Island** *island* Antarctica
66 *M8* **Charcot Seamounts** *undersea feature* E Atlantic Ocean
Chardara *see* Shardara
151 *P17* **Chardarinskoye Vodokhranilishche** ⊠ S Kazakhstan
33 *U11* **Chardon** Ohio, N USA *41.33N 81.10W*
46 *K9* **Chardonnières** SW Haiti *18.17N 74.09W*
152 *K12* **Chardzhev** ***prev.*** Chardzhou, Chardzhui, Leninsk-Turkmenski, ***Turkm.*** Chärjew. Lebapskiy Velayat, E Turkmenistan *39.07N 63.30E*
Chardzhevskaya Oblast' *see* Lebapskiy Velayat
Chardzhou/Chardzhui *see* Chardzhev
104 *L11* **Charente** ◈ *department* W France
104 *J11* **Charente** ≈ W France
104 *J10* **Charente-Maritime** ◈ *department* W France
143 *U12* **Ch'arents'avan** C Armenia *40.23N 44.41E*
80 *I12* **Chari** ***var.*** Shari. ≈ Central African Republic/Chad
80 *G11* **Chari-Baguirmi** ***off.*** Préfecture du Chari-Baguirmi. ◈ *prefecture* SW Chad
155 *Q4* **Chārīkār** Parwān, NE Afghanistan *35.01N 69.10E*
31 *V15* **Chariton** Iowa, C USA *41.00N 93.18W*
29 *U3* **Chariton River** ≈ Missouri, C USA
57 *T7* **Charity** NW Guyana *7.22N 58.34W*
33 *R7* **Charity Island** *island* Michigan, N USA
Chärjew *see* Chardzhev
Chärjew Oblasty *see* Lebapskiy Velayat
Charkhlik/Charkhliq *see* Ruoqiang
101 *G20* **Charleroi** Hainaut, S Belgium *50.25N 4.27E*
9 *V12* **Charles** Manitoba, C Canada *55.27N 100.58W*
13 *R10* **Charlesbourg** Quebec, SE Canada *46.49N 71.14W*
23 *Y7* **Charles, Cape** *headland* Virginia, NE USA *37.09N 75.57W*
31 *W12* **Charles City** Iowa, C USA *43.04N 92.40W*
23 *W6* **Charles City** Virginia, NE USA *37.19N 77.01W*
105 *O5* **Charles de Gaulle** ✈ (Paris) Seine-et-Marne, N France *49.04N 2.36E*
10 *K1* **Charles Island** *island* Nunavut, NE Canada
Charles Island *see* Santa María, Isla
18 *Mm5* **Charles-Lindbergh** ✈ (Minneapolis/Saint Paul) Minnesota, N USA *44.47N 93.12W*
32 *K9* **Charles Mound** *hill* Illinois, N USA *42.30N 90.14W*
193 *A22* **Charles Sound** *sound* South Island, NZ
193 *G15* **Charleston** West Coast, South Island, NZ *41.54S 171.25E*
29 *S11* **Charleston** Arkansas, C USA *35.18N 94.02W*
32 *M14* **Charleston** Illinois, N USA *39.30N 88.10W*
24 *L3* **Charleston** Mississippi, S USA *34.00N 90.03W*
29 *Z7* **Charleston** Missouri, C USA *36.55N 89.21W*
23 *T15* **Charleston** South Carolina, SE USA *32.48N 79.57W*
23 *Q5* **Charleston** *state capital* West Virginia, NE USA *38.21N 81.37W*
12 *L14* **Charleston Lake** ⊛ Ontario, SE Canada
37 *W11* **Charleston Peak** ▲ Nevada, W USA *36.16N 115.40W*
47 *W10* **Charlestown** Nevis, Saint Kitts and Nevis *17.05N 62.35W*
33 *P16* **Charlestown** Indiana, N USA *38.27N 85.40W*
20 *M9* **Charlestown** New Hampshire, NE USA *43.14N 72.23W*
23 *V3* **Charles Town** West Virginia, NE USA *39.17N 77.51W*
189 *W9* **Charleville** Queensland, E Australia *26.24S 146.18E*
105 *R3* **Charleville-Mézières** Ardennes, N France *49.45N 4.43E*
33 *P5* **Charlevoix** Michigan, N USA *45.19N 85.15W*
33 *Q6* **Charlevoix, Lake** ⊛ Michigan, N USA
41 *T9* **Charley River** ≈ Alaska, USA
66 *J6* **Charlie-Gibbs Fracture Zone** *tectonic feature* N Atlantic Ocean
105 *Q10* **Charlieu** Loire, E France *46.11N 4.10E*
33 *Q9* **Charlotte** Michigan, N USA *42.33N 84.50W*
23 *R10* **Charlotte** North Carolina, SE USA *35.13N 80.50W*
22 *I8* **Charlotte** Tennessee, S USA *36.11N 87.18W*
27 *R13* **Charlotte** Texas, SW USA *28.51N 98.42W*
23 *R10* **Charlotte** ✈ North Carolina, SE USA *35.12N 80.54W*
47 *T9* **Charlotte Amalie** ***prev.*** Saint Thomas. ○ (Virgin Islands (US)) Saint Thomas, N Virgin Islands (US) *18.22N 64.55W*
23 *U7* **Charlotte Court House** Virginia, NE USA *37.04N 78.37W*
25 *W14* **Charlotte Harbor** *inlet* Florida, SE USA
Charlotte Island *see* Abaiang
97 *J15* **Charlottenberg** Värmland, C Sweden *59.52N 12.16E*
Charlottenhof *see* Aegviidu
23 *U5* **Charlottesville** Virginia, NE USA *38.01N 78.28W*
Charlotte Town *see* Roseau, Dominica
Charlotte Town *see* Gouyave, Grenada
11 *Q14* **Charlottetown** Prince Edward Island, Prince Edward Island, SE Canada *46.13N 63.09W*
47 *Z16* **Charlotteville** Tobago, Trinidad and Tobago *11.16N 60.33W*
190 *M11* **Charlton** Victoria, SE Australia *36.18S 143.19E*
10 *H10* **Charlton Island** *island* Nunavut, C Canada
105 *T6* **Charmes** Vosges, NE France *48.19N 6.19E*
121 *F19* **Charnawchytsy** ***Rus.*** Chernavchitsy. Brestskaya Voblasts', SW Belarus *52.13N 23.43E*
13 *R10* **Charny** Quebec, SE Canada *46.43N 71.14W*
155 *T5* **Chārsadda** North-West Frontier Province, NW Pakistan *34.12N 71.46E*
152 *M14* **Charshanga** ***prev.*** Charshangy, ***Turkm.*** Charshangngy. Lebapskiy Velayat, E Turkmenistan *37.31N 65.58E*
Charshangngy/Charshangy *see* Charshanga
Charsk *see* Shar
189 *W6* **Charters Towers** Queensland, NE Australia *20.01S 146.19E*
13 *R12* **Chartierville** Quebec, SE Canada *45.19N 71.13W*
104 *M6* **Chartres** ***anc.*** Autricum, Civitas Carnutum. Eure-et-Loir, C France *48.27N 1.27E*
151 *W15* **Charyn** ***Kaz.*** Sharyn. Almaty, SE Kazakhstan *43.48N 79.22E*
63 *D21* **Chascomús** Buenos Aires, E Argentina *35.34S 58.01W*
9 *N16* **Chase** British Columbia, SW Canada *50.49N 119.40W*
23 *U7* **Chase City** Virginia, NE USA *36.48N 78.27W*
21 *S4* **Chase, Mount** ▲ Maine, NE USA *46.06N 68.30W*
120 *M13* **Chashniki** ***Rus.*** Chashniki. Vitsyebskaya Voblasts', N Belarus *54.51N 29.09E*
117 *D15* **Chásia** ▲▲ C Greece
31 *V9* **Chaska** Minnesota, N USA *44.47N 93.36W*
193 *D25* **Chaslands Mistake** *headland* South Island, NZ *46.37S 169.21E*
129 *R11* **Chasovo** Respublika Komi, NW Russian Federation *61.58N 50.34E*
Chasovo *see* Vazhgort
128 *H14* **Chastova** Novgorodskaya Oblast', NW Russian Federation *58.37N 32.04E*
149 *R3* **Chāt** Golestān, N Iran *37.52N 55.27E*
Chatak *see* Chhatak
41 *R9* **Chatanika** Alaska, USA *65.06N 147.28W*
41 *R9* **Chatanika River** ≈ Alaska, USA
153 *T8* **Chat-Bazar** Talasskaya Oblast', NW Kyrgyzstan *42.29N 72.37E*
47 *Y14* **Chateaubelair** Saint Vincent, W Saint Vincent and the Grenadines *13.16N 61.14W*
104 *J7* **Châteaubriant** Loire-Atlantique, NW France *47.43N 1.22W*
105 *Q8* **Château-Chinon** Nièvre, C France *47.04N 3.50E*
110 *C10* **Château d'Oex** Vaud, W Switzerland *46.28N 7.09E*
104 *L7* **Château-du-Loir** Sarthe, NW France *47.40N 0.25E*
104 *M6* **Châteaudun** Eure-et-Loir, C France *48.04N 1.19E*
104 *K7* **Château-Gontier** Mayenne, NW France *47.49N 0.42W*
13 *O13* **Châteauguay** Quebec, SE Canada *45.21N 73.46W*
104 *F6* **Châteaulin** Finistère, NW France *48.12N 4.07W*
105 *N9* **Châteaumeillant** Cher, C France *46.33N 2.10E*
104 *K11* **Châteauneuf-sur-Charente** Charente, W France *45.34N 0.33W*
104 *M7* **Château-Renault** Indre-et-Loire, C France *47.34N 0.52E*
105 *N9* **Châteauroux** ***prev.*** Indreville. Indre, C France *46.50N 1.42E*
105 *T5* **Château-Salins** Moselle, NE France *48.50N 6.29E*
105 *P4* **Château-Thierry** Aisne, N France *49.03N 3.24E*
101 *H21* **Châtelet** Hainaut, S Belgium *50.24N 4.31E*
Châtelherault *see* Châtellerault
104 *L9* **Châtellerault** ***var.*** Châtelherault. Vienne, W France *46.49N 0.33E*
31 *X10* **Chatfield** Minnesota, N USA *43.51N 92.11W*
11 *O14* **Chatham** New Brunswick, SE Canada *47.01N 65.30W*
12 *D17* **Chatham** Ontario, S Canada *42.24N 82.10W*
99 *P22* **Chatham** SE England, UK *51.22N 0.31E*
32 *K14* **Chatham** Illinois, N USA *39.40N 89.42W*
23 *T7* **Chatham** Virginia, NE USA *36.49N 79.24W*
65 *F22* **Chatham, Isla** *island* S Chile
183 *R12* **Chatham Island** *island* Chatham Islands, NZ
Chatham Island *see* San Cristóbal, Isla
Chatham Island Rise *see* Chatham Rise
199 *Jj14* **Chatham Islands** *island group* NZ, SW Pacific Ocean
183 *Q12* **Chatham Rise** ***var.*** Chatham Island Rise. *undersea feature* S Pacific Ocean
41 *X13* **Chatham Strait** *strait* Alaska, USA
Chathóir, Rinn *see* Cahore Point
104 *M9* **Châtillon-sur-Indre** Indre, C France *46.58N 1.10E*
105 *Q7* **Châtillon-sur-Seine** Côte d'Or, C France *47.51N 4.30E*
153 *S8* **Chatkal** ***Uzb.*** Chotqol. ≈ Kyrgyzstan/Uzbekistan
153 *R9* **Chatkal Range** ***Rus.*** Chatkal'skiy Khrebet. ▲▲ Kyrgyzstan/Uzbekistan
Chatkal'skiy Khrebet *see* Chatkal Range
25 *N7* **Chatom** Alabama, S USA *31.28N 88.15W*
Chatrapur *see* Chhatrapur

◆ Country
● Country Capital
◇ Dependent Territory
○ Dependent Territory Capital
◈ Administrative Region
✈ International Airport
▲ Mountain
▲▲ Mountain Range
⛰ Volcano
≈ River
⊛ Lake
⊠ Reservoir

149 S10 **Chatrūd** Kermān, C Iran *30.39N 56.57E*
25 S2 **Chatsworth** Georgia, SE USA *34.46N 84.46W*
Chattagām *see* Chittagong
25 S8 **Chattahoochee** Florida, SE USA *30.40N 84.51W*
25 R8 **Chattahoochee River** ≈ SE USA
22 L10 **Chattanooga** Tennessee, S USA *35.05N 85.16W*
153 V10 **Chatyr-Kël', Ozero** ◎ C Kyrgyzstan
153 W9 **Chatyr-Tash** Narynskaya Oblast', C Kyrgyzstan *40.54N 76.22E*
13 R12 **Chaudière** ≈ Quebec, SE Canada
178 J14 **Châu Đôc** *var.* Chauphu, Chau Phu. An Giang, S Vietnam *10.52N 105.07E*
158 D13 **Chauhtan** *prev.* Chohtan. Rājasthān, NW India *25.27N 71.07E*
117 Ff5 **Chauk** Magwe, W Myanmar *20.52N 94.49E*
105 R6 **Chaumont** *prev.* Chaumont-en-Bassigny. Haute-Marne, N France *48.07N 5.07E*
Chaumont-en-Bassigny *see* Chaumont
127 O4 **Chaunskaya Guba** *bay* NE Russian Federation
105 P3 **Chauny** Aisne, N France *49.37N 3.13E*
Châu Ô *see* Binh Sơn
Chau Phu *see* Châu Đôc
104 I5 **Chausey, Îles** *island group* N France
Chausy *see* Chavusy
20 C11 **Chautauqua Lake** ◎ New York, NE USA
104 L9 **Chauvigny** Vienne, W France *46.35N 0.37E*
128 L6 **Chavan'ga** Murmanskaya Oblast', NW Russian Federation *66.07N 37.44E*
12 K10 **Chavannes, Lac** ◎ Quebec, SE Canada
Chavantes, Represa de *see* Xavantes, Represa de
63 D15 **Chavarría** Corrientes, NE Argentina *28.57S 58.34W*
131 P4 **Chavash Respubliki** *var.* Chuvashskaya Respublika, *Eng.* Chuvashia. ◈ *autonomous republic* W Russian Federation
106 I5 **Chaves** *anc.* Aquae Flaviae. Vila Real, N Portugal *41.43N 7.28W*
Chávez, Isla *see* Santa Cruz, Isla
84 G13 **Chavuma** North Western, NW Zambia *13.04S 22.43E*
121 O16 **Chavusy** *Rus.* Chausy. Mahilyowskaya Voblasts', E Belarus *53.49N 30.59E*
151 Q16 **Chayan** Yuzhnyy Kazakhstan, S Kazakhstan *42.55N 69.32E*
153 U8 **Chayek** Narynskaya Oblast', C Kyrgyzstan *41.54N 74.28E*
145 T6 **Chāy Khānah** E Iraq *34.19N 44.33E*
129 T16 **Chaykovskiy** Permskaya Oblast', NW Russian Federation *56.45N 54.09E*
178 K12 **Chbar** Môndól Kiri, E Cambodia *12.46N 107.10E*
25 Q4 **Cheaha Mountain** ▲ Alabama, S USA *33.29N 85.48W*
Cheatharlach *see* Carlow
23 S2 **Cheat River** ≈ NE USA
113 A16 **Cheb** *Ger.* Eger. Karlovarský Kraj, W Czech Republic *50.04N 12.23E*
131 Q3 **Cheboksary** Chavash Respubliki, W Russian Federation *56.06N 47.14E*
33 Q5 **Cheboygan** Michigan, N USA *45.40N 84.28W*
Chechaouèn *see* Chefchaouen
Chechenia *see* Chechenskaya Respublika
131 O15 **Chechenskaya Respublika** *Eng.* Chechenia, Chechnia, *Rus.* Chechnya. ◈ *autonomous republic* SW Russian Federation
69 N4 **Chech, Erg** *desert* Algeria/Mali
Chechersk *see* Chachersk
Chechevichi *see* Chachevichy
Che-chiang *see* Zhejiang
Chechnia/Chechnya *see* Chechenskaya Respublika
169 Y15 **Chech'ŏn** *Jap.* Teisen. N South Korea *37.06N 128.15E*
113 L15 **Chęciny** Świętokrzyskie, S Poland *50.51N 20.31E*
29 Q10 **Checotah** Oklahoma, C USA *35.28N 95.31W*
11 R15 **Chedabucto Bay** *inlet* Nova Scotia, E Canada
177 F7 **Cheduba Island** *island* W Myanmar
39 T5 **Cheesman Lake** ⊞ Colorado, C USA
205 S16 **Cheetham, Cape** *headland* Antarctica *70.25S 162.40E*
76 G5 **Chefchaouen** *var.* Chaouèn, Chechaouèn, *Sp.* Xauen. N Morocco *35.09N 5.16W*
Chefoo *see* Yantai
40 M12 **Chefornak** Alaska, USA *60.09N 164.09W*
126 Mm15 **Chegdomyn** Khabarovskiy Kray, SE Russian Federation *51.09N 132.58E*
78 M4 **Chegga** Tiris Zemmour, NE Mauritania *25.27N 5.49W*
Cheghcheran *see* Chaghcharān
34 G9 **Chehalis** Washington, NW USA *46.39N 122.57W*
34 G9 **Chehalis River** ≈ Washington, NW USA
154 M6 **Chehel Abdālān, Kūh-e** *var.* Chalap Dalan, *Pash.* Chalap Dalan. ▲▲ C Afghanistan
117 D14 **Cheimadítis, Límni** ◎ N Greece
105 U15 **Cheiron, Mont** ▲ SE France *43.49N 7.00E*
169 X17 **Cheju** *Jap.* Saishū. S South Korea *33.31N 126.34E*
169 Y17 **Cheju** ✈ S South Korea *33.31N 126.28E*
169 Y17 **Cheju-do** *Jap.* Saishū; *prev.* Quelpart. *island* S South Korea
169 X17 **Cheju-haehyŏp** *strait* S South Korea
Chekiang *see* Zhejiang
Chekichler *see* Chekishlyar
152 B13 **Chekishlyar** *Turkm.* Chekichler. Balkanskiy Velayat, W Turkmenistan *37.35N 53.52E*
196 F8 **Chelab** Babeldaob, N Palau
153 N11 **Chelak** *Rus.* Chelek. Samarqand Viloyati, C Uzbekistan *39.55N 66.45E*
34 J7 **Chelan, Lake** ⊞ Washington, NW USA
Chelek *see* Chelak
152 A11 **Cheleken** Balkanskiy Velayat, W Turkmenistan *39.25N 53.07E*
Chélif/Chéliff *see* Chelif, Oued
76 J5 **Chelif, Oued** *var.* Chélif, Chéliff, Chellif, Shellif. ≈ N Algeria
150 K12 **Chelkar** Aktyubinsk, W Kazakhstan *47.49N 59.28E*
Chelkar, Ozero *see* Shalkar, Ozero
Chellif *see* Chelif, Oued
113 P14 **Chełm** *Rus.* Kholm. Lubelskie, SE Poland *51.07N 23.28E*
112 I9 **Chełmno** *Ger.* Culm, Kulm. Kujawski-pomorskie, C Poland *53.21N 18.27E*
12 F10 **Chelmsford** Ontario, S Canada *46.33N 81.16W*
99 P21 **Chelmsford** E England, UK *51.43N 0.28E*
112 J9 **Chełmża** *Ger.* Culmsee, Kulmsee. Kujawski-pomorskie, C Poland *53.12N 18.36E*
29 Q8 **Chelsea** Oklahoma, C USA *36.32N 95.25W*
20 M8 **Chelsea** Vermont, NE USA *43.57N 72.24W*
99 L21 **Cheltenham** C England, UK *51.54N 2.04W*
107 R9 **Chelva** País Valenciano, E Spain *39.45N 1.00W*
125 Ee12 **Chelyabinsk** Chelyabinskaya Oblast', C Russian Federation *55.12N 61.25E*
125 E12 **Chelyabinskaya Oblast'** ◈ *province* C Russian Federation
126 Jj4 **Chelyuskin, Mys** *headland* N Russian Federation *77.42N 104.13E*
126 H15 **Chemal** Altayskiy Kray, S Russian Federation *51.22N 85.08E*
43 Y12 **Chemax** Yucatán, SE Mexico *20.41N 87.54W*
85 N16 **Chemba** Sofala, C Mozambique *17.10S 34.52E*
84 J13 **Chembe** Luapula, NE Zambia *11.58S 28.45E*
152 J17 **Chemenibit** Maryyskiy Velayat, S Turkmenistan *35.27N 62.19E*
Chemerisy *see* Chamyarysy
118 K7 **Chemerivtsi** Khmel'nyts'ka Oblast', W Ukraine *49.00N 26.21E*
104 J8 **Chemillé** Maine-et-Loire, NW France *47.15N 0.42W*
181 X17 **Chemin Grenier** S Mauritius *20.28S 57.28E*
103 N16 **Chemnitz** *prev.* Karl-Marx-Stadt. Sachsen, E Germany *50.49N 12.55E*
Chemulpo *see* Inch'ŏn
34 H14 **Chemult** Oregon, NW USA *43.14N 121.48W*
20 G12 **Chemung River** ≈ New York/Pennsylvania, NE USA
155 U8 **Chenāb** ≈ India/Pakistan
41 S9 **Chena Hot Springs** Alaska, USA *65.06N 146.02W*
20 I11 **Chenango River** ≈ New York, NE USA
174 Gg3 **Chenderoh, Tasik** ◎ Peninsular Malaysia
13 Q11 **Chêne, Rivière du** ≈ Quebec, SE Canada
34 L8 **Cheney** Washington, NW USA *47.29N 117.34W*
28 M6 **Cheney Reservoir** ⊞ Kansas, C USA
Chengchiatun *see* Liaoyuan
Ch'eng-chou/Chengchow *see* Zhengzhou
167 P1 **Chengde** *var.* Jehol. Hebei, E China *41.00N 117.57E*
166 I9 **Chengdu** *var.* Chengtu, Ch'eng-tu. Sichuan, C China *30.40N 104.03E*
167 Q14 **Chenghai** Guangdong, S China *23.33N 116.42E*
Chenghsien *see* Zhengzhou
166 L17 **Chengmai** Hainan, S China *19.45N 109.56E*
Chengtu/Ch'eng-tu *see* Chengdu
165 W12 **Chengxian** *var.* Cheng Xian. Gansu, C China *33.42N 105.45E*
Chenkiang *see* Zhenjiang
161 J19 **Chennai** *prev.* Madras. Tamil Nādu, S India *13.04N 80.18E*
161 J19 **Chennai** ✈ Tamil Nādu, S India *13.07N 80.13E*
105 R8 **Chenôve** Côte d'Or, C France *47.16N 5.00E*
Chenstokhov *see* Częstochowa
166 L11 **Chenxi** Hunan, S China *28.01N 110.15E*
Chen Xian/Chenxian/Chen Xiang *see* Chenzhou
167 N12 **Chenzhou** *var.* Chenxian, Chen Xian, Chen Xiang. Hunan, S China *25.51N 113.01E*
178 Kk12 **Cheo Reo** *var.* A Yun Pa. Gia Lai, S Vietnam *13.19N 108.27E*
116 I11 **Chepelare** Smolyan, S Bulgaria *41.43N 24.40E*
116 I11 **Chepelarska Reka** ≈ S Bulgaria
58 B11 **Chepén** La Libertad, C Peru *7.12S 79.24W*
64 J10 **Chepes** La Rioja, C Argentina *31.23S 66.34W*
167 O15 **Chep Lap Kok** ✈ (Hong Kong) S China *22.23N 114.11E*
45 U14 **Chepo** Panamá, C Panama *9.10N 79.05W*
Chepping Wycombe *see* High Wycombe
129 R14 **Cheptsa** ≈ NW Russian Federation
32 K3 **Chequamegon Point** *headland* Wisconsin, N USA *46.42N 90.45W*
105 O8 **Cher** ◈ *department* C France
104 M8 **Cher** ≈ C France
Cherangani Hills *see* Cherangany Hills
83 H17 **Cherangany Hills** *var.* Cherangani Hills. ▲▲ W Kenya
23 S11 **Cheraw** South Carolina, SE USA *34.42N 79.52W*
104 J3 **Cherbourg** *anc.* Carusbur. Manche, N France *49.39N 1.36W*
131 R5 **Cherdakly** Ul'yanovskaya Oblast', W Russian Federation *54.21N 48.54E*
129 U12 **Cherdyn'** Permskaya Oblast', NW Russian Federation *60.21N 56.39E*
128 J14 **Cherekha** ≈ W Russian Federation
126 J15 **Cheremkhovo** Irkutskaya Oblast', S Russian Federation *53.16N 102.44E*
126 Hh15 **Cheremushki** Respublika Khakasiya, S Russian Federation *52.48N 91.20E*
Cheren *see* Keren
128 K14 **Cherepovets** Vologodskaya Oblast', NW Russian Federation *59.09N 37.49E*
129 O11 **Cherevkovo** Arkhangel'skaya Oblast', NW Russian Federation *61.45N 45.16E*
76 I6 **Chergui, Chott ech** *salt lake* NW Algeria
Cherikov *see* Cherykaw
119 P6 **Cherkas'ka Oblast'** *var.* Cherkasy, *Rus.* Cherkasskaya Oblast'. ◈ *province* C Ukraine
Cherkasskaya Oblast' *see* Cherkas'ka Oblast'
Cherkassy *see* Cherkasy
119 Q6 **Cherkasy** *Rus.* Cherkassy. Cherkas'ka Oblast', C Ukraine *49.25N 32.04E*
Cherkasy *see* Cherkas'ka Oblast'
130 M15 **Cherkessk** Karachayevo-Cherkesskaya Respublika, SW Russian Federation *44.12N 42.06E*
125 G13 **Cherlak** Omskaya Oblast', C Russian Federation *54.06N 74.59E*
125 Ff14 **Cherlakskiy** Omskaya Oblast', C Russian Federation *54.42N 74.23E*
129 U13 **Chermoz** Permskaya Oblast', NW Russian Federation *58.49N 56.07E*
Chernavchitsy *see* Charnawchytsy
129 T3 **Chernaya** Nenetskiy Avtonomnyy Okrug, NW Russian Federation *68.36N 56.34E*
129 T4 **Chernaya** ≈ NW Russian Federation
Chernigov *see* Chernihiv
Chernigovskaya Oblast' *see* Chernihivs'ka Oblast'
119 Q2 **Chernihiv** *Rus.* Chernigov. Chernihivs'ka Oblast', NE Ukraine *48.18N 25.59E*
Chernihiv *see* Chernihivs'ka Oblast'
119 V9 **Chernihivka** Zaporiz'ka Oblast', SE Ukraine *47.11N 36.10E*
119 P2 **Chernihivs'ka Oblast'** *var.* Chernihiv, *Rus.* Chernigovskaya Oblast'. ◈ *province* NE Ukraine
116 I9 **Cherni Osŭm** ≈ N Bulgaria
118 J8 **Chernivets'ka Oblast'** *var.* Chernivtsi, *Rus.* Chernovitskaya Oblast'. ◈ *province* W Ukraine
116 J9 **Cherni Vit** ≈ NW Bulgaria
116 G10 **Cherni Vrŭkh** ▲ W Bulgaria *42.33N 23.18E*
118 K8 **Chernivtsi** *Ger.* Czernowitz, *Rom.* Cernăuţi, *Rus.* Chernovtsy. Chernivets'ka Oblast', W Ukraine *48.18N 25.55E*
118 M7 **Chernivtsi** Vinnyts'ka Oblast', C Ukraine *48.33N 28.06E*
Chernivtsi *see* Chernivets'ka Oblast'
Chernobyl' *see* Chornobyl'
126 Hh15 **Chernogorsk** Respublika Khakasiya, S Russian Federation *53.48N 91.03E*
Cherno More *see* Black Sea
Chernomorskoye *see* Chornomors'ke
151 T7 **Chernoretskoye** Pavlodar, NE Kazakhstan *52.51N 76.37E*
Chernovitskaya Oblast' *see* Chernivets'ka Oblast'
Chernovtsy *see* Chernivtsi
151 U8 **Chernoye** Pavlodar, NE Kazakhstan *51.40N 77.33E*
Chernoye More *see* Black Sea
129 U16 **Chernushka** Permskaya Oblast', NW Russian Federation *56.30N 56.07E*
119 N4 **Chernyakhiv** *Rus.* Chernyakhov. Zhytomyrs'ka Oblast', N Ukraine *50.31N 28.38E*
Chernyakhov *see* Chernyakhiv
121 C14 **Chernyakhovsk** *Ger.* Insterburg. Kaliningradskaya Oblast', W Russian Federation *54.36N 21.49E*
130 K8 **Chernyanka** Belgorodskaya Oblast', W Russian Federation *50.59N 37.54E*
129 V5 **Chernyshëva, Gryada** ▲▲ NW Russian Federation
150 J14 **Chernyshëva, Zaliv** *gulf* SW Kazakhstan
126 L15 **Chernyshevsk** Chitinskaya Oblast', S Russian Federation *52.28N 116.52E*
126 K11 **Chernyshevskiy** Respublika Sakha (Yakutiya), NE Russian Federation *62.57N 112.29E*
131 P13 **Chërnyye Zemli** *plain* SW Russian Federation
Chërnyy Irtysh *see* Ertix He
131 V7 **Chërnyy Otrog** Orenburgskaya Oblast', W Russian Federation *52.03N 56.09E*
31 T12 **Cherokee** Iowa, C USA *42.45N 95.33W*
28 M8 **Cherokee** Oklahoma, C USA *36.45N 98.22W*
27 R9 **Cherokee** Texas, SW USA *30.56N 98.42W*
23 O8 **Cherokee Lake** ⊞ Tennessee, S USA
Cherokees, Lake O' The *see* Grand Lake O' The Cherokees
46 H1 **Cherokee Sound** Great Abaco, N Bahamas *26.16N 77.03W*
159 V13 **Cherrapunji** Meghālaya, NE India *25.16N 91.42E*
30 L9 **Cherry Creek** ≈ South Dakota, N USA
20 J16 **Cherry Hill** New Jersey, NE USA *39.55N 75.01W*
29 Q7 **Cherryvale** Kansas, C USA *37.16N 95.33W*
23 Q10 **Cherryville** North Carolina, SE USA *35.22N 81.22W*
Cherski Range *see* Cherskogo, Khrebet
127 O5 **Cherskiy** Respublika Sakha (Yakutiya), NE Russian Federation *68.45N 161.15E*
126 Mm8 **Cherskogo, Khrebet** *var.* Cherski Range. ▲▲ NE Russian Federation
Cherso *see* Cres
130 L10 **Chertkovo** Rostovskaya Oblast', SW Russian Federation *49.22N 40.10E*
Cherven' *see* Chervyen'
116 H8 **Cherven Bryag** Pleven, N Bulgaria *43.17N 24.06E*
118 M4 **Chervonoarmiys'k** Zhytomyrs'ka Oblast', N Ukraine *50.27N 28.15E*
Chervonograd *see* Chervonohrad
118 I4 **Chervonohrad** *Rus.* Chervonograd. L'vivs'ka Oblast', NW Ukraine *50.27N 24.11E*
119 W6 **Chervonooskil's'ke Vodoskhovyshche** *Rus.* Krasnoosol'skoye Vodokhranilishche. ⊞ NE Ukraine
Chervonoye, Ozero *see* Chyrvonaye, Vozyera
119 S4 **Chervonozavods'ke** Poltavs'ka Oblast', C Ukraine *50.24N 33.22E*
121 L16 **Chervyen'** *Rus.* Cherven'. Minskaya Voblasts', C Belarus *53.42N 28.23E*
121 P16 **Cherykaw** *Rus.* Cherikov. Mahilyowskaya Voblasts', E Belarus *53.34N 31.19E*
33 R9 **Chesaning** Michigan, N USA *43.10N 84.07W*
23 X5 **Chesapeake Bay** *inlet* NE USA
Cheshevlya *see* Tsyeshawlya
99 K18 **Cheshire** *cultural region* C England, UK
129 P5 **Chëshskaya Guba** *var.* Archangel Bay, Chesha Bay, Dvina Bay. *bay* NW Russian Federation
12 F14 **Chesley** Ontario, S Canada *44.17N 81.06W*
23 Q10 **Chesnee** South Carolina, SE USA *35.09N 81.51W*
99 K18 **Chester** *Wel.* Caerleon; *hist.* Legaceaster, *Lat.* Deva, Devana Castra. C England, UK *53.12N 2.54W*
37 O4 **Chester** California, W USA *40.18N 121.14W*
32 K16 **Chester** Illinois, N USA *37.54N 89.49W*
35 S7 **Chester** Montana, NW USA *48.30N 110.59W*
20 I16 **Chester** Pennsylvania, NE USA *39.51N 75.21W*
23 R1 **Chester** South Carolina, SE USA *34.42N 81.12W*
27 X9 **Chester** Texas, SW USA *30.55N 94.36W*
23 W6 **Chester** Virginia, NE USA *37.22N 77.27W*
23 R11 **Chester** West Virginia, NE USA *40.34N 80.33W*
99 M18 **Chesterfield** C England, UK *53.15N 1.25W*
23 S11 **Chesterfield** South Carolina, SE USA *34.44N 80.05W*
23 W6 **Chesterfield** Virginia, NE USA *37.22N 77.31W*
199 I10 **Chesterfield, Îles** *island group* NW New Caledonia
15 Ll6 **Chesterfield Inlet** Nunavut, NW Canada *63.19N 90.57W*
15 L6 **Chesterfield Inlet** *inlet* Nunavut, N Canada
23 Y3 **Chester River** ≈ Delaware/Maryland, NE USA
23 X3 **Chestertown** Maryland, NE USA *39.12N 76.04W*
21 R4 **Chesuncook Lake** ◎ Maine, NE USA
32 J5 **Chetek** Wisconsin, N USA *45.19N 91.39W*
11 R14 **Chéticamp** Nova Scotia, SE Canada *46.13N 61.19W*
29 Q8 **Chetopa** Kansas, C USA *37.02N 95.05W*
43 Y14 **Chetumal** *var.* Payo Obispo. Quintana Roo, SE Mexico *18.32N 88.15W*
Chetumal, Bahia/Chetumal, Bahía de *see* Chetumal Bay
44 G1 **Chetumal Bay** *var.* Bahia Chetumal, Bahía de Chetumal. *bay* Belize/Mexico
8 M13 **Chetwynd** British Columbia, W Canada *55.42N 121.36W*
40 M11 **Chevak** Alaska, USA *61.31N 165.35W*
38 M12 **Chevelon Creek** ≈ Arizona, SW USA
193 J17 **Cheviot** Canterbury, South Island, NZ *42.48S 173.17E*
98 L13 **Cheviot Hills** *hill range* England/Scotland, UK
98 L13 **Cheviot, The** ▲ NE England, UK *55.28N 2.10W*
12 M11 **Chevreuil, Lac du** ◎ Quebec, SE Canada
83 I16 **Ch'ew Bahir** *var.* Lake Stefanie. ◎ Ethiopia/Kenya
34 L7 **Chewelah** Washington, NW USA *48.16N 117.42W*
28 K10 **Cheyenne** Oklahoma, C USA *35.38N 99.40W*
35 Z17 **Cheyenne** *state capital* Wyoming, C USA *41.08N 104.45W*
28 L5 **Cheyenne Bottoms** ◎ Kansas, C USA
18 Kk6 **Cheyenne River** ≈ South Dakota/Wyoming, N USA
39 W5 **Cheyenne Wells** Colorado, C USA *38.49N 102.21W*
110 C9 **Cheyres** Vaud, W Switzerland *46.48N 6.48E*
Chezdi-Oşorheiu *see* Târgu Secuiesc
159 P13 **Chhapra** *prev.* Chapra. Bihār, N India *25.49N 84.42E*
159 V13 **Chhatak** *var.* Chatak. Chittagong, NE Bangladesh *25.02N 91.33E*
160 J9 **Chhatarpur** Madhya Pradesh, C India *24.54N 79.34E*
160 N13 **Chhatrapur** *prev.* Chatrapur; Orissa, E India *19.25N 85.01E*
160 L12 **Chhattīsgarh** *plain* C India
160 I11 **Chhindwāra** Madhya Pradesh, C India *22.04N 78.58E*
159 T12 **Chhukha** SW Bhutan *27.01N 89.36E*
167 S14 **Chiai** *var.* Chia-i, Chiayi, Kiayi, Jiayi, *Jap.* Kagi. C Taiwan *23.28N 120.27E*
Chia-mu-ssu *see* Jiamusi
85 B15 **Chiange** *Port.* Vila de Almoster. Huíla, SW Angola *15.49S 13.52E*
Chiang-hsi *see* Jiangxi
167 S12 **Chiang Kai-shek** ✈ (T'aipei) N Taiwan *25.09N 121.20E*
178 I8 **Chiang Khan** Loei, E Thailand *17.51N 101.43E*
178 H7 **Chiang Mai** *var.* Chiangmai, Chiengmai, Kiangmai. Chiang Mai, NW Thailand *18.48N 98.58E*
178 H7 **Chiang Mai** ✈ Chiang Mai, NW Thailand *18.44N 98.53E*
178 Hh6 **Chiang Rai** *var.* Chianpai, Chienrai, Muang Chiang Rai. Chiang Rai, NW Thailand *19.55N 99.51E*
Chiang-su *see* Jiangsu
Chianning/Chian-ning *see* Nanjing
Chianpai *see* Chiang Rai
108 G12 **Chianti** *cultural region* C Italy
Chiapa *see* Chiapa de Corzo
43 U16 **Chiapa de Corzo** *var.* Chiapa. Chiapas, SE Mexico *16.42N 92.58W*
43 V16 **Chiapas** ◈ *state* SE Mexico
108 J12 **Chiaravalle** Marche, C Italy *43.36N 13.19E*
109 N22 **Chiaravalle Centrale** Calabria, SW Italy *38.40N 16.25E*
108 E7 **Chiari** Lombardia, N Italy *45.33N 10.00E*
110 H12 **Chiasso** Ticino, S Switzerland *45.51N 9.01E*
143 S9 **Chiat'ura** C Georgia *42.13N 43.11E*
43 P15 **Chiautla** *var.* Chiautla de Tapia. Puebla, S Mexico *18.16N 98.31W*
Chiautla de Tapia *see* Chiautla
108 D10 **Chiavari** Liguria, NW Italy *44.19N 9.19E*
108 E6 **Chiavenna** Lombardia, N Italy *46.19N 9.22E*
Chiayi *see* Chiai
Chiazza *see* Piazza Armerina
172 Ss12 **Chiba** *var.* Tiba. Chiba, Honshū, S Japan *35.37N 140.05E*
171 K17 **Chiba** *off.* Chiba-ken, *var.* Tiba. ◈ *prefecture* Honshū, S Japan
85 M18 **Chibabava** Sofala, C Mozambique *20.16S 33.39E*
85 B15 **Chibia** *Port.* João de Almeida, Vila João de Almeida. Huíla, SW Angola *15.09S 13.45E*
85 M18 **Chiboma** Sofala, C Mozambique *20.06S 33.54E*
84 J12 **Chibondo** Luapula, N Zambia *10.42S 28.42E*
84 K11 **Chibote** Luapula, NE Zambia *9.52S 29.33E*
10 K12 **Chibougamau** Quebec, SE Canada *49.55N 74.24W*
170 Ff11 **Chiburi-jima** *island* Oki-shotō, SW Japan
85 M20 **Chibuto** Gaza, S Mozambique *24.40S 33.33E*
33 N11 **Chicago** Illinois, N USA *41.51N 87.39W*
33 N11 **Chicago Heights** Illinois, N USA *41.30N 87.38W*
13 W6 **Chic-Chocs, Monts** *Eng.* Shickshock Mountains. ▲▲ Quebec, SE Canada
41 W13 **Chichagof Island** *island* Alexander Archipelago, Alaska, USA
59 K20 **Chichas, Cordillera de** ▲▲ SW Bolivia
43 X12 **Chichén-Itzá, Ruinas** *ruins* Yucatán, SE Mexico *20.35N 88.34W*
99 N23 **Chichester** SE England, UK *50.50N 0.48W*
171 Jj16 **Chichibu** *var.* Titibu. Saitama, Honshū, S Japan *35.58N 139.06E*
44 C5 **Chichicastenango** Quiché, W Guatemala *14.55N 91.06W*
44 I9 **Chichigalpa** Chinandega, NW Nicaragua *12.34N 87.04W*
Ch'i-ch'i-ha-erh *see* Qiqihar
172 T16 **Chichijima-rettō** *Eng.* Beechy Group. *island group* SE Japan
56 K4 **Chichiriviche** Falcón, N Venezuela *10.58N 68.16W*
41 R11 **Chickaloon** Alaska, USA *61.48N 148.27W*
22 L10 **Chickamauga Lake** ⊞ Tennessee, S USA
25 N7 **Chickasawhay River** ≈ Mississippi, S USA
28 M11 **Chickasha** Oklahoma, C USA *35.03N 97.56W*
41 T9 **Chicken** Alaska, USA *64.04N 141.56W*
106 J16 **Chiclana de la Frontera** Andalucía, S Spain *36.25N 6.09W*
58 B11 **Chiclayo** Lambayeque, NW Peru *6.46S 79.46W*
37 N5 **Chico** California, W USA *39.42N 121.51W*
85 L15 **Chicoa** Tete, NW Mozambique *15.45S 32.25E*
85 M20 **Chicomo** Gaza, S Mozambique *24.29S 34.15E*
20 M11 **Chicopee** Massachusetts, NE USA *42.08N 72.34W*
65 I19 **Chico, Río** ≈ SE Argentina
65 I21 **Chico, Río** ≈ S Argentina
29 W14 **Chicot, Lake** ◎ Arkansas, C USA
13 R7 **Chicoutimi** Quebec, SE Canada *48.24N 71.04W*
13 Q8 **Chicoutimi** ≈ Quebec, SE Canada
85 L19 **Chicualacuala** Gaza, SW Mozambique *22.06S 31.42E*
85 B14 **Chicuma** Benguela, C Angola *13.33S 14.41E*
161 J21 **Chidambaram** Tamil Nādu, SE India *11.25N 79.42E*
206 K13 **Chidley, Cape** *headland* Newfoundland and Labrador, E Canada *60.25N 64.39W*
103 N24 **Chiemsee** ◎ SE Germany
Chiengmai *see* Chiang Mai
Chienrai *see* Chiang Rai
108 B8 **Chieri** Piemonte, NW Italy *45.01N 7.49E*
108 F8 **Chiese** ≈ N Italy
109 K14 **Chieti** *var.* Teate. Abruzzo, C Italy *42.22N 14.10E*
101 E19 **Chièvres** Hainaut, SW Belgium *50.34N 3.49E*
169 S12 **Chifeng** *var.* Ulanhad. Nei Mongol Zizhiqu, N China *42.16N 118.58E*
84 F13 **Chifumage** ≈ E Angola
84 M13 **Chifunda** Eastern, NE Zambia *11.57S 32.36E*
151 S14 **Chiganak** *var.* Čiganak. Zhambyl, SE Kazakhstan *45.10N 73.55E*
41 P15 **Chiginagak, Mount** ▲ Alaska, USA *57.10N 157.00W*
Chigirin *see* Chyhyryn
43 P13 **Chignahuapan** Puebla, S Mexico *19.52N 98.03W*
41 O15 **Chignik** Alaska, USA *56.18N 158.24W*
85 M19 **Chigombe** ≈ S Mozambique
56 D7 **Chigorodó** Antioquia, NW Colombia *7.42N 76.45W*
85 M19 **Chigubo** Gaza, S Mozambique *22.50S 33.30E*
168 D6 **Chihertey** Bayan-Ölgiy, W Mongolia *48.10N 89.35E*
Chih-fu *see* Yantai
Chihli *see* Hebei
Chihli, Gulf of *see* Bo Hai
42 J6 **Chihuahua** Chihuahua, NW Mexico *28.40N 106.06W*
42 I6 **Chihuahua** ◈ *state* N Mexico
151 O15 **Chiili** Kzylorda, S Kazakhstan *44.09N 66.44E*
28 M7 **Chikaskia River** ≈ Kansas/Oklahoma, C USA
161 H19 **Chik Ballāpur** Karnātaka, W India *13.28N 77.42E*
128 G15 **Chikhachevo** Pskovskaya Oblast', W Russian Federation *57.17N 29.51E*
161 F19 **Chikmagalūr** Karnātaka, W India *13.19N 75.46E*
133 V7 **Chikoy** ≈ C Russian Federation
85 J15 **Chikumbi** Lusaka, C Zambia *15.16S 28.18E*
84 M13 **Chikwa** Eastern, NE Zambia *11.39S 32.45E*
Chikwana *see* Chikwawa
85 N15 **Chikwawa** *var.* Chikwana. Southern, S Malawi *16.03S 34.51E*
161 J16 **Chilakalūrupet** Andhra Pradesh, E India *16.09N 80.13E*
152 L14 **Chilan** Lebapskiy Velayat, E Turkmenistan *37.57N 64.58E*
Chilapa *see* Chilapa de Alvarez
43 P16 **Chilapa de Alvarez** *var.* Chilapa. Guerrero, S Mexico *17.36N 99.09W*
161 J25 **Chilaw** North Western Province, W Sri Lanka *7.34N 79.49E*
59 D15 **Chilca** Lima, W Peru *12.33S 76.44W*
25 Q4 **Childersburg** Alabama, S USA *33.16N 86.21W*
27 P4 **Childress** Texas, SW USA *34.25N 100.13W*
65 G14 **Chile** *off.* Republic of Chile. ◆ *republic* SW South America
49 R10 **Chile Basin** *undersea feature* E Pacific Ocean
65 H20 **Chile Chico** Aisén, W Chile *46.34S 71.43W*
64 I9 **Chilecito** La Rioja, NW Argentina *29.10S 67.30W*
64 H12 **Chilecito** Mendoza, W Argentina *33.52S 69.03W*
85 L14 **Chilembwe** Eastern, E Zambia *13.54S 31.38E*
200 O13 **Chile Rise** *undersea feature* SE Pacific Ocean
119 N13 **Chilia Braţul** ≈ SE Romania
Chilia-Nouă *see* Kiliya
151 V15 **Chilik** Almaty, SE Kazakhstan *43.35N 78.17E*
151 V15 **Chilik** ≈ SE Kazakhstan
160 O13 **Chilika Lake** *var.* Chilka Lake. ◎ E India
84 J13 **Chililabombwe** Copperbelt, C Zambia *12.19S 27.52E*
Chi-lin *see* Jilin
Chilka Lake *see* Chilika Lake
8 H9 **Chilkoot Pass** *pass* British Columbia, W Canada *59.41N 135.13W*
Chill Ala, Cuan *see* Killala Bay
64 G13 **Chillán** Bío Bío, C Chile *36.37S 72.10W*
63 C22 **Chillar** Buenos Aires, E Argentina *37.16S 59.58W*
Chill Chiaráin, Cuan *see* Kilkieran Bay
32 K12 **Chillicothe** Illinois, N USA *40.55N 89.29W*
29 S3 **Chillicothe** Missouri, C USA *39.48N 93.33W*
33 S14 **Chillicothe** Ohio, N USA *39.19N 82.58W*
27 Q4 **Chillicothe** Texas, SW USA *34.15N 99.31W*
8 M17 **Chilliwack** British Columbia, SW Canada *49.09N 121.54W*
Chill Mhantáin, Ceann *see* Wicklow Head
Chill Mhantáin, Sléibhte *see* Wicklow Mountains
110 C10 **Chillon** Vaud, W Switzerland *46.24N 6.56E*
152 C11 **Chil'mamedkum, Peski** *Turkm.* Chilmämetgum. *desert* W Turkmenistan
Chilmämetgum *see* Chil'mamedkum, Peski
65 F17 **Chiloé, Isla de** *var.* Isla Grande de Chiloé. *island* W Chile
34 H15 **Chiloquin** Oregon, NW USA *42.33N 121.33W*
43 O16 **Chilpancingo** *var.* Chilpancingo de los Bravos. Guerrero, S Mexico *17.33N 99.30W*
Chilpancingo de los Bravos *see* Chilpancingo
99 N21 **Chiltern Hills** *hill range* S England, UK
32 M7 **Chilton** Wisconsin, N USA *44.04N 88.10W*
84 F11 **Chiluage** Lunda Sul, NE Angola *9.32S 21.48E*
84 N12 **Chilumba** *prev.* Deep Bay. Northern, N Malawi *10.27S 34.12E*
167 T12 **Chilung** *var.* Keelung, *Jap.* Kirun, Kirun'; *prev. Sp.* Santissima Trinidad. N Taiwan *25.10N 121.43E*
85 N15 **Chilwa, Lake** *var.* Lago Chirua, Lake Shirwa. ◎ SE Malawi
178 J10 **Chi, Mae Nam** ≈ E Thailand
44 C6 **Chimaltenango** Chimaltenango, C Guatemala *14.37N 90.48W*
44 A2 **Chimaltenango** *off.* Departamento de Chimaltenango. ◈ *department* S Guatemala
45 V15 **Chimán** Panamá, E Panama *8.41N 78.37W*
85 M17 **Chimanimani** *prev.* Mandidzudzure, Melsetter. Manicaland, E Zimbabwe *19.48S 32.52E*
101 G22 **Chimay** Hainaut, S Belgium *50.03N 4.19E*
39 S10 **Chimayo** New Mexico, SW USA *36.00N 105.55W*
Chimbay *see* Chimboy
58 A13 **Chimborazo** ◈ *province* C Ecuador
58 C7 **Chimborazo** ⛰ C Ecuador *1.29S 78.50W*
58 C12 **Chimbote** Ancash, W Peru *9.04S 78.34W*
152 H7 **Chimboy** *Rus.* Chimbay. Qoraqalpog'iston Respublikasi, NW Uzbekistan *43.03N 59.52E*
194 H12 **Chimbu** ◈ *province* C PNG
56 F6 **Chimichagua** Cesar, N Colombia *9.19N 73.51W*
Chimishliya *see* Cimişlia
Chimkent *see* Shymkent
Chimkentskaya Oblast' *see* Yuzhnyy Kazakhstan
30 I14 **Chimney Rock** *rock* Nebraska, C USA *41.40N 103.21W*
85 M17 **Chimoio** Manica, C Mozambique *19.07S 33.28E*
84 K11 **Chimpembe** Northern, NE Zambia *9.33S 29.30E*
43 O8 **China** Nuevo León, NE Mexico *25.44N 99.09W*
162 M9 **China** *off.* People's Republic of China, *Chin.* Chung-hua Jen-min Kung-ho-kuo, Zhonghua Renmin Gongheguo; *prev.* Chinese Empire. ◆ *republic* E Asia
21 Q7 **China Lake** ◎ Maine, NE USA
44 F8 **Chinameca** San Miguel, E El Salvador *13.28N 88.21W*
Chi-nan/Chinan *see* Jinan
44 H9 **Chinandega** Chinandega, NW Nicaragua *12.37N 87.07W*
44 H9 **Chinandega** ◈ *department* NW Nicaragua
China, People's Republic of *see* China
China, Republic of *see* Taiwan
26 J11 **Chinati Mountains** ▲▲ Texas, SW USA
Chinaz *see* Chinoz
59 E15 **Chincha Alta** Ica, SW Peru *13.25S 76.08W*
9 N11 **Chinchaga** ≈ Alberta, SW Canada
Chin-chiang *see* Quanzhou
Chinchilla *see* Chinchilla de Monte Aragón
107 Q11 **Chinchilla de Monte Aragón** *var.* Chinchilla. Castilla-La Mancha, C Spain *38.55N 1.43W*
56 D10 **Chinchiná** Caldas, W Colombia *4.58N 75.37W*
107 O8 **Chinchón** Madrid, C Spain *40.07N 3.25W*
43 Z14 **Chinchorro, Banco** *island* SE Mexico
Chin-chou/Chinchow *see* Jinzhou
23 Z5 **Chincoteague** Assateague Island, Virginia, NE USA *37.55N 75.22W*
85 O17 **Chinde** Zambézia, NE Mozambique *18.34S 36.25E*
169 X17 **Chin-do** *Jap.* Chin-tō. *island* SW South Korea
165 R13 **Chindu** Qinghai, C China *33.19N 97.08E*
177 G2 **Chindwin** ≈ N Myanmar
Chinese Empire *see* China
Ch'ing Hai *see* Qinghai Hu
Chinghai *see* Qinghai
Chingildi *see* Shengeldi
150 H9 **Chingirlau** *Kaz.* Shyngghyrlaū. Zapadnyy Kazakhstan, W Kazakhstan *51.10N 53.44E*
84 J13 **Chingola** Copperbelt, C Zambia *12.31S 27.52E*
Ching-Tao/Ch'ing-tao *see* Qingdao
84 C13 **Chinguar** Huambo, C Angola *12.33S 16.22E*
78 I7 **Chinguețți** *var.* Chinguetti. Adrar, C Mauritania *20.25N 12.24W*
169 Z16 **Chinhae** *Jap.* Chinkai. S South Korea *35.06N 128.48E*
177 Ff4 **Chin Hills** ▲▲ W Myanmar
85 K16 **Chinhoyi** *prev.* Sinoia. Mashonaland West, N Zimbabwe *17.19S 30.06E*
Chinhsien *see* Jinzhou
41 Q14 **Chiniak, Cape** *headland* Kodiak Island, Alaska, USA *57.37N 152.10W*
12 G10 **Chiniguchi Lake** ◎ Ontario, S Canada
155 U8 **Chiniot** Punjab, NE Pakistan *31.40N 73.00E*
169 Y16 **Chinju** *Jap.* Shinshū. S South Korea *35.11N 128.06E*
Chinkai *see* Chinhae
80 M13 **Chinko** ≈ E Central African Republic
39 O9 **Chinle** Arizona, SW USA *36.09N 109.33W*
167 R13 **Chinmen Tao** *var.* Jinmen Dao, Quemoy. *island* W Taiwan
Chinnchâr *see* Shinshār
Chinnereth *see* Tiberias, Lake
171 J15 **Chino** *var.* Tino. Nagano, Honshū, S Japan *36.00N 138.10E*

◆ Country
● Country Capital
◇ Dependent Territory
○ Dependent Territory Capital
◈ Administrative Region
✈ International Airport
▲ Mountain
▲▲ Mountain Range
⛰ Volcano
≈ River
◎ Lake
⊞ Reservoir

104 *L8* **Chinon** Indre-et-Loire, C France *47.10N 0.15E*
35 *T7* **Chinook** Montana, NW USA *48.35N 109.13W*
Chinook State *see* Washington
199 *Jj3* **Chinook Trough** *undersea feature* N Pacific Ocean
38 *K11* **Chino Valley** Arizona, SW USA *34.45N 112.27W*
153 *P10* **Chinoz** ***Rus.*** Chinaz. Toshkent Viloyati, E Uzbekistan *40.58N 68.46E*
84 *L12* **Chinsali** Northern, NE Zambia *10.33S 32.04E*
177 *F4* **Chin State** ◈ *state* W Myanmar
Chinsura *see* Chunchura
Chin-tō *see* Chin-do
56 *E6* **Chinú** Córdoba, NW Colombia *9.07N 75.25W*
101 *K24* **Chiny, Forêt de** *forest* SE Belgium
85 *M15* **Chioco** Tete, NW Mozambique *16.22S 32.50E*
108 *H8* **Chioggia** ***anc.*** Fossa Claudia. Veneto, NE Italy *45.13N 12.16E*
116 *H12* **Chionótrypa** ▲ NE Greece *41.16N 24.06E*
117 *L18* **Chíos** ***var.*** Hios, Khíos, ***It.*** Scio, ***Turk.*** Sakiz-Adasi. Chíos, E Greece *38.22N 26.07E*
117 *K18* **Chíos** ***var.*** Khíos. *island* E Greece
85 *M14* **Chipata** ***prev.*** Fort Jameson. Eastern, E Zambia *13.40S 32.42E*
85 *C14* **Chipindo** Huíla, C Angola *13.53S 15.47E*
25 *R8* **Chipley** Florida, SE USA *30.46N 85.32W*
161 *D15* **Chiplūn** Mahārāshtra, W India *17.31N 73.31E*
83 *H22* **Chipogolo** Dodoma, C Tanzania *6.52S 36.03E*
25 *R8* **Chipola River** ≈ Florida, SE USA
99 *L22* **Chippenham** S England, UK *51.28N 2.07W*
32 *J6* **Chippewa Falls** Wisconsin, N USA *44.55N 91.25W*
32 *J4* **Chippewa, Lake** ▣ Wisconsin, N USA
33 *Q8* **Chippewa River** ≈ Michigan, N USA
32 *I6* **Chippewa River** ≈ Wisconsin, N USA
Chipping Wycombe *see* High Wycombe
116 *G8* **Chiprovtsi** Montana, NW Bulgaria *43.23N 22.53E*
21 *T4* **Chiputneticook Lakes** *lakes* Canada/USA
58 *D13* **Chiquián** Ancash, W Peru *10.03S 77.11W*
43 *Y11* **Chiquilá** Quintana Roo, SE Mexico *21.25N 87.20W*
44 *E6* **Chiquimula** Chiquimula, SE Guatemala *14.45N 89.31W*
44 *A3* **Chiquimula** ***off.*** Departamento de Chiquimula. ◈ *department* SE Guatemala
44 *D7* **Chiquimulilla** Santa Rosa, S Guatemala *14.06N 90.22W*
56 *F9* **Chiquinquirá** Boyacá, C Colombia *5.37N 73.51W*
161 *J17* **Chīrāla** Andhra Pradesh, E India *15.49N 80.21E*
155 *N4* **Chīras** Ghowr, N Afghanistan *35.15N 65.39E*
158 *H11* **Chirāwa** Rājasthān, N India *28.15N 75.42E*
Chirchik *see* Chirchiq
153 *Q9* **Chirchiq** ***Rus.*** Chirchik. Toshkent Viloyati, E Uzbekistan *41.30N 69.31E*
153 *P10* **Chirchiq** ≈ E Uzbekistan
Chire *see* Shire
85 *L18* **Chiredzi** Masvingo, SE Zimbabwe *21.03S 31.40E*
27 *X8* **Chireno** Texas, SW USA *31.30N 94.21W*
79 *X7* **Chirfa** Agadez, NE Niger *21.01N 12.41E*
39 *O16* **Chiricahua Mountains** ▲▲ Arizona, SW USA
39 *O16* **Chiricahua Peak** ▲ Arizona, SW USA *31.51N 109.17W*
56 *F6* **Chiriguaná** Cesar, N Colombia *9.24N 73.37W*
41 *P15* **Chirikof Island** *island* Alaska, USA
45 *P16* **Chiriquí** ***off.*** Provincia de Chiriquí. ◈ *province* SW Panama
45 *P17* **Chiriquí, Golfo de** ***Eng.*** Chiriqui Gulf. *gulf* SW Panama
45 *P15* **Chiriquí Grande** Bocas del Toro, W Panama *8.55N 82.08W*
Chiriqui Gulf *see* Chiriquí, Golfo de
45 *P15* **Chiriquí, Laguna de** *lagoon* NW Panama
45 *O16* **Chiriquí Viejo, Río** ≈ W Panama
Chiriquí, Volcán de *see* Barú, Volcán
85 *N15* **Chiromo** Southern, S Malawi *16.32S 35.07E*
116 *J10* **Chirpan** Stara Zagora, C Bulgaria *42.13N 25.22E*
45 *N14* **Chirripó Atlántico, Río** ≈ E Costa Rica
Chirripó, Cerro *see* Chirripó Grande, Cerro
45 *N14* **Chirripó Grande, Cerro** ***var.*** Cerro Chirripó. ▲ SE Costa Rica *9.31N 83.28W*
45 *N13* **Chirripó, Río** ***var.*** Río Chirripó del Pacífico. ≈ NE Costa Rica
Chirua, Lago *see* Chilwa, Lake
85 *J15* **Chirundu** Southern, S Zambia *16.01S 28.52E*
31 *W8* **Chisago City** Minnesota, N USA *45.22N 92.53W*
85 *J14* **Chisamba** Central, C Zambia *14.58S 28.21E*
41 *T10* **Chisana** Alaska, USA *62.09N 142.07W*
84 *I13* **Chisasa** North Western, NW Zambia *12.09S 25.30E*
10 *I9* **Chisasibi** Quebec, C Canada *53.45N 79.01W*
44 *D4* **Chisec** Alta Verapaz, C Guatemala *15.47N 90.13W*
131 *U5* **Chishmy** Respublika Bashkortostan, W Russian Federation *54.33N 55.21E*
31 *V4* **Chisholm** Minnesota, N USA *47.29N 92.52W*
166 *I11* **Chishui He** ≈ C China
Chisimaio/Chisimayu *see* Kismaayo
119 *N10* **Chişinău** ***Rus.*** Kishinev. ● (Moldova) C Moldova *47.00N 28.50E*
119 *N10* **Chişinău** ✕ S Moldova *46.54N 28.56E*
Chişinău-Criş *see* Chişineu-Criş
118 *F10* **Chişineu-Criş** ***Hung.*** Kşjenő; ***prev.*** Chişinău-Criş. Arad, W Romania *46.33N 21.29E*
85 *K14* **Chisomo** Central, C Zambia *13.30S 30.37E*
108 *A8* **Chisone** ≈ NW Italy
26 *K12* **Chisos Mountains** ▲▲ Texas, SW USA
155 *U10* **Chistiān Mandi** Punjab, E Pakistan *29.52N 72.46E*
41 *T10* **Chistochina** Alaska, USA *62.34N 144.39W*
131 *R4* **Chistopol'** Respublika Tatarstan, W Russian Federation *55.20N 50.39E*
151 *O8* **Chistopol'ye** Severnyy Kazakhstan, N Kazakhstan *52.37N 67.13E*
126 *Kk16* **Chita** Chitinskaya Oblast', S Russian Federation *52.03N 113.34E*
85 *B16* **Chitado** Cunene, SW Angola *17.16S 13.54E*
Chitaldroog/Chitaldrug *see* Chitradurga
85 *C15* **Chitanda** ≈ S Angola
Chitangwiza *see* Chitungwiza
84 *F10* **Chitato** Lunda Norte, NE Angola *7.23S 20.45E*
85 *C14* **Chitembo** Bié, C Angola *13.31S 16.44E*
41 *T11* **Chitina** Alaska, USA *61.31N 144.26W*
41 *T11* **Chitina River** ≈ Alaska, USA
126 *Kk14* **Chitinskaya Oblast'** ◈ *province* S Russian Federation
84 *M11* **Chitipa** Northern, NW Malawi *9.40S 33.19E*
172 *Oo6* **Chitose** ***var.*** Titose. Hokkaidō, NE Japan *42.50N 141.39E*
161 *G18* **Chitradurga** ***prev.*** Chitaldroog, Chitaldrug. Karnātaka, W India *14.15N 76.24E*
155 *T3* **Chitrāl** North-West Frontier Province, NW Pakistan *35.51N 71.46E*
45 *S16* **Chitré** Herrera, S Panama *7.57N 80.25W*
159 *V16* **Chittagong** ***Ben.*** Chāttagām. Chittagong, SE Bangladesh *22.19N 91.48E*
159 *U16* **Chittagong** ◈ *division* E Bangladesh
159 *Q15* **Chittaranjan** West Bengal, NE India *23.52N 86.40E*
158 *G14* **Chittaurgarh** Rājasthān, N India *24.54N 74.42E*
161 *I19* **Chittoor** Andhra Pradesh, E India *13.13N 79.06E*
161 *G21* **Chittūr** Kerala, SW India *10.42N 76.46E*
85 *K16* **Chitungwiza** ***prev.*** Chitangwiza. Mashonaland East, NE Zimbabwe *18.00S 31.06E*
64 *H4* **Chíuchíu** Antofagasta, N Chile *22.13S 68.34W*
84 *F12* **Chiumbe** ***var.*** Tshiumbe. ≈ Angola/Dem. Rep. Congo
85 *F15* **Chiume** Moxico, E Angola *15.08S 21.09E*
84 *K13* **Chiundaponde** Northern, NE Zambia *12.14S 30.40E*
108 *H13* **Chiusi** Toscana, C Italy *43.00N 11.56E*
56 *J5* **Chivacoa** Yaracuy, N Venezuela *10.10N 68.54W*
108 *B8* **Chivasso** Piemonte, NW Italy *45.13N 7.54E*
85 *L17* **Chivhu** ***prev.*** Enkeldoorn. Midlands, C Zimbabwe *19.01S 30.54E*
63 *C20* **Chivilcoy** Buenos Aires, E Argentina *34.55S 60.00W*
84 *N12* **Chiweta** Northern, N Malawi *10.36S 34.09E*
44 *D4* **Chixoy, Río** ***var.*** Río Negro, Río Salinas. ≈ Guatemala/Mexico
84 *H13* **Chizela** North Western, NW Zambia *13.11S 24.59E*
129 *O5* **Chizha** Nenetskiy Avtonomnyy Okrug, NW Russian Federation *67.04N 44.19E*
170 *G13* **Chizu** Tottori, Honshū, SW Japan *35.15N 134.14E*
Chkalov *see* Orenburg
76 *J5* **Chlef** ***var.*** Ech Cheliff, Ech Chleff; ***prev.*** Al-Asnam, El Asnam, Orléansville. NW Algeria *36.10N 1.21E*
117 *G18* **Chlómo** ▲ C Greece *38.36N 22.57E*
113 *M15* **Chmielnik** Świętokrzyskie, C Poland *50.37N 20.43E*
178 *J11* **Chŏâm Khsant** Preăh Vihéar, N Cambodia *14.13N 104.55E*
64 *G10* **Choapa, Río** ***var.*** Choapo. ≈ C Chile
Choapas *see* Las Choapas
Choarta *see* Chwārtā
85 *H17* **Chobe** ◈ *district* NE Botswana
69 *T13* **Chobe** ≈ N Botswana
12 *K8* **Chochocouane** ≈ Quebec, SE Canada
112 *E13* **Chocianów** ***Ger.*** Kotzenan. Dolnośląskie, SW Poland *51.23N 15.55E*
56 *C9* **Chocó** ***off.*** Departamento del Chocó. ◈ *province* W Colombia
37 *X16* **Chocolate Mountains** ▲▲ California, W USA
23 *W9* **Chocowinity** North Carolina, SE USA *35.33N 77.03W*
29 *N10* **Choctaw** Oklahoma, C USA *35.30N 97.16W*
25 *Q8* **Choctawhatchee Bay** *bay* Florida, SE USA
25 *Q8* **Choctawhatchee River** ≈ Florida, SE USA
Chodau *see* Chodov
169 *V14* **Chŏ-do** *island* SW North Korea
Chodorów *see* Khodoriv
113 *A16* **Chodov** ***Ger.*** Chodau. Karlovarský Kraj, W Czech Republic *50.15N 12.45E*
112 *G10* **Chodzież** Wielkopolskie, C Poland *53.00N 16.55E*
65 *J15* **Choele Choel** Río Negro, C Argentina *39.18S 65.42W*
85 *L14* **Chofombo** Tete, NW Mozambique *14.43S 31.48E*
Chohtan *see* Chauhtan
9 *U14* **Choiceland** Saskatchewan, C Canada *53.28N 104.26W*
195 *U13* **Choiseul** ***var.*** Lauru. *island* NW Solomon Islands
65 *M23* **Choiseul Sound** *sound* East Falkland, Falkland Islands
42 *H7* **Choix** Sinaloa, C Mexico *26.43N 108.20W*
112 *D10* **Chojna** Zachodniopomorskie, W Poland *52.56N 14.25E*
112 *H8* **Chojnice** ***Ger.*** Konitz. Pomorskie, N Poland *53.41N 17.34E*
113 *F14* **Chojnów** ***Ger.*** Hainau, Haynau. Dolnośląskie, SW Poland *51.16N 15.55E*
171 *Ll11* **Chōkai-san** ▲ Honshū, C Japan *39.06N 140.02E*
178 *I11* **Chok Chai** Nakhon Ratchasima, C Thailand *14.45N 102.10E*
82 *I12* **Ch'ok'ē** ***var.*** Choke Mountains. ▲▲ NW Ethiopia
27 *R13* **Choke Canyon Lake** ▣ Texas, SW USA
Choke Mountains *see* Ch'ok'ē
151 *T15* **Chokpar** ***Kaz.*** Shoqpar. Zhambyl, S Kazakhstan *43.49N 74.25E*
153 *W7* **Chok-Tal** ***var.*** Choktal. Issyk-Kul'skaya Oblast', E Kyrgyzstan *42.37N 76.45E*
Chókué *see* Chokwé
126 *Mm6* **Chokurdakh** Respublika Sakha (Yakutiya), NE Russian Federation *70.38N 148.18E*
85 *L20* **Chokwé** ***var.*** Chókué. Gaza, S Mozambique *24.36S 33.06E*
196 *F8* **Chol** Babeldaob, N Palau
166 *E8* **Chola Shan** ▲▲ C China
104 *J8* **Cholet** Maine-et-Loire, NW France *47.03N 0.52W*
65 *H17* **Cholila** Chubut, W Argentina *42.33S 71.28W*
Cholo *see* Thyolo
153 *V8* **Cholpon** Narynskaya Oblast', C Kyrgyzstan *42.07N 75.25E*
153 *X7* **Cholpon-Ata** Issyk-Kul'skaya Oblast', E Kyrgyzstan *42.39N 77.05E*
43 *P14* **Cholula** Puebla, S Mexico *19.03N 98.19W*
44 *I8* **Choluteca** Choluteca, S Honduras *13.16N 87.11W*
44 *H8* **Choluteca** ◈ *department* S Honduras
44 *G6* **Choluteca, Río** ≈ SW Honduras
85 *I15* **Choma** Southern, S Zambia *16.47S 26.58E*
159 *T11* **Chomo Lhari** ▲ NW Bhutan *27.59N 89.24E*
178 *H7* **Chom Thong** Chiang Mai, NW Thailand *18.28N 98.41E*
113 *B15* **Chomutov** ***Ger.*** Komotau. Ústecký Kraj, NW Czech Republic *50.28N 13.24E*
126 *K12* **Chona** ≈ C Russian Federation
169 *X15* **Ch'ŏnan** ***Jap.*** Tenan. W South Korea *36.51N 127.10E*
178 *Hh12* **Chon Buri** ***prev.*** Bang Pla Soi. Chon Buri, S Thailand *13.17N 100.58E*
58 *B6* **Chone** Manabí, W Ecuador *0.41S 80.06W*
169 *W13* **Ch'ŏngch'ŏn-gang** ≈ W North Korea
169 *Y11* **Ch'ŏngjin** NE North Korea *41.48N 129.43E*
169 *W13* **Chŏngju** W North Korea *39.43N 125.13E*
167 *S8* **Chongming Dao** *island* E China
166 *J10* **Chongqing** ***var.*** Ch'ung-ching, Ch'ung-ch'ing, Chungking, Pahsien, Tchongking, Yuzhou. Chongqing Shi, C China *29.34N 106.27E*
Chŏngup *see* Chŏnju
167 *O10* **Chongyang** Hubei, C China *29.34N 114.03E*
169 *Y16* **Chŏnju** ***prev.*** Chŏngup, ***Jap.*** Seiyu. SW South Korea *35.51N 127.08E*
169 *Y15* **Chŏnju** ***Jap.*** Zenshū. SW South Korea *35.51N 127.08E*
Chonnacht *see* Connaught
169 *Q9* **Chonogol** Sühbaatar, E Mongolia *45.55N 115.19E*
65 *F19* **Chonos, Archipiélago de los** *island group* S Chile
44 *K10* **Chontales** ◈ *department* S Nicaragua
178 *Jj14* **Chơn Thanh** Sông Be, S Vietnam *11.25N 106.37E*
164 *K17* **Cho Oyu** ***var.*** Qowowuyag. ▲ China/Nepal *28.07N 86.37E*
118 *G7* **Chop** ***Cz.*** Čop, ***Hung.*** Csap. Zakarpats'ka Oblast', W Ukraine *48.25N 22.13E*
23 *Y3* **Choptank River** ≈ Maryland, NE USA
Chorcaí, Cuan *see* Cork Harbour
45 *P15* **Chorcha, Cerro** ▲ W Panama *8.39N 82.07W*
Chorku *see* Chorkŭh
153 *R11* **Chorkŭh** ***Rus.*** Chorku. N Tajikistan *40.04N 70.30E*
99 *K17* **Chorley** NW England, UK *53.40N 2.37W*
Chorne More *see* Black Sea
119 *R5* **Chornobay** Cherkas'ka Oblast', C Ukraine *49.40N 32.20E*
119 *O3* **Chornobyl'** ***Rus.*** Chernobyl'. Kyyivs'ka Oblast', N Ukraine *51.16N 30.15E*
119 *R12* **Chornomors'ke** ***Rus.*** Chernomorskoye. Respublika Krym, S Ukraine *45.29N 32.45E*
119 *R4* **Chornukhy** Poltavs'ka Oblast', C Ukraine *50.15N 32.57E*
Chorokh/Chorokhi *see* Çoruh Nehri
112 *O9* **Choroszcz** Podlaskie, NE Poland *53.09N 22.59E*
118 *K6* **Chortkiv** ***Rus.*** Chortkov. Ternopil's'ka Oblast', W Ukraine *49.01N 25.45E*
Chortkov *see* Chortkiv
Chorum *see* Çorum
112 *M9* **Chorzele** Mazowieckie, C Poland *53.16N 20.53E*
113 *J16* **Chorzów** ***Ger.*** Königshütte; ***prev.*** Królewska Huta. Śląskie, S Poland *50.17N 18.57E*
169 *W12* **Ch'osan** N North Korea *40.45N 125.52E*
Chōsen-kaikyō *see* Korea Strait
171 *Kk17* **Chōshi** ***var.*** Tyôsi. Chiba, Honshū, S Japan *35.43N 140.48E*
65 *H14* **Chos Malal** Neuquén, W Argentina *37.22S 70.16W*
Chosŏn-minjujuŭi-inmin-kanghwaguk *see* North Korea
112 *E9* **Choszczno** ***Ger.*** Arnswalde. Zachodniopomorskie, NW Poland *53.10N 15.24E*
159 *O15* **Chota Nāgpur** *plateau* N India
35 *R8* **Choteau** Montana, NW USA *47.48N 112.40W*
Chotqol *see* Chatkal
12 *M8* **Chouart** ≈ Quebec, SE Canada
78 *I7* **Choûm** Adrar, C Mauritania *21.18N 12.58W*
29 *Q9* **Chouteau** Oklahoma, C USA *36.11N 95.20W*
23 *X8* **Chowan River** ≈ North Carolina, SE USA
37 *Q10* **Chowchilla** California, W USA *37.06N 120.15W*
169 *P7* **Choybalsan** Dornod, E Mongolia *48.02N 114.31E*
168 *M9* **Choyr** Dornogovĭ, C Mongolia *46.20N 108.21E*
193 *I19* **Christchurch** Canterbury, South Island, NZ *43.31S 172.39E*
99 *M24* **Christchurch** S England, UK *50.43N 1.45W*
193 *I18* **Christchurch** ✕ Canterbury, South Island, NZ *43.28S 172.33E*
46 *J12* **Christiana** C Jamaica *18.13N 77.28W*
85 *H22* **Christiana** Free State, C South Africa *27.55S 25.10E*
117 *J23* **Christiáni** *island* Kykládes, Greece, Aegean Sea
Christiania *see* Oslo
12 *G13* **Christian Island** *island* Ontario, S Canada
203 *P16* **Christian, Point** *headland* Pitcairn Island, Pitcairn Islands *25.04S 130.07E*
40 *M11* **Christian River** ≈ Alaska, USA
Christiansand *see* Kristiansand
23 *S7* **Christiansburg** Virginia, NE USA *37.07N 80.24W*
97 *G23* **Christiansfeld** Sønderjylland, SW Denmark *55.21N 9.30E*
Christianshåb *see* Qasigiannguit
41 *X14* **Christian Sound** *inlet* Alaska, USA
47 *T9* **Christiansted** Saint Croix, S Virgin Islands (US) *17.43N 64.42W*
Christiansund *see* Kristiansund
27 *R13* **Christine** Texas, SW USA *28.47N 98.30W*
181 *U7* **Christmas Island** ◇ *Australian external territory* E Indian Ocean
133 *T17* **Christmas Island** *island* E Indian Ocean
Christmas Island *see* Kiritimati
199 *K8* **Christmas Ridge** *undersea feature* C Pacific Ocean
32 *L16* **Christopher** Illinois, N USA *37.58N 89.03W*
27 *P9* **Christoval** Texas, SW USA *31.09N 100.30W*
113 *F17* **Chrudim** Pardubický Kraj, C Czech Republic *49.58N 15.49E*
117 *K25* **Chrýsi** *island* SE Greece
123 *Mm3* **Chrysochoú, Kólpos** ***var.*** Khrysokhou Bay. *bay* E Mediterranean Sea
116 *I13* **Chrysoúpoli** ***var.*** Hrisoupoli; ***prev.*** Khrisoúpolis. Anatolikí Makedonía kai Thráki, NE Greece *40.58N 24.42E*
113 *K16* **Chrzanów** ***var.*** Chrzanow, ***Ger.*** Zaumgarten. Śląskie, S Poland *50.09N 19.18E*
133 *Q7* **Chu** ***Kaz.*** Shū. ≈ Kazakhstan/Kyrgyzstan
44 *C5* **Chuacús, Sierra de** ▲▲ W Guatemala
159 *S15* **Chuadanga** Khulna, W Bangladesh *23.37N 88.52E*
Chuan *see* Sichuan
Ch'uan-chou *see* Quanzhou
41 *O11* **Chuathbaluk** Alaska, USA *61.36N 159.14W*
194 *I12* **Chuave** Chimbu, W PNG *6.06S 145.06E*
Chubek *see* Moskva
65 *I17* **Chubut** ***off.*** Provincia de Chubut. ◈ *province* S Argentina
65 *I17* **Chubut, Río** ≈ SE Argentina
45 *V15* **Chucanti, Cerro** ▲ E Panama *8.48N 78.27W*
Ch'u-chiang *see* Shaoguan
45 *W15* **Chucunaque, Río** ≈ E Panama
Chudin *see* Chudzin
118 *M5* **Chudniv** Zhytomyrs'ka Oblast', N Ukraine *50.02N 28.06E*
128 *H13* **Chudovo** Novgorodskaya Oblast', W Russian Federation *59.07N 31.42E*
Chudskoye Ozero *see* Peipus, Lake
121 *J18* **Chudzin** ***Rus.*** Chudin. Brestskaya Voblasts', SW Belarus *52.43N 26.56E*
41 *Q13* **Chugach Islands** *island group* Alaska, USA
41 *S11* **Chugach Mountains** ▲▲ Alaska, USA
170 *Ee12* **Chūgoku-sanchi** ▲▲ Honshū, SW Japan
Chuguyev *see* Chuhuyiv
119 *V5* **Chuhuyiv** ***var.*** Chuguyev. Kharkivs'ka Oblast', E Ukraine *49.51N 36.44E*
63 *H19* **Chuí** Rio Grande do Sul, S Brazil *33.40S 53.24W*
Chuí *see* Chuy
151 *S15* **Chu-Iliyskiye Gory** ***Kaz.*** Shū-Ile Taūlary. ▲▲ S Kazakhstan
Chukai *see* Cukai
Chukchi Avtonomnyy Okrug *see* Chukotskiy Avtonomnyy Okrug
Chukchi Peninsula *see* Chukotskiy Poluostrov
207 *R6* **Chukchi Plain** *undersea feature* Arctic Ocean
207 *R6* **Chukchi Plateau** *undersea feature* Arctic Ocean
207 *R4* **Chukchi Sea** ***Rus.*** Chukotskoye More. *sea* Arctic Ocean
129 *N14* **Chukhloma** Kostromskaya Oblast', NW Russian Federation *58.42N 42.39E*
Chukotka *see* Chukotskiy Avtonomnyy Okrug
Chukot Range *see* Anadyrskiy Khrebet
127 *Oo5* **Chukotskiy Avtonomnyy Okrug** ***var.*** Chukchi Avtonomnyy Okrug, Chukotka. ◈ *autonomous district* NE Russian Federation
127 *Q4* **Chukotskiy, Mys** *headland* NE Russian Federation *64.15N 173.03W*
127 *Pp4* **Chukotskiy Poluostrov** ***Eng.*** Chukchi Peninsula. *peninsula* NE Russian Federation
Chukotskoye More *see* Chukchi Sea
Chukurkak *see* Chuqurqoq
Chulakkurgan *see* Shollakorgan
37 *U17* **Chula Vista** California, W USA *32.38N 117.04W*
126 *Ll13* **Chul'man** Respublika Sakha (Yakutiya), NE Russian Federation *56.50N 124.47E*
58 *B9* **Chulucanas** Piura, NW Peru *5.07S 80.10W*
126 *Gg14* **Chulym** Novosibirskaya Oblast', C Russian Federation *55.03N 80.53E*
126 *H13* **Chulym** ≈ C Russian Federation
158 *K6* **Chumar** Jammu and Kashmir, N India *32.37N 78.36E*
116 *K9* **Chumerna** ▲ C Bulgaria *42.45N 25.58E*
127 *N13* **Chumikan** Khabarovskiy Kray, E Russian Federation *54.41N 135.12E*
178 *I9* **Chum Phae** Khon Kaen, C Thailand *16.31N 102.09E*
178 *Gg14* **Chumphon** ***var.*** Jumporn. Chumphon, SW Thailand *10.30N 99.10E*
178 *Hh10* **Chumsaeng** ***var.*** Chum Saeng. Nakhon Sawan, C Thailand *15.52N 100.20E*
126 *H14* **Chumysh** ≈ S Russian Federation
126 *Ii13* **Chuna** ≈ C Russian Federation
167 *R9* **Chun'an** ***var.*** Pailing. Zhejiang, SE China *29.37N 118.59E*
167 *S13* **Chunan** N Taiwan *24.44N 120.51E*
169 *Y14* **Ch'unch'ŏn** ***Jap.*** Shunsen. N South Korea *37.52N 127.48E*
159 *S16* **Chunchura** ***prev.*** Chinsura. West Bengal, NE India *22.54N 88.19E*
151 *W15* **Chundzha** Almaty, SE Kazakhstan *43.31N 79.28E*
Ch'ung-ch'ing/Ch'ung-ching *see* Chongqing
Chung-hua Jen-min Kung-ho-kuo *see* China
169 *Y15* **Ch'ungju** ***Jap.*** Chūshū. C South Korea *36.57N 127.49E*
Chungking *see* Chongqing
167 *T14* **Chungyang Shanmo** ***Chin.*** Taiwan Shan. ▲▲ C Taiwan
155 *V9* **Chūniān** Punjab, E Pakistan *30.57N 74.01E*
126 *Ii14* **Chunskiy** Irkutskaya Oblast', S Russian Federation *56.10N 99.15E*
126 *J11* **Chunya** ≈ C Russian Federation
128 *J6* **Chupa** Respublika Kareliya, NW Russian Federation *66.15N 33.02E*
129 *P8* **Chuprovo** Respublika Komi, NW Russian Federation *64.16N 46.27E*
59 *G17* **Chuquibamba** Arequipa, SW Peru *15.54S 72.37W*
64 *H4* **Chuquicamata** Antofagasta, N Chile *22.19S 68.55W*
59 *L21* **Chuquisaca** ◈ *department* S Bolivia
Chuquisaca *see* Sucre
152 *I8* **Chuqurqoq** ***Rus.*** Chukurkak. Qoraqalpog'iston Respublikasi, NW Uzbekistan *42.44N 61.33E*
131 *T2* **Chur** Udmurtskaya Respublika, NW Russian Federation *57.06N 52.57E*
110 *I9* **Chur** ***Fr.*** Coire, ***It.*** Coira, ***Rmsch.*** Cuera, Quera; ***anc.*** Curia Rhaetorum. Graubünden, E Switzerland *46.52N 9.31E*
126 *M11* **Churapcha** Respublika Sakha (Yakutiya), NE Russian Federation *61.59N 132.06E*
9 *V16* **Churchbridge** Saskatchewan, S Canada *50.55N 101.53W*
23 *O8* **Church Hill** Tennessee, S USA *36.31N 82.42W*
9 *X9* **Churchill** Manitoba, C Canada *58.46N 94.10W*
9 *X10* **Churchill** ≈ Manitoba/Saskatchewan, C Canada
11 *P9* **Churchill** ≈ Newfoundland and Labrador, E Canada
9 *Y9* **Churchill, Cape** *headland* Manitoba, C Canada *58.42N 93.12W*
11 *P9* **Churchill Falls** Newfoundland and Labrador, E Canada *53.38N 64.00W*
9 *S12* **Churchill Lake** ◎ Saskatchewan, C Canada
21 *Q3* **Churchill Lake** ▣ Maine, NE USA
204 *I5* **Churchill Peninsula** *peninsula* Antarctica
24 *H8* **Church Point** Louisiana, S USA *30.24N 92.13W*
31 *O3* **Churchs Ferry** North Dakota, N USA *48.15N 99.12W*
152 *G12* **Churchuri** Akhalskiy Velayat, C Turkmenistan *38.55N 59.13E*
23 *T5* **Churchville** Virginia, NE USA *38.13N 79.10W*
158 *G10* **Chūru** Rājasthān, NW India *28.18N 75.00E*
56 *J4* **Churuguara** Falcón, N Venezuela *10.48N 69.30W*
150 *J12* **Chushkakul, Gory** ▲▲ SW Kazakhstan
Chūshū *see* Ch'ungju
39 *O9* **Chuska Mountains** ▲▲ Arizona/New Mexico, SW USA
Chu, Sông *see* Sam, Nam
125 *Ee11* **Chusovaya** ≈ W Russian Federation
129 *V14* **Chusovoy** Permskaya Oblast', NW Russian Federation *58.17N 57.54E*
153 *R10* **Chust** Namangan Viloyati, E Uzbekistan *40.58N 71.12E*
Chust *see* Khust
13 *U6* **Chute-aux-Outardes** Quebec, SE Canada *49.07N 68.25W*
119 *U5* **Chutove** Poltavs'ka Oblast', C Ukraine *49.45N 35.11E*
201 *O15* **Chuuk** ***var.*** Truk. ◈ *state* C Micronesia
201 *P15* **Chuuk Islands** ***var.*** Hogoley Islands; ***prev.*** Truk Islands. *island group* Caroline Islands, C Micronesia
Chuvashia *see* Chavash Respubliki
Chuvashskaya Respublika *see* Chavash Respubliki
Chuwārtah *see* Chwārtā
Chu Xian/Chuxian *see* Chuzhou
166 *G13* **Chuxiong** Yunnan, SW China *25.01N 101.31E*
153 *V7* **Chuy** Chuyskaya Oblast', N Kyrgyzstan *42.45N 75.11E*
63 *H19* **Chuy** ***var.*** Chuí. Rocha, E Uruguay *33.42S 53.27W*
126 *K12* **Chuya** Respublika Sakha (Yakutiya), NE Russian Federation *59.30N 112.26E*
Chüy Oblasty *see* Chuyskaya Oblast'
153 *U8* **Chuyskaya Oblast'** ***Kir.*** Chüy Oblasty. ◈ *province* N Kyrgyzstan
167 *Q7* **Chuzhou** ***var.*** Chuxian, Chu Xian. Anhui, E China *32.21N 118.15E*
145 *U3* **Chwārtā** ***var.*** Choarta, Chuwārtah. NE Iraq *35.10N 45.58E*
121 *N16* **Chyhirynskaye Vodaskhovishcha** ▣ E Belarus
119 *R6* **Chyhyryn** ***Rus.*** Chigirin. Cherkas'ka Oblast', N Ukraine *49.03N 32.40E*
Chyrvonaya Slabada *see* Krasnaya Slabada
121 *L19* **Chyrvonaye, Vozyera** ***Rus.*** Ozero Chervonoye. ◎ SE Belarus
178 *K12* **Chư Sê** Gia Lai, C Vietnam *13.38N 108.06E*
119 *N11* **Ciadîr-Lunga** ***var.*** Ceadâr-Lunga, ***Rus.*** Chadyr-Lunga. S Moldova *46.03N 28.50E*
174 *K15* **Ciamis** ***prev.*** Tjiamis. Jawa, C Indonesia *7.19S 108.21E*
109 *I16* **Ciampino** ✕ Lazio, C Italy *41.48N 12.36W*
174 *J14* **Cianjur** ***prev.*** Tjiandjoer. Jawa, C Indonesia *6.49S 107.09E*
62 *H10* **Cianorte** Paraná, S Brazil *23.37S 52.38W*
Ciarraí *see* Kerry
114 *N13* **Ćićevac** Serbia, E Serbia and Montenegro (Yugoslavia) *43.44N 21.25E*
197 *K14* **Cicia** ***prev.*** Thithia. *island* Lau Group, E Fiji
107 *P4* **Cidacos** ≈ N Spain
142 *I10* **Cide** Kastamonu, N Turkey *41.52N 33.01E*
112 *L10* **Ciechanów** ***prev.*** Zichenau. Mazowieckie, C Poland *52.53N 20.36E*
112 *O10* **Ciechanowiec** ***Ger.*** Rudelstadt. Podlaskie, E Poland *52.43N 22.30E*
112 *J10* **Ciechocinek** Kujawskio-pomorskie, C Poland *52.52N 18.48E*
46 *F6* **Ciego de Ávila** Ciego de Ávila, C Cuba *21.50N 78.44W*
56 *F4* **Ciénaga** Magdalena, N Colombia *10.58N 74.15W*
56 *E6* **Ciénaga de Oro** Córdoba, NW Colombia *8.52N 75.37W*
46 *E5* **Cienfuegos** Cienfuegos, C Cuba *22.10N 80.27W*
106 *F4* **Cíes, Illas** *island group* NW Spain
113 *P16* **Cieszanów** Podkarpackie, SE Poland *50.15N 23.09E*
113 *J17* **Cieszyn** ***Cz.*** Těšín, ***Ger.*** Teschen. Śląskie, S Poland *49.45N 18.37E*
107 *R12* **Cieza** Murcia, SE Spain *38.13N 1.25W*
142 *F13* **Çifteler** Eskişehir, W Turkey *39.25N 31.00E*
107 *P7* **Cifuentes** Castilla-La Mancha, C Spain *40.46N 2.37W*
Čiganak *see* Chiganak
107 *P9* **Cigüela** ≈ C Spain
142 *H14* **Cihanbeyli** Konya, C Turkey *38.40N 32.55E*
142 *H14* **Cihanbeyli Yaylası** *plateau* C Turkey
106 *L10* **Cíjara, Embalse de** ▣ C Spain
174 *K15* **Cikalong** Jawa, S Indonesia *7.46S 108.13E*
174 *Ii14* **Cikawung** Jawa, S Indonesia *6.49S 105.29E*
197 *K12* **Cikobia** ***prev.*** Thikombia. *island* N Fiji
174 *K15* **Cilacap** ***prev.*** Tjilatjap. Jawa, C Indonesia *07.44S 109.00E*
181 *O16* **Cilaos** C Réunion *21.07S 55.28E*
143 *S11* **Çıldır** Ardahan, NE Turkey *41.07N 43.07E*
143 *S11* **Çıldır Gölü** ◎ NE Turkey
174 *K14* **Ciledug** ***prev.*** Tjiledoeg. Jawa, SW Indonesia *6.55S 108.43E*
166 *M10* **Cili** Hunan, S China *29.27N 111.03E*
124 *R12* **Cilicia Trough** *undersea feature* E Mediterranean Sea
Cill Airne *see* Killarney
Cill Chainnigh *see* Kilkenny
Cill Chaoi *see* Kilkee
Cill Choca *see* Kilcock
Cill Dara *see* Kildare
107 *N3* **Cilleruelo de Bezana** Castilla-León, N Spain *42.58N 3.50W*
Cilli *see* Celje
Cill Mhantáin *see* Wicklow
Cill Rois *see* Kilrush
28 *J6* **Cimarron** Kansas, C USA *37.49N 100.20W*
39 *T9* **Cimarron** New Mexico, SW USA *36.30N 104.55W*
28 *M9* **Cimarron River** ≈ Kansas/Oklahoma, C USA
119 *N11* **Cimişlia** ***Rus.*** Chimishliya. S Moldova *46.31N 28.45E*
Cîmpia Turzii *see* Câmpia Turzii
Cîmpina *see* Câmpina
Cîmpulung *see* Câmpulung
Cîmpulung Moldovenesc *see* Câmpulung Moldovenesc
143 *P15* **Çınar** Dıyarbakır, SE Turkey *37.45N 40.22E*
56 *J8* **Cinaruco, Río** ≈ Colombia/Venezuela
Cina Selatan, Laut *see* South China Sea
107 *T5* **Cinca** ≈ NE Spain
114 *G13* **Cincar** ▲ SW Bosnia and Herzegovina *43.55N 17.05E*
33 *Q15* **Cincinnati** Ohio, N USA *39.04N 84.33W*
23 *M4* **Cincinnati** ✕ Kentucky, S USA *39.03N 84.39W*
Cinco de Outubro *see* Xá-Muteba
142 *C15* **Çine** Aydın, SW Turkey *37.37N 28.03E*
101 *J21* **Ciney** Namur, SE Belgium *50.16N 5.06E*
106 *H6* **Cinfães** Viseu, N Portugal *41.04N 8.06W*
108 *J12* **Cingoli** Marche, C Italy *43.25N 13.09E*
43 *U16* **Cintalapa** ***var.*** Cintalapa de Figueroa. Chiapas, SE Mexico *16.42N 93.40W*
Cintalapa de Figueroa *see* Cintalapa
105 *X14* **Cinto, Monte** ▲ Corse, France, C Mediterranean Sea *42.22N 8.57E*
Cintra *see* Sintra
107 *Q5* **Cintruénigo** Navarra, N Spain *42.04N 1.49W*
Cionn tSáile *see* Kinsale
118 *K13* **Ciorani** Prahova, SE Romania *44.48N 26.25E*
115 *E14* **Čiovo** ***It.*** Bua. *island* S Croatia
174 *J14* **Cipanas** Jawa, S Indonesia
Cipiúr *see* Kippure
65 *I15* **Cipolletti** Río Negro, C Argentina *38.55S 68.00W*
123 *L8* **Circeo, Capo** *headland* C Italy *41.15N 13.03E*
41 *S8* **Circle** ***var.*** Circle City. Alaska, USA *65.51N 144.04W*
35 *X8* **Circle** Montana, NW USA *47.25N 105.32W*
Circle City *see* Circle
33 *S14* **Circleville** Ohio, N USA *39.36N 82.57W*
38 *K6* **Circleville** Utah, W USA *38.10N 112.16W*
174 *K14* **Cirebon** ***prev.*** Tjirebon. Jawa, S Indonesia *6.46S 108.33E*
99 *L21* **Cirencester** ***anc.*** Corinium, Corinium Dobunorum. C England, UK *51.43N 1.58W*
Cirkvenica *see* Crikvenica
109 *O20* **Ciro** Calabria, SW Italy *39.22N 17.02E*
109 *O20* **Ciro Marina** Calabria, S Italy *39.21N 17.07E*
104 *K14* **Ciron** ≈ SW France
Cirquenizza *see* Crikvenica
27 *R7* **Cisco** Texas, SW USA *32.23N 98.58W*
118 *I12* **Cisnădie** ***Ger.*** Heltau, ***Hung.*** Nagydisznód. Sibiu, SW Romania *45.42N 24.08E*
65 *G18* **Cisnes, Río** ≈ S Chile
27 *T11* **Cistern** Texas, SW USA *29.46N 97.12W*
106 *L3* **Cistierna** Castilla-León, N Spain *42.46N 5.07W*
174 *Ii14* **Citeureup** Jawa, S Indonesia *6.34S 105.41E*
Citharista *see* la Ciotat
Citlaltépetl *see* Orizaba, Volcán Pico de
57 *X10* **Citron** NW French Guiana *4.49N 53.56W*
25 *N7* **Citronelle** Alabama, S USA *31.05N 88.13W*
37 *O7* **Citrus Heights** California, W USA *38.42N 121.18W*
108 *H7* **Cittadella** Veneto, NE Italy *45.37N 11.46E*
108 *H13* **Città della Pieve** Umbria, C Italy *42.57N 12.01E*
108 *H12* **Città di Castello** Umbria, C Italy *43.27N 12.13E*
109 *I14* **Cittaducale** Lazio, C Italy *42.24N 12.55E*
109 *N22* **Cittanova** Calabria, SW Italy *38.21N 16.04E*
Cittavecchia *see* Starigrad
118 *G10* **Ciucea** ***Hung.*** Csucsa. Cluj, NW Romania *46.57N 22.51E*
118 *M13* **Ciucurova** Tulcea, SE Romania *44.57N 28.24E*
Ciudad Acuña *see* Villa Acuña
43 *N15* **Ciudad Altamirano** Guerrero, S Mexico *18.22N 100.39W*
44 *G7* **Ciudad Barrios** San Miguel, NE El Salvador *13.46N 88.13W*
56 *I7* **Ciudad Bolívar** Barinas, NW Venezuela *8.23N 70.34W*
57 *N7* **Ciudad Bolívar** ***prev.*** Angostura. Bolívar, E Venezuela *8.07N 63.31W*
42 *K6* **Ciudad Camargo** Chihuahua, N Mexico *27.42N 105.10W*
42 *E8* **Ciudad Constitución** Baja California Sur, W Mexico *25.06N 111.42W*
Ciudad Cortés *see* Cortés
43 *V17* **Ciudad Cuauhtémoc** Chiapas, SE Mexico *15.23N 91.11W*
44 *J9* **Ciudad Darío** ***var.*** Dario. Matagalpa, W Nicaragua *12.42N 86.06W*
Ciudad de Dolores Hidalgo *see* Dolores Hidalgo
44 *C6* **Ciudad de Guatemala** ***Eng.*** Guatemala City; ***prev.*** Santiago de los Caballeros. ● (Guatemala) Guatemala, C Guatemala *14.37N 90.29W*
Ciudad del Carmen *see* Carmen
64 *Q6* **Ciudad del Este** ***prev.*** Cuidad Presidente Stroessner, Presidente Stroessner, Puerto Presidente Stroessner. Alto Paraná, SE Paraguay *25.34S 54.40W*
64 *K5* **Ciudad de Libertador General San Martín** ***var.*** Libertador General San Martín. Jujuy, C Argentina *23.49S 64.45W*

◆ COUNTRY
● COUNTRY CAPITAL
◇ DEPENDENT TERRITORY
○ DEPENDENT TERRITORY CAPITAL
◈ ADMINISTRATIVE REGION
✕ INTERNATIONAL AIRPORT
▲ MOUNTAIN
▲▲ MOUNTAIN RANGE
VOLCANO
≈ RIVER
◎ LAKE
▣ RESERVOIR

Ciudad Delicias *see* Delicias
43 O11 **Ciudad del Maíz** San Luis Potosí, C Mexico *22.25N 99.36W*
Ciudad de México *see* México
56 J7 **Ciudad de Nutrias** Barinas, NW Venezuela *8.03N 69.17W*
Ciudad de Panamá *see* Panamá
57 P7 **Ciudad Guayana** *prev.* San Tomé de Guayana, Santo Tomé de Guayana. Bolívar, NE Venezuela *8.22N 62.37W*
42 K14 **Ciudad Guzmán** Jalisco, SW Mexico *19.40N 103.30W*
43 V17 **Ciudad Hidalgo** Chiapas, SE Mexico *14.45N 92.13W*
43 N14 **Ciudad Hidalgo** Michoacán de Ocampo, SW Mexico *19.40N 100.34W*
42 J3 **Ciudad Juárez** Chihuahua, N Mexico *31.39N 106.25W*
42 L8 **Ciudad Lerdo** Durango, C Mexico *25.34N 103.30W*
43 Q11 **Ciudad Madero** *var.* Villa Cecilia. Tamaulipas, C Mexico *22.18N 97.55W*
43 P11 **Ciudad Mante** Tamaulipas, C Mexico *22.43N 99.01W*
44 F2 **Ciudad Melchor de Mencos** *var.* Melchor de Mencos. Petén, NE Guatemala *17.03N 89.12W*
43 P8 **Ciudad Miguel Alemán** Tamaulipas, C Mexico *26.19N 98.55W*
Ciudad Mutis *see* Bahía Solano
42 G6 **Ciudad Obregón** Sonora, NW Mexico *27.32N 109.52W*
56 I5 **Ciudad Ojeda** Zulia, NW Venezuela *10.09N 71.15W*
57 P7 **Ciudad Piar** Bolívar, E Venezuela *7.25N 63.19W*
Ciudad Porfirio Díaz *see* Piedras Negras
Ciudad Quesada *see* Quesada
107 N11 **Ciudad Real** Castilla-La Mancha, C Spain *38.58N 3.55W*
107 N11 **Ciudad Real** ◆ *province* Castilla-La Mancha, C Spain
106 J7 **Ciudad-Rodrigo** Castilla-León, N Spain *40.36N 6.33W*
44 A6 **Ciudad Tecún Umán** San Marcos, SW Guatemala *14.40N 92.06W*
Ciudad Trujillo *see* Santo Domingo
43 P12 **Ciudad Valles** San Luis Potosí, C Mexico *21.58N 99.00W*
43 O10 **Ciudad Victoria** Tamaulipas, C Mexico *23.43N 99.07W*
44 C6 **Ciudad Vieja** Suchitepéquez, S Guatemala *14.30N 90.46W*
118 L8 **Ciuhuru** *var.* Reuţel. N Moldova
Ciutadella *see* Ciutadella de Menorca
107 Z8 **Ciutadella de Menorca** *var.* Ciutadella. Menorca, Spain, W Mediterranean Sea *40.00N 3.50E*
142 L11 **Civa Burnu** *headland* N Turkey *41.22N 36.39E*
108 J7 **Cividale del Friuli** Friuli-Venezia Giulia, NE Italy *46.06N 13.25E*
109 H14 **Civita Castellana** Lazio, C Italy *42.16N 12.24E*
108 J12 **Civitanova Marche** Marche, C Italy *43.18N 13.40E*
Civitas Altae Ripae *see* Brzeg
Civitas Carnutum *see* Chartres
Civitas Eburovicum *see* Évreux
Civitas Nemetum *see* Speyer
109 G15 **Civitavecchia** *anc.* Centum Cellae, Trajani Portus. Lazio, C Italy *42.04N 11.46E*
104 L10 **Civray** Vienne, W France *46.10N 0.18E*
142 E14 **Çivril** Denizli, W Turkey *38.18N 29.43E*
167 O5 **Cixian** Hebei, E China *36.19N 114.22E*
143 R16 **Cizre** Şırnak, SE Turkey *37.21N 42.10E*
Clacton *see* Clacton-on-Sea
99 Q21 **Clacton-on-Sea** *var.* Clacton. E England, UK *51.48N 1.09E*
24 H5 **Claiborne, Lake** Louisiana, S USA
104 L10 **Clain** W France
99 Q11 **Claire, Lake** Alberta, C Canada
27 O6 **Clairemont** Texas, SW USA *33.09N 100.45W*
36 M3 **Clair Engle Lake** California, W USA
20 B15 **Clairton** Pennsylvania, NE USA *40.17N 79.52W*
34 F7 **Clallam Bay** Washington, NW USA *48.13N 124.16W*
105 P8 **Clamecy** Nièvre, C France *47.28N 3.30E*
25 P5 **Clanton** Alabama, S USA *32.50N 86.37W*
63 D17 **Clara** Entre Ríos, E Argentina *31.49S 58.48W*
99 E18 **Clara** *Ir.* Clóirtheach. C Ireland *53.19N 7.36W*
31 T9 **Clara City** Minnesota, N USA *44.57N 95.22W*
63 D23 **Claraz** Buenos Aires, E Argentina *37.55S 59.18W*
Clár Chlainne Mhuiris *see* Claremorris
190 I8 **Clare** South Australia *33.49S 138.35E*
99 C19 **Clare** *Ir.* An Clár. *cultural region* W Ireland
99 C18 **Clare** W Ireland
99 A16 **Clare Island** *Ir.* Cliara. *island* W Ireland
46 J12 **Claremont** C Jamaica *18.22N 77.10W*
31 W10 **Claremont** Minnesota, N USA *44.01N 93.00W*
21 N9 **Claremont** New Hampshire, NE USA *43.21N 72.18W*
29 Q9 **Claremore** Oklahoma, C USA *36.18N 95.37W*
99 C17 **Claremorris** *Ir.* Clár Chlainne Mhuiris. W Ireland *53.47N 9.00W*
193 J16 **Clarence** Canterbury, South Island, NZ *42.07S 173.54E*
193 J16 **Clarence** South Island, NZ
67 F15 **Clarence Bay** *bay* Ascension Island, C Atlantic Ocean
65 H25 **Clarence, Isla** *island* S Chile
204 H2 **Clarence Island** *island* South Shetland Islands, Antarctica
191 V5 **Clarence River** New South Wales, SE Australia
46 J5 **Clarence Town** Long Island, C Bahamas *23.03N 74.57W*
29 W12 **Clarendon** Arkansas, C USA *34.41N 91.18W*
27 O3 **Clarendon** Texas, SW USA *34.56N 100.53W*
11 U12 **Clarenville** Newfoundland and Labrador, SE Canada *48.12N 54.01W*
9 Q17 **Claresholm** Alberta, SW Canada *50.01N 113.33W*
31 T16 **Clarinda** Iowa, C USA *40.44N 95.02W*
57 N5 **Clarines** Anzoátegui, NE Venezuela *9.55N 65.10W*
31 V12 **Clarion** Iowa, C USA *42.43N 93.43W*
20 C13 **Clarion** Pennsylvania, NE USA *41.11N 79.21W*
199 L7 **Clarion Fracture Zone** *tectonic feature* NE Pacific Ocean
20 D13 **Clarion River** Pennsylvania, NE USA
31 Q9 **Clark** South Dakota, N USA *44.50N 97.44W*
38 K11 **Clarkdale** Arizona, SW USA *34.46N 112.03W*
13 W4 **Clarke City** Quebec, SE Canada *50.09N 66.36W*
191 Q15 **Clarke Island** *island* Furneaux Group, Tasmania, SE Australia
189 X6 **Clarke Range** Queensland, E Australia
25 T2 **Clarkesville** Georgia, SE USA *34.36N 83.31W*
31 S9 **Clarkfield** Minnesota, N USA *44.48N 95.49W*
35 N7 **Clark Fork** Idaho, NW USA *48.06N 116.10W*
35 N8 **Clark Fork** Idaho/Montana, NW USA
41 Q12 **Clark, Lake** Alaska, USA
37 W12 **Clark Mountain** ▲ California, W USA *35.30N 115.34W*
39 S3 **Clark Peak** ▲ Colorado, C USA *40.36N 105.57W*
12 D14 **Clark, Point** *headland* Ontario, S Canada *44.04N 81.45W*
23 S3 **Clarksburg** West Virginia, NE USA *39.16N 80.19W*
24 K2 **Clarksdale** Mississippi, S USA *34.12N 90.34W*
35 U12 **Clarks Fork Yellowstone River** Montana/Wyoming, NW USA
23 P13 **Clark Hill Lake** *var.* J.Storm Thurmond Reservoir. Georgia/South Carolina, SE USA
31 R14 **Clarkson** Nebraska, C USA *41.42N 97.07W*
41 O13 **Clarks Point** Alaska, USA *58.50N 158.33W*
20 I13 **Clarks Summit** Pennsylvania, NE USA *41.29N 75.42W*
34 M10 **Clarkston** Washington, NW USA *46.25N 117.02W*
46 J12 **Clark's Town** C Jamaica *18.25N 77.32W*
29 T10 **Clarksville** Arkansas, C USA *35.28N 93.28W*
33 P13 **Clarksville** Indiana, N USA *40.01N 85.54W*
22 I8 **Clarksville** Tennessee, S USA *36.31N 87.21W*
27 W5 **Clarksville** Texas, SW USA *33.36N 95.03W*
23 U8 **Clarksville** Virginia, NE USA *36.36N 78.36W*
23 U11 **Clarkton** North Carolina, SE USA *34.28N 78.39W*
63 C24 **Claromecó** *var.* Balneario Claromecó. Buenos Aires, E Argentina *38.51S 60.01W*
27 N3 **Claude** Texas, SW USA *35.06N 101.21W*
Clausentum *see* Southampton
179 P7 **Claveria** Luzon, N Philippines *18.36N 121.04E*
101 J20 **Clavier** Liège, E Belgium *50.27N 5.21E*
25 W6 **Claxton** Georgia, SE USA *32.09N 81.54W*
23 R4 **Clay** West Virginia, NE USA *38.28N 81.04W*
29 N3 **Clay Center** Kansas, C USA *39.22N 97.08W*
31 P16 **Clay Center** Nebraska, C USA *40.31N 98.03W*
23 Y2 **Claymont** Delaware, NE USA *39.48N 75.27W*
38 M14 **Claypool** Arizona, SW USA *33.24N 110.50W*
25 R6 **Clayton** Alabama, S USA *31.52N 85.27W*
25 T1 **Clayton** Georgia, SE USA *34.52N 83.24W*
24 J5 **Clayton** Louisiana, S USA *31.43N 91.32W*
29 X5 **Clayton** Missouri, C USA *38.39N 90.21W*
39 V9 **Clayton** New Mexico, SW USA *36.27N 103.12W*
23 V9 **Clayton** North Carolina, SE USA *35.39N 78.27W*
29 Q12 **Clayton** Oklahoma, C USA *34.35N 95.21W*
190 I4 **Clayton River** *seasonal river* South Australia
23 R7 **Claytor Lake** Virginia, NE USA
29 P13 **Clear Boggy Creek** Oklahoma, C USA
99 B22 **Clear, Cape** *var.* The Bill of Cape Clear, *Ir.* Ceann Cléire. *headland* SW Ireland *51.25N 9.31W*
38 M12 **Clear Creek** Arizona, SW USA
41 S12 **Cleare, Cape** *headland* Montague Island, Alaska, USA *59.46N 147.54W*
20 E13 **Clearfield** Pennsylvania, NE USA *41.01N 78.27W*
38 L2 **Clearfield** Utah, W USA *41.06N 112.03W*
27 Q6 **Clear Fork Brazos River** Texas, SW USA
33 T12 **Clear Fork Reservoir** Ohio, N USA
9 N12 **Clear Hills** Alberta, SW Canada
31 V12 **Clear Lake** Iowa, C USA *43.07N 93.27W*
31 R9 **Clear Lake** South Dakota, N USA *44.45N 96.40W*
36 M6 **Clear Lake** California, W USA
24 G6 **Clear Lake** Louisiana, S USA
36 M6 **Clearlake** California, W USA *38.57N 122.38W*
37 P1 **Clear Lake Reservoir** California, W USA
9 N16 **Clearwater** British Columbia, SW Canada *51.37N 120.01W*
25 U12 **Clearwater** Florida, SE USA *27.58N 82.46W*
9 R12 **Clearwater** Alberta/Saskatchewan, C Canada
29 W7 **Clearwater Lake** Missouri, C USA
35 N10 **Clearwater Mountains** Idaho, NW USA
35 N10 **Clearwater River** Idaho, NW USA
31 S4 **Clearwater River** Minnesota, N USA
27 T7 **Cleburne** Texas, SW USA *32.21N 97.23W*
34 I9 **Cle Elum** Washington, NW USA *47.12N 120.56W*
99 O17 **Cleethorpes** E England, UK *53.34N 0.01W*
Cléire, Ceann *see* Clear, Cape
23 O11 **Clemson** South Carolina, SE USA *34.40N 82.50W*
23 Q4 **Clendenin** West Virginia, NE USA *38.29N 81.21W*
28 M9 **Cleo Springs** Oklahoma, C USA *36.25N 98.25W*
Clerk Island *see* Onotoa
189 X8 **Clermont** Queensland, E Australia *22.46S 147.40E*
13 S8 **Clermont** Quebec, SE Canada *47.41N 70.15W*
105 O4 **Clermont** Oise, N France *49.22N 2.25E*
31 X12 **Clermont** Iowa, C USA *43.00N 91.39W*
105 P11 **Clermont-Ferrand** Puy-de-Dôme, C France *45.46N 3.04E*
105 Q15 **Clermont-l'Hérault** Hérault, S France *43.37N 3.25E*
101 M22 **Clervaux** Diekirch, N Luxembourg *50.03N 6.01E*
108 G6 **Cles** Trentino-Alto Adige, N Italy *46.22N 11.04E*
190 H8 **Cleve** South Australia *33.43S 136.30E*
Cleve *see* Kleve
25 T2 **Cleveland** Georgia, SE USA *34.36N 83.45W*
24 K3 **Cleveland** Mississippi, S USA *33.45N 90.43W*
33 T11 **Cleveland** Ohio, N USA *41.30N 81.42W*
29 O9 **Cleveland** Oklahoma, C USA *36.18N 96.27W*
22 L10 **Cleveland** Tennessee, S USA *35.09N 84.52W*
27 W10 **Cleveland** Texas, SW USA *30.19N 95.06W*
33 N7 **Cleveland** Wisconsin, N USA *43.58N 87.45W*
33 O4 **Cleveland Cliffs Basin** Michigan, N USA
33 U11 **Cleveland Heights** Ohio, N USA *41.31N 81.33W*
35 P6 **Cleveland, Mount** ▲ Montana, NW USA *48.55N 113.51W*
Cleves *see* Kleve
99 B16 **Clew Bay** *Ir.* Cuan Mó. *inlet* W Ireland
25 Y14 **Clewiston** Florida, SE USA *26.45N 80.55W*
Cliara *see* Clare Island
99 A17 **Clifden** *Ir.* An Clochán. W Ireland *53.28N 10.13W*
39 O14 **Clifton** Arizona, SW USA *33.03N 109.18W*
20 K14 **Clifton** New Jersey, NE USA *40.50N 74.28W*
27 S8 **Clifton** Texas, SW USA *31.43N 97.36W*
23 S6 **Clifton Forge** Virginia, NE USA *37.49N 79.49W*
190 I1 **Clifton Hills** South Australia *27.03S 138.49E*
9 S17 **Climax** Saskatchewan, S Canada *49.12N 108.22W*
23 O8 **Clinch River** Tennessee/Virginia, S USA
27 P12 **Cline** Texas, SW USA *29.14N 100.07W*
23 N10 **Clingmans Dome** ▲ North Carolina/Tennessee, SE USA *35.33N 83.30W*
26 H8 **Clint** Texas, SW USA *31.35N 106.13W*
8 M16 **Clinton** British Columbia, SW Canada *51.06N 121.31W*
12 E15 **Clinton** Ontario, S Canada *43.37N 81.31W*
29 U10 **Clinton** Arkansas, C USA *35.36N 92.26W*
32 L10 **Clinton** Illinois, N USA *40.09N 88.57W*
31 Z14 **Clinton** Iowa, C USA *41.50N 90.11W*
22 G7 **Clinton** Kentucky, S USA *36.39N 89.00W*
24 J8 **Clinton** Louisiana, S USA *30.52N 91.01W*
21 N11 **Clinton** Massachusetts, NE USA *42.25N 71.40W*
33 R10 **Clinton** Michigan, N USA *42.04N 83.58W*
24 K5 **Clinton** Mississippi, S USA *32.22N 90.22W*
29 S5 **Clinton** Missouri, C USA *38.22N 93.51W*
23 V10 **Clinton** North Carolina, SE USA *35.00N 78.19W*
28 L10 **Clinton** Oklahoma, C USA *35.31N 98.58W*
23 Q12 **Clinton** South Carolina, SE USA *34.28N 81.52W*
23 M9 **Clinton** Tennessee, S USA *36.06N 84.07W*
15 J7 **Clinton-Colden Lake** Northwest Territories, NW Canada
8 H5 **Clinton Creek** Yukon Territory, NW Canada *64.24N 140.35W*
32 L13 **Clinton Lake** Illinois, N USA
29 Q4 **Clinton Lake** Kansas, N USA
23 T11 **Clio** South Carolina, SE USA *34.34N 79.33W*
199 L17 **Clipperton Fracture Zone** *tectonic feature* E Pacific Ocean
200 N7 **Clipperton Island** ◇ *French dependency of French Polynesia* E Pacific Ocean
48 K6 **Clipperton Island** *island* E Pacific Ocean
(0) F16 **Clipperton Seamounts** *undersea feature* E Pacific Ocean
104 J8 **Clisson** Loire-Atlantique, NW France *47.06N 1.19W*
64 K7 **Clodomira** Santiago del Estero, N Argentina *27.33S 64.07W*
Cloich na Coillte *see* Clonakilty
Clóirtheach *see* Clara
99 C21 **Clonakilty** *Ir.* Cloich na Coillte. SW Ireland *51.37N 8.54W*
189 T6 **Cloncurry** Queensland, C Australia *20.44S 140.30E*
99 F18 **Clondalkin** *Ir.* Cluain Dolcáin. E Ireland *53.19N 6.24W*
99 E16 **Clones** *Ir.* Cluain Eois. N Ireland *54.10N 7.13W*
99 D20 **Clonmel** *Ir.* Cluain Meala. S Ireland *52.21N 7.42W*
102 G11 **Cloppenburg** Niedersachsen, NW Germany *52.51N 8.03E*
31 W6 **Cloquet** Minnesota, N USA *46.43N 92.27W*
39 S14 **Cloudcroft** New Mexico, SW USA *32.57N 105.44W*
35 W12 **Cloud Peak** ▲ Wyoming, C USA *44.22N 107.10W*
193 K14 **Cloudy Bay** *inlet* South Island, NZ
23 R10 **Clover** South Carolina, SE USA *35.06N 81.13W*
36 M6 **Cloverdale** California, W USA *38.49N 123.03W*
22 J5 **Cloverport** Kentucky, S USA *37.50N 86.37W*
37 Q10 **Clovis** California, W USA *36.48N 119.43W*
39 W12 **Clovis** New Mexico, SW USA *34.22N 103.12W*
12 K13 **Cloyne** Ontario, SE Canada *44.48N 77.09W*
Cluain Dolcáin *see* Clondalkin
Cluain Eois *see* Clones
Cluainín *see* Manorhamilton
Cluain Meala *see* Clonmel
118 H10 **Cluj** ◆ *county* NW Romania
Cluj *see* Cluj-Napoca
118 H10 **Cluj-Napoca** *Ger.* Klausenburg, *Hung.* Kolozsvár; *prev.* Cluj. Cluj, NW Romania *46.47N 23.36E*
Clunia *see* Feldkirch
105 R10 **Cluny** Saône-et-Loire, C France *46.25N 4.38E*
105 T10 **Cluses** Haute-Savoie, E France *46.04N 6.34E*
108 E7 **Clusone** Lombardia, N Italy *45.56N 10.00E*
27 W12 **Clute** Texas, SW USA *29.01N 95.24W*
193 D23 **Clutha** South Island, NZ
99 J18 **Clwyd** *cultural region* NE Wales, UK
193 D22 **Clyde** Otago, South Island, NZ *45.12S 169.21E*
29 N3 **Clyde** Kansas, C USA *39.35N 97.24W*
31 P2 **Clyde** North Dakota, N USA *48.44N 98.51W*
33 S11 **Clyde** Ohio, N USA *41.18N 82.58W*
27 Q7 **Clyde** Texas, SW USA *32.24N 99.29W*
12 K13 **Clyde** Ontario, SE Canada
98 J13 **Clyde** W Scotland, UK
98 H12 **Clydebank** S Scotland, UK *55.54N 4.24W*
98 H13 **Clyde, Firth of** *inlet* S Scotland, UK
35 S11 **Clyde Park** Montana, NW USA *45.56N 110.39W*
106 I7 **Côa, Rio** N Portugal
37 W16 **Coachella** California, W USA *33.38N 116.10W*
37 W16 **Coachella Canal** *canal* California, W USA
42 I9 **Coacoyole** Durango, C Mexico *24.30N 106.33W*
27 N7 **Coahoma** Texas, SW USA *32.18N 101.18W*
8 K8 **Coal** Yukon Territory, NW Canada
42 L14 **Coalcomán** *var.* Coalcomán de Matamoros. Michoacán de Ocampo, S Mexico *18.49N 103.13W*
Coalcomán de Matamoros *see* Coalcomán
41 T8 **Coal Creek** Alaska, USA *65.21N 143.08W*
9 Q17 **Coaldale** Alberta, SW Canada *49.42N 112.36W*
29 P12 **Coalgate** Oklahoma, C USA *34.33N 96.14W*
37 P11 **Coalinga** California, W USA *36.08N 120.21W*
8 L9 **Coal River** British Columbia, W Canada *59.38N 126.45W*
23 Q6 **Coal River** West Virginia, NE USA
38 M2 **Coalville** Utah, W USA *40.56N 111.22W*
60 E13 **Coari** Amazonas, N Brazil *4.07S 63.07W*
61 D14 **Coari, Rio** NW Brazil
83 J20 **Coast** ◆ *province* SE Kenya
Coast *see* Pwani
14 F11 **Coast Mountains** *Fr.* Chaîne Côtière. Canada/USA
17 Ff3 **Coast Ranges** W USA
98 I12 **Coatbridge** S Scotland, UK *55.52N 4.01W*
44 B6 **Coatepeque** Quezaltenango, SW Guatemala *14.42N 91.49W*
20 H16 **Coatesville** Pennsylvania, NE USA *39.58N 75.47W*
13 Q13 **Coaticook** Quebec, SE Canada *45.07N 71.46W*
15 Mm6 **Coats Island** *island* Nunavut, NE Canada
205 O4 **Coats Land** *physical region* Antarctica
43 T14 **Coatzacoalcos** *var.* Quetzalcoalco; *prev.* Puerto México. Veracruz-Llave, E Mexico *18.06N 94.25W*
43 S14 **Coatzacoalcos, Río** SE Mexico
118 M15 **Cobadin** Constanţa, SW Romania *44.02N 28.29E*
12 H9 **Cobalt** Ontario, S Canada *47.23N 79.40W*
44 D5 **Cobán** Alta Verapaz, C Guatemala *15.28N 90.19W*
191 O6 **Cobar** New South Wales, SE Australia *31.31S 145.50E*
20 F12 **Cobb Hill** ▲ Pennsylvania, NE USA *41.52N 77.52W*
(0) D8 **Cobb Seamount** *undersea feature* E Pacific Ocean *47.00N 131.00W*
12 K12 **Cobden** Ontario, SE Canada *45.36N 76.54W*
99 D21 **Cobh** *Ir.* An Cóbh; *prev.* Cove of Cork, Queenstown. SW Ireland *51.51N 8.16W*
59 J14 **Cobija** Pando, NW Bolivia *11.04S 68.49W*
Coblence/Coblenz *see* Koblenz
20 J10 **Cobleskill** New York, NE USA *42.40N 74.29W*
12 I15 **Cobourg** Ontario, SE Canada *43.57N 78.06W*
189 P1 **Cobourg Peninsula** *headland* Northern Territory, N Australia *11.27S 132.33E*
191 O10 **Cobram** Victoria, SE Australia *35.56S 145.36E*
84 N13 **Cóbuè** Niassa, N Mozambique *12.08S 34.46E*
103 K18 **Coburg** Bayern, SE Germany *50.16N 10.58E*
21 Q5 **Coburn Mountain** ▲ Maine, NE USA *45.28N 70.07W*
Coca *see* Puerto Francisco de Orellana
59 H18 **Cocachacra** Arequipa, SW Peru *17.09S 71.46W*
61 J17 **Cocalinho** Mato Grosso, W Brazil *14.22S 51.00W*
Cocanada *see* Kākināda
107 S11 **Cocentaina** País Valenciano, E Spain *38.44N 0.27W*
59 L18 **Cochabamba** *hist.* Oropeza. Cochabamba, C Bolivia *17.23S 66.10W*
59 K18 **Cochabamba** ◆ *department* C Bolivia
59 L18 **Cochabamba, Cordillera de** C Bolivia
103 E18 **Cochem** Rheinland-Pfalz, W Germany *50.09N 7.09E*
39 R6 **Cochetopa Hills** Colorado, C USA
161 G22 **Cochin** *var.* Kochi. Kerala, SW India *9.56N 76.15E*
46 D5 **Cochinos, Bahía de** *Eng.* Bay of Pigs. *bay* SE Cuba
39 O16 **Cochise Head** ▲ Arizona, SW USA *32.03N 109.19W*
25 U5 **Cochran** Georgia, SE USA *32.23N 83.21W*
9 P16 **Cochrane** Alberta, SW Canada *51.15N 114.25W*
10 G12 **Cochrane** Ontario, S Canada *49.04N 81.01W*
65 G20 **Cochrane** Aisén, S Chile *47.16S 72.33W*
9 U10 **Cochrane** Manitoba/Saskatchewan, C Canada
Cochrane, Lago *see* Pueyrredón, Lago
Cocibolca *see* Nicaragua, Lago de
Cockade State *see* Maryland
46 M6 **Cockburn Harbour** South Caicos, S Turks and Caicos Islands *21.28N 71.30W*
12 C11 **Cockburn Island** *island* Ontario, S Canada
46 J3 **Cockburn Town** San Salvador, E Bahamas *24.01N 74.30W*
23 X2 **Cockeysville** Maryland, NE USA *39.29N 76.34W*
189 N12 **Cocklebiddy** Western Australia *32.02S 125.54E*
46 I12 **Cockpit Country, The** *physical region* W Jamaica
45 S16 **Coclé** *off.* Provincia de Coclé. ◆ *province* C Panama
45 S15 **Coclé del Norte** Colón, C Panama *9.04N 80.32W*
25 Y12 **Cocoa** Florida, SE USA *28.23N 80.44W*
25 Y12 **Cocoa Beach** Florida, SE USA *28.19N 80.36W*
81 D17 **Cocobeach** Estuaire, NW Gabon *0.58N 9.34E*
46 G5 **Coco, Cayo** *island* C Cuba
157 Q19 **Coco Channel** *strait* Andaman Sea/Bay of Bengal
181 N6 **Coco-de-Mer Seamounts** *undersea feature* W Indian Ocean
38 K10 **Coconino Plateau** *plain* Arizona, SW USA
45 N6 **Coco, Río** *var.* Río Wanki, Segoviao Wangkí. Honduras/Nicaragua
181 T8 **Cocos (Keeling) Islands** ◇ *Australian external territory* E Indian Ocean
181 T7 **Cocos Basin** *undersea feature* E Indian Ocean
196 B17 **Cocos Island** *island* S Guam
Cocos Island Ridge *see* Cocos Ridge
133 S17 **Cocos Islands** *island group* E Indian Ocean
(0) G15 **Cocos Plate** *tectonic feature*
200 Oo8 **Cocos Ridge** *var.* Cocos Island Ridge. *undersea feature* E Pacific Ocean
42 K13 **Cocula** Jalisco, SW Mexico *20.25N 103.52W*
109 D17 **Coda Cavallo, Capo** *headland* Sardegna, Italy, C Mediterranean Sea *40.49N 9.43E*
60 E13 **Codajás** Amazonas, N Brazil *3.49S 62.12W*
Codazzi *see* Agustín Codazzi
21 Q12 **Cod, Cape** *headland* Massachusetts, NE USA *41.50N 69.56W*
193 B25 **Codfish Island** *island* SW NZ
108 H9 **Codigoro** Emilia-Romagna, N Italy *44.49N 12.07E*
11 P5 **Cod Island** *island* Newfoundland and Labrador, E Canada
118 J12 **Codlea** *Ger.* Zeiden, *Hung.* Feketehalom. Braşov, C Romania *45.42N 25.27E*
60 M13 **Codó** Maranhão, E Brazil *4.28S 43.51W*
108 E8 **Codogno** Lombardia, N Italy *45.10N 9.42E*
118 M10 **Codrii** *hill range* C Moldova
47 W9 **Codrington** Barbuda, Antigua and Barbuda *17.37N 61.49W*
108 J7 **Codroipo** Friuli-Venezia Giulia, NE Italy *45.58N 13.00E*
30 M12 **Cody** Nebraska, C USA *42.54N 101.13W*
35 U12 **Cody** Wyoming, C USA *43.31N 109.04W*
23 P7 **Coeburn** Virginia, NE USA *36.56N 82.27W*
56 E10 **Coello** Tolima, W Colombia *4.16N 74.54W*
Coemba *see* Cuemba
189 V2 **Coen** Queensland, NE Australia *14.03S 143.16E*
103 E14 **Coesfeld** Nordrhein-Westfalen, W Germany *51.55N 7.10E*
34 M8 **Coeur d'Alene** Idaho, NW USA *47.40N 116.46W*
34 M8 **Coeur d'Alene Lake** Idaho, NW USA
100 O8 **Coevorden** Drenthe, NE Netherlands *52.39N 6.45E*
8 H6 **Coffee Creek** Yukon Territory, W Canada *62.52N 139.05W*
32 L15 **Coffeen Lake** Illinois, N USA
24 L3 **Coffeeville** Mississippi, S USA *33.58N 89.40W*
29 Q8 **Coffeyville** Kansas, C USA *37.02N 95.37W*
190 G9 **Coffin Bay** South Australia *34.39S 135.30E*
190 F9 **Coffin Bay Peninsula** *peninsula* South Australia
191 V5 **Coffs Harbour** New South Wales, SE Australia *30.18S 153.07E*
107 R10 **Cofrentes** País Valenciano, E Spain *39.13N 1.04W*
Cogilnic *see* Kohyl'nyk
104 K11 **Cognac** *anc.* Compniacum. Charente, W France *45.42N 0.19W*
108 B7 **Cogne** Valle d'Aosta, NW Italy *45.37N 7.27E*
105 U16 **Cogolin** Var, SE France *43.15N 6.30E*
107 O7 **Cogolludo** Castilla-La Mancha, C Spain *40.58N 3.05W*
Cohalm *see* Rupea
94 L8 **Čohkarášša** *var.* Cuokkarašša. ▲ N Norway *69.57N 24.38E*
F11 **Cohocton River** New York, NE USA
20 L10 **Cohoes** New York, NE USA *42.46N 73.42W*
191 N10 **Cohuna** Victoria, SE Australia *35.51S 144.15E*
45 P17 **Coiba, Isla de** *island* SW Panama
65 H23 **Coig, Río** S Argentina
65 G19 **Coihaique** *var.* Coyhaique. Aisén, S Chile *45.31S 72.00W*
161 G21 **Coimbatore** Tamil Nādu, S India *11.00N 76.57E*
106 G8 **Coimbra** *anc.* Conimbria, Conimbriga. Coimbra, W Portugal *40.12N 8.25W*
106 G8 **Coimbra** ◆ *district* N Portugal
106 L15 **Coín** Andalucía, S Spain *36.40N 4.45W*
59 J20 **Coipasa, Laguna** W Bolivia
59 J20 **Coipasa, Salar de** *salt lake* W Bolivia
Coira/Coire *see* Chur
Coirib, Loch *see* Corrib, Lough
56 K6 **Cojedes** *off.* Estado Cojedes. ◆ *state* N Venezuela
44 F7 **Cojutepeque** Cuscatlán, C El Salvador *13.44N 88.55W*
35 S16 **Cokeville** Wyoming, C USA *42.03N 110.55W*
190 M13 **Colac** Victoria, SE Australia *38.22S 143.37E*
61 O20 **Colatina** Espírito Santo, SE Brazil *19.34S 40.37W*
29 O13 **Colbert** Oklahoma, C USA *33.51N 96.30W*
102 L12 **Colbitz-Letzinger Heide** *heathland* N Germany
28 I3 **Colby** Kansas, C USA *39.24N 101.03W*
59 H17 **Colca, Río** SW Peru
99 P21 **Colchester** *hist.* Colneceaste, *anc.* Camulodunum. E England, UK *51.54N 0.54E*
21 N13 **Colchester** Connecticut, NE USA *41.34N 72.17W*
40 M16 **Cold Bay** Alaska, USA *55.11N 162.43W*
9 R14 **Cold Lake** Alberta, SW Canada *54.25N 110.16W*
9 R13 **Cold Lake** Alberta/Saskatchewan, S Canada
31 U8 **Cold Spring** Minnesota, N USA *45.27N 94.25W*
27 W10 **Coldspring** Texas, SW USA *30.35N 95.07W*
9 N17 **Coldstream** British Columbia, SW Canada *50.13N 119.09W*
98 L13 **Coldstream** SE Scotland, UK *55.39N 2.19W*
12 H13 **Coldwater** Ontario, S Canada *44.43N 79.36W*
28 K7 **Coldwater** Kansas, C USA *37.13N 99.18W*
33 Q10 **Coldwater** Michigan, N USA *41.56N 85.00W*
27 N1 **Coldwater Creek** Oklahoma/Texas, SW USA
24 K2 **Coldwater River** Mississippi, S USA
191 O9 **Coleambally** New South Wales, SE Australia *34.48S 145.54E*
21 O6 **Colebrook** New Hampshire, NE USA *44.52N 71.27W*
29 T5 **Cole Camp** Missouri, C USA *38.27N 93.12W*
41 T6 **Coleen River** Alaska, USA
9 P17 **Coleman** Alberta, SW Canada *49.36N 114.26W*
27 Q8 **Coleman** Texas, SW USA *31.49N 99.25W*
Çölemerik *see* Hakkâri
85 K22 **Colenso** KwaZulu/Natal, E South Africa *28.39S 29.49E*
190 L12 **Coleraine** Victoria, SE Australia *37.39S 141.42E*
99 F14 **Coleraine** *Ir.* Cúil Raithin. N Northern Ireland, UK *55.07N 6.40W*
193 G18 **Coleridge, Lake** South Island, NZ
85 H24 **Colesberg** Northern Cape, C South Africa *30.41S 25.08E*
24 H7 **Colfax** Louisiana, S USA *31.31N 92.42W*
34 L9 **Colfax** Washington, NW USA *46.52N 117.21W*
32 J6 **Colfax** Wisconsin, N USA *45.00N 91.44W*
65 I19 **Colhué Huapí, Lago** S Argentina
47 Z6 **Colibris, Pointe des** *headland* Grande Terre, E Guadeloupe *16.15N 61.10W*
108 D6 **Colico** Lombardia, N Italy *46.08N 9.24E*
101 E14 **Colijnsplaat** Zeeland, SW Netherlands *51.36N 3.47E*
42 L14 **Colima** Colima, S Mexico *19.12N 103.45W*
42 K14 **Colima** ◆ *state* SW Mexico
42 L14 **Colima, Nevado de** C Mexico *19.36N 103.36W*
61 M14 **Colinas** Maranhão, E Brazil *6.01S 44.15W*
98 F10 **Coll** *island* W Scotland, UK
107 N7 **Collado Villalba** *var.* Villalba. Madrid, C Spain *40.37N 3.58W*
191 R4 **Collarenebri** New South Wales, SE Australia *29.31S 148.33E*
39 P5 **Collbran** Colorado, C USA *39.14N 107.57W*
108 G12 **Colle di Val d'Elsa** Toscana, C Italy *43.26N 11.06E*
41 R9 **College** Alaska, USA *64.49N 148.06W*
34 K10 **College Place** Washington, NW USA *46.03N 118.23W*
27 U10 **College Station** Texas, SW USA *30.36N 96.21W*
191 P4 **Collerina** New South Wales, SE Australia *29.41S 146.36E*
188 I13 **Collie** Western Australia *33.19S 116.06E*
188 L4 **Collier Bay** *bay* Western Australia
23 F10 **Collierville** Tennessee, S USA *35.02N 89.39W*
108 F11 **Collina, Passo della** *pass* C Italy *44.02N 10.55E*
12 G14 **Collingwood** Ontario, S Canada *44.28N 80.12W*
192 I13 **Collingwood** Tasman, South Island, NZ *40.40S 172.40E*
194 M15 **Collingwood Bay** *bay* SE PNG
24 L7 **Collins** Mississippi, S USA *31.39N 89.33W*
32 K15 **Collinsville** Illinois, N USA *38.40N 89.58W*
29 P9 **Collinsville** Oklahoma, C USA *36.21N 95.50W*
22 H10 **Collinwood** Tennessee, S USA *35.10N 87.44W*
Collipo *see* Leiria
65 G14 **Collipulli** Araucanía, C Chile *37.55S 72.30W*
99 D16 **Collooney** *Ir.* Cúil Mhuine. NW Ireland *54.10N 8.28W*
31 R10 **Colman** South Dakota, N USA *43.58N 96.48W*
105 U6 **Colmar** *Ger.* Kolmar. Haut-Rhin, NE France *48.04N 7.21E*
106 M15 **Colmenar** Andalucía, S Spain *36.54N 4.19W*
Colmenar *see* Colmenar de Oreja
107 O9 **Colmenar de Oreja** *var.* Colmenar. Madrid, C Spain *40.06N 3.25W*
107 N7 **Colmenar Viejo** Madrid, C Spain *40.39N 3.46W*
27 X9 **Colmesneil** Texas, SW USA *30.54N 94.25W*
Cöln *see* Köln
Colneceaste *see* Colchester
42 C3 **Colnet** Baja California, NW Mexico
61 G15 **Colniza** Mato Grosso, W Brazil *9.16S 59.25W*
Cologne *see* Köln
44 B6 **Colomba** Quezaltenango, SW Guatemala *14.45N 91.39W*
Colomb-Béchar *see* Béchar
56 E11 **Colombia** Huila, C Colombia *3.24N 74.49W*
56 G10 **Colombia** *off.* Republic of Colombia. ◆ *republic* N South America
66 E12 **Colombian Basin** *undersea feature* SW Caribbean Sea
Colombie-Britannique *see* British Columbia
13 T6 **Colombier** Quebec, SE Canada *48.51N 68.52W*
161 J25 **Colombo** ● (Sri Lanka) Western Province, W Sri Lanka *6.55N 79.52E*
161 J25 **Colombo** ✕ Western Province, SW Sri Lanka *6.50N 79.59E*
31 N11 **Colome** South Dakota, N USA *43.13N 99.42W*
63 D18 **Colon** Entre Ríos, E Argentina *32.13S 58.15W*
63 B19 **Colón** Buenos Aires, E Argentina *33.53S 61.06W*
46 D5 **Colón** Matanzas, C Cuba *22.42N 80.54W*
45 T14 **Colón** *prev.* Aspinwall. Colón, C Panama *9.04N 80.32W*
44 K5 **Colón** ◆ *department* NE Honduras
45 S15 **Colón** *off.* Provincia de Colón. ◆ *province* N Panama
59 A16 **Colón, Archipiélago de** *var.* Islas de los Galápagos, *Eng.* Galapagos Islands, Tortoise Islands. *island group* Ecuador, E Pacific Ocean
46 K5 **Colonel Hill** Crooked Island, SE Bahamas *22.43N 74.12W*
42 B3 **Colonet, Cabo** *headland* NW Mexico *30.57N 116.19W*
196 G14 **Colonia** Yap, W Micronesia *9.29N 138.06E*
63 D19 **Colonia** ◆ *department* SW Uruguay
Colonia *see* Kolonia, Micronesia
Colonia *see* Colonia del Sacramento, Uruguay
Colonia Agrippina *see* Köln
63 D20 **Colonia del Sacramento** *var.* Colonia. Colonia, SW Uruguay *34.28S 57.48W*
64 L8 **Colonia Dora** Santiago del Estero, N Argentina *28.34S 62.58W*
Colonia Julia Fanestris *see* Fano

◆ Country
● Country Capital
◇ Dependent Territory
○ Dependent Territory Capital
◆ Administrative Region
✕ International Airport
▲ Mountain
▲ Mountain Range
Volcano
River
Lake
Reservoir

23 W5 **Colonial Beach** Virginia, NE USA 38.15N 76.57W
23 V6 **Colonial Heights** Virginia, NE USA 37.15N 77.24W
200 Oo8 **Colón Ridge** undersea feature E Pacific Ocean
98 F12 **Colonsay** island W Scotland, UK
59 K22 **Colorada, Laguna** ◎ SW Bolivia
39 R6 **Colorado** off. State of Colorado; also known as Centennial State, Silver State. ◆ state C USA
65 H22 **Colorado, Cerro** ▲ S Argentina 49.58S 71.38W
27 O7 **Colorado City** Texas, SW USA 32.23N 100.51W
38 M7 **Colorado Plateau** plateau W USA
63 A24 **Colorado, Río** ⁓ E Argentina
45 N12 **Colorado, Río** ⁓ NE Costa Rica
Colorado, Río see Colorado River
18 Hh10 **Colorado River** var. Río Colorado. ⁓ Mexico/USA
18 Ll15 **Colorado River** ⁓ Texas, SW USA
37 W15 **Colorado River Aqueduct** aqueduct California, W USA
46 A4 **Colorados, Archipiélago de los** island group NW Cuba
64 J9 **Colorados, Desagües de los** ◎ W Argentina
39 T5 **Colorado Springs** Colorado, C USA 38.49N 104.46W
42 L11 **Colotlán** Jalisco, SW Mexico 22.07N 103.15W
59 L19 **Colquechaca** Potosí, C Bolivia 18.39S 66.12W
25 S7 **Colquitt** Georgia, SE USA 31.10N 84.43W
31 R11 **Colton** South Dakota, N USA 43.47N 96.55W
34 M10 **Colton** Washington, NW USA 46.34N 117.10W
37 P8 **Columbia** California, W USA 38.01N 120.22W
32 K16 **Columbia** Illinois, N USA 38.26N 90.12W
22 L7 **Columbia** Kentucky, S USA 37.06N 85.18W
24 I6 **Columbia** Louisiana, S USA 32.05N 92.03W
23 W3 **Columbia** Maryland, NE USA 39.11N 76.52W
24 L7 **Columbia** Mississippi, S USA 31.15N 89.50W
29 U4 **Columbia** Missouri, C USA 38.55N 92.19W
23 Y9 **Columbia** North Carolina, SE USA 35.53N 76.16W
20 G16 **Columbia** Pennsylvania, NE USA 40.01N 76.30W
23 Q12 **Columbia** state capital South Carolina, SE USA 34.00N 81.00W
22 I9 **Columbia** Tennessee, S USA 35.37N 87.02W
(0) F9 **Columbia** ⁓ Canada/USA
34 K9 **Columbia Basin** basin Washington, NW USA
207 Q10 **Columbia, Cape** headland Ellesmere Island, Nunavut, NE Canada
33 Q12 **Columbia City** Indiana, N USA 41.09N 85.29W
23 W3 **Columbia, District of** ◆ federal district NE USA
35 P7 **Columbia Falls** Montana, NW USA 48.22N 114.10W
9 O15 **Columbia Icefield** icefield Alberta/British Columbia, S Canada
9 O15 **Columbia, Mount** ▲ Alberta/British Columbia, SW Canada 52.07N 117.30W
9 N15 **Columbia Mountains** ▲ British Columbia, SW Canada
25 P4 **Columbiana** Alabama, S USA 33.10N 86.36W
33 V12 **Columbiana** Ohio, N USA 40.53N 80.41W
34 M14 **Columbia Plateau** plateau Idaho/Oregon, NW USA
31 P7 **Columbia Road Reservoir** ⊠ South Dakota, N USA
67 K16 **Columbia Seamount** undersea feature C Atlantic Ocean 20.30S 32.00W
85 D25 **Columbine, Cape** headland SW South Africa 32.50S 17.39E
107 U9 **Columbretes, Islas** island group E Spain
25 R5 **Columbus** Georgia, SE USA 32.28N 84.58W
33 P14 **Columbus** Indiana, N USA 39.12N 85.55W
29 R7 **Columbus** Kansas, C USA 37.10N 94.50W
25 N4 **Columbus** Mississippi, S USA 33.30N 88.25W
35 U11 **Columbus** Montana, NW USA 45.38N 109.15W
31 Q15 **Columbus** Nebraska, C USA 41.25N 97.22W
39 Q16 **Columbus** New Mexico, SW USA 31.49N 107.38W
23 P10 **Columbus** North Carolina, SE USA 35.15N 82.09W
30 K2 **Columbus** North Dakota, N USA 48.52N 102.47W
33 S13 **Columbus** state capital Ohio, N USA 39.57N 83.00W
27 U11 **Columbus** Texas, SW USA 29.42N 96.32W
32 L8 **Columbus** Wisconsin, N USA 43.21N 89.00W
33 R12 **Columbus Grove** Ohio, N USA 40.55N 84.03W
31 Y15 **Columbus Junction** Iowa, C USA 41.16N 91.21W
46 J3 **Columbus Point** headland Cat Island, C Bahamas 24.07N 75.19W
37 T8 **Columbus Salt Marsh** salt marsh Nevada, W USA
37 N6 **Colusa** California, W USA 39.10N 122.03W
34 L7 **Colville** Washington, NW USA 48.33N 117.54W
192 M5 **Colville, Cape** headland North Island, NZ 36.28S 175.20E
192 M5 **Colville Channel** channel North Island, NZ
41 P6 **Colville River** ⁓ Alaska, USA
99 J18 **Colwyn Bay** N Wales, UK 53.18N 3.43W
108 H9 **Comacchio** var. Commachio; anc. Comactium. Emilia-Romagna, N Italy 44.40N 12.10E
108 H9 **Comacchio, Valli di** lagoon Adriatic Sea, N Mediterranean Sea
Comactium see Comacchio
43 V17 **Comalapa** Chiapas, SE Mexico 15.42N 92.06W
43 U15 **Comalcalco** Tabasco, SE Mexico 18.16N 93.05W
65 H16 **Comallo** Río Negro, SW Argentina 40.58S 70.13W
28 M12 **Comanche** Oklahoma, C USA 34.22N 97.57W
27 R8 **Comanche** Texas, SW USA 31.54N 98.36W
204 H2 **Comandante Ferraz** Brazilian research station Antarctica 61.57S 58.23W
64 N6 **Comandante Fontana** Formosa, N Argentina 25.19S 59.42W
65 I22 **Comandante Luis Peidra Buena** Santa Cruz, S Argentina 50.04S 68.55W
61 O18 **Comandatuba** Bahia, SE Brazil 15.13S 39.00W
118 K11 **Comănești** Hung. Kománfalva. Bacău, SW Romania 46.24N 26.27E
59 M19 **Comarapa** Santa Cruz, C Bolivia 17.52S 64.34W
118 J13 **Comarnic** Prahova, SE Romania 45.13N 25.36E
44 H6 **Comayagua** Comayagua, W Honduras 14.33N 87.37W
44 H6 **Comayagua** ◆ department W Honduras
44 I6 **Comayagua, Montañas de** ▲ C Honduras
23 R15 **Combahee River** ⁓ South Carolina, SE USA
64 G10 **Combarbalá** Coquimbo, C Chile 31.15S 71.03W
105 S7 **Combeaufontaine** Haute-Saône, E France 47.43N 5.52E
99 G15 **Comber** Ir. An Comar. Northern Ireland, UK 54.33N 5.45W
101 K20 **Comblain-au-Pont** Liège, E Belgium 50.29N 5.36E
104 I6 **Combourg** Ille-et-Vilaine, NW France 48.21N 1.44W
46 M9 **Comendador** prev. Elías Piña. W Dominican Republic 18.51N 71.40W
Comer See see Como, Lago di
27 R11 **Comfort** Texas, SW USA 29.58N 98.54W
159 V15 **Comilla** Ben. Kumillā. Chittagong, E Bangladesh 23.28N 91.10E
101 B18 **Comines** Hainaut, W Belgium 50.46N 2.58E
123 J16 **Comino** Malt. Kemmuna. island C Malta
109 D18 **Comino, Capo** headland Sardegna, Italy, C Mediterranean Sea 40.32N 9.49E
109 K25 **Comiso** Sicilia, Italy, C Mediterranean Sea 36.57N 14.37E
43 V16 **Comitán** var. Comitán de Domínguez. Chiapas, SE Mexico 16.14N 92.06W
Comitán de Domínguez see Comitán
Commachio see Comacchio
Commander Islands see Komandorskiye Ostrova
105 O10 **Commentry** Allier, C France 46.18N 2.46E
25 T2 **Commerce** Georgia, SE USA 34.12N 83.27W
29 R8 **Commerce** Oklahoma, C USA 36.55N 94.52W
27 V5 **Commerce** Texas, SW USA 33.16N 95.52W
39 T4 **Commerce City** Colorado, C USA 39.45N 104.54W
105 S5 **Commercy** Meuse, NE France 48.46N 5.36E
57 W9 **Commewijne** var. Commewyne. ◆ district NE Suriname
Commewyne see Commewijne
13 P8 **Commissaires, Lac des** ◎ Québec, SE Canada
66 A12 **Commissioner's Point** headland W Bermuda
15 Ll3 **Committee Bay** bay Nunavut, N Canada
108 D7 **Como** anc. Comum. Lombardia, N Italy 45.48N 9.04E
65 J19 **Comodoro Rivadavia** Chubut, SE Argentina 45.49S 67.30W
108 D6 **Como, Lago di** var. Lario, Eng. Lake Como, Ger. Comer See. ◎ N Italy
Como, Lake see Como, Lago di
42 E7 **Comondú** Baja California Sur, W Mexico 26.01N 111.50W
118 F12 **Comorâște** Hung. Komornok. Caraș-Severin, SW Romania 45.13N 21.34E
Comores, République Fédérale Islamique des see Comoros
161 G24 **Comorin, Cape** headland SE India 8.00N 77.10E
180 M8 **Comoro Basin** undersea feature SW Indian Ocean
180 K14 **Comoro Islands** island group W Indian Ocean
180 H13 **Comoros** off. Federal Islamic Republic of the Comoros, Fr. République Fédérale Islamique des Comores. ◆ republic W Indian Ocean
8 L17 **Comox** Vancouver Island, British Columbia, SW Canada 49.40N 124.55W
105 O4 **Compiègne** Oise, N France 49.25N 2.49E
Complutum see Alcalá de Henares
Compniacum see Cognac
42 K12 **Compostela** Nayarit, C Mexico 21.14N 104.52W
Compostella see Santiago
62 L11 **Comprida, Ilha** island S Brazil
119 N11 **Comrat** Rus. Komrat. S Moldova 46.18N 28.40E
27 O11 **Comstock** Texas, SW USA 29.39N 101.10W
33 P9 **Comstock Park** Michigan, N USA 43.00N 85.40W
199 Kk3 **Comstock Seamount** undersea feature N Pacific Ocean 48.15N 156.55W
Comum see Como
165 N17 **Cona** Xizang Zizhiqu, W China 27.58N 91.54E
78 H14 **Conakry** ● (Guinea) Conakry, SW Guinea 9.31N 13.43W
78 H14 **Conakry** ✕ Conakry, SW Guinea 9.37N 13.32W
Conamara see Connemara
Conca see Cuenca
27 Q12 **Concan** Texas, SW USA 29.27N 99.43W
104 F6 **Concarneau** Finistère, NW France 47.52N 3.55W
85 O17 **Conceição** Sofala, C Mozambique 18.47S 36.18E
61 K15 **Conceição do Araguaia** Pará, NE Brazil 8.15S 49.15W
60 F10 **Conceição do Maú** Roraima, W Brazil 3.34N 59.52W
63 D14 **Concepción** var. Concepcion. Corrientes, NE Argentina 28.25S 57.54W
64 J8 **Concepción** Tucumán, N Argentina 27.19S 65.34W
59 O17 **Concepción** Santa Cruz, E Bolivia 16.15S 62.07W
64 G13 **Concepción** Bío Bío, C Chile 36.47S 73.01W
56 E14 **Concepción** Putumayo, S Colombia 0.03N 75.39W
64 O5 **Concepción** var. Villa Concepción. Concepción, C Paraguay 23.26S 57.23W
64 O5 **Concepción** off. Departamento de Concepción. ◆ department E Paraguay
Concepción see La Concepción
Concepción de la Vega see La Vega
43 N9 **Concepción del Oro** Zacatecas, C Mexico 24.37N 101.25W
63 D18 **Concepción del Uruguay** Entre Ríos, E Argentina 32.30S 58.15W
44 K11 **Concepción, Volcán** ▲ SW Nicaragua 11.31N 85.37W
46 J4 **Conception Island** island C Bahamas
37 P14 **Conception, Point** headland California, W USA 34.27N 120.28W
56 H6 **Concha** Zulia, W Venezuela 9.01N 71.45W
62 L9 **Conchas** São Paulo, S Brazil 23.00S 47.58W
39 U11 **Conchas Dam** New Mexico, SW USA 35.21N 104.11W
39 U10 **Conchas Lake** ⊠ New Mexico, SW USA
104 M5 **Conches-en-Ouche** Eure, N France 49.00N 1.00E
39 N12 **Concho** Arizona, SW USA 34.28N 109.33W
42 J5 **Conchos, Río** ⁓ NW Mexico
43 O8 **Conchos, Río** ⁓ C Mexico
110 C8 **Concise** Vaud, W Switzerland 46.52N 6.40E
37 N8 **Concord** California, W USA 37.58N 122.01W
21 O9 **Concord** state capital New Hampshire, NE USA 43.10N 71.31W
23 R10 **Concord** North Carolina, SE USA 35.30N 80.34W
63 D17 **Concordia** Entre Ríos, E Argentina 31.25S 58.00W
56 D9 **Concordia** Antioquia, W Colombia 6.03N 75.57W
42 J10 **Concordia** Sinaloa, C Mexico 23.18N 106.03W
59 I19 **Concordia** Tacna, SW Peru 18.12S 70.19W
29 N3 **Concordia** Kansas, C USA 39.34N 97.39W
29 S4 **Concordia** Missouri, C USA 38.58N 93.34W
62 I13 **Concórdia** Santa Catarina, S Brazil 27.13S 52.01W
178 J7 **Con Cuông** Nghê An, N Vietnam 19.02N 104.54E
178 Jj16 **Côn Đao** var. Con Son. island S Vietnam
Condate see St-Claude, Jura, France
Condate see Rennes, Ille-et-Vilaine, France
Condate see Montereau-Faut-Yonne, Seine-St-Denis, France
31 P8 **Conde** South Dakota, N USA 45.08N 98.07W
44 J8 **Condega** Estelí, NW Nicaragua 13.21N 86.23W
105 P2 **Condé-sur-l'Escaut** Nord, N France 50.27N 3.36E
104 K5 **Condé-sur-Noireau** Calvados, N France 48.52N 0.31W
Condivincum see Nantes
191 P8 **Condobolin** New South Wales, SE Australia 33.04S 147.08E
104 L15 **Condom** Gers, S France 43.56N 0.23E
34 J11 **Condon** Oregon, NW USA 45.13N 120.11W
56 D9 **Condoto** Chocó, W Colombia 5.06N 76.37W
25 P7 **Conecuh River** ⁓ Alabama/Florida, SE USA
108 H7 **Conegliano** Veneto, NE Italy 45.52N 12.18E
63 C19 **Conesa** Buenos Aires, E Argentina 33.36S 60.21W
12 F15 **Conestogo** ⁓ Ontario, S Canada
195 O17 **Conflict Group** island group SE PNG
Confluentes see Koblenz
104 L10 **Confolens** Charente, W France 46.00N 0.40E
38 J4 **Confusion Range** ▲ Utah, W USA
64 N6 **Confuso, Río** ⁓ C Paraguay
23 R12 **Congaree River** ⁓ South Carolina, SE USA
Công Hoa Xa Hôi Chu Nghia Viêt Nam see Vietnam
166 K12 **Congjiang** prev. Bingmei. Guizhou, S China 25.48N 108.55E
81 K19 **Congo** off. Democratic Republic of Congo; prev. Zaire, Belgian Congo, Congo (Kinshasa). ◆ republic C Africa
81 G18 **Congo** off. Republic of the Congo, Fr. Moyen-Congo; prev. Middle Congo. ◆ republic C Africa
69 T11 **Congo** var. Kongo, Fr. Zaire. ⁓ C Africa
Congo see Zaire (province, Angola)
Congo/Congo (Kinshasa) see Congo (Democratic Republic of)
70 G12 **Congo Basin** drainage basin W Dem. Rep. Congo
69 Q11 **Congo Canyon** var. Congo Seavalley, Congo Submarine Canyon. undersea feature E Atlantic Ocean
Congo Cone see Congo Fan
67 P15 **Congo Fan** var. Congo Cone. undersea feature E Atlantic Ocean
Coni see Cuneo
65 H18 **Cónico, Cerro** ▲ SW Argentina 43.12S 71.42W
Conimbria/Conimbriga see Coimbra
Conjeeveram see Kānchīpuram
9 R13 **Conklin** Alberta, C Canada 55.36N 111.06W
26 M1 **Conlen** Texas, SW USA 36.16N 102.10W
Con, Loch see Conn, Lough
Connacht see Connaught
99 B17 **Connaught** var. Connacht, Ir. Chonnacht, Cúige. cultural region W Ireland
33 V10 **Conneaut** Ohio, N USA 41.56N 80.32W
20 L13 **Connecticut** off. State of Connecticut; also known as Blue Law State, Constitution State, Land of Steady Habits, Nutmeg State. ◆ state NE USA
21 N8 **Connecticut** ⁓ Canada/USA
21 O6 **Connecticut Lakes** lakes New Hampshire, NE USA
34 K9 **Connell** Washington, NW USA 46.39N 118.51W
99 B17 **Connemara** Ir. Conamara. region W Ireland
33 Q14 **Connersville** Indiana, N USA 39.38N 85.15W
99 B16 **Conn, Lough** Ir. Loch Con. ◎ W Ireland
37 X6 **Connors Pass** pass Nevada, W USA 39.01N 114.37W
189 X7 **Connors Range** ▲ Queensland, E Australia
58 E7 **Cononaco, Río** ⁓ E Ecuador
31 W13 **Conrad** Iowa, C USA 42.13N 92.52W
35 R7 **Conrad** Montana, NW USA 48.10N 111.58W
27 W10 **Conroe** Texas, SW USA 30.18N 95.27W
27 V10 **Conroe, Lake** ⊠ Texas, SW USA
63 C17 **Conscripto Bernardi** Entre Ríos, E Argentina 31.03S 59.04W
61 M20 **Conselheiro Lafaiete** Minas Gerais, SE Brazil 20.40S 43.48W
Consentia see Cosenza
99 L14 **Consett** N England, UK 54.49N 1.52W
46 B5 **Consolación del Sur** Pinar del Río, W Cuba 22.29N 83.31W
Con Son see Côn Đao
9 R15 **Consort** Alberta, SW Canada 51.58N 110.44W
Constance see Konstanz
110 I6 **Constance, Lake** Ger. Bodensee. ◎ C Europe
106 G9 **Constância** Santarém, C Portugal 39.28N 8.22W
119 N14 **Constanța** var. Küstendje, Eng. Constanza, Ger. Konstanza, Turk. Küstence. Constanța, SE Romania 44.09N 28.36E
118 L14 **Constanța** ◆ county SE Romania
Constantia see Coutances, France
Constantia see Konstanz, Germany
106 K13 **Constantina** Andalucía, S Spain 37.54N 5.36W
76 L5 **Constantine** var. Qacentina, Ar. Qoussantîna. NE Algeria 36.22N 6.43E
41 O14 **Constantine, Cape** headland Alaska, USA 58.23N 158.53W
Constantinople see İstanbul
Constantiola see Oltenița
Constanz see Konstanz
Constanza see Constanța
64 G13 **Constitución** Maule, C Chile 35.25S 72.19W
63 D17 **Constitución** Salto, N Uruguay 31.04S 57.51W
Constitution State see Connecticut
107 N10 **Consuegra** Castilla-La Mancha, C Spain 39.28N 3.43W
189 X9 **Consuelo Peak** ▲ Queensland, E Australia 24.45S 148.01E
58 E11 **Contamana** Loreto, N Peru 7.19S 75.04W
Contrasto, Colle del see Contrasto, Portella del
109 K23 **Contrasto, Portella del** var. Colle del Contrasto. pass Sicilia, Italy, C Mediterranean Sea 37.51N 14.22E
56 G8 **Contratación** Santander, C Colombia 6.18N 73.27W
104 M8 **Contres** Loir-et-Cher, C France 47.24N 1.30E
109 O17 **Conversano** Puglia, SE Italy 40.58N 17.07E
29 U11 **Conway** Arkansas, C USA 35.05N 92.26W
21 O8 **Conway** New Hampshire, NE USA 43.58N 71.05W
23 U13 **Conway** South Carolina, SE USA 33.50N 79.03W
27 N2 **Conway** Texas, SW USA 35.10N 101.23W
29 U11 **Conway, Lake** ⊠ Arkansas, C USA
29 N7 **Conway Springs** Kansas, C USA 37.23N 97.38W
99 J18 **Conwy** N Wales, UK 53.16N 3.51W
25 T3 **Conyers** Georgia, SE USA 33.40N 84.01W
Coo see Kos
190 F4 **Coober Pedy** South Australia 29.01S 134.46E
189 P2 **Cooinda** Northern Territory, N Australia 12.54S 132.31E
190 B6 **Cook** South Australia 30.37S 130.26E
31 W4 **Cook** Minnesota, N USA 47.51N 92.41W
203 N6 **Cook, Baie de** bay Moorea, W French Polynesia
8 J16 **Cook, Cape** headland Vancouver Island, British Columbia, SW Canada 50.04N 127.52W
39 Q15 **Cookes Peak** ▲ New Mexico, SW USA 32.32N 107.43W
22 L8 **Cookeville** Tennessee, S USA 36.09N 85.30W
183 P9 **Cook Fracture Zone** tectonic feature S Pacific Ocean
Cook, Grand Récif de see Cook, Récif de
41 Q12 **Cook Inlet** inlet Alaska, USA
203 X2 **Cook Island** island Line Islands, E Kiribati
202 J14 **Cook Islands** ◇ territory in free association with NZ S Pacific Ocean
193 E19 **Cook, Mount** prev. Aoraki, Aorangi. ▲ South Island, NZ 43.38S 170.05E
197 G4 **Cook, Récif de** var. Grand Récif de Cook. reef S New Caledonia
12 G14 **Cookstown** Ontario, S Canada 44.12N 79.39W
99 F15 **Cookstown** Ir. An Chorr Chríochach. C Northern Ireland, UK 54.39N 6.45W
193 K14 **Cook Strait** var. Raukawa. strait NZ
189 W3 **Cooktown** Queensland, NE Australia 15.28S 145.15E
191 P6 **Coolabah** New South Wales, SE Australia 31.03S 146.42E
190 J11 **Coola Coola Swamp** wetland South Australia
191 S7 **Coolah** New South Wales, SE Australia 31.49S 149.43E
191 P9 **Coolamon** New South Wales, SE Australia 34.49S 147.13E
191 T4 **Coolatai** New South Wales, SE Australia 29.16S 150.45E
188 K12 **Coolgardie** Western Australia 31.00S 121.12E
38 L14 **Coolidge** Arizona, SW USA 32.58N 111.29W
27 U8 **Coolidge** Texas, SW USA 31.45N 96.39W
191 Q11 **Cooma** New South Wales, SE Australia 36.16S 149.09E
Coomassie see Kumasi
191 R6 **Coonabarabran** New South Wales, SE Australia 31.19S 149.18E
190 J10 **Coonalpyn** South Australia 35.43S 139.50E
191 R6 **Coonamble** New South Wales, SE Australia 30.56S 148.22E
Coondapoor see Kundāpura
161 G21 **Coonoor** Tamil Nādu, SE India 11.21N 76.46E
31 U14 **Coon Rapids** Iowa, C USA 41.52N 94.40W
31 V8 **Coon Rapids** Minnesota, N USA 45.12N 93.18W
27 V5 **Cooper** Texas, SW USA 33.22N 95.41W
189 U9 **Cooper Creek** var. Barcoo, Cooper's Creek. seasonal river Queensland/South Australia
41 R12 **Cooper Landing** Alaska, USA 60.27N 149.59W
23 T14 **Cooper River** ⁓ South Carolina, SE USA
Cooper's Creek see Cooper Creek
46 H1 **Coopers Town** Great Abaco, N Bahamas 26.46N 77.27W
20 J10 **Cooperstown** New York, NE USA 42.43N 74.55W
31 P4 **Cooperstown** North Dakota, N USA 47.26N 98.07W
33 P9 **Coopersville** Michigan, N USA 43.03N 85.55W
190 D7 **Coorabie** South Australia 31.57S 132.18E
25 Q3 **Coosa River** ⁓ Alabama/Georgia, S USA
34 E14 **Coos Bay** Oregon, NW USA 43.22N 124.13W
191 Q9 **Cootamundra** New South Wales, SE Australia 34.40S 148.03E
99 E16 **Cootehill** Ir. Muinchille. N Ireland 54.04N 7.04W
Čop see Chop
59 J17 **Copacabana** La Paz, W Bolivia 16.11S 69.02W
65 H14 **Copahué, Volcán** ▲ C Chile 37.56S 71.04W
43 U16 **Copainalá** Chiapas, SE Mexico 17.04N 93.13W
34 F8 **Copalis Beach** Washington, NW USA 47.05N 124.11W
44 F6 **Copán** ◆ department W Honduras
Copán see Copán Ruinas
27 T14 **Copano Bay** bay NW Gulf of Mexico
44 F6 **Copán Ruinas** var. Copán. Copán, W Honduras 14.51N 89.07W
Copenhagen see København
109 Q19 **Copertino** Puglia, SE Italy 40.16N 18.03E
64 H7 **Copiapó** Atacama, N Chile 27.17S 70.25W
64 G8 **Copiapó, Bahía** bay N Chile
64 G7 **Copiapó, Río** ⁓ N Chile
116 M12 **Çöpköy** Edirne, NW Turkey 41.14N 26.51E
190 I5 **Copley** South Australia 30.36S 138.26E
108 H9 **Copparo** Emilia-Romagna, C Italy 44.53N 11.53E
57 V10 **Coppename Rivier** var. Koppename. ⁓ C Suriname
27 S9 **Copperas Cove** Texas, SW USA 31.07N 97.54W
84 J13 **Copperbelt** ◆ province C Zambia
41 S11 **Copper Center** Alaska, USA 61.57N 145.21W
Coppermine see Kugluktuk
15 J5 **Coppermine** ⁓ Northwest Territories/Nunavut, N Canada
41 T11 **Copper River** ⁓ Alaska, USA
Copper State see Arizona
118 I11 **Copșa Mică** Ger. Kleinkopisch, Hung. Kiskapus. Sibiu, C Romania 45.48N 24.08E
164 J14 **Coqên** Xizang Zizhiqu, W China 31.13N 85.12E
Coquilhatville see Mbandaka
34 E14 **Coquille** Oregon, NW USA 43.10N 124.11W
64 G9 **Coquimbo** Coquimbo, N Chile 29.59S 71.18W
64 G9 **Coquimbo** off. Región de Coquimbo. ◆ region C Chile
118 I15 **Corabia** Olt, S Romania 43.46N 24.31E
59 F17 **Coracora** Ayacucho, SW Peru 15.07S 73.45W
Cora Droma Rúisc see Carrick-on-Shannon
46 K9 **Corail** SW Haiti 18.32N 73.54W
191 V4 **Coraki** New South Wales, SE Australia 29.01S 153.15E
188 G8 **Coral Bay** Western Australia 23.02S 113.51E
25 Y16 **Coral Gables** Florida, SE USA 25.43N 80.16W
15 M5 **Coral Harbour** Southampton Island, Northwest Territories, NE Canada 64.10N 83.15W
199 I10 **Coral Sea** sea SW Pacific Ocean
182 M7 **Coral Sea Basin** undersea feature N Coral Sea
199 Hh10 **Coral Sea Islands** ◇ Australian external territory SW Pacific Ocean
190 M12 **Corangamite, Lake** ◎ Victoria, SE Australia
Corantijn Rivier see Courantyne River
20 B14 **Coraopolis** Pennsylvania, NE USA 40.28N 80.08W
109 N17 **Corato** Puglia, SE Italy 41.09N 16.25E
105 O17 **Corbières** ▲ S France
105 P8 **Corbigny** Nièvre, C France 47.15N 3.42E
23 N7 **Corbin** Kentucky, S USA 36.57N 84.06W
106 L14 **Corbones** ⁓ SW Spain
Corcaigh see Cork
37 R11 **Corcoran** California, W USA 36.06N 119.33W
49 T14 **Corcovado, Golfo** gulf S Chile
65 G18 **Corcovado, Volcán** ▲ S Chile 43.13S 72.45W
106 F3 **Corcubión** Galicia, NW Spain 42.55N 9.12W
Corcyra Nigra see Korčula
62 Q9 **Cordeiro** Rio de Janeiro, SE Brazil 22.01S 42.20W
25 T6 **Cordele** Georgia, SE USA 31.58N 83.49W
28 L11 **Cordell** Oklahoma, C USA 35.18N 98.58W
105 N14 **Cordes** Tarn, S France 44.03N 1.57E
64 O6 **Cordillera** off. Departamento de la Cordillera. ◆ department C Paraguay
190 K1 **Cordillo Downs** South Australia 26.44S 140.37E
64 K10 **Córdoba** Córdoba, C Argentina 31.25S 64.10W
43 R14 **Córdoba** Veracruz-Llave, E Mexico 18.52N 96.48W
106 M13 **Córdoba** var. Cordoba, Eng. Cordova; anc. Corduba. Andalucía, SW Spain 37.52N 4.46W
64 K11 **Córdoba** off. Provincia de Córdoba. ◆ province C Argentina
56 D7 **Córdoba** off. Departamento de Córdoba. ◆ province NW Colombia
106 L13 **Córdoba** ◆ province Andalucía, S Spain
64 K10 **Córdoba, Sierras de** ▲ C Argentina
25 O3 **Cordova** Alabama, S USA 33.45N 87.10W
41 S12 **Cordova** Alaska, USA 60.32N 145.45W
Cordova/Corduba see Córdoba
Corentyne River see Courantyne River
Corfu see Kérkyra
106 J9 **Coria** Extremadura, W Spain 39.58N 6.31W
106 J14 **Coria del Río** Andalucía, S Spain 37.18N 6.04W
191 S8 **Coricudgy, Mount** ▲ New South Wales, SE Australia 32.49S 150.28E
109 N20 **Corigliano Calabro** Calabria, SW Italy 39.35N 16.30E
Corinium/Corinium Dobunorum see Cirencester
25 N1 **Corinth** Mississippi, S USA 34.56N 88.29W
Corinth see Kórinthos
Corinth Canal see Dióryga Korinthou
Corinth, Gulf of/Corinthiacus Sinus see Korinthiakós Kólpos
Corinthus see Kórinthos
44 I9 **Corinto** Chinandega, NW Nicaragua 12.28N 87.10W
99 C21 **Cork** Ir. Corcaigh. S Ireland 51.54N 7.06W
99 C21 **Cork** Ir. Corcaigh. cultural region SW Ireland
99 C21 **Cork** ✕ SW Ireland 51.52N 8.25W
99 D21 **Cork Harbour** Ir. Cuan Chorcaí. inlet SW Ireland
109 I23 **Corleone** Sicilia, Italy, C Mediterranean Sea 37.49N 13.18E
116 N13 **Çorlu** Tekirdağ, NW Turkey 41.10N 27.48E
116 N12 **Çorlu Çayı** ⁓ NW Turkey
Cormaiore see Courmayeur
9 V13 **Cormorant** Manitoba, C Canada 54.12N 100.33W
25 T2 **Cornelia** Georgia, SE USA 34.30N 83.31W
62 J10 **Cornélio Procópio** Paraná, S Brazil 23.07S 50.40W
57 V9 **Corneliskondre** Sipaliwini, N Suriname 5.21N 56.10W
32 J5 **Cornell** Wisconsin, N USA 45.09N 91.10W
11 S12 **Corner Brook** Newfoundland and Labrador, E Canada 48.58N 57.58W
Corner Rise Seamounts see Corner Seamounts
66 I9 **Corner Seamounts** var. Corner Rise Seamounts. undersea feature NW Atlantic Ocean
118 M9 **Cornești** Rus. Korneshty. C Moldova 47.23N 28.00E
Corneto see Tarquinia
Cornhusker State see Nebraska
29 X8 **Corning** Arkansas, C USA 36.25N 90.35W
37 N5 **Corning** California, W USA 39.54N 122.12W
31 U15 **Corning** Iowa, C USA 40.58N 94.46W
20 G11 **Corning** New York, NE USA 42.08N 77.03W
Corn Islands see Maíz, Islas del
109 J14 **Corno Grande** ▲ C Italy 42.26N 13.29E
13 N13 **Cornwall** Ontario, SE Canada 45.01N 74.45W
99 H25 **Cornwall** cultural region SW England, UK
99 G25 **Cornwall, Cape** headland SW England, UK 50.11N 5.39W
56 J4 **Coro** prev. Santa Ana de Coro. Falcón, NW Venezuela 11.27N 69.40W
59 J18 **Corocoro** La Paz, W Bolivia 17.10S 68.28W
59 K17 **Coroico** La Paz, W Bolivia 16.09S 67.41W
192 M5 **Coromandel** Waikato, North Island, NZ 36.47S 175.30E
161 K20 **Coromandel Coast** coast E India
192 M5 **Coromandel Peninsula** peninsula North Island, NZ
192 M6 **Coromandel Range** ▲ North Island, NZ
179 P12 **Coron** Busuanga Island, W Philippines 12.02N 120.10E
37 T15 **Corona** California, W USA 33.52N 117.34W
39 T12 **Corona** New Mexico, SW USA 34.15N 105.36W
9 U17 **Coronach** Saskatchewan, S Canada 49.07N 105.33W
37 U17 **Coronado** California, W USA 32.41N 117.10W
45 N15 **Coronado, Bahía de** bay S Costa Rica
9 R15 **Coronation** Alberta, SW Canada 52.06N 111.25W
15 Ii4 **Coronation Gulf** gulf Nunavut, N Canada
204 I1 **Coronation Island** island Antarctica
41 X14 **Coronation Island** island Alexander Archipelago, Alaska, USA
63 B18 **Coronda** Santa Fe, C Argentina 31.58S 60.55W
65 F14 **Coronel** Bío Bío, C Chile 37.01S 73.07W
63 D20 **Coronel Brandsen** var. Brandsen. Buenos Aires, E Argentina 35.07S 58.15W
64 K4 **Coronel Cornejo** Salta, N Argentina 22.46S 63.49W
63 B24 **Coronel Dorrego** Buenos Aires, E Argentina 38.38S 61.15W
64 P6 **Coronel Oviedo** Caaguazú, SE Paraguay 25.30S 56.27W
63 B23 **Coronel Pringles** Buenos Aires, E Argentina 37.58S 61.26W
63 B23 **Coronel Suárez** Buenos Aires, E Argentina 37.27S 61.57W
63 E22 **Coronel Vidal** Buenos Aires, E Argentina 37.28S 57.45W
57 V9 **Coronie** ◆ district NW Suriname
59 G17 **Coropuna, Nevado** ▲ S Peru 15.31S 72.31W
Çorovoda see Çorovodë
115 L22 **Çorovodë** var. Çorovoda. Berat, S Albania 40.29N 20.15E
191 P11 **Corowa** New South Wales, SE Australia 36.01S 146.22E
44 G1 **Corozal** Corozal, N Belize 18.22N 88.22W
56 E6 **Corozal** Sucre, NW Colombia 9.18N 75.19W
44 G1 **Corozal** ◆ district N Belize
27 T14 **Corpus Christi** Texas, SW USA 27.48N 97.24W
27 T14 **Corpus Christi Bay** inlet Texas, SW USA
27 R14 **Corpus Christi, Lake** ⊠ Texas, SW USA
65 F16 **Corral** Los Lagos, C Chile 39.55S 73.30W
107 O9 **Corral de Almaguer** Castilla-La Mancha, C Spain 39.45N 3.10W
106 K6 **Corrales** Castilla-León, N Spain 41.22N 5.43W
39 R11 **Corrales** New Mexico, SW USA 35.11N 106.37W
Corrán Tuathail see Carrauntoohil
108 F9 **Correggio** Emilia-Romagna, C Italy 44.47N 10.46E
179 P11 **Corregidor Island** island NW Philippines
61 M16 **Corrente** Piauí, E Brazil 10.28S 45.10W
61 I19 **Correntes, Rio** ⁓ SW Brazil
105 N12 **Corrèze** ◆ department C France
99 C17 **Corrib, Lough** Ir. Loch Coirib. ◎ W Ireland
63 C14 **Corrientes** Corrientes, NE Argentina 27.28S 58.42W
63 D15 **Corrientes** off. Provincia de Corrientes. ◆ province NE Argentina
46 A5 **Corrientes, Cabo** headland W Cuba 21.48N 84.30W
42 I13 **Corrientes, Cabo** headland SW Mexico 20.25N 105.42W
Corrientes, Provincia de see Corrientes
63 C16 **Corrientes, Río** ⁓ NE Argentina
58 E8 **Corrientes, Río** ⁓ Ecuador/Peru
27 W9 **Corrigan** Texas, SW USA 31.00N 94.49W
57 U9 **Corriverton** E Guyana 5.55N 57.09W
Corriza see Korçë
191 Q11 **Corryong** Victoria, SE Australia 36.14S 147.54E
105 Y12 **Corse** Eng. Corsica. ◆ region France, C Mediterranean Sea
105 X13 **Corse** Eng. Corsica. island France, C Mediterranean Sea
105 Y13 **Corse, Cap** headland Corse, France, C Mediterranean Sea 43.01N 9.25E
105 X15 **Corse-du-Sud** ◆ department Corse, France, C Mediterranean Sea
31 P11 **Corsica** South Dakota, N USA 43.25N 98.24W
Corsica see Corse
27 U7 **Corsicana** Texas, SW USA 32.04N 96.27W

105 Y15 **Corte** Corse, France, C Mediterranean Sea *42.19N 9.09E*
65 G16 **Corte Alto** Los Lagos, S Chile *40.58S 73.04W*
106 I13 **Cortegana** Andalucía, S Spain *37.55N 6.49W*
45 N15 **Cortés** *var.* Ciudad Cortés. Puntarenas, SE Costa Rica *8.59N 83.32W*
44 G5 **Cortés** ◆ *department* NW Honduras
39 P8 **Cortez** Colorado, C USA *37.22N 108.36W*
Cortez, Sea of *see* California, Golfo de
108 H6 **Cortina d'Ampezzo** Veneto, NE Italy *46.33N 12.09E*
20 H11 **Cortland** New York, NE USA *42.34N 76.09W*
33 V11 **Cortland** Ohio, N USA *41.19N 80.43W*
108 H12 **Cortona** Toscana, C Italy *43.15N 12.01E*
78 H13 **Corubal, Rio** ⛰ E Guinea-Bissau
106 G10 **Coruche** Santarém, C Portugal *38.58N 8.31W*
Çoruh *see* Rize
143 R11 **Çoruh Nehri** *Geor.* Chorokhi, *Rus.* Chorokh. ⛰ Georgia/Turkey
142 K12 **Çorum** *var.* Chorum. Çorum, N Turkey *40.31N 34.57E*
142 J12 **Çorum** *var.* Chorum. ◆ *province* N Turkey
61 H19 **Corumbá** Mato Grosso do Sul, S Brazil *19.00S 57.35W*
12 D16 **Corunna** Ontario, S Canada *42.49N 82.25W*
Corunna *see* A Coruña
34 F12 **Corvallis** Oregon, NW USA *44.34N 122.36W*
66 M1 **Corvo** *var.* Ilha do Corvo. *island* Azores, Portugal, NE Atlantic Ocean
Corvo, Ilha do *see* Corvo
33 O16 **Corydon** Indiana, N USA *38.12N 86.07W*
31 V16 **Corydon** Iowa, C USA *40.45N 93.19W*
Cos *see* Kos
42 I9 **Cosalá** Sinaloa, C Mexico *24.25N 106.39W*
43 R15 **Cosamaloapan** *var.* Cosamaloapan de Carpio. Veracruz-Llave, E Mexico *18.21N 95.50W*
Cosamaloapan de Carpio *see* Cosamaloapan
109 N21 **Cosenza** *anc.* Consentia. Calabria, SW Italy *39.16N 16.15E*
33 T13 **Coshocton** Ohio, N USA *40.16N 81.51W*
44 H9 **Cosigüina, Punta** *headland* NW Nicaragua *12.53N 87.42W*
31 T9 **Cosmos** Minnesota, N USA *44.56N 94.42W*
105 O8 **Cosne-sur-Loire** Nièvre, C France *47.25N 2.56E*
110 B9 **Cossonay** Vaud, W Switzerland *46.37N 6.28E*
Cossyra *see* Pantelleria
49 R4 **Costa, Cordillera de la** *var.* Cordillera de Venezuela. ▲ N Venezuela
44 K13 **Costa Rica** *off.* Republic of Costa Rica. ◆ *republic* Central America
45 N15 **Costeña, Fila** ▲ S Costa Rica
Costermansville *see* Bukavu
118 I14 **Costeşti** Argeş, SW Romania *44.38N 24.52E*
39 S8 **Costilla** New Mexico, SW USA *36.58N 105.31W*
37 O7 **Cosumnes River** ⛰ California, W USA
103 O16 **Coswig** Sachsen, E Germany *51.07N 13.36E*
103 M14 **Coswig** Sachsen-Anhalt, E Germany *51.53N 12.26E*
Cosyra *see* Pantelleria
179 R16 **Cotabato** Mindanao, S Philippines *7.13N 124.12E*
58 C5 **Cotacachi** ▲ N Ecuador *0.29N 78.17W*
59 L21 **Cotagaita** Potosí, S Bolivia *20.46S 65.40W*
105 V15 **Côte d'Azur** *prev.* Nice. ✈ (Nice) Alpes-Maritimes, SE France *43.40N 7.12E*
Côte d'Ivoire *see* Ivory Coast
105 R8 **Côte d'Or** *cultural region* C France
105 R7 **Côte d'Or** ◆ *department* E France
Côte Française des Somalis *see* Djibouti
104 J4 **Cotentin** *peninsula* N France
104 G6 **Côtes d'Armor** *prev.* Côtes-du-Nord. ◆ *department* NW France
Côtes-du Nord *see* Côtes d'Armor
Cöthen *see* Köthen
Côtière, Chaîne *see* Coast Mountains
42 M13 **Cotija** *var.* Cotija de la Paz. Michoacán de Ocampo, SW Mexico *19.49N 102.39W*
Cotija de la Paz *see* Cotija
79 R16 **Cotonou** *var.* Kotonu. S Benin *6.24N 2.25E*
79 R16 **Cotonou** ✈ S Benin *6.31N 2.18E*
58 B6 **Cotopaxi** *prev.* León. ◆ *province* C Ecuador
58 C6 **Cotopaxi** ⛰ N Ecuador *0.42S 78.24W*
Cotrone *see* Crotone
99 L21 **Cotswold Hills** *var.* Cotswolds. *hill range* S England, UK
Cotswolds *see* Cotswold Hills
34 F13 **Cottage Grove** Oregon, NW USA *43.48N 123.03W*
23 S14 **Cottageville** South Carolina, SE USA *32.55N 80.28W*
103 P14 **Cottbus** *prev.* Kottbus. Brandenburg, E Germany *51.42N 14.22E*
29 U9 **Cotter** Arkansas, C USA *36.16N 92.30W*
108 A9 **Cottian Alps** *Fr.* Alpes Cottiennes, *It.* Alpi Cozie. ▲ France/Italy
Cottiennes, Alpes *see* Cottian Alps
Cotton State, The *see* Alabama
24 G4 **Cotton Valley** Louisiana, S USA *32.49N 93.25W*
38 L12 **Cottonwood** Arizona, SW USA *34.43N 112.00W*
34 M10 **Cottonwood** Idaho, NW USA *46.01N 116.20W*
31 S9 **Cottonwood** Minnesota, N USA *44.37N 95.41W*
27 Q7 **Cottonwood** Texas, SW USA *32.12N 99.14W*
29 O5 **Cottonwood Falls** Kansas, C USA *38.22N 96.32W*
38 L3 **Cottonwood Heights** Utah, W USA *40.37N 111.48W*
31 S10 **Cottonwood River** ⛰ Minnesota, N USA
47 O9 **Cotuí** C Dominican Republic *19.04N 70.10W*
27 Q13 **Cotulla** Texas, SW USA *28.26N 99.13W*
Cotyora *see* Ordu
104 I11 **Coubre, Pointe de la** *headland* W France *45.39N 1.23W*
20 E12 **Coudersport** Pennsylvania, NE USA *41.45N 78.00W*
13 S9 **Coudres, Île aux** *island* Quebec, SE Canada
190 G11 **Couedic, Cape de** *headland* South Australia *36.04S 136.43E*
Couentrey *see* Coventry
104 I6 **Couesnon** ⛰ NW France
34 H10 **Cougar** Washington, NW USA *46.03N 122.18W*
104 L10 **Couhé** Vienne, W France *46.18N 0.10E*
34 K8 **Coulee City** Washington, NW USA *47.36N 119.18W*
205 Q15 **Coulman Island** *island* Antarctica
105 P5 **Coulommiers** Seine-et-Marne, N France *48.49N 3.04E*
12 K11 **Coulonge** ⛰ Quebec, SE Canada
12 K11 **Coulonge Est** ⛰ Quebec, SE Canada
37 Q9 **Coulterville** California, W USA *37.41N 120.10W*
40 M9 **Council** Alaska, USA *64.54N 163.40W*
34 M12 **Council** Idaho, NW USA *44.45N 116.26W*
31 S15 **Council Bluffs** Iowa, C USA *41.15N 95.51W*
29 O5 **Council Grove** Kansas, C USA *38.37N 96.27W*
29 O5 **Council Grove Lake** ⊠ Kansas, C USA
34 G7 **Coupeville** Washington, NW USA *48.13N 122.41W*
57 U12 **Courantyne River** *var.* Corantijn Rivier, Corentyne River. ⛰ Guyana/Suriname
101 G21 **Courcelles** Hainaut, S Belgium *50.28N 4.22E*
110 C7 **Courgenay** Jura, NW Switzerland *47.24N 7.09E*
130 B2 **Courland Lagoon** *Ger.* Kurisches Haff, *Rus.* Kurskiy Zaliv. *lagoon* Lithuania/Russian Federation
120 B12 **Courland Spit** *Lith.* Kuršių Nerija, *Rus.* Kurshskaya Kosa. *spit* Lithuania/Russian Federation
108 A6 **Courmayeur** *prev.* Cormaiore. Valle d'Aosta, NW Italy *45.48N 7.00E*
110 D7 **Courroux** Jura, NW Switzerland *47.22N 7.22E*
8 K17 **Courtenay** Vancouver Island, British Columbia, SW Canada *49.40N 124.58W*
23 W7 **Courtland** Virginia, NE USA *36.41N 77.01W*
27 V10 **Courtney** Texas, SW USA *30.16N 96.04W*
32 J4 **Court Oreilles, Lac** ⊚ Wisconsin, N USA
Courtrai *see* Kortrijk
101 H19 **Court-Saint-Étienne** Wallon Brabant, C Belgium *50.38N 4.34E*
24 G6 **Coushatta** Louisiana, S USA *32.00N 93.20W*
180 I16 **Cousin** *island* Inner Islands, NE Seychelles
180 I16 **Cousine** *island* Inner Islands, NE Seychelles
104 J4 **Coutances** *anc.* Constantia. Manche, N France *49.04N 1.27W*
104 K12 **Coutras** Gironde, SW France *45.01N 0.07W*
47 U14 **Couva** Trinidad, Trinidad and Tobago *10.25N 61.27W*
110 B8 **Couvet** Neuchâtel, W Switzerland *46.57N 6.41E*
101 H22 **Couvin** Namur, S Belgium *50.03N 4.30E*
118 K12 **Covasna** *Ger.* Kowasna, *Hung.* Kovászna. Covasna, E Romania *45.51N 26.09E*
118 J11 **Covasna** ◆ *county* E Romania
12 E12 **Cove Island** *island* Ontario, S Canada
36 M5 **Covelo** California, W USA *39.46N 123.16W*
99 M20 **Coventry** *anc.* Couentrey. C England, UK *52.25N 1.30W*
Cove of Cork *see* Cobh
23 U5 **Covesville** Virginia, NE USA *37.52N 78.41W*
106 I8 **Covilhã** Castelo Branco, E Portugal *40.16N 7.30W*
25 T3 **Covington** Georgia, SE USA *33.34N 83.52W*
33 N13 **Covington** Indiana, N USA *40.08N 87.23W*
22 M3 **Covington** Kentucky, S USA *39.04N 84.30W*
24 K8 **Covington** Louisiana, S USA *30.28N 90.06W*
33 Q13 **Covington** Ohio, N USA *40.07N 84.21W*
22 F9 **Covington** Tennessee, S USA *35.33N 89.39W*
23 S6 **Covington** Virginia, NE USA *37.47N 79.59W*
191 Q8 **Cowal, Lake** *seasonal lake* New South Wales, SE Australia
9 W15 **Cowan** Manitoba, S Canada *51.59N 100.36W*
20 F12 **Cowanesque River** ⛰ New York/Pennsylvania, NE USA
188 L12 **Cowan, Lake** ⊚ Western Australia
13 P13 **Cowansville** Quebec, SE Canada *45.13N 72.43W*
190 H8 **Cowell** South Australia *33.43S 136.53E*
99 M23 **Cowes** S England, UK *50.45N 1.19W*
29 Q10 **Coweta** Oklahoma, C USA *35.57N 95.39W*
(0) D6 **Cowie Seamount** *undersea feature* NE Pacific Ocean *54.15N 149.30W*
34 G10 **Cowlitz River** ⛰ Washington, NW USA
23 Q11 **Cowpens** South Carolina, SE USA *35.01N 81.48W*
191 R8 **Cowra** New South Wales, SE Australia *33.52S 148.36E*
Coxen Hole *see* Roatán
61 I19 **Coxim** Mato Grosso do Sul, S Brazil *18.28S 54.45W*
61 I19 **Coxim, Rio** ⛰ SW Brazil
Coxin Hole *see* Roatán
159 V17 **Cox's Bazar** Chittagong, S Bangladesh *21.25N 92.01E*
78 H14 **Coyah** Conakry, W Guinea *9.45N 13.25W*
42 K5 **Coyame** Chihuahua, N Mexico *29.28N 105.01W*
26 L9 **Coyanosa Draw** ⛰ Texas, SW USA
Coyhaique *see* Coihaique
44 C7 **Coyolate, Río** ⛰ S Guatemala
Coyote State *see* South Dakota
42 I10 **Coyotitán** Sinaloa, C Mexico *23.44N 106.34W*
43 N15 **Coyuca** *var.* Coyuca de Catalán. Guerrero, S Mexico *18.21N 100.39W*
43 O16 **Coyuca** *var.* Coyuca de Benítez. Guerrero, S Mexico *16.57N 100.01W*
Coyuca de Benítez/Coyuca de Catalán *see* Coyuca
31 N15 **Cozad** Nebraska, C USA *40.52N 99.58W*
Cozie, Alpi *see* Cottian Alps
Cozmeni *see* Kitsman'
42 E3 **Cozón, Cerro** ▲ NW Mexico *31.16N 112.29W*
43 Z12 **Cozumel** Quintana Roo, E Mexico *20.28N 86.54W*
43 Z12 **Cozumel, Isla** *island* SE Mexico
34 K8 **Crab Creek** ⛰ Washington, NW USA
46 H12 **Crab Pond Point** *headland* W Jamaica *18.07N 78.01W*
Cracovia/Cracow *see* Małopolskie
85 I25 **Cradock** Eastern Cape, S South Africa *32.06S 25.37E*
41 Y14 **Craig** Prince of Wales Island, Alaska, USA *55.29N 133.04W*
39 Q3 **Craig** Colorado, C USA *40.31N 107.33W*
99 F15 **Craigavon** C Northern Ireland, UK *54.28N 6.25W*
23 T5 **Craigsville** Virginia, NE USA *38.07N 79.21W*
103 J21 **Crailsheim** Baden-Württemberg, S Germany *49.07N 10.04E*
118 H14 **Craiova** Dolj, SW Romania *44.19N 23.49E*
8 K12 **Cranberry Junction** British Columbia, SW Canada *55.35N 128.21W*
20 J8 **Cranberry Lake** ⊚ New York, NE USA
9 V13 **Cranberry Portage** Manitoba, C Canada *54.34N 101.22W*
9 P17 **Cranbrook** British Columbia, SW Canada *49.28N 115.48W*
32 M5 **Crandon** Wisconsin, N USA *45.34N 88.54W*
34 K14 **Crane** Oregon, NW USA *43.24N 118.35W*
26 M9 **Crane** Texas, SW USA *31.24N 102.21W*
Crane *see* The Crane
27 S8 **Cranfills Gap** Texas, SW USA *31.46N 97.49W*
21 O12 **Cranston** Rhode Island, NE USA *41.46N 71.26W*
Cranz *see* Zelenogradsk
61 L15 **Craolândia** Tocantins, E Brazil *7.17S 47.23W*
104 J7 **Craon** Mayenne, NW France *47.52N 0.57W*
205 V16 **Crary, Cape** *headland* Antarctica
Crasna *see* Kraszna
34 G14 **Crater Lake** ⊚ Oregon, NW USA
194 I13 **Crater Mount** ▲ C PNG *6.23S 145.18E*
35 P14 **Craters of the Moon National Monument** *national park* Idaho, NW USA
61 O14 **Crateús** Ceará, E Brazil *5.10S 40.39W*
Crathis *see* Crati
109 N20 **Crati** *anc.* Crathis. ⛰ S Italy
9 U16 **Craven** Saskatchewan, S Canada *50.43N 104.49W*
56 I8 **Cravo Norte** Arauca, E Colombia *6.17N 70.15W*
30 J12 **Crawford** Nebraska, C USA *42.40N 103.24W*
27 T8 **Crawford** Texas, SW USA *31.31N 97.26W*
9 O17 **Crawford Bay** British Columbia, SW Canada *49.39N 116.44W*
67 M19 **Crawford Seamount** *undersea feature* S Atlantic Ocean *40.30S 10.00W*
33 O13 **Crawfordsville** Indiana, N USA *40.02N 86.52W*
25 S9 **Crawfordville** Florida, SE USA *30.10N 84.22W*
99 O23 **Crawley** SE England, UK *51.07N 0.12W*
35 S10 **Crazy Mountains** ▲ Montana, NW USA
9 T11 **Cree** ⛰ Saskatchewan, C Canada
39 R7 **Creede** Colorado, C USA *37.51N 106.55W*
42 I6 **Creel** Chihuahua, N Mexico *27.45N 107.36W*
9 S11 **Cree Lake** ⊚ Saskatchewan, C Canada
9 V13 **Creighton** Saskatchewan, C Canada *54.46N 101.54W*
31 Q13 **Creighton** Nebraska, C USA *42.28N 97.54W*
105 O4 **Creil** Oise, N France *49.16N 2.28E*
108 E8 **Crema** Lombardia, N Italy *45.22N 9.40E*
108 E8 **Cremona** Lombardia, N Italy *45.07N 10.01E*
Creole State *see* Louisiana
114 M10 **Crepaja** *Hung.* Cserépalja. Serbia, N Serbia and Montenegro (Yugoslavia) *45.02N 20.36E*
105 O4 **Crépy-en-Valois** Oise, N France *49.13N 2.54E*
114 B10 **Cres** *It.* Cherso. Primorje-Gorski Kotar, NW Croatia *44.57N 14.24E*
114 A11 **Cres** *It.* Cherso; *anc.* Crexa. *island* W Croatia
34 H14 **Crescent** Oregon, NW USA *43.27N 121.40W*
36 K1 **Crescent City** California, W USA *41.45N 124.13W*
25 W10 **Crescent City** Florida, SE USA *29.25N 81.30W*
178 M10 **Crescent Group** *island group* C Paracel Islands
25 W10 **Crescent Lake** ⊚ Florida, SE USA
31 X11 **Cresco** Iowa, C USA *43.22N 92.06W*
63 B18 **Crespo** Entre Ríos, E Argentina *32.02S 60.22W*
56 E5 **Crespo** ✈ (Cartagena) Bolívar, NW Colombia *10.27N 75.31W*
105 R13 **Crest** Drôme, E France *44.45N 5.00E*
39 R5 **Crested Butte** Colorado, C USA *38.52N 106.59W*
33 S12 **Crestline** Ohio, N USA *40.47N 82.44W*
9 O17 **Creston** British Columbia, SW Canada *49.04N 116.31W*
31 U15 **Creston** Iowa, C USA *41.03N 94.21W*
35 V16 **Creston** Wyoming, C USA *41.40N 107.43W*
39 S7 **Crestone Peak** ▲ Colorado, C USA *37.58N 105.34W*
25 P8 **Crestview** Florida, SE USA *30.43N 86.34W*
123 Gg10 **Cretan Trough** *undersea feature* Aegean Sea, C Mediterranean Sea
31 R16 **Crete** Nebraska, C USA *40.36N 96.58W*
Crete *see* Kríti
105 O5 **Créteil** Val-de-Marne, N France *48.46N 2.28E*
Crete, Sea of/Creticum, Mare *see* Kritikó Pélagos
107 X4 **Creus, Cap de** *headland* NE Spain *42.18N 3.18E*
105 N10 **Creuse** ◆ *department* C France
104 L9 **Creuse** ⛰ C France
105 T4 **Creutzwald** Moselle, NE France *49.13N 6.41E*
107 S12 **Crevillente** País Valenciano, E Spain *38.12N 0.47W*
99 L18 **Crewe** C England, UK *53.04N 2.27W*
23 V7 **Crewe** Virginia, NE USA *37.10N 78.07W*
Crexa *see* Cres
45 Q15 **Cricamola, Río** ⛰ NW Panama
63 K14 **Criciúma** Santa Catarina, S Brazil *28.39S 49.22W*
98 J11 **Crieff** C Scotland, UK *56.22N 3.49W*
114 B10 **Crikvenica** *It.* Cirquenizza; *prev.* Cirkvenica, Crjkvenica. Primorje-Gorski Kotar, NW Croatia *45.12N 14.40E*
Crimea/Crimean Oblast *see* Krym, Respublika
103 M16 **Crimmitschau** *var.* Krimmitschau. Sachsen, E Germany *50.48N 12.22E*
118 G11 **Crişcior** *Hung.* Kristyor. Hunedoara, W Romania *46.09N 22.54E*
23 Y5 **Crisfield** Maryland, NE USA *37.58N 75.51W*
33 P3 **Crisp Point** *headland* Michigan, N USA *46.45N 85.15W*
61 L19 **Cristalina** Goiás, C Brazil *16.43S 47.37W*
46 J7 **Cristal, Sierra del** ▲ E Cuba
45 T14 **Cristóbal** Colón, C Panama *9.18N 79.52W*
56 F4 **Cristóbal Colón, Pico** ▲ N Colombia *10.52N 73.46W*
Cristur/Cristuru Săcuiesc *see* Cristuru Secuiesc
118 I11 **Cristuru Secuiesc** *prev.* Cristur, Cristuru Săcuiesc, Sitaş Cristuru, *Ger.* Kreutz, *Hung.* Székelykeresztúr, Szitás-Keresztúr. Harghita, C Romania *46.16N 25.01E*
118 F10 **Crişul Alb** *var.* Weisse Kreisch, *Ger.* Weisse Körös, *Hung.* Fehér-Körös. ⛰ Hungary/Romania
118 F10 **Crişul Negru** *Ger.* Schwarze Körös, *Hung.* Fekete-Körös. ⛰ Hungary/Romania
118 G10 **Crişul Repede** *var.* Schnelle Kreisch, *Ger.* Schnelle Körös, *Hung.* Sebes-Körös. ⛰ Hungary/Romania
119 N10 **Criuleni** *Rus.* Kriulyany. C Moldova *47.12N 29.09E*
Crivadia Vulcanului *see* Vulcan
Crjkvenica *see* Crikvenica
115 O17 **Crna Gora** ▲ FYR Macedonia/Serbia and Montenegro (Yugoslavia)
Crna Gora *see* Montenegro
115 O20 **Crna Reka** ⛰ S FYR Macedonia
Crni Drim *see* Black Drin
111 V10 **Črni vrh** ▲ NE Slovenia *46.28N 15.14E*
111 V13 **Črnomelj** *Ger.* Tschernembl. SE Slovenia *45.32N 15.12E*
99 A17 **Croagh Patrick** *Ir.* Cruach Phádraig. ▲ W Ireland *53.45N 9.39W*
114 D9 **Croatia** *off.* Republic of Croatia, *Ger.* Kroatien, *SCr.* Hrvatska. ◆ *republic* SE Europe
Croce, Picco di *see* Wilde Kreuzspitze
13 P8 **Croche** ⛰ Quebec, SE Canada
175 Nn3 **Crocker, Banjaran** *var.* Crocker Range. ▲ East Malaysia
Crocker Range *see* Crocker, Banjaran
27 V9 **Crockett** Texas, SW USA *31.19N 95.27W*
69 V14 **Crocodile** *var.* Krokodil. ⛰ N South Africa
Crocodile *see* Limpopo
22 I7 **Crofton** Kentucky, S USA *37.01N 87.25W*
31 Q12 **Crofton** Nebraska, C USA *42.43N 97.30W*
Croia *see* Krujë
105 R16 **Croisette, Cap** *headland* SE France *43.12N 5.21E*
104 G8 **Croisic, Pointe du** *headland* NW France *47.16N 2.42W*
105 S13 **Croix Haute, Col de la** *pass* E France *44.43N 5.39E*
13 U5 **Croix, Pointe à la** *headland* Quebec, SE Canada *49.16N 67.46W*
12 F13 **Croker, Cape** *headland* Ontario, S Canada *44.56N 80.57W*
189 P1 **Croker Island** *island* Northern Territory, N Australia
98 I8 **Cromarty** N Scotland, UK *57.40N 4.01W*
101 M21 **Crombach** Liège, E Belgium *50.14N 6.07E*
99 Q18 **Cromer** E England, UK *52.55N 1.06E*
193 D22 **Cromwell** Otago, South Island, NZ *45.03S 169.13E*
193 H16 **Cronadun** West Coast, South Island, NZ *42.03S 171.52E*
41 O11 **Crooked Creek** Alaska, USA *61.52N 158.06W*
46 K5 **Crooked Island** *island* SE Bahamas
46 J5 **Crooked Island Passage** *channel* SE Bahamas
34 I13 **Crooked River** ⛰ Oregon, NW USA
31 R4 **Crookston** Minnesota, N USA *47.46N 96.36W*
30 I10 **Crooks Tower** ▲ South Dakota, N USA *44.09N 103.55W*
33 T14 **Crooksville** Ohio, N USA *39.46N 82.05W*
191 R9 **Crookwell** New South Wales, SE Australia *34.28S 149.27E*
12 L14 **Crosby** Ontario, SE Canada *44.39N 76.13W*
99 K17 **Crosby** *var.* Great Crosby. NW England, UK *53.30N 3.01W*
31 U6 **Crosby** Minnesota, N USA *46.30N 93.58W*
30 K2 **Crosby** North Dakota, N USA *48.54N 103.17W*
27 O5 **Crosbyton** Texas, SW USA *33.39N 101.14W*
79 V16 **Cross** ⛰ Cameroon/Nigeria
25 U10 **Cross City** Florida, SE USA *29.37N 83.08W*
Crossen *see* Krosno Odrzańskie
29 V14 **Crossett** Arkansas, C USA *33.08N 91.58W*
99 K15 **Cross Fell** ▲ N England, UK *54.42N 2.30W*
9 P16 **Crossfield** Alberta, SW Canada *51.24N 114.03W*
23 Q12 **Cross Hill** South Carolina, SE USA *34.18N 81.58W*
21 U6 **Cross Island** *island* Maine, NE USA
9 X13 **Cross Lake** Manitoba, C Canada *54.37N 97.34W*
24 F5 **Cross Lake** ⊠ Louisiana, S USA
38 I12 **Crossman Peak** ▲ Arizona, SW USA *34.33N 114.09W*
27 Q7 **Cross Plains** Texas, SW USA *32.07N 99.10W*
79 V17 **Cross River** ◆ *state* SE Nigeria
22 L9 **Crossville** Tennessee, S USA *35.57N 85.01W*
33 S8 **Croswell** Michigan, N USA *43.16N 82.37W*
12 K13 **Crotch Lake** ⊚ Ontario, SE Canada
Croton/Crotona *see* Crotone
109 O21 **Crotone** *var.* Cotrone; *anc.* Croton, Crotona. Calabria, SW Italy *39.04N 17.07E*
35 V11 **Crow Agency** Montana, NW USA *45.35N 107.28W*
191 U7 **Crowdy Head** *headland* New South Wales, SE Australia *31.52S 152.45E*
27 Q4 **Crowell** Texas, SW USA *33.58N 99.43W*
191 O6 **Crowl Creek** *seasonal river* New South Wales, SE Australia
24 H9 **Crowley** Louisiana, S USA *30.11N 92.21W*
37 S9 **Crowley, Lake** ⊠ California, W USA
29 X10 **Crowleys Ridge** *hill range* Arkansas, C USA
194 J11 **Crown Island** *island* N Papau New Guinea
33 N11 **Crown Point** Indiana, N USA *41.25N 87.22W*
39 P10 **Crownpoint** New Mexico, SW USA *35.40N 108.09W*
35 R10 **Crow Peak** ▲ Montana, NW USA *46.17N 111.54W*
9 P17 **Crowsnest Pass** *pass* Alberta/British Columbia, SW Canada *49.38N 114.43W*
31 T6 **Crow Wing River** ⛰ Minnesota, N USA
99 O22 **Croydon** SE England, UK *51.21N 0.06W*
181 P11 **Crozet Basin** *undersea feature* S Indian Ocean
181 O12 **Crozet Islands** *island group* French Southern and Antarctic Territories
181 N12 **Crozet Plateau** *var.* Crozet Plateaus. *undersea feature* SW Indian Ocean
Crozet Plateaus *see* Crozet Plateau
104 E6 **Crozon** Finistère, NW France *48.14N 4.31W*
Cruacha Dubha, Na *see* Macgillycuddy's Reeks
Cruach Phádraig *see* Croagh Patrick
118 M14 **Crucea** Constanţa, SE Romania *44.30N 28.18E*
46 E5 **Cruces** Cienfuegos, C Cuba *22.18N 80.18W*
109 O20 **Crucoli Torretta** Calabria, SW Italy *39.26N 17.03E*
43 P9 **Cruillas** Tamaulipas, C Mexico *24.43N 98.26W*
66 K9 **Cruiser Tablemount** *undersea feature* E Atlantic Ocean *32.00N 28.00W*
63 G14 **Cruz Alta** Rio Grande do Sul, S Brazil *28.37S 53.37W*
46 G8 **Cruz, Cabo** *headland* S Cuba *19.50N 77.43W*
62 N9 **Cruzeiro** São Paulo, S Brazil *22.33S 44.55W*
62 H10 **Cruzeiro do Oeste** Paraná, S Brazil *23.45S 53.03W*
61 A15 **Cruzeiro do Sul** Acre, W Brazil *7.40S 72.39W*
25 U11 **Crystal Bay** *bay* Florida, SE USA
190 I8 **Crystal Brook** South Australia *33.24S 138.10E*
9 X17 **Crystal City** Manitoba, S Canada *49.07N 98.54W*
29 X5 **Crystal City** Missouri, C USA *38.13N 90.22W*
27 P13 **Crystal City** Texas, SW USA *28.40N 99.49W*
32 M4 **Crystal Falls** Michigan, N USA *46.06N 88.19W*
25 Q8 **Crystal Lake** Florida, SE USA *30.26N 85.41W*
33 O6 **Crystal Lake** ⊚ Michigan, N USA
25 V11 **Crystal River** Florida, SE USA *28.54N 82.35W*
39 Q5 **Crystal River** ⛰ Colorado, C USA
24 K6 **Crystal Springs** Mississippi, S USA *31.59N 90.21W*
Csaca *see* Čadca
Csakathurn/Csáktornya *see* Čakovec
Csap *see* Chop
Csepén *see* Čepin
Cserépalja *see* Crepaja
Csermő *see* Cermei
Csíkszereda *see* Miercurea-Ciuc
113 L24 **Csongrád** Csongrád, SE Hungary *46.42N 20.05E*
113 L24 **Csongrád** *off.* Csongrád Megye. ◆ *county* SE Hungary
113 H22 **Csorna** Győr-Moson-Sopron, NW Hungary *47.37N 17.13E*
Csucsa *see* Ciucea
113 G25 **Csurgó** Somogy, SW Hungary *46.16N 17.09E*
Csurog *see* Čurug
56 L5 **Cúa** Miranda, N Venezuela *10.07N 66.53W*
84 C11 **Cuale** Malanje, NW Angola *8.13S 16.11E*
69 T12 **Cuando** *var.* Kwando. ⛰ S Africa
85 E15 **Cuando Cubango** *var.* Kuando-Kubango. ◆ *province* SE Angola
85 E16 **Cuangar** Cuando Cubango, S Angola *17.34S 18.39E*
84 D11 **Cuango** Lunda Norte, NE Angola *9.09S 18.01E*
84 C10 **Cuango** Uíge, NW Angola *6.17S 16.41E*
84 C10 **Cuango** *var.* Kwango. ⛰ Angola/Dem. Rep. Congo
see also Kwango
Cuan, Loch *see* Strangford Lough
84 C12 **Cuanza** *var.* Kwanza. ⛰ C Angola
84 B11 **Cuanza Norte** *var.* Kuanza Norte. ◆ *province* NE Angola
84 B12 **Cuanza Sul** *var.* Kuanza Sul. ◆ *province* NE Angola
63 E16 **Cuareim, Río** *var.* Rio Quaraí. ⛰ Brazil/Uruguay *see also* Quaraí, Rio
85 D15 **Cuatir** ⛰ S Angola
42 M7 **Cuatro Ciénegas** *var.* Cuatro Ciénegas de Carranza. Coahuila de Zaragoza, NE Mexico *26.59N 102.04W*
Cuatro Ciénegas de Carranza *see* Cuatro Ciénegas
42 I6 **Cuauhtémoc** Chihuahua, N Mexico *28.22N 106.51W*
43 P14 **Cuautla** Morelos, S Mexico *18.47N 98.56W*
106 H12 **Cuba** Beja, S Portugal *38.10N 7.54W*
29 W6 **Cuba** Missouri, C USA *38.03N 91.24W*
39 R10 **Cuba** New Mexico, SW USA *36.01N 106.57W*
46 E6 **Cuba** *off.* Republic of Cuba. ◆ *republic* W West Indies
49 O2 **Cuba** *island* W West Indies
84 B13 **Cubal** Benguela, W Angola *12.58S 14.16E*
85 C15 **Cubango** *var.* Kuvango, *Port.* Vila Artur de Paiva, Vila da Ponte. Huíla, SW Angola *14.27S 16.17E*
85 D16 **Cubango** *var.* Kavango, Kavengo, Kubango, Okavango, Okavanggo. ⛰ S Africa *see also* Okavango
56 H8 **Cubará** Boyacá, N Colombia *7.01N 72.07W*
142 I12 **Çubuk** Ankara, N Turkey *40.13N 33.01E*
85 D14 **Cuchi** Cuando Cubango, C Angola *14.40S 16.58E*
44 C5 **Cuchumatanes, Sierra de los** ▲ W Guatemala
Cuculaya, Rio *see* Kukalaya, Rio
84 E12 **Cucumbi** *prev.* Trás-os-Montes. Lunda Sul, NE Angola *10.13S 19.04E*
56 G7 **Cúcuta** *var.* San José de Cúcuta. Norte de Santander, N Colombia *7.55N 72.31W*
33 N9 **Cudahy** Wisconsin, N USA *42.54N 87.51W*
161 J21 **Cuddalore** Tamil Nādu, SE India *11.43N 79.46E*
161 I18 **Cuddapah** Andhra Pradesh, S India *14.30N 78.49E*
106 M6 **Cuéllar** Castilla-León, N Spain *41.24N 4.19W*
84 D13 **Cuemba** *var.* Coemba. Bié, C Angola *12.09S 18.07E*
58 B8 **Cuenca** Azuay, S Ecuador *02.54S 79.00W*
107 Q9 **Cuenca** *anc.* Conca. Castilla-La Mancha, C Spain *40.04N 2.07W*
107 P9 **Cuenca** ◆ *province* Castilla-La Mancha, C Spain
42 L9 **Cuencamé** *var.* Cuencamé de Ceniceros. Durango, C Mexico *24.51N 103.42W*
Cuencamé de Ceniceros *see* Cuencamé
107 Q8 **Cuenca, Serranía de** ▲ C Spain
Cuera *see* Chur
107 P5 **Cuerda del Pozo, Embalse de la** ⊠ N Spain
43 O14 **Cuernavaca** Morelos, S Mexico *18.57N 99.15W*
27 T12 **Cuero** Texas, SW USA *29.04N 97.16W*
46 I7 **Cueto** Holguín, E Cuba *20.39N 75.55W*
43 Q13 **Cuetzalán** *var.* Cuetzalán del Progreso. Puebla, S Mexico *20.00N 97.27W*
Cuetzalán del Progreso *see* Cuetzalán
107 Q14 **Cuevas de Almanzora** Andalucía, S Spain *37.19N 1.52W*
107 T8 **Cuevas de Vinromá** País Valenciano, E Spain *40.18N 0.07E*
118 H12 **Cugir** *Hung.* Kudzsir. Alba, SW Romania *45.48N 23.24E*
61 H18 **Cuiabá** *prev.* Cuyabá. *state capital* Mato Grosso, SW Brazil *15.31S 56.04W*
61 H19 **Cuiabá, Rio** ⛰ SW Brazil
43 R15 **Cuicatlán** *var.* San Juan Bautista Cuicatlán. Oaxaca, SE Mexico *17.48N 96.57W*
203 W16 **Cuidado, Punta** *headland* Easter Island, Chile, E Pacific Ocean *27.07S 109.18W*
Cuidad Presidente Stroessner *see* Ciudad del Este
Cúige *see* Connaught
Cúige Laighean *see* Leinster
Cúige Mumhan *see* Munster
100 L13 **Cuijck** Noord-Brabant, SE Netherlands *51.40N 5.55E*
Cúil an tSúdaire *see* Portarlington
44 D7 **Cuilapa** Santa Rosa, S Guatemala *14.15N 90.17W*
44 B5 **Cuilco, Río** ⛰ W Guatemala
Cúil Mhuine *see* Collooney
Cúil Raithin *see* Coleraine
85 C14 **Cuima** Huambo, C Angola *13.16S 15.39E*
85 E16 **Cuito** *var.* Kwito. ⛰ SE Angola
85 E15 **Cuíto Cuanavale** Cuando Cubango, E Angola *15.01S 19.07E*
43 N14 **Cuitzeo, Lago de** ⊚ C Mexico
29 W4 **Cuivre River** ⛰ Missouri, C USA
Çuka *see* Çukë
174 Hh4 **Cukai** *var.* Chukai, Kemaman. Terengganu, Peninsular Malaysia *4.15N 103.25E*
115 L23 **Çukë** *var.* Çuka. Vlorë, S Albania *39.50N 20.01E*
Cularo *see* Grenoble
179 Pp13 **Culasi** Panay Island, C Philippines *11.21N 122.05E*
35 Y7 **Culbertson** Montana, NW USA *48.09N 104.30W*
30 M16 **Culbertson** Nebraska, C USA *40.13N 100.50W*
191 P10 **Culcairn** New South Wales, SE Australia *35.41S 147.01E*
47 W5 **Culebra** *var.* Dewey. E Puerto Rico *18.19N 65.17W*
47 W6 **Culebra, Isla de** *island* E Puerto Rico
39 T8 **Culebra Peak** ▲ Colorado, C USA *37.07N 105.11W*
106 J5 **Culebra, Sierra de la** ▲ NW Spain
100 J12 **Culemborg** Gelderland, C Netherlands *51.57N 5.17E*
143 V14 **Culfa** *Rus.* Dzhul'fa. SW Azerbaijan *38.58N 45.37E*
191 P4 **Culgoa River** ⛰ New South Wales/Queensland, SE Australia
42 I9 **Culiacán** *var.* Culiacán Rosales, Culiacán-Rosales. Sinaloa, C Mexico *24.48N 107.25W*
Culiacán-Rosales/Culiacán Rosales *see* Culiacán
179 P13 **Culion Island** *island* Calamian Group, W Philippines
107 P14 **Cúllar-Baza** Andalucía, S Spain *37.34N 2.34W*
107 S10 **Cullera** País Valenciano, E Spain *39.10N 0.15W*
25 P3 **Cullman** Alabama, S USA *34.10N 86.50W*
110 B10 **Cully** Vaud, W Switzerland *46.58N 6.46E*
Culm *see* Chełmno
Culmsee *see* Chełmża
23 V4 **Culpeper** Virginia, NE USA *38.28N 78.00W*
193 I17 **Culverden** Canterbury, South Island, NZ *42.46S 172.51E*
57 N5 **Cumaná** Sucre, NE Venezuela *10.28N 64.12W*
57 O5 **Cumanacoa** Sucre, NE Venezuela *10.16N 63.58W*
56 C13 **Cumbal, Nevado de** *elevation* S Colombia *0.51N 77.58W*
23 O7 **Cumberland** Kentucky, S USA *36.55N 83.00W*
23 U2 **Cumberland** Maryland, NE USA *39.39N 78.45W*
23 V6 **Cumberland** Virginia, NE USA *37.30N 78.13W*
197 A11 **Cumberland, Cape** *var.* Cape Nahoi. *headland* Espiritu Santo, N Vanuatu *14.39S 166.35E*
9 V14 **Cumberland House** Saskatchewan, C Canada *53.57N 102.21W*
25 W8 **Cumberland Island** *island* Georgia, SE USA
22 L7 **Cumberland, Lake** ⊠ Kentucky, S USA
16 O1 **Cumberland Peninsula** *peninsula* Baffin Island, Nunavut, NE Canada
2 N9 **Cumberland Plateau** *plateau* E USA
32 L1 **Cumberland Point** *headland* Michigan, N USA *47.51N 89.14W*
23 O7 **Cumberland River** ⛰ Kentucky/Tennessee, S USA
16 O2 **Cumberland Sound** *inlet* Baffin Island, Nunavut, NE Canada
98 I12 **Cumbernauld** S Scotland, UK *55.57N 4.00W*
99 K15 **Cumbria** *cultural region* NW England, UK
99 K15 **Cumbrian Mountains** ▲ NW England, UK
25 S2 **Cumming** Georgia, SE USA *34.12N 84.08W*
Cummin in Pommern *see* Kamień Pomorski
190 G9 **Cummins** South Australia *34.17S 135.43E*
98 I13 **Cumnock** W Scotland, UK *55.31N 4.28W*
42 G4 **Cumpas** Sonora, NW Mexico *30.00N 109.48W*
142 H16 **Çumra** Konya, C Turkey *37.32N 32.52E*
65 G15 **Cunco** Araucanía, C Chile *38.57S 72.13W*

56 E9 **Cundinamarca** *off.* Departamento de Cundinamarca. ◈ *province* C Colombia
43 U15 **Cunduacán** Tabasco, SE Mexico 18.00N 93.07W
85 C16 **Cunene** ◈ *province* S Angola
85 A16 **Cunene** *var.* Kunene. ⤳ Angola/Namibia *see also* Kunene
108 A9 **Cuneo** *Fr.* Coni. Piemonte, NW Italy 44.22N 7.31E
85 E15 **Cunjamba** Cuando Cubango, E Angola 15.22S 20.07E
189 V10 **Cunnamulla** Queensland, E Australia 28.09S 145.43E
Cuokkarašša *see* Čohkarášša
108 B7 **Cuorgne** Piemonte, NE Italy 45.23N 7.34E
98 K11 **Cupar** E Scotland, UK 56.19N 3.01W
118 L8 **Cupcina** *Rus.* Kupchino; *prev.* Calinisc, Kalinisk. N Moldova 48.07N 27.22E
56 C8 **Cupica** Chocó, W Colombia 6.43N 77.31W
56 C8 **Cupica, Golfo de** *gulf* W Colombia
114 N13 **Ćuprija** Serbia, E Serbia and Montenegro (Yugoslavia) 43.57N 21.21E
Cura *see* Villa de Cura
47 P16 **Curaçao** *island* Netherlands Antilles
58 H13 **Curanja, Río** ⤳ E Peru
58 F7 **Curaray, Rio** ⤳ Ecuador/Peru
118 K14 **Curcani** Călărași, SE Romania 44.04N 26.39E
190 H4 **Curdimurka** South Australia 29.27S 136.56E
105 P7 **Cure** ⤳ C France
181 Y16 **Curepipe** C Mauritius 20.19S 57.31E
57 R6 **Curiapo** Delta Amacuro, NE Venezuela 10.03N 63.05W
Curia Rhaetorum *see* Chur
64 G12 **Curicó** Maule, C Chile 35.00S 71.15W
Curieta *see* Krk
180 I15 **Curieuse** *island* Inner Islands, NE Seychelles
61 C16 **Curitiba** Acre, W Brazil 10.08S 69.00W
62 K12 **Curitiba** *prev.* Curytiba. *state capital* Paraná, S Brazil 25.25S 49.25W
62 J13 **Curitibanos** Santa Catarina, S Brazil 27.18S 50.34W
191 S6 **Curlewis** New South Wales, SE Australia 31.09S 150.18E
190 J6 **Curnamona** South Australia 31.39S 139.35E
85 A15 **Curoca** ⤳ SW Angola
191 T6 **Currabubula** New South Wales, SE Australia 31.17S 150.43E
61 Q14 **Currais Novos** Rio Grande do Norte, E Brazil 6.12S 36.30W
37 W7 **Currant** Nevada, W USA 38.43N 115.27W
37 W6 **Currant Mountain** ▲ Nevada, W USA 38.56N 115.19W
46 H2 **Current** Eleuthera Island, C Bahamas 25.24N 76.44W
29 W8 **Current River** ⤳ Arkansas/Missouri, C USA
190 M14 **Currie** Tasmania, SE Australia 39.59S 143.51E
23 Y8 **Currituck** North Carolina, SE USA 36.27N 76.02W
23 Y8 **Currituck Sound** *sound* North Carolina, SE USA
41 R11 **Curry** Alaska, USA 62.36N 150.00W
Curtbunar *see* Tervel
118 I13 **Curtea de Argeș** *var.* Curtea-de-Arges. Argeș, S Romania 45.06N 24.40E
118 E10 **Curtici** *Ger.* Kurtitsch, *Hung.* Kürtös. Arad, W Romania 46.21N 21.17E
30 M16 **Curtis** Nebraska, C USA 40.36N 100.27W
106 H2 **Curtis-Estación** Galicia, NW Spain 43.09N 8.10W
191 O14 **Curtis Group** *island group* Tasmania, SE Australia
189 Y8 **Curtis Island** *island* Queensland, SE Australia
60 K11 **Curuá, Ilha do** *island* NE Brazil
49 U7 **Curuá, Rio** ⤳ N Brazil
61 A14 **Curuçá, Rio** ⤳ NW Brazil
114 L9 **Čurug** *Hung.* Csurog. Serbia, N Serbia and Montenegro (Yugoslavia) 45.30N 20.02E
63 D16 **Curuzú Cuatiá** Corrientes, NE Argentina 29.45S 58.01W
61 M19 **Curvelo** Minas Gerais, SE Brazil 18.45S 44.27W
20 E14 **Curwensville** Pennsylvania, NE USA 40.57N 78.29W
32 M3 **Curwood, Mount** ▲ Michigan, N USA 46.42N 88.14W
Curytiba *see* Curitiba
Curzola *see* Korčula
44 A10 **Cuscatlán** ◈ *department* C El Salvador
59 H15 **Cusco** *var.* Cuzco. Cusco, C Peru 13.34S 72.01W
59 H15 **Cusco** *off.* Departamento de Cusco; *var.* Cuzco. ◈ *department* C Peru
29 O9 **Cushing** Oklahoma, C USA 36.01N 96.46W
27 W8 **Cushing** Texas, SW USA 31.48N 94.50W
42 I6 **Cusihuiriachic** Chihuahua, N Mexico 28.16N 106.46W
105 P10 **Cusset** Allier, C France 46.07N 3.27E
25 S6 **Cusseta** Georgia, SE USA 32.18N 84.46W
30 J10 **Custer** South Dakota, N USA 43.46N 103.36W
Cüstrin *see* Kostrzyn
35 Q7 **Cut Bank** Montana, NW USA 48.37N 112.19W
Cutch, Gulf of *see* Kachchh, Gulf of
25 S6 **Cuthbert** Georgia, SE USA 31.46N 84.47W
9 S15 **Cut Knife** Saskatchewan, S Canada 52.40N 108.54W
25 Y16 **Cutler Ridge** Florida, SE USA 25.34N 80.21W
24 K10 **Cut Off** Louisiana, S USA 29.32N 90.20W
65 I15 **Cutral-Có** Neuquén, C Argentina 38.55S 69.13W
109 O21 **Cutro** Calabria, SW Italy 39.01N 16.59E
191 O4 **Cuttaburra Channels** *seasonal river* New South Wales, SE Australia
160 O12 **Cuttack** Orissa, E India 20.28N 85.52E
85 C15 **Cuvelai** Cunene, SW Angola 15.40S 15.48E
81 G18 **Cuvette** *var.* Région de la Cuvette. ◈ *province* C Congo
181 V9 **Cuvier Basin** *undersea feature* E Indian Ocean
181 U9 **Cuvier Plateau** *undersea feature* E Indian Ocean
84 B12 **Cuvo** ⤳ W Angola
102 H9 **Cuxhaven** Niedersachsen, NW Germany 53.51N 8.42E
Cuyabá *see* Cuiabá
179 Pp13 **Cuyo East Pass** *passage* C Philippines
179 P13 **Cuyo West Pass** *passage* C Philippines
Cuyuni, Río *see* Cuyuni River
57 S8 **Cuyuni River** *var.* Río Cuyuni. ⤳ Guyana/Venezuela
Cuzco *see* Cusco
99 K22 **Cwmbran** *Wel.* Cwmbrân. SW Wales, UK 51.39N 3.00W
30 K15 **C.W.McConaughy, Lake** ⊠ Nebraska, C USA
83 D20 **Cyangugu** SW Rwanda 2.27S 29.00E
112 D11 **Cybinka** *Ger.* Ziebingen. Lubuskie, W Poland 52.11N 14.46E
Cyclades *see* Kykládes
Cydonia *see* Chaniá
Cymru *see* Wales
22 M5 **Cynthiana** Kentucky, S USA 38.23N 84.17W
9 S17 **Cypress Hills** ▲▲ Alberta/Saskatchewan, SW Canada
Cypro-Syrian Basin *see* Cyprus Basin
123 Mm1 **Cyprus** *off.* Republic of Cyprus, *Gk.* Kypros, *Turk.* Kıbrıs, Kıbrıs Cumhuriyeti. ◆ *republic* E Mediterranean Sea
86 L14 **Cyprus** *Gk.* Kypros, *Turk.* Kıbrıs. *island* E Mediterranean Sea
123 Gg10 **Cyprus Basin** *var.* Cypro-Syrian Basin. *undersea feature* E Mediterranean Sea
Cythera *see* Kýthira
Cythnos *see* Kýthnos
112 F9 **Czaplinek** *Ger.* Tempelburg. Zachodniopomorskie, NW Poland 53.33N 16.14E
Czarna Woda *see* Wda
112 G8 **Czarne** Pomorskie, N Poland 53.40N 17.00E
112 G10 **Czarnków** Wielkopolskie, C Poland 52.52N 16.31E
113 E17 **Czech Republic** *Cz.* Česká Republika. ◆ *republic* C Europe
Czegléd *see* Cegléd
112 G12 **Czempiń** Wielkolpolskie, C Poland 52.10N 16.46E
Czenstochau *see* Częstochowa
Czerkow *see* Čerchov
Czernowitz *see* Chernivtsi
112 I8 **Czersk** Pomorskie, N Poland 53.48N 17.58E
113 J15 **Częstochowa** *Ger.* Czenstochau, Tschenstochau, *Rus.* Chenstokhov. Śląskie, S Poland 50.51N 19.09E
112 F10 **Człopa** *Ger.* Schloppe. Zachodniopomorskie, NW Poland 53.04N 16.04E
112 H8 **Człuchów** *Ger.* Schlochau. Pomorskie, NW Poland 53.40N 17.19E

D

169 V9 **Da'an** *var.* Dalai. Jilin, NE China 45.28N 124.18E
13 S10 **Daaquam** Quebec, SE Canada 46.36N 70.03W
Daawo, Webi *see* Dawa Wenz
56 I4 **Dabajuro** Falcón, NW Venezuela 11.00N 70.41W
79 N15 **Dabakala** NE Ivory Coast 8.19N 4.24W
Daban *see* Bairin Youqi
113 K23 **Dabas** Pest, C Hungary 47.13N 19.18E
166 L8 **Daba Shan** ▲▲ C China
146 J5 **Dabbāgh, Jabal** ▲ NW Saudi Arabia 27.52N 35.48E
56 D8 **Dabeiba** Antioquia, NW Colombia 6.57N 76.13W
160 E11 **Dabhoi** Gujarāt, W India 22.07N 73.28E
167 P8 **Dabie Shan** ▲▲ C China
78 J13 **Dabola** Haute-Guinée, C Guinea 10.48N 11.01W
79 N17 **Dabou** S Ivory Coast 5.19N 4.22W
112 P8 **Dąbrowa Białostocka** Podlaskie, NE Poland 53.38N 23.18E
113 M16 **Dąbrowa Tarnowska** Małopolskie, S Poland 50.10N 21.00E
121 M20 **Dabryn'** *Rus.* Dobryn'. Homyel'skaya Voblasts', SE Belarus 51.46N 29.12E
165 P10 **Dabsan Hu** ◎ C China
167 Q13 **Dabu** *prev.* Huliao. Guangdong, S China 24.19N 116.07E
118 H15 **Dăbuleni** Dolj, SW Romania 43.47N 24.05E
Dacca *see* Dhaka
103 L23 **Dachau** Bayern, SE Germany 48.16N 11.25E
166 K8 **Dachuan** *prev.* Daxian, Da Xian. Sichuan, C China 31.16N 107.31E
Dacia Bank *see* Dacia Seamount
66 M10 **Dacia Seamount** *var.* Dacia Bank. *undersea feature* E Atlantic Ocean 31.10N 13.42W
39 T3 **Dacono** Colorado, C USA 40.04N 104.56W
Đắc Tô *see* Đak Tô
Dacura *see* Dákura
25 W12 **Dade City** Florida, SE USA 28.21N 82.12W
158 L10 **Dadeldhura** *var.* Dandeldhura. Far Western, W Nepal 29.12N 80.31E
25 Q5 **Dadeville** Alabama, S USA 32.49N 85.45W
105 N15 **Dadou** ⤳ S France
160 D12 **Dādra and Nagar Haveli** ◈ *union territory* W India
155 P14 **Dādu** Sind, SE Pakistan 26.42N 67.48E
178 K11 **Da Du Bǒloc** Kon Tum, C Vietnam 14.06N 107.40E
166 G9 **Dadu He** ⤳ C China
Daegu *see* Taegu
Daerah Istimewa Aceh *see* Aceh
179 Q11 **Daet** Luzon, N Philippines 14.06N 122.57E
166 I11 **Dafang** Guizhou, S China 27.07N 105.40E
159 W11 **Dafla Hills** ▲▲ NE India
9 U15 **Dafoe** Saskatchewan, S Canada 51.46N 104.11W
78 G10 **Dagana** N Senegal 16.28N 15.35W
Dagana *see* Dahana, Tajikistan
Dagana *see* Massakory, Chad
120 K11 **Dagda** Krāslava, SE Latvia 56.06N 27.36E
Dagden *see* Hiiumaa
Dagden-Sund *see* Soela Väin
131 P16 **Dagestan, Respublika** *prev.* Dagestanskaya ASSR, *Eng.* Daghestan. ◈ *autonomous republic* SW Russian Federation
Dagestanskaya ASSR *see* Dagestan, Respublika
131 R17 **Dagestanskiye Ogni** Respublika Dagestan, SW Russian Federation 42.09N 48.08E
193 A23 **Dagg Sound** *sound* South Island, NZ
Daghestan *see* Dagestan, Respublika
147 Y8 **Daghmar** NE Oman 23.09N 59.01E
Dağliq Qarabağ *see* Nagornyy Karabakh
Dagö *see* Hiiumaa
56 D11 **Dagua** Valle del Cauca, W Colombia 3.37N 76.42W
166 H11 **Daguan** Yunnan, SW China 27.42N 103.51E
179 P9 **Dagupan** *off.* Dagupan City. Luzon, N Philippines 16.04N 120.21E
165 N16 **Dagzê** Xizang Zizhiqu, W China 29.38N 91.15E
153 Q13 **Dahana** *Rus.* Dagana, Dakhana. SW Tajikistan 38.03N 69.51E
169 V10 **Dahei Shan** ▲▲ N China
169 T7 **Da Hinggan Ling** *Eng.* Great Khingan Range. ▲▲ NE China
Dahlac Archipelago *see* Dahlak Archipelago
82 K9 **Dahlak Archipelago** *var.* Dahlac Archipelago. *island group* E Eritrea
25 T2 **Dahlonega** Georgia, SE USA 34.31N 83.59W
103 O14 **Dahme** Brandenburg, E Germany 52.10N 13.47E
102 O13 **Dahme** ⤳ E Germany
147 O14 **Dahm, Ramlat** *desert* NW Yemen
160 E10 **Dāhod** *prev.* Dohad. Gujarāt, W India 22.48N 74.18E
Dahomey *see* Benin
164 G10 **Dahongliutan** Xinjiang Uygur Zizhiqu, NW China 35.59N 79.12E
Dahra *see* Dara
145 R2 **Dahūk** *var.* Dohuk, *Kurd.* Dihōk. N Iraq 36.52N 43.01E
118 J15 **Daia** Giurgiu, S Romania 44.00N 25.59E
171 L15 **Daigo** Ibaraki, Honshū, S Japan 36.43N 140.22E
169 O13 **Dai Hai** ◎ N China
Daihoku *see* T'aipei
195 X14 **Dai Island** *island* N Solomon Islands
177 G8 **Daik-u** Pegu, SW Myanmar 17.46N 96.40E
144 H9 **Dā'īl** Dar'ā, S Syria 32.45N 36.07E
178 Kk12 **Dai Lanh** Khanh Hoa, S Vietnam 12.49N 109.20E
167 Q13 **Daimao Shan** ▲▲ SE China
107 N11 **Daimiel** Castilla-La Mancha, C Spain 39.04N 3.37W
117 F22 **Daimonía** Pelopónnisos, S Greece 36.38N 22.54E
Dainan *see* T'ainan
27 W6 **Daingerfield** Texas, SW USA 33.01N 94.43W
Daingin, Bá an *see* Dingle Bay
165 R13 **Dainkognubma** Xizang Zizhiqu, W China 32.26N 97.58E
171 Hh17 **Daiō-zaki** *headland* Honshū, SW Japan 34.15N 136.50E
Dairbhre *see* Valencia Island
63 B22 **Daireaux** Buenos Aires, E Argentina 36.36S 61.42W
Dairen *see* Dalian
77 W9 **Dairûț** *var.* Dayrûț. C Egypt 27.31N 30.46E
170 Ff12 **Dai-sen** ▲ Kyūshū, SW Japan 35.22N 133.33E
27 X10 **Daisetta** Texas, SW USA 30.06N 94.38W
199 Gg5 **Daitō-jima** *island group* SW Japan
199 Gg5 **Daitō Ridge** *undersea feature* N Philippine Sea
167 N3 **Daixian** *var.* Dai Xian. Shanxi, C China 39.07N 112.54E
167 Q12 **Daiyun Shan** ▲▲ SE China
46 M8 **Dajabón** NW Dominican Republic 19.29N 71.40W
166 G6 **Dajin Chuan** ⤳ C China
154 J6 **Dak** ◎ W Afghanistan
78 F11 **Dakar** ● (Senegal) W Senegal 14.43N 17.27W
78 F11 **Dakar** ✕ W Senegal 14.42N 17.27W
178 K11 **Đak Glây** Kon Tum, C Vietnam 15.05N 107.42E
Dakhana *see* Dahana
159 U16 **Dakhin Shahbazpur Island** *island* S Bangladesh
Dakhla *see* Ad Dakhla
78 F7 **Dakhlet Nouâdhibou** ◈ *region* NW Mauritania
Đak Lap *see* Kiên Đưc
178 K13 **Đak Nông** Đăc Lăc, S Vietnam 11.58N 107.42E
79 U11 **Dakoro** Maradi, S Niger 14.28N 6.45E
31 U12 **Dakota City** Iowa, C USA 42.42N 94.13W
31 R13 **Dakota City** Nebraska, C USA 42.25N 96.25W
115 M17 **Đakovica** *var.* Djakovica, *Alb.* Gjakovë. Serbia, S Serbia and Montenegro (Yugoslavia) 42.22N 20.30E
114 I10 **Đakovo** *var.* Djakovo, *Hung.* Diakovár. Osijek-Baranja, E Croatia 45.18N 18.24E
Dakshin *see* Deccan
178 K11 **Đak Tô** *var.* Đăc Tô. Kon Tum, C Vietnam 14.35N 107.55E
45 N7 **Dákura** *var.* Dacura. Región Autónoma Atlántico Norte, NE Nicaragua 14.22N 83.13W
97 I14 **Dal** Akershus, S Norway 60.19N 11.16E
84 E12 **Dala** Lunda Sul, E Angola 11.03S 20.12E
110 J8 **Dalaas** Vorarlberg, W Austria 47.08N 10.03E
78 I13 **Dalaba** Moyenne-Guinée, W Guinea 10.46N 12.12W
Dalai *see* Da'an
Dalain Hob *see* Ejin Qi
Dalai Nor *see* Hulun Nur
169 Q11 **Dalai Nur** *salt lake* N China
Dala-Jarna *see* Järna
97 M14 **Dalälven** ⤳ C Sweden
142 C16 **Dalaman** Muğla, SW Turkey 36.46N 28.46E
142 C16 **Dalaman** ✕ Muğla, SW Turkey 36.37N 28.51E
142 D16 **Dalaman Çayı** ⤳ SW Turkey
168 K11 **Dalandzadgad** Ömnögovĭ, S Mongolia 43.35N 104.23E
97 D17 **Dalane** *physical region* S Norway
201 Z2 **Dalap-Uliga-Djarrit** *var.* Delap-Uliga-Darrit, D-U-D. *island group* Ratak Chain, SE Marshall Islands
96 J12 **Dalarna** *prev.* Kopparberg ◈ *county* C Sweden
96 L13 **Dalarna** *prev. Eng.* Dalecarlia. *cultural region* C Sweden
97 P16 **Dalarö** Stockholm, C Sweden 59.07N 18.25E
178 Kk13 **Đa Lat** Lâm Đông, S Vietnam 11.55N 108.25E
168 J11 **Dalay** Ömnögovĭ, S Mongolia 43.27N 103.30E
154 L12 **Dālbandīn** *var.* Dāl Bandin. Baluchistān, SW Pakistan 28.48N 64.08E
97 J17 **Dalbosjön** *lake bay* S Sweden
189 Y10 **Dalby** Queensland, E Australia 27.14S 151.16E
96 D13 **Dale** Hordaland, S Norway 60.34N 5.48E
96 C12 **Dale** Sogn og Fjordane, S Norway 61.22N 5.24E
34 K12 **Dale** Oregon, NW USA 44.58N 118.56W
27 T11 **Dale** Texas, SW USA 29.56N 97.34W
Dalecarlia *see* Dalarna
23 W4 **Dale City** Virginia, NE USA 38.38N 77.18W
22 L8 **Dale Hollow Lake** ⊠ Kentucky/Tennessee, S USA
100 O8 **Dalen** Drenthe, NE Netherlands 52.42N 6.45E
97 E15 **Dalen** Telemark, S Norway 59.25N 7.58E
177 F4 **Daletme** Chin State, W Myanmar 21.44N 92.48E
25 Q7 **Daleville** Alabama, S USA 31.18N 85.42W
100 M9 **Dalfsen** Overijssel, E Netherlands 52.31N 6.16E
26 M1 **Dalhart** Texas, SW USA 36.04N 102.31W
11 O13 **Dalhousie** New Brunswick, SE Canada 48.03N 66.22W
158 I6 **Dalhousie** Himāchal Pradesh, N India 32.31N 76.01E
166 F12 **Dali** *var.* Xiaguan. Yunnan, SW China 25.33N 100.10E
Dali *see* Idálion
169 U14 **Dalian** *var.* Dairen, Dalien, Lüda, Ta-lien, *Rus.* Dalny. Liaoning, NE China 38.53N 121.36E
107 O15 **Dalías** Andalucía, S Spain 36.49N 2.50W
Dalien *see* Dalian
Dalijan *see* Delijān
114 J9 **Dalj** *Hung.* Dalja. Osijek-Baranja, E Croatia 45.29N 19.00E
Dalja *see* Dalj
34 F12 **Dallas** Oregon, NW USA 44.55N 123.19W
27 U6 **Dallas** Texas, SW USA 32.46N 96.48W
27 T7 **Dallas-Fort Worth** ✕ Texas, SW USA 32.37N 97.16W
160 K12 **Dalli Rājhara** Madhya Pradesh, C India 20.33N 81.04E
41 X15 **Dall Island** *island* Alexander Archipelago, Alaska, USA
40 M12 **Dall Lake** ◎ Alaska, USA
79 S12 **Dallol Bosso** *seasonal river* W Niger
147 U7 **Dalmā** *island* W UAE
115 E14 **Dalmacija** *Eng.* Dalmatia, *Ger.* Dalmatien, *It.* Dalmazia. *cultural region* S Croatia
Dalmatia/Dalmatien/Dalmazia *see* Dalmacija
127 Nn17 **Dal'negorsk** Primorskiy Kray, SE Russian Federation 44.27N 135.30E
127 Nn17 **Dal'nerechensk** Primorskiy Kray, SE Russian Federation 45.57N 133.42E
Dalny *see* Dalian
78 M16 **Daloa** C Ivory Coast 6.52N 6.28W
166 J11 **Dalou Shan** ▲▲ S China
189 X7 **Dalrymple Lake** ◎ Queensland, E Australia
12 H14 **Dalrymple Lake** ◎ Ontario, S Canada
189 X7 **Dalrymple, Mount** ▲ Queensland, E Australia 21.01S 148.34E
95 K20 **Dalsbruk** *Fin.* Taalintehdas. Länsi-Suomi, W Finland 60.01N 22.33E
97 K19 **Dalsjöfors** Västra Götaland, S Sweden 57.43N 13.04E
97 J17 **Dals Långed** *var.* Långed. Västra Götaland, S Sweden 58.54N 12.20E
159 O15 **Dāltenganj** *prev.* Daltonganj. Bihār, N India 23.59N 84.07E
25 R2 **Dalton** Georgia, SE USA 34.46N 84.58W
Daltonganj *see* Dāltenganj
205 X14 **Dalton Iceberg Tongue** *ice feature* Antarctica
94 J1 **Dalvík** Nordhurland Eystra, N Iceland 65.58N 18.31W
37 N8 **Daly City** California, W USA 37.44N 122.27W
189 P2 **Daly River** ⤳ Northern Territory, N Australia
189 Q3 **Daly Waters** Northern Territory, N Australia 16.21S 133.21E
121 F20 **Damachava** *var.* Damachova, *Pol.* Domaczewo, *Rus.* Domachëvo. Brestskaya Voblasts', SW Belarus 51.45N 23.36E
Damachova *see* Damachava
79 W11 **Damagaram Takaya** Zinder, S Niger 14.02N 9.28E
160 D12 **Damān** Damān and Diu, W India 20.25N 72.58E
160 B12 **Damān and Diu** ◈ *union territory* W India
77 V7 **Damanhûr** *anc.* Hermopolis Parva. N Egypt 31.02N 30.34E
Damão *see* Damān
167 O1 **Damaqun Shan** ▲▲ E China
81 I15 **Damara** Ombella-Mpoko, S Central African Republic 5.00N 18.45E
85 D18 **Damaraland** *physical region* C Namibia
175 T15 **Damar, Kepulauan** *var.* Baraf Daja Islands, Kepulauan Barat Daya. *island group* C Indonesia
174 Gg4 **Damar Laut** Perak, Peninsular Malaysia 4.13N 100.36E
175 Tt15 **Damar, Pulau** *island* Maluku, E Indonesia
Damas *see* Dimashq
79 Y12 **Damasak** Borno, NE Nigeria 13.10N 12.40E
Damasco *see* Dimashq
23 Q8 **Damascus** Virginia, NE USA 36.37N 81.46W
Damascus *see* Dimashq
79 X13 **Damaturu** Yobe, NE Nigeria 11.44N 11.58E
175 Ss4 **Damau** Pulau Kaburuang, N Indonesia 3.46N 126.49E
149 O5 **Damāvand, Qolleh-ye** ▲ N Iran 35.59N 52.06E
84 B10 **Damba** Uíge, NW Angola 6.42S 15.07E
116 M12 **Dambaslar** Tekirdağ, NW Turkey 41.13N 27.13E
118 J13 **Dâmbovița** *prev.* Dîmbovița. ◈ *county* SE Romania
118 J13 **Dâmbovița** *prev.* Dîmbovița. ⤳ S Romania
181 Y15 **D'Ambre, Île** *island* NE Mauritius
161 K24 **Dambulla** Central Province, C Sri Lanka 7.51N 80.40E
46 K9 **Dame-Marie** SW Haiti 18.31N 74.24W
46 J9 **Dame Marie, Cap** *headland* SW Haiti 18.37N 74.24W
149 Q4 **Dāmghān** Semnān, N Iran 36.13N 54.22E
Damietta *see* Dumyāt
144 G10 **Dāmiyā** Al Balqā', NW Jordan 32.07N 35.33E
152 G11 **Damla** Dashkhovuzskiy Velayat, N Turkmenistan 40.05N 59.15E
Dammām *see* Ad Dammān
102 G12 **Damme** Niedersachsen, NW Germany 52.31N 8.12E
159 R15 **Dāmodar** ⤳ NE India
160 J9 **Damoh** Madhya Pradesh, C India 23.50N 79.24E
79 P15 **Damongo** NW Ghana 9.06N 1.49W
144 G7 **Damoûr** *var.* Ad Dāmūr. W Lebanon 33.36N 35.30E
175 Pp7 **Dampal, Teluk** *bay* Sulawesi, C Indonesia
188 H7 **Dampier** Western Australia 20.40S 116.40E
188 H6 **Dampier Archipelago** *island group* Western Australia
176 Uu9 **Dampier, Selat** *strait* Papua, E Indonesia
194 L12 **Dampier Strait** *strait* NE PNG
147 U14 **Damqawt** *var.* Damqut. E Yemen 16.35N 52.39E
165 O13 **Dam Qu** ⤳ C China
Damqut *see* Damqawt
178 Ii13 **Dâmrei, Chuŏr Phmun** *Fr.* Chaîne de l'Éléphant. ▲▲ SW Cambodia
110 C7 **Damvant** Jura, NW Switzerland 47.22N 6.55E
Damwâld *see* Damwoude
100 L5 **Damwoude** *Fris.* Damwâld. Friesland, N Netherlands 53.18N 5.59E
165 N15 **Damxung** Xizang Zizhiqu, W China 30.28N 91.01E
82 K11 **Danakil Desert** *var.* Afar Depression, Danakil Plain. *desert* E Africa
Danakil Plain *see* Danakil Desert
37 R8 **Dana, Mount** ▲ California, W USA 37.54N 119.13W
78 L16 **Danané** W Ivory Coast 7.16N 8.09W
178 Kk10 **Đà Nẵng** *prev.* Tourane. Quang Nam-Da Nẵng, C Vietnam 16.04N 108.13E
179 Qq13 **Danao** *var.* Danao City. Cebu, C Philippines 10.34N 124.00E
166 G9 **Danba** Sichuan, C China 30.54N 101.49E
Danborg *see* Daneborg
20 L13 **Danbury** Connecticut, NE USA 41.21N 73.27W
27 W12 **Danbury** Texas, SW USA 29.13N 95.20W
37 X15 **Danby Lake** ◎ California, W USA 34.13N 115.07W
204 H4 **Danco Coast** *physical region* Antarctica
84 B11 **Dande** ⤳ NW Angola
Dandeldhura *see* Dadeldhura
161 E17 **Dandeli** Karnātaka, W India 15.18N 74.42E
191 O12 **Dandenong** Victoria, SE Australia 38.01S 145.13E
169 V13 **Dandong** *var.* Tan-tung; *prev.* An-tung. Liaoning, NE China 40.09N 124.23E
207 Q14 **Daneborg** *var.* Danborg. Tunu, N Greenland 74.34N 19.51W
118 I14 **Draganești-Olt** Olt, S Romania 44.06N 25.00E
27 V12 **Danevang** Texas, SW USA 29.03N 96.11W
Dänew *see* Deynau
12 L12 **Danford Lake** Quebec, SE Canada 45.55N 76.12W
21 T4 **Danforth** Maine, NE USA 45.39N 67.54W
39 P3 **Danforth Hills** ▲▲ Colorado, C USA
Dangara *see* Danghara
165 V12 **Dangchang** Gansu, C China 34.01N 104.19E
Dangchengwan *see* Subei
84 B10 **Dange** Uíge, NW Angola 7.55S 15.01E
Dangerous Archipelago *see* Tuamotu, Îles
85 E26 **Danger Point** *headland* SW South Africa 34.37S 19.20E
153 Q13 **Danghara** *Rus.* Dangara. SW Tajikistan 38.04N 69.14E
165 P8 **Danghe Nanshan** ▲▲ W China
82 I12 **Dangila** *var.* Dāngilā. Amhara, NW Ethiopia 11.08N 36.51E
165 P8 **Dangjin Shankou** *pass* N China 39.22N 94.19E
Dangla *see* Tanggula Shan
Dāngilā *see* Dangila, NW Ethiopia
Dangme Chu *see* Manās
159 Y11 **Dāngori** Assam, NE India 27.40N 95.34E
Dang Raek, Phanom/Dangrek, Chaîne des *see* Dângrêk, Chuŏr Phnum
178 Ii11 **Dângrêk, Chuŏr Phnum** *var.* Phanom Dang Raek, Phanom Dong Rak, *Fr.* Chaîne des Dangrek. ▲▲ Cambodia/Thailand
44 G3 **Dangriga** *prev.* Stann Creek. Stann Creek, E Belize 16.58N 88.13W
167 P6 **Dangshan** Anhui, E China 34.28N 116.24E
35 T15 **Daniel** Wyoming, C USA 42.49N 110.04W
85 H22 **Daniëlskuil** Northern Cape, N South Africa 28.07S 23.35E
21 N12 **Danielson** Connecticut, NE USA 41.48N 71.53W
128 M15 **Danilov** Yaroslavskaya Oblast', W Russian Federation 58.11N 40.11E
131 O9 **Danilovka** Volgogradskaya Oblast', SW Russian Federation 50.21N 44.03E
Danish West Indies *see* Virgin Islands (US)
166 L7 **Dan Jiang** ⤳ C China
166 M7 **Danjiangkou Shuiku** ⊠ C China
147 W8 **Dank** *var.* Dhank. NW Oman 23.34N 56.16E
158 J7 **Dankhar** Himāchal Pradesh, N India 32.07N 78.12E
130 L6 **Dankov** Lipetskaya Oblast', W Russian Federation 53.17N 39.07E
44 J7 **Danlí** El Paraíso, S Honduras 14.02N 86.34W
Danmark *see* Denmark
Danmarksstraedet *see* Denmark Strait
97 O14 **Dannemora** Uppsala, C Sweden 60.13N 17.49E
20 L6 **Dannemora** New York, NE USA 44.42N 73.42W
102 K11 **Dannenberg** Niedersachsen, N Germany 53.05N 11.06E
192 N12 **Dannevirke** Manawatu-Wanganui, North Island, NZ 40.13S 176.04E
23 U8 **Dan River** ⤳ Virginia, NE USA
178 Hh9 **Dan Sai** Loei, C Thailand 17.15N 101.04E
20 F10 **Dansville** New York, NE USA 42.34N 77.40W
Dantzig *see* Gdańsk
88 E12 **Danube** *Bul.* Dunav, *Cz.* Dunaj, *Ger.* Donau, *Hung.* Duna, *Rom.* Dunărea. ⤳ C Europe
Danubian Plain *see* Dunavska Ravnina
177 Ff8 **Danubyu** Irrawaddy, SW Myanmar 17.15N 95.34E
Danum *see* Doncaster
21 P11 **Danvers** Massachusetts, NE USA 42.34N 70.54W
29 T11 **Danville** Arkansas, C USA 35.03N 93.23W
33 N13 **Danville** Illinois, N USA 40.10N 87.37W
33 O14 **Danville** Indiana, N USA 39.45N 86.31W
31 Y15 **Danville** Iowa, C USA 40.52N 91.18W
22 M6 **Danville** Kentucky, S USA 37.39N 84.46W
20 G14 **Danville** Pennsylvania, NE USA 40.57N 76.36W
23 T6 **Danville** Virginia, NE USA 36.35N 79.24W
Danxian/Dan Xian *see* Danzhou
166 L17 **Danzhou** *prev.* Danxian, Dan Xian, Nada. Hainan, S China 19.31N 109.31E
Danzig *see* Gdańsk
Danziger Bucht *see* Danzig, Gulf of
112 J6 **Danzig, Gulf of** *var.* Gulf of Gdańsk, *Ger.* Danziger Bucht, *Pol.* Zakota Gdańska, *Rus.* Gdan'skaya Bukhta. *gulf* N Poland
166 F10 **Daocheng** Sichuan, C China 29.05N 100.14E
Daokou *see* Huaxian
106 H7 **Dão, Rio** ⤳ N Portugal
Daosa *see* Dausa
79 Y7 **Dao Timmi** Agadez, NE Niger 20.31N 13.34E
166 M13 **Daoxian** *var.* Dao Xian. Hunan, S China 25.30N 111.37E
79 Q14 **Dapaong** N Togo 10.52N 0.12E
25 N8 **Daphne** Alabama, S USA 30.36N 87.54W
179 Qq15 **Dapitan** Mindanao, S Philippines 8.39N 123.25E
165 P9 **Da Qaidam** Qinghai, C China 37.49N 95.18E
169 V8 **Daqing** Heilongjiang, NE China 46.29N 125.07E
169 O13 **Daqing Shan** ▲▲ N China
Daqm *see* Duqm
145 T5 **Dāqūq** *var.* Tāwūq. N Iraq 35.07N 44.27E
78 G10 **Dara** *var.* Dahra. NW Senegal 15.20N 15.28W
144 H9 **Dar'ā** *var.* Der'a, *Fr.* Déraa. Dar'ā, SW Syria 32.37N 36.06E
144 H8 **Dar'ā** *off.* Muḥāfaẓat Dar'ā, *var.* Darā, Derá, Derrá. ◈ *governorate* S Syria
149 Q12 **Dārāb** Fārs, S Iran 28.52N 54.25E
118 K8 **Darabani** Botoșani, NW Romania 48.10N 26.40E
Daraj *see* Dirj
148 M8 **Dārān** Eṣfahān, W Iran 33.02N 50.27E
178 Kk12 **Đa Răng, Sông** *var.* Ba. ⤳ S Vietnam
126 Kk16 **Darasun** Chitinskaya Oblast', S Russian Federation 51.36N 113.58E
Daraut-Kurgan *see* Daroot-Korgon
79 W13 **Darazo** Bauchi, E Nigeria 11.01N 10.27E
145 S3 **Darband** N Iraq 36.15N 44.17E
145 V4 **Darband-i Khān, Sadd** *dam* NE Iraq 35.07N 45.42E
145 N1 **Darbāsīyah** *var.* Derbisīye. Al Ḥasakah, N Syria 37.06N 40.42E
120 C11 **Darbėnai** Kretinga, NW Lithuania 56.02N 21.16E
159 Q13 **Darbhanga** Bihār, N India 26.10N 85.54E
40 M9 **Darby, Cape** *headland* Alaska, USA 64.19N 162.46W
114 I9 **Darda** *Hung.* Dárda. Osijek-Baranja, E Croatia 45.37N 18.41E
29 T11 **Dardanelle** Arkansas, C USA 35.13N 93.09W
29 S11 **Dardanelle, Lake** ⊠ Arkansas, C USA
Dardanelles *see* Çanakkale Boğazı
Dardanelli *see* Çanakkale
Dar-el-Beida *see* Casablanca
142 M14 **Darende** Malatya, C Turkey 38.33N 37.31E
83 J22 **Dar es Salaam** Dar es Salaam, E Tanzania 6.51S 39.18E
83 J22 **Dar es Salaam** ✕ Pwani, E Tanzania 6.57S 39.17E
193 H18 **Darfield** Canterbury, South Island, NZ 43.28S 172.07E
108 F7 **Darfo** Lombardia, N Italy 45.54N 10.12E
82 B10 **Darfur** *var.* Darfur Massif. *cultural region* W Sudan
Darfur Massif *see* Darfur
152 J10 **Dargan-Ata** *var.* Darganata. Lebapskiy Velayat, NE Turkmenistan 40.30N 62.09E
Darganata *see* Dargan-Ata
149 T3 **Dargaz** *var.* Darreh Gaz; *prev.* Moḥammadābād. Khorāsān, NE Iran 37.28N 59.08E
145 U4 **Dargazayn** NE Iraq 35.39N 45.00E
191 P12 **Dargo** Victoria, SE Australia 37.29S 147.15E
168 K7 **Darhan** Bulgan, C Mongolia 48.07N 103.54E
169 N8 **Darhan** Hentiy, C Mongolia 46.38N 109.25E
168 L6 **Darhan** Selenge, N Mongolia 49.24N 105.57E
169 N12 **Darhan Muminggan Lianheqi** *var.* Bailingmiao. Nei Mongol Zizhiqu, N China 41.41N 110.25E
25 W7 **Darien** Georgia, SE USA 31.22N 81.25W
45 W16 **Darién** *off.* Provincia del Darién. ◈ *province* SE Panama
Darién, Golfo del *see* Darien, Gulf of
45 X14 **Darien, Gulf of** *Sp.* Golfo del Darién. *gulf* S Caribbean Sea
Darien, Isthmus of *see* Panamá, Istmo de
44 K9 **Dariense, Cordillera** ▲▲ C Nicaragua
45 W15 **Darién, Serranía del** ▲▲ Colombia/Panama
Dario *see* Ciudad Darío
Dariorigum *see* Vannes
Dariv *see* Darvi
Darj *see* Dirj
Darjeeling *see* Darjiling
159 S12 **Darjiling** *prev.* Darjeeling. West Bengal, NE India 27.00N 88.13E
Darkehnen *see* Ozersk
165 S12 **Darlag** Qinghai, C China 33.43N 99.42E
191 T3 **Darling Downs** *hill range* Queensland, E Australia
30 M2 **Darling, Lake** ⊠ North Dakota, N USA
188 I12 **Darling Range** ▲▲ Western Australia
190 L8 **Darling River** ⤳ New South Wales, SE Australia
99 M15 **Darlington** N England, UK 54.31N 1.34W
23 T12 **Darlington** South Carolina, SE USA 34.18N 79.52W
32 K9 **Darlington** Wisconsin, N USA 42.40N 90.07W
112 G7 **Darłowo** Zachodniopomorskie, NW Poland 54.24N 16.21E
103 G19 **Darmstadt** Hessen, SW Germany 49.52N 8.39E
77 S7 **Darnah** *var.* Dérna. NE Libya 32.46N 22.39E
105 S6 **Darney** Vosges, NE France 48.06N 5.58E
190 M7 **Darnick** New South Wales, SE Australia 32.52S 143.38E
205 Y6 **Darnley, Cape** *headland* Antarctica 67.36S 70.04E
107 R7 **Daroca** Aragón, NE Spain 41.07N 1.25W
153 S11 **Daroot-Korgon** *var.* Daraut-Kurgan. Oshskaya Oblast', SW Kyrgyzstan 39.34N 72.13E
63 A23 **Darregueira** *var.* Darreguéira. Buenos Aires, E Argentina 37.40S 63.12W
Darreguéira *see* Darregueira
Darreh Gaz *see* Dargaz
148 K7 **Darreh Shahr** *var.* Darreh-ye Shahr. Īlām, W Iran 33.10N 47.18E
Darreh-ye Shahr *see* Darreh Shahr
34 I7 **Darrington** Washington, NW USA 48.15N 121.36W
27 P1 **Darrouzett** Texas, SW USA 36.27N 100.19W

◆ Country ● Country Capital ◇ Dependent Territory ○ Dependent Territory Capital ◈ Administrative Region ✕ International Airport ▲ Mountain ▲▲ Mountain Range Volcano ⤳ River ◎ Lake ⊠ Reservoir

159 S15 **Darsana** *var.* Darshana. Khulna, N Bangladesh *23.31N 88.49E*
Darshana *see* Darsana
102 M7 **Darss** *peninsula* NE Germany
102 M7 **Darsser Ort** *headland* NE Germany *54.28N 12.31E*
99 J24 **Dart** ⁂ SW England, UK
Dartang *see* Baqên
99 P22 **Dartford** SE England, UK *51.27N 0.13E*
190 L12 **Dartmoor** Victoria, SE Australia *37.56S 141.18E*
99 I24 **Dartmoor** *moorland* SW England, UK
11 Q15 **Dartmouth** Nova Scotia, SE Canada *44.40N 63.34W*
99 J24 **Dartmouth** SW England, UK *50.20N 3.34W*
13 Y6 **Dartmouth** ⁂ Quebec, SE Canada
191 Q11 **Dartmouth Reservoir** ⊚ Victoria, SE Australia
Dartuch, Cabo *see* Artrutx, Cap d'
194 G15 **Daru** Western, SW PNG *9.04S 143.12E*
114 G9 **Daruvar** *Hung.* Daruvár. Bjelovar-Bilogora, NE Croatia *45.34N 17.12E*
152 F10 **Darvaza** *Turkm.* Derweze. Akhalskiy Velayat, C Turkmenistan *40.10N 58.27E*
Darvaza *see* Darvoza
Darvazskiy Khrebet *see* Darvoz, Qatorkŭhi
168 F8 **Darvi** *var.* Dariv. Govĭ-Altay, W Mongolia *46.20N 94.11E*
154 L9 **Darvīshān** *var.* Darweshan, Garmser. Helmand, S Afghanistan *31.01N 64.12E*
153 R13 **Darvoz, Qatorkŭhi** *Rus.* Darvazskiy Khrebet. ▲ C Tajikistan
153 O10 **Darvoza** *Rus.* Darvaza. Jizzax Viloyati, C Uzbekistan *40.59N 67.19E*
Darweshan *see* Darvīshān
65 J15 **Darwin** Río Negro, S Argentina *39.13S 65.41W*
189 O1 **Darwin** *prev.* Palmerston, Port Darwin. *territory capital* Northern Territory, N Australia *12.27S 130.52E*
67 D24 **Darwin** *var.* Darwin Settlement. East Falkland, Falkland Islands *51.51S 58.55W*
64 H8 **Darwin, Cordillera** ▲ N Chile
59 B17 **Darwin, Volcán** ⁂ Galapagos Islands, Ecuador, E Pacific Ocean *0.12S 91.17W*
155 S8 **Darya Khān** Punjab, E Pakistan *31.48N 71.05E*
151 O15 **Dar'yalyktakyr, Ravnina** *plain* S Kazakhstan
149 T11 **Dārzīn** Kermān, S Iran *29.10N 58.09E*
166 L8 **Dashennongjia** ▲ C China *31.24N 110.16E*
Dashhowuz *see* Dashkhovuz
Dashhowuz Welayaty *see* Dashkhovuzskiy Velayat
121 O16 **Dashkawka** *Rus.* Dashkovka. Mahilyowskaya Voblasts', E Belarus *53.42N 30.17E*
152 H8 **Dashkhovuz** *Turkm.* Dashhowuz; *prev.* Tashauz. Dashkhovuzskiy Velayat, N Turkmenistan *41.51N 59.52E*
Dashkhovuz *see* Dashkhovuzskiy Velayat
152 E9 **Dashkhovuzskiy Velayat** *var.* Dashkhovuz, *Turkm.* Dashhowuz Welayaty. ◆ *province* N Turkmenistan
Dashköpri *see* Tashkepri
Dashkovka *see* Dashkawka
154 J15 **Dasht** ⁂ SW Pakistan
Dashtidzhum *see* Dashtijum
153 R13 **Dashtijum** *Rus.* Dashtidzhum. SW Tajikistan *38.06N 70.11E*
155 W7 **Daska** Punjab, NE Pakistan *32.21N 74.20E*
Đa, Sông *see* Black River
79 R15 **Dassa** *var.* Dassa-Zoumé. S Benin *7.46N 2.15E*
Dassa-Zoumé *see* Dassa
31 U8 **Dassel** Minnesota, N USA *45.06N 94.18W*
158 H3 **Dastegil Sar** *var.* Disteghil Sār. ▲ N India
142 C16 **Datça** Muğla, SW Turkey *36.46N 27.40E*
172 Nn6 **Date** Hokkaidō, NE Japan *42.28N 140.51E*
160 I8 **Datia** *prev.* Duttia. Madhya Pradesh, C India *25.40N 78.28E*
165 T10 **Datong** Qinghai, C China *37.01N 101.33E*
167 N2 **Datong** *var.* Tatung, Ta-t'ung. Shanxi, C China *40.09N 113.16E*
165 S9 **Datong He** ⁂ C China
165 S9 **Datong Shan** ▲ C China
174 Kk6 **Datu, Tanjung** *headland* Indonesia/Malaysia *2.01N 109.37E*
Daua *see* Dawa Wenz
180 H16 **Dauban, Mount** ▲ Silhouette, NE Seychelles
155 T7 **Dāūd Khel** Punjab, E Pakistan *32.52N 71.34E*
121 G15 **Daugai** Alytus, S Lithuania *54.22N 24.20E*
Daugava *see* Western Dvina
120 J11 **Daugavpils** *Ger.* Dünaburg; *prev. Rus.* Dvinsk. *municipality* Daugvapils, SE Latvia *55.53N 26.33E*
Dauka *see* Dawkah
Daulatabad *see* Malāyer
103 D18 **Daun** Rheinland-Pfalz, W Germany *50.13N 6.50E*
161 E14 **Daund** *prev.* Dhond. Mahārāshtra, W India *18.28N 74.37E*
178 Gg12 **Daung Kyun** *island* S Myanmar
9 W15 **Dauphin** Manitoba, S Canada *51.09N 100.04W*
105 S13 **Dauphiné** *cultural region* E France
25 N9 **Dauphin Island** *island* Alabama, S USA
9 X15 **Dauphin River** Manitoba, S Canada *51.55N 98.03W*
79 V12 **Daura** Katsina, N Nigeria *13.03N 8.18E*
158 H12 **Dausa** *prev.* Daosa. Rājasthān, N India *26.54N 76.18E*
Dauwa *see* Dawwah
143 Y10 **Däväçi** *Rus.* Divichi. NE Azerbaijan *41.15N 48.58E*
161 F18 **Dāvangere** Karnātaka, W India *14.30N 75.52E*
179 Rr16 **Davao** *off.* Davao City. Mindanao, S Philippines *7.06N 125.35E*
179 Rr16 **Davao Gulf** *gulf* Mindanao, S Philippines
13 Q11 **Daveluyville** Quebec, SE Canada *46.12N 72.07W*
31 Z14 **Davenport** Iowa, C USA *41.31N 90.34W*
34 L8 **Davenport** Washington, NW USA *47.39N 118.09W*
45 P16 **David** Chiriquí, W Panama *8.25N 82.25W*
13 O11 **David** ⁂ Quebec, SE Canada
31 R15 **David City** Nebraska, C USA *41.15N 97.07W*
David-Gorodok *see* Davyd-Haradok
9 T16 **Davidson** Saskatchewan, S Canada *51.15N 105.58W*
23 R10 **Davidson** North Carolina, SE USA *35.29N 80.49W*
28 K12 **Davidson** Oklahoma, C USA *34.15N 99.06W*
41 S6 **Davidson Mountains** ▲ Alaska, USA
180 M8 **Davie Ridge** *undersea feature* W Indian Ocean
190 A1 **Davies, Mount** ▲ South Australia *26.14S 129.14E*
37 O7 **Davis** California, W USA *38.31N 121.46W*
29 N12 **Davis** Oklahoma, C USA *34.30N 97.07W*
205 Y7 **Davis** *Australian research station* Antarctica *68.30S 78.15E*
204 H3 **Davis Coast** *physical region* Antarctica
20 C16 **Davis, Mount** ▲ Pennsylvania, NE USA *39.47N 79.10W*
26 K9 **Davis Mountains** ▲ Texas, SW USA
205 Z9 **Davis Sea** *sea* Antarctica
67 O20 **Davis Seamounts** *undersea feature* S Atlantic Ocean
206 M13 **Davis Strait** *strait* Baffin Bay/Labrador Sea
131 U5 **Davlekanovo** Respublika Bashkortostan, W Russian Federation *54.13N 55.06E*
110 J9 **Davos** *Rmsch.* Tavau. Graubünden, E Switzerland *46.48N 9.50E*
121 J20 **Davyd-Haradok** *Pol.* Dawidgródek, *Rus.* David-Gorodok. Brestskaya Voblasts', SW Belarus *52.03N 27.13E*
169 U12 **Dawa** Liaoning, NE China *40.55N 122.02E*
147 O11 **Dawāsir, Wādī ad** *dry watercourse* S Saudi Arabia
83 K15 **Dawa Wenz** *var.* Daua, Webi Daawo. ⁂ E Africa
Dawaymah, Birkat ad *see* Umm al Baqar, Hawr
Dawei *see* Tavoy
121 K14 **Dawhinava** *Rus.* Dolginovo. Minskaya Voblasts', N Belarus *54.39N 27.28E*
Dawidgródek *see* Davyd-Haradok
147 V12 **Dawkah** *var.* Dauka. SW Oman *18.32N 54.03E*
Dawlat Qaṭar *see* Qatar
26 M3 **Dawn** Texas, SW USA *34.54N 102.10W*
146 M11 **Daws** Al Bāḩah, SW Saudi Arabia *20.19N 41.12E*
8 H5 **Dawson** *var.* Dawson City. Yukon Territory, NW Canada *64.04N 139.24W*
25 S6 **Dawson** Georgia, SE USA *31.46N 84.27W*
31 S9 **Dawson** Minnesota, N USA *44.55N 96.03W*
Dawson City *see* Dawson
9 N13 **Dawson Creek** British Columbia, W Canada *55.48N 120.18W*
8 H7 **Dawson Range** ▲ Yukon Territory, W Canada
189 Y9 **Dawson River** ⁂ Queensland, E Australia
8 J15 **Dawsons Landing** British Columbia, SW Canada *51.33N 127.38W*
22 I7 **Dawson Springs** Kentucky, S USA *37.10N 87.41W*
25 S2 **Dawsonville** Georgia, SE USA *34.28N 84.07W*
166 G8 **Dawu** Sichuan, C China *30.55N 101.08E*
Dawu *see* Maqên
Dawukou *see* Shizuishan
147 Y10 **Dawwah** *var.* Dauwa. W Oman *20.36N 58.52E*
104 J15 **Dax** *var.* Ax; *anc.* Aquae Augustae, Aquae Tarbelicae. Landes, SW France *43.43N 1.03W*
Da Xian/Daxian *see* Dachuan
166 G9 **Daxue Shan** ▲ C China
166 G12 **Dayao** Yunnan, SW China *25.41N 101.23E*
Dayishan *see* Gaoyou
191 N12 **Daylesford** Victoria, SE Australia *37.24S 144.07E*
37 U10 **Daylight Pass** *pass* California, W USA *36.44N 116.55W*
63 D17 **Daymán, Río** ⁂ N Uruguay
Dayr *see* Ad Dayr
144 G10 **Dayr 'Allā** *var.* Deir 'Alla. Al Balqā', N Jordan *32.39N 36.06E*
145 N4 **Dayr az Zawr** *var.* Deir ez Zor. Dayr az Zawr, E Syria *35.12N 40.12E*
144 M5 **Dayr az Zawr** *off.* Muḩāfaẓat Dayr az Zawr, *var.* Dayr Az-Zor. ◆ *governorate* E Syria
Dayr Az-Zor *see* Dayr az Zawr
Dayrūṭ *see* Dairûṭ
9 Q15 **Daysland** Alberta, SW Canada *52.53N 112.19W*
33 R14 **Dayton** Ohio, N USA *39.45N 84.11W*
22 L10 **Dayton** Tennessee, S USA *35.30N 85.01W*
27 W11 **Dayton** Texas, SW USA *30.03N 94.53W*
34 L10 **Dayton** Washington, NW USA *46.19N 117.58W*
25 X10 **Daytona Beach** Florida, SE USA *29.12N 81.03W*
175 N10 **Dayu** Borneo, C Indonesia *1.58S 115.04E*
167 O13 **Dayu Ling** ▲ S China
167 R7 **Da Yunhe** *Eng.* Grand Canal. *canal* E China
167 S11 **Dayu Shan** *island* SE China
166 J9 **Dazhu** Sichuan, C China *30.45N 107.10E*
166 J9 **Dazu** Chongqing Shi, C China *29.48N 105.46E*
85 H24 **De Aar** Northern Cape, C South Africa *30.40S 24.01E*
204 K5 **Deacon, Cape** *headland* Antarctica
41 R5 **Deadhorse** Alaska, USA *70.15N 148.28W*
35 T12 **Dead Indian Peak** ▲ Wyoming, C USA *44.36N 109.45W*
25 R9 **Dead Lake** ⊚ Florida, SE USA
46 J4 **Deadman's Cay** Long Island, C Bahamas *23.09N 75.06W*
144 G11 **Dead Sea** *var.* Bahret Lut, Lacus Asphaltites, *Ar.* Al Baḩr al Mayyit, Baḩrat Lūṭ, *Heb.* Yam HaMelaḩ. *salt lake* Israel/Jordan
30 J9 **Deadwood** South Dakota, N USA *44.22N 103.43W*
99 Q22 **Deal** SE England, UK *51.14N 1.22E*
85 I22 **Dealesville** Free State, C South Africa *28.40S 25.46E*
Dealnu *see* Tana/Teno
167 P10 **De'an** Jiangxi, S China *29.24N 115.46E*
64 K9 **Deán Funes** Córdoba, C Argentina *30.25S 64.22W*
204 L12 **Dean Island** *island* Antarctica
33 S10 **Dearborn** Michigan, N USA *42.16N 83.13W*
29 R3 **Dearborn** Missouri, C USA *39.31N 94.46W*
34 K9 **Deary** Idaho, NW USA *46.46N 118.33W*
34 M9 **Deary** Washington, NW USA *46.42N 116.36W*
8 J10 **Dease** ⁂ British Columbia, W Canada
8 J10 **Dease Lake** British Columbia, W Canada *58.28N 130.04W*
37 U11 **Death Valley** California, W USA *36.25N 116.50W*
37 U11 **Death Valley** *valley* California, W USA
104 L4 **Deauville** Calvados, N France *49.21N 0.06E*
119 X7 **Debal'tseve** *Rus.* Debal'tsevo. Donets'ka Oblast', SE Ukraine *48.21N 38.25E*
Debal'tsevo *see* Debal'tseve
115 M19 **Debar** *Ger.* Dibra, *Turk.* Debre. W FYR Macedonia *41.32N 20.33E*
41 O9 **Debauch Mountain** ▲ Alaska, USA *64.31N 159.52W*
De Behagle *see* Laï
27 X7 **De Berry** Texas, SW USA *32.18N 94.09W*
131 T2 **Debessy** Udmurtskaya Respublika, NW Russian Federation *57.41N 53.56E*
113 N16 **Dębica** Podkarpackie, SE Poland *50.03N 21.24E*
De Bildt *see* De Bilt
100 J11 **De Bilt** *var.* De Bildt. Utrecht, C Netherlands *52.06N 5.10E*
127 O9 **Debin** Magadanskaya Oblast', E Russian Federation *62.18N 150.42E*
112 N13 **Dęblin** *Rus.* Ivangorod. Lubelskie, E Poland *51.34N 21.49E*
112 D10 **Dębno** Zachodniopomorskie, NW Poland *52.44N 14.42E*
41 S10 **Deborah, Mount** ▲ Alaska, USA *63.38N 147.13W*
35 N8 **De Borgia** Montana, NW USA *47.23N 115.24W*
Debra Birhan *see* Debre Birhan
Debra Marcos *see* Debre Mark'os
Debra Tabor *see* Debre Tabor
Debre *see* Debar
82 J13 **Debre Birhan** *var.* Debra Birhan. Amhara, N Ethiopia *9.45N 39.40E*
113 N22 **Debrecen** *Ger.* Debreczin, *Rom.* Debreţin; *prev.* Debreczen. Hajdú-Bihar, E Hungary *47.31N 21.37E*
Debreczen/Debreczin *see* Debrecen
82 I12 **Debre Mark'os** *var.* Debra Marcos. Amhara, N Ethiopia *10.18N 37.48E*
115 N19 **Debrešte** SW FYR Macedonia *41.29N 21.20E*
82 J11 **Debre Tabor** *var.* Debra Tabor. Amhara, N Ethiopia *11.46N 38.06E*
Debreţin *see* Debrecen
82 J13 **Debre Zeyt** Oromo, C Ethiopia *8.41N 39.00E*
115 L16 **Dečani** Serbia, S Serbia and Montenegro (Yugoslavia) *42.33N 20.18E*
25 P2 **Decatur** Alabama, S USA *34.36N 86.58W*
25 S3 **Decatur** Georgia, SE USA *33.46N 84.18W*
32 L13 **Decatur** Illinois, N USA *39.50N 88.57W*
33 Q12 **Decatur** Indiana, N USA *40.48N 84.55W*
24 M5 **Decatur** Mississippi, S USA *32.26N 89.06W*
31 S14 **Decatur** Nebraska, C USA *42.00N 96.19W*
27 S6 **Decatur** Texas, SW USA *33.14N 97.32W*
22 H9 **Decaturville** Tennessee, S USA *35.34N 88.07W*
105 O13 **Decazeville** Aveyron, S France *44.34N 2.18E*
161 H17 **Deccan** *Hind.* Dakshin. *plateau* C India
12 J8 **Decelles, Réservoir** ⊠ Quebec, SE Canada
10 K2 **Déception** Quebec, NE Canada *62.06N 74.36W*
166 G11 **Dechang** Sichuan, C China *27.24N 102.09E*
113 C15 **Děčín** *Ger.* Tetschen. Ústecký Kraj, NW Czech Republic *50.48N 14.15E*
105 P9 **Decize** Nièvre, C France *46.51N 3.25E*
100 I6 **De Cocksdorp** Noord-Holland, NW Netherlands *53.09N 4.52E*
31 X11 **Decorah** Iowa, C USA *43.18N 91.47W*
Dedeagaç/Dedeagach *see* Alexandroúpoli
196 C15 **Dededo** N Guam *13.30N 144.51E*
100 N9 **Dedemsvaart** Overijssel, E Netherlands *52.36N 6.28E*
21 O11 **Dedham** Massachusetts, NE USA *42.14N 71.10W*
65 H19 **Dedo, Cerro** ▲ SW Argentina *44.46S 71.48W*
79 O13 **Dédougou** W Burkina *12.25N 3.27W*
128 G15 **Dedovichi** Pskovskaya Oblast', W Russian Federation *57.31N 29.53E*
169 V6 **Dedu** *var.* Qingshan. Heilongjiang, NE China *48.30N 126.17E*
161 J24 **Deduru Oya** ⁂ W Sri Lanka
85 N14 **Dedza** Central, S Malawi *14.24S 34.15E*
85 N14 **Dedza Mountain** ▲ C Malawi *14.22S 34.16E*
99 J19 **Dee** *Wel.* Afon Dyfrdwy. ⁂ England/Wales, UK
98 K9 **Dee** ⁂ NE Scotland, UK
Deep Bay *see* Chilumba
23 T3 **Deep Creek Lake** ⊠ Maryland, NE USA
38 J4 **Deep Creek Range** ▲ Utah, W USA
29 P10 **Deep Fork** ⁂ Oklahoma, C USA
12 J11 **Deep River** Ontario, SE Canada *46.05N 77.28W*
23 T10 **Deep River** ⁂ North Carolina, SE USA
191 U4 **Deepwater** New South Wales, SE Australia *29.27S 151.52E*
33 S14 **Deer Creek Lake** ⊚ Ohio, N USA
25 Z15 **Deerfield Beach** Florida, SE USA *26.19N 80.06W*
41 N8 **Deering** Alaska, USA *66.04N 162.43W*
40 M16 **Deer Island** *island* Alaska, USA
21 S7 **Deer Isle** *island* Maine, NE USA
11 S11 **Deer Lake** Newfoundland and Labrador, SE Canada *49.10N 57.18W*
101 D18 **Deerlijk** West-Vlaanderen, W Belgium *50.52N 3.21E*
35 Q10 **Deer Lodge** Montana, NW USA *46.24N 112.43W*
34 L8 **Deer Park** Washington, NW USA *47.55N 117.28W*
31 U5 **Deer River** Minnesota, N USA *47.19N 93.47W*
Deés *see* Dej
33 R11 **Defiance** Ohio, N USA *41.16N 84.21W*
25 Q8 **De Funiak Springs** Florida, SE USA *30.43N 86.07W*
97 L23 **Degeberga** Skåne, S Sweden *55.48N 14.06E*
106 H12 **Degebe, Ribeira** ⁂ S Portugal
82 M13 **Degeh Bur** Somali, E Ethiopia *8.08N 43.35E*
13 U9 **Dégelis** Quebec, SE Canada *47.30N 68.38W*
79 U17 **Degema** Rivers, S Nigeria *4.46N 6.47E*
97 L16 **Degerfors** Örebro, C Sweden *59.13N 14.25E*
200 N16 **De Gerlache Seamounts** *undersea feature* SE Pacific Ocean
103 N21 **Deggendorf** Bayern, SE Germany *48.49N 12.58E*
124 Nn2 **Değirmenlik** *Gk.* Kythréa. N Cyprus *35.14N 33.28E*
82 I11 **Degoma** Amhara, N Ethiopia *12.22N 37.36E*
De Gordyk *see* Gorredijk
29 T12 **De Gray Lake** ⊠ Arkansas, C USA
188 J6 **De Grey River** ⁂ Western Australia
130 M10 **Degtevo** Rostovskaya Oblast', SW Russian Federation *49.12N 40.39E*
149 X13 **Dehak** Sīstān va Balūchestān, SE Iran *27.10N 62.34E*
149 R9 **Deh 'Alī** Kermān, C Iran *31.40N 56.10E*
149 S13 **Dehbārez** *var.* Rūdān. Hormozgān, S Iran *27.30N 57.10E*
149 P10 **Deh Bīd** Fārs, C Iran *30.37N 53.11E*
148 M10 **Deh Dasht** Kohkīlūyeh va Būyer Aḩmadī, SW Iran *30.49N 50.36E*
77 N8 **Dehibat** SE Tunisia *31.58N 10.43E*
Dehli *see* Delhi
148 K8 **Dehlorān** Īlām, W Iran *32.40N 47.18E*
153 N13 **Dehqonobod** *Rus.* Dekhkanabad. Qashqadaryo Viloyati, S Uzbekistan *38.24N 66.31E*
158 J9 **Dehra Dūn** Uttar Pradesh, N India *30.18N 78.03E*
159 O14 **Dehri** Bihār, N India *24.55N 84.10E*
154 K10 **Deh Shū** *var.* Deshu. Helmand, S Afghanistan *30.28N 63.21E*
101 D17 **Deinze** Oost-Vlaanderen, NW Belgium *50.58N 3.31E*
Deir 'Alla *see* Dayr 'Allā
Deir ez Zor *see* Dayr az Zawr
Deirgeirt, Loch *see* Derg, Lough
118 H9 **Dej** *Hung.* Dés; *prev.* Deés. Cluj, NW Romania *47.08N 23.55E*
97 K15 **Deje** Värmland, C Sweden *59.34N 13.28E*
176 Y14 **De Jongs, Tanjung** *headland* Papua, SE Indonesia *6.55S 138.31E*
De Jouwer *see* Joure
32 M10 **De Kalb** Illinois, N USA *41.55N 88.45W*
24 M5 **De Kalb** Mississippi, S USA *32.46N 88.39W*
27 W5 **De Kalb** Texas, SW USA *33.30N 94.34W*
Dekéleia *see* Dhekélia
81 K20 **Dekese** Kasai Occidental, C Dem. Rep. Congo *3.28S 21.24E*
Dekhkanabad *see* Dehqonobod
81 I14 **Dékoa** Kémo, C Central African Republic *6.17N 19.07E*
100 H6 **De Koog** Noord-Holland, NW Netherlands *53.06N 4.43E*
32 M9 **Delafield** Wisconsin, N USA *43.03N 88.22W*
63 C23 **De La Garma** Buenos Aires, E Argentina *37.58S 60.25W*
12 K10 **Delahey, Lac** ⊚ Quebec, SE Canada
82 E11 **Delami** Southern Kordofan, C Sudan *11.51N 30.30E*
25 X11 **De Land** Florida, SE USA *29.01N 81.18W*
37 R12 **Delano** California, W USA *35.46N 119.15W*
31 V8 **Delano** Minnesota, N USA *45.03N 93.46W*
38 K6 **Delano Peak** ▲ Utah, W USA *38.22N 112.21W*
Delap-Uliga-Darrit *see* Dalap-Uliga-Djarrit
154 L7 **Delārām** Farāh, SW Afghanistan *32.10N 63.27E*
40 F17 **Delarof Islands** *island group* Aleutian Islands, Alaska, USA
32 M9 **Delavan** Wisconsin, N USA *42.37N 88.37W*
33 S13 **Delaware** Ohio, N USA *40.18N 83.04W*
20 I17 **Delaware** *off.* State of Delaware; also known as Blue Hen State, Diamond State, First State. ◆ *state* NE USA
20 I17 **Delaware Bay** *bay* NE USA
26 J8 **Delaware Mountains** ▲ Texas, SW USA
20 I12 **Delaware River** ⁂ NE USA
29 Q3 **Delaware River** ⁂ Kansas, C USA
20 J14 **Delaware Water Gap** *valley* New Jersey/Pennsylvania, NE USA
103 G14 **Delbrück** Nordrhein-Westfalen, W Germany *51.46N 8.34E*
9 Q15 **Delburne** Alberta, SW Canada *52.09N 113.11W*
180 M12 **Del Cano Rise** *undersea feature* SW Indian Ocean
115 Q18 **Delčevo** NE FYR Macedonia *41.57N 22.45E*
Delcommune, Lac *see* Nzilo, Lac
100 O10 **Delden** Overijssel, E Netherlands *52.16N 6.40E*
191 R12 **Delegate** New South Wales, SE Australia *37.04S 148.57E*
De Lemmer *see* Lemmer
110 D7 **Delémont** *Ger.* Delsberg. Jura, NW Switzerland *47.22N 7.21E*
27 R7 **De Leon** Texas, SW USA *32.06N 98.33W*
117 F18 **Delfoí** Stereá Ellás, C Greece *38.28N 22.31E*
100 G12 **Delft** Zuid-Holland, W Netherlands *52.01N 4.22E*
161 J23 **Delft** *island* NW Sri Lanka
100 O5 **Delfzijl** Groningen, NE Netherlands *53.19N 6.55E*
(0) E9 **Delgada Fan** *undersea feature* NE Pacific Ocean
44 F7 **Delgado** San Salvador, SW El Salvador *13.44N 89.07W*
84 Q12 **Delgado, Cabo** *headland* N Mozambique *10.41S 40.40E*
82 E6 **Delgo** Northern, N Sudan *20.07N 30.34E*
165 R10 **Delhi** *var.* Delingha. Qinghai, C China *37.19N 97.22E*
158 I10 **Delhi** *var.* Dehli, *Hind.* Dilli; *hist.* Shahjahanabad. Delhi, N India *28.40N 77.11E*
24 J5 **Delhi** Louisiana, S USA *32.28N 91.29W*
20 J11 **Delhi** New York, NE USA *42.16N 74.55W*
158 I10 **Delhi** ◆ *union territory* NW India
142 J17 **Deli Burnu** *headland* S Turkey *36.43N 34.55E*
57 X10 **Délices** C French Guiana *4.46N 53.42W*
142 J12 **Delice Çayı** ⁂ C Turkey
42 J6 **Delicias** *var.* Ciudad Delicias. Chihuahua, N Mexico *28.08N 105.22W*
149 N7 **Delījān** *var.* Dalijan, Dilijan. Markazī, W Iran *34.01N 50.39E*
114 P12 **Deli Jovan** ▲ E Serbia and Montenegro (Yugoslavia)
Déli-Kárpátok *see* Carpaţii Meridionali
15 H6 **Déljne** *prev.* Fort Franklin. Northwest Territories, NW Canada *65.10N 123.30W*
Delingha *see* Delhi
13 Q7 **Delisle** Quebec, SE Canada *48.39N 71.42W*
9 T15 **Delisle** Saskatchewan, S Canada *51.54N 107.01W*
103 M15 **Delitzsch** Sachsen, E Germany *51.31N 12.19E*
35 Q12 **Dell** Montana, NW USA *44.41N 112.42W*
26 I7 **Dell City** Texas, SW USA *31.56N 105.12W*
105 U7 **Delle** Territoire-de-Belfort, E France *47.30N 7.00E*
38 J9 **Dellenbaugh, Mount** ▲ Arizona, SW USA *36.06N 113.32W*
31 R11 **Dell Rapids** South Dakota, N USA *43.50N 96.42W*
23 Y4 **Delmar** Maryland, NE USA *38.26N 75.32W*
20 K11 **Delmar** New York, NE USA *42.37N 73.49W*
102 G11 **Delmenhorst** Niedersachsen, NW Germany *53.03N 8.37E*
114 C9 **Delnice** Primorje-Gorski Kotar, NW Croatia *45.24N 14.49E*
39 R7 **Del Norte** Colorado, C USA *37.40N 106.21W*
41 N6 **De Long Mountains** ▲ Alaska, USA
191 P16 **Deloraine** Tasmania, SE Australia *41.34S 146.43E*
9 W17 **Deloraine** Manitoba, S Canada *49.12N 100.28W*
33 O12 **Delphi** Indiana, N USA *40.35N 86.40W*
33 Q12 **Delphos** Ohio, N USA *40.49N 84.20W*
25 Z15 **Delray Beach** Florida, SE USA *26.27N 80.04W*
27 O12 **Del Rio** Texas, SW USA *29.22N 100.55W*
Delsberg *see* Delémont
96 N11 **Delsbo** Gävleborg, C Sweden *61.49N 16.34E*
39 P6 **Delta** Colorado, C USA *38.44N 108.04W*
38 K5 **Delta** Utah, W USA *39.21N 112.34W*
79 T17 **Delta** ◆ *state* S Nigeria
57 Q6 **Delta Amacuro** *off.* Territorio Delta Amacuro. ◆ *federal district* NE Venezuela
41 S9 **Delta Junction** Alaska, USA *64.02N 145.43W*
25 X11 **Deltona** Florida, SE USA *28.54N 81.15W*
191 T5 **Delungra** New South Wales, SE Australia *29.40S 150.49E*
160 C12 **Delvāda** Gujarāt, W India *20.46N 71.01E*
63 B21 **Del Valle** Buenos Aires, E Argentina *35.55S 60.42W*
Delvina *see* Delvinë
117 C15 **Delvináki** *var.* Dhelvinákion; *prev.* Pogónion. Ípeiros, W Greece *39.56N 20.27E*
115 L23 **Delvinë** *var.* Delvina, *It.* Delvino. Vlorë, S Albania *39.56N 20.07E*
Delvino *see* Delvinë
118 I7 **Delyatyn** Ivano-Frankivs'ka Oblast', W Ukraine *48.32N 24.38E*
131 U5 **Dëma** ⁂ W Russian Federation
107 O5 **Demanda, Sierra de la** ▲ W Spain
41 T5 **Demarcation Point** *headland* Alaska, USA *69.40N 141.19W*
81 K21 **Demba** Kasai Occidental, C Dem. Rep. Congo *5.24S 22.16E*
180 H13 **Dembéni** Grande Comore, NW Comoros *11.49S 43.25E*
81 M15 **Dembia** Mbomou, SE Central African Republic *5.08N 24.25E*
Dembidollo *see* Dembī Dolo
82 H13 **Dembī Dolo** *var.* Dembidollo. Oromo, C Ethiopia *8.33N 34.49E*
158 K6 **Demchok** *var.* Dêmqog. China/India *see also* Dêmqog *32.30N 79.42E*
158 L6 **Demchok** *var.* Dêmqog. *disputed region* China/India *see also* Dêmqog
100 I12 **De Meern** Utrecht, C Netherlands *52.06N 5.00E*
101 I17 **Demer** ⁂ C Belgium
66 H12 **Demerara Plain** *undersea feature* W Atlantic Ocean
66 H12 **Demerara Plateau** *undersea feature* W Atlantic Ocean
57 T9 **Demerara River** ⁂ NE Guyana
130 H3 **Demidov** Smolenskaya Oblast', W Russian Federation *55.15N 31.30E*
39 Q15 **Deming** New Mexico, SW USA *32.13N 107.46W*
34 H6 **Deming** Washington, NW USA *48.49N 122.13W*
60 E10 **Demini, Rio** ⁂ NW Brazil
142 D13 **Demirci** Manisa, W Turkey *39.03N 28.40E*
115 P19 **Demir Kapija** *prev.* Železna Vrata. SE FYR Macedonia *41.25N 22.15E*
116 N11 **Demirköy** Kırklareli, NW Turkey *41.49N 27.47E*
102 N9 **Demmin** Mecklenburg-Vorpommern, NE Germany *53.53N 13.03E*
25 O5 **Demopolis** Alabama, S USA *32.31N 87.50W*
33 N11 **Demotte** Indiana, N USA *41.13N 87.07W*
164 F13 **Dêmqog** *var.* Demchok. China/India *see also* Demchok *32.36N 79.28E*
158 L6 **Dêmqog** *var.* Demchok. *disputed region* China/India *see also* Demchok
176 Yy10 **Demta** Papua, E Indonesia *2.19S 140.06E*
125 G11 **Dem'yanka** ⁂ C Russian Federation
128 H15 **Demyansk** Novgorodskaya Oblast', W Russian Federation *57.39N 32.31E*
125 Ff11 **Dem'yanskoye** Tyumenskaya Oblast', C Russian Federation *59.39N 69.15E*
105 P2 **Denain** Nord, N France *50.19N 3.24E*
41 S10 **Denali** Alaska, USA *63.08N 147.33W*
Denali *see* McKinley, Mount
83 M14 **Denan** Somali, E Ethiopia *6.40N 43.31E*
Denau *see* Denov
99 J18 **Denbigh** *Wel.* Dinbych. NE Wales, UK *53.10N 3.25W*
99 J18 **Denbigh** *cultural region* N Wales, UK
100 I6 **Den Burg** Noord-Holland, NW Netherlands *53.03N 4.46E*
101 F18 **Dender** *Fr.* Dendre. ⁂ W Belgium
101 F18 **Denderleeuw** Oost-Vlaanderen, NW Belgium *50.52N 4.04E*
101 F17 **Dendermonde** *Fr.* Termonde. Oost-Vlaanderen, NW Belgium *51.01N 4.07E*
Dendre *see* Dender
204 J9 **Dendtler Island** *island* Antarctica
100 P10 **Denekamp** Overijssel, E Netherlands *52.23N 7.00E*
79 W12 **Dengas** Zinder, S Niger *13.15N 9.43E*
Dêngkagoin *see* Têwo
168 L13 **Dengkou** *var.* Bayan Gol. Nei Mongol Zizhiqu, N China *40.15N 106.58E*
165 Q14 **Dêngqên** Xizang Zizhiqu, W China *31.28N 95.28E*
Deng Xian *see* Dengzhou
166 M7 **Dengzhou** *prev.* Deng Xian. Henan, C China *32.43N 112.02E*
Dengzhou *see* Penglai
Den Haag *see* 's-Gravenhage
100 N9 **Den Ham** Overijssel, E Netherlands *52.30N 6.30E*
188 H10 **Denham** Western Australia *25.56S 113.35E*
46 J12 **Denham, Mount** ▲ C Jamaica *18.13N 77.33W*
24 J8 **Denham Springs** Louisiana, S USA *30.29N 90.57W*
100 I7 **Den Helder** Noord-Holland, NW Netherlands *52.54N 4.45E*
107 T11 **Denia** País Valenciano, E Spain *38.51N 0.07E*
201 Q8 **Denig** W Nauru
191 N10 **Deniliquin** New South Wales, SE Australia *35.33S 144.58E*
31 T14 **Denison** Iowa, C USA *42.00N 95.22W*
27 U5 **Denison** Texas, SW USA *33.45N 96.32W*
150 L8 **Denisovka** *prev.* Ordzhonikidze. Kostanay, N Kazakhstan *52.24N 61.40E*
142 D15 **Denizli** Denizli, SW Turkey *37.46N 29.04E*
142 D15 **Denizli** ◆ *province* SW Turkey
Denjong *see* Sikkim
191 S7 **Denman** New South Wales, SE Australia *32.24S 150.43E*
205 Y10 **Denman Glacier** *glacier* Antarctica
23 R14 **Denmark** South Carolina, SE USA *33.19N 81.08W*
97 G23 **Denmark** *off.* Kingdom of Denmark, *Dan.* Danmark; *anc.* Hafnia. ◆ *monarchy* N Europe
94 H1 **Denmark Strait** *var.* Danmarksstraedet. *strait* Greenland/Iceland
47 T11 **Dennery** E Saint Lucia *13.55N 60.53W*
100 I7 **Den Oever** Noord-Holland, NW Netherlands *52.56N 5.01E*
153 O13 **Denov** *Rus.* Denau. Surkhondaryo Viloyati, S Uzbekistan *38.19N 67.48E*
175 N16 **Denpasar** *prev.* Paloe. Bali, C Indonesia *8.40S 115.13E*
118 E12 **Denta** Timiş, W Romania *45.18N 21.14E*
23 Y3 **Denton** Maryland, NE USA *38.52N 75.49W*
27 T6 **Denton** Texas, SW USA *33.10N 97.08W*
195 O15 **D'Entrecasteaux Islands** *island group* SE PNG
39 T4 **Denver** *state capital* Colorado, C USA *39.44N 105.00W*
18 K8 **Denver** ✕ Colorado, C USA *39.57N 104.38W*
26 L6 **Denver City** Texas, SW USA *32.57N 102.49W*
158 J9 **Deoband** Uttar Pradesh, N India *29.40N 77.40E*
Deoghar *see* Devghar
160 E13 **Deolāli** Mahārāshtra, W India *19.55N 73.49E*
160 I10 **Deori** Madhya Pradesh, C India *23.09N 78.39E*
159 O12 **Deoria** Uttar Pradesh, N India *26.31N 83.48E*
101 A17 **De Panne** West-Vlaanderen, W Belgium *51.06N 2.34E*
56 M5 **Dependencia Federal** *off.* Territorio Dependencia Federal. ◆ *federal dependency* N Venezuela
Dependencia Federal, Territorio *see* Dependencia Federal
32 M7 **De Pere** Wisconsin, N USA *44.26N 88.03W*
20 D10 **Depew** New York, NE USA *42.54N 78.41W*
101 E17 **De Pinte** Oost-Vlaanderen, NW Belgium *51.00N 3.37E*
27 V5 **Deport** Texas, SW USA *33.31N 95.19W*
126 M7 **Deputatskiy** Respublika S akha (Yakutiya), NE Russian Federation *69.18N 139.48E*
29 S13 **De Queen** Arkansas, C USA *34.02N 94.20W*
24 G8 **De Quincy** Louisiana, S USA *30.27N 93.25W*
83 J20 **Dera** *spring/well* S Kenya *2.39S 39.52E*
Der'a/Derá/Déraa *see* Dar'ā
155 S10 **Dera Ghāzi Khān** *var.* Dera Ghāzikhān. Punjab, C Pakistan *30.01N 70.37E*
155 S8 **Dera Ismāīl Khān** North-West Frontier Province, C Pakistan *31.51N 70.55E*
115 L16 **Đeravica** ▲ S Serbia and Montenegro (Yugoslavia) *42.33N 20.08E*
118 L6 **Derazhnya** Khmel'nyts'ka Oblast', W Ukraine *49.16N 27.24E*
131 R17 **Derbent** Respublika Dagestan, SW Russian Federation *42.01N 48.16E*
153 N13 **Derbent** Surkhondaryo Viloyati, S Uzbekistan *38.15N 66.59E*
Derbisīye *see* Darbāsīyah
81 M15 **Derbissaka** Mbomou, SE Central African Republic *5.43N 24.48E*
188 L4 **Derby** Western Australia *17.18S 123.36E*
99 M19 **Derby** C England, UK *52.55N 1.30W*
29 N7 **Derby** Kansas, C USA *37.33N 97.16W*
99 L18 **Derbyshire** *cultural region* C England, UK
114 O11 **Đerdap** *physical region* E Serbia and Montenegro (Yugoslavia)
Derelí *see* Gónnoi
176 X11 **Derew** ⁂ Papua, E Indonesia
131 R8 **Dergachi** Saratovskaya Oblast', W Russian Federation *51.15N 48.58E*
Dergachi *see* Derhachi
99 C19 **Derg, Lough** *Ir.* Loch Deirgeirt. ⊚ W Ireland
119 V5 **Derhachi** *Rus.* Dergachi. Kharkivs'ka Oblast', E Ukraine *50.08N 36.10E*
24 G8 **De Ridder** Louisiana, S USA *30.51N 93.18W*
143 P16 **Derik** Mardin, SE Turkey *37.22N 40.16E*
85 E20 **Derm** Hardap, C Namibia *23.38S 18.12E*
150 M14 **Dermentobe** *prev.* Dyurmen'tyube. Kzylorda, S Kazakhstan *45.46N 63.42E*
29 W14 **Dermott** Arkansas, C USA *33.31N 91.26W*
Dérna *see* Darnah
Dernberg, Cape *see* Dolphin Head
24 J11 **Dernieres, Isles** *island group* Louisiana, S USA
Dernis *see* Drniš
104 I4 **Déroute, Passage de la** *strait* Channel Islands/France
Derrá *see* Dar'ā
Derry *see* Londonderry
Dertona *see* Tortona
Dertosa *see* Tortosa
82 H8 **Derudeb** Red Sea, NE Sudan *17.28N 36.04E*

◆ Country
● Country Capital
◇ Dependent Territory
○ Dependent Territory Capital
◆ Administrative Region
✕ International Airport
▲ Mountain
▲ Mountain Range
⁂ Volcano
⁂ River
⊚ Lake
⊠ Reservoir

114 H10 **Derventa** Republika Srpska, N Bosnia and Herzegovina 44.57N 17.55E
191 O16 **Derwent Bridge** Tasmania, SE Australia 42.10S 146.13E
191 O17 **Derwent, River** ⁂ Tasmania, SE Australia
Derweze see Darvaza
Deržavinsk see Derzhavinsk
151 O9 **Derzhavinsk** var. Deržavinsk. Akmola, C Kazakhstan 51.04N 66.19E
Dés see Dej
59 J18 **Desaguadero** Puno, S Peru 16.31S 69.01W
59 J18 **Desaguadero, Río** ⁂ Bolivia/Peru
203 W9 **Désappointement, Îles du** island group Îles Tuamotu, C French Polynesia
29 W11 **Des Arc** Arkansas, C USA 34.58N 91.30W
12 C10 **Desbarats** Ontario, S Canada 46.20N 83.52W
64 H13 **Descabezado Grande, Volcán** ▲ C Chile 35.34S 70.40W
42 B2 **Descanso** Baja California, NW Mexico 32.08N 116.51W
104 L9 **Descartes** Indre-et-Loire, C France 46.58N 0.40E
9 T13 **Deschambault Lake** ◎ Saskatchewan, C Canada
Deschnaer Koppe see Velká Deštná
34 I11 **Deschutes River** ⁂ Oregon, NW USA
82 J12 **Desē** var. Desse, It. Dessie. Amhara, N Ethiopia 11.01N 39.39E
65 I20 **Deseado, Río** ⁂ S Argentina
108 F8 **Desenzano del Garda** Lombardia, N Italy 45.28N 10.31E
38 K3 **Deseret Peak** ▲ Utah, W USA 40.27N 112.37W
66 P6 **Deserta Grande** island Madeira, Portugal, NE Atlantic Ocean
66 P6 **Desertas, Ilhas** island group Madeira, Portugal, NE Atlantic Ocean
37 X16 **Desert Center** California, W USA 33.42N 115.22W
37 V15 **Desert Hot Springs** California, W USA 33.57N 116.33W
12 K10 **Désert, Lac** ◎ Quebec, SE Canada
38 J2 **Desert Peak** ▲ Utah, W USA 41.03N 113.22W
33 R11 **Deshler** Ohio, N USA 41.12N 83.55W
Deshu see Deh Shū
Desiderii Fanum see St-Dizier
108 D7 **Desio** Lombardia, N Italy 45.37N 9.12E
117 E15 **Deskáti** var. Dheskáti. Dytikí Makedonía, N Greece 39.55N 21.49E
30 L2 **Des Lacs River** ⁂ North Dakota, N USA
29 X6 **Desloge** Missouri, C USA 37.52N 90.31W
9 Q12 **Desmarais** Alberta, W Canada 55.58N 113.55W
31 Q10 **De Smet** South Dakota, N USA 44.23N 97.33W
31 V14 **Des Moines** state capital Iowa, C USA 41.36N 93.36W
19 N8 **Des Moines River** ⁂ C USA
119 P4 **Desna** ⁂ Russian Federation/Ukraine
118 G14 **Desnățui** ⁂ S Romania
65 F24 **Desolación, Isla** island S Chile
31 V14 **De Soto** Iowa, C USA 41.31N 94.00W
25 Q4 **De Soto Falls** waterfall Alabama, S USA 33.22N 86.12W
85 I25 **Despatch** Eastern Cape, S South Africa 33.48S 25.28E
107 N12 **Despeñaperros, Desfiladero de** pass S Spain 38.25N 3.26W
33 N10 **Des Plaines** Illinois, N USA 42.01N 87.52W
117 J21 **Despotikó** island Kykládes, Greece, Aegean Sea
114 N12 **Despotovac** Serbia, E Serbia and Montenegro (Yugoslavia) 44.06N 21.25E
103 M14 **Dessau** Sachsen-Anhalt, E Germany 51.51N 12.15E
Desse see Desē
101 J16 **Dessel** Antwerpen, N Belgium 51.15N 5.07E
Dessie see Desē
Destêrro see Florianópolis
25 P9 **Destin** Florida, SE USA 30.23N 86.30W
Deštná see Velká Deštná
200 Oo11 **Desventurados, Islas de los** island group W Chile
105 N1 **Desvres** Pas-de-Calais, N France 50.41N 1.48E
118 E12 **Deta** Ger. Detta. Timiș, W Romania 45.22N 21.13E
103 H14 **Detmold** Nordrhein-Westfalen, W Germany 51.55N 8.52E
33 S10 **Detroit** Michigan, N USA 42.19N 83.03W
27 W5 **Detroit** Texas, SW USA 33.39N 95.16W
33 S10 **Detroit** ⁂ Canada/USA
31 S6 **Detroit Lakes** Minnesota, N USA 46.49N 95.49W
33 S10 **Detroit Metropolitan** ✕ Michigan, N USA 42.12N 83.16W
Detta see Deta
178 J11 **Det Udom** Ubon Ratchathani, E Thailand 14.54N 105.03E
113 K20 **Detva** Hung. Gyeva. Banskobystrický Kraj, C Slovakia 48.34N 19.25E
160 G13 **Deūlgaon Rāja** Mahārāshtra, C India 20.04N 76.08E
101 L15 **Deurne** Noord-Brabant, SE Netherlands 51.28N 5.46E
101 H16 **Deurne** ✕ (Antwerpen) Antwerpen, N Belgium 51.10N 4.28E
Deutsch-Brod see Havlíčkův Brod
Deutschendorf see Poprad
Deutsch-Eylau see Iława
111 Y6 **Deutschkreutz** Burgenland, E Austria 47.36N 16.38E
Deutsch Krone see Wałcz
Deutschland/Deutschland, Bundesrepublik see Germany
111 V9 **Deutschlandsberg** Steiermark, SE Austria 46.52N 15.13E
Deutsch-Südwestafrika see Namibia
111 Y3 **Deutsch-Wagram** Niederösterreich, E Austria 48.19N 16.33E
Deux-Ponts see Zweibrücken
12 I11 **Deux Rivieres** Ontario, SE Canada 46.13N 78.16W
104 K9 **Deux-Sèvres** ◆ department W France
118 G11 **Deva** Ger. Diemrich, Hung. Déva. Hunedoara, W Romania 45.55N 22.54E
Deva see Chester
Devana see Aberdeen
Devana Castra see Chester
Devđelija see Gevgelija
142 L12 **Deveci Dağları** ▲ N Turkey
143 P15 **Devegeçidi Barajı** ⊠ SE Turkey
142 K15 **Develi** Kayseri, C Turkey 38.22N 35.28E
100 M11 **Deventer** Overijssel, E Netherlands 52.15N 6.10E
13 O10 **Devenyns, Lac** ◎ Quebec, SE Canada
98 K8 **Deveron** ⁂ NE Scotland, UK
159 R14 **Devghar** prev. Deoghar. Bihār, NE India
29 R10 **Devil's Den** plateau Arkansas, C USA
37 R7 **Devils Gate** pass California, W USA 38.20N 119.23W
32 J2 **Devils Island** island Apostle Islands, Wisconsin, N USA
Devil's Island see Diable, Île du
31 P3 **Devils Lake** North Dakota, N USA 48.07N 98.49W
33 R10 **Devils Lake** ◎ Michigan, N USA
31 O3 **Devils Lake** ◎ North Dakota, N USA
37 W13 **Devils Playground** desert California, W USA
27 O11 **Devils River** ⁂ Texas, SW USA
35 Y12 **Devils Tower** ▲ Wyoming, C USA 44.33N 104.45W
116 I11 **Devin** prev. Dovlen. Smolyan, SW Bulgaria 41.45N 24.24E
27 R12 **Devine** Texas, SW USA 29.08N 98.54W
158 H13 **Devli** Rājasthān, N India 25.46N 75.22E
Devne see Devnya
116 N8 **Devnya** prev. Devne. Varna, E Bulgaria 43.13N 27.36E
33 U14 **Devola** Ohio, N USA 39.28N 81.28W
Devoll see Devollit, Lumi i
115 M21 **Devollit, Lumi i** var. Devoll. ⁂ SE Albania
9 Q14 **Devon** Alberta, SW Canada 53.21N 113.47W
99 I23 **Devon** cultural region SW England, UK
207 N10 **Devon Island** prev. North Devon Island. island Parry Islands, Nunavut, NE Canada
191 O16 **Devonport** Tasmania, SE Australia 41.14S 146.20E
142 H11 **Devrek** Zonguldak, N Turkey 41.13N 31.57E
160 G10 **Dewās** Madhya Pradesh, C India 22.58N 76.03E
De Westerein see Zwaagwesteinde
29 P8 **Dewey** Oklahoma, C USA 36.48N 95.56W
Dewey see Culebra
100 M8 **De Wijk** Drenthe, NE Netherlands 52.41N 6.13E
29 W12 **De Witt** Arkansas, C USA 34.17N 91.20W
31 Z14 **De Witt** Iowa, C USA 41.49N 90.32W
31 R16 **De Witt** Nebraska, C USA 40.23N 96.55W
99 M17 **Dewsbury** N England, UK 53.42N 1.37W
167 Q10 **Dexing** Jiangxi, S China 28.49N 117.37E
29 Y8 **Dexter** Missouri, C USA 36.48N 89.57W
39 U14 **Dexter** New Mexico, SW USA 33.12N 104.25W
166 I8 **Deyang** Sichuan, C China 31.07N 104.22E
190 C4 **Dey-Dey, Lake** salt lake South Australia
149 S7 **Deyhūk** Khorāsān, E Iran 33.18N 57.30E
152 K12 **Deynau** var. Dyanev, Turkm. Dänew. Lebapskiy Velayat, NE Turkmenistan 39.16N 63.09E
148 L8 **Dezfūl** var. Dizful. Khūzestān, SW Iran 32.22N 48.28E
133 X4 **Dezhneva, Mys** headland NE Russian Federation 66.07N 69.40W
167 P4 **Dezhou** Shandong, E China 37.28N 116.18E
Dezh Shāhpūr see Marīvān
Dhahran see Az̧ Z̧ahrān
Dhahran Al Khobar see Az̧ Z̧ahrān al Khubar
159 U14 **Dhaka** prev. Dacca. ● (Bangladesh) Dhaka, C Bangladesh 23.42N 90.22E
159 T15 **Dhaka** ◆ division C Bangladesh
Dhali see Idálion
147 O15 **Dhamār** W Yemen 14.31N 44.25E
Dhambul see Taraz
160 K12 **Dhamtari** Madhya Pradesh, C India 20.43N 81.36E
159 Q15 **Dhanbād** Bihār, NE India 23.48N 86.27E
158 L10 **Dhangadhi** var. Dhangarhi. Far Western, W Nepal 28.45N 80.38E
Dhangarhi see Dhangadhi
Dhank see Ḍank
159 R12 **Dhankuta** Eastern, E Nepal 27.06N 87.21E
158 I6 **Dhaola Dhār** ▲ NE India
160 F10 **Dhār** Madhya Pradesh, C India 22.36N 75.23E
159 R12 **Dharan** var. Dharan Bazar. Eastern, E Nepal 26.51N 87.18E
161 H21 **Dhārāpuram** Tamil Nādu, SE India 10.45N 77.33E
161 H20 **Dharmapuri** Tamil Nādu, SE India 12.10N 78.07E
161 H18 **Dharmavaram** Andhra Pradesh, E India 14.27N 77.43E
160 M11 **Dharmjaygarh** Madhya Pradesh, C India 22.27N 83.16E
Dharmsāla see Dharmshāla
158 I7 **Dharmshāla** prev. Dharmsāla. Himāchal Pradesh, N India 32.13N 76.24E
161 F17 **Dhārwād** prev. Dharwar. Karnātaka, SW India 15.30N 75.04E
Dharwar see Dhārwād
159 O10 **Dhaulāgiri** ▲ C Nepal 28.45N 83.27E
83 L18 **Dheere Laaq** var. Lak Dera, It. Lach Dera. seasonal river Kenya/Somalia
124 O3 **Dhekéleia Sovereign Base Area** UK military installation E Cyprus 34.59N 33.45E
124 O3 **Dhekélia** Eng. Dhekelia. Gk. Dekéleia. UK air base SE Cyprus 35.00N 33.45E
Dhelvinákion see Delvinákí
115 M22 **Dhëmbelit, Majae** ▲ S Albania 40.10N 20.22E
160 O12 **Dhenkānāl** Orissa, E India 20.40N 85.36E
Dheskáti see Deskáti
144 G11 **Dhībān** Al 'Āşimah, NW Jordan 31.30N 35.46E
Dhidhimótikhon see Didymóteicho
Dhíkti Ori see Díkti
144 I12 **Dhirwah, Wādī adh** dry watercourse C Jordan
Dhístomon see Dístomo
Dhodhekánisos see Dodekánisos
Dhodhóni see Dodóni
Dhofar see Z̧ufār
Dhomokós see Domokós
Dhond see Daund
161 H17 **Dhone** Andhra Pradesh, C India 15.25N 77.52E
160 B11 **Dhorāji** Gujarāt, W India 21.43N 70.27E
Dhráma see Dráma
160 C10 **Dhrāngadhra** Gujarāt, W India 22.58N 71.31E
Dhrepanon, Akrotírio see Drépano, Akrotírio
159 T13 **Dhuburi** Assam, NE India 26.06N 89.55E
160 F12 **Dhule** prev. Dhulia. Mahārāshtra, C India 20.54N 74.46E
Dhulia see Dhule
Dhún Dealgan, Cuan see Dundalk Bay
Dhún Droma, Cuan see Dundrum Bay
Dhún na nGall, Bá see Donegal Bay
Dhū Shaykh see Qazānīyah
82 Q13 **Dhuudo** Bari, NE Somalia 9.21N 50.19E
83 N15 **Dhuusa Marreeb** var. Dusa Marreb, It. Dusa Mareb. Galguduud, C Somalia 5.33N 46.24E
117 J24 **Día** island SE Greece
57 Y9 **Diable, Île du** var. Devil's Island. island N French Guiana
13 N12 **Diable, Rivière du** ⁂ Quebec, SE Canada
37 N8 **Diablo, Mount** ▲ California, W USA 37.52N 121.57W
37 O9 **Diablo Range** ▲ California, W USA
26 I8 **Diablo, Sierra** ▲ Texas, SW USA
47 O11 **Diablotins, Morne** ▲ N Dominica 15.30N 61.23W
79 N11 **Diafarabé** Mopti, C Mali 14.12N 5.01W
79 N11 **Diaka** ⁂ SW Mali
Diakovár see Đakovo
78 I12 **Dialakoto** S Senegal 13.21N 13.19W
63 B18 **Diamante** Entre Ríos, E Argentina 32.04S 60.40W
64 I12 **Diamante, Río** ⁂ C Argentina
61 M19 **Diamantina** Minas Gerais, SE Brazil 18.16S 43.37W
61 N17 **Diamantina, Chapada** ▲ E Brazil
181 U11 **Diamantina Fracture Zone** tectonic feature E Indian Ocean
189 T8 **Diamantina River** ⁂ Queensland/South Australia
40 D9 **Diamond Head** headland Oahu, Hawaii, USA, C Pacific Ocean 21.15N 157.48W
39 P2 **Diamond Peak** ▲ Colorado, C USA 40.56N 108.56W
37 W5 **Diamond Peak** ▲ Nevada, W USA 39.34N 115.46W
Diamond State see Delaware
78 J11 **Diamou** Kayes, SW Mali 14.04N 11.16W
97 I23 **Dianalund** Vestsjælland, C Denmark 55.31N 11.30E
67 G25 **Diana's Peak** ▲ C Saint Helena
166 M16 **Dianbai** Guangdong, S China 21.33N 110.58E
166 G13 **Dian Chi** ◎ SW China
108 B10 **Diano Marina** Liguria, NW Italy 43.55N 8.06E
79 R13 **Diapaga** E Burkina 12.04N 1.47E
Diarbekr see Diyarbakır
109 J15 **Diavolo, Passo del** pass C Italy 41.55N 13.42E
63 B18 **Díaz** Santa Fe, C Argentina 32.22S 61.04W
147 W6 **Dibā al Ḩişn** var. Dibāh, Dibba. Ash Shāriqah, NE UAE 25.34N 56.16E
145 S3 **Dībaga** N Iraq 35.51N 43.49E
Dibāh see Dibā al Ḩişn
81 L22 **Dibaya** Kasai Occidental, S Dem. Rep. Congo 6.31S 22.57E
Dibba see Dibā al Ḩişn
205 W15 **Dibble Iceberg Tongue** ice feature Antarctica
115 L19 **Dibër** ◆ district E Albania
85 I20 **Dibete** Central, SE Botswana 23.45S 26.29E
27 W9 **Diboll** Texas, SW USA 31.11N 94.46W
Dibra see Debar
159 X11 **Dibrugarh** Assam, NE India 27.29N 94.49E
56 G4 **Dibulla** La Guajira, N Colombia 11.14N 73.22W
27 O5 **Dickens** Texas, SW USA 33.37N 100.50W
21 R2 **Dickey** Maine, NE USA 47.04N 69.05W
32 K9 **Dickeyville** Wisconsin, N USA 42.37N 90.36W
30 K5 **Dickinson** North Dakota, N USA 46.54N 102.48W
(0) E6 **Dickins Seamount** undersea feature NE Pacific Ocean
29 O13 **Dickson** Oklahoma, C USA 34.11N 96.58W
22 I9 **Dickson** Tennessee, S USA 36.04N 87.23W
Dicle see Tigris
Dicsőszentmárton see Târnăveni
100 M12 **Didam** Gelderland, E Netherlands 51.55N 6.07E
169 Y8 **Didao** Heilongjiang, NE China 45.20N 130.54E
78 L12 **Didiéni** Koulikoro, W Mali 13.48N 8.01W
Didimo see Dídymo
Didimotiho see Didymóteicho
83 K17 **Didimtu** spring/well NE Kenya 2.58N 40.07E
69 U9 **Didinga Hills** ▲ S Sudan
9 Q16 **Didsbury** Alberta, SW Canada 51.39N 114.09W
158 G11 **Dīdwāna** Rājasthān, N India 27.22N 74.36E
117 G20 **Dídymo** var. Didimo. ▲ S Greece 37.28N 23.12E
116 L12 **Didymóteicho** var. Dhidhimótikhon, Didimotiho. Anatolikí Makedonía kai Thráki, NE Greece 41.22N 26.28E
105 S13 **Die** Drôme, E France 44.46N 5.21E
79 O13 **Diébougou** SW Burkina 11.00N 3.12W
Diedenhofen see Thionville
9 S16 **Diefenbaker, Lake** ◎ Saskatchewan, S Canada
64 H7 **Diego de Almagro** Atacama, N Chile 26.24S 70.10W
65 F23 **Diego de Almagro, Isla** island S Chile
63 A20 **Diego de Alvear** Santa Fe, C Argentina 34.24S 62.04W
181 Q7 **Diego Garcia** island S British Indian Ocean Territory
Diégo-Suarez see Antsirañana
101 M23 **Diekirch** Diekirch, C Luxembourg 49.52N 6.10E
101 L23 **Diekirch** ◆ district N Luxembourg
78 K11 **Diéma** Kayes, W Mali 14.28N 9.10W
103 H15 **Diemel** ⁂ W Germany
100 I10 **Diemen** Noord-Holland, C Netherlands 52.21N 4.58E
Diemrich see Deva
178 Ii6 **Điện Biên** var. Bien Bien, Dien Bien Phu. Lai Châu, N Vietnam 21.22N 103.01E
Dien Bien Phu see Điện Biên
178 Jj8 **Diễn Châu** Nghê An, N Vietnam 18.54N 105.35E
101 K18 **Diepenbeek** Limburg, NE Belgium 50.54N 5.25E
100 N11 **Diepenheim** Overijssel, E Netherlands 52.10N 6.37E
100 M10 **Diepenveen** Overijssel, E Netherlands 52.18N 6.09E
102 G12 **Diepholz** Niedersachsen, NW Germany 52.36N 8.22E
104 M3 **Dieppe** Seine-Maritime, N France 49.55N 1.04E
100 M12 **Dieren** Gelderland, E Netherlands 52.03N 6.06E
29 S13 **Dierks** Arkansas, C USA 34.07N 94.01W
101 J17 **Diest** Vlaams Brabant, C Belgium 50.58N 5.03E
110 F7 **Dietikon** Zürich, NW Switzerland 47.24N 8.25E
105 R13 **Dieulefit** Drôme, E France 44.30N 5.01E
105 T5 **Dieuze** Moselle, NE France 48.49N 6.41E
121 H15 **Dieveniškės** Šalčininkai, SE Lithuania 54.12N 25.38E
100 N7 **Diever** Drenthe, NE Netherlands 52.49N 6.19E
103 F17 **Diez** Rheinland-Pfalz, W Germany 50.22N 8.01E
79 Y12 **Diffa** Diffa, SE Niger 13.20N 12.39E
79 Y10 **Diffa** ◆ department SE Niger
101 L25 **Differdange** Luxembourg, SW Luxembourg 49.31N 5.52E
11 O16 **Digby** Nova Scotia, SE Canada 44.37N 65.46W
28 I5 **Dighton** Kansas, C USA 38.28N 100.28W
Dignano d'Istria see Vodnjan
105 T14 **Digne** var. Digne-les-Bains. Alpes-de-Haute-Provence, SE France 44.04N 6.13E
Digne-les-Bains see Digne
Digoel see Digul, Sungai
105 Q10 **Digoin** Saône-et-Loire, C France 46.30N 3.59E
179 Rr16 **Digos** Mindanao, S Philippines 6.46N 125.21E
155 Q16 **Digri** Sind, SE Pakistan 25.10N 69.10E
176 Z13 **Digul Barat, Sungai** ⁂ Papua, E Indonesia
176 Z14 **Digul, Sungai** prev. Digoel. ⁂ Papua, E Indonesia
176 Z13 **Digul Timur, Sungai** ⁂ Papua, E Indonesia
Dihang see Brahmaputra
159 X10 **Dihāng** ⁂ NE India
Dihōk see Dahūk
83 L17 **Diinsoor** Bay, S Somalia 2.28N 43.00E
Dijlah see Tigris
101 H17 **Dijle** ⁂ C Belgium
105 R8 **Dijon** anc. Dibio. Côte d'Or, C France 47.21N 5.03E
95 H14 **Dikanäs** Västerbotten, N Sweden 65.15N 16.00E
82 L12 **Dikhil** SW Djibouti 11.07N 42.18E
142 B13 **Dikili** İzmir, W Turkey 39.04N 26.52E
101 B17 **Diksmuide** var. Dixmuide, Fr. Dixmude. West-Vlaanderen, W Belgium 51.01N 2.52E
126 Hh6 **Dikson** Taymyrskiy (Dolgano-Nenetskiy) Avtonomnyy Okrug, N Russian Federation 73.30N 80.35E
117 K25 **Díkti** var. Dhíkti Ori. ▲ Kríti, Greece, E Mediterranean Sea
79 Z13 **Dikwa** Borno, NE Nigeria 12.00N 13.57E
83 J15 **Dīla** Southern, S Ethiopia 6.19N 38.16E
101 G18 **Dilbeek** Vlaams Brabant, C Belgium 50.51N 4.16E
175 S16 **Dili** var. Dilli, Dilly. ● (East Timor) N East Timor 8.33S 125.34E
79 Y11 **Dilia** var. Dillia. ⁂ SE Niger
Dilijan see Delijan
178 K13 **Di Linh** Lâm Đông, S Vietnam 11.34N 108.04E
103 G16 **Dillenburg** Hessen, W Germany 50.45N 8.16E
27 Q13 **Dilley** Texas, SW USA 28.40N 99.10W
Dilli see Delhi, India
Dilli see Dili, East Timor
Dillia see Dilia
82 E11 **Dilling** var. Ad Dalanj. Southern Kordofan, C Sudan 12.01N 29.40E
103 D20 **Dillingen** Saarland, SW Germany 49.20N 6.43E
Dillingen see Dillingen an der Donau
103 J22 **Dillingen an der Donau** var. Dillingen. Bayern, S Germany 48.34N 10.29E
41 O13 **Dillingham** Alaska, USA 59.03N 158.30W
35 Q12 **Dillon** Montana, NW USA 45.13N 112.37W
23 T12 **Dillon** South Carolina, SE USA 34.25N 79.22W
33 T13 **Dillon Lake** ⊠ Ohio, N USA
Dilly see Dili
Dilman see Salmās
81 K24 **Dilolo** Katanga, S Dem. Rep. Congo 10.42S 22.21E
117 J20 **Dílos** island Kykládes, Greece, Aegean Sea
147 Y11 **Ḑil', Ra's aḑ** headland E Oman 19.12N 57.53E
31 R5 **Dilworth** Minnesota, N USA 46.53N 96.38W
144 H7 **Dimashq** var. Ash Shām, Esh Sham, Eng. Damascus, Fr. Damas, It. Damasco. ● (Syria) Dimashq, SW Syria 33.30N 36.19E
144 I8 **Dimashq** off. Muḩāfaz̧at Dimashq, var. Damascus, Ar. Ash Sham, Ash Shām, Damasco, Esh Sham, Fr. Damas. ◆ governorate S Syria
144 I7 **Dimashq** ✕ Dimashq, S Syria 33.30N 36.19E
81 L21 **Dimbelenge** Kasai Occidental, C Dem. Rep. Congo 5.36S 23.04E
79 N16 **Dimbokro** E Ivory Coast 6.43N 4.43W
190 L11 **Dimboola** Victoria, SE Australia 36.29S 142.03E
Dimbovița see Dâmbovița
Dimitrov see Dymytrov
116 K11 **Dimitrovgrad** Khaskovo, S Bulgaria 42.03N 25.36E
131 R5 **Dimitrovgrad** Ul'yanovskaya Oblast', W Russian Federation 54.14N 49.37E
115 Q15 **Dimitrovgrad** prev. Caribrod. Serbia, SE Serbia and Montenegro (Yugoslavia) 43.01N 22.46E
Dimitrovo see Pernik
Dimlang see Vogel Peak
26 M3 **Dimmitt** Texas, SW USA 34.33N 102.18W
116 F7 **Dimovo** Vidin, NW Bulgaria 43.46N 22.46E
61 A16 **Dimpolis** Acre, W Brazil 9.52S 71.51W
117 O23 **Dimyliá** Ródos, Dodekánisos, Greece, Aegean Sea 36.17N 27.59E
179 R13 **Dinagat** Dinagat Island, S Philippines 10.00N 125.36E
179 Rr13 **Dinagat Island** island S Philippines
159 S13 **Dinajpur** Rajshahi, NW Bangladesh 25.37N 88.39E
104 I6 **Dinan** Côtes d'Armor, NW France 48.27N 2.01W
101 I21 **Dinant** Namur, S Belgium 50.16N 4.55E
142 E15 **Dinar** Afyon, SW Turkey 38.04N 30.09E
114 F13 **Dinara** ▲ W Croatia 43.49N 16.42E
Dinara see Dinaric Alps
104 I5 **Dinard** Ille-et-Vilaine, NW France 48.38N 2.04W
114 F13 **Dinaric Alps** var. Dinara. ▲ Bosnia and Herzegovina/Croatia
149 N10 **Dīnār, Kūh-e** ▲ C Iran 30.51N 51.36E
Dinbych see Denbigh
161 H22 **Dindigul** Tamil Nādu, SE India 10.23N 78.00E
85 M19 **Dindiza** Gaza, S Mozambique 23.22S 33.28E
155 V7 **Dinga** Punjab, E Pakistan 32.37N 73.45E
81 H21 **Dinga** Bandundu, SW Dem. Rep. Congo 5.00S 16.29E
164 L16 **Dinggyê** Xizang Zizhiqu, W China 28.18N 88.06E
99 A20 **Dingle** Ir. An Daingean. SW Ireland 52.08N 10.16W
99 A20 **Dingle Bay** Ir. Bá an Daingin. bay SW Ireland
20 I13 **Dingmans Ferry** Pennsylvania, NE USA 41.12N 74.51W
103 N22 **Dingolfing** Bayern, SE Germany 48.37N 12.28E
179 P8 **Dingras** Luzon, N Philippines 18.06N 120.43E
78 J13 **Dinguiraye** Haute-Guinée, N Guinea 11.19N 10.49W
98 I8 **Dingwall** N Scotland, UK 57.36N 4.25W
165 V10 **Dingxi** Gansu, C China 35.36N 104.33E
167 Q7 **Dingyuan** Anhui, E China 32.30N 117.40E
167 O3 **Dingzhou** prev. Ding Xian. Hebei, E China 38.31N 114.52E
178 K6 **Đinh Lâp** Lang Sơn, N Vietnam 21.33N 107.03E
178 K14 **Đinh Quan** Đông Nai, S Vietnam 11.11N 107.20E
102 E13 **Dinkel** ⁂ Germany/Netherlands
103 J21 **Dinkelsbühl** Bayern, S Germany 49.06N 10.18E
103 D14 **Dinslaken** Nordrhein-Westfalen, W Germany 51.34N 6.43E
37 R11 **Dinuba** California, W USA 36.32N 119.23W
23 W7 **Dinwiddie** Virginia, NE USA 37.04N 77.34W
100 N13 **Dinxperlo** Gelderland, E Netherlands 51.51N 6.30E
117 F14 **Dió** anc. Dium. site of ancient city Kentrikí Makedonía, N Greece 40.13N 22.30E
Diófás see Nucet
78 M12 **Dioïla** Koulikoro, W Mali 12.28N 6.43W
117 G19 **Dióryga Korinthou** Eng. Corinth Canal. canal S Greece
78 G12 **Diouloulou** SW Senegal 13.00N 16.34W
79 N11 **Dioura** Mopti, W Mali 14.48N 5.20W
78 G11 **Diourbel** W Senegal 14.38N 16.12W
158 L10 **Dipayal** Far Western, W Nepal 29.09N 80.46E
124 Oo2 **Dipkarpaz** Gk. Rizokarpaso, Rizokárpason. NE Cyprus 35.36N 34.23E
155 R17 **Diplo** Sind, SE Pakistan 24.29N 69.36E
179 Qq15 **Dipolog** var. Dipolog City. Mindanao, S Philippines 8.31N 123.20E
193 C23 **Dipton** Southland, South Island, NZ 45.55S 168.21E
79 O10 **Diré** Tombouctou, C Mali 16.12N 3.31W
82 L13 **Dirē Dawa** Dirē Dawa, E Ethiopia 9.34N 41.53E
Dirfis see Dírfys
117 H18 **Dírfys** var. Dirfis. ▲ Évvioa, C Greece
77 N9 **Dirj** var. Daraj, Darj. W Libya 30.09N 10.25E
188 G10 **Dirk Hartog Island** island Western Australia
79 Y8 **Dirkou** Agadez, NE Niger 18.45N 13.00E
189 X11 **Dirranbandi** Queensland, E Australia 28.37S 148.13E
83 O16 **Dirri** Galguduud, C Somalia 4.15N 46.31E
Dirschau see Tczew
39 N6 **Dirty Devil River** ⁂ Utah, W USA
34 E10 **Disappointment, Cape** headland Washington, NW USA 46.16N 124.06W
188 L8 **Disappointment, Lake** salt lake Western Australia
191 R12 **Disaster Bay** bay New South Wales, SE Australia
46 J11 **Discovery Bay** C Jamaica 18.27N 77.23W
190 K13 **Discovery Bay** inlet SE Australia
69 Y15 **Discovery II Fracture Zone** tectonic feature SW Indian Ocean
Discovery Seamount/Discovery Seamounts see Discovery Tablemount
67 O19 **Discovery Tablemount** var. Discovery Seamount, Discovery Seamounts. undersea feature SW Indian Ocean 42.00S 0.10E
110 G9 **Disentis** Rmsch. Mustér. Graubünden, S Switzerland 46.43N 8.52E
41 O10 **Dishna River** ⁂ Alaska, USA
205 X4 **Dismal Mountains** ▲ Antarctica
30 M14 **Dismal River** ⁂ Nebraska, C USA
Disna see Dzisna
101 L19 **Dison** Liège, E Belgium 50.37N 5.52E
159 V12 **Dispur** Assam, NE India 26.03N 91.52E
13 R11 **Disraeli** Quebec, SE Canada 45.58N 71.21W
117 F18 **Dístomo** prev. Dhístomon. Stereá Ellás, C Greece 38.25N 22.40E
117 H18 **Dístos, Límni** ◎ Évvoia, C Greece
61 L18 **Distrito Federal** Eng. Federal District. ◆ federal district C Brazil
43 P14 **Distrito Federal** ◆ federal district S Mexico
56 L4 **Distrito Federal** off. Territorio Distrito Federal. ◆ federal district N Venezuela
Distrito Federal, Territorio see Distrito Federal
118 J10 **Ditrău** Hung. Ditró. Harghita, C Romania 46.47N 25.30E
Ditró see Ditrău
160 B12 **Diu** Damān and Diu, W India 20.42N 70.58E
179 Rr14 **Diuata Mountains** ▲ Mindanao, S Philippines
Dium see Dió
111 S13 **Divača** SW Slovenia 45.40N 13.58E
104 K5 **Dives** ⁂ N France
Divichi see Dāvăçi
35 Q11 **Divide** Montana, NW USA 45.44N 112.47W
Divin see Dzivin
85 N18 **Divinhe** Sofala, E Mozambique 20.41S 34.46E
61 L20 **Divinópolis** Minas Gerais, SE Brazil 20.07S 44.55W
131 N13 **Divnoye** Stavropol'skiy Kray, SW Russian Federation 45.54N 43.18E
78 M17 **Divo** S Ivory Coast 5.49N 5.22W
Divodurum Mediomatricum see Metz
143 N13 **Divriği** Sivas, C Turkey 39.22N 38.06E
Diwaniyah see Ad Dīwānīyah
12 J10 **Dix Milles, Lac** ◎ Quebec, SE Canada
12 M8 **Dix Milles, Lac des** ◎ Quebec, SE Canada
Dixmude/Dixmuide see Diksmuide
37 N7 **Dixon** California, W USA 38.19N 121.49W
32 L10 **Dixon** Illinois, N USA 41.51N 89.26W
22 I6 **Dixon** Kentucky, S USA 37.30N 87.39W
29 V6 **Dixon** Missouri, C USA 37.59N 92.05W
39 S9 **Dixon** New Mexico, SW USA 36.10N 105.49W
41 Y15 **Dixon Entrance** strait Canada/USA
20 D14 **Dixonville** Pennsylvania, NE USA 40.43N 79.01W
143 T13 **Diyadin** Ağrı, E Turkey 39.33N 43.40E
145 V5 **Diyālá, Nahr** var. Rudkhaneh-ye Sīrvān, Sirwan. ⁂ Iran/Iraq see also Sīrvān, Rudkhaneh-ye
143 P15 **Diyarbakır** var. Diarbekr; anc. Amida. Diyarbakır, SE Turkey 37.55N 40.13E
143 P15 **Diyarbakır** var. Diarbekr. ◆ province SE Turkey
Dizful see Dezfūl
81 F16 **Dja** ⁂ SE Cameroon
Djadié see Zadié
79 X7 **Djado** Agadez, NE Niger 21.00N 12.11E
79 X6 **Djado, Plateau du** ▲ NE Niger
Djailolo see Halmahera, Pulau
Djajapura see Jayapura
Djakarta see Jakarta
Djakovica see Đakovica
Djakovo see Đakovo
81 G20 **Djambala** Plateaux, C Congo 2.31S 14.43E
Djambi see Jambi
Djambi see Hari, Batang, Sumatera, W Indonesia
76 M9 **Djanet** E Algeria 28.43N 8.57E
76 M11 **Djanet** prev. Fort Charlet. SE Algeria 24.34N 9.33E
Djatiwangi see Jatiwangi
Djaul see Dyaul Island
Djawa see Jawa
Djéblé see Jablah
80 I10 **Djédaa** Batha, C Chad 13.31N 18.34E
76 J6 **Djelfa** var. El Djelfa. N Algeria 34.42N 3.16E
81 M14 **Djéma** Haut-Mbomou, E Central African Republic 6.03N 25.19E
Djeneponto see Jeneponto
79 N12 **Djenné** var. Jenné. Mopti, C Mali 13.55N 4.34W
Djérablous see Jarābulus
Djerba see Jerba, Île de
81 F15 **Djérem** ⁂ C Cameroon
Djevdjelija see Gevgelija
79 P11 **Djibo** N Burkina 14.09N 1.37W
82 L12 **Djibouti** var. Jibuti. ● (Djibouti) E Djibouti 11.32N 42.55E
82 L12 **Djibouti** off. Republic of Djibouti, var. Jibuti; prev. French Somaliland, French Territory of the Afars and Issas, Fr. Côte Française des Somalis, Territoire Français des Afars et des Issas. ◆ republic E Africa
82 L12 **Djibouti** ✕ C Djibouti 11.29N 42.54E
Djidjel/Djidjelli see Jijel
57 W10 **Djoemoe** Sipaliwini, C Suriname 4.00N 55.27W
Djokjakarta see Yogyakarta
81 K21 **Djoku-Punda** Kasai Occidental, S Dem. Rep. Congo 5.27S 20.58E
81 K18 **Djolu** Equateur, N Dem. Rep. Congo 0.42N 22.23E
Djorče Petrov see Đorče Petrov
81 F17 **Djoua** ⁂ Congo/Gabon
79 R14 **Djougou** W Benin 9.42N 1.38E
81 F16 **Djoum** Sud, S Cameroon 2.38N 12.51E
80 I8 **Djourab, Erg du** dunes N Chad
81 P17 **Djugu** Orientale, NE Dem. Rep. Congo 1.55N 30.31E
Djumbir see Ďumbier
94 L3 **Djúpivogur** Austurland, SE Iceland 64.39N 14.18W
96 L13 **Djura** Dalarna, C Sweden 60.37N 15.00E
Djurdjevac see Đurđevac
85 G18 **D'Kar** Ghanzi, NW Botswana 21.31S 21.55E
207 U6 **Dmitriya Lapteva, Proliv** strait N Russian Federation
130 J7 **Dmitriyev-L'govskiy** Kurskaya Oblast', W Russian Federation 52.08N 35.09E
Dmitriyevsk see Makiyivka
130 K3 **Dmitrov** Moskovskaya Oblast', W Russian Federation 56.23N 37.30E
Dmitrovichi see Dzmitravichy
130 J6 **Dmitrovsk-Orlovskiy** Orlovskaya Oblast', W Russian Federation 52.28N 35.01E
119 R3 **Dmytrivka** Chernihivs'ka Oblast', N Ukraine 50.56N 32.57E
Dnepr see Dnieper
Dneprodzerzhinsk see Dniprodzerzhyns'k
Dneprodzerzhinskoye Vodokhranilishche see Dniprodzerzhyns'ke Vodoskhovyshche
Dnepropetrovsk see Dnipropetrovs'k
Dnepropetrovskaya Oblast' see Dnipropetrovs'ka Oblast'
Dneprorudnoye see Dniprorudne
Dneprovskiy Liman see Dniprovs'kyy Lyman
Dneprovsko-Bugskiy Kanal see Dnyaprowska-Buhski, Kanal
Dnestr see Dniester
Dnestrovskiy Liman see Dnistrovs'kyy Lyman
88 H11 **Dnieper** Bel. Dnyapro, Rus. Dnepr, Ukr. Dnipro. ⁂ E Europe
119 P3 **Dnieper Lowland** Bel. Prydnyaprowskaya Nizina, Ukr. Prydniprovs'ka Nyzovyna. lowlands Belarus/Ukraine
118 M8 **Dniester** Rom. Nistru, Rus. Dnestr, Ukr. Dnister; anc. Tyras. ⁂ Moldova/Ukraine
Dnipro see Dnieper
119 T7 **Dniprodzerzhyns'k** Rus. Dneprodzerzhinsk; prev. Kamenskoye. Dnipropetrovs'ka Oblast', E Ukraine 48.30N 34.35E
119 T7 **Dniprodzerzhyns'ke Vodoskhovyshche** Rus. Dneprodzerzhinskoye Vodokhranilishche. ⊠ C Ukraine
119 U7 **Dnipropetrovs'k** Rus. Dnepropetrovsk; prev. Yekaterinoslav. Dnipropetrovs'ka Oblast', E Ukraine 48.28N 34.59E

◆ Country ● Country Capital ◇ Dependent Territory ○ Dependent Territory Capital ◆ Administrative Region ✕ International Airport ▲ Mountain ▲ Mountain Range ▲ Volcano ⁂ River ◎ Lake ⊠ Reservoir

119 U8 **Dnipropetrovs'k** ✕ Dnipropetrovs'ka Oblast', S Ukraine 48.20N 35.04E
Dnipropetrovs'k see Dnipropetrovs'ka Oblast'
119 T7 **Dnipropetrovs'ka Oblast'** var. Dnipropetrovs'k, Rus. Dnepropetrovskaya Oblast'. ◈ province E Ukraine
119 U9 **Dniprorudne** Rus. Dneprorudnoye. Zaporiz'ka Oblast', SE Ukraine 47.21N 35.00E
119 Q11 **Dniprovs'kyy Lyman** Rus. Dneprovskiy Liman. bay S Ukraine
Dnister see Dniester
119 O11 **Dnistrovs'kyy Lyman** Rus. Dnestrovskiy Liman. inlet S Ukraine
128 G14 **Dno** Pskovskaya Oblast', W Russian Federation 57.48N 29.58E
Dnyapro see Dnieper
121 H20 **Dnyaprowska-Buhski, Kanal** Rus. Dneprovsko-Bugskiy Kanal. canal SW Belarus
11 O14 **Doaktown** New Brunswick, SE Canada 46.34N 66.06W
80 H13 **Doba** Logone-Oriental, S Chad 8.40N 16.49E
120 E9 **Dobele** Ger. Doblen. Dobele, W Latvia 56.36N 23.14E
103 N16 **Döbeln** Sachsen, E Germany 51.07N 13.07E
176 Vv9 **Doberai, Jazirah** Dut. Vogelkop. peninsula Papua, E Indonesia
112 F10 **Dobiegniew** Ger. Lubuskie, W Poland 52.58N 15.43E
Doblen see Dobele
83 K18 **Dobli** spring/well SW Somalia 0.24N 41.18E
176 W13 **Dobo** Pulau Wamar, E Indonesia 5.45S 134.12E
114 H11 **Doboj** Republika Srpska, N Bosnia and Herzegovina 44.45N 18.03E
112 L8 **Dobre Miasto** Ger. Guttstadt. Warmińsko-Mazurskie, NE Poland 53.59N 20.25E
116 N7 **Dobrich** Rom. Bazargic; prev. Tolbukhin. Dobrich, NE Bulgaria 43.34N 27.49E
116 N7 **Dobrich** ◈ province NE Bulgaria
130 M8 **Dobrinka** Lipetskaya Oblast', W Russian Federation 52.10N 40.30E
130 M7 **Dobrinka** Volgogradskaya Oblast', SW Russian Federation 50.52N 41.48E
Dobrla Vas see Eberndorf
113 I15 **Dobrodzień** Ger. Guttentag. Opolskie, S Poland 50.43N 18.24E
Dobrogea see Dobruja
119 W7 **Dobropillya** Rus. Dobropol'ye. Donets'ka Oblast', SE Ukraine 48.29N 37.06E
Dobropol'ye see Dobropillya
119 P8 **Dobrovelychkivka** Kirovohrads'ka Oblast', C Ukraine 48.22N 31.12E
Dobrudja/Dobrudzha see Dobruja
116 O7 **Dobruja** var. Dobrudja, Bul. Dobrudzha, Rom. Dobrogea. physical region Bulgaria/Romania
121 P19 **Dobrush** Homyel'skaya Voblasts', SE Belarus 52.25N 31.21E
129 U14 **Dobryanka** Permskaya Oblast', NW Russian Federation 58.28N 56.27E
119 P2 **Dobryanka** Chernihivs'ka Oblast', N Ukraine 52.03N 31.09E
Dobryn' see Dabryn'
23 R8 **Dobson** North Carolina, SE USA 36.30N 80.54W
61 N20 **Doce, Rio** ≈ SE Brazil
95 I16 **Dockstа** Västernorrland, C Sweden 63.06N 18.22E
43 N10 **Doctor Arroyo** Nuevo León, NE Mexico 23.40N 100.09W
64 L4 **Doctor Pedro P. Peña** Boquerón, W Paraguay 22.22S 62.22W
175 T7 **Dodaga** Pulau Halmahera, E Indonesia 1.06N 128.10E
161 G21 **Dodda Betta** ▲ S India 11.28N 76.44E
Dodecanese see Dodekánisos
117 M22 **Dodekánisos** var. Nóties Sporádes, Eng. Dodecanese; prev. Dhodhekánisos. island group SE Greece
28 J6 **Dodge City** Kansas, C USA 37.45N 100.01W
32 K9 **Dodgeville** Wisconsin, N USA 42.57N 90.07W
99 H25 **Dodman Point** headland SW England, UK 50.13N 4.47W
83 J14 **Dodola** Oromo, C Ethiopia 7.00N 39.15E
83 H22 **Dodoma** ● (Tanzania) Dodoma, C Tanzania 6.10S 35.45E
83 H22 **Dodoma** ◈ region C Tanzania
117 C16 **Dodóni** var. Dhodhóni. site of ancient city Ípeiros, W Greece 39.33N 20.47E
35 U7 **Dodson** Montana, NW USA 48.25N 108.18W
27 P3 **Dodson** Texas, SW USA 34.46N 100.01W
100 M12 **Doesburg** Gelderland, E Netherlands 52.01N 6.07E
100 N12 **Doetinchem** Gelderland, E Netherlands 51.58N 6.16E
164 L12 **Dogai Coring** var. Lake Montcalm. ◎ W China
143 N15 **Doğanşehir** Malatya, C Turkey 38.06N 37.52E
86 E9 **Dogger Bank** undersea feature C North Sea
25 S10 **Dog Island** island Florida, SE USA
12 C7 **Dog Lake** ◎ Ontario, S Canada
108 B9 **Dogliani** Piemonte, NE Italy 44.33N 7.55E
170 G11 **Dōgo** island Oki-shotō, SW Japan
Do Gonbadān see Dow Gonbadān
79 S12 **Dogondoutchi** Dosso, SW Niger 13.37N 4.03E
Dōgo-san see Dōgo-yama
170 F13 **Dōgo-yama** var. Dōgo-san. ▲ Kyūshū, SW Japan 35.03N 133.12E
Dogrular see Pravda
143 T13 **Doğubayazıt** Ağrı, E Turkey 39.33N 44.07E
143 P12 **Doğu Karadeniz Dağları** var. Anadolu Dağları. ▲▲ NE Turkey
Doha see Ad Dawḩah
Dohad see Dāhod
Dohuk see Dahūk
165 N16 **Doilungdêqên** Xizang Zizhiqu, W China 29.41N 90.58E
116 F12 **Doïranis, Límnis** Bul. Ezero Doyransko. ◎ N Greece
Doire see Londonderry
101 H22 **Doische** Namur, S Belgium 50.09N 4.43E
61 P17 **Dois de Julho** ✕ (Salvador) Bahia, NE Brazil 12.04S 38.58W
62 H12 **Dois Vizinhos** Paraná, S Brazil 25.47S 53.03W
82 H10 **Doka** Gedaref, E Sudan 13.30N 35.46E
Doka see Kéita, Bahr
145 T3 **Dokan** var. Dūkān. E Iraq 35.55N 44.58E
96 H13 **Dokka** Oppland, S Norway 60.49N 10.04E
100 L5 **Dokkum** Friesland, N Netherlands 53.20N 6.00E
100 L5 **Dokkumer Ee** ≈ N Netherlands
78 K13 **Doko** Haute-Guinée, NE Guinea 11.46N 8.58W
Dokshitsy see Dokshytsy
120 K13 **Dokshytsy** Rus. Dokshitsy. Vitsyebskaya Voblasts', N Belarus 54.54N 27.46E
119 X8 **Dokuchayevs'k** var. Dokuchayevsk. Donets'ka Oblast', SE Ukraine 47.43N 37.40E
Dolak, Pulau see Yos Sudarso, Pulau
31 P9 **Doland** South Dakota, N USA 44.51N 98.06W
65 J18 **Dolavón** Chaco, S Argentina 43.20S 65.42W
13 P6 **Dolbeau** Quebec, SE Canada 48.52N 72.15W
104 I5 **Dol-de-Bretagne** Ille-et-Vilaine, NW France 48.33N 1.45W
66 J13 **Doldrums Fracture Zone** tectonic feature W Atlantic Ocean
105 S8 **Dôle** Jura, E France 47.04N 5.30E
99 J19 **Dolgellau** NW Wales, UK 52.44N 3.54W
Dolginovo see Dawhinava
Dolgi, Ostrov see Dolgiy, Ostrov
129 U2 **Dolgiy, Ostrov** var. Ostrov Dolgi. island NW Russian Federation
168 J9 **Dölgöön** Övörhangay, C Mongolia 45.57N 103.14E
109 C20 **Dolianova** Sardegna, Italy, C Mediterranean Sea 39.23N 9.08E
Dolina see Dolyna
127 Oo15 **Dolinsk** Ostrov Sakhalin, Sakhalinskaya Oblast', SE Russian Federation 47.20N 142.52E
Dolinskaya see Dolyns'ka
81 F21 **Dolisie** prev. Loubomo. Le Niari, S Congo 4.12S 12.40E
118 G14 **Dolj** ◈ county SW Romania
100 P5 **Dollard** bay NW Germany
204 J5 **Dolleman Island** island Antarctica
116 I8 **Dolni Dŭbnik** Pleven, N Bulgaria 43.24N 24.25E
116 F8 **Dolni Lom** Vidin, NW Bulgaria 43.31N 22.46E
Dolnja Lendava see Lendava
116 K9 **Dolno Panicherevo** var. Panicherevo. Sliven, C Bulgaria 42.36N 25.51E
113 F14 **Dolnośląskie** ◈ province SW Poland
113 K18 **Dolný Kubín** Hung. Alsókubin. Žilinský Kraj, N Slovakia 49.13N 19.16E
108 H8 **Dolo** Veneto, NE Italy 45.25N 12.06E
Dolomites/Dolomiti see Dolomitiche, Alpi
108 H6 **Dolomitiche, Alpi** var. Dolomiti, Eng. Dolomites. ▲▲ NE Italy
Dolonnur see Duolun
168 K10 **Doloon** Ömnögovĭ, S Mongolia 44.28N 105.22E
63 E21 **Dolores** Buenos Aires, E Argentina 36.21S 57.39W
44 E3 **Dolores** Petén, N Guatemala 16.33N 89.25W
179 R12 **Dolores** Samar, C Philippines 12.01N 125.27E
107 S12 **Dolores** País Valenciano, E Spain 38.09N 0.45W
63 D19 **Dolores** Soriano, SW Uruguay 33.34S 58.15W
43 N12 **Dolores Hidalgo** var. Ciudad de Dolores Hidalgo. Guanajuato, C Mexico 21.10N 100.55W
15 Hh3 **Dolphin and Union Strait** strait Northwest Territories / Nunavut, N Canada
67 D23 **Dolphin, Cape** headland East Falkland, Falkland Islands 51.15S 58.57W
46 H12 **Dolphin Head** hill W Jamaica 18.21N 78.08W
85 B21 **Dolphin Head** var. Cape Dernberg. headland SW Namibia 25.33S 14.36E
112 G12 **Dolsk** Ger. Dolzig. Wielkolpolskie, C Poland 51.59N 17.03E
178 J8 **Đô Lương** Nghê An, N Vietnam 18.51N 105.19E
118 I6 **Dolyna** Rus. Dolina. Ivano-Frankivs'ka Oblast', W Ukraine 48.58N 24.01E
119 R8 **Dolyns'ka** Rus. Dolinskaya. Kirovohrads'ka Oblast', S Ukraine 48.06N 32.46E
Dolzig see Dolsk
Domachëvo/Domaczewo see Damachava
119 P9 **Domanivka** Mykolayivs'ka Oblast', S Ukraine 47.40N 30.56E
159 S13 **Domar** Rajshahi, N Bangladesh 26.09N 88.49E
110 I9 **Domat/Ems** Graubünden, SE Switzerland 46.49N 9.28E
113 A18 **Domažlice** Ger. Taus. Plzeňský Kraj, W Czech Republic 49.25N 12.55E
131 X8 **Dombarovskiy** Orenburgskaya Oblast', W Russian Federation 50.53N 59.18E
96 G10 **Dombås** Oppland, S Norway 62.04N 9.07E
85 M17 **Dombe** Manica, C Mozambique 19.59S 33.24E
84 A13 **Dombe Grande** Benguela, C Angola 12.57S 13.07E
105 R10 **Dombes** physical region E France
176 Xx10 **Dombo** Papua, E Indonesia 1.52S 137.09E
113 I25 **Dombóvár** Tolna, S Hungary 46.24N 18.09E
101 D14 **Domburg** Zeeland, SW Netherlands 51.34N 3.30E
60 L13 **Dom Eliseu** Pará, NE Brazil 4.02S 47.31W
Domel Island see Letsôk-aw Kyun
105 O11 **Dôme, Puy de** ▲ C France 45.46N 3.00E
38 H13 **Dome Rock Mountains** ▲▲ Arizona, SW USA
Domesnes, Cape see Kolkasrags
64 G8 **Domeyko** Atacama, N Chile 28.57S 70.54W
64 H5 **Domeyko, Cordillera** ▲▲ N Chile
104 K5 **Domfront** Orne, N France 48.35N 0.39W
176 Xx10 **Dom, Gunung** ▲ Papua, E Indonesia 2.41S 137.00E
47 X11 **Dominica** off. Commonwealth of Dominica. ◆ republic E West Indies
49 S3 **Dominica** island Dominica
Dominica Channel see Martinique Passage
45 N15 **Dominical** Puntarenas, SE Costa Rica 9.16N 83.52W
47 Q8 **Dominican Republic** ◆ republic C West Indies
47 X11 **Dominica Passage** passage E Caribbean Sea
101 K14 **Dommel** ≈ S Netherlands
83 O14 **Domo** Somali, E Ethiopia 7.53N 46.55E
130 L4 **Domodedovo** ✕ (Moskva) Moskovskaya Oblast', W Russian Federation 55.19N 37.55E
108 C6 **Domodossola** Piemonte, NE Italy 46.07N 8.20E
117 F17 **Domokós** var. Dhomokós. Stereá Ellás, C Greece 39.07N 22.18E
180 I14 **Domoni** Anjouan, SE Comoros 12.15S 44.39E
63 G16 **Dom Pedrito** Rio Grande do Sul, S Brazil 30.55S 54.39W
Dompoe see Dompu
175 Oo16 **Dompu** prev. Dompoe. Sumbawa, C Indonesia 8.30S 118.28E
Domschale see Domžale
64 H13 **Domuyo, Volcán** ⊼ W Argentina 36.36S 70.22W
111 U11 **Domžale** Ger. Domschale. C Slovenia 46.09N 14.33E
131 O10 **Don** var. Duna, Tanais. ≈ SW Russian Federation
98 K9 **Don** ≈ NE Scotland, UK
190 M11 **Donald** Victoria, SE Australia 36.27S 143.03E
24 J9 **Donaldsonville** Louisiana, S USA 30.06N 90.59W
25 S8 **Donalsonville** Georgia, SE USA 31.02N 84.52W
Donau see Danube
103 G23 **Donaueschingen** Baden-Württemberg, SW Germany 47.57N 8.30E
103 K22 **Donaumoos** wetland S Germany
103 K22 **Donauwörth** Bayern, S Germany 48.43N 10.46E
111 U7 **Donawitz** Steiermark, SE Austria 47.23N 15.00E
119 X7 **Donbass** industrial region Russian Federation/Ukraine
106 K11 **Don Benito** Extremadura, W Spain 38.57N 5.52W
99 M17 **Doncaster** anc. Danum. N England, UK 53.31N 1.07W
46 K12 **Don Christophers Point** headland C Jamaica 18.19N 76.48W
57 V9 **Donderkamp** Sipaliwini, NW Suriname 5.18N 56.22W
84 B12 **Dondo** Cuanza Norte, NW Angola 9.40S 14.24E
175 Q9 **Dondo** Sulawesi, N Indonesia 0.54S 121.33E
85 N17 **Dondo** Sofala, C Mozambique 19.36S 34.46E
175 Pp7 **Dondo, Teluk** bay Sulawesi, N Indonesia
161 K26 **Dondra Head** headland S Sri Lanka 5.57N 80.33E
Donduşani see Donduşeni
118 M8 **Donduşeni** var. Donduşani, Rus. Dondyushany. N Moldova 48.13N 27.38E
Dondyushany see Donduşeni
99 D15 **Donegal** Ir. Dún na nGall. NW Ireland 54.39N 8.06W
99 D14 **Donegal** Ir. Dún na nGall. cultural region NW Ireland
99 C15 **Donegal Bay** Ir. Bá Dhún na nGall. bay NW Ireland
86 K10 **Donets** ≈ Russian Federation/Ukraine
119 X8 **Donets'k** Rus. Donetsk; prev. Stalino. Donets'ka Oblast', E Ukraine 47.58N 37.49E
119 W8 **Donets'k** ✕ Donets'ka Oblast', E Ukraine 48.03N 37.44E
Donets'k see Donets'ka Oblast'
119 W8 **Donets'ka Oblast'** var. Donets'k, Rus. Donetskaya Oblast'; prev. Rus. Stalinskaya Oblast'. ◈ province SE Ukraine
Donetskaya Oblast' see Donets'ka Oblast'
69 P8 **Donga** ≈ Cameroon/Nigeria
163 O13 **Dongchuan** Yunnan, SW China 26.09N 103.10E
101 I14 **Dongen** Noord-Brabant, S Netherlands 51.37N 4.55E
166 K17 **Dongfang** var. Basuo. Hainan, S China 19.05N 108.40E
169 Z7 **Dongfanghong** Heilongjiang, NE China 46.13N 133.13E
169 W11 **Dongfeng** Jilin, NE China 42.39N 125.33E
175 P9 **Donggala** Sulawesi, C Indonesia 0.40S 119.43E
169 V13 **Donggou** Liaoning, NE China 39.52N 124.07E
167 O14 **Dongguan** Guangdong, S China 23.03N 113.43E
178 K9 **Đông Hà** Quang Tri, C Vietnam 16.45N 107.10E
Dong Hai see East China Sea
166 M16 **Donghai Dao** island S China
178 Jj9 **Đông Hơi** Quang Binh, C Vietnam 17.30N 106.34E
110 H10 **Dongio** Ticino, S Switzerland 46.27N 8.58E
Dongkan see Binhai
166 L11 **Dongkou** Hunan, S China 27.06N 110.34E
Dongliao see Liaoyuan
Dong-nai see Đông Nai, Sông
178 K13 **Đông Nai, Sông** var. Dong-nai, Dong Noi, Donnai. ≈ S Vietnam
167 O14 **Dongnan Qiuling** plateau SE China
169 Y9 **Dongning** Heilongjiang, NE China 44.01N 131.03E
Dong Noi see Đông Nai, Sông
85 C14 **Dongo** Huíla, C Angola 14.35S 15.51E
82 E7 **Dongola** var. Donqola, Dunqulah. Northern, N Sudan 19.10N 30.27E
81 I17 **Dongou** La Likouala, NE Congo 2.04N 18.00E
178 Jj13 **Đông Phu** Sông Be, S Vietnam 11.31N 106.55E
Dong Rak, Phanom see Dângrêk, Chuŏr Phnum
167 Q14 **Dongshan Dao** island SE China
169 N14 **Dongsheng** Nei Mongol Zizhiqu, N China 39.51N 110.00E
167 R7 **Dongtai** Jiangsu, E China 32.52N 120.13E
167 N10 **Dongting Hu** var. Tung-t'ing Hu. ◎ S China
167 P10 **Dongxiang** Jiangxi, S China 28.17N 116.36E
167 Q4 **Dongying** Shandong, E China 37.27N 118.01E
29 X8 **Doniphan** Missouri, C USA 36.37N 90.49W
8 G7 **Donjek** ≈ Yukon Territory, W Canada
114 E11 **Donji Lapac** Lika-Senj, W Croatia 44.33N 15.58E
114 H8 **Donji Miholjac** Osijek-Baranja, NE Croatia 45.45N 18.10E
114 P12 **Donji Milanovac** Serbia, E Serbia and Montenegro (Yugoslavia) 44.27N 22.06E
114 G12 **Donji Vakuf** var. Srbobran, Federacija Bosna I Hercegovina, C Bosnia & Herzegovina 44.08N 17.23E
100 M6 **Donkerbroek** Friesland, N Netherlands 52.58N 5.15E
178 Hh11 **Don Muang** ✕ (Krung Thep) Nonthaburi, C Thailand 13.51N 100.40E
27 S17 **Donna** Texas, SW USA 26.10N 98.03W
13 Q10 **Donnacona** Quebec, SE Canada 46.41N 71.46W
Donnai see Đông Nai, Sông
31 Y16 **Donnellson** Iowa, C USA 40.38N 91.33W
9 O13 **Donnelly** Alberta, W Canada 55.42N 117.06W
37 P6 **Donner Pass** pass California, W USA 39.19N 120.19W
103 F19 **Donnersberg** ▲ W Germany 49.37N 7.54E
Donoso see Miguel de la Borda
107 P2 **Donostia-San Sebastián** País Vasco, N Spain 43.19N 1.58W
117 K21 **Donoúsa** island Kykládes, Greece, Aegean Sea
37 P8 **Don Pedro Reservoir** ▣ California, W USA
Donqola see Dongola
130 L5 **Donskoy** Tul'skaya Oblast', W Russian Federation 54.02N 38.27E
179 Q11 **Donsol** Luzon, N Philippines 12.56N 123.34E
83 L16 **Doolow** Somali, E Ethiopia 4.10N 42.04E
41 Q7 **Doonerak, Mount** ▲ Alaska, USA 67.54N 150.33W
100 J12 **Doorn** Utrecht, C Netherlands 52.01N 5.21E
Doornik see Tournai
33 N6 **Door Peninsula** peninsula Wisconsin, N USA
82 P13 **Dooxo Nugaaleed** var. Nogal Valley. valley E Somalia
166 G8 **Do Qu** ≈ C China
108 B7 **Dora Baltea** anc. Duria Major. ≈ NW Italy
188 K7 **Dora, Lake** salt lake Western Australia
108 A8 **Dora Riparia** anc. Duria Minor. ≈ NW Italy
Dorbiljin see Emin
169 V8 **Dorbod** var. Dorbod Mongolzu Zizhixian, Talkang. Heilongjiang, NE China 46.50N 124.25E
Dorbod Mongolzu Zizhixian see Dorbod
115 N18 **Đorče Petrov** var. Djorče Petrov, Gorče Petrov. N FYR Macedonia 42.01N 21.21E
12 F16 **Dorchester** Ontario, S Canada 43.00N 81.04W
99 L24 **Dorchester** anc. Durnovaria. S England, UK 50.43N 2.25W
15 Mm4 **Dorchester, Cape** headland Baffin Island, Nunavut, NE Canada 65.25N 77.25W
85 D19 **Dordabis** Khomas, C Namibia 22.57S 17.39E
104 L12 **Dordogne** ◈ department SW France
105 N12 **Dordogne** ≈ W France
100 H13 **Dordrecht** var. Dordt, Dort. Zuid-Holland, SW Netherlands 51.48N 4.40E
Dordt see Dordrecht
105 P11 **Dore** ≈ C France
9 S13 **Doré Lake** Saskatchewan, C Canada 54.37N 107.36W
105 O12 **Dore, Monts** ▲ C France
103 M23 **Dorfen** Bayern, SE Germany 48.16N 12.06E
109 D18 **Dorgali** Sardegna, Italy, C Mediterranean Sea 40.18N 9.34E
168 F7 **Dörgön Nuur** ◎ NW Mongolia
79 Q12 **Dori** N Burkina 14.03N 0.01W
85 E24 **Doring** ≈ S South Africa
103 E16 **Dormagen** Nordrhein-Westfalen, W Germany 51.06N 6.49E
105 P4 **Dormans** Marne, N France 49.03N 3.44E
110 E6 **Dornach** Solothurn, NW Switzerland 47.28N 7.37E
Dorna Watra see Vatra Dornei
110 J7 **Dornbirn** Vorarlberg, W Austria 47.25N 9.46E
98 I7 **Dornoch** N Scotland, UK 57.52N 4.00W
98 J7 **Dornoch Firth** inlet N Scotland, UK
169 P7 **Dornod** ◈ province E Mongolia
169 N10 **Dornogovĭ** ◈ province SE Mongolia
79 P10 **Doro** Tombouctou, S Mali 16.07N 0.57W
118 L14 **Dorobanţu** Călăraşi, S Romania 44.15N 26.55E
113 J22 **Dorog** Komárom-Esztergom, N Hungary 47.42N 18.44E
130 I4 **Dorogobuzh** Smolenskaya Oblast', W Russian Federation 54.56N 33.16E
118 K8 **Dorohoi** Botoşani, NE Romania 47.57N 26.24E
95 H15 **Dorotea** Västerbotten, N Sweden 64.16N 16.30E
Dorpat see Tartu
188 G10 **Dorre Island** island Western Australia
191 U5 **Dorrigo** New South Wales, SE Australia 30.22S 152.43E
37 N1 **Dorris** California, W USA 41.58N 121.54W
12 H13 **Dorset** Ontario, SE Canada 45.12N 78.52W
99 K23 **Dorset** cultural region S England, UK
103 E14 **Dorsten** Nordrhein-Westfalen, W Germany 51.40N 6.58E
Dort see Dordrecht
103 F15 **Dortmund** Nordrhein-Westfalen, W Germany 51.31N 7.28E
102 F12 **Dortmund-Ems-Kanal** canal W Germany
142 L17 **Dörtyol** Hatay, S Turkey 36.51N 36.10E
148 L7 **Do Rūd** var. Dow Rūd, Durud. Lorestān, W Iran 33.31N 49.03E
81 O15 **Doruma** Orientale, N Dem. Rep. Congo 4.35N 27.43E
13 O12 **Dorval** ✕ (Montréal) Quebec, SE Canada 45.27N 73.46W
47 T5 **Dos Bocas, Lago** ◎ C Puerto Rico
106 K14 **Dos Hermanas** Andalucía, S Spain 37.16N 5.55W
Dospad Dagh see Rhodope Mountains
37 P10 **Dos Palos** California, W USA 37.00N 120.39W
116 I11 **Dospat** Smolyan, S Bulgaria 41.39N 24.10E
116 H11 **Dospat, Yazovir** ▣ SW Bulgaria
102 M11 **Dosse** ≈ NE Germany
79 S12 **Dosso** Dosso, SW Niger 12.59N 3.13E
79 S12 **Dosso** ◈ department SW Niger
150 G12 **Dossor** Atyrau, SW Kazakhstan 47.32N 52.58E
153 O10 **Do'stlik** Jizzax Viloyati, C Uzbekistan 40.37N 67.59E
153 V9 **Dostuk** Narynskaya Oblast', C Kyrgyzstan 41.19N 75.40E
151 X13 **Dostyk** prev. Druzhba. Almaty, SE Kazakhstan 45.15N 82.28E
25 R7 **Dothan** Alabama, S USA 31.13N 85.23W
41 T9 **Dot Lake** Alaska, USA 63.39N 144.10W
120 F12 **Dotnuva** Kėdainiai, C Lithuania 55.22N 23.52E
101 D19 **Dottignies** Hainaut, W Belgium 50.43N 3.16E
105 P2 **Douai** prev. Douay, anc. Duacum. Nord, N France 50.22N 3.04E
12 L9 **Douaire, Lac** ◎ Quebec, SE Canada
81 D16 **Douala** var. Duala. Littoral, W Cameroon 4.04N 9.43E
81 D16 **Douala** ✕ Littoral, W Cameroon 3.57N 9.48E
104 F6 **Douarnenez** Finistère, NW France 48.04N 4.19W
104 E6 **Douarnenez, Baie de** bay NW France
Douay see Douai
27 O6 **Double Mountain Fork Brazos River** ≈ Texas, SW USA
25 O3 **Double Springs** Alabama, S USA 34.09N 87.24W
105 T8 **Doubs** ◈ department E France
110 C8 **Doubs** ≈ France/Switzerland
193 A22 **Doubtful Sound** sound South Island, NZ
192 J2 **Doubtless Bay** bay North Island, NZ
27 X9 **Doucette** Texas, SW USA 30.48N 94.25W
104 K8 **Doué-la-Fontaine** Maine-et-Loire, NW France 47.12N 0.16W
79 O11 **Douentza** Mopti, S Mali 14.59N 2.57W
40 L9 **Douglas** East Falkland, Falkland Islands
99 I16 **Douglas** ○ (Isle of Man) E Isle of Man 54.09N 4.28W
85 H23 **Douglas** Northern Cape, C South Africa 29.03S 23.46E
41 X13 **Douglas** Alexander Archipelago, Alaska, USA 58.12N 134.18W
39 O17 **Douglas** Arizona, SW USA 31.20N 109.32W
25 U7 **Douglas** Georgia, SE USA 31.30N 82.51W
35 Y15 **Douglas** Wyoming, C USA 42.48N 105.22W
23 O7 **Douglas, Cape** headland Alaska USA 64.59N 166.41W
8 J14 **Douglas Channel** channel British Columbia, W Canada
190 G3 **Douglas Creek** seasonal river South Australia
33 P5 **Douglas Lake** ◎ Michigan, N USA
23 O9 **Douglas Lake** ▣ Tennessee, S USA
41 Q13 **Douglas, Mount** ▲ Alaska, USA 58.51N 153.31W
204 J6 **Douglas Range** ▲▲ Alexander Island, Antarctica
124 N10 **Doukáto, Akrotírio** headland Lefkáda, W Greece 38.35N 20.33E
105 O2 **Doullens** Somme, N France 50.09N 2.21E
Douma see Dūmā
81 F15 **Doumé** Est, E Cameroon 4.13N 13.27E
101 E21 **Dour** Hainaut, S Belgium 50.24N 3.46E
61 K18 **Dourada, Serra** ▲▲ S Brazil
61 I21 **Dourados** Mato Grosso do Sul, S Brazil 22.09S 54.52W
105 N5 **Dourdan** Essonne, N France 48.33N 1.58E
106 I6 **Douro** Sp. Duero. ≈ Portugal/Spain see also Duero
106 G6 **Douro Litoral** former province N Portugal
Douvres see Dover
104 K15 **Douze** ≈ SW France
191 P17 **Dover** Tasmania, SE Australia 43.19S 147.01E
99 Q22 **Dover** Fr. Douvres; Lat. Dubris Portus. SE England, UK 51.08N 3.00W
19 Rr8 **Dover** state capital Delaware, NE USA 39.09N 75.31W
21 P9 **Dover** New Hampshire, NE USA 43.10N 70.50W
20 J14 **Dover** New Jersey, NE USA 40.51N 74.33W
33 U12 **Dover** Ohio, N USA 40.31N 81.28W
22 H8 **Dover** Tennessee, S USA 36.29N 87.50W
99 Q23 **Dover, Strait of** var. Straits of Dover, Fr. Pas de Calais. strait England, UK/France
Dover, Straits of see Dover, Strait of
Dovlen see Devin
96 G11 **Dovre** Oppland, S Norway 61.59N 9.16E
96 G10 **Dovrefjell** plateau S Norway
Dovsk see Dowsk
85 M14 **Dowa** Central, C Malawi 13.42S 33.55E
33 O10 **Dowagiac** Michigan, N USA 41.58N 86.06W
149 N10 **Dow Gonbadān** var. Do Gonbadān, Gonbadān. Kohkīlūyeh va Būyer Aḩmadī, SW Iran 30.24N 50.45E
154 M2 **Dowlatābād** Fāryāb, N Afghanistan 36.30N 64.51E
99 G16 **Down** cultural region SE Northern Ireland, UK
35 R16 **Downey** Idaho, NW USA 42.25N 112.06W
37 P5 **Downieville** California, W USA 39.33N 120.49W
99 G16 **Downpatrick** Ir. Dún Pádraig. SE Northern Ireland, UK 54.19N 5.43W
28 M3 **Downs** Kansas, C USA 39.30N 98.33W
20 J12 **Downsville** New York, NE USA 42.03N 74.59W
Dow Rūd see Do Rūd
31 V12 **Dows** Iowa, C USA 42.39N 93.30W
121 O17 **Dowsk** Rus. Dovsk. Homyel'skaya Voblasts', SE Belarus 53.09N 30.27E
37 Q4 **Doyle** California, W USA 40.00N 120.06W
20 I15 **Doylestown** Pennsylvania, NE USA 40.18N 75.07W
Doyransko, Ezero see Doïranis, Límnis
116 I8 **Doyrentsi** Lovech, N Bulgaria 43.13N 24.46E
170 Ff11 **Dōzen** island Oki-shotō, SW Japan
12 K9 **Dozois, Réservoir** ▣ Quebec, SE Canada
76 D9 **Drâa** seasonal river S Morocco
Drâa, Hammada du see Dra, Hamada du
Drabble see José Enrique Rodó
119 Q5 **Drabiv** Cherkas'ka Oblast', C Ukraine 49.57N 32.10E
Drable see José Enrique Rodó
105 S13 **Drac** ≈ E France
Drač/Drač see Durrës
62 I8 **Dracena** São Paulo, S Brazil 21.27S 51.30W
100 M6 **Drachten** Friesland, N Netherlands 53.07N 6.06E
94 H11 **Drag** Nordland, C Norway 68.02N 16.00E
118 L14 **Dragalina** Călăraşi, SE Romania 44.25N 27.17E
118 J14 **Drăgăneşti-Vlaşca** Teleorman, S Romania 44.05N 25.39E
118 I13 **Drăgăşani** Vâlcea, SW Romania 44.40N 24.16E
116 G9 **Dragoman** Sofiya, W Bulgaria 42.57N 22.53E
117 L25 **Dragonáda** island SE Greece
Dragonera, Isla see Sa Dragonera
47 T14 **Dragon's Mouths, The** strait Trinidad and Tobago/Venezuela
97 J23 **Dragør** København, E Denmark 55.36N 12.42E
116 F10 **Dragovishtsa** Kyustendil, W Bulgaria 42.22N 22.39E
105 U15 **Draguignan** Var, SE France 43.31N 6.31E
76 E9 **Dra, Hamada du** var. Hammada du Drâa, Haut Plateau du Dra. plateau W Algeria
Dra, Haut Plateau du see Dra, Hamada du
121 H19 **Drahichyn** Pol. Drohiczyn Poleski, Rus. Drogichin. Brestskaya Voblasts', SW Belarus 52.10N 25.10E
31 N4 **Drake** North Dakota, N USA 47.54N 100.23W
85 K23 **Drakensberg** ▲▲ Lesotho/South Africa
204 F3 **Drake Passage** passage Atlantic Ocean/Pacific Ocean
116 L8 **Dralfa** Türgovishte, N Bulgaria 43.17N 26.25E
116 I12 **Dráma** var. Dhráma. Anatolikí Makedonía kai Thráki, NE Greece 41.09N 24.10E
Dramburg see Drawsko Pomorskie
97 H15 **Drammen** Buskerud, S Norway 59.43N 10.12E
97 H15 **Drammensfjorden** fjord S Norway
94 H1 **Drangajökull** ▲ NW Iceland 66.13N 22.18W
97 F16 **Drangedal** Telemark, S Norway 59.04N 9.01E
94 I2 **Drangsnes** Vestfirdhir, NW Iceland 65.42N 21.27W
Drann see Dravinja
111 T10 **Drau** var. Drava, Eng. Drave, Hung. Dráva. ≈ C Europe see also Drava
86 I11 **Drava** var. Drau, Eng. Drave, Hung. Dráva. ≈ C Europe see also Drau
Dráva see Drau/Drava
Drave see Drau/Drava
111 W10 **Dravinja** Ger. Drann. ≈ NE Slovenia
111 V9 **Dravograd** Ger. Unterdrauburg; prev. Spodnji Dravograd. N Slovenia 46.36N 15.00E
112 F10 **Drawa** ≈ NW Poland
112 F9 **Drawno** Zachodniopomorskie, NW Poland 53.12N 15.44E
112 F9 **Drawsko Pomorskie** Ger. Dramburg. Zachodniopomorskie, NW Poland 53.31N 15.48E
31 R3 **Drayton** North Dakota, N USA 48.34N 97.10W
9 P14 **Drayton Valley** Alberta, SW Canada 53.15N 115.00W
194 F10 **Dreikikir** East Sepik, NW PNG 3.34S 142.44E
Dreikirchen see Teiuş
100 N7 **Drenthe** ◈ province NE Netherlands
117 H15 **Drépano, Akrotírio** var. Akra Dhrepanon. headland N Greece 39.56N 23.57E
Drepanum see Trapani
12 D17 **Dresden** Ontario, S Canada 42.34N 82.09W
103 O16 **Dresden** Sachsen, E Germany 51.02N 13.43E
22 G8 **Dresden** Tennessee, S USA 36.17N 88.42W
120 M11 **Dretun'** Rus. Dretun'. Vitsyebskaya Voblasts', N Belarus 55.42N 29.12E
104 M5 **Dreux** anc. Drocae, Durocasses. Eure-et-Loir, C France 48.43N 1.22E
96 I11 **Drevsjø** Hedmark, S Norway 61.52N 12.01E
24 K3 **Drew** Mississippi, S USA 33.48N 90.31W
112 F10 **Drezdenko** Ger. Driesen. Lubuskie, W Poland 52.51N 15.49E
100 J12 **Driebergen** var. Driebergen-Rijsenburg. Utrecht, C Netherlands 52.03N 5.16E
Driebergen-Rijsenburg see Driebergen
Driesen see Drezdenko
99 N16 **Driffield** E England, UK 54.00N .28W
67 D25 **Driftwood Point** headland East Falkland, Falkland Islands 52.15S 59.00W
35 S14 **Driggs** Idaho, NW USA 43.44N 111.06W
Drin see Drinit, Lumi i
114 K12 **Drina** ≈ Bosnia and Herzegovina/Serbia and Montenegro (Yugoslavia)
Drin, Gulf of see Drinit, Gjiri i
115 K18 **Drinit, Gjiri i** var. Pellg i Drinit, Eng. Gulf of Drin. gulf NW Albania
115 L17 **Drinit, Lumi i** var. Drin. ≈ NW Albania
Drinit, Pellg i see Drinit, Gjiri i
Drinit të Zi, Lumi i see Black Drin
115 L22 **Drino** var. Drinos, Pótamos, Alb. Lumi i Drinos. ≈ Albania/Greece
Drinos, Lumi i/Drínos Pótamos see Drino
27 S11 **Dripping Springs** Texas, SW USA 30.11N 98.04W
27 S15 **Driscoll** Texas, SW USA 27.40N 97.45W
24 H5 **Driskill Mountain** ▲ Louisiana, S USA 32.25N 92.54W
Drissa see Drysa
96 G10 **Driva** ≈ S Norway
114 E13 **Drniš** It. Šibenik-Knin, S Croatia 43.51N 16.10E
97 H15 **Drøbak** Akershus, S Norway 59.40N 10.37E
118 G13 **Drobeta-Turnu Severin** prev. Turnu Severin. Mehedinţi, SW Romania 44.39N 22.39E
Drocae see Dreux
118 M8 **Drochia** Rus. Drokiya. N Moldova 48.02N 27.46E
99 F17 **Drogheda** Ir. Droichead Átha. NE Ireland 53.43N 6.21W
Drogichin see Drahichyn
Drogobych see Drohobych
Drohiczyn Poleski see Drahichyn
118 H6 **Drohobych** Pol. Drohobycz, Rus. Drogobych. L'vivs'ka Oblast', NW Ukraine 49.22N 23.34E
Drohobycz see Drohobych
Droichead Átha see Drogheda
Droicheadna Bandan see Bandon
Droichead na Banna see Banbridge
Droim Mór see Dromore
Drokiya see Drochia
105 R13 **Drôme** ◈ department E France
105 S13 **Drôme** ≈ E France
99 G15 **Dromore** Ir. Droim Mór. SE Northern Ireland, UK 54.25N 6.09W
108 A9 **Dronero** Piemonte, NE Italy 44.28N 7.25E
104 L12 **Dronne** ≈ SW France
205 Q3 **Dronning Maud Land** physical region Antarctica
100 K6 **Dronrijp** Fris. Dronryp. Friesland, N Netherlands 53.12N 5.37E
Dronryp see Dronrijp
100 L9 **Dronten** Flevoland, C Netherlands 52.31N 5.40E
Drontheim see Trondheim
104 L13 **Dropt** ≈ SW France
155 T4 **Drosh** North-West Frontier Province, NW Pakistan 35.33N 71.48E
Drossen see Ośno Lubuskie
Drug see Durg
Drujba see Pitnak
120 I12 **Drūkšiai** ◎ NE Lithuania
Druk-yul see Bhutan
9 Q16 **Drumheller** Alberta, SW Canada 51.28N 112.42W

◆ Country ● Country Capital ◇ Dependent Territory ○ Dependent Territory Capital ◈ Administrative Region ✕ International Airport ▲ Mountain ▲▲ Mountain Range ⊼ Volcano ≈ River ◎ Lake ▣ Reservoir

35 Q10 **Drummond** Montana, NW USA 46.39N 113.12W
33 R4 **Drummond Island** *island* Michigan, N USA
Drummond Island *see* Tabiteuea
23 X7 **Drummond, Lake** ◎ Virginia, NE USA
13 P12 **Drummondville** Quebec, SE Canada 45.52N 72.28W
41 T11 **Drum, Mount** ▲ Alaska, USA 62.11N 144.37W
29 O9 **Drumright** Oklahoma, C USA 35.59N 96.36W
101 J14 **Drunen** Noord-Brabant, S Netherlands 51.40N 5.07E
Druskienniki *see* Druskininkai
121 F15 **Druskininkai** *Pol.* Druskienniki. Druskininkai, S Lithuania 54.00N 24.00E
100 K13 **Druten** Gelderland, SE Netherlands 51.52N 5.37E
120 K11 **Druya** Vitsyebskaya Voblasts', NW Belarus 55.48N 27.27E
119 S2 **Druzhba** Sums'ka Oblast', NE Ukraine 52.01N 33.56E
Druzhba *see* Dostyk, Kazakhstan
Druzhba *see* Pitnak, Uzbekistan
126 Mm7 **Druzhina** Respublika Sakha (Yakutiya), NE Russian Federation 68.01N 144.58E
119 X7 **Druzhkivka** Donets'ka Oblast', E Ukraine 48.38N 37.31E
114 E12 **Drvar** Federacija Bosna I Hercegovina, Bosnia and Herzegovina 44.21N 16.24E
115 G15 **Drvenik** Split-Dalmacija, SE Croatia 43.10N 17.13E
116 K9 **Dryanovo** Gabrovo, N Bulgaria 42.58N 25.28E
28 G7 **Dry Cimarron River** ⁓ Kansas/Oklahoma, C USA
10 B11 **Dryden** Ontario, C Canada 49.48N 92.48W
26 M11 **Dryden** Texas, SW USA 30.01N 102.06W
205 Q14 **Drygalski Ice Tongue** *ice feature* Antarctica
120 L11 **Drysa** *Rus.* Drissa. ⁓ N Belarus
25 V17 **Dry Tortugas** *island* Florida, SE USA
81 D15 **Dschang** Ouest, W Cameroon 5.28N 10.01E
56 J5 **Duaca** Lara, N Venezuela 10.16N 69.12W
Duacum *see* Douai
Duala *see* Douala
47 N9 **Duarte, Pico** ▲ C Dominican Republic 19.02N 70.57W
146 J5 **Ḍubā** Tabūk, NW Saudi Arabia 27.25N 35.42E
Dubai *see* Dubayy
119 N9 **Dubăsari** *Rus.* Dubossary. NE Moldova 47.16N 29.07E
119 N9 **Dubăsari Reservoir** ▣ NE Moldova
15 Jj8 **Dubawnt** ⁓ Nunavut, NW Canada
15 K7 **Dubawnt Lake** ◎ Northwest Territories/Nunavut, N Canada
32 L6 **Du Bay, Lake** ▣ Wisconsin, N USA
147 U7 **Dubayy** *Eng.* Dubai. Dubayy, NE UAE 25.10N 55.18E
147 W7 **Dubayy** *Eng.* Dubai. ✕ Dubayy, NE UAE 25.15N 55.22E
191 R7 **Dubbo** New South Wales, SE Australia 32.16S 148.40E
110 G7 **Dübendorf** Zürich, NW Switzerland 47.24N 8.36E
99 F18 **Dublin** *Ir.* Baile Átha Cliath; *anc.* Eblana. ● (Ireland), E Ireland 53.19N 6.15W
25 U5 **Dublin** Georgia, SE USA 32.32N 82.54W
27 R7 **Dublin** Texas, SW USA 32.05N 98.20W
99 G18 **Dublin** *Ir.* Baile Átha Cliath; *anc.* Eblana. *cultural region* E Ireland
99 G18 **Dublin Airport** ✕ E Ireland 53.25N 6.18W
201 V12 **Dublon** *var.* Tonoas. *island* Chuuk Islands, C Micronesia
130 K2 **Dubna** Moskovskaya Oblast', W Russian Federation 56.45N 37.09E
113 G19 **Dubňany** *Ger.* Dubnian. Brněnský Kraj, SE Czech Republic 48.54N 17.00E
Dubnian *see* Dubňany
113 I19 **Dubnica nad Váhom** *Hung.* Máriatölgyes; *prev.* Dubnicz. Trenčiansky Kraj, W Slovakia 48.58N 18.10E
Dubnicz *see* Dubnica nad Váhom
118 K4 **Dubno** Rivnens'ka Oblast', NW Ukraine 50.27N 25.39E
20 D13 **Du Bois** Pennsylvania, NE USA 41.07N 78.45W
35 R13 **Dubois** Idaho, NW USA 44.10N 112.13W
35 T14 **Dubois** Wyoming, C USA 43.31N 109.37W
Dubossary *see* Dubăsari
131 O10 **Dubovka** Volgogradskaya Oblast', SW Russian Federation 49.10N 48.49E
78 H14 **Dubréka** Guinée-Maritime, SW Guinea 9.48N 13.31W
12 B7 **Dubreuilville** Ontario, S Canada 48.21N 84.31W
Dubris Portus *see* Dover
121 L20 **Dubrova** *Rus.* Dubrova. Homyel'skaya Voblasts', SE Belarus 51.46N 28.13E
130 I5 **Dubrovka** Bryanskaya Oblast', W Russian Federation 53.44N 33.27E
115 H16 **Dubrovnik** *It.* Ragusa. Dubrovnik-Neretva, SE Croatia 42.39N 18.06E
115 I16 **Dubrovnik** ✕ Dubrovnik-Neretva, SE Croatia 42.34N 18.17E
115 F16 **Dubrovnik-Neretva** *off.* Dubrovačko-Neretvanska Županija. ◈ *province* SE Croatia
Dubrovno *see* Dubrowna
118 L2 **Dubrovytsya** Rivnens'ka Oblast', NW Ukraine 51.34N 26.37E
121 O14 **Dubrowna** *Rus.* Dubrovno. Vitsyebskaya Voblasts', N Belarus 54.34N 30.40E
31 Z13 **Dubuque** Iowa, C USA 42.30N 90.39W
120 E12 **Dubysa** ⁓ C Lithuania
178 K12 **Đưc Cơ** Gia Lai, C Vietnam 13.48N 107.41E
203 V12 **Duc de Gloucester, Îles du** *Eng.* Duke of Gloucester Islands. *island group* C French Polynesia
113 C15 **Duchcov** *Ger.* Dux. Ústecký Kraj, NW Czech Republic 50.37N 13.40E
39 N3 **Duchesne** Utah, W USA 40.09N 110.24W
203 P17 **Ducie Island** *atoll* E Pitcairn Islands
9 W15 **Duck Bay** Manitoba, S Canada 52.11N 100.08W
25 X17 **Duck Key** *island* Florida Keys, Florida, SE USA
9 T14 **Duck Lake** Saskatchewan, S Canada 52.52N 106.12W
9 V15 **Duck Mountain** ▲▲ Manitoba, S Canada
22 I9 **Duck River** ⁓ Tennessee, S USA
22 M10 **Ducktown** Tennessee, S USA 35.01N 84.24W
178 Kk11 **Đưc Phô** Quang Ngai, C Vietnam 14.55N 108.55E
178 Jj8 **Đưc Tho** Ha Tinh, N Vietnam 18.30N 105.36E
178 Kk13 **Đưc Trong** *var.* Liên Nghia. Lâm Đông, S Vietnam 11.45N 108.24E
D-U-D *see* Dalap-Uliga-Djarrit
101 M25 **Dudelange** *var.* Forge du Sud, *Ger.* Dudelingen. Luxembourg, S Luxembourg 49.28N 6.04E
Dudelingen *see* Dudelange
103 J15 **Duderstadt** Niedersachsen, C Germany 51.31N 10.16E
159 N15 **Dūdhi** Uttar Pradesh, N India 24.13N 83.18E
126 I8 **Dudinka** Taymyrskiy (Dolgano-Nenetskiy) Avtonomnyy Okrug, N Russian Federation 69.27N 86.13E
99 L20 **Dudley** C England, UK 52.30N 2.04W
160 G13 **Dudna** ⁓ C India
78 L16 **Duékoué** W Ivory Coast 6.45N 7.21W
106 M5 **Dueñas** Castilla-León, N Spain 41.52N 4.33W
106 K4 **Duerna** ⁓ NW Spain
107 O6 **Duero** *Port.* Douro. ⁓ Portugal/Spain *see also* Douro
Duesseldorf *see* Düsseldorf
23 P12 **Due West** South Carolina, SE USA 34.19N 82.23W
205 P11 **Dufek Coast** *physical region* Antarctica
101 H17 **Duffel** Antwerpen, C Belgium 51.06N 4.30E
37 S2 **Duffer Peak** ▲ Nevada, W USA 41.40N 118.45W
195 X7 **Duff Islands** *island group* E Solomon Islands
Dufour, Pizzo/Dufour, Punta *see* Dufour Spitze
110 E12 **Dufour Spitze** *It.* Pizzo Dufour, Punta Dufour. ▲ Italy/Switzerland 45.54N 7.50E
114 D9 **Duga Resa** Karlovac, C Croatia 45.25N 15.30E
24 H5 **Dugdemona River** ⁓ Louisiana, S USA
160 J12 **Duggipar** Mahārāshtra, C India 21.06N 80.10E
114 B13 **Dugi Otok** *var.* Isola Grossa, *It.* Isola Lunga. *island* W Croatia
115 F14 **Dugopolje** Split-Dalmacija, S Croatia 43.35N 16.35E
166 L8 **Du He** ⁓ C China
56 M11 **Duida, Cerro** ▲ S Venezuela 3.21N 65.45W
Duinekerke *see* Dunkerque
103 E15 **Duisburg** *prev.* Duisburg-Hamborn. Nordrhein-Westfalen, W Germany 51.24N 6.47E
Duisburg-Hamborn *see* Duisburg
101 F14 **Duiveland** *island* SW Netherlands
100 M12 **Duiven** Gelderland, E Netherlands 51.57N 6.02E
145 W10 **Dujaylah, Hawr ad** ◎ S Iraq
83 L18 **Dujuuma** Shabeellaha Hoose, S Somalia 1.04N 42.37E
Dūkān *see* Dokan
41 Z14 **Duke Island** *island* Alexander Archipelago, Alaska, USA
Dukelský Priesmy/Dukelský Průsmyk *see* Dukla Pass
Duke of Gloucester Islands *see* Duc de Gloucester, Îles du
83 F14 **Duk Faiwil** Jonglei, SE Sudan 7.30N 31.27E
147 T7 **Dukhān** C Qatar 25.29N 50.48E
Dukhan Heights *see* Dukhān, Jabal
149 N16 **Dukhān, Jabal** *var.* Dukhan Heights. *hill range* S Qatar
131 Q7 **Dukhovnitskoye** Saratovskaya Oblast', W Russian Federation 52.31N 48.32E
130 H4 **Dukhovshchina** Smolenskaya Oblast', W Russian Federation 55.15N 32.22E
Dukielska, Przełęcz *see* Dukla Pass
113 N17 **Dukla** Podkarpackie, SE Poland 49.33N 21.40E
Duklai Hág *see* Dukla Pass
113 N18 **Dukla Pass** *Cz.* Dukelský Průsmyk, *Ger.* Dukla-Pass, *Hung.* Duklai Hág, *Pol.* Przełęcz Dukielska, *Slvk.* Dukelský Priesmy. *pass* Poland/Slovakia 49.25N 21.42E
Dukou *see* Panzhihua
120 I12 **Dūkštas** Ignalina, E Lithuania 55.32N 26.21E
168 M8 **Dulaan** Hentiy, C Mongolia 47.09N 108.48E
165 R10 **Dulan** *var.* Qagan Us. Qinghai, C China 36.11N 97.51E
39 R8 **Dulce** New Mexico, SW USA 36.55N 107.00W
45 N16 **Dulce, Golfo** *gulf* S Costa Rica
Dulce, Golfo *see* Izabal, Lago de
44 K6 **Dulce Nombre de Culmí** Olancho, C Honduras 15.04N 85.35W
64 L9 **Dulce, Río** ⁓ C Argentina
126 M9 **Dulgalakh** ⁓ NE Russian Federation
116 M8 **Dŭlgopol** Varna, E Bulgaria 43.05N 27.24E
159 V14 **Dullabchara** Assam, NE India 24.25N 92.22E
22 D3 **Dulles** ✕ (Washington DC) Virginia, NE USA 39.00N 77.27W
103 E14 **Dülmen** Nordrhein-Westfalen, W Germany 51.51N 7.17E
116 M7 **Dulovo** Silistra, NE Bulgaria 43.50N 27.10E
31 W5 **Duluth** Minnesota, N USA 46.46N 92.06W
144 H7 **Dūmā** *Fr.* Douma. Dimashq, SW Syria 33.33N 36.24E
179 Pp16 **Dumagasa Point** *headland* Mindanao, S Philippines 7.01N 121.54E
179 Qq14 **Dumaguete** *var.* Dumaguete City. Negros, C Philippines 9.16N 123.17E
174 Gg6 **Dumai** Sumatera, W Indonesia 1.40N 101.27E
191 T4 **Dumaresq River** ⁓ New South Wales/Queensland, SE Australia
29 W13 **Dumas** Arkansas, C USA 33.53N 91.29W
27 N1 **Dumas** Texas, SW USA 35.51N 101.57W
144 I7 **Ḍumayr** Dimashq, W Syria 33.36N 36.28E
98 I12 **Dumbarton** W Scotland, UK 55.57N 4.34W
98 I12 **Dumbarton** *cultural region* C Scotland, UK
197 J7 **Dumbéa** Province Sud, S New Caledonia 22.11S 166.27E
113 K19 **Ďumbier** *Ger.* Djumbir, *Hung.* Gyömbér. ▲ C Slovakia 48.54N 19.36E
118 I11 **Dumbrăveni** *Ger.* Elisabethstedt, *Hung.* Erzsébetváros; *prev.* Ebesfalva, Eppeschdorf, Ibașfalău. Sibiu, C Romania 45.48N 24.08E
118 L12 **Dumbrăveni** Vrancea, E Romania 45.30N 27.08E
99 J14 **Dumfries** S Scotland, UK 55.04N 3.37W
99 J14 **Dumfries** *cultural region* SW Scotland, UK
159 R15 **Dumka** Bihār, NE India 24.16N 87.15E
Dümmer *see* Dümmersee
102 G12 **Dümmersee** *var.* Dümmer. ◎ NW Germany
12 J11 **Dumoine** ⁓ Quebec, SE Canada
12 J10 **Dumoine, Lac** ◎ Quebec, SE Canada
205 V16 **Dumont d'Urville** *French research station* Antarctica 66.24S 139.38E
205 W15 **Dumont d'Urville Sea** S Pacific Ocean
12 K11 **Dumont, Lac** ◎ Quebec, SE Canada
77 W7 **Dumyât** *Eng.* Damietta. N Egypt 31.25N 31.48E
Duna *see* Don, Russian Federation
Duna *see* Danube, C Europe
Düna *see* Western Dvina
Dünaburg *see* Daugavpils
113 J24 **Dunaföldvár** Tolna, C Hungary 46.16N 18.54E
Dunaj *see* Wien, Austria
Dunaj *see* Danube, C Europe
113 L18 **Dunajec** ⁓ S Poland
113 H21 **Dunajská Streda** *Hung.* Dunaszerdahely. Trnavský Kraj, W Slovakia 48.00N 17.27E
Dunapentele *see* Dunaújváros
Dunărea *see* Danube
118 M13 **Dunărea Veche, Braţul** ⁓ SE Romania
119 N13 **Dunării, Delta** *delta* SE Romania
Dunaszerdahely *see* Dunajská Streda
113 J23 **Dunaújváros** *prev.* Dunapentele, Sztálinváros. Fejér, C Hungary 47.00N 18.55E
Dunav *see* Danube
116 J8 **Dunavska Ravnina** *Eng.* Danubian Plain. *plain* N Bulgaria
116 G7 **Dunavtsi** Vidin, NW Bulgaria 43.56N 22.49E
127 N17 **Dunay** Primorskiy Kray, SE Russian Federation 42.53N 132.20E
Dunayevtsy *see* Dunayivtsi
118 L7 **Dunayivtsi** *Rus.* Dunayevtsy. Khmel'nyts'ka Oblast', NW Ukraine 48.54N 26.51E
193 F22 **Dunback** Otago, South Island, NZ 45.22S 170.37E
8 L17 **Duncan** Vancouver Island, British Columbia, SW Canada 48.46N 123.10W
39 O15 **Duncan** Arizona, SW USA 32.43N 109.06W
28 M12 **Duncan** Oklahoma, C USA 34.30N 97.57W
Duncan Island *see* Pinzón, Isla
157 Q20 **Duncan Passage** *strait* Andaman Sea/Bay of Bengal
98 K6 **Duncansby Head** *headland* N Scotland, UK 58.37N 3.01W
12 G12 **Dunchurch** Ontario, S Canada 45.36N 79.54W
120 D7 **Dundaga** Talsi, NW Latvia 57.29N 22.19E
12 G14 **Dundalk** Ontario, S Canada 44.11N 80.22W
99 F16 **Dundalk** *Ir.* Dún Dealgan. NE Ireland 54.01N 6.25W
23 X3 **Dundalk** Maryland, NE USA 39.15N 76.31W
99 F16 **Dundalk Bay** *Ir.* Cuan Dhún Dealgan. *bay* NE Ireland
12 G16 **Dundas** Ontario, S Canada 43.16N 79.55W
188 L12 **Dundas, Lake** *salt lake* Western Australia
169 O7 **Dundbürd** Hentiy, E Mongolia 47.55N 111.37E
Dún Dealgan *see* Dundalk
13 N13 **Dundee** Quebec, SE Canada 45.01N 74.27W
85 K22 **Dundee** KwaZulu/Natal, E South Africa 28.08S 30.12E
98 K11 **Dundee** E Scotland, UK 56.28N 3.00W
33 R10 **Dundee** Michigan, N USA 41.57N 83.39W
27 R5 **Dundee** Texas, SW USA 33.43N 98.52W
204 H3 **Dundee Island** *island* Antarctica
168 L9 **Dundgovĭ** ◈ *province* C Mongolia
99 G16 **Dundrum Bay** *Ir.* Cuan Dhún Droma. *inlet* NW Irish Sea
176 Y11 **Dundu** ⁓ Papua, E Indonesia
9 T15 **Dundurn** Saskatchewan, S Canada 51.43N 106.27W
168 E6 **Dund-Us** Hovd, W Mongolia 48.06N 91.22E
193 F23 **Dunedin** Otago, South Island, NZ 45.52S 170.31E
191 R7 **Dunedoo** New South Wales, SE Australia 32.04S 149.23E
99 D14 **Dunfanaghy** *Ir.* Dún Fionnachaidh. NW Ireland 55.10N 7.58W
98 J12 **Dunfermline** C Scotland, UK 56.04N 3.28W
Dún Fionnachaidh *see* Dunfanaghy
155 V10 **Dunga Bunga** Punjab, E Pakistan 29.51N 73.19E
99 F15 **Dungannon** *Ir.* Dún Geanainn. C Northern Ireland, UK 54.31N 6.46W
Dun Garbháin *see* Dungarvan
158 F15 **Dūngarpur** Rājasthān, N India 23.53N 73.39E
99 E21 **Dungarvan** *Ir.* Dun Garbháin. S Ireland 52.04N 7.37W
103 N21 **Dungau** *cultural region* SE Germany
Dún Geanainn *see* Dungannon
99 P23 **Dungeness** *headland* SE England, UK 50.55N 0.58E
65 I23 **Dungeness, Punta** *headland* S Argentina 52.25S 68.25W
Dungloe *see* Dunglow
99 D14 **Dunglow** *var.* Dungloe, *Ir.* An Clochán Liath. NW Ireland 54.57N 8.22W
191 T7 **Dungog** New South Wales, SE Australia 32.24S 151.45E
81 O16 **Dungu** Orientale, NE Dem. Rep. Congo 3.40N 28.31E
174 Hh3 **Dungun** *var.* Kuala Dungun. Terengganu, Peninsular Malaysia 4.46N 103.25E
82 I6 **Dungūnab** Red Sea, NE Sudan 21.06N 37.06E
13 P13 **Dunham** Quebec, SE Canada 45.08N 72.48W
Dunheved *see* Launceston
Dunholme *see* Durham
169 X10 **Dunhua** Jilin, NE China 43.22N 128.12E
165 P8 **Dunhuang** Gansu, N China 40.10N 94.43E
190 L12 **Dunkeld** Victoria, SE Australia 37.41S 142.19E
105 O1 **Dunkerque** *Eng.* Dunkirk, *Flem.* Duinekerke; *prev.* Dunquerque. Nord, N France 51.06N 2.34E
99 K23 **Dunkery Beacon** ▲ SW England, UK 51.10N 3.36W
20 C11 **Dunkirk** New York, NE USA 42.28N 79.19W
Dunkirk *see* Dunkerque
79 P17 **Dunkwa** SW Ghana 5.58N 1.45W
99 G18 **Dún Laoghaire** *Eng.* Dunleary; *prev.* Kingstown. E Ireland 53.16N 6.07W
31 S14 **Dunlap** Iowa, C USA 41.51N 95.36W
22 L10 **Dunlap** Tennessee, S USA 35.22N 85.23W
Dunleary *see* Dún Laoghaire
Dún Mánmhaí *see* Dunmanway
99 B21 **Dunmanway** *Ir.* Dún Mánmhaí. SW Ireland 51.43N 9.07W
20 I13 **Dunmore** Pennsylvania, NE USA 41.25N 75.37W
23 U10 **Dunn** North Carolina, SE USA 35.18N 78.36W
Dún na nGall *see* Donegal
25 V11 **Dunnellon** Florida, SE USA 29.03N 82.27W
98 J6 **Dunnet Head** *headland* N Scotland, UK 58.40N 3.27W
31 N14 **Dunning** Nebraska, C USA 41.49N 100.04W
67 B24 **Dunnose Head Settlement** West Falkland, Falkland Islands 51.24S 60.28W
12 G17 **Dunnville** Ontario, S Canada 42.54N 79.36W
Dún Pádraig *see* Downpatrick
Dunquerque *see* Dunkerque
Dunqulah *see* Dongola
98 L12 **Duns** SE Scotland, UK 55.46N 2.13W
31 N2 **Dunseith** North Dakota, N USA 48.48N 100.03W
37 N2 **Dunsmuir** California, W USA 41.12N 122.19W
99 N21 **Dunstable** *Lat.* Durocobrivae. E England, UK 51.52N 0.31W
193 D21 **Dunstan Mountains** ▲▲ South Island, NZ
105 O9 **Dun-sur-Auron** Cher, C France 46.52N 2.40E
193 F21 **Duntroon** Canterbury, South Island, NZ 44.52S 170.40E
155 T10 **Dunyāpur** Punjab, E Pakistan 29.48N 71.48E
169 U5 **Duobukur He** ⁓ NE China
169 R12 **Duolun** *var.* Dolonnur. Nei Mongol Zizhiqu, N China 42.11N 116.30E
178 Ii14 **Dương Đông** Kiên Giang, S Vietnam 10.15N 103.58E
116 G10 **Dupnitsa** *prev.* Marek, Stanke Dimitrov. Kyustendil, W Bulgaria 42.15N 23.09E
30 L8 **Dupree** South Dakota, N USA 45.03N 101.36W
35 Q7 **Dupuyer** Montana, NW USA 48.13N 112.34W
147 Y11 **Duqm** *var.* Daqm. E Oman 19.42N 57.39E
65 F23 **Duque de York, Isla** *island* S Chile
189 N4 **Durack Range** ▲▲ Western Australia
142 K10 **Durağan** Sinop, N Turkey 41.25N 35.03E
105 S15 **Durance** ⁓ SE France
33 R9 **Durand** Michigan, N USA 42.54N 83.58W
32 I6 **Durand** Wisconsin, N USA 44.37N 91.55W
197 L7 **Durand, Récif** *reef* SE New Caledonia
42 K10 **Durango** *var.* Victoria de Durango. Durango, W Mexico 24.03N 104.37W
107 P3 **Durango** País Vasco, N Spain 43.10N 2.37W
39 Q8 **Durango** Colorado, C USA 37.13N 107.51W
42 J9 **Durango** ◈ *state* C Mexico
116 O7 **Durankulak** *Rom.* Răcari; *prev.* Blatnitsa, Duranulac. Dobrich, NE Bulgaria 43.41N 28.31E
24 L4 **Durant** Mississippi, S USA 33.04N 89.51W
29 P13 **Durant** Oklahoma, C USA 33.59N 96.22W
Duranulac *see* Durankulak
107 N6 **Duratón** ⁓ N Spain
63 E19 **Durazno** *var.* San Pedro de Durazno. Durazno, C Uruguay 33.24S 56.28W
63 E19 **Durazno** ◈ *department* C Uruguay
Durazzo *see* Durrës
85 K23 **Durban** *var.* Port Natal. KwaZulu/Natal, E South Africa 29.51S 31.00E
85 K23 **Durban** ✕ KwaZulu/Natal, E South Africa 29.55S 31.01E
120 C9 **Durbe** *Ger.* Durben. Liepāja, W Latvia 56.34N 21.22E
Durben *see* Durbe
101 K21 **Durbuy** Luxembourg, SE Belgium 50.21N 5.27E
107 N15 **Dúrcal** Andalucía, S Spain 37.00N 3.24W
114 F8 **Đurđevac** *Ger.* Sankt Georgen, *Hung.* Szentgyörgy; *prev.* Djurdjevac, Gjurgjevac. Koprivnica-Križevci, N Croatia 46.02N 17.03E
115 K15 **Đurđevica Tara** Montenegro, SW Serbia and Montenegro (Yugoslavia) 43.09N 19.18E
99 L24 **Durdle Door** *natural arch* S England, UK
164 L3 **Düre** Xinjiang Uygur Zizhiqu, W China 46.30N 88.25E
103 D16 **Düren** *anc.* Marcodurum. Nordrhein-Westfalen, W Germany 50.48N 6.28E
160 K12 **Durg** *prev.* Drug. Madhya Pradesh, C India 21.12N 81.19E
159 U13 **Durgapur** Dhaka, N Bangladesh 25.10N 90.41E
159 R15 **Durgāpur** West Bengal, NE India 23.30N 87.19E
12 F14 **Durham** Ontario, S Canada 44.10N 80.48W
99 M14 **Durham** *hist.* Dunholme. N England, UK 54.46N 1.34W
23 U9 **Durham** North Carolina, SE USA 35.59N 78.54W
99 L15 **Durham** *cultural region* N England, UK
174 Gg7 **Duri** Sumatera, W Indonesia 1.13N 101.13E
Duria Major *see* Dora Baltea
Duria Minor *see* Dora Riparia
Durlas *see* Thurles
147 P8 **Ḍurmā** Ar Riyāḍ, C Saudi Arabia 24.37N 46.06E
115 J15 **Durmitor** ▲ N Serbia and Montenegro (Yugoslavia) 43.06N 19.00E
98 H6 **Durness** N Scotland, UK 58.34N 4.45W
111 Y3 **Dürnkrut** Niederösterreich, E Austria 48.28N 16.50E
Durnovaria *see* Dorchester
Durobrivae *see* Rochester
Durocasses *see* Dreux
Durocobrivae *see* Dunstable
Durocortorum *see* Reims
Durostorum *see* Silistra
Durovernum *see* Canterbury
115 K20 **Durrës** *var.* Durrësi, Dursi, *It.* Durazzo, *SCr.* Drač, *Turk.* Draç. Durrës, W Albania 41.19N 19.25E
115 K19 **Durrës** ◈ *district* W Albania
Durrësi *see* Durrës
99 A21 **Dursey Island** *Ir.* Oileán Baoi. *island* SW Ireland
Dursi *see* Durrës
Durud *see* Do Rūd
116 P12 **Dursunbey** Balıkesir, NW Turkey 41.18N 28.41E
116 O12 **Dursun Gölü** ◎ NW Turkey
144 I9 **Durūz, Jabal ad** ▲ SW Syria 37.00N 32.30E
192 K13 **D'Urville Island** *island* C NZ
176 Xx9 **D'Urville, Tanjung** *headland* Papua, E Indonesia 1.26S 137.52E
Dusa Mareb/Dusa Marreb *see* Dhuusa Marreeb
120 I11 **Dusetos** Zarasai, NE Lithuania 55.44N 25.49E
152 H14 **Dushak** Akhalskiy Velayat, S Turkmenistan 37.15N 59.57E
166 K12 **Dushan** Guizhou, S China 25.45N 107.33E
153 P13 **Dushanbe** *var.* Dyushambe; *prev.* Stalinabad, *Taj.* Stalinobod. ● (Tajikistan) W Tajikistan 38.35N 68.43E
153 P13 **Dushanbe** ✕ W Tajikistan 38.31N 68.49E
143 T9 **Dushet'i** E Georgia 42.07N 44.44E
20 H13 **Dushore** Pennsylvania, NE USA 41.30N 76.23W
193 A23 **Dusky Sound** *sound* South Island, NZ
103 E15 **Düsseldorf** *var.* Duesseldorf. Nordrhein-Westfalen, W Germany 51.13N 6.49E
153 P14 **Dūsti** *Rus.* Dusti. SW Tajikistan 37.22N 68.41E
204 I9 **Dustin Island** *island* Antarctica
Dutch East Indies *see* Indonesia
Dutch Guiana *see* Suriname
40 L17 **Dutch Harbor** Unalaska Island, Alaska, USA 53.50N 166.33W
38 J3 **Dutch Mount** ▲ Utah, W USA 40.16N 113.56W
Dutch New Guinea *see* Papua
Dutch West Indies *see* Netherlands Antilles
85 H20 **Dutlwe** Kweneng, S Botswana 23.56S 23.53E
69 V16 **Du Toit Fracture Zone** *tectonic feature* SW Indian Ocean
129 U8 **Dutovo** Respublika Komi, NW Russian Federation 63.45N 56.38E
79 V13 **Dutsan Wai** *var.* Dutsen Wai. Kaduna, C Nigeria 10.49N 8.15E
79 W13 **Dutse** Jigawa, N Nigeria 11.43N 9.25E
Dutsen Wai *see* Dutsan Wai
Duttia *see* Datia
12 E17 **Dutton** Ontario, S Canada 42.40N 81.28W
38 L7 **Dutton, Mount** ▲ Utah, W USA 38.00N 112.10W
168 E7 **Duut** Hovd, W Mongolia 47.28N 91.52E
12 K11 **Duval, Lac** ◎ Quebec, SE Canada
131 W3 **Duvan** Respublika Bashkortostan, W Russian Federation 55.42N 57.56E
144 L9 **Duwaykhilat Satiḥ ar Ruwayshid** *seasonal river* SE Jordan
Dux *see* Duchcov
166 J13 **Duyang Shan** ▲▲ S China
178 Jj15 **Duyên Hai** Tra Vinh, S Vietnam 9.39N 106.28E
166 K12 **Duyun** Guizhou, S China 26.16N 107.28E
142 G11 **Düzce** Bolu, NW Turkey 40.51N 31.09E
Duzdab *see* Zāhedān
Duzenkyr, Khrebet *see* Duzkyr, Khrebet
152 I16 **Duzkyr, Khrebet** *prev.* Khrebet Duzenkyr. ▲▲ S Turkmenistan
Dvina Bay *see* Chëshskaya Guba
Dvinsk *see* Daugavpils
128 L7 **Dvinskaya Guba** *bay* NW Russian Federation
114 E10 **Dvor** Sisak-Moslavina, C Croatia 45.05N 16.22E
119 W5 **Dvorichna** Kharkivs'ka Oblast', E Ukraine 49.52N 37.43E
113 F16 **Dvůr Králové nad Labem** *Ger.* Königinhof an der Elbe. Hradecký Kraj, NE Czech Republic 50.25N 15.48E
160 A10 **Dwārka** Gujarāt, W India 22.13N 68.58E
32 M12 **Dwight** Illinois, N USA 41.05N 88.25W
100 N8 **Dwingeloo** Drenthe, NE Netherlands 52.49N 6.20E
35 N10 **Dworshak Reservoir** ▣ Idaho, NW USA
Dyal *see* Dyaul Island
Dyanev *see* Deynau
Dyatlovo *see* Dzyatlava
195 N9 **Dyaul Island** *var.* Djaul, Dyal. *island* NE PNG
22 G8 **Dyer** Tennessee, S USA 36.04N 88.59W
16 O1 **Dyer, Cape** *headland* Baffin Island, Nunavut, NE Canada 66.37N 61.13W
22 F8 **Dyersburg** Tennessee, S USA 36.01N 89.23W
31 Y13 **Dyersville** Iowa, C USA 42.29N 91.07W
99 I21 **Dyfed** *cultural region* SW Wales, UK
Dyfrdwy, Afon *see* Dee
Dyhernfurth *see* Brzeg Dolny
113 E19 **Dyje** *var.* Thaya. ⁓ Austria/Czech Republic *see also* Thaya
119 T5 **Dykanska** Poltavs'ka Oblast', C Ukraine 49.48N 34.33E
194 L15 **Dyke Ackland Bay** *inlet* E PNG
131 N16 **Dykhtau** ▲ SW Russian Federation 43.01N 42.56E
113 A16 **Dyleń** *Ger.* Tillenberg. ▲ NW Czech Republic 49.58N 12.31E
112 K9 **Dylewska Góra** ▲ N Poland 53.33N 19.57E
119 O4 **Dymer** Kyyivs'ka Oblast', N Ukraine 50.50N 30.21E
119 W7 **Dymytrov** *Rus.* Dimitrov. Donets'ka Oblast', SE Ukraine 48.18N 37.19E
113 O17 **Dynów** Podkarpackie, SE Poland 49.49N 22.14E
31 X13 **Dysart** Iowa, C USA 42.10N 92.18W
Dysna *see* Dzisna
117 D18 **Dytikí Ellás** *Eng.* Greece West. ◈ *region* C Greece
117 C14 **Dytikí Makedonía** *Eng.* Macedonia West. ◈ *region* N Greece
Dyurment'yube *see* Dermentobe
131 U4 **Dyurtyuli** Respublika Bashkortostan, W Russian Federation 55.31N 54.49E
Dyushambe *see* Dushanbe
168 I7 **Dzaanhushuu** Arhangay, C Mongolia 47.36N 101.06E
Dza Chu *see* Mekong
168 I8 **Dzadgay** Bayanhongor, C Mongolia 46.12N 99.29E
168 H8 **Dzag** Bayanhongor, C Mongolia 46.54N 99.11E
168 H10 **Dzalaa** Bayanhongor, C Mongolia 44.29N 99.19E
180 J14 **Dzaoudzi** E Mayotte 12.48S 45.18E
Dzaudzhikau *see* Vladikavkaz
168 G7 **Dzavhan** ◈ *province* NW Mongolia
168 G7 **Dzavhan Gol** ⁓ NW Mongolia
168 J7 **Dzegstey** Arhangay, C Mongolia 47.38N 102.31E
131 O3 **Dzerzhinsk** Nizhegorodskaya Oblast', W Russian Federation 56.20N 43.22E
Dzerzhinsk *see* Dzyarzhynsk, Belarus
Dzerzhinsk *see* Dzerzhyns'k, Ukraine
Dzerzhinskiy *see* Nar'yan-Mar
Dzerzhinskoye *see* Tokzhaylau
119 X7 **Dzerzhyns'k** *Rus.* Dzerzhinsk. Donets'ka Oblast', SE Ukraine 48.21N 37.50E
118 M5 **Dzerzhyns'k** Zhytomyrs'ka Oblast', N Ukraine 50.07N 27.56E
Dzhailgan *see* Jayilgan
151 N14 **Dzhalagash** *Kaz.* Zhalashash. Kzylorda, S Kazakhstan 45.06N 64.40E
153 T10 **Dzhalal-Abad** *Kir.* Jalal-Abad. Dzhalal-Abadskaya Oblast', W Kyrgyzstan 40.55N 73.00E
153 S9 **Dzhalal-Abadskaya Oblast'** *Kir.* Jalal-Abad Oblasty. ◈ *province* W Kyrgyzstan
Dzhalilabad *see* Cālilabad
126 Ll15 **Dzhalinda** Amurskaya Oblast', SE Russian Federation 53.29N 123.53E
Dzhambeyty *see* Zhympity
Dzhambulskaya Oblast' *see* Zhambyl
Dzhankel'dy *see* Jongeldi
119 T12 **Dzhankoy** Respublika Krym, S Ukraine 45.42N 34.24E
151 V14 **Dzhansugurov** *Kaz.* Zhansügirov. Almaty, SE Kazakhstan 45.25N 79.23E
153 R9 **Dzhany-Bazar** *var.* Yangibazar. Dzhalal-Abadskaya Oblast', W Kyrgyzstan 41.40N 70.49E
Dzhanybek *see* Zhanibek
126 L8 **Dzhardzhan** Respublika Sakha (Yakutiya), NE Russian Federation 68.47N 123.51E
Dzharkurgan *see* Jarqo'rg'on
119 S11 **Dzharylhats'ka Zatoka** *gulf* S Ukraine
Dzhayilgan *see* Jayilgan
152 B11 **Dzhebel** *Turkm.* Jebel. Balkanskiy Velayat, W Turkmenistan 39.42N 54.10E
153 T14 **Dzhelandy** SE Tajikistan 37.34N 72.34E
153 Y7 **Dzhergalan** *Kir.* Jyrgalan. Issyk-Kul'skaya Oblast', NE Kyrgyzstan 42.37N 78.55E
Zhitikara *see* Dzhetygara
Dzhetysay *see* Zhetysay.
Dzhezkazgan *see* Zhezkazgan
152 J10 **Dzhigirbent** *Turkm.* Jigerbent. Lebapskiy Velayat, NE Turkmenistan 40.44N 61.56E
Dzhirgatal' *see* Jirgatol
Dzhizak *see* Jizzax
Dzhizakskaya Oblast' *see* Jizzax Viloyati
127 N12 **Dzhugdzhur, Khrebet** ▲▲ E Russian Federation
Dzhul'fa *see* Culfa
Dzhuma *see* Juma
151 W14 **Dzhungarskiy Alatau** ▲▲ China/Kazakhstan
150 M14 **Dzhusaly** *Kaz.* Zholsaly. Kzylorda, SW Kazakhstan 45.28N 64.04E
152 J12 **Dzhynlykum, Peski** *desert* E Turkmenistan
112 L9 **Działdowo** Warmińsko-Mazurskie, C Poland 53.13N 20.11E
113 L16 **Działoszyce** Świętokrzyskie, C Poland 50.21N 20.19E
43 X11 **Dzidzantún** Yucatán, E Mexico
113 G15 **Dzierżoniów** *Ger.* Reichenbach. Dolnośląskie, SW Poland 50.43N 16.40E
43 X11 **Dzilam de Bravo** Yucatán, E Mexico 21.24N 88.52W
120 L12 **Dzisna** *Rus.* Disna. Vitsyebskaya Voblasts', N Belarus 55.33N 28.13E
120 K12 **Dzisna** *Lith.* Dysna, *Rus.* Disna. ⁓ Belarus/Lithuania
121 G20 **Dzivin** *Rus.* Divin. Brestskaya Voblasts', SW Belarus 51.58N 24.33E
121 M15 **Dzmitravichy** *Rus.* Dmitrovichi. Minskaya Voblasts', C Belarus 53.58N 29.14E
168 M8 **Dzogsool** Töv, C Mongolia 46.46N 107.18E
133 S8 **Dzungaria** *var.* Sungaria, Zungaria. *physical region* W China
Dzungarian Basin *see* Junggar Pendi
168 G5 **Dzür** Dzavhan, W Mongolia 49.36N 95.46E
169 Q8 **Dzüünbulag** Dornod, E Mongolia 46.48N 115.21E
169 O8 **Dzüünbulag** Sühbaatar, E Mongolia 46.30N 112.22E
168 H7 **Dzuunmod** Dzavhan, C Mongolia 48.09N 97.22E
168 L8 **Dzuunmod** Töv, C Mongolia 47.45N 107.00E
Dzüün Soyonĭ Nuruu *see* Eastern Sayans
168 F8 **Dzüyl** Govĭ-Altay, SW Mongolia 46.09N 93.55E
Dzvina *see* Western Dvina
121 J16 **Dzyarzhynsk** *Rus.* Dzerzhinsk; *prev.* Kaydanovo. Minskaya Voblasts', C Belarus 53.41N 27.09E
121 H17 **Dzyatlava** *Pol.* Zdzięcioł, *Rus.* Dyatlovo. Hrodzyenskaya Voblasts', W Belarus 53.27N 25.23E

E

E *see* Hubei
Éadan Doire *see* Edenderry
39 W6 **Eads** Colorado, C USA 38.28N 102.46W
39 O13 **Eagar** Arizona, SW USA 34.05N 109.17W
41 T8 **Eagle** Alaska, USA 64.47N 141.12W
11 S8 **Eagle** ⁓ Newfoundland and Labrador, E Canada
8 I3 **Eagle** ⁓ Yukon Territory, NW Canada
31 T7 **Eagle Bend** Minnesota, N USA 46.10N 95.02W
30 M8 **Eagle Butte** South Dakota, N USA 44.58N 101.13W
31 V12 **Eagle Grove** Iowa, C USA 42.39N 93.54W
21 R2 **Eagle Lake** Maine, NE USA 47.01N 68.35W
27 U11 **Eagle Lake** Texas, SW USA 29.35N 96.19W
10 A11 **Eagle Lake** ◎ Ontario, S Canada
37 P3 **Eagle Lake** ◎ California, W USA
21 R3 **Eagle Lake** ◎ Maine, NE USA
31 Y3 **Eagle Mountain** ▲ Minnesota, N USA 47.54N 90.33W
27 T6 **Eagle Mountain Lake** ▣ Texas, SW USA
39 S9 **Eagle Nest Lake** ▣ New Mexico, SW USA
27 P13 **Eagle Pass** Texas, SW USA 28.43N 100.31W
67 C25 **Eagle Passage** *passage* SW Atlantic Ocean
37 R8 **Eagle Peak** ▲ California, W USA 38.11N 119.22W
37 Q2 **Eagle Peak** ▲ California, W USA 41.16N 120.12W
39 P13 **Eagle Peak** ▲ New Mexico, SW USA 33.39N 109.36W
8 I4 **Eagle Plain** Yukon Territory, NW Canada 66.23N 136.42W
34 G15 **Eagle Point** Oregon, NW USA 42.28N 122.48W
195 N17 **Eagle Point** *headland* SE PNG 10.31S 149.53E

◆ Country ● Country Capital ◇ Dependent Territory ○ Dependent Territory Capital ◈ Administrative Region ✕ International Airport ▲ Mountain ▲▲ Mountain Range 🜂 Volcano ⁓ River ◎ Lake ▣ Reservoir

41 R11 **Eagle River** Alaska, USA 61.18N 149.38W
32 M2 **Eagle River** Michigan, N USA 47.24N 88.18W
32 L4 **Eagle River** Wisconsin, N USA 45.55N 89.15W
23 S6 **Eagle Rock** Virginia, NE USA 37.40N 79.46W
38 J13 **Eagletail Mountains** ▲▲ Arizona, SW USA
178 Kk12 **Ea Hleo** Đăc Lăc, S Vietnam 13.09N 108.14E
178 Kk12 **Ea Kar** Đăc Lăc, S Vietnam 12.47N 108.26E
Eanjum *see* Anjum
Eanodat *see* Enontekiö
10 B10 **Ear Falls** Ontario, C Canada 50.37N 93.13W
29 X10 **Earle** Arkansas, C USA 35.16N 90.28W
37 R12 **Earlimart** California, W USA 35.52N 119.17W
22 I6 **Earlington** Kentucky, S USA 37.16N 87.30W
12 H8 **Earlton** Ontario, S Canada 47.41N 79.46W
31 T13 **Early** Iowa, C USA 42.27N 95.09W
98 J11 **Earn** ~ N Scotland, UK
193 C21 **Earnslaw, Mount** ▲ South Island, NZ 44.34S 168.26E
26 M4 **Earth** Texas, SW USA 34.13N 102.24W
23 P11 **Easley** South Carolina, SE USA 34.49N 82.36W
East *see* Est
East Açores Fracture Zone *see* East Azores Fracture Zone
99 P19 **East Anglia** *physical region* E England, UK
13 Q12 **East Angus** Quebec, SE Canada 45.29N 71.39W
East Antarctica *see* Greater Antarctica
20 E10 **East Aurora** New York, NE USA 42.44N 78.36W
East Australian Basin *see* Tasman Basin
East Azerbaijan *see* Āzarbāyān-e Shariqī
66 L9 **East Azores Fracture Zone** *var.* East Açores Fracture Zone. *tectonic feature* E Atlantic Ocean
24 M11 **East Bay** *bay* Louisiana, S USA
27 V11 **East Bernard** Texas, SW USA 29.31N 96.04W
31 V8 **East Bethel** Minnesota, N USA 45.24N 93.14W
East Borneo *see* Kalimantan Timur
99 P23 **Eastbourne** SE England, UK 50.46N 0.16E
13 R11 **East-Broughton** Quebec, SE Canada 46.13N 71.03W
46 M6 **East Caicos** *island* E Turks and Caicos Islands
192 R7 **East Cape** *headland* North Island, NZ 37.40S 178.31E
182 M4 **East Caroline Basin** *undersea feature* SW Pacific Ocean
198 G5 **East China Sea** *Chin.* Dong Hai. *sea* W Pacific Ocean
99 P19 **East Dereham** E England, UK 52.40N 0.55E
32 J9 **East Dubuque** Illinois, N USA 42.29N 90.38W
9 S17 **Eastend** Saskatchewan, S Canada 49.29N 108.48W
200 Nn11 **Easter Fracture Zone** *tectonic feature* E Pacific Ocean
Easter Island *see* Pascua, Isla de
83 J18 **Eastern** ◆ *province* Kenya
159 Q12 **Eastern** ◆ *zone* E Nepal
84 L13 **Eastern** ◆ *province* E Zambia
85 H24 **Eastern Cape** *off.* Eastern Cape Province, *Afr.* Oos-Kaap. ◆ *province* SE South Africa
Eastern Desert *see* Sahara el Sharqîya
83 F15 **Eastern Equatoria** ◆ *state* SE Sudan
Eastern Euphrates *see* Murat Nehri
161 J17 **Eastern Ghats** ▲▲ SE India
194 I13 **Eastern Highlands** ◆ *province* C PNG
161 K25 **Eastern Province** ◆ *province* E Sri Lanka
Eastern Region *see* Ash Sharqīyah
126 I15 **Eastern Sayans** *Mong.* Dzüün Soyonï Nuruu, *Rus.* Vostochnyy Sayan. ▲▲ Mongolia/Russian Federation
Eastern Scheldt *see* Oosterschelde
Eastern Sierra Madre *see* Madre Oriental, Sierra
Eastern Transvaal *see* Mpumalanga
9 W14 **Easterville** Manitoba, C Canada 53.06N 99.52W
Easterwâlde *see* Oosterwolde
65 M23 **East Falkland** *var.* Isla Soledad. *island* E Falkland Islands
21 P12 **East Falmouth** Massachusetts, NE USA 41.34N 70.31W
East Fayu *see* Fayu
East Flanders *see* Oost Vlaanderen
41 S6 **East Fork Chandalar River** ~ Alaska, USA
31 U12 **East Fork Des Moines River** ~ Iowa/Minnesota, C USA
East Frisian Islands *see* Ostfriesische Inseln
20 K10 **East Glenville** New York, NE USA 42.53N 73.55W
31 R4 **East Grand Forks** Minnesota, N USA 47.54N 97.59W
99 O23 **East Grinstead** SE England, UK 51.07N 0.00W
20 M12 **East Hartford** Connecticut, NE USA 41.45N 72.36W
20 M13 **East Haven** Connecticut, NE USA 41.16N 72.52W
181 T9 **East Indiaman Ridge** *undersea feature* E Indian Ocean
133 V16 **East Indies** *island group* SE Asia
East Java *see* Jawa Timur
33 Q6 **East Jordan** Michigan, N USA 45.09N 85.07W
East Kalimantan *see* Kalimantan Timur
East Kazakhstan *see* Vostochnyy Kazakhstan
98 I12 **East Kilbride** S Scotland, UK 55.46N 4.10W
27 R7 **Eastland** Texas, SW USA 32.24N 98.49W
33 Q9 **East Lansing** Michigan, N USA 42.44N 84.28W
37 X11 **East Las Vegas** Nevada, W USA 36.05N 115.02W
99 M23 **Eastleigh** S England, UK 50.58N 1.22W
33 V12 **East Liverpool** Ohio, N USA 40.37N 80.34W
85 J25 **East London** *Afr.* Oos-Londen; *prev.* Emonti, Port Rex. Eastern Cape, S South Africa 33.00S 27.54E
98 K12 **East Lothian** *cultural region* SE Scotland, UK
10 I10 **Eastmain** Quebec, E Canada 52.11N 78.27W
10 J10 **Eastmain** ~ Quebec, C Canada
13 P13 **Eastman** Quebec, SE Canada 45.19N 72.18W
25 U6 **Eastman** Georgia, SE USA 32.12N 83.10W
183 O3 **East Mariana Basin** *undersea feature* W Pacific Ocean
32 K11 **East Moline** Illinois, N USA 41.30N 90.26W
195 O12 **East New Britain** ◆ *province* E PNG
31 T15 **East Nishnabotna River** ~ Iowa, C USA
207 V12 **East Novaya Zemlya Trough** *var.* Novaya Zemlya Trough. *undersea feature* W Kara Sea
East Nusa Tenggara *see* Nusa Tenggara Timur
23 X4 **Easton** Maryland, NE USA 38.46N 76.04W
20 I14 **Easton** Pennsylvania, NE USA 40.40N 75.13W
200 N8 **East Pacific Rise** *undersea feature* E Pacific Ocean
East Pakistan *see* Bangladesh
33 V12 **East Palestine** Ohio, N USA 40.49N 80.32W
32 L12 **East Peoria** Illinois, N USA 40.40N 89.34W
25 S3 **East Point** Georgia, SE USA 33.40N 84.26W
21 U6 **Eastport** Maine, NE USA 44.54N 66.59W
29 Z8 **East Prairie** Missouri, C USA 36.46N 89.23W
21 O12 **East Providence** Rhode Island, NE USA 41.48N 71.20W
22 L11 **East Ridge** Tennessee, S USA 35.00N 85.15W
99 N16 **East Riding** *cultural region* N England, UK
20 F9 **East Rochester** New York, NE USA 43.06N 77.29W
32 K15 **East Saint Louis** Illinois, N USA 38.35N 90.07W
67 K21 **East Scotia Basin** *undersea feature* SE Scotia Sea
East Sea *see* Japan, Sea of
194 F11 **East Sepik** ◆ *province* NW PNG
181 N4 **East Sheba Ridge** *undersea feature* W Arabian Sea
East Siberian Sea *see* Vostochno-Sibirskoye More
20 I14 **East Stroudsburg** Pennsylvania, NE USA 41.00N 75.10W
East Tasmanian Rise/East Tasmania Plateau/East Tasmania Rise *see* East Tasman Plateau
199 Hh13 **East Tasman Plateau** *var.* East Tasmanian Rise, East Tasmania Plateau, East Tasmania Rise. *undersea feature* SW Tasman Sea
66 L7 **East Thulean Rise** *undersea feature* N Atlantic Ocean
175 S16 **East Timor** *var* Loro Sae *prev.* Portuguese Timor, Timor Timur ◆ *country* SE Asia
23 Y6 **Eastville** Virginia, NE USA 37.18N 75.57W
37 R7 **East Walker River** ~ California/Nevada, W USA
190 D1 **Eateringinna Creek** ~ South Australia
39 T3 **Eaton** Colorado, C USA 40.31N 104.42W
13 Q12 **Eaton** ~ Quebec, SE Canada
9 S16 **Eatonia** Saskatchewan, S Canada 51.13N 109.22W
33 Q10 **Eaton Rapids** Michigan, N USA 42.30N 84.39W
25 U4 **Eatonton** Georgia, SE USA 33.19N 83.23W
34 H9 **Eatonville** Washington, NW USA 46.51N 122.19W
32 J6 **Eau Claire** Wisconsin, N USA 44.49N 91.30W
Eau Claire, Lac à L' *see* St.Clair, Lake
10 J7 **Eau Claire, Lac à l'** ◎ Quebec, SE Canada
32 L6 **Eau Claire River** ~ Wisconsin, N USA
196 J16 **Eauripik Atoll** *atoll* Caroline Islands, C Micronesia
199 H8 **Eauripik Rise** *undersea feature* W Pacific Ocean
104 K15 **Eauze** Gers, S France 43.52N 0.06E
43 P11 **Ébano** San Luis Potosí, C Mexico 22.13N 98.22W
99 K21 **Ebbw Vale** SE Wales, UK 51.48N 3.13W
81 E17 **Ebebiyin** NE Equatorial Guinea 2.08N 11.15E
97 H22 **Ebeltoft** Århus, C Denmark 56.10N 10.42E
111 X5 **Ebenfurth** Niederösterreich, E Austria 47.51N 16.21E
20 D14 **Ebensburg** Pennsylvania, NE USA 40.28N 78.42W
111 S5 **Ebensee** Oberösterreich, N Austria 47.48N 13.45E
103 H20 **Eberbach** Baden-Württemberg, SW Germany 49.28N 8.58E
124 Q9 **Eber Gölü** *salt lake* C Turkey
111 U9 **Eberndorf** *Slvn.* Dobrla Vas. Kärnten, S Austria 46.33N 14.35E
111 R4 **Eberschwang** Oberösterreich, N Austria 48.09N 13.37E
102 O11 **Eberswalde-Finow** Brandenburg, E Germany 52.49N 13.48E
Ebesfalva *see* Dumbrăveni
172 Oo5 **Ebetsu** *var.* Ebetu. Hokkaidō, NE Japan 43.08N 141.37E
Ebetu *see* Ebetsu
Ebinayon *see* Evinayong
164 I4 **Ebinur Hu** ◎ NW China
144 I3 **Ebla** *Ar.* Tell Mardīkh. *site of ancient city* Idlib, NW Syria
Eblana *see* Dublin
110 H7 **Ebnat** Sankt Gallen, NE Switzerland 47.16N 9.07E
109 L18 **Eboli** Campania, S Italy 40.39N 15.01E
81 E16 **Ebolowa** Sud, S Cameroon 2.55N 11.10E
81 N21 **Ebombo** Kasai Oriental, C Dem. Rep. Congo 5.42S 26.07E
201 T9 **Ebon Atoll** *var.* Epoon. *atoll* Ralik Chain, S Marshall Islands
Ebora *see* Évora
Eboracum *see* York
Eborodunum *see* Yverdon
103 J19 **Ebrach** Bayern, C Germany 49.49N 10.30E
111 X5 **Ebreichsdorf** Niederösterreich, E Austria 47.58N 16.24E
107 S6 **Ebro** ~ NE Spain
107 N3 **Ebro, Embalse del** ▣ N Spain
123 Hh8 **Ebro Fan** *undersea feature* W Mediterranean Sea
Eburacum *see* York
Ebusus *see* Eivissa
101 F20 **Écaussinnes-d'Enghien** Hainaut, SW Belgium 50.34N 4.10E
Ecbatana *see* Hamadān
23 Q6 **Eccles** West Virginia, NE USA 37.46N 81.16W
117 L14 **Eceabat** Çanakkale, NW Turkey 40.12N 26.22E
179 P9 **Echague** Luzon, N Philippines 16.42N 121.37E
Ech Cheliff/Ech Chleff *see* Chlef
Echeng *see* Ezhou
171 Kk13 **Echigo-sanmyaku** ▲▲ Honshū, C Japan
117 C18 **Echinádes** *island group* W Greece
116 J12 **Echínos** *var.* Ehinos, Ekhínos. Anatolikí Makedonía kai Thráki, NE Greece 41.16N 25.00E
171 H13 **Echizen-misaki** *headland* Honshū, SW Japan 35.59N 135.57E
Echmiadzin *see* Ejmiatsin
15 Hh5 **Echo Bay** Northwest Territories, NW Canada 66.04N 118.00W
37 Y11 **Echo Bay** Nevada, W USA 36.19N 114.27W
38 L9 **Echo Cliffs** *cliff* Arizona, SW USA
12 C10 **Echo Lake** ◎ Ontario, S Canada
37 Q7 **Echo Summit** ▲ California, W USA 38.47N 120.06W
12 L8 **Échouani, Lac** ◎ Quebec, SE Canada
101 L17 **Echt** Limburg, SE Netherlands 51.07N 5.52E
103 H22 **Echterdingen** ✈ (Stuttgart) Baden-Württemberg, SW Germany 48.40N 9.13E
101 N24 **Echternach** Grevenmacher, E Luxembourg 49.49N 6.25E
191 N11 **Echuca** Victoria, SE Australia 36.10S 144.46E
106 L14 **Ecija** *anc.* Astigi. Andalucía, SW Spain 37.33N 5.04W
Eckengraf *see* Viesīte
102 I7 **Eckernförde** Schleswig-Holstein, N Germany 54.28N 9.49E
102 J7 **Eckernförder Bucht** *inlet* N Germany
104 L7 **Écommoy** Sarthe, NW France 47.51N 0.15E
12 L10 **Écorce, Lac de l'** ◎ Quebec, SE Canada
13 Q8 **Écorces, Rivière aux** ~ Quebec, SE Canada
58 C7 **Ecuador** *off.* Republic of Ecuador. ◆ *republic* NW South America
82 L10 **Ed** *var.* Edd. SE Eritrea 13.54N 41.39E
97 I17 **Ed** Västra Götaland, S Sweden 58.55N 11.55E
100 I9 **Edam** Noord-Holland, C Netherlands 52.31N 5.03E
98 K4 **Eday** *island* NE Scotland, UK
27 S17 **Edcouch** Texas, SW USA 26.17N 97.57W
Edd *see* Ed
82 C11 **Ed Da'ein** Southern Darfur, W Sudan 11.25N 26.07E
82 G11 **Ed Damazin** *var.* Ad Damazīn. Blue Nile, E Sudan 11.45N 34.20E
82 G8 **Ed Damer** *var.* Ad Damar, Ad Dāmir. River Nile, NE Sudan 17.37N 33.58E
82 E8 **Ed Debba** Northern, N Sudan 18.01N 30.55E
82 F10 **Ed Dueim** *var.* Ad Duwaym, Ad Duwēm. White Nile, C Sudan 13.38N 32.36E
191 Q16 **Eddystone Point** *headland* Tasmania, SE Australia 41.01S 148.18E
99 I25 **Eddystone Rocks** *rocks* SW England, UK
31 W15 **Eddyville** Iowa, C USA 41.09N 92.37W
22 H7 **Eddyville** Kentucky, S USA 37.05N 88.04W
100 L12 **Ede** Gelderland, C Netherlands 52.03N 5.40E
79 T16 **Ede** Osun, SW Nigeria 7.40N 4.21E
81 D16 **Edéa** Littoral, SW Cameroon 3.46N 10.07E
113 M20 **Edelény** Borsod-Abaúj-Zemplén, NE Hungary 48.19N 20.44E
191 R12 **Eden** New South Wales, SE Australia 37.04S 149.51E
23 T8 **Eden** North Carolina, SE USA 36.29N 79.46W
27 P9 **Eden** Texas, SW USA 31.13N 99.51W
99 K14 **Eden** ~ NW England, UK
85 I23 **Edenburg** Free State, C South Africa 29.43S 25.54E
193 D24 **Edendale** Southland, South Island, NZ 46.18S 168.48E
99 E18 **Edenderry** *Ir.* Éadan Doire. C Ireland 53.21N 7.03W
190 L11 **Edenhope** Victoria, SE Australia 37.04S 141.15E
23 X8 **Edenton** North Carolina, SE USA 36.06N 76.46W
103 G16 **Eder** ~ NW Germany
176 Yy14 **Ederah** ~ Papua, E Indonesia
103 H15 **Edersee** ◎ W Germany
Edessa *see* Şanlıurfa
116 E13 **Édessa** *var.* Édhessa. Kentrikí Makedonía, N Greece 40.48N 22.03E
Edfu *see* Idfu
31 P16 **Edgar** Nebraska, C USA 40.22N 97.58W
21 P13 **Edgartown** Martha's Vineyard, Massachusetts, NE USA 41.22N 70.30W
41 X13 **Edgecumbe, Mount** ▲ Baranof Island, Alaska, USA 57.03N 135.45W
23 Q13 **Edgefield** South Carolina, SE USA 33.47N 81.55W
31 P6 **Edgeley** North Dakota, N USA 46.19N 98.42W
30 I11 **Edgemont** South Dakota, N USA 43.18N 103.49W
94 O3 **Edgeøya** *island* S Svalbard
29 Q4 **Edgerton** Kansas, C USA 38.45N 95.00W
31 S10 **Edgerton** Minnesota, N USA 43.52N 96.07W
23 X3 **Edgewood** Maryland, NE USA 39.20N 76.21W
27 V6 **Edgewood** Texas, SW USA 32.42N 95.53W
Édhessa *see* Édessa
31 V9 **Edina** Minnesota, N USA 44.53N 93.21W
29 U2 **Edina** Missouri, C USA 40.10N 92.10W
27 S17 **Edinburg** Texas, SW USA 26.18N 98.09W
67 M24 **Edinburgh** *var.* Settlement of Edinburgh. ○ (Tristan da Cunha) NW Tristan da Cunha 37.03S 12.18W
98 J12 **Edinburgh** ◐ S Scotland, UK 55.57N 3.13W
33 P14 **Edinburgh** Indiana, N USA 39.19N 86.00W
98 J12 **Edinburgh** ✈ S Scotland, UK 55.57N 3.22W
118 L8 **Edineț** *var.* Edineți, *Rus.* Yedintsy. NW Moldova 48.10N 27.18E
Edineți *see* Edineț
Edingen *see* Enghien
142 B9 **Edirne** *Eng.* Adrianople; *anc.* Adrianopolis, Hadrianopolis. Edirne, NW Turkey 41.40N 26.34E
142 B11 **Edirne** ◆ *province* NW Turkey
20 K15 **Edison** New Jersey, NE USA 40.31N 74.24W
23 S15 **Edisto Island** South Carolina, SE USA 32.34N 80.17W
23 R14 **Edisto River** ~ South Carolina, SE USA
35 S10 **Edith, Mount** ▲ Montana, NW USA 46.25N 111.10W
29 N10 **Edmond** Oklahoma, C USA 35.40N 97.27W
34 H8 **Edmonds** Washington, NW USA 47.48N 122.22W
9 Q14 **Edmonton** Alberta, SW Canada 53.34N 113.25W
22 K7 **Edmonton** Kentucky, S USA 36.57N 85.37W
9 Q14 **Edmonton** ✈ Alberta, SW Canada 53.22N 113.43W
31 P3 **Edmore** North Dakota, N USA 48.22N 98.26W
11 N13 **Edmundston** New Brunswick, SE Canada 47.22N 68.19W
27 U12 **Edna** Texas, SW USA 28.58N 96.39W
41 X14 **Edna Bay** Kosciusko Island, Alaska, USA 55.54N 133.40W
79 U16 **Edo** ◆ *state* S Nigeria
108 F6 **Edolo** Lombardia, N Italy 46.12N 10.19E
66 L6 **Edoras Bank** *undersea feature* C Atlantic Ocean
98 G7 **Edrachillis Bay** *bay* NW Scotland, UK
142 B12 **Edremit** Balıkesir, NW Turkey 39.34N 27.01E
142 B12 **Edremit Körfezi** *gulf* NW Turkey
97 P14 **Edsbro** Stockholm, C Sweden 59.54N 18.30E
97 N18 **Edsbruk** Kalmar, S Sweden 58.01N 16.30E
96 M12 **Edsbyn** Gävleborg, C Sweden 61.22N 15.45E
9 O14 **Edson** Alberta, SW Canada 53.36N 116.28W
64 K13 **Eduardo Castex** La Pampa, C Argentina 35.52S 64.15W
60 F12 **Eduardo Gomes** ✈ (Manaus) Amazonas, NW Brazil 5.55S 35.15W
Edwardesabad *see* Bannu
69 U9 **Edward, Lake** *var.* Albert Edward Nyanza, Edward Nyanza, Lac Idi Amin, Lake Rutanzige. ◎ Uganda/Dem. Rep. Congo
Edward Nyanza *see* Edward, Lake
24 K5 **Edwards** Mississippi, S USA 32.19N 90.36W
27 O10 **Edwards Plateau** *plain* Texas, SW USA
32 J11 **Edwards River** ~ Illinois, N USA
32 K15 **Edwardsville** Illinois, N USA 38.48N 89.57W
205 O13 **Edward VII Peninsula** *peninsula* Antarctica
205 X4 **Edward VIII Gulf** *bay* Antarctica
8 J11 **Edziza, Mount** ▲ British Columbia, W Canada 57.43N 130.39W
25 H16 **Edzo** *prev.* Rae-Edzo. Northwest Territories, NW Canada 62.43N 115.55W
41 N12 **Eek** Alaska, USA 60.13N 162.01W
101 D16 **Eeklo** *var.* Eekloo. Oost-Vlaanderen, NW Belgium 51.10N 3.34E
Eekloo *see* Eeklo
41 N12 **Eek River** ~ Alaska, USA
100 N6 **Eelde** Drenthe, NE Netherlands 53.07N 6.30E
36 L5 **Eel River** ~ California, W USA
33 P12 **Eel River** ~ Indiana, N USA
Eems *see* Ems
100 O4 **Eemshaven** Groningen, NE Netherlands 53.27N 6.50E
100 O5 **Eems Kanaal** *canal* NE Netherlands
100 M11 **Eerbeek** Gelderland, E Netherlands 52.07N 6.04E
101 C17 **Eernegem** West-Vlaanderen, W Belgium 51.08N 3.03E
101 J15 **Eersel** Noord-Brabant, S Netherlands 51.22N 5.19E
Eesti Vabariik *see* Estonia
197 C14 **Efate** *var.* Éfaté, Fr. Vaté *prev.* Sandwich Island. *island* C Vanuatu
111 S4 **Eferding** Oberösterreich, N Austria 48.18N 14.00E
32 M15 **Effingham** Illinois, N USA 39.07N 88.32W
119 N15 **Eforie-Nord** Constanța, SE Romania 44.04N 28.37E
119 N15 **Eforie Sud** Constanța, E Romania 44.00N 28.38E
Efyrnwy, Afon *see* Vyrnwy
169 N7 **Eg** Hentiy, N Mongolia 48.42N 110.07E
109 G23 **Egadi, Isole** *island group* S Italy
37 X6 **Egan Range** ▲▲ Nevada, W USA
12 K12 **Eganville** Ontario, SE Canada 45.33N 77.03W
Ege Denizi *see* Aegean Sea
41 O14 **Egegik** Alaska, USA 58.13N 157.22W
113 L21 **Eger** *Ger.* Erlau. Heves, NE Hungary 47.54N 20.21E
Eger *see* Cheb, Czech Republic
Eger *see* Ohre, Czech Republic/Germany
181 P8 **Egeria Fracture Zone** *tectonic feature* W Indian Ocean
97 C17 **Egersund** Rogaland, S Norway 58.27N 6.01E
110 J7 **Egg** Vorarlberg, NW Austria 47.27N 9.55E
103 H14 **Egge-gebirge** ▲▲ C Germany
111 Q4 **Eggelsberg** Oberösterreich, N Austria 48.04N 13.00E
111 W2 **Eggenburg** Niederösterreich, NE Austria 48.36N 15.49E
103 N22 **Eggenfelden** Bayern, SE Germany 48.24N 12.45E
20 J17 **Egg Harbor City** New Jersey, NE USA 39.31N 74.39W
67 G25 **Egg Island** *island* W Saint Helena
191 N14 **Egg Lagoon** Tasmania, SE Australia 39.42S 143.57E
101 I20 **Éghezèe** Namur, C Belgium 50.36N 4.55E
94 L2 **Egilsstadhir** Austurland, E Iceland 65.14N 14.21W
Egina *see* Aígina
Egindibulaq *see* Yegindybulak
Egio *see* Aígio
105 N12 **Égletons** Corrèze, C France 45.24N 2.01E
100 H9 **Egmond aan Zee** Noord-Holland, NW Netherlands 52.37N 4.37E
Egmont *see* Taranaki, Mount
192 J10 **Egmont, Cape** *headland* North Island, NZ 39.18S 173.44E
Egoli *see* Johannesburg
Eğri Palanka *see* Kriva Palanka
97 G23 **Egtved** Vejle, C Denmark 55.34N 9.18E
127 Pp4 **Egvekinot** Chukotskiy Avtonomnyy Okrug, NE Russian Federation 66.13N 178.55W
77 V9 **Egypt** *off.* Arab Republic of Egypt, *Ar.* Jumhūrīyah Mişr al 'Arabīyah; *prev.* United Arab Republic, *anc.* Aegyptus. ◆ *republic* NE Africa
32 L17 **Egypt, Lake Of** ▣ Illinois, N USA
Ehen Hudag *see* Alxa Zuoqi
170 E15 **Ehime** *off.* Ehime-ken. ◆ *prefecture* Shikoku, SW Japan
103 I23 **Ehingen** Baden-Württemberg, S Germany 48.16N 9.43E
Ehinos *see* Echínos
23 R14 **Ehrhardt** South Carolina, SE USA 33.06N 81.00W
110 L7 **Ehrwald** Tirol, W Austria 47.24N 10.52E
203 W6 **Eiao** *island* Îles Marquises, NE French Polynesia
107 P2 **Eibar** País Vasco, N Spain 43.10N 2.28W
100 O11 **Eibergen** Gelderland, E Netherlands 52.06N 6.39E
111 V9 **Eibiswald** Steiermark, SE Austria 46.40N 15.15E
111 P8 **Eichham** ▲ SW Austria 47.04N 12.24E
103 J15 **Eichsfeld** *hill range* C Germany
103 K21 **Eichstätt** Bayern, SE Germany 48.53N 11.11E
102 H8 **Eider** ~ N Germany
96 E13 **Eidfjord** Hordaland, S Norway 60.26N 7.05E
96 D13 **Eidfjorden** *fjord* S Norway
96 F9 **Eidsvåg** Møre og Romsdal, S Norway 62.46N 8.00E
97 I14 **Eidsvoll** Akershus, S Norway 60.19N 11.16E
94 N2 **Eidsvollfjellet** ▲ NW Svalbard 79.13N 13.23E
Eier-Berg *see* Suur Munamägi
103 D18 **Eifel** *plateau* W Germany
110 E9 **Eiger** ▲ C Switzerland 46.33N 8.02E
98 G10 **Eigg** *island* W Scotland, UK
161 D24 **Eight Degree Channel** *channel* India/Maldives
46 G1 **Eight Mile Rock** Grand Bahama Island, N Bahamas 26.28N 78.43W
204 J9 **Eights Coast** *physical region* Antarctica
188 K6 **Eighty Mile Beach** *beach* Western Australia
101 L18 **Eijsden** Limburg, SE Netherlands 50.47N 5.41E
97 G15 **Eikeren** ◎ S Norway
Eil *see* Eyl
Eilat *see* Elat
191 O12 **Eildon** Victoria, SE Australia 37.17S 145.57E
191 O12 **Eildon, Lake** ◎ Victoria, SE Australia
82 E8 **Eilei** Northern Kordofan, C Sudan 16.33N 30.54E
103 N15 **Eilenburg** Sachsen, E Germany 51.28N 12.37E
96 H13 **Eina** Oppland, S Norway 60.37N 10.37E
Ein 'Avedat *see* En 'Avedat
103 I14 **Einbeck** Niedersachsen, C Germany 51.49N 9.52E
101 K15 **Eindhoven** Noord-Brabant, S Netherlands 51.25N 5.30E
110 G8 **Einsiedeln** Schwyz, NE Switzerland 47.06N 8.44E
Eipel *see* Ipel'
Éire *see* Ireland, Republic of
Éireann, Muir *see* Irish Sea
Eirik Outer Ridge *see* Eirik Ridge
66 I6 **Eirik Ridge** *var.* Eirik Outer Ridge. *undersea feature* E Labrador Sea
94 I3 **Eiríksjökull** ▲ C Iceland 64.47N 20.23W
61 B14 **Eirunepé** Amazonas, N Brazil 6.37S 69.52W
101 L17 **Eisden** Limburg, NE Belgium 51.05N 5.42E
85 F18 **Eiseb** ~ Botswana/Namibia
Eisen *see* Yŏngch'ŏn
103 J16 **Eisenach** Thüringen, C Germany 50.58N 10.19E
Eisenburg *see* Vasvár
111 U6 **Eisenerz** Steiermark, SE Austria 47.33N 14.52E
102 Q13 **Eisenhüttenstadt** Brandenburg, E Germany 52.09N 14.36E
111 U10 **Eisenkappel** *Slvn.* Železna Kapela. Kärnten, S Austria 46.27N 14.33E
Eisenmarkt *see* Hunedoara
111 Y5 **Eisenstadt** Burgenland, E Austria 47.49N 16.31E
Eishū *see* Yŏngju
121 H15 **Eišiškes** Šalčininkai, SE Lithuania 54.10N 24.59E
103 L15 **Eisleben** Sachsen-Anhalt, C Germany 51.31N 11.33E
202 I3 **Eita** Tarawa, W Kiribati 1.21N 173.04E
Eitape *see* Aitape
107 V11 **Eivissa** *var.* Iviza, *Cast.* Ibiza; *anc.* Ebusus. Eivissa, Spain, W Mediterranean Sea 38.54N 1.25E
107 V10 **Eivissa** *var.* Iviza, *Cast.* Ibiza; *anc.* Ebusus. *island* Islas Baleares, Spain, W Mediterranean Sea
107 R4 **Ejea de los Caballeros** Aragón, NE Spain 42.07N 1.09W
42 E8 **Ejido Insurgentes** Baja California Sur, W Mexico 25.14N 111.45W
168 I12 **Ejin Qi** *var.* Dalain Hob. Nei Mongol Zizhiqu, N China 41.59N 101.04E
Ejmiadzın *see* Ejmiatsin
143 T12 **Ejmiatsin** *var.* Ejmiadzın, Etchmiadzin, *Rus.* Echmiadzin. W Armenia 40.10N 44.17E
79 P16 **Ejura** C Ghana 7.22N 1.22W
43 R16 **Ejutla** *var.* Ejutla de Crespo. Oaxaca, SE Mexico 16.30N 96.40W
Ejutla de Crespo *see* Ejutla
35 Y10 **Ekalaka** Montana, NW USA 45.52N 104.32W
Ekapa *see* Cape Town
130 **Ekaterinodar** *see* Krasnodar
95 L20 **Ekenäs** *Fin.* Tammisaari. Etelä-Suomi, SW Finland 60.00N 23.30E
Ekerem *see* Okarem
192 M13 **Eketahuna** Manawatu-Wanganui, North Island, NZ 40.41S 175.40E
Ekhínos *see* Echínos
127 P3 **Ekiatapskiy Khrebet** ▲▲ NE Russian Federation
151 T8 **Ekibastuz** Pavlodar, NE Kazakhstan 51.45N 75.22E
127 N14 **Ekimchan** Amurskaya Oblast', SE Russian Federation 53.04N 132.56E
97 O15 **Ekoln** ◎ C Sweden
82 I7 **Ekowit** Red Sea, NE Sudan 18.46N 37.07E
97 L19 **Eksjö** Jönköping, S Sweden 57.40N 15.00E
95 I15 **Ekträsk** Västerbotten, N Sweden 64.28N 19.49E
41 O13 **Ekuk** Alaska, USA 58.48N 158.25W
10 F9 **Ekwan** ~ Ontario, C Canada
41 O13 **Ekwok** Alaska, USA 59.21N 157.28W
177 G6 **Ela** Mandalay, C Myanmar 19.37N 96.15E
El Aaiun *see* El Ayoun
83 N15 **Ēl Ābrēd** Somali, E Ethiopia 5.33N 45.12E
117 F22 **Elafónisos** *island* S Greece
117 F22 **Elafonísou, Porthmós** *strait* S Greece
El-Aïoun *see* El Ayoun
77 U8 **El 'Alamein** *var.* Al 'Alamayn. N Egypt 30.46N 28.58E
43 Q12 **El Alazán** Veracruz-Llave, C Mexico 21.06N 97.43W
59 J18 **El Alto** *var.* La Paz. ✈ (La Paz) La Paz, W Bolivia 16.31S 68.07W
Elam *see* Īlām
El Amparo *see* El Amparo de Apure
56 I8 **El Amparo de Apure** *var.* El Amparo. Apure, C Venezuela 7.03N 70.46W
175 Ss12 **Elara** Pulau Ambelau, E Indonesia 3.49S 127.10E
El Araïch/El Araïche *see* Larache
42 D6 **El Arco** Baja California, NW Mexico 28.03N 113.25W
77 X7 **El 'Arîsh** *var.* Al 'Arīsh. NE Egypt 33.00N 31.00E
117 L25 **Elása** *island* SE Greece
El Asnam *see* Chlef
Elassón *see* Elassóna
117 E15 **Elassóna** *prev.* Elassón. Thessalía, C Greece 39.54N 22.11E
107 N2 **El Astillero** Cantabria, N Spain 43.23N 3.45W
144 F14 **Elat** *var.* Eilat, Elath. Southern, S Israel 29.33N 34.57E
Elat, Gulf of *see* Aqaba, Gulf of
Elath *see* Elat, Israel
Elath *see* Al 'Aqabah, Jordan
117 C17 **Eláti** ▲ Lefkáda, Iónioi Nísoi, Greece, C Mediterranean Sea 38.43N 20.38E
196 L16 **Elato Atoll** *atoll* Caroline Islands, C Micronesia
82 C7 **El'Atrun** Northern Darfur, NW Sudan 18.10N 26.40E
76 H6 **El Ayoun** *var.* El Aaiun, El-Aïoun, La Youne. NE Morocco 34.38N 2.28W
143 N14 **Elâzığ** *var.* Elâziz. Elâzığ, E Turkey 38.40N 39.13E
143 O14 **Elâzığ** *var.* Elâziz. ◆ *province* C Turkey
Elâziz *see* Elâzığ
Azraq, Bahr el *see* Blue Nile
25 Q7 **Elba** Alabama, S USA 31.24N 86.04W
108 E13 **Elba, Isola d'** *island* Archipelago Toscano, C Italy
127 Nn15 **El'ban** Khabarovskiy Kray, E Russian Federation 50.03N 136.34E
56 F6 **El Banco** Magdalena, N Colombia 9.00N 74.01W
El Barco *see* O Barco
106 L8 **El Barco de Ávila** Castilla-León, N Spain 40.21N 5.31W
El Barco de Valdeorras *see* O Barco
144 H7 **El Barouk, Jabal** ▲▲ C Lebanon
115 L20 **Elbasan** *var.* Elbasani. Elbasan, C Albania 41.07N 20.04E
115 L20 **Elbasan** ◆ *district* C Albania
Elbasani *see* Elbasan
56 K6 **El Baúl** Cojedes, C Venezuela 8.55N 68.17W
88 D11 **Elbe** *Cz.* Labe. ~ Czech Republic/Germany
102 L13 **Elbe-Havel-Kanal** *canal* E Germany
102 K9 **Elbe-Lübeck-Kanal** *canal* N Germany
El Beni *see* Beni
144 H7 **El Beqaa** *var.* Al Biqā', Bekaa Valley. *valley* E Lebanon
27 R6 **Elbert** Texas, SW USA 33.15N 98.58W
39 R5 **Elbert, Mount** ▲ Colorado, C USA 39.07N 106.26W
25 U3 **Elberton** Georgia, SE USA 34.06N 82.52W
102 K11 **Elbe-Seiten-Kanal** *canal* N Germany
104 M4 **Elbeuf** Seine-Maritime, N France 49.16N 1.01E
Elbing *see* Elbląg
142 M15 **Elbistan** Kahramanmaraş, S Turkey 38.13N 37.10E
112 K7 **Elbląg** *var.* Elblag, *Ger.* Elbing. Warmińsko-Mazurskie, NE Poland 54.10N 19.25E
45 N10 **El Bluff** Región Autónoma Atlántico Sur, SE Nicaragua 12.01N 83.41W
65 H17 **El Bolsón** Río Negro, W Argentina 41.57S 71.33W
107 P11 **El Bonillo** Castilla-La Mancha, C Spain 38.57N 2.31W
El Bordo *see* Patía
El Boulaida/El Boulaïda *see* Blida
9 T16 **Elbow** Saskatchewan, S Canada 51.07N 106.30W
31 S7 **Elbow Lake** Minnesota, N USA 45.59N 95.58W
131 N16 **El'brus** *var.* Gora El'brus. ▲ SW Russian Federation 43.18N 42.21E
El'brus, Gora *see* El'brus
130 M15 **El'brusskiy** Karachayevo-Cherkesskaya Respublika, SW Russian Federation 43.36N 42.06E
83 D14 **El Buhayrat** *var.* Lakes State. ◆ *state* S Sudan
El Bur *see* Ceel Buur
100 L10 **Elburg** Gelderland, E Netherlands 52.27N 5.46E
107 O6 **El Burgo de Osma** Castilla-León, C Spain 41.36N 3.04W
Elburz Mountains *see* Alborz, Reshteh-ye Kūhhā-ye
37 V17 **El Cajon** California, W USA 32.46N 116.52W
65 H22 **El Calafate** *var.* Calafate. Santa Cruz, S Argentina 50.19S 72.12W
57 Q8 **El Callao** Bolívar, E Venezuela 7.18N 61.48W
27 U12 **El Campo** Texas, SW USA 29.12N 96.16W
56 I7 **El Cantón** Barinas, W Venezuela 7.25N 71.16W
37 Q8 **El Capitan** ▲ California, W USA 37.46N 119.39W
56 H5 **El Carmelo** Zulia, NW Venezuela 10.21N 71.46W
64 J5 **El Carmen** Jujuy, NW Argentina 24.24S 65.16W
56 E5 **El Carmen de Bolívar** Bolívar, NW Colombia 9.45N 75.11W
57 O8 **El Casabe** Bolívar, SE Venezuela 6.25N 63.34W
44 M12 **El Castillo de La Concepción** Río San Juan, SE Nicaragua 10.58N 84.24W
El Cayo *see* San Ignacio
37 X17 **El Centro** California, W USA 32.47N 115.33W
57 N6 **El Chaparro** Anzoátegui, NE Venezuela 9.08N 65.01W
107 S12 **Elche** *var.* Elx-Elche; *anc.* Ilici, *Lat.* Illicis. País Valenciano, E Spain 38.16N 0.40W
107 Q12 **Elche de la Sierra** Castilla-La Mancha, C Spain 38.27N 2.03W
43 U15 **El Chichonal, Volcán** ⩙ SE Mexico 17.20N 93.12W
42 C2 **El Chinero** Baja California, NW Mexico
189 R1 **Elcho Island** *island* Wessel Islands, Northern Territory, N Australia
65 H18 **El Corcovado** Chubut, SW Argentina 43.31S 71.30W
107 R12 **Elda** País Valenciano, E Spain 38.28N 0.46W
102 M10 **Elde** ~ NE Germany
100 L12 **Elden** Gelderland, E Netherlands 51.57N 5.53E
83 J16 **El Der** *spring/well* S Ethiopia 3.55N 39.48E
El Dere *see* Ceel Dheere
42 E3 **El Desemboque** Sonora, NW Mexico 30.33N 112.59W
56 F5 **El Difícil** *var.* Ariguaní. Magdalena, N Colombia 9.49N 74.16W
126 Mm11 **El'dikan** Respublika Sakha (Yakutiya), NE Russian Federation 60.46N 135.04E
El Djazaïr *see* Alger
El Djelfa *see* Djelfa
31 X15 **Eldon** Iowa, C USA 40.55N 92.13W
29 U5 **Eldon** Missouri, C USA 38.21N 92.34W

◆ Country
● Country Capital
◇ Dependent Territory
○ Dependent Territory Capital
◆ Administrative Region
✈ International Airport
▲ Mountain
▲▲ Mountain Range
⩙ Volcano
~ River
◎ Lake
▣ Reservoir

56 E13 **El Doncello** Caquetá, S Colombia *1.43N 75.16W*
31 W13 **Eldora** Iowa, C USA *42.21N 93.06W*
62 G12 **Eldorado** Misiones, NE Argentina *26.22S 54.33W*
42 I9 **El Dorado** Sinaloa, C Mexico *24.19N 107.22W*
29 U14 **El Dorado** Arkansas, C USA *33.12N 92.40W*
32 M17 **Eldorado** Illinois, N USA *37.48N 88.26W*
29 O6 **El Dorado** Kansas, C USA *37.49N 96.51W*
28 K12 **Eldorado** Oklahoma, C USA *34.28N 99.39W*
27 O9 **Eldorado** Texas, SW USA *30.51N 100.36W*
57 Q8 **El Dorado** Bolívar, E Venezuela *6.45N 61.37W*
56 F10 **El Dorado** ✕ (Bogotá) Cundinamarca, C Colombia *1.15N 71.52W*
El Dorado *see* California
29 O6 **El Dorado Lake** ⊠ Kansas, C USA
29 S6 **El Dorado Springs** Missouri, C USA *37.53N 94.01W*
83 H18 **Eldoret** Rift Valley, W Kenya *0.31N 35.16E*
31 Z14 **Eldridge** Iowa, C USA *41.39N 90.34W*
97 J21 **Eldsberga** Halland, S Sweden *56.36N 13.00E*
27 R4 **Electra** Texas, SW USA *34.01N 98.55W*
39 Q7 **Electra Lake** ⊠ Colorado, C USA
40 B8 **Eleele** *Haw.* 'Ele'ele. Kauai, Hawaii, USA, C Pacific Ocean *21.54N 159.35W*
Elefantes *see* Olifants
117 H19 **Elefsína** *prev.* Elevsís. Attikí, C Greece *38.02N 23.33E*
117 G19 **Eléftheres** *anc.* Eleutherae. *site of ancient city* Attikí/Stereá Ellás, C Greece *38.12N 23.24E*
116 I13 **Eleftheroúpoli** *prev.* Elevtheroúpolis. Anatolikí Makedonía kai Thráki, NE Greece *40.56N 24.16E*
76 F10 **El Eglab** ⛰ SW Algeria
120 F10 **Eleja** Jelgava, C Latvia *56.24N 23.41E*
Elek *see* Ilek
121 G14 **Elektrėnai** Kaišiadorys, SE Lithuania *54.47N 24.35E*
130 L3 **Elektrostal'** Moskovskaya Oblast', W Russian Federation *55.46N 38.23E*
83 H15 **Elemi Triangle** *disputed region* Kenya/Sudan
56 G16 **El Encanto** Amazonas, S Colombia *1.45S 73.12W*
39 R14 **Elephant Butte Reservoir** ⊠ New Mexico, SW USA
Éléphant, Chaîne de l' *see* Dâmrei, Chuŏr Phmun
204 G2 **Elephant Island** *island* South Shetland Islands, Antarctica
Elephant River *see* Olifants
El Escorial *see* San Lorenzo de El Escorial
Élesd *see* Aleşd
116 F11 **Eleshnitsa** ≈ W Bulgaria
143 S13 **Eleşkirt** Ağrı, E Turkey *39.22N 42.48E*
44 F5 **El Estor** Izabal, E Guatemala *15.31N 89.19W*
Eleutherae *see* Eléftheres
46 I2 **Eleuthera Island** *island* N Bahamas
39 S5 **Elevenmile Canyon Reservoir** ⊠ Colorado, C USA
29 W8 **Eleven Point River** ≈ Arkansas/Missouri, C USA
Elevsís *see* Elefsína
Elevtheroúpolis *see* Eleftheroúpoli
77 W8 **El Faiyûm** *var.* Al Fayyūm. N Egypt *29.24N 30.52E*
82 B10 **El Fasher** *var.* Al Fāshir. Northern Darfur, W Sudan *13.37N 25.22E*
77 W8 **El Fashn** *var.* Al Fashn. C Egypt *28.49N 30.54E*
El Ferrol/El Ferrol del Caudillo *see* Ferrol
41 W13 **Elfin Cove** Chichagof Island, Alaska, USA *58.09N 136.16W*
107 W4 **El Fluvià** ≈ NE Spain
42 H7 **El Fuerte** Sinaloa, W Mexico *26.28N 108.34W*
82 D11 **El Fula** Western Kordofan, C Sudan *11.43N 28.19E*
El Gedaref *see* Gedaref
82 A10 **El Geneina** *var.* Ajjinena, Al-Genain, Al Junaynah. Western Darfur, W Sudan *13.27N 22.30E*
98 J8 **Elgin** NE Scotland, UK *57.39N 3.19W*
32 M10 **Elgin** Illinois, N USA *42.02N 88.16W*
31 P14 **Elgin** Nebraska, C USA *41.58N 98.04W*
37 Y9 **Elgin** Nevada, W USA *37.19N 114.30W*
30 L6 **Elgin** North Dakota, N USA *46.24N 101.51W*
28 M12 **Elgin** Oklahoma, C USA *34.46N 98.17W*
27 T10 **Elgin** Texas, SW USA *30.21N 97.22W*
127 N9 **El'ginskiy** Respublika Sakha (Yakutiya), NE Russian Federation *64.27N 141.57E*
77 W8 **El Gîza** *var.* Al Jīzah, Gîza, Gizeh. N Egypt *30.01N 31.13E*
76 J8 **El Goléa** *var.* Al Golea. C Algeria *30.35N 2.58E*
42 D2 **El Golfo de Santa Clara** Sonora, NW Mexico *31.44N 114.34W*
83 G18 **Elgon, Mount** ▲ E Uganda *1.07N 34.29E*
96 I10 **Elgpiggen** ▲ S Norway *62.13N 11.18E*
107 T4 **El Grado** Aragón, NE Spain *42.09N 0.13E*
42 L6 **El Guaje, Laguna** ⊠ NE Mexico
56 H6 **El Guayabo** Zulia, W Venezuela *8.37N 72.19W*
79 O6 **El Guettâra** *oasis* N Mali *22.01N 3.00W*
78 J6 **El Ḥammâmi** *desert* N Mauritania
78 M5 **El Ḥank** *cliff* N Mauritania
El Haseke *see* Al Ḥasakah
82 H10 **El Hawata** Gedaref, E Sudan *13.25N 34.42E*
El Higo *see* Higos
176 Uu16 **Eliase** Pulau Selaru, E Indonesia *8.16S 130.49E*
Elías Piña *see* Comendador
27 R6 **Eliasville** Texas, SW USA *32.55N 98.46W*
Elichpur *see* Achalpur
39 V13 **Elida** New Mexico, SW USA *33.57N 103.39W*
117 F18 **Elikónas** ⛰ C Greece
69 T10 **Elila** ≈ W Dem. Rep. Congo
41 N9 **Elim** Alaska, USA *64.37N 162.15W*
Elimberrum *see* Auch
Eliocroca *see* Lorca
63 B16 **Elisa** Santa Fe, C Argentina *30.42S 61.04W*
Elisabethstedt *see* Dumbrăveni
Élisabethville *see* Lubumbashi
131 O13 **Elista** Respublika Kalmykiya, SW Russian Federation *46.17N 44.09E*
190 I9 **Elizabeth** South Australia *34.44S 138.39E*
23 Q3 **Elizabeth** West Virginia, NE USA *39.03N 81.22W*
21 Q9 **Elizabeth, Cape** *headland* Maine, NE USA *43.34N 70.12W*
23 Y8 **Elizabeth City** North Carolina, SE USA *36.18N 76.13W*
23 P8 **Elizabethton** Tennessee, S USA *36.21N 82.12W*
32 M17 **Elizabethtown** Illinois, N USA *37.24N 88.21W*
22 K6 **Elizabethtown** Kentucky, S USA *37.41N 85.51W*
20 L7 **Elizabethtown** New York, NE USA *44.13N 73.37W*
23 U11 **Elizabethtown** North Carolina, SE USA *34.37N 78.36W*
20 G15 **Elizabethtown** Pennsylvania, NE USA *40.08N 76.36W*
76 E6 **El-Jadida** *prev.* Mazagan. W Morocco *33.15N 8.27W*
El Jafr *see* Jafr, Qā' al
82 F11 **El Jebelein** White Nile, E Sudan *12.37N 32.51E*
112 N8 **Ełk** *Ger.* Lyck. Warmińsko-Mazurskie, NE Poland *53.51N 22.19E*
112 O8 **Ełk** ≈ NE Poland
31 Y12 **Elkader** Iowa, C USA *42.51N 91.24W*
82 G9 **El Kamlin** Gezira, C Sudan *15.01N 33.02E*
35 N11 **Elk City** Idaho, NW USA *45.50N 115.28W*
28 K10 **Elk City** Oklahoma, C USA *35.24N 99.24W*
29 P7 **Elk City Lake** ⊠ Kansas, C USA
36 M5 **Elk Creek** California, W USA *39.34N 122.34W*
30 J10 **Elk Creek** ≈ South Dakota, N USA
76 M5 **El Kef** *var.* Al Kāf, Le Kef. NW Tunisia *36.13N 8.44E*
76 F7 **El Kelâa Srarhna** *var.* Kal al Sraghna. C Morocco *32.05N 7.20W*
El Kerak *see* Al Karak
9 P17 **Elkford** British Columbia, SW Canada *49.58N 114.57W*
El Khalil *see* Hebron
82 E7 **El Khandaq** Northern, N Sudan *18.34N 30.34E*
77 W10 **El Khârga** *var.* Al Khārijah. C Egypt *25.31N 30.36E*
33 P11 **Elkhart** Indiana, N USA *41.40N 85.58W*
28 H7 **Elkhart** Kansas, C USA *37.00N 101.51W*
27 V8 **Elkhart** Texas, SW USA *31.37N 95.34W*
32 M7 **Elkhart Lake** ◎ Wisconsin, N USA
El Khartûm *see* Khartoum
39 Q3 **Elkhead Mountains** ⛰ Colorado, C USA
20 I12 **Elk Hill** ▲ Pennsylvania, NE USA *41.42N 75.33W*
144 G8 **El Khiyam** *var.* Al Khiyām, Khiam. S Lebanon *33.12N 35.42E*
31 S15 **Elkhorn** Nebraska, C USA *41.17N 96.13W*
32 M9 **Elkhorn** Wisconsin, N USA *42.40N 88.34W*
31 R14 **Elkhorn River** ≈ Nebraska, C USA
131 O16 **El'khotovo** Respublika Severnaya Osetiya, SW Russian Federation *43.18N 44.17E*
116 L10 **Elkhovo** *prev.* Kizilagach. Yambol, E Bulgaria *42.12N 26.36E*
23 R8 **Elkin** North Carolina, SE USA *36.14N 80.51W*
23 S4 **Elkins** West Virginia, NE USA *38.55N 79.51W*
205 X3 **Elkins, Mount** ▲ Antarctica *66.25S 53.54E*
12 G8 **Elk Lake** Ontario, S Canada *47.44N 80.19W*
33 P6 **Elk Lake** ◎ Michigan, N USA
20 F12 **Elkland** Pennsylvania, NE USA *41.59N 77.16W*
37 W3 **Elko** Nevada, W USA *40.48N 115.46W*
9 R14 **Elk Point** Alberta, SW Canada *53.52N 110.49W*
31 R12 **Elk Point** South Dakota, N USA *42.42N 96.37W*
31 V8 **Elk River** Minnesota, N USA *45.18N 93.34W*
22 J10 **Elk River** ≈ Alabama/Tennessee, S USA
23 R4 **Elk River** ≈ West Virginia, NE USA
22 I7 **Elkton** Kentucky, S USA *36.48N 87.07W*
23 Y2 **Elkton** Maryland, NE USA *39.36N 75.49W*
31 R10 **Elkton** South Dakota, N USA *44.14N 96.28W*
22 I10 **Elkton** Tennessee, S USA *35.01N 86.51W*
23 U5 **Elkton** Virginia, NE USA *38.22N 78.35W*
El Kuneitra *see* Al Qunayṭirah
83 L15 **El Kure** Somali, E Ethiopia *5.37N 42.05E*
82 D12 **El Lagowa** Western Kordofan, C Sudan *11.22N 29.10E*
41 S12 **Ellamar** Alaska, USA *60.54N 146.37W*
Ellás *see* Greece
25 S6 **Ellaville** Georgia, SE USA *32.14N 84.18W*
207 P9 **Ellef Ringnes Island** *island* Nunavut, N Canada
31 V10 **Ellendale** Minnesota, N USA *43.53N 93.19W*
31 P7 **Ellendale** North Dakota, N USA *46.00N 98.31W*
38 M6 **Ellen, Mount** ▲ Utah, W USA *38.06N 110.48W*
34 I9 **Ellensburg** Washington, NW USA *47.00N 120.34W*
20 K12 **Ellenville** New York, NE USA *41.43N 74.24W*
Ellep *see* Lib
23 T10 **Ellerbe** North Carolina, SE USA *35.04N 79.45W*
207 P10 **Ellesmere Island** *island* Queen Elizabeth Islands, Nunavut, N Canada
193 H19 **Ellesmere, Lake** ◎ South Island, NZ
99 K18 **Ellesmere Port** C England, UK *53.16N 2.54W*
33 O14 **Ellettsville** Indiana, N USA *39.13N 86.37W*
101 E19 **Ellezelles** Hainaut, SW Belgium *50.44N 3.40E*
15 Jj4 **Ellice** ≈ Nunavut, NE Canada
Ellice Islands *see* Tuvalu
Ellichpur *see* Achalpur
23 W3 **Ellicott City** Maryland, NE USA *39.16N 76.48W*
25 S2 **Ellijay** Georgia, SE USA *34.42N 84.28W*
29 W7 **Ellington** Missouri, C USA *37.14N 90.58W*
28 L5 **Ellinwood** Kansas, C USA *38.21N 98.34W*
85 J24 **Elliot** Eastern Cape, SE South Africa *31.19S 27.51E*
12 D10 **Elliot Lake** Ontario, S Canada *46.24N 82.37W*
189 X6 **Elliot, Mount** ▲ Queensland, E Australia *19.36S 147.02E*
23 T5 **Elliott Knob** ▲ Virginia, NE USA *38.10N 79.18W*
28 K4 **Ellis** Kansas, C USA *38.56N 99.33W*
190 F8 **Elliston** South Australia *33.39S 134.56E*
24 M7 **Ellisville** Mississippi, S USA *31.36N 89.12W*
107 V5 **El Llobregat** ≈ NE Spain
98 L9 **Ellon** NE Scotland, UK *57.22N 2.06W*
Ellore *see* Elūru
23 S13 **Elloree** South Carolina, SE USA *33.34N 80.37W*
28 M4 **Ellsworth** Kansas, C USA *38.43N 98.13W*
21 S7 **Ellsworth** Maine, NE USA *44.32N 68.25W*
32 I6 **Ellsworth** Wisconsin, N USA *44.43N 92.28W*
28 M11 **Ellsworth, Lake** ⊠ Oklahoma, C USA
204 K9 **Ellsworth Land** *physical region* Antarctica
204 L9 **Ellsworth Mountains** ⛰ Antarctica
103 J21 **Ellwangen** Baden-Württemberg, S Germany *48.58N 10.07E*
20 B14 **Ellwood City** Pennsylvania, NE USA *40.49N 80.15W*
110 H8 **Elm** Glarus, NE Switzerland *46.55N 9.09E*
34 G9 **Elma** Washington, NW USA *47.00N 123.24W*
124 Qq15 **El Maḥalla el Kubra** *var.* Al Maḥallah al Kubrá, Mahalla el Kubra. N Egypt *30.58N 31.10E*
76 E9 **El Mahbas** *var.* Mahbés. SW Western Sahara *27.25N 9.09W*
65 H17 **El Maitén** Chubut, W Argentina *42.03S 71.10W*
142 E16 **Elmalı** Antalya, SW Turkey *36.40N 29.54E*
82 G10 **El Manaqil** Gezira, C Sudan *14.12N 33.01E*
56 M12 **El Mango** Amazonas, S Venezuela *1.55N 66.34W*
77 W7 **El Manṣûra** *var.* Al Manṣūrah, Manṣûra. N Egypt *31.02N 31.30E*
57 P8 **El Manteco** Bolívar, E Venezuela *7.17N 62.31W*
31 O16 **Elm Creek** Nebraska, C USA *40.43N 99.22W*
El Mediyya *see* Médéa
79 V9 **Elméki** Agadez, C Niger *17.52N 8.07E*
110 K7 **Elmen** Tirol, W Austria *47.22N 10.34E*
20 I16 **Elmer** New Jersey, NE USA *39.34N 75.09W*
144 G6 **El Mina** *var.* Al Mīnā'. N Lebanon *34.28N 35.49E*
77 W9 **El Minya** *var.* Al Minyā, Minya. C Egypt *28.06N 30.40E*
12 F15 **Elmira** Ontario, S Canada *43.35N 80.34W*
20 G11 **Elmira** New York, NE USA *42.06N 76.49W*
38 K13 **El Mirage** Arizona, SW USA *33.36N 112.19W*
31 O7 **Elm Lake** ⊠ South Dakota, N USA
El Moján *see* San Rafael
107 N7 **El Molar** Madrid, C Spain *40.43N 3.34W*
78 L7 **El Mrâyer** *well* C Mauritania *21.40N 7.50W*
78 L5 **El Mreïti** *well* N Mauritania *23.40N 7.23W*
78 L8 **El Mreyyé** *desert* E Mauritania
31 P8 **Elm River** ≈ North Dakota/South Dakota, N USA
102 I9 **Elmshorn** Schleswig-Holstein, N Germany *53.45N 9.39E*
82 D12 **El Muglad** Western Kordofan, C Sudan *11.01N 27.43E*
El Muwaqqar *see* Al Muwaqqar
12 G14 **Elmvale** Ontario, S Canada *44.34N 79.53W*
32 K12 **Elmwood** Illinois, N USA *40.46N 89.58W*
28 J8 **Elmwood** Oklahoma, C USA *36.37N 100.31W*
105 P17 **Elne** *anc.* Illiberis. Pyrénées-Orientales, S France *42.36N 2.58E*
56 F11 **El Nevado, Cerro** *elevation* C Colombia *3.56N 74.20W*
179 Oo13 **El Nido** Palawan, W Philippines *11.10N 119.25E*
64 I12 **El Nihuil** Mendoza, W Argentina *35.05S 68.38W*
77 W7 **El Nouzha** ✕ (Alexandria) N Egypt *31.06N 29.58E*
82 E10 **El Obeid** *var.* Al Obayyid, Al Ubayyiḍ. Northern Kordofan, C Sudan *13.10N 30.10E*
43 O13 **El Oro** México, S Mexico *19.51N 100.07W*
58 B8 **El Oro** ◈ *province* SW Ecuador
63 B19 **Elortondo** Santa Fe, C Argentina *33.42S 61.37W*
56 J8 **Elorza** Apure, C Venezuela *7.01N 69.30W*
El Ouâdi *see* El Oued
76 L7 **El Oued** *var.* Al Oued, El Ouâdi, El Wad. NE Algeria *33.19N 6.52E*
38 L15 **Eloy** Arizona, SW USA *32.47N 111.33W*
57 Q7 **El Palmar** Bolívar, E Venezuela *8.03N 61.51W*
42 K8 **El Palmito** Durango, W Mexico *25.40N 104.58W*
57 P7 **El Pao** Bolívar, E Venezuela *8.02N 62.38W*
56 K5 **El Pao** Cojedes, N Venezuela *9.42N 68.12W*
44 J7 **El Paraíso** El Paraíso, S Honduras *13.52N 86.32W*
44 I7 **El Paraíso** ◈ *department* SE Honduras
32 L12 **El Paso** Illinois, N USA *40.44N 89.01W*
26 G8 **El Paso** Texas, SW USA *31.45N 106.30W*
26 G8 **El Paso** ✕ Texas, SW USA *31.48N 106.24W*
107 U7 **El Perello** Cataluña, NE Spain *40.52N 0.43E*
57 P5 **El Pilar** Sucre, NE Venezuela *10.33N 63.13W*
44 F7 **El Pital, Cerro** ▲ El Salvador/Honduras *14.19N 89.06W*
37 Q9 **El Portal** California, W USA *37.40N 119.46W*
42 J3 **El Porvenir** Chihuahua, N Mexico *31.13N 105.51W*
45 U14 **El Porvenir** San Blas, N Panama *9.33N 78.55W*
107 W6 **El Prat de Llobregat** Cataluña, NE Spain *41.19N 2.04E*
44 H5 **El Progreso** Yoro, NW Honduras *15.25N 87.49W*
44 A2 **El Progreso** *off.* Departamento de El Progreso. ◈ *department* C Guatemala
El Progreso *see* Guastatoya
106 L9 **El Puente del Arzobispo** Castilla-La Mancha, C Spain *39.48N 5.10W*
106 J15 **El Puerto de Santa María** Andalucía, S Spain *36.36N 6.13W*
64 I8 **El Puesto** Catamarca, NW Argentina *27.57S 67.37W*
El Qâhira *see* Cairo
77 V10 **El Qaṣr** *var.* Al Qaṣr. C Egypt *25.39N 28.54E*
El Qatrani *see* Al Qaṭrānah
42 I10 **El Quelite** Sinaloa, C Mexico *23.37N 106.26W*
64 G9 **Elqui, Río** ≈ N Chile
El Quneitra *see* Al Qunayṭirah
El Quseir *see* Al Quṣayr
El Quweira *see* Al Quwayrah
147 O15 **El-Rahaba** ✕ (Ṣan'ā') W Yemen *15.28N 44.12E*
44 M10 **El Rama** Región Autónoma Atlántico Sur, SE Nicaragua *12.12N 84.13W*
45 W16 **El Real** *var.* El Real de Santa María. Darién, SE Panama *8.07N 77.42W*
El Real de Santa María *see* El Real
28 M10 **El Reno** Oklahoma, C USA *35.31N 97.57W*
42 K9 **El Rodeo** Durango, C Mexico *25.08N 104.34W*
106 J13 **El Ronquillo** Andalucía, S Spain *37.43N 6.09W*
9 S16 **Elrose** Saskatchewan, S Canada *51.07N 107.59W*
32 K8 **Elroy** Wisconsin, N USA *43.43N 90.16W*
27 S17 **Elsa** Texas, SW USA *26.17N 97.59W*
77 W8 **El Ṣaff** *var.* Aṣ Ṣaff. N Egypt *29.26N 31.19E*
42 J10 **El Salto** Durango, C Mexico *23.46N 105.22W*
44 D8 **El Salvador** *off.* Republica de El Salvador. ◆ *republic* Central America
56 K7 **El Samán de Apure** Apure, C Venezuela *7.51N 68.47W*
12 D7 **Elsas** Ontario, S Canada *48.31N 82.53W*
42 F3 **El Sásabe** *var.* Aduana del Sásabe. Sonora, NW Mexico *31.27N 111.31W*
Elsass *see* Alsace
42 J5 **El Sáuz** Chihuahua, N Mexico *29.03N 106.15W*
29 W4 **Elsberry** Missouri, C USA *39.10N 90.46W*
47 P9 **El Seibo** *var.* Santa Cruz de El Seibo, Santa Cruz del Seibo. E Dominican Republic *18.45N 69.04W*
44 B7 **El Semillero Barra Nahualate** Escuintla, SW Guatemala *14.01N 91.28W*
Elsene *see* Ixelles
165 N11 **Elsen Nur** ◎ C China
38 L6 **Elsinore** Utah, W USA *38.40N 112.09W*
Elsinore *see* Helsingør
101 L18 **Elsloo** Limburg, SE Netherlands *50.57N 5.46E*
62 G13 **El Soberbio** Misiones, NE Argentina *27.15S 54.04W*
57 N6 **El Socorro** Guárico, C Venezuela *9.00N 65.42W*
56 L6 **El Sombrero** Guárico, N Venezuela *9.25N 67.06W*
100 L10 **Elspeet** Gelderland, E Netherlands *52.19N 5.47E*
100 L12 **Elst** Gelderland, E Netherlands *51.55N 5.51E*
103 O15 **Elsterwerda** Brandenburg, E Germany *51.27N 13.32E*
42 J4 **El Sueco** Chihuahua, N Mexico *29.52N 106.23W*
El Suweida *see* As Suwaydā'
El Suweis *see* Suez
56 D12 **El Tambo** Cauca, SW Colombia *2.25N 76.49W*
183 T13 **Eltanin Fracture Zone** *tectonic feature* SE Pacific Ocean
107 X5 **El Ter** ≈ NE Spain
192 K11 **Eltham** Taranaki, North Island, NZ *39.25S 174.17E*
57 O6 **El Tigre** Anzoátegui, NE Venezuela *8.55N 64.15W*
El Tigrito *see* San José de Guanipa
56 J5 **El Tocuyo** Lara, N Venezuela *9.47N 69.48W*
131 Q10 **El'ton** Volgogradskaya Oblast', SW Russian Federation *49.07N 46.50E*
34 K10 **Eltopia** Washington, NW USA *46.33N 118.59W*
63 A18 **El Trébol** Santa Fe, C Argentina *32.12S 61.40W*
42 J13 **El Tuito** Jalisco, SW Mexico *20.20N 105.19W*
77 X8 **El Ṭûr** *var.* Aṭ Ṭūr. NE Egypt *28.18N 33.37E*
161 K16 **Elūru** *prev.* Ellore. Andhra Pradesh, E India *16.45N 81.10E*
120 H13 **Elva** *Ger.* Elwa. Tartumaa, SE Estonia *58.13N 26.27E*
39 R9 **El Vado Reservoir** ⊠ New Mexico, SW USA
45 S15 **El Valle** Coclé, C Panama *8.39N 80.07W*
106 I11 **Elvas** Portalegre, C Portugal *38.52N 7.10W*
56 K7 **El Venado** Apure, C Venezuela *7.25N 68.46W*
107 V6 **El Vendrell** Cataluña, NE Spain *41.13N 1.31E*
96 I13 **Elverum** Hedmark, S Norway *60.52N 11.34E*
44 I9 **El Viejo** Chinandega, NW Nicaragua *12.37N 87.09W*
56 G7 **El Viejo, Cerro** ▲ C Colombia *7.31N 72.56W*
56 H6 **El Vigía** Mérida, NW Venezuela *8.37N 71.39W*
107 Q4 **El Villar de Arnedo** La Rioja, N Spain *42.19N 2.05W*
61 A14 **Elvira** Amazonas, W Brazil *7.12S 69.56W*
Elwa *see* Elva
El Wad *see* El Oued
83 K17 **El Wak** North Eastern, NE Kenya *2.46N 40.57E*
35 R7 **Elwell, Lake** ⊠ Montana, NW USA
33 P13 **Elwood** Indiana, N USA *40.16N 85.50W*
29 R3 **Elwood** Kansas, C USA *39.43N 94.52W*
31 N16 **Elwood** Nebraska, C USA *40.35N 99.51W*
Elx-Elche *see* Elche
99 O20 **Ely** E England, UK *52.23N 0.15E*
31 X4 **Ely** Minnesota, N USA *47.54N 91.52W*
37 X6 **Ely** Nevada, W USA *39.15N 114.53W*
El Yopal *see* Yopal
33 T11 **Elyria** Ohio, N USA *41.22N 82.06W*
47 S9 **El Yunque** ▲ E Puerto Rico *18.15N 65.46W*
103 I22 **Elz** ≈ SW Germany
197 C14 **Emae** *island* Shepherd Islands, C Vanuatu
120 I5 **Emajõgi** *Ger.* Embach. ≈ SE Estonia
Emāmrūd *see* Shāhrūd
155 Q2 **Emām Ṣāḥeb** *var.* Emam Saheb, Hazarat Imam. Kunduz, NE Afghanistan *37.10N 68.55E*
Emāmshahr *see* Shāhrūd
97 M20 **Emån** ≈ S Sweden
197 D14 **Emao** *island* C Vanuatu
150 J11 **Emba** *Kaz.* Embi. Aktyubinsk, W Kazakhstan *48.49N 58.10E*
150 H12 **Emba** *Kaz.* Zhem. ≈ W Kazakhstan
Embach *see* Emajõgi
64 K5 **Embarcación** Salta, N Argentina *23.15S 64.04W*
32 M15 **Embarras River** ≈ Illinois, N USA
Embi *see* Emba
83 I19 **Embu** Eastern, C Kenya *0.30N 37.30E*
102 E10 **Emden** Niedersachsen, NW Germany *53.22N 7.12E*
31 Q4 **Emerado** North Dakota, N USA *47.55N 97.21W*
189 X8 **Emerald** Queensland, E Australia *23.33S 148.10E*
Emerald Isle *see* Montserrat
59 J15 **Emero, Río** ≈ W Bolivia
9 Y17 **Emerson** Manitoba, S Canada *49.01N 97.07W*
31 T15 **Emerson** Iowa, C USA *41.00N 95.22W*
31 R13 **Emerson** Nebraska, C USA *42.16N 96.43W*
38 M5 **Emery** Utah, W USA *38.54N 111.16W*
Emesa *see* Ḥimṣ
142 E13 **Emet** Kütahya, W Turkey *39.21N 29.15E*
194 G14 **Emeti** Western, SW PNG *7.51S 143.14E*
37 V3 **Emigrant Pass** *pass* Nevada, W USA *40.39N 116.15W*
80 I6 **Emi Koussi** ▲ N Chad *19.52N 18.34E*
Emilia *see* Emilia-Romagna
43 V15 **Emiliano Zapata** Chiapas, SE Mexico *17.45N 91.45W*
108 E9 **Emilia-Romagna** *prev.* Emilia, *anc.* Æmilia. ◈ *region* N Italy
164 J3 **Emin** *var.* Dorbiljin. Xinjiang Uygur Zizhiqu, NW China *46.31N 83.35E*
155 W8 **Eminābād** Punjab, E Pakistan *32.01N 73.51E*
23 L5 **Eminence** Kentucky, S USA *38.22N 85.10W*
29 W7 **Eminence** Missouri, C USA *37.09N 91.21W*
116 N9 **Emine, Nos** *headland* E Bulgaria *42.43N 27.53E*
164 I3 **Emin He** ≈ NW China
195 N8 **Emirau Island** *island* N PNG
142 F13 **Emirdağ** Afyon, W Turkey *39.01N 31.09E*
97 M21 **Emmaboda** Kalmar, S Sweden *56.36N 15.30E*
120 E5 **Emmaste** Hiiumaa, W Estonia *58.43N 22.36E*
20 I15 **Emmaus** Pennsylvania, NE USA *40.32N 75.28W*
191 U4 **Emmaville** New South Wales, SE Australia *29.26S 151.38E*
110 E9 **Emme** ≈ W Switzerland
100 L8 **Emmeloord** Flevoland, N Netherlands *52.43N 5.46E*
100 O8 **Emmen** Drenthe, NE Netherlands *52.48N 6.57E*
110 F8 **Emmen** Luzern, C Switzerland *47.03N 8.14E*
103 F23 **Emmendingen** Baden-Württemberg, SW Germany *48.07N 7.51E*
100 P8 **Emmer-Compascuum** Drenthe, NE Netherlands *52.47N 7.03E*
103 D14 **Emmerich** Nordrhein-Westfalen, W Germany *51.49N 6.16E*
31 U12 **Emmetsburg** Iowa, C USA *43.06N 94.40W*
34 M14 **Emmett** Idaho, NW USA *43.52N 116.30W*
40 M10 **Emmonak** Alaska, USA *62.46N 164.31W*
Emona *see* Ljubljana
Emonti *see* East London
26 L12 **Emory Peak** ▲ Texas, SW USA *29.15N 103.18W*
42 F6 **Empalme** Sonora, NW Mexico *27.57N 110.49W*
85 L23 **Empangeni** KwaZulu/Natal, E South Africa *28.40S 31.57E*
63 C14 **Empedrado** Corrientes, NE Argentina *27.57S 58.46W*
199 Ii3 **Emperor Seamounts** *undersea feature* NW Pacific Ocean
199 J3 **Emperor Trough** *undersea feature* N Pacific Ocean
37 R4 **Empire** Nevada, W USA *40.26N 119.21W*
Empire State of the South *see* Georgia
Emplawas *see* Amplawas
108 F11 **Empoli** Toscana, C Italy *43.43N 10.57E*
29 P5 **Emporia** Kansas, C USA *38.24N 96.10W*
23 W7 **Emporia** Virginia, NE USA *36.41N 77.32W*
20 E13 **Emporium** Pennsylvania, NE USA *41.31N 78.13W*
195 S12 **Empress Augusta Bay** *inlet* Bougainville Island, PNG
Empty Quarter *see* Ar Rub' al Khālī
102 E10 **Ems** *Dut.* Eems. ≈ NW Germany
102 F13 **Emsdetten** Nordrhein-Westfalen, NW Germany *52.10N 7.31E*
Ems-Hunte Canal *see* Küstenkanal
102 F10 **Ems-Jade-Kanal** *canal* NW Germany
102 F11 **Emsland** *cultural region* NW Germany
190 D3 **Emu Junction** South Australia *28.39S 132.13E*
169 T3 **Emur He** ≈ NE China
57 R8 **Enachu Landing** NW Guyana *6.09N 60.01W*
95 F16 **Enafors** Jämtland, C Sweden *63.16N 12.24E*
96 N11 **Enånger** Gävleborg, C Sweden *61.30N 17.10E*
98 G7 **Enard Bay** *bay* NW Scotland, UK *58.06N 5.20W*
Enareträsk *see* Inarijärvi
176 X12 **Enarotali** Papua, E Indonesia *3.55S 136.21E*
171 I15 **Ena-san** ▲ Honshū, S Japan *35.27N 137.36E*
144 E12 **En 'Avedat** *var.* Ein 'Avedat, *well* S Israel
172 P2 **Enbetsu** Hokkaidō, NE Japan *44.44N 141.47E*
63 H16 **Encantadas, Serra das** ⛰ S Brazil
42 E7 **Encantado, Cerro** ▲ NW Mexico *26.46N 112.33W*
64 P7 **Encarnación** Itapúa, S Paraguay *27.19S 55.49W*
42 M12 **Encarnación de Díaz** Jalisco, SW Mexico *21.33N 102.13W*
79 O17 **Enchi** SW Ghana *5.52N 2.48W*
27 Q14 **Encinal** Texas, SW USA *28.02N 99.21W*
37 U17 **Encinitas** California, W USA *33.02N 117.17W*
27 S16 **Encino** Texas, SW USA *26.58N 98.06W*
56 H6 **Encontrados** Zulia, NW Venezuela *9.01N 72.16W*
190 I10 **Encounter Bay** *inlet* South Australia
63 F15 **Encruzilhada** Rio Grande do Sul, S Brazil *28.58S 55.31W*
63 H16 **Encruzilhada do Sul** Rio Grande do Sul, S Brazil *30.30S 52.31W*
113 M20 **Encs** Borsod-Abaúj-Zemplén, NE Hungary *48.21N 21.09E*
199 M3 **Endeavour Seamount** *undersea feature* N Pacific Ocean *48.15N 129.04W*
189 V1 **Endeavour Strait** *strait* Queensland, NE Australia
175 Q16 **Endeh** Flores, S Indonesia *8.48S 121.37E*
97 G23 **Endelave** *island* C Denmark
203 T4 **Enderbury Island** *atoll* Phoenix Islands, C Kiribati
9 N16 **Enderby** British Columbia, SW Canada *50.34N 119.09W*
205 W4 **Enderby Land** *physical region* Antarctica
181 N14 **Enderby Plain** *undersea feature* S Indian Ocean
31 Q6 **Enderlin** North Dakota, N USA *46.37N 97.36W*
Endersdorf *see* Jędrzejów
30 K16 **Enders Reservoir** ⊠ Nebraska, C USA
20 H11 **Endicott** New York, NE USA *42.06N 76.03W*
41 P7 **Endicott Mountains** ⛰ Alaska, USA
120 I5 **Endla Raba** *wetland* C Estonia
119 T9 **Enerhodar** Zaporiz'ka Oblast', SE Ukraine *47.30N 34.40E*
59 F14 **Ene, Río** ≈ C Peru
201 N4 **Enewetak Atoll** *var.* Ānewetak, Eniwetok. *atoll* Ralik Chain, W Marshall Islands
116 L13 **Enez** Edirne, NW Turkey *40.43N 26.04E*
23 W8 **Enfield** North Carolina, SE USA *36.10N 77.40W*
194 G12 **Enga** ◈ *province* W PNG
47 Q9 **Engaño, Cabo** *headland* E Dominican Republic *18.36N 68.19W*
172 Q5 **Engaru** Hokkaidō, NE Japan *44.06N 143.30E*
144 F11 **'En Gedi** Southern, E Israel *31.23N 35.21E*
110 F9 **Engelberg** Unterwalden, C Switzerland *46.51N 8.25E*
23 Y9 **Engelhard** North Carolina, SE USA *35.30N 76.00W*
131 P8 **Engel's** Saratovskaya Oblast', W Russian Federation *51.27N 46.09E*
103 G24 **Engen** Baden-Württemberg, SW Germany *47.52N 8.46E*
Engeten *see* Aiud
174 H13 **Enggano, Pulau** *island* W Indonesia
82 J8 **Enghershatu** ▲ N Eritrea *16.41N 38.21E*
101 F19 **Enghien** *Dut.* Edingen. Hainaut, SW Belgium *50.42N 4.03E*
29 V12 **England** Arkansas, C USA *34.32N 91.58W*
99 M20 **England** *Lat.* Anglia. *national region* UK
15 L2 **Englefield, Cape** *headland* Nunavut, NE Canada *69.51N 85.31W*
12 H8 **Englehart** Ontario, S Canada *47.49N 79.52W*
39 T4 **Englewood** Colorado, C USA *39.39N 104.59W*
33 O16 **English** Indiana, N USA *38.19N 86.28W*
41 Q13 **English Bay** Alaska, USA *59.21N 151.55W*
English Bazar *see* Ingrāj Bāzār
99 N25 **English Channel** *var.* The Channel, *Fr.* la Manche. *channel* NW Europe
204 J7 **English Coast** *physical region* Antarctica
107 S11 **Enguera** País Valenciano, E Spain *38.58N 0.42W*
120 E8 **Engure** Tukums, W Latvia *57.09N 23.13E*
120 E8 **Engures Ezers** ◎ NW Latvia
143 R9 **Enguri** *Rus.* Inguri. ≈ NW Georgia
Engyum *see* Gangi
28 M9 **Enid** Oklahoma, C USA *36.24N 97.52W*
24 L3 **Enid Lake** ⊠ Mississippi, S USA
201 Y2 **Enigu** *island* Ratak Chain, SE Marshall Islands
Enikale Strait *see* Kerch Strait
153 Z8 **Enil'chek** Issyk-Kul'skaya Oblast', E Kyrgyzstan *42.04N 79.01E*
117 F17 **Enipéfs** ≈ C Greece
172 O6 **Eniwa** Hokkaidō, NE Japan *42.54N 141.33E*
172 O6 **Eniwa-dake** △ Hokkaidō, NE Japan *42.48N 141.15E*
Eniwetok *see* Enewetak Atoll
Enkeldoorn *see* Chivhu
127 Nn11 **Enkan, Mys** *headland* NE Russian Federation *58.29N 141.27E*
100 J8 **Enkhuizen** Noord-Holland, NW Netherlands *52.34N 5.03E*
111 Q4 **Enknach** ≈ N Austria
97 N15 **Enköping** Uppsala, C Sweden *59.39N 17.07E*
109 K24 **Enna** *var.* Castrogiovanni, Henna. Sicilia, Italy, C Mediterranean Sea *37.34N 14.18E*
82 D11 **En Nahud** Western Kordofan, C Sudan *12.40N 28.28E*
144 F8 **En Nâqoûra** *var.* An Nāqūrah. SW Lebanon *33.06N 33.30E*
En Nazira *see* Nazerat
80 K8 **Ennedi** *plateau* E Chad
103 E15 **Ennepetal** Nordrhein-Westfalen, W Germany *51.18N 7.22E*
191 P4 **Enngonia** New South Wales, SE Australia *29.19S 145.52E*
99 C19 **Ennis** *Ir.* Inis. W Ireland *52.49N 8.58W*
35 R11 **Ennis** Montana, NW USA *45.21N 111.45W*
27 U7 **Ennis** Texas, SW USA *32.19N 96.37W*
99 F20 **Enniscorthy** *Ir.* Inis Córthaidh. SE Ireland *52.30N 6.34W*
99 E15 **Enniskillen** *var.* Inniskilling, *Ir.* Inis Ceithleann. SW Northern Ireland, UK *54.21N 7.37W*
99 B19 **Ennistimon** *Ir.* Inis Díomáin. W Ireland *52.56N 9.17W*
111 T4 **Enns** Oberösterreich, N Austria *48.12N 14.29E*
111 T4 **Enns** ≈ C Austria
95 O16 **Eno** Itä-Suomi, E Finland *62.45N 30.15E*
26 M5 **Enochs** Texas, SW USA *33.51N 102.46W*
95 N17 **Enonkoski** Isä-Suomi, E Finland *62.04N 28.53E*
94 K10 **Enontekiö** *Lapp.* Eanodat. Lappi, N Finland *68.25N 23.40E*
23 Q11 **Enoree** South Carolina, SE USA *34.39N 81.58W*
23 P11 **Enoree River** ≈ South Carolina, SE USA
20 M6 **Enosburg Falls** Vermont, NE USA *44.54N 72.50W*
175 P11 **Enrekang** Sulawesi, C Indonesia *3.33S 119.46E*
47 N10 **Enriquillo** SW Dominican Republic *17.53N 71.13W*
47 N9 **Enriquillo, Lago** ◎ SW Dominican Republic
100 L9 **Ens** Flevoland, N Netherlands *52.39N 5.49E*
100 P11 **Enschede** Overijssel, E Netherlands *52.13N 6.55E*
42 B2 **Ensenada** Baja California, NW Mexico *31.52N 116.31W*
103 E20 **Ensheim** ✕ (Saarbrücken) Saarland, W Germany *49.13N 7.09E*
166 L9 **Enshi** Hubei, C China *30.16N 109.25E*

◆ Country ● Country Capital ◇ Dependent Territory ○ Dependent Territory Capital ◈ Administrative Region ✕ International Airport ▲ Mountain ⛰ Mountain Range △ Volcano ≈ River ◎ Lake ⊠ Reservoir

171 Hh17 **Enshū-nada** gulf SW Japan
25 O8 **Ensley** Florida, SE USA 30.31N 87.16W
Enso see Svetogorsk
83 F18 **Entebbe** S Uganda 0.07N 32.29E
83 F18 **Entebbe** ✕ C Uganda 0.04N 32.29E
103 M18 **Entenbühl** ▲ Czech Republic/Germany 50.09N 12.10E
100 N10 **Enter** Overijssel, E Netherlands 52.19N 6.34E
25 Q7 **Enterprise** Alabama, S USA 31.19N 85.50W
34 L11 **Enterprise** Oregon, NW USA 45.25N 117.16W
38 J7 **Enterprise** Utah, W USA 37.33N 113.42W
34 J8 **Entiat** Washington, NW USA 47.39N 120.15W
107 P15 **Entinas, Punta de las** headland S Spain 36.40N 2.44W
110 F8 **Entlebuch** Luzern, W Switzerland 47.02N 8.04E
110 F8 **Entlebuch** valley C Switzerland
65 I22 **Entrada, Punta** headland S Argentina
105 O13 **Entraygues-sur-Truyère** Aveyron, S France 44.39N 2.36E
197 G3 **Entrecasteaux, Récifs d'** reef N New Caledonia
63 C17 **Entre Ríos** off. Provincia de Entre Ríos. ◐ province NE Argentina
44 K7 **Entre Ríos, Cordillera** ▲▲ Honduras/Nicaragua
106 G9 **Entroncamento** Santarém, C Portugal 39.28N 8.28W
176 Z10 **Entrop** Papua, E Indonesia 2.37S 140.43E
79 V16 **Enugu** Enugu, S Nigeria 6.24N 7.24E
79 U16 **Enugu** ◐ state SE Nigeria
127 Pp3 **Enurmino** Chukotskiy Avtonomnyy Okrug, NE Russian Federation 66.46N 171.40W
56 E9 **Envigado** Antioquia, W Colombia 6.09N 75.37W
61 B15 **Envira** Amazonas, W Brazil 7.12S 69.58W
Enyélé see Enyellé
81 I16 **Enyellé** var. Enyélé. La Likouala, NE Congo 2.48N 18.01E
103 H21 **Enz** ≈ SW Germany
171 J16 **Enzan** Yamanashi, Honshū, S Japan 35.42N 138.43E
106 I2 **Eo** ≈ NW Spain
Eochaill see Youghal
Eochaille, Cuan see Youghal Bay
109 K22 **Eolie, Isole** var. Isole Lipari, Eng. Aeolian Islands, Lipari Islands. island group S Italy
201 U12 **Eot** island Chuuk, C Micronesia
117 J25 **Epáno Archánes** var. Áno Arkhánai; prev. Epáno Arkhánai. Kríti, Greece, E Mediterranean Sea 35.12N 25.10E
Epáno Arkhánai see Epáno Archánes
117 G14 **Epanomí** Kentrikí Makedonía, N Greece 40.25N 22.55E
100 M10 **Epe** Gelderland, E Netherlands 52.21N 5.58E
79 S16 **Epe** Lagos, S Nigeria 6.37N 4.01E
81 I17 **Epéna** La Likouala, NE Congo 1.27N 17.28E
Eperies/Eperjes see Prešov
105 Q4 **Épernay** anc. Sparnacum. Marne, N France 49.01N 3.58E
38 L5 **Ephraim** Utah, W USA 39.21N 111.35W
20 H15 **Ephrata** Pennsylvania, NE USA 40.09N 76.08W
34 J8 **Ephrata** Washington, NW USA 47.19N 119.33W
197 C13 **Epi** var. Épi island C Vanuatu
107 R6 **Épila** Aragón, NE Spain 41.34N 1.19W
105 T6 **Épinal** Vosges, NE France 48.10N 6.28E
Epiphania see Ḩamāh
Epirus see Ípeiros
124 N4 **Episkopí** SW Cyprus 34.37N 32.53E
Episkopi Bay see Episkopí, Kólpos
124 N4 **Episkopí, Kólpos** var. Episkopi Bay. bay SE Cyprus
Epitoli see Pretoria
Epoon see Ebon Atoll
Eporedia see Ivrea
Eppeschdorf see Dumbrăveni
103 H21 **Eppingen** Baden-Württemberg, SW Germany 49.09N 8.54E
85 E18 **Epukiro** Omaheke, E Namibia 21.40S 19.09E
31 Y13 **Epworth** Iowa, C USA 42.27N 90.55W
149 O10 **Eqlīd** var. Iqlid. Fārs, C Iran 30.54N 52.43E
Equality State see Wyoming
81 J18 **Equateur** off. Région de l' Equateur. ◐ region N Dem. Rep. Congo
157 K22 **Equatorial Channel** channel S Maldives
81 B17 **Equatorial Guinea** off. Republic of Equatorial Guinea. ◆ republic C Africa
194 H14 **Era** ≈ S PNG
124 R13 **Eratosthenes Tablemount** undersea feature E Mediterranean Sea 33.48N 32.53E
Erautini see Johannesburg
194 H13 **Erave** Southern Highlands, W PNG 6.36S 143.55E
142 L12 **Erbaa** Tokat, N Turkey 40.39N 36.37E
103 E19 **Erbeskopf** ▲ W Germany 49.43N 7.04E
Erbil see Arbīl
124 Nn3 **Ercan** ✕ (Nicosia) N Cyprus 35.07N 33.30E
Ercegnovi see Herceg-Novi
143 T14 **Erçek Gölü** ⊚ E Turkey
143 S14 **Erciş** Van, E Turkey 39.02N 43.21E
142 K14 **Erciyes Dağı** anc. Argaeus. ▲ C Turkey 38.35N 35.27E
113 J22 **Érd** Ger. Hanselbeck. Pest, C Hungary 47.22N 18.55E
Erdaobaihe see Baihe
165 O12 **Erdaogou** Qinghai, W China 34.30N 92.49E
169 X11 **Erdao Jiang** ▲▲ NE China
Erdăt-Sângeorz see Sângeorgiu de Pădure
142 C11 **Erdek** Balıkesir, NW Turkey 40.25N 27.49E
Erdély see Transylvania
Erdélyi-Havasok see Carpaţii Meridionali
142 J17 **Erdemli** İçel, S Turkey 36.39N 34.18E
168 K6 **Erdenet** Bulgan, N Mongolia 49.01N 104.06E
168 I8 **Erdenetsogt** Bayanhongor, C Mongolia 46.27N 100.53E
80 K7 **Erdi** plateau NE Chad
80 L7 **Erdi Ma** desert NE Chad
103 M23 **Erding** Bayern, SE Germany 48.18N 11.54E
Erdőszáda see Ardusat
Erdőszentgyörgy see Sângeorgiu de Pădure
104 I7 **Erdre** ≈ NW France
205 R13 **Erebus, Mount** ▲ Ross Island, Antarctica 78.11S 165.09E
63 H14 **Erechim** Rio Grande do Sul, S Brazil 27.34S 52.15W
169 O7 **Ereen Davaanï Nuruu** ▲▲ NE Mongolia
169 Q6 **Ereentsav** Dornod, NE Mongolia 49.51N 115.41E
142 I16 **Ereğli** Konya, S Turkey 37.30N 34.01E
142 I15 **Ereğli Gölü** ⊚ W Turkey
117 A15 **Ereíkoussa** island Iónioi Nísoi, Greece, C Mediterranean Sea
169 O11 **Erenhot** var. Erlian. Nei Mongol Zizhiqu, NE China 43.35N 112.00E
106 M6 **Eresma** ≈ N Spain
117 K17 **Eresós** var. Eressós. Lésvos, E Greece 39.10N 25.57E
Eressós see Eresós
Erevan see Yerevan
Ereymentaū see Yereymentau
101 K21 **Érezée** Luxembourg, SE Belgium 50.16N 5.34E
76 G7 **Erfoud** SE Morocco 31.29N 4.18W
103 D16 **Erft** ≈ W Germany
103 K16 **Erfurt** Thüringen, C Germany 50.59N 11.02E
143 P15 **Ergani** Dıyarbakır, SE Turkey 38.16N 39.43E
169 N11 **Ergel** Dornogovĭ, SE Mongolia 43.10N 109.13E
Ergene Irmağı see Ergene Çayı
168 L11 **Ergenetsogt** Ömnögovĭ, S Mongolia 42.54N 106.16E
142 C10 **Ergene Çayı** var. Ergene Irmağı. ≈ NW Turkey
120 I9 **Ērgļi** Madona, C Latvia 56.54N 25.37E
80 H11 **Erguig, Bahr** ≈ SW Chad
Ergun He see Argun
169 S5 **Ergun Youqi** Nei Mongol Zizhiqu, N China 50.13N 120.09E
169 T5 **Ergun Zuoqi** Nei Mongol Zizhiqu, N China 50.48N 121.30E
166 F12 **Er Hai** ⊠ SW China
104 G4 **Er, Îles d'** island group NW France
106 K4 **Ería** ≈ NW Spain
82 H8 **Eriba** Kassala, NE Sudan 16.37N 36.04E
98 I6 **Eriboll, Loch** inlet NW Scotland, UK
67 Q18 **Erica Seamount** undersea feature SW Indian Ocean 38.15S 14.30E
109 H23 **Erice** Sicilia, Italy, C Mediterranean Sea 38.02N 12.35E
106 E10 **Ericeira** Lisboa, C Portugal 38.58N 9.25W
98 H10 **Ericht, Loch** ⊚ C Scotland, UK
28 J11 **Erick** Oklahoma, C USA 35.13N 99.52W
20 B11 **Erie** Pennsylvania, NE USA 42.06N 80.03W
20 E9 **Erie Canal** canal New York, NE USA
Érié, Lac see Erie, Lake
33 T10 **Erie, Lake** Fr. Lac Érié. ⊚ Canada/USA
Erigabo see Ceerigaabo
79 N8 **'Erîgât** desert N Mali
Erigavo see Ceerigaabo
94 P2 **Erik Eriksenstretet** strait E Svalbard
9 X15 **Eriksdale** Manitoba, S Canada 50.52N 98.07W
201 V6 **Erikub Atoll** var. Ādkup. atoll Ratak Chain, C Marshall Islands
Erimanthos see Erýmanthos
172 P8 **Erimo** Hokkaidō, NE Japan 42.01N 143.07E
172 Oo8 **Erimo-misaki** headland Hokkaidō, NE Japan 41.57N 143.12E
22 H8 **Erin** Tennessee, S USA 36.19N 87.41W
98 E9 **Eriskay** island NW Scotland, UK
Erithraí see Erythrés
82 I9 **Eritrea** off. State of Eritrea, Tig. Ērtra. ◆ transitional government E Africa
Erivan see Yerevan
103 D16 **Erkelenz** Nordrhein-Westfalen, W Germany 51.04N 6.19E
97 P15 **Erken** ⊚ C Sweden
103 K19 **Erlangen** Bayern, S Germany 49.35N 11.00E
166 G9 **Erlang Shan** ▲ C China 29.56N 102.24E
Erlau see Eger
111 V5 **Erlauf** ≈ NE Austria
189 Q8 **Erldunda Roadhouse** Northern Territory, N Australia 25.13S 133.13E
Erlian see Erenhot
29 T15 **Erling, Lake** ⊠ Arkansas, USA
111 O8 **Erlsbach** Tirol, W Austria 46.54N 12.15E
Ermak see Aksu
100 K10 **Ermelo** Gelderland, C Netherlands 52.18N 5.37E
85 K21 **Ermelo** Mpumalanga, NE South Africa 26.31S 29.58E
142 H17 **Ermenek** Karaman, S Turkey 36.37N 32.55E
Érmihályfalva see Valea lui Mihai
117 G20 **Ermióni** Pelopónnisos, S Greece 37.24N 23.15E
117 J20 **Ermoúpoli** var. Hermoupolis; prev. Ermoúpolis. Sýros, Kykládes, Greece, Aegean Sea 37.26N 24.55E
Ermoúpolis see Ermoúpoli
Ernabella see Pukatja
161 G22 **Ernākulam** Kerala, SW India 10.04N 76.18E
104 J6 **Ernée** Mayenne, NW France 48.18N 0.54W
63 H14 **Ernestina, Barragem** ⊠ S Brazil
56 E4 **Ernesto Cortissoz** ✕ (Barranquilla) Atlántico, N Colombia
161 H21 **Erode** Tamil Nādu, SE India 11.21N 77.43E
Eroj see Iroj
85 C19 **Erongo** ◐ district W Namibia
101 F21 **Erquelinnes** Hainaut, S Belgium 50.18N 4.07E
76 G7 **Er-Rachidia** var. Ksar al Soule. E Morocco 31.58N 4.22W
82 E11 **Er Rahad** var. Ar Rahad. Northern Kordofan, C Sudan 12.42N 30.33E
Er Ramle see Ramla
85 O15 **Errego** Zambézia, NE Mozambique 16.02S 37.12E
Errenteria see Rentería
Er Rif/Er Riff see Rif
99 D14 **Errigal Mountain** Ir. An Earagail. ▲ N Ireland 55.03N 8.09W
99 A15 **Erris Head** Ir. Ceann Iorrais. headland W Ireland 54.18N 10.01W
197 D15 **Erromango** island S Vanuatu
Error Guyot see Error Tablemount
181 O4 **Error Tablemount** var. Error Guyot. undersea feature W Indian Ocean 10.19N 56.04E
82 G11 **Er Roseires** Blue Nile, E Sudan 11.52N 34.22E
Erseka see Ersekë
115 M22 **Ersekë** var. Erseka, Kolonjë. Korçë, SE Albania 40.19N 20.39E
Érsekújvár see Nové Zámky
31 S4 **Erskine** Minnesota, N USA 47.42N 96.00W
105 V6 **Erstein** Bas-Rhin, NE France 48.24N 7.39E
110 G9 **Erstfeld** Uri, C Switzerland 46.49N 8.41E
164 M3 **Ertai** Xinjiang Uygur Zizhiqu, NW China 46.04N 90.06E
130 M7 **Ertil'** Voronezhskaya Oblast', W Russian Federation 51.51N 40.46E
Ertis see Irtysh, C Asia
Ertis see Irtyshsk, Kazakhstan
164 K2 **Ertix He** Rus. Chërnyy Irtysh. ≈ China/Kazakhstan
Ērtra see Eritrea
23 P9 **Erwin** North Carolina, SE USA 35.19N 78.40W
116 L12 **Erydropótamos** Bul. Byala Reka. ≈ Bulgaria/Greece
117 E19 **Erýmanthos** var. Erimanthos. ▲ S Greece 37.57N 21.51E
117 G19 **Erythrés** prev. Erithraí. Stereá Ellás, C Greece 38.19N 23.20E
166 F12 **Eryuan** Yunnan, SW China 26.09N 100.01E
111 U6 **Erzbach** ≈ W Austria
Erzerum see Erzurum
103 N17 **Erzgebirge** Cz. Krušné Hory, Eng. Ore Mountains. ▲▲ Czech Republic/Germany see also Krušné Hory
126 I16 **Erzin** Respublika Tyva, S Russian Federation 50.17N 95.03E
143 O13 **Erzincan** var. Erzinjan. Erzincan, E Turkey 39.43N 39.30E
143 N13 **Erzincan** var. Erzinjan. ◐ province NE Turkey
Erzinjan see Erzincan
Erzsébetváros see Dumbrăveni
143 Q13 **Erzurum** prev. Erzerum. Erzurum, NE Turkey 39.57N 41.16E
143 Q12 **Erzurum** prev. Erzerum. ◐ province NE Turkey
195 N16 **Esa'ala** Normanby Island, SE PNG 9.45S 150.47E
172 Nn7 **Esan-misaki** headland Hokkaidō, N Japan 41.49N 141.12E
172 Pp3 **Esashi** Hokkaidō, NE Japan 44.57N 142.32E
171 M11 **Esashi** var. Esasi. Iwate, Honshū, C Japan 39.13N 141.08E
171 Mm6 **Esasho** Hokkaidō, N Japan
Esasi see Esashi
97 F23 **Esbjerg** Ribe, W Denmark 55.28N 8.28E
Esbo see Espoo
38 L7 **Escalante** Utah, W USA 37.46N 111.36W
38 M7 **Escalante River** ≈ Utah, W USA
12 L12 **Escalier, Réservoir l'** ⊠ Quebec, SE Canada
42 K7 **Escalón** Chihuahua, N Mexico 26.43N 104.20W
106 M8 **Escalona** Castilla-La Mancha, C Spain 40.10N 4.24W
25 O8 **Escambia River** ≈ Florida, SE USA
33 N5 **Escanaba** Michigan, N USA 45.45N 87.03W
33 N4 **Escanaba River** ≈ Michigan, N USA
107 R8 **Escandón, Puerto de** pass E Spain 40.17N 0.57W
43 W14 **Escárcega** Campeche, SE Mexico 18.33N 90.41W
179 Pp7 **Escarpada Point** headland Luzon, N Philippines 18.28N 122.10E
25 N8 **Escatawpa River** ≈ Alabama/Mississippi, S USA
105 P2 **Escaut** ≈ N France
Escaut see Scheldt
101 M25 **Esch-sur-Alzette** Luxembourg, S Luxembourg 49.30N 5.58E
103 J15 **Eschwege** Hessen, C Germany 51.10N 10.03E
103 D16 **Eschweiler** Nordrhein-Westfalen, W Germany 50.48N 6.15E
Esclaves, Grand Lac des see Great Slave Lake
47 O8 **Escocesa, Bahía** bay N Dominican Republic
45 W15 **Escocés, Punta** headland NE Panama 8.50N 77.37W
37 U17 **Escondido** California, W USA 33.07N 117.05W
44 M10 **Escondido, Río** ≈ SE Nicaragua
13 S7 **Escoumins, Rivière des** ≈ Quebec, SE Canada
39 O13 **Escudilla Mountain** ▲ Arizona, SW USA 33.57N 109.07W
42 J11 **Escuinapa** var. Escuinapa de Hidalgo. Sinaloa, C Mexico 22.49N 105.46W
Escuinapa de Hidalgo see Escuinapa
44 C6 **Escuintla** Escuintla, S Guatemala 14.16N 90.46W
43 V17 **Escuintla** Chiapas, SE Mexico 15.15N 92.39W
44 A2 **Escuintla** off. Departamento de Escuintla. ◐ department S Guatemala
13 W7 **Escuminac** ≈ Quebec, SE Canada
81 D16 **Eséka** Centre, SW Cameroon 3.40N 10.48E
142 I12 **Esenboğa** ✕ (Ankara) Ankara, C Turkey 40.05N 33.01E
Esenguly see Gasan-Kuli
142 D17 **Eşen Çayı** ≈ SW Turkey
107 T4 **Ésera** ≈ NE Spain
149 N8 **Eşfahān** Eng. Isfahan; anc. Aspadana. Eşfahān, C Iran 32.40N 51.40E
149 O7 **Eşfahān** off. Ostān-e Eşfahān. ◐ province C Iran
107 N5 **Esgueva** ≈ N Spain
155 Q3 **Eshkamesh** Takhār, NE Afghanistan 36.25N 69.10E
155 T2 **Eshkāshem** Badakhshān, NE Afghanistan 36.43N 71.34E
85 L23 **Eshowe** KwaZulu/Natal, E South Africa 28.49S 31.29E
149 T5 **'Eshqābād** Khorāsān, NE Iran 36.00N 59.01E
Esh Sham see Dimashq
Esh Sharā see Ash Sharāh
Esik see Yesik
Esil see Ishim, Kazakhstan/Russian Federation
Esil see Yesil', Kazakhstan
191 V2 **Esk** Queensland, E Australia 27.15S 152.22E
192 O11 **Eskdale** Hawke's Bay, North Island, NZ 39.24S 176.51E
Eski Dzhumaya see Tŭrgovishte
94 L2 **Eskifjördhur** Austurland, E Iceland 65.04N 14.01W
145 S3 **Eski Kaļak** var. Askī Kalak, Kalak. N Iraq 36.16N 43.40E
97 N16 **Eskilstuna** Södermanland, C Sweden 59.22N 16.31E
14 G2 **Eskimo Lakes** lakes Northwest Territories, NW Canada
15 L8 **Eskimo Point** headland Nunavut, E Canada 61.19N 93.49W
Eskimo Point see Arviat
145 Q2 **Eski Mosul** N Iraq 36.31N 42.45E
153 T10 **Eski-Nookat** var. Iski-Nauket. Oshskaya Oblast', SW Kyrgyzstan 40.18N 72.29E
142 F12 **Eskişehir** var. Eskishehr. Eskişehir, W Turkey 39.46N 30.30E
142 F13 **Eskişehir** var. Eski shehr. ◐ province NW Turkey
Eskishehr see Eskişehir
106 K5 **Esla** ≈ NW Spain
148 J6 **Eslāmābād** var. Eslāmābād-e Gharb; prev. Harunabad, Shāhābād. Kermānshāhān, W Iran 34.07N 46.34E
Eslāmābād-e Gharb see Eslāmābād
154 J4 **Eslām Qal'eh** Pash. Islam Qala. Herāt, W Afghanistan 34.41N 61.03E
97 K23 **Eslöv** Skåne, S Sweden 55.49N 13.19E
149 S12 **Esmā'īlābād** Kermān, S Iran 28.48N 56.39E
149 U8 **Esmā'īlābād** Khorāsān, E Iran 35.19N 60.30E
142 D14 **Eşme** Uşak, W Turkey 38.25N 28.58E
46 G6 **Esmeralda** Camagüey, E Cuba 21.51N 78.10W
65 F21 **Esmeralda, Isla** island S Chile
58 B5 **Esmeraldas** Esmeraldas, N Ecuador 0.55N 79.40W
58 B5 **Esmeraldas** ◐ province NW Ecuador
Esna see Isna
12 B6 **Esnagi Lake** ⊚ Ontario, S Canada
149 V14 **Espakeh** Sīstān va Balūchestān, SE Iran 26.54N 60.09E
105 O13 **Espalion** Aveyron, S France 44.31N 2.45E
España see Spain
12 E11 **Espanola** Ontario, S Canada 46.15N 81.46W
39 S10 **Espanola** New Mexico, SW USA 35.59N 106.04W
59 C18 **Española, Isla** var. Hood Island. island Galapagos Islands, Ecuador, E Pacific Ocean
106 M13 **Espejo** Andalucía, S Spain 37.40N 4.34W
96 C13 **Espeland** Hordaland, S Norway 60.22N 5.27E
102 G12 **Espelkamp** Nordrhein-Westfalen, NW Germany 52.22N 8.37E
40 M8 **Espenberg, Cape** headland Alaska, USA 66.33N 163.36W
188 L13 **Esperance** Western Australia 33.49S 121.52E
195 W15 **Esperance, Cape** headland Guadacanal, C Solomon Islands 9.09S 159.38E
59 P18 **Esperancita** Santa Cruz, E Bolivia
63 B17 **Esperanza** Santa Fe, C Argentina 31.25S 60.59W
42 G6 **Esperanza** Sonora, NW Mexico 27.37N 109.51W
26 H9 **Esperanza** Texas, SW USA 31.09N 105.40W
204 H3 **Esperanza** Argentinian research station Antarctica 63.29S 56.53W
106 E12 **Espichel, Cabo** headland S Portugal 38.25N 9.15W
56 E10 **Espinal** Tolima, C Colombia 4.09N 74.54W
50 K10 **Espinhaço, Serra do** ▲▲ SE Brazil
106 G6 **Espinho** Aveiro, N Portugal 41.01N 8.37W
61 N18 **Espinosa** Minas Gerais, SE Brazil 14.58S 42.49W
105 O15 **Espinouse** ▲▲ S France
62 Q8 **Espírito Santo** off. Estado do Espírito Santo. ◐ state E Brazil
197 B12 **Espiritu Santo** var. Santo. island W Vanuatu
43 Z13 **Espíritu Santo, Bahía del** bay SE Mexico
42 F9 **Espíritu Santo, Isla del** island W Mexico
43 Y12 **Espita** Yucatán, SE Mexico 21.00N 88.17W
13 Y7 **Espoir, Cap d'** headland Quebec, SE Canada 48.24N 64.21W
Esponsede/Esponsende see Esposende
95 L20 **Espoo** Swe. Esbo. Etelä-Suomi, S Finland 60.10N 24.42E
106 G5 **Esposende** var. Esponsede, Esponsende. Braga, N Portugal 41.30N 8.46W
85 M18 **Espungabera** Manica, SW Mozambique 20.27S 32.48E
65 H17 **Esquel** Chubut, SW Argentina 42.55S 71.19W
8 L17 **Esquimalt** Vancouver Island, British Columbia, SW Canada 48.25N 123.27W
63 C16 **Esquina** Corrientes, NE Argentina 30.00S 59.30W
44 E6 **Esquipulas** Chiquimula, SE Guatemala 14.34N 89.20W
44 K9 **Esquipulas** Matagalpa, C Nicaragua 12.39N 85.48W
96 I8 **Essandjøen** ⊚ S Norway
76 E7 **Essaouira** prev. Mogador. W Morocco 31.33N 9.40W
Esseg see Osijek
Es Semara see Smara
101 G15 **Essen** Antwerpen, N Belgium 51.28N 4.28E
103 E15 **Essen** var. Essen an der Ruhr. Nordrhein-Westfalen, W Germany 51.28N 7.01E
Essen an der Ruhr see Essen
76 I5 **Es Senia** ✕ (Oran) NW Algeria 35.34N 0.42W
57 T8 **Essequibo Islands** island group N Guyana
57 T11 **Essequibo River** ≈ C Guyana
12 C18 **Essex** Ontario, S Canada 42.06N 82.52W
31 T16 **Essex** Iowa, C USA 40.49N 95.18W
99 P21 **Essex** cultural region E England, UK
33 R8 **Essexville** Michigan, N USA 43.37N 83.50W
103 H22 **Esslingen** var. Esslingen am Neckar. Baden-Württemberg, SW Germany 48.45N 9.18E
Esslingen am Neckar see Esslingen
105 N6 **Essonne** ◐ department N France
Es Suweida see As Suwaydā'
81 F16 **Est** Eng. East. ◐ province SE Cameroon
106 I1 **Estaca de Bares, Punta da** point NW Spain 43.46N 7.40W
26 M5 **Estacado, Llano** plain New Mexico/Texas, SW USA
65 K25 **Estados, Isla de los** prev. Eng. Staten Island. island S Argentina
149 P12 **Eşţahbān** Fārs, S Iran
12 F11 **Estaire** Ontario, S Canada 46.19N 80.47W
39 S12 **Estancia** New Mexico, SW USA 34.45N 106.03W
61 P16 **Estância** Sergipe, E Brazil 11.15S 37.28W
106 G7 **Estarreja** Aveiro, N Portugal 40.45N 8.34W
104 M17 **Estats, Pic d'** Sp. Pico d'Estats. ▲ France/Spain 42.39N 1.24E
Estats, Pico d' see Estats, Pic d'
85 K23 **Estcourt** KwaZulu/Natal, E South Africa 28.58S 29.54E
108 H8 **Este** anc. Ateste. Veneto, NE Italy 45.14N 11.40E
44 J9 **Estelí** Estelí, NW Nicaragua 13.04N 86.21W
44 J9 **Estelí** ◐ department NW Nicaragua
Estella see Estella-Lizarra
107 Q4 **Estella-Lizarra** Bas. Lizarra var Estella Navarra, N Spain 42.40N 2.01W
31 R9 **Estelline** South Dakota, N USA 44.34N 96.54W
27 P4 **Estelline** Texas, SW USA 34.33N 100.26W
106 L14 **Estepa** Andalucía, S Spain 37.16N 4.52W
106 L16 **Estepona** Andalucía, S Spain 36.25N 5.09W
41 R9 **Ester** Alaska, USA 64.49N 148.03W
9 V16 **Esterhazy** Saskatchewan, S Canada 50.40N 102.01W
39 S3 **Estes Park** Colorado, C USA 40.22N 105.31W
9 V17 **Estevan** Saskatchewan, S Canada 49.07N 103.04W
31 T11 **Estherville** Iowa, C USA 43.24N 94.49W
23 R15 **Estill** South Carolina, SE USA 32.45N 81.14W
105 Q6 **Estissac** Aube, N France 48.17N 3.51E
13 T9 **Est, Lac de l'** ⊚ Quebec, SE Canada
Estland see Estonia
9 S16 **Eston** Saskatchewan, S Canada 51.09N 108.41W
120 G5 **Estonia** off. Republic of Estonia, Est. Eesti Vabariik, Ger. Estland, Latv. Igaunija; prev. Estonian SSR, Rus. Estonskaya SSR. ◆ republic NE Europe
Estonskaya SSR see Estonia
106 E11 **Estoril** Lisboa, W Portugal 38.42N 9.22W
61 L14 **Estreito** Maranhão, E Brazil 6.34S 47.22W
106 I8 **Estrela, Serra da** ▲▲ C Portugal
42 D3 **Estrella, Punta** headland NW Mexico 30.53N 114.45W
Estremadura see Extremadura
106 F10 **Estremadura** cultural and historical region W Portugal
106 H11 **Estremoz** Évora, S Portugal 38.49N 7.34W
81 D18 **Estuaire** off. Province de l'Estuaire, var. L'Estuaire. ◐ province NW Gabon
Eszék see Osijek
113 I22 **Esztergom** Ger. Gran; anc. Strigonium. Komárom-Esztergom, N Hungary 47.46N 18.44E
158 K11 **Etah** Uttar Pradesh, N India 27.33N 78.39E
201 R17 **Etal Atoll** atoll Mortlock Islands, C Micronesia
101 K24 **Étalle** Luxembourg, SE Belgium 49.40N 5.36E
105 N6 **Étampes** Essonne, N France 48.25N 2.10E
190 J1 **Etamunbanie, Lake** salt lake South Australia
105 N1 **Étaples** Pas-de-Calais, N France 50.31N 1.37E
158 K12 **Etāwah** Uttar Pradesh, N India 26.46N 79.01E
13 R10 **Etchemin** ≈ Quebec, SE Canada
Etchmiadzin see Ejmiatsin
42 G7 **Etchojoa** Sonora, NW Mexico 26.54N 109.37W
95 L19 **Etelä-Suomi** ◐ province S Finland
85 B16 **Etengua** Kunene, NW Namibia 17.24S 13.05E
101 K25 **Éthe** Luxembourg, SE Belgium 49.34N 5.32E
9 W15 **Ethelbert** Manitoba, S Canada 51.30N 100.22W
82 H12 **Ethiopia** off. Federal Democratic Republic of Ethiopia; prev. Abyssinia, People's Democratic Republic of Ethiopia. ◆ republic E Africa
82 I13 **Ethiopian Highlands** var. Ethiopian Plateau. plateau N Ethiopia
Ethiopian Plateau see Ethiopian Highlands
36 M2 **Etna** California, W USA 41.25N 122.53W
20 B14 **Etna** Pennsylvania, NE USA 40.29N 79.55W
96 G12 **Etna** ≈ S Norway
109 L24 **Etna, Monte** Eng. Mount Etna. ⊼ Sicilia, Italy, C Mediterranean Sea 37.46N 15.00E
Etna, Mount see Etna, Monte
97 C15 **Etne** Hordaland, S Norway 59.40N 5.55E
Etoliko see Aitolikó
41 Y14 **Etolin Island** island Alexander Archipelago, Alaska, USA
40 L12 **Etolin Strait** strait Alaska, USA
85 C17 **Etosha Pan** salt lake N Namibia
81 G18 **Etoumbi** Cuvette, NW Congo 0.01N 14.57E
22 M10 **Etowah** Tennessee, S USA 35.19N 84.31W
25 S2 **Etowah River** ≈ Georgia, SE USA
Etrek see Atrak
104 L3 **Étretat** Seine-Maritime, N France 49.46N 0.23E
116 H9 **Etropole** Sofiya, W Bulgaria 42.50N 24.00E
Etsch see Adige
Et Tafila see Aţ Ţafilah
101 M23 **Ettelbrück** Diekirch, C Luxembourg 49.51N 6.06E
201 V12 **Etten** atoll Chuuk Islands, C Micronesia
101 H14 **Etten-Leur** Noord-Brabant, S Netherlands 51.34N 4.37E
78 G7 **Et Tîdra** var. Ile Tîdra. island Dakhlet Nouâdhibou, NW Mauritania
103 G21 **Ettlingen** Baden-Württemberg, SW Germany 48.57N 8.25E
104 M2 **Eu** Seine-Maritime, N France 50.01N 1.24E
200 Rr16 **'Eua** prev. Middleburg Island. island Tongatapu Group, SE Tonga
200 R15 **Eua Iki** island Tongatapu Group, S Tonga
Euboea see Évvoia
189 O12 **Eucla** Western Australia 31.40S 128.50E
33 U11 **Euclid** Ohio, N USA 41.35N 81.31W
29 W14 **Eudora** Arkansas, C USA 33.06N 91.15W
29 Q4 **Eudora** Kansas, C USA 38.56N 95.06W
190 J9 **Eudunda** South Australia 34.11S 139.03E
25 R6 **Eufaula** Alabama, S USA 31.53N 85.09W
29 Q11 **Eufaula** Oklahoma, C USA 35.17N 95.34W
29 Q11 **Eufaula Lake** var. Eufaula Reservoir. ⊠ Oklahoma, C USA
Eufaula Reservoir see Eufaula Lake
34 F13 **Eugene** Oregon, NW USA 44.03N 123.05W
42 B6 **Eugenia, Punta** headland W Mexico 27.48N 115.03W
191 Q8 **Eugowra** New South Wales, SE Australia 33.28S 148.21E
106 I2 **Eume** ≈ NW Spain
106 H2 **Eume, Embalse do** ⊠ NW Spain
Eumolpias see Plovdiv
61 O18 **Eunápolis** Bahia, SE Brazil 16.19S 39.36W
24 H8 **Eunice** Louisiana, S USA 30.29N 92.25W
39 W15 **Eunice** New Mexico, SW USA 32.26N 103.09W
101 M19 **Eupen** Liège, E Belgium 50.37N 6.01E
138 Jj9 **Euphrates** Ar. Al Furāt, Turk. Firat Nehri. ≈ SW Asia
144 L3 **Euphrates Dam** dam N Syria 35.52N 38.34E
24 M4 **Eupora** Mississippi, S USA 33.32N 89.16W
95 K19 **Eura** Länsi-Suomi, W Finland 61.06N 22.12E
95 K19 **Eurajoki** Länsi-Suomi, W Finland 61.13N 21.44E
0-1 **Eurasian Plate** tectonic feature
104 L4 **Eure** ◐ department N France
104 M4 **Eure** ≈ N France
104 M6 **Eure-et-Loir** ◐ department C France
36 K3 **Eureka** California, W USA 40.47N 124.12W
29 P6 **Eureka** Kansas, C USA 37.47N 96.15W
35 O6 **Eureka** Montana, NW USA 48.52N 115.03W
37 V5 **Eureka** Nevada, W USA 39.30N 115.58W
31 O7 **Eureka** South Dakota, N USA 45.46N 99.37W
38 L4 **Eureka** Utah, W USA 39.57N 112.07W
34 K10 **Eureka** Washington, NW USA 46.21N 118.41W
29 S9 **Eureka Springs** Arkansas, C USA 36.25N 93.43W
190 K6 **Eurinilla Creek** seasonal river South Australia
191 O11 **Euroa** Victoria, SE Australia 36.46S 145.35E
180 M9 **Europa** island W Madagascar
106 L3 **Europa, Picos de** ▲▲ N Spain
106 L16 **Europa Point** headland S Gibraltar 36.07N 5.20W
86-87 **Europe** continent
100 F12 **Europoort** Zuid-Holland, W Netherlands 51.59N 4.08E
Euskadi see País Vasco
103 D17 **Euskirchen** Nordrhein-Westfalen, W Germany 50.40N 6.47E
25 W11 **Eustis** Florida, SE USA 28.51N 81.41W
190 M9 **Euston** New South Wales, SE Australia 34.34S 142.45E
25 N5 **Eutaw** Alabama, S USA 32.50N 87.53W
102 K8 **Eutin** Schleswig-Holstein, N Germany 54.07N 10.37E
8 K14 **Eutsuk Lake** ⊠ British Columbia, SW Canada
Euxine Sea see Black Sea
85 C16 **Evale** Cunene, SW Angola 16.36S 15.46E
39 T3 **Evans** Colorado, C USA 40.22N 104.41W
9 P14 **Evansburg** Alberta, SW Canada 53.34N 114.57W
31 X13 **Evansdale** Iowa, C USA 42.28N 92.16W
191 V4 **Evans Head** New South Wales, SE Australia 29.07S 153.27E
10 J11 **Evans, Lac** ⊚ Quebec, SE Canada
39 S5 **Evans, Mount** ▲ Colorado, C USA 39.15N 106.10W
15 Mm6 **Evans Strait** strait Nunavut, N Canada
33 N10 **Evanston** Illinois, N USA 42.02N 87.41W
35 S17 **Evanston** Wyoming, C USA 41.16N 110.57W
12 D11 **Evansville** Manitoulin Island, Ontario, S Canada 45.48N 82.34W
33 N16 **Evansville** Indiana, N USA 37.58N 87.33W
32 L9 **Evansville** Wisconsin, N USA 42.46N 89.16W
27 S8 **Evant** Texas, SW USA 31.28N 98.09W
149 P13 **Evaz** Fārs, S Iran 27.48N 53.58E
31 W4 **Eveleth** Minnesota, N USA 47.27N 92.32W
190 E3 **Evelyn Creek** seasonal river South Australia
189 Q2 **Evelyn, Mount** ▲ Northern Territory, N Australia 13.28S 132.50E
126 I11 **Evenkiyskiy Avtonomnyy Okrug** ◐ autonomous district N Russian Federation
191 R13 **Everard, Cape** headland Victoria, SE Australia 37.48S 149.21E
190 F6 **Everard, Lake** salt lake South Australia
190 C2 **Everard Ranges** ▲▲ South Australia
159 R11 **Everest, Mount** Chin. Qomolangma Feng, Nep. Sagarmatha. ▲ China/Nepal 27.58N 86.57E
20 E15 **Everett** Pennsylvania, NE USA 40.00N 78.22W
34 H7 **Everett** Washington, NW USA 47.58N 122.12W
101 E17 **Evergem** Oost-Vlaanderen, NW Belgium 51.07N 3.43E
25 X16 **Everglades City** Florida, SE USA 25.51N 81.22W
25 Y16 **Everglades, The** wetland Florida, SE USA
25 P7 **Evergreen** Alabama, S USA 31.25N 86.55W
39 T4 **Evergreen** Colorado, C USA 39.37N 105.19W
Evergreen State see Washington
99 L21 **Evesham** C England, UK 52.06N 1.57W
105 T10 **Évian-les-Bains** Haute-Savoie, E France 46.22N 6.34E
95 K16 **Evijärvi** Länsi-Suomi, W Finland 63.22N 23.30E
81 D17 **Evinayong** var. Ebinayon, Evinayoung. C Equatorial Guinea 1.28N 10.17E
Evinayoung see Evinayong
117 E18 **Évinos** ≈ C Greece
97 E17 **Evje** Aust-Agder, S Norway 58.34N 7.49E
Evmolpia see Plovdiv
106 H11 **Évora** anc. Ebora, Lat. Liberalitas Julia. Évora, C Portugal 38.34N 7.54W
106 G11 **Évora** ◐ district S Portugal
104 M4 **Évreux** anc. Civitas Eburovicum. Eure, N France 49.01N 1.09E
104 K6 **Évron** Mayenne, NW France 48.10N 0.24W
116 L13 **Évros** Bul. Maritsa, Turk. Meriç; anc. Hebrus. ≈ SE Europe see also Maritsa/Meriç
117 F21 **Evrótas** ≈ S Greece
105 O5 **Évry** Essonne, N France 48.38N 2.27E
27 O8 **E.V.Spence Reservoir** ⊠ Texas, SW USA
117 I18 **Évvoia** Lat. Euboea. island C Greece
40 D9 **Ewa Beach** Oahu, Hawaii, USA, C Pacific Ocean 21.19N 158.00W
34 L9 **Ewan** Washington, NW USA 47.06N 117.46W
46 K12 **Ewarton** C Jamaica 18.10N 77.04W
83 J18 **Ewaso Ng'iro** var. Nyiro. ≈ C Kenya
194 E13 **Ewe** ≈ W PNG
31 P13 **Ewing** Nebraska, C USA 42.13N 98.20W
204 J5 **Ewing Island** island Antarctica
67 P17 **Ewing Seamount** undersea feature E Atlantic Ocean 23.19S 8.45E
164 L6 **Ewirgol** Xinjiang Uygur Zizhiqu, W China 42.55N 87.39E
81 G19 **Ewo** Cuvette, W Congo 0.55S 14.49E
29 S3 **Excelsior Springs** Missouri, C USA 39.20N 94.13W
99 J23 **Exe** ≈ SW England, UK

◆ Country
● Country Capital
◇ Dependent Territory
○ Dependent Territory Capital
◐ Administrative Region
✕ International Airport
▲ Mountain
▲▲ Mountain Range
⊼ Volcano
≈ River
⊚ Lake
⊠ Reservoir

204 *L12* **Executive Committee Range** ▲ Antarctica
12 *E16* **Exeter** Ontario, S Canada 43.19N 81.26W
99 *J24* **Exeter** *anc.* Isca Damnoniorum. SW England, UK 50.43N 3.31W
37 *R11* **Exeter** California, W USA 36.17N 119.08W
21 *P10* **Exeter** New Hampshire, NE USA 42.57N 70.55W
Exin *see* Kcynia
31 *T14* **Exira** Iowa, C USA 41.36N 94.55W
99 *J23* **Exmoor** *moorland* SW England, UK
23 *Y6* **Exmore** Virginia, NE USA 37.31N 75.48W
188 *G8* **Exmouth** Western Australia 22.00S 114.06E
99 *J24* **Exmouth** SW England, UK 50.36N 3.24W
188 *G8* **Exmouth Gulf** *gulf* Western Australia
181 *V8* **Exmouth Plateau** *undersea feature* E Indian Ocean
117 *J20* **Exompourgo** *ancient monument* Tínos, Kykládes, Greece, Aegean Sea 37.34N 25.12E
106 *I10* **Extremadura** *var.* Estremadura. ◆ *autonomous community* W Spain
80 *F12* **Extrême-Nord** *Eng.* Extreme North. ◆ *province* N Cameroon
Extreme North *see* Extrême-Nord
46 *I3* **Exuma Cays** *islets* C Bahamas
46 *I3* **Exuma Sound** *sound* C Bahamas
83 *H20* **Eyasi, Lake** ◎ N Tanzania
97 *F17* **Eydehavn** Aust-Agder, S Norway 58.31N 8.52E
98 *L12* **Eyemouth** SE Scotland, UK 55.51N 2.06W
98 *G7* **Eye Peninsula** *peninsula* NW Scotland, UK
82 *Q13* **Eyl** *It.* Eil. Nugaal, E Somalia 8.03N 49.49E
105 *N11* **Eymoutiers** Haute-Vienne, C France 45.45N 1.43E
Eyo (lower course) *see* Uolo, Río
31 *X10* **Eyota** Minnesota, N USA 44.00N 92.13W
190 *H2* **Eyre Basin, Lake** *salt lake* South Australia
190 *I1* **Eyre Creek** *seasonal river* Northern Territory/South Australia
182 *L9* **Eyre, Lake** *salt lake* South Australia
193 *C22* **Eyre Mountains** ▲ South Island, NZ
190 *H3* **Eyre North, Lake** *salt lake* South Australia
190 *G7* **Eyre Peninsula** *peninsula* South Australia
190 *H4* **Eyre South, Lake** *salt lake* South Australia
97 *B18* **Eysturoy** *Dan.* Østerø *Island* Faeroe Islands 62.15N 6.55W
63 *D20* **Ezeiza** ✕ (Buenos Aires) Buenos Aires, E Argentina 34.49S 58.30W
Ezeres *see* Ezeriş
118 *F12* **Ezeriş** *Hung.* Ezeres. Caraş-Severin, W Romania 45.21N 21.55E
167 *O9* **Ezhou** *prev.* Echeng. Hubei, C China 30.22N 114.52E
129 *R11* **Ezhva** Respublika Komi, NW Russian Federation 61.45N 50.43E
142 *B12* **Ezine** Çanakkale, NW Turkey 39.46N 26.19E
Ezo *see* Hokkaidō
Ezra/Ezraa *see* Izra'

F

203 *P7* **Faaa** Tahiti, W French Polynesia 17.31S 149.36W
203 *P7* **Faaa** ✕ (Papeete) Tahiti, W French Polynesia 17.31S 149.36W
97 *H24* **Faaborg** *var.* Fåborg. Fyn, C Denmark 55.06N 10.15E
157 *K19* **Faadhippolhu Atoll** *var.* Fadiffolu, Lhaviyani Atoll. *atoll* N Maldives
203 *U10* **Faaite** *atoll* Îles Tuamotu, C French Polynesia
203 *Q8* **Faaone** Tahiti, W French Polynesia 17.39S 149.18W
26 *H8* **Fabens** Texas, SW USA 31.30N 106.09W
96 *H12* **Fåberg** Oppland, S Norway 61.15N 10.21E
Fåborg *see* Faaborg
108 *I12* **Fabriano** Marche, C Italy 43.19N 15.52E
151 *U16* **Fabrichnyy** Almaty, SE Kazakhstan 43.12N 76.19E
56 *F10* **Facatativá** Cundinamarca, C Colombia 4.52N 74.27W
79 *X9* **Fachi** Agadez, C Niger 18.01N 11.36E
196 *B16* **Facpi Point** *headland* W Guam
20 *I13* **Factoryville** Pennsylvania, NE USA 41.34N 75.45W
80 *K8* **Fada** Borkou-Ennedi-Tibesti, E Chad 17.13N 21.31E
79 *Q13* **Fada-Ngourma** E Burkina 12.07N 0.26E
126 *Jj4* **Faddeya, Zaliv** *bay* N Russian Federation
126 *M4* **Faddeyevskiy, Ostrov** *island* Novosibirskiye Ostrova, NE Russian Federation
147 *W12* **Fadhī** S Oman 17.54N 55.30E
108 *H10* **Faenza** *anc.* Faventia. Emilia-Romagna, N Italy 44.16N 11.52E
66 *M5* **Faeroe-Iceland Ridge** *undersea feature* NW Norwegian Sea
66 *M5* **Faeroe Islands** *Dan.* Færøerne, *Faer.* Føroyar. ◇ *Danish external territory* N Atlantic Ocean
88 *C8* **Faeroe Islands** *island group* N Atlantic Ocean
Færøerne *see* Faeroe Islands
66 *N6* **Faeroe-Shetland Trough** *undersea feature* NE Atlantic Ocean
106 *H6* **Fafe** Braga, N Portugal 41.27N 8.10W
82 *K13* **Fafen Shet'** ↝ E Ethiopia
200 *Qq15* **Fafo** *island* Tongatapu Group, S Tonga
198 *Bb8* **Fagaloa Bay** *bay* Upolu, E Samoa
198 *B7* **Fagamālo** Savai'i, N Samoa 13.27S 172.22W
118 *I12* **Făgăraş** *Ger.* Fogarasch, *Hung.* Fogaras. Braşov, C Romania 45.49N 24.58E
97 *M20* **Fagerhult** Kalmar, S Sweden 57.07N 15.40E
96 *G13* **Fagernes** Oppland, S Norway 60.58N 9.13E
94 *I9* **Fagernes** Troms, N Norway 69.31N 19.16E
97 *M14* **Fagersta** Västmanland, C Sweden 59.58N 15.49E
79 *W13* **Faggo** *var.* Foggo. Bauchi, N Nigeria 11.22N 9.55E
Faghman *see* Fughmah
Fagibina, Lake *see* Faguibine, Lac
65 *J25* **Fagnano, Lago** ◎ S Argentina
101 *G22* **Fagne** *hill range* S Belgium
79 *N10* **Faguibine, Lac** *var.* Lake Fagibina. ◎ NW Mali
Fahaheel *see* Al Fuḥayḥīl
Fahlun *see* Falun
149 *U12* **Fahraj** Kermān, SE Iran 29.03N 58.54E
66 *P5* **Faial** Madeira, Portugal, NE Atlantic Ocean 32.46N 16.52W
66 *N2* **Faial** *var.* Ilha do Faial. *island* Azores, Portugal, NE Atlantic Ocean
Faial, Ilha do *see* Faial
110 *G10* **Faido** Ticino, S Switzerland 46.30N 8.48E
Faifo *see* Hôi An
Failaka Island *see* Faylakah
202 *G12* **Faioa, Île** *island* N Wallis and Futuna
189 *W8* **Fairbairn Reservoir** ⊞ Queensland, E Australia
41 *R9* **Fairbanks** Alaska, USA 64.48N 147.47W
23 *U12* **Fair Bluff** North Carolina, SE USA 34.18N 79.02W
33 *R14* **Fairborn** Ohio, N USA 39.49N 84.01W
25 *S3* **Fairburn** Georgia, SE USA 33.34N 84.34W
32 *M12* **Fairbury** Illinois, N USA 40.45N 88.30W
31 *Q17* **Fairbury** Nebraska, C USA 40.08N 97.10W
31 *T9* **Fairfax** Minnesota, N USA 44.31N 94.43W
29 *O8* **Fairfax** Oklahoma, C USA 36.34N 96.42W
23 *R14* **Fairfax** South Carolina, SE USA 32.57N 81.14W
37 *N8* **Fairfield** California, W USA 38.14N 122.03W
35 *O14* **Fairfield** Idaho, NW USA 43.20N 114.45W
32 *M16* **Fairfield** Illinois, N USA 38.22N 88.22W
31 *X15* **Fairfield** Iowa, C USA 41.00N 91.57W
35 *R8* **Fairfield** Montana, NW USA 47.36N 111.59W
33 *Q14* **Fairfield** Ohio, N USA 39.21N 84.33W
27 *U8* **Fairfield** Texas, SW USA 31.43N 96.10W
29 *T7* **Fair Grove** Missouri, C USA 37.22N 93.09W
21 *P12* **Fairhaven** Massachusetts, NE USA 41.38N 70.51W
25 *N8* **Fairhope** Alabama, S USA 30.31N 87.54W
98 *L4* **Fair Isle** *island* NE Scotland, UK
193 *F20* **Fairlie** Canterbury, South Island, NZ 44.05S 170.50E
31 *U11* **Fairmont** Minnesota, N USA 43.40N 94.27W
31 *Q16* **Fairmont** Nebraska, C USA 40.37N 97.36W
23 *S3* **Fairmont** West Virginia, NE USA 39.29N 80.08W
33 *P13* **Fairmount** Indiana, N USA 40.25N 85.39W
20 *H10* **Fairmount** New York, NE USA 43.03N 76.14W
31 *R7* **Fairmount** North Dakota, N USA 46.02N 96.36W
39 *S5* **Fairplay** Colorado, C USA 39.13N 106.00W
20 *F9* **Fairport** New York, NE USA 43.06N 77.26W
9 *O12* **Fairview** Alberta, W Canada 56.03N 118.28W
28 *L9* **Fairview** Oklahoma, C USA 36.16N 98.28W
38 *L4* **Fairview** Utah, W USA 39.37N 111.26W
37 *T6* **Fairview Peak** ▲ Nevada, W USA 39.13N 118.09W
196 *H14* **Fais** *atoll* Caroline Islands, W Micronesia
155 *U8* **Faisalābād** *prev.* Lyallpur. Punjab, NE Pakistan 31.25N 73.06E
Faisaliya *see* Fayşalīyah
30 *L8* **Faith** South Dakota, N USA 45.01N 102.02W
159 *N12* **Faizābād** Uttar Pradesh, N India 26.46N 82.07E
Faizabad/Faizābād *see* Feyzābād
47 *S9* **Fajardo** E Puerto Rico 18.20N 65.39W
145 *R9* **Fajj, Wādī al** *dry watercourse* S Iraq
146 *K4* **Fajr, Bi'r** *well* NW Saudi Arabia 28.46N 37.51E
203 *W10* **Fakahina** *atoll* Îles Tuamotu, C French Polynesia
202 *L10* **Fakaofo Atoll** *island* SE Tokelau
203 *U10* **Fakarava** *atoll* Îles Tuamotu, C French Polynesia
131 *T2* **Fakel** Udmurtskaya Respublika, NW Russian Federation 57.35N 53.00E
99 *P19* **Fakenham** E England, UK 52.50N 0.51E
176 *V11* **Fakfak** Papua, E Indonesia 2.55S 132.16E
176 *V11* **Fakfak, Pegunungan** ▲ Papua, E Indonesia
159 *T12* **Fakīragrām** Assam, NE India 26.22N 90.15E
116 *M10* **Fakiyska Reka** ↝ SE Bulgaria
97 *J24* **Fakse** Storstrøm, SE Denmark 55.16N 12.08E
97 *J24* **Fakse Bugt** *bay* SE Denmark
97 *J24* **Fakse Ladeplads** Storstrøm, SE Denmark 55.13N 12.10E
169 *V11* **Faku** Liaoning, NE China 42.30N 123.27E
78 *J14* **Falaba** N Sierra Leone 9.54N 11.22W
104 *K5* **Falaise** Calvados, N France 48.52N 0.12W
116 *H12* **Falakró** ▲ NE Greece
201 *T12* **Falalu** *island* Chuuk, C Micronesia
177 *Ff4* **Falam** Chin State, W Myanmar 22.58N 93.45E
149 *N8* **Falāvarjān** Eşfahān, C Iran 32.33N 51.28E
118 *M11* **Fălciu** Vaslui, E Romania 46.19N 28.10E
56 *I4* **Falcón** *off.* Estado Falcón. ◆ *state* NW Venezuela
108 *J12* **Falconara Marittima** Marche, C Italy 43.37N 13.22E
Falcone, Capo del *see* Falcone, Punta del
109 *A16* **Falcone, Punta del** *var.* Capo del Falcone. *headland* Sardegna, Italy, C Mediterranean Sea 40.57N 8.12E
9 *Y16* **Falcon Lake** Manitoba, S Canada 49.43N 95.18W
Falcon Lake *see* Falcón, Presa/Falcon Reservoir
43 *O7* **Falcón, Presa** *var.* Falcon Lake, Falcon Reservoir. ⊞ Mexico/USA *see also* Falcon Reservoir
27 *Q16* **Falcon Reservoir** *var.* Falcon Lake, Presa Falcón. ⊞ Mexico/USA *see also* Falcón, Presa
202 *L10* **Fale** *island* Fakaofo Atoll, SE Tokelau
198 *Aa7* **Faleālupo** Savai'i, NW Samoa 13.30S 172.46W
202 *B10* **Falefatu** *island* Funafuti Atoll, C Tuvalu
198 *Aa7* **Fālelima** Savai'i, NW Samoa 13.30S 172.40W
97 *N18* **Falerum** Östergötland, S Sweden 58.07N 16.15E
Faleshty *see* Făleşti
118 *M9* **Făleşti** *Rus.* Faleshty. NW Moldova 47.33N 27.43E
27 *S15* **Falfurrias** Texas, SW USA 27.13N 98.08W
9 *O13* **Falher** Alberta, W Canada 55.45N 117.18W
Falkenau an der Eger *see* Sokolov
97 *J21* **Falkenberg** Halland, S Sweden 56.55N 12.30E
Falkenberg *see* Niemodlin
Falkenburg in Pommern *see* Złocieniec
102 *N12* **Falkensee** Brandenburg, NE Germany 52.34N 13.04E
98 *J12* **Falkirk** C Scotland, UK 56.00N 3.48W
67 *I20* **Falkland Escarpment** *undersea feature* SW Atlantic Ocean
65 *K24* **Falkland Islands** *var.* Falklands, Islas Malvinas. ◇ *UK dependent territory* SW Atlantic Ocean
49 *W14* **Falkland Islands** *island group* SW Atlantic Ocean
67 *I20* **Falkland Plateau** *var.* Argentine Rise. *undersea feature* SW Atlantic Ocean
Falklands *see* Falkland Islands
65 *M23* **Falkland Sound** *var.* Estrecho de San Carlos. *strait* C Falkland Islands
Falknov nad Ohří *see* Sokolov
117 *H21* **Falkonéra** *island* S Greece
97 *K18* **Falköping** Västra Götaland, S Sweden 58.10N 13.31E
145 *U8* **Fallāḥ** E Iraq 32.58N 45.09E
37 *U16* **Fallbrook** California, W USA 33.22N 117.15W
201 *U12* **Falleallej Pass** *passage* Chuuk Islands, C Micronesia
95 *J14* **Fällfors** Västerbotten, N Sweden 65.07N 20.46E
204 *I6* **Fallières Coast** *physical region* Antarctica
102 *I11* **Fallingbostel** Niedersachsen, NW Germany 52.52N 9.42E
35 *X9* **Fallon** Montana, NW USA 46.49N 105.07W
37 *S5* **Fallon** Nevada, W USA 39.28N 118.46W
21 *O12* **Fall River** Massachusetts, NE USA 41.42N 71.09W
29 *P6* **Fall River Lake** ⊞ Kansas, C USA
37 *O3* **Fall River Mills** California, W USA 41.00N 121.28W
23 *W4* **Falls Church** Virginia, NE USA 38.53N 77.11W
31 *S17* **Falls City** Nebraska, C USA 40.03N 95.36W
27 *S12* **Falls City** Texas, SW USA 28.58N 98.01W
Fallūja *see* Al Fallūjah
79 *S12* **Falmey** Dosso, SW Niger 12.29N 2.58E
47 *W10* **Falmouth** Antigua, Antigua and Barbuda 16.59N 61.48W
46 *J11* **Falmouth** W Jamaica 18.28N 77.39W
99 *H25* **Falmouth** SW England, UK 50.07N 5.04W
22 *M4* **Falmouth** Kentucky, S USA 38.40N 84.19W
21 *P13* **Falmouth** Massachusetts, NE USA 41.31N 70.36W
23 *W5* **Falmouth** Virginia, NE USA 38.19N 77.28W
201 *U12* **Falos** *island* Chuuk, C Micronesia
85 *E26* **False Bay** *Afr.* Valsbaai. *bay* SW South Africa
161 *K17* **False Divi Point** *headland* E India 15.46N 80.43E
40 *M16* **False Pass** Unimak Island, Alaska, USA 54.52N 163.15W
160 *P12* **False Point** *headland* E India 20.23N 86.52E
107 *U6* **Falset** Cataluña, NE Spain 41.07N 0.49E
97 *I25* **Falster** *island* SE Denmark
97 *J23* **Falsterbo** Skåne, S Sweden 55.22N 12.49E
118 *K9* **Fălticeni** *Hung.* Falticsén. Suceava, NE Romania 47.27N 26.18E
Falticsén *see* Fălticeni
96 *M13* **Falun** *var.* Fahlun. Dalarna, C Sweden 60.36N 15.36E
Famagusta *see* Gazimağusa
Famagusta Bay *see* Gazimağusa Körfezi
64 *I8* **Famatina** La Rioja, NW Argentina 28.53S 67.31W
101 *J21* **Famenne** *physical region* SE Belgium
115 *D22* **Fan** *var.* Fani. ↝ N Albania
79 *X15* **Fan** ↝ E Nigeria
78 *M12* **Fana** Koulikoro, SW Mali 12.45N 6.55W
117 *K19* **Fána** *ancient harbor* Chíos, SE Greece 38.11N 25.35E
201 *V13* **Fanan** *island* Chuuk, C Micronesia
201 *U12* **Fanapanges** *island* Chuuk, C Micronesia
117 *L20* **Fanári, Akrotírio** *headland* Ikaría, Dodekánisos, Greece, Aegean Sea 37.40N 26.21E
47 *Q13* **Fancy** Saint Vincent, Saint Vincent and the Grenadines 13.22N 61.10W
180 *I5* **Fandriana** Fianarantsoa, SE Madagascar 20.13S 47.21E
178 *H6* **Fang** Chiang Mai, NW Thailand 19.55N 99.13E
82 *E13* **Fangak** Jonglei, SE Sudan 9.04N 30.52E
203 *W10* **Fangatau** *atoll* Îles Tuamotu, C French Polynesia
203 *X12* **Fangataufa** *island* Îles Tuamotu, SE French Polynesia
200 *Qq15* **Fanga Uta** *bay* S Tonga
167 *N7* **Fangcheng** Henan, C China 33.18N 113.03E
166 *K15* **Fangchenggang** *var.* Fangcheng Gezu Zizhixian; *prev.* Fangcheng. Guangxi Zhuangzu Zizhiqu, S China 21.49N 108.21E
167 *S15* **Fangshan** S Taiwan 22.19N 120.41E
169 *X8* **Fangzheng** Heilongjiang, NE China 45.49N 128.49E
Fani *see* Fan
121 *K16* **Fanipal'** *Rus.* Fanipol'. Minskaya Voblasts', C Belarus 53.43N 27.17E
Fanipol' *see* Fanipal'
27 *T13* **Fannin** Texas, SW USA 28.41N 97.13W
Fanning Island *see* Tabuaeran
96 *G8* **Fannrem** Sør-Trøndelag, S Norway 63.16N 9.48E
108 *I11* **Fano** *anc.* Colonia Julia Fanestris, Fanum Fortunae. Marche, C Italy 43.51N 13.01E
97 *E23* **Fanø** *island* W Denmark
178 *Ii5* **Fan Si Pan** ▲ N Vietnam 22.18N 103.36E
Fanum Fortunae *see* Fano
Fao *see* Al Fāw
147 *W7* **Faq'** *var.* Al Faqa. Dubayy, E UAE 24.42N 55.37E
152 *K12* **Farab** *Turkm.* Farap. Lebapskiy Velayat, NE Turkmenistan 39.15N 63.32E
204 *H5* **Faraday** *UK research station* Antarctica 65.35S 64.09W
193 *G16* **Faraday, Mount** ▲ South Island, NZ 42.01S 171.37E
81 *P16* **Faradje** Orientale, NE Dem. Rep. Congo 3.45N 29.43E
Faradofay *see* Tôlañaro
180 *I7* **Farafangana** Fianarantsoa, SE Madagascar 22.49S 47.49E
154 *J7* **Farāh** *var.* Farah, Fararud. Farāh, W Afghanistan 32.22N 62.07E
154 *K7* **Farāh** ◆ *province* W Afghanistan
154 *J7* **Farāh Rūd** ↝ W Afghanistan
196 *K7* **Farallon de Medinilla** *island* C Northern Mariana Islands
196 *J2* **Farallon de Pajaros** *var.* Uracas. *island* N Northern Mariana Islands
78 *J14* **Faranah** Haute-Guinée, S Guinea 10.01N 10.43W
Farap *see* Farab
Fararud *see* Farāh
146 *M13* **Farasān, Jazā'ir** *island group* SW Saudi Arabia
180 *I5* **Faratsiho** Antananarivo, C Madagascar 19.24S 46.57E
196 *K15* **Faraulep Atoll** *atoll* Caroline Islands, C Micronesia
101 *H20* **Farciennes** Hainaut, S Belgium 50.25N 4.33E
107 *O14* **Fardes** ↝ S Spain
203 *S10* **Fare** Huahine, W French Polynesia 16.42S 151.01W
99 *M23* **Fareham** S England, UK 50.51N 1.10W
41 *P11* **Farewell** Alaska, USA 62.35N 153.59W
193 *H13* **Farewell, Cape** *headland* South Island, NZ 40.30S 172.39E
Farewell, Cape *see* Nunap Isua
192 *I13* **Farewell Spit** *spit* South Island, NZ
97 *I17* **Färgelanda** Västra Götaland, S Sweden 58.34N 11.58E
Farghona Valley *see* Fergana Valley
Farghona, Wodii/Farghona Wodiysi *see* Fergana Valley
25 *V8* **Fargo** Georgia, SE USA 30.42N 82.33W
31 *R5* **Fargo** North Dakota, N USA 46.52N 96.47W
153 *S10* **Farg'ona** *Rus.* Fergana; *prev.* Novyy Margilan. Farg'ona Viloyati, E Uzbekistan 40.27N 71.43E
153 *R10* **Farg'ona Viloyati** *Rus.* Ferganskaya Oblast'. ◆ *province* E Uzbekistan
31 *V10* **Faribault** Minnesota, N USA 44.18N 93.16W
158 *J11* **Farīdābād** Haryāna, N India 28.25N 77.18E
158 *H8* **Farīdkot** Punjab, NW India 30.42N 74.46E
159 *T15* **Faridpur** Dhaka, C Bangladesh 23.28N 89.49E
124 *N16* **Fārigh, Wādī al** ↝ N Libya
180 *I4* **Farihy Alaotra** ◎ C Madagascar
96 *M11* **Färila** Gävleborg, C Sweden 61.48N 15.55E
106 *E9* **Farilhões** *island* C Portugal
78 *G12* **Farim** NW Guinea-Bissau 12.29N 15.14W
Farish *see* Forish
147 *T11* **Fāris, Qalamat** *well* SE Saudi Arabia 19.59N 50.57E
97 *N21* **Färjestaden** Kalmar, S Sweden 56.37N 16.30E
155 *R2* **Farkhār** Takhār, NE Afghanistan 36.39N 69.43E
153 *Q14* **Farkhor** *Rus.* Parkhar. SW Tajikistan 37.31N 69.21E
118 *F12* **Fârliug** *prev.* Firliug, *Hung.* Furluk. Caraş-Severin, SW Romania 45.21N 21.55E
117 *M21* **Farmakonísi** *island* Dodekánisos, Greece, Aegean Sea
32 *M13* **Farmer City** Illinois, N USA 40.14N 88.38W
33 *N14* **Farmersburg** Indiana, N USA 39.14N 87.21W
27 *U6* **Farmersville** Texas, SW USA 33.09N 96.21W
24 *H5* **Farmerville** Louisiana, S USA 32.46N 92.24W
31 *X16* **Farmington** Iowa, C USA 40.37N 91.43W
21 *Q6* **Farmington** Maine, NE USA 44.40N 70.09W
31 *V9* **Farmington** Minnesota, N USA 44.39N 93.09W
29 *X6* **Farmington** Missouri, C USA 37.46N 90.25W
21 *O9* **Farmington** New Hampshire, NE USA 43.23N 71.04W
39 *P9* **Farmington** New Mexico, SW USA 36.43N 108.13W
38 *L2* **Farmington** Utah, W USA 40.58N 111.53W
23 *W9* **Farmville** North Carolina, SE USA 35.37N 77.36W
23 *U6* **Farmville** Virginia, NE USA 37.18N 78.23W
99 *N22* **Farnborough** S England, UK 51.16N 0.46W
99 *N22* **Farnham** S England, UK 51.13N 0.49W
8 *J7* **Faro** Yukon Territory, W Canada 62.15N 133.30W
106 *G14* **Faro** Faro, S Portugal 37.01N 7.55W
106 *G14* **Faro** ◆ *district* S Portugal
106 *G14* **Faro** ✕ Faro, S Portugal 37.02N 8.01W
80 *F13* **Faro** ↝ Cameroon/Nigeria
97 *Q18* **Fårö** Gotland, SE Sweden 57.55N 19.10E
Faro, Punta del *see* Peloro, Capo
97 *Q18* **Fårösund** Gotland, SE Sweden 57.51N 19.02E
181 *N7* **Farquhar Group** *island group* S Seychelles
20 *B13* **Farrell** Pennsylvania, NE USA 41.12N 80.28W
158 *K11* **Farrukhābād** Uttar Pradesh, N India 27.24N 79.34E
149 *P11* **Fārs** *off.* Ostān-e Fārs; *anc.* Persis. ◆ *province* S Iran
117 *F16* **Fársala** Thessalía, C Greece 39.18N 22.22E
149 *R4* **Fārsīān** Golestān, N Iran
Fars, Khalīj-e *see* Persian Gulf
97 *G21* **Farsø** Nordjylland, N Denmark 56.46N 9.21E
97 *D18* **Farsund** Vest-Agder, S Norway 58.04N 6.48E
147 *U14* **Fartak, Ra's** *headland* E Yemen 15.34N 52.19E
62 *H13* **Fartura, Serra da** ▲ S Brazil
Farvel, Kap *see* Nunap Isua
26 *L4* **Farwell** Texas, SW USA 34.22N 103.02W
204 *I9* **Farwell Island** *island* Antarctica
158 *L9* **Far Western** ◆ *zone* W Nepal
154 *M3* **Fāryāb** ◆ *province* N Afghanistan
149 *P12* **Fasā** Fārs, S Iran 28.55N 53.39E
147 *U12* **Fasad, Ramlat** *desert* SW Oman
109 *P17* **Fasano** Puglia, SE Italy 40.49N 17.21E
94 *L3* **Fáskrúðsfjördhur** Austurland, E Iceland 64.55N 14.01W
119 *O5* **Fastiv** *Rus.* Fastov. Kyyivs'ka Oblast', NW Ukraine 50.08N 29.59E
99 *B22* **Fastnet Rock** *Ir.* Carraig Aonair. *island* SW Ireland
Fastov *see* Fastiv
202 *C9* **Fatato** *island* Funafuti Atoll, C Tuvalu
158 *K12* **Fatehgarh** Uttar Pradesh, N India 27.22N 79.37E
155 *U6* **Fatehjang** Punjab, E Pakistan 33.33N 72.39E
158 *G11* **Fatehpur** Rājasthān, N India 27.58N 74.58E
158 *L13* **Fatehpur** Uttar Pradesh, N India 25.55N 80.55E
130 *J7* **Fatezh** Kurskaya Oblast', W Russian Federation 52.01N 35.51E
78 *G11* **Fatick** W Senegal 14.20N 16.29W
106 *G9* **Fátima** Santarém, W Portugal 39.37N 8.39W
142 *M11* **Fatsa** Ordu, N Turkey 41.01N 37.31E
Fatshan *see* Foshan
202 *D12* **Fatua, Pointe** *var.* Pointe Nord. *headland* Île Futuna, S Wallis and Futuna
203 *X7* **Fatu Hiva** *island* Îles Marquises, NE French Polynesia
Fatunda *see* Fatundu
81 *H21* **Fatundu** *var.* Fatunda. Bandundu, W Dem. Rep. Congo 4.07S 17.13E
31 *O8* **Faulkton** South Dakota, N USA 45.02N 99.07W
118 *L13* **Făurei** *prev.* Filimon Sîrbu. Brăila, SE Romania 45.04N 27.15E
195 *T13* **Fauro** *island* Shortland Islands, NW Solomon Islands
94 *G12* **Fauske** Nordland, C Norway 67.15N 15.27E
9 *P13* **Faust** Alberta, W Canada 55.19N 115.33W
101 *L23* **Fauvillers** Luxembourg, SE Belgium 49.52N 5.40E
109 *J24* **Favara** Sicilia, Italy, C Mediterranean Sea 37.19N 13.39E
Faventia *see* Faenza
109 *G23* **Favignana, Isola** *island* Isole Egadi, S Italy
10 *D8* **Fawn** ↝ Ontario, SE Canada
Faxa Bay *see* Faxaflói
94 *H3* **Faxaflói** *Eng.* Faxa Bay. *bay* W Iceland
80 *I7* **Faya** *prev.* Faya-Largeau, Largeau. Borkou-Ennedi-Tibesti, N Chad 17.58N 19.06E
Faya-Largeau *see* Faya
197 *J5* **Fayaoué** Province des Îles Loyauté, C New Caledonia 20.41S 166.31E
144 *M5* **Faydāt** *hill range* E Syria
25 *O3* **Fayette** Alabama, S USA 33.40N 87.49W
31 *X12* **Fayette** Iowa, C USA 42.50N 91.48W
24 *J6* **Fayette** Mississippi, S USA 31.42N 91.03W
29 *U4* **Fayette** Missouri, C USA 39.09N 92.40W
29 *S9* **Fayetteville** Arkansas, C USA 36.03N 94.09W
23 *U10* **Fayetteville** North Carolina, SE USA 35.03N 78.52W
22 *J10* **Fayetteville** Tennessee, S USA 35.09N 86.34W
27 *U11* **Fayetteville** Texas, SW USA 29.52N 96.40W
23 *R5* **Fayetteville** West Virginia, NE USA 38.03N 81.06W
147 *R4* **Faylakah** *var.* Failaka Island. *island* E Kuwait
145 *T10* **Fayşalīya** *var.* Faisaliya. S Iraq 31.48N 44.36E
201 *P15* **Fayu** *var.* East Fayu. *island* Hall Islands, C Micronesia
158 *G8* **Fāzilka** Punjab, NW India 30.25N 74.04E
Fdérick *see* Fdérik
78 *I6* **Fdérik** *var.* Fdérick, *Fr.* Fort Gouraud. Tiris Zemmour, NW Mauritania 22.40N 12.40W
Feabhail, Loch *see* Foyle, Lough
99 *B20* **Feale** ↝ SW Ireland
23 *V12* **Fear, Cape** *headland* Bald Head Island, North Carolina, SE USA 33.50N 77.57W
37 *O6* **Feather River** ↝ California, W USA
193 *M14* **Featherston** Wellington, North Island, NZ 41.07S 175.19E
104 *L3* **Fécamp** Seine-Maritime, N France 49.45N 0.22E
Fédala *see* Mohammedia
63 *D17* **Federación** Entre Ríos, E Argentina 30.57S 58.04W
63 *D17* **Federal** Entre Ríos, E Argentina 30.53S 58.45W
79 *T15* **Federal Capital District** ◆ *capital territory* C Nigeria
Federal Capital Territory *see* Australian Capital Territory
Federal District *see* Distrito Federal
23 *Y4* **Federalsburg** Maryland, NE USA 38.41N 75.46W
76 *M6* **Fedjaj, Chott el** *var.* Chott el Fejaj, Shaṭṭ al Fijāj. *salt lake* C Tunisia
96 *B13* **Fedje** *island* S Norway
150 *M7* **Fedorovka** Kostanay, N Kazakhstan 51.12N 52.00E
131 *U6* **Fedorovka** Respublika Bashkortostan, W Russian Federation 53.09N 55.07E
Fëdory *see* Fyadory
119 *U11* **Fedotova Kosa** *spit* SE Ukraine
201 *V13* **Fefan** *atoll* Chuuk Islands, C Micronesia
113 *O21* **Fehérgyarmat** Szabolcs-Szatmár-Bereg, E Hungary 47.58N 22.28E
Fehér-Körös *see* Crişul Alb
Fehértemplom *see* Bela Crkva
Fehérvölgy *see* Albac
102 *L7* **Fehmarn** *island* N Germany
Fehmarnbelt *see* Fehmarn Belt
97 *H25* **Fehmarn Belt** *Dan.* Femern Bælt, *Ger.* Fehmarnbelt. *strait* Denmark/Germany
111 *X8* **Fehring** Steiermark, SE Austria 46.56N 16.00E
61 *B15* **Feijó** Acre, W Brazil 8.07S 70.27W
192 *M12* **Feilding** Manawatu-Wanganui, North Island, NZ 40.14S 175.34E
Feira *see* Feira de Santana
61 *O17* **Feira de Santana** *var.* Feira. Bahia, E Brazil 12.16S 38.52W
111 *X7* **Feistritz** ↝ SE Austria
Feistritz *see* Ilirska Bistrica
167 *P8* **Feixi** *prev.* Shangpaihe. Anhui, E China 31.40N 117.08E
Fejaj, Chott el *see* Fedjaj, Chott el
113 *I23* **Fejér** *off.* Fejér Megye. ◆ *county* W Hungary
97 *I24* **Fejø** *island* SE Denmark
142 *K15* **Feke** Adana, S Turkey 37.49N 35.55E
Feketehalom *see* Codlea
Fekete-Körös *see* Crişul Negru
111 *T3* **Feldaist** ↝ N Austria
111 *W8* **Feldbach** Steiermark, SE Austria 46.57N 15.52E
103 *F24* **Feldberg** ▲ SW Germany 47.52N 8.01E
118 *J12* **Feldioara** *Ger.* Marienburg, *Hung.* Földvár. Braşov, C Romania 45.48N 25.37E
110 *I7* **Feldkirch** *anc.* Clunia. Vorarlberg, W Austria 47.15N 9.37E
111 *S9* **Feldkirchen in Kärnten** *Slvn.* Trg. Kärnten, S Austria 46.42N 14.01E
Félegyháza *see* Kiskunfélegyháza
198 *B8* **Feleolo** ✕ (Āpia) Upolu, C Samoa 13.49S 171.59W
106 *H6* **Felgueiras** Porto, N Portugal 41.22N 8.12W
Felicitas Julia *see* Lisboa
180 *J16* **Félicité** *island* Inner Islands, NE Seychelles
157 *K20* **Felidhu Atoll** *atoll* C Maldives
43 *Y13* **Felipe Carrillo Puerto** Quintana Roo, SE Mexico 19.33N 88.01W
99 *Q21* **Felixstowe** E England, UK 51.58N 1.19E
105 *N11* **Felletin** Creuse, C France 45.53N 2.12E
Fellin *see* Viljandi
Felsőbánya *see* Baia Sprie
Felsőmuzslya *see* Mužlja
Felsővisó *see* Vişeu de Sus
37 *N10* **Felton** California, W USA 37.03N 122.04W
108 *H7* **Feltre** Veneto, NE Italy 46.01N 11.55E
Femern Bælt *see* Fehmarn Belt
97 *I24* **Femø** *island* SE Denmark
96 *I10* **Femunden** ◎ S Norway
106 *H2* **Fene** Galicia, NW Spain 43.28N 8.10W
12 *I14* **Fenelon Falls** Ontario, SE Canada 44.34N 78.43W
201 *U13* **Feneppi** *atoll* Chuuk Islands, C Micronesia
143 *O11* **Fener Burnu** *headland* N Turkey 41.07N 39.26E
117 *J14* **Fengári** ▲ Samothráki, E Greece 40.27N 25.37E
169 *V13* **Fengcheng** *var.* Feng-cheng, Fenghwangcheng. Liaoning, NE China 40.28N 124.01E
166 *K11* **Fenggang** *prev.* Longquan. Guizhou, S China 27.57N 107.42E
167 *S9* **Fenghua** Zhejiang, SE China 29.38N 121.23E
Fenghwangcheng *see* Fengcheng
166 *L9* **Fengjie** Sichuan, C China 31.03N 109.29E
166 *M14* **Fengkai** *prev.* Jiankou. Guangdong, S China 23.26N 111.28E
167 *T13* **Fenglin** *Jap.* Hōrin. C Taiwan 23.52N 121.30E
167 *P1* **Fengning** *prev.* Dagezhen. Hebei, E China 41.12N 116.37E
166 *E13* **Fengqing** Yunnan, SW China 24.38N 99.54E
167 *O6* **Fengqiu** Henan, C China 35.01N 114.24E
167 *Q2* **Fengrun** Hebei, E China 39.49N 118.10E
169 *T4* **Fengshui Shan** ▲ NE China 52.20N 123.22E
167 *P14* **Fengshun** Guangdong, S China 23.51N 116.11E
Fengtien *see* Liaoning, China
Fengtien *see* Shenyang, China
166 *J7* **Fengxian** *var.* Feng Xian; *prev.* Shuangshipu. Shaanxi, C China 33.50N 106.33E
Fengxiang *see* Luobei
169 *P13* **Fengzhen** Nei Mongol Zizhiqu, N China 40.25N 113.09E
166 *M6* **Fen He** ↝ C China
159 *V15* **Feni** Chittagong, E Bangladesh 23.00N 91.24E
195 *Q10* **Feni Islands** *island group* NE PNG
40 *H17* **Fenimore Pass** *strait* Aleutian Islands, Alaska, USA
86 *B9* **Feni Ridge** *undersea feature* N Atlantic Ocean
Fennern *see* Vändra
32 *J9* **Fennimore** Wisconsin, N USA 42.58N 90.39W
180 *J4* **Fenoarivo** Toamasina, E Madagascar 20.52S 46.52E
97 *I24* **Fensmark** Storstrøm, SE Denmark 55.16N 11.48E
99 *O19* **Fens, The** *wetland* E England, UK
33 *R9* **Fenton** Michigan, N USA 42.48N 83.42W
202 *K10* **Fenua Fala** *island* SE Tokelau
202 *F12* **Fenuafo'ou, Île** *island* E Wallis and Futuna
202 *L10* **Fenua Loa** *island* Fakaofo Atoll, E Tokelau
166 *M4* **Fenyang** Shanxi, C China 37.14N 111.40E
119 *U13* **Feodosiya** *var.* Kefe, *It.* Kaffa; *anc.* Theodosia. Respublika Krym, S Ukraine 45.03N 35.23E
96 *I10* **Feragen** ◎ S Norway
76 *L5* **Fer, Cap de** *headland* NE Algeria 37.05N 7.10E
33 *O16* **Ferdinand** Indiana, N USA 38.13N 86.51W
Ferdinand *see* Montana, Bulgaria
Ferdinand *see* Mihail Kogălniceanu, Romania
Ferdinandsberg *see* Oţelu Roşu
149 *T7* **Ferdows** *var.* Firdaus; *prev.* Tūn. Khorāsān, E Iran 34.00N 58.09E
105 *Q5* **Fère-Champenoise** Marne, N France 48.45N 3.59E
Ferencz-Jósef Csúcs *see* Gerlachovský štít
109 *J16* **Ferentino** Lazio, C Italy 41.40N 13.16E
116 *L13* **Féres** Anatolikí Makedonía kai Thráki, NE Greece 40.54N 26.12E
Fergana *see* Farg'ona
153 *S10* **Fergana Valley** *var.* Farghona Valley, *Rus.* Ferganskaya Dolina, *Taj.* Wodii Farghona, *Uzb.* Farghona Wodiysi. *basin* Tajikistan/Uzbekistan
Ferganskaya Dolina *see* Fergana Valley
Ferganskaya Oblast' *see* Farg'ona Viloyati
153 *U9* **Ferganskiy Khrebet** ▲ C Kyrgyzstan
12 *F15* **Fergus** Ontario, S Canada 43.42N 80.22W
31 *S6* **Fergus Falls** Minnesota, N USA 46.15N 96.02W
195 *N15* **Fergusson Island** *var.* Kaluwawa. *island* SE PNG
113 *K22* **Ferihegy** ✕ (Budapest) Budapest, C Hungary 47.25N 19.13E
Ferizaj *see* Uroševac
79 *N14* **Ferkessédougou** N Ivory Coast 9.36N 5.12W
111 *T10* **Ferlach** *Slvn.* Borovlje. Kärnten, S Austria 46.31N 14.18E
99 *E16* **Fermanagh** *cultural region* SW Northern Ireland, UK
108 *J13* **Fermo** *anc.* Firmum Picenum. Marche, C Italy 43.09N 13.43E
106 *J6* **Fermoselle** Castilla-León, N Spain 41.19N 6.24W
99 *D20* **Fermoy** *Ir.* Mainistir Fhear Maí. SW Ireland 52.07N 8.16W
25 *W8* **Fernandina Beach** Amelia Island, Florida, SE USA 30.40N 81.27W
59 *A17* **Fernandina, Isla** *var.* Narborough Island. *island* Galapagos Islands, Ecuador, E Pacific Ocean
49 *Y5* **Fernando de Noronha** *island* E Brazil
Fernando Po/Fernando Póo *see* Bioco, Isla de
62 *J7* **Fernandópolis** São Paulo, S Brazil 20.12S 50.14W
106 *M13* **Fernán Núñez** Andalucía, S Spain 37.40N 4.43W
85 *Q14* **Fernão Veloso, Baia de** *bay* NE Mozambique
36 *K3* **Ferndale** California, W USA 40.34N 124.16W
34 *H6* **Ferndale** Washington, NW USA 48.51N 122.35W
9 *P17* **Fernie** British Columbia, SW Canada 49.30N 115.00W
37 *R5* **Fernley** Nevada, W USA 39.35N 119.15W
Ferozepore *see* Fīrozpur
109 *N18* **Ferrandina** Basilicata, S Italy 40.30N 16.25E

108 G9 **Ferrara** *anc.* Forum Alieni. Emilia-Romagna, N Italy *44.49N 11.36E*
123 H11 **Ferrat, Cap** *headland* NW Algeria *35.52N 0.24W*
109 D20 **Ferrato, Capo** *headland* Sardegna, Italy, C Mediterranean Sea *39.18N 9.37E*
106 G12 **Ferreira do Alentejo** Beja, S Portugal *38.04N 8.06W*
58 B11 **Ferreñafe** Lambayeque, W Peru *6.37S 79.45W*
110 C12 **Ferret** Valais, SW Switzerland *45.57N 7.04E*
104 I13 **Ferret, Cap** *headland* W France *44.37N 1.15W*
24 I6 **Ferriday** Louisiana, S USA *31.37N 91.33W*
Ferro *see* Hierro
109 D16 **Ferro, Capo** *headland* Sardegna, Italy, C Mediterranean Sea *41.09N 9.31E*
106 H2 **Ferrol** *var.* El Ferrol; *prev.* El Ferrol del Caudillo. Galicia, NW Spain *43.28N 8.13W*
58 B12 **Ferrol, Península de** *peninsula* W Peru
38 M5 **Ferron** Utah, W USA *39.05N 111.07W*
23 S7 **Ferrum** Virginia, NE USA *36.54N 80.01W*
25 O8 **Ferry Pass** Florida, SE USA *30.30N 87.12W*
Ferryville *see* Menzel Bourguiba
31 S4 **Fertile** Minnesota, N USA *47.32N 96.16W*
Fertő *see* Neusiedler See
100 L5 **Ferwerd** *Fris.* Ferwert. Friesland, N Netherlands *53.21N 5.46E*
Ferwert *see* Ferwerd
76 G6 **Fès** *Eng.* Fez. N Morocco *34.06N 4.57W*
81 I22 **Feshi** Bandundu, SW Dem. Rep. Congo *6.07S 18.12E*
31 O4 **Fessenden** North Dakota, N USA *47.36N 99.37W*
Festenberg *see* Twardogóra
29 X5 **Festus** Missouri, C USA *38.13N 90.24W*
118 M14 **Fetești** Ialomița, SE Romania *44.22N 27.51E*
142 D17 **Fethiye** Muğla, SW Turkey *36.37N 29.07E*
98 M1 **Fetlar** *island* NE Scotland, UK
97 I15 **Fetsund** Akershus, S Norway *59.55N 11.03E*
10 L5 **Feuilles, Lac aux** ◎ Quebec, E Canada
10 L5 **Feuilles, Rivière aux** ≈ Quebec, E Canada
101 M23 **Feulen** Diekirch, C Luxembourg *49.52N 6.03E*
105 Q11 **Feurs** Loire, E France *45.44N 4.14E*
97 F18 **Fevik** Aust-Agder, S Norway *58.22N 8.40E*
126 Mm14 **Fevral'sk** Amurskaya Oblast', SE Russian Federation *52.25N 131.06E*
155 S2 **Feyzābād** *var.* Faizabad, Faizābād, Feyzābād, Fyzabad. Badakhshān, NE Afghanistan *37.06N 70.34E*
Fez *see* Fès
99 J19 **Ffestiniog** NW Wales, UK *52.55N 3.54W*
Fhóid Duibh, Cuan an *see* Blacksod Bay
64 I8 **Fiambalá** Catamarca, NW Argentina *27.45S 67.37W*
180 I6 **Fianarantsoa** Fianarantsoa, C Madagascar *21.27S 47.05E*
180 H6 **Fianarantsoa** ◈ *province* SE Madagascar
80 G12 **Fianga** Mayo-Kébbi, SW Chad *9.57N 15.09E*
Ficce *see* Fiché
82 J12 **Fiché** *It.* Ficce. Oromo, C Ethiopia *9.48N 38.43E*
103 N17 **Fichtelberg** ▲ Czech Republic/Germany *50.26N 12.57E*
103 M18 **Fichtelgebirge** ▲▲ SE Germany
103 M19 **Fichtelnaab** ≈ SE Germany
108 E9 **Fidenza** Emilia-Romagna, N Italy *44.52N 10.04E*
115 K21 **Fier** *var.* Fieri. Fier, SW Albania *40.44N 19.34E*
115 K21 **Fier** ◈ *district* W Albania
Fieri *see* Fier
Fierza *see* Fierzë
115 L17 **Fierzë** *var.* Fierza. Shkodër, N Albania *42.15N 20.02E*
115 L17 **Fierzës, Liqeni i** ◎ N Albania
110 F10 **Fiesch** Valais, SW Switzerland *46.25N 8.09E*
108 G11 **Fiesole** Toscana, C Italy *43.50N 11.18E*
144 G12 **Fifah** Aț Țafilah, W Jordan *30.55N 35.25E*
98 K11 **Fife** *var.* Kingdom of Fife. *cultural region* E Scotland, UK
98 K11 **Fife Ness** *headland* E Scotland, UK *56.16N 2.35W*
Fifteen Twenty Fracture Zone *see* Barracuda Fracture Zone
105 N13 **Figeac** Lot, S France *44.37N 2.01E*
97 N19 **Figeholm** Kalmar, SE Sweden *57.12N 16.34E*
Figig *see* Figuig
85 J18 **Figtree** Matabeleland South, SW Zimbabwe *20.20S 28.20E*
106 F8 **Figueira da Foz** Coimbra, W Portugal *40.09N 8.51W*
107 X4 **Figueres** Cataluña, E Spain *42.16N 2.57E*
76 H7 **Figuig** *var.* Figig. E Morocco *32.09N 1.13W*
Fijāj, Shaṭṭ al *see* Fedjaj, Chott el
197 J14 **Fiji** *off.* Sovereign Democratic Republic of Fiji, *Fij.* Viti. ◆ *republic* SW Pacific Ocean
197 J13 **Fiji** *island group* SW Pacific Ocean
183 Q8 **Fiji Plate** *tectonic feature*
107 P14 **Filabres, Sierra de los** ▲▲ SE Spain
85 K18 **Filabusi** Matabeleland South, S Zimbabwe *20.31S 29.16E*
44 K13 **Filadelfia** Guanacaste, W Costa Rica *10.24N 85.33W*
113 K20 **Fiľakovo** *Hung.* Fülek. Banskobystrický Kraj, C Slovakia *48.15N 19.53E*
205 N5 **Filchner Ice Shelf** *ice shelf* Antarctica
12 J11 **Fildegrand** ≈ Quebec, SE Canada
35 O15 **Filer** Idaho, NW USA *42.34N 114.36W*
Filevo *see* Vŭrbitsa
118 H14 **Filiași** Dolj, SW Romania *44.32N 23.30E*
117 B16 **Filiátes** Ípeiros, W Greece *39.36N 20.19E*
117 D21 **Filiatrá** Pelopónnisos, S Greece *37.10N 21.35E*
109 K22 **Filicudi, Isola** *island* Isole Eolie, S Italy
147 Y10 **Filim** E Oman *20.37N 58.11E*
Filimon Sîrbu *see* Făurei
79 S11 **Filingué** Tillabéri, W Niger *14.21N 3.16E*
116 K13 **Filiourí** ≈ NE Greece
116 I13 **Filippoi** *anc.* Philippi. *site of ancient city* Anatolikí Makedonía kai Thráki, NE Greece *41.01N 24.15E*
97 L15 **Filipstad** Värmland, C Sweden *59.43N 14.10E*
110 I9 **Filisur** Graubünden, S Switzerland *46.40N 9.43E*
96 E12 **Fillefjell** ▲▲ S Norway
37 R14 **Fillmore** California, W USA *34.23N 118.56W*
38 K5 **Fillmore** Utah, W USA *38.57N 112.19W*
12 J10 **Fils, Lac du** ◎ Quebec, SE Canada
142 H11 **Filyos Çayı** ≈ N Turkey
205 Q2 **Fimbulheimen** *physical region* Antarctica
205 Q1 **Fimbul Ice Shelf** *ice shelf* Antarctica
108 G9 **Finale Emilia** Emilia-Romagna, C Italy *44.50N 11.17E*
108 C10 **Finale Ligure** Liguria, NW Italy *44.11N 8.21E*
107 P14 **Fiñana** Andalucía, S Spain *37.09N 2.47W*
180 I6 **Finandrahana** Fianarantsoa, SE Madagascar
23 S6 **Fincastle** Virginia, NE USA *37.29N 79.51W*
101 M25 **Findel** ✈ (Luxembourg) Luxembourg, C Luxembourg *49.39N 6.16E*
98 J9 **Findhorn** ≈ N Scotland, UK
33 R12 **Findlay** Ohio, N USA *41.02N 83.39W*
20 G11 **Finger Lakes** *lakes* New York, NE USA
85 L14 **Fingoè** Tete, NW Mozambique *15.01S 31.52E*
142 E17 **Finike** Antalya, SW Turkey *36.18N 30.07E*
104 F6 **Finistère** ◈ *department* NW France
194 J12 **Finisterre, Mount** ▲ C PNG *5.58S 146.30E*
194 J12 **Finisterre Range** ▲▲ N PNG
189 Q8 **Finke** Northern Territory, N Australia *25.37S 134.35E*
111 S10 **Finkenstein** Kärnten, S Austria *46.34N 13.53E*
201 Y15 **Finkol, Mount** *var.* Mount Crozer. ▲ Kosrae, E Micronesia *5.18N 163.00E*
95 L17 **Finland** *off.* Republic of Finland, *Fin.* Suomen Tasavalta, Suomi. ◆ *republic* N Europe
128 F12 **Finland, Gulf of** *Est.* Soome Laht, *Fin.* Suomenlahti, *Ger.* Finnischer Meerbusen, *Rus.* Finskiy Zaliv, *Swe.* Finska Viken. *gulf* E Baltic Sea
8 L11 **Finlay** ≈ British Columbia, W Canada
191 O10 **Finley** New South Wales, SE Australia *35.41S 145.33E*
31 Q4 **Finley** North Dakota, N USA *47.30N 97.50W*
Finnischer Meerbusen *see* Finland, Gulf of
94 K9 **Finnmark** ◈ *county* N Norway
94 K9 **Finnmarksvidda** *physical region* N Norway
94 I9 **Finnsnes** Troms, N Norway *69.13N 17.58E*
194 K13 **Finschhafen** Morobe, C PNG *6.38S 147.49E*
96 E13 **Finse** Hordaland, S Norway *60.35N 7.33E*
Finska Viken/Finskiy Zaliv *see* Finland, Gulf of
97 M17 **Finspång** Östergötland, S Sweden *58.42N 15.45E*
110 F10 **Finsteraarhorn** ▲ Switzerland *46.33N 8.07E*
103 O14 **Finsterwalde** Brandenburg, E Germany *51.37N 13.43E*
193 A23 **Fiordland** *physical region* South Island, NZ
108 E9 **Fiorenzuola d'Arda** Emilia-Romagna, C Italy *44.57N 9.53E*
Firat Nehri *see* Euphrates
Firdaus *see* Ferdows
20 M14 **Fire Island** *island* New York, NE USA
108 G11 **Firenze** *Eng.* Florence; *anc.* Florentia. Toscana, C Italy *43.46N 11.15E*
108 G10 **Firenzuola** Toscana, C Italy *44.07N 11.22E*
12 C6 **Fire River** Ontario, S Canada *48.46N 83.34W*
Firliug *see* Fârliug
63 B19 **Firmat** Santa Fe, C Argentina *33.28S 61.28W*
105 Q12 **Firminy** Loire, E France *45.22N 4.18E*
Firmum Picenum *see* Fermo
158 J12 **Firozābād** Uttar Pradesh, N India *27.09N 78.24E*
158 G8 **Firozpur** *var.* Ferozepore. Punjab, NW India *30.55N 74.37E*
First State *see* Delaware
149 O12 **Fīrūzābād** Fārs, S Iran *28.51N 52.34E*
Fischamend *see* Fischamend Markt
111 Y4 **Fischamend Markt** *var.* Fischamend. Niederösterreich, NE Austria *48.06N 16.37E*
111 W6 **Fischbacher Alpen** ▲▲ E Austria
Fischhausen *see* Primorsk
85 D21 **Fish** *var.* Vis. ≈ S Namibia
85 F24 **Fish** *Afr.* Vis. ≈ SW South Africa
9 X15 **Fisher Branch** Manitoba, S Canada *51.09N 97.34W*
9 X15 **Fisher River** Manitoba, S Canada *51.25N 97.23W*
21 N13 **Fishers Island** *island* New York, NE USA
39 U8 **Fishers Peak** ▲ Colorado, C USA *37.06N 104.27W*
15 M6 **Fisher Strait** *strait* Nunavut, N Canada
99 H21 **Fishguard** *Wel.* Abergwaun. SW Wales, UK *51.58N 4.49W*
21 R2 **Fish River Lake** ◎ Maine, NE USA
204 K6 **Fiske, Cape** *headland* Antarctica *74.27S 60.28W*
105 P4 **Fismes** Marne, N France *49.19N 3.41E*
106 F3 **Fisterra, Cabo** *headland* NW Spain *42.53N 9.16W*
21 N11 **Fitchburg** Massachusetts, NE USA *42.34N 71.48W*
98 L3 **Fitful Head** *headland* NE Scotland, UK *59.57N 1.24W*
97 C14 **Fitjar** Hordaland, S Norway *59.55N 5.19E*
198 Bb8 **Fito** ▲ Upolu, C Samoa *13.57S 171.42W*
25 U6 **Fitzgerald** Georgia, SE USA *31.42N 83.15W*
188 M5 **Fitzroy Crossing** Western Australia *18.10S 125.40E*
65 G21 **Fitzroy, Monte** *var.* Cerro Chaltel. ▲ S Argentina *49.18S 73.06W*
189 Y8 **Fitzroy River** ≈ Queensland, E Australia
188 L5 **Fitzroy River** ≈ Western Australia
12 E12 **Fitzwilliam Island** *island* Ontario, S Canada
109 J15 **Fiuggi** Lazio, C Italy *41.47N 13.16E*
Fiume *see* Rijeka
109 H15 **Fiumicino** Lazio, C Italy *41.46N 12.13E*
Fiumicino *see* Leonardo da Vinci
108 E10 **Fivizzano** Toscana, C Italy *44.13N 10.06E*
81 O21 **Fizi** Sud Kivu, E Dem. Rep. Congo *4.15S 28.57E*
Fizuli *see* Füzuli
94 I11 **Fjällåsen** Norrbotten, N Sweden *67.31N 20.07E*
97 G20 **Fjerritslev** Nordjylland, N Denmark *57.06N 9.16E*
F.J.S. *see* Franz Josef Strauss
97 L16 **Fjugesta** Örebro, C Sweden *59.10N 14.50E*
Fladstrand *see* Frederikshavn
39 V5 **Flagler** Colorado, C USA *39.17N 103.04W*
25 X10 **Flagler Beach** Florida, SE USA *29.28N 81.07W*
38 L11 **Flagstaff** Arizona, SW USA *35.12N 111.39W*
67 H24 **Flagstaff Bay** *bay* Saint Helena, C Atlantic Ocean
21 P5 **Flagstaff Lake** ◎ Maine, NE USA
96 E13 **Flåm** Sogn og Fjordane, S Norway *60.51N 7.06E*
13 O8 **Flamand** ≈ Quebec, SE Canada
32 J5 **Flambeau River** ≈ Wisconsin, N USA
99 O16 **Flamborough Head** *headland* E England, UK *54.06N 0.03W*
102 N13 **Fläming** *hill range* NE Germany
18 Ii7 **Flaming Gorge Reservoir** ▣ Utah/Wyoming, NW USA
176 Xx13 **Flamingo, Teluk** *bay* N Arafura Sea
101 B18 **Flanders** *Dut.* Vlaanderen, *Fr.* Flandre. *cultural region* Belgium/France
Flandre *see* Flanders
31 R10 **Flandreau** South Dakota, N USA *44.03N 96.36W*
98 D6 **Flannan Isles** *island group* NW Scotland, UK
30 M6 **Flasher** North Dakota, N USA *46.25N 101.12W*
95 G15 **Flåsjön** ◎ N Sweden
41 O11 **Flat** Alaska, USA *62.27N 158.00W*
14 G7 **Flat** ≈ Northwest Territories, NW Canada
94 H1 **Flateyri** Vestfirdhir, NW Iceland *66.03N 23.28W*
35 P8 **Flathead Lake** ◎ Montana, NW USA
181 Y15 **Flat Island** *Fr.* Île Plate. *island* N Mauritius
179 N14 **Flat Island** *island* NE Spratly Islands
27 T11 **Flatonia** Texas, SW USA *29.41N 97.06W*
193 M14 **Flat Point** *headland* North Island, NZ *41.12S 176.03E*
29 X6 **Flat River** Missouri, C USA *37.51N 90.31W*
33 P8 **Flat River** ≈ Michigan, N USA
33 P14 **Flatrock River** ≈ Indiana, N USA
34 E6 **Flattery, Cape** *headland* Washington, NW USA *48.22N 124.43W*
66 B12 **Flatts Village** *var.* The Flatts Village. C Bermuda *32.19N 64.43W*
110 H7 **Flawil** Sankt Gallen, NE Switzerland *47.25N 9.12E*
99 N22 **Fleet** S England, UK *51.16N 0.49W*
99 K16 **Fleetwood** NW England, UK *53.55N 3.01W*
20 H15 **Fleetwood** Pennsylvania, NE USA *40.27N 75.49W*
97 D18 **Flekkefjord** Vest-Agder, S Norway *58.16N 6.40E*
23 N5 **Flemingsburg** Kentucky, S USA *38.25N 83.43W*
20 J15 **Flemington** New Jersey, NE USA *40.30N 74.51W*
66 I7 **Flemish Cap** *undersea feature* NW Atlantic Ocean
97 N16 **Flen** Södermanland, C Sweden *59.03N 16.37E*
102 I6 **Flensburg** Schleswig-Holstein, N Germany *54.46N 9.25E*
102 J6 **Flensburger Förde** *inlet* Denmark/Germany
104 K5 **Flers** Orne, N France *48.45N 0.34W*
97 C14 **Flesland** ✈ (Bergen) Hordaland, S Norway *60.18N 5.15E*
Flessingue *see* Vlissingen
23 P10 **Fletcher** North Carolina, SE USA *35.24N 82.29W*
33 R6 **Fletcher Pond** ◎ Michigan, N USA
104 L15 **Fleurance** Gers, S France *43.50N 0.39E*
110 B8 **Fleurier** Neuchâtel, W Switzerland *46.55N 6.37E*
101 H20 **Fleurus** Hainaut, S Belgium *50.28N 4.33E*
105 N7 **Fleury-les-Aubrais** Loiret, C France *47.55N 1.55E*
100 K10 **Flevoland** ◈ *province* C Netherlands
Flickertail State *see* North Dakota
110 H9 **Flims** Glarus, NE Switzerland *46.50N 9.16E*
190 F8 **Flinders Island** *island* Investigator Group, South Australia
191 P14 **Flinders Island** *island* Furneaux Group, Tasmania, SE Australia
190 I6 **Flinders Ranges** ▲▲ South Australia
189 U5 **Flinders River** ≈ Queensland, NE Australia
9 V13 **Flin Flon** Manitoba, C Canada *54.46N 101.51W*
99 K18 **Flint** NE Wales, UK *53.15N 3.09W*
33 R9 **Flint** Michigan, N USA *43.00N 83.41W*
99 J18 **Flint** *cultural region* NE Wales, UK
29 O7 **Flint Hills** *hill range* Kansas, C USA
203 Y6 **Flint Island** *island* Line Islands, E Kiribati
25 S4 **Flint River** ≈ Georgia, SE USA
33 R9 **Flint River** ≈ Michigan, N USA
201 X12 **Flipper Point** *headland* C Wake Island *19.18N 166.37E*
96 I13 **Flisa** Hedmark, S Norway *60.36N 12.01E*
96 J13 **Flisa** ≈ S Norway
126 Hh4 **Flissingskiy, Mys** *headland* Novaya Zemlya, NW Russian Federation *76.43N 69.01E*
Flitsch *see* Bovec
107 U6 **Flix** Cataluña, NE Spain *41.13N 0.32E*
97 J19 **Floda** Västra Götaland, S Sweden *57.46N 12.19E*
103 O16 **Flöha** ≈ E Germany
27 O4 **Flomot** Texas, SW USA *34.13N 100.58W*
31 V5 **Floodwood** Minnesota, N USA *46.55N 92.55W*
32 M15 **Flora** Illinois, N USA *38.40N 88.29W*
105 P14 **Florac** Lozère, S France *44.18N 3.35E*
25 Q8 **Florala** Alabama, S USA *31.00N 86.19W*
105 S4 **Florange** Moselle, NE France *49.21N 6.06E*
Floreana, Isla *see* Santa María, Isla
25 O2 **Florence** Alabama, S USA *34.48N 87.40W*
38 L14 **Florence** Arizona, SW USA *33.01N 111.23W*
39 T6 **Florence** Colorado, C USA *38.20N 105.06W*
29 O5 **Florence** Kansas, C USA *38.13N 96.56W*
22 M4 **Florence** Kentucky, S USA *39.00N 84.37W*
34 E13 **Florence** Oregon, NW USA *43.58N 124.06W*
23 T12 **Florence** South Carolina, SE USA *34.12N 79.45W*
27 S9 **Florence** Texas, SW USA *30.50N 97.47W*
Florence *see* Firenze
56 E13 **Florencia** Caquetá, S Colombia *1.37N 75.37W*
101 H21 **Florennes** Namur, S Belgium *50.15N 4.36E*
Florentia *see* Firenze
65 J18 **Florentino Ameghino, Embalse** ◎ S Argentina
101 J24 **Florenville** Luxembourg, SE Belgium *49.42N 5.19E*
44 E3 **Flores** Petén, N Guatemala *16.54N 89.55W*
63 E19 **Flores** ◈ *department* S Uruguay
175 Pp16 **Flores** *island* Nusa Tenggara, C Indonesia
66 M1 **Flores** *island* Azores, Portugal, NE Atlantic Ocean
Floreshty *see* Florești
Flores, Lago de *see* Petén Itzá, Lago
Flores, Laut *see* Flores Sea
175 P15 **Flores Sea** *Ind.* Laut Flores. *sea* C Indonesia
118 M8 **Florești** *Rus.* Floreshty. N Moldova *47.52N 28.19E*
27 S12 **Floresville** Texas, SW USA *29.07N 98.09W*
61 N14 **Floriano** Piauí, E Brazil *06.45S 43.00W*
63 K14 **Florianópolis** *prev.* Destêrro. *state capital* Santa Catarina, S Brazil *27.34S 48.31W*
46 G6 **Florida** Camagüey, C Cuba *21.31N 78.13W*
63 F19 **Florida** Florida, S Uruguay *34.04S 56.13W*
63 F19 **Florida** ◈ *department* S Uruguay
25 U9 **Florida** *off.* State of Florida; *also known as* Peninsular State, Sunshine State. ◈ *state* SE USA
25 Y17 **Florida Bay** *bay* Florida, SE USA
56 G8 **Floridablanca** Santander, N Colombia *7.04N 73.06W*
195 X15 **Florida Islands** *island group* C Solomon Islands
25 Y17 **Florida Keys** *island group* Florida, SE USA
39 Q16 **Florida Mountains** ▲▲ New Mexico, SW USA
66 D10 **Florida, Straits of** *strait* Atlantic Ocean/Gulf of Mexico
116 D13 **Flórina** *var.* Phlórina. Dytikí Makedonía, N Greece *40.48N 21.25E*
29 X4 **Florissant** Missouri, C USA *38.47N 90.19W*
96 C11 **Florø** Sogn og Fjordane, S Norway *61.34N 5.01E*
117 L22 **Floúda, Akrotírio** *headland* Astypálaia, Kykládes, Greece, Aegean Sea *36.38N 26.23E*
23 S7 **Floyd** Virginia, NE USA *36.53N 80.21W*
27 N4 **Floydada** Texas, SW USA *33.58N 101.20W*
Flüela Wisshorn *see* Weisshorn
100 K7 **Fluessen** ◎ N Netherlands
107 S5 **Flúmen** ≈ NE Spain
109 C20 **Flumendosa** ≈ Sardegna, Italy, C Mediterranean Sea
33 R9 **Flushing** Michigan, N USA *43.03N 83.51W*
Flushing *see* Vlissingen
27 O6 **Fluvanna** Texas, SW USA *32.54N 101.06W*
194 F14 **Fly** ≈ Indonesia/PNG
204 I10 **Flying Fish, Cape** *headland* Thurston Island, Antarctica *72.00S 102.25W*
Flylân *see* Vlieland
200 Ss13 **Foa** *island* Ha'apai Group, C Tonga
9 U15 **Foam Lake** Saskatchewan, S Canada *51.37N 103.31W*
115 J14 **Foča** *var* Srbinje, Republika Srpska, Bosnia and Herzegovina *43.32N 18.45E*
118 L12 **Focșani** Vrancea, E Romania *45.45N 27.13E*
Fogaras/Fogarasch *see* Făgăraș
109 M16 **Foggia** Puglia, SE Italy *41.28N 15.31E*
Foggo *see* Faggo
78 D10 **Fogo** *island* Ilhas de Sotavento, SW Cape Verde
11 U11 **Fogo Island** *island* Newfoundland and Labrador, E Canada
111 U7 **Fohnsdorf** Steiermark, SE Austria *47.13N 14.40E*
102 G7 **Föhr** *island* NW Germany
106 F14 **Fóia** ▲ S Portugal *37.19N 8.39W*
12 I10 **Foins, Lac aux** ◎ Quebec, SE Canada
105 N17 **Foix** Ariège, S France *42.58N 1.39E*
130 I5 **Fokino** Bryanskaya Oblast', W Russian Federation *53.22N 34.22E*
127 N17 **Fokino** Primorskiy Kray, SE Russian Federation *42.58N 132.25E*
Fola, Cnoc *see* Bloody Foreland
96 E13 **Folarskardnuten** ▲ S Norway *60.34N 7.18E*
94 G11 **Foldafjorden** *fjord* C Norway
95 E14 **Foldafjorden** *fjord* C Norway
Földvár *see* Feldioara
95 F14 **Foldereid** Nord-Trøndelag, C Norway *64.58N 12.09E*
117 J22 **Folégandros** *island* Kykládes, Greece, Aegean Sea
25 O9 **Foley** Alabama, S USA *30.24N 87.40W*
31 U7 **Foley** Minnesota, N USA *45.39N 93.54W*
12 E7 **Foleyet** Ontario, S Canada *48.15N 82.25W*
97 D14 **Folgefonni** *glacier* S Norway
108 I13 **Foligno** Umbria, C Italy *42.58N 12.40E*
99 Q23 **Folkestone** SE England, UK *51.04N 1.10E*
25 W8 **Folkston** Georgia, SE USA *30.49N 82.00W*
96 H10 **Folldal** Hedmark, S Norway *62.08N 10.00E*
27 P1 **Follett** Texas, SW USA *36.25N 100.08W*
108 F13 **Follonica** Toscana, C Italy *42.55N 10.45E*
23 T15 **Folly Beach** South Carolina, SE USA *32.39N 79.56W*
37 O7 **Folsom** California, W USA *38.40N 121.11W*
118 M12 **Foltești** Galați, E Romania *45.45N 28.00E*
180 H14 **Fomboni** Mohéli, S Comoros *12.18S 43.46E*
20 K10 **Fonda** New York, NE USA *42.57N 74.24W*
9 S10 **Fond-du-Lac** Saskatchewan, C Canada *59.19N 107.09W*
32 M8 **Fond du Lac** Wisconsin, N USA *43.48N 88.27W*
9 T10 **Fond-du-Lac** ≈ Saskatchewan, C Canada
202 C9 **Fongafale** *var.* Funafuti. ● (Tuvalu) Funafuti Atoll, SE Tuvalu *8.31N 179.11E*
202 G8 **Fongafale** *atoll* C Tuvalu
109 C18 **Fonni** Sardegna, Italy, C Mediterranean Sea *40.07N 9.17E*
201 V12 **Fono** *island* Chuuk, C Micronesia
56 G4 **Fonseca** La Guajira, N Colombia *10.54N 72.54W*
Fonseca, Golfo de *see* Fonseca, Gulf of
44 H8 **Fonseca, Gulf of** *Sp.* Golfo de Fonseca. *gulf* Central America
105 O6 **Fontainebleau** Seine-et-Marne, N France *48.24N 2.42E*
65 G19 **Fontana, Lago** ◎ W Argentina
23 N10 **Fontana Lake** ▣ North Carolina, SE USA
109 L24 **Fontanarossa** ✈ (Catania) Sicilia, Italy, C Mediterranean Sea *37.28N 15.04E*
9 N11 **Fontas** ≈ British Columbia, W Canada
60 D12 **Fonte Boa** Amazonas, N Brazil *2.31S 66.01W*
104 J10 **Fontenay-le-Comte** Vendée, NW France *46.28N 0.48W*
35 T16 **Fontenelle Reservoir** ▣ Wyoming, C USA
200 Ss12 **Fonualei** *island* Vava'u Group, N Tonga
113 H24 **Fonyód** Somogy, W Hungary *46.43N 17.31E*
Foochow *see* Fuzhou
41 Q10 **Foraker, Mount** ▲ Alaska, USA *62.57N 151.24W*
197 D14 **Forari** Éfaté, C Vanuatu *17.42S 168.33E*
105 U4 **Forbach** Moselle, NE France *49.10N 6.54E*
191 Q8 **Forbes** New South Wales, SE Australia *33.24S 148.00E*
79 T17 **Forcados** Delta, S Nigeria *5.16N 5.25E*
105 S14 **Forcalquier** Alpes-de-Haute-Provence, SE France *43.57N 5.46E*
103 K19 **Forchheim** Bayern, SE Germany *49.43N 11.07E*
176 V14 **Fordate, Pulau** *island* Kepulauan Tanimbar, E Indonesia
37 R13 **Ford City** California, W USA *35.09N 119.27W*
96 D11 **Førde** Sogn og Fjordane, S Norway *61.27N 5.49E*
33 N4 **Ford River** ≈ Michigan, N USA
191 O4 **Fords Bridge** New South Wales, SE Australia *29.44S 145.25E*
22 J6 **Fordsville** Kentucky, S USA *37.36N 86.39W*
29 U13 **Fordyce** Arkansas, C USA *33.49N 92.24W*
78 I14 **Forécariah** Guinée-Maritime, SW Guinea *9.28N 13.06W*
207 O14 **Forel, Mont** ▲ SE Greenland *66.55N 36.45W*
9 R17 **Foremost** Alberta, SW Canada *49.30N 111.34W*
12 D16 **Forest** Ontario, S Canada *43.05N 82.00W*
24 L5 **Forest** Mississippi, S USA *32.22N 89.30W*
33 S12 **Forest** Ohio, N USA *40.47N 83.26W*
31 V11 **Forest City** Iowa, C USA *43.15N 93.38W*
23 Q10 **Forest City** North Carolina, SE USA *35.19N 81.52W*
34 G11 **Forest Grove** Oregon, NW USA *45.31N 123.06W*
191 P17 **Forestier Peninsula** *peninsula* Tasmania, SE Australia
31 V8 **Forest Lake** Minnesota, N USA *45.16N 92.59W*
25 S3 **Forest Park** Georgia, SE USA *33.37N 84.22W*
31 Q3 **Forest River** ≈ North Dakota, N USA
13 T6 **Forestville** Quebec, SE Canada *48.45N 69.04W*
105 Q11 **Forez, Monts du** ▲▲ C France
98 K10 **Forfar** E Scotland, UK *56.37N 2.54W*
28 J8 **Forgan** Oklahoma, C USA *36.54N 100.32W*
Forge du Sud *see* Dudelange
103 J24 **Forggensee** ◎ S Germany
153 N10 **Forish** *Rus.* Farish. Jizzax Viloyati, C Uzbekistan *40.33N 66.52E*
22 F9 **Forked Deer River** ≈ Tennessee, S USA
34 F7 **Forks** Washington, NW USA *47.57N 124.22W*
94 N2 **Forlandsundet** *sound* W Svalbard
108 H10 **Forlì** *anc.* Forum Livii. Emilia-Romagna, N Italy *44.13N 12.01E*
31 Q7 **Forman** North Dakota, N USA *46.07N 97.39W*
99 K17 **Formby** NW England, UK *53.34N 3.04W*
107 V11 **Formentera** *anc.* Ophiusa, *Lat.* Frumentum. *island* Islas Baleares, Spain, W Mediterranean Sea
Formentor, Cabo de *see* Formentor, Cap de
107 Y9 **Formentor, Cap de** *var.* Cabo de Formentor, Cape Formentor. *headland* Mallorca, Spain, W Mediterranean Sea *39.57N 3.12E*
Formentor, Cape *see* Formentor, Cap de
109 J16 **Formia** Lazio, C Italy *41.16N 13.37E*
64 O7 **Formosa** Formosa, NE Argentina *26.07S 58.13W*
64 M6 **Formosa** *off.* Provincia de Formosa. ◈ *province* NE Argentina
Formosa/Formo'sa *see* Taiwan
61 I17 **Formosa, Serra** ▲▲ C Brazil
Formosa Strait *see* Taiwan Strait
97 H15 **Fornebu** ✈ (Oslo) Akershus, S Norway *59.54N 10.37E*
27 U6 **Forney** Texas, SW USA *32.45N 96.28W*
97 H21 **Fornæs** *headland* C Denmark *56.26N 10.57E*
108 E9 **Fornovo di Taro** Emilia-Romagna, C Italy *44.42N 10.07E*
119 T14 **Foros** Respublika Krym, S Ukraine *44.24N 33.47E*
Føroyar *see* Faeroe Islands
98 J8 **Forres** NE Scotland, UK *57.32N 3.37W*
29 X11 **Forrest City** Arkansas, C USA *35.01N 90.48W*
41 Y15 **Forrester Island** *island* Alexander Archipelago, Alaska, USA
27 N7 **Forsan** Texas, SW USA *32.06N 101.22W*
189 V5 **Forsayth** Queensland, NE Australia *18.31S 143.37E*
97 L19 **Forserum** Jönköping, S Sweden *57.42N 14.28E*
97 K15 **Forshaga** Värmland, C Sweden *59.33N 13.28E*
95 L19 **Forssa** Etelä-Suomi, S Finland *60.49N 23.40E*
103 Q14 **Forst** *Lus.* Baršć Łužyca. Brandenburg, E Germany *51.43N 14.38E*
191 U7 **Forster-Tuncurry** New South Wales, SE Australia *32.13S 152.31E*
25 T4 **Forsyth** Georgia, SE USA *33.00N 83.57W*
29 T8 **Forsyth** Missouri, C USA *36.41N 93.07W*
35 W10 **Forsyth** Montana, NW USA *46.16N 106.40W*
155 U11 **Fort Abbās** Punjab, E Pakistan *29.11N 72.54E*
10 G10 **Fort Albany** Ontario, C Canada *52.15N 81.34W*
58 L13 **Fortaleza** Pando, N Bolivia *9.48S 65.28W*
60 P13 **Fortaleza** *prev.* Ceará. *state capital* Ceará, NE Brazil *3.45S 38.34W*
61 D16 **Fortaleza** Rondônia, W Brazil *8.45S 64.06W*
58 C13 **Fortaleza, Río** ≈ W Peru
Fort-Archambault *see* Sarh
23 U3 **Fort Ashby** West Virginia, NE USA *39.30N 78.46W*
98 I9 **Fort Augustus** N Scotland, UK *57.13N 4.37W*
Fort-Bayard *see* Zhanjiang
35 S8 **Fort Benton** Montana, NW USA *47.49N 110.40W*
37 Q1 **Fort Bidwell** California, W USA *41.50N 120.07W*
36 L5 **Fort Bragg** California, W USA *39.25N 123.48W*
33 N16 **Fort Branch** Indiana, N USA *38.15N 87.34W*
Fort-Bretonnet *see* Bousso
35 T17 **Fort Bridger** Wyoming, C USA *41.18N 110.19W*
Fort-Cappolani *see* Tidjikja
Fort Charlet *see* Djanet
Fort-Chimo *see* Kuujjuaq
9 R10 **Fort Chipewyan** Alberta, C Canada *58.42N 111.07W*
Fort Cobb Lake *see* Fort Cobb Reservoir
28 L11 **Fort Cobb Reservoir** *var.* Fort Cobb Lake. ▣ Oklahoma, C USA
39 T3 **Fort Collins** Colorado, C USA *40.35N 105.04W*
12 K12 **Fort-Coulonge** Quebec, SE Canada *45.51N 76.43W*
Fort-Crampel *see* Kaga Bandoro
Fort-Dauphin *see* Tôlañaro
26 K10 **Fort Davis** Texas, SW USA *30.34N 103.55W*
39 O10 **Fort Defiance** Arizona, SW USA *35.44N 109.04W*
47 Q12 **Fort-de-France** *prev.* Fort-Royal. ○ (Martinique) W Martinique *14.36N 61.04W*
47 P12 **Fort-de-France, Baie de** *bay* W Martinique
Fort de Kock *see* Bukittinggi
25 P6 **Fort Deposit** Alabama, S USA *31.58N 86.34W*
31 U13 **Fort Dodge** Iowa, C USA *42.30N 94.10W*
11 S10 **Forteau** Quebec, E Canada *51.30N 56.55W*
108 E11 **Forte dei Marmi** Toscana, C Italy *43.59N 10.10E*
12 H17 **Fort Erie** Ontario, S Canada *42.55N 78.55W*
188 H7 **Fortescue River** ≈ Western Australia
21 S2 **Fort Fairfield** Maine, NE USA *46.45N 67.51W*
Fort-Foureau *see* Kousséri
10 A11 **Fort Frances** Ontario, S Canada *48.37N 93.22W*
Fort Franklin *see* Déljne
25 R7 **Fort Gaines** Georgia, SE USA *31.36N 85.03W*
39 T8 **Fort Garland** Colorado, C USA *37.22N 105.24W*
23 P5 **Fort Gay** West Virginia, NE USA *38.06N 82.35W*
Fort George *see* La Grande Rivière
29 Q10 **Fort Gibson** Oklahoma, C USA *35.48N 95.15W*
29 Q9 **Fort Gibson Lake** ▣ Oklahoma, C USA
15 Gg5 **Fort Good Hope** *var.* Good Hope. Northwest Territories, NW Canada *66.16N 128.37W*
25 V4 **Fort Gordon** Georgia, SE USA *33.25N 82.09W*
Fort Gouraud *see* Fdérik
98 I11 **Forth** ≈ C Scotland, UK
Fort Hall *see* Murang'a
26 H8 **Fort Hancock** Texas, SW USA *31.18N 105.49W*
Fort Hertz *see* Putao
98 K12 **Forth, Firth of** *estuary* E Scotland, UK
12 L14 **Forthton** Ontario, SE Canada *44.43N 75.31W*
12 M8 **Fortier** ≈ Quebec, SE Canada
Fortín General Eugenio Garay *see* General Eugenio A. Garay
Fort Jameson *see* Chipata
Fort Johnston *see* Mangochi
21 R1 **Fort Kent** Maine, NE USA *47.15N 68.33W*
Fort-Lamy *see* Ndjamena
25 Z15 **Fort Lauderdale** Florida, SE USA *26.07N 80.08W*
23 R11 **Fort Lawn** South Carolina, SE USA *34.43N 80.46W*
15 Gg9 **Fort Liard** *var.* Liard. Northwest Territories, W Canada *60.13N 123.28W*
46 M8 **Fort-Liberté** NE Haiti *19.37N 71.51W*
23 N9 **Fort Loudoun Lake** ▣ Tennessee, S USA
39 T3 **Fort Lupton** Colorado, C USA *40.04N 104.48W*
9 R12 **Fort MacKay** Alberta, C Canada *57.12N 111.40W*
9 Q17 **Fort Macleod** *var.* MacLeod. Alberta, SW Canada *49.43N 113.24W*
31 Y16 **Fort Madison** Iowa, C USA *40.37N 91.15W*
Fort Manning *see* Mchinji
27 P9 **Fort McKavett** Texas, SW USA *30.50N 100.07W*
9 R12 **Fort McMurray** Alberta, C Canada *56.43N 111.22W*
14 Ff3 **Fort McPherson** *var.* McPherson. Northwest Territories, NW Canada *67.28N 134.49W*
23 R11 **Fort Mill** South Carolina, SE USA *35.00N 80.57W*
Fort-Millot *see* Ngouri
39 U3 **Fort Morgan** Colorado, C USA *40.13N 103.48W*
25 W14 **Fort Myers** Florida, SE USA *26.39N 81.52W*
25 W15 **Fort Myers Beach** Florida, SE USA *26.27N 81.57W*
8 M10 **Fort Nelson** British Columbia, W Canada *58.48N 122.43W*
8 M10 **Fort Nelson** ≈ British Columbia, W Canada
Fort Norman *see* Tulita.
25 Q2 **Fort Payne** Alabama, S USA *34.23N 85.43W*
35 W7 **Fort Peck** Montana, NW USA *48.00N 106.28W*
35 V8 **Fort Peck Lake** ▣ Montana, NW USA
25 Y13 **Fort Pierce** Florida, SE USA *27.28N 80.19W*
31 N10 **Fort Pierre** South Dakota, N USA *44.21N 100.22W*
83 E18 **Fort Portal** SW Uganda *0.39N 30.16E*
15 Hh8 **Fort Providence** *var.* Providence. Northwest Territories, W Canada *61.21N 117.39W*
9 U16 **Fort Qu'Appelle** Saskatchewan, S Canada *50.49N 103.52W*
Fort-Repoux *see* Akjoujt
15 I8 **Fort Resolution** *var.* Resolution. Northwest Territories, W Canada *61.10N 113.39W*
35 T13 **Fortress Mountain** ▲ Wyoming, C USA *44.20N 109.51W*
Fort Rosebery *see* Mansa

◆ Country ● Country Capital ◇ Dependent Territory ○ Dependent Territory Capital ◈ Administrative Region ✈ International Airport ▲ Mountain ▲▲ Mountain Range Volcano ≈ River ◎ Lake ▣ Reservoir

Fort-Rousset see Owando
Fort-Royal see Fort-de-France
10 I10 **Fort Rupert** prev. Rupert House. Quebec, SE Canada 51.30N 79.45W
14 G12 **Fort St.James** British Columbia, SW Canada 54.25N 124.15W
9 N12 **Fort St.John** British Columbia, W Canada 56.16N 120.51W
Fort Sandeman see Zhob
9 Q14 **Fort Saskatchewan** Alberta, SW Canada 53.42N 113.12W
29 R6 **Fort Scott** Kansas, C USA 37.49N 94.42W
10 E6 **Fort Severn** Ontario, C Canada 56.00N 87.40W
33 R12 **Fort Shawnee** Ohio, N USA 40.41N 84.08W
150 E14 **Fort-Shevchenko** Mangistau, W Kazakhstan 44.28N 50.16E
Fort-Sibut see Sibut
15 H8 **Fort Simpson** var. Simpson. Northwest Territories, W Canada 61.52N 121.22W
15 I9 **Fort Smith** district capital Northwest Territories, W Canada 60.01N 111.55W
29 R10 **Fort Smith** Arkansas, C USA 35.23N 94.24W
39 T13 **Fort Stanton** New Mexico, SW USA 33.28N 105.31W
26 L9 **Fort Stockton** Texas, SW USA 30.54N 102.54W
39 U12 **Fort Sumner** New Mexico, SW USA 34.28N 104.15W
28 K8 **Fort Supply** Oklahoma, C USA 36.34N 99.34W
28 K8 **Fort Supply Lake** ▣ Oklahoma, C USA
31 O10 **Fort Thompson** South Dakota, N USA 44.01N 99.22W
Fort-Trinquet see Bîr Mogreïn
107 R12 **Fortuna** Murcia, SE Spain 38.10N 1.07W
36 K3 **Fortuna** California, W USA 40.35N 124.07W
30 J2 **Fortuna** North Dakota, N USA 48.53N 103.46W
25 T5 **Fort Valley** Georgia, SE USA 32.33N 83.53W
9 P11 **Fort Vermilion** Alberta, W Canada 58.22N 115.58W
Fort Victoria see Masvingo
33 P13 **Fortville** Indiana, N USA 39.55N 85.51W
25 P9 **Fort Walton Beach** Florida, SE USA 30.24N 86.37W
33 P12 **Fort Wayne** Indiana, N USA 41.07N 85.07W
98 H10 **Fort William** N Scotland, UK 56.49N 5.07W
27 T6 **Fort Worth** Texas, SW USA 32.43N 97.19W
30 M7 **Fort Yates** North Dakota, N USA 46.05N 100.37W
41 S7 **Fort Yukon** Alaska, USA 66.35N 145.05W
Forum Alieni see Ferrara
Forum Julii see Fréjus
Forum Livii see Forlì
149 Q15 **Forūr, Jazīreh-ye** island S Iran
96 H7 **Fosen** physical region S Norway
167 N14 **Foshan** var. Fatshan, Fo-shan, Namhoi. Guangdong, S China 23.03N 113.05E
Fossa Claudia see Chioggia
108 B9 **Fossano** Piemonte, NW Italy 44.33N 7.43E
101 H21 **Fosses-la-Ville** Namur, S Belgium 50.24N 4.42E
34 J12 **Fossil** Oregon, NW USA 45.00N 120.15W
Foss Lake see Foss Reservoir
108 I11 **Fossombrone** Marche, C Italy 43.42N 12.48E
28 K10 **Foss Reservoir** var. Foss Lake. ▣ Oklahoma, C USA
31 S4 **Fosston** Minnesota, N USA 47.34N 95.45W
191 O13 **Foster** Victoria, SE Australia 38.40S 146.15E
9 T12 **Foster Lakes** ◎ Saskatchewan, C Canada
33 S12 **Fostoria** Ohio, N USA 41.09N 83.25W
81 D19 **Fougamou** Ngounié, C Gabon 1.15S 10.37E
104 J6 **Fougères** Ille-et-Vilaine, NW France 48.21N 1.12W
Fou-hsin see Fuxin
29 S14 **Fouke** Arkansas, C USA 33.15N 93.53W
98 K2 **Foula** island NE Scotland, UK
67 D24 **Foul Bay** bay East Falkland, Falkland Islands
99 P21 **Foulness Island** island SE England, UK
193 F15 **Foulwind, Cape** headland South Island, NZ 41.45S 171.28E
81 E15 **Foumban** Ouest, NW Cameroon 5.43N 10.49E
180 H13 **Foumbouni** Grande Comore, NW Comoros 11.49S 43.30E
205 N8 **Foundation Ice Stream** glacier Antarctica
39 T6 **Fountain** Colorado, C USA 38.40N 104.42W
38 L4 **Fountain Green** Utah, W USA 39.37N 111.37W
23 P11 **Fountain Inn** South Carolina, SE USA 34.41N 82.12W
29 S11 **Fourche LaFave River** ≈ Arkansas, C USA
35 Z13 **Four Corners** Wyoming, C USA 44.04N 104.08W
105 Q2 **Fourmies** Nord, N France 50.01N 4.03E
40 J17 **Four Mountains, Islands of** island group Aleutian Islands, Alaska, USA
181 P17 **Fournaise, Piton de la** ▲ SE Réunion 21.13S 55.43E
12 J8 **Fournière, Lac** ◎ Quebec, SE Canada
117 L20 **Foúrnoi** island Dodekánisos, Greece, Aegean Sea
66 K13 **Four North Fracture Zone** tectonic feature W Atlantic Ocean
Fouron-Saint-Martin see Sint-Martens-Voeren
32 L3 **Fourteen Mile Point** headland Michigan, N USA 46.59N 89.07W
78 I13 **Fouta Djallon** var. Futa Jallon. ▲▲ W Guinea
193 C25 **Foveaux Strait** strait S NZ
37 Q11 **Fowler** California, W USA 36.35N 119.40W
39 U6 **Fowler** Colorado, C USA 38.07N 104.01W
33 N12 **Fowler** Indiana, N USA 40.36N 87.20W
190 D7 **Fowlers Bay** bay South Australia
27 R13 **Fowlerton** Texas, SW USA 28.27N 98.48W
148 M3 **Fowman** var. Fuman, Fumen. Gīlān, NW Iran 37.15N 49.19E
67 C25 **Fox Bay East** West Falkland, Falkland Islands
67 C25 **Fox Bay West** West Falkland, Falkland Islands
12 J14 **Foxboro** Ontario, SE Canada 44.16N 77.23W
9 O14 **Fox Creek** Alberta, W Canada 54.25N 116.57W
66 G5 **Foxe Basin** sea Nunavut, N Canada
66 G5 **Foxe Channel** channel Nunavut, N Canada
97 I16 **Foxen** ◎ C Sweden
16 N4 **Foxe Peninsula** peninsula Baffin Island, Nunavut, NE Canada
193 E19 **Fox Glacier** West Coast, South Island, NZ 43.28S 170.00E
40 L17 **Fox Islands** island Aleutian Islands, Alaska, USA
32 M10 **Fox Lake** Illinois, N USA 42.24N 88.10W
9 V12 **Fox Mine** Manitoba, C Canada 56.36N 101.48W
37 R3 **Fox Mountain** ▲ Nevada, W USA 41.01N 119.30W
67 E25 **Fox Point** headland East Falkland, Falkland Islands 51.55S 58.24W
32 M11 **Fox River** ≈ Illinois/Wisconsin, N USA
32 L7 **Fox River** ≈ Wisconsin, N USA
192 L13 **Foxton** Manawatu-Wanganui, North Island, NZ 40.30S 175.17E
9 S16 **Fox Valley** Saskatchewan, S Canada 50.28N 109.28W
9 W16 **Foxwarren** Manitoba, S Canada 50.30N 101.09W
99 E14 **Foyle, Lough** Ir. Loch Feabhail. inlet N Ireland
204 H5 **Foyn Coast** physical region Antarctica
106 I2 **Foz** Galicia, NW Spain 43.33N 7.16W
62 I12 **Foz do Areia, Represa de** ▣ S Brazil
61 A16 **Foz do Breu** Acre, W Brazil 9.21S 72.40W
85 A16 **Foz do Cunene** Namibe, SW Angola 17.11S 11.52E
62 G12 **Foz do Iguaçu** Paraná, S Brazil 25.33S 54.31W
60 C12 **Foz do Mamoriá** Amazonas, NW Brazil 2.28S 66.06W
107 T6 **Fraga** Aragón, NE Spain 41.31N 0.21E
46 F5 **Fragoso, Cayo** island C Cuba
63 G18 **Fraile Muerto** Cerro Largo, NE Uruguay 32.30S 54.30W
101 H21 **Fraire** Namur, S Belgium 50.16N 4.30E
101 L21 **Fraiture, Baraque de** hill SE Belgium 50.22N 5.50E
Frakštát see Hlohovec
207 S10 **Fram Basin** var. Amundsen Basin. undersea feature Arctic Ocean
101 F20 **Frameries** Hainaut, S Belgium 50.25N 3.40E
21 O11 **Framingham** Massachusetts, NE USA 42.15N 71.24W
62 L7 **Franca** São Paulo, S Brazil 20.33S 47.27W
197 G4 **Français, Récif des** reef W New Caledonia
109 K14 **Francavilla al Mare** Abruzzo, C Italy 42.25N 14.16E
109 P18 **Francavilla Fontana** Puglia, SE Italy 40.31N 17.34E
104 M8 **France** off. French Republic, It./Sp. Francia; prev. Gaul, Gaule, Lat. Gallia. ◆ republic W Europe
47 O8 **Francés Viejo, Cabo** headland NE Dominican Republic 19.39N 69.57W
81 F19 **Franceville** var. Massoukou, Masuku. Haut-Ogooué, E Gabon 1.40S 13.31E
81 F19 **Franceville** ✕ Haut-Ogooué, E Gabon 1.38S 13.24E
Francfort see Frankfurt am Main
105 T8 **Franche-Comté** ◈ region E France
Francia see France
31 O11 **Francis Case, Lake** ▣ South Dakota, N USA
62 H12 **Francisco Beltrão** Paraná, S Brazil 26.04S 53.04W
Francisco I. Madero see Villa Madero
63 A21 **Francisco Madero** Buenos Aires, E Argentina 35.52S 62.03W
44 H6 **Francisco Morazán** prev. Tegucigalpa. ◈ department C Honduras
85 J18 **Francistown** North East, NE Botswana 21.08S 27.31E
Franconian Forest see Frankenwald
Franconian Jura see Fränkische Alb
100 K6 **Franeker** Fris. Frjentsjer. Friesland, N Netherlands 53.10N 5.33E
Frankenalb see Fränkische Alb
103 H16 **Frankenberg** Hessen, C Germany 51.04N 8.49E
103 J20 **Frankenhöhe** hill range C Germany
33 R8 **Frankenmuth** Michigan, N USA 43.19N 83.44W
103 F20 **Frankenstein** hill W Germany 49.24N 8.04E
Frankenstein/Frankenstein in Schlesien see Ząbkowice Śląskie
103 G20 **Frankenthal** Rheinland-Pfalz, W Germany 49.33N 8.21E
103 L18 **Frankenwald** Eng. Franconian Forest. ▲▲ C Germany
46 J12 **Frankfield** C Jamaica 18.07N 77.22W
12 J14 **Frankford** Ontario, SE Canada 44.12N 77.36W
33 O13 **Frankfort** Indiana, N USA 40.16N 86.30W
29 O3 **Frankfort** Kansas, C USA 39.42N 96.25W
22 L5 **Frankfort** state capital Kentucky, S USA 38.12N 84.52W
Frankfort on the Main see Frankfurt am Main
Frankfurt see Słubice, Poland
Frankfurt see Frankfurt am Main, Germany
103 G18 **Frankfurt am Main** var. Frankfurt, Fr. Francfort; prev. Eng. Frankfort on the Main. Hessen, SW Germany 50.07N 8.40E
102 Q12 **Frankfurt an der Oder** Brandenburg, E Germany 52.19N 14.31E
103 L21 **Fränkische Alb** var. Frankenalb, Eng. Franconian Jura. ▲▲ S Germany
103 I18 **Fränkische Saale** ≈ C Germany
103 L19 **Fränkische Schweiz** hill range C Germany
25 R4 **Franklin** Georgia, SE USA 33.15N 85.06W
33 P14 **Franklin** Indiana, N USA 39.28N 86.01W
22 J7 **Franklin** Kentucky, S USA 36.43N 86.34W
24 I9 **Franklin** Louisiana, S USA 29.48N 91.30W
31 O17 **Franklin** Nebraska, C USA 40.06N 98.57W
23 N10 **Franklin** North Carolina, SE USA 35.07N 83.22W
20 C13 **Franklin** Pennsylvania, NE USA 41.24N 79.49W
22 J9 **Franklin** Tennessee, S USA 35.55N 86.52W
27 U9 **Franklin** Texas, SW USA 31.01N 96.29W
23 X7 **Franklin** Virginia, NE USA 36.40N 76.55W
23 T4 **Franklin** West Virginia, NE USA 38.39N 79.19W
32 M9 **Franklin** Wisconsin, N USA 42.53N 88.00W
15 H2 **Franklin Bay** inlet Northwest Territories, N Canada
34 K7 **Franklin D.Roosevelt Lake** ▣ Washington, NW USA
37 W4 **Franklin Lake** ◎ Nevada, W USA
193 B22 **Franklin Mountains** ▲▲ South Island, NZ
41 R5 **Franklin Mountains** ▲▲ Alaska, USA
41 N4 **Franklin, Point** headland Alaska, USA 70.54N 158.48W
191 O17 **Franklin River** ≈ Tasmania, SE Australia
15 K2 **Franklin Strait** strait Nunavut, N Canada
24 K8 **Franklinton** Louisiana, S USA 30.51N 90.09W
23 U9 **Franklinton** North Carolina, SE USA 36.06N 78.27W
Frankstadt see Frenštát pod Radhoštěm
27 V7 **Frankston** Texas, SW USA 32.03N 95.30W
35 U12 **Frannie** Wyoming, C USA 44.57N 108.37W
13 U5 **Franquelin** Quebec, SE Canada 49.17N 67.52W
13 U5 **Franquelin** ≈ Quebec, SE Canada
85 C18 **Fransfontein** Kunene, NW Namibia 20.10S 15.03E
95 H17 **Fränsta** Västernorrland, C Sweden 62.30N 16.06E
126 H1 **Frantsa-Iosifa, Zemlya** Eng. Franz Josef Land. island group N Russian Federation
193 E18 **Franz Josef Glacier** West Coast, South Island, NZ 43.22S 170.11E
Franz Josef Land see Frantsa-Iosifa, Zemlya
Franz-Josef Spitze see Gerlachovský štít
103 L23 **Franz Josef Strauss** abbrev. F.J.S. ✕ (München) Bayern, SE Germany 48.07N 11.43E
109 A19 **Frasca, Capo della** headland Sardegna, Italy, C Mediterranean Sea 39.46N 8.27E
109 I15 **Frascati** Lazio, C Italy 41.48N 12.40E
9 N14 **Fraser** ≈ British Columbia, SW Canada
85 G24 **Fraserburg** Western Cape, SW South Africa 31.49S 21.29E
98 L8 **Fraserburgh** NE Scotland, UK 57.41N 2.19W
189 Z9 **Fraser Island** var. Great Sandy Island. island Queensland, E Australia
8 L14 **Fraser Lake** British Columbia, SW Canada 54.00N 124.45W
8 L15 **Fraser Plateau** plateau British Columbia, SW Canada
192 P10 **Frasertown** Hawke's Bay, North Island, NZ 38.58S 177.25E
101 E19 **Frasnes-lez-Buissenal** Hainaut, SW Belgium 50.40N 3.37E
110 I7 **Frastanz** Vorarlberg, NW Austria 47.13N 9.37E
12 B8 **Frater** Ontario, S Canada 47.19N 84.28W
Frauenbach see Baia Mare
Frauenburg see Saldus, Latvia
Frauenburg see Frombork, Poland
110 H6 **Frauenfeld** Thurgau, NE Switzerland 47.34N 8.54E
111 Z5 **Frauenkirchen** Burgenland, E Austria 47.49N 16.57E
63 D19 **Fray Bentos** Río Negro, W Uruguay 33.09S 58.14W
63 F19 **Fray Marcos** Florida, S Uruguay 34.13S 55.43W
31 S6 **Frazee** Minnesota, N USA 46.42N 95.40W
106 M5 **Frechilla** Castilla-León, N Spain 42.07N 4.49W
32 I4 **Frederic** Wisconsin, N USA 45.42N 92.30W
97 G23 **Fredericia** Vejle, C Denmark 55.34N 9.46E
23 W3 **Frederick** Maryland, NE USA 39.24N 77.24W
28 L12 **Frederick** Oklahoma, C USA 34.23N 99.01W
31 P7 **Frederick** South Dakota, N USA 45.49N 98.31W
31 X12 **Fredericksburg** Iowa, C USA 42.58N 92.12W
27 R10 **Fredericksburg** Texas, SW USA 30.16N 98.52W
23 W5 **Fredericksburg** Virginia, NE USA 38.16N 77.27W
41 X13 **Frederick Sound** sound Alaska, USA
29 X6 **Fredericktown** Missouri, C USA 37.33N 90.17W
62 H13 **Frederico Westphalen** Rio Grande do Sul, S Brazil 27.22S 53.20W
11 O15 **Fredericton** New Brunswick, SE Canada 45.57N 66.40W
97 I22 **Frederiksborg** off. Frederiksborgs Amt. ◈ county E Denmark
Frederikshåb see Paamiut
97 H19 **Frederikshavn** prev. Fladstrand. Nordjylland, N Denmark 57.28N 10.33E
97 J22 **Frederikssund** Frederiksborg, E Denmark 55.51N 12.04E
47 T9 **Frederiksted** Saint Croix, S Virgin Islands (US) 17.41N 64.51W
97 I22 **Frederiksværk** var. Frederiksværk og Hanehoved. Frederiksborg, E Denmark 55.58N 12.01E
Frederiksværk og Hanehoved see Frederiksværk
56 E9 **Fredonia** Antioquia, W Colombia 5.57N 75.42W
38 K8 **Fredonia** Arizona, SW USA 36.57N 112.31W
29 P7 **Fredonia** Kansas, C USA 37.31N 95.49W
20 C11 **Fredonia** New York, NE USA 42.26N 79.19W
37 P4 **Fredonyer Pass** pass California, W USA 40.21N 120.52W
95 I15 **Fredrika** Västerbotten, N Sweden 64.03N 18.25E
97 L14 **Fredriksberg** Dalarna, C Sweden 60.07N 14.22E
Fredrikshald see Halden
Fredrikshamn see Hamina
97 H16 **Fredrikstad** Østfold, S Norway 59.12N 10.57E
32 K16 **Freeburg** Illinois, N USA 38.25N 89.54W
20 K15 **Freehold** New Jersey, NE USA 40.14N 74.14W
20 H14 **Freeland** Pennsylvania, NE USA 41.01N 75.54W
190 J5 **Freeling Heights** ▲ South Australia 30.09S 139.24E
37 Q7 **Freel Peak** ▲ California, W USA 38.52N 119.52W
16 T7 **Freels, Cape** headland Newfoundland and Labrador, E Canada 49.16N 53.30W
31 Q11 **Freeman** South Dakota, N USA 43.21N 97.26W
46 G1 **Freeport** Grand Bahama Island, N Bahamas 26.28N 78.43W
32 L10 **Freeport** Illinois, N USA 42.18N 89.37W
27 W12 **Freeport** Texas, SW USA 28.57N 95.21W
46 G1 **Freeport** ✕ Grand Bahama Island, N Bahamas 26.31N 78.48W
27 R14 **Freer** Texas, SW USA 27.52N 98.37W
85 I22 **Free State** off. Free State Province; prev. Orange Free State, Afr. Oranje Vrystaat. ◈ province C South Africa
Free State see Maryland
78 G15 **Freetown** ● (Sierra Leone) W Sierra Leone 8.27N 13.16W
180 J16 **Frégate** island Inner Islands, NE Seychelles
106 J12 **Fregenal de la Sierra** Extremadura, W Spain 38.10N 6.39W
190 C2 **Fregon** South Australia 26.44S 132.03E
104 H5 **Fréhel, Cap** headland NW France 48.41N 2.21W
96 F8 **Frei** Møre og Romsdal, S Norway 63.02N 7.47E
103 O16 **Freiberg** Sachsen, E Germany 50.55N 13.21E
103 O16 **Freiberger Mulde** ≈ E Germany
Freiburg see Fribourg, Switzerland
Freiburg see Freiburg im Breisgau, Germany
103 F23 **Freiburg im Breisgau** var. Freiburg, Fr. Fribourg-en-Brisgau. Baden-Württemberg, SW Germany 48.00N 7.52E
Freiburg in Schlesien see Świebodzice
Freie Hansestadt Bremen see Bremen
Freie und Hansestadt Hamburg see Brandenburg
103 L22 **Freising** Bayern, SE Germany 48.24N 11.45E
111 T3 **Freistadt** Oberösterreich, N Austria 48.30N 14.27E
Freistadtl see Hlohovec
103 O16 **Freital** Sachsen, E Germany 51.00N 13.40E
Freiwaldau see Jeseník
106 J6 **Freixo de Espada à Cinta** Bragança, N Portugal 41.04N 6.49W
105 U15 **Fréjus** anc. Forum Julii. Var, SE France 43.25N 6.43E
188 I13 **Fremantle** Western Australia 32.07S 115.43E
37 N9 **Fremont** California, W USA 37.32N 121.56W
33 Q11 **Fremont** Indiana, N USA 41.43N 84.54W
31 W15 **Fremont** Iowa, C USA 41.12N 92.26W
33 P8 **Fremont** Michigan, N USA 43.28N 85.56W
31 R15 **Fremont** Nebraska, C USA 41.25N 96.30W
33 S11 **Fremont** Ohio, N USA 41.21N 83.07W
35 T14 **Fremont Peak** ▲ Wyoming, C USA 43.07N 109.37W
38 M6 **Fremont River** ≈ Utah, W USA
23 O9 **French Broad River** ≈ Tennessee, S USA
23 N5 **Frenchburg** Kentucky, S USA 37.57N 83.41W
20 C12 **French Creek** ≈ Pennsylvania, NE USA
34 K15 **Frenchglen** Oregon, NW USA 42.49N 118.55W
57 Y10 **French Guiana** var. Guiana, Guyane. ◇ French overseas department N South America
French Guinea see Guinea
33 O15 **French Lick** Indiana, N USA 38.33N 86.37W
193 J14 **French Pass** Marlborough, South Island, NZ 40.57S 173.49E
203 T11 **French Polynesia** ◇ French overseas territory C Polynesia
French Republic see France
12 F11 **French River** ≈ Ontario, S Canada
French Somaliland see Djibouti
181 P12 **French Southern and Antarctic Territories** Fr. Terres Australes et Antarctiques Françaises. ◇ French overseas territory S Indian Ocean
French Sudan see Mali
French Territory of the Afars and Issas see Djibouti
French Togoland see Togo
76 J6 **Frenda** NW Algeria 35.06N 1.03E
113 I18 **Frenštát pod Radhoštěm** Ger. Frankstadt. Ostravský Kraj E Czech Republic 49.33N 18.10E
78 M17 **Fresco** S Ivory Coast 5.05N 5.34W
205 U16 **Freshfield, Cape** headland Antarctica
42 L10 **Fresnillo** var. Fresnillo de González Echeverría. Zacatecas, C Mexico 23.10N 102.52W
Fresnillo de González Echeverría see Fresnillo
37 Q10 **Fresno** California, W USA 36.44N 119.48W
Freu, Cabo del see Freu, Cap des
107 Y9 **Freu, Cap des** var. Cabo del Freu. headland Mallorca, Spain, W Mediterranean Sea 39.44N 3.28E
103 G22 **Freudenstadt** Baden-Württemberg, SW Germany 48.28N 8.25E
Freudenthal see Bruntál
191 Q17 **Freycinet Peninsula** peninsula Tasmania, SE Australia
78 H14 **Fria** Guinée-Maritime, W Guinea 10.27N 13.37W
85 A17 **Fria, Cape** headland NW Namibia 18.32S 12.00E
37 Q10 **Friant** California, W USA 36.56N 119.44W
64 K8 **Frías** Catamarca , N Argentina 28.40S 65.00W
110 D9 **Fribourg** Ger. Freiburg. Fribourg, W Switzerland 46.49N 7.10E
110 C9 **Fribourg** Ger. Freiburg. ◈ canton W Switzerland
Fribourg-en-Brisgau see Freiburg im Breisgau
34 G7 **Friday Harbor** San Juan Islands, Washington, NW USA 48.31N 123.01W
194 F11 **Frieda** ≈ NW PNG
Friedau see Ormož
103 K23 **Friedberg** Bayern, S Germany 48.21N 10.58E
103 H18 **Friedberg** Hessen, W Germany 50.19N 8.46E
Friedeberg Neumark see Strzelce Krajeńskie
Friedek-Mistek see Frýdek-Místek
Friedland see Pravdinsk
103 I24 **Friedrichshafen** Baden-Württemberg, S Germany 47.39N 9.28E
Friedrichstadt see Jaunjelgava
31 Q16 **Friend** Nebraska, C USA 40.37N 97.16W
Friendly Islands see Tonga
57 V9 **Friendship** Coronie, N Suriname 5.49N 56.16W
32 L7 **Friendship** Wisconsin, N USA 43.58N 89.48W
111 T8 **Friesach** Kärnten, S Austria 46.58N 14.24E
Friesche Eilanden see Frisian Islands
103 F22 **Friesenheim** Baden-Württemberg, SW Germany 48.27N 7.56E
Friesische Inseln see Frisian Islands
100 K6 **Friesland** ◈ province N Netherlands
62 Q10 **Frio, Cabo** headland SE Brazil 23.01S 41.59W
26 M3 **Friona** Texas, SW USA 34.38N 102.43W
44 L12 **Frío, Río** ≈ N Costa Rica
27 R13 **Frio River** ≈ Texas, SW USA
101 M25 **Frisange** Luxembourg, S Luxembourg 49.31N 6.12E
Frisches Haff see Vistula Lagoon
38 J6 **Frisco Peak** ▲ Utah, W USA 38.31N 113.17W
86 F9 **Frisian Islands** Dut. Friesche Eilanden, Ger. Friesische Inseln. island group N Europe
20 L12 **Frissell, Mount** ▲ Connecticut, NE USA 42.01N 73.25W
97 J19 **Fristad** Västra Götaland, S Sweden 57.49N 13.01E
27 N2 **Fritch** Texas, SW USA 35.38N 101.36W
97 J19 **Fritsla** Västra Götaland, S Sweden 57.33N 12.46E
103 H16 **Fritzlar** Hessen, C Germany 51.09N 9.16E
108 H6 **Friuli-Venezia Giulia** ◈ region NE Italy
Frjentsjer see Franeker
206 L13 **Frobisher Bay** inlet Baffin Island, Nunavut, NE Canada
Frobisher Bay see Iqaluit
9 S12 **Frobisher Lake** ◎ Saskatchewan, C Canada
96 G7 **Frohavet** sound C Norway
Frohenbruck see Veselí nad Lužnicí
111 V7 **Frohnleiten** Steiermark, SE Austria 47.16N 15.19E
101 G22 **Froidchapelle** Hainaut, S Belgium 50.10N 4.18E
131 O9 **Frolovo** Volgogradskaya Oblast', SW Russian Federation 49.46N 43.38E
112 K7 **Frombork** Ger. Frauenburg. Warmińsko-Mazurskie, NE Poland 54.21N 19.40E
99 L22 **Frome** SW England, UK 51.15N 2.21W
190 I4 **Frome Creek** seasonal river South Australia
190 J6 **Frome Downs** South Australia 31.17S 139.48E
190 J5 **Frome, Lake** salt lake South Australia
Fronicken see Wronki
106 H10 **Fronteira** Portalegre, C Portugal 39.03N 7.39W
42 M7 **Frontera** Coahuila de Zaragoza, NE Mexico 26.55N 101.27W
43 U14 **Frontera** Tabasco, SE Mexico 18.32N 92.35W
42 G3 **Fronteras** Sonora, NW Mexico 30.51N 109.36W
105 Q16 **Frontignan** Hérault, S France 43.27N 3.45E
56 D8 **Frontino** Antioquia, NW Colombia 6.46N 76.10W
23 V4 **Front Royal** Virginia, NE USA 38.52N 78.09W
109 J16 **Frosinone** anc. Frusino. Lazio, C Italy 41.37N 13.19E
109 K16 **Frosolone** Molise, C Italy 41.34N 14.25E
27 U7 **Frost** Texas, SW USA 32.04N 96.48W
23 U2 **Frostburg** Maryland, NE USA 39.39N 78.55W
25 X13 **Frostproof** Florida, SE USA 27.45N 81.31W
Frostviken see Kvarnbergsvattnet
97 M15 **Frövi** Örebro, C Sweden 59.28N 15.24E
96 F7 **Frøya** island W Norway
39 P5 **Fruita** Colorado, C USA 39.10N 108.42W
30 J9 **Fruitdale** South Dakota, N USA 44.39N 103.38W
25 W11 **Fruitland Park** Florida, SE USA 28.51N 81.54W
Frumentum see Formentera
153 S11 **Frunze** Oshskaya Oblast', SW Kyrgyzstan 40.07N 71.40E
Frunze see Bishkek
119 O9 **Frunzivka** Odes'ka Oblast', SW Ukraine 47.19N 29.46E
Frusino see Frosinone
110 E9 **Frutigen** Bern, W Switzerland 46.35N 7.38E
113 I17 **Frýdek-Místek** Ger. Friedek-Mistek. Ostravský Kraj, E Czech Republic 49.40N 18.22E
200 Qq16 **Fua'amotu** Tongatapu, S Tonga 21.15S 175.08W
202 A9 **Fuafatu** island Funafuti Atoll, C Tuvalu
202 A9 **Fuagea** island Funafuti Atoll, C Tuvalu
202 B8 **Fualifeke** atoll C Tuvalu
202 A8 **Fualopa** island Funafuti Atoll, C Tuvalu
157 K22 **Fuammulah** var. Gnaviyani Atoll. atoll S Maldives
167 R11 **Fu'an** Fujian, SE China 27.11N 119.42E
Fu-chien see Fujian
Fu-chou see Fuzhou
170 F13 **Fuchū** var. Hutyû. Hiroshima, Honshū, SW Japan 34.33N 133.16E
166 M13 **Fuchuan** Guangxi Zhuangzu Zizhiqu, S China 24.56N 111.15E
172 N11 **Fudai** Iwate, Honshū, C Japan 39.59N 141.50E
167 S11 **Fuding** Fujian, SE China 27.21N 120.10E
83 J20 **Fudua** spring/well S Kenya 2.13S 39.43E
106 M16 **Fuengirola** Andalucía, S Spain 36.31N 4.37W
106 J12 **Fuente de Cantos** Extremadura, W Spain 38.15N 6.18W
106 J11 **Fuente del Maestre** Extremadura, W Spain 38.31N 6.26W
106 L12 **Fuente Obejuna** Andalucía, S Spain 38.15N 5.25W
106 L6 **Fuentesaúco** Castilla-León, N Spain 41.13N 5.30W
64 O3 **Fuerte Olimpo** var. Olimpo. Alto Paraguay, NE Paraguay 21.01S 57.51W
42 H8 **Fuerte, Río** ≈ C Mexico
66 Q11 **Fuerteventura** island Islas Canarias, Spain, NE Atlantic Ocean
147 S14 **Fughmah** var. Faghman, Fugma. C Yemen 16.07N 49.22E
94 M2 **Fuglehuken** headland W Svalbard 78.54N 10.30E
97 B18 **Fugloy** Dan. Fuglø Island Faeroe Islands 62.21N 6.16W
207 T15 **Fugløya Bank** undersea feature E Norwegian Sea
166 E11 **Fugong** Yunnan, SW China 27.00N 98.48E
Fugma see Fughmah
83 K16 **Fugugo** spring/well NE Kenya 3.19N 39.39E
164 L2 **Fuhai** var. Burultokay. Xinjiang Uygur Zizhiqu, NW China 47.15N 87.39E
167 P10 **Fu He** ≈ S China
Fuhkien see Fujian
102 J9 **Fuhlsbüttel** ✕ (Hamburg) Hamburg, N Germany 53.37N 9.57E
103 L14 **Fuhne** ≈ C Germany
Fu-hsin see Fuxin
Fujairah see Al Fujayrah
171 J17 **Fuji** var. Huzi. Shizuoka, Honshū, S Japan 35.08N 138.39E
167 Q12 **Fujian** var. Fu-chien, Fuhkien, Fujian Sheng, Fukien, Min. ◈ province SE China
166 I9 **Fu Jiang** ≈ C China
Fujian Sheng see Fujian
171 I17 **Fujieda** var. Huzieda. Shizuoka, Honshū, S Japan 34.54N 138.15E
Fuji, Mount/Fujiyama see Fuji-san
169 Y7 **Fujin** Heilongjiang, NE China 47.12N 132.01E
171 J16 **Fujinomiya** var. Huzinomiya. Shizuoka, Honshū, S Japan 35.19N 138.34E
171 J16 **Fuji-san** var. Fujiyama, Eng. Mount Fuji. ▲ Honshū, SE Japan 35.23N 138.44E
171 Jj17 **Fujisawa** var. Huzisawa. Kanagawa, Honshū, S Japan 35.22N 139.28E
171 J16 **Fuji-Yoshida** var. Huziyosida. Yamanashi, Honshū, S Japan 35.30N 138.48E
172 Oo4 **Fukagawa** var. Hukagawa. Hokkaidō, NE Japan 43.44N 142.01E
164 L5 **Fukang** Xinjiang Uygur Zizhiqu, W China 44.07N 87.55E
171 M8 **Fukaura** Aomori, Honshū, C Japan 40.38N 139.55E
200 R15 **Fukave** island Tongatapu Group, S Tonga
Fukien see Fujian
171 Gg14 **Fukuchiyama** var. Hukutiyama. Kyōto, Honshū, SW Japan 35.16N 135.07E
170 B12 **Fukue** var. Hukue. Nagasaki, Fukue-jima, SW Japan 32.40N 128.46E
170 B12 **Fukue-jima** island Gotō-rettō, SW Japan
171 Hh13 **Fukui** var. Hukui. Fukui, Honshū, SW Japan 36.03N 136.12E
171 Hh14 **Fukui** off. Fukui-ken, var. Hukui. ◈ prefecture Honshū, SW Japan
170 C12 **Fukuoka** var. Hukuoka; hist. Najima. Fukuoka, Kyūshū, SW Japan 33.36N 130.24E
170 Cc13 **Fukuoka** off. Fukuoka-ken, var. Hukuoka. ◈ prefecture Kyūshū, SW Japan
171 L13 **Fukushima** var. Hukusima. Fukushima, Honshū, C Japan 37.46N 140.27E
171 Mm7 **Fukushima** Hokkaidō, NE Japan 41.27N 140.14E
171 Kk14 **Fukushima** off. Fukushima-ken, var. Hukusima. ◈ prefecture Honshū, C Japan
170 F14 **Fukuyama** var. Hukuyama. Hiroshima, Honshū, SW Japan 34.28N 133.23E
78 G13 **Fulacunda** C Guinea-Bissau 11.46N 15.09W
133 P8 **Fūlādī, Kūh-e** ▲ E Afghanistan 34.37N 67.31E
197 K16 **Fulaga** island Lau Group, E Fiji
103 I17 **Fulda** Hessen, C Germany 50.33N 9.40E
31 S10 **Fulda** Minnesota, N USA 43.52N 95.36W
103 I16 **Fulda** ≈ C Germany
Fülek see Fil'akovo
Fulin see Hanyuan
166 K10 **Fuling** Chongqing Shi, C China 29.45N 107.23E
37 T15 **Fullerton** California, SE USA 33.52N 117.55W
31 P15 **Fullerton** Nebraska, C USA 41.21N 97.58W
110 M8 **Fulpmes** Tirol, W Austria 47.11N 11.22E
22 G8 **Fulton** Kentucky, S USA 36.31N 88.52W
25 N2 **Fulton** Mississippi, S USA 34.16N 88.24W
29 V4 **Fulton** Missouri, C USA 38.51N 91.57W
20 H9 **Fulton** New York, NE USA 43.18N 76.22W
Fuman/Fumen see Fowman
105 R3 **Fumay** Ardennes, N France 49.58N 4.42E
104 M13 **Fumel** Lot-et-Garonne, SW France 44.31N 0.58E
171 K17 **Funabashi** var. Hunabasi. Chiba, Honshū, S Japan 35.40N 139.57E
202 B10 **Funafara** atoll C Tuvalu
202 C9 **Funafuti** ✕ Funafuti Atoll, C Tuvalu 8.30S 179.12E
Funafuti see Fongafale
202 F8 **Funafuti Atoll** atoll C Tuvalu
202 B9 **Funangongo** atoll C Tuvalu
95 F17 **Funäsdalen** Jämtland, C Sweden 62.33N 12.33E
66 O6 **Funchal** Madeira, Portugal, NE Atlantic Ocean 32.40N 16.55W
66 P5 **Funchal** ✕ Madeira, Portugal, NE Atlantic Ocean 32.37N 16.52W
56 F5 **Fundación** Magdalena, N Colombia 10.28N 74.10W
106 I8 **Fundão** var. Fundão. Castelo Branco, C Portugal 40.07N 7.30W
11 O16 **Fundy, Bay of** bay Canada/USA
Fünen see Fyn
56 C13 **Fúnes** Nariño, SW Colombia 0.58N 77.27W
Fünfkirchen see Pécs
85 M19 **Funhalouro** Inhambane, S Mozambique 23.04S 34.24E
167 R6 **Funing** Jiangsu, E China 33.43N 119.47E
166 I14 **Funing** Yunnan, SW China 23.39N 105.41E
166 M7 **Funiu Shan** ▲▲ C China
79 U13 **Funtua** Katsina, N Nigeria 11.31N 7.19E
167 R12 **Fuqing** Fujian, SE China 25.40N 119.23E
85 M14 **Furancungo** Tete, NW Mozambique 14.49S 33.32E
172 P5 **Furano** var. Hurano. Hokkaidō, NE Japan 43.22N 142.25E
118 I15 **Furculeşti** Teleorman, S Romania 43.51N 25.07E
Füred see Balatonfüred
172 Qq7 **Füren-ko** ◎ Hokkaidō, NE Japan
149 R12 **Fürg** Fārs, S Iran 28.16N 55.13E
Furluk see Fârliug
Fürmanov/Furmanovka see Moyynkum
Furmanovo see Zhalpaktal
61 L20 **Furnas, Represa de** ▣ SE Brazil
191 Q14 **Furneaux Group** island group Tasmania, SE Australia
Furnes see Veurne
166 J10 **Furong Jiang** ≈ S China
144 I5 **Furqlus** Ḥimṣ, W Syria 34.40N 37.02E
102 F12 **Fürstenau** Niedersachsen, NW Germany 52.30N 7.40E
111 X8 **Fürstenfeld** Steiermark, SE Austria 47.03N 16.01E
103 L23 **Fürstenfeldbruck** Bayern, S Germany 48.10N 11.16E
102 P12 **Fürstenwalde** Brandenburg, NE Germany 52.22N 14.04E

◆ Country ● Country Capital ◇ Dependent Territory ○ Dependent Territory Capital ◈ Administrative Region ✕ International Airport ▲ Mountain ▲▲ Mountain Range Volcano ≈ River ◎ Lake ▣ Reservoir

103 *K20* **Fürth** Bayern, S Germany *49.28N 10.58E*
111 *W3* **Furth bei Göttweig** Niederösterreich, NW Austria *48.22N 15.33E*
172 *O4* **Furubira** Hokkaidō, NE Japan *43.14N 140.38E*
96 *L12* **Furudal** Dalarna, C Sweden *61.10N 15.07E*
171 *Ii14* **Furukawa** Gifu, Honshū, SW Japan *36.13N 137.11E*
171 *M12* **Furukawa** *var.* Hurukawa. Miyagi, Honshū, C Japan *38.36N 140.56E*
56 *F10* **Fusagasugá** Cundinamarca, C Colombia *4.22N 74.21W*
Fusan *see* Pusan
Fushë-Arëzi/Fushë-Arrësi *see* Fushë-Arrëz
115 *L18* **Fushë-Arrëz** *var.* Fushë-Arëzi, Fushë-Arrësi. Shkodër, N Albania *42.05N 20.01E*
Fushë-Kruja *see* Fushë-Krujë
115 *K19* **Fushë-Krujë** *var.* Fushë-Kruja. Durrës, C Albania *41.30N 19.43E*
169 *V12* **Fushun** *var.* Fou-shan, Fu-shun. Liaoning, NE China *41.49N 123.54E*
Fusin *see* Fuxin
110 *G10* **Fusio** Ticino, S Switzerland *46.27N 8.39E*
169 *X11* **Fusong** Jilin, NE China *42.19N 127.16E*
103 *K24* **Füssen** Bayern, S Germany *47.34N 10.42E*
166 *K15* **Fusui** *prev.* Funan. Guangxi Zhuangzu Zizhiqu, S China *22.39N 107.49E*
Futa Jallon *see* Fouta Djallon
65 *G18* **Futaleufú** Los Lagos, S Chile *43.12S 71.53W*
114 *K10* **Futog** Serbia, NW Serbia and Montenegro (Yugoslavia) *45.15N 19.43E*
171 *K17* **Futtsu** *var.* Huttu. Chiba, Honshū, S Japan *35.11N 139.52E*
197 *E16* **Futuna** *island* S Vanuatu
202 *D12* **Futuna, Île** *island* S Wallis and Futuna
167 *Q11* **Futun Xi** ≈ SE China
166 *L5* **Fuxian** *var.* Fu Xian. Shaanxi, C China *36.03N 109.19E*
Fuxian *see* Wafangdian
166 *G13* **Fuxian Hu** ⊠ SW China
169 *U12* **Fuxin** *var.* Fou-hsin, Fu-hsin, Fusin. Liaoning, NE China *41.59N 121.39E*
Fuxing *see* Wangmo
167 *P7* **Fuyang** Anhui, E China *32.54N 115.47E*
167 *O4* **Fuyang He** ≈ E China
169 *U7* **Fuyu** Heilongjiang, NE China *47.48N 124.25E*
Fuyu/Fu-yü *see* Songyuan
169 *Z6* **Fuyuan** Heilongjiang, NE China *48.20N 134.22E*
164 *M3* **Fuyun** *var.* Koktokay. Xinjiang Uygur Zizhiqu, NW China *46.57N 89.29E*
113 *L22* **Füzesabony** Heves, E Hungary *47.44N 20.23E*
167 *R12* **Fuzhou** *var.* Foochow, Fu-chou. Fujian, SE China *26.09N 119.16E*
Fuzhou *see* Linchuan
143 *W13* **Füzuli** *Rus.* Fizuli. SW Azerbaijan *39.33N 47.09E*
121 *I20* **Fyadory** *Rus.* Fëdory. Brestskaya Voblasts', SW Belarus *51.56N 26.21E*
97 *G24* **Fyn** *off.* Fyns Amt, *var.* Fünen. ◈ *county* C Denmark
97 *G23* **Fyn** *Ger.* Fünen. *island* C Denmark
98 *H12* **Fyne, Loch** *inlet* W Scotland, UK
97 *E16* **Fyresvatnet** ◎ S Norway
FYR Macedonia/FYROM *see* Macedonia, FYR
Fyzabad *see* Feyẕābād

G

83 *O14* **Gaalkacyo** *var.* Galka'yo, *It.* Galcaio. Mudug, C Somalia *6.42N 47.24E*
Gabakly *see* Kabakly
116 *H8* **Gabare** Vratsa, NW Bulgaria *43.20N 23.57E*
104 *K15* **Gabas** ≈ SW France
37 *T7* **Gabbs** Nevada, W USA *38.51N 117.55W*
84 *B12* **Gabela** Cuanza Sul, W Angola *10.49S 14.21E*
Gaberones *see* Gaborone
201 *X14* **Gabert** *island* Caroline Islands, E Micronesia
76 *M7* **Gabès** *var.* Qābis. E Tunisia *33.53N 10.03E*
76 *M6* **Gabès, Golfe de** *Ar.* Khalīj Qābis. *gulf* E Tunisia
Gablonz an der Neisse *see* Jablonec nad Nisou
Gablös *see* Cavalese
81 *E18* **Gabon** *off.* Gabonese Republic. ◆ *republic* C Africa
85 *I20* **Gaborone** *prev.* Gaberones. ● (Botswana) South East, SE Botswana *24.42S 25.49E*
85 *I20* **Gaborone** ✕ South East, SE Botswana *24.45S 25.49E*
106 *K8* **Gabriel y Galán, Embalse de** ⊠ W Spain
149 *U15* **Gābrīk, Rūd-e** ≈ SE Iran
116 *J9* **Gabrovo** Gabrovo, N Bulgaria *42.54N 25.19E*
116 *J9* **Gabrovo** ◈ *province* N Bulgaria
78 *H12* **Gabú** *prev.* Nova Lamego. E Guinea-Bissau *12.16N 14.09W*
31 *O6* **Gackle** North Dakota, N USA *46.34N 99.07W*
115 *I15* **Gacko** Republika Srpska, Bosnia and Herzegovina *43.08N 18.29E*
161 *F17* **Gadag** Karnātaka, W India *15.25N 75.37E*
95 *G15* **Gäddede** Jämtland, C Sweden *64.30N 14.15E*
165 *S12* **Gadê** Qinghai, C China *33.56N 99.49E*
Gades/Gadier/Gadir/Gadire *see* Cádiz
107 *P15* **Gádor, Sierra de** ▲▲ S Spain
155 *S15* **Gadra** Sind, SE Pakistan *25.39N 70.28E*
25 *Q3* **Gadsden** Alabama, S USA *34.00N 86.00W*
38 *H15* **Gadsden** Arizona, SW USA *32.33N 114.45W*
Gadyach *see* Hadyach
81 *H15* **Gadzi** Mambéré-Kadéï, SW Central African Republic *4.46N 16.42E*
118 *J13* **Găeşti** Dâmboviţa, S Romania *44.41N 25.18E*
109 *J17* **Gaeta** Lazio, C Italy *41.12N 13.34E*
109 *J17* **Gaeta, Golfo di** *var.* Gulf of Gaeta. *gulf* C Italy
196 *L14* **Gaferut** *atoll* Caroline Islands, W Micronesia
23 *Q10* **Gaffney** South Carolina, SE USA *35.04N 81.39W*
Gäfle *see* Gävle
Gäfleborg *see* Gävleborg
76 *M6* **Gafsa** *var.* Qafşah. W Tunisia *34.24N 8.51E*
Gafurov *see* Ghafurov
153 *O10* **Gagarin** Jizzax Viloyati, C Uzbekistan *40.40N 68.04E*
103 *G21* **Gaggenau** Baden-Württemberg, SW Germany *48.48N 8.19E*
196 *F16* **Gagil Tamil** *var.* Gagil-Tomil. *island* Caroline Islands, W Micronesia
Gagil-Tomil *see* Gagil Tamil
131 *O4* **Gagino** Nizhegorodskaya Oblast', W Russian Federation *55.18N 45.01E*
109 *Q19* **Gagliano del Capo** Puglia, SE Italy *39.49N 18.22E*
96 *L13* **Gagnef** Dalarna, C Sweden *60.34N 15.04E*
78 *M17* **Gagnoa** C Ivory Coast *6.10N 5.56W*
11 *N10* **Gagnon** Quebec, E Canada *51.55N 68.16W*
Gago Coutinho *see* Lumbala N'Guimbo
175 *Tt8* **Gag, Pulau** *island* E Indonesia
143 *P8* **Gagra** NW Georgia *43.17N 40.17E*
33 *S13* **Gahanna** Ohio, N USA *40.01N 82.52W*
149 *R13* **Gahkom** Hormozgān, S Iran *28.14N 55.48E*
Gahnpa *see* Ganta
59 *Q19* **Gaíba, Laguna** ◎ E Bolivia
159 *T13* **Gaibanda** *var.* Gaibandah. Rajshahi, NW Bangladesh *25.15N 89.32E*
Gaibandah *see* Gaibanda
Gaibhlte, Cnoc Mór na n *see* Galtymore Mountain
111 *R9* **Gail** ≈ S Austria
103 *I21* **Gaildorf** Baden-Württemberg, S Germany *48.41N 10.08E*
105 *N15* **Gaillac** *var.* Gaillac-sur-Tarn. Tarn, S France *43.54N 1.54E*
Gaillac-sur-Tarn *see* Gaillac
Gaillimh *see* Galway
Gaillimhe, Cuan na *see* Galway Bay
111 *Q9* **Gailtaler Alpen** ▲▲ S Austria
65 *J17* **Gaimán** Chaco, S Argentina *43.15S 65.30W*
22 *K8* **Gainesboro** Tennessee, S USA *36.21N 85.39W*
25 *V10* **Gainesville** Florida, SE USA *29.39N 82.19W*
25 *T2* **Gainesville** Georgia, SE USA *34.18N 83.49W*
29 *U8* **Gainesville** Missouri, C USA *36.36N 92.25W*
27 *T5* **Gainesville** Texas, SW USA *33.37N 97.09W*
111 *X5* **Gainfarn** Niederösterreich, NE Austria *47.59N 16.11E*
99 *N18* **Gainsborough** E England, UK *53.24N 0.48W*
190 *G6* **Gairdner, Lake** *salt lake* South Australia
Gaissane *see* Gáissát
94 *L8* **Gáissát** *var.* Gaissane ▲▲ N Norway
45 *T15* **Gaital, Cerro** ▲ C Panama *8.37N 80.04W*
23 *W3* **Gaithersburg** Maryland, NE USA *39.07N 77.07W*
169 *U13* **Gaizhou** Liaoning, NE China *40.24N 122.16E*
Gaiziņ *see* Gaizina Kalns
120 *I9* **Gaizina Kalns** *var.* Gaiziņ. ▲ E Latvia *56.51N 25.58E*
Gajac *see* Villeneuve-sur-Lot
174 *L15* **Gajahmungkur, Danau** ◎ Jawa, S Indonesia
41 *S10* **Gakona** Alaska, USA *62.21N 145.16W*
Galaassiya *see* Galaosiyo
Galāğil *see* Jalājil
Galam, Pulau *see* Gelam, Pulau
64 *J6* **Galán, Cerro** ▲ NW Argentina *25.54S 66.45W*
113 *H21* **Galanta** *Hung.* Galánta. Trnavský Kraj, W Slovakia *48.11N 17.45E*
152 *L11* **Galaosiyo** *Rus.* Galaassiya. Buxoro Viloyati, C Uzbekistan *39.53N 64.25E*
59 *B17* **Galápagos** *off.* Provincia de Galápagos. ◈ *province* Ecuador, E Pacific Ocean
199 *M9* **Galapagos Fracture Zone** *tectonic feature* E Pacific Ocean
200 *O10* **Galapagos Rise** *undersea feature* E Pacific Ocean
98 *K13* **Galashiels** SE Scotland, UK *55.37N 2.49W*
118 *M12* **Galaţi** *Ger.* Galatz. Galaţi, E Romania *45.27N 28.00E*
118 *L12* **Galaţi** ◈ *county* E Romania
109 *Q19* **Galatina** Puglia, SE Italy *40.10N 18.10E*
109 *Q19* **Galatone** Puglia, SE Italy *40.09N 18.04E*
Galatz *see* Galaţi
23 *R8* **Galax** Virginia, NE USA *36.39N 80.55W*
Galaymor *see* Kala-i-Mor
Galcaio *see* Gaalkacyo
66 *P11* **Gáldar** Gran Canaria, Islas Canarias, NE Atlantic Ocean *28.09N 15.40W*
96 *F11* **Galdhøpiggen** ▲ S Norway *61.30N 8.08E*
42 *I4* **Galeana** Chihuahua, N Mexico *30.07N 107.35W*
43 *O9* **Galeana** Nuevo León, NE Mexico *24.45N 99.59W*
62 *P9* **Galeão** ✕ (Rio de Janeiro) Rio de Janeiro, SE Brazil *22.48S 43.16W*
175 *T6* **Galela** Pulau Halmahera, E Indonesia *1.52N 127.48E*
41 *O9* **Galena** Alaska, USA *64.43N 156.55W*
32 *K10* **Galena** Illinois, N USA *42.25N 90.25W*
29 *R7* **Galena** Kansas, C USA *37.04N 94.38W*
29 *T8* **Galena** Missouri, C USA *36.45N 93.30W*
47 *V15* **Galeota Point** *headland* Trinidad, Trinidad and Tobago *10.07N 60.59W*
107 *P13* **Galera** Andalucía, S Spain *37.45N 2.33W*
47 *Y16* **Galera Point** *headland* Trinidad, Trinidad and Tobago *10.49N 60.54W*
58 *A5* **Galera, Punta** *headland* NW Ecuador *0.49N 80.03W*
32 *K12* **Galesburg** Illinois, N USA *40.57N 90.22W*
32 *J7* **Galesville** Wisconsin, N USA *44.04N 91.21W*
20 *F12* **Galeton** Pennsylvania, NE USA *41.43N 77.38W*
118 *H9* **Gâlgău** *Hung.* Galgó; *prev.* Gîlgău. Sălaj, NW Romania *47.15N 23.44E*
Galgó *see* Gâlgău
Galgóc *see* Hlohovec
83 *N15* **Galguduud** *off.* Gobolka Galguduud. ◈ *region* E Somalia
143 *Q9* **Gali** W Georgia *42.40N 41.39E*
129 *N14* **Galich** Kostromskaya Oblast', NW Russian Federation *58.21N 42.21E*
116 *H7* **Galiche** Vratsa, NW Bulgaria *43.36N 23.53E*
106 *H3* **Galicia** *anc.* Gallaecia. ◈ *autonomous community* NW Spain
66 *M8* **Galicia Bank** *undersea feature* E Atlantic Ocean
Galilee *see* HaGalil
189 *W7* **Galilee, Lake** ◎ Queensland, NE Australia
Galilee, Sea of *see* Tiberias, Lake
108 *E11* **Galileo Galilei** ✕ (Pisa) Toscana, C Italy *43.40N 10.22E*
33 *S12* **Galion** Ohio, N USA *40.43N 82.47W*
Galka'yo *see* Gaalkacyo
82 *H11* **Gallabat** Gedaref, E Sudan *12.56N 36.08E*
Gallaecia *see* Galicia
153 *O11* **G'allaorol** Jizzax Viloyati, C Uzbekistan *40.01N 67.30E*
108 *C7* **Gallarate** Lombardia, NW Italy *45.39N 8.46E*
29 *S2* **Gallatin** Missouri, C USA *39.54N 93.57W*
22 *J8* **Gallatin** Tennessee, S USA *36.23N 86.27W*
35 *R11* **Gallatin Peak** ▲ Montana, NW USA *45.22N 111.21W*
35 *R12* **Gallatin River** ≈ Montana/Wyoming, NW USA
161 *J26* **Galle** *prev.* Point de Galle. Southern Province, SW Sri Lanka *6.04N 80.11E*
107 *S5* **Gállego** ≈ NE Spain
200 *N9* **Gallego Rise** *undersea feature* E Pacific Ocean
Gallegos *see* Río Gallegos
65 *H23* **Gallegos, Río** ≈ Argentina/Chile
Gallia *see* France
24 *K10* **Galliano** Louisiana, S USA *29.26N 90.18W*
116 *G13* **Gallikós** ≈ N Greece
39 *S12* **Gallinas Peak** ▲ New Mexico, SW USA *34.14N 105.47W*
56 *H3* **Gallinas, Punta** *headland* NE Colombia *12.27N 71.43W*
39 *T11* **Gallinas River** ≈ New Mexico, SW USA
109 *Q19* **Gallipoli** Puglia, SE Italy *40.07N 18.00E*
Gallipoli *see* Gelibolu
Gallipoli Peninsula *see* Gelibolu Yarımadası
33 *T15* **Gallipolis** Ohio, N USA *38.45N 82.13W*
94 *J12* **Gällivare** Norrbotten, N Sweden *67.08N 20.39E*
111 *T4* **Gallneukirchen** Oberösterreich, N Austria *48.21N 14.22E*
107 *Q7* **Gallo** ≈ C Spain
95 *G17* **Gällö** Jämtland, C Sweden *62.57N 15.15E*
109 *I23* **Gallo, Capo** *headland* Sicilia, Italy, C Mediterranean Sea *38.13N 13.18E*
39 *P13* **Gallo Mountains** ▲▲ New Mexico, SW USA
20 *G8* **Galloo Island** *island* New York, NE USA
99 *H15* **Galloway, Mull of** *headland* S Scotland, UK *54.37N 4.54W*
39 *P10* **Gallup** New Mexico, SW USA *35.31N 108.45W*
107 *R5* **Gallur** Aragón, NE Spain *41.51N 1.21W*
Gâlma *see* Guelma
37 *O8* **Galt** California, W USA *38.13N 121.19W*
76 *C10* **Galtat-Zemmour** C Western Sahara *25.07N 12.21W*
97 *G22* **Galten** Århus, C Denmark *56.09N 9.54E*
99 *D20* **Galtymore Mountain** *Ir.* Cnoc Mór na nGaibhlte. ▲ S Ireland *52.21N 8.09W*
99 *D20* **Galty Mountains** *Ir.* Na Gaibhlte. ▲▲ S Ireland
32 *K11* **Galva** Illinois, N USA *41.10N 90.02W*
27 *X12* **Galveston** Texas, SW USA *29.16N 94.48W*
27 *W11* **Galveston Bay** *inlet* Texas, SW USA
27 *W12* **Galveston Island** *island* Texas, SW USA
63 *B18* **Gálvez** Santa Fe, C Argentina *31.57S 61.13W*
99 *C18* **Galway** *Ir.* Gaillimh. W Ireland *53.16N 9.03W*
99 *B18* **Galway** *Ir.* Gaillimh. *cultural region* W Ireland
99 *B18* **Galway Bay** *Ir.* Cuan na Gaillimhe. *bay* W Ireland
85 *F18* **Gam** Otjozondjupa, NE Namibia *20.10S 20.51E*
194 *G14* **Gama** ≈ SW PNG
171 *Hh16* **Gamagōri** Aichi, Honshū, SW Japan *34.49N 137.12E*
56 *F7* **Gamarra** Cesar, N Colombia *8.21N 73.46W*
Gámas *see* Kaamanen
164 *L17* **Gamba** Xizang Zizhiqu, W China *28.13N 88.31E*
79 *P14* **Gambaga** NE Ghana *10.32N 0.28W*
82 *G13* **Gambēla** Gambēla, W Ethiopia *8.09N 34.15E*
83 *H14* **Gambēla** ◈ *region*, W Ethiopia *8.09N 34.15E*
40 *K10* **Gambell** Saint Lawrence Island, Alaska, USA *63.43N 171.40W*
78 *E12* **Gambia** *off.* Republic of The Gambia, The Gambia. ◆ *republic* W Africa
78 *I12* **Gambia** *Fr.* Gambie. ≈ W Africa
66 *K12* **Gambia Plain** *undersea feature* E Atlantic Ocean
Gambie *see* Gambia
33 *T13* **Gambier** Ohio, N USA *40.22N 82.24W*
203 *Y13* **Gambier, Îles** *island group* E French Polynesia
190 *G10* **Gambier Islands** *island group* South Australia
81 *H19* **Gamboma** Plateaux, E Congo *1.52S 15.51E*
81 *G16* **Gamboula** Mambéré-Kadéï, SW Central African Republic *4.09N 15.12E*
39 *P10* **Gamerco** New Mexico, SW USA *35.34N 108.45W*
143 *V12* **Gamiş Dağı** ▲ W Azerbaijan *40.18N 46.15E*
Gamlakarleby *see* Kokkola
97 *N18* **Gamleby** Kalmar, S Sweden *57.54N 16.25E*
Gammelstad *see* Gammelstaden
95 *J14* **Gammelstaden** *var.* Gammelstad. Norrbotten, N Sweden *65.37N 22.04E*
Gammouda *see* Sidi Bouzid
161 *J25* **Gampaha** Western Province, W Sri Lanka *07.05N 80.00E*
161 *K25* **Gampola** Central Province, C Sri Lanka *7.10N 80.34E*
176 *Uu8* **Gam, Pulau** *island* E Indonesia
178 *Jj5* **Gâm, Sông** ≈ N Vietnam
94 *L7* **Gamvik** Finnmark, N Norway *71.04N 28.08E*
156 *H13* **Gan** Addu Atoll, C Maldives
Gan *see* Gansu, China
Gan *see* Jiangxi, China
Ganaane *see* Juba
39 *O10* **Ganado** Arizona, SW USA *35.42N 109.31W*
27 *U12* **Ganado** Texas, SW USA *29.02N 96.30W*
12 *L14* **Gananoque** Ontario, SE Canada *44.19N 76.10W*
Ganāveh *see* Bandar-e Gonāveh
143 *V11* **Gäncä** *Rus.* Gyandzha; *prev.* Kirovabad, Yelisavetpol. W Azerbaijan *40.41N 46.22E*
Ganchi *see* Ghonchí
Gand *see* Gent
84 *B13* **Ganda** *var.* Mariano Machado, *Port.* Vila Mariano Machado. Benguela, W Angola *12.59S 14.37E*
81 *L22* **Gandajika** Kasai Oriental, S Dem. Rep. Congo *6.42S 24.00E*
159 *O12* **Gandak** *Nep.* Nārāyāni. ≈ India/Nepal
11 *U11* **Gander** Newfoundland and Labrador, SE Canada *48.55N 54.33W*
11 *U11* **Gander** ✕ Newfoundland and Labrador, E Canada *49.03N 54.49W*
102 *G11* **Ganderkesee** Niedersachsen, NW Germany *53.01N 8.33E*
107 *T7* **Gandesa** Cataluña, NE Spain *41.03N 0.25E*
160 *B10* **Gāndhīdhām** Gujarāt, W India *23.07N 70.05E*
160 *D10* **Gāndhīnagar** Gujarāt, W India *23.12N 72.37E*
160 *F9* **Gāndhi Sāgar** ◎ C India
107 *T11* **Gandía** País Valenciano, E Spain *38.58N 0.10W*
165 *O10* **Gang** Qinghai, W China
158 *G9* **Gangānagar** Rājasthān, NW India *29.54N 73.55E*
158 *I12* **Gangāpur** Rājasthān, N India *26.30N 76.49E*
159 *S17* **Ganga Sāgar** West Bengal, NE India *21.39N 88.04E*
Gangavathi *see* Gangāwati
161 *G17* **Gangāwati** *var.* Gangavathi. Karnātaka, C India *15.26N 76.35E*
165 *S9* **Gangca** *var.* Shaliuhe. Qinghai, C China *37.21N 100.09E*
164 *H14* **Gangdisê Shan** *Eng.* Kailas Range. ▲▲ W China
105 *Q15* **Ganges** Hérault, S France *43.57N 3.42E*
159 *P13* **Ganges** *Ben.* Padma. ≈ Bangladesh/India *see also* Padma
Ganges Cone *see* Ganges Fan
181 *S3* **Ganges Fan** *var.* Ganges Cone. *undersea feature* N Bay of Bengal
159 *U17* **Ganges, Mouths of the** *delta* Bangladesh/India
109 *K23* **Gangi** *anc.* Engyum. Sicilia, Italy, C Mediterranean Sea *37.48N 14.13E*
158 *K8* **Gangotri** Uttar Pradesh, N India *30.55N 79.01E*
Gangra *see* Çankırı
159 *S11* **Gangtok** Sikkim, N India *27.19N 88.39E*
165 *W11* **Gangu** Gansu, C China *34.46N 105.21E*
169 *U5* **Gan He** ≈ NE China
175 *T9* **Gani** Pulau Halmahera, E Indonesia *0.45S 128.13E*
167 *O12* **Gan Jiang** ≈ S China
152 *H15* **Gannaly** Akhalskiy Velayat, S Turkmenistan *37.02N 60.43E*
169 *U7* **Gannan** Heilongjiang, NE China *47.58N 123.36E*
105 *P10* **Gannat** Allier, C France *46.06N 3.12E*
35 *T14* **Gannett Peak** ▲ Wyoming, C USA *43.10N 109.39W*
31 *O10* **Gannvalley** South Dakota, N USA *44.01N 98.59W*
111 *Y3* **Gänserndorf** Niederösterreich, NE Austria *48.22N 16.43E*
Gansos, Lago dos *see* Goose Lake
165 *T9* **Gansu** *var.* Gan, Gansu Sheng, Kansu. ◈ *province* N China
Gansu Sheng *see* Gansu
78 *K16* **Ganta** *var.* Gahnpa. NE Liberia *7.15N 8.58W*
190 *H11* **Gantheaume, Cape** *headland* South Australia *36.04S 137.28E*
Gantsevichi *see* Hantsavichy
167 *Q6* **Ganyu** *var.* Qingkou. Jiangsu, E China *34.55N 119.06E*
150 *D12* **Ganyushkino** Atyrau, SW Kazakhstan *46.35N 49.15E*
167 *O12* **Ganzhou** Jiangxi, S China *25.51N 114.58E*
79 *Q10* **Gao** Gao, E Mali *16.15N 0.03E*
79 *R10* **Gao** ◈ *region* SE Mali
167 *O10* **Gao'an** Jiangxi, S China *28.24N 115.27E*
167 *N5* **Gaoping** Shanxi, C China *35.51N 112.55E*
165 *S8* **Gaotai** Gansu, N China *39.22N 99.44E*
Gaoth Dobhair *see* Gweedore
79 *O14* **Gaoua** SW Burkina *10.18N 3.12W*
78 *I13* **Gaoual** Moyenne-Guinée, N Guinea *11.43N 13.13W*
Gaoxiong *see* Kaohsiung
167 *R7* **Gaoyou** *var.* Dayishan. Jiangsu, E China *32.45N 119.30E*
167 *R7* **Gaoyou Hu** ◎ E China
166 *M15* **Gaozhou** Guangdong, S China *21.56N 110.49E*
105 *T13* **Gap** *anc.* Vapincum. Hautes-Alpes, SE France *44.33N 6.04E*
164 *G13* **Gar** *var.* Gar Xincun. Xizang Zizhiqu, W China *32.04N 80.01E*
Garabekevyul/Garabekewül *see* Karabekaul
Garabogazköl *see* Kara-Bogaz-Gol
45 *V16* **Garachiné** Darién, SE Panama *8.03N 78.22W*
45 *V16* **Garachiné, Punta** *headland* SE Panama *8.05N 78.23W*
Garagan *see* Karagan
56 *G10* **Garagoa** Boyacá, C Colombia *5.04N 73.19W*
Garagöl *see* Karagel'
Garagum *see* Garagumy
Garagum Kanaly *see* Garagumskiy Kanal
152 *E12* **Garagumskiy Kanal** *var.* Kara Kum Canal, Karakumskiy Kanal, *Turkm.* Garagum Kanaly. *canal* C Turkmenistan
152 *F12* **Garagumy** *var.* Qara Qum, *Eng.* Black Sand Desert, Kara Kum, *Turkm.* Garagum; *prev.* Peski Karakumy. *desert* C Turkmenistan
191 *S4* **Garah** New South Wales, SE Australia *29.07S 149.37E*
66 *O11* **Garajonay** ▲ Gomera, Islas Canarias, NE Atlantic Ocean *28.07N 17.13W*
116 *M8* **Gara Khitrino** Shumen, NE Bulgaria *43.26N 26.55E*
78 *L13* **Garalo** Sikasso, SW Mali *10.58N 7.26W*
Garam *see* Hron
Garamäbnyyaz *see* Karamet-Niyaz
Garamszentkereszt *see* Žiar nad Hronom
79 *Q13* **Garango** S Burkina *11.45N 0.30W*
61 *Q15* **Garanhuns** Pernambuco, E Brazil *8.52S 36.28W*
196 *H5* **Garapan** Saipan, S Northern Mariana Islands *15.12S 145.43E*
Gárassavon *see* Kaaresuvanto
80 *J13* **Garba** Bamingui-Bangoran, N Central African Republic *9.09N 20.24E*
83 *L16* **Garbahaarrey** *It.* Garba Harre. Gedo, SW Somalia *3.14N 42.18E*
Garba Harre *see* Garbahaarrey
83 *J18* **Garba Tula** Eastern, C Kenya *0.31N 38.35E*
29 *N9* **Garber** Oklahoma, C USA *36.26N 97.35W*
36 *L4* **Garberville** California, W USA *40.07N 123.48W*
102 *I12* **Garbsen** Niedersachsen, N Germany *52.24N 9.36E*
62 *K9* **Garça** São Paulo, S Brazil *22.13S 49.36W*
106 *L10* **García de Solá, Embalse de** ⊠ C Spain
105 *Q14* **Gard** ◈ *department* S France
105 *Q14* **Gard** ≈ S France
108 *F7* **Garda, Lago di** *var.* Benaco, *Eng.* Lake Garda, *Ger.* Gardasee. ◎ NE Italy
Garda, Lake *see* Garda, Lago di
Gardan Divāl *see* Gardan Dīwāl
155 *Q5* **Gardan Dīwāl** *var.* Gardan Divāl. Wardag, C Afghanistan *34.30N 68.15E*
105 *S15* **Gardanne** Bouches-du-Rhône, SE France *43.27N 5.28E*
Gardasee *see* Garda, Lago di
102 *L12* **Gardelegen** Sachsen-Anhalt, C Germany *52.31N 11.25E*
12 *B10* **Garden** ≈ Ontario, S Canada
25 *X6* **Garden City** Georgia, SE USA *32.06N 81.09W*
28 *I6* **Garden City** Kansas, C USA *37.58N 100.52W*
29 *S5* **Garden City** Missouri, C USA *38.34N 94.12W*
27 *N8* **Garden City** Texas, SW USA *31.50N 101.29W*
25 *P3* **Gardendale** Alabama, S USA *33.39N 86.48W*
33 *P5* **Garden Island** *island* Michigan, N USA
24 *M11* **Garden Island Bay** *bay* Louisiana, S USA
33 *O5* **Garden Peninsula** *peninsula* Michigan, N USA
Garden State *see* New Jersey
97 *I14* **Gardermoen** Akershus, S Norway *60.10N 11.04E*
Gardeyz *see* Gardēz
155 *Q6* **Gardēz** *var.* Gardeyz, Gordiaz. Paktīā, E Afghanistan *33.34N 69.14E*
95 *G14* **Gardiken** ◎ N Sweden
21 *Q7* **Gardiner** Maine, NE USA *44.13N 69.46W*
35 *S12* **Gardiner** Montana, NW USA *45.02N 110.42W*
21 *N13* **Gardiners Island** *island* New York, NE USA
Gardner Island *see* Nikumaroro
21 *T6* **Gardner Lake** ◎ Maine, NE USA
37 *Q6* **Gardnerville** Nevada, W USA *38.55N 119.44W*
Gardo *see* Qardho
108 *F7* **Gardone Val Trompia** Lombardia, N Italy *45.40N 10.11E*
Garegegasnjárga *see* Karigasniemi
40 *F17* **Gareloi Island** *island* Aleutian Islands, Alaska, USA
108 *B10* **Garessio** Piemonte, NE Italy *44.14N 8.01E*
34 *M9* **Garfield** Washington, NW USA *47.00N 117.07W*
33 *U11* **Garfield Heights** Ohio, N USA *41.25N 81.36W*
Gargaliani *see* Gargaliánoi
117 *D21* **Gargaliánoi** *var.* Gargaliani. Pelopónnisos, S Greece *37.04N 21.37E*
109 *N15* **Gargano, Promontorio del** *headland* SE Italy *41.51N 16.11E*
110 *J8* **Gargellen** Graubünden, W Switzerland *46.57N 9.55E*
95 *I14* **Gargnäs** Västerbotten, N Sweden *65.19N 18.00E*
120 *C11* **Gargždai** Gargždai, W Lithuania *55.42N 21.24E*
160 *J13* **Garhchiroli** Mahārāshtra, C India *20.14N 79.58E*
159 *O15* **Garhwa** Bihār, N India *24.07N 83.52E*
176 *Ww11* **Gariau** Papua, E Indonesia *3.43S 134.54E*
85 *E24* **Garies** Northern Cape, W South Africa *30.25S 17.55E*
109 *K17* **Garigliano** ≈ C Italy
83 *K19* **Garissa** Coast, E Kenya *0.27S 39.39E*
23 *V11* **Garland** North Carolina, SE USA *34.45N 78.25W*
27 *T6* **Garland** Texas, SW USA *32.54N 96.36W*
38 *L1* **Garland** Utah, W USA *41.43N 112.07W*
108 *D8* **Garlasco** Lombardia, N Italy *45.12N 8.59E*
121 *F14* **Garliava** Kaunas, S Lithuania *54.49N 23.52E*
Garm *see* Gharm
148 *M9* **Garm, Āb-e** *var.* Rūd-e Khersān. ≈ SW Iran
103 *K25* **Garmisch-Partenkirchen** Bayern, S Germany *47.30N 11.06E*
149 *O5* **Garmsār** *prev.* Qishlaq. Semnān, N Iran *35.18N 52.21E*
Garmser *see* Darvīshān
31 *V12* **Garner** Iowa, C USA *43.06N 93.36W*
23 *U9* **Garner** North Carolina, SE USA *35.42N 78.36W*
29 *Q5* **Garnett** Kansas, C USA *38.16N 95.14W*
101 *M25* **Garnich** Luxembourg, SW Luxembourg *49.37N 5.57E*
190 *M8* **Garnpung, Lake** *salt lake* New South Wales, SE Australia
Garoe *see* Garoowe
Garoet *see* Garut
159 *U13* **Gāro Hills** *hill range* NE India
104 *K13* **Garonne** *anc.* Garumna. ≈ S France
82 *P13* **Garoowe** *var.* Garoe. Nugaal, N Somalia *8.24N 48.29E*
80 *F12* **Garoua** *var.* Garua. Nord, N Cameroon *9.16N 13.22E*
81 *G14* **Garoua Boulaï** Est, E Cameroon *5.54N 14.33E*
79 *O10* **Garou, Lac** ◎ C Mali
194 *M11* **Garove Island** *island* Witu Islands, C PNG
97 *L16* **Garphyttan** Örebro, C Sweden *59.18N 14.54E*
31 *R11* **Garretson** South Dakota, N USA *43.43N 96.30W*
33 *Q11* **Garrett** Indiana, N USA *41.21N 85.08W*
35 *Q10* **Garrison** Montana, NW USA *46.32N 112.46W*
30 *M4* **Garrison** North Dakota, N USA *47.36N 101.25W*
27 *X8* **Garrison** Texas, SW USA *31.49N 94.29W*
30 *L4* **Garrison Dam** *dam* North Dakota, N USA *47.29N 101.24W*
106 *J9* **Garrovillas** Extremadura, W Spain *39.43N 6.33W*
Garrygala *see* Kara-Kala
15 *Jj6* **Garry Lake** ◎ Nunavut, N Canada
Gars *see* Gars am Kamp
111 *W3* **Gars am Kamp** *var.* Gars. Niederösterreich, NE Austria *48.35N 15.40E*
83 *K20* **Garsen** Coast, S Kenya *2.16S 40.07E*
Garshy *see* Karshi
12 *F10* **Garson** Ontario, S Canada *46.33N 80.51Wß*
111 *T5* **Garsten** Oberösterreich, N Austria *48.00N 14.24E*
Gartar *see* Qianning
104 *M10* **Gartempe** ≈ C France
Gartog *see* Markam
Garua *see* Garoua
85 *D21* **Garub** Karas, SW Namibia *26.33S 16.00E*
Garumna *see* Garonne
174 *Jj15* **Garut** *prev.* Garoet. Jawa, C Indonesia *7.15S 107.55E*
193 *C20* **Garvie Mountains** ▲▲ South Island, NZ
112 *N12* **Garwolin** Mazowieckie, E Poland *51.53N 21.36E*
27 *U12* **Garwood** Texas, SW USA *29.25N 96.25W*
Gar Xincun *see* Gar
33 *N11* **Gary** Indiana, N USA *41.35N 87.21W*
27 *X7* **Gary** Texas, SW USA *32.00N 94.21W*
170 *E12* **Garyū-san** ▲ Kyūshū, SW Japan *34.40N 132.12E*
164 *G13* **Gar Zangbo** ≈ W China
166 *F8* **Garzê** Sichuan, C China *31.40N 99.58E*
56 *E12* **Garzón** Huila, S Colombia *2.13N 75.37W*
152 *B13* **Gasan-Kuli** *var.* Esenguly. Balkanskiy Velayat, W Turkmenistan *37.29N 53.56E*
33 *P13* **Gas City** Indiana, N USA *40.29N 85.36W*
104 *K15* **Gascogne** *Eng.* Gascony. *cultural region* S France
Gascogne, Golfe de *see* Gascony, Gulf of
28 *V5* **Gasconade River** ≈ Missouri, C USA
Gascony *see* Gascogne
188 *H9* **Gascoyne Junction** Western Australia *25.06S 115.10E*
181 *V8* **Gascoyne Plain** *undersea feature* E Indian Ocean
188 *H9* **Gascoyne River** ≈ Western Australia
199 *I12* **Gascoyne Tablemount** *undersea feature* N Tasman Sea *36.30S 156.30E*
69 *U6* **Gash** *var.* Nahr al Qāsh. ≈ W Sudan
155 *X3* **Gasherbrum** ▲ NE Pakistan *35.39N 76.34E*
165 *N9* **Gas Hu** ◎ C China
79 *X12* **Gashua** Yobe, NE Nigeria *12.55N 11.10E*
176 *Uu9* **Gasim** Papua, E Indonesia *1.21S 131.27E*
195 *N12* **Gasmata** New Britain, E PNG *6.12S 150.25E*
25 *V14* **Gasparilla Island** *island* Florida, SE USA
174 *Jj11* **Gaspar, Selat** *strait* W Indonesia
13 *Y6* **Gaspé** Quebec, SE Canada *48.50N 64.33W*
13 *Z6* **Gaspé, Cap de** *headland* Quebec, SE Canada *48.45N 64.10W*
13 *X6* **Gaspé, Péninsule de** *var.* Péninsule de la Gaspésie. *peninsula* Quebec, SE Canada
Gaspésie, Péninsule de la *see* Gaspé, Péninsule de
171 *Ll12* **Gas-san** ▲ Honshū, C Japan *38.33N 140.02E*
79 *W15* **Gassol** Taraba, E Nigeria *8.28N 10.24E*
Gastein *see* Badgastein
23 *R10* **Gastonia** North Carolina, SE USA *35.15N 81.11W*
23 *V8* **Gaston, Lake** ⊠ North Carolina/Virginia, SE USA
117 *D19* **Gastoúni** Dytikí Ellás, S Greece *37.51N 21.15E*
65 *I17* **Gastre** Chubut, S Argentina *42.20S 69.10W*
Gat *see* Ghāt
107 *P15* **Gata, Cabo de** *headland* S Spain *36.43N 2.11W*
Gata, Cape *see* Gátas, Akrotíri
107 *T11* **Gata de Gorgos** País Valenciano, E Spain *38.45N 0.06E*
118 *E12* **Gătaia** *Ger.* Gataja, *Hung.* Gátalja; *prev.* Gáttája. Timiş, W Romania *45.24N 21.25E*
Gataja/Gátalja *see* Gătaia
124 *Nn4* **Gátas, Akrotíri** *var.* Cape Gata. *headland* S Cyprus *34.34N 33.03E*
106 *J8* **Gata, Sierra de** ▲▲ W Spain
128 *G13* **Gatchina** Leningradskaya Oblast', NW Russian Federation *59.33N 30.06E*
23 *P8* **Gate City** Virginia, NE USA *36.38N 82.34W*
99 *M14* **Gateshead** NE England, UK *54.57N 1.37W*
15 *Jj2* **Gateshead Island** *island* Nunavut, N Canada
23 *X8* **Gatesville** North Carolina, SE USA *36.23N 76.43W*
27 *S8* **Gatesville** Texas, SW USA *31.26N 97.44W*
12 *L12* **Gatineau** Quebec, SE Canada *45.28N 75.40W*
12 *L11* **Gatineau** ≈ Ontario/Quebec, SE Canada
23 *N9* **Gatlinburg** Tennessee, S USA *35.42N 83.30W*
Gatooma *see* Kadoma
Gáttája *see* Gătaia
45 *T14* **Gatún, Lago** ⊠ C Panama
61 *N14* **Gaturiano** Piauí, NE Brazil *6.53S 41.45W*
99 *O22* **Gatwick** ✕ (London) SE England, UK *51.10N 0.12W*
197 *J15* **Gau** *prev.* Ngau. *island* C Fiji
197 *C11* **Gaua** *var* Santa Maria, *island* Banks Islands, N Vanuatu
106 *L16* **Gaucín** Andalucía, S Spain *36.31N 5.19W*
Gauhāti *see* Guwāhāti
120 *I8* **Gauja** *Ger.* Aa. ≈ Estonia/Latvia
120 *I7* **Gaujiena** Alūksne, NE Latvia *57.31N 26.24E*
Gaul/Gaule *see* France
96 *H9* **Gauldalen** *valley* S Norway
23 *R5* **Gauley River** ≈ West Virginia, NE USA
101 *D19* **Gaurain-Ramecroix** Hainaut, SW Belgium *50.35N 3.31E*
97 *F15* **Gaustatoppen** ▲ S Norway *59.50N 8.39E*
85 *J21* **Gauteng** *off.* Gauteng Province; *prev.* Pretoria-Witwatersrand-Vereeniging. ◈ *province* NE South Africa
Gauteng *see* Germiston, South Africa
Gauteng *see* Johannesburg, South Africa
176 *Y10* **Gauttier, Pegunungan** ▲▲ Papua, E Indonesia
149 *P14* **Gāvbandī** Hormozgān, S Iran *27.07N 53.21E*
117 *H25* **Gavdopoúla** *island* SE Greece
117 *H26* **Gávdos** *island* SE Greece
104 *K16* **Gave de Pau** *var.* Gave-de-Pay. ≈ SW France
Gave-de-Pay *see* Gave de Pau
104 *J16* **Gave d'Oloron** ≈ SW France
101 *E18* **Gavere** Oost-Vlaanderen, NW Belgium *50.56N 3.40E*
96 *N13* **Gävle** *var.* Gäfle; *prev.* Gefle. Gävleborg, C Sweden *60.40N 17.09E*
96 *M11* **Gävleborg** *var.* Gäfleborg, Gefleborg. ◈ *county* C Sweden
96 *O13* **Gävlebukten** *bay* C Sweden
128 *L16* **Gavrilov-Yam** Yaroslavskaya Oblast', W Russian Federation *57.19N 39.52E*
195 *P15* **Gawa Island** *island* SE Papau New Guinea
190 *I9* **Gawler** South Australia *34.37S 138.43E*
190 *G7* **Gawler Ranges** *hill range* South Australia
Gawso *see* Goaso
168 *H11* **Gaxun Nur** ◎ N China
159 *P14* **Gaya** Bihār, N India *24.48N 85.00E*
79 *S13* **Gaya** Dosso, SW Niger *11.54N 3.25E*
Gaya *see* Kyjov
33 *Q6* **Gaylord** Michigan, N USA *45.01N 84.40W*

◆ Country ● Country Capital ◇ Dependent Territory ○ Dependent Territory Capital ◈ Administrative Region ✕ International Airport ▲ Mountain ▲▲ Mountain Range Volcano ≈ River ◎ Lake ⊠ Reservoir

31 U9 **Gaylord** Minnesota, N USA 44.33N 94.13W
189 Y9 **Gayndah** Queensland, E Australia 25.37S 151.30E
129 T12 **Gayny** Komi-Permyatskiy Avtonomnyy Okrug, NW Russian Federation 60.19N 54.15E
Gaysin see Haysyn
Gayvorno see Hayvoron
144 E11 **Gaza** *Ar.* Ghazzah, *Heb.* 'Azza. NE Gaza Strip 31.30N 34.00E
85 L20 **Gaza** *off.* Província de Gaza. ◆ province SW Mozambique
152 I9 **Gaz-Achak** *Turkm.* Gazojak. Lebapskiy Velayat, NE Turkmenistan 41.12N 61.24E
Gazalkent see G'azalkent
153 Q9 **G'azalkent** *Rus.* Gazalkent. Toshkent Viloyati, E Uzbekistan 41.30N 69.46E
152 C11 **Gazandzhyk** *Turkm.* Gazanjyk; *prev.* Kazandzhik. Balkanskiy Velayat, W Turkmenistan 39.16N 55.27E
Gazanjyk see Gazandzhyk
79 V12 **Gazaoua** Maradi, S Niger 13.28N 7.54E
144 E11 **Gaza Strip** *Ar.* Qiṭā' Ghazzah. disputed region SW Asia
195 P11 **Gazelle Peninsula** headland New Britain, E PNG 4.32S 151.56E
197 J5 **Gazelle, Récif de la** reef C New Caledonia
Gazgan see G'ozg'on
Gazi Antep see Gaziantep
142 M16 **Gaziantep** *var.* Gazi Antep; *prev.* Aintab, Antep. Gaziantep, S Turkey 37.04N 37.21E
142 M17 **Gaziantep** *var.* Gazi Antep. ◆ province S Turkey
116 M13 **Gaziköy** Tekirdağ, NW Turkey 40.45N 27.18E
124 O3 **Gazimağusa** *var.* Famagusta, *Gk.* Ammóchostos. E Cyprus 35.06N 33.57E
124 Nn2 **Gazimağusa Körfezi** *var.* Famagusta Bay, *Gk.* Kólpos Ammóchostos. bay E Cyprus
152 K11 **Gazli** Buxoro Viloyati, C Uzbekistan 40.09N 63.28E
Gazojak see Gaz-Achak
81 K15 **Gbadolite** Equateur, NW Dem. Rep. Congo 4.18N 20.55E
76 K16 **Gbanga** *var.* Gbarnga. N Liberia 7.01N 9.30W
Gbarnga see Gbanga
79 S14 **Gbéroubouè** *var.* Béroubouay. N Benin 10.35N 2.47E
79 W16 **Gboko** Benue, S Nigeria 7.21N 8.57E
Gcuwa see Butterworth
110 J7 **Gdańsk** *Fr.* Dantzig, *Ger.* Danzig. Pomorskie, N Poland 54.21N 18.35E
Gdan'skaya Bukhta/Gdańsk, Gulf of see Danzig, Gulf of
Gdańska, Zakota see Danzig, Gulf of
Gdingen see Gdynia
128 F13 **Gdov** Pskovskaya Oblast', W Russian Federation 58.43N 27.51E
112 I6 **Gdynia** *Ger.* Gdingen. Pomorskie, N Poland 54.31N 18.30E
28 M10 **Geary** Oklahoma, C USA 35.37N 98.19W
Geavvú see Kevo
78 H12 **Gêba, Rio** ⟿ C Guinea-Bissau
175 Tt8 **Gebe, Pulau** island E Indonesia
142 E11 **Gebze** Kocaeli, NW Turkey 40.48N 29.25E
124 O2 **Geçitkale** *Gk.* Lefkonico, Lefkónikon. NE Cyprus 35.16N 33.44E
82 H10 **Gedaref** *var.* Al Qaḍārif, El Gedaref. Gedaref, E Sudan 14.03N 35.24E
82 H10 **Gedaref** ◆ state E Sudan
82 B11 **Gedid Ras el Fil** Southern Darfur, W Sudan 12.48N 25.42E
101 I23 **Gedinne** Namur, SE Belgium 49.57N 4.55E
142 E13 **Gediz** Kütahya, W Turkey 39.04N 29.25E
142 C14 **Gediz Nehri** ⟿ W Turkey
83 N14 **Gedlegubē** Somali, E Ethiopia 6.53N 45.08E
83 L17 **Gedo** *off.* Gobolka Gedo. ◆ region SW Somalia
97 I25 **Gedser** Storstrøm, SE Denmark 54.34N 11.57E
101 I16 **Geel** *var.* Gheel. Antwerpen, N Belgium 51.10N 4.58E
191 N13 **Geelong** Victoria, SE Australia 38.09S 144.20E
Ge'e'mu see Golmud
101 I14 **Geertruidenberg** Noord-Brabant, S Netherlands 51.43N 4.52E
102 H10 **Geeste** ⟿ NW Germany
102 J10 **Geesthacht** Schleswig-Holstein, N Germany 53.25N 10.22E
191 P17 **Geeveston** Tasmania, SE Australia 43.12S 146.54E
Gefle see Gävle
Gefleborg see Gävleborg
164 G13 **Gê'gyai** Xizang Zizhiqu, W China 32.28N 81.03E
79 X12 **Geidam** Yobe, NE Nigeria 12.52N 11.55E
9 T11 **Geikie** ⟿ Saskatchewan, C Canada
96 F13 **Geilo** Buskerud, S Norway 60.31N 8.13E
96 E10 **Geiranger** Møre og Romsdal, S Norway 62.07N 7.12E
103 I22 **Geislingen** *var.* Geislingen an der Steige. Baden-Württemberg, SW Germany 48.35N 9.52E
Geislingen an der Steige see Geislingen
83 F20 **Geita** Mwanza, NW Tanzania 2.52S 32.12E
97 G15 **Geithus** Buskerud, S Norway 59.55N 9.57E
166 H14 **Gejiu** *var.* Kochiu. Yunnan, S China 23.21N 103.07E
Gëkdepe see Geok-Tepe
152 E9 **Geklengkui, Solonchak** *var.* Solonchak Goklenkuy. salt marsh NW Turkmenistan
83 D14 **Gel** ⟿ W Sudan
109 K25 **Gela** *prev.* Terranova di Sicilia. Sicilia, Italy, C Mediterranean Sea 37.04N 14.15E
Gëladaindong see Gladaindong
83 N14 **Geladī** Somali, E Ethiopia 6.58N 46.24E
174 Kk11 **Gelam, Pulau** *var.* Pulau Galam. island N Indonesia
100 L11 **Gelderland** *prev. Eng.* Guelders. ◆ province E Netherlands
100 J13 **Geldermalsen** Gelderland, C Netherlands 51.52N 5.16E
103 D14 **Geldern** Nordrhein-Westfalen, W Germany 51.31N 6.19E
101 K15 **Geldrop** Noord-Brabant, SE Netherlands 51.25N 5.31E
101 L17 **Geleen** Limburg, SE Netherlands 50.57N 5.49E
130 K14 **Gelendzhik** Krasnodarskiy Kray, SW Russian Federation 44.34N 38.06E
Gelib see Jilib
142 B11 **Gelibolu** *Eng.* Gallipoli. Çanakkale, NW Turkey 40.25N 26.40E
117 L14 **Gelibolu Yarımadası** *Eng.* Gallipoli Peninsula. peninsula NW Turkey
Gelinting, Teluk see Geliting, Teluk
175 Qq16 **Geliting, Teluk** *var.* Teluk Gelinting. bay Nusa Tenggara, S Indonesia
83 O14 **Gellinsor** Mudug, C Somalia 6.25N 46.44E
103 H18 **Gelnhausen** Hessen, C Germany 50.12N 9.12E
103 E14 **Gelsenkirchen** Nordrhein-Westfalen, W Germany 51.33N 7.06E
85 C20 **Geluk** Hardap, SW Namibia 24.35S 15.48E
101 H20 **Gembloux** Namur, Belgium 50.34N 4.42E
194 I12 **Gembogl** Chimbu, C PNG 5.52S 145.06E
81 J16 **Gemena** Equateur, NW Dem. Rep. Congo 3.13N 19.49E
101 L14 **Gemert** Noord-Brabant, SE Netherlands 51.33N 5.40E
142 E11 **Gemlik** Bursa, NW Turkey 40.25N 29.10E
Gem of the Mountains see Idaho
108 J6 **Gemona del Friuli** Friuli-Venezia Giulia, NE Italy 46.18N 13.11E
Gem State see Idaho
Genalē Wenz see Juba
174 Ll7 **Genali, Danau** ◎ Borneo, N Indonesia
101 G19 **Genappe** Wallon Brabant, C Belgium 50.39N 4.27E
143 P14 **Genç** Bingöl, E Turkey 38.45N 40.31E
Genck see Genk
100 M9 **Genemuiden** Overijssel, E Netherlands 52.38N 6.03E
65 K14 **General Acha** La Pampa, C Argentina 37.24S 64.34W
63 C21 **General Alvear** Buenos Aires, E Argentina 36.03S 60.01W
64 I12 **General Alvear** Mendoza, W Argentina 34.58S 67.40W
63 B20 **General Arenales** Buenos Aires, E Argentina 34.21S 61.19W
63 D21 **General Belgrano** Buenos Aires, E Argentina 35.46S 58.30W
204 H3 **General Bernardo O'Higgins** Chilean research station Antarctica 63.09S 57.13W
43 O8 **General Bravo** Nuevo León, NE Mexico 25.47N 99.04W
64 M7 **General Capdevila** Chaco, N Argentina 27.25S 61.30W
General Carrera, Lago see Buenos Aires, Lago
43 N9 **General Cepeda** Coahuila de Zaragoza, NE Mexico 25.18N 101.24W
65 K15 **General Conesa** Río Negro, E Argentina 40.07S 64.32W
63 G18 **General Enrique Martínez** Treinta y Tres, E Uruguay 33.13S 53.46W
64 L3 **General Eugenio A. Garay** *var.* Fortín General Eugenio Garay; *prev.* Yrendagüé. Nueva Asunción, NW Paraguay 20.31S 62.09W
63 C18 **General Galarza** Entre Ríos, E Argentina 32.43S 59.24W
63 E22 **General Guido** Buenos Aires, E Argentina 36.36S 57.45W
General José F.Uriburu see Zárate
63 E22 **General Juan Madariaga** Buenos Aires, E Argentina 37.02S 57.06W
43 O16 **General Juan N Alvarez** ✕ (Acapulco) Guerrero, S Mexico 16.47N 99.47W
63 B22 **General La Madrid** Buenos Aires, E Argentina 37.13S 61.10W
63 E21 **General Lavalle** Buenos Aires, E Argentina 36.25S 56.55W
General Machado see Camacupa
64 I8 **General Manuel Belgrano, Cerro** ▲ W Argentina 29.05S 67.05W
43 O8 **General Mariano Escobero** ✕ (Monterrey) Nuevo León, NE Mexico 25.47N 100.00W
63 B20 **General O'Brien** Buenos Aires, E Argentina 34.54S 60.45W
64 K13 **General Pico** La Pampa, C Argentina 35.40S 63.44W
64 M7 **General Pinedo** Chaco, N Argentina 27.16S 61.19W
63 B20 **General Pinto** Buenos Aires, E Argentina 34.45S 61.49W
63 E22 **General Pirán** Buenos Aires, E Argentina 37.16S 57.46W
45 N15 **General, Río** ⟿ S Costa Rica
65 I15 **General Roca** Río Negro, C Argentina 39.00S 67.35W
179 Rr17 **General Santos** *off.* General Santos City. Mindanao, S Philippines 6.09N 125.10E
43 O9 **General Terán** Nuevo León, NE Mexico 25.17N 99.37W
116 N7 **General Toshevo** *Rom.* I.G.Duca, *prev.* Casim, Kasimköj. Dobrich, NE Bulgaria 43.43N 28.04E
63 B20 **General Viamonte** Buenos Aires, E Argentina 35.01S 61.00W
63 A20 **General Villegas** Buenos Aires, E Argentina 35.01S 63.01W
Gênes see Genova
20 E11 **Genesee River** ⟿ New York/Pennsylvania, NE USA
32 K11 **Geneseo** Illinois, N USA 41.27N 90.08W
20 F10 **Geneseo** New York, NE USA 42.48N 77.46W
59 L14 **Geneshuaya, Río** ⟿ N Bolivia
25 Q8 **Geneva** Alabama, S USA 31.01N 85.51W
32 M10 **Geneva** Illinois, N USA 41.53N 88.18W
31 Q16 **Geneva** Nebraska, C USA 40.31N 97.36W
20 G10 **Geneva** New York, NE USA 42.52N 76.58W
33 U10 **Geneva** Ohio, NE USA 41.48N 80.53W
Geneva see Genève
110 B10 **Geneva, Lake** *Fr.* Lac de Genève, Lac Léman, le Léman, *Ger.* Genfer See. ◎ France/Switzerland
110 A10 **Genève** *Eng.* Geneva, *Ger.* Genf, *It.* Ginevra. Genève, SW Switzerland 46.13N 6.09E
110 A11 **Genève** *Eng.* Geneva, *Ger.* Genf, *It.* Ginevra. ◆ canton SW Switzerland
110 A10 **Genève** *var.* Geneva. ✕ Vaud, SW Switzerland 46.13N 6.06E
Genève, Lac de see Geneva, Lake
Genf see Genève
Genfer See see Geneva, Lake
169 S5 **Gen He** ⟿ NE China
Genichesk see Heniches'k
106 L14 **Genil** ⟿ S Spain
101 K18 **Genk** *var.* Genck. Limburg, NE Belgium 50.58N 5.30E
170 Cc12 **Genkai-nada** gulf Kyūshū, SW Japan
109 C19 **Gennargentu, Monti del** ▲ Sardegna, Italy, C Mediterranean Sea 40.01N 9.14E
101 M14 **Gennep** Limburg, SE Netherlands 51.43N 5.58E
32 M10 **Genoa** Illinois, N USA 42.06N 88.41W
31 Q15 **Genoa** Nebraska, C USA 41.27N 97.43W
Genoa see Genova
Genoa, Gulf of see Genova, Golfo di
108 D10 **Genova** *Eng.* Genoa, *Fr.* Gênes; *anc.* Genua. Liguria, NW Italy 44.28N 9.00E
108 D10 **Genova, Golfo di** *Eng.* Gulf of Genoa. gulf NW Italy
59 C17 **Genovesa, Isla** *var.* Tower Island. island Galapagos Islands, Ecuador, E Pacific Ocean
Genshū see Wŏnju
101 E17 **Gent** *Eng.* Ghent, *Fr.* Gand. Oost-Vlaanderen, NW Belgium 51.01N 3.42E
174 J15 **Genteng** Jawa, C Indonesia 7.21S 106.19E
102 M12 **Genthin** Sachsen-Anhalt, E Germany 52.24N 12.10E
29 R9 **Gentry** Arkansas, C USA 36.16N 94.28W
Genua see Genova
109 I15 **Genzano di Roma** Lazio, C Italy 41.42N 12.42E
Geokchay see Göyçay
152 F13 **Geok-Tepe** *var.* Gëkdepe, *Turkm.* Gökdepe. Akhalskiy Velayat, C Turkmenistan 38.05N 58.07E
126 Gg1 **Georga, Zemlya** *Eng.* George Land. island Zemlya Frantsa-Iosifa, N Russian Federation
85 G26 **George** Western Cape, S South Africa 33.51S 22.28E
31 S11 **George** Iowa, C USA 43.20N 96.00W
11 O5 **George** ⟿ Newfoundland and Labrador/Quebec, E Canada
47 T11 **George F L Charles** *prev.* Vigie. ✕ (Castries). NE Saint Lucia 14.01N 60.59W
67 C25 **George Island** island S Falkland Islands
191 R10 **George, Lake** ◎ New South Wales, SE Australia
83 E18 **George, Lake** ◎ SW Uganda
25 W10 **George, Lake** ◎ Florida, SE USA
20 L8 **George, Lake** ⊠ New York, NE USA
George Land see Georga, Zemlya
Georgenburg see Jurbarkas
George River see Kangiqsualujjuaq
66 G8 **Georges Bank** undersea feature W Atlantic Ocean
193 A21 **George Sound** sound South Island, NZ
67 F15 **Georgetown** ○ (Ascension Island) NW Ascension Island 17.55S 14.25W
189 V5 **Georgetown** Queensland, NE Australia 18.17S 143.37E
191 P15 **George Town** Tasmania, SE Australia 41.07S 146.50E
46 I4 **George Town** Great Exuma Island, C Bahamas 23.28N 75.47W
46 D8 **George Town** *var.* Georgetown. ○ (Cayman Islands) Grand Cayman, SW Cayman Islands 19.15N 81.22W
78 H12 **Georgetown** E Gambia 13.33N 14.49W
57 T8 **Georgetown** ● (Guyana) N Guyana 6.46N 58.10W
173 Ff3 **George Town** *var.* Penang, Pinang. Pinang, Peninsular Malaysia 5.28N 100.19E
47 Y14 **Georgetown** Saint Vincent, Saint Vincent and the Grenadines 13.14N 61.07W
23 Y4 **Georgetown** Delaware, NE USA 38.39N 75.22W
25 R6 **Georgetown** Georgia, SE USA 31.52N 85.04W
22 M5 **Georgetown** Kentucky, S USA 38.13N 84.33W
23 T13 **Georgetown** South Carolina, SE USA 33.22N 79.17W
27 S10 **Georgetown** Texas, SW USA 30.37N 97.40W
57 T8 **Georgetown** ✕ N Guyana 6.46N 58.10W
205 U16 **George V Coast** physical region Antarctica
205 T15 **George V Land** physical region Antarctica
204 J7 **George VI Ice Shelf** ice shelf Antarctica
204 J6 **George VI Sound** sound Antarctica
27 S14 **George West** Texas, SW USA 28.19N 98.07W
143 R9 **Georgia** *off.* Republic of Georgia, *Geor.* Sak'art'velo, *Rus.* Gruzinskaya SSR, Gruziya; *prev.* Georgian SSR. ◆ republic SW Asia
25 S5 **Georgia** *off.* State of Georgia; also known as Empire State of the South, Peach State. ◆ state SE USA
12 F12 **Georgian Bay** lake bay Ontario, S Canada
8 L17 **Georgia, Strait of** strait British Columbia, W Canada
Georgi Dimitrov see Kostenets
Georgi Dimitrov, Yazovir see Koprinka, Yazovir
116 M9 **Georgi Traykov, Yazovir** ⊠ NE Bulgaria
Georgiu-Dezh see Liski
151 W10 **Georgiyevka** Vostochnyy Kazakhstan, E Kazakhstan 49.19N 81.34E
Georgiyevka see Korday,
131 N15 **Georgiyevsk** Stavropol'skiy Kray, SW Russian Federation 44.07N 43.22E
102 G13 **Georgsmarienhütte** Niedersachsen, NW Germany 52.12N 8.04E
205 O1 **Georg von Neumayer** German research station Antarctica 70.41S 8.18W
103 M16 **Gera** Thüringen, E Germany 50.51N 12.13E
103 K16 **Gera** ⟿ C Germany
101 E19 **Geraardsbergen** Oost-Vlaanderen, SW Belgium 50.46N 3.52E
117 F21 **Geráki** Pelopónnisos, S Greece 36.56N 22.46E
29 W5 **Gerald** Missouri, C USA 38.24N 91.20W
49 V8 **Geral de Goiás, Serra** ▲ E Brazil
193 G20 **Geraldine** Canterbury, South Island, NZ 44.06S 171.13E
188 H11 **Geraldton** Western Australia 28.47S 114.39E
10 E11 **Geraldton** Ontario, S Canada 49.43N 86.58W
62 J12 **Geral, Serra** ▲ S Brazil
175 P16 **Gerampi** Sumbawa, S Indonesia 8.47S 118.51E
105 U6 **Gérardmer** Vosges, NE France 48.05N 6.54E
Gerasa see Jarash
Gerdauen see Zheleznodorozhnyy
41 Q11 **Gerdine, Mount** ▲ Alaska, USA 61.40N 152.21W
142 H11 **Gerede** Bolu, N Turkey 40.48N 32.13E
142 H11 **Gerede Çayı** ⟿ N Turkey
154 M8 **Gereshk** Helmand, SW Afghanistan 31.49N 64.31E
103 L24 **Geretsried** Bayern, S Germany 47.51N 11.28E
107 P14 **Gérgal** Andalucía, S Spain 37.07N 2.34W
194 K13 **Gerhards, Cape** headland C PNG 6.43S 147.21E
30 I14 **Gering** Nebraska, C USA 41.49N 103.39W
37 R3 **Gerlach** Nevada, W USA 40.38N 119.21W
Gerlachfalvi Csúcs/Gerlachovka see Gerlachovský štít
113 L18 **Gerlachovský štít** *var.* Gerlachovka, *Ger.* Gerlsdorfer Spitze, *Hung.* Gerlachfalvi Csúcs; *prev.* Stalinov Štít, *Ger.* Franz-Josef Spitze, *Hung.* Ferencz-Jósef Csúcs. ▲ N Slovakia 49.12N 20.09E
110 E8 **Gerlafingen** Solothurn, NW Switzerland 47.10N 7.34E
Gerlsdorfer Spitze see Gerlachovský štít
145 V3 **Germak** E Iraq 35.49N 46.09E
German East Africa see Tanzania
Germanicopolis see Çankırı
Germanicum, Mare/German Ocean see North Sea
Germanovichi see Hyermanavichy
German Southwest Africa see Namibia
22 E10 **Germantown** Tennessee, S USA 35.06N 89.51W
103 I15 **Germany** *off.* Federal Republic of Germany, *Ger.* Bundesrepublik Deutschland, Deutschland. ◆ federal republic N Europe
103 L23 **Germering** Bayern, SE Germany 48.07N 11.22E
85 J21 **Germiston** *var.* Gauteng. Gauteng, NE South Africa 26.15S 28.10E
Gernika see Gernika-Lumo
107 P2 **Gernika-Lumo** *var.* Gernika, Guernica, Guernica y Lumo. País Vasco, N Spain 43.19N 2.40W
171 Ii15 **Gero** Gifu, Honshū, SW Japan 35.48N 137.15E
117 F22 **Geroliménas** Pelopónnisos, S Greece 36.28N 22.25E
Gerona see Girona
101 H21 **Gerpinnes** Hainaut, S Belgium 50.20N 4.38E
104 L15 **Gers** ◆ department S France
104 L14 **Gers** ⟿ S France
Gerunda see Girona
142 K10 **Gerze** Sinop, N Turkey 41.48N 35.13E
164 I13 **Gêrzê** Xizang Zizhiqu, W China 32.19N 84.05E
Gesoriacum/Gessoriacum see Boulogne-sur-Mer
101 J21 **Gesves** Namur, SE Belgium 50.24N 5.04E
95 J20 **Geta** Åland, SW Finland 60.22N 19.49E
107 N8 **Getafe** Madrid, C Spain 40.18N 3.43W
97 J21 **Getinge** Halland, S Sweden 56.46N 12.42E
20 F16 **Gettysburg** Pennsylvania, NE USA 39.49N 77.13W
31 N8 **Gettysburg** South Dakota, N USA 45.00N 99.57W
204 K12 **Getz Ice Shelf** ice shelf Antarctica
143 S15 **Gevaş** Van, SE Turkey 38.16N 43.04E
Gevgeli see Gevgelija
115 Q20 **Gevgelija** *var.* Đevđelija, Djevdjelija, *Turk.* Gevgeli. SE FYR Macedonia 41.09N 22.30E
105 T10 **Gex** Ain, E France 46.21N 6.02E
94 I3 **Geysir** physical region SW Iceland
142 F11 **Geyve** Sakarya, NW Turkey 40.31N 30.18E
82 G10 **Gezira** ◆ state E Sudan
111 V3 **Gföhl** Niederösterreich, N Austria 48.30N 15.27E
85 H22 **Ghaap Plateau** *Afr.* Ghaapplato. plateau C South Africa
Ghaapplato see Ghaap Plateau
Ghaba see Al Ghābah
144 J8 **Ghāb, Tall** ▲ SE Syria 33.09N 37.48E
145 Q9 **Ghadaf, Wādī al** dry watercourse C Iraq
Ghadamès see Ghadāmis
76 M9 **Ghadāmis** *var.* Ghadamès, Rhadames. W Libya 30.07N 9.30E
147 Y10 **Ghadan** E Oman 20.20N 57.58E
77 O10 **Ghaddūwah** C Libya 26.36N 14.26E
153 Q11 **Ghafurov** *Rus.* Gafurov; *prev.* Sovetabad. NW Tajikistan 40.13N 69.42E
159 N12 **Ghāghara** ⟿ S Asia
155 P13 **Ghaibi Dero** Sind, SE Pakistan 27.34N 67.42E
147 Y10 **Ghalat** E Oman 21.06N 58.51E
145 W11 **Ghamūkah, Hawr** ◎ S Iraq
79 P15 **Ghana** *off.* Republic of Ghana. ◆ republic W Africa
147 X12 **Ghānah** spring/well S Oman 18.35N 56.34E
Ghanongga see Ranongga
Ghansi/Ghansiland see Ghanzi
85 F18 **Ghanzi** *var.* Khanzi. Ghanzi, W Botswana 21.39S 21.38E
85 G19 **Ghanzi** *var.* Ghansi, Ghansiland, Khanzi. ◆ district C Botswana
69 T14 **Ghanzi** *var.* Knanzi. ⟿ Botswana/South Africa
Ghap'an see Kapan
144 F13 **Gharandal** Ma'ān, SW Jordan 30.12N 35.18E
Gharbt, Jabal al see Liban, Jebel
76 K7 **Ghardaïa** N Algeria 32.29N 3.44E
145 U14 **Gharibīyah, Sha'īb al** ⟿ S Iraq
153 R12 **Gharm** *Rus.* Garm. C Tajikistan 39.03N 70.25E
155 P17 **Gharo** Sind, SE Pakistan 24.43N 67.34E
145 W10 **Gharrāf, Shaṭṭ al** ⟿ S Iraq
Gharvān see Gharyān
77 O7 **Gharyān** *var.* Gharvān. NW Libya 32.10N 13.01E
76 M11 **Ghāt** *var.* Gat. SW Libya 24.58N 10.10E
Ghawdex see Gozo
147 U8 **Ghayathi** Abū Ẓaby, W UAE 23.51N 53.01E
Ghazāl, Baḥr al see Ghazal, Bahr el
80 H9 **Ghazal, Bahr el** *var.* Soro. seasonal river C Chad
82 E13 **Ghazal, Bahr el** *var.* Baḥr al Ghazāl. ⟿ S Sudan
76 H6 **Ghazaouet** NW Algeria 35.05N 1.52W
158 J10 **Ghāziābād** Uttar Pradesh, N India 28.42N 77.28E
159 O13 **Ghāzīpur** Uttar Pradesh, N India 25.38N 83.33E
155 Q6 **Ghaznī** *var.* Ghazni. Ghaznī, E Afghanistan 33.31N 68.24E
155 P7 **Ghaznī** ◆ province SE Afghanistan
Ghazzah see Gaza
Gheel see Geel
Ghelizâne see Relizane
Ghent see Gent
Gheorghe Braţul see Sfântu Gheorghe, Braţul
Gheorghe Gheorghiu-Dej see Oneşti
118 J10 **Gheorgheni** *prev.* Gheorghieni, Sînt-Miclăuş, *Ger.* Niklasmarkt, *Hung.* Gyergyószentmiklós. Harghita, C Romania 46.43N 25.34E
Gheorghieni see Gheorgheni
118 H10 **Gherla** *Ger.* Neuschliss, *Hung.* Szamosújvár; *prev.* Armenierstadt. Cluj, NW Romania 47.02N 23.55E
Gheweifat see Ghuwayfāt
Ghilan see Gīlān
109 C18 **Ghilarza** Sardegna, Italy, C Mediterranean Sea 40.09N 8.50E
Ghilizane see Relizane
Ghimbi see Gīmbī
Ghiriş see Câmpia Turzii
105 Y15 **Ghisonaccia** Corse, France, C Mediterranean Sea 42.00N 9.25E
Ghizo see Gizo
153 Q11 **Ghonchí** *Rus.* Ganchi. NW Tajikistan 39.57N 69.10E
Ghor see Ghowr
159 T13 **Ghoraghat** Rajshahi, NW Bangladesh 25.17N 89.16E
155 R13 **Ghotki** Sind, SE Pakistan 28.00N 69.21E
154 M5 **Ghowr** *var.* Ghor. ◆ province C Afghanistan
153 T13 **Ghūdara** *var.* Gudara, *Rus.* Kudara. SE Tajikistan 38.28N 72.39E
159 R13 **Ghugri** ⟿ N India
153 S14 **Ghund** *Rus.* Gunt. ⟿ SE Tajikistan
Ghurdaqah see Hurghada
154 J5 **Ghūriān** Herāt, W Afghanistan 34.19N 61.25E
147 T8 **Ghuwayfāt** *var.* Gheweifat. Abū Ẓaby, W UAE 24.06N 51.40E
123 Mm17 **Ghuzayyil, Sabkhat** salt lake N Libya
117 G17 **Giáltra** Évvoia, C Greece 38.21N 22.58E
Giamame see Jamaame
116 F13 **Giannitsá** *var.* Yiannitsá. Kentrikí Makedonía, N Greece 40.48N 22.24E
109 F14 **Giannutri, Isola di** island Archipelago Toscano, C Italy
98 F13 **Giant's Causeway** *Ir.* Clochán an Aifir. lava flow N Northern Ireland, UK
178 J15 **Gia Rai** Minh Hai, S Vietnam 9.16N 105.25E
109 L24 **Giarre** Sicilia, Italy, C Mediterranean Sea 37.43N 15.12E
46 I7 **Gibara** Holguín, E Cuba 21.05N 76.08W
31 O16 **Gibbon** Nebraska, C USA 40.45N 98.50W
34 K11 **Gibbon** Oregon, NW USA 45.40N 118.22W
35 P11 **Gibbonsville** Idaho, NW USA 45.33N 113.55W
66 A13 **Gibb's Hill** hill S Bermuda 32.15N 64.51W
94 I9 **Gibostad** Troms, N Norway 69.21N 18.01E
106 I14 **Gibraleón** Andalucía, S Spain 37.22N 6.58W
106 L16 **Gibraltar** ○ (Gibraltar) S Gibraltar 36.08N 5.21W
106 L16 **Gibraltar** ◇ UK dependent territory SW Europe
Gibraltar, Détroit de/Gibraltar, Estrecho de see Gibraltar, Strait of
106 J17 **Gibraltar, Strait of** *Fr.* Détroit de Gibraltar, *Sp.* Estrecho de Gibraltar. strait Atlantic Ocean/Mediterranean Sea
33 S11 **Gibsonburg** Ohio, N USA 41.22N 83.19W
32 M13 **Gibson City** Illinois, N USA 40.27N 88.24W
188 L8 **Gibson Desert** desert Western Australia
8 L17 **Gibsons** British Columbia, SW Canada 49.24N 123.31W
155 N12 **Gīdār** Baluchistān, SW Pakistan 28.16N 66.00E
161 I17 **Giddalūr** Andhra Pradesh, E India 15.24N 78.54E
27 U10 **Giddings** Texas, SW USA 30.10N 96.56W
29 Y8 **Gideon** Missouri, C USA 36.27N 89.55W
83 I15 **Gīdolē** Southern, S Ethiopia 5.31N 37.26E
120 H13 **Giedraičiai** Molėtai, E Lithuania 55.05N 25.16E
105 O7 **Gien** Loiret, C France 47.40N 2.37E
103 G17 **Giessen** Hessen, W Germany 50.34N 8.40E
100 O6 **Gieten** Drenthe, NE Netherlands 53.00N 6.43E
25 Y13 **Gifford** Florida, SE USA 27.40N 80.24W
15 Ll1 **Gifford** ⟿ Baffin Island, Nunavut, NE Canada
102 J12 **Gifhorn** Niedersachsen, N Germany 52.28N 10.33E
9 P13 **Gift Lake** Alberta, W Canada 55.49N 115.57W
171 Hh15 **Gifu** *var.* Gihu. Gifu, Honshū, SW Japan 35.23N 136.46E
171 I14 **Gifu** *off.* Gifu-ken, *var.* Gihu. ◆ prefecture Honshū, SW Japan
130 M13 **Gigant** Rostovskaya Oblast', SW Russian Federation 46.29N 41.18E
42 E8 **Giganta, Sierra de la** ▲ W Mexico
56 E12 **Gigante** Huila, S Colombia 2.24N 75.34W
116 I7 **Gigen** Pleven, N Bulgaria 43.40N 24.31E
Giggiga see Jijiga
98 G12 **Gigha Island** island SW Scotland, UK
109 E14 **Giglio, Isola del** island Archipelago Toscano, C Italy
Gihu see Gifu
152 L11 **G'ijduvon** *Rus.* Gizhduvan. Buxoro Viloyati, C Uzbekistan 40.06N 64.38E
106 L2 **Gijón** *var.* Xixón. Asturias, NW Spain 43.31N 5.40W
83 D20 **Gikongoro** SW Rwanda 2.30S 29.32E
38 K14 **Gila Bend** Arizona, SW USA 32.57N 112.43W
38 J14 **Gila Bend Mountains** ▲ Arizona, SW USA
39 N14 **Gila Mountains** ▲ Arizona, SW USA
38 I15 **Gila Mountains** ▲ Arizona, SW USA
148 M4 **Gīlān** *off.* Ostān-e Gīlān; *var.* Ghilan, Guilan. ◆ province NW Iran
Gilani see Gnjilane
38 L14 **Gila River** ⟿ Arizona, SW USA
31 W4 **Gilbert** Minnesota, N USA 47.29N 92.27W
Gilbert Islands see Tungaru
8 L16 **Gilbert, Mount** ▲ British Columbia, SW Canada 50.49N 124.03W
189 U4 **Gilbert River** ⟿ Queensland, NE Australia
(0) C6 **Gilbert Seamounts** undersea feature NE Pacific Ocean
35 S7 **Gildford** Montana, NW USA 48.34N 110.21W
85 P15 **Gilé** Zambézia, NE Mozambique 16.04S 38.16E
32 K4 **Gile Flowage** ◎ Wisconsin, N USA
190 G7 **Giles, Lake** salt lake South Australia
77 U12 **Gilf Kebir Plateau** *Ar.* Haḍabat al Jilf al Kabīr. plateau SW Egypt
191 R6 **Gilgandra** New South Wales, SE Australia 31.43S 148.39E
Gilgău see Gâlgău
83 I19 **Gilgil** Rift Valley, SW Kenya 0.33S 36.18E
191 S4 **Gil Gil Creek** ⟿ New South Wales, SE Australia
155 V3 **Gilgit** Jammu and Kashmir, NE Pakistan 35.54N 74.19E
155 V3 **Gilgit** ⟿ N Pakistan
9 X11 **Gillam** Manitoba, C Canada 56.25N 94.45W
97 J22 **Gilleleje** Frederiksborg, E Denmark 56.05N 12.17E
32 K14 **Gillespie** Illinois, N USA 39.07N 89.49W
29 W13 **Gillett** Arkansas, C USA 34.07N 91.22W
35 X12 **Gillette** Wyoming, C USA 44.17N 105.30W
99 P22 **Gillingham** SE England, UK 51.24N 0.33E
205 X6 **Gillock Island** island Antarctica
181 O16 **Gillot** ✕ (St-Denis) N Réunion 20.52S 55.31E
67 H25 **Gill Point** headland E Saint Helena 15.58S 5.37W
32 M12 **Gilman** Illinois, N USA 40.44N 87.58W
27 W6 **Gilmer** Texas, SW USA 32.43N 94.56W
Gilolo see Halmahera, Pulau
83 G14 **Gilo Wenz** ⟿ SW Ethiopia
37 O10 **Gilroy** California, W USA 37.00N 121.34W
194 H12 **Giluwe, Mount** ▲ W PNG 6.03S 143.52E
126 M14 **Gilyuy** ⟿ SE Russian Federation
101 I14 **Gilze** Noord-Brabant, S Netherlands 51.33N 4.55E
172 O14 **Gima** Okinawa, Kume-jima, SW Japan
82 H13 **Gīmbī** *It.* Ghimbi. Oromo, C Ethiopia 9.13N 35.39E
47 T12 **Gimie, Mount** ▲ C Saint Lucia 13.51N 61.00W
9 X16 **Gimli** Manitoba, S Canada 50.39N 97.00W
Gimma see Jīma
97 O14 **Gimo** Uppsala, C Sweden 60.10N 18.12E
104 L15 **Gimone** ⟿ S France
Gimpoe see Gimpu
175 Pp9 **Gimpu** *prev.* Gimpoe. Sulawesi, C Indonesia 1.38S 120.00E
190 F5 **Gina** South Australia 29.56S 134.33E
Ginevra see Genève
101 J19 **Gingelom** Limburg, NE Belgium 50.46N 5.09E
188 I12 **Gingin** Western Australia 31.22S 115.51E
179 R14 **Gingoog** Mindanao, S Philippines 8.47N 125.05E
83 K14 **Ginīr** Oromo, C Ethiopia 7.12N 40.43E
Giohar see Jawhar
109 O17 **Gioia del Colle** Puglia, SE Italy 40.46N 16.55E
109 M22 **Gioia, Golfo di** gulf S Italy
Giona see Gkióna
117 I16 **Gioúra** island Vóreioi Sporádes, Greece, Aegean Sea
109 O17 **Giovinazzo** Puglia, SE Italy 41.10N 16.40E
Gipeswic see Ipswich
Gipuzkoa see Guipúzcoa
Giran see Ilan
32 K14 **Girard** Illinois, N USA 39.27N 89.46W
29 R7 **Girard** Kansas, C USA 37.30N 94.50W
27 O6 **Girard** Texas, SW USA 33.18N 100.38W
56 E10 **Girardot** Cundinamarca, C Colombia 4.19N 74.46W
180 M7 **Giraud Seamount** undersea feature SW Indian Ocean 9.57S 46.55E
85 A15 **Giraul** ⟿ SW Angola
98 L9 **Girdle Ness** headland NE Scotland, UK 57.09N 2.04W
143 N11 **Giresun** *var.* Kerasunt; *anc.* Cerasus, Pharnacia. Giresun, NE Turkey 40.55N 38.34E
143 N12 **Giresun** *var.* Kerasunt. ◆ province NE Turkey
143 N12 **Giresun Dağları** ▲ N Turkey
77 X10 **Girga** *var.* Girgeh, Jirjā. C Egypt 26.19N 31.49E
Girgeh see Girga
Girgenti see Agrigento
194 H10 **Girgir, Cape** headland NW PNG 3.48S 144.29E
159 Q15 **Girīdīh** Bihār, NE India 24.10N 86.19E
191 P6 **Girilambone** New South Wales, SE Australia 31.19S 146.57E
Girin see Jilin
124 R12 **Girne** *Gk.* Kerýneia, Kyrenia. N Cyprus 35.19N 33.19E
107 X5 **Girona** *var.* Gerona; *anc.* Gerunda. Cataluña, NE Spain 41.58N 2.49E
107 W5 **Girona** *var.* Gerona ◆ province Cataluña, NE Spain
104 J12 **Gironde** ◆ department SW France
104 J11 **Gironde** estuary SW France
107 V5 **Gironella** Cataluña, NE Spain 42.01N 1.52E
105 N15 **Girou** ⟿ S France
99 H14 **Girvan** W Scotland, UK 55.14N 4.53W
26 M9 **Girvin** Texas, SW USA 31.05N 102.24W
192 Q9 **Gisborne** Gisborne, North Island, NZ 38.41S 178.01E
192 P9 **Gisborne** *off.* Gisborne District. ◆ unitary authority North Island, NZ
Giseifu see Üijŏngbu
Gisenye see Gisenyi
83 D19 **Gisenyi** *var.* Gisenye. NW Rwanda 1.42S 29.18E
97 K20 **Gislaved** Jönköping, S Sweden 57.19N 13.30E
105 N4 **Gisors** Eure, N France 49.18N 1.46E
Gissar see Hisor
153 P12 **Gissar Range** *Rus.* Gissarskiy Khrebet. ▲ Tajikistan/Uzbekistan
Gissarskiy Khrebet see Gissar Range
101 B16 **Gistel** West-Vlaanderen, W Belgium 51.09N 2.58E
110 F9 **Giswil** Unterwalden, C Switzerland 46.49N 8.11E
117 B16 **Gitánes** ancient monument Ípeiros, W Greece 39.34N 20.19E
83 E20 **Gitarama** C Rwanda 2.05S 29.45E
83 E20 **Gitega** C Burundi 3.20S 29.56E
Githio see Gýtheio
110 H11 **Giubiasco** Ticino, S Switzerland 46.10N 9.01E
108 K13 **Giulianova** Abruzzo, C Italy 42.45N 13.58E
Giulie, Alpi see Julian Alps
Giumri see Gyumri
118 M13 **Giurgeni** Ialomiţa, SE Romania 44.46N 27.51E
118 J15 **Giurgiu** Giurgiu, S Romania 43.54N 25.58E
118 J14 **Giurgiu** ◆ county SE Romania
97 F22 **Give** Vejle, C Denmark 55.51N 9.15E
105 R2 **Givet** Ardennes, N France 50.08N 4.50E
105 R11 **Givors** Rhône, E France 45.36N 4.46E
85 K19 **Giyani** Limpopo, NE South Africa 23.19S 30.37E
82 I13 **Giyon** Oromo, C Ethiopia 8.31N 37.56E
Gīza/Gīzeh see El Gîza

◆ Country ● Country Capital ◇ Dependent Territory ○ Dependent Territory Capital ◆ Administrative Region ✕ International Airport ▲ Mountain ▲ Mountain Range Volcano ⟿ River ◎ Lake ⊠ Reservoir

77 V8 **Giza, Pyramids of** *ancient monument* N Egypt *29.46N 31.03E*
Gizhduvan *see* G'ijduvon
127 Oo8 **Gizhiga** Magadanskaya Oblast', E Russian Federation *61.57N 160.16E*
127 Oo8 **Gizhiginskaya Guba** *bay* E Russian Federation
195 T14 **Gizo** Gizo, NW Solomon Islands *8.03S 156.49E*
195 T14 **Gizo** *var.* Ghizo. *island* NW Solomon Islands
112 N7 **Giżycko** *Ger.* Warmińsko-Mazurskie, NE Poland *54.03N 21.48E*
Gizymałów *see* Hrymayliv
Gjakovë *see* Đakovica
96 F12 **Gjende** ◎ S Norway
97 F17 **Gjerstad** Aust-Agder, S Norway *58.54N 9.03E*
Gjilan *see* Gnjilane
Gjinokastër *see* Gjirokastër
115 L23 **Gjirokastër** *var.* Gjirokastra; *prev.* Gjinokastër, *Gk.* Argyrokastron, *It.* Argirocastro. Gjirokastër, S Albania *40.04N 20.09E*
115 L22 **Gjirokastër** ◈ *district* S Albania
15 K3 **Gjoa Haven** King William Island, Nunavut, NW Canada *68.37N 95.57W*
96 H13 **Gjøvik** Oppland, S Norway *60.46N 10.40E*
115 J22 **Gjuhëzës, Kepi i** *headland* SW Albania *40.25N 19.19E*
Gjurgjevac *see* Đurđevac
117 E18 **Gkióna** *var.* Giona. ▲▲ C Greece
124 Oo3 **Gkréko, Akrotíri** *var.* Cape Greco, Pidálion. *headland* E Cyprus *34.57N 34.06E*
101 I18 **Glabbeek-Zuurbemde** Vlaams Brabant, C Belgium *50.54N 4.58E*
11 R14 **Glace Bay** Cape Breton Island, Nova Scotia, SE Canada *46.12N 59.57W*
9 O16 **Glacier** British Columbia, SW Canada *51.12N 117.33W*
41 W12 **Glacier Bay** *inlet* Alaska, USA
34 I7 **Glacier Peak** ▲ Washington, NW USA *48.06N 121.06W*
165 N13 **Gladaindong** *var.* Gèladaindong. ▲ C China *33.24N 91.00E*
23 Q7 **Glade Spring** Virginia, NE USA *36.47N 81.46W*
45 W7 **Gladewater** Texas, SW USA *32.32N 94.57W*
189 Y8 **Gladstone** Queensland, E Australia *23.52S 151.16E*
190 I8 **Gladstone** South Australia *33.16S 138.21E*
9 X16 **Gladstone** Manitoba, S Canada *50.12N 98.56W*
33 O5 **Gladstone** Michigan, N USA *45.51N 87.01W*
29 R4 **Gladstone** Missouri, C USA *39.12N 94.33W*
33 Q7 **Gladwin** Michigan, N USA *43.58N 84.29W*
97 J15 **Glafsfjorden** ◎ C Sweden
94 H2 **Gláma** *physical region* NW Iceland
96 I12 **Gláma** *var.* Glommen, Glomma. ≈ S Norway
114 F13 **Glamoč** Federacija Bosna I Hercegovina, NE Bosnia and Herzegovina *44.01N 16.51E*
99 J22 **Glamorgan** *cultural region* S Wales, UK
97 G24 **Glamsbjerg** Fyn, C Denmark *55.16N 10.07E*
179 Rr17 **Glan** Mindanao, S Philippines *5.49N 125.11E*
97 M17 **Glan** ◎ S Sweden
111 T9 **Glan** ≈ SE Austria
103 F19 **Glan** ≈ W Germany
Glaris *see* Glarus
110 H9 **Glarner Alpen** *Eng.* Glarus Alps. ▲▲ E Switzerland
110 H8 **Glarus** Glarus, E Switzerland *47.03N 9.04E*
110 H9 **Glarus** *Fr.* Glaris. ◈ *canton* C Switzerland
Glarus Alps *see* Glarner Alpen
29 N3 **Glasco** Kansas, C USA *39.21N 97.50W*
98 I12 **Glasgow** S Scotland, UK *55.52N 4.15W*
22 K7 **Glasgow** Kentucky, S USA *37.00N 85.54W*
29 T4 **Glasgow** Missouri, C USA *39.13N 92.51W*
35 W7 **Glasgow** Montana, NW USA *48.12N 106.37W*
23 T6 **Glasgow** Virginia, NE USA *37.37N 79.27W*
98 I12 **Glasgow** ✈ W Scotland, UK *55.52N 4.27W*
9 S14 **Glaslyn** Saskatchewan, S Canada *53.20N 108.18W*
20 I16 **Glassboro** New Jersey, NE USA *39.40N 75.05W*
26 L10 **Glass Mountains** ▲▲ Texas, SW USA
99 K23 **Glastonbury** SW England, UK *51.09N 2.43W*
Glatz *see* Kłodzko
103 N16 **Glauchau** Sachsen, E Germany *50.48N 12.31E*
Glavn'a Morava *see* Velika Morava
115 N16 **Glavnik** Serbia, S Serbia and Montenegro (Yugoslavia) *42.53N 21.10E*
131 T1 **Glazov** Udmurtskaya Respublika, NW Russian Federation *58.05N 52.38E*
Głda *see* Gwda
111 U8 **Gleinalpe** ▲▲ SE Austria
111 W8 **Gleisdorf** Steiermark, SE Austria *47.07N 15.43E*
Gleiwitz *see* Gliwice
41 S11 **Glenallen** Alaska, USA *62.06N 145.33W*
104 F7 **Glénan, Îles** *island group* NW France
193 G21 **Glenavy** Canterbury, South Island, NZ *44.53S 171.04E*
8 H5 **Glenboyle** Yukon Territory, NW Canada *63.55N 138.43W*
23 X3 **Glen Burnie** Maryland, NE USA *39.09N 76.37W*
38 L8 **Glen Canyon** *canyon* Utah, W USA
38 L8 **Glen Canyon Dam** *dam* Arizona, SW USA *36.56N 111.28W*
32 K15 **Glen Carbon** Illinois, N USA *38.45N 89.58W*
12 E17 **Glencoe** Ontario, S Canada *42.44N 81.42W*
85 K22 **Glencoe** KwaZulu/Natal, E South Africa *28.09S 30.12E*
31 U9 **Glencoe** Minnesota, N USA *44.46N 94.09W*
98 H10 **Glen Coe** *valley* N Scotland, UK
38 K13 **Glendale** Arizona, SW USA *33.32N 112.11W*
37 S15 **Glendale** California, W USA *34.09N 118.17W*
190 G5 **Glendambo** South Australia *30.59S 135.45E*
35 Y8 **Glendive** Montana, NW USA *47.07N 104.42W*
35 Y15 **Glendo** Wyoming, C USA *42.27N 105.01W*
57 S10 **Glendor Mountains** ▲▲ C Guyana
190 K12 **Glenelg River** ≈ South Australia/Victoria, SE Australia
31 P4 **Glenfield** North Dakota, N USA *47.25N 98.33W*
27 V12 **Glen Flora** Texas, SW USA *29.22N 96.12W*
189 P7 **Glen Helen** Northern Territory, N Australia *23.45S 132.46E*
191 U5 **Glen Innes** New South Wales, SE Australia *29.42S 151.45E*
33 P6 **Glen Lake** ◎ Michigan, N USA
8 I7 **Glenlyon Peak** ▲ Yukon Territory, W Canada *62.32N 134.51W*
39 N16 **Glenn, Mount** ▲ Arizona, SW USA *31.55N 110.00W*
35 N15 **Glenns Ferry** Idaho, NW USA *42.57N 115.18W*
25 W6 **Glennville** Georgia, SE USA *31.56N 81.55W*
8 J10 **Glenora** British Columbia, W Canada *57.52N 131.16W*
190 M11 **Glenorchy** Victoria, SE Australia *36.56S 142.39E*
191 V5 **Glenreagh** New South Wales, SE Australia *30.04S 153.00E*
35 X15 **Glenrock** Wyoming, C USA *42.51N 105.52W*
98 K11 **Glenrothes** E Scotland, UK *56.11N 3.09W*
20 L9 **Glens Falls** New York, NE USA *43.18N 73.38W*
99 D14 **Glenties** *Ir.* Na Gleannta. NW Ireland *54.46N 8.16W*
30 L5 **Glen Ullin** North Dakota, N USA *46.49N 101.49W*
23 R4 **Glenville** West Virginia, NE USA *38.55N 80.50W*
29 T12 **Glenwood** Arkansas, C USA *34.19N 93.33W*
31 S15 **Glenwood** Iowa, C USA *41.03N 95.44W*
31 T7 **Glenwood** Minnesota, N USA *45.39N 95.23W*
38 L5 **Glenwood** Utah, W USA *38.45N 111.59W*
32 I5 **Glenwood City** Wisconsin, N USA *45.04N 92.11W*
39 Q4 **Glenwood Springs** Colorado, C USA *39.33N 107.21W*
110 F10 **Gletsch** Valais, S Switzerland *46.34N 8.21E*
Glevum *see* Gloucester
31 U14 **Glidden** Iowa, C USA *42.03N 94.43W*
114 E9 **Glina** Sisak-Moslavina, NE Croatia *45.19N 16.07E*
96 F11 **Glittertind** ▲ S Norway *61.24N 8.19E*
113 J16 **Gliwice** *Ger.* Gleiwitz. Śląskie, S Poland *50.19N 18.49E*
38 M14 **Globe** Arizona, SW USA *33.24N 110.47W*
Globino *see* Hlobyne
110 L9 **Glockturm** ▲ SW Austria *46.54N 10.42E*
118 L9 **Glodeni** *Rus.* Glodyany. N Moldova *47.47N 27.33E*
111 S9 **Glödnitz** Kärnten, S Austria *46.57N 14.03E*
Glodyany *see* Glodeni
Glogau *see* Głogów
111 W6 **Gloggnitz** Niederösterreich, E Austria *47.41N 15.57E*
112 F13 **Głogów** *Ger.* Glogau, Glogow. Dolnośląskie, SW Poland *51.39N 16.04E*
113 I16 **Głogówek** *Ger.* Oberglogau. Opolskie, S Poland *50.21N 17.51E*
94 G12 **Glomfjord** Nordland, C Norway *66.48N 13.57E*
Glommen *see* Gláma
95 I14 **Glommersträsk** Norrbotten, N Sweden *65.16N 19.40E*
180 I1 **Glorieuses, Nosy** *island group* N Madagascar
67 C25 **Glorious Hill** *hill* East Falkland, Falkland Islands
40 J12 **Glory of Russia Cape** *headland* Saint Matthew Island, Alaska, USA *60.36N 172.57W*
24 J7 **Gloster** Mississippi, S USA *31.12N 91.01W*
191 U7 **Gloucester** New South Wales, SE Australia *32.01S 152.00E*
194 L12 **Gloucester** New Britain, E PNG *5.28S 148.28E*
99 L21 **Gloucester** *hist.* Caer Glou, *Lat.* Glevum. C England, UK *51.52N 2.13W*
21 P10 **Gloucester** Massachusetts, NE USA *42.36N 70.36W*
23 X6 **Gloucester** Virginia, NE USA *37.23N 76.30W*
99 K21 **Gloucestershire** *cultural region* C England, UK
33 T14 **Glouster** Ohio, N USA *39.30N 82.04W*
44 H3 **Glovers Reef** *reef* E Belize
20 K10 **Gloversville** New York, NE USA *43.03N 74.20W*
112 K12 **Głowno** Łódź, C Poland *51.58N 19.43E*
113 H16 **Głubczyce** *Ger.* Leobschütz. Opolskie, S Poland *50.11N 17.49E*
130 L11 **Glubokiy** Rostovskaya Oblast', SW Russian Federation *48.34N 40.16E*
151 W9 **Glubokoye** Vostochnyy Kazakhstan, E Kazakhstan *50.10N 82.16E*
Glubokoye *see* Hlybokaye
113 H16 **Głuchołazy** *Ger.* Ziegenhais. Opolskie, S Poland *50.18N 17.22E*
102 I9 **Glückstadt** Schleswig-Holstein, N Germany *53.47N 9.25E*
Glukhov *see* Hlukhiv
Glushkevichi *see* Hlushkavichy
Glusk/Glussk *see* Hlusk
Glybokaya *see* Hlyboka
97 F21 **Glyngøre** Viborg, NW Denmark *56.45N 8.55E*
131 Q9 **Gmelinka** Volgogradskaya Oblast', SW Russian Federation *50.50N 46.51E*
111 R8 **Gmünd** Kärnten, S Austria *46.56N 13.32E*
111 U2 **Gmünd** Niederösterreich, N Austria *48.45N 14.57E*
Gmünd *see* Schwäbisch Gmünd
111 S5 **Gmunden** Oberösterreich, N Austria *47.54N 13.46E*
Gmundner See *see* Traunsee
96 N10 **Gnarp** Gävleborg, C Sweden *62.03N 17.19E*
111 W8 **Gnas** Steiermark, SE Austria *46.53N 15.48E*
Gnesen *see* Gniezno
97 O16 **Gnesta** Södermanland, C Sweden *59.02N 17.19E*
112 H11 **Gniezno** *Ger.* Gnesen. Wielkopolskie, C Poland *52.33N 17.35E*
115 O17 **Gnjilane** *var.* Gilani, *Alb.* Gjilan. Serbia, S Serbia and Montenegro (Yugoslavia) *42.27N 21.28E*
97 K20 **Gnosjö** Jönköping, S Sweden *57.22N 13.43E*
161 E17 **Goa** *prev.* Old Goa, Vela Goa, Velha Goa. Goa, W India *15.31N 73.55E*
161 E17 **Goa** *var.* Old Goa. ◈ *state* W India
44 H7 **Goascorán, Río** ≈ El Salvador/Honduras
79 O16 **Goaso** *var.* Gawso. W Ghana *6.49N 2.27W*
83 K14 **Goba** *It.* Oromo, S Ethiopia *7.02N 39.58E*
85 C20 **Gobabed** Erongo, W Namibia *23.36S 15.03E*
85 E19 **Gobabis** Omaheke, E Namibia *22.24S 18.58E*
Gobannium *see* Abergavenny
66 M7 **Goban Spur** *undersea feature* NW Atlantic Ocean
Gobbà *see* Goba
65 H21 **Gobernador Gregores** Santa Cruz, S Argentina *48.43S 70.21W*
63 F14 **Gobernador Ingeniero Virasoro** Corrientes, NE Argentina
168 L12 **Gobi** *desert* China/Mongolia
170 G16 **Gobō** Wakayama, Honshū, SW Japan *33.52N 135.09E*
103 D14 **Goch** Nordrhein-Westfalen, W Germany *51.41N 6.10E*
85 E20 **Gochas** Hardap, S Namibia *24.54S 18.43E*
161 I14 **Godāvari** *var.* Godavari. ≈ C India
161 L16 **Godāvari, Mouths of the** *delta* E India
13 V5 **Godbout** Quebec, SE Canada *49.19N 67.37W*
13 U5 **Godbout** ≈ Quebec, SE Canada
13 U5 **Godbout Est** ≈ Quebec, SE Canada
29 N6 **Goddard** Kansas, C USA *37.39N 97.34W*
12 E15 **Goderich** Ontario, S Canada *43.45N 81.42W*
Godhavn *see* Qeqertarsuaq
160 E10 **Godhra** Gujarāt, W India *22.49N 73.40E*
Göding *see* Hodonín
113 K22 **Gödöllő** Pest, N Hungary *47.36N 19.19E*
64 H11 **Godoy Cruz** Mendoza, W Argentina *32.58S 68.49W*
9 Y11 **Gods** ≈ Manitoba, C Canada
9 Y13 **Gods Lake** Manitoba, C Canada *54.29N 94.21W*
9 X13 **Gods Lake** ◎ Manitoba, C Canada
Godthaab/Godthåb *see* Nuuk
Godwin Austen, Mount *see* K2
Goede Hoop, Kaap de *see* Good Hope, Cape of
Goedgegun *see* Nhlangano
Goeie Hoop, Kaap die *see* Good Hope, Cape of
11 O7 **Goélands, Lac aux** ◎ Quebec, SE Canada
100 E13 **Goeree** *island* SW Netherlands
101 F15 **Goes** Zeeland, SW Netherlands *51.30N 3.55E*
Goettingen *see* Göttingen
21 O10 **Goffstown** New Hampshire, NE USA *43.01N 71.34W*
12 E8 **Gogama** Ontario, S Canada *47.42N 81.43W*
170 Ee12 **Gō-gawa** ≈ Honshū, SW Japan
32 L3 **Gogebic, Lake** ◎ Michigan, N USA
32 K3 **Gogebic Range** *hill range* Michigan/Wisconsin, N USA
143 V13 **Gogi, Mount** *Arm.* Gogi Lerr, *Az.* Küküdağ. ▲ Armenia/Azerbaijan *39.33N 45.35E*
128 F12 **Gogland, Ostrov** *island* NW Russian Federation
113 I15 **Gogolin** Opolskie, S Poland *50.28N 18.04E*
Gogonou *see* Gogounou
79 S14 **Gogounou** *var.* Gogonou. N Benin *10.49N 2.49E*
158 I10 **Gohāna** Haryāna, N India *29.06N 76.43E*
61 K18 **Goianésia** Goiás, C Brazil *15.21S 49.01W*
61 K18 **Goiânia** *prev.* Goyania. *state capital* Goiás, C Brazil *16.43S 49.18W*
61 K18 **Goiás** Goiás, C Brazil *15.57S 50.07W*
61 J18 **Goiás** *off.* Estado de Goiás; *prev.* Goiaz, Goyaz. ◈ *state* C Brazil
Goiaz *see* Goiás
165 R14 **Goinsargoin** Xizang Zizhiqu, W China *31.55N 98.04E*
62 H10 **Goio-Erê** Paraná, SW Brazil *24.08S 53.07W*
101 I15 **Goirle** Noord-Brabant, S Netherlands *51.31N 5.04E*
106 H8 **Góis** Coimbra, N Portugal *40.10N 8.06W*
171 Gg16 **Gojō** *var.* Gozyô. Nara, Honshū, SW Japan *34.21N 135.42E*
171 M10 **Gojōme** Akita, Honshū, NW Japan *39.55N 140.07E*
155 U9 **Gojra** Punjab, E Pakistan *31.09N 72.39E*
170 D15 **Gokase-gawa** ≈ Kyūshū, SW Japan
142 A11 **Gökçeada** *var.* Imroz Adası, *Gk.* Imbros. *island* NW Turkey
Gökçeada *see* Imroz
Gökdepe *see* Geok-Tepe
142 I10 **Gökırmak** ≈ N Turkey
Goklenkuy, Solonchak *see* Geklengkui, Solonchak
142 C16 **Gökova Körfezi** *gulf* SW Turkey
142 K15 **Göksu** ≈ S Turkey
142 L15 **Göksun** Kahramanmaraş, C Turkey *38.03N 36.30E*
142 I17 **Göksu Nehri** ≈ S Turkey
85 J16 **Gokwe** Midlands, NW Zimbabwe *18.10S 28.54E*
96 F13 **Gol** Buskerud, S Norway *60.42N 8.57E*
159 X12 **Golāghāt** Assam, NE India *26.31N 93.54E*
112 H10 **Gołańcz** Wielkopolskie, C Poland *52.57N 17.17E*
144 G8 **Golan Heights** *Ar.* Al Jawlān, *Heb.* HaGolan. ▲▲ SW Syria
Golārā *see* Ārān
Golaya Pristan *see* Hola Prystan'
149 T11 **Golbāf** Kermān, C Iran *29.51N 57.43E*
142 M15 **Gölbaşı** Adıyaman, S Turkey *37.46N 37.40E*
111 P9 **Gölbner** ▲ SW Austria *46.51N 12.31E*
32 M17 **Golconda** Illinois, N USA *37.18N 88.30W*
37 T3 **Golconda** Nevada, W USA *40.56N 117.29W*
142 E11 **Gölcük** Kocaeli, NW Turkey *40.42N 29.50E*
110 I7 **Goldach** Sankt Gallen, NE Switzerland *47.28N 9.28E*
112 N7 **Gołdap** *Ger.* Goldap. Warmińsko-Mazurskie, NE Poland *54.18N 22.30E*
34 E15 **Gold Beach** Oregon, NW USA *42.24N 124.25W*
Goldberg *see* Złotoryja
70 D11 **Gold Coast** *coastal region* S Ghana
191 V3 **Gold Coast** *cultural region* Queensland, E Australia
41 R10 **Gold Creek** Alaska, USA *62.48N 149.40W*
9 O16 **Golden** British Columbia, SW Canada *51.19N 116.58W*
39 T4 **Golden** Colorado, C USA *39.40N 105.12W*
192 I13 **Golden Bay** *bay* South Island, NZ
29 R7 **Golden City** Missouri, C USA *37.23N 94.05W*
34 I11 **Goldendale** Washington, NW USA *45.49N 120.49W*
Goldener Tisch *see* Zlatý Stôl
46 L13 **Golden Grove** E Jamaica *17.55N 76.16W*
12 J12 **Golden Lake** ◎ Ontario, SE Canada
24 K10 **Golden Meadow** Louisiana, S USA *29.22N 90.15W*
47 V10 **Golden Rock** ✈ (Basseterre) Saint Kitts, Saint Kitts and Nevis *17.16N 62.43W*
Golden State, The *see* California
85 K16 **Golden Valley** Mashonaland West, N Zimbabwe *18.15S 29.46E*
37 U9 **Goldfield** Nevada, W USA *37.40N 117.13W*
Goldingen *see* Kuldīga
Goldmarkt *see* Zlatna
8 K17 **Gold River** Vancouver Island, British Columbia, SW Canada *49.48N 126.01W*
23 V10 **Goldsboro** North Carolina, SE USA *35.22N 77.59W*
26 M8 **Goldsmith** Texas, SW USA *31.58N 102.36W*
27 R8 **Goldthwaite** Texas, SW USA *31.27N 98.34W*
143 R11 **Göle** Ardahan, NE Turkey *40.46N 42.36E*
Golema Ada *see* Ostrovo
116 H9 **Golema Planina** ▲▲ W Bulgaria
116 F9 **Golemi Vrŭkh** ▲ W Bulgaria *42.41N 22.38E*
112 D8 **Goleniów** *Ger.* Gollnow. Zachodniopomorskie, NW Poland *53.33N 14.48E*
149 R3 **Golestān** ◈ *province* N Iran
37 Q14 **Goleta** California, W USA *34.25N 119.51W*
45 O16 **Golfito** Puntarenas, SE Costa Rica *8.37N 83.07W*
27 T13 **Goliad** Texas, SW USA *28.40N 97.23W*
115 L14 **Golija** ▲▲ SW Serbia and Montenegro (Yugoslavia)
115 O16 **Goljak** ▲▲ SE Serbia and Montenegro (Yugoslavia)
142 M12 **Gölköy** Ordu, N Turkey *40.42N 37.37E*
Gollel *see* Lavumisa
111 X3 **Göllersbach** ≈ NE Austria
Gollnow *see* Goleniów
Golmo *see* Golmud
165 P10 **Golmud** *var.* Ge'e'mu, Golmo, *Chin.* Ko-erh-mu. Qinghai, C China *36.22N 94.56E*
105 Y14 **Golo** ≈ Corse, France, C Mediterranean Sea
Golovanevsk *see* Holovanivs'k
Golovchin *see* Halowchyn
41 N9 **Golovin** Alaska, USA *64.33N 162.54W*
148 M7 **Golpāyegān** *var.* Gulpaigan. Eşfahān, W Iran *33.22N 50.18E*
Golshan *see* Ţabas
Gol'shany *see* Hal'shany
98 J7 **Golspie** N Scotland, UK *57.58N 3.55W*
114 O11 **Golubac** Serbia, NE Serbia and Montenegro (Yugoslavia) *44.38N 21.36E*
112 J9 **Golub-Dobrzyń** Kujawski-pomorskie, C Poland *53.06N 19.03E*
151 S7 **Golubovka** Pavlodar, N Kazakhstan *53.07N 74.11E*
84 B11 **Golungo Alto** Cuanza Norte, NW Angola *9.10S 14.45E*
116 M8 **Golyama Kamchiya** ≈ E Bulgaria
116 L8 **Golyama Reka** ≈ N Bulgaria
116 H11 **Golyama Syutkya** ▲ SW Bulgaria *41.55N 24.03E*
116 I12 **Golyam Perelik** ▲ S Bulgaria *41.37N 24.34E*
116 I11 **Golyam Persenk** ▲ S Bulgaria *41.50N 24.33E*
125 F12 **Golyshmanovo** Tyumenskaya Oblast', C Russian Federation *56.22N 68.25E*
81 P19 **Goma** Nord Kivu, NE Dem. Rep. Congo *1.36S 29.07E*
171 Gg16 **Gomadan-zan** ▲ Honshū, SW Japan *34.03N 135.34E*
Gomati *see* Gumti
79 X14 **Gombe** Gombe, E Nigeria *10.19N 11.02E*
69 U10 **Gombe** *var.* Igombe. ≈ E Tanzania
79 Y14 **Gombi** Adamawa, E Nigeria *10.07N 12.45E*
Gombroon *see* Bandar-e 'Abbās
Gomel' *see* Homyel'
Gomel'skaya Oblast' *see* Homyel'skaya Voblasts'
66 N11 **Gomera** *island* Islas Canarias, Spain, NE Atlantic Ocean
42 I5 **Gómez Farias** Chihuahua, N Mexico *29.25N 107.46W*
42 L8 **Gómez Palacio** Durango, C Mexico *25.39N 103.30W*
164 J13 **Gomo** Xizang Zizhiqu, W China *33.37N 86.40E*
175 T11 **Gomumu, Pulau** *see* Gomumu, Pulau
149 T6 **Gonābād** *var.* Gunabad. Khorāsān, NE Iran *36.21N 58.38E*
46 L8 **Gonaïves** *var.* Les Gonaïves. N Haiti *19.26N 72.40W*
126 M13 **Gonam** ≈ NE Russian Federation
46 L9 **Gonâve, Canal de la** *var.* Canal de Sud. *channel* N Caribbean Sea
46 K9 **Gonâve, Golfe de la** *gulf* N Caribbean Sea
Gonâveh *see* Bandar-e Gonāveh
46 K9 **Gonâve, Île de la** *island* C Haiti
Gonbadān *see* Dow Gonbadān
149 Q3 **Gonbad-e Kāvūs** *var.* Gunbad-i-Qawus. Golestān, N Iran *37.15N 55.10E*
158 M12 **Gonda** Uttar Pradesh, N India *27.07N 81.58E*
Gondar *see* Gonder
82 I11 **Gonder** *var.* Gondar. Amhara, N Ethiopia *12.35N 37.27E*
80 J13 **Gondey** Moyen-Chari, S Chad *9.07N 19.10E*
160 J12 **Gondia** Mahārāshtra, C India *21.27N 80.12E*
106 G6 **Gondomar** Porto, NW Portugal *41.10N 8.34W*
142 C12 **Gönen** Balıkesir, W Turkey *40.06N 27.39E*
142 C12 **Gönen Çayı** ≈ NW Turkey
165 O15 **Gongbo'gyamda** Xizang Zizhiqu, W China *30.03N 93.10E*
165 N16 **Gonggar** Xizang Zizhiqu, W China *29.18N 90.56E*
166 G9 **Gongga Shan** ▲ C China *29.49N 101.55E*
165 T10 **Gonghe** Qinghai, C China *36.22N 100.44E*
164 I5 **Gongliu** *var.* Tokkuztara. Xinjiang Uygur Zizhiqu, NW China *43.29N 82.16E*
79 W14 **Gongola** ≈ E Nigeria
Gongoleh State *see* Jonglei
191 P5 **Gongolgon** New South Wales, SE Australia *30.19S 146.57E*
165 Q6 **Gongpoquan** Gansu, N China *41.45N 100.27E*
166 I10 **Gongxian** *var.* Gong Xian. Sichuan, C China *28.25N 104.51E*
163 V10 **Gongzhuling** *prev.* Huaide. Jilin, NE China *43.30N 124.48E*
165 S14 **Gonjo** Xizang Zizhiqu, W China *30.51N 98.16E*
109 B20 **Gonnesa** Sardegna, Italy, C Mediterranean Sea *39.15N 8.27E*
Gonni/Gónnos *see* Gónnoi
117 F15 **Gónnoi** *var.* Gonni, Gónnos; *prev.* Dereli. Thessalía, C Greece *39.52N 22.27E*
172 N9 **Gonohe** Aomori, Honshū, C Japan *40.34N 141.18E*
170 Cc11 **Gōnoura** Nagasaki, Iki, SW Japan *33.44N 129.41E*
37 O11 **Gonzales** California, W USA *36.30N 121.26W*
24 J9 **Gonzales** Louisiana, S USA *30.14N 90.55W*
27 T12 **Gonzales** Texas, SW USA *29.30N 97.27W*
43 P11 **González** Tamaulipas, C Mexico *22.52N 98.25W*
23 V6 **Goochland** Virginia, NE USA *37.40N 77.53W*
195 N16 **Goodenough Bay** *inlet* SE PNG
205 X14 **Goodenough, Cape** *headland* Antarctica *66.15S 126.34E*
195 N15 **Goodenough Island** *var.* Morata. *island* SE PNG
Good Hope *see* Fort Good Hope
41 N8 **Goodhope Bay** *bay* Alaska, USA
85 D26 **Good Hope, Cape of** *Afr.* Kaap de Goede Hoop, Kaap die Goeie Hoop. *headland* SW South Africa *34.19S 18.25E*
8 K10 **Good Hope Lake** British Columbia, W Canada *59.15N 129.18W*
85 E23 **Goodhouse** Northern Cape, W South Africa *28.54S 18.13E*
35 O15 **Gooding** Idaho, NW USA *42.56N 114.42W*
28 H3 **Goodland** Kansas, C USA *39.21N 101.42W*
181 Y15 **Goodlands** NW Mauritius *20.01S 57.39E*
22 J8 **Goodlettsville** Tennessee, S USA *36.19N 86.42W*
41 N13 **Goodnews** Alaska, USA *59.07N 161.35W*
27 O3 **Goodnight** Texas, SW USA *35.00N 101.07W*
191 Q4 **Goodooga** New South Wales, SE Australia *29.09S 147.30E*
31 N4 **Goodrich** North Dakota, N USA *47.24N 100.07W*
27 W10 **Goodrich** Texas, SW USA *30.36N 94.57W*
31 X10 **Goodview** Minnesota, N USA *44.04N 91.42W*
28 H8 **Goodwell** Oklahoma, C USA *36.36N 101.38W*
99 N17 **Goole** E England, UK *53.43N 0.46W*
191 O8 **Goolgowi** New South Wales, SE Australia *34.00S 145.43E*
190 I10 **Goolwa** South Australia *35.31S 138.43E*
189 Y11 **Goondiwindi** Queensland, E Australia *28.33S 150.22E*
100 O11 **Goor** Overijssel, E Netherlands *52.13N 6.33E*
Goose Bay *see* Happy Valley-Goose Bay
35 V13 **Gooseberry Creek** ≈ Wyoming, C USA
23 S14 **Goose Creek** South Carolina, SE USA *32.58N 80.01W*
65 M23 **Goose Green** *var.* Prado del Ganso. East Falkland, Falkland Islands *51.52S 59.00W*
17 G6 **Goose Lake** *var.* Lago dos Gansos. ◎ California/Oregon, W USA
31 Q4 **Goose River** ≈ North Dakota, N USA
159 T16 **Gopalganj** Dhaka, S Bangladesh *23.03N 89.52E*
159 O12 **Gopālganj** Bihār, N India *26.28N 84.25E*
Gopher State *see* Minnesota
103 I22 **Göppingen** Baden-Württemberg, SW Germany *48.42N 9.39E*
112 G13 **Góra** *Ger.* Guhrau. Dolnośląskie, SW Poland *51.40N 16.30E*
112 M12 **Góra Kalwaria** Mazowieckie, C Poland *52.00N 21.14E*
159 O12 **Gorakhpur** Uttar Pradesh, N India *26.45N 83.22E*
Gorany *see* Harany
115 J14 **Goražde** Federacija Bosna I Hercegovina, Bosnia and Herzegovina *43.39N 18.58E*
Gorbovichi *see* Harbavichy
Gorče Petrov *see* Đorče Petrov
(0) E9 **Gorda Ridges** *undersea feature* NE Pacific Ocean
Gordiaz *see* Gardēz
80 K12 **Gordil** Vakaga, N Central African Republic *9.37N 21.42E*
25 U5 **Gordon** Georgia, SE USA *32.52N 83.19W*
30 K12 **Gordon** Nebraska, C USA *42.48N 102.12W*
27 R7 **Gordon** Texas, SW USA *32.32N 98.21W*
30 L13 **Gordon Creek** ≈ Nebraska, C USA
65 I25 **Gordon, Isla** *island* S Chile
191 O17 **Gordon, Lake** ◎ Tasmania, SE Australia
191 O17 **Gordon River** ≈ Tasmania, SE Australia
23 V5 **Gordonsville** Virginia, NE USA *38.08N 78.11W*
82 H13 **Gorē** Oromo, C Ethiopia *8.08N 35.33E*
193 D24 **Gore** Southland, South Island, NZ *46.06S 168.58E*
80 H13 **Goré** Logone-Oriental, S Chad *7.55N 16.37E*
12 D11 **Gore Bay** Manitoulin Island, Ontario, S Canada *45.54N 82.28W*
27 Q5 **Goree** Texas, SW USA *33.28N 99.31W*
143 O11 **Görele** Giresun, NE Turkey *41.00N 39.00E*
21 N6 **Gore Mountain** ▲ Vermont, NE USA *44.55N 71.47W*
41 R13 **Gore Point** *headland* Alaska, USA *59.12N 150.57W*
39 R4 **Gore Range** ▲▲ Colorado, C USA
99 F19 **Gorey** *Ir.* Guaire. SE Ireland *52.40N 6.18W*
149 R12 **Gorgāb** Kermān, S Iran
149 Q4 **Gorgān** *var.* Astarabad, Astrabad, Gurgan; *prev.* Asterābād, *anc.* Hyrcania. Golestān, N Iran *36.53N 54.28E*
149 Q4 **Gorgān, Rūd-e** ≈ N Iran
78 I10 **Gorgol** ◈ *region* S Mauritania
108 D12 **Gorgona, Isola di** *island* Archipelago Toscano, C Italy
21 P8 **Gorham** Maine, NE USA *43.41N 70.27W*
143 T10 **Gori** C Georgia *42.00N 44.07E*
100 I13 **Gorinchem** *var.* Gorkum. Zuid-Holland, C Netherlands *51.49N 4.58E*
143 V13 **Goris** SE Armenia *39.31N 46.20E*
128 K16 **Goritsy** Tverskaya Oblast', W Russian Federation *57.09N 36.44E*
108 J7 **Gorizia** *Ger.* Görz. Friuli-Venezia Giulia, NE Italy *45.55N 13.37E*
118 G13 **Gorj** ◈ *county* SW Romania
111 W12 **Gorjanci** *var.* Uskočke Planine, Žumberak, Žumberačko Gorje, *Ger.* Uskokengebirge; *prev.* Sichelburger Gerbirge. ▲▲ Croatia/Slovenia *see also* Žumberačko Gorje
Görkau *see* Jirkov
Gorki *see* Horki
Gor'kiy *see* Nizhniy Novgorod
Gor'kiy Reservoir *see* Gor'kovskoye Vodokhranilishche
125 D9 **Gor'kovskoye Vodokhranilishche** *Eng.* Gor'kiy Reservoir. ▣ W Russian Federation
Gorkum *see* Gorinchem
97 I23 **Gørlev** Vestsjælland, E Denmark *55.33N 11.13E*
113 M17 **Gorlice** Małopolskie, S Poland *49.37N 21.08E*
103 Q15 **Görlitz** Sachsen, E Germany *51.09N 14.57E*
Görlitz *see* Zgorzelec
Gorlovka *see* Horlivka
27 R7 **Gorman** Texas, SW USA *32.12N 98.40W*
23 T3 **Gormania** West Virginia, NE USA *39.16N 79.18W*
Gorna Dzhumaya *see* Blagoevgrad
116 K8 **Gorna Oryakhovitsa** Veliko Tŭrnovo, N Bulgaria *43.12N 25.38E*
116 J8 **Gorna Studena** Veliko Tŭrnovo, N Bulgaria *43.26N 25.21E*
Gornja Mužlja *see* Mužlja
111 X9 **Gornja Radgona** *Ger.* Oberradkersburg. NE Slovenia *46.39N 16.00E*
114 M13 **Gornji Milanovac** Serbia, C Serbia and Montenegro (Yugoslavia) *44.01N 20.26E*
114 G13 **Gornji Vakuf** *var.* Uskoplje. Federacija Bosna I Hercegovina, W Bosnia and Herzegovina *43.55N 17.34E*
126 H15 **Gorno-Altaysk** Respublika Altay, S Russian Federation *51.58N 85.55E*
Gorno-Altayskaya Respublika *see* Altay, Respublika
126 K13 **Gorno-Chuyskiy** Irkutskaya Oblast', C Russian Federation *57.33N 111.38E*
129 V14 **Gornozavodsk** Permskaya Oblast', NW Russian Federation *58.21N 58.24E*
127 O16 **Gornozavodsk** Ostrov Sakhalin, Sakhalinskaya Oblast', SE Russian Federation *46.34N 141.52E*
126 Gg15 **Gornyak** Altayskiy Kray, S Russian Federation *50.58N 81.24E*
126 K15 **Gornyy** Chitinskaya Oblast', S Russian Federation *51.42N 48.26E*
131 R8 **Gornyy** Saratovskaya Oblast', W Russian Federation *51.42N 48.26E*
Gornyy Altay *see* Altay, Respublika
131 O10 **Gornyy Balykley** Volgogradskaya Oblast', SW Russian Federation *49.37N 45.03E*
82 I13 **Goroch'an** ▲ W Ethiopia *9.09N 37.16E*
Gorodenka *see* Horodenka
131 O3 **Gorodets** Nizhegorodskaya Oblast', W Russian Federation *56.36N 43.27E*
Gorodets *see* Haradzyets
Gorodeya *see* Haradzyeya
131 P6 **Gorodishche** Penzenskaya Oblast', W Russian Federation *53.17N 45.39E*
Gorodishche *see* Horodyshche
Gorodnya *see* Horodnya
Gorodok *see* Haradok
Gorodok/Gorodok Yagellonski *see* Horodok
130 M13 **Gorodovikovsk** Respublika Kalmykiya, SW Russian Federation *46.07N 41.56E*
194 I12 **Goroka** Eastern Highlands, C PNG *6.03S 145.22E*
Gorokhov *see* Horokhiv
131 N3 **Gorokhovets** Vladimirskaya Oblast', W Russian Federation *56.12N 42.40E*
79 Q11 **Gorom-Gorom** NE Burkina *14.27N 0.13W*
176 V12 **Gorong, Kepulauan** *island group* E Indonesia
85 M17 **Gorongosa** Sofala, C Mozambique *18.40S 34.03E*
176 Uu12 **Gorong, Pulau** *island* Kepulauan Gorong, E Indonesia
175 R8 **Gorontalo** Sulawesi, C Indonesia *0.33N 123.04E*
175 Qq8 **Gorontalo, Teluk** *bay* Sulawesi, C Indonesia
Gorontalo, Teluk *see* Tomini, Gulf of
112 L7 **Górowo Iławeckie** *Ger.* Landsberg. Warmińsko-Mazurskie, NE Poland, *54.18N 20.30E*
100 M7 **Gorredijk** *Fris.* De Gordyk. Friesland, N Netherlands *53.00N 6.04E*
86 C14 **Gorringe Ridge** *undersea feature* E Atlantic Ocean
100 M11 **Gorssel** Gelderland, E Netherlands *52.12N 6.13E*
111 T8 **Görtschitz** ≈ S Austria
Goryn *see* Horyn'
Görz *see* Gorizia
112 E10 **Gorzów Wielkopolski** *Ger.* Landsberg, Landsberg an der Warthe. Lubuskie, W Poland *52.43N 15.12E*
110 G9 **Göschenen** Uri, C Switzerland *46.40N 8.36E*
195 N16 **Goschen Strait** *strait* SE PNG
171 Kk13 **Gosen** Niigata, Honshū, C Japan *37.43N 139.11E*
191 T8 **Gosford** New South Wales, SE Australia *33.25S 151.22E*
33 P11 **Goshen** Indiana, N USA *41.34N 85.49W*
20 K13 **Goshen** New York, NE USA *41.24N 74.17W*
Goshoba *see* Koshoba
171 Mm8 **Goshogawara** *var.* Gosyogawara. Aomori, Honshū, C Japan *40.46N 140.24E*
Goshquduq Qum *see* Tosquduq Qumlari
103 J14 **Goslar** Niedersachsen, C Germany *51.55N 10.25E*
29 Y9 **Gosnell** Arkansas, C USA *35.57N 89.58W*
114 C11 **Gospić** Lika-Senj, C Croatia *44.32N 15.21E*
99 N23 **Gosport** S England, UK *50.48N 1.07W*
96 D9 **Gossa** *island* S Norway
110 H7 **Gossau** Sankt Gallen, NE Switzerland *47.25N 9.16E*
101 G20 **Gosselies** *var.* Goss'lies. Hainaut, S Belgium *50.28N 4.25E*
79 P10 **Gossi** Tombouctou, C Mali *15.44N 1.19W*
Goss'lies *see* Gosselies
115 N18 **Gostivar** W FYR Macedonia *41.48N 20.55E*
Gostomel' *see* Hostomel'
112 G12 **Gostyń** *var.* Gostyn. Wielkopolskie, C Poland *51.53N 16.59E*
112 K11 **Gostynin** Mazowieckie, C Poland *52.25N 19.27E*
Gosyogawara *see* Goshogawara
97 J18 **Göta Älv** ≈ S Sweden
97 N17 **Göta kanal** *canal* S Sweden
97 K18 **Götaland** *cultural region* S Sweden
97 H17 **Göteborg** *Eng.* Gothenburg. Västra Götaland, S Sweden *57.43N 11.58E*
79 X16 **Gotel Mountains** ▲▲ E Nigeria
97 K17 **Götene** Västra Götaland, S Sweden *58.31N 13.28E*
Gotera *see* San Francisco
103 K16 **Gotha** Thüringen, C Germany *50.57N 10.43E*
31 N15 **Gothenburg** Nebraska, C USA *40.57N 100.09W*

◆ Country ● Country Capital ◇ Dependent Territory ○ Dependent Territory Capital ◈ Administrative Region ✈ International Airport ▲ Mountain ▲▲ Mountain Range Volcano ≈ River ◎ Lake ▣ Reservoir

Gothenburg see Göteborg
79 R12 **Gothèye** Tillabéri, SW Niger 13.52N 1.27E
Gothland see Gotland
97 P19 **Gotland** var. Gothland, Gottland. ◈ county SE Sweden
97 O18 **Gotland** island SE Sweden
170 B12 **Gotō-rettō** island group SW Japan
116 H12 **Gotse Delchev** prev. Nevrokop. Blagoevgrad, SW Bulgaria 41.35N 23.43E
97 P17 **Gotska Sandön** island SE Sweden
170 Ee12 **Gōtsu** var. Gôtu. Shimane, Honshū, SW Japan 35.00N 132.13E
103 I15 **Göttingen** var. Goettingen. Niedersachsen, C Germany 51.33N 9.55E
Gottland see Gotland
95 I16 **Gottne** Västernorrland, C Sweden 63.27N 18.25E
Gottschee see Kočevje
Gottwaldov see Zlín
Gôtu see Gōtsu
Goturdepe see Koturdepe
110 I7 **Götzis** Vorarlberg, NW Austria 47.21N 9.40E
100 H12 **Gouda** Zuid-Holland, C Netherlands 52.01N 4.42E
78 I11 **Goudiri** var. Goudiry. E Senegal 14.12N 12.40W
Goudiry see Goudiri
79 X12 **Goudoumaria** Diffa, S Niger 13.28N 11.15E
13 R9 **Gouffre, Rivière du** ↝ Quebec, SE Canada
67 M19 **Gough Fracture Zone** tectonic feature S Atlantic Ocean
67 M19 **Gough Island** island Tristan da Cunha, S Atlantic Ocean
13 N8 **Gouin, Réservoir** ⊠ Quebec, SE Canada
12 B10 **Goulais River** Ontario, S Canada 46.41N 84.22W
191 R9 **Goulburn** New South Wales, SE Australia 34.45S 149.43E
191 O11 **Goulburn River** ↝ Victoria, SE Australia
205 O10 **Gould Coast** physical region Antarctica
Goulimime see Guelmime
116 F13 **Gouménissa** Kentrikí Makedonía, N Greece 40.55N 22.27E
79 O10 **Goundam** Tombouctou, NW Mali 16.25N 3.41W
80 H12 **Goundi** Moyen-Chari, S Chad 9.18N 17.21E
80 G12 **Gounou-Gaya** Mayo-Kébbi, SW Chad 9.37N 15.30E
79 O12 **Gourci** var. Gourcy. NW Burkina 13.14N 2.22W
Gourcy see Gourci
104 M13 **Gourdon** Lot, S France 44.45N 1.22E
79 W11 **Gouré** Zinder, SE Niger 13.58N 10.16E
104 G6 **Gourin** Morbihan, NW France 48.07N 3.37W
79 P10 **Gourma-Rharous** Tombouctou, C Mali 16.54N 1.55W
105 N4 **Gournay-en-Bray** Seine-Maritime, N France 49.29N 1.42E
80 J6 **Gouro** Borkou-Ennedi-Tibesti, N Chad 19.26N 19.36E
106 H8 **Gouveia** Guarda, N Portugal 40.28N 7.34W
20 I7 **Gouverneur** New York, NE USA 44.20N 75.27W
101 L21 **Gouvy** Luxembourg, E Belgium 50.10N 5.55E
47 R14 **Gouyave** var. Charlotte Town. NW Grenada 12.10N 61.43W
Goverla, Gora see Hoverla, Hora
61 N20 **Governador Valadares** Minas Gerais, SE Brazil 18.51S 41.57W
179 Rr16 **Governor Generoso** Mindanao, S Philippines 6.36N 126.06E
46 I2 **Governor's Harbour** Eleuthera Island, C Bahamas 25.11N 76.15W
168 F9 **Govĭ-Altay** ◈ province SW Mongolia
168 I10 **Govĭ Altayn Nuruu** ▲ S Mongolia
160 L9 **Govind Ballabh Pant Sāgar** ⊠ C India
158 I7 **Govind Sāgar** ⊠ NE India
153 N14 **Govurdak** Turkm. Gowurdak; prev. Guardak. Lebapskiy Velayat, E Turkmenistan 37.50N 66.06E
20 D11 **Gowanda** New York, NE USA 42.25N 78.55W
154 J10 **Gowd-e Zereh, Dasht-e** var. Guad-i-Zirreh. marsh SW Afghanistan
12 F8 **Gowganda** Ontario, S Canada 47.39N 80.43W
12 G8 **Gowganda Lake** ◎ Ontario, S Canada
31 U13 **Gowrie** Iowa, C USA 42.16N 94.17W
Gowurdak see Govurdak
63 C15 **Goya** Corrientes, NE Argentina 29.10S 59.15W
Goyania see Goiânia
143 X11 **Göyçay** Rus. Geokchay. C Azerbaijan 40.38N 47.44E
Goymat see Koymat
Goymatdag see Koymatdag, Gory
142 F12 **Göynük** Bolu, NW Turkey 40.24N 30.45E
172 N12 **Goyō-san** ▲ Honshū, C Japan 39.12N 141.40E
80 K11 **Goz Beïda** Ouaddaï, SE Chad 12.06N 21.22E
152 M10 **G'ozg'on** Rus. Gazgan. Navoiy Viloyati, C Uzbekistan 40.36N 65.29E
164 H11 **Gozha Co** ◎ W China
123 J15 **Gozo** Malt. Ghawdex. island N Malta
82 H9 **Gōz Regeb** Kassala, NE Sudan 16.03N 35.33E
Gozyō see Gojō
85 H25 **Graaff-Reinet** Eastern Cape, S South Africa 32.16S 24.31E
Graasten see Gråsten
78 L17 **Grabo** SW Ivory Coast 4.57N 7.30W
114 P11 **Grabovica** Serbia, E Serbia and Montenegro (Yugoslavia) 44.30N 22.29E
112 I13 **Grabów nad Prosną** Wielkopolskie, C Poland 51.30N 18.06E
110 I8 **Grabs** Sankt Gallen, NE Switzerland 47.10N 9.27E
114 D12 **Gračac** Zadar, C Croatia 44.18N 15.52E
114 I11 **Gračanica** Federacija Bosna I Hercegovina, NE Bosnia and Herzegovina 44.41N 18.20E
12 L11 **Gracefield** Quebec, SE Canada 46.06N 76.03W
101 K19 **Grâce-Hollogne** Liège, E Belgium 50.38N 5.30E
25 R8 **Graceville** Florida, SE USA 30.57N 85.31W
31 R8 **Graceville** Minnesota, N USA 45.34N 96.25W
44 G6 **Gracias** Lempira, W Honduras 14.34N 88.34W
Gracias see Lempira
44 L5 **Gracias a Dios** ◈ department E Honduras
45 O6 **Gracias a Dios, Cabo de** headland Honduras/Nicaragua 15.00N 83.10W
66 O2 **Graciosa** var. Ilha Graciosa. island Azores, Portugal, NE Atlantic Ocean
66 Q11 **Graciosa** island Islas Canarias, Spain, NE Atlantic Ocean
Graciosa, Ilha see Graciosa
114 I11 **Gradačac** Federacija Bosna I Hercegovina, N Bosnia and Herzegovina 44.51N 18.24E
61 J15 **Gradaús, Serra dos** ▲ C Brazil
106 L3 **Gradefes** Castilla-León, N Spain 42.37N 5.13W
Gradiška see Bosanska Gradiška
Gradizhsk see Hradyz'k
108 J7 **Grado** Friuli-Venezia Giulia, NE Italy 45.41N 13.24E
106 K2 **Grado** Asturias, N Spain 43.22N 6.04W
115 P19 **Gradsko** C FYR Macedonia 41.34N 21.56E
39 V11 **Grady** New Mexico, SW USA 34.49N 103.19W
31 T12 **Graettinger** Iowa, C USA 43.14N 94.45W
103 M23 **Grafing** Bayern, SE Germany 48.01N 11.57E
27 S6 **Graford** Texas, SW USA 32.56N 98.15W
191 V5 **Grafton** New South Wales, SE Australia 29.41S 152.55E
31 Q3 **Grafton** North Dakota, N USA 48.24N 97.24W
23 S3 **Grafton** West Virginia, NE USA 39.20N 80.01W
23 T9 **Graham** North Carolina, SE USA 36.04N 79.24W
27 R6 **Graham** Texas, SW USA 33.06N 98.34W
Graham Bell Island see Greem-Bell, Ostrov
8 I13 **Graham Island** island Queen Charlotte Islands, British Columbia, SW Canada
21 S6 **Graham Lake** ◎ Maine, NE USA
204 H4 **Graham Land** physical region Antarctica
39 N15 **Graham, Mount** ▲ Arizona, SW USA 32.42N 109.52W
Grahamstad see Grahamstown
85 I25 **Grahamstown** Afr. Grahamstad. Eastern Cape, S South Africa 33.18S 26.31E
Grahovo see Bosansko Grahovo
70 C11 **Grain Coast** coastal region S Liberia
174 Mm16 **Grajagan** Jawa, S Indonesia 8.33S 114.13E
174 Mm16 **Grajagan, Teluk** bay Jawa, S Indonesia
61 L14 **Grajaú** Maranhão, E Brazil 5.49S 45.12W
60 M13 **Grajaú, Rio** ↝ NE Brazil
112 O8 **Grajewo** Podlaskie, NE Poland 53.38N 22.25E
97 F24 **Gram** Sønderjylland, SW Denmark 55.18N 9.03E
105 N13 **Gramat** Lot, S France 44.45N 1.45E
24 H5 **Grambling** Louisiana, S USA 32.31N 92.43W
117 C14 **Grámmos** ▲ Albania/Greece
98 I9 **Grampian Mountains** ▲ C Scotland, UK
190 L12 **Grampians, The** ▲ Victoria, SE Australia
100 O9 **Gramsbergen** Overijssel, E Netherlands 52.37N 6.39E
115 L21 **Gramsh** var. Gramshi. Elbasan, C Albania 40.52N 20.12E
Gramshi see Gramsh
Gran see Hron, Slovakia
Gran see Esztergom, N Hungary
56 F11 **Granada** Meta, C Colombia 3.36N 73.44W
44 J10 **Granada** Granada, SW Nicaragua 11.55N 85.58W
107 N14 **Granada** Andalucía, S Spain 37.13N 3.40W
39 W6 **Granada** Colorado, C USA 38.00N 102.18W
44 J11 **Granada** ◈ department SW Nicaragua
107 N14 **Granada** ◈ province Andalucía, S Spain
65 I21 **Gran Altiplanicie Central** plain S Argentina
99 E17 **Granard** Ir. Gránard. C Ireland 53.46N 7.30W
65 J20 **Gran Bajo** basin S Argentina
65 J15 **Gran Bajo del Gualicho** basin E Argentina
65 I21 **Gran Bajo de San Julián** basin SE Argentina
27 S7 **Granbury** Texas, SW USA 32.26N 97.47W
13 P12 **Granby** Quebec, SE Canada 45.24N 72.40W
29 S8 **Granby** Missouri, C USA 36.55N 94.14W
39 S3 **Granby, Lake** ⊠ Colorado, C USA
66 O12 **Gran Canaria** var. Grand Canary. island Islas Canarias, Spain, NE Atlantic Ocean
49 T11 **Gran Chaco** var. Chaco. lowland plain South America
47 R14 **Grand Anse** SW Grenada 12.01N 61.45W
Grand-Anse see Portsmouth
46 G1 **Grand Bahama Island** island N Bahamas
Grand Balé see Tui
105 U7 **Grand Ballon** Ger. Ballon de Guebwiller. ▲ NE France 47.53N 7.06E
11 T13 **Grand Bank** Newfoundland and Labrador, SE Canada 47.04N 55.46W
66 I7 **Grand Banks of Newfoundland and Labrador** undersea feature NW Atlantic Ocean
Grand Bassa see Buchanan
79 N17 **Grand-Bassam** var. Bassam. SE Ivory Coast 5.13N 3.46W
12 E16 **Grand Bend** Ontario, S Canada 43.17N 81.46W
78 L17 **Grand-Bérébi** var. Grand-Béréby. SW Ivory Coast 4.37N 6.55W
Grand-Béréby see Grand-Bérébi
47 X11 **Grand-Bourg** Marie-Galante, SE Guadeloupe 15.53N 61.18W
46 M6 **Grand Caicos** var. Middle Caicos. island C Turks and Caicos Islands
12 K12 **Grand Calumet, Île du** island Quebec, SE Canada
99 E18 **Grand Canal** Ir. An Chanáil Mhór. canal C Ireland
Grand Canary see Gran Canaria
38 K10 **Grand Canyon** Arizona, SW USA 36.01N 112.10W
38 J9 **Grand Canyon** canyon Arizona, SW USA
Grand Canyon State see Arizona
46 D8 **Grand Cayman** island SW Cayman Islands
9 R14 **Grand Centre** Alberta, SW Canada 54.25N 110.13W
78 L17 **Grand Cess** SE Liberia 4.36N 8.12W
110 D12 **Grand Combin** ▲ S Switzerland 45.58N 7.27E
34 K8 **Grand Coulee** Washington, NW USA 47.56N 119.00W
34 J8 **Grand Coulee** valley Washington, NW USA
47 X5 **Grand Cul-de-Sac Marin** bay N Guadeloupe
Grand Duchy of Luxembourg see Luxembourg
65 I22 **Grande, Bahía** bay S Argentina
9 N14 **Grande Cache** Alberta, W Canada 53.52N 119.07W
105 U12 **Grande Casse** ▲ E France 45.22N 6.50E
180 G12 **Grande Comore** var. Njazidja, Great Comoro. island NW Comoros
63 G18 **Grande, Cuchilla** hill range E Uruguay
47 S5 **Grande de Añasco, Río** ↝ W Puerto Rico
Grande de Chiloé, Isla see Chiloé, Isla de
60 J12 **Grande de Gurupá, Ilha** river island NE Brazil
59 K21 **Grande de Lipez, Río** ↝ SW Bolivia
47 U6 **Grande de Loíza, Río** ↝ E Puerto Rico
47 T5 **Grande de Manatí, Río** ↝ C Puerto Rico
44 L9 **Grande de Matagalpa, Río** ↝ C Nicaragua
42 K12 **Grande de Santiago, Río** var. Santiago. ↝ C Mexico
45 O15 **Grande de Térraba, Río** var. Río Térraba. ↝ SE Costa Rica
10 J9 **Grande Deux, Réservoir la** ⊠ Quebec, SE Canada
62 O10 **Grande, Ilha** island SE Brazil
9 O13 **Grande Prairie** Alberta, W Canada 55.10N 118.52W
76 I8 **Grand Erg Occidental** desert W Algeria
76 L9 **Grand Erg Oriental** desert Algeria/Tunisia
61 J20 **Grande, Rio** ↝ S Brazil
2 F15 **Grande, Rio** var. Río Bravo, Sp. Río Bravo del Norte, Bravo del Norte. ↝ Mexico/USA
59 M18 **Grande, Río** ↝ C Bolivia
13 Y7 **Grande-Rivière** Quebec, SE Canada 48.27N 64.37W
13 Y6 **Grande Rivière** ↝ Quebec, SE Canada
46 M8 **Grande-Rivière-du-Nord** N Haiti 19.28N 72.07W
64 K9 **Grande, Salina** var. Gran Salitral. salt lake C Argentina
13 S7 **Grandes-Bergeronnes** Quebec, SE Canada 48.16N 69.32W
49 W6 **Grande, Serra** ▲ W Brazil
42 K4 **Grande, Sierra** ▲ N Mexico
105 S12 **Grandes Rousses** ▲ E France
65 K17 **Grandes, Salinas** salt lake E Argentina
47 Y5 **Grande Terre** island E West Indies
13 X5 **Grande-Vallée** Quebec, SE Canada 49.12N 65.08W
47 Y5 **Grande Vigie, Pointe de la** headland Grande Terre, N Guadeloupe 16.31N 61.27W
11 N14 **Grand Falls** New Brunswick, SE Canada 47.01N 67.46W
11 T11 **Grand Falls** Newfoundland and Labrador, SE Canada 48.57N 55.48W
26 L9 **Grandfalls** Texas, SW USA 31.20N 102.51W
23 P9 **Grandfather Mountain** ▲ North Carolina, SE USA 36.06N 81.48W
28 L13 **Grandfield** Oklahoma, C USA 34.15N 98.40W
9 N17 **Grand Forks** British Columbia, SW Canada 49.01N 118.30W
31 R4 **Grand Forks** North Dakota, N USA 47.54N 97.02W
33 O9 **Grand Haven** Michigan, N USA 43.03N 86.13W
Grandichi see Hrandzichy
31 P15 **Grand Island** Nebraska, C USA 40.55N 98.20W
33 O3 **Grand Island** island Michigan, N USA
24 K10 **Grand Isle** Louisiana, S USA 29.12N 90.00W
67 A23 **Grand Jason** island Jason Islands, NW Falkland Islands
39 P5 **Grand Junction** Colorado, C USA 39.03N 108.33W
22 F10 **Grand Junction** Tennessee, S USA 35.03N 89.11W
12 J9 **Grand-Lac-Victoria** Quebec, SE Canada 47.33N 77.28W
12 J9 **Grand lac Victoria** ◎ Quebec, SE Canada
79 N17 **Grand-Lahou** var. Grand Lahu. S Ivory Coast 5.09N 5.01W
Grand Lahu see Grand-Lahou
39 S3 **Grand Lake** Colorado, C USA 40.15N 105.49W
11 S11 **Grand Lake** ◎ Newfoundland and Labrador, E Canada
24 G9 **Grand Lake** ◎ Louisiana, S USA
33 R5 **Grand Lake** ◎ Michigan, N USA
33 Q13 **Grand Lake** ⊠ Ohio, N USA
29 R9 **Grand Lake O' The Cherokees** var. Lake O' The Cherokees. ⊠ Oklahoma, C USA
33 Q9 **Grand Ledge** Michigan, N USA 42.45N 84.45W
104 I8 **Grand-Lieu, Lac de** ◎ NW France
21 U6 **Grand Manan Channel** channel Canada/USA
11 O15 **Grand Manan Island** island New Brunswick, SE Canada
31 Y4 **Grand Marais** Minnesota, N USA 47.45N 90.19W
13 P10 **Grand-Mère** Quebec, SE Canada 46.36N 72.41W
39 P5 **Grand Mesa** ▲ Colorado, C USA
110 C10 **Grand Muveran** ▲ W Switzerland 46.16N 7.12E
106 G12 **Grândola** Setúbal, S Portugal 38.10N 8.34W
Grand Paradis see Gran Paradiso
197 G4 **Grand Passage** passage N New Caledonia
79 R16 **Grand-Popo** S Benin 6.19N 1.49E
31 Z3 **Grand Portage** Minnesota, N USA 48.00N 89.36W
27 T6 **Grand Prairie** Texas, SW USA 32.45N 97.00W
9 W14 **Grand Rapids** Manitoba, C Canada 53.12N 99.19W
33 P9 **Grand Rapids** Michigan, N USA 42.57N 86.40W
31 V5 **Grand Rapids** Minnesota, N USA 47.14N 93.31W
197 G5 **Grand Récif de Koumac** reef W New Caledonia
197 J8 **Grand Récif Sud** reef S New Caledonia
12 L10 **Grand-Remous** Quebec, SE Canada 46.36N 75.53W
12 F15 **Grand River** ↝ Ontario, S Canada
33 P9 **Grand River** ↝ Michigan, N USA
29 T3 **Grand River** ↝ Missouri, C USA
30 M7 **Grand River** ↝ South Dakota, N USA
47 Q11 **Grand' Rivière** N Martinique 14.51N 61.12W
34 F11 **Grand Ronde** Oregon, NW USA 45.03N 123.43W
34 L11 **Grand Ronde River** ↝ Oregon/Washington, NW USA
Grand-Saint-Bernard, Col du see Great Saint Bernard Pass
27 V6 **Grand Saline** Texas, SW USA 32.40N 95.42W
57 X10 **Grand-Santi** W French Guiana 4.19N 54.24W
Grandsee see Grandson
110 B9 **Grandson** prev. Grandsee. Vaud, W Switzerland 46.49N 6.39E
180 J16 **Grand Sœur** island Les Sœurs, NE Seychelles
35 S14 **Grand Teton** ▲ Wyoming, C USA 43.44N 110.48W
33 P5 **Grand Traverse Bay** lake bay Michigan, N USA
47 N6 **Grand Turk** ○ (Turks and Caicos Islands) Grand Turk Island, S Turks and Caicos Islands 21.24N 71.08W
47 N6 **Grand Turk Island** island SE Turks and Caicos Islands
105 S13 **Grand Veymont** ▲ E France 44.51N 5.32E
9 W15 **Grandview** Manitoba, S Canada 51.10N 100.40W
29 R4 **Grandview** Missouri, C USA 38.53N 94.31W
38 I10 **Grand Wash Cliffs** cliff Arizona, SW USA
12 J8 **Granet, Lac** ◎ Quebec, SE Canada
97 L14 **Grangärde** Dalarna, C Sweden 60.15N 15.00E
46 H12 **Grange Hill** W Jamaica 18.18N 78.10W
98 J12 **Grangemouth** C Scotland, UK 56.01N 3.43W
27 T10 **Granger** Texas, SW USA 30.43N 97.26W
34 J10 **Granger** Washington, NW USA 46.20N 120.11W
35 T17 **Granger** Wyoming, C USA 41.37N 109.58W
Granges see Grenchen
97 L14 **Grängesberg** Dalarna, C Sweden 60.06N 15.00E
35 N11 **Grangeville** Idaho, NW USA 45.55N 116.07W
8 K13 **Granisle** British Columbia, SW Canada 54.55N 126.13W
32 K15 **Granite City** Illinois, N USA 38.42N 90.09W
31 S9 **Granite Falls** Minnesota, N USA 44.48N 95.33W
23 Q9 **Granite Falls** North Carolina, SE USA 35.48N 81.25W
38 K12 **Granite Mountain** ▲ Arizona, SW USA 34.38N 112.34W
35 T12 **Granite Peak** ▲ Montana, NW USA 45.09N 109.48W
37 T2 **Granite Peak** ▲ Nevada, W USA 41.40N 117.35W
38 J3 **Granite Peak** ▲ Utah, W USA 40.09N 113.18W
Granite State see New Hampshire
109 H24 **Granitola, Capo** headland Sicilia, Italy, C Mediterranean Sea 37.33N 12.39E
193 H15 **Granity** West Coast, South Island, NZ 41.37S 171.53E
Gran Lago see Nicaragua, Lago de
65 J18 **Gran Laguna Salada** ◎ S Argentina
Gran Malvina, Isla see West Falkland
97 L18 **Gränna** Jönköping, S Sweden 58.01N 14.30E
107 W5 **Granollers** var. Granollérs. Cataluña, NE Spain 41.37N 2.18E
108 A7 **Gran Paradiso** Fr. Grand Paradis. ▲ NW Italy 45.31N 7.13E
Gran Pilastro see Hochfeiler
Gran Salitral see Grande, Salina
Gran San Bernardo, Passo di see Great Saint Bernard Pass
Gran Santiago see Santiago
109 J14 **Gran Sasso d'Italia** ▲ C Italy
102 N11 **Gransee** Brandenburg, NE Germany 53.00N 13.10E
30 L15 **Grant** Nebraska, C USA 40.50N 101.43W
29 R1 **Grant City** Missouri, C USA 40.29N 94.24W
99 N19 **Grantham** E England, UK 52.55N 0.39W
67 D24 **Grantham Sound** sound East Falkland, Falkland Islands
204 K13 **Grant Island** island Antarctica
47 Z14 **Grantley Adams** ✈ (Bridgetown) SE Barbados 13.04N 59.29W
37 S7 **Grant, Mount** ▲ Nevada, W USA 38.34N 118.47W
98 J9 **Grantown-on-Spey** N Scotland, UK 57.11N 3.52W
37 W8 **Grant Range** ▲ Nevada, W USA
39 Q11 **Grants** New Mexico, SW USA 35.09N 107.50W
32 I4 **Grantsburg** Wisconsin, N USA 45.46N 92.40W
34 F15 **Grants Pass** Oregon, NW USA 42.26N 123.19W
38 K3 **Grantsville** Utah, W USA 40.36N 112.27W
23 R4 **Grantsville** West Virginia, NE USA 38.54N 81.04W
104 I5 **Granville** Manche, N France 48.49N 1.34W
9 V12 **Granville Lake** ◎ Manitoba, C Canada
27 V8 **Grapeland** Texas, SW USA 31.29N 95.28W
27 T6 **Grapevine** Texas, SW USA 32.55N 97.04W
85 K20 **Graskop** Mpumalanga, NE South Africa 24.58S 30.49E
97 P14 **Gräsö** Uppsala, C Sweden 60.22N 18.30E
95 I19 **Gräsö** island C Sweden
105 U15 **Grasse** Alpes-Maritimes, SE France 43.42N 6.52E
20 E14 **Grassflat** Pennsylvania, NE USA 41.00N 78.04W
35 U9 **Grassrange** Montana, NW USA 47.02N 108.48W
20 J6 **Grass River** ↝ New York, NE USA
37 P6 **Grass Valley** California, W USA 39.12N 121.04W
191 N14 **Grassy** Tasmania, SE Australia 40.03S 144.04E
30 K4 **Grassy Butte** North Dakota, N USA 47.20N 103.13W
23 R5 **Grassy Knob** ▲ West Virginia, NE USA 38.04N 80.31W
97 G24 **Gråsten** var. Graasten. Sønderjylland, SW Denmark 54.55N 9.37E
97 J18 **Grästorp** Västra Götaland, S Sweden 58.19N 12.45E
Gratianopolis see Grenoble
111 V8 **Gratwein** Steiermark, SE Austria 47.06N 15.18E
Gratz see Graz
110 I9 **Graubünden** Fr. Grisons, It. Grigioni. ◈ canton SE Switzerland
Graudenz see Grudziądz
105 N15 **Graulhet** Tarn, S France 43.45N 1.58E
107 T4 **Graus** Aragón, NE Spain 42.11N 0.21E
63 I16 **Gravataí** Rio Grande do Sul, S Brazil 29.55S 51.00W
100 L13 **Grave** Noord-Brabant, SE Netherlands 51.45N 5.45E
9 T17 **Gravelbourg** Saskatchewan, S Canada 49.52N 106.33W
105 N1 **Gravelines** Nord, N France 51.00N 2.07E
Graven see Grez-Doiceau
12 H13 **Gravenhurst** Ontario, S Canada 44.55N 79.22W
35 O10 **Grave Peak** ▲ Idaho, NW USA 46.24N 114.43W
104 I11 **Grave, Pointe de** headland W France 45.33N 1.24W
191 S4 **Gravesend** New South Wales, SE Australia 29.37S 150.15E
99 P22 **Gravesend** SE England, UK 51.27N 0.24E
109 N17 **Gravina di Puglia** Eng. Gravina in Puglia. Puglia, SE Italy 40.48N 16.25E
Gravina in Puglia see Gravina di Puglia
105 S8 **Gray** Haute-Saône, E France 47.28N 5.34E
25 T4 **Gray** Georgia, SE USA 33.00N 83.31W
205 V16 **Gray, Cape** headland Antarctica, 67.30S 143.30E
34 F9 **Grayland** Washington, NW USA 46.46N 124.07W
41 N10 **Grayling** Alaska, USA 62.55N 160.07W
33 Q6 **Grayling** Michigan, N USA 44.40N 84.43W
34 F9 **Grays Harbor** inlet Washington, NW USA
23 O5 **Grayson** Kentucky, S USA 38.19N 82.57W
39 S4 **Grays Peak** ▲ Colorado, C USA 39.37N 105.49W
32 M16 **Grayville** Illinois, N USA 38.15N 87.59W
111 V8 **Graz** prev. Gratz. Steiermark, SE Austria 47.04N 15.23E
106 L15 **Grazalema** Andalucía, S Spain 36.46N 5.22W
115 P15 **Grdelica** Serbia, SE Serbia and Montenegro (Yugoslavia) 42.54N 22.05E
46 H1 **Great Abaco** var. Abaco Island. island N Bahamas
Great Admiralty Island see Manus Island
Great Alfold see Great Hungarian Plain
Great Ararat see Büyükağrı Dağı
189 U8 **Great Artesian Basin** lowlands Queensland, C Australia
197 I15 **Great Astrolabe Reef** reef Kadavu, SW Fiji
189 O12 **Great Australian Bight** bight S Australia
66 E11 **Great Bahama Bank** undersea feature E Gulf of Mexico
192 M4 **Great Barrier Island** island N NZ
189 X4 **Great Barrier Reef** reef Queensland, NE Australia
20 L11 **Great Barrington** Massachusetts, NE USA 42.11N 73.20W
(0) F10 **Great Basin** basin W USA
15 H5 **Great Bear Lake** Fr. Grand Lac de l'Ours. ◎ Northwest Territories, NW Canada
Great Belt see Storebælt
28 L5 **Great Bend** Kansas, C USA 38.21N 98.45W
Great Bermuda see Bermuda
99 A20 **Great Blasket Island** Ir. An Blascaod Mór. island SW Ireland
Great Britain see Britain
157 Q23 **Great Channel** channel Andaman Sea/Indian Ocean
177 F10 **Great Coco Island** island SW Myanmar
Great Crosby see Crosby
23 X7 **Great Dismal Swamp** wetland North Carolina/Virginia, SE USA
35 V16 **Great Divide Basin** basin Wyoming, C USA
189 W7 **Great Dividing Range** ▲ NE Australia
12 D12 **Great Duck Island** island Ontario, S Canada
Great Elder Reservoir see Waconda Lake
205 V8 **Greater Antarctica** var. East Antarctica. physical region Antarctica
46 G8 **Greater Antilles** island group West Indies
133 V16 **Greater Sunda Islands** var. Sunda Islands. island group Indonesia
192 I1 **Great Exhibition Bay** inlet North Island, NZ
46 H4 **Great Exuma Island** island C Bahamas
35 R8 **Great Falls** Montana, NW USA 47.30N 111.18W
23 R11 **Great Falls** South Carolina, SE USA 34.34N 80.54W
86 F9 **Great Fisher Bank** undersea feature C North Sea
Great Glen see Mor, Glen
Great Grimsby see Grimsby
46 I4 **Great Guana Cay** island C Bahamas
66 I5 **Great Hellefiske Bank** undersea feature N Atlantic Ocean
113 L24 **Great Hungarian Plain** var. Great Alfold, Plain of Hungary, Hung. Alföld. plain SE Europe
46 L7 **Great Inagua** var. Inagua Islands. island S Bahamas
Great Indian Desert see Thar Desert
85 G25 **Great Karoo** var. Great Karroo, High Veld, Afr. Groot Karoo, Hoë Karoo. plateau region S South Africa
Great Karroo see Great Karoo
Great Kei see Groot-Kei
Great Khingan Range see Da Hinggan Ling
12 E11 **Great La Cloche Island** island Ontario, S Canada
191 P16 **Great Lake** ◎ Tasmania, SE Australia
Great Lake see Tônlé Sap
16 O16 **Great Lakes** lakes Ontario, Canada/USA
Great Lakes State see Michigan
99 L20 **Great Malvern** W England, UK 52.07N 2.19W
192 M5 **Great Mercury Island** island N NZ
Great Meteor Seamount see Great Meteor Tablemount
66 K10 **Great Meteor Tablemount** var. Great Meteor Seamount. undersea feature E Atlantic Ocean 30.00N 28.30W
33 Q14 **Great Miami River** ↝ Ohio, N USA
157 Q24 **Great Nicobar** island Nicobar Islands, India, NE Indian Ocean
99 O19 **Great Ouse** var. Ouse. ↝ E England, UK
191 Q17 **Great Oyster Bay** bay Tasmania, SE Australia
46 I13 **Great Pedro Bluff** headland W Jamaica 17.51N 77.44W
23 T12 **Great Pee Dee River** ↝ North Carolina/South Carolina, SE USA
133 W9 **Great Plain of China** plain E China
(0) F12 **Great Plains** var. High Plains. plains Canada/USA
39 W6 **Great Plains Reservoirs** ⊠ Colorado, C USA
21 Q13 **Great Point** headland Nantucket Island, Massachusetts, NE USA 41.23N 70.03W
70 I13 **Great Rift Valley** var. Rift Valley. depression Asia/Africa
83 I23 **Great Ruaha** ↝ S Tanzania
20 K10 **Great Sacandaga Lake** ⊠ New York, NE USA
110 C12 **Great Saint Bernard Pass** Fr. Col du Grand-Saint-Bernard, It. Passo di Gran San Bernardo. pass Italy/Switzerland 45.52N 7.10E
46 F1 **Great Sale Cay** island N Bahamas
Great Salt Desert see Kavīr, Dasht-e
38 K1 **Great Salt Lake** salt lake Utah, W USA
38 J3 **Great Salt Lake Desert** plain Utah, W USA
28 M8 **Great Salt Plains Lake** ⊠ Oklahoma, C USA
77 T9 **Great Sand Sea** desert Egypt/Libya
188 L6 **Great Sandy Desert** desert Western Australia
Great Sandy Desert see Ar Rub' al Khālī
Great Sandy Island see Fraser Island
197 I13 **Great Sea Reef** reef Vanua Levu, N Fiji
40 H17 **Great Sitkin Island** island Aleutian Islands, Alaska, USA
15 I8 **Great Slave Lake** Fr. Grand Lac des Esclaves. ◎ Northwest Territories, NW Canada
23 O10 **Great Smoky Mountains** ▲ North Carolina/Tennessee, SE USA
8 L11 **Great Snow Mountain** ▲ British Columbia, W Canada 57.22N 124.08W
66 A12 **Great Sound** bay Bermuda, NW Atlantic Ocean
188 M10 **Great Victoria Desert** desert South Australia/Western Australia
204 H2 **Great Wall** Chinese research station South Shetland Islands, Antarctica 61.57S 58.23W
21 T7 **Great Wass Island** island Maine, NE USA
99 Q19 **Great Yarmouth** var. Yarmouth. E England, UK 52.37N 1.43E
145 S1 **Great Zab** Ar. Az Zāb al Kabīr, Kurd. Zē-i Bādinān, Turk. Büyükzap Suyu. ↝ Iraq/Turkey
97 I17 **Grebbestad** Västra Götaland, S Sweden 58.42N 11.15E
Grebenka see Hrebinka
44 M13 **Grecia** Alajuela, C Costa Rica 10.04N 84.19W
63 E18 **Greco** Río Negro, W Uruguay 32.49S 57.03W
Greco, Cape see Gkréko, Akrotíri
106 L8 **Gredos, Sierra de** ▲ W Spain
20 F9 **Greece** New York, NE USA 43.12N 77.41W
117 E17 **Greece** off. Hellenic Republic, Gk. Elláș; anc. Hellas. ◆ republic SE Europe
Greece Central see Stereá Ellás
Greece West see Dytikí Ellás
39 T3 **Greeley** Colorado, C USA 40.21N 104.41W
31 P14 **Greeley** Nebraska, C USA 41.33N 98.31W
126 Hh1 **Greem-Bell, Ostrov** Eng. Graham Bell Island. island Zemlya Frantsa-Iosifa, N Russian Federation
32 M6 **Green Bay** Wisconsin, N USA 44.32N 88.00W
33 N6 **Green Bay** lake bay Michigan/Wisconsin, N USA
23 S5 **Greenbrier River** ↝ West Virginia, NE USA
31 S2 **Greenbush** Minnesota, N USA 48.42N 96.10W
191 R12 **Green Cape** headland New South Wales, SE Australia 37.15S 150.03E
33 O14 **Greencastle** Indiana, N USA 39.38N 86.51W
20 F16 **Greencastle** Pennsylvania, NE USA 39.47N 77.43W
29 T2 **Green City** Missouri, C USA 40.16N 92.57W
23 O9 **Greeneville** Tennessee, S USA 36.09N 82.49W
37 O11 **Greenfield** California, W USA 36.19N 121.15W
33 P14 **Greenfield** Indiana, N USA 39.47N 85.46W
31 U15 **Greenfield** Iowa, C USA 41.18N 94.27W
20 M11 **Greenfield** Massachusetts, NE USA 42.33N 72.34W
29 S7 **Greenfield** Missouri, C USA 37.25N 93.50W
33 S14 **Greenfield** Ohio, N USA 39.21N 83.22W
22 G8 **Greenfield** Tennessee, S USA 36.09N 88.48W
32 M9 **Greenfield** Wisconsin, N USA 42.55N 87.59W
29 T9 **Green Forest** Arkansas, C USA 36.19N 93.24W
39 T7 **Greenhorn Mountain** ▲ Colorado, C USA 37.50N 104.59W
Green Island see Lü Tao
195 R10 **Green Islands** var. Nissan Islands. island group NE PNG
9 S14 **Green Lake** Saskatchewan, C Canada 54.15N 107.51W
32 L8 **Green Lake** ◎ Wisconsin, N USA
207 O14 **Greenland** Dan. Grønland, Inuit Kalaallit Nunaat. ◇ Danish external territory NE North America
86 D4 **Greenland** island NE North America
207 R13 **Greenland Plain** undersea feature N Greenland Sea
207 R14 **Greenland Sea** sea Arctic Ocean
39 R4 **Green Mountain Reservoir** ⊠ Colorado, C USA
20 M8 **Green Mountains** ▲ Vermont, NE USA
Green Mountain State see Vermont
98 H12 **Greenock** W Scotland, UK 55.57N 4.45W
41 T5 **Greenough, Mount** ▲ Alaska, USA 69.15N 141.37W
194 E10 **Green River** Sandaun, NW PNG 3.46S 141.10E
39 N5 **Green River** Utah, W USA 39.00N 110.07W
35 U17 **Green River** Wyoming, C USA 41.33N 109.27W
18 Ii7 **Green River** ↝ W USA
32 K11 **Green River** ↝ Illinois, N USA
22 J7 **Green River** ↝ Kentucky, S USA
30 K5 **Green River** ↝ North Dakota, N USA
39 N6 **Green River** ↝ Utah, W USA
35 T16 **Green River** ↝ Wyoming, C USA
22 L7 **Green River Lake** ⊠ Kentucky, S USA
25 O5 **Greensboro** Alabama, S USA 32.42N 87.36W
25 U3 **Greensboro** Georgia, SE USA 33.34N 83.10W
23 T9 **Greensboro** North Carolina, SE USA 36.04N 79.47W
33 P14 **Greensburg** Indiana, N USA 39.20N 85.28W
28 K6 **Greensburg** Kansas, C USA 37.36N 99.17W
22 L7 **Greensburg** Kentucky, S USA 37.15N 85.28W
20 C15 **Greensburg** Pennsylvania, NE USA 40.18N 79.32W
39 O13 **Greens Peak** ▲ Arizona, SW USA 34.06N 109.34W

23 V12 **Green Swamp** *wetland* North Carolina, SE USA
23 O4 **Greenup** Kentucky, S USA 38.34N 82.49W
38 M16 **Green Valley** Arizona, SW USA 31.49N 111.00W
78 K17 **Greenville** *var.* Sino, Sinoe. SE Liberia 5.01N 9.03W
25 P6 **Greenville** Alabama, S USA 31.49N 86.37W
25 T8 **Greenville** Florida, SE USA 30.28N 83.37W
25 S4 **Greenville** Georgia, SE USA 33.03N 84.42W
32 L15 **Greenville** Illinois, N USA 38.53N 89.24W
22 I7 **Greenville** Kentucky, S USA 37.12N 87.10W
21 Q5 **Greenville** Maine, NE USA 45.26N 69.36W
33 P9 **Greenville** Michigan, N USA 43.10N 85.15W
24 J4 **Greenville** Mississippi, S USA 33.24N 91.03W
23 W9 **Greenville** North Carolina, SE USA 35.36N 77.22W
33 Q13 **Greenville** Ohio, N USA 40.06N 84.37W
21 O12 **Greenville** Rhode Island, NE USA 41.52N 71.33W
23 P11 **Greenville** South Carolina, SE USA 34.51N 82.23W
27 U6 **Greenville** Texas, SW USA 33.08N 96.06W
33 T12 **Greenwich** Ohio, N USA 41.01N 82.31W
29 S11 **Greenwood** Arkansas, C USA 35.13N 94.15W
33 O14 **Greenwood** Indiana, N USA 39.38N 86.06W
24 K4 **Greenwood** Mississippi, S USA 33.30N 90.11W
23 P12 **Greenwood** South Carolina, SE USA 34.12N 82.09W
23 Q12 **Greenwood, Lake** ⊠ South Carolina, SE USA
23 P11 **Greer** South Carolina, SE USA 34.56N 82.13W
29 V10 **Greers Ferry Lake** ⊠ Arkansas, C USA
29 S13 **Greeson, Lake** ⊠ Arkansas, C USA
31 O12 **Gregory** South Dakota, N USA 43.11N 99.26W
190 J3 **Gregory, Lake** *salt lake* South Australia
188 J9 **Gregory Lake** ◎ Western Australia
189 V5 **Gregory Range** ▲▲ Queensland, E Australia
Greifenberg/Greifenberg in Pommern *see* Gryfice
Greifenhagen *see* Gryfino
102 O8 **Greifswald** Mecklenburg-Vorpommern, NE Germany 54.04N 13.24E
102 O8 **Greifswalder Bodden** *bay* NE Germany
111 U4 **Grein** Oberösterreich, N Austria 48.14N 14.50E
103 M17 **Greiz** Thüringen, C Germany 50.40N 12.10E
Gremicha/Gremiha *see* Gremikha
128 M4 **Gremikha** *var.* Gremicha, Gremiha. Murmanskaya Oblast', NW Russian Federation 68.01N 39.31E
129 V14 **Gremyachinsk** Permskaya Oblast', NW Russian Federation 58.33N 57.52E
97 H21 **Grenaa** *var.* Grenå. Århus, C Denmark 56.25N 10.52E
Grenå *see* Grenaa
24 L3 **Grenada** Mississippi, S USA 33.46N 89.48W
47 W15 **Grenada** ◆ *commonwealth republic* SE West Indies
49 S4 **Grenada** *island* Grenada
49 R4 **Grenada Basin** *undersea feature* W Atlantic Ocean
24 L3 **Grenada Lake** ⊠ Mississippi, S USA
47 Y14 **Grenadines, The** *island group* Grenada/St Vincent and the Grenadines
110 D7 **Grenchen** *Fr.* Granges. Solothurn, NW Switzerland 47.12N 7.30E
191 Q9 **Grenfell** New South Wales, SE Australia 33.54S 148.09E
9 V16 **Grenfell** Saskatchewan, S Canada 50.24N 102.55W
94 J1 **Grenivík** Nordhurland Eystra, N Iceland 65.57N 18.10W
105 S12 **Grenoble** *anc.* Cularo, Gratianopolis. Isère, E France 45.10N 5.41E
30 J2 **Grenora** North Dakota, N USA 48.36N 103.57W
94 N8 **Grense-Jakobselv** Finnmark, N Norway 69.46N 30.39E
47 S14 **Grenville** E Grenada 12.07N 61.37W
34 G11 **Gresham** Oregon, NW USA 45.30N 122.25W
Gresk *see* Hresk
108 B7 **Gressoney-St-Jean** Valle d'Aosta, NW Italy 45.48N 7.49E
24 K9 **Gretna** Louisiana, S USA 29.54N 90.03W
23 T7 **Gretna** Virginia, NE USA 36.57N 79.21W
100 F13 **Grevelingen** *inlet* S North Sea
103 F13 **Greven** Nordrhein-Westfalen, NW Germany 52.06N 7.37E
117 D15 **Grevená** Dytikí Makedonía, N Greece 40.06N 21.26E
103 D16 **Grevenbroich** Nordrhein-Westfalen, W Germany 51.06N 6.34E
101 N24 **Grevenmacher** Grevenmacher, E Luxembourg 49.40N 6.27E
101 M24 **Grevenmacher** ◆ *district* E Luxembourg
102 K9 **Grevesmühlen** Mecklenburg-Vorpommern, N Germany 53.52N 11.12E
193 H16 **Grey** ≈ South Island, NZ
35 V12 **Greybull** Wyoming, C USA 44.29N 108.03W
35 U13 **Greybull River** ≈ Wyoming, C USA
67 A24 **Grey Channel** *sound* Falkland Islands
Greyerzer See *see* Gruyère, Lac de la
11 T10 **Grey Islands** *island group* Newfoundland and Labrador, E Canada
20 L10 **Greylock, Mount** ▲ Massachusetts, NE USA 42.38N 73.09W
193 G17 **Greymouth** West Coast, South Island, NZ 42.28S 171.13E
189 U10 **Grey Range** ▲▲ New South Wales/Queensland, E Australia
99 G18 **Greystones** *Ir.* Na Clocha Liatha. E Ireland 53.07N 6.04W
193 M14 **Greytown** Wellington, North Island, NZ 41.05S 175.25E
85 K23 **Greytown** KwaZulu/Natal, E South Africa 29.04S 30.34E
Greytown *see* San Juan del Norte
101 H19 **Grez-Doiceau** *Dut.* Graven. Wallon Brabant, C Belgium 50.43N 4.41E
117 J19 **Griá, Akrotírio** *headland* Ándros, Kykládes, Greece, Aegean Sea 37.54N 24.57E
131 N8 **Gribanovskiy** Voronezhskaya Oblast', W Russian Federation 51.27N 41.53E
80 I13 **Gribingui** ≈ N Central African Republic
37 O6 **Gridley** California, W USA 39.21N 121.41W
85 G23 **Griekwastad** Northern Cape, C South Africa 28.50S 23.16E
25 S4 **Griffin** Georgia, SE USA 33.15N 84.16W
191 O9 **Griffith** New South Wales, SE Australia 34.18S 146.01E
12 F13 **Griffith Island** *island* Ontario, S Canada
23 W10 **Grifton** North Carolina, SE USA 35.22N 77.26W
Grigioni *see* Graubünden
121 H14 **Grigiškes** Trakai, SE Lithuania 54.42N 25.00E
119 N10 **Grigoriopol** C Moldova 47.09N 29.18E
153 X7 **Grigor'yevka** Issyk-Kul'skaya Oblast', E Kyrgyzstan 42.43N 77.27E
200 Oo9 **Grijalva Ridge** *undersea feature* E Pacific Ocean
43 U15 **Grijalva, Río** *var.* Tabasco. ≈ Guatemala/Mexico
100 N5 **Grijpskerk** Groningen, NE Netherlands 53.15N 6.18E
85 C22 **Grillenthal** Karas, SW Namibia 26.55S 15.24E
81 J15 **Grimari** Ouaka, C Central African Republic 5.44N 20.02E
Grimaylov *see* Hrymayliv
101 G18 **Grimbergen** Vlaams Brabant, C Belgium 50.55N 4.22E
191 N15 **Grim, Cape** *headland* Tasmania, SE Australia 40.42S 144.42E
102 N8 **Grimmen** Mecklenburg-Vorpommern, NE Germany 54.06N 13.03E
12 G16 **Grimsby** Ontario, S Canada 43.10N 79.34W
99 O17 **Grimsby** *prev.* Great Grimsby. E England, UK 53.34N 0.04W
94 J1 **Grímsey** *var.* Grimsey. *island* N Iceland
9 O12 **Grimshaw** Alberta, W Canada 56.12N 117.37W
97 F18 **Grimstad** Aust-Agder, S Norway 58.19N 8.34E
94 H4 **Grindavík** Reykjanes, W Iceland 65.57N 18.10W
110 F9 **Grindelwald** Bern, S Switzerland 46.37N 8.04E
97 F23 **Grindsted** Ribe, W Denmark 55.46N 8.55E
31 W14 **Grinnell** Iowa, C USA 41.44N 92.43W
111 U10 **Grintovec** ▲ N Slovenia 46.21N 14.31E
190 H1 **Griselda, Lake** *salt lake* South Australia
Grisons *see* Graubünden
97 P14 **Grisslehamn** Stockholm, C Sweden 60.04N 18.49E
31 T15 **Griswold** Iowa, C USA 41.14N 95.08W
104 M1 **Griz Nez, Cap** *headland* N France 50.51N 1.34E
114 P13 **Grljan** Serbia, E Serbia and Montenegro (Yugoslavia) 43.52N 22.18E
114 E11 **Grmeč** ▲▲ NW Bosnia and Herzegovina
101 H16 **Grobbendonk** Antwerpen, N Belgium 51.12N 4.41E
Grobin *see* Grobiņa
120 C10 **Grobiņa** *Ger.* Grobin. Liepāja, W Latvia 56.32N 21.12E
85 K20 **Groblersdal** Mpumalanga, NE South Africa 25.15S 29.25E
85 G23 **Groblershoop** Northern Cape, W South Africa 28.51S 22.01E
Gródek Jagielloński *see* Horodok
111 Q6 **Grödig** Salzburg, W Austria 47.42N 13.06E
113 H15 **Grodków** Opolskie, S Poland 50.42N 17.23E
Grodnenskaya Oblast' *see* Hrodzyenskaya Voblasts'
Grodno *see* Hrodna
112 L12 **Grodzisk Mazowiecki** Mazowieckie, C Poland 52.07N 20.40E
112 F12 **Grodzisk Wielkopolski** Wielkopolskie, C Poland 52.13N 16.21E
Grodzyanka *see* Hradzyanka
100 O12 **Groenlo** Gelderland, E Netherlands 52.01N 6.36E
85 E22 **Groenrivier** Karas, SE Namibia 27.27S 18.52E
27 U8 **Groesbeck** Texas, SW USA 31.31N 96.34W
100 L13 **Groesbeek** Gelderland, SE Netherlands 51.46N 5.55E
104 G7 **Groix, Îles de** *island group* NW France
112 M12 **Grójec** Mazowieckie, C Poland 51.51N 20.52E
67 K15 **Gröll Seamount** *undersea feature* C Atlantic Ocean 12.54S 33.24W
102 E13 **Gronau** *var.* Gronau in Westfalen. Nordrhein-Westfalen, NW Germany 52.12N 7.01E
Gronau in Westfalen *see* Gronau
95 F15 **Grong** Nord-Trøndelag, C Norway 64.29N 12.19E
97 N22 **Grönhögen** Kalmar, S Sweden 56.16N 16.09E
100 N5 **Groningen** Groningen, NE Netherlands 53.13N 6.34E
57 W9 **Groningen** Saramacca, N Suriname 5.45N 55.31W
100 N5 **Groningen** ◆ *province* NE Netherlands
Grønland *see* Greenland
110 H11 **Grono** Graubünden, S Switzerland 46.15N 9.07E
97 M20 **Grönskåra** Kalmar, S Sweden 57.04N 15.45E
27 O2 **Groom** Texas, SW USA 35.12N 101.06W
37 W9 **Groom Lake** ◎ Nevada, W USA
85 H25 **Groot** ≈ S South Africa
189 S2 **Groote Eylandt** *island* Northern Territory, N Australia
100 M6 **Grootegast** Groningen, NE Netherlands 53.11N 6.12E
85 D17 **Grootfontein** Otjozondjupa, N Namibia 19.31S 18.04E
85 E22 **Groot Karasberge** ▲▲ S Namibia
Groot Karoo *see* Great Karoo
85 J25 **Groot-Kei** *Eng.* Great Kei. ≈ S South Africa
47 T10 **Gros Islet** N Saint Lucia 14.04N 60.57W
46 L8 **Gros-Morne** NW Haiti 19.37N 72.39W
11 S11 **Gros Morne** ▲ Newfoundland and Labrador, E Canada 49.38N 57.45W
105 R9 **Grosne** ≈ C France
47 S12 **Gros Piton** ▲ SW Saint Lucia 13.48N 61.04W
Grossa, Isola *see* Dugi Otok
Grossbetschkerek *see* Zrenjanin
Grosse Isper *see* Grosse Ysper
Grosse Kokel *see* Târnava Mare
103 M21 **Grosse Laaber** *var.* Grosse Laber. ≈ SE Germany
Grosse Laber *see* Grosse Laaber
Grosse Morava *see* Velika Morava
103 O15 **Grossenhain** Sachsen, E Germany 51.18N 13.31E
111 Y4 **Grossenzersdorf** Niederösterreich, NE Austria 48.11N 16.34E
103 O21 **Grosser Arber** ▲ SE Germany 49.07N 13.10E
103 K17 **Grosser Beerberg** ▲ C Germany 50.39N 10.45E
103 G18 **Grosser Feldberg** ▲ W Germany 50.13N 8.28E
111 O8 **Grosser Löffler** *It.* Monte Lovello. ▲ Austria/Italy 47.02N 11.56E
111 N8 **Grosser Möseler** *var.* Mesule. ▲ Austria/Italy 47.01N 11.52E
102 J8 **Grosser Plöner See** ◎ N Germany
103 O21 **Grosser Rachel** ▲ SE Germany 48.59N 13.23E
Grosser Sund *see* Suur Väin
13 V6 **Grosses-Roches** Quebec, SE Canada 48.55N 67.06W
111 P8 **Grosses Weiesbachhorn** *var.* Wiesbachhorn. ▲ W Austria 47.09N 12.44E
108 F13 **Grosseto** Toscana, C Italy 42.45N 11.07E
103 M22 **Grosse Vils** ≈ SE Germany
111 U4 **Grosse Ysper** *var.* Grosse Isper. ≈ N Austria
103 G19 **Gross-Gerau** Hessen, W Germany 49.55N 8.28E
111 U3 **Gross Gerungs** Niederösterreich, N Austria 48.33N 14.58E
111 P8 **Grossglockner** ▲ W Austria 47.05N 12.39E
Grosskanizsa *see* Nagykanizsa
Gross-Karol *see* Carei
Grosskikinda *see* Kikinda
111 W9 **Grossklein** Steiermark, SE Austria 46.43N 15.24E
Grosskoppe *see* Velká Deštná
Grossmeseritsch *see* Velké Meziříčí
Grossmichel *see* Michalovce
103 H19 **Grossostheim** Bayern, C Germany 49.54N 9.03E
111 X7 **Grosspetersdorf** Burgenland, SE Austria 47.15N 16.19E
111 T5 **Grossraming** Oberösterreich, C Austria 47.54N 14.34E
103 P14 **Grossräschen** Brandenburg, E Germany 51.34N 14.00E
Grossrauschenbach *see* Revúca
Gross-Sankt-Johannis *see* Suure-Jaani
Gross-Schlatten *see* Abrud
111 V2 **Gross-Siegharts** Niederösterreich, N Austria 48.48N 15.25E
Gross-Skaisgirren *see* Bol'shakovo
Gross-Steffelsdorf *see* Rimavská Sobota
Gross Strehlitz *see* Strzelce Opolskie
111 O8 **Grossvenediger** ▲ W Austria 47.07N 12.19E
Grosswardein *see* Oradea
Gross Wartenberg *see* Syców
111 U11 **Grosuplje** C Slovenia 46.00N 14.36E
101 H17 **Grote Nete** ≈ N Belgium
96 E10 **Grotli** Oppland, S Norway 62.02N 7.36E
21 N13 **Groton** Connecticut, NE USA 41.20N 72.03W
31 P8 **Groton** South Dakota, N USA 45.27N 98.06W
109 P18 **Grottaglie** Puglia, SE Italy 40.31N 17.25E
109 L17 **Grottaminarda** Campania, S Italy 41.04N 15.02E
108 K13 **Grottammare** Marche, C Italy 43.00N 13.52E
23 U5 **Grottoes** Virginia, NE USA 38.16N 78.49W
Grou *see* Grouw
11 N10 **Groulx, Monts** ▲▲ Quebec, E Canada
12 E7 **Groundhog** ≈ Ontario, S Canada
38 J1 **Grouse Creek** Utah, W USA 41.41N 113.52W
38 J1 **Grouse Creek Mountains** ▲▲ Utah, W USA
100 L6 **Grouw** *Fris.* Grou. Friesland, N Netherlands 53.07N 5.51E
29 R8 **Grove** Oklahoma, C USA 36.35N 94.46W
33 S13 **Grove City** Ohio, N USA 39.52N 83.05W
20 B13 **Grove City** Pennsylvania, NE USA 41.09N 80.02W
25 O6 **Grove Hill** Alabama, S USA 31.42N 87.46W
35 S15 **Grover** Wyoming, C USA 42.48N 110.57W
37 P13 **Grover City** California, W USA 35.08N 120.37W
27 Y11 **Groves** Texas, SW USA 29.57N 93.55W
21 O7 **Groveton** New Hampshire, NE USA 44.35N 71.28W
27 W9 **Groveton** Texas, SW USA 31.03N 95.07W
38 J15 **Growler Mountains** ▲▲ Arizona, SW USA
Grozdovo *see* Bratya Daskalovi
131 P16 **Groznyy** Chechenskaya Respublika, SW Russian Federation 43.20N 45.42E
Grubeshov *see* Hrubieszów
114 G9 **Grubišno Polje** Bjelovar-Bilogora, NE Croatia 45.42N 17.09E
Grudovo *see* Sredets
112 J9 **Grudziądz** *Ger.* Graudenz. Kujawsko-pomorskie, C Poland 53.28N 18.45E
27 R17 **Grulla** *var.* La Grulla. Texas, SW USA 26.15N 98.37W
42 K14 **Grullo** Jalisco, SW Mexico 19.45N 104.15W
69 V10 **Grumeti** ≈ N Tanzania
97 K16 **Grums** Värmland, C Sweden 59.22N 13.10E
111 S5 **Grünau im Almtal** Oberösterreich, N Austria 47.51N 13.56E
103 H17 **Grünberg** Hessen, W Germany 50.36N 8.57E
Grünberg/Grünberg in Schlesien *see* Zielona Góra
Grünberg in Schlesien *see* Zielona Góra
94 H3 **Grundarfjördhur** Vestfirdhir, W Iceland 64.55N 23.15W
23 P7 **Grundy** Virginia, NE USA 37.16N 82.06W
31 W13 **Grundy Center** Iowa, C USA 42.21N 92.46W
Grüneberg *see* Zielona Góra
27 N1 **Gruver** Texas, SW USA 36.16N 101.24W
110 C9 **Gruyère, Lac de la** *Ger.* Greyerzer See. ◎ SW Switzerland
110 C9 **Gruyères** Fribourg, W Switzerland 46.34N 7.04E
120 E11 **Gruzdiai** Šiauliai, N Lithuania 56.06N 23.15E
Gruzinskaya SSR/Gruziya *see* Georgia
152 C10 **Gryada Akkyr** *Turkm.* Akgyr Erezi. *hill range* NW Turkmenistan
130 L7 **Gryazi** Lipetskaya Oblast', W Russian Federation 52.27N 39.56E
128 M14 **Gryazovets** Vologodskaya Oblast', NW Russian Federation 58.52N 40.12E
113 M17 **Grybów** Małopolskie, SE Poland 49.35N 20.54E
96 M13 **Grycksbo** Dalarna, C Sweden 60.40N 15.30E
112 E8 **Gryfice** *Ger.* Greifenberg, Greifenberg in Pommern. Zachodniopomorskie, NW Poland 53.55N 15.10E
112 D9 **Gryfino** *Ger.* Greifenhagen. Zachodniopomorskie, NW Poland 53.15N 14.30E
94 H9 **Gryllefjord** Troms, N Norway 69.21N 17.07E
97 L15 **Grythyttan** Örebro, C Sweden 59.52N 14.31E
110 D10 **Gstaad** Bern, W Switzerland 46.30N 7.16E
45 P14 **Guabito** Bocas del Toro, NW Panama 9.30N 82.35W
46 G7 **Guacanayabo, Golfo de** *gulf* S Cuba
42 I7 **Guachochi** Chihuahua, N Mexico
106 J11 **Guadajira** ≈ SW Spain
106 M13 **Guadajoz** ≈ S Spain
42 L13 **Guadalajara** Jalisco, C Mexico 20.43N 103.23W
107 O8 **Guadalajara** *Ar.* Wad Al-Hajarah; *anc.* Arriaca. Castilla-La Mancha, C Spain 40.37N 3.10W
107 O7 **Guadalajara** ◆ *province* Castilla-La Mancha, C Spain
106 K12 **Guadalcanal** Andalucía, S Spain 38.06N 5.49W
195 W16 **Guadalcanal** *off.* Guadalcanal Province. ◆ *province* C Solomon Islands
195 W16 **Guadalcanal** *island* C Solomon Islands
107 O12 **Guadalén** ≈ S Spain
107 R13 **Guadalentín** ≈ SE Spain
106 K15 **Guadalete** ≈ SW Spain
107 O13 **Guadalimar** ≈ S Spain
107 P12 **Guadalmena** ≈ S Spain
106 L11 **Guadalmez** ≈ W Spain
107 S7 **Guadalope** ≈ E Spain
106 K13 **Guadalquivir** ≈ W Spain
106 J14 **Guadalquivir, Marismas del** *var.* Las Marismas. *wetland* SW Spain
42 M11 **Guadalupe** Zacatecas, C Mexico 22.44N 102.27W
59 E16 **Guadalupe** Ica, W Peru 13.59S 75.49W
106 L10 **Guadalupe** Extremadura, W Spain 39.26N 5.18W
38 L14 **Guadalupe** Arizona, SW USA 33.20N 111.57W
37 P13 **Guadalupe** California, W USA 34.55N 120.34W
199 Mm5 **Guadalupe** *island* NW Mexico
Guadalupe *see* Canelones
42 J3 **Guadalupe Bravos** Chihuahua, N Mexico 31.22N 106.04W
42 A4 **Guadalupe, Isla** *island* NW Mexico
39 U15 **Guadalupe Mountains** ▲▲ New Mexico/Texas, SW USA
26 J8 **Guadalupe Peak** ▲ Texas, SW USA 31.53N 104.51W
27 R11 **Guadalupe River** ≈ SW USA
106 K10 **Guadalupe, Sierra de** ▲▲ W Spain
42 K9 **Guadalupe Victoria** Durango, C Mexico 24.30N 104.03W
42 I8 **Guadalupe y Calvo** Chihuahua, N Mexico 26.04N 106.58W
107 N7 **Guadarrama** Madrid, C Spain 40.40N 4.06W
107 N7 **Guadarrama** ≈ C Spain
106 M7 **Guadarrama, Puerto de** *pass* C Spain 40.41N 4.14W
107 N9 **Guadarrama, Sierra de** ▲▲ C Spain
107 Q9 **Guadazaón** ≈ C Spain
47 X10 **Guadeloupe** ◇ *French overseas department* E West Indies
49 S3 **Guadeloupe** *island group* E West Indies
47 W10 **Guadeloupe Passage** *passage* E Caribbean Sea
106 H13 **Guadiana** ≈ Portugal/Spain
107 O13 **Guadiana Menor** ≈ S Spain
107 Q8 **Guadiela** ≈ C Spain
107 O14 **Guadix** Andalucía, S Spain 37.19N 3.07W
Guad-i-Zirreh *see* Gowd-e Zereh, Dasht-e
200 O13 **Guafo Fracture Zone** *tectonic feature* SE Pacific Ocean
65 F18 **Guafo, Isla** *island* S Chile
44 I6 **Guaimaca** Francisco Morazán, C Honduras 14.33N 86.49W
56 J12 **Guainía** *off.* Comisaría del Guainía. ◆ *province* E Colombia
56 K12 **Guainía, Río** ≈ Colombia/Venezuela
57 O9 **Guaiquinima, Cerro** *elevation* SE Venezuela 5.45N 63.46W
64 O7 **Guairá** *off.* Departamento del Guairá. ◆ *department* S Paraguay
62 G10 **Guaíra** Paraná, S Brazil 24.04S 54.15W
62 L7 **Guaíra** São Paulo, S Brazil 20.17S 48.21W
Guaire *see* Gorey
65 F18 **Guaiteca, Isla** *island* S Chile
46 G6 **Guajaba, Cayo** *headland* C Cuba 21.50N 77.33W
61 D16 **Guajará-Mirim** Rondônia, W Brazil 10.49S 65.21W
Guajira *see* La Guajira
56 H3 **Guajira, Península de la** *peninsula* N Colombia
44 J6 **Gualaco** Olancho, C Honduras 15.00N 86.03W
36 L7 **Gualala** California, W USA 38.45N 123.33W
44 E5 **Gualán** Zacapa, C Guatemala 15.06N 89.20W
63 C19 **Gualeguay** Entre Ríos, E Argentina 33.09S 59.19W
63 D18 **Gualeguaychú** Entre Ríos, E Argentina 32.58S 58.30W
63 C18 **Gualeguay, Río** ≈ E Argentina
65 K16 **Gualicho, Salina del** *salt lake* E Argentina
196 B15 **Guam** ◇ *US unincorporated territory* W Pacific Ocean
65 F19 **Guamblin, Isla** *island* Archipiélago de los Chonos, S Chile
63 A22 **Guaminí** Buenos Aires, E Argentina 37.04S 62.22W
42 H8 **Guamúchil** Sinaloa, C Mexico 25.23N 108.00W
56 H4 **Guana** *var.* Misión de Guana. Zulia, NW Venezuela 11.07N 72.17W
46 C4 **Guanabacoa** La Habana, W Cuba 23.01N 82.12W
44 K13 **Guanacaste** *off.* Provincia de Guanacaste. ◆ *province* NW Costa Rica
44 K12 **Guanacaste, Cordillera de** ▲▲ NW Costa Rica
42 J8 **Guanaceví** Durango, C Mexico 25.55N 105.51W
46 A5 **Guanahacabibes, Golfo de** *gulf* W Cuba
44 K4 **Guanaja, Isla de** *island* Islas de la Bahía, N Honduras
46 C4 **Guanajay** La Habana, W Cuba 22.52N 82.39W
43 N12 **Guanajuato** Guanajuato, C Mexico 21.00N 101.16W
42 M12 **Guanajuato** ◆ *state* C Mexico
56 J6 **Guanare** Portuguesa, N Venezuela 9.04N 69.45W
56 K7 **Guanare, Río** ≈ W Venezuela
56 J6 **Guanarito** Portuguesa, NW Venezuela 8.39N 69.12W
166 M3 **Guancen Shan** ▲▲ C China
64 I9 **Guandacol** La Rioja, W Argentina 29.31S 68.30W
46 A5 **Guane** Pinar del Río, W Cuba 22.12N 84.05W
167 N14 **Guangdong** *var.* Guangdong Sheng, Kuang-tung, Kwangtung, Yue. ◆ *province* S China
Guangdong Sheng *see* Guangdong
Guanghua *see* Laohekou
Guangju *see* Kwangju
166 I13 **Guangnan** Yunnan, SW China 24.07N 104.54E
167 N8 **Guangshui** *prev.* Yingshan. Hubei, C China 31.41N 113.53E
Guangxi *see* Guangxi Zhuangzu Zizhiqu
166 K14 **Guangxi Zhuangzu Zizhiqu** *var.* Guangxi, Gui, Kuang-hsi, Kwangsi, *Eng.* Kwangsi Chuang Autonomous Region. ◆ *autonomous region* S China
166 J8 **Guangyuan** *var.* Kuang-yuan, Kwangyuan. Sichuan, C China 32.27N 105.49E
167 N14 **Guangzhou** *var.* Kuang-chou, Kwangchow, *Eng.* Canton. Guangdong, S China 23.10N 113.19E
61 N19 **Guanhães** Minas Gerais, SE Brazil 18.46S 42.58W
166 I12 **Guanling** *var.* Guanling Bouyeizu Miaozu Zizhixian. Guizhou, S China 25.56N 105.36E
Guanling Bouyeizu Miaozu Zizhixian *see* Guanling
57 N5 **Guanta** Anzoátegui, NE Venezuela 10.15N 64.37W
46 J8 **Guantánamo** Guantánamo, SE Cuba 20.06N 75.16W
46 J8 **Guantánamo, Bahía de** *Eng.* Guantánamo Bay. *US military installation*, SE Cuba 20.06N 75.16W
Guantánamo Bay *see* Bahía de Guantánamo
166 H9 **Guanxian** *var.* Guan Xian. Sichuan, C China 31.01N 103.40E
167 Q6 **Guanyun** Jiangsu, E China 34.19N 119.16E
56 C12 **Guapí** Cauca, SW Colombia 2.36N 77.54W
45 N13 **Guápiles** Limón, NE Costa Rica 10.11N 83.45W
63 I15 **Guaporé** Rio Grande do Sul, S Brazil 28.55S 51.53W
49 S8 **Guaporé, Río** *var.* Río Iténez. ≈ Bolivia/Brazil *see also* Iténez, Río
58 B7 **Guaranda** Bolívar, C Ecuador 1.34S 78.58W
62 H11 **Guaraniaçu** Paraná, S Brazil 25.05S 52.52W
61 O20 **Guarapari** Espírito Santo, SE Brazil 20.39S 40.31W
62 I12 **Guarapuava** Paraná, S Brazil 25.22S 51.28W
62 J8 **Guararapes** São Paulo, S Brazil 21.16S 50.37W
107 S4 **Guara, Sierra de** ▲▲ NE Spain
62 N10 **Guaratinguetá** São Paulo, S Brazil 22.44S 45.16W
106 I7 **Guarda** Guarda, N Portugal 40.31N 7.16W
106 I7 **Guarda** ◆ *district* N Portugal
Guardak *see* Govurdak
106 M3 **Guardo** Castilla-León, N Spain 42.48N 4.49W
106 K11 **Guareña** Extremadura, W Spain 38.51N 6.06W
62 J11 **Guaricana, Pico** ▲ S Brazil 25.13S 48.50W
56 L6 **Guárico** *off.* Estado Guárico. ◆ *state* N Venezuela
46 J7 **Guarico, Punta** *headland* E Cuba 20.36N 74.43W
56 L7 **Guárico, Río** ≈ C Venezuela
62 M10 **Guarujá** São Paulo, SE Brazil 23.50S 46.27W
63 L22 **Guarulhos** ✕ (São Paulo) São Paulo, S Brazil 23.23S 46.32W
45 R17 **Guarumal** Veraguas, S Panama 7.48N 81.15W
Guasapa *see* Guasopa
42 H8 **Guasave** Sinaloa, C Mexico 25.33N 108.28W
56 I8 **Guasdualito** Apure, C Venezuela 7.13N 70.45W
57 Q7 **Guasipati** Bolívar, E Venezuela 7.29N 61.54W
195 Q15 **Guasopa** *var.* Guasapa. Woodlark Island, SE PNG 9.12S 152.55E
108 F9 **Guastalla** Emilia-Romagna, C Italy 44.54N 10.38E
44 D6 **Guastatoya** *var.* El Progreso. El Progreso, C Guatemala 14.51N 90.02W
44 D5 **Guatemala** *off.* Republic of Guatemala. ◆ *republic* Central America
44 A2 **Guatemala** *off.* Departamento de Guatemala. ◆ *department* S Guatemala
200 O7 **Guatemala Basin** *undersea feature* E Pacific Ocean
Guatemala City *see* Ciudad de Guatemala
47 V14 **Guatuaro Point** *headland* Trinidad, Trinidad and Tobago 10.19N 60.58W
194 G14 **Guavi** ≈ SW PNG
56 G13 **Guaviare** *off.* Comisaría Guaviare. ◆ *province* S Colombia
56 J11 **Guaviare, Río** ≈ E Colombia
63 E15 **Guaviravi** Corrientes, NE Argentina 29.19S 56.49W
56 G12 **Guayabero, Río** ≈ SW Colombia
47 U6 **Guayama** E Puerto Rico 17.58N 66.07W
44 J7 **Guayambre, Río** ≈ S Honduras
Guayanas, Macizo de las *see* Guiana Highlands
47 V6 **Guayanés, Punta** *headland* E Puerto Rico 18.03N 65.48W
44 J6 **Guayape, Río** ≈ C Honduras
58 B7 **Guayaquil** *var.* Santiago de Guayaquil. Guayas, SW Ecuador 2.13S 79.54W
Guayaquil *see* Simon Bolivar
58 A8 **Guayaquil, Golfo de** *var.* Gulf of Guayaquil. *gulf* SW Ecuador
Guayaquil, Gulf of *see* Guayaquil, Golfo de
58 A7 **Guayas** ◆ *province* W Ecuador
64 N7 **Guaycurú, Río** ≈ NE Argentina
42 F6 **Guaymas** Sonora, NW Mexico 27.56N 110.54W
47 U5 **Guaynabo** E Puerto Rico 18.19N 66.05W
82 H12 **Guba** Benishangul, W Ethiopia 11.11N 35.21E
152 H8 **Gubadag** *Turkm.* Tel'man; *prev.* Tel'mansk. Dashkhovuzskiy Velayat, N Turkmenistan 42.07N 59.55E
129 T1 **Guba Dolgaya** Nenetskiy Avtonomnyy Okrug, NW Russian Federation 70.16N 58.45E
129 V13 **Gubakha** Permskaya Oblast', NW Russian Federation 58.52N 57.35E
108 I12 **Gubbio** Umbria, C Italy 43.27N 12.34E
102 Q13 **Guben** *var.* Wilhelm-Pieck-Stadt. Brandenburg, E Germany 51.58N 14.42E
Guben *see* Gubin
112 D12 **Gubin** *Ger.* Guben. Lubuskie, W Poland 51.58N 14.43E
130 K8 **Gubkin** Belgorodskaya Oblast', W Russian Federation 51.16N 37.32E
Gudara *see* Ghūdara
107 S8 **Gúdar, Sierra de** ▲▲ E Spain
143 P8 **Gudaut'a** NW Georgia 43.06N 40.35E
96 G12 **Gudbrandsdalen** *valley* S Norway
97 G21 **Gudenå** *var.* Gudenaa. ≈ C Denmark
Gudenaa *see* Gudenå
131 P16 **Gudermes** Chechenskaya Respublika, SW Russian Federation 43.23N 46.06E
161 J18 **Gūdūr** Andhra Pradesh, E India 14.10N 79.51E
152 B13 **Gudurolum** Balkanskiy Velayat, W Turkmenistan 37.28N 54.30E
96 D13 **Gudvangen** Sogn og Fjordane, S Norway 60.54N 6.49E
105 U7 **Guebwiller** Haut-Rhin, NE France 47.55N 7.13E
Guéckédou *see* Guékédou
12 K8 **Guéguen, Lac** ◎ Quebec, SE Canada
78 J15 **Guékédou** *var.* Guéckédou. Guinée-Forestière, S Guinea 8.33N 10.08W
43 R16 **Guelatao** Oaxaca, SE Mexico
Guelders *see* Gelderland
80 G11 **Guélengdeng** Mayo-Kébbi, W Chad 10.55N 15.31E
76 L5 **Guelma** *var.* Gâlma. NE Algeria 36.28N 7.25E
76 D8 **Guelmime** *var.* Goulimime. SW Morocco 28.59N 10.10W
12 G15 **Guelph** Ontario, S Canada 43.33N 80.12W
104 I7 **Guémené-Penfao** Loire-Atlantique, NW France 47.37N 1.49W
104 I7 **Guer** Morbihan, NW France 47.54N 2.07W
80 I11 **Guéra** *off.* Préfecture du Guéra. ◆ *prefecture* S Chad
104 H8 **Guérande** Loire-Atlantique, NW France 47.19N 2.25W
80 K9 **Guéréda** Biltine, E Chad 14.30N 22.04E
105 N10 **Guéret** Creuse, C France 46.10N 1.52E
Guernica/Guernica y Lumo *see* Gernika-Lumo
35 Z15 **Guernsey** Wyoming, C USA 42.16N 104.44W
99 K25 **Guernsey** *island* Channel Islands, NW Europe
78 J10 **Guérou** Assaba, S Mauritania 16.48N 11.40W
27 R16 **Guerra** Texas, SW USA 26.54N 98.53W
43 O15 **Guerrero** ◆ *state* S Mexico
42 D6 **Guerrero Negro** Baja California Sur, NW Mexico 27.55N 114.04W
105 P9 **Gueugnon** Saône-et-Loire, C France 46.36N 4.03E
78 M17 **Guéyo** S Ivory Coast 5.25N 6.04W
109 L15 **Guglionesi** Molise, C Italy 41.54N 14.54E
196 K5 **Guguan** *island* C Northern Mariana Islands
Guhrau *see* Góra
Gui *see* Guangxi Zhuangzu Zizhiqu
Guiana *see* French Guiana
49 V4 **Guiana Basin** *undersea feature* W Atlantic Ocean
50 G6 **Guiana Highlands** *var.* Macizo de las Guayanas. ▲▲ N South America
Guiba *see* Juba
104 I7 **Guichen** Ille-et-Vilaine, NW France 47.57N 1.47W
63 E18 **Guichón** Paysandú, W Uruguay 32.21S 57.12W
79 U12 **Guidan-Roumji** Maradi, S Niger 13.40N 6.41E
Guidder *see* Guider
165 T10 **Guide** Qinghai, C China 36.06N 101.25E
80 F12 **Guider** *var.* Guidder. Nord, N Cameroon 9.55N 13.58E
78 I11 **Guidimaka** ◆ *region* S Mauritania
79 W12 **Guidimouni** Zinder, S Niger 13.40N 9.31E
78 G10 **Guier, Lac de** *var.* Lac de Guiers. ◎ N Senegal
166 L14 **Guigang** *prev.* Guixian, Gui Xian. Guangxi Zhuangzu Zizhiqu, S China 23.06N 109.36E
78 L16 **Guiglo** W Ivory Coast 6.33N 7.28W
56 L5 **Güigüe** Carabobo, N Venezuela 10.04N 67.48W
85 M20 **Guijá** Gaza, S Mozambique 24.30S 33.07E
44 E7 **Güija, Lago de** ◎ El Salvador/Guatemala
106 K8 **Guijuelo** Castilla-León, N Spain 40.34N 5.40W
Guilan *see* Gīlān
99 N22 **Guildford** SE England, UK 51.13N 0.34W
21 R5 **Guildford** Maine, NE USA 45.10N 69.22W
21 O7 **Guildhall** Vermont, NE USA 44.34N 71.36W
105 R13 **Guilherand** Ardèche, E France 44.57N 4.49E
166 L13 **Guilin** *var.* Kuei-lin, Kweilin. Guangxi Zhuangzu Zizhiqu, S China 25.15N 110.16E
10 J6 **Guillaume-Delisle, Lac** ◎ Quebec, NE Canada
105 U13 **Guillestre** Hautes-Alpes, SE France 44.41N 6.39E
106 H6 **Guimarães** *var.* Guimaráes. Braga, N Portugal 41.25N 8.19W
60 D11 **Guimarães Rosas, Pico** ▲ NW Brazil
25 N3 **Guin** Alabama, S USA 33.58N 87.54W
Güina *see* Wina
78 I14 **Guinea** *off.* Republic of Guinea, *var.* Guinée; *prev.* French Guinea, People's Revolutionary Republic of Guinea. ◆ *republic* W Africa
66 N13 **Guinea Basin** *undersea feature* E Atlantic Ocean
78 E12 **Guinea-Bissau** *off.* Republic of Guinea-Bissau, *Fr.* Guinée-Bissau, *Port.* Guiné-Bissau; *prev.* Portuguese Guinea. ◆ *republic* W Africa
68 K7 **Guinea Fracture Zone** *tectonic feature* E Atlantic Ocean
66 O13 **Guinea, Gulf of** *Fr.* Golfe de Guinée. *gulf* E Atlantic Ocean
Guiné-Bissau *see* Guinea-Bissau
Guinée *see* Guinea
Guinée-Bissau *see* Guinea-Bissau
78 K15 **Guinée-Forestière** ◆ *state* SE Guinea
Guinée, Golfe de *see* Guinea, Gulf of
78 H13 **Guinée-Maritime** ◆ *state* W Guinea
46 C4 **Güines** La Habana, W Cuba 22.50N 82.02W
104 G5 **Guingamp** Côtes d'Armor, NW France 48.34N 3.09W
107 P3 **Guipúzcoa** *Basq.* Gipuzkoa. ◆ *province* País Vasco, N Spain

◆ Country ● Country Capital ◇ Dependent Territory ○ Dependent Territory Capital ◆ Administrative Region ✕ International Airport ▲ Mountain ▲▲ Mountain Range ▲ Volcano ≈ River ◎ Lake ⊠ Reservoir

46 C5 **Güira de Melena** La Habana, W Cuba 22.43N 82.31W
76 G8 **Guir, Hamada du** *desert* Algeria/Morocco
57 P5 **Güiria** Sucre, NE Venezuela 10.37N 62.21W
166 L14 **Gui Shui** ∽ S China
106 H2 **Guitiriz** Galicia, NW Spain 43.10N 7.52W
79 N17 **Guitri** S Ivory Coast 5.31N 5.13W
179 R13 **Guiuan** Samar, C Philippines 11.02N 125.45E
Gui Xian/Guixian *see* Guigang
166 J12 **Guiyang** *var.* Kuei-Yang, Kuei-yang, Kueyang, Kweiyang; *prev.* Kweichu. Guizhou, S China 26.33N 106.44E
166 J12 **Guizhou** *var.* Guizhou Sheng, Kuei-chou, Kweichow, Qian. ◈ *province* S China
Guizhou Sheng *see* Guizhou
104 J13 **Gujan-Mestras** Gironde, SW France 44.39N 1.04W
160 B10 **Gujarāt** *var.* Gujerat. ◈ *state* W India
155 V6 **Gūjar Khān** Punjab, E Pakistan 33.15N 73.18E
Gujerat *see* Gujarāt
155 V7 **Gujrānwāla** Punjab, NE Pakistan 32.11N 74.08E
155 V7 **Gujrāt** Punjab, E Pakistan 32.33N 74.03E
165 U9 **Gulang** Gansu, C China 37.31N 102.55E
191 R6 **Gulargambone** New South Wales, SE Australia 31.19S 148.31E
161 G15 **Gulbarga** Karnātaka, C India 17.22N 76.46E
120 J8 **Gulbene** *Ger.* Alt-Schwanenburg. Gulbene, NE Latvia 57.10N 26.44E
153 U10 **Gul'cha** *Kir.* Gülchö. Oshskaya Oblast', SW Kyrgyzstan 40.16N 73.27E
Gülchö *see* Gul'cha
181 T10 **Gulden Draak Seamount** *undersea feature* E Indian Ocean 33.45S 101.00E
142 J16 **Gülek Boğazı** *var.* Cilician Gates. *pass* S Turkey 37.19N 34.49E
194 I14 **Gulf** ◈ *province* S PNG
25 O9 **Gulf Breeze** Florida, SE USA 30.21N 87.09W
25 V13 **Gulfport** Florida, SE USA 27.45N 82.42W
24 M9 **Gulfport** Mississippi, S USA 30.22N 89.05W
25 O9 **Gulf Shores** Alabama, S USA 30.15N 87.40W
Gulf, The *see* Persian Gulf
191 R7 **Gulgong** New South Wales, SE Australia 32.22S 149.31E
166 I11 **Gulin** Sichuan, C China 28.06N 105.47E
176 V12 **Gulir** Pulau Kasiui, E Indonesia 4.27S 131.41E
Gulistan *see* Guliston
153 P10 **Guliston** *Rus.* Gulistan. Sirdaryo Viloyati, E Uzbekistan 40.28N 68.45E
169 T6 **Guliya Shan** ▲ NE China 49.42N 122.22E
Gulja *see* Yining
41 S11 **Gulkana** Alaska, USA 62.17N 145.25W
9 S17 **Gull Lake** Saskatchewan, S Canada 50.04N 108.30W
33 P10 **Gull Lake** ◎ Michigan, N USA
31 T6 **Gull Lake** ◎ Minnesota, N USA
97 L16 **Gullspång** Västra Götaland, S Sweden 58.58N 14.04E
158 H5 **Gulmarg** Jammu and Kashmir, NW India 34.04N 74.25E
Gulpaigan *see* Golpāyegān
101 L18 **Gulpen** Limburg, SE Netherlands 50.48N 5.53E
151 S13 **Gul'shad** *Kaz.* Gulshat. Zhezkazgan, E Kazakhstan 46.37N 74.21E
Gulshat *see* Gul'shad
83 F17 **Gulu** N Uganda 2.46N 32.21E
116 K10 **Gŭlŭbovo** Stara Zagora, C Bulgaria 42.10N 25.52E
116 I7 **Gulyantsi** Pleven, N Bulgaria 43.37N 24.40E
Gulyaypole *see* Hulyaypole
Guma *see* Pishan
81 K16 **Gumba** Equateur, NW Dem. Rep. Congo 2.58N 21.23E
Gumbinnen *see* Gusev
83 H24 **Gumbiro** Ruvuma, S Tanzania 10.19S 35.40E
152 B11 **Gumdag** *prev.* Kum-Dag. Balkanskiy Velayat, W Turkmenistan 39.13N 54.35E
79 W12 **Gumel** Jigawa, N Nigeria 12.37N 9.23E
107 N5 **Gumiel de Hizán** Castilla-León, N Spain 41.46N 3.42W
194 I12 **Gumine** *var.* Gumire. Chimbu, C PNG 6.12S 144.53E
Gumire *see* Gumine
159 P16 **Gumla** Bihār, N India 23.03N 84.36E
Gumma *see* Gunma
103 F16 **Gummersbach** Nordrhein-Westfalen, W Germany 51.01N 7.34E
79 T13 **Gummi** Zamfara, NW Nigeria 12.07N 5.07E
Gumpolds *see* Humpolec
159 N13 **Gumti** *var.* Gomati. ∽ N India
Gümülcine/Gümüljina *see* Komotiní
Gümüşane *see* Gümüşhane
143 O12 **Gümüşhane** *var.* Gümüşane, Gumushkhane. Gümüşhane, NE Turkey 40.30N 39.27E
143 O12 **Gümüşhane** *var.* Gümüşane, Gumushkhane. ◈ *province* NE Turkey
Gumushkhane *see* Gümüşhane
176 W13 **Gumzai** Pulau Kola, E Indonesia 5.27S 134.38E
160 H9 **Guna** Madhya Pradesh, C India 24.39N 77.21E
Gunabad *see* Gonābād
Gunbad-i-Qawus *see* Gonbad-e Kāvūs
191 O9 **Gunbar** New South Wales, SE Australia 34.03S 145.32E
191 O9 **Gun Creek** *seasonal river* New South Wales, SE Australia
191 Q10 **Gundagai** New South Wales, SE Australia 35.06S 148.03E
81 K17 **Gundji** Equateur, N Dem. Rep. Congo 2.13N 21.31E
161 G20 **Gundlupet** Karnātaka, W India 11.48N 76.42E
142 G16 **Gündoğmuş** Antalya, S Turkey 36.52N 32.01E
143 O14 **Güney Doğu Toroslar** ▲▲ SE Turkey
81 J21 **Gungu** Bandundu, SW Dem. Rep. Congo 5.43S 19.19E
131 P17 **Gunib** Respublika Dagestan, SW Russian Federation 42.24N 46.55E
114 J11 **Gunja** Vukovar-Srijem, E Croatia 44.53N 18.51E
33 P9 **Gun Lake** ◎ Michigan, N USA
171 Jj15 **Gunma** *off.* Gunma-ken, *var.* Gumma. ◈ *prefecture* Honshū, S Japan
207 P15 **Gunnbjørn Fjeld** *var.* Gunnbjörns Bjerge. ▲ C Greenland 69.03N 29.36W
191 S6 **Gunnedah** New South Wales, SE Australia 30.58S 150.15E
181 Y15 **Gunner's Quoin** *var.* Coin de Mire. *island* N Mauritius
39 R6 **Gunnison** Colorado, C USA 38.33N 106.55W
38 L5 **Gunnison** Utah, W USA 39.09N 111.49W
39 P5 **Gunnison River** ∽ Colorado, C USA
23 X2 **Gunpowder River** ∽ Maryland, NE USA
Güns *see* Kőszeg
Gunsan *see* Kunsan
111 S4 **Gunskirchen** Oberösterreich, N Austria 48.07N 13.54E
Gunt *see* Ghund
161 H17 **Guntakal** Andhra Pradesh, C India 15.10N 77.24E
25 Q2 **Guntersville** Alabama, S USA 34.21N 86.17W
25 Q2 **Guntersville Lake** ⊠ Alabama, S USA
111 X4 **Guntramsdorf** Niederösterreich, E Austria 48.03N 16.19E
161 J16 **Guntūr** *var.* Guntur. Andhra Pradesh, SE India 16.19N 80.27E
173 F7 **Gunungsitoli** Pulau Nias, W Indonesia 1.11N 97.35E
161 M14 **Gunupur** Orissa, E India 19.04N 83.52E
103 J23 **Günz** ∽ S Germany
Gunzan *see* Kunsan
103 J22 **Günzburg** Bayern, S Germany 48.26N 10.18E
103 K21 **Gunzenhausen** Bayern, S Germany 49.07N 10.45E
Guovdageaidnu *see* Kautokeino
167 P7 **Guoyang** Anhui, E China 33.29N 116.14E
118 G11 **Gurahonț** *Hung.* Honctő. Arad, W Romania 46.16N 22.20E
Gurahumora *see* Gura Humorului
118 K9 **Gura Humorului** *Ger.* Gurahumora. Suceava, NE Romania 47.31N 26.00E
164 K4 **Gurbantünggüt Shamo** *desert* W China
158 H7 **Gurdāspur** Punjab, N India 32.02N 75.23E
29 T13 **Gurdon** Arkansas, C USA 33.55N 93.09W
Gurdzhaani *see* Gurjaani
Gurgan *see* Gorgān
158 I10 **Gurgaon** Haryāna, N India 28.24N 76.59E
61 M15 **Gurguéia, Rio** ∽ NE Brazil
57 Q7 **Guri, Embalse de** ⊠ E Venezuela
143 V10 **Gurjaani** *Rus.* Gurdzhaani. E Georgia 41.42N 45.47E
111 T8 **Gurk** Kärnten, S Austria 46.52N 14.17E
111 T9 **Gurk** *Slvn.* Krka. ∽ S Austria
Gurkfeld *see* Krško
116 K9 **Gurkovo** *prev.* Kolupchii. Stara Zagora, C Bulgaria 42.42N 25.46E
111 S9 **Gurktaler Alpen** ▲▲ S Austria
152 H8 **Gurlan** *Rus.* Gurlen. Xorazm Viloyati, W Uzbekistan 41.54N 60.18E
Gurlen *see* Gurlan
85 M16 **Guro** Manica, C Mozambique 17.25S 33.23E
142 M14 **Gürün** Sivas, C Turkey 38.43N 37.15E
61 K16 **Gurupi** Tocantins, C Brazil 11.43S 49.01W
60 L12 **Gurupi, Rio** ∽ NE Brazil
158 E14 **Guru Sikhar** ▲ NW India 24.45N 72.51E
Gur'yev/Gur'yevskaya Oblast' *see* Atyrau
79 U13 **Gusau** Zamfara, NW Nigeria 12.18N 6.27E
130 C3 **Gusev** *Ger.* Gumbinnen. Kaliningradskaya Oblast', W Russian Federation 54.36N 22.13E
152 J17 **Gushgy** *prev.* Kushka. Maryyskiy Velayat, S Turkmenistan 35.18N 62.17E
Gushiago *see* Gushiegu
79 Q14 **Gushiegu** *var.* Gushiago. NE Ghana 9.54N 0.12W
172 P15 **Gushikawa** Okinawa, Okinawa, SW Japan 26.21N 127.49E
115 L16 **Gusinje** Montenegro, SW Serbia and Montenegro (Yugoslavia) 42.34N 19.51E
126 Jj16 **Gusinoozersk** Respublika Buryatiya, S Russian Federation 51.18N 106.28E
130 M4 **Gus'-Khrustal'nyy** Vladimirskaya Oblast', W Russian Federation 55.39N 40.42E
109 B19 **Guspini** Sardegna, Italy, C Mediterranean Sea 39.33N 8.39E
111 X8 **Güssing** Burgenland, SE Austria 47.04N 16.18E
111 V6 **Gusswerk** Steiermark, E Austria 47.43N 15.18E
94 O2 **Gustav Adolf Land** *physical region* NE Svalbard
205 X5 **Gustav Bull Mountains** ▲▲ Antarctica
41 W13 **Gustavus** Alaska, USA 58.24N 135.44W
94 O1 **Gustav V Land** *physical region* NE Svalbard
37 P9 **Gustine** California, W USA 37.14N 121.00W
27 R8 **Gustine** Texas, SW USA 31.51N 98.24W
102 M9 **Güstrow** Mecklenburg-Vorpommern, NE Germany 53.48N 12.11E
97 N18 **Gusum** Östergötland, S Sweden 58.15N 16.30E
Guta/Gúta *see* Kolárovo
Gutenstein *see* Ravne na Koroškem
103 G14 **Gütersloh** Nordrhein-Westfalen, W Germany 51.54N 8.22E
29 N10 **Guthrie** Oklahoma, C USA 35.52N 97.25W
27 P5 **Guthrie** Texas, SW USA 33.37N 100.21W
31 U14 **Guthrie Center** Iowa, C USA 41.40N 94.30W
43 Q13 **Gutiérrez Zamora** Veracruz-Llave, E Mexico 20.29N 97.07W
Gutta *see* Kolárovo
31 Y12 **Guttenberg** Iowa, C USA 42.47N 91.06W
Guttentag *see* Dobrodzień
Guttstadt *see* Dobre Miasto
168 G8 **Guulin** Govĭ-Altay, C Mongolia 46.33N 97.21E
159 V12 **Guwāhāti** *prev.* Gauhāti. Assam, NE India 26.09N 91.42E
145 R3 **Guwēr** *var.* Al Kuwayr, Al Quwayr, Quwair. N Iraq 36.03N 43.30E
Guwlumayak *see* Kuuli-Mayak
57 R9 **Guyana** *off.* Cooperative Republic of Guyana; *prev.* British Guiana. ◆ *republic* N South America
23 P5 **Guyandotte River** ∽ West Virginia, NE USA
Guyane *see* French Guiana
Guyi *see* Sanjiang
28 H8 **Guymon** Oklahoma, C USA 36.40N 101.28W
152 K12 **Guynuk** Lebapskiy Velayat, NE Turkmenistan 39.18N 63.00E
23 O9 **Guyot, Mount** ▲ North Carolina/Tennessee, SE USA 35.42N 83.15W
191 U5 **Guyra** New South Wales, SE Australia 30.13S 151.42E
165 W10 **Guyuan** Ningxia, N China 35.57N 106.13E
Guzar *see* G'uzor
124 N3 **Güzelyurt** *Gk.* Mórfou, Morphou. W Cyprus 35.11N 33.00E
124 N2 **Güzelyurt Körfezi** *var.* Morfou Bay, Morphou Bay, *Gk.* Kólpos Mórfou. *bay* W Cyprus
42 I3 **Guzmán** Chihuahua, N Mexico 31.13N 107.27W
153 N13 **G'uzor** *Rus.* Guzar. Qashqadaryo Viloyati, S Uzbekistan 38.41N 66.12E
121 B14 **Gvardeysk** *Ger.* Tapaiu. Kaliningradskaya Oblast', W Russian Federation 54.39N 21.02E
Gvardeyskoye *see* Hvardiys'ke
191 R5 **Gwabegar** New South Wales, SE Australia 30.34S 148.58E
154 J16 **Gwādar** *var.* Gwadur. Baluchistān, SW Pakistan 25.09N 62.21E
154 J16 **Gwādar East Bay** *bay* SW Pakistan
154 J16 **Gwādar West Bay** *bay* SW Pakistan
Gwadur *see* Gwādar
85 J17 **Gwai** Matabeleland North, W Zimbabwe 19.17S 27.37E
160 I7 **Gwalior** Madhya Pradesh, C India 26.15N 78.12E
85 J18 **Gwanda** Matabeleland South, SW Zimbabwe 20.56S 29.00E
81 N15 **Gwane** Orientale, N Dem. Rep. Congo 4.40N 25.51E
85 I17 **Gwayi** ∽ W Zimbabwe
112 G8 **Gwda** *var.* Głda, *Ger.* Küddow. ∽ NW Poland
99 C14 **Gweebarra Bay** *Ir.* Béal an Bheara. *inlet* W Ireland
99 D14 **Gweedore** *Ir.* Gaoth Dobhair. NW Ireland 55.03N 8.13W
Gwelo *see* Gweru
99 K21 **Gwent** *cultural region* S Wales, UK
85 K17 **Gweru** *prev.* Gwelo. Midlands, C Zimbabwe 19.27S 29.49E
31 Q7 **Gwinner** North Dakota, N USA 46.10N 97.42W
79 Y13 **Gwoza** Borno, NE Nigeria 11.07N 13.40E
Gwy *see* Wye
191 R4 **Gwydir River** ∽ New South Wales, SE Australia
99 I19 **Gwynedd** *var.* Gwyneth. *cultural region* NW Wales, UK
Gwyneth *see* Gwynedd
165 O16 **Gyaca** Xizang Zizhiqu, W China 29.06N 92.37E
Gya'gya *see* Saga
117 M22 **Gyalí** *var.* Yialí. *island* Dodekánisos, Greece, Aegean Sea
Gyandzha *see* Gäncä
164 M16 **Gyangzê** Xizang Zizhiqu, W China 28.49N 89.37E
164 L14 **Gyaring Co** ◎ W China
165 Q12 **Gyaring Hu** ◎ C China
117 I20 **Gyáros** *var.* Yioúra. *island* Kykládes, Greece, Aegean Sea
126 Hh7 **Gyda** Yamalo-Nenetskiy Avtonomnyy Okrug, N Russian Federation 70.55N 78.34E
126 H7 **Gydanskiy Poluostrov** *Eng.* Gyda Peninsula. *peninsula* N Russian Federation
Gyda Peninsula *see* Gydanskiy Poluostrov
Gyéres *see* Câmpia Turzii
Gyergyószentmiklós *see* Gheorgheni
Gyergyótölgyes *see* Tulgheş
Gyertyámos *see* Cărpiniş
Gyeva *see* Detva
Gyigang *see* Zayü
97 I23 **Gyldenløves Høy** *hill range* C Denmark
189 Z10 **Gympie** Queensland, E Australia 26.04S 152.40E
177 Ff7 **Gyobingauk** Pegu, SW Myanmar 18.13N 95.39E
113 M23 **Gyomaendrőd** Békés, SE Hungary 46.55N 20.49E
Gyömbér *see* Ďumbier
113 L22 **Gyöngyös** Heves, NE Hungary 47.43N 19.48E
113 H22 **Győr** *Ger.* Raab; *Lat.* Arrabona. Győr-Moson-Sopron, NW Hungary 47.40N 17.40E
113 G22 **Győr-Moson-Sopron** *off.* Győr-Moson-Sopron Megye. ◈ *county* NW Hungary
9 X15 **Gypsumville** Manitoba, S Canada 51.46N 98.37W
10 M4 **Gyrfalcon Islands** *island group* Nunavut, NE Canada
97 N14 **Gysinge** Gävleborg, C Sweden 60.16N 16.55E
117 F22 **Gýtheio** *var.* Githio; *prev.* Ýthion. Pelopónnisos, S Greece 36.46N 22.34E
152 L13 **Gyuichbirleshik** Lebapskiy Velayat, E Turkmenistan 38.10N 64.33E
113 N24 **Gyula** *Rom.* Jula. Békés, SE Hungary 46.37N 21.19E
Gyulafehérvár *see* Alba Iulia
Gyulovo *see* Roza
143 T11 **Gyumri** *var.* Giumri, *Rus.* Kumayri; *prev.* Aleksandropol', Leninakan. W Armenia 40.48N 43.51E
152 D13 **Gyunuzyndag, Gora** ▲ W Turkmenistan 38.15N 56.25E
152 D12 **Gyzylarbat** *prev.* Kizyl-Arvat. Balkanskiy Velayat, W Turkmenistan 39.01N 56.14E
Gyzylbaydak *see* Krasnoye Znamya
Gyzyletrek *see* Kizyl-Atrek
Gyzylgaya *see* Kizyl-Kaya
Gyzylsu *see* Kizyl-Su
130 J3 **Gzhatsk** Smolenskaya Oblast', W Russian Federation 55.33N 35.00E

H

159 T12 **Ha** W Bhutan 27.16N 89.22E
Haabai *see* Ha'apai Group
101 H17 **Haacht** Vlaams Brabant, C Belgium 50.58N 4.37E
111 T4 **Haag** Niederösterreich, NE Austria 48.07N 14.32E
204 L8 **Haag Nunataks** ▲ Antarctica
94 N2 **Haakon VII Land** *physical region* NW Svalbard
100 O11 **Haaksbergen** Overijssel, E Netherlands 52.09N 6.45E
101 E14 **Haamstede** Zeeland, SW Netherlands 51.43N 3.45E
200 Ss13 **Ha'ano** *island* Ha'apai Group, C Tonga
200 Ss13 **Ha'apai Group** *var.* Haabai. *island group* C Tonga
95 L15 **Haapajärvi** Oulu, C Finland 63.45N 25.19E
95 L17 **Haapamäki** Länsi-Suomi, W Finland 62.11N 24.32E
95 L15 **Haapavesi** Oulu, C Finland 64.09N 25.25E
203 N7 **Haapiti** Moorea, W French Polynesia 17.33S 149.52W
120 F4 **Haapsalu** *Ger.* Hapsal. Läänemaa, W Estonia 58.57N 23.32E
Ha'Arava *see* 'Arabah, Wādī al
97 G24 **Haarby** *var.* Hårby. Fyn, C Denmark 55.13N 10.07E
100 H10 **Haarlem** *prev.* Harlem. Noord-Holland, W Netherlands 52.22N 4.39E
193 D19 **Haast** West Coast, South Island, NZ 43.53S 169.01E
193 C20 **Haast** ∽ South Island, NZ
193 D20 **Haast Pass** *pass* South Island, NZ 44.07S 169.18E
200 R16 **Ha'atua** 'Eau, E Tonga 21.23S 174.57W
155 P15 **Hab** ∽ SW Pakistan
147 W7 **Haba** *var.* Al Haba. Dubayy, NE UAE 25.01N 55.37E
164 K2 **Habahe** *var.* Kaba. Xinjiang Uygur Zizhiqu, NW China 48.04N 86.20E
147 U13 **Ḩabarūt** *var.* Habrut. SW Oman 17.19N 52.45E
83 J18 **Habaswein** North Eastern, NE Kenya 1.01N 39.27E
101 L24 **Habay-la-Neuve** Luxembourg, SE Belgium 49.43N 5.38E
145 S8 **Ḩabbānīyah, Buḩayrat** ◎ C Iraq
Habelschwerdt *see* Bystrzyca Kłodzka
159 V14 **Habiganj** Chittagong, NE Bangladesh 24.22N 91.25E
169 Q12 **Habirag** Nei Mongol Zizhiqu, N China 42.18N 115.40E
97 L19 **Habo** Västra Götaland, S Sweden 57.55N 14.04E
127 P16 **Habomai Islands** *island group* Kuril'skiye Ostrova, SE Russian Federation
172 P3 **Haboro** Hokkaidō, NE Japan 44.19N 141.42E
159 S16 **Habra** West Bengal, NE India 22.39N 88.17E
Habrut *see* Ḩabarūt
149 P17 **Ḩabshān** Abū Ẓaby, C UAE 23.51N 53.34E
56 E14 **Hacha** Putumayo, S Colombia 00.02S 75.30W
172 Ss13 **Hachijō** Tōkyō, Hachijō-jima, SE Japan 33.50N 139.19E
172 Ss13 **Hachijō-jima** *var.* Hatizyô Zima. *island* Izu-shotō, SE Japan
171 I14 **Hachiman** Gifu, Honshū, SW Japan 35.46N 136.57E
171 M9 **Hachimori** Akita, Honshū, C Japan 40.22N 139.59E
172 N10 **Hachinohe** Aomori, Honshū, C Japan 40.30N 141.28E
171 Jj16 **Hachiōji** *var.* Hatiôzi. Tōkyō, Honshū, S Japan 35.39N 139.17E
95 G17 **Hackås** Jämtland, C Sweden 62.55N 14.31E
20 K14 **Hackensack** New Jersey, NE USA 40.51N 73.57W
Hadama *see* Nazrēt
171 J16 **Hadano** Kanagawa, Honshū, S Japan 35.23N 139.13E
147 W13 **Ḩadbaram** S Oman 17.27N 55.13E
145 U13 **Ḩaddānīyah** *well* S Iraq 30.27N 44.40E
98 K12 **Haddington** SE Scotland, UK 55.59N 2.45W
147 Z8 **Ḩadd, Ra's al** *headland* NE Oman 22.28N 59.58E
Haded *see* Xadeed
79 W12 **Hadejia** Jigawa, N Nigeria 12.22N 10.02E
79 W12 **Hadejia** ∽ N Nigeria
144 F9 **Ḩadera** *var.* Khadera. Haifa, C Israel 32.25N 34.55E
Hadersleben *see* Haderslev
97 G24 **Haderslev** *Ger.* Hadersleben. Sønderjylland, SW Denmark 55.15N 9.30E
157 J21 **Hadhdhunmathi Atoll** *var.* Haddummati Atoll, Laamu Atoll. *atoll* S Maldives
Hadhramaut *see* Ḩaḑramawt
147 W17 **Hadīboh** Suquṭrā, SE Yemen 12.37N 54.04E
164 K9 **Hadilik** Xinjiang Uygur Zizhiqu, W China 37.51N 86.10E
142 H16 **Hadım** Konya, S Turkey 36.58N 32.27E
146 K7 **Hadīyah** Al Madīnah, W Saudi Arabia 25.36N 38.31E
15 J1 **Hadley Bay** *bay* Victoria Island, Nunavut, N Canada
178 Jj6 **Ha Đông** *var.* Hadong. Ha Tây, N Vietnam 20.58N 105.46E
147 R15 **Ḩaḑramawt** *Eng.* Hadhramaut. ▲▲ S Yemen
Hadria *see* Adria
Hadrianopolis *see* Edirne
Hadria Picena *see* Apricena
97 G22 **Hadsten** Århus, C Denmark 56.19N 10.03E
97 G21 **Hadsund** Nordjylland, N Denmark 56.43N 10.07E
119 S4 **Hadyach** *Rus.* Gadyach. Poltavs'ka Oblast', NE Ukraine 50.21N 34.00E
114 I13 **Hadžići** Federacija Bosna I Hercegovina, SE Bosnia and Herzegovina 43.49N 18.12E
169 W14 **Haeju** S North Korea 38.04N 125.40E
Haerbin/Haerhpin/Ha-erh-pin *see* Harbin
147 P5 **Ḩafar al Bāṭin** Ash Sharqīyah, N Saudi Arabia 28.25N 45.58E
9 T15 **Hafford** Saskatchewan, S Canada 52.43N 107.19W
142 M13 **Hafik** Sivas, N Turkey 39.52N 37.24E
155 V8 **Hāfizābād** Punjab, E Pakistan 32.05N 73.37E
94 H4 **Hafnarfjördhur** Reykjanes, W Iceland 64.03N 21.57W
Hafnia *see* København, Denmark
Hafnia *see* Denmark
Hafren *see* Severn
Hafun *see* Xaafuun
Hafun, Ras *see* Xaafuun, Raas
82 G10 **Hag 'Abdullah** Sinnar, E Sudan 13.58N 33.34E
83 K18 **Hagadera** North Eastern, E Kenya 0.06N 40.23E
144 G8 **HaGalil** *Eng.* Galilee. ▲▲ N Israel
12 G10 **Hagar** Ontario, S Canada 46.27N 80.22W
161 G18 **Hagari** *var.* Vedāvati. ∽ W India
196 B16 **Hagåtña** *var.* Agana, Agaña. ○ (Guam) NW Guam 13.27N 144.45E
102 M13 **Hagelberg** *hill* NE Germany 52.03N 12.33E
41 N14 **Hagemeister Island** *island* Alaska, USA
103 F15 **Hagen** Nordrhein-Westfalen, W Germany 51.21N 7.27E
102 K10 **Hagenow** Mecklenburg-Vorpommern, N Germany 53.27N 11.10E
8 K15 **Hagensborg** British Columbia, SW Canada 52.24N 126.24W
82 I13 **Hägere Hiywet** *var.* Agere Hiywet, Ambo. Oromo, C Ethiopia 9.00N 37.55E
35 O15 **Hagerman** Idaho, NW USA 42.48N 114.53W
39 U14 **Hagerman** New Mexico, SW USA 33.07N 104.19W
23 V2 **Hagerstown** Maryland, NE USA 39.38N 77.43W
12 G16 **Hagersville** Ontario, S Canada 42.58N 80.03W
104 J15 **Hagetmau** Landes, SW France 43.40N 0.36W
97 K14 **Hagfors** Värmland, C Sweden 60.03N 13.45E
95 G16 **Häggenås** Jämtland, C Sweden 63.24N 14.53E
170 Dd12 **Hagi** Yamaguchi, Honshū, SW Japan 34.24N 131.22E
178 J5 **Ha Giang** Ha Giang, N Vietnam 22.49N 104.58E
Hagios Evstrátios *see* Ágios Efstrátios
HaGolan *see* Golan Heights
105 T4 **Hagondange** Moselle, NE France 49.15N 6.06E
99 B18 **Hag's Head** *Ir.* Ceann Caillí. *headland* W Ireland 52.56N 9.29W
104 I3 **Hague, Cap de la** *headland* N France 49.43N 1.56W
105 V5 **Haguenau** Bas-Rhin, NE France 48.49N 7.46E
172 T16 **Hahajima-rettō** *island group* SE Japan
13 R8 **Há Há, Lac** ◎ Quebec, SE Canada
180 H13 **Hahaya** ✕ (Moroni) Grande Comore, NW Comoros
24 K9 **Hahnville** Louisiana, S USA 29.58N 90.24W
85 E22 **Haib** Karas, S Namibia 28.12S 18.19E
Haibak *see* Āybak
155 N15 **Haibo** ∽ SW Pakistan
169 U12 **Haicheng** Liaoning, NE China 40.52N 122.45E
Haida *see* Nový Bor
Haidarabad *see* Hyderābād
Haidenschaft *see* Ajdovščina
178 Jj6 **Hai Dương** Hai Hưng, N Vietnam 20.55N 106.21E
144 F9 **Haifa** ◈ *district* NW Israel
Haifa *see* Ḩefa
Haifa, Bay of *see* Ḩefa, Mifraẓ
167 P14 **Haifeng** Guangdong, S China 22.58N 115.16E
Haifong *see* Hai Phong
167 P3 **Hai He** ∽ E China
Haikang *see* Leizhou
166 L17 **Haikou** *var.* Hai-k'ou, Hoihow, *Fr.* Hoï-Hao. Hainan, S China 20.00N 110.16E
146 M6 **Ḩā'il** Ḩā'il, NW Saudi Arabia 27.00N 42.50E
147 N5 **Ḩā'il** *off.* Minṭaqah Ḩā'il. ◈ *province* N Saudi Arabia
Hai-la-erh *see* Hailar
169 S6 **Hailar** *var.* Hai-la-erh; *prev.* Hulun. Nei Mongol Zizhiqu, N China 49.15N 119.40E
169 S6 **Hailar He** ∽ NE China
35 P14 **Hailey** Idaho, NW USA 43.31N 114.18W
12 H9 **Haileybury** Ontario, S Canada 47.27N 79.39W
169 X9 **Hailin** Heilongjiang, NE China 44.37N 129.24E
Ḩā'il, Minṭaqah *see* Ḩā'il
Hailong *see* Meihekou
95 K14 **Hailuoto** *Swe.* Karlö. *island* W Finland
Haima *see* Haymā'
Haimen *see* Taizhou
166 M17 **Hainan** *var.* Hainan Sheng, Qiong. ◈ *province* S China
166 K17 **Hainan Dao** *island* S China
Hainan Sheng *see* Hainan
Hainan Strait *see* Qiongzhou Haixia
Hainasch *see* Ainaži
Hainau *see* Chojnów
101 E20 **Hainaut** ◈ *province* SW Belgium
Hainburg *see* Hainburg an der Donau
111 Z4 **Hainburg an der Donau** *var.* Hainburg. Niederösterreich, NE Austria 48.08N 16.57E
41 W12 **Haines** Alaska, USA 59.13N 135.27W
34 L12 **Haines** Oregon, NW USA 44.53N 117.56W
25 W12 **Haines City** Florida, SE USA 28.06N 81.37W
8 H8 **Haines Junction** Yukon Territory, W Canada 60.45N 137.30W
111 W4 **Hainfeld** Niederösterreich, NE Austria 48.01N 15.45E
103 N16 **Hainichen** Sachsen, E Germany 50.58N 13.07E
178 K6 **Hai Phong** *var.* Haifong, Haiphong. N Vietnam 20.49N 106.40E
Haiphong *see* Hai Phong
167 S12 **Haitan Dao** *island* SE China
46 K8 **Haiti** *off.* Republic of Haiti. ◆ *republic* C West Indies
37 T11 **Haiwee Reservoir** ⊠ California, W USA
82 I7 **Haiya** Red Sea, NE Sudan 18.16N 36.21E
165 T10 **Haiyan** Qinghai, W China 36.55N 100.54E
166 M13 **Haiyang Shan** ▲▲ S China
165 V10 **Haiyuan** Ningxia, N China 36.32N 105.31E
Hajda *see* Nový Bor
113 M22 **Hajdú-Bihar** *off.* Hajdú-Bihar Megye. ◈ *county* E Hungary
113 N22 **Hajdúböszörmény** Hajdú-Bihar, E Hungary 47.39N 21.32E
113 N22 **Hajdúhadház** Hajdú-Bihar, E Hungary 47.40N 21.40E
113 N21 **Hajdúnánás** Hajdú-Bihar, E Hungary 47.49N 21.25E
113 N22 **Hajdúszoboszló** Hajdú-Bihar, E Hungary 47.27N 21.23E
148 I3 **Ḩājī Ebrāhīm, Kūh-e** ▲ Iran/Iraq 36.53N 44.56E
171 Kk11 **Hajiki-zaki** *headland* Sado, C Japan 38.19N 138.28E
Hajine *see* Abū Ḩardān
159 P13 **Hājīpur** Bihār, N India 25.40N 85.13E
147 N14 **Ḩajjah** W Yemen 15.43N 43.33E
145 U11 **Ḩajjama** S Iraq 31.24N 45.20E
149 R12 **Ḩājjīābād** Hormozgān, C Iran 28.19N 55.55E
145 U14 **Ḩajj, Thaqb al** *well* S Iraq 29.58N 44.32E
115 L16 **Hajla** ▲ SW Serbia and Montenegro (Yugoslavia)
112 P10 **Hajnówka** *Ger.* Hermhausen. Podlaskie, NE Poland 52.43N 23.37E
177 Ff4 **Haka** Chin State, W Myanmar 22.42N 93.40E
Hakapehi *see* Punaauia
Hakâri *see* Hakkâri
143 T16 **Hakkâri** *var.* Çölemerik, Hakâri. Hakkâri, SE Turkey 37.36N 43.45E
143 T16 **Hakkâri** *var.* Hakkari. ◈ *province* SE Turkey
94 J12 **Hakkas** Norrbotten, N Sweden 66.52N 21.36E
171 Gg16 **Hakken-zan** ▲ Honshū, SW Japan 34.11N 135.57E
172 N9 **Hakkōda-san** ▲ Honshū, C Japan 40.40N 140.49E
172 Pp3 **Hako-dake** ▲ Hokkaidō, NE Japan 44.40N 142.22E
172 N7 **Hakodate** Hokkaidō, NE Japan 41.46N 140.42E
171 Ii12 **Hakui** Ishikawa, Honshū, SW Japan 36.52N 136.45E
202 B16 **Hakupu** SE Niue 19.06S 169.49E
171 I14 **Haku-san** ▲ Honshū, SW Japan 36.07N 136.45E
Hal *see* Halle
155 Q15 **Hāla** Sind, SE Pakistan 25.46N 68.28E
144 I3 **Ḩalab** *Eng.* Aleppo, *Fr.* Alep; *anc.* Beroea. Ḩalab, NW Syria 36.13N 37.10E
144 I3 **Ḩalab** *off.* Muḩāfaẓat Ḩalab, *var.* Aleppo, Halab. ◈ *governorate* NW Syria
144 I3 **Ḩalab** ✕ Ḩalab, NW Syria 36.12N 37.10E
147 O8 **Ḩalabān** *var.* Halibān. Ar Riyāḑ, C Saudi Arabia 23.28N 44.19E
145 V4 **Ḩalabja** NE Iraq 35.10N 45.58E
202 A16 **Halagigie Point** *headland* W Niue
77 Z11 **Halaib** SE Egypt 22.10N 36.33E
202 G12 **Halalo** Île Uvea, N Wallis and Futuna 13.21S 176.10W
Halandri *see* Chalándri
147 X13 **Ḩalānīyāt, Juzur al** *var.* Jazā'ir Bin Ghalfān, *Eng.* Kuria Muria Islands. *island group* S Oman
147 W13 **Ḩalānīyāt, Khalīj al** *Eng.* Kuria Muria Bay. *bay* S Oman
Halas *see* Kiskunhalas
40 G11 **Halawa** *Haw.* Hālawa. Hawaii, USA, C Pacific Ocean 20.13N 155.46W
40 F9 **Halawa, Cape** *headland* Molokai, Hawaii, USA, C Pacific Ocean 21.09N 156.43W
168 H6 **Halban** Hövsgöl, N Mongolia 49.30N 97.33E
103 K14 **Halberstadt** Sachsen-Anhalt, C Germany 51.54N 11.04E
192 M12 **Halcombe** Manawatu-Wanganui, North Island, NZ 40.09S 175.30E
97 I16 **Halden** *prev.* Fredrikshald. Østfold, S Norway 59.07N 11.19E
102 L13 **Haldensleben** Sachsen-Anhalt, C Germany 52.18N 11.25E
Háldi *see* Halti
159 S17 **Haldia** West Bengal, NE India 22.07N 88.06E
158 K10 **Haldwāni** Uttar Pradesh, N India 29.13N 79.31E
40 F10 **Haleakala** *crater* Maui, Hawaii, USA, C Pacific Ocean 20.45N 156.12W
27 N4 **Hale Center** Texas, SW USA 34.03N 101.50W
101 J18 **Halen** Limburg, NE Belgium 50.35N 5.08E
25 O2 **Haleyville** Alabama, S USA 34.13N 87.37W
79 O17 **Half Assini** SW Ghana 5.03N 2.57W
37 R8 **Half Dome** ▲ California, W USA 37.46N 119.27W
193 C25 **Halfmoon Bay** *var.* Oban. Stewart Island, Southland, NZ 46.52S 168.08E
190 E5 **Half Moon Lake** *salt lake* South Australia
169 R7 **Halhgol** Dornod, E Mongolia 47.57N 118.07E
Haliacmon *see* Aliákmonas
Halibān *see* Ḩalabān
12 I13 **Haliburton** Ontario, SE Canada 45.03N 78.32W
12 I12 **Haliburton Highlands** *var.* Madawaska Highlands. *hill range* Ontario, SE Canada
11 Q15 **Halifax** Nova Scotia, SE Canada 44.37N 63.34W
99 L17 **Halifax** N England, UK 53.43N 1.52W
23 W8 **Halifax** North Carolina, SE USA 36.18N 77.35W
23 U7 **Halifax** Virginia, NE USA 36.46N 78.55W
11 Q15 **Halifax** ✕ Nova Scotia, SE Canada 44.33N 63.48W
149 T13 **Ḩalīl Rūd** *seasonal river* SE Iran
144 I6 **Ḩalīmah** ▲ Lebanon/Syria 34.12N 36.37E
168 G8 **Haliun** Govĭ-Altay, W Mongolia 45.55N 96.06E
120 I3 **Haljala** *Ger.* Halljal. Lääne-Virumaa, N Estonia 59.25N 26.18E
41 Q4 **Halkett, Cape** *headland* Alaska, USA 70.48N 152.11W
Halkida *see* Chalkída
98 J6 **Halkirk** N Scotland, UK 58.30N 3.29W
13 X7 **Hall** ∽ Quebec, SE Canada
Hall *see* Schwäbisch Hall
95 H15 **Hälla** Västerbotten, N Sweden 63.55N 17.19E
98 J6 **Halladale** ∽ N Scotland, UK
97 J21 **Halland** ◈ *county* S Sweden
25 Z15 **Hallandale** Florida, SE USA 25.58N 80.09W
97 K22 **Hallandsås** *physical region* S Sweden
15 M2 **Hall Beach** Nunavut, N Canada 68.10N 81.55W
101 G19 **Halle** *Fr.* Hal. Vlaams Brabant, C Belgium 50.43N 4.13E
103 M15 **Halle** *var.* Halle an der Saale. Sachsen-Anhalt, C Germany 51.28N 11.58E
Halle an der Saale *see* Halle
37 W3 **Halleck** Nevada, W USA 40.57N 115.27W
97 L15 **Hällefors** Örebro, C Sweden 59.48N 14.27E
97 N16 **Hälleforsnäs** Södermanland, C Sweden 59.10N 16.30E
111 Q6 **Hallein** Salzburg, N Austria 47.40N 13.06E
103 L15 **Halle-Neustadt** Sachsen-Anhalt, C Germany 51.28N 11.54E
27 U12 **Hallettsville** Texas, SW USA 29.27N 96.57W
205 N4 **Halley** *UK research station* Antarctica 75.42S 26.30W
30 L4 **Halliday** North Dakota, N USA 47.19N 102.19W
39 S2 **Halligan Reservoir** ⊠ Colorado, C USA
102 G7 **Halligen** *island group* N Germany
96 G13 **Hallingdal** *valley* S Norway
40 J12 **Hall Island** *island* Alaska, USA
Hall Island *see* Maiana
201 P15 **Hall Islands** *island group* C Micronesia
120 H6 **Halliste** ∽ S Estonia
Halljal *see* Haljala
95 I15 **Hällnäs** Västerbotten, N Sweden 64.19N 19.41E
31 R2 **Hallock** Minnesota, N USA 48.47N 96.56W
16 Oo3 **Hall Peninsula** *peninsula* Baffin Island, Nunavut, NE Canada
22 F9 **Halls** Tennessee, S USA 35.52N 89.24W
97 M16 **Hallsberg** Örebro, C Sweden 59.04N 15.07E
189 N5 **Halls Creek** Western Australia 18.17S 127.39E
190 L12 **Halls Gap** Victoria, SE Australia 37.09S 142.30E
97 N15 **Hallstahammar** Västmanland, C Sweden 59.25N 16.16E
111 R6 **Hallstatt** Salzburg, W Austria 47.32N 13.39E
Hallstatter See ◎ C Austria
97 P14 **Hallstavik** Stockholm, C Sweden 60.12N 18.45E
27 X7 **Hallsville** Texas, SW USA 32.31N 94.30W
105 P1 **Halluin** Nord, N France 50.46N 3.07E
Halmahera, Laut *see* Halmahera Sea
175 T7 **Halmahera, Pulau** *prev.* Djailolo, Gilolo, Jailolo. *island* E Indonesia
175 Tt8 **Halmahera Sea** *Ind.* Laut Halmahera. *sea* E Indonesia
97 J21 **Halmstad** Halland, S Sweden 56.41N 12.48E
175 T11 **Halong** Pulau Ambon, E Indonesia 3.39S 128.13E

◆ Country ● Country Capital ◇ Dependent Territory ○ Dependent Territory Capital ◈ Administrative Region ✕ International Airport ▲ Mountain ▲▲ Mountain Range Volcano ∽ River ◎ Lake ⊠ Reservoir

121 N15 **Halowchyn** *Rus.* Golovchin. Mahilyowskaya Voblasts', E Belarus 54.03N 29.52E
97 H20 **Hals** Nordjylland, N Denmark 57.00N 10.19E
96 F8 **Halsa** Møre og Romsdal, S Norway 63.04N 8.13E
121 I15 **Hal'shany** *Rus.* Gol'shany. Hrodzyenskaya Voblasts', W Belarus 54.15N 26.01E
Hälsingborg *see* Helsingborg
31 R5 **Halstad** Minnesota, N USA 47.21N 96.49W
29 N6 **Halstead** Kansas, C USA 38.00N 97.30W
101 G15 **Halsteren** Noord-Brabant, S Netherlands 51.31N 4.16E
95 L16 **Halsua** Länsi-Suomi, W Finland 63.28N 24.10E
103 E14 **Haltern** Nordrhein-Westfalen, W Germany 51.45N 7.10E
94 J9 **Halti** *var.* Haltiatunturi, *Lapp.* Háldi. ▲ Finland/Norway 69.18N 21.19E
Haltiatunturi *see* Halti
118 J6 **Halych** Ivano-Frankivs'ka Oblast', W Ukraine 49.08N 24.44E
Halycus *see* Platani
105 P3 **Ham** Somme, N France 49.46N 3.03E
Hama *see* Ḥamāh
170 Ee12 **Hamada** Shimane, Honshū, SW Japan 34.54N 132.07E
148 L6 **Hamadān** *anc.* Ecbatana. Hamadān, W Iran 34.50N 48.31E
148 L6 **Hamadān** *off.* Ostān-e Hamadān. ◈ *province* W Iran
144 I5 **Ḥamāh** *var.* Hama; *anc.* Epiphania, *Bibl.* Hamath. Ḥamāh, W Syria 35.09N 36.43E
144 I5 **Ḥamāh** *off.* Muḥāfaẓat Ḥamāh, *var.* Hama. ◈ *governorate* C Syria
171 I17 **Hamakita** Shizuoka, Honshū, S Japan 34.46N 137.46E
172 O4 **Hamamasu** Hokkaidō, NE Japan 43.37N 141.24E
171 I17 **Hamamatsu** *var.* Hamamatu. Shizuoka, Honshū, S Japan 34.43N 137.45E
Hamamatu *see* Hamamatsu
172 Qq7 **Hamanaka** Hokkaidō, NE Japan 43.05N 145.05E
171 I17 **Hamana-ko** ◎ Honshū, S Japan
96 I13 **Hamar** *prev.* Storhammer. Hedmark, S Norway 60.48N 11.04E
147 U10 **Ḥamārīr al Kidan, Qalamat** *well* E Saudi Arabia 21.40N 53.13E
170 G12 **Hamasaka** Hyōgo, Honshū, SW Japan 35.37N 134.27E
Hamath *see* Ḥamāh
172 Pp2 **Hamatonbetsu** Hokkaidō, NE Japan 45.07N 142.21E
161 K26 **Hambantota** Southern Province, SE Sri Lanka 6.11N 81.10E
194 G10 **Hambili** ≈ NW PNG
Hambourg *see* Hamburg
102 J9 **Hamburg** Hamburg, N Germany 53.33N 10.02E
29 V14 **Hamburg** Arkansas, C USA 33.13N 91.48W
31 S16 **Hamburg** Iowa, C USA 40.36N 95.39W
20 D10 **Hamburg** New York, NE USA 42.40N 78.49W
102 I10 **Hamburg** *Fr.* Hambourg. ◈ *state* N Germany
154 K5 **Hamdam Āb, Dasht-e** *Pash.* Dasht-i Hamdamab. ▲▲ W Afghanistan
Hamdamab, Dasht-i *see* Hamdam Āb, Dasht-e
20 M13 **Hamden** Connecticut, NE USA 41.22N 72.55W
146 K6 **Ḥamḍ, Wādī al** *dry watercourse* W Saudi Arabia
95 K18 **Hämeenkyrö** Länsi-Suomi, W Finland 61.39N 23.10E
95 L19 **Hämeenlinna** *Swe.* Tavastehus. Etelä-Suomi, S Finland 61.00N 24.25E
HaMelaẖ, Yam *see* Dead Sea
Hamelin *see* Hameln
102 I13 **Hameln** *Eng.* Hamelin. Niedersachsen, N Germany 52.05N 9.21E
188 I8 **Hamersley Range** ▲▲ Western Australia
169 Y12 **Hamgyŏng-sanmaek** ▲▲ N North Korea
169 X13 **Hamhŭng** C North Korea 39.53N 127.31E
165 O6 **Hami** *var.* Ha-mi, *Uigh.* Kumul, Qomul. Xinjiang Uygur Zizhiqu, NW China 42.48N 93.27E
145 X10 **Ḥāmid Amīn** E Iraq 32.06N 46.53E
147 W11 **Hamīdān, Khawr** *oasis* SE Saudi Arabia 20.25N 54.43E
144 H5 **Ḥamīdīyah** *var.* Hamîdîyé. Ṭarṭūs, W Syria 34.43N 35.58E
116 L12 **Hamidiye** Edirne, NW Turkey 41.09N 26.40E
Hamîdîyé *see* Ḥamīdīyah
190 L12 **Hamilton** Victoria, SE Australia 37.45S 142.04E
66 B12 **Hamilton** ○ (Bermuda) C Bermuda 32.18N 64.48W
12 G16 **Hamilton** Ontario, S Canada 43.15N 79.49W
192 M7 **Hamilton** Waikato, North Island, NZ 37.48S 175.15E
98 I12 **Hamilton** S Scotland, UK 55.46N 4.03W
25 N3 **Hamilton** Alabama, S USA 34.08N 87.59W
40 M10 **Hamilton** Alaska, USA 62.54N 163.53W
32 J13 **Hamilton** Illinois, N USA 40.24N 91.20W
29 S3 **Hamilton** Missouri, C USA 39.44N 94.00W
35 P10 **Hamilton** Montana, NW USA 46.15N 114.09W
27 S8 **Hamilton** Texas, SW USA 31.42N 98.07W
12 G16 **Hamilton** ✕ Ontario, SE Canada 43.12N 79.54W
66 I6 **Hamilton Bank** *undersea feature* SE Labrador Sea
190 E1 **Hamilton Creek** *seasonal river* South Australia
11 R8 **Hamilton Inlet** *inlet* Newfoundland and Labrador, E Canada
29 T12 **Hamilton, Lake** ⊠ Arkansas, C USA
37 W6 **Hamilton, Mount** ▲ Nevada, W USA 39.15N 115.30W
77 S8 **Ḥamīm, Wādī al** ≈ NE Libya
95 N19 **Hamina** *Swe.* Fredrikshamn. Etelä-Suomi, S Finland 60.33N 27.15E
9 W16 **Hamiota** Manitoba, S Canada 50.13N 100.37W
158 L13 **Hamīrpur** Uttar Pradesh, N India 25.57N 80.07E
Hamīs Musait *see* Khamīs Mushayt
23 T11 **Hamlet** North Carolina, SE USA 34.52N 79.41W
27 P6 **Hamlin** Texas, SW USA 32.52N 100.07W
23 P5 **Hamlin** West Virginia, NE USA 38.16N 82.06W
33 O7 **Hamlin Lake** ◎ Michigan, N USA
103 F14 **Hamm** *var.* Hamm in Westfalen. Nordrhein-Westfalen, W Germany 51.39N 7.49E
Ḥammāmāt, Khalīj al *see* Hammamet, Golfe de
77 N5 **Hammamet, Golfe de** *Ar.* Khalīj al Ḥammāmāt. *gulf* NE Tunisia
145 R3 **Ḥammān al 'Alīl** N Iraq 36.07N 43.15E
145 X12 **Ḥammār, Hawr al** ◎ SE Iraq
95 J20 **Hammarland** Åland, SW Finland 60.13N 19.45E
95 H16 **Hammarstrand** Jämtland, C Sweden 63.07N 16.27E
95 O17 **Hammaslahti** Itä-Suomi, E Finland 62.26N 29.58E
101 F17 **Hamme** Oost-Vlaanderen, NW Belgium 51.06N 4.07E
102 H10 **Hamme** ≈ NW Germany
97 G22 **Hammel** Århus, C Denmark 56.15N 9.52E
103 I18 **Hammelburg** Bayern, C Germany 50.06N 9.50E
101 H18 **Hamme-Mille** Wallon Brabant, C Belgium 50.48N 4.42E
102 H10 **Hamme-Oste-Kanal** *canal* NW Germany
95 G16 **Hammerdal** Jämtland, C Sweden 63.34N 15.19E
94 K8 **Hammerfest** Finnmark, N Norway 70.40N 23.40E
103 D14 **Hamminkeln** Nordrhein-Westfalen, W Germany 51.43N 6.36E
Hamm in Westfalen *see* Hamm
28 K10 **Hammon** Oklahoma, C USA 35.37N 99.22W
33 N11 **Hammond** Indiana, N USA 41.35N 87.30W
24 K8 **Hammond** Louisiana, S USA 30.30N 90.27W
101 K20 **Hamoir** Liège, E Belgium 50.28N 5.35E
101 J21 **Hamois** Namur, SE Belgium 50.21N 5.09E
101 K16 **Hamont** Limburg, NE Belgium 51.15N 5.33E
193 F22 **Hampden** Otago, South Island, NZ 45.18S 170.49E
21 R6 **Hampden** Maine, NE USA 44.44N 68.51W
99 M23 **Hampshire** *cultural region* S England, UK
11 O15 **Hampton** New Brunswick, SE Canada 45.30N 65.49W
29 U14 **Hampton** Arkansas, C USA 33.33N 92.28W
31 V12 **Hampton** Iowa, C USA 42.44N 93.12W
21 P10 **Hampton** New Hampshire, NE USA 42.55N 70.48W
23 R14 **Hampton** South Carolina, SE USA 32.52N 81.06W
23 P8 **Hampton** Tennessee, S USA 36.16N 82.10W
23 X7 **Hampton** Virginia, NE USA 37.01N 76.21W
96 L11 **Hamra** Gävleborg, C Sweden 61.40N 15.00E
82 D10 **Hamrat esh Sheikh** Northern Kordofan, C Sudan 14.37N 27.55E
145 S5 **Ḥamrīn, Jabal** ▲▲ N Iraq
123 Jj16 **Hamrun** C Malta 35.53N 14.28E
178 K14 **Ham Thuân Nam** Binh Thuân, S Vietnam 10.49N 107.49E
176 Ww11 **Hamuku** Papua, E Indonesia 3.18S 135.00E
Hāmūn, Daryācheh-ye *see* Şāberī, Hāmūn-e/Sīstān, Daryācheh-ye
Hamwih *see* Southampton
40 G10 **Hana** *Haw.* Hāna. Maui, Hawaii, USA, C Pacific Ocean 20.45N 155.59W
23 S14 **Hanahan** South Carolina, SE USA 32.55N 80.01W
40 B8 **Hanalei** Kauai, Hawaii, USA, C Pacific Ocean 22.12N 159.30W
178 Kk10 **Ha Nam** Quang Nam-Đa Năng, C Vietnam 15.42N 108.24E
171 Mm11 **Hanamaki** Iwate, Honshū, C Japan 39.25N 141.04E
40 F10 **Hanamanioa, Cape** *headland* Maui, Hawaii, USA, C Pacific Ocean 20.34N 156.22W
202 B16 **Hanan** ✕ (Alofi) SW Niue
103 H18 **Hanau** Hessen, W Germany 50.06N 8.56E
15 J7 **Hanbury** ≈ Northwest Territories, NW Canada
Hânceşti *see* Hînceşti
8 M15 **Hanceville** British Columbia, SW Canada 51.54N 122.56W
25 P3 **Hanceville** Alabama, S USA 34.03N 86.46W
Hancewicze *see* Hantsavichy
166 L6 **Hancheng** Shaanxi, C China 35.22N 110.27E
23 V2 **Hancock** Maryland, NE USA 39.42N 78.10W
32 M3 **Hancock** Michigan, N USA 47.07N 88.34W
31 S8 **Hancock** Minnesota, N USA 45.30N 95.47W
20 I12 **Hancock** New York, NE USA 41.57N 75.15W
82 Q12 **Handa** Bari, NE Somalia 10.35N 51.09E
167 O5 **Handan** *var.* Han-tan. Hebei, E China 36.34N 114.28E
97 P16 **Handen** Stockholm, C Sweden 59.12N 18.09E
83 J22 **Handeni** Tanga, E Tanzania 5.25S 38.04E
39 Q7 **Handies Peak** ▲ Colorado, C USA 37.54N 107.30W
113 J19 **Handlová** *Ger.* Krickerhäu, *Hung.* Nyitrabánya; *prev. Ger.* Kriegerhaj. Trenčiansky Kraj, W Slovakia 48.45N 18.45E
171 K17 **Haneda** ✕ (Tōkyō) Tōkyō, Honshū, S Japan 35.33N 139.45E
144 F13 **HaNegev** *Eng.* Negev. *desert* S Israel
37 Q11 **Hanford** California, W USA 36.19N 119.39W
203 V16 **Hanga Roa** Easter Island, Chile, E Pacific Ocean 27.09S 109.25W
168 H7 **Hangayn Nuruu** ▲▲ C Mongolia
Hang-chou/Hangchow *see* Hangzhou
97 K20 **Hånger** Jönköping, S Sweden 57.06N 13.58E
Hangö *see* Hanko
167 R9 **Hangzhou** *var.* Hang-chou, Hangchow. Zhejiang, SE China 30.18N 120.07E
168 F5 **Hanhöhiy Uul** ▲▲ NW Mongolia
Hanhowuz *see* Khauz-Khan
143 P15 **Hani** Dıyarbakır, SE Turkey 38.25N 40.22E
Hania *see* Chaniá
147 R11 **Ḥanīsh al Kabīr, Jazīrat al** *island* SW Yemen
Hanka, Lake *see* Khanka, Lake
95 M17 **Hankasalmi** Länsi-Suomi, W Finland 62.25N 26.27E
31 R7 **Hankinson** North Dakota, N USA 46.04N 96.54W
95 K20 **Hanko** *Swe.* Hangö. Etelä-Suomi, SW Finland 59.50N 23.00E
Han-kou/Han-k'ou/Hankow *see* Wuhan
38 M6 **Hanksville** Utah, W USA 38.21N 110.43W
158 K6 **Hanle** Jammu and Kashmir, NW India 32.46N 79.01E
193 I17 **Hanmer Springs** Canterbury, South Island, NZ 42.30S 172.48E
9 R16 **Hanna** Alberta, SW Canada 51.37N 111.55W
29 V3 **Hannibal** Missouri, C USA 39.42N 91.23W
188 M3 **Hann, Mount** ▲ Western Australia 15.53S 125.46E
102 I12 **Hannover** *Eng.* Hanover. Niedersachsen, NW Germany 52.23N 9.43E
101 J19 **Hannut** Liège, C Belgium 50.40N 5.04E
97 L22 **Hanöbukten** *bay* S Sweden
178 Jj6 **Ha Nôi** *Eng.* Hanoi, *Fr.* Ha noï. ● (Vietnam) N Vietnam 21.01N 105.52E
12 F14 **Hanover** Ontario, S Canada 44.22N 81.01W
33 P15 **Hanover** Indiana, N USA 38.42N 85.28W
20 G16 **Hanover** Pennsylvania, NE USA 39.46N 76.57W
23 W6 **Hanover** Virginia, NE USA 37.44N 77.21W
Hanover *see* Hannover
65 G23 **Hanover, Isla** *island* S Chile
Hanselbeck *see* Érd
205 X5 **Hansen Mountains** ▲▲ Antarctica
166 M8 **Han Shui** ≈ C China
158 H10 **Hānsi** Haryāna, NW India 29.07N 75.58E
97 F20 **Hanstholm** Viborg, NW Denmark 57.05N 8.39E
Han-tan *see* Handan
164 H6 **Hantengri Feng** *var.* Pik Khan-Tengri. ▲ China/Kazakhstan *see also* Khan-Tengri, Pik 42.17N 80.11E
121 I18 **Hantsavichy** *Pol.* Hancewicze, *Rus.* Gantsevichi. Brestskaya Voblasts', SW Belarus 52.45N 26.27E
16 N2 **Hantzsch** ≈ Baffin Island, Nunavut, NE Canada
158 G9 **Hanumāngarh** Rājasthān, NW India 29.33N 74.21E
191 O9 **Hanwood** New South Wales, SE Australia 34.19S 146.03E
Hanyang *see* Caidian
Hanyang *see* Wuhan
166 H10 **Hanyuan** *var.* Fulin. Sichuan, C China 29.22N 102.39E
166 J7 **Hanzhong** Shaanxi, C China 33.12N 106.59E
203 W11 **Hao** *atoll* Îles Tuamotu, C French Polynesia
159 S16 **Hāora** *prev.* Howrah. West Bengal, NE India 22.34N 88.19E
80 K8 **Haouach, Ouadi** *dry watercourse* E Chad
94 K13 **Haparanda** Norrbotten, N Sweden 65.49N 24.04E
27 N3 **Happy** Texas, SW USA 34.44N 101.51W
36 M1 **Happy Camp** California, W USA 41.48N 123.24W
11 Q9 **Happy Valley-Goose Bay** *prev.* Goose Bay. Newfoundland and Labrador, E Canada 53.19N 60.24W
Hapsal *see* Haapsalu
158 J10 **Hāpur** Uttar Pradesh, N India 28.43N 77.46E
144 F12 **HaQatan, HaMakhtesh** ▲▲ S Israel
146 I4 **Ḥaql** Tabūk, NW Saudi Arabia 29.18N 34.58E
176 Vv13 **Har** Pulau Kai Besar, E Indonesia 5.21S 133.09E
168 M8 **Haraat** Dundgovĭ, C Mongolia 46.30N 107.39E
147 R8 **Ḥaraḍ** *var.* Haradh. Ash Sharqīyah, E Saudi Arabia 24.08N 49.01E
Haradh *see* Ḥaraḍ
120 N12 **Haradok** *Rus.* Gorodok. Vitsyebskaya Voblasts', N Belarus 55.27N 30.00E
94 J13 **Harads** Norrbotten, N Sweden 66.04N 21.04E
121 G19 **Haradzyets** *Rus.* Gorodets. Brestskaya Voblasts', SW Belarus 52.11N 24.41E
121 J17 **Haradzyeya** *Rus.* Gorodeya. Minskaya Voblasts', C Belarus 53.18N 26.33E
203 V10 **Haraiki** *atoll* Îles Tuamotu, C French Polynesia
171 Ll14 **Haramachi** Fukushima, Honshū, E Japan 37.39N 140.55E
120 M12 **Harany** *Rus.* Gorany. Vitsyebskaya Voblasts', N Belarus 55.25N 29.03E
85 L16 **Harare** *prev.* Salisbury. ● (Zimbabwe) Mashonaland East, NE Zimbabwe 17.47S 31.03E
85 L16 **Harare** ✕ Mashonaland East, NE Zimbabwe 17.51S 31.06E
80 J10 **Haraz-Djombo** Batha, C Chad 14.10N 19.35E
121 O16 **Harbavichy** *Rus.* Gorbovichi. Mahilyowskaya Voblasts', E Belarus 53.51N 30.42E
78 J16 **Harbel** W Liberia 6.19N 10.19W
169 W8 **Harbin** *var.* Haerbin, Ha-erh-pin, Kharbin; *prev.* Haerhpin, Pingkiang, Pinkiang. Heilongjiang, NE China 45.45N 126.40E
33 S7 **Harbor Beach** Michigan, N USA 43.50N 82.39W
11 T13 **Harbour Breton** Newfoundland and Labrador, E Canada 47.28N 55.49W
67 D25 **Harbours, Bay of** *bay* East Falkland, Falkland Islands
Hårby *see* Haarby
38 I13 **Harcuvar Mountains** ▲▲ Arizona, SW USA
110 I7 **Hard** Vorarlberg, NW Austria 47.28N 9.42E
160 H11 **Harda Khās** Madhya Pradesh, C India 22.22N 77.06E
97 D14 **Hardanger** *physical region* S Norway
97 D14 **Hardangerfjorden** *fjord* S Norway
96 E13 **Hardangerjøkulen** *glacier* S Norway
97 E14 **Hardangervidda** *plateau* S Norway
85 D20 **Hardap** ◈ *district* S Namibia
23 R15 **Hardeeville** South Carolina, SE USA 32.18N 81.04W
100 L5 **Hardegarijp** *Fris.* Hurdegaryp. Friesland, N Netherlands 53.13N 5.57E
100 O9 **Hardenberg** Overijssel, E Netherlands 52.34N 6.37E
191 Q9 **Harden-Murrumburrah** New South Wales, SE Australia 34.33S 148.22E
100 K10 **Harderwijk** Gelderland, C Netherlands 52.21N 5.36E
32 J14 **Hardin** Illinois, N USA 39.10N 90.37W
35 V11 **Hardin** Montana, NW USA 45.43N 107.34W
25 R5 **Harding, Lake** ⊠ Alabama/Georgia, SE USA
22 J6 **Hardinsburg** Kentucky, S USA 37.46N 86.27W
100 I13 **Hardinxveld-Giessendam** Zuid-Holland, C Netherlands 51.52N 4.49E
9 R15 **Hardisty** Alberta, SW Canada 52.42N 111.22W
158 L12 **Hardoi** Uttar Pradesh, N India 27.22N 80.06E
25 U4 **Hardwick** Georgia, SE USA 33.03N 83.13W
29 W9 **Hardy** Arkansas, C USA 36.19N 91.28W
96 D10 **Hareid** Møre og Romsdal, S Norway 62.22N 6.01E
15 Gg5 **Hare Indian** ≈ Northwest Territories, NW Canada
101 D18 **Harelbeke** *var.* Harlebeke. West-Vlaanderen, W Belgium 50.51N 3.19E
Harem *see* Ḥārim
102 E11 **Haren** Niedersachsen, NW Germany 52.47N 7.16E
100 N6 **Haren** Groningen, NE Netherlands 53.09N 6.36E
82 L13 **Hārer** Hārer, E Ethiopia 9.17N 42.18E
97 P14 **Harg** Uppsala, C Sweden 60.13N 18.25E
Hargeisa *see* Hargeysa
82 M13 **Hargeysa** *var.* Hargeisa. Woqooyi Galbeed, NW Somalia 9.31N 44.06E
118 J10 **Harghita** ◈ *county* NE Romania
27 S17 **Hargill** Texas, SW USA 26.26N 98.00W
168 J8 **Harhorin** Övörhangay, C Mongolia 47.13N 102.48E
165 Q9 **Har Hu** ◎ C China
Hariana *see* Haryāna
147 P15 **Ḥarīb** W Yemen 15.08N 45.35E
174 I9 **Hari, Batang** *prev.* Djambi. ≈ Sumatera, W Indonesia
158 J9 **Haridwār** *prev.* Hardwar. Uttar Pradesh, N India 29.58N 78.09E
161 F18 **Harihar** Karnātaka, W India 14.33N 75.43E
193 F18 **Harihari** West Coast, South Island, NZ 43.09S 170.35E
144 I3 **Ḥārim** *var.* Harem. Idlib, W Syria 36.30N 36.30E
170 G14 **Harima-nada** *sea* S Japan
100 F13 **Haringvliet** *channel* SW Netherlands
100 F13 **Haringvlietdam** *dam* SW Netherlands 51.49N 4.04E
155 U5 **Harīpur** North-West Frontier Province, NW Pakistan 34.00N 73.01E
154 J4 **Harīrūd** *var.* Tedzhen, *Turkm.* Tejen. ≈ Afghanistan/Iran *see also* Tedzhen
Härjåhågnen *see* Østrehogna
Härjahågnen *see* Østrehogna
95 K18 **Harjavalta** Länsi-Suomi, W Finland 61.17N 22.04E
Härjehågna *see* Østrehogna
120 G4 **Harjumaa** *off.* Harju Maakond. ◈ *province* NW Estonia
23 X11 **Harkers Island** North Carolina, SE USA 34.42N 76.33W
145 S1 **Harki** N Iraq 37.03N 43.39E
31 T14 **Harlan** Iowa, C USA 41.40N 95.19W
23 O7 **Harlan** Kentucky, S USA 36.50N 83.19W
31 N17 **Harlan County Lake** ⊠ Nebraska, C USA
118 L9 **Hârlău** *var.* Hîrlău. Iaşi, NE Romania 47.24N 26.56E
Harlebeke *see* Harelbeke
35 U7 **Harlem** Montana, NW USA 48.31N 108.46W
Harlem *see* Haarlem
97 G22 **Harlev** Århus, C Denmark 56.08N 10.00E
100 K6 **Harlingen** *Fris.* Harns. Friesland, N Netherlands 53.10N 5.25E
27 T17 **Harlingen** Texas, SW USA 26.12N 97.43W
99 O21 **Harlow** E England, UK 51.46N 0.07E
35 T10 **Harlowton** Montana, NW USA 46.26N 109.49W
96 N11 **Harmånger** Gävleborg, C Sweden 61.55N 17.19E
100 I11 **Harmelen** Utrecht, C Netherlands 52.06N 4.58E
31 X11 **Harmony** Minnesota, N USA 43.33N 92.00W
34 J14 **Harney Basin** *basin* Oregon, NW USA
(0) F9 **Harney Basin** ▲▲ Oregon, NW USA
34 J14 **Harney Lake** ◎ Oregon, NW USA
30 J10 **Harney Peak** ▲ South Dakota, N USA 43.52N 103.31W
95 H17 **Härnösand** *var.* Hernösand. Västernorrland, C Sweden 62.37N 17.55E
Harns *see* Harlingen
168 F6 **Har Nuur** ◎ NW Mongolia
107 P4 **Haro** La Rioja, N Spain 42.34N 2.52W
42 F6 **Haro, Cabo** *headland* NW Mexico 27.50N 110.55W
96 D9 **Harøy** *island* S Norway
99 N21 **Harpenden** E England, UK 51.49N 0.22W
78 L18 **Harper** *var.* Cape Palmas. NE Liberia 4.25N 7.43W
28 M7 **Harper** Kansas, C USA 37.17N 98.01W
34 L13 **Harper** Oregon, NW USA 43.51N 117.37W
27 Q10 **Harper** Texas, SW USA 30.18N 99.18W
37 U13 **Harper Lake** *salt flat* California, W USA
41 T9 **Harper, Mount** ▲ Alaska, USA 64.18N 143.54W
97 J21 **Harplinge** Halland, S Sweden 56.45N 12.45E
38 J13 **Harquahala Mountains** ▲▲ Arizona, SW USA
147 T15 **Ḥarrah** SE Yemen 15.02N 50.22E
10 H11 **Harricana** ≈ Quebec, SE Canada
22 M9 **Harriman** Tennessee, S USA 35.57N 84.33W
11 R11 **Harrington Harbour** Quebec, E Canada 50.34N 59.29W
66 B12 **Harrington Sound** *bay* Bermuda, NW Atlantic Ocean
98 F8 **Harris** *physical region* NW Scotland, UK
29 X10 **Harrisburg** Arkansas, C USA 35.33N 90.43W
32 M17 **Harrisburg** Illinois, N USA 37.44N 88.32W
30 I14 **Harrisburg** Nebraska, C USA 41.31N 103.43W
34 F12 **Harrisburg** Oregon, NW USA 44.16N 123.10W
20 G15 **Harrisburg** *state capital* Pennsylvania, NE USA 40.16N 76.52W
190 F6 **Harris, Lake** ◎ South Australia
25 W11 **Harris, Lake** ◎ Florida, SE USA
85 J22 **Harrismith** Free State, E South Africa 28.16S 29.06E
29 T9 **Harrison** Arkansas, C USA 36.13N 93.06W
33 Q7 **Harrison** Michigan, N USA 44.01N 84.49W
30 I12 **Harrison** Nebraska, C USA 42.39N 103.53W
41 Q5 **Harrison Bay** *inlet* Alaska, USA
24 I6 **Harrisonburg** Louisiana, S USA 31.44N 91.51W
23 U4 **Harrisonburg** Virginia, NE USA 38.27N 78.52W
11 R7 **Harrison, Cape** *headland* Newfoundland and Labrador, E Canada 54.55N 57.48W
29 R5 **Harrisonville** Missouri, C USA 38.39N 94.21W
Harris Ridge *see* Lomonosov Ridge
199 K3 **Harris Seamount** *undersea feature* N Pacific Ocean 46.09N 161.25W
98 F8 **Harris, Sound of** *strait* NW Scotland, UK
33 R6 **Harrisville** Michigan, N USA 44.39N 83.19W
23 R3 **Harrisville** West Virginia, NE USA 39.12N 81.03W
22 M6 **Harrodsburg** Kentucky, S USA 37.45N 84.50W
99 M16 **Harrogate** N England, UK 54.00N 1.33W
27 Q4 **Harrold** Texas, SW USA 34.05N 99.02W
29 S5 **Harry S.Truman Reservoir** ⊠ Missouri, C USA
102 G13 **Harsewinkel** Nordrhein-Westfalen, W Germany 51.58N 8.13E
118 M14 **Hârşova** *prev.* Hîrşova. Constanţa, SE Romania 44.40N 27.58E
94 H10 **Harstad** Troms, N Norway 68.48N 16.31E
33 O8 **Hart** Michigan, N USA 43.43N 86.22W
26 M4 **Hart** Texas, SW USA 34.23N 102.07W
8 I5 **Hart** ≈ Yukon Territory, NW Canada
85 F23 **Hartbees** ≈ C South Africa
111 X7 **Hartberg** Steiermark, SE Austria 47.15N 15.55E
190 I10 **Hart, Cape** *headland* South Australia 35.54S 138.01E
97 E14 **Hårteigen** ▲ S Norway 60.11N 7.01E
25 Q7 **Hartford** Alabama, S USA 31.06N 85.42W
29 R11 **Hartford** Arkansas, C USA 35.01N 94.22W
20 M12 **Hartford** *state capital* Connecticut, NE USA 41.45N 72.41W
22 J6 **Hartford** Kentucky, S USA 37.24N 86.52W
33 P10 **Hartford** Michigan, N USA 42.12N 85.54W
31 R11 **Hartford** South Dakota, N USA 43.37N 96.56W
32 M8 **Hartford** Wisconsin, N USA 43.19N 88.25W
33 P13 **Hartford City** Indiana, N USA 40.27N 85.22W
31 Q13 **Hartington** Nebraska, C USA 42.37N 97.15W
11 N14 **Hartland** New Brunswick, SE Canada 46.18N 67.31W
99 H23 **Hartland Point** *headland* SW England, UK 51.01N 4.33W
99 M15 **Hartlepool** N England, UK 54.40N 1.13W
31 T12 **Hartley** Iowa, C USA 43.10N 95.28W
26 M1 **Hartley** Texas, SW USA 35.52N 102.24W
34 J15 **Hart Mountain** ▲ Oregon, NW USA 42.24N 119.46W
181 U10 **Hartog Ridge** *undersea feature* W Indian Ocean
95 M18 **Hartola** Etelä-Suomi, S Finland 61.34N 26.04E
69 U14 **Harts** *var.* Hartz. ≈ N South Africa
25 P2 **Hartselle** Alabama, S USA 34.26N 86.56W
25 S3 **Hartsfield Atlanta** ✕ Georgia, SE USA 33.38N 84.24W
29 Q11 **Hartshorne** Oklahoma, C USA 34.51N 95.33W
23 S12 **Hartsville** South Carolina, SE USA 34.22N 80.04W
22 K8 **Hartsville** Tennessee, S USA 36.23N 86.10W
29 U7 **Hartville** Missouri, C USA 37.15N 92.30W
25 U2 **Hartwell** Georgia, SE USA 34.21N 82.55W
23 O11 **Hartwell Lake** ⊠ Georgia/South Carolina, SE USA
Hartz *see* Harts
Harunabad *see* Eslāmābād
168 E6 **Har-Us** Hovd, W Mongolia 48.30N 91.25E
168 E6 **Har Us Nuur** ◎ NW Mongolia
32 M10 **Harvard** Illinois, N USA 42.25N 88.36W
31 P16 **Harvard** Nebraska, C USA 40.37N 98.06W
39 R5 **Harvard, Mount** ▲ Colorado, C USA 38.55N 106.19W
33 N11 **Harvey** Illinois, N USA 41.36N 87.39W
31 N4 **Harvey** North Dakota, N USA 47.43N 99.55W
99 Q21 **Harwich** E England, UK 51.55N 1.16E
158 H10 **Haryāna** *var.* Hariana. ◈ *state* N India
147 Y9 **Ḥaryān, Ṭawī al** *spring/well* NE Oman 21.56N 58.33E
103 J14 **Harz** ▲▲ C Germany
Hasakah *see* Al Ḥasakah
171 M12 **Hasama** Miyagi, Honshū, C Japan 38.42N 141.09E
142 J15 **Hasan Dağı** ▲ C Turkey 38.09N 34.15E
145 T9 **Ḥasan Ibn Ḥassūn** C Iraq 32.24N 44.13E
155 R6 **Ḥasan Khēl** *var.* Ahmad Khel. Paktīā, SE Afghanistan 33.46N 69.37E
102 F12 **Hase** ≈ NW Germany
Haselberg *see* Krasnoznamensk
102 F12 **Haselünne** Niedersachsen, NW Germany 52.40N 7.28E
168 K9 **Hashaat** Dundgovĭ, C Mongolia 45.09N 104.51E
Hashemite Kingdom of Jordan *see* Jordan
145 V8 **Hāshimah** E Iraq 33.22N 45.56E
171 Gg16 **Hashimoto** *var.* Hasimoto. Wakayama, Honshū, SW Japan 34.18N 135.34E
147 W13 **Ḥāsik** S Oman 17.22N 55.18E
155 U10 **Hāsilpur** Punjab, E Pakistan 29.44N 72.33E
Hasimoto *see* Hashimoto
29 Q10 **Haskell** Oklahoma, C USA 35.49N 95.40W
27 Q6 **Haskell** Texas, SW USA 33.09N 99.43W
116 M11 **Hasköy** Edirne, NW Turkey 41.37N 26.51E
97 L24 **Hasle** Bornholm, E Denmark 55.12N 14.43E
99 N23 **Haslemere** SE England, UK 51.06N 0.45W
104 I16 **Hasparren** Pyrénées-Atlantiques, SW France 43.22N 1.18W
Hassakeh *see* Al Ḥasakah
161 G19 **Hassan** Karnātaka, W India 13.01N 76.03E
38 J13 **Hassayampa River** ≈ Arizona, SW USA
103 J18 **Hassberge** *hill range* C Germany
96 N10 **Hassela** Gävleborg, C Sweden 62.06N 16.45E
101 J18 **Hasselt** Limburg, NE Belgium 50.55N 5.19E
100 M9 **Hasselt** Overijssel, E Netherlands 52.36N 6.06E
Hassetché *see* Al Ḥasakah
103 J18 **Hassfurt** Bayern, C Germany 50.02N 10.32E
76 L9 **Hassi Bel Guebbour** E Algeria 28.41N 6.29E
76 L8 **Hassi Messaoud** E Algeria 31.41N 6.10E
97 K22 **Hässleholm** Skåne, S Sweden 56.09N 13.45E
Hasta Colonia/Hasta Pompeia *see* Asti
191 O13 **Hastings** Victoria, SE Australia 38.18S 145.12E
192 O11 **Hastings** Hawke's Bay, North Island, NZ 39.39S 176.51E
99 P23 **Hastings** SE England, UK 50.51N 0.36E
33 P9 **Hastings** Michigan, N USA 42.37N 85.16W
31 W9 **Hastings** Minnesota, N USA 44.44N 92.51W
31 P16 **Hastings** Nebraska, C USA 40.35N 98.23W
97 K22 **Hästveda** Skåne, S Sweden 56.16N 13.55E
94 J8 **Hasvik** Finnmark, N Norway 70.29N 22.08E
39 V6 **Haswell** Colorado, C USA 38.27N 103.09W
168 I10 **Hatansuudal** Bayanhongor, C Mongolia 44.34N 100.41E
169 P9 **Hatavch** Sühbaatar, E Mongolia 46.10N 112.57E
142 K17 **Hatay** ◈ *province* S Turkey
39 R15 **Hatch** New Mexico, SW USA 32.40N 107.10W
38 K7 **Hatch** Utah, W USA 37.39N 112.25W
22 F9 **Hatchie River** ≈ Tennessee, S USA
118 G12 **Haţeg** *Ger.* Wallenthal, *Hung.* Hátszeg; *prev.* Hatzeg, Hötzing. Hunedoara, SW Romania 45.35N 22.57E
172 Oo17 **Hateruma-jima** *island* Yaeyama-shotō, SW Japan
191 N8 **Hatfield** New South Wales, SE Australia 33.54S 143.43E
168 I5 **Hatgal** Hövsgöl, N Mongolia 50.24N 100.12E
159 V16 **Hathazari** Chittagong, SE Bangladesh 22.30N 91.46E
147 T13 **Hathūt, Hiṣā'** *oasis* NE Yemen 17.46N 51.14E
178 Ii14 **Ha Tiên** Kiên Giang, S Vietnam 10.24N 104.30E
178 Jj8 **Ha Tinh** Ha Tinh, N Vietnam 18.21N 105.55E
Hatiôzi *see* Hachiōji
144 F12 **Ḫatira, Haré** *hill range* S Israel
178 J6 **Hat Lot** Sơn La, N Vietnam 21.07N 104.10E
47 P16 **Hato Airport** ✕ (Willemstad) Curaçao, SW Netherlands Antilles 12.10N 68.56W
56 H9 **Hato Corozal** Casanare, C Colombia 6.07N 71.45W
Hato del Volcán *see* Volcán
47 P9 **Hato Mayor** E Dominican Republic 18.44N 69.16W
Hatra *see* Al Ḥaḍr
Hatria *see* Adria
Hátszeg *see* Haţeg
149 R16 **Ḥattá** Dubayy, NE UAE 24.50N 56.06E
190 L9 **Hattah** Victoria, SE Australia 34.49S 142.18E
100 M9 **Hattem** Gelderland, E Netherlands 52.28N 6.04E
23 Z10 **Hatteras** Hatteras Island, North Carolina, SE USA 35.13N 75.39W
23 Rr10 **Hatteras, Cape** *headland* North Carolina, SE USA 35.29N 75.33W
23 Z9 **Hatteras Island** *island* North Carolina, SE USA
66 F10 **Hatteras Plain** *undersea feature* W Atlantic Ocean
95 G14 **Hattfjelldal** Troms, N Norway 65.37N 13.58E
24 M7 **Hattiesburg** Mississippi, S USA 31.19N 89.17W
31 Q4 **Hatton** North Dakota, N USA 47.38N 97.27W
Hatton Bank *see* Hatton Ridge
66 L6 **Hatton Ridge** *var.* Hatton Bank. *undersea feature* N Atlantic Ocean
203 W6 **Hatutu** *island* Îles Marquises, NE French Polynesia
113 K22 **Hatvan** Heves, NE Hungary 47.40N 19.38E
178 H17 **Hat Yai** *var.* Ban Hat Yai. Songkhla, SW Thailand 7.01N 100.27E
Hatzeg *see* Haţeg
Hatzfeld *see* Jimbolia
82 N13 **Haud** *plateau* Ethiopia/Somalia
97 D18 **Hauge** Rogaland, S Norway 58.19N 6.16E
97 C15 **Haugesund** Rogaland, S Norway 59.24N 5.16E
111 X2 **Haugsdorf** Niederösterreich, NE Austria 48.41N 16.04E
192 M9 **Hauhungaroa Range** ▲▲ North Island, NZ
97 E15 **Haukeligrend** Telemark, S Norway 59.45N 7.33E
95 L14 **Haukipudas** Oulu, C Finland 65.11N 25.21E
95 M17 **Haukivesi** ◎ SE Finland
95 M17 **Haukivuori** Isä-Suomi, E Finland 62.02N 27.11E
Hauptkanal *see* Havelländ Grosse
195 Z17 **Hauraha** San Cristobal, SE Solomon Islands 10.47S 162.00E
192 L5 **Hauraki Gulf** *gulf* North Island, NZ
193 B24 **Hauroko, Lake** ◎ South Island, NZ
178 Jj15 **Hâu, Sông** ≈ S Vietnam
94 N12 **Hautajärvi** Lappi, NE Finland 66.30N 29.01E
76 F7 **Haut Atlas** *Eng.* High Atlas. ▲▲ C Morocco
81 M17 **Haut-Congo** *off.* Région du Haut-Congo; *prev.* Haut-Zaïre. ◈ *region* NE Dem. Rep. Congo
105 Y14 **Haute-Corse** ◈ *department* Corse, France, C Mediterranean Sea
104 L16 **Haute-Garonne** ◈ *department* S France
78 J13 **Haute-Guinée** ◈ *state* NE Guinea
81 K14 **Haute-Kotto** ◈ *prefecture* E Central African Republic
105 P12 **Haute-Loire** ◈ *department* C France
105 R6 **Haute-Marne** ◈ *department* N France
104 M3 **Haute-Normandie** ◈ *region* N France
13 U6 **Hauterive** Quebec, SE Canada 49.10N 68.16W
105 T13 **Hautes-Alpes** ◈ *department* SE France
105 S7 **Haute-Saône** ◈ *department* E France
105 T10 **Haute-Savoie** ◈ *department* E France
101 M20 **Hautes Fagnes** *Ger.* Hohes Venn. ▲▲ E Belgium
104 K16 **Hautes-Pyrénées** ◈ *department* S France
101 L23 **Haute Sûre, Lac de la** ⊠ NW Luxembourg
104 M11 **Haute-Vienne** ◈ *department* C France
21 S8 **Haut, Isle au** *island* Maine, NE USA
81 M14 **Haut-Mbomou** ◈ *préfecture* SE Central African Republic
105 Q2 **Hautmont** Nord, N France 50.15N 3.55E

◆ Country
● Country Capital
◇ Dependent Territory
○ Dependent Territory Capital
◈ Administrative Region
✕ International Airport
▲ Mountain
▲▲ Mountain Range
Volcano
≈ River
◎ Lake
⊠ Reservoir

81 F19 **Haut-Ogooué** *off.* Province du Haut-Ogooué, *var.* Le Haut-Ogooué. ◈ *province* SE Gabon

Haut-Ogooué, Le *see* Haut-Ogooué

105 U7 **Haut-Rhin** ◈ *department* NE France

76 I6 **Hauts Plateaux** *plateau* Algeria/Morocco

40 D9 **Hauula** *Haw.* Hau'ula. Oahu, Hawaii, USA, C Pacific Ocean *21.36N 157.54W*

103 O22 **Hauzenberg** Bayern, SE Germany *48.39N 13.37E*

32 K13 **Havana** Illinois, N USA *40.18N 90.03W*

Havana *see* La Habana

99 N23 **Havant** S England, UK *50.51N 0.58W*

37 Y14 **Havasu, Lake** ▣ Arizona/California, W USA

97 J23 **Havdrup** Roskilde, E Denmark *55.33N 12.07E*

102 N10 **Havel** ≈ NE Germany

101 J21 **Havelange** Namur, SE Belgium *50.23N 5.14E*

102 M11 **Havelberg** Sachsen-Anhalt, NE Germany *52.49N 12.05E*

155 U5 **Haveliān** North-West Frontier Province, NW Pakistan *34.07N 73.12E*

102 N12 **Havelländ Grosse** *var.* Hauptkanal. *canal* NE Germany

12 J14 **Havelock** Ontario, SE Canada *44.22N 77.57W*

193 J14 **Havelock** Marlborough, South Island, NZ *41.17S 173.46E*

23 X11 **Havelock** North Carolina, SE USA *34.52N 76.54W*

192 O11 **Havelock North** Hawke's Bay, North Island, NZ *39.40S 176.53E*

100 M8 **Havelte** Drenthe, NE Netherlands *52.46N 6.14E*

29 N6 **Haven** Kansas, C USA *37.54N 97.46W*

99 H21 **Haverfordwest** SW Wales, UK *51.49N 4.57W*

99 P20 **Haverhill** E England, UK *52.04N 0.26E*

21 O10 **Haverhill** Massachusetts, NE USA *42.46N 71.02W*

95 G17 **Haverö** Västernorrland, C Sweden *62.25N 15.04E*

113 I17 **Havířov** Ostravský Kraj, E Czech Republic *49.47N 18.30E*

113 E17 **Havlíčkův Brod** *Ger.* Deutsch-Brod; *prev.* Německý Brod. Jihlavský Kraj, C Czech Republic *49.41N 15.47E*

94 K7 **Havøysund** Finnmark, N Norway *70.59N 24.39E*

35 T7 **Havre** Montana, NW USA *48.33N 109.40W*

Havre *see* le Havre

101 F20 **Havré** Hainaut, S Belgium *50.28N 4.03E*

11 P11 **Havre-St-Pierre** Quebec, E Canada *50.16N 63.36W*

142 B10 **Havsa** Edirne, NW Turkey *41.33N 26.49E*

40 D8 **Hawaii** *off.* State of Hawaii; also known as Aloha State, Paradise of the Pacific. ◈ *state* USA, C Pacific Ocean

40 G12 **Hawaii** *Haw.* Hawai'i. *island* Hawaiian Islands, USA, C Pacific Ocean

199 K5 **Hawaiian Islands** *prev.* Sandwich Islands. *island group* Hawaii, USA, C Pacific Ocean

199 Jj6 **Hawaiian Ridge** *undersea feature* N Pacific Ocean

199 Kk6 **Hawaiian Trough** *undersea feature* N Pacific Ocean

31 R12 **Hawarden** Iowa, C USA *43.00N 96.29W*

Hawash *see* Āwash

145 P6 **Hawbayn al Gharbīyah** C Iraq *34.24N 42.06E*

193 D21 **Hawea, Lake** ◎ South Island, NZ

192 K11 **Hawera** Taranaki, North Island, NZ *39.36S 174.16E*

22 J5 **Hawesville** Kentucky, S USA *37.53N 86.44W*

40 G11 **Hawi** *Haw.* Hāwī. Hawaii, USA, C Pacific Ocean *20.13N 155.49W*

98 K13 **Hawick** SE Scotland, UK *55.24N 2.49W*

145 S4 **Ḥawījah** C Iraq *35.15N 43.54E*

145 Y10 **Ḥawīzah, Hawr al** ◎ S Iraq

193 E21 **Hawkdun Range** ▲▲ South Island, NZ

192 P10 **Hawke Bay** *bay* North Island, NZ

190 I6 **Hawker** South Australia *31.54S 138.25E*

192 N11 **Hawke's Bay** *off.* Hawkes Bay Region. ◈ *region* North Island, NZ

155 O16 **Hawkes Bay** *bay* SE Pakistan

13 N12 **Hawkesbury** Ontario, SE Canada *45.35N 74.37W*

Hawkeye State *see* Iowa

25 T5 **Hawkinsville** Georgia, SE USA *32.16N 83.28W*

12 B7 **Hawk Junction** Ontario, S Canada *48.05N 84.34W*

23 N10 **Haw Knob** ▲ North Carolina/Tennessee, SE USA *35.18N 84.01W*

23 Q9 **Hawksbill Mountain** ▲ North Carolina, SE USA *35.54N 81.53W*

35 Z16 **Hawk Springs** Wyoming, C USA *41.48N 104.17W*

Hawlēr *see* Arbīl

31 S5 **Hawley** Minnesota, N USA *46.53N 96.18W*

27 P7 **Hawley** Texas, SW USA *32.36N 99.47W*

147 R14 **Ḥawrā'** C Yemen *15.39N 48.20E*

145 P7 **Ḥawrān, Wadi** *dry watercourse* W Iraq

23 T9 **Haw River** ≈ North Carolina, SE USA

145 U5 **Hawshqūrah** E Iraq *34.34N 45.33E*

37 S7 **Hawthorne** Nevada, W USA *38.30N 118.38W*

39 W3 **Haxtun** Colorado, C USA *40.36N 102.38W*

191 N9 **Hay** New South Wales, SE Australia *34.31S 144.50E*

9 O10 **Hay** ≈ W Canada

176 U11 **Haya** Pulau Seram, E Indonesia *3.22S 129.31E*

172 N11 **Hayachine-san** ▲ Honshū, C Japan *39.31N 141.28E*

105 S4 **Hayange** Moselle, NE France *49.19N 6.04E*

HaYarden *see* Jordan

Hayastani Hanrapetut'yun *see* Armenia

Hayasui-seto *see* Hōyo-kaikyō

41 N9 **Haycock** Alaska, USA *65.12N 161.10W*

38 M14 **Hayden** Arizona, SW USA *33.00N 110.46W*

39 Q3 **Hayden** Colorado, C USA *40.29N 107.15W*

30 M10 **Hayes** South Dakota, N USA *44.20N 101.01W*

9 X13 **Hayes** ≈ Manitoba, C Canada

15 Kk11 **Hayes** ≈ Nunavut, NE Canada

30 M16 **Hayes Center** Nebraska, C USA *40.28N 101.01W*

41 S10 **Hayes, Mount** ▲ Alaska, USA *63.37N 146.43W*

23 N11 **Hayesville** North Carolina, SE USA *35.15N 84.15W*

37 X10 **Hayford Peak** ▲ Nevada, W USA *36.40N 115.10W*

36 M3 **Hayfork** California, W USA *40.33N 123.10W*

Hayir, Qasr al *see* Ḥayr al Gharbī, Qaṣr al

169 P8 **Haylaastay** Sühbaatar, E Mongolia *46.44N 113.51E*

12 I12 **Hay Lake** ◎ Ontario, SE Canada

147 X11 **Haymā'** *var.* Haima. C Oman *19.58N 56.20E*

142 H13 **Haymana** Ankara, C Turkey *39.25N 32.30E*

144 J7 **Ḥaymūr, Jabal** ▲▲ W Syria

Haynau *see* Chojnów

24 G4 **Haynesville** Louisiana, S USA *32.57N 93.08W*

25 P6 **Hayneville** Alabama, S USA *32.13N 86.34W*

116 M12 **Hayrabolu** Tekirdağ, NW Turkey *41.12N 27.08E*

142 C10 **Hayrabolu Deresi** ≈ NW Turkey

144 J6 **Ḥayr al Gharbī, Qaṣr al** *var.* Qasr al Hayir, Qasr al Hir al Gharbi. *ruins* Ḥimṣ, C Syria *34.23N 37.40E*

144 L5 **Ḥayr ash Sharqī, Qaṣr al** *var.* Qasr al Hir Ash Sharqī. *ruins* Ḥimṣ, C Syria *35.07N 39.06E*

15 Hh9 **Hay River** Northwest Territories, W Canada *60.51N 115.42W*

28 K4 **Hays** Kansas, C USA *38.52N 99.19W*

30 K12 **Hay Springs** Nebraska, C USA *42.40N 102.41W*

67 H25 **Haystack, The** ▲ NE Saint Helena *15.55S 5.40W*

29 N7 **Haysville** Kansas, C USA *37.34N 97.21W*

119 O7 **Haysyn** *Rus.* Gaysin. Vinnyts'ka Oblast', C Ukraine *48.49N 29.29E*

29 Y9 **Hayti** Missouri, C USA *36.13N 89.45W*

31 Q9 **Hayti** South Dakota, N USA *44.39N 97.11W*

119 O8 **Hayvoron** *Rus.* Gayvorno. Kirovohrads'ka Oblast', C Ukraine *48.19N 29.54E*

37 N9 **Hayward** California, W USA *37.40N 122.07W*

32 J4 **Hayward** Wisconsin, N USA *46.01N 91.25W*

99 O23 **Haywards Heath** SE England, UK *51.00N 0.06W*

149 S11 **Hazārān, Kūh-e** *var.* Kūh-e ā Hazr. ▲ SE Iran *29.26N 57.15E*

Hazarat Imam *see* Emām Şāḩeb

23 O7 **Hazard** Kentucky, S USA *37.15N 83.11W*

143 O15 **Hazar Gölü** ◎ C Turkey

159 P15 **Hazārībāg** *var.* Hazāribāgh. Bihār, N India *24.00N 85.23E*

Hazāribāgh *see* Hazārībāg

105 O1 **Hazebrouck** Nord, N France *50.43N 2.33E*

32 K9 **Hazel Green** Wisconsin, N USA *42.33N 90.26W*

199 Ii10 **Hazel Holme Bank** *undersea feature* S Pacific Ocean *12.49S 174.30E*

8 K13 **Hazelton** British Columbia, SW Canada *55.15N 127.37W*

31 N6 **Hazelton** North Dakota, N USA *46.27N 100.17W*

37 R5 **Hazen** Nevada, W USA *39.33N 119.02W*

30 L5 **Hazen** North Dakota, N USA *47.18N 101.37W*

40 L12 **Hazen Bay** *bay* E Bering Sea

145 S5 **Hazīm, Bi'r** *well* C Iraq *34.50N 43.25E*

25 V6 **Hazlehurst** Georgia, SE USA *31.51N 82.35W*

24 K6 **Hazlehurst** Mississippi, S USA *31.51N 90.24W*

20 K15 **Hazlet** New Jersey, NE USA *40.24N 74.10W*

152 I9 **Hazorasp** *Rus.* Khazarosp. Xorazm Viloyati, W Uzbekistan *41.21N 61.01E*

153 R13 **Hazratishoh, Qatorkŭhi** *var.* Khrebet Khazretishi, *Rus.* Khrebet Khozretishi. ▲▲ S Tajikistan

Hazr, Kūh-e ā *see* Hazārān, Kūh-e

155 U6 **Hazro** Punjab, E Pakistan *33.55N 72.33E*

25 R7 **Headland** Alabama, S USA *31.21N 85.20W*

190 C6 **Head of Bight** *headland* South Australia *31.33S 131.05E*

35 N10 **Headquarters** Idaho, NW USA *46.38N 115.52W*

36 M7 **Healdsburg** California, W USA *38.36N 122.52W*

29 N13 **Healdton** Oklahoma, C USA *34.13N 97.29W*

191 O12 **Healesville** Victoria, SE Australia *37.41S 145.31E*

41 R10 **Healy** Alaska, USA *63.51N 148.58W*

181 R13 **Heard and McDonald Islands** ◇ *Australian external territory* S Indian Ocean

181 R13 **Heard Island** *island* Heard and McDonald Islands, S Indian Ocean

27 U9 **Hearne** Texas, SW USA *30.52N 96.35W*

10 F12 **Hearst** Ontario, S Canada *49.42N 83.40W*

204 J5 **Hearst Island** *island* Antarctica

Heart of Dixie *see* Alabama

30 L5 **Heart River** ≈ North Dakota, N USA

33 T13 **Heath** Ohio, N USA *40.01N 82.26W*

191 N11 **Heathcote** Victoria, SE Australia *36.57S 144.43E*

99 N22 **Heathrow** ✕ (London)SE England, UK *51.28N 0.27W*

23 X5 **Heathsville** Virginia, NE USA *37.54N 76.25W*

29 R11 **Heavener** Oklahoma, C USA *34.53N 94.36W*

27 R15 **Hebbronville** Texas, SW USA *27.18N 98.40W*

169 Q13 **Hebei** *var.* Hebei Sheng, Hopeh, Hopei, Ji; *prev.* Chihli. ◈ *province* E China

Hebei Sheng *see* Hebei

176 U9 **Hebera** Papua, E Indonesia *1.08S 129.54E*

38 M3 **Heber City** Utah, W USA *40.29N 111.24W*

29 V10 **Heber Springs** Arkansas, C USA *35.30N 91.58W*

167 N5 **Hebi** Henan, C China *35.57N 114.07E*

34 F11 **Hebo** Oregon, NW USA *45.10N 123.55W*

98 F9 **Hebrides, Sea of the** *sea* NW Scotland, UK

11 P5 **Hebron** Newfoundland and Labrador, E Canada *58.15N 62.45W*

33 N11 **Hebron** Indiana, N USA *41.19N 87.12W*

31 Q17 **Hebron** Nebraska, C USA *40.10N 97.35W*

30 L5 **Hebron** North Dakota, N USA *46.54N 102.03W*

144 F11 **Hebron** *var.* Al Khalīl, El Khalil, *Heb.* Hevron; *anc.* Kiriath-Arba. S West Bank *31.30N 35.00E*

Hebrus *see* Évros/Maritsa/Meriç

97 N14 **Heby** Västmanland, C Sweden *59.55N 16.52E*

8 I14 **Hecate Strait** *strait* British Columbia, W Canada

43 W12 **Hecelchakán** Campeche, SE Mexico *20.09N 90.04W*

166 K13 **Hechi** *var.* Jinchengjiang. Guangxi Zhuangzu Zizhiqu, S China *24.40N 108.05E*

103 H23 **Hechingen** Baden-Württemberg, S Germany *48.20N 8.58E*

101 K17 **Hechtel** Limburg, NE Belgium *51.07N 5.24E*

166 J9 **Hechuan** Chongqing Shi, C China *30.01N 106.15E*

31 P7 **Hecla** South Dakota, N USA *45.52N 98.09W*

31 T9 **Hector** Minnesota, N USA *44.44N 94.43W*

95 F17 **Hede** Jämtland, C Sweden *62.25N 13.33E*

97 M14 **Hedemora** Dalarna, C Sweden *60.18N 15.58E*

94 K13 **Hedenäset** Norrbotten, N Sweden *66.12N 23.40E*

97 G23 **Hedensted** Vejle, C Denmark *55.46N 9.43E*

97 N14 **Hedesunda** Gävleborg, C Sweden *60.25N 17.00E*

97 N14 **Hedesundafjord** ◎ C Sweden

27 O3 **Hedley** Texas, SW USA *34.52N 100.39W*

96 I12 **Hedmark** ◈ *county* S Norway

172 Pp14 **Hedo-misaki** *headland* Okinawa, SW Japan *26.55N 128.15E*

31 X15 **Hedrick** Iowa, C USA *41.10N 92.18W*

101 L16 **Heel** Limburg, SE Netherlands *51.12N 6.01E*

201 Y12 **Heel Point** *point* Wake Island *19.18N 166.39E*

100 H9 **Heemskerk** Noord-Holland, W Netherlands *52.31N 4.40E*

100 M10 **Heerde** Gelderland, E Netherlands *52.24N 6.01E*

100 L7 **Heerenveen** *Fris.* It Hearrenfean. Friesland, N Netherlands *52.57N 5.55E*

100 I8 **Heerhugowaard** Noord-Holland, NW Netherlands *52.40N 4.49E*

94 O3 **Heer Land** *physical region* C Svalbard

101 M18 **Heerlen** Limburg, SE Netherlands *50.55N 6.00E*

101 J19 **Heers** Limburg, NE Belgium *50.46N 5.17E*

Heerwegen *see* Polkowice

100 K13 **Heesch** Noord-Brabant, S Netherlands *51.43N 5.31E*

101 K15 **Heeze** Noord-Brabant, SE Netherlands *51.22N 5.34E*

144 F8 **Ḥefa** *var.* Haifa; *hist.* Caiffa, Caiphas, *anc.* Sycaminum. Haifa, N Israel *32.49N 34.58E*

144 F8 **Ḥefa, Mifraẓ** *Eng.* Bay of Haifa. *bay* N Israel

167 Q8 **Hefei** *var.* Hofei; *hist.* Luchow. Anhui, E China *31.51N 117.20E*

25 R3 **Heflin** Alabama, S USA *33.39N 85.35W*

169 X7 **Hegang** Heilongjiang, NE China *47.18N 130.15E*

171 Ii11 **Hegura-jima** *island* SW Japan

Heguri-jima *see* Heigun-tō

Hei *see* Heilongjiang

102 H8 **Heide** Schleswig-Holstein, N Germany *54.12N 9.06E*

103 G20 **Heidelberg** Baden-Württemberg, SW Germany *49.24N 8.40E*

85 J21 **Heidelberg** Gauteng, NE South Africa *26.27S 28.21E*

24 M6 **Heidelberg** Mississippi, S USA *31.53N 88.58W*

Heidenheim *see* Heidenheim an der Brenz

103 J22 **Heidenheim an der Brenz** *var.* Heidenheim. Baden-Württemberg, S Germany *48.40N 10.09E*

111 U2 **Heidenreichstein** Niederösterreich, N Austria *48.53N 15.07E*

170 E14 **Heigun-tō** *var.* Heguri-jima. *island* SW Japan

169 W5 **Heihe** *prev.* Ai-hun. Heilongjiang, NE China *50.13N 127.29E*

Hei-ho *see* Nagqu

85 J22 **Heilbron** Free State, N South Africa *27.16S 27.58E*

103 H21 **Heilbronn** Baden-Württemberg, SW Germany *49.09N 9.13E*

Heiligenbeil *see* Mamonovo

111 Q8 **Heiligenblut** Tirol, W Austria *47.04N 12.50E*

102 K7 **Heiligenhafen** Schleswig-Holstein, N Germany *54.22N 10.57E*

Heiligenkreuz *see* Žiar nad Hronom

103 J15 **Heiligenstadt** Thüringen, C Germany *51.22N 10.09E*

Heilong Jiang *see* Amur

169 W8 **Heilongjiang** *var.* Hei, Heilongjiang Sheng, Hei-lung-chiang, Heilungkiang. ◈ *province* NE China

Heilongjiang Sheng *see* Heilongjiang

100 H9 **Heiloo** Noord-Holland, NW Netherlands *52.36N 4.43E*

Heilsberg *see* Lidzbark Warmiński

Hei-lung-chiang/Heilungkiang *see* Heilongjiang

94 I4 **Heimaey** *var.* Heimaæy. *island* S Iceland

96 H8 **Heimdal** Sør-Trøndelag, S Norway *63.21N 10.22E*

Heinaste *see* Ainaži

95 N17 **Heinävesi** Itä-Suomi, E Finland *62.22N 28.42E*

101 M22 **Heinerscheid** Diekirch, N Luxembourg *50.06N 6.04E*

100 M10 **Heino** Overijssel, E Netherlands *52.26N 6.13E*

95 M18 **Heinola** Etelä-Suomi, S Finland *61.13N 26.04E*

103 C16 **Heinsberg** Nordrhein-Westfalen, W Germany *51.02N 6.01E*

169 U12 **Heishan** Liaoning, NE China *41.43N 122.12E*

166 H8 **Heishui** Sichuan, C China *32.08N 102.54E*

101 H17 **Heist-op-den-Berg** Antwerpen, C Belgium *51.04N 4.43E*

Heitō *see* P'ingtung

176 Y14 **Heitske** Papua, E Indonesia *7.02S 138.45E*

Hejanah *see* Al Hījānah

Hejaz *see* Al Ḥijāz

166 M14 **He Jiang** ≈ S China

164 K6 **Hejing** Xinjiang Uygur Zizhiqu, NW China *42.21N 86.19E*

Héjjasfalva *see* Vânători

165 S11 **Heka** Qinghai, W China *35.49N 99.49E*

143 N14 **Hekimhan** Malatya, C Turkey *38.49N 37.55E*

94 J4 **Hekla** ▲ S Iceland *63.56N 19.42W*

112 J6 **Hel** *Ger.* Hela. Pomorskie, N Poland *54.35N 18.48E*

Hela *see* Hel

95 F17 **Helagsfjället** ▲ C Sweden *62.57N 12.31E*

165 W8 **Helan** *var.* Xigang. Ningxia, N China *38.33N 106.21E*

168 K14 **Helan Shan** ▲▲ N China

101 M16 **Helden** Limburg, SE Netherlands *51.20N 6.00E*

29 X12 **Helena** Arkansas, C USA *34.32N 90.34W*

35 R10 **Helena** *state capital* Montana, NW USA *46.35N 112.02W*

98 H12 **Helensburgh** W Scotland, UK *56.00N 4.45W*

192 K5 **Helensville** Auckland, North Island, NZ *36.42S 174.25E*

97 L20 **Helgasjön** ◎ S Sweden

102 G8 **Helgoland** *Eng.* Heligoland. *island* NW Germany

Helgoland Bay *see* Helgoländer Bucht

102 G8 **Helgoländer Bucht** *var.* Helgoland Bay, Heligoland Bight. *bay* NW Germany

Heligoland *see* Helgoland

Heligoland Bight *see* Helgoländer Bucht

Heliopolis *see* Baalbek

94 I4 **Hella** Sudhurland, SW Iceland *63.51N 20.24W*

Hellas *see* Greece

149 N11 **Ḥelleh, Rūd-e** ≈ S Iran

100 N10 **Hellendoorn** Overijssel, E Netherlands *52.22N 6.27E*

Hellenic Republic *see* Greece

123 Gg10 **Hellenic Trough** *undersea feature* Aegean Sea, C Mediterranean Sea

96 E10 **Hellesylt** Møre og Romsdal, S Norway *62.06N 6.51E*

100 F13 **Hellevoetsluis** Zuid-Holland, SW Netherlands *51.49N 4.07E*

107 Q12 **Hellín** Castilla-La Mancha, C Spain *38.31N 1.43W*

117 H19 **Hellinikon** ✕ (Athína) Attikí, C Greece *37.53N 23.43E*

34 M12 **Hells Canyon** *valley* Idaho/Oregon, NW USA

154 L9 **Helmand** ◈ *province* S Afghanistan

154 K10 **Helmand, Daryā-ye** *var.* Rūd-e Hīrmand. ≈ Afghanistan/Iran *see also* Hīrmand, Rūd-e

Helmantica *see* Salamanca

103 K15 **Helme** ≈ C Germany

101 L15 **Helmond** Noord-Brabant, S Netherlands *51.28N 5.40E*

98 J7 **Helmsdale** N Scotland, UK *58.06N 3.36W*

102 K13 **Helmstedt** Niedersachsen, N Germany *52.13N 11.01E*

169 Y10 **Helong** Jilin, NE China *42.38N 129.01E*

38 M4 **Helper** Utah, W USA *39.40N 110.52W*

102 O10 **Helpter Berge** *hill* NE Germany *53.29N 13.37E*

97 J22 **Helsingborg** *prev.* Hälsingborg. Skåne, S Sweden *55.59N 12.48E*

Helsingfors *see* Helsinki

97 J22 **Helsingør** *Eng.* Elsinore. Frederiksborg, E Denmark *56.03N 12.37E*

95 M20 **Helsinki** *Swe.* Helsingfors. ● (Finland) Etelä-Suomi, S Finland *60.18N 24.58E*

99 H25 **Helston** SW England, UK *50.04N 5.16W*

Heltau *see* Cisnădie

63 C17 **Helvecia** Santa Fe, C Argentina *31.09S 60.09W*

99 K15 **Helvellyn** ▲ NW England, UK *54.31N 3.00W*

Helvetia *see* Switzerland

77 W8 **Helwân** *var.* Hilwân, Hulwan, Hulwân. N Egypt *29.51N 31.19E*

99 N21 **Hemel Hempstead** E England, UK *51.46N 0.28W*

37 U16 **Hemet** California, W USA *33.45N 116.58W*

30 J13 **Hemingford** Nebraska, C USA *42.18N 103.02W*

23 T13 **Hemingway** South Carolina, SE USA *33.45N 79.25W*

94 G13 **Hemnesberget** Nordland, C Norway *66.13N 13.33E*

27 Y8 **Hemphill** Texas, SW USA *31.20N 93.51W*

27 V11 **Hempstead** Texas, SW USA *30.06N 96.04W*

97 P20 **Hemse** Gotland, SE Sweden *57.12N 18.22E*

96 F13 **Hemsedal** *valley* S Norway

165 T11 **Henan** *var.* Henan Mongolzu Zizhixian, Yêgainnyin. Qinghai, C China *34.42N 101.36E*

167 N6 **Henan** *var.* Henan Sheng, Honan, Yu. ◈ *province* C China

192 L4 **Hen and Chickens** *island group* N NZ

Henan Mongolzu Zizhixian/Henan Sheng *see* Henan

107 O7 **Henares** ≈ C Spain

171 M8 **Henashi-zaki** *headland* Honshū, C Japan *40.37N 139.51E*

104 I16 **Hendaye** Pyrénées-Atlantiques, SW France *43.22N 1.46W*

142 F11 **Hendek** Sakarya, NW Turkey *40.49N 30.40E*

63 B21 **Henderson** Buenos Aires, E Argentina *36.18S 61.43W*

22 I5 **Henderson** Kentucky, S USA *37.50N 87.35W*

37 X11 **Henderson** Nevada, W USA *36.02N 114.58W*

23 V8 **Henderson** North Carolina, SE USA *36.19N 78.24W*

22 G10 **Henderson** Tennessee, S USA *35.25N 88.37W*

27 W7 **Henderson** Texas, SW USA *32.09N 94.48W*

32 J12 **Henderson Creek** ≈ Illinois, N USA

195 X16 **Henderson Field** ✕ (Honiara) Guadalcanal, C Solomon Islands *9.28S 160.02E*

203 O17 **Henderson Island** *atoll* N Pitcairn Islands

23 O10 **Hendersonville** North Carolina, SE USA *35.19N 82.27W*

22 J8 **Hendersonville** Tennessee, S USA *36.18N 86.37W*

149 O14 **Hendorābī, Jazīreh-ye** *island* S Iran

57 V10 **Hendrik Top** *var.* Hendriktop. *elevation* C Suriname *4.14N 56.07W*

Hendū Kosh *see* Hindu Kush

12 L12 **Heney, Lac** ◎ Quebec, SE Canada

194 I12 **Henganofi** Eastern Highlands, C PNG *6.13S 145.31E*

Hengchow *see* Hengyang

167 S15 **Hengchun** S Taiwan *22.09N 120.43E*

165 R16 **Hengduan Shan** ▲▲ SW China

100 N12 **Hengelo** Gelderland, E Netherlands *52.02N 6.18E*

100 O10 **Hengelo** Overijssel, E Netherlands *52.15N 6.48E*

Hengnan *see* Hengyang

167 N11 **Hengshan** Hunan, S China *27.17N 112.51E*

166 L4 **Hengshan** Shaanxi, C China *37.57N 109.17E*

167 O4 **Hengshui** Hebei, E China *37.42N 115.39E*

167 N12 **Hengyang** *var.* Hengnan, Heng-yang; *prev.* Hengchow. Hunan, S China *26.54N 112.33E*

119 U11 **Heniches'k** *Rus.* Genichesk. Khersons'ka Oblast', S Ukraine *46.10N 34.49E*

23 Z4 **Henlopen, Cape** *headland* Delaware, NE USA *38.48N 75.06W*

Henna *see* Enna

96 M10 **Hennan** Gävleborg, C Sweden *62.01N 15.55E*

104 G7 **Hennebont** Morbihan, NW France *47.48N 3.16W*

32 L11 **Hennepin** Illinois, N USA *41.13N 89.21W*

28 M9 **Hennessey** Oklahoma, C USA *36.06N 97.54W*

102 N12 **Hennigsdorf** *var.* Hennigsdorf bei Berlin. Brandenburg, NE Germany *52.37N 13.13E*

Hennigsdorf bei Berlin *see* Hennigsdorf

21 N9 **Henniker** New Hampshire, NE USA *43.10N 71.47W*

27 S5 **Henrietta** Texas, SW USA *33.49N 98.12W*

Henrique de Carvalho *see* Saurimo

32 L12 **Henry** Illinois, N USA *41.06N 89.21W*

23 Y7 **Henry, Cape** *headland* Virginia, NE USA *36.55N 76.01W*

29 P10 **Henryetta** Oklahoma, C USA *35.26N 95.58W*

204 M7 **Henry Ice Rise** *ice cap* Antarctica

16 N1 **Henry Kater, Cape** *headland* Baffin Island, Nunavut, NE Canada *69.09N 66.45W*

35 R13 **Henrys Fork** ≈ Idaho, NW USA

12 E15 **Hensall** Ontario, S Canada *43.25N 81.28W*

102 J9 **Henstedt-Ulzburg** Schleswig-Holstein, N Germany *53.45N 9.59E*

169 N7 **Hentiy** ◈ *province* N Mongolia

168 M7 **Hentiyn Nuruu** ▲▲ N Mongolia

191 P10 **Henty** New South Wales, SE Australia *35.33S 147.03E*

177 Ff8 **Henzada** Irrawaddy, SW Myanmar *17.36N 95.25E*

103 G19 **Heppenheim** Hessen, W Germany *49.39N 8.38E*

34 J11 **Heppner** Oregon, NW USA *45.21N 119.33W*

166 L15 **Hepu** *prev.* Lianzhou. Guangxi Zhuangzu Zizhiqu, S China *21.40N 109.12E*

94 J2 **Heradhsvötn** ≈ C Iceland

Herakleion *see* Irákleio

154 K5 **Herāt** *var.* Herat; *anc.* Aria. Herāt, W Afghanistan *34.22N 62.11E*

154 J5 **Herāt** ◈ *province* W Afghanistan

105 P14 **Hérault** ◈ *department* S France

105 P15 **Hérault** ≈ S France

9 T16 **Herbert** Saskatchewan, S Canada *50.27N 107.09W*

193 F22 **Herbert** Otago, South Island, NZ *45.14S 170.48E*

40 J17 **Herbert Island** *island* Aleutian Islands, Alaska, USA

194 I12 **Herbert, Mount** ▲ C PNG *5.44S 145.00E*

Herbertshöhe *see* Kokopo

13 Q7 **Hérbertville** Quebec, SE Canada *48.22N 71.42W*

103 G17 **Herborn** Hessen, W Germany *50.40N 8.18E*

115 I17 **Herceg-Novi** *It.* Castelnuovo; *prev.* Ercegnovi. Montenegro, SW Serbia and Montenegro (Yugoslavia) *42.28N 18.35E*

9 X10 **Herchmer** Manitoba, C Canada *57.25N 94.12W*

194 K14 **Hercules Bay** *bay* E PNG

94 K2 **Herdhubreidh** ▲ C Iceland *65.12N 16.26W*

44 M13 **Heredia** Heredia, C Costa Rica *10.00N 84.06W*

44 M12 **Heredia** *off.* Provincia de Heredia. ◈ *province* N Costa Rica

99 K21 **Hereford** W England, UK *52.04N 2.43W*

26 M3 **Hereford** Texas, SW USA *34.49N 102.25W*

13 Q13 **Hereford, Mont** ▲ Quebec, SE Canada *45.04N 71.38W*

99 K21 **Herefordshire** *cultural region* W England, UK

203 U11 **Hereheretue** *atoll* Îles Tuamotu, C French Polynesia

107 N10 **Herencia** Castilla-La Mancha, C Spain *39.19N 3.19W*

101 H18 **Herent** Vlaams Brabant, C Belgium *50.54N 4.40E*

101 I16 **Herentals** *var.* Herenthals. Antwerpen, N Belgium *51.10N 4.49E*

Herenthals *see* Herentals

101 H17 **Herenthout** Antwerpen, N Belgium *51.09N 4.45E*

97 J23 **Herfølge** Roskilde, E Denmark *55.25N 12.09E*

102 G13 **Herford** Nordrhein-Westfalen, NW Germany *52.07N 8.40E*

29 O5 **Herington** Kansas, C USA *38.37N 96.55W*

110 H7 **Herisau** *Fr.* Hérisau. Appenzell Ausser Rhoden, NE Switzerland *47.22N 9.16E*

Héristal *see* Herstal

101 J18 **Herk-de-Stad** Limburg, NE Belgium *50.57N 5.12E*

Herkulesbad/Herkulesfürdő *see* Băile Herculane

Herlen Gol/Herlen He *see* Kerulen

37 Q4 **Herlong** California, W USA *40.07N 120.06W*

99 L26 **Herm** *island* Channel Islands

111 R9 **Hermagor** *Slvn.* Šmohor. Kärnten, S Austria *46.37N 13.24E*

31 S7 **Herman** Minnesota, N USA *45.49N 96.08W*

98 L1 **Herma Ness** *headland* NE Scotland, UK *60.51N 0.55W*

29 V4 **Hermann** Missouri, C USA *38.40N 91.25W*

189 Q8 **Hermannsburg** Northern Territory, N Australia *23.59S 132.55E*

Hermannstadt *see* Sibiu

96 E12 **Hermansverk** Sogn og Fjordane, S Norway *61.10N 6.52E*

144 H6 **Hermel** *var.* Hirmil. NE Lebanon *34.23N 36.19E*

Hermhausen *see* Hajnówka

191 P6 **Hermidale** New South Wales, SE Australia *31.36S 146.42E*

57 X9 **Herminadorp** Sipaliwini, NE Suriname *5.05N 54.22W*

34 K11 **Hermiston** Oregon, NW USA *45.50N 119.17W*

29 T6 **Hermitage** Missouri, C USA *37.57N 93.21W*

194 I8 **Hermit Islands** *island group* N PNG

27 O7 **Hermleigh** Texas, SW USA *32.37N 100.44W*

144 G7 **Hermon, Mount** *Ar.* Jabal ash Shaykh. ▲ S Syria *35.30N 33.30E*

Hermopolis Parva *see* Damanhûr

30 J10 **Hermosa** South Dakota, N USA *43.49N 103.12W*

42 F5 **Hermosillo** Sonora, NW Mexico *28.58N 110.53W*

Hermoupolis *see* Ermoúpoli

113 N20 **Hernád** *var.* Hornád, *Ger.* Kundert. ≈ Hungary/Slovakia

63 C18 **Hernández** Entre Ríos, E Argentina *32.21S 60.01W*

25 V11 **Hernando** Florida, SE USA *28.54N 82.22W*

24 L1 **Hernando** Mississippi, S USA *34.49N 89.59W*

107 Q2 **Hernani** País Vasco, N Spain *43.16N 1.58W*

101 F19 **Herne** Vlaams Brabant, C Belgium *50.45N 4.03E*

103 E14 **Herne** Nordrhein-Westfalen, W Germany *51.33N 7.13E*

97 F22 **Herning** Ringkøbing, W Denmark *56.07N 8.58E*

Hernösand *see* Härnösand

124 Q13 **Herodotus Basin** *undersea feature* E Mediterranean Sea

124 Nn14 **Herodotus Trough** *undersea feature* C Mediterranean Sea

31 T11 **Heron Lake** Minnesota, N USA *43.48N 95.18W*

Herowābād *see* Khalkhāl

97 G16 **Herre** Telemark, S Norway *59.06N 9.34E*

31 N7 **Herreid** South Dakota, N USA *45.49N 100.04W*

103 H22 **Herrenberg** Baden-Württemberg, S Germany *48.36N 8.52E*

106 L14 **Herrera** Andalucía, S Spain *37.22N 4.49W*

45 R17 **Herrera** *off.* Provincia de Herrera. ◈ *province* S Panama

106 L10 **Herrera del Duque** Extremadura, W Spain *39.10N 5.03W*

106 M4 **Herrera de Pisuerga** Castilla-León, N Spain *42.34N 4.19W*

43 Z13 **Herrero, Punta** *headland* SE Mexico *19.15N 87.28W*

191 P16 **Herrick** Tasmania, SE Australia *41.07S 147.53E*

32 L17 **Herrin** Illinois, N USA *37.48N 89.01W*

22 M6 **Herrington Lake** ▣ Kentucky, S USA

97 K18 **Herrljunga** Västra Götaland, S Sweden *58.04N 13.01E*

105 N16 **Hers** ≈ S France

8 I1 **Herschel Island** *island* Yukon Territory, NW Canada

101 I17 **Herselt** Antwerpen, C Belgium *51.03N 4.52E*

20 G15 **Hershey** Pennsylvania, NE USA *40.17N 76.39W*

101 K19 **Herstal** *Fr.* Héristal. Liège, E Belgium *50.40N 5.37E*

99 O21 **Hertford** E England, UK *51.48N 0.04W*

23 X8 **Hertford** North Carolina, SE USA *36.11N 76.28W*

99 O21 **Hertfordshire** *cultural region* E England, UK

189 Z9 **Hervey Bay** Queensland, E Australia *25.17S 152.48E*

103 O14 **Herzberg** Brandenburg, E Germany *51.42N 13.15E*

101 E18 **Herzele** Oost-Vlaanderen, NW Belgium *50.52N 3.52E*

103 K20 **Herzogenaurach** Bayern, SE Germany *49.34N 10.52E*

111 W4 **Herzogenburg** Niederösterreich, NE Austria *48.18N 15.43E*

Herzogenbusch *see* 's-Hertogenbosch

105 N2 **Hesdin** Pas-de-Calais, N France *50.21N 2.00E*

166 K14 **Heshan** Guangxi Zhuangzu Zizhiqu, S China *23.45N 108.58E*

165 X10 **Heshui** *var.* Xihuachi. Gansu, C China *35.42N 108.06E*

101 M25 **Hespérange** Luxembourg, SE Luxembourg *49.34N 6.10E*

37 U14 **Hesperia** California, W USA *34.25N 117.17W*

39 P7 **Hesperus Mountain** ▲ Colorado, C USA *37.27N 108.05W*

8 J6 **Hess** ≈ Yukon Territory, NW Canada

Hesse *see* Hessen

103 J21 **Hesselberg** ▲ S Germany *49.04N 10.32E*

97 I22 **Hesselo** *island* E Denmark

103 H17 **Hessen** *Eng./Fr.* Hesse. ◈ *state* C Germany

199 Jj6 **Hess Tablemount** *undersea feature* C Pacific Ocean *17.49N 174.15W*

29 N6 **Hesston** Kansas, C USA *38.08N 97.25W*

95 G15 **Hestskjøltoppen** ▲ C Norway *64.21N 13.57E*

99 K18 **Heswall** NW England, UK *53.19N 3.06W*

159 P12 **Hetauda** Central, C Nepal

Hétfalu *see* Săcele

30 K7 **Hettinger** North Dakota, N USA *46.00N 102.38W*

103 L14 **Hettstedt** Sachsen-Anhalt, C Germany *51.39N 11.31E*

94 P3 **Heuglin, Kapp** *headland* SE Svalbard *78.15N 22.49E*

195 Y16 **Heuru** San Cristobal, SE Solomon Islands *10.13S 161.25E*

101 J17 **Heusden** Limburg, NE Belgium *51.01N 5.16E*

100 J13 **Heusden** Noord-Brabant, S Netherlands *51.43N 5.05E*

104 K3 **Hève, Cap de la** *headland* N France *49.28N 0.13W*

101 H18 **Heverlee** Vlaams Brabant, C Belgium *50.52N 4.41E*

113 L22 **Heves** Heves, NE Hungary *47.37N 20.17E*

113 L22 **Heves** *off.* Heves Megye. ◈ *county* NE Hungary

Hevron *see* Hebron

47 Y13 **Hewanorra** ✕ (Saint Lucia) S Saint Lucia *13.44N 60.57W*

166 M13 **Hexian** *var.* Babu, He Xian. Guangxi Zhuangzu Zizhiqu, S China *24.25N 111.31E*

166 L6 **Heyang** Shaanxi, C China *35.03N 109.55E*

Heydebrech *see* Kędzierzyn-Kozle

Heydekrug *see* Šilutė

99 K16 **Heysham** NW England, UK *54.02N 2.54W*

167 O14 **Heyuan** Guangdong, S China *23.50N 114.43E*

190 L12 **Heywood** Victoria, SE Australia *38.09S 141.38E*

188 K3 **Heywood Islands** *island group* Western Australia

167 O6 **Heze** *var.* Caozhou. Shandong, E China *35.16N 115.27E*

165 U11 **Hezheng** Gansu, C China *35.24N 103.21E*

165 U11 **Hezuozhen** Gansu, C China *34.55N 102.49E*

25 Z16 **Hialeah** Florida, SE USA *25.51N 80.16W*

29 Q3 **Hiawatha** Kansas, C USA *39.48N 95.31W*

38 M4 **Hiawatha** Utah, W USA *39.28N 111.00W*

31 V4 **Hibbing** Minnesota, N USA *47.24N 92.55W*

191 N17 **Hibbs, Point** *headland* Tasmania, SE Australia *42.37S 145.15E*

Hibernia *see* Ireland

170 D12 **Hibiki-nada** *inlet* SW Japan

22 F8 **Hickman** Kentucky, S USA *36.34N 89.11W*

23 Q9 **Hickory** North Carolina, SE USA *35.44N 81.20W*

23 Q9 **Hickory, Lake** ◎ North Carolina, SE USA

192 Q7 **Hicks Bay** Gisborne, North Island, NZ *37.36S 178.18E*

27 S8 **Hico** Texas, SW USA *31.58N 98.01W*

172 Oo6 **Hidaka** Hokkaidō, NE Japan *42.53N 142.24E*

171 Gg13 **Hidaka** Hyōgo, Honshū, SW Japan *35.27N 134.43E*

172 P7 **Hidaka-sanmyaku** ▲▲ Hokkaidō, NE Japan

43 O6 **Hidalgo** *var.* Villa Hidalgo. Coahuila de Zaragoza, NE Mexico *27.46N 99.54W*

◆ Country
● Country Capital
◇ Dependent Territory
○ Dependent Territory Capital
◈ Administrative Region
✕ International Airport
▲ Mountain
▲▲ Mountain Range
Volcano
≈ River
◎ Lake
▣ Reservoir

43 N8 Hidalgo Nuevo León, NE Mexico 29.58N 100.27W
43 O10 Hidalgo Tamaulipas, C Mexico 24.17N 99.21W
43 O13 Hidalgo ◆ state C Mexico
42 J7 Hidalgo del Parral var. Parral. Chihuahua, N Mexico 26.58N 105.40W
171 J14 Hida-sanmyaku ▲ Honshū, S Japan
102 N7 Hiddensee island NE Germany
82 G6 Hidiglib, Wadi ≈ NE Sudan
111 U6 Hieflau Salzburg, E Austria 47.36N 14.34E
197 H5 Hienghène Province Nord, C New Caledonia 20.43S 164.54E
Hierosolyma see Jerusalem
66 N12 Hierro var. Ferro. island Islas Canarias, Spain, NE Atlantic Ocean
170 Ee13 Higashi-Hiroshima var. Higashihirosima. Hiroshima, Honshū, SW Japan 34.25N 132.45E
171 J18 Higashi-Izu Shizuoka, Honshū, S Japan 34.43N 138.58E
171 Ll12 Higashine var. Higasine. Yamagata, Honshū, C Japan 38.26N 140.23E
170 C11 Higashi-suidō strait SW Japan
Higashihirosima see Higashi-Hiroshima
Higasine see Higashine
27 P1 Higgins Texas, SW USA 36.06N 100.01W
33 P7 Higgins Lake ◎ Michigan, N USA
29 S4 Higginsville Missouri, C USA 39.04N 93.43W
High Atlas see Haut Atlas
32 M5 High Falls Reservoir ▣ Wisconsin, N USA
46 K12 Highgate C Jamaica 18.15N 76.53W
27 X11 High Island Texas, SW USA 29.35N 94.24W
33 O5 High Island island Michigan, N USA
32 K15 Highland Illinois, N USA 38.44N 89.40W
33 N10 Highland Park Illinois, N USA 42.10N 87.48W
23 O10 Highlands North Carolina, SE USA 35.04N 83.10W
9 O11 High Level Alberta, W Canada 58.31N 117.07W
31 O9 Highmore South Dakota, N USA 44.29N 99.26W
179 Oo10 High Peak ▲ Luzon, N Philippines 15.28N 120.07E
High Plains see Great Plains
23 S9 High Point North Carolina, SE USA 35.58N 80.00W
20 J13 High Point hill New Jersey, NE USA 41.19N 74.38W
9 P13 High Prairie Alberta, W Canada 55.27N 116.28W
9 Q16 High River Alberta, SW Canada 50.34N 113.49W
23 S9 High Rock Lake ▣ North Carolina, SE USA
25 V9 High Springs Florida, SE USA 29.49N 82.36W
High Veld see Great Karoo
99 J24 High Willhays ▲ SW England, UK 50.39N 3.58W
99 N22 High Wycombe prev. Chepping Wycombe, Chipping Wycombe. SE England, UK 51.37N 0.46W
43 P12 Higos var. El Higo. Veracruz-Llave, E Mexico 21.47N 98.28W
104 I16 Higuer, Cap headland NE Spain 43.23N 1.46W
47 R5 Higüero, Punta headland W Puerto Rico 18.21N 67.15W
47 P9 Higüey var. Salvaleón de Higüey. E Dominican Republic 18.34N 68.43W
202 G11 Hihifo ✈ (Matā'utu) Île Uvea, N Wallis and Futuna
83 N16 Hiiraan off. Gobolka Hiiraan. ◆ region C Somalia
120 E4 Hiiumaa off. Hiiumaa Maakond. ◆ province W Estonia
120 D4 Hiiumaa Ger. Dagden, Swe. Dagö. island W Estonia
Hijanah see Al Hījānah
107 S6 Híjar Aragón, NE Spain 41.10N 0.27W
170 E13 Hikari Yamaguchi, Honshū, SW Japan 33.55N 131.58E
170 Ff15 Hiketa Kagawa, Shikoku, SW Japan 34.15N 134.20E
171 Hh15 Hikone Shiga, Honshū, SW Japan 35.15N 136.14E
170 D13 Hiko-san ▲ Kyūshū, SW Japan 33.27N 130.55E
203 V10 Hikueru atoll Îles Tuamotu, C French Polynesia
192 K3 Hikurangi Northland, North Island, NZ 35.37S 174.16E
192 Q8 Hikurangi ▲ North Island, NZ 37.55S 177.59E
199 J13 Hikurangi Trench var. Hikurangi Trough. undersea feature SW Pacific Ocean
Hikurangi Trough see Hikurangi Trench
202 B15 Hikutavake NW Niue
124 Nn14 Hilāl, Ra's al headland N Libya 32.55N 22.09E
63 A24 Hilario Ascasubi Buenos Aires, E Argentina 39.22S 62.39W
103 K17 Hildburghausen Thüringen, C Germany 50.26N 10.44E
103 E15 Hilden Nordrhein-Westfalen, W Germany 51.10N 6.55E
102 I13 Hildesheim Niedersachsen, N Germany 52.09N 9.57E
35 T9 Hilger Montana, NW USA 47.15N 109.18W
Hili see Hilli
Hilla see Al Ḥillah
47 O14 Hillaby, Mount ▲ N Barbados 13.12N 59.34W
97 K19 Hillared Västra Götaland, S Sweden 57.37N 13.10E
205 R12 Hillary Coast physical region Antarctica
44 G2 Hill Bank Orange Walk, N Belize 17.36N 88.43W
35 O14 Hill City Idaho, NW USA 43.18N 115.03W
28 K3 Hill City Kansas, C USA 39.21N 99.51W
31 V5 Hill City Minnesota, N USA 46.59N 93.36W
30 J10 Hill City South Dakota, N USA 43.54N 103.33W
67 C24 Hill Cove Settlement West Falkland, Falkland Islands
100 H10 Hillegom Zuid-Holland, W Netherlands 52.18N 4.34E
97 J22 Hillerød Frederiksborg, E Denmark 55.55N 12.19E
38 M7 Hillers, Mount ▲ Utah, W USA 37.53N 110.42W
159 S13 Hilli var. Hili. Rajshahi, NW Bangladesh 25.17N 89.02E
31 R11 Hills Minnesota, N USA 43.31N 96.21W
32 L14 Hillsboro Illinois, N USA 39.09N 89.29W
29 N5 Hillsboro Kansas, C USA 38.21N 97.12W
29 X5 Hillsboro Missouri, C USA 38.13N 90.33W
21 N10 Hillsboro New Hampshire, NE USA 43.06N 71.52W
39 Q14 Hillsboro New Mexico, SW USA 32.55N 107.33W
31 R4 Hillsboro North Dakota, N USA 47.25N 97.03W
33 R14 Hillsboro Ohio, N USA 39.12N 83.36W
34 G11 Hillsboro Oregon, NW USA 45.31N 122.59W
27 T8 Hillsboro Texas, SW USA 32.01N 97.08W
32 K8 Hillsboro Wisconsin, N USA 43.40N 90.21W
25 Y14 Hillsboro Canal canal Florida, SE USA
47 Y15 Hillsborough Carriacou, N Grenada 12.28N 61.28W
99 G15 Hillsborough E Northern Ireland, UK 54.27N 6.06W
23 U9 Hillsborough North Carolina, SE USA 36.04N 79.06W
33 Q10 Hillsdale Michigan, N USA 41.55N 84.37W
191 O8 Hillston New South Wales, SE Australia 33.30S 145.33E
23 R7 Hillsville Virginia, NE USA 36.45N 80.44W
98 L2 Hillswick NE Scotland, UK 60.28N 1.37W
Hill Tippera see Tripura
40 H11 Hilo Hawaii, USA, C Pacific Ocean 19.42N 155.04W
20 F9 Hilton New York, NE USA 43.17N 77.47W
12 C10 Hilton Beach Ontario, S Canada 46.14N 83.51W
23 R16 Hilton Head Island South Carolina, SE USA 32.13N 80.45W
23 R16 Hilton Head Island island South Carolina, SE USA
101 J15 Hilvarenbeek Noord-Brabant, S Netherlands 51.28N 5.07E
100 J11 Hilversum Noord-Holland, C Netherlands 52.13N 5.10E
Hilwān see Helwân
158 J7 Himāchal Pradesh ◆ state NW India
Himalaya/Himalaya Shan see Himalayas
158 M9 Himalayas var. Himalaya, Chin. Himalaya Shan. ▲ S Asia
179 Q14 Himamaylan Negros, C Philippines 10.04N 122.52E
95 K15 Himanka Länsi-Suomi, W Finland 64.03N 24.40E
Himara see Himarë
115 L23 Himarë var. Himara. Vlorë, S Albania 40.06N 19.45E
144 M2 Ḥimār, Wādī al dry watercourse N Syria
160 D9 Himatnagar Gujarāt, W India 23.37N 73.01E
111 Y4 Himberg Niederösterreich, E Austria 48.03N 16.27E
171 J14 Hime-gawa ≈ Honshū, S Japan
170 G14 Himeji var. Himezi. Hyōgo, Honshū, SW Japan 34.47N 134.32E
170 Dd13 Hime-jima island SW Japan
Himezi see Himeji
171 Ii13 Himi Toyama, Honshū, SW Japan 36.52N 136.59E
111 S9 Himmelberg Kärnten, S Austria 46.45N 14.01E
144 I5 Ḥimş var. Homs; anc. Emesa. Ḥimş, C Syria 34.43N 36.43E
144 K6 Ḥimş off. Muḥāfaẓat Ḥimş, var. Homs. ◆ governorate C Syria
144 I5 Ḥimş, Buḥayrat var. Buḥayrat Qaṭṭīnah. ◎ W Syria
179 Rr15 Hinatuan Mindanao, S Philippines 8.21N 126.19E
119 N10 Hinceşti var. Hânceşti; prev. Kotovsk. C Moldova 46.48N 28.33E
46 M9 Hinche C Haiti 19.07N 72.00W
189 X5 Hinchinbrook Island island Queensland, NE Australia
41 S12 Hinchinbrook Island island Alaska, USA
99 M19 Hinckley C England, UK 52.33N 1.21W
31 V7 Hinckley Minnesota, N USA 46.01N 92.57W
38 K5 Hinckley Utah, W USA 39.21N 112.39W
20 J9 Hinckley Reservoir ▣ New York, NE USA
158 I12 Hindaun Rājasthān, N India 26.43N 77.01E
Hindenburg/Hindenburg in Oberschlesien see Zabrze
Hindiya see Al Hindīyah
23 O6 Hindman Kentucky, S USA 37.20N 82.58W
190 L10 Hindmarsh, Lake ◎ Victoria, SE Australia
193 G19 Hinds Canterbury, South Island, NZ 44.00S 171.33E
193 G19 Hinds ≈ South Island, NZ
97 H23 Hindsholm island C Denmark
155 S4 Hindu Kush Per. Hendū Kosh. ▲ Afghanistan/Pakistan
161 H19 Hindupur Andhra Pradesh, E India 13.46N 77.33E
9 O12 Hines Creek Alberta, W Canada 56.14N 118.36W
25 W6 Hinesville Georgia, SE USA 31.51N 81.36W
160 I12 Hinganghāt Mahārāshtra, C India 20.31N 78.52E
155 N15 Hingol ≈ SW Pakistan
160 H13 Hingoli Mahārāshtra, C India 19.45N 77.08E
143 R13 Hınıs Erzurum, E Turkey 39.22N 41.43E
94 O2 Hinlopenstretet strait N Svalbard
94 G10 Hinnøya island C Norway
170 D15 Hinokage Miyazaki, Kyūshū, SW Japan 32.39N 131.20E
170 F11 Hino-misaki headland Honshū, SW Japan 35.25N 132.37E
110 H10 Hinterrhein ≈ SW Switzerland
9 O14 Hinton Alberta, SW Canada 53.24N 117.34W
28 M10 Hinton Oklahoma, C USA 35.28N 98.21W
23 R6 Hinton West Virginia, NE USA 37.40N 80.53W
Hios see Chíos
43 N8 Hipolito Coahuila de Zaragoza, NE Mexico 25.42N 101.22W
Hipponium see Vibo Valentia
170 C12 Hirado Nagasaki, Hirado-shima, SW Japan 33.22N 129.32E
170 C12 Hirado-shima island SW Japan
171 Gg15 Hirakata Ōsaka, Honshū, SW Japan 34.48N 135.37E
172 P17 Hirakubo-saki headland Ishigaki-jima, SW Japan 24.36N 124.19E
160 M11 Hirākud Reservoir ▣ E India
Hir al Gharbi, Qasr al see Ḥayr al Gharbī, Qaşr al
172 N9 Hiranai Aomori, Honshū, C Japan 40.56N 140.55E
172 Pp16 Hirara Okinawa, Miyako-jima, SW Japan 24.48N 125.16E
Qasr al Hir Ash Sharqi see Ḥayr ash Sharqī, Qaşr al
170 F12 Hirata Shimane, Honshū, SW Japan 35.26N 132.50E
171 Jj17 Hiratsuka var. Hiratuka. Kanagawa, Honshū, S Japan 35.20N 139.20E
Hiratuka see Hiratsuka
142 I13 Hirfanlı Barajı ▣ C Turkey
161 G18 Hiriyūr Karnātaka, W India 13.58N 76.33E
Hîrlău see Hârlău
154 K10 Hirmand, Rūd-e var. Daryā-ye Helmand. ≈ Afghanistan/Iran see also Helmand, Daryā-ye
Hirmil see Hermel
172 P8 Hiroo Hokkaidō, NE Japan 42.16N 143.16E
171 Mm9 Hirosaki Aomori, Honshū, C Japan 40.34N 140.28E
170 E13 Hiroshima var. Hirosima. Hiroshima, Honshū, SW Japan 34.22N 132.25E
170 Ee13 Hiroshima off. Hiroshima-ken, var. Hirosima. ◆ prefecture Honshū, SW Japan
Hirosima see Hiroshima
Hirschberg/Hirschberg im Riesengebirge/Hirschberg in Schlesien see Jelenia Góra
105 Q3 Hirson Aisne, N France 49.55N 4.04E
Hîrşova see Hârşova
97 G19 Hirtshals Nordjylland, N Denmark 57.34N 9.58E
171 H16 Hisai Mie, Honshū, SW Japan 34.38N 136.27E
158 H10 Hisār Haryāna, NW India 29.10N 75.45E
194 J15 Hisiu Central, SW PNG 9.01S 146.49E
153 P13 Hisor Rus. Gissar. W Tajikistan 38.34N 68.29E
Hispalis see Sevilla
Hispana/Hispania see Spain
46 M7 Hispaniola island Dominion Republic/Haiti
66 F11 Hispaniola Basin var. Hispaniola Trough. undersea feature SW Atlantic Ocean
Hispaniola Trough see Hispaniola Basin
Histonium see Vasto
145 R7 Hīt SW Iraq 33.38N 42.50E
170 D14 Hita Ōita, Kyūshū, SW Japan 33.20N 130.55E
171 L16 Hitachi var. Hitati. Ibaraki, Honshū, S Japan 36.40N 140.42E
171 L15 Hitachi-Ōta var. Hitatiôta. Ibaraki, Honshū, S Japan 36.31N 140.31E
Hitati see Hitachi
Hitatiôta see Hitachi-Ōta
99 O21 Hitchin E England, UK 51.57N 0.16W
203 Q7 Hitiaa Tahiti, W French Polynesia 17.34S 149.16W
170 Cc15 Hitoyoshi var. Hitoyosi. Kumamoto, Kyūshū, SW Japan 32.12N 130.45E
Hitoyosi see Hitoyoshi
96 F7 Hitra prev. Hitteren. island S Norway
Hitteren see Hitra
197 B10 Hiu island Torres Islands, N Vanuatu
171 K14 Hiuchiga-take ▲ Honshū, C Japan 36.57N 139.18E
203 X7 Hiva Oa island Îles Marquises, N French Polynesia
22 M10 Hiwassee Lake ▣ North Carolina, SE USA
22 M10 Hiwassee River ≈ SE USA
97 H20 Hjallerup Nordjylland, N Denmark 57.10N 10.10E
97 M16 Hjälmaren Eng. Lake Hjalmar. ◎ C Sweden
Hjalmar, Lake see Hjälmaren
97 C14 Hjellestad Hordaland, S Norway 60.15N 5.13E
97 D16 Hjelmeland Rogaland, S Norway 59.12N 6.07E
96 G10 Hjerkinn Oppland, S Norway 62.13N 9.37E
97 L18 Hjo Västra Götaland, S Sweden 58.16N 14.07E
97 G19 Hjørring Nordjylland, N Denmark 57.28N 9.58E
178 H1 Hkakabo Razi ▲ Myanmar/China 28.17N 97.28E
178 H1 Hkring Bum ▲ N Myanmar 27.05N 97.16E
85 L21 Hlathikulu var. Hlatikulu. S Swaziland 26.57S 31.19E
Hlatikulu see Hlathikulu
Hliboka see Hlyboka
113 F17 Hlinsko var. Hlinsko v Čechách. Pardubický Kraj, C Czech Republic 49.46N 15.54E
Hlinsko v Čechách see Hlinsko
119 S6 Hlobyne Rus. Globino. Poltavs'ka Oblast', NE Ukraine 49.24N 33.16E
113 H20 Hlohovec Ger. Freistadtl, Hung. Galgóc; prev. Frakštát. Trnavský Kraj, W Slovakia 48.27N 17.47E
85 J23 Hlotse var. Leribe. NW Lesotho 28.55S 28.01E
113 I17 Hlučín Ger. Hultschin, Pol. Hulczyn. Ostravský Kraj, E Czech Republic 49.54N 18.10E
119 S2 Hlukhiv Rus. Glukhov. Sums'ka Oblast', NE Ukraine 51.39N 33.52E
121 K21 Hlushkavichy Rus. Glushkevichi. Homyel'skaya Voblasts', SE Belarus 51.33N 27.48E
121 L18 Hlusk Rus. Glusk, Glussk. Mahilyowskaya Voblasts', E Belarus 52.54N 28.40E
118 K8 Hlyboka Ger. Hliboka, Rus. Glybokaya. Chernivets'ka Oblast', W Ukraine 48.04N 25.55E
120 K13 Hlybokaye Rus. Glubokoye. Vitsyebskaya Voblasts', N Belarus 55.08N 27.40E
79 Q16 Ho SE Ghana 6.36N 0.28E
178 Jj6 Hoa Binh Hoa Binh, N Vietnam 20.49N 105.19E
85 E20 Hoachanas Hardap, C Namibia 23.52S 18.02E
Hoai Nhơn see Bông Sơn
178 Jj8 Hoa Lac Quang Binh, C Vietnam 17.54N 106.24E
178 J5 Hoang Liên Sơn ▲ N Vietnam
85 B17 Hoanib ≈ NW Namibia
35 S15 Hoback Peak ▲ Wyoming, C USA 43.04N 110.34W
191 P17 Hobart prev. Hobarton, Hobart Town. state capital Tasmania, SE Australia 42.54S 147.18E
28 L11 Hobart Oklahoma, C USA 35.01N 99.05W
191 P17 Hobart ✈ Tasmania, SE Australia 42.52S 147.28E
Hobarton/Hobart Town see Hobart
39 W14 Hobbs New Mexico, SW USA 32.42N 103.08W
204 L12 Hobbs Coast physical region Antarctica
25 Z14 Hobe Sound Florida, SE USA 27.03N 80.08W
Hobicaurikány see Uricani
56 E12 Hobo Huila, S Colombia 2.34N 75.28W
101 G16 Hoboken Antwerpen, N Belgium 51.12N 4.22E
164 K3 Hoboksar var. Hoboksar Mongol Zizhixian. Xinjiang Uygur Zizhiqu, NW China 46.48N 85.42E
Hoboksar Mongol Zizhixian see Hoboksar
97 G21 Hobro Nordjylland, N Denmark 56.39N 9.51E
23 X10 Hobucken North Carolina, SE USA 35.15N 76.31W
97 O20 Hoburgen headland SE Sweden 56.54N 18.07E
83 P15 Hobyo It. Obbia. Mudug, E Somalia 5.16N 48.24E
111 R8 Hochalmspitze ▲ SW Austria 47.00N 13.19E
111 Q4 Hochburg Oberösterreich, N Austria 48.10N 12.57E
110 F8 Hochdorf Luzern, N Switzerland 47.10N 8.16E
111 N8 Hochfeiler It. Gran Pilastro. ▲ Austria/Italy 46.59N 11.42E
178 Jj14 Hô Chi Minh var. Ho Chi Minh City; prev. Saigon. S Vietnam 10.46N 106.43E
Ho Chi Minh City see Hô Chi Minh
110 I7 Höchst Vorarlberg, NW Austria 47.28N 9.40E
Höchstadt see Höchstadt an der Aisch
103 K19 Höchstadt an der Aisch var. Höchstadt. Bayern, C Germany 49.43N 10.48E
110 L9 Hochwilde It. L'Altissima. ▲ Austria/Italy 46.45N 11.00E
111 S7 Hochwildstelle ▲ C Austria 47.21N 13.53E
33 T14 Hocking River ≈ Ohio, N USA
Hoctúm see Hoctún
43 X12 Hoctún var. Hoctúm. Yucatán, E Mexico 20.48N 89.13W
Hodeida see Al Ḥudaydah
22 K6 Hodgenville Kentucky, S USA 37.34N 85.44W
9 T17 Hodgeville Saskatchewan, S Canada 50.06N 106.55W
78 L9 Hodh ech Chargui ◆ region E Mauritania
Hodh el Garbi see Hodh el Gharbi
78 J10 Hodh el Gharbi var. Hodh el Garbi. ◆ region S Mauritania
113 L25 Hódmezővásárhely Csongrád, SE Hungary 46.27N 20.17E
76 J6 Hodna, Chott El var. Chott el-Hodna, Ar. Shatt al-Hodna. salt lake N Algeria
Hodna, Shatt al- see Hodna, Chott El
113 G19 Hodonín Ger. Göding. Brněnský Kraj, SE Czech Republic 48.51N 17.07E
168 G6 Hödrögö Dzavhan, N Mongolia 48.51N 96.48E
Hodság/Hodschag see Odžaci
41 R7 Hodzana River ≈ Alaska, USA
Hoei see Huy
101 H19 Hoeilaart Vlaams Brabant, C Belgium 50.46N 4.28E
Hoë Karoo see Great Karoo
100 F12 Hoek van Holland Eng. Hook of Holland. Zuid-Holland, W Netherlands 52.00N 4.07E
100 L11 Hoenderloo Gelderland, E Netherlands 52.08N 5.46E
101 L18 Hoensbroek Limburg, SE Netherlands 50.55N 5.55E
169 Y11 Hoeryŏng NE North Korea 42.23N 129.46E
101 K18 Hoeselt Limburg, NE Belgium 50.49N 5.30E
100 K11 Hoevelaken Gelderland, C Netherlands 52.10N 5.27E
Hoey see Huy
103 M18 Hof Bayern, SE Germany 50.19N 11.55E
Höfdhakaupstadhur see Skagaströnd
Hofei see Hefei
103 G18 Hofheim am Taunus Hessen, W Germany 50.04N 8.27E
Hofmarkt see Odorheiu Secuiesc
94 L3 Höfn Austurland, SE Iceland 64.14N 15.17W
96 N13 Hofors Gävleborg, C Sweden 60.33N 16.21E
94 J6 Hofsjökull glacier C Iceland
94 J1 Hofsós Nordhurland Vestra, N Iceland 65.54N 19.25W
170 Dd13 Hōfu Yamaguchi, Honshū, SW Japan 34.01N 131.34E
Hofuf see Al Hufūf
97 J22 Höganäs Skåne, S Sweden 56.11N 12.39E
191 P14 Hogan Group island group Tasmania, SE Australia
25 R4 Hogansville Georgia, SE USA 33.10N 84.55W
41 P8 Hogatza River ≈ Alaska, USA
30 I14 Hogback Mountain ▲ Nebraska, C USA 41.40N 103.44W
97 G14 Høgevarde ▲ S Norway 60.19N 9.27E
Högfors see Karkkila
33 P5 Hog Island island Michigan, N USA
23 Y6 Hog Island island Virginia, NE USA
Hogoley Islands see Chuuk Islands
97 N20 Högsby Kalmar, S Sweden 57.10N 16.03E
38 K1 Hogup Mountains ▲ Utah, W USA
103 E17 Hohe Acht ▲ W Germany 50.23N 7.00E
Hohenelbe see Vrchlabí
110 I7 Hohenems Vorarlberg, W Austria 47.22N 9.43E
Hohenmauth see Vysoké Mýto
Hohensalza see Inowrocław
Hohenstadt see Zábřeh
Hohenstein in Ostpreussen see Olsztynek
22 I9 Hohenwald Tennessee, S USA 35.33N 87.33W
103 L17 Hohenwarte-Stausee ▣ C Germany
Hohes Venn see Hautes Fagnes
111 Q8 Hohe Tauern ▲ W Austria
169 O13 Hohhot var. Huhehot, Huhuohaote, Mong. Kukukhoto; prev. Kweisui, Kwesui. Nei Mongol Zizhiqu, N China 40.49N 111.37E
105 U6 Hohneck ▲ NE France 48.04N 7.01E
79 Q16 Hohoe E Ghana 7.07N 0.31E
170 D12 Hōhoku Yamaguchi, Honshū, SW Japan 34.15N 130.56E
165 O11 Hoh Sai Hu ◎ C China
165 N11 Hoh Xil Hu ◎ C China
164 L11 Hoh Xil Shan ▲ W China
178 Kk10 Hôi An prev. Faifo. Quang Nam-Đa Năng, C Vietnam 15.54N 108.19E
Hoï-Hao/Hoihow see Haikou
83 F17 Hoima W Uganda 1.25N 31.22E
28 L5 Hoisington Kansas, C USA 38.31N 98.46W
Hojagala see Khodzhakala
Hojambaz see Khodzhambas
97 H23 Højby Fyn, C Denmark 55.19N 10.27E
97 F24 Højer Sønderjylland, SW Denmark 54.57N 8.43E
170 Ee14 Hōjō var. Hôzyô. Ehime, Shikoku, SW Japan 33.58N 132.47E
192 J3 Hokianga Harbour inlet SE Tasman Sea
193 F17 Hokitika West Coast, South Island, NZ 42.43S 170.58E
172 P5 Hokkai-dō ◆ territory Hokkaidō, NE Japan
172 Oo5 Hokkaidō prev. Ezo, Yeso, Yezo. island NE Japan
97 G15 Hokksund Buskerud, S Norway 59.46N 9.54E
149 S4 Hokmābād Khorāsān, N Iran 36.37N 57.34E
Hokō see P'ohang
Hoko-guntō/Hoko-shotō see P'enghu Liehtao
Hoktemberyan see Armavir
96 F13 Hol Buskerud, S Norway 60.36N 8.18E
119 R11 Hola Prystan' Rus. Golaya Pristan. Khersons'ka Oblast', S Ukraine 46.31N 32.31E
97 I23 Holbæk Vestsjælland, E Denmark 55.42N 11.42E
168 G6 Holboo Dzavhan, W Mongolia 48.35N 95.25E
191 P10 Holbrook New South Wales, SE Australia 35.45S 147.18E
39 N11 Holbrook Arizona, SW USA 34.54N 110.09W
29 S5 Holden Missouri, C USA 38.42N 93.59W
38 K5 Holden Utah, W USA 39.06N 112.16W
29 O11 Holdenville Oklahoma, C USA 35.04N 96.24W
31 O16 Holdrege Nebraska, C USA 40.28N 99.28W
37 X3 Hole in the Mountain Peak ▲ Nevada, W USA 40.54N 115.06W
161 G20 Hole Narsipur Karnātaka, W India 12.46N 76.13E
113 H18 Holešov Ger. Holleschau. Zlínský Kraj, E Czech Republic 49.19N 17.34E
47 N14 Holetown prev. Jamestown. W Barbados 13.09N 59.37W
33 Q12 Holgate Ohio, N USA 41.12N 84.06W
46 I7 Holguín Holguín, SE Cuba 20.51N 76.16W
25 V12 Holiday Florida, SE USA 28.11N 82.44W
41 O12 Holitna River ≈ Alaska, USA
96 J13 Höljes Värmland, C Sweden 60.54N 12.34E
111 X3 Hollabrunn Niederösterreich, NE Austria 48.33N 16.06E
38 L3 Holladay Utah, W USA 40.39N 111.49W
9 X16 Holland Manitoba, S Canada 49.36N 98.52W
33 O9 Holland Michigan, N USA 42.47N 86.06W
27 T9 Holland Texas, SW USA 30.52N 97.24W
Holland see Netherlands
24 K4 Hollandale Mississippi, S USA 33.10N 90.51W
Hollandia see Jayapura
Hollandsch Diep see Hollands Diep
101 H14 Hollands Diep var. Hollandsch Diep. channel SW Netherlands
Holleschau see Holešov
27 R5 Holliday Texas, SW USA 33.49N 98.41W
20 E15 Hollidaysburg Pennsylvania, NE USA 40.24N 78.22W
23 S6 Hollins Virginia, NE USA 37.20N 79.56W
28 J12 Hollis Oklahoma, C USA 34.42N 99.54W
37 O10 Hollister California, W USA 36.51N 121.25W
29 T8 Hollister Missouri, C USA 36.37N 93.13W
95 M19 Hollola Etelä-Suomi, S Finland 60.59N 25.31E
100 K4 Hollum Friesland, N Netherlands 53.27N 5.38E
97 J23 Höllviksnäs Skåne, S Sweden 55.25N 12.57E
39 W6 Holly Colorado, C USA 38.03N 102.07W
33 R9 Holly Michigan, N USA 42.47N 83.37W
23 S14 Holly Hill South Carolina, SE USA 33.19N 80.24W
23 W11 Holly Ridge North Carolina, SE USA 34.31N 77.31W
24 L1 Holly Springs Mississippi, S USA 34.46N 89.25W
25 Z15 Hollywood Florida, SE USA 26.00N 80.09W
15 I2 Holman Victoria Island, Northwest Territories, N Canada 70.42N 117.45W
94 I2 Hólmavík Vestfirdhir, NW Iceland 65.42N 21.43W
32 J7 Holmen Wisconsin, N USA 43.57N 91.14W
25 R8 Holmes Creek ≈ Alabama/Florida, SE USA
97 H16 Holmestrand Vestfold, S Norway 59.28N 10.19E
95 J16 Holmön island N Sweden
97 E22 Holmsland Klit beach W Denmark
95 J16 Holmsund Västerbotten, N Sweden 63.42N 20.25E
97 Q18 Holmudden headland SE Sweden 57.59N 19.14E
194 L15 Holnicote Bay headland SW PNG 8.30S 148.18E
144 F10 Ḥolon var. Kholon. Tel Aviv, C Israel 32.01N 34.46E
119 P8 Holovanivs'k Rus. Golovanevsk. Kirovohrads'ka Oblast', C Ukraine 48.21N 30.26E
97 F21 Holstebro Ringkøbing, W Denmark 56.22N 8.37E
97 F23 Holsted Ribe, W Denmark 55.30N 8.54E
31 T13 Holstein Iowa, C USA 42.29N 95.32W
Holsteinborg/Holsteinsborg/Holstenborg/Holstensborg see Sisimiut
23 O8 Holston River ≈ Tennessee, S USA
33 Q9 Holt Michigan, N USA 42.38N 84.31W
100 N10 Holten Overijssel, E Netherlands 52.16N 6.25E
29 P3 Holton Kansas, C USA 39.28N 95.44W
29 U5 Holts Summit Missouri, C USA 38.38N 92.07W
37 X17 Holtville California, W USA 32.48N 115.22W
100 L5 Holwerd Fris. Holwert. Friesland, N Netherlands 53.22N 5.51E
Holwert see Holwerd
41 O11 Holy Cross Alaska, USA 62.12N 159.46W
39 R4 Holy Cross, Mount Of The ▲ Colorado, C USA 39.28N 106.28W
99 I18 Holyhead Wel. Caer Gybi. NW Wales, UK 53.19N 4.37W
99 H18 Holy Island island NW Wales, UK
98 L12 Holy Island island NE England, UK
39 W3 Holyoke Colorado, C USA 40.31N 102.18W
20 M11 Holyoke Massachusetts, NE USA 42.12N 72.37W
103 I14 Holzminden Niedersachsen, C Germany 51.49N 9.27E
83 G19 Homa Bay Nyanza, W Kenya 0.31S 34.30E
Homāyūnshahr see Khomeynīshahr
79 P11 Hombori Mopti, S Mali 15.13N 1.39W
103 E20 Homburg Saarland, SW Germany 49.19N 7.19E
16 Nn1 Home Bay bay Baffin Bay, Nunavut, NE Canada
Homenau see Humenné
41 Q13 Homer Alaska, USA 59.38N 151.33W
24 H4 Homer Louisiana, S USA 32.47N 93.03W
20 H10 Homer New York, NE USA 42.38N 76.10W
25 V7 Homerville Georgia, SE USA 31.02N 82.45W
25 Y16 Homestead Florida, SE USA 25.28N 80.28W
29 O9 Hominy Oklahoma, C USA 36.24N 96.24W
96 H8 Hommelvik Sør-Trøndelag, S Norway 63.24N 10.46E
97 C16 Hommersåk Rogaland, S Norway 58.55N 5.51E
161 H15 Homnābād Karnātaka, C India 17.46N 77.08E
24 J7 Homochitto River ≈ Mississippi, S USA
85 N20 Homoine Inhambane, SE Mozambique 23.51S 35.04E
114 O12 Homoljske Planine ▲ E Serbia and Montenegro (Yugoslavia)
Homonna see Humenné
Homs see Al Khums, Libya
Homs see Ḥimş, Syria
121 P19 Homyel' Rus. Gomel'. Homyel'skaya Voblasts', SE Belarus 52.24N 31.00E
120 L12 Homyel' Vitsyebskaya Voblasts', N Belarus 55.20N 28.52E
121 L19 Homyel'skaya Voblasts' prev. Rus. Gomel'skaya Oblast'. ◆ province SE Belarus
Honan see Henan, China
Honan see Luoyang, China
172 Pp6 Honbetsu Hokkaidō, NE Japan 43.09N 143.46E
Honctő see Gurahonț
56 E9 Honda Tolima, C Colombia 5.12N 74.45W
85 D24 Hondeklip Afr. Hondeklipbaai. Northern Cape, W South Africa 30.15S 17.17E
Hondeklipbaai see Hondeklip
9 Q13 Hondo Alberta, W Canada 54.43N 113.14W
170 C14 Hondo Kumamoto, Shimo-jima, SW Japan 32.27N 130.10E
27 Q12 Hondo Texas, SW USA 29.21N 99.08W
44 G1 Hondo ≈ Central America
Hondo see Honshū
44 G6 Honduras off. Republic of Honduras. ◆ republic Central America
Honduras, Golfo de see Honduras, Gulf of
44 H4 Honduras, Gulf of Sp. Golfo de Honduras. gulf W Caribbean Sea
9 V12 Hone Manitoba, C Canada 56.13N 101.12W
23 P12 Honea Path South Carolina, SE USA 34.27N 82.23W
97 H14 Hønefoss Buskerud, S Norway 60.10N 10.15E
33 S12 Honey Creek ≈ Ohio, N USA
27 V5 Honey Grove Texas, SW USA 33.34N 95.54W
37 Q4 Honey Lake ◎ California, W USA
104 L4 Honfleur Calvados, N France 49.25N 0.13E
Hon Gai see Hông Gai
167 O8 Hong'an prev. Huang'an. Hubei, C China 31.20N 114.43E
Hongay see Hông Gai
178 K6 Hông Gai var. Hon Gai, Hongay. Quang Ninh, N Vietnam 20.57N 107.06E
167 O15 Honghai Wan bay N South China Sea
Hông Hà, Sông see Red River
167 O7 Hong He ≈ C China
167 N9 Hong Hu ◎ C China
166 L11 Hongjiang Hunan, S China 27.09N 109.58E
167 O15 Hong Kong Chin. Xianggang. S China 22.16N 114.09E
165 P7 Hongliuyuan Gansu, N China 41.01N 95.24E
169 O9 Hongor Dornogovi, SE Mongolia 45.49N 111.20E
167 S8 Hongqiao ✈ (Shanghai) Shanghai Shi, E China 31.28N 121.08E
166 K14 Hongshui He ≈ S China
166 M5 Hongtong Shanxi, C China 36.30N 111.42E
170 G16 Hongū Wakayama, Honshū, SW Japan 33.50N 135.42E
Honguedo, Détroit d' see Honguedo Passage
13 Y5 Honguedo Passage var. Honguedo Strait, Fr. Détroit d'Honguedo. strait Quebec, E Canada
Honguedo Strait see Honguedo Passage
Hongwan see Sunan
169 X13 Hongwŏn E North Korea 40.03N 127.54E
166 H7 Hongyuan prev. Hurama. Sichuan, C China 32.49N 102.40E
167 Q7 Hongze Hu var. Hung-tse Hu. ◎ E China
195 W16 Honiara ● (Solomon Islands) Guadalcanal, C Solomon Islands 9.27S 159.55E
171 Ll11 Honjō var. Honzyô. Akita, Honshū, C Japan 39.22N 140.03E
95 K18 Honkajoki Länsi-Suomi, W Finland 62.00N 22.15E
171 Ii16 Honkawane Shizuoka, Honshū, S Japan 35.07N 138.07E
94 K7 Honningsvåg Finnmark, N Norway 70.58N 25.58E
97 I19 Hönö Västra Götaland, S Sweden 57.42N 11.39E
40 G11 Honokaa Haw. Honoka'a. Hawaii, USA, C Pacific Ocean 20.04N 155.27W
40 G11 Honokohau Haw. Honokōhau. Hawaii, USA, C Pacific Ocean 19.40N 156.01W
40 D9 Honolulu ● Oahu, Hawaii, USA, C Pacific Ocean 21.18N 157.51W
40 H11 Honomu Haw. Honomū. Hawaii, USA, C Pacific Ocean 19.51N 155.06W
107 P10 Honrubia Castilla-La Mancha, C Spain 39.36N 2.16W
171 I15 Honshū var. Hondo, Honsyû. island SW Japan
Honsyû see Honshū
Honte see Westerschelde
Honzyô see Honjō
15 E5 Hood ≈ Nunavut, NW Canada
Hood Island see Española, Isla
34 H11 Hood, Mount ▲ Oregon, NW USA 45.22N 121.41W
194 K16 Hood Point headland S PNG 10.04S 147.42E
34 H11 Hood River Oregon, NW USA 45.42N 121.31W
100 H10 Hoofddorp Noord-Holland, W Netherlands 52.18N 4.40E
101 G15 Hoogerheide Noord-Brabant, S Netherlands 51.25N 4.19E
100 N8 Hoogeveen Drenthe, NE Netherlands 52.43N 6.30E
100 O6 Hoogezand-Sappemeer Groningen, NE Netherlands 53.10N 6.46E

◆ Country ● Country Capital ◇ Dependent Territory ○ Dependent Territory Capital ◆ Administrative Region ✈ International Airport ▲ Mountain ▲ Mountain Range ⚠ Volcano ≈ River ◎ Lake ▣ Reservoir

100 J8 **Hoogkarspel** Noord-Holland, NW Netherlands 52.42N 4.59E
100 N5 **Hoogkerk** Groningen, NE Netherlands 53.13N 6.30E
100 G13 **Hoogvliet** Zuid-Holland, SW Netherlands 51.51N 4.23E
28 I8 **Hooker** Oklahoma, C USA 36.51N 101.12W
99 E21 **Hook Head** *Ir.* Rinn Duáin. *headland* SE Ireland 52.07N 6.55W
Hook of Holland *see* Hoek van Holland
168 J9 **Hoolt** Övörhangay, C Mongolia 45.31N 103.06E
41 W13 **Hoonah** Chichagof Island, Alaska, USA 58.05N 135.21W
40 L11 **Hooper Bay** Alaska, USA 61.31N 166.06W
33 N13 **Hoopeston** Illinois, N USA 40.28N 87.40W
97 K22 **Höör** Skåne, S Sweden 55.55N 13.33E
100 I9 **Hoorn** Noord-Holland, NW Netherlands 52.38N 5.04E
20 L10 **Hoosic River** ~ New York, NE USA
Hoosier State *see* Indiana
37 Y11 **Hoover Dam** *dam* Arizona/Nevada, W USA 36.01N 114.44W
168 I9 **Höövör** Övörhangay, C Mongolia 45.10N 101.19E
143 Q11 **Hopa** Artvin, NE Turkey 41.23N 41.27E
20 J14 **Hopatcong** New Jersey, NE USA 40.55N 74.39W
8 M17 **Hope** British Columbia, SW Canada 49.21N 121.28W
41 R12 **Hope** Alaska, USA 60.55N 149.38W
29 T14 **Hope** Arkansas, C USA 33.40N 93.35W
33 P14 **Hope** Indiana, N USA 39.18N 85.46W
31 Q5 **Hope** North Dakota, N USA 47.18N 97.42W
11 Q7 **Hopedale** Newfoundland and Labrador, NE Canada 55.25N 60.14W
Hopeh/Hopei *see* Hebei
188 K13 **Hope, Lake** *salt lake* Western Australia
43 X13 **Hopelchén** Campeche, SE Mexico 19.44N 89.52W
23 U11 **Hope Mills** North Carolina, SE USA 34.58N 78.57W
191 O7 **Hope, Mount** New South Wales, SE Australia 32.49S 145.55E
94 P4 **Hopen** *island* SE Svalbard
207 Q4 **Hope, Point** *headland* Alaska, USA
10 M3 **Hopes Advance, Cap** *headland* Quebec, NE Canada 61.07N 69.30W
190 L10 **Hopetoun** Victoria, SE Australia 35.46S 142.23E
85 H23 **Hopetown** Northern Cape, W South Africa 29.38S 24.06E
23 W6 **Hopewell** Virginia, NE USA 37.16N 77.15W
111 O7 **Hopfgarten-im-Brixental** Tirol, W Austria 47.28N 12.14E
189 N8 **Hopkins Lake** *salt lake* Western Australia
190 M12 **Hopkins River** ~ Victoria, SE Australia
22 I7 **Hopkinsville** Kentucky, S USA 36.52N 87.29W
36 M6 **Hopland** California, W USA 38.58N 123.09W
97 G24 **Hoptrup** Sønderjylland, SW Denmark 55.09N 9.27E
34 F9 **Hoquiam** Washington, NW USA 46.58N 123.53W
31 R6 **Horace** North Dakota, N USA 46.44N 96.54W
143 R12 **Horasan** Erzurum, NE Turkey 40.03N 42.10E
103 G22 **Horb am Neckar** Baden-Württemberg, S Germany 48.27N 8.42E
97 K23 **Hörby** Skåne, S Sweden 55.50N 13.42E
45 P16 **Horconcitos** Chiriquí, W Panama 8.17N 82.10W
97 C14 **Hordaland** ◆ *county* S Norway
118 H13 **Horezu** Vâlcea, SW Romania 45.06N 24.00E
110 G7 **Horgen** Zürich, N Switzerland 47.16N 8.36E
168 I7 **Horgo** Arhangay, C Mongolia 48.06N 99.52E
Hōrin *see* Fenglin
169 O13 **Horinger** Nei Mongol Zizhiqu, N China 40.23N 111.48E
168 I9 **Horiult** Bayanhongor, C Mongolia 45.09N 100.50E
9 U17 **Horizon** Saskatchewan, S Canada 49.33N 105.05W
199 J10 **Horizon Bank** *undersea feature* S Pacific Ocean
199 J11 **Horizon Deep** *undersea feature* W Pacific Ocean
97 L14 **Hörken** Örebro, S Sweden 60.03N 14.55E
121 O15 **Horki** *Rus.* Gorki. Mahilyowskaya Voblasts', E Belarus 54.17N 30.59E
205 O10 **Horlick Mountains** ▲▲ Antarctica
119 X7 **Horlivka** *Rom.* Adâncata, *Rus.* Gorlovka. Donets'ka Oblast', E Ukraine 48.19N 38.04E
149 V11 **Ḩormak** Sīstān va Balūchestān, SE Iran 30.00N 60.50E
149 R13 **Hormozgān** *off.* Ostān-e Hormozgān. ◆ *province* S Iran
Hormoz, Tangeh-ye *see* Hormuz, Strait of
147 W6 **Hormuz, Strait of** *var.* Strait of Ormuz, *Per.* Tangeh-ye Hormoz. *strait* Iran/Oman
111 W2 **Horn** Niederösterreich, NE Austria 48.39N 15.37E
97 M18 **Horn** Östergötland, S Sweden 57.54N 15.49E
15 Hh8 **Horn** ~ Northwest Territories, NW Canada
Hornád *see* Hernád
15 H3 **Hornaday** ~ Northwest Territories, NW Canada
94 H13 **Hornavan** ◎ N Sweden
67 C24 **Hornby Mountains** *hill range* West Falkland, Falkland Islands
Horn, Cape *see* Hornos, Cabo de
99 O18 **Horncastle** E England, UK 53.12N 0.07W
97 N14 **Horndal** Dalarna, C Sweden 60.16N 16.25E
95 I16 **Hörnefors** Västerbotten, N Sweden 63.37N 19.54E
20 F11 **Hornell** New York, NE USA 42.19N 77.38W
Horné Nové Mesto *see* Kysucké Nové Mesto
10 F12 **Hornepayne** Ontario, S Canada 49.13N 84.48W
96 D10 **Hornindalsvatnet** ◎ S Norway
103 G22 **Hornisgrinde** ▲ SW Germany 48.37N 8.13E
24 M9 **Horn Island** *island* Mississippi, S USA
65 J26 **Hornos, Cabo de** *Eng.* Cape Horn. *headland* S Chile 55.52S 67.00W
119 S10 **Hornostayivka** Khersons'ka Oblast', S Ukraine 47.00N 33.42E
191 T9 **Hornsby** New South Wales, SE Australia 33.44S 151.08E
99 O16 **Hornsea** E England, UK 53.54N 0.09W
96 O11 **Hornslandet** *peninsula* C Sweden
97 H22 **Hornslet** Århus, C Denmark 56.19N 10.19E
94 O4 **Hornsundtind** ▲ S Svalbard 76.54N 16.07E
Horochów *see* Horokhiv
118 J7 **Horodenka** *Rus.* Gorodenka. Ivano-Frankivs'ka Oblast', W Ukraine 48.41N 25.28E
119 Q2 **Horodnya** *Rus.* Gorodnya. Chernihivs'ka Oblast', NE Ukraine 51.54N 31.30E
118 K6 **Horodok** Khmel'nyts'ka Oblast', W Ukraine 49.10N 26.34E
118 H5 **Horodok** *Pol.* Gródek Jagielloński, *Rus.* Gorodok, Gorodok Yagellonski. L'vivs'ka Oblast', NW Ukraine 49.48N 23.39E
119 Q6 **Horodyshche** *Rus.* Gorodishche. Cherkas'ka Oblast', C Ukraine 49.18N 31.27E
172 P4 **Horokanai** Hokkaidō, NE Japan 44.02N 142.08E
118 J4 **Horokhiv** *Pol.* Horochów, *Rus.* Gorokhov. Volyns'ka Oblast', NW Ukraine 50.31N 24.50E
172 P7 **Horoshiri-dake** *var.* Horosiri Dake. ▲ Hokkaidō, N Japan 42.43N 142.41E
Horosiri Dake *see* Horoshiri-dake
113 C17 **Hořovice** *Ger.* Horowitz. Středočeský Kraj, W Czech Republic 49.49N 13.53E
Horowitz *see* Hořovice
169 T9 **Horqin Youyi Zhongqi** Nei Mongol Zizhiqu, NE China 45.02N 121.33E
169 U11 **Horqin Zuoyi Houqi** Nei Mongol Zizhiqu, N China 42.53N 122.22E
169 T9 **Horqin Zuoyi Zhongqi** Nei Mongol Zizhiqu, N China 45.02N 121.28E
64 O5 **Horqueta** Concepción, C Paraguay 23.23S 57.04W
57 O12 **Horqueta Minas** Amazonas, S Venezuela 2.19N 63.31W
97 J20 **Horred** Västra Götaland, S Sweden 57.22N 12.25E
157 J19 **Horsburgh Atoll** *atoll* N Maldives
22 K7 **Horse Cave** Kentucky, S USA 37.10N 85.54W
39 V6 **Horse Creek** ~ Colorado, C USA
29 S6 **Horse Creek** ~ Missouri, C USA
20 G11 **Horseheads** New York, NE USA 42.10N 76.49W
39 P13 **Horse Mount** ▲ New Mexico, SW USA 33.58N 108.10W
97 G22 **Horsens** Vejle, C Denmark 55.52N 9.52E
67 F25 **Horse Pasture Point** *headland* W Saint Helena 15.57S 5.46W
35 N13 **Horseshoe Bend** Idaho, NW USA 43.55N 116.11W
38 L13 **Horseshoe Reservoir** ▣ Arizona, SW USA
66 M9 **Horseshoe Seamounts** *undersea feature* E Atlantic Ocean
190 L11 **Horsham** Victoria, SE Australia 36.44S 142.13E
99 O23 **Horsham** SE England, UK 51.01N 0.21W
101 M15 **Horst** Limburg, SE Netherlands 51.29N 6.04E
66 N2 **Horta** Faial, Azores, Portugal, NE Atlantic Ocean 38.31N 28.39W
97 H16 **Horten** Vestfold, S Norway 59.25N 10.24E
113 M23 **Hortobágy-Berettyó** ~ E Hungary
29 Q3 **Horton** Kansas, C USA 39.39N 95.31W
15 H3 **Horton** ~ Northwest Territories, NW Canada
97 I23 **Hørve** Vestsjælland, E Denmark 55.46N 11.28E
97 L22 **Hörvik** Blekinge, S Sweden 56.01N 14.45E
144 E11 **Horvot Haluza** *var.* Khorvot Khalutsa. *ruins* Southern, S Israel 30.49N 34.50E
12 E7 **Horwood Lake** ◎ Ontario, S Canada
118 K4 **Horyn'** *Rus.* Goryn. ~ NW Ukraine
83 I14 **Hosa'ina** *var.* Hosseina, *It.* Hosanna. Southern, S Ethiopia 7.38N 37.58E
Hosanna *see* Hosa'ina
103 H18 **Hösbach** Bayern, C Germany 50.00N 9.12E
Hose Mountains *see* Hose, Pegunungan
174 Mm6 **Hose, Pegunungan** *var.* Hose Mountains. ▲▲ East Malaysia
154 L15 **Hoshāb** Baluchistān, SW Pakistan 26.01N 63.51E
160 H10 **Hoshangābād** Madhya Pradesh, C India 22.43N 77.45E
118 L4 **Hoshcha** Rivnens'ka Oblast', NW Ukraine 50.37N 26.38E
158 I7 **Hoshiārpur** Punjab, NW India 31.35N 75.57E
168 J7 **Höshööt** Arhangay, C Mongolia 48.06N 102.34E
101 M23 **Hosingen** Diekirch, NE Luxembourg 50.01N 6.04E
195 N12 **Hoskins** New Britain, E PNG 5.28S 150.25E
161 G17 **Hospet** Karnātaka, C India 15.16N 76.19E
106 K4 **Hospital de Orbigo** Castilla-León, N Spain 42.27N 5.52W
Hospitalet *see* L'Hospitalet de Llobregat
94 N13 **Hossa** Oulu, E Finland 65.28N 29.36E
Hosseina *see* Hosa'ina
Hosszúmezjő *see* Câmpulung Moldovenesc
65 I25 **Hoste, Isla** *island* S Chile
119 O4 **Hostomel'** *Rus.* Gostomel'. Kyyivs'ka Oblast', N Ukraine 50.40N 30.15E
161 H20 **Hosūr** Tamil Nādu, SE India 12.45N 77.51E
178 H8 **Hot** Chiang Mai, NW Thailand 18.07N 98.35E
164 G10 **Hotan** *var.* Khotan, *Chin.* Ho-t'ien. Xinjiang Uygur Zizhiqu, NW China 37.10N 79.51E
164 H9 **Hotan He** ~ NW China
85 G22 **Hotazel** Northern Cape, N South Africa 27.12S 22.58E
39 Q5 **Hotchkiss** Colorado, C USA 38.47N 107.43W
37 V7 **Hot Creek Range** ▲▲ Nevada, W USA
Hote *see* Hoti
176 U11 **Hoti** *var.* Hote. Pulau Seram, E Indonesia 2.58S 130.19E
Ho-t'ien *see* Hotan
Hotin *see* Khotyn
95 H15 **Hoting** Jämtland, C Sweden 64.07N 16.14E
168 L14 **Hotong Qagan Nur** ◎ N China
168 J8 **Hotont** Arhangay, C Mongolia 47.21N 102.27E
29 T12 **Hot Springs** Arkansas, C USA 34.30N 93.03W
30 J11 **Hot Springs** South Dakota, N USA 43.25N 103.28W
23 S5 **Hot Springs** Virginia, NE USA 38.00N 79.50W
37 Q4 **Hot Springs Peak** ▲ California, W USA 40.23N 120.06W
29 T12 **Hot Springs Village** Arkansas, C USA 34.39N 93.03W
Hotspur Bank *see* Hotspur Seamount
67 J16 **Hotspur Seamount** *var.* Hotspur Bank. *undersea feature* C Atlantic Ocean 18.00S 35.00W
15 Hh6 **Hottah Lake** ◎ Northwest Territories, NW Canada
46 K9 **Hotte, Massif de la** ▲▲ SW Haiti
101 K21 **Hotton** Luxembourg, SE Belgium 50.18N 5.25E
Hötzing *see* Haţeg
197 I6 **Houaïlou** Province Nord, C New Caledonia 21.17S 165.37E
76 K5 **Houari Boumediène** ✕ (Alger) N Algeria 36.38N 3.15E
178 Hh6 **Houayxay** *var.* Ban Houayxay, Ban Houei Sai. Bokèo, N Laos 20.16N 100.27E
105 N5 **Houdan** Yvelines, N France 48.48N 1.36E
101 F20 **Houdeng-Goegnies** *var.* Houdeng-Gœgnies. Hainaut, S Belgium 50.28N 4.10E
104 K14 **Houeillès** Lot-et-Garonne, SW France 44.15N 0.02E
101 L22 **Houffalize** Luxembourg, SE Belgium 50.08N 5.47E
32 M3 **Houghton** Michigan, N USA 47.06N 88.34W
33 Q7 **Houghton Lake** Michigan, N USA 44.18N 84.45W
33 Q7 **Houghton Lake** ◎ Michigan, N USA
21 T3 **Houlton** Maine, NE USA 46.09N 67.49W
166 M5 **Houma** Shanxi, C China 35.33N 111.19E
200 Q15 **Houma** 'Eua, C Tonga 21.10S 175.17W
200 R16 **Houma** Tongatapu, S Tonga 21.18S 174.55W
24 J10 **Houma** Louisiana, S USA 29.34N 90.43W
200 Qq16 **Houma Taloa** *headland* Tongatapu, S Tonga 21.16S 175.07W
79 O13 **Houndé** SW Burkina 11.34N 3.31W
104 J12 **Hourtin-Carcans, Lac d'** ◎ SW France
38 J5 **House Range** ▲▲ Utah, W USA
8 K13 **Houston** British Columbia, SW Canada 54.24N 126.39W
41 R11 **Houston** Alaska, USA 61.37N 149.50W
31 X10 **Houston** Minnesota, N USA 43.45N 91.34W
24 M3 **Houston** Mississippi, S USA 33.54N 89.00W
29 V7 **Houston** Missouri, C USA 37.19N 91.57W
27 W11 **Houston** Texas, SW USA 29.45N 95.21W
27 W11 **Houston** ✕ Texas, SW USA 30.03N 95.18W
100 J12 **Houten** Utrecht, C Netherlands 52.01N 5.10E
101 K17 **Houthalen** Limburg, NE Belgium 51.01N 5.22E
101 I22 **Houyet** Namur, SE Belgium 50.10N 5.00E
97 H22 **Hov** Århus, C Denmark 55.54N 10.13E
97 L17 **Hova** Västra Götaland, S Sweden 58.52N 14.13E
168 E6 **Hovd** *var.* Khovd. Hovd, W Mongolia 47.58N 91.40E
168 J10 **Hovd** Övörhangay, C Mongolia 44.43N 102.08E
168 E7 **Hovd** ◆ *province* W Mongolia
168 C5 **Hovd Gol** ~ NW Mongolia
99 O23 **Hove** SE England, UK 50.49N 0.10W
31 N8 **Hoven** South Dakota, N USA 45.12N 99.47W
118 I8 **Hoverla, Hora** *Rus.* Gora Goverla. ▲ W Ukraine 48.09N 24.30E
168 H8 **Höviyn Am** Bayanhongor, C Mongolia 47.08N 98.41E
97 M21 **Hovmantorp** Kronoberg, S Sweden 56.46N 15.07E
169 N11 **Hövsgöl** Dornogovĭ, SE Mongolia 43.35N 109.40E
168 I5 **Hövsgöl** ◆ *province* N Mongolia
Hövsgöl, Lake *see* Hövsgöl Nuur
168 J5 **Hövsgöl Nuur** *var.* Lake Hovsgol. ◎ N Mongolia
80 L9 **Howa, Ouadi** *var.* Wādi Howar. ~ Chad/Sudan *see also* Howar, Wādi
29 P7 **Howard** Kansas, C USA 37.28N 96.15W
31 Q10 **Howard** South Dakota, N USA 43.58N 97.31W
27 N10 **Howard Draw** *valley* Texas, SW USA
31 U8 **Howard Lake** Minnesota, N USA 45.03N 94.03W
82 B8 **Howar, Wādi** *var.* Ouadi Howa. ~ Chad/Sudan *see also* Howa, Ouadi
27 U5 **Howe** Texas, SW USA 33.29N 96.38W
191 R12 **Howe, Cape** *headland* New South Wales/Victoria, SE Australia 37.30S 149.58E
33 R9 **Howell** Michigan, N USA 42.36N 83.55W
30 L9 **Howes** South Dakota, N USA 44.34N 102.03W
85 K23 **Howick** KwaZulu/Natal, E South Africa 29.29S 30.13E
Howrah *see* Hāora
29 W9 **Hoxie** Arkansas, C USA 36.03N 90.58W
28 J3 **Hoxie** Kansas, C USA 39.21N 100.26W
103 I14 **Höxter** Nordrhein-Westfalen, W Germany 51.46N 9.22E
164 K6 **Hoxud** Xinjiang Uygur Zizhiqu, NW China 42.18N 86.51E
98 J5 **Hoy** *island* N Scotland, UK
45 S17 **Hoya, Cerro** ▲ S Panama 7.22N 80.38W
96 D12 **Høyanger** Sogn og Fjordane, S Norway 61.13N 6.04E
103 P15 **Hoyerswerda** Sachsen, E Germany 51.27N 14.17E
170 Dd15 **Hōyo-kaikyō** *var.* Hayasui-seto. *strait* SW Japan
106 J8 **Hoyos** Extremadura, W Spain 40.10N 6.43W
31 W4 **Hoyt Lakes** Minnesota, N USA 47.31N 92.08W
89 V2 **Hoyvík** Streymoy, N Faeroe Islands
143 O14 **Hozat** Tunceli, E Turkey 39.09N 39.13E
Hōzyō *see* Hōjō
113 F16 **Hradec Králové** *Ger.* Königgrätz. Hradecký Kraj, N Czech Republic 50.13N 15.49E
113 E16 **Hradecký Kraj** ◆ *region* N Czech Republic
113 B16 **Hradiště** *Ger.* Burgstadlberg. ▲ NW Czech Republic 50.12N 13.04E
119 R6 **Hradyz'k** *Rus.* Gradizhsk. Poltavs'ka Oblast', NE Ukraine 49.12N 33.08E
121 M16 **Hradzyanka** *Rus.* Grodzyanka. Mahilyowskaya Voblasts', E Belarus 53.36N 28.47E
121 F16 **Hrandzichy** *Rus.* Grandichi. Hrodzyenskaya Voblasts', W Belarus 53.43N 23.50E
113 H18 **Hranice** *Ger.* Mährisch-Weisskirchen. Olomoucký Kraj, E Czech Republic 49.34N 17.45E
114 I13 **Hrasnica** Federacija Bosna I Hercegovina, SE Bosnia and Herzegovina 43.48N 18.19E
111 V11 **Hrastnik** C Slovenia 46.09N 15.08E
143 U12 **Hrazdan** *Rus.* Razdan. C Armenia 40.30N 44.50E
143 T12 **Hrazdan** *var.* Zanga, *Rus.* Razdan. ~ C Armenia
119 R5 **Hrebinka** *Rus.* Grebenka. Poltavs'ka Oblast', NE Ukraine 50.08N 32.27E
121 K17 **Hresk** *Rus.* Gresk. Minskaya Voblasts', C Belarus 53.10N 27.28E
Hrisoupoli *see* Chrysoúpoli
121 F16 **Hrodna** *Pol.* Grodno. Hrodzyenskaya Voblasts', W Belarus 53.40N 23.50E
121 F16 **Hrodzyenskaya Voblasts'** *prev. Rus.* Grodnenskaya Oblast'. ◆ *province* W Belarus
113 J21 **Hron** *Ger.* Gran, *Hung.* Garam. ~ C Slovakia
113 Q14 **Hrubieszów** *Rus.* Grubeshov. Lubelskie, E Poland 50.48N 23.54E
114 F13 **Hrvace** Split-Dalmacija, SE Croatia 43.46N 16.35E
Hrvatska *see* Croatia
114 F10 **Hrvatska Kostajnica** *var.* Kostajnica. Sisak-Moslavina, C Croatia 45.14N 16.35E
Hrvatsko Grahovo *see* Bosansko Grahovo
118 K6 **Hrymayliv** *Pol.* Gízymałów, *Rus.* Grimaylov. Ternopil's'ka Oblast', W Ukraine 49.18N 26.02E
178 H4 **Hsenwi** Shan State, E Myanmar 23.20N 97.59E
Hsia-men *see* Xiamen
Hsiang-t'an *see* Xiangtan
Hsi Chiang *see* Xi Jiang
178 Gg6 **Hsihseng** Shan State, C Myanmar 20.07N 97.16E
167 S13 **Hsinchu** *municipality* N Taiwan 24.51N 121.01E
Hsing-k'ai Hu *see* Khanka, Lake
Hsi-ning/Hsining *see* Xining
Hsinking *see* Changchun
Hsin-yang *see* Xinyang
167 S14 **Hsinying** *var.* Sinying, *Jap.* Shinei. C Taiwan 23.12N 120.15E
178 Gg4 **Hsipaw** Shan State, C Myanmar 22.36N 97.16E
Hsu-chou *see* Xuzhou
167 S13 **Hsüeh Shan** ▲ N Taiwan
Hu *see* Shanghai Shi
85 B18 **Huab** ~ W Namibia
59 M21 **Huacaya** Chuquisaca, S Bolivia 20.55S 63.24W
59 J19 **Huachacalla** Oruro, SW Bolivia 19.01S 68.22W
165 X9 **Huachi** *var.* Rouyuanchengzi. Gansu, C China 36.24N 107.58E
59 N16 **Huachi, Laguna** ◎ N Bolivia
59 D14 **Huacho** Lima, W Peru 11.09S 77.37W
169 Y8 **Huachuan** Heilongjiang, NE China 46.21N 130.43E
169 P12 **Huade** Nei Mongol Zizhiqu, N China 41.52N 113.58E
169 W10 **Huadian** Jilin, NE China 42.58N 126.37E
58 E13 **Huagaruncho, Cordillera** ▲▲ C Peru
Hua Hin *see* Ban Hua Hin
203 S10 **Huahine** *island* Îles Sous le Vent, W French Polynesia
Huahua, Rio *see* Wawa, Río
178 Ii9 **Huai** ~ E Thailand
167 P6 **Huaibei** Anhui, E China 34.00N 116.48E
Huaide *see* Gongzhuling
163 T10 **Huai He** ~ C China
166 L11 **Huaihua** Hunan, S China 27.36N 109.56E
167 N14 **Huaiji** Guangdong, S China 23.54N 112.12E
167 O2 **Huailai** *prev.* Shacheng. Hebei, E China 40.22N 115.34E
167 P7 **Huainan** *var.* Huai-nan, Hwainan. Anhui, E China 32.36N 116.56E
167 N2 **Huairen** Shanxi, C China 35.28N 110.29E
167 O7 **Huaiyang** Henan, C China 33.39N 114.34E
167 Q7 **Huaiyin** *var.* Qingjiang. Jiangsu, E China 33.33N 119.03E
178 Gg16 **Huai Yot** Trang, SW Thailand 7.45N 99.36E
43 Q15 **Huajuapan** *var.* Huajuapan de León. Oaxaca, SE Mexico 17.49N 97.48W
Huajuapan de León *see* Huajuapan
43 O9 **Hualahuises** Nuevo León, NE Mexico 24.55N 99.44W
38 I11 **Hualapai Mountains** ▲▲ Arizona, SW USA
38 I11 **Hualapai Peak** ▲ Arizona, SW USA 35.04N 113.54W
64 J7 **Hualfín** Catamarca, N Argentina 27.15S 66.52W
167 T13 **Hualien** *var.* Hwalien, *Jap.* Karen. C Taiwan 23.58N 121.34E
58 E10 **Huallaga, Río** ~ N Peru
58 C11 **Huamachuco** La Libertad, C Peru 7.50S 78.03W
43 Q14 **Huamantla** Tlaxcala, S Mexico 19.18N 97.57W
84 C13 **Huambo** *Port.* Nova Lisboa. Huambo, C Angola 12.48S 15.45E
84 B13 **Huambo** ◆ *province* C Angola
43 P15 **Huamuxtitlán** Guerrero, S Mexico 17.49N 98.34W
65 H17 **Huancache, Sierra** ▲▲ SW Argentina
59 I17 **Huancané** Puno, SE Peru 15.15S 69.47W
59 F16 **Huancapi** Ayacucho, C Peru 13.36S 74.09W
59 E15 **Huancavelica** Huancavelica, SW Peru 12.45S 75.03W
59 E15 **Huancavelica** *off.* Departamento de Huancavelica. ◆ *department* W Peru
59 E14 **Huancayo** Junín, C Peru 12.03S 75.13W
59 K20 **Huanchaca, Cerro** ▲ S Bolivia 20.12S 66.35W
58 C12 **Huandoy, Nevado** ▲ W Peru 8.48S 77.33W
167 O8 **Huangchuan** Henan, C China 32.08N 115.03E
Huang Hai *see* Yellow Sea
163 Q8 **Huang He** *var.* Yellow River. ~ C China
167 Q4 **Huanghe Kou** *delta* E China
166 L5 **Huangling** Shaanxi, C China 35.34N 109.12E
167 O9 **Huangpi** Hubei, C China 30.53N 114.16E
169 P13 **Huangqi Hai** ◎ N China
167 Q9 **Huang Shan** ▲ Anhui, E China 29.43N 118.19E
167 Q9 **Huangshan** *var.* Tunxi. Anhui, E China 29.48N 118.17E
167 O9 **Huangshi** *var.* Huang-shih, Hwangshih. Hubei, C China 30.14N 115.00E
Huang-shih *see* Huangshi
166 L5 **Huangtu Gaoyuan** *plateau* C China
63 B22 **Huanguelén** Buenos Aires, E Argentina 37.01S 61.57W
167 S10 **Huangyan** Zhejiang, SE China 28.42N 121.13E
165 T10 **Huangyuan** Qinghai, C China 36.40N 101.12E
165 T10 **Huangzhong** Qinghai, C China 36.31N 101.32E
169 W12 **Huanren** Liaoning, NE China 41.16N 125.25E
59 F15 **Huanta** Ayacucho, C Peru 12.54S 74.13W
58 E13 **Huánuco** Huánuco, C Peru 9.57S 76.15W
58 D13 **Huánuco** *off.* Departamento de Huánuco. ◆ *department* C Peru
59 K19 **Huanuni** Oruro, W Bolivia 18.15S 66.54W
165 X9 **Huan Xian** Gansu, C China 36.30N 107.20E
167 S12 **Huap'ing Yu** *island* N Taiwan
64 H3 **Huara** Tarapacá, N Chile 19.59S 69.42W
59 D14 **Huaral** Lima, W Peru 11.28S 77.12W
Huarás *see* Huaraz
58 D13 **Huaraz** *var.* Huarás. Ancash, W Peru 9.30S 77.31W
59 I16 **Huari Huari, Río** ~ S Peru
58 C13 **Huarmey** Ancash, W Peru 10.03S 78.09W
42 H4 **Huásabas** Sonora, NW Mexico 29.46N 109.18W
58 D8 **Huasaga, Río** ~ Ecuador/Peru
178 H16 **Hua Sai** Nakhon Si Thammarat, SW Thailand 8.01N 100.18E
58 D12 **Huascarán, Nevado** ▲ W Peru 9.01S 77.27W
64 G8 **Huasco** Atacama, N Chile 28.28S 71.12W
64 G8 **Huasco, Río** ~ C Chile
165 S11 **Huashikia** Qinghai, W China
42 G7 **Huatabampo** Sonora, NW Mexico 26.49N 109.40W
165 W10 **Huating** Gansu, C China 35.13N 106.39E
178 Jj7 **Huatt, Phou** ▲ N Vietnam 19.45N 104.48E
43 Q14 **Huatusco** *var.* Huatusco de Chicuellar. Veracruz-Llave, C Mexico 19.13N 96.57W
Huatusco de Chicuellar *see* Huatusco
43 P13 **Huauchinango** Puebla, S Mexico 20.12N 98.03W
Huaunta *see* Wounta
43 R15 **Huautla** *var.* Huautla de Jiménez. Oaxaca, SE Mexico 18.10N 96.51W
Huautla de Jiménez *see* Huautla
167 O5 **Huaxian** *var.* Daokou, Hua Xian. Henan, C China 35.33N 114.30E
31 V13 **Hubbard** Iowa, C USA 42.18N 93.18W
27 U8 **Hubbard** Texas, SW USA 31.52N 96.43W
27 Q6 **Hubbard Creek Lake** ◎ Texas, SW USA
33 R6 **Hubbard Lake** ◎ Michigan, N USA
166 M9 **Hubei** *var.* E, Hubei Sheng, Hupeh, Hupei. ◆ *province* C China
Hubei Sheng *see* Hubei
111 P8 **Huben** Tirol, W Austria 46.55N 12.35E
33 R13 **Huber Heights** Ohio, N USA 39.50N 84.07W
161 F17 **Hubli** Karnātaka, SW India 15.19N 75.13E
169 X12 **Huch'ang** N North Korea 41.24N 127.04E
99 M18 **Hucknall** C England, UK 53.01N 1.10W
99 L17 **Huddersfield** N England, UK 53.39N 1.46W
97 O16 **Huddinge** Stockholm, C Sweden 59.15N 17.57E
96 N11 **Hudiksvall** Gävleborg, C Sweden 61.45N 17.12E
31 W13 **Hudson** Iowa, C USA 42.24N 92.27W
21 O11 **Hudson** Massachusetts, NE USA 42.24N 71.34W
33 Q11 **Hudson** Michigan, N USA 41.51N 84.21W
32 H6 **Hudson** Wisconsin, N USA 44.58N 92.43W
9 V14 **Hudson Bay** Saskatchewan, S Canada 58.13N 90.48W
10 G6 **Hudson Bay** *bay* NE Canada
205 T16 **Hudson, Cape** *headland* Antarctica 68.15S 154.00E
Hudson, Détroit d' *see* Hudson Strait
29 Q9 **Hudson, Lake** ▣ Oklahoma, C USA
20 K9 **Hudson River** ~ New Jersey/New York, NE USA
8 M12 **Hudson's Hope** British Columbia, W Canada 56.03N 121.58W
10 L2 **Hudson Strait** *Fr.* Détroit d'Hudson. *strait* Nunavut/Quebec, NE Canada
Hudūd ash Shamālīyah, Minṭaqat al *see* Al Ḥudūd ash Shamālīyah
Hudur *see* Xuddur
178 K9 **Huê** Thưa Thiên-Huê, C Vietnam 16.28N 107.34E
106 J7 **Huebra** ~ W Spain
26 H8 **Hueco Mountains** ▲▲ Texas, SW USA
118 G10 **Huedin** *Hung.* Bánffyhunyad. Cluj, NW Romania 46.51N 23.01E
42 J10 **Huehuento, Cerro** ▲ C Mexico 24.04N 105.42W
44 B5 **Huehuetenango** Huehuetenango, W Guatemala 15.19N 91.25W
44 B4 **Huehuetenango** *off.* Departamento de Huehuetenango. ◆ *department* W Guatemala
42 L11 **Huejuquilla** Jalisco, SW Mexico 22.40N 103.52W
43 P12 **Huejutla** *var.* Huejutla de Reyes. Hidalgo, C Mexico 21.08N 98.16W
Huejutla de Reyes *see* Huejutla
104 G6 **Huelgoat** Finistère, NW France 48.22N 3.45W
107 O13 **Huelma** Andalucía, S Spain 37.39N 3.28W
106 I14 **Huelva** *anc.* Onuba. Andalucía, SW Spain 37.15N 6.55W
106 I13 **Huelva** ◆ *province* Andalucía, SW Spain
106 J13 **Huelva** ~ SW Spain
107 Q14 **Huercal-Overa** Andalucía, S Spain 37.22N 1.55W
39 Q9 **Huerfano Mountain** ▲ New Mexico, SW USA 36.25N 107.50W
39 T7 **Huerfano River** ~ Colorado, C USA
107 S12 **Huertas, Cabo** *headland* SE Spain 38.21N 0.25W
107 R6 **Huerva** ~ N Spain
107 S4 **Huesca** *anc.* Osca. Aragón, NE Spain 42.07N 0.25W
107 T4 **Huesca** ◆ *province* Aragón, NE Spain
107 P13 **Huéscar** Andalucía, S Spain 37.39N 2.31W
43 N15 **Huetamo** *var.* Huetamo de Núñez. Michoacán de Ocampo, SW Mexico 18.37N 100.53W
Huetamo de Núñez *see* Huetamo
107 P8 **Huete** Castilla-La Mancha, C Spain 40.07N 2.40W
25 P4 **Hueytown** Alabama, S USA 33.27N 87.00W
30 L16 **Hugh Butler Lake** ▣ Nebraska, C USA
189 V6 **Hughenden** Queensland, NE Australia 20.56S 144.15E
190 A6 **Hughes** South Australia 30.41S 129.31E
41 P8 **Hughes** Alaska, USA 66.03N 154.15W
29 X11 **Hughes** Arkansas, C USA 34.57N 90.28W
27 W6 **Hughes Springs** Texas, SW USA 33.00N 94.37W
39 V5 **Hugo** Colorado, C USA 39.08N 103.28W
29 Q13 **Hugo** Oklahoma, C USA 34.01N 95.31W
29 Q13 **Hugo Lake** ▣ Oklahoma, C USA
28 H7 **Hugoton** Kansas, C USA 37.10N 101.21W
Huhehot/Huhuohaote *see* Hohhot
167 R13 **Hui'an** Fujian, SE China 25.06N 118.45E
192 O9 **Huiarau Range** ▲▲ North Island, NZ
85 D22 **Huib-Hoch Plateau** *plateau* S Namibia
43 O13 **Huichapán** Hidalgo, C Mexico 20.22N 99.42W
Huicheng *see* Shexian
169 W13 **Hŭich'ŏn** C North Korea 40.09N 126.17E
56 E12 **Huila** *off.* Departamento del Huila. ◆ *province* S Colombia
85 B15 **Huíla** ◆ *province* SW Angola
56 D11 **Huila, Nevado del** *elevation* C Colombia 2.56N 75.59W
85 B15 **Huíla Plateau** *plateau* S Angola
166 G12 **Huili** Sichuan, C China 26.39N 102.13E
167 P4 **Huimin** Shandong, E China 37.28N 117.30E
169 W11 **Huinan** *var.* Chaoyang. Jilin, NE China 42.40N 126.03E
64 K12 **Huinca Renancó** Córdoba, C Argentina 34.51S 64.22W
165 V10 **Huining** Gansu, C China 35.42N 105.01E
166 J12 **Huishui** Guizhou, S China 26.07N 106.39E
104 L6 **Huisne** ~ NW France
100 L12 **Huissen** Gelderland, SE Netherlands 51.57N 5.57E
165 N11 **Huiten Nur** ◎ C China
95 K19 **Huittinen** Länsi-Suomi, W Finland 61.10N 22.40E
43 O15 **Huitzuco** *var.* Huitzuco de los Figueroa. Guerrero, S Mexico 18.18N 99.22W
Huitzuco de los Figueroa *see* Huitzuco
165 W11 **Huixian** *var.* Hui Xian. Gansu, C China 33.48N 106.02E
43 V17 **Huixtla** Chiapas, SE Mexico 15.07N 92.29W
166 H12 **Huize** Yunnan, SW China 26.28N 103.18E
100 J10 **Huizen** Noord-Holland, C Netherlands 52.16N 5.15E
167 O14 **Huizhou** Guangdong, S China 23.05N 114.22E
168 J6 **Hujirt** Arhangay, C Mongolia 48.49N 101.20E
168 J8 **Hujirt** Övörhangay, C Mongolia 46.50N 102.38E
168 K8 **Hujrt** Töv, C Mongolia 46.41N 104.40E
Hukagawa *see* Fukagawa
Hŭksan-chedo *see* Hŭksan-gundo
169 W17 **Hŭksan-gundo** *var.* Hŭksan-chedo. *island group* SW South Korea
Hukue *see* Fukue
Hukui *see* Fukui
85 G20 **Hukuntsi** Kgalagadi, SW Botswana 23.58S 21.43E
Hukuoka *see* Fukuoka
Hukusima *see* Fukushima
Hukutiyama *see* Fukuchiyama
Hukuyama *see* Fukuyama
169 W8 **Hulan** Heilongjiang, NE China 45.58N 126.37E
169 W8 **Hulan He** ~ NE China
33 Q4 **Hulbert Lake** ◎ Michigan, N USA
Hulczyn *see* Hlučín
169 Z8 **Hulin** Heilongjiang, NE China 45.48N 133.06E
169 S9 **Hulingol** *prev.* Huolin Gol. Nei Mongol Zizhiqu, N China 45.35N 119.53E
12 L12 **Hull** Quebec, SE Canada 45.25N 75.45W
31 S12 **Hull** Iowa, C USA 43.11N 96.07W
Hull *see* Kingston upon Hull
Hull Island *see* Orona
101 F16 **Hulst** Zeeland, SW Netherlands 51.16N 4.03E
169 Q7 **Hulstay** Dornod, NE Mongolia 48.25N 114.56E
Hultschin *see* Hlučín
97 M19 **Hultsfred** Kalmar, S Sweden 57.30N 15.49E
Hulun *see* Hailar
Hu-lun Ch'ih *see* Hulun Nur
169 Q6 **Hulun Nur** *var.* Hu-lun Ch'ih; *prev.* Dalai Nor. ◎ NE China
Hulwan/Hulwân *see* Helwân
119 V8 **Hulyaypole** *Rus.* Gulyaypole. Zaporiz'ka Oblast', SE Ukraine 47.41N 36.10E
169 V4 **Huma** Heilongjiang, NE China 51.40N 126.38E
47 V6 **Humacao** E Puerto Rico 18.09N 65.49W
169 U4 **Huma He** ~ NE China
64 J5 **Humahuaca** Jujuy, N Argentina 23.13S 65.19W
61 E14 **Humaitá** Amazonas, N Brazil 7.33S 63.01W
64 N7 **Humaitá** Ñeembucú, S Paraguay 27.06S 58.28W
85 H26 **Humansdorp** Eastern Cape, S South Africa 34.01S 24.45E
29 S6 **Humansville** Missouri, C USA 37.47N 93.34W
42 I8 **Humaya, Río** ~ C Mexico
85 C16 **Humbe** Cunene, SW Angola 16.37S 14.52E
99 N17 **Humber** *estuary* E England, UK
99 N17 **Humberside** *cultural region* E England, UK
Humberto *see* Umberto
27 W11 **Humble** Texas, SW USA 29.58N 95.15W
9 U15 **Humboldt** Saskatchewan, S Canada 52.13N 105.09W
31 U12 **Humboldt** Iowa, C USA 42.42N 94.13W
29 Q6 **Humboldt** Kansas, C USA 37.48N 95.26W
31 S17 **Humboldt** Nebraska, C USA 40.09N 95.56W
37 S3 **Humboldt** Nevada, W USA 40.36N 118.15W
22 G9 **Humboldt** Tennessee, S USA 35.49N 88.55W
36 K3 **Humboldt Bay** *bay* California, W USA
37 S4 **Humboldt Lake** ◎ Nevada, W USA

◆ Country ● Country Capital ◇ Dependent Territory ○ Dependent Territory Capital ◆ Administrative Region ✕ International Airport ▲ Mountain ▲▲ Mountain Range Volcano ~ River ◎ Lake ▣ Reservoir

197 J7 **Humboldt, Mont** ▲ S New Caledonia 21.57S 166.24E
37 S4 **Humboldt River** ≈ Nevada, W USA
37 T5 **Humboldt Salt Marsh** *wetland* Nevada, W USA
191 P11 **Hume, Lake** ◎ New South Wales/Victoria, SE Australia
113 N19 **Humenné** *Ger.* Homenau, *Hung.* Homonna. Prešovský Kraj, E Slovakia 48.57N 21.54E
31 V15 **Humeston** Iowa, C USA 40.51N 93.30W
56 J5 **Humocaro Bajo** Lara, N Venezuela 9.42N 70.02W
31 Q14 **Humphrey** Nebraska, C USA 41.38N 97.29W
37 S9 **Humphreys, Mount** ▲ California, W USA 37.11N 118.39W
38 L11 **Humphreys Peak** ▲ Arizona, SW USA 35.18N 111.40W
113 E17 **Humpolec** *Ger.* Gumpolds, Humpoletz. Jihlavský Kraj, C Czech Republic 49.33N 15.22E
Humpoletz *see* Humpolec
95 K19 **Humppila** Etelä-Suomi, S Finland 60.54N 23.21E
34 F8 **Humptulips** Washington, NW USA 47.13N 123.57W
44 H7 **Humuya, Río** ≈ W Honduras
77 P9 **Hūn** N Libya 29.06N 15.56E
Hunabasi *see* Funabashi
94 I1 **Húnaflói** *bay* NW Iceland
166 M11 **Hunan** *var.* Hunan Sheng, Xiang. ◐ *province* S China
Hunan Sheng *see* Hunan
169 Y10 **Hunchun** Jilin, NE China 42.51N 130.21E
97 I22 **Hundested** Frederiksborg, E Denmark 55.58N 11.52E
Hundred Mile House *see* 100 Mile House
118 G12 **Hunedoara** *Ger.* Eisenmarkt, *Hung.* Vajdahunyad. Hunedoara, SW Romania 45.45N 22.54E
118 G12 **Hunedoara** ◐ *county* W Romania
103 I17 **Hünfeld** Hessen, C Germany 50.40N 9.46E
113 H23 **Hungary** *off.* Republic of Hungary, *Ger.* Ungarn, *Hung.* Magyarország, *Rom.* Ungaria, *SCr.* Madarska, *Ukr.* Uhorshchyna; *prev.* Hungarian People's Republic. ◆ *republic* C Europe
Hungary, Plain of *see* Great Hungarian Plain
168 F6 **Hungiy** Dzavhan, W Mongolia 48.31N 94.15E
169 X13 **Hŭngnam** E North Korea 39.50N 127.36E
35 P8 **Hungry Horse Reservoir** ⊠ Montana, NW USA
Hungt'ou *see* Lan Yü
Hung-tse Hu *see* Hongze Hu
178 Jj6 **Hưng Yên** Hai Hưng, N Vietnam 20.37N 106.04E
Hunjiang *see* Baishan
97 I18 **Hunnebostrand** Västra Götaland, S Sweden 58.26N 11.19E
103 E19 **Hunsrück** ▲▲ W Germany
99 P18 **Hunstanton** E England, UK 52.57N 0.28E
161 G20 **Hunsūr** Karnātaka, E India 12.18N 76.15E
168 I7 **Hunt** Arhangay, C Mongolia 47.49N 99.24E
102 G12 **Hunte** ≈ NW Germany
31 Q5 **Hunter** North Dakota, N USA 47.10N 97.11W
27 S11 **Hunter** Texas, SW USA 29.47N 98.01W
193 D20 **Hunter** ≈ South Island, NZ
191 N15 **Hunter Island** *island* Tasmania, SE Australia
20 K11 **Hunter Mountain** ▲ New York, NE USA 42.10N 74.13W
193 B23 **Hunter Mountains** ▲▲ South Island, NZ
191 S7 **Hunter River** ≈ New South Wales, SE Australia
34 L7 **Hunters** Washington, NW USA 48.07N 118.13W
193 F20 **Hunters Hills, The** *hill range* South Island, NZ
192 M12 **Hunterville** Manawatu-Wanganui, North Island, NZ 39.55S 175.34E
33 N16 **Huntingburg** Indiana, N USA 38.18N 86.57W
99 O20 **Huntingdon** E England, UK 52.19N 0.12W
20 E15 **Huntingdon** Pennsylvania, NE USA 40.28N 78.00W
22 G9 **Huntingdon** Tennessee, S USA 36.00N 88.25W
99 O20 **Huntingdonshire** *cultural region* C England, UK
33 P12 **Huntington** Indiana, N USA 40.52N 85.30W
34 L13 **Huntington** Oregon, NW USA 44.22N 117.18W
27 X9 **Huntington** Texas, SW USA 31.16N 94.34W
38 M5 **Huntington** Utah, W USA 39.19N 110.57W
23 P5 **Huntington** West Virginia, NE USA 38.24N 82.27W
37 T16 **Huntington Beach** California, W USA 33.39N 118.00W
37 W4 **Huntington Creek** ≈ Nevada, W USA
192 L7 **Huntly** Waikato, North Island, NZ 37.33S 175.09E
98 K8 **Huntly** NE Scotland, UK 57.25N 2.48W
8 K8 **Hunt, Mount** ▲ Yukon Territory, NW Canada 61.29N 129.10W
12 H12 **Huntsville** Ontario, S Canada 45.18N 79.12W
25 P2 **Huntsville** Alabama, S USA 34.43N 86.35W
29 S9 **Huntsville** Arkansas, C USA 36.05N 93.43W
29 U3 **Huntsville** Missouri, C USA 39.26N 92.33W
22 M8 **Huntsville** Tennessee, S USA 36.25N 84.30W
27 V10 **Huntsville** Texas, SW USA 30.43N 95.34W
38 L2 **Huntsville** Utah, W USA 41.16N 111.47W
43 W12 **Hunucmá** Yucatán, SE Mexico 20.59N 89.55W
155 W3 **Hunza** *var.* Karīmābād. Jammu and Kashmir, NE Pakistan 36.22N 74.43E
155 W3 **Hunza** ≈ NE Pakistan
Hunze *see* Oostermoers Vaart
164 H4 **Huocheng** *var.* Shuiding. Xinjiang Uygur Zizhiqu, NW China 44.03N 80.49E
167 N6 **Huojia** Henan, C China 35.13N 113.37E
Huolin Gol *see* Hulingol
197 F3 **Huon** *reef* N New Caledonia
194 K13 **Huon Gulf** *gulf* E PNG
194 K13 **Huon Peninsula** *headland* C PNG 6.24S 147.50E
Huoshao Dao *see* Lü Tao
Huoshao Tao *see* Lan Yü
Hupeh/Hupei *see* Hubei
Hurano *see* Furano
97 H14 **Hurdalsjøen** ◎ S Norway
12 E13 **Hurd, Cape** *headland* Ontario, S Canada 45.12N 81.43W
Hurdegaryp *see* Hardegarijp
31 N4 **Hurdsfield** North Dakota, N USA 47.24N 99.55W
168 J7 **Hüremt** Bulgan, C Mongolia 48.40N 102.33E
168 J8 **Hüremt** Övörhangay, C Mongolia 46.18N 102.27E
77 X9 **Hurghada** *var.* Al Ghurdaqah, Ghurdaqah. E Egypt 27.16N 33.46E
67 V9 **Huri Hills** ▲▲ NW Kenya
39 P15 **Hurley** New Mexico, SW USA 32.42N 108.07W
32 K4 **Hurley** Wisconsin, N USA 46.25N 90.15W
23 Y4 **Hurlock** Maryland, NE USA 38.37N 75.51W
31 P10 **Huron** South Dakota, N USA 44.19N 98.13W
33 S6 **Huron, Lake** ◎ Canada/USA
33 N3 **Huron Mountains** *hill range* Michigan, N USA
38 J8 **Hurricane** Utah, W USA 37.10N 113.18W
23 P5 **Hurricane** West Virginia, NE USA 38.25N 82.01W
38 J8 **Hurricane Cliffs** *cliff* Arizona, SW USA
25 V6 **Hurricane Creek** ≈ Georgia, SE USA
96 E12 **Hurrungane** ▲ S Norway 61.25N 7.48E
103 E16 **Hürth** Nordrhein-Westfalen, W Germany 50.52N 6.52E
Hurukawa *see* Furukawa
193 I17 **Hurunui** ≈ South Island, NZ
97 F21 **Hurup** Viborg, NW Denmark 56.46N 8.25E
119 T14 **Hurzuf** Respublika Krym, S Ukraine 44.33N 34.18E
Huş *see* Huşi
97 B19 **Húsavík** *Dan.* Husevig Faeroe Islands 61.19N 6.41W
94 K1 **Húsavík** Nordhurland Eystra, NE Iceland 66.03N 17.19W
118 M10 **Huşi** *var.* Huş. Vaslui, E Romania 46.40N 28.05E
97 L19 **Huskvarna** Jönköping, S Sweden 57.46N 14.15E
41 P8 **Huslia** Alaska, USA 65.42N 156.24W
Husn *see* Al Ḩuşn
97 C15 **Husnes** Hordaland, S Norway 59.52N 5.46E
96 D8 **Hustadvika** *sea area* S Norway
Husté *see* Khust
102 H7 **Husum** Schleswig-Holstein, N Germany 54.28N 9.04E
95 I16 **Husum** Västernorrland, C Sweden 63.21N 19.12E
118 K6 **Husyatyn** Ternopil's'ka Oblast', W Ukraine 49.04N 26.10E
Huszt *see* Khust
168 K6 **Hutag** Bulgan, N Mongolia 49.22N 102.50E
28 M6 **Hutchinson** Kansas, C USA 38.03N 97.55W
31 U9 **Hutchinson** Minnesota, N USA 44.53N 94.22W
25 Y13 **Hutchinson Island** *island* Florida, SE USA
38 L11 **Hutch Mountain** ▲ Arizona, SW USA 34.49N 111.22W
147 O14 **Ḩūth** NW Yemen 16.13N 44.00E
195 R11 **Hutjena** Buka Island, NE PNG 5.19S 154.40E
111 T8 **Hüttenberg** Kärnten, S Austria 46.58N 14.33E
27 T10 **Hutto** Texas, SW USA 30.32N 97.33W
Huttu *see* Futtsu
110 E8 **Huttwil** Bern, W Switzerland 47.06N 7.48E
164 K5 **Hutubi** Xinjiang Uygur Zizhiqu, NW China 44.10N 86.51E
167 N4 **Hutuo He** ≈ C China
Hutyû *see* Fuchū
193 E20 **Huxley, Mount** ▲ South Island, NZ 44.02S 169.42E
101 J20 **Huy** *Dut.* Hoei, Hoey. Liège, E Belgium 50.31N 5.13E
167 R8 **Huzhou** *var.* Wuxing. Zhejiang, SE China 30.54N 120.04E
Huzi *see* Fuji
Huzieda *see* Fujieda
Huzinomiya *see* Fujinomiya
Huzisawa *see* Fujisawa
Huziyosida *see* Fuji-Yoshida
94 I2 **Hvammstangi** Nordhurland Vestra, N Iceland 65.22N 20.54W
94 K4 **Hvannadalshnúkur** ▲ S Iceland 64.01N 16.39W
115 E15 **Hvar** *It.* Lesina. Split-Dalmacija, S Croatia 43.10N 16.27E
115 F15 **Hvar** *It.* Lesina; *anc.* Pharus. *island* S Croatia
119 T13 **Hvardiys'ke** *Rus.* Gvardeyskoye. Respublika Krym, S Ukraine 45.07N 34.01E
94 I4 **Hveragerdhi** Sudhurland, SW Iceland 64.00N 21.13W
97 E22 **Hvide Sande** Ringkøbing, W Denmark 56.00N 8.08E
94 I3 **Hvitá** ≈ C Iceland
97 G15 **Hvittingfoss** Buskerud, S Norway 59.28N 10.00E
94 I4 **Hvolsvöllur** Sudhurland, SW Iceland 63.44N 20.12W
Hwach'ŏn-chŏsuji *see* P'aro-ho
Hwainan *see* Huainan
Hwalien *see* Hualien
85 I16 **Hwange** *prev.* Wankie. Matabeleland North, W Zimbabwe 18.18S 26.30E
Hwang-Hae *see* Yellow Sea
Hwangshih *see* Huangshi
85 L17 **Hwedza** Mashonaland East, E Zimbabwe 18.15S 29.48E
65 G20 **Hyades, Cerro** ▲ S Chile 46.57S 73.09W
21 Q12 **Hyannis** Massachusetts, NE USA 41.38N 70.15W
30 L13 **Hyannis** Nebraska, C USA 41.58N 101.45W
168 F6 **Hyargas Nuur** ◎ NW Mongolia
Hybla/Hybla Major *see* Paternò
41 Y14 **Hydaburg** Prince of Wales Island, Alaska, USA 55.10N 132.44W
193 F22 **Hyde** Otago, South Island, NZ 45.17S 170.17E
23 O7 **Hyden** Kentucky, S USA 37.07N 83.22W
20 K12 **Hyde Park** New York, NE USA 41.46N 73.52W
41 Z14 **Hyder** Alaska, USA 55.55N 130.01W
161 I15 **Hyderābād** *var.* Haidarabad. Andhra Pradesh, C India 17.22N 78.25E
155 Q16 **Hyderābād** *var.* Haidarabad. Sind, SE Pakistan 25.25N 68.21E
105 T16 **Hyères** Var, SE France 43.07N 6.07E
105 T16 **Hyères, Îles d'** *island group* S France
120 K12 **Hyermanavichy** *Rus.* Germanovichi. Vitsyebskaya Voblasts', N Belarus 55.25N 27.43E
169 X12 **Hyesan** NE North Korea 41.17N 128.13E
8 K8 **Hyland** ≈ Yukon Territory, NW Canada
97 K20 **Hyltebruk** Halland, S Sweden 57.00N 13.14E
20 D16 **Hyndman** Pennsylvania, NE USA 39.49N 78.42W
35 P14 **Hyndman Peak** ▲ Idaho, NW USA 43.45N 114.07W
170 G13 **Hyōgo** *off.* Hyōgo-ken. ◐ *prefecture* Honshū, SW Japan
170 G13 **Hyōno-sen** ▲ Kyūshū, SW Japan 35.21N 134.30E
Hypanis *see* Kuban'
Hypsas *see* Belice
Hyrcania *see* Gorgān
38 L1 **Hyrum** Utah, W USA 41.37N 111.51W
95 N14 **Hyrynsalmi** Oulu, C Finland 64.40N 28.30E
35 V10 **Hysham** Montana, NW USA 46.16N 107.14W
9 N13 **Hythe** Alberta, W Canada 55.18N 119.44W
99 Q23 **Hythe** SE England, UK 51.04N 1.04E
170 D15 **Hyūga** Miyazaki, Kyūshū, SW Japan 32.24N 131.34E
Hyvinge *see* Hyvinkää
95 L19 **Hyvinkää** *Swe.* Hyvinge. Etelä-Suomi, S Finland 60.37N 24.49E

I

118 J9 **Iacobeni** *Ger.* Jakobeny. Suceava, NE Romania 47.24N 25.19E
Iader *see* Zadar
180 I7 **Iakora** Fianarantsoa, SE Madagascar 23.04S 46.40E
194 H12 **Ialibu** Southern Highlands, W PNG 6.15S 143.55E
118 K14 **Ialomiţa** *var.* Jalomitsa. ◐ *county* SE Romania
118 K14 **Ialomiţa** ≈ SE Romania
119 N10 **Ialoveni** *Rus.* Yaloveny. C Moldova 46.57N 28.47E
119 N11 **Ialpug** *var.* Ialpugul Mare, *Rus.* Yalpug. ≈ Moldova/Ukraine
Ialpugul Mare *see* Ialpug
25 T8 **Iamonia, Lake** ◎ Florida, SE USA
118 L13 **Ianca** Brăila, SE Romania 45.06N 27.29E
118 M10 **Iaşi** *Ger.* Jassy. Iaşi, NE Romania 47.08N 27.38E
118 L9 **Iaşi** *Ger.* Jassy, Yassy. ◐ *county* NE Romania
116 J13 **Íasmos** Anatolikí Makedonía kai Thráki, NE Greece 41.07N 25.12E
24 H6 **Iatt, Lake** ⊠ Louisiana, S USA
60 B11 **Iauaretê** Amazonas, NW Brazil 0.37N 69.10W
179 Oo10 **Iba** Luzon, N Philippines 15.25N 119.55E
79 S16 **Ibadan** Oyo, SW Nigeria 7.21N 4.01E
56 E10 **Ibagué** Tolima, C Colombia 4.27N 75.13W
62 J10 **Ibaiti** Paraná, S Brazil 23.52S 50.09W
179 Pp12 **Ibajay** Panay Island, C Philippines 11.42N 122.17E
38 J4 **Ibapah Peak** ▲ Utah, W USA 39.51N 113.55W
115 M15 **Ibar** *Alb.* Ibër. ≈ C Serbia and Montenegro (Yugoslavia)
170 F14 **Ibara** Okayama, Honshū, SW Japan 34.36N 133.27E
171 Kk16 **Ibaraki** *off.* Ibaraki-ken. ◐ *prefecture* Honshū, S Japan
58 C5 **Ibarra** *var.* San Miguel de Ibarra. Imbabura, N Ecuador 0.22N 78.07W
Ibaşfalău *see* Dumbrăveni
147 O16 **Ibb** W Yemen 13.55N 44.10E
102 F13 **Ibbenbüren** Nordrhein-Westfalen, NW Germany 52.17N 7.43E
81 H16 **Ibenga** ≈ N Congo
Ibër *see* Ibar
59 I14 **Iberia** Madre de Dios, E Peru 11.21S 69.36W
Iberia *see* Spain
68 M1 **Iberian Basin** *undersea feature* E Atlantic Ocean
Iberian Mountains *see* Ibérico, Sistema
86 D12 **Iberian Peninsula** *physical region* Portugal/Spain
66 M8 **Iberian Plain** *undersea feature* E Atlantic Ocean
Ibérica, Cordillera *see* Ibérico, Sistema
107 P6 **Ibérico, Sistema** *var.* Cordillera Ibérica, *Eng.* Iberian Mountains. ▲▲ NE Spain
10 K7 **Iberville Lac d'** ◎ Quebec, NE Canada
79 T14 **Ibeto** Niger, W Nigeria 10.30N 5.07E
79 W15 **Ibi** Taraba, C Nigeria 8.13N 9.46E
107 S11 **Ibi** País Valenciano, E Spain 38.37N 0.34W
61 L20 **Ibiá** Minas Gerais, SE Brazil 19.30S 46.31W
63 F15 **Ibicuí, Rio** ≈ S Brazil
63 C19 **Ibicuy** Entre Ríos, E Argentina 33.46S 59.07W
63 F16 **Ibirapuitã** ≈ S Brazil
Ibiza *see* Eivissa
144 J4 **Ibn Wardān, Qaşr** *ruins* Ḩamāh, C Syria 35.19N 37.13E
Ibo *see* Sassandra
196 E9 **Ibobang** Babeldaob, N Palau
176 Vv11 **Ibonma** Papua, E Indonesia 3.27S 133.30E
61 N17 **Ibotirama** Bahia, E Brazil 12.13S 43.12W
147 Y8 **Ibrā** NE Oman 22.45N 58.30E
131 Q4 **Ibresi** Chavash Respubliki, W Russian Federation 55.22N 47.04E
147 X8 **'Ibrī** NW Oman 23.12N 56.28E
170 Bb16 **Ibusuki** Kagoshima, Kyūshū, SW Japan 31.13N 130.37E
59 E16 **Ica** Ica, SW Peru 14.01S 75.48W
59 E16 **Ica** *off.* Departamento de Ica. ◐ *department* SW Peru
60 C11 **Içana** Amazonas, NW Brazil 0.22N 67.25W
Icaria *see* Ikaría
60 B13 **Içá, Rio** *var.* Río Putumayo. ≈ NW South America *see also* Putumayo, Río
142 I17 **İçel** *var.* Ichili. ◐ *province* S Turkey
94 I3 **Iceland** *off.* Republic of Iceland, *Dan.* Island, *Icel.* Ísland. ◆ *republic* N Atlantic Ocean
88 B7 **Iceland** *island* N Atlantic Ocean
66 L5 **Iceland Basin** *undersea feature* N Atlantic Ocean
Icelandic Plateau *see* Iceland Plateau
207 Q15 **Iceland Plateau** *var.* Icelandic Plateau. *undersea feature* S Greenland Sea
161 E16 **Ichalkaranji** Mahārāshtra, W India 16.42N 74.28E
170 Cc15 **Ichifusa-yama** ▲ Kyūshū, SW Japan 32.18N 131.05E
171 K17 **Ichihara** *var.* Itihara. Chiba, Honshū, S Japan 35.30N 140.08E
Ichili *see* İçel
171 I15 **Ichinomiya** *var.* Itinomiya. Aichi, Honshū, SW Japan 35.19N 136.47E
171 Mm12 **Ichinoseki** *var.* Itinoseki. Iwate, Honshū, C Japan 38.25N 141.06E
119 R3 **Ichnya** Chernihivs'ka Oblast', NE Ukraine 50.52N 32.24E
59 L17 **Ichoa, Río** ≈ C Bolivia
I-ch'un *see* Yichun
Iconium *see* Konya
Iculisma *see* Angoulême
41 U12 **Icy Bay** *inlet* Alaska, USA
41 N5 **Icy Cape** *headland* Alaska, USA 70.19N 161.52W
41 W13 **Icy Strait** *strait* Alaska, USA
29 R13 **Idabel** Oklahoma, C USA 33.54N 94.49W
31 T13 **Ida Grove** Iowa, C USA 42.21N 95.28W
79 U16 **Idah** Kogi, S Nigeria 7.06N 6.45E
35 N13 **Idaho** *off.* State of Idaho; also known as Gem of the Mountains, Gem State. ◐ *state* NW USA
35 N14 **Idaho City** Idaho, NW USA 43.48N 115.51W
35 R14 **Idaho Falls** Idaho, NW USA 43.28N 112.01W
124 Nn3 **Idálion** *var.* Dali, Dhali. C Cyprus 35.00N 33.25E
27 N5 **Idalou** Texas, SW USA 33.40N 101.40W
106 I9 **Idanha-a-Nova** Castelo Branco, C Portugal 39.55N 7.15W
103 E19 **Idar-Oberstein** Rheinland-Pfalz, SW Germany 49.43N 7.19E
120 J3 **Ida-Virumaa** *off.* Ida-Viru Maakond. ◐ *province* NE Estonia
128 J8 **Idel'** Respublika Kareliya, NW Russian Federation 64.08N 34.12E
81 C15 **Idenao** Sud-Ouest, SW Cameroon 4.04N 9.01E
Idenburg-rivier *see* Taritatu, Sungai
Idensalmi *see* Iisalmi
168 I6 **Ider** Hövsgöl, C Mongolia 48.45N 99.52E
77 X10 **Idfu** *var.* Edfu. SE Egypt 24.57N 32.51E
Ídhi Óros *see* Ídi
Ídhra *see* Ýdra
173 F3 **Idi** Sumatera, W Indonesia 5.00N 98.00E
117 I25 **Ídi** *var.* Ídhi Óros. ▲ Kríti, Greece, E Mediterranean Sea
Idi Amin, Lac *see* Edward, Lake
108 G10 **Idice** ≈ N Italy
78 G9 **Idini** Trarza, W Mauritania 17.58N 15.40W
81 J21 **Idiofa** Bandundu, SW Dem. Rep. Congo 5.00S 19.38E
41 O10 **Iditarod River** ≈ Alaska, USA
97 M14 **Idkerberget** Dalarna, C Sweden 60.22N 15.15E
144 I3 **Idlib** Idlib, NW Syria 35.57N 36.37E
144 I4 **Idlib** *off.* Muḩāfaẓat Idlib. ◐ *governorate* NW Syria
Idra *see* Ýdra
96 J11 **Idre** Dalarna, C Sweden 61.52N 12.45E
Idria *see* Idrija
111 S11 **Idrija** *It.* Idria. W Slovenia 46.00N 14.59E
103 G18 **Idstein** Hessen, W Germany 50.10N 8.16E
85 J25 **Idutywa** Eastern Cape, SE South Africa 32.06S 28.19E
Idzhevan *see* Ijevan
120 G9 **Iecava** Bauska, S Latvia 56.36N 24.10E
172 P14 **Ie-jima** *var.* Ii-shima. *island* Nansei-shotō, SW Japan
101 B18 **Ieper** *Fr.* Ypres. West-Vlaanderen, W Belgium 50.51N 2.52E
117 K25 **Ierápetra** Kríti, Greece, E Mediterranean Sea 35.00N 25.45E
117 G22 **Iérax, Akrotírio** *headland* S Greece 36.45N 23.06E
Ierisós *see* Ierissós
117 H14 **Ierissós** *var.* Ierisós. Kentrikí Makedonía, N Greece 40.24N 23.52E
118 I11 **Iernut** *Hung.* Radnót. Mureş, C Romania 46.27N 24.18E
108 J12 **Iesi** *var.* Jesi. Marche, C Italy 43.33N 13.16E
94 K9 **Iešjávri** *var.* Jiesjavrre. ◎ N Norway
Iesolo *see* Jesolo
196 K16 **Ifalik Atoll** *atoll* Caroline Islands, C Micronesia
180 I6 **Ifanadiana** Fianarantsoa, SE Madagascar 21.19S 47.39E
79 T16 **Ife** Osun, SW Nigeria 7.25N 4.31E
79 V8 **Iferouâne** Agadez, N Niger 19.08N 8.21E
Iferten *see* Yverdon
94 L8 **Ifjord** Finnmark, N Norway 70.27N 27.06E
79 R8 **Ifôghas, Adrar des** *var.* Adrar des Iforas. ▲▲ NE Mali
Iforas, Adrar des *see* Ifôghas, Adrar des
190 D6 **Ifould lake** *salt lake* South Australia
76 G6 **Ifrane** C Morocco 33.31N 5.09W
175 T7 **Iga** Pulau Halmahera, E Indonesia 1.23N 128.17E
83 G18 **Iganga** SE Uganda 0.34N 33.27E
62 L7 **Igarapava** São Paulo, S Brazil 20.01S 47.46W
126 Hh9 **Igarka** Krasnoyarskiy Kray, N Russian Federation 67.31N 86.33E
Igaunija *see* Estonia
I.G.Duca *see* General Toshevo
Igel *see* Jihlava
143 T12 **Iğdır** ◐ *province* E Turkey
96 N11 **Iggesund** Gävleborg, C Sweden 61.37N 17.15E
41 P7 **Igikpak, Mount** ▲ Alaska, USA 67.28N 154.55W
41 P13 **Igiugig** Alaska, USA 59.19N 155.53W
Iglau/Iglawa/Igława *see* Jihlava
109 B20 **Iglesias** Sardegna, Italy, C Mediterranean Sea 39.19N 8.33E
131 V4 **Iglino** Respublika Bashkortostan, W Russian Federation 54.51N 56.29E
Igló *see* Spišská Nová Ves
15 Ll2 **Igloolik** Nunavut, N Canada 69.24N 81.55W
10 B11 **Ignace** Ontario, S Canada 49.25N 91.40W
120 I12 **Ignalina** Ignalina, E Lithuania 55.20N 26.10E
131 Q5 **Ignatovka** Ul'yanovskaya Oblast', W Russian Federation 53.56N 47.40E
128 K12 **Ignatovo** Vologodskaya Oblast', NW Russian Federation 60.47N 37.51E
116 N11 **İğneada** Kırklareli, NW Turkey 41.54N 27.58E
124 P7 **İğneada Burnu** *headland* NW Turkey 41.54N 28.03E
Igombe *see* Gombe
117 B16 **Igoumenítsa** Ípeiros, W Greece 39.30N 20.16E
131 T2 **Igra** Udmurtskaya Respublika, NW Russian Federation 57.30N 53.01E
125 Ff9 **Igrim** Khanty-Mansiyskiy Avtonomnyy Okrug, N Russian Federation 63.09N 64.33E
62 G12 **Iguaçu, Rio** *Sp.* Río Iguazú. ≈ Argentina/Brazil *see also* Iguazú, Río
61 I22 **Iguaçu, Salto do** *Sp.* Cataratas del Iguazú; *prev.* Victoria Falls. *waterfall* Argentina/Brazil *see also* Iguazú, Cataratas del 25.37S 54.28W
43 O15 **Iguala** *var.* Iguala de la Independencia. Guerrero, S Mexico 18.21N 99.33W
107 V5 **Igualada** Cataluña, NE Spain 41.34N 1.37E
Iguala de la Independencia *see* Iguala
62 G12 **Iguazú, Cataratas del** *Port.* Salto do Iguaçu, *prev.* Victoria Falls. *waterfall* Argentina/Brazil *see also* Iguaçu, Salto do 25.40S 54.25W
64 Q6 **Iguazú, Río** *Port.* Rio Iguaçu. ≈ Argentina/Brazil *see also* Iguaçu, Rio
81 D19 **Iguéla** Ogooué-Maritime, SW Gabon 2.00S 9.23E
Iguid, Erg *see* Iguîdi, 'Erg
69 M5 **Iguîdi, 'Erg** *var.* Erg Iguid. *desert* Algeria/Mauritania
180 K2 **Iharaña** *prev.* Vohémar. Antsirañana, NE Madagascar 13.22S 50.00E
157 K18 **Ihavandippolhu Atoll** *var.* Ihavandiffulu Atoll. *atoll* N Maldives
168 M11 **Ih Bulag** Ömnögovĭ, S Mongolia 43.04N 107.43E
172 Pp14 **Iheya-jima** *island* Nansei-shotō, SW Japan
168 L8 **Ihhayrhan** Töv, C Mongolia 46.57N 105.51E
180 I6 **Ihosy** Fianarantsoa, S Madagascar 22.22S 46.09E
168 L7 **Ihsüüj** Töv, C Mongolia 48.12N 106.23E
95 L14 **Ii** Oulu, C Finland 65.18N 25.23E
171 Ii16 **Iida** Nagano, Honshū, S Japan 35.30N 137.48E
171 L13 **Iide-san** ▲ Honshū, C Japan 38.03N 139.39E
95 M14 **Iijoki** ≈ C Finland
120 J4 **Iisaku** *Ger.* Isaak. Ida-Virumaa, NE Estonia 59.07N 27.18E
95 M16 **Iisalmi** *var.* Idensalmi. Itä-Suomi, C Finland 63.31N 27.10E
171 Jj14 **Iiyama** Nagano, Honshū, S Japan 36.52N 138.22E
170 D13 **Iizuka** Fukuoka, Kyūshū, SW Japan 33.37N 130.40E
79 S16 **Ijebu-Ode** Ogun, SW Nigeria 6.46N 3.57E
143 U11 **Ijevan** *Rus.* Idzhevan. N Armenia 40.53N 45.07E
100 H9 **IJmuiden** Noord-Holland, W Netherlands 52.28N 4.34E
100 M12 **IJssel** *var.* Yssel. ≈ Netherlands/Germany
100 J8 **IJsselmeer** *prev.* Zuider Zee. ◎ N Netherlands
100 L9 **IJsselmuiden** Overijssel, E Netherlands 52.34N 5.55E
100 I12 **IJsselstein** Utrecht, C Netherlands 52.01N 5.01E
63 G14 **Ijuí** Rio Grande do Sul, S Brazil 28.22S 53.55W
63 G14 **Ijuí, Rio** ≈ S Brazil
201 R8 **Ijuw** NE Nauru 0.30S 166.57E
101 E16 **IJzendijke** Zeeland, SW Netherlands 51.20N 3.36E
101 A18 **Ijzer** ≈ W Belgium
95 K18 **Ikaalinen** Länsi-Suomi, W Finland 61.46N 23.04E
180 I6 **Ikalamavony** Fianarantsoa, SE Madagascar 21.10S 46.34E
193 G16 **Ikamatua** West Coast, South Island, NZ 42.16S 171.42E
79 U16 **Ikare** Ondo, SW Nigeria 7.36N 5.52E
117 L20 **Ikaría** *var.* Kariot, Nicaria, Nikaria; *anc.* Icaria. *island* Dodekánisos, Greece, Aegean Sea
97 F22 **Ikast** Ringkøbing, W Denmark 56.09N 9.10E
192 O9 **Ikawhenua Range** ▲▲ North Island, NZ
172 Pp7 **Ikeda** Hokkaidō, NE Japan 42.54N 143.25E
170 F15 **Ikeda** Tokushima, Shikoku, SW Japan 34.00N 133.47E
79 S16 **Ikeja** Lagos, SW Nigeria 6.36N 3.16E
81 L19 **Ikela** Equateur, C Dem. Rep. Congo 1.10S 23.16E
116 H10 **Ikhtiman** Sofiya, W Bulgaria 42.25N 23.49E
170 Cc12 **Iki** *island* SW Japan
131 O13 **Iki Burul** Respublika Kalmykiya, SW Russian Federation 45.48N 44.44E
170 C12 **Iki-suidō** *strait* SW Japan
170 Bb12 **Ikitsuki-shima** *island* SW Japan
143 P11 **Ikizdere** Rize, NE Turkey 40.46N 40.34E
41 P14 **Ikolik, Cape** *headland* Kodiak Island, Alaska, USA 57.12N 154.46W
79 V17 **Ikom** Cross River, SE Nigeria 5.57N 8.43E
180 I6 **Ikongo** *prev.* Fort-Carnot. Fianarantsoa, SE Madagascar 21.52S 47.27E
41 P5 **Ikpikpuk River** ≈ Alaska, USA
202 H1 **Iku** *prev.* Lone Tree Islet. *atoll* Tungaru, W Kiribati
171 Gg14 **Ikuno** Hyōgo, Honshū, SW Japan 35.13N 134.48E
202 H16 **Ikurangi** ▲ Rarotonga, S Cook Islands 21.12S 159.45W
176 Xx12 **Ilaga** Papua, E Indonesia 3.54S 137.30E
179 Pp8 **Ilagan** Luzon, N Philippines 17.07N 121.54E
159 R12 **Ilam** Eastern, E Nepal 26.52N 87.58E
148 J7 **Īlām** *var.* Elam. Īlām, W Iran 33.40N 46.24E
148 J8 **Īlām** *off.* Ostān-e Īlām. ◐ *province* W Iran
167 T13 **Ilan** *Jap.* Giran. N Taiwan 24.46N 121.46E
152 G9 **Ilanly Obvodnitel'nyy Kanal** *canal* N Turkmenistan
126 Ii14 **Ilanskiy** Krasnoyarskiy Kray, S Russian Federation 56.16N 95.59E
110 H9 **Ilanz** Graubünden, S Switzerland 46.46N 9.10E
79 S16 **Ilaro** Ogun, SW Nigeria 6.52N 3.01E
59 I17 **Ilave** Puno, S Peru 16.07S 69.37W
112 K8 **Iława** *Ger.* Deutsch-Eylau. Warmińsko-Mazurskie, NE Poland, 53.36N 19.34E
126 Ll11 **Il'benge** Respublika Sakha (Yakutiya), NE Russian Federation 62.52N 124.13E
Ile *see* Ili
9 S13 **Ile-à-la-Crosse** Saskatchewan, C Canada 55.29N 108.00W
81 J21 **Ilebo** *prev.* Port-Francqui. Kasai Occidental, W Dem. Rep. Congo 4.19S 20.31E
105 N5 **Île-de-France** ◐ *region* N France
150 I9 **Ilek** *Kaz.* Elek. ≈ Kazakhstan/Russian Federation
Ilerda *see* Lleida
79 T16 **Ilesha** Osun, SW Nigeria 7.35N 4.49E
197 J5 **Îles Loyauté, Province des** ◐ *province* E New Caledonia
9 X12 **Ilford** Manitoba, C Canada 56.02N 95.48W
99 I23 **Ilfracombe** SW England, UK 51.12N 4.09W
142 I11 **Ilgaz Dağları** ▲▲ N Turkey
142 G15 **Ilgın** Konya, W Turkey 38.16N 31.57E
62 I7 **Ilha Solteira** São Paulo, S Brazil 20.28S 51.19W
106 G7 **Ílhavo** Aveiro, N Portugal 40.36N 8.40W
61 O18 **Ilhéus** Bahia, E Brazil 14.49S 39.06W
133 R7 **Ili** *Kaz.* Ile, *Rus.* Reka Ili. ≈ China/Kazakhstan
Ili *see* Ili He
118 G11 **Ilia** *Hung.* Marosillye. Hunedoara, SW Romania 45.57N 22.39E
41 P13 **Iliamna** Alaska, USA 59.42N 154.49W
41 P13 **Iliamna Lake** ◎ Alaska, USA
143 N13 **İliç** Erzincan, C Turkey 39.27N 38.34E
Il'ichevsk *see* Şärur, Azerbaijan
Il'ichevsk *see* Illichivs'k, Ukraine
Ilici *see* Elche
39 V2 **Iliff** Colorado, C USA 40.46N 103.04W
179 R15 **Iligan** *off.* Iligan City. Mindanao, S Philippines 8.12N 124.15E
179 R15 **Iligan Bay** *bay* S Philippines
164 I5 **Ili He** *Rus.* Ili. ≈ China/Kazakhstan
58 C6 **Iliniza** ▲ N Ecuador 0.37S 78.41W
Ilinski *see* Il'inskiy
129 U14 **Il'inskiy** *Perm.* Ilinski. Permskaya Oblast', NW Russian Federation 58.33N 55.31E
127 Oo15 **Il'inskiy** Ostrov Sakhalin, Sakhalinskaya Oblast', SE Russian Federation 47.59N 142.14E
20 I10 **Ilion** New York, NE USA 43.01N 75.02W
40 E9 **Ilio Point** *headland* Molokai, Hawaii, USA, C Pacific Ocean 21.13N 157.15W
111 T13 **Ilirska Bistrica** *prev.* Bistrica, *Ger.* Feistritz, Illyrisch-Feistritz, *It.* Villa del Nevoso. SW Slovenia 45.34N 14.12E
143 Q16 **Ilisu Barajı** ⊠ SE Turkey
161 G17 **Ilkal** Karnātaka, C India 15.59N 76.08E
99 M19 **Ilkeston** C England, UK 52.58N 1.18W
123 Jj17 **Il-Kullana** *headland* SW Malta 35.49N 14.26E
110 J8 **Ill** ≈ W Austria
105 U6 **Ill** ≈ NE France
64 G10 **Illapel** Coquimbo, C Chile 31.40S 71.13W
Illaue Fartak Trench *see* Alula-Fartak Trench
190 C2 **Illbillee, Mount** ▲ South Australia 27.01S 132.13E
104 I6 **Ille-et-Vilaine** ◐ *department* NW France
79 T11 **Illéla** Tahoua, SW Niger 14.25N 5.10E
103 J24 **Iller** ≈ S Germany
103 J23 **Illertissen** Bayern, S Germany 48.13N 10.08E
107 N8 **Illescas** Castilla-La Mancha, C Spain 40.07N 3.51W
Ille-sur-Tet *see* Ille-sur-Têt
105 O17 **Ille-sur-Têt** *var.* Ille-sur-Tet. Pyrénées-Orientales, S France 42.40N 2.37E
Illiberis *see* Elne
119 P11 **Illichivs'k** *Rus.* Il'ichevsk. Odes'ka Oblast', SW Ukraine 46.18N 30.36E
Illicis *see* Elche
104 M6 **Illiers-Combray** Eure-et-Loir, C France 48.19N 1.14E
32 K12 **Illinois** *off.* State of Illinois; also known as Prairie State, Sucker State. ◐ *state* C USA
32 J13 **Illinois River** ≈ Illinois, N USA
119 N6 **Illintsi** Vinnyts'ka Oblast', C Ukraine 49.07N 29.13E
Illiturgis *see* Andújar
76 M10 **Illizi** SE Algeria 26.30N 8.28E
29 Y7 **Illmo** Missouri, C USA 37.13N 89.30W
Illur co *see* Lorca
Illuro *see* Mataró
Illyrisch-Feistritz *see* Ilirska Bistrica
103 K16 **Ilm** ≈ C Germany
103 K17 **Ilmenau** Thüringen, C Germany 50.40N 10.55E
128 H14 **Il'men', Ozero** ◎ NW Russian Federation
59 H18 **Ilo** Moquegua, SW Peru 17.39S 71.22W
179 Q13 **Iloilo** *off.* Iloilo City. Panay Island, C Philippines 10.42N 122.34E
114 K10 **Ilok** *Hung.* Újlak. Serbia, NW Serbia and Montenegro (Yugoslavia) 45.12N 19.22E
95 O16 **Ilomantsi** Itä-Suomi, E Finland 62.40N 30.55E
44 F8 **Ilopango, Lago de** *volcanic lake* C El Salvador
79 T15 **Ilorin** Kwara, W Nigeria 8.32N 4.34E
119 X8 **Ilovays'k** *Rus.* Ilovaysk. Donets'ka Oblast', SE Ukraine 47.54N 38.13E
131 O10 **Ilovlya** Volgogradskaya Oblast', SW Russian Federation 49.45N 44.18E
131 O10 **Ilovlya** ≈ SW Russian Federation
127 P8 **Il'pyrskoye** Koryakskiy Avtonomnyy Okrug, E Russian Federation 60.00N 164.16E
130 K14 **Il'skiy** Krasnodarskiy Kray, SW Russian Federation 44.52N 38.26E
190 B2 **Iltur** South Australia 27.33S 130.31E
176 Y11 **Ilugwa** Papua, E Indonesia 3.42S 139.09E
Iluh *see* Batman
120 I11 **Ilūkste** Daugvapils, SE Latvia 55.58N 26.21E
176 Uu12 **Ilur** Pulau Gorong, E Indonesia 4.00S 131.25E
34 F10 **Ilwaco** Washington, NW USA 46.19N 124.03W
152 H8 **Il'yaly** *var.* Ylanly. Dashkhovuzskiy Velayat, N Turkmenistan 41.56N 59.42E
Ilyasbaba Burnu *see* Tekke Burnu
129 U9 **Ilych** ≈ NW Russian Federation
103 O21 **Ilz** ≈ SE Germany
113 M14 **Iłża** Radom, SE Poland 51.09N 21.15E
170 Ee14 **Imabari** *var.* Imaharu. Ehime, Shikoku, SW Japan 34.04N 132.58E
172 N5 **Imagane** Hokkaidō, NE Japan 42.26N 140.00E
Imaharu *see* Imabari
171 K15 **Imaichi** *var.* Imaiti. Tochigi, Honshū, S Japan 36.43N 139.40E
Imaiti *see* Imaichi
171 Hh14 **Imajō** Fukui, Honshū, SW Japan 35.45N 136.10E
145 R9 **Imām Ibn Hāshim** C Iraq 32.46N 43.21E
145 T11 **Imān 'Abd Allāh** S Iraq 31.36N 44.34E
128 J4 **Imandra, Ozero** ◎ NW Russian Federation
170 E16 **Imano-yama** ▲ Shikoku, SW Japan 32.51N 132.48E
170 C13 **Imari** Saga, Kyūshū, SW Japan 33.16N 129.51E
Imarssuak Mid-Ocean Seachannel *see* Imarssuak Seachannel
66 J6 **Imarssuak Seachannel** *var.* Imarssuak Mid-Ocean Seachannel. *channel* N Atlantic Ocean
95 N18 **Imatra** Etelä-Suomi, S Finland 61.13N 28.49E
171 H14 **Imazu** Shiga, Honshū, SW Japan 35.25N 136.00E
58 C6 **Imbabura** ◐ *province* N Ecuador
57 R9 **Imbaimadai** W Guyana 5.44N 60.23W
63 K14 **Imbituba** Santa Catarina, S Brazil 28.15S 48.43W
29 W9 **Imboden** Arkansas, C USA 36.12N 91.10W

◆ Country ● Country Capital ◇ Dependent Territory ○ Dependent Territory Capital ◐ Administrative Region ✕ International Airport ▲ Mountain ▲▲ Mountain Range Volcano ≈ River ◎ Lake ⊠ Reservoir

Imbros see Gökçeada
152 B11 **Imeni 26 Bakinskikh Komissarov** Turkm. 26 Baku Komissarlary Adyndaky. Balkanskiy Velayat, W Turkmenistan 39.24N 54.04E
Imeni 26 Bakinskikh Komissarov see 26 Bakı Komissarı
129 N13 **Imeni Babushkina** Vologodskaya Oblast', NW Russian Federation 59.40N 43.04E
130 J7 **Imeni Karla Libknekhta** Kurskaya Oblast', W Russian Federation 51.36N 35.28E
152 I14 **Imeni Mollanepesa** Maryyskiy Velayat, S Turkmenistan 37.36N 61.54E
127 N14 **Imeni Poliny Osipenko** Khabarovskiy Kray, SE Russian Federation 52.21N 136.17E
152 J15 **Imeni S.A.Niyazova** Maryyskiy Velayat, S Turkmenistan 36.44N 62.23E
Imeni Sverdlova Rudnik see Sverdlovs'k
196 E9 **Imeong** Babeldaob, N Palau
83 L14 **Īmī** Somali, E Ethiopia 6.27N 42.10E
117 M21 **Imia** Turk. Kardak. island Dodekánisos, Greece, Aegean Sea
Imishli see İmişli
143 X12 **İmişli** Rus. Imishli. C Azerbaijan 39.54N 48.04E
169 X14 **Imjin-gang** River North Korea/South Korea
37 S3 **Imlay** Nevada, W USA 40.39N 118.10W
33 S9 **Imlay City** Michigan, N USA 43.01N 83.04W
25 X15 **Immokalee** Florida, SE USA 26.24N 81.25W
79 U17 **Imo** ◆ state SE Nigeria
108 G10 **Imola** Emilia-Romagna, N Italy 44.22N 11.43E
194 E9 **Imonda** Sandaun, NW PNG 3.19S 141.10E
Imoschi see Imotski
115 G14 **Imotski** It. Imoschi. Split-Dalmacija, SE Croatia 43.28N 17.13E
61 L14 **Imperatriz** Maranhão, NE Brazil 5.31S 47.28W
108 B10 **Imperia** Liguria, NW Italy 43.52N 8.03E
59 E15 **Imperial** Lima, W Peru 13.04S 76.20W
37 X17 **Imperial** California, W USA 32.51N 115.34W
30 L16 **Imperial** Nebraska, C USA 40.30N 101.37W
26 M9 **Imperial** Texas, SW USA 31.15N 102.40W
37 Y17 **Imperial Dam** dam California, W USA 32.52N 114.27W
81 I17 **Impfondo** La Likouala, NE Congo 1.40N 18.02E
159 X14 **Imphāl** Manipur, NE India 24.46N 93.55E
105 P9 **Imphy** Nièvre, C France 46.55N 3.16E
108 G11 **Impruneta** Toscana, C Italy 43.42N 11.16E
117 K15 **Imroz** var. Gökçeada. Çanakkale, NW Turkey 40.11N 25.53E
Imroz Adası see Gökçeada
110 L7 **Imst** Tirol, W Austria 47.13N 10.40E
42 F3 **Imuris** Sonora, NW Mexico 30.48N 110.52W
179 P11 **Imus** Luzon, N Philippines 14.27N 120.55E
171 J15 **Ina** Nagano, Honshū, S Japan 35.55N 137.59E
67 M18 **Inaccessible Island** island W Tristan da Cunha
117 F20 **Ínachos** River S Greece
196 H6 **I Naftan, Puntan** headland Saipan, S Northern Mariana Islands
Inagua Islands see Great Inagua/Little Inagua
193 H15 **Inangahua** West Coast, South Island, NZ 41.51S 171.58E
176 V10 **Inanwatan** Papua, E Indonesia 2.06S 132.07E
59 I14 **Iñapari** Madre de Dios, E Peru 11.00S 69.34W
196 B17 **Inarajan** SE Guam 13.16N 144.45E
94 L10 **Inari** Lapp. Anár, Aanaar. Lappi, N Finland 68.54N 27.06E
94 L10 **Inarijärvi** Lapp. Aanaarjävri, Swe. Enareträsk. Lake N Finland
94 L9 **Inarijoki** Lapp. Anárjohka. River Finland/Norway
Inău see Ineu
171 L14 **Inawashiro-ko** var. Inawasiro Ko. Lake Honshū, C Japan
Inawasiro Ko see Inawashiro-ko
64 H7 **Inca de Oro** Atacama, N Chile 26.45S 69.54W
117 J15 **İnce Burnu** headland NW Turkey 40.08N 25.39E
142 K9 **İnce Burnu** headland N Turkey 42.06N 34.57E
142 I17 **İncekum Burnu** headland S Turkey 36.13N 33.57E
78 G7 **Inchiri** ◆ region NW Mauritania
169 X15 **Inch'ŏn** off. Inch'ŏn-gwangyŏksi, Jap. Jinsen; prev. Chemulpo. NW South Korea 37.27N 126.40E
85 M17 **Inchope** Manica, C Mozambique 19.09S 33.54E
Incoronata see Kornat
105 Y15 **Incudine, Monte** ▲ Corse, France, C Mediterranean Sea 41.52N 9.13E
62 M10 **Indaiatuba** São Paulo, S Brazil 23.03S 47.14W
95 H17 **Indal** Västernorrland, C Sweden 62.36N 17.06E
95 H17 **Indalsälven** River C Sweden
42 K8 **Inde** Durango, C Mexico 25.55N 105.10W
Indefatigable Island see Santa Cruz, Isla
37 S10 **Independence** California, W USA 36.48N 118.12W
31 X13 **Independence** Iowa, C USA 42.28N 91.42W
29 P7 **Independence** Kansas, C USA 37.13N 95.42W
22 M4 **Independence** Kentucky, S USA 38.56N 84.32W
29 R4 **Independence** Missouri, C USA 39.05N 94.25W
23 R8 **Independence** Virginia, NE USA 36.37N 81.09W
32 J7 **Independence** Wisconsin, N USA 44.21N 91.25W
207 R12 **Independence Fjord** fjord N Greenland
Independence Island see Malden Island
37 W2 **Independence Mountains** ▲ Nevada, W USA
59 K18 **Independencia** Cochabamba, C Bolivia 17.07S 66.52W
59 E16 **Independencia, Bahía de la** bay W Peru
Independencia, Monte see Adam, Mount
118 M12 **Independenţa** Galaţi, SE Romania 45.27N 27.45E
Inderagiri see Indragiri, Sungai
Inderbor see Inderborskiy
150 F11 **Inderborskiy** Kaz. İnderbor. Atyrau, W Kazakhstan 48.35N 51.45E
157 I14 **India** off. Republic of India, var. Indian Union, Union of India, Hind. Bhārat. ◆ republic S Asia
India see Indija
20 D14 **Indiana** Pennsylvania, NE USA 40.37N 79.09W
33 N13 **Indiana** off. State of Indiana; also known as The Hoosier State. ◆ state N USA
33 O14 **Indianapolis** state capital Indiana, N USA 39.46N 86.09W
9 O10 **Indian Cabins** Alberta, W Canada 59.51N 117.06W
44 G1 **Indian Church** Orange Walk, N Belize 17.47N 88.39W
Indian Desert see Thar Desert
9 U16 **Indian Head** Saskatchewan, S Canada 50.31N 103.40W
33 O4 **Indian Lake** Lake Michigan, N USA
20 K9 **Indian Lake** Lake New York, NE USA
33 R13 **Indian Lake** Reservoir Ohio, N USA
180-181 **Indian Ocean** ocean
31 V15 **Indianola** Iowa, C USA 41.21N 93.33W
24 K4 **Indianola** Mississippi, S USA 33.27N 90.39W
38 J6 **Indian Peak** ▲ Utah, W USA 38.18N 113.52W
25 Y13 **Indian River** lagoon Florida, SE USA
37 W10 **Indian Springs** Nevada, W USA 36.33N 115.40W
25 Y14 **Indiantown** Florida, SE USA 27.01N 80.29W
61 K19 **Indiara** Goiás, S Brazil 17.12S 50.09W
129 Q4 **Indiga** Nenetskiy Avtonomnyy Okrug, NW Russian Federation 67.40N 49.01E
126 Mm6 **Indigirka** River NE Russian Federation
114 L10 **Inđija** Hung. India; prev. Indjija. Serbia, N Serbia and Montenegro (Yugoslavia) 45.03N 20.04E
37 V16 **Indio** California, W USA 33.42N 116.13W
44 M12 **Indio, Río** River SE Nicaragua
158 I10 **Indira Gandhi International** ✕ (Delhi) Delhi, N India
157 Q23 **Indira Point** headland Andaman and Nicobar Islands, India, NE Indian Ocean 6.54N 93.54E
195 X15 **Indispensable Strait** strait C Solomon Islands
Indjija see Inđija
133 Q13 **Indo-Australian Plate** tectonic feature
181 N11 **Indomed Fracture Zone** tectonic feature SW Indian Ocean
175 Nn12 **Indonesia** off. Republic of Indonesia, Ind. Republik Indonesia; prev. Dutch East Indies, Netherlands East Indies, United States of Indonesia. ◆ republic SE Asia
Indonesian Borneo see Kalimantan
160 G10 **Indore** Madhya Pradesh, C India 22.42N 75.50E
174 Hh8 **Indragiri, Sungai** var. Batang Kuantan, Inderagiri. River Sumatera, W Indonesia
Indramajoe/Indramaju see Indramayu
174 K14 **Indramayu** prev. Indramajoe, Indramaju. Jawa, C Indonesia 6.22S 108.19E
161 K14 **Indrāvati** River S India
105 N9 **Indre** ◆ department C France
104 M8 **Indre** River C France
104 L8 **Indre-et-Loire** ◆ department C France
Indreville see Châteauroux
158 G3 **Indus** Chin. Yindu He; prev. Yin-tu Ho. River S Asia
Indus Cone see Indus Fan
181 P3 **Indus Fan** var. Indus Cone. undersea feature N Arabian Sea
155 P17 **Indus, Mouths of the** delta S Pakistan
85 I24 **Indwe** Eastern Cape, SE South Africa 31.28S 27.19E
142 I10 **İnebolu** Kastamonu, N Turkey 41.57N 33.45E
79 P8 **I-n-Échaï** oasis C Mali 20.04N 2.00W
116 M13 **İnecik** Tekirdağ, NW Turkey 40.55N 27.16E
142 E12 **İnegöl** Bursa, NW Turkey 40.06N 29.31E
Inessa see Biancavilla
118 F10 **Ineu** Hung. Borosjenő; prev. Inău. Arad, W Romania 46.25N 21.50E
Ineul/Ineu, Vîrful see Ineu, Vârful
118 J9 **Ineu, Vârful** var. Ineul; prev. Vîrful Ineu. ▲ N Romania 47.31N 24.52E
23 P6 **Inez** Kentucky, S USA 37.53N 82.33W
76 E8 **Inezgane** ✕ (Agadir) W Morocco 30.35N 9.27W
43 T17 **Inferior, Laguna** lagoon S Mexico
42 M15 **Infiernillo, Presa del** Reservoir S Mexico
106 L2 **Infiesto** Asturias, N Spain 43.21N 5.21W
95 L20 **Ingå** Fin. Inkoo. Etelä-Suomi, S Finland 60.01N 24.05E
79 U10 **Ingal** var. I-n-Gall. Agadez, C Niger 16.52N 6.57E
I-n-Gall see Ingal
101 C18 **Ingelmunster** West-Vlaanderen, W Belgium 50.12N 3.15E
81 I18 **Ingende** Equateur, W Dem. Rep. Congo 0.15S 18.58E
64 L5 **Ingeniero Guillermo Nueva Juárez** Formosa, N Argentina 23.55S 61.49W
65 H16 **Ingeniero Jacobacci** Río Negro, C Argentina 41.21S 69.46W
12 F16 **Ingersoll** Ontario, S Canada 43.03N 80.52W
168 K6 **Ingettolgoy** Bulgan, N Mongolia 49.27N 103.59E
189 W5 **Ingham** Queensland, NE Australia 18.34S 146.12E
152 M11 **Ingichka** Samarqand Viloyati, C Uzbekistan 39.46N 65.56E
99 L16 **Ingleborough** ▲ N England, UK 54.07N 2.22W
27 T14 **Ingleside** Texas, SW USA 27.52N 97.12W
192 K10 **Inglewood** Taranaki, North Island, NZ 39.10S 174.12E
37 S15 **Inglewood** California, W USA 33.57N 118.21W
126 Kk16 **Ingoda** River S Russian Federation
103 L21 **Ingolstadt** Bayern, S Germany 48.46N 11.25E
35 V9 **Ingomar** Montana, NW USA 46.34N 107.21W
11 R14 **Ingonish Beach** Cape Breton Island, Nova Scotia, SE Canada 46.42N 60.22W
159 S14 **Ingrāj Bāzār** prev. English Bazar. West Bengal, NE India 25.00N 88.10E
27 Q11 **Ingram** Texas, SW USA 30.04N 99.14W
205 X7 **Ingrid Christensen Coast** physical region Antarctica
76 K14 **I-n-Guezzam** S Algeria 19.35N 5.49E
Ingulets see Inhulets'
Inguri see Enguri
Ingushetia/Ingushetiya, Respublika see Ingushskaya Respublika
131 O15 **Ingushskaya Respublika** var. Respublika Ingushetiya, Eng. Ingushetia. ◆ autonomous republic SW Russian Federation
85 N20 **Inhambane** Inhambane, SE Mozambique 23.52S 35.31E
85 M20 **Inhambane** off. Província de Inhambane. ◆ province S Mozambique
85 N17 **Inhaminga** Sofala, C Mozambique 18.22S 35.02E
85 N20 **Inharrime** Inhambane, SE Mozambique 24.28S 35.01E
85 M18 **Inhassoro** Inhambane, E Mozambique 21.31S 35.13E
119 S9 **Inhulets'** Rus. Ingulets. Dnipropetrovs'ka Oblast', E Ukraine 47.40N 33.15E
119 R10 **Inhulets'** Rus. Ingulets. River S Ukraine
107 Q10 **Iniesta** Castilla-La Mancha, C Spain 39.27N 1.45W
I-ning see Yining
56 K11 **Inírida, Río** River E Colombia
Inis see Ennis
Inis Ceithleann see Enniskillen
Inis Córthaidh see Enniscorthy
Inis Díomáin see Ennistimon
99 A17 **Inishbofin** Ir. Inis Bó Finne. island W Ireland
99 B18 **Inisheer** var. Inishere, Ir. Inis Oírr. island W Ireland
Inishere see Inisheer
99 B18 **Inishmaan** Ir. Inis Meáin. island W Ireland
99 A18 **Inishmore** Ir. Árainn. island W Ireland
98 E13 **Inishtrahull** Ir. Inis Trá Tholl. island NW Ireland
99 A17 **Inishturk** Ir. Inis Toirc. island W Ireland
Inkoo see Ingå
193 J16 **Inland Kaikoura Range** ▲ South Island, NZ
Inland Sea see Seto-naikai
23 P11 **Inman** South Carolina, SE USA 35.03N 82.05W
110 L7 **Inn** River C Europe
207 O11 **Innaanganeq** var. Kap York. headland NW Greenland 75.54N 66.27W
190 K2 **Innamincka** South Australia 27.47S 140.45E
94 G12 **Inndyr** Nordland, C Norway 67.01N 14.00E
44 G3 **Inner Channel** inlet SE Belize
98 F11 **Inner Hebrides** island group W Scotland, UK
180 H15 **Inner Islands** var. Central Group. island group NE Seychelles
Inner Mongolia/Inner Mongolian Autonomous Region see Nei Mongol Zizhiqu
98 G8 **Inner Sound** strait NW Scotland, UK
102 J13 **Innerste** River C Germany
189 W5 **Innisfail** Queensland, NE Australia 17.29S 146.03E
9 Q15 **Innisfail** Alberta, SW Canada 52.01N 113.58W
Inniskilling see Enniskillen
41 O11 **Innoko River** River Alaska, USA
170 F14 **Innoshima** var. Innosima. Hiroshima, SW Japan 34.18N 133.09E
Innosima see Innoshima
Innsbruch see Innsbruck
110 M7 **Innsbruck** var. Innsbruch. Tirol, W Austria 47.16N 11.25E
81 I19 **Inongo** Bandundu, W Dem. Rep. Congo 1.55S 18.19E
Inoucdjouac see Inukjuak
Inowrazlaw see Inowrocław
112 I10 **Inowrocław** Ger. Hohensalza; prev. Inowrazlaw. Kujawski-pomorskie, C Poland 52.47N 18.15E
59 K18 **Inquisivi** La Paz, W Bolivia 17.01S 67.03W
Inrin see Yüanlin
79 O8 **I-n-Sâkâne, 'Erg** desert N Mali
76 J10 **I-n-Salah** var. In Salah. C Algeria 27.10N 2.31E
131 O5 **Insar** Respublika Mordoviya, W Russian Federation 53.52N 44.26E
201 X15 **Insiaf** Kosrae, E Micronesia
96 L13 **Insjön** Dalarna, C Sweden 60.40N 15.05E
Insterburg see Chernyakhovsk
Insula see Lille
118 L13 **Însurăţei** Brăila, SE Romania 44.55N 27.40E
129 V6 **Inta** Respublika Komi, NW Russian Federation 66.00N 60.09E
79 R9 **I-n-Tebezas** Kidal, E Mali 17.58N 1.51E
Interamna see Teramo
Interamna Nahars see Terni
30 L11 **Interior** South Dakota, N USA 43.42N 101.57W
110 E9 **Interlaken** Bern, SW Switzerland 46.40N 7.51E
31 V2 **International Falls** Minnesota, N USA 48.37N 93.25W
178 Gg7 **Inthanon, Doi** ▲ NW Thailand 18.33N 98.29E
44 G7 **Intibucá** ◆ department SW Honduras
44 G8 **Intipucá** La Unión, SE El Salvador 13.10N 88.03W
63 B15 **Intiyaco** Santa Fe, C Argentina 28.43S 60.04W
118 K12 **Întorsura Buzăului** Ger. Bozau, Hung. Bodzafordulő. Covasna, E Romania 45.49N 26.10E
24 H9 **Intracoastal Waterway** inland waterway system Louisiana, S USA
27 V13 **Intracoastal Waterway** inland waterway system Texas, SW USA
110 G11 **Intragna** Ticino, S Switzerland 46.12N 8.42E
171 Kk17 **Inubō-zaki** headland Honshū, S Japan 35.42N 140.51E
170 D14 **Inukai** Ōita, Kyūshū, SW Japan 33.05N 131.37E
10 I5 **Inukjuak** var. Inoucdjouac; prev. Port Harrison. Quebec, NE Canada 58.28N 77.58W
65 I24 **Inútil, Bahía** bay S Chile
Inuuvik see Inuvik
14 G3 **Inuvik** var. Inuuvik. Northwest Territories, NW Canada 68.25N 133.34W
171 I15 **Inuyama** Aichi, Honshū, SW Japan 35.22N 136.55E
58 G13 **Inuya, Río** River E Peru
129 U13 **In'va** River NW Russian Federation
98 H11 **Inveraray** W Scotland, UK 56.13N 5.04W
193 C24 **Invercargill** Southland, South Island, NZ 46.25S 168.22E
191 T5 **Inverell** New South Wales, SE Australia 29.49S 151.07E
98 I8 **Invergordon** N Scotland, UK 57.42N 4.01W
9 P16 **Invermere** British Columbia, SW Canada 50.30N 116.00W
11 R14 **Inverness** Cape Breton Island, Nova Scotia, SE Canada 46.13N 61.19W
98 I8 **Inverness** N Scotland, UK 57.27N 4.15W
25 V11 **Inverness** Florida, SE USA 28.50N 82.19W
98 I9 **Inverness** cultural region NW Scotland, UK
98 K9 **Inverurie** NE Scotland, UK 57.13N 2.13W
190 F8 **Investigator Group** island group South Australia
181 T7 **Investigator Ridge** undersea feature E Indian Ocean
190 H10 **Investigator Strait** strait South Australia
31 R11 **Inwood** Iowa, C USA 43.16N 96.25W
126 H16 **Inya** Respublika Altay, S Russian Federation 50.27N 86.45E
127 Nn10 **Inya** River E Russian Federation
Inyanga see Nyanga
85 M16 **Inyangani** ▲ NE Zimbabwe 18.22S 32.57E
85 J17 **Inyathi** Matabeleland North, SW Zimbabwe 19.36S 28.52E
37 T12 **Inyokern** California, W USA 35.37N 117.48W
37 T10 **Inyo Mountains** ▲ California, W USA
131 P6 **Inza** Ul'yanovskaya Oblast', W Russian Federation 53.51N 46.21E
131 W5 **Inzer** Respublika Bashkortostan, W Russian Federation 54.11N 57.37E
131 N7 **Inzhavino** Tambovskaya Oblast', W Russian Federation 52.18N 42.28E
117 C16 **Ioánnina** var. Janina, Yannina. Ípeiros, W Greece 39.39N 20.52E
170 B17 **Iō-jima** var. Iwojima. island Nansei-shotō, SW Japan
128 L4 **Iokan'ga** River NW Russian Federation
29 Q6 **Iola** Kansas, C USA 37.55N 95.24W
Iolcus see Iolkós
117 G16 **Iolkós** anc. Iolcus. site of ancient city Thessalía, C Greece 39.24N 22.56E
Iolotan' see Yëloten
85 A16 **Iona** Namibe, SW Angola 16.54S 12.39E
98 F11 **Iona** island W Scotland, UK
118 M15 **Ion Corvin** Constanţa, SE Romania 44.06N 27.49E
37 P7 **Ione** California, W USA 38.21N 120.55W
118 I13 **Ioneşti** Vâlcea, SW Romania 44.51N 24.12E
33 Q9 **Ionia** Michigan, N USA 42.59N 85.04W
Ionia Basin see Ionian Basin
123 Mm12 **Ionian Basin** var. Ionia Basin. undersea feature Ionian Sea, C Mediterranean Sea
Ionian Islands see Iónioi Nísoi
123 Mm11 **Ionian Sea** Gk. Iónio Pélagos, It. Mar Ionio. sea C Mediterranean Sea
117 B17 **Iónioi Nísoi** Eng. Ionian Islands. ◆ region W Greece
117 B17 **Iónioi Nísoi** Eng. Ionian Islands. island group W Greece
Ionio, Mar/Iónio Pélagos see Ionian Sea
Iordan see Yordan
143 U10 **Iori** var. Qabırrı. River Azerbaijan/Georgia
Iorrais, Ceann see Erris Head
117 J22 **Íos** Íos, Kykládes, Greece, Aegean Sea 36.42N 25.16E
117 J22 **Íos** var. Nio. island Kykládes, Greece, Aegean Sea
24 G9 **Iowa** Louisiana, S USA 30.12N 93.00W
31 V13 **Iowa** off. State of Iowa; also known as The Hawkeye State. ◆ state C USA
31 Y14 **Iowa City** Iowa, C USA 41.39N 91.31W
31 V13 **Iowa Falls** Iowa, C USA 42.31N 93.15W
27 R4 **Iowa Park** Texas, SW USA 33.57N 98.40W
31 Y14 **Iowa River** River Iowa, C USA
121 M19 **Ipa** Rus. Ipa. River SE Belarus
61 N20 **Ipatinga** Minas Gerais, SE Brazil 19.31S 42.30W
131 N13 **Ipatovo** Stavropol'skiy Kray, SW Russian Federation 45.40N 42.51E
117 C16 **Ípeiros** Eng. Epirus. ◆ region W Greece
Ipek see Peć
113 J21 **Ipel'** var. Ipoly, Ger. Eipel. River Hungary/Slovakia
56 C13 **Ipiales** Nariño, SW Colombia 0.50N 77.42W
201 V14 **Ipis** atoll Chuuk Islands, C Micronesia
61 A14 **Ipixuna** Amazonas, W Brazil 6.57S 71.42W
174 Gg4 **Ipoh** Perak, Peninsular Malaysia 4.36N 101.01E
Ipoly see Ipel'
197 D15 **Ipota** Erromango, S Vanuatu 18.54S 169.19E
81 K14 **Ippy** Ouaka, C Central African Republic 6.17N 21.13E
116 L13 **İpsala** Edirne, NW Turkey 40.55N 26.24E
Ipsario see Ypsário
191 V3 **Ipswich** Queensland, E Australia 27.36S 152.49E
99 Q20 **Ipswich** hist. Gipeswic. E England, UK 52.05N 1.08E
31 O8 **Ipswich** South Dakota, N USA 45.24N 99.00W
Iput' see Iputs'
121 P18 **Iputs'** Rus. Iput'. River Belarus/Russian Federation
16 O3 **Iqaluit** prev. Frobisher Bay. Baffin Island, Nunavut, NE Canada 63.43N 68.28W
165 P9 **Iqe** Qinghai, W China 38.03N 94.45E
165 P9 **Iqe He** River C China
Iqlid see Eqlīd
64 G3 **Iquique** Tarapacá, N Chile 20.15S 70.07W
58 G8 **Iquitos** Loreto, N Peru 3.51S 73.13W
27 N9 **Iraan** Texas, SW USA 30.52N 101.54W
81 K14 **Ira Banda** Haute-Kotto, E Central African Republic 5.57N 22.05E
172 Pp16 **Irabu-jima** island Miyako-shotō, SW Japan
57 Y9 **Iracoubo** N French Guiana 5.28N 53.15W
171 Hh17 **Irago-misaki** headland Honshū, SW Japan 34.35N 137.00E
62 H13 **Iraí** Rio Grande do Sul, S Brazil 27.15S 53.16W
116 G12 **Irákleia** Kentrikí Makedonía, N Greece 41.09N 23.16E
117 J21 **Irákleia** island Kykládes, Greece, Aegean Sea
117 J25 **Irákleio** var. Herakleion, Eng. Candia; prev. Iráklion. Kríti, Greece, E Mediterranean Sea 35.19N 25.07E
117 J25 **Irákleio** ✕ Kríti, Greece, E Mediterranean Sea 35.20N 25.10E
117 F15 **Irákleio** anc. Heracleum. castle Kentrikí Makedonía, N Greece 40.02N 22.34E
Iráklion see Irákleio
149 O7 **Iran** off. Islamic Republic of Iran; prev. Persia. ◆ republic SW Asia
60 F13 **Iranduba** Amazonas, NW Brazil 3.19S 60.09W
87 P13 **Iranian Plate** tectonic feature
149 Q9 **Iranian Plateau** var. Plateau of Iran. plateau N Iran
175 N6 **Iran, Pegunungan** var. Iran Mountains. ▲ Indonesia/Malaysia
Iran, Plateau of see Iranian Plateau
149 W13 **Īrānshahr** Sīstān va Balūchestān, SE Iran 27.14N 60.40E
57 P5 **Irapa** Sucre, NE Venezuela 10.33N 62.37W
43 N13 **Irapuato** Guanajuato, C Mexico 20.40N 101.22W
145 R7 **Iraq** off. Republic of Iraq, Ar. 'Irāq. ◆ republic SW Asia
62 J12 **Irati** Paraná, S Brazil 25.25S 50.37W
107 R3 **Irati** River N Spain
129 T8 **Irayel'** Respublika Komi, NW Russian Federation 64.28N 55.20E
45 N13 **Irazú, Volcán** ✕ C Costa Rica 9.57N 83.52W
Irbenskiy Zaliv/Irbes Šaurums see Irbe Strait
120 D7 **Irbe Strait** Est. Kura Kurk, Latv. Irbes Šaurums, Rus. Irbenskiy Zaliv; prev. Est. Irbe Väin. strait Estonia/Latvia
Irbe Väin see Irbe Strait
144 G9 **Irbid** Irbid, N Jordan 32.33N 35.51E
144 G9 **Irbid** off. Muḥāfaẓat Irbid. ◆ governorate N Jordan
Irbīl see Arbīl
125 F11 **Irbit** Sverdlovskaya Oblast', C Russian Federation 57.37N 63.10E
111 S6 **Irdning** Steiermark, SE Austria 47.29N 14.04E
81 I18 **Irebu** Equateur, W Dem. Rep. Congo 0.32S 17.44E
86 C9 **Ireland** Lat. Hibernia. island Ireland/UK
99 D17 **Ireland** off. Ireland, var. Republic of Ireland, Ir. Éire. ◆ republic NW Europe
66 A12 **Ireland Island North** island W Bermuda
66 A12 **Ireland Island South** island W Bermuda
Ireland, Republic of see Ireland
129 V15 **Iren'** River NW Russian Federation
193 A22 **Irene, Mount** ▲ South Island, NZ 45.04S 167.24E
Irgalem see Yirga 'Alem
150 L11 **Irgiz** Aktyubinsk, C Kazakhstan 48.37N 61.12E
Irian see New Guinea
Irian Barat see Papua
Irian, Teluk see Cenderawasih, Teluk
80 K9 **Iriba** Biltine, NE Chad 15.10N 22.10E
179 Q11 **Iriga** Luzon, N Philippines 13.25N 123.24E
131 X7 **Iriklinskoye Vodokhranilishche** Reservoir W Russian Federation
Isbarta see Isparta
83 H23 **Iringa** Iringa, C Tanzania 7.49S 35.39E
83 H23 **Iringa** ◆ region S Tanzania
172 O17 **Iriomote-jima** island Sakishima-shotō, SW Japan
44 L4 **Iriona** Colón, NE Honduras 15.53N 85.08W
49 U7 **Iriri** River N Brazil
60 I13 **Iriri, Rio** River C Brazil
Iris see Yeşilırmak
37 W9 **Irish, Mount** ▲ Nevada, W USA 37.39N 115.22W
99 H17 **Irish Sea** Ir. Muir Éireann. sea C British Isles
145 U12 **Irjal ash Shaykhīyah** S Iraq 30.49N 44.58E
153 U11 **Irkeshtam** Oshskaya Oblast', SW Kyrgyzstan 39.39N 73.49E
126 J16 **Irkut** River S Russian Federation
126 Jj16 **Irkutsk** Irkutskaya Oblast', S Russian Federation 52.18N 104.15E
126 Jj13 **Irkutskaya Oblast'** ◆ province S Russian Federation
Irlir, Gora see Irlir Toghi
152 K8 **Irlir Togʻi** var. Gora Irlir. ▲ N Uzbekistan 42.43N 63.24E
Irminger Basin see Reykjanes Basin
23 R12 **Irmo** South Carolina, SE USA 34.05N 81.10W
104 E6 **Iroise** sea NW France
201 X2 **Iroj** var. Eroj. island Ratak Chain, SE Marshall Islands
190 H7 **Iron Baron** South Australia 33.01S 137.13E
195 X15 **Iron Bottom Sound** sound C Solomon Islands
12 C10 **Iron Bridge** Ontario, S Canada 46.16N 83.12W
22 H10 **Iron City** Tennessee, S USA 35.01N 87.34W
12 I13 **Irondale** River Ontario, SE Canada
190 H7 **Iron Knob** South Australia 32.46S 137.08E
32 M5 **Iron Mountain** Michigan, N USA 45.51N 88.03W
32 M4 **Iron River** Michigan, N USA 46.05N 88.38W
32 J3 **Iron River** Wisconsin, N USA 46.34N 91.22W
29 X6 **Ironton** Missouri, C USA 37.36N 90.37W
33 S15 **Ironton** Ohio, N USA 38.32N 82.40W
32 K4 **Ironwood** Michigan, N USA 46.27N 90.10W
10 H12 **Iroquois Falls** Ontario, S Canada 48.46N 80.40W
33 N12 **Iroquois River** River Illinois/Indiana, N USA
171 Ii18 **Irō-zaki** headland Honshū, S Japan 34.36N 138.49E
Irpen' see Irpin'
119 O4 **Irpin'** Rus. Irpen'. Kyyivs'ka Oblast', N Ukraine 50.31N 30.15E
119 O4 **Irpin'** Rus. Irpen'. River N Ukraine
147 Q16 **'Irqah** SW Yemen 13.42N 47.21E
177 Ff8 **Irrawaddy** var. Ayeyarwady. ◆ division SW Myanmar
177 G6 **Irrawaddy** var. Ayeyarwady. River W Myanmar
177 Ff9 **Irrawaddy, Mouths of the** delta SW Myanmar
119 N4 **Irsha** River N Ukraine
118 H7 **Irshava** Zakarpats'ka Oblast', W Ukraine 48.19N 23.03E
109 N18 **Irsina** Basilicata, S Italy 40.42N 16.18E
Irtish see Irtysh
133 R5 **Irtysh** var. Irtish, Kaz. Ertis. River C Asia
151 S7 **Irtyshsk** Kaz. Ertis. Pavlodar, NE Kazakhstan 53.21N 75.27E
81 P17 **Irumu** Orientale, E Dem. Rep. Congo 1.27N 29.52E
107 Q2 **Irún** País Vasco, N Spain 43.19N 1.48W
Iruña see Pamplona
107 Q3 **Irurtzun** Navarra, N Spain 42.55N 1.49W
98 I13 **Irvine** W Scotland, UK 55.37N 4.40W
23 N6 **Irvine** Kentucky, S USA 37.42N 83.58W
27 T6 **Irving** Texas, SW USA 32.48N 96.57W
22 K5 **Irvington** Kentucky, S USA 37.52N 86.16W
Isaak see Iisaku
30 L8 **Isabel** South Dakota, N USA 45.21N 101.25W
195 W14 **Isabel** off. Isabel Province. ◆ province N Solomon Islands
179 Q17 **Isabela** Basilan Island, SW Philippines 6.41N 122.00E
47 S5 **Isabela** W Puerto Rico 18.30N 67.01W
47 N8 **Isabela, Cabo** headland NW Dominican Republic 19.54N 71.03W
59 A18 **Isabela, Isla** var. Albemarle Island. island Galapagos Islands, Ecuador, E Pacific Ocean
42 I12 **Isabela, Isla** island C Mexico
44 K9 **Isabella, Cordillera** ▲ NW Nicaragua
37 S12 **Isabella Lake** Reservoir California, W USA
33 N2 **Isabelle, Point** headland Michigan, N USA 47.20N 87.56W
Isabel Segunda see Vieques
118 M13 **Isaccea** Tulcea, E Romania 45.16N 28.28E
94 H1 **Ísafjarðardjúp** inlet NW Iceland
94 H1 **Ísafjörður** Vestfirðir, NW Iceland 66.04N 23.09W
170 C13 **Isahaya** Nagasaki, Kyūshū, SW Japan 32.51N 130.04E
155 S7 **Isa Khel** Punjab, E Pakistan 32.39N 71.12E
180 H7 **Isalo** var. Massif de L'Isalo. ▲ SW Madagascar
Isalo, Massif de L' see Isalo
81 K20 **Isandja** Kasai Occidental, C Dem. Rep. Congo 3.03S 21.57E
197 D16 **Isangel** Tanna, S Vanuatu 19.34S 169.17E
81 M18 **Isangi** Orientale, C Dem. Rep. Congo 0.46N 24.15E
103 L24 **Isar** River Austria/Germany
103 M23 **Isar-Kanal** canal SE Germany
Isca Damnoniorum see Exeter
109 K18 **Ischia** var. Isola d'Ischia; anc. Aenaria. Campania, S Italy 40.43N 13.57E
109 J18 **Ischia, Isola d'** island S Italy
56 B12 **Iscuandé** var. Santa Bárbara. Nariño, SW Colombia 2.31N 78.04W
171 Hh16 **Ise** Mie, Honshū, SW Japan 34.28N 136.42E
97 I23 **Isefjord** fjord E Denmark
Iseghem see Izegem
199 Jj17 **Iselin Seamount** undersea feature S Pacific Ocean 72.30S 179.00W
Isenhof see Püssi
108 E7 **Iseo** Lombardia, N Italy 45.40N 10.03E
105 U12 **Iseran, Col de l'** pass E France 45.26N 7.00E
105 S11 **Isère** ◆ department E France
105 S12 **Isère** River E France
103 F15 **Iserlohn** Nordrhein-Westfalen, W Germany 51.22N 7.42E
109 K16 **Isernia** var. Æsernia. Molise, C Italy 41.34N 14.13E
171 Jj15 **Isesaki** Gunma, Honshū, S Japan 36.19N 139.10E
133 Q5 **Iset'** River C Russian Federation
171 Hh16 **Ise-wan** bay S Japan
79 S15 **Iseyin** Oyo, W Nigeria 7.56N 3.33E
Isfahan see Eşfahān
153 Q11 **Isfana** Oshskaya Oblast', SW Kyrgyzstan 39.51N 69.31E
153 R11 **Isfara** N Tajikistan 40.06N 70.34E
155 O4 **Isfi Maidān** Ghowr, N Afghanistan 35.09N 66.16E
94 O3 **Isfjorden** fjord W Svalbard
Isha Baydhabo see Baydhabo
129 V11 **Isherim, Gora** ▲ NW Russian Federation 61.06N 59.09E
131 Q5 **Isheyevka** Ul'yanovskaya Oblast', W Russian Federation 54.27N 48.18E
172 Oo17 **Ishigaki** Okinawa, Ishigaki-jima, SW Japan 24.19N 124.09E
172 P17 **Ishigaki-jima** var. Isigaki Zima. island Sakishima-shotō, SW Japan
172 O5 **Ishikari** Hokkaidō, NE Japan 43.12N 141.21E
172 Oo5 **Ishikari-gawa** var. Isikari Gawa. River Hokkaidō, NE Japan
172 O4 **Ishikari-wan** bay Hokkaidō, NE Japan
171 L14 **Ishikawa** Fukushima, Honshū, C Japan 37.08N 140.26E
172 Oo14 **Ishikawa** var. Isikawa. Okinawa, Okinawa, SW Japan 26.25N 127.46E
171 I13 **Ishikawa** off. Ishikawa-ken, var. Isikawa. ◆ prefecture Honshū, SW Japan
125 Ff12 **Ishim** Tyumenskaya Oblast', C Russian Federation 56.12N 69.25E
133 R6 **Ishim** Kaz. Esil. River Kazakhstan/Russian Federation
131 V6 **Ishimbay** Respublika Bashkortostan, W Russian Federation 53.21N 56.03E
151 O9 **Ishimskoye** Akmola, C Kazakhstan 51.22N 67.07E
171 M13 **Ishinomaki** var. Isinomaki. Miyagi, Honshū, C Japan 38.25N 141.16E
171 Kk16 **Ishioka** var. Isioka. Ibaraki, Honshū, S Japan 36.12N 140.18E
170 Ee15 **Ishizuchi-san** ▲ Shikoku, SW Japan 33.44N 133.07E
Ishkashim see Ishkoshim
Ishkashimskiy Khrebet see Ishkoshim, Qatorkŭhi
153 S15 **Ishkoshim** Rus. Ishkashim. S Tajikistan 36.46N 71.35E
153 S15 **Ishkoshim, Qatorkŭhi** Rus. Ishkashimskiy Khrebet. ▲ SE Tajikistan
33 N4 **Ishpeming** Michigan, N USA 46.29N 87.40W
153 N11 **Ishtixon** Rus. Ishtykhan. Samarqand Viloyati, C Uzbekistan 39.59N 66.28E
Ishtykhan see Ishtixon
159 T15 **Ishurdi** var. Iswardi. Rajshahi, W Bangladesh 24.10N 89.04E
63 G17 **Isidoro Noblia** Cerro Largo, NE Uruguay 31.58S 54.09W
104 J4 **Isigny-sur-Mer** Calvados, N France 49.20N 1.06W
Isikari Gawa see Ishikari-gawa
Isikawa see Ishikawa
142 C11 **Işıklar Dağı** ▲ NW Turkey
109 C19 **Isili** Sardegna, Italy, C Mediterranean Sea 39.46N 9.06E
125 Ff13 **Isil'kul'** Omskaya Oblast', C Russian Federation 54.52N 71.07E
Isinomaki see Ishinomaki
Isioka see Ishioka
83 I18 **Isiolo** Eastern, C Kenya 0.21N 37.33E
81 O16 **Isiro** Orientale, NE Dem. Rep. Congo 2.51N 27.46E
94 P2 **Isispynten** headland NE Svalbard 79.51N 26.44E
126 Ll11 **Isit** Respublika Sakha (Yakutiya), NE Russian Federation 60.53N 125.32E
155 O2 **Iskabad Canal** canal N Afghanistan
153 Q9 **Iskandar** Rus. Iskander. Toshkent Viloyati, E Uzbekistan 41.32N 69.46E
Iskander see Iskandar

◆ Country
● Country Capital
◇ Dependent Territory
○ Dependent Territory Capital
◆ Administrative Region
✕ International Airport
▲ Mountain
▲ Mountain Range
✕ Volcano
River
Lake
Reservoir

Iskăr see Iskŭr
124 O2 Iskele var. Trikomo, Gk. Tríkomon. E Cyprus 35.16N 33.54E
142 K17 İskenderun Eng. Alexandretta. Hatay, S Turkey 36.34N 36.10E
144 H2 İskenderun Körfezi Eng. Gulf of Alexandretta. gulf S Turkey
142 J11 İskilip Çorum, N Turkey 40.45N 34.28E
Iski-Nauket see Eski-Nookat
126 Gg14 Iskitim Novosibirskaya Oblast', C Russian Federation 54.36N 83.05E
116 J11 Iskra prev. Popovo. Kŭrdzhali, S Bulgaria 41.55N 25.12E
116 G10 Iskŭr var. Iskăr. ≈ NW Bulgaria
116 H10 Iskŭr, Yazovir prev. Yazovir Stalin. ▣ W Bulgaria
43 S15 Isla Veracruz-Llave, SE Mexico 18.01N 95.30W
121 J15 Islach Rus. Isloch'. ≈ C Belarus
106 H14 Isla Cristina Andalucía, S Spain 37.12N 7.19W
Isla de León see San Fernando
155 U6 Islāmābād ● (Pakistan) Federal Capital Territory Islāmābād, NE Pakistan 33.40N 73.07E
155 V6 Islāmābād ✈ Federal Capital Territory Islāmābād, NE Pakistan 33.40N 73.07E
Islamabad see Anantnāg
155 R17 Islāmkot Sind, SE Pakistan 24.37N 70.04E
25 Y17 Islamorada Florida Keys, Florida, SE USA 24.55N 80.37W
159 P14 Islāmpur Bihār, N India 25.09N 85.13E
Islam Qala see Eslām Qal'eh
Island/Ísland see Iceland
20 K16 Island Beach spit New Jersey, NE USA
21 S4 Island Falls Maine, NE USA 45.59N 68.16W
190 H6 Island Lagoon ◎ South Australia
9 Y13 Island Lake ◎ Manitoba, C Canada
31 W5 Island Lake Reservoir ▣ Minnesota, N USA
35 R13 Island Park Idaho, NW USA 44.27N 111.21W
21 N6 Island Pond Vermont, NE USA 44.48N 71.51W
192 K2 Islands, Bay of inlet North Island, NZ
105 R7 Is-sur-Tille Côte d'Or, C France 47.34N 5.03E
44 J3 Islas de la Bahía ◈ department N Honduras
67 L20 Islas Orcadas Rise undersea feature S Atlantic Ocean
98 F12 Islay island SW Scotland, UK
118 I15 Islaz Teleorman, S Romania 43.43N 24.52E
31 V7 Isle Minnesota, N USA 46.08N 93.28W
104 M12 Isle ≈ W France
99 I16 Isle of Man ◇ UK crown dependency NW Europe
23 X7 Isle of Wight Virginia, NE USA 36.54N 76.41W
99 M24 Isle of Wight cultural region S England, UK
203 Y3 Isles Lagoon ◎ Kiritimati, E Kiribati
39 R11 Isleta Pueblo New Mexico, SW USA 34.54N 106.40W
Isloch' see Islach
63 E19 Ismael Cortinas Flores, S Uruguay 33.57S 57.04W
Ismailia see Ismâ'ilîya
77 W7 Ismâ'ilîya var. Ismailia. N Egypt 30.31N 32.13E
Ismid see İzmit
77 X10 Isna var. Esna. SE Egypt 25.16N 32.24E
95 K18 Isojoki Länsi-Suomi, W Finland 62.07N 22.00E
84 M12 Isoka Northern, NE Zambia 10.07S 32.42E
Isola d'Ischia see Ischia
Isola d'Istria see Izola
Isonzo see Soča
13 U4 Isoukustouc ≈ Québec, SE Canada
142 F15 Isparta var. Isbarta. Isparta, SW Turkey 37.46N 30.31E
142 F15 Isparta var. Isbarta. ◈ province SW Turkey
116 M7 Isperikh prev. Kemanlar. Razgrad, N Bulgaria 43.43N 26.49E
109 L26 Ispica Sicilia, Italy, C Mediterranean Sea 36.46N 14.55E
154 J14 Ispikān Baluchistān, SW Pakistan 26.21N 62.15E
143 Q12 İspir Erzurum, NE Turkey 40.28N 41.01E
144 E12 Israel off. State of Israel, var. Medinat Israel, Heb. Yisrael, Yisra'el. ◆ republic SW Asia
Issa see Vis
57 S9 Issano C Guyana 5.49N 59.28W
78 M16 Issia SW Ivory Coast 6.33N 6.33W
Issiq Köl see Issyk-Kul', Ozero
105 P11 Issoire Puy-de-Dôme, C France 45.33N 3.15E
105 N9 Issoudun anc. Uxellodunum. Indre, C France 46.57N 1.58E
83 H22 Issuna Singida, C Tanzania 5.24S 34.48E
Issyk see Yesik
Issyk-Kul' see Balykchy
153 X7 Issyk-Kul', Ozero var. Issiq Köl, Kir. Ysyk-Köl. ◎ E Kyrgyzstan
153 X7 Issyk-Kul'skaya Oblast' Kir. Ysyk-Köl Oblasty. ◈ province E Kyrgyzstan
155 Q7 Istādeh-ye Moqor, Āb-e- var. Āb-i-Istāda. ◎ SE Afghanistan
142 D11 İstanbul Bul. Tsarigrad, Eng. Istanbul; prev. Constantinople, anc. Byzantium. İstanbul, NW Turkey 41.01N 28.57E
116 P12 İstanbul ◈ province NW Turkey
116 P12 İstanbul Boğazı var. Bosporus Thracius, Eng. Bosphorus, Bosporus, Turk. Karadeniz Boğazı. strait NW Turkey
Istarska Županija see Istra
117 G19 Isthmía Pelopónnisos, S Greece 37.55N 23.02E
117 G17 Istiaía Évvoia, C Greece 38.57N 23.09E
56 D9 Istmina Chocó, W Colombia 5.09N 76.42W
25 W13 Istokpoga, Lake ◎ Florida, SE USA
114 A9 Istra off. Istarska županija. ◈ province NW Croatia
114 I10 Istra Eng. Istria, Ger. Istrien. cultural region NW Croatia
105 R15 Istres Bouches-du-Rhône, SE France 43.30N 4.58E
Istria/Istrien see Istra
179 R16 Isulan Mindanao, S Philippines 6.36N 124.36E
194 I11 Isumrud Strait strait NE PNG
Iswardi see Ishurdi
131 V7 Isyangulovo Respublika Bashkortostan, W Russian Federation 52.10N 56.38E
64 O6 Itá Central, S Paraguay 25.28S 57.21W
61 O17 Itaberaba Bahia, E Brazil 12.34S 40.21W
61 M20 Itabira prev. Presidente Vargas. Minas Gerais, SE Brazil 19.39S 43.13W
61 O18 Itabuna Bahia, E Brazil 14.48S 39.18W
61 J18 Itacaiu Mato Grosso, S Brazil 14.49S 51.21W
60 G12 Itacoatiara Amazonas, N Brazil 3.06S 58.22W
56 D9 Itagüí Antioquia, W Colombia 6.12N 75.40W
62 D13 Itá Ibaté Corrientes, NE Argentina 27.27S 57.24W
62 G11 Itaipú, Represa de ▣ Brazil/Paraguay
60 H13 Itaituba Pará, NE Brazil 4.15S 55.56W
62 K13 Itajaí Santa Catarina, S Brazil 26.49S 48.39W
Italia/Italiana, Republica/Italian Republic, The see Italy
Italian Somaliland see Somalia
27 T7 Italy Texas, SW USA 32.10N 96.52W
108 G12 Italy off. The Italian Republic, It. Italia, Republica Italiana. ◆ republic S Europe
61 O19 Itamaraju Bahia, E Brazil 16.58S 39.31W
61 C14 Itamarati Amazonas, W Brazil 6.12S 68.16W
61 M19 Itambé, Pico de ▲ SE Brazil 18.22S 43.21W
171 Gg15 Itami ✈ (Ōsaka) Ōsaka, Honshū, SW Japan 34.47N 135.24E
117 H15 Ítamos ▲ N Greece 40.06N 23.51E
159 W11 Itānagar Arunāchal Pradesh, NE India 27.09N 93.35E
Itany see Litani
61 N19 Itaobim Minas Gerais, SE Brazil 16.34S 41.27W
61 P15 Itaparica, Represa de ▣ E Brazil
60 M13 Itapecuru-Mirim Maranhão, E Brazil 3.24S 44.19W
62 Q8 Itaperuna Rio de Janeiro, SE Brazil 21.13S 41.51W
61 O18 Itapetinga Bahia, E Brazil 15.16S 40.16W
62 L10 Itapetininga São Paulo, S Brazil 23.33S 48.03W
62 K10 Itapeva São Paulo, S Brazil 23.58S 48.54W
49 W6 Itapicuru, Rio ≈ NE Brazil
60 O13 Itapipoca Ceará, E Brazil 3.28S 39.34W
62 M9 Itapira São Paulo, S Brazil 22.25S 46.46W
62 K8 Itápolis São Paulo, S Brazil 21.36S 48.43W
62 K10 Itaporanga São Paulo, S Brazil 23.43S 49.28W
64 P7 Itapúa off. Departamento de Itapúa. ◈ department SE Paraguay
61 E15 Itapuã do Oeste Rondônia, W Brazil 9.21S 63.07W
63 E15 Itaqui Rio Grande do Sul, S Brazil 29.10S 56.28W
62 K10 Itararé São Paulo, S Brazil 24.07S 49.16W
62 K10 Itararé, Rio ≈ S Brazil
160 H11 Itārsi Madhya Pradesh, C India 22.42N 77.55E
27 T7 Itasca Texas, SW USA 32.09N 97.09W
Itassi see Vieille Case
95 N17 Itä-Suomi ◈ province E Finland
62 D13 Itatí Corrientes, NE Argentina 27.16S 58.15W
62 K10 Itatinga São Paulo, S Brazil 23.08S 48.36W
117 F18 Itéas, Kólpos gulf C Greece
59 N15 Iténez, Río var. Rio Guaporé. ≈ Bolivia/Brazil see also Guaporé, Rio
56 H11 Iteviate, Río ≈ C Colombia
102 I13 Ith hill range C Germany
33 Q8 Ithaca Michigan, N USA 43.17N 84.36W
20 H11 Ithaca New York, NE USA 42.25N 76.30W
117 C18 Itháki Itháki, Iónioi Nísoi, Greece, C Mediterranean Sea 38.22N 20.43E
117 C18 Itháki island Iónioi Nísoi, Greece, C Mediterranean Sea
It Hearrenfean see Heerenveen
Ithiara see Ichihara
81 L17 Itimbiri ≈ N Dem. Rep. Congo
Itinomiya see Ichinomiya
Itinoseki see Ichinoseki
41 Q5 Itkilik River ≈ Alaska, USA
171 J17 Itō Shizuoka, Honshū, S Japan 34.59N 139.03E
171 J13 Itoigawa Niigata, Honshū, C Japan 37.01N 137.52E
13 R6 Itomamo, Lac ◎ Québec, SE Canada
172 Oo15 Itoman Okinawa, SW Japan 26.04N 127.40E
104 M5 Iton ≈ N France
59 M16 Itonamas Río ≈ NE Bolivia
Itoupé, Mont see Sommet Tabulaire
Itseqqortoormiit see Ittoqqortoormiit
24 K4 Itta Bena Mississippi, S USA 33.30N 90.19W
109 B17 Ittiri Sardegna, Italy, C Mediterranean Sea 40.36N 8.34E
207 Q14 Ittoqqortoormiit var. Itseqqortoormiit, Dan. Scoresbysund, Eng. Scoresby Sound. Tunu, C Greenland 70.33N 21.52W
62 M10 Itu São Paulo, S Brazil 23.17S 47.16W
178 Mm14 Itu Aba Island island W Spratly Islands
56 D8 Ituango Antioquia, NW Colombia 7.06N 75.51W
61 A14 Ituí, Rio ≈ NW Brazil
81 O20 Itula Sud Kivu, E Dem. Rep. Congo 3.30S 27.49E
61 K19 Itumbiara Goiás, C Brazil 18.25S 49.15W
57 T9 Ituni E Guyana 5.24N 58.18W
43 X13 Iturbide Campeche, SE Mexico 19.41N 89.29W
Ituri see Aruwimi
127 Pp16 Iturup, Ostrov island Kuril'skiye Ostrova, SE Russian Federation
62 L7 Ituverava São Paulo, S Brazil 20.22S 47.48W
61 C15 Ituxi, Rio ≈ W Brazil
63 E14 Ituzaingó Corrientes, NE Argentina 27.34S 56.43W
103 K18 Itz ≈ C Germany
102 I9 Itzehoe Schleswig-Holstein, N Germany 53.55N 9.31E
25 N2 Iuka Mississippi, S USA 34.48N 88.11W
62 I11 Ivaiporã Paraná, S Brazil 24.16S 51.46W
62 I11 Ivaí, Rio ≈ S Brazil
94 L10 Ivalo Lapp. Avveel, Avvil. Lappi, N Finland 68.34N 27.29E
94 L10 Ivalojoki Lapp. Avveel. ≈ N Finland
121 H20 Ivanava Pol. Janów, Janów Poleski, Rus. Ivanovo. Brestskaya Voblasts', SW Belarus 52.07N 25.31E
Ivangorod see Dęblin
Ivangrad see Berane
191 N7 Ivanhoe New South Wales, SE Australia 32.54S 144.20E
31 S9 Ivanhoe Minnesota, N USA 44.27N 96.15W
12 D8 Ivanhoe ≈ Ontario, S Canada
114 E8 Ivanić-Grad Sisak-Moslavina, N Croatia 45.43N 16.23E
119 T10 Ivanivka Khersons'ka Oblast', S Ukraine 46.43N 34.28E
119 P10 Ivanivka Odes'ka Oblast', SW Ukraine 46.57N 30.26E
115 L14 Ivanjica Serbia, C Serbia and Montenegro (Yugoslavia) 43.36N 20.14E
114 G11 Ivanjska var. Potkozarje. Republika Srpska, NW Bosnia & Herzegovina 44.54N 17.04E
113 H21 Ivanka ✈ (Bratislava) Bratislavský Kraj, W Slovakia 48.10N 17.13E
119 O3 Ivankiv Rus. Ivankov. Kyyivs'ka Oblast', N Ukraine 50.55N 29.53E
Ivankov see Ivankiv
41 O15 Ivanof Bay Alaska, USA 55.55N 159.28W
118 J7 Ivano-Frankivs'k Ger. Stanislau, Pol. Stanisławów, Rus. Ivano-Frankovsk; prev. Stanislav. Ivano-Frankivs'ka Oblast', W Ukraine 48.55N 24.45E
Ivano-Frankivs'k see Ivano-Frankivs'ka Oblast'
118 I7 Ivano-Frankivs'ka Oblast' var. Ivano-Frankivs'k, Rus. Ivano-Frankovskaya Oblast'; prev. Stanislavskaya Oblast'. ◈ province W Ukraine
Ivano-Frankovsk see Ivano-Frankivs'k
Ivano-Frankovskaya Oblast' see Ivano-Frankivs'ka Oblast'
128 M16 Ivanovo Ivanovskaya Oblast', W Russian Federation 57.01N 40.58E
Ivanovo see Ivanava
125 A16 Ivanovskaya Oblast' ◈ province W Russian Federation
37 X12 Ivanpah Lake ◎ California, W USA
114 E7 Ivanščica ▲ NE Croatia
116 M8 Ivanski Shumen, NE Bulgaria 43.09N 27.02E
131 R7 Ivanteyevka Saratovskaya Oblast', W Russian Federation 52.13N 49.06E
Ivantsevichi/Ivatsevichi see Ivatsevichy
118 I4 Ivanychi Volyns'ka Oblast', NW Ukraine 50.37N 24.22E
121 H18 Ivatsevichy Pol. Iwacewicze, Rus. Ivantsevichi, Ivatsevichi. Brestskaya Voblasts', SW Belarus 52.43N 25.21E
116 L12 Ivaylovgrad Khaskovo, S Bulgaria 41.32N 26.06E
116 K11 Ivaylovgrad, Yazovir ▣ S Bulgaria
125 F10 Ivdel' Sverdlovskaya Oblast', C Russian Federation 60.42N 60.07E
Ivenets see Ivyanyets
118 L12 Ivești Galați, E Romania 45.27N 28.00E
Ivigtut see Ivittuut
81 F18 Ivindo ≈ Congo/Gabon
61 I21 Ivinheima Mato Grosso do Sul, SW Brazil 22.16S 53.52W
206 M15 Ivittuut var. Ivigtut. Kitaa, S Greenland 61.28N 48.33W
Iviza see Eivissa
180 I6 Ivohibe Fianarantsoa, SE Madagascar 22.28S 46.52E
Ivoire, Côte d' see Ivory Coast
194 I14 Ivori ≈ S PNG
78 L15 Ivory Coast off. Republic of the Ivory Coast, Fr. Côte d'Ivoire, République de la Côte d'Ivoire. ◆ republic W Africa
70 C11 Ivory Coast Fr. Côte d'Ivoire. coastal region S Ivory Coast
97 L22 Ivösjön ◎ S Sweden
108 B7 Ivrea anc. Eporedia. Piemonte, NW Italy 45.28N 7.52E
10 J2 Ivujivik Québec, NE Canada 62.25N 77.49W
121 J16 Ivyanyets Rus. Ivenets. Minskaya Voblasts', C Belarus 53.52N 26.45E
Iv'ye see Iwye
Iwacewicze see Ivatsevichy
172 N11 Iwaizumi Iwate, Honshū, NE Japan 39.48N 141.46E
171 Ll15 Iwaki Fukushima, Honshū, N Japan 37.01N 140.52E
171 Mm9 Iwaki-san ▲ Honshū, C Japan 40.39N 140.20E
171 E13 Iwakuni Yamaguchi, Honshū, SW Japan 34.07N 132.06E
172 Oo5 Iwamizawa Hokkaidō, NE Japan 43.11N 141.43E
172 Nn5 Iwanai Hokkaidō, NE Japan 42.51N 140.21E
171 Ll13 Iwanuma Miyagi, Honshū, C Japan 38.07N 140.49E
171 I17 Iwata Shizuoka, Honshū, S Japan 34.42N 137.49E
172 N10 Iwate Iwate, Honshū, N Japan 40.02N 141.12E
171 Mm11 Iwate off. Iwate-ken. ◈ prefecture Honshū, C Japan
171 Mm10 Iwate-san ▲ Honshū, C Japan 39.52N 140.59E
Iwje see Iwye
79 S16 Iwo Oyo, SW Nigeria 7.21N 3.58E
Iwojima see Iō-jima
121 I16 Iwye Pol. Iwje, Rus. Iv'ye. Hrodzyenskaya Voblasts', W Belarus 53.55N 25.46E
44 C4 Ixcán, Río ≈ Guatemala/Mexico
101 G18 Ixelles Dut. Elsene. Brussels, C Belgium 50.49N 4.21E
59 J16 Ixiamas La Paz, NW Bolivia 13.43S 68.10W
43 O13 Ixmiquilpan var. Ixmiquilpán. Hidalgo, C Mexico 20.28N 99.11W
85 K23 Ixopo KwaZulu/Natal, E South Africa 30.07S 30.03E
Ixtacihuatal, Volcán see Iztaccíhuatl, Volcán
42 M16 Ixtapa Guerrero, S Mexico 17.37N 101.29W
43 S16 Ixtepec Oaxaca, SE Mexico 16.32N 95.03W
42 K12 Ixtlán var. Ixtlán del Río. Nayarit, C Mexico 21.03N 104.23W
Ixtlán del Río see Ixtlán
125 F12 Iyevlevo Tyumenskaya Oblast', C Russian Federation 57.36N 67.20E
170 E14 Iyo Ehime, Shikoku, SW Japan 33.44N 132.42E
170 F15 Iyomishima var. Iyomisima. Ehime, Shikoku, SW Japan 33.58N 133.31E
Iyomisima see Iyomishima
170 Dd14 Iyo-nada sea S Japan
44 E4 Izabal off. Departamento de Izabal. ◈ department E Guatemala
44 F5 Izabal, Lago de prev. Golfo Dulce. ◎ E Guatemala
149 O9 Izad Khvāst Fārs, C Iran 31.31N 52.08E
43 X12 Izamal Yucatán, SE Mexico 20.58N 89.00W
131 Q16 Izberbash Respublika Dagestan, SW Russian Federation 42.32N 47.51E
101 C18 Izegem prev. Iseghem. West-Vlaanderen, W Belgium 50.55N 3.13E
148 M9 Īzeh Khūzestān, SW Iran 31.48N 49.52E
172 P14 Izena-jima island Nansei-shotō, SW Japan
116 N10 Izgrev Burgas, E Bulgaria 42.09N 27.49E
131 T2 Izhevsk prev. Ustinov. Udmurtskaya Respublika, NW Russian Federation 56.48N 53.12E
129 S7 Izhma Respublika Komi, NW Russian Federation 64.56N 53.52E
129 S7 Izhma ≈ NW Russian Federation
147 X8 Izkī NE Oman 22.45N 57.35E
Izmail see Izmayil
119 N13 Izmayil Rus. Izmail. Odes'ka Oblast', SW Ukraine 45.19N 28.48E
142 B14 İzmir prev. Smyrna. İzmir, W Turkey 38.25N 27.10E
142 C14 İzmir prev. Smyrna. ◈ province W Turkey
142 E11 İzmit var. Ismid; anc. Astacus. Kocaeli, NW Turkey 40.46N 29.55E
106 M14 Iznájar Andalucía, S Spain 37.17N 4.16W
106 M14 Iznajar, Embalse de ▣ S Spain
107 N14 Iznalloz Andalucía, S Spain 37.23N 3.31W
142 E11 İznik Bursa, NW Turkey 40.27N 29.43E
142 E12 İznik Gölü ◎ NW Turkey
130 M14 Izobil'nyy Stavropol'skiy Kray, SW Russian Federation 45.22N 41.40E
111 S13 Izola It. Isola d'Istria. SW Slovenia 45.31N 13.40E
144 H9 Izra' var. Ezra, Ezraa. Dar'ā, S Syria 32.52N 36.15E
43 P14 Iztaccíhuatl, Volcán var. Volcán Ixtaccihuatl. ♨ S Mexico 19.07N 98.37W
44 C7 Iztapa Escuintla, SE Guatemala 13.55N 90.45W
Izúcar de Matamoros see Matamoros
171 J17 Izu-hantō peninsula Honshū, S Japan
170 C11 Izuhara Nagasaki, Tsushima, SW Japan 34.11N 129.16E
170 C15 Izumi Kagoshima, Kyūshū, SW Japan 32.05N 130.22E
171 Gg15 Izumiōtsu Ōsaka, Honshū, SW Japan 34.29N 135.25E
171 Gg15 Izumi-Sano Ōsaka, Honshū, SW Japan 34.24N 135.19E
170 F12 Izumo Shimane, Honshū, SW Japan 35.22N 132.45E
Izu Shichito see Izu-shotō
172 Ss13 Izu-shotō var. Izu Shichito. island group S Japan
199 H4 Izu Trench undersea feature NW Pacific Ocean
126 I4 Izvestiy TsIK, Ostrova island N Russian Federation
116 G10 Izvor Pernik, W Bulgaria 42.27N 22.53E
118 L5 Izyaslav Khmel'nyts'ka Oblast', W Ukraine 50.08N 26.53E
119 W6 Izyum Kharkivs'ka Oblast', E Ukraine 49.12N 37.18E

J

95 M18 Jaala Etelä-Suomi, S Finland 61.04N 26.30E
146 J5 Jabal ash Shifā desert NW Saudi Arabia
147 U8 Jabal az Ẓannah var. Jebel Dhanna. Abū Ẓaby, W UAE 24.10N 52.36E
144 E11 Jabaliya var. Jabāliyah. NE Gaza Strip 31.30N 34.25E
Jabāliyah see Jabaliya
107 N11 Jabalón ≈ C Spain
160 J10 Jabalpur prev. Jubbulpore. Madhya Pradesh, C India 23.10N 79.58E
147 N15 Jabal Zuuqar, Jazīrat var. Az Zuqur. island SW Yemen
Jabat see Jabwot
144 J3 Jabbūl, Sabkhat al salt flat NW Syria
189 P1 Jabiru Northern Territory, N Australia 12.44S 132.48E
144 H4 Jablah var. Jeble, Fr. Djéblé. Al Lādhiqīyah, W Syria 35.00N 36.00E
114 C11 Jablanac Lika-Senj, W Croatia 44.43N 14.54E
115 H14 Jablanica Federacija Bosna I Hercegovina, SW Bosnia and Herzegovina 43.39N 17.43E
115 M20 Jablanica Alb. Mali i Jabllanicës, var. Malet e Jabllanicës. ▲▲ Albania/FYR Macedonia see also Jabllanicës, Mali i
Jabllanicës, Malet e see Jablanica/Jabllanicës, Mali i
115 M20 Jabllanicës, Mali i var. Malet e Jabllanicës, Mac. Jablanica. ▲▲ Albania/FYR Macedonia see also Jablanica
113 E15 Jablonec nad Nisou Ger. Gablonz an der Neisse. Liberecký Kraj, N Czech Republic 50.43N 15.10E
Jabłonków/Jablunkau see Jablunkov
112 J9 Jabłonowo Pomorskie Kujawski-pomorskie, C Poland 53.24N 19.08E
113 J17 Jablunkov Ger. Jablunkau, Pol. Jabłonków. Ostravský Kraj, E Czech Republic 49.34N 18.45E
61 Q15 Jaboatão Pernambuco, E Brazil 08.05S 35.00W
62 L8 Jaboticabal São Paulo, S Brazil 21.15S 48.16W
201 U7 Jabwot var. Jabat, Jebat, Jōwat. island Ralik Chain, S Marshall Islands
107 S4 Jaca Aragón, NE Spain 42.34N 0.33W
44 B4 Jacaltenango Huehuetenango, W Guatemala 15.39N 91.46W
61 G14 Jacaré-a-Canga Pará, NE Brazil 5.58S 57.31W
62 N10 Jacareí São Paulo, S Brazil 23.18S 45.55W
61 I18 Jaciara Mato Grosso, W Brazil 15.58S 54.57W
61 E15 Jaciparaná Rondônia, W Brazil 9.20S 64.27W
21 P5 Jackman Maine, NE USA 45.35N 70.14W
37 X1 Jackpot Nevada, W USA 41.57N 114.41W
22 M8 Jacksboro Tennessee, S USA 36.19N 84.10W
27 S6 Jacksboro Texas, SW USA 33.13N 98.10W
25 N7 Jackson Alabama, S USA 31.30N 87.53W
37 P7 Jackson California, W USA 38.19N 120.46W
23 O6 Jackson Kentucky, S USA 37.30N 83.22W
24 J8 Jackson Louisiana, S USA 30.50N 91.13W
33 Q10 Jackson Michigan, N USA 42.15N 84.24W
31 T11 Jackson Minnesota, N USA 43.38N 95.00W
24 K5 Jackson state capital Mississippi, S USA 32.19N 90.12W
29 Y7 Jackson Missouri, C USA 37.22N 89.40W
23 W8 Jackson North Carolina, SE USA 36.24N 77.22W
33 T15 Jackson Ohio, NE USA 39.03N 82.40W
22 G9 Jackson Tennessee, S USA 35.37N 88.49W
35 S14 Jackson Wyoming, C USA 43.28N 110.45W
193 C19 Jackson Bay bay South Island, NZ
194 K16 Jackson Field ✈ (Port Moresby) Central/National Capital District, S PNG 9.28S 147.12E
193 C20 Jackson Head headland South Island, NZ 43.57S 168.38E
25 S8 Jackson, Lake ◎ Florida, SE USA
35 S13 Jackson Lake ◎ Wyoming, C USA
204 J6 Jackson, Mount ▲ Antarctica 71.43S 63.45W
39 U3 Jackson Reservoir ◎ Colorado, C USA
25 Q3 Jacksonville Alabama, S USA 33.48N 85.45W
29 V11 Jacksonville Arkansas, C USA 34.52N 92.06W
25 W8 Jacksonville Florida, SE USA 30.19N 81.39W
32 K14 Jacksonville Illinois, N USA 39.43N 90.13W
23 W11 Jacksonville North Carolina, SE USA 34.45N 77.25W
27 W7 Jacksonville Texas, SW USA 31.57N 95.16W
25 X9 Jacksonville Beach Florida, SE USA 30.17N 81.23W
46 L9 Jacmel var. Jaquemel. S Haiti 18.13N 72.33W
Jacob see Nkayi
155 Q12 Jacobābād Sind, SE Pakistan 28.16N 68.30E
57 T11 Jacobs Ladder Falls waterfall S Guyana 2.57N 58.06W
47 O11 Jaco, Pointe headland N Dominica 15.38N 61.25W
13 Q9 Jacques-Cartier ≈ Québec, SE Canada
11 P11 Jacques-Cartier, Détroit de var. Jacques-Cartier Passage. strait Gulf of St. Lawrence/St. Lawrence River
13 W6 Jacques-Cartier, Mont ▲ Québec, SE Canada 48.58N 66.00W
Jacques-Cartier Passage see Jacques-Cartier, Détroit de
195 O12 Jacquinot Bay inlet New Britain, PNG
63 H16 Jacuí, Rio ≈ S Brazil
62 L11 Jacupiranga São Paulo, S Brazil 24.42S 48.00W
102 G10 Jade ≈ NW Germany
102 G10 Jadebusen bay NW Germany
Jadotville see Likasi
Jadransko More/Jadransko Morje see Adriatic Sea
107 O7 Jadraque Castilla-La Mancha, C Spain 40.55N 2.55W
58 C10 Jaén Cajamarca, N Peru 5.43S 78.46W
107 N13 Jaén Andalucía, SW Spain 37.46N 3.48W
107 N13 Jaén ◈ province Andalucía, S Spain
161 J23 Jaffna Northern Province, N Sri Lanka 9.42N 80.03E
161 K23 Jaffna Lagoon lagoon N Sri Lanka
21 N10 Jaffrey New Hampshire, NE USA 42.46N 72.00W
144 H13 Jafr, Qā' al var. El Jafr. salt pan S Jordan
158 J9 Jagādhri Haryāna, N India 30.10N 77.18E
120 H4 Jägala var. Jägala Jõgi, Ger. Jaggowal. ≈ NW Estonia
Jägala Jõgi see Jägala
Jagannath see Puri
161 L14 Jagdalpur Madhya Pradesh, C India 19.07N 82.04E
169 U5 Jagdaqi Nei Mongol Zizhiqu, N China 50.25N 124.02E
Jägerndorf see Krnov
Jaggowal see Jägala
145 O2 Jaghjaghah, Nahr ≈ N Syria
179 Qq14 Jagna Bohol, C Philippines 9.37N 124.16E
114 N13 Jagodina prev. Svetozarevo. Serbia, C Serbia and Montenegro (Yugoslavia) 43.59N 21.15E
114 K12 Jagodnja ▲ W Serbia and Montenegro (Yugoslavia)
103 I20 Jagst ≈ SW Germany
161 I14 Jagtiāl Andhra Pradesh, C India 18.49N 78.53E
63 H18 Jaguarão Rio Grande do Sul, S Brazil 32.32S 53.20W
63 H18 Jaguarão, Rio var. Río Yaguarón. ≈ Brazil/Uruguay
62 K11 Jaguariaíva Paraná, S Brazil 24.15S 49.43W
46 D5 Jagüey Grande Matanzas, W Cuba 22.31N 81.09W
159 P14 Jahānābād Bihār, N India 25.13N 84.58E
Jahra see Al Jahrā'
149 P12 Jahrom var. Jahrum. Fārs, S Iran 28.34N 53.32E
Jahrum see Jahrom
Jailolo see Halmahera, Pulau
175 Tt8 Jailolo, Selat strait E Indonesia
Jainat see Chai Nat
Jainti see Jayanti
158 H12 Jaipur prev. Jeypore. Rājasthān, N India 26.54N 75.46E
159 T14 Jaipur Hat Rajshahi, NW Bangladesh 25.04N 89.03E
158 D11 Jaisalmer Rājasthān, NW India 26.55N 70.56E
160 O12 Jājapur Orissa, E India 18.54N 82.36E
149 R4 Jājarm Khorāsān, NE Iran 36.58N 56.25E
114 G12 Jajce Federacija Bosna I Hercegovina, W Bosnia and Herzegovina 44.20N 17.16E
Jaji see 'Alī Kheyl
85 D17 Jakalsberg Otjozondjupa, N Namibia 19.22S 17.28E
174 J14 Jakarta prev. Djakarta, Dut. Batavia. ● (Indonesia) Jawa, C Indonesia 6.07S 106.45E
8 I8 Jakes Corner Yukon Territory, W Canada 60.18N 134.00W
158 H9 Jākhal Haryāna, NW India 29.46N 75.51E
Jakobeny see Iacobeni
95 K16 Jakobstad Fin. Pietarsaari. Länsi-Suomi, W Finland 63.40N 22.40E
Jakobstadt see Jēkabpils
115 O18 Jakupica ▲ C FYR Macedonia
39 W15 Jal New Mexico, SW USA 32.07N 103.10W
147 P7 Jalājil var. Ğalāğil. Ar Riyāḍ, C Saudi Arabia 25.42N 45.22E
Jalal-Abad see Dzhalal-Abad, Dzhalal-Abadskaya Oblast', W Kyrgyzstan
155 S5 Jalālābād var. Jalalabad, Jelalabad. Nangarhār, E Afghanistan 34.25N 70.28E
Jalal-Abad Oblasty see Dzhalal-Abadskaya Oblast'
155 V7 Jalālpur Punjab, E Pakistan 32.39N 74.10E
155 T11 Jalālpur Pīrwāla Punjab, E Pakistan 29.30N 71.19E
158 H8 Jalandhar prev. Jullundur. Punjab, N India 31.19N 75.36E
44 J7 Jalán, Río ≈ S Honduras
44 E6 Jalapa Jalapa, C Guatemala 14.39N 89.58W
44 J7 Jalapa Nueva Segovia, NW Nicaragua 13.57N 86.09W
44 A3 Jalapa off. Departamento de Jalapa. ◈ department SE Guatemala
44 E6 Jalapa, Río ≈ SE Guatemala
149 X13 Jālaq Sīstān va Balūchestān, SE Iran
95 K17 Jalasjärvi Länsi-Suomi, W Finland 62.30N 22.49E
155 O8 Jaldak Zābul, SE Afghanistan 32.00N 66.45E
62 J7 Jales São Paulo, S Brazil 20.15S 50.34W
160 P11 Jaleshwar var. Jaleswar. Orissa, NE India 21.51N 87.15E
Jaleswar see Jaleshwar
160 F12 Jalgaon Mahārāshtra, C India 21.01N 75.34E
145 W12 Jalībah S Iraq 30.37N 46.31E
145 W13 Jalīb Shahāb S Iraq 30.25N 46.08E
79 X15 Jalingo Taraba, E Nigeria 8.54N 11.22E
42 K13 Jalisco ◈ state SW Mexico
160 G13 Jālna Mahārāshtra, W India 19.52N 75.55E
Jalomitsa see Ialomița
107 R5 Jalón ≈ N Spain
158 E13 Jālor Rājasthān, N India 25.21N 72.43E
114 K11 Jalovik Serbia, W Serbia and Montenegro (Yugoslavia) 44.37N 19.48E
42 L12 Jalpa Zacatecas, C Mexico 21.40N 103.00W
159 S12 Jalpāiguri West Bengal, NE India 26.43N 88.24E
43 O12 Jalpán var. Jalpan. Querétaro de Arteaga, C Mexico 21.13N 99.28W
69 P2 Jalta island N Tunisia
77 S9 Jālū var. Jūlā. NE Libya 29.01N 21.33E
201 U8 Jaluit Atoll var. Jālwōj. atoll Ralik Chain, S Marshall Islands
Jālwōj see Jaluit Atoll
83 L18 Jamaame It. Giamame; prev. Margherita. Jubbada Hoose, S Somalia 0.00N 42.43E
79 W13 Jamaare ≈ NE Nigeria
46 G9 Jamaica ◆ commonwealth republic W West Indies
49 P3 Jamaica island W West Indies
46 I9 Jamaica Channel channel Haiti/Jamaica
159 T14 Jamalpur Dhaka, N Bangladesh 24.54N 89.57E
159 Q14 Jamālpur Bihār, NE India 25.19N 86.30E
174 I6 Jamaluang var. Jemaluang. Johor, Peninsular Malaysia 2.13N 103.48E
61 I14 Jamanxim, Rio ≈ C Brazil
58 B8 Jambelí, Canal de channel S Ecuador
101 I20 Jambes Namur, SE Belgium 50.26N 4.51E
174 Hh9 Jambi var. Telanaipura; prev. Djambi. Sumatera, W Indonesia 1.34S 103.37E
174 H9 Jambi off. Propinsi Jambi, var. Djambi. ◈ province W Indonesia
Jamdena see Yamdena, Pulau
10 H8 James Bay bay Ontario/Quebec, E Canada
65 F19 James, Isla island Archipiélago de los Chonos, S Chile
189 Q8 James Ranges ▲▲ Northern Territory, C Australia
31 P8 James River ≈ North Dakota/South Dakota, N USA
23 X7 James River ≈ Virginia, NE USA
204 H4 James Ross Island island Antarctica
190 I8 Jamestown South Australia 33.13S 138.36E
67 G25 Jamestown ○ (Saint Helena) NW Saint Helena 15.55S 5.43W
37 P8 Jamestown California, W USA 37.57N 120.25W
22 L7 Jamestown Kentucky, S USA 36.58N 85.03W
20 D11 Jamestown New York, NE USA 42.04N 79.15W
31 P5 Jamestown North Dakota, N USA 46.54N 98.42W
22 L8 Jamestown Tennessee, S USA 36.25N 84.57W
Jamestown see Holetown
13 N10 Jamet ≈ Québec, SE Canada
43 Q17 Jamiltepec var. Santiago Jamiltepec. Oaxaca, SE Mexico 16.16N 97.50W
97 F20 Jammerbugten bay Skagerrak, E North Sea
158 H6 Jammu prev. Jummoo. Jammu and Kashmir, NW India 32.43N 74.54E
158 I5 Jammu and Kashmir var. Jammu-Kashmir, Kashmir. ◈ state NW India
155 V4 Jammu and Kashmir disputed region India/Pakistan
160 B10 Jāmnagar prev. Navanagar. Gujarāt, W India 22.28N 70.06E
155 S11 Jāmpur Punjab, E Pakistan 29.39N 70.34E
95 L18 Jämsä Länsi-Suomi, W Finland 61.51N 25.10E
95 L18 Jämsänkoski Länsi-Suomi, W Finland 61.54N 25.10E
159 Q16 Jamshedpur Bihār, NE India 22.46N 86.12E
96 K9 Jämtland ◈ county C Sweden
159 Q14 Jamūi Bihār, NE India 24.57N 86.13E
159 T14 Jamuna ≈ N Bangladesh
Jamuna see Brahmaputra
Jamundá see Nhamundá, Rio
56 D11 Jamundí Valle del Cauca, SW Colombia 3.16N 76.31W
159 Q12 Janakpur Central, C Nepal 26.45N 85.55E
61 N18 Janaúba Minas Gerais, SE Brazil 15.46S 43.16W
60 K11 Janaucu, Ilha island NE Brazil
149 Q7 Jandaq Eşfahān, C Iran 34.04N 54.25E
66 Q11 Jandia, Punta de headland Fuerteventura, Islas Canarias, Spain, NE Atlantic Ocean 28.03N 14.31W
61 B14 Jandiatuba, Rio ≈ NW Brazil
107 N12 Jándula ≈ S Spain
31 V10 Janesville Minnesota, N USA 44.07N 93.43W
32 L9 Janesville Wisconsin, N USA 42.42N 89.01W
155 N13 Jangal Baluchistān, SW Pakistan 28.00N 65.48E
85 N20 Jangamo Inhambane, SE Mozambique 24.04S 35.25E
161 J14 Jangaon Andhra Pradesh, C India 18.47N 79.25E
159 S14 Jangipur West Bengal, NE India 24.31N 88.03E
Janina see Ioánnina
Janischken see Joniškis
114 J11 Janja Republika Srpska, NE Bosnia and Herzegovina 44.40N 19.15E
Jankovac see Jánoshalma
207 Q15 Jan Mayen ◇ Norwegian dependency N Atlantic Ocean
86 D5 Jan Mayen island N Atlantic Ocean

◆ Country
● Country Capital
◇ Dependent Territory
○ Dependent Territory Capital
◈ Administrative Region
✈ International Airport
▲ Mountain
▲▲ Mountain Range
♨ Volcano
≈ River
◎ Lake
▣ Reservoir

207 R15 **Jan Mayen Fracture Zone** *tectonic feature* Greenland Sea/Norwegian Sea
207 R15 **Jan Mayen Ridge** *undersea feature* Greenland Sea/Norwegian Sea
42 H3 **Janos** Chihuahua, N Mexico 30.45N 108.21W
113 K25 **Jánoshalma** SCr. Jankovac. Bács-Kiskun, S Hungary 46.18N 19.16E
Janow/Janów *see* Jonava, Lithuania
Janów *see* Ivanava, Belarus
112 H10 **Janowiec Wielkopolski** Ger. Janowitz. Kujawski-pomorskie, C Poland 52.47N 17.30E
Janowitz *see* Janowiec Wielkopolski
113 O15 **Janów Lubelski** Lubelskie, E Poland 50.43N 22.24E
Janów Poleski *see* Ivanava
85 H25 **Jansenville** Eastern Cape, S South Africa 32.55S 24.40E
176 W12 **Jantan** Papua, E Indonesia 3.53S 134.20E
61 M18 **Januária** Minas Gerais, SE Brazil 15.28S 44.22W
Janūbīyah, Al Bādiyah al *see* Ash Shāmīyah
104 I7 **Janzé** Ille-et-Vilaine, NW France 47.55N 1.28W
160 F10 **Jaora** Madhya Pradesh, C India 23.40N 75.10E
171 H12 **Japan** var. Nippon, Jap. Nihon. ◆ *monarchy* E Asia
133 Y9 **Japan** *island group* E Asia
199 H3 **Japan Basin** *undersea feature* N Sea of Japan
133 Y8 **Japan, Sea of** var. East Sea, Rus. Yapanskoye More. *sea* NW Pacific Ocean
199 H4 **Japan Trench** *undersea feature* NW Pacific Ocean
Japen *see* Yapen, Pulau
61 A15 **Japiim** var. Mâncio Lima. Acre, W Brazil 8.00S 73.39W
60 D12 **Japurá** Amazonas, N Brazil 1.43S 66.14W
60 C12 **Japurá, Rio** var. Río Caquetá, Yapurá. ⟿ Brazil/Colombia *see also* Caquetá, Río
45 W17 **Jaqué** Darién, SE Panama 7.30N 78.09W
Jaquemel *see* Jacmel
Jarablos *see* Jarābulus
144 K2 **Jarābulus** var. Jarablos, Jerablus, Fr. Djérablous. Ḥalab, N Syria 36.51N 38.02E
62 K13 **Jaraguá do Sul** Santa Catarina, S Brazil 26.28S 49.07W
106 K9 **Jaraicejo** Extremadura, W Spain 39.40N 5.49W
106 K9 **Jaráiz de la Vera** Extremadura, W Spain 40.04N 5.45W
107 O7 **Jarama** ⟿ C Spain
65 J20 **Jaramillo** Santa Cruz, SE Argentina 47.10S 67.07W
Jarandilla de la Vega *see* Jarandilla de la Vera
106 K8 **Jarandilla de la Vera** var. Jarandilla de la Vega. Extremadura, W Spain 40.07N 5.39W
155 V9 **Jarānwāla** Punjab, E Pakistan 31.19N 73.25E
144 G9 **Jarash** var. Jerash; anc. Gerasa. Irbid, NW Jordan 32.16N 35.54E
Jarbah, Jazīrat *see* Jerba, Île de
96 N13 **Järbo** Gävleborg, C Sweden 60.43N 16.40E
Jardan *see* Yordan
46 F7 **Jardines de la Reina, Archipiélago de los** *island group* C Cuba
168 J7 **Jargalant** Arhangay, C Mongolia 47.46N 101.56E
168 I8 **Jargalant** Bayanhongor, C Mongolia 47.14N 99.43E
168 D7 **Jargalant** Bayan-Ölgiy, W Mongolia 46.56N 91.07E
168 K6 **Jargalant** Bulgan, N Mongolia 49.09N 104.19E
168 G9 **Jargalant** Govĭ-Altay, W Mongolia 45.39N 97.10E
Jarīd, Shaṭṭ al *see* Jerid, Chott el
61 I11 **Jari, Rio** var. Jary. ⟿ N Brazil
147 N7 **Jarīr, Wādī al** *dry watercourse* C Saudi Arabia
Jarja *see* Yur'ya
96 L13 **Järna** var. Dala-Jarna. Dalarna, C Sweden 60.31N 14.22E
97 O16 **Järna** Stockholm, C Sweden 59.04N 17.34E
104 K11 **Jarnac** Charente, W France 45.41N 0.10W
112 H12 **Jarocin** Wielkopolskie, C Poland 51.58N 17.30E
113 F16 **Jaroměř** Ger. Jermer. Hradecký Kraj, N Czech Republic 50.22N 15.55E
Jaroslau *see* Jarosław
113 O16 **Jarosław** Ger. Jaroslau, Rus. Yaroslav. Podkarpackie, SE Poland 50.01N 22.41E
95 F16 **Järpen** Jämtland, C Sweden 63.21N 13.30E
153 O14 **Jarqo'rg'on** Rus. Dzharkurgan. Surkhondaryo Viloyati, S Uzbekistan 37.31N 67.20E
145 P2 **Jarrāh, Wadi** *dry watercourse* NE Syria
Jars, Plain of *see* Xiangkhoang, Plateau de
168 K14 **Jartai Yanchi** ◎ N China
61 E16 **Jaru** Rondônia, W Brazil 10.24S 62.45W
169 T10 **Jarud Qi** Nei Mongol Zizhiqu, N China 44.25N 121.12E
120 I4 **Järva-Jaani** Ger. Sankt-Johannis. Järvamaa, N Estonia 59.02N 25.52E
120 G5 **Järvakandi** Ger. Jerwakant. Raplamaa, NW Estonia 58.47N 24.49E
120 H4 **Järvamaa** off. Järva Maakond. ◆ *province* N Estonia
95 L19 **Järvenpää** Etelä-Suomi, S Finland 60.28N 25.03E
12 G17 **Jarvis** Ontario, S Canada 42.53N 80.06W
185 R8 **Jarvis Island** ◇ *US unincorporated territory* C Pacific Ocean
96 M11 **Järvsö** Gävleborg, C Sweden 61.43N 16.25E
Jary *see* Jari, Rio
114 M9 **Jaša Tomić** Serbia, NE Serbia and Montenegro (Yugoslavia) 45.27N 20.51E
114 D12 **Jasenice** Zadar, SW Croatia 44.15N 15.33E
144 I11 **Jashshat al 'Adlah, Wādī al** *dry watercourse* C Jordan
79 Q16 **Jasikan** E Ghana 7.24N 0.28E
149 T15 **Jāsk** Hormozgān, SE Iran 25.35N 58.06E
152 F6 **Jasliq** Rus. Zhaslyk. Qoraqalpog'iston Respublikasi, NW Uzbekistan 43.57N 57.30E
113 N17 **Jasło** Podkarpackie, SE Poland 49.45N 21.28E
9 U16 **Jasmin** Saskatchewan, S Canada 51.11N 103.34W
67 A23 **Jason Islands** *island group* NW Falkland Islands
204 I4 **Jason Peninsula** *peninsula* Antarctica
33 N15 **Jasonville** Indiana, N USA 39.09N 87.12W
9 O15 **Jasper** Alberta, SW Canada 52.55N 118.04W
12 L13 **Jasper** Ontario, SE Canada 44.50N 75.57W
25 O3 **Jasper** Alabama, S USA 33.49N 87.16W
29 T9 **Jasper** Arkansas, C USA 36.00N 93.11W
25 U8 **Jasper** Florida, SE USA 30.31N 82.57W
33 N16 **Jasper** Indiana, N USA 38.22N 86.57W
31 R11 **Jasper** Minnesota, N USA 43.51N 96.24W
29 S7 **Jasper** Missouri, C USA 37.20N 94.18W
22 K10 **Jasper** Tennessee, S USA 35.04N 85.37W
27 Y9 **Jasper** Texas, SW USA 30.55N 94.00W
9 O15 **Jasper National Park** *national park* Alberta/British Columbia, SW Canada
Jassy *see* Iaşi
115 N14 **Jastrebac** ▲ SE Serbia and Montenegro (Yugoslavia)
114 D9 **Jastrebarsko** Zagreb, N Croatia 45.40N 15.40E
Jastrow *see* Jastrowie
112 G9 **Jastrowie** Ger. Jastrow. Wielkopolskie, C Poland 53.25N 16.48E
113 J17 **Jastrzębie-Zdrój** Śląskie, S Poland 49.58N 18.34E
113 L22 **Jászapáti** Jász-Nagykun-Szolnok, E Hungary 47.31N 20.09E
113 L22 **Jászberény** Jász-Nagykun-Szolnok, E Hungary 47.30N 19.54E
113 L23 **Jász-Nagykun-Szolnok** off. Jász-Nagykun-Szolnok Megye. ◆ *county* E Hungary
61 J19 **Jataí** Goiás, C Brazil 17.58S 51.45W
60 G12 **Jatapu, Serra do** ▲ N Brazil
43 W16 **Jatate, Río** ⟿ SE Mexico
155 P17 **Jāti** Sind, SE Pakistan 24.19N 68.18E
46 F6 **Jatibonico** Sancti Spíritus, C Cuba 21.55N 79.12W
174 Jj14 **Jatiluhur, Danau** ◎ Jawa, S Indonesia
Jativa *see* Xátiva
174 K14 **Jatiwangi** prev. Djatiwangi. Jawa, C Indonesia 6.45S 108.12E
155 S11 **Jattoi** Punjab, E Pakistan 29.22N 70.55E
62 L9 **Jaú** São Paulo, S Brazil 22.17S 48.32W
60 F11 **Jauaperi, Rio** ⟿ N Brazil
101 I19 **Jauche** Wallon Brabant, C Belgium 50.42N 4.55E
Jauer *see* Jawor
Jauf *see* Al Jawf
155 U7 **Jauharābād** Punjab, E Pakistan 32.19N 72.15E
59 E14 **Jauja** Junín, C Peru 11.44S 75.30W
43 O10 **Jaumave** Tamaulipas, C Mexico 23.28N 99.22W
120 H10 **Jaunjelgava** Ger. Friedrichstadt. Aizkraukle, S Latvia 56.36N 25.06E
Jaunlatgale *see* Pytalovo
120 I8 **Jaunpiebalga** Gulbene, NE Latvia 57.10N 26.02E
120 E9 **Jaunpils** Tukums, C Latvia 56.45N 23.03E
159 N13 **Jaunpur** Uttar Pradesh, N India 25.43N 82.40E
31 N8 **Java** South Dakota, N USA 45.29N 99.54W
Java *see* Jawa
107 R9 **Javalambre** ▲ E Spain 40.02N 1.06W
181 V7 **Java Ridge** *undersea feature* E Indian Ocean
61 A14 **Javari, Rio** var. Yavarí. ⟿ Brazil/Peru
169 O7 **Javarthushuu** Dornod, NE Mongolia 49.05N 112.40E
174 Kk13 **Java Sea** Ind. Laut Jawa. *sea* W Indonesia
181 U7 **Java Trench** var. Sunda Trench. *undersea feature* E Indian Ocean
107 T11 **Jávea** var. Xàbia. País Valenciano, E Spain 38.48N 0.10E
169 O7 **Javhlant** Hentiy, E Mongolia 47.46N 112.06E
65 G20 **Javier, Isla** *island* S Chile
115 L14 **Javor** ▲ Bosnia and Herzegovina/Serbia and Montenegro (Yugoslavia)
113 K20 **Javorie** Hung. Jávoros. ▲ S Slovakia 48.26N 19.16E
Jávoros *see* Javorie
95 J14 **Jävre** Norrbotten, N Sweden 65.07N 21.31E
174 K14 **Jawa** Eng. Java; prev. Djawa. *island* C Indonesia
174 J15 **Jawa Barat** off. Propinsi Jawa Barat, Eng. West Java. ◆ *province* S Indonesia
Jawa, Laut *see* Java Sea
145 R3 **Jawān** NW Iraq 35.57N 43.03E
174 Kk15 **Jawa Tengah** off. Propinsi Jawa Tengah, Eng. Central Java. ◆ *province* S Indonesia
174 L15 **Jawa Timur** off. Propinsi Jawa Timur, Eng. East Java. ◆ *province* S Indonesia
83 N17 **Jawhar** var. Johwar, It. Giohar. Shabeellaha Dhexe, S Somalia 2.36N 45.30E
113 F14 **Jawor** Ger. Jauer. Dolnośląskie, SW Poland 51.01N 16.10E
Jaworów *see* Yavoriv
113 J16 **Jaworzno** Śląskie, S Poland 50.13N 19.07E
Jaxartes *see* Syr Darya
29 R9 **Jay** Oklahoma, C USA 36.25N 94.48W
Jayabum *see* Chaiyaphum
Jayanath *see* Chai Nat
159 T12 **Jayanti** prev. Jainti. West Bengal, NE India 26.43N 89.43E
176 Xx12 **Jaya, Puncak** prev. Puntjak Carstensz, Puntjak Sukarno. ▲ Papua, E Indonesia 4.00S 137.10E
176 Z10 **Jayapura** var. Djajapura, Dut. Hollandia; prev. Kotabaru, Sukarnapura. Papua, E Indonesia 2.37S 140.39E
176 Y12 **Jayawijaya, Pegunungan** ▲ Papua, E Indonesia
Jay Dairen *see* Dalian
Jayhawker State *see* Kansas
153 S12 **Jayilgan** Rus. Dzhailgan, Dzhayilgan. C Tajikistan 39.17N 71.32E
161 L14 **Jaypur** var. Jeypore, Jeypur. Orissa, E India 18.54N 82.36E
27 O6 **Jayton** Texas, SW USA 33.15N 100.34W
149 U13 **Jaz Murian, Hāmūn-e** ◎ SE Iran
144 M4 **Jazrah** Ar Raqqah, C Syria 35.56N 39.02E
144 G6 **Jbaïl** var. Jebeil, Jubayl, Jubeil; anc. Biblical Gebal, Bybles. W Lebanon 34.00N 35.45E
27 O7 **J.B.Thomas, Lake** ⊠ Texas, SW USA
Jdaïdé *see* Judaydah
37 X12 **Jean** Nevada, W USA 35.45N 115.20W
24 I9 **Jeanerette** Louisiana, S USA 29.54N 91.39W
46 L8 **Jean-Rabel** NW Haiti 19.49N 73.12W
149 T12 **Jebāl Bārez, Kūh-e** ▲ SE Iran
Jebat *see* Jabwot
79 T15 **Jebba** Kwara, W Nigeria 9.04N 4.50E
Jebeil *see* Jbaïl
118 E12 **Jebel** Hung. Széphely; prev. Hung. Zsebely. Timiş, W Romania 45.33N 21.13E
Jebel *see* Dzhebel
Jebel, Bahr el *see* White Nile
Jebel Dhanna *see* Jabal az Zannah
Jeble *see* Jablah
98 K13 **Jedburgh** SE Scotland, UK 55.28N 2.34W
Jedda *see* Jiddah
113 L15 **Jędrzejów** Ger. Endersdorf. Świętokrzyskie, C Poland 50.39N 20.18E
102 K12 **Jeetze** var. Jeetzel. ⟿ C Germany
Jeetzel *see* Jeetze
31 U14 **Jefferson** Iowa, C USA 42.01N 94.22W
23 Q8 **Jefferson** North Carolina, SE USA 36.24N 81.33W
27 X6 **Jefferson** Texas, SW USA 32.45N 94.21W
32 M9 **Jefferson** Wisconsin, N USA 43.01N 88.48W
29 U5 **Jefferson City** *state capital* Missouri, C USA 38.33N 92.12W
35 R10 **Jefferson City** Montana, NW USA 46.24N 112.01W
22 M9 **Jefferson City** Tennessee, S USA 36.07N 83.29W
37 U7 **Jefferson, Mount** ▲ Nevada, W USA 38.49N 116.54W
34 H12 **Jefferson, Mount** ▲ Oregon, NW USA 44.40N 121.48W
22 L5 **Jeffersontown** Kentucky, S USA 38.11N 85.33W
33 P16 **Jeffersonville** Indiana, N USA 38.16N 85.45W
35 V15 **Jeffrey City** Wyoming, C USA 42.29N 107.49W
79 T13 **Jega** Kebbi, NW Nigeria 12.15N 4.21E
Jehol *see* Chengde
64 P5 **Jejui-Guazú, Río** ⟿ E Paraguay
120 I10 **Jēkabpils** Ger. Jakobstadt. Jēkabpils, S Latvia 56.30N 25.56E
25 W7 **Jekyll Island** *island* Georgia, SE USA
174 L11 **Jelai, Sungai** ⟿ Borneo, N Indonesia
Jelalabad *see* Jalālābād
113 H14 **Jelcz-Laskowice** Dolnośląskie, SW Poland 51.01N 17.24E
113 E14 **Jelenia Góra** Ger. Hirschberg, Hirschberg im Riesengebirge, Hirschberg im Riesengebirge, Hirschberg in Schlesien. Dolnośląskie, SW Poland 50.54N 15.48E
159 S11 **Jelep La** *pass* N India 27.24N 88.51E
120 F9 **Jelgava** Ger. Mitau. Jelgava, C Latvia 56.38N 23.47E
114 L13 **Jelica** ▲ C Serbia and Montenegro (Yugoslavia)
22 M8 **Jellico** Tennessee, S USA 36.33N 84.06W
97 G23 **Jelling** Vejle, C Denmark 55.45N 9.24E
174 Ii5 **Jemaja, Pulau** *island* W Indonesia
Jemaluang *see* Jamaluang
101 E20 **Jemappes** Hainaut, S Belgium 50.27N 3.52E
174 M16 **Jember** prev. Djember. Jawa, C Indonesia 8.07S 113.45E
101 I20 **Jemeppe-sur-Sambre** Namur, S Belgium 50.27N 4.41E
39 R10 **Jemez Pueblo** New Mexico, SW USA 35.36N 106.43W
164 K2 **Jeminay** Xinjiang Uygur Zizhiqu, NW China 47.28N 85.49E
201 U5 **Jemo Island** *atoll* Ratak Chain, C Marshall Islands
175 Nn8 **Jempang, Danau** ◎ Borneo, N Indonesia
103 L16 **Jena** Thüringen, C Germany 50.55N 11.34E
24 I6 **Jena** Louisiana, S USA 31.40N 92.07W
110 I8 **Jenaz** Graubünden, SE Switzerland 46.56N 9.43E
111 N7 **Jenbach** Tirol, W Austria 47.23N 11.47E
175 P13 **Jeneponto** prev. Djeneponto. Sulawesi, C Indonesia 5.40S 119.42E
144 F9 **Jenīn** N West Bank 32.28N 35.17E
23 P7 **Jenkins** Kentucky, S USA 37.10N 82.37W
29 P9 **Jenks** Oklahoma, C USA 36.01N 95.58W
Jenné *see* Djenné
111 X8 **Jennersdorf** Burgenland, SE Austria 46.57N 16.08E
24 H9 **Jennings** Louisiana, S USA 30.13N 92.39W
15 Jj4 **Jenny Lind Island** *island* Nunavut, N Canada
25 Y13 **Jensen Beach** Florida, SE USA 27.15N 80.13W
15 M2 **Jens Munk Island** *island* Nunavut, NE Canada
61 O17 **Jequié** Bahia, E Brazil 13.52S 40.06W
61 O18 **Jequitinhonha, Rio** ⟿ E Brazil
Jerablus *see* Jarābulus
76 H6 **Jerada** NE Morocco 34.16N 2.07W
Jerash *see* Jarash
77 N7 **Jerba, Île de** var. Djerba, Jazīrat Jarbah. *island* E Tunisia
46 K9 **Jérémie** SW Haiti 18.38N 74.10W
Jerez *see* Jeréz de la Frontera, Spain
Jeréz *see* Jerez de García Salinas, Mexico
42 L11 **Jerez de García Salinas** var. Jeréz. Zacatecas, C Mexico 22.40N 103.00W
106 J15 **Jeréz de la Frontera** var. Jerez; prev. Xeres. Andalucía, SW Spain 36.40N 6.07W
106 I12 **Jeréz de los Caballeros** Extremadura, W Spain 38.19N 6.45W
Jergucati *see* Jorgucat
144 G10 **Jericho** Ar. Arīḥā, Heb. Yeriḥo. E West Bank 31.51N 35.27E
76 M7 **Jerid, Chott el** var. Shaṭṭ al Jarīd. *salt lake* SW Tunisia
191 O10 **Jerilderie** New South Wales, SE Australia 35.24S 145.43E
Jerischmarkt *see* Câmpia Turzii
94 K11 **Jerisjärvi** ◎ NW Finland
Jermentau *see* Yereymentau
Jermer *see* Jaroměř
38 K11 **Jerome** Arizona, SW USA 34.45N 112.06W
35 O15 **Jerome** Idaho, NW USA 42.43N 114.31W
99 L26 **Jersey** *island* Channel Islands, NW Europe
20 K14 **Jersey City** New Jersey, NE USA 40.42N 74.01W
20 F13 **Jersey Shore** Pennsylvania, NE USA 41.12N 77.13W
32 K14 **Jerseyville** Illinois, N USA 39.07N 90.19W
106 K8 **Jerte** ⟿ W Spain
144 F10 **Jerusalem** Ar. Al Quds, Al Quds ash Sharīf, Heb. Yerushalayim; anc. Hierosolyma. ● (Israel) Jerusalem, NE Israel 31.46N 35.13E
144 G10 **Jerusalem** ◆ *district* E Israel
191 S10 **Jervis Bay** New South Wales, SE Australia 35.09S 150.42E
191 S10 **Jervis Bay Territory** ◇ *territory* SE Australia
Jerwakant *see* Järvakandi
111 S10 **Jesenice** Ger. Assling. NW Slovenia 46.26N 14.00E
113 H16 **Jeseník** Ger. Freiwaldau. Olomoucký Kraj, E Czech Republic 50.14N 17.12E
Jesi *see* Iesi
108 I8 **Jesolo** var. Iesolo. Veneto, NE Italy 45.32N 12.37E
Jesselton *see* Kota Kinabalu
97 I14 **Jessheim** Akershus, S Norway 60.07N 11.10E
159 T15 **Jessore** Khulna, W Bangladesh 23.10N 89.12E
25 W6 **Jesup** Georgia, SE USA 31.36N 81.54W
43 S15 **Jesús Carranza** Veracruz-Llave, SE Mexico 17.30N 95.01W
64 K10 **Jesús María** Córdoba, C Argentina 30.58S 64.04W
28 K6 **Jetmore** Kansas, C USA 38.04N 99.53W
105 Q2 **Jeumont** Nord, N France 50.18N 4.06E
97 H14 **Jevnaker** Oppland, S Norway 60.13N 10.22E
Jewe *see* Jõhvi
27 V9 **Jewett** Texas, SW USA 31.21N 96.08W
21 N12 **Jewett City** Connecticut, NE USA 41.36N 71.58W
Jewish Autonomous Oblast *see* Yevreyskaya Avtonomnaya Oblast'
Jeypore/Jeypur *see* Jaypur, Orissa, India
Jeypore *see* Jaipur, Rājasthān, India
115 L17 **Jezercës, Maja e** ▲ N Albania 42.27N 19.49E
113 B18 **Jezerní Hora** ▲ SW Czech Republic 49.10N 13.11E
160 F10 **Jhābua** Madhya Pradesh, C India 22.47N 74.36E
158 H14 **Jhālāwār** Rājasthān, N India 24.33N 76.10E
Jhang/Jhang Sadar *see* Jhang Sadr
155 U9 **Jhang Sadr** var. Jhang, Jhang Sadar. Punjab, NE Pakistan 31.16N 72.19E
158 J13 **Jhānsi** Uttar Pradesh, N India 25.27N 78.34E
160 M11 **Jhārsuguda** Orissa, E India 21.54N 84.09E
155 V7 **Jhelum** Punjab, NE Pakistan 32.55N 73.42E
133 P9 **Jhelum** ⟿ E Pakistan
Jhenaidaha *see* Jhenida
159 T15 **Jhenida** var. Jhenaidaha. Dhaka, W Bangladesh 23.34N 89.39E
155 P16 **Jhimpir** Sind, SE Pakistan 25.01N 67.59E
Jhind *see* Jind
155 R16 **Jhudo** Sind, SE Pakistan 24.58N 69.23E
Jhumra *see* Chak Jhumra
158 H11 **Jhunjhunūn** Rājasthān, N India 28.07N 75.21E
Ji *see* Hebei, China
Ji *see* Jilin, China
159 S14 **Jiāganj** West Bengal, NE India 24.18N 88.07E
166 J7 **Jialing Jiang** ⟿ C China
169 Y7 **Jiamusi** var. Chia-mu-ssu, Kiamusze. Heilongjiang, NE China 46.45N 130.19E
167 O11 **Ji'an** Jiangxi, S China 27.06N 114.57E
169 W12 **Ji'an** Jilin, NE China 41.04N 126.07E
169 T13 **Jianchang** Liaoning, NE China 40.48N 119.51E
166 F11 **Jianchuan** Yunnan, SW China 26.28N 99.49E
164 M4 **Jiangjunmiao** Xinjiang Uygur Zizhiqu, W China 44.42N 90.06E
166 K11 **Jiangkou** Guizhou, S China 27.46N 108.53E
167 Q12 **Jiangle** Fujian, SE China 26.44N 117.26E
167 N15 **Jiangmen** Guangdong, S China 22.34N 113.01E
167 Q10 **Jiangshan** Zhejiang, SE China 28.41N 118.33E
167 Q7 **Jiangsu** var. Chiang-su, Jiangsu Sheng, Kiangsu, Su. ◆ *province* E China
Jiangsu Sheng *see* Jiangsu
167 O11 **Jiangxi** var. Chiang-hsi, Gan, Jiangxi Sheng, Kiangsi. ◆ *province* S China
Jiangxi Sheng *see* Jiangxi
166 I8 **Jiangyou** prev. Zhongba. Sichuan, C China 31.52N 104.52E
167 N9 **Jianli** Hubei, C China 29.48N 112.45E
167 Q11 **Jian'ou** Fujian, SE China 27.04N 118.19E
169 S12 **Jianping** Liaoning, NE China 41.13N 119.37E
166 L9 **Jianshi** Hubei, C China 30.37N 109.42E
133 V11 **Jian Xi** ⟿ SE China
167 Q11 **Jianyang** Fujian, SE China 27.24N 118.06E
166 I9 **Jianyang** Sichuan, C China 30.22N 104.31E
169 X10 **Jiaohe** Jilin, NE China 43.41N 127.20E
Jiaojiang *see* Taizhou
167 N6 **Jiaozuo** Henan, C China 35.13N 113.13E
Jiashan *see* Mingguang
164 F8 **Jiashi** var. Payzawat. Xinjiang Uygur Zizhiqu, NW China 39.27N 76.45E
160 L9 **Jiāwān** Madhya Pradesh, C India 24.19N 82.16E
167 S9 **Jiaxing** Zhejiang, SE China 30.43N 120.46E
Jiayi *see* Chiai
169 X6 **Jiayin** var. Chaoyang. Heilongjiang, NE China 48.51N 130.24E
165 R8 **Jiayuguan** Gansu, N China 39.49N 98.27E
144 M4 **Jibli** Ar Raqqah, C Syria 35.49N 39.23E
118 H9 **Jibou** Hung. Zsibó. Sălaj, NW Romania 47.13N 23.17E
147 Z9 **Jibsh, Ra's al** *headland* E Oman 21.20N 59.23E
Jibuti *see* Djibouti
113 E15 **Jičín** Ger. Jitschin. Hradecký Kraj, N Czech Republic 50.27N 15.20E
146 K10 **Jiddah** Eng. Jedda. Makkah, W Saudi Arabia 21.33N 39.13E
147 W11 **Jiddat al Ḥarāsīs** *desert* C Oman
Jiesjavrre *see* Iešjávri
166 M4 **Jiexiu** Shanxi, C China 37.00N 111.50E
167 P14 **Jieyang** Guangdong, S China 23.33N 116.21E
121 F14 **Jieznas** Prienai, S Lithuania 54.37N 24.10E
Jifa', Bi'r *see* Jif'īyah, Bi'r
147 P15 **Jif'īyah, Bi'r** var. Bi'r Jifā'. *well* C Yemen 14.48N 46.00E
79 W13 **Jigawa** ◆ *state* N Nigeria
Jigerbent *see* Dzhigirbent
46 I7 **Jiguaní** Granma, E Cuba 20.24N 76.25W
165 T12 **Jigzhi** Qinghai, C China 33.23N 101.25E
Jih-k'a-tse *see* Xigazê
113 E18 **Jihlava** Ger. Iglau, Pol. Igława. Jihlavský Kraj, C Czech Republic 49.22N 15.36E
113 E18 **Jihlava** var. Igel, Ger. Iglawa. ⟿ S Czech Republic
113 E18 **Jihlavský kraj** ◆ *region* C Czech Republic
76 L5 **Jijel** var. Djidjel; prev. Djidjelli. NE Algeria 36.49N 5.43E
118 L9 **Jijia** ⟿ N Romania
82 L13 **Jijiga** It. Giggiga. Somali, E Ethiopia 9.21N 42.53E
107 S12 **Jijona** var. Xixona. País Valenciano, E Spain 38.34N 0.29W
Jilf al Kabīr, Haḍabat al *see* Gilf Kebir Plateau
83 L18 **Jilib** It. Gelib. Jubbada Dhexe, S Somalia 0.18N 42.48E
169 W10 **Jilin** var. Chi-lin, Girin, Kirin; prev. Yungki, Yunki. Jilin, NE China 43.46N 126.31E
169 W10 **Jilin** var. Chi-lin, Girin, Ji, Jilin Sheng, Kirin. ◆ *province* NE China
169 W11 **Jilin Hada Ling** ▲ NE China
Jilin Sheng *see* Jilin
169 S4 **Jiliu He** ⟿ NE China
107 Q6 **Jiloca** ⟿ N Spain
83 I14 **Jīma** var. Jimma, It. Gimma. Oromo, C Ethiopia 7.41N 36.51E
46 M9 **Jimaní** W Dominican Republic 18.27N 71.51W
118 E11 **Jimbolia** Ger. Hatzfeld, Hung. Zsombolya. Timiş, W Romania 45.47N 20.43E
106 K16 **Jimena de la Frontera** Andalucía, S Spain 36.27N 5.28W
42 K7 **Jiménez** Chihuahua, N Mexico 27.09N 104.54W
43 N5 **Jiménez** Coahuila de Zaragoza, NE Mexico 29.04N 100.43W
43 P9 **Jiménez** var. Santander Jiménez. Tamaulipas, C Mexico 24.11N 98.29W
42 L10 **Jiménez del Teul** Zacatecas, C Mexico 23.13N 103.46W
79 Y14 **Jimeta** Adamawa, E Nigeria 9.16N 12.25E
Jimma *see* Jīma
164 M5 **Jimsar** Xinjiang Uygur Zizhiqu, NW China 44.05N 88.48E
20 I14 **Jim Thorpe** Pennsylvania, NE USA 40.51N 75.43W
Jin *see* Shanxi, China
Jin *see* Tianjin Shi, China
167 P5 **Jinan** var. Chinan, Chi-nan, Tsinan. Shandong, E China 36.42N 116.57E
165 T8 **Jinchang** Gansu, N China 38.31N 102.07E
167 N5 **Jincheng** Shanxi, C China 35.33N 112.51E
Jinchengjiang *see* Hechi
158 I9 **Jīnd** prev. Jhind. Haryāna, NW India 29.25N 76.14E
191 Q11 **Jindabyne** New South Wales, SE Australia 36.28S 148.36E
113 O18 **Jindřichův Hradec** Ger. Neuhaus. Budějovický Kraj, S Czech Republic 49.09N 15.01E
Jing *see* Beijing Shi, China
Jing *see* Jinghe, China
165 X10 **Jingchuan** Gansu, C China 35.19N 107.23E
167 Q10 **Jingdezhen** Jiangxi, S China 29.18N 117.18E
167 O12 **Jinggangshan** Jiangxi, S China 26.36N 114.11E
167 P3 **Jinghai** Tianjin Shi, E China 38.53N 116.45E
166 K6 **Jing He** ⟿ C China
164 I4 **Jinghe** var. Jing. Xinjiang Uygur Zizhiqu, NW China 44.35N 82.55E
166 F15 **Jinghong** var. Yunjinghong. Yunnan, SW China 22.03N 100.55E
166 M9 **Jingmen** Hubei, C China 30.58N 112.09E
169 X10 **Jingpo Hu** ◎ NE China
166 M8 **Jing Shan** ▲ C China
165 V9 **Jingtai** var. Yitiaoshan. Gansu, C China 37.12N 104.06E
166 J14 **Jingxi** Guangxi Zhuangzu Zizhiqu, S China 23.10N 106.22E
Jing Xian *see* Jingzhou
169 W11 **Jingyu** Jilin, NE China 42.23N 126.48E
165 V10 **Jingyuan** Gansu, C China 36.34N 104.43E
166 L12 **Jingzhou** var. Jing Xian. Hunan, S China 26.34N 109.40E
166 M9 **Jingzhou** prev. Shahi, Sha-shih, Shasi. Hubei, C China 30.21N 112.09E
167 R10 **Jinhua** Zhejiang, SE China 29.15N 119.36E
169 P13 **Jining** Nei Mongol Zizhiqu, N China 40.58N 113.08E
167 P5 **Jining** Shandong, E China 35.25N 116.35E
83 G18 **Jinja** S Uganda 0.27N 33.13E
167 O11 **Jin Jiang** ⟿ S China
167 R13 **Jinjiang** var. Qingyang. Fujian, SE China 24.45N 118.35E
176 W14 **Jin, Kepulauan** *island group* E Indonesia
Jinmen Dao *see* Chinmen Tao
44 J9 **Jinotega** Jinotega, NW Nicaragua 13.03N 85.59W
44 K7 **Jinotega** ◆ *department* N Nicaragua
44 J11 **Jinotepe** Carazo, SW Nicaragua 11.49N 86.11W
166 L13 **Jinping** prev. Sanjiang. Guizhou, S China 26.42N 109.13E
166 H14 **Jinping** Yunnan, SW China 22.47N 103.12E
Jinsen *see* Inch'ŏn
166 J11 **Jinsha** Guizhou, S China 27.24N 106.16E
163 N12 **Jinsha Jiang** ⟿ SW China
166 M10 **Jinshi** Hunan, S China 29.42N 111.46E
165 R7 **Jinta** Gansu, N China 40.01N 98.57E
179 Q12 **Jintotolo Channel** *channel* C Philippines
167 Q12 **Jin Xi** ⟿ SE China
Jinxi *see* Lianshan
Jinxian *see* Jinzhou
167 P6 **Jinxiang** Shandong, E China 35.07N 116.19E
167 P8 **Jinzhai** prev. Meishan. Anhui, E China 31.42N 115.47E
169 U14 **Jinzhou** prev. Jinxian. Liaoning, NE China 39.04N 121.45E
169 T12 **Jinzhou** var. Chin-chou, Chinchow; prev. Chinhsien. Liaoning, NE China 41.07N 121.06E
144 H12 **Jinz, Qā' al** ◎ C Jordan
49 S8 **Jiparaná, Rio** ⟿ W Brazil
58 A7 **Jipijapa** Manabí, W Ecuador 1.22S 80.34W
44 F8 **Jiquilisco** Usulután, S El Salvador 13.19N 88.34W
153 S12 **Jirgatol** Rus. Dzhirgatal'. C Tajikistan 39.13N 71.09E
Jirjā *see* Girga
113 B15 **Jirkov** Ger. Görkau. Ústecký Kraj, NW Czech Republic 50.30N 13.28E
Jiroft *see* Sabzvārān
166 L11 **Jishou** Hunan, S China 28.20N 109.43E
Jisr ash Shadadi *see* Ash Shadādah
118 I14 **Jitaru** Olt, S Romania 44.27N 24.32E
Jitschin *see* Jičín
118 H14 **Jiu** Ger. Schil, Schyl, Hung. Zsil, Zsily. ⟿ S Romania
167 R11 **Jiufeng Shan** ▲ SE China
167 P9 **Jiujiang** Jiangxi, S China 29.45N 115.58E
167 O10 **Jiuling Shan** ▲ S China
166 G10 **Jiulong** Sichuan, C China 29.00N 101.30E
167 Q13 **Jiulong Jiang** ⟿ SE China
167 Q12 **Jiulong Xi** ⟿ SE China
165 R8 **Jiuquan** Gansu, N China 39.42N 98.36E
166 K17 **Jiusuo** Hainan, S China 18.25N 109.55E
169 W10 **Jiutai** Jilin, NE China 44.01N 125.51E
166 K13 **Jiuwan Dashan** ▲ S China
154 I16 **Jiwani** Baluchistān, SW Pakistan 25.05N 61.46E
169 Y8 **Jixi** Heilongjiang, NE China 45.16N 131.01E
169 Y7 **Jixian** Heilongjiang, NE China 46.43N 131.10E
166 M5 **Jixian** var. Ji Xian. Shanxi, C China 36.15N 110.41E
Jiza *see* Al Jīzah
147 N13 **Jīzān** var. Qīzān. Jīzān, SW Saudi Arabia 17.49N 42.49E
147 N13 **Jīzān** var. Minṭaqat Jīzān. ◆ *province* SW Saudi Arabia
146 K6 **Jizl, Wādī al** *dry watercourse* W Saudi Arabia
170 Ff12 **Jizō-zaki** *headland* Honshū, SW Japan 35.34N 133.16E
147 U14 **Jiz', Wādī al** *dry watercourse* E Yemen
153 O11 **Jizzax** Rus. Dzhizak. Jizzax Viloyati, C Uzbekistan 40.07N 67.47E
153 N10 **Jizzax Viloyati** Rus. Dzhizakskaya Oblast'. ◆ *province* C Uzbekistan
62 I13 **Joaçaba** Santa Catarina, S Brazil 27.08S 51.30W
Joal *see* Joal-Fadiout
78 F11 **Joal-Fadiout** prev. Joal. W Senegal 14.16N 16.51W
78 E10 **João Barrosa** Boa Vista, E Cape Verde 16.01N 22.44W
João Belo *see* Xai-Xai
João de Almeida *see* Chibia
61 Q15 **João Pessoa** prev. Paraíba. *state capital* Paraíba, E Brazil 7.06S 34.52W
27 X7 **Joaquin** Texas, SW USA 31.58N 94.03W
64 K6 **Joaquín V.González** Salta, N Argentina 25.03S 64.06W
Joazeiro *see* Juazeiro
Jo'burg *see* Johannesburg
111 O7 **Jochberger Ache** ⟿ W Austria
Jo-ch'iang *see* Ruoqiang
94 K12 **Jock** Norrbotten, N Sweden 66.40N 22.45E
44 I5 **Jocón** Yoro, N Honduras 15.17N 86.55W
107 O13 **Jódar** Andalucía, S Spain 37.51N 3.18W
158 F12 **Jodhpur** Rājasthān, NW India 26.16N 73.01E
101 I19 **Jodoigne** Wallon Brabant, C Belgium 50.43N 4.52E
97 I22 **Jægerspris** Frederiksborg, E Denmark 55.52N 11.58E
95 O16 **Joensuu** Itä-Suomi, E Finland 62.36N 29.45E
97 C17 **Jæren** *physical region* S Norway
39 W4 **Joes** Colorado, C USA 39.36N 102.40W
203 Z3 **Joe's Hill** *hill* Kiritimati, NE Kiribati 1.48N 157.19W
171 Jj13 **Jōetsu** var. Zyôetu. Niigata, Honshū, C Japan 37.09N 138.13E
85 M18 **Jofane** Inhambane, S Mozambique 21.16S 34.21E
159 R12 **Jogbani** Bihār, NE India 26.22N 87.16E
120 I5 **Jõgeva** Ger. Laisholm. Jõgevamaa, E Estonia 58.46N 26.23E
120 I4 **Jõgevamaa** off. Jõgeva Maakond. ◆ *province* E Estonia
161 E18 **Jog Falls** *waterfall* Karnātaka, W India 14.16N 74.44E
149 S4 **Joghatāy** Khorāsān, NE Iran 36.34N 57.00E
159 U12 **Jogīghopa** Assam, NE India 26.13N 90.34E
158 I7 **Jogindarnagar** Himāchal Pradesh, N India 31.51N 76.55E
Jogjakarta *see* Yogyakarta
171 Ii13 **Jōhana** Toyama, Honshū, SW Japan 36.30N 136.53E
85 J21 **Johannesburg** var. Egoli, Erautini, Gauteng, abbrev. Jo'burg. Gauteng, NE South Africa 26.10S 28.01E
37 T13 **Johannesburg** California, W USA 35.20N 117.37W
85 I21 **Johannesburg** ✕ Gauteng, NE South Africa 26.08S 28.01E
Johannisburg *see* Pisz
155 P14 **Johi** Sind, SE Pakistan 26.46N 67.28E
57 T13 **Johi Village** S Guyana 1.48N 58.33W
34 K13 **John Day** Oregon, NW USA 44.25N 118.57W
34 I11 **John Day River** ⟿ Oregon, NW USA
20 L14 **John F Kennedy** ✕ (New York) Long Island, New York, NE USA 40.39N 73.45W
23 V8 **John H.Kerr Reservoir** var. Buggs Island Lake, Kerr Lake. ⊠ North Carolina/Virginia, SE USA
39 V6 **John Martin Reservoir** ⊠ Colorado, C USA
98 K6 **John o'Groats** N Scotland, UK 58.37N 3.03W
29 P5 **John Redmond Reservoir** ⊠ Kansas, C USA
41 Q7 **John River** ⟿ Alaska, USA
28 H6 **Johnson** Kansas, C USA 37.33N 101.46W
20 M7 **Johnson** Vermont, NE USA 44.39N 72.40W
20 D13 **Johnsonburg** Pennsylvania, NE USA 41.28N 78.37W
20 H11 **Johnson City** New York, NE USA 42.06N 75.54W
23 P8 **Johnson City** Tennessee, S USA 36.18N 82.21W
27 R10 **Johnson City** Texas, SW USA 30.16N 98.24W
37 S12 **Johnsondale** California, W USA 35.58N 118.32W
8 I8 **Johnsons Crossing** Yukon Territory, W Canada 60.30N 133.15W
23 T13 **Johnsonville** South Carolina, SE USA 33.50N 79.26W
23 Q13 **Johnston** South Carolina, SE USA 33.49N 81.48W
199 K6 **Johnston Atoll** ◇ *US unincorporated territory* C Pacific Ocean
183 Q3 **Johnston Atoll** *atoll* C Pacific Ocean
32 L17 **Johnston City** Illinois, N USA 37.49N 88.55W
188 K12 **Johnston, Lake** *salt lake* Western Australia
33 S13 **Johnstown** Ohio, N USA 40.08N 82.39W
20 D15 **Johnstown** Pennsylvania, NE USA 40.19N 78.55W
174 Hh6 **Johor** var. Johore. ◆ *state* Peninsular Malaysia
Johor Baharu *see* Johor Bahru
174 I6 **Johor Bahru** var. Johor Baharu, Johore Bahru. Johor, Peninsular Malaysia 1.28N 103.43E
Johore *see* Johor
Johore Bahru *see* Johor Bahru

◆ Country ● Country Capital ◇ Dependent Territory ○ Dependent Territory Capital ◆ Administrative Region ✕ International Airport ▲ Mountain ▲ Mountain Range Volcano ⟿ River ◎ Lake ⊠ Reservoir

120 K3 **Jõhvi** *Ger.* Jewe. Ida-Virumaa, NE Estonia 59.21N 27.25E
105 P7 **Joigny** Yonne, C France 47.58N 3.24E
Joinvile *see* Joinville
62 K12 **Joinville** *var.* Joinvile. Santa Catarina, S Brazil 26.19S 48.55W
105 R6 **Joinville** Haute-Marne, N France 48.26N 5.07E
204 H3 **Joinville Island** *island* Antarctica
43 O15 **Jojutla** *var.* Jojutla de Juárez. Morelos, S Mexico 18.36N 99.11W
Jojutla de Juárez *see* Jojutla
94 I12 **Jokkmokk** Norrbotten, N Sweden 66.35N 19.56E
94 L2 **Jökulsá á Dal** ~ E Iceland
94 K2 **Jökulsá á Fjöllum** ~ NE Iceland
Jokyakarta *see* Yogyakarta
32 M11 **Joliet** Illinois, N USA 41.33N 88.04W
13 O11 **Joliette** Quebec, SE Canada 46.01N 73.27W
179 Pp17 **Jolo** Jolo Island, SW Philippines 6.02N 121.00E
96 D11 **Jølstervatnet** ◎ S Norway
174 Ll15 **Jombang** *prev.* Djombang. Jawa, S Indonesia 7.33S 112.13E
165 R14 **Jomda** Xizang Zizhiqu, W China 31.26N 98.09E
58 A6 **Jome, Punta de** *headland* W Ecuador 0.57S 80.49W
120 G13 **Jonava** *Ger.* Janow, *Pol.* Janów. Jonava, C Lithuania 55.04N 24.19E
152 L11 **Jondor** *Rus.* Zhondor. Buxoro Viloyati, C Uzbekistan 39.46N 64.11E
165 V11 **Jonê** Gansu, C China 34.36N 103.39E
152 K10 **Jongeldi** *Rus.* Dzhankel'dy. Buxoro Viloyati, C Uzbekistan 40.50N 63.16E
29 X9 **Jonesboro** Arkansas, C USA 35.50N 90.42W
25 S4 **Jonesboro** Georgia, SE USA 33.31N 84.21W
32 L17 **Jonesboro** Illinois, N USA 37.25N 89.19W
24 H5 **Jonesboro** Louisiana, S USA 32.14N 92.43W
23 P8 **Jonesboro** Tennessee, S USA 36.17N 82.28W
21 T6 **Jonesport** Maine, NE USA 44.33N 67.35W
(0) J4 **Jones Sound** *channel* Nunavut, N Canada
24 I6 **Jonesville** Louisiana, S USA 31.37N 91.49W
33 Q10 **Jonesville** Michigan, N USA 41.58N 84.39W
23 Q11 **Jonesville** South Carolina, SE USA 34.49N 81.38W
83 F14 **Jonglei** Jonglei, SE Sudan 6.54N 31.19E
83 F14 **Jonglei** *var.* Gongoleh State. ◈ *state* SE Sudan
83 F14 **Jonglei Canal** *canal* S Sudan
120 F11 **Joniškėlis** Pasvalys, N Lithuania 56.02N 24.10E
120 F10 **Joniškis** *Ger.* Janischken. Joniškis, N Lithuania 56.15N 23.36E
97 L19 **Jönköping** Jönköping, S Sweden 57.45N 14.10E
97 K20 **Jönköping** ◈ *county* S Sweden
13 Q7 **Jonquière** Quebec, SE Canada 48.25N 71.16W
43 V15 **Jonuta** Tabasco, SE Mexico 18.04N 92.03W
104 K12 **Jonzac** Charente-Maritime, W France 45.26N 0.25W
29 R7 **Joplin** Missouri, C USA 37.04N 94.30W
35 W8 **Jordan** Montana, NW USA 47.18N 106.54W
144 H12 **Jordan** *off.* Hashemite Kingdom of Jordan, *Ar.* Al Mamlakah al Urdunīyah al Hāshimīyah, Al Urdunn; *prev.* Transjordan. ◆ *monarchy* SW Asia
144 G9 **Jordan** *Ar.* Urdunn, *Heb.* HaYarden. ~ SW Asia
Jordan Lake *see* B.Everett Jordan Reservoir
113 K17 **Jordanów** Małopolskie, S Poland 49.39N 19.51E
34 M15 **Jordan Valley** Oregon, NW USA 42.59N 117.03W
144 G9 **Jordan Valley** *valley* N Israel
59 D15 **Jorge Chávez International** *var.* Lima. ✈ (Lima) Lima, W Peru 12.07S 77.01W
115 L23 **Jorgucat** *var.* Jergucati, Jorgucati. Gjirokastër, S Albania 39.57N 20.14E
Jorgucati *see* Jorgucat
159 X12 **Jorhāt** Assam, NE India 26.45N 94.09E
95 J14 **Jörn** Västerbotten, N Sweden 65.02N 20.04E
39 R14 **Jornada Del Muerto** *valley* New Mexico, SW USA
95 N17 **Joroinen** Isä-Suomi, E Finland 62.10N 27.49E
97 C16 **Jørpeland** Rogaland, S Norway 59.01N 6.01E
79 W14 **Jos** Plateau, C Nigeria 9.58N 8.57E
179 Rr17 **Jose Abad Santos** *var.* Trinidad. Mindanao, S Philippines 5.51N 125.35E
63 F19 **José Batlle y Ordóñez** *var.* Batlle y Ordóñez. Florida, C Uruguay 33.28S 55.07W
65 H18 **José de San Martín** Chubut, S Argentina 44.03S 70.27W
63 E19 **José Enrique Rodó** *var.* Rodó, José E.Rodo; *prev.* Drabble, Drable. Soriano, SW Uruguay 33.43S 57.33W
José E.Rodo *see* José Enrique Rodó
Josefsdorf *see* Žabalj
46 C4 **José Martí** ✈ (La Habana) Cuidad de La Habana, N Cuba 23.03N 82.22W
63 F19 **José Pedro Varela** *var.* José P.Varela. Lavalleja, S Uruguay 33.30S 54.28W
189 N2 **Joseph Bonaparte Gulf** *gulf* N Australia
39 N11 **Joseph City** Arizona, SW USA 34.56N 110.18W
11 O9 **Joseph, Lake** ◎ Newfoundland and Labrador, E Canada
12 G13 **Joseph, Lake** ◎ Ontario, S Canada
194 I11 **Josephstaal** Madang, N PNG 4.42S 144.59E
José P.Varela *see* José Pedro Varela
61 J14 **José Rodrigues** Pará, N Brazil 5.45S 51.19W
158 K9 **Joshīmath** Uttar Pradesh, N India 30.33N 79.34E
27 T7 **Joshua** Texas, SW USA 32.27N 97.23W
37 V15 **Joshua Tree** California, W USA 34.07N 116.18W
79 V14 **Jos Plateau** *plateau* C Nigeria
104 H6 **Josselin** Morbihan, NW France 47.57N 2.35W
Jos Sudarso *see* Yos Sudarso, Pulau
96 E11 **Jostedalsbreen** *glacier* S Norway
96 F12 **Jotunheimen** ▲▲ S Norway
144 G7 **Joûnié** *var.* Junīyah. W Lebanon 33.54N 33.36E
27 R13 **Jourdanton** Texas, SW USA 28.55N 98.33W
100 L7 **Joure** *Fris.* De Jouwer. Friesland, N Netherlands 52.58N 5.48E
95 M18 **Joutsa** Länsi-Suomi, W Finland 61.46N 26.09E
95 N18 **Joutseno** Etelä-Suomi, S Finland 61.06N 28.30E
94 M12 **Joutsijärvi** Lappi, NE Finland 66.40N 28.00E
110 A9 **Joux, Lac de** ◎ W Switzerland
46 D5 **Jovellanos** Matanzas, W Cuba 22.49N 81.14W
159 V13 **Jowai** Meghālaya, NE India 25.25N 92.21E
Jōwat *see* Jabwot
Jowhar *see* Jawhar
149 O12 **Jowkān** Fārs, S Iran
149 Q10 **Jowzam** Kermān, C Iran
155 N2 **Jowzjān** ◈ *province* N Afghanistan
Józseffalva *see* Žabalj
J.Storm Thurmond Reservoir *see* Clark Hill Lake
47 T6 **Juana Díaz** C Puerto Rico 18.03N 66.30W
42 L9 **Juan Aldama** Zacatecas, C Mexico 24.18N 103.23W
(0) E9 **Juan de Fuca Plate** *tectonic feature*
34 F7 **Juan de Fuca, Strait of** *strait* Canada/USA
Juan Fernandez Islands *see* Juan Fernández, Islas
200 Oo12 **Juan Fernández, Islas** *Eng.* Juan Fernandez Islands. *island group* W Chile
57 O4 **Juangriego** Nueva Esparta, NE Venezuela 11.03N 63.58W
58 D11 **Juanjuí** *var.* Juanjuy. San Martín, N Peru 7.12S 76.45W
Juanjuy *see* Juanjuí
95 N16 **Juankoski** Itä-Suomi, C Finland 63.01N 28.24E
Juan Lacaze *see* Juan L.Lacaze
63 E20 **Juan L.Lacaze** *var.* Juan Lacaze, Puerto Sauce; *prev.* Sauce. Colonia, SW Uruguay 34.25S 57.25W
64 L5 **Juan Solá** Salta, N Argentina 23.30S 62.42W
65 F21 **Juan Stuven, Isla** *island* S Chile
61 H16 **Juará** Mato Grosso, W Brazil 11.10S 57.28W
43 N7 **Juárez** *var.* Villa Juárez. Coahuila de Zaragoza, NE Mexico 27.39N 100.43W
42 C2 **Juárez, Sierra de** ▲▲ NW Mexico
61 O15 **Juazeiro** *prev.* Joazeiro. Bahia, E Brazil 9.25S 40.30W
61 P14 **Juazeiro do Norte** Ceará, E Brazil 7.10S 39.18W
83 F15 **Juba** *var.* Jūbā. Bahr el Gabel, S Sudan 4.49N 31.34E
83 L17 **Juba** *Amh.* Genalē Wenz, *It.* Guiba, *Som.* Ganaane, Webi Jubba. ~ Ethiopia/Somalia
204 H2 **Jubany** *Argentinian research station* Antarctica 61.57S 58.23W
Jubayl *see* Jbaïl
83 L18 **Jubbada Dhexe** *off.* Gobolka Jubbada Dhexe. ◈ *region* SW Somalia
83 K18 **Jubbada Hoose** ◈ *region* SW Somalia
Jubba, Webi *see* Juba
Jubbulpore *see* Jabalpur
Jubeil *see* Jbaïl
76 B9 **Juby, Cap** *headland* SW Morocco 27.58N 12.56W
107 R10 **Júcar** *var.* Jucar. ~ C Spain
42 L12 **Juchipila** Zacatecas, C Mexico 21.25N 103.06W
43 S16 **Juchitán** *var.* Juchitán de Zaragosa. Oaxaca, SE Mexico 16.27N 95.00W
Juchitán de Zaragosa *see* Juchitán
144 G11 **Judaea** *cultural region* Israel/West Bank
144 F11 **Judaean Hills** *Heb.* Haré Yehuda. *hill range* E Israel
144 H8 **Judaydah** *Fr.* Jdaïdé. Dimashq, W Syria 33.17N 36.15E
145 P11 **Judayyidat Hāmir** S Iraq 31.29N 41.25E
111 U8 **Judenburg** Steiermark, C Austria 47.09N 14.42E
35 T8 **Judith River** ~ Montana, NW USA
29 V11 **Judsonia** Arkansas, C USA 35.16N 91.38W
147 P14 **Jufrah, Wādī al** *dry watercourse* NW Yemen
Jugoslavija/Jugoslavija, Savezna Republika *see* Serbia and Montenegro (Yugoslavia)
44 K10 **Juigalpa** Chontales, S Nicaragua 12.04N 85.21W
167 T13 **Juishui** C Taiwan 23.43N 121.28E
102 E9 **Juist** *island* NW Germany
61 M21 **Juiz de Fora** Minas Gerais, SE Brazil 21.46S 43.22W
64 J5 **Jujuy** *off.* Provincia de Jujuy. ◈ *province* N Argentina
Jujuy *see* San Salvador de Jujuy
94 J11 **Jukkasjärvi** Norrbotten, N Sweden 67.52N 20.39E
Jula *see* Gyula, Hungary
Jūlā *see* Jālū, Libya
39 W2 **Julesburg** Colorado, C USA 40.59N 102.15W
Julia Beterrae *see* Béziers
59 I17 **Juliaca** Puno, SE Peru 15.32S 70.10W
189 U6 **Julia Creek** Queensland, C Australia 20.40S 141.49E
37 V17 **Julian** California, W USA 33.04N 116.36W
100 H7 **Julianadorp** Noord-Holland, NW Netherlands 52.53N 4.43E
111 S11 **Julian Alps** *Ger.* Julische Alpen, *It.* Alpi Giulie, *Slvn.* Julijske Alpe. ▲▲ Italy/Slovenia
57 V11 **Juliana Top** ▲ C Suriname 3.39N 56.36W
Julianehåb *see* Qaqortoq
Julijske Alpe *see* Julian Alps
42 J6 **Julimes** Chihuahua, N Mexico 28.29N 105.21W
Julio Briga *see* Bragança, Portugal
Juliobriga *see* Logroño, Spain
63 G15 **Júlio de Castilhos** Rio Grande do Sul, S Brazil 29.14S 53.42W
Juliomagus *see* Angers
Julische Alpen *see* Julian Alps
Jullundur *see* Jalandhar
153 N11 **Juma** *Rus.* Dzhuma. Samarqand Viloyati, C Uzbekistan 39.43N 66.37E
167 O3 **Juma He** ~ E China
83 L18 **Jumboo** Jubbada Hoose, S Somalia 0.12S 42.34E
37 Y11 **Jumbo Peak** ▲ Nevada, W USA 36.12N 114.09W
107 R12 **Jumilla** Murcia, SE Spain 38.28N 1.19W
159 N10 **Jumla** Mid Western, NW Nepal 29.22N 82.13E
Jummoo *see* Jammu
Jumna *see* Yamuna
Jumporn *see* Chumphon
32 K5 **Jump River** ~ Wisconsin, N USA
160 B11 **Jūnāgadh** *var.* Junagarh. Gujarāt, W India 21.31N 70.31E
Junagarh *see* Jūnāgadh
167 Q6 **Junan** *prev.* Shizilu. Shandong, E China 35.11N 118.47E
64 G11 **Juncal, Cerro** ▲ C Chile 33.03S 70.02W
27 Q10 **Junction** Texas, SW USA 30.29N 99.46W
38 K6 **Junction** Utah, W USA 38.14N 112.13W
29 O4 **Junction City** Kansas, C USA 39.01N 96.49W
34 F13 **Junction City** Oregon, NW USA 44.13N 123.12W
62 M10 **Jundiaí** São Paulo, S Brazil 23.10S 46.54W
194 E13 **June** ~ W PNG
41 X12 **Juneau** *state capital* Alaska, USA 58.13N 134.11W
32 M8 **Juneau** Wisconsin, N USA 43.22N 88.42W
107 U6 **Juneda** Cataluña, NE Spain 41.33N 0.49E
191 Q9 **Junee** New South Wales, SE Australia 34.51S 147.33E
37 R8 **June Lake** California, W USA 37.46N 119.04W
Jungbunzlau *see* Mladá Boleslav
164 L4 **Junggar Pendi** *Eng.* Dzungarian Basin. *basin* NW China
101 N24 **Junglinster** Grevenmacher, C Luxembourg 49.43N 6.15E
20 F14 **Juniata River** ~ Pennsylvania, NE USA
63 B20 **Junín** Buenos Aires, E Argentina 34.36S 61.01W
59 E14 **Junín** Junín, C Peru 11.13S 76.01W
59 F14 **Junín** *off.* Departamento de Junín. ◈ *department* C Peru
65 H15 **Junín de los Andes** Neuquén, W Argentina 39.57S 71.04W
59 D14 **Junín, Lago de** ◎ C Peru
Junīyah *see* Joûnié
Junkseylon *see* Phuket
166 I11 **Junlian** Sichuan, C China 28.11N 104.31E
27 O11 **Juno** Texas, SW USA 30.09N 101.07W
94 J11 **Junosuando** Norrbotten, N Sweden 67.25N 22.28E
95 H16 **Junsele** Västernorrland, C Sweden 63.42N 16.54E
Junten *see* Sunch'ŏn
34 L14 **Juntura** Oregon, NW USA 43.43N 118.05W
95 N14 **Juntusranta** Oulu, E Finland 65.12N 29.30E
120 H11 **Juodupė** Rokiškis, NE Lithuania 56.07N 25.37E
121 H14 **Juozapinės Kalnas** ▲ SE Lithuania 54.29N 25.27E
101 K19 **Juprelle** Liège, E Belgium 50.43N 5.31E
82 D13 **Jur** ~ C Sudan
105 S9 **Jura** ◈ *department* E France
110 C7 **Jura** ◈ *canton* NW Switzerland
110 B8 **Jura** *var.* Jura Mountains. ▲▲ France/Switzerland
98 G12 **Jura** *island* SW Scotland, UK
Juraciszki *see* Yuratsishki
56 C8 **Juradó** Chocó, NW Colombia 7.07N 77.45W
Jura Mountains *see* Jura
98 G12 **Jura, Sound of** *strait* W Scotland, UK
145 V15 **Juraybīyāt, Bi'r** *well* S Iraq 29.13N 45.28E
120 E13 **Jurbarkas** *Ger.* Georgenburg, Jurburg. Jurbarkas, W Lithuania 55.04N 22.45E
101 F20 **Jurbise** Hainaut, SW Belgium 50.33N 3.54E
Jurburg *see* Jurbarkas
120 F9 **Jūrmala** Rīga, C Latvia 56.56N 23.42E
176 Ww13 **Jursian, Pulau** *island* E Indonesia
60 D13 **Juruá** Amazonas, NW Brazil 3.08S 65.59W
50 F7 **Juruá, Rio** *var.* Río Yuruá. ~ Brazil/Peru
61 G16 **Juruena** Mato Grosso, W Brazil 10.32S 58.38W
61 G16 **Juruena** ~ W Brazil
171 Mm8 **Jūsan-ko** ◎ Honshū, C Japan
27 O6 **Justiceburg** Texas, SW USA 32.57N 101.07W
Justinianopolis *see* Kirşehir
64 K11 **Justo Daract** San Luis, C Argentina 33.52S 65.12W
61 C14 **Jutaí** Amazonas, W Brazil 5.10S 68.45W
60 C13 **Jutaí, Rio** ~ NW Brazil
102 N13 **Jüterbog** Brandenburg, E Germany 51.58N 13.06E
44 E6 **Jutiapa** Jutiapa, S Guatemala 14.18N 89.52W
44 A3 **Jutiapa** *off.* Departamento de Jutiapa. ◈ *department* SE Guatemala
44 J6 **Juticalpa** Olancho, C Honduras 14.39N 86.12W
84 I13 **Jutila** North Western, NW Zambia 12.33S 26.09E
Jutland *see* Jylland
86 F8 **Jutland Bank** *undersea feature* SE North Sea
95 N16 **Juuka** Itä-Suomi, E Finland 63.12N 29.16E
95 N17 **Juva** Isä-Suomi, SE Finland 61.55N 27.54E
Juvavum *see* Salzburg
46 A6 **Juventud, Isla de la** *var.* Isla de Pinos, *Eng.* Isle of Youth; *prev.* The Isle of the Pines. *island* W Cuba
Ju Xian *see* Juxian
167 Q5 **Juxian** *var.* Ju Xian. Shandong, E China 35.33N 118.45E
167 P6 **Juye** Shandong, E China 35.25N 116.04E
115 O15 **Južna Morava** *Ger.* Südliche Morava. ~ SE Serbia and Montenegro (Yugoslavia)
97 I23 **Jyderup** Vestsjælland, E Denmark 55.40N 11.25E
97 F22 **Jylland** *Eng.* Jutland. *peninsula* W Denmark
Jyrgalan *see* Dzhergalan
95 M17 **Jyväskylä** Länsi-Suomi, W Finland 62.07N 25.47E

K

155 X3 **K2** *Chin.* Qogir Feng, *Eng.* Mount Godwin Austen. ▲ China/Pakistan 35.55N 76.30E
40 D9 **Kaaawa** *Haw.* Ka'a'wa. Oahu, Hawaii, USA, C Pacific Ocean 21.33N 157.51W
83 G16 **Kaabong** NE Uganda 3.30N 34.07E
Kaaden *see* Kadaň
57 V9 **Kaaimanston** Sipaliwini, N Suriname 5.06N 56.04W
152 G14 **Kaakhka** *var.* Kaka. Akhalskiy Velayat, S Turkmenistan 37.19N 59.36E
Kaala *see* Caála
197 H5 **Kaala-Gomen** Province Nord, W New Caledonia 20.40S 164.24E
94 L9 **Kaamanen** *Lapp.* Gámas. Lappi, N Finland 69.04N 27.16E
Kaapstad *see* Cape Town
Kaarasjoki *see* Karasjok
Kaaresuanto *see* Karesuando
94 J10 **Kaaresuvanto** *Lapp.* Gárassavon. Lappi, N Finland 68.28N 22.29E
95 K19 **Kaarina** Länsi-Suomi, W Finland 60.24N 22.25E
101 I14 **Kaatsheuvel** Noord-Brabant, S Netherlands 51.39N 5.01E
95 N16 **Kaavi** Itä-Suomi, C Finland 62.58N 28.30E
Ka'a'wa *see* Kaaawa
176 Y15 **Kaba** Papua, E Indonesia 7.34S 138.27E
Kaba *see* Habahe
175 Q13 **Kabaena, Pulau** *island* C Indonesia
175 Q13 **Kabaena, Selat** *strait* Sulawesi, C Indonesia
152 J11 **Kabakly** *Turkm.* Gabakly. Lebapskiy Velayat, NE Turkmenistan 39.45N 62.30E
78 J14 **Kabala** N Sierra Leone 9.40N 11.36W
83 E19 **Kabale** SW Uganda 1.15S 29.58E
57 U10 **Kabalebo Rivier** ~ W Suriname
81 N22 **Kabalo** Katanga, SE Dem. Rep. Congo 6.01S 26.55E
151 W13 **Kabanbay** *Kaz.* Qabanbay *prev.* Andreyevka, *Kaz.* Andreevka. Almaty, SE Kazakhstan 45.49N 80.34E
81 O21 **Kabambare** Maniema, E Dem. Rep. Congo 4.40S 27.40E
197 K15 **Kabara** *prev.* Kambara. *island* Lau Group, E Fiji
Kabardino-Balkaria *see* Kabardino-Balkarskaya Respublika
130 M15 **Kabardino-Balkarskaya Respublika** *Eng.* Kabardino-Balkaria. ◈ *autonomous republic* SW Russian Federation
81 O19 **Kabare** Sud Kivu, E Dem. Rep. Congo 2.13S 28.40E
176 Uu8 **Kabarei** Papua, E Indonesia 0.01S 130.58E
179 Q16 **Kabasalan** Mindanao, S Philippines 7.46N 122.49E
79 U15 **Kabba** Kogi, S Nigeria 7.48N 6.07E
94 I13 **Kåbdalis** Norrbotten, N Sweden 66.08N 20.03E
144 M6 **Kabd aş Şārim** *hill range* E Syria
12 B7 **Kabenung Lake** ◎ Ontario, S Canada
31 W3 **Kabetogama Lake** ◎ Minnesota, N USA
Kabia, Pulau *see* Kabin, Pulau
81 M22 **Kabinda** Kasai Oriental, SE Dem. Rep. Congo 6.09S 24.28E
Kabinda *see* Cabinda
175 P13 **Kabin, Pulau** *var.* Pulau Kabia. *island* W Indonesia
175 Rr16 **Kabir** Pulau Pantar, S Indonesia 8.15S 124.12E
155 T10 **Kabīrwāla** Punjab, E Pakistan 30.24N 71.51E
176 U8 **Kable Bet** Papua, E Indonesia 0.24S 129.54E
80 I13 **Kabo** Ouham, NW Central African Republic 7.43N 18.38E
Kābol *see* Kābul
85 H14 **Kabompo** North Western, W Zambia 13.36S 24.10E
85 H14 **Kabompo** ~ W Zambia
81 M22 **Kabongo** Katanga, SE Dem. Rep. Congo 7.19S 25.34E
123 Kk12 **Kaboudia, Rass** *headland* E Tunisia 35.13N 11.09E
149 U4 **Kabūd Gonbad** Khorāsān, NE Iran 37.01N 59.46E
148 L5 **Kabūd Rāhang** Hamadān, W Iran 35.12N 48.43E
84 L12 **Kabuko** Northern, NE Zambia 11.31S 31.16E
155 Q5 **Kābul** *var.* Kabul, *Per.* Kābol. ● (Afghanistan) Kābul, E Afghanistan 34.34N 69.07E
155 Q5 **Kābul** *Eng.* Kabul, *Per.* Kābol. ◈ *province* E Afghanistan
155 Q5 **Kābul** ✈ Kābul, E Afghanistan 34.31N 69.10E
155 R5 **Kabul** *var.* Daryā-ye Kābul. ~ Afghanistan/Pakistan *see also* Kābul, Daryā-ye
155 S5 **Kābul, Daryā-ye** *var.* Kabul. ~ Afghanistan/Pakistan *see also* Kabul
81 O25 **Kabunda** Katanga, SE Dem. Rep. Congo 12.21S 29.14E
175 Ss4 **Kaburuang, Pulau** *island* Kepulauan Talaud, N Indonesia
82 G8 **Kabushiya** River Nile, NE Sudan 16.54N 33.40E
85 J14 **Kabwe** Central, C Zambia 14.28S 28.25E
194 K12 **Kabwum** Morobe, C PNG 6.07S 147.11E
115 N17 **Kačanik** Serbia, S Serbia and Montenegro (Yugoslavia) 42.13N 21.16E
176 U8 **Kacepi** Pulau Gebe, E Indonesia 0.05S 129.30E
120 F13 **Kačerginė** Kaunas, C Lithuania 54.55N 23.40E
119 S13 **Kacha** Respublika Krym, S Ukraine 44.46N 33.33E
160 A10 **Kachchh, Gulf of** *var.* Gulf of Cutch, Gulf of Kutch. *gulf* W India
160 I11 **Kachchhīdhāna** Madhya Pradesh, C India 21.33N 78.54E
155 Q11 **Kachchh, Rann of** *var.* Rann of Kachh, Rann of Kutch. *salt marsh* India/Pakistan
41 Q13 **Kachemak Bay** *bay* Alaska, USA
Kachh, Rann of *see* Kachchh, Rann of
79 V14 **Kachia** Kaduna, C Nigeria 9.52N 8.00E
178 Gg2 **Kachin State** ◈ *state* N Myanmar
151 T7 **Kachiry** Pavlodar, NE Kazakhstan 53.04N 76.05E
126 Jj15 **Kachug** Irkutskaya Oblast', S Russian Federation 53.52N 105.54E
143 Q11 **Kaçkar Dağları** ▲▲ NE Turkey
161 C21 **Kadamatt Island** *island* Lakshadweep, India, N Indian Ocean
113 B15 **Kadaň** *Ger.* Kaaden.Ústecký Kraj, NW Czech Republic 50.22N 13.14E
178 Gg12 **Kadan Kyun** *prev.* King Island. *island* Mergui Archipelago, S Myanmar
197 I16 **Kadavu** *prev.* Kandavu. *island* S Fiji
197 I15 **Kadavu Passage** *channel* S Fiji
81 G16 **Kadéï** ~ Cameroon/Central African Republic
Kadhimain *see* Al Kāẓimīyah
Kadijica *see* Kadiytsa
116 M13 **Kadıköy Barajı** ⊠ NW Turkey
190 I8 **Kadina** South Australia 33.59S 137.43E
142 H15 **Kadınhanı** Konya, C Turkey 38.15N 32.13E
78 M14 **Kadiolo** Sikasso, S Mali 10.30N 5.43W
142 L16 **Kadirli** Osmaniye, S Turkey 37.22N 36.04E
116 G11 **Kadiytsa** | Mac. Kadijica. ▲ Bulgaria/FYR Macedonia 41.48N 22.58E
30 L10 **Kadoka** South Dakota, N USA 43.49N 101.30W
131 N5 **Kadom** Ryazanskaya Oblast', W Russian Federation 54.35N 42.27E
85 K16 **Kadoma** *prev.* Gatooma. Mashonaland West, C Zimbabwe 18.18S 29.55E
82 E12 **Kadugli** Southern Kordofan, S Sudan 11.00N 29.44E
79 V14 **Kaduna** Kaduna, C Nigeria 10.32N 7.25E
79 V14 **Kaduna** ◈ *state* C Nigeria
79 V15 **Kaduna** ~ N Nigeria
128 K14 **Kaduy** Vologodskaya Oblast', NW Russian Federation 59.10N 37.11E
160 E13 **Kadwa** ~ W India
127 Nn9 **Kadykchan** Magadanskaya Oblast', E Russian Federation 62.54N 146.53E
Kadzharan *see* K'ajaran
129 T7 **Kadzherom** Respublika Komi, NW Russian Federation 64.42N 55.51E
153 X8 **Kadzhi-Say** *Kir.* Kajisay. Issyk-Kul'skaya Oblast', NE Kyrgyzstan 42.07N 77.10E
78 I10 **Kaédi** Gorgol, S Mauritania 16.12N 13.31W
80 G12 **Kaélé** Extrême-Nord, N Cameroon 10.09N 14.25E
40 C9 **Kaena Point** *headland* Oahu, Hawaii, USA, C Pacific Ocean 21.34N 158.16W
192 J2 **Kaeo** Northland, North Island, NZ 35.03S 173.40E
169 X14 **Kaesŏng** *var.* Kaesŏng-si. S North Korea 37.57N 126.30E
Kaesŏng-si *see* Kaesŏng
Kaewieng *see* Kavieng
81 L24 **Kafakumba** Katanga, S Dem. Rep. Congo 9.39S 23.43E
Kafan *see* Kapan
79 V14 **Kafanchan** Kaduna, C Nigeria 9.32N 8.18E
Kaffa *see* Feodosiya
78 G11 **Kaffrine** C Senegal 14.07N 15.27W
Kafiau *see* Kofiau, Pulau
117 I19 **Kafiréas, Akrotírio** *headland* Évvoia, C Greece 38.10N 24.35E
117 I19 **Kafiréos, Stenó** *strait* Évvoia/Kykládes, Greece, Aegean Sea
Kafirnigan *see* Kofarnihon
Kafo *see* Kafu
Kafr ash Shaykh/Kafrel Sheik *see* Kafr el Sheikh
77 W7 **Kafr el Sheikh** *var.* Kafr ash Shaykh, Kafrel Sheik. N Egypt 31.08N 30.58E
83 F17 **Kafu** *var.* Kafo. ~ W Uganda
85 J15 **Kafue** Lusaka, SE Zambia 15.43S 28.10E
85 I14 **Kafue** ~ C Zambia
69 T13 **Kafue Flats** *plain* C Zambia
171 I13 **Kaga** Ishikawa, Honshū, SW Japan 36.18N 136.19E
81 J14 **Kaga Bandoro** *prev.* Fort-Crampel. Nana-Grébizi, C Central African Republic 6.54N 19.09E
83 E18 **Kagadi** W Uganda 0.57N 30.52E
40 H17 **Kagalaska Island** *island* Aleutian Islands, Alaska, USA
Kagan *see* Kogon
Kaganovichabad *see* Kolkhozobod
Kagarlyk *see* Kaharlyk
170 F15 **Kagawa** *off.* Kagawa-ken. ◈ *prefecture* Shikoku, SW Japan
160 J13 **Kagaznagar** Andhra Pradesh, C India 19.25N 79.30E
95 J14 **Kåge** Västerbotten, N Sweden 64.49N 21.00E
83 E19 **Kagera** *var.* Ziwa Magharibi, *Eng.* West Lake. ◈ *region* NW Tanzania
83 E19 **Kagera** *var.* Akagera. ~ Rwanda/Tanzania *see also* Akagera
78 L5 **Kâgheț** *var.* Karet. *physical region* N Mauritania
Kagi *see* Chiai
143 S12 **Kağızman** Kars, NE Turkey 40.08N 43.10E
196 I6 **Kagman Point** *headland* Saipan, S Northern Mariana Islands
170 Bb15 **Kagoshima** *var.* Kagosima. Kagoshima, Kyūshū, SW Japan 31.36N 130.33E
172 Qq14 **Kagoshima** *off.* Kagoshima-ken, *var.* Kagosima. ◈ *prefecture* Kyūshū, SW Japan
170 Bb16 **Kagoshima-wan** *bay* SW Japan
Kagosima *see* Kagoshima
194 H12 **Kagua** Southern Highlands, W PNG 6.25S 143.48E
Kagul *see* Cahul
Kagul, Ozero *see* Kahul, Ozero
40 B8 **Kahala Point** *headland* Kauai, Hawaii, USA, C Pacific Ocean 22.08N 159.17W
40 G12 **Kahaluu** *Haw.* Kahalu'u. Hawaii, USA, C Pacific Ocean 19.34N 155.58W
83 F21 **Kahama** Shinyanga, NW Tanzania 3.48S 32.36E
119 P5 **Kaharlyk** *Rus.* Kagarlyk. Kyyivs'ka Oblast', N Ukraine 49.49N 30.49E
174 Mm10 **Kahayan, Sungai** ~ Borneo, C Indonesia
81 I22 **Kahemba** Bandundu, SW Dem. Rep. Congo 7.20S 19.00E
193 A23 **Kaherekoau Mountains** ▲▲ South Island, NZ
149 W14 **Kahīrī** *var.* Kūhīrī. Sīstān va Balūchestān, SE Iran 26.55N 61.04E
103 L16 **Kahla** Thüringen, C Germany 50.49N 11.33E
103 G15 **Kahler Asten** ▲ W Germany 51.11N 8.32E
155 Q4 **Kahmard, Daryā-ye** *prev.* Darya-i-Surkhab. ~ NE Afghanistan
149 T13 **Kahnūj** Kermān, SE Iran 27.59N 57.40E
29 V1 **Kahoka** Missouri, C USA 40.25N 91.43W
40 E10 **Kahoolawe** *island* Hawaii, USA, C Pacific Ocean
142 M16 **Kahramanmaraş** *var.* Kahraman Maraş, Maraş, Marash. Kahramanmaraş, S Turkey 37.34N 36.54E
142 L15 **Kahramanmaraş** *var.* Kahraman Maraş, Maraş, Marash. ◈ *province* C Turkey
Kahror/Kahror Pakka *see* Karor Pacca
143 N15 **Kâhta** Adıyaman, S Turkey 37.48N 38.34E
40 D8 **Kahuku** Oahu, Hawaii, USA, C Pacific Ocean 21.40N 157.57W
40 D8 **Kahuku Point** *headland* Oahu, Hawaii, USA, C Pacific Ocean 21.42N 157.59W
118 M12 **Kahul, Ozero** *var.* Lacul Cahul, *Rus.* Ozero Kagul. ◎ Moldova/Ukraine
149 V11 **Kahūrak** Sīstān va Balūchestān, SE Iran 29.25N 59.37E
192 G13 **Kahurangi Point** *headland* South Island, NZ 40.41S 171.57E
155 V6 **Kahūta** Punjab, E Pakistan 33.34N 73.22E
79 S14 **Kaiama** Kwara, W Nigeria 9.37N 3.58E
194 J12 **Kaiapit** Morobe, C PNG 6.16S 146.13E
193 I18 **Kaiapoi** Canterbury, South Island, NZ 43.22S 172.39E
38 K9 **Kaibab Plateau** *plain* Arizona, SW USA
171 Gg14 **Kaibara** Hyōgo, Honshū, SW Japan 35.06N 135.03E
176 Vv13 **Kai Besar, Pulau** *island* Kepulauan Kai, E Indonesia
38 L9 **Kaibito Plateau** *plain* Arizona, SW USA
164 K6 **Kaidu He** *var.* Karaxahar. ~ NW China
57 S10 **Kaieteur Falls** *waterfall* C Guyana 5.04N 59.32W
167 O6 **Kaifeng** Henan, C China 34.46N 114.19E
192 J3 **Kaihu** Northland, North Island, NZ 35.47S 173.39E
176 V13 **Kai Kecil, Pulau** *island* Kepulauan Kai, E Indonesia
176 V14 **Kai, Kepulauan** *prev.* Kei Islands. *island group* Maluku, SE Indonesia
192 J3 **Kaikohe** Northland, North Island, NZ 35.25S 173.48E
193 J16 **Kaikoura** Canterbury, South Island, NZ 42.21S 173.40E
193 J16 **Kaikoura Peninsula** *peninsula* South Island, NZ
Kailas Range *see* Gangdisê Shan
166 K12 **Kaili** Guizhou, S China 26.34N 107.58E
40 F10 **Kailua** Maui, Hawaii, USA, C Pacific Ocean 20.53N 156.13W
40 G11 **Kailua** *var.* Kailua-Kona, Kona. Hawaii, USA, C Pacific Ocean 19.43N 155.58W
Kailua-Kona *see* Kailua
194 E13 **Kaim** ~ W PNG
176 Y13 **Kaima** Papua, E Indonesia 5.36S 138.39E
192 M7 **Kaimai Range** ▲▲ North Island, NZ
116 E13 **Kaïmaktsalán** ▲ Greece/FYR Macedonia 40.57N 21.48E
193 C20 **Kaimanawa Mountains** ▲▲ North Island, NZ
120 E4 **Käina** *Ger.* Keinis; *prev.* Keina. Hiiumaa, W Estonia 58.49N 22.45E
111 V7 **Kainach** ~ SE Austria
170 G16 **Kainan** Tokushima, Shikoku, SW Japan 33.36N 134.20E
170 Ff16 **Kainan** Wakayama, Honshū, SW Japan 34.10N 135.11E
194 J12 **Kainantu** Eastern Highlands, C PNG 6.16S 145.49E
153 U7 **Kaindy** *Kir.* Kayyngdy. Chuyskaya Oblast', N Kyrgyzstan 42.48N 73.39E
79 T14 **Kainji Dam** *dam* W Nigeria 9.52N 4.36E
Kainji Lake *see* Kainji Reservoir
79 T14 **Kainji Reservoir** *var.* Kainji Lake. ⊠ W Nigeria
194 J14 **Kaintiba** *var.* Kamina. Gulf, S PNG 7.29S 146.04E
94 K12 **Kainulaisjärvi** Norrbotten, N Sweden 67.00N 22.31E
192 K5 **Kaipara Harbour** *harbor* North Island, NZ
158 I10 **Kairāna** Uttar Pradesh, N India 29.24N 77.10E
194 G9 **Kairiru Island** *island* NW PNG
76 M6 **Kairouan** *var.* Al Qayrawān. E Tunisia 35.45N 10.11E
Kaisaria *see* Kayseri
103 F20 **Kaiserslautern** Rheinland-Pfalz, SW Germany 49.27N 7.46E
120 G13 **Kaišiadorys** Kaišiadorys, S Lithuania 54.51N 24.27E
192 I2 **Kaitaia** Northland, North Island, NZ 35.07S 173.13E
193 E24 **Kaitangata** Otago, South Island, NZ 46.15S 169.49E
158 I9 **Kaithal** Haryāna, NW India 29.46N 76.20E
174 J11 **Kait, Tanjung** *headland* Sumatera, W Indonesia 3.13S 106.03E
40 E9 **Kaiwi Channel** *channel* Hawaii, USA, C Pacific Ocean
166 K9 **Kaixian** *var.* Kai Xian. Sichuan, C China 31.13N 108.25E
169 V11 **Kaiyuan** *var.* K'ai-yüan. Liaoning, NE China 42.36N 124.03E
166 H14 **Kaiyuan** Yunnan, SW China 23.42N 103.13E
41 O9 **Kaiyuh Mountains** ▲▲ Alaska, USA
95 M15 **Kajaani** *Swe.* Kajana. Oulu, C Finland 64.16N 27.46E
155 N7 **Kajakī, Band-e** ◎ C Afghanistan
Kajan *see* Kayan, Sungai
Kajana *see* Kajaani
143 V13 **K'ajaran** *Rus.* Kadzharan. SE Armenia 39.10N 46.09E
Kajisay *see* Kadzhi-Say
115 O20 **Kajmakčalan** ▲ S FYR Macedonia 40.57N 21.48E
Kajnar *see* Kaynar
155 N6 **Kajrān** Urūzgān, C Afghanistan 33.12N 65.28E
155 N5 **Kaj Rūd** ~ C Afghanistan
Kaka *see* Kaakhka
10 C12 **Kakabeka Falls** Ontario, S Canada 48.24N 89.40W
85 F23 **Kakamas** Northern Cape, W South Africa 28.45S 20.33E
83 H18 **Kakamega** Western, W Kenya 0.13N 34.43E
114 H13 **Kakanj** Federacija Bosna I Hercegovina, Bosnia and Herzegovina 44.06N 18.07E
193 F22 **Kakanui Mountains** ▲▲ South Island, NZ
192 K11 **Kakaramea** Taranaki, North Island, NZ 39.42S 174.27E
78 J16 **Kakata** C Liberia 6.34N 10.19W
192 M11 **Kakatahi** Manawatu-Wanganui, North Island, NZ 39.40S 175.20E
115 M23 **Kakavi** Gjirokastër, S Albania 39.55N 20.19E
153 O14 **Kakaydi** Surkhondaryo Viloyati, S Uzbekistan 37.37N 67.30E
170 Ee13 **Kake** Hiroshima, Honshū, SW Japan 34.37N 132.17E
41 X13 **Kake** Kupreanof Island, Alaska, USA 56.58N 133.57W
175 R12 **Kakea** Pulau Wowoni, C Indonesia 4.09S 123.06E
171 Ii17 **Kakegawa** Shizuoka, Honshū, S Japan 34.58N 138.21E
172 Qq13 **Kakeromajima** Kagoshima, SW Japan
149 T6 **Kākhak** *var.* Kākhk. Khorāsān, E Iran
120 L11 **Kakhanavichy** *Rus.* Kokhanovichi. Vitsyebskaya Voblasts', N Belarus 55.57N 28.06E
41 P13 **Kakhonak** Alaska, USA 59.26N 154.48W
119 S10 **Kakhovka** Khersons'ka Oblast', S Ukraine 46.48N 33.30E
119 U9 **Kakhovs'ka Vodoskhovyshche** *Rus.* Kakhovskoye Vodokhranilishche. ⊠ SE Ukraine
Kakhovskoye Vodokhranilishche *see* Kakhovs'ka Vodoskhovyshche
119 T11 **Kakhovs'kyy Kanal** *canal* S Ukraine
Kakia *see* Khakhea
161 L16 **Kākināda** *prev.* Cocanada. Andhra Pradesh, E India 16.55N 82.13E
Kākisalmi *see* Priozersk
170 G14 **Kakogawa** Hyōgo, Honshū, SW Japan 34.49N 134.52E
83 F18 **Kakoge** C Uganda 1.03N 32.30E
151 O7 **Kak, Ozero** ◎ N Kazakhstan
Ka-Krem *see* Malyy Yenisey
Kakshaal-Too, Khrebet *see* Kokshaal-Tau
41 S5 **Kaktovik** Alaska, USA 70.07N 143.37W
171 Ll13 **Kakuda** Miyagi, Honshū, C Japan 37.59N 140.47E
171 M11 **Kakunodate** Akita, Honshū, C Japan 39.36N 140.38E
Kalaallit Nunaat *see* Greenland
155 T7 **Kālābāgh** Punjab, E Pakistan 32.58N 71.30E
175 Rr16 **Kalabahi** Pulau Alor, S Indonesia 8.13S 124.31E

◆ Country
● Country Capital
◇ Dependent Territory
○ Dependent Territory Capital
◈ Administrative Region
✈ International Airport
▲ Mountain
▲▲ Mountain Range
Volcano
~ River
◎ Lake
⊠ Reservoir

196 I5 **Kalabera** Saipan, S Northern Mariana Islands
85 G14 **Kalabo** Western, W Zambia 14.52S 22.33E
130 M9 **Kalach** Voronezhskaya Oblast', W Russian Federation 50.24N 41.00E
125 G13 **Kalachinsk** Omskaya Oblast', C Russian Federation 55.03N 74.30E
131 N10 **Kalach-na-Donu** Volgogradskaya Oblast', SW Russian Federation 48.45N 43.29E
177 F5 **Kaladan** ~ W Myanmar
12 K14 **Kaladar** Ontario, SE Canada 44.38N 77.06W
40 G13 **Ka Lae** *var.* South Cape, South Point. *headland* Hawaii, USA, C Pacific Ocean 18.54N 155.40W
85 G19 **Kalahari Desert** *desert* Southern Africa
40 B8 **Kalaheo** *Haw.* Kalāheo. Kauai, Hawaii, USA, C Pacific Ocean 21.55N 159.31W
Kalaikhum *see* Qal'aikhum
152 J16 **Kala-i-Mor** *Turkm.* Galaymor. Maryyskiy Velayat, S Turkmenistan 35.40N 62.28E
95 K15 **Kalajoki** Oulu, W Finland 64.15N 24.00E
Kalak *see* Eski Kaļak
Kal al Sraghna *see* El Kelâa Srarhna
34 G10 **Kalama** Washington, NW USA 46.00N 122.50W
Kalámai *see* Kalámata
117 G14 **Kalamariá** Kentrikí Makedonía, N Greece 40.36N 22.58E
117 E21 **Kalámata** *prev.* Kalámai. Pelopónnisos, S Greece 37.01N 22.07E
33 P10 **Kalamazoo** Michigan, N USA 42.17N 85.35W
33 P9 **Kalamazoo River** ~ Michigan, N USA
Kalambaka *see* Kalampáka
119 S13 **Kalamits'ka Zatoka** *Rus.* Kalamitskiy Zaliv. *gulf* S Ukraine
Kalamitskiy Zaliv *see* Kalamits'ka Zatoka
117 H18 **Kálamos** Attikí, C Greece 38.16N 23.51E
117 C18 **Kálamos** *island* Iónioi Nísoi, Greece, C Mediterranean Sea
117 D15 **Kalampáka** *var.* Kalambaka. Thessalía, C Greece 39.43N 21.36E
Kalan *see* Călan, Romania
Kalan *see* Tunceli, Turkey
119 S11 **Kalanchak** Khersons'ka Oblast', S Ukraine 46.14N 33.19E
175 Pp15 **Kalao, Pulau** *island* Kepulauan Bonerate, W Indonesia
175 Q15 **Kalaotoa, Pulau** *island* W Indonesia
161 J24 **Kala Oya** ~ NW Sri Lanka
Kalarash *see* Călărași
95 H17 **Kälarne** Jämtland, C Sweden 63.00N 16.10E
149 V15 **Kalar Rūd** ~ SE Iran
178 Ii9 **Kalasin** *var.* Muang Kalasin. Kalasin, E Thailand 16.28N 103.31E
155 O8 **Kalāt** *Per.* Qalāt. Zābul, S Afghanistan 32.10N 66.54E
155 O11 **Kālat** *var.* Kelat, Khelat. Baluchistān, SW Pakistan 29.02N 66.34E
117 J14 **Kalathriá, Akrotírio** *headland* Samothráki, NE Greece 40.24N 25.34E
200 R17 **Kalau** *island* Tongatapu Group, SE Tonga
40 E9 **Kalaupapa** Molokai, Hawaii, USA, C Pacific Ocean 21.11N 156.59W
131 N13 **Kalaus** ~ SW Russian Federation
Kalávrita *see* Kalávryta
117 E19 **Kalávryta** *var.* Kalávrita. Dytikí Ellás, S Greece 38.01N 22.06E
147 Y10 **Kalbān** W Oman 20.19N 58.40E
188 H11 **Kalbarri** Western Australia 27.43S 114.08E
151 X10 **Kalbinskiy Khrebet** *Kaz.* Qalba Zhotasy. ▲ E Kazakhstan
150 G10 **Kaldygayty** ~ W Kazakhstan
142 I12 **Kalecik** Ankara, N Turkey 40.08N 33.27E
175 R13 **Kaledupa, Pulau** *island* Kepulauan Tukangbesi, C Indonesia
81 O19 **Kalehe** Sud Kivu, E Dem. Rep. Congo 2.04S 28.52E
81 P22 **Kalemie** *prev.* Albertville. Katanga, SE Dem. Rep. Congo 5.55S 29.09E
177 Ff3 **Kalemyo** Sagaing, W Myanmar 23.11N 94.03E
84 H12 **Kalene Hill** North Western, NW Zambia 11.10S 24.12E
Kale Sultanie *see* Çanakkale
128 I7 **Kalevala** Respublika Kareliya, NW Russian Federation 65.12N 31.16E
177 Ff3 **Kalewa** Sagaing, C Myanmar 23.15N 94.19E
Kalgan *see* Zhangjiakou
41 Q12 **Kalgin Island** *island* Alaska, USA
188 L12 **Kalgoorlie** Western Australia 30.51S 121.27E
Kali *see* Sārda
117 E17 **Kaliakoúda** ▲ C Greece 38.47N 21.42E
116 O8 **Kaliakra, Nos** *headland* NE Bulgaria 43.22N 28.28E
117 F19 **Kaliánoi** Pelopónnisos, S Greece 37.55N 22.28E
179 Q13 **Kalibo** Panay Island, C Philippines 11.40N 122.21E
117 N24 **Kali Limni** ▲ Kárpathos, SE Greece 35.34N 27.08E
81 N20 **Kalima** Maniema, E Dem. Rep. Congo 2.33S 26.27E
174 M8 **Kalimantan** *Eng.* Indonesian Borneo. *geopolitical region* Borneo, C Indonesia
174 L8 **Kalimantan Barat** *off.* Propinsi Kalimantan Barat, *Eng.* West Borneo, West Kalimantan. ◆ *province* N Indonesia
174 Mm11 **Kalimantan Selatan** *off.* Propinsi Kalimantan Selatan, *Eng.* South Borneo, South Kalimantan. ◆ *province* N Indonesia
174 M9 **Kalimantan Tengah** *off.* Propinsi Kalimantan Tengah, *Eng.* Central Borneo, Central Kalimantan. ◆ *province* N Indonesia
175 N7 **Kalimantan Timur** *off.* Propinsi Kalimantan Timur, *Eng.* East Borneo, East Kalimantan. ◆ *province* N Indonesia
Kálimnos *see* Kálymnos
159 S12 **Kālimpang** West Bengal, NE India 27.05N 88.25E
Kalinin *see* Tver', Russian Federation
Kalinin *see* Boldumsaz, Turkmenistan
Kalininabad *see* Kalininobod
130 B3 **Kaliningrad** Kaliningradskaya Oblast', W Russian Federation 54.48N 21.33E
Kaliningrad *see* Kaliningradskaya Oblast'
130 A3 **Kaliningradskaya Oblast'** *var.* Kaliningrad. ◆ *province and enclave* W Russian Federation
Kalinino *see* Tashir
153 P14 **Kalininobod** *Rus.* Kalininabad. SW Tajikistan 37.49N 68.55E
131 O8 **Kalininsk** Saratovskaya Oblast', W Russian Federation 51.31N 44.25E
Kalininsk *see* Boldumsaz
Kalinisk *see* Cupcina
121 M19 **Kalinkavichy** *Rus.* Kalinkovichi. Homyel'skaya Voblasts', SE Belarus 52.07N 29.19E
Kalinkovichi *see* Kalinkavichy
83 G18 **Kaliro** SE Uganda 0.54N 33.30E
Kalisch/Kalish *see* Kalisz
35 O7 **Kalispell** Montana, NW USA 48.12N 114.18W
112 I13 **Kalisz** *Ger.* Kalisch, *Rus.* Kalish; *anc.* Calisia. Wielkopolskie, C Poland 51.46N 18.04E
112 F9 **Kalisz Pomorski** *Ger.* Kallies. Zachodniopomorskie, NW Poland 53.55N 15.55E
130 M10 **Kalitva** ~ SW Russian Federation
83 F21 **Kaliua** Tabora, C Tanzania 5.03S 31.48E
94 K13 **Kalix** Norrbotten, N Sweden 65.51N 23.13E
94 J11 **Kalixfors** Norrbotten, N Sweden 67.45N 20.20E
151 T8 **Kalkaman** Pavlodar, NE Kazakhstan 51.57N 75.58E
Kalkandelen *see* Tetovo
189 O4 **Kalkarindji** Northern Territory, N Australia 17.31S 130.40E
33 P6 **Kalkaska** Michigan, N USA 44.43N 85.12W
95 F16 **Kall** Jämtland, C Sweden 63.30N 13.15E
201 X2 **Kallalen** *var.* Calalen. *island* Ratak Chain, SE Marshall Islands
120 J5 **Kallaste** *Ger.* Krasnogor. Tartumaa, SE Estonia 58.37N 27.12E
95 N16 **Kallavesi** ⊚ SE Finland
117 F17 **Kallídromo** ▲ C Greece
Kallies *see* Kalisz Pomorski
97 M22 **Kallinge** Blekinge, S Sweden 56.13N 15.16E
117 L16 **Kalloní** Lésvos, E Greece 39.14N 26.15E
95 F16 **Kallsjön** ⊚ C Sweden
97 N21 **Kalmar** *var.* Calmar. Kalmar, S Sweden 56.40N 16.22E
97 M19 **Kalmar** *var.* Calmar. ◆ *county* S Sweden
97 N20 **Kalmarsund** *strait* S Sweden
154 L16 **Kalmat, Khor** *Eng.* Kalmat Lagoon. *lagoon* SW Pakistan
Kalmat Lagoon *see* Kalmat, Khor
119 X9 **Kal'mius** ~ E Ukraine
101 H15 **Kalmthout** Antwerpen, N Belgium 51.24N 4.27E
Kalmykia/Kalmykiya-Khal'mg Tangch, Respublika *see* Kalmykiya, Respublika
131 O12 **Kalmykiya, Respublika** *var.* Respublika Kalmykiya-Khal'mg Tangch, *Eng.* Kalmykia; *prev.* Kalmytskaya ASSR. ◆ *autonomous republic* SW Russian Federation
Kalmytskaya ASSR *see* Kalmykiya, Respublika
120 F9 **Kalnciems** Jelgava, C Latvia 56.46N 23.37E
116 L10 **Kalnitsa** ~ SE Bulgaria
113 J24 **Kalocsa** Bács-Kiskun, S Hungary 46.31N 19.00E
116 J9 **Kalofer** Plovdiv, C Bulgaria 42.36N 25.00E
40 E10 **Kalohi Channel** *channel* C Pacific Ocean
85 I16 **Kalomo** Southern, S Zambia 17.04S 26.27E
31 X14 **Kalona** Iowa, C USA 41.28N 91.42W
117 K22 **Kalotási, Akrotírio** *headland* Amorgós, Kykládes, Greece, Aegean Sea 36.47N 25.45E
158 J8 **Kalpa** Himāchal Pradesh, N India 31.33N 78.16E
117 C15 **Kalpáki** Ípeiros, W Greece 39.53N 20.38E
161 C22 **Kalpeni Island** *island* Lakshadweep, India, N Indian Ocean
158 K13 **Kālpi** Uttar Pradesh, N India 26.07N 79.43E
164 G7 **Kalpin** Xinjiang Uygur Zizhiqu, NW China 40.35N 78.52E
155 P16 **Kalri Lake** ⊚ SE Pakistan
149 R5 **Kāl Shūr** ~ N Iran
41 N11 **Kalskag** Alaska, USA 61.32N 160.15W
97 B18 **Kalsoy** *Dan.* Kalsø *Island* Faeroe Islands 62.20N 6.46W
41 O9 **Kaltag** Alaska, USA 64.19N 158.43W
110 H7 **Kaltbrunn** Sankt Gallen, NE Switzerland 47.11N 9.00E
Kaltdorf *see* Pruszków
79 X14 **Kaltungo** Gombe, E Nigeria 9.49N 11.22E
130 K4 **Kaluga** Kaluzhskaya Oblast', W Russian Federation 54.31N 36.16E
161 J26 **Kalu Ganga** ~ S Sri Lanka
84 J13 **Kalulushi** Copperbelt, C Zambia 12.52S 28.06E
188 M2 **Kalumburu** Western Australia 14.11S 126.40E
97 H23 **Kalundborg** Vestsjælland, E Denmark 55.42N 11.06E
84 K11 **Kalungwishi** ~ N Zambia
155 T8 **Kalūr Kot** Punjab, E Pakistan 32.07N 71.19E
118 I6 **Kalush** *Pol.* Kałusz. Ivano-Frankivs'ka Oblast', W Ukraine 49.01N 24.21E
Kałusz *see* Kalush
112 N11 **Kałuszyn** Mazowieckie, C Poland 52.12N 21.43E
161 J26 **Kalutara** Western Province, SW Sri Lanka 6.34N 79.58E
Kaluwawa *see* Fergusson Island
130 I5 **Kaluzhskaya Oblast'** ◆ *province* W Russian Federation
121 E14 **Kalvarija** *Pol.* Kalwaria. Marijampolė, S Lithuania 54.25N 23.13E
95 K15 **Kälviä** Länsi-Suomi, W Finland 63.50N 23.31E
111 U6 **Kalwang** Steiermark, E Austria 47.25N 14.48E
Kalwaria *see* Kalvarija
160 D13 **Kalyān** Mahārāshtra, W India 19.16N 73.10E
128 K16 **Kalyazin** Tverskaya Oblast', W Russian Federation 57.15N 37.53E
117 D18 **Kalydón** *anc.* Calydon. *site of ancient city* Dytikí Ellás, C Greece 38.24N 21.31E
117 M21 **Kálymnos** *var.* Kálimnos. Kálymnos, Dodekánisos, Greece, Aegean Sea 36.57N 26.58E
117 M21 **Kálymnos** *var.* Kálimnos. *island* Dodekánisos, Greece, Aegean Sea
119 O5 **Kalynivka** Kyyivs'ka Oblast', N Ukraine 50.14N 30.16E
119 N6 **Kalynivka** Vinnyts'ka Oblast', C Ukraine 49.27N 28.32E
44 M10 **Kama** *var.* Cama. Región Autónoma Atlántico Sur, SE Nicaragua 12.06N 83.55W
125 E9 **Kama** ~ NW Russian Federation
172 N12 **Kamaishi** *var.* Kamaisi. Iwate, Honshū, C Japan 39.17N 141.51E
Kamaisi *see* Kamaishi
120 H13 **Kamajai** Molėtai, E Lithuania 55.49N 25.30E
120 H11 **Kamajai** Rokiškis, NE Lithuania 55.16N 25.30E
171 Jj17 **Kamakura** Kanagawa, Honshū, S Japan 35.17N 139.31E
155 U9 **Kamālia** Punjab, NE Pakistan 30.43N 72.39E
85 I14 **Kamalondo** North Western, NW Zambia 13.42S 25.38E
142 I13 **Kaman** Kirşehir, C Turkey 39.22N 33.43E
81 O20 **Kamanyola** Sud Kivu, E Dem. Rep. Congo 2.54S 29.04E
147 N14 **Kamarān** *island* W Yemen
57 R9 **Kamarang** W Guyana 5.49N 60.38W
Kāmāreddi/Kamareddy *see* Rāmāreddi
Kama Reservoir *see* Kamskoye Vodokhranilishche
154 K13 **Kamarod** Baluchistān, SW Pakistan 27.34N 63.36E
175 R13 **Kamaru** Pulau Buton, C Indonesia 5.10S 123.03E
79 S13 **Kamba** Kebbi, NW Nigeria 11.50N 3.44E
Kambaeng Petch *see* Kamphaeng Phet
188 L12 **Kambalda** Western Australia 31.15S 121.33E
155 P13 **Kambar** *var.* Qambar. Sind, SE Pakistan 27.34N 68.03E
Kambara *see* Kabara
78 I14 **Kambia** W Sierra Leone 9.09N 12.52W
175 S16 **Kambing, Pulau** *island* W East Timor
Kambos *see* Kámpos
81 N25 **Kambove** Katanga, SE Dem. Rep. Congo 10.49S 26.39E
Kambryk *see* Cambrai
127 Pp10 **Kamchatka** ~ E Russian Federation
Kamchatka *see* Kamchatka, Poluostrov
Kamchatka Basin *see* Komandorskaya Basin
127 P11 **Kamchatka, Poluostrov** *Eng.* Kamchatka. *peninsula* E Russian Federation
127 Pp11 **Kamchatskaya Oblast'** ◆ *province* E Russian Federation
127 Pp10 **Kamchatskiy Zaliv** *gulf* E Russian Federation
116 N9 **Kamchiya** ~ E Bulgaria
116 L9 **Kamchiya, Yazovir** ⊠ E Bulgaria
Kamdesh *see* Kāmdeysh
155 T4 **Kāmdeysh** *var.* Kamdesh. Kunar, E Afghanistan 35.25N 71.25E
170 Ee14 **Kamega-mori** ▲ Shikoku, SW Japan 33.45N 133.12E
120 M13 **Kamen'** *Rus.* Kamen'. Vitsyebskaya Voblasts', N Belarus 55.01N 28.52E
Kamenets *see* Kamyanets
Kamenets-Podol'skaya Oblast' *see* Khmel'nyts'ka Oblast'
Kamenets-Podol'skiy *see* Kam"yanets'-Podil's'kyy
115 Q18 **Kamenica** NE FYR Macedonia 42.03N 22.34E
114 A11 **Kamenjak, Rt** *headland* NW Croatia
150 F8 **Kamenka** Zapadnyy Kazakhstan, NW Kazakhstan 51.06N 51.16E
129 O6 **Kamenka** Arkhangel'skaya Oblast', NW Russian Federation 65.55N 44.01E
130 O6 **Kamenka** Penzenskaya Oblast', W Russian Federation 53.12N 44.00E
131 L8 **Kamenka** Voronezhskaya Oblast', W Russian Federation 50.44N 39.31E
Kamenka *see* Camenca, Moldova
Kamenka *see* Kam"yanka, Ukraine
Kamenka-Bugskaya *see* Kam"yanka-Buz'ka
Kamenka Dneprovskaya *see* Kam"yanka-Dniprovs'ka
Kamen Kashirskiy *see* Kamin'-Kashyrs'kyy
126 Gg14 **Kamen'-na-Obi** Altayskiy Kray, S Russian Federation 53.42N 81.04E
130 L15 **Kamennomostskiy** Respublika Adygeya, SW Russian Federation 44.13N 40.12E
130 L11 **Kamenolomni** Rostovskaya Oblast', SW Russian Federation 47.36N 40.18E
131 P8 **Kamenskiy** Saratovskaya Oblast', W Russian Federation 50.56N 45.32E
127 P7 **Kamenskoye** Koryakskiy Avtonomnyy Okrug, E Russian Federation 62.29N 166.16E
Kamenskoye *see* Dniprodzerzhyns'k
130 L11 **Kamensk-Shakhtinskiy** Rostovskaya Oblast', SW Russian Federation 48.18N 40.16E
125 Ee11 **Kamensk-Ural'skiy** Sverdlovskaya Oblast', C Russian Federation 56.30N 61.45E
103 P15 **Kamenz** Sachsen, E Germany 51.15N 14.06E
171 Gg14 **Kameoka** Kyōto, Honshū, SW Japan 35.02N 135.35E
130 M3 **Kameshkovo** Vladimirskaya Oblast', W Russian Federation 56.21N 41.01E
171 H15 **Kameyama** Mie, Honshū, SW Japan 34.52N 136.25E
170 Cc10 **Kami-Agata** Nagasaki, Tsushima, SW Japan 34.40N 129.27E
35 N10 **Kamiah** Idaho, NW USA 46.13N 116.01W
Kamień Koszyrski *see* Kamin'-Kashyrs'kyy
112 H9 **Kamień Krajeński** *Ger.* Kamin in Westpreussen. Kujawsko-pomorskie, C Poland 53.31N 17.31E
113 F15 **Kamienna Góra** *Ger.* Landeshut, Landeshut in Schlesien. Dolnośląskie, SW Poland 50.48N 16.00E
112 D8 **Kamień Pomorski** *Ger.* Cummin in Pommern. Zachodniopomorskie, NW Poland 53.57N 14.44E
172 N7 **Kamiiso** Hokkaidō, NE Japan 41.50N 140.38E
81 L22 **Kamiji** Kasai Oriental, S Dem. Rep. Congo 6.35S 23.18E
172 Pp5 **Kamikawa** Hokkaidō, NE Japan 43.51N 142.47E
170 Bb15 **Kami-Koshiki-jima** *island* SW Japan
81 M23 **Kamina** Katanga, S Dem. Rep. Congo 8.42S 25.01E
Kamina *see* Kaintiba
44 C6 **Kaminaljuyú** *ruins* Guatemala, C Guatemala 14.34N 90.36W
Kamin in Westpreussen *see* Kamień Krajeński
118 J2 **Kamin'-Kashyrs'kyy** *Pol.* Kamień Koszyrski, *Rus.* Kamen Kashirskiy. Volyns'ka Oblast', NW Ukraine 51.39N 24.59E
172 N6 **Kaminokuni** Hokkaidō, NE Japan 41.48N 140.05E
171 Ll13 **Kaminoyama** Yamagata, Honshū, C Japan 38.09N 140.15E
171 Ii14 **Kamioka** Gifu, Honshū, SW Japan 36.20N 137.18E
41 Q13 **Kamishak Bay** *bay* Alaska, USA
172 Pp6 **Kami-Shihoro** Hokkaidō, NE Japan 43.14N 143.18E
Kamishli *see* Al Qāmishlī
Kamissar *see* Kamsar
170 Cc10 **Kami-Tsushima** Nagasaki, Tsushima, SW Japan 34.40N 129.27E
81 O20 **Kamituga** Sud Kivu, E Dem. Rep. Congo 3.07S 28.10E
170 B17 **Kamiyaku** Kagoshima, Yaku-shima, SW Japan 30.24N 130.32E
9 N16 **Kamloops** British Columbia, SW Canada 50.39N 120.24W
109 G25 **Kamma** Sicilia, Italy, C Mediterranean Sea 36.46N 12.03E
199 Ii4 **Kammu Seamount** *undersea feature* N Pacific Ocean 32.09N 173.00E
111 U11 **Kamnik** *Ger.* Stein. C Slovenia 46.13N 14.34E
Kamniške Alpe *see* Kamniško-Savinjske Alpe
111 T10 **Kamniško-Savinjske Alpe** *var.* Kamniške Alpe, Sanntaler Alpen, *Ger.* Steiner Alpen. ▲ N Slovenia
171 Kk13 **Kamo** Niigata, Honshū, C Japan 37.42N 139.03E
171 K17 **Kamogawa** Chiba, Honshū, S Japan 35.05N 140.04E
155 W8 **Kāmoke** Punjab, E Pakistan 31.58N 74.13E
84 L13 **Kamoto** Eastern, E Zambia 13.16S 32.04E
111 V3 **Kamp** ~ N Austria
83 F18 **Kampala** ● (Uganda) S Uganda 0.21N 32.28E
174 H8 **Kampar, Sungai** ~ Sumatera, W Indonesia
174 Ii10 **Kampa, Teluk** *bay* Pulau Bangka, W Indonesia
100 L9 **Kampen** Overijssel, E Netherlands 52.33N 5.55E
81 N20 **Kampene** Maniema, E Dem. Rep. Congo 3.34S 26.40E
31 Q9 **Kampeska, Lake** ⊚ South Dakota, N USA
178 Gg9 **Kamphaeng Phet** *var.* Kambaeng Petch. Kamphaeng Phet, W Thailand 16.28N 99.31E
Kampo *see* Campo, Cameroon
Kampo *see* Ntem, Cameroon/Equatorial Guinea
178 J13 **Kâmpóng Cham** *prev.* Kompong Cham. Kâmpóng Cham, C Cambodia 12.00N 105.27E
178 J13 **Kâmpóng Chhnăng** *prev.* Kompong. Kâmpóng Chhnăng, C Cambodia 12.15N 104.40E
178 Ii12 **Kâmpóng Khleăng** *prev.* Kompong Kleang. Siĕmréab, NW Cambodia 13.04N 104.07E
178 I14 **Kâmpóng Saôm** *prev.* Kompong Som, Sihanoukville. Kâmpóng Saôm, SW Cambodia 10.37N 103.30E
178 J13 **Kâmpóng Spoe** *prev.* Kompong Speu. Kâmpóng Spœ, S Cambodia 11.28N 104.29E
124 N3 **Kámpos** *var.* Kambos. NW Cyprus 35.03N 32.44E
178 Ii14 **Kâmpôt** Kâmpôt, SW Cambodia 10.37N 104.10E
Kamptee *see* Kāmthi
79 O14 **Kampti** SW Burkina 10.07N 3.22W
Kampuchea *see* Cambodia
174 Ll5 **Kampung Sirik** Sarawak, East Malaysia 2.42N 111.28E
176 Y13 **Kampung, Sungai** ~ Papua, E Indonesia
176 Vv12 **Kamrau, Teluk** *bay* Papua, E Indonesia
9 V15 **Kamsack** Saskatchewan, S Canada 51.34N 101.51W
78 H13 **Kamsar** *var.* Kamissar. Guinée-Maritime, W Guinea 10.36N 14.34W
131 R4 **Kamskoye Ust'ye** Respublika Tatarstan, W Russian Federation 55.13N 49.11E
129 U14 **Kamskoye Vodokhranilishche** *var.* Kama Reservoir. ⊠ NW Russian Federation
160 I12 **Kāmthi** *prev.* Kamptee. Mahārāshtra, C India 21.19N 79.11E
Kamuela *see* Waimea
172 Nn5 **Kamuenai** Hokkaidō, NE Japan 43.07N 140.25E
172 P7 **Kamui-dake** ▲ Hokkaidō, NE Japan 42.24N 142.57E
172 Nn4 **Kamui-misaki** *headland* Hokkaidō, NE Japan 43.20N 140.20E
45 O15 **Kámuk, Cerro** ▲ SE Costa Rica 9.15N 83.01W
176 Vv9 **Kamundan, Sungai** ~ Papua, E Indonesia
176 X12 **Kamura, Sungai** ~ Papua, E Indonesia
118 K7 **Kam"yanets'-Podil's'kyy** *Rus.* Kamenets-Podol'skiy. Khmel'nyts'ka Oblast', W Ukraine 48.42N 26.36E
119 Q6 **Kam"yanka** *Rus.* Kamenka. Cherkas'ka Oblast', C Ukraine 49.03N 32.06E
118 I5 **Kam"yanka-Buz'ka** *Rus.* Kamenka-Bugskaya. L'vivs'ka Oblast', NW Ukraine 50.03N 24.20E
119 T9 **Kam"yanka-Dniprovs'ka** *Rus.* Kamenka Dneprovskaya. Zaporiz'ka Oblast', SE Ukraine 47.28N 34.24E
121 F19 **Kamyanyets** *Rus.* Kamenets. Brestskaya Voblasts', SW Belarus 52.24N 23.50E
131 P9 **Kamyshin** Volgogradskaya Oblast', SW Russian Federation 50.06N 45.20E
125 Ee11 **Kamyshlov** Sverdlovskaya Oblast', C Russian Federation 56.55N 62.37E
131 Q13 **Kamyzyak** Astrakhanskaya Oblast', SW Russian Federation 46.07N 48.03E
10 K8 **Kanaaupscow** ~ Quebec, C Canada
38 K8 **Kanab** Utah, W USA 37.03N 112.31W
38 K9 **Kanab Creek** ~ Arizona/Utah, SW USA
197 J13 **Kanacea** *prev.* Kanathea. Taveuni, N Fiji 16.59S 179.54E
197 K14 **Kanacea** *island* Lau Group, E Fiji
40 G17 **Kanaga Island** *island* Aleutian Islands, Alaska, USA
40 G17 **Kanaga Volcano** ▲ Kanaga Island, Alaska, USA 51.55N 177.09W
171 J17 **Kanagawa** *off.* Kanagawa-ken. ◆ *prefecture* Honshū, S Japan
11 Q8 **Kanairiktok** ~ Newfoundland and Labrador, E Canada
Kanaky *see* New Caledonia
81 K22 **Kananga** *prev.* Luluabourg. Kasai Occidental, S Dem. Rep. Congo 5.51S 22.22E
Kananur *see* Cannanore
Kanara *see* Karnātaka
38 J7 **Kanarraville** Utah, W USA 37.32N 113.10W
131 Q4 **Kanash** Chuvashskaya Respublika, W Russian Federation 55.30N 47.27E
Kanathea *see* Kanacea
23 Q4 **Kanawha River** ~ West Virginia, NE USA
171 I15 **Kanayama** Gifu, Honshū, SW Japan 35.46N 137.15E
171 I12 **Kanazawa** Ishikawa, Honshū, SW Japan 36.34N 136.40E
177 G4 **Kanbalu** Sagaing, C Myanmar 23.10N 95.31E
177 Ff8 **Kanbe** Yangon, SW Myanmar 16.40N 96.01E
178 H11 **Kanchanaburi** Kanchanaburi, W Thailand 14.01N 99.31E
Känchenjunga *see* Kangchenjunga
151 V11 **Kanchingiz, Khrebet** ▲ E Kazakhstan
161 J19 **Kānchipuram** *prev.* Conjeeveram. Tamil Nādu, SE India 12.49N 79.43E
155 N8 **Kandahār** *Per.* Qandahār. Kandahār, S Afghanistan 31.36N 65.48E
155 N9 **Kandahār** *Per.* Qandahār. ◆ *province* SE Afghanistan
Kandalakša *see* Kandalaksha
128 I5 **Kandalaksha** *var.* Kandalakša, *Fin.* Kantalahti. Murmanskaya Oblast', NW Russian Federation 67.09N 32.13E
Kandalaksha Gulf / Kandalakshskaya Guba *see* Kandalakshskiy Zaliv
128 K6 **Kandalakshskiy Zaliv** *var.* Kandalakshskaya Guba, *Eng.* Kandalaksha Gulf. *bay* NW Russian Federation
Kandalangodi *see* Kandalengoti
85 G17 **Kandalengoti** *var.* Kandalangodi. Ngamiland, NW Botswana 19.25S 22.12E
175 N10 **Kandangan** Borneo, C Indonesia 2.49S 115.15E
Kandau *see* Kandava
120 E8 **Kandava** *Ger.* Kandau. Tukums, W Latvia 57.02N 22.48E
Kandavu *see* Kadavu
79 R14 **Kandé** *var.* Kanté. NE Togo 9.55N 1.01E
103 F23 **Kandel** ▲ SW Germany 48.03N 8.00E
194 G12 **Kandep** Enga, W PNG 5.50S 143.26E
155 R12 **Kandh Kot** Sind, SE Pakistan 28.15N 69.18E
79 S13 **Kandi** N Benin 11.04N 2.58E
155 P14 **Kandiāro** Sind, SE Pakistan 27.01N 68.16E
142 F11 **Kandıra** Kocaeli, NW Turkey 41.04N 30.07E
191 S8 **Kandos** New South Wales, SE Australia 32.52S 149.58E
154 M16 **Kandrāch** *var.* Kanrach. Baluchistān, SW Pakistan 25.26N 65.28E
180 I4 **Kandreho** Mahajanga, C Madagascar 17.27S 46.06E
194 M12 **Kandrian** New Britain, E PNG 6.10S 149.33E
Kandukur *see* Kondukür
161 K25 **Kandy** Central Province, C Sri Lanka 7.16N 80.40E
150 I10 **Kandyagash** *Kaz.* Qandyaghash; *prev.* Oktyabr'sk. Aktyubinsk, W Kazakhstan 49.25N 57.24E
20 D12 **Kane** Pennsylvania, NE USA 41.39N 78.47W
66 I11 **Kane Fracture Zone** *tectonic feature* NW Atlantic Ocean
Kaněka *see* Kanëvka
80 G9 **Kanem** *off.* Préfecture du Kanem. ◆ *prefecture* W Chad
40 D9 **Kaneohe** *Haw.* Kāne'ohe. Oahu, Hawaii, USA, C Pacific Ocean 21.25N 157.48W
Kanestron, Akrotírio *see* Palioúri, Akrotírio
Kanëv *see* Kaniv
128 M5 **Kanëvka** *var.* Kanëka. Murmanskaya Oblast', NW Russian Federation 67.07N 39.43E
130 K13 **Kanevskaya** Krasnodarskiy Kray, SW Russian Federation 46.07N 38.57E
Kanevskoye Vodokhranilishche *see* Kanivs'ke Vodoskhovyshche
171 Ll12 **Kaneyama** Yamagata, Honshū, C Japan 38.54N 140.20E
85 G20 **Kang** Kgalagadi, C Botswana 23.40S 22.49E
78 L13 **Kangaba** Koulikoro, SW Mali 11.57N 8.24W
142 M13 **Kangal** Sivas, C Turkey 39.15N 37.22E
149 O13 **Kangān** Būshehr, S Iran 25.50N 57.30E
149 S15 **Kangān** Hormozgān, SE Iran 27.49N 52.04E
173 G2 **Kangar** Perlis, Peninsular Malaysia 6.28N 100.10E
78 L13 **Kangaré** Sikasso, S Mali 11.39N 8.10W
190 F10 **Kangaroo Island** *island* South Australia
95 M17 **Kangasniemi** Itä-Suomi, E Finland 61.58N 26.36E
148 K6 **Kangāvar** *var.* Kangāwar. Kermānshāh, W Iran 34.30N 47.53E
Kangāwar *see* Kangāvar
159 S11 **Kangchenjunga** *var.* Kānchenjunga. ▲ NE India 27.36N 88.06E
166 G9 **Kangding** Sichuan, C China 30.03N 101.56E
175 Nn14 **Kangean, Kepulauan** *island group* S Indonesia
175 N14 **Kangean, Pulau** *island* Kepulauan Kangean, S Indonesia
69 U8 **Kangen** *var.* Kengen. ~ SE Sudan
207 N14 **Kangerlussuaq** *Dan.* Sondre Strømfjord. ✕ Kitaa, W Greenland 66.59N 50.28W
207 Q15 **Kangertittivaq** *Dan.* Scoresby Sund. *fjord* E Greenland
178 H2 **Kangfang** Kachin State, N Myanmar 26.09N 98.36E
176 Z13 **Kanggup** Papua, E Indonesia 5.56S 140.49E
169 X12 **Kanggye** N North Korea 40.57N 126.37E
207 P15 **Kangikajik** *var.* Kap Brewster. *headland* E Greenland 70.10N 22.00W
11 N5 **Kangiqsualujjuaq** *prev.* George River, Port-Nouveau-Québec. Quebec, E Canada 58.34N 65.58W
10 L2 **Kangiqsujuaq** *prev.* Maricourt, Wakeham Bay. Quebec, NE Canada 61.35N 72.00W
10 M4 **Kangirsuk** *prev.* Bellin, Payne. Quebec, E Canada 60.00N 70.01W
164 J15 **Kangmar** Xizang Zizhiqu, W China 30.45N 85.43E
164 M16 **Kangmar** Xizang Zizhiqu, W China 28.34N 89.40E
169 Y14 **Kangnŭng** *Jap.* Kōryō. NE South Korea 37.47N 128.51E
81 D18 **Kango** Estuaire, NW Gabon 0.17N 10.00E
158 I7 **Kāngra** Himāchal Pradesh, NW India 32.04N 76.16E
159 Q16 **Kangsabati Reservoir** ⊠ N India
165 O17 **Kangto** ▲ China/India 27.54N 92.33E
165 W12 **Kangxian** *var.* Kang Xian, Zuitaizi. Gansu, C China 33.21N 105.40E
177 Ff4 **Kani** Sagaing, C Myanmar 22.24N 94.55E
78 M15 **Kani** NW Ivory Coast 8.24N 6.38W
81 M23 **Kaniama** Katanga, S Dem. Rep. Congo 7.31S 24.10E
Kanibadam *see* Konibodom
175 O2 **Kanibongan** Sabah, East Malaysia 6.40N 117.12E
193 F17 **Kaniere** West Coast, South Island, NZ 42.45S 171.00E
193 G17 **Kaniere, Lake** ⊚ South Island, NZ
196 E17 **Kanifaay** Yap, W Micronesia
129 O4 **Kanin Kamen'** ▲ NW Russian Federation
129 N3 **Kanin Nos** Nenetskiy Avtonomnyy Okrug, NW Russian Federation 68.38N 43.19E
129 N3 **Kanin Nos, Mys** *headland* NW Russian Federation 68.39N 43.14E
129 O5 **Kanin, Poluostrov** *peninsula* NW Russian Federation
145 V8 **Kāni Sakht** E Iraq 33.19N 46.04E
145 T3 **Kāni Sulaymān** N Iraq 35.54N 44.35E
172 N8 **Kanita** Aomori, Honshū, C Japan 41.04N 140.36E
119 Q5 **Kaniv** *Rus.* Kanëv. Cherkas'ka Oblast', C Ukraine 49.46N 31.28E
190 K11 **Kaniva** Victoria, SE Australia 36.25S 141.13E
119 Q5 **Kanivs'ke Vodoskhovyshche** *Rus.* Kanevskoye Vodokhranilishche. ⊠ C Ukraine
114 L8 **Kanjiža** *Ger.* Altkanischa, *Hung.* Magyarkanizsa, Ókanizsa; *prev.* Stara Kanjiža. Serbia, N Serbia and Montenegro (Yugoslavia) 46.03N 20.03E
95 K18 **Kankaanpää** Länsi-Suomi, W Finland 61.46N 22.25E
32 M12 **Kankakee** Illinois, N USA 41.07N 87.51W
33 O11 **Kankakee River** ~ Illinois/Indiana, N USA
78 K14 **Kankan** Haute-Guinée, E Guinea 10.25N 9.19W
160 K13 **Kānker** Madhya Pradesh, C India 20.19N 81.29E
78 J10 **Kankossa** Assaba, S Mauritania 15.54N 11.31W
178 Gg13 **Kanmaw Kyun** *var.* Kisseraing, Kithareng. *island* Mergui Archipelago, S Myanmar
170 E13 **Kanmuri-yama** ▲ Kyūshū, SW Japan 34.28N 132.03E
23 R10 **Kannapolis** North Carolina, SE USA 35.29N 80.37W
95 L16 **Kannonkoski** Länsi-Suomi, W Finland 62.58N 25.19E
Kannur *see* Cannanore
95 K15 **Kannus** Länsi-Suomi, W Finland 63.51N 23.55E
79 V13 **Kano** Kano, N Nigeria 11.56N 8.30E
79 V13 **Kano** ◆ *state* N Nigeria
79 V13 **Kano** ✕ Kano, N Nigeria 11.56N 8.26E
170 F14 **Kan'onji** *var.* Kanonzi. Kagawa, Shikoku, SW Japan 34.10N 133.38E
Kanonzi *see* Kan'onji
28 M5 **Kanopolis Lake** ⊠ Kansas, C USA
38 K5 **Kanosh** Utah, W USA 38.48N 112.26W
174 Ll6 **Kanowit** Sarawak, East Malaysia 2.03N 112.15E
170 Bb17 **Kanoya** Kagoshima, Kyūshū, SW Japan 31.21N 130.49E
158 L13 **Kānpur** *Eng.* Cawnpore. Uttar Pradesh, N India 26.28N 80.21E
Kanrach *see* Kandrāch
171 Gg15 **Kansai** ✕ (Ōsaka) Ōsaka, Honshū, SW Japan 34.25N 135.13E
29 R9 **Kansas** Oklahoma, C USA 36.14N 94.46W
28 L5 **Kansas** *off.* State of Kansas; *also known as* Jayhawker State, Sunflower State. ◆ *state* C USA
29 R4 **Kansas City** Kansas, C USA 39.06N 94.37W
29 R4 **Kansas City** Missouri, C USA 39.06N 94.34W
29 R3 **Kansas City** ✕ Missouri, C USA 39.18N 94.45W
29 P4 **Kansas River** ~ Kansas, C USA
126 I14 **Kansk** Krasnoyarskiy Kray, S Russian Federation 56.11N 95.32E
Kansu *see* Gansu
153 V7 **Kant** Chuyskaya Oblast', N Kyrgyzstan 42.54N 74.47E
Kantalahti *see* Kandalaksha
178 Gg16 **Kantang** *var.* Ban Kantang. Trang, SW Thailand 7.25N 99.30E
117 H25 **Kántanos** Kríti, Greece, E Mediterranean Sea 35.20N 23.42E
79 R12 **Kantchari** E Burkina 12.28N 1.31E
Kanté *see* Kandé
Kantemir *see* Cantemir
130 L9 **Kantemirovka** Voronezhskaya Oblast', W Russian Federation 49.43N 39.53E
178 J11 **Kantharalak** Si Sa Ket, E Thailand 14.32N 104.37E
Kantipur *see* Kathmandu
41 Q9 **Kantishna River** ~ Alaska, USA
171 K16 **Kantō** *physical region* Honshū, SW Japan
203 S3 **Kanton** *var.* Abariringa, Canton Island; *prev.* Mary Island. *atoll* Phoenix Islands, C Kiribati
171 Jj15 **Kantō-sanchi** ▲ Honshū, S Japan
99 C20 **Kanturk** *Ir.* Ceann Toirc. SW Ireland 52.12N 8.54W
57 T11 **Kanuku Mountains** ▲ S Guyana
171 Kk15 **Kanuma** Tochigi, Honshū, S Japan 36.36N 139.46E
85 H20 **Kanye** Southern, SE Botswana 24.55S 25.14E
85 H17 **Kanyu** Ngamiland, C Botswana 20.07S 24.36E
177 G7 **Kanyutkwin** Pegu, C Myanmar 18.19N 96.30E
81 M24 **Kanzenze** Katanga, SE Dem. Rep. Congo 10.33S 25.28E
200 Ss13 **Kao** *island* Kotu Group, W Tonga
167 S14 **Kaohsiung** *var.* Gaoxiong, *Jap.* Takao, Takow. S Taiwan 22.36N 120.16E
167 S14 **Kaohsiung** ✕ S Taiwan 22.26N 120.32E
Kaokoana *see* Kirakira
85 B17 **Kaoko Veld** ▲ N Namibia
78 G11 **Kaolack** *var.* Kaolak. W Senegal 14.09N 16.07W
Kaolak *see* Kaolack
Kaolan *see* Lanzhou
195 W15 **Kaolo** San Jorge, N Solomon Islands 8.24S 159.35E
85 H14 **Kaoma** Western, W Zambia 14.43S 24.46E
40 B8 **Kapaa** *Haw.* Kapa'a. Kauai, Hawaii, USA, C Pacific Ocean 22.04N 159.19W
115 J16 **Kapa Moračka** ▲ SW Serbia and Montenegro (Yugoslavia) 42.53N 19.01E
143 V13 **Kapan** *Rus.* Kafan; *prev.* Ghap'an. SE Armenia 39.13N 46.25E
84 L13 **Kapandashila** Northern, NE Zambia 12.43S 31.00E

◆ Country ● Country Capital ◇ Dependent Territory ○ Dependent Territory Capital ◆ Administrative Region ✕ International Airport ▲ Mountain ▲ Mountain Range ▲ Volcano ~ River ⊚ Lake ⊠ Reservoir

81 L23 **Kapanga** Katanga, S Dem. Rep. Congo *8.22S 22.37E*

151 U15 **Kapchagay** *Kaz.* Kapshaghay. Almaty, SE Kazakhstan *43.52N 77.05E*

151 V15 **Kapchagayskoye Vodokhranilishche** *Kaz.* Qapshagay Böyeni. ▣ SE Kazakhstan

101 F15 **Kapelle** Zeeland, SW Netherlands *51.28N 3.58E*

101 G16 **Kapellen** Antwerpen, N Belgium *51.19N 4.25E*

97 P15 **Kapellskär** Stockholm, C Sweden *59.43N 19.03E*

83 H18 **Kapenguria** Rift Valley, W Kenya *1.13N 35.07E*

111 V6 **Kapfenberg** Steiermark, C Austria *47.27N 15.15E*

85 J14 **Kapiri Mposhi** Central, C Zambia *13.54S 28.40E*

155 R4 **Kāpīsā** ◆ *province* E Afghanistan

10 G10 **Kapiskau** ≈ Ontario, C Canada

192 K13 **Kapiti Island** *island* C NZ

80 K9 **Kapka, Massif du** ▲▲ E Chad

Kaplamada *see* Kaubalatmada, Gunung

24 H9 **Kaplan** Louisiana, S USA *30.00N 92.16W*

152 E9 **Kaplangky, Plato** *ridge* Turkmenistan/Uzbekistan

113 D19 **Kaplice** *Ger.* Kaplitz. Budějovický Kraj , S Czech Republic *48.42N 14.27E*

Kaplitz *see* Kaplice

Kapoche *see* Capoche

176 U10 **Kapocol** Papua, E Indonesia *1.59S 130.11E*

178 Gg14 **Kapoe** Ranong, SW Thailand *9.33N 98.37E*

Kapoeas *see* Kapuas, Sungai

83 G15 **Kapoeta** Eastern Equatoria, SE Sudan *4.49N 33.34E*

113 I25 **Kapos** ≈ S Hungary

113 H25 **Kaposvár** Somogy, SW Hungary *46.22N 17.54E*

96 H13 **Kapp** Oppland, S Norway *60.42N 10.49E*

102 I7 **Kappeln** Schleswig-Holstein, N Germany *54.40N 9.56E*

Kaproncza *see* Koprivnica

111 P7 **Kaprun** Salzburg, C Austria *47.15N 12.48E*

Kapshaghay *see* Kapchagay

Kapstad *see* Cape Town

Kapsukas *see* Marijampolė

176 Yy10 **Kaptiau** Papua, E Indonesia *2.23S 139.51E*

121 L19 **Kaptsevichy** *Rus.* Koptsevichi. Homyel'skaya Voblasts', SE Belarus *52.13N 28.19E*

Kapuas Hulu, Banjaran/ Kapuas Hulu, Pegunungan *see* Kapuas Mountains

174 M7 **Kapuas Mountains** *Ind.* Banjaran Kapuas Hulu, Pegunungan Kapuas Hulu. ▲▲ Indonesia/Malaysia

174 Kk8 **Kapuas, Sungai** ≈ Borneo, N Indonesia

175 N10 **Kapuas, Sungai** *prev.* Kapoeas. ≈ Borneo, C Indonesia

190 J9 **Kapunda** South Australia *34.23S 138.51E*

158 H8 **Kapūrthala** Punjab, N India *31.22N 75.15E*

174 L14 **Kapur Utara, Pegugungan** ▲▲ Jawa, S Indonesia

10 G12 **Kapuskasing** Ontario, S Canada *49.25N 82.25W*

12 D6 **Kapuskasing** ≈ Ontario, S Canada

131 P11 **Kapustin Yar** Astrakhanskaya Oblast', SW Russian Federation *48.36N 45.49E*

84 K11 **Kaputa** Northern, NE Zambia *8.27S 29.35E*

113 G22 **Kapuvár** Győr-Moson-Sopron, NW Hungary *47.35N 17.01E*

Kapydzhik, Gora *see* Qapiciğ Dağı

121 J17 **Kapyl'** *Rus.* Kopyl'. Minskaya Voblasts', C Belarus *53.09N 27.04E*

45 N9 **Kara** *var.* Cara. Región Autónoma Atlántico Sur, E Nicaragua *12.52N 83.35W*

79 R14 **Kara** *var.* Lama-Kara. NE Togo *9.36N 1.12E*

79 Q14 **Kara** ≈ N Togo

153 U7 **Kara-Balta** Chuyskaya Oblast', N Kyrgyzstan *42.50N 73.51E*

150 L7 **Karabalyk** *Kaz.* Komsomol, *prev.* Komsomolets. Kostanay, N Kazakhstan *53.48N 61.58E*

150 G11 **Karabau** Atyrau, W Kazakhstan *48.29N 53.05E*

152 E7 **Karabaur', Uval** *Kaz.* Korabavur Pastligi, *Uzb.* Qorabowur Kirlari. *physical region* Kazakhstan/Uzbekistan

152 L13 **Karabekaul** *var.* Garabekevyul, *Turkm.* Garabekewül. Lebapskiy Velayat, E Turkmenistan *38.31N 64.04E*

152 K15 **Karabil', Vozvyshennost'** ▲▲ S Turkmenistan

152 A9 **Kara-Bogaz-Gol** *Turkm.* Garabogazköl. Balkanskiy Velayat, NW Turkmenistan *41.03N 52.52E*

152 B9 **Kara-Bogaz-Gol, Zaliv** *bay* NW Turkmenistan

151 R15 **Karaboget** *Kaz.* Qaraböget. Zhambyl, S Kazakhstan *44.36N 72.03E*

142 H11 **Karabük** Karabük, NW Turkey *41.12N 32.36E*

142 H11 **Karabük** ◆ *province* NW Turkey

126 Ii13 **Karabula** Krasnoyarskiy Kray, C Russian Federation *58.01N 97.17E*

151 V14 **Karabulak** *Kaz.* Qarabulaq. Almaty, SE Kazakhstan *44.54N 78.29E*

151 Y11 **Karabulak** *Kaz.* Qarabulaq. Vostochnyy Kazakhstan, E Kazakhstan *47.33N 84.38E*

151 Q17 **Karabulak** *Kaz.* Qarabulaq. Yuzhnyy Kazakhstan, S Kazakhstan *42.31N 69.46E*

142 C17 **Kara Burnu** *headland* SW Turkey *36.34N 28.00E*

150 K10 **Karabutak** *Kaz.* Qarabutaq. Aktyubinsk, W Kazakhstan *49.58N 60.06E*

142 D12 **Karacabey** Bursa, NW Turkey *40.13N 28.22E*

116 O12 **Karacaköy** İstanbul, NW Turkey *41.24N 28.21E*

116 M12 **Karacaoğlan** Kırklareli, NW Turkey *41.30N 27.06E*

Karachay-Cherkessia *see* Karachayevo-Cherkesskaya Respublika

130 L15 **Karachayevo-Cherkesskaya Respublika** *Eng.* Karachay-Cherkessia. ◆ *autonomous republic* SW Russian Federation

130 M15 **Karachayevsk** Karachayevo-Cherkesskaya Respublika, SW Russian Federation *43.43N 41.53E*

130 J6 **Karachev** Bryanskaya Oblast', W Russian Federation *53.07N 35.56E*

155 O16 **Karāchi** Sind, SE Pakistan *24.51N 67.01E*

155 O16 **Karāchi** ✈ Sind, S Pakistan *24.51N 67.01E*

Karácsonkő *see* Piatra-Neamț

161 E15 **Karād** Mahārāshtra, W India *17.19N 74.15E*

142 H16 **Karadağ** ▲ S Turkey *37.00N 33.00E*

153 T10 **Karadar'ya** *Uzb.* Qoradaryo. ≈ Kyrgyzstan/Uzbekistan

Karadeniz *see* Black Sea

Karadeniz Boğazı *see* İstanbul Boğazı

152 B13 **Karadepe** Balkanskiy Velayat, W Turkmenistan *38.04N 54.01E*

Karadzhar *see* Qorajar

Karaferiye *see* Véroia

152 E13 **Karagan** *Turkm.* Garagan. Akhalskiy Velayat, C Turkmenistan *38.16N 57.34E*

151 R10 **Karaganda** *Kaz.* Qaraghandy. Karaganda, C Kazakhstan *49.52N 73.07E*

151 R10 **Karaganda** *off.* Karagandinskaya Oblast', *Kaz.* Qaraghandy Oblysy. ◆ *province* C Kazakhstan

Karagandinskaya Oblast' *see* Karaganda

151 T10 **Karagayly** *Kaz.* Qaraghayly. Karaganda, C Kazakhstan *49.25N 75.31E*

152 A11 **Karagel'** *Turkm.* Garagöl. Balkanskiy Velayat, W Turkmenistan *39.24N 53.13E*

127 Pp8 **Karaginskiy, Ostrov** *island* E Russian Federation

207 T1 **Karaginskiy Zaliv** *bay* E Russian Federation

143 P13 **Karagöl Dağları** ▲▲ NE Turkey

116 L13 **Karahisar** Edirne, NW Turkey *40.47N 26.34E*

131 V3 **Karaidel'** Respublika Bashkortostan, W Russian Federation *55.50N 56.55E*

131 V3 **Karaidel'skiy** Respublika Bashkortostan, W Russian Federation *55.51N 57.09E*

116 L13 **Karaidemir Barajı** ▣ NW Turkey

161 J21 **Kāraikāl** Pondicherry, SE India *10.58N 79.49E*

161 I22 **Kāraikkudi** Tamil Nādu, SE India *10.04N 78.46E*

151 Y11 **Kara Irtysh** *Rus.* Chërnyy Irtysh. ≈ NE Kazakhstan

149 N5 **Karaj** Tehrān, N Iran *35.43N 51.25E*

174 H5 **Karak** Pahang, Peninsular Malaysia *3.24N 101.58E*

Karak *see* Al Karak

153 T11 **Kara-Kabak** Oshskaya Oblast', SW Kyrgyzstan *39.40N 72.45E*

152 D12 **Kara-Kala** *var.* Garrygala. Balkanskiy Velayat, W Turkmenistan *38.27N 56.15E*

Karakala *see* Oqqal'a

Karakalpakstan, Respublika *see* Qoraqalpog'iston Respublikasi

Karakalpakya *see* Qoraqalpog'iston

Karakax *see* Moyu

164 G10 **Karakax He** ≈ NW China

124 S9 **Karakaya Barajı** ▣ C Turkey

175 Ss4 **Karakelang, Pulau** *island* N Indonesia

Karakılısse *see* Ağrı

Karak, Muḩāfaẓat al *see* Al Karak

Kara-Köl *see* Kara-Kul'

153 Y7 **Karakol** *prev.* Przheval'sk. Issyk-Kul'skaya Oblast', NE Kyrgyzstan *42.31N 78.20E*

153 X8 **Karakol** *var.* Karakolka. Issyk-Kul'skaya Oblast', NE Kyrgyzstan *41.30N 77.18E*

Karakolka *see* Karakol

155 W2 **Karakoram Highway** *road* China/Pakistan

155 Z3 **Karakoram Pass** *Chin.* Karakoram Shankou. *pass* C Asia *35.23N 77.45E*

158 I3 **Karakoram Range** ▲▲ C Asia

Karakoram Shankou *see* Karakoram Pass

Karaköse *see* Ağrı

151 P14 **Karakoyyn, Ozero** *Kaz.* Qaraqoyyn. ◎ C Kazakhstan

85 F19 **Karakubis** Ghanzi, W Botswana *22.03S 20.36E*

153 T9 **Kara-Kul'** *Kir.* Kara-Köl. Dzhalal-Abadskaya Oblast', W Kyrgyzstan *40.35N 73.36E*

Karakul' *see* Qorako'l, Uzbekistan

Karakul' *see* Qarokŭl, Tajikistan

153 U10 **Kara-Kul'dzha** Oshskaya Oblast', SW Kyrgyzstan *40.32N 73.50E*

131 T3 **Karakulino** Udmurtskaya Respublika, NW Russian Federation *56.02N 53.45E*

Karakul', Ozero *see* Qarokŭl

Kara Kum *see* Garagumy

Kara Kum Canal/Karakumskiy Kanal *see* Garagumskiy Kanal

Karakumy, Peski *see* Garagumy

85 E17 **Karakuwisa** Okavango, NE Namibia *18.55S 19.40E*

126 Jj14 **Karam** Irkutskaya Oblast', S Russian Federation *55.07N 107.21E*

Karamai *see* Karamay

175 N13 **Karamain, Pulau** *island* N Indonesia

142 I16 **Karaman** Karaman, S Turkey *37.10N 33.13E*

142 H16 **Karaman** ◆ *province* S Turkey

116 M8 **Karamandere** ≈ NE Bulgaria

164 J4 **Karamay** *var.* Karamai, Kelamayi, *prev. Chin.* K'o-la-ma-i. Xinjiang Uygur Zizhiqu, NW China *45.33N 84.45E*

175 Nn11 **Karambu** Borneo, N Indonesia *3.48S 116.06E*

193 H14 **Karamea** West Coast, South Island, NZ *41.15S 172.07E*

193 H14 **Karamea** ≈ South Island, NZ

193 G15 **Karamea Bight** *gulf* South Island, NZ

152 L14 **Karamet-Niyaz** *Turkm.* Garamäbnyyaz. Lebapskiy Velayat, E Turkmenistan *37.45N 64.28E*

164 K10 **Karamiran He** ≈ NW China

176 Yy11 **Karamor, Pengunungan** ▲▲ Papua, E Indonesia

153 S11 **Karamyk** Oshskaya Oblast', SW Kyrgyzstan *39.28N 71.45E*

175 Nn16 **Karangasem** Bali, S Indonesia *8.24S 115.40E*

160 H12 **Kāranja** Mahārāshtra, C India *20.30N 77.26E*

Karanpur *see* Karanpura

158 F9 **Karanpura** *var.* Karanpur. Rājasthān, NW India *29.46N 73.30E*

Karánsebes/Karansebesch *see* Caransebeș

151 T14 **Karaoy** *Kaz.* Qaraoy. Almaty, SE Kazakhstan *45.52N 74.44E*

116 N7 **Karapelit** *Rom.* Stejarul. Dobrich, NE Bulgaria *43.40N 27.33E*

142 I15 **Karapınar** Konya, C Turkey *37.43N 33.34E*

85 D22 **Karas** ◆ *district* S Namibia

153 Y8 **Kara-Say** Issyk-Kul'skaya Oblast', NE Kyrgyzstan *41.34N 77.55E*

85 E22 **Karasburg** Karas, S Namibia *27.59S 18.45E*

Kara Sea *see* Karskoye More

94 K9 **Kárášjohka** *var.* Karašjokka. ≈ N Norway

94 L9 **Karasjok** *Fin.* Kaarasjoki, *Lapp.* Kárášjohka. Finnmark, N Norway *69.27N 25.28S*

Kárášjohka *see* Karasjok

Karašjokka *see* Kárášjohka

Kara Strait *see* Karskiye Vorota, Proliv

Kara Su *see* Mesta/Néstos

151 N8 **Karasu** *Kaz.* Qarasū. Kostanay, N Kazakhstan *52.43N 65.28E*

142 F11 **Karasu** Sakarya, NW Turkey *41.03N 30.39E*

Karasubazar *see* Bilohirs'k

125 G14 **Karasuk** Novosibirskaya Oblast', C Russian Federation *53.41N 78.04E*

151 U13 **Karatal** *Kaz.* Qaratal. ≈ SE Kazakhstan

142 K17 **Karataş** Adana, S Turkey *36.37N 35.24E*

151 Q16 **Karatau** *Kaz.* Qarataū. Zhambyl, S Kazakhstan *43.09N 70.28E*

Karatau *see* Karatau, Khrebet

151 P16 **Karatau, Khrebet** *var.* Karatau, *Kaz.* Qarataū. ▲▲ S Kazakhstan

150 G13 **Karaton** *Kaz.* Qaraton. Atyrau, W Kazakhstan *46.33N 53.31E*

170 C12 **Karatsu** *var.* Karatu. Saga, Kyūshū, SW Japan *33.27N 129.55E*

Karatu *see* Karatsu

126 Hh7 **Karaul** Taymyrskiy (Dolgano-Nenetskiy) Avtonomnyy Okrug, N Russian Federation *70.07N 83.12E*

Karaulbazar *see* Qorovulbozor

Karauzyak *see* Qorao'zak

117 D16 **Karáva** ▲ C Greece *39.19N 21.33E*

Karavanke *see* Karawanken

117 F22 **Karavás** Kýthira, S Greece *36.21N 22.57E*

115 J20 **Karavastasë, Laguna e** *var.* Kënet' e Karavastas, Kravasta Lagoon. *lagoon* W Albania

Karavastas, Kënet' e *see* Karavastasë, Laguna e

120 I5 **Karavere** Tartumaa, E Estonia *58.25N 26.29E*

117 L23 **Karavonísia** *island* Kykládes, Greece, Aegean Sea

174 Jj14 **Karawang** *prev.* Krawang. Jawa, C Indonesia *6.13S 107.16E*

111 T10 **Karawanken** *Slvn.* Karavanke. ▲▲ Austria/Serbia and Montenegro (Yugoslavia)

Karaxahar *see* Kaidu He

143 R13 **Karayazı** Erzurum, NE Turkey *39.40N 42.09E*

151 Q12 **Karazhal** Zhezkazgan, C Kazakhstan *48.02N 70.52E*

145 S9 **Karbalā'** *var.* Kerbala, Kerbela. S Iraq *32.37N 44.03E*

96 L11 **Kårböle** Gävleborg, C Sweden *61.59N 15.16E*

113 M23 **Karcag** Jász-Nagykun-Szolnok, E Hungary *47.21N 20.51E*

Kardak *see* Imia

116 N7 **Kardam** Dobrich, NE Bulgaria *43.45N 28.06E*

117 M22 **Kardámaina** Kos, Dodekánisos, Greece, Aegean Sea *36.46N 27.08E*

Kardamila *see* Kardámyla

117 L18 **Kardámyla** *var.* Kardamila, Kardhámila. Chíos, E Greece *38.33N 26.04E*

Kardeljevo *see* Ploče

Kardh *see* Qardho

Kardhámila *see* Kardámyla

Kardhítsa *see* Kardítsa

117 E16 **Kardítsa** *var.* Kardhítsa. Thessalía, C Greece *39.22N 21.55E*

120 E4 **Kärdla** *Ger.* Kertel. Hiiumaa, W Estonia *59.00N 22.42E*

Karelia *see* Kareliya, Respublika

121 I16 **Karelichy** *Pol.* Korelicze, *Rus.* Korelichi. Hrodzyenskaya Voblasts', W Belarus *53.34N 26.07E*

128 I10 **Kareliya, Respublika** *prev.* Karel'skaya ASSR, *Eng.* Karelia. ◆ *autonomous republic* NW Russian Federation

Karel'skaya ASSR *see* Kareliya, Respublika

83 E22 **Karema** Rukwa, W Tanzania *6.49S 30.25E*

Karen *see* Hualien

85 I14 **Karenda** Central, C Zambia *14.42S 26.52E*

178 Gg8 **Karen State** *var.* Kawthule State, Kayin State. ◆ *state* S Myanmar

94 J10 **Karesuando** *Lapp.* Kaaresuanto. Norrbotten, N Sweden *68.25N 22.28E*

Karet *see* Kâgheț

Kareyz-e-Elyās/Kārez Iliās *see* Kārīz-e Elyās

126 Gg12 **Kargasok** Tomskaya Oblast', C Russian Federation *59.01N 80.34E*

126 Gg14 **Kargat** Novosibirskaya Oblast', C Russian Federation *55.07N 80.19E*

142 J11 **Kargı** Çorum, N Turkey *41.09N 34.31E*

158 I5 **Kargil** Jammu and Kashmir, NW India *34.34N 76.06E*

Kargilik *see* Yecheng

128 L11 **Kargopol'** Arkhangel'skaya Oblast', NW Russian Federation *61.30N 38.53E*

112 F12 **Kargowa** *Ger.* Unruhstadt. Lubuskie, W Poland *52.05N 15.50E*

79 X13 **Kari** Bauchi, E Nigeria *11.13N 10.34E*

85 J15 **Kariba** Mashonaland West, N Zimbabwe *16.28S 28.47E*

85 J16 **Kariba, Lake** ▣ Zambia/Zimbabwe

172 Nn5 **Kariba-yama** ▲ Hokkaidō, NE Japan *42.36N 139.55E*

85 C19 **Karibib** Erongo, C Namibia *21.56S 15.51E*

Karies *see* Karyés

94 L9 **Karigasniemi** *Lapp.* Garegegasnjárga. Lappi, N Finland *69.24N 25.52E*

172 P6 **Karikachi-tōge** *pass* Hokkaidō, NE Japan *43.08N 142.46E*

192 J2 **Karikari, Cape** *headland* North Island, NZ *34.47S 173.24E*

Karīmābād *see* Hunza

174 K10 **Karimata, Kepulauan** *island group* N Indonesia

174 K9 **Karimata, Pulau** *island* Kepulauan Karimata, N Indonesia

174 K10 **Karimata, Selat** *strait* W Indonesia

161 I14 **Karīmnagar** Andhra Pradesh, C India *18.28N 79.09E*

194 I13 **Karimui** Chimbu, C PNG *6.19S 144.48E*

174 L13 **Karimunjawa, Pulau** *island* S Indonesia

82 N12 **Karin** Woqooyi Galbeed, N Somalia *10.48N 45.46E*

Kariot *see* Ikaría

95 L20 **Karis** *Fin.* Karjaa. Etelä-Suomi, SW Finland *60.05N 23.39E*

Káristos *see* Kárystos

154 J4 **Kārīz-e Elyās** *var.* Kareyz-e-Elyās, Kārez Iliās. Herāt, NW Afghanistan *35.26N 61.24E*

Karjaa *see* Karis

151 T10 **Karkaralinsk** *Kaz.* Qarqaraly. Karaganda, E Kazakhstan *49.31N 75.53E*

194 J11 **Karkar Island** *island* N PNG

149 N7 **Karkas, Kūh-e** ▲▲ C Iran

148 K8 **Karkheh, Rūd-e** ≈ SW Iran

117 L20 **Karkinágrio** Ikaría, Dodekánisos, Greece, Aegean Sea *37.31N 26.01E*

119 R12 **Karkinits'ka Zatoka** *Rus.* Karkinitskiy Zaliv. *gulf* S Ukraine

Karkinitskiy Zaliv *see* Karkinits'ka Zatoka

95 L19 **Karkkila** *Swe.* Högfors. Etelä-Suomi, S Finland *60.31N 24.10E*

95 M19 **Kärkölä** Etelä-Suomi, S Finland *60.52N 25.17E*

190 G9 **Karkoo** South Australia *34.03S 135.45E*

Karkūk *see* Kirkūk

120 D5 **Kärla** *Ger.* Kergel. Saaremaa, W Estonia *58.19N 22.15E*

Karleby *see* Kokkola

112 F7 **Karlino** *Ger.* Körlin an der Persante. Zachodniopomorskie, NW Poland *54.02N 15.52E*

143 Q13 **Karlıova** Bingöl, E Turkey *39.16N 41.01E*

119 U6 **Karlivka** Poltavs'ka Oblast', C Ukraine *49.27N 35.08E*

Karl-Marx-Stadt *see* Chemnitz

Karlö *see* Hailuoto

114 C11 **Karlobag** *It.* Carlopago. Lika-Senj, W Croatia *44.31N 15.06E*

114 D9 **Karlovac** *Ger.* Karlstadt, *Hung.* Károlyváros. Karlovac, C Croatia *45.28N 15.31E*

114 C10 **Karlovac** *off.* Karlovačka Županija. ◆ *province* C Croatia

Karlovačka Županija *see* Karlovac

113 A16 **Karlovarský Kraj** ◆ W Czech Republic

116 J9 **Karlovo** *prev.* Levskigrad. Plovdiv, C Bulgaria *42.39N 24.49E*

113 A16 **Karlovy Vary** *Ger.* Karlsbad; *prev. Eng.* Carlsbad. Karlovarský Kraj, W Czech Republic *50.13N 12.51E*

Karlsbad *see* Karlovy Vary

97 L17 **Karlsborg** Västra Götaland, S Sweden *58.31N 14.31E*

Karlsburg *see* Alba Iulia

97 L22 **Karlshamn** Blekinge, S Sweden *56.10N 14.49E*

97 L16 **Karlskoga** Örebro, C Sweden *59.19N 14.33E*

97 M22 **Karlskrona** Blekinge, S Sweden *56.11N 15.38E*

103 G21 **Karlsruhe** *var.* Carlsruhe. Baden-Württemberg, SW Germany *49.01N 8.24E*

97 K16 **Karlstad** Värmland, C Sweden *59.22N 13.36E*

31 R3 **Karlstad** Minnesota, N USA *48.34N 96.31W*

103 I18 **Karlstadt** Bayern, C Germany *49.58N 9.46E*

Karlstadt *see* Karlovac

41 Q14 **Karluk** Kodiak Island, Alaska, USA *57.34N 154.27W*

Karluk *see* Qarluq

121 O17 **Karma** *Rus.* Korma. Homyel'skaya Voblasts', SE Belarus *53.07N 30.48E*

161 F14 **Karmāla** Mahārāshtra, W India *18.26N 75.08E*

152 M11 **Karmana** Navoiy Viloyati, C Uzbekistan *40.09N 65.18E*

144 G8 **Karmi'él** *var.* Carmiel. Northern, N Israel *32.55N 35.21E*

97 B16 **Karmøy** *island* S Norway

158 I9 **Karnāl** Haryāna, N India *29.40N 76.58E*

159 W15 **Karnaphuli Reservoir** ▣ NE India

161 F17 **Karnātaka** *var.* Kanara; *prev.* Maisur, Mysore. ◆ *state* W India

27 S13 **Karnes City** Texas, SW USA *28.52N 97.54W*

111 P9 **Karnische Alpen** *It.* Alpi Carniche. ▲▲ Austria/Italy

116 M9 **Karnobat** Burgas, E Bulgaria *42.39N 26.58E*

111 Q9 **Kärnten** *off.* Land Kärnten, *Eng.* Carinthi, *Slvn.* Koroška. ◆ *state* S Austria

Karnul *see* Kurnool

85 K16 **Karoi** Mashonaland West, N Zimbabwe *16.49S 29.40E*

Karol *see* Carei

Károly-Fehérvár *see* Alba Iulia

Károlyváros *see* Karlovac

179 Qq15 **Karomatan** Mindanao, S Philippines *7.47N 123.48E*

84 M12 **Karonga** Northern, N Malawi *9.56S 33.54E*

153 W10 **Karool-Tëbë** Narynskaya Oblast', C Kyrgyzstan *40.33N 75.52E*

190 J9 **Karoonda** South Australia *35.04S 139.58E*

155 S9 **Karor Lāl Esan** Punjab, E Pakistan *31.15N 70.54E*

155 T11 **Karor Pacca** *var.* Kahror, Kahror Pakka. Punjab, E Pakistan *29.37N 71.58E*

175 P10 **Karosa** Sulawesi, C Indonesia *1.38S 119.21E*

Karpasía/Karpas Peninsula *see* Kırpaşa

Karpaten *see* Carpathian Mountains

117 L22 **Karpáthio Pélagos** *sea* Dodekánisos, Greece, Aegean Sea

117 N24 **Kárpathos** Kárpathos, SE Greece *35.30N 27.13E*

117 N24 **Kárpathos** *It.* Scarpanto; *anc.* Carpathos, Carpathus. *island* SE Greece

Karpathos Strait *see* Karpathou, Stenó

117 N24 **Karpathou, Stenó** *var.* Karpathos Strait, Scarpanto Strait. *strait* Dodekánisos, Greece, Aegean Sea

Karpaty *see* Carpathian Mountains

117 E17 **Karpenísi** *prev.* Karpenísion. Stereá Ellás, C Greece *38.55N 21.45E*

Karpenísion *see* Karpenísi

Karpilovka *see* Aktsyabrski

129 O8 **Karpogory** Arkhangel'skaya Oblast', NW Russian Federation *64.01N 44.22E*

188 I7 **Karratha** Western Australia *20.43S 116.52E*

143 S12 **Kars** *var.* Qars. Kars, NE Turkey *40.34N 43.04E*

143 S12 **Kars** *var.* Qars. ◆ *province* NE Turkey

151 O12 **Karsakpay** *Kaz.* Qarsaqbay. Zhezkazgan, C Kazakhstan *47.51N 66.42E*

95 L15 **Kärsämäki** Oulu, C Finland *63.58N 25.49E*

Karsau *see* Kārsava

120 K9 **Kārsava** *Ger.* Karsau; *prev. Rus.* Korsovka. Ludza, E Latvia *56.46N 27.39E*

152 A9 **Karshi** *Turkm.* Garshy. Balkanskiy Velayat, NW Turkmenistan *40.45N 52.50E*

Karshi *see* Qarshi

Karshinskaya Step *see* Qarshi Cho'li

Karshinskiy Kanal *see* Qarshi Kanali

86 I5 **Karskiye Vorota, Proliv** *Eng.* Kara Strait. *strait* N Russian Federation

126 Gg5 **Karskoye More** *Eng.* Kara Sea. *sea* Arctic Ocean

95 L17 **Karstula** Länsi-Suomi, W Finland *62.52N 24.48E*

131 Q5 **Karsun** Ul'yanovskaya Oblast', W Russian Federation *54.12N 47.00E*

125 E12 **Kartaly** Chelyabinskaya Oblast', C Russian Federation *53.02N 60.42E*

20 E13 **Karthaus** Pennsylvania, NE USA *41.06N 78.03W*

112 I7 **Kartuzy** Pomorskie, NW Poland *54.21N 18.10E*

172 N10 **Karumai** Iwate, Honshū, C Japan *40.19N 141.27E*

189 U4 **Karumba** Queensland, NE Australia *17.31S 140.51E*

148 L10 **Kārūn** *var.* Rūd-e Kārūn. ≈ SW Iran

94 K13 **Karungi** Norrbotten, N Sweden *66.03N 23.55E*

94 K13 **Karunki** Lappi, N Finland *66.01N 24.06E*

Kārūn, Rūd-e *see* Kārūn

161 H21 **Karūr** Tamil Nādu, SE India *10.58N 78.03E*

95 K17 **Karvia** Länsi-Suomi, W Finland *62.07N 22.34E*

113 J17 **Karviná** *Ger.* Karwin, *Pol.* Karwina; *prev.* Nová Karvinná. Ostravský Kraj, E Czech Republic *49.51N 18.33E*

161 E17 **Kārwār** Karnātaka, W India *14.49N 74.09E*

110 M7 **Karwendelgebirge** ▲▲ Austria/Germany

Karwin/Karwina *see* Karviná

117 I14 **Karyés** *var.* Karies. Ágion Óros, N Greece *40.15N 24.15E*

126 Kk16 **Karymskoye** Chitinskaya Oblast', S Russian Federation *51.36N 114.02E*

117 I19 **Kárystos** *var.* Káristos. Évvoia, C Greece *38.01N 24.25E*

142 E17 **Kaş** Antalya, SW Turkey *36.12N 29.37E*

41 Y14 **Kasaan** Prince of Wales Island, Alaska, USA *55.32N 132.24W*

170 G14 **Kasai** Hyōgo, Honshū, SW Japan *34.56N 134.49E*

81 K21 **Kasai** *var.* Cassai, Kassai. ≈ Angola/Dem. Rep. Congo

81 K22 **Kasai Occidental** *off.* Région Kasai Occidental. ◆ *region* S Dem. Rep. Congo

81 L21 **Kasai Oriental** *off.* Région Kasai Oriental. ◆ *region* C Dem. Rep. Congo

81 L24 **Kasaji** Katanga, S Dem. Rep. Congo *10.22S 23.29E*

171 Kk16 **Kasama** Ibaraki, Honshū, S Japan *36.21N 140.15E*

84 L12 **Kasama** Northern, N Zambia *10.13S 31.12E*

Kasan *see* Koson

85 H16 **Kasane** Chobe, NE Botswana *17.48S 25.06E*

83 E23 **Kasanga** Rukwa, W Tanzania *8.27S 31.10E*

81 G21 **Kasangulu** Bas-Congo, W Dem. Rep. Congo *4.33S 15.12E*

Kasansay *see* Kosonsoy

Kasargen *see* Kasari

161 E20 **Kāsaragod** Kerala, SW India *12.30N 75.01E*

120 P13 **Kasari** *var.* Kasari Jõgi, *Ger.* Kasargen. ≈ W Estonia

Kasari Jõgi *see* Kasari

15 K9 **Kasba Lake** ◎ Northwest Territories/Nunavut, N Canada

Kaschau *see* Košice

170 Bb16 **Kaseda** Kagoshima, Kyūshū, SW Japan *31.23N 130.18E*

85 I14 **Kasempa** North Western, NW Zambia *13.27S 25.49E*

81 O24 **Kasenga** Katanga, SE Dem. Rep. Congo *10.22S 28.37E*

81 P17 **Kasenye** *var.* Kasenyi. Orientale, NE Dem. Rep. Congo *1.22N 30.25E*

Kasenyi *see* Kasenye

83 E18 **Kasese** SW Uganda *0.10N 30.06E*

81 O19 **Kasese** Maniema, E Dem. Rep. Congo *1.36S 27.31E*

158 J11 **Kāsganj** Uttar Pradesh, N India *27.48N 78.36E*

149 U4 **Kashaf Rūd** ≈ NE Iran

149 N7 **Kāshān** Eşfahān, C Iran *33.57N 51.30E*

130 M10 **Kashary** Rostovskaya Oblast', SW Russian Federation *49.02N 40.58E*

41 O12 **Kashegelok** Alaska, USA *60.57N 157.46W*

Kashgar *see* Kashi

164 E7 **Kashi** *Chin.* Kaxgar, K'o-shih, *Uigh.* Kashgar. Xinjiang Uygur Zizhiqu, NW China *39.32N 75.58E*

171 Gg16 **Kashihara** *var.* Kasihara. Nara, Honshū, SW Japan *34.31N 135.49E*

171 Kk17 **Kashima** Ibaraki, Honshū, S Japan *35.59N 140.37E*

170 C13 **Kashima** *var.* Kasima. Saga, Kyūshū, SW Japan *33.09N 130.07E*

171 L16 **Kashima-nada** *gulf* S Japan

128 K15 **Kashin** Tverskaya Oblast', W Russian Federation *57.20N 37.34E*

158 K10 **Kāshīpur** Uttar Pradesh, N India *29.13N 78.58E*

130 L4 **Kashira** Moskovskaya Oblast', W Russian Federation *54.53N 38.13E*

171 K17 **Kashiwa** *var.* Kasiwa. Chiba, Honshū, S Japan *35.50N 139.59E*

171 Jj13 **Kashiwazaki** *var.* Kasiwazaki. Niigata, Honshū, C Japan *37.22N 138.33E*

Kashkadar'inskaya Oblast' *see* Qashqadaryo Viloyati

149 T5 **Kāshmar** *var.* Turshiz; *prev.* Solṭānābād, Torshiz. Khorāsān, NE Iran *35.15N 58.28E*

Kashmir *see* Jammu and Kashmir

155 R12 **Kashmor** Sind, SE Pakistan *28.23N 69.43E*

155 S5 **Kashmūnd Ghar** *Eng.* Kashmund Range. ▲▲ E Afghanistan

Kashmund Range *see* Kashmūnd Ghar

Kasi *see* Vārānasi

159 O12 **Kasia** Uttar Pradesh, N India *26.45N 83.55E*

41 N12 **Kasigluk** Alaska, USA *60.54N 162.31W*

Kasihara *see* Kashihara

41 R12 **Kasilof** Alaska, USA *60.20N 151.16W*

Kasima *see* Kashima

Kasimköj *see* General Toshevo

130 M4 **Kasimov** Ryazanskaya Oblast', W Russian Federation *54.59N 41.22E*

81 P18 **Kasindi** Nord Kivu, E Dem. Rep. Congo *0.07N 29.41E*

175 Ss8 **Kasiruta, Pulau** *island* Kepulauan Bacan, E Indonesia

84 M12 **Kasitu** ≈ N Malawi

176 V12 **Kasiui, Pulau** *island* Kepulauan Watubela, E Indonesia

Kasiwa *see* Kashiwa

Kasiwazaki *see* Kashiwazaki

32 L14 **Kaskaskia River** ≈ Illinois, N USA

95 J17 **Kaskinen** *Swe.* Kaskö. Länsi-Suomi, W Finland *62.19N 21.15E*

Kaskö *see* Kaskinen

Kas Kong *see* Kŏng, Kaôh

9 O17 **Kaslo** British Columbia, SW Canada *49.54N 116.57W*

Käsmark *see* Kežmarok

174 M10 **Kasongan** Borneo, C Indonesia *2.01S 113.21E*

81 N21 **Kasongo** Maniema, E Dem. Rep. Congo *4.22S 26.42E*

81 H22 **Kasongo-Lunda** Bandundu, SW Dem. Rep. Congo *6.30S 16.51E*

117 M24 **Kásos** *island* S Greece

Kasos Strait *see* Kasou, Stenó

117 M25 **Kasou, Stenó** *var.* Kasos Strait. *strait* Dodekánisos/Kríti, Greece, Aegean Sea

143 T10 **Kaspi** C Georgia *41.54N 44.25E*

116 M8 **Kaspichan** Shumen, NE Bulgaria *43.18N 27.09E*

Kaspīy Mangy Oypaty *see* Caspian Depression

131 Q16 **Kaspiysk** Respublika Dagestan, SW Russian Federation *42.52N 47.40E*

Kaspiyskiy *see* Lagan'

Kaspiyskoye More/Kaspiy Tengizi *see* Caspian Sea

Kassa *see* Košice

Kassai *see* Kasai

82 I9 **Kassala** Kassala, E Sudan *15.24N 36.25E*

82 H9 **Kassala** ◆ *state* NE Sudan

117 G15 **Kassándra** *prev.* Pallíni; *anc.* Pallene. *peninsula* NE Greece

117 G15 **Kassándras, Akrotírio** *headland* N Greece *39.58N 23.22E*

117 H15 **Kassándras, Kólpos** *var.* Kólpos Toronaíos. *gulf* N Greece

145 Y11 **Kassārah** E Iraq *31.21N 47.25E*

103 I15 **Kassel** *prev.* Cassel. Hessen, C Germany *51.19N 9.30E*

76 M6 **Kasserine** *var.* Al Qaşrayn. W Tunisia *35.15N 8.52E*

12 J14 **Kasshabog Lake** ◎ Ontario, SE Canada

145 O5 **Kassīr, Sabkhat al** ◎ E Syria

31 W10 **Kasson** Minnesota, N USA *44.00N 92.42W*

117 C17 **Kassópi** *site of ancient city* Ípeiros, W Greece *39.08N 20.38E*

117 N24 **Kastállou, Akrotírio** *headland* Kárpathos, SE Greece *35.24N 27.08E*

142 I11 **Kastamonu** *var.* Castamoni, Kastamuni. Kastamonu, N Turkey *41.22N 33.46E*

142 I10 **Kastamonu** *var.* Kastamuni. ◆ *province* N Turkey

Kastamuni *see* Kastamonu

117 E14 **Kastaneá** Kentrikí Makedonía, N Greece *40.25N 22.09E*

117 H24 **Kastélli** Kríti, Greece, E Mediterranean Sea *35.30N 23.39E*

Kastellórizon *see* Megísti

97 N21 **Kastlösa** Kalmar, S Sweden *56.25N 16.25E*

117 D14 **Kastoría** Dytikí Makedonía, N Greece *40.30N 21.16E*

130 K7 **Kastornoye** Kurskaya Oblast', W Russian Federation *51.49N 38.07E*

117 I21 **Kástro** Sífnos, Kykládes, Greece, Aegean Sea *36.58N 24.45E*

97 J23 **Kastrup** ✈ (København) København, E Denmark *55.36N 12.39E*

121 Q17 **Kastsyukovichy** *Rus.* Kostyukovichi. Mahilyowskaya Voblasts', E Belarus *53.19N 32.03E*

121 O18 **Kastsyukowka** *Rus.* Kostyukovka. Homyel'skaya Voblasts', SE Belarus *52.32N 30.54E*

170 Cc12 **Kasuga** Fukuoka, Kyūshū, SW Japan *33.31N 130.27E*

171 I15 **Kasugai** Aichi, Honshū, SW Japan *35.15N 136.57E*

83 E21 **Kasulu** Kigoma, W Tanzania *4.33S 30.06E*

171 Gg13 **Kasumi** Hyōgo, Honshū, SW Japan *35.36N 134.37E*

171 Kk16 **Kasumiga-ura** ◎ Honshū, S Japan

131 R17 **Kasumkent** Respublika Dagestan, SW Russian Federation *41.39N 48.09E*

84 M13 **Kasungu** Central, C Malawi *13.01S 33.30E*

155 W9 **Kasūr** Punjab, E Pakistan *31.07N 74.30E*

85 G15 **Kataba** Western, W Zambia *15.28S 23.25E*

21 R4 **Katahdin, Mount** ▲ Maine, NE USA *45.55N 68.52W*

81 M20 **Katako-Kombe** Kasai Oriental, C Dem. Rep. Congo *3.24S 24.25E*

41 T12 **Katalla** Alaska, USA *60.12N 144.31W*

Katana *see* Qaṭanā

81 L24 **Katanga** *off.* Région du Katanga; *prev.* Shaba. ◆ *region* SE Dem. Rep. Congo

126 J12 **Katanga** ≈ C Russian Federation

160 J11 **Katangi** Madhya Pradesh, C India *21.46N 79.49E*

188 J13 **Katanning** Western Australia *33.44S 117.33E*

189 P8 **Kata Tjuta** *var.* Mount Olga ▲ Northern Territory, C Australia *25.20S 130.47E*

Katawaz *see* Zarghūn Shahr

157 Q22 **Katchall Island** *island* Nicobar Islands, India, NE Indian Ocean

117 F14 **Kateríni** Kentrikí Makedonía, N Greece *40.17N 22.30E*

119 P7 **Katerynopil'** Cherkas'ka Oblast', C Ukraine *49.00N 30.59E*

178 Gg3 **Katha** Sagaing, N Myanmar *24.10N 96.19E*

189 P2 **Katherine** Northern Territory, N Australia *14.28S 132.19E*

160 B11 **Kāthiāwār Peninsula** *peninsula* W India

159 P11 **Kathmandu** *prev.* Kantipur. ● (Nepal) Central, C Nepal *27.46N 85.16E*

158 H7 **Kathua** Jammu and Kashmir, NW India *32.24N 75.33E*

78 L12 **Kati** Koulikoro, SW Mali *12.45N 8.06W*

159 R13 **Katihār** Bihār, NE India *25.33N 87.34E*

192 N7 **Katikati** Bay of Plenty, North Island, NZ *37.33S 175.55E*

85 H16 **Katima Mulilo** Caprivi, NE Namibia *17.31S 24.19E*

79 N15 **Katiola** C Ivory Coast *8.12N 5.04W*

203 V10 **Katiu** *atoll* Îles Tuamotu, C French Polynesia

119 N12 **Katlabukh, Ozero** ◎ SW Ukraine

41 P14 **Katmai, Mount** ▲ Alaska, USA *58.16N 154.57W*

160 J9 **Katni** Madhya Pradesh, C India *23.46N 80.28E*

117 D19 **Káto Achaïa** *var.* Kato Ahaia, Káto Akhaía. Dytikí Ellás, S Greece *38.08N 21.35E*

Kato Ahaia/Káto Akhaía *see* Káto Achaïa

124 Nn3 **Kato Lakatámeia** *var.* Kato Lakatamia. C Cyprus *35.07N 33.20E*

Kato Lakatamia *see* Kato Lakatámeia

81 N22 **Katompi** Katanga, SE Dem. Rep. Congo *6.10S 26.19E*

85 K14 **Katondwe** Lusaka, C Zambia *15.08S 30.10E*

116 H12 **Káto Nevrokópi** *prev.* Káto Nevrokópion. Anatolikí Makedonía kai Thráki, NE Greece *41.21N 23.52E*

Káto Nevrokópion *see* Káto Nevrokópi

83 E18 **Katonga** ≈ S Uganda

117 F15 **Káto Ólympos** ▲▲ C Greece

117 D17 **Katoúna** Dytikí Ellás, C Greece *38.46N 21.07E*

◆ Country
● Country Capital
◇ Dependent Territory
○ Dependent Territory Capital
◆ Administrative Region
✈ International Airport
▲ Mountain
▲▲ Mountain Range
Volcano
≈ River
◎ Lake
▣ Reservoir

117 E19 **Káto Vlasiá** Dytikí Makedonía, S Greece 38.02N 21.54E
113 J16 **Katowice** Ger. Kattowitz. Śląskie, S Poland 50.14N 19.00E
159 S15 **Kātoya** West Bengal, NE India 23.39N 88.10E
142 E16 **Katrançık Dağı** ▲ SW Turkey
97 N16 **Katrineholm** Södermanland, C Sweden 58.58N 16.15E
98 I11 **Katrine, Loch** ◎ C Scotland, UK
79 V12 **Katsina** Katsina, N Nigeria 12.58N 7.33E
79 U12 **Katsina** ◈ state N Nigeria
69 P8 **Katsina Ala** ∼ S Nigeria
170 C11 **Katsumoto** Nagasaki, Iki, SW Japan 33.49N 129.42E
171 L16 **Katsuta** var. Katuta. Ibaraki, Honshū, S Japan 36.24N 140.31E
171 K17 **Katsuura** var. Katuura. Chiba, Honshū, S Japan 35.09N 140.16E
171 I14 **Katsuyama** var. Katuyama. Fukui, Honshū, SW Japan 36.03N 136.28E
170 Ff13 **Katsuyama** Okayama, Honshū, SW Japan 35.06N 133.43E
Kattakurgan see Kattaqo'rg'on
153 N11 **Kattaqo'rg'on** Rus. Kattakurgan. Samarqand Viloyati, C Uzbekistan 39.55N 66.11E
117 O23 **Kattavía** Ródos, Dodekánisos, Greece, Aegean Sea 35.56N 27.47E
97 I21 **Kattegat** Dan. Kattegatt. strait N Europe
Kattegatt see Kattegat
97 P19 **Katthammarsvik** Gotland, SE Sweden 57.27N 18.54E
Kattowitz see Katowice
127 N17 **Katun'** ∼ S Russian Federation
Katuta see Katsuta
Katuura see Katsuura
Katuyama see Katsuyama
Katwijk see Katwijk aan Zee
100 G11 **Katwijk aan Zee** var. Katwijk. Zuid-Holland, W Netherlands 52.12N 4.24E
40 B8 **Kauai** Haw. Kaua'i. island Hawaiian Islands, Hawaii, USA, C Pacific Ocean
40 C8 **Kauai Channel** channel Hawaii, USA, C Pacific Ocean
175 Ss11 **Kaubalatmada, Gunung** var. Kaplamada. ▲ Pulau Buru, E Indonesia 3.16S 126.17E
203 U10 **Kauehi** atoll Îles Tuamotu, C French Polynesia
Kauen see Kaunas
103 K24 **Kaufbeuren** Bayern, S Germany 47.52N 10.37E
27 U7 **Kaufman** Texas, SW USA 32.35N 96.18W
103 I15 **Kaufungen** Hessen, C Germany 51.16N 9.39E
95 K17 **Kauhajoki** Länsi-Suomi, W Finland 62.24N 22.12E
95 K16 **Kauhava** Länsi-Suomi, W Finland 63.06N 23.07E
32 M7 **Kaukauna** Wisconsin, N USA 44.18N 88.18W
94 L11 **Kaukonen** Lappi, N Finland 67.28N 24.49E
40 A8 **Kaulakahi Channel** channel Hawaii, USA, C Pacific Ocean
40 E9 **Kaunakakai** Molokai, Hawaii, USA, C Pacific Ocean 21.05N 157.01W
40 F12 **Kauna Point** headland Hawaii, USA, C Pacific Ocean 19.02N 155.52W
120 F13 **Kaunas** Ger. Kauen, Pol. Kowno; prev. Rus. Kovno. Kaunas, C Lithuania 54.54N 23.57E
194 H10 **Kaup** East Sepik, NW PNG 3.48S 143.56E
79 U12 **Kaura Namoda** Zamfara, NW Nigeria 12.43N 6.17E
Kaushany see Căuşeni
95 K16 **Kaustinen** Länsi-Suomi, W Finland 63.33N 23.40E
175 T7 **Kau, Teluk** bay Pulau Halmahera, E Indonesia
101 M23 **Kautenbach** Diekirch, NE Luxembourg 49.57N 6.01E
94 K10 **Kautokeino** Lapp. Guovdageaidnu. Finnmark, N Norway 69.00N 23.01E
Kavadar see Kavadarci
115 P19 **Kavadarci** Turk. Kavadar. C FYR Macedonia 41.25N 22.00E
Kavaja see Kavajë
115 K20 **Kavajë** It. Cavaia, Kavaja. Tiranë, W Albania 41.11N 19.33E
116 M13 **Kavak Çayı** ∼ NW Turkey
Kavakli see Topolovgrad
116 I13 **Kavála** prev. Kaválla. Anatolikí Makedonía kai Thráki, NE Greece 40.57N 24.25E
116 I13 **Kaválas, Kólpos** gulf Aegean Sea, NE Mediterranean Sea
127 Nn17 **Kavalerovo** Primorskiy Kray, SE Russian Federation 44.17N 135.06E
161 J17 **Kāvali** Andhra Pradesh, E India 15.04N 80.02E
Kaválla see Kavála
Kavango see Cubango/Okavango
161 C21 **Kavaratti** Lakshadweep, SW India 10.33N 72.37E
116 O8 **Kavarna** Dobrich, NE Bulgaria 43.26N 28.21E
120 G12 **Kavarskas** Anykščiai, E Lithuania 55.27N 24.55E
78 I13 **Kavendou** ▲ C Guinea 10.49N 12.14W
Kavengo see Cubango/Okavango
161 F20 **Kāveri** var. Cauvery. ∼ S India
195 N9 **Kavieng** var. Kaewieng. NE PNG 2.34S 150.48E
85 H16 **Kavimba** Chobe, NE Botswana 18.03S 24.30E
85 I15 **Kavingu** Southern, S Zambia 15.39S 26.03E
149 Q6 **Kavīr, Dasht-e** var. Great Salt Desert. salt pan N Iran
Kavirondo Gulf see Winam Gulf
Kavkaz see Caucasus
97 K23 **Kävlinge** Skåne, S Sweden 55.46N 13.04E
197 I15 **Kavukavu Reef** var. Beqa Barrier Reef, Cakaubalavu Reef. reef Viti Levu, SW Fiji
84 G12 **Kavungo** Moxico, E Angola 11.31S 22.59E
171 M10 **Kawabe** Akita, Honshū, C Japan 39.39N 140.14E
171 K15 **Kawagoe** Saitama, Honshū, S Japan 35.55N 139.30E
171 K16 **Kawaguchi** var. Kawaguti. Saitama, Honshū, S Japan 35.49N 139.40E
Kawaguti see Kawaguchi
172 N11 **Kawai** Iwate, Honshū, C Japan 39.36N 141.40E
40 A8 **Kawaihoa Point** headland Niihau, Hawaii, USA, C Pacific Ocean 21.47N 160.12W
192 K3 **Kawakawa** Northland, North Island, NZ 35.23S 174.03E
84 I13 **Kawama** North Western, NW Zambia 13.04S 25.59E
84 K11 **Kawambwa** Luapula, N Zambia 9.48S 29.04E
170 F14 **Kawanoe** Ehime, Shikoku, SW Japan 34.01N 133.32E
160 K11 **Kawardha** Madhya Pradesh, C India 21.59N 81.12E
12 I14 **Kawartha Lakes** ◎ Ontario, SE Canada
171 K17 **Kawasaki** Kanagawa, Honshū, S Japan 35.33N 139.40E
175 T9 **Kawassi** Pulau Obi, E Indonesia 1.32S 127.25E
172 N8 **Kawauchi** Aomori, Honshū, C Japan 41.11N 141.00E
192 L5 **Kawau Island** island N NZ
192 N10 **Kaweka Range** ▲ North Island, NZ
Kawelecht see Puhja
176 Z13 **Kawentinkim** Papua, E Indonesia 5.04S 140.55E
192 O8 **Kawerau** Bay of Plenty, North Island, NZ 38.06S 176.42E
192 L8 **Kawhia** Waikato, North Island, NZ 38.04S 174.49E
192 K8 **Kawhia Harbour** inlet North Island, NZ
37 V8 **Kawich Peak** ▲ Nevada, W USA 38.00N 116.27W
37 V9 **Kawich Range** ▲ Nevada, W USA
12 G12 **Kawigamog Lake** ◎ Ontario, S Canada
175 Rr3 **Kawio, Kepulauan** island group N Indonesia
178 Gg9 **Kawkareik** Karen State, S Myanmar 16.34N 98.14E
29 O8 **Kaw Lake** ⊠ Oklahoma, C USA
177 G3 **Kawlin** Sagaing, N Myanmar 23.48N 95.40E
Kawm Umbū see Kôm Ombo
Kawthule State see Karen State
Kaxgar see Kashi
164 D7 **Kaxgar He** ∼ NW China
164 J5 **Kax He** ∼ NW China
79 P12 **Kaya** C Burkina 13.04N 1.09W
178 Gg7 **Kayah State** ◈ state C Myanmar
126 J7 **Kayak** Taymyrskiy (Dolgano-Nenetskiy) Avtonomnyy Okrug, N Russian Federation 71.27N 103.21E
41 T12 **Kayak Island** island Alaska, USA
116 M11 **Kayalıköy Barajı** ⊠ NW Turkey
161 G23 **Kāyankulam** Kerala, SW India 9.10N 76.31E
177 G8 **Kayan** Yangon, SW Myanmar 16.54N 96.34E
175 N6 **Kayan, Sungai** prev. Kajan. ∼ Borneo, C Indonesia
150 F14 **Kaydak, Sor** salt flat SW Kazakhstan
Kaydanovo see Dzyarzhynsk
39 N9 **Kayenta** Arizona, SW USA 36.43N 110.15W
78 J11 **Kayes** Kayes, W Mali 14.25N 11.21W
78 J11 **Kayes** ◈ region SW Mali
Kayin State see Karen State
151 U10 **Kaynar** var. Kajnar. Vostochnyy Kazakhstan, E Kazakhstan 49.13N 77.27E
Kaynary see Căinari
85 H15 **Kayoya** Western, W Zambia 16.13S 24.09E
Kayrakkum see Qayroqqum
Kayrakkumskoye Vodokhranilishche see Qayroqqum, Obanbori
142 K14 **Kayseri** var. Kaisaria; anc. Caesarea Mazaca, Mazaca. Kayseri, C Turkey 38.42N 35.28E
142 K14 **Kayseri** var. Kaisaria. ◈ province C Turkey
38 L2 **Kaysville** Utah, W USA 41.10N 111.55W
126 Hh8 **Kayyerkan** Taymyrskiy (Dolgano-Nenetskiy) Avtonomnyy Okrug, N Russian Federation 69.26N 87.31E
Kayyngdy see Kaindy
12 L11 **Kazabazua** Quebec, SE Canada 45.58N 76.00W
12 L12 **Kazabazua** ∼ Quebec, SE Canada
126 M7 **Kazach'ye** Respublika Sakha (Yakutiya), NE Russian Federation 70.38N 135.54E
Kazakdar'ya see Qozoqdaryo
150 F9 **Kazakhlyshor, Solonchak** var. Solonchak Shorkazakhly. salt marsh NW Turkmenistan
Kazakhskaya SSR/Kazakh Soviet Socialist Republic see Kazakhstan
151 R9 **Kazakhskiy Melkosopochnik** Eng. Kazakh Uplands, Kirghiz Steppe, Kaz. Saryarqa. uplands C Kazakhstan
150 L12 **Kazakhstan** off. Republic of Kazakhstan, var. Kazakstan, Kaz. Qazaqstan, Qazaqstan Respublikasy; prev. Kazakh Soviet Socialist Republic, Rus. Kazakhskaya SSR. ◆ republic C Asia
Kazakh Uplands see Kazakhskiy Melkosopochnik
Kazakstan see Kazakhstan
150 L14 **Kazalinsk** Kzylorda, S Kazakhstan 45.51N 62.08E
131 R4 **Kazan'** Respublika Tatarstan, W Russian Federation 55.43N 49.07E
131 R4 **Kazan'** ✕ Respublika Tatarstan, W Russian Federation 55.46N 49.21E
15 K8 **Kazan** ∼ Nunavut, NW Canada
Kazandzhik see Gazandzhyk
119 R8 **Kazanka** Mykolayivs'ka Oblast', S Ukraine 47.49N 32.50E
Kazanketken see Qozonketkan
Kazanlik see Kazanlŭk
116 J9 **Kazanlŭk** prev. Kazanlik. Stara Zagora, C Bulgaria 42.38N 25.24E
172 T17 **Kazan-rettō** Eng. Volcano Islands. island group SE Japan
125 F12 **Kazanskoye** Tyumenskaya Oblast', C Russian Federation 55.39N 69.06E
119 V12 **Kazantip, Mys** headland S Ukraine 45.27N 35.50E
153 U9 **Kazarman** Narynskaya Oblast', C Kyrgyzstan 41.21N 74.03E
Kazatin see Kozyatyn
Kazbegi see Kazbek
Kazbegi see Qazbegi
143 T9 **Kazbek** var. Kazbegi, Geor. Mqinvartsveri. ▲ N Georgia 42.43N 44.28E
84 M13 **Kazembe** Eastern, NE Zambia 12.06S 32.45E
149 N11 **Kāzerūn** Fārs, S Iran 29.40N 51.38E
129 R12 **Kazhym** Respublika Komi, NW Russian Federation 60.19N 51.26E
Kazi Ahmad see Qāzi Ahmad
Kazi Magomed see Qazimämmäd
142 H16 **Kazımkarabekir** Karaman, S Turkey 37.13N 32.58E
113 M20 **Kazincbarcika** Borsod-Abaúj-Zemplén, NE Hungary 48.15N 20.40E
121 H17 **Kazlowshchyna** Pol. Kozłowszczyzna, Rus. Kozlovshchina. Hrodzyenskaya Voblasts', W Belarus 53.19N 25.18E
121 E14 **Kazlų Rūda** Marijampolė, S Lithuania 54.45N 23.28E
150 E9 **Kaztalovka** Zapadnyy Kazakhstan, W Kazakhstan 49.47N 48.40E
81 K22 **Kazumba** Kasai Occidental, S Dem. Rep. Congo 6.19S 21.57E
171 Mm10 **Kazuno** Akita, Honshū, C Japan 40.08N 140.47E
Kazvin see Qazvīn
120 J12 **Kaz'yany** Rus. Koz'yany. Vitsyebskaya Voblasts', NW Belarus 55.19N 26.52E
125 Ff9 **Kazym** ∼ N Russian Federation
112 H10 **Kcynia** Ger. Exin. Kujawsko-pomorskie, C Poland 53.00N 17.29E
117 I20 **Kéa** Kéa, Kykládes, Greece, Aegean Sea 37.22N 24.21E
117 I20 **Kéa** prev. Kéos, anc. Ceos. island Kykládes, Greece, Aegean Sea
40 H11 **Keaau** Haw. Kea'au. Hawaii, USA, C Pacific Ocean 19.36N 155.01W
40 F11 **Keahole Point** headland Hawaii, USA, C Pacific Ocean 19.43N 156.03W
40 G12 **Kealakekua** Hawaii, USA, C Pacific Ocean 19.31N 155.55W
40 H11 **Kea, Mauna** ▲ Hawaii, USA, C Pacific Ocean 19.50N 155.30W
39 N10 **Keams** Arizona, SW USA 35.47N 110.09W
Kéamu see Aneityum
31 O16 **Kearney** Nebraska, C USA 40.42N 99.06W
38 L3 **Kearns** Utah, W USA 40.39N 112.00W
117 H20 **Kéas, Stenó** strait SE Greece
143 O14 **Keban Barajı** dam C Turkey 38.49N 38.46E
143 O14 **Keban Barajı** ⊠ C Turkey
79 S13 **Kebbi** ◈ state NW Nigeria
78 G10 **Kébémèr** NW Senegal 15.24N 16.25W
76 M7 **Kebili** var. Qibilī. C Tunisia 33.42N 9.06E
144 H4 **Kebir, Nahr el** ∼ NW Syria
82 A10 **Kebkabiya** Northern Darfur, W Sudan 13.39N 24.04E
94 I11 **Kebnekaise** ▲ N Sweden 68.01N 18.24E
83 M14 **K'ebrī Dehar** Somali, E Ethiopia 6.43N 44.15E
154 K10 **Kech** ∼ SW Pakistan
8 K10 **Kechika** ∼ British Columbia, W Canada
113 K23 **Kecskemét** Bács-Kiskun, C Hungary 46.54N 19.41E
174 Gg2 **Kedah** ◈ state Peninsular Malaysia
120 F12 **Kėdainiai** Kėdainiai, C Lithuania 55.19N 24.00E
Kedder see Kehra
11 N13 **Kedgwick** New Brunswick, SE Canada 47.37N 67.21W
174 Ll15 **Kediri** Jawa, C Indonesia 7.45S 112.01E
176 Y10 **Kedir Sarmi** Papua, E Indonesia 2.00S 139.01E
169 V7 **Kedong** Heilongjiang, NE China 48.00N 126.15E
78 I12 **Kédougou** SE Senegal 12.34N 12.09W
126 Gg13 **Kedrovyy** Tomskaya Oblast', C Russian Federation 57.31N 79.45E
113 H16 **Kędzierzyn-Kozle** Ger. Heydebrech. Opolskie, S Poland 50.20N 18.12E
14 G6 **Keele** ∼ Northwest Territories, NW Canada
8 K6 **Keele Peak** ▲ Yukon Territory, NW Canada 63.31N 130.21W
Keelung see Chilung
21 N10 **Keene** New Hampshire, NE USA 42.55N 72.14W
101 H17 **Keerbergen** Vlaams Brabant, C Belgium 51.01N 4.39E
85 E21 **Keetmanshoop** Karas, S Namibia 26.36S 18.07E
10 A11 **Keewatin** Ontario, S Canada 49.46N 94.30W
31 V4 **Keewatin** Minnesota, N USA 47.24N 93.04W
117 B18 **Kefallinía** var. Kefallonía. island Iónioi Nísoi, Greece, C Mediterranean Sea
Kefallonía see Kefallinía
117 M22 **Kéfalos** Kos, Dodekánisos, Greece, Aegean Sea 36.44N 26.58E
175 Rr17 **Kefamenanu** Timor, C Indonesia 9.31S 124.28E
144 F10 **Kefar Sava** var. Kfar Saba. Central, C Israel 32.12N 34.58E
Kefe see Feodosiya
79 V15 **Keffi** Nassarawa, C Nigeria 8.52N 7.54E
94 H4 **Keflavík** ✕ (Reykjavík) Reykjanes, W Iceland 63.58N 22.37W
94 H4 **Keflavík** Reykjanes, W Iceland 64.01N 22.35W
Kegalee see Kegalla
161 J25 **Kegalla** var. Kegalee, Kegalle. Sabaragamuwa Province, C Sri Lanka 7.13N 80.21E
Kegalle see Kegalla
Kegayli see Kegeyli
Kegel see Keila
151 W16 **Kegen** Almaty, SE Kazakhstan 42.57N 79.15E
152 H7 **Kegeyli** Prev. Kegayli. Qoraqalpog'iston Respublikasi, W Uzbekistan 42.46N 59.49E
103 F22 **Kehl** Baden-Württemberg, SW Germany 48.34N 7.49E
120 H3 **Kehra** Ger. Kedder. Harjumaa, NW Estonia 59.19N 25.22E
119 U6 **Kehychivka** Kharkivs'ka Oblast', E Ukraine 49.18N 35.46E
99 L17 **Keighley** N England, UK 53.51N 1.53W
Kei Islands see Kai, Kepulauan
Keijō see Sŏul
120 G3 **Keila** Ger. Kegel. Harjumaa, NW Estonia 59.19N 24.28E
Keilberg see Klínovec
85 F23 **Keimoes** Northern Cape, W South Africa 28.41S 20.57E
Keina/Keinis see Käina
176 Yy14 **Keisak** Papua, E Indonesia 7.01S 140.02E
Keishū see Kyŏngju
79 T11 **Keïta** Tahoua, C Niger 14.43N 5.45E
80 J12 **Kéita, Bahr** var. Doka. ∼ S Chad
95 M16 **Keitele** ◎ C Finland
190 K10 **Keith** South Australia 36.01S 140.22E
98 K8 **Keith** NE Scotland, UK 57.33N 2.57W
28 K3 **Keith Sebelius Lake** ⊠ Kansas, C USA
34 G11 **Keizer** Oregon, NW USA 44.59N 123.01W
40 A8 **Kekaha** Kauai, Hawaii, USA, C Pacific Ocean 21.58N 159.43W
153 U10 **Këk-Art** prev. Alaykel', Alay-Kuu. Oshskaya Oblast', SW Kyrgyzstan 40.15N 74.21E
153 W10 **Këk-Aygyr** var. Keyaygyr. Narynskaya Oblast', C Kyrgyzstan 40.42N 75.37E
153 V9 **Këk-Dzhar** Narynskaya Oblast', C Kyrgyzstan 41.28N 74.48E
12 L8 **Kékek** ∼ Quebec, SE Canada
193 K15 **Kekerengu** Canterbury, South Island, NZ 41.55S 174.05E
113 L21 **Kékes** ▲ N Hungary 47.53N 19.59E
175 Rr17 **Kekneno, Gunung** ▲ Timor, S Indonesia
153 S9 **Këk-Tash** Kir. Kök-Tash. Dzhalal-Abadskaya Oblast', W Kyrgyzstan 41.08N 72.25E
83 M15 **K'elafo** Somali, E Ethiopia 5.36N 44.12E
175 O6 **Kelai, Sungai** ∼ Borneo, N Indonesia
Kelamayi see Karamay
Kelang see Klang
174 H3 **Kelantan** ◈ state Peninsular Malaysia
Kelantan see Kelantan, Sungai
174 H3 **Kelantan, Sungai** var. Kelantan. ∼ Peninsular Malaysia
Kelat see Kālat
Këlcyra see Këlcyrë
115 L22 **Këlcyrë** var. Këlcyra. Gjirokastër, S Albania 40.19N 20.10E
152 L14 **Kelifskiy Uzboy** salt marsh E Turkmenistan
143 O12 **Kelkit** Gümüşhane, NE Turkey 40.05N 39.25E
142 M12 **Kelkit Çayı** ∼ N Turkey
79 W11 **Kellé** Zinder, S Niger 14.10N 10.10E
81 G18 **Kéllé** Cuvette, W Congo 0.04S 14.33E
151 P7 **Kellerovka** Severnyy Kazakhstan, N Kazakhstan 53.51N 69.15E
15 H1 **Kellett, Cape** headland Banks Island, Northwest Territories, NW Canada 71.57N 125.55W
33 S11 **Kelleys Island** island Ohio, N USA
35 N8 **Kellogg** Idaho, NW USA 47.30N 116.07W
94 M12 **Kelloselkä** Lappi, N Finland 66.55N 28.52E
99 F17 **Kells** Ir. Ceanannas. E Ireland 53.43N 6.52W
120 E12 **Kelmė** Kelmė, C Lithuania 55.39N 22.57E
101 M19 **Kelmis** var. La Calamine. Liège, E Belgium 50.43N 6.01E
80 H12 **Kélo** Tandjilé, SW Chad 9.21N 15.49E
85 I14 **Kelongwa** North Western, NW Zambia 13.41S 26.19E
9 N17 **Kelowna** British Columbia, SW Canada 49.49N 119.28W
9 X12 **Kelsey** Manitoba, C Canada 56.02N 96.31W
36 M6 **Kelseyville** California, W USA 38.58N 122.51W
98 K13 **Kelso** SE Scotland, UK 55.36N 2.27W
34 G10 **Kelso** Washington, NW USA 46.09N 122.54W
205 W15 **Keltie, Cape** headland Antarctica
Keltsy see Kielce
174 Hh6 **Keluang** var. Kluang. Johor, Peninsular Malaysia 2.01N 103.18E
174 I8 **Kelume** Pulau Lingga, W Indonesia 0.12S 104.27E
9 U15 **Kelvington** Saskatchewan, S Canada 52.10N 103.30W
128 J7 **Kem'** Respublika Kareliya, NW Russian Federation 64.55N 34.17E
128 I7 **Kem'** ∼ NW Russian Federation
143 O13 **Kemah** Erzincan, E Turkey 39.34N 39.01E
143 N13 **Kemaliye** Erzincan, C Turkey 39.17N 38.30E
Kemaman see Cukai
Kemanlar see Isperikh
8 K14 **Kemano** British Columbia, SW Canada 53.39N 127.58W
Kemarat see Khemmarat
175 Qq9 **Kembani** Pulau Peleng, N Indonesia 1.32S 122.57E
142 F17 **Kemer** Antalya, SW Turkey 36.39N 30.33E
126 H14 **Kemerovo** prev. Shcheglovsk. Kemerovskaya Oblast', C Russian Federation 55.25N 86.04E
126 H14 **Kemerovskaya Oblast'** ◈ province S Russian Federation
94 L13 **Kemi** Lappi, NW Finland 65.46N 24.34E
94 M12 **Kemijärvi** Swe. Kemiträsk. Lappi, N Finland 66.41N 27.24E
94 M12 **Kemijärvi** ◎ N Finland
94 L13 **Kemijoki** ∼ NW Finland
153 V7 **Kemin** prev. Bystrovka. Chuyskaya Oblast', N Kyrgyzstan
94 L13 **Keminmaa** Lappi, NW Finland 65.49N 24.34E
Kemins Island see Nikumaroro
Kemiö see Kimito
Kemiträsk see Kemijärvi
131 P5 **Kemlya** Respublika Mordoviya, W Russian Federation 54.42N 45.16E
101 B18 **Kemmel** West-Vlaanderen, W Belgium 50.42N 2.51E
35 S16 **Kemmerer** Wyoming, C USA 41.47N 110.32W
Kemmuna see Comino
81 I14 **Kémo** ◈ prefecture S Central African Republic
27 U7 **Kemp** Texas, SW USA 32.26N 96.13W
95 L14 **Kempele** Oulu, C Finland 64.55N 25.25E
103 D15 **Kempen** Nordrhein-Westfalen, W Germany 51.22N 6.25E
27 Q5 **Kemp, Lake** ◎ Texas, SW USA
205 W5 **Kemp Land** physical region Antarctica
27 S9 **Kempner** Texas, SW USA 31.03N 98.01W
46 H3 **Kemp's Bay** Andros Island, W Bahamas 24.02N 77.32W
191 U6 **Kempsey** New South Wales, SE Australia 31.04S 152.49E
103 J24 **Kempten** Bayern, S Germany 47.43N 10.19E
13 N9 **Kempt, Lac** ◎ Quebec, SE Canada
191 P17 **Kempton** Tasmania, SE Australia 42.34S 147.13E
160 J9 **Ken** ∼ C India
41 R12 **Kenai** Alaska, USA 60.33N 151.15W
(0) D5 **Kenai Mountains** ▲ Alaska, USA
41 R12 **Kenai Peninsula** peninsula Alaska, USA
23 V11 **Kenansville** North Carolina, SE USA 34.57N 77.54W
124 Pp15 **Kenâyis, Râs el-** headland N Egypt 31.13N 27.53E
99 K16 **Kendal** NW England, UK 54.19N 2.45W
25 Y16 **Kendall** Florida, SE USA 25.39N 80.18W
15 Ll6 **Kendall, Cape** headland Nunavut, E Canada 63.31N 87.09W
20 J15 **Kendall Park** New Jersey, NE USA 40.25N 74.33W
33 Q11 **Kendallville** Indiana, N USA 41.24N 85.10W
175 Qq12 **Kendari** Sulawesi, C Indonesia 3.57S 122.36E
174 L10 **Kendawangan** Borneo, C Indonesia 2.31S 110.13E
174 Ll15 **Kendeng, Pegunungan** ▲ Jawa, S Indonesia
160 O12 **Kendrāpāra** var. Kendrāparha. Orissa, E India 20.29N 86.25E
Kendrāparha see Kendrāpāra
160 O11 **Kendujhargarh** prev. Keonjihargarh. Orissa, E India 21.42N 85.36E
27 S13 **Kenedy** Texas, SW USA 28.49N 97.51W
152 E13 **Kënekesir** Turkm. Könekesir. Balkanskiy Velayat, W Turkmenistan 38.16N 56.51E
78 J15 **Kenema** SE Sierra Leone 7.55N 11.12W
31 P16 **Kenesaw** Nebraska, C USA 40.37N 98.39W
152 G8 **Këneurgench** Turkm. Köneürgench; prev. Kunya-Urgench. Dashkhovuzskiy Velayat, N Turkmenistan 42.20N 59.09E
81 H21 **Kenge** Bandundu, SW Dem. Rep. Congo 4.52S 16.58E
Kengen see Kangen
178 Hh5 **Keng Tung** var. Kentung. Shan State, E Myanmar 21.18N 99.36E
85 F23 **Kenhardt** Northern Cape, W South Africa 29.20S 21.10E
78 J12 **Kéniéba** Kayes, W Mali 12.47N 11.16W
Kenimekh see Konimex
175 Nn3 **Keningau** Sabah, East Malaysia 5.21N 116.10E
76 F6 **Kénitra** prev. Port-Lyautey. NW Morocco 34.19N 6.29W
23 V9 **Kenly** North Carolina, SE USA 35.39N 78.16W
99 B21 **Kenmare** Ir. Neidín. S Ireland 51.52N 9.34W
30 L2 **Kenmare** North Dakota, N USA 48.40N 102.04W
99 A21 **Kenmare River** Ir. An Ribhéar. inlet NE Atlantic Ocean
20 D10 **Kenmore** New York, NE USA 42.58N 78.52W
27 W8 **Kennard** Texas, SW USA 31.21N 95.10W
31 N10 **Kennebec** South Dakota, N USA 43.53N 99.52W
21 Q7 **Kennebec River** ∼ Maine, NE USA
21 P9 **Kennebunk** Maine, NE USA 43.22N 70.33W
41 R13 **Kennedy Entrance** strait Alaska, USA
177 Ff3 **Kennedy Peak** ▲ W Myanmar 23.18N 93.52E
24 K9 **Kenner** Louisiana, S USA 29.57N 90.15W
188 I8 **Kenneth Range** ▲ Western Australia
29 Y9 **Kennett** Missouri, C USA 36.14N 90.03W
20 I16 **Kennett Square** Pennsylvania, NE USA 39.50N 75.40W
34 K10 **Kennewick** Washington, NW USA 46.12N 119.08W
10 E11 **Kenogami** ∼ Ontario, S Canada
13 Q7 **Kénogami, Lac** ◎ Quebec, SE Canada
12 G8 **Kenogami Lake** Ontario, S Canada 48.04N 80.10W
12 F7 **Kenogamissi Lake** ◎ Ontario, S Canada
8 I6 **Keno Hill** Yukon Territory, NW Canada 63.54N 135.18W
10 A11 **Kenora** Ontario, S Canada 49.46N 94.25W
33 N9 **Kenosha** Wisconsin, N USA 42.34N 87.49W
11 P14 **Kensington** Prince Edward Island, SE Canada 46.25N 63.39W
28 L3 **Kensington** Kansas, C USA 39.46N 99.01W
34 I11 **Kent** Oregon, NW USA 45.14N 120.43W
26 J9 **Kent** Texas, SW USA 31.03N 104.13W
34 H8 **Kent** Washington, NW USA 47.22N 122.13W
99 P22 **Kent** cultural region SE England, UK
151 P16 **Kentau** Yuzhnyy Kazakhstan, S Kazakhstan 43.28N 68.40E
191 P14 **Kent Group** island group Tasmania, SE Australia
33 N12 **Kentland** Indiana, N USA 40.46N 87.25W
33 R12 **Kenton** Ohio, N USA 40.39N 83.36W
15 J4 **Kent Peninsula** peninsula Nunavut, N Canada
117 F14 **Kentrikí Makedonía** Eng. Macedonia Central. ◈ region N Greece
22 J6 **Kentucky** off. Commonwealth of Kentucky; also known as The Bluegrass State. ◈ state C USA
22 H8 **Kentucky Lake** ⊠ Kentucky/Tennessee, S USA
Kentung see Keng Tung
11 P15 **Kentville** Nova Scotia, SE Canada 45.04N 64.30W
24 K8 **Kentwood** Louisiana, S USA 30.56N 90.30W
33 P9 **Kentwood** Michigan, N USA 42.52N 85.33W
83 H17 **Kenya** off. Republic of Kenya. ◆ republic E Africa
Kenya, Mount see Kirinyaga
174 Hh3 **Kenyir, Tasik** var. Tasek Kenyir. ◎ Peninsular Malaysia
31 W10 **Kenyon** Minnesota, N USA 44.16N 92.59W
31 Y16 **Keokuk** Iowa, C USA 40.24N 91.22W
Keonjihargarh see Kendujhargarh
Kéos see Kéa
31 X16 **Keosauqua** Iowa, C USA 40.43N 91.58W
31 X15 **Keota** Iowa, C USA 41.21N 91.57W
23 O11 **Keowee, Lake** ⊠ South Carolina, SE USA
128 I7 **Kepa** var. Kepe. Respublika Kareliya, NW Russian Federation 65.09N 32.15E
Kepe see Kepa
201 O13 **Kepirohi Falls** waterfall Pohnpei, E Micronesia
193 B22 **Kepler Mountains** ▲ South Island, NZ
113 I14 **Kępno** Wielkopolskie, C Poland 51.17N 17.56E
67 C24 **Keppel Island** island N Falkland Islands
Keppel Island see Niuatoputapu
67 C23 **Keppel Sound** sound N Falkland Islands
142 D12 **Kepsut** Balıkesir, NW Turkey 39.40N 28.09E
176 W12 **Kerai** Papua, E Indonesia 3.53S 134.30E
Kerak see Al Karak
161 F22 **Kerala** ◈ state S India
194 H10 **Keram** ∼ N PNG
172 O14 **Kerama-rettō** island group SW Japan
191 N10 **Kerang** Victoria, SE Australia 35.46S 144.01E
Kerasunt see Giresun
117 H19 **Keratéa** var. Keratea. Attikí, C Greece 37.48N 23.58E
95 M19 **Kerava** Swe. Kervo. Etelä-Suomi, S Finland 60.22N 25.01E
Kerbala/Kerbela see Karbalā'
34 F15 **Kerby** Oregon, NW USA 42.10N 123.39W
119 W12 **Kerch** Rus. Kerch'. Respublika Krym, SE Ukraine 45.22N 36.30E
Kerchens'ka Protska/Kerchenskiy Proliv see Kerch Strait
119 V13 **Kerchens'kyy Pivostriv** peninsula S Ukraine
124 R4 **Kerch Strait** var. Bosporus Cimmerius, Enikale Strait, Rus. Kerchenskiy Proliv, Ukr. Kerchens'ka Protska. strait Black Sea/Sea of Azov
158 K8 **Kerdārnāth** Uttar Pradesh, N India 30.43N 79.03E
Kerdilio see Kerdýlio
116 H13 **Kerdýlio** var. Kerdilio. ▲ N Greece 40.46N 23.37E
194 J14 **Kerema** Gulf, S PNG 7.58S 145.46E
Keremitlik see Lyulyakovo
142 I9 **Kerempe Burnu** headland N Turkey 42.01N 33.20E
82 J9 **Keren** var. Cheren. C Eritrea 15.45N 38.22E
27 U7 **Kerens** Texas, SW USA 32.07N 96.13W
192 M6 **Kerepehi** Waikato, North Island, NZ 37.18S 175.33E
151 P10 **Kerey, Ozero** ◎ C Kazakhstan
Kergel see Kärla
181 Q12 **Kerguelen** island C French Southern and Antarctic Territories
181 Q13 **Kerguelen Plateau** undersea feature S Indian Ocean
117 C20 **Kerí** Zákynthos, Iónioi Nísoi, Greece, C Mediterranean Sea 37.40N 20.48E
83 H19 **Kericho** Rift Valley, W Kenya 0.21S 35.16E
192 K2 **Kerikeri** Northland, North Island, NZ 35.13S 173.57E
95 O17 **Kerimäki** Isä-Suomi, E Finland 61.55N 29.18E
174 Gg10 **Kerinci, Danau** ◎ Sumatera, W Indonesia
174 Gg9 **Kerinci, Gunung** ▲ Sumatera, W Indonesia 2.00S 101.40E
Keriya see Yutian
164 H9 **Keriya He** ∼ NW China
100 J9 **Kerkbuurt** Noord-Holland, C Netherlands 52.29N 5.08E
100 J13 **Kerkdriel** Gelderland, C Netherlands 51.46N 5.21E
77 N6 **Kerkenah, Îles de** var. Kerkenna Islands, Ar. Juzur Qarqannah. island group E Tunisia
Kerkenna Islands see Kerkenah, Îles de
117 M20 **Kerketévs** ▲ Sámos, Dodekánisos, Greece, Aegean Sea 37.44N 26.39E
31 T8 **Kerkhoven** Minnesota, N USA 45.12N 95.18W
152 M14 **Kerki** Lebapskiy Velayat, E Turkmenistan 37.51N 65.06E
152 M14 **Kerkichi** Lebapskiy Velayat, E Turkmenistan 37.46N 65.18E
117 F16 **Kerkíneo** prehistoric site Thessalía, C Greece 39.32N 22.42E
116 G12 **Kerkinitis, Límni** ◎ N Greece
Kérkira see Kérkyra
101 M18 **Kerkrade** Limburg, SE Netherlands 50.52N 6.04E
Kerkuk see Kirkūk
117 B16 **Kerkyra** ✕ Kérkyra, Iónioi Nísoi, Greece, C Mediterranean Sea 39.36N 19.55E
117 B16 **Kérkyra** var. Kérkira, Eng. Corfu. Kérkyra, Iónioi Nísoi, Greece, C Mediterranean Sea 39.36N 19.55E
117 A16 **Kérkyra** var. Kérkira, Eng. Corfu. island Iónioi Nísoi, Greece, C Mediterranean Sea
199 Jj12 **Kermadec Islands** island group NZ, SW Pacific Ocean
183 R10 **Kermadec Ridge** undersea feature SW Pacific Ocean
183 R11 **Kermadec Trench** undersea feature SW Pacific Ocean
149 S10 **Kermān** var. Kirman; anc. Carmana. Kermān, C Iran 30.18N 57.04E
149 R11 **Kermān** off. Ostān-e Kermān, var. Kirman; anc. Carmania. ◈ province SE Iran
149 U12 **Kermān, Biābān-e** var. Kerman Desert. desert SE Iran
149 Q9 **Kermānshāh** Yazd, C Iran 34.19N 47.04E
148 J6 **Kermānshāh** off. Ostān-e Kermānshāh; prev. Bākhtarān, Kermānshāhān. ◈ province W Iran
Kermānshāhān see Kermānshāh
116 L10 **Kermen** Sliven, C Bulgaria 42.30N 26.12E
26 L8 **Kermit** Texas, SW USA 31.51N 103.05W
23 P6 **Kermit** West Virginia, NE USA 37.51N 82.24W
23 S9 **Kernersville** North Carolina, SE USA 36.12N 80.13W
37 S12 **Kern River** ∼ California, W USA
37 S12 **Kernville** California, W USA 35.44N 118.25W
117 K21 **Kéros** island Kykládes, Greece, Aegean Sea
78 K14 **Kérouané** Haute-Guinée, SE Guinea 9.16N 9.00W
103 D16 **Kerpen** Nordrhein-Westfalen, W Germany 50.51N 6.40E
152 I11 **Kerpichli** Lebapskiy Velayat, NE Turkmenistan 40.12N 61.09E
26 M1 **Kerrick** Texas, SW USA 36.29N 102.14W
Kerr Lake see John H.Kerr Reservoir
9 S15 **Kerrobert** Saskatchewan, S Canada 51.55N 109.09W
27 Q11 **Kerrville** Texas, SW USA 30.03N 99.06W
99 B20 **Kerry** Ir. Ciarraí. cultural region SW Ireland
23 S11 **Kershaw** South Carolina, SE USA 34.33N 80.34W
Kertel see Kärdla
97 H23 **Kerteminde** Fyn, C Denmark 55.27N 10.40E
169 Q7 **Kerulen** Chin. Herlen He, Mong. Herlen Gol. ∼ China/Mongolia
Kervo see Kerava
Kerýneia see Girne
10 H11 **Kesagami Lake** ◎ Ontario, SE Canada
95 O17 **Kesälahti** Itä-Suomi, E Finland 61.54N 29.49E
142 B11 **Keşan** Edirne, NW Turkey 40.52N 26.38E
171 Mm12 **Kesennuma** Miyagi, Honshū, C Japan 38.54N 141.34E
169 V7 **Keshan** Heilongjiang, NE China 48.00N 125.46E
32 M6 **Keshena** Wisconsin, N USA 44.54N 88.37W
142 I13 **Keskin** Kırıkkale, C Turkey 39.40N 33.36E
Késmárk see Kežmarok
128 I6 **Kesten'ga** var. Kest Enga. Respublika Kareliya, NW Russian Federation 65.53N 31.47E
100 K12 **Kesteren** Gelderland, C Netherlands 51.55N 5.34E
12 H14 **Keswick** Ontario, S Canada 44.15N 79.26W
99 K15 **Keswick** NW England, UK 54.30N 3.03W
113 H24 **Keszthely** Zala, SW Hungary 46.46N 17.16E
126 Hh13 **Ket'** ∼ C Russian Federation
79 R17 **Keta** SE Ghana 5.54N 1.02E
174 Kk10 **Ketapang** Borneo, C Indonesia 1.49S 109.58E
131 O12 **Ketchenery** prev. Sovetskoye. Respublika Kalmykiya, SW Russian Federation 47.18N 44.31E
41 Y14 **Ketchikan** Revillagigedo Island, Alaska, USA 55.20N 131.39W
35 O14 **Ketchum** Idaho, NW USA 43.40N 114.24W
Kete/Kete Krakye see Kete-Krachi
79 Q15 **Kete-Krachi** var. Kete, Kete Krakye. E Ghana 7.49N 0.03W
100 L9 **Ketelmeer** channel E Netherlands
155 P17 **Keti Bandar** Sind, SE Pakistan 23.55N 67.31E
151 W16 **Ketmen', Khrebet** ▲ SE Kazakhstan
79 S16 **Kétou** SE Benin 7.25N 2.36E
112 M7 **Kętrzyn** Ger. Rastenburg. Warmińsko-Mazurskie, NE Poland, 54.03N 21.22E

◆ Country ● Country Capital ◇ Dependent Territory ○ Dependent Territory Capital ◈ Administrative Region ✕ International Airport ▲ Mountain ▲ Mountain Range Volcano ∼ River ◎ Lake ⊠ Reservoir

99 N20 **Kettering** C England, UK 52.24N 0.43W
33 R14 **Kettering** Ohio, N USA 39.41N 84.10W
20 F13 **Kettle Creek** ≈ Pennsylvania, NE USA
34 L7 **Kettle Falls** Washington, NW USA 48.36N 118.03W
12 D16 **Kettle Point** headland Ontario, S Canada 43.12N 82.01W
31 V6 **Kettle River** ≈ Minnesota, N USA
194 E12 **Ketu** ≈ W PNG
20 G10 **Keuka Lake** ◎ New York, NE USA
Keupriya see Primorsko
95 L17 **Keuruu** Länsi-Suomi, W Finland 62.15N 24.34E
Kevevára see Kovin
94 L9 **Kevo** Lapp. Geavvú. Lappi, N Finland 69.42N 27.08E
46 M6 **Kew** North Caicos, N Turks and Caicos Islands 21.52N 71.57W
32 K11 **Kewanee** Illinois, N USA 41.15N 89.55W
33 N7 **Kewaunee** Wisconsin, N USA 44.27N 87.31W
32 M3 **Keweenaw Bay** ◎ Michigan, N USA
33 N2 **Keweenaw Peninsula** peninsula Michigan, N USA 47.15N 88.19W
33 N2 **Keweenaw Point** headland Michigan, N USA 47.24N 87.42W
31 N12 **Keya Paha River** ≈ Nebraska/South Dakota, N USA
Keyaygyr see Këk-Aygyr
25 Z16 **Key Biscayne** Florida, SE USA 25.41N 80.09W
28 G8 **Keyes** Oklahoma, C USA 36.48N 102.15W
25 Y17 **Key Largo** Key Largo, Florida, SE USA 25.06N 80.24W
23 U3 **Keyser** West Virginia, NE USA 39.26N 78.58W
29 O9 **Keystone Lake** ⊠ Oklahoma, C USA
38 L16 **Keystone Peak** ▲ Arizona, SW USA 31.52N 111.12W
Keystone State see Pennsylvania
23 U7 **Keysville** Virginia, NE USA 37.02N 78.28W
29 T3 **Keytesville** Missouri, C USA 39.25N 92.56W
25 W17 **Key West** Florida Keys, Florida, SE USA 24.34N 81.48W
131 T1 **Kez** Udmurtskaya Respublika, NW Russian Federation 57.55N 53.42E
Kezdivásárhely see Târgu Secuiesc
126 J13 **Kezhma** Krasnoyarskiy Kray, C Russian Federation 58.57N 101.00E
113 L18 **Kežmarok** Ger. Käsmark, Hung. Késmárk. Prešovský Kraj, E Slovakia 49.09N 20.25E
Kfar Saba see Kefar Sava
85 F20 **Kgalagadi** ◆ district SW Botswana
85 I20 **Kgatleng** ◆ district SE Botswana
196 F8 **Kgkeklau** Babeldaob, N Palau
129 R6 **Khabarikha** var. Chabaricha. Respublika Komi, NW Russian Federation 65.52N 52.19E
127 N16 **Khabarovsk** Khabarovskiy Kray, SE Russian Federation 48.31N 135.07E
126 Mm12 **Khabarovskiy Kray** ◆ territory E Russian Federation
147 W7 **Khabb** Abū Ẓaby, E UAE 24.39N 55.43E
Khabour, Nahr al see Khābūr, Nahr al
Khabura see Al Khābūrah
145 N2 **Khābūr, Nahr al** var. Nahr al Khabour. ≈ Syria/Turkey
Khachmas see Xaçmaz
82 B12 **Khadari** ≈ W Sudan
Khadera see Hadera
147 X12 **Khādhil** var. Khudal. SE Oman 18.48N 56.48E
161 E14 **Khadki** prev. Kirkee. Mahārāshtra, W India 18.34N 73.52E
130 L14 **Khadyzhensk** Krasnodarskiy Kray, SW Russian Federation 44.26N 39.31E
116 N9 **Khadzhiyska Reka** ≈ E Bulgaria
119 P10 **Khadzhybeys'kyy Lyman** ◎ SW Ukraine
144 K3 **Khafsah** Ḥalab, N Syria 36.16N 38.03E
158 M13 **Khāga** Uttar Pradesh, N India 25.46N 81.04E
159 Q13 **Khagaria** Bihār, NE India 25.31N 86.27E
155 Q13 **Khairpur** Sind, SE Pakistan 27.30N 68.49E
126 Hh15 **Khakasiya, Respublika** prev. Khakasskaya Avtonomnaya Oblast', Eng. Khakassia. ◆ autonomous republic C Russian Federation
Khakassia/Khakasskaya Avtonomnaya Oblast' see Khakasiya, Respublika
178 H9 **Kha Khaeng, Khao** ▲ W Thailand 16.13N 99.03E
85 G20 **Khakhea** var. Kakia. Southern, S Botswana 24.40S 23.28E
152 L13 **Khalach** Lebapskiy Velayat, E Turkmenistan 38.05N 64.46E
Khalándrion see Chalándri
131 W7 **Khalilovo** Orenburgskaya Oblast', W Russian Federation 51.25N 58.13E
Khalkabad see Xalqobod
148 L3 **Khalkhāl** prev. Herowābād. Ardabīl, NW Iran 37.40N 48.34E
Khalkidhikí see Chalkidikí
Khalkís see Chalkída
129 W3 **Khal'mer-Yu** Respublika Komi, NW Russian Federation 68.00N 64.45E
121 M14 **Khalopyenichy** Rus. Kholopenichi. Minskaya Voblasts', NE Belarus 54.31N 28.58E
Khalturin see Orlov
147 Y10 **Khalūf** var. Al Khaluf. E Oman 20.27N 57.58E
160 K10 **Khamaria** Madhya Pradesh, C India 23.07N 80.54E
160 D11 **Khambhāt** Gujarāt, W India 22.19N 72.39E
160 C12 **Khambhāt, Gulf of** Eng. Gulf of Cambay. gulf W India
178 K10 **Khâm Đưc** Quang Nam-Đa Năng, C Vietnam 15.28N 107.49E
160 G12 **Khāmgaon** Mahārāshtra, C India 20.40N 76.34E
147 O14 **Khamir** var. Khamr. W Yemen 16.00N 43.56E
147 N12 **Khamīs Mushayt** var. Hamīs Musait. 'Asīr, SW Saudi Arabia 18.19N 42.41E
126 L10 **Khampa** Respublika Sakha (Yakutiya), NE Russian Federation 63.43N 123.02E
Khamr see Khamir
85 C19 **Khan** ≈ W Namibia
155 Q2 **Khānābād** Kunduz, NE Afghanistan 36.42N 69.07E
Khân Abou Châmâte/Khan Abou Ech Cham see Khān Abū Shāmāt
144 I7 **Khān Abū Shāmāt** var. Khân Abou Châmâte, Khan Abou Ech Cham. Dimashq, W Syria 33.43N 36.56E
Khān al Baghdādī see Al Baghdādī
Khān al Maḩāwīl see Al Maḩāwīl
145 T7 **Khān al Mashāhidah** C Iraq 33.40N 44.15E
145 T10 **Khān al Muşallá** S Iraq 32.09N 44.19E
145 U6 **Khānaqīn** E Iraq 34.22N 45.22E
145 T11 **Khān ar Ruḩbah** S Iraq 31.42N 44.18E
145 P2 **Khān as Sūr** N Iraq 36.28N 41.36E
145 T8 **Khān Āzād** C Iraq 33.07N 44.21E
160 N13 **Khandaparha** prev. Khandpara. Orissa, E India 20.15N 85.10E
Khandpara see Khandaparha
155 T2 **Khandūd** var. Khandud, Wakhan. Badakhshān, NE Afghanistan 36.57N 72.19E
160 G11 **Khandwa** Madhya Pradesh, C India 21.49N 76.22E
126 Mm10 **Khandyga** Respublika Sakha (Yakutiya), NE Russian Federation 62.39N 135.30E
155 T10 **Khānewāl** Punjab, NE Pakistan 30.18N 71.55E
155 S10 **Khāngarh** Punjab, E Pakistan 29.56N 71.10E
Khanh Hung see Soc Trăng
Khaniá see Chaniá
Khanka see Xonqa
169 Z8 **Khanka, Lake** var. Hsing-k'ai Hu, Lake Hanka, Chin. Xingkai Hu, Rus. Ozero Khanka. ◎ China/Russian Federation
Khanka, Ozero see Khanka, Lake
Khankendi see Xankändi
Khanlar see Xanlar
126 Kk10 **Khannya** ≈ NE Russian Federation
155 S12 **Khānpur** Punjab, SE Pakistan 23.37N 70.40E
155 S12 **Khānpur** Punjab, E Pakistan 28.31N 70.30E
144 I4 **Khān Shaykhūn** var. Khan Sheikhun. Idlib, NW Syria 35.27N 36.37E
Khan Sheikhun see Khān Shaykhūn
151 S15 **Khantau** Zhambyl, S Kazakhstan 44.13N 73.47E
151 W16 **Khan Tengri, Pik** ▲ SE Kazakhstan 42.13N 80.13E
178 J9 **Khanthabouli** prev. Savannakhét. Savannakhét, S Laos 16.37N 104.48E
125 Ff10 **Khanty-Mansiysk** prev. Ostyako-Voguls'k. Khanty-Mansiyskiy Avtonomnyy Okrug, C Russian Federation 61.01N 69.00E
129 V8 **Khanty-Mansiyskiy Avtonomnyy Okrug** ◆ autonomous district C Russian Federation
145 R4 **Khānūqah** C Iraq 35.25N 43.15E
144 E11 **Khān Yūnis** var. Khān Yūnus. S Gaza Strip 31.23N 34.19E
Khān Yūnus see Khān Yūnis
Khanzi see Ghanzi
145 U5 **Khān Zūr** E Iraq 35.03N 45.08E
178 H10 **Khao Laem Reservoir** ⊠ W Thailand
126 Kk17 **Khapcheranga** Chitinskaya Oblast', S Russian Federation 49.46N 112.21E
131 Q12 **Kharabali** Astrakhanskaya Oblast', SW Russian Federation 47.28N 47.14E
159 R16 **Kharagpur** West Bengal, NE India 22.30N 87.19E
145 V11 **Kharā'ib 'Abd al Karīm** S Iraq 31.07N 45.33E
149 Q8 **Kharānaq** Yazd, C Iran 31.54N 54.21E
Kharbin see Harbin
152 H13 **Khardzhagaz** Akhalskiy Velayat, C Turkmenistan 37.54N 60.10E
Khārga Oasis see Great Oasis, The
160 F11 **Khargon** Madhya Pradesh, C India 21.49N 75.39E
155 V7 **Khāriān** Punjab, NE Pakistan 32.52N 73.52E
119 X8 **Kharisyz'k** Donets'ka Oblast', E Ukraine 48.01N 38.10E
119 V5 **Kharkiv** Rus. Khar'kov. Kharkivs'ka Oblast', NE Ukraine 50.00N 36.14E
119 V5 **Kharkiv** ✕ Kharkivs'ka Oblast', E Ukraine 49.54N 36.20E
Kharkiv see Kharkivs'ka Oblast'
119 U5 **Kharkivs'ka Oblast'** var. Kharkiv, Rus. Khar'kovskaya Oblast'. ◆ province E Ukraine
Khar'kov see Kharkiv
Khar'kovskaya Oblast' see Kharkivs'ka Oblast'
128 L3 **Kharlovka** Murmanskaya Oblast', NW Russian Federation 68.47N 37.09E
116 K11 **Kharmanli** Khaskovo, S Bulgaria 41.55N 25.54E
116 K11 **Kharmanliyska Reka** ≈ S Bulgaria
128 M13 **Kharovsk** Vologodskaya Oblast', NW Russian Federation 59.57N 40.05E
82 F9 **Khartoum** var. El Khartûm, Khartum. ● (Sudan) Khartoum, C Sudan 15.33N 32.31E
82 F9 **Khartoum** ◆ state NE Sudan
82 F9 **Khartoum** ✕ Khartoum, C Sudan 15.36N 32.37E
82 F9 **Khartoum North** Khartoum, C Sudan 15.37N 32.33E
119 X8 **Khartsyz'k** Rus. Khartsyzsk. Donets'ka Oblast', SE Ukraine 48.01N 38.10E
Khartsyzsk see Khartsyz'k
Khartum see Khartoum
Khasab see Al Khaşab
127 N18 **Khasan** Primorskiy Kray, SE Russian Federation 42.24N 130.45E
131 P16 **Khasavyurt** Respublika Dagestan, SW Russian Federation 43.16N 46.33E
149 W12 **Khāsh** prev. Vāsht. Sīstān va Balūchestān, SE Iran 28.15N 61.11E
154 K8 **Khāsh, Dasht-e** Eng. Khash Desert. desert SW Afghanistan
Khash Desert see Khāsh, Dasht-e
Khashim Al Qirba/Khashm al Qirbah see Khashm el Girba
82 H9 **Khashm el Girba** var. Khashim Al Qirba, Khashm al Qirbah. Kassala, E Sudan 15.00N 35.59E
144 G14 **Khashsh, Jabal al** ▲▲ S Jordan
143 S10 **Khashuri** C Georgia 41.59N 43.36E
159 V13 **Khāsi Hills** hill range NE India
116 K11 **Khaskovo** Khaskovo, S Bulgaria 41.56N 25.34E
116 K11 **Khaskovo** ◆ province S Bulgaria
126 J7 **Khatanga** Taymyrskiy (Dolgano-Nenetskiy) Avtonomnyy Okrug, N Russian Federation 71.55N 102.17E
126 J7 **Khatanga** ≈ N Russian Federation
Khatanga, Gulf of see Khatangskiy Zaliv
126 Jj6 **Khatangskiy Zaliv** var. Gulf of Khatanga. bay N Russian Federation
147 W7 **Khatmat al Malāḩah** N Oman 24.56N 56.22E
149 S16 **Khaţmat al Malāḩah** Ash Shāriqah, E UAE
127 Q6 **Khatyrka** Chukotskiy Avtonomnyy Okrug, NE Russian Federation 62.03N 175.09E
152 I14 **Khauz-Khan** Turkm. Hanhowuz. Akhalskiy Velayat, S Turkmenistan 37.15N 61.12E
152 I14 **Khauzkhanskoye Vodokhranilishche** ⊠ S Turkmenistan
Khavaling see Khovaling
Khavast see Xovos
145 W10 **Khawrah, Nahr al** ≈ S Iraq
Khawr Barakah see Baraka
147 W7 **Khawr Fakkān** var. Khor Fakkan. Ash Shāriqah, NE UAE 25.21N 56.19E
146 L6 **Khaybar** Al Madīnah, NW Saudi Arabia 25.52N 39.15E
Khaybar, Kowtal-e see Khyber Pass
153 S11 **Khaydarkan** var. Khaydarken. Oshskaya Oblast', SW Kyrgyzstan 39.56N 71.16E
Khaydarken see Khaydarkan
129 U2 **Khaypudyrskaya Guba** bay NW Russian Federation
145 S1 **Khayrūzuk** E Iraq 36.58N 44.19E
Khazar, Baḩr-e/Khazar, Daryā-ye see Caspian Sea
Khazarosp see Hazorasp
Khazretishi, Khrebet see Hazratishoh, Qatorkŭhi
Khelat see Kālat
76 F6 **Khemisset** NW Morocco 33.52N 6.04W
178 J10 **Khemmarat** var. Kemarat. Ubon Ratchathani, E Thailand 16.03N 105.10E
76 L6 **Khenchela** var. Khenchla. NE Algeria 35.22N 7.09E
Khenchla see Khenchela
76 G7 **Khénifra** C Morocco 32.59N 5.37W
Khersān, Rūd-e see Garm, Āb-e
119 R10 **Kherson** Khersons'ka Oblast', S Ukraine 46.39N 32.37E
Kherson see Khersons'ka Oblast'
119 S14 **Khersones, Mys** Rus. Mys Khersonesskiy. headland S Ukraine 44.34N 33.24E
Khersonesskiy, Mys see Khersones, Mys
119 R10 **Khersons'ka Oblast'** var. Kherson, Rus. Khersonskaya Oblast'. ◆ province S Ukraine
Khersonskaya Oblast' see Khersons'ka Oblast'
126 J7 **Kheta** Taymyrskiy (Dolgano-Nenetskiy) Avtonomnyy Okrug, N Russian Federation 71.33N 99.40E
126 J7 **Kheta** ≈ N Russian Federation
178 Jj8 **Khe Ve** Quang Binh, C Vietnam 17.52N 105.49E
155 U7 **Khewra** Punjab, E Pakistan 32.40N 73.04E
Khiam see El Khiyam
128 J4 **Khibiny** ▲▲ NW Russian Federation
126 K16 **Khilok** Chitinskaya Oblast', S Russian Federation 51.26N 110.25E
126 K16 **Khilok** ≈ S Russian Federation
130 K3 **Khimki** Moskovskaya Oblast', W Russian Federation 55.57N 37.48E
153 S12 **Khingov** Rus. Obi-Khingou. ≈ C Tajikistan
Khíos see Chíos
155 R15 **Khipro** Sind, SE Pakistan 25.50N 69.18E
145 S10 **Khirr, Wādī al** dry watercourse S Iraq
116 I10 **Khisarya** Plovdiv, C Bulgaria 42.33N 24.43E
Khiva see Xiva
Khiwa see Xiva
178 H9 **Khlong Khlung** Kamphaeng Phet, W Thailand 16.15N 99.41E
178 Gg16 **Khlong Thom** Krabi, SW Thailand 7.55N 99.09E
178 I12 **Khlung** Chantaburi, S Thailand 12.25N 102.12E
Khmel'nik see Khmil'nyk
Khmel'nitskaya Oblast' see Khmel'nyts'ka Oblast'
Khmel'nitskiy see Khmel 'nyts'kyy
118 K5 **Khmel'nyts'ka Oblast'** var. Khmel'nyts'kyy, Rus. Khmel'nitskaya Oblast'; prev. Kamenets-Podol'skaya Oblast'. ◆ province NW Ukraine
118 L6 **Khmel 'nyts'kyy** Rus. Khmel'nitskiy; prev. Proskurov. Khmel'nyts'ka Oblast', W Ukraine 49.24N 26.59E
Khmel'nyts'kyy see Khmel'nyts'ka Oblast'
118 M6 **Khmil'nyk** Rus. Khmel'nik. Vinnyts'ka Oblast', C Ukraine 49.36N 27.59E
143 R9 **Khobi** W Georgia 42.20N 41.54E
121 P15 **Khodasy** Rus. Khodosy. Mahilyowskaya Voblasts', E Belarus 53.56N 31.28E
118 I6 **Khodoriv** Pol. Chodorów, Rus. Khodorov. L'vivs'ka Oblast', NW Ukraine 49.19N 24.19E
Khodorov see Khodoriv
Khodosy see Khodasy
152 D12 **Khodzhakala** Turkm. Hojagala. Balkanskiy Velayat, W Turkmenistan 38.46N 56.14E
152 M13 **Khodzhambas** Turkm. Hojambaz. Lebapskiy Velayat, E Turkmenistan 38.11N 64.33E
Khodzhent see Khŭjand
Khodzheyli see Xo'jayli
Khoi see Khvoy
Khojend see Khŭjand
Khokand see Qo'qon
130 L8 **Khokhol'skiy** Voronezhskaya Oblast', W Russian Federation 51.33N 38.43E
178 Hh10 **Khok Samrong** Lop Buri, C Thailand 15.03N 100.43E
155 P2 **Kholm** var. Tashqurghan, Pash. Khulm. Balkh, N Afghanistan 36.42N 67.40E
128 H15 **Kholm** Novgorodskaya Oblast', W Russian Federation 57.10N 31.06E
Kholm see Chełm
Kholmech' see Kholmyech
127 Oo16 **Kholmsk** Ostrov Sakhalin, Sakhalinskaya Oblast', SE Russian Federation 46.57N 142.10E
121 O19 **Kholmyech** Rus. Kholmech'. Homyel'skaya Voblasts', SE Belarus 52.09N 30.37E
Kholon see Holon
Kholopenichi see Khalopyenichy
85 D19 **Khomas** ◆ district C Namibia
85 D19 **Khomas Hochland** var. Khomasplato. plateau C Namibia
Khomasplato see Khomas Hochland
Khomein see Khomeyn
148 M7 **Khomeyn** var. Khomein, Khumain. Markazī, W Iran 33.37N 50.03E
149 N8 **Khomeynīshahr** prev. Homāyūnshahr. Eşfahān, C Iran 32.39N 51.34E
Khoms see Al Khums
Khong Sedone see Muang Khôngxédôn
178 Ii9 **Khon Kaen** var. Muang Khon Kaen. Khon Kaen, E Thailand 16.25N 102.49E
Khonqa see Xonqa
178 I9 **Khon San** Khon Kaen, E Thailand 16.40N 101.51E
127 N8 **Khonuu** Respublika Sakha (Yakutiya), NE Russian Federation 66.24N 143.15E
131 N8 **Khopër** var. Khoper. ≈ SW Russian Federation
127 Nn16 **Khor** Khabarovskiy Kray, SE Russian Federation 47.43N 134.48E
127 Nn16 **Khor** ≈ SE Russian Federation
149 S6 **Khorāsān** off. Ostān-e Khorāsān, var. Khorassan, Khurasan. ◆ province NE Iran
Khorassan see Khorāsān
Khorat see Nakhon Ratchasima
160 O13 **Khordha** prev. Khurda. Orissa, E India 20.13N 85.39E
129 U4 **Khorey-Ver** Nenetskiy Avtonomnyy Okrug, NW Russian Federation 67.25N 58.05E
Khorezmskaya Oblast' see Xorazm Viloyati
Khor Fakkan see Khawr Fakkān
151 W15 **Khorgos** Almaty, SE Kazakhstan 44.13N 80.22E
126 K16 **Khorinsk** Respublika Buryatiya, S Russian Federation 52.13N 109.52E
85 C18 **Khorixas** Kunene, NW Namibia 20.22S 14.55E
147 O17 **Khormaksar** var. Aden. ✕ ('Adan) SW Yemen 12.56N 45.00E
Khormal see Khurmāl
Khormuj see Khvormūj
Khorog see Khorugh
119 S5 **Khorol** Poltavs'ka Oblast', NE Ukraine 49.49N 33.16E
148 L7 **Khorramābād** var. Khurramabad. Lorestān, W Iran 33.28N 48.21E
148 K10 **Khorramshahr** var. Khurramshahr, Muhammerah; prev. Mohammerah. Khūzestān, SW Iran 30.29N 48.09E
153 S14 **Khorugh** Rus. Khorog. S Tajikistan 37.29N 71.31E
131 Q12 **Khosheutovo** Astrakhanskaya Oblast', SW Russian Federation 47.04N 47.49E
Khotan see Hotan
Khorvot Khalutsa see Horvot Haluza
Khotimsk see Khotsimsk
Khotin see Khotyn
121 R16 **Khotsimsk** Rus. Khotimsk. Mahilyowskaya Voblasts', E Belarus 53.24N 32.34E
118 K7 **Khotyn** Rom. Hotin, Rus. Khotin. Chernivets'ka Oblast', W Ukraine 48.29N 26.30E
76 F7 **Khouribga** C Morocco 32.54N 6.51W
153 Q13 **Khovaling** Rus. Khavaling. SW Tajikistan 38.22N 69.54E
Khovd see Hovd
155 R6 **Khowst** Paktīā, E Afghanistan 33.22N 69.57E
Khoy see Khvoy
121 N20 **Khoyniki** Rus. Khoyniki. Homyel'skaya Voblasts', SE Belarus 51.53N 29.58E
Khozretishi, Khrebet see Hazratishoh, Qatorkŭhi
Khrisoúpolis see Chrysoúpoli
126 Mm6 **Khroma** ≈ NE Russian Federation
150 J10 **Khromtau** Kaz. Khromtaū. Aktyubinsk, W Kazakhstan 50.14N 58.22E
Khrysokhou Bay see Chrysochoú, Kólpos
119 O7 **Khrystynivka** Cherkas'ka Oblast', C Ukraine 48.49N 29.55E
178 J10 **Khuang Nai** Ubon Ratchathani, E Thailand 15.22N 104.33E
Khudal see Khādhil
Khudat see Xudat
155 W9 **Khudiān** Punjab, E Pakistan 30.58N 74.19E
Khudzhand see Khŭjand
153 O13 **Khufar** Surkhondaryo Viloyati, S Uzbekistan 38.31N 67.45E
85 G21 **Khuis** Kgalagadi, SW Botswana 26.37S 21.50E
153 Q11 **Khŭjand** var. Khodzhent, Khojend, Rus. Khudzhand; prev. Leninabad, Taj. Leninobod. N Tajikistan 40.16N 69.37E
178 Ii11 **Khukhan** Si Sa Ket, E Thailand 14.38N 104.12E
Khulm see Kholm
159 T16 **Khulna** Khulna, SW Bangladesh 22.48N 89.31E
159 T16 **Khulna** ◆ division SW Bangladesh
Khumain see Khomeyn
Khums see Al Khums
155 W2 **Khunjerāb Pass** Chin. Kunjirap Daban. pass China/Pakistan see also Kunjirap Daban 36.46N 75.16E
159 P16 **Khunti** Bihār, N India 23.01N 85.19E
178 Gg7 **Khun Yuam** Mae Hong Son, NW Thailand 18.54N 97.54E
Khurais see Khurayş
Khurasan see Khorāsān
147 R7 **Khurayş** var. Khurais. Ash Sharqīyah, C Saudi Arabia 25.06N 48.02E
Khurda see Khordha
158 J11 **Khurja** Uttar Pradesh, N India 28.15N 77.51E
145 V4 **Khurmāl** var. Khormal. NE Iraq 35.19N 46.06E
Khurramabad see Khorramābād
Khurramshahr see Khorramshahr
155 U7 **Khushāb** Punjab, NE Pakistan 32.16N 72.18E
118 H8 **Khust** Cz. Chust, Husté, Hung. Huszt. Zakarpats'ka Oblast', W Ukraine 48.10N 23.19E
82 D11 **Khuwei** Western Kordofan, C Sudan 13.01N 29.13E
155 O13 **Khuzdār** Baluchistān, SW Pakistan 27.49N 66.33E
148 L9 **Khūzestān** off. Ostān-e Khūzestān, var. Khuzistan; prev. Arabistan, anc. Susiana. ◆ province SW Iran
126 Jj15 **Khuzhir** Respublika Buryatiya, S Russian Federation 53.10N 107.18E
Khuzistan see Khūzestān
155 R2 **Khvājeh Ghār** var. Khwajaghar, Khwaja-i-Ghar. Takhār, NE Afghanistan 37.05N 69.28E
131 Q7 **Khvalynsk** Saratovskaya Oblast', W Russian Federation 52.30N 48.06E
149 N12 **Khvormūj** var. Khormuj. Būshehr, S Iran 28.32N 51.22E
148 I2 **Khvoy** var. Khoi, Khoy. Āžarbāyjān-e Bākhtarī, NW Iran 38.36N 45.03E
Khwajaghar/Khwaja-i-Ghar see Khvājeh Ghār
155 S5 **Khyber Pass** var. Kowtal-e Khaybar. pass Afghanistan/Pakistan 34.07N 71.05E
195 V14 **Kia** Santa Isabel, N Solomon Islands 7.34S 158.31E
191 S10 **Kiama** New South Wales, SE Australia 34.40S 150.49E
179 R17 **Kiamba** Mindanao, S Philippines 5.59N 124.36E
81 O22 **Kiambi** Katanga, SE Dem. Rep. Congo 7.15S 28.01E
29 Q12 **Kiamichi Mountains** ▲▲ Oklahoma, C USA
29 Q12 **Kiamichi River** ≈ Oklahoma, C USA
12 M10 **Kiamika, Réservoir** ⊠ Quebec, SE Canada
Kiamusze see Jiamusi
41 N7 **Kiana** Alaska, USA 66.58N 160.25W
Kiangmai see Chiang Mai
Kiang-ning see Nanjing
Kiangsi see Jiangxi
Kiangsu see Jiangsu
95 M14 **Kiantajärvi** ◎ E Finland
117 F19 **Kiáto** prev. Kiáton. Pelopónnisos, S Greece 38.01N 22.45E
Kiáton see Kiáto
Kiayi see Chiai
69 T9 **Kibali** var. Uele (upper course). ≈ NE Dem. Rep. Congo
81 E20 **Kibangou** Le Niari, SW Congo 3.27S 12.21E
Kibarty see Kybartai
94 M8 **Kiberg** Finnmark, N Norway 70.17N 30.47E
97 F22 **Kibæk** Ringkøbing, W Denmark 56.03N 8.52E
81 N20 **Kibombo** Maniema, E Dem. Rep. Congo 3.52S 25.59E
83 E20 **Kibondo** Kigoma, NW Tanzania 3.34S 30.40E
83 J15 **Kibre Mengist** var. Adola. Oromo, C Ethiopia 5.50N 39.06E
Kıbrıs/Kıbrıs Cumhuriyeti see Cyprus
83 E20 **Kibungo** var. Kibungu. SE Rwanda 2.09S 30.30E
Kibungu see Kibungo
115 N19 **Kičevo** SW FYR Macedonia 41.31N 20.57E
129 P13 **Kichmengskiy Gorodok** Vologodskaya Oblast', NW Russian Federation 60.00N 45.52E
32 J8 **Kickapoo River** ≈ Wisconsin, N USA
9 P16 **Kicking Horse Pass** pass Alberta/British Columbia, SW Canada 51.27N 116.13W
79 R9 **Kidal** Kidal, C Mali 18.22N 1.21E
79 Q8 **Kidal** ◆ region NE Mali
179 R16 **Kidapawan** Mindanao, S Philippines 7.02N 125.04E
99 L20 **Kidderminster** C England, UK 52.22N 2.13W
78 I11 **Kidira** E Senegal 14.27N 12.18W
192 O11 **Kidnappers, Cape** headland North Island, NZ 41.13S 175.15E
102 J8 **Kiel** Schleswig-Holstein, N Germany 54.21N 10.04E
113 L15 **Kielce** Rus. Keltsy. Świętokrzyskie, C Poland 50.52N 20.39E
102 K7 **Kieler Bucht** bay N Germany
102 J7 **Kieler Förde** inlet N Germany
178 K13 **Kiên Đưc** var. Đak Lap. Đăc Lăc, S Vietnam 11.59N 107.30E
81 N24 **Kienge** Katanga, SE Dem. Rep. Congo 10.33S 27.33E
195 S12 **Kieta** Bougainville Island, NE PNG 6.13S 155.39E
102 Q12 **Kietz** Brandenburg, NE Germany 52.33N 14.36E
Kiev see Kyyiv
Kiev Reservoir see Kyyivs'ke Vodoskhovyshche
78 J10 **Kiffa** Assaba, S Mauritania 16.37N 11.22W
117 H19 **Kifisiá** Attikí, C Greece 38.04N 23.49E
117 F18 **Kifisós** ≈ C Greece
145 U5 **Kifrī** N Iraq 34.43N 44.58E
83 D20 **Kigali** ● (Rwanda) C Rwanda 1.58S 30.02E
83 E20 **Kigali** ✕ C Rwanda 1.43S 30.01E
143 P13 **Kiğı** Bingöl, E Turkey 39.19N 40.19E
83 E21 **Kigoma** Kigoma, W Tanzania 4.52S 29.36E
83 E21 **Kigoma** ◆ region W Tanzania
40 F10 **Kihei** Haw. Kīhei. Maui, Hawaii, USA, C Pacific Ocean 20.47N 156.28W
95 K17 **Kihniö** Länsi-Suomi, W Finland 62.10N 23.10E
120 F6 **Kihnu** var. Kihnu Saar, Ger. Kühnö. island SW Estonia
Kihnu Saar see Kihnu
40 A8 **Kii Landing** Niihau, Hawaii, USA, C Pacific Ocean 21.58N 160.03W
95 L14 **Kiiminki** Oulu, C Finland 65.05N 25.46E
171 H16 **Kii-Nagashima** var. Nagashima. Mie, Honshū, SW Japan 34.10N 136.18E
171 Gg16 **Kii-sanchi** ▲▲ Honshū, SW Japan
94 L11 **Kiistala** Lappi, N Finland 67.52N 25.19E
170 Ff16 **Kii-suidō** strait S Japan
172 R14 **Kikai-shima** var. Kikaiga-shima. island Nansei-shotō, SW Japan
114 M8 **Kikinda** Ger. Grosskikinda, Hung. Nagykikinda; prev. Velika Kikinda. Serbia, N Serbia and Montenegro (Yugoslavia) 45.48N 20.29E
Kikládhes see Kykládes
172 N7 **Kikonai** Hokkaidō, NE Japan 41.40N 140.25E
194 H14 **Kikori** Gulf, S PNG 7.31S 144.16E
194 G13 **Kikori** ≈ W PNG
170 Cc14 **Kikuchi** var. Kikuti. Kumamoto, Kyūshū, SW Japan 33.00N 130.49E
Kikuti see Kikuchi
131 N8 **Kikvidze** Volgogradskaya Oblast', SW Russian Federation 50.47N 42.58E
12 I10 **Kikwissi, Lac** ◎ Quebec, SE Canada
81 I21 **Kikwit** Bandundu, W Dem. Rep. Congo 4.59S 18.53E
97 K15 **Kil** Värmland, C Sweden 59.30N 13.19E
96 N12 **Kilafors** Gävleborg, C Sweden 61.13N 16.34E
40 B8 **Kilauea** Haw. Kīlauea. Kauai, Hawaii, USA, C Pacific Ocean 22.12N 159.24W
40 H12 **Kilauea Caldera** crater Hawaii, USA, C Pacific Ocean 19.25N 155.16W
111 V4 **Kilb** Niederösterreich, C Austria 48.06N 15.21E
41 O12 **Kilbuck Mountains** ▲▲ Alaska, USA
169 Y12 **Kilchu** NE North Korea 40.57N 129.22E
99 F18 **Kilcock** Ir. Cill Choca. E Ireland 53.25N 6.40W
191 V2 **Kilcoy** Queensland, E Australia 26.58S 152.30E
99 F18 **Kildare** Ir. Cill Dara. E Ireland 53.10N 6.55W
99 F18 **Kildare** Ir. Cill Dara. cultural region E Ireland
128 K2 **Kil'din, Ostrov** island NW Russian Federation
27 W7 **Kilgore** Texas, SW USA 32.23N 94.52W
Kilien Mountains see Qilian Shan
116 K9 **Kilifarevo** Veliko Tŭrnovo, N Bulgaria 43.00N 25.36E
83 K20 **Kilifi** Coast, SE Kenya 3.37S 39.49E
201 U9 **Kili Island** var. Kōle. island Ralik Chain, S Marshall Islands
155 V2 **Kilik Pass** pass Afghanistan/China 37.03N 74.31E
Kilimane see Quelimane
83 I21 **Kilimanjaro** ◆ region E Tanzania
83 I20 **Kilimanjaro** var. Uhuru Peak. ▲ NE Tanzania 3.01S 37.14E
Kilimbangara see Kolombangara
Kilinailau Islands see Tulun Islands
83 K23 **Kilindoni** Pwani, E Tanzania 7.55S 39.40E
120 H6 **Kilingi-Nõmme** Ger. Kurkund. Pärnumaa, SW Estonia 58.07N 24.00E
142 M17 **Kilis** Kilis, S Turkey 36.43N 37.07E
142 M16 **Kilis** ◆ province S Turkey
119 N12 **Kiliya** Rom. Chilia-Nouă. Odes'ka Oblast', SW Ukraine 45.29N 29.16E
99 B19 **Kilkee** Ir. Cill Chaoi. W Ireland 52.40N 9.37W
99 E19 **Kilkenny** Ir. Cill Chainnigh. S Ireland 52.39N 7.15W
99 E19 **Kilkenny** Ir. Cill Chainnigh. cultural region S Ireland
99 B18 **Kilkieran Bay** Ir. Cuan Chill Chiaráin. bay W Ireland
116 G13 **Kilkís** Kentrikí Makedonía, N Greece 40.59N 22.54E
99 C15 **Killala Bay** Ir. Cuan Chill Ala. inlet NW Ireland
9 R15 **Killam** Alberta, SW Canada 52.45N 111.46W
191 U3 **Killarney** Queensland, E Australia 28.18S 152.15E
9 W17 **Killarney** Manitoba, S Canada 49.12N 99.40W
12 E11 **Killarney** Ontario, S Canada 45.58N 81.27W
99 B20 **Killarney** Ir. Cill Airne. SW Ireland 52.03N 9.30W
30 K4 **Killdeer** North Dakota, N USA 47.21N 102.45W
30 J4 **Killdeer Mountains** ▲▲ North Dakota, N USA
47 V15 **Killdeer River** ≈ Trinidad, Trinidad and Tobago
27 S9 **Killeen** Texas, SW USA 31.07N 97.43W
41 P6 **Killik River** ≈ Alaska, USA
16 P4 **Killinek Island** island Nunavut, NE Canada
Killini see Kyllíni
117 C19 **Killínis, Akrotírio** headland S Greece 37.55N 21.07E
99 D15 **Killybegs** Ir. Na Cealla Beaga. NW Ireland 54.37N 8.27W
Kilmain see Quelimane
98 I13 **Kilmarnock** W Scotland, UK 55.37N 4.30W
23 X6 **Kilmarnock** Virginia, NE USA 37.42N 76.22W
129 S16 **Kil'mez'** Kirovskaya Oblast', NW Russian Federation 56.55N 51.03E
131 S2 **Kil'mez'** Udmurtskaya Respublika, NW Russian Federation 57.04N 51.22E
129 R16 **Kil'mez'** ≈ NW Russian Federation
69 V11 **Kilombero** ≈ S Tanzania
94 J10 **Kilpisjarvi** Lappi, N Finland 69.03N 20.49E
99 B19 **Kilrush** Ir. Cill Rois. W Ireland 52.39N 9.28W
81 O24 **Kilwa** Katanga, SE Dem. Rep. Congo 9.22S 28.19E
Kilwa see Kilwa Kivinje
83 J24 **Kilwa Kivinje** var. Kilwa. Lindi, SE Tanzania 8.45S 39.21E
83 J24 **Kilwa Masoko** Lindi, SE Tanzania 8.55S 39.31E
176 Uu11 **Kilwo** Pulau Seram, E Indonesia 3.36S 130.48E
116 P12 **Kilyos** İstanbul, NW Turkey 41.15N 29.01E
39 V8 **Kim** Colorado, C USA 37.12N 103.22W
175 N3 **Kimanis, Teluk** bay Sabah, East Malaysia
190 H8 **Kimba** South Australia 33.09S 136.26E
30 I15 **Kimball** Nebraska, C USA 41.16N 103.40W
31 O11 **Kimball** South Dakota, N USA 43.45N 98.57W
81 I21 **Kimbao** Bandundu, SW Dem. Rep. Congo 5.27S 17.40E
195 N12 **Kimbe** New Britain, E PNG 5.36S 150.10E
195 N11 **Kimbe Bay** inlet New Britain, E PNG
9 P17 **Kimberley** British Columbia, SW Canada 49.40N 115.58W
85 H23 **Kimberley** Northern Cape, C South Africa 28.45S 24.46E
188 M4 **Kimberley Plateau** plateau Western Australia
35 P15 **Kimberly** Idaho, NW USA 42.31N 114.21W
169 Y12 **Kimch'aek** prev. Sŏngjin. E North Korea 40.42N 129.12E
169 Y15 **Kimch'ŏn** C South Korea 36.08N 128.06E
169 Z16 **Kim Hae** var. Pusan. ✕ (Pusan) SE South Korea 35.10N 128.57E
Kími see Kými
95 K20 **Kimito** Swe. Kemiö. Länsi-Suomi, W Finland 60.10N 22.45E
172 O6 **Kimobetsu** Hokkaidō, NE Japan 42.47N 140.55E
117 I21 **Kímolos** island Kykládes, Greece, Aegean Sea
117 I21 **Kímolou Sífnou, Stenó** strait Kykládes, Greece, Aegean Sea
130 L5 **Kimovsk** Tul'skaya Oblast', W Russian Federation 53.59N 38.34E
169 X15 **Kimpo** ✕ (Sŏul) NW South Korea 37.37N 126.42E
Kimpolung see Câmpulung Moldovenesc
128 K16 **Kimry** Tverskaya Oblast', W Russian Federation 56.52N 37.21E
81 H21 **Kimvula** Bas-Congo, SW Dem. Rep. Congo 5.38S 15.51E
175 Nn2 **Kinabalu, Gunung** ▲ East Malaysia 5.52N 116.08E
Kinabatangan see Kinabatangan, Sungai
175 Oo3 **Kinabatangan, Sungai** var. Kinabatangan. ≈ East Malaysia
117 L21 **Kínaros** island Kykládes, Greece, Aegean Sea
9 O15 **Kinbasket Lake** ⊠ British Columbia, SW Canada
98 I7 **Kinbrace** N Scotland, UK 58.16N 2.59W
12 E14 **Kincardine** Ontario, S Canada 44.10N 81.35W
98 K10 **Kincardine** cultural region E Scotland, UK
81 K21 **Kinda** Kasai Occidental, SE Dem. Rep. Congo 4.48S 21.49E
81 M24 **Kinda** Katanga, SE Dem. Rep. Congo 9.19S 25.06E
177 Ff3 **Kindat** Sagaing, N Myanmar 23.42N 94.28E
111 V6 **Kindberg** Steiermark, C Austria 47.31N 15.27E

Key
◆ Country
● Country Capital
◇ Dependent Territory
○ Dependent Territory Capital
◆ Administrative Region
✕ International Airport
▲ Mountain
▲▲ Mountain Range
⌇ Volcano
≈ River
◎ Lake
⊠ Reservoir

24 H8 **Kinder** Louisiana, S USA 30.29N 92.51W
100 H13 **Kinderdijk** Zuid-Holland, SW Netherlands 51.52N 4.37E
99 M17 **Kinder Scout** ▲ C England, UK 53.25N 1.52W
9 S16 **Kindersley** Saskatchewan, S Canada 51.28N 109.08W
78 I14 **Kindia** Guinée-Maritime, SW Guinea 10.12N 12.26W
66 B11 **Kindley Field** air base E Bermuda
31 R6 **Kindred** North Dakota, N USA 46.39N 97.01W
81 N20 **Kindu** prev. Kindu-Port-Empain. Maniema, C Dem. Rep. Congo 2.57S 25.54E
Kindu-Port-Empain see Kindu
131 S6 **Kinel'** Samarskaya Oblast', W Russian Federation 53.14N 50.40E
129 N15 **Kineshma** Ivanovskaya Oblast', W Russian Federation 57.28N 42.07E
King see King William's Town
146 K10 **King Abdul Aziz** ✈ (Makkah) Makkah, W Saudi Arabia 21.44N 39.08E
23 X6 **King and Queen Court House** Virginia, NE USA 37.40N 76.49W
King Charles Islands see Kong Karls Land
King Christian IX Land see Kong Christian IX Land
King Christian X Land see Kong Christian X Land
37 O11 **King City** California, W USA 36.12N 121.09W
29 R2 **King City** Missouri, C USA 40.03N 94.31W
40 M16 **King Cove** Alaska, USA 55.03N 162.19W
28 M10 **Kingfisher** Oklahoma, C USA 35.49N 97.56W
King Frederik VI Coast see Kong Frederik VI Kyst
King Frederik VIII Land see Kong Frederik VIII Land
67 B24 **King George Bay** bay West Falkland, Falkland Islands
204 G3 **King George Island** var. King George Land. island South Shetland Islands, Antarctica
10 I6 **King George Islands** island group Nunavut, C Canada
King George Land see King George Island
128 G13 **Kingisepp** Leningradskaya Oblast', NW Russian Federation 59.23N 28.37E
191 N14 **King Island** island Tasmania, SE Australia
8 J15 **King Island** island British Columbia, SW Canada
King Island see Kadan Kyun
Kingissepp see Kuressaare
147 Q7 **King Khalid** ✈ (Ar Riyāḍ) Ar Riyāḍ, C Saudi Arabia 25.00N 46.40E
37 S2 **King Lear Peak** ▲ Nevada, W USA 41.13N 118.30W
205 Y8 **King Leopold and Queen Astrid Land** physical region Antarctica
188 M4 **King Leopold Ranges** ▲▲ Western Australia
38 I11 **Kingman** Arizona, SW USA 35.12N 114.02W
28 M6 **Kingman** Kansas, C USA 37.39N 98.06W
199 K7 **Kingman Reef** ◇ US territory C Pacific Ocean
81 N20 **Kingombe** Maniema, E Dem. Rep. Congo 2.37S 26.39E
190 F5 **Kingoonya** South Australia 30.56S 135.20E
204 J10 **King Peninsula** peninsula Antarctica
41 P13 **King Salmon** Alaska, USA 58.41N 156.39W
37 Q6 **Kings Beach** California, W USA 39.13N 120.02W
37 R11 **Kingsburg** California, W USA 36.30N 119.33W
190 I10 **Kingscote** South Australia 35.41S 137.36E
King's County see Offaly
204 H2 **King Sejong** South Korean research station Antarctica 61.57S 58.23W
191 T9 **Kingsford Smith** ✈ (Sydney) New South Wales, SE Australia 33.58S 151.09E
9 P17 **Kingsgate** British Columbia, SW Canada 48.58N 116.09W
25 W8 **Kingsland** Georgia, SE USA 30.48N 81.41W
31 S13 **Kingsley** Iowa, C USA 42.35N 95.58W
99 O19 **King's Lynn** var. Bishop's Lynn, Kings Lynn, Lynn, Lynn Regis. E England, UK 52.45N 0.24E
23 Q10 **Kings Mountain** North Carolina, SE USA 35.15N 81.20W
188 K4 **King Sound** sound Western Australia
39 N2 **Kings Peak** ▲ Utah, W USA 40.43N 110.27W
23 O8 **Kingsport** Tennessee, S USA 36.32N 82.31W
37 R11 **Kings River** ≈ California, W USA
191 P17 **Kingston** Tasmania, SE Australia 42.58S 147.18E
12 K14 **Kingston** Ontario, SE Canada 44.13N 76.30W
46 K13 **Kingston** ● (Jamaica) E Jamaica 17.58N 76.48W
193 C22 **Kingston** Otago, South Island, NZ 45.20S 168.45E
21 P12 **Kingston** Massachusetts, NE USA 41.59N 70.43W
29 S3 **Kingston** Missouri, C USA 39.36N 94.02W
20 K12 **Kingston** New York, NE USA 41.55N 74.00W
33 S14 **Kingston** Ohio, N USA 39.28N 82.54W
21 O13 **Kingston** Rhode Island, NE USA 41.28N 71.31W
22 M9 **Kingston** Tennessee, S USA 35.52N 84.30W
37 W12 **Kingston Peak** ▲ California, W USA 35.43N 115.54W
190 J11 **Kingston Southeast** South Australia 36.51S 139.53E
99 N17 **Kingston upon Hull** var. Hull. E England, UK 53.45N 0.19W
99 N22 **Kingston upon Thames** SE England, UK 51.25N 0.18W
47 P14 **Kingstown** ● (Saint Vincent and the Grenadines) Saint Vincent, Saint Vincent and the Grenadines 13.09N 61.13W
Kingstown see Dún Laoghaire
23 T13 **Kingstree** South Carolina, SE USA 33.40N 79.49W
66 L8 **Kings Trough** undersea feature E Atlantic Ocean
12 C18 **Kingsville** Ontario, S Canada 42.03N 82.43W
27 S15 **Kingsville** Texas, SW USA 27.31N 97.52W
23 W6 **King William** Virginia, NE USA 37.42N 77.03W
15 K3 **King William Island** island Nunavut, N Canada Arctic Ocean
85 I25 **King William's Town** var. King, Kingwilliamstown. Eastern Cape, S South Africa 32.51S 27.20E
23 T3 **Kingwood** West Virginia, NE USA 39.28N 79.40W
142 C13 **Kınık** İzmir, W Turkey 39.04N 27.25E
81 G21 **Kinkala** Le Pool, S Congo 4.18S 14.49E
171 Mm14 **Kinka-san** headland Honshū, C Japan 38.17N 141.34E
192 M8 **Kinleith** Waikato, North Island, NZ 38.16S 175.53E
97 J19 **Kinna** Västra Götaland, S Sweden 57.31N 12.42E
98 L8 **Kinnaird Head** var. Kinnairds Head. headland NE Scotland, UK 58.39N 3.22W
97 K20 **Kinnared** Halland, S Sweden 57.01N 13.04E
Kinneret, Yam see Tiberias, Lake
161 K24 **Kinniyai** Eastern Province, NE Sri Lanka 8.30N 81.10E
95 L16 **Kinnula** Länsi-Suomi, W Finland 63.24N 25.00E
12 I8 **Kinojévis** ≈ Quebec, SE Canada
170 G16 **Kino-kawa** ≈ Honshū, SW Japan
9 U11 **Kinoosao** Saskatchewan, C Canada 57.06N 101.01W
101 L17 **Kinrooi** Limburg, NE Belgium 51.09N 5.47E
98 J11 **Kinross** C Scotland, UK 56.13N 3.26W
98 J11 **Kinross** cultural region C Scotland, UK
99 C21 **Kinsale** Ir. Cionn tSáile. SW Ireland 51.42N 8.31W
97 D14 **Kinsarvik** Hordaland, S Norway 60.22N 6.43E
81 G21 **Kinshasa** prev. Léopoldville. ● (Zaire) Kinshasa, W Dem. Rep. Congo 4.21S 15.16E
81 G21 **Kinshasa** off. Ville de Kinshasa, var. Kinshasa City. ◈ region SW Dem. Rep. Congo
81 G21 **Kinshasa** ✈ Kinshasa, SW Dem. Rep. Congo 4.23S 15.30E
Kinshasa City see Kinshasa
119 U9 **Kins'ka** ≈ SE Ukraine
28 K6 **Kinsley** Kansas, C USA 37.52N 99.25W
23 W10 **Kinston** North Carolina, SE USA 35.15N 77.34W
79 P15 **Kintampo** W Ghana 6.36N 0.28E
190 B1 **Kintore, Mount** ▲ South Australia 26.30S 130.24E
98 G13 **Kintyre** peninsula W Scotland, UK
98 G13 **Kintyre, Mull of** headland W Scotland, UK 55.16N 5.46W
177 G4 **Kin-u** Sagaing, C Myanmar 22.46N 95.36E
10 G8 **Kinushseo** ≈ Ontario, C Canada
9 P13 **Kinuso** Alberta, W Canada 55.19N 115.23W
160 I13 **Kinwat** Mahārāshtra, C India 19.37N 78.12E
83 F16 **Kinyeti** ▲ S Sudan 3.56N 32.52E
103 I17 **Kinzig** ≈ SW Germany
197 J13 **Kioa** island N Fiji
Kioga, Lake see Kyoga, Lake
28 M8 **Kiowa** Kansas, C USA 37.01N 98.29W
29 P12 **Kiowa** Oklahoma, C USA 34.43N 95.54W
Kiparissía see Kyparissía
12 H10 **Kipawa, Lac** ◎ Quebec, SE Canada
83 G24 **Kipengere Range** ▲▲ SW Tanzania
83 E23 **Kipili** Rukwa, W Tanzania 7.30S 30.39E
83 K20 **Kipini** Coast, SE Kenya 2.30S 40.30E
9 V16 **Kipling** Saskatchewan, S Canada 50.04N 102.45W
40 M13 **Kipnuk** Alaska, USA 59.56N 164.02W
99 F18 **Kippure** Ir. Cipiúr. ▲ E Ireland 53.10N 6.22W
81 N25 **Kipushi** Katanga, SE Dem. Rep. Congo 11.45S 27.19E
195 Y17 **Kirakira** var. Kaokaona. San Cristobal, SE Solomon Islands 10.28S 161.54E
161 K14 **Kirandul** var. Bailādila. Madhya Pradesh, C India 18.46N 81.18E
161 I21 **Kīranūr** Tamil Nādu, SE India 11.37N 79.10E
121 N21 **Kiraw** Rus. Kirovo. Homyel'skaya Voblasts', SE Belarus 51.30N 29.25E
121 M17 **Kirawsk** Rus. Kirovsk; prev. Startsy. Mahilyowskaya Voblasts', E Belarus 53.16N 29.28E
120 F5 **Kirbla** Läänemaa, W Estonia 58.45N 23.57E
27 Y9 **Kirbyville** Texas, SW USA 30.39N 93.53W
116 M12 **Kırcasalih** Edirne, NW Turkey 41.24N 26.48E
111 W8 **Kirchbach** var. Kirchbach in Steiermark. Steiermark, SE Austria 46.55N 15.40E
Kirchbach in Steiermark see Kirchbach
110 H7 **Kirchberg** Sankt Gallen, NE Switzerland 47.24N 9.03E
111 S5 **Kirchdorf an der Krems** Oberösterreich, N Austria 47.54N 14.06E
Kirchheim see Kirchheim unter Teck
103 I22 **Kirchheim unter Teck** var. Kirchheim. Baden-Württemberg, SW Germany 48.39N 9.27E
Kirdzhali see Kŭrdzhali
126 Jj14 **Kirenga** ≈ S Russian Federation
126 Jj13 **Kirensk** Irkutskaya Oblast', C Russian Federation 57.37N 107.54E
Kirghizia see Kyrgyzstan
151 S16 **Kirghiz Range** Rus. Kirgizskiy Khrebet; prev. Alexander Range. ▲▲ Kazakhstan/Kyrgyzstan
Kirghiz SSR see Kyrgyzstan
Kirghiz Steppe see Kazakhskiy Melkosopochnik
Kirgizskaya SSR see Kyrgyzstan
Kirgizskiy Khrebet see Kirghiz Range
81 I19 **Kiri** Bandundu, W Dem. Rep. Congo 1.29S 19.00E
Kiriath-Arba see Hebron
203 R3 **Kiribati** off. Republic of Kiribati. ◆ republic C Pacific Ocean
142 L17 **Kırıkhan** Hatay, S Turkey 36.30N 36.19E
142 I13 **Kırıkkale** Kırıkkale, C Turkey 39.50N 33.31E
142 C10 **Kırıkkale** ◈ province C Turkey
128 L13 **Kirillov** Vologodskaya Oblast', NW Russian Federation 59.52N 38.24E
Kirin see Jilin
83 I18 **Kirinyaga** prev. Mount Kenya. ⛰ C Kenya 0.02S 37.19E
128 H13 **Kirishi** var. Kirisi. Leningradskaya Oblast', NW Russian Federation 59.28N 32.02E
170 C16 **Kirishima-yama** ▲ Kyūshū, SW Japan 31.58N 130.51E
Kirisi see Kirishi
203 Y2 **Kiritimati** ✈ Kiritimati, E Kiribati 2.00N 157.30W
203 Y2 **Kiritimati** prev. Christmas Island. atoll Line Islands, E Kiribati
195 O15 **Kiriwina Island** Eng. Trobriand Island. island SE PNG
195 O15 **Kiriwina Islands** var. Trobriand Islands. island group S PNG
98 K12 **Kirkcaldy** E Scotland, UK 56.07N 3.10W
99 I14 **Kirkcudbright** S Scotland, UK 54.49N 4.03W
99 I14 **Kirkcudbright** cultural region S Scotland, UK
Kirkee see Khadki
94 M8 **Kirkenes** var. Kirkkoniemi. Finnmark, N Norway 69.43N 30.01E
97 I14 **Kirkenær** Hedmark, S Norway 60.27N 12.04E
94 J4 **Kirkjubæjarklaustur** Sudhurland, S Iceland 63.46N 18.03W
Kirk-Kilissa see Kırklareli
Kirkkoniemi see Kirkenes
95 L20 **Kirkkonummi** Swe. Kyrkslätt. Etelä-Suomi, S Finland 60.06N 24.25E
12 G7 **Kirkland Lake** Ontario, S Canada 48.10N 80.01W
142 C9 **Kırklareli** prev. Kirk-Kilissa. Kırklareli, NW Turkey 41.45N 27.12E
142 I13 **Kırklareli** ◈ province NW Turkey
193 F20 **Kirkliston Range** ▲▲ South Island, NZ
12 D10 **Kirkpatrick Lake** ◎ Ontario, S Canada
205 Q11 **Kirkpatrick, Mount** ▲ Antarctica 84.37S 164.36E
29 U2 **Kirksville** Missouri, C USA 40.11N 92.34W
145 T4 **Kirkūk** var. Karkūk, Kerkuk. N Iraq 35.28N 44.25E
145 U7 **Kir Kush** E Iraq 33.42N 45.15E
98 K5 **Kirkwall** NE Scotland, UK
85 H25 **Kirkwood** Eastern Cape, S South Africa 33.23S 25.19E
29 X5 **Kirkwood** Missouri, C USA 38.34N 90.24W
Kirman see Kermān
Kir Moab/Kir of Moab see Al Karak
130 I5 **Kirov** Kaluzhskaya Oblast', W Russian Federation 54.01N 34.16E
129 R14 **Kirov** prev. Vyatka. Kirovskaya Oblast', NW Russian Federation 58.34N 49.38E
Kīrov see Balpyk Bi, Kazakhstan
Kīrov see Kopbirlick
Kirova see Kopbirlick
Kirovabad see Gäncä, Azerbaijan
Kirovabad see Panj, Tajikistan
Kirovakan see Vanadzor
Kirovo see Kiraw, Belarus
Kirovo/Kirovograd see Kirovohrad, Ukraine
Kirovo see Beshariq, Uzbekistan
129 R14 **Kirovo-Chepetsk** Kirovskaya Oblast', NW Russian Federation 58.33N 50.06E
Kirovogradskaya Oblast'/Kirovohrad see Kirovohrads'ka Oblast'
119 R7 **Kirovohrad** Rus. Kirovograd; prev. Kirovo, Yelizavetgrad, Zinov'yevsk. Kirovohrads'ka Oblast', C Ukraine 48.30N 31.17E
119 P7 **Kirovohrads'ka Oblast'** var. Kirovohrad, Rus. Kirovogradskaya Oblast'. ◈ province C Ukraine
128 J4 **Kirovsk** Murmanskaya Oblast', NW Russian Federation 67.37N 33.38E
Kirovsk see Babadaykhan, Turkmenistan
Kirovsk see Kirawsk, Belarus
119 X7 **Kirovs'k** Luhans'ka Oblast', E Ukraine 48.40N 38.39E
125 Dd9 **Kirovskaya Oblast'** ◈ province NW Russian Federation
119 X8 **Kirov'ske** Donets'ka Oblast', E Ukraine 48.12N 38.19E
119 U13 **Kirovs'ke** Rus. Kirovskoye. Respublika Krym, S Ukraine 45.13N 35.12E
Kirovskiy see Balpyk Bi
Kirovskoye see Kyzyl-Adyr
Kirovskoye see Kirovs'ke
124 Oo2 **Kırpaşa** var. Karpas Peninsula, Gk. Karpasía. peninsula NE Cyprus
152 E11 **Kirpili** Akhalskiy Velayat, C Turkmenistan 39.31N 57.13E
98 K10 **Kirriemuir** E Scotland, UK 56.37N 3.00W
129 S13 **Kirs** Kirovskaya Oblast', NW Russian Federation 59.22N 52.20E
131 N7 **Kirsanov** Tambovskaya Oblast', W Russian Federation 52.40N 42.48E
142 J14 **Kırşehir** anc. Justinianopolis. Kirşehir, C Turkey 39.09N 34.07E
142 I13 **Kırşehir** ◈ province C Turkey
155 P4 **Kīrthar Range** ▲▲ S Pakistan
39 P9 **Kirtland** New Mexico, SW USA 36.43N 108.21W
Kirun/Kirun' see Chilung
94 J11 **Kiruna** Norrbotten, N Sweden 67.50N 20.16E
81 M18 **Kirundu** Orientale, NE Dem. Rep. Congo 0.45S 25.28E
28 L3 **Kirwin Reservoir** ⊠ Kansas, C USA
131 Q4 **Kirya** Chavash Respubliki, W Russian Federation 55.04N 46.50E
Kiryat Gat see Qiryat Gat
171 K15 **Kiryū** Gunma, Honshū, S Japan 36.24N 139.19E
97 M18 **Kisa** Östergötland, S Sweden 58.00N 15.39E
171 Ll11 **Kisakata** Akita, Honshū, C Japan 39.12N 139.55E
Kisalföld see Little Alföld
81 L18 **Kisangani** prev. Stanleyville. Orientale, NE Dem. Rep. Congo 0.30N 25.13E
41 N12 **Kisaralik River** ≈ Alaska, USA
171 K17 **Kisarazu** Chiba, Honshū, S Japan 35.19N 139.51E
113 I22 **Kisbér** Komárom-Esztergom, NW Hungary 47.30N 18.00E
9 V17 **Kisbey** Saskatchewan, S Canada 49.41N 102.39W
126 H14 **Kiselevsk** Kemerovskaya Oblast', S Russian Federation 54.00N 86.38E
159 R13 **Kishanganj** Bihār, NE India 26.06N 87.57E
158 G12 **Kishangarh** Rājasthān, N India 26.33N 74.52E
Kishegyes see Mali Iđoš
79 S15 **Kishi** Oyo, W Nigeria 9.01N 3.53E
Kishinev see Chişinău
Kishiözen see Malyy Uzen'
171 Gg15 **Kishiwada** var. Kisiwada. Ōsaka, Honshū, SW Japan 34.28N 135.22E
149 P14 **Kīsh, Jazīreh-ye** var. Qeys. island S Iran
151 R7 **Kishkenekol'** prev. Kzyltu. Kaz. Qyzyltu; Severnyy Kazakhstan, N Kazakhstan 53.39N 72.22E
158 I6 **Kishtwār** Jammu and Kashmir, NW India 33.19N 75.49E
83 H19 **Kisii** Nyanza, SW Kenya 0.40S 34.46E
83 J23 **Kisiju** Pwani, E Tanzania 7.25S 39.19E
Kisiwada see Kishiwada
Kisjenő see Chişineu-Criş
40 E17 **Kiska Island** island Aleutian Islands, Alaska, USA
Kiskapus see Copşa Mică
113 M22 **Kiskörei-víztároló** ⊠ E Hungary
Kis-Küküllo see Târnava Mică
113 L24 **Kiskunfélegyháza** var. Félegyháza. Bács-Kiskun, C Hungary 46.42N 19.52E
113 K25 **Kiskunhalas** var. Halas. Bács-Kiskun, S Hungary 46.25N 19.28E
113 K24 **Kiskunmajsa** Bács-Kiskun, S Hungary 46.31N 19.45E
131 N15 **Kislovodsk** Stavropol'skiy Kray, SW Russian Federation 43.55N 42.44E
83 L18 **Kismaayo** var. Chisimayu, Kismayu, It. Chisimaio. Jubbada Hoose, S Somalia 0.04S 42.34E
Kismayu see Kismaayo
171 Ii15 **Kiso-sanmyaku** ▲▲ Honshū, S Japan
Kisseraing see Kanmaw Kyun
78 K14 **Kissidougou** Guinée-Forestière, S Guinea 9.15N 10.07W
25 X12 **Kissimmee** Florida, SE USA 28.17N 81.24W
25 X12 **Kissimmee, Lake** ◎ Florida, SE USA
25 X13 **Kissimmee River** ≈ Florida, SE USA
9 V13 **Kississing Lake** ◎ Manitoba, C Canada
113 L24 **Kistelek** Csongrád, SE Hungary 46.27N 19.58E
Kistna see Krishna
113 M23 **Kisújszállás** Jász-Nagykun-Szolnok, E Hungary 47.13N 20.43E
170 F12 **Kisuki** Shimane, Honshū, SW Japan 35.25N 133.15E
83 H18 **Kisumu** prev. Port Florence. Nyanza, W Kenya 0.02N 34.42E
Kisutzaneustadtl see Kysucké Nové Mesto
113 O20 **Kisvárda** Ger. Kleinwardein. Szabolcs-Szatmár-Bereg, E Hungary 48.13N 22.03E
83 J24 **Kiswere** Lindi, SE Tanzania 9.24S 39.37E
Kiszucaújhely see Kysucké Nové Mesto
78 K12 **Kita** Kayes, W Mali 13.04N 9.29W
207 N14 **Kitaa** ◈ province W Greenland
Kitab see Kitob
172 N5 **Kitahiyama** Hokkaidō, NE Japan 42.25N 139.55E
171 L15 **Kita-Ibaraki** Ibaraki, Honshū, S Japan 36.48N 140.43E
172 Ss17 **Kita-Iō-jima** Eng. San Alessandro. island SE Japan
171 Mm11 **Kitakami** Iwate, Honshū, C Japan 39.16N 141.06E
171 M13 **Kitakami-gawa** ≈ Honshū, C Japan
172 N11 **Kitakami-sanchi** ▲▲ Honshū, C Japan
171 L13 **Kitakata** Fukushima, Honshū, C Japan 37.38N 139.51E
170 D12 **Kitakyūshū** var. Kitakyûsyû. Fukuoka, Kyūshū, SW Japan 33.51N 130.49E
Kitakyûsyû see Kitakyūshū
83 H18 **Kitale** Rift Valley, W Kenya 1.01N 35.01E
172 Q5 **Kitami** Hokkaidō, NE Japan 43.51N 143.50E
172 Pp4 **Kitami-sanchi** ▲▲ Hokkaidō, NE Japan
171 Kk17 **Kita-ura** ◎ Honshū, S Japan
195 O15 **Kitava Island** island Kiriwina Islands, SE PNG
39 W5 **Kit Carson** Colorado, C USA 38.45N 102.47W
188 M12 **Kitchener** Western Australia 31.03S 124.00E
12 F16 **Kitchener** Ontario, S Canada 43.28N 80.27W
95 O17 **Kitee** Itä-Suomi, E Finland 62.06N 30.09E
83 G16 **Kitgum** N Uganda 3.16N 32.54E
Kithareng see Kanmaw Kyun
Kíthira see Kýthira
Kíthnos see Kýthnos
8 J13 **Kitimat** British Columbia, SW Canada 54.04N 128.37W
94 L11 **Kitinen** ≈ N Finland
153 N12 **Kitob** Rus. Kitab. Qashqadaryo Viloyati, S Uzbekistan 39.06N 66.46E
118 K7 **Kitsman'** Ger. Kotzman, Rom. Cozmeni, Rus. Kitsman. Chernivets'ka Oblast', W Ukraine 48.27N 25.46E
170 Dd14 **Kitsuki** var. Kituki. Ōita, Kyūshū, SW Japan 33.25N 131.37E
20 C14 **Kittanning** Pennsylvania, NE USA 40.48N 79.28W
21 P10 **Kittery** Maine, NE USA 43.05N 70.44W
94 L11 **Kittilä** Lappi, N Finland 67.39N 24.52E
111 Z4 **Kittsee** Burgenland, E Austria 48.05N 17.05E
83 J19 **Kitui** Eastern, S Kenya 1.25S 38.00E
Kituki see Kitsuki
83 G22 **Kitunda** Tabora, C Tanzania 6.47S 33.13E
8 K13 **Kitwanga** British Columbia, SW Canada 55.07N 128.03W
84 J13 **Kitwe** var. Kitwe-Nkana. Copperbelt, C Zambia 12.48S 28.13E
Kitwe-Nkana see Kitwe
111 O7 **Kitzbühel** Tirol, W Austria 47.27N 12.22E
111 O7 **Kitzbüheler Alpen** ▲▲ W Austria
103 J19 **Kitzingen** Bayern, SE Germany 49.43N 10.10E
159 Q14 **Kiul** Bihār, NE India 25.10N 86.06E
194 E12 **Kiunga** Western, SW PNG 6.06S 141.12E
95 M16 **Kiuruvesi** Itä-Suomi, C Finland 63.37N 26.40E
40 M7 **Kivalina** Alaska, USA 67.43N 164.31W
94 L13 **Kivalo** ridge C Finland
118 J3 **Kivertsi** Pol. Kiwerce, Rus. Kivertsy. Volyns'ka Oblast', NW Ukraine 50.49N 25.31E
Kivertsy see Kivertsi
95 L16 **Kivijärvi** Länsi-Suomi, W Finland 63.09N 25.04E
97 L23 **Kivik** Skåne, S Sweden 55.40N 14.15E
120 J3 **Kiviõli** Ida-Virumaa, NE Estonia 59.20N 27.00E
Kivu, Lac see Kivu, Lake
69 U10 **Kivu, Lake** Fr. Lac Kivu. ◎ Rwanda/Dem. Rep. Congo
194 G15 **Kiwai Island** island SW PNG
41 N8 **Kiwalik** Alaska, USA 66.01N 161.50W
Kiwerce see Kivertsi
Kiyev see Kyyiv
151 R10 **Kiyevka** Karaganda, C Kazakhstan 50.15N 71.33E
Kiyevskaya Oblast' see Kyyivs'ka Oblast'
Kiyevskoye Vodokhranilishche see Kyyivs'ke Vodoskhovyshche
142 D10 **Kıyıköy** Kırklareli, NW Turkey 41.37N 28.07E
151 O9 **Kiyma** Akmola, C Kazakhstan 51.37N 67.31E
129 V13 **Kizel** Permskaya Oblast', NW Russian Federation 58.59N 57.37E
129 O12 **Kizema** var. Kizëma. Arkhangel'skaya Oblast', NW Russian Federation 61.06N 44.51E
Kizilagach see Elkhovo
142 H12 **Kızılcahamam** Ankara, N Turkey 40.28N 32.37E
142 J10 **Kızıl Irmak** ≈ C Turkey
Kızılkoca see Şefaatli
Kizil Kum see Kyzyl Kum
143 P16 **Kızıltepe** Mardin, SE Turkey 37.12N 40.36E
Ki Zil Uzen see Qezel Owzan
131 Q16 **Kizilyurt** Respublika Dagestan, SW Russian Federation 43.13N 46.54E
131 Q15 **Kizlyar** Respublika Dagestan, SW Russian Federation 43.51N 46.39E
131 S3 **Kizner** Udmurtskaya Respublika, NW Russian Federation 56.19N 51.37E
Kizyl-Arvat see Gyzylarbat
152 B13 **Kizyl-Atrek** Turkm. Gyzyletrek. Balkanskiy Velayat, W Turkmenistan 37.40N 54.44E
152 D10 **Kizyl-Kaya** Turkm. Gyzylgaya. Balkanskiy Velayat, NW Turkmenistan 40.37N 55.15E
152 A10 **Kizyl-Su** Turkm. Gyzylsu. Balkanskiy Velayat, W Turkmenistan 39.49N 53.00E
97 H16 **Kjerkøy** island S Norway
Kjølen see Kölen
94 L7 **Kjøllefjord** Finnmark, N Norway 70.55N 27.19E
94 H11 **Kjøpsvik** Nordland, C Norway 68.07N 16.22E
174 Ii9 **Klabat, Teluk** bay Pulau Bangka, W Indonesia
114 I12 **Kladanj** Federacija Bosan I Hercegovina, C Bosnia and Herzegovina 44.14N 18.42E
176 Xx16 **Kladar** Papua, E Indonesia 8.14S 137.46E
113 C16 **Kladno** Středočeský Kraj, NW Czech Republic 50.10N 14.04E
114 P11 **Kladovo** Serbia, E Serbia and Montenegro (Yugoslavia) 44.37N 22.36E
178 Hh12 **Klaeng** Rayong, S Thailand 12.48N 101.41E
111 T9 **Klagenfurt** Slvn. Celovec. Kärnten, S Austria 46.37N 14.19E
120 B11 **Klaipėda** Ger. Memel. Klaipėda, NW Lithuania 55.42N 21.09E
174 M15 **Klakah** Jawa, C Indonesia 7.55S 113.12E
97 B18 **Klaksvík** Dan. Klaksvig Faeroe Islands 62.13N 6.43W
36 L2 **Klamath** California, W USA 41.31N 124.02W
34 H16 **Klamath Falls** Oregon, NW USA 42.13N 121.46W
36 M1 **Klamath Mountains** ▲▲ California/Oregon, W USA
36 L2 **Klamath River** ≈ California/Oregon, W USA
174 Gg5 **Klang** var. Kelang; prev. Port Swettenham. Selangor, Peninsular Malaysia 3.01N 101.27E
96 J13 **Klarälven** ≈ Norway/Sweden
113 B15 **Klášterec nad Ohří** Ger. Klösterle an der Eger. Ústecký Kraj, NW Czech Republic 50.24N 13.10E
174 L15 **Klaten** Jawa, C Indonesia 7.40S 110.31E
113 B18 **Klatovy** Ger. Klattau. Plzeňský Kraj, W Czech Republic 49.24N 13.16E
Klattau see Klatovy
Klausenburg see Cluj-Napoca
41 Y14 **Klawock** Prince of Wales Island, Alaska, USA 55.33N 133.06W
100 P8 **Klazienaveen** Drenthe, NE Netherlands 52.43N 7.00E
Kleck see Klyetsk
112 H11 **Kłecko** Wielkolpolskie, C Poland 52.37N 17.27E
112 I11 **Kleczew** Wielkopolskie, C Poland 52.22N 18.12E
8 L15 **Kleena Kleene** British Columbia, SW Canada 51.55N 124.54W
85 D20 **Klein Aub** Hardap, C Namibia 23.48S 16.39E
Kleine Donau see Mosoni-Duna
103 O14 **Kleine Elster** ≈ E Germany
Kleine Kokel see Târnava Mică
101 I16 **Kleine Nete** ≈ N Belgium
Kleines Ungarisches Tiefland see Little Alföld
85 E22 **Klein Karas** Karas, S Namibia 27.37S 18.05E
Kleinkopisch see Copşa Mică
Klein-Marien see Väike-Maarja
Kleinschlatten see Zlatna
85 D23 **Kleinsee** Northern Cape, W South Africa 29.43S 17.03E
Kleinwardein see Kisvárda
117 C16 **Kleisoúra** Ípeiros, W Greece 39.21N 20.52E
97 C17 **Klepp** Rogaland, S Norway 58.46N 5.39E
85 I22 **Klerksdorp** North-West, N South Africa 26.52S 26.39E
130 I5 **Kletnya** Bryanskaya Oblast', W Russian Federation 53.25N 32.58E
Kletsk see Klyetsk
103 D14 **Kleve** Eng. Cleves, Fr. Clèves; prev. Cleve. Nordrhein-Westfalen, W Germany 51.46N 6.07E
115 J16 **Kličevo** Montenegro, SW Serbia and Montenegro (Yugoslavia) 42.45N 18.58E
121 M16 **Klichaw** Rus. Klichev. Mahilyowskaya Voblasts', E Belarus 53.28N 29.21E
Klichev see Klichaw
121 Q16 **Klimavichy** Rus. Klimovichi. Mahilyowskaya Voblasts', E Belarus 53.37N 31.58E
116 M7 **Kliment** Shumen, NE Bulgaria 43.37N 27.00E
Klimovichi see Klimavichy
95 G14 **Klimpfjäll** Västerbotten, N Sweden 65.04N 14.49E
130 K3 **Klin** Moskovskaya Oblast', W Russian Federation 56.19N 36.45E
115 M16 **Klina** Serbia, S Serbia and Montenegro (Yugoslavia) 42.38N 20.35E
113 B15 **Klínovec** Ger. Keilberg. ▲ NW Czech Republic 50.23N 12.57E
97 P19 **Klintehamn** Gotland, SE Sweden 57.22N 18.15E
131 R8 **Klintsovka** Saratovskaya Oblast', W Russian Federation 51.42N 49.17E
130 H6 **Klintsy** Bryanskaya Oblast', W Russian Federation 52.46N 32.20E
97 K22 **Klippan** Skåne, S Sweden 56.07N 13.10E
94 G13 **Klippen** Västerbotten, N Sweden 65.50N 15.07E
124 Nn3 **Klírou** W Cyprus 35.01N 33.11E
116 I9 **Klisura** Plovdiv, C Bulgaria 42.42N 24.28E
97 F20 **Klitmøller** Viborg, NW Denmark 57.01N 8.29E
114 F11 **Ključ** Federacija Bosna I Hercegovina, NW Bosnia and Herzegovina 44.32N 16.46E
113 J14 **Kłobuck** Śląskie, S Poland 50.55N 18.54E
112 J11 **Kłodawa** Wielkopolskie, C Poland 52.14N 18.55E
113 G16 **Kłodzko** Ger. Glatz. Dolnośląskie, SW Poland 50.27N 16.37E
97 I14 **Kløfta** Akershus, S Norway 60.04N 11.09E
114 P12 **Klokočevac** Serbia, E Serbia and Montenegro (Yugoslavia) 44.19N 22.11E
120 G3 **Klooga** Ger. Lodensee. Harjumaa, NW Estonia 59.18N 24.15E
101 F15 **Kloosterzande** Zeeland, SW Netherlands 51.22N 4.01E
115 L19 **Klos** var. Klosi. Dibër, C Albania 41.30N 20.07E
Klosi see Klos
Klösterle an der Eger see Klášterec nad Ohří
111 X3 **Klosterneuburg** Niederösterreich, NE Austria 48.19N 16.19E
110 J9 **Klosters** Graubünden, SE Switzerland 46.54N 9.52E
110 G7 **Kloten** Zürich, N Switzerland 47.27N 8.34E
110 G7 **Kloten** ✈ (Zürich) Zürich, N Switzerland 47.25N 8.36E
102 K12 **Klötze** Sachsen-Anhalt, C Germany 52.37N 11.09E
10 K3 **Klotz, Lac** ◎ Quebec, NE Canada
103 O15 **Klotzsche** ✈ (Dresden) Sachsen, E Germany 51.06N 13.44E
8 H7 **Kluane Lake** ◎ Yukon Territory, W Canada
Kluang see Keluang
113 I14 **Kluczbork** Ger. Kreuzburg, Kreuzburg in Oberschlesien. Opolskie, S Poland 50.59N 18.13E
41 W12 **Klukwan** Alaska, USA 59.24N 135.49W
Klyastitsy see Klyastsitsy
120 L11 **Klyastsitsy** Rus. Klyastitsy. Vitsyebskaya Voblasts', N Belarus 55.54N 28.38E
131 T5 **Klyavlino** Samarskaya Oblast', W Russian Federation 54.21N 52.12E
86 K9 **Klyaz'in** ≈ W Russian Federation
131 N3 **Klyaz'ma** ≈ W Russian Federation
121 J17 **Klyetsk** Pol. Kleck, Rus. Kletsk. Minskaya Voblasts', SW Belarus 53.04N 26.38E
153 S8 **Klyuchevka** Talasskaya Oblast', NW Kyrgyzstan 42.33N 71.45E
127 Pp10 **Klyuchevskaya Sopka, Vulkan** ⛰ E Russian Federation 56.03N 160.37E
127 Pp10 **Klyuchi** Kamchatskaya Oblast', E Russian Federation 56.18N 160.44E
97 D17 **Knaben** Vest-Agder, S Norway 58.46N 7.04E
Knanzi see Ghanzi
97 K21 **Knäred** Halland, S Sweden 56.30N 13.21E
99 M16 **Knaresborough** N England, UK 54.01N 1.35W
116 H8 **Knezha** Vratsa , NW Bulgaria 43.29N 24.04E
27 O9 **Knickerbocker** Texas, SW USA 31.18N 100.35W
30 K5 **Knife River** ≈ North Dakota, N USA
8 K16 **Knight Inlet** inlet British Columbia, W Canada
41 S12 **Knight Island** island Alaska, USA
99 K20 **Knighton** E Wales, UK 52.20N 3.00W
37 O7 **Knights Landing** California, W USA 38.47N 121.43W
114 E13 **Knin** Šibenik-Knin, S Croatia 44.03N 16.12E
27 Q12 **Knippal** Texas, SW USA
111 U7 **Knittelfeld** Steiermark, C Austria 47.13N 14.51E
97 O15 **Knivsta** Uppsala, C Sweden 59.43N 17.49E
115 P14 **Knjaževac** Serbia, E Serbia and Montenegro (Yugoslavia) 43.34N 22.16E
29 S4 **Knob Noster** Missouri, C USA 38.47N 93.33W
101 D15 **Knokke-Heist** West-Vlaanderen, NW Belgium 51.21N 3.19E
97 H20 **Knøsen** hill N Denmark 57.09N 10.15E
Knosós see Knossos
117 J25 **Knossos** Gk. Knosós. prehistoric site Kríti, Greece, E Mediterranean Sea 35.17N 25.10E
27 N7 **Knott** Texas, SW USA 32.21N 101.35W
204 K5 **Knowles, Cape** headland Antarctica 71.45S 60.19W
33 O11 **Knox** Indiana, N USA 41.16N 86.37W
31 O3 **Knox** North Dakota, N USA 48.19N 99.43W
20 C13 **Knox** Pennsylvania, NE USA 41.13N 79.33W
201 X8 **Knox Atoll** var. Ņadikdik, Narikrik. atoll Ratak Chain, SE Marshall Islands
8 H13 **Knox, Cape** headland Graham Island, British Columbia, SW Canada 54.05N 133.02W
27 P5 **Knox City** Texas, SW USA 33.25N 99.49W
205 Y11 **Knox Coast** physical region Antarctica
33 T12 **Knox Lake** ⊠ Ohio, N USA
25 T5 **Knoxville** Georgia, SE USA 32.44N 83.58W
32 K12 **Knoxville** Illinois, N USA 40.54N 90.16W
31 W15 **Knoxville** Iowa, C USA 41.19N 93.06W
23 N9 **Knoxville** Tennessee, S USA 35.57N 83.55W
207 P11 **Knud Rasmussen Land** physical region N Greenland
Knüll see Knüllgebirge
103 I16 **Knüllgebirge** var. Knüll. ▲▲ C Germany
Knyazhevo see Sredishte
Knyazhitsy see Knyazhytsy
121 O15 **Knyazhytsy** Rus. Knyazhitsy. Mahilyowskaya Voblasts', E Belarus 54.10N 30.27E
85 G26 **Knysna** Western Cape, SW South Africa 34.01S 23.05E
176 V10 **Koagas** Papua, E Indonesia 2.40S 132.16E
Koartac see Quaqtaq
174 J10 **Koba** Pulau Bangka, W Indonesia 2.29S 106.22E
170 C16 **Kobayashi** var. Kobayasi. Miyazaki, Kyūshū, SW Japan 32.01N 130.55E
Kobayasi see Kobayashi
171 Gg14 **Kōbe** Hyōgo, Honshū, SW Japan 34.39N 135.10E
Kobelyaki see Kobelyaky
119 T6 **Kobelyaky** Rus. Kobelyaki. Poltavs'ka Oblast', NE Ukraine 49.10N 34.13E
97 J22 **København** Eng. Copenhagen; anc. Hafnia. ● (Denmark) Sjælland, København, E Denmark 55.43N 12.34E
97 J23 **København** off. Københavns Amt. ◈ county E Denmark
78 K10 **Kobenni** Hodh el Gharbi, S Mauritania 15.58N 9.24W
176 U11 **Kobi** Pulau Seram, E Indonesia 2.56S 129.53E
103 F17 **Koblenz** prev. Coblenz, Fr. Coblence, anc. Confluentes. Rheinland-Pfalz, W Germany 50.21N 7.36E

110 F6 **Koblenz** Aargau, N Switzerland 47.34N 8.16E
176 Ww11 **Kobowre, Pegunungan** ▲▲ Papua, E Indonesia
128 J14 **Kobozha** Novgorodskaya Oblast', W Russian Federation 58.48N 35.00E
Kobrin see Kobryn
176 W14 **Kobroor, Pulau** island Kepulauan Aru, E Indonesia
121 G19 **Kobryn** Pol. Kobryn, Rus. Kobrin. Brestskaya Voblasts', SW Belarus 52.13N 24.21E
41 O7 **Kobuk** Alaska, USA 66.54N 156.52W
41 O7 **Kobuk River** ∽ Alaska, USA
143 Q10 **K'obulet'i** W Georgia 41.47N 41.46E
126 Ll10 **Kobyay** Respublika Sakha (Yakutiya), NE Russian Federation 63.36N 126.33E
142 E11 **Kocaeli** ❖ province NW Turkey
115 P18 **Kočani** NE FYR Macedonia 41.55N 22.25E
114 K12 **Koceljevo** Serbia, W Serbia and Montenegro (Yugoslavia) 44.28N 19.49E
111 U12 **Kočevje** Ger. Gottschee. S Slovenia 45.41N 14.47E
159 T12 **Koch Bihār** West Bengal, NE India 26.19N 89.25E
126 J10 **Kochechum** ∽ N Russian Federation
103 I20 **Kocher** ∽ SW Germany
129 T13 **Kochevo** Komi-Permyatskiy Avtonomnyy Okrug, NW Russian Federation 59.37N 54.16E
170 Ee15 **Kōchi** var. Kôti. Kōchi, Shikoku, SW Japan 33.31N 133.30E
170 Ee15 **Kōchi** off. Kōchi-ken, var. Kôti. ❖ prefecture Shikoku, SW Japan
Kochi see Cochin
Kochiu see Gejiu
Kochkor see Kochkorka
153 V8 **Kochkorka** Kir. Kochkor. Narynskaya Oblast', C Kyrgyzstan 42.09N 75.42E
129 V5 **Kochmes** Respublika Komi, NW Russian Federation 66.10N 60.46E
131 P15 **Kochubey** Respublika Dagestan, SW Russian Federation 44.25N 46.33E
117 I17 **Kochýlas** ▲ Skýros, Vóreioi Sporádes, Greece, Aegean Sea 38.50N 24.35E
112 O13 **Kock** Lubelskie, E Poland 51.39N 22.26E
83 J19 **Kodacho** spring/well S Kenya 1.52S 39.22E
161 K24 **Koddiyar Bay** bay NE Sri Lanka
41 Q14 **Kodiak** Kodiak Island, Alaska, USA 57.47N 152.24W
41 Q14 **Kodiak Island** island Alaska, USA
160 B12 **Kodīnār** Gujarāt, W India 20.43N 70.46E
128 M9 **Kodino** Arkhangel'skaya Oblast', NW Russian Federation 63.36N 39.54E
126 Ii13 **Kodinsk** Krasnoyarskiy Kray, C Russian Federation 58.37N 99.18E
82 F12 **Kodok** Upper Nile, SE Sudan 9.51N 32.07E
119 N8 **Kodyma** Odes'ka Oblast', SW Ukraine 48.05N 29.09E
101 B17 **Koekelare** West-Vlaanderen, W Belgium 51.07N 2.58E
Koeln see Köln
Koepang see Kupang
Ko-erh-mu see Golmud
101 J17 **Koersel** Limburg, NE Belgium 51.04N 5.17E
85 E21 **Koës** Karas, SE Namibia 25.57S 19.04E
Koetai see Mahakam, Sungai
Koetaradja see Bandaaceh
38 I14 **Kofa Mountains** ▲▲ Arizona, SW USA
176 Z15 **Kofarau** Papua, E Indonesia 7.29S 140.28E
153 P13 **Kofarnihon** Rus. Kofarnikhon; prev. Ordzhonikidzeabad, Taj. Orjonikidzeobod, Yangi-Bazar. W Tajikistan 38.32N 68.56E
153 P14 **Kofarnihon** Rus. Kafirnigan. ∽ SW Tajikistan
Kofarnikhon see Kofarnihon
116 M11 **Kofçaz** Kırklareli, NW Turkey 41.57N 27.07E
176 U9 **Kofiau, Pulau** var. Kafiau. island Kepulauan Raja Ampat, E Indonesia
117 J25 **Kófinas** ▲ Kríti, Greece, E Mediterranean Sea 34.58N 25.03E
124 Nn4 **Kofinou** var. Kophinou. S Cyprus 34.49N 33.24E
111 V8 **Köflach** Steiermark, SE Austria 47.04N 15.04E
79 Q17 **Koforidua** SE Ghana 6.04N 0.17W
170 Ff12 **Kōfu** Tottori, Honshū, SW Japan 35.16N 133.31E
171 J15 **Kōfu** var. Kôhu. Yamanashi, Honshū, S Japan 35.40N 138.33E
171 K16 **Koga** Ibaraki, Honshū, S Japan 36.12N 139.42E
83 F22 **Koga** Tabora, C Tanzania 6.08S 32.20E
Kogălniceanu see Mihail Kogălniceanu
11 P6 **Kogaluk** ∽ Newfoundland and Labrador, E Canada
10 J4 **Kogaluk** ∽ Quebec, NE Canada
126 Gg10 **Kogalym** Khanty-Mansiyskiy Avtonomnyy Okrug, C Russian Federation 62.13N 74.34E
97 J23 **Køge** Roskilde, E Denmark 55.28N 12.12E
97 J23 **Køge Bugt** bay E Denmark
79 U16 **Kogi** ❖ state C Nigeria
152 L11 **Kogon** Rus. Kagan. Buxoro Viloyati, C Uzbekistan 39.46N 64.28E
169 Y17 **Kōgūm-do** island S South Korea
Kōhalom see Rupea
155 T6 **Kohāt** North-West Frontier Province, NW Pakistan 33.37N 71.30E
120 G4 **Kohila** Ger. Koil. Raplamaa, NW Estonia 59.07N 24.45E
159 X13 **Kohīma** Nāgāland, E India 25.40N 94.07E
Koh I Noh see Büyükağrı Dağı
148 L10 **Kohkīlūyeh va Būyer Aḩmadī** off. Ostān-e Kohkīlūyeh va Būyer Aḩmadī, var. Boyer Ahmadī va Kohkīlūyeh. ❖ province SW Iran
Kohsān see Kūhestān
120 J3 **Kohtla-Järve** Ida-Virumaa, NE Estonia 59.22N 27.21E
Kōhu see Kōfu
119 N10 **Kohyl'nyk** Rom. Cogîlnic. ∽ Moldova/Ukraine
171 K13 **Koide** Niigata, Honshū, C Japan 37.13N 138.58E
8 G7 **Koidern** Yukon Territory, W Canada 61.55N 140.22W
78 J15 **Koidu** E Sierra Leone 8.39N 11.01W
120 I4 **Koigi** Järvamaa, C Estonia 58.51N 25.45E
Koil see Kohila
180 H13 **Koimbani** Grande Comore, NW Comoros 11.37S 43.22E
145 T3 **Koi Sanjaq** var. Koysanjaq, Küysanjaq. N Iraq 36.04N 44.37E
95 O16 **Koitere** ◎ E Finland
Koivisto see Primorsk
169 Z16 **Kōje-do** Jap. Kyōsai-tō. island S South Korea
82 J13 **K'ok'a Hāyk'** ◎ C Ethiopia
Kokand see Qo'qon
190 F6 **Kokatha** South Australia 31.17S 135.16E
Kokcha see Ko'kcha
152 M10 **Ko'kcha** Rus. Kokcha. Buxoro Viloyati, C Uzbekistan 40.30N 64.58E
Kokchetav see Kokshetau
95 K18 **Kokemäenjoki** ∽ SW Finland
176 X12 **Kokenau** var. Kokonau. Papua, E Indonesia 4.38S 136.24E
85 E22 **Kokerboom** Karas, SE Namibia 28.10S 19.25E
121 N14 **Kokhanava** Rus. Kokhanovo. Vitsyebskaya Voblasts', NE Belarus 54.28N 29.58E
Kokhanovichi see Kakhanavichy
Kokhanovo see Kokhanava
Kök-Janggak see Kok-Yangak
95 K16 **Kokkola** Swe. Karleby; prev. Swe. Gamlakarleby. Länsi-Suomi, W Finland 63.49N 23.10E
164 L3 **Kok Kuduk** well N China 46.03N 87.34E
120 H9 **Koknese** Aizkraukle, C Latvia 56.38N 25.27E
79 T13 **Koko** Kebbi, W Nigeria 11.25N 4.33E
194 K15 **Kokoda** Northern, S PNG 8.51S 147.37E
78 K12 **Kokofata** Kayes, W Mali 12.48N 9.56W
41 N6 **Kokolik River** ∽ Alaska, USA
33 O13 **Kokomo** Indiana, N USA 40.29N 86.07W
Kokonau see Kokenau
Koko Nor see Qinghai Hu, China
Koko Nor see Qinghai, China
195 P10 **Kokopo** var. Kopopo; prev. Herbertshöhe. New Britain, E PNG 4.19S 152.13E
151 X10 **Kokpekti** Kaz. Kökpekti. Vostochnyy Kazakhstan, E Kazakhstan 48.45N 82.24E
151 X11 **Kokpekti** ∽ E Kazakhstan
41 P9 **Kokrines** Alaska, USA 64.57N 154.42W
41 P9 **Kokrines Hills** ▲▲ Alaska, USA
151 P17 **Koksaray** Yuzhnyy Kazakhstan, S Kazakhstan 42.40N 68.09E
153 X9 **Kokshaal-Tau** Rus. Khrebet Kakshaal-Too. ▲▲ China/Kyrgyzstan
151 P7 **Kokshetau** Kaz. Kökshetaū; prev. Kokchetav. Akmola, N Kazakhstan 53.18N 69.25E
101 A17 **Koksijde** West-Vlaanderen, W Belgium 51.07N 2.39E
10 M5 **Koksoak** ∽ Quebec, E Canada
85 K24 **Kokstad** KwaZulu/Natal, E South Africa 30.23S 29.22E
151 W15 **Koktal** Kaz. Köktal. Almaty, SE Kazakhstan 44.04N 79.43E
151 Q12 **Koktas** ∽ C Kazakhstan
Kök-Tash see Kek-Tash
Koktokay see Fuyun
170 C16 **Kokubu** Kagoshima, Kyūshū, SW Japan 31.44N 130.44E
126 L15 **Kokuy** Chitinskaya Oblast', S Russian Federation 52.13N 117.18E
153 T9 **Kok-Yangak** Kir. Kök-Janggak. Dzhalal-Abadskaya Oblast', W Kyrgyzstan 41.02N 73.11E
164 F9 **Kokyar** Xinjiang Uygur Zizhiqu, W China 37.24N 77.15E
155 O13 **Kolāchi** var. Kulachi. ∽ SW Pakistan
78 J15 **Kolahun** N Liberia 8.24N 10.01W
175 Q12 **Kolaka** Sulawesi, C Indonesia 4.04S 121.37E
Kolam see Quilon
K'o-la-ma-i see Karamay
Kola Peninsula see Kol'skiy Poluostrov
161 H19 **Kolār** Karnātaka, E India 13.10N 78.10E
161 H19 **Kolār Gold Fields** Karnātaka, E India 12.56N 78.16E
94 K11 **Kolari** Lappi, NW Finland 67.19N 23.51E
113 I21 **Kolárovo** Ger. Gutta; prev. Guta, Hung. Gúta. Nitriansky Kraj, SW Slovakia 47.54N 18.00E
115 K16 **Kolašin** Montenegro, SW Serbia and Montenegro (Yugoslavia) 42.49N 19.32E
158 F11 **Kolāyat** Rājasthān, NW India 27.55N 73.01E
97 N15 **Kolbäck** Västmanland, C Sweden 59.33N 16.15E
Kolbcha see Kowbcha
207 Q15 **Kolbeinsey Ridge** undersea feature Denmark Strait/Norwegian Sea
Kolberg see Kołobrzeg
97 H15 **Kolbotn** Akershus, S Norway 62.15N 10.24E
113 N16 **Kolbuszowa** Podkarpackie, SE Poland 50.12N 22.07E
130 L3 **Kol'chugino** Vladimirskaya Oblast', W Russian Federation 56.19N 39.24E
78 H12 **Kolda** S Senegal 12.58N 14.58W
97 G23 **Kolding** Vejle, C Denmark 55.28N 9.30E
81 M17 **Kole** Orientale, N Dem. Rep. Congo 2.09N 25.17E
81 K20 **Kole** Kasai Oriental, SW Dem. Rep. Congo 3.27S 22.28E
Kōle see Kili Island
86 F6 **Kölen** Nor. Kjølen. ▲▲ Norway/Sweden
Kolepom, Pulau see Yos Sudarso, Pulau
120 H3 **Kolga Laht** Ger. Kolko-Wiek. bay N Estonia
129 Q3 **Kolguyev, Ostrov** island NW Russian Federation
161 E16 **Kolhāpur** Mahārāshtra, SW India 16.42N 74.13E
157 K21 **Kolhumadulu Atoll** var. Kolumadulu Atoll, Thaa Atoll. atoll S Maldives
95 O16 **Koli** var. Kolinkylä. Itä-Suomi, E Finland 63.06N 29.45E
41 O13 **Koliganek** Alaska, USA 59.43N 157.16W
113 E16 **Kolín** Ger. Kolin. Středočeský Kraj, C Czech Republic 50.01N 15.10E
Kolinkylä see Koli
202 E12 **Koliu** Île Futuna, W Wallis and Futuna
120 E7 **Kolka** Talsi, NW Latvia 57.43N 22.33E
120 E7 **Kolkasrags** prev. Eng. Cape Domesnes. headland NW Latvia 57.45N 22.35E
Kolkata see Calcutta
Kolkhozabad see Kolkhozobod
153 P14 **Kolkhozobod** Rus. Kolkhozabad; prev. Kaganovichabad, Tugalan. SW Tajikistan 37.33N 68.34E
Kolki/Kołki see Kolky
Kolko-Wiek see Kolga Laht
118 K3 **Kolky** Pol. Kołki, Rus. Kolki. Volyns'ka Oblast', NW Ukraine 51.05N 25.40E
Kollam see Quilon
161 G20 **Kollegāl** Karnātaka, W India 12.07N 77.06E
100 M5 **Kollum** Friesland, N Netherlands 53.16N 6.09E
Kolmar see Colmar
103 E16 **Köln** var. Koeln, Eng./Fr. Cologne; prev. Cöln, anc. Colonia Agrippina, Oppidum Ubiorum. Nordrhein-Westfalen, W Germany 50.57N 6.57E
112 N9 **Kolno** Podlaskie, NE Poland 53.24N 21.57E
112 J12 **Koło** Wielkopolskie, C Poland 52.10N 18.39E
40 B8 **Koloa** Haw. Kōloa. Kauai, Hawaii, USA, C Pacific Ocean 21.54N 159.28W
112 E7 **Kołobrzeg** Ger. Kolberg. Zachodniopomorskie, NW Poland 54.10N 15.33E
130 H4 **Kolodnya** Smolenskaya Oblast', W Russian Federation 54.57N 32.22E
202 E13 **Kolofau, Mont** Ѫ Île Alofi, S Wallis and Futuna 14.21S 178.01W
129 O14 **Kologriv** Kostromskaya Oblast', NW Russian Federation 58.49N 44.22E
78 L12 **Kolokani** Koulikoro, W Mali 13.34N 8.01W
79 N13 **Koloko** W Burkina 11.06N 5.18W
195 U14 **Kolombangara** var. Kilimbangara, Nduke. island New Georgia Islands, NW Solomon Islands
Kolomea see Kolomyya
130 L4 **Kolomna** Moskovskaya Oblast', W Russian Federation 55.02N 38.52E
118 J7 **Kolomyya** Ger. Kolomea. Ivano-Frankivs'ka Oblast', W Ukraine 48.31N 25.00E
78 M13 **Kolondiéba** Sikasso, SW Mali 11.04N 6.55W
200 R15 **Kolonga** Tongatapu, S Tonga 21.07S 175.04W
201 U16 **Kolonia** var. Colonia. Pohnpei, E Micronesia 6.57N 158.12E
Kolonja see Kolonjë
115 K21 **Kolonjë** var. Kolonja. Fier, C Albania 40.49N 19.37E
Kolonjë see Ersekë
Kolotambu see Avuavu
200 Q15 **Kolovai** Tongatapu, S Tonga 21.05S 175.20W
175 R13 **Kolowanawatobo, Teluk** bay Pulau Buton, C Indonesia
Kolozsvár see Cluj-Napoca
164 C9 **Kolpa** Ger. Kulpa, SCr. Kupa. ∽ Croatia/Slovenia
126 H12 **Kolpashevo** Tomskaya Oblast', C Russian Federation 58.21N 82.44E
128 H13 **Kolpino** Leningradskaya Oblast', NW Russian Federation 59.43N 30.39E
102 M10 **Kölpinsee** ◎ NE Germany
152 K8 **Ko'lquduq** Rus. Kulkuduk. Navoiy Viloyati, N Uzbekistan 42.36N 63.24E
128 K5 **Kol'skiy Poluostrov** Eng. Kola Peninsula. peninsula NW Russian Federation
131 T6 **Koltubanovskiy** Orenburgskaya Oblast', W Russian Federation 53.00N 52.00E
114 L11 **Kolubara** ∽ C Serbia and Montenegro (Yugoslavia)
Kolupchii see Gurkovo
112 K13 **Koluszki** Łodzkie, C Poland 51.43N 19.49E
129 T6 **Kolva** ∽ NW Russian Federation
95 E14 **Kolvereid** Nord-Trøndelag, W Norway 64.47N 11.22E
154 L15 **Kolwa** Balūchistān, SW Pakistan 26.03N 64.00E
81 M24 **Kolwezi** Katanga, S Dem. Rep. Congo 10.43S 25.29E
127 Nn7 **Kolyma** ∽ NE Russian Federation
Kolyma Lowland see Kolymskaya Nizmennost'
Kolyma Range/Kolymskiy, Khrebet see Kolymskoye Nagor'ye
127 Nn6 **Kolymskaya Nizmennost'** Eng. Kolyma Lowland. lowlands NE Russian Federation
127 Nn6 **Kolymskoye** Respublika Sakha (Yakutiya), NE Russian Federation 68.42N 158.46E
127 N17 **Kolymskoye Nagor'ye** var. Khrebet Kolymskiy, Eng. Kolyma Range. ▲▲ E Russian Federation
127 N17 **Kolyuchinskaya Guba** bay NE Russian Federation
151 W15 **Kol'zhat** Almaty, SE Kazakhstan 43.30N 80.37E
116 G8 **Kom** ▲ NW Bulgaria 43.10N 23.02E
82 I13 **Koma** Oromo, C Ethiopia 8.19N 36.48E
79 X12 **Komadugu Gana** ∽ NE Nigeria
171 Ii15 **Komagane** Nagano, Honshū, S Japan 35.46N 137.56E
81 P17 **Komanda** Orientale, NE Dem. Rep. Congo 1.23N 29.44E
207 U1 **Komandorskaya Basin** var. Kamchatka Basin. undersea feature SW Bering Sea
129 Pp9 **Komandorskiye Ostrova** Eng. Commander Islands. island group E Russian Federation
Komanfalva see Comănești
113 I22 **Komárno** Ger. Komorn, Hung. Komárom. Nitriansky Kraj, SW Slovakia 47.46N 18.07E
113 I22 **Komárom** Komárom-Esztergom, NW Hungary 47.44N 18.06E
Komárom see Komárno
113 I22 **Komárom-Esztergom** off. Komárom-Esztergom Megye. ❖ county N Hungary
171 I13 **Komatsu** var. Komatu. Ishikawa, Honshū, SW Japan 36.24N 136.27E
170 Ff15 **Komatsushima** Tokushima, Shikoku, SW Japan 34.00N 134.36E
Komatu see Komatsu
85 D17 **Kombat** Otjozondjupa, N Namibia 19.42S 17.45E
Kombissiguiri see Kombissiri
79 P13 **Kombissiri** var. Kombissiguiri. C Burkina 12.03N 1.14W
196 E10 **Komebail Lagoon** lagoon N Palau
83 F20 **Kome Island** island N Tanzania
Komeyo see Wandai
176 W13 **Komfane** Pulau Wokam, E Indonesia 5.36S 134.42E
119 P10 **Kominternivs'ke** Odes'ka Oblast', SW Ukraine 46.52N 30.56E
129 R12 **Komi-Permyatskiy Avtonomnyy Okrug** ❖ autonomous district W Russian Federation
129 R8 **Komi, Respublika** ❖ autonomous republic NW Russian Federation
113 I25 **Komló** Baranya, SW Hungary 46.11N 18.19E
Kommunarsk see Alchevs'k
153 S12 **Kommunizm, Qullai** ▲ E Tajikistan
194 G12 **Komo** Southern Highlands, W PNG 6.06S 142.52E
175 P16 **Komodo** Pulau Komodo, S Indonesia 8.35S 119.27E
175 P16 **Komodo, Pulau** island Nusa Tenggara, S Indonesia
79 N15 **Komoé** var. Komoé Fleuve. ∽ E Ivory Coast
Komoé Fleuve see Komoé
77 X11 **Kôm Ombo** var. Kawm Umbū. SE Egypt 24.23N 32.58E
81 F20 **Komono** La Lékoumou, SW Congo 3.15S 13.13E
176 Y16 **Komoran** Papua, E Indonesia 8.14S 138.51E
176 Y16 **Komoran, Pulau** island E Indonesia
Komorn see Komárno
Komornok see Comoraște
171 J14 **Komoro** Nagano, Honshū, S Japan 36.22N 138.25E
Komosolabad see Komsomolobod
Komotau see Chomutov
116 K13 **Komotiní** var. Gümüljina, Turk. Gümülcine. Anatolikí Makedonía kai Thráki, NE Greece 41.06N 25.27E
115 K16 **Komovi** ▲ SW Serbia and Montenegro (Yugoslavia)
119 R8 **Kompaniyivka** Kirovohrads'ka Oblast', C Ukraine 48.16N 32.12E
194 H12 **Kompiam** Enga, W PNG 5.23S 143.54E
Kompong see Kâmpóng Chhnăng
Kompong Cham see Kâmpóng Cham
Kompong Kleang see Kâmpóng Khleăng
Kompong Som see Kâmpóng Saôm
Kompong Speu see Kâmpóng Spoe
Komrat see Comrat
Komsomol see Komsomol'skiy, Atyrau, Kazakhstan
Komsomol see Karabalyk
Komsomolets see Karabalyk
126 Ii2 **Komsomolets, Ostrov** island Severnaya Zemlya, N Russian Federation
150 F13 **Komsomolets, Zaliv** lake gulf SW Kazakhstan
153 Q12 **Komsomolobod** Rus. Komosolabad. C Tajikistan 38.51N 69.54E
128 M16 **Komsomol'sk** Ivanovskaya Oblast', W Russian Federation 56.58N 40.15E
119 S6 **Komsomol's'k** Poltavs'ka Oblast', C Ukraine 49.01N 33.37E
152 M11 **Komsomol'sk** Navoiy Viloyati, N Uzbekistan 40.14N 65.10E
150 G12 **Komsomol'skiy** Kaz. Komsomol. Atyrau, W Kazakhstan 47.18N 53.37E
129 W4 **Komsomol'skiy** Respublika Komi, NW Russian Federation 67.33N 64.00E
127 Nn15 **Komsomol'sk-na-Amure** Khabarovskiy Kray, SE Russian Federation 50.31N 136.58E
Komsomol'sk-na-Ustyurte see Kubla-Ustyurt
150 K10 **Komsomol'skoye** Aktyubinsk, NW Kazakhstan
131 Q8 **Komsomol'skoye** Saratovskaya Oblast', W Russian Federation 50.45N 47.00E
151 P10 **Kon** ∽ C Kazakhstan
Kona see Kailua
128 K16 **Konakovo** Tverskaya Oblast', W Russian Federation 56.42N 36.44E
149 V15 **Konārak** Sīstān va Balūchestān, SE Iran 25.26N 60.22E
Konarhā see Kunar
29 O11 **Konawa** Oklahoma, C USA 34.57N 96.45W
176 V9 **Konda** Papua, E Indonesia 1.34S 131.58E
125 Ff11 **Konda** ∽ C Russian Federation
160 L13 **Kondagaon** Madhya Pradesh, C India 19.38N 81.41E
12 K10 **Kondiaronk, Lac** ◎ Quebec, SE Canada
188 J13 **Kondinin** Western Australia 32.31S 118.15E
83 H21 **Kondoa** Dodoma, C Tanzania 4.54S 35.46E
131 P6 **Kondol'** Penzenskaya Oblast', W Russian Federation 52.49N 45.03E
116 N10 **Kondolovo** Burgas, E Bulgaria 42.07N 27.43E
176 Z16 **Kondomirat** Papua, E Indonesia 8.57S 140.55E
128 J10 **Kondopoga** Respublika Kareliya, NW Russian Federation 62.12N 34.16E
Kondoz see Kunduz
161 J17 **Kondukūr** var. Kandukur. Andhra Pradesh, E India 15.17N 79.49E
Kondūz see Kunduz
197 H6 **Koné** Province Nord, W New Caledonia 21.04S 164.51E
Könekesir see Kënekesir
Köneürgench see Këneurgench
79 N15 **Kong** N Ivory Coast 9.06N 4.34W
41 S5 **Kongakut River** ∽ Alaska, USA
207 O14 **Kong Christian IX Land** Eng. King Christian IX Land. physical region SE Greenland
207 P13 **Kong Christian X Land** Eng. King Christian X Land. physical region E Greenland
207 N13 **Kong Frederik IX Land** Eng. King Frederik IX Land. physical region SW Greenland
207 Q12 **Kong Frederik VIII Land** Eng. King Frederik VIII Land. physical region NE Greenland
207 N15 **Kong Frederik VI Kyst** Eng. King Frederik VI Coast. physical region SE Greenland
178 I13 **Kõng, Kaôh** prev. Kas Kong. island SW Cambodia
94 P2 **Kong Karls Land** Eng. King Charles Islands. island group SE Svalbard
83 G14 **Kong Kong** ∽ SE Sudan
Kongo see Congo (river)
85 G16 **Kongola** Caprivi, NE Namibia 17.47S 23.24E
81 N21 **Kongolo** Katanga, E Dem. Rep. Congo 5.20S 26.57E
83 F14 **Kongor** Jonglei, SE Sudan 7.09N 31.44E
207 Q14 **Kong Oscar Fjord** fjord E Greenland
79 P12 **Kongoussi** N Burkina 13.19N 1.31W
97 G15 **Kongsberg** Buskerud, S Norway 59.39N 9.37E
94 Q2 **Kongsøya** island Kong Karls Land, E Svalbard
97 I14 **Kongsvinger** Hedmark, S Norway 60.10N 12.00E
178 Jj11 **Kông, Tônle** Lao. Xê Kong. ∽ Cambodia/Laos
164 E8 **Kongur Shan** ▲ NW China 38.39N 75.21E
83 I22 **Kongwa** Dodoma, C Tanzania 6.13S 36.28E
Kong, Xê see Kông, Tônle
Konia see Konya
153 R11 **Konibodom** Rus. Kanibadam. N Tajikistan 40.16N 70.20E
113 K15 **Koniecpol** Śląskie, S Poland 50.47N 19.45E
Konieh see Konya
Königgrätz see Hradec Králové
Königinhof an der Elbe see Dvůr Králové nad Labem
103 K23 **Königsbrunn** Bayern, S Germany 48.16N 10.52E
Königshütte see Chorzów
103 O24 **Königssee** ◎ SE Germany
111 S8 **Königstuhl** ▲ S Austria 46.57N 13.47E
111 U3 **Königswiesen** Oberösterreich, N Austria 48.25N 14.48E
103 E17 **Königswinter** Nordrhein-Westfalen, W Germany 50.40N 7.12E
152 M11 **Konimex** Rus. Kenimekh. Navoiy Viloyati, N Uzbekistan 40.14N 65.10E
112 I12 **Konin** Ger. Kuhnau. Wielkopolskie, C Poland 52.13N 18.16E
Koninkrijk der Nederlanden see Netherlands
115 L24 **Konispol** var. Konispoli. Vlorë, S Albania 39.40N 20.10E
Konispoli see Konispol
117 C15 **Kónitsa** Ípeiros, W Greece 40.04N 20.48E
Konitz see Chojnice
110 D8 **Köniz** Bern, W Switzerland 46.55N 7.26E
115 H14 **Konjic** Federacija Bosna I Hercegovina, C Bosnia and Herzegovina 43.39N 17.55E
94 J10 **Könkämäälven** ∽ Finland/Sweden
161 D14 **Konkan** W India
85 D22 **Konkiep** ∽ S Namibia
78 I14 **Konkouré** ∽ W Guinea
79 O11 **Konna** Mopti, S Mali 14.58N 3.49W
195 P10 **Konogaiang, Mount** ▲ New Ireland, NE PNG 4.05S 152.43E
195 P10 **Konogogo** New Ireland, NE PNG 3.25S 152.09E
110 E9 **Konolfingen** Bern, W Switzerland 46.53N 7.36E
79 P16 **Konongo** C Ghana 6.39N 1.06W
195 O9 **Konos** New Ireland, NE PNG 3.07S 151.43E
128 M12 **Konosha** Arkhangel'skaya Oblast', NW Russian Federation 60.58N 40.09E
119 R3 **Konotop** Sums'ka Oblast', NE Ukraine 51.15N 33.13E
164 L7 **Konqi He** ∽ NW China
113 L14 **Końskie** Świętokrzyskie, C Poland 51.12N 20.26E
Konstantinovka see Kostyantynivka
130 M11 **Konstantinovsk** Rostovskaya Oblast', SW Russian Federation 47.37N 41.07E
103 H24 **Konstanz** var. Constanz, Eng. Constance; hist. Kostnitz, anc. Constantia. Baden-Württemberg, S Germany 47.40N 9.10E
Konstanza see Constanța
79 T14 **Kontagora** Niger, W Nigeria 10.25N 5.29E
80 E13 **Kontcha** Nord, N Cameroon 8.00N 12.13E
101 G17 **Kontich** Antwerpen, N Belgium 51.07N 4.27E
95 O16 **Kontiolahti** Itä-Suomi, E Finland 62.46N 29.51E
95 M15 **Kontiomäki** Oulu, C Finland 64.20N 28.09E
178 K11 **Kon Tum** var. Kontum. Kon Tum, C Vietnam 14.23N 108.00E
Konur see Sulakyurt
142 H15 **Konya** var. Konieh; prev. Konia, anc. Iconium. Konya, C Turkey 37.51N 32.30E
142 H15 **Konya** var. Konia, Konieh. ❖ province C Turkey
151 T13 **Konyrat** var. Kounradskiy, Kaz. Qongyrat. Karaganda, C Kazakhstan 46.58N 74.54E
151 W15 **Konyrolen** Almaty, SE Kazakhstan 44.16N 79.18E
83 I19 **Konza** Eastern, S Kenya 1.44S 37.07E
100 I9 **Koog aan den Zaan** Noord-Holland, C Netherlands 52.28N 4.49E
190 E7 **Koonibba** South Australia 31.55S 133.23E
33 O11 **Koontz Lake** Indiana, N USA 41.25N 86.24W
176 V8 **Koor** Papua, E Indonesia 0.21S 132.28E
191 R9 **Koorawatha** New South Wales, SE Australia 34.03S 148.33E
120 J5 **Koosa** Tartumaa, E Estonia 58.31N 27.06E
35 N7 **Kootenai** var. Kootenay. ∽ Canada/USA see also Kootenay
9 P17 **Kootenay** var. Kootenai. ∽ Canada/USA see also Kootenai
85 F24 **Kootjieskolk** Northern Cape, W South Africa 31.16S 20.21E
115 M15 **Kopaonik** ▲▲ S Serbia and Montenegro (Yugoslavia)
Kopar see Koper
94 K1 **Kópasker** Nordhurland Eystra, N Iceland 66.15N 16.23W
94 H4 **Kópavogur** Reykjanes, W Iceland 64.06N 21.47W
151 U13 **Kopbirlick** Kaz. Kīrov, prev. Kirova. Almaty, SE Kazakhstan 46.24N 77.16E
111 S13 **Koper** It. Capodistria; prev. Kopar. SW Slovenia 45.32N 13.42E
97 C16 **Kopervik** Rogaland, S Norway 59.16N 5.18E
Kopetdag, Khrebet see Koppeh Dāgh
125 Ee12 **Kopeysk** Kurganskaya Oblast', C Russian Federation 55.06N 61.31E
Kophinou see Kofinou
190 G8 **Kopi** South Australia 33.24S 135.40E
Kopiago see Lake Copiago
159 W12 **Kopili** ∽ NE India
97 M15 **Köping** Västmanland, C Sweden 59.31N 16.00E
115 K17 **Koplik** var. Kopliku. Shkodër, NW Albania 42.12N 19.26E
Kopliku see Koplik
Kopopo see Kokopo
96 I11 **Koppang** Hedmark, S Norway 61.34N 11.01E
Kopparberg see Dalarna
149 S3 **Koppeh Dāgh** var. Khrebet Kopetdag. ▲▲ Iran/Turkmenistan
Koppename see Coppename Rivier
97 J15 **Koppom** Värmland, C Sweden 59.42N 12.07E
Kopreinitz see Koprivnica
116 K9 **Koprinka, Yazovir** prev. Yazovir Georgi Dimitrov. ⊠ C Bulgaria
114 F7 **Koprivnica** Ger. Kopreinitz, Hung. Kaproncza. Koprivnica-Križevci, N Croatia 46.10N 16.49E
114 F8 **Koprivnica-Križevci** off. Koprivničko-Križevačka Županija. ❖ province N Croatia
113 I17 **Kopřivnice** Ger. Nesselsdorf. Ostravský Kraj, E Czech Republic 49.36N 18.09E
Köprülü see Veles
Koptsevichi see Kaptsevichy
Kopyl' see Kapyl'
121 O14 **Kopys'** Rus. Kopys'. Vitsyebskaya Voblasts', NE Belarus 54.21N 30.21E
115 M18 **Korab** ▲ Albania/FYR Macedonia 41.48N 20.33E
Korabavur Pastligi see Karabaur', Uval
83 M14 **K'orahē** Somali, E Ethiopia 6.36N 44.21E
117 L16 **Kórakas, Akrotírio** headland Lésvos, E Greece 39.20N 26.20E
114 D9 **Korana** ∽ C Croatia
161 L14 **Korāput** Orissa, E India 18.49N 82.43E
Korat see Nakhon Ratchasima
178 Ii9 **Korat Plateau** plateau E Thailand
145 T1 **Korāwa, Sar-i** ▲ NE Iraq 37.07N 44.39E
160 L11 **Korba** Madhya Pradesh, C India 22.25N 82.43E
103 H15 **Korbach** Hessen, C Germany 51.16N 8.52E
Korça see Korçë
115 M21 **Korçë** var. Korça, Gk. Korytsa, It. Corrizza; prev. Koritsa. Korçë, SE Albania 40.37N 20.46E
115 M21 **Korçë** ❖ district SE Albania
115 G15 **Korčula** It. Curzola. Dubrovnik-Neretva, S Croatia 42.57N 17.08E
115 F15 **Korčula** It. Curzola; anc. Corcyra Nigra. island S Croatia
115 F15 **Korčulanski Kanal** channel S Croatia
151 T6 **Korday** prev. Georgiyevka. Zhambyl, SE Kazakhstan 43.06N 74.42E
148 J5 **Kordestān** off. Ostān-e Kordestān, var. Kurdestan. ❖ province W Iran
149 P4 **Kord Kūy** var. Kurd Kui. Golestān, N Iran 36.49N 54.04E
169 V13 **Korea Bay** bay China/North Korea
Korea, Democratic People's Republic of see North Korea
176 Uu15 **Koreare** Pulau Yamdena, E Indonesia 7.33S 131.13E
Korea, Republic of see South Korea
169 Z17 **Korea Strait** Jap. Chōsen-kaikyō, Kor. Taehan-haehyŏp. channel Japan/South Korea
Korelichi/Korelicze see Karelichy
82 J11 **Korem** Tigray, N Ethiopia 12.32N 39.29E
79 U11 **Korén Adoua** ∽ C Niger
130 J7 **Korenevo** Kurskaya Oblast', W Russian Federation 51.21N 34.53E
130 L13 **Korenovsk** Krasnodarskiy Kray, SW Russian Federation 45.28N 39.25E
118 L4 **Korets'** Pol. Korzec, Rus. Korets. Rivnens'ka Oblast', NW Ukraine 50.38N 27.12E
127 Pp8 **Korf** Koryakskiy Avtonomnyy Okrug, E Russian Federation 60.20N 165.37E
204 L7 **Korff Ice Rise** ice cap Antarctica
151 Q10 **Korgalzhyn** var. Kurgal'dzhinsky, Kaz. Qorgazhyn. prev. Kurgal'dzhino. Akmola, C Kazakhstan 50.33N 69.58E
94 G13 **Korgen** Troms, N Norway 66.04N 13.51E
153 R9 **Korgon-Dēbē** Dzhalal-Abadskaya Oblast', W Kyrgyzstan 41.51N 70.52E
78 M14 **Korhogo** N Ivory Coast 9.28N 5.38W
117 F19 **Korinthiakós Kólpos** Eng. Gulf of Corinth; anc. Corinthiacus Sinus. gulf C Greece
117 F19 **Kórinthos** Eng. Corinth; anc. Corinthus. Pelopónnisos, S Greece 37.55N 22.55E
115 M18 **Koritnik** ▲ S Serbia and Montenegro (Yugoslavia) 42.06N 20.34E
Koritsa see Korçë
171 L14 **Kōriyama** Fukushima, Honshū, C Japan 37.25N 140.20E
142 E16 **Korkuteli** Antalya, SW Turkey 37.04N 30.12E
164 K6 **Korla** Chin. K'u-erh-lo. Xinjiang Uygur Zizhiqu, NW China 41.48N 86.10E
126 H11 **Korliki** Khanty-Mansiyskiy Avtonomnyy Okrug, C Russian Federation 61.28N 82.12E
Körlin an der Persante see Karlino
Korma see Karma
12 D8 **Kormak** Ontario, S Canada 47.38N 83.00W
Kormakíti, Akrotíri/Kormakiti, Cape/Kormakítis see Koruçam Burnu
113 G23 **Körmend** Vas, W Hungary 47.01N 16.34E
145 T5 **Kōrmōr** E Iraq 35.06N 44.47E
114 C13 **Kornat** It. Incoronata. island W Croatia
Korneshty see Cornești
111 X3 **Korneuburg** Niederösterreich, NE Austria 48.22N 16.20E
151 P7 **Korneyevka** Severnyy Kazakhstan, N Kazakhstan 54.01N 68.30E
97 I17 **Kornsjø** Østfold, S Norway 58.55N 11.40E
79 O11 **Koro** Mopti, S Mali 14.05N 3.06W
197 J14 **Koro** island C Fiji
194 F12 **Koroba** Southern Highlands, W PNG 5.46S 142.48E
130 K8 **Korocha** Belgorodskaya Oblast', W Russian Federation 50.49N 37.08E
142 H12 **Köroğlu Dağları** ▲▲ C Turkey
191 V6 **Korogoro Point** headland New South Wales, SE Australia 31.03S 153.04E
83 J21 **Korogwe** Tanga, E Tanzania 5.12S 38.26E
190 L13 **Koroit** Victoria, SE Australia 38.17S 142.22E
197 H15 **Korolevu** Viti Levu, W Fiji 18.12S 177.44E
202 I17 **Koromiri** island S Cook Islands
179 R16 **Koronadal** Mindanao, S Philippines 6.23N 124.54E
117 E22 **Koróni** Pelopónnisos, S Greece 36.46N 21.57E
116 G13 **Korónia, Límni** ◎ N Greece
112 I9 **Koronowo** Ger. Krone an der Brahe. Kujawski-pomorskie, C Poland 53.18N 17.56E
119 R2 **Korop** Chernihivs'ka Oblast', N Ukraine 51.35N 32.57E
117 H19 **Koropí** Attikí, C Greece 37.54N 23.52E
Koror see Oreor
Kőrös see Križevci
113 L23 **Kőrös** ∽ E Hungary
Kőrösbánya see Baia de Criș
197 J14 **Koro Sea** sea C Fiji
Koroška see Kärnten
119 N3 **Korosten'** Zhytomyrs'ka Oblast', NW Ukraine 50.56N 28.39E
Korostyshev see Korostyshiv
119 N4 **Korostyshiv** Rus. Korostyshev. Zhytomyrs'ka Oblast', N Ukraine 50.18N 29.04E
129 V3 **Korotaikha** ∽ NW Russian Federation
126 H9 **Korotchayevo** Yamalo-Nenetskiy Avtonomnyy Okrug, N Russian Federation 66.00N 78.11E
80 I8 **Koro Toro** Borkou-Ennedi-Tibesti, N Chad 16.01N 18.27E
41 N16 **Korovin Island** island Shumagin Islands, Alaska, USA
197 I14 **Korovou** Viti Levu, W Fiji 17.48S 178.32E
95 M17 **Korpilahti** Länsi-Suomi, W Finland 62.01N 25.34E
94 K12 **Korpilombolo** Norrbotten, N Sweden 66.51N 23.00E

◆ Country ● Country Capital ◇ Dependent Territory ○ Dependent Territory Capital ❖ Administrative Region ✈ International Airport ▲ Mountain ▲▲ Mountain Range Ѫ Volcano ∽ River ◎ Lake ⊠ Reservoir

27 Oo16 **Korsakov** Ostrov Sakhalin, Sakhalinskaya Oblast', SE Russian Federation 46.41N 142.45E
95 J16 **Korsholm** *Fin.* Mustasaari. Länsi-Suomi, W Finland 63.07N 21.45E
97 I23 **Korsør** Vestsjælland, E Denmark 55.19N 11.09E
Korsovka *see* Kārsava
119 P6 **Korsun'-Shevchenkivs'kyy** *Rus.* Korsun'-Shevchenkovskiy. Cherkas'ka Oblast', C Ukraine 49.25N 31.15E
Korsun'-Shevchenkovskiy *see* Korsun'-Shevchenkivs'kyy
101 C17 **Kortemark** West-Vlaanderen, W Belgium 51.03N 3.03E
101 H18 **Kortenberg** Vlaams Brabant, C Belgium 50.52N 4.33E
101 K18 **Kortessem** Limburg, NE Belgium 50.52N 5.22E
101 E14 **Kortgene** Zeeland, SW Netherlands 51.34N 3.48E
82 F8 **Korti** Northern, N Sudan 18.06N 31.33E
101 C18 **Kortrijk** *Fr.* Courtrai. West-Vlaanderen, W Belgium 50.49N 3.16E
124 N2 **Koruçam Burnu** *var.* Cape Kormakiti, Kormakítis, *Gk.* Akrotíri Kormakíti. *headland* N Cyprus 35.24N 32.55E
191 O13 **Korumburra** Victoria, SE Australia 38.27S 145.48E
Koryak Range *see* Koryakskoye Nagor'ye
127 P8 **Koryakskiy Avtonomnyy Okrug** ◈ *autonomous district* E Russian Federation
Koryakskiy Khrebet *see* Koryakskoye Nagor'ye
127 Pp7 **Koryakskoye Nagor'ye** *var.* Koryakskiy Khrebet, *Eng.* Koryak Range. ▲▲ NE Russian Federation
129 P11 **Koryazhma** Arkhangel'skaya Oblast', NW Russian Federation 61.16N 47.06E
Kōryō *see* Kangnŭng
Korytsa *see* Korçë
119 Q2 **Koryukivka** Chernihivs'ka Oblast', N Ukraine 51.45N 32.16E
Korzec *see* Korets'
117 N21 **Kos** Kos, Dodekánisos, Greece, Aegean Sea 36.53N 27.18E
117 M21 **Kos** *It.* Coo; *anc.* Cos. *island* Dodekánisos, Greece, Aegean Sea
129 T12 **Kosa** Komi-Permyatskiy Avtonomnyy Okrug, NW Russian Federation 59.55N 54.54E
129 T13 **Kosa** ≈ NW Russian Federation
170 C11 **Kō-saki** *headland* Nagasaki, Tsushima, SW Japan 34.06N 129.13E
169 X13 **Kosan** SE North Korea 38.50N 127.26E
121 H18 **Kosava** *Rus.* Kosovo. Brestskaya Voblasts', SW Belarus 52.45N 25.16E
Kosch *see* Kose
150 G12 **Koschagyl** *Kaz.* Qosshaghyl. Atyrau, W Kazakhstan 46.52N 53.46E
112 G12 **Kościan** *Ger.* Kosten. Wielkopolskie, C Poland 52.04N 16.37E
112 I7 **Kościerzyna** Pomorskie, NW Poland 54.06N 17.55E
24 L4 **Kosciusko** Mississippi, S USA 33.03N 89.35W
Kosciusko, Mount *see* Kosciuszko, Mount
191 R11 **Kosciuszko, Mount** *prev.* Mount Kosciusko ▲ New South Wales, SE Australia 36.28S 148.15E
120 H4 **Kose** *Ger.* Kosch. Harjumaa, NW Estonia 59.10N 25.10E
116 G6 **Koshava** Vidin, NW Bulgaria 44.03N 23.00E
153 U9 **Kosh-Dëbë** *var.* Koshtebë. Narynskaya Oblast', C Kyrgyzstan 41.03N 74.08E
171 K16 **Koshigaya** *var.* Kosigaya. Saitama, Honshū, S Japan 35.54N 139.46E
K'o-shih *see* Kashi
170 B15 **Koshikijima-rettō** *var.* Kosikizima Rettô. *island group* SW Japan
151 W13 **Koshkarkol', Ozero** ◎ SE Kazakhstan
32 L9 **Koshkonong, Lake** ◎ Wisconsin, N USA
152 B10 **Koshoba** *Turkm.* Goshoba. Balkanskiy Velayat, NW Turkmenistan 40.28N 54.11E
171 J14 **Kōshoku** *var.* Kôsyoku. Nagano, Honshū, S Japan 36.31N 138.07E
Koshtebë *see* Kosh-Dëbë
Kōshū *see* Kwangju
113 N19 **Košice** *Ger.* Kaschau, *Hung.* Kassa. Košický Kraj, E Slovakia 48.43N 21.15E
113 M20 **Košický Kraj** ◈ *region* E Slovakia
Kosigaya *see* Koshigaya
Kosikizima Rettô *see* Koshikijima-retto
159 R12 **Kosi Reservoir** ▧ E Nepal
118 J8 **Kosiv** Ivano-Frankivs'ka Oblast', W Ukraine 48.19N 25.04E
151 O11 **Koskol'** Zhezkazgan, C Kazakhstan 49.34N 67.03E
129 Q9 **Koslan** Respublika Komi, NW Russian Federation 63.27N 48.52E
Köslin *see* Koszalin
152 M12 **Koson** *Rus.* Kasan. Qashqadaryo Viloyati, S Uzbekistan 39.03N 65.34E
169 Y13 **Kosŏng** SE North Korea 38.40N 128.13E
153 S9 **Kosonsoy** *Rus.* Kasansay. Namangan Viloyati, E Uzbekistan 41.15N 71.28E
115 M16 **Kosovo** *prev.* Autonomous Province of Kosovo and Metohija. *region* S Serbia and Montenegro (Yugoslavia)
Kosovo *see* Kosava
Kosovo and Metohija, Autonomous Province of *see* Kosovo
115 N16 **Kosovo Polje** Serbia, S Serbia and Montenegro (Yugoslavia) 42.40N 21.07E
115 O16 **Kosovska Kamenica** Serbia, SE Serbia and Montenegro (Yugoslavia) 42.37N 21.33E
115 M16 **Kosovska Mitrovica** *Alb.* Mitrovicë; *prev.* Mitrovica, Titova Mitrovica. Serbia, S Serbia and Montenegro (Yugoslavia) 42.54N 20.52E
201 X17 **Kosrae** ◈ *state* E Micronesia
201 Y14 **Kosrae** *prev.* Kusaie. *island* Caroline Islands, E Micronesia
27 U9 **Kosse** Texas, SW USA 31.16N 96.38W
111 P6 **Kössen** Tirol, W Austria 47.40N 12.24E
78 M16 **Kossou, Lac de** ◎ C Ivory Coast
Kossukavak *see* Krumovgrad
Kostajnica *see* Hrvatska Kostajnica
150 M7 **Kostanay** *var.* Kustanay, *Kaz.* Qostanay. N Kazakhstan 53.15N 63.34E
150 L8 **Kostanay** *var.* Kostanayskaya Oblast, *Kaz.* Qostanay Oblysy. ◈ *province* N Kazakhstan
Kostanayskaya Oblast *see* Kostanay
Kostamus *see* Kostomuksha
Kosten *see* Kościan
116 H10 **Kostenets** *prev.* Georgi Dimitrov. Sofiya, W Bulgaria 42.17N 23.52E
82 F10 **Kosti** White Nile, C Sudan 13.10N 32.37E
Kostnitz *see* Konstanz
128 H7 **Kostomuksha** *Fin.* Kostamus. Respublika Kareliya, NW Russian Federation 64.33N 30.28E
118 K3 **Kostopil'** *Rus.* Kostopol'. Rivnens'ka Oblast', NW Ukraine 50.20N 26.28E
Kostopol' *see* Kostopil'
128 M15 **Kostroma** Kostromskaya Oblast', NW Russian Federation 57.46N 40.59E
129 N14 **Kostroma** ≈ NW Russian Federation
129 N14 **Kostromskaya Oblast'** ◈ *province* NW Russian Federation
112 D11 **Kostrzyn** *Ger.* Cüstrin, Küstrin. Lubuskie, W Poland 52.35N 14.39E
112 H11 **Kostrzyn** Wielkolpolskie, C Poland 52.23N 17.13E
119 X7 **Kostyantynivka** *Rus.* Konstantinovka. Donets'ka Oblast', SE Ukraine 48.30N 37.45E
Kostyukovichi *see* Kastsyukovichy
Kostyukovka *see* Kastsyukowka
Kôsyoku *see* Kōshoku
129 U6 **Kos'yu** Respublika Komi, NW Russian Federation 65.39N 59.01E
129 U6 **Kos'yu** ≈ NW Russian Federation
112 F7 **Koszalin** *Ger.* Köslin. Koszalin, NW Poland 54.11N 16.10E
113 F22 **Kőszeg** *Ger.* Güns. Vas, W Hungary 47.24N 16.33E
158 H13 **Kota** *prev.* Kotah. Rājasthān, N India 25.13N 75.51E
174 H9 **Kota Baru** Sumatera, W Indonesia 1.07S 101.43E
175 Nn11 **Kotabaru** Pulau Laut, C Indonesia 3.15S 116.15E
Kotabaru *see* Jayapura
174 H2 **Kota Bharu** *var.* Kota Baharu, Kota Bahru. Kelantan, Peninsular Malaysia 6.07N 102.15E
Kotaboemi *see* Kotabumi
174 Ii12 **Kotabumi** *prev.* Kotaboemi. Sumatera, W Indonesia 4.49S 104.54E
155 S10 **Kot Addu** Punjab, E Pakistan 30.25N 70.54E
Kotah *see* Kota
175 Nn2 **Kota Kinabalu** *prev.* Jesselton. Sabah, East Malaysia 5.58N 116.04E
175 Nn2 **Kota Kinabalu** ✕ Sabah, East Malaysia 5.58N 116.04E
94 M12 **Kotala** Lappi, N Finland 67.01N 29.00E
Kotamobagoe *see* Kotamobagu
175 Rr7 **Kotamobagu** *prev.* Kotamobagoe. Sulawesi, C Indonesia 0.46N 124.21E
161 L14 **Kotapad** *var.* Kotapārh. Orissa, E India 19.10N 82.23E
Kotapārh *see* Kotapad
178 Gg17 **Ko Ta Ru Tao** *island* SW Thailand
174 L11 **Kotawaringin, Teluk** *bay* Borneo, C Indonesia
155 Q13 **Kot Dīji** Sind, SE Pakistan 27.16N 68.43E
158 K9 **Kotdwāra** Uttar Pradesh, N India 29.43N 78.33E
129 Q14 **Kotel'nich** Kirovskaya Oblast', NW Russian Federation 58.19N 48.12E
131 N12 **Kotel'nikovo** Volgogradskaya Oblast', SW Russian Federation 47.37N 43.07E
126 Ll4 **Kotel'nyy, Ostrov** *island* Novosibirskiye Ostrova, N Russian Federation
119 T5 **Kotel'va** Poltavs'ka Oblast', C Ukraine 50.04N 34.46E
103 M14 **Köthen** *var.* Cöthen. Sachsen-Anhalt, C Germany 51.46N 11.58E
Kôti *see* Kōchi
83 G17 **Kotido** NE Uganda 3.03N 34.07E
95 N19 **Kotka** Etelä-Suomi, S Finland 60.28N 26.54E
129 P11 **Kotlas** Arkhangel'skaya Oblast', NW Russian Federation 61.13N 46.43E
40 M10 **Kotlik** Alaska, USA 63.01N 163.33W
79 Q17 **Kotoka** ✕ (Accra) S Ghana 5.41N 0.10W
Kotonu *see* Cotonou
115 J17 **Kotor** *It.* Cattaro. Montenegro, SW Serbia and Montenegro (Yugoslavia) 42.25N 18.47E
Kotor *see* Kotoriba
114 F7 **Kotoriba** *Hung.* Kotor. Međimurje, N Croatia 46.20N 16.47E
115 I17 **Kotorska, Boka** *It.* Bocche di Cattaro. *bay* Montenegro, SW Serbia and Montenegro (Yugoslavia)
114 H11 **Kotorsko** Republika Srpska, N Bosnia and Herzegovina 44.50N 18.03E
114 G11 **Kotor Varoš** Republika Srpska, N Bosnia and Herzegovina 44.37N 17.24E
Koto Sho/Kotosho *see* Lan Yü
130 M7 **Kotovsk** Tambovskaya Oblast', W Russian Federation 52.39N 41.31E
119 O9 **Kotovs'k** *Rus.* Kotovsk. Odes'ka Oblast', SW Ukraine 47.42N 29.30E
Kotovsk *see* Hînceşti
121 G16 **Kotra** *Rus.* Kotra. ≈ W Belarus
155 P16 **Kotri** Sind, SE Pakistan 25.22N 68.16E
111 Q9 **Kötschach** Kärnten, S Austria 46.41N 12.57E
161 K15 **Kottagūdem** Andhra Pradesh, E India 17.36N 80.40E
161 F21 **Kottappadi** Kerala, SW India 11.38N 76.03E
161 G23 **Kottayam** Kerala, SW India 9.37N 76.31E
Kottbus *see* Cottbus
Kotte *see* Sri Jayawardanapura
81 K15 **Kotto** ≈ Central African Republic/Dem. Rep. Congo
200 S13 **Kotu Group** *island group* W Tonga
152 B11 **Koturdepe** *Turkm.* Goturdepe. Balkanskiy Velayat, W Turkmenistan 39.32N 53.39E
126 J9 **Kotuy** ≈ N Russian Federation
85 M16 **Kotwa** Mashonaland East, NE Zimbabwe 16.58S 32.46E
41 N7 **Kotzebue** Alaska, USA 66.54N 162.36W
40 M7 **Kotzebue Sound** *inlet* Alaska, USA
Kotzenan *see* Chocianów
Kotzman *see* Kitsman'
79 R14 **Kouandé** NW Benin 10.19N 1.42E
81 J15 **Kouango** Ouaka, S Central African Republic 5.00N 20.01E
79 O13 **Koudougou** C Burkina 12.15N 2.22W
100 K7 **Koudum** Friesland, N Netherlands 52.55N 5.26E
117 L25 **Koufonísi** *island* SE Greece
117 K21 **Koufonísi** *island* Kykládes, Greece, Aegean Sea
40 M8 **Kougarok Mountain** ▲ Alaska, USA 65.41N 165.29W
81 E20 **Kouilou** ≈ S Congo
16 N3 **Koukdjuak** ≈ Baffin Island, Nunavut, NE Canada
124 N4 **Koúklia** SW Cyprus 34.42N 32.35E
81 E19 **Koulamoutou** Ogooué-Lolo, C Gabon 1.06S 12.26E
78 L12 **Koulikoro** Koulikoro, SW Mali 12.55N 7.35W
78 L11 **Koulikoro** ◈ *region* SW Mali
197 H5 **Koumac** Province Nord, W New Caledonia 20.34S 164.18E
171 J15 **Koumi** Nagano, Honshū, S Japan 36.06N 138.27E
80 I13 **Koumra** Moyen-Chari, S Chad 8.55N 17.31E
Kounadougou *see* Koundougou
78 M15 **Kounahiri** C Ivory Coast 7.47N 5.51W
78 I12 **Koundâra** Moyenne-Guinée, NW Guinea 12.28N 13.15W
79 N13 **Koundougou** *var.* Kounadougou. C Burkina 11.43N 4.40W
78 H11 **Koungheul** C Senegal 14.00N 14.48W
Kounradskiy *see* Konyrat
27 X10 **Kountze** Texas, SW USA 30.22N 94.18W
79 Q13 **Koupéla** C Burkina 12.09N 0.23W
79 N13 **Kouri** Sikasso, SW Mali 12.09N 4.46W
57 Y9 **Kourou** N French Guiana 5.07N 52.37W
116 J12 **Kouroú** ≈ NE Greece
78 K14 **Kouroussa** Haute-Guinée, C Guinea 10.40N 9.49W
Kousseir *see* Al Quşayr
80 G11 **Kousséri** *prev.* Fort-Foureau. Extrême-Nord, NE Cameroon 12.01N 15.03E
Kouteifé *see* Al Quţayfah
78 M13 **Koutiala** Sikasso, S Mali 12.24N 5.30W
78 M14 **Kouto** NW Ivory Coast 9.51N 6.25W
95 M19 **Kouvola** Etelä-Suomi, S Finland 60.50N 26.48E
81 G18 **Kouyou** ≈ C Congo
114 M10 **Kovačica** *Hung.* Antafalva; *prev.* Kovacsicza. Serbia, N Serbia and Montenegro (Yugoslavia) 45.08N 20.36E
Kovacsicza *see* Kovačica
Kővárhosszúfalu *see* Satulung
Kovászna *see* Covasna
128 I4 **Kovdor** Murmanskaya Oblast', NW Russian Federation 67.32N 30.27E
128 I5 **Kovdozero, Ozero** ◎ NW Russian Federation
118 J3 **Kovel'** *Pol.* Kowel. Volyns'ka Oblast', NW Ukraine 51.13N 24.42E
114 M11 **Kovin** *Hung.* Kevevára; *prev.* Temes-Kubin. Serbia, NE Serbia and Montenegro (Yugoslavia) 44.45N 20.59E
Kovno *see* Kaunas
131 N3 **Kovrov** Vladimirskaya Oblast', W Russian Federation 56.24N 41.21E
131 O5 **Kovylkino** Respublika Mordoviya, W Russian Federation 54.03N 43.52E
112 J11 **Kowal** Kujawsko-pomorskie, C Poland 52.31N 19.08E
112 J9 **Kowalewo Pomorskie** *Ger.* Schönsee. Kujawsko-pomorskie, C Poland 53.07N 18.48E
Kowasna *see* Covasna
121 M16 **Kowbcha** *Rus.* Kolbcha. Mahilyowskaya Voblasts', E Belarus 53.40N 29.13E
Koweit *see* Kuwait
Kowel *see* Kovel'
193 F17 **Kowhitirangi** West Coast, South Island, NZ 42.54S 171.01E
167 O15 **Kowloon** *Chin.* Jiulong. Hong Kong, S China
Kowno *see* Kaunas
165 N7 **Kox Kuduk** *well* NW China 40.32N 92.30E
142 D16 **Köyceğiz** Muğla, SW Turkey 36.58N 28.38E
129 N6 **Koyda** Arkhangel'skaya Oblast', NW Russian Federation 66.22N 42.42E
152 D10 **Koymat** *Turkm.* Goymat. Balkanskiy Velayat, NW Turkmenistan 40.23N 55.45E
152 D10 **Koymatdag, Gory** *Turkm.* Goymatdag. *hill range* NW Turkmenistan
Koyna Reservoir *see* Shivāji Sāgar
171 M11 **Koyoshi-gawa** ≈ Honshū, C Japan
Koysanjaq *see* Koi Sanjaq
Koytash *see* Qo'ytosh
41 N9 **Koyuk** Alaska, USA 64.55N 161.09W
41 N9 **Koyuk River** ≈ Alaska, USA
41 O9 **Koyukuk** Alaska, USA 64.52N 157.42W
41 O9 **Koyukuk River** ≈ Alaska, USA
142 J13 **Kozaklı** Nevşehir, C Turkey 39.13N 34.51E
170 F13 **Kōzan** Hiroshima, Honshū, SW Japan 34.35N 133.02E
142 K16 **Kozan** Adana, S Turkey 37.27N 35.46E
117 E14 **Kozáni** Dytikí Makedonía, N Greece 40.18N 21.48E
114 F10 **Kozara** ▲▲ NW Bosnia and Herzegovina
Kozarska Dubica *see* Bosanska Dubica
119 P3 **Kozelets'** *Rus.* Kozelets. Chernihivs'ka Oblast', NE Ukraine 50.54N 31.09E
119 S6 **Kozel'shchyna** Poltavs'ka Oblast', C Ukraine 49.13N 33.49E
130 J5 **Kozel'sk** Kaluzhskaya Oblast', W Russian Federation 54.04N 35.51E
Kozhikode *see* Calicut
129 V9 **Kozhimiz, Gora** ▲ NW Russian Federation 63.13N 58.54E
128 L9 **Kozhozero, Ozero** ◎ NW Russian Federation
129 T7 **Kozhva** *var.* Kozya. Respublika Komi, NW Russian Federation 65.06N 57.00E
129 T7 **Kozhva** ≈ NW Russian Federation
129 U6 **Kozhim** Respublika Komi, NW Russian Federation 65.43N 59.25E
112 N13 **Kozienice** Mazowieckie, C Poland 51.37N 21.30E
111 S13 **Kozina** SW Slovenia 45.36N 13.56E
116 H7 **Kozloduy** Vratsa, NW Bulgaria 43.47N 23.42E
131 Q3 **Kozlovka** Chavash Respubliki, W Russian Federation 55.53N 48.07E
Kozlovshchina/Kozlowszczyzna *see* Kazlowshchyna
131 P3 **Koz'modem'yansk** Respublika Mariy El, W Russian Federation 56.19N 46.33E
118 J6 **Kozova** Ternopil's'ka Oblast', W Ukraine 49.25N 25.09E
115 P20 **Kožuf** ▲ S FYR Macedonia 41.10N 22.14E
172 S13 **Kōzu-shima** *island* E Japan
Kozya *see* Kozhva
Koz'yany *see* Kaz'yany
119 N5 **Kozyatyn** *Rus.* Kazatin. Vinnyts'ka Oblast', C Ukraine 49.40N 28.48E
79 Q16 **Kpalimé** *var.* Palimé. SW Togo 6.54N 0.37E
79 Q16 **Kpandu** E Ghana 7.00N 0.18E
101 F15 **Krabbendijke** Zeeland, SW Netherlands 51.25N 4.07E
178 Gg16 **Krabi** *var.* Muang Krabi. Krabi, SW Thailand 8.04N 98.52E
178 Gg14 **Kra Buri** Ranong, SW Thailand 10.25N 98.48E
178 Jj13 **Krâchéh** *prev.* Kratie. Krâchéh, E Cambodia 12.28N 106.01E
97 G17 **Kragerø** Telemark, S Norway 58.53N 9.22E
114 M13 **Kragujevac** Serbia, C Serbia and Montenegro (Yugoslavia) 44.01N 20.54E
Krainburg *see* Kranj
178 Gg14 **Kra, Isthmus of** *isthmus* Malaysia/Thailand
114 D12 **Krajina** *cultural region* SW Croatia
Krakatau, Pulau *see* Rakata, Pulau
Krakau *see* Małopolskie
113 L16 **Kraków** *Eng.* Cracow, *Ger.* Krakau; *anc.* Cracovia. Małopolskie, S Poland 50.03N 19.57E
102 L9 **Krakower See** ◎ NE Germany
178 Ii12 **Krâlănh** Siĕmréab, NW Cambodia 13.35N 103.27E
47 Q16 **Kralendijk** Bonaire, E Netherlands Antilles 12.07N 68.13W
114 B10 **Kraljevica** *It.* Porto Re. Primorje-Gorski Kotar, NW Croatia 45.15N 14.36E
114 M13 **Kraljevo** *prev.* Rankovićevo. Serbia, C Serbia and Montenegro (Yugoslavia) 43.44N 20.40E
Kralup an der Moldau *see* Kralupy nad Vltavou
113 C16 **Kralupy nad Vltavou** *Ger.* Kralup an der Moldau. Středočeský Kraj, NW Czech Republic 50.13N 14.17E
119 W7 **Kramators'k** *Rus.* Kramatorsk. Donets'ka Oblast', SE Ukraine 48.43N 37.34E
95 H17 **Kramfors** Västernorrland, C Sweden 62.55N 17.49E
117 D15 **Kranéa** Dytikí Makedonía, N Greece 39.54N 21.21E
110 M7 **Kranebitten** ✕ (Innsbruck) Tirol, W Austria 47.18N 11.21E
117 G20 **Kranídi** Pelopónnisos, S Greece 37.21N 23.09E
111 T11 **Kranj** *Ger.* Krainburg. NW Slovenia 46.16N 14.16E
117 F16 **Krannón** *battleground* Thessalía, C Greece 39.32N 22.20E
Kranz *see* Zelenogradsk
114 D7 **Krapina** Krapina-Zagorje, N Croatia 46.12N 15.52E
114 E8 **Krapina** ≈ N Croatia
114 D8 **Krapina-Zagorje** *off.* Krapinsko-Zagorska Županija. ◈ *province* N Croatia
116 L7 **Krapinets** ≈ NE Bulgaria
113 I15 **Krapkowice** *Ger.* Krappitz. Opolskie, S Poland 50.28N 17.55E
Krappitz *see* Krapkowice
129 O12 **Krasavino** Vologodskaya Oblast', NW Russian Federation 60.56N 46.27E
125 Ff5 **Krasino** Novaya Zemlya, Arkhangel'skaya Oblast', N Russian Federation 70.45N 54.16E
127 N18 **Kraskino** Primorskiy Kray, SE Russian Federation 42.40N 130.51E
120 J11 **Krāslava** Krāslava, SE Latvia 55.56N 27.08E
121 M14 **Krasnaluki** *Rus.* Krasnoluki. Vitsyebskaya Voblasts', N Belarus 54.37N 28.49E
121 P17 **Krasnapollye** *Rus.* Krasnopol'ye. Mahilyowskaya Voblasts', E Belarus 53.19N 31.24E
130 L15 **Krasnaya Polyana** Krasnodarskiy Kray, SW Russian Federation 43.40N 40.13E
121 J18 **Krasnaya Slabada** *var.* Chyrvonaya Slabada, *Rus.* Krasnaya Sloboda. Minskaya Voblasts', S Belarus 52.51N 27.10E
Krasnaya Sloboda *see* Krasnaya Slabada
121 J15 **Krasnaye** *Rus.* Krasnoye. Minskaya Voblasts', C Belarus 54.13N 27.04E
113 O14 **Kraśnik** *Ger.* Kratznick. Lubelskie, E Poland 50.55N 22.13E
113 O14 **Kraśnik Fabryczny** Lubelskie, SE Poland 50.57N 22.07E
119 O9 **Krasni Okny** Odes'ka Oblast', SW Ukraine 47.33N 29.28E
151 P7 **Krasnoarmeysk** Severnyy Kazakhstan, N Kazakhstan 53.52N 69.51E
131 P8 **Krasnoarmeysk** Saratovskaya Oblast', W Russian Federation 51.01N 45.42E
Krasnoarmeysk *see* Krasnoarmiys'k/Tayynsha
127 Oo4 **Krasnoarmeyskiy** Chukotskiy Avtonomnyy Okrug, NE Russian Federation 69.30N 171.44E
119 W7 **Krasnoarmiys'k** *Rus.* Krasnoarmeysk. Donets'ka Oblast', SE Ukraine 48.16N 37.13E
129 P11 **Krasnoborsk** Arkhangel'skaya Oblast', NW Russian Federation 61.31N 45.57E
130 K14 **Krasnodar** *prev.* Ekaterinodar, Yekaterinodar. Krasnodarskiy Kray, SW Russian Federation 45.02N 39.00E
130 K13 **Krasnodarskiy Kray** ◈ *territory* SW Russian Federation
119 Z7 **Krasnodon** Luhans'ka Oblast', E Ukraine 48.16N 39.45E
Krasnogor *see* Kallaste
131 T2 **Krasnogorskoye** *Latv.* Sarkaņi. Udmurtskaya Respublika, NW Russian Federation 57.42N 52.29E
Krasnograd *see* Krasnohrad
Krasnogvardeysk *see* Bulung'ur
130 M13 **Krasnogvardeyskoye** Stavropol'skiy Kray, SW Russian Federation 45.49N 41.31E
Krasnogvardeyskoye *see* Krasnohvardiys'ke
119 U6 **Krasnohrad** *Rus.* Krasnograd. Kharkivs'ka Oblast', E Ukraine 49.22N 35.27E
119 S12 **Krasnohvardiys'ke** *Rus.* Krasnogvardeyskoye. Respublika Krym, S Ukraine 45.30N 34.19E
126 L16 **Krasnokamensk** Chitinskaya Oblast', S Russian Federation 50.03N 118.01E
129 U14 **Krasnokamsk** Permskaya Oblast', W Russian Federation 58.07N 55.48E
131 U8 **Krasnokholm** Orenburgskaya Oblast', W Russian Federation 51.34N 54.11E
119 U5 **Krasnokuts'k** *Rus.* Krasnokutsk. Kharkivs'ka Oblast', E Ukraine 50.01N 35.03E
130 L7 **Krasnolesnyy** Voronezhskaya Oblast', W Russian Federation 51.53N 39.37E
Krasnoluki *see* Krasnaluki
Krasnoosol'skoye Vodokhranilishche *see* Chervonooskil's'ke Vodoskhovyshche
119 S11 **Krasnoperekops'k** *Rus.* Krasnoperekopsk. Respublika Krym, S Ukraine 45.56N 33.46E
119 U4 **Krasnopillya** Sums'ka Oblast', NE Ukraine 50.46N 35.17E
Krasnopol'ye *see* Krasnapollye
126 H9 **Krasnosel'kup** Yamalo-Nenetskiy Avtonomnyy Okrug, N Russian Federation 65.46N 82.11E
128 L5 **Krasnoshchel'ye** Murmanskaya Oblast', NW Russian Federation 67.22N 37.03E
131 O5 **Krasnoslobodsk** Respublika Mordoviya, W Russian Federation 54.24N 43.51E
131 T2 **Krasnoslobodsk** Volgogradskaya Oblast', SW Russian Federation 48.41N 44.34E
Krasnostav *see* Krasnystaw
125 F10 **Krasnotur'insk** Sverdlovskaya Oblast', C Russian Federation 59.45N 60.19E
125 E11 **Krasnoufimsk** Sverdlovskaya Oblast', C Russian Federation 56.43N 57.39E
125 Ee10 **Krasnoural'sk** Sverdlovskaya Oblast', C Russian Federation 58.24N 59.44E
131 V5 **Krasnousol'skiy** Respublika Bashkortostan, W Russian Federation 53.55N 56.22E
129 U12 **Krasnovishersk** Permskaya Oblast', NW Russian Federation 60.22N 57.04E
Krasnovodsk *see* Turkmenbashi
152 A10 **Krasnovodskiy Zaliv** *Turkm.* Krasnowodsk Aylagy. *lake gulf* W Turkmenistan
152 B10 **Krasnovodskoye Plato** *Turkm.* Krasnowodsk Platosy. *plateau* NW Turkmenistan
Krasnowodsk Aylagy *see* Krasnovodskiy Zaliv
Krasnowodsk Platosy *see* Krasnovodskoye Plato
126 Hh14 **Krasnoyarsk** Krasnoyarskiy Kray, S Russian Federation 56.04N 92.46E
131 X7 **Krasnoyarskiy** Orenburgskaya Oblast', W Russian Federation 51.56N 59.54E
126 I12 **Krasnoyarskiy Kray** ◈ *territory* C Russian Federation
126 I14 **Krasnoyarskoye Vodokhranilishche** ▧ S Russian Federation
Krasnoye *see* Krasnaye
152 J15 **Krasnoye Znamya** *Turkm.* Gyzylbaydak. Maryyskiy Velayat, S Turkmenistan 36.51N 62.24E
129 R11 **Krasnozatonskiy** Respublika Komi, NW Russian Federation 61.39N 51.00E
120 D13 **Krasnoznamensk** *prev.* Lasdehnen, *Ger.* Haselberg. Kaliningradskaya Oblast', W Russian Federation 54.57N 22.28E
130 K3 **Krasnoznamensk** Moskovskaya Oblast', W Russian Federation 55.40N 37.05E
119 R11 **Krasnoznam"yans'kyy Kanal** *canal* S Ukraine
113 P14 **Krasnystaw** *Rus.* Krasnostav. Lubelskie, SE Poland 51.00N 23.10E
130 H4 **Krasnyy** Smolenskaya Oblast', W Russian Federation 54.36N 31.27E
131 P2 **Krasnyye Baki** Nizhegorodskaya Oblast', W Russian Federation 57.07N 45.12E
131 Q13 **Krasnyye Barrikady** Astrakhanskaya Oblast', SW Russian Federation 46.14N 47.48E
128 K15 **Krasnyy Kholm** Tverskaya Oblast', W Russian Federation 58.04N 37.05E
131 Q8 **Krasnyy Kut** Saratovskaya Oblast', W Russian Federation 50.54N 46.58E
Krasnyy Liman *see* Krasnyy Lyman
119 Y7 **Krasnyy Luch** *prev.* Krindachevka. Luhans'ka Oblast', E Ukraine 48.08N 38.52E
119 X6 **Krasnyy Lyman** *Rus.* Krasnyy Liman. Donets'ka Oblast', SE Ukraine 49.00N 37.50E
131 R3 **Krasnyy Steklovar** Respublika Mariy El, W Russian Federation 56.14N 48.49E
131 P8 **Krasnyy Tekstil'shchik** Saratovskaya Oblast', W Russian Federation 51.35N 45.49E
131 R13 **Krasnyy Yar** Astrakhanskaya Oblast', SW Russian Federation 46.33N 48.21E
Krassóvár *see* Caraşova
118 L5 **Krasyliv** Khmel'nyts'ka Oblast', W Ukraine 49.38N 26.59E
113 O21 **Kraszna** *Rom.* Crasna. ≈ Hungary/Romania
Kratie *see* Krâchéh
194 I13 **Kratke Range** ▲▲ C PNG
115 P17 **Kratovo** NE FYR Macedonia 42.04N 22.08E
Kratznick *see* Kraśnik
176 Yy11 **Krau** Papua, E Indonesia 3.15S 140.07E
178 Ii13 **Krâvanh, Chuŏr Phnum** *Eng.* Cardamom Mountains, *Fr.* Chaîne des Cardamomes. ▲▲ W Cambodia
Kravasta Lagoon *see* Karavastasë, Laguna e
Krawang *see* Karawang
Kraxatau *see* Rakata, Pulau
131 Q15 **Kraynovka** Respublika Dagestan, SW Russian Federation 43.58N 47.24E
120 D12 **Kražiai** Kelmė, C Lithuania 55.36N 22.41E
29 P11 **Krebs** Oklahoma, C USA 34.55N 95.43W
103 D15 **Krefeld** Nordrhein-Westfalen, W Germany 51.19N 6.34E
Kreisstadt *see* Krosno Odrzańskie
117 D17 **Kremastón, Technití Límni** ▧ C Greece
Kremenchug *see* Kremenchuk
Kremenchugskoye Vodokhranilishche/Kremenchuk Reservoir *see* Kremenchuts'ke Vodoskhovyshche
119 S6 **Kremenchuk** *Rus.* Kremenchug. Poltavs'ka Oblast', NE Ukraine 49.03N 33.27E
119 R6 **Kremenchuts'ke Vodoskhovyshche** *Eng.* Kremenchuk Reservoir, *Rus.* Kremenchugskoye Vodokhranilishche. ▧ C Ukraine
118 K5 **Kremenets'** *Pol.* Krzemieniec, *Rus.* Kremenets. Ternopil's'ka Oblast', W Ukraine 50.05N 25.43E
Kremennaya *see* Kreminna
119 X6 **Kreminna** *Rus.* Kremennaya. Luhans'ka Oblast', E Ukraine 49.03N 38.14E
39 R4 **Kremmling** Colorado, C USA 40.03N 106.23W
111 V3 **Krems** ≈ NE Austria
Krems *see* Krems an der Donau
111 W3 **Krems an der Donau** *var.* Krems. Niederösterreich, N Austria 48.25N 15.34E
Kremsier *see* Kroměříž
111 S4 **Kremsmünster** Oberösterreich, N Austria 48.04N 14.08E
40 M17 **Krenitzin Islands** *island* Aleutian Islands, Alaska, USA
Kresena *see* Kresna
116 G11 **Kresna** *var.* Kresena. Blagoevgrad, SW Bulgaria 41.43N 23.12E
114 O12 **Krespoljin** Serbia, E Serbia and Montenegro (Yugoslavia) 44.37N 21.36E
27 N4 **Kress** Texas, SW USA 34.21N 101.43W
127 Pp4 **Kresta, Zaliv** *bay* E Russian Federation
117 D20 **Kréstena** *prev.* Selinoús. Dytikí Ellás, S Greece 37.36N 21.36E
128 H14 **Kresttsy** Novgorodskaya Oblast', W Russian Federation 58.15N 32.28E
126 Kk11 **Krestyakh** Respublika Sakha (Yakutiya), NE Russian Federation 62.10N 116.24E
Kretikon Delagos *see* Kritikó Pélagos
120 C11 **Kretinga** *Ger.* Krottingen. Kretinga, NW Lithuania 55.53N 21.13E
Kreutz *see* Cristuru Secuiesc
Kreuz *see* Križevci, Croatia
Kreuz *see* Risti, Estonia
Kreuzburg/Kreuzburg in Oberschlesien *see* Kluczbork
Kreuzingen *see* Bol'shakovo
110 H6 **Kreuzlingen** Thurgau, NE Switzerland 47.37N 9.10E
103 K25 **Kreuzspitze** ▲ S Germany 47.30N 10.55E
103 F16 **Kreuztal** Nordrhein-Westfalen, W Germany 50.58N 8.00E
121 I15 **Kreva** *Rus.* Krevo. Hrodzyenskaya Voblasts', W Belarus 54.19N 26.16E
Krevo *see* Kreva
Kría Vrísi *see* Krýa Vrýsi
81 D16 **Kribi** Sud, SW Cameroon 2.53N 9.57E
Krichëv *see* Krychaw
Krickerhäu/Kriegerhaj *see* Handlová
111 W6 **Krieglach** Steiermark, E Austria 47.33N 15.37E
110 F8 **Kriens** Luzern, W Switzerland 47.01N 8.16E
Krimmitschau *see* Crimmitschau
100 H12 **Krimpen aan den IJssel** Zuid-Holland, SW Netherlands 51.56N 4.39E
Krindachevka *see* Krasnyy Luch
117 G25 **Kríos, Akrotírio** *headland* Kríti, Greece, E Mediterranean Sea 35.17N 23.31E
161 J16 **Krishna** *prev.* Kistna. ≈ C India
161 H20 **Krishnagiri** Tamil Nādu, SE India 12.33N 78.10E
161 K17 **Krishna, Mouths of the** *delta* SE India
159 S15 **Krishnanagar** West Bengal, N India 23.22N 88.31E
161 G20 **Krishnarājāsāgara Reservoir** ▧ W India
97 N19 **Kristdala** Kalmar, S Sweden 57.24N 16.12E
Kristiania *see* Oslo
97 E18 **Kristiansand** *var.* Christiansand. Vest-Agder, S Norway 58.07N 7.52E
97 L22 **Kristianstad** Skåne, S Sweden 56.01N 14.10E
96 F8 **Kristiansund** *var.* Christiansund. Møre og Romsdal, S Norway 63.07N 7.45E
Kristiinankaupunki *see* Kristinestad
95 I14 **Kristineberg** Västerbotten, N Sweden 65.07N 18.36E
97 L16 **Kristinehamn** Värmland, C Sweden 59.16N 14.09E
95 J17 **Kristinestad** *Fin.* Kristiinankaupunki. Länsi-Suomi, W Finland 62.15N 21.24E
Kristyor *see* Crişcior
117 J25 **Kríti** *Eng.* Crete. ◈ *region* Greece, Aegean Sea
117 J24 **Kríti** *Eng.* Crete. *island* Greece, Aegean Sea
117 J23 **Kritikó Pélagos** *var.* Kretikon Delagos, *Eng.* Sea of Crete; *anc.* Mare Creticum. *sea* Greece, Aegean Sea
Kriulyany *see* Criuleni
114 I12 **Krivaja** ≈ NE Bosnia and Herzegovina
Krivaja *see* Mali Iđoš
115 P17 **Kriva Palanka** *Turk.* Eğri Palanka. NE FYR Macedonia 42.13N 22.19E
Krivichi *see* Kryvychy
116 H8 **Krivodol** Vratsa, NW Bulgaria 43.23N 23.30E
130 M10 **Krivorozh'ye** Rostovskaya Oblast', SW Russian Federation 48.51N 40.49E
Krivoshin *see* Kryvoshyn
Krivoy Rog *see* Kryvyy Rih
114 F7 **Križevci** *Ger.* Kreuz, *Hung.* Kőrös. Varaždin, NE Croatia 46.02N 16.32E
114 B10 **Krk** *It.* Veglia. Primorje-Gorski Kotar, NW Croatia 45.01N 14.36E
114 B10 **Krk** *It.* Veglia; *anc.* Curieta. *island* NW Croatia
111 V12 **Krka** ≈ SE Slovenia
Krka *see* Gurk
111 R11 **Krn** ▲ NW Slovenia 46.15N 13.37E
113 H16 **Krnov** *Ger.* Jägerndorf. Ostravský Kraj, E Czech Republic 50.05N 17.42E
Kroatien *see* Croatia
97 G14 **Krøderen** Buskerud, S Norway 60.06N 9.48E
97 G14 **Krøderen** ◎ S Norway
Kroi *see* Krui
97 N17 **Krokek** Östergötland, S Sweden 58.40N 16.25E
Krokodil *see* Crocodile
95 G16 **Krokom** Jämtland, C Sweden 63.19N 14.30E
119 S2 **Krolevets'** *Rus.* Krolevets. Sums'ka Oblast', NE Ukraine 51.34N 33.24E
Królewska Huta *see* Chorzów
113 H18 **Kroměříž** *Ger.* Kremsier. Zlínský Kraj, E Czech Republic 49.18N 17.24E
100 I9 **Krommenie** Noord-Holland, C Netherlands 52.30N 4.46E
130 J6 **Kromy** Orlovskaya Oblast', W Russian Federation 52.41N 35.45E
103 L18 **Kronach** Bayern, E Germany 50.14N 11.19E
Krone an der Brahe *see* Koronowo
178 I13 **Krŏng Kaôh Kŏng** Kaôh Kông, SW Cambodia 11.37N 102.58E
97 K21 **Kronoberg** ◈ *county* S Sweden
127 Pp11 **Kronotskiy Zaliv** *bay* E Russian Federation
205 O2 **Kronprinsesse Märtha Kyst** *physical region* Antarctica
205 V3 **Kronprins Olav Kyst** *physical region* Antarctica
128 G12 **Kronshtadt** Leningradskaya Oblast', NW Russian Federation 60.01N 29.42E
Kronstadt *see* Braşov
85 I22 **Kroonstad** Free State, C South Africa 27.40S 27.15E
126 Kk13 **Kropotkin** Irkutskaya Oblast', C Russian Federation 58.30N 115.21E
130 L14 **Kropotkin** Krasnodarskiy Kray, SW Russian Federation 45.28N 40.30E
112 J11 **Krośniewice** Łódzkie, C Poland 52.14N 19.10E
113 N17 **Krosno** *Ger.* Krossen. Podkarpackie, SE Poland 49.40N 21.46E
112 E12 **Krosno Odrzańskie** *Ger.* Crossen, Kreisstadt. Lubuskie, W Poland 52.02N 15.06E
Krossen *see* Krosno
Krotoschin *see* Krotoszyn
112 H13 **Krotoszyn** *Ger.* Krotoschin. Wielkopolskie, C Poland 51.43N 17.24E

◆ Country
● Country Capital
◇ Dependent Territory
○ Dependent Territory Capital
◈ Administrative Region
✕ International Airport
▲ Mountain
▲▲ Mountain Range
Volcano
≈ River
◎ Lake
▧ Reservoir

Krottingen see Kretinga
Krousón see Krousónas
117 J25 **Krousónas** prev. Krousón, Kroussón. Kríti, Greece, E Mediterranean Sea 35.13N 24.58E
Kroussón see Krousónas
Krraba see Krrabë
115 L20 **Krrabë** var. Krraba. Tiranë, C Albania 41.15N 19.56E
115 L17 **Krrabit, Mali i** ▲ N Albania
111 W12 **Krško** Ger. Gurkfeld; prev. Videm-Krško. E Slovenia 45.57N 15.31E
85 K19 **Kruger National Park** national park Northern, N South Africa
85 J21 **Krugersdorp** Gauteng, NE South Africa 26.04S 27.46E
40 D16 **Krugloi Point** headland Agattu Island, Alaska, USA 52.30N 173.46E
Krugloye see Kruhlaye
121 N15 **Kruhlaye** Rus. Krugloye. Mahilyowskaya Voblasts', E Belarus 54.15N 29.48E
174 I13 **Krui** var. Kroi. Sumatera, SW Indonesia 5.11S 103.55E
101 G16 **Kruibeke** Oost-Vlaanderen, N Belgium 51.10N 4.18E
85 G25 **Kruidfontein** Western Cape, SW South Africa 32.50S 21.59E
101 F15 **Kruiningen** Zeeland, SW Netherlands 51.28N 4.01E
Kruja see Krujë
115 L19 **Krujë** var. Kruja, It. Croia. Durrës, C Albania 41.30N 19.48E
Krulevshchina see Krulewshchyna
120 K13 **Krulewshchyna** Rus. Krulevshchina. Vitsyebskaya Voblasts', N Belarus 55.01N 27.46E
27 T6 **Krum** Texas, SW USA 33.15N 97.14W
103 J23 **Krumbach** Bayern, S Germany 48.12N 10.21E
115 M17 **Krumë** Kukës, NE Albania 42.11N 20.25E
Krummau see Český Krumlov
116 K12 **Krumovgrad** prev. Kossukavak. Kŭrdzhali, S Bulgaria 41.27N 25.40E
116 K12 **Krumovitsa** ⚠ S Bulgaria
116 L10 **Krumovo** Yambol, E Bulgaria 42.16N 26.25E
178 Hh11 **Krung Thep** var. Krung Thep Mahanakhon, Eng. Bangkok. ● (Thailand) Bangkok, C Thailand 13.43N 100.30E
178 Hh12 **Krung Thep, Ao** var. Bight of Bangkok. bay S Thailand
Krung Thep Mahanakhon see Krung Thep
Krupa/Krupa na Uni see Bosanska Krupa
121 M15 **Krupki** Rus. Krupki. Minskaya Voblasts', C Belarus 54.19N 29.07E
97 G24 **Kruså** var. Krusaa. Sønderjylland, SW Denmark 54.49N 9.25E
Krusaa see Kruså
15 I4 **Krusenstern, Cape** headland Nunavut, NW Canada 68.17N 114.00W
115 N14 **Kruševac** Serbia, C Serbia and Montenegro (Yugoslavia) 43.36N 21.19E
115 N19 **Kruševo** SW FYR Macedonia 41.22N 21.15E
113 A15 **Krušné Hory** Eng. Ore Mountains, Ger. Erzgebirge. ▲ Czech Republic/Germany see also Erzgebirge
41 W13 **Kruzof Island** island Alexander Archipelago, Alaska, USA
116 F13 **Krýa Vrýsi** var. Kría Vrísi. Kentrikí Makedonía, N Greece 40.40N 22.18E
121 P16 **Krychaw** Rus. Krichëv. Mahilyowskaya Voblasts', E Belarus 53.42N 31.43E
66 K11 **Krylov Seamount** undersea feature E Atlantic Ocean 17.34N 30.07W
Krym see Krym, Respublika
119 S13 **Krym, Respublika** var. Krym, Eng. Crimea, Crimean Oblast; prev. Rus. Krymskaya ASSR, Krymskaya Oblast'. ◆ province SE Ukraine
130 K14 **Krymsk** Krasnodarskiy Kray, SW Russian Federation 44.56N 38.02E
Krymskaya ASSR/Krymskaya Oblast' see Krym, Respublika
119 T13 **Kryms'ki Hory** ▲ S Ukraine
119 T13 **Kryms'kyy Pivostriv** peninsula S Ukraine
113 M18 **Krynica** Ger. Tannenhof. Małopolskie, S Poland 49.26N 20.57E
119 P8 **Kryve Ozero** Odes'ka Oblast', SW Ukraine 47.54N 30.19E
121 I18 **Kryvoshyn** Rus. Krivoshin. Brestskaya Voblasts', SW Belarus 52.52N 26.07E
121 K14 **Kryvychy** Rus. Krivichi. Minskaya Voblasts', C Belarus 54.43N 27.16E
119 S8 **Kryvyy Rih** Rus. Krivoy Rog. Dnipropetrovs'ka Oblast', SE Ukraine 47.53N 33.24E
119 N8 **Kryzhopil'** Vinnyts'ka Oblast', C Ukraine 48.22N 28.51E
Krzemieniec see Kremenets'
113 J14 **Krzepice** Śląskie, S Poland 50.58N 18.42E
112 F10 **Krzyż Wielkoplski** Wielkopolskie, C Poland 52.52N 16.03E
Ksar al Kabir see Ksar-el-Kebir
Ksar al Soule see Er-Rachidia
76 J5 **Ksar El Boukhari** N Algeria 35.57N 2.49E
76 G5 **Ksar-el-Kebir** var. Alcázar, Ksar al Kabir, Ksar-el-Kébir, Ar. Al-Kasr al-Kebir, Al-Qsar al-Kbir, Sp. Alcazarquivir. NW Morocco 35.04N 5.55W
112 H12 **Książ Wielkopolski** Ger. Xions. Wielkolpolskie, C Poland 52.03N 17.10E
131 O3 **Kstovo** Nizhegorodskaya Oblast', W Russian Federation 56.07N 44.12E
174 Mm4 **Kuala Belait** W Brunei 4.48N 114.12E
Kuala Dungun see Dungun
174 M7 **Kualakerian** Borneo, C Indonesia
174 M10 **Kualakuayan** Borneo, C Indonesia 2.01S 112.34E
174 H4 **Kuala Lipis** Pahang, Peninsular Malaysia 4.11N 102.00E
174 H5 **Kuala Lumpur** ● (Malaysia) Kuala Lumpur, Peninsular Malaysia 3.07N 101.42E
Kuala Pelabohan Kelang see Pelabuhan Klang
175 Nn3 **Kuala Penyu** Sabah, East Malaysia 5.37N 115.36E
40 E9 **Kualapuu** Haw. Kualapu'u. Molokai, Hawaii, USA, C Pacific Ocean 21.09N 157.02W
173 G6 **Kuala, Sungai** ⚠ Sumatera, W Indonesia
174 Hh3 **Kuala Terengganu** var. Kuala Trengganu. Terengganu, Peninsular Malaysia 5.19N 103.07E
174 Hh9 **Kualatungkal** Sumatera, W Indonesia 0.49S 103.22E
175 O3 **Kuamut, Sungai** ⚠ East Malaysia
175 Qq7 **Kuandang** Sulawesi, N Indonesia 0.50N 122.55E
175 Qq7 **Kuandang, Teluk** bay Sulawesi, N Indonesia
169 V12 **Kuandian** Liaoning, NE China 40.41N 124.46E
Kuando-Kubango see Cuando Cubango
Kuang-chou see Guangzhou
Kuang-hsi see Guangxi Zhuangzu Zizhiqu
Kuang-tung see Guangdong
Kuang-yuan see Guangyuan
174 Hh4 **Kuantan** Pahang, Peninsular Malaysia 3.49N 103.19E
Kuantan, Batang see Indragiri, Sungai
Kuanza Norte see Cuanza Norte
Kuanza Sul see Cuanza Sul
Kuba see Quba
125 Aa12 **Kuban'** var. Hypanis. ⚠ SW Russian Federation
Kubango see Cubango/Okavango
147 X8 **Kubārah** NW Oman 23.03N 56.52E
95 H16 **Kubbe** Västernorrland, C Sweden 63.31N 18.04E
82 A11 **Kubbum** Southern Darfur, W Sudan 11.46N 23.46E
128 L13 **Kubenskoye, Ozero** ⊚ NW Russian Federation
152 G6 **Kubla-Ustyurt** Rus. Komsomol'sk-na-Ustyurte. Qoraqalpog'iston Respublikasi, NW Uzbekistan 44.06N 58.14E
170 Ee16 **Kubokawa** Kōchi, Shikoku, SW Japan 33.22N 133.14E
116 L7 **Kubrat** prev. Balbunar. Razgrad, N Bulgaria 43.48N 26.31E
175 Oo15 **Kubu** Sumbawa, S Indonesia 8.15S 115.30E
114 O13 **Kučajske Planine** ▲ E Serbia and Montenegro (Yugoslavia)
172 Pp2 **Kuccharo-ko** ⊚ Hokkaidō, N Japan
114 O11 **Kučevo** Serbia, NE Serbia and Montenegro (Yugoslavia) 44.29N 21.42E
Kuchan see Qūchān
174 L6 **Kuching** prev. Sarawak. Sarawak, East Malaysia 1.31N 110.19E
174 L7 **Kuching** ✕ Sarawak, East Malaysia 1.31N 110.19E
170 Aa17 **Kuchinoerabu-jima** island Nansei-shotō, SW Japan
170 C13 **Kuchinotsu** Nagasaki, Kyūshū, SW Japan 32.36N 130.11E
111 Q6 **Kuchl** Salzburg, NW Austria 47.37N 13.12E
154 L9 **Kūchnay Darweyshān** Helmand, S Afghanistan 31.01N 64.09E
Kuchurgan see Kuchurhan
119 O9 **Kuchurhan** Rus. Kuchurgan. ⚠ NE Ukraine
Kuçova see Kuçovë
115 L21 **Kuçovë** var. Kuçova; prev. Qyteti Stalin. Berat, C Albania 40.48N 19.55E
142 D11 **Küçük Çekmece** İstanbul, NW Turkey 41.01N 28.46E
170 Dd13 **Kudamatsu** var. Kudamatu. Yamaguchi, Honshū, SW Japan 34.00N 131.53E
Kudamatu see Kudamatsu
Kudara see Ghŭdara
175 O1 **Kudat** Sabah, East Malaysia 6.54N 116.46E
Küddow see Gwda
161 G17 **Kūdligi** Karnātaka, W India 14.58N 76.24E
Kudowa see Kudowa-Zdrój
113 F16 **Kudowa-Zdrój** Ger. Kudowa. Wałbrzych, SW Poland 50.27N 16.13E
119 P9 **Kudryavtsivka** Mykolayivs'ka Oblast', S Ukraine 47.18N 31.02E
174 L14 **Kudus** prev. Koedoes. Jawa, C Indonesia 6.46S 110.48E
129 T13 **Kudymkar** Komi-Permyatskiy Avtonomnyy Okrug, NW Russian Federation 59.01N 54.40E
Kudzsir see Cugir
Kuei-chou see Guizhou
Kuei-lin see Guilin
Kuei-yang see Guiyang
K'u-erh-lo see Korla
Kueyang see Guiyang
Kufa see Al Kūfah
142 E14 **Küfiçayı** ⚠ C Turkey
111 O6 **Kufstein** Tirol, W Austria 47.36N 12.10E
151 V14 **Kugaly** Kaz. Qoghaly. Almaty, SE Kazakhstan 44.30N 78.40E
15 I4 **Kugluktuk** var. Qurlurtuuq prev. Coppermine. Nunavut, NW Canada 67.49N 115.12W
149 Y13 **Kūhak** Sīstān va Balūchestān, SE Iran 27.10N 63.15E
149 R9 **Kūhbonān** Kermān, C Iran 31.22N 56.16E
154 J5 **Kūhestān** var. Kohsān. Herāt, W Afghanistan 34.40N 61.10E
95 N15 **Kuhmo** Oulu, E Finland 64.04N 29.34E
95 L18 **Kuhmoinen** Länsi-Suomi, W Finland 61.32N 25.09E
Kuhnau see Konin
Kühnö see Kihnu
149 O8 **Kūhpāyeh** Eşfahān, C Iran 32.42N 52.25E
178 H13 **Kui Buri** var. Ban Kui Nua. Prachuap Khiri Khan, SW Thailand 12.10N 99.49E
Kuibyshev see Kuybyshevskoye Vodokhranilishche
84 D13 **Kuito** Port. Silva Porto. Bié, C Angola 12.21S 16.54E
41 X14 **Kuiu Island** island Alexander Archipelago, Alaska, USA
94 L13 **Kuivaniemi** Oulu, C Finland 65.34N 25.13E
79 V14 **Kujama** Kaduna, C Nigeria 10.27N 7.39E
112 I10 **Kujawsko-pomorskie** ◆ province, C Poland
172 N10 **Kuji** var. Kuzi. Iwate, Honshū, C Japan 40.12N 141.47E
Kujto, Ozero see Kuyto, Ozero
Kujū-renzan see Kujū-san
170 D14 **Kujū-san** var. Kujū-renzan. ▲ Kyūshū, SW Japan 33.07N 131.13E
45 N7 **Kukalaya, Rio** var. Rio Cuculaya, Rio Kukulaya. ⚠ NE Nicaragua
115 O16 **Kukavica** var. Vlajna. ▲ SE Serbia and Montenegro (Yugoslavia) 42.46N 21.58E
115 M18 **Kukës** var. Kukësi. Kukës, NE Albania 42.03N 20.25E
115 L18 **Kukës** ◆ district NE Albania
Kukësi see Kukës
194 J14 **Kukipi** Gulf, S PNG 8.10S 146.09E
131 S3 **Kukmor** Respublika Tatarstan, W Russian Federation 56.11N 50.56E
Kukong see Shaoguan
41 N6 **Kukpowruk River** ⚠ Alaska, USA
40 M6 **Kukpuk River** ⚠ Alaska, USA
Kukukhoto see Hohhot
Kukulaya, Rio see Kukalaya, Rio
174 Hh7 **Kukup** Johor, Peninsular Malaysia 1.18N 103.27E
201 W12 **Kuku Point** headland NW Wake Island 19.19N 166.36E
152 G11 **Kukurtli** Akhalskiy Velayat, C Turkmenistan 39.58N 58.47E
Kül see Kül, Rūd-e
116 F7 **Kula** Vidin, NW Bulgaria 43.55N 22.32E
142 D14 **Kula** Manisa, W Turkey 38.33N 28.36E
114 K9 **Kula** Serbia, NW Serbia and Montenegro (Yugoslavia) 45.37N 19.31E
155 S8 **Kulāchi** North-West Frontier Province, NW Pakistan 31.58N 70.30E
Kulachi see Kolāchi
150 F11 **Kulagino** Kaz. Külagino. Atyrau, W Kazakhstan 48.30N 51.33E
174 Hh6 **Kulai** Johor, Peninsular Malaysia 1.40N 103.33E
116 M7 **Kulak** ⚠ NE Bulgaria
159 T11 **Kula Kangri** var. Kulhakangri. ▲ Bhutan/China 28.06N 90.19E
150 E13 **Kulaly, Ostrov** island SW Kazakhstan
153 V9 **Kulanak** Narynskaya Oblast', C Kyrgyzstan 41.18N 75.38E
152 B8 **Kulandag** ▲ W Turkmenistan
151 S16 **Kulan** Kaz. Qulan; prev. Lugovoy, Lugovoye. Zhambyl, S Kazakhstan 42.55N 72.49E
159 V14 **Kulaura** Chittagong, NE Bangladesh 24.31N 92.01E
120 D9 **Kuldīga** Ger. Goldingen. Kuldīga, W Latvia 56.57N 21.59E
Kuldja see Yining
Kul'dzhuktau, Gory see Quljuqtov Tog'lari
131 N4 **Kulebaki** Nizhegorodskaya Oblast', W Russian Federation 55.25N 42.31E
114 E11 **Kulen Vakuf** var. Spasovo, Federacija Bosna I Hercegovina, NW Bosnia and Herzegovina 44.32N 16.05E
189 Q9 **Kulgera Roadhouse** Northern Territory, N Australia 25.49S 133.30E
Kulhakangri see Kula Kangri
131 T1 **Kuliga** Udmurtskaya Respublika, NW Russian Federation 58.14N 53.49E
Kulkuduk see Ko'lquduq
120 G4 **Kullamaa** Läänemaa, W Estonia 58.52N 24.05E
207 O12 **Kullorsuaq** var. Kuvdlorssuak. Kitaa, C Greenland 74.57N 57.07W
31 O6 **Kulm** North Dakota, N USA 46.18N 98.57W
Kulm see Chełmno
152 D12 **Kul'mach** Balkanskiy Velayat, W Turkmenistan 39.04N 55.49E
103 L18 **Kulmbach** Bayern, SE Germany 50.07N 11.27E
Kulmsee see Chełmża
153 Q14 **Kŭlob** Rus. Kulyab. SW Tajikistan 37.55N 68.46E
94 M13 **Kuloharju** Lappi, N Finland 65.51N 28.10E
129 N7 **Kuloy** Arkhangel'skaya Oblast', NW Russian Federation 64.55N 43.35E
129 N7 **Kuloy** ⚠ NW Russian Federation
143 Q14 **Kulp** Dıyarbakır, SE Turkey 38.31N 41.01E
Kulpa see Kolpa
79 P14 **Kulpawn** ⚠ N Ghana
149 R13 **Kūl, Rūd-e** var. Kül. ⚠ S Iran
150 G12 **Kul'sary** Kaz. Qulsary. Atyrau, W Kazakhstan 46.58N 53.58E
159 R15 **Kulti** West Bengal, NE India 23.45N 86.49E
95 G14 **Kultsjön** ⊚ N Sweden
142 I14 **Kulu** Konya, W Turkey 39.06N 33.01E
127 Nn10 **Kulu** ⚠ E Russian Federation
125 G14 **Kulunda** Altayskiy Kray, S Russian Federation 52.33N 79.04E
151 T7 **Kulunda Steppe** Kaz. Qulyndy Zhazyghy, Rus. Kulundinskaya Ravnina. grassland Kazakhstan/Russian Federation
Kulundinskaya Ravnina see Kulunda Steppe
190 M9 **Kulwin** Victoria, SE Australia 35.04S 142.37E
Kulyab see Kŭlob
119 Q3 **Kulykivka** Chernihivs'ka Oblast', N Ukraine 51.23N 31.39E
Kum see Qom
170 Ee15 **Kuma** Ehime, Shikoku, SW Japan 33.36N 132.53E
131 P14 **Kuma** ⚠ SW Russian Federation
Kumafa see Kumawa, Pegunungan
171 K15 **Kumagaya** Saitama, Honshū, S Japan 36.10N 139.22E
172 N6 **Kumaishi** Hokkaidō, NE Japan 42.08N 139.57E
174 Ll11 **Kumai, Teluk** bay Borneo, C Indonesia
131 Y7 **Kumak** Orenburgskaya Oblast', W Russian Federation 51.16N 60.06E
176 Y9 **Kumamba, Kepulauan** island group E Indonesia
170 Cc14 **Kumamoto** Kumamoto, Kyūshū, SW Japan 32.49N 130.40E
170 C14 **Kumamoto** off. Kumamoto-ken. ◆ prefecture Kyūshū, SW Japan
171 Gg17 **Kumano** Mie, Honshū, SW Japan 33.53N 136.03E
Kumanova see Kumanovo
115 O17 **Kumanovo** Turk. Kumanova. N FYR Macedonia 42.08N 21.42E
193 G17 **Kumara** West Coast, South Island, NZ 42.39S 171.12E
188 J8 **Kumarina Roadhouse** Western Australia 24.46S 119.39E
159 T15 **Kumarkhali** Khulna, W Bangladesh 23.54N 89.13E
79 P16 **Kumasi** prev. Coomassie. C Ghana 6.40N 1.39W
176 Vv11 **Kumawa, Pegunungan** var. Kumafa. ▲ Papua, E Indonesia
Kumayri see Gyumri
81 D15 **Kumba** Sud-Ouest, W Cameroon 4.39N 9.25E
116 N13 **Kumbağ** Tekirdağ, NW Turkey 40.51N 27.26E
161 J21 **Kumbakonam** Tamil Nādu, SE India 10.58N 79.24E
176 Z16 **Kumbe, Sungai** ⚠ Papua, E Indonesia
Kum-Dag see Gumdag
172 O14 **Kume-jima** island Nansei-shotō, SW Japan
131 V6 **Kumertau** Respublika Bashkortostan, W Russian Federation 52.48N 55.48E
125 F11 **Kuminskiy** Khanty-Mansiyskiy Avtonomnyy Okrug, C Russian Federation 58.42N 65.56E
37 R4 **Kumiva Peak** ▲ Nevada, W USA 40.24N 119.16W
165 N8 **Kum Kuduk** well NW China 40.21N 91.43E
165 N7 **Kumkuduk** Xinjiang Uygur Zizhiqu, W China 40.15N 91.55E
Kumkurgan see Qumqo'rg'on
97 M16 **Kumla** Örebro, C Sweden 59.51N 16.40E
142 E17 **Kumluca** Antalya, SW Turkey 36.22N 30.16E
102 N9 **Kummerower See** ⊚ NE Germany
79 X14 **Kumo** Gombe, E Nigeria 10.03N 11.13E
151 O13 **Kumola** ⚠ C Kazakhstan
178 H1 **Kumon Range** ▲ N Myanmar
126 K14 **Kumora** Respublika Buryatiya, S Russian Federation 55.43N 110.47E
85 F22 **Kums** Karas, SE Namibia 28.07S 19.40E
161 E18 **Kumta** Karnātaka, W India 14.25N 74.24E
164 L6 **Kümük** Xinjiang Uygur Zizhiqu, W China
40 H12 **Kumukahi, Cape** headland Hawaii, USA, C Pacific Ocean 19.31N 154.48W
131 Q17 **Kumukh** Respublika Dagestan, SW Russian Federation 42.10N 47.07E
Kumul see Hami
131 N9 **Kumylzhenskaya** Volgogradskaya Oblast', SW Russian Federation 49.54N 42.35E
147 W6 **Kumzār** N Oman 26.19N 56.26E
155 S4 **Kunar** Per. Konarhā. ◆ province E Afghanistan
Kunashiri see Kunashir, Ostrov
127 Pf16 **Kunashir, Ostrov** var. Kunashiri. island Kuril'skiye Ostrova, SE Russian Federation
120 I3 **Kunda** Lääne-Virumaa, NE Estonia 59.31N 26.32E
158 M13 **Kunda** Uttar Pradesh, N India 25.43N 81.31E
161 E19 **Kundāpura** var. Coondapoor. Karnātaka, W India 13.39N 74.41E
81 O24 **Kundelungu, Monts** ▲ S Dem. Rep. Congo
Kundert see Hernád
194 I12 **Kundiawa** Chimbu, W PNG 06.00S 144.57E
Kundla see Sāvarkundla
174 Hh7 **Kundur, Pulau** island W Indonesia
155 Q2 **Kunduz** var. Kondoz, Kundūz, Qondūz, Per. Kondūz. Kunduz, NE Afghanistan 36.48N 68.50E
155 Q2 **Kunduz** Per. Kondūz. ◆ province NE Afghanistan
Kuneitra see Al Qunayţirah
85 B18 **Kunene** ◆ district NE Namibia
85 A16 **Kunene** var. Cunene. ⚠ Angola/Namibia see also Cunene
Künes see Xinyuan
164 J5 **Künes He** ⚠ NW China
97 I19 **Kungälv** Västra Götaland, S Sweden 57.54N 12.00E
153 W7 **Kungei Ala-Tau** Rus. Khrebet Kyungëy Ala-Too, Kir. Küngöy Ala-Too. ▲ Kazakhstan/Kyrgyzstan
Küngöy Ala-Too see Kungei Ala-Tau
Kungrad see Qo'ng'irot
97 J19 **Kungsbacka** Halland, S Sweden 57.30N 12.04E
97 I18 **Kungshamn** Västra Götaland, S Sweden 58.21N 11.15E
97 M16 **Kungsör** Västmanland, C Sweden 59.25N 16.21E
81 J16 **Kungu** Equateur, NW Dem. Rep. Congo 2.46N 19.12E
129 V15 **Kungur** Permskaya Oblast', NW Russian Federation 57.24N 56.56E
177 G9 **Kungyangon** Yangon, SW Myanmar 16.27N 96.00E
113 M22 **Kunhegyes** Jász-Nagykun-Szolnok, E Hungary 47.23N 20.37E
178 H5 **Kunhing** Shan State, E Myanmar 21.17N 98.26E
170 Cc15 **Kunimi-dake** ▲ Kyūshū, SW Japan 32.31N 131.01E
164 D9 **Kunjirap Daban** var. Khūnjerāb Pass. pass China/Pakistan see also Khūnjerāb Pass 36.46N 75.16E
Kunlun Mountains see Kunlun Shan
164 H10 **Kunlun Shan** Eng. Kunlun Mountains. ▲ NW China
165 P11 **Kunlun Shankou** pass C China 35.45N 93.59E
166 G13 **Kunming** var. K'un-ming; prev. Yunnan. Yunnan, SW China 25.04N 102.40E
172 N6 **Kunnui** Hokkaidō, NE Japan 42.26N 140.18E
97 B18 **Kunoy** Dan. Kunø Island Faeroe Islands 62.18N 6.40W
169 X16 **Kunsan** var. Gunsan, Jap. Gunzan. W South Korea 35.58N 126.42E
113 L24 **Kunszentmárton** Jász-Nagykun-Szolnok, E Hungary 46.49N 20.15E
113 J23 **Kunszentmiklós** Bács-Kiskun, C Hungary 47.02N 19.05E
189 N3 **Kununurra** Western Australia 15.49S 128.43E
Kunya-Urgench see Këneurgench
Kunyé see Pins, Île des
174 Mm8 **Kunyi** Borneo, C Indonesia 3.22S 119.19E
103 I20 **Künzelsau** Baden-Württemberg, S Germany 49.22N 9.43E
167 S10 **Kuocang Shan** ▲ SE China
128 H5 **Kuoloyarvi** var. Luolajarvi. Murmanskaya Oblast', NW Russian Federation 66.58N 29.13E
95 N16 **Kuopio** Itä-Suomi, C Finland 62.54N 27.41E
95 K17 **Kuortane** Länsi-Suomi, W Finland 62.48N 23.30E
95 M18 **Kuortti** Itä-Suomi, E Finland 61.25N 26.25E
Kupa see Kolpa
175 R17 **Kupang** prev. Koepang. Timor, C Indonesia 10.13S 123.37E
41 Q5 **Kuparuk River** ⚠ Alaska, USA
Kupchino see Cupcina
194 L16 **Kupiano** Central, S PNG 10.04S 148.16E
188 M4 **Kupingarri** Western Australia 16.46S 125.57E
125 G14 **Kupino** Novosibirskaya Oblast', C Russian Federation 54.22N 77.09E
120 H11 **Kupiškis** Kupiškis, NE Lithuania 55.51N 24.58E
116 L13 **Küplü** Edirne, NW Turkey 41.06N 26.23E
41 X13 **Kupreanof Island** island Alexander Archipelago, Alaska, USA
41 O16 **Kupreanof Point** headland Alaska, USA 55.34N 159.36W
114 G13 **Kupres** Federacija Bosna I Hercegovina, SW Bosnia and Herzegovina 44.00N 17.15E
119 W5 **Kup"yans'k** Rus. Kupyansk. Kharkivs'ka Oblast', E Ukraine 49.42N 37.36E
119 W5 **Kup"yans'k-Vuzlovyy** Kharkivs'ka Oblast', E Ukraine 49.40N 37.41E
164 I6 **Kuqa** Xinjiang Uygur Zizhiqu, NW China 41.43N 82.58E
Kür see Kura
143 W11 **Kura** Az. Kür, Geor. Mtkvari, Turk. Kura Nehri. ⚠ SW Asia
57 R8 **Kuracki** NW Guyana 6.52N 60.13W
170 Ee13 **Kurahashi-jima** island SW Japan
Kura Kurk see Irbe Strait
153 Q10 **Kurama Range** Rus. Kuraminskiy Khrebet. ▲ Tajikistan/Uzbekistan
Kuraminskiy Khrebet see Kurama Range
Kura Nehri see Kura
176 Ww10 **Kuran, Kepulauan** island group E Indonesia
121 J14 **Kuranyets** Rus. Kurenets. Minskaya Voblasts', C Belarus 54.34N 26.58E
170 Ff14 **Kurashiki** var. Kurasiki. Okayama, Honshū, SW Japan 34.35N 133.44E
160 L10 **Kurasia** Madhya Pradesh, C India 23.11N 82.16E
Kurasiki see Kurashiki
170 G12 **Kurayoshi** var. Kurayosi. Tottori, Honshū, SW Japan 35.25N 133.51E
Kurayosi see Kurayoshi
169 X6 **Kurbin He** ⚠ NE China
151 X10 **Kurchum** Kaz. Kürshim. Vostochnyy Kazakhstan, E Kazakhstan 48.35N 83.37E
151 Y10 **Kurchum** ⚠ E Kazakhstan
143 X11 **Kürdämir** Rus. Kyurdamir. C Azerbaijan 40.21N 48.08E
Kurdestan see Kordestān
145 S1 **Kurdistan** cultural region SW Asia
Kurd Kui see Kord Küy
161 F15 **Kurduvādi** Mahārāshtra, W India 18.06N 75.31E
116 J11 **Kŭrdzhali** var. Kirdzhali. Kŭrdzhali, S Bulgaria 41.39N 25.23E
116 J11 **Kŭrdzhali** ◆ province S Bulgaria
116 J11 **Kŭrdzhali, Yazovir** ⊠ S Bulgaria
170 Ee13 **Kure** Hiroshima, Honshū, SW Japan 34.15N 132.33E
199 J5 **Kure Atoll** var. Ocean Island. atoll Hawaiian Islands, Hawaii, USA, C Pacific Ocean
142 J10 **Küre Dağları** ▲ N Turkey
Kurenets see Kuranyets
120 E6 **Kuressaare** Ger. Arensburg; prev. Kingissepp. Saaremaa, W Estonia 58.14N 22.27E
126 I9 **Kureyka** Krasnoyarskiy Kray, N Russian Federation 66.22N 87.21E
126 I9 **Kureyka** ⚠ N Russian Federation
151 P10 **Kurgal'dzhin, Ozero** ⊚ C Kazakhstan
Kurgal'dzhinskiy see Korgalzhyn
Kurgal'dzhino see Korgalzhyn
125 F12 **Kurgan** Kurganskaya Oblast', C Russian Federation 55.30N 65.19E
130 L14 **Kurganinsk** Krasnodarskiy Kray, SW Russian Federation 44.55N 40.45E
125 Ee12 **Kurganskaya Oblast'** ◆ province C Russian Federation
Kurgan-Tyube see Qŭrghonteppa
203 O2 **Kuria** prev. Woodle Island. island Tungaru, W Kiribati
Kuria Muria Bay see Ḩalānīyāt, Khalīj al
Kuria Muria Islands see Ḩalānīyāt, Juzur al
159 T13 **Kurigram** Rajshahi, N Bangladesh 25.49N 89.37E
176 Yy16 **Kurik** Papua, E Indonesia 8.12S 140.15E
95 K17 **Kurikka** Länsi-Suomi, W Finland 62.36N 22.25E
171 M12 **Kurikoma-yama** ▲ Honshū, C Japan 38.57N 140.44E
199 Hh3 **Kurile Basin** undersea feature NW Pacific Ocean
Kurile Islands see Kuril'skiye Ostrova
Kurile-Kamchatka Depression see Kurile Trench
199 Hh3 **Kurile Trench** var. Kurile-Kamchatka Depression. undersea feature NW Pacific Ocean
131 Q9 **Kurilovka** Saratovskaya Oblast', W Russian Federation 50.39N 48.02E
127 P15 **Kuril'sk** Kuril'skiye Ostrova, Sakhalinskaya Oblats', SE Russian Federation 45.10N 147.51E
127 Pp15 **Kuril'skiye Ostrova** Eng. Kurile Islands. island group SE Russian Federation
44 M9 **Kurinwas, Río** ⚠ E Nicaragua
Kurisches Haff see Courland Lagoon
Kurkund see Kilingi-Nõmme
130 M4 **Kurlovskiy** Vladimirskaya Oblast', W Russian Federation 55.25N 40.39E
82 G12 **Kurmuk** Blue Nile, SE Sudan 10.36N 34.16E
Kurna see Al Qurnah
161 H17 **Kurnool** var. Karnul. Andhra Pradesh, S India 15.51N 78.01E
171 J13 **Kurobe** Toyama, Honshū, SW Japan 36.52N 137.26E
170 Cc13 **Kurogi** Fukuoka, Kyūshū, SW Japan 33.09N 130.45E
171 Mm9 **Kuroishi** var. Kuroisi. Aomori, Honshū, C Japan 40.40N 140.34E
Kuroisi see Kuroishi
171 Kk14 **Kuroiso** Tochigi, Honshū, S Japan 36.58N 140.01E
172 N5 **Kuromatsunai** Hokkaidō, NE Japan 42.40N 140.18E
172 Oo17 **Kuro-shima** island SW Japan
171 H16 **Kuroso-yama** ▲ Honshū, SW Japan 34.31N 136.10E
193 F21 **Kurow** Canterbury, South Island, NZ 44.44S 170.29E
176 Uu13 **Kur, Pulau** island E Indonesia
131 N15 **Kursavka** Stavropol'skiy Kray, SW Russian Federation 44.28N 42.31E
120 E11 **Kuršėnai** Šiauliai, N Lithuania 56.00N 22.56E
Kürshim see Kurchum
Kurshskaya Kosa/Kuršių Nerija see Courland Spit
130 J7 **Kursk** Kurskaya Oblast', W Russian Federation 51.43N 36.46E
130 I7 **Kurskaya Oblast'** ◆ province W Russian Federation
Kurskiy Zaliv see Courland Lagoon
115 N15 **Kuršumlija** Serbia, S Serbia and Montenegro (Yugoslavia) 43.09N 21.16E
143 R15 **Kurtalan** Siirt, SE Turkey 37.56N 41.43E
125 Ee12 **Kurtamysh** Kurganskaya Oblast', C Russian Federation 54.51N 64.46E
Kurtbunar see Tervel
Kurt-Dere see Vŭlchidol
Kurtitsch/Kürtös see Curtici
151 U15 **Kurtty** ⚠ SE Kazakhstan
95 L18 **Kuru** Länsi-Suomi, W Finland 61.51N 23.46E
82 C13 **Kuru** ⚠ W Sudan
116 M13 **Kuru Dağı** ▲ NW Turkey
164 L7 **Kuruktag** ▲ NW China
85 G22 **Kuruman** Northern Cape, N South Africa 27.28S 23.27E
69 T14 **Kuruman** ⚠ W South Africa
170 Cc13 **Kurume** Fukuoka, Kyūshū, SW Japan 33.15N 130.27E
126 K15 **Kurumkan** Respublika Buryatiya, S Russian Federation 54.13N 110.21E
161 J25 **Kurunegala** North Western Province, C Sri Lanka 7.28N 80.22E
57 T10 **Kurupukari** C Guyana 4.39N 58.39W
129 U10 **Kur"ya** Respublika Komi, NW Russian Federation 61.38N 57.12E
150 E15 **Kuryk** prev. Yeraliyev. Mangistau, SW Kazakhstan 43.12N 51.43E
142 B15 **Kuşadası** Aydın, SW Turkey 37.51N 27.15E
117 M19 **Kuşadası Körfezi** gulf SW Turkey
170 Aa16 **Kusagaki-guntō** island SW Japan
Kusaie see Kosrae
151 T12 **Kusak** ⚠ C Kazakhstan
Kusary see Qusar
178 Hh8 **Ku Sathan, Doi** ▲ NW Thailand 18.22N 100.31E
171 H15 **Kusatsu** var. Kusatu. Shiga, Honshū, SW Japan 35.02N 135.58E
Kusatu see Kusatsu
144 F11 **Kuseifa** Southern, C Israel 31.15N 35.01E
142 C12 **Kuş Gölü** ⊚ NW Turkey
130 L12 **Kushchevskaya** Krasnodarskiy Kray, SW Russian Federation 46.35N 39.40E
171 H16 **Kushida-gawa** ⚠ Honshū, SW Japan
170 Bb15 **Kushikino** var. Kusikino. Kagoshima, Kyūshū, SW Japan 31.42N 130.13E
170 C17 **Kushima** var. Kusima. Miyazaki, Kyūshū, SW Japan 31.27N 131.11E
170 G17 **Kushimoto** Wakayama, Honshū, SW Japan 33.28N 135.45E
172 Q7 **Kushiro** var. Kusiro. Hokkaidō, NE Japan 42.58N 144.24E
154 K4 **Kūshk** Herāt, W Afghanistan 34.54N 62.09E
152 J17 **Kushka** ⚠ S Turkmenistan
Kushka see Gushgy
151 N8 **Kushmurun** Kaz. Qusmuryn. Kostanay, N Kazakhstan 52.27N 64.31E
151 N8 **Kushmurun, Ozero** Kaz. Qusmuryn. ⊚ N Kazakhstan
131 U4 **Kushnarenkovo** Respublika Bashkortostan, W Russian Federation 55.07N 55.24E
Kushrabat see Qo'shrabot
159 T15 **Kushtia** var. Kustia. Khulna, W Bangladesh 23.54N 89.07E
125 Ee10 **Kushva** Sverdlovskaya Oblast', C Russian Federation 58.14N 59.36E
Kusikino see Kushikino
Kusima see Kushima
Kusiro see Kushiro
40 M13 **Kuskokwim Bay** bay Alaska, USA
41 P11 **Kuskokwim Mountains** ▲ Alaska, USA
41 N12 **Kuskokwim River** ⚠ Alaska, USA
110 G7 **Küsnacht** Zürich, N Switzerland 47.21N 8.32E
172 Qq6 **Kussharo-ko** var. Kussyaro. ⊚ Hokkaidō, NE Japan
Küssnacht see Küssnacht am Rigi
110 F8 **Küssnacht am Rigi** var. Küssnacht. Schwyz, C Switzerland 47.03N 8.25E
Kussyaro see Kussharo-ko
Kustanay see Kostanay
Küstence/Küstendje see Constanţa
102 F11 **Küstenkanal** var. Ems-Hunte Canal. canal NW Germany
Küstrin see Kostrzyn
Kustia see Kushtia
175 T7 **Kusu** Pulau Halmahera, E Indonesia 0.51N 127.41E
175 Nn16 **Kuta** Pulau Lombok, S Indonesia 8.52S 116.15E
145 T4 **Kutabān** N Iraq 35.21N 44.45E
142 E13 **Kütahya** prev. Kutaia. Kütahya, W Turkey 39.25N 29.55E
142 E13 **Kütahya** var. Kutaia. ◆ province W Turkey
Kutai see Mahakam, Sungai
Kutaia see Kütahya
143 R9 **K'ut'aisi** W Georgia 42.15N 42.42E
Kūt al 'Amārah see Al Kūt
Kut al Hai/Kūt al Ḩayy see Al Ḩayy
Kut al Imara see Al Kūt
126 M12 **Kutana** Respublika Sakha (Yakutiya), NE Russian Federation 59.05N 131.43E
Kutaradja/Kutaraja see Bandaaceh
172 Nn5 **Kutchan** Hokkaidō, NE Japan 42.54N 140.46E
Kutch, Gulf of see Kachchh, Gulf of
Kutch, Rann of see Kachchh, Rann of
114 F9 **Kutina** Sisak-Moslavina, NE Croatia 45.29N 16.45E
114 H9 **Kutjevo** Požega-Slavonija, NE Croatia 45.26N 17.54E
113 E17 **Kutná Hora** Ger. Kuttenberg. Středočeský Kraj, C Czech Republic 49.57N 15.15E
112 K12 **Kutno** Łódzkie, C Poland 52.13N 19.23E
Kuttenberg see Kutná Hora
81 I20 **Kutu** Bandundu, W Dem. Rep. Congo 2.42S 18.07E
159 V17 **Kutubdia Island** island SE Bangladesh
82 B10 **Kutum** Northern Darfur, W Sudan 14.10N 24.40E
153 Y7 **Kuturgu** Issyk-Kul'skaya Oblast', E Kyrgyzstan 42.45N 78.04E
10 M5 **Kuujjuaq** prev. Fort-Chimo. Quebec, E Canada 58.10N 68.15W
10 I7 **Kuujjuarapik** Quebec, C Canada 55.07N 78.09W
152 A10 **Kuuli-Mayak** Turkm. Guwlumayak. Balkanskiy Velayat, NW Turkmenistan 40.14N 52.43E
120 I6 **Kuulse magi** ▲ S Estonia
94 N13 **Kuusamo** Oulu, E Finland 65.57N 29.15E
95 M19 **Kuusankoski** Etelä-Suomi, S Finland 60.51N 26.40E
131 W7 **Kuvandyk** Orenburgskaya Oblast', W Russian Federation 51.27N 57.18E
Kuvango see Cubango
Kuvasay see Quwasoy
Kuvdlorssuak see Kullorsuaq
128 I16 **Kuvshinovo** Tverskaya Oblast', W Russian Federation 57.03N 34.09E
147 Q4 **Kuwait** off. State of Kuwait, var. Dawlat al Kuwait, Koweit, Kuweit. ◆ monarchy SW Asia
Kuwait see Al Kuwayt
Kuwait Bay see Kuwayt, Jūn al
Kuwait City see Al Kuwayt
Kuwait, Dawlat al see Kuwait
Kuwajleen see Kwajalein Atoll
171 H15 **Kuwana** Mie, Honshū, SW Japan 35.03N 136.40E
176 V9 **Kuwawin** Papua, E Indonesia 1.10S 132.40E
145 X9 **Kuwayt** E Iraq 32.26N 47.12E
148 K11 **Kuwayt, Jūn al** var. Kuwait Bay. bay E Kuwait
Kuweit see Kuwait
119 P10 **Kuyal'nyts'kyy Lyman** ⊚ SW Ukraine
125 G13 **Kuybyshev** Novosibirskaya Oblast', C Russian Federation 55.28N 77.55E
Kuybyshev see Bolgar, Respublika Tatarstan, Russian Federation
Kuybyshev see Samara
119 W9 **Kuybysheve** Rus. Kuybyshevo. Zaporiz'ka Oblast', SE Ukraine 47.20N 36.41E
Kuybyshevo see Kuybysheve
Kuybyshev Reservoir see Kuybyshevskoye Vodokhranilishche
Kuybyshevskaya Oblast' see Samarskaya Oblast'
151 O7 **Kuybyshevskiy** Severnyy Kazakhstan, N Kazakhstan 53.16N 66.53E
131 R4 **Kuybyshevskoye Vodokhranilishche** var. Kuibyshev, Eng. Kuybyshev Reservoir. ⊠ W Russian Federation
127 N9 **Kuydusun** Respublika Sakha (Yakutiya), NE Russian Federation 63.15N 143.10E
129 U16 **Kuyeda** Permskaya Oblast', NW Russian Federation 56.23N 55.19E
Kuyjsanjaq see Koi Sanjaq
128 I7 **Kuyto, Ozero** var. Ozero Kujto. ⊚ NW Russian Federation
164 J4 **Kuytun** Xinjiang Uygur Zizhiqu, NW China 44.25N 84.55E

◆ Country ● Country Capital ◇ Dependent Territory ○ Dependent Territory Capital ◆ Administrative Region ✕ International Airport ▲ Mountain ▲ Mountain Range 🌋 Volcano ⚠ River ⊚ Lake ⊠ Reservoir

126 J15 Kuytun Irkutskaya Oblast', S Russian Federation 54.18N 101.28E
126 Ii12 Kuyumba Evenkiyskiy Avtonomnyy Okrug, C Russian Federation 61.00N 97.07E
57 S12 Kuyuwini Landing S Guyana 2.06N 59.14W
Kuzi see Kuji
40 M9 Kuzitrin River ⇝ Alaska, USA
131 P6 Kuznetsk Penzenskaya Oblast', W Russian Federation 53.06N 46.27E
118 K3 Kuznetsovs'k Rivnens'ka Oblast', NW Ukraine 51.21N 25.51E
128 K6 Kuzomen' Murmanskaya Oblast', NW Russian Federation 66.16N 36.47E
172 N10 Kuzumaki Iwate, Honshū, C Japan 40.04N 141.26E
94 H9 Kvaløya island N Norway
94 K8 Kvalsund Finnmark, N Norway 70.30N 23.56E
96 G11 Kvam Oppland, S Norway 61.42N 9.43E
131 X7 Kvarkeno Orenburgskaya Oblast', W Russian Federation 52.09N 59.44E
95 G15 Kvarnbergsvattnet var. Frostviken. ◎ N Sweden
114 A11 Kvarner var. Carnaro, It. Quarnero. gulf W Croatia
114 B11 Kvarnerič channel W Croatia
41 O14 Kvichak Bay bay Alaska, USA
94 H12 Kvikkjokk Norrbotten, N Sweden 66.58N 17.45E
97 D17 Kvina ⇝ S Norway
94 Q1 Kvitøya island NE Svalbard
97 F16 Kvitseid Telemark, S Norway 59.23N 8.31E
97 H24 Kværndrup Fyn, C Denmark 55.10N 10.31E
81 H20 Kwa ⇝ W Dem. Rep. Congo
79 Q15 Kwadwokurom C Ghana 7.49N 0.15W
195 X14 Kwailibesi Malaita, N Solomon Islands 8.25S 160.48E
201 S6 Kwajalein Atoll var. Kuwajleen. atoll Ralik Chain, C Marshall Islands
57 W9 Kwakoegron Brokopondo, N Suriname 5.13N 55.19W
83 J21 Kwale Coast, S Kenya 4.11S 39.30E
79 U17 Kwale Delta, S Nigeria 5.51N 6.29E
81 H20 Kwamouth Bandundu, W Dem. Rep. Congo 3.10S 16.16E
Kwando see Cuando
Kwangchow see Guangzhou
Kwangchu see Kwangju
169 X16 Kwangju off. Kwangju-gwangyŏksi, var. Guangju, Kwangchu, Jap. Kōshū. SW South Korea 35.09N 126.52E
81 H20 Kwango Port. Cuango. ⇝ Angola/Dem. Rep. Congo see also Cuango
Kwangsi/Kwangsi Chuang Autonomous Region see Guangxi Zhuangzu Zizhiqu
Kwangtung see Guangdong
Kwangyuan see Guangyuan
83 F17 Kwania, Lake ◎ C Uganda
Kwanza see Cuanza
79 S15 Kwara ◆ state SW Nigeria
176 Ww11 Kwatisore Papua, E Indonesia 3.14S 134.57E
85 K22 KwaZulu/Natal off. KwaZulu/Natal Province; prev. Natal. ◆ province E South Africa
Kweichow see Guizhou
Kweichu see Guiyang
Kweilin see Guilin
Kweisui see Hohhot
Kweiyang see Guiyang
85 K17 Kwekwe prev. Que Que. Midlands, C Zimbabwe 18.55S 29.48E
85 G20 Kweneng ◆ district S Botswana
Kwesui see Hohhot
41 N12 Kwethluk Alaska, USA 60.48N 161.26W
41 N12 Kwethluk River ⇝ Alaska, USA
112 J8 Kwidzyń Ger. Marienwerder. Pomorskie, N Poland 53.44N 18.55E
40 M13 Kwigillingok Alaska, USA 59.51N 163.07W
194 K16 Kwikila Central, S PNG 9.48S 147.37E
81 I20 Kwilu ⇝ W Dem. Rep. Congo
Kwito see Cuito
176 V8 Kwoka, Gunung ▲ Papua, E Indonesia 0.34S 132.25E
80 I12 Kyabé Moyen-Chari, S Chad 9.28N 18.54E
191 O11 Kyabram Victoria, SE Australia 36.21S 145.04E
178 Gg9 Kyaikkami prev. Amherst. Mon State, S Myanmar 16.02N 97.36E
177 Ff9 Kyaiklat Irrawaddy, SW Myanmar 16.25N 95.42E
177 G8 Kyaikto Mon State, S Myanmar 17.16N 97.01E
126 Jj16 Kyakhta Respublika Buryatiya, S Russian Federation 50.24N 106.12E
190 G8 Kyancutta South Australia 33.10S 135.33E
177 Ff7 Kyangin Irrawaddy, SW Myanmar 18.19N 95.15E
178 Jj8 Ky Anh Ha Tinh, N Vietnam 18.05N 106.16E
177 Ff5 Kyaukpadaung Mandalay, C Myanmar 20.49N 95.07E
177 F6 Kyaukpyu Arakan State, W Myanmar 19.27N 93.33E
177 G5 Kyaukse Mandalay, C Myanmar 21.34N 96.12E
177 Ff8 Kyaunggon Irrawaddy, SW Myanmar 17.04N 95.12E
121 E14 Kybartai Pol. Kibarty. Vilkaviškis, S Lithuania 54.37N 22.44E
158 I7 Kyelang Himāchal Pradesh, NW India 32.33N 77.03E
113 G19 Kyjov Ger. Gaya. Brněnský Kraj, SE Czech Republic 49.00N 17.07E
117 J21 Kykládes var. Kikládhes, Eng. Cyclades. island group SE Greece
27 S11 Kyle Texas, SW USA 29.59N 97.52W
98 G9 Kyle of Lochalsh N Scotland, UK 57.17N 5.39W
103 D18 Kyll ⇝ W Germany
117 F19 Kyllíni var. Killini. ▲ S Greece
95 M19 Kymijoki ⇝ S Finland
117 H18 Kými, Akrotírio headland Évvoia, C Greece 38.39N 24.08E
129 W14 Kyn Permskaya Oblast', NW Russian Federation 57.48N 58.38E
191 N12 Kyneton Victoria, SE Australia 37.14S 144.28E
83 G17 Kyoga, Lake var. Lake Kioga. ◎ C Uganda
171 H13 Kyōga-misaki headland Honshū, SW Japan 35.46N 135.13E
191 V4 Kyogle New South Wales, SE Australia 28.37S 153.00E
169 W15 Kyŏnggi-man bay NW South Korea
169 Z16 Kyŏngju Jap. Keishū. SE South Korea 35.49N 129.09E
Kyŏngsŏng see Sŏul
Kyōsai-tō see Kōje-do
83 F19 Kyotera S Uganda 0.37S 31.34E
171 H15 Kyōto Kyōto, Honshū, SW Japan 35.01N 135.46E
171 H14 Kyōto off. Kyōto-fu, var. Kyōto Hu. ◆ urban prefecture Honshū, SW Japan
Kyōto-fu/Kyōto Hu see Kyōto
117 D21 Kyparissía var. Kiparissía. Pelopónnisos, S Greece 37.13N 21.39E
117 D20 Kyparissiakós Kólpos gulf S Greece
Kyperounda see Kyperoúnta
124 N3 Kyperoúnta var. Kyperounda. C Cyprus 34.57N 33.02E
Kypros see Cyprus
117 H16 Kyrá Panagía island Vóreioi Sporádes, Greece, Aegean Sea
Kyrenia see Girne
Kyrenia Mountains see Beşparmak Dağları
Kyrgyz Republic see Kyrgyzstan
153 U9 Kyrgyzstan off. Kyrgyz Republic, var. Kirghizia; prev. Kirgizskaya SSR, Kirghiz SSR, Republic of Kyrgyzstan. ◆ republic C Asia
102 M11 Kyritz Brandenburg, NE Germany 52.56N 12.24E
Kyrkslätt see Kirkkonummi
96 G8 Kyrksæterøra Sør-Trøndelag, S Norway 63.16N 9.04E
129 U8 Kyrta Respublika Komi, NW Russian Federation 64.03N 57.41E
125 Ee12 Kyshtym Chelyabinskaya Oblast', S Russian Federation 55.39N 60.31E
113 J18 Kysucké Nové Mesto prev. Horné Nové Mesto, Ger. Kisutzaneustadtl, Oberneustadtl, Hung. Kiszucaújhely. Žilinský Kraj, N Slovakia 49.19N 18.47E
119 N12 Kytay, Ozero ◎ SW Ukraine
117 F23 Kýthira var. Kíthira, It. Cerigo; Lat. Cythera. Kýthira, S Greece 36.09N 22.58E
117 F23 Kýthira var. Kíthira, It. Cerigo; Lat. Cythera. island S Greece
117 I20 Kýthnos Kýthnos, Kykládes, Greece, Aegean Sea 37.24N 24.28E
117 I20 Kýthnos var. Kíthnos, Thermiá, It. Termia; anc. Cythnos. island Kykládes, Greece, Aegean Sea
117 I20 Kýthnou, Stenó strait Kykládes, Greece, Aegean Sea
Kythréa see Değirmenlik
Kyungëy Ala-Too, Khrebet see Kungei Ala-Tau
Kyurdamir see Kürdämir
152 C11 Kyuren, Gora ▲ W Turkmenistan 39.05N 55.09E
172 C15 Kyūshū var. Kyûsyû. island SW Japan
199 Gg6 Kyushu-Palau Ridge var. Kyusyu-Palau Ridge. undersea feature W Pacific Ocean
170 Cc15 Kyūshū-sanchi ▲▲ Kyūshū, SW Japan
116 F10 Kyustendil anc. Pautalia. Kyustendil, W Bulgaria 42.17N 22.42E
116 G11 Kyustendil ◆ province W Bulgaria
Kyûsyû see Kyūshū
Kyusyu-Palau Ridge see Kyushu-Palau Ridge
126 L7 Kyusyur Respublika Sakha (Yakutiya), NE Russian Federation 70.36N 127.19E
191 P10 Kywong New South Wales, SE Australia 34.59S 146.42E
119 P4 Kyyiv Eng. Kiev, Rus. Kiyev. ● (Ukraine) Kyyivs'ka Oblast', N Ukraine 50.26N 30.31E
Kyyiv see Kyyivs'ka Oblast'
119 O4 Kyyivs'ka Oblast' var. Kyyiv, Rus. Kiyevskaya Oblast'. ◆ province N Ukraine
119 P3 Kyyivs'ke Vodoskhovyshche Eng. Kiev Reservoir, Rus. Kiyevskoye Vodokhranilishche. ⊠ N Ukraine
95 L16 Kyyjärvi Länsi-Suomi, W Finland 63.01N 24.34E
126 I16 Kyzyl Respublika Tyva, C Russian Federation 51.45N 94.28E
153 S8 Kyzyl-Adyr prev. Kirovskoye. Talasskaya Oblast', NW Kyrgyzstan 42.37N 71.34E
151 V14 Kyzylagash Almaty, SE Kazakhstan 45.19N 78.45E
152 C13 Kyzylbair Balkanskiy Velayat, W Turkmenistan 38.13N 55.38E
Kyzyl-Dzhiik, Pereval see Uzbel Shankou
151 S7 Kyzylkak, Ozero ◎ NE Kazakhstan
151 X11 Kyzylkesek Vostochnyy Kazakhstan, E Kazakhstan 47.55N 82.01E
153 S10 Kyzyl-Kiya Kir. Kyzyl-Kyya. Oshskaya Oblast', SW Kyrgyzstan 40.15N 72.07E
150 L11 Kyzylkol', Ozero ◎ C Kazakhstan
151 N15 Kyzylorda var. Kzyl-Orda, Qizil Orda Kaz. Qyzylorda; prev. Perovsk. Kzylorda, S Kazakhstan 44.54N 65.30E
150 L14 Kyzylorda off. Kyzylordinskaya Oblast' Kaz. Qyzylorda Oblysy. ◆ province S Kazakhstan
138 L19 Kyzyl Kum var. Kizil Kum, Qizil Qum, Uzb. Qizilqum. desert Kazakhstan/Uzbekistan
Kyzyl-Kyya see Kyzyl-Kiya
Kyzylrabat see Qizilravote
Kyzylrabot see Qizilrabot
Kyzylsu see Kyzyl-Suu
153 X7 Kyzyl-Suu prev. Pokrovka. Issyk-Kul'skaya Oblast', NE Kyrgyzstan 42.19N 77.55E
153 S12 Kyzyl-Suu var. Kyzylsu. ⇝ Kyrgyzstan/Tajikistan
153 X8 Kyzyl-Tuu Issyk-Kul'skaya Oblast', E Kyrgyzstan 42.06N 76.54E
151 Q12 Kyzylzhar Kaz. Qyzylzhar. Zhezkazgan, C Kazakhstan 48.22N 70.00E
Kzyl-Orda see Kyzylorda
Kzyylordinskaya Oblast' see Kyzylorda
Kzyltu see Kishkenekol'

— L —

111 X2 Laa an der Thaya Niederösterreich, NE Austria 48.42N 16.22E
65 K15 La Adela La Pampa, SE Argentina 38.57S 64.02W
Laagen see Numedalslågen
111 S5 Laakirchen Oberösterreich, N Austria 47.59N 13.49E
Laaland see Lolland
106 I11 La Albuera Extremadura, W Spain 38.43N 6.49W
107 O7 La Alcarria physical region C Spain
106 K14 La Algaba Andalucía, S Spain 37.27N 6.01W
107 P9 La Almarcha Castilla-La Mancha, C Spain 39.40N 2.22W
107 R6 La Almunia de Doña Godina Aragón, NE Spain 41.28N 1.22W
43 N5 La Amistad, Presa ⊠ NW Mexico
120 F4 Läänemaa off. Lääne Maakond. ◆ province NW Estonia
120 I3 Lääne-Virumaa off. Lääne-Viru Maakond. ◆ province NE Estonia
64 J9 La Antigua, Salina salt lake W Argentina
101 E17 Laarne Oost-Vlaanderen, NW Belgium 51.03N 3.49E
82 O13 Laas Caanood Nugaal, N Somalia 8.33N 47.44E
43 O9 La Ascensión Nuevo León, NE Mexico 24.15N 99.53W
82 N12 Laas Dhaareed Woqooyi Galbeed, N Somalia 10.12N 46.09E
57 O4 La Asunción Nueva Esparta, NE Venezuela 11.06N 63.53W
Laatokka see Ladozhskoye Ozero
102 I13 Laatzen Niedersachsen, NW Germany 52.19N 9.46E
40 E9 Laau Point headland Molokai, Hawaii, USA, C Pacific Ocean 21.06N 157.18W
44 D6 La Aurora ✈ (Ciudad de Guatemala) Guatemala, C Guatemala 14.33N 90.30W
76 C9 Laâyoune var. Aaiún. ○ (Western Sahara) NW Western Sahara 27.10N 13.10W
130 L14 Laba ⇝ SW Russian Federation
42 M6 La Babia Coahuila de Zaragoza, NE Mexico 28.36N 102.04W
13 R7 La Baie Quebec, SE Canada 48.20N 70.54W
175 R16 Labala Pulau Lomblen, S Indonesia 8.30S 123.27E
64 K8 La Banda Santiago del Estero, N Argentina 27.43S 64.13W
La Banda Oriental see Uruguay
106 K4 La Bañeza Castilla-León, N Spain 42.18N 5.54W
42 M13 La Barca Jalisco, SW Mexico 20.18N 102.30W
42 K14 La Barra de Navidad Jalisco, C Mexico 19.12N 104.38W
197 J13 Labasa prev. Lambasa. Vanua Levu, N Fiji 16.25S 179.24E
179 Q15 Labason Mindanao, S Philippines 8.03N 122.31E
104 H8 la Baule-Escoublac Loire-Atlantique, NW France 47.16N 2.24W
Labe see Elbe
78 I13 Labé Moyenne-Guinée, NW Guinea 11.19N 12.16W
25 X14 La Belle Florida, SE USA 26.45N 81.26W
13 N11 Labelle Quebec, SE Canada 46.15N 74.43W
8 H7 Laberge, Lake ◎ Yukon Territory, W Canada
Labes see Łobez
Labiau see Polessk
114 A10 Labin It. Albona. Istra, NW Croatia 45.05N 14.07E
130 L14 Labinsk Krasnodarskiy Kray, SW Russian Federation 44.39N 40.43E
107 X5 La Bisbal d'Empordà Cataluña, NE Spain 41.58N 3.02E
121 P16 Labkovichy Rus. Lobkovichi. Mahilyowskaya Voblasts', E Belarus 53.49N 31.43E
13 S4 La Blache, Lac de ◎ Quebec, SE Canada
179 Q11 Labo Luzon, N Philippines 14.10N 122.47E
Laboehanbadjo see Labuhanbajo
Laborca see Laborec
113 N18 Laborec Hung. Laborca. ⇝ E Slovakia
110 D11 La Borgne ⇝ S Switzerland
47 T12 Laborie SW Saint Lucia 13.45N 61.00W
81 F21 La Bouenza ◆ province S Congo
104 J14 Labouheyre Landes, SW France 44.12N 0.55W
64 L12 Laboulaye Córdoba, C Argentina 34.05S 63.20W
11 Q7 Labrador cultural region Newfoundland and Labrador, SW Canada
66 I6 Labrador Basin var. Labrador Sea Basin. undersea feature Labrador Sea
11 N9 Labrador City Newfoundland and Labrador, E Canada 52.55N 66.52W
11 Q5 Labrador Sea sea NW Atlantic Ocean
Labrador Sea Basin see Labrador Basin
Labrang see Xiahe
56 G9 Labranzagrande Boyacá, C Colombia 5.30N 72.33W
47 U15 La Brea Trinidad, Trinidad and Tobago 10.13N 61.36W
61 D14 Lábrea Amazonas, N Brazil 7.19S 64.46W
13 S6 Labrieville Quebec, SE Canada 49.15N 69.31W
104 K14 Labrit Landes, SW France 44.03N 0.29W
110 C9 La Broye ⇝ SW Switzerland
105 N15 Labruguière Tarn, S France 43.31N 2.15E
174 I8 Labu Pulau Singkep, W Indonesia 0.34S 104.24E
175 N3 Labuan var. Victoria. Labuan, East Malaysia 5.19N 115.13E
175 N3 Labuan ◆ federal territory East Malaysia
Labuan see Labuan, Pulau
175 N3 Labuan, Pulau var. Labuan. island East Malaysia
175 Pp16 Labuhanbajo prev. Laboehanbadjo. Flores, S Indonesia 8.29S 119.54E
173 G6 Labuhanbilik Sumatera, N Indonesia 2.33N 100.09E
173 Ee5 Labuhanhaji Sumatera, W Indonesia 3.31N 97.00E
Labuk see Labuk, Sungai
Labuk Bay see Labuk, Teluk
175 O2 Labuk, Sungai var. Labuk. ⇝ East Malaysia
175 Oo2 Labuk, Teluk var. Labuk Bay, Telukan Labuk. bay S Sulu Sea
Labuk, Telukan see Labuk, Teluk
177 Ff9 Labutta Irrawaddy, SW Myanmar 16.07N 94.45E
125 G8 Labytnangi Yamalo-Nenetskiy Avtonomnyy Okrug, N Russian Federation 66.39N 66.26E
80 F10 Lac off. Préfecture du Lac. ◆ prefecture W Chad
115 K19 Laç var. Laci. Lezhë, C Albania 41.37N 19.37E
59 K19 Lacajahuira, Rio ⇝ W Bolivia
La Calamine see Kelmis
64 G11 La Calera Valparaíso, C Chile 32.48S 71.13W
11 P11 Lac-Allard Quebec, E Canada 50.37N 63.26W
106 L13 La Campana Andalucía, S Spain 37.35N 5.24W
104 J12 Lacanau Gironde, SW France 44.59N 1.04W
44 C2 Lacandón, Sierra del ▲▲ Guatemala/Mexico
La Cañiza see A Cañiza
43 W16 Lacantún, Río ⇝ SE Mexico
105 Q3 la Capelle Aisne, N France 49.58N 3.55E
114 K10 Laćarak Serbia, NW Serbia and Montenegro (Yugoslavia) 45.00N 19.34E
64 L11 La Carlota Córdoba, C Argentina 33.27S 63.16W
179 Q13 La Carlota Negros, S Philippines 10.21N 122.55E
106 L13 La Carlota Andalucía, S Spain 37.40N 4.55W
107 N12 La Carolina Andalucía, S Spain 38.15N 3.37W
105 O15 Lacaune Tarn, S France 43.42N 2.42E
13 P7 Lac-Bouchette Quebec, SE Canada 48.14N 72.11W
Laccadive Islands/Laccadive Minicoy and Amindivi Islands, the see Lakshadweep
9 Y16 Lac du Bonnet Manitoba, S Canada 50.13N 96.04W
32 L4 Lac du Flambeau Wisconsin, N USA 45.58N 89.51W
13 P8 Lac-Édouard Quebec, SE Canada 47.39N 72.16W
44 I4 La Ceiba Atlántida, N Honduras 15.45N 86.28W
56 E9 La Ceja Antioquia, W Colombia 6.08N 75.21W
190 J11 Lacepede Bay bay South Australia
34 G9 Lacey Washington, NW USA 47.01N 122.49W
105 P12 la Chaise-Dieu Haute-Loire, C France 45.19N 3.41E
116 G13 Lachanás Kentrikí Makedonía, N Greece 40.57N 23.15E
128 I11 Lacha, Ozero ◎ NW Russian Federation
105 O8 la Charité-sur-Loire Nièvre, C France 47.10N 2.59E
105 N9 la Châtre Indre, C France 46.34N 1.58E
110 C8 La Chaux-de-Fonds Neuchâtel, W Switzerland 47.07N 6.51E
Lach Dera see Dheere Laaq
110 G8 Lachen Schwyz, C Switzerland 47.11N 8.49E
191 Q8 Lachlan River ⇝ New South Wales, SE Australia
45 T15 La Chorrera Panamá, C Panama 8.51N 79.46W
13 V7 Lac-Humqui Quebec, SE Canada 48.21N 67.32W
13 N12 Lachute Quebec, SE Canada 45.39N 74.21W
Lachyn see Laçın
Laci see Laç
143 W13 Laçın Rus. Lachyn. SW Azerbaijan 39.36N 46.34E
105 S16 la Ciotat anc. Citharista. Bouches-du-Rhône, SE France 43.10N 5.36E
20 D10 Lackawanna New York, NE USA 42.49N 78.49W
9 Q13 Lac La Biche Alberta, SW Canada 54.46N 111.58W
Lac La Martre see Wha Ti
13 R12 Lac-Mégantic var. Mégantic. Quebec, SE Canada 45.34N 70.52W
Lacobriga see Lagos
42 G5 La Colorada Sonora, NW Mexico 28.46N 110.29W
9 Q15 Lacombe Alberta, SW Canada 52.30N 113.42W
32 L12 Lacon Illinois, N USA 41.01N 89.24W
45 P16 La Concepción var. Concepción. Chiriquí, W Panama 8.30N 82.37W
56 H5 La Concepción Zulia, NW Venezuela 10.22N 71.46W
56 H5 La Concepción Zulia, NW Venezuela 10.37N 71.51W
109 C19 Laconi Sardegna, Italy, C Mediterranean Sea 39.52N 9.02E
21 O9 Laconia New Hampshire, NE USA 43.31N 71.28W
63 H19 La Coronilla Rocha, E Uruguay 33.54S 53.32W
La Coruña see A Coruña
105 O11 la Courtine Creuse, C France 45.42N 2.18E
104 J16 Lacq Pyrénées-Atlantiques, SW France 43.25N 0.37W
13 P9 La Croche Quebec, SE Canada 47.38N 72.42W
31 X3 la Croix, Lac ◎ Canada/USA
28 K5 La Crosse Kansas, C USA 38.31N 99.18W
23 V7 La Crosse Virginia, NE USA 36.41N 78.03W
34 L9 La Crosse Washington, NW USA 46.48N 117.51W
32 J7 La Crosse Wisconsin, N USA 43.45N 91.12W
56 C13 La Cruz Nariño, SW Colombia 1.31N 77.01W
44 K12 La Cruz Guanacaste, NW Costa Rica 11.04N 85.37W
42 I10 La Cruz Sinaloa, W Mexico 23.52N 106.52W
63 F19 La Cruz Florida, S Uruguay 33.54S 56.10W
44 M9 La Cruz de Río Grande Región Autónoma Atlántico Sur, E Nicaragua 13.04N 84.07W
56 J4 La Cruz de Taratara Falcón, N Venezuela 11.03N 69.43W
13 Q10 Lac-St-Charles Quebec, SE Canada 46.56N 71.24W
42 M6 La Cuesta Coahuila de Zaragoza, NE Mexico 28.43N 102.33W
59 A17 La Cumbra, Volcán ♖ Galapagos Islands, Ecuador, E Pacific Ocean 0.21S 91.30W
158 J5 Ladākh Range ▲▲ NE India
28 I5 Ladder Creek ⇝ Kansas, C USA
47 X10 la Désirade atoll E Guadeloupe
Lādhiqīyah, Muḥāfaẓat al see Al Lādhiqīyah
85 F25 Ladismith Western Cape, SW South Africa 33.27S 21.15E
158 G11 Lādnūn Rājasthān, NW India 27.36N 74.25E
Ladoga, Lake see Ladozhskoye Ozero
117 E19 Ládon ⇝ S Greece
56 E9 La Dorada Caldas, C Colombia 5.28N 74.40W
128 H11 Ladozhskoye Ozero Eng. Lake Ladoga, Fin. Laatokka. ◎ NW Russian Federation
39 R12 Ladron Peak ▲ New Mexico, SW USA 34.25N 107.04W
128 J11 Ladva-Vetka Respublika Kareliya, NW Russian Federation 61.18N 34.24E
191 Q15 Lady Barron Tasmania, SE Australia 40.12S 148.12E
12 G9 Lady Evelyn Lake ◎ Ontario, S Canada
25 W11 Lady Lake Florida, SE USA 28.55N 81.55W
8 L17 Ladysmith Vancouver Island, British Columbia, SW Canada 48.55N 123.45W
85 J22 Ladysmith KwaZulu/Natal, E South Africa 28.34S 29.46E
32 J5 Ladysmith Wisconsin, N USA 45.27N 91.07W
151 P9 Ladyzhenka Akmola, C Kazakhstan 50.58N 68.44E
194 K13 Lae Morobe, W PNG 6.45S 146.55E
201 R6 Lae Atoll atoll Ralik Chain, W Marshall Islands
42 C3 La Encantada, Cerro de ▲ NW Mexico 31.03N 115.25W
96 E12 Lærdalsøyri Sogn og Fjordane, S Norway 61.04N 7.24E
57 N11 La Esmeralda Amazonas, S Venezuela 3.10N 65.33W
44 G7 La Esperanza Intibucá, SW Honduras 14.18N 88.10W
32 K8 La Farge Wisconsin, N USA 43.36N 90.39W
25 R5 Lafayette Alabama, S USA 32.54N 85.24W
39 T4 Lafayette Colorado, C USA 39.59N 105.06W
25 R2 La Fayette Georgia, SE USA 34.42N 85.16W
33 O13 Lafayette Indiana, N USA 40.25N 86.52W
24 I9 Lafayette Louisiana, S USA 30.13N 92.01W
22 K8 Lafayette Tennessee, S USA 36.31N 86.01W
21 N7 Lafayette, Mount ▲ New Hampshire, NE USA 44.09N 71.37W
La Fe see Santa Fé
105 P3 la Fère Aisne, N France 49.41N 3.20E
104 L6 la Ferté-Bernard Sarthe, NW France 48.13N 0.40E
104 K5 la Ferté-Macé Orne, N France 48.35N 0.21W
105 N7 la Ferté-St-Aubin Loiret, C France 47.42N 1.57E
105 P5 la Ferté-sous-Jouarre Seine-et-Marne, N France 48.57N 3.07E
79 V15 Lafia Nassarawa, C Nigeria 8.29N 8.34E
79 T15 Lafiagi Kwara, W Nigeria 8.52N 5.25E
9 T17 Lafleche Saskatchewan, S Canada 49.40N 106.28W
104 K7 la Flèche Sarthe, NW France 47.42N 0.04W
111 X7 Lafnitz Hung. Lapines. ⇝ Austria/Hungary
197 I6 La Foa Province Sud, S New Caledonia 21.46S 165.49E
22 M8 La Follette Tennessee, S USA 36.22N 84.07W
13 N12 Lafontaine Quebec, SE Canada 45.52N 74.01W
24 K10 Lafourche, Bayou ⇝ Louisiana, S USA
64 K6 La Fragua Santiago del Estero, N Argentina 26.06S 64.06W
56 H7 La Fría Táchira, NW Venezuela 8.13N 72.15W
106 J7 La Fuente de San Esteban Castilla-León, N Spain 40.48N 6.14W
194 G11 Lagaip ⇝ W PNG
63 B15 La Gallareta Santa Fe, C Argentina 29.34S 60.22W
131 Q14 Lagan' prev. Kaspiyskiy. Respublika Kalmykiya, SW Russian Federation 45.25N 47.19E
97 L20 Lagan Kronoberg, S Sweden 56.55N 14.01E
97 K21 Lågan ⇝ S Sweden
94 L2 Lagarfljót var. Lögurinn. ◎ E Iceland
39 R7 La Garita Mountains ▲▲ Colorado, C USA
179 P9 Lagawe Luzon, N Philippines 16.46N 121.06E
80 F13 Lagdo Nord, N Cameroon 9.12N 13.43E
80 F13 Lagdo, Lac de ◎ N Cameroon
102 H13 Lage Nordrhein-Westfalen, W Germany 52.00N 8.48E
96 H12 Lågen ⇝ S Norway
63 J14 Lages Santa Catarina, S Brazil 27.45S 50.16W
Laghj see Laḥij
155 R4 Laghmān ◆ province E Afghanistan
76 J6 Laghouat N Algeria 33.49N 2.59E
107 Q10 La Gineta Castilla-La Mancha, C Spain 39.08N 2.00W
117 E21 Lagkáda var. Langada. Pelopónnisos, S Greece 36.49N 22.19E
116 G13 Lagkadás var. Langades, Langadhás. Kentrikí Makedonía, N Greece 40.45N 23.04E
117 E20 Lagkádia var. Langádhia, Langadia. Pelopónnisos, S Greece 37.39N 22.03E
56 F6 La Gloria Cesar, N Colombia 8.37N 73.49W
43 O7 La Gloria Nuevo León, NE Mexico
94 N3 Lågneset headland W Svalbard 77.46N 13.44E
106 G14 Lagoa Faro, S Portugal 37.07N 8.27W
La Goagira see La Guajira
63 I14 Lagoa Vermelha Rio Grande do Sul, S Brazil 28.13S 51.31W
143 V10 Lagodekhi SE Georgia 41.49N 46.15E
44 C7 La Gomera Escuintla, S Guatemala 14.04N 91.03W
Lagone see Logone
109 M19 Lagonegro Basilicata, S Italy 40.06N 15.42E
65 G16 Lago Ranco Los Lagos, S Chile 40.21S 72.29W
79 S16 Lagos Lagos, SW Nigeria 6.24N 3.16E
106 F14 Lagos anc. Lacobriga. Faro, S Portugal 37.04N 8.40W
79 S16 Lagos ◆ state SW Nigeria
42 M12 Lagos de Moreno Jalisco, SW Mexico 21.21N 101.55W
Lagosta see Lastovo
76 A12 Lagouira SW Western Sahara 20.55N 17.04W
94 O1 Lågøya island N Svalbard
34 L11 La Grande Oregon, NW USA 45.21N 118.04W
105 Q14 la Grande-Combe Gard, S France 44.13N 4.01E
10 K9 La Grande Rivière var. Fort George. ⇝ Quebec, SE Canada
25 R4 La Grange Georgia, SE USA 33.01N 85.01W
33 P11 Lagrange Indiana, N USA 41.38N 85.25W
22 L5 La Grange Kentucky, S USA 38.22N 85.07W
29 V2 La Grange Missouri, C USA 40.00N 91.31W
23 V10 La Grange North Carolina, SE USA 35.18N 77.47W
27 U11 La Grange Texas, SW USA 29.54N 96.52W
107 N7 La Granja Castilla-León, N Spain 40.53N 4.01W
57 Q9 La Gran Sabana grassland E Venezuela
56 H7 La Grita Táchira, NW Venezuela 8.09N 71.58W
La Grulla see Grulla
13 R11 La Guadeloupe Quebec, SE Canada 45.57N 70.56W
66 F12 La Guaira Distrito Federal, N Venezuela 10.35N 66.52W
56 G4 La Guajira off. Departamento de La Guajira, var. Guajira, La Goagira. ◆ province NE Colombia
196 I4 Lagua Lichan, Punta headland Saipan, S Northern Mariana Islands
20 K14 La Guardia ✈ (New York) Long Island, New York, NE USA 40.44N 73.51W
La Guardia/Laguardia see A Guardia
107 P4 Laguardia País Vasco, N Spain 42.32N 2.31W
La Gudiña see A Gudiña
105 O9 la Guerche-sur-l'Aubois Cher, C France 46.55N 3.00E
105 O13 Laguiole Aveyron, S France 34.49S 20.01E
85 F26 L'Agulhas var. Agulhas. W Cape, SW South Africa 33.32N 117.46W
63 K14 Laguna Santa Catarina, S Brazil 28.28S 48.45W
39 Q11 Laguna New Mexico, SW USA 35.03N 107.30W
37 T16 Laguna Beach California, W USA 33.32N 117.46W
37 Y17 Laguna Dam dam Arizona/California, W USA 32.49N 114.30W
42 L7 Laguna El Rey Coahuila de Zaragoza, N Mexico
37 V17 Laguna Mountains ▲▲ California, W USA
63 B17 Laguna Paiva Santa Fe, C Argentina 31.21S 60.40W
64 H3 Lagunas Tarapacá, N Chile 21.01S 69.36W
58 E9 Lagunas Loreto, N Peru 5.16S 75.40W
59 M20 Lagunillas Santa Cruz, SE Bolivia 19.37S 63.39W
56 H6 Lagunillas Mérida, NW Venezuela 8.31N 71.24W
46 C4 La Habana var. Havana. ● (Cuba) Ciudad de La Habana, W Cuba 23.07N 82.25W
175 Oo3 Lahad Datu Sabah, East Malaysia 5.01N 118.19E
175 Oo3 Lahad Datu, Teluk var. Telukan Lahad Datu, Teluk Darvel, Teluk Datu; prev. Darvel Bay. bay Sabah, East Malaysia
40 F10 Lahaina Maui, Hawaii, USA, C Pacific Ocean 20.52N 156.40W
174 Hh12 Lahat Sumatera, W Indonesia 3.46S 103.31E
La Haye see 's-Gravenhage
Lahej see Laḥij
64 G9 La Higuera Coquimbo, N Chile 29.33S 71.15W
147 S13 Laḥī, Ḥisā' al spring/well NE Yemen 17.28N 50.05E
147 O16 Laḥij var. Laḥj, Eng. Lahej. SW Yemen 13.03N 44.55E
148 M3 Lāhījān Gīlān, NW Iran 37.15N 50.03E
121 I19 Lahishyn Pol. Lohiszyn, Rus. Logishin. Brestskaya Voblasts', SW Belarus 52.19N 25.59E
Laḥj see Laḥij
103 F18 Lahn ⇝ W Germany
Lähn see Wleń
97 J21 Laholm Halland, S Sweden 56.30N 13.04E
97 J21 Laholmsbukten bay S Sweden
37 R6 Lahontan Reservoir ⊠ Nevada, W USA
155 W8 Lahore Punjab, NE Pakistan 31.35N 74.18E
155 W8 Lahore ✈ Punjab, E Pakistan 31.34N 74.22E
57 Q6 La Horqueta Delta Amacuro, NE Venezuela 9.13N 62.02W
121 K15 Lahoysk Rus. Logoysk. Minskaya Voblasts', C Belarus 54.12N 27.53E
103 F22 Lahr Baden-Württemberg, S Germany 48.21N 7.51E
95 M19 Lahti Swe. Lahtis. Etelä-Suomi, S Finland 61.00N 25.40E
Lahtis see Lahti
42 M14 La Huacana Michoacán de Ocampo, SW Mexico 18.56N 101.52W
42 K14 La Huerta Jalisco, SW Mexico 19.29N 104.40W
80 H12 Laï prev. Behagle, De Behagle. Tandjilé, S Chad 9.22N 16.13E
194 G12 Laiagam Enga, W PNG 5.31S 143.28E
Laibach see Ljubljana
178 Ii5 Lai Châu Lai Châu, N Vietnam 22.04N 103.10E
40 D9 Laie Haw. Lā'ie. Oahu, Hawaii, USA, C Pacific Ocean 21.39N 157.55W
104 L5 l'Aigle Orne, N France 48.46N 0.37E
105 Q7 Laignes Côte d'Or, C France 47.51N 4.24E
95 K17 Laihia Länsi-Suomi, W Finland 62.58N 22.00E
Laila see Laylā
85 F25 Laingsburg Western Cape, SW South Africa 33.09S 20.48E
111 U2 Lainsitz Cz. Lužnice. ⇝ Austria/Czech Republic
98 I7 Lairg N Scotland, UK 58.02N 4.22W
83 I17 Laisamis Eastern, N Kenya 1.35N 37.49E
Laisberg see Leisi
131 R4 Laishevo Respublika Tatarstan, W Russian Federation 55.26N 49.27E
Laisholm see Jõgeva
94 H13 Laisvall Norrbotten, N Sweden 66.07N 17.10E
95 K19 Laitila Länsi-Suomi, W Finland 60.52N 21.40E
167 P5 Laiwu Shandong, E China 36.12N 117.36E
167 R4 Laixi var. Shuiji. Shandong, E China 36.53N 120.33E
167 R4 Laiyang Shandong, E China 37.03N 120.48E
167 O3 Laiyuan Hebei, E China 39.19N 114.43E
167 R4 Laizhou var. Ye Xian. Shandong, E China 37.12N 120.01E
167 Q4 Laizhou Wan var. Laichow Bay. bay E China
39 S8 La Jara Colorado, C USA 37.16N 105.57W
63 I15 Lajeado Rio Grande do Sul, S Brazil 29.28S 52.00W
114 L12 Lajkovac Serbia, C Serbia and Montenegro (Yugoslavia) 44.22N 20.12E
113 K23 Lajosmizse Bács-Kiskun, C Hungary 47.03N 19.29E
Lajta see Leitha
42 I6 La Junta Chihuahua, N Mexico 28.27N 107.21W
39 V7 La Junta Colorado, C USA 37.58N 103.34W
94 J13 Lakaträsk Norrbotten, N Sweden 66.16N 21.10E
Lak Dera see Dheere Laaq
Lakeamu see Lakekamu
31 P12 Lake Andes South Dakota, N USA 43.08N 98.33W
24 H9 Lake Arthur Louisiana, S USA 30.04N 92.40W
197 L15 Lakeba prev. Lakemba. island Lau Group, E Fiji
197 L14 Lakeba Passage channel E Fiji
31 S10 Lake Benton Minnesota, N USA 44.15N 96.17W
25 V9 Lake Butler Florida, SE USA 30.01N 82.20W
191 P8 Lake Cargelligo New South Wales, SE Australia 33.21S 146.25E
24 G9 Lake Charles Louisiana, S USA 30.13N 93.13W
29 X9 Lake City Arkansas, C USA 35.49N 90.25W
39 Q7 Lake City Colorado, C USA 38.01N 107.18W
25 V9 Lake City Florida, SE USA 30.12N 82.39W
31 U13 Lake City Iowa, C USA 42.16N 94.43W
33 P7 Lake City Michigan, N USA 44.18N 85.13W
31 W9 Lake City Minnesota, N USA 44.27N 92.16W
23 T13 Lake City South Carolina, SE USA 33.52N 79.45W
31 Q7 Lake City South Dakota, N USA 45.42N 97.22W
22 M8 Lake City Tennessee, S USA 36.13N 84.09W
194 F12 Lake Copiago var. Kopiago. Southern Highlands, W PNG 5.28S 142.30E
8 L17 Lake Cowichan Vancouver Island, British Columbia, SW Canada 48.49N 124.04W
31 U10 Lake Crystal Minnesota, N USA 44.07N 94.13W
27 T6 Lake Dallas Texas, SW USA 33.06N 97.01W
99 K15 Lake District physical region NW England, UK
20 D10 Lake Erie Beach New York, NE USA 42.37N 79.04W
31 T11 Lakefield Minnesota, N USA 43.40N 95.10W
27 V6 Lake Fork Reservoir ◎ Texas, SW USA
32 M9 Lake Geneva Wisconsin, N USA 42.36N 88.25W

20 L9 **Lake George** New York, NE USA 43.25N 73.45W
16 O4 **Lake Harbour** Baffin Island, Nunavut, NE Canada 62.48N 69.49W
38 I12 **Lake Havasu City** Arizona, SW USA 34.26N 114.20W
27 W12 **Lake Jackson** Texas, SW USA 29.01N 95.25W
194 J14 **Lakekamu** *var.* Lakeamu. ≈ S PNG
188 K13 **Lake King** Western Australia 33.09S 119.46E
194 F12 **Lake Kutubu** ⊚ W PNG
25 V12 **Lakeland** Florida, SE USA 28.03N 81.57W
25 U7 **Lakeland** Georgia, SE USA 31.02N 83.04W
189 W4 **Lakeland Downs** Queensland, NE Australia 15.54S 144.54E
9 P16 **Lake Louise** Alberta, SW Canada 51.25N 116.10W
Lakemba *see* Lakeba
31 V11 **Lake Mills** Iowa, C USA 43.25N 93.31W
41 Q10 **Lake Minchumina** Alaska, USA 63.55N 152.25W
Lakemti *see* Nek'emtē
194 E13 **Lake Murray** Western, SW PNG 6.45S 141.25E
82 F5 **Lake Nasser** *var.* Buhayrat Nasir, Buḥayrat Nāṣir, Buḥeiret Nâṣir. ⊚ Egypt/Sudan
33 R9 **Lake Orion** Michigan, N USA 42.46N 83.14W
202 B16 **Lakepa** NE Niue 18.58S 169.48E
31 T11 **Lake Park** Iowa, C USA 43.27N 95.19W
20 K7 **Lake Placid** New York, NE USA 44.16N 73.57W
20 K9 **Lake Pleasant** New York, NE USA 43.27N 74.24W
36 M6 **Lakeport** California, W USA 39.03N 122.55W
31 Q10 **Lake Preston** South Dakota, N USA 44.21N 97.22W
24 J5 **Lake Providence** Louisiana, S USA 32.48N 91.10W
193 E20 **Lake Pukaki** Canterbury, South Island, NZ 44.12S 170.10E
191 Q12 **Lakes Entrance** Victoria, SE Australia 37.52S 147.58E
39 N12 **Lakeside** Arizona, SW USA 34.09N 109.58W
37 V17 **Lakeside** California, W USA 32.50N 116.55W
25 S9 **Lakeside** Florida, SE USA 30.22N 84.18W
30 K13 **Lakeside** Nebraska, C USA 42.01N 102.27W
34 E13 **Lakeside** Oregon, NW USA 43.34N 124.10W
23 W6 **Lakeside** Virginia, NE USA 37.36N 77.28W
Lakes State *see* El Buhayrat
Lake State *see* Michigan
193 F20 **Lake Tekapo** Canterbury, South Island, NZ 44.01S 170.29E
23 O10 **Lake Toxaway** North Carolina, SE USA 35.06N 82.57W
31 T13 **Lake View** Iowa, C USA 42.18N 95.04W
34 I16 **Lakeview** Oregon, NW USA 42.13N 120.21W
27 O3 **Lakeview** Texas, SW USA 34.38N 100.36W
29 W14 **Lake Village** Arkansas, C USA 33.19N 91.16W
25 W12 **Lake Wales** Florida, SE USA 27.54N 81.35W
39 T4 **Lakewood** Colorado, C USA 39.38N 105.07W
20 K15 **Lakewood** New Jersey, NE USA 40.04N 74.11W
20 C11 **Lakewood** New York, NE USA 42.03N 79.19W
33 T11 **Lakewood** Ohio, N USA 41.28N 81.48W
25 Y13 **Lakewood Park** Florida, SE USA 27.32N 80.24W
25 Z14 **Lake Worth** Florida, SE USA 26.37N 80.03W
158 H4 **Lake Wular** ⊚ NE India
128 H11 **Lakhdenpokh'ya** Respublika Kareliya, NW Russian Federation 61.25N 30.05E
158 L11 **Lakhīmpur** Uttar Pradesh, N India 27.57N 80.46E
160 J11 **Lakhnādon** Madhya Pradesh, C India 22.36N 79.36E
Lakhnau *see* Lucknow
160 A9 **Lakhpat** Gujarāt, W India 23.49N 68.54E
121 K19 **Lakhva** *Rus.* Lakhva. Brestskaya Voblasts', SW Belarus 52.13N 27.15E
28 I6 **Lakin** Kansas, C USA 37.56N 101.18W
155 S7 **Lakki Marwat** North-West Frontier Province, NW Pakistan 32.36N 70.55E
117 F21 **Lakonía** *historical region* S Greece
117 F22 **Lakonikós Kólpos** *gulf* S Greece
78 M17 **Lakota** S Ivory Coast 5.52N 5.42W
31 U11 **Lakota** Iowa, C USA 43.22N 94.04W
31 P3 **Lakota** North Dakota, N USA 48.02N 98.20W
Lak Sao *see* Ban Lakxao
94 L8 **Laksefjorden** *fjord* N Norway
94 K8 **Lakselv** Finnmark, N Norway 70.01N 24.57E
161 B21 **Lakshadweep** *prev.* the Laccadive, Minicoy and Amindivi Islands. ◈ *union territory* India, N Indian Ocean
161 C22 **Lakshadweep** *Eng.* Laccadive Islands. *island group* India, N Indian Ocean
159 S17 **Lakshmikāntapur** West Bengal, NE India 22.04N 88.19E
114 G11 **Laktaši** Republika Srpska, N Bosnia and Herzegovina 44.54N 17.16E
155 V7 **Lāla Mūsa** Punjab, NE Pakistan 32.40N 74.01E
la Laon *see* Laon
116 M11 **Lalapaşa** Edirne, NW Turkey 41.52N 26.43E
85 P14 **Lalaua** Nampula, N Mozambique 14.21S 38.16E
107 S10 **L'Alcúdia** *var.* L'Alcudia. País Valenciano, E Spain 39.10N 0.30W
82 J11 **Lalibela** Amhara, N Ethiopia, 12.01N 39.05E
159 T12 **Lalmanirhat** Rajshahi, N Bangladesh 25.51N 89.34E
81 F20 **La Lékoumou** ◈ *province* SW Congo
44 E8 **La Libertad** La Libertad, SW El Salvador 13.28N 89.17W
44 E3 **La Libertad** Petén, N Guatemala 16.46N 90.07W
44 H6 **La Libertad** Comayagua, SW Honduras 14.44N 87.37W
42 E4 **La Libertad** *var.* Puerto Libertad. Sonora, NW Mexico 29.52N 112.39W
44 K10 **La Libertad** Chontales, S Nicaragua 12.14N 85.15W
44 A9 **La Libertad** ◈ *department* SW El Salvador
58 B11 **La Libertad** *off.* Departamento de La Libertad. ◈ *department* W Peru
64 G11 **La Ligua** Valparaíso, C Chile 32.23S 71.16W
145 U5 **La'lī Khān** E Iraq 34.58N 45.36E
81 H16 **La Likouala** ◈ *province* NE Congo
106 H3 **Lalín** Galicia, NW Spain 42.40N 8.06W
104 L13 **Lalinde** Dordogne, SW France 44.52N 0.42E
106 K16 **La Línea** *var.* La Línea de la Concepción. Andalucía, S Spain 36.10N 5.21W
La Línea de la Concepción *see* La Línea
158 J14 **Lalitpur** Uttar Pradesh, N India 24.42N 78.24E
159 P11 **Lalitpur** Central, C Nepal 27.45N 85.17E
158 K10 **Lālkua** Uttar Pradesh, N India 29.04N 79.31E
9 R12 **La Loche** Saskatchewan, C Canada 56.31N 109.27W
104 M6 **la Loupe** Eure-et-Loir, C France 48.30N 1.04E
101 G20 **La Louvière** Hainaut, S Belgium 50.28N 4.15E
L'Altissima *see* Hochwilde
106 L14 **La Luisiana** Andalucía, S Spain 37.30N 5.14W
39 S14 **La Luz** New Mexico, SW USA 32.58N 105.56W
109 D16 **la Maddalena** Sardegna, Italy, C Mediterranean Sea 41.13N 9.25E
64 J7 **La Madrid** Tucumán, N Argentina 27.37S 65.16W
Lama-Kara *see* Kara
175 R16 **Lamakera, Selat** *strait* Nusa Tenggara, S Indonesia
13 S8 **La Malbaie** Quebec, SE Canada 47.39N 70.10W
178 Ij10 **Lamam** Xékong, S Laos 15.22N 106.40E
107 P10 **La Mancha** *physical region* C Spain
la Manche *see* English Channel
197 C13 **Lamap** Malekula, C Vanuatu 16.26S 167.47E
39 W6 **Lamar** Colorado, C USA 38.03N 102.36W
29 S7 **Lamar** Missouri, C USA 37.30N 94.16W
23 S12 **Lamar** South Carolina, SE USA 34.10N 80.03W
109 C19 **La Marmora, Punta** ▲ Sardegna, Italy, C Mediterranean Sea 39.58N 9.20E
15 H7 **La Martre, Lac** ⊚ Northwest Territories, NW Canada
58 D10 **Lamas** San Martín, N Peru 6.27S 76.32W
44 I5 **La Masica** Atlántida, NW Honduras 15.37N 87.04W
105 R12 **Lamastre** Ardèche, E France 45.00N 4.32E
La Matepec *see* Santa Ana, Volcán de
46 I7 **La Maya** Santiago de Cuba, E Cuba 20.09N 75.40W
111 S5 **Lambach** Oberösterreich, N Austria 48.06N 13.52E
173 Ff8 **Lambak** Pulau Pini, W Indonesia 0.08N 98.36E
104 H5 **Lamballe** Côtes d'Armor, NW France 48.28N 2.31W
81 D18 **Lambaréné** Moyen-Ogooué, W Gabon 0.40S 10.13E
Lambasa *see* Labasa
175 Q12 **Lambasina Besar, Pulau** *island* C Indonesia
58 B11 **Lambayeque** Lambayeque, W Peru 6.39S 79.54W
58 A10 **Lambayeque** *off.* Departamento de Lambayeque. ◈ *department* NW Peru
99 G17 **Lambay Island** *Ir.* Reachrainn. *island* E Ireland
195 O10 **Lambert, Cape** *headland* New Britain, E PNG 4.15S 151.31E
205 W6 **Lambert Glacier** *glacier* Antarctica
31 T10 **Lamberton** Minnesota, N USA 44.14N 95.15W
29 X4 **Lambert-Saint Louis** ✈ Missouri, C USA 38.43N 90.19W
33 R11 **Lambertville** Michigan, N USA 41.46N 83.37W
20 J15 **Lambertville** New Jersey, NE USA 40.20N 74.55W
175 Pp9 **Lambogo** Sulawesi, N Indonesia 0.57S 120.23E
108 D8 **Lambro** ≈ N Italy
15 H2 **Lambton, Cape** *headland* Banks Island, Northwest Territories, NW Canada 71.04N 123.07W
35 W11 **Lame Deer** Montana, NW USA 45.37N 106.37W
106 H6 **Lamego** Viseu, N Portugal 41.04N 7.49W
197 C13 **Lamen Bay** Épi, C Vanuatu 16.36S 168.10E
47 X6 **Lamentin** Basse Terre, N Guadeloupe 16.16N 61.37W
Lamentin *see* le Lamentin
190 K10 **Lameroo** South Australia 35.22S 140.30E
56 F10 **La Mesa** Cundinamarca, C Colombia 4.39N 74.24W
37 U17 **La Mesa** California, W USA 32.44N 117.00W
39 R16 **La Mesa** New Mexico, SW USA 32.03N 106.41W
27 N6 **Lamesa** Texas, SW USA 32.43N 101.57W
197 I15 **Lami** Viti Levu, C Fiji 18.07S 178.25E
117 F17 **Lamía** Stereá Ellás, C Greece 38.54N 22.26E
179 Q17 **Lamitan** Basilan Island, SW Philippines 6.40N 122.07E
197 J14 **Lamiti** Gau, C Fiji 18.00S 179.20E
176 Uu8 **Lamlam** Papua, E Indonesia 0.03S 130.46E
196 B16 **Lamlam, Mount** ▲ SW Guam 13.19N 144.40E
111 Q6 **Lammer** ≈ E Austria
193 E23 **Lammerlaw Range** ▲▲ South Island, NZ
97 L20 **Lammhult** Kronoberg, S Sweden 57.09N 14.34E
95 L18 **Lammi** Etelä-Suomi, S Finland 61.06N 25.00E
201 U11 **Lamoil** *island* Chuuk, C Micronesia
37 W3 **Lamoille** Nevada, W USA 40.47N 115.37W
20 M7 **Lamoille River** ≈ Vermont, NE USA
32 J13 **La Moine River** ≈ Illinois, N USA
179 Pp10 **Lamon Bay** *bay* Luzon, N Philippines
31 V16 **Lamoni** Iowa, C USA 40.37N 93.56W
37 R13 **Lamont** California, W USA 35.15N 118.54W
29 N8 **Lamont** Oklahoma, C USA 36.41N 97.33W
56 E13 **La Montañita** *var.* Montañita. Caquetá, S Colombia 1.23N 75.28W
45 N8 **La Mosquitia** *var.* Miskito Coast, *Eng.* Mosquito Coast. *coastal region* E Nicaragua
104 I9 **la Mothe-Achard** Vendée, NW France 46.37N 1.37W
196 L15 **Lamotrek Atoll** *atoll* Caroline Islands, C Micronesia
31 P6 **La Moure** North Dakota, N USA 46.21N 98.17W
178 H8 **Lampang** *var.* Muang Lampang. Lampang, NW Thailand 18.16N 99.30E
178 Ii9 **Lam Pao Reservoir** ⊠ E Thailand
27 S9 **Lampasas** Texas, SW USA 31.03N 98.10W
27 S9 **Lampasas River** ≈ Texas, SW USA
43 N7 **Lampazos** *var.* Lampazos de Naranjo. Nuevo León, NE Mexico 27.00N 100.28W
Lampazos de Naranjo *see* Lampazos
117 E19 **Lámpeia** Dytikí Ellás, S Greece 37.51N 21.48E
103 G19 **Lampertheim** Hessen, W Germany 49.36N 8.28E
99 I20 **Lampeter** SW Wales, UK 52.07N 4.03W
178 H7 **Lamphun** *var.* Lampun, Muang Lamphun. Lamphun, NW Thailand 18.36N 99.01E
9 X10 **Lamprey** Manitoba, C Canada 58.18N 94.06W
Lampun *see* Lamphun
174 I13 **Lampung** *off.* Propinsi Lampung. ◈ *province* SW Indonesia
174 Ii13 **Lampung, Teluk** *bay* Sumatera, SW Indonesia
130 K6 **Lamskoye** Lipetskaya Oblast', W Russian Federation 52.57N 38.04E
83 K20 **Lamu** Coast, SE Kenya 2.17S 40.49E
45 N14 **La Muerte, Cerro** ▲ C Costa Rica 9.33N 83.47W
105 S13 **la Mure** Isère, E France 44.54N 5.48E
39 S10 **Lamy** New Mexico, SW USA 35.27N 105.52W
121 J18 **Lan'** *Rus.* Lan'. ≈ C Belarus
40 B8 **Lanai** *Haw.* Lāna'i. *island* Hawaii, USA, C Pacific Ocean
40 E10 **Lanai City** Lanai, Hawaii, USA, C Pacific Ocean 20.49N 156.55W
101 L18 **Lanaken** Limburg, NE Belgium 50.52N 5.39E
179 R15 **Lanao, Lake** *var.* Lake Sultan Alonto. ⊚ Mindanao, S Philippines
98 J12 **Lanark** S Scotland, UK 55.38N 4.24W
98 I13 **Lanark** *cultural region* C Scotland, UK
106 L9 **La Nava de Ricomalillo** Castilla-La Mancha, C Spain 39.40N 4.58W
178 Gg13 **Lanbi Kyun** *prev.* Sullivan Island. *island* Mergui Archipelago, S Myanmar
Lancang Jiang *see* Mekong
99 K17 **Lancashire** *cultural region* NW England, UK
13 N13 **Lancaster** Ontario, SE Canada 45.10N 74.31W
99 K16 **Lancaster** NW England, UK 54.03N 2.48W
37 T14 **Lancaster** California, W USA 34.42N 118.08W
22 M6 **Lancaster** Kentucky, S USA 37.35N 84.34W
29 U1 **Lancaster** Missouri, C USA 40.30N 92.31W
21 O7 **Lancaster** New Hampshire, NE USA 44.28N 71.34W
20 D10 **Lancaster** New York, NE USA 42.54N 78.40W
33 T14 **Lancaster** Ohio, N USA 39.42N 82.36W
20 H16 **Lancaster** Pennsylvania, NE USA 40.03N 76.18W
23 R11 **Lancaster** South Carolina, SE USA 34.43N 80.46W
27 U7 **Lancaster** Texas, SW USA 32.35N 96.45W
23 X5 **Lancaster** Virginia, NE USA 37.45N 76.25W
32 J9 **Lancaster** Wisconsin, N USA 42.52N 90.43W
207 N10 **Lancaster Sound** *sound* Nunavut, N Canada
Lan-chou/Lan-chow/Lanchow *see* Lanzhou
109 K14 **Lanciano** Abruzzo, C Italy 42.15N 14.22E
113 O16 **Łańcut** Podkarpackie, SE Poland 50.04N 22.13E
174 Kk8 **Landak, Sungai** ≈ Borneo, N Indonesia
Landao *see* Lantau Island
Landau *see* Landau an der Isar, Bayern, Germany
Landau *see* Landau in der Pfalz, Rheinland-Pfalz, Germany
103 N22 **Landau an der Isar** *var.* Landau. Bayern, SE Germany 48.40N 12.41E
103 F20 **Landau in der Pfalz** *var.* Landau. Rheinland-Pfalz, SW Germany 49.12N 8.07E
Land Burgenland *see* Burgenland
110 K8 **Landeck** Tirol, W Austria 47.09N 10.34E
101 J19 **Landen** Vlaams Brabant, C Belgium 50.45N 5.04E
35 U15 **Lander** Wyoming, C USA 42.49N 108.43W
104 F5 **Landerneau** Finistère, NW France 48.27N 4.16W
97 K20 **Landeryd** Halland, S Sweden 57.04N 13.15E
104 J15 **Landes** ◈ *department* SW France
Landeshut/Landeshut in Schlesien *see* Kamienna Góra
107 R9 **Landete** Castilla-La Mancha, C Spain 39.54N 1.22W
101 M18 **Landgraaf** Limburg, SE Netherlands 50.55N 6.04E
104 F5 **Landivisiau** Finistère, NW France 48.31N 4.03W
Land of Enchantment *see* New Mexico
Land of Opportunity *see* Arkansas
Land of Steady Habits *see* Connecticut
Land of the Midnight Sun *see* Alaska
110 I8 **Landquart** Graubünden, SE Switzerland 46.58N 9.35E
110 J9 **Landquart** ≈ Austria/Switzerland
23 P10 **Landrum** South Carolina, SE USA 35.10N 82.11W
Landsberg *see* Górowo Iławeckie, Warmińsko-Mazurskie, NE Poland
Landsberg *see* Gorzów Wielkopolski, Gorzów, Poland
103 K23 **Landsberg am Lech** Bayern, S Germany 48.03N 10.52E
Landsberg an der Warthe *see* Gorzów Wielkopolski
99 G25 **Land's End** *headland* SW England, UK 50.02N 5.41W
103 M22 **Landshut** Bayern, SE Germany 48.31N 12.09E
Landskron *see* Lanškroun
97 J22 **Landskrona** Skåne, S Sweden 55.52N 12.52E
100 I10 **Landsmeer** Noord-Holland, C Netherlands 52.25N 4.55E
97 J19 **Landvetter** ✈ (Göteborg) Västra Götaland, S Sweden 57.39N 12.22E
Landwarów *see* Lentvaris
25 R5 **Lanett** Alabama, S USA 32.52N 85.11W
110 C8 **La Neuveville** *var.* Neuveville, *Ger.* Neuenstadt. Neuchâtel, W Switzerland 47.05N 7.03E
97 G21 **Langå** *var.* Langaa. Århus, C Denmark 56.23N 9.55E
Langaa *see* Langå
164 G14 **La'nga Co** ⊚ W China
Langada *see* Lagkáda
Langades/Langadhás *see* Lagkadás
Langádhia/Langadia *see* Lagkádia
153 T14 **Langar** *Rus.* Lyangar. SE Tajikistan 37.04N 72.39E
152 M10 **Langar** *Rus.* Lyangar. Navoiy Viloyati, C Uzbekistan 40.27N 65.54E
148 M3 **Langarūd** Gīlān, NW Iran 37.12N 50.10E
9 V16 **Langbank** Saskatchewan, S Canada 50.01N 102.16W
31 P2 **Langdon** North Dakota, N USA 48.45N 98.22W
105 P12 **Langeac** Haute-Loire, C France 45.06N 3.31E
104 L8 **Langeais** Indre-et-Loire, C France 47.22N 0.27E
82 I8 **Langeb, Wadi** ≈ NE Sudan
Långed *see* Dals Långed
97 G25 **Langeland** *island* S Denmark
101 B18 **Langemark** West-Vlaanderen, W Belgium 50.55N 2.55E
103 G18 **Langen** Hessen, W Germany 49.58N 8.40E
103 J22 **Langenau** Baden-Württemberg, S Germany 48.30N 10.08E
9 V16 **Langenburg** Saskatchewan, S Canada 50.49N 101.43W
103 E16 **Langenfeld** Nordrhein-Westfalen, W Germany 51.06N 6.57E
110 L8 **Längenfeld** Tirol, W Austria 47.04N 10.59E
102 I12 **Langenhagen** Niedersachsen, N Germany 52.25N 9.43E
102 I12 **Langenhagen** ✈ (Hannover) Niedersachsen, NW Germany 52.28N 9.40E
111 W3 **Langenlois** Niederösterreich, NE Austria 48.28N 15.42E
110 E7 **Langenthal** Bern, NW Switzerland 47.13N 7.46E
111 W6 **Langenwang** Steiermark, E Austria 47.34N 15.39E
111 X3 **Langenzersdorf** Niederösterreich, E Austria 48.19N 16.22E
102 F9 **Langeoog** *island* NW Germany
126 Gg11 **Langepas** Khanty-Mansiyskiy Avtonomnyy Okrug, C Russian Federation 61.12N 75.24E
97 H23 **Langeskov** Fyn, C Denmark 55.22N 10.36E
97 G16 **Langesund** Telemark, S Norway 59.00N 9.43E
97 G17 **Langesundsfjorden** *fjord* S Norway
96 D10 **Langevågen** Møre og Romsdal, S Norway 62.25N 6.13E
167 P3 **Langfang** Hebei, E China 39.30N 116.39E
96 E9 **Langfjorden** *fjord* S Norway
31 Q8 **Langford** South Dakota, N USA 45.36N 97.48W
173 G6 **Langgapayung** Sumatera, W Indonesia 1.42N 99.57E
108 E9 **Langhirano** Emilia-Romagna, C Italy 44.37N 10.16E
99 K14 **Langholm** S Scotland, UK 55.13N 3.11W
94 I3 **Langjökull** *glacier* C Iceland
173 Ff2 **Langkawi, Pulau** *island* Peninsular Malaysia
175 R13 **Langkesi, Kepulauan** *island group* C Indonesia
178 Gg15 **Langkha Tuk, Khao** ▲ SW Thailand 9.19N 98.39E
12 L8 **Langlade** Quebec, SE Canada 48.13N 75.58W
8 M17 **Langley** British Columbia, SW Canada 49.07N 122.39W
178 Jj7 **Lang Mô** Thanh Hoa, N Vietnam 19.36N 105.30E
Langnau *see* Langnau im Emmental
110 E8 **Langnau im Emmental** *var.* Langnau. Bern, W Switzerland 46.57N 7.46E
105 Q13 **Langogne** Lozère, S France 44.40N 3.52E
164 K16 **Langoi Kangri** ▲ W China 28.51N 87.28E
104 K13 **Langon** Gironde, SW France 47.43N 1.49W
La Ngounié *see* Ngounié
94 G10 **Langøya** *island* C Norway
164 G14 **Langqên Zangbo** ≈ China/India
106 K2 **Langreo** *var.* Sama de Langreo. Asturias, N Spain 43.18N 5.40W
105 S7 **Langres** Haute-Marne, N France 47.52N 5.19E
105 R8 **Langres, Plateau de** *plateau* C France
173 F4 **Langsa** Sumatera, W Indonesia 4.29N 97.53E
95 H16 **Långsele** Västernorrland, C Sweden 63.10N 17.04E
168 L12 **Lang Shan** ▲▲ N China
97 M14 **Långshyttan** Dalarna, C Sweden 60.25N 16.01E
178 K5 **Lang Sơn** *var.* Langson. Lang Sơn, N Vietnam 21.49N 106.45E
178 Gg14 **Lang Suan** Chumphon, SW Thailand 9.52N 99.03E
95 J14 **Långträsk** Norrbotten, N Sweden 65.22N 20.19E
27 N11 **Langtry** Texas, SW USA 29.46N 101.25W
105 P16 **Languedoc** *cultural region* S France
105 P15 **Languedoc-Roussillon** ◈ *region* S France
29 X10 **L'Anguille River** ≈ Arkansas, C USA
95 I16 **Långviksmon** Västernorrland, N Sweden 63.39N 18.45E
103 K22 **Langweid** Bayern, S Germany 48.29N 10.50E
166 J8 **Langzhong** Sichuan, C China 31.46N 105.55E
Lan Hsü *see* Lan Yü
9 U15 **Lanigan** Saskatchewan, S Canada 51.49N 105.01W
118 K5 **Lanivtsi** Ternopil's'ka Oblast', W Ukraine 49.52N 26.05E
143 Y13 **Länkäran** *Rus.* Lenkoran'. S Azerbaijan 38.46N 48.50E
104 L16 **Lannemezan** Hautes-Pyrénées, S France 43.07N 0.22E
104 G5 **Lannion** Côtes d'Armor, NW France 48.43N 3.27W
12 M11 **L'Annonciation** Quebec, SE Canada 46.22N 74.51W
107 V5 **L'Anoia** ≈ NE Spain
20 I15 **Lansdale** Pennsylvania, NE USA 40.14N 75.13W
12 L14 **Lansdowne** Ontario, SE Canada 44.25N 76.00W
158 K9 **Lansdowne** Uttar Pradesh, N India 29.49N 78.42E
32 M3 **L'Anse** Michigan, N USA 46.45N 88.27W
13 S7 **L'Anse-St-Jean** Quebec, SE Canada 48.14N 70.13W
95 K18 **Länsi-Suomi** ◈ *province* W Finland
31 Y11 **Lansing** Iowa, C USA 43.22N 91.11W
29 R4 **Lansing** Kansas, C USA 39.15N 94.54W
33 Q9 **Lansing** *state capital* Michigan, N USA 42.43N 84.33W
94 J12 **Lansjärv** Norrbotten, N Sweden 66.39N 22.10E
113 G17 **Lanškroun** *Ger.* Landskron. Pardubický Kraj, C Czech Republic 49.53N 16.34E
178 Gg16 **Lanta, Ko** *island* S Thailand
167 O15 **Lantau Island** *Cant.* Tai Yue Shan, *Chin.* Landao. *island* Hong Kong, S China
Lan-ts'ang Chiang *see* Mekong
175 Q7 **Lanu** Sulawesi, N Indonesia 1.00N 121.33E
109 D19 **Lanusei** Sardegna, Italy, C Mediterranean Sea 39.55N 9.31E
104 H7 **Lanvaux, Landes de** *physical region* NW France
169 W8 **Lanxi** Heilongjiang, NE China 46.18N 126.49E
167 R10 **Lanxi** Zhejiang, SE China 29.13N 119.30E
La Nyanga *see* Nyanga
167 T15 **Lan Yü** *var.* Huoshao Tao, *var.* Hungt'ou, Lan Hsü, Lanyü, *Eng.* Orchid Island; *prev.* Kotosho, Koto Sho. *island* SE Taiwan
66 P11 **Lanzarote** *island* Islas Canarias, Spain, NE Atlantic Ocean
165 V10 **Lanzhou** *var.* Lan-chou, Lanchow, Lan-chow; *prev.* Kaolan. Gansu, C China 36.01N 103.52E
108 B8 **Lanzo Torinese** Piemonte, NE Italy 45.18N 7.26E
179 P8 **Laoag** Luzon, N Philippines 18.11N 120.34E
179 R12 **Laoang** Samar, C Philippines 12.29N 125.01E
178 J5 **Lao Cai** Lao Cai, N Vietnam 22.29N 104.00E
Laodicea/Laodicea ad Mare *see* Al Lādhiqīyah
Laoet *see* Laut, Pulau
169 T11 **Laoha He** ≈ NE China
166 M8 **Laohekou** *prev.* Guanghua. Hubei, C China 32.21N 111.40E
Laoi, An *see* Lee
99 E19 **Laois** *prev.* Leix, Queen's County. *cultural region* C Ireland
Laojunmiao *see* Yumen
169 W12 **Lao Ling** ▲▲ N China
66 Q11 **La Oliva** *var.* Oliva. Fuerteventura, Islas Canarias, Spain, NE Atlantic Ocean 28.36N 13.52W
Lao, Loch *see* Belfast Lough
Lao Mangnai *see* Mangnai
105 P3 **Laon** *var.* la Laon; *anc.* Laudunum. Aisne, N France 49.34N 3.37E
Lao People's Democratic Republic *see* Laos
56 M3 **La Orchila, Isla** *island* N Venezuela
66 O11 **La Orotava** Tenerife, Islas Canarias, Spain, NE Atlantic Ocean 28.22N 16.31W
59 E14 **La Oroya** Junín, C Peru 11.29S 75.57W
178 Ii7 **Laos** *off.* Lao People's Democratic Republic. ◆ *republic* SE Asia
167 R5 **Laoshan Wan** *bay* E China
169 Y10 **Laoye Ling** ▲▲ NE China
62 J12 **Lapa** Paraná, S Brazil 25.46S 49.44W
105 P10 **Lapalisse** Allier, C France 46.13N 3.39E
56 F9 **La Palma** Cundinamarca, C Colombia 5.22N 74.24W
44 F7 **La Palma** Chalatenango, N El Salvador 14.19N 89.10W
45 W16 **La Palma** Darién, SE Panama 8.24N 78.09W
66 N11 **La Palma** *island* Islas Canarias, Spain, NE Atlantic Ocean
106 J14 **La Palma del Condado** Andalucía, S Spain 37.22N 6.33W
63 F18 **La Paloma** Durazno, C Uruguay 34.37S 54.07W
63 G20 **La Paloma** Rocha, E Uruguay 34.37S 54.07W
63 A21 **La Pampa** *off.* Provincia de La Pampa. ◈ *province* C Argentina
57 P8 **La Paragua** Bolívar, E Venezuela 6.53N 63.16W
121 O16 **Lapatsichy** *Rus.* Lopatichi. Mahilyowskaya Voblasts', E Belarus 53.34N 30.53E
63 C16 **La Paz** Entre Ríos, E Argentina 30.45S 59.36W
64 I11 **La Paz** Mendoza, C Argentina 33.27S 67.35W
59 J18 **La Paz** *var.* La Paz de Ayacucho. ● (Bolivia-legislative and administrative capital) La Paz, W Bolivia 16.30S 68.12W
44 H6 **La Paz** La Paz, SW Honduras 14.27N 87.41W
42 F9 **La Paz** Baja California Sur, NW Mexico 24.06N 110.18W
63 F20 **La Paz** Canelones, S Uruguay 34.46S 56.13W
59 J16 **La Paz** ◈ *department* W Bolivia
44 B9 **La Paz** ◈ *department* S El Salvador
44 G7 **La Paz** ◈ *department* SW Honduras
La Paz *see* El Alto, Bolivia
La Paz *see* Robles, Colombia
La Paz *see* La Paz Centro, Nicaragua
42 F9 **La Paz, Bahía de** *bay* W Mexico
44 I10 **La Paz Centro** *var.* La Paz. León, W Nicaragua 12.19N 86.40W
La Paz de Ayacucho *see* La Paz
56 J15 **La Pedrera** Amazonas, SE Colombia 1.19S 69.31W
33 S9 **Lapeer** Michigan, N USA 43.03N 83.19W
42 K6 **La Perla** Chihuahua, N Mexico 28.11N 104.28W
172 Pp1 **La Perouse Strait** *Jap.* Sōya-kaikyō, *Rus.* Proliv Laperuza. *strait* Japan/Russian Federation
65 I14 **La Perra, Salitral de** *salt lake* C Argentina
Laperuza, Proliv *see* La Perouse Strait
43 Q10 **La Pesca** Tamaulipas, C Mexico 23.49N 97.45W
42 M13 **La Piedad Cavadas** Michoacán de Ocampo, C Mexico 20.19N 102.01W
Lapines *see* Lafnitz
95 M16 **Lapinlahti** Itä-Suomi, C Finland 63.21N 27.25E
Lápithos *see* Lapta
24 K9 **Laplace** Louisiana, S USA 30.04N 90.28W
47 X12 **La Plaine** SE Dominica 15.19N 61.15W
181 P16 **la Plaine-des-Palmistes** C Réunion
94 K11 **Lapland** *Fin.* Lappi, *Swe.* Lappland. *cultural region* N Europe
30 M8 **La Plant** South Dakota, N USA 45.06N 100.40W
63 D20 **La Plata** Buenos Aires, E Argentina 34.56S 57.55W
56 D12 **La Plata** Huila, SW Colombia 2.25N 75.47W
23 W4 **La Plata** Maryland, NE USA 38.28N 76.55W
La Plata *see* Sucre
47 U6 **la Plata, Río de** ≈ C Puerto Rico
107 W4 **La Pobla de Lillet** Cataluña, NE Spain 42.15N 1.57E
107 U4 **La Pobla de Segur** Cataluña, NE Spain 42.15N 0.58E
13 S9 **La Pocatière** Quebec, SE Canada 47.17N 70.04W
106 L3 **La Pola de Gordón** Castilla-León, N Spain 42.50N 5.38W
33 O11 **La Porte** Indiana, N USA 41.36N 86.43W
20 H13 **Laporte** Pennsylvania, NE USA 41.25N 76.28W
31 X13 **La Porte City** Iowa, C USA 42.19N 92.11W
64 J8 **La Posta** Catamarca, C Argentina 27.59S 65.32W
42 E8 **La Poza Grande** Baja California Sur, W Mexico 25.45N 111.58W
95 K16 **Lappajärvi** Länsi-Suomi, W Finland 63.11N 23.37E
95 L16 **Lappajärvi** ⊚ W Finland
95 N18 **Lappeenranta** *Swe.* Villmanstrand. Etelä-Suomi, S Finland 61.04N 28.15E
95 J17 **Lappfjärd** *Fin.* Lapväärtti. Länsi-Suomi, W Finland 62.13N 21.34E
94 L12 **Lappi** *Swe.* Lappland. ◈ *province* N Finland
Lappi *see* Lapland
Lappland *see* Lappi
Lappland *see* Lapland, N Europe
Lappo *see* Lapua
63 C23 **Laprida** Buenos Aires, E Argentina 37.33S 60.46W
27 P13 **La Pryor** Texas, SW USA 28.56N 99.51W
142 B11 **Lâpseki** Çanakkale, NW Turkey 40.22N 26.42E
124 Nn2 **Lapta** *Gk.* Lápithos. NW Cyprus 35.19N 33.11E
Laptev Sea *see* Laptevykh, More
126 Kk5 **Laptevykh, More** *Eng.* Laptev Sea. *sea* Arctic Ocean
95 K16 **Lapua** *Swe.* Lappo. Länsi-Suomi, W Finland 62.57N 23.00E
107 P3 **La Puebla de Arganzón** País Vasco, N Spain 42.45N 2.49W
106 L14 **La Puebla de Cazalla** Andalucía, S Spain 37.13N 5.18W
106 M9 **La Puebla de Montalbán** Castilla-La Mancha, C Spain 39.52N 4.22W
56 I6 **La Puerta** Trujillo, NW Venezuela 9.09N 70.44W
179 Qq13 **Lapu-Lapu** C Philippines 10.18N 123.58E
Lapurdum *see* Bayonne
42 E7 **La Purísima** Baja California Sur, W Mexico 26.10N 112.04W
Lapväärtti *see* Lappfjärd
112 O10 **Łapy** Podlaskie, NE Poland 53.00N 22.50E
82 D6 **Laqiya Arba'in** Northern, NW Sudan 20.01N 28.01E
64 J4 **La Quiaca** Jujuy, N Argentina 22.12S 65.36W
109 J14 **L'Aquila** *var.* Aquila, Aquila degli Abruzzo. Abruzzo, C Italy 42.21N 13.24E
149 Q13 **Lār** Fārs, S Iran 27.42N 54.19E
56 J5 **Lara** *off.* Estado Lara. ◈ *state* NW Venezuela
106 G2 **Laracha** Galicia, NW Spain 43.14N 8.34W
76 G5 **Larache** *var.* al Araïch, El Araïch, El Araïche, *anc.* Lixus. NW Morocco 35.16N 6.07W
105 T14 **Laragne-Montéglin** Hautes-Alpes, SE France 44.21N 5.46E
106 M13 **La Rambla** Andalucía, S Spain 37.37N 4.44W
35 Y17 **Laramie** Wyoming, C USA 41.18N 105.35W
35 X15 **Laramie Mountains** ▲▲ Wyoming, C USA
35 Y16 **Laramie River** ≈ Wyoming, C USA
62 H12 **Laranjeiras do Sul** Paraná, S Brazil 25.22S 52.22W
Larantoeka *see* Larantuka
175 Qq16 **Larantuka** *prev.* Larantoeka. Flores, C Indonesia 8.20S 123.00E
176 V15 **Larat** Pulau Larat, E Indonesia 7.07S 131.46E
176 V15 **Larat, Pulau** *island* Kepulauan Tanimbar, E Indonesia
97 P19 **Lärbro** Gotland, SE Sweden 57.46N 18.49E
108 A9 **Larche, Col de** *pass* France/Italy 44.26N 6.54E
12 H8 **Larder Lake** Ontario, S Canada 48.06N 79.43W
107 O2 **Laredo** Cantabria, N Spain 43.22N 3.22W
27 Q15 **Laredo** Texas, SW USA 27.30N 99.30W
42 H9 **La Reforma** Sinaloa, W Mexico 25.04N 108.03W
100 N11 **Laren** Gelderland, E Netherlands 52.12N 6.22E
100 J11 **Laren** Noord-Holland, C Netherlands 52.15N 5.13E
104 K13 **la Réole** Gironde, SW France 44.34N 0.00W
La Réunion *see* Réunion
Largeau *see* Faya
105 U13 **l'Argentière-la-Bessée** Hautes-Alpes, SE France 44.49N 6.34E
155 O4 **Lar Gerd** *var.* Largird. Balkh, N Afghanistan 35.36N 66.48E
Largird *see* Lar Gerd
25 V12 **Largo** Florida, SE USA 27.54N 82.47W
39 Q9 **Largo, Canon** *valley* New Mexico, SW USA
46 D6 **Largo, Cayo** *island* W Cuba
25 Z17 **Largo, Key** *island* Florida Keys, Florida, SE USA
98 H12 **Largs** W Scotland, UK 55.47N 4.50W
104 I16 **la Rhune** *var.* Larrún. ▲ France/Spain *see also* Larrún 43.19N 1.36W
la Riege *see* Ariège
31 Q4 **Larimore** North Dakota, N USA 47.54N 97.37W
109 L15 **Larino** Molise, C Italy 41.46N 14.50E
Lario *see* Como, Lago di
64 I9 **La Rioja** La Rioja, NW Argentina 29.25S 66.49W
64 I9 **La Rioja** *off.* Provincia de La Rioja. ◈ *province* NW Argentina
107 O4 **La Rioja** ◈ *autonomous community* N Spain
117 F16 **Lárisa** *var.* Larissa. Thessalía, C Greece 39.38N 22.27E
Larissa *see* Lárisa
155 Q13 **Lārkāna** *var.* Larkhana. Sind, SE Pakistan 27.31N 68.18E
Larkhana *see* Lārkāna
Larnaca *see* Lárnaka
124 Nn3 **Lárnaka** *var.* Larnaca, Larnax. SE Cyprus 34.54N 33.38E
124 Nn3 **Lárnaka** ✈ SE Cyprus 34.52N 33.38E
Larnax *see* Lárnaka
99 G14 **Larne** *Ir.* Latharna. E Northern Ireland, UK 54.51N 5.49W
28 L5 **Larned** Kansas, C USA 38.10N 99.06W
106 L3 **La Robla** Castilla-León, N Spain 42.48N 5.37W
106 J10 **La Roca de la Sierra** Extremadura, W Spain 39.06N 6.41W
101 K22 **La Roche-en-Ardenne** Luxembourg, SE Belgium 50.11N 5.35E
104 L11 **la Rochefoucauld** Charente, W France 45.43N 0.23E
104 J10 **la Rochelle** *anc.* Rupella. Charente-Maritime, W France 46.09N 1.07W
104 I9 **la Roche-sur-Yon** *prev.* Bourbon Vendée, Napoléon-Vendée. Vendée, NW France 46.40N 1.25W
107 Q10 **La Roda** Castilla-La Mancha, C Spain 39.13N 2.10W
106 L14 **La Roda de Andalucía** Andalucía, S Spain 37.12N 4.45W
47 P9 **La Romana** E Dominican Republic 18.25N 69.00W
9 T13 **La Ronge** Saskatchewan, C Canada 55.07N 105.18W
9 U13 **La Ronge, Lac** ⊚ Saskatchewan, C Canada
24 K10 **Larose** Louisiana, S USA 29.34N 90.22W
44 M7 **La Rosita** Región Autónoma Atlántico Norte, NE Nicaragua 13.55N 84.23W
189 Q3 **Larrimah** Northern Territory, N Australia 15.30S 133.12E

◆ Country ● Country Capital ◇ Dependent Territory ○ Dependent Territory Capital ◈ Administrative Region ✈ International Airport ▲ Mountain ▲▲ Mountain Range ⛰ Volcano ≈ River ⊚ Lake ⊠ Reservoir

64 N11 Larroque Entre Ríos, E Argentina 33.05S 59.06W
107 Q2 Larrún Fr. la Rhune. ▲ France/Spain see also la Rhune 43.18N 1.35W
205 X6 Lars Christensen Coast physical region Antarctica
41 Q14 Larsen Bay Kodiak Island, Alaska, USA 57.32N 153.58W
204 I5 Larsen Ice Shelf ice shelf Antarctica
15 K3 Larsen Sound sound Nunavut, N Canada
La Rúa see A Rúa
104 K16 Laruns Pyrénées-Atlantiques, SW France 43.00N 0.25W
97 G16 Larvik Vestfold, S Norway 59.03N 10.01E
126 H11 Lar'yak Khanty-Mansiyskiy Avtonomnyy Okrug, C Russian Federation 61.09N 80.01E
La-sa see Lhasa
175 Tt11 Lasahata Pulau Seram, E Indonesia 2.52S 128.27E
Lasahau see Lasihao
39 O6 La Sal Utah, W USA 38.19N 109.14W
12 C17 La Salle Ontario, S Canada 42.13N 83.05W
32 L11 La Salle Illinois, N USA 41.19N 89.06W
47 O9 Las Americas ✕ (Santo Domingo) S Dominican Republic 18.24N 69.38W
81 G17 La Sangha ◈ province N Congo
39 V6 Las Animas Colorado, C USA 38.04N 103.13W
110 D10 La Sarine var. Sarine. ≈ SW Switzerland
110 B9 La Sarraz Vaud, W Switzerland 46.40N 6.32E
10 H12 La Sarre Quebec, SE Canada 48.49N 79.12W
56 L3 Las Aves, Islas var. Islas de Aves. island group N Venezuela
57 N7 Las Bonitas Bolívar, C Venezuela 7.50N 65.40W
106 K15 Las Cabezas de San Juan Andalucía, S Spain 36.58N 5.55W
63 G19 Lascano Rocha, E Uruguay 33.40S 54.12W
64 I5 Lascar, Volcán ▲ N Chile 23.22S 67.33W
43 T15 Las Choapas var. Choapas. Veracruz-Llave, SE Mexico 17.51N 94.00W
39 R15 Las Cruces New Mexico, SW USA 32.19N 106.49W
Lasdehnen see Krasnoznamensk
107 V4 La See d'Urgel var. La Seu d'Urgell, Seo de Urgel. Cataluña, NE Spain 42.22N 1.27E
La Selle see Selle, Pic de la
64 G9 La Serena Coquimbo, C Chile 29.54S 71.18W
106 K11 La Serena physical region W Spain
La Seu d'Urgell see La See d'Urgel
105 T16 la Seyne-sur-Mer Var, SE France 43.07N 5.52E
63 D21 Las Flores Buenos Aires, E Argentina 36.03S 59.07W
64 H9 Las Flores San Juan, W Argentina 30.14S 69.10W
9 S14 Lashburn Saskatchewan, S Canada 53.09N 109.37W
64 I11 Las Heras Mendoza, W Argentina 32.46S 68.51W
178 Gg4 Lashio Shan State, E Myanmar 22.58N 97.48E
154 M8 Lashkar Gāh var. Lash-Kar-Gar'. Helmand, S Afghanistan 31.34N 64.21E
Lash-Kar-Gar' see Lashkar Gāh
175 Qq13 Lasihao var. Lasahau. Pulau Muna, C Indonesia 5.01S 122.23E
109 N21 La Sila ▲ SW Italy
65 H23 La Silueta, Cerro ▲ S Chile 52.22S 72.09W
44 L9 La Sirena Región Autónoma Atlántico Sur, E Nicaragua 12.58N 84.42W
112 J13 Łask Łódzkie, C Poland 51.36N 19.06E
111 V11 Laško Ger. Tüffer. C Slovenia 46.08N 15.13E
65 H14 Las Lajas Neuquén, W Argentina 38.31S 70.22W
65 H15 Las Lajas, Cerro ▲ W Argentina 38.49S 70.42W
64 M6 Las Lomitas Formosa, N Argentina 24.45S 60.34W
43 V16 Las Margaritas Chiapas, SE Mexico 16.15N 91.58W
Las Marismas see Guadalquivir, Marismas del
56 M6 Las Mercedes Guárico, N Venezuela 9.06N 66.22W
44 F6 Las Minas, Cerro ▲ W Honduras 14.33N 88.41W
107 O11 La Solana Castilla-La Mancha, C Spain 38.55N 3.13W
47 Q14 La Soufrière ※ Saint Vincent, Saint Vincent and the Grenadines 13.20N 61.11W
104 M10 la Souterraine Creuse, C France 46.15N 1.28E
64 N7 Las Palmas Chaco, N Argentina 27.07S 58.45W
45 Q16 Las Palmas Veraguas, W Panama 8.09N 81.28W
66 P12 Las Palmas var. Las Palmas de Gran Canaria. Gran Canaria, Islas Canarias, Spain, NE Atlantic Ocean 28.08N 15.27W
66 P12 Las Palmas ◈ province Islas Canarias, Spain, NE Atlantic Ocean
66 Q12 Las Palmas ✕ Gran Canaria, Islas Canarias, Spain, NE Atlantic Ocean
Las Palmas de Gran Canaria see Las Palmas
42 D6 Las Palomas Baja California Sur, W Mexico 31.43N 107.37W
107 P10 Las Pedroñeras Castilla-La Mancha, C Spain 39.27N 2.40W
108 E10 La Spezia Liguria, NW Italy 44.07N 9.49E
63 F20 Las Piedras Canelones, S Uruguay 34.42S 56.13W
65 J18 Las Plumas Chubut, S Argentina 43.46S 67.15W
63 B18 Las Rosas Santa Fe, C Argentina 32.27S 61.30W
Lassa see Lhasa
37 O4 Lassen Peak ▲ California, W USA 40.27N 121.28W
204 K6 Lassiter Coast physical region Antarctica
111 V9 Lassnitz ≈ SE Austria
13 O12 L'Assomption Quebec, SE Canada 45.48N 73.27W
13 N11 L'Assomption ≈ Quebec, SE Canada
45 S17 Las Tablas Los Santos, S Panama 7.45N 80.17W
Lastarria, Volcán see Azufre, Volcán
39 V4 Last Chance Colorado, C USA 39.41N 103.34W
Last Frontier, The see Alaska
9 U16 Last Mountain Lake ◎ Saskatchewan, S Canada
64 H9 Las Tórtolas, Cerro ▲ W Argentina 29.57S 69.49W
63 C14 Las Toscas Santa Fe, C Argentina 28.22S 59.19W
81 F19 Lastoursville Ogooué-Lolo, E Gabon 0.49S 12.43E
115 F16 Lastovo It. Lagosta. island SW Croatia
115 F16 Lastovski Kanal channel SW Croatia
42 E6 Las Tres Vírgenes, Volcán ※ W Mexico 27.27N 112.34W
42 F4 Las Trincheras Sonora, NW Mexico 30.21N 111.27W
57 N8 Las Trincheras Bolívar, E Venezuela 6.57N 64.49W
46 H7 Las Tunas var. Victoria de las Tunas. Las Tunas, E Cuba 20.58N 76.58W
La Suisse see Switzerland
42 I5 Las Varas Chihuahua, N Mexico 29.35N 108.01W
42 J12 Las Varas Nayarit, C Mexico 21.11N 105.09W
64 L10 Las Varillas Córdoba, E Argentina 31.54S 62.45W
37 X11 Las Vegas Nevada, W USA 36.09N 115.10W
39 T10 Las Vegas New Mexico, SW USA 35.35N 105.15W
195 W8 Lata Nendō, Solomon Islands 10.45S 165.43E
11 R10 La Tabatière Quebec, E Canada 50.51N 58.58W
58 C6 Latacunga Cotopaxi, C Ecuador 0.58S 78.36W
204 I7 Latady Island island Antarctica
56 E14 La Tagua Putumayo, S Colombia 0.04S 74.39W
Latakia see Al Lādhiqīyah
94 J10 Lätäseno ≈ NW Finland
12 H9 Latchford Ontario, S Canada 47.20N 79.45W
12 J13 Latchford Bridge Ontario, SE Canada 45.16N 77.29W
200 Ss12 Late island Vava'u Group, N Tonga
159 P15 Lātehār Bihār, N India 23.48N 84.28E
13 R7 Laterrière Quebec, SE Canada 48.17N 71.10W
104 J13 la Teste Gironde, SW France 44.37N 1.04W
27 V8 Latexo Texas, SW USA 31.24N 95.28W
20 L10 Latham New York, NE USA 42.45N 73.45W
Latharna see Larne
110 B9 La Thielle var. Thièle. ≈ W Switzerland
29 R3 Lathrop Missouri, C USA 39.33N 94.19W
109 I16 Latina prev. Littoria. Lazio, C Italy 41.28N 12.52E
43 R14 La Tinaja Veracruz-Llave, S Mexico
108 J7 Latisana Friuli-Venezia Giulia, NE Italy 45.47N 13.01E
Latium see Lazio
117 K25 Lató site of ancient city Kríti, Greece, E Mediterranean Sea 35.09N 25.40E
197 J7 La Tontouta ✕ (Noumea) Province Sud, S New Caledonia 22.06S 166.12E
57 N4 La Tortuga, Isla var. Isla Tortuga. island N Venezuela
110 C10 La Tour-de-Peilz var. La Tour de Peilz. Vaud, SW Switzerland 46.28N 6.52E
105 S11 la Tour-du-Pin Isère, E France 45.34N 5.25E
104 J11 la Tremblade Charente-Maritime, W France 45.45N 1.07W
104 L10 la Trimouille Vienne, W France 46.27N 1.02E
44 J9 La Trinidad Estelí, NW Nicaragua 12.57N 86.13W
179 P9 La Trinidad Luzon, N Philippines 16.30N 120.39E
43 V16 La Trinitaria Chiapas, SE Mexico 16.02N 92.00W
47 Q11 la Trinité E Martinique 14.43N 60.57W
13 U7 La Trinité-des-Monts Quebec, SE Canada 48.07N 68.31W
20 C15 Latrobe Pennsylvania, NE USA 40.18N 79.19W
191 P13 La Trobe River ≈ Victoria, SE Australia
Lattakia/Lattaquié see Al Lādhiqīyah
175 Tt11 Latu Pulau Seram, E Indonesia 3.24S 128.37E
13 P9 La Tuque Quebec, SE Canada 47.25N 72.46W
161 G14 Lātūr Mahārāshtra, C India 18.24N 76.34E
120 G8 Latvia off. Republic of Latvia, Ger. Lettland, Latv. Latvija, Latvijas Republika; prev. Latvian SSR, Rus. Latviyskaya SSR. ◆ republic NE Europe
Latvian SSR/Latvija/Latvijas Republika/Latviyskaya SSR see Latvia
195 O12 Lau New Britain, E PNG 5.46S 151.21E
183 R9 Lau Basin undersea feature S Pacific Ocean
103 O15 Lauchhammer Brandenburg, E Germany 51.27N 13.32E
Laudunum see Laon
Laudus see St-Lô
Lauenburg/Lauenburg in Pommern see Lębork
103 L20 Lauf an der Pegnitz Bayern, SE Germany 49.31N 11.16E
110 D7 Laufen Basel, NW Switzerland 47.25N 7.31E
111 P5 Lauffen Salzburg, NW Austria 47.54N 12.57E
94 I2 Laugarbakki Nordhurland Vestra, N Iceland 65.18N 20.51W
94 I4 Laugarvatn Sudhurland, SW Iceland 64.09N 20.43W
33 O3 Laughing Fish Point headland Michigan, N USA 46.31N 87.01W
197 L14 Lau Group island group E Fiji
Lauis see Lugano
95 M17 Laukaa Länsi-Suomi, W Finland 62.27N 25.58E
120 D12 Laukuva Šilalė, W Lithuania 55.37N 22.12E
Laun see Louny
191 P16 Launceston Tasmania, SE Australia 41.25S 147.07E
99 I24 Launceston anc. Dunheved. SW England, UK 50.37N 4.21W
56 C13 La Unión Nariño, SW Colombia 1.34N 77.09W
44 H8 La Unión La Unión, SE El Salvador 13.19N 87.52W
44 I6 La Unión Olancho, C Honduras 15.02N 86.40W
42 M15 La Unión Guerrero, S Mexico 17.59N 101.48W
43 Y14 La Unión Quintana Roo, E Mexico 18.00N 101.48W
107 S13 La Unión Murcia, SE Spain 37.37N 0.53W
56 L7 La Unión Barinas, C Venezuela 8.12N 67.46W
44 B10 La Unión ◈ department E El Salvador
40 H11 Laupahoehoe Haw. Laupāhoehoe. Hawaii, USA, C Pacific Ocean 20.00N 155.15W
103 I23 Laupheim Baden-Württemberg, S Germany 48.13N 9.54E
189 W3 Laura Queensland, NE Australia 15.37S 144.34E
201 X2 Laura atoll Majuro Atoll, SE Marshall Islands
Laurana see Lovran
56 L8 La Urbana Bolívar, C Venezuela 7.05N 66.58W
23 Y4 Laurel Delaware, NE USA 38.33N 75.34W
25 V14 Laurel Florida, SE USA 27.07N 82.27W
23 W3 Laurel Maryland, NE USA 39.06N 76.51W
24 M6 Laurel Mississippi, S USA 31.41N 89.10W
35 U11 Laurel Montana, NW USA 45.40N 108.46W
31 R13 Laurel Nebraska, C USA 42.25N 97.04W
20 H15 Laureldale Pennsylvania, NE USA 40.24N 75.52W
20 C16 Laurel Hill ridge Pennsylvania, NE USA
31 T12 Laurens Iowa, C USA 42.51N 94.51W
23 P11 Laurens South Carolina, SE USA 34.29N 82.01W
Laurentian Highlands see Laurentian Mountains
13 P10 Laurentian Mountains var. Laurentian Highlands, Fr. Les Laurentides. plateau Newfoundland and Labrador/Quebec, Canada
13 O12 Laurentides Quebec, SE Canada 45.51N 73.49W
Laurentides, Les see Laurentian Mountains
109 M19 Lauria Basilicata, S Italy 40.03N 15.49E
204 I1 Laurie Island island Antarctica
23 T11 Laurinburg North Carolina, SE USA 34.51N 79.40W
32 M2 Laurium Michigan, N USA 47.14N 88.26W
Lauru see Choiseul
110 B9 Lausanne It. Losanna. Vaud, SW Switzerland 46.31N 6.39E
103 Q16 Lausche Cz. Luže. ▲ Czech Republic/Germany see also Luže 50.52N 14.39E
103 Q16 Lausitzer Bergland var. Lausitzer Gebirge, Cz. Gory Lużyckie, Lužické Hory, Eng. Lusatian Mountains. ▲▲ E Germany
Lausitzer Gebirge see Lausitzer Bergland
Lausitzer Neisse see Neisse
105 T12 Lautaret, Col du pass SE France 45.03N 6.23E
65 G15 Lautaro Araucanía, C Chile 38.31S 72.27W
103 F21 Lauter ≈ W Germany
110 I7 Lauterach Vorarlberg, NW Austria 47.28N 9.43E
103 I17 Lauterbach Hessen, C Germany 50.37N 9.24E
110 E9 Lauterbrunnen Bern, C Switzerland 46.36N 7.52E
175 Nn12 Laut Kecil, Kepulauan island group N Indonesia
197 H14 Lautoka Viti Levu, W Fiji 17.40S 177.25E
175 Nn11 Laut, Pulau prev. Laoet. island Borneo, C Indonesia
174 Jj4 Laut, Pulau island Kepulauan Natuna, W Indonesia
175 Nn11 Laut, Selat strait Borneo, C Indonesia
173 F4 Laut Tawar, Danau ◎ Sumatera, NW Indonesia
201 V14 Lauvergne Island island Chuuk, C Micronesia
100 M5 Lauwers Meer ◎ N Netherlands
100 M4 Lauwersoog Groningen, NE Netherlands 53.25N 6.14E
104 M14 Lauzerte Tarn-et-Garonne, S France 44.15N 1.08E
27 U13 Lavaca Bay bay Texas, SW USA
27 U12 Lavaca River ≈ Texas, SW USA
13 O12 Laval Quebec, SE Canada 45.32N 73.44W
104 J6 Laval Mayenne, NW France 48.04N 0.46W
13 T6 Laval ≈ Quebec, SE Canada
63 F19 Lavalleja ◈ department S Uruguay
13 O12 Lavaltrie Quebec, SE Canada 45.56N 73.14W
195 X17 Lavanggu Rennell, S Solomon Islands 11.39S 160.13E
149 O14 Lāvān, Jazīreh-ye island S Iran
111 U8 Lavant ≈ S Austria
120 G5 Lavassaare Ger. Lawassaar. Pärnumaa, SW Estonia 58.31N 24.22E
106 L3 La Vecilla de Curueño Castilla-León, N Spain 42.51N 5.24W
47 N8 La Vega var. Concepción de la Vega. C Dominican Republic 19.15N 70.32W
La Vela see La Vela de Coro
56 J4 La Vela de Coro var. La Vela. Falcón, N Venezuela 11.26N 69.35W
105 N17 Lavelanet Ariège, S France 42.55N 1.49E
109 M17 Lavello Basilicata, S Italy 41.03N 15.48E
38 J8 La Verkin Utah, W USA 37.12N 113.16W
28 J8 Laverne Oklahoma, C USA 36.42N 99.53W
27 S12 La Vernia Texas, SW USA 29.19N 98.07W
95 K18 Lavia Länsi-Suomi, W Finland 61.36N 22.34E
12 I12 Lavieille, Lake ◎ Ontario, SE Canada
96 C12 Lavik Sogn og Fjordane, S Norway 61.06N 5.25E
La Vila Jojosa see Villajoyosa
35 U10 Lavina Montana, NW USA 46.18N 108.55W
204 H5 Lavoisier Island island Antarctica
25 U2 Lavonia Georgia, SE USA 34.26N 83.06W
105 R13 la Voulte-sur-Rhône Ardèche, E France 44.49N 4.46E
127 Q3 Lavrentiya Chukotskiy Avtonomnyy Okrug, NE Russian Federation 65.33N 171.12W
117 H20 Lávrio prev. Lávrion. Attikí, C Greece 37.43N 24.03E
Lávrion see Lávrio
85 L22 Lavumisa prev. Gollel. SE Swaziland 27.20S 31.51E
155 T4 Lawarai Pass pass N Pakistan 35.22N 71.48E
Lawassaar see Lavassaare
147 P16 Lawdar SW Yemen 13.49N 45.54E
27 Q7 Lawn Texas, SW USA 32.07N 99.45W
205 Y4 Law Promontory headland Antarctica
79 O14 Lawra NW Ghana 10.40N 2.55W
193 E23 Lawrence Otago, South Island, NZ 45.53S 169.43E
33 P14 Lawrence Indiana, N USA 39.49N 86.01W
29 Q4 Lawrence Kansas, C USA 38.58N 95.14W
21 O10 Lawrence Massachusetts, NE USA 42.42N 71.09W
22 L5 Lawrenceburg Kentucky, S USA 38.02N 84.54W
22 I10 Lawrenceburg Tennessee, S USA 35.14N 87.19W
25 T3 Lawrenceville Georgia, SE USA 33.57N 83.59W
33 N15 Lawrenceville Illinois, N USA 38.43N 87.40W
23 V7 Lawrenceville Virginia, NE USA 36.45N 77.51W
29 S3 Lawson Missouri, C USA 39.26N 94.12W
28 L12 Lawton Oklahoma, C USA 34.35N 98.19W
146 I4 Lawz, Jabal al ▲ NW Saudi Arabia 28.45N 35.20E
97 L16 Laxå Örebro, C Sweden 59.00N 14.37E
129 T5 Laya ≈ NW Russian Federation
59 I19 La Yarada Tacna, SW Peru 18.14S 70.30W
147 S15 Layjūn C Yemen 15.27N 49.16E
147 Q9 Laylā var. Laila. Ar Riyāḍ, C Saudi Arabia 22.13N 46.39E
25 P4 Lay Lake ▣ Alabama, S USA
47 P14 Layou Saint Vincent, Saint Vincent and the Grenadines 13.11N 61.16W
La Youne see El Ayoun
199 Jj5 Laysan Island island Hawaiian Islands, Hawaii, USA, C Pacific Ocean
38 L2 Layton Utah, W USA 41.03N 112.00W
36 L5 Laytonville California, W USA 39.39N 123.30W
180 H17 Lazare, Pointe headland Mahé, NE Seychelles 4.46S 55.28E
127 O14 Lazarev Khabarovskiy Kray, SE Russian Federation 52.11N 141.18E
114 L12 Lazarevac Serbia, C Serbia and Montenegro (Yugoslavia) 44.25N 20.17E
67 N22 Lazarev Sea sea Antarctica
42 M15 Lázaro Cárdenas Michoacán de Ocampo, SW Mexico 17.55N 102.12W
121 F15 Lazdijai Lazdijai, S Lithuania 54.13N 23.33E
109 H15 Lazio anc. Latium. ◈ region C Italy
113 A16 Lázně Kynžvart Ger. Bad Königswart. Karlovarský Kraj, W Czech Republic 50.00N 12.40E
Lazovsk see Sîngerei
178 Ii13 Leach Poŭthĭsăt, W Cambodia 12.19N 103.45E
29 X9 Leachville Arkansas, C USA 35.56N 90.15W
30 I9 Lead South Dakota, N USA 44.21N 103.45W
9 S16 Leader Saskatchewan, S Canada 50.55N 109.31W
21 S6 Lead Mountain ▲ Maine, NE USA 44.53N 68.07W
39 R5 Leadville Colorado, C USA 39.15N 106.17W
9 V12 Leaf Rapids Manitoba, C Canada 56.30N 100.01W
24 M7 Leaf River ≈ Mississippi, S USA
27 W11 League City Texas, SW USA 29.30N 95.05W
25 N7 Leakesville Mississippi, S USA 31.09N 88.33W
27 Q11 Leakey Texas, SW USA 29.43N 99.45W
Leal see Lihula
85 G15 Lealui Western, W Zambia 15.12S 22.58E
Leamhcán see Lucan
12 C18 Leamington Ontario, S Canada 42.03N 82.34W
Leamington/Leamington Spa see Royal Leamington Spa
Leammi see Lemmenjoki
27 S10 Leander Texas, SW USA 30.34N 97.51W
63 F13 Leandro N.Alem Misiones, NE Argentina 27.34S 55.15W
99 A20 Leane, Lough Ir. Loch Léin. ◎ SW Ireland
188 G8 Learmouth Western Australia 22.17S 114.03E
Leau see Zoutleeuw
L'Eau d'Heure see Plate Taille, Lac de la
202 D12 Leava Île Futuna, S Wallis and Futuna
29 R3 Leavenworth Kansas, C USA 39.17N 94.55W
34 I8 Leavenworth Washington, NW USA 47.36N 120.39W
94 L8 Leavvajohka var. Levajok, Lœvvajok. Finnmark, N Norway 69.57N 26.18E
29 R4 Leawood Kansas, C USA 38.57N 94.37W
112 H6 Łeba Ger. Leba. Pomorskie, N Poland 54.45N 17.31E
112 I6 Łeba Ger. Leba. ≈ N Poland
103 D20 Lebach Saarland, SW Germany 49.25N 6.54E
Łeba, Jezioro see Łebsko, Jezioro
179 R17 Lebak Mindanao, S Philippines 6.28N 124.03E
175 Oo11 Lebani,Teluk bay Sulawesi, C Indonesia
33 O13 Lebanon Indiana, N USA 40.03N 86.28W
22 L6 Lebanon Kentucky, S USA 37.34N 85.15W
29 U6 Lebanon Missouri, C USA 37.40N 92.39W
21 N9 Lebanon New Hampshire, NE USA 43.40N 72.15W
34 G12 Lebanon Oregon, NW USA 44.32N 122.54W
20 H15 Lebanon Pennsylvania, NE USA 40.20N 76.24W
22 J8 Lebanon Tennessee, S USA 36.13N 86.16W
23 P7 Lebanon Virginia, NE USA 36.54N 82.04W
144 G6 Lebanon off. Republic of Lebanon, Ar. Al Lubnān, Fr. Liban. ◆ republic SW Asia
22 K6 Lebanon Junction Kentucky, S USA 37.49N 85.43W
Lebanon, Mount see Liban, Jebel
152 J10 Lebap Lebapskiy Velayat, NE Turkmenistan 41.04N 61.49E
152 H11 Lebapskiy Velayat Turkm. Lebap Welayaty; prev. Rus. Chardzhevskaya Oblast', Turkm. Chärjew Oblasty. ◈ province E Turkmenistan
Lebap Welayaty see Lebapskiy Velayat
Lebasee see Łebsko, Jezioro
101 F17 Lebbeke Oost-Vlaanderen, NW Belgium 51.00N 4.08E
37 S14 Lebec California, W USA 34.51N 118.52W
Lebedin see Lebedyn
126 Ll12 Lebedinyy Respublika Sakha (Yakutiya), NE Russian Federation 58.23N 125.24E
130 L6 Lebedyan' Lipetskaya Oblast', W Russian Federation 53.00N 39.11E
119 T4 Lebedyn Rus. Lebedin. Sums'ka Oblast', NE Ukraine 50.36N 34.30E
10 I12 Lebel-sur-Quévillon Quebec, SE Canada 49.01N 76.55W
94 L8 Lebesby Finnmark, N Norway 70.31N 27.00E
104 M9 le Blanc Indre, C France 46.38N 1.04E
29 P5 Lebo Kansas, C USA 38.22N 95.50W
81 L15 Lebo Orientale, N Dem. Rep. Congo 4.30N 23.58E
112 H6 Lębork var. Lėbork, Ger. Lauenburg, Lauenburg in Pommern. Pomorskie, N Poland 54.31N 17.43E
105 O17 le Boulou Pyrénées-Orientales, S France 42.31N 2.49E
110 A9 Le Brassus Vaud, W Switzerland 46.35N 6.14E
106 J15 Lebrija Andalucía, S Spain 36.55N 6.04W
112 G6 Łebsko, Jezioro Ger. Lebasee; prev. Jezioro Łeba. ◎ N Poland
65 F14 Lebu Bío Bío, C Chile 37.34S 73.37W
Lebyazh'ye see Akku
106 F6 Leça da Palmeira Porto, N Portugal 41.12N 8.43W
105 U15 le Cannet Alpes-Maritimes, SE France 43.35N 7.00E
Le Cap see Cap-Haïtien
105 P2 le Cateau-Cambrésis Nord, N France 50.05N 3.32E
109 Q18 Lecce Puglia, SE Italy 40.22N 18.10E
108 D7 Lecco Lombardia, N Italy 45.49N 9.27E
31 V10 Le Center Minnesota, N USA 44.23N 93.43W
110 J7 Lech Vorarlberg, W Austria 47.14N 10.10E
103 K22 Lech ≈ Austria/Germany
117 D19 Lechainá var. Lehena, Lekhainá. Dytikí Ellás, S Greece 37.56N 21.16E
104 J11 le Château d'Oléron Charente-Maritime, W France 45.53N 1.12W
105 R3 le Chesne Ardennes, N France 49.33N 4.42E
105 R13 le Cheylard Ardèche, E France 44.55N 4.25E
110 K7 Lechtaler Alpen ▲▲ W Austria
102 H6 Leck Schleswig-Holstein, N Germany 54.45N 9.00E
12 L9 Lecointre, Lac ◎ Quebec, SE Canada
24 H7 Lecompte Louisiana, S USA 31.05N 92.24W
105 Q9 le Creusot Saône-et-Loire, C France 46.48N 4.25E
Leculberri see Lekunberri
112 P13 Łęczna Lubelskie, E Poland 51.19N 22.52E
112 J12 Łęczyca Ger. Lentschiza, Rus. Lenchitsa. Łódzkie, C Poland 52.03N 19.10E
102 F10 Leda ≈ NW Germany
111 Y9 Ledava ≈ NE Slovenia
101 F17 Lede Oost-Vlaanderen, NW Belgium 50.58N 3.58E
106 K6 Ledesma Castilla-León, N Spain 41.05N 6.00W
47 Q12 le Diamant SW Martinique 14.28N 61.02W
180 J16 Le Digue island Inner Islands, NE Seychelles
105 Q10 le Donjon Allier, C France 46.19N 3.50E
104 M10 le Dorat Haute-Vienne, C France 46.14N 1.05E
Ledo Salinarius see Lons-le-Saunier
9 Q14 Leduc Alberta, SW Canada 53.16N 113.30W
127 Pp7 Ledyanaya, Gora ▲ E Russian Federation 61.51N 171.03E
99 C21 Lee Ir. An Laoi. ≈ SW Ireland
31 U5 Leech Lake ◎ Minnesota, N USA
28 K10 Leedey Oklahoma, C USA 35.54N 99.21W
99 M17 Leeds N England, UK 53.49N 1.34W
25 P4 Leeds Alabama, S USA 33.33N 86.32W
31 O3 Leeds North Dakota, N USA 48.19N 99.43W
100 N6 Leek Groningen, NE Netherlands 53.10N 6.24E
101 K15 Leende Noord-Brabant, SE Netherlands 51.21N 5.34E
102 F10 Leer Niedersachsen, NW Germany 53.14N 7.25E
100 J13 Leerdam Zuid-Holland, C Netherlands 51.54N 5.06E
100 K12 Leersum Utrecht, C Netherlands 52.01N 5.25E
25 W11 Leesburg Florida, SE USA 28.48N 81.52W
23 V3 Leesburg Virginia, NE USA 39.07N 77.33W
29 R4 Lees Summit Missouri, C USA 38.55N 94.21W
24 G7 Leesville Louisiana, S USA 31.08N 93.15W
27 S12 Leesville Texas, SW USA 29.22N 97.45W
33 U13 Leesville Lake ▣ Ohio, N USA
Leesville Lake see Smith Mountain Lake
191 P9 Leeton New South Wales, SE Australia 34.33S 146.24E
100 L6 Leeuwarden Fris. Ljouwert. Friesland, N Netherlands 53.15N 5.48E
188 I14 Leeuwin, Cape headland Western Australia 34.18S 115.03E
37 R8 Lee Vining California, W USA 37.57N 119.07W
47 V8 Leeward Islands island group E West Indies
Leeward Islands see Vent, Îles Sous le, W French Polynesia
Leeward Islands see Sotavento, Ilhas de, Cape Verde
81 G20 Léfini ≈ SE Congo
Léfka see Lefke
117 C17 Lefkáda prev. Levkás. Lefkáda, Iónioi Nísoi, Greece, C Mediterranean Sea 38.50N 20.43E
117 B17 Lefkáda It. Santa Maura; prev. Levkás, anc. Leucas. island Iónioi Nísoi, Greece, C Mediterranean Sea
117 H25 Lefká Óri ▲▲ Kríti, Greece, E Mediterranean Sea
124 N3 Lefke Gk. Léfka. W Cyprus 35.06N 32.52E
117 B16 Lefkímmi var. Levkímmi. Kérkyra, Iónioi Nísoi, Greece, C Mediterranean Sea 39.25N 20.03E
Lefkonico/Lefkónikon see Geçitkale
Lefkoşa/Lefkosía see Nicosia
27 O2 Lefors Texas, SW USA 35.26N 100.48W
47 R12 le François E Martinique 14.36N 60.54W
188 L12 Lefroy, Lake salt lake Western Australia
Legaceaster see Chester
107 N8 Leganés Madrid, C Spain 40.19N 3.46W
179 Q11 Legaspi off. Legaspi City. Luzon, N Philippines 13.06N 123.43E
Leghorn see Livorno
112 M11 Legionowo Mazowieckie, C Poland 52.23N 20.55E
101 K24 Léglise Luxembourg, SE Belgium 49.48N 5.31E
108 G8 Legnago Lombardia, NE Italy 45.13N 11.18E
108 D7 Legnano Veneto, NE Italy 45.36N 8.54E
113 F14 Legnica Ger. Liegnitz. Dolnośląskie, SW Poland 51.12N 16.11E
37 Q9 Le Grand California, W USA 37.12N 120.15W
105 Q15 le Grau-du-Roi Gard, S France 43.32N 4.10E
191 U3 Legume New South Wales, SE Australia 28.24S 152.20E
104 L4 le Havre Eng. Havre; prev. le Havre-de-Grâce. Seine-Maritime, N France 49.30N 0.07E
le Havre-de-Grâce see le Havre
Lehena see Lechainá
38 L3 Lehi Utah, W USA 40.23N 111.51W
20 I14 Lehighton Pennsylvania, NE USA 40.49N 75.42W
31 O6 Lehr North Dakota, N USA 46.15N 99.21W
40 A8 Lehua Island island Hawaiian Islands, Hawaii, USA, C Pacific Ocean
155 S9 Leiah Punjab, NE Pakistan 30.58N 70.53E
111 W9 Leibnitz Steiermark, SE Austria 46.48N 15.33E
99 M19 Leicester Lat. Batae Coritanorum. C England, UK 52.37N 1.04W
99 M19 Leicestershire cultural region C England, UK
100 H11 Leiden prev. Leyden, anc. Lugdunum Batavorum. Zuid-Holland, W Netherlands 52.09N 4.30E
100 H11 Leiderdorp Zuid-Holland, W Netherlands 52.07N 4.31E
100 G11 Leidschendam Zuid-Holland, W Netherlands 52.04N 4.24E
101 D18 Leie Fr. Lys. ≈ Belgium/France
Leifear see Lifford
192 L4 Leigh Auckland, North Island, NZ 36.17S 174.48E
99 K17 Leigh NW England, UK 53.30N 2.33W
190 I5 Leigh Creek South Australia 30.27S 138.23E
25 O2 Leighton Alabama, S USA 34.42N 87.31W
99 M21 Leighton Buzzard E England, UK 51.55N 0.40W
Léim an Bhradáin see Leixlip
Léim an Mhadaidh see Limavady
Léime, Ceann see Loop Head, Ireland
Léime, Ceann see Slyne Head, Ireland
103 G20 Leimen Baden-Württemberg, SW Germany 49.21N 8.40E
102 I13 Leine ≈ NW Germany
103 J15 Leinefelde Thüringen, C Germany 51.22N 10.19E
Léin, Loch see Leane, Lough
99 D19 Leinster Ir. Cúige Laighean. cultural region E Ireland
99 F19 Leinster, Mount Ir. Stua Laighean. ▲ SE Ireland 52.36N 6.45W
121 F15 Leipalingis Lazdijai, S Lithuania 54.05N 23.52E
94 J12 Leipojärvi Norrbotten, N Sweden 67.03N 21.15E
33 R12 Leipsic Ohio, N USA 41.06N 83.58W
Leipsic see Leipzig
117 M20 Leipsoí island Dodekánisos, Greece, Aegean Sea
103 M15 Leipzig Pol. Lipsk; hist. Leipsic, anc. Lipsia. Sachsen, E Germany 51.19N 12.24E
103 M15 Leipzig Halle ✕ Sachsen, E Germany 51.26N 12.14E
106 G9 Leiria anc. Collipo. Leiria, C Portugal 39.45N 8.49W
106 F9 Leiria ◈ district C Portugal
97 C15 Leirvik Hordaland, S Norway 59.48N 5.26E
120 E5 Leisi Ger. Laisberg. Saaremaa, W Estonia 58.35N 22.42E
106 J3 Leitariegos, Puerto de pass NW Spain 43.02N 6.26W
22 J6 Leitchfield Kentucky, S USA 37.28N 86.17W
111 Y5 Leitha Hung. Lajta. ≈ Austria/Hungary
Leitir Ceanainn see Letterkenny
Leitmeritz see Litoměřice
Leitomischl see Litomyšl
99 D16 Leitrim Ir. Liatroim. cultural region NW Ireland
117 F18 Leivádia prev. Levádhia. Stereá Ellás, C Greece 38.24N 22.51E
Leix see Laois
99 F18 Leixlip Eng. Salmon Leap, Ir. Léim an Bhradáin. E Ireland 53.22N 6.31W
66 N8 Leixões Porto, N Portugal 41.10N 8.40W
167 N12 Leiyang Hunan, S China 26.23N 112.49E
166 L16 Leizhou var. Haikang. Guangdong, S China 20.54N 110.04E
166 L16 Leizhou Bandao var. Luichow Peninsula. peninsula S China
100 H13 Lek ≈ SW Netherlands
116 I13 Lekánis ▲▲ NE Greece
180 H13 Le Kartala ▲ Grande Comore, NW Comoros
Le Kef see El Kef
81 G20 Lékéti, Monts de la ▲▲ S Congo
Lekhainá see Lechainá
116 H8 Lekhchevo Montana, NW Bulgaria 43.32N 23.31E
94 G11 Leknes Nordland, C Norway 68.07N 13.36E
81 E21 Lékoumou ◈ province SW Congo
96 L13 Leksand Dalarna, C Sweden 60.44N 15.00E
128 H8 Leksozero, Ozero ◎ NW Russian Federation
107 Q3 Lekunberri var. Lecumberri. Navarra, N Spain 43.00N 1.54W
175 Tt6 Lelai, Tanjung headland Pulau Halmahera, N Indonesia 1.31N 128.43E
47 Q12 le Lamentin var. Lamentin. C Martinique 14.37N 61.01W
47 Q12 le Lamentin ✕ (Fort-de-France) C Martinique 14.34N 61.00W
33 P6 Leland Michigan, N USA 44.59N 85.45W
24 J4 Leland Mississippi, S USA 33.24N 90.54W
97 J16 Lelång var. Lelången. ◎ S Sweden
Lelången see Lelång
Lel'chitsy see Lyel'chytsy
Le Léman see Geneva, Lake
27 O3 Lelia Lake Texas, SW USA 34.52N 100.42W
115 I14 Lelija ▲ SE Bosnia and Herzegovina 43.25N 18.31E
110 C8 Le Locle Neuchâtel, W Switzerland 47.04N 6.45E
201 Y14 Lelu Kosrae, E Micronesia
Lelu see Lelu Island
201 Y14 Lelu Island var. Lelu. island Kosrae, E Micronesia
57 W9 Lelydorp Wanica, N Suriname 5.36N 55.04W
100 K9 Lelystad Flevoland, C Netherlands 52.30N 5.25E
65 K25 Le Maire, Estrecho de strait S Argentina
174 Hh7 Lemang Pulau Rangsang, W Indonesia 1.04N 102.44E
195 R11 Lemankoa Buka Island, NE PNG 5.04S 154.37E
Léman, Lac see Geneva, Lake
104 L6 le Mans Sarthe, NW France 48.00N 0.12E
31 S12 Le Mars Iowa, C USA 42.47N 96.10W
174 I11 Lematan, Air ≈ Sumatera, W Indonesia
111 S3 Lembach im Mühlkreis Oberösterreich, N Austria 48.28N 13.53E
103 G23 Lemberg ▲ SW Germany 48.09N 8.47E
Lemberg see L'viv
Lemdiyya see Médéa
124 Qq12 Lemesós var. Limassol. SW Cyprus 34.40N 33.02E
102 H13 Lemgo Nordrhein-Westfalen, W Germany 52.01N 8.54E
35 P13 Lemhi Range ▲▲ Idaho, NW USA
16 Oo2 Lemieux Islands island group Nunavut, NE Canada

◆ Country
● Country Capital
◇ Dependent Territory
○ Dependent Territory Capital
◈ Administrative Region
✕ International Airport
▲ Mountain
▲▲ Mountain Range
※ Volcano
≈ River
◎ Lake
▣ Reservoir

175 Q7 **Lemito** Sulawesi, N Indonesia 0.34N 121.31E
94 L10 **Lemmenjoki** Lapp. Leammi. ≈ NE Finland
100 L7 **Lemmer** Fris. De Lemmer. Friesland, N Netherlands 52.49N 5.43E
30 L7 **Lemmon** South Dakota, N USA 45.54N 102.08W
38 M15 **Lemmon, Mount** ▲ Arizona, SW USA 32.26N 110.47W
Lemnos see Límnos
33 O14 **Lemon, Lake** ◎ Indiana, N USA
104 J5 **le Mont St-Michel** castle Manche, N France 48.37N 1.31W
37 Q11 **Lemoore** California, W USA 36.16N 119.48W
201 T13 **Lemotol Bay** bay Chuuk Islands, C Micronesia
47 Y5 **le Moule** var. Moule. Grande Terre, NE Guadeloupe 16.20N 61.20W
Lemovices see Limoges
Le Moyen-Ogooué see Moyen-Ogooué
10 M6 **le Moyne, Lac** ◎ Quebec, E Canada
95 L18 **Lempäälä** Länsi-Suomi, W Finland 61.13N 23.46E
44 E7 **Lempa, Río** ≈ Central America
44 F7 **Lempira** prev. Gracias. ◈ department SW Honduras
Lemsalu see Limbaži
109 N17 **Le Murge** ▲▲ SE Italy
129 V6 **Lemva** ≈ NW Russian Federation
97 F21 **Lemvig** Ringkøbing, W Denmark 56.31N 8.19E
177 Ff8 **Lemyethna** Irrawaddy, SW Myanmar 17.36N 95.07E
32 K10 **Lena** Illinois, N USA 42.22N 89.49W
133 V4 **Lena** ≈ NE Russian Federation
181 N13 **Lena Tablemount** undersea feature S Indian Ocean 51.06S 56.54E
Lenchitsa see Łęczyca
61 N17 **Lençóis** Bahia, E Brazil 12.36S 41.24W
62 K9 **Lençóis Paulista** São Paulo, S Brazil 22.35S 48.51W
178 Mm15 **Len Dao** island S Spratly Islands
111 Y9 **Lendava** Hung. Lendva, Ger. Unterlimbach; prev. Dolnja Lendava. NE Slovenia 46.33N 16.27E
85 F20 **Lendepas** Hardap, SE Namibia 24.41S 19.58E
128 H9 **Lendery** Respublika Kareliya, NW Russian Federation 63.20N 31.18E
Lendum see Lens
Lendva see Lendava
29 R4 **Lenexa** Kansas, C USA 38.57N 94.43W
111 Q5 **Lengau** Oberösterreich, N Austria 48.01N 13.17E
151 Q17 **Lenger** Yuzhnyy Kazakhstan, S Kazakhstan 42.10N 69.54E
165 O9 **Lenghu** Qinghai, C China 38.50N 93.25E
165 T9 **Lenglong Ling** ▲ N China 37.40N 102.13E
110 D7 **Lengnau** Bern, W Switzerland 47.12N 7.22E
166 M12 **Lengshuitan** Hunan, S China 26.31N 111.38E
97 M20 **Lenhovda** Kronoberg, S Sweden 57.00N 15.16E
81 E20 **Le Niari** ◈ province SW Congo
Lenīn see Leninskoye, Kazakhstan
Lenin see Akdepe, Turkmenistan
Leninabad see Khŭjand
Leninakan see Gyumri
Lenina, Pik see Lenin Peak
119 V12 **Lenine** Rus. Lenino. Respublika Krym, S Ukraine 45.18N 35.47E
Leningor see Leninogorsk
153 Q13 **Leningrad** Rus. Leningradskiy; prev. Mŭ'minobod, Rus. Muminabad. SW Tajikistan 38.03N 69.50E
Leningrad see Sankt-Peterburg
130 L13 **Leningradskaya** Krasnodarskiy Kray, SW Russian Federation 46.19N 39.23E
205 S16 **Leningradskaya** Russian research station Antarctica 69.30S 159.51E
128 H12 **Leningradskaya Oblast'** ◈ province NW Russian Federation
Leningradskiy see Leningrad
Lenino see Lenine, Ukraine
Lenino see Lyenina, Belarus
Leninobod see Khŭjand
151 X9 **Leninogorsk** Kaz. Leningor. Vostochnyy Kazakhstan, E Kazakhstan 50.20N 83.33E
131 T5 **Leninogorsk** Respublika Tatarstan, W Russian Federation 54.34N 52.27E
153 T12 **Lenin Peak** Rus. Pik Lenina, Taj. Qullai Lenin. ▲ Kyrgyzstan/Tajikistan 39.20N 72.50E
153 S8 **Leninpol'** Talasskaya Oblast', NW Kyrgyzstan 42.29N 71.54E
Lenin, Qullai see Lenin Peak
131 P11 **Leninsk** Volgogradskaya Oblast', SW Russian Federation 48.41N 45.18E
Leninsk see Akdepe, Turkmenistan
Leninsk see Asaka, Uzbekistan
Leninsk see Baykonyr, Kazakhstan
151 T8 **Leninskiy** Pavlodar, E Kazakhstan 52.18N 76.48E
126 H14 **Leninsk-Kuznetskiy** Kemerovskaya Oblast', S Russian Federation 54.42N 86.16E
151 N7 **Leninskoye** Kaz. Lenīn. Kostanay, N Kazakhstan 54.04N 65.22E
129 P15 **Leninskoye** Kirovskaya Oblast', NW Russian Federation 58.19N 47.03E
Leninsk-Turkmenski see Chardzhev
Leninváros see Tiszaújváros
Lenkoran' see Länkäran
103 F15 **Lenne** ≈ W Germany
103 G16 **Lennestadt** Nordrhein-Westfalen, W Germany 51.07N 8.04E
31 R11 **Lennox** South Dakota, N USA 43.21N 96.53W
65 J25 **Lennox, Isla** Eng. Lennox Island. island S Chile
Lennox Island see Lennox, Isla
23 Q9 **Lenoir** North Carolina, SE USA 35.54N 81.32W
22 M9 **Lenoir City** Tennessee, S USA 35.48N 84.15W
110 C7 **Le Noirmont** Jura, NW Switzerland 47.14N 6.57E
12 L9 **Lenôtre, Lac** ◎ Quebec, SE Canada
31 U15 **Lenox** Iowa, C USA 40.52N 94.33W
105 O2 **Lens** anc. Lendum, Lentium. Pas-de-Calais, N France 50.25N 2.49E
126 Kk12 **Lensk** Respublika Sakha (Yakutiya), NE Russian Federation 60.43N 115.16E
113 F24 **Lenti** Zala, SW Hungary 46.38N 16.30E
Lentia see Linz
95 N14 **Lentiira** Oulu, E Finland 64.22N 29.52E
109 L25 **Lentini** anc. Leontini. Sicilia, Italy, C Mediterranean Sea 37.17N 15.00E
Lentium see Lens
Lentschiza see Łęczyca
95 N15 **Lentua** ◎ E Finland
121 H14 **Lentvaris** Pol. Landwarów. Trakai, SE Lithuania 24.39N 24.58E
110 F7 **Lenzburg** Aargau, N Switzerland 47.24N 8.09E
111 R5 **Lenzing** Oberösterreich, N Austria 47.58N 13.34E
79 P13 **Léo** SW Burkina 11.09N 2.04W
111 V7 **Leoben** Steiermark, C Austria 47.22N 15.06E
Leobschütz see Głubczyce
46 L9 **Léogâne** S Haiti 18.28N 72.39W
175 Q7 **Leok** Sulawesi, N Indonesia 1.10N 121.20E
31 O7 **Leola** South Dakota, N USA 45.41N 98.58W
99 K20 **Leominster** W England, UK 52.09N 2.18W
21 N11 **Leominster** Massachusetts, NE USA 42.29N 71.43W
31 V16 **Leon** Iowa, C USA 40.44N 93.45W
42 M12 **León** var. León de los Aldamas. Guanajuato, C Mexico 21.05N 101.43W
44 I10 **León** León, NW Nicaragua 12.24N 86.52W
106 L4 **León** Castilla-León, NW Spain 42.34N 5.33W
44 I9 **León** ◈ department W Nicaragua
106 K4 **León** ◈ province Castilla-León, NW Spain
León see Cotopaxi
104 I15 **Léon** Landes, SW France 43.54N 1.17W
27 V9 **Leona** Texas, SW USA 31.09N 95.58W
188 K11 **Leonara** Western Australia 28.52S 121.16E
27 U5 **Leonard** Texas, SW USA 33.22N 96.15W
Leonard Murray Mountains see Murray Range
109 H15 **Leonardo da Vinci** prev. Fiumicino. ✈ (Roma) Lazio, C Italy 41.48N 12.15E
23 X5 **Leonardtown** Maryland, NE USA 38.17N 76.35W
27 Q13 **Leona River** ≈ Texas, SW USA
43 Z11 **Leona Vicario** Quintana Roo, SE Mexico 20.57N 87.06W
103 H21 **Leonberg** Baden-Württemberg, SW Germany 48.48N 9.01E
64 M3 **León, Cerro** ▲ NW Paraguay 20.21S 60.16W
León de los Aldamas see León
111 T4 **Leonding** Oberösterreich, N Austria 48.17N 14.15E
109 I14 **Leonessa** Lazio, C Italy 42.36N 12.56E
109 K24 **Leonforte** Sicilia, Italy, C Mediterranean Sea 37.37N 14.22E
191 O13 **Leongatha** Victoria, SE Australia 38.30S 145.56E
117 F21 **Leonídi** Pelopónnisos, S Greece 37.10N 22.50E
106 J4 **León, Montes de** ▲▲ NW Spain
27 S8 **Leon River** ≈ Texas, SW USA
Leontini see Lentini
Léopold II, Lac see Mai-Ndombe, Lac
101 J17 **Leopoldsburg** Limburg, NE Belgium 51.07N 5.16E
Léopoldville see Kinshasa
28 I5 **Leoti** Kansas, C USA 38.28N 101.21W
118 M11 **Leova** Rus. Leovo. SW Moldova 46.31N 28.16E
Leovo see Leova
104 G8 **le Palais** Morbihan, NW France 47.20N 3.08W
29 X10 **Lepanto** Arkansas, C USA 35.34N 90.21W
174 J11 **Lepar, Pulau** island W Indonesia
106 I14 **Lepe** Andalucía, S Spain 37.15N 7.12W
Lepel' see Lyepyel'
85 I19 **Lephepe** Kweneng, SE Botswana 23.17S 25.48E
167 Q10 **Leping** Jiangxi, S China 29.01N 117.07E
Lépontiennes, Alpes/Lepontine, Alpi see Lepontine Alps
110 G10 **Lepontine Alps** Fr. Alpes Lépontiennes, It. Alpi Lepontine. ▲▲ Italy/Switzerland
81 G20 **Le Pool** ◈ province S Congo
181 O16 **le Port** NW Réunion
105 N1 **le Portel** Pas-de-Calais, N France 50.42N 1.34E
95 N17 **Leppävirta** Itä-Suomi, C Finland 62.30N 27.49E
47 Q11 **le Prêcheur** NW Martinique 14.48N 61.13W
Lepsi see Lepsy
151 V13 **Lepsy** Kaz. Lepsi. Almaty, SE Kazakhstan 46.13N 78.55E
151 V13 **Lepsy** Kaz. Lepsi. ≈ SE Kazakhstan
Le Puglie see Puglia
105 Q12 **le Puy** prev. le Puy-en-Velay, hist. Anicium, Podium Anicensis. Haute-Loire, C France 45.03N 3.52E
le Puy-en-Velay see le Puy
Le Raizet see le Raizet
47 X11 **le Raizet** var. Le Raizet. ✈ (Pointe-à-Pitre) Grande Terre, C Guadeloupe 16.16N 61.31W
109 J24 **Lercara Friddi** Sicilia, Italy, C Mediterranean Sea 37.45N 13.37E
80 G12 **Léré** Mayo-Kébbi, SW Chad 9.40N 14.16E
Leribe see Hlotse
108 E10 **Lerici** Liguria, NW Italy 44.06N 9.53E
56 I14 **Lérida** Vaupés, SE Colombia 0.01S 70.28W
Lérida see Lleida
107 N5 **Lerma** Castilla-León, N Spain 42.01N 3.46W
42 M13 **Lerma, Río** ≈ C Mexico
117 F20 **Lérna** prehistoric site Pelopónnisos, S Greece 37.31N 22.43E
47 R11 **le Robert** E Martinique 14.40N 60.56W
117 M21 **Léros** island Dodekánisos, Greece, Aegean Sea
32 L13 **Le Roy** Illinois, N USA 40.21N 88.45W
29 Q6 **Le Roy** Kansas, C USA 38.04N 95.37W
31 W11 **Le Roy** Minnesota, N USA 43.30N 92.30W
20 E10 **Le Roy** New York, NE USA 42.58N 77.58W
Lerrnayin Gharabakh see Nagornyy Karabakh
97 J19 **Lerum** Västra Götaland, S Sweden 57.46N 12.12E
98 M2 **Lerwick** NE Scotland, UK 60.09N 1.09W
47 Y6 **les Abymes** var. Abymes. Grande Terre, C Guadeloupe 16.16N 61.30W
les Albères see Albères, Chaîne des
104 M4 **les Andelys** Eure, N France 49.15N 1.27E
47 Q12 **les Anses-d'Arlets** SW Martinique 14.29N 61.05W
107 U6 **Les Borges Blanques** var. Borjas Blancas. Cataluña, NE Spain 41.31N 0.52E
Lesbos see Lésvos
Les Cayes see Cayes
33 Q4 **Les Cheneaux Islands** island Michigan, N USA
105 T12 **les Écrins** ▲ E France 44.54N 6.25E
110 C10 **Le Sépey** Vaud, W Switzerland 46.21N 7.04E
13 T7 **Les Escoumins** Quebec, SE Canada 48.21N 69.25W
Les Gonaïves see Gonaïves
Lesh/Leshi see Lezhë
166 H9 **Leshan** Sichuan, C China 29.42N 103.43E
110 D11 **Les Haudères** Valais, SW Switzerland 46.02N 7.27E
104 J9 **les Herbiers** Vendée, NW France 46.52N 1.01W
129 O8 **Leshukonskoye** Arkhangel'skaya Oblast', NW Russian Federation 64.54N 45.48E
Lesina see Hvar
109 M15 **Lesina, Lago di** ◎ SE Italy
116 K13 **Lesítse** ▲▲ NE Greece
96 G10 **Lesja** Oppland, S Norway 62.07N 8.56E
97 L15 **Lesjöfors** Värmland, C Sweden 59.57N 14.12E
113 O18 **Lesko** Podkarpackie, SE Poland 49.28N 22.19E
115 O15 **Leskovac** Serbia, SE Serbia and Montenegro (Yugoslavia) 43.00N 21.58E
115 M22 **Leskovik** var. Leskoviku. Korçë, S Albania 40.09N 20.39E
Leskoviku see Leskovik
35 P14 **Leslie** Idaho, NW USA 43.51N 113.28W
33 Q10 **Leslie** Michigan, N USA 42.27N 84.25W
Leśna/Lesnaya see Lyasnaya
104 F5 **Lesneven** Finistère, NW France 48.35N 4.19W
114 J11 **Lešnica** Serbia, W Serbia and Montenegro (Yugoslavia) 44.40N 19.18E
125 Ee10 **Lesnoy** Sverdlovskaya Oblast', C Russian Federation 58.40N 59.48E
129 S13 **Lesnoy** Kirovskaya Oblast', NW Russian Federation 59.49N 52.07E
126 I13 **Lesosibirsk** Krasnoyarskiy Kray, C Russian Federation 58.13N 92.22E
85 J23 **Lesotho** off. Kingdom of Lesotho; prev. Basutoland. ◆ monarchy S Africa
127 Nn17 **Lesozavodsk** Primorskiy Kray, SE Russian Federation 45.23N 133.15E
104 J12 **Lesparre-Médoc** Gironde, SW France 45.18N 0.57W
110 C8 **Les Ponts-de-Martel** Neuchâtel, W Switzerland 47.00N 6.45E
104 I9 **les Sables-d'Olonne** Vendée, NW France 46.30N 1.46W
105 P1 **Lesquin** ✈ Nord, N France 50.34N 3.07E
111 S7 **Lessach** var. Lessachbach. ≈ E Austria
Lessachbach see Lessach
47 W11 **les Saintes** var. Îles des Saintes. island group S Guadeloupe
76 L5 **Les Salines** ✈ (Annaba) NE Algeria 36.45N 7.57E
101 J22 **Lesse** ≈ SE Belgium
97 M21 **Lessebo** Kronoberg, S Sweden 56.45N 15.19E
204 M10 **Lesser Antarctica** var. West Antarctica. physical region Antarctica
47 P15 **Lesser Antilles** island group E West Indies
143 T10 **Lesser Caucasus** Rus. Malyy Kavkaz. ▲▲ SW Asia
Lesser Khingan Range see Xiao Hinggan Ling
9 P13 **Lesser Slave Lake** ◎ Alberta, W Canada
Lesser Sunda Islands see Nusa Tenggara
101 E19 **Lessines** Hainaut, SW Belgium 50.43N 3.49E
105 R16 **les Stes-Maries-de-la-Mer** Bouches-du-Rhône, SE France 43.27N 4.26E
12 G15 **Lester B.Pearson** var. Toronto. ✈ (Toronto) Ontario, S Canada 43.59N 81.30W
31 U9 **Lester Prairie** Minnesota, N USA 44.52N 94.02W
95 L16 **Lestijärvi** Länsi-Suomi, W Finland 63.29N 24.41E
L'Estuaire see Estuaire
31 U9 **Le Sueur** Minnesota, N USA 44.27N 93.53W
110 B8 **Les Verrières** Neuchâtel, W Switzerland 46.54N 6.29E
117 L17 **Lésvos** anc. Lesbos. island E Greece
112 G12 **Leszno** Ger. Lissa. Wielkopolskie, C Poland 51.51N 16.34E
85 L20 **Letaba** Limpopo, NE South Africa 23.44S 31.29E
181 P17 **le Tampon** SW Réunion
99 O21 **Letchworth** E England, UK 51.58N 0.13W
113 G25 **Letenye** Zala, SW Hungary 46.25N 16.42E
9 Q17 **Lethbridge** Alberta, SW Canada 49.43N 112.48W
57 S11 **Lethem** S Guyana 3.24N 59.45W
85 H18 **Letiahau** ≈ W Botswana
56 J18 **Leticia** Amazonas, S Colombia 4.09S 69.57W
175 T15 **Leti, Kepulauan** island group E Indonesia
85 I18 **Letlhakane** Central, C Botswana 21.28S 25.39E
85 H20 **Letlhakeng** Kweneng, SE Botswana 24.04S 25.03E
116 J8 **Letnitsa** Lovech, N Bulgaria 43.19N 25.02E
105 N1 **le Touquet-Paris-Plage** Pas-de-Calais, N France 50.31N 1.34E
177 G8 **Letpadan** Pegu, SW Myanmar 17.22N 94.10E
177 Ff6 **Letpan** Arakan State, W Myanmar 19.22N 94.11E
104 M2 **le Tréport** Seine-Maritime, N France 50.03N 1.21E
178 Gg13 **Letsôk-aw Kyun** var. Letsutan Island; prev. Domel Island. island Mergui Archipelago, S Myanmar
Letsutan Island see Letsôk-aw Kyun
99 E14 **Letterkenny** Ir. Leitir Ceanainn. NW Ireland 54.57N 7.43W
Lettland see Latvia
118 M6 **Letychiv** Khmel'nyts'ka Oblast', W Ukraine 49.24N 27.39E
Lëtzebuerg see Luxembourg
118 H14 **Leu** Dolj, SW Romania 44.10N 24.01E
Leucas see Lefkáda
105 P17 **Leucate** Aude, S France 42.55N 3.03E
105 P17 **Leucate, Étang de** ◎ S France
110 E10 **Leuk** Valais, SW Switzerland 46.18N 7.46E
110 E10 **Leukerbad** Valais, SW Switzerland 46.22N 7.47E
Leusden see Leusden-Centrum
100 K11 **Leusden-Centrum** var. Leusden. Utrecht, C Netherlands 52.07N 5.25E
Leutensdorf see Litvínov
Leutschau see Levoča
101 H18 **Leuven** Fr. Louvain, Ger. Löwen. Vlaams Brabant, C Belgium 50.52N 4.42E
101 I20 **Leuze** Namur, C Belgium 50.33N 4.55E
Leuze see Leuze-en-Hainaut
101 E19 **Leuze-en-Hainaut** var. Leuze. Hainaut, SW Belgium 50.36N 3.37E
Léva see Levice
Levádhia see Leivádia
Levajok see Leavvajohka
38 L4 **Levan** Utah, W USA 39.33N 111.51W
95 E16 **Levanger** Nord-Trøndelag, C Norway 63.45N 11.18E
124 P14 **Levantine Basin** undersea feature E Mediterranean Sea
108 D10 **Levanto** Liguria, W Italy 44.12N 9.33E
109 H23 **Levanzo, Isola di** island Isole Egadi, S Italy
131 Q17 **Levashi** Respublika Dagestan, SW Russian Federation 42.27N 47.19E
26 M5 **Levelland** Texas, SW USA 33.35N 102.22W
41 P13 **Levelock** Alaska, USA 59.07N 156.51W
103 E16 **Leverkusen** Nordrhein-Westfalen, W Germany 51.01N 7.00E
113 J21 **Levice** Ger. Lewentz, Lewenz, Hung. Léva. Nitriansky Kraj, SW Slovakia 48.13N 18.37E
108 G6 **Levico Terme** Trentino-Alto Adige, N Italy 46.02N 11.19E
117 E20 **Levídi** Pelopónnisos, S Greece 37.39N 22.13E
105 P14 **le Vigan** Gard, S France 43.00N 3.36E
192 L13 **Levin** Manawatu-Wanganui, North Island, NZ 40.37S 175.17E
13 R10 **Lévis** var. Levis. Quebec, SE Canada 46.46N 71.10W
23 P6 **Levisa Fork** ≈ Kentucky/Virginia, S USA
117 L21 **Levítha** island Kykládes, Greece, Aegean Sea
20 L14 **Levittown** Long Island, New York, NE USA 40.42N 73.29W
20 J15 **Levittown** Pennsylvania, NE USA 40.09N 74.50W
Levkás see Lefkáda
Levkímmi see Lefkímmi
113 L19 **Levoča** Ger. Leutschau, Hung. Locse. Prešovský Kraj, E Slovakia 49.01N 20.34E
Lévrier, Baie du see Nouâdhibou, Dakhlet
105 N9 **Levroux** Indre, C France 47.00N 1.37E
116 J8 **Levski** Pleven, N Bulgaria 43.22N 25.10E
Levskigrad see Karlovo
130 L6 **Lev Tolstoy** Lipetskaya Oblast', W Russian Federation 53.12N 39.28E
197 I14 **Levuka** Ovalau, C Fiji 17.42S 178.49E
177 G6 **Lewe** Mandalay, C Myanmar 19.40N 96.04E
Lewentz/Lewenz see Levice
99 O23 **Lewes** SE England, UK 50.52N 0.01E
23 Z4 **Lewes** Delaware, NE USA 38.46N 75.08W
31 Q12 **Lewis and Clark Lake** ⊠ Nebraska/South Dakota, N USA
20 G14 **Lewisburg** Pennsylvania, NE USA 40.57N 76.52W
22 J10 **Lewisburg** Tennessee, S USA 35.27N 86.47W
23 S6 **Lewisburg** West Virginia, NE USA 37.48N 80.27W
98 F6 **Lewis, Butt of** headland NW Scotland, UK 58.31N 6.18W
98 F7 **Lewis, Isle of** island NW Scotland, UK
37 U4 **Lewis, Mount** ▲ Nevada, W USA 40.22N 116.50W
193 H16 **Lewis Pass** pass South Island, NZ 42.23S 172.21E
35 P7 **Lewis Range** ▲▲ Montana, NW USA
25 O3 **Lewis Smith Lake** ⊠ Alabama, S USA
34 M10 **Lewiston** Idaho, NW USA 46.25N 117.01W
21 P7 **Lewiston** Maine, NE USA 44.07N 70.13W
31 X10 **Lewiston** Minnesota, N USA 43.58N 91.52W
20 D9 **Lewiston** New York, NE USA 43.10N 79.02W
38 L1 **Lewiston** Utah, W USA 41.58N 111.52W
32 K13 **Lewistown** Illinois, N USA 40.23N 90.09W
35 T9 **Lewistown** Montana, NW USA 47.04N 109.25W
29 T14 **Lewisville** Arkansas, C USA 33.21N 93.34W
27 T6 **Lewisville** Texas, SW USA 33.00N 96.57W
27 T6 **Lewisville, Lake** ⊠ Texas, SW USA
Le Woleu-Ntem see Woleu-Ntem
25 U3 **Lexington** Georgia, SE USA 33.51N 83.04W
22 M5 **Lexington** Kentucky, S USA 38.03N 84.30W
24 L4 **Lexington** Mississippi, S USA 33.06N 90.03W
29 S4 **Lexington** Missouri, C USA 39.10N 93.52W
31 N16 **Lexington** Nebraska, C USA 40.46N 99.44W
22 S9 **Lexington** North Carolina, SE USA 35.49N 80.15W
29 N11 **Lexington** Oklahoma, C USA 35.00N 97.20W
23 R12 **Lexington** South Carolina, SE USA 33.58N 81.14W
22 G9 **Lexington** Tennessee, S USA 35.39N 88.23W
27 T10 **Lexington** Texas, SW USA 30.25N 97.00W
23 T6 **Lexington** Virginia, NE USA 37.46N 79.26W
23 X5 **Lexington Park** Maryland, NE USA 38.16N 76.27W
Leyden see Leiden
104 J14 **Leyre** ≈ SW France
179 R13 **Leyte** island C Philippines
179 R13 **Leyte Gulf** gulf E Philippines
113 O16 **Leżajsk** Podkarpackie, SE Poland 50.15N 22.24E
Lezha see Lezhë
115 K18 **Lezhë** var. Lezha; prev. Lesh, Leshi. Lezhë, NW Albania 41.46N 19.40E
115 K18 **Lezhë** ◈ district NW Albania
105 O16 **Lézignan-Corbières** Aude, S France 43.12N 2.46E
130 J7 **L'gov** Kurskaya Oblast', W Russian Federation 51.38N 35.17E
165 P15 **Lhari** Xizang Zizhiqu, W China 30.34N 93.40E
165 N16 **Lhasa** var. La-sa, Lassa. Xizang Zizhiqu, W China 29.40N 91.10E
165 O15 **Lhasa He** ≈ W China
164 K16 **Lhazê** Xizang Zizhiqu, W China 29.07N 87.32E
164 K14 **Lhazhong** Xizang Zizhiqu, W China 31.58N 86.43E
173 F3 **Lhoksukon** Sumatera, W Indonesia 5.04N 97.19E
165 Q15 **Lhorong** Xizang Zizhiqu, W China 30.51N 95.41E
107 W6 **L'Hospitalet de Llobregat** var. Hospitalet. Cataluña, NE Spain 41.21N 2.06E
159 R11 **Lhotse** ▲ China/Nepal 28.00N 86.55E
165 N17 **Lhozhag** Xizang Zizhiqu, W China 28.21N 90.47E
165 O16 **Lhünzê** Xizang Zizhiqu, W China 28.25N 92.30E
165 N15 **Lhünzhub** var. Poindo. Xizang Zizhiqu, W China 30.14N 91.20E
178 H8 **Li** Lamphun, NW Thailand 17.46N 98.54E
Liancheng see Qinglong
179 Rr14 **Lianga** Mindanao, S Philippines 8.36N 126.04E
167 P12 **Liangcheng** Fujian, SE China 25.47N 116.42E
166 K9 **Liangping** Chongqing Shi, C China 30.40N 107.46E
Liangzhou see Wuwei
167 O9 **Liangzi Hu** ◎ C China
167 R12 **Lianjiang** Fujian, SE China 26.13N 119.33E
166 L15 **Lianjiang** Guangdong, S China 21.41N 110.12E
167 O13 **Lianping** Guangdong, S China 24.22N 114.23E
169 T13 **Lianshan** prev. Jinxi. Liaoning, NE China 40.42N 120.52E
Lian Xian see Lianzhou
166 M11 **Lianyuan** prev. Lantian. Hunan, S China 27.51N 111.44E
167 Q6 **Lianyungang** var. Xinpu. Jiangsu, E China 34.37N 119.12E
167 N13 **Lianzhou** var. Linxian; prev. Lian Xian. Guangdong, S China 24.48N 112.20E
Liao see Liaoning
167 P5 **Liaocheng** Shandong, E China 36.31N 115.59E
169 U13 **Liaodong Bandao** var. Liaotung Peninsula. peninsula NE China
169 T13 **Liaodong Wan** Eng. Gulf of Lantung, Gulf of Liaotung. gulf NE China
169 U11 **Liao He** ≈ NE China
169 W12 **Liao Ling** ▲▲ NE China
169 U12 **Liaoning** var. Liao, Liaoning Sheng, Shengking; hist. Fengtien, Shenking. ◈ province NE China
Liaoning Sheng see Liaoning
Liaotung, Gulf of see Liaodong Wan
Liaotung Peninsula see Liaodong Bandao
169 V12 **Liaoyang** var. Liao-yang. Liaoning, NE China 41.16N 123.12E
169 V11 **Liaoyuan** var. Dongliao, Shuang-liao, Jap. Chengchiatun. Jilin, NE China 42.51N 125.09E
169 U12 **Liaozhong** Liaoning, NE China 41.33N 122.54E
Liaqatabad see Piplān
8 M10 **Liard** ≈ W Canada
Liard see Fort Liard
8 L10 **Liard River** British Columbia, W Canada 59.22N 126.04W
155 O15 **Liāri** Baluchistān, SW Pakistan 25.43N 66.28E
Liatroim see Leitrim
201 S6 **Lib** var. Ellep. island Ralik Chain, C Marshall Islands
Liban see Lebanon
144 H6 **Liban, Jebel** Ar. Jabal al Gharbt, Jabal Lubnān, Eng. Mount Lebanon. ▲▲ C Lebanon
Libau see Liepāja
35 N7 **Libby** Montana, NW USA 48.25N 115.33W
81 I16 **Libenge** Equateur, NW Dem. Rep. Congo 3.39N 18.39E
28 I7 **Liberal** Kansas, C USA 37.01N 100.55W
29 R7 **Liberal** Missouri, C USA 37.33N 94.31W
Liberalitas Julia see Évora
113 D15 **Liberec** Ger. Reichenberg. Liberecký Kraj, N Czech Republic 50.44N 15.04E
113 D15 **Liberecký Kraj** ◈ region N Czech Republic
44 K12 **Liberia** Guanacaste, NW Costa Rica 10.36N 85.26W
78 K17 **Liberia** off. Republic of Liberia. ◆ republic W Africa
63 D16 **Libertad** Corrientes, NE Argentina 30.01S 57.51W
63 E20 **Libertad** San José, S Uruguay 34.37S 56.39W
56 I7 **Libertad** Barinas, NW Venezuela 8.21N 69.39W
56 K6 **Libertad** Cojedes, N Venezuela 9.19N 68.43W
64 G12 **Libertador** off. Región del Libertador General Bernardo O'Higgins. ◈ region C Chile
Libertador General San Martín see Ciudad de Libertador General San Martín
22 L6 **Liberty** Kentucky, S USA 37.19N 84.54W
24 J7 **Liberty** Mississippi, S USA 31.09N 90.49W
29 R4 **Liberty** Missouri, C USA 39.15N 94.22W
20 J12 **Liberty** New York, NE USA 41.48N 74.45W
23 T9 **Liberty** North Carolina, SE USA 35.49N 79.34W
Libian Desert see Libyan Desert
101 J23 **Libin** Luxembourg, SE Belgium 50.01N 5.13E
166 K13 **Libo** Guizhou, S China 25.28N 107.52E
Libohova see Libohovë
115 L23 **Libohovë** var. Libohova. Gjirokastër, S Albania 40.03N 20.13E
83 K18 **Liboi** North Eastern, E Kenya 0.23N 40.55E
104 K13 **Libourne** Gironde, SW France 44.55N 0.13W
101 K23 **Libramont** Luxembourg, SE Belgium 49.55N 5.21E
115 M20 **Librazhd** var. Librazhdi. Elbasan, E Albania 41.10N 20.22E
Librazhdi see Librazhd
81 C18 **Libreville** ● (Gabon) Estuaire, NW Gabon 0.25N 9.29E
179 Rr15 **Libuganon** ≈ Mindanao, S Philippines
77 P10 **Libya** off. Socialist People's Libyan Arab Jamahiriya, Ar. Al Jamāhīrīyah al 'Arabīyah al Lībīyah ash Sha'bīyah al Ishtirākīyah; prev. Libyan Arab Republic. ◆ Islamic state N Africa
77 T11 **Libyan Desert** var. Libian Desert, Ar. Aş Şahrā' al Lībīyah. desert N Africa
77 T8 **Libyan Plateau** var. Aḍ Diffah. plateau Egypt/Libya
Lībīyah, Aş Şahrā' al see Libyan Desert
64 G12 **Licantén** Maule, C Chile 35.00S 72.00W
109 J25 **Licata** anc. Phintias. Sicilia, Italy, C Mediterranean Sea 37.07N 13.56E
143 P14 **Lice** Dıyarbakır, SE Turkey 38.28N 40.39E
99 L19 **Lichfield** C England, UK 52.42N 1.48W
85 N14 **Lichinga** Niassa, N Mozambique 13.17S 35.15E
111 V3 **Lichtenau** Niederösterreich, N Austria 48.29N 15.24E
85 I21 **Lichtenburg** North-West, N South Africa 26.06S 26.08E
103 K18 **Lichtenfels** Bayern, SE Germany 50.09N 11.03E
100 O12 **Lichtenvoorde** Gelderland, E Netherlands 51.58N 6.34E
Lichtenwald see Sevnica
101 C17 **Lichtervelde** West-Vlaanderen, W Belgium 51.01N 3.09E
166 L9 **Lichuan** Hubei, C China 30.19N 108.55E
29 V7 **Licking** Missouri, C USA 37.30N 91.51W
22 M4 **Licking River** ≈ Kentucky, S USA
114 C11 **Lički Osik** Lika-Senj, C Croatia 44.36N 15.24E
Ličko-Senjska Županija see Lika-Senj
109 K19 **Licosa, Punta** headland S Italy 40.15N 14.54E
121 H16 **Lida** Rus. Lida. Hrodzyenskaya Voblasts', W Belarus 53.53N 25.19E
95 H17 **Liden** Västernorrland, C Sweden 62.43N 16.49E
31 R7 **Lidgerwood** North Dakota, N USA 46.04N 97.09W
Lidhorikíon see Lidoríki
97 K21 **Lidhult** Kronoberg, S Sweden 56.49N 13.25E
97 P16 **Lidingö** Stockholm, C Sweden 59.22N 18.10E
97 K17 **Lidköping** Västra Götaland, S Sweden 58.30N 13.10E
Lido di Iesolo see Lido di Jesolo
108 I8 **Lido di Jesolo** var. Lido di Iesolo. Veneto, NE Italy 45.30N 12.37E
109 H15 **Lido di Ostia** Lazio, C Italy 41.42N 12.19E
Lidokhorikion see Lidoríki
117 E18 **Lidoríki** prev. Lidhorikíon, Lidokhorikion. Stereá Ellás, C Greece 38.31N 22.12E
112 K9 **Lidzbark** Warmińsko-Mazurskie, NE Poland 53.15N 19.49E
112 L7 **Lidzbark Warmiński** Ger. Heilsberg. Warmińsko-Mazurskie, NE Poland, 54.07N 20.34E
111 U3 **Liebenau** Oberösterreich, N Austria 48.33N 14.48E
189 P7 **Liebig, Mount** ▲ Northern Territory, C Australia 23.19S 131.30E
111 V8 **Lieboch** Steiermark, SE Austria 47.00N 15.21E
110 I8 **Liechtenstein** off. Principality of Liechtenstein. ◆ principality C Europe
101 F18 **Liedekerke** Vlaams Brabant, C Belgium 50.51N 4.05E
101 K19 **Liège** Dut. Luik, Ger. Lüttich. Liège, E Belgium 50.37N 5.34E
101 K20 **Liège** Dut. Luik. ◈ province E Belgium
Liegnitz see Legnica
95 O16 **Lieksa** Itä-Suomi, E Finland 63.20N 30.00E
120 F10 **Lielupe** ≈ Latvia/Lithuania
120 G9 **Lielvārde** Ogre, C Latvia 56.45N 24.48E
178 Kk14 **Liên Hương** var. Tuy Phong. Bình Thuận, S Vietnam 11.13N 108.40E
Liên Nghia see Đưc Trong
111 P9 **Lienz** Tirol, W Austria 46.49N 12.45E
120 B10 **Liepāja** Ger. Libau. Liepāja, W Latvia 56.31N 21.02E
101 H17 **Lier** Fr. Lierre. Antwerpen, N Belgium 51.07N 4.34E
97 H15 **Lierbyen** Buskerud, S Norway 59.46N 10.13E
101 L21 **Lierneux** Liège, E Belgium 50.12N 5.51E
Lierre see Lier
103 D18 **Lieser** ≈ W Germany
111 U7 **Liesing** ≈ E Austria
110 E6 **Liestal** Basel-Land, N Switzerland 47.28N 7.43E
Lietuva see Lithuania
Lievenhof see Līvāni
105 O2 **Liévin** Pas-de-Calais, N France 50.25N 2.48E
12 M9 **Lièvre, Rivière du** ≈ Quebec, SE Canada
111 T6 **Liezen** Steiermark, C Austria 47.34N 14.12E
99 E14 **Lifford** Ir. Leifear. NW Ireland 54.49N 7.28W
197 K5 **Lifou** island Îles Loyauté, E New Caledonia
200 Ss13 **Lifuka** island Ha'apai Group, C Tonga
179 Q11 **Ligao** Luzon, N Philippines 13.16N 123.30E
Liger see Loire
44 H2 **Lighthouse Reef** reef E Belize
191 Q4 **Lightning Ridge** New South Wales, SE Australia 29.29S 148.00E
105 N9 **Lignières** Cher, C France 46.45N 2.10E
105 S5 **Ligny-en-Barrois** Meuse, NE France 48.42N 5.22E
85 P15 **Ligonha** ≈ NE Mozambique
33 P11 **Ligonier** Indiana, N USA 41.25N 85.33W
83 I25 **Ligunga** Ruvuma, S Tanzania 10.51S 37.10E
108 D9 **Ligure, Appennino** Eng. Ligurian Mountains. ▲▲ NW Italy
Ligure, Mar see Ligurian Sea
108 C9 **Liguria** ◈ region NW Italy
Ligurian Mountains see Ligure, Appennino
123 K6 **Ligurian Sea** Fr. Mer Ligurienne, It. Mar Ligure. sea N Mediterranean Sea
Ligurienne, Mer see Ligurian Sea
195 P9 **Lihir Group** island group NE PNG
195 P9 **Lihir Island** island Lihir Group, N PNG
40 B8 **Lihue** Haw. Līhu'e. Kauai, Hawaii, USA, C Pacific Ocean 21.58N 159.22W
120 F5 **Lihula** Ger. Leal. Läänemaa, W Estonia 58.43N 23.52E
128 I2 **Liinakhamari** var. Linacmamari. Murmanskaya Oblast', NW Russian Federation 69.40N 31.27E
Liivi Laht see Riga, Gulf of
166 F11 **Lijiang** var. Dayan, Lijiang Naxizu Zizhixian. Yunnan, SW China 26.52N 100.10E
114 C11 **Lika-Senj** off. Ličko-Senjska Županija. ◈ province W Croatia
81 N25 **Likasi** prev. Jadotville. Katanga, SE Dem. Rep. Congo 11.01S 26.51E
81 L16 **Likati** Orientale, N Dem. Rep. Congo 3.28N 23.45E
8 M15 **Likely** British Columbia, SW Canada 52.40N 121.34W
159 Y11 **Likhapāni** Assam, NE India 27.24N 95.51E
128 J16 **Likhoslavl'** Tverskaya Oblast', W Russian Federation 57.08N 35.27E
201 U5 **Likiep Atoll** atoll Ratak Chain, C Marshall Islands
97 D18 **Liknes** Vest-Agder, S Norway 58.19N 6.58E
81 H18 **Likouala** ≈ N Congo
81 H18 **Likouala aux Herbes** ≈ E Congo
202 B16 **Liku** E Niue 19.01S 169.46E
Likupang, Selat see Bangka, Selat
29 Y8 **Lilbourn** Missouri, C USA 36.35N 89.37W
105 X14 **l'Île-Rousse** Corse, France, C Mediterranean Sea 42.39N 8.59E
111 W5 **Lilienfeld** Niederösterreich, NE Austria 48.01N 15.36E
167 N11 **Liling** Hunan, S China 27.42N 113.49E
97 J18 **Lilla Edet** Västra Götaland, S Sweden 58.07N 12.07E

◆ Country ● Country Capital ◇ Dependent Territory ○ Dependent Territory Capital ◈ Administrative Region ✈ International Airport ▲ Mountain ▲▲ Mountain Range Volcano ≈ River ◎ Lake ⊠ Reservoir

105 P1 Lille var. l'Isle, Dut. Rijssel, Flem. Ryssel; prev. Lisle, anc. Insula. Nord, N France 50.37N 3.04E
97 G24 Lillebælt var. Lille Bælt, Eng. Little Belt. strait S Denmark
104 L3 Lillebonne Seine-Maritime, N France 49.30N 0.34E
96 H12 Lillehammer Oppland, S Norway 61.07N 10.28E
105 O1 Lillers Pas-de-Calais, N France 50.34N 2.26E
97 F18 Lillesand Aust-Agder, S Norway 58.13N 8.22E
97 I15 Lillestrøm Akershus, S Norway 59.58N 11.04E
95 F18 Lillhärdal Jämtland, C Sweden 61.51N 14.04E
23 U10 Lillington North Carolina, SE USA 35.24N 78.49W
107 O9 Lillo Castilla-La Mancha, C Spain 39.43N 3.19W
8 M16 Lillooet British Columbia, SW Canada 50.40N 121.58W
85 M14 Lilongwe ● (Malawi) Central, W Malawi 13.58S 33.48E
85 M14 Lilongwe ✕ Central, W Malawi 13.46S 33.44E
85 M14 Lilongwe ≈ W Malawi
179 Q15 Liloy Mindanao, S Philippines 8.04N 122.42E
Lilybaeum see Marsala
190 J7 Lilydale South Australia 32.57S 140.00E
191 P16 Lilydale Tasmania, SE Australia 41.17S 147.13E
115 J14 Lim ≈ Bosnia and Herzegovina/Serbia and Montenegro (Yugoslavia)
59 D15 Lima ● (Peru) Lima, W Peru 12.06S 78.00W
96 K13 Lima Dalarna, C Sweden 60.55N 13.19E
33 R12 Lima Ohio, NE USA 40.43N 84.06W
59 D14 Lima ◈ department W Peru
Lima see Jorge Chávez International
106 G5 Lima, Rio Sp. Limia ≈ Portugal/Spain see also Limia
113 L17 Limanowa Małopolskie, S Poland 49.43N 20.25E
174 I8 Limas Pulau Sebangka, W Indonesia 0.09N 104.31E
Limassol see Lemesós
99 F14 Limavady Ir. Léim an Mhadaidh. NW Northern Ireland, UK 55.03N 6.57W
65 J14 Limay Mahuida La Pampa, C Argentina 37.09S 66.40W
65 H15 Limay, Río ≈ W Argentina
103 N16 Limbach-Oberfrohna Sachsen, E Germany 50.52N 12.46E
83 F22 Limba Limba ≈ C Tanzania
109 C17 Limbara, Monte ▲ Sardegna, Italy, C Mediterranean Sea 40.50N 9.10E
120 G7 Limbaži Est. Lemsalu. Limbaži, N Latvia 57.33N 24.46E
81 M8 Limbé N Haiti 19.40N 72.25W
175 Qq7 Limboto, Danau ◎ Sulawesi, N Indonesia
101 L19 Limbourg Liège, E Belgium 50.37N 5.55E
101 K17 Limburg ◈ province NE Belgium
101 L16 Limburg ◈ province SE Netherlands
103 F17 Limburg an der Lahn Hessen, W Germany 50.22N 8.04E
96 K13 Limedsforsen Dalarna, C Sweden 60.52N 13.25E
62 L9 Limeira São Paulo, S Brazil 22.34S 47.25W
99 C19 Limerick Ir. Luimneach. SW Ireland 52.40N 8.37W
99 C20 Limerick Ir. Luimneach. cultural region SW Ireland
21 S2 Limestone Maine, NE USA 46.52N 67.49W
27 U9 Limestone, Lake ◎ Texas, SW USA
41 P12 Lime Village Alaska, USA 61.21N 155.26W
97 F20 Limfjorden fjord N Denmark
97 J23 Limhamn Skåne, S Sweden 55.34N 12.57E
106 H5 Limia Port. Rio Lima ≈ Portugal/Spain see also Lima, Rio
95 L14 Liminka Oulu, C Finland 64.48N 25.19E
Limín Vathéos see Sámos
117 G17 Límni Évvoia, C Greece 38.46N 23.20E
117 J15 Límnos anc. Lemnos. island E Greece
104 M11 Limoges anc. Augustoritum Lemovicensium, Lemovices. Haute-Vienne, C France 45.50N 1.16E
39 U5 Limon Colorado, C USA 39.15N 103.41W
45 O13 Limón var. Puerto Limón. Limón, E Costa Rica 9.59N 83.02W
44 K4 Limón Colón, NE Honduras 15.51N 85.30W
45 N13 Limón off. Provincia de Limón. ◈ province E Costa Rica
108 A10 Limone Piemonte Piemonte, NE Italy 44.12N 7.37E
Limones see Valdéz
Limonum see Poitiers
105 N11 Limousin ◈ region C France
105 N16 Limoux Aude, S France 43.03N 2.13E
85 L19 Limpopo var. Crocodile. ≈ S Africa
85 J20 Limpopo off. Limpopo Province; prev. Northern, Northern Transvaal. ◈ province NE South Africa
166 K17 Limu Ling ▲▲ S China
115 M20 Lin var. Lini. Elbasan, E Albania 41.03N 20.37E
Linacmamari see Liinakhamari
179 P13 Linapacan Island island W Philippines
64 G13 Linares Maule, C Chile 35.49S 71.37W
56 C13 Linares Nariño, SW Colombia 1.23N 77.33W
43 O9 Linares Nuevo León, NE Mexico 24.50N 99.33W
107 N12 Linares Andalucía, S Spain 38.04N 3.37W
109 G15 Linaro, Capo headland C Italy 42.01N 11.49E
108 D8 Linate ✕ (Milano) Lombardia, N Italy 45.27N 9.18E
166 F13 Lincang Yunnan, SW China 23.55N 100.03E
167 P11 Linchuan var. Fuzhou. Jiangxi, S China 27.58N 116.19E
63 B20 Lincoln Buenos Aires, E Argentina 34.50S 61.32W
193 H19 Lincoln Canterbury, South Island, NZ 43.37S 172.30E
99 N18 Lincoln anc. Lindum, Lindum Colonia. E England, UK 53.13N 0.33W
37 O6 Lincoln California, W USA 38.52N 121.18W
32 L13 Lincoln Illinois, N USA 40.09N 89.21W
28 M4 Lincoln Kansas, C USA 39.03N 98.09W
21 S5 Lincoln Maine, NE USA 45.22N 68.30W
29 T5 Lincoln Missouri, C USA 38.23N 93.19W
31 R16 Lincoln state capital Nebraska, C USA 40.46N 96.42W
34 F11 Lincoln City Oregon, NW USA 44.57N 124.01W
178 M10 Lincoln Island island E Paracel Islands
207 Q11 Lincoln Sea sea Arctic Ocean
99 N18 Lincolnshire cultural region E England, UK
23 R10 Lincolnton North Carolina, SE USA 35.28N 81.15W
27 V7 Lindale Texas, SW USA 32.31N 95.24W
103 I25 Lindau var. Lindau am Bodensee. Bayern, S Germany 47.33N 9.40E
Lindau am Bodensee see Lindau
126 L9 Linde ≈ NE Russian Federation
57 T9 Linden E Guyana 5.58N 58.11W
25 O6 Linden Alabama, S USA 32.18N 87.48W
22 H9 Linden Tennessee, S USA 35.37N 87.50W
27 X6 Linden Texas, SW USA 33.01N 94.22W
20 J16 Lindenwold New Jersey, NE USA 39.47N 74.58W
97 M15 Lindesberg Örebro, C Sweden 59.36N 15.15E
97 D18 Lindesnes headland S Norway 57.58N 7.03E
Líndhos see Líndos
83 K24 Lindi Lindi, SE Tanzania 10.00S 39.41E
83 J24 Lindi ◈ region SE Tanzania
83 N17 Lindi ≈ NE Dem. Rep. Congo
169 V7 Lindian Heilongjiang, NE China 47.10N 124.51E
193 E21 Lindis Pass pass South Island, NZ 44.33S 169.40E
85 J22 Lindley Free State, C South Africa 27.48S 27.57E
97 J19 Lindome Västra Götaland, S Sweden 57.34N 12.04E
Lindong see Bairin Zuoqi
117 O23 Líndos var. Líndhos. Ródos, Dodekánisos, Greece, Aegean Sea 36.04N 28.04E
12 I14 Lindsay Ontario, SE Canada 44.21N 78.43W
37 R11 Lindsay California, W USA 36.11N 119.06W
35 X8 Lindsay Montana, NW USA 47.13N 105.10W
29 N11 Lindsay Oklahoma, C USA 34.50N 97.37W
29 N5 Lindsborg Kansas, C USA 38.34N 97.39W
97 N21 Lindsdal Kalmar, S Sweden 56.43N 16.18E
175 Pp9 Lindu, Danau ◎ Sulawesi, N Indonesia
Lindum/Lindum Colonia see Lincoln
203 W3 Line Islands island group E Kiribati
Linëvo see Linova
165 M5 Linfen var. Lin-fen. Shanxi, C China 36.07N 111.34E
161 F18 Linganamakki Reservoir ⊠ SW India
166 L17 Lingao Hainan, S China 19.44N 109.23E
179 Oo9 Lingayen Luzon, N Philippines 16.00N 120.12E
179 Oo9 Lingayen Gulf gulf Luzon, N Philippines
166 M6 Lingbao var. Guolüezhen. Henan, C China 34.34N 110.50E
96 N12 Lingbo Gävleborg, C Sweden 61.04N 16.45E
Lingeh see Bandar-e Langeh
102 E12 Lingen var. Lingen an der Ems. Niedersachsen, NW Germany 52.31N 7.19E
Lingen an der Ems see Lingen
174 Ii8 Lingga, Kepulauan island group W Indonesia
174 I8 Lingga, Pulau island Kepulauan Lingga, W Indonesia
12 J14 Lingham Lake ◎ Ontario, SE Canada
96 M13 Linghed Dalarna, C Sweden 60.48N 15.55E
35 Z15 Lingle Wyoming, C USA 42.07N 104.21W
20 G15 Linglestown Pennsylvania, NE USA 40.20N 76.46W
81 K18 Lingomo II Equateur, NW Dem. Rep. Congo 0.42N 21.59E
166 L15 Lingshan Guangxi Zhuangzu Zizhiqu, S China 22.28N 109.19E
166 L17 Lingshui Hainan, S China 18.35N 110.03E
161 G16 Lingsugūr Karnātaka, C India 16.13N 76.33E
109 L23 Linguaglossa Sicilia, Italy, C Mediterranean Sea 37.51N 15.06E
78 H10 Linguère N Senegal 15.24N 15.06W
165 W8 Lingwu Ningxia, N China 38.04N 106.21E
Lingxi see Yongshun
167 O12 Lingxian var. Ling Xian. Hunan, S China 26.32N 113.48E
169 S12 Lingyuan Liaoning, NE China 41.09N 119.24E
169 U4 Linhai Heilongjiang, NE China 51.30N 124.18E
167 S10 Linhai var. Taizhou. Zhejiang, SE China 28.53N 121.10E
61 O20 Linhares Espírito Santo, SE Brazil 19.22S 40.04W
168 M13 Linhe Nei Mongol Zizhiqu, N China 40.46N 107.27E
Lini see Lin
145 S1 Linik, Chiyā-ē ▲ N Iraq
97 M18 Linköping Östergötland, S Sweden 58.25N 15.37E
169 Y8 Linkou Heilongjiang, NE China 45.18N 130.16E
120 F11 Linkuva Pakruojis, N Lithuania 56.06N 23.58E
29 V5 Linn Missouri, C USA 38.29N 91.51W
27 S16 Linn Texas, SW USA 26.32N 98.06W
29 T2 Linneus Missouri, C USA 39.53N 93.10W
98 H10 Linnhe, Loch inlet W Scotland, UK
121 G19 Linova Rus. Linëvo. Brestskaya Voblasts', SW Belarus 52.28N 24.33E
167 O5 Linqing Shandong, E China 36.49N 115.39E
167 N6 Linruzhen Henan, C China 34.10N 112.51E
62 K8 Lins São Paulo, S Brazil 21.40S 49.43W
95 F17 Linsell Jämtland, C Sweden 62.10N 14.00E
166 J9 Linshui Sichuan, C China 30.24N 106.54E
46 K12 Linstead C Jamaica 18.07N 77.01W
165 U11 Lintan Gansu, N China 34.43N 101.27E
165 V11 Lintao Gansu, C China 35.23N 103.54E
13 S12 Lintère ≈ Quebec, SE Canada
110 H8 Linth ≈ NW Switzerland
110 H8 Linthal Glarus, NE Switzerland 46.59N 8.57E
33 N15 Linton Indiana, N USA 39.01N 87.10W
31 N6 Linton North Dakota, N USA 46.16N 100.13W
169 R11 Linxi Nei Mongol Zizhiqu, N China 43.29N 117.59E
165 U11 Linxia var. Linxia Huizu Zizhizhou. Gansu, C China 35.33N 103.08E
Linxia Huizu Zizhizhou see Linxia
Linxian see Lianzhou
167 Q6 Linyi Shandong, E China 37.12N 116.54E
167 P4 Linyi Shandong, E China 37.13N 116.50E
166 M6 Linyi Shanxi, C China 35.10N 110.45E
111 T4 Linz anc. Lentia. Oberösterreich, N Austria 48.19N 14.18E
165 S8 Linze var. Shahepu. Gansu, N China 39.06N 100.03E
46 J13 Lionel Town C Jamaica 17.49N 77.13W
105 Q16 Lion, Golfe du Eng. Gulf of Lion, Gulf of Lions; anc. Sinus Gallicus. gulf S France
Lion, Gulf of/Lions, Gulf of see Lion, Golfe du
85 K16 Lions Den Mashonaland West, N Zimbabwe 17.16S 30.00E
12 F13 Lion's Head Ontario, S Canada 44.59N 81.16W
Lios Ceannúir, Bá see Liscannor Bay
Lios Mór see Lismore
Lios na gCearrbhach see Lisburn
Lios Tuathail see Listowel
81 G17 Liouesso La Sangha, N Congo 1.01N 15.43E
Liozno see Lyozna
179 P11 Lipa off. Lipa City. Luzon, N Philippines 13.57N 121.10E
27 S7 Lipan Texas, SW USA 32.31N 98.03W
Lipari Islands/Lipari, Isole see Eolie, Isole
109 L22 Lipari, Isola island Isole Eolie, S Italy
118 L8 Lipcani Rus. Lipkany. N Moldova 48.16N 26.47E
95 N17 Liperi Itä-Suomi, E Finland 62.30N 29.25E
130 L7 Lipetsk Lipetskaya Oblast', W Russian Federation 52.37N 39.37E
130 K6 Lipetskaya Oblast' ◈ province W Russian Federation
59 K22 Lipez, Cordillera de ▲▲ SW Bolivia
112 E10 Lipiany Ger. Lippehne. Zachodniopomorskie, W Poland 53.00N 14.58E
114 G9 Lipik Požega-Slavonija, NE Croatia 45.24N 17.08E
128 L12 Lipin Bor Vologodskaya Oblast', NW Russian Federation 60.12N 38.04E
166 L12 Liping Guizhou, S China 26.16N 109.07E
Lipkany see Lipcani
121 H15 Lipnishki Rus. Lipnishki. Hrodzyenskaya Voblasts', W Belarus 54.01N 25.39E
112 J10 Lipno Kujawsko-pomorskie, C Poland 52.51N 19.11E
118 F11 Lipova Hung. Lippa. Arad, W Romania 46.06N 21.40E
Lipovets see Lypovets'
Lippa see Lipova
103 E14 Lippe ≈ W Germany
Lippehne see Lipiany
103 G14 Lippstadt Nordrhein-Westfalen, W Germany 51.40N 8.21E
27 P1 Lipscomb Texas, SW USA 36.12N 100.13W
Lipsia/Lipsk see Leipzig
Liptau-Sankt-Nikolaus/Liptószentmiklós see Liptovský Mikuláš
113 K19 Liptovský Mikuláš Ger. Liptau-Sankt-Nikolaus, Hung. Liptószentmiklós. Žilinský Kraj, N Slovakia 49.06N 19.36E
191 O13 Liptrap, Cape headland Victoria, SE Australia 38.55S 145.58E
166 L13 Lipu Guangxi Zhuangzu Zizhiqu, S China 24.29N 110.24E
147 X12 Liqbi S Oman 18.27N 56.37E
83 G17 Lira N Uganda 2.15N 32.55E
59 F15 Lircay Huancavelica, C Peru 12.58S 74.43W
109 J15 Liri ≈ C Italy
150 M8 Lisakovsk Kostanay, NW Kazakhstan 52.37N 62.34E
81 K17 Lisala Equateur, N Dem. Rep. Congo 2.10N 21.28E
106 F11 Lisboa Eng. Lisbon; anc. Felicitas Julia, Olisipo. ● (Portugal) Lisboa, W Portugal 38.43N 9.07W
106 F10 Lisboa ◈ Eng. Lisbon. district C Portugal
21 N7 Lisbon New Hampshire, NE USA 44.11N 71.52W
31 Q6 Lisbon North Dakota, N USA 46.27N 97.42W
Lisbon see Lisboa
21 Q8 Lisbon Falls Maine, NE USA 44.00N 70.03W
99 G15 Lisburn Ir. Lios na gCearrbhach. E Northern Ireland, UK 54.31N 6.03W
40 L6 Lisburne, Cape headland Alaska, USA 68.52N 166.13W
99 B19 Liscannor Bay Ir. Bá Lios Ceannúir. inlet W Ireland
115 Q18 Lisec ▲ E FYR Macedonia 41.46N 22.30E
166 F13 Lishe Jiang ≈ SW China
166 M4 Lishi Shanxi, C China 37.27N 111.05E
169 V10 Lishu Jilin, NE China 43.25N 124.19E
167 R10 Lishui Zhejiang, SE China 28.27N 119.25E
199 Jj5 Lisianski Island island Hawaiian Islands, Hawaii, USA, C Pacific Ocean
Lisichansk see Lysychans'k
104 L4 Lisieux anc. Noviomagus. Calvados, N France 49.09N 0.13E
130 L8 Liski prev. Georgiu-Dezh. Voronezhskaya Oblast', W Russian Federation 51.00N 39.36E
L'Isle/l'Isle see Lille
105 N4 l'Isle-Adam Val-d'Oise, N France 49.07N 2.13E
105 R15 l'Isle-sur-la-Sorgue Vaucluse, SE France 43.55N 5.03E
13 S9 L'Islet Quebec, SE Canada 47.07N 70.18W
190 M12 Lismore Victoria, SE Australia 37.59S 143.18E
99 D20 Lismore Ir. Lios Mór. S Ireland 52.10N 7.10W
Lissa see Vis, Croatia
Lissa see Leszno, Poland
100 H11 Lisse Zuid-Holland, W Netherlands 52.15N 4.33E
97 D18 Lista peninsula S Norway
97 D18 Listafjorden fjord S Norway
205 R13 Lister, Mount ▲ Antarctica 78.12S 161.46E
130 M8 Listopadovka Voronezhskaya Oblast', W Russian Federation 51.54N 41.08E
12 F15 Listowel Ontario, S Canada 43.44N 80.57W
99 B20 Listowel Ir. Lios Tuathail. SW Ireland 52.27N 9.28W
166 L14 Litang Guangxi Zhuangzu Zizhiqu, S China 23.09N 109.07E
166 F9 Litang Sichuan, C China 30.03N 100.12E
166 F10 Litang Qu ≈ C China
57 X12 Litani var. Itany. ≈ French Guiana/Suriname
144 G8 Līṭānī, Nahr el var. Nahr al Litant. ≈ C Lebanon
Litant, Nahr al see Līṭānī, Nahr el
Litauen see Lithuania
32 K14 Litchfield Illinois, N USA 39.17N 89.52W
31 U8 Litchfield Minnesota, N USA 45.09N 94.31W
38 K13 Litchfield Park Arizona, SW USA 33.29N 112.21W
191 S8 Lithgow New South Wales, SE Australia 33.30S 150.09E
117 I26 Líthino, Akrotírio headland Kríti, Greece, E Mediterranean Sea 34.55N 24.43E
120 D12 Lithuania off. Republic of Lithuania, Ger. Litauen, Lith. Lietuva, Pol. Litwa, Rus. Litva; prev. Lithuanian SSR, Rus. Litovskaya SSR. ◆ republic NE Europe
Lithuanian SSR see Lithuania
111 U11 Litija Ger. Littai. C Slovenia 46.03N 14.50E
20 H15 Lititz Pennsylvania, NE USA 40.09N 76.18W
117 F15 Litóchoro var. Litohoro, Litókhoron. Kentrikí Makedonía, N Greece 40.06N 22.30E
Litohoro/Litókhoron see Litóchoro
113 C15 Litoměřice Ger. Leitmeritz. Ústecký Kraj, NW Czech Republic 50.32N 14.09E
113 F17 Litomyšl Ger. Leitomischl. Pardubický Kraj, C Czech Republic 49.52N 16.16E
113 G17 Litovel Ger. Littau. Olomoucký Kraj, E Czech Republic 49.42N 17.04E
127 Nn15 Litovko Khabarovskiy Kray, SE Russian Federation 49.22N 135.10E
Litovskaya SSR see Lithuania
Littai see Litija
Littau see Litovel
46 G1 Little Abaco var. Abaco Island. island N Bahamas
113 I21 Little Alföld Ger. Kleines Ungarisches Tiefland, Hung. Kisalföld, Slvk. Podunajská Rovina. plain Hungary/Slovakia
157 Q20 Little Andaman island Andaman Islands, India, NE Indian Ocean
28 M5 Little Arkansas River ≈ Kansas, C USA
192 L4 Little Barrier Island island N NZ
Little Belt see Lillebælt
40 M11 Little Black River ≈ Alaska, USA
29 O2 Little Blue River ≈ Kansas/Nebraska, C USA
46 D8 Little Cayman island E Cayman Islands
9 X11 Little Churchill ≈ Manitoba, C Canada
177 Ee10 Little Coco Island island SW Myanmar
38 L10 Little Colorado River ≈ Arizona, SW USA
12 E11 Little Current Manitoulin Island, Ontario, S Canada 45.57N 81.55W
10 E11 Little Current ≈ Ontario, S Canada
40 L8 Little Diomede Island island Alaska, USA
46 I4 Little Exuma island C Bahamas
31 U7 Little Falls Minnesota, N USA 45.59N 94.21W
20 J10 Little Falls New York, NE USA 43.02N 74.51W
26 M5 Littlefield Texas, SW USA 33.55N 102.19W
31 V3 Littlefork Minnesota, N USA 48.24N 93.33W
31 V3 Little Fork River ≈ Minnesota, N USA
9 N16 Little Fort British Columbia, SW Canada 51.27N 120.15W
9 Y14 Little Grand Rapids Manitoba, C Canada 52.06N 95.29W
99 N23 Littlehampton SE England, UK 50.48N 0.33W
37 T2 Little Humboldt River ≈ Nevada, W USA
46 K6 Little Inagua var. Inagua Islands. island S Bahamas
23 Q4 Little Kanawha River ≈ West Virginia, NE USA
85 F25 Little Karoo plateau S South Africa
41 O16 Little Koniuji Island island Shumagin Islands, Alaska, USA
46 H12 Little London W Jamaica 18.14N 78.13W
11 R10 Little Mecatina Fr. Rivière du Petit Mécatina. ≈ Newfoundland and Labrador/Quebec, E Canada
98 F8 Little Minch, The strait NW Scotland, UK
29 T13 Little Missouri River ≈ Arkansas, USA
30 J7 Little Missouri River ≈ NW USA
30 J3 Little Muddy River ≈ North Dakota, N USA
157 Q22 Little Nicobar island Nicobar Islands, India, NE Indian Ocean
29 R6 Little Osage River ≈ Missouri, C USA
99 P20 Little Ouse ≈ E England, UK
155 V2 Little Pamir Pash. Pāmīr-e Khord, Rus. Malyy Pamir. ▲▲ Afghanistan/Tajikistan
23 U12 Little Pee Dee River ≈ North Carolina/South Carolina, SE USA
29 V10 Little Red River ≈ Arkansas, C USA
Little Rhody see Rhode Island
193 I19 Little River Canterbury, South Island, NZ 43.45S 172.49E
23 U12 Little River South Carolina, SE USA 33.52N 78.36W
29 Y9 Little River ≈ Arkansas/Missouri, C USA
29 R13 Little River ≈ Arkansas/Oklahoma, USA
25 T7 Little River ≈ Georgia, SE USA
24 H6 Little River ≈ Louisiana, S USA
27 T10 Little River ≈ Texas, SW USA
29 V12 Little Rock state capital Arkansas, C USA 34.45N 92.17W
33 N8 Little Sable Point headland Michigan, N USA 43.38N 86.32W
105 U11 Little Saint Bernard Pass Fr. Col du Petit St-Bernard, It. Colle di Piccolo San Bernardo. pass France/Italy 45.41N 6.54E
36 K7 Little Salt Lake ◎ Utah, W USA
188 K8 Little Sandy Desert desert Western Australia
31 S13 Little Sioux River ≈ Iowa, C USA
40 E17 Little Sitkin Island island Aleutian Islands, Alaska, USA
9 O13 Little Smoky Alberta, W Canada 54.35N 117.06W
9 O14 Little Smoky ≈ Alberta, W Canada
39 P3 Little Snake River ≈ Colorado, C USA
66 A12 Little Sound bay Bermuda, NW Atlantic Ocean
39 T4 Littleton Colorado, C USA 39.36N 105.01W
21 N7 Littleton New Hampshire, NE USA 44.18N 71.46W
20 D11 Little Valley New York, NE USA 42.15N 78.46W
32 M15 Little Wabash River ≈ Illinois, N USA
12 D10 Little White River ≈ Ontario, S Canada
30 M12 Little White River ≈ South Dakota, N USA
27 R5 Little Wichita River ≈ Texas, SW USA
148 I4 Little Zab Ar. Nahraz Zāb aş Şaghīr, Kurd. Zē-i Kōya, Per. Rūdkhāneh-ye Zāb-e Kūchek. ≈ Iran/Iraq
81 D15 Littoral ◈ province W Cameroon
Littoria see Latina
Litva/Litwa see Lithuania
113 B15 Litvínov Ger. Leutensdorf. Ústecký Kraj, NW Czech Republic 50.37N 13.37E
118 M6 Lityn Vinnyts'ka Oblast', C Ukraine 49.19N 28.06E
Liu-chou/Liuchow see Liuzhou
169 W11 Liuhe Jilin, NE China 42.15N 125.49E
Liukang Tenggaya, Kepulauan see Sabalana, Kepulauan
85 Q15 Liúpo Nampula, NE Mozambique 15.36S 39.57E
85 G14 Liuwa Plain plain W Zambia
166 L13 Liuzhou var. Liu-chou, Liuchow. Guangxi Zhuangzu Zizhiqu, S China 24.09N 108.55E
118 H8 Livada Hung. Sárköz. Satu Mare, NW Romania 47.52N 23.03E
117 J20 Liváda, Akrotírio headland Tínos, Kykládes, Greece, Aegean Sea 37.36N 25.15E
117 L21 Livádi island Kykládes, Greece, Aegean Sea
Livanátai see Livanátes
117 G18 Livanátes prev. Livanátai. Stereá Ellás, C Greece 38.43N 23.01E
120 I10 Līvāni Ger. Lievenhof. Preiļi, SE Latvia 56.22N 26.12E
67 E25 Lively Island island SE Falkland Islands
67 D25 Lively Sound sound SE Falkland Islands
41 R8 Livengood Alaska, USA 65.31N 148.32W
108 I7 Livenza ≈ NE Italy
37 O6 Live Oak California, W USA 39.17N 121.41W
25 U9 Live Oak Florida, SE USA 30.18N 82.59W
37 O9 Livermore California, W USA 37.40N 121.46W
22 I6 Livermore Kentucky, S USA 37.31N 87.08W
21 Q7 Livermore Falls Maine, NE USA 44.30N 70.09W
26 J10 Livermore, Mount ▲ Texas, SW USA 30.37N 104.10W
11 P16 Liverpool Nova Scotia, SE Canada 44.03N 64.43W
99 K17 Liverpool NW England, UK 53.25N 2.55W
191 S7 Liverpool Range ▲▲ New South Wales, SE Australia
98 J12 Livingston C Scotland, UK 55.51N 3.31W
25 N5 Livingston Alabama, S USA 32.34N 88.12W
37 P9 Livingston California, W USA 37.22N 120.45W
24 J8 Livingston Louisiana, S USA 30.30N 90.45W
35 S11 Livingston Montana, NW USA 45.40N 110.33W
22 L8 Livingston Tennessee, S USA 36.22N 85.19W
27 W9 Livingston Texas, SW USA 30.42N 94.55W
44 F4 Lívingston Izabal, E Guatemala 15.49N 88.46W
85 I16 Livingstone var. Maramba. Southern, S Zambia 17.51S 25.48E
193 B22 Livingstone Mountains ▲▲ South Island, NZ
82 K13 Livingstone Mountains ▲▲ S Tanzania
84 N12 Livingstonia Northern, N Malawi 10.29S 34.06E
204 G4 Livingston Island island Antarctica
27 W9 Livingston, Lake ⊠ Texas, SW USA
114 F13 Livno Federacija Bosna I Hercegovina, SW Bosnia and Herzegovina 43.49N 17.00E
130 K7 Livny Orlovskaya Oblast', W Russian Federation 52.25N 37.42E
95 M14 Livojoki ≈ C Finland
33 R10 Livonia Michigan, N USA 42.22N 83.22W
108 E11 Livorno Eng. Leghorn. Toscana, C Italy 43.31N 10.18E
Livramento see Santana do Livramento
147 U8 Liwā var. Al Liwā'. oasis region S UAE
83 I24 Liwale Lindi, SE Tanzania 9.46S 37.55E
165 W9 Liwangbu Ningxia, N China 36.42N 106.04E
85 N15 Liwonde Southern, S Malawi 15.04S 35.12E
165 V11 Lixian var. Li Xian. Gansu, C China 34.15N 105.07E
166 H8 Lixian var. Li Xian; prev. Zagunao. Sichuan, C China 31.27N 103.06E
Lixian Jiang see Black River
117 B18 Lixoúri prev. Lixoúrion. Kefallinía, Iónioi Nísoi, Greece, C Mediterranean Sea 38.12N 20.25E
Lixoúrion see Lixoúri
Lixus see Larache
Lizarra see Estella-Lizarra
35 U15 Lizard Head Peak ▲ Wyoming, C USA 42.47N 109.12W
99 H25 Lizard Point headland SW England, UK 49.57N 5.12W
114 L12 Ljig Serbia, C Serbia and Montenegro (Yugoslavia) 44.14N 20.16E
Ljouwert see Leeuwarden
Ljubelj see Loibl Pass
111 U11 Ljubljana Ger. Laibach, It. Lubiana; anc. Aemona, Emona. ● (Slovenia) C Slovenia 46.03N 14.28E
111 T11 Ljubljana ✕ C Slovenia 46.14N 14.26E
115 N17 Ljuboten ▲ S Serbia and Montenegro (Yugoslavia) 42.12N 21.06E
97 P19 Ljugarn Gotland, SE Sweden 57.23N 18.45E
86 G7 Ljungan ≈ N Sweden
95 F17 Ljungan ≈ C Sweden
97 K21 Ljungby Kronoberg, S Sweden 56.49N 13.55E
97 M17 Ljungsbro Östergötland, S Sweden 58.31N 15.30E
97 I18 Ljungskile Västra Götaland, S Sweden 58.13N 11.55E
96 M11 Ljusdal Gävleborg, C Sweden 61.49N 16.10E
96 M11 Ljusnan ≈ C Sweden
96 N12 Ljusne Gävleborg, C Sweden 61.11N 17.07E
97 P15 Ljusterö Stockholm, C Sweden 59.31N 18.40E
111 X9 Ljutomer Ger. Luttenberg. NE Slovenia 46.31N 16.12E
65 G15 Llaima, Volcán ▲ S Chile 39.01S 71.38W
107 X4 Llançà var. Llansá. Cataluña, NE Spain 42.23N 3.08E
99 J21 Llandovery C Wales, UK 52.01N 3.47W
99 J20 Llandrindod Wells E Wales, UK 52.15N 3.22W
99 J18 Llandudno N Wales, UK 53.19N 3.49W
99 I21 Llanelli prev. Llanelly. SW Wales, UK 51.41N 4.11W
Llanelly see Llanelli
106 M2 Llanes Asturias, N Spain 43.25N 4.46W
99 K19 Llangollen NE Wales, UK 52.58N 3.10W
27 R10 Llano Texas, SW USA 30.45N 98.41W
27 Q10 Llano River ≈ Texas, SW USA
56 I9 Llanos physical region Colombia/Venezuela
65 G16 Llanquihue, Lago ◎ S Chile
Llansá see Llançà
107 U5 Lleida Cast. Lérida; anc. Ilerda. Cataluña, NE Spain 41.37N 0.36E
107 U5 Lleida Cast. Lérida ◈ province Cataluña, NE Spain
106 K12 Llerena Extremadura, W Spain 38.13N 6.00W
107 S9 Llíria País Valenciano, E Spain 39.37N 0.36W
107 W4 Llivia Cataluña, NE Spain 42.27N 2.00E
107 O3 Llodio País Vasco, N Spain 43.07N 2.58W
107 X5 Lloret de Mar Cataluña, NE Spain 41.42N 2.51E
Llorri see Tossal de l'Orri
8 L11 Lloyd George, Mount ▲ British Columbia, W Canada 57.46N 124.57W
9 R14 Lloydminster Alberta/Saskatchewan, SW Canada 53.18N 110.00W
38 L6 Loa Utah, W USA 38.24N 111.38W
174 Mm4 Loagan Bunut ◎ East Malaysia
178 Mm14 Loaita Island island W Spratly Islands
40 G12 Loa, Mauna ▲ Hawaii, USA, C Pacific Ocean 19.28N 155.39W
Loanda see Luanda
81 J22 Loange ≈ S Dem. Rep. Congo
81 E21 Loango Le Kouilou, S Congo 4.37S 11.49E
108 B10 Loano Liguria, NW Italy 44.07N 8.15E
64 H4 Loa, Río ≈ N Chile
85 I20 Lobatse var. Lobatsi. Kgatleng, SE Botswana 25.10S 25.40E
Lobatsi see Lobatse
103 Q15 Löbau Sachsen, E Germany 51.06N 14.39E
81 H16 Lobaye ◈ prefecture SW Central African Republic
81 I16 Lobaye ≈ SW Central African Republic
101 G21 Lobbes Hainaut, S Belgium 50.21N 4.16E
63 D23 Lobería Buenos Aires, E Argentina 38.07S 58.48W
112 F8 Łobez Ger. Labes. Zachodniopomorskie, NW Poland 53.39N 15.39E
84 A13 Lobito Benguela, W Angola 12.19S 13.34E
Lobkovichi see Labkovichy
Lob Nor see Lop Nur
176 W11 Lobo Papua, E Indonesia 3.41S 134.06E
106 J11 Lobón Extremadura, W Spain 38.51N 6.37W
63 D20 Lobos Buenos Aires, E Argentina 35.10S 59.07W
42 E4 Lobos, Cabo headland NW Mexico 29.53N 112.43W
42 F6 Lobos, Isla island NW Mexico
Lobositz see Lovosice
Lobsens see Łobżenica
Loburi see Lop Buri
112 H9 Łobżenica Ger. Lobsens. Wielkopolskie, C Poland 53.19N 17.11E
110 G11 Locarno Ger. Luggarus. Ticino, S Switzerland 46.10N 8.47E
98 E9 Lochboisdale NW Scotland, UK 57.08N 7.17W
100 N11 Lochem Gelderland, E Netherlands 52.10N 6.25E
104 M8 Loches Indre-et-Loire, C France 47.08N 1.00E
Loch Garman see Wexford
98 H12 Lochgilphead W Scotland, UK 56.02N 5.27W
98 H7 Lochinver N Scotland, UK 58.10N 5.14W
98 F8 Lochmaddy NW Scotland, UK 57.35N 7.10W
98 J10 Lochnagar ▲ C Scotland, UK 56.58N 3.09W
101 E17 Lochristi Oost-Vlaanderen, NW Belgium 51.07N 3.49E
98 H9 Lochy, Loch ◎ N Scotland, UK
190 G8 Lock South Australia 33.37S 135.45E
99 J14 Lockerbie S Scotland, UK 55.10N 3.27W
29 S13 Lockesburg Arkansas, C USA 33.58N 94.10W
191 P10 Lockhart New South Wales, SE Australia 35.15S 146.43E
27 S11 Lockhart Texas, SW USA 29.52N 97.40W
20 F13 Lock Haven Pennsylvania, NE USA 41.08N 77.27W
27 N4 Lockney Texas, SW USA 34.06N 101.27W
102 O12 Löcknitz ≈ NE Germany
20 E9 Lockport New York, NE USA 43.09N 78.40W
178 Jj13 Lôc Ninh Sông Be, S Vietnam 11.51N 106.34E
109 N23 Locri Calabria, SW Italy 38.16N 16.16E
Locse see Levoča
29 T2 Locust Creek ≈ Missouri, C USA
25 P3 Locust Fork ≈ Alabama, S USA
29 Q9 Locust Grove Oklahoma, C USA 36.12N 95.10W
96 E11 Lodalskåpa ▲ S Norway 61.47N 7.10E
191 N10 Loddon River ≈ Victoria, SE Australia
Lodensee see Klooga
105 P15 Lodève anc. Luteva. Hérault, S France 43.43N 3.19E
128 I12 Lodeynoye Pole Leningradskaya Oblast', NW Russian Federation 60.41N 33.29E
35 V11 Lodge Grass Montana, NW USA 45.19N 107.20W
30 J15 Lodgepole Creek ≈ Nebraska/Wyoming, C USA
155 T11 Lodhrān Punjab, E Pakistan 29.36N 71.34E
108 D8 Lodi Lombardia, NW Italy 45.19N 9.36E
37 O8 Lodi California, W USA 38.07N 121.17W
33 T12 Lodi Ohio, N USA 41.00N 82.01W
94 H10 Lødingen Nordland, C Norway 68.24N 15.55E
81 L20 Lodja Kasai Oriental, C Dem. Rep. Congo 3.28S 23.24E
39 O3 Lodore, Canyon of canyon Colorado, C USA
107 Q4 Lodosa Navarra, N Spain 42.25N 2.04W
83 H16 Lodwar Rift Valley, NW Kenya 3.06N 35.37E
112 K13 Łódź Rus. Lodz. Łódź, C Poland 51.51N 19.26E
112 J13 Łódzkie ◈ province C Poland 51.51N 19.26E

◆ Country
● Country Capital
◇ Dependent Territory
○ Dependent Territory Capital
◈ Administrative Region
✕ International Airport
▲ Mountain
▲▲ Mountain Range
Volcano
≈ River
◎ Lake
⊠ Reservoir

178 I8 **Loei** *var.* Loey, Muang Loei. Loei, C Thailand *17.28N 101.42E*
100 I11 **Loenen** Utrecht, C Netherlands *52.13N 5.01E*
178 J9 **Loeng Nok Tha** Yasothon, E Thailand *16.12N 104.31E*
85 F24 **Loeriesfontein** Northern Cape, W South Africa *30.53S 19.28E*
97 H20 **Læsø** *island* N Denmark
Loewoek *see* Luwuk
Loey *see* Loei
78 J16 **Lofa** ∽ N Liberia
111 P6 **Lofer** Salzburg, C Austria *47.37N 12.42E*
94 F11 **Lofoten** *var.* Lofoten Islands. *island group* C Norway
Lofoten Islands *see* Lofoten
97 N18 **Loftahammar** Kalmar, S Sweden *57.55N 16.45E*
131 O10 **Log** Volgogradskaya Oblast', SW Russian Federation *49.32N 43.52E*
79 S12 **Loga** Dosso, SW Niger *13.33N 3.18E*
31 S14 **Logan** Iowa, C USA *41.38N 95.47W*
28 K3 **Logan** Kansas, C USA *39.39N 99.34W*
33 T14 **Logan** Ohio, N USA *39.32N 82.24W*
38 L1 **Logan** Utah, W USA *41.45N 111.50W*
23 P6 **Logan** West Virginia, NE USA *37.51N 81.59W*
37 Y10 **Logandale** Nevada, W USA *36.36N 114.28W*
21 O11 **Logan International** ✕ (Boston) Massachusetts, NE USA *42.22N 71.00W*
9 N16 **Logan Lake** British Columbia, SW Canada *50.28N 120.42W*
25 Q4 **Logan Martin Lake** ⊠ Alabama, S USA
8 G8 **Logan, Mount** ▲ Yukon Territory, W Canada *60.32N 140.34W*
34 I7 **Logan, Mount** ▲ Washington, NW USA *48.32N 120.57W*
35 P7 **Logan Pass** *pass* Montana, NW USA *48.43N 113.44W*
33 O12 **Logansport** Indiana, N USA *40.44N 86.25W*
24 F6 **Logansport** Louisiana, S USA *31.58N 94.00W*
Logar *see* Lowgar
69 R11 **Loge** ∽ NW Angola
Logishin *see* Lahishyn
Log na Coille *see* Lugnaquillia Mountain
80 G11 **Logone** *var.* Lagone. ∽ Cameroon/Chad
80 G13 **Logone-Occidental** *off.* Préfecture du Logone-Occidental. ◈ *prefecture* SW Chad
80 H13 **Logone Occidental** ∽ SW Chad
80 G13 **Logone-Oriental** *off.* Préfecture du Logone-Oriental. ◈ *prefecture* SW Chad
80 H13 **Logone Oriental** ∽ SW Chad
Logone Oriental *see* Pendé
L'Ogooué-Ivindo *see* Ogooué-Ivindo
L'Ogooué-Lolo *see* Ogooué-Lolo
L'Ogooué-Maritime *see* Ogooué-Maritime
Logoysk *see* Lahoysk
107 P4 **Logroño** *anc.* Vareia, *Lat.* Juliobriga. La Rioja, N Spain *42.28N 2.25W*
106 L10 **Logrosán** Extremadura, W Spain *39.21N 5.28W*
97 G20 **Løgstør** Nordjylland, N Denmark *56.57N 9.19E*
97 H22 **Løgten** Århus, C Denmark *56.16N 10.19E*
97 F24 **Løgumkloster** Sønderjylland, SW Denmark *55.04N 8.58E*
Lögurinn *see* Lagarfljót
197 B10 **Loh** *island* Torres Islands, N Vanuatu
159 P15 **Lohārdaga** Bihār, N India *23.27N 84.42E*
158 H10 **Lohāru** Haryāna, N India *28.27N 75.53E*
103 D15 **Lohausen** ✕ (Düsseldorf) Nordrhein-Westfalen, W Germany *51.18N 6.51E*
201 O14 **Lohd** Pohnpei, E Micronesia
194 I14 **Lohiki** ∽ S PNG
94 L12 **Lohiniva** Lappi, N Finland *67.09N 25.04E*
Lohiszyn *see* Lahishyn
95 L20 **Lohja** *var.* Lojo. Etelä-Suomi, S Finland *60.14N 24.07E*
175 O8 **Lohjanan** Borneo, C Indonesia
27 Q9 **Lohn** Texas, SW USA *31.15N 99.22W*
102 G12 **Lohne** Niedersachsen, NW Germany *52.40N 8.13E*
Lohr *see* Lohr am Main
103 I18 **Lohr am Main** *var.* Lohr. Bayern, C Germany *50.00N 9.30E*
111 T10 **Loibl Pass** *Ger.* Loiblpass, *Slvn.* Ljubelj. *pass* Austria/Slovenia *46.25N 14.15E*
178 Gg6 **Loi-Kaw** Kayah State, C Myanmar *19.40N 97.12E*
95 K19 **Loimaa** Länsi-Suomi, W Finland *60.51N 23.03E*
105 O6 **Loing** ∽ C France
178 Ii6 **Loi, Phou** ▲ N Laos *20.18N 103.14E*
104 L7 **Loir** ∽ C France
105 Q11 **Loire** ◈ *department* E France
104 M7 **Loire** *var.* Liger. ∽ C France
104 I7 **Loire-Atlantique** ◈ *department* NW France
105 O7 **Loiret** ◈ *department* C France
104 M8 **Loir-et-Cher** ◈ *department* C France
103 L24 **Loisach** ∽ SE Germany
58 B9 **Loja** Loja, S Ecuador *3.58S 79.16W*
107 N14 **Loja** Andalucía, S Spain *37.10N 4.09W*
58 B9 **Loja** ◈ *province* S Ecuador
Lojo *see* Lohja
118 J4 **Lokachi** Volyns'ka Oblast', NW Ukraine *50.44N 24.39E*
81 M20 **Lokandu** Maniema, C Dem. Rep. Congo *2.34S 25.43E*
94 M11 **Lokan Tekojärvi** ◎ NE Finland
143 Z11 **Lökbatan** *Rus.* Lokbatan. E Azerbaijan *40.21N 49.43E*
101 F17 **Lokeren** Oost-Vlaanderen, NW Belgium *51.06N 3.58E*
Lokhvitsa *see* Lokhvytsya
119 S4 **Lokhvytsya** *Rus.* Lokhvitsa. Poltavs'ka Oblast', NE Ukraine *50.21N 33.15E*
83 H17 **Lokichar** Rift Valley, NW Kenya *2.22N 35.40E*
83 G16 **Lokichokio** Rift Valley, NW Kenya *4.16N 34.22E*
83 H16 **Lokitaung** Rift Valley, NW Kenya *4.15N 35.45E*
94 M11 **Lokka** Lappi, N Finland *67.47N 27.40E*
96 G8 **Løkken Verk** Sør-Trøndelag, S Norway *63.07N 9.40E*
128 G16 **Loknya** Pskovskaya Oblast', W Russian Federation *56.48N 30.08E*
79 V15 **Loko** Nassarawa, C Nigeria *8.00N 7.48E*
79 U15 **Lokoja** Kogi, C Nigeria *7.47N 6.44E*
125 E12 **Lokomotivnyy** Chelyabinskaya Oblast', C Russian Federation *53.00N 60.35E*
83 H17 **Lokori** Rift Valley, W Kenya *1.55N 36.03E*
79 R16 **Lokossa** S Benin *6.37N 1.43E*
120 I3 **Loksa** *Ger.* Loxa. Harjumaa, NW Estonia *59.36N 25.43E*
16 P3 **Loks Land** *island* Nunavut, NE Canada
82 C13 **Lol** ∽ S Sudan
78 K15 **Lola** Guinée-Forestière, SE Guinea *7.52N 8.28W*
37 Q5 **Lola, Mount** ▲ California, W USA *39.27N 120.20W*
83 H20 **Loliondo** Arusha, NE Tanzania *2.03S 35.46E*
97 H25 **Lolland** *prev.* Laaland. *island* S Denmark
195 O11 **Lolobau Island** *island* E PNG
175 T6 **Loloda Utara, Kepulauan** *island group* E Indonesia
81 E16 **Lolodorf** Sud, SW Cameroon *3.16N 10.49E*
116 G7 **Lom** *prev.* Lom-Palanka. Oblast Montana, NW Bulgaria *43.48N 23.16E*
116 G7 **Lom** ∽ Montana, NW Bulgaria
81 M19 **Lomami** ∽ C Dem. Rep. Congo
59 F17 **Lomas** Arequipa, SW Peru *15.29S 74.54W*
65 I23 **Lomas, Bahía** *bay* S Chile
63 D20 **Lomas de Zamora** Buenos Aires, E Argentina *34.52S 58.26W*
63 D20 **Loma Verde** Buenos Aires, E Argentina *35.16S 58.24W*
188 K4 **Lombadina** Western Australia *16.39S 122.54E*
108 E6 **Lombardia** *Eng.* Lombardy. ◈ *region* N Italy
Lombardy *see* Lombardia
104 M15 **Lombez** Gers, S France *43.28N 0.54E*
175 R15 **Lomblen, Pulau** *island* Nusa Tenggara, S Indonesia
181 W7 **Lombok Basin** *undersea feature* E Indian Ocean
175 Nn16 **Lombok, Pulau** *island* Nusa Tenggara, C Indonesia
175 Nn16 **Lombok, Selat** *strait* S Indonesia
79 Q16 **Lomé** ● (Togo) S Togo *6.08N 1.13E*
79 Q16 **Lomé** ✕ S Togo *6.08N 1.13E*
81 L19 **Lomela** Kasai Oriental, C Dem. Rep. Congo *2.19S 23.15E*
27 R9 **Lometa** Texas, SW USA *31.13N 98.23W*
81 F16 **Lomié** Est, SE Cameroon *3.09N 13.34E*
32 M8 **Lomira** Wisconsin, N USA *43.36N 88.26W*
97 K23 **Lomma** Skåne, S Sweden *55.40N 13.04E*
101 J16 **Lommel** Limburg, N Belgium *51.13N 5.19E*
98 I11 **Lomond, Loch** ◎ C Scotland, UK
207 R9 **Lomonosov Ridge** *var.* Harris Ridge, *Rus.* Khrebet Lomonsova. *undersea feature* Arctic Ocean
Lomonsova, Khrebet *see* Lomonosov Ridge
Lom-Palanka *see* Lom
Lomphat *see* Lumphăt
37 P14 **Lompoc** California, W USA *34.39N 120.29W*
178 Hh9 **Lom Sak** *var.* Muang Lom Sak. Phetchabun, C Thailand *16.45N 101.12E*
112 N9 **Łomża** *Rus.* Lomzha. Podlaskie, NE Poland *53.10N 22.04E*
Lomzha *see* Łomża
161 D14 **Lonāvale** *prev.* Lonaula. Mahārāshtra, W India *18.45N 73.27E*
65 G15 **Loncoche** Araucanía, C Chile *39.21S 72.34W*
65 H14 **Loncopue** Neuquén, W Argentina *38.06S 70.36W*
101 G17 **Londerzeel** Vlaams Brabant, C Belgium *51.00N 4.19E*
Londinium *see* London
12 E16 **London** Ontario, S Canada *42.59N 81.12W*
203 Y2 **London** Kiritimati, E Kiribati *02.00N 157.28W*
99 O22 **London** *anc.* Augusta, *Lat.* Londinium. ● (UK) SE England, UK *51.30N 0.10W*
23 N7 **London** Kentucky, S USA *37.06N 84.03W*
33 S13 **London** Ohio, NE USA *39.52N 83.27W*
27 Q10 **London** Texas, SW USA *30.40N 99.33W*
99 O22 **London City** ✕ SE England, UK *51.31N 0.07E*
99 E14 **Londonderry** *var.* Derry, *Ir.* Doire. NW Northern Ireland, UK *55.00N 7.19W*
99 F14 **Londonderry** *cultural region* NW Northern Ireland, UK
188 M2 **Londonderry, Cape** *headland* Western Australia *13.46S 126.56E*
65 H25 **Londonderry, Isla** *island* S Chile
45 O7 **Londres, Cayos** *reef* NE Nicaragua
62 I10 **Londrina** Paraná, S Brazil *23.18S 51.13W*
29 N13 **Lone Grove** Oklahoma, C USA *34.11N 97.15W*
12 E12 **Lonely Island** *island* Ontario, S Canada
37 T8 **Lone Mountain** ▲ Nevada, W USA *38.01N 117.28W*
27 V6 **Lone Oak** Texas, SW USA *33.02N 95.58W*
37 T11 **Lone Pine** California, W USA *36.36N 118.04W*
Lone Star State *see* Texas
85 D14 **Longa** Cuando Cubango, C Angola *14.37S 18.27E*
84 B12 **Longa** ∽ W Angola
85 E15 **Longa** ∽ SE Angola
169 W11 **Longang Shan** ▲▲ NE China
207 S4 **Longa, Proliv** *Eng.* Long Strait. *strait* NE Russian Federation
46 J13 **Long Bay** *bay* W Jamaica
23 V13 **Long Bay** *bay* North Carolina/South Carolina, E USA
37 T16 **Long Beach** California, W USA *33.46N 118.11W*
24 M9 **Long Beach** Mississippi, S USA *30.21N 89.09W*
20 L14 **Long Beach** Long Island, New York, NE USA *40.34N 73.38W*
34 F9 **Long Beach** Washington, NW USA *46.21N 124.03W*
20 K16 **Long Beach Island** *island* New Jersey, NE USA
67 M25 **Longbluff** *headland* SW Tristan da Cunha
25 U13 **Longboat Key** *island* Florida, SE USA
20 K15 **Long Branch** New Jersey, NE USA *40.18N 73.59W*
46 J5 **Long Cay** *island* SE Bahamas
167 P14 **Longchuan** *prev.* Laolong. Guangdong, S China *24.07N 115.10E*
Longchuan Jiang *see* Shweli
34 K12 **Long Creek** Oregon, NW USA *44.40N 119.07W*
165 W10 **Longde** Ningxia, N China *35.37N 106.07E*
191 P16 **Longford** Tasmania, SE Australia *41.41S 147.03E*
99 D17 **Longford** *Ir.* An Longfort. C Ireland *53.44N 7.49W*
99 E17 **Longford** *Ir.* An Longfort. *cultural region* C Ireland
167 P1 **Longhua** Hebei, E China *41.18N 117.43E*
175 Nn8 **Longiram** Borneo, C Indonesia *0.01S 115.36E*
46 J4 **Long Island** *island* C Bahamas
10 H8 **Long Island** *island* Nunavut, C Canada
194 K11 **Long Island** *var.* Arop Island. *island* N PNG
20 L14 **Long Island** *island* New York, NE USA
Long Island *see* Bermuda
20 M14 **Long Island Sound** *sound* NE USA
166 K13 **Long Jiang** ∽ S China
169 U7 **Longjiang** Heilongjiang, NE China *47.20N 123.09E*
169 Y10 **Longjing** *var.* Yanji. Jilin, NE China *42.48N 129.26E*
167 R4 **Longkou** Shandong, E China *37.40N 120.21E*
10 E11 **Longlac** Ontario, S Canada *49.46N 86.34W*
21 S1 **Long Lake** ◎ Maine, NE USA
33 O6 **Long Lake** ◎ Michigan, N USA
33 R5 **Long Lake** ◎ Michigan, N USA
31 N6 **Long Lake** ◎ North Dakota, N USA
32 J4 **Long Lake** ⊠ Wisconsin, N USA
101 K23 **Longlier** Luxembourg, SE Belgium *49.51N 5.27E*
166 I13 **Longlin** *var.* Longlin Gezu Zizhixian. Guangxi Zhuangzu Zizhiqu, S China *24.46N 105.19E*
39 T3 **Longmont** Colorado, C USA *40.09N 105.07W*
31 N13 **Long Pine** Nebraska, C USA *42.32N 99.42W*
Longping *see* Luodian
12 F17 **Long Point** *headland* Ontario, S Canada *42.33N 80.15W*
12 K15 **Long Point** *headland* Ontario, SE Canada *43.56N 76.53W*
192 P10 **Long Point** *headland* North Island, NZ *39.07S 177.41E*
32 L2 **Long Point** *headland* Michigan, N USA *47.50N 89.09W*
12 G17 **Long Point Bay** *lake bay* Ontario, S Canada
31 T7 **Long Prairie** Minnesota, N USA *45.58N 94.52W*
11 S11 **Long Range Mountains** *hill range* Newfoundland and Labrador, E Canada
67 H25 **Long Range Point** *headland* SE Saint Helena *16.00S 05.41W*
189 V8 **Longreach** Queensland, E Australia *23.31S 144.18E*
166 H7 **Longriba** Sichuan, C China *32.32N 102.20E*
166 L10 **Longshan** Hunan, S China *29.25N 109.28E*
39 S3 **Longs Peak** ▲ Colorado, C USA *40.15N 105.37W*
Long Strait *see* Longa, Proliv
104 K8 **Longué** Maine-et-Loire, NW France *47.23N 0.07W*
11 P11 **Longue-Pointe** Quebec, E Canada *50.20N 64.13W*
105 S4 **Longuyon** Meurthe-et-Moselle, NE France *49.25N 5.37E*
27 W7 **Longview** Texas, SW USA *32.30N 94.44W*
34 G10 **Longview** Washington, NW USA *46.08N 122.56W*
67 H25 **Longwood** C Saint Helena
27 P7 **Longworth** Texas, SW USA *32.37N 100.20W*
105 S3 **Longwy** Meurthe-et-Moselle, NE France *49.31N 5.46E*
165 V11 **Longxi** Gansu, C China *35.00N 104.34E*
178 J14 **Long Xuyên** *var.* Longxuyen. An Giang, S Vietnam *10.22N 105.25E*
167 Q13 **Longyan** Fujian, SE China *25.06N 117.01E*
94 O3 **Longyearbyen** ○ (Svalbard) Spitsbergen, W Svalbard *78.12N 15.39E*
166 J15 **Longzhou** Guangxi Zhuangzu Zizhiqu, S China *22.22N 106.46E*
102 F12 **Löningen** Niedersachsen, NW Germany *52.43N 7.42E*
29 V11 **Lonoke** Arkansas, C USA *34.46N 91.54W*
97 L21 **Lönsboda** Skåne, S Sweden *56.24N 14.19E*
105 S9 **Lons-le-Saunier** *anc.* Ledo Salinarius. Jura, E France *46.40N 5.31E*
33 O15 **Loogootee** Indiana, N USA *38.40N 86.54W*
33 Q9 **Looking Glass River** ∽ Michigan, N USA
23 X11 **Lookout, Cape** *headland* North Carolina, SE USA *34.36N 76.31W*
41 O6 **Lookout Ridge** *ridge* Alaska, USA
189 N11 **Loongana** Western Australia *30.53S 127.15E*
101 I14 **Loon op Zand** Noord-Brabant, S Netherlands *51.37N 5.04E*
99 A19 **Loop Head** *Ir.* Ceann Léime. *headland* W Ireland *52.33N 10.33W*
111 V4 **Loosdorf** Niederösterreich, NE Austria *48.13N 15.25E*
164 G10 **Lop** Xinjiang Uygur Zizhiqu, NW China *37.06N 80.12E*
114 J11 **Lopare** Republika Srpska, NE Bosnia and Herzegovina *44.39N 18.49E*
Lopatichi *see* Lapatsichy
131 Q15 **Lopatin** Respublika Dagestan, SW Russian Federation *43.52N 47.40E*
131 P7 **Lopatino** Penzenskaya Oblast', W Russian Federation *52.38N 45.46E*
178 Hh10 **Lop Buri** *var.* Loburi. Lop Buri, C Thailand *14.46N 100.40E*
27 R16 **Lopeno** Texas, SW USA *26.42N 99.06W*
197 D13 **Lopevi** *var.* Ulveah. *island* C Vanuatu
81 C18 **Lopez, Cap** *headland* W Gabon *0.39S 8.44E*
100 I12 **Lopik** Utrecht, C Netherlands *51.58N 4.57E*
Lop Nor *see* Lop Nur
164 M7 **Lop Nur** *var.* Lob Nor, Lop Nor, Lo-pu Po. *seasonal lake* NW China
Lopnur *see* Yuli
81 K17 **Lopori** ∽ NW Dem. Rep. Congo
100 O5 **Loppersum** Groningen, NE Netherlands *53.19N 6.45E*
94 I8 **Lopphavet** *sound* N Norway
Lo-pu Po *see* Lop Nur
Lora *see* Lowrah
190 F3 **Lora Creek** *seasonal river* South Australia
106 K13 **Lora del Río** Andalucía, S Spain *37.39N 5.31W*
154 M11 **Lora, Hāmūn-i** *wetland* SW Pakistan
33 T11 **Lorain** Ohio, N USA *41.27N 82.10W*
27 O7 **Loraine** Texas, SW USA *32.24N 100.42W*
33 R13 **Loramie, Lake** ⊠ Ohio, N USA
107 Q13 **Lorca** *Ar.* Lurka; *anc.* Eliocroca, *Lat.* Illur co. Murcia, S Spain *37.40N 1.40W*
199 I12 **Lord Howe Island** *island* E Australia
Lord Howe Island *see* Ontong Java Atoll
183 O10 **Lord Howe Rise** *undersea feature* SW Pacific Ocean
199 I12 **Lord Howe Seamounts** *undersea feature* W Pacific Ocean
39 P15 **Lordsburg** New Mexico, SW USA *32.19N 108.42W*
194 K8 **Lorengau** *var.* Lorungau. Manus Island, N PNG *2.03S 147.16E*
27 N5 **Lorenzo** Texas, SW USA *33.40N 101.31W*
148 K7 **Lorestān** *off.* Ostān-e Lorestān, *var.* Luristan. ◈ *province* W Iran
59 M17 **Loreto** Beni, N Bolivia *15.19S 64.40W*
108 J12 **Loreto** Marche, C Italy *43.25N 13.37E*
42 F8 **Loreto** Baja California Sur, W Mexico *25.59N 111.21W*
42 M11 **Loreto** Zacatecas, C Mexico *22.15N 102.00W*
58 E9 **Loreto** *off.* Departamento de Loreto. ◈ *department* NE Peru
83 K18 **Lorian Swamp** *swamp* E Kenya
56 E6 **Lorica** Córdoba, NW Colombia *9.13N 75.49W*
104 G7 **Lorient** *prev.* l'Orient. Morbihan, NW France *47.45N 3.22W*
113 K22 **Lőrinci** Heves, NE Hungary *47.43N 19.39E*
12 G11 **Loring** Ontario, S Canada *45.55N 79.59W*
35 V6 **Loring** Montana, NW USA *48.49N 107.48W*
105 R13 **Loriol-sur-Drôme** Drôme, E France *44.46N 4.51E*
23 U12 **Loris** South Carolina, SE USA *34.03N 78.53W*
59 I18 **Loriscota, Laguna** ◎ S Peru
191 N13 **Lorne** Victoria, SE Australia *38.33S 143.57E*
98 G11 **Lorn, Firth of** *inlet* W Scotland, UK
Loro Sae *see* East Timor
103 F24 **Lörrach** Baden-Württemberg, S Germany *47.37N 7.40E*
105 T5 **Lorraine** ◈ *region* NE France
Lorungau *see* Lorengau
97 L16 **Los** Gävleborg, C Sweden *61.42N 15.15E*
37 P14 **Los Alamos** California, W USA *34.44N 120.16W*
39 S10 **Los Alamos** New Mexico, SW USA *35.52N 106.17W*
44 F5 **Los Amates** Izabal, E Guatemala *15.16N 89.07W*
37 S15 **Los Angeles** California, W USA *34.03N 118.14W*
65 G14 **Los Ángeles** Bío Bío, C Chile *37.29S 72.18W*
37 S15 **Los Angeles** ✕ California, W USA *33.54N 118.24W*
37 T13 **Los Angeles Aqueduct** *aqueduct* California, W USA
Losanna *see* Lausanne
65 H20 **Los Antiguos** Santa Cruz, SW Argentina *46.36S 71.31W*
201 Q16 **Losap Atoll** *atoll* C Micronesia
37 P10 **Los Banos** California, W USA *37.00N 120.39W*
106 K16 **Los Barrios** Andalucía, S Spain *36.10N 5.30W*
64 L5 **Los Blancos** Salta, N Argentina *23.39S 62.36W*
44 L12 **Los Chiles** Alajuela, NW Costa Rica *11.00N 84.42W*
107 O2 **Los Corrales de Buelna** Cantabria, N Spain *43.15N 4.04W*
27 T17 **Los Fresnos** Texas, SW USA *26.03N 97.28W*
37 N9 **Los Gatos** California, W USA *37.13N 121.58W*
112 O11 **Łosice** Mazowieckie, E Poland *52.13N 22.42E*
114 B11 **Lošinj** *Ger.* Lussin, *It.* Lussino. *island* W Croatia
Los Jardines *see* Ngetik Atoll
65 G15 **Los Lagos** Los Lagos, C Chile *39.52S 72.52W*
65 F17 **Los Lagos** *off.* Región de los Lagos. ◈ *region* C Chile
Loslau *see* Wodzisław Śląski
66 N11 **Los Llanos** *var.* Los Llanos de Aridane. La Palma, Islas Canarias, Spain, NE Atlantic Ocean *28.39N 17.54W*
Los Llanos de Aridane *see* Los Llanos
39 R11 **Los Lunas** New Mexico, SW USA *34.48N 106.43W*
65 I16 **Los Menucos** Río Negro, C Argentina *40.52S 68.07W*
42 H8 **Los Mochis** Sinaloa, C Mexico *25.48N 108.57W*
37 N4 **Los Molinos** California, W USA *40.00N 122.05W*
106 M9 **Los Navalmorales** Castilla-La Mancha, C Spain *39.43N 4.37W*
27 S15 **Los Olmos Creek** ∽ Texas, SW USA
Losonc/Losontz *see* Lučenec
178 Jj5 **Lô, Sông** *Chin.* Panlong Jiang. ∽ China/Vietnam
46 B5 **Los Palacios** Pinar del Río, W Cuba *22.30N 83.19W*
106 K14 **Los Palacios y Villafranca** Andalucía, S Spain *37.10N 5.55W*
175 Ss16 **Lospalos** E East Timor *8.28S 126.56E*
39 R12 **Los Pinos Mountains** ▲▲ New Mexico, SW USA
39 R11 **Los Ranchos De Albuquerque** New Mexico, SW USA *35.09N 106.37W*
42 M14 **Los Reyes** Michoacán de Ocampo, SW Mexico *19.36N 102.29W*
58 B7 **Los Ríos** ◈ *province* C Ecuador
66 O11 **Los Rodeos** ✕ (Santa Cruz de Ternerife) Tenerife, Islas Canarias, Spain, NE Atlantic Ocean *28.27N 16.19W*
56 L4 **Los Roques, Islas** *island group* N Venezuela
45 S17 **Los Santos** Los Santos, S Panama *7.55N 80.25W*
45 S17 **Los Santos** *off.* Provincia de Los Santos. ◈ *province* S Panama
Los Santos *see* Los Santos de Maimona
106 J12 **Los Santos de Maimona** *var.* Los Santos. Extremadura, W Spain *38.27N 6.22W*
100 P10 **Losser** Overijssel, E Netherlands *52.16N 7.01E*
98 J8 **Lossiemouth** NE Scotland, UK *57.43N 3.18W*
63 B14 **Los Tábanos** Santa Fe, C Argentina *28.27S 59.57W*
56 J4 **Los Taques** Falcón, N Venezuela *11.49N 70.16W*
12 G11 **Lost Channel** Ontario, S Canada *45.54N 80.20W*
56 L5 **Los Teques** Miranda, N Venezuela *10.23N 67.01W*
37 Q12 **Lost Hills** California, W USA *35.35N 119.40W*
38 I7 **Lost Peak** ▲ Utah, W USA *37.30N 113.57W*
35 P11 **Lost Trail Pass** *pass* Montana, NW USA *45.40N 113.58W*
195 N15 **Losuia** Kiriwina Island, SE PNG *8.30S 151.04E*
64 G10 **Los Vilos** Coquimbo, C Chile *31.52S 71.28W*
107 N10 **Los Yébenes** Castilla-La Mancha, C Spain *39.34N 3.52W*
105 N13 **Lot** ◈ *department* S France
105 N13 **Lot** ∽ S France
65 F14 **Lota** Bío Bío, C Chile *37.08S 73.07W*
83 G15 **Lotagipi Swamp** *wetland* Kenya/Sudan
104 K14 **Lot-et-Garonne** ◈ *department* SW France
85 K21 **Lothair** Mpumalanga, NE South Africa *26.22S 30.25E*
35 R7 **Lothair** Montana, NW USA *48.28N 111.15W*
81 L20 **Loto** Kasai Oriental, C Dem. Rep. Congo *2.48S 22.30E*
198 B8 **Lotofagā** Upolu, SE Samoa *13.57S 171.51W*
110 D10 **Lötschbergtunnel** *tunnel* Valais, SW Switzerland
27 T9 **Lott** Texas, SW USA *31.12N 97.02W*
128 H3 **Lotta** *var.* Lutto. ∽ Finland/Russian Federation
192 Q7 **Lottin Point** *headland* North Island, NZ *37.26S 178.07E*
Lötzen *see* Giżycko
Loualaba *see* Lualaba
178 I6 **Louangnamtha** *var.* Luong Nam Tha. Louang Namtha, N Laos *20.55N 101.24E*
178 I7 **Louangphabang** *var.* Louangphrabang, Luang Prabang. Louangphabang, N Laos *19.51N 102.08E*
Louangphrabang *see* Louangphabang
204 H5 **Loubet Coast** *physical region* Antarctica
Loubomo *see* Dolisie
Louch *see* Loukhi
104 H6 **Loudéac** Côtes d'Armor, NW France *48.10N 2.45W*
166 M11 **Loudi** Hunan, S China *27.51N 111.58E*
81 F21 **Loudima** La Bouenza, S Congo *4.06S 13.04E*
22 M9 **Loudon** Tennessee, S USA *35.43N 84.19W*
33 T12 **Loudonville** Ohio, N USA *40.38N 82.13W*
104 L8 **Loudun** Vienne, W France *47.01N 0.04E*
104 K7 **Loué** Sarthe, NW France *48.00N 0.14W*
78 G10 **Louga** NW Senegal *15.36N 16.14W*
99 M19 **Loughborough** C England, UK *52.46N 1.10W*
99 C18 **Loughrea** *Ir.* Baile Locha Riach. W Ireland *53.12N 8.34W*
105 S9 **Louhans** Saône-et-Loire, C France *46.38N 5.12E*
23 P5 **Louisa** Kentucky, S USA *38.06N 82.40W*
23 V5 **Louisa** Virginia, NE USA *38.02N 78.00W*
23 V9 **Louisburg** North Carolina, SE USA *36.05N 78.18W*
27 U12 **Louise** Texas, SW USA *29.07N 96.22W*
13 P11 **Louiseville** Quebec, SE Canada *46.15N 72.54W*
195 Q17 **Louisiade Archipelago** *island group* SE PNG
29 W3 **Louisiana** Missouri, C USA *39.25N 91.03W*
24 G8 **Louisiana** *off.* State of Louisiana; *also known as* Creole State, Pelican State. ◈ *state* S USA
194 K9 **Lou Island** *island* N PNG
85 K19 **Louis Trichardt** Limpopo, NE South Africa *23.06S 29.55E*
25 V4 **Louisville** Georgia, SE USA *33.00N 82.24W*
32 M15 **Louisville** Illinois, N USA *38.46N 88.32W*
22 K5 **Louisville** Kentucky, S USA *38.15N 85.45W*
24 M4 **Louisville** Mississippi, S USA *33.07N 89.03W*
31 S15 **Louisville** Nebraska, C USA *41.00N 96.09W*
199 Jj12 **Louisville Ridge** *undersea feature* S Pacific Ocean
128 J6 **Loukhi** *var.* Louch. Respublika Kareliya, NW Russian Federation *66.05N 33.04E*
81 H19 **Loukoléla** Cuvette, E Congo *1.04S 17.10E*
106 G14 **Loulé** Faro, S Portugal *37.07N 8.01W*
113 C16 **Louny** *Ger.* Laun. Ústecký kraj NW Czech Republic *50.22N 13.49E*
31 O15 **Loup City** Nebraska, C USA *41.16N 98.58W*
31 P15 **Loup River** ∽ Nebraska, C USA
13 S9 **Loup, Rivière du** ∽ Quebec, SE Canada
10 K7 **Loups Marins, Lacs des** *lakes* Quebec, NE Canada
104 K16 **Lourdes** Hautes-Pyrénées, S France *43.06N 0.03W*
Lourenço Marques *see* Maputo
106 F11 **Loures** Lisboa, C Portugal *38.49N 9.10W*
106 F10 **Lourinhã** Lisboa, C Portugal *39.13N 9.19W*
117 C16 **Loúros** ∽ W Greece
106 G8 **Lousã** Coimbra, N Portugal *40.07N 8.15W*
166 M10 **Lou Shui** ∽ C China
191 O5 **Louth** New South Wales, SE Australia *30.34S 145.07E*
99 O18 **Louth** E England, UK *53.18N 0.00W*
99 F17 **Louth** *Ir.* Lú. *cultural region* NE Ireland
117 H15 **Loutrá** Kentrikí Makedonía, N Greece *39.55N 23.37E*
117 G19 **Loutráki** Pelopónnisos, S Greece *37.55N 22.55E*
Louvain *see* Leuven
101 H19 **Louvain-la Neuve** Wallon Brabant, C Belgium *50.39N 4.36E*
12 J8 **Louvicourt** Quebec, SE Canada *48.04N 77.22W*
104 M4 **Louviers** Eure, N France *49.13N 1.10E*
32 K14 **Lou Yaeger, Lake** ⊠ Illinois, N USA
95 J15 **Lövånger** Västerbotten, N Sweden *64.22N 21.19E*
128 J14 **Lovat'** ∽ NW Russian Federation
115 J17 **Lovćen** ▲ S Serbia and Montenegro (Yugoslavia) *42.22N 18.49E*
116 I8 **Lovech** Lovech, N Bulgaria *43.09N 24.42E*
116 I9 **Lovech** ◈ *province* N Bulgaria
27 V9 **Lovelady** Texas, SW USA *31.07N 95.27W*
39 T3 **Loveland** Colorado, C USA *40.24N 105.04W*
35 U12 **Lovell** Wyoming, C USA *44.50N 108.23W*
Lovello, Monte *see* Grosser Löffler
37 S4 **Lovelock** Nevada, W USA *40.11N 118.30W*
108 E7 **Lovere** Lombardia, N Italy *45.51N 10.06E*
32 L10 **Loves Park** Illinois, N USA *42.19N 89.03W*
28 M2 **Lovewell Reservoir** ⊠ Kansas, C USA
95 M19 **Loviisa** *Swe.* Lovisa. Etelä-Suomi, S Finland *60.27N 26.15E*
39 V15 **Loving** New Mexico, SW USA *32.17N 104.06W*
23 U6 **Lovingston** Virginia, NE USA *37.45N 78.47W*
39 V14 **Lovington** New Mexico, SW USA *32.56N 103.21W*
Lovisa *see* Loviisa
113 C15 **Lovosice** *Ger.* Lobositz. Ústecký Kraj, NW Czech Republic *50.29N 14.01E*
128 K4 **Lovozero** Murmanskaya Oblast', NW Russian Federation *68.00N 35.03E*
128 K4 **Lovozero, Ozero** ◎ NW Russian Federation
114 B9 **Lovran** *It.* Laurana. Primorje-Gorski Kotar, NW Croatia *45.16N 14.15E*
118 E11 **Lovrin** *Ger.* Lowrin. Timiş, W Romania *45.58N 20.48E*
84 E10 **Lóvua** Lunda Norte, NE Angola *7.21S 20.09E*
84 G12 **Lóvua** Moxico, E Angola *11.33S 23.35E*
67 D25 **Low Bay** *bay* East Falkland, Falkland Islands
15 M6 **Low, Cape** *headland* Nunavut, E Canada *63.05N 85.27W*
35 N10 **Lowell** Idaho, NW USA *46.07N 115.36W*
21 O10 **Lowell** Massachusetts, NE USA *42.37N 71.19W*
Löwen *see* Leuven
Löwenberg in Schlesien *see* Lwówek Śląski
Lower Austria *see* Niederösterreich
Lower Bann *see* Bann
Lower California *see* Baja California
Lower Danube *see* Niederösterreich
193 L14 **Lower Hutt** Wellington, North Island, NZ *41.13S 174.51E*
41 N11 **Lower Kalskag** Alaska, USA *61.30N 160.28W*
37 O1 **Lower Klamath Lake** ◎ California, W USA
37 Q2 **Lower Lake** ◎ California/Nevada, W USA
99 E15 **Lower Lough Erne** ◎ SW Northern Ireland, UK
Lower Lusatia *see* Niederlausitz
Lower Normandy *see* Basse-Normandie, France
8 K9 **Lower Post** British Columbia, W Canada *59.53N 128.19W*
31 T4 **Lower Red Lake** ◎ Minnesota, N USA
Lower Rhine *see* Neder Rijn
Lower Saxony *see* Niedersachsen
Lower Tunguska *see* Nizhnyaya Tunguska
99 Q19 **Lowestoft** E England, UK *52.28N 1.45E*
155 Q5 **Lowgar** *var.* Logar. ◈ *province* E Afghanistan
190 H7 **Low Hill** South Australia *32.17S 136.46E*
112 K12 **Łowicz** Łódzkie, C Poland *52.06N 19.55E*
35 N13 **Lowman** Idaho, NW USA *44.04N 115.37W*
155 P8 **Lowrah** *var.* Lora. ∽ SE Afghanistan
Lowrin *see* Lovrin
191 N17 **Low Rocky Point** *headland* Tasmania, SE Australia *42.59S 145.28E*
20 I8 **Lowville** New York, NE USA *43.47N 75.29W*
Loxa *see* Loksa
190 K9 **Loxton** South Australia *34.30S 140.36E*
83 G21 **Loya** Tabora, C Tanzania *4.57S 33.53E*
32 K6 **Loyal** Wisconsin, N USA *44.45N 90.30W*
20 G13 **Loyalsock Creek** ∽ Pennsylvania, NE USA
37 Q5 **Loyalton** California, W USA *39.39N 120.16W*
Lo-yang *see* Luoyang
197 J6 **Loyauté, Îles** *island group* S New Caledonia
Loyev *see* Loyew
121 O20 **Loyew** *Rus.* Loyev. Homyel'skaya Voblasts', SE Belarus *51.55N 30.48E*
129 S13 **Loyno** Kirovskaya Oblast', NW Russian Federation *59.44N 52.42E*
105 P13 **Lozère** ◈ *department* S France
105 Q14 **Lozère, Mont** ▲ S France *44.27N 3.44E*
114 J11 **Loznica** Serbia, W Serbia and Montenegro (Yugoslavia) *44.32N 19.13E*
119 V7 **Lozova** *Rus.* Lozovaya. Kharkivs'ka Oblast', E Ukraine *48.54N 36.22E*
Lozovaya *see* Lozova
107 N7 **Lozoyuela** Madrid, C Spain *40.55N 3.36W*
Lœvvajok *see* Leavvajohka
Lu *see* Shandong, China
Lú *see* Louth, Ireland
84 F12 **Luacano** Moxico, E Angola *11.19S 21.30E*
81 N21 **Lualaba** *Fr.* Loualaba. ∽ SE Dem. Rep. Congo
85 H14 **Luampa** Western, NW Zambia *15.02S 24.27E*
85 H15 **Luampa Kuta** Western, W Zambia *15.22S 24.40E*
167 P8 **Lu'an** Anhui, E China *31.46N 116.31E*
106 K2 **Luanco** Asturias, N Spain *43.36N 5.48W*
84 A11 **Luanda** *var.* Loanda, *Port.* São Paulo de Loanda. ● (Angola) Luanda, NW Angola *8.48S 13.17E*
84 A11 **Luanda** ◈ *province* NW Angola
84 A11 **Luanda** ✕ Luanda, NW Angola *8.49S 13.16E*
84 D12 **Luando** ∽ C Angola
Luang *see* Tapi, Mae Nam
85 G14 **Luanginga** *var.* Luanguinga. ∽ Angola/Zambia
178 Gg15 **Luang, Khao** ▲ SW Thailand *8.21N 99.46E*
Luang Prabang *see* Louangphabang
178 I8 **Luang Prabang Range** *Th.* Thiukhaoluang Phrahang. ▲▲ Laos/Thailand
178 H16 **Luang, Thale** *lagoon* S Thailand
Luangua, Rio *see* Luangwa
84 E11 **Luangue** ∽ NE Angola
Luanguinga *see* Luanginga
85 K15 **Luangwa** *var.* Aruângua. Lusaka, C Zambia *15.36S 30.27E*
85 K14 **Luangwa** *var.* Aruângua, Rio Luangua. ∽ Mozambique/Zambia
167 Q2 **Luan He** ∽ E China
202 G11 **Luaniva, Île** *island* E Wallis and Futuna
167 P2 **Luanping** *var.* Anjiangying. Hebei, E China *40.55N 117.19E*
84 J13 **Luanshya** Copperbelt, C Zambia *13.09S 28.24E*
64 K13 **Luan Toro** La Pampa, C Argentina *36.14S 65.08W*
167 Q2 **Luanxian** *var.* Luan Xian. Hebei, E China *39.47N 118.46E*
84 J12 **Luapula** ◈ *province* N Zambia
81 O25 **Luapula** ∽ Dem. Rep. Congo/Zambia
106 J2 **Luarca** Asturias, N Spain *43.33N 6.31W*
174 Ll7 **Luar, Danau** ◎ Borneo, N Indonesia
81 L25 **Luashi** Katanga, S Dem. Rep. Congo *10.54S 23.55E*
84 G12 **Luau** *Port.* Vila Teixeira de Sousa. Moxico, NE Angola *10.43S 22.07E*
81 C16 **Luba** *prev.* San Carlos. Isla de Bioco, NW Equatorial Guinea *3.26N 8.36E*
44 F4 **Lubaantun** *ruins* Toledo, S Belize *16.18N 88.57W*
113 P16 **Lubaczów** *var.* Lubaczów. Podkarpackie, SE Poland *50.09N 23.08E*
Lubale *see* Lubalo

◆ Country ● Country Capital ◇ Dependent Territory ○ Dependent Territory Capital ◈ Administrative Region ✕ International Airport ▲ Mountain ▲▲ Mountain Range ⛰ Volcano ∽ River ◎ Lake ⊠ Reservoir

84 E11 Lubalo Lunda Norte, NE Angola 9.02S 19.11E
84 E11 Lubalo var. Lubale. ≈ Angola/Zaire
120 J9 Lubāna Madona, E Latvia 56.55N 29.43E
Lubānas Ezers see Lubāns
179 P11 Lubang Island island N Philippines
85 B15 Lubango Port. Sá da Bandeira. Huíla, SW Angola 14.54S 13.33E
120 J9 Lubāns var. Lubānas Ezers. ◎ E Latvia
81 M21 Lubao Kasai Oriental, C Dem. Rep. Congo 5.21S 25.42E
112 O13 Lubartów Ger. Qumälisch. Lubelskie, E Poland 51.26N 22.36E
102 G13 Lübbecke Nordrhein-Westfalen, NW Germany 52.18N 8.37E
102 O13 Lübben Brandenburg, E Germany 51.55N 13.51E
103 P14 Lübbenau Brandenburg, E Germany 51.52N 13.57E
27 N5 Lubbock Texas, SW USA 33.34N 101.51W
Lubcz see Lyubcha
21 U6 Lubec Maine, NE USA 44.49N 67.00W
102 K9 Lübeck Schleswig-Holstein, N Germany 53.52N 10.40E
102 K8 Lübecker Bucht bay N Germany
81 M21 Lubefu Kasai Oriental, C Dem. Rep. Congo 4.43S 24.25E
113 O14 Lubelska, Wyżyna plateau SE Poland
113 O14 Lubelskie ⬖ province E Poland
Lubembe see Luembe
Lüben see Lubin
150 H9 Lubenka Zapadnyy Kazakhstan, W Kazakhstan 50.27N 54.07E
81 P18 Lubero Nord Kivu, E Dem. Rep. Congo 0.10S 29.12E
81 L22 Lubi ≈ S Dem. Rep. Congo
Lubiana see Ljubljana
112 J11 Lubień Kujawski Kujawsko-pomorskie, C Poland 52.25N 19.10E
69 T11 Lubilandji ≈ S Dem. Rep. Congo
112 F13 Lubin Ger. Lüben. Dolnośląskie, SW Poland 51.22N 16.12E
113 O14 Lublin Rus. Lyublin. Lubelskie, E Poland 51.15N 22.33E
113 J15 Lubliniec Śląskie, S Poland 50.40N 18.40E
Lubnān, Jabal see Liban, Jebel
119 R5 Lubny Poltavs'ka Oblast', NE Ukraine 50.00N 33.00E
Luboml see Lyuboml'
112 G11 Luboń Ger. Peterhof. Wielkolpolskie, C Poland 52.22N 16.54E
112 D12 Lubsko Ger. Sommerfeld. Lubuskie, W Poland 51.46N 14.56E
81 N24 Lubudi Katanga, SE Dem. Rep. Congo 9.57S 25.58E
174 Hh11 Lubuklinggau Sumatera, W Indonesia 3.15S 102.51E
81 N25 Lubumbashi prev. Élisabethville. Katanga, SE Dem. Rep. Congo 11.39S 27.31E
85 I14 Lubungu Central, C Zambia 14.28S 26.30E
112 E12 Lubuskie ⬖ province W Poland
81 N18 Lubutu Maniema, E Dem. Rep. Congo 0.42S 26.31E
Luca see Lucca
84 C11 Lucala ≈ W Angola
12 E16 Lucan Ontario, S Canada 43.10N 81.22W
99 F18 Lucan Ir. Leamhcán. E Ireland 53.22N 6.27W
Lucanian Mountains see Lucano, Appennino
109 M18 Lucano, Appennino Eng. Lucanian Mountains. ▲▲ S Italy
84 F11 Lucapa var. Lukapa. Lunda Norte, NE Angola 8.23S 20.42E
31 V15 Lucas Iowa, C USA 41.01N 93.26W
63 C18 Lucas González Entre Ríos, E Argentina 32.25S 59.33W
67 C25 Lucas Point headland West Falkland, Falkland Islands 52.10S 60.22W
33 S15 Lucasville Ohio, N USA 38.52N 83.00W
108 F11 Lucca anc. Luca. Toscana, C Italy 43.49N 10.30E
46 H12 Lucea W Jamaica 18.26N 78.10W
99 H15 Luce Bay inlet SW Scotland, UK
24 M8 Lucedale Mississippi, S USA 30.55N 88.35W
179 Pp11 Lucena off. Lucena City. Luzon, N Philippines 13.57N 121.38E
106 M14 Lucena Andalucía, S Spain 37.25N 4.28W
107 S8 Lucena del Cid País Valenciano, E Spain 40.07N 0.15W
113 D15 Lučenec Ger. Losontz, Hung. Losonc. Banskobystrický Kraj, C Slovakia 48.21N 19.36E
Lucentum see Alicante
109 M16 Lucera Puglia, SE Italy 41.30N 15.19E
Lucerna/Lucerne see Luzern
Lucerne, Lake of see Vierwaldstätter See
42 J4 Lucero Chihuahua, N Mexico 30.51N 106.27W
127 Nn17 Luchegorsk Primorskiy Kray, SE Russian Federation 46.26N 134.10E
107 Q13 Luchena ≈ SE Spain
84 N13 Lucheringo var. Luchulingo. ≈ N Mozambique
Luchesa see Luchosa
Luchin see Luchyn
120 N13 Luchosa Rus. Luchesa. ≈ N Belarus
Luchow see Hefei
102 K11 Lüchow Mecklenburg-Vorpommern, N Germany 52.57N 11.10E
Luchulingo see Lucheringo
121 N17 Luchyn Rus. Luchin. Homyel'skaya Voblasts', SE Belarus 53.01N 30.01E
57 U11 Lucie Rivier ≈ W Suriname
190 K11 Lucindale South Australia 36.57S 140.20E
175 T13 Lucipara, Kepulauan island group E Indonesia
85 A14 Lucira Namibe, SW Angola 13.51S 12.35E
Łuck see Luts'k
103 O14 Luckau Brandenburg, E Germany 51.50N 13.42E
102 N13 Luckenwalde Brandenburg, E Germany 52.06N 13.11E
12 E15 Lucknow Ontario, S Canada 43.58N 81.30W
158 L12 Lucknow var. Lakhnau. Uttar Pradesh, N India 26.49N 80.54E
104 J10 Luçon Vendée, NW France 46.27N 1.10W
46 I7 Lucrecia, Cabo headland E Cuba 21.00N 75.34W
84 F13 Lucusse Moxico, E Angola 12.32S 20.46E
Lüda see Dalian
116 M9 Luda Kamchiya ≈ E Bulgaria
Ludasch see Luduş
116 I10 Luda Yana ≈ C Bulgaria
114 F7 Ludbreg Varaždin, N Croatia 46.15N 16.36E
31 P7 Ludden North Dakota, N USA 45.58N 98.07W
103 F15 Lüdenscheid Nordrhein-Westfalen, W Germany 51.13N 7.37E
85 C21 Lüderitz prev. Angra Pequena. Karas, SW Namibia 26.37S 15.10E
158 H8 Ludhiāna Punjab, N India 30.55N 75.52E
33 O7 Ludington Michigan, N USA 43.58N 86.27W
99 K20 Ludlow W England, UK 52.19N 2.27W
37 W14 Ludlow California, W USA 34.43N 116.07W
30 J7 Ludlow South Dakota, N USA 45.48N 103.21W
20 M9 Ludlow Vermont, NE USA 43.24N 72.39W
116 L7 Ludogorie physical region NE Bulgaria
25 W6 Ludowici Georgia, SE USA 31.42N 81.44W
Ludsan see Ludza
118 I10 Luduş Ger. Ludasch, Hung. Marosludas. Mureş, C Romania 46.27N 24.04E
97 M14 Ludvika Dalarna, C Sweden 60.07N 15.13E
103 H21 Ludwigsburg Baden-Württemberg, SW Germany 48.54N 9.12E
102 O13 Ludwigsfelde Brandenburg, NE Germany 52.17N 13.15E
103 G20 Ludwigshafen var. Ludwigshafen am Rhein. Rheinland-Pfalz, W Germany 49.28N 8.24E
Ludwigshafen am Rhein see Ludwigshafen
103 L20 Ludwigskanal canal SE Germany
102 L10 Ludwigslust Mecklenburg-Vorpommern, N Germany 53.19N 11.28E
120 K10 Ludza Ger. Ludsan. Ludza, E Latvia 56.32N 27.41E
81 K21 Luebo Kasai Occidental, SW Dem. Rep. Congo 5.19S 21.21E
27 Q6 Lueders Texas, SW USA 32.46N 99.38W
81 N20 Lueki Maniema, C Dem. Rep. Congo 3.25S 25.49E
84 F10 Luembe var. Lubembe. ≈ Angola/Dem. Rep. Congo
84 E13 Luena var. Lwena, Port. Luso. Moxico, E Angola 11.46S 19.52E
81 M24 Luena Katanga, SE Dem. Rep. Congo 9.28S 25.45E
84 K12 Luena Northern, NE Zambia 10.31S 30.12E
84 F13 Luena ≈ E Angola
85 F16 Luengue ≈ SE Angola
69 V13 Luenha ≈ W Mozambique
85 G15 Lueti ≈ Angola/Zambia
166 J7 Lüeyang Shaanxi, C China 33.12N 106.31E
167 P14 Lufeng Guangdong, S China 22.58N 115.36E
81 N24 Lufira ≈ SE Dem. Rep. Congo
81 N25 Lufira, Lac de Retenue de la var. Lac Tshangalele. ⊠ SE Dem. Rep. Congo
27 W8 Lufkin Texas, SW USA 31.20N 94.43W
84 L11 Lufubu ≈ N Zambia
128 G14 Luga Leningradskaya Oblast', NW Russian Federation 58.43N 29.46E
128 G13 Luga ≈ NW Russian Federation
Luganer See see Lugano, Lago di
110 H11 Lugano Ger. Lauis. Ticino, S Switzerland 46.01N 8.57E
110 H12 Lugano, Lago di var. Ceresio, Ger. Luganer See. ◎ S Switzerland
Lugansk see Luhans'k
197 B12 Luganville Espiritu Santo, C Vanuatu 15.31S 167.12E
Lugdunum see Lyon
Lugdunum Batavorum see Leiden
85 O15 Lugela Zambézia, NE Mozambique 16.27S 36.47E
85 O16 Lugela ≈ C Mozambique
84 P13 Lugenda, Rio ≈ N Mozambique
Luggarus see Locarno
Lugh Ganana see Luuq
99 G19 Lugnaquillia Mountain Ir. Log na Coille. ▲ E Ireland 52.58N 6.27W
108 H10 Lugo Emilia-Romagna, N Italy 44.25N 11.52E
106 I3 Lugo anc. Lugus Augusti. Galicia, NW Spain 43.00N 7.33W
106 I3 Lugo ⬖ province Galicia, NW Spain
23 R12 Lugoff South Carolina, SE USA 34.13N 80.41W
118 F12 Lugoj Ger. Lugosch, Hung. Lugos. Timiş, W Romania 45.40N 21.56E
Lugos/Lugosch see Lugoj
Lugovoy/Lugovoye see Kulan
164 I13 Lugu Xizang Zizhiqu, W China 33.26N 84.10E
Lugus Augusti see Lugo
Luguvallium/Luguvallum see Carlisle
119 Y7 Luhans'k Rus. Lugansk; prev. Voroshilovgrad. Luhans'ka Oblast', E Ukraine 48.32N 39.21E
119 Y7 Luhans'k ✕ Luhans'ka Oblast', E Ukraine 48.25N 39.24E
119 X6 Luhans'ka Oblast' var. Luhans'k; prev. Voroshilovgrad, Rus. Voroshilovgradskaya Oblast'. ⬖ province E Ukraine
167 Q7 Luhe Jiangsu, E China 32.22N 118.51E
175 T11 Luhu Pulau Seram, E Indonesia 3.20S 127.58E
166 G8 Luhuo var. Zhaggo. Sichuan, C China 31.25N 100.39E
118 M3 Luhyny Zhytomyrs'ka Oblast', N Ukraine 51.06N 28.24E
85 G15 Lui ≈ W Zambia
85 G16 Luiana ≈ SE Angola
85 L15 Luia, Rio var. Ruya. ≈ Mozambique/Zimbabwe
Luichow Peninsula see Leizhou Bandao
Luik see Liège
84 C13 Luimbale Huambo, C Angola 12.15S 15.19E
Luimneach see Limerick
108 D6 Luino Lombardia, N Italy 46.00N 8.45E
84 E13 Luio ≈ E Angola
94 L11 Luiro ≈ NE Finland
81 N25 Luishia Katanga, SE Dem. Rep. Congo 11.18S 27.08E
61 M19 Luislândia do Oeste Minas Gerais, SE Brazil 17.59S 45.35W
42 K5 Luis L.León, Presa ⊠ N Mexico
Luis Muñoz Marin see San Juan
205 N5 Luitpold Coast physical region Antarctica
81 K22 Luiza Kasai Occidental, S Dem. Rep. Congo 7.10S 22.27E
63 D20 Luján Buenos Aires, E Argentina 34.34S 59.07W
81 N24 Lukafu Katanga, SE Dem. Rep. Congo 10.28S 27.31E
Lukapa see Lucapa
114 I11 Lukavac Federacija Bosna I Hercegovina, NE Bosnia and Herzegovina 44.33N 18.31E
81 I20 Lukenie ≈ C Dem. Rep. Congo
81 H19 Lukolela Equateur, W Dem. Rep. Congo 1.03S 17.07E
121 M14 Lukoml'skaye, Vozyera Rus. Ozero Lukoml'skoye. ◎ N Belarus
Lukoml'skoye, Ozero see Lukoml'skaye, Vozyera
116 I8 Lukovit Lovech, N Bulgaria 43.13N 24.10E
112 O12 Łuków Ger. Bogendorf. Lubelskie, E Poland 51.57N 22.22E
131 O4 Lukoyanov Nizhegorodskaya Oblast', W Russian Federation 55.02N 44.26E
81 N22 Lukuga ≈ SE Dem. Rep. Congo
81 F21 Lukula Bas-Congo, SW Dem. Rep. Congo 5.22S 12.57E
85 G14 Lukulu Western, NW Zambia 14.24S 23.12E
201 R17 Lukunor Atoll atoll Mortlock Islands, C Micronesia
84 J12 Lukwesa Luapula, NE Zambia 10.03S 28.42E
95 K14 Luleå Norrbotten, N Sweden 65.34N 22.10E
94 J13 Luleälven ≈ N Sweden
142 C10 Lüleburgaz Kırklareli, NW Turkey 41.25N 27.22E
166 M4 Lüliang Shan ▲▲ C China
81 O21 Lulimba Maniema, E Dem. Rep. Congo 4.42S 28.37E
24 K9 Luling Louisiana, S USA 29.55N 90.22W
27 T11 Luling Texas, SW USA 29.40N 97.39W
81 I18 Lulonga ≈ NW Dem. Rep. Congo
81 K22 Lulua ≈ S Dem. Rep. Congo
Luluabourg see Kananga
198 Dd8 Luma Ta'ū, E American Samoa 14.15S 169.30W
174 M16 Lumajang Jawa, C Indonesia 8.06S 113.13E
164 G12 Lumajangdong Co ◎ W China
84 G13 Lumbala Kaquengue Moxico, E Angola 12.40S 22.34E
85 F14 Lumbala N'Guimbo var. Nguimbo, Port. Gago Coutinho, Vila Gago Coutinho. Moxico, E Angola 14.04S 21.25E
23 T11 Lumber River ≈ North Carolina/South Carolina, SE USA
Lumber State see Maine
24 L8 Lumberton Mississippi, S USA 31.00N 89.27W
23 U11 Lumberton North Carolina, SE USA 34.37N 79.00W
107 R4 Lumbier Navarra, N Spain 42.39N 1.19W
85 Q15 Lumbo Nampula, NE Mozambique 15.00S 40.40E
128 M4 Lumbovka Murmanskaya Oblast', NW Russian Federation 67.41N 40.31E
106 J7 Lumbrales Castilla-León, N Spain 40.57N 6.43W
159 W13 Lumding Assam, NE India 25.46N 93.10E
84 F12 Lumege var. Lumeje. Moxico, E Angola 11.30S 20.57E
Lumeje see Lumege
194 F10 Lumi Sandaun, NW PNG 3.30S 142.04E
101 J17 Lummen Limburg, NE Belgium 50.58N 5.12E
95 J20 Lumparland Åland, SW Finland 60.06N 20.15E
178 K12 Lumphăt prev. Lomphat. Rôtânôkiri, NE Cambodia 13.32N 106.57E
9 U16 Lumsden Saskatchewan, S Canada 50.39N 104.52W
193 C23 Lumsden Southland, South Island, NZ 45.43S 168.26E
174 J11 Lumut, Tanjung headland Sumatera, W Indonesia 3.47S 105.55E
163 P4 Lün Töv, C Mongolia 47.51N 105.11E
166 H13 Lunan var. Lunan Yizu Zizhixian. Yunnan, SW China 24.46N 103.12E
Lunan Yizu Zizhixian see Lunan
118 I13 Lunca Corbului Argeş, S Romania 44.41N 24.46E
97 K23 Lund Skåne, S Sweden 55.42N 13.10E
37 X6 Lund Nevada, W USA 38.50N 115.00W
84 D11 Lunda Norte ⬖ province NE Angola
84 E12 Lunda Sul ⬖ province NE Angola
84 M13 Lundazi Eastern, NE Zambia 12.19S 33.10E
97 G16 Lunde Telemark, S Norway 61.31N 6.37E
Lundenburg see Břeclav
97 C17 Lundevatnet ◎ S Norway
Lundi see Runde
99 I23 Lundy island SW England, UK
102 J10 Lüneburg Niedersachsen, N Germany 53.15N 10.25E
102 J11 Lüneburger Heide heathland NW Germany
105 Q15 Lunel Hérault, S France 43.40N 4.08E
103 F14 Lünen Nordrhein-Westfalen, W Germany 51.37N 7.31E
11 P16 Lunenburg Nova Scotia, SE Canada 44.22N 64.21W
23 V7 Lunenburg Virginia, NE USA 36.56N 78.15W
105 T5 Lunéville Meurthe-et-Moselle, NE France 48.34N 6.30E
85 I14 Lunga ≈ C Zambia
Lunga, Isola see Dugi Otok
164 H12 Lungdo Xizang Zizhiqu, W China 33.45N 82.09E
164 I14 Lunggar Xizang Zizhiqu, W China 31.10N 84.01E
78 I15 Lungi ✕ (Freetown) W Sierra Leone 8.36N 13.10W
Lungkiang see Qiqihar
Lungleh see Lunglei
159 W15 Lunglei prev. Lungleh. Mizoram, NE India 22.55N 92.49E
164 L15 Lungsang Xizang Zizhiqu, W China 29.49N 88.27E
84 E13 Lungué-Bungo var. Lungwebungu. ≈ Angola/Zambia see also Lungwebungu
85 G14 Lungwebungu var. Lungué-Bungo. ≈ Angola/Zambia see also Lungué-Bungo
158 F12 Lūni Rājasthān, N India 26.03N 73.00E
158 F12 Lūni ≈ N India
Luninets see Luninyets
37 S7 Luning Nevada, W USA 38.29N 118.10W
Łuniniec see Luninyets
131 P6 Lunino Penzenskaya Oblast', W Russian Federation 53.35N 45.12E
121 J19 Luninyets Pol. Łuniniec, Rus. Luninets. Brestskaya Voblasts', SW Belarus 52.15N 26.49E
158 F10 Lūnkaransar Rājasthān, NW India 28.31N 73.49E
121 G17 Lunna Pol. Łunna, Rus. Lunna. Hrodzyenskaya Voblasts', W Belarus 53.27N 24.16E
78 I15 Lunsar W Sierra Leone 8.40N 12.31W
85 K14 Lunsemfwa ≈ C Zambia
164 J6 Luntai var. Bügür. Xinjiang Uygur Zizhiqu, NW China 41.48N 84.14E
100 K11 Lunteren Gelderland, C Netherlands 52.04N 5.37E
175 O16 Lunyuk Sumbawa, S Indonesia 8.56S 117.15E
111 U5 Lunz am See Niederösterreich, C Austria 47.54N 15.01E
169 Y7 Luobei var. Fengxiang. Heilongjiang, NE China 47.35N 130.51E
166 J13 Luodian var. Longping. Guizhou, S China 25.25N 106.49E
166 M15 Luoding Guangdong, S China 22.44N 111.28E
166 M6 Luo He ≈ C China
166 L5 Luo He ≈ C China
167 N7 Luohe Henan, C China 33.37N 114.00E
Luolajarvi see Kuoloyarvi
Luong Nam Tha see Louangnamtha
166 L13 Luoqing Jiang ≈ S China
167 O8 Luoshan Henan, C China 32.12N 114.30E
167 O12 Luoxiao Shan ▲▲ S China
167 N6 Luoyang var. Honan, Lo-yang. Henan, C China 34.40N 112.25E
167 R12 Luoyuan Fujian, SE China 26.29N 119.32E
81 F21 Luozi Bas-Congo, W Dem. Rep. Congo 4.57S 14.07E
85 J17 Lupane Matabeleland North, W Zimbabwe 18.46S 27.47E
166 I12 Lupanshui prev. Shuicheng. Guizhou, S China 26.38N 104.49E
174 Ll7 Lupar, Batang ≈ East Malaysia
Lupatia see Altamura
118 G12 Lupeni Hung. Lupény. Hunedoara, SW Romania 45.20N 23.07E
Lupény see Lupeni
84 N13 Lupiliche Niassa, N Mozambique 11.36S 35.15E
85 E14 Lupire Cuando Cubango, E Angola 14.39S 19.39E
179 Rr16 Lupon Mindanao, S Philippines 6.53N 126.00E
81 L22 Luputa Kasai Oriental, S Dem. Rep. Congo 7.07S 23.43E
123 Jj17 Luqa ✕ (Valletta) S Malta 35.53N 14.27E
165 U11 Luqu Gansu, C China 34.34N 102.27E
47 U5 Luquillo, Sierra de ▲▲ E Puerto Rico
28 L4 Luray Kansas, C USA 39.06N 98.41W
23 U4 Luray Virginia, NE USA 38.40N 78.27W
105 T7 Lure Haute-Saône, E France 47.42N 6.30E
84 D11 Luremo Lunda Norte, NE Angola 8.32S 17.55E
99 F15 Lurgan Ir. An Lorgain. S Northern Ireland, UK 54.28N 6.19W
59 K18 Luribay La Paz, W Bolivia 17.09S 67.39W
85 Q14 Lúrio Nampula, NE Mozambique 13.32S 40.33E
85 P14 Lúrio, Rio ≈ NE Mozambique
Luristan see Lorestān
Lurka see Lorca
85 J15 Lusaka ● (Zambia) Lusaka, SE Zambia 15.23S 28.16E
85 J15 Lusaka ⬖ province C Zambia
85 J15 Lusaka ✕ Lusaka, C Zambia 15.10S 28.22E
81 L21 Lusambo Kasai Oriental, C Dem. Rep. Congo 4.54S 23.25E
195 N14 Lusancay Islands and Reefs island group SE PNG
81 I21 Lusanga Bandundu, SW Dem. Rep. Congo 4.55S 18.40E
81 N21 Lusangi Maniema, E Dem. Rep. Congo 4.39S 27.10E
Lusatian Mountains see Lausitzer Bergland
Lushnja see Lushnjë
115 K21 Lushnjë var. Lushnja. Fier, C Albania 40.54N 19.43E
83 J21 Lushoto Tanga, E Tanzania 4.48S 38.19E
104 L10 Lusignan Vienne, W France 46.25N 0.06E
35 Z15 Lusk Wyoming, C USA 42.45N 104.27W
Luso see Luena
104 L10 Lussac-les-Châteaux Vienne, W France 46.23N 0.44E
Lussin/Lussino see Lošinj
Lussinpiccolo see Mali Lošinj
110 I7 Lustenau Vorarlberg, W Austria 47.26N 9.39E
167 T14 Lü Tao var. Huoshao Dao, Lütao, Eng. Green Island. island SE Taiwan
Lūt, Baḩrat/Lut, Bahret see Dead Sea
24 K9 Lutcher Louisiana, S USA 30.02N 90.42W
149 T9 Lūt, Dasht-e var. Kavīr-e Lūt. desert E Iran
85 F14 Lutembo Moxico, E Angola 13.30S 21.21E
Lutetia/Lutetia Parisiorum see Paris
Luteva see Lodève
12 G15 Luther Lake ◎ Ontario, S Canada
195 U13 Luti Choiseul Island, NW Solomon Islands 7.13S 157.01E
Lūt, Kavīr-e see Lūt, Dasht-e
99 N21 Luton SE England, UK 51.52N 0.25W
99 N21 Luton ✕ (London) SE England, UK 51.54N 0.24W
110 B10 Lutry Vaud, SW Switzerland 46.31N 6.31E
15 Ii8 Łutselk'e prev. Snowdrift. Northwest Territories, W Canada 62.24N 110.42W
31 Y4 Lutsen Minnesota, N USA 47.39N 90.37W
118 J4 Luts'k Pol. Łuck, Rus. Lutsk. Volyns'ka Oblast', NW Ukraine 50.45N 25.22E
Luttenberg see Ljutomer
Lüttich see Liège
85 G25 Luttig Western Cape, SW South Africa 32.33S 22.13E
Lutto see Lotta
84 E13 Lutuai Moxico, E Angola 12.38S 20.06E
119 Y7 Lutuhyne Luhans'ka Oblast', E Ukraine 48.24N 39.12E
176 Ww13 Lutur, Pulau island Kepulauan Aru, E Indonesia
25 V12 Lutz Florida, SE USA 28.09N 82.27W
Lutzow-Holm Bay see Lützow Holmbukta
205 V2 Lützow Holmbukta var. Lutzow-Holm Bay. bay Antarctica
83 L16 Luuq It. Lugh Ganana. Gedo, SW Somalia 3.42N 42.34E
94 M12 Luusua Lappi, NE Finland 66.28N 27.16E
25 Q6 Luverne Alabama, S USA 31.43N 86.15W
31 S11 Luverne Minnesota, N USA 43.39N 96.12W
81 O22 Luvua ≈ SE Dem. Rep. Congo
84 F13 Luvuei Moxico, E Angola 13.08S 21.09E
83 H24 Luwego ≈ S Tanzania
84 K12 Luwingu Northern, NE Zambia 10.13S 29.55E
175 Qq9 Luwuk prev. Loewoek. Sulawesi, C Indonesia 0.55S 122.46E
25 N3 Luxapallila Creek ≈ Alabama/Mississippi, S USA
101 M25 Luxembourg ● (Luxembourg) Luxembourg, S Luxembourg 49.37N 6.07E
101 M25 Luxembourg off. Grand Duchy of Luxembourg, var. Lëtzebuerg, Luxemburg. ◆ monarchy NW Europe
101 J23 Luxembourg ⬖ province SE Belgium
101 L24 Luxembourg ⬖ district S Luxembourg
33 N6 Luxemburg Wisconsin, N USA 44.32N 87.42W
Luxemburg see Luxembourg
105 U7 Luxeuil-les-Bains Haute-Saône, E France 47.49N 6.22E
166 E13 Luxi prev. Mangshi. Yunnan, SW China 24.27N 98.31E
84 E10 Luxico ≈ Angola/Dem. Rep. Congo
77 X10 Luxor Ar. Al Uqşur. E Egypt 25.39N 32.39E
77 X10 Luxor ✕ C Egypt 25.39N 32.48E
166 M4 Luya Shan ▲▲ C China
104 J15 Luy de Béarn ≈ SW France
104 J15 Luy de France ≈ SW France
129 P12 Luza Kirovskaya Oblast', NW Russian Federation 60.37N 47.13E
129 Q12 Luza ≈ NW Russian Federation
106 I16 Luz, Costa de la coastal region SW Spain
113 K20 Luže var. Lausche. ▲ Czech Republic/Germany see also Lausche 50.51N 14.40E
110 F8 Luzern Fr. Lucerne, It. Lucerna. Luzern, C Switzerland 47.03N 8.16E
110 E8 Luzern Fr. Lucerne. ⬖ canton C Switzerland
166 L13 Luzhai Guangxi Zhuangzu Zizhiqu, S China 24.33N 109.46E
120 K12 Luzhki Rus. Luzhki. Vitsyebskaya Voblasts', N Belarus 55.20N 27.54E
166 I10 Luzhou Sichuan, C China 28.55N 105.28E
Lužická Nisa see Neisse
Lužické Hory see Lausitzer Bergland
Lužnice see Lainsitz
179 Pp9 Luzon island N Philippines
179 Oo6 Luzon Strait strait Philippines/Taiwan
118 I5 L'viv Ger. Lemberg, Pol. Lwów, Rus. L'vov. L'vivs'ka Oblast', W Ukraine 49.48N 24.04E
L'viv see L'vivs'ka Oblast'
118 I4 L'vivs'ka Oblast' var. L'viv, Rus. L'vovskaya Oblast'. ⬖ province NW Ukraine
L'vov see L'viv
L'vovskaya Oblast' see L'vivs'ka Oblast'
Lwena see Luena
Lwów see L'viv
112 F11 Lwówek Ger. Neustadt bei Pinne. Wielkolpolskie, C Poland 52.27N 16.10E
113 E14 Lwówek Śląski Ger. Löwenberg in Schlesien. Dolnośląskie, SW Poland 51.06N 15.35E
121 I18 Lyakhavichy Rus. Lyakhovichi. Brestskaya Voblasts', SW Belarus 53.01N 26.15E
Lyakhovichi see Lyakhavichy
193 B22 Lyall, Mount ▲ South Island, NZ 45.14S 167.31E
Lyallpur see Faisalābād
125 G10 Lyamin ≈ C Russian Federation
Lyangar see Langar
125 G10 Lyantor Khanty-Mansiyskiy Avtonomnyy Okrug, C Russian Federation 61.40N 72.21E
128 H11 Lyaskelya Respublika Kareliya, NW Russian Federation 61.42N 31.06E
121 I18 Lyasnaya Rus. Lesnaya. Brestskaya Voblasts', SW Belarus 52.58N 25.46E
121 F19 Lyasnaya Pol. Leśna, Rus. Lesnaya. ≈ SW Belarus
128 H15 Lychkovo Novgorodskaya Oblast', W Russian Federation 57.55N 32.24E
Lyck see Ełk
95 I15 Lycksele Västerbotten, N Sweden 64.34N 18.40E
20 G13 Lycoming Creek ≈ Pennsylvania, NE USA
Lycopolis see Asyût
205 N3 Lyddan Island island Antarctica
85 K20 Lydenburg Mpumalanga, NE South Africa 25.01S 30.27E
121 L20 Lyel'chytsy Rus. Lel'chitsy. Homyel'skaya Voblasts', SE Belarus 51.46N 28.19E
121 P14 Lyenina Rus. Lenino. Mahilyowskaya Voblasts', E Belarus 54.26N 31.07E
120 L13 Lyepyel' Rus. Lepel'. Vitsyebskaya Voblasts', N Belarus 54.54N 28.43E
27 S17 Lyford Texas, SW USA 26.24N 97.47W
97 E17 Lygna ≈ S Norway
20 G14 Lykens Pennsylvania, NE USA 40.33N 76.42W
117 E21 Lykódimo ▲ S Greece 36.56N 21.49E
99 K24 Lyme Bay bay S England, UK
99 K24 Lyme Regis S England, UK 50.44N 2.55W
112 L7 Łyna Ger. Alle. ≈ N Poland
31 P12 Lynch Nebraska, C USA 42.49N 98.27W
22 J10 Lynchburg Tennessee, S USA 35.15N 86.22W
23 T6 Lynchburg Virginia, NE USA 37.24N 79.08W
23 T12 Lynches River ≈ South Carolina, SE USA
34 H6 Lynden Washington, NW USA 48.57N 122.27W
190 I5 Lyndhurst South Australia 30.19S 138.20E
29 Q5 Lyndon Kansas, C USA 38.37N 95.40W
21 N7 Lyndonville Vermont, NE USA 44.31N 71.58W
97 D18 Lyngdal Vest-Agder, S Norway 58.07N 7.04E
94 I9 Lyngen inlet Arctic Ocean
97 G17 Lyngør Aust-Agder, S Norway 58.38N 9.05E
94 I9 Lyngseidet Troms, N Norway 69.36N 20.07E
21 P11 Lynn Massachusetts, NE USA 42.28N 70.57W
Lynn see King's Lynn
25 R9 Lynn Haven Florida, SE USA 30.15N 85.39W
9 V11 Lynn Lake Manitoba, C Canada 56.51N 101.01W
Lynn Regis see King's Lynn
120 I13 Lyntupy Rus. Lyntupy. Vitsyebskaya Voblasts', NW Belarus 55.03N 26.19E
105 R11 Lyon Eng. Lyons; anc. Lugdunum. Rhône, E France 45.46N 4.49E
15 H3 Lyon, Cape headland Northwest Territories, NW Canada 69.47N 123.10W
20 K6 Lyon Mountain ▲ New York, NE USA 44.42N 73.52W
105 Q11 Lyonnais, Monts du ▲▲ C France
67 N25 Lyon Point headland SE Tristan da Cunha 37.06S 12.13W
190 E5 Lyons South Australia 30.40S 133.50E
39 T3 Lyons Colorado, C USA 40.13N 105.16W
25 V6 Lyons Georgia, SE USA 32.12N 82.19W
28 M5 Lyons Kansas, C USA 38.21N 98.12W
31 R14 Lyons Nebraska, C USA 41.56N 96.28W
20 G10 Lyons New York, NE USA 43.03N 76.58W
Lyons see Lyon
120 O13 Lyozna Rus. Liozno. Vitsyebskaya Voblasts', NE Belarus 55.01N 30.48E
119 S4 Lypova Dolyna Sums'ka Oblast', NE Ukraine 50.36N 33.50E
119 N6 Lypovets' Rus. Lipovets. Vinnyts'ka Oblast', C Ukraine 49.13N 29.06E
Lys see Leie
113 I18 Lysá Hora ▲ E Czech Republic 49.31N 18.27E
97 D16 Lysefjorden fjord S Norway
97 I18 Lysekil Västra Götaland, S Sweden 58.16N 11.25E
Lysi see Akdoğan
35 V14 Lysite Wyoming, C USA 43.16N 107.42W
131 P3 Lyskovo Nizhegorodskaya Oblast', W Russian Federation 56.04N 45.01E
110 D8 Lyss Bern, W Switzerland 47.04N 7.19E
97 H22 Lystrup Århus, C Denmark 56.14N 10.14E
129 V14 Lys'va Permskaya Oblast', NW Russian Federation 58.04N 57.48E
119 P6 Lysyanka Cherkas'ka Oblast', C Ukraine 49.15N 30.50E
119 X6 Lysychans'k Rus. Lisichansk. Luhans'ka Oblast', E Ukraine 48.52N 38.27E
99 K17 Lytham St Anne's NW England, UK 53.45N 3.01W
193 I19 Lyttelton Canterbury, South Island, NZ 43.35S 172.44E
8 M17 Lytton British Columbia, SW Canada 50.12N 121.34W
121 L18 Lyuban' Rus. Lyuban'. Minskaya Voblasts', S Belarus 52.48N 28.00E
121 L18 Lyubanskaye Vodaskhovishcha ⊠ C Belarus
118 M5 Lyubar Zhytomyrs'ka Oblast', N Ukraine 49.54N 27.48E
Lyubashëvka see Lyubashivka
119 O8 Lyubashivka Rus. Lyubashëvka. Odes'ka Oblast', SW Ukraine 47.49N 30.18E
121 I16 Lyubcha Pol. Lubcz, Rus. Lyubcha. Hrodzyenskaya Voblasts', W Belarus 53.46N 26.04E
130 L4 Lyubertsy Moskovskaya Oblast', W Russian Federation 55.37N 38.02E
118 K2 Lyubeshiv Volyns'ka Oblast', NW Ukraine 51.46N 25.33E
128 M14 Lyubim Yaroslavskaya Oblast', NW Russian Federation 58.21N 40.46E
116 K11 Lyubimets Khaskovo, S Bulgaria 41.51N 26.03E
Lyublin see Lublin
118 I3 Lyuboml' Pol. Luboml. Volyns'ka Oblast', NW Ukraine 51.12N 24.01E
Lyubotin see Lyubotyn
119 U5 Lyubotyn Rus. Lyubotin. Kharkivs'ka Oblast', E Ukraine 49.57N 35.57E
130 I5 Lyudinovo Kaluzhskaya Oblast', W Russian Federation 53.52N 34.28E
131 T2 Lyuk Udmurtskaya Respublika, NW Russian Federation 56.55N 52.45E
116 M9 Lyulyakovo prev. Keremitlik. Burgas, E Bulgaria 42.53N 27.05E
121 I18 Lyusina Rus. Lyusino. Brestskaya Voblasts', SW Belarus 52.37N 26.31E
Lyusino see Lyusina

M

144 G9 Ma'ād Irbid, N Jordan 32.37N 35.36E
Maalahti see Malax
Maale see Male'
144 G13 Ma'ān Ma'ān, SW Jordan 30.10N 35.45E
144 H13 Ma'ān off. Muḩāfaẓat Ma'ān, var. Ma'an, Ma'ān. ⬖ governorate S Jordan
95 M16 Maaninka Itä-Suomi, C Finland 63.10N 27.19E
168 K7 Maanĭt Bulgan, C Mongolia 48.17N 103.29E
168 M8 Maanĭt Töv, C Mongolia 47.14N 107.34E
95 N15 Maanselkä Oulu, C Finland 63.53N 28.27E
167 Q8 Ma'anshan Anhui, E China 31.45N 118.31E
196 F16 Maap island Caroline Islands, W Micronesia
120 H3 Maardu Ger. Maart. Harjumaa, NW Estonia 59.28N 25.01E
Ma'aret-en-Nu'man see Ma'arrat an Nu'mān
101 K16 Maarheeze Noord-Brabant, SE Netherlands 51.19N 5.37E
Maarianhamina see Mariehamn
144 I4 Ma'arrat an Nu'mān var. Ma'aret-en-Nu'man, Fr. Maarret enn Naamâne. Idlib, NW Syria 35.40N 36.40E
Maarret enn Naamâne see Ma'arrat an Nu'mān
100 I11 Maarssen Utrecht, C Netherlands 52.07N 5.03E
Maart see Maardu
101 L17 Maas Fr. Meuse. ≈ W Europe see also Meuse
101 M15 Maasbree Limburg, SE Netherlands 51.22N 6.03E
101 L17 Maaseik prev. Maeseyck. Limburg, NE Belgium 51.04N 5.48E
179 R13 Maasin Leyte, C Philippines 10.10N 124.55E
101 L17 Maasmechelen Limburg, NE Belgium 50.58N 5.42E
100 G12 Maassluis Zuid-Holland, SW Netherlands 51.55N 4.15E
101 L18 Maastricht var. Maestricht; anc. Traietum ad Mosam, Traiectum Tungorum. Limburg, SE Netherlands 50.51N 5.42E
191 N18 Maatsuyker Group island group Tasmania, SE Australia
Maba see Qujiang
85 L20 Mabalane Gaza, S Mozambique 23.43S 32.37E
27 V7 Mabank Texas, SW USA 32.22N 96.06W
172 N10 Mabechi-gawa var. Mabuchi-gawa. ≈ Honshū, C Japan
99 O18 Mablethorpe E England, UK 53.20N 0.14E
176 W9 Maboi Papua, E Indonesia 1.00S 134.02E
85 M19 Mabote Inhambane, S Mozambique 22.03S 34.09E
34 J10 Mabton Washington, NW USA 46.13N 120.00W
Mabuchi-gawa see Mabechi-gawa
85 H20 Mabutsane Southern, S Botswana 24.22S 23.34E
65 G19 Macá, Cerro ▲ S Chile 45.07S 73.11W
62 Q9 Macaé Rio de Janeiro, SE Brazil 22.21S 41.48W
84 N13 Macaloge Niassa, N Mozambique 12.30S 35.25E
Macan see Bonerate, Kepulauan
167 N15 Macao Chin. Aomen, Port. Macau. S China
106 H9 Mação Santarém, C Portugal 39.33N 8.00W
60 J11 Macapá state capital Amapá, N Brazil 0.04N 51.04W
45 S17 Macaracas Los Santos, S Panama 7.43N 80.33W
57 P6 Macare, Caño ≈ NE Venezuela
57 Q6 Macareo, Caño ≈ NE Venezuela
Macarsca see Makarska

MacArthur *see* Ormoc
190 *L12* **Macarthur** Victoria, SE Australia *38.04S 142.02E*
58 *C7* **Macas** Morona Santiago, SE Ecuador *2.22S 78.07W*
Macassar *see* Ujungpandang
61 *Q14* **Macau** Rio Grande do Norte, E Brazil *5.04S 36.37W*
Macau *see* Macao
Macău *see* Makó, Hungary
67 *E24* **Macbride Head** *headland* East Falkland, Falkland Islands *51.25S 57.55W*
25 *V9* **Macclenny** Florida, SE USA *30.16N 82.07W*
99 *L18* **Macclesfield** C England, UK *53.16N 2.07W*
198 *F6* **Macclesfield Bank** *undersea feature* N South China Sea
MacCluer Gulf *see* Berau, Teluk
189 *N7* **Macdonald, Lake** *salt lake* Western Australia
189 *Q7* **Macdonnell Ranges** ⛰ Northern Territory, C Australia
98 *K8* **Macduff** NE Scotland, UK *57.39N 2.28W*
106 *I6* **Macedo de Cavaleiros** Bragança, N Portugal *41.31N 6.57W*
Macedonia Central *see* Kentrikí Makedonía
Macedonia East and Thrace *see* Anatolikí Makedonía kai Thráki
115 *O19* **Macedonia, FYR** ***off.*** the Former Yugoslav Republic of Macedonia, ***var.*** Macedonia, Mac. Makedonija, ***abbrev.*** FYR Macedonia, FYROM. ◆ *republic* SE Europe
Macedonia West *see* Dytikí Makedonía
61 *Q16* **Maceió** *state capital* Alagoas, E Brazil *9.40S 35.43W*
78 *K15* **Macenta** Guinée-Forestière, SE Guinea *8.31N 9.31W*
108 *J12* **Macerata** Marche, C Italy *43.19N 13.28E*
9 *S11* **MacFarlane** ≈ Saskatchewan, C Canada
190 *H7* **Macfarlane, Lake** ***var.*** Lake Mcfarlane. ◎ South Australia
Macgillicuddy's Reeks Mountains *see* Macgillycuddy's Reeks
99 *B21* **Macgillycuddy's Reeks** ***var.*** Macgillicuddy's Reeks Mountains, ***Ir.*** Na Cruacha Dubha. ⛰ SW Ireland
9 *X16* **MacGregor** Manitoba, S Canada *49.58N 98.49W*
155 *O10* **Mach** Baluchistān, SW Pakistan *29.52N 67.19E*
58 *C6* **Machachi** Pichincha, C Ecuador *0.33S 78.34W*
85 *M19* **Machaila** Gaza, S Mozambique *22.15S 32.57E*
Machaire Fíolta *see* Magherafelt
Machaire Rátha *see* Maghera
83 *I19* **Machakos** Eastern, S Kenya *1.33S 37.17E*
58 *B8* **Machala** El Oro, SW Ecuador *3.19S 79.57W*
85 *J19* **Machaneng** Central, SE Botswana *23.12S 27.28E*
85 *M18* **Machanga** Sofala, E Mozambique *20.55S 35.03E*
82 *G13* **Machar Marshes** *wetland* SE Sudan
104 *I8* **Machecoul** Loire-Atlantique, NW France *46.59N 1.51W*
167 *O8* **Macheng** Hubei, C China *31.10N 115.00E*
161 *J16* **Mācherla** Andhra Pradesh, C India *16.28N 79.25E*
159 *O11* **Machhapuchhre** ▲ C Nepal *28.30N 83.57E*
21 *T6* **Machias** Maine, NE USA *44.43N 67.28W*
21 *R3* **Machias River** ≈ Maine, NE USA
21 *T6* **Machias River** ≈ Maine, NE USA
66 *P5* **Machico** Madeira, Portugal, NE Atlantic Ocean *32.43N 16.46W*
161 *K16* **Machilīpatnam** ***var.*** Bandar Masulipatnam. Andhra Pradesh, E India *16.12N 81.10E*
56 *G5* **Machiques** Zulia, NW Venezuela *10.01N 72.40W*
59 *G15* **Machupicchu** Cusco, C Peru *13.07S 72.30W*
85 *M20* **Macia** ***var.*** Vila de Macia. Gaza, S Mozambique *25.01S 33.05E*
Macías Nguema Biyogo *see* Bioco, Isla de
118 *M13* **Măcin** Tulcea, SE Romania *45.15N 28.09E*
191 *T4* **Macintyre River** ≈ New South Wales/Queensland, SE Australia
189 *Y7* **Mackay** Queensland, NE Australia *21.10S 149.10E*
189 *O7* **Mackay, Lake** *salt lake* Northern Territory/Western Australia
8 *M13* **Mackenzie** British Columbia, W Canada *55.18N 123.09W*
15 *Gg6* **Mackenzie** ≈ Northwest Territories, NW Canada
205 *Y6* **Mackenzie Bay** *bay* Antarctica
8 *J1* **Mackenzie Bay** *bay* NW Canada
2 *D9* **Mackenzie Delta** *delta* Northwest Territories, NW Canada
207 *P8* **Mackenzie King Island** *island* Queen Elizabeth Islands, Northwest Territories, N Canada
14 *G5* **Mackenzie Mountains** ⛰ Northwest Territories, NW Canada
33 *Q5* **Mackinac, Straits of** ◎ Michigan, N USA
204 *K5* **Mackintosh, Cape** *headland* Antarctica *72.52S 60.00W*
9 *R15* **Macklin** Saskatchewan, S Canada *52.19N 109.51W*
191 *V6* **Macksville** New South Wales, SE Australia *30.39S 152.54E*
191 *V5* **Maclean** New South Wales, SE Australia *29.30S 153.15E*
85 *J24* **Maclear** Eastern Cape, SE South Africa *31.04S 28.22E*
191 *U6* **Macleay River** ≈ New South Wales, SE Australia
MacLeod *see* Fort Macleod
188 *G9* **Macleod, Lake** ◎ Western Australia
8 *I6* **Macmillan** ≈ Yukon Territory, NW Canada
32 *J12* **Macomb** Illinois, N USA *40.27N 90.40W*
109 *B18* **Macomer** Sardegna, Italy, C Mediterranean Sea *40.14N 8.46E*
84 *Q13* **Macomia** Cabo Delgado, NE Mozambique *12.15S 40.06E*
25 *T5* **Macon** Georgia, SE USA *32.48N 83.41W*
25 *N4* **Macon** Mississippi, S USA *33.06N 88.33W*
29 *U3* **Macon** Missouri, C USA *39.44N 92.28W*
105 *R10* **Mâcon** ***anc.*** Matisco, Matisco Ædourum. Saône-et-Loire, C France *46.19N 4.48E*
24 *J6* **Macon, Bayou** ≈ Arkansas/Louisiana, S USA
84 *G13* **Macondo** Moxico, E Angola *12.31S 23.45E*
85 *M16* **Macossa** Manica, C Mozambique *17.51S 33.54E*
9 *T12* **Macoun Lake** ◎ Saskatchewan, C Canada
32 *K14* **Macoupin Creek** ≈ Illinois, N USA
Macouria *see* Tonate
85 *N18* **Macovane** Inhambane, SE Mozambique *21.30S 35.07E*
191 *N17* **Macquarie Harbour** *inlet* Tasmania, SE Australia
199 *Ii15* **Macquarie Island** *island* NZ, SW Pacific Ocean
191 *T8* **Macquarie, Lake** *lagoon* New South Wales, SE Australia
191 *Q6* **Macquarie Marshes** *wetland* New South Wales, SE Australia
183 *O13* **Macquarie Ridge** *undersea feature* SW Pacific Ocean
191 *Q6* **Macquarie River** ≈ New South Wales, SE Australia
191 *P17* **Macquarie River** ≈ Tasmania, SE Australia
205 *V5* **Mac. Robertson Land** *physical region* Antarctica
99 *C21* **Macroom** ***Ir.*** Maigh Chromtha. SW Ireland *51.54N 8.57W*
44 *G5* **Macuelizo** Santa Bárbara, NW Honduras *15.21N 88.31W*
190 *G2* **Macumba River** ≈ South Australia
59 *I16* **Macusani** Puno, S Peru *14.07S 70.27W*
58 *E8* **Macusari, Río** ≈ N Peru
43 *U15* **Macuspana** Tabasco, SE Mexico *17.43N 92.36W*
144 *G10* **Ma'dabā** ***var.*** Mādabā, Madeba; ***anc.*** Medeba. Al 'Āşimah NW Jordan *31.43N 35.48E*
180 *G2* **Madagascar** ***off.*** Democratic Republic of Madagascar, ***Malg.*** Madagasikara; ***prev.*** Malagasy Republic. ◆ *republic* W Indian Ocean
180 *I5* **Madagascar** *island* W Indian Ocean
132 *L17* **Madagascar Basin** *undersea feature* W Indian Ocean
132 *L16* **Madagascar Plain** *undersea feature* W Indian Ocean
69 *Y14* **Madagascar Plateau** ***var.*** Madagascar Ridge, Madagascar Rise, ***Rus.*** Madagaskarskiy Khrebet. *undersea feature* W Indian Ocean
Madagascar Ridge/Madagascar Rise *see* Madagascar Plateau
Madagasikara *see* Madagascar
Madagaskarskiy Khrebet *see* Madagascar Plateau
66 *N2* **Madalena** Pico, Azores, Portugal, NE Atlantic Ocean *38.31N 28.15W*
79 *Y6* **Madama** Agadez, NE Niger *21.54N 13.43E*
116 *J12* **Madan** Smolyan, S Bulgaria *41.30N 24.58E*
161 *I19* **Madanapalle** Andhra Pradesh, E India *13.33N 78.31E*
194 *I11* **Madang** Madang, N PNG *5.09S 145.48E*
194 *I11* **Madang** ⬗ *province* N PNG
152 *G7* **Madaniyat** ***Rus.*** Madeniyet. Qoraqalpog'iston Respublikasi, W Uzbekistan *42.48N 59.00E*
Madanīyīn *see* Médenine
79 *U11* **Madaoua** Tahoua, SW Niger *14.06N 6.01E*
Madaras *see* Vtáčnik
159 *U15* **Madaripur** Dhaka, C Bangladesh *23.09N 90.10E*
79 *U12* **Madarounfa** Maradi, S Niger *13.16N 7.07E*
Mađarska *see* Hungary
152 *B13* **Madau** ***Turkm.*** Madaw. Balkanskiy Velayat, W Turkmenistan *38.11N 54.46E*
195 *P15* **Madau Island** *island* SE PNG
Madaw *see* Madau
21 *S1* **Madawaska** Maine, NE USA *47.19N 68.19W*
12 *J13* **Madawaska** ≈ Ontario, SE Canada
Madawaska Highlands *see* Haliburton Highlands
177 *G4* **Madaya** Mandalay, C Myanmar *22.12N 96.04E*
109 *K17* **Maddaloni** Campania, S Italy *41.03N 14.22E*
31 *O3* **Maddock** North Dakota, N USA *47.57N 99.31W*
101 *I14* **Made** Noord-Brabant, S Netherlands *51.40N 4.48E*
Madeba *see* Ma'dabā
66 *L9* **Madeira** ***var.*** Ilha de Madeira. *island* Madeira, Portugal, NE Atlantic Ocean
Madeira, Ilha de *see* Madeira
66 *O5* **Madeira Islands** ***Port.*** Região Autoónoma da Madeira. ⬗ *autonomous region* Madeira, Portugal, NE Atlantic Ocean
66 *L9* **Madeira Plain** *undersea feature* E Atlantic Ocean
66 *L9* **Madeira Ridge** *undersea feature* E Atlantic Ocean
61 *F14* **Madeira, Rio** ***Sp.*** Río Madera. ≈ Bolivia/Brazil ***see also*** Madera, Río
103 *J25* **Mädelegabel** ▲ Austria/Germany *47.18N 10.19E*
13 *X6* **Madeleine** ≈ Quebec, SE Canada
13 *X5* **Madeleine, Cap de la** *headland* Quebec, SE Canada *49.13N 65.20W*
11 *Q13* **Madeleine, Îles de la** ***Eng.*** Magdalen Islands. *island group* Quebec, E Canada
31 *U10* **Madelia** Minnesota, N USA *44.03N 94.26W*
37 *P3* **Madeline** California, W USA *41.02N 120.28W*
32 *K3* **Madeline Island** *island* Apostle Islands, Wisconsin, N USA
143 *O15* **Maden** Elâzığ, SE Turkey *38.24N 39.42E*
151 *V12* **Madeniyet** Vostochnyy Kazakhstan, E Kazakhstan *47.51N 78.37E*
Madeniyet *see* Madaniyat
42 *H5* **Madera** Chihuahua, N Mexico *29.10N 108.10W*
37 *Q10* **Madera** California, W USA *36.57N 120.02W*
58 *L13* **Madera, Río** ***Port.*** Rio Madeira. ≈ Bolivia/Brazil ***see also*** Madeira, Rio
108 *D6* **Madesimo** Lombardia, N Italy *46.20N 9.26E*
147 *O14* **Madhāb, Wādī** *dry watercourse* NW Yemen
159 *R13* **Madhepura** ***prev.*** Madhipure. Bihār, NE India *25.55N 86.48E*
Madhipure *see* Madhepura
159 *Q13* **Madhubani** Bihār, N India *26.21N 86.04E*
159 *Q15* **Madhupur** Bihār, NE India *24.16N 86.37E*
158 *K15* **Madhya Pradesh** ***prev.*** Central Provinces and Berar. ⬗ *state* C India
59 *K15* **Madidi, Río** ≈ W Bolivia
161 *F20* **Madikeri** ***prev.*** Mercara. Karnātaka, W India *12.28N 75.40E*
29 *O13* **Madill** Oklahoma, C USA *34.05N 96.46W*
81 *G21* **Madimba** Bas-Congo, SW Dem. Rep. Congo *4.58S 15.07E*
144 *M4* **Ma'dīn** Ar Raqqah, C Syria *35.45N 39.36E*
Madīnah, Minţaqat al *see* Al Madīnah
78 *M14* **Madinani** NW Ivory Coast *9.37N 6.57W*
147 *O17* **Madīnat ash Sha'b** ***prev.*** Al Ittiḩād. SW Yemen *12.52N 44.55E*
144 *K3* **Madīnat ath Thawrah** ***var.*** Ath Thawrah. Ar Raqqah, N Syria Asia *35.36N 39.00E*
181 *O6* **Madingley Rise** *undersea feature* W Indian Ocean
81 *E21* **Madingo-Kayes** Le Kouilou, S Congo *4.22S 11.40E*
81 *F21* **Madingou** La Bouenza, S Congo *4.10S 13.33E*
Madioen *see* Madiun
25 *U8* **Madison** Florida, SE USA *30.27N 83.24W*
25 *T3* **Madison** Georgia, SE USA *33.37N 83.28W*
33 *P15* **Madison** Indiana, N USA *38.44N 85.22W*
29 *P6* **Madison** Kansas, C USA *38.08N 96.08W*
21 *Q6* **Madison** Maine, NE USA *44.48N 69.52W*
31 *S9* **Madison** Minnesota, N USA *45.00N 96.12W*
24 *K5* **Madison** Mississippi, S USA *32.27N 90.07W*
31 *Q14* **Madison** Nebraska, C USA *41.49N 97.27W*
31 *R10* **Madison** South Dakota, N USA *44.00N 97.06W*
23 *V5* **Madison** Virginia, NE USA *38.24N 78.12W*
23 *Q5* **Madison** West Virginia, NE USA *38.04N 81.49W*
32 *L9* **Madison** *state capital* Wisconsin, N USA *43.04N 89.22W*
23 *T6* **Madison Heights** Virginia, NE USA *37.25N 79.07W*
22 *I6* **Madisonville** Kentucky, S USA *37.19N 87.30W*
22 *M10* **Madisonville** Tennessee, S USA *35.31N 84.21W*
27 *V9* **Madisonville** Texas, SW USA *30.57N 95.54W*
174 *Ll15* **Madiun** ***prev.*** Madioen. Jawa, C Indonesia *7.37S 111.33E*
Madjene *see* Majene
12 *J14* **Madoc** Ontario, SE Canada *44.31N 77.27W*
Madoera *see* Madura, Pulau
83 *J18* **Mado Gashi** North Eastern, E Kenya *0.40N 39.09E*
165 *R11* **Madoi** Qinghai, C China *34.53N 98.07E*
201 *O13* **Madolenihmw** Pohnpei, E Micronesia
120 *I9* **Madona** ***Ger.*** Modohn. Madona, E Latvia *56.51N 26.10E*
109 *J23* **Madonie** ⛰ Sicilia, Italy, C Mediterranean Sea
147 *Y11* **Madrakah, Ra's** *headland* E Oman *18.56N 57.54E*
34 *I12* **Madras** Oregon, NW USA *44.37N 121.07W*
Madras *see* Chennai
59 *H14* **Madre de Dios** ***off.*** Departamento de Madre de Dios. ⬗ *department* E Peru
65 *F22* **Madre de Dios, Isla** *island* S Chile
59 *J14* **Madre de Dios, Río** ≈ Bolivia/Peru
27 *T16* **Madre, Laguna** ◎ Texas, SW USA
43 *Q9* **Madre, Laguna** *lagoon* NE Mexico
39 *Q12* **Madre Mount** ▲ New Mexico, SW USA *34.18N 107.54W*
107 *N8* **Madrid** ● (Spain) Madrid, C Spain *40.25N 3.43W*
31 *V14* **Madrid** Iowa, C USA *41.52N 93.49W*
107 *N7* **Madrid** ⬗ *autonomous community* C Spain
107 *N10* **Madridejos** Castilla-La Mancha, C Spain *39.28N 3.31W*
106 *L7* **Madrigal de las Altas Torres** Castilla-León, N Spain *41.05N 5.00W*
106 *K10* **Madrigalejo** Extremadura, W Spain *39.08N 5.36W*
36 *L3* **Mad River** ≈ California, W USA
44 *J8* **Madriz** ⬗ *department* NW Nicaragua
106 *K10* **Madroñera** Extremadura, W Spain *39.25N 5.46W*
189 *N12* **Madura** Western Australia *31.52S 127.01E*
Madura *see* Madurai
161 *H22* **Madurai** ***prev.*** Madura, Mathurai. Tamil Nādu, S India *9.55N 78.07E*
174 *M15* **Madura, Pulau** ***prev.*** Madoera. *island* C Indonesia
174 *Mm15* **Madura, Selat** *strait* C Indonesia
131 *Q17* **Madzhalis** Respublika Dagestan, SW Russian Federation *42.12N 47.46E*
116 *K12* **Madzharovo** Khaskovo, S Bulgaria *41.36N 25.52E*
85 *M14* **Madzimoyo** Eastern, E Zambia *13.39S 32.31E*
171 *K15* **Maebashi** ***var.*** Maebasi, Mayebashi. Gunma, Honshū, S Japan *36.24N 139.01E*
Maebasi *see* Maebashi
178 *Hh6* **Mae Chan** Chiang Rai, NW Thailand *20.13N 99.52E*
178 *Gg7* **Mae Hong Son** ***var.*** Maehongson, Muai To. Mae Hong Son, NW Thailand *19.16N 97.55E*
Mae Nam Khong *see* Mekong
178 *Hh7* **Mae Nam Nan** ≈ NW Thailand
178 *H10* **Mae Nam Tha Chin** ≈ W Thailand
178 *Hh7* **Mae Nam Yom** ≈ W Thailand
178 *H7* **Mae Sariang** Mae Hong Son, NW Thailand *18.07N 97.57E*
39 *O3* **Maeser** Utah, W USA *40.28N 109.35W*
Maeseyck *see* Maaseik
178 *Gg9* **Mae Sot** ***var.*** Ban Mae Sot. Tak, W Thailand *16.43N 98.31E*
Maestricht *see* Maastricht
178 *H7* **Mae Suai** ***var.*** Ban Mae Suai. Chiang Rai, NW Thailand *19.36N 99.32E*
178 *H7* **Mae Tho, Doi** ▲ NW Thailand *18.56N 99.20E*
180 *I4* **Maevatanana** Mahajanga, C Madagascar *16.57S 46.49E*
197 *C12* **Maéwo** ***prev.*** Aurora. *island* C Vanuatu
175 *T8* **Mafa** Pulau Halmahera, E Indonesia *0.01N 127.49E*
85 *I23* **Mafeteng** W Lesotho *29.48S 27.15E*
101 *J21* **Maffe** Namur, SE Belgium *50.21N 5.19E*
176 *Y10* **Maffin** Papua, E Indonesia *1.57S 138.48E*
191 *P12* **Maffra** Victoria, SE Australia *37.59S 147.03E*
83 *K23* **Mafia** *island* E Tanzania
83 *J23* **Mafia Channel** *sea waterway* E Tanzania
85 *I21* **Mafikeng** North-West, N South Africa *25.52S 25.39E*
62 *J12* **Mafra** Santa Catarina, S Brazil *26.07S 49.46W*
106 *F10* **Mafra** Lisboa, C Portugal *38.57N 9.19W*
149 *Q17* **Mafraq** Abū Z̧aby, C UAE *24.21N 54.33E*
Mafraq/Mafraq, Muḩāfaz̧at al *see* Al Mafraq
127 *O10* **Magadan** Magadanskaya Oblast', E Russian Federation *59.37N 150.49E*
127 *Nn8* **Magadanskaya Oblast'** ⬗ *province* E Russian Federation
110 *G11* **Magadino** Ticino, S Switzerland *46.09N 8.50E*
65 *G23* **Magallanes** ***off.*** Región de Magallanes y de la Antártica Chilena. ⬗ *region* S Chile
Magallanes *see* Punta Arenas
Magallanes, Estrecho de *see* Magellan, Strait of
12 *I10* **Maganasipi, Lac** ◎ Quebec, SE Canada
56 *F6* **Magangué** Bolívar, N Colombia *9.13N 74.46W*
Magareva *see* Mangareva
79 *V12* **Magaria** Zinder, S Niger *13.00N 8.55E*
194 *M16* **Magarida** Central, SW PNG *10.13S 149.17E*
179 *Pp9* **Magat** ≈ Luzon, N Philippines
29 *T11* **Magazine Mountain** ▲ Arkansas, C USA *35.10N 93.38W*
78 *I15* **Magburaka** C Sierra Leone *8.43N 11.57W*
126 *M14* **Magdagachi** Amurskaya Oblast', SE Russian Federation *53.25N 125.41E*
64 *O12* **Magdalena** Buenos Aires, E Argentina *35.04S 57.30W*
59 *M15* **Magdalena** Beni, N Bolivia *13.22S 64.07W*
42 *F4* **Magdalena** Sonora, NW Mexico *30.37N 110.58W*
39 *Q13* **Magdalena** New Mexico, SW USA *34.07N 107.14W*
56 *F5* **Magdalena** ***off.*** Departamento del Magdalena. ⬗ *province* N Colombia
42 *E9* **Magdalena, Bahía** *bay* W Mexico
65 *G19* **Magdalena, Isla** *island* Archipiélago de los Chonos, S Chile
42 *D8* **Magdalena, Isla** *island* W Mexico
49 *P6* **Magdalena, Río** ≈ C Colombia
42 *F4* **Magdalena, Río** ≈ NW Mexico
Magdalen Islands *see* Madeleine, Îles de la
102 *L13* **Magdeburg** Sachsen-Anhalt, C Germany *52.07N 11.39E*
24 *L6* **Magee** Mississippi, S USA *31.52N 89.43W*
174 *Kk15* **Magelang** Jawa, C Indonesia *7.28S 110.10E*
199 *J7* **Magellan Rise** *undersea feature* C Pacific Ocean
65 *H24* **Magellan, Strait of** ***Sp.*** Estrecho de Magallanes. *strait* Argentina/Chile
108 *D7* **Magenta** Lombardia, NW Italy *45.28N 8.52E*
Magerøy *see* Magerøya
94 *K7* **Magerøya** ***var.*** Magerøy. *island* N Norway
170 *B17* **Mage-shima** *island* Nansei-shotō, SW Japan
110 *G11* **Maggia** Ticino, S Switzerland *46.15N 8.42E*
110 *G10* **Maggia** ≈ SW Switzerland
Maggiore, Lago *see* Maggiore, Lake
108 *C6* **Maggiore, Lake** ***It.*** Lago Maggiore. ◎ Italy/Switzerland
46 *I12* **Maggotty** W Jamaica *18.09N 77.46W*
78 *I10* **Maghama** Gorgol, S Mauritania *15.31N 12.49W*
99 *F14* **Maghera** ***Ir.*** Machaire Rátha. C Northern Ireland, UK *54.51N 6.40W*
99 *F15* **Magherafelt** ***Ir.*** Machaire Fíolta. C Northern Ireland, UK *54.45N 6.36W*
196 *H6* **Magicienne Bay** *bay* Saipan, S Northern Mariana Islands
107 *O13* **Magina** ▲ S Spain *37.43N 3.24W*
83 *H24* **Magingo** Ruvuma, S Tanzania *9.57S 35.23E*
126 *Jj14* **Magistral'nyy** Irkutskaya Oblast', S Russian Federation *56.18N 107.27E*
114 *H11* **Maglaj** Federacija Bosna I Hercegovina, N Bosnia and Herzegovina *44.32N 18.03E*
109 *Q19* **Maglie** Puglia, SE Italy *40.07N 18.18E*
38 *L2* **Magna** Utah, W USA *40.42N 112.06W*
Magnesia *see* Manisa
12 *G12* **Magnetawan** ≈ Ontario, S Canada
125 *Dd12* **Magnitogorsk** Chelyabinskaya Oblast', C Russian Federation *53.28N 59.06E*
29 *T14* **Magnolia** Arkansas, C USA *33.16N 93.14W*
24 *K7* **Magnolia** Mississippi, S USA *31.08N 90.27W*
27 *V10* **Magnolia** Texas, SW USA *30.12N 95.46W*
Magnolia State *see* Mississippi
97 *J15* **Magnor** Hedmark, S Norway *59.57N 12.14E*
197 *K14* **Mago** ***prev.*** Mango. *island* Lau Group, E Fiji
85 *L15* **Màgoé** Tete, NW Mozambique *15.51S 31.49E*
13 *Q13* **Magog** Quebec, SE Canada *45.16N 72.09W*
85 *J15* **Magoye** Southern, S Zambia *16.01S 27.37E*
43 *Q12* **Magozal** Veracruz-Llave, C Mexico *21.33N 97.57W*
12 *B7* **Magpie** ≈ Ontario, S Canada
9 *Q17* **Magrath** Alberta, SW Canada *49.27N 112.52W*
107 *R10* **Magro** ≈ E Spain
78 *I9* **Magṭa' Laḥjar** ***var.*** Magta Lahjar, Magta' Lahjar, Magtá Lahjar. Brakna, SW Mauritania *17.27N 13.07W*
85 *L20* **Magude** Maputo, S Mozambique *25.01S 32.40E*
79 *Y12* **Magumeri** Borno, NE Nigeria *12.07N 12.48E*
201 *O14* **Magur Islands** *island group* Caroline Islands, C Micronesia
Magway *see* Magwe
177 *Ff6* **Magwe** ***var.*** Magway. Magwe, W Myanmar *20.07N 94.59E*
177 *Ff6* **Magwe** ***var.*** Magway. ⬗ *division* C Myanmar
Magyar-Becse *see* Bečej
Magyarkanizsa *see* Kanjiža
Magyarország *see* Hungary
Magyarzsombor *see* Zimbor
148 *J4* **Mahābād** ***var.*** Mehabad; ***prev.*** Sāūjbulāgh. Āzarbāyjān-e Bākhtarī, NW Iran *36.43N 45.43E*
180 *H5* **Mahabo** Toliara, W Madagascar *20.22S 44.39E*
Maha Chai *see* Samut Sakhon
161 *D14* **Mahād** Mahārāshtra, W India *18.04N 73.21E*
83 *N17* **Mahadday Weyne** Shabeellaha Dhexe, C Somalia *2.55N 45.30E*
81 *Q17* **Mahagi** Orientale, NE Dem. Rep. Congo *2.16N 30.58E*
Mahāil *see* Muhāyil
180 *I4* **Mahajamba** *seasonal river* NW Madagascar
158 *G10* **Mahājan** Rājasthān, NW India *28.46N 73.49E*
180 *I3* **Mahajanga** ***var.*** Majunga. Mahajanga, NW Madagascar *15.40S 46.19E*
180 *I3* **Mahajanga** ⬗ *province* W Madagascar
180 *I3* **Mahajanga** ✈ Mahajanga, NW Madagascar *15.40S 46.19E*
175 *N7* **Mahakam, Sungai** ***var.*** Koetai, Kutai. ≈ Borneo, C Indonesia
85 *I19* **Mahalapye** ***var.*** Mahalatswe. Central, SE Botswana *23.01S 26.52E*
Mahalatswe *see* Mahalapye
Mahalla el Kubra *see* El Maḥalla el Kubra
175 *Q10* **Mahalona** Sulawesi, C Indonesia *2.37S 121.26E*
Mahameru *see* Semeru, Gunung
149 *S11* **Mahān** Kermān, E Iran *30.07N 57.15E*
160 *N12* **Mahānadi** ≈ E India
180 *J5* **Mahanoro** Toamasina, E Madagascar *19.52S 48.48E*
159 *P13* **Mahārājganj** Bihār, N India *26.07N 84.31E*
160 *G13* **Mahārāshtra** ⬗ *state* W India
180 *I4* **Mahavavy** *seasonal river* N Madagascar
161 *K24* **Mahaweli Ganga** ≈ C Sri Lanka
Mahbés *see* El Mahbas
161 *J15* **Mahbūbābād** Andhra Pradesh, E India *17.35N 80.00E*
161 *H16* **Mahbūbnagar** Andhra Pradesh, C India *16.45N 78.01E*
146 *M8* **Mahd adh Dhahab** Al Madīnah, W Saudi Arabia *23.33N 40.56E*
57 *S9* **Mahdia** C Guyana *5.16N 59.08W*
77 *N6* **Mahdia** ***var.*** Al Mahdīyah, Mehdia. NE Tunisia *35.14N 11.06E*
161 *F20* **Mahe** ***Fr.*** Mahé; ***prev.*** Mayyali. Pondicherry, SW India *11.44N 75.33E*
180 *I16* **Mahé** ✈ Mahé, NE Seychelles *4.37S 55.27E*
180 *H16* **Mahé** *island* Inner Islands, NE Seychelles
181 *Y17* **Mahebourg** SE Mauritius *20.24S 57.42E*
158 *L10* **Mahendranagar** Far Western, W Nepal *28.58N 80.13E*
83 *I23* **Mahenge** Morogoro, SE Tanzania *8.40S 36.40E*
193 *F22* **Maheno** Otago, South Island, NZ *45.10S 170.51E*
160 *D9* **Mahesāna** Gujarāt, W India *23.37N 72.28E*
160 *F11* **Maheshwar** Madhya Pradesh, C India *22.12N 75.40E*
157 *F14* **Mahi** ≈ N India
192 *Q10* **Mahia Peninsula** *peninsula* North Island, NZ
121 *O16* **Mahilyow** ***Rus.*** Mogilëv. Mahilyowskaya Voblasts', E Belarus *53.54N 30.23E*
121 *M16* **Mahilyowskaya Voblasts'** ***prev. Rus.*** Mogilëvskaya Oblast'. ⬗ *province* E Belarus
203 *P7* **Mahina** Tahiti, W French Polynesia *17.28S 149.27W*
193 *E23* **Mahinerangi, Lake** ◎ South Island, NZ
85 *L22* **Mahlabatini** KwaZulu/Natal, E South Africa *28.10S 31.27E*
177 *G5* **Mahlaing** Mandalay, C Myanmar *21.03N 95.43E*
111 *X8* **Mahldorf** Steiermark, SE Austria *46.54N 15.55E*
Mahmūd-e 'Erāqī *see* Maḩmūd-e Rāqī
155 *R4* **Maḩmūd-e Rāqī** ***var.*** Mahmūd-e 'Erāqī. Kāpīsā, NE Afghanistan *35.01N 69.19E*
Mahmudiya *see* Al Maḩmūdīyah
31 *S5* **Mahnomen** Minnesota, N USA *47.19N 95.58W*
158 *K14* **Mahoba** Uttar Pradesh, N India *25.18N 79.52E*
107 *Z9* **Mahón** ***Cat.*** Maó, ***Eng.*** Port Mahon; ***anc.*** Portus Magonis. Menorca, Spain, W Mediterranean Sea *39.54N 4.15E*
20 *D14* **Mahoning Creek Lake** ⊠ Pennsylvania, NE USA
107 *Q10* **Mahora** Castilla-La Mancha, C Spain *39.13N 1.43W*
Mähren *see* Moravia
Mährisch-Budwitz *see* Moravské Budějovice
Mährisch-Kromau *see* Moravský Krumlov
Mährisch-Neustadt *see* Uničov
Mährisch-Schönberg *see* Šumperk
Mährisch-Trübau *see* Moravská Třebová
Mährisch-Weisskirchen *see* Hranice
Māh-Shahr *see* Bandar-e Māhshahr
81 *N19* **Mahulu** Maniema, E Dem. Rep. Congo *1.04S 27.10E*
160 *C12* **Mahuva** Gujarāt, W India *21.06N 71.46E*
116 *N11* **Mahya Dağı** ▲ NW Turkey *41.47N 27.34E*
107 *T6* **Maials** ***var.*** Mayals. Cataluña, NE Spain *41.22N 0.30E*
203 *O2* **Maiana** ***prev.*** Hall Island. *atoll* Tungaru, W Kiribati
203 *S11* **Maiao** ***var.*** Tapuaemanu, Tubuai-Manu. *island* Îles du Vent, W French Polynesia
56 *H4* **Maicao** La Guajira, N Colombia *11.25N 72.15W*
Mai Ceu/Mai Chio *see* Maych'ew
105 *U8* **Maîche** Doubs, E France *47.15N 6.43E*
99 *N22* **Maidenhead** S England, UK *51.31N 0.43W*
9 *S15* **Maidstone** Saskatchewan, S Canada *53.06N 109.21W*
99 *P22* **Maidstone** SE England, UK *51.16N 0.31E*
79 *Y13* **Maiduguri** Borno, NE Nigeria *11.51N 13.09E*
110 *I8* **Maienfeld** Sankt Gallen, NE Switzerland *47.01N 9.30E*
118 *J12* **Măieruş** ***Hung.*** Szászmagyarós. Braşov, C Romania *45.55N 25.30E*
Maigh Chromtha *see* Macroom
Maigh Eo *see* Mayo
57 *N9* **Maigualida, Sierra** ⛰ S Venezuela
160 *K9* **Maihar** Madhya Pradesh, C India *24.18N 80.46E*
160 *K11* **Maikala Range** ⛰ C India
69 *T10* **Maiko** ≈ W Dem. Rep. Congo
Mailand *see* Milano
158 *L11* **Mailāni** Uttar Pradesh, N India *28.16N 80.19E*
155 *U10* **Māilsi** Punjab, E Pakistan *29.46N 72.15E*
153 *R8* **Maimak** Talasskaya Oblast', NW Kyrgyzstan *42.40N 71.12E*
Maimāna *see* Meymaneh
Maimansingh *see* Mymensingh
176 *Vv11* **Maimawa** Papua, E Indonesia *3.21S 133.36E*
Maimuna *see* Al Maymūnah
103 *G18* **Main** ≈ C Germany
117 *F22* **Maïna** *ancient monument* Pelopónnisos, S Greece *36.24N 22.28E*
117 *E20* **Maínalo** ⛰ S Greece
103 *L22* **Mainburg** Bayern, SE Germany *48.40N 11.48E*
Main Camp *see* Banana
12 *E12* **Main Channel** *lake channel* Ontario, S Canada
81 *I20* **Mai-Ndombe, Lac** ***prev.*** Lac Léopold II. ◎ W Dem. Rep. Congo
103 *K20* **Main-Donau-Kanal** *canal* SE Germany
21 *R6* **Maine** ***off.*** State of Maine; also known as Lumber State, Pine Tree State. ⬗ *state* NE USA
104 *K6* **Maine** *cultural region* NW France
104 *J7* **Maine-et-Loire** ⬗ *department* NW France
21 *Q9* **Maine, Gulf of** *gulf* NE USA
79 *X12* **Maïné-Soroa** Diffa, SE Niger *13.13N 12.05E*
178 *Gg1* **Maingkwan** ***var.*** Mungkawn. Kachin State, N Myanmar *26.19N 96.37E*
Main Island *see* Bermuda
Mainistir Fhear Maí *see* Fermoy
Mainistirna Búille *see* Boyle
Mainistir na Corann *see* Midleton
Mainistir na Féile *see* Abbeyfeale
98 *J5* **Mainland** *island* Orkney, N Scotland, UK
98 *L2* **Mainland** *island* Shetland, NE Scotland, UK
165 *P16* **Mainling** Xizang Zizhiqu, W China *29.12N 94.06E*
158 *K12* **Mainpuri** Uttar Pradesh, N India *27.13N 79.01E*
105 *N5* **Maintenon** Eure-et-Loir, C France *48.35N 1.34E*
180 *H4* **Maintirano** Mahajanga, W Madagascar *18.01S 44.03E*
95 *M15* **Mainua** Oulu, C Finland *64.05N 27.28E*
103 *G18* **Mainz** ***Fr.*** Mayence. Rheinland-Pfalz, SW Germany *50.00N 8.16E*
78 *I9* **Maio** ***var.*** Vila do Maio. Maio, S Cape Verde *15.07N 23.12W*
78 *E10* **Maio** ***var.*** Mayo. *island* Ilhas de Sotavento, SE Cape Verde
64 *G12* **Maipo, Río** ≈ C Chile
64 *H12* **Maipo, Volcán** ▲ W Argentina *34.09S 69.51W*
63 *E22* **Maipú** Buenos Aires, E Argentina *36.52S 57.52W*
64 *I11* **Maipú** Mendoza, E Argentina *33.00S 68.46W*
64 *H11* **Maipú** Santiago, C Chile *33.30S 70.52W*
56 *L5* **Maiquetía** Distrito Federal, N Venezuela *10.36N 66.57W*
110 *I10* **Maira** ***It.*** Mera. ≈ Italy/Switzerland
108 *A9* **Maira** ≈ NW Italy
159 *V12* **Mairābari** Assam, NE India *26.28N 92.22E*
46 *K7* **Maisí** Guantánamo, E Cuba *20.13N 74.08W*
120 *H13* **Maišiagala** Vilnius, SE Lithuania *54.52N 25.03E*
159 *V17* **Maiskhal Island** *island* SE Bangladesh
178 *Gg13* **Mai Sombun** Chumphon, SW Thailand *10.49N 99.13E*
Maisur *see* Karnātaka, India
Maisur *see* Mysore, India
191 *T8* **Maitland** New South Wales, SE Australia *32.47S 151.31E*
190 *I9* **Maitland** South Australia *34.21S 137.42E*
12 *F15* **Maitland** ≈ Ontario, S Canada
205 *R1* **Maitri** *Indian research station* Antarctica *70.03S 8.59E*
165 *N15* **Maizhokunggar** Xizang Zizhiqu, W China *29.49N 91.40E*
45 *O10* **Maíz, Islas del** ***var.*** Corn Islands. *island group* SE Nicaragua
171 *H14* **Maizuru** Kyōto, Honshū, SW Japan *35.28N 135.21E*
56 *F6* **Majagual** Sucre, N Colombia *8.36N 74.30W*
43 *Z13* **Majahual** Quintana Roo, E Mexico *18.43N 87.43W*
Majardah, Wādī *see* Medjerda, Oued/Mejerda
Mājeej *see* Mejit Island
175 *P11* **Majene** ***prev.*** Madjene. Sulawesi, C Indonesia *3.33S 118.58E*
45 *V15* **Majé, Serranía de** ⛰ E Panama
114 *I11* **Majevica** ⛰ NE Bosnia and Herzegovina
83 *H15* **Majī** Southern, S Ethiopia *6.11N 35.32E*
147 *X7* **Majīs** NW Oman *24.25N 56.34E*
Majorca *see* Mallorca
Mājro *see* Majuro Atoll
Majunga *see* Mahajanga
201 *Y3* **Majuro** ✈ Majuro Atoll, SE Marshall Islands *7.04N 171.07E*
201 *Y2* **Majuro Atoll** ***var.*** Mājro. *atoll* Ratak Chain, SE Marshall Islands
201 *X2* **Majuro Lagoon** *lagoon* Majuro Atoll, SE Marshall Islands
78 *H11* **Maka** C Senegal *13.39N 14.25W*
81 *F20* **Makabana** Le Niari, SW Congo *3.28S 12.36E*
40 *D9* **Makaha** ***Haw.*** Mākaha. Oahu, Hawaii, USA, C Pacific Ocean *21.28N 158.13W*
40 *B8* **Makahuena Point** *headland* Kauai, Hawaii, USA, C Pacific Ocean *21.52N 159.28W*
40 *D9* **Makakilo City** Oahu, Hawaii, USA, C Pacific Ocean *21.21N 158.05W*
85 *H18* **Makalamabedi** Central, C Botswana *20.18S 23.52E*
Makale *see* Mek'elē
164 *K17* **Makalu** ***Chin.*** Makaru Shan. ▲ China/Nepal *27.53N 87.09E*
83 *G23* **Makampi** Mbeya, S Tanzania *8.00S 33.17E*
151 *X12* **Makanchi** ***Kaz.*** Maqanshy. Vostochnyy Kazakhstan, E Kazakhstan *46.47N 82.00E*
44 *M8* **Makantaka** Región Autónoma Atlántico Norte, NE Nicaragua *13.13N 84.04W*
202 *B16* **Makapu Point** *headland* W Niue *18.58S 169.55E*
193 *C24* **Makarewa** Southland, South Island, NZ *46.17S 168.16E*
119 *O4* **Makariv** Kyyivs'ka Oblast', N Ukraine *50.28N 29.49E*
193 *D20* **Makarora** ≈ South Island, NZ
127 *Oo15* **Makarov** Ostrov Sakhalin, Sakhalinskaya Oblast', SE Russian Federation *48.24N 142.37E*
207 *R9* **Makarov Basin** *undersea feature* Arctic Ocean
199 *Hh4* **Makarov Seamount** *undersea feature* W Pacific Ocean *29.30N 153.30E*
115 *F15* **Makarska** ***It.*** Macarsca. Split-Dalmacija, SE Croatia *43.18N 17.00E*
Makaru Shan *see* Makalu
129 *O15* **Makar'yev** Kostromskaya Oblast', NW Russian Federation *57.52N 43.46E*
84 *L11* **Makasa** Northern, NE Zambia *9.42S 31.54E*
Makasar *see* Ujungpandang
Makasar, Selat *see* Makassar Straits
Makassar *see* Ujungpandang
198 *Ff8* **Makassar Straits** ***Ind.*** Selat Makasar. *strait* C Indonesia
150 *G12* **Makat** ***Kaz.*** Maqat. Atyrau, SW Kazakhstan *47.41N 53.24E*
203 *T10* **Makatea** *island* Îles Tuamotu, C French Polynesia
145 *U7* **Makātū** E Iraq *33.55N 45.25E*
180 *H6* **Makay** ***var.*** Massif du Makay. ⛰ SW Madagascar
116 *J12* **Makaza** *pass* Bulgaria/Greece *41.16N 25.26E*
176 *Uu9* **Makbon** Papua, E Indonesia *0.43S 131.30E*
Makedonija *see* Macedonia, FYR
202 *B16* **Makefu** W Niue *18.58S 169.55W*
203 *V10* **Makemo** *atoll* Îles Tuamotu, C French Polynesia
78 *I15* **Makeni** C Sierra Leone *8.57N 12.01W*
Makenzen *see* Orlyak
Makeyevka *see* Makiyivka

◆ Country ● Country Capital ◇ Dependent Territory ○ Dependent Territory Capital ⬗ Administrative Region ✈ International Airport ▲ Mountain ⛰ Mountain Range ⩙ Volcano ≈ River ◎ Lake ⊠ Reservoir

131 Q16 **Makhachkala** *prev.* Petrovsk-Port. Respublika Dagestan, SW Russian Federation *42.58N 47.30E*
150 F11 **Makhambet** Atyrau, W Kazakhstan *47.35N 51.35E*
Makharadze *see* Ozurget'i
145 W13 **Makhfar Al Buşayyah** S Iraq *30.09N 46.09E*
145 R4 **Makhmūr** N Iraq *35.46N 43.31E*
144 I11 **Makhrūq, Wadi al** *dry watercourse* E Jordan
145 R4 **Makḥūl, Jabal** ▲ C Iraq
147 R13 **Makhyah, Wādī** *dry watercourse* N Yemen
176 W11 **Maki** Papua, E Indonesia *3.00S 134.10E*
175 Ss8 **Makian, Pulau** *island* Maluku, E Indonesia
193 G21 **Makikihi** Canterbury, South Island, NZ *44.36S 171.09E*
203 O2 **Makin** *prev.* Pitt Island. *atoll* Tungaru, W Kiribati
83 I20 **Makindu** Eastern, S Kenya *2.15S 37.49E*
151 Q8 **Makinsk** Akmola, N Kazakhstan *52.37N 70.26E*
195 Y17 **Makira** *off.* Makira Province. ◈ *province* SE Solomon Islands
Makira *see* San Cristobal
119 X8 **Makiyivka** *Rus.* Makeyevka; *prev.* Dmitriyevsk. Donets'ka Oblast', E Ukraine *47.57N 37.47E*
146 L10 **Makkah** *Eng.* Mecca. Makkah, W Saudi Arabia *21.27N 39.50E*
146 M10 **Makkah** *var.* Minţaqat Makkah. ◈ *province* W Saudi Arabia
11 R7 **Makkovik** Newfoundland and Labrador, NE Canada *55.06N 59.06W*
100 K6 **Makkum** Friesland, N Netherlands *53.03N 5.25E*
Mako *see* Makung
113 M25 **Makó** *Rom.* Macău. Csongrád, SE Hungary *46.14N 20.28E*
12 G9 **Makobe Lake** ◎ Ontario, S Canada
197 I14 **Makogai** *island* C Fiji
81 F18 **Makokou** Ogooué-Ivindo, NE Gabon *0.37N 12.46E*
83 G23 **Makongolosi** Mbeya, S Tanzania *8.24S 33.09E*
83 E19 **Makota** SW Uganda *0.37S 30.12E*
81 G18 **Makoua** Cuvette, C Congo *0.01S 15.40E*
112 M10 **Maków Mazowiecki** Mazowieckie, C Poland *52.51N 21.06E*
113 K17 **Maków Podhalański** Małopolskie, S Poland *49.43N 19.40E*
149 V14 **Makran** *cultural region* Iran/Pakistan
158 G12 **Makrāna** Rājasthān, N India *27.01N 74.43E*
149 U15 **Makran Coast** *coastal region* SE Iran
121 F20 **Makrany** *Rus.* Mokrany. Brestskaya Voblasts', SW Belarus *51.49N 24.15E*
Makrinoros *see* Makrynóros
117 H20 **Makrónisosi** *island* Kykládes, Greece, Aegean Sea
117 D17 **Makrynóros** *var.* Makrinoros. ▲ C Greece
117 G19 **Makryplági** ▲ C Greece *38.00N 23.06E*
Maksamaa *see* Maxmo
128 J15 **Maksatikha** *var.* Maksatha, Maksaticha. Tverskaya Oblast', W Russian Federation *57.49N 35.46E*
160 G10 **Maksi** Madhya Pradesh, C India *23.18N 76.09E*
148 I1 **Mākū** Āzarbāyjān-e Bākhtarī, NW Iran *39.16N 44.33E*
159 Y11 **Mākum** Assam, NE India *27.28N 95.28E*
Makun *see* Makung
167 R14 **Makung** *prev.* Mako, Makun. W Taiwan *23.34N 119.34E*
170 Bb16 **Makurazaki** Kagoshima, Kyūshū, SW Japan *31.15N 130.15E*
79 V15 **Makurdi** Benue, C Nigeria *7.41N 8.35E*
125 F12 **Makushino** Kurganskaya Oblast', C Russian Federation *55.11N 67.16E*
40 L17 **Makushin Volcano** ▲ Unalaska Island, Alaska, USA *53.53N 166.55W*
85 K16 **Makwiro** Mashonaland West, N Zimbabwe *17.52S 30.24E*
59 D15 **Mala** Lima, W Peru *12.45S 76.38W*
Mala *see* Mallow, Ireland
Mala *see* Malaita, Solomon Islands
95 I14 **Malå** Västerbotten, N Sweden *65.12N 18.45E*
202 G12 **Mala'atoli** Île Uvea, E Wallis and Futuna
179 Qq15 **Malabang** E Mindanao, S Philippines *7.37N 124.04E*
161 E21 **Malabār Coast** *coast* SW India
81 C16 **Malabo** *prev.* Santa Isabel. ● (Equatorial Guinea) Isla de Bioco, NW Equatorial Guinea *3.43N 8.51E*
81 C16 **Malabo** ✕ Isla de Bioco, N Equatorial Guinea *3.44N 8.51E*
Malaca *see* Málaga
Malacca *see* Melaka
173 G4 **Malacca, Strait of** *Ind.* Selat Malaka. *strait* Indonesia/Malaysia
Malacka *see* Malacky
113 G20 **Malacky** *Hung.* Malacka. Bratislavský Kraj, W Slovakia *48.25N 17.01E*
35 R16 **Malad City** Idaho, NW USA *42.10N 112.16W*
119 Q4 **Mala Divytsya** Chernihivs'ka Oblast', N Ukraine *50.40N 32.13E*
121 J15 **Maladzyechna** *Pol.* Molodeczno, *Rus.* Molodechno. Minskaya Voblasts', C Belarus *54.19N 26.51E*
202 D12 **Malaee** Île Futuna, N Wallis and Futuna
39 V15 **Malaga** New Mexico, SW USA *32.10N 104.04W*
56 G8 **Málaga** Santander, C Colombia *6.42N 72.43W*
106 M15 **Málaga** *anc.* Malaca. Andalucía, S Spain *36.43N 4.25W*
106 L15 **Málaga** ◈ *province* Andalucía, S Spain
106 M15 **Málaga** ✕ Andalucía, S Spain *36.38N 4.36W*
Malagasy Republic *see* Madagascar
107 N10 **Malagón** Castilla-La Mancha, C Spain *39.10N 3.51W*
99 G18 **Malahide** *Ir.* Mullach Íde. E Ireland *53.27N 6.09W*
195 Y14 **Malaita** *off.* Malaita Province. ◈ *province* N Solomon Islands
195 Y15 **Malaita** *var.* Mala. *island* N Solomon Islands
82 F13 **Malakal** Upper Nile, S Sudan *9.31N 31.40E*
114 C10 **Mala Kapela** ▲ NW Croatia
27 V7 **Malakoff** Texas, SW USA *32.10N 96.00W*
Malakula *see* Malekula
155 V7 **Malakwāl** *var.* Mālikwāla. Punjab, E Pakistan *32.31N 73.18E*
194 J12 **Malalamai** Madang, W PNG *5.47S 146.40E*
194 J14 **Malalaua** Gulf, S PNG *8.04S 146.09E*
175 Q11 **Malamala** Sulawesi, C Indonesia *3.21S 120.58E*
174 M15 **Malang** Jawa, C Indonesia *7.58S 112.45E*
85 O14 **Malanga** Niassa, N Mozambique *13.27S 36.05E*
Malange *see* Malanje
94 I9 **Malangen** *sound* N Norway
84 C11 **Malanje** *var.* Malange. Malanje, NW Angola *9.33S 16.25E*
84 C11 **Malanje** *var.* Malange. ◈ *province* N Angola
154 M16 **Malān, Rās** *headland* SW Pakistan *25.13N 63.31E*
79 S13 **Malanville** NE Benin *11.49N 3.22E*
Malapane *see* Ozimek
161 F21 **Malappuram** Kerala, SW India *11.00N 76.02E*
45 T17 **Mala, Punta** *headland* S Panama *7.28N 79.58W*
97 N16 **Mälaren** ◎ C Sweden
64 H13 **Malargüe** Mendoza, W Argentina *35.31S 69.34W*
12 J8 **Malartic** Quebec, SE Canada *48.09N 78.09W*
121 F20 **Malaryta** *Pol.* Maloryta, *Rus.* Malorita. Brestskaya Voblasts', SW Belarus *51.46N 24.04E*
65 J19 **Malaspina** Chubut, SE Argentina *44.56S 66.52W*
41 U12 **Malaspina Glacier** *glacier* Alaska, USA
143 N15 **Malatya** *anc.* Melitene. Malatya, SE Turkey *38.22N 38.18E*
142 M14 **Malatya** ◈ *province* C Turkey
119 Q7 **Mala Vyska** *Rus.* Malaya Viska. Kirovohrads'ka Oblast', S Ukraine *48.37N 31.36E*
85 M14 **Malawi** *off.* Republic of Malaŵi; *prev.* Nyasaland, Nyasaland Protectorate. ◆ *republic* S Africa
Malawi, Lake *see* Nyasa, Lake
95 J17 **Malax** *Fin.* Maalahti. Länsi-Suomi, W Finland *62.55N 21.30E*
128 H14 **Malaya Vishera** Novgorodskaya Oblast', W Russian Federation *58.52N 32.12E*
Malaya Viska *see* Mala Vyska
179 R15 **Malaybalay** Mindanao, S Philippines *8.10N 125.08E*
148 L6 **Malāyer** *prev.* Daulatabad. Hamadān, W Iran *34.19N 48.46E*
174 Gg3 **Malay Peninsula** *peninsula* Malaysia/Thailand
174 I3 **Malaysia** *var.* Federation of Malaysia; *prev.* the separate territories of Federation of Malaya, Sarawak and Sabah (North Borneo) and Singapore. ◆ *monarchy* SE Asia
143 R14 **Malazgirt** Muş, E Turkey *39.09N 42.30E*
13 R8 **Malbaie** ≈ Quebec, SE Canada
79 T12 **Malbaza** Tahoua, S Niger *13.57N 5.32E*
112 J7 **Malbork** *Ger.* Marienburg, Marienburg in Westpreussen. Pomorskie, N Poland *54.01N 19.02E*
102 N9 **Malchin** Mecklenburg-Vorpommern, N Germany *53.43N 12.46E*
102 M9 **Malchiner See** ◎ NE Germany
101 D16 **Maldegem** Oost-Vlaanderen, NW Belgium *51.12N 3.27E*
100 L13 **Malden** Gelderland, SE Netherlands *51.46N 5.51E*
21 O11 **Malden** Massachusetts, NE USA *42.25N 71.04W*
29 Y8 **Malden** Missouri, C USA *36.33N 89.58W*
203 X4 **Malden Island** *prev.* Independence Island. *atoll* E Kiribati
181 Q6 **Maldives** *off.* Maldivian Divehi, Republic of Maldives. ◆ *republic* N Indian Ocean
Maldivian Divehi *see* Maldives
99 P21 **Maldon** E England, UK *51.43N 0.40E*
63 G20 **Maldonado** Maldonado, S Uruguay *34.57S 54.58W*
63 G20 **Maldonado** ◈ *department* S Uruguay
43 P17 **Maldonado, Punta** *headland* S Mexico *16.18N 98.31W*
157 K19 **Male'** *Div.* Maale ● (Maldives) Male' Atoll, C Maldives *4.10N 73.29E*
108 G6 **Malè** Trentino-Alto Adige, N Italy *46.21N 10.51E*
78 K13 **Maléa** *var.* Maléya. Haute-Guinée, NE Guinea *11.46N 9.43W*
117 G22 **Maléas, Akrotírio** *headland* S Greece *36.25N 23.11E*
117 L17 **Maléas, Akrotírio** *headland* Lésvos, E Greece *39.01N 26.36E*
157 K19 **Male' Atoll** *var.* Kaafu Atoll. *atoll* C Maldives
Malebo, Pool *see* Stanley Pool
160 E12 **Mālegaon** Mahārāshtra, W India *20.33N 74.31E*
83 F15 **Malek** Jonglei, S Sudan *6.04N 31.36E*
197 B13 **Malekula** *var.* Malakula; *prev.* Mallicolo. *island* W Vanuatu
201 Y15 **Malem** Kosrae, E Micronesia *5.16N 163.01E*
85 O15 **Malema** Nampula, N Mozambique *14.57S 37.28E*
81 N23 **Malemba-Nkulu** Katanga, SE Dem. Rep. Congo *8.01S 26.48E*
195 Q10 **Malendok Island** *island* Tanga Islands, NE PNG
128 K9 **Malen'ga** Respublika Kareliya, NW Russian Federation *63.50N 36.21E*
97 M20 **Målerås** Kalmar, S Sweden *56.55N 15.34E*
105 O6 **Malesherbes** Loiret, C France *48.18N 2.25E*
117 G18 **Malesína** Stereá Ellás, E Greece *38.37N 23.15E*
Maléya *see* Maléa
131 O15 **Malgobek** Chechenskaya Respublika, SW Russian Federation *43.34N 44.34E*
107 X5 **Malgrat de Mar** Cataluña, NE Spain *41.39N 2.45E*
82 C9 **Malha** Northern Darfur, W Sudan *15.07N 26.00E*
145 Q5 **Malḥāt** C Iraq *34.44N 42.41E*
34 K14 **Malheur Lake** ◎ Oregon, NW USA
34 L14 **Malheur River** ≈ Oregon, NW USA
78 I13 **Mali** Moyenne-Guinée, NW Guinea *12.07N 12.28W*
79 O9 **Mali** *off.* Republic of Mali, *Fr.* République du Mali; *prev.* French Sudan, Sudanese Republic. ◆ *republic* W Africa
175 S16 **Maliana** W East Timor *8.57S 125.25E*
178 H1 **Mali Hka** ≈ N Myanmar
Mali Idjoš *see* Mali Iđoš
114 K8 **Mali Iđoš** *var.* Mali Idjoš, *Hung.* Kishegyes; *prev.* Krivaja. Serbia, N Serbia and Montenegro (Yugoslavia) *45.43N 19.40E*
114 K9 **Mali Kanal** *canal* N Serbia and Montenegro (Yugoslavia)
175 R8 **Maliku** Sulawesi, N Indonesia *0.36S 123.13E*
Malik, Wadi al *see* Milk, Wadi el
Mālikwāla *see* Malakwāl
178 Gg12 **Mali Kyun** *var.* Tavoy Island. *island* Mergui Archipelago, S Myanmar
97 M19 **Målilla** Kalmar, S Sweden *57.24N 15.49E*
114 B11 **Mali Lošinj** *It.* Lussinpiccolo. Primorje-Gorski Kotar, W Croatia *44.31N 14.28E*
Malin *see* Malyn
179 Q15 **Malindang, Mount** ▲ Mindanao, S Philippines *8.12N 123.37E*
83 K20 **Malindi** Coast, SE Kenya *3.13S 40.04E*
Malines *see* Mechelen
98 E13 **Malin Head** *Ir.* Cionn Mhálanna. *headland* NW Ireland *55.37N 7.37W*
175 Pp7 **Malino, Gunung** ▲ Sulawesi, N Indonesia *0.44N 120.45E*
115 M21 **Maliq** *var.* Maliqi. Korçë, SE Albania *40.45N 20.45E*
Maliqi *see* Maliq
179 Rr16 **Malita** Mindanao, S Philippines *6.13N 125.39E*
160 G12 **Malkāpur** Mahārāshtra, C India *20.52N 76.18E*
142 B10 **Malkara** Tekirdağ, NW Turkey *40.55N 26.56E*
121 J19 **Mal'kavichy** *Rus.* Mal'kovichi. Brestskaya Voblasts', SW Belarus *52.28N 26.39E*
Malkiye *see* Al Mālikīyah
116 L11 **Malko Sharkovo, Yazovir** ▣ SE Bulgaria
116 N11 **Malko Tŭrnovo** Burgas, E Bulgaria *42.00N 27.33E*
Mal'kovichi *see* Mal'kavichy
191 R12 **Mallacoota** Victoria, SE Australia *37.34S 149.45E*
98 G10 **Mallaig** N Scotland, UK *57.03N 5.48W*
190 I9 **Mallala** South Australia *34.29S 138.30E*
77 W9 **Mallawi** C Egypt *27.49N 30.43E*
107 R5 **Mallén** Aragón, NE Spain *41.52N 1.25W*
108 F5 **Malles Venosta** Trentino-Alto Adige, N Italy *46.40N 10.37E*
Mallicolo *see* Malekula
111 Q8 **Mallnitz** Salzburg, S Austria *46.58N 13.09E*
107 W9 **Mallorca** *Eng.* Majorca; *anc.* Baleares Major. *island* Islas Baleares, Spain, W Mediterranean Sea
99 C20 **Mallow** *Ir.* Mala. SW Ireland *52.07N 8.39W*
95 E15 **Malm** Nord-Trøndelag, C Norway *64.04N 11.12E*
97 L19 **Malmbäck** Jönköping, S Sweden *57.34N 14.30E*
94 J12 **Malmberget** Norrbotten, N Sweden *67.09N 20.39E*
101 M20 **Malmédy** Liège, E Belgium *50.25N 6.01E*
85 E25 **Malmesbury** Western Cape, SW South Africa *33.28S 18.43E*
97 N16 **Malmköping** Södermanland, C Sweden *59.07N 16.49E*
97 K23 **Malmö** Skåne, S Sweden *55.35N 13.00E*
97 K23 **Malmo** ✕ Skåne, S Sweden *55.33N 13.23E*
47 Q16 **Malmok** *headland* Bonaire, S Netherlands Antilles *12.16N 68.21W*
97 M18 **Malmslätt** Östergötland, S Sweden *58.25N 15.30E*
129 R16 **Malmyzh** Kirovskaya Oblast', NW Russian Federation *56.30N 50.37E*
197 B12 **Malo** *island* W Vanuatu
130 J7 **Maloarkhangel'sk** Orlovskaya Oblast', W Russian Federation *52.25N 36.37E*
Maloelap *see* Maloelap Atoll
201 V6 **Maloelap Atoll** *var.* Maloelap. *atoll* E Marshall Islands
Maloenda *see* Malunda
110 I10 **Maloja** Graubünden, S Switzerland *46.25N 9.42E*
84 L12 **Malole** Northern, NE Zambia *10.05S 31.37E*
197 H13 **Malolo** *island* Mamanuca Group, W Fiji
197 H13 **Malolo Barrier Reef** *var.* Ro Ro Reef. *reef* W Fiji
179 P10 **Malolos** Luzon, N Philippines *14.51N 120.49E*
20 K6 **Malone** New York, NE USA *44.51N 74.18W*
81 K25 **Malonga** Katanga, S Dem. Rep. Congo *10.30S 23.06E*
113 L15 **Małopolska** *plateau* S Poland
113 K17 **Małopolskie** ◈ *province* S Poland
Malorita/Maloryta *see* Malaryta
128 K9 **Maloshuyka** Arkhangel'skaya Oblast', NW Russian Federation *63.43N 37.20E*
116 G10 **Mal'ovitsa** ▲ W Bulgaria *42.12N 23.19E*
151 V15 **Malovodnoye** Almaty, SE Kazakhstan *43.31N 77.42E*
96 C10 **Måløy** Sogn og Fjordane, S Norway *61.55N 5.06E*
130 K4 **Maloyaroslavets** Kaluzhskaya Oblast', W Russian Federation *55.03N 36.31E*
125 F6 **Malozemel'skaya Tundra** *physical region* NW Russian Federation
106 J10 **Malpartida de Cáceres** Extremadura, W Spain *39.25N 6.30W*
106 K9 **Malpartida de Plasencia** Extremadura, W Spain *39.58N 6.03W*
108 C7 **Malpensa** ✕ (Milano) Lombardia, N Italy *45.41N 8.40E*
78 J6 **Malqteïr** *desert* N Mauritania
120 J10 **Malta** Rēzekne, SE Latvia *56.19N 27.11E*
35 V7 **Malta** Montana, NW USA *48.21N 107.52W*
123 Jj14 **Malta** *off.* Republic of Malta. ◆ *republic* C Mediterranean Sea
111 R8 **Malta** *var.* Maltabach. ≈ S Austria
123 L11 **Malta** *island* C Mediterranean Sea
Maltabach *see* Malta
Malta, Canale di *see* Malta Channel
123 L12 **Malta Channel** *It.* Canale di Malta. *strait* Italy/Malta
85 D20 **Maltahöhe** Hardap, SW Namibia *24.49S 16.58E*
99 N16 **Malton** N England, UK *54.07N 0.49W*
175 T11 **Maluku** *off.* Propinsi Maluku, *Dut.* Molukken, *Eng.* Moluccas. ◈ *province* E Indonesia
175 Ss9 **Maluku** *Dut.* Molukken, *Eng.* Moluccas; *prev.* Spice Islands. *island group* E Indonesia
Maluku, Laut *see* Molucca Sea
79 V13 **Malumfashi** Katsina, N Nigeria *11.51N 7.39E*
175 P11 **Malunda** *prev.* Maloenda. Sulawesi, C Indonesia *2.58S 118.52E*
96 K13 **Malung** Dalarna, C Sweden *60.40N 13.45E*
96 K13 **Malungsfors** Dalarna, C Sweden *60.43N 13.34E*
195 X14 **Maluu** *var.* Malu'u. Malaita, N Solomon Islands *8.22S 160.39E*
161 D16 **Mālvan** Mahārāshtra, W India *16.05N 73.28E*
Malventum *see* Benevento
29 U12 **Malvern** Arkansas, C USA *34.21N 92.48W*
31 S15 **Malvern** Iowa, C USA *40.59N 95.36W*
46 I13 **Malvern** ▲ W Jamaica *17.59N 77.42W*
Malvinas, Islas *see* Falkland Islands
119 N4 **Malyn** *Rus.* Malin. Zhytomyrs'ka Oblast', N Ukraine *50.46N 29.14E*
127 O5 **Malyy Anyuy** ≈ NE Russian Federation
131 O11 **Malyye Derbety** Respublika Kalmykiya, SW Russian Federation *47.57N 44.39E*
Malyy Kavkaz *see* Lesser Caucasus
126 M5 **Malyy Lyakhovskiy, Ostrov** *island* NE Russian Federation
Malyy Pamir *see* Little Pamir
126 Jj4 **Malyy Taymyr, Ostrov** *island* Severnaya Zemlya, N Russian Federation
150 E10 **Malyy Uzen'** *Kaz.* Kishiözen. ≈ Kazakhstan/Russian Federation
126 I16 **Malyy Yenisey** *var.* Ka-Krem. ≈ S Russian Federation
126 K13 **Mama** Irkutskaya Oblast', C Russian Federation *58.13N 112.45E*
131 S3 **Mamadysh** Respublika Tatarstan, W Russian Federation *55.46N 51.22E*
119 N14 **Mamaia** Constanța, E Romania *44.13N 28.37E*
197 G14 **Mamanuca Group** *island group* Yasawa Group, W Fiji
152 L13 **Mamash** Lebapskiy Velayat, E Turkmenistan *38.24N 64.12E*
176 W11 **Mamasiware** Papua, E Indonesia *2.46S 134.26E*
194 L14 **Mambare** ≈ S PNG
81 O17 **Mambasa** Orientale, NE Dem. Rep. Congo *1.22N 29.02E*
176 Xx10 **Mamberamo, Sungai** ≈ Papua, E Indonesia
81 G15 **Mambéré** ≈ SW Central African Republic
81 G15 **Mambéré-Kadéï** ◈ *prefecture* SW Central African Republic
176 X9 **Mambetaloi** Papua, E Indonesia *1.38S 136.12E*
Mambij *see* Manbij
81 H18 **Mambili** ≈ W Congo
85 N18 **Mambone** *var.* Nova Mambone. Inhambane, E Mozambique *20.59S 35.04E*
179 P11 **Mamburao** Mindoro, N Philippines *13.16N 120.36E*
180 I16 **Mamelles** *island* Inner Islands, NE Seychelles
101 M25 **Mamer** Luxembourg, SW Luxembourg *49.37N 6.01E*
104 L6 **Mamers** Sarthe, NW France *48.21N 0.22E*
81 D15 **Mamfe** Sud-Ouest, W Cameroon *5.46N 9.18E*
151 P6 **Mamlyutka** Severnyy Kazakhstan, N Kazakhstan *54.55N 68.31E*
38 M15 **Mammoth** Arizona, SW USA *32.43N 110.38W*
35 S12 **Mammoth Hot Springs** Wyoming, C USA *44.57N 110.40W*
Mamoedjoe *see* Mamuju
121 A14 **Mamonovo** *Ger.* Heiligenbeil. Kaliningradskaya Oblast', W Russian Federation *54.28N 19.57E*
59 L14 **Mamoré, Rio** ≈ Bolivia/Brazil
78 I14 **Mamou** Moyenne-Guinée, W Guinea *10.34N 12.45W*
24 H8 **Mamou** Louisiana, S USA *30.37N 92.25W*
180 I14 **Mamoudzou** ○ (Mayotte) C Mayotte *12.48S 45.00E*
180 I3 **Mampikony** Mahajanga, N Madagascar *16.03S 47.39E*
79 P16 **Mampong** C Ghana *7.01N 1.36W*
112 M7 **Mamry, Jezioro** *Ger.* Mauersee. ◎ NE Poland
175 P10 **Mamuju** *prev.* Mamoedjoe. Sulawesi, S Indonesia *2.40S 118.51E*
175 Oo10 **Mamuju, Teluk** *bay* Sulawesi, C Indonesia
85 F19 **Mamuno** Ghanzi, W Botswana *22.15S 20.01E*
115 K19 **Mamuras** *var.* Mamurasi, Mamurras. Lezhë, C Albania *41.34N 19.42E*
Mamurasi/Mamurras *see* Mamuras
78 L16 **Man** W Ivory Coast *7.24N 7.33W*
57 X9 **Mana** NW French Guiana *5.40N 53.49W*
58 A6 **Manabí** ◈ *province* W Ecuador
44 G4 **Manabique, Punta** *var.* Cabo Tres Puntas. *headland* E Guatemala *15.57N 88.37W*
56 G11 **Manacacías, Río** ≈ C Colombia
60 F13 **Manacapuru** Amazonas, N Brazil *3.16S 60.37W*
175 Rr6 **Manado** *prev.* Menado. Sulawesi, C Indonesia *1.31N 124.55E*
196 H5 **Managaha** *island* S Northern Mariana Islands
101 G20 **Manage** Hainaut, S Belgium *50.30N 4.13E*
44 J10 **Managua** ● (Nicaragua) Managua, W Nicaragua *12.07N 86.15W*
44 J10 **Managua** ◈ *department* W Nicaragua
44 J10 **Managua** ✕ Managua, W Nicaragua *12.07N 86.11W*
44 J10 **Managua, Lago de** *var.* Xolotlán. ◎ W Nicaragua
Manah *see* Bilād Manaḥ
20 K16 **Manahawkin** New Jersey, NE USA *39.39N 74.12W*
192 K11 **Manaia** Taranaki, North Island, NZ *39.32S 174.04E*
180 J6 **Manakara** Fianarantsoa, SE Madagascar *22.09S 48.00E*
158 J7 **Manāli** Himāchal Pradesh, NW India *32.18N 77.12E*
133 U12 **Ma, Nam** *Vtn.* Sông Mã. ≈ Laos/Vietnam
Manama *see* Al Manāmah
194 I10 **Manam Island** *island* N PNG
69 Y13 **Mananara** ≈ SE Madagascar
190 M9 **Manangatang** Victoria, SE Australia *35.04S 142.53E*
180 J6 **Mananjary** Fianarantsoa, SE Madagascar *21.13S 48.19E*
78 L14 **Manankoro** Sikasso, SW Mali *10.33N 7.25W*
78 J12 **Manantali, Lac de** ▣ W Mali
Manáos *see* Manaus
193 B23 **Manapouri** Southland, South Island, NZ *45.33S 167.38E*
193 B23 **Manapouri, Lake** ◎ South Island, NZ
60 F13 **Manaquiri** Amazonas, NW Brazil *3.27S 60.37W*
Manar *see* Mannar
164 K5 **Manas** Xinjiang Uygur Zizhiqu, NW China *44.16N 86.12E*
159 U12 **Manās** *var.* Dangme Chu. ≈ Bhutan/India
153 R8 **Manas, Gora** ▲ Kyrgyzstan/Uzbekistan *42.17N 71.04E*
164 K3 **Manas Hu** ◎ NW China
159 P10 **Manaslu** ▲ C Nepal *28.33N 84.33E*
39 S8 **Manassa** Colorado, C USA *37.10N 105.56W*
23 W4 **Manassas** Virginia, NE USA *38.45N 77.28W*
47 T5 **Manatí** C Puerto Rico *18.26N 66.29W*
175 S16 **Manatuto** N East Timor *8.31S 126.00E*
194 L14 **Manau** Northern, S PNG *8.05S 147.57E*
56 H4 **Manaure** La Guajira, N Colombia *11.46N 72.28W*
60 F12 **Manaus** *prev.* Manáos. *state capital* Amazonas, NW Brazil *03.06S 60.00W*
142 G17 **Manavgat** Antalya, SW Turkey *36.46N 31.28E*
192 M13 **Manawatu** ≈ North Island, NZ
192 L11 **Manawatu-Wanganui** *off.* Manawatu-Wanganui Region. ◈ *region* North Island, NZ
176 Uu12 **Manawoka, Pulau** *island* Kepulauan Gorong, E Indonesia
179 Rr16 **Manay** Mindanao, S Philippines *7.12N 126.29E*
144 K2 **Manbij** *var.* Mambij, *Fr.* Membidj. Ḥalab, N Syria *36.31N 37.55E*
107 N13 **Mancha Real** Andalucía, S Spain *37.46N 3.37W*
104 I4 **Manche** ◈ *department* N France
99 L17 **Manchester** *Lat.* Mancunium. NW England, UK *53.30N 2.15W*
25 S5 **Manchester** Georgia, SE USA *32.51N 84.37W*
31 Y13 **Manchester** Iowa, C USA *42.28N 91.27W*
23 N7 **Manchester** Kentucky, S USA *37.10N 83.40W*
21 O10 **Manchester** New Hampshire, NE USA *42.58N 71.25W*
22 K10 **Manchester** Tennessee, S USA *35.28N 86.05W*
20 M9 **Manchester** Vermont, NE USA *43.09N 73.03W*
99 L18 **Manchester** ✕ NW England, UK *53.21N 2.16W*
155 P15 **Manchhar Lake** ◎ SE Pakistan
Man-chou-li *see* Manzhouli
133 X7 **Manchurian Plain** *plain* NE China
Máncio Lima *see* Japiim
Mancunium *see* Manchester
154 J15 **Mand** Balūchistān, SW Pakistan *26.06N 61.58E*
Mand *see* Mand, Rūd-e
83 H25 **Manda** Iringa, SW Tanzania *10.25S 34.38E*
180 H6 **Mandabe** Toliara, W Madagascar *21.01S 44.55E*
168 I5 **Mandal** Hövsgöl, N Mongolia *49.55N 99.21E*
168 L7 **Mandal** Töv, C Mongolia *48.24N 106.47E*
97 E18 **Mandal** Vest-Agder, S Norway *58.01N 7.27E*
177 G5 **Mandalay** Mandalay, C Myanmar *21.57N 96.04E*
177 G6 **Mandalay** ◈ *division* C Myanmar
168 L9 **Mandalgovĭ** Dundgovĭ, C Mongolia *45.47N 106.18E*
145 V7 **Mandalī** E Iraq *33.43N 45.33E*
97 E18 **Mandalselva** ≈ S Norway
30 M5 **Mandan** North Dakota, N USA *46.49N 100.53W*
Mandargiri Hill *see* Mandār Hill
159 R14 **Mandār Hill** *prev.* Mandargiri Hill. Bihār, NE India *24.51N 87.03E*
175 P11 **Mandar, Teluk** *bay* Sulawesi, C Indonesia
109 C19 **Mandas** Sardegna, Italy, C Mediterranean Sea *39.40N 9.07E*
Mandasor *see* Mandsaur
83 L16 **Mandera** North Eastern, NE Kenya *3.55N 41.52E*
35 V13 **Manderson** Wyoming, C USA *44.13N 107.55W*
46 J12 **Mandeville** C Jamaica *18.01N 77.31W*
24 K9 **Mandeville** Louisiana, S USA *30.21N 90.04W*
158 I7 **Mandi** Himāchal Pradesh, NW India *31.40N 76.58E*
78 K14 **Mandiana** Haute-Guinée, E Guinea *10.37N 8.39W*
155 U10 **Mandi Būrewāla** *var.* Būrewāla. Punjab, E Pakistan *30.04N 72.46E*
158 G9 **Mandi Dabwāli** Haryāna, NW India *29.55N 74.40E*
Mandidzudzure *see* Chimanimani
85 M15 **Mandié** Manica, NW Mozambique *16.27S 33.28E*
85 N14 **Mandimba** Niassa, N Mozambique *14.21S 35.40E*
175 Ss9 **Mandioli, Pulau** *island* Kepulauan Bacan, E Indonesia
59 Q19 **Mandioré, Laguna** ◎ E Bolivia
160 J10 **Mandla** Madhya Pradesh, C India *22.39N 80.21E*
85 M20 **Mandlakazi** *var.* Manjacaze. Gaza, S Mozambique *24.43S 33.57E*
97 E24 **Mandø** *var.* Manø. *island* W Denmark
176 Ww9 **Mandori** Papua, E Indonesia *1.01S 134.58E*
Mandoúdhion/Mandoudi *see* Mantoúdi
117 G19 **Mándra** Attikí, C Greece *38.04N 23.31E*
180 I7 **Mandrare** ≈ S Madagascar
116 M10 **Mandra, Yazovir** *salt lake* SE Bulgaria
109 L23 **Mandrazzi, Portella** *pass* Sicilia, Italy, C Mediterranean Sea *37.57N 15.02E*
180 J3 **Mandritsara** Mahajanga, N Madagascar *15.49S 48.49E*
149 O13 **Mand, Rūd-e** *var.* Mand. ≈ S Iran
160 F9 **Mandsaur** *prev.* Mandasor. Madhya Pradesh, C India *24.05N 75.04E*
160 F11 **Māndu** Madhya Pradesh, C India *22.22N 75.24E*
175 Oo5 **Mandul, Pulau** *island* N Indonesia
85 G15 **Mandundu** Western, W Zambia *16.34S 22.18E*
188 I13 **Mandurah** Western Australia *32.31S 115.40E*
109 P18 **Manduria** Puglia, SE Italy *40.24N 17.37E*
161 G20 **Mandya** Karnātaka, C India *12.34N 76.55E*
79 P12 **Mané** C Burkina *12.59N 1.21W*
108 E8 **Manerbio** Lombardia, NW Italy *45.22N 10.09E*
Manevichi *see* Manevychi
118 K3 **Manevychi** *Pol.* Maniewicze, *Rus.* Manevichi. Volyns'ka Oblast', NW Ukraine *51.18N 25.29E*
109 N16 **Manfredonia** Puglia, SE Italy *41.38N 15.54E*
109 N16 **Manfredonia, Golfo di** *gulf* Adriatic Sea, N Mediterranean Sea
79 P13 **Manga** C Burkina *11.40N 1.04W*
61 L16 **Mangabeiras, Chapada das** ▲ E Brazil
81 J20 **Mangai** Bandundu, W Dem. Rep. Congo *3.57S 19.32E*
202 L17 **Mangaia** *island group* S Cook Islands
192 M9 **Mangakino** Waikato, North Island, NZ *38.22S 175.45E*
118 M15 **Mangalia** *anc.* Callatis. Constanța, SE Romania *43.48N 28.34E*
80 J11 **Mangalmé** Guéra, SE Chad *12.25N 19.37E*
161 E19 **Mangalore** Karnātaka, W India *12.54N 74.51E*
203 Y13 **Mangareva** *var.* Magareva. *island* Îles Tuamotu, SE French Polynesia
85 I23 **Mangaung** Free State, C South Africa *29.10S 26.19E*
Mangaung *see* Bloemfontein
160 K9 **Mangawān** Madhya Pradesh, C India *24.39N 81.33E*
192 M11 **Mangaweka** Manawatu-Wanganui, North Island, NZ *39.49S 175.47E*
192 N11 **Mangaweka** ▲ North Island, NZ *39.51S 176.06E*
81 P17 **Mangbwalu** Orientale, NE Dem. Rep. Congo *2.06N 30.04E*
103 L24 **Mangfall** ≈ SE Germany
174 K11 **Manggar** Pulau Belitung, W Indonesia *2.52S 108.14E*
176 Vv12 **Manggawitu** Papua, E Indonesia *4.11S 133.28E*
177 G2 **Mangin Range** ▲ N Myanmar
145 R1 **Mangish** N Iraq *37.03N 43.04E*
150 E13 **Mangistau** *Kaz.* Mangqystaū Oblysy; *prev.* Mangyshlakskaya. ◈ *province* SW Kazakhstan
Mangit *see* Mang'it
152 H8 **Mang'it** *Rus.* Mangit. Qoraqalpog'iston Respublikasi, W Uzbekistan *42.06N 60.02E*
56 A13 **Manglares, Cabo** *headland* SW Colombia *1.36N 79.01W*
155 V6 **Mangla Reservoir** ▣ NE Pakistan
165 N9 **Mangnai** *var.* Lao Mangnai. Qinghai, C China *37.52N 91.39E*
Mango *see* Mago, Fiji
Mango *see* Sansanné-Mango, Togo
Mangoche *see* Mangochi
85 N14 **Mangochi** *var.* Mangoche; *prev.* Fort Johnston. Southern, SE Malawi *14.27S 35.15E*
79 N14 **Mangodara** SW Burkina *9.49N 4.22W*
180 H6 **Mangoky** ≈ W Madagascar
175 S10 **Mangole, Pulau** *island* Kepulauan Sula, E Indonesia
192 J2 **Mangonui** Northland, North Island, NZ *35.00S 173.30E*
Mangqystaū Oblysy *see* Mangistau
Mangqystaū Shyghanaghy *see* Mangyshlakskiy Zaliv
106 H7 **Mangualde** Viseu, N Portugal *40.36N 7.46W*
63 H18 **Mangueira, Lagoa** ◎ S Brazil
79 X6 **Manguéni, Plateau du** ▲ NE Niger
28 K11 **Mangum** Oklahoma, C USA *34.52N 99.30W*
81 O18 **Mangurdjipa** Nord Kivu, E Dem. Rep. Congo *0.28N 28.33E*
85 L16 **Mangwendi** Mashonaland East, E Zimbabwe *18.22S 31.24E*
150 F15 **Mangyshlak, Plato** *plateau* SW Kazakhstan
150 E14 **Mangyshlakskiy Zaliv** *Kaz.* Mangqystaū Shyghanaghy. *gulf* SW Kazakhstan
Mangyshlakskaya *see* Mangistau
168 I5 **Manhan** Hövsgöl, N Mongolia *50.05N 100.01E*
29 O4 **Manhattan** Kansas, C USA *39.11N 96.33W*
101 L21 **Manhay** Luxembourg, SE Belgium *50.13N 5.43E*
85 L21 **Manhiça** *prev.* Vila de Manhiça. Maputo, S Mozambique *25.20S 32.49E*
85 L21 **Manhoca** Maputo, S Mozambique *26.47S 32.37E*
61 N20 **Manhuaçu** Minas Gerais, SE Brazil *20.16S 42.01W*
149 R11 **Mānī** Kermān, C Iran
56 H10 **Maní** Casanare, C Colombia *4.49N 72.15W*
58 A6 **Mania, Bahía de** *bay* W Ecuador
85 M17 **Manica** *var.* Vila de Manica. Manica, W Mozambique *18.51S 32.50E*
85 M17 **Manica** *off.* Província de Manica. ◈ *province* W Mozambique
85 L17 **Manicaland** ◈ *province* E Zimbabwe
13 U5 **Manic Deux, Réservoir** ▣ Quebec, SE Canada
Manich *see* Manych
61 F14 **Manicoré** Amazonas, N Brazil *5.48S 61.16W*
11 N11 **Manicouagan** Quebec, SE Canada *50.40N 68.46W*
11 N11 **Manicouagan** ≈ Quebec, SE Canada
13 U6 **Manicouagan, Péninsule de** *peninsula* Quebec, SE Canada
11 N11 **Manicouagan, Réservoir** ◎ Quebec, SE Canada
13 T4 **Manic Trois, Réservoir** ▣ Quebec, SE Canada
81 M20 **Maniema** *off.* Région du Maniema. ◈ *region* E Dem. Rep. Congo
Maniewicze *see* Manevychi
166 F8 **Maniganggo** Sichuan, C China *32.01N 99.04E*
9 Y15 **Manigotagan** Manitoba, S Canada *51.06N 96.18W*
159 R13 **Manihāri** Bihār, N India *25.21N 87.37E*
203 U9 **Manihi** *island* Îles Tuamotu, C French Polynesia
202 L13 **Manihiki** *atoll* N Cook Islands
183 U8 **Manihiki Plateau** *undersea feature* C Pacific Ocean
206 M14 **Maniitsoq** *var.* Manitsoq, *Dan.* Sukkertoppen. Kita, S Greenland *65.12N 52.05W*
159 T15 **Manikganj** Dhaka, C Bangladesh *23.52N 90.00E*
158 M14 **Mānikpur** Uttar Pradesh, N India *25.04N 81.06E*
179 P11 **Manila** *off.* City of Manila. ● (Philippines) Luzon, N Philippines *14.34N 120.58E*
29 Y9 **Manila** Arkansas, C USA *35.52N 90.10W*
201 N16 **Manila Reef** *reef* W Micronesia
191 T6 **Manilla** New South Wales, SE Australia *30.44S 150.43E*
200 Qq14 **Maniloa** *island* Tongatapu Group, S Tonga
127 P7 **Manily** Koryakskiy Avtonomnyy Okrug, E Russian Federation *62.33N 165.03E*
176 Ww9 **Manim, Pulau** *island* E Indonesia
173 Ff8 **Maninjau, Danau** ◎ Sumatera, W Indonesia
159 W13 **Manipur** ◈ *state* NE India
159 X14 **Manipur Hills** *hill range* E India
142 C14 **Manisa** *var.* Manissa; *prev.* Saruhan, *anc.* Magnesia. Manisa, W Turkey *38.36N 27.28E*
142 C13 **Manisa** *var.* Manissa. ◈ *province* W Turkey
Manissa *see* Manisa
33 O7 **Manistee** Michigan, N USA *44.14N 86.19W*
33 P7 **Manistee River** ≈ Michigan, N USA
33 O4 **Manistique** Michigan, N USA *45.57N 86.15W*
33 P4 **Manistique Lake** ◎ Michigan, N USA
9 W13 **Manitoba** ◈ *province* S Canada
9 X16 **Manitoba, Lake** ◎ Manitoba, S Canada
9 X17 **Manitou** Manitoba, S Canada *49.12N 98.28W*
33 N2 **Manitou Island** *island* Michigan, N USA
12 H11 **Manitou Lake** ◎ Ontario, SE Canada
10 G15 **Manitoulin Island** *island* Ontario, S Canada
39 T5 **Manitou Springs** Colorado, C USA *38.51N 104.56W*
12 G12 **Manitouwabing Lake** ◎ Ontario, S Canada
10 E12 **Manitouwadge** Ontario, S Canada *49.13N 85.51W*
10 G15 **Manitowaning** Manitoulin Island, Ontario, S Canada *45.43N 81.49W*

◆ COUNTRY ● COUNTRY CAPITAL ◇ DEPENDENT TERRITORY ○ DEPENDENT TERRITORY CAPITAL ◈ ADMINISTRATIVE REGION ✕ INTERNATIONAL AIRPORT ▲ MOUNTAIN ▲ MOUNTAIN RANGE ▲ VOLCANO ≈ RIVER ◎ LAKE ▣ RESERVOIR

12 B7 Manitowik Lake ◎ Ontario, S Canada
33 N7 Manitowoc Wisconsin, N USA 44.04N 87.40W
Manîtsoq see Maniitsoq
145 O7 Mānī', Wādī al dry watercourse W Iraq
10 J14 Maniwaki Quebec, SE Canada 46.24N 75.58W
176 X11 Maniwori Papua, E Indonesia 2.49S 136.00E
56 E10 Manizales Caldas, W Colombia 5.03N 73.52W
114 F11 Manjača ▲ NW Bosnia and Herzegovina
Manjacaze see Mandlakazi
188 J14 Manjimup Western Australia 34.18S 116.14E
111 V4 Mank Niederösterreich, C Austria 48.06N 15.13E
81 I17 Mankanza Equateur, NW Dem. Rep. Congo 1.40N 19.08E
159 N12 Mankāpur Uttar Pradesh, N India 27.03N 82.12E
28 M3 Mankato Kansas, C USA 39.45N 98.10W
31 U10 Mankato Minnesota, N USA 44.10N 94.00W
119 O7 Man'kivka Cherkas'ka Oblast', C Ukraine 48.58N 30.10E
78 M15 Mankono C Ivory Coast 8.06N 6.07W
9 T17 Mankota Saskatchewan, S Canada 49.25N 107.04W
161 K23 Mankulam Northern Province, N Sri Lanka 9.09N 80.27E
41 Q9 Manley Hot Springs Alaska, USA 65.00N 150.37W
20 H10 Manlius New York, NE USA 43.00N 75.58W
107 W5 Manlleu Cataluña, NE Spain 41.58N 2.16E
31 V11 Manly Iowa, C USA 43.17N 93.12W
160 E13 Manmād Mahārāshtra, W India 20.15N 74.28E
190 J7 Mannahill South Australia 32.29S 139.58E
161 J23 Mannar var. Manar. Northern Province, NW Sri Lanka 9.01N 79.53E
161 I24 Mannar, Gulf of gulf India/Sri Lanka
161 J23 Mannar Island island N Sri Lanka
Mannersdorf see Mannersdorf am Leithagebirge
111 Y5 Mannersdorf am Leithagebirge var. Mannersdorf. Niederösterreich, E Austria 47.58N 16.36E
111 Y6 Mannersdorf an der Rabnitz Burgenland, E Austria 47.25N 16.32E
103 G20 Mannheim Baden-Württemberg, SW Germany 49.28N 8.29E
9 O12 Manning Alberta, W Canada 56.52N 117.39W
31 T14 Manning Iowa, C USA 41.54N 95.03W
30 K5 Manning North Dakota, N USA 47.13N 102.46W
23 S13 Manning South Carolina, SE USA 33.42N 80.12W
203 Y2 Manning, Cape headland Kiritimati, NE Kiribati 2.01N 157.25W
195 V13 Manning Strait strait NW Solomon Islands
23 S3 Mannington West Virginia, NE USA 39.31N 80.20W
190 A1 Mann Ranges ▲ South Australia
109 C19 Mannu ≈ Sardegna, Italy, C Mediterranean Sea
9 R14 Mannville Alberta, SW Canada 53.19N 111.08W
78 J15 Mano ≈ Liberia/Sierra Leone
Manø see Mandø
41 O13 Manokotak Alaska, USA 59.00N 158.58W
176 W9 Manokwari Papua, E Indonesia 0.49S 134.04E
81 N22 Manono Shabo, SE Dem. Rep. Congo 7.18S 27.25E
27 T10 Manor Texas, SW USA 30.20N 97.33W
99 D16 Manorhamilton Ir. Cluainín. NW Ireland 54.18N 8.10W
105 S15 Manosque Alpes-de-Haute-Provence, SE France 43.49N 5.46E
10 L11 Manouane, Lac ◎ Quebec, SE Canada
169 W12 Manp'o var. Manp'ojin. NW North Korea 41.10N 126.24E
Manp'ojin see Manp'o
203 T4 Manra prev. Sydney Island. atoll Phoenix Islands, C Kiribati
107 V5 Manresa Cataluña, NE Spain 41.44N 1.52E
158 H9 Mānsa Punjab, NW India 30.00N 75.25E
84 J12 Mansa prev. Fort Rosebery. Luapula, N Zambia 11.13S 28.55E
78 G12 Mansa Konko C Gambia 13.26N 15.29W
13 Q11 Manseau Quebec, SE Canada 46.23N 71.59W
155 U5 Mānsehra North-West Frontier Province, NW Pakistan 34.22N 73.18E
15 Mm6 Mansel Island island Nunavut, NE Canada
191 O12 Mansfield Victoria, SE Australia 37.04S 146.06E
99 M18 Mansfield C England, UK 53.09N 1.10W
29 S11 Mansfield Arkansas, C USA 35.03N 94.15W
24 G6 Mansfield Louisiana, S USA 32.02N 93.42W
21 O12 Mansfield Massachusetts, NE USA 42.00N 71.11W
33 T12 Mansfield Ohio, N USA 40.45N 82.31W
20 G12 Mansfield Pennsylvania, NE USA 41.46N 77.02W
20 M7 Mansfield, Mount ▲ Vermont, NE USA 44.31N 72.49W
61 M16 Mansidão Bahia, E Brazil 10.46S 44.03W
104 L11 Mansle Charente, W France 45.52N 0.11E
78 G12 Mansôa C Guinea-Bissau 12.07N 15.18W
49 V8 Manso, Rio ≈ C Brazil
Manşûra see El Manşûra
Mansurabad see Mehrān, Rūd-e
58 A6 Manta Manabí, W Ecuador 0.57S 80.39W
59 F14 Mantaro, Río ≈ C Peru
37 O8 Manteca California, W USA 37.48N 121.13W
56 J7 Mantecal Apure, C Venezuela 7.34N 69.07W
33 N11 Manteno Illinois, N USA 41.15N 87.49W
23 Y9 Manteo Roanoke Island, North Carolina, SE USA 35.53N 75.39W
Mantes-Gassicourt see Mantes-la-Jolie
105 N5 Mantes-la-Jolie prev. Mantes-Gassicourt, Mantes-sur-Seine, anc. Medunta. Yvelines, N France 48.58N 1.42E
Mantes-sur-Seine see Mantes-la-Jolie
38 L5 Manti Utah, W USA 39.16N 111.38W
Mantinea see Mantíneia
117 F20 Mantíneia anc. Mantinea. site of ancient city Pelopónnisos, S Greece 37.36N 22.22E
61 M21 Mantiqueira, Serra da ▲ S Brazil
31 W10 Mantorville Minnesota, N USA 44.04N 92.45W
117 G17 Mantoúdi var. Mandoudi; prev. Mandoúdhion. Évvoia, C Greece 38.46N 23.28E
Mantoue see Mantova
108 F8 Mantova Eng. Mantua, Fr. Mantoue. Lombardia, NW Italy 45.10N 10.46E
95 M19 Mäntsälä Etelä-Suomi, S Finland 60.38N 25.21E
95 L17 Mänttä Länsi-Suomi, W Finland 62.00N 24.36E
Mantua see Mantova
129 O14 Manturovo Kostromskaya Oblast', NW Russian Federation 58.19N 44.42E
95 M18 Mäntyharju Ita-Suomi, SE Finland 61.25N 26.52E
94 M13 Mäntyjärvi Lappi, N Finland 66.00N 27.35E
202 L16 Manuae island S Cook Islands
203 Q10 Manuae atoll Îles Sous le Vent, W French Polynesia
198 Dd8 Manua Islands island group E American Samoa
42 L5 Manuel Benavides Chihuahua, N Mexico 29.07N 103.52W
63 D21 Manuel J.Cobo Buenos Aires, E Argentina 35.49S 57.54W
60 M12 Manuel Luís, Recife reef E Brazil
63 F15 Manuel Viana Rio Grande do Sul, S Brazil 29.33S 55.28W
61 I14 Manuel Zinho Pará, N Brazil 7.21S 54.47W
203 V11 Manuhangi atoll Îles Tuamotu, C French Polynesia
193 E22 Manuherikia ≈ South Island, NZ
175 R11 Manui, Pulau island N Indonesia
Manukau see Manurewa
192 L6 Manukau Harbour harbor North Island, NZ
174 K14 Manuk, Ci ≈ Jawa, S Indonesia
176 U12 Manuk, Pulau island Maluku, E Indonesia
203 Z2 Manulu Lagoon ◎ Kiritimati, E Kiribati
190 J7 Manunda Creek seasonal river South Australia
59 K15 Manupari, Río ≈ N Bolivia
192 L6 Manurewa var. Manukau. Auckland, North Island, NZ 37.03S 174.55E
59 K15 Manurimi, Río ≈ NW Bolivia
194 J8 Manus ◈ province N PNG
194 J8 Manus Island var. Great Admiralty Island. island N PNG
176 U15 Manuwui Pulau Babar, E Indonesia 7.47S 129.39E
31 Q3 Manvel North Dakota, N USA 48.07N 97.15W
35 Z14 Manville Wyoming, C USA 42.45N 104.38W
24 G6 Many Louisiana, S USA 31.34N 93.28W
83 H21 Manyara, Lake ◎ NE Tanzania
130 L12 Manych var. Manich. ≈ SW Russian Federation
131 N13 Manych-Gudilo, Ozero salt lake SW Russian Federation
85 H14 Manyinga North Western, NW Zambia 13.28S 24.18E
107 O11 Manzanares Castilla-La Mancha, C Spain 39.00N 3.23W
46 H7 Manzanillo Granma, E Cuba 20.21N 77.07W
42 K14 Manzanillo Colima, SW Mexico 19.00N 104.18W
42 K14 Manzanillo, Bahía bay SW Mexico
39 S11 Manzano Mountains ▲ New Mexico, SW USA
39 R12 Manzano Peak ▲ New Mexico, SW USA 34.35N 106.27W
169 R6 Manzhouli var. Man-chou-li. Nei Mongol Zizhiqu, N China 49.36N 117.28E
Manzil Bū Ruqaybah see Menzel Bourguiba
145 X9 Manzilīyah E Iraq 32.26N 47.01E
85 L21 Manzini prev. Bremersdorp. C Swaziland 26.30S 31.33E
85 L21 Manzini ✈ (Mbabane) C Swaziland 26.36S 31.25E
80 G10 Mao Kanem, W Chad 14.06N 15.16E
47 N8 Mao NW Dominican Republic 19.33N 71.09W
Maó see Mahón
Maoemere see Maumere
165 W9 Maojing Gansu, N China 36.25N 106.36E
176 Xx12 Maoke, Pegunungan Dut. Sneeuw-gebergte, Eng. Snow Mountains. ▲ Papua, E Indonesia
Maol Réidh, Caoc see Mweelrea
166 M15 Maoming Guangdong, S China 21.45N 110.50E
166 H8 Maoxian var. Mao Xian; prev. Fengyizhen. Sichuan, C China 31.42N 103.48E
85 L19 Mapai Gaza, SW Mozambique 22.52S 32.00E
164 H15 Mapam Yumco ◎ W China
85 I15 Mapanza Southern, S Zambia 16.16S 26.54E
56 J4 Mapararí Falcón, N Venezuela 10.47N 69.26W
43 U17 Mapastepec Chiapas, SE Mexico 15.24N 92.55W
175 O5 Mapat, Pulau island N Indonesia
176 Yy14 Mapi Papua, E Indonesia 7.02S 139.24E
176 Vv7 Mapia, Kepulauan island group E Indonesia
42 L8 Mapimí Durango, C Mexico 25.50N 103.50W
85 N19 Mapinhane Inhambane, SE Mozambique 22.14S 35.07E
57 N7 Mapire Monagas, NE Venezuela 7.48N 64.40W
9 S17 Maple Creek Saskatchewan, S Canada 49.55N 109.28W
33 Q9 Maple River ≈ Michigan, N USA
31 P7 Maple River ≈ North Dakota/South Dakota, N USA
31 S13 Mapleton Iowa, C USA 42.10N 95.47W
31 U10 Mapleton Minnesota, N USA 43.55N 93.57W
31 R5 Mapleton North Dakota, N USA 46.51N 97.04W
34 F13 Mapleton Oregon, NW USA 44.01N 123.56W
38 L3 Mapleton Utah, W USA 40.07N 111.37W
199 Ii5 Mapmaker Seamounts undersea feature N Pacific Ocean
194 G10 Maprik East Sepik, NW PNG 3.35S 143.03E
85 L21 Maputo prev. Lourenço Marques. ● (Mozambique) Maputo, S Mozambique 25.58S 32.34E
85 L21 Maputo ◈ province S Mozambique
85 L21 Maputo ✈ Maputo, S Mozambique 25.47S 32.36E
69 V14 Maputo ≈ S Mozambique
Maqanshy see Makanchi
Maqat see Makat
115 K19 Maqë ≈ NW Albania
115 M19 Maqellarë Dibër, C Albania 41.36N 20.29E
165 S12 Maqên var. Dawu. Qinghai, C China 34.32N 100.17E
165 S11 Maqên Gangri ▲ C China 34.44N 99.25E
165 U12 Maqu Gansu, C China 34.02N 102.00E
106 M9 Maqueda Castilla-La Mancha, C Spain 40.04N 4.22W
84 B9 Maquela do Zombo Uíge, NW Angola 6.03S 15.05E
65 I16 Maquinchao Río Negro, C Argentina 41.19S 68.46W
31 Z13 Maquoketa Iowa, C USA 42.03N 90.42W
31 Y13 Maquoketa River ≈ Iowa, C USA
12 F13 Mar Ontario, S Canada 44.48N 81.12W
97 F14 Mår ◎ S Norway
83 G19 Mara ◈ region N Tanzania
203 P8 Maraa Tahiti, W French Polynesia 17.43S 149.34W
60 D12 Maraã Amazonas, NW Brazil 1.48S 65.21W
203 O8 Maraa, Pointe headland Tahiti, W French Polynesia 17.43S 149.34W
61 K14 Marabá Pará, NE Brazil 5.22S 49.10W
56 H5 Maracaibo Zulia, NW Venezuela 10.39N 71.39W
Maracaibo, Gulf of see Venezuela, Golfo de
56 H5 Maracaibo, Lago de var. Lake Maracaibo. inlet NW Venezuela
Maracaibo, Lake see Maracaibo, Lago de
60 K10 Maracá, Ilha de island NE Brazil
61 H20 Maracaju, Serra de ▲ S Brazil
60 I11 Maracanaquará, Planalto ▲ NE Brazil
56 L5 Maracay Aragua, N Venezuela 10.15N 67.36W
Marada see Marādah
77 R9 Marādah var. Marada. N Libya 29.15N 19.28E
79 U12 Maradi Maradi, S Niger 13.30N 7.05E
79 U11 Maradi ◈ department S Niger
83 E21 Maragarazi var. Muragarazi. ≈ Burundi/Tanzania
Maragha see Marāgheh
148 J3 Marāgheh var. Maragha. Āżarbāyjān-e Khāvarī, NW Iran 37.21N 46.13E
147 P7 Marāh var. Marrāt. Ar Riyāḍ, C Saudi Arabia 25.04N 45.30E
57 N11 Marahuaca, Cerro ▲ S Venezuela 3.37N 65.25W
29 R5 Marais des Cygnes River ≈ Kansas/Missouri, C USA
60 L11 Marajó, Baía de bay N Brazil
61 K12 Marajó, Ilha de island N Brazil
202 O2 Marakei atoll Tungaru, W Kiribati
Marakesh see Marrakech
83 I18 Maralal Rift Valley, C Kenya 1.04N 36.42E
85 G21 Maralaleng Kgalagadi, S Botswana 25.42S 22.39E
151 U8 Maraldy, Ozero ◎ NE Kazakhstan
189 C5 Maralinga South Australia 30.16S 131.35E
179 R15 Maramag Mindanao, S Philippines 7.45N 124.58E
Máramarossziget see Sighetu Marmației
195 Y16 Maramasike var. Small Malaita. island N Solomon Islands
Maramba see Livingstone
204 H3 Marambio Argentinian research station Antarctica 64.22S 57.18W
118 H9 Maramureș ◈ county NW Romania
38 L15 Marana Arizona, SW USA 32.24N 111.12W
107 P7 Maranchón Castilla-La Mancha, C Spain 41.01N 2.10W
148 J2 Marand var. Merend. Āżarbāyjān-e Khāvarī, NW Iran 38.23N 45.48E
Marandellas see Marondera
60 L13 Maranhão off. Estado do Maranhão. ◈ state E Brazil
106 H10 Maranhão, Barragem do ▣ C Portugal
155 O11 Mārān, Koh-i ▲ SW Pakistan 29.24N 66.50E
108 J7 Marano, Laguna di lagoon NE Italy
58 E9 Marañón, Río ≈ N Peru
104 J10 Marans Charente-Maritime, W France 46.19N 0.58W
85 M20 Marão Inhambane, S Mozambique 24.15S 34.09E
193 B23 Mararoa ≈ South Island, NZ
Maraş/Marash see Kahramanmaraş
109 M19 Maratea Basilicata, S Italy 39.57N 15.44E
106 G11 Marateca Setúbal, S Portugal 38.34N 8.40W
117 B20 Marathiá, Akrotírio headland Zákynthos, Iónioi Nísoi, Greece, C Mediterranean Sea 37.39N 20.49E
10 E12 Marathon Ontario, S Canada 48.43N 86.22W
25 Y17 Marathon Florida Keys, Florida, SE USA 24.42N 81.05W
26 L10 Marathon Texas, SW USA 30.10N 103.14W
Marathón see Marathónas
117 H19 Marathónas prev. Marathón. Attikí, C Greece 38.09N 23.58E
175 Oo6 Maratua, Pulau island N Indonesia
61 O18 Maraú Bahia, SE Brazil 14.07S 39.02W
149 R3 Marāveh Tappeh Golestān, N Iran 37.52N 55.57E
26 L11 Maravillas Creek ≈ Texas, SW USA
194 J13 Marawaka Eastern Highlands, C PNG 6.56S 145.54E
179 R15 Marawi Mindanao, S Philippines 7.58N 124.16E
Marbat see Mirbāţ
106 L16 Marbella Andalucía, S Spain 36.31N 4.49W
188 J7 Marble Bar Western Australia 21.13S 119.48E
38 L9 Marble Canyon canyon Arizona, SW USA
27 S10 Marble Falls Texas, SW USA 30.34N 98.16W
29 Y7 Marble Hill Missouri, C USA 37.18N 89.58W
35 T15 Marbleton Wyoming, C USA 45.31N 110.06W
Marburg see Maribor
Marburg see Marburg an der Lahn, Germany
103 H16 Marburg an der Lahn hist. Marburg. Hessen, W Germany 50.49N 8.46E
113 H23 Marcal ≈ W Hungary
44 G7 Marcala La Paz, SW Honduras 14.13N 88.02W
113 H24 Marcali Somogy, SW Hungary 46.33N 17.24E
85 A16 Marca, Ponta da headland SW Angola 16.31S 11.42E
61 I16 Marcelândia Mato Grosso, W Brazil 11.18S 54.49W
29 T3 Marceline Missouri, C USA 39.42N 92.57W
62 I13 Marcelino Ramos Rio Grande do Sul, S Brazil 27.31S 51.57W
57 Y12 Marcel, Mont ▲ S French Guiana 2.32N 53.00W
99 O19 March E England, UK 52.37N 0.13E
111 Z3 March var. Morava. ≈ C Europe see also Morava
108 I12 Marche Eng. Marches. ◈ region C Italy
105 N11 Marche cultural region C France
101 J21 Marche-en-Famenne Luxembourg, SE Belgium 50.13N 5.21E
106 K14 Marchena Andalucía, S Spain 37.19N 5.24W
59 B17 Marchena, Isla var. Bindloe Island. island Galapagos Islands, Ecuador, E Pacific Ocean
Marches see Marche
101 J20 Marchin Liège, E Belgium 50.30N 5.17E
189 S1 Marchinbar Island island Wessel Islands, Northern Territory, N Australia
64 L9 Mar Chiquita, Laguna ◎ C Argentina
105 Q10 Marcigny Saône-et-Loire, C France 46.16N 4.04E
25 W16 Marco Florida, SE USA 25.56N 81.43W
Marcodurum see Düren
61 O15 Marcolândia Pernambuco, E Brazil 7.21S 40.40W
108 I8 Marco Polo ✈ (Venezia) Veneto, NE Italy 45.30N 12.21E
Marcq see Mark
118 M8 Mărculeşti Rus. Markuleshty. N Moldova 47.54N 28.14E
31 S12 Marcus Iowa, C USA 42.49N 95.48W
41 S11 Marcus Baker, Mount ▲ Alaska, USA 61.26N 147.45W
199 Hh5 Marcus Island var. Minami Tori Shima. island E Japan
20 K8 Marcy, Mount ▲ New York, NE USA 44.06N 73.55W
155 T5 Mardān North-West Frontier Province, N Pakistan 34.13N 71.59E
65 N14 Mar del Plata Buenos Aires, E Argentina 37.59S 57.31W
143 Q16 Mardin Mardin, SE Turkey 37.19N 40.43E
143 Q16 Mardin ◈ province SE Turkey
143 Q16 Mardin Dağları ▲ SE Turkey
168 J9 Mardzad Övörhangay, C Mongolia 45.58N 102.06E
197 L6 Maré island Îles Loyauté, E New Caledonia
Marea Neagră see Black Sea
107 Z8 Mare de Déu del Toro ▲ Menorca, Spain, W Mediterranean Sea 39.59N 4.06E
189 W4 Mareeba Queensland, NE Australia 17.03S 145.30E
98 G8 Maree, Loch ◎ N Scotland, UK
Mareeq see Mereeg
Marek see Dupnitsa
78 J11 Maréna Kayes, W Mali 14.36N 10.57W
202 I2 Marenanuka atoll Tungaru, W Kiribati
31 X14 Marengo Iowa, C USA 41.48N 92.04W
104 J11 Marennes Charente-Maritime, W France 45.47N 1.04W
109 G23 Marettimo, Isola island Isole Egadi, S Italy
26 K10 Marfa Texas, SW USA 30.18N 104.01W
59 P17 Marfil, Laguna ◎ E Bolivia
Marganets see Marhanets'
27 Q4 Margaret Texas, SW USA 34.00N 99.38W
188 I14 Margaret River Western Australia 33.58S 115.10E
194 G12 Margarima Southern Highlands, W PNG 5.57S 143.22E
57 N4 Margarita, Isla de island N Venezuela
117 I25 Margarítes Kríti, Greece, E Mediterranean Sea 35.19N 24.40E
99 Q22 Margate prev. Mergate. SE England, UK 51.24N 1.24E
25 Z15 Margate Florida, SE USA 26.14N 80.12W
Margelan see Marg'ilon
105 P13 Margeride, Montagnes de la ▲ C France
Margherita see Jamaame
109 N16 Margherita di Savoia Puglia, SE Italy 41.22N 16.09E
Margherita, Lake see Ābaya Hāyk'
83 E18 Margherita Peak Fr. Pic Marguerite. ▲ Uganda/Dem. Rep. Congo 0.28N 29.58E
155 O4 Marghī Bāmīān, N Afghanistan 35.10N 66.26E
118 G9 Marghita Hung. Margitta. Bihor, NW Romania 47.20N 22.19E
Margilan see Marg'ilon
118 K8 Marginea Suceava, NE Romania 47.49N 25.47E
Margitta see Marghita
153 S10 Marg'ilon var. Margelan, Rus. Margilan. Farg'ona Viloyati, E Uzbekistan 40.29N 71.43E
154 K9 Mārgow, Dasht-e desert SW Afghanistan
101 L18 Margraten Limburg, SE Netherlands 50.49N 5.49E
8 M15 Marguerite British Columbia, SW Canada 52.17N 122.10W
204 I6 Marguerite Bay bay Antarctica
Marguerite, Pic see Margherita Peak
119 T9 Marhanets' Rus. Marganets. Dnipropetrovs'ka Oblast', E Ukraine 47.34N 34.37E
194 E15 Mari Western, SW PNG 9.10S 141.39E
203 R12 Maria island Îles Australes, SW French Polynesia
203 Y12 Maria atoll Groupe Actéon, SE French Polynesia
42 I12 María Cleofas, Isla island C Mexico
64 H4 María Elena var. Oficina María Elena. Antofagasta, N Chile 22.18S 69.40W
97 G21 Mariager Århus, C Denmark 56.39N 9.58E
63 C22 María Ignacia Buenos Aires, E Argentina 37.24S 59.30W
191 P17 Maria Island island Tasmania, SE Australia
42 H12 María Madre, Isla island C Mexico
42 I12 María Magdalena, Isla island C Mexico
199 H6 Mariana Islands island group Guam/Northern Mariana Islands
183 N3 Mariana Trench var. Challenger Deep. undersea feature W Pacific Ocean
159 X12 Mariāni Assam, NE India 26.39N 94.18E
29 X11 Marianna Arkansas, C USA 34.46N 90.45W
25 R8 Marianna Florida, SE USA 30.46N 85.13W
180 J16 Marianne island Inner Islands, NE Seychelles
97 M19 Mariannelund Jönköping, S Sweden 57.37N 15.33E
63 D15 Mariano I.Loza Corrientes, NE Argentina 29.22S 58.12W
Mariano Machado see Ganda
113 A16 Mariánské Lázně Ger. Marienbad. Karlovarský Kraj, W Czech Republic 49.57N 12.42E
Máriaradna see Radna
35 S7 Marias River ≈ Montana, NW USA
Maria-Theresiopel see Subotica
Máriatölgyes see Dubnica nad Váhom
192 H1 Maria van Diemen, Cape headland North Island, NZ 34.27S 172.38E
111 V5 Mariazell Steiermark, E Austria 47.45N 15.17E
147 P15 Ma'rib W Yemen 15.28N 45.25E
97 I25 Maribo Storstrøm, S Denmark 54.46N 11.30E
111 W9 Maribor Ger. Marburg. NE Slovenia 46.33N 15.40E
Marica see Maritsa
37 R13 Maricopa California, W USA 35.03N 119.24W
Maricourt see Kangiqsujuaq
83 D15 Maridi Western Equatoria, SW Sudan 4.55N 29.30E
204 M11 Marie Byrd Land physical region Antarctica
199 Ll16 Marie Byrd Seamount undersea feature N Amundsen Sea 70.00S 118.00W
47 X11 Marie-Galante var. Ceyre to the Caribs. island SE Guadeloupe
47 Y6 Marie-Galante, Canal de channel S Guadeloupe
95 J20 Mariehamn Fin. Maarianhamina. Åland, SW Finland 60.04N 19.55E
46 C4 Mariel La Habana, W Cuba 22.58N 82.49W
101 H22 Mariembourg Namur, S Belgium 50.07N 4.30E
Marienbad see Mariánské Lázně
Marienburg see Alūksne, Latvia
Marienburg see Malbork, Poland
Marienburg see Feldioara, Romania
Marienburg in Westpreussen see Malbork
Marienhausen see Viļaka
85 D20 Mariental Hardap, SW Namibia 24.35S 17.55E
20 D13 Marienville Pennsylvania, NE USA 41.27N 79.07W
Marienwerder see Kwidzyń
60 C12 Marié, Rio ≈ NW Brazil
97 K17 Mariestad Västra Götaland, S Sweden 58.42N 13.49E
25 S3 Marietta Georgia, SE USA 33.57N 84.34W
33 U14 Marietta Ohio, N USA 39.25N 81.27W
29 N13 Marietta Oklahoma, C USA 33.56N 97.07W
83 H18 Marigat Rift Valley, W Kenya 0.28S 35.58E
105 S16 Marignane Bouches-du-Rhône, SE France 43.25N 5.12E
Marignano see Melegnano
47 O11 Marigot NE Dominica 15.31N 61.17W
126 Hh14 Mariinsk Kemerovskaya Oblast', S Russian Federation 56.13N 87.27E
131 Q3 Mariinskiy Posad Respublika Mariy El, W Russian Federation 56.07N 47.44E
121 E14 Marijampolė prev. Kapsukas. Marijampolė, S Lithuania 54.33N 23.21E
116 G12 Marikostenovo Blagoevgrad, SW Bulgaria 41.25N 23.21E
62 J9 Marília São Paulo, S Brazil 22.13S 49.58W
84 D11 Marimba Malanje, NW Angola 8.18S 16.58E
145 T1 Marī Mīlā E Iraq 36.58N 44.42E
106 G4 Marín Galicia, NW Spain 42.22N 8.42W
37 N10 Marina California, W USA 36.40N 121.48W
Marina di Catanzaro see Catanzaro Marina
Mar"ina Gorka see Mar"ina Horka
121 L17 Mar"ina Horka Rus. Mar'ina Gorka. Minskaya Voblasts', C Belarus 53.30N 28.09E
179 Pp11 Marinduque island C Philippines
33 S9 Marine City Michigan, N USA 42.43N 82.29W
33 N6 Marinette Wisconsin, N USA 45.06N 87.37W
62 I10 Maringá Paraná, S Brazil 23.25S 51.55W
85 N16 Maringuè Sofala, C Mozambique 17.57S 34.23E
106 F9 Marinha Grande Leiria, C Portugal 39.45N 8.55W
109 I15 Marino Lazio, C Italy 41.46N 12.40E
61 A15 Mário Lobão Acre, W Brazil 8.21S 72.58W
25 O5 Marion Alabama, S USA 32.37N 87.19W
29 Y11 Marion Arkansas, C USA 35.12N 90.12W
32 L17 Marion Illinois, N USA 37.43N 88.55W
33 P13 Marion Indiana, N USA 40.31N 85.40W
31 X13 Marion Iowa, C USA 42.01N 91.36W
29 O5 Marion Kansas, C USA 38.21N 97.01W
22 H6 Marion Kentucky, S USA 37.19N 88.04W
23 P9 Marion North Carolina, SE USA 35.43N 82.00W
33 S12 Marion Ohio, N USA 40.34N 83.07W
23 T12 Marion South Carolina, SE USA 34.10N 79.24W
23 Q7 Marion Virginia, NE USA 36.49N 81.31W
29 O5 Marion Lake ▣ Kansas, C USA
23 S13 Marion, Lake ▣ South Carolina, SE USA
29 S8 Marionville Missouri, C USA 37.00N 93.38W
57 N7 Maripa Bolívar, E Venezuela 7.27N 65.10W
57 X11 Maripasoula W French Guiana 3.43N 54.04W
37 Q9 Mariposa California, W USA 37.28N 119.59W
63 G19 Mariscala Lavalleja, S Uruguay 34.03S 54.46W
64 M4 Mariscal Estigarribia Boquerón, NW Paraguay 22.02S 60.39W
58 C6 Mariscal Sucre var. Quito. ✈ (Quito) Pichincha, C Ecuador 0.21S 78.37W
32 K16 Marissa Illinois, N USA 38.15N 89.45W
105 U14 Maritime Alps Fr. Alpes Maritimes, It. Alpi Marittime. ▲ France/Italy
Maritimes, Alpes see Maritime Alps
Maritime Territory see Primorskiy Kray
116 K11 Maritsa var. Marica, Gk. Évros, Turk. Meriç; anc. Hebrus. ≈ SW Europe see also Évros/Meriç
Maritsa see Simeonovgrad
Marittime, Alpi see Maritime Alps
Maritzburg see Pietermaritzburg
119 X9 Mariupol' prev. Zhdanov. Donets'ka Oblast', SE Ukraine 47.06N 37.33E
57 Q6 Mariusa, Caño ≈ NE Venezuela
148 J5 Marīvān prev. Dezh Shāhpūr. Kordestān, W Iran 35.30N 46.09E
125 A16 Mariy El, Respublika prev. Mariyskaya ASSR. ◈ autonomous republic W Russian Federation
131 R3 Mariyets Respublika Mariy El, W Russian Federation 56.31N 49.48E
Mariyskaya ASSR see Mariy El, Respublika
120 G4 Märjamaa Ger. Merjama. Raplamaa, NW Estonia 58.53N 24.24E
101 I15 Mark Fr. Marcq. ≈ Belgium/Netherlands
83 N17 Marka var. Merca. Shabeellaha Hoose, S Somalia 1.43N 44.45E
151 Z10 Markakol', Ozero Kaz. Marqaköl. ◎ E Kazakhstan
78 M12 Markala Ségou, W Mali 13.38N 6.07W
165 S15 Markam var. Gartog. Xizang Zizhiqu, W China 29.40N 98.33E
97 K21 Markaryd Kronoberg, S Sweden 56.25N 13.34E
148 L7 Markazī off. Ostān-e Markazī. ◈ province W Iran
12 F14 Markdale Ontario, S Canada 44.19N 80.37W
29 X10 Marked Tree Arkansas, C USA 35.31N 90.25W
100 N11 Markelo Overijssel, E Netherlands 52.15N 6.30E
100 J9 Markermeer ◎ C Netherlands
99 N20 Market Harborough C England, UK 52.30N 0.57W
99 N18 Market Rasen E England, UK 53.23N 0.21W
126 Kk10 Markha ≈ NE Russian Federation
10 H16 Markham Ontario, S Canada 43.53N 79.13W
27 V12 Markham Texas, SW USA 28.57N 96.04W
194 J13 Markham ≈ C PNG
205 Q11 Markham, Mount ▲ Antarctica 82.58S 163.30E
112 M11 Marki Mazowieckie, C Poland 52.19N 21.07E
164 F8 Markit Xinjiang Uygur Zizhiqu, NW China 38.55N 77.40E
119 Y5 Markivka Rus. Markovka. Luhans'ka Oblast', E Ukraine 49.34N 39.35E
37 Q7 Markleeville California, W USA 38.41N 119.47W
100 L8 Marknesse Flevoland, N Netherlands 52.44N 5.54E
81 H14 Markounda var. Marcounda. Ouham, NW Central African Republic 7.37N 17.00E
Markovka see Markivka
127 P6 Markovo Chukotskiy Avtonomnyy Okrug, NE Russian Federation 64.43N 170.13E
131 P8 Marks Saratovskaya Oblast', W Russian Federation 51.40N 46.44E
24 K2 Marks Mississippi, S USA 34.15N 90.16W
24 I7 Marksville Louisiana, S USA 31.07N 92.04W
103 I19 Marktheidenfeld Bayern, C Germany 49.50N 9.36E
103 J24 Marktoberdorf Bayern, S Germany 47.45N 10.36E
103 M18 Marktredwitz Bayern, E Germany 50.00N 12.04E
Markt-Übelbach see Übelbach
29 V3 Mark Twain Lake ▣ Missouri, C USA
Markuleshty see Mărculeşti
103 E14 Marl Nordrhein-Westfalen, W Germany 51.40N 7.06E
190 E2 Marla South Australia 27.19S 133.35E
189 Y8 Marlborough Queensland, E Australia 22.55S 150.07E
99 M22 Marlborough S England, UK 51.25N 1.44W
193 I15 Marlborough off. Marlborough District. ◈ unitary authority South Island, NZ
105 P3 Marle Aisne, N France 49.54N 3.48E
33 S8 Marlette Michigan, N USA 43.20N 83.05W
27 T9 Marlin Texas, SW USA 31.18N 96.54W
23 S5 Marlinton West Virginia, NE USA 38.13N 80.05W
28 M12 Marlow Oklahoma, C USA 34.39N 97.57W
161 E17 Marmagao Goa, W India 15.22N 73.53E
Marmanda see Marmande
104 L13 Marmande anc. Marmanda. Lot-et-Garonne, SW France 44.30N 0.10E
142 C11 Marmara Balıkesir, NW Turkey 40.36N 27.34E
142 D11 Marmara Denizi Eng. Sea of Marmara. sea NW Turkey
116 N13 Marmaraereğlisi Tekirdağ, NW Turkey 40.58N 27.57E
Marmara, Sea of see Marmara Denizi
142 C16 Marmaris Muğla, SW Turkey 36.52N 28.16E
30 J6 Marmarth North Dakota, N USA 46.17N 103.55W
23 Q5 Marmet West Virginia, NE USA 38.12N 81.31W
108 H5 Marmolada, Monte ▲ N Italy 46.36N 11.58E
106 M13 Marmolejo Andalucía, S Spain 38.03N 4.10W
12 J14 Marmora Ontario, SE Canada 44.29N 77.40W
41 Q14 Marmot Bay bay Alaska, USA
105 Q4 Marne ◈ department N France
105 Q4 Marne ≈ N France
143 U10 Marneuli prev. Borchalo, Sarvani. S Georgia 41.28N 44.45E
80 I13 Maro Moyen-Chari, S Chad 8.25N 18.46E
56 L12 Maroa Amazonas, S Venezuela 2.40N 67.33W
180 J3 Maroantsetra Toamasina, NE Madagascar 15.22S 49.43E
203 W11 Marokau atoll Îles Tuamotu, C French Polynesia
180 J5 Marolambo Toamasina, E Madagascar 20.03S 48.07E
180 J2 Maromokotro ▲ N Madagascar
85 L16 Marondera prev. Marandellas. Mashonaland East, NE Zimbabwe 18.10S 31.33E
57 X9 Maroni Dut. Marowijne. ≈ French Guiana/Suriname
191 V2 Maroochydore-Mooloolaba Queensland, E Australia 26.36S 153.04E
175 P13 Maros Sulawesi, C Indonesia 4.58S 119.34E
118 H11 Maros var. Mureş, Mureşul, Ger. Marosch, Mieresch. ≈ Hungary/Romania see also Mureş
Marosch see Maros/Mureş
Maroshévíz see Toplița
Marosillye see Ilia
Marosludas see Luduş
Marosújvár/Marosújvárakna see Ocna Mureş
Marosvásárhely see Târgu Mureş
203 V14 Marotiri var. Îlots de Bass, Morotiri. island group Îles Australes, SW French Polynesia
80 G12 Maroua Extrême-Nord, N Cameroon 10.34N 14.19E
57 X12 Marouini Rivier ≈ SE Suriname
180 I3 Marovoay Mahajanga, NW Madagascar 16.04S 46.40E
57 W9 Marowijne ◈ district NE Suriname
Marowijne see Maroni
Marqaköl see Markakol', Ozero

◆ Country ● Country Capital ◇ Dependent Territory ○ Dependent Territory Capital ◈ Administrative Region ✈ International Airport ▲ Mountain ▲ Mountain Range ⋏ Volcano ≈ River ◎ Lake ▣ Reservoir

199 M9 Marquesas Fracture Zone tectonic feature E Pacific Ocean
Marquesas Islands see Marquises, Îles
25 W17 Marquesas Keys island group Florida, SE USA
31 Y12 Marquette Iowa, C USA 43.02N 91.10W
33 N3 Marquette Michigan, N USA 46.32N 87.24W
105 N1 Marquise Pas-de-Calais, N France 50.49N 1.42E
203 X7 Marquises, Îles Eng. Marquesas Islands. island group N French Polynesia
191 Q6 Marra Creek ≈ New South Wales, SE Australia
82 B10 Marra Hills plateau W Sudan
82 B11 Marra, Jebel ▲ W Sudan 12.59N 24.16E
76 E7 Marrakech var. Marakesh, Eng. Marrakesh; prev. Morocco. W Morocco 31.39N 7.57W
Marrakesh see Marrakech
Marrāt see Marāh
191 N15 Marrawah Tasmania, SE Australia 40.55S 144.41E
190 I4 Marree South Australia 29.39S 138.06E
83 L17 Marrehan ▲▲ SW Somalia
85 N17 Marromeu Sofala, C Mozambique 18.18S 35.58E
106 J17 Marroquí, Punta headland SW Spain 36.01N 5.39W
191 N8 Marrowie Creek seasonal river New South Wales, SE Australia
85 O14 Marrupa Niassa, N Mozambique 13.13S 37.30E
190 D1 Marryat South Australia 26.22S 133.22E
77 Y10 Marsa ʿAlam SE Egypt 25.01N 34.52E
77 R8 Marsá al Burayqah var. Al Burayqah. N Libya 30.21N 19.37E
83 J17 Marsabit Eastern, N Kenya 2.19N 37.58E
109 H23 Marsala anc. Lilybaeum. Sicilia, Italy, C Mediterranean Sea 37.48N 12.26E
123 Jj17 Marsaxlokk Bay bay SE Malta
67 G15 Mars Bay Ascension Island, C Atlantic Ocean
103 H15 Marsberg Nordrhein-Westfalen, W Germany 51.28N 8.51E
9 R15 Marsden Saskatchewan, S Canada 52.50N 109.45W
100 H7 Marsdiep strait NW Netherlands
105 R16 Marseille Eng. Marseilles; anc. Massilia. Bouches-du-Rhône, SE France 43.19N 5.21E
Marseille-Marignane see Provence
32 M11 Marseilles Illinois, N USA 41.19N 88.42W
Marseilles see Marseille
78 J16 Marshall W Liberia 6.10N 10.22W
41 N11 Marshall Alaska, USA 61.52N 162.04W
29 U9 Marshall Arkansas, C USA 35.54N 92.37W
33 N14 Marshall Illinois, N USA 39.23N 87.41W
33 Q10 Marshall Michigan, N USA 42.16N 84.57W
31 S9 Marshall Minnesota, N USA 44.26N 95.48W
29 T4 Marshall Missouri, C USA 39.07N 93.12W
23 O9 Marshall North Carolina, SE USA 35.49N 82.41W
27 X6 Marshall Texas, SW USA 32.32N 94.22W
201 S4 Marshall Islands off. Republic of the Marshall Islands. ◆ republic W Pacific Ocean
183 Q3 Marshall Islands island group W Pacific Ocean
199 I7 Marshall Seamounts undersea feature SW Pacific Ocean
31 W13 Marshalltown Iowa, C USA 42.01N 92.54W
21 P12 Marshfield Massachusetts, NE USA 42.04N 70.40W
29 T7 Marshfield Missouri, C USA 37.20N 92.54W
32 K6 Marshfield Wisconsin, N USA 44.41N 90.12W
46 H1 Marsh Harbour Great Abaco, W Bahamas 26.31N 77.03W
21 S3 Mars Hill Maine, NE USA 46.31N 67.51W
23 P9 Mars Hill North Carolina, SE USA 35.49N 82.33W
24 H10 Marsh Island island Louisiana, S USA
23 S11 Marshville North Carolina, SE USA 34.59N 80.22W
13 W5 Marsoui Quebec, SE Canada 49.12N 65.58W
13 R8 Mars, Rivière à ≈ Quebec, SE Canada
97 O15 Märsta Stockholm, C Sweden 59.37N 17.52E
97 H24 Marstal Fyn, C Denmark 54.52N 10.31E
97 I19 Marstrand Västra Götaland, S Sweden 57.54N 11.31E
27 U8 Mart Texas, SW USA 31.32N 96.49W
178 Gg9 Martaban var. Moktama. Mon State, S Myanmar 16.31N 97.34E
177 G9 Martaban, Gulf of gulf S Myanmar
109 Q19 Martano Puglia, SE Italy 40.12N 18.19E
Martapoera see Martapura
175 N11 Martapura prev. Martapoera. Borneo, C Indonesia 3.25S 114.51E
101 L23 Martelange Luxembourg, SE Belgium 49.50N 5.43E
116 L7 Marten Ruse, N Bulgaria 43.57N 26.08E
12 H10 Marten River Ontario, S Canada 46.43N 79.45W
9 T15 Martensville Saskatchewan, S Canada 52.15N 106.42W
Marteskirch see Târnăveni
Martes Tolosane see Martres-Tolosane
117 K25 Mártha Kríti, Greece, E Mediterranean Sea 35.03N 25.22E
191 Q6 Marthaguy Creek ≈ New South Wales, SE Australia
21 P13 Martha's Vineyard island Massachusetts, NE USA
110 C11 Martigny Valais, SW Switzerland 46.04N 7.03E
105 R16 Martigues Bouches-du-Rhône, SE France 43.24N 5.03E
113 J19 Martin Ger. Sankt Martin, Hung. Turócszentmárton; prev. Turčianský Svätý Martin. Žilinský Kraj, N Slovakia 49.03N 18.54E
30 L11 Martin South Dakota, N USA 43.10N 101.43W
22 G8 Martin Tennessee, S USA 36.20N 88.51W
107 S7 Martín ≈ E Spain
109 P18 Martina Franca Puglia, SE Italy 40.42N 17.19E
193 M14 Martinborough Wellington, North Island, NZ 41.15S 175.28E
27 S11 Martindale Texas, SW USA 29.49N 97.49W
37 N8 Martinez California, W USA 38.00N 122.12W
25 V3 Martinez Georgia, SE USA 33.31N 82.04W
43 Q13 Martínez de La Torre Veracruz-Llave, E Mexico 20.06N 97.03W
47 Y12 Martinique ◇ French overseas department E West Indies
1 O15 Martinique island E West Indies
Martinique Channel see Martinique Passage
47 X12 Martinique Passage var. Dominica Channel, Martinique Channel. channel Dominica/Martinique
25 Q5 Martin Lake ▣ Alabama, S USA
117 G18 Martíno prev. Martínon. Stereá Ellás, C Greece 38.34N 23.13E
Martínon see Martíno
204 J11 Martin Peninsula peninsula Antarctica
41 S5 Martin Point headland Alaska, USA 70.06N 143.04W
111 V3 Martinsberg Niederösterreich, NE Austria 48.23N 15.09E
23 V3 Martinsburg West Virginia, NE USA 39.25N 77.55W
33 V13 Martins Ferry Ohio, N USA 40.06N 80.43W
Martinskirch see Târnăveni
33 O14 Martinsville Indiana, N USA 39.25N 86.25W
23 S8 Martinsville Virginia, NE USA 36.41N 79.52W
67 K16 Martin Vaz, Ilhas island group E Brazil
Martōk see Martuk
192 M12 Marton Manawatu-Wanganui, North Island, NZ 40.05S 175.22E
107 N13 Martos Andalucía, S Spain 37.43N 3.58W
104 M16 Martres-Tolosane var. Martes Tolosane. Haute-Garonne, S France 43.13N 1.00E
94 M11 Martti Lappi, NE Finland 67.28N 28.19E
150 I9 Martuk Kaz. Martök. Aktyubinsk, NW Kazakhstan 50.45N 56.30E
143 U12 Martuni E Armenia 40.07N 45.20E
60 L11 Marudá Pará, E Brazil 5.25S 49.04W
175 O2 Marudu, Teluk bay East Malaysia
155 O8 Maʿrūf Kandahār, SE Afghanistan 31.37N 67.08E
170 F14 Marugame Kagawa, Shikoku, SW Japan 34.16N 133.46E
193 H16 Maruia ≈ South Island, NZ
100 M6 Marum Groningen, NE Netherlands 53.07N 6.16E
197 C13 Marum, Mount ▲ Ambrym, C Vanuatu 16.15S 168.07E
81 P23 Marungu ▲▲ SE Dem. Rep. Congo
203 Y12 Marutea atoll Groupe Actéon, C French Polynesia
149 O11 Marv Dasht var. Mervdasht. Fārs, S Iran 29.51N 52.44E
105 P13 Marvejols Lozère, S France 44.35N 3.16E
29 X12 Marvell Arkansas, C USA 34.33N 90.52W
38 L6 Marvine, Mount ▲ Utah, W USA 38.40N 111.38W
145 Q7 Marwānīyah C Iraq 33.58N 42.31E
158 F13 Mārwār var. Marwar Junction. Rājasthān, N India 25.43N 73.39E
Marwar Junction see Mārwār
9 R14 Marwayne Alberta, SW Canada 53.30N 110.25W
152 I14 Mary prev. Merv. Maryyskiy Velayat, S Turkmenistan 37.24N 61.48E
Mary see Maryyskiy Velayat
189 Z9 Maryborough Queensland, E Australia 25.31S 152.36E
190 M11 Maryborough Victoria, SE Australia 37.04S 143.43E
Maryborough see Port Laoise
85 G23 Marydale Northern Cape, W South Africa 29.25S 22.06E
119 W8 Mar"yinka Donets'ka Oblast', E Ukraine 47.57N 37.27E
Mary Island see Kanton
23 W4 Maryland off. State of Maryland; also known as America in Miniature, Cockade State, Free State, Old Line State. ◈ state NE USA
27 P7 Maryneal Texas, SW USA 32.12N 100.25W
99 J15 Maryport NW England, UK 54.44N 3.28W
11 U13 Marystown Newfoundland and Labrador, SE Canada 47.10N 55.10W
38 K6 Marysvale Utah, W USA 38.26N 112.14W
37 O6 Marysville California, W USA 39.07N 121.35W
29 O3 Marysville Kansas, C USA 39.48N 96.37W
33 S13 Marysville Michigan, N USA 42.54N 82.29W
33 S9 Marysville Ohio, NE USA 40.13N 83.22W
34 H7 Marysville Washington, NW USA 48.03N 122.10W
29 R2 Maryville Missouri, C USA 40.20N 94.52W
23 N9 Maryville Tennessee, S USA 35.45N 83.58W
Mary Welayaty see Maryyskiy Velayat
152 I15 Maryyskiy Velayat var. Mary, Turkm. Mary Welayaty. ◈ province S Turkmenistan
Marzūq see Murzuq
176 V11 Mas Papua, E Indonesia 3.28S 132.40E
44 J11 Masachapa var. Puerto Masachapa. Managua, W Nicaragua 11.47N 86.31W
83 G19 Masai Mara National Reserve reserve C Kenya
83 I21 Masai Steppe grassland NW Tanzania
83 F19 Masaka SW Uganda 0.19S 31.46E
175 N13 Masalembo Besar, Pulau island S Indonesia
143 Y13 Masallı Rus. Masally. S Azerbaijan 39.03N 48.39E
Masally see Masallı
175 Pp10 Masamba Sulawesi, C Indonesia 2.33S 120.19E
Masampo see Masan
169 Y16 Masan prev. Masampo. S South Korea 35.10N 128.36E
Masandam Peninsula see Musandam Peninsula
83 J25 Masasi Mtwara, SE Tanzania 10.43S 38.48E
Masawa see Massawa
44 J10 Masaya Masaya, W Nicaragua 11.58N 86.06W
44 J10 Masaya ◈ department W Nicaragua
179 Q12 Masbate Masbate, N Philippines 12.21N 123.34E
179 Qq12 Masbate island C Philippines
76 I6 Mascara var. Mouaskar. NW Algeria 35.25N 0.10E
181 O7 Mascarene Basin undersea feature W Indian Ocean
181 O9 Mascarene Islands island group W Indian Ocean
181 N9 Mascarene Plain undersea feature W Indian Ocean
181 O7 Mascarene Plateau undersea feature W Indian Ocean
204 H5 Mascart, Cape headland Adelaide Island, Antarctica
64 J10 Mascasín, Salinas de salt lake C Argentina
42 K13 Mascota Jalisco, C Mexico 20.31N 104.46W
13 O12 Mascouche Quebec, SE Canada 45.46N 73.37W
128 J9 Masel'gskaya Respublika Kareliya, NW Russian Federation 63.09N 34.22E
85 J23 Maseru ● (Lesotho) W Lesotho 29.21S 27.34E
85 J23 Maseru ✕ W Lesotho 29.27S 27.37E
Mashaba see Mashava
166 K14 Mashan Guangxi Zhuangzu Zizhiqu, S China 23.40N 108.10E
85 K17 Mashava prev. Mashaba. Masvingo, SE Zimbabwe 20.03S 30.28E
149 U4 Mashhad var. Meshed. Khorāsān, NE Iran 36.16N 59.34E
172 Oo4 Mashike Hokkaidō, NE Japan 43.51N 141.30E
Mashiz see Bardsīr
155 N14 Mashkai ≈ SW Pakistan
149 X13 Māshkel var. Rūd-i Māshkel, Rūd-e Māshkīd. ≈ Iran/Pakistan
154 K12 Māshkel, Hāmūn-i salt marsh SW Pakistan
Māshkel, Rūd-i/Māshkīd, Rūd-e see Māshkel
85 K15 Mashonaland Central ◈ province N Zimbabwe
85 K16 Mashonaland East ◈ province NE Zimbabwe
85 J16 Mashonaland West ◈ province NW Zimbabwe
Mashtagi see Maştağa
172 Qq6 Mashū-ko var. Masyû Ko. ◎ Hokkaidō, NE Japan
147 S14 Masīlah, Wādī al dry watercourse SE Yemen
81 I21 Masi-Manimba Bandundu, SW Dem. Rep. Congo 4.44S 17.56E
83 F17 Masindi W Uganda 1.40N 31.45E
83 I19 Masinga Reservoir ▣ S Kenya
179 Oo10 Masinloc Luzon, N Philippines 15.35N 119.57E
Masīra see Maşīrah, Jazīrat
Masira, Gulf of see Maşīrah, Khalīj
147 Y10 Maşīrah, Jazīrat var. Masīra. island E Oman
147 Y10 Maşīrah, Khalīj var. Gulf of Masira. bay E Oman
Masis see Büyükağrı Dağı
81 O19 Masisi Nord Kivu, E Dem. Rep. Congo 1.25S 28.49E
176 U11 Masiwang ≈ Pulau Seram, E Indonesia
Masjed-e Soleymān see Masjed Soleymān
148 L9 Masjed Soleymān var. Masjed-e Soleymān, Masjid-i Sulaiman. Khūzestān, SW Iran 31.58N 49.17E
Masjid-i Sulaiman see Masjed Soleymān
Maskat see Masqaţ
145 Q7 Maskhān C Iraq 33.41N 42.46E
147 X8 Maskin var. Miskin. NW Oman 23.28N 56.46E
99 B17 Mask, Lough Ir. Loch Measca. ◎ W Ireland
116 N10 Maslen Nos headland E Bulgaria 42.19N 27.47E
180 K3 Masoala, Tanjona headland NE Madagascar 15.58N 50.13E
Masohi see Amahai
33 Q9 Mason Michigan, N USA 42.33N 84.25W
33 R14 Mason Ohio, N USA 39.21N 84.18W
27 Q10 Mason Texas, SW USA 30.44N 99.15W
23 P4 Mason West Virginia, NE USA 39.01N 82.01W
193 B25 Mason Bay bay Stewart Island, NZ
32 K13 Mason City Illinois, N USA 40.12N 89.42W
31 V12 Mason City Iowa, C USA 43.09N 93.12W
Mă, Sông see Ma, Nam
20 B16 Masontown Pennsylvania, NE USA 39.49N 79.53W
147 Y8 Masqaţ var. Maskat, Eng. Muscat. ● (Oman) NE Oman 23.34N 58.36E
108 E10 Massa Toscana, C Italy 44.01N 10.07E
20 M11 Massachusetts off. Commonwealth of Massachusetts; also known as Bay State, Old Bay State, Old Colony State. ◈ state NE USA
21 P11 Massachusetts Bay bay Massachusetts, NE USA
37 R2 Massacre Lake ◎ Nevada, W USA
109 O18 Massafra Puglia, SE Italy 40.35N 17.05E
110 G11 Massagno Ticino, S Switzerland 46.01N 8.55E
80 G11 Massaguet Chari-Baguirmi, W Chad 12.28N 15.25E
Massakori see Massakory
80 G10 Massakory var. Massakori; prev. Dagana. Chari-Baguirmi, W Chad 13.01N 15.43E
80 H11 Massalassef Chari-Baguirmi, SW Chad 11.37N 17.09E
108 F13 Massa Marittima Toscana, C Italy 43.03N 10.55E
84 B11 Massangano Cuanza Norte, NW Angola 9.36S 14.19E
85 M18 Massangena Gaza, S Mozambique 21.34S 32.57E
82 J9 Massawa var. Masawa, Amh. Mitsʼiwa. E Eritrea 15.37N 39.27E
82 K9 Massawa Channel channel E Eritrea
20 J6 Massena New York, NE USA 44.55N 74.53W
80 H11 Massenya Chari-Baguirmi, SW Chad 11.21N 16.09E
8 I13 Masset Graham Island, British Columbia, SW Canada 54.00N 132.09W
104 L16 Masseube Gers, S France 43.26N 0.33E
12 E11 Massey Ontario, S Canada 46.13N 82.06W
105 P12 Massiac Cantal, C France 45.16N 3.13E
105 P12 Massif Central plateau C France
Massilia see Marseille
33 U12 Massillon Ohio, N USA 40.48N 81.31W
79 N12 Massina Ségou, W Mali 13.58N 5.24W
85 N19 Massinga Inhambane, SE Mozambique 23.16S 35.23E
85 L20 Massingir Gaza, SW Mozambique 23.57S 32.12E
205 Z10 Masson Island island Antarctica
Massoukou see Franceville
143 Z11 Maştağa Rus. Mashtagi, Mastaga. E Azerbaijan 40.31N 50.01E
Mastanli see Momchilgrad
192 M13 Masterton Wellington, North Island, NZ 40.56S 175.39E
20 M14 Mastic Long Island, New York, NE USA 40.48N 72.50W
155 O10 Mastung Baluchistān, SW Pakistan 29.46N 66.48E
121 J20 Mastva Rus. Mostva. ≈ SW Belarus
121 G17 Masty Rus. Mosty. Hrodzyenskaya Voblastsʼ, W Belarus 53.25N 24.30E
170 E12 Masuda Shimane, Honshū, SW Japan 34.40N 131.50E
94 J11 Masugnsbyn Norrbotten, N Sweden 67.28N 22.01E
Masuku see Franceville
85 K17 Masvingo prev. Fort Victoria, Nyanda, Victoria. Masvingo, SE Zimbabwe 20.04S 30.49E
85 K18 Masvingo prev. Victoria. ◈ province SE Zimbabwe
176 W10 Maswaar, Pulau island East Indies
144 H5 Maşyāf Fr. Misiaf. Ḩamāh, C Syria 35.04N 36.21E
Masyû Ko see Mashū-ko
112 E9 Maszewo Zachodniopomorskie, NW Poland 53.29N 15.01E
85 I17 Matabeleland North ◈ province W Zimbabwe
85 J18 Matabeleland South ◈ province S Zimbabwe
84 O13 Mataca Niassa, N Mozambique 12.27S 36.13E
197 G13 Matacawa Levu island Yasawa Group, NW Fiji
12 G8 Matachewan Ontario, S Canada 47.57N 80.39W
81 F22 Matadi Bas-Congo, W Dem. Rep. Congo 5.49S 13.31E
27 O4 Matador Texas, SW USA 34.01N 100.50W
44 J9 Matagalpa Matagalpa, C Nicaragua 12.53N 85.55W
44 K9 Matagalpa ◈ department W Nicaragua
10 I12 Matagami Quebec, S Canada 49.46N 77.37W
27 U13 Matagorda Texas, SW USA 28.40N 96.57W
27 U13 Matagorda Bay inlet Texas, SW USA
27 U14 Matagorda Island island Texas, SW USA
27 V13 Matagorda Peninsula headland Texas, SW USA 28.34N 96.01W
203 Q8 Mataiea Tahiti, W French Polynesia 17.46S 149.25W
203 T9 Mataiva atoll Îles Tuamotu, C French Polynesia
191 O7 Matakana New South Wales, SE Australia 32.59S 145.53E
192 N7 Matakana Island island NE NZ
85 C15 Matala Huíla, SW Angola 14.45S 15.01E
202 G12 Matalaʿa Pointe headland Île Uvea, N Wallis and Futuna 13.19S 176.07W
161 K25 Matale Central Province, C Sri Lanka 7.28N 80.37E
202 E12 Matalesina, Pointe headland Île Alofi, W Wallis and Futuna
78 I10 Matam NE Senegal 15.40N 13.18W
192 M8 Matamata Waikato, North Island, NZ 37.49S 175.45E
79 V12 Matamey Zinder, S Niger 13.27N 8.27E
42 L8 Matamoros Coahuila de Zaragoza, NE Mexico 25.34N 103.12W
43 P15 Matamoros var. Izúcar de Matamoros. Puebla, S Mexico 18.36N 98.30W
43 Q8 Matamoros Tamaulipas, C Mexico 25.49N 97.31W
175 Q10 Matana, Danau ◎ Sulawesi, C Indonesia
77 S13 Maʿṭan as Sārah SE Libya 21.45N 21.55E
84 J12 Matanda Luapula, N Zambia 11.24S 28.25E
83 J24 Matandu ≈ S Tanzania
13 V6 Matane Quebec, SE Canada 48.48N 67.31W
13 V6 Matane ≈ Quebec, SE Canada
79 S12 Matankari Dosso, SW Niger 13.39N 4.03E
41 R11 Matanuska River ≈ Alaska, USA
56 G7 Matanza Santander, N Colombia 7.22N 73.01W
46 D4 Matanzas Matanzas, NW Cuba 23.00N 81.32W
13 V7 Matapédia ≈ Quebec, SE Canada
13 V6 Matapédia, Lac ◎ Quebec, SE Canada
202 B17 Mata Point headland SE Niue 19.07S 169.51E
202 D12 Matapu, Pointe headland Île Futuna, W Wallis and Futuna
64 G12 Mataquito, Río ≈ C Chile
161 K26 Matara Southern Province, S Sri Lanka 5.57N 80.33E
117 D18 Matarágka var. Mataránga. Dytikí Ellás, C Greece 38.31N 21.32E
175 Nn16 Mataram Pulau Lombok, C Indonesia 8.36S 116.07E
Mataránga see Matarágka
189 Q3 Mataranka Northern Territory, N Australia 14.55S 133.03E
107 W6 Mataró anc. Illuro. Cataluña, E Spain 41.31N 2.27E
192 O8 Matata Bay of Plenty, North Island, NZ 37.54S 176.45E
198 Cc8 Matātula, Cape headland Tutuila, W American Samoa 14.15S 170.34W
193 D24 Mataura Southland, South Island, NZ 46.11S 168.53E
193 D24 Mataura ≈ South Island, NZ
Mata Uta see Matāʿutu
202 G11 Matāʿutu var. Mata Uta. ○ (Wallis and Futuna) Île Uvea, Wallis and Futuna 13.22S 176.12W
198 B8 Matāutu Upolu, C Samoa 13.57S 171.55W
202 G12 Matāʿutu, Baie de bay Île Uvea, Wallis and Futuna
203 P7 Matavai, Baie de bay Tahiti, W French Polynesia
202 I16 Matavera Rarotonga, S Cook Islands 21.13S 159.43W
203 V16 Mataveri Easter Island, Chile, E Pacific Ocean 27.10S 109.27W
203 V17 Mataveri ✕ (Easter Island) Easter Island, Chile, E Pacific Ocean 27.10S 109.27W
192 P9 Matawai Gisborne, North Island, NZ 38.23S 177.31E
13 O10 Matawin ≈ Quebec, SE Canada
151 V13 Matay Almaty, SE Kazakhstan 45.52N 78.45E
12 K8 Matchi-Manitou, Lac ◎ Quebec, SE Canada
43 O10 Matehuala San Luis Potosí, C Mexico 23.40N 100.37W
47 V13 Matelot Trinidad, Trinidad and Tobago 10.48N 61.06W
85 M15 Matenge Tete, NW Mozambique 15.22S 33.47E
109 O18 Matera Basilicata, S Italy 40.39N 16.34E
113 O21 Mátészalka Szabolcs-Szatmár-Bereg, E Hungary 47.57N 22.16E
176 Y10 Matewar Papua, E Indonesia 1.44S 138.26E
95 H17 Matfors Västernorrland, C Sweden 62.22N 16.59E
104 K11 Matha Charente-Maritime, W France 45.50N 0.13W
(0) F15 Mathematicians Seamounts undersea feature E Pacific Ocean
23 X6 Mathews Virginia, NE USA 37.24N 76.17W
27 S14 Mathis Texas, SW USA 28.05N 97.49W
158 J11 Mathura prev. Muttra. Uttar Pradesh, N India 27.30N 77.42E
Mathurai see Madurai
179 Rr16 Mati Mindanao, S Philippines 6.58N 126.11E
Matianus see Orūmīyeh, Daryācheh-ye
Matiara see Matiāri
155 Q15 Matiāri var. Matiara. Sind, SE Pakistan 25.37N 68.28E
43 S16 Matías Romero Oaxaca, SE Mexico 16.52N 94.57W
45 O13 Matina Limón, E Costa Rica 10.02N 83.15W
12 D10 Matinenda Lake ◎ Ontario, S Canada
21 R8 Matinicus Island island Maine, NE USA
Matisco/Matisco Ædourum see Mâcon
155 Q16 Mātli Sind, SE Pakistan 25.06N 68.37E
99 M18 Matlock C England, UK 53.07N 1.31W
61 F18 Mato Grosso prev. Vila Bela da Santissima Trindade. Mato Grosso, W Brazil 14.52S 59.58W
61 G17 Mato Grosso off. Estado de Mato Grosso; prev. Matto Grosso. ◈ state W Brazil
62 H8 Mato Grosso do Sul off. Estado de Mato Grosso do Sul. ◈ state S Brazil
61 I18 Mato Grosso, Planalto de plateau C Brazil
106 G6 Matosinhos prev. Matozinhos. Porto, NW Portugal 41.10N 8.42W
57 Z10 Matoury NE French Guiana 4.49N 52.17W
Matozinhos see Matosinhos
113 L21 Mátra ▲▲ N Hungary
147 Y8 Maţraḩ var. Mutrah. NE Oman 23.35N 58.30E
118 L12 Mătrașești Vrancea, E Romania 45.52N 27.13E
110 M8 Matrei Am Brenner Tirol, W Austria 47.09N 11.28E
111 P8 Matrei in Osttirol Tirol, W Austria 47.04N 12.31E
78 I15 Matru SW Sierra Leone 7.37N 12.07W
77 U7 Maţrūḩ var. Mersa Maţrūḩ; anc. Paraetonium. NW Egypt 31.20N 27.15E
172 Q13 Matsubara var. Matubara. Kagoshima, Tokuno-shima, SW Japan 32.58N 129.55E
171 K16 Matsudo var. Matudo. Chiba, Honshū, S Japan 35.45N 139.49E
170 F11 Matsue var. Matsuye, Matue. Shimane, Honshū, SW Japan 35.27N 133.03E
171 Mm7 Matsumae Hokkaidō, NE Japan 41.27N 140.04E
171 J14 Matsumoto var. Matumoto. Nagano, Honshū, S Japan 36.18N 137.58E
171 H16 Matsusaka var. Matsuzaka, Matusaka. Mie, Honshū, SW Japan 34.34N 136.30E
167 S12 Matsu Tao Chin. Mazu Dao. island NW Taiwan
Matsutō see Mattō
170 C12 Matsuura var. Matuura. Nagasaki, Kyūshū, SW Japan 33.21N 129.40E
170 Ee14 Matsuyama var. Matuyama. Ehime, Shikoku, SW Japan 33.49N 132.46E
Matsuye see Matsue
Matsuzaka see Matsusaka
171 J17 Matsuzaki Shizuoka, Honshū, S Japan 34.43N 138.45E
12 F8 Mattagami ≈ Ontario, S Canada
12 F8 Mattagami Lake ◎ Ontario, S Canada
64 K12 Mattaldi Córdoba, C Argentina 34.32S 64.18W
23 Y9 Mattamuskeet, Lake ◎ North Carolina, SE USA
23 W6 Mattaponi River ≈ Virginia, NE USA
12 I11 Mattawa Ontario, SE Canada 46.19N 78.42W
12 I11 Mattawa ≈ Ontario, SE Canada
21 S5 Mattawamkeag Maine, NE USA 45.30N 68.20W
21 S4 Mattawamkeag Lake ◎ Maine, NE USA
110 D11 Matterhorn It. Monte Cervino. ▲ Italy/Switzerland see also Cervino, Monte 45.58N 7.36E
37 W1 Matterhorn ▲ Nevada, W USA 41.48N 115.22W
34 L12 Matterhorn var. Sacajawea Peak. ▲ Oregon, NW USA 45.12N 117.18W
37 R8 Matterhorn Peak ▲ California, W USA 38.06N 119.19W
111 Y5 Mattersburg Burgenland, E Austria 47.44N 16.23E
110 E11 Matter Vispa ≈ S Switzerland
57 R7 Matthews Ridge N Guyana 7.30N 60.07W
46 K7 Matthew Town Great Inagua, S Bahamas 20.56N 73.40W
111 Q4 Mattighofen Oberösterreich, NW Austria 48.07N 13.09E
109 N16 Mattinata Puglia, SE Italy 41.41N 16.01E
147 T9 Maţţī, Sabkhat salt flat Saudi Arabia/UAE
20 M14 Mattituck Long Island, New York, NE USA 40.59N 72.31W
171 I13 Mattō var. Matsutō. Ishikawa, Honshū, SW Japan 36.31N 136.34E
Matto Grosso see Mato Grosso
32 M14 Mattoon Illinois, N USA 39.28N 88.22W
59 L16 Mattos, Río ≈ C Bolivia
Mattu see Metu
174 Ll5 Matu Sarawak, East Malaysia 2.39N 111.31E
59 E14 Matucana Lima, W Peru 11.53S 76.23W
Matudo see Matsudo
Matue see Matsue
197 J16 Matuku island S Fiji
114 B9 Matulji Primorje-Gorski Kotar, NW Croatia 45.21N 14.18E
Matumoto see Matsumoto
57 P5 Maturín Monagas, NE Venezuela 9.45N 63.10W
Matusaka see Matsusaka
Matuura see Matsuura
Matuyama see Matsuyama
130 K11 Matveyev Kurgan Rostovskaya Oblastʼ, SW Russian Federation 47.31N 38.55E
131 O8 Matyshevo Volgogradskaya Oblastʼ, SW Russian Federation 50.53N 44.09E
159 O13 Mau var. Maunāth Bhanjan. Uttar Pradesh, N India 25.57N 83.33E
85 O14 Maúa Niassa, N Mozambique 13.54S 37.13E
104 M17 Maubermé, Pic de var. Tuc de Moubermé, Sp. Pico Mauberme; prev. Tuc de Maubermé. ▲ France/Spain see also Moubermé, Tuc de 42.48N 0.54E
Mauberme, Pico see Maubermé, Pic de/Moubermé, Tuc de
Maubermé, Tuc de see Maubermé, Pic de/Moubermé, Tuc de
105 Q2 Maubeuge Nord, N France 50.16N 4.00E
177 Ff8 Maubin Irrawaddy, SW Myanmar 16.43N 95.37E
158 L13 Maudaha Uttar Pradesh, N India 25.40N 80.07E
191 N9 Maude New South Wales, SE Australia 34.30S 144.20E
205 P3 Maudheimvidda physical region Antarctica
67 N22 Maud Rise undersea feature S Atlantic Ocean
111 Q4 Mauerkirchen Oberösterreich, NW Austria 48.10N 13.07E
Mauersee see Mamry, Jezioro
196 K2 Maug Islands island group N Northern Mariana Islands
105 Q15 Mauguio Hérault, S France 43.37N 4.01E
199 Kk6 Maui island Hawaii, USA, C Pacific Ocean
202 M16 Mauke atoll S Cook Islands
64 G13 Maule off. Región del Maule. ◈ region C Chile
104 J9 Mauléon Deux-Sèvres, W France 46.55N 0.45W
104 J16 Mauléon-Licharre Pyrénées-Atlantiques, SW France 43.14N 0.51W
64 G13 Maule, Río ≈ C Chile
65 G17 Maullín Los Lagos, S Chile 41.37S 73.34W
Maulmain see Moulmein
33 R11 Maumee Ohio, N USA 41.34N 83.40W
33 Q12 Maumee River ≈ Indiana/Ohio, N USA
29 U11 Maumelle Arkansas, C USA 34.51N 92.24W
29 T11 Maumelle, Lake ▣ Arkansas, C USA
175 Qq16 Maumere prev. Maoemere. Flores, S Indonesia 8.34S 122.13E
85 G17 Maun Ngamiland, C Botswana 20.00S 23.25E
Maunāth Bhanjan see Mau
Maunawai see Waimea
202 H16 Maungaroa ▲ Rarotonga, S Cook Islands 21.13S 159.48W
192 K3 Maungatapere Northland, North Island, NZ 35.46S 174.10E
192 K4 Maungaturoto Northland, North Island, NZ 36.06S 174.21E
203 R10 Maupiti var. Maurua. island Îles Sous le Vent, W French Polynesia
158 K14 Mau Rānīpur Uttar Pradesh, N India 25.13N 79.07E
24 K9 Maurepas, Lake ◎ Louisiana, S USA
105 T16 Maures ▲▲ SE France
105 O12 Mauriac Cantal, C France 45.13N 2.21E
Maurice see Mauritius
67 J20 Maurice Ewing Bank undersea feature SW Atlantic Ocean
190 C4 Maurice, Lake salt lake South Australia
20 I17 Maurice River ≈ New Jersey, NE USA
27 Y10 Mauriceville Texas, SW USA 30.13N 93.52W
100 K12 Maurik Gelderland, C Netherlands 51.57N 5.25E
78 H8 Mauritania off. Islamic Republic of Mauritania, Ar. Mūrītānīyah. ◆ republic W Africa
181 W15 Mauritius off. Republic of Mauritius, Fr. Maurice. ◆ republic W Indian Ocean
132 M17 Mauritius island W Indian Ocean
181 N9 Mauritius Trench undersea feature W Indian Ocean
104 H6 Mauron Morbihan, NW France 48.06N 2.16W
105 N13 Maurs Cantal, C France 44.45N 2.12E
Maurua see Maupiti
Maury Mid-Ocean Channel see Maury Seachannel
66 L6 Maury Seachannel var. Maury Mid-Ocean Channel. undersea feature N Atlantic Ocean
32 K8 Mauston Wisconsin, N USA 43.45N 90.01W
111 R8 Mauterndorf Salzburg, NW Austria 47.09N 13.39E
111 T4 Mauthausen Oberösterreich, N Austria 48.13N 14.30E
111 Q9 Mauthen Kärnten, S Austria 46.39N 12.58E
85 F15 Mavinga Cuando Cubango, SE Angola 15.49S 20.23E
85 M17 Mavita Manica, W Mozambique 19.31S 33.09E
117 K22 Mavrópetra, Akrotírio headland Thíra, Kykládes, Greece, Aegean Sea 36.28N 25.22E
117 F16 Mavrovoúni ▲ C Greece 39.37N 22.45E
192 Q8 Mawhai Point headland North Island, NZ 38.08S 178.24E
177 Ff3 Mawlaik Sagaing, C Myanmar 23.40N 94.25E
Mawlamyine see Moulmein
147 N14 Mawr, Wādī dry watercourse NW Yemen
205 X5 Mawson Australian research station Antarctica 67.24S 63.16E
205 X5 Mawson Coast physical region Antarctica
30 M4 Max North Dakota, N USA 47.48N 101.18W
43 W12 Maxcanú Yucatán, SE Mexico 20.35N 90.00W
Maxesibebi see Mount Ayliff
111 Q5 Maxglan ✕ (Salzburg) Salzburg, W Austria 47.46N 13.00E
95 K16 Maxmo Fin. Maksamaa. Länsi-Suomi, W Finland 63.13N 22.04E
23 T11 Maxton North Carolina, SE USA 34.47N 79.34W
27 R8 May Texas, SW USA 31.58N 98.54W
194 E10 May ≈ NW PNG
127 N17 Maya ≈ E Russian Federation
157 Q19 Māyābandar Andaman and Nicobar Islands, India, E Indian Ocean 12.43N 92.52E
Mayadin see Al Mayādīn
46 L5 Mayaguana island SE Bahamas
46 L5 Mayaguana Passage passage SE Bahamas
47 S6 Mayagüez W Puerto Rico 18.12N 67.08W
47 R6 Mayagüez, Bahía de bay W Puerto Rico
Mayals see Maials
81 G20 Mayama Le Pool, SE Congo 3.49S 14.52E
39 V8 Maya, Mesa De ▲ Colorado, C USA 37.06N 103.30W
149 R4 Mayamey Semnān, N Iran 36.26N 55.49E
44 F3 Maya Mountains Sp. Montañas Mayas. ▲▲ Belize/Guatemala
46 I7 Mayarí Holguín, E Cuba 20.40N 75.42W
Mayas, Montañas see Maya Mountains
20 I17 May, Cape headland New Jersey, NE USA 38.55N 74.57W
82 J11 Maych'ew var. Mai Chio, It. Mai Ceu, Tigray, N Ethiopia 12.55N 39.30E
144 I2 Maydān Ikbiz Ḩalab, N Syria 36.51N 36.40E
155 Q5 Maydān Shahr Wardag, E Afghanistan 34.27N 68.48E
82 O12 Maydh Sanaag, N Somalia 10.57N 47.07E
Maydī see Midī
Mayebashi see Maebashi
Mayence see Mainz
104 K6 Mayenne Mayenne, NW France 48.18N 0.37W

◆ Country ● Country Capital ◇ Dependent Territory ○ Dependent Territory Capital ◈ Administrative Region ✕ International Airport ▲ Mountain ▲▲ Mountain Range ⛰ Volcano ≈ River ◎ Lake ▣ Reservoir

104 J6 **Mayenne** ◈ *department* NW France
104 J7 **Mayenne** ≈ N France
38 K12 **Mayer** Arizona, SW USA *34.25N 112.15W*
24 J4 **Mayersville** Mississippi, S USA *32.54N 91.04W*
9 P14 **Mayerthorpe** Alberta, SW Canada *53.58N 115.06W*
23 S12 **Mayesville** South Carolina, SE USA *34.00N 80.10W*
193 G19 **Mayfield** Canterbury, South Island, NZ *43.50S 171.24E*
35 N14 **Mayfield** Idaho, NW USA *43.24N 115.56W*
22 G7 **Mayfield** Kentucky, S USA *36.44N 88.38W*
38 L5 **Mayfield** Utah, W USA *39.06N 111.42W*
168 K9 **Mayhan** Övörhangay, C Mongolia *46.02N 104.00E*
39 T14 **Mayhill** New Mexico, SW USA *32.52N 105.28W*
151 T9 **Maykain** *Kaz.* Mayqayyng. Pavlodar, NE Kazakhstan *51.24N 75.46E*
130 L14 **Maykop** Respublika Adygeya, SW Russian Federation *44.36N 40.06E*
Maylibash *see* Maylybas
Mayli-Say *see* Mayluu-Suu
153 T9 **Mayluu-Suu** *prev.* Mayli-Say, *Kir.* Mayly-Say. Dzhalal-Abadskaya Oblast', W Kyrgyzstan *41.16N 72.27E*
150 L14 **Maylybas** *prev.* Maylibash. Kyzylorda, S Kazakhstan *45.51N 62.37E*
Mayly-Say *see* Mayluu-Suu
Maymana *see* Meymaneh
178 Gg5 **Maymyo** Mandalay, C Myanmar *22.03N 96.30E*
127 P6 **Mayn** ≈ NE Russian Federation
131 Q5 **Mayna** Ul'yanovskaya Oblast', W Russian Federation *54.04N 47.20E*
23 N8 **Maynardville** Tennessee, S USA *36.15N 83.48W*
12 J13 **Maynooth** Ontario, SE Canada *45.14N 77.54W*
8 I6 **Mayo** Yukon Territory, NW Canada *63.37N 135.48W*
25 U9 **Mayo** Florida, SE USA *30.03N 83.10W*
99 B16 **Mayo** *Ir.* Maigh Eo. *cultural region* W Ireland
Mayo *see* Maio
80 G12 **Mayo-Kébbi** *off.* Préfecture du Mayo-Kébbu, *var.* Mayo-Kébi. ◈ *prefecture* SW Chad
Mayo-Kébi *see* Mayo-Kébbi
81 F19 **Mayoko** Le Niari, SW Congo *2.18S 12.45E*
179 Q11 **Mayon Volcano** ⛰ Luzon, N Philippines *13.15N 123.40E*
63 A24 **Mayor Buratovich** Buenos Aires, E Argentina *39.12S 62.41W*
106 L4 **Mayorga** Castilla-León, N Spain *42.10N 5.16W*
192 N6 **Mayor Island** *island* NE NZ
Mayor Pablo Lagerenza *see* Capitán Pablo Lagerenza
181 I14 **Mayotte** ◇ *French territorial collectivity* E Africa
Mayoumba *see* Mayumba
46 J13 **May Pen** C Jamaica *17.58N 77.15W*
Mayqayyng *see* Maykain
179 P7 **Mayraira Point** *headland* Luzon, N Philippines *18.36N 120.47E*
111 N8 **Mayrhofen** Tirol, W Austria *47.09N 11.52E*
194 F10 **May River** East Sepik, NW PNG *4.10S 141.51E*
126 Mm15 **Mayskiy** Amurskaya Oblast', SE Russian Federation *52.13N 129.30E*
131 O15 **Mayskiy** Kabardino-Balkarskaya Respublika, SW Russian Federation *43.37N 44.04E*
151 U9 **Mayskoye** Pavlodar, NE Kazakhstan *50.55N 78.11E*
20 J17 **Mays Landing** New Jersey, NE USA *39.27N 74.43W*
23 N4 **Maysville** Kentucky, S USA *38.39N 83.44W*
29 R2 **Maysville** Missouri, C USA *39.53N 94.21W*
176 Y14 **Mayu** *channel* Papua, E Indonesia
81 D20 **Mayumba** *var.* Mayoumba. Nyanga, S Gabon *3.22S 10.37E*
175 Ss7 **Mayu, Pulau** *island* Maluku, E Indonesia
33 S8 **Mayville** Michigan, N USA *43.18N 83.16W*
20 C11 **Mayville** New York, NE USA *42.15N 79.31W*
31 Q4 **Mayville** North Dakota, N USA *47.27N 97.17W*
126 M11 **Mayya** Respublika Sakha (Yakutiya), NE Russian Federation *61.45N 130.16E*
Mayyali *see* Mahe
Mayyit, Al Baḩr al *see* Dead Sea
85 J15 **Mazabuka** Southern, S Zambia *15.52S 27.46E*
Mazaca *see* Kayseri
Mazagan *see* El-Jadida
34 J7 **Mazama** Washington, NW USA *48.34N 120.26W*
105 O15 **Mazamet** Tarn, S France *43.30N 2.21E*
149 O4 **Māzandarān** *off.* Ostān-e Māzandarān. ◈ *province* N Iran
162 F7 **Mazar** Xinjiang Uygur Zizhiqu, NW China *36.31N 76.59E*
109 H24 **Mazara del Vallo** Sicilia, Italy, C Mediterranean Sea *37.39N 12.36E*
155 O2 **Mazār-e Sharīf** *var.* Mazār-i Sharif. Balkh, N Afghanistan *36.44N 67.06E*
Mazār-i Sharif *see* Mazār-e Sharīf
107 R13 **Mazarrón** Murcia, SE Spain *37.36N 1.19W*
107 R14 **Mazarrón, Golfo de** *gulf* SE Spain
57 S9 **Mazaruni River** ≈ N Guyana
44 B6 **Mazatenango** Suchitepéquez, SW Guatemala *14.31N 91.28W*
42 I10 **Mazatlán** Sinaloa, C Mexico *23.15N 106.24W*
38 L12 **Mazatzal Mountains** ▲▲ Arizona, SW USA
120 D10 **Mažeikiai** Mažeikiai, NW Lithuania *56.19N 22.21E*
120 D7 **Mazirbe** Talsi, NW Latvia *57.39N 22.16E*
42 G5 **Mazocahui** Sonora, NW Mexico *29.34N 110.07W*
59 I18 **Mazocruz** Puno, S Peru *16.41S 69.42W*
Mazoe, Rio *see* Mazowe
81 N21 **Mazomeno** Maniema, E Dem. Rep. Congo *4.54S 27.13E*
165 Q6 **Mazong Shan** ▲ N China *41.40N 97.10E*
85 L16 **Mazowe** *var.* Rio Mazoe. ≈ Mozambique/Zimbabwe
112 L11 **Mazowieckie** ◈ *province* C Poland
Mazra'a *see* Al Mazra'ah
144 G6 **Mazraat Kfar Debiâne** C Lebanon *34.00N 35.51E*
120 H7 **Mazsalaca** *Est.* Väike-Salatsi, *Ger.* Salisburg. Valmiera, N Latvia *57.52N 25.03E*
112 L9 **Mazury** *physical region* NE Poland
121 M20 **Mazyr** *Rus.* Mozyr'. Homyel'skaya Voblasts', SE Belarus *52.03N 29.14E*
109 K25 **Mazzarino** Sicilia, Italy, C Mediterranean Sea *37.18N 14.13E*
Mba *see* Ba
85 L21 **Mbabane** ● (Swaziland) NW Swaziland *26.24S 31.13E*
Mbacké *see* Mbaké
79 N16 **Mbahiakro** E Ivory Coast *7.25N 4.18W*
81 I16 **Mbaïki** *var.* M'Baiki. Lobaye, SW Central African Republic *3.52N 17.58E*
81 F14 **Mbakaou, Lac de** ◎ C Cameroon
78 G11 **Mbaké** *var.* Mbacké. W Senegal *14.50N 15.52W*
84 L11 **Mbala** *prev.* Abercorn. Northern, NE Zambia *8.49S 31.22E*
85 J18 **Mbalabala** *prev.* Balla Balla. Matabeleland South, SW Zimbabwe *20.27S 29.03E*
83 G18 **Mbale** E Uganda *1.04N 34.12E*
81 E16 **Mbalmayo** *var.* M'Balmayo. Centre, S Cameroon *3.30N 11.31E*
83 H25 **Mbamba Bay** Ruvuma, S Tanzania *11.15S 34.44E*
81 I18 **Mbandaka** *prev.* Coquilhatville. Equateur, NW Dem. Rep. Congo *0.07N 18.11E*
84 B9 **M'Banza Congo** *var.* Mbanza Congo; *prev.* São Salvador, São Salvador do Congo. Zaire, NW Angola *6.10S 14.16E*
81 G21 **Mbanza-Ngungu** Bas-Congo, W Dem. Rep. Congo *5.19S 14.45E*
69 V11 **Mbarangandu** ≈ E Tanzania
83 E19 **Mbarara** SW Uganda *0.36S 30.40E*
81 L15 **Mbari** ≈ SE Central African Republic
83 I24 **Mbarika Mountains** ▲▲ S Tanzania
85 J24 **Mbashe** ≈ S South Africa
Mbatiki *see* Batiki
80 F13 **Mbé** Nord, N Cameroon *7.51N 13.36E*
83 J24 **Mbemkuru** *var.* Mbwemkuru. ≈ S Tanzania
Mbengga *see* Beqa
180 H13 **Mbéni** Grande Comore, NW Comoros
85 K18 **Mberengwa** Midlands, S Zimbabwe *20.25S 29.57E*
83 G24 **Mbeya** Mbeya, SW Tanzania *8.54S 33.28E*
83 G23 **Mbeya** ◈ *region* S Tanzania
81 E19 **Mbigou** Ngounié, C Gabon *01.54S 12.00E*
Mbilua *see* Vella Lavella
81 F19 **Mbinda** Le Niari, SW Congo *2.07S 12.52E*
81 D17 **Mbini** W Equatorial Guinea *1.34N 9.39E*
Mbini *see* Uolo, Río
85 L18 **Mbizi** Masvingo, SE Zimbabwe *21.21S 30.58E*
83 G23 **Mbogo** Mbeya, W Tanzania *7.24S 33.26E*
81 N15 **Mboki** Haut-Mbomou, SE Central African Republic *5.18N 25.52E*
81 G18 **Mbomo** Cuvette, NW Congo *0.25N 14.42E*
81 L15 **Mbomou** ◈ *prefecture* SE Central African Republic
Mbomou/M'Bomu/Mbomu *see* Bomu
78 F11 **Mbour** W Senegal *14.24N 16.58W*
78 I10 **Mbout** Gorgol, S Mauritania *16.01N 12.37W*
81 J14 **Mbrès** *var.* Mbrés. Nana-Grébizi, C Central African Republic *6.40N 19.46E*
81 L22 **Mbuji-Mayi** *prev.* Bakwanga. Kasai Oriental, S Dem. Rep. Congo *6.04S 23.30E*
194 J9 **M'buke Islands** *island group* N PNG
83 H21 **Mbulu** Arusha, N Tanzania *3.45S 35.33E*
194 K8 **M'bunai** *var.* Bunai. Manus Island, N PNG *2.09S 147.11E*
64 N8 **Mburucuyá** Corrientes, NE Argentina *28.03S 58.15W*
Mbutha *see* Buca
Mbwemkuru *see* Mbemkuru
83 G21 **Mbwikwe** Singida, C Tanzania *5.19S 34.09E*
11 O15 **McAdam** New Brunswick, SE Canada *45.34N 67.19W*
27 O5 **McAdoo** Texas, SW USA *33.41N 100.58W*
37 V2 **McAfee Peak** ▲ Nevada, W USA *41.31N 115.57W*
29 P11 **McAlester** Oklahoma, C USA *34.55N 95.46W*
27 S17 **McAllen** Texas, SW USA *26.12N 98.13W*
23 S11 **McBee** South Carolina, SE USA *34.30N 80.12W*
9 N14 **McBride** British Columbia, SW Canada *53.21N 120.19W*
26 M9 **McCamey** Texas, SW USA *31.08N 102.13W*
35 R15 **McCammon** Idaho, NW USA *42.38N 112.10W*
37 X11 **McCarran** ✈ (Las Vegas) Nevada, W USA *36.04N 115.07W*
41 T11 **McCarthy** Alaska, USA *61.25N 142.55W*
32 M5 **McCaslin Mountain** *hill* Wisconsin, N USA *45.24N 88.24W*
27 O2 **McClellan Creek** ≈ Texas, SW USA
23 T14 **McClellanville** South Carolina, SE USA *33.07N 79.27W*
15 Jj2 **McClintock Channel** *channel* Nunavut, N Canada
205 R12 **McClintock, Mount** ▲ Antarctica *80.09S 156.42E*
37 N2 **McCloud** California, W USA *41.15N 122.09W*
37 N3 **McCloud River** ≈ California, W USA
37 Q9 **McClure, Lake** ⊠ California, W USA
207 O8 **McClure Strait** *strait* Northwest Territories, N Canada
31 N4 **McClusky** North Dakota, N USA *47.27N 100.25W*
23 T11 **McColl** South Carolina, SE USA *34.40N 79.33W*
24 K7 **McComb** Mississippi, S USA *31.14N 90.27W*
20 E16 **McConnellsburg** Pennsylvania, NE USA *39.56N 78.00W*
33 T14 **McConnelsville** Ohio, N USA *39.39N 81.51W*
30 M17 **McCook** Nebraska, C USA *40.12N 100.37W*
23 P13 **McCormick** South Carolina, SE USA *33.54N 82.17W*
9 W16 **McCreary** Manitoba, S Canada *50.48N 99.34W*
29 W11 **McCrory** Arkansas, C USA *35.15N 91.12W*
27 T10 **McDade** Texas, SW USA *30.15N 97.15W*
25 O8 **McDavid** Florida, SE USA *30.51N 87.18W*
37 T1 **McDermitt** Nevada, W USA *41.57N 117.43W*
25 S4 **McDonough** Georgia, SE USA *33.27N 84.09W*
38 L12 **McDowell Mountains** ▲▲ Arizona, SW USA
22 H8 **McEwen** Tennessee, S USA *36.06N 87.37W*
37 R12 **McFarland** California, W USA *35.41N 119.14W*
Mcfarlane, Lake *see* Macfarlane, Lake
29 P12 **McGee Creek Lake** ⊠ Oklahoma, C USA
29 W13 **McGehee** Arkansas, C USA *33.37N 91.24W*
37 X5 **Mcgill** Nevada, W USA *39.24N 114.46W*
12 K11 **McGillivray, Lac** ◎ Quebec, SE Canada
41 P10 **Mcgrath** Alaska, USA *62.57N 155.36W*
27 T8 **McGregor** Texas, SW USA *31.26N 97.24W*
35 O12 **McGuire, Mount** ▲ Idaho, NW USA *45.10N 114.36W*
85 M14 **Mchinji** *prev.* Fort Manning. Central, W Malawi *13.47S 32.51E*
30 M7 **McIntosh** South Dakota, N USA *45.52N 101.19W*
16 O3 **McKeand** ≈ Baffin Island, Nunavut, NE Canada
203 R4 **McKean Island** *island* Phoenix Islands, C Kiribati
32 J13 **McKee Creek** ≈ Illinois, N USA
20 C15 **Mckeesport** Pennsylvania, NE USA *40.18N 79.48W*
23 V7 **McKenney** Virginia, NE USA *36.57N 77.42W*
22 G8 **McKenzie** Tennessee, S USA *36.07N 88.31W*
193 B20 **McKerrow, Lake** ◎ South Island, NZ
41 Q10 **McKinley, Mount** *var.* Denali. ▲ Alaska, USA *63.04N 151.00W*
41 R10 **McKinley Park** Alaska, USA *63.42N 149.01W*
36 K3 **McKinleyville** California, W USA *40.56N 124.06W*
27 U6 **McKinney** Texas, SW USA *33.12N 96.37W*
28 I5 **McKinney, Lake** ◎ Kansas, C USA
30 M7 **McLaughlin** South Dakota, N USA *45.48N 100.48W*
27 O2 **McLean** Texas, SW USA *35.13N 100.36W*
32 M16 **Mcleansboro** Illinois, N USA *38.05N 88.32W*
9 O13 **McLennan** Alberta, W Canada *55.42N 116.49W*
12 L9 **McLennan, Lac** ◎ Quebec, SE Canada
8 M13 **McLeod Lake** British Columbia, W Canada *55.03N 123.02W*
29 N10 **McLoud** Oklahoma, C USA *35.26N 97.05W*
34 G15 **McLoughlin, Mount** ▲ Oregon, NW USA *42.27N 122.18W*
39 U15 **McMillan, Lake** ⊠ New Mexico, SW USA
34 G11 **McMinnville** Oregon, NW USA *45.13N 123.12W*
22 K9 **McMinnville** Tennessee, S USA *35.42N 85.46W*
205 R13 **McMurdo** *US research station* Antarctica *77.40S 167.16E*
26 H9 **McNary** Texas, SW USA *31.15N 105.46W*
39 N13 **Mcnary** Arizona, SW USA *34.04N 109.51W*
29 N5 **McPherson** Kansas, C USA *38.22N 97.39W*
McPherson *see* Fort McPherson
25 U6 **McRae** Georgia, SE USA *32.04N 82.54W*
31 P4 **McVille** North Dakota, N USA *47.45N 98.10W*
85 J25 **Mdantsane** Eastern Cape, SE South Africa *32.54S 27.39E*
178 Jj6 **Me** Ninh Binh, N Vietnam *20.21N 105.49E*
28 J7 **Meade** Kansas, C USA *37.14N 100.20W*
41 O5 **Meade River** ≈ Alaska, USA
37 Y11 **Mead, Lake** ⊠ Arizona/Nevada, W USA
26 M5 **Meadow** Texas, SW USA *33.20N 102.12W*
9 S14 **Meadow Lake** Saskatchewan, C Canada *55.08N 108.25W*
37 Y10 **Meadow Valley Wash** ≈ Nevada, W USA
24 J7 **Meadville** Mississippi, S USA *31.28N 90.51W*
20 B12 **Meadville** Pennsylvania, NE USA *41.38N 80.09W*
12 F14 **Meaford** Ontario, S Canada *44.35N 80.35W*
Meáin, Inis *see* Inishmaan
106 G8 **Mealhada** Aveiro, N Portugal *40.22N 8.27W*
11 R8 **Mealy Mountains** ▲▲ Newfoundland and Labrador, E Canada
9 O10 **Meander River** Alberta, W Canada *59.01N 117.42W*
34 E11 **Meares, Cape** *headland* Oregon, NW USA *45.29N 123.59W*
49 V6 **Mearim, Rio** ≈ NE Brazil
Measca, Loch *see* Mask, Lough
99 F17 **Meath** *Ir.* An Mhí. *cultural region* E Ireland
9 T14 **Meath Park** Saskatchewan, S Canada *53.25N 105.18W*
105 O5 **Meaux** Seine-et-Marne, N France *48.58N 2.54E*
23 T9 **Mebane** North Carolina, SE USA *36.06N 79.16W*
176 W9 **Mebo, Gunung** ▲ Papua, E Indonesia *1.10S 133.53E*
96 I8 **Mebonden** Sør-Trøndelag, S Norway *63.13N 11.00E*
84 A10 **Mebridege** ≈ NW Angola
37 W16 **Mecca** California, W USA *33.34N 116.04W*
Mecca *see* Makkah
31 Y14 **Mechanicsville** Iowa, C USA *41.54N 91.15W*
20 L10 **Mechanicville** New York, NE USA *42.54N 73.41W*
101 H17 **Mechelen** *Eng.* Mechlin, *Fr.* Malines. Antwerpen, C Belgium *51.01N 4.28E*
196 C8 **Mecherchar** *var.* Eil Malk. *island* Palau Islands, Palau
103 D17 **Mechernich** Nordrhein-Westfalen, W Germany *50.36N 6.39E*
130 L12 **Mechetinskaya** Rostovskaya Oblast', SW Russian Federation *46.46N 40.30E*
116 J11 **Mechka** ≈ S Bulgaria
Mechlin *see* Mechelen
63 D23 **Mechongué** Buenos Aires, E Argentina *38.09S 58.13W*
117 L14 **Mecidiye** Edirne, NW Turkey *40.39N 26.33E*
103 I24 **Meckenbeuren** Baden-Württemberg, S Germany *47.42N 9.34E*
102 L8 **Mecklenburger Bucht** *bay* N Germany
102 M10 **Mecklenburgische Seenplatte** *wetland* NE Germany
102 L9 **Mecklenburg-Vorpommern** ◈ *state* NE Germany
85 Q15 **Meconta** Nampula, NE Mozambique *15.01S 39.52E*
113 I25 **Mecsek** ▲▲ SW Hungary
85 P14 **Mecubúri** ≈ N Mozambique
85 Q14 **Mecúfi** Cabo Delgado, NE Mozambique *13.18S 40.33E*
84 O13 **Mecula** Niassa, N Mozambique *12.03S 37.37E*
173 Ff5 **Medan** Sumatera, E Indonesia *3.34N 98.39E*
63 A24 **Médanos** *var.* Medanos. Buenos Aires, E Argentina *38.51S 62.44W*
63 C19 **Médanos** Entre Ríos, E Argentina *33.25S 59.03W*
161 K24 **Medawachchiya** North Central Province, N Sri Lanka *8.32N 80.30E*
108 C8 **Mede** Lombardia, N Italy *45.06N 8.43E*
76 J5 **Médéa** *var.* El Mediyya, Lemdiyya. N Algeria *36.24N 2.42E*
Medeba *see* Ma'dabā
56 E8 **Medellín** Antioquia, NW Colombia *6.15N 75.36W*
102 H9 **Medem** ≈ NW Germany
100 J8 **Medemblik** Noord-Holland, NW Netherlands *52.46N 5.06E*
77 N7 **Médenine** *var.* Madanīyīn. SE Tunisia *33.23N 10.30E*
78 G9 **Mederdra** Trarza, SW Mauritania *16.55N 15.40W*
Medeshamstede *see* Peterborough
44 F4 **Medesto Mendez** Izabal, NE Guatemala *15.54N 89.13W*
21 O11 **Medford** Massachusetts, NE USA *42.25N 71.08W*
29 N8 **Medford** Oklahoma, C USA *36.49N 97.45W*
34 G15 **Medford** Oregon, NW USA *42.19N 122.52W*
32 K6 **Medford** Wisconsin, N USA *45.07N 90.22W*
41 P10 **Medfra** Alaska, USA *63.06N 154.42W*
118 M14 **Medgidia** Constanța, SE Romania *44.16N 28.13E*
Medgyes *see* Mediaș
45 O5 **Media Luna, Arrecifes de la** *reef* E Honduras
62 G11 **Medianeira** Paraná, S Brazil *25.15S 54.07W*
31 Y15 **Mediapolis** Iowa, C USA *41.00N 91.09W*
118 I11 **Mediaș** *Ger.* Mediasch, *Hung.* Medgyes. Sibiu, C Romania *46.09N 24.20E*
43 S15 **Medias Aguas** Veracruz-Llave, SE Mexico *17.40N 95.01W*
Mediasch *see* Mediaș
108 G10 **Medicina** Emilia-Romagna, C Italy *44.29N 11.41E*
35 X16 **Medicine Bow** Wyoming, C USA *41.52N 106.11W*
39 S2 **Medicine Bow Mountains** ▲▲ Colorado/Wyoming, C USA
35 X16 **Medicine Bow River** ≈ Wyoming, C USA
9 R17 **Medicine Hat** Alberta, SW Canada *50.03N 110.40W*
28 L7 **Medicine Lodge** Kansas, C USA *37.14N 98.33W*
28 L7 **Medicine Lodge River** ≈ Kansas/Oklahoma, C USA
114 E7 **Međimurje** *off.* Međimurska Županija. ◈ *province* N Croatia
Međimurska Županija *see* Međimurje
56 G10 **Medina** Cundinamarca, C Colombia *4.31N 73.21W*
20 E9 **Medina** New York, NE USA *43.13N 78.23W*
31 O5 **Medina** North Dakota, N USA *46.53N 99.18W*
33 T11 **Medina** Ohio, N USA *41.08N 81.51W*
27 Q11 **Medina** Texas, SW USA *29.46N 99.14W*
Medina *see* Al Madīnah
123 Ll12 **Medina Bank** *undersea feature* C Mediterranean Sea
107 P6 **Medinaceli** Castilla-León, N Spain *41.10N 2.25W*
106 L6 **Medina del Campo** Castilla-León, N Spain *41.18N 4.55W*
106 L5 **Medina de Ríoseco** Castilla-León, N Spain *41.52N 5.03W*
Médina Gonassé *see* Médina Gounas
78 H12 **Médina Gounas** *var.* Médina Gonassé. S Senegal *13.06N 13.49W*
27 S12 **Medina River** ≈ Texas, SW USA
106 K16 **Medina Sidonia** Andalucía, S Spain *36.28N 5.55W*
Medinat Israel *see* Israel
121 H14 **Medininkai** Vilnius, SE Lithuania *54.31N 25.39E*
159 R16 **Medinīpur** West Bengal, NE India *22.27N 87.19E*
Mediolanum *see* Saintes, France
Mediolanum *see* Milano, Italy
Mediomatrica *see* Metz
124 O13 **Mediterranean Ridge** *undersea feature* C Mediterranean Sea
123 L11 **Mediterranean Sea** *Fr.* Mer Méditerranée. *sea* Africa/Asia/Europe
Méditerranée, Mer *see* Mediterranean Sea
81 N17 **Medje** Orientale, NE Dem. Rep. Congo *2.27N 27.14E*
123 K11 **Medjerda, Oued** *var.* Mejerda, Wādī Majardah. ≈ Algeria/Tunisia *see also* Mejerda
116 G7 **Medkovets** Montana, NW Bulgaria *43.39N 23.22E*
95 J15 **Medle** Västerbotten, N Sweden *64.45N 20.45E*
131 W7 **Mednogorsk** Orenburgskaya Oblast', W Russian Federation *51.24N 57.37E*
127 Qq9 **Mednyy, Ostrov** *island* E Russian Federation
104 J12 **Médoc** *cultural region* SW France
165 Q16 **Mêdog** Xizang Zizhiqu, W China *29.25N 95.25E*
30 J5 **Medora** North Dakota, N USA *46.52N 103.32W*
81 E17 **Médouneu** Woleu-Ntem, N Gabon *0.58N 10.49E*
108 I7 **Meduna** ≈ NE Italy
Medunta *see* Mantes-la-Jolie
Medvedica *see* Medveditsa
128 J16 **Medveditsa** *var.* Medvedica. ≈ W Russian Federation
131 O9 **Medveditsa** ≈ SW Russian Federation
114 E8 **Medvednica** ▲▲ NE Croatia
129 R15 **Medvedok** Kirovskaya Oblast', NW Russian Federation *57.23N 50.01E*
127 Nn5 **Medvezh'i, Ostrova** *island group* NE Russian Federation
128 J9 **Medvezh'yegorsk** Respublika Kareliya, NW Russian Federation *62.56N 34.26E*
111 T11 **Medvode** *Ger.* Zwischenwässern. NW Slovenia *46.09N 14.21E*
130 J4 **Medyn'** Kaluzhskaya Oblast', W Russian Federation *54.59N 35.52E*
188 J10 **Meekatharra** Western Australia *26.36S 118.34E*
39 Q4 **Meeker** Colorado, C USA *40.02N 107.54W*
11 T12 **Meelpaeg Lake** ◎ Newfoundland and Labrador, E Canada
Meenen *see* Menen
103 M16 **Meerane** Sachsen, E Germany *50.49N 12.28E*
103 D15 **Meerbusch** Nordrhein-Westfalen, W Germany *51.19N 6.43E*
100 I12 **Meerkerk** Zuid-Holland, C Netherlands *51.55N 5.00E*
101 L18 **Meerssen** *var.* Mersen. Limburg, SE Netherlands *50.52N 5.45E*
158 J10 **Meerut** Uttar Pradesh, N India *29.01N 77.40E*
35 U13 **Meeteetse** Wyoming, C USA *44.10N 108.53W*
101 K17 **Meeuwen** Limburg, NE Belgium *51.04N 5.36E*
83 J16 **Mēga** Oromo, C Ethiopia *4.03N 38.15E*
83 J16 **Mēga Escarpment** *escarpment* S Ethiopia
Megála Kalívia *see* Megála Kalývia
117 E16 **Megála Kalývia** *var.* Megála Kalívia. Thessalía, C Greece *39.30N 21.48E*
117 H14 **Megáli Panagiá** *var.* Megáli Panayía. Kentrikí Makedonía, N Greece *40.24N 23.42E*
Megáli Panayía *see* Megáli Panagiá
Megáli Préspa, Límni *see* Prespa, Lake
116 K12 **Megálo Livádi** ▲ Bulgaria/Greece *41.18N 25.51E*
117 E20 **Megalópoli** *prev.* Megalópolis. Pelopónnisos, S Greece *37.23N 22.08E*
Megalópolis *see* Megalópoli
176 V9 **Megamo** Papua, E Indonesia *0.55S 131.46E*
117 C18 **Meganísi** *island* Iónioi Nísoi, Greece, C Mediterranean Sea
Meganom, Mys *see* Mehanom, Mys
Mégantic *see* Lac-Mégantic
13 R12 **Mégantic, Mont** ▲ Quebec, SE Canada *45.27N 71.09W*
117 G19 **Mégara** Attikí, C Greece *38.00N 23.20E*
27 R5 **Megargel** Texas, SW USA *33.27N 98.55W*
100 K13 **Megen** Noord-Brabant, S Netherlands *51.49N 5.34E*
159 U13 **Meghālaya** ◈ *state* NE India
159 U16 **Meghna** ≈ S Bangladesh
143 V14 **Meghri** *Rus.* Megri. SE Armenia *38.57N 46.15E*
126 Gg11 **Megion** Khanty-Mansiyskiy Avtonomnyy Okrug, C Russian Federation *61.01N 76.15E*
117 Q23 **Megísti** *var.* Kastellórizon. *island* SE Greece
Megri *see* Meghri
Mehabad *see* Mahābād
118 F13 **Mehadia** *Hung.* Mehádia. Caraș-Severin, SW Romania *44.53N 22.20E*
94 L7 **Mehamn** Finnmark, N Norway *71.01N 27.46E*
119 U13 **Mehanom, Mys** *Rus.* Mys Meganom. *headland* S Ukraine *44.48N 35.04E*
155 P14 **Mehar** Sind, SE Pakistan *27.10N 67.56E*
188 J8 **Meharry, Mount** ▲ Western Australia *23.17S 118.48E*
Mehdia *see* Mahdia
118 G14 **Mehedinți** ◈ *county* SW Romania
159 S15 **Meherpur** Khulna, W Bangladesh *23.46N 88.40E*
23 W8 **Meherrin River** ≈ North Carolina/Virginia, SE USA
Meheso *see* Mī'ēso
203 T11 **Mehetia** *island* Îles du Vent, W French Polynesia
120 K6 **Mehikoorma** Tartumaa, E Estonia *58.14N 27.29E*
Me Hka *see* Nmai Hka
149 N5 **Mehrabad** ✈ (Tehrān) Tehrān, N Iran *35.46N 51.07E*
148 J7 **Mehrān** Īlām, W Iran *33.07N 46.10E*
149 Q14 **Mehrān, Rūd-e** *prev.* Mansurabad. ≈ W Iran
149 Q9 **Mehrīz** Yazd, C Iran *31.31N 54.28E*
155 R5 **Mehtarlām** *var.* Mehtar Lām, Meterlam, Methariam, Metharlam. Laghmān, E Afghanistan *34.39N 70.10E*
105 N8 **Mehun-sur-Yèvre** Cher, C France *47.09N 2.15E*
81 G14 **Meiganga** Adamaoua, NE Cameroon *6.31N 14.07E*
166 H10 **Meigu** Sichuan, C China *28.22N 103.07E*
169 W11 **Meihekou** *var.* Hailong. Jilin, NE China *42.31N 125.40E*
101 L15 **Meijel** Limburg, SE Netherlands *51.22N 5.52E*
177 G5 **Meiktila** Mandalay, C Myanmar *20.52N 95.54E*
Meilbhe, Loch *see* Melvin, Lough
110 G7 **Meilen** Zürich, N Switzerland *47.16N 8.39E*
Meilu *see* Wuchuan
167 T12 **Meinhua Yu** *island* N Taiwan
103 J17 **Meiningen** Thüringen, C Germany *50.34N 10.25E*
110 F9 **Meiringen** Bern, S Switzerland *46.42N 8.13E*
103 O15 **Meissen** *var.* Meißen. Sachsen, E Germany *51.10N 13.28E*
103 I15 **Meissner** ▲ C Germany *51.13N 9.52E*
101 K25 **Meix-devant-Virton** Luxembourg, SE Belgium *49.36N 5.27E*
Mei Xian *see* Meizhou
167 P13 **Meizhou** *var.* Meixian, Mei Xian. Guangdong, S China *24.21N 116.05E*
69 P2 **Mejerda** *var.* Oued Medjerda, Wādī Majardah. ≈ Algeria/Tunisia *see also* Medjerda, Oued
44 F7 **Mejicanos** San Salvador, C El Salvador *13.50N 89.13W*
Méjico *see* Mexico
64 G5 **Mejillones** Antofagasta, N Chile *23.03S 70.25W*
201 V5 **Mejit Island** *var.* Mājeej. *island* Ratak Chain, NE Marshall Islands
81 F17 **Mékambo** Ogooué-Ivindo, NE Gabon *1.03N 13.49E*
82 J10 **Mek'elē** *var.* Makale. Tigray, N Ethiopia *13.36N 39.28E*
76 I10 **Mekerrhane, Sebkha** *var.* Sebkha Meqerghane, Sebkra Mekerrhane. *salt flat* C Algeria
Mekerrhane, Sebkra *see* Mekerrhane, Sebkha
78 G10 **Mékhé** NW Senegal *15.08N 16.42W*
152 G14 **Mekhinli** Akhalskiy Velayat, C Turkmenistan *37.28N 59.20E*
13 P9 **Mékinac, Lac** ◎ Quebec, SE Canada
Meklong *see* Samut Songhram
76 G6 **Meknès** N Morocco *33.54N 5.27W*
133 U12 **Mekong** *var.* Lan-ts'ang Chiang, *Cam.* Mékôngk, *Chin.* Lancang Jiang, *Lao.* Mènam Khong, *Th.* Mae Nam Khong, *Tib.* Dza Chu, *Vtn.* Sông Tiên Giang. ≈ SE Asia
Mekongga, Pegunungan *see* Mengkoka, Pegunungan
Mékôngk *see* Mekong
178 K15 **Mekong, Mouths of the** *delta* S Vietnam
40 L12 **Mekoryuk** Nunivak Island, Alaska, USA *60.23N 166.11W*
79 R14 **Mékrou** ≈ N Benin
174 H6 **Melaka** *var.* Malacca. Melaka, Peninsular Malaysia *2.13N 102.13E*
174 H6 **Melaka** *var.* Malacca. ◈ *state* Peninsular Malaysia
Melaka, Selat *see* Malacca, Strait of
183 O6 **Melanesia** *island group* W Pacific Ocean
183 P5 **Melanesian Basin** *undersea feature* W Pacific Ocean
175 Ss4 **Melanguane** Pulau Karakelang, N Indonesia *4.02N 126.43E*
174 Ll8 **Melawi, Sungai** ≈ Borneo, N Indonesia
191 N12 **Melbourne** *state capital* Victoria, SE Australia *37.51S 144.56E*
29 V9 **Melbourne** Arkansas, C USA *36.03N 91.54W*
25 Y12 **Melbourne** Florida, SE USA *28.04N 80.36W*
31 W14 **Melbourne** Iowa, C USA *41.57N 93.07W*
94 G10 **Melbu** Nordland, C Norway *68.30N 14.46E*
Melchor de Mencos *see* Ciudad Melchor de Mencos
65 F19 **Melchor, Isla** *island* Archipiélago de los Chonos, S Chile
42 M9 **Melchor Ocampo** Zacatecas, C Mexico *24.45N 101.38W*
12 C11 **Meldrum Bay** Manitoulin Island, Ontario, S Canada *45.55N 83.06W*
Meleda *see* Mljet
108 D8 **Melegnano** *prev.* Marignano. Lombardia, N Italy *45.22N 9.19E*
196 F9 **Melekeok** *var.* Melekeiok. Babeldaob, N Palau *7.30N 134.39E*
114 L9 **Melenci** *Hung.* Melencze. Serbia, N Serbia and Montenegro (Yugoslavia) *45.32N 20.18E*
Melencze *see* Melenci
131 N4 **Melenki** Vladimirskaya Oblast', W Russian Federation *55.21N 41.37E*
131 V6 **Meleuz** Respublika Bashkortostan, W Russian Federation *52.55N 55.54E*
10 L6 **Mélèzes, Rivière aux** ≈ Quebec, C Canada
80 I11 **Melfi** Guéra, S Chad *11.04N 17.57E*
109 M17 **Melfi** Basilicata, S Italy *41.00N 15.33E*
9 U14 **Melfort** Saskatchewan, S Canada *52.52N 104.37W*
106 H4 **Melgaço** Viana do Castelo, N Portugal *42.07N 8.15W*
107 N4 **Melgar de Fernamental** Castilla-León, N Spain *42.24N 4.15W*
76 L6 **Melghir, Chott** *var.* Chott Melrhir. *salt lake* E Algeria
96 H8 **Melhus** Sør-Trøndelag, S Norway *63.16N 10.16E*
106 H3 **Melide** Galicia, NW Spain *42.54N 8.01W*
Meligalá *see* Meligalás
117 E21 **Meligalás** *prev.* Meligalá. Pelopónnisos, S Greece *37.13N 21.58E*
62 L12 **Mel, Ilha do** *island* S Brazil
122 G11 **Melilla** *anc.* Rusaddir, Russadir. Melilla, Spain, N Africa *35.18N 2.55W*
73 N1 **Melilla** *enclave* Spain, N Africa
65 G18 **Melimoyu, Monte** ▲ S Chile *44.06S 72.49W*
175 N8 **Melintang, Danau** ◎ Borneo, N Indonesia
119 U7 **Melioratyvne** Dnipropetrovs'ka Oblast', E Ukraine *48.35N 35.18E*
64 G11 **Melipilla** Santiago, C Chile *33.33S 71.34W*
117 I25 **Mélissa, Akrotírio** *headland* Kríti, Greece, E Mediterranean Sea *35.06N 24.33E*
15 Kk16 **Melita** Manitoba, S Canada *49.16N 100.58W*
Melita *see* Mljet
Melitene *see* Malatya
109 M23 **Melito di Porto Salvo** Calabria, SW Italy *37.55N 15.48E*
119 U10 **Melitopol'** Zaporiz'ka Oblast', SE Ukraine *46.49N 35.22E*
111 V4 **Melk** Niederösterreich, NE Austria *48.12N 15.20E*
97 K15 **Mellan-Fryken** ◎ C Sweden
101 E17 **Melle** Oost-Vlaanderen, NW Belgium *51.00N 3.48E*
102 G13 **Melle** Niedersachsen, NW Germany *52.12N 8.19E*
97 J17 **Mellerud** Västra Götaland, S Sweden *58.42N 12.27E*
104 K10 **Melle-sur-Bretonne** Deux-Sèvres, W France *46.13N 0.07W*
31 P8 **Mellette** South Dakota, N USA *45.07N 98.29W*
123 J16 **Mellieha** E Malta *35.58N 14.21E*
82 B10 **Mellit** Northern Darfur, W Sudan *14.07N 25.34E*
77 N7 **Mellita** ✈ SE Tunisia *33.47N 10.51E*
65 G21 **Mellizo Sur, Cerro** ▲ S Chile *48.27S 73.10W*
102 G9 **Mellum** *island* NW Germany
85 L22 **Melmoth** KwaZulu/Natal, E South Africa *28.30S 31.23E*
113 D16 **Mělník** *Ger.* Melnik. Středočeský Kraj, NW Czech Republic *50.21N 14.30E*
126 H13 **Mel'nikovo** Tomskaya Oblast', C Russian Federation *56.35N 84.11E*
63 G18 **Melo** Cerro Largo, NE Uruguay *32.22S 54.10W*
Melodunum *see* Melun
Melrhir, Chott *see* Melghir, Chott
191 P7 **Melrose** New South Wales, SE Australia *32.41S 146.58E*
190 I7 **Melrose** South Australia *32.52S 138.16E*
31 T7 **Melrose** Minnesota, N USA *45.40N 94.46W*
35 Q11 **Melrose** Montana, NW USA *45.33N 112.41W*
39 V12 **Melrose** New Mexico, SW USA *34.25N 103.37W*
110 I8 **Mels** Sankt Gallen, NE Switzerland *47.03N 9.25E*
Melsetter *see* Chimanimani
35 V9 **Melstone** Montana, NW USA *46.37N 107.49W*
103 I16 **Melsungen** Hessen, C Germany *51.07N 9.33E*
94 L12 **Meltaus** Lappi, NW Finland *66.54N 25.18E*
99 N19 **Melton Mowbray** C England, UK *52.46N 1.03W*
84 Q13 **Meluco** Cabo Delgado, NE Mozambique *12.39S 39.35E*
105 O5 **Melun** *anc.* Melodunum. Seine-et-Marne, N France *48.31N 2.40E*
82 F12 **Melut** Upper Nile, SE Sudan *10.27N 32.13E*
29 P5 **Melvern Lake** ⊠ Kansas, C USA
9 V16 **Melville** Saskatchewan, S Canada *50.57N 102.49W*
Melville Bay/Melville Bugt *see* Qimusseriarsuaq
47 O11 **Melville Hall** ✈ (Dominica) NE Dominica *15.33N 61.19W*
189 O1 **Melville Island** *island* Northern Territory, N Australia
207 O8 **Melville Island** *island* Parry Islands, Northwest Territories, NW Canada
16 R7 **Melville, Lake** ◎ Newfoundland and Labrador, E Canada
15 Ll2 **Melville Peninsula** *peninsula* Nunavut, NE Canada
Melville Sound *see* Viscount Melville Sound
27 Q9 **Melvin** Texas, SW USA *31.12N 99.34W*
99 D15 **Melvin, Lough** *Ir.* Loch Meilbhe. ◎ S Northern Ireland, UK/Ireland
174 M9 **Memala** Borneo, C Indonesia *1.43S 112.36E*
115 L22 **Memaliaj** Gjirokastër, S Albania *40.21N 19.56E*
85 Q14 **Memba** Nampula, NE Mozambique *14.07S 40.33E*
85 Q14 **Memba, Baia de** *inlet* NE Mozambique
Membidj *see* Manbij
Memel *see* Neman, NE Europe
Memel *see* Klaipėda, Lithuania

◆ Country
● Country Capital
◇ Dependent Territory
○ Dependent Territory Capital
◈ Administrative Region
✈ International Airport
▲ Mountain
▲▲ Mountain Range
⛰ Volcano
≈ River
◎ Lake
⊠ Reservoir

103 J23 Memmingen Bayern, S Germany 47.58N 10.10E
29 U1 Memphis Missouri, C USA 40.27N 92.10W
22 E10 Memphis Tennessee, S USA 35.09N 90.03W
27 P3 Memphis Texas, SW USA 34.43N 100.31W
22 E10 Memphis ✈ Tennessee, S USA 35.02N 89.57W
13 Q13 Memphrémagog, Lac var. Lake Memphremagog. ◎ Canada/USA see also Memphremagog, Lake
21 N6 Memphremagog, Lake var. Lac Memphrémagog. ◎ Canada/USA see also Memphrémagog, Lac
119 Q2 Mena Chernihivs'ka Oblast', NE Ukraine 51.30N 32.15E
29 S12 Mena Arkansas, C USA 34.35N 94.14W
Menaam see Menaldum
Menado see Manado
108 D6 Menaggio Lombardia, N Italy 46.03N 9.14E
31 T6 Menahga Minnesota, N USA 46.45N 95.06W
79 R10 Ménaka Goa, E Mali 15.54N 2.25E
100 K5 Menaldum Fris. Menaam. Friesland, N Netherlands 53.13N 5.37E
Mènam Khong see Mekong
76 E7 Menara ✈ (Marrakech) C Morocco 31.36N 8.00W
27 Q9 Menard Texas, SW USA 30.55N 99.47W
199 M14 Menard Fracture Zone tectonic feature E Pacific Ocean
32 M7 Menasha Wisconsin, N USA 44.13N 88.25W
Mencezi Garagum see Tsentral'nyye Nizmennyye Garagumy
200 O10 Mendaña Fracture Zone tectonic feature E Pacific Ocean
174 M10 Mendawai, Sungai ~ Borneo, C Indonesia
105 P13 Mende anc. Mimatum. Lozère, S France 44.31N 3.30E
83 J14 Mendebo ▲▲ C Ethiopia
82 J9 Mendefera prev. Adi Ugri. S Eritrea 14.53N 38.51E
207 S7 Mendeleyev Ridge undersea feature Arctic Ocean
131 T3 Mendeleyevsk Respublika Tatarstan, W Russian Federation 55.54N 52.19E
103 F15 Menden Nordrhein-Westfalen, W Germany 51.25N 7.48E
24 L6 Mendenhall Mississippi, S USA 31.57N 89.52W
40 L13 Mendenhall, Cape headland Nunivak Island, Alaska, USA 59.45N 166.10W
43 P9 Méndez var. Villa de Méndez. Tamaulipas, C Mexico 25.06N 98.32W
82 H13 Mendī Oromo, C Ethiopia 9.43N 35.07E
194 G12 Mendi Southern Highlands, W PNG 6.07S 143.39E
99 K22 Mendip Hills var. Mendips. hill range S England, UK
Mendips see Mendip Hills
36 L6 Mendocino California, W USA 39.18N 123.48W
36 J3 Mendocino, Cape headland California, W USA 40.26N 124.24W
(0) B8 Mendocino Fracture Zone tectonic feature NE Pacific Ocean
37 P10 Mendota California, W USA 36.44N 120.24W
32 L11 Mendota Illinois, N USA 41.32N 89.04W
32 K8 Mendota, Lake ◎ Wisconsin, N USA
64 I11 Mendoza Mendoza, W Argentina 33.00S 68.47W
64 I12 Mendoza off. Provincia de Mendoza. ◈ province W Argentina
110 H12 Mendrisio Ticino, S Switzerland 45.52N 8.58E
174 Hh7 Mendung Pulau Mendol, W Indonesia 0.33N 103.09E
56 I5 Mene de Mauroa Falcón, NW Venezuela 10.39N 71.04W
56 I5 Mene Grande Zulia, NW Venezuela 9.51N 70.57W
142 B14 Menemen İzmir, W Turkey 38.34N 27.03E
101 C18 Menen var. Meenen, Fr. Menin. West-Vlaanderen, W Belgium 50.48N 3.07E
169 Q8 Menengiyn Tal plain E Mongolia
201 R9 Meneng Point headland SW Nauru 0.33S 166.57E
94 L10 Menešjärvi Lapp. Menešjávri. Lappi, N Finland 68.39N 26.22E
Menešjávri see Menešjärvi
109 I24 Menfi Sicilia, Italy, C Mediterranean Sea 37.34N 12.58E
167 P7 Mengcheng Anhui, E China 33.17N 116.31E
166 F15 Menghai Yunnan, SW China 22.02N 100.18E
175 Q11 Mengkoka, Pegunungan var. Pegunungan Mekongga. ▲▲ Sulawesi, C Indonesia
166 F15 Mengla Yunnan, SW China 21.30N 101.33E
67 F24 Menguera Point headland East Falkland, Falkland Islands
166 M13 Mengzhu Ling ▲▲ S China
166 H14 Mengzi Yunnan, SW China 23.20N 103.32E
Menin see Menen
190 L7 Menindee New South Wales, SE Australia 32.24S 142.25E
190 L7 Menindee Lake ◎ New South Wales, SE Australia
190 J10 Meningie South Australia 35.43S 139.20E
105 O5 Mennecy Essonne, N France 48.34N 2.25E
31 Q12 Menno South Dakota, N USA 43.14N 97.34W
116 H13 Menoïkio ▲▲ NE Greece
33 N5 Menominee Michigan, N USA 45.06N 87.36W
32 M5 Menominee River ~ Michigan/Wisconsin, N USA
32 M8 Menomonee Falls Wisconsin, N USA 43.11N 88.09W
32 I6 Menomonie Wisconsin, N USA 44.52N 91.55W
85 D14 Menongue var. Vila Serpa Pinto, Port. Serpa Pinto. Cuando Cubango, C Angola 14.38S 17.38E
123 I8 Menorca Eng. Minorca; anc. Balearis Minor. island Islas Baleares, Spain, W Mediterranean Sea
107 S13 Menor, Mar lagoon SE Spain
41 S10 Mentasta Lake ◎ Alaska, USA
41 S10 Mentasta Mountains ▲▲ Alaska, USA
173 Ff10 Mentawai, Kepulauan island group W Indonesia
173 G10 Mentawai, Selat strait W Indonesia
174 Ii10 Mentok Pulau Bangka, W Indonesia 2.01S 105.10E
105 V15 Menton It. Mentone. Alpes-Maritimes, SE France 43.46N 7.30E
26 K8 Mentone Texas, SW USA 31.42N 103.36W
Mentone see Menton
33 U11 Mentor Ohio, N USA 41.40N 81.20W
175 Nn7 Menyapa, Gunung ▲ Borneo, N Indonesia 1.04N 116.01E
165 T9 Menyuan var. Menyuan Huizu Zizhixian. Qinghai, C China 37.27N 101.33E
Menyuan Huizu Zizhixian see Menyuan
76 M5 Menzel Bourguiba var. Manzil Bū Ruqaybah; prev. Ferryville. N Tunisia 37.09N 9.51E
142 M15 Menzelet Barajı ▣ C Turkey
131 T4 Menzelinsk Respublika Tatarstan, W Russian Federation 55.44N 53.00E
188 K11 Menzies Western Australia 29.42S 121.04E
205 V6 Menzies, Mount ▲ Antarctica 73.32S 61.02E
42 J6 Meoqui Chihuahua, N Mexico 28.19N 105.30W
85 N14 Meponda Niassa, NE Mozambique 13.19S 34.52E
100 M8 Meppel Drenthe, NE Netherlands 52.42N 6.12E
102 E12 Meppen Niedersachsen, NW Germany 52.42N 7.18E
Meqerghane, Sebkha see Mekerrhane, Sebkha
107 T6 Mequinenza, Embalse de ▣ NE Spain
32 M8 Mequon Wisconsin, N USA 43.13N 87.57W
Mera see Maira
190 D3 Meramangye, Lake salt lake South Australia
29 W5 Meramec River ~ Missouri, C USA
Meran see Merano
174 H10 Merangin ~ Sumatera, W Indonesia
108 G5 Merano Ger. Meran. Trentino-Alto Adige, N Italy 46.40N 11.10E
174 H4 Merapuh Lama Pahang, Peninsular Malaysia 4.37N 101.58E
108 D7 Merate Lombardia, N Italy 45.42N 9.26E
175 Nn11 Meratus, Pegunungan ▲▲ Borneo, N Indonesia
176 Z16 Merauke Papua, E Indonesia 8.28S 140.28E
176 Z16 Merauke, Sungai ~ Papua, E Indonesia
190 L9 Merbein Victoria, SE Australia 34.11S 142.03E
101 F21 Merbes-le-Château Hainaut, S Belgium 50.19N 4.09E
Merca see Marka
56 C13 Mercaderes Cauca, SW Colombia 1.47N 77.10W
Mercara see Madikeri
37 P9 Merced California, W USA 37.17N 120.30W
63 C20 Mercedes Buenos Aires, E Argentina 34.42S 59.30W
63 D15 Mercedes Corrientes, NE Argentina 29.09S 58.04W
64 J11 Mercedes prev. Villa Mercedes. San Luis, C Argentina 33.40S 65.24W
63 D19 Mercedes Soriano, SW Uruguay 33.16S 58.01W
27 S17 Mercedes Texas, SW USA 26.09N 97.54W
37 R9 Merced Peak ▲ California, W USA 37.34N 119.30W
37 P9 Merced River ~ California, W USA
20 B13 Mercer Pennsylvania, NE USA 41.13N 80.13W
101 G18 Merchtem Vlaams Brabant, C Belgium 50.57N 4.13E
13 O13 Mercier Quebec, SE Canada 45.15N 73.45W
27 Q9 Mercury Texas, SW USA 31.23N 99.09W
192 M5 Mercury Islands island group N NZ
21 O9 Meredith New Hampshire, NE USA 43.36N 71.28W
67 B25 Meredith, Cape var. Cabo Belgrano headland West Falkland, Falkland Islands 52.15S 60.40W
39 V6 Meredith, Lake ◎ Colorado, C USA
27 N2 Meredith, Lake ▣ Texas, SW USA
83 O16 Mereeg var. Mareeq, It. Meregh. Galguduud, E Somalia 3.47N 47.19E
119 V5 Merefa Kharkivs'ka Oblast', E Ukraine 49.48N 36.04E
Meregh see Mereeg
197 C11 Mere Lava island Banks Islands, N Vanuatu
101 E17 Merelbeke Oost-Vlaanderen, NW Belgium 51.00N 3.45E
Merend see Marand
127 Oo9 Merenga Magadanskaya Oblast', E Russian Federation 61.43N 156.02E
178 K12 Mereuch Mōndól Kiri, E Cambodia 13.01N 107.26E
Mergate see Margate
150 F9 Mergenevo Zapadnyy Kazakhstan, NW Kazakhstan 49.58N 51.19E
178 Gg12 Mergui Tenasserim, S Myanmar 12.25N 98.34E
177 G12 Mergui Archipelago island group S Myanmar
116 L12 Meriç Edirne, NW Turkey 41.12N 26.24E
116 L12 Meriç Bul. Maritsa, Gk. Évros; anc. Hebrus. ~ SE Europe see also Évros/Maritsa
43 X12 Mérida Yucatán, SW Mexico 20.58N 89.35W
106 J11 Mérida anc. Augusta Emerita. Extremadura, W Spain 38.55N 6.19W
56 I6 Mérida Mérida, W Venezuela 8.36N 71.07W
56 H7 Mérida off. Estado Mérida. ◈ state W Venezuela
20 M13 Meriden Connecticut, NE USA 41.32N 72.48W
24 M5 Meridian Mississippi, S USA 32.24N 88.43W
27 S8 Meridian Texas, SW USA 31.55N 97.39W
104 J13 Mérignac Gironde, SW France 44.50N 0.39W
104 J13 Mérignac ✈ (Bordeaux) Gironde, SW France 44.51N 0.44W
95 J18 Merikarvia Länsi-Suomi, W Finland 61.51N 21.30E
191 R12 Merimbula New South Wales, SE Australia 36.52S 149.51E
190 L9 Meringur Victoria, SE Australia 34.26S 141.19E
Merín, Laguna see Mirim Lagoon
99 I19 Merioneth cultural region W Wales, UK
196 A11 Merir island Palau Islands, N Palau
196 B17 Merizo SW Guam 13.15N 144.40E
Merjama see Märjamaa
151 S16 Merke Zhambyl, S Kazakhstan 42.52N 73.09E
27 P7 Merkel Texas, SW USA 32.28N 100.00W
121 F15 Merkinė Varėna, S Lithuania 54.09N 24.11E
101 G16 Merksem Antwerpen, N Belgium 51.17N 4.26E
101 I15 Merksplas Antwerpen, N Belgium 51.22N 4.54E
Merkulovichi see Myerkulavichy
121 G15 Merkys ~ S Lithuania
34 F15 Merlin Oregon, NW USA 42.34N 123.23W
63 C20 Merlo Buenos Aires, E Argentina 34.39S 58.45W
144 G8 Meron, Haré ▲ N Israel 35.06N 33.00E
76 K6 Merouane, Chott salt lake NE Algeria
82 F7 Merowe Northern, N Sudan 18.28N 31.49E
188 J12 Merredin Western Australia 31.31S 118.18E
99 I14 Merrick ▲ S Scotland, UK 55.09N 4.28W
34 H16 Merrill Oregon, NW USA 42.00N 121.37W
32 L5 Merrill Wisconsin, N USA 45.12N 89.43W
33 N11 Merrillville Indiana, N USA 41.28N 87.19W
21 O10 Merrimack River ~ Massachusetts/New Hampshire, NE USA
30 L12 Merriman Nebraska, C USA 42.54N 101.42W
9 N17 Merritt British Columbia, SW Canada 50.09N 120.49W
25 Y12 Merritt Island Florida, SE USA 28.21N 80.42W
25 Y11 Merritt Island island Florida, SE USA
30 M12 Merritt Reservoir ▣ Nebraska, C USA
191 S7 Merriwa New South Wales, SE Australia 32.09S 150.24E
191 O8 Merriwagga New South Wales, SE Australia 33.51S 145.38E
24 G8 Merryville Louisiana, S USA 30.45N 93.32W
82 K9 Mersa Fatma E Eritrea 14.52N 40.16E
104 M7 Mer St-Aubin Loir-et-Cher, C France 47.42N 1.31E
Mersa Maṭrûḥ see Maṭrûḥ
101 M24 Mersch Luxembourg, C Luxembourg 49.45N 6.06E
103 M15 Merseburg Sachsen-Anhalt, C Germany 51.22N 12.00E
Mersen see Meerssen
99 K18 Mersey ~ NW England, UK
142 J17 Mersin İçel, S Turkey 36.49N 34.39E
174 I6 Mersing Johor, Peninsular Malaysia 2.25N 103.49E
120 E8 Mērsrags Talsi, NW Latvia 57.21N 23.05E
158 G12 Merta var. Merta City. Rājasthān, N India 26.40N 74.04E
Merta City see Merta
158 F12 Merta Road Rājasthān, N India 26.45N 73.59E
99 J21 Merthyr Tydfil S Wales, UK 51.46N 3.22W
106 H13 Mértola Beja, S Portugal 37.37N 7.40W
205 V16 Mertz Glacier glacier Antarctica
101 M24 Mertzig Diekirch, C Luxembourg 49.50N 6.00E
27 O9 Mertzon Texas, SW USA 31.15N 100.49W
83 I18 Meru Eastern, C Kenya 0.03N 37.37E
105 N4 Méru Oise, N France 49.15N 2.07E
83 I20 Meru, Mount ▲ NE Tanzania 3.12S 36.45E
Merv see Mary
Mervdasht see Marv Dasht
142 K11 Merzifon Amasya, N Turkey 40.52N 35.28E
103 D20 Merzig Saarland, SW Germany 49.27N 6.39E
38 L14 Mesa Arizona, SW USA 33.25N 111.49W
31 V4 Mesabi Range ▲▲ Minnesota, N USA
56 H6 Mesa Bolívar Mérida, NW Venezuela 8.30N 71.37W
109 Q18 Mesagne Puglia, SE Italy 40.33N 17.49E
41 P12 Mesa Mountain ▲ Alaska, USA 60.26N 155.14W
117 J25 Mesará lowland Kríti, Greece, E Mediterranean Sea
39 S14 Mescalero New Mexico, SW USA 33.09N 105.46W
103 G15 Meschede Nordrhein-Westfalen, W Germany 51.21N 8.16E
143 Q12 Mescit Dağları ▲▲ NE Turkey
201 V13 Mesegon island Chuuk, C Micronesia
Meseritz see Międzyrzecz
56 F11 Mesetas Meta, C Colombia 3.14N 74.09W
Meshchera Lowland see Meshcherskaya Nizina
130 M4 Meshcherskaya Nizina Eng. Meshchera Lowland. basin W Russian Federation
130 J5 Meshchovsk Kaluzhskaya Oblast', W Russian Federation 54.21N 35.23E
129 R9 Meshchura Respublika Komi, NW Russian Federation 63.18N 50.56E
Meshed see Mashhad
Meshed-i-Sar see Bābolsar
82 E13 Meshra'er Req Warab, S Sudan 8.30N 29.27E
39 R15 Mesilla New Mexico, SW USA 32.15N 106.49W
110 H10 Mesocco Ger. Misox. Ticino, S Switzerland 46.18N 9.13E
117 D18 Mesolóngi prev. Mesolóngion. Dytikí Ellás, W Greece 38.22N 21.26E
Mesolóngion see Mesolóngi
12 E8 Mesomikenda Lake ◎ Ontario, S Canada
63 D15 Mesopotamia var. Mesopotamia Argentina. physical region NE Argentina
Mesopotamia Argentina see Mesopotamia
37 Y10 Mesquite Nevada, W USA 36.47N 114.04W
84 Q13 Messalo, Rio var. Mualo. ~ NE Mozambique
Messana/Messene see Messina
101 L25 Messancy Luxembourg, SE Belgium 49.36N 5.49E
109 M23 Messina var. Messana, Messene; anc. Zancle. Sicilia, Italy, C Mediterranean Sea 38.11N 15.33E
Messina see Musina
Messina, Strait of see Messina, Stretto di
109 M23 Messina, Stretto di Eng. Strait of Messina. strait SW Italy
117 E21 Messíni Pelopónnisos, S Greece 37.03N 22.00E
117 E21 Messinía peninsula S Greece
117 E22 Messiniakós Kólpos gulf S Greece
126 H8 Messoyakha ~ N Russian Federation
116 H11 Mesta Gk. Néstos, Turk. Kara Su. ~ Bulgaria/Greece see also Néstos
Mestghanem see Mostaganem
143 R8 Mestia var. Mestiya. N Georgia 43.03N 42.49E
Mestiya see Mestia
117 K18 Mestón, Akrotírio headland Chíos, E Greece 38.15N 25.52E
108 H8 Mestre Veneto, NE Italy 45.30N 12.13E
61 M16 Mestre, Espigão ▲▲ E Brazil
174 Ii11 Mesuji ~ Sumatera, W Indonesia
Mesule see Grosser Möseler
8 J10 Meszah Peak ▲ British Columbia, W Canada 58.31N 131.28W
56 G11 Meta off. Departamento del Meta. ◈ province C Colombia
13 Q8 Metabetchouane ~ Quebec, SE Canada
16 O4 Meta Incognita Peninsula peninsula Baffin Island, Nunavut, NE Canada
24 K9 Metairie Louisiana, S USA 29.58N 90.09W
34 M6 Metaline Falls Washington, NW USA 48.51N 117.21W
64 K6 Metán Salta, N Argentina 25.25S 64.52W
84 N13 Metangula Niassa, N Mozambique 12.40S 34.49E
44 E7 Metapán Santa Ana, NW El Salvador 14.19N 89.30W
56 K9 Meta, Río ~ Colombia/Venezuela
108 I11 Metauro ~ C Italy
82 H11 Metema Amhara, N Ethiopia 12.53N 36.10E
117 D15 Metéora religious building Thessalía, C Greece 39.45N 21.37E
67 O20 Meteor Rise undersea feature SW Indian Ocean
195 N9 Meteran New Hanover, NE PNG 2.36S 150.09E
Meterlam/Methariam/Metharlam see Mehtarlām
117 G20 Methanon peninsula S Greece
34 J6 Methow River ~ Washington, NW USA
21 O10 Methuen Massachusetts, NE USA 42.43N 71.10W
193 G19 Methven Canterbury, South Island, NZ 43.37S 171.38E
Metis see Metz
115 G15 Metković Dubrovnik-Neretva, SE Croatia 43.02N 17.37E
41 Y14 Metlakatla Annette Island, Alaska, USA 55.07N 131.34W
111 V13 Metlika Ger. Möttling. SE Slovenia 45.38N 15.18E
111 T8 Metnitz Kärnten, S Austria 46.58N 14.09E
29 W12 Meto, Bayou ~ Arkansas, C USA
174 Ii13 Metro Sumatera, W Indonesia 5.05S 105.17E
32 M17 Metropolis Illinois, N USA 37.09N 88.43W
Metropolitan see Santiago
37 N8 Metropolitan Oakland ✈ California, W USA 37.42N 122.13W
117 D15 Métsovo prev. Métsovon. Ípeiros, C Greece 39.47N 21.12E
Métsovon see Métsovo
25 V5 Metter Georgia, SE USA 32.24N 82.03W
101 H21 Mettet Namur, S Belgium 50.19N 4.43E
103 D20 Mettlach Saarland, SW Germany 49.28N 6.37E
Mettu see Metu
82 H13 Metu var. Mattu, Mettu. Oromo, C Ethiopia 8.18N 35.39E
175 N7 Metulang Borneo, N Indonesia 1.28N 114.40E
144 G8 Metulla Northern, N Israel 33.16N 35.35E
150 G14 Mertvyy Kultuk, Sor salt flat SW Kazakhstan
105 T4 Metz anc. Divodurum Mediomatricum, Mediomatrica, Metis. Moselle, NE France 49.07N 6.09E
103 H22 Metzingen Baden-Württemberg, S Germany 48.31N 9.16E
173 E4 Meulaboh Sumatera, W Indonesia 4.10N 96.09E
101 D18 Meulebeke West-Vlaanderen, W Belgium 50.57N 3.18E
105 U6 Meurthe ~ NE France
105 S5 Meurthe-et-Moselle ◈ department NE France
105 S4 Meuse ◈ department NE France
86 F10 Meuse Dut. Maas. ~ W Europe see also Maas
195 O11 Mevelo ~ New Britain, C Papau New Guinea
Mexcala, Río see Balsas, Río
27 U8 Mexia Texas, SW USA 31.40N 96.28W
60 K11 Mexiana, Ilha island NE Brazil
42 C1 Mexicali Baja California, NW Mexico 32.34N 115.26W
29 V4 Mexico Missouri, C USA 39.10N 91.52W
20 H9 Mexico New York, NE USA 43.27N 76.14W
42 L7 Mexico off. United Mexican States, var. Méjico, México, Sp. Estados Unidos Mexicanos. ◆ federal republic N Central America
43 O14 México var. Ciudad de México, Eng. Mexico City. ● (Mexico) México, C Mexico 19.24N 99.04W
43 O13 México ◈ state S Mexico
(0) J13 Mexico Basin var. Sigsbee Deep. undersea feature C Gulf of Mexico
Mexico City see México
México, Golfo de see Mexico, Gulf of
46 B4 Mexico, Gulf of Sp. Golfo de México. gulf W Atlantic Ocean
Meyadine see Al Mayādīn
41 Y14 Meyers Chuck Etolin Island, Alaska, USA 55.44N 132.15W
154 M3 Meymaneh var. Maimāna, Maymana. Fāryāb, NW Afghanistan 35.57N 64.48E
149 N7 Meymeh Eşfahān, C Iran 33.28N 51.09E
127 Pp6 Meynypil'gyno Chukotskiy Avtonomnyy Okrug, NE Russian Federation 62.33N 177.00E
110 A10 Meyrin Genève, SW Switzerland 46.13N 6.04E
177 Ff8 Mezaligon Irrawaddy, SW Myanmar 17.53N 95.12E
43 O15 Mezcala Guerrero, S Mexico 17.55N 99.34W
116 H8 Mezdra Vratsa, NW Bulgaria 43.09N 23.44E
105 P16 Mèze Hérault, S France 43.25N 3.37E
129 O6 Mezen' Arkhangel'skaya Oblast', NW Russian Federation 65.54N 44.10E
129 P8 Mezen' ~ NW Russian Federation
Mezen, Bay of see Mezenskaya Guba
105 Q13 Mézenc, Mont ▲ C France 44.57N 4.15E
129 O8 Mezenskaya Guba var. Bay of Mezen. bay NW Russian Federation
125 Bb7 Mezha ~ W Russian Federation
Mezha see Myazha
126 Hh15 Mezhdurechensk Kemerovskaya Oblast', S Russian Federation 53.37N 87.59E
125 F4 Mezhdusharskiy, Ostrov island Novaya Zemlya, N Russian Federation
Mezhëvo see Myezhava
Mezhgor'ye see Mizhhir"ya
131 W5 Mezhgor'ye Respublika Bashkortostan, W Russian Federation 54.10N 57.55E
119 V8 Mezhova Dnipropetrovs'ka Oblast', E Ukraine 48.15N 36.44E
8 J12 Meziadin Junction British Columbia, W Canada 56.06N 129.15W
113 G16 Mezileské sedlo var. Przełęcz Międzyleska. pass Czech Republic/Poland 50.05N 16.40E
104 L14 Mézin Lot-et-Garonne, SW France 44.03N 0.16E
113 M24 Mezőberény Békés, SE Hungary 46.49N 21.00E
113 M25 Mezőhegyes Békés, SE Hungary 46.19N 20.51E
113 M25 Mezőkovácsháza Békés, SE Hungary 46.25N 20.52E
113 M21 Mezőkövesd Borsod-Abaúj-Zemplén, NE Hungary 47.48N 20.34E
Mezőtelegd see Tileagd
113 M23 Mezőtúr Jász-Nagykun-Szolnok, E Hungary 47.00N 20.37E
42 K10 Mezquital Durango, C Mexico 23.29N 104.24W
108 G6 Mezzolombardo Trentino-Alto Adige, N Italy 46.13N 11.08E
84 L13 Mfuwe Northern, N Zambia 13.00S 31.45E
123 J16 Mġarr Gozo, N Malta 36.01N 14.18E
130 H6 Mglin Bryanskaya Oblast', W Russian Federation 53.01N 32.54E
Mhálanna, Cionn see Malin Head
160 G10 Mhow Madhya Pradesh, C India 22.36N 75.47E
Miadzioł Nowy see Myadzyel
179 Q13 Miagao Panay Island, C Philippines 10.40N 122.15E
43 R17 Miahuatlán var. Miahuatlán de Porfirio Díaz. Oaxaca, SE Mexico 16.21N 96.36W
Miahuatlán de Porfirio Díaz see Miahuatlán
106 K10 Miajadas Extremadura, W Spain 39.10N 5.54W
Miajlar see Myājlār
38 M14 Miami Arizona, SW USA 33.23N 110.53W
25 Z16 Miami Florida, SE USA 25.46N 80.11W
29 R8 Miami Oklahoma, C USA 36.52N 94.52W
27 O2 Miami Texas, SW USA 35.41N 100.38W
25 Z16 Miami ✈ Florida, SE USA 25.47N 80.16W
25 Z16 Miami Beach Florida, SE USA 25.47N 80.07W
25 Y15 Miami Canal canal Florida, SE USA
33 R14 Miamisburg Ohio, N USA 39.38N 84.17W
155 U10 Miān Channūn Punjab, E Pakistan 30.27N 72.24E
148 J4 Miāndowāb var. Mianduab, Miyāndoāb. Āžarbāyjān-e Bākhtarī, NW Iran 36.58N 46.06E
180 H5 Miandrivazo Toliara, C Madagascar 19.31S 45.28E
Mianduab see Miāndowāb
148 K3 Mīāneh var. Miyāneh. Āžarbāyjān-e Khāvarī, NW Iran 37.25N 47.43E
155 O16 Miāni Hōr lagoon S Pakistan
166 G10 Mianning Sichuan, C China 28.34N 102.12E
155 T7 Miānwāli Punjab, NE Pakistan 32.31N 71.33E
166 J7 Mianxian var. Mian Xian. Shaanxi, C China 33.12N 106.36E
166 I8 Mianyang Sichuan, C China 31.28N 104.43E
Mianyang see Xiantao
167 R3 Miaodao Qundao island group E China
167 S13 Miaoli N Taiwan 24.33N 120.48E
125 E12 Miass Chelyabinskaya Oblast', C Russian Federation 55.00N 59.55E
112 G8 Miastko Ger. Rummelsburg in Pommern. Pomorskie, N Poland 54.00N 16.58E
Miava see Myjava
9 O15 Mica Creek British Columbia, SW Canada 51.58N 118.29W
166 J7 Micang Shan ▲▲ C China
194 I12 Michael, Mount ▲ C PNG 6.24S 145.18E
Mi Chai see Nong Khai
113 O19 Michalovce Ger. Grossmichel, Hung. Nagymihály. Košický Kraj, E Slovakia 48.46N 21.54E
101 M20 Michel, Baraque hill E Belgium 50.38N 6.09E
41 S5 Michelson, Mount ▲ Alaska, USA 69.19N 144.16W
47 P9 Miches E Dominican Republic 18.56N 69.04W
32 M4 Michigamme, Lake ◎ Michigan, N USA
32 M4 Michigamme Reservoir ▣ Michigan, N USA
33 N4 Michigamme River ~ Michigan, N USA
33 O7 Michigan off. State of Michigan; also known as Great Lakes State, Lake State, Wolverine State. ◈ state N USA
33 O11 Michigan City Indiana, N USA 41.43N 86.52W
33 O8 Michigan, Lake ◎ N USA
33 P2 Michipicoten Bay lake bay Ontario, N Canada
12 A8 Michipicoten Island island Ontario, S Canada
12 B7 Michipicoten River Ontario, S Canada 47.56N 84.48W
Michurin see Tsarevo
130 M6 Michurinsk Tambovskaya Oblast', W Russian Federation 52.56N 40.30E
Mico, Punta/Mico, Punto see Monkey Point
44 L10 Mico, Río ~ SE Nicaragua
47 T12 Micoud SE Saint Lucia 13.49N 60.54W
201 N16 Micronesia off. Federated States of Micronesia. ◆ federation W Pacific Ocean
183 P4 Micronesia island group W Pacific Ocean
174 Jj5 Midai, Pulau island Kepulauan Natuna, W Indonesia
Mid-Atlantic Cordillera see Mid-Atlantic Ridge
67 M17 Mid-Atlantic Ridge var. Mid-Atlantic Cordillera, Mid-Atlantic Rise, Mid-Atlantic Swell. undersea feature Atlantic Ocean
Mid-Atlantic Rise/Mid-Atlantic Swell see Mid-Atlantic Ridge
101 E15 Middelburg Zeeland, SW Netherlands 51.30N 3.36E
85 H24 Middelburg Eastern Cape, S South Africa 31.28S 25.01E
85 K21 Middelburg Mpumalanga, NE South Africa 25.46S 29.28E
97 G23 Middelfart Fyn, C Denmark 55.30N 9.43E
100 G13 Middelharnis Zuid-Holland, SW Netherlands 51.45N 4.10E
101 B16 Middelkerke West-Vlaanderen, W Belgium 51.11N 2.51E
100 I9 Middenbeemster Noord-Holland, C Netherlands 52.33N 4.55E
100 I8 Middenmeer Noord-Holland, NW Netherlands 52.48N 4.58E
37 Q2 Middle Alkali Lake ◎ California, W USA
200 Nn6 Middle America Trench undersea feature E Pacific Ocean
157 P19 Middle Andaman island Andaman Islands, India, NE Indian Ocean
Middle Atlas see Moyen Atlas
23 R3 Middlebourne West Virginia, NE USA 39.29N 80.54W
25 W9 Middleburg Florida, SE USA 30.03N 81.55W
Middleburg Island see 'Eua
Middle Caicos see Grand Caicos
27 N8 Middle Concho River ~ Texas, SW USA
Middle Congo see Congo (Republic of)
41 R6 Middle Fork Chandalar River ~ Alaska, USA
41 Q7 Middle Fork Koyukuk River ~ Alaska, USA
35 O12 Middle Fork Salmon River ~ Idaho, NW USA
9 T15 Middle Lake Saskatchewan, S Canada 52.31N 105.16W
30 L13 Middle Loup River ~ Nebraska, C USA
193 E22 Middlemarch Otago, South Island, NZ 45.30S 170.07E
33 T15 Middleport Ohio, N USA 39.00N 82.03W
31 U14 Middle Raccoon River ~ Iowa, C USA
31 R3 Middle River ~ Minnesota, N USA
23 N8 Middlesboro Kentucky, S USA 36.37N 83.42W
99 M15 Middlesbrough N England, UK 54.34N 1.13W
44 G3 Middlesex Stann Creek, C Belize 17.00N 88.31W
99 N22 Middlesex cultural region SE England, UK
11 P15 Middleton Nova Scotia, SE Canada 44.54N 65.01W
22 F10 Middleton Tennessee, S USA 35.05N 88.57W
32 L9 Middleton Wisconsin, N USA 43.06N 89.30W
41 S13 Middleton Island island Alaska, USA
36 M7 Middletown California, W USA 38.44N 122.39W
23 Y2 Middletown Delaware, NE USA 39.25N 75.39W
20 K15 Middletown New Jersey, NE USA 40.22N 74.07W
20 K13 Middletown New York, NE USA 41.27N 74.25W
33 R14 Middletown Ohio, N USA 39.33N 84.19W
20 G15 Middletown Pennsylvania, NE USA 40.11N 76.42W
147 N14 Mīdī var. Maydī. NW Yemen 16.18N 42.51E
105 O16 Midi, Canal du canal S France
104 K17 Midi de Bigorre, Pic du ▲ S France 42.57N 0.08E
104 K17 Midi d'Ossau, Pic du ▲ SW France 42.51N 0.27W
181 R7 Mid-Indian Basin undersea feature N Indian Ocean
181 P7 Mid-Indian Ridge var. Central Indian Ridge. undersea feature C Indian Ocean
105 N14 Midi-Pyrénées ◈ region S France
27 N8 Midkiff Texas, SW USA 31.35N 101.51W
12 G13 Midland Ontario, S Canada 44.43N 79.51W
33 R8 Midland Michigan, N USA 43.37N 84.15W
30 M10 Midland South Dakota, N USA 44.04N 101.07W
26 M8 Midland Texas, SW USA 32.00N 102.04W
85 K17 Midlands ◈ province C Zimbabwe
99 D21 Midleton Ir. Mainistir na Corann. SW Ireland 51.55N 8.10W
27 T7 Midlothian Texas, SW USA 32.28N 96.59W
98 K12 Midlothian cultural region S Scotland, UK
180 I7 Midongy Fianarantsoa, S Madagascar 21.58S 47.46E
104 K15 Midou ~ SW France
199 Ii6 Mid-Pacific Mountains var. Mid-Pacific Seamounts. undersea feature NW Pacific Ocean
Mid-Pacific Seamounts see Mid-Pacific Mountains
179 R16 Midsayap Mindanao, S Philippines 7.12N 124.31E
38 L3 Midway Utah, W USA 40.30N 111.28W
199 Jj5 Midway Islands ◇ US territory C Pacific Ocean
35 X14 Midwest Wyoming, C USA 43.24N 106.15W
29 N10 Midwest City Oklahoma, C USA 35.27N 97.24W
158 M10 Mid Western ◈ zone W Nepal
100 P5 Midwolda Groningen, NE Netherlands 53.12N 7.00E
143 Q16 Midyat Mardin, SE Turkey 37.25N 41.19E
116 F8 Midžhur SCr. Midžor. ▲ Bulgaria/Serbia and Montenegro (Yugoslavia) see also Midžor 43.24N 22.41E
115 Q14 Midžor Bul. Midzhur. ▲ Bulgaria/Serbia and Montenegro (Yugoslavia) see also Midzhur 43.24N 22.40E
171 H16 Mie off. Mie-ken. ◈ prefecture Honshū, SW Japan
113 L16 Miechów Małopolskie, S Poland 50.20N 20.00E
112 F11 Międzychód Ger. Mitteldorf. Wielkopolskie, C Poland 52.36N 15.52E
Międzyleska, Przełęcz see Mezileské Sedlo
112 O12 Międzyrzec Podlaski Lubelskie, E Poland 52.00N 22.47E
112 E11 Międzyrzecz Ger. Meseritz. Lubelskie, W Poland 52.26N 15.33E
Mie-ken see Mie
104 L16 Miélan Gers, S France 43.25N 0.18E
113 N16 Mielec Podkarpackie, SE Poland 50.18N 21.27E
97 L21 Mien ◎ S Sweden
43 O8 Mier Tamaulipas, C Mexico 26.25N 99.10W
118 J11 Miercurea-Ciuc Ger. Szeklerburg, Hung. Csíkszereda. Harghita, C Romania 46.23N 25.47E
Mieresch see Maros/Mureș
Mieres del Camín see Mieres del Camino
106 K2 Mieres del Camino var. Mieres del Camín. Asturias, NW Spain 43.15N 5.46W
101 K15 Mierlo Noord-Brabant, SE Netherlands 51.27N 5.37E
43 O10 Mier y Noriega Nuevo León, NE Mexico 23.24N 100.06W
Mies see Stříbro
82 K13 Mī'ēso var. Meheso, Oromo. C Ethiopia 9.13N 40.47E
Miesso see Mī'ēso
112 D10 Mieszkowice Ger. Bärwalde Neumark. Zachodniopomorskie, W Poland 52.45N 14.24E
20 G14 Mifflinburg Pennsylvania, NE USA 40.55N 77.03W
20 F14 Mifflintown Pennsylvania, NE USA 40.34N 77.24W
43 R15 Miguel Alemán, Presa ▣ SE Mexico

◆ Country ● Country Capital ◇ Dependent Territory ○ Dependent Territory Capital ◈ Administrative Region ✈ International Airport ▲ Mountain ▲▲ Mountain Range ⛰ Volcano ~ River ◎ Lake ▣ Reservoir

42 L9 **Miguel Asua** var. Miguel Auza. Zacatecas, C Mexico 24.16N 103.28W
Miguel Auza see Miguel Asua
45 S15 **Miguel de la Borda** var. Donoso. Colón, C Panama 9.06N 80.19W
43 N13 **Miguel Hidalgo** ✈ (Guadalajara) Jalisco, SW Mexico 20.52N 101.09W
42 H7 **Miguel Hidalgo, Presa** ▣ W Mexico
118 J14 **Mihăileşti** Giurgiu, S Romania 44.19N 25.54E
118 M14 **Mihail Kogălniceanu** var. Kogălniceanu; prev. Caramurat, Ferdinand. Constanţa, SE Romania 44.23N 28.24E
119 N14 **Mihai Viteazu** Constanţa, SE Romania 44.37N 28.41E
142 G12 **Mihalıççık** Eskişehir, NW Turkey 39.52N 31.30E
170 Ee13 **Mihara** Hiroshima, Honshū, SW Japan 34.24N 133.03E
171 Jj17 **Mihara-yama** ⛰ Miyako-jima, SE Japan 34.43N 139.22E
107 S8 **Mijares** ≈ E Spain
100 I11 **Mijdrecht** Utrecht, C Netherlands 52.12N 4.52E
172 Oo5 **Mikasa** Hokkaidō, NE Japan 43.19N 141.54E
Mikashevichi see Mikashevichy
121 K19 **Mikashevichy** Pol. Mikaszewicze, Rus. Mikashevichi. Brestskaya Voblasts', SW Belarus 52.13N 27.28E
Mikaszewicze see Mikashevichy
171 Hh16 **Mikawa-wan** bay S Japan
130 L5 **Mikhaylov** Ryazanskaya Oblast', W Russian Federation 54.12N 39.03E
Mikhaylovgrad see Montana
205 Z8 **Mikhaylov Island** island Antarctica
151 T6 **Mikhaylovka** Pavlodar, N Kazakhstan 53.49N 76.31E
131 N9 **Mikhaylovka** Volgogradskaya Oblast', SW Russian Federation 50.06N 43.17E
Mikhaylovka see Mykhaylivka
170 G14 **Miki** Hyōgo, Honshū, SW Japan 34.46N 135.00E
83 K24 **Mikindani** Mtwara, SE Tanzania 10.16S 40.04E
95 N18 **Mikkeli** Swe. Sankt Michel. Itä-Suomi, E Finland 61.41N 27.14E
112 M8 **Mikołajki** Ger. Nikolaiken. Warmińsko-Mazurskie, NE Poland 53.49N 21.31E
Míkonos see Mýkonos
116 I9 **Mikre** Lovech, N Bulgaria 43.02N 24.32E
116 C13 **Mikrí Préspa, Límni** ◎ N Greece
129 P4 **Mikulkin, Mys** headland NW Russian Federation 67.50N 46.36E
83 I23 **Mikumi** Morogoro, SE Tanzania 7.22S 37.00E
129 R10 **Mikun'** Respublika Komi, NW Russian Federation 62.20N 50.02E
171 Hh13 **Mikuni** Fukui, Honshū, SW Japan 36.12N 136.09E
171 Jj14 **Mikuni-tōge** pass Honshū, C Japan 36.48N 138.47E
172 Ss13 **Mikura-jima** island E Japan
31 V7 **Milaca** Minnesota, N USA 45.45N 93.40W
64 J10 **Milagro** La Rioja, C Argentina 31.00S 66.01W
58 B7 **Milagro** Guayas, SW Ecuador 2.08S 79.34W
33 P4 **Milakokia Lake** ◎ Michigan, N USA
32 J1 **Milan** Illinois, N USA 41.27N 90.33W
33 R10 **Milan** Michigan, N USA 42.05N 83.40W
29 T2 **Milan** Missouri, C USA 40.12N 93.07W
39 Q11 **Milan** New Mexico, SW USA 35.10N 107.53W
22 G9 **Milan** Tennessee, S USA 35.55N 88.45W
Milan see Milano
97 F15 **Miland** Telemark, S Norway 59.57N 8.48E
85 N15 **Milange** Zambézia, NE Mozambique 16.08S 35.51E
108 D8 **Milano** Eng. Milan, Ger. Mailand; anc. Mediolanum. Lombardia, N Italy 45.28N 9.10E
27 U10 **Milano** Texas, SW USA 30.42N 96.51W
142 C15 **Milas** Muğla, SW Turkey 37.16N 27.46E
121 K21 **Milashavichy** Rus. Milashevichi. Homyel'skaya Voblasts', SE Belarus 51.38N 27.54E
Milashevichi see Milashavichy
121 I18 **Milavidy** Rus. Milovidy. Brestskaya Voblasts', SW Belarus 52.54N 25.51E
109 L23 **Milazzo** anc. Mylae. Sicilia, Italy, C Mediterranean Sea 38.13N 15.15E
31 R8 **Milbank** South Dakota, N USA 45.12N 96.36W
21 T7 **Milbridge** Maine, NE USA 44.31N 67.55W
102 L11 **Milde** ≈ C Germany
12 F14 **Mildmay** Ontario, S Canada 44.03N 81.07W
190 L9 **Mildura** Victoria, SE Australia 34.13S 142.09E
143 X12 **Mil Düzü** Rus. Mil'skaya Ravnina, Mil'skaya Step'. physical region C Azerbaijan
166 H13 **Mile** Yunnan, SW China 24.28N 103.25E
Mile see Mili Atoll
189 Y10 **Miles** Queensland, E Australia 26.41S 150.15E
27 P8 **Miles** Texas, SW USA 31.36N 100.10W
35 X9 **Miles City** Montana, NW USA 46.24N 105.48W
9 U17 **Milestone** Saskatchewan, S Canada 50.00N 104.24W
109 N22 **Mileto** Calabria, SW Italy 38.35N 16.03E
109 K16 **Miletto, Monte** ▲ C Italy 41.28N 14.21E
20 M13 **Milford** Connecticut, NE USA 41.12N 73.01W
23 Y3 **Milford** var. Milford City. Delaware, NE USA 38.54N 75.25W
31 T11 **Milford** Iowa, C USA 43.19N 95.09W
21 S6 **Milford** Maine, NE USA 44.57N 68.37W
31 R16 **Milford** Nebraska, C USA 40.46N 97.03W
21 O10 **Milford** New Hampshire, NE USA 42.49N 71.38W
20 J13 **Milford** Pennsylvania, NE USA 41.19N 74.48W
27 T7 **Milford** Texas, SW USA 32.07N 96.57W
38 K6 **Milford** Utah, W USA 38.22N 112.57W
Milford see Milford Haven
Milford City see Milford
99 H21 **Milford Haven** prev. Milford. SW Wales, UK 51.43N 5.01W
29 O4 **Milford Lake** ▣ Kansas, C USA
193 B21 **Milford Sound** Southland, South Island, NZ 44.40S 167.57E
193 B21 **Milford Sound** inlet South Island, NZ
Milhau see Millau
Milḥ, Baḥr al see Razāzah, Buḥayrat ar
145 T10 **Milḥ, Wādī al** dry watercourse S Iraq
201 W8 **Mili Atoll** var. Mile. atoll Ratak Chain, SE Marshall Islands
112 H13 **Milicz** Dolnośląskie, SW Poland 51.31N 17.18E
109 L25 **Militello in Val di Catania** Sicilia, Italy, C Mediterranean Sea 37.16N 14.46E
127 Pp11 **Mil'kovo** Kamchatskaya Oblast', E Russian Federation 54.39N 158.35E
9 R17 **Milk River** Alberta, SW Canada 49.10N 112.06W
46 J13 **Milk River** ≈ C Jamaica
35 W7 **Milk River** ≈ Montana, NW USA
82 D9 **Milk, Wadi el** var. Wadi al Malik. ≈ C Sudan
101 L14 **Mill** Noord-Brabant, SE Netherlands 51.42N 5.46E
105 P14 **Millau** var. Milhau; anc. Æmilianum. Aveyron, S France 44.06N 3.04E
12 I14 **Millbrook** Ontario, SE Canada 44.09N 78.26W
25 U4 **Milledgeville** Georgia, SE USA 33.04N 83.13W
10 C12 **Mille Lacs, Lac des** ◎ Ontario, S Canada
31 V6 **Mille Lacs Lake** ◎ Minnesota, N USA
25 V4 **Millen** Georgia, SE USA 32.50N 81.56W
203 Y5 **Millennium Island** prev. Caroline Island, Thornton Island. atoll Line Islands, E Kiribati
31 O9 **Miller** South Dakota, N USA 44.31N 98.59W
32 K5 **Miller Dam Flowage** ◎ Wisconsin, N USA
41 U12 **Miller, Mount** ▲ Alaska, USA 60.29N 142.16W
130 L10 **Millerovo** Rostovskaya Oblast', SW Russian Federation 48.57N 40.25E
39 N17 **Miller Peak** ▲ Arizona, SW USA 31.23N 110.17W
33 T12 **Millersburg** Ohio, N USA 40.33N 81.55W
20 G15 **Millersburg** Pennsylvania, NE USA 40.31N 76.56W
193 D23 **Millers Flat** Otago, South Island, NZ 45.42S 169.25E
27 Q8 **Millersview** Texas, SW USA 31.26N 99.44W
108 B10 **Millesimo** Piemonte, NE Italy 44.24N 8.09E
15 Mm15 **Milles Lacs, Lac des** ◎ Ontario, SW Canada
27 Q13 **Millett** Texas, SW USA 28.33N 99.10W
105 N11 **Millevaches, Plateau de** plateau C France
190 K12 **Millicent** South Australia 37.37S 140.21E
100 M13 **Millingen aan den Rijn** Gelderland, SE Netherlands 51.52N 6.02E
22 E10 **Millington** Tennessee, S USA 35.20N 89.54W
21 R4 **Millinocket** Maine, NE USA 45.38N 68.45W
21 R4 **Millinocket Lake** ◎ Maine, NE USA
205 Z11 **Mill Island** island Antarctica
191 T3 **Millmerran** Queensland, E Australia 27.52S 151.15E
111 R9 **Millstatt** Kärnten, S Austria 46.45N 13.36E
99 B19 **Milltown Malbay** Ir. Sráid na Cathrach. W Ireland 52.51N 9.23W
20 J17 **Millville** New Jersey, NE USA 39.24N 75.01W
29 S13 **Millwood Lake** ▣ Arkansas, C USA
Milne Bank see Milne Seamounts
195 O17 **Milne Bay** ◆ province SE PNG
195 N17 **Milne Bay** bay SE PNG
66 J8 **Milne Seamounts** var. Milne Bank. undersea feature N Atlantic Ocean
31 Q6 **Milnor** North Dakota, N USA 46.15N 97.27W
21 R5 **Milo** Maine, NE USA 45.15N 69.01W
117 I22 **Mílos** Mílos, Kykládes, Greece, Aegean Sea 36.45N 24.26E
117 I22 **Mílos** island Kykládes, Greece, Aegean Sea
112 H11 **Miłosław** Wielkolpolskie, C Poland 52.13N 17.28E
115 K19 **Milot** var. Miloti. Lezhë, C Albania 41.42N 19.43E
Miloti see Milot
119 Z5 **Milove** Luhans'ka Oblast', E Ukraine 49.22N 40.09E
Milovidy see Milavidy
190 L4 **Milparinka** New South Wales, SE Australia 29.48S 141.57E
37 N9 **Milpitas** California, W USA 37.25N 121.54W
Mil'skaya Ravnina/Mil'skaya Step' see Mil Düzü
12 G15 **Milton** Ontario, S Canada 43.31N 79.52W
193 E24 **Milton** Otago, South Island, NZ 46.07S 169.59E
23 Y4 **Milton** Delaware, NE USA 38.48N 75.21W
25 P8 **Milton** Florida, SE USA 30.37N 87.02W
20 G14 **Milton** Pennsylvania, NE USA 41.01N 76.49W
20 L7 **Milton** Vermont, NE USA 44.37N 73.04W
34 K11 **Milton-Freewater** Oregon, NW USA 45.54N 118.24W
99 N21 **Milton Keynes** SE England, UK 52.00N 0.43W
29 N3 **Miltonvale** Kansas, C USA 39.21N 97.27W
167 N10 **Miluo** Hunan, S China 28.52N 113.00E
32 M9 **Milwaukee** Wisconsin, N USA 43.03N 87.55W
Milyang see Miryang
Mimatum see Mende
39 Q15 **Mimbres Mountains** ▲▲ New Mexico, SW USA
190 D2 **Mimili** South Australia 27.01S 132.33E
104 J14 **Mimizan** Landes, SW France 44.12N 1.12W
Mimmaya see Minmaya
81 E19 **Mimongo** Ngounié, C Gabon 1.36S 11.43E
Min see Fujian
37 T7 **Mina** Nevada, W USA 38.23N 118.07W
149 S14 **Mīnāb** Hormozgān, SE Iran 27.08N 57.02E
Mînâ Baranîs see Berenice
155 R9 **Mīna Bāzār** Baluchistān, SW Pakistan 30.58N 69.11E
170 C15 **Minamata** Kumamoto, Kyūshū, SW Japan 32.12N 130.23E
172 Ss17 **Minami-Iō-jima** Eng. San Augustine. island SE Japan
172 Nn7 **Minami-Kayabe** Hokkaidō, NE Japan 41.54N 140.58E
170 B17 **Minamitane** Kagoshima, Tanega-shima, SW Japan 30.23N 130.54E
Minami Tori Shima see Marcus Island
64 J4 **Mina Pirquitas** Jujuy, NW Argentina 22.48S 66.24W
181 O3 **Mīnā' Qābūs** NE Oman
63 F19 **Minas** Lavalleja, S Uruguay 34.19S 55.15W
11 P15 **Minas Basin** bay Nova Scotia, SE Canada
63 F17 **Minas de Corrales** Rivera, NE Uruguay 31.34S 55.19W
46 A5 **Minas de Matahambre** Pinar del Río, W Cuba 22.34N 83.57W
106 J13 **Minas de Ríotinto** Andalucía, S Spain 37.40N 6.36W
62 K7 **Minas Gerais** off. Estado de Minas Gerais. ◆ state E Brazil
44 E5 **Minas, Sierra de las** ▲▲ E Guatemala
43 T15 **Minatitlán** Veracruz-Llave, E Mexico 17.58N 94.31W
177 Ff6 **Minbu** Magwe, W Myanmar 20.09N 94.52E
155 V10 **Minchinābād** Punjab, E Pakistan 30.10N 73.40E
65 G17 **Minchinmávida, Volcán** ▲ S Chile 42.51S 72.23W
98 G7 **Minch, The** var. North Minch. strait NW Scotland, UK
108 F8 **Mincio** anc. Mincius. ≈ N Italy
Mincius see Mincio
28 M11 **Minco** Oklahoma, C USA 35.18N 97.56W
179 Rr16 **Mindanao** island S Philippines
Mindanao Sea see Bohol Sea
103 J23 **Mindel** ≈ S Germany
103 J23 **Mindelheim** Bayern, S Germany 48.03N 10.29E
Mindello see Mindelo
78 C9 **Mindelo** var. Mindello; prev. Porto Grande. São Vicente, N Cape Verde 16.54N 25.01W
12 I13 **Minden** Ontario, SE Canada 44.54N 78.41W
102 H13 **Minden** anc. Minthun. Nordrhein-Westfalen, NW Germany 52.18N 8.55E
24 G5 **Minden** Louisiana, S USA 32.37N 93.17W
31 O16 **Minden** Nebraska, C USA 40.30N 98.57W
37 Q6 **Minden** Nevada, W USA 38.58N 119.46W
190 L8 **Mindona Lake** seasonal lake New South Wales, SE Australia
179 Pp12 **Mindoro** island N Philippines
179 P12 **Mindoro Strait** strait W Philippines
165 S9 **Mine** Gansu, N China
170 Dd12 **Mine** Yamaguchi, Honshū, SW Japan 34.10N 131.12E
99 E21 **Mine Head** Ir. Mionn Ard. headland S Ireland 51.58N 7.36W
99 J23 **Minehead** SW England, UK 51.13N 3.28W
61 J19 **Mineiros** Goiás, C Brazil 17.34S 52.33W
27 V6 **Mineola** Texas, SW USA 32.39N 95.29W
27 S13 **Mineral** Texas, SW USA 28.32N 97.54W
131 N15 **Mineral'nyye Vody** Stavropol'skiy Kray, SW Russian Federation 44.13N 43.06E
32 K9 **Mineral Point** Wisconsin, N USA 42.54N 90.09W
27 S6 **Mineral Wells** Texas, SW USA 32.48N 98.06W
38 K6 **Minersville** Utah, W USA 38.12N 112.56W
33 U12 **Minerva** Ohio, N USA 40.43N 81.06W
109 N17 **Minervino Murge** Puglia, SE Italy 41.06N 16.04E
105 O16 **Minervois** physical region S France
164 I10 **Minfeng** var. Niya. Xinjiang Uygur Zizhiqu, NW China 37.07N 82.43E
81 O25 **Minga** Katanga, SE Dem. Rep. Congo 11.06S 27.57E
143 W11 **Mingäçevir** Rus. Mingechaur, Mingechevir. C Azerbaijan 40.46N 47.02E
143 W11 **Mingäçevir Su Anbarı** Rus. Mingechaurskoye Vodokhranilishche, Mingechevirskoye Vodokhranilishche. ▣ NW Azerbaijan
177 G8 **Mingaladon** ✈ (Yangon) Yangon, SW Myanmar 16.55N 96.11E
11 P11 **Mingan** Quebec, E Canada 50.19N 64.01W
155 U5 **Mingāora** var. Mingora, Mongora. North-West Frontier Province, N Pakistan 34.46N 72.22E
152 K8 **Mingbuloq** Rus. Mynbulak. Navoiy Viloyati, N Uzbekistan 42.18N 62.53E
152 K9 **Mingbuloq Botig'I** Rus. Vpadina Mynbulak. depression N Uzbekistan
Mingechaur/Mingechevir see Mingäçevir
Mingechaurskoye Vodokhranilishche/Mingechevirskoye Vodokhranilishche see Mingäçevir Su Anbarı
167 Q7 **Mingguang** prev. Jiashan. Anhui, S China 32.45N 117.58E
177 Ff4 **Mingin** Sagaing, C Myanmar 22.51N 94.30E
107 Q10 **Minglanilla** Castilla-La Mancha, C Spain 39.31N 1.36W
33 V13 **Mingo Junction** Ohio, N USA 40.19N 80.36W
Mingora see Mingāora
169 V7 **Mingshui** Heilongjiang, NE China 47.10N 125.52E
Mingteke Daban see Mintaka Pass
85 Q14 **Minguri** Nampula, NE Mozambique 14.30S 40.37E
165 U10 **Minhe** var. Shangchuankou. Qinghai, C China 36.21N 102.40E
177 Ff6 **Minhla** Magwe, W Myanmar 19.57N 94.58E
178 J15 **Minh Lương** Kiên Giang, S Vietnam 9.52N 105.10E
106 G5 **Minho, Rio** Sp. Miño. ≈ Portugal/Spain see also Miño
106 G5 **Minho** former province N Portugal
161 C24 **Minicoy Island** island SW India
35 P15 **Minidoka** Idaho, NW USA 42.45N 113.29W
120 C11 **Minija** ≈ W Lithuania
188 G9 **Minilya** Western Australia 23.45S 114.03E
12 E8 **Minisinakwa Lake** ◎ Ontario, S Canada
47 T12 **Ministre Point** headland S Saint Lucia 13.42N 60.57W
9 V15 **Minitonas** Manitoba, S Canada 52.07N 101.02W
Minius see Miño
167 R12 **Min Jiang** ≈ SE China
166 H10 **Min Jiang** ≈ C China
190 H9 **Minlaton** South Australia 34.52S 137.33E
172 N8 **Minmaya** var. Mimmaya. Aomori, Honshū, C Japan 41.10N 140.24E
79 U14 **Minna** Niger, C Nigeria 9.33N 6.33E
172 Pp16 **Minna-jima** island Sakishima-shotō, SW Japan
29 N4 **Minneapolis** Kansas, C USA 39.07N 97.42W
31 U9 **Minneapolis** Minnesota, N USA 44.58N 93.15W
31 V8 **Minneapolis-Saint Paul** ✈ Minnesota, N USA 44.53N 93.13W
15 Kk15 **Minnedosa** Manitoba, S Canada 50.13N 99.49W
28 J7 **Minneola** Kansas, C USA 37.26N 100.00W
31 S7 **Minnesota** off. State of Minnesota; also known as Gopher State, New England of the West, North Star State. ◆ state N USA
31 S9 **Minnesota River** ≈ Minnesota/South Dakota, N USA
31 V9 **Minnetonka** Minnesota, N USA 44.55N 93.28W
31 O3 **Minnewaukan** North Dakota, N USA 48.03N 99.15W
190 F7 **Minnipa** South Australia 32.52S 135.07E
106 H2 **Miño** Galicia, NW Spain 43.21N 8.12W
106 G5 **Miño** var. Mino, Minius, Port. Rio Minho. ≈ Portugal/Spain see also Minho, Rio
171 Ii16 **Minobu** Yamanashi, Honshū, S Japan 35.22N 138.30E
32 L4 **Minocqua** Wisconsin, N USA 45.53N 89.42W
171 I15 **Minokamo** Gifu, Honshū, SW Japan 35.24N 136.57E
32 L12 **Minonk** Illinois, N USA 40.54N 89.01W
Minorca see Menorca
30 M3 **Minot** North Dakota, N USA 48.15N 101.19W
165 U8 **Minqin** Gansu, N China 38.35N 103.07E
121 J16 **Minsk** ● (Belarus) Minskaya Voblasts', C Belarus 53.52N 27.34E
121 L16 **Minsk** ✈ Minskaya Voblasts', C Belarus 53.52N 27.58E
Minskaya Oblast' see Minskaya Voblasts'
121 K16 **Minskaya Voblasts'** prev. Rus. Minskaya Oblast'. ◆ province C Belarus
121 J16 **Minskaya Wzvyshsha** ▲▲ C Belarus
112 N12 **Mińsk Mazowiecki** var. Nowo-Minsk. Mazowieckie, C Poland 52.11N 21.33E
33 Q13 **Minster** Ohio, N USA 40.23N 84.22W
81 F15 **Minta** Centre, C Cameroon 4.34N 12.54E
155 W2 **Mintaka Pass** Chin. Mingteke Daban. pass China/Pakistan 36.59N 75.04E
117 D20 **Mínthi** ▲▲ S Greece
Minthun see Minden
11 O14 **Minto** New Brunswick, SE Canada 46.04N 66.04W
8 H6 **Minto** Yukon Territory, W Canada 62.33N 136.45W
41 R9 **Minto** Alaska, USA 65.07N 149.22W
31 Q3 **Minto** North Dakota, N USA 48.17N 97.22W
10 K6 **Minto, Lac** ◎ Quebec, C Canada
205 R16 **Minto, Mount** ▲ Antarctica 71.38S 169.11E
9 U17 **Minton** Saskatchewan, S Canada 49.12N 104.33W
201 R15 **Minto Reef** atoll Caroline Islands, C Micronesia
39 R4 **Minturn** Colorado, C USA 39.34N 106.21W
109 J16 **Minturno** Lazio, C Italy 41.15N 13.47E
126 Hh15 **Minusinsk** Krasnoyarskiy Kray, S Russian Federation 53.37N 91.49E
110 G11 **Minusio** Ticino, S Switzerland 46.11N 8.47E
81 E17 **Minvoul** Woleu-Ntem, N Gabon 2.07N 12.12E
147 R13 **Minwakh** N Yemen 16.54N 48.04E
165 V11 **Minxian** var. Min Xian. Gansu, C China 34.22N 104.02E
Minya see El Minya
33 R6 **Mio** Michigan, N USA 44.40N 84.09W
Mionn Ard see Mine Head
176 Ww9 **Mios Num, Selat** strait Papua, E Indonesia
164 L5 **Miquan** Xinjiang Uygur Zizhiqu, NW China 44.04N 87.40E
121 I17 **Mir** Hrodzyenskaya Voblasts', W Belarus 53.25N 26.28E
108 H8 **Mira** Veneto, NE Italy 45.25N 12.07E
106 G13 **Mira, Rio** ≈ S Portugal
10 K15 **Mirabel** var. Montreal. ✈ (Montréal) Quebec, SE Canada 45.27N 73.47W
62 Q8 **Miracema** Rio de Janeiro, SE Brazil 21.24S 42.10W
56 G9 **Miraflores** Boyacá, C Colombia 5.07N 73.09W
42 G10 **Miraflores** Baja California Sur, W Mexico 23.24N 109.45W
46 L9 **Miragoâne** S Haiti 18.25N 73.07W
161 E16 **Miraj** Mahārāshtra, W India 16.51N 74.42E
63 E23 **Miramar** Buenos Aires, E Argentina 38.15S 57.49W
105 R15 **Miramas** Bouches-du-Rhône, SE France 43.34N 4.58E
104 K12 **Mirambeau** Charente-Maritime, W France 45.23N 0.33W
104 L13 **Miramont-de-Guyenne** Lot-et-Garonne, SW France 44.34N 0.20E
117 L25 **Mirampéllou Kólpos** gulf Krití, Greece, E Mediterranean Sea
164 L8 **Miran** Xinjiang Uygur Zizhiqu, NW China 39.13N 88.58E
56 M5 **Miranda** off. Estado Miranda. ◆ state N Venezuela
Miranda de Corvo see Miranda do Corvo
107 O3 **Miranda de Ebro** La Rioja, N Spain 42.40N 2.57W
106 G8 **Miranda do Corvo** var. Miranda de Corvo. Coimbra, N Portugal 40.04N 8.19W
106 J6 **Miranda do Douro** Bragança, N Portugal 41.30N 6.16W
104 L15 **Mirande** Gers, S France 43.31N 0.25E
106 I6 **Mirandela** Bragança, N Portugal 41.28N 7.10W
27 R15 **Mirando City** Texas, SW USA 27.24N 99.00W
108 G9 **Mirandola** Emilia-Romagna, N Italy 44.52N 11.04E
62 I8 **Mirandópolis** São Paulo, S Brazil 21.10S 51.03W
62 K8 **Mirassol** São Paulo, S Brazil 20.50S 49.30W
106 J3 **Miravalles** ▲ NW Spain 42.52N 6.45W
44 L12 **Miravalles, Volcán** ⛰ NW Costa Rica 10.43N 85.07W
147 W13 **Mirbāṭ** var. Marbat. S Oman 17.03N 54.44E
46 M9 **Mirebalais** C Haiti 18.46N 72.03W
105 T6 **Mirecourt** Vosges, NE France 48.19N 6.04E
105 N16 **Mirepoix** Ariège, S France 43.04N 1.52E
Mirgorod see Myrhorod
145 W10 **Mīr Ḥājī Khalīl** E Iraq 32.11N 46.19E
174 Mm4 **Miri** Sarawak, East Malaysia 4.22N 113.58E
79 W12 **Miria** Zinder, S Niger 13.39N 9.15E
190 F5 **Mirikata** South Australia 29.56S 135.13E
56 K4 **Mirimire** Falcón, N Venezuela 11.07N 68.36W
63 H18 **Mirim Lagoon** var. Lake Mirim, Sp. Laguna Merín. lagoon Brazil/Uruguay
Mirim, Lake see Mirim Lagoon
Mírina see Mýrina
180 H14 **Miringoni** Mohéli, S Comoros 12.16S 93.39E
149 W11 **Mīrjāveh** Sīstān va Balūchestān, SE Iran 29.04N 61.23E
205 Z9 **Mirny** Russian research station Antarctica 66.25S 93.09E
128 M10 **Mirnyy** Arkhangel'skaya Oblast', NW Russian Federation 62.50N 40.20E
126 Kk11 **Mirnyy** Respublika Sakha (Yakutiya), NE Russian Federation 62.30N 113.58E
Mironovka see Myronivka
112 F9 **Mirosławiec** Zachodniopomorskie, NW Poland 53.21N 16.04E
Mirovo see Vrattsa
102 N10 **Mirow** Mecklenburg-Vorpommern, N Germany 53.16N 12.48E
158 G6 **Mīrpur** Jammu and Kashmir, NW India 33.06N 73.49E
Mīrpur see New Mīrpur
155 P17 **Mīrpur Batoro** Sind, SE Pakistan 24.40N 68.15E
155 Q16 **Mīrpur Khās** Sind, SE Pakistan 25.31N 69.00E
155 P17 **Mīrpur Sakro** Sind, SE Pakistan 24.31N 67.37E
149 T14 **Mīr Shahdād** Hormozgān, S Iran 26.15N 58.28E
Mirtoan Sea see Mirtóo Pélagos
117 G21 **Mirtóo Pélagos** Eng. Mirtoan Sea; anc. Myrtoum Mare. sea S Greece
169 Z16 **Miryang** var. Milyang, Jap. Mitsuō. SE South Korea 35.30N 128.46E
Mirzachirla see Murzechirla
170 Dd14 **Misaki** Ehime, Shikoku, SW Japan 33.22N 132.04E
43 Q13 **Misantla** Veracruz-Llave, E Mexico 19.54N 96.51W
172 N9 **Misawa** Aomori, Honshū, C Japan 40.41N 141.22E
59 G14 **Mishagua, Río** ≈ C Peru
169 Z8 **Mishan** Heilongjiang, NE China 45.30N 131.53E
33 O11 **Mishawaka** Indiana, N USA 41.40N 86.10W
41 N6 **Misheguk Mountain** ▲ Alaska, USA 68.13N 161.11W
171 Jj17 **Mishima** var. Misima. Shizuoka, Honshū, S Japan 35.07N 138.55E
170 Dd11 **Mi-shima** island SW Japan
131 V4 **Mishkino** Respublika Bashkortostan, W Russian Federation 55.31N 55.57E
159 Y10 **Mishmi Hills** hill range NE India
167 N11 **Mi Shui** ≈ S China
Misiaf see Maşyāf
109 J23 **Misilmeri** Sicilia, Italy, C Mediterranean Sea 38.03N 13.27E
Misima see Mishima
195 P17 **Misima Island** island SE PNG
Misión de Guana see Guana
62 F13 **Misiones** off. Provincia de Misiones. ◆ province NE Argentina
64 P8 **Misiones** off. Departamento de las Misiones. ◆ department S Paraguay
Misión San Fernando see San Fernando
Miskin see Maskin
Miskito Coast see La Mosquitia
45 O7 **Miskitos, Cayos** island group NE Nicaragua
113 M21 **Miskolc** Borsod-Abaúj-Zemplén, NE Hungary 48.04N 20.46E
175 Tt10 **Misool, Pulau** island Maluku, E Indonesia
Misox see Mesocco
31 Y3 **Misquah Hills** hill range Minnesota, N USA
77 P7 **Mişrātah** var. Misurata. NW Libya 32.22N 15.06E
123 Ll15 **Mişrātah, Râs** headland N Libya 32.22N 15.16E
12 C7 **Missanabie** Ontario, S Canada 48.18N 84.04W
60 E10 **Missão Catrimani** Roraima, N Brazil 1.25N 62.05W
12 D6 **Missinaibi** ≈ Ontario, S Canada
12 C7 **Missinaibi Lake** ◎ Ontario, S Canada
9 T13 **Missinipe** Saskatchewan, C Canada 55.36N 104.45W
30 M11 **Mission** South Dakota, N USA 43.16N 100.38W
27 S17 **Mission** Texas, SW USA 26.13N 98.19W
10 F10 **Missisa Lake** ◎ Ontario, C Canada
20 M6 **Missisquoi Bay** lake bay Canada/USA
12 C10 **Mississagi** ≈ Ontario, S Canada
12 G15 **Mississauga** Ontario, S Canada 43.36N 79.34W
33 P12 **Mississinewa Lake** ▣ Indiana, N USA
33 P12 **Mississinewa River** ≈ Indiana/Ohio, N USA
24 K4 **Mississippi** off. State of Mississippi; also known as Bayou State, Magnolia State. ◆ state SE USA
12 K13 **Mississippi** ≈ Ontario, SE Canada
24 M10 **Mississippi Delta** delta Louisiana, S USA
49 N1 **Mississippi Fan** undersea feature N Gulf of Mexico
12 L13 **Mississippi Lake** ◎ Ontario, SE Canada
(0) J11 **Mississippi River** ≈ C USA
24 M9 **Mississippi Sound** sound Alabama/Mississippi, S USA
35 P9 **Missoula** Montana, NW USA 46.54N 114.03W
29 T5 **Missouri** off. State of Missouri; also known as Bullion State, Show Me State. ◆ state C USA
27 V11 **Missouri City** Texas, SW USA 29.37N 95.32W
(0) J10 **Missouri River** ≈ C USA
13 Q6 **Mistassibi** ≈ Quebec, SE Canada
13 P6 **Mistassini** Quebec, SE Canada 48.54N 72.13W
13 P6 **Mistassini** ≈ Quebec, SE Canada
10 J11 **Mistassini, Lac** ◎ Quebec, SE Canada
111 Y3 **Mistelbach an der Zaya** Niederösterreich, NE Austria 48.33N 16.33E
109 L24 **Misterbianco** Sicilia, Italy, C Mediterranean Sea 37.31N 15.01E
97 N19 **Misterhult** Kalmar, S Sweden 57.28N 16.34E
59 H17 **Misti, Volcán** ▲ S Peru 16.20S 71.22W
Mistras see Mystrás
109 K23 **Mistretta** anc. Amestratus. Sicilia, Italy, C Mediterranean Sea 37.55N 14.22E
170 C14 **Misumi** Kumamoto, Kyūshū, SW Japan 32.37N 130.29E
170 Ee12 **Misumi** Shimane, Honshū, SW Japan 34.47N 132.00E
Misurata see Mişrātah
85 O14 **Mitande** Niassa, N Mozambique 14.06S 36.03E
42 J13 **Mita, Punta de** headland C Mexico 20.46N 105.31W
57 W12 **Mitaraka, Massif du** ▲ NE South America 2.18N 54.31W
Mitau see Jelgava
189 X9 **Mitchell** Queensland, E Australia 26.29S 148.00E
12 E15 **Mitchell** Ontario, S Canada 43.28N 81.11W
30 I13 **Mitchell** Nebraska, C USA 41.56N 103.48W
34 J12 **Mitchell** Oregon, NW USA 44.34N 120.09W
31 P11 **Mitchell** South Dakota, N USA 43.42N 98.01W
25 P5 **Mitchell Lake** ▣ Alabama, S USA
33 P7 **Mitchell, Lake** ◎ Michigan, N USA
23 P9 **Mitchell, Mount** ▲ North Carolina, SE USA 35.46N 82.16W
189 V3 **Mitchell River** ≈ Queensland, NE Australia
99 D20 **Mitchelstown** Ir. Baile Mhistéala. SW Ireland 52.19N 8.16W
12 M9 **Mitchinamécus, Lac** ◎ Quebec, SE Canada
Mitèmboni see Mitemele, Río
81 D17 **Mitemele, Río** var. Mitèmboni, Temboni, Utamboni. ≈ S Equatorial Guinea
155 S12 **Mithānkot** Punjab, E Pakistan 28.57N 70.21E
155 T7 **Mitha Tiwāna** Punjab, E Pakistan 32.16N 72.07E
155 R17 **Mithi** Sind, SE Pakistan 24.43N 69.52E
Míthimna see Míthymna
Mi Tho see My Tho
117 L16 **Míthymna** var. Míthimna. Lésvos, E Greece 39.22N 26.11E
202 L16 **Mitiaro** island S Cook Islands
Mitilíni see Mytilíni
13 U7 **Mitis** ≈ Quebec, SE Canada
43 R16 **Mitla** Oaxaca, SE Mexico 16.55N 96.19W
171 Kk16 **Mito** Ibaraki, Honshū, S Japan 36.21N 140.25E
94 N2 **Mitra, Kapp** headland W Svalbard 79.07N 11.11E
192 M13 **Mitre** ▲ North Island, NZ 40.46S 175.27E
193 B21 **Mitre Peak** ▲ South Island, NZ 44.37S 167.45E
41 O15 **Mitrofania Island** island Alaska, USA
Mitrovica/Mitrowitz see Sremska Mitrovica, Serbia, Serbia and Montenegro (Yugoslavia)
Mitrovica/Mitrovicë see Kosovska Mitrovica, Serbia, Serbia and Montenegro (Yugoslavia)
180 H12 **Mitsamiouli** Grande Comore, NW Comoros 11.22S 43.19E
180 I3 **Mitsinjo** Mahajanga, NW Madagascar 16.00S 45.52E
Mits'iwa see Massawa
180 H13 **Mitsoudjé** Grande Comore, NW Comoros
Mitspe Ramon see Mizpé Ramon
172 Oo7 **Mitsuishi** Hokkaidō, NE Japan 42.12N 142.40E
171 K13 **Mitsuke** var. Mituke. Niigata, Honshū, C Japan 37.33N 138.57E
Mitsuō see Miryang
170 Cc10 **Mitsushima** Nagasaki, Tsushima, SW Japan 34.16N 129.18E
102 G12 **Mittelandkanal** canal NW Germany
110 J7 **Mittelberg** Vorarlberg, NW Austria 47.19N 10.09E
Mitteldorf see Międzychód
Mittelstadt see Baia Sprie
Mitterburg see Pazin
111 P7 **Mittersill** Salzburg, NW Austria 47.16N 12.27E
103 N16 **Mittweida** Sachsen, E Germany 50.59N 12.57E
56 J13 **Mitú** Vaupés, SE Colombia 1.07N 70.04W
Mituke see Mitsuke
Mitumba, Chaîne des/Mitumba Range see Mitumba, Monts
81 O22 **Mitumba, Monts** var. Chaîne des Mitumba, Mitumba Range. ▲▲ E Dem. Rep. Congo
81 N23 **Mitwaba** Katanga, SE Dem. Rep. Congo 8.37S 27.19E
81 E18 **Mitzic** Woleu-Ntem, N Gabon 0.48N 11.30E
84 K11 **Miueru Wantipa, Lake** ◎ N Zambia
171 Jj17 **Miura** Kanagawa, Honshū, S Japan 35.07N 139.37E
171 M13 **Miyagi** off. Miyagi-ken. ◆ prefecture Honshū, C Japan
144 M7 **Miyāh, Wādī al** dry watercourse E Syria
172 Ss13 **Miyake** Tōkyō, Miyako-jima, SE Japan 34.34N 135.33E
172 N11 **Miyako** Iwate, Honshū, C Japan 39.39N 141.57E
172 Q16 **Miyako-jima** island Sakishima-shotō, SW Japan
170 C16 **Miyakonojō** var. Miyakonzyô. Miyazaki, Kyūshū, SW Japan 31.42N 131.03E
Miyakonzyô see Miyakonojō
172 Pp16 **Miyako-shotō** island group SW Japan
150 G11 **Miyaly** Atyrau, W Kazakhstan 48.52N 53.55E
Miyāndoāb see Mīāndowāb
Miyāneh see Mīāneh
170 C15 **Miyanojō** Kagoshima, Kyūshū, SW Japan 31.55N 130.29E
170 Cc16 **Miyazaki** Miyazaki, Kyūshū, SW Japan 31.55N 131.23E
170 C15 **Miyazaki** off. Miyazaki-ken. ◆ prefecture Kyūshū, SW Japan
171 H13 **Miyazu** Kyōto, Honshū, SW Japan 35.28N 135.21E
Miyory see Myory
170 F13 **Miyoshi** var. Miyosi. Hiroshima, Honshū, SW Japan 34.48N 132.51E
Miyosi see Miyoshi
Miza see Mizë
83 H14 **Mīzan Teferī** Southern, S Ethiopia 6.57N 35.30E
Mizda see Mizdah
77 O8 **Mizdah** var. Mizda. NW Libya 31.25N 12.58E
115 K20 **Mizë** var. Miza. Fier, W Albania 40.58N 19.32E
99 A22 **Mizen Head** Ir. Carn Uí Néid. headland SW Ireland 51.26N 9.50W
118 H7 **Mizhhir"ya** Rus. Mezhgor'ye. Zakarpats'ka Oblast', W Ukraine 48.28N 23.31E
166 L4 **Mizhi** Shaanxi, C China 37.43N 110.13E
118 K13 **Mizil** Prahova, SE Romania 45.00N 26.29E
116 H7 **Miziya** Vratsa, NW Bulgaria 43.42N 23.52E
159 W15 **Mizo Hills** hill range E India
159 W15 **Mizoram** ◆ state NE India
144 F12 **Mizpé Ramon** var. Mitspe Ramon. Southern, S Israel 30.37N 34.46E
59 L19 **Mizque** Cochabamba, C Bolivia 17.58S 65.18W
59 M19 **Mizque, Río** ≈ C Bolivia
171 I15 **Mizunami** Gifu, Honshū, SW Japan 35.19N 137.12E
171 Mm12 **Mizusawa** Iwate, Honshū, C Japan 39.09N 141.07E
97 M18 **Mjölby** Östergötland, S Sweden 58.19N 15.10E
97 G15 **Mjøndalen** Buskerud, S Norway 59.45N 9.58E
97 J19 **Mjörn** ◎ S Sweden
96 I13 **Mjøsa** var. Mjøsen. ◎ S Norway
Mjøsen see Mjøsa
83 G21 **Mkalama** Singida, C Tanzania 4.09S 34.34E
82 K13 **Mkata** ≈ C Tanzania

◆ Country
● Country Capital
◇ Dependent Territory
○ Dependent Territory Capital
◆ Administrative Region
✈ International Airport
▲ Mountain
▲▲ Mountain Range
⛰ Volcano
≈ River
◎ Lake
▣ Reservoir

85 K14 **Mkushi** Central, C Zambia 13.37S 29.27E
85 L22 **Mkuze** KwaZulu/Natal, E South Africa 27.40S 32.05E
83 J22 **Mkwaja** Tanga, E Tanzania 5.42S 38.48E
113 D16 **Mladá Boleslav** *Ger.* Jungbunzlau. Středočeský Kraj, N Czech Republic 50.24N 14.55E
114 M12 **Mladenovac** Serbia, C Serbia and Montenegro (Yugoslavia) 44.27N 20.42E
116 L11 **Mladinovo** Khaskovo, S Bulgaria 41.57N 26.13E
115 O17 **Mlado Nagoričane** N FYR Macedonia 42.11N 21.49E
Mlanje *see* Mulanje
114 N12 **Mlava** ⁂ E Serbia and Montenegro (Yugoslavia)
112 L9 **Mława** Mazowieckie, C Poland 53.07N 20.23E
115 G16 **Mljet** *It.* Meleda; *anc.* Melita. *island* S Croatia
118 K4 **Mlyniv** Rivnens'ka Oblast', NW Ukraine 50.31N 25.36E
85 I21 **Mmabatho** North-West, N South Africa 25.51S 25.37E
85 I19 **Mmashoro** Central, E Botswana 21.56S 26.39E
46 J7 **Moa** Holguín, E Cuba 20.38N 74.36W
78 J15 **Moa** ⁂ Guinea/Sierra Leone
39 O6 **Moab** Utah, W USA 38.34N 109.34W
189 V1 **Moa Island** *island* Queensland, NE Australia
197 J15 **Moala** *island* S Fiji
85 L21 **Moamba** Maputo, SW Mozambique 25.33S 32.15E
81 F19 **Moanda** *var.* Mouanda. Haut-Ogooué, SE Gabon 1.31S 13.07E
175 T16 **Moa, Pulau** *island* Kepulauan Leti, E Indonesia
85 M15 **Moatize** Tete, NW Mozambique 16.03S 33.49E
81 P22 **Moba** Katanga, E Dem. Rep. Congo 7.03S 29.51E
171 K17 **Mobara** Chiba, Honshū, S Japan 35.25N 140.19E
Mobay *see* Montego Bay
81 K15 **Mobaye** Basse-Kotto, S Central African Republic 4.19N 21.17E
81 K15 **Mobayi-Mbongo** Equateur, NW Dem. Rep. Congo 4.19N 21.18E
27 P2 **Mobeetie** Texas, SW USA 35.33N 100.25W
29 U3 **Moberly** Missouri, C USA 39.25N 92.26W
25 N8 **Mobile** Alabama, S USA 30.41N 88.02W
25 N9 **Mobile Bay** *bay* Alabama, S USA
25 N8 **Mobile River** ⁂ Alabama, S USA
31 N8 **Mobridge** South Dakota, N USA 45.32N 100.25W
Mobutu Sese Seko, Lac *see* Albert, Lake
47 N8 **Moca** N Dominican Republic 19.23N 70.31W
Moçâmedes *see* Namibe
178 J6 **Môc Châu** Sơn La, N Vietnam 20.52N 104.38E
197 L15 **Moce** *island* Lau Group, E Fiji
85 Q15 **Moçambique** Nampula, NE Mozambique 15.00S 40.44E
Mocha *see* Al Mukhā
200 Oo13 **Mocha Fracture Zone** *tectonic feature* SE Pacific Ocean
65 F14 **Mocha, Isla** *island* C Chile
58 C12 **Moche, Río** ⁂ W Peru
178 J14 **Môc Hoa** Long An, S Vietnam 10.46N 105.55E
85 I20 **Mochudi** Kgatleng, SE Botswana 24.25S 26.07E
84 Q13 **Mocímboa da Praia** *var.* Vila de Mocímboa da Praia. Cabo Delgado, N Mozambique 11.16S 40.21E
96 L13 **Mockfjärd** Dalarna, C Sweden 60.30N 14.57E
23 R9 **Mocksville** North Carolina, SE USA 35.53N 80.33W
34 F8 **Moclips** Washington, NW USA 47.11N 124.13W
84 C13 **Môco** *var.* Morro de Môco. ▲ W Angola 12.36S 15.09E
56 D13 **Mocoa** Putumayo, SW Colombia 1.07N 76.37W
62 M8 **Mococa** São Paulo, S Brazil 21.30S 47.00W
Môco, Morro de *see* Môco
42 H8 **Mocorito** Sinaloa, C Mexico 25.24N 107.55W
42 J4 **Moctezuma** Chihuahua, N Mexico 30.10N 106.24W
43 N11 **Moctezuma** San Luis Potosí, C Mexico 22.44N 101.04W
42 G4 **Moctezuma** Sonora, NW Mexico 29.49N 109.40W
43 P12 **Moctezuma, Río** ⁂ C Mexico
Mó, Cuan *see* Clew Bay
85 O16 **Mocuba** Zambézia, NE Mozambique 16.49S 37.01E
105 U12 **Modane** Savoie, E France 45.14N 6.41E
108 F9 **Modena** *anc.* Mutina. Emilia-Romagna, N Italy 44.39N 10.55E
38 I7 **Modena** Utah, W USA 37.46N 113.54W
37 O9 **Modesto** California, W USA 37.38N 121.01W
109 L25 **Modica** *anc.* Motyca. Sicilia, Italy, C Mediterranean Sea 36.52N 14.45E
85 J20 **Modimolle** prev. Nylstroom. Limpopo, NE South Africa 24.39S 28.23E
81 K17 **Modjamboli** Equateur, N Dem. Rep. Congo 2.27N 22.03E
111 X4 **Mödling** Niederösterreich, NE Austria 48.07N 16.15E
Modohn *see* Madona
169 N8 **Modot** Hentiy, C Mongolia 47.45N 109.03E
176 W12 **Modowi** Papua, E Indonesia 4.05S 134.39E
114 I12 **Modračko Jezero** ▣ NE Bosnia and Herzegovina
114 I10 **Modriča** Republika Srpska, N Bosnia and Herzegovina 44.57N 18.17E
191 O13 **Moe** Victoria, SE Australia 38.10S 146.18E
Moearatewe *see* Muaratewe
Moei, Mae Nam *see* Thaungyin
96 H13 **Moelv** Hedmark, S Norway 60.55N 10.47E
94 I10 **Moen** Troms, N Norway 69.08N 18.35E
Moen *see* Weno, Micronesia
Möen *see* Møn, Denmark
Moena *see* Muna, Pulau
38 M10 **Moenkopi Wash** ⁂ Arizona, SW USA
193 F22 **Moeraki Point** *headland* South Island, NZ 45.23S 170.52E
101 F16 **Moerbeke** Oost-Vlaanderen, NW Belgium 51.11N 3.57E
101 H14 **Moerdijk** Noord-Brabant, S Netherlands 51.42N 4.37E
Moero, Lac *see* Mweru, Lake
103 D15 **Moers** *var.* Mörs. Nordrhein-Westfalen, W Germany 51.27N 6.37E
Moesi *see* Musi, Air
Moeskroen *see* Mouscron
98 J13 **Moffat** S Scotland, UK 55.28N 3.36W
193 C22 **Moffat Peak** ▲ South Island, NZ 44.57S 168.10E
158 H8 **Moga** Punjab, N India 30.49N 75.13E
81 N19 **Moga** Sud Kivu, E Dem. Rep. Congo 2.16S 26.54E
Mogadiscio/Mogadishu *see* Muqdisho
Mogador *see* Essaouira
106 J6 **Mogadouro** Bragança, N Portugal 41.19N 6.43W
171 Ll12 **Mogami-gawa** ⁂ Honshū, C Japan
178 Gg2 **Mogaung** Kachin State, N Myanmar 25.19N 96.54E
112 L13 **Mogielnica** Mazowieckie, C Poland 51.40N 20.42E
Mogilëv *see* Mahilyow
Mogilev-Podol'skiy *see* Mohyliv-Podil's'kyy
Mogilëvskaya Oblast' *see* Mahilyowskaya Voblasts'
112 I11 **Mogilno** Kujawsko-pomorskie, C Poland 52.39N 17.58E
62 L9 **Mogi-Mirim** *var.* Moji-Mirim. São Paulo, S Brazil 22.26S 46.55W
85 Q15 **Mogincual** Nampula, NE Mozambique 15.33S 40.28E
116 E13 **Mogilenitsas** ⁂ N Greece
108 H8 **Mogliano Veneto** Veneto, NE Italy 45.34N 12.13E
115 M21 **Moglicë** Korçë, SE Albania 40.43N 20.22E
126 L15 **Mogocha** Chitinskaya Oblast', S Russian Federation 53.39N 119.47E
126 H13 **Mogochin** Tomskaya Oblast', C Russian Federation 57.42N 83.24E
82 F13 **Mogogh** Jonglei, SE Sudan 8.25N 31.19E
176 Vv10 **Mogoi** Papua, E Indonesia 1.44S 133.13E
178 Gg4 **Mogok** Mandalay, C Myanmar 22.55N 96.28E
39 P14 **Mogollon Mountains** ▲▲ New Mexico, SW USA
38 M12 **Mogollon Rim** *cliff* Arizona, SW USA
63 E23 **Mogotes, Punta** *headland* E Argentina 38.03S 57.31W
44 J8 **Mogotón** ▲ NW Nicaragua 13.45N 86.22W
106 I14 **Moguer** Andalucía, S Spain 37.15N 6.52W
113 J26 **Mohács** Baranya, SW Hungary 46.00N 18.40E
193 C20 **Mohaka** ⁂ North Island, NZ
30 M2 **Mohall** North Dakota, N USA 48.45N 101.30W
Moḥammadābād *see* Dargaz
76 F6 **Mohammedia** *prev.* Fédala. NW Morocco 33.46N 7.16W
76 F6 **Mohammed V** ✕ (Casablanca) W Morocco 33.07N 8.28W
Mohammerah *see* Khorramshahr
38 H10 **Mohave, Lake** ▣ Arizona/Nevada, W USA
38 I12 **Mohave Mountains** ▲▲ Arizona, SW USA
38 I15 **Mohawk Mountains** ▲▲ Arizona, SW USA
20 J10 **Mohawk River** ⁂ New York, NE USA
169 T3 **Mohe** Heilongjiang, NE China 53.00N 122.33E
97 L20 **Moheda** Kronoberg, S Sweden 57.00N 14.34E
180 H13 **Mohéli** *var.* Mwali, Mohilla, Mohila, *Fr.* Moili. *island* S Comoros
158 I11 **Mohendergarh** Haryāna, N India 28.16N 76.13E
40 K12 **Mohican, Cape** *headland* Nunivak Island, Alaska, USA 60.12N 167.25W
Mohn *see* Muhu
103 G15 **Möhne** ⁂ W Germany
103 G15 **Möhne-Stausee** ▣ W Germany
94 P2 **Mohn, Kapp** *headland* NW Svalbard 79.26N 25.44E
207 S14 **Mohns Ridge** *undersea feature* Greenland Sea/Norwegian Sea
59 I17 **Moho** Puno, SW Peru 15.21S 69.32W
Mohokare *see* Caledon
97 L17 **Moholm** Västra Götaland, S Sweden 58.37N 14.04E
38 J11 **Mohon Peak** ▲ Arizona, SW USA 34.55N 113.07W
83 J23 **Mohoro** Pwani, E Tanzania 8.09S 39.10E
Mohra *see* Moravice
Mohrungen *see* Morąg
118 M7 **Mohyliv-Podil's'kyy** *Rus.* Mogilev-Podol'skiy. Vinnyts'ka Oblast', C Ukraine 48.28N 27.49E
97 D17 **Moi** Rogaland, S Norway 58.27N 6.31E
197 I6 **Moindou** Province Sud, C New Caledonia 21.42S 165.40E
118 K11 **Moineşti** *Hung.* Mojnest. Bacău, E Romania 46.27N 26.31E
Móinteach Mílic *see* Mountmellick
12 J14 **Moira** ⁂ Ontario, SE Canada
94 G13 **Mo i Rana** Nordland, C Norway 66.19N 14.10E
159 X14 **Moirāng** Manipur, NE India 24.28N 93.45E
117 J25 **Moíres** Kríti, Greece, E Mediterranean Sea 35.03N 24.51E
120 H6 **Mõisaküla** *Ger.* Moiseküll. Viljandimaa, S Estonia 58.05N 25.11E
Moiseküll *see* Mõisaküla
13 W4 **Moisie** Quebec, E Canada 50.12N 66.06W
13 W3 **Moisie** ⁂ Quebec, SE Canada
104 M14 **Moissac** Tarn-et-Garonne, S France 44.07N 1.04E
80 I13 **Moïssala** Moyen-Chari, S Chad 8.21N 17.46E
57 O7 **Moitaco** Bolívar, E Venezuela 8.00N 64.22W
97 P15 **Möja** Stockholm, C Sweden 59.25N 18.55E
107 Q14 **Mojácar** Andalucía, S Spain 37.09N 1.49W
37 T13 **Mojave** California, W USA 35.03N 118.10W
37 V13 **Mojave Desert** *plain* California, W USA
37 V13 **Mojave River** ⁂ California, W USA
Moji-Mirim *see* Mogi-Mirim
115 K15 **Mojkovac** Montenegro, SW Serbia and Montenegro (Yugoslavia) 42.57N 19.34E
Mojnest *see* Moineşti
174 Ll15 **Mojokerto** *prev.* Modjokerto. Jawa, C Indonesia 7.25S 112.31E
Mōka *see* Mooka
159 Q13 **Mokāma** *prev.* Mokameh, Mukama. Bihār, N India 25.24N 85.55E
81 O25 **Mokambo** Katanga, SE Dem. Rep. Congo 12.23S 28.21E
Mokameh *see* Mokāma
40 D9 **Mokapu Point** *headland* Oahu, Hawaii, USA, C Pacific Ocean 21.27N 157.43W
192 L9 **Mokau** Waikato, North Island, NZ 38.42S 174.37E
192 L9 **Mokau** ⁂ North Island, NZ
37 P7 **Mokelumne River** ⁂ California, W USA
85 J23 **Mokhotlong** NE Lesotho 29.19S 29.06E
Mokil Atoll *see* Mwokil Atoll
97 N14 **Möklinta** Västmanland, C Sweden 60.04N 16.34E
192 L4 **Mokohinau Islands** *island group* N NZ
159 X12 **Mokokchūng** Nāgāland, NE India 26.19N 94.30E
80 F12 **Mokolo** Extrême-Nord, N Cameroon 10.49N 13.54E
193 D24 **Mokoreta** ⁂ South Island, NZ
85 J20 **Mokopane** *prev.* Potgietersrus. Limpopo, NE South Africa 24.09S 28.58E
169 X17 **Mokp'o** *Jap.* Moppo. SW South Korea 34.49N 126.26E
115 L16 **Mokra Gora** ▲▲ S Serbia and Montenegro (Yugoslavia)
Mokrany *see* Makrany
131 O5 **Moksha** ⁂ W Russian Federation
Moktama *see* Martaban
79 T14 **Mokwa** Niger, W Nigeria 9.19N 5.01E
101 J16 **Mol** *prev.* Moll. Antwerpen, N Belgium 51.10N 5.07E
109 O17 **Mola di Bari** Puglia, SE Italy 41.03N 17.04E
Molai *see* Moláoi
43 P13 **Molango** Hidalgo, C Mexico 20.48N 98.43W
117 F22 **Moláoi** *var.* Molai. Pelopónnisos, S Greece 36.47N 22.50E
43 Z12 **Molas del Norte, Punta** *var.* Punta Molas. *headland* SE Mexico 20.34N 86.43W
Molas, Punta *see* Molas del Norte, Punta
107 R11 **Molatón** ▲ C Spain 38.58N 1.19W
99 K18 **Mold** NE Wales, UK 53.10N 3.07W
Moldau *see* Moldova
Moldau *see* Vltava, Czech Republic
Moldavia *see* Moldova
Moldavian SSR/Moldavskaya SSR *see* Moldova
96 E9 **Molde** Møre og Romsdal, S Norway 62.43N 7.07E
Moldotau, Khrebet *see* Moldo-Too, Khrebet
153 V9 **Moldo-Too, Khrebet** *prev.* Khrebet Moldotau. ▲▲ C Kyrgyzstan
118 K9 **Moldova** ⁂ N Romania
118 K9 **Moldova** *Eng.* Moldavia, *Ger.* Moldau. *former province* NE Romania
118 L9 **Moldova** *off.* Republic of Moldova, *var.* Moldavia; *prev.* Moldavian SSR, *Rus.* Moldavskaya SSR. ◆ *republic* SE Europe
118 F13 **Moldova Nouă** *Ger.* Neumoldowa, *Hung.* Újmoldova. Caraş-Severin, SW Romania 44.45N 21.39E
118 F13 **Moldova Veche** *Ger.* Altmoldowa, *Hung.* Ómoldova. Caraş-Severin, SW Romania 44.45N 21.13E
Moldoveanul *see* Vârful Moldoveanu
85 I20 **Molepolole** Kweneng, SE Botswana 24.25S 25.30E
46 L8 **Môle-St-Nicolas** NW Haiti 19.46N 73.19W
120 H13 **Molėtai** Molėtai, E Lithuania 55.14N 25.25E
109 O17 **Molfetta** Puglia, SE Italy 41.12N 16.34E
175 R8 **Molibagu** Sulawesi, N Indonesia 0.25N 123.57E
64 G12 **Molina** Maule, C Chile 35.06S 71.18W
107 Q7 **Molina de Aragón** Castilla-La Mancha, C Spain 40.49N 1.54W
107 R13 **Molina de Segura** Murcia, SE Spain 38.03N 1.10W
32 J11 **Moline** Illinois, N USA 41.30N 90.31W
29 P7 **Moline** Kansas, C USA 37.21N 96.18W
81 P23 **Moliro** Katanga, SE Dem. Rep. Congo 8.10S 30.31E
109 K16 **Molise** ◆ *region* S Italy
97 K15 **Molkom** Värmland, C Sweden 59.36N 13.43E
Moll *see* Mol
111 Q9 **Möll** ⁂ S Austria
97 J22 **Mölle** Skåne, S Sweden 56.15N 12.19E
59 H18 **Mollendo** Arequipa, SW Peru 17.01S 72.01W
107 U5 **Mollerussa** Cataluña, NE Spain 41.37N 0.52E
110 H8 **Mollis** Glarus, NE Switzerland 47.05N 9.03E
97 J19 **Mölndal** Västra Götaland, S Sweden 57.39N 12.05E
97 J19 **Mölnlycke** Västra Götaland, S Sweden 57.42N 12.19E
119 U9 **Molochans'k** *Rus.* Molochansk. Zaporiz'ka Oblast', SE Ukraine 47.10N 35.38E
119 U10 **Molochna** *Rus.* Molochnaya. ⁂ S Ukraine
Molochnaya *see* Molochna
119 U10 **Molochnyy Lyman** *bay* N Black Sea
Molodechno/Molodeczno *see* Maladzyechna
205 V3 **Molodezhnaya** *Russian research station* Antarctica 67.33S 46.12E
128 J14 **Mologa** ⁂ NW Russian Federation
40 E9 **Molokai** *Haw.* Moloka'i. *island* Hawaii, USA, C Pacific Ocean
183 X3 **Molokai Fracture Zone** *tectonic feature* NE Pacific Ocean
128 K15 **Molokovo** Tverskaya Oblast', W Russian Federation 58.10N 36.43E
129 Q14 **Moloma** ⁂ NW Russian Federation
191 R8 **Molong** New South Wales, SE Australia 33.07S 148.52E
85 H21 **Molopo** *seasonal river* Botswana/South Africa
117 F17 **Mólos** Stereá Ellás, C Greece 38.48N 22.40E
175 Q7 **Molosipat** Sulawesi, N Indonesia 0.28N 121.08E
Molotov *see* Severodvinsk, Arkhangel'skaya Oblast', Russian Federation
Molotov *see* Perm', Permskaya Oblast', Russian Federation
81 G17 **Moloundou** Est, SE Cameroon 2.03N 15.13E
105 U5 **Molsheim** Bas-Rhin, NE France 48.33N 7.30E
15 L12 **Molson Lake** ◎ Manitoba, C Canada
Moluccas *see* Maluku
175 Rr8 **Molucca Sea** *Ind.* Laut Maluku. *sea* E Indonesia
Molukken *see* Maluku
85 O15 **Molumbo** Zambézia, N Mozambique 15.33S 36.19E
176 Uu14 **Molu, Pulau** *island* Maluku, E Indonesia
85 P16 **Moma** Nampula, NE Mozambique 16.42S 39.12E
176 Xx13 **Momats** ⁂ Papua, E Indonesia
44 J11 **Mombacho, Volcán** ⁂ SW Nicaragua 11.49N 85.58W
83 K21 **Mombasa** Coast, SE Kenya 4.04N 39.40E
83 J21 **Mombasa** ✕ Coast, SE Kenya 4.01S 39.31E
Mombetsu *see* Monbetsu
176 Y16 **Mombum** Papua, E Indonesia 8.16S 138.51E
116 J12 **Momchilgrad** *prev.* Mastanli. Kŭrdzhali, S Bulgaria 41.33N 25.25E
101 F23 **Momignies** Hainaut, S Belgium 50.02N 4.10E
56 E6 **Momil** Córdoba, NW Colombia 9.15N 75.40W
44 I10 **Momotombo, Volcán** ⁂ W Nicaragua 12.25N 86.33W
58 B5 **Mompiche, Ensenada de** *bay* NW Ecuador
81 K18 **Mompono** Equateur, NW Dem. Rep. Congo 0.11N 21.31E
56 F6 **Mompós** Bolívar, NW Colombia 9.10N 74.21W
97 J24 **Møn** *prev.* Möen. *island* SE Denmark
38 L4 **Mona** Utah, W USA 39.49N 111.52W
Mona, Canal de la *see* Mona Passage
98 E8 **Monach Islands** *island group* NW Scotland, UK
105 V14 **Monaco** *var.* Monaco-Ville; *anc.* Monoecus. ● (Monaco) S Monaco 43.46N 7.22E
105 V14 **Monaco** *off.* Principality of Monaco. ◆ *monarchy* W Europe
Monaco *see* München
Monaco Basin *see* Canary Basin
Monaco-Ville *see* Monaco
98 I9 **Monadhliath Mountains** ▲▲ N Scotland, UK
57 O6 **Monagas** *off.* Estado Monagas. ◆ *state* NE Venezuela
99 F16 **Monaghan** *Ir.* Muineachán. N Ireland 54.15N 6.58W
99 E16 **Monaghan** *Ir.* Muineachán. *cultural region* N Ireland
45 S16 **Monagrillo** Herrera, S Panama 7.58N 80.23W
26 L8 **Monahans** Texas, SW USA 31.33N 102.52W
47 Q9 **Mona, Isla** *island* W Puerto Rico
47 Q9 **Mona Passage** *Sp.* Canal de la Mona. *channel* Dominican Republic/Puerto Rico
45 O14 **Mona, Punta** *headland* E Costa Rica 9.44N 82.48W
161 K25 **Monaragala** Uva Province, SE Sri Lanka 6.52N 81.22E
35 S9 **Monarch** Montana, NW USA 47.04N 110.51W
14 Ff14 **Monarch Mountain** ▲ British Columbia, SW Canada 51.59N 125.56W
Monasterio *see* Monesterio
Monasterzyska *see* Monastyrys'ka
Monastir *see* Bitola
Monastyriska *see* Monastyrys'ka
119 O7 **Monastyrshche** Cherkas'ka Oblast', C Ukraine 48.59N 29.47E
118 J6 **Monastyrys'ka** *Pol.* Monasterzyska, *Rus.* Monastyriska. Ternopil's'ka Oblast', W Ukraine 49.04N 25.10E
81 E15 **Monatélé** Centre, SW Cameroon 4.16N 11.12E
172 Q4 **Monbetsu** *var.* Mombetsu, Monbetu. Hokkaidō, NE Japan 44.22N 143.22E
Monbetu *see* Monbetsu
108 B8 **Moncalieri** Piemonte, NW Italy 45.00N 7.41E
106 G4 **Monção** Viana do Castelo, N Portugal 42.03N 8.29W
107 Q5 **Moncayo** ▲ N Spain 41.43N 1.51W
107 Q5 **Moncayo, Sierra del** ▲▲ N Spain
128 J4 **Monchegorsk** Murmanskaya Oblast', NW Russian Federation 67.55N 32.46E
103 D15 **Mönchengladbach** *prev.* München-Gladbach. Nordrhein-Westfalen, W Germany 51.12N 6.25E
106 F14 **Monchique** Faro, S Portugal 37.19N 8.33W
106 G14 **Monchique, Serra de** ▲▲ S Portugal
23 S14 **Moncks Corner** South Carolina, SE USA 33.12N 80.00W
43 N7 **Monclova** Coahuila de Zaragoza, NE Mexico 26.55N 101.25W
Moncorvo *see* Torre de Moncorvo
11 P14 **Moncton** New Brunswick, SE Canada 46.04N 64.49W
106 F8 **Mondego, Cabo** *headland* N Portugal 40.10N 8.58W
106 G8 **Mondego, Rio** ⁂ N Portugal
106 I2 **Mondoñedo** Galicia, NW Spain 43.25N 7.22W
101 N25 **Mondorf-les-Bains** Grevenmacher, SE Luxembourg 49.30N 6.16E
104 M7 **Mondoubleau** Loir-et-Cher, C France 48.00N 0.49E
32 J6 **Mondovi** Wisconsin, N USA 44.34N 91.40W
108 B9 **Mondovì** Piemonte, NW Italy 44.22N 7.55E
107 P3 **Mondragón** *var.* Arrasate. País Vasco, N Spain 43.04N 2.30W
109 J17 **Mondragone** Campania, S Italy 41.07N 13.52E
111 R5 **Mondsee** ◎ N Austria
126 J16 **Mondy** Respublika Buryatiya, S Russian Federation 51.41N 101.03E
117 G22 **Monemvasía** Pelopónnisos, S Greece 36.22N 23.03E
20 B15 **Monessen** Pennsylvania, NE USA 40.07N 79.51W
106 J12 **Monesterio** *var.* Monasterio. Extremadura, W Spain 38.04N 6.16W
12 L8 **Monet** Quebec, SE Canada 48.09N 75.37W
29 S8 **Monett** Missouri, C USA 36.55N 93.55W
29 X9 **Monette** Arkansas, C USA 35.53N 90.20W
12 G11 **Monetville** Ontario, S Canada 46.08N 80.24W
108 J7 **Monfalcone** Friuli-Venezia Giulia, NE Italy 45.49N 13.31E
106 H10 **Monforte** Portalegre, C Portugal 39.03N 7.25W
106 I4 **Monforte** Galicia, NW Spain 42.31N 7.30W
83 I24 **Monga** Lindi, SE Tanzania 9.05S 37.51E
81 L16 **Monga** Orientale, N Dem. Rep. Congo 4.12N 22.49E
83 F15 **Mongalla** Bahr el Gabel, S Sudan 5.12N 31.42E
159 U11 **Mongar** E Bhutan 27.16N 91.07E
178 K6 **Mong Cai** Quang Ninh, N Vietnam 21.33N 107.56E
188 I11 **Mongers Lake** *salt lake* Western Australia
195 U14 **Mongga** Kolombangara, NW Solomon Islands 7.51S 157.00E
178 Hh6 **Mong Hpayak** Shan State, E Myanmar 20.56N 100.00E
Monghyr *see* Munger
108 B10 **Mongioie** ▲ NW Italy 44.13N 7.46E
178 Gg5 **Möng Küng** Shan State, E Myanmar 21.39N 97.31E
Mongla *see* Mungla
196 C15 **Mongmong** C Guam
178 Gg6 **Möng Nai** Shan State, E Myanmar 20.28N 97.51E
80 I11 **Mongo** Guéra, C Chad 12.11N 18.39E
78 I14 **Mongo** ⁂ N Sierra Leone
169 I8 **Mongolia** *Mong.* Mongol Uls. ◆ *republic* E Asia
133 V8 **Mongolia, Plateau of** *plateau* E Mongolia
Mongolküre *see* Zhaosu
Mongol Uls *see* Mongolia
81 E17 **Mongomo** E Equatorial Guinea 1.39N 11.18E
79 Y12 **Mongonu** *var.* Monguno. Borno, NE Nigeria 12.42N 13.37E
Mongora *see* Mingāora
80 K11 **Mongororo** Ouaddaï, SE Chad 12.03N 22.26E
Mongos, Chaîne des *see* Bongo, Massif des
81 I16 **Mongoumba** Lobaye, SW Central African Republic 3.39N 18.30E
Mongrove, Punta *see* Cayacal, Punta
85 G15 **Mongu** Western, W Zambia 15.13S 23.09E
78 I10 **Mônguel** Gorgol, SW Mauritania 16.25N 13.07W
Monguno *see* Mongonu
178 H4 **Möng Yai** Shan State, E Myanmar 22.25N 98.02E
178 Hh5 **Möng Yang** Shan State, E Myanmar 21.52N 99.31E
178 H3 **Möng Yu** Shan State, E Myanmar 24.00N 97.57E
168 K8 **Mönhbulag** Övörhangay, C Mongolia 46.48N 103.25E
Mönh Sarïdag *see* Munku-Sardyk, Gora
194 L15 **Moni** ⁂ S Papau New Guinea
117 I15 **Moní Megístis Lávras** *monastery* Kentrikí Makedonía, N Greece 40.10N 24.22E
117 F18 **Moní Osíou Loúkas** *monastery* Stereá Ellás, C Greece 38.22N 22.42E
56 F9 **Moniquirá** Boyacá, C Colombia 5.57N 73.35W
105 Q12 **Monistrol-sur-Loire** Haute-Loire, C France 45.19N 4.12E
37 V7 **Monitor Range** ▲▲ Nevada, W USA
117 I14 **Moní Vatopedíou** *monastery* Kentrikí Makedonía, N Greece 40.19N 24.13E
179 Rr15 **Monkayo** Mindanao, S Philippines 7.45N 125.58E
Monkchester *see* Newcastle upon Tyne
85 N14 **Monkey Bay** Southern, SE Malawi 14.09S 34.53E
45 N11 **Monkey Point** *var.* Punta Mico, Punte Mono, Punto Mico. *headland* SE Nicaragua 11.37N 83.39W
Monkey River *see* Monkey River Town
44 G3 **Monkey River Town** *var.* Monkey River. Toledo, SE Belize 16.22N 88.28W
12 M13 **Monkland** Ontario, SE Canada 45.11N 74.51W
81 J19 **Monkoto** Equateur, NW Dem. Rep. Congo 1.35S 20.43E
99 K21 **Monmouth** *Wel.* Trefynwy. SE Wales, UK 51.49N 2.43W
32 J12 **Monmouth** Illinois, N USA 40.54N 90.39W
34 F12 **Monmouth** Oregon, NW USA 44.51N 123.13W
99 K21 **Monmouth** *cultural region* SE Wales, UK
100 I10 **Monnickendam** Noord-Holland, C Netherlands 52.28N 5.01E
79 R15 **Mono** ⁂ C Togo
Monoecus *see* Monaco
37 R8 **Mono Lake** ◎ California, W USA
117 O23 **Monólithos** Ródos, Dodekánisos, Greece, Aegean Sea 36.08N 27.45E
21 Q12 **Monomoy Island** *island* Massachusetts, NE USA
33 O12 **Monon** Indiana, N USA 40.52N 86.54W
31 Y12 **Monona** Iowa, C USA 43.03N 91.23W
32 L9 **Monona** Wisconsin, N USA 43.03N 89.18W
20 B15 **Monongahela** Pennsylvania, NE USA 40.10N 79.54W
20 B16 **Monongahela River** ⁂ NE USA
109 P17 **Monopoli** Puglia, SE Italy 40.57N 17.18E
Mono, Punte *see* Monkey Point
113 K23 **Monor** Pest, C Hungary 47.19N 19.28E
Monostor *see* Beli Manastir
80 K8 **Monou** Borkou-Ennedi-Tibesti, NE Chad 16.22N 22.15E
107 S12 **Monóvar** País Valenciano, E Spain 38.25N 0.49W
107 R7 **Monreal del Campo** Aragón, NE Spain 40.46N 1.19W
109 I23 **Monreale** Sicilia, Italy, C Mediterranean Sea 38.04N 13.16E
25 T3 **Monroe** Georgia, SE USA 33.47N 83.42W
31 W14 **Monroe** Iowa, C USA 41.31N 93.06W
24 I5 **Monroe** Louisiana, S USA 32.31N 92.06W
33 S10 **Monroe** Michigan, N USA 41.55N 83.24W
20 K13 **Monroe** New York, NE USA 41.18N 74.09W
23 S11 **Monroe** North Carolina, SE USA 34.59N 80.33W
38 L6 **Monroe** Utah, W USA 38.37N 112.07W
34 H7 **Monroe** Washington, NW USA 47.51N 121.58W
32 L9 **Monroe** Wisconsin, N USA 42.34N 89.39W
29 V3 **Monroe City** Missouri, C USA 39.39N 91.43W
33 O15 **Monroe Lake** ▣ Indiana, N USA
25 O7 **Monroeville** Alabama, S USA 31.31N 87.19W
20 C15 **Monroeville** Pennsylvania, NE USA 40.24N 79.44W
78 J16 **Monrovia** ● (Liberia) W Liberia 6.18N 10.48W
78 J16 **Monrovia** ✕ W Liberia 6.22N 10.50W
107 T7 **Monroyo** Aragón, NE Spain 40.46N 0.03W
101 F20 **Mons** *Dut.* Bergen. Hainaut, S Belgium 50.28N 3.58E
106 I8 **Monsanto** Castelo Branco, C Portugal 40.01N 7.07W
108 H8 **Monselice** Veneto, NE Italy 45.15N 11.47E
178 Gg9 **Mon State** ◆ *state* S Myanmar
100 G12 **Monster** Zuid-Holland, W Netherlands 52.01N 4.10E
97 N20 **Mönsterås** Kalmar, S Sweden 57.03N 16.27E
103 F17 **Montabaur** Rheinland-Pfalz, W Germany 50.25N 7.48E
108 G8 **Montagnana** Veneto, NE Italy 45.14N 11.31E
37 N1 **Montague** California, W USA 41.43N 122.31W
27 S5 **Montague** Texas, SW USA 33.39N 97.41W
191 S11 **Montague Island** *island* New South Wales, SE Australia
41 S12 **Montague Island** *island* Alaska, USA
41 S13 **Montague Strait** *strait* N Gulf of Alaska
104 J8 **Montaigu** Vendée, NW France 46.58N 1.18W
Montaigu *see* Scherpenheuvel
107 S7 **Montalbán** Aragón, NE Spain 40.49N 0.48W
108 G13 **Montalcino** Toscana, C Italy 43.01N 11.34E
106 H5 **Montalegre** Vila Real, N Portugal 41.49N 7.48W
116 G8 **Montana** *prev.* Ferdinand, Mikhaylovgrad. Montana, NW Bulgaria 43.25N 23.14E
110 D10 **Montana** Valais, SW Switzerland 46.23N 7.29E
41 R11 **Montana** Alaska, USA 62.06N 150.03W
116 G8 **Montana** ◆ *province* NW Bulgaria
35 T9 **Montana** *off.* State of Montana; also known as Mountain State, Treasure State. ◆ *state* NW USA
106 J10 **Montánchez** Extremadura, W Spain 39.15N 6.07W
Montañita *see* La Montañita
13 Q8 **Mont-Apica** Quebec, SE Canada 47.57N 71.24W
106 G10 **Montargil** Portalegre, C Portugal 39.04N 8.10W
106 G10 **Montargil, Barragem de** ▣ C Portugal
105 O7 **Montargis** Loiret, C France 48.00N 2.43E
105 O4 **Montataire** Oise, N France 49.16N 2.24E
104 M14 **Montauban** Tarn-et-Garonne, S France 44.01N 1.19E
21 N14 **Montauk** Long Island, New York, NE USA 41.01N 71.58W
21 N14 **Montauk Point** *headland* Long Island, New York, NE USA 41.04N 71.51W
105 Q7 **Montbard** Côte d'Or, C France 47.35N 4.25E
105 U7 **Montbéliard** Doubs, E France 47.31N 6.49E
27 W11 **Mont Belvieu** Texas, SW USA 29.51N 94.53W
107 U6 **Montblanc** *var.* Montblanch. Cataluña, NE Spain 41.22N 1.10E
Montblanch *see* Montblanc
105 Q11 **Montbrison** Loire, E France 45.37N 4.04E
Montcalm, Lake *see* Dogai Coring
105 Q9 **Montceau-les-Mines** Saône-et-Loire, C France 46.40N 4.19E
105 U12 **Mont Cenis, Col du** *pass* E France 45.16N 6.54E
104 K15 **Mont-de-Marsan** Landes, SW France 43.54N 0.30W
105 O3 **Montdidier** Somme, N France 49.39N 2.34E
197 J7 **Mont-Dore** Province Sud, S New Caledonia 22.18S 166.34E
22 K10 **Monteagle** Tennessee, S USA 35.15N 85.47W
59 M20 **Monteagudo** Chuquisaca, S Bolivia 19.48S 63.57W
43 R16 **Monte Albán** *ruins* Oaxaca, S Mexico 17.01N 96.46W
107 R11 **Montealegre del Castillo** Castilla-La Mancha, C Spain 38.48N 1.18W
61 N18 **Monte Azul** Minas Gerais, SE Brazil 15.13S 42.52W
12 M12 **Montebello** Quebec, SE Canada 45.40N 74.55W
108 H7 **Montebelluna** Veneto, NE Italy 45.46N 12.03E
62 G13 **Montecarlo** Misiones, NE Argentina 26.37S 54.45W
63 D16 **Monte Caseros** Corrientes, NE Argentina 30.15S 57.39W
62 J13 **Monte Castelo** Santa Catarina, S Brazil 26.34S 50.12W
108 F11 **Montecatini Terme** Toscana, C Italy 43.52N 10.46E
44 H7 **Montecillos, Cordillera de** ▲▲ W Honduras
64 I12 **Monte Comén** Mendoza, W Argentina 34.34S 67.52W
46 M8 **Monte Cristi** *var.* San Fernando de Monte Cristi. NW Dominican Republic 19.52N 71.39W
60 C13 **Monte Cristo** Amazonas, W Brazil 3.13S 68.00W
109 E14 **Montecristo, Isola di** *island* Archipelago Toscano, C Italy
Monte Croce Carnico, Passo di *see* Plöcken Pass
60 J12 **Monte Dourado** Pará, NE Brazil 0.48S 52.32W
42 L11 **Monte Escobedo** Zacatecas, C Mexico 22.19N 103.30W
108 I13 **Montefalco** Umbria, C Italy 42.54N 12.40E
109 H14 **Montefiascone** Lazio, C Italy 42.33N 12.01E
107 N14 **Montefrío** Andalucía, S Spain 37.19N 4.00W
46 I11 **Montego Bay** *var.* Mobay. W Jamaica 18.28N 77.55W
Montego Bay *see* Sangster
106 J8 **Montehermoso** Extremadura, W Spain 40.04N 6.19W
106 F10 **Montejunto, Serra de** ▲ C Portugal 39.10N 9.01W
Monteleone di Calabria *see* Vibo Valentia
56 E7 **Montelíbano** Córdoba, NW Colombia 7.58N 75.24W
105 R13 **Montélimar** *anc.* Acunum Acusio, Montilium Adhemari. Drôme, E France 44.33N 4.45E
106 K15 **Montellano** Andalucía, S Spain 37.00N 5.34W
37 Y2 **Montello** Nevada, W USA 41.18N 114.10W
32 L8 **Montello** Wisconsin, N USA 43.46N 89.19W
65 J18 **Montemayor, Meseta de** *plain* SE Argentina
43 O9 **Montemorelos** Nuevo León, NE Mexico 25.10N 99.51W
106 G11 **Montemor-o-Novo** Évora, S Portugal 38.37N 8.13W
106 G8 **Montemor-o-Velho** *var.* Montemor-o-Vélho. Coimbra, N Portugal 40.10N 8.40W
106 H7 **Montemuro, Serra de** ▲ N Portugal 40.59N 7.59W
104 K12 **Montendre** Charente-Maritime, W France 45.17N 0.24W
63 I15 **Montenegro** Rio Grande do Sul, S Brazil 29.40S 51.32W
115 J16 **Montenegro** *Serb.* Crna Gora. ◆ *republic* SW Serbia and Montenegro (Yugoslavia)
64 G10 **Monte Patria** Coquimbo, N Chile 30.40S 71.00W
47 O9 **Monte Plata** E Dominican Republic 18.46N 69.43W
85 P14 **Montepuez** Cabo Delgado, N Mozambique 13.09S 39.00E
85 P14 **Montepuez** ⁂ N Mozambique
108 G13 **Montepulciano** Toscana, C Italy 43.02N 11.51E
64 L6 **Monte Quemado** Santiago del Estero, N Argentina 25.46S 62.51W
105 O6 **Montereau-Faut-Yonne** *anc.* Condate. Seine-St-Denis, N France 48.22N 2.57E
37 N11 **Monterey** California, W USA 36.36N 121.53W
22 L9 **Monterey** Tennessee, S USA 36.09N 85.16W
23 T5 **Monterey** Virginia, NE USA 38.24N 79.33W
Monterey *see* Monterrey
37 N10 **Monterey Bay** *bay* California, W USA
56 D6 **Montería** Córdoba, NW Colombia 8.45N 75.54W
59 N18 **Montero** Santa Cruz, C Bolivia 17.19S 63.15W

◆ Country ● Country Capital ◇ Dependent Territory ○ Dependent Territory Capital ◆ Administrative Region ✕ International Airport ▲ Mountain ▲▲ Mountain Range ⁂ Volcano ⁂ River ◎ Lake ▣ Reservoir

64 J7 **Monteros** Tucumán, C Argentina 27.12S 65.30W
106 I5 **Monterrei** Galicia, NW Spain 41.55N 7.27W
43 O8 **Monterrey** *var.* Monterey. Nuevo León, NE Mexico 25.40N 100.16W
34 F9 **Montesano** Washington, NW USA 46.58N 123.37W
109 M19 **Montesano sulla Marcellana** Campania, S Italy 40.15N 15.41E
109 N16 **Monte Sant' Angelo** Puglia, SE Italy 41.43N 15.58E
61 O16 **Monte Santo** Bahia, E Brazil 10.25S 39.18W
109 D18 **Monte Santu, Capo di** *headland* Sardegna, Italy, C Mediterranean Sea 40.05N 9.43E
61 M19 **Montes Claros** Minas Gerais, SE Brazil 16.45S 43.52W
109 K14 **Montesilvano Marina** Abruzzo, C Italy 42.28N 14.07E
25 P4 **Montevallo** Alabama, S USA 33.06N 86.51W
108 G12 **Montevarchi** Toscana, C Italy 43.31N 11.34E
31 S9 **Montevideo** Minnesota, N USA 44.56N 95.43W
63 F20 **Montevideo** ● (Uruguay) Montevideo, S Uruguay 34.55S 56.10W
39 S7 **Monte Vista** Colorado, C USA 37.33N 106.08W
25 T5 **Montezuma** Georgia, SE USA 32.18N 84.01W
31 W14 **Montezuma** Iowa, C USA 41.35N 92.31W
28 J6 **Montezuma** Kansas, C USA 37.33N 100.25W
105 U12 **Montgenèvre, Col de** *pass* France/Italy 44.56N 6.45E
99 K20 **Montgomery** E Wales, UK 52.37N 3.05W
25 Q5 **Montgomery** *state capital* Alabama, S USA 32.22N 86.18W
31 V9 **Montgomery** Minnesota, N USA 44.26N 93.34W
20 G13 **Montgomery** Pennsylvania, NE USA 41.08N 76.52W
23 Q5 **Montgomery** West Virginia, NE USA 38.07N 81.19W
99 K19 **Montgomery** *cultural region* E Wales, UK
Montgomery *see* Sāhīwāl
29 V4 **Montgomery City** Missouri, C USA 38.58N 91.30W
37 S8 **Montgomery Pass** *pass* Nevada, W USA 37.57N 118.21W
104 K12 **Montguyon** Charente-Maritime, W France 45.12N 0.13W
110 C10 **Monthey** Valais, SW Switzerland 46.15N 6.55E
29 V13 **Monticello** Arkansas, C USA 33.37N 91.44W
25 T4 **Monticello** Florida, SE USA 30.33N 83.52W
25 T8 **Monticello** Georgia, SE USA 33.18N 83.40W
32 M13 **Monticello** Illinois, N USA 40.01N 88.34W
33 O12 **Monticello** Indiana, N USA 40.45N 86.46W
31 Y13 **Monticello** Iowa, C USA 42.14N 91.11W
22 L7 **Monticello** Kentucky, S USA 36.51N 84.51W
31 V8 **Monticello** Minnesota, N USA 45.19N 93.45W
24 K7 **Monticello** Mississippi, S USA 31.33N 90.06W
29 V2 **Monticello** Missouri, C USA 40.07N 91.42W
20 J12 **Monticello** New York, NE USA 41.39N 74.41W
39 O7 **Monticello** Utah, W USA 37.52N 109.20W
108 F8 **Montichiari** Lombardia, N Italy 45.24N 10.27E
104 M12 **Montignac** Dordogne, SW France 45.24N 0.54E
101 G21 **Montignies-le-Tilleul** *var.* Montigny-le-Tilleul. Hainaut, S Belgium 50.22N 4.22E
12 J8 **Montigny, Lac de** ◎ Quebec, SE Canada
105 S6 **Montigny-le-Roi** Haute-Marne, N France 48.02N 5.28E
Montigny-le-Tilleul *see* Montignies-le-Tilleul
45 R16 **Montijo** Veraguas, S Panama 7.58N 81.12W
106 F11 **Montijo** Setúbal, W Portugal 38.42N 8.58W
106 J11 **Montijo** Extremadura, W Spain 38.55N 6.37W
Montilium Adhemari *see* Montélimar
106 M13 **Montilla** Andalucía, S Spain 37.36N 4.39W
104 L3 **Montivilliers** Seine-Maritime, N France 49.31N 0.10E
13 U7 **Mont-Joli** Quebec, SE Canada 48.33N 68.12W
12 M10 **Mont-Laurier** Quebec, SE Canada 46.33N 75.31W
13 X5 **Mont-Louis** Quebec, SE Canada 49.13N 65.44W
105 N17 **Mont-Louis** *var.* Mont Louis. Pyrénées-Orientales, S France 42.30N 2.07E
105 O10 **Montluçon** Allier, C France 46.21N 2.37E
13 R10 **Montmagny** Quebec, SE Canada 47.00N 70.31W
105 S3 **Montmédy** Meuse, NE France 49.31N 5.21E
105 P5 **Montmirail** Marne, N France 48.53N 3.31E
13 R9 **Montmorency** ≈ Quebec, SE Canada
104 M10 **Montmorillon** Vienne, W France 46.25N 0.52E
109 J14 **Montorio al Vomano** Abruzzo, C Italy 42.31N 13.39E
106 M13 **Montoro** Andalucía, S Spain 38.00N 4.21W
35 S16 **Montpelier** Idaho, NW USA 42.19N 111.18W
31 P6 **Montpelier** North Dakota, N USA 46.40N 98.34W
20 M7 **Montpelier** *state capital* Vermont, NE USA 44.15N 72.32W
105 Q15 **Montpellier** Hérault, S France 43.37N 3.52E
104 L12 **Montpon-Ménestérol** Dordogne, SW France 45.01N 0.10E
12 G8 **Montreal** ≈ Ontario, S Canada
12 C8 **Montreal** ≈ Ontario, S Canada
Montreal *see* Mirabel
10 K15 **Montréal** *Eng.* Montreal. Quebec, SE Canada 45.30N 73.36W
9 T14 **Montreal Lake** ◎ Saskatchewan, C Canada
12 B9 **Montreal River** Ontario, S Canada 47.13N 84.36W
105 N2 **Montreuil** Pas-de-Calais, N France 50.28N 1.46E
104 K8 **Montreuil-Bellay** Maine-et-Loire, NW France 47.07N 0.10W
110 C10 **Montreux** Vaud, SW Switzerland 46.27N 6.55E
110 B9 **Montricher** Vaud, W Switzerland 46.37N 6.24E
98 K10 **Montrose** E Scotland, UK 56.43N 2.28W
29 W14 **Montrose** Arkansas, C USA 33.18N 91.29W
39 Q6 **Montrose** Colorado, C USA 38.28N 107.52W
31 Y16 **Montrose** Iowa, C USA 40.31N 91.24W
20 H12 **Montrose** Pennsylvania, NE USA 41.49N 75.52W
23 X5 **Montross** Virginia, NE USA 38.04N 76.50W
13 O12 **Mont-St-Hilaire** Quebec, SE Canada 45.34N 73.10W
105 S3 **Mont-St-Martin** Meurthe-et-Moselle, NE France 49.31N 5.51E
47 V10 **Montserrat** *var.* Emerald Isle. ◇ *UK dependent territory* E West Indies
107 V5 **Montserrat** ▲ NE Spain 41.39N 1.44E
106 M7 **Montuenga** Castilla-León, N Spain 41.04N 4.37W
101 M19 **Montzen** Liège, E Belgium 50.42N 5.59E
39 N8 **Monument Valley** *valley* Arizona/Utah, SW USA
177 G4 **Monywa** Sagaing, C Myanmar 22.04N 95.12E
108 D7 **Monza** Lombardia, N Italy 45.34N 9.16E
85 J15 **Monze** Southern, S Zambia 16.19S 27.29E
107 T5 **Monzón** Aragón, NE Spain 41.54N 0.12E
27 T9 **Moody** Texas, SW USA 31.18N 97.21W
100 L13 **Mook** Limburg, SE Netherlands 51.45N 5.52E
171 Kk15 **Mooka** *var.* Mōka. Tochigi, Honshū, S Japan 36.28N 140.01E
190 K3 **Moomba** South Australia 28.07S 140.12E
12 G13 **Moon** ≈ Ontario, S Canada
Moon *see* Muhu
189 Y10 **Moonie** Queensland, E Australia 27.45S 150.22E
198 B10 **Moonless Mountains** *undersea feature* E Pacific Ocean
190 L13 **Moonlight Head** *headland* Victoria, SE Australia 38.47S 143.12E
Moon-Sund *see* Väinameri
190 H8 **Moonta** South Australia 34.03S 137.36E
Moor *see* Mór
188 I12 **Moora** Western Australia 30.22S 116.04E
100 H12 **Moordrecht** Zuid-Holland, C Netherlands 51.58N 4.40E
35 T9 **Moore** Montana, NW USA 47.00N 109.40W
29 N11 **Moore** Oklahoma, C USA 35.20N 97.29W
27 R12 **Moore** Texas, SW USA 29.03N 99.01W
203 S10 **Moorea** *island* Îles du Vent, W French Polynesia
23 U3 **Moorefield** West Virginia, NE USA 39.03N 78.58W
25 X14 **Moore Haven** Florida, SE USA 26.49N 81.05W
188 J11 **Moore, Lake** ◎ Western Australia
21 N7 **Moore Reservoir** ⊠ New Hampshire/Vermont, NE USA
46 G1 **Moores Island** *island* N Bahamas
23 R10 **Mooresville** North Carolina, SE USA 35.34N 80.48W
31 R5 **Moorhead** Minnesota, N USA 46.51N 96.43W
24 K4 **Moorhead** Mississippi, S USA 33.27N 90.30W
176 Ww10 **Moor, Kepulauan** *island group* E Indonesia
101 F18 **Moorsel** Oost-Vlaanderen, C Belgium 50.58N 4.06E
101 C18 **Moorslede** West-Vlaanderen, W Belgium 50.53N 3.03E
20 L8 **Moosalamoo, Mount** ▲ Vermont, NE USA 43.55N 73.03W
103 M22 **Moosburg** Bayern, SE Germany 48.28N 11.55E
35 S14 **Moose** Wyoming, C USA 43.38N 110.42W
10 H11 **Moose** ≈ Ontario, S Canada
10 H10 **Moose Factory** Ontario, S Canada 51.16N 80.31W
21 Q4 **Moosehead Lake** ◎ Maine, NE USA
9 U16 **Moose Jaw** Saskatchewan, S Canada 50.25N 105.29W
9 V14 **Moose Lake** Manitoba, C Canada 53.42N 100.22W
31 W6 **Moose Lake** Minnesota, N USA 46.28N 92.46W
21 P6 **Mooselookmeguntic Lake** ◎ Maine, NE USA
41 R12 **Moose Pass** Alaska, USA 60.28N 149.21W
21 P5 **Moose River** ≈ Maine, NE USA
20 J9 **Moose River** ≈ New York, NE USA
9 V16 **Moosomin** Saskatchewan, S Canada 50.09N 101.40W
10 H10 **Moosonee** Ontario, SE Canada 51.18N 80.40W
21 N12 **Moosup** Connecticut, NE USA 41.42N 71.51W
85 N16 **Mopeia** Zambézia, NE Mozambique 17.58S 35.43E
85 H18 **Mopipi** Central, C Botswana 21.10S 24.54E
Moppo *see* Mokp'o
79 N11 **Mopti** Mopti, C Mali 14.30N 4.15W
79 O11 **Mopti** ◈ *region* S Mali
59 H18 **Moquegua** Moquegua, SE Peru 17.12S 70.55W
59 H18 **Moquegua** *off.* Departamento de Moquegua. ◈ *department* S Peru
113 I23 **Mór** *Ger.* Moor. Fejér, C Hungary 47.21N 18.13E
80 G11 **Mora** Extrême-Nord, N Cameroon 11.01N 14.07E
106 G11 **Mora** Évora, S Portugal 38.55N 8.10W
107 N9 **Mora** Castilla-La Mancha, C Spain 39.40N 3.46W
96 L12 **Mora** Dalarna, C Sweden 61.00N 14.30E
31 V7 **Mora** Minnesota, N USA 45.52N 93.18W
39 T10 **Mora** New Mexico, SW USA 35.56N 105.16W
115 J17 **Morača** ≈ SW Serbia and Montenegro (Yugoslavia)
158 K10 **Morādābād** Uttar Pradesh, N India 28.49N 78.45E
107 U6 **Móra d'Ebre** *var.* Mora de Ebro. Cataluña, NE Spain 41.04N 0.37E
Mora de Ebro *see* Móra d'Ebre
107 S8 **Mora de Rubielos** Aragón, NE Spain 40.15N 0.45W
180 H4 **Morafenobe** Mahajanga, W Madagascar 17.49S 44.54E
112 K8 **Morąg** *Ger.* Mohrungen. Warmińsko-Mazurskie, NE Poland, 53.55N 19.55E
113 L25 **Mórahalom** Csongrád, S Hungary 46.13N 19.51E
107 N11 **Moral de Calatrava** Castilla-La Mancha, C Spain 38.49N 3.34W
65 G19 **Moraleda, Canal** *strait* SE Pacific Ocean
56 J3 **Morales** Bolívar, N Colombia 8.16N 73.52W
56 D12 **Morales** Cauca, SW Colombia 2.43N 76.36W
44 F5 **Morales** Izabal, E Guatemala 15.29N 88.46W
180 J5 **Moramanga** Toamasina, E Madagascar 18.57S 48.13E
29 Q6 **Moran** Kansas, C USA 37.55N 95.10W
27 Q7 **Moran** Texas, SW USA 32.33N 99.10W
189 X7 **Moranbah** Queensland, NE Australia 22.01S 148.07E
46 L13 **Morant Bay** E Jamaica 17.52N 76.24W
98 G10 **Morar, Loch** ◎ N Scotland, UK
Morata *see* Goodenough Island
107 Q12 **Moratalla** Murcia, SE Spain 38.10N 1.52W
110 C8 **Morat, Lac de** *Ger.* Murtensee. ◎ W Switzerland
86 I11 **Morava** *var.* March. ≈ C Europe *see also* March
Morava *see* Moravia, Czech Republic
Morava *see* Velika Morava, Serbia and Montenegro (Yugoslavia)
31 W15 **Moravia** Iowa, C USA 40.53N 92.49W
113 F18 **Moravia** *Cz.* Morava, *Ger.* Mähren. *cultural region* E Czech Republic
113 H17 **Moravice** *Ger.* Mohra. ≈ NE Czech Republic
118 E12 **Moravița** Timiș, SW Romania 45.15N 21.17E
113 G17 **Moravská Třebová** *Ger.* Mährisch-Trübau. Pardubický Kraj, C Czech Republic 49.45N 16.40E
113 E19 **Moravské Budějovice** *Ger.* Mährisch-Budwitz. Jihlavský Kraj, C Czech Republic 49.03N 15.48E
113 F19 **Moravský Krumlov** *Ger.* Mährisch-Kromau. Brněnský Kraj, SE Czech Republic 48.58N 16.30E
98 J8 **Moray** *cultural region* N Scotland, UK
98 J8 **Moray Firth** *inlet* N Scotland, UK
44 B10 **Morazán** ◈ *department* NE El Salvador
160 C10 **Morbi** Gujarāt, W India 22.51N 70.49E
104 G7 **Morbihan** ◈ *department* NW France
Mörbisch *see* Mörbisch am See
111 Y5 **Mörbisch am See** *var.* Mörbisch. Burgenland, E Austria 47.43N 16.40E
97 N21 **Mörbylånga** Kalmar, S Sweden 56.31N 16.25E
104 J14 **Morcenx** Landes, SW France 44.04N 0.55W
Morcheh Khort *see* Mürcheh Khvort
15 L16 **Morden** Manitoba, S Canada 49.12N 98.04W
Mordovskaya ASSR/Mordvinia *see* Mordoviya, Respublika
131 N5 **Mordoviya, Respublika** *prev.* Mordovskaya ASSR, *Eng.* Mordovia, Mordvinia. ◈ *autonomous republic* W Russian Federation
130 M7 **Mordovo** Tambovskaya Oblast', W Russian Federation 52.05N 40.49E
Morea *see* Pelopónnisos
30 K8 **Moreau River** ≈ South Dakota, N USA
99 K16 **Morecambe** NW England, UK 54.04N 2.52W
99 K16 **Morecambe Bay** *inlet* NW England, UK
191 S4 **Moree** New South Wales, SE Australia 29.28S 149.52E
194 E15 **Morehead** Western, SW PNG 8.42S 141.37E
23 N5 **Morehead** Kentucky, S USA 38.13N 83.25W
194 E15 **Morehead** ≈ SW PNG
23 X11 **Morehead City** North Carolina, SE USA 34.43N 76.43W
29 Y8 **Morehouse** Missouri, C USA 36.51N 89.41W
110 E10 **Mörel** Valais, SW Switzerland 46.22N 8.03E
56 D13 **Morelia** Caquetá, S Colombia 1.27N 75.46W
43 N14 **Morelia** Michoacán de Ocampo, S Mexico 19.40N 101.10W
107 T7 **Morella** País Valenciano, E Spain 40.37N 0.06W
42 I7 **Morelos** Chihuahua, N Mexico 26.37N 107.37W
43 O15 **Morelos** ◈ *state* S Mexico
160 H7 **Morena** Madhya Pradesh, C India 26.35N 77.59E
106 L12 **Morena, Sierra** ▲ S Spain
39 O14 **Morenci** Arizona, SW USA 33.05N 109.21W
33 R11 **Morenci** Michigan, N USA 41.43N 84.13W
118 J13 **Moreni** Dâmbovița, S Romania 44.58N 25.39E
96 D9 **Møre og Romsdal** ◈ *county* S Norway
14 Ee12 **Moresby Island** *island* Queen Charlotte Islands, British Columbia, SW Canada
191 W2 **Moreton Island** *island* Queensland, E Australia
105 O3 **Moreuil** Somme, N France 49.47N 2.28E
37 V7 **Morey Peak** ▲ Nevada, W USA 38.40N 116.16W
129 U4 **More-Yu** ≈ NW Russian Federation
105 T9 **Morez** Jura, E France 46.33N 6.01E
Mórfou *see* Güzelyurt
Morfou Bay/Mórfou, Kólpos *see* Güzelyurt Körfezi
190 J8 **Morgan** South Australia 34.02S 139.39E
25 S7 **Morgan** Georgia, SE USA 31.31N 84.34W
27 S8 **Morgan** Texas, SW USA 32.01N 97.36W
24 J10 **Morgan City** Louisiana, S USA 29.42N 91.12W
22 H6 **Morganfield** Kentucky, S USA 37.40N 87.55W
37 O10 **Morgan Hill** California, W USA 37.05N 121.38W
23 Q9 **Morganton** North Carolina, SE USA 35.45N 81.41W
22 J7 **Morgantown** Kentucky, S USA 37.13N 86.40W
23 S2 **Morgantown** West Virginia, NE USA 39.37N 79.57W
110 B10 **Morges** Vaud, SW Switzerland 46.30N 6.24E
154 M4 **Morghāb, Daryā-ye** *var.* Murgab, Murghab, *Turkm.* Murgap Deryasy. ≈ Afghanistan/Turkmenistan *see also* Murgab
Morghāb, Daryā-ye *see* Murgab
98 I9 **Mor, Glen** *var.* Glen Albyn, Great Glen. *valley* N Scotland, UK
105 T5 **Morhange** Moselle, NE France 48.56N 6.37E
164 M5 **Mori** *var.* Mori Kazak Zizhixian. Xinjiang Uygur Zizhiqu, NW China 43.48N 90.21E
172 Nn6 **Mori** Hokkaidō, NE Japan 42.04N 140.35E
37 Y6 **Moriah, Mount** ▲ Nevada, W USA 39.16N 114.10W
39 S11 **Moriarty** New Mexico, SW USA 34.59N 106.03W
56 J12 **Morichal** Guaviare, E Colombia 2.18N 69.54W
194 H14 **Morigio Island** *island* S PNG
Mori Kazak Zizhixian *see* Mori
169 U7 **Morin Dawa** *var.* Morin Dawa Daurzu Zizhiqi. Nei Mongol Zizhiqu, N China 48.21N 124.32E
Morin Dawa Daurzu Zizhiqi *see* Morin Dawa
15 I13 **Morinville** Alberta, SW Canada 53.48N 113.37W
171 Mm11 **Morioka** Iwate, Honshū, C Japan 39.42N 141.08E
191 T8 **Morisset** New South Wales, SE Australia 33.07S 151.32E
171 Mm10 **Moriyoshi-yama** ▲ Honshū, C Japan 39.58N 140.32E
94 K13 **Morjärv** Norrbotten, N Sweden 66.03N 22.45E
131 R3 **Morki** Respublika Mariy El, W Russian Federation 56.27N 49.01E
126 K10 **Morkoka** ≈ NE Russian Federation
104 F5 **Morlaix** Finistère, NW France 48.34N 3.49W
97 M20 **Mörlunda** Kalmar, S Sweden 57.19N 15.52E
109 N19 **Mormanno** Calabria, SW Italy 39.54N 15.58E
38 L11 **Mormon Lake** ◎ Arizona, SW USA
37 Y10 **Mormon Peak** ▲ Nevada, W USA 36.59N 114.25W
Mormon State *see* Utah
47 Y5 **Morne-à-l'Eau** Grande Terre, N Guadeloupe 16.20N 61.28W
31 Y15 **Morning Sun** Iowa, C USA 41.06N 91.15W
200 O14 **Mornington Abyssal Plain** *undersea feature* SE Pacific Ocean
65 F22 **Mornington, Isla** *island* S Chile
189 T4 **Mornington Island** *island* Wellesley Islands, Queensland, N Australia
117 E18 **Mórnos** ≈ C Greece
155 P14 **Moro** Sind, SE Pakistan 26.36N 67.58E
34 I11 **Moro** Oregon, NW USA 45.28N 120.44W
194 K14 **Morobe** Morobe, C PNG 7.46S 147.35E
194 J14 **Morobe** ◈ *province* C PNG
33 N12 **Morocco** Indiana, N USA 40.57N 87.27W
76 E8 **Morocco** *off.* Kingdom of Morocco, *Ar.* Al Mamlakah. ◆ *monarchy* N Africa
Morocco *see* Marrakech
83 I22 **Morogoro** Morogoro, E Tanzania 6.49S 37.40E
83 H24 **Morogoro** ◈ *region* SE Tanzania
179 Qq16 **Moro Gulf** *gulf* S Philippines
43 N13 **Moroleón** Guanajuato, C Mexico 20.00N 101.13W
180 H6 **Morombe** Toliara, W Madagascar 21.46S 43.21E
46 G5 **Morón** Ciego de Ávila, C Cuba 22.04N 78.39W
56 K5 **Morón** Carabobo, N Venezuela 10.28N 68.10W
Morón *see* Morón de la Frontera
169 N8 **Mörön** Hentiy, C Mongolia 47.21N 110.21E
168 I6 **Mörön** Hövsgöl, N Mongolia 49.38N 100.07E
58 D8 **Morona, Río** ≈ N Peru
58 C8 **Morona Santiago** ◈ *province* E Ecuador
180 H5 **Morondava** Toliara, W Madagascar 20.19S 44.16E
106 K14 **Morón de la Frontera** *var.* Morón. Andalucía, S Spain 37.07N 5.27W
180 G13 **Moroni** ● (Comoros) Grande Comore, NW Comoros 11.40S 43.16E
175 Tt6 **Morotai, Pulau** *island* Maluku, E Indonesia
175 T6 **Morotai, Selat** *strait* Maluku, E Indonesia
Morotiri *see* Marotiri
83 H17 **Moroto** NE Uganda 2.31N 34.40E
Morozov *see* Bratan
130 M11 **Morozovsk** Rostovskaya Oblast', SW Russian Federation 48.21N 41.54E
99 L14 **Morpeth** N England, UK 55.10N 1.40W
Morphou *see* Güzelyurt
Morphou Bay *see* Güzelyurt Körfezi
30 I13 **Morrill** Nebraska, C USA 41.57N 103.55W
29 U11 **Morrilton** Arkansas, C USA 35.09N 92.44W
9 Q16 **Morrin** Alberta, SW Canada 51.40N 112.45W
192 M7 **Morrinsville** Waikato, North Island, NZ 37.40S 175.32E
9 X16 **Morris** Manitoba, S Canada 49.21N 97.21W
32 M11 **Morris** Illinois, N USA 41.21N 88.25W
31 S8 **Morris** Minnesota, N USA 45.31N 95.52W
12 M13 **Morrisburg** Ontario, SE Canada 44.55N 75.07W
207 R11 **Morris Jesup, Kap** *headland* N Greenland 83.33N 32.40W
190 B1 **Morris, Mount** ▲ South Australia 26.04S 131.03E
32 K10 **Morrison** Illinois, N USA 41.48N 89.58W
38 K13 **Morristown** Arizona, SW USA 33.48N 112.34W
20 J14 **Morristown** New Jersey, NE USA 40.48N 74.28W
23 O8 **Morristown** Tennessee, S USA 36.12N 83.18W
44 L11 **Morrito** Río San Juan, SW Nicaragua 11.37N 85.03W
37 P13 **Morro Bay** California, W USA 35.21N 120.51W
97 L22 **Mörrum** Blekinge, S Sweden 56.10N 14.45E
85 N16 **Morrumbala** Zambézia, NE Mozambique 17.16S 35.34E
85 N20 **Morrumbene** Inhambane, SE Mozambique 23.38S 35.22E
97 F21 **Mors** *island* NW Denmark
Mörs *see* Moers
27 N1 **Morse** Texas, SW USA 36.03N 101.28W
131 N6 **Morshansk** Tambovskaya Oblast', W Russian Federation 53.27N 41.46E
104 L5 **Mortagne-au-Perche** Orne, N France 48.32N 0.31E
104 J8 **Mortagne-sur-Sèvre** Vendée, NW France 47.00N 0.57W
106 G8 **Mortágua** Viseu, N Portugal 40.24N 8.13W
104 J5 **Mortain** Manche, N France 48.39N 0.51W
108 C8 **Mortara** Lombardia, N Italy 45.15N 8.43E
61 J17 **Mortes, Rio das** ≈ C Brazil
190 M12 **Mortlake** Victoria, SE Australia 38.06S 142.48E
Mortlock Group *see* Takuu Islands
201 Q17 **Mortlock Islands** *prev.* Nomoi Islands. *island group* C Micronesia
31 T9 **Morton** Minnesota, N USA 44.33N 94.58W
24 L5 **Morton** Mississippi, S USA 32.21N 89.39W
26 M5 **Morton** Texas, SW USA 33.40N 102.45W
34 H9 **Morton** Washington, NW USA 46.33N 122.16W
(0) D7 **Morton Seamount** *undersea feature* NE Pacific Ocean 50.15N 142.45W
47 U15 **Moruga** Trinidad, Trinidad and Tobago 10.04N 61.16W
191 P9 **Morundah** New South Wales, SE Australia 34.57S 146.18E
Moruroa *see* Mururoa
191 S11 **Moruya** New South Wales, SE Australia 35.55S 150.04E
105 Q8 **Morvan** *physical region* C France
193 G21 **Morven** Canterbury, South Island, NZ 44.51S 171.07E
191 O13 **Morwell** Victoria, SE Australia 38.13S 146.25E
129 N6 **Morzhovets, Ostrov** *island* NW Russian Federation
106 G4 **Mos** Galicia, NW Spain 42.10N 8.37W
130 J4 **Mosal'sk** Kaluzhskaya Oblast', W Russian Federation 54.30N 34.55E
103 H20 **Mosbach** Baden-Württemberg, SW Germany 49.21N 9.06E
97 E18 **Mosby** Vest-Agder, S Norway 58.12N 7.55E
35 V9 **Mosby** Montana, NW USA 46.58N 107.53W
34 M9 **Moscow** Idaho, NW USA 46.43N 117.00W
22 F10 **Moscow** Tennessee, S USA 35.04N 89.27W
Moscow *see* Moskva
103 D19 **Mosel** *Fr.* Moselle. ≈ W Europe *see also* Moselle
105 T4 **Moselle** ◈ *department* NE France
105 T6 **Moselle** *Ger.* Mosel. ≈ W Europe *see also* Mosel
34 K9 **Moses Lake** ◎ Washington, NW USA
85 I18 **Mosetse** Central, E Botswana 20.40S 26.37E
94 H4 **Mosfellsbær** Sudhurland, SW Iceland 65.09N 21.43W
193 F23 **Mosgiel** Otago, South Island, NZ 45.51S 170.21E
128 M11 **Mosha** ≈ NW Russian Federation
83 I20 **Moshi** Kilimanjaro, NE Tanzania 3.21S 37.19E
112 G12 **Mosina** Wielkolpolskie, C Poland 52.13N 16.48E
32 L6 **Mosinee** Wisconsin, N USA 44.45N 89.39W
94 F13 **Mosjøen** Nordland, C Norway 65.49N 13.12E
127 Nn13 **Moskal'vo** Ostrov Sakhalin, Sakhalinskaya Oblast', SE Russian Federation 53.36N 142.31E
94 I13 **Moskosel** Norrbotten, N Sweden 65.52N 19.30E
130 K4 **Moskovskaya Oblast'** ◈ *province* W Russian Federation
Moskovskiy *see* Moskva
130 J3 **Moskva** *Eng.* Moscow. ● (Russian Federation) Gorod Moskva, W Russian Federation 55.45N 37.42E
153 Q14 **Moskva** *Rus.* Moskovskiy; *prev.* Chubek. SW Tajikistan 37.41N 69.33E
130 L4 **Moskva** ≈ W Russian Federation
85 I20 **Mosomane** Kgatleng, SE Botswana 24.03S 26.16E
Moson and Magyaróvár *see* Mosonmagyaróvár
113 H21 **Mosoni-Duna** *Ger.* Kleine Donau. ≈ NW Hungary
113 H21 **Mosonmagyaróvár** *Ger.* Wieselburg-Ungarisch-Altenburg; *prev.* Moson and Magyaróvár, *Ger.* Wieselburg and Ungarisch-Altenburg. Győr-Moson-Sopron, NW Hungary 47.51N 17.15E
Mospino *see* Mospyne
119 X8 **Mospyne** *Rus.* Mospino. Donets'ka Oblast', E Ukraine 47.53N 38.03E
56 B12 **Mosquera** Nariño, SW Colombia 2.31N 78.24W
39 U10 **Mosquero** New Mexico, SW USA 35.46N 103.57W
Mosquito Coast *see* La Mosquitia
33 U11 **Mosquito Creek Lake** ⊠ Ohio, N USA
Mosquito Gulf *see* Mosquitos, Golfo de los
25 X11 **Mosquito Lagoon** *wetland* Florida, SE USA
45 N10 **Mosquito, Punta** *headland* E Nicaragua 12.18N 83.38W
45 W14 **Mosquito, Punta** *headland* NE Panama 9.06N 77.52W
45 Q15 **Mosquitos, Golfo de los** *Eng.* Mosquito Gulf. *gulf* N Panama
97 H16 **Moss** Østfold, S Norway 59.25N 10.40E
Mossâmedes *see* Namibe
24 G8 **Moss Bluff** Louisiana, S USA 30.18N 93.11W
193 C23 **Mossburn** Southland, South Island, NZ 45.40S 168.15E
85 G26 **Mosselbaai** *var.* Mosselbai, *Eng.* Mossel Bay. Western Cape, SW South Africa 34.10S 22.07E
Mosselbai/Mossel Bay *see* Mosselbaai
81 F20 **Mossendjo** Le Niari, SW Congo 2.57S 12.39E
191 N8 **Mossgiel** New South Wales, SE Australia 33.16S 144.34E
103 H22 **Mössingen** Baden-Württemberg, S Germany 48.22N 9.01E
189 W4 **Mossman** Queensland, NE Australia 16.34S 145.27E
61 P14 **Mossoró** Rio Grande do Norte, NE Brazil 5.10S 37.19W
25 N9 **Moss Point** Mississippi, S USA 30.24N 88.31W
191 S9 **Moss Vale** New South Wales, SE Australia 34.33S 150.22E
34 G9 **Mossyrock** Washington, NW USA 46.32N 122.30W
113 B15 **Most** *Ger.* Brüx. Ústecký Kraj, NW Czech Republic 50.30N 13.37E
123 Jj16 **Mosta** *var.* Musta. C Malta 35.54N 14.25E
76 I5 **Mostaganem** *var.* Mestghanem. NW Algeria 35.55N 0.08E
115 H14 **Mostar** Federacija Bosna I Hercegovina, S Bosnia and Herzegovina 43.20N 17.47E
63 J17 **Mostardas** Rio Grande do Sul, S Brazil 31.06S 50.52W
118 K14 **Mostiştea** ≈ S Romania
Mostva *see* Mastva
Mosty *see* Masty
118 H5 **Mostys'ka** L'vivs'ka Oblast', W Ukraine 49.47N 23.09E
Mosul *see* Al Mawşil
97 F15 **Møsvatnet** ◎ S Norway
82 J12 **Mot'a** Amhara, N Ethiopia 11.03N 38.03E
197 C10 **Mota** *island* Banks Islands, N Vanuatu
81 H16 **Motaba** ≈ N Congo
107 O10 **Mota del Cuervo** Castilla-La Mancha, C Spain 39.30N 2.52W
106 L5 **Mota del Marqués** Castilla-León, N Spain 41.37N 5.10W
44 F5 **Motagua, Río** ≈ Guatemala/Honduras
121 H19 **Motal'** Brestskaya Voblasts', SW Belarus 52.13N 25.34E
97 L17 **Motala** Östergötland, S Sweden 58.33N 15.05E
197 C10 **Mota Lava** *island* Banks Islands, N Vanuatu
203 X7 **Motane** *var.* Mohotani. *island* Îles Marquises, NE French Polynesia
158 K13 **Moth** Uttar Pradesh, N India 25.43N 78.58E
Mother of Presidents/Mother of States *see* Virginia
98 I12 **Motherwell** C Scotland, UK 55.48N 4.00W
159 P12 **Motīhāri** Bihār, N India 26.40N 84.55E
107 Q10 **Motilla del Palancar** Castilla-La Mancha, C Spain 39.34N 1.55W
192 N7 **Motiti Island** *island* NE NZ
67 E25 **Motley Island** *island* SE Falkland Islands
85 J19 **Motloutse** ≈ E Botswana
43 V17 **Motozintla de Mendoza** Chiapas, SE Mexico 15.22N 92.11W
107 N15 **Motril** Andalucía, S Spain 36.45N 3.29W
118 G13 **Motru** Gorj, SW Romania 44.49N 22.55E
171 Mm5 **Motsuta-misaki** *headland* Hokkaidō, NE Japan 42.36N 139.48E
30 L6 **Mott** North Dakota, N USA 46.21N 102.17W
Möttling *see* Metlika
109 O18 **Mottola** Puglia, SE Italy 40.37N 17.01E
192 P8 **Motu** ≈ North Island, NZ
193 I14 **Motueka** Tasman, South Island, NZ 41.08S 173.01E
193 I14 **Motueka** ≈ South Island, NZ
Motu Iti *see* Tupai
43 X12 **Motul** *var.* Motul de Felipe Carrillo Puerto. Yucatán, SE Mexico 21.06N 89.16W
Motul de Felipe Carrillo Puerto *see* Motul
203 U17 **Motu Nui** *island* Easter Island, Chile, E Pacific Ocean
203 Q10 **Motu One** *var.* Bellingshausen. *atoll* Îles Sous le Vent, W French Polynesia
202 I16 **Motutapu** *island* E Cook Islands
200 R15 **Motu Tapu** *island* Tongatapu Group, S Tonga
192 L5 **Motutapu Island** *island* N NZ
Motyca *see* Modica
126 I13 **Motygino** Krasnoyarskiy Kray, C Russian Federation 58.09N 94.35E
Mouanda *see* Moanda
Mouaskar *see* Mascara
107 U3 **Moubermé, Tuc de** *Fr.* Pic de Maubermé, *Sp.* Pico Mauberme; *prev.* Tuc de Maubermé. ▲ France/Spain *see also* Maubermé, Pic de 42.48N 0.57E
47 N7 **Mouchoir Passage** *passage* SE Turks and Caicos Islands
78 I9 **Moudjéria** Tagant, SW Mauritania 17.52N 12.19W
110 C9 **Moudon** Vaud, W Switzerland 46.41N 6.49E
Mouhoun *see* Black Volta
81 E19 **Mouila** Ngounié, C Gabon 1.49S 11.01E
81 K14 **Mouka** Haute-Kotto, C Central African Republic 7.12N 21.52E
Moukden *see* Shenyang
191 N10 **Moulamein** New South Wales, SE Australia 35.06S 144.03E
Moulamein Creek *see* Billabong Creek
76 F6 **Moulay-Bousselham** NW Morocco 34.54N 6.15W
Moule *see* le Moule
82 M11 **Moulhoulé** N Djibouti 12.34N 43.06E
105 P9 **Moulins** Allier, C France 46.34N 3.19E
178 Gg9 **Moulmein** *var.* Maulmain, Mawlamyine. Mon State, S Myanmar 16.30N 97.39E
177 F9 **Moulmeingyun** Irrawaddy, SW Myanmar 16.24N 95.15E
76 G6 **Moulouya** *var.* Mulucha, Muluya, Mulwiya. *seasonal river* NE Morocco
25 O2 **Moulton** Alabama, S USA 34.28N 87.16W
31 W16 **Moulton** Iowa, C USA 40.41N 92.40W
27 T11 **Moulton** Texas, SW USA 29.34N 97.08W
25 T7 **Moultrie** Georgia, SE USA 31.10N 83.47W
23 S14 **Moultrie, Lake** ⊠ South Carolina, SE USA
24 K3 **Mound Bayou** Mississippi, S USA 33.52N 90.43W
32 L17 **Mound City** Illinois, N USA 37.06N 89.09W
29 R6 **Mound City** Kansas, C USA 38.08N 94.48W
29 Q2 **Mound City** Missouri, C USA 40.07N 95.13W
31 N7 **Mound City** South Dakota, N USA 45.42N 100.04W
80 H13 **Moundou** Logone-Occidental, SW Chad 8.34N 16.01E
29 P10 **Mounds** Oklahoma, C USA 35.52N 96.03W
23 R2 **Moundsville** West Virginia, NE USA 39.55N 80.44W
178 Ii12 **Moŭng Roessei** Bătdâmbâng, W Cambodia 12.46N 103.28E
Moun Hou *see* Black Volta
14 G5 **Mountain** ≈ Northwest Territories, NW Canada
39 S12 **Mountainair** New Mexico, SW USA 34.31N 106.14W
37 V1 **Mountain City** Nevada, W USA 41.48N 115.58W
23 Q8 **Mountain City** Tennessee, S USA 36.28N 81.48W
29 U7 **Mountain Grove** Missouri, C USA 37.07N 92.15W
29 U9 **Mountain Home** Arkansas, C USA 36.19N 92.24W
35 N15 **Mountain Home** Idaho, NW USA 43.07N 115.42W
27 Q11 **Mountain Home** Texas, SW USA 30.11N 99.19W
31 W4 **Mountain Iron** Minnesota, N USA 47.31N 92.37W
31 T10 **Mountain Lake** Minnesota, N USA 43.57N 94.54W
25 S3 **Mountain Park** Georgia, SE USA 34.04N 84.24W
37 W12 **Mountain Pass** *pass* California, W USA 35.28N 115.31W
29 T12 **Mountain Pine** Arkansas, C USA 34.34N 93.10W
41 Y14 **Mountain Point** Annette Island, Alaska, USA 55.17N 131.31W
Mountain State *see* Montana, USA
Mountain State *see* West Virginia, USA
29 V7 **Mountain View** Arkansas, C USA 35.52N 92.07W
40 H12 **Mountain View** Hawaii, USA, C Pacific Ocean 19.31N 155.03W
29 V10 **Mountain View** Missouri, C USA 37.00N 91.42W
40 M11 **Mountain Village** Alaska, USA 62.06N 163.42W
23 R8 **Mount Airy** North Carolina, SE USA 36.30N 80.36W
85 K24 **Mount Ayliff** *Xh.* Maxesibebi. Eastern Cape, SE South Africa 30.48S 29.22E
31 U16 **Mount Ayr** Iowa, C USA 40.42N 94.14W
190 J9 **Mount Barker** South Australia 35.06S 138.52E
188 J14 **Mount Barker** Western Australia 34.42S 117.40E
191 P11 **Mount Beauty** Victoria, SE Australia 36.47S 147.12E
12 E16 **Mount Brydges** Ontario, S Canada 42.54N 81.29W
33 N16 **Mount Carmel** Illinois, N USA 38.23N 87.46W
32 K10 **Mount Carroll** Illinois, N USA 42.04N 89.58W

◆ Country ● Country Capital ◇ Dependent Territory ○ Dependent Territory Capital ◈ Administrative Region ✕ International Airport ▲ Mountain ▲ Mountain Range Volcano ≈ River ◎ Lake ⊠ Reservoir

33 S9 **Mount Clemens** Michigan, N USA 42.36N 82.52W
193 E19 **Mount Cook** Canterbury, South Island, NZ 43.46S 170.06E
85 L16 **Mount Darwin** Mashonaland Central, NE Zimbabwe 16.45S 31.32E
21 S7 **Mount Desert Island** island Maine, NE USA
25 W11 **Mount Dora** Florida, SE USA 28.48N 81.38W
190 G5 **Mount Eba** South Australia 30.11S 135.40E
27 W8 **Mount Enterprise** Texas, SW USA 31.53N 94.40W
190 J4 **Mount Fitton** South Australia 29.55S 139.26E
85 J24 **Mount Fletcher** Eastern Cape, SE South Africa 30.40S 28.30E
12 F15 **Mount Forest** Ontario, S Canada 43.58N 80.43W
190 K12 **Mount Gambier** South Australia 37.47S 140.48E
189 W5 **Mount Garnet** Queensland, NE Australia 17.41S 145.07E
23 P6 **Mount Gay** West Virginia, NE USA 37.49N 82.00W
33 S12 **Mount Gilead** Ohio, N USA 40.33N 82.49W
194 H12 **Mount Hagen** Western Highlands, C PNG 5.53S 144.12E
20 J16 **Mount Holly** New Jersey, NE USA 39.59N 74.46W
23 R10 **Mount Holly** North Carolina, SE USA 35.18N 81.01W
29 T12 **Mount Ida** Arkansas, C USA 34.33N 93.37W
189 T6 **Mount Isa** Queensland, C Australia 20.48S 139.32E
23 U4 **Mount Jackson** Virginia, NE USA 38.45N 78.38W
20 D12 **Mount Jewett** Pennsylvania, NE USA 41.43N 78.37W
20 L13 **Mount Kisco** New York, NE USA 41.12N 73.42W
20 B15 **Mount Lebanon** Pennsylvania, NE USA 40.21N 80.03W
190 J8 **Mount Lofty Ranges** ▲ South Australia
188 J10 **Mount Magnet** Western Australia 28.09S 117.52E
192 N7 **Mount Maunganui** Bay of Plenty, North Island, NZ 37.39S 176.11E
99 E18 **Mountmellick** Ir. Móinteach Mílic. C Ireland 53.07N 7.19W
32 L10 **Mount Morris** Illinois, N USA 42.03N 89.25W
33 R9 **Mount Morris** Michigan, N USA 43.07N 83.42W
20 F10 **Mount Morris** New York, NE USA 42.43N 77.51W
20 B16 **Mount Morris** Pennsylvania, NE USA 39.43N 80.06W
32 K15 **Mount Olive** Illinois, N USA 39.04N 89.43W
23 V10 **Mount Olive** North Carolina, SE USA 35.12N 78.03W
23 N4 **Mount Olivet** Kentucky, S USA 38.32N 84.01W
31 Y15 **Mount Pleasant** Iowa, C USA 40.57N 91.33W
33 Q8 **Mount Pleasant** Michigan, N USA 43.36N 84.46W
20 C15 **Mount Pleasant** Pennsylvania, NE USA 40.07N 79.33W
23 T14 **Mount Pleasant** South Carolina, SE USA 32.47N 79.51W
22 I9 **Mount Pleasant** Tennessee, S USA 35.32N 87.11W
27 W6 **Mount Pleasant** Texas, SW USA 33.10N 94.49W
38 L4 **Mount Pleasant** Utah, W USA 39.33N 111.27W
65 N23 **Mount Pleasant** ✕ (Stanley) East Falkland, Falkland Islands
99 G25 **Mount's Bay** inlet SW England, UK
37 N2 **Mount Shasta** California, W USA 41.18N 122.19W
32 J13 **Mount Sterling** Illinois, N USA 39.59N 90.44W
23 N5 **Mount Sterling** Kentucky, S USA 38.03N 83.56W
20 E15 **Mount Union** Pennsylvania, NE USA 40.21N 77.51W
25 V6 **Mount Vernon** Georgia, SE USA 32.10N 82.35W
32 L16 **Mount Vernon** Illinois, N USA 38.19N 88.54W
22 M6 **Mount Vernon** Kentucky, S USA 37.22N 84.22W
29 S7 **Mount Vernon** Missouri, C USA 37.06N 93.49W
33 T13 **Mount Vernon** Ohio, N USA 40.23N 82.29W
34 K13 **Mount Vernon** Oregon, NW USA 44.22N 119.07W
27 W6 **Mount Vernon** Texas, SW USA 33.11N 95.13W
34 H7 **Mount Vernon** Washington, NW USA 48.25N 122.19W
22 L5 **Mount Washington** Kentucky, S USA 38.03N 85.33W
190 F8 **Mount Wedge** South Australia 33.29S 135.08E
32 L14 **Mount Zion** Illinois, N USA 39.46N 88.52W
189 Y9 **Moura** Queensland, NE Australia 24.34S 149.57E
60 F12 **Moura** Amazonas, NW Brazil 1.32S 61.43W
106 H12 **Moura** Beja, S Portugal 38.07N 7.27W
106 I12 **Mourão** Évora, S Portugal 38.22N 7.19W
78 L11 **Mourdiah** Koulikoro, W Mali 14.28N 7.31W
80 K7 **Mourdi, Dépression du** desert lowland Chad/Sudan
104 J16 **Mourenx** Pyrénées-Atlantiques, SW France 43.24N 0.37W
Mourgana see Mourgkána
117 C15 **Mourgkána** var. Mourgana. ▲ Albania/Greece 39.48N 20.24E
99 G16 **Mourne Mountains** Ir. Beanna Boirche. ▲ SE Northern Ireland, UK
117 I15 **Moúrtzeflos, Akrotírio** headland Límnos, E Greece 40.00N 25.02E
101 C19 **Mouscron** Dut. Moeskroen. Hainaut, W Belgium 50.43N 3.13E
Mouse River see Souris River
80 H10 **Moussoro** Kanem, W Chad 13.40N 16.31E
105 T11 **Moûtiers** Savoie, E France 45.28N 6.31E
180 J14 **Moutsamoudou** var. Mutsamudu. Anjouan, SE Comoros 12.10S 44.25E
76 K11 **Mouydir, Monts de** ▲ S Algeria
81 F20 **Mouyondzi** La Bouenza, S Congo 3.58S 13.57E
117 E16 **Mouzáki** prev. Mouzákion. Thessalía, C Greece 39.25N 21.40E
Mouzákion see Mouzáki
31 S13 **Moville** Iowa, C USA 42.30N 96.04W
84 E13 **Moxico** ◈ province E Angola
180 I14 **Moya** Anjouan, SE Comoros 12.18S 44.27E
42 L12 **Moyahua** Zacatecas, C Mexico 21.19N 103.10W
83 J16 **Moyalē** Oromo, C Ethiopia 3.34N 38.58E
78 I15 **Moyamba** W Sierra Leone 8.04N 12.30W
76 G7 **Moyen Atlas** Eng. Middle Atlas. ▲ N Morocco
80 H13 **Moyen-Chari** off. Préfecture du Moyen-Chari. ◈ prefecture S Chad
Moyen-Congo see Congo (Republic of)
85 J24 **Moyeni** var. Quthing. SW Lesotho 30.25S 27.43E
78 H13 **Moyenne-Guinée** ◈ state NW Guinea
81 D18 **Moyen-Ogooué** off. Province du Moyen-Ogooué, var. Le Moyen-Ogooué. ◈ province C Gabon
105 S4 **Moyeuvre-Grande** Moselle, NE France 49.15N 6.03E
35 N7 **Moyie Springs** Idaho, NW USA 48.43N 116.15W
152 G6 **Mo'ynoq** Rus. Muynak. Qoraqalpog'iston Respublikasi, NW Uzbekistan 43.45N 59.03E
151 S15 **Moynnkum** prev. Fumanovka, Kaz. Fūrmanov. Zhambyl, S Kazakhstan 44.15N 72.55E
83 F16 **Moyo** NW Uganda 3.37N 31.43E
58 D10 **Moyobamba** San Martín, NW Peru 6.04S 76.55W
175 O16 **Moyo, Pulau** island S Indonesia
80 H10 **Moyto** Chari-Baguirmi, W Chad 12.34N 16.33E
164 G9 **Moyu** var. Karakax. Xinjiang Uygur Zizhiqu, NW China 37.16N 79.39E
126 Jj9 **Moyyero** ≈ N Russian Federation
151 Q15 **Moyynkum, Peski** Kaz. Moyynqum. desert S Kazakhstan
Moyynqum see Moyynkum, Peski
151 S12 **Moyynty** Zhezkazgan, C Kazakhstan 47.10N 73.24E
151 S12 **Moyynty** ≈ C Kazakhstan
Mozambika, Lakandranon' i see Mozambique Channel
85 M18 **Mozambique** off. Republic of Mozambique; prev. People's Republic of Mozambique, Portuguese East Africa. ◆ republic S Africa
Mozambique Basin see Natal Basin
Mozambique, Canal de see Mozambique Channel
85 P17 **Mozambique Channel** Fr. Canal de Mozambique, Mal. Lakandranon' i Mozambika. strait W Indian Ocean
180 L11 **Mozambique Escarpment** var. Mozambique Scarp. undersea feature SW Indian Ocean
180 L10 **Mozambique Plateau** var. Mozambique Rise. undersea feature SW Indian Ocean
Mozambique Rise see Mozambique Plateau
Mozambique Scarp see Mozambique Escarpment
131 O15 **Mozdok** Respublika Severnaya Osetiya, SW Russian Federation 43.48N 44.42E
59 K17 **Mozetenes, Serranías de** ▲ C Bolivia
130 J4 **Mozhaysk** Moskovskaya Oblast', W Russian Federation 55.31N 36.01E
131 T3 **Mozhga** Udmurtskaya Respublika, NW Russian Federation 56.24N 52.13E
Mozyr' see Mazyr
81 P22 **Mpala** Katanga, E Dem. Rep. Congo 6.43S 29.28E
81 G19 **Mpama** ≈ C Congo
83 E22 **Mpanda** Rukwa, W Tanzania 6.21S 31.01E
84 L11 **Mpande** Northern, NE Zambia 9.13S 31.42E
85 J18 **Mphoengs** Matabeleland South, SW Zimbabwe 21.04S 27.56E
83 F18 **Mpigi** S Uganda 0.13N 32.19E
85 L13 **Mpika** Northern, NE Zambia 11.49S 31.27E
85 J14 **Mpima** Central, C Zambia 14.25S 28.34E
84 J13 **Mpongwe** Copperbelt, C Zambia 13.25S 28.13E
84 K11 **Mporokoso** Northern, N Zambia 9.22S 30.06E
81 H20 **Mpouya** Plateaux, SE Congo 2.39S 16.12E
79 P16 **Mpraeso** C Ghana 6.46N 0.41W
84 L11 **Mpulungu** Northern, N Zambia 8.47S 31.09E
85 K21 **Mpumalanga** prev. Eastern Transvaal, Afr. Oos-Transvaal. ◈ province NE South Africa
85 D16 **Mpungu** Okavango, N Namibia 17.36S 18.16E
83 I22 **Mpwapwa** Dodoma, C Tanzania 6.21S 36.28E
Mqinvartsveri see Kazbek
112 M8 **Mrągowo** Ger. Sensburg. Warmińsko-Mazurskie, NE Poland, 53.52N 21.19E
131 V6 **Mrakovo** Respublika Bashkortostan, W Russian Federation 52.43N 56.36E
180 I13 **Mramani** Anjouan, E Comoros 12.18S 44.39E
114 F12 **Mrkonjić Grad** Republika Srpska, W Bosnia and Herzegovina 44.25N 17.04E
112 H9 **Mrocza** Kujawsko-pomorskie, NW Poland 53.15N 17.38E
128 I14 **Msta** ≈ NW Russian Federation
Mtkvari see Kura
Mtoko see Mutoko
130 K6 **Mtsensk** Orlovskaya Oblast', W Russian Federation 53.17N 36.34E
83 K24 **Mtwara** Mtwara, SE Tanzania 10.16S 40.10E
83 J25 **Mtwara** ◈ region SE Tanzania
106 G14 **Mu** ▲ S Portugal 37.24N 8.04W
200 Qq15 **Mu'a** Tongatapu, S Tonga 21.11S 175.07W
Muai To see Mae Hong Son
85 P16 **Mualama** Zambézia, NE Mozambique 16.51S 38.21E
Mualo see Messalo, Rio
81 E22 **Muanda** Bas-Congo, SW Dem. Rep. Congo 5.53S 12.17E
Muang Chiang Rai see Chiang Rai
178 J6 **Muang Ham** Houaphan, N Laos 20.19N 104.00E
178 J9 **Muang Hinboun** Khammouan, C Laos 17.37N 104.37E
Muang Kalasin see Kalasin
Muang Khammouan see Thakhèk
178 Jj11 **Muang Không** Champasak, S Laos 14.08N 105.48E
178 Jj10 **Muang Khôngxédôn** var. Khong Sedone. Salavan, S Laos 15.34N 105.46E
Muang Khon Kaen see Khon Kaen
178 Ii6 **Muang Khoua** Phôngsali, N Laos 21.07N 102.31E
Muang Krabi see Krabi
Muang Lampang see Lampang
Muang Lamphun see Lamphun
Muang Loei see Loei
Muang Lom Sak see Lom Sak
Muang Nakhon Sawan see Nakhon Sawan
178 I6 **Muang Namo** Oudômxai, N Laos 20.58N 101.46E
Muang Nan see Nan
178 Ii6 **Muang Ngoy** Louangphabang, N Laos 20.43N 102.42E
178 I5 **Muang Ou Tai** Phôngsali, N Laos 22.06N 101.59E
Muang Pak Lay see Pak Lay
Muang Pakxan see Pakxan
178 Jj10 **Muang Pakxong** Champasak, S Laos 15.10N 106.17E
178 Jj9 **Muang Phalan** var. Muang Phalane. Savannakhét, S Laos 16.40N 105.33E
Muang Phalane see Muang Phalan
Muang Phan see Phan
Muang Phayao see Phayao
Muang Phichit see Phichit
178 Jj9 **Muang Phin** Savannakhét, S Laos 16.31N 106.01E
Muang Phitsanulok see Phitsanulok
Muang Phrae see Phrae
Muang Roi Et see Roi Et
Muang Sakon Nakhon see Sakon Nakhon
Muang Samut Prakan see Samut Prakan
178 I6 **Muang Sing** Louang Namtha, N Laos 21.12N 101.09E
Muang Ubon see Ubon Ratchathani
Muang Uthai Thani see Uthai Thani
178 I7 **Muang Vangviang** Viangchan, C Laos 18.53N 102.27E
Muang Xaignabouri see Xaignabouli
Muang Xay see Xai
178 Jj9 **Muang Xépôn** var. Sepone. Savannakhét, S Laos 16.40N 106.15E
174 H6 **Muar** var. Bandar Maharani. Johor, Peninsular Malaysia 2.01N 102.34E
173 Ff6 **Muara** Sumatera, W Indonesia 2.18N 98.54E
174 Hh11 **Muarabeliti** Sumatera, W Indonesia 3.13S 103.00E
174 H9 **Muarabungo** Sumatera, W Indonesia 1.36S 103.37E
174 I11 **Muaraenim** Sumatera, W Indonesia 3.36S 103.43E
174 Mm8 **Muarajuloi** Borneo, C Indonesia 0.12S 114.03E
175 Nn9 **Muarakaman** Borneo, C Indonesia 0.09S 116.43E
173 Ff9 **Muarasigep** Pulau Siberut, W Indonesia 1.01S 98.48E
174 Hh9 **Muaratembesi** Sumatera, W Indonesia 1.42S 103.07E
175 N9 **Muaratewe** var. Muarateweh; prev. Moearatewe. Borneo, C Indonesia 0.58S 114.52E
Muarateweh see Muaratewe
175 O7 **Muarawahau** Borneo, N Indonesia 1.03N 116.48E
144 G13 **Mubārak, Jabal** ▲ S Jordan 29.19N 35.13E
159 N13 **Mubārakpur** Uttar Pradesh, N India 26.05N 83.19E
Mubarek see Muborak
83 F18 **Mubende** SW Uganda 0.34N 31.24E
79 Y14 **Mubi** Adamawa, NE Nigeria 10.15N 13.18E
152 M12 **Muborak** Rus. Mubarek. Qashqadaryo Viloyati, S Uzbekistan 39.17N 65.10E
176 Vv9 **Mubrani** Papua, E Indonesia 0.42S 133.25E
69 U12 **Muchinga Escarpment** escarpment NE Zambia
131 N7 **Muchkapskiy** Tambovskaya Oblast', W Russian Federation 51.51N 42.25E
98 G10 **Muck** island W Scotland, UK
83 Q13 **Mucojo** Cabo Delgado, N Mozambique 12.04S 40.30E
84 F12 **Muconda** Lunda Sul, NE Angola 10.37S 21.19E
56 I10 **Muco, Río** ≈ E Colombia
85 O16 **Mucubela** Zambézia, NE Mozambique 16.51S 37.48E
44 J5 **Mucupina, Monte** ▲ N Honduras 15.07N 86.36W
142 J14 **Mucur** Kirşehir, C Turkey 39.04N 34.25E
149 U8 **Mūd** Khorāsān, E Iran 32.40N 59.30E
169 Y9 **Mudanjiang** var. Mu-tan-chiang. Heilongjiang, NE China 44.33N 129.40E
169 Y9 **Mudan Jiang** ≈ NE China
142 D11 **Mudanya** Bursa, NW Turkey 40.22N 28.52E
30 K8 **Mud Butte** South Dakota, N USA 45.00N 102.51W
161 G16 **Muddebihāl** Karnātaka, C India 16.26N 76.07E
29 P12 **Muddy Boggy Creek** ≈ Oklahoma, C USA
38 M6 **Muddy Creek** ≈ Utah, W USA
39 V7 **Muddy Creek Reservoir** ▣ Colorado, C USA
35 W15 **Muddy Gap** Wyoming, C USA 42.21N 107.27W
37 Y11 **Muddy Peak** ▲ Nevada, W USA 36.17N 114.40W
191 R7 **Mudgee** New South Wales, SE Australia 32.37S 149.34E
31 S3 **Mud Lake** ◎ Minnesota, N USA
31 P7 **Mud Lake Reservoir** ▣ South Dakota, N USA
178 Gg9 **Mudon** Mon State, S Myanmar 16.14N 97.46E
83 O14 **Mudug** off. Gobolka Mudug. ◈ region NE Somalia
83 O14 **Mudug** var. Mudugh. plain N Somalia
Mudugh see Mudug
85 Q15 **Muecate** Nampula, NE Mozambique 14.56S 39.38E
84 Q13 **Mueda** Cabo Delgado, NE Mozambique 11.40S 39.36E
44 L10 **Muelle de los Bueyes** Región Autónoma Atlántico Sur, SE Nicaragua 12.03N 84.34W
Muenchen see München
85 M14 **Muende** Tete, NW Mozambique 14.22S 33.00E
27 T5 **Muenster** Texas, SW USA 33.39N 97.22W
Muenster see Münster
45 O6 **Muerto, Cayo** reef NE Nicaragua
43 T17 **Muerto, Mar** lagoon SE Mexico
66 F11 **Muertos Trough** undersea feature N Caribbean Sea
85 H14 **Mufaya Kuta** Western, NW Zambia 14.30S 24.18E
84 J13 **Mufulira** Copperbelt, C Zambia 12.33S 28.15E
167 O10 **Mufu Shan** ▲ C China
Mugalzhar Taūlary see Mugodzhary, Gory
143 Y12 **Muğan Düzü** Rus. Muganskaya Ravnina, Muganskaya Step'. physical region S Azerbaijan
Muganskaya Ravnina/Muganskaya Step' see Muğan Düzü
108 K8 **Muggia** Friuli-Venezia Giulia, NE Italy 45.36N 13.48E
159 N14 **Mughal Sarāi** Uttar Pradesh, N India 25.18N 83.07E
Mughla see Muğla
147 W11 **Mughshin** var. Muqshin. S Oman 19.25N 54.38E
153 S12 **Mughsu** Rus. Muksu. ≈ C Tajikistan
170 Ff16 **Mugi** Tokushima, Shikoku, SW Japan 33.39N 134.24E
142 C16 **Muğla** var. Mughla. Muğla, SW Turkey 37.13N 28.22E
142 C16 **Muğla** var. Mughla. ◈ province SW Turkey
150 J11 **Mugodzhary, Gory** Kaz. Mugalzhar Taūlary. ▲ W Kazakhstan
85 O15 **Mugulama** Zambézia, NE Mozambique 16.01S 37.33E
145 U9 **Muḩammad** E Iraq 32.46N 45.14E
145 R8 **Muḩammadīyah** C Iraq 33.22N 42.48E
82 I6 **Muhammad Qol** Red Sea, NE Sudan 20.52N 37.09E
77 Y9 **Muhammad, Râs** headland E Egypt 27.45N 34.18E
Muhammerah see Khorramshahr
146 M12 **Muḩāyil** var. Mahāil. 'Asīr, SW Saudi Arabia 18.34N 42.01E
145 O7 **Muḩaywir** W Iraq 33.34N 41.06E
103 H21 **Mühlacker** Baden-Württemberg, SW Germany 48.57N 8.51E
Mühlbach see Sebeş
Mühldorf see Mühldorf am Inn
103 N23 **Mühldorf am Inn** var. Mühldorf. Bayern, SE Germany 48.14N 12.32E
103 J15 **Mühlhausen** var. Mühlhausen in Thüringen. Thüringen, C Germany 51.13N 10.28E
Mühlhausen in Thüringen see Mühlhausen
205 Q2 **Mühlig-Hofmann Mountains** ▲ Antarctica
95 L14 **Muhos** Oulu, C Finland 64.48N 26.00E
144 K6 **Muḩ, Sabkhat al** ◎ C Syria
120 E5 **Muhu** Ger. Mohn, Moon. island W Estonia
83 F19 **Muhutwe** Kagera, NW Tanzania 1.31S 31.40E
Muhu Väin see Väinameri
100 J10 **Muiden** Noord-Holland, C Netherlands 52.19N 5.04E
200 R15 **Mui Hopohoponga** headland Tongatapu, S Tonga 21.09S 175.01W
171 K14 **Muika** var. Muikamachi. Niigata, Honshū, C Japan 37.04N 138.53E
Muikamachi see Muika
Muinchille see Cootehill
Muineachán see Monaghan
99 F19 **Muine Bheag** Eng. Bagenalstown. SE Ireland 52.42N 6.57W
58 B5 **Muisne** Esmeraldas, NW Ecuador 0.34N 79.58W
85 P14 **Muite** Nampula, NE Mozambique 14.02S 39.06E
43 Z11 **Mujeres, Isla** island E Mexico
118 G7 **Mukacheve** Hung. Munkács, Rus. Mukachevo. Zakarpats'ka Oblast', W Ukraine 48.26N 22.44E
Mukachevo see Mukacheve
174 Ll5 **Mukah** Sarawak, East Malaysia 2.55N 112.01E
Mukalla see Al Mukallā
Mukama see Mokāma
Mukāshafa/Mukashshafah see Mukayshīfah
172 Oo6 **Mu-kawa** ≈ Hokkaidō, NE Japan
145 S6 **Mukayshīfah** var. Mukāshafa, Mukashshafah. N Iraq 34.24N 43.44E
178 J9 **Mukdahan** Mukdahan, E Thailand 16.31N 104.43E
Mukden see Shenyang
172 Ss16 **Mukojima-rettō** Eng. Parry group. island group SE Japan
152 M14 **Mukry** Lebapskiy Velayat, E Turkmenistan 37.39N 65.37E
Muksu see Mughsu
159 U14 **Muktagacha** var. Muktagachha Dhaka, N Bangladesh 24.46N 90.16E
Muktagachha see Muktagacha
84 K13 **Mukuku** Central, C Zambia 12.10S 29.50E
84 K11 **Mukupa Kaoma** Northern, NE Zambia 9.55S 30.19E
83 I18 **Mukutan** Rift Valley, W Kenya 1.06N 36.16E
85 F16 **Mukwe** Caprivi, NE Namibia 18.01S 21.24E
107 R13 **Mula** Murcia, SE Spain 38.01N 1.28W
157 K20 **Mulaku Atoll** var. Meemu Atoll. atoll C Maldives
85 J15 **Mulalika** Lusaka, C Zambia 15.37S 28.48E
169 X8 **Mulan** Heilongjiang, NE China 45.57N 128.00E
85 N15 **Mulanje** var. Mlanje. Southern, S Malawi 16.04S 35.35E
42 H5 **Mulatos** Sonora, NW Mexico 28.42N 108.44W
25 P3 **Mulberry Fork** ≈ Alabama, S USA
41 P12 **Mulchatna River** ≈ Alaska, USA
129 W4 **Mul'da** Respublika Komi, NW Russian Federation 67.29N 63.55E
103 M14 **Mulde** ≈ E Germany
29 R10 **Muldrow** Oklahoma, C USA 35.25N 94.34W
42 E7 **Mulegé** Baja California Sur, W Mexico 26.54N 112.00W
110 I10 **Mulegns** Graubünden, S Switzerland 46.30N 9.36E
81 M21 **Mulenda** Kasai Oriental, C Dem. Rep. Congo 4.19S 24.55E
26 M4 **Muleshoe** Texas, SW USA 34.13N 102.43W
85 O15 **Mulevala** Zambézia, NE Mozambique 16.18S 37.40E
191 P5 **Mulgoa Creek** seasonal river New South Wales, SE Australia
107 O15 **Mulhacén** var. Cerro de Mulhacén. ▲ S Spain 37.07N 3.11W
Mulhacén, Cerro de see Mulhacén
Mülhausen see Mulhouse
103 E24 **Müllheim** Baden-Württemberg, SW Germany 47.49N 7.36E
103 E15 **Mülheim** var. Mulheim an der Ruhr. Nordrhein-Westfalen, W Germany 51.25N 6.52E
Mulheim an der Ruhr see Mülheim
105 U7 **Mulhouse** Ger. Mülhausen. Haut-Rhin, NE France 47.45N 7.19E
166 G11 **Muli** var. Bowa, Muli Zangzu Zizhixian. Sichuan, C China 27.49N 101.10E
176 Y15 **Muli** channel Papua, E Indonesia
169 Y9 **Muling** Heilongjiang, NE China 44.54N 130.35E
Mullach Íde see Malahide
Mullaitivu see Mullaittivu
161 K23 **Mullaittivu** var. Mullaitivu. Northern Province, N Sri Lanka 9.15N 80.48E
35 N8 **Mullan** Idaho, NW USA 47.28N 115.48W
30 M13 **Mullen** Nebraska, C USA 42.02N 101.01W
191 Q6 **Mullengudgery** New South Wales, SE Australia 31.42S 147.24E
23 Q6 **Mullens** West Virginia, NE USA 37.34N 81.22W
Müller-gerbergte see Muller, Pegunungan
174 Mm7 **Muller, Pegunungan** Dut. Müller-gerbergte. ▲ Borneo, C Indonesia
194 F12 **Muller Range** ▲ W PNG
33 Q5 **Mullett Lake** ◎ Michigan, N USA
20 J16 **Mullica River** ≈ New Jersey, NE USA
27 R8 **Mullin** Texas, SW USA 31.33N 98.40W
99 E17 **Mullingar** Ir. An Muileann gCearr. C Ireland 53.31N 7.19W
23 T12 **Mullins** South Carolina, SE USA 34.12N 79.15W
98 G11 **Mull, Isle of** island W Scotland, UK
131 R5 **Mullovka** Ul'yanovskaya Oblast', W Russian Federation 54.13N 49.19E
97 K19 **Mullsjö** Västra Götaland, S Sweden 57.55N 13.55E
191 V4 **Mullumbimby** New South Wales, SE Australia 28.34S 153.28E
85 H15 **Mulobezi** Western, SW Zambia 16.48S 25.10E
85 C15 **Mulondo** Huíla, SW Angola 15.41S 15.09E
85 G15 **Mulonga Plain** plain W Zambia
81 N23 **Mulongo** Katanga, SE Dem. Rep. Congo 7.44S 26.57E
155 T10 **Multān** Punjab, E Pakistan 30.12N 71.29E
95 L17 **Multia** Länsi-Suomi, W Finland 62.27N 24.49E
Mulucha see Moulouya
85 J14 **Mulungushi** Central, C Zambia 14.15S 28.27E
85 K14 **Mulungwe** Central, C Zambia 13.57S 29.51E
Muluya see Moulouya
29 N7 **Mulvane** Kansas, C USA 37.28N 97.14W
191 O10 **Mulwala** New South Wales, SE Australia 35.59S 146.00E
Mulwiya see Moulouya
190 K6 **Mulyungarie** South Australia 31.29S 140.45E
160 D13 **Mumbai** prev. Bombay. Mahārāshtra, W India 18.55N 72.51E
160 D13 **Mumbai** ✕ Mahārāshtra, W India 19.10N 72.51E
85 D14 **Mumbué** Bié, C Angola 13.52S 17.15E
194 J13 **Mumeng** Morobe, C PNG 6.57S 146.37E
176 W9 **Mumi** Papua, E Indonesia 1.33S 134.09E
Muminabad/Mŭ'minobod see Leningrad
131 Q13 **Mumra** Astrakhanskaya Oblast', SW Russian Federation 45.46N 47.46E
43 X12 **Muna** Yucatán, SE Mexico 20.28N 89.45W
126 Kk9 **Muna** ≈ NE Russian Federation
158 C12 **Munābāo** Rājasthān, NW India 25.46N 70.19E
Munamägi see Suur Munamägi
175 Qq13 **Muna, Pulau** prev. Moena. island C Indonesia
175 Qq13 **Muna, Selat** strait Sulawesi, C Indonesia
103 L18 **Münchberg** Bayern, E Germany 50.10N 11.49E
103 L23 **München** var. Muenchen, Eng. Munich, It. Monaco. Bayern, SE Germany 48.08N 11.34E
München-Gladbach see Mönchengladbach
110 E6 **Münchenstein** Basel-Land, NW Switzerland 47.31N 7.37E
8 L10 **Muncho Lake** British Columbia, W Canada 58.52N 125.40W
33 P13 **Muncie** Indiana, N USA 40.10N 85.22W
20 G13 **Muncy** Pennsylvania, NE USA 41.10N 76.46W
195 U14 **Munda** New Georgia, NW Solomon Islands 8.15S 157.15E
9 Q14 **Mundare** Alberta, SW Canada 53.34N 112.20W
27 Q5 **Munday** Texas, SW USA 33.27N 99.37W
33 N10 **Mundelein** Illinois, N USA 42.15N 88.00W
103 I15 **Münden** Niedersachsen, C Germany 52.16N 8.54E
107 Q12 **Mundo** ≈ S Spain
194 L11 **Mundua Island** island Witu Islands, C PNG
84 B12 **Munenga** Cuanza Sul, NW Angola 10.05S 14.35E
107 P11 **Munera** Castilla-La Mancha, C Spain 39.03N 2.28W
22 E9 **Munford** Tennessee, S USA 35.27N 89.49W
22 K7 **Munfordville** Kentucky, S USA 37.15N 85.53W
190 D5 **Mungala** South Australia 30.36S 132.57E
85 M16 **Mungári** Manica, C Mozambique 17.09S 33.33E
81 O16 **Mungbere** Orientale, NE Dem. Rep. Congo 2.37N 28.30E
159 Q13 **Munger** prev. Monghyr. Bihār, NE India 25.22N 86.28E
190 I2 **Mungeranie** South Australia 28.02S 138.42E
Mu Nggava see Rennell
174 K6 **Mungguresak, Tanjung** headland Borneo, N Indonesia 1.57N 109.19E
Mungiki see Bellona
191 R4 **Mungindi** New South Wales, SE Australia 28.59S 149.00E
Mungkawn see Maingkwan
159 T16 **Mungla** var. Mongla. Khulna, S Bangladesh 22.18N 89.34E
84 C13 **Mungo** Huambo, W Angola 11.46S 16.13E
196 F16 **Munguy Bay** bay Yap, W Micronesia
84 E13 **Munhango** Bié, C Angola 12.12S 18.34E
197 L14 **Munia** island Lau Group, E Fiji
Munich see München
107 S7 **Muniesa** Aragón, NE Spain 41.01N 0.49W
33 O4 **Munising** Michigan, N USA 46.24N 86.39W
Munkács see Mukacheve
97 I17 **Munkedal** Västra Götaland, S Sweden 58.28N 11.37E
97 K15 **Munkfors** Värmland, C Sweden 59.49N 13.34E
126 J16 **Munku-Sardyk, Gora** var. Mönh Sarĭdag. ▲ Mongolia/Russian Federation 51.45N 100.22E
101 E18 **Munkzwalm** Oost-Vlaanderen, NW Belgium 50.53N 3.44E
178 J10 **Mun, Mae Nam** ≈ E Thailand
159 U15 **Munshiganj** Dhaka, C Bangladesh 23.31N 90.31E
110 D8 **Münsingen** Bern, W Switzerland 46.52N 7.36E
105 U6 **Munster** Haut-Rhin, NE France 48.03N 7.09E
102 J11 **Munster** Niedersachsen, NW Germany 52.58N 10.06E
99 B20 **Munster** Ir. Cúige Mumhan. cultural region S Ireland
102 F13 **Münster** var. Muenster, Münster in Westfalen. Nordrhein-Westfalen, W Germany 51.58N 7.37E
110 F10 **Münster** Valais, S Switzerland 46.31N 8.18E
Münsterberg in Schlesien see Ziębice
Münster in Westfalen see Münster
102 E13 **Münsterland** cultural region NW Germany
102 F13 **Münster-Osnabruck** ✕ Nordrhein-Westfalen, NW Germany 52.08N 7.41E
33 R4 **Munuscong Lake** ◎ Michigan, N USA
85 K17 **Munyati** ≈ C Zimbabwe
111 R3 **Münzkirchen** Oberösterreich, N Austria 48.29N 13.37E
94 K11 **Muodoslompolo** Norrbotten, N Sweden 67.57N 23.31E
94 M13 **Muojärvi** ◎ NE Finland
178 J6 **Mường Khến** Hoa Binh, N Vietnam 20.34N 105.18E
Muong Sai see Xai
178 I7 **Muong Xiang Ngeun** var. Xieng Ngeun. Louangphabang, N Laos 19.43N 102.09E
94 K11 **Muonio** Lappi, N Finland 67.58N 23.40E
Muonioälv/Muoniojoki see Muonionjoki
94 K11 **Muonionjoki** var. Muoniojoki, Swe. Muonioälv. ≈ Finland/Sweden
85 N17 **Mupa** ≈ C Mozambique
85 E16 **Mupini** Okavango, NE Namibia 17.55S 19.34E
82 F8 **Muqaddam, Wadi** ≈ N Sudan
144 K9 **Muqāt** Al Mafraq, E Jordan 32.28N 38.04E
147 X7 **Muqaz** N Oman 24.13N 56.48E
83 N17 **Muqdisho** Eng. Mogadishu, It. Mogadiscio. ● (Somalia) Banaadir, S Somalia 2.06N 45.27E
83 N17 **Muqdisho** ✕ Banaadir, E Somalia 1.58N 45.18E
Muqshin see Mughshin
111 T8 **Mur** SCr. Mura. ≈ C Europe
Mura see Mur
111 X9 **Mura** ≈ NE Slovenia
143 T14 **Muradiye** Van, E Turkey 39.00N 43.44E
Muragarazi see Maragarazi
171 L12 **Murakami** Niigata, Honshū, C Japan 38.13N 139.28E
65 G22 **Murallón, Cerro** ▲ S Argentina 49.49S 73.25W
83 E20 **Muramvya** C Burundi 3.18S 29.41E
83 I19 **Murang'a** prev. Fort Hall. Central, SW Kenya 0.43S 37.10E
83 H16 **Murangering** Rift Valley, NW Kenya 3.48N 35.29E
Murapara see Murupara
146 M5 **Murār, Bi'r al** well NW Saudi Arabia 27.20N 40.21E
129 Q13 **Murashi** Kirovskaya Oblast', NW Russian Federation 59.27N 48.02E
105 O12 **Murat** Cantal, C France 45.07N 2.52E
116 N12 **Muratlı** Tekirdağ, NW Turkey 41.12N 27.30E
143 R14 **Murat Nehri** var. Eastern Euphrates; anc. Arsanias. ≈ NE Turkey
109 D20 **Muravera** Sardegna, Italy, C Mediterranean Sea 39.24N 9.34E
171 Ll12 **Murayama** Yamagata, Honshū, C Japan 38.29N 140.21E
124 Oo15 **Muraysah, Ra's al** headland N Libya 31.58N 25.00E
106 I6 **Murça** Vila Real, N Portugal 41.24N 7.28W
82 Q11 **Murcanyo** Bari, NE Somalia 11.39N 50.27E
149 N8 **Mürcheh Khvort** var. Morcheh Khort. Eşfahān, C Iran 33.07N 51.26E
193 H15 **Murchison** Tasman, South Island, NZ 41.48S 172.19E
193 B22 **Murchison Mountains** ▲ South Island, NZ
188 I10 **Murchison River** ≈ Western Australia
107 R13 **Murcia** Murcia, SE Spain 37.58N 1.07W
107 Q13 **Murcia** ◈ autonomous community SE Spain
105 O13 **Mur-de-Barrez** Aveyron, S France 44.48N 2.39E
190 G8 **Murdinga** South Australia 33.46S 135.46E
30 M10 **Murdo** South Dakota, N USA 43.53N 100.42W
13 X6 **Murdochville** Quebec, SE Canada 48.57N 65.30W
111 W9 **Mureck** Steiermark, SE Austria 46.42N 15.46E
116 M13 **Mürefte** Tekirdağ, NW Turkey 40.40N 27.15E
118 I10 **Mureş** ◈ county N Romania
86 J11 **Mureş** var. Maros, Mureşul, Ger. Marosch, Mieresch. ≈ Hungary/Romania see also Maros
Mureşul see Maros/Mureş
104 M16 **Muret** Haute-Garonne, S France 43.28N 1.19E
29 T13 **Murfreesboro** Arkansas, C USA 34.03N 93.41W
23 W8 **Murfreesboro** North Carolina, SE USA 36.26N 77.06W
22 J9 **Murfreesboro** Tennessee, S USA 35.51N 86.23W
152 I14 **Murgab** prev. Murgap see also Morghāb, Daryā-ye. Maryyskiy Velayat, S Turkmenistan 37.19N 61.48E
152 J16 **Murgab** var. Murghab, Pash. Daryā-ye Morghāb, Turkm. Murgap Deryasy. ≈ Afghanistan/Turkmenistan see also Morghāb, Daryā-ye
Murgab see Murghob
Murgap see Murgab
Murgap Deryasy see Morghāb, Daryā-ye/Murgab
116 H9 **Murgash** ▲ W Bulgaria 42.51N 23.58E
Murghab see Morghāb, Daryā-ye/Murgab
153 U13 **Murghob** Rus. Murgab. SE Tajikistan 38.11N 73.59E
153 U13 **Murghob** Rus. Murgab. ≈ SE Tajikistan
189 Z10 **Murgon** Queensland, E Australia 26.07S 152.03E
202 I16 **Muri** Rarotonga, S Cook Islands 21.15S 159.43W
110 F7 **Muri** Aargau, W Switzerland 47.16N 8.21E
110 D8 **Muri** var. Muri bei Bern. Bern, W Switzerland 46.55N 7.30E
106 K3 **Murias de Paredes** Castilla-León, N Spain 42.51N 6.11W
Muri bei Bern see Muri
84 F11 **Muriege** Lunda Sul, NE Angola 9.55S 21.12E
201 P14 **Murilo Atoll** atoll Hall Islands, C Micronesia
Mūrītānīyah see Mauritania
102 N10 **Müritz** var. Müritzee. ◎ NE Germany
Müritzee see Müritz
102 L10 **Müritz-Elde-Kanal** canal N Germany
192 K6 **Muriwai Beach** Auckland, North Island, NZ 36.56S 174.28E
94 J13 **Murjek** Norrbotten, N Sweden 66.27N 20.54E
128 J3 **Murmansk** Murmanskaya Oblast', NW Russian Federation 68.58N 33.07E
128 I4 **Murmanskaya Oblast'** ◈ province NW Russian Federation
207 V14 **Murmansk Rise** undersea feature SW Barents Sea
128 J3 **Murmashi** Murmanskaya Oblast', NW Russian Federation 68.49N 32.42E
130 M5 **Murmino** Ryazanskaya Oblast', W Russian Federation 54.31N 40.01E
103 K24 **Murnau** Bayern, SE Germany 47.41N 11.12E

105 *X16* **Muro, Capo di** *headland* Corse, France, C Mediterranean Sea *41.45N 8.40E*
109 *M18* **Muro Lucano** Basilicata, S Italy *40.48N 15.33E*
131 *N4* **Murom** Vladimirskaya Oblast', W Russian Federation *55.33N 42.03E*
125 *G13* **Muromtsevo** Omskaya Oblast', C Russian Federation *56.18N 75.15E*
172 *Nn6* **Muroran** Hokkaidō, NE Japan *42.19N 140.58E*
106 *G3* **Muros** Galicia, NW Spain *42.46N 9.03W*
106 *F3* **Muros e Noia, Ría de** *estuary* NW Spain
170 *F16* **Muroto** Kōchi, Shikoku, SW Japan *33.18N 134.07E*
170 *F16* **Muroto-zaki** *headland* Shikoku, SW Japan *33.15N 134.09E*
118 *L7* **Murovani Kurylivtsi** Vinnyts'ka Oblast', C Ukraine *48.43N 27.31E*
112 *G11* **Murowana Goślina** Wielkolpolskie, C Poland *52.33N 16.59E*
34 *M14* **Murphy** Idaho, NW USA *43.14N 116.36W*
23 *N10* **Murphy** North Carolina, SE USA *35.05N 84.01W*
37 *P8* **Murphys** California, W USA *38.07N 120.27W*
32 *L17* **Murphysboro** Illinois, N USA *37.45N 89.20W*
31 *V15* **Murray** Iowa, C USA *41.03N 93.56W*
22 *H8* **Murray** Kentucky, S USA *36.36N 88.18W*
190 *J10* **Murray Bridge** South Australia *35.06S 139.15E*
183 *X2* **Murray Fracture Zone** *tectonic feature* NE Pacific Ocean
194 *E13* **Murray, Lake** ◎ SW PNG
23 *P12* **Murray, Lake** ⊠ South Carolina, SE USA
8 *K8* **Murray, Mount** ▲ Yukon Territory, NW Canada *60.49N 128.57W*
194 *H13* **Murray Range** *var.* Leonard Murray Mountains. ▲▲ W PNG
Murray Range *see* Murray Ridge
181 *O3* **Murray Ridge** *var.* Murray Range. *undersea feature* N Arabian Sea
191 *N10* **Murray River** ≈ SE Australia
190 *K10* **Murrayville** Victoria, SE Australia *35.17S 141.12E*
155 *U5* **Murree** Punjab, E Pakistan *33.55N 73.25E*
103 *I21* **Murrhardt** Baden-Württemberg, S Germany *49.00N 9.34E*
191 *O9* **Murrumbidgee River** ≈ New South Wales, SE Australia
85 *P15* **Murrupula** Nampula, NE Mozambique *15.26S 38.46E*
191 *T7* **Murrurundi** New South Wales, SE Australia *31.47S 150.51E*
111 *X9* **Murska Sobota** *Ger.* Olsnitz. NE Slovenia *46.40N 16.09E*
160 *G12* **Murtajāpur** *prev.* Murtazapur. Mahārāshtra, C India *20.43N 77.28E*
79 *S16* **Murtala Muhammed** ✕ (Lagos) Ogun, SW Nigeria *6.31N 3.12E*
Murtazapur *see* Murtajāpur
110 *C8* **Murten** Neuchâtel, W Switzerland *46.55N 7.06E*
Murtensee *see* Morat, Lac de
190 *L11* **Murtoa** Victoria, SE Australia *36.39S 142.27E*
94 *N13* **Murtovaara** Oulu, E Finland *65.40N 29.25E*
Murua Island *see* Woodlark Island
161 *D14* **Murud** Mahārāshtra, W India *18.27N 72.56E*
192 *O9* **Murupara** *var.* Murapara. Bay of Plenty, North Island, NZ *38.27S 176.40E*
203 *X12* **Mururoa** *var.* Moruroa. *atoll* Îles Tuamotu, SE French Polynesia
Murviedro *see* Sagunto
160 *J9* **Murwāra** Madhya Pradesh, N India *23.50N 80.23E*
191 *V4* **Murwillumbah** New South Wales, SE Australia *28.19S 153.24E*
152 *H11* **Murzechirla** *prev.* Mirzachirla. Akhalskiy Velayat, C Turkmenistan *39.33N 60.02E*
Murzuk *see* Murzuq
77 *O11* **Murzuq** *var.* Marzūq, Murzuk. SW Libya *25.55N 13.55E*
Murzuq, Edeyin *see* Murzuq, Idhān
77 *N11* **Murzuq, Ḥamādat** *plateau* W Libya
77 *O11* **Murzuq, Idhān** *var.* Edeyin Murzuq. *desert* SW Libya
111 *W6* **Mürzzuschlag** Steiermark, E Austria *47.34N 15.40E*
143 *Q14* **Muş** *var.* Mush. Muş, E Turkey *38.45N 41.30E*
143 *Q14* **Muş** *var.* Mush. ◈ *province* E Turkey
194 *L16* **Musa** ≈ S PNG
120 *G11* **Mūša** ≈ Latvia/Lithuania
77 *X8* **Mûsa, Gebel** ▲ NE Egypt *28.33N 33.51E*
Musaiyib *see* Al Musayyib
Musa Khel *see* Mūsā Khel Bazār
155 *R9* **Mūsā Khel Bazār** *var.* Musa Khel. Baluchistān, SW Pakistan *30.52N 69.46E*
116 *H10* **Musala** ▲ W Bulgaria *42.12N 23.36E*
173 *F6* **Musala, Pulau** *island* W Indonesia
85 *I15* **Musale** Southern, S Zambia *15.27S 26.50E*
147 *Y9* **Muşalla** NE Oman *22.19N 58.03E*
147 *W6* **Musandam Peninsula** *Ar.* Masandam Peninsula. *peninsula* N Oman
Musay'id *see* Umm Sa'īd
Muscat *see* Masqaţ
Muscat and Oman *see* Oman
31 *Y14* **Muscatine** Iowa, C USA *41.25N 91.03W*
Muscat Sīb Airport *see* Seeb
33 *O15* **Muscatuck River** ≈ Indiana, N USA
194 *G10* **Muschu Island** *island* NW PNG
32 *K8* **Muscoda** Wisconsin, N USA *43.11N 90.27W*
193 *F19* **Musgrave, Mount** ▲ South Island, NZ *43.48S 170.43E*
189 *P9* **Musgrave Ranges** ▲▲ South Australia
Mush *see* Muş
144 *H12* **Mushayyish, Qaşr al** *castle* Ma'ān, C Jordan *30.58N 36.41E*
81 *H20* **Mushie** Bandundu, W Dem. Rep. Congo *3.00S 16.55E*
174 *I11* **Musi, Air** *prev.* Moesi. ≈ Sumatera, W Indonesia
199 *K5* **Musicians Seamounts** *undersea feature* N Pacific Ocean
85 *K19* **Musina** *prev.* Messina. Limpopo, NE South Africa *22.18S 30.02E*
56 *D8* **Musinga, Alto** ▲ NW Colombia *6.49N 76.24W*
31 *T2* **Muskeg Bay** *lake bay* Minnesota, N USA
33 *O8* **Muskegon** Michigan, N USA *43.13N 86.15W*
33 *O8* **Muskegon Heights** Michigan, N USA *43.12N 86.14W*
33 *P8* **Muskegon River** ≈ Michigan, N USA
33 *T14* **Muskingum River** ≈ Ohio, N USA
97 *P16* **Muskö** Stockholm, C Sweden *58.58N 18.10E*
Muskogean *see* Tallahassee
29 *Q10* **Muskogee** Oklahoma, C USA *35.45N 95.22W*
12 *H13* **Muskoka, Lake** ◎ Ontario, S Canada
82 *H8* **Musmar** Red Sea, NE Sudan *18.13N 35.40E*
85 *K14* **Musofu** Central, C Zambia *13.31S 29.03E*
83 *G19* **Musoma** Mara, N Tanzania *1.31S 33.49E*
84 *L13* **Musoro** Central, C Zambia *13.21S 31.04E*
194 *M8* **Mussau Island** *island* NE PNG
100 *P7* **Musselkanaal** Groningen, NE Netherlands *52.55N 7.01E*
35 *V9* **Musselshell River** ≈ Montana, NW USA
84 *C12* **Mussende** Cuanza Sul, NW Angola *10.33S 16.01E*
104 *L12* **Mussidan** Dordogne, SW France *45.03N 0.22E*
101 *L25* **Musson** Luxembourg, SE Belgium *49.33N 5.42E*
158 *J9* **Mussoorie** Uttar Pradesh, N India *30.25N 78.04E*
Musta *see* Mosta
158 *M13* **Mustafābād** Uttar Pradesh, N India *25.54N 81.16E*
142 *D12* **Mustafakemalpaşa** Bursa, NW Turkey *40.03N 28.25E*
Mustafa-Pasha *see* Svilengrad
83 *M15* **Mustahīl** Somali, E Ethiopia *5.18N 44.34E*
26 *M7* **Mustang Draw** *valley* Texas, SW USA
27 *T14* **Mustang Island** *island* Texas, SW USA
Mustasaari *see* Korsholm
Mustér *see* Disentis
65 *I19* **Musters, Lago** ◎ S Argentina
47 *Y14* **Mustique** *island* C Saint Vincent and the Grenadines
120 *I6* **Mustla** Viljandimaa, S Estonia *58.12N 25.51E*
120 *J4* **Mustvee** *Ger.* Tschorna. Jõgevamaa, E Estonia *58.51N 26.57E*
44 *L9* **Musún, Cerro** ▲ NE Nicaragua *13.01N 85.02W*
191 *T7* **Muswellbrook** New South Wales, SE Australia *32.16S 150.55E*
113 *M18* **Muszyna** Małopolskie, SE Poland *49.21N 20.54E*
142 *I17* **Mut** İçel, S Turkey *36.37N 33.27E*
77 *V10* **Mût** *var.* Mut. C Egypt *25.34N 28.58E*
111 *V9* **Muta** N Slovenia *46.37N 15.09E*
202 *B15* **Mutalau** N Niue *18.55S 169.49E*
Mu-tan-chiang *see* Mudanjiang
84 *I13* **Mutanda** North Western, NW Zambia *12.22S 26.15E*
61 *O17* **Mutá, Ponta do** *headland* E Brazil *13.54S 38.54W*
85 *L17* **Mutare** *var.* Mutari; *prev.* Umtali. Manicaland, E Zimbabwe *18.54S 32.36E*
Mutari *see* Mutare
56 *D8* **Mutatá** Antioquia, NW Colombia *7.16N 76.31W*
Mutina *see* Modena
176 *Z15* **Muting** Papua, E Indonesia *7.10S 140.41E*
85 *L16* **Mutoko** *prev.* Mtoko. Mashonaland East, NE Zimbabwe *17.24S 32.13E*
83 *J20* **Mutomo** Eastern, S Kenya *1.49S 38.13E*
126 *J12* **Mutoray** Evenkiyskiy Avtonomnyy Okrug, C Russian Federation *61.30N 101.00E*
Mutrah *see* Maţraḩ
81 *M24* **Mutshatsha** Katanga, S Dem. Rep. Congo *10.40S 24.25E*
172 *Nn8* **Mutsu** *var.* Mutu. Aomori, Honshū, N Japan *41.18N 141.11E*
172 *N8* **Mutsu-wan** *bay* N Japan
110 *E6* **Muttenz** Basel-Land, NW Switzerland *47.31N 7.39E*
193 *A26* **Muttonbird Islands** *island group* SW NZ
Mutu *see* Mutsu
85 *O15* **Mutuáli** Nampula, N Mozambique *14.51S 37.01E*
84 *D13* **Mutumbo** Bié, C Angola *13.10S 17.22E*
201 *Y14* **Mutunte, Mount** *var.* Mount Buache. ▲ Kosrae, E Micronesia *5.21N 163.00E*
161 *K24* **Mutur** Eastern Province, E Sri Lanka *8.27N 81.15E*
94 *L13* **Muurola** Lappi, NW Finland *66.21N 25.19E*
168 *M14* **Mu Us Shamo** *var.* Ordos Desert. *desert* N China
84 *B11* **Muxima** Bengo, NW Angola *9.27S 13.58E*
128 *I8* **Muyezerskiy** Respublika Kareliya, NW Russian Federation *63.54N 32.00E*
83 *E20* **Muyinga** NE Burundi *2.54S 30.19E*
44 *K9* **Muy Muy** Matagalpa, C Nicaragua *12.43N 85.37W*
Muynak *see* Mo'ynoq
81 *N22* **Muyumba** Katanga, SE Dem. Rep. Congo *7.13S 27.02E*
155 *V5* **Muzaffarābād** Jammu and Kashmir, NE Pakistan *34.24N 73.30E*
155 *S10* **Muzaffargarh** Punjab, E Pakistan *30.04N 71.10E*
158 *J9* **Muzaffarnagar** Uttar Pradesh, N India *29.28N 77.42E*
159 *P13* **Muzaffarpur** Bihār, N India *26.07N 85.22E*
164 *H6* **Muzat He** ≈ W China
85 *L15* **Muze** Tete, NW Mozambique *15.05S 31.16E*
125 *Ff8* **Muzhi** Yamalo-Nenetskiy Avtonomnyy Okrug, N Russian Federation *65.25N 64.28E*
104 *H7* **Muzillac** Morbihan, NW France *47.34N 2.30W*
Muzkol, Khrebet *see* Muzqūl, Qatorkūhi
114 *L9* **Mužlja** *Hung.* Felsőmuzslya; *prev.* Gornja Mužlja. Serbia, N Serbia and Montenegro (Yugoslavia) *45.21N 20.25E*
56 *F9* **Muzo** Boyacá, C Colombia *5.34N 74.07W*
85 *J15* **Muzoka** Southern, S Zambia *16.39S 27.21E*
41 *Y15* **Muzon, Cape** *headland* Dall Island, Alaska, USA *54.39N 132.41W*
42 *M6* **Múzquiz** Coahuila de Zaragoza, NE Mexico *27.52N 101.31W*
153 *U13* **Muzqŭl, Qatorkŭhi** *Rus.* Khrebet Muzkol. ▲▲ SE Tajikistan
164 *G10* **Muztag** ▲ NW China *36.02N 80.13E*
164 *D8* **Muztagata** ▲ NW China *38.16N 75.03E*
164 *K10* **Muztag Feng** *var.* Ulugh Muztag. ▲ W China *36.26N 87.15E*
85 *K17* **Mvuma** *prev.* Umvuma. Midlands, C Zimbabwe *19.16S 30.31E*
84 *L13* **Mwanya** Eastern, E Zambia *12.40S 32.15E*
83 *G20* **Mwanza** Mwanza, NW Tanzania *2.31S 32.55E*
81 *N23* **Mwanza** Katanga, SE Dem. Rep. Congo *7.49S 26.49E*
83 *F20* **Mwanza** ◈ *region* N Tanzania
84 *M13* **Mwase Lundazi** Eastern, E Zambia *12.26S 33.20E*
99 *B17* **Mweelrea** *Ir.* Caoc Maol Réidh. ▲ W Ireland *53.37N 9.47W*
81 *K21* **Mweka** Kasai Occidental, C Dem. Rep. Congo *4.51S 21.37E*
84 *K12* **Mwenda** Luapula, N Zambia *10.25S 29.10E*
81 *L22* **Mwene-Ditu** Kasai Oriental, S Dem. Rep. Congo *7.05S 23.33E*
85 *L18* **Mwenezi** ≈ S Zimbabwe
81 *O20* **Mwenga** Sud Kivu, E Dem. Rep. Congo *3.00S 28.28E*
84 *K11* **Mweru, Lake** *var.* Lac Moero. ◎ Dem. Rep. Congo/Zambia
84 *H13* **Mwinilunga** North Western, NW Zambia *11.43S 24.24E*
201 *V16* **Mwokil Atoll** *var.* Mokil Atoll. *atoll* Caroline Islands, E Micronesia
Myadel' *see* Myadzyel
120 *J13* **Myadzyel** *Pol.* Miadzioł Nowy, *Rus.* Myadel'. Minskaya Voblasts', N Belarus *54.51N 26.51E*
158 *C12* **Myājlār** *var.* Miajlar. Rājasthān, NW India *26.16N 70.21E*
127 *O9* **Myakit** Magadanskaya Oblast', E Russian Federation *61.23N 151.58E*
25 *W13* **Myakka River** ≈ Florida, SE USA
128 *L14* **Myaksa** Vologodskaya Oblast', NW Russian Federation *58.54N 38.15E*
191 *U8* **Myall Lake** ◎ New South Wales, SE Australia
177 *Ff7* **Myanaung** Irrawaddy, SW Myanmar *18.16N 95.19E*
178 *Gg4* **Myanmar** *off.* Union of Myanmar, *Eng.* Burma. ◆ *military dictatorship* SE Asia
177 *F9* **Myaungmya** Irrawaddy, SW Myanmar *16.33N 94.55E*
120 *N11* **Myazha** *Rus.* Mezha. Vitsyebskaya Voblasts', NE Belarus *55.40N 30.25E*
121 *O18* **Myerkulavichy** *Rus.* Merkulovichi. Homyel'skaya Voblasts', SE Belarus *52.57N 30.33E*
121 *N14* **Myezhava** *Rus.* Mezhëvo. Vitsyebskaya Voblasts', NE Belarus *54.39N 30.18E*
177 *Ff5* **Myingyan** Mandalay, C Myanmar *21.25N 95.19E*
177 *G5* **Myinmu** Sagaing, C Myanmar *21.58N 95.34E*
178 *Gg2* **Myitkyina** Kachin State, N Myanmar *25.24N 97.25E*
177 *G5* **Myittha** Mandalay, C Myanmar *21.21N 96.06E*
113 *H19* **Myjava** *Hung.* Miava. Trenčiansky Kraj, W Slovakia *48.48N 17.31E*
Myjeldino *see* Myyëldino
119 *U9* **Mykhaylivka** *Rus.* Mikhaylovka. Zaporiz'ka Oblast', SE Ukraine *47.16N 35.14E*
97 *A18* **Mykines** *Dan.* Myggenaes *Island* Faeroe Islands *62.07N 7.38W*
118 *I5* **Mykolayiv** L'vivs'ka Oblast', W Ukraine *49.34N 23.58E*
119 *Q10* **Mykolayiv** *Rus.* Nikolayev. Mykolayivs'ka Oblast', S Ukraine *46.57N 31.58E*
119 *Q10* **Mykolayiv** ✕ Mykolayivs'ka Oblast', S Ukraine *47.02N 31.54E*
Mykolayiv *see* Mykolayivs'ka Oblast'
119 *P9* **Mykolayivka** Odes'ka Oblast', SW Ukraine *47.34N 30.48E*
119 *S13* **Mykolayivka** Respublika Krym, S Ukraine *44.58N 33.37E*
119 *P9* **Mykolayivs'ka Oblast'** *var.* Mykolayiv, *Rus.* Nikolayevskaya Oblast'. ◈ *province* S Ukraine
117 *J20* **Mýkonos** Mýkonos, Kykládes, Greece, Aegean Sea *37.27N 25.20E*
117 *K20* **Mýkonos** *var.* Míkonos. *island* Kykládes, Greece, Aegean Sea
129 *R7* **Myla** Respublika Komi, NW Russian Federation *65.24N 50.51E*
Mylae *see* Milazzo
95 *M19* **Myllykoski** Etelä-Suomi, S Finland *60.45N 26.52E*
Mymensing *see* Mymensingh
159 *U14* **Mymensingh** *var.* Maimansingh, Mymensing; *prev.* Nasirābād. Dhaka, N Bangladesh *24.45N 90.22E*
95 *K19* **Mynämäki** Länsi-Suomi, W Finland *60.41N 22.00E*
151 *S14* **Mynaral** *Kaz.* Myngaral. Zhambyl, S Kazakhstan *45.25N 73.37E*
Mynbulak *see* Mingbuloq
Mynbulak, Vpadina *see* Mingbuloq Botig'I
Myngaral *see* Mynaral
177 *F5* **Myohaung** Arakan State, W Myanmar *20.34N 93.12E*
169 *W13* **Myohyang-sanmaek** ▲▲ C North Korea
171 *Jj13* **Myōkō-san** ▲ Honshū, S Japan *36.54N 138.05E*
85 *J15* **Myooye** Central, C Zambia *15.10S 27.24E*
120 *K12* **Myory** *prev.* Miyory. Vitsyebskaya Voblasts', N Belarus *55.39N 27.39E*
94 *J4* **Mýrdalsjökull** *glacier* S Iceland
94 *G10* **Myre** Nordland, C Norway *68.54N 15.04E*
119 *S5* **Myrhorod** *Rus.* Mirgorod. Poltavs'ka Oblast', NE Ukraine *49.57N 33.36E*
117 *J15* **Mýrina** *var.* Mírina. Límnos, SE Greece *39.52N 25.04E*
119 *P5* **Myronivka** *Rus.* Mironovka. Kyyivs'ka Oblast', N Ukraine *49.40N 30.58E*
23 *U13* **Myrtle Beach** South Carolina, SE USA *33.41N 78.53W*
34 *F14* **Myrtle Creek** Oregon, NW USA *43.01N 123.19W*
191 *P11* **Myrtleford** Victoria, SE Australia *36.34S 146.45E*
34 *E14* **Myrtle Point** Oregon, NW USA *43.04N 124.08W*
117 *K25* **Mýrtos** Kríti, Greece, E Mediterranean Sea *35.00N 25.34E*
Myrtoum Mare *see* Mirtóo Pélagos
95 *G17* **Myrviken** Jämtland, C Sweden *62.59N 14.19E*
97 *I15* **Mysen** Østfold, S Norway *59.33N 11.19E*
128 *L15* **Myshkin** Yaroslavskaya Oblast', NW Russian Federation *57.47N 38.28E*
113 *K17* **Myślenice** Małopolskie, S Poland *49.49N 19.55E*
112 *D10* **Myślibórz** Zachodniopomorskie, NW Poland *52.55N 14.51E*
161 *G20* **Mysore** *var.* Maisur. Karnātaka, W India *12.18N 76.37E*
Mysore *see* Karnātaka
117 *F21* **Mystrás** *var.* Mistras. Pelopónnisos, S Greece *37.03N 22.22E*
129 *T12* **Mysy** Komi-Permyatskiy Avtonomnyy Okrug, NW Russian Federation *60.40N 53.59E*
113 *K15* **Myszków** Śląskie, S Poland *50.35N 19.16E*
178 *Jj14* **My Tho** *var.* Mi Tho. Tiên Giang, S Vietnam *10.21N 106.21E*
Mytilene *see* Mytilíni
117 *L17* **Mytilíni** *var.* Mitilíni; *anc.* Mytilene. Lésvos, E Greece *39.05N 26.33E*
130 *K3* **Mytishchi** Moskovskaya Oblast', W Russian Federation *56.00N 37.51E*
39 *N3* **Myton** Utah, W USA *40.11N 110.03W*
94 *K2* **Mývatn** ◎ C Iceland
129 *T11* **Myyëldino** *var.* Myjeldino. Respublika Komi, NW Russian Federation *61.46N 54.48E*
84 *M13* **Mzimba** Northern, NW Malawi *11.56S 33.36E*
84 *M12* **Mzuzu** Northern, N Malawi *11.23S 34.03E*
178 *Jj6* **Mương Khên** Hoa Binh, N Vietnam *20.34N 105.18E*

N

103 *M19* **Naab** ≈ SE Germany
100 *G12* **Naaldwijk** Zuid-Holland, W Netherlands *52.00N 4.13E*
40 *G12* **Naalehu** *var.* Nā'ālehu. Hawaii, USA, C Pacific Ocean *19.04N 155.36W*
95 *K19* **Naantali** *Swe.* Nådendal. Länsi-Suomi, W Finland *60.25N 22.10E*
100 *J10* **Naarden** Noord-Holland, C Netherlands *52.18N 5.10E*
111 *U4* **Naarn** ≈ N Austria
99 *F18* **Naas** *Ir.* An Nás, Nás na Ríogh. C Ireland *53.13N 6.39W*
94 *M9* **Näätämöjoki** *Lapp.* Njávdám. ≈ NE Finland
85 *E23* **Nababeep** *var.* Nababiep. Northern Cape, W South Africa *29.36S 17.46E*
Nababiep *see* Nababeep
Nabadwip *see* Navadwīp
171 *H16* **Nabari** Mie, Honshū, SW Japan *34.37N 136.06E*
Nabatié *see* Nabatîyé
144 *G8* **Nabatîyé** *var.* An Nabatīyah at Taḩtā, Nabatié, Nabatiyet et Tahta. SW Lebanon *33.18N 35.36E*
Nabatiyet et Tahta *see* Nabatîyé
197 *I13* **Nabavatu** Vanua Levu, N Fiji *16.35S 178.55E*
202 *I2* **Nabeina** *island* Tungaru, W Kiribati
131 *T4* **Naberezhnyye Chelny** *prev.* Brezhnev. Respublika Tatarstan, W Russian Federation *55.43N 52.21E*
41 *T10* **Nabesna** Alaska, USA *62.22N 143.00W*
41 *T10* **Nabesna River** ≈ Alaska, USA
77 *N5* **Nabeul** *var.* Nābul. NE Tunisia *36.32N 10.45E*
158 *I9* **Nābha** Punjab, NW India *30.22N 76.12E*
176 *Ww11* **Nabire** Papua, E Indonesia *3.22S 135.31E*
147 *O15* **Nabī Shu'ayb, Jabal an** ▲ W Yemen *15.24N 44.04E*
197 *I13* **Nabiti** Vanua Levu, N Fiji *16.37S 178.54E*
144 *F10* **Nablus** *var.* Nābulus, *Heb.* Shekhem; *anc.* Neapolis, *Bibl.* Shechem. N West Bank *32.14N 35.16E*
197 *I13* **Nabouwalu** Vanua Levu, N Fiji *17.00S 178.43E*
Nābul *see* Nabeul
Nābulus *see* Nablus
197 *J13* **Nabuna** Vanua Levu, N Fiji *16.13S 179.46E*
179 *Rr15* **Nabunturan** Mindanao, S Philippines *7.34N 125.54E*
85 *Q14* **Nacala** Nampula, NE Mozambique *14.30S 40.37E*
44 *H8* **Nacaome** Valle, S Honduras *13.30N 87.31W*
Na Cealla Beaga *see* Killybegs
Na-ch'ii *see* Nagqu
171 *Gg17* **Nachikatsuura** *var.* Nachi-Katsuura. Wakayama, Honshū, SE Japan *33.37N 135.54E*
83 *J24* **Nachingwea** Lindi, SE Tanzania *10.21S 38.46E*
113 *F16* **Náchod** Hradecký Kraj, N Czech Republic *50.25N 16.09E*
Na Clocha Liatha *see* Greystones
42 *G3* **Naco** Sonora, NW Mexico *31.16N 109.56W*
27 *X8* **Nacogdoches** Texas, SW USA *31.36N 94.40W*
42 *G4* **Nacozari de García** Sonora, NW Mexico *30.27N 109.43W*
197 *H13* **Nacula** *prev.* Nathula. *island* Yasawa Group, NW Fiji
Nada *see* Danzhou
79 *O14* **Nadawli** NW Ghana *10.30N 2.40W*
106 *I3* **Nadela** Galicia, NW Spain *42.58N 7.33W*
Nådendal *see* Naantali
150 *M7* **Nadezhdinka** *prev.* Nadezhdinskiy. Kostanay, N Kazakhstan *53.46N 63.43E*
Nadezhdinskiy *see* Nadezhdinka
Nadgan *see* Nadqān, Qalamat
197 *H14* **Nadi** *prev.* Nandi. Viti Levu, W Fiji *17.48S 177.25E*
197 *H14* **Nadi** *prev.* Nandi. ✕ Viti Levu, W Fiji *17.46S 177.28E*
160 *D10* **Nadiād** Gujarāt, W India *22.42N 72.54E*
Nadikdik *see* Knox Atoll
118 *E11* **Nădlac** *Ger.* Nadlak, *Hung.* Nagylak. Arad, W Romania *46.10N 20.47E*
Nadlak *see* Nădlac
76 *H6* **Nador** *prev.* Villa Nador. NE Morocco *35.15N 2.56W*
147 *S9* **Nadqān, Qalamat** *var.* Nadgan. *well* E Saudi Arabia *23.10N 50.08E*
113 *N22* **Nádudvar** Hajdú-Bihar, E Hungary *47.26N 21.09E*
123 *J16* **Nadur** Gozo, N Malta *36.03N 14.18E*
197 *J13* **Naduri** *prev.* Nanduri. Vanua Levu, N Fiji *16.27S 179.10E*
118 *I7* **Nadvirna** *Pol.* Nadwórna, *Rus.* Nadvornaya. Ivano-Frankivs'ka Oblast', W Ukraine *48.27N 24.30E*
128 *J8* **Nadvoitsy** Respublika Kareliya, NW Russian Federation *63.52N 34.17E*
Nadvornaya/Nadwórna *see* Nadvirna
126 *Gg9* **Nadym** Yamalo-Nenetskiy Avtonomnyy Okrug, N Russian Federation *65.25N 72.40E*
126 *Gg9* **Nadym** ≈ C Russian Federation
194 *J13* **Nadzab** Morobe, C PNG *6.36S 146.45E*
79 *X13* **Nafada** Gombe, E Nigeria *11.02N 11.18E*
110 *H8* **Näfels** Glarus, NE Switzerland *47.06N 9.04E*
117 *E18* **Náfpaktos** *var.* Návpaktos. Dytikí Ellás, C Greece *38.22N 21.49E*
117 *F20* **Náfplio** *prev.* Návplion. Pelopónnisos, S Greece *37.33N 22.50E*
145 *U6* **Naft Khāneh** E Iraq *34.01N 45.26E*
155 *N13* **Nāg** Baluchistān, SW Pakistan *27.43N 65.31E*
179 *Q11* **Naga** *off.* Naga City; *prev.* Nueva Caceres. Luzon, N Philippines *13.36N 123.10E*
Nagaarzê *see* Nagarzê
10 *F11* **Nagagami** ≈ Ontario, S Canada
170 *E14* **Nagahama** Ehime, Shikoku, SW Japan *33.36N 132.29E*
171 *Hh14* **Nagahama** Shiga, Honshū, SW Japan *35.22N 136.16E*
159 *X12* **Nāga Hills** ▲▲ NE India
171 *Ll13* **Nagai** Yamagata, Honshū, C Japan *38.07N 140.02E*
Na Gaibhlte *see* Galty Mountains
41 *N16* **Nagai Island** *island* Shumagin Islands, Alaska, USA
159 *X12* **Nāgāland** ◈ *state* NE India
171 *Jj13* **Nagano** Nagano, Honshū, S Japan *36.39N 138.10E*
171 *J14* **Nagano** *off.* Nagano-ken. ◈ *prefecture* Honshū, S Japan
171 *K13* **Nagaoka** Niigata, Honshū, C Japan *37.26N 138.48E*
159 *W12* **Nagaon** *prev.* Nowgong. Assam, NE India *26.21N 92.41E*
161 *J21* **Nāgappattinam** *var.* Negapatam, Negapattinam. Tamil Nādu, SE India *10.45N 79.49E*
Nagara Nayok *see* Nakhon Nayok
Nagara Panom *see* Nakhon Phanom
Nagara Pathom *see* Nakhon Pathom
Nagara Sridharmaraj *see* Nakhon Si Thammarat
Nagara Svarga *see* Nakhon Sawan
161 *H16* **Nāgārjuna Sāgar** ⊠ E India
44 *I10* **Nagarote** León, SW Nicaragua *12.16N 86.33W*
164 *M16* **Nagarzê** *var.* Nagaarzê. Xizang Zizhiqu, W China *28.57N 90.25E*
170 *Bb13* **Nagasaki** Nagasaki, Kyūshū, SW Japan *32.45N 129.52E*
170 *Bb12* **Nagasaki** *off.* Nagasaki-ken. ◈ *prefecture* Kyūshū, SW Japan
170 *Bb14* **Naga-shima** *island* SW Japan
170 *Dd13* **Naga-shima** *island* SW Japan
Nagashima *see* Kii-Nagashima
170 *Dd12* **Nagato** Yamaguchi, Honshū, SW Japan *34.22N 131.10E*
158 *F11* **Nāgaur** Rājasthān, NW India *27.12N 73.43E*
160 *F10* **Nāgda** Madhya Pradesh, C India *23.28N 75.27E*
100 *L8* **Nagele** Flevoland, N Netherlands *52.39N 5.43E*
161 *H24* **Nāgercoil** Tamil Nādu, SE India *8.10N 77.30E*
159 *X12* **Nāginimāra** Nāgāland, NE India *26.43N 94.51E*
Na Gleannta *see* Glenties
172 *P14* **Nago** Okinawa, Okinawa, SW Japan *26.36N 127.58E*
160 *K9* **Nāgod** Madhya Pradesh, C India *24.36N 80.35E*
161 *J26* **Nagoda** Southern Province, S Sri Lanka *6.13N 80.13E*
103 *G22* **Nagold** Baden-Württemberg, SW Germany *48.33N 8.43E*
Nagorno-Karabakhskaya Avtonomnaya Oblast *see* Nagornyy Karabakh
126 *Ll13* **Nagornyy** Respublika Sakha (Yakutiya), NE Russian Federation *55.53N 124.58E*
143 *V12* **Nagornyy Karabakh** *var.* Nagorno-Karabakhskaya Avtonomnaya Oblast , *Arm.* Lerrnayin Gharabakh, *Az.* Dağliq Qarabağ. *former autonomous region* SW Azerbaijan
129 *R13* **Nagorsk** Kirovskaya Oblast', NW Russian Federation *59.18N 50.49E*
171 *Hh15* **Nagoya** Aichi, Honshū, SW Japan *35.10N 136.52E*
160 *I12* **Nāgpur** Mahārāshtra, C India *21.09N 79.06E*
162 *K10* **Nagqu** *Chin.* Na-ch'ii; *prev.* Hei-ho. Xizang Zizhiqu, W China *31.30N 91.57E*
158 *J8* **Nāg Tibba Range** ▲▲ N India
47 *O8* **Nagua** NE Dominican Republic *19.18N 69.48W*
113 *H25* **Nagyatád** Somogy, SW Hungary *46.14N 17.19E*
Nagybánya *see* Baia Mare
Nagybecskerek *see* Zrenjanin
Nagydisznód *see* Cisnădie
Nagyenyed *see* Aiud
113 *N21* **Nagykálló** Szabolcs-Szatmár-Bereg, E Hungary *47.49N 21.47E*
113 *G25* **Nagykanizsa** *Ger.* Grosskanizsa. Zala, SW Hungary *46.27N 17.00E*
Nagykároly *see* Carei
113 *K22* **Nagykáta** Pest, C Hungary *47.24N 19.43E*
Nagykikinda *see* Kikinda
113 *K23* **Nagykőrös** Pest, C Hungary *47.04N 19.45E*
Nagy-Küküllő *see* Târnava Mare
Nagylak *see* Nădlac
Nagymihály *see* Michalovce
Nagyrőce *see* Revúca
Nagysomkút *see* Şomcuta Mare
Nagysurány *see* Šurany
Nagyszalonta *see* Salonta
Nagyszeben *see* Sibiu
Nagyszentmiklós *see* Sânnicolau Mare
Nagyszöllös *see* Vynohradiv
Nagyszombat *see* Trnava
Nagytapolcsány *see* Topoľčany
Nagyvárad *see* Oradea
172 *Oo15* **Naha** Okinawa, Okinawa, SW Japan *26.10N 127.40E*
158 *J8* **Nāhan** Himāchal Pradesh, NW India *30.33N 77.18E*
Nahang, Rūd-e *see* Nihing
Nahariya *see* Nahariyya
144 *F8* **Nahariyya** *var.* Nahariya. Northern, N Israel *33.01N 35.04E*
148 *L6* **Nahāvand** *var.* Nehavend. Hamadān, W Iran *34.13N 48.21E*
103 *F19* **Nahe** ≈ SW Germany
Na h-Iarmhidhe *see* Westmeath
201 *O13* **Nahnalaud** ▲ Pohnpei, E Micronesia
Nahoi, Cape *see* Cumberland, Cape
65 *H16* **Nahuel Huapi, Lago** ◎ W Argentina
25 *W7* **Nahunta** Georgia, SE USA *31.11N 81.58W*
42 *J6* **Naica** Chihuahua, N Mexico *27.53N 105.30W*
9 *U15* **Naicam** Saskatchewan, S Canada *52.26N 104.30W*
169 *T11* **Naiman Qi** Nei Mongol Zizhiqu, N China *42.51N 120.41E*
164 *M4* **Naimin Bulak** *spring* NW China *44.57N 90.29E*
11 *P6* **Nain** Newfoundland and Labrador, NE Canada *56.33N 61.45W*
149 *P8* **Nā'īn** Eşfahān, C Iran *32.52N 53.04E*
158 *K10* **Naini Tāl** Uttar Pradesh, N India *29.22N 79.25E*
160 *J11* **Nainpur** Madhya Pradesh, C India *22.25N 80.10E*
197 *J14* **Nairai** *island* C Fiji
98 *J8* **Nairn** N Scotland, UK *57.36N 3.51W*
98 *I8* **Nairn** *cultural region* NE Scotland, UK
83 *I19* **Nairobi** ● (Kenya) Nairobi Area, S Kenya *1.16S 36.49E*
83 *I19* **Nairobi** ✕ Nairobi Area, S Kenya *1.21S 37.01E*
84 *P13* **Nairoto** Cabo Delgado, NE Mozambique *12.22S 39.05E*
120 *G3* **Naissaar** *island* N Estonia
Naissus *see* Niš
197 *K13* **Naitaba** *var.* Naitauba; *prev.* Naitamba. *island* Lau Group, E Fiji
Naitamba/Naitauba *see* Naitaba
83 *I19* **Naivasha** Rift Valley, SW Kenya *0.43S 36.25E*
83 *H19* **Naivasha, Lake** ◎ SW Kenya
Najaf *see* An Najaf
149 *N8* **Najafābād** *var.* Nejafabad. Eşfahān, C Iran *32.37N 51.22E*
147 *N7* **Najd** *var.* Nejd. *cultural region* C Saudi Arabia
107 *O4* **Nájera** La Rioja, N Spain *42.25N 2.45W*
107 *P4* **Najerilla** ≈ N Spain
158 *J9* **Najībābād** Uttar Pradesh, N India *29.37N 78.19E*
Najima *see* Fukuoka
169 *Y11* **Najin** NE North Korea *42.13N 130.15E*
145 *T9* **Najm al Ḩassūn** C Iraq *32.24N 44.13E*
147 *O13* **Najrān** *var.* Abā as Su'ūd. Najrān, S Saudi Arabia *17.31N 44.08E*
147 *P12* **Najrān** *off.* Minţaqat al Najrān. ◈ *province* S Saudi Arabia
170 *Bb12* **Nakadōri-jima** *island* Gotō-rettō, SW Japan
172 *Pp3* **Nakagawa** Hokkaidō, NE Japan *44.49N 142.04E*
171 *Kk15* **Naka-gawa** ≈ Honshū, S Japan
40 *F9* **Nakalele Pont** *headland* Maui, Hawaii, USA, C Pacific Ocean *21.01N 156.35W*
170 *D12* **Nakama** Fukuoka, Kyūshū, SW Japan *33.49N 130.42E*
Nakambé *see* White Volta
Nakamti *see* Nek'emtē
170 *E15* **Nakamura** Kōchi, Shikoku, SW Japan *33.00N 132.54E*
195 *O12* **Nakanai Mountains** ▲▲ New Britain, E PNG
171 *Jj14* **Nakano** Nagano, Honshū, S Japan *36.43N 138.22E*
170 *Ff11* **Nakano-shima** *island* Oki-shotō, SW Japan
170 *Ff12* **Nakano-umi** *var.* Naka-umi. ◎ Honshū, SW Japan
171 *Mm8* **Nakasato** Aomori, Honshū, C Japan *40.58N 140.26E*
172 *P7* **Nakasatsunai** Hokkaidō, NE Japan *42.42N 143.09E*
172 *Qq7* **Nakashibetsu** Hokkaidō, NE Japan *43.31N 144.58E*
83 *F18* **Nakasongola** C Uganda *1.19N 32.28E*
172 *Pp3* **Nakatonbetsu** Hokkaidō, NE Japan *44.58N 142.18E*
170 *D13* **Nakatsu** *var.* Nakatu. Ōita, Kyūshū, SW Japan *33.34N 131.12E*
171 *I15* **Nakatsugawa** *var.* Nakatugawa. Gifu, Honshū, SW Japan *35.30N 137.29E*
Nakatu *see* Nakatsu
Nakatugawa *see* Nakatsugawa
Naka-umi *see* Nakano-umi
172 *O5* **Nakayama-tōge** *pass* Hokkaidō, NE Japan *42.51N 141.05E*
Nakdong *see* Naktong-gang
Nakel *see* Nakło nad Notecią
82 *J8* **Nakfa** N Eritrea *16.38N 38.26E*
Nakhichevan' *see* Naxçıvan
127 *Nn18* **Nakhodka** Primorskiy Kray, SE Russian Federation *42.46N 132.47E*
126 *H8* **Nakhodka** Yamalo-Nenetskiy Avtonomnyy Okrug, N Russian Federation *67.48N 77.48E*
Nakhon Navok *see* Nakhon Nayok
178 *Hh11* **Nakhon Nayok** *var.* Nagara Nayok, Nakhon Navok. Nakhon Nayok, C Thailand *14.12N 101.08E*
178 *H11* **Nakhon Pathom** *var.* Nagara Pathom, Nakorn Pathom. Nakhon Pathom, W Thailand *13.49N 100.06E*
178 *J9* **Nakhon Phanom** *var.* Nagara Panom. Nakhon Phanom, E Thailand *17.22N 104.46E*
178 *Hh10* **Nakhon Ratchasima** *var.* Khorat, Korat. Nakhon Ratchasima, E Thailand *15.00N 102.06E*
178 *H10* **Nakhon Sawan** *var.* Muang Nakhon Sawan, Nagara Svarga. Nakhon Sawan, W Thailand *15.42N 100.06E*
178 *H15* **Nakhon Si Thammarat** *var.* Nagara Sridharmaraj, Nakhon Sithamnaraj. Nakhon Si Thammarat, SW Thailand *8.24N 99.58E*
Nakhon Sithamnaraj *see* Nakhon Si Thammarat
145 *Y11* **Nakhrash** SE Iraq *31.13N 47.24E*
8 *I9* **Nakina** British Columbia, W Canada *59.12N 132.48W*
112 *H9* **Nakło nad Notecią** *Ger.* Nakel. Kujawsko-pomorskie, C Poland *53.07N 17.34E*
41 *P13* **Naknek** Alaska, USA *58.45N 157.01W*
158 *H8* **Nakodar** Punjab, NW India *31.06N 75.31E*
84 *M11* **Nakonde** Northern, NE Zambia *9.22S 32.45E*
Nakorn Pathom *see* Nakhon Pathom
97 *H24* **Nakskov** Storstrøm, SE Denmark *54.50N 11.05E*
169 *Y15* **Naktong-gang** *var.* Nakdong, *Jap.* Rakutō-kō. ≈ C South Korea
83 *H18* **Nakuru** Rift Valley, SW Kenya *0.16S 36.04E*
83 *H19* **Nakuru, Lake** ◎ Rift Valley, C Kenya
9 *O17* **Nakusp** British Columbia, SW Canada *50.13N 117.48W*
155 *N15* **Nāl** ≈ W Pakistan
168 *M7* **Nalayh** Töv, C Mongolia *47.48N 107.17E*
159 *V12* **Nalbāri** Assam, NE India *26.36N 91.49E*
65 *G19* **Nalcayec, Isla** *island* Archipiélago de los Chonos, S Chile
131 *N15* **Nal'chik** Kabardino-Balkarskaya Respublika, SW Russian Federation *43.29N 43.39E*
161 *I16* **Nalgonda** Andhra Pradesh, C India *17.04N 79.15E*
159 *S14* **Nalhāti** West Bengal, NE India *24.19N 87.52E*
159 *U14* **Nalitabari** Dhaka, N Bangladesh *25.06N 90.10E*
161 *I17* **Nallamala Hills** ▲▲ E India
142 *G12* **Nallıhan** Ankara, NW Turkey *40.12N 31.22E*
106 *K2* **Nalón** ≈ NW Spain
178 *Gg3* **Nalong** Kachin State, N Myanmar *24.42N 97.27E*
77 *N8* **Nālūt** NW Libya *31.52N 10.58E*
176 *Uu12* **Nama** Pulau Manawoka, E Indonesia *4.07S 131.22E*
201 *Q16* **Nama** *island* C Micronesia
85 *O16* **Namacurra** Zambézia, NE Mozambique *17.31S 37.03E*
196 *F9* **Namai Bay** *bay* Babeldaob, N Palau
31 *W2* **Namakan Lake** ◎ Canada/USA
149 *O6* **Namak, Daryācheh-ye** *marsh* N Iran
149 *T6* **Namak, Kavīr-e** *salt pan* NE Iran
178 *H6* **Namaklwe** Shan State, E Myanmar *19.45N 99.01E*
Namaksār, Kowl-e/Namakzār, Daryācheh-ye *see* Namakzar
154 *I5* **Namakzar** *Pash.* Daryācheh-ye Namakzār, Kowl-e Namaksār. *marsh* Afghanistan/Iran
176 *W13* **Namalau** Pulau Jursian, E Indonesia *5.50S 134.43E*
83 *I20* **Namanga** Rift Valley, S Kenya *2.33S 36.48E*

◆ Country
● Country Capital
◇ Dependent Territory
○ Dependent Territory Capital
◈ Administrative Region
✕ International Airport
▲ Mountain
▲▲ Mountain Range
Volcano
≈ River
◎ Lake
⊠ Reservoir

153 S10 **Namangan** Namangan Viloyati, E Uzbekistan 40.59N 71.33E
Namanganskaya Oblast' *see* Namangan Viloyati
153 R10 **Namangan Viloyati** *Rus.* Namanganskaya Oblast'. ◈ *province* E Uzbekistan
85 Q14 **Namapa** Nampula, NE Mozambique 13.43S 39.48E
85 C21 **Namaqualand** *physical region* S Namibia
83 G18 **Namasagali** C Uganda 1.01N 32.58E
195 P10 **Namatanai** New Ireland, NE PNG 3.42S 152.28E
85 I14 **Nambala** Central, C Zambia 15.06S 27.03E
83 J23 **Nambanje** Lindi, SE Tanzania 8.37S 38.21E
176 Ww9 **Namber** Papua, E Indonesia 0.58S 134.51E
85 G16 **Nambiya** Ngamiland, N Botswana 18.09S 23.08E
191 V2 **Nambour** Queensland, E Australia 26.43S 152.54E
191 V6 **Nambucca Heads** New South Wales, SE Australia 30.37S 153.00E
165 N15 **Nam Co** ◎ W China
178 Ii5 **Nâm Cum** Lai Châu, N Vietnam 22.37N 103.12E
Namdik *see* Namorik Atoll
178 Jj6 **Nam Định** Nam Ha, N Vietnam 20.25N 106.12E
175 Tt11 **Namea, Tanjung** *headland* Pulau Seram, SE Indonesia
101 I20 **Namêche** Namur, SE Belgium 50.29N 5.02E
32 J4 **Namekagon Lake** ◎ Wisconsin, N USA
196 F10 **Namekakl Passage** *passage* Babeldaob, N Palau
Namen *see* Namur
85 P15 **Nametil** Nampula, NE Mozambique 15.46S 39.21E
169 X14 **Nam-gang** ≈ C North Korea
169 Y16 **Nam-gang** ≈ S South Korea
169 Y17 **Namhae-do** *Jap.* Nankai-tō. *island* S South Korea
Namhoi *see* Foshan
85 C19 **Namib Desert** *desert* W Namibia
85 A15 **Namibe** *Port.* Moçâmedes, Mossâmedes. Namibe, SW Angola 15.10S 12.09E
85 A15 **Namibe** ◈ *province* SE Angola
85 C18 **Namibia** *off.* Republic of Namibia, *var.* South West Africa, *Afr.* Suidwes-Afrika, *Ger.* Deutsch-Südwestafrika; *prev.* German Southwest Africa, South-West Africa. ◆ *republic* S Africa
67 O17 **Namibia Plain** *undersea feature* S Atlantic Ocean
171 Ll14 **Namie** Fukushima, Honshū, C Japan 37.29N 140.58E
171 Mm8 **Namioka** Aomori, Honshū, C Japan 40.43N 140.34E
42 I5 **Namiquipa** Chihuahua, N Mexico 29.15N 107.25W
165 P15 **Namjagbarwa Feng** ▲ W China 29.39N 95.00E
175 Ss11 **Namlea** Pulau Buru, E Indonesia 3.12S 127.06E
164 L16 **Namling** Xizang Zizhiqu, W China 29.40N 88.58E
Namnetes *see* Nantes
178 Ii8 **Nam Ngum** ≈ C Laos
Namo *see* Namu Atoll
191 R5 **Namoi River** ≈ New South Wales, SE Australia
201 Q17 **Namoluk Atoll** *atoll* Mortlock Islands, C Micronesia
201 O15 **Namonuito Atoll** *atoll* Caroline Islands, C Micronesia
201 T9 **Namorik Atoll** *var.* Namdik. *atoll* Ralik Chain, S Marshall Islands
178 Ii6 **Nam Ou** ≈ N Laos
34 M14 **Nampa** Idaho, NW USA 43.32N 116.33W
78 M11 **Nampala** Ségou, W Mali 15.21N 5.32W
169 W14 **Namp'o** SW North Korea 38.45N 125.25E
85 P15 **Nampula** Nampula, NE Mozambique 15.09S 39.13E
85 P15 **Nampula** *off.* Província de Nampula. ◈ *province* NE Mozambique
169 W13 **Namsan-ni** NW North Korea 40.25N 125.01E
Namslau *see* Namysłów
95 E15 **Namsos** Nord-Trøndelag, C Norway 64.28N 11.31E
95 F14 **Namsskogan** Nord-Trøndelag, C Norway 64.57N 13.04E
178 H6 **Nam Teng** ≈ E Myanmar
178 I6 **Nam Tha** ≈ N Laos
126 M10 **Namtsy** Respublika Sakha (Yakutiya), NE Russian Federation 62.42N 129.30E
178 Gg4 **Namtu** Shan State, E Myanmar 23.04N 97.25E
8 J15 **Namu** British Columbia, SW Canada 51.46N 127.49W
201 T7 **Namu Atoll** *var.* Namo. *atoll* Ralik Chain, C Marshall Islands
197 K15 **Namuka-i-lau** *island* Lau Group, E Fiji
85 O15 **Namuli, Mont** ▲ NE Mozambique 15.15S 37.33E
85 P14 **Namuno** Cabo Delgado, N Mozambique 13.36S 38.52E
101 I20 **Namur** *Dut.* Namen. Namur, SE Belgium 50.28N 4.52E
101 H21 **Namur** *Dut.* Namen. ◈ *province* S Belgium
85 D17 **Namutoni** Kunene, N Namibia 18.47S 16.48E
169 Y16 **Namwŏn** *Jap.* Nangen. S South Korea 35.24N 127.20E
178 Mm14 **Namyit Island** *island* S Spratly Islands
113 H14 **Namysłów** *Ger.* Namslau. Opolskie, S Poland 51.05N 17.41E
178 Hh7 **Nan** *var.* Muang Nan. Nan, NW Thailand 18.47N 100.46E
81 G15 **Nana** ≈ W Central African Republic
172 Nn7 **Nanae** Hokkaidō, NE Japan 41.55N 140.40E
81 I14 **Nana-Grébizi** ◈ *prefecture* N Central African Republic
8 L17 **Nanaimo** Vancouver Island, British Columbia, SW Canada 49.07N 123.58W
40 C9 **Nanakuli** *Haw.* Nānākuli. Oahu, Hawaii, USA, C Pacific Ocean 21.23N 158.09W
81 G15 **Nana-Mambéré** ◈ *prefecture* W Central African Republic
167 R13 **Nan'an** Fujian, SE China 24.57N 118.22E
191 U2 **Nanango** Queensland, E Australia 26.42S 151.58E
171 Ii12 **Nanao** Ishikawa, Honshū, SW Japan 37.02N 136.57E
167 Q14 **Nan'ao Dao** *island* S China
171 Ii11 **Nanatsu-shima** *island* SW Japan
58 F8 **Nanay, Río** ≈ NE Peru
166 J8 **Nanbu** Sichuan, C China 31.19N 106.02E
169 X7 **Nancha** Heilongjiang, NE China 47.09N 129.16E
167 P10 **Nanchang** *var.* Nan-ch'ang, Nanch'ang-hsien. Jiangxi, S China 28.38N 115.57E
Nanch'ang-hsien *see* Nanchang
167 P11 **Nancheng** Jiangxi, S China 27.37N 116.37E
Nan-ching *see* Nanjing
166 J9 **Nanchong** Sichuan, C China 30.46N 106.03E
166 J10 **Nanchuan** Chongqing Shi, C China 29.06N 107.13E
105 T5 **Nancy** Meurthe-et-Moselle, NE France 48.40N 6.10E
193 A22 **Nancy Sound** *sound* South Island, NZ
158 L9 **Nanda Devi** ▲ NW India 30.27N 80.00E
44 J11 **Nandaime** Granada, SW Nicaragua 11.46N 86.03W
166 K13 **Nandan** Guangxi Zhuangzu Zizhiqu, S China 25.03N 107.31E
161 H14 **Nānded** Mahārāshtra, C India 19.10N 77.21E
170 G15 **Nanden** Hyōgo, Awaji-shima, SW Japan 34.19N 134.53E
191 S5 **Nandewar Range** ▲▲ New South Wales, SE Australia
Nandi *see* Nadi
166 E13 **Nanding He** ≈ China/Vietnam
Nándorhgy *see* Oțelu Roșu
160 E11 **Nandurbār** Mahārāshtra, W India 21.22N 74.18E
Nanduri *see* Naduri
161 I17 **Nandyāl** Andhra Pradesh, E India 15.30N 78.28E
167 P11 **Nanfeng** Jiangxi, S China 27.15N 116.30E
Nang *see* Nang Xian
81 E15 **Nanga Eboko** Centre, C Cameroon 4.37N 12.21E
155 W4 **Nanga Parbat** ▲ India/Pakistan 35.15N 74.36E
174 L8 **Nangapinoh** Borneo, C Indonesia 0.21S 111.43E
155 R5 **Nangarhār** ◈ *province* E Afghanistan
174 M8 **Nangaserawai** *var.* Nangah Serawai. Borneo, C Indonesia 0.19S 112.25E
174 L9 **Nangatayap** Borneo, C Indonesia 1.30S 110.33E
Nangen *see* Namwŏn
105 P5 **Nangis** Seine-et-Marne, N France 48.36N 3.02E
169 X13 **Nangnim-sanmaek** ▲▲ C North Korea
167 O4 **Nangong** Hebei, E China 37.24N 115.24E
165 Q14 **Nangqên** Qinghai, C China 32.05N 96.28E
178 I11 **Nang Rong** Buri Ram, E Thailand 14.37N 102.48E
165 O16 **Nang Xian** *var.* Nang. Xizang Zizhiqu, W China 29.04N 93.03E
Nan Hai *see* South China Sea
166 L8 **Nan He** ≈ C China
166 F12 **Nanhua** Yunnan, SW China 25.15N 101.15E
Naniwa *see* Ōsaka
161 G20 **Nanjangūd** Karnātaka, W India 12.07N 76.40E
167 Q8 **Nanjing** *var.* Nan-ching, Nanking; *prev.* Chianning, Chian-ning, Kiang-ning. Jiangsu, E China 32.03N 118.46E
Nankai-tō *see* Namhae-do
167 O12 **Nankang** Jiangxi, S China 25.40N 114.40E
Nanking *see* Nanjing
170 F15 **Nankoku** Kōchi, Shikoku, SW Japan 33.34N 133.37E
167 N13 **Nan Ling** ▲▲ S China
166 L15 **Nanliu Jiang** ≈ S China
201 P13 **Nan Madol** *ruins* Temwen Island, E Micronesia
166 K15 **Nanning** *var.* Nan-ning; *prev.* Yung-ning. Guangxi Zhuangzu Zizhiqu, S China 22.49N 108.19E
206 M15 **Nanortalik** Kitaa, S Greenland 60.12N 44.53W
Nanouki *see* Aranuka
166 H13 **Nanpan Jiang** ≈ S China
158 M11 **Nānpāra** Uttar Pradesh, N India 27.51N 81.30E
167 Q12 **Nanping** *var.* Nan-p'ing; *prev.* Yenping. Fujian, SE China 26.40N 118.07E
166 I7 **Nanping** Sichuan, C China 33.25N 104.05E
167 R12 **Nanri Dao** *island* SE China
172 Q13 **Nansei-shotō** *Eng.* Ryukyu Islands. *island group* SW Japan
Nansei Syotō Trench *see* Ryukyu Trench
207 T10 **Nansen Basin** *undersea feature* Arctic Ocean
207 T10 **Nansen Cordillera** *var.* Arctic-Mid Oceanic Ridge, Nansen Ridge. *undersea feature* Arctic Ocean
Nansen Ridge *see* Nansen Cordillera
133 T9 **Nan Shan** ▲▲ C China
179 Nn14 **Nanshan Island** *island* E Spratly Islands
Nansha Qundao *see* Spratly Islands
10 K3 **Nantais, Lac** ◎ Quebec, NE Canada
105 N5 **Nanterre** Hauts-de-Seine, N France 48.52N 2.13E
104 I8 **Nantes** *Bret.* Naoned; *anc.* Condivincum, Namnetes. Loire-Atlantique, NW France 47.12N 1.31W
12 G17 **Nanticoke** Ontario, S Canada 42.49N 80.04W
20 H13 **Nanticoke** Pennsylvania, NE USA 41.12N 76.00W
23 Y4 **Nanticoke River** ≈ Delaware/Maryland, NE USA
9 Q17 **Nanton** Alberta, SW Canada 50.21N 113.46W
167 S8 **Nantong** Jiangsu, E China 32.00N 120.52E
167 S13 **Nant'ou** W Taiwan 23.54N 120.33E
105 S10 **Nantua** Ain, E France 46.10N 5.34E
21 Q13 **Nantucket** Nantucket Island, Massachusetts, NE USA 41.15N 70.05W
21 Q13 **Nantucket Island** *island* Massachusetts, NE USA
21 Q13 **Nantucket Sound** *sound* Massachusetts, NE USA
84 P13 **Nantulo** Cabo Delgado, N Mozambique 12.30S 39.03E
201 O12 **Nanuh** Pohnpei, E Micronesia
197 K13 **Nanuku Passage** *channel* NE Fiji
202 D6 **Nanumaga** *var.* Nanumanga. *atoll* NW Tuvalu
Nanumanga *see* Nanumaga
202 D5 **Nanumea Atoll** *atoll* NW Tuvalu
61 O19 **Nanuque** Minas Gerais, SE Brazil 17.49S 40.21W
175 Ss4 **Nanusa, Kepulauan** *island group* N Indonesia
169 U4 **Nanweng He** ≈ NE China
166 I10 **Nanxi** Sichuan, C China 28.54N 104.58E
167 N10 **Nanxian** *var.* Nan Xian. Hunan, S China 29.23N 112.18E
167 N7 **Nanyang** *var.* Nan-yang. Henan, C China 32.58N 112.29E
167 P6 **Nanyang Hu** ◎ E China
171 L13 **Nan'yō** Yamagata, Honshū, C Japan 38.05N 140.07E
83 I18 **Nanyuki** Central, C Kenya 0.01N 37.04E
166 M8 **Nanzhang** Hubei, C China 31.47N 111.48E
107 T11 **Nao, Cabo de La** *headland* E Spain 38.43N 0.13E
10 M9 **Naococane, Lac** ◎ Quebec, E Canada
159 S14 **Naogaon** Rajshahi, NW Bangladesh 24.49N 88.58E
Naokot *see* Naukot
197 C12 **Naone** Maewo, C Vanuatu 15.03S 168.06E
Naoned *see* Nantes
117 E14 **Náousa** Kentrikí Makedonía, N Greece 40.38N 22.06E
37 N8 **Napa** California, W USA 38.15N 122.17W
41 O11 **Napaimiut** Alaska, USA 61.32N 158.46W
41 N12 **Napakiak** Alaska, USA 60.42N 161.57W
126 H7 **Napalkovo** Yamalo-Nenetskiy Avtonomnyy Okrug, N Russian Federation 70.06N 73.43E
10 I16 **Napanee** Ontario, SE Canada 44.13N 76.57W
176 Ww11 **Napanwainami** Papua, E Indonesia 3.01S 135.51E
176 W11 **Napan-Yaur** Papua, E Indonesia 2.55S 134.50E
41 N12 **Napaskiak** Alaska, USA 60.42N 161.46W
178 Jj5 **Na Phac** Cao Băng, N Vietnam 22.24N 105.54E
176 Ww9 **Napido** Papua, E Indonesia 0.41S 135.27E
192 O11 **Napier** Hawke's Bay, North Island, NZ 39.30S 176.55E
205 X3 **Napier Mountains** ▲▲ Antarctica
13 O13 **Napierville** Quebec, SE Canada 45.12N 73.25W
25 W15 **Naples** Florida, SE USA 26.08N 81.48W
27 W5 **Naples** Texas, SW USA 33.12N 94.40W
Naples *see* Napoli
166 I14 **Napo** Guangxi Zhuangzu Zizhiqu, S China 23.21N 105.47E
58 D6 **Napo** ◈ *province* NE Ecuador
31 O6 **Napoleon** North Dakota, N USA 46.30N 99.46W
33 R11 **Napoleon** Ohio, N USA 41.23N 84.07W
Napoléon-Vendée *see* la Roche-sur-Yon
24 J9 **Napoleonville** Louisiana, S USA 29.55N 91.01W
109 K17 **Napoli** *Eng.* Naples, *Ger.* Neapel; *anc.* Neapolis. Campania, S Italy 40.52N 14.15E
109 J18 **Napoli, Golfo di** *gulf* S Italy
59 F7 **Napo, Río** ≈ Ecuador/Peru
203 W9 **Napuka** *island* Îles Tuamotu, C French Polynesia
148 J3 **Naqadeh** Āžarbāyjān-e Bākhtarī, NW Iran 36.57N 45.24E
145 U6 **Naqnah** E Iraq 34.13N 45.33E
Nar *see* Nera
171 H15 **Nara** Nara, Honshū, SW Japan 34.40N 135.49E
78 L11 **Nara** Koulikoro, W Mali 15.04N 7.19W
171 Gg16 **Nara** *off.* Nara-ken. ◈ *prefecture* Honshū, SW Japan
155 R14 **Nāra Canal** *irrigation canal* S Pakistan
190 K11 **Naracoorte** South Australia 37.01S 140.45E
191 P8 **Naradhan** New South Wales, SE Australia 33.37S 146.19E
Naradhivas *see* Narathiwat
58 B8 **Naranjal** Guayas, W Ecuador 2.39S 79.34W
59 Q19 **Naranjos** Santa Cruz, E Bolivia
43 Q12 **Naranjos** Veracruz-Llave, E Mexico 21.20N 97.42W
165 Q6 **Naran Sebstein Bulag** *spring* NW China 42.40N 96.58E
149 X12 **Narānū** Sīstān va Balūchestān, SE Iran
170 Bb12 **Narao** Nagasaki, Nakadōri-jima, SW Japan 32.40N 129.03E
161 J16 **Narasaraopet** Andhra Pradesh, E India 16.16N 80.06E
164 J5 **Narat** Xinjiang Uygur Zizhiqu, W China 43.19N 84.01E
178 Hh17 **Narathiwat** *var.* Naradhivas. Narathiwat, SW Thailand 6.25N 101.48E
39 V10 **Nara Visa** New Mexico, SW USA 35.35N 103.06W
Nārāyāni *see* Gandak
Narbada *see* Narmada
Narbo Martius *see* Narbonne
105 P16 **Narbonne** *anc.* Narbo Martius. Aude, S France 43.11N 3.00E
Narborough Island *see* Fernandina, Isla
106 J2 **Narcea** ≈ NW Spain
158 J9 **Narendranagar** Uttar Pradesh, N India 30.10N 78.21E
Nares Abyssal Plain *see* Nares Plain
66 G11 **Nares Plain** *var.* Nares Abyssal Plain. *undersea feature* NW Atlantic Ocean
207 P10 **Nares Strait** *Dan.* Nares Stræde. *strait* Canada/Greenland
Nares Stræde *see* Nares Strait
112 O9 **Narew** ≈ E Poland
161 F17 **Nargund** Karnātaka, W India 15.43N 75.23E
85 D20 **Narib** Hardap, S Namibia 24.10S 17.46E
Narikrik *see* Knox Atoll
56 B13 **Nariño** *off.* Departamento de Nariño. ◈ *province* SW Colombia
171 Kk17 **Narita** Chiba, Honshū, S Japan 35.46N 140.17E
171 Kk17 **Narita** ✈ (Tōkyō) Chiba, Honshū, S Japan 35.45N 140.23E
Narıya *see* An Nu'ayrīyah
158 J8 **Nārkanda** Himāchal Pradesh, NW India 31.13N 77.27E
94 L13 **Narkaus** Lappi, NW Finland 66.13N 26.09E
160 E11 **Narmada** *var.* Narbada. ≈ C India
158 H11 **Narnaul** *var.* Nārnaul. Haryāna, N India 28.05N 76.12E
109 I14 **Narni** Umbria, C Italy 42.31N 12.31E
109 J24 **Naro** Sicilia, Italy, C Mediterranean Sea 37.18N 13.48E
Narodichi *see* Narodychi
129 V7 **Narodnaya, Gora** ▲ NW Russian Federation 65.04N 60.12E
119 N3 **Narodychi** *Rus.* Narodichi. Zhytomyrs'ka Oblast', N Ukraine 51.11N 29.01E
130 J4 **Naro-Fominsk** Moskovskaya Oblast', W Russian Federation 55.25N 36.41E
83 H19 **Narok** Rift Valley, SW Kenya 1.04S 35.54E
106 H2 **Narón** Galicia, NW Spain 43.31N 8.08W
191 S11 **Narooma** New South Wales, SE Australia 36.16S 150.08E
Narova *see* Narva
Narovlya *see* Narowlya
155 W8 **Nārowāl** Punjab, E Pakistan 32.04N 74.54E
121 N20 **Narowlya** *Rus.* Narovlya. Homyel'skaya Voblasts', SE Belarus 51.49N 29.30E
95 J17 **Närpes** *Fin.* Närpiö. Länsi-Suomi, W Finland 62.28N 21.19E
Närpiö *see* Närpes
191 S5 **Narrabri** New South Wales, SE Australia 30.21S 149.48E
191 P9 **Narrandera** New South Wales, SE Australia 34.46S 146.32E
191 Q4 **Narran Lake** ◎ New South Wales, SE Australia
191 Q4 **Narran River** ≈ New South Wales/Queensland, SE Australia
188 J13 **Narrogin** Western Australia 32.52S 117.16E
191 Q7 **Narromine** New South Wales, SE Australia 32.16S 148.15E
23 R6 **Narrows** Virginia, NE USA 37.19N 80.48W
206 M15 **Narsarsuaq** ✈ Kitaa, S Greenland 61.07N 45.03W
160 I10 **Narsimhapur** Madhya Pradesh, C India 22.58N 79.15E
Narsingdi *see* Narsinghdi
159 U15 **Narsinghdi** *var.* Narsingdi. Dhaka, C Bangladesh 23.55N 90.40E
160 H9 **Narsinghgarh** Madhya Pradesh, C India 23.45N 77.04E
169 Q11 **Nart** Nei Mongol Zizhiqu, N China 42.54N 115.55E
Nartës, Gjol i/Nartës, Laguna e *see* Nartës, Liqeni i
115 J22 **Nartës, Liqeni i** *var.* Gjol i Nartës, Laguna e Nartës. ◎ SW Albania
117 F17 **Nartháki** ▲ C Greece 39.12N 22.24E
131 O15 **Nartkala** Kabardino-Balkarskaya Respublika, SW Russian Federation 43.34N 43.55E
170 Ff15 **Naruto** Tokushima, Shikoku, SW Japan 34.09N 134.34E
120 K3 **Narva** Ida-Virumaa, NE Estonia 59.22N 28.12E
120 K4 **Narva** *prev.* Narova. ≈ Estonia/Russian Federation
120 J3 **Narva Bay** *Est.* Narva Laht, *Ger.* Narwa-Bucht, *Rus.* Narvskiy Zaliv. *bay* Estonia/Russian Federation
Narva Laht *see* Narva Bay
128 F13 **Narva Reservoir** *Est.* Narva Veehoidla, *Rus.* Narvskoye Vodokhranilishche. ⊞ Estonia/Russian Federation
Narva Veehoidla *see* Narva Reservoir
94 H10 **Narvik** Nordland, C Norway 68.25N 17.24E
Narvskiy Zaliv *see* Narva Bay
Narvskoye Vodokhranilishche *see* Narva Reservoir
Narwa-Bucht *see* Narva Bay
158 I9 **Narwāna** Haryāna, NW India 29.40N 76.10E
129 R4 **Nar'yan-Mar** *prev.* Beloshchel'ye, Dzerzhinskiy. Nenetskiy Avtonomnyy Okrug, NW Russian Federation 67.38N 53.00E
126 H12 **Narym** Tomskaya Oblast', C Russian Federation 58.59N 81.20E
151 Y10 **Narymskiy Khrebet** *Kaz.* Naryn Zhotasy. ▲▲ E Kazakhstan
153 W9 **Naryn** Narynskaya Oblast', C Kyrgyzstan 41.24N 75.59E
153 U8 **Naryn** ≈ Kyrgyzstan/Uzbekistan
151 W16 **Narynkol** *Kaz.* Narynqol. Almaty, SE Kazakhstan 42.41N 80.10E
Naryn Oblasty *see* Narynskaya Oblast'
Narynqol *see* Narynkol
153 V9 **Narynskaya Oblast'** *Kir.* Naryn Oblasty. ◈ *province* C Kyrgyzstan
Naryn Zhotasy *see* Narymskiy Khrebet
130 J6 **Naryshkino** Orlovskaya Oblast', W Russian Federation 53.00N 35.41E
97 L14 **Nås** Dalarna, C Sweden 60.28N 14.30E
94 G13 **Nasafjället** ▲ C Norway 66.29N 15.23E
95 H16 **Näsåker** Västernorrland, C Sweden 63.27N 16.55E
197 J14 **Nasau** Koro, C Fiji 17.20S 179.26E
118 I9 **Năsăud** *Ger.* Nussdorf, *Hung.* Naszód. Bistrița-Năsăud, N Romania 47.16N 24.24E
105 P13 **Nasbinals** Lozère, S France 44.40N 3.03E
Na Sceirí *see* Skerries
Nase *see* Naze
193 E22 **Naseby** Otago, South Island, NZ 45.02S 170.09E
149 R10 **Nāșerīyeh** Kermān, C Iran
27 X5 **Nash** Texas, SW USA 33.26N 94.04W
160 E13 **Nāshik** *prev.* Nāsik. Mahārāshtra, W India 20.04N 73.48E
58 E7 **Nashiño, Río** ≈ Ecuador/Peru
31 W12 **Nashua** Iowa, C USA 42.57N 92.32W
35 W7 **Nashua** Montana, NW USA 48.06N 106.16W
21 O10 **Nashua** New Hampshire, NE USA 42.45N 71.26W
29 S13 **Nashville** Arkansas, C USA 33.57N 93.51W
25 U7 **Nashville** Georgia, SE USA 31.12N 83.15W
32 L16 **Nashville** Illinois, N USA 38.20N 89.22W
33 O14 **Nashville** Indiana, N USA 39.13N 86.15W
23 V9 **Nashville** North Carolina, SE USA 35.58N 77.58W
22 J8 **Nashville** *state capital* Tennessee, S USA 36.10N 86.48W
22 J9 **Nashville** ✈ Tennessee, S USA 36.06N 86.44W
66 H10 **Nashville Seamount** *undersea feature* NW Atlantic Ocean 30.00N 57.20W
114 H9 **Našice** Osijek-Baranja, E Croatia 45.29N 18.05E
112 M11 **Nasielsk** Mazowieckie, C Poland 52.33N 20.46E
95 K18 **Näsijärvi** ◎ SW Finland
Nāsik *see* Nāshik
82 G13 **Nasir** Upper Nile, SE Sudan 8.37N 33.06E
155 Q12 **Nasīrābād** Baluchistān, SW Pakistan 28.29N 68.24E
154 K15 **Nasīrābād** Baluchistān, SW Pakistan 28.25N 68.28E
Nasīrābād *see* Mymensingh
Nasir, Buhayrat/Nâșir, Buḥeiret *see* Nasser, Lake
Nāsiri *see* Ahvāz
Nasiriya *see* An Nāșirīyah
Nás na Ríogh *see* Naas
109 L23 **Naso** Sicilia, Italy, C Mediterranean Sea 38.07N 14.46E
Nasratabad *see* Zābol
8 J11 **Nass** ≈ British Columbia, SW Canada
79 V15 **Nassarawa** Nassarawa, C Nigeria 8.33N 7.42E
46 H2 **Nassau** ● (Bahamas) New Providence, N Bahamas 25.03N 77.20W
46 H2 **Nassau** ✈ New Providence, C Bahamas 25.00N 77.26W
202 J13 **Nassau** *island* N Cook Islands
25 W8 **Nassau Sound** *sound* Florida, SE USA
110 L7 **Nassereith** Tirol, W Austria 47.19N 10.51E
97 L19 **Nässjö** Jönköping, S Sweden 57.39N 14.40E
101 K22 **Nassogne** Luxembourg, SE Belgium 50.08N 5.19E
10 J6 **Nastapoka Islands** *island group* Nunavut, C Canada
95 M19 **Nastola** Etelä-Suomi, S Finland 60.57N 25.55E
171 L14 **Nasu-dake** ▲ Honshū, S Japan 37.07N 139.57E
179 P11 **Nasugbu** Luzon, N Philippines 14.03N 120.39E
96 N11 **Näsviken** Gävleborg, C Sweden 61.46N 16.55E
Naszód *see* Năsăud
85 I17 **Nata** Central, NE Botswana 20.10S 26.10E
56 E11 **Natagaima** Tolima, C Colombia 3.30N 75.06W
61 Q14 **Natal** Rio Grande do Norte, E Brazil 5.46S 35.15W
173 Ff8 **Natal** Sumatera, N Indonesia 0.25N 99.09E
Natal *see* KwaZulu/Natal
181 L10 **Natal Basin** *var.* Mozambique Basin. *undersea feature* W Indian Ocean
27 R12 **Natalia** Texas, SW USA 29.11N 98.51W
69 W15 **Natal Valley** *undersea feature* SW Indian Ocean
Natanya *see* Netanya
149 O7 **Naṭanz** Eșfahān, C Iran 33.31N 51.55E
11 Q11 **Natashquan** Quebec, E Canada 50.10N 61.49W
11 Q10 **Natashquan** ≈ Newfoundland and Labrador/Quebec, E Canada
24 J7 **Natchez** Mississippi, S USA 31.33N 91.24W
24 G6 **Natchitoches** Louisiana, S USA 31.45N 93.05W
110 E10 **Naters** Valais, S Switzerland 46.22N 8.00E
Nathanya *see* Netanya
94 O3 **Nathorst Land** *physical region* W Svalbard
Nathula *see* Nacula
194 J15 **National Capital District** ◈ *province* S PNG
37 U17 **National City** California, W USA 32.40N 117.06W
192 M10 **National Park** Manawatu-Wanganui, North Island, NZ 39.11S 175.22E
79 R14 **Natitingou** NW Benin 10.21N 1.25E
42 B5 **Natividad, Isla** *island* W Mexico
171 M13 **Natori** Miyagi, Honshū, C Japan 38.11N 140.52E
20 C14 **Natrona Heights** Pennsylvania, NE USA 40.37N 79.42W
83 H20 **Natron, Lake** ◎ Kenya/Tanzania
Natsrat *see* Naẓerat
177 Ff7 **Nattalin** Pegu, C Myanmar 18.25N 95.34E
94 J12 **Nattavaara** Norrbotten, N Sweden 66.45N 20.58E
111 S3 **Natternbach** Oberösterreich, N Austria 48.26N 13.44E
97 M22 **Nättraby** Blekinge, S Sweden 56.12N 15.30E
174 K4 **Natuna Besar, Pulau** *island* Kepulauan Natuna, W Indonesia
174 **Natuna Islands** *see* Natuna, Kepulauan
174 Jj5 **Natuna, Kepulauan** *var.* Natuna Islands. *island group* W Indonesia
174 J6 **Natuna, Laut** *sea* W Indonesia
23 N6 **Natural Bridge** *tourist site* Kentucky, C USA 37.44N 83.37W
181 V11 **Naturaliste Fracture Zone** *tectonic feature* E Indian Ocean
182 J10 **Naturaliste Plateau** *undersea feature* E Indian Ocean
Nau *see* Nov
105 O14 **Naucelle** Aveyron, S France 44.10N 2.19E
85 D20 **Nauchas** Hardap, C Namibia 23.36S 16.21E
110 K9 **Nauders** Tirol, W Austria 46.52N 10.31E
Naugard *see* Nowogard
120 F12 **Naujamiestis** Panevėžys, C Lithuania 55.42N 24.10E
120 E10 **Naujoji Akmenė** Akmenė, NW Lithuania 56.20N 22.57E
155 R16 **Naukot** *var.* Naokot. Sind, SE Pakistan 24.52N 69.27E
103 L16 **Naumburg** *var.* Naumburg an der Saale. Sachsen-Anhalt, C Germany 51.09N 11.48E
Naumburg am Queis *see* Nowogrodziec
Naumburg an der Saale *see* Naumburg
203 W15 **Naunau** *ancient monument* Easter Island, Chile, E Pacific Ocean
144 G10 **Nā'ūr** Al 'Āșimah, W Jordan 31.52N 35.49E
201 Q8 **Nauru** *off.* Republic of Nauru; *prev.* Pleasant Island. ◆ *republic* W Pacific Ocean
183 P5 **Nauru** *island* W Pacific Ocean
201 Q9 **Nauru International** ✈ S Nauru
Nausari *see* Navsāri
21 Q12 **Nauset Beach** *beach* Massachusetts, NE USA
Naushahra *see* Nowshera
155 P14 **Naushahro Fīroz** Sind, SE Pakistan 26.53N 68.12E
Nauṣhara *see* Nowshera
197 I14 **Nausori** Viti Levu, W Fiji 17.48S 177.35E
58 F9 **Nauta** Loreto, N Peru 4.31S 73.35W
159 O12 **Nautanwa** Uttar Pradesh, N India 27.25N 83.25E
43 R13 **Nautla** Veracruz-Llave, E Mexico 20.12N 96.46W
Nauzad *see* Now Zād
43 N6 **Nava** Coahuila de Zaragoza, NE Mexico 28.28N 100.45W
Navabad *see* Navobod
106 L6 **Nava del Rey** Castilla-León, N Spain 41.19N 5.04W
159 S15 **Navadwīp** *prev.* Nabadwip. West Bengal, NE India 23.24N 88.22E
197 J14 **Navaga** Koro, W Fiji 17.21S 179.22E
106 M9 **Navahermosa** Castilla-La Mancha, C Spain 39.39N 4.25W
121 I16 **Navahrudak** *Pol.* Nowogródek, *Rus.* Novogrudok. Hrodzyenskaya Voblasts', W Belarus 53.34N 25.54E
121 I16 **Navahrudskaye Wzvyshsha** ▲▲ W Belarus
38 M8 **Navajo Mount** ▲ Utah, W USA 37.00N 110.52W
39 Q9 **Navajo Reservoir** ⊞ New Mexico, SW USA
179 Qq12 **Naval** Biliran Island, C Philippines 11.32N 124.26E
106 K9 **Navalmoral de la Mata** Extremadura, W Spain 39.54N 5.33W
106 K10 **Navalvillar de Pelea** Extremadura, W Spain 39.05N 5.27W
99 F17 **Navan** *Ir.* An Uaimh. E Ireland 53.39N 6.40W
Navanagar *see* Jāmnagar
120 L12 **Navapolatsk** *Rus.* Novopolotsk. Vitsyebskaya Voblasts', N Belarus 55.33N 28.34E
155 P6 **Nāvar, Dasht-e** *Pash.* Dasht-i-Nawar. *desert* C Afghanistan
127 Q5 **Navarin, Mys** *headland* NE Russian Federation 62.18N 179.06E
65 I25 **Navarino, Isla** *island* S Chile
107 Q4 **Navarra** *Eng./Fr.* Navarre. ◈ *autonomous community* N Spain
Navarre *see* Navarra
107 P4 **Navarrete** La Rioja, N Spain 42.25N 2.34W
63 C20 **Navarro** Buenos Aires, E Argentina 35.01S 59.18W
107 O12 **Navas de San Juan** Andalucía, S Spain 38.10N 3.19W
27 V10 **Navasota** Texas, SW USA 30.23N 96.05W
27 U9 **Navasota River** ≈ Texas, SW USA
46 I9 **Navassa Island** ◇ *US unincorporated territory* C West Indies
121 L19 **Navasyolki** *Rus.* Novosëlki. Homyel'skaya Voblasts', SE Belarus 52.24N 28.27E
121 H17 **Navayel'nya** *Pol.* Nowojelnia, *Rus.* Novoyel'nya. Hrodzyenskaya Voblasts', W Belarus 53.26N 25.36E
176 Yy11 **Naver** Papua, E Indonesia 3.27S 139.45E
120 H5 **Navesti** ≈ C Estonia
106 J2 **Navia** Asturias, N Spain 43.33N 6.43W
106 J2 **Navia** ≈ NW Spain
61 I21 **Naviraí** Mato Grosso do Sul, SW Brazil 23.01S 54.09W
197 G14 **Naviti** *island* Yasawa Group, NW Fiji
130 I6 **Navlya** Bryanskaya Oblast', W Russian Federation 52.47N 34.28E
197 J13 **Navoalevu** Vanua Levu, N Fiji 16.22S 179.28E
153 R12 **Navobod** *Rus.* Navabad, Novabad. C Tajikistan 39.00N 70.06E
153 P13 **Navobod** *Rus.* Navabad. W Tajikistan 38.37N 68.42E
Navoi *see* Navoiy
152 M11 **Navoiy** *Rus.* Navoi. Navoiy Viloyati, C Uzbekistan 40.05N 65.22E
Navoiyskaya Oblast' *see* Navoiy Viloyati
152 K8 **Navoiy Viloyati** *Rus.* Navoiyskaya Oblast'. ◈ *province* N Uzbekistan
42 G7 **Navojoa** Sonora, NW Mexico 27.04N 109.28W
Navolat *see* Navolato
42 H9 **Navolato** *var.* Navolat. Sinaloa, C Mexico 24.46N 167.42W
197 C12 **Navonda** Ambae, C Vanuatu 15.21S 167.58E
Návpaktos *see* Náfpaktos
Návplion *see* Náfplio
79 P14 **Navrongo** N Ghana 10.54N 1.03W
160 D12 **Navsāri** *var.* Nausari. Gujarāt, W India 20.55N 72.55E
197 I15 **Navua** Viti Levu, W Fiji 18.13S 178.10E
144 H8 **Nawá** Dar'ā, S Syria 32.52N 36.03E
Nawabashah *see* Nawābshāh
159 S14 **Nawabganj** Rajshahi, NW Bangladesh 24.36N 88.17E
159 S14 **Nawābganj** Uttar Pradesh, N India 26.52N 82.09E
155 Q15 **Nawābshāh** *var.* Nawabashah. Sind, S Pakistan 26.15N 68.25E
159 P14 **Nawāda** Bihār, N India 24.54N 85.33E
158 H11 **Nawalgarh** Rājasthān, N India 27.51N 75.16E
Nawāl, Sabkhat an *see* Noual, Sebkhet en
Nawar, Dasht-i- *see* Nāvar, Dasht-e
178 Gg4 **Nawnghkio** *var.* Nawngkio. Shan State, C Myanmar 22.21N 96.48E
Nawngkio *see* Nawnghkio
143 U13 **Naxçıvan** *Rus.* Nakhichevan'. SW Azerbaijan 39.13N 45.24E
166 I10 **Naxi** Sichuan, C China 28.48N 105.25E
117 K21 **Náxos** *var.* Naxos. Náxos, Kykládes, Greece, Aegean Sea 37.06N 25.22E
117 K21 **Náxos** *island* Kykládes, Greece, Aegean Sea
42 J11 **Nayarit** ◈ *state* C Mexico
197 K14 **Nayau** *island* Lau Group, E Fiji
149 S8 **Nāy Band** Khorāsān, E Iran 32.26N 57.30E
172 Pp4 **Nayoro** Hokkaidō, NE Japan 44.21N 142.27E
106 F9 **Nazaré** *var.* Nazare. Leiria, C Portugal 39.36N 9.04W
26 M4 **Nazareth** Texas, SW USA 34.32N 102.06W
Nazareth *see* Naẓerat
181 O8 **Nazareth Bank** *undersea feature* W Indian Ocean
126 Hh14 **Nazarovo** Krasnoyarskiy Kray, S Russian Federation 56.00N 89.33E
42 K9 **Nazas** Durango, C Mexico 25.16N 104.04W
59 F16 **Nazca** Ica, S Peru 14.52S 75.01W
(0) L17 **Nazca Plate** *tectonic feature*
200 Oo11 **Nazca Ridge** *undersea feature* E Pacific Ocean
172 R13 **Naze** *var.* Nase. Kagoshima, Amami-ōshima, SW Japan 28.21N 129.30E
144 G9 **Naẓerat** *var.* Natsrat, *Ar.* En Nazira, *Eng.* Nazareth. Northern, N Israel 32.42N 35.18E
143 R14 **Nazik Gölü** ◎ E Turkey
142 C15 **Nazilli** Aydın, SW Turkey 37.55N 28.19E
143 P14 **Nazimiye** Tunceli, E Turkey 39.12N 39.51E
126 Gg11 **Nazino** Tomskaya Oblast', C Russian Federation 60.02N 78.51E
Nazinon *see* Red Volta
8 L15 **Nazko** British Columbia, SW Canada 52.57N 123.44W
131 O16 **Nazran'** Ingushskaya Respublika, SW Russian Federation 43.15N 44.52E
82 J13 **Nazrēt** *var.* Adama, Hadama. Oromo, C Ethiopia 8.31N 39.20E
Nazwāh *see* Nizwá
125 Ff13 **Nazyvayevsk** Omskaya Oblast', C Russian Federation 55.35N 71.13E
84 J13 **Nchanga** Copperbelt, C Zambia 12.30S 27.52E
84 J11 **Nchelenge** Luapula, N Zambia 9.24S 28.45E
Ncheu *see* Ntcheu
Ndaghamcha, Sebkra de *see* Te-n-Dghâmcha, Sebkhet
83 G21 **Ndala** Tabora, C Tanzania 4.45S 33.15E
84 B11 **N'Dalatando** *Port.* Salazar, Vila Salazar. Cuanza Norte, NW Angola 9.18S 14.48E
79 S14 **Ndali** C Benin 9.52N 2.44E
83 E18 **Ndeke** SW Uganda 0.11S 30.04E
80 J13 **Ndélé** Bamingui-Bangoran, N Central African Republic 8.24N 20.40E
81 E19 **Ndendé** Ngounié, S Gabon 2.21S 11.19E
81 E20 **Ndindi** Nyanga, S Gabon 3.46S 11.06E
80 G11 **Ndjamena** *var.* N'Djamena; *prev.* Fort-Lamy. ● (Chad) Chari-Baguirmi, W Chad 12.08N 15.01E
80 G11 **Ndjamena** ✈ Chari-Baguirmi, W Chad 12.09N 15.00E
81 D18 **Ndjolé** Moyen-Ogooué, W Gabon 0.07S 10.45E
84 J13 **Ndola** Copperbelt, C Zambia 12.58S 28.35E
Ndrhamcha, Sebkha de *see* Te-n-Dghâmcha, Sebkhet
81 L15 **Ndu** Orientale, N Dem. Rep. Congo 4.46N 22.54E
83 H21 **Nduguti** Singida, C Tanzania 4.19S 34.40E
195 X16 **Nduindui** Guadalcanal, C Solomon Islands 9.46S 159.54E
Nduke *see* Kolombangara
117 F16 **Néa Anchiálos** *var.* Nea Anhialos, Néa Ankhíalos. Thessalía, C Greece 39.18N 22.49E
Nea Anhialos/Néa Ankhíalos *see* Néa Anchiálos
117 H18 **Néa Artáki** Évvoia, C Greece 38.31N 23.39E
99 F15 **Neagh, Lough** ◎ E Northern Ireland, UK
34 F7 **Neah Bay** Washington, NW USA 48.21N 124.39W
117 J22 **Nea Kaméni** *island* Kykládes, Greece, Aegean Sea
189 O8 **Neale, Lake** ◎ Northern Territory, C Australia
190 G2 **Neales River** *seasonal river* South Australia

◆ Country · ● Country Capital · ◇ Dependent Territory · ○ Dependent Territory Capital · ◈ Administrative Region · ✈ International Airport · ▲ Mountain · ▲▲ Mountain Range · Volcano · ≈ River · ◎ Lake · ⊞ Reservoir

117 G14 Néa Moudanía var. Néa Moudhaniá. Kentrikí Makedonía, N Greece 40.15N 23.19E
Néa Moudhaniá see Néa Moudanía
118 K10 Neamţ ◆ county NE Romania
Neapel see Napoli
117 D14 Neápoli prev. Neápolis. Dytikí Makedonía, N Greece 40.18N 21.23E
117 K25 Neápoli Kríti, Greece, E Mediterranean Sea 35.15N 25.37E
117 G22 Neápoli Pelopónnisos, S Greece 36.29N 23.05E
Neapolis see Napoli, Italy
Neapolis see Nablus, West Bank
Neápolis see Neápoli, Greece
40 D16 Near Islands island group Aleutian Islands, Alaska, USA
99 J21 Neath S Wales, UK 51.39N 3.48W
116 H13 Néa Zíchni var. Néa Zíkhni; prev. Néa Zíkhna. Kentrikí Makedonía, NE Greece 41.02N 23.51E
Néa Zíkhna/Néa Zíkhni see Néa Zíchni
44 C5 Nebaj Quiché, W Guatemala 15.25N 91.05W
79 P13 Nebbou S Burkina 11.22N 1.49W
152 B11 Nebitdag Balkanskiy Velayat, W Turkmenistan 39.33N 54.19E
56 M13 Neblina, Pico da ▲ NW Brazil 0.49N 66.31W
128 I13 Nebolchi Novgorodskaya Oblast', W Russian Federation 59.08N 33.19E
38 L4 Nebo, Mount ▲ Utah, W USA 39.47N 111.46W
30 L14 Nebraska off. State of Nebraska; also known as Blackwater State, Cornhusker State, Tree Planters State. ◆ state C USA
31 S16 Nebraska City Nebraska, C USA 40.38N 95.52W
109 K23 Nebrodi, Monti var. Monti Caronie. ▲ Sicilia, Italy, C Mediterranean Sea
8 L14 Nechako ∽ British Columbia, SW Canada
31 Q2 Neche North Dakota, N USA 48.57N 97.33W
27 V8 Neches Texas, SW USA 31.51N 95.28W
27 W8 Neches River ∽ Texas, SW USA
103 H20 Neckar ∽ SW Germany
103 H20 Neckarsulm Baden-Württemberg, SW Germany 49.12N 9.13E
199 K5 Necker Island island C British Virgin Islands
183 U3 Necker Ridge undersea feature N Pacific Ocean
63 D23 Necochea Buenos Aires, E Argentina 38.33S 58.42W
106 H2 Neda Galicia, NW Spain 43.28N 8.09W
117 E20 Nédas ∽ S Greece
27 Y11 Nederland Texas, SW USA 29.58N 93.59W
Nederland see Netherlands
100 K12 Neder Rijn Eng. Lower Rhine. ∽ C Netherlands
101 L16 Nederweert Limburg, SE Netherlands 51.16N 5.45E
97 G16 Nedre Tokke ◎ S Norway
Nedrigaylov see Nedryhayliv
119 S3 Nedryhayliv Rus. Nedrigaylov. Sums'ka Oblast', NE Ukraine 50.51N 33.52E
100 O11 Neede Gelderland, E Netherlands 52.07N 6.36E
35 T13 Needle Mountain ▲ Wyoming, C USA 44.03N 109.33W
37 Y14 Needles California, W USA 34.50N 114.37W
99 M24 Needles, The rocks Isle of Wight, S England, UK
64 O7 Ñeembucú off. Departamento de Ñeembucú. ◆ department SW Paraguay
32 M7 Neenah Wisconsin, N USA 44.09N 88.26W
9 W16 Neepawa Manitoba, S Canada 50.13N 99.28W
101 K16 Neerpelt Limburg, NE Belgium 51.13N 5.25E
76 M6 Nefta ✕ W Tunisia 34.03N 8.05E
130 L15 Neftegorsk Krasnodarskiy Kray, SW Russian Federation 44.21N 39.40E
131 U3 Neftekamsk Respublika Bashkortostan, W Russian Federation 56.06N 54.12E
131 O14 Neftekumsk Stavropol'skiy Kray, SW Russian Federation 44.45N 45.00E
125 G11 Nefteyugansk Khanty-Mansiyskiy Avtonomnyy Okrug, C Russian Federation 61.07N 72.18E
Neftezavodsk see Seydi
84 C10 Negage var. N'Gage. Uíge, NW Angola 7.46S 15.27E
Negapatam/Negapattinam see Nāgappattinam
175 N16 Negara Bali, Indonesia 8.21S 114.34E
175 N10 Negara Borneo, C Indonesia 2.40S 115.04E
Negara Brunei Darussalam see Brunei
33 N4 Negaunee Michigan, N USA 46.30N 87.36W
83 J15 Negēlē var. Negelli, It. Neghelli. Oromo, C Ethiopia 5.13N 39.43E
Negelli see Negēlē
Negeri Pahang Darul Makmur see Pahang
Negeri Selangor Darul Ehsan see Selangor
174 H5 Negeri Sembilan var. Negri Sembilan. ◆ state Peninsular Malaysia
94 P3 Negerpynten headland S Svalbard 77.15N 22.40E
Negev see HaNegev
Neghelli see Negēlē
118 I12 Negoiu var. Negoiul. ▲ S Romania 45.34N 24.34E
Negoiul see Negoiu
84 P13 Negomane var. Negomano. Cabo Delgado, N Mozambique 11.22S 38.32E
Negomano see Negomane
161 J25 Negombo Western Province, SW Sri Lanka 7.13N 79.51E
Negoreloye see Nyeharelaye
114 P12 Negotin Serbia, E Serbia and Montenegro (Serbia and Montenegro (Yugoslavia)) 44.13N 22.31E
115 P19 Negotino C FYR Macedonia 41.29N 22.04E
58 A10 Negra, Punta headland NW Peru 6.03S 81.08W
106 G3 Negreira Galicia, NW Spain 42.54N 8.46W
118 L10 Negreşti Vaslui, E Romania 46.49N 27.28E
Negreşti see Negreşti-Oaş
118 H8 Negreşti-Oaş Hung. Avasfelsőfalu; prev. Negreşti. Satu Mare, NE Romania 47.56N 23.21E
46 H12 Negril W Jamaica 18.16N 78.21W
Negri Sembilan see Negeri Sembilan
65 K15 Negro, Río ∽ E Argentina
64 N7 Negro, Río ∽ NE Argentina
59 N17 Negro, Río ∽ E Bolivia
64 O5 Negro, Río ∽ C Paraguay
50 F6 Negro, Río ∽ N South America
63 E18 Negro, Río ∽ Brazil/Uruguay
Negro, Río see Sico Tinto, Río, Honduras
Negro, Río see Chixoy, Río, Guatemala/Mexico
179 Q14 Negros island C Philippines
118 M15 Negru Vodă Constanţa, SE Romania 43.47N 28.10E
11 P13 Neguac New Brunswick, SE Canada 47.16N 65.04W
12 B7 Negwazu, Lake ◎ Ontario, S Canada
Négyfalu see Săcele
34 F10 Nehalem Oregon, NW USA 45.42N 123.55W
34 F10 Nehalem River ∽ Oregon, NW USA
Nehavend see Nahāvand
149 V9 Nehbandān Khorāsān, E Iran 31.33N 60.01E
169 V6 Nehe Heilongjiang, NE China 48.28N 124.52E
200 Ss12 Neiafu 'Uta Vava'u, N Tonga 18.36S 173.58W
47 N9 Neiba var. Neyba. SW Dominican Republic 18.27N 71.28W
Néid, Carn Uí see Mizen Head
94 M9 Neiden Finnmark, N Norway 69.40N 29.22E
Neidín see Kenmare
Néifinn see Nephin
105 S10 Neige, Crêt de la ▲ E France 46.18N 5.58E
181 O16 Neiges, Piton des ▲ C Réunion 21.04S 55.28E
13 R9 Neiges, Rivière des ∽ Quebec, SE Canada
166 I10 Neijiang Sichuan, C China 29.31N 105.03E
32 K6 Neillsville Wisconsin, N USA 44.34N 90.36W
Nei Monggol Zizhiqu/Nei Mongol see Nei Mongol Zizhiqu
169 Q10 Nei Mongol Gaoyuan plateau NE China
169 O12 Nei Mongol Zizhiqu var. Nei Mongol, Eng. Inner Mongolia, Inner Mongolian Autonomous Region; prev. Nei Monggol Zizhiqu. ◆ autonomous region N China
167 O4 Neiqiu Hebei, E China 37.22N 114.34E
Neiriz see Neyrīz
103 Q16 Neisse Cz. Lužická Nisa, Ger. Lausitzer Neisse, Pol. Nisa, Nysa Łużycka. ∽ C Europe
Neisse see Nysa
56 E11 Neiva Huila, S Colombia 2.58N 75.15W
166 M7 Neixiang Henan, C China 33.07N 111.49E
Nejafabad see Najafābād
9 V9 Nejanilini Lake ◎ Manitoba, C Canada
Nejd see Najd
82 I13 Nek'emtē var. Lakemti, Nakamti. Oromo, C Ethiopia 9.06N 36.31E
130 M9 Nekhayevskiy Volgogradskaya Oblast', SW Russian Federation 50.25N 41.44E
32 K7 Nekoosa Wisconsin, N USA 44.19N 89.54W
Neksø see Nexø
117 C16 Nekyomanteío ancient monument Ípeiros, W Greece 39.13N 20.31E
106 H7 Nelas Viseu, N Portugal 40.31N 7.52W
128 H16 Nelidovo Tverskaya Oblast', W Russian Federation 56.13N 32.45E
31 P13 Neligh Nebraska, C USA 42.07N 98.01W
127 N12 Nel'kan Khabarovskiy Kray, E Russian Federation 57.44N 136.09E
94 M10 Nellim var. Nellimö, Lapp. Njellim. Lappi, N Finland 68.49N 28.18E
Nellimö see Nellim
161 J18 Nellore Andhra Pradesh, E India 14.29N 80.00E
127 O16 Nel'ma Khabarovskiy Kray, SE Russian Federation 47.43N 139.08E
63 B17 Nelson Santa Fe, C Argentina 31.16S 60.45W
9 O17 Nelson British Columbia, SW Canada 49.29N 117.13W
193 I14 Nelson Nelson, South Island, NZ 41.16S 173.16E
99 L17 Nelson NW England, UK 53.51N 2.13W
31 P17 Nelson Nebraska, C USA 40.12N 98.04W
193 J14 Nelson ◆ unitary authority South Island, NZ
9 X12 Nelson ∽ Manitoba, C Canada
191 U8 Nelson Bay New South Wales, SE Australia 32.45S 152.09E
190 K13 Nelson, Cape headland Victoria, SE Australia 38.25S 141.33E
194 M15 Nelson, Cape headland S PNG 8.57S 149.19E
65 G23 Nelson, Estrecho strait SE Pacific Ocean
9 W12 Nelson House Manitoba, C Canada 55.49N 98.51W
32 J4 Nelson Lake ◎ Wisconsin, N USA
33 T14 Nelsonville Ohio, N USA 39.27N 82.13W
29 S2 Nelsoon River ∽ Iowa/Missouri, C USA
85 K21 Nelspruit Mpumalanga, NE South Africa 25.28S 30.58E
78 L10 Néma Hodh ech Chargui, SE Mauritania 16.31N 7.12W
120 D13 Neman Ger. Ragnit. Kaliningradskaya Oblast', W Russian Federation 55.01N 22.00E
86 I9 Neman Bel. Nyoman, Ger. Memel, Lith. Nemunas, Pol. Niemen, Rus. Neman. ∽ NE Europe
Nemausus see Nîmes
117 F19 Neméa Pelopónnisos, S Greece 37.49N 22.40E
Německý Brod see Havlíčkův Brod
12 D7 Nemegosenda ∽ Ontario, S Canada
12 D8 Nemegosenda Lake ◎ Ontario, S Canada
121 H14 Nemenčinė Vilnius, SE Lithuania 54.50N 25.29E
Nemetocenna see Arras
Nemirov see Nemyriv
105 O6 Nemours Seine-et-Marne, N France 48.16N 2.40E
Nemunas see Neman
172 R7 Nemuro Hokkaidō, NE Japan 43.19N 145.34E
172 R7 Nemuro-hantō peninsula Hokkaidō, NE Japan
172 R6 Nemuro-kaikyō strait Japan/Russian Federation
172 R7 Nemuro-wan bay N Japan
118 H5 Nemyriv Rus. Nemirov. L'vivs'ka Oblast', NW Ukraine 50.07N 23.27E
119 N7 Nemyriv Rus. Nemirov. Vinnyts'ka Oblast', C Ukraine 48.57N 28.51E
99 D19 Nenagh Ir. An tAonach. C Ireland 52.52N 8.12W
41 R9 Nenana Alaska, USA 64.33N 149.05W
41 R9 Nenana River ∽ Alaska, USA
195 W8 Nendö var. Swallow Island. island Santa Cruz Islands, E Solomon Islands
99 O19 Nene ∽ E England, UK
129 R4 Nenetskiy Avtonomnyy Okrug ◆ autonomous district NW Russian Federation
203 W11 Nengonengo atoll Îles Tuamotu, C French Polynesia
169 U6 Nen Jiang var. Nonni. ∽ NE China
169 V6 Nenjiang Heilongjiang, NE China 49.10N 125.18E
201 P16 Neoch atoll Caroline Islands, C Micronesia
117 D18 Neochóri Dytikí Ellás, C Greece 38.23N 21.14E
29 Q7 Neodesha Kansas, C USA 37.25N 95.40W
31 S14 Neola Iowa, C USA 41.27N 95.40W
117 M19 Néon Karlovási var. Néon Karlovásion. Sámos, Dodekánisos, Greece, Aegean Sea 37.48N 26.42E
Néon Karlovásion see Néon Karlovási
117 E16 Néon Monastíri Thessalía, C Greece 39.22N 21.55E
29 R8 Neosho Missouri, C USA 36.52N 94.22W
29 Q7 Neosho River ∽ Kansas/Oklahoma, C USA
127 N17 Nepa ∽ C Russian Federation
159 N10 Nepal off. Kingdom of Nepal. ◆ monarchy S Asia
158 M11 Nepalganj Mid Western, SW Nepal 28.04N 81.37E
12 L13 Nepean Ontario, SE Canada 45.19N 75.53W
38 L4 Nephi Utah, W USA 39.43N 111.49W
99 B16 Nephin Ir. Néifinn. ▲ W Ireland 54.00N 9.21W
69 T9 Nepoko ∽ NE Dem. Rep. Congo
20 K15 Neptune New Jersey, NE USA 40.10N 74.03W
190 G10 Neptune Islands island group South Australia
109 I14 Nera anc. Nar. ∽ C Italy
104 L14 Nérac Lot-et-Garonne, SW France 44.07N 0.21E
113 D16 Neratovice Ger. Neratowitz. Středočeský Kraj, C Czech Republic 50.16N 14.31E
Neratowitz see Neratovice
126 L15 Nercha ∽ S Russian Federation
126 L15 Nerchinsk Chitinskaya Oblast', S Russian Federation 52.01N 116.25E
126 L16 Nerchinskiy Zavod Chitinskaya Oblast', S Russian Federation 51.13N 119.25E
128 M15 Nerekhta Kostromskaya Oblast', NW Russian Federation 57.27N 40.33E
120 H10 Nereta Aizkraukle, S Latvia 56.12N 25.18E
108 K13 Nereto Abruzzo, C Italy 42.49N 13.50E
115 H15 Neretva ∽ Bosnia and Herzegovina/Croatia
117 C17 Nerikós ruins Lefkáda, Iónioi Nísoi, Greece, C Mediterranean Sea 38.48N 20.43E
120 B12 Neringa Ger. Nidden; prev. Nida. Neringa, SW Lithuania 55.19N 21.00E
85 F15 Neriquinha Cuando Cubango, SE Angola 15.44S 21.34E
120 I13 Neris Bel. Viliya, Pol. Wilia; prev. Pol. Wilja. ∽ Belarus/Lithuania
Neris see Viliya
107 N15 Nerja Andalucía, S Spain 36.45N 3.34W
128 L16 Nerl' ∽ W Russian Federation
176 Vv13 Nerong, Selat strait Kepulauan Kai, E Indonesia
107 P12 Nerpio Castilla-La Mancha, C Spain 38.08N 2.18W
106 J13 Nerva Andalucía, S Spain 37.39N 6.31W
126 Ll13 Neryungri Respublika Sakha (Yakutiya), NE Russian Federation 56.37N 124.19E
100 L4 Nes Friesland, N Netherlands 53.28N 5.46E
96 G13 Nesbyen Buskerud, S Norway 60.34N 9.34E
94 L2 Neskaupstadhur Austurland, E Iceland 65.08N 13.45W
94 F13 Nesna Nordland, C Norway 66.11N 12.54E
28 K5 Ness City Kansas, C USA 38.27N 99.54W
Nesselsdorf see Kopřivnice
110 H7 Nesslau Sankt Gallen, NE Switzerland 47.13N 9.12E
98 I9 Ness, Loch ◎ N Scotland, UK
Nesterov see Zhovkva
116 I12 Néstos Bul. Mesta, Turk. Kara Su. ∽ Bulgaria/Greece see also Mesta
97 C14 Nesttun Hordaland, S Norway 60.19N 5.16E
Nesvizh see Nyasvizh
144 F9 Netanya var. Natanya, Nathanya. Central, C Israel 32.19N 34.51E
100 I9 Netherlands off. Kingdom of the Netherlands, var. Holland, Dut. Koninkrijk der Nederlanden, Nederland. ◆ monarchy NW Europe
47 S9 Netherlands Antilles prev. Dutch West Indies. ◇ Dutch autonomous region S Caribbean Sea
Netherlands East Indies see Indonesia
Netherlands Guiana see Suriname
Netherlands New Guinea see Papua
118 L4 Netishyn Khmel'nyts'ka Oblast', W Ukraine 50.20N 26.38E
144 E11 Netivot Southern, S Israel 31.25N 34.36E
109 O21 Neto ∽ S Italy
16 N2 Nettilling Lake ◎ Baffin Island, Nunavut, N Canada
31 V3 Nett Lake ◎ Minnesota, N USA
109 I16 Nettuno Lazio, C Italy 41.26N 12.40E
Netum see Noto
43 U16 Netzahualcóyotl, Presa ⊠ SE Mexico
Netze see Noteć
Neu Amerika see Puławy
Neubetsche see Novi Bečej
Neubidschow see Nový Bydžov
Neubistritz see Nová Bystřice
102 N9 Neubrandenburg Mecklenburg-Vorpommern, NE Germany 53.33N 13.16E
103 K22 Neuburg an der Donau Bayern, S Germany 48.43N 11.10E
110 C8 Neuchâtel Ger. Neuenburg. Neuchâtel, W Switzerland 46.58N 6.55E
110 C8 Neuchâtel Ger. Neuenburg. ◆ canton W Switzerland
110 C8 Neuchâtel, Lac de Ger. Neuenburger See. ◎ W Switzerland
Neudorf see Spišská Nová Ves
102 L10 Neue Elde canal N Germany
Neuenburg see Neuchâtel
Neuenburg an der Elbe see Nymburk
Neuenburger See see Neuchâtel, Lac de
110 F7 Neuenhof Aargau, N Switzerland 47.27N 8.17E
102 H11 Neuenland ✕ (Bremen) Bremen, NW Germany 53.03N 8.46E
Neuenstadt see La Neuveville
103 C18 Neuerburg Rheinland-Pfalz, W Germany 50.01N 6.13E
101 K24 Neufchâteau Luxembourg, SE Belgium 49.49N 5.25E
105 S6 Neufchâteau Vosges, NE France 48.21N 5.42E
104 M3 Neufchâtel-en-Bray Seine-Maritime, N France 49.44N 1.26E
111 S3 Neufelden Oberösterreich, N Austria 48.27N 14.01E
Neugradisk see Nova Gradiška
Neuhaus see Jindřichův Hradec
Neuhäusel see Nové Zámky
110 G6 Neuhausen var. Neuhausen am Rheinfall. Schaffhausen, N Switzerland 47.24N 8.37E
Neuhausen am Rheinfall see Neuhausen
103 I17 Neuhof Hessen, C Germany 50.26N 9.34E
Neuhof see Zgierz
Neukuhren see Pionerskiy
Neu-Langenburg see Tukuyu
111 W4 Neulengbach Niederösterreich, NE Austria 48.10N 15.53E
115 G15 Neum Federacija Bosna I Hercegovina, S Bosnia and Herzegovina 42.57N 17.33E
Neumark see Nowy Targ, Nowy Sącz, Poland
Neumark see Nowe Miasto Lubawskie, Toruń, Poland
Neumarkt see Neumarkt im Hausruckkreis, Oberösterreich, Austria
Neumarkt see Neumarkt Am Wallersee, Salzburg, Austria
Neumarkt see Środa Śląska, Wrocław, Poland
Neumarkt see Târgu Secuiesc, Covasna, Romania
Neumarkt see Târgu Mureş, Mureş, Romania
111 Q5 Neumarkt am Wallersee var. Neumarkt. Salzburg, NW Austria 47.55N 13.16E
111 R4 Neumarkt im Hausruckkreis var. Neumarkt. Oberösterreich, N Austria 48.16N 13.40E
103 L20 Neumarkt in der Oberpfalz Bayern, SE Germany 49.16N 11.28E
Neumarktl see Tržič
Neumoldowa see Moldova Nouă
102 J8 Neumünster Schleswig-Holstein, N Germany 54.04N 9.58E
111 X5 Neunkirchen var. Neunkirchen am Steinfeld. Niederösterreich, E Austria 47.43N 16.04E
103 E20 Neunkirchen Saarland, SW Germany 49.21N 7.10E
Neunkirchen am Steinfeld see Neunkirchen
Neuoderberg see Bohumín
65 I15 Neuquén Neuquén, SE Argentina 39.03S 68.36W
65 H14 Neuquén off. Provincia de Neuquén. ◆ province W Argentina
65 H14 Neuquén, Río ∽ W Argentina
Neurode see Nowa Ruda
102 N11 Neuruppin Brandenburg, NE Germany 52.55N 12.49E
Neusalz an der Oder see Nowa Sól
Neu Sandec/Neusandez see Małopolskie
103 K22 Neusäss Bayern, S Germany 48.24N 10.49E
Neusatz see Novi Sad
Neuschliss see Gherla
23 N8 Neuse River ∽ North Carolina, SE USA
111 Z5 Neusiedl am See Burgenland, E Austria 47.56N 16.51E
113 G22 Neusiedler See Hung. Fertő. ◎ Austria/Hungary
Neusohl see Banská Bystrica
103 D15 Neuss anc. Novaesium, Novesium. Nordrhein-Westfalen, W Germany 51.12N 6.40E
Neuss see Nyon
Neustadt see Neustadt an der Aisch, Bayern, Germany
Neustadt see Neustadt bei Coburg, Bayern, Germany
Neustadt see Prudnik, Opole, Poland
Neustadt see Baia Mare, Maramureş, Romania
102 I12 Neustadt am Rübenberge Niedersachsen, N Germany 52.30N 9.28E
103 J19 Neustadt an der Aisch var. Neustadt. Bayern, C Germany 49.34N 10.36E
Neustadt an der Haardt see Neustadt an der Weinstrasse
103 F20 Neustadt an der Weinstrasse prev. Neustadt an der Haardt, hist. Niewenstat, anc. Nova Civitas. Rheinland-Pfalz, SW Germany 49.21N 8.09E
103 K18 Neustadt bei Coburg var. Neustadt. Bayern, C Germany 50.19N 11.06E
Neustadt bei Pinne see Lwówek
Neustadt in Oberschlesien see Prudnik
Neustadtl see Novo mesto
Neustadtl in Mähren see Nové Město na Moravě
Neustettin see Szczecinek
110 M8 Neustift im Stubaital var. Stubaital. Tirol, W Austria 47.07N 11.26E
102 N10 Neustrelitz Mecklenburg-Vorpommern, NE Germany 53.22N 13.04E
Neutitschein see Nový Jičín
Neutra see Nitra
103 J22 Neu-Ulm Bayern, S Germany 48.23N 10.01E
Neuveville see La Neuveville
105 N12 Neuvic Corrèze, C France 45.23N 2.16E
Neuwarp see Nowe Warpno
102 G9 Neuwerk island NW Germany
103 E17 Neuwied Rheinland-Pfalz, W Germany 50.25N 7.28E
Neuzen see Terneuzen
128 H12 Neva ∽ NW Russian Federation
31 V14 Nevada Iowa, C USA 42.01N 93.27W
29 R6 Nevada Missouri, C USA 37.50N 94.21W
37 R5 Nevada off. State of Nevada; also known as Battle Born State, Sagebrush State, Silver State. ◆ state W USA
37 P6 Nevada City California, W USA 39.15N 121.02W
128 G16 Nevel' Pskovskaya Oblast', W Russian Federation 56.01N 29.54E
127 Oo16 Nevel'sk Ostrov Sakhalin, Sakhalinskaya Oblast', SE Russian Federation 46.41N 141.54E
126 Ll14 Never Amurskaya Oblast', SE Russian Federation 53.58N 124.04E
131 Q6 Neverkino Penzenskaya Oblast', W Russian Federation 52.53N 46.46E
105 P9 Nevers anc. Noviodunum. Nièvre, C France 47.00N 3.09E
20 J12 Neversink River ∽ New York, NE USA
191 Q6 Nevertire New South Wales, SE Australia 31.52S 147.42E
115 H15 Nevesinje Republika Srpska, S Bosnia and Herzegovina 43.15N 18.09E
120 G12 Nevežis ∽ C Lithuania
130 M14 Nevinnomyssk Stavropol'skiy Kray, SW Russian Federation 44.39N 41.57E
47 W10 Nevis island Saint Kitts and Nevis
Nevoso, Monte see Veliki Snežnik
Nevrokop see Gotse Delchev
142 J14 Nevşehir var. Nevshehr. Nevşehir, C Turkey 38.37N 34.43E
142 J14 Nevşehir var. Nevshehr. ◆ province C Turkey
Nevshehr see Nevşehir
125 Ee11 Nev'yansk Sverdlovskaya Oblast', C Russian Federation 57.26N 60.15E
83 J25 Newala Mtwara, SE Tanzania 10.58S 39.18E
33 P16 New Albany Indiana, N USA 38.16N 85.49W
24 M2 New Albany Mississippi, S USA 34.29N 89.00W
31 Y11 New Albin Iowa, C USA 43.30N 91.17W
57 U8 New Amsterdam E Guyana 6.17N 57.30W
191 Q4 New Angledool New South Wales, SE Australia 29.06S 147.54E
23 Y2 Newark Delaware, NE USA 39.40N 75.45W
20 K14 Newark New Jersey, NE USA 40.42N 74.12W
20 G10 Newark New York, NE USA 43.01N 77.04W
33 T13 Newark Ohio, N USA 40.03N 82.24W
Newark see Newark-on-Trent
37 W5 Newark Lake ◎ Nevada, W USA
99 N18 Newark-on-Trent var. Newark. C England, UK 53.04N 0.49W
24 M7 New Augusta Mississippi, S USA 31.12N 89.03W
21 P12 New Bedford Massachusetts, NE USA 41.37N 70.55W
34 G11 Newberg Oregon, NW USA 45.18N 122.58W
23 X10 New Bern North Carolina, SE USA 35.07N 77.03W
22 F8 Newbern Tennessee, S USA 36.06N 89.15W
33 P4 Newberry Michigan, N USA 46.21N 85.30W
23 Q12 Newberry South Carolina, SE USA 34.16N 81.37W
20 F15 New Bloomfield Pennsylvania, NE USA 40.24N 77.08W
27 X5 New Boston Texas, SW USA 33.27N 94.25W
27 S11 New Braunfels Texas, SW USA 29.43N 98.09W
33 Q13 New Bremen Ohio, N USA 40.26N 84.22W
99 F18 Newbridge Ir. An Droichead Nua. C Ireland 53.10N 6.48W
20 B14 New Brighton Pennsylvania, NE USA 40.44N 80.18W
20 M12 New Britain Connecticut, NE USA 41.37N 72.45W
195 N13 New Britain island E PNG
199 Hh9 New Britain Trench undersea feature W Pacific Ocean
20 J15 New Brunswick New Jersey, NE USA 40.29N 74.27W
13 V8 New Brunswick Fr. Nouveau-Brunswick. ◆ province SE Canada
20 K13 Newburgh New York, NE USA 41.30N 74.00W
99 M22 Newbury S England, UK 51.25N 1.19W
21 P10 Newburyport Massachusetts, NE USA 42.49N 70.53W
79 T14 New Bussa Niger, W Nigeria 9.50N 4.32E
197 J4 New Caledonia var. Kanaky, Fr. Nouvelle-Calédonie. ◇ French overseas territory SW Pacific Ocean
197 H5 New Caledonia island SW Pacific Ocean
183 O10 New Caledonia Basin undersea feature W Pacific Ocean
191 T8 Newcastle New South Wales, SE Australia 32.55S 151.46E
11 O14 Newcastle New Brunswick, SE Canada 47.01N 65.36W
12 I15 Newcastle Ontario, SE Canada 43.55N 78.35W
99 C20 Newcastle Ir. An Caisleán Nua. SW Ireland 52.25N 9.04W
85 K22 Newcastle KwaZulu/Natal, E South Africa 27.45S 29.59E
99 G16 Newcastle Ir. An Caisleán Nua. SE Northern Ireland, UK 54.12N 5.54W
33 P13 New Castle Indiana, N USA 39.55N 85.21W
22 L5 New Castle Kentucky, S USA 38.22N 85.09W
29 N11 Newcastle Oklahoma, C USA 35.15N 97.36W
20 B13 New Castle Pennsylvania, NE USA 40.59N 80.19W
27 R6 Newcastle Texas, SW USA 33.11N 98.44W
38 J7 Newcastle Utah, W USA 37.40N 113.31W
23 S6 New Castle Virginia, NE USA 37.29N 80.06W
35 Z13 Newcastle Wyoming, C USA 43.52N 104.13W
47 W10 Newcastle ✕ Nevis, Saint Kitts and Nevis 17.08N 62.36W
99 L14 Newcastle ✕ NE England, UK 55.03N 1.42W
Newcastle see Newcastle upon Tyne
99 L18 Newcastle-under-Lyme C England, UK 53.00N 2.14W
99 M14 Newcastle upon Tyne var. Newcastle; hist. Monkchester, Lat. Pons Aelii. NE England, UK 54.58N 1.34W
189 Q4 Newcastle Waters Northern Territory, N Australia 17.20S 133.26E
Newchwang see Yingkou
20 K13 New City New York, NE USA 41.08N 73.57W
33 U13 Newcomerstown Ohio, N USA 40.16N 81.36W
20 G15 New Cumberland Pennsylvania, NE USA 40.13N 76.52W
23 R1 New Cumberland West Virginia, NE USA 40.30N 80.35W
158 I10 New Delhi ● (India) Delhi, N India 28.34N 77.14E
9 O17 New Denver British Columbia, SW Canada 49.58N 117.21W
30 J9 Newell South Dakota, N USA 44.42N 103.25W
23 Q13 New Ellenton South Carolina, SE USA 33.25N 81.41W
24 J6 Newellton Louisiana, S USA 32.04N 91.14W
30 K6 New England North Dakota, N USA 46.32N 102.52W
21 P8 New England cultural region NE USA
New England of the West see Minnesota
191 U5 New England Range ▲ New South Wales, SE Australia
66 G9 New England Seamounts var. Bermuda-New England Seamount Arc. undersea feature W Atlantic Ocean
40 M14 Newenham, Cape headland Alaska, USA 58.39N 162.10W
144 F11 Newé Zohar Southern, E Israel 31.07N 35.23E
20 D9 Newfane New York, NE USA 43.16N 78.40W
99 M23 New Forest physical region S England, UK
16 S8 Newfoundland Fr. Terre-Neuve. island Newfoundland and Labrador, SE Canada
11 R9 Newfoundland and Labrador Fr. Terre Neuve. ◆ province E Canada
67 J8 Newfoundland Basin undersea feature NW Atlantic Ocean
66 I8 Newfoundland Ridge undersea feature NW Atlantic Ocean
66 J8 Newfoundland Seamounts undersea feature N Sargasso Sea
20 G16 New Freedom Pennsylvania, NE USA 39.43N 76.41W
195 U14 New Georgia island New Georgia Islands, NW Solomon Islands
195 T15 New Georgia Islands island group NW Solomon Islands
195 U14 New Georgia Sound var. The Slot. sound E Solomon Sea
32 L9 New Glarus Wisconsin, N USA 42.50N 89.38W
11 Q15 New Glasgow Nova Scotia, SE Canada 45.36N 62.37W
New Goa see Panaji
194 D11 New Guinea Dut. Nieuw Guinea, Ind. Irian. island Indonesia/PNG
199 H9 New Guinea Trench undersea feature SW Pacific Ocean
34 I6 Newhalem Washington, NW USA 48.40N 121.18W
41 P13 Newhalen Alaska, USA 59.43N 154.54W
31 X13 Newhall Iowa, C USA 42.00N 91.58W
12 F16 New Hamburg Ontario, S Canada 43.24N 80.37W
21 N9 New Hampshire off. State of New Hampshire; also known as The Granite State. ◆ state NE USA
31 W12 New Hampton Iowa, C USA 43.03N 92.19W
195 N9 New Hanover island NE PNG
20 M13 New Haven Connecticut, NE USA 41.18N 72.55W
33 Q12 New Haven Indiana, N USA 41.02N 84.59W
29 W5 New Haven Missouri, C USA 38.34N 91.15W
99 P23 Newhaven SE England, UK 50.48N 0.00W
8 K13 New Hazelton British Columbia, SW Canada 55.15N 127.30W
New Hebrides see Vanuatu
183 P9 New Hebrides Trench undersea feature N Coral Sea
20 H15 New Holland Pennsylvania, NE USA 40.06N 76.05W
24 I9 New Iberia Louisiana, S USA 30.00N 91.51W
195 N10 New Ireland ◆ province NE PNG
195 P10 New Ireland island NE PNG
67 A24 New Island island W Falkland Islands
20 J15 New Jersey off. State of New Jersey; also known as The Garden State. ◆ state NE USA
20 C14 New Kensington Pennsylvania, NE USA 40.33N 79.45W
23 W6 New Kent Virginia, NE USA 37.31N 76.58W
29 O8 Newkirk Oklahoma, C USA 36.52N 97.03W
23 Q9 Newland North Carolina, SE USA 36.04N 81.50W
30 L6 New Leipzig North Dakota, N USA 46.21N 101.54W
12 H9 New Liskeard Ontario, S Canada 47.31N 79.40W
24 G7 Newllano Louisiana, S USA 31.06N 93.16W
21 N13 New London Connecticut, NE USA 41.21N 72.04W
31 Y15 New London Iowa, C USA 40.55N 91.24W
31 T8 New London Minnesota, N USA 45.18N 94.56W
29 V3 New London Missouri, C USA 39.35N 91.24W
32 M7 New London Wisconsin, N USA 44.25N 88.44W
29 Y8 New Madrid Missouri, C USA 36.35N 89.31W
188 J8 Newman Western Australia 23.18S 119.45E
204 M13 Newman Island island Antarctica
12 H15 Newmarket Ontario, S Canada 44.03N 79.26W
99 P20 Newmarket E England, UK 52.17N 0.28E
21 P10 Newmarket New Hampshire, NE USA 43.04N 70.53W
23 U4 New Market Virginia, NE USA 38.39N 78.40W
23 R2 New Martinsville West Virginia, NE USA 39.37N 80.48W
33 U14 New Matamoras Ohio, N USA 39.32N 81.04W
34 M12 New Meadows Idaho, NW USA 44.57N 116.16W
28 R12 New Mexico off. State of New Mexico; also known as Land of Enchantment, Sunshine State. ◆ state SW USA
155 V6 New Mirpur var. Mīrpur. Sind, SE Pakistan 33.09N 73.42E
157 T17 New Moore Island island E India
25 S4 Newnan Georgia, SE USA 33.22N 84.48W
191 P17 New Norfolk Tasmania, SE Australia 42.46S 147.01E
24 K9 New Orleans Louisiana, S USA 30.00N 90.00W
24 K9 New Orleans ✕ Louisiana, S USA 29.59N 90.17W
20 K12 New Paltz New York, NE USA 41.44N 74.04W
33 U12 New Philadelphia Ohio, N USA 40.29N 81.27W
192 K10 New Plymouth Taranaki, North Island, NZ 39.04S 174.06E
99 M24 Newport S England, UK 50.42N 1.18W
99 K22 Newport SE Wales, UK 51.35N 3.00W
29 W10 Newport Arkansas, C USA 35.36N 91.16W
33 N13 Newport Indiana, N USA 39.52N 87.24W
22 M3 Newport Kentucky, S USA 39.05N 84.30W
31 W9 Newport Minnesota, N USA 44.52N 93.00W
34 F12 Newport Oregon, NW USA 44.38N 124.03W
21 O13 Newport Rhode Island, NE USA 41.29N 71.17W
23 O9 Newport Tennessee, S USA 35.58N 83.11W
21 N6 Newport Vermont, NE USA 44.55N 72.13W
34 M7 Newport Washington, NW USA 48.08N 117.05W
23 X7 Newport News Virginia, NE USA 36.58N 76.25W
99 N20 Newport Pagnell SE England, UK 52.04N 0.43W
25 U12 New Port Richey Florida, SE USA 28.14N 82.42W
31 V9 New Prague Minnesota, N USA 44.32N 93.34W
46 H3 New Providence island N Bahamas
99 H24 Newquay SW England, UK 50.27N 5.03W
99 I20 New Quay SW Wales, UK 52.13N 4.22W
31 V10 New Richland Minnesota, N USA 43.53N 93.29W
13 X7 New-Richmond Quebec, SE Canada 48.10N 65.54W
33 R15 New Richmond Ohio, N USA 38.57N 84.16W
32 I5 New Richmond Wisconsin, N USA 45.09N 92.31W
44 G1 New River ∽ N Belize

◆ Country ● Country Capital ◇ Dependent Territory ○ Dependent Territory Capital ◆ Administrative Region ✕ International Airport ▲ Mountain ▲ Mountain Range ⚠ Volcano ∽ River ◎ Lake ⊠ Reservoir

57 T12 **New River** SE Guyana
23 R6 **New River** West Virginia, NE USA
44 G1 **New River Lagoon** ◎ N Belize
24 J8 **New Roads** Louisiana, S USA *30.42N 91.26W*
20 L14 **New Rochelle** New York, NE USA *40.55N 73.44W*
31 O4 **New Rockford** North Dakota, N USA *47.40N 99.08W*
99 P23 **New Romney** SE England, UK *50.58N 0.57E*
99 F20 **New Ross** *Ir.* Ros Mhic Thriúin. SE Ireland *52.24N 6.55W*
99 F16 **Newry** *Ir.* An tIúr. SE Northern Ireland, UK *54.10N 6.19W*
30 M5 **New Salem** North Dakota, N USA *46.51N 101.24W*
New Sarum *see* Salisbury
31 W14 **New Sharon** Iowa, C USA *41.28N 92.39W*
New Siberian Islands *see* Novosibirskiye Ostrova
25 X11 **New Smyrna Beach** Florida, SE USA *29.01N 80.55W*
191 O7 **New South Wales** ◈ *state* SE Australia
41 O13 **New Stuyahok** Alaska, USA *59.27N 95.18W*
23 N8 **New Tazewell** Tennessee, S USA *36.26N 83.36W*
40 M12 **Newtok** Alaska, USA *60.56N 164.37W*
25 S7 **Newton** Georgia, SE USA *31.18N 84.20W*
31 W14 **Newton** Iowa, C USA *41.42N 93.03W*
29 N6 **Newton** Kansas, C USA *38.03N 97.20W*
21 O11 **Newton** Massachusetts, NE USA *42.19N 71.10W*
24 M5 **Newton** Mississippi, S USA *32.19N 89.09W*
20 J14 **Newton** New Jersey, NE USA *41.03N 74.45W*
23 R9 **Newton** North Carolina, SE USA *35.40N 81.13W*
27 Y9 **Newton** Texas, SW USA *30.51N 93.45W*
99 J24 **Newton Abbot** SW England, UK *50.33N 3.34W*
98 K13 **Newton St Boswells** SE Scotland, UK *55.34N 2.40W*
99 I14 **Newton Stewart** S Scotland, UK *54.58N 4.30W*
94 O2 **Newtontoppen** ▲ C Svalbard *78.57N 17.34E*
30 K3 **New Town** North Dakota, N USA *47.58N 102.30W*
99 J20 **Newtown** E Wales, UK *52.31N 3.19W*
99 G15 **Newtownabbey** *Ir.* Baile na Mainistreach. E Northern Ireland, UK *54.40N 5.57W*
99 G15 **Newtownards** *Ir.* Baile Nua na hArda. SE Northern Ireland, UK *54.36N 5.40W*
31 U10 **New Ulm** Minnesota, N USA *44.20N 94.28W*
30 K10 **New Underwood** South Dakota, N USA *44.05N 102.46W*
27 V10 **New Waverly** Texas, SW USA *30.32N 95.28W*
20 K14 **New York** New York, NE USA *40.44N 73.57W*
20 G10 **New York** ◈ *state* NE USA
37 X13 **New York Mountains** ▲▲ California, W USA
192 K12 **New Zealand** *abbrev.* NZ. ◆ *commonwealth republic* SW Pacific Ocean
97 M24 **Nexø** *var.* Neksø Bornholm, E Denmark *55.04N 15.05E*
129 O15 **Neya** Kostromskaya Oblast', NW Russian Federation *58.19N 43.51E*
Neyba *see* Neiba
149 Q12 **Neyrīz** *var.* Neiriz, Niriz. Fārs, S Iran *29.13N 54.18E*
149 T4 **Neyshābūr** *var.* Nishapur. Khorāsān, NE Iran *36.14N 58.46E*
161 J21 **Neyveli** Tamil Nādu, SE India *11.36N 79.25E*
Nezhin *see* Nizhyn
35 N10 **Nezperce** Idaho, NW USA *46.14N 116.15W*
24 H8 **Nezpique, Bayou** Louisiana, S USA
176 W14 **Ngabordamlu, Tanjung** *headland* Pulau Trangan, SE Indonesia *6.58S 134.13E*
79 Y13 **Ngadda** NE Nigeria
N'Gage *see* Negage
193 G16 **Ngahere** West Coast, South Island, NZ *42.22S 171.29E*
79 Z12 **Ngala** Borno, NE Nigeria *12.19N 14.11E*
85 G17 **Ngamiland** ◈ *district* N Botswana
164 K16 **Ngamring** Xizang Zizhiqu, W China *29.16N 87.10E*
83 K19 **Ngangerabeli Plain** *plain* SE Kenya
164 I14 **Ngangla Ringco** ◎ W China
164 G13 **Nganglong Kangri** ▲ W China *32.55N 81.00E*
164 K15 **Ngangzê Co** ◎ W China
81 F14 **Ngaoundéré** *var.* N'Gaoundéré. Adamaoua, N Cameroon *7.19N 13.34E*
83 E20 **Ngara** Kagera, NW Tanzania *2.30S 30.40E*
196 F8 **Ngardmau Bay** *bay* Babeldaob, N Palau
196 F7 **Ngaregur** *island* Palau Islands, N Palau
192 L7 **Ngaruawahia** Waikato, North Island, NZ *37.41S 175.09E*
192 N11 **Ngaruroro** North Island, NZ
202 I16 **Ngatangiia** Rarotonga, S Cook Islands *21.13S 159.43W*
192 M6 **Ngatea** Waikato, North Island, NZ *37.16S 175.29E*
177 F8 **Ngathainggyaung** Irrawaddy, SW Myanmar *17.22N 95.04E*
Ngatik *see* Ngetik Atoll
Ngau *see* Gau
174 Ll15 **Ngawi** Jawa, S Indonesia *7.22S 111.22E*
196 C7 **Ngcheangel** *var.* Kayangel Islands. *island* Palau Islands, N Palau
196 E10 **Ngchemiangel** Babeldaob, N Palau
196 C8 **Ngeaur** *var.* Angaur. *island* Palau Islands, S Palau
196 E10 **Ngerkeai** Babeldaob, N Palau
196 F9 **Ngermechau** Babeldaob, N Palau *7.34N 134.39E*
196 C8 **Ngeruktabel** *prev.* Urukthapel. *island* Palau Islands, S Palau
196 F8 **Ngetbong** Babeldaob, N Palau *7.37N 134.34E*
201 T17 **Ngetik Atoll** *var.* Ngatik; *prev.* Los Jardines. *atoll* Caroline Islands, E Micronesia
196 E10 **Ngetkip** Babeldaob, N Palau
Nggamea *see* Qamea
195 V15 **Nggatokae** *island* New Georgia Islands, NW Solomon Islands
85 C16 **N'Giva** *var.* Ondjiva, *Port.* Vila Pereira de Eça. Cunene, S Angola *17.01S 15.41E*
81 G20 **Ngo** Plateaux, SE Congo *2.28S 15.43E*
178 Jj7 **Ngoc Lac** Thanh Hoa, N Vietnam *20.06N 105.21E*
81 G17 **Ngoko** Cameroon/Congo
176 W14 **Ngoni, Tanjung** *headland* Maluku, Kepulauan Aru, SE Indonesia *6.10S 134.04E*
83 H19 **Ngorengore** Rift Valley, SW Kenya *1.01S 35.26E*
165 Q11 **Ngoring Hu** ◎ C China
Ngorolaka *see* Banifing
83 H20 **Ngorongoro Crater** *crater* N Tanzania *3.10S 35.34E*
81 D19 **Ngounié** *off.* Province de la Ngounié, *var.* La Ngounié. ◈ *province* S Gabon
81 D19 **Ngounié** Congo/Gabon
80 H10 **Ngoura** *var.* NGoura. Chari-Baguirmi, W Chad *12.52N 16.27E*
80 G10 **Ngouri** *var.* NGouri; *prev.* Fort-Millot. Lac, W Chad *13.40N 15.24E*
79 Y10 **Ngourti** Diffa, E Niger *15.22N 13.13E*
79 Y11 **Nguigmi** *var.* N'Guigmi. Diffa, SE Niger *14.16N 13.07E*
Nguimbo *see* Lumbala N'Guimbo
196 F15 **Ngulu Atoll** *atoll* Caroline Islands, W Micronesia
197 C14 **Nguna** *island* C Vanuatu
N'Gunza *see* Sumbe
175 N16 **Ngurah Rai** ✕ (Bali) Bali, S Indonesia
79 W12 **Nguru** Yobe, NE Nigeria *12.55N 10.30E*
Ngwaketze *see* Southern
85 I16 **Ngweze** S Zambia
85 M17 **Nhamatanda** Sofala, C Mozambique *19.16S 34.10E*
60 G12 **Nhamundá, Rio** *var.* Jamundá, Yamundá. N Brazil
62 J7 **Nhandeara** São Paulo, S Brazil *20.40S 50.03W*
N'Harea *see* Nharêa
84 D12 **Nharêa** *var.* N'Harea, Nhareia. Bié, W Angola *11.28S 16.57E*
Nhareia *see* Nharêa
178 Kk13 **Nha Trang** Khanh Hoa, S Vietnam *12.15N 109.10E*
190 L11 **Nhill** Victoria, SE Australia *36.21S 141.38E*
85 L22 **Nhlangano** *prev.* Goedgegun. SW Swaziland *27.01S 31.11E*
189 S1 **Nhulunbuy** Northern Territory, N Australia *12.15S 136.46E*
79 N10 **Niafounké** Tombouctou, W Mali *15.54N 3.58W*
33 N5 **Niagara** Wisconsin, N USA *45.45N 87.57W*
12 H16 **Niagara** Ontario, S Canada
12 G15 **Niagara Escarpment** *hill range* Ontario, S Canada
12 H16 **Niagara Falls** Ontario, S Canada *43.04N 79.06W*
20 D9 **Niagara Falls** New York, NE USA *43.06N 79.04W*
16 Pp17 **Niagara Falls** *waterfall* Canada/USA *43.04N 79.04W*
78 K12 **Niagassola** *var.* Nyagassola. Haute-Guinée, NE Guinea *12.22N 9.07W*
79 R12 **Niamey** ● (Niger) Niamey, SW Niger *13.28N 2.03E*
79 R12 **Niamey** ✕ Niamey, SW Niger *13.28N 2.14E*
79 R14 **Niamtougou** N Togo *9.49N 1.07E*
81 O16 **Niangara** Orientale, NE Dem. Rep. Congo *3.45N 27.54E*
79 O10 **Niangay, Lac** ◎ E Mali
79 N14 **Niangoloko** SW Burkina *10.15N 4.53W*
29 U6 **Niangua River** Missouri, C USA
81 O17 **Nia-Nia** Orientale, NE Dem. Rep. Congo *1.26N 27.38E*
21 N13 **Niantic** Connecticut, NE USA *41.19N 72.11W*
169 U7 **Nianzishan** Heilongjiang, NE China *47.31N 122.52E*
173 F7 **Nias, Pulau** *island* W Indonesia
84 O13 **Niassa** *off.* Província do Niassa. ◈ *province* N Mozambique
203 U10 **Niau** *island* Îles Tuamotu, C French Polynesia
97 G20 **Nibe** Nordjylland, N Denmark *56.58N 9.39E*
201 Q8 **Nibok** N Nauru *0.31S 166.55E*
120 C10 **Nīca** Liepāja, W Latvia *56.21N 21.03E*
Nicaea *see* Nice
44 J9 **Nicaragua** *off.* Republic of Nicaragua. ◆ *republic* Central America
44 K11 **Nicaragua, Lago de** *var.* Cocibolca, Gran Lago, *Eng.* Lake Nicaragua. ◎ S Nicaragua
Nicaragua, Lake *see* Nicaragua, Lago de
66 D11 **Nicaraguan Rise** *undersea feature* NW Caribbean Sea
Nicaria *see* Ikaría
109 N21 **Nicastro** Calabria, SW Italy *38.58N 16.19E*
105 V15 **Nice** *It.* Nizza; *anc.* Nicaea. Alpes-Maritimes, SE France *43.43N 7.13E*
Nice *see* Côte d'Azur
Nicephorium *see* Ar Raqqah
10 M9 **Nichicun, Lac** ◎ Quebec, E Canada
170 C17 **Nichinan** *var.* Nitinan. Miyazaki, Kyūshū, SW Japan *31.36N 131.22E*
46 E4 **Nicholas Channel** *channel* N Cuba
Nicholas II Land *see* Severnaya Zemlya
155 U2 **Nicholas Range** *Pash.* Selseleh-ye Kūh-e Vākhān, *Taj.* Qatorkŭhi Vakhon. ▲▲ Afghanistan/Tajikistan
22 M6 **Nicholasville** Kentucky, S USA *37.52N 84.34W*
46 G2 **Nicholls Town** Andros Island, NW Bahamas *25.07N 78.01W*
23 U12 **Nichols** South Carolina, SE USA *34.13N 79.09W*
57 U9 **Nickerie** ◈ *district* NW Suriname
57 V9 **Nickerie Rivier** NW Suriname
157 P22 **Nicobar Islands** *island group* India, E Indian Ocean
118 L9 **Nicolae Bălcescu** Botoşani, NE Romania *47.33N 26.52E*
13 P11 **Nicolet** Quebec, SE Canada *46.13N 72.37W*
13 Q12 **Nicolet** Quebec, SE Canada
33 Q4 **Nicolet, Lake** ◎ Michigan, N USA
31 U10 **Nicollet** Minnesota, N USA *44.16N 94.11W*
63 F19 **Nico Pérez** Florida, S Uruguay *33.30S 55.10W*
Nicopolis *see* Nikopol, Bulgaria
Nicopolis *see* Nikópoli, Greece
124 R12 **Nicosia** *Gk.* Lefkosía, *Turk.* Lefkoşa. ● (Cyprus) C Cyprus *35.10N 33.22E*
109 K24 **Nicosia** Sicilia, Italy, C Mediterranean Sea *37.45N 14.24E*
109 N22 **Nicotera** Calabria, SW Italy *38.33N 15.55E*
44 K13 **Nicoya** Guanacaste, W Costa Rica *10.06N 85.26W*
44 L14 **Nicoya, Golfo de** *gulf* W Costa Rica
44 L14 **Nicoya, Península de** *peninsula* NW Costa Rica
Nictheroy *see* Niterói
113 L15 **Nida** S Poland
Nida *see* Neringa
Nidaros *see* Trondheim
110 D8 **Nidau** Bern, W Switzerland *47.07N 7.15E*
103 H17 **Nidda** W Germany
Nidden *see* Neringa
97 F17 **Nidelva** S Norway
126 J10 **Nidym** Evenkiyskiy Avtonomnyy Okrug, N Russian Federation *64.08N 99.52E*
112 L9 **Nidzica** *Ger.* Niedenburg. Warmińsko-Mazurskie, NE Poland, *53.22N 20.27E*
102 H6 **Niebüll** Schleswig-Holstein, N Germany *54.47N 8.51E*
Niedenburg *see* Nidzica
101 N25 **Niederanven** Luxembourg, C Luxembourg *49.39N 6.15E*
105 V4 **Niederbronn-les-Bains** Bas-Rhin, NE France *48.57N 7.37E*
Niederdonau *see* Niederösterreich
111 S7 **Niedere Tauern** ▲▲ C Austria
103 P14 **Niederlausitz** *Eng.* Lower Lusatia. *physical region* E Germany
111 U5 **Niederösterreich** *off.* Land Niederösterreich, *Eng.* Lower Austria, *Ger.* Niederdonau; *prev.* Lower Danube. ◈ *state* NE Austria
102 G12 **Niedersachsen** *Eng.* Lower Saxony, *Fr.* Basse-Saxe. ◈ *state* NW Germany
81 D17 **Niefang** *var.* Sevilla de Niefang. NW Equatorial Guinea *1.52N 10.12E*
85 G23 **Niekerkshoop** Northern Cape, W South Africa *29.21S 22.49E*
101 G17 **Niel** Antwerpen, N Belgium *51.07N 4.19E*
Niélé *see* Niellé
78 M14 **Niellé** *var.* Niélé. N Ivory Coast *10.12N 5.37W*
81 O22 **Niemba** Katanga, E Dem. Rep. Congo *5.58S 28.24E*
113 G15 **Niemcza** *Ger.* Nimptsch. Dolnośląskie, SW Poland *50.45N 16.52E*
Niemen *see* Neman
94 J13 **Niemisel** Norrbotten, N Sweden *66.00N 22.00E*
113 H15 **Niemodlin** *Ger.* Falkenberg. Opolskie, S Poland *50.37N 17.45E*
78 M13 **Niéna** Sikasso, SW Mali *11.24N 6.20W*
102 H12 **Nienburg** Niedersachsen, N Germany *52.37N 9.12E*
102 N13 **Nieplitz** NE Germany
113 L16 **Niepołomice** Małopolskie, S Poland *50.02N 20.12E*
103 D14 **Niers** Germany/Netherlands
103 Q15 **Niesky** *Lus.* Niska. Sachsen, E Germany *51.16N 14.49E*
Nieśwież *see* Nyasvizh
Nieuport *see* Nieuwpoort
100 O8 **Nieuw-Amsterdam** Drenthe, NE Netherlands *52.43N 6.52E*
57 W9 **Nieuw Amsterdam** Commewijne, NE Suriname *5.52N 55.04W*
101 M14 **Nieuw-Bergen** Limburg, SE Netherlands *51.36N 6.04E*
100 O7 **Nieuw-Buinen** Drenthe, NE Netherlands *52.57N 6.55E*
100 J12 **Nieuwegein** Utrecht, C Netherlands *52.03N 5.06E*
100 P6 **Nieuwe Pekela** Groningen, NE Netherlands *53.04N 6.58E*
100 P5 **Nieuweschans** Groningen, NE Netherlands *53.10N 7.10E*
Nieuw Guinea *see* New Guinea
100 I11 **Nieuwkoop** Zuid-Holland, C Netherlands *52.09N 4.46E*
100 M9 **Nieuwleusen** Overijssel, S Netherlands *52.34N 6.16E*
100 J11 **Nieuw-Loosdrecht** Utrecht, C Netherlands *52.12N 5.07E*
57 U9 **Nieuw Nickerie** Nickerie, NW Suriname *05.52N 57.00W*
100 P5 **Nieuwolda** Groningen, NE Netherlands *53.15N 6.58E*
101 B17 **Nieuwpoort** *var.* Nieuport. West-Vlaanderen, W Belgium *51.07N 2.45E*
101 G14 **Nieuw-Vossemeer** Noord-Brabant, S Netherlands *51.34N 4.13E*
100 P7 **Nieuw-Weerdinge** Drenthe, NE Netherlands *52.51N 7.00E*
42 L10 **Nieves** Zacatecas, C Mexico *24.00N 102.57W*
66 O11 **Nieves, Pico de las** ▲ Gran Canaria, Islas Canarias, Spain, NE Atlantic Ocean *27.58N 15.34W*
105 P8 **Nièvre** ◈ *department* C France
Niewenstat *see* Neustadt an der Weinstrasse
142 J15 **Niğde** Niğde, C Turkey *37.58N 34.42E*
142 J15 **Niğde** ◈ *province* C Turkey
85 J21 **Nigel** Gauteng, NE South Africa *26.25S 28.28E*
79 V10 **Niger** *off.* Republic of Niger. ◆ *republic* W Africa
79 T14 **Niger** ◈ *state* C Nigeria
69 P8 **Niger** W Africa
Niger Cone *see* Niger Fan
69 P9 **Niger Delta** *delta* S Nigeria
69 P9 **Niger Fan** *var.* Niger Cone. *undersea feature* E Atlantic Ocean
79 T13 **Nigeria** *off.* Federal Republic of Nigeria. ◆ *federal republic* W Africa
79 T17 **Niger, Mouths of the** *delta* S Nigeria
193 C24 **Nightcaps** Southland, South Island, NZ *45.58S 168.03E*
12 F7 **Night Hawk Lake** ◎ Ontario, S Canada
67 M19 **Nightingale Island** *island* S Tristan da Cunha, S Atlantic Ocean
40 M12 **Nightmute** Alaska, USA *60.28N 164.43W*
116 G13 **Nigríta** Kentrikí Makedonía, NE Greece *40.54N 23.28E*
154 J15 **Nihing** *Per.* Rūd-e Nahang. Iran/Pakistan
203 V10 **Nihiru** *atoll* Îles Tuamotu, C French Polynesia
Nihommatsu *see* Nihonmatsu
Nihon *see* Japan
171 L13 **Nihonmatsu** *var.* Nihommatsu, Nihonmatu. Fukushima, Honshū, C Japan *37.35N 140.22E*
Nihonmatu *see* Nihonmatsu
64 I12 **Nihuil, Embalse del** ◎ W Argentina
171 K12 **Niigata** Niigata, Honshū, C Japan *37.55N 139.01E*
171 K13 **Niigata** *off.* Niigata-ken. ◈ *prefecture* Honshū, C Japan
170 F15 **Niihama** Ehime, Shikoku, SW Japan *33.57N 133.15E*
40 A8 **Niihau** *island* Hawaii, USA, C Pacific Ocean
172 Ss13 **Nii-jima** *island* E Japan
170 Ff13 **Niimi** Okayama, Honshū, SW Japan *35.00N 133.27E*
171 Kk13 **Niitsu** *var.* Niitu. Niigata, Honshū, C Japan *37.48N 139.06E*
Niitu *see* Niitsu
107 P15 **Nijar** Andalucía, S Spain *36.57N 2.13W*
100 K11 **Nijkerk** Gelderland, C Netherlands *52.13N 5.30E*
101 H16 **Nijlen** Antwerpen, N Belgium *51.10N 4.40E*
100 L13 **Nijmegen** *Ger.* Nimwegen; *anc.* Noviomagus. Gelderland, SE Netherlands *51.49N 5.52E*
100 N10 **Nijverdal** Overijssel, E Netherlands *52.22N 6.28E*
202 G16 **Nikao** Rarotonga, S Cook Islands
Nikaria *see* Ikaría
128 I2 **Nikel'** Murmanskaya Oblast', NW Russian Federation *69.24N 30.12E*
175 Rr17 **Nikiniki** Timor, S Indonesia *10.00S 124.30E*
133 Q15 **Nikitin Seamount** *undersea feature* E Indian Ocean *5.48S 84.48E*
79 S14 **Nikki** E Benin *9.55N 3.12E*
171 Kk15 **Nikkō** *var.* Nikko. Tochigi, Honshū, S Japan *36.45N 139.37E*
Niklasmarkt *see* Gheorgheni
41 P10 **Nikolai** Alaska, USA *63.00N 154.22W*
Nikolaiken *see* Mikołajki
Nikolainkaupunki *see* Länsi-Suomi
Nikolayev *see* Mykolayiv
Nikolayevka *see* Zhetigen
151 O6 **Nikolayevka** Severnyy Kazakhstan, N Kazakhstan
131 P9 **Nikolayevsk** Volgogradskaya Oblast', SW Russian Federation *50.03N 45.30E*
Nikolayevskaya Oblast' *see* Mykolayivs'ka Oblast'
127 Nn14 **Nikolayevsk-na-Amure** Khabarovskiy Kray, SE Russian Federation *53.04N 140.39E*
131 P6 **Nikol'sk** Penzenskaya Oblast', W Russian Federation *53.46N 46.03E*
129 O13 **Nikol'sk** Vologodskaya Oblast', NW Russian Federation *59.35N 45.31E*
Nikol'sk *see* Ussuriysk
40 K17 **Nikolski** Umnak Island, Alaska, USA *52.56N 168.52W*
Nikol'skiy *see* Satpayev
131 V7 **Nikol'skoye** Orenburgskaya Oblast', W Russian Federation *52.01N 55.48E*
Nikol'sk-Ussuriyskiy *see* Ussuriysk
116 J7 **Nikopol** *anc.* Nicopolis. Pleven, N Bulgaria *43.43N 24.55E*
119 S9 **Nikopol'** Dnipropetrovs'ka Oblast', SE Ukraine *47.34N 34.23E*
117 C17 **Nikópoli** *anc.* Nicopolis. *site of ancient city* Ípeiros, W Greece *39.01N 20.43E*
142 M12 **Niksar** Tokat, N Turkey *40.36N 36.54E*
149 V14 **Nīkshahr** Sīstān va Balūchestān, SE Iran *26.15N 60.10E*
115 J16 **Nikšić** Montenegro, SW Serbia and Montenegro (Yugoslavia) *42.46N 18.56E*
203 R4 **Nikumaroro** *prev.* Gardner Island, Kemins Island. *atoll* Phoenix Islands, C Kiribati
203 P3 **Nikunau** *var.* Nukunau; *prev.* Byron Island. *atoll* Tungaru, W Kiribati
161 G21 **Nilambūr** Kerala, SW India *11.16N 76.15E*
37 X16 **Niland** California, W USA *33.14N 115.31W*
69 T3 **Nile** *Ar.* Nahr an Nīl. N Africa
82 G8 **Nile** *former province* NW Uganda
77 W7 **Nile Delta** *delta* N Egypt
69 T3 **Nile Fan** *undersea feature* E Mediterranean Sea
33 O11 **Niles** Michigan, N USA *41.49N 86.15W*
33 V11 **Niles** Ohio, N USA *41.10N 80.46W*
161 F20 **Nīleswaram** Kerala, SW India *12.18N 75.07E*
12 K10 **Nilgaut, Lac** ◎ Quebec, SE Canada
164 I5 **Nilka** Xinjiang Uygur Zizhiqu, NW China *43.46N 82.33E*
Nīl, Nahr an *see* Nile
95 N16 **Nilsiä** Itä-Suomi, C Finland *63.13N 28.00E*
160 F9 **Nimach** Madhya Pradesh, C India *24.30N 74.51E*
158 G14 **Nimbāhera** Rājasthān, N India *24.37N 74.45E*
78 L15 **Nimba, Monts** *var.* Nimba Mountains. ▲▲ W Africa
Nimba Mountains *see* Nimba, Monts
Nimburg *see* Nymburk
105 Q15 **Nîmes** *anc.* Nemausus, Nismes. Gard, S France *43.49N 4.19E*
158 H11 **Nīm ka Thāna** Rājasthān, N India *27.44N 75.44E*
191 R11 **Nimmitabel** New South Wales, SE Australia *36.34S 149.18E*
Nimptsch *see* Niemcza
205 R11 **Nimrod Glacier** *glacier* Antarctica
Nimroze *see* Nīmrūz
154 K8 **Nīmrūz** *var.* Nimroze; *prev.* Chakhānsūr. ◈ *province* SW Afghanistan
83 F16 **Nimule** Eastern Equatoria, S Sudan *3.33N 32.06E*
Nimwegen *see* Nijmegen
161 C23 **Nine Degree Channel** *channel* India/Maldives
20 G9 **Ninemile Point** *headland* New York, NE USA *43.31N 76.22W*
181 S8 **Ninetyeast Ridge** *undersea feature* E Indian Ocean
191 P13 **Ninety Mile Beach** *beach* Victoria, SE Australia
192 I2 **Ninety Mile Beach** *beach* North Island, NZ
23 P12 **Ninety Six** South Carolina, SE USA *34.10N 82.01W*
169 Y9 **Ning'an** Heilongjiang, NE China *44.20N 129.28E*
167 S9 **Ningbo** *var.* Ning-po, Yin-hsien; *prev.* Ninghsien. Zhejiang, SE China *29.54N 121.33E*
167 U12 **Ningde** Fujian, SE China *26.48N 119.33E*
167 P12 **Ningdu** Jiangxi, S China *26.28N 115.58E*
194 E12 **Ningerum** Western, SW PNG *5.43S 141.09E*
167 R9 **Ningguo** Anhui, E China *30.33N 118.58E*
167 S9 **Ninghai** Zhejiang, SE China *29.19N 121.22E*
Ning-hsia *see* Ningxia
Ninghsien *see* Ningbo
166 J15 **Ningming** Guangxi Zhuangzu Zizhiqu, S China *22.07N 106.43E*
166 H11 **Ningnan** Sichuan, C China *26.59N 102.49E*
Ning-po *see* Ningbo
Ningsia/Ningsia Hui/Ningsia Hui Autonomous Region *see* Ningxia
166 J5 **Ningxia** *off.* Ningxia Huizu Zizhiqu, *var.* Ning-hsia, Ningsia, *Eng.* Ningsia Hui, Ningsia Hui Autonomous Region. ◈ *autonomous region* N China
165 X10 **Ningxian** Gansu, N China *35.30N 108.04E*
178 Jj7 **Ninh Binh** Ninh Binh, N Vietnam *20.12N 105.58E*
178 Kk13 **Ninh Hoa** Khanh Hoa, S Vietnam *12.28N 109.07E*
194 H7 **Ninigo Group** *island group* N PNG
41 Q12 **Ninilchik** Alaska, USA *60.03N 151.40W*
29 N7 **Ninnescah River** Kansas, C USA
205 U16 **Ninnis Glacier** *glacier* Antarctica
172 N10 **Ninohe** Iwate, Honshū, C Japan *40.17N 141.18E*
101 F18 **Ninove** Oost-Vlaanderen, C Belgium *50.49N 4.01E*
179 P11 **Ninoy Aquino** ✕ (Manila) Luzon, N Philippines *14.26N 121.00E*
Nio *see* Íos
31 P12 **Niobrara** Nebraska, C USA *42.43N 97.59W*
30 M12 **Niobrara River** Nebraska/Wyoming, C USA
81 I20 **Nioki** Bandundu, W Dem. Rep. Congo *2.44S 17.42E*
78 M11 **Niono** Ségou, C Mali *14.15N 5.57W*
78 K11 **Nioro** *var.* Nioro du Sahel. Kayes, W Mali *15.13N 9.38W*
78 G11 **Nioro du Rip** SW Senegal *13.44N 15.48W*
Nioro du Sahel *see* Nioro
104 K10 **Niort** Deux-Sèvres, W France *46.21N 0.24W*
180 H14 **Nioumachoua** Mohéli, S Comoros *12.21S 43.43E*
194 G12 **Nipa** Southern Highlands, W PNG *6.12S 143.29E*
9 U14 **Nipawin** Saskatchewan, S Canada *53.21N 103.55W*
10 D12 **Nipigon** Ontario, S Canada *49.01N 88.15W*
10 D11 **Nipigon, Lake** ◎ Ontario, S Canada
9 S13 **Nipin** Saskatchewan, C Canada
12 G11 **Nipissing, Lake** ◎ Ontario, S Canada
37 P13 **Nipomo** California, W USA *35.02N 120.28W*
Nippon *see* Japan
144 K6 **Niqniqīyah, Jabal an** ▲▲ C Syria
64 I9 **Niquivil** San Juan, W Argentina *30.25S 68.42W*
176 Yy10 **Nirabotong** Papua, E Indonesia *2.35S 140.08E*
171 J16 **Nirasaki** Yamanashi, Honshū, S Japan *35.43N 138.24E*
Niriz *see* Neyrīz
161 I14 **Nirmal** Andhra Pradesh, C India *19.04N 78.21E*
159 Q13 **Nirmāli** Bihār, NE India *26.18N 86.34E*
115 O14 **Niš** *Eng.* Nish, *Ger.* Nisch; *anc.* Naissus. Serbia, SE Serbia and Montenegro (Yugoslavia) *43.20N 21.52E*
106 H9 **Nisa** Portalegre, C Portugal *39.31N 7.39W*
Nisa *see* Neisse
147 P4 **Nişab** Al Ḩudūd ash Shamālīyah, N Saudi Arabia *29.10N 44.43E*
147 Q15 **Nişāb** *var.* Anşāb. SW Yemen *14.24N 46.47E*
115 P14 **Nišava** *Bul.* Nishava. Bulgaria/Serbia and Montenegro (Yugoslavia) ***see also*** Nishava
109 K25 **Niscemi** Sicilia, Italy, C Mediterranean Sea *37.09N 14.22E*
Nisch/Nish *see* Niš
172 Nn5 **Niseko** Hokkaidō, NE Japan *42.50N 140.43E*
Nishapur *see* Neyshābūr
116 G9 **Nishava** *var.* Nišava. Bulgaria/Serbia and Montenegro (Yugoslavia) ***see also*** Nišava
120 L11 **Nishcha** *Rus.* Nishcha. N Belarus
172 Qq7 **Nishibetsu-gawa** Hokkaidō, NE Japan
170 E13 **Nishi-gawa** Honshū, SW Japan
170 Ee13 **Nishi-Nōmi-jima** *var.* Nōmi-jima. *island* SW Japan
170 Bb17 **Nishinoomote** Kagoshima, Tanega-shima, SW Japan *30.42N 130.59E*
172 Ss16 **Nishino-shima** *Eng.* Rosario. *island* Ogasawara-shotō, SE Japan
171 Hh16 **Nishio** *var.* Nisio. Aichi, Honshū, SW Japan *34.52N 137.01E*
170 C13 **Nishi-Sonogi-hantō** *peninsula* Kyūshū, SW Japan
171 Gg14 **Nishiwaki** *var.* Nisiwaki. Hyōgo, Honshū, SW Japan *35.02N 134.57E*
147 U14 **Nishtūn** SE Yemen *15.47N 52.08E*
Nisiros *see* Nísyros
Nisiwaki *see* Nishiwaki
Niska *see* Niesky
115 O14 **Niška Banja** Serbia, SE Serbia and Montenegro (Yugoslavia) *43.18N 22.01E*
10 D6 **Niskibi** Ontario, C Canada
113 O15 **Nisko** Podkarpackie, SE Poland *50.31N 22.09E*
8 H7 **Nisling** Yukon Territory, W Canada
101 H22 **Nismes** Namur, S Belgium *50.04N 4.31E*
Nismes *see* Nîmes
118 M10 **Nisporeni** *Rus.* Nisporeny. W Moldova *47.04N 28.10E*
Nisporeny *see* Nisporeni
97 K20 **Nissan** S Sweden
195 R11 **Nissan Island** *island* Green Islands, NE PNG
Nissan Islands *see* Green Islands
97 F16 **Nisser** ◎ S Norway
97 E21 **Nissum Bredning** *inlet* NW Denmark
31 U6 **Nisswa** Minnesota, N USA *46.31N 94.17W*
Nistru *see* Dniester
117 M22 **Nísyros** *var.* Nisiros. *island* Dodekánisos, Greece, Aegean Sea
120 H8 **Nītaure** Cēsis, C Latvia *57.05N 25.12E*
62 P10 **Niterói** *prev.* Nictheroy. Rio de Janeiro, SE Brazil *22.54S 43.06W*
12 F16 **Nith** Ontario, S Canada
98 J13 **Nith** S Scotland, UK
Nitinan *see* Nichinan
113 I21 **Nitra** *Ger.* Neutra, *Hung.* Nyitra. Nitriansky Kraj, SW Slovakia *48.19N 18.04E*
113 I20 **Nitra** *Ger.* Neutra, *Hung.* Nyitra. W Slovakia
113 I21 **Nitriansky Kraj** ◈ *region* SW Slovakia
23 Q5 **Nitro** West Virginia, NE USA *38.24N 81.50W*
125 F11 **Nitsa** C Russian Federation
97 H14 **Nittedal** Akershus, S Norway *60.08N 10.45E*
Niuatobutabu *see* Niuatoputapu
200 S11 **Niuatoputapu** *var.* Niuatobutabu; *prev.* Keppel Island. *island* N Tonga
200 Q15 **Niu'Aunofa** *headland* Tongatapu, S Tonga *21.03S 175.19W*
Niuchwang *see* Yingkou
202 B16 **Niue** ◇ *self-governing territory in free association with NZ* S Pacific Ocean
202 F10 **Niulakita** *var.* Nurakita. *atoll* S Tuvalu
202 E6 **Niutao** *atoll* NW Tuvalu
95 L15 **Nivala** Oulu, C Finland *63.56N 25.00E*
104 I15 **Nive** SW France
101 G19 **Nivelles** Wallon Brabant, C Belgium *50.36N 4.04E*
105 P8 **Nivernais** *cultural region* C France
13 N8 **Niverville, Lac** ◎ Quebec, SE Canada
29 T7 **Nixa** Missouri, C USA *37.02N 93.17W*
37 R5 **Nixon** Nevada, W USA *39.48N 119.24W*
27 S12 **Nixon** Texas, SW USA *29.16N 97.45W*
Niya *see* Minfeng
152 K12 **Niyazov** Lebapskiy Velayat, NE Turkmenistan *39.13N 63.16E*
161 H14 **Nizāmābād** Andhra Pradesh, C India *18.40N 78.04E*
161 H15 **Nizām Sāgar** ◎ C India
129 N16 **Nizhegorodskaya Oblast'** ◈ *province* W Russian Federation
126 K14 **Nizhneangarsk** Respublika Buryatiya, S Russian Federation *55.47N 109.39E*
Nizhnegorskiy *see* Nyzhn'ohirs'kyy
131 S4 **Nizhnekamsk** Respublika Tatarstan, W Russian Federation *55.36N 51.45E*
131 U3 **Nizhnekamskoye Vodokhranilishche** ▣ W Russian Federation
127 O5 **Nizhnekolymsk** Respublika Sakha (Yakutiya), NE Russian Federation *68.32N 161.00E*
127 N16 **Nizhneleninskoye** Yevreyskaya Avtonomnaya Oblast', SE Russian Federation *47.50N 132.30E*
126 Ii14 **Nizhneudinsk** Irkutskaya Oblast', S Russian Federation *54.48N 98.51E*
126 Gg11 **Nizhnevartovsk** Khanty-Mansiyskiy Avtonomnyy Okrug, C Russian Federation *60.57N 76.40E*
126 Ll6 **Nizhneyansk** Respublika Sakha (Yakutiya), NE Russian Federation *71.25N 135.59E*
131 Q11 **Nizhniy Baskunchak** Astrakhanskaya Oblast', SW Russian Federation *48.15N 46.49E*
126 M11 **Nizhniy Bestyakh** Respublika Sakha (Yakutiya), NE Russian Federation *61.55N 130.07E*
131 O6 **Nizhniy Lomov** Penzenskaya Oblast', W Russian Federation *53.32N 43.39E*
131 P3 **Nizhniy Novgorod** *prev.* Gor'kiy. Nizhegorodskaya Oblast', W Russian Federation *56.17N 43.59E*
129 T8 **Nizhniy Odes** Respublika Komi, NW Russian Federation *63.42N 54.58E*
Nizhniy Pyandzh *see* Panji Poyon
125 Ee11 **Nizhniy Tagil** Sverdlovskaya Oblast', C Russian Federation *57.57N 59.51E*
129 T9 **Nizhnyaya-Omra** Respublika Komi, NW Russian Federation *62.46N 55.54E*
129 P5 **Nizhnyaya Pesha** Nenetskiy Avtonomnyy Okrug, NW Russian Federation *66.54N 47.37E*
125 F11 **Nizhnyaya Tavda** Tyumenskaya Oblast', C Russian Federation *57.41N 65.54E*
126 Jj12 **Nizhnyaya Tunguska** *Eng.* Lower Tunguska. N Russian Federation
119 Q3 **Nizhyn** *Rus.* Nezhin. Chernihivs'ka Oblast', NE Ukraine *51.03N 31.54E*
142 M17 **Nizip** Gaziantep, S Turkey *37.01N 37.46E*
147 X8 **Nizwá** *var.* Nazwāh. NE Oman *22.50N 57.27E*
Nizza *see* Nice
108 C9 **Nizza Monferrato** Piemonte, NE Italy *44.47N 8.22E*
Njávdám *see* Näätämöjoki
Njellim *see* Nellim
83 H24 **Njombe** Iringa, S Tanzania *9.19S 34.46E*
83 G23 **Njombe** C Tanzania
94 I10 **Njunis** ▲ N Norway *68.47N 19.24E*
95 H17 **Njurunda** Västernorrland, C Sweden *62.15N 17.24E*
96 N11 **Njutånger** Gävleborg, C Sweden *61.37N 17.04E*
81 D14 **Nkambe** Nord-Ouest, NW Cameroon *6.34N 10.43E*
Nkata Bay *see* Nkhata Bay
81 F21 **Nkayi** *prev.* Jacob. La Bouenza, S Congo *4.10S 13.17E*
85 J17 **Nkayi** Matabeleland North, W Zimbabwe *19.02S 28.55E*
84 N13 **Nkhata Bay** *var.* Nkata Bay. Northern, N Malawi *11.36S 34.16E*
83 E22 **Nkonde** Kigoma, N Tanzania *6.16S 30.17E*
81 D15 **Nkongsamba** *var.* N'Kongsamba. Littoral, W Cameroon *4.58N 9.52E*
85 E16 **Nkurenkuru** Okavango, N Namibia *17.39S 18.37E*
79 Q15 **Nkwanta** E Ghana *8.18N 0.27E*
178 H1 **Nmai Hka** *var.* Me Hka. N Myanmar
Noardwâlde *see* Noordwolde
41 N7 **Noatak** Alaska, USA *67.34N 162.58W*
41 N7 **Noatak River** Alaska, USA
Nobeji *see* Noheji
170 D15 **Nobeoka** Miyazaki, Kyūshū, SW Japan *32.34N 131.37E*
29 N11 **Noble** Oklahoma, C USA *35.08N 97.23W*
33 P13 **Noblesville** Indiana, N USA *40.03N 86.00W*
172 O6 **Noboribetsu** *var.* Noboribetu. Hokkaidō, NE Japan *42.27N 141.08E*
Noboribetu *see* Noboribetsu
61 H18 **Nobres** Mato Grosso, W Brazil *14.43S 56.15W*
109 N21 **Nocera Terinese** Calabria, S Italy *39.03N 16.10E*
43 Q16 **Nochixtlán** *var.* Asunción Nochixtlán. Oaxaca, SE Mexico *17.28N 97.18W*
27 S5 **Nocona** Texas, SW USA *33.47N 97.43W*
65 K21 **Nodales, Bahía de los** *bay* S Argentina
29 Q2 **Nodaway River** Iowa/Missouri, C USA
29 R8 **Noel** Missouri, C USA *36.33N 94.29W*
97 C17 **Nærbø** Rogaland, S Norway *58.40N 5.39E*
97 I24 **Næstved** Storstrøm, SE Denmark *55.12N 11.47E*
42 H3 **Nogales** Chihuahua, NW Mexico *18.49N 97.12W*
42 F3 **Nogales** Sonora, NW Mexico *31.16N 110.52W*
38 M17 **Nogales** Arizona, SW USA *31.20N 110.55W*
Nogal Valley *see* Dooxo Nugaaleed
104 K15 **Nogaro** Gers, S France *43.46N 0.01W*
112 J7 **Nogat** N Poland
170 D12 **Nōgata** Fukuoka, Kyūshū, SW Japan *33.42N 130.43E*
131 P15 **Nogayskaya Step'** *steppe* SW Russian Federation
104 M6 **Nogent-le-Rotrou** Eure-et-Loir, C France *48.19N 0.49E*
105 O4 **Nogent-sur-Oise** Oise, N France *49.16N 2.28E*
105 P6 **Nogent-sur-Seine** Aube, N France *48.30N 3.31E*
126 I10 **Noginsk** Evenkiyskiy Avtonomnyy Okrug, N Russian Federation *64.28N 91.09E*
130 L3 **Noginsk** Moskovskaya Oblast', W Russian Federation *55.51N 38.23E*
127 O14 **Nogliki** Ostrov Sakhalin, Sakhalinskaya Oblast', SE Russian Federation *51.44N 143.14E*
171 I14 **Nōgōhaku-san** ▲ Honshū, SW Japan *35.46N 136.30E*
168 D5 **Nogoonnuur** Bayan-Ölgiy, NW Mongolia *49.31N 89.48E*
63 C18 **Nogoyá** Entre Ríos, E Argentina *32.25S 59.49W*
113 K21 **Nógrád** *off.* Nógrád Megye. ◈ *county* N Hungary
107 U5 **Noguera Pallaresa** NE Spain
107 U4 **Noguera Ribagorçana** NE Spain

◆ Country
● Country Capital
◇ Dependent Territory
○ Dependent Territory Capital
◈ Administrative Region
✕ International Airport
▲ Mountain
▲▲ Mountain Range
Volcano
River
◎ Lake
▣ Reservoir

172 N9 **Noheji** var. Nobeji. Aomori, Honshū, C Japan 40.51N 141.07E
103 E19 **Nohfelden** Saarland, SW Germany 49.35N 7.08E
40 A8 **Nohili Point** headland Kauai, Hawaii, USA, C Pacific Ocean 22.03N 159.48W
106 G3 **Noia** Galicia, NW Spain 42.48N 8.52W
105 N16 **Noire, Montagne** ▲▲ S France
13 P12 **Noire, Rivière** ≈ Quebec, SE Canada
12 J10 **Noire, Rivière** ≈ Quebec, SE Canada
Noire, Rivière see Black River
104 G6 **Noires, Montagnes** ▲▲ NW France
104 H8 **Noirmoutier-en-l'Île** Vendée, NW France 47.00N 2.15W
104 H8 **Noirmoutier, Île de** island NW France
171 Jj17 **Nojima-zaki** headland Honshū, S Japan 34.54N 139.54E
195 W8 **Noka** Nendō, E Solomon Islands 10.42S 165.57E
85 G17 **Nokaneng** Ngamiland, NW Botswana 19.40S 22.12E
95 L18 **Nokia** Länsi-Suomi, W Finland 61.28N 23.30E
154 K11 **Nok Kundi** Baluchistān, SW Pakistan 28.49N 62.39E
32 L14 **Nokomis** Illinois, N USA 39.18N 89.17W
32 K5 **Nokomis, Lake** ⊠ Wisconsin, N USA
80 G9 **Nokou** Kanem, W Chad 14.36N 14.45E
197 B12 **Nokuku** Espiritu Santo, W Vanuatu 14.56S 166.34E
97 J18 **Nol** Västra Götaland, S Sweden 57.55N 12.03E
81 H16 **Nola** Sangha-Mbaéré, SW Central African Republic 3.28N 16.05E
27 P7 **Nolan** Texas, SW USA 32.15N 100.15W
129 R15 **Nolinsk** Kirovskaya Oblast', NW Russian Federation 57.34N 49.54E
97 B19 **Nólsoy** Dan. Nolsø Island Faeroe Islands 61.59N 6.39W
194 F12 **Nomad** Western, SW Papau New Guinea 6.11S 142.13E
170 B15 **Noma-zaki** headland Kyūshū, SW Japan 31.24N 130.07E
42 K10 **Nombre de Dios** Durango, C Mexico 23.51N 104.13W
44 I5 **Nombre de Dios, Cordillera** ▲▲ N Honduras
40 M9 **Nome** Alaska, USA 64.30N 165.24W
31 Q6 **Nome** North Dakota, N USA 46.39N 97.49W
40 M9 **Nome, Cape** headland Alaska, USA 64.25N 165.00W
Nōmi-jima see Nishi-Nōmi-jima
12 M11 **Nominingue, Lac** ⊚ Quebec, SE Canada
Nomoi Islands see Mortlock Islands
170 Bb13 **Nomo-zaki** headland Kyūshū, SW Japan 32.34N 129.45E
200 S13 **Nomuka** island Nomuka Group, C Tonga
200 S14 **Nomuka Group** island group W Tonga
201 Q15 **Nomwin Atoll** atoll Hall Islands, C Micronesia
15 Ii8 **Nonacho Lake** ⊚ Northwest Territories, NW Canada
Nondaburi see Nonthaburi
41 P12 **Nondalton** Alaska, USA 59.58N 154.51W
169 V10 **Nong'an** Jilin, NE China 44.23N 125.04E
178 I10 **Nong Bua Khok** Nakhon Ratchasima, C Thailand 15.23N 101.51E
178 I9 **Nong Bua Lamphu** Udon Thani, E Thailand 17.11N 102.27E
178 J7 **Nông Hèt** Xiangkhoang, N Laos 19.27N 104.02E
Nongkaya see Nong Khai
178 I8 **Nong Khai** var. Mi Chai, Nongkaya. Nong Khai, E Thailand 17.52N 102.43E
178 Gg15 **Nong Met** Surat Thani, SW Thailand 9.27N 99.09E
85 L22 **Nongoma** KwaZulu/Natal, E South Africa 27.54S 31.40E
178 Hh10 **Nong Phai** Phetchabun, C Thailand 15.58N 101.02E
159 U13 **Nongstoin** Meghālaya, NE India 25.24N 91.19E
85 C19 **Nonidas** Erongo, N Namibia 22.36S 14.40E
Nonni see Nen Jiang
42 I7 **Nonoava** Chihuahua, N Mexico 27.24N 106.18W
203 O3 **Nonouti** prev. Sydenham Island. atoll Tungaru, W Kiribati
178 Hh11 **Nonthaburi** var. Nondaburi, Nontha Buri. Nonthaburi, C Thailand 13.55N 100.33E
104 L11 **Nontron** Dordogne, SW France 45.34N 0.41E
189 P1 **Noonamah** Northern Territory, N Australia 12.46S 131.08E
30 K2 **Noonan** North Dakota, N USA 48.51N 102.57W
101 E14 **Noord-Beveland** var. North Beveland. island SW Netherlands
101 J14 **Noord-Brabant** Eng. North Brabant. ◈ province S Netherlands
100 H7 **Noorder Haaks** spit NW Netherlands
100 H9 **Noord-Holland** Eng. North Holland. ◈ province NW Netherlands
Noordhollandsch Kanaal see Noordhollands Kanaal
100 H8 **Noordhollands Kanaal** var. Noordhollandsch Kanaal. canal NW Netherlands
Noord-Kaap see Northern Cape
100 L8 **Noordoostpolder** island N Netherlands
47 P16 **Noordpunt** headland Curaçao, C Netherlands Antilles 12.21N 69.08W
100 I8 **Noord-Scharwoude** Noord-Holland, NW Netherlands 52.42N 4.48E
Noordwes see North-West
100 G11 **Noordwijk aan Zee** Zuid-Holland, W Netherlands 52.15N 4.25E
100 H11 **Noordwijkerhout** Zuid-Holland, W Netherlands 52.16N 4.30E
100 M7 **Noordwolde** Fris. Noardwâlde. Friesland, N Netherlands 52.54N 6.10E
Noordzee see North Sea
100 H10 **Noordzee-Kanaal** canal NW Netherlands
95 K18 **Noormarkku** Swe. Norrmark. Länsi-Suomi, W Finland 61.34N 21.54E
41 N8 **Noorvik** Alaska, USA 66.50N 161.01W
8 J17 **Nootka Sound** inlet British Columbia, W Canada
84 A9 **Nóqui** Zaire, NW Angola 5.53S 13.26E
97 L15 **Nora** Örebro, C Sweden 59.31N 15.01E
153 Q13 **Norak** Rus. Nurek. W Tajikistan 38.23N 69.13E
16 P14 **Noranda** Quebec, SE Canada 48.16N 79.03W
31 W12 **Nora Springs** Iowa, C USA 43.08N 93.00W
97 M14 **Norberg** Västmanland, C Sweden 60.04N 15.34E
12 K13 **Norcan Lake** ⊚ Ontario, SE Canada
207 R12 **Nord** Avannaarsua, N Greenland 81.38N 12.51W
80 F13 **Nord** Eng. North. ◈ province N Cameroon
105 P2 **Nord** ◈ department N France
94 P1 **Nordaustlandet** island NE Svalbard
97 G24 **Nordborg** Ger. Nordburg. Sønderjylland, SW Denmark 55.04N 9.40E
Nordburg see Nordborg
97 F23 **Nordby** Ribe, W Denmark 55.27N 8.25E
9 P15 **Nordegg** Alberta, SW Canada 52.27N 116.06W
102 E9 **Norden** Niedersachsen, NW Germany 53.36N 7.12E
102 G10 **Nordenham** Niedersachsen, NW Germany 53.28N 8.27E
126 Ii4 **Nordenshel'da, Arkhipelag** island group N Russian Federation
94 O3 **Nordenskiold Land** physical region W Svalbard
102 E9 **Norderney** island NW Germany
102 J9 **Norderstedt** Schleswig-Holstein, N Germany 53.42N 9.58E
96 C11 **Nordfjord** physical region S Norway
96 D11 **Nordfjord** fjord S Norway
96 D11 **Nordfjordeid** Sogn og Fjordane, S Norway 61.54N 6.01E
94 G11 **Nordfold** Nordland, C Norway 67.48N 15.16E
Nordfriesische Inseln see North Frisian Islands
102 H7 **Nordfriesland** cultural region N Germany
103 K15 **Nordhausen** Thüringen, C Germany 51.31N 10.48E
27 T13 **Nordheim** Texas, SW USA 28.55N 97.36W
96 C13 **Nordhordland** physical region S Norway
102 E12 **Nordhorn** Niedersachsen, NW Germany 52.25N 7.04E
94 I1 **Nordhurfjördhur** Vestfirdhir, NW Iceland 66.01N 21.33W
94 J1 **Nordhurland Eystra** ◈ region N Iceland
94 I2 **Nordhurland Vestra** ◈ region N Iceland
180 H16 **Nord, Île du** island Inner Islands, NE Seychelles
97 F20 **Nordjylland** off. Nordjyllands Amt. ◈ county N Denmark
94 K7 **Nordkapp** Eng. North Cape. headland N Norway 71.10N 25.42E
94 O1 **Nordkapp** headland N Svalbard 80.31N 19.58E
94 L7 **Nordkinn** headland N Norway 71.07N 27.40E
81 N19 **Nord Kivu** off. Région du Nord Kivu. ◈ region E Dem. Rep. Congo
94 G12 **Nordland** ◈ county C Norway
103 J21 **Nördlingen** Bayern, S Germany 48.49N 10.28E
95 I16 **Nordmaling** Västerbotten, N Sweden 63.34N 19.30E
97 K15 **Nordmark** Värmland, C Sweden 59.52N 14.04E
Nord, Mer du see North Sea
96 F8 **Nordmøre** physical region S Norway
102 I8 **Nord-Ostee-Kanal** canal N Germany
(0) J3 **Nordostrundingen** headland NE Greenland 83.00N 10.00W
81 D14 **Nord-Ouest** Eng. North-West. ◈ province NW Cameroon
Nord-Ouest, Territoires du see Northwest Territories
105 N2 **Nord-Pas-de-Calais** ◈ region N France
103 F19 **Nordpfälzer Bergland** ▲▲ W Germany
Nord, Pointe see Fatua, Pointe
197 H5 **Nord, Province** ◈ province C New Caledonia
103 D14 **Nordrhein-Westfalen** Eng. North Rhine-Westphalia, Fr. Rhénanie du Nord-Westphalie. ◈ state W Germany
Nordsee/Nordsjøen/Nordsøen see North Sea
102 H7 **Nordstrand** island N Germany
95 E15 **Nord-Trøndelag** ◈ county C Norway
99 E19 **Nore** Ir. An Fheoir. ≈ S Ireland
31 Q14 **Norfolk** Nebraska, C USA 42.01N 97.25W
23 X7 **Norfolk** Virginia, NE USA 36.51N 76.17W
99 P19 **Norfolk** cultural region E England, UK
199 Ii11 **Norfolk Island** ◇ Australian external territory SW Pacific Ocean
183 P9 **Norfolk Ridge** undersea feature W Pacific Ocean
29 U8 **Norfork Lake** ⊠ Arkansas/Missouri, C USA
100 N6 **Norg** Drenthe, NE Netherlands 53.04N 6.28E
Norge see Norway
97 D14 **Norheimsund** Hordaland, S Norway 60.22N 6.09E
27 S16 **Norias** Texas, SW USA 26.47N 97.45W
171 J14 **Norikura-dake** ▲ Honshū, S Japan 36.06N 137.33E
126 I8 **Noril'sk** Taymyrskiy (Dolgano-Nenetskiy) Avtonomnyy Okrug, N Russian Federation 69.21N 88.01E
12 I13 **Norland** Ontario, SE Canada 44.46N 78.48W
23 V8 **Norlina** North Carolina, SE USA 36.26N 78.11W
32 L13 **Normal** Illinois, N USA 40.30N 88.59W
29 N11 **Norman** Oklahoma, C USA 35.13N 97.27W
Norman see Tulita
195 O16 **Normanby Island** island SE PNG
Normandes, Îles see Channel Islands
60 G9 **Normandia** Roraima, N Brazil 3.57N 59.39W
104 L5 **Normandie** Eng. Normandy. cultural region N France
104 J5 **Normandie, Collines de** hill range NW France
Normandy see Normandie
27 V9 **Normangee** Texas, SW USA 31.01N 96.06W
23 Q10 **Norman, Lake** ⊠ North Carolina, SE USA
46 K13 **Norman Manley** ✈ (Kingston) E Jamaica 17.55N 76.46W
189 U5 **Norman River** ≈ Queensland, NE Australia
189 U4 **Normanton** Queensland, NE Australia 17.48S 141.07E
15 Gg5 **Norman Wells** Northwest Territories, NW Canada 65.18N 126.42W
10 H12 **Normétal** Quebec, S Canada 48.58N 79.22W
9 V15 **Norquay** Saskatchewan, S Canada 51.51N 102.04W
96 N11 **Norra Dellen** ⊚ C Sweden
95 G15 **Norråker** Jämtland, C Sweden 64.25N 15.40E
96 N12 **Norrala** Gävleborg, C Sweden 61.22N 17.04E
Norra Ny see Stöllet
94 G13 **Norra Storjfjället** ▲ N Sweden 65.57N 15.15E
94 I13 **Norrbotten** ◈ county N Sweden
97 G23 **Nørre Aaby** var. Nørre Åby. Fyn, C Denmark 55.28N 9.52E
Nørre Åby see Nørre Aaby
97 I24 **Nørre Alslev** Storstrøm, SE Denmark 54.54N 11.52E
97 E23 **Nørre Nebel** Ribe, W Denmark 55.45N 8.16E
97 G20 **Nørresundby** Nordjylland, N Denmark 57.05N 9.55E
23 N8 **Norris Lake** ⊠ Tennessee, S USA
20 I15 **Norristown** Pennsylvania, NE USA 40.07N 75.20W
97 N17 **Norrköping** Östergötland, S Sweden 58.34N 16.10E
Norrmark see Noormarkku
96 N13 **Norrsundet** Gävleborg, C Sweden 60.55N 17.09E
97 P15 **Norrtälje** Stockholm, C Sweden 59.45N 18.42E
188 L12 **Norseman** Western Australia 32.16S 121.45E
95 I14 **Norsjö** Västerbotten, N Sweden 64.55N 19.30E
97 G16 **Norsjø** ⊚ S Norway
126 Mm15 **Norsk** Amurskaya Oblast', SE Russian Federation 52.20N 129.57E
Norske Havet see Norwegian Sea
197 C13 **Norsup** Malekula, C Vanuatu 16.05S 167.24E
203 V15 **Norte, Cabo** headland Easter Island, Chile, E Pacific Ocean 27.03S 109.24W
56 F7 **Norte de Santander** off. Departamento de Norte de Santander. ◈ province N Colombia
63 E21 **Norte, Punta** headland E Argentina 36.17S 56.46W
23 R13 **North** South Carolina, SE USA 33.37N 81.06W
North see Nord
20 L10 **North Adams** Massachusetts, NE USA 42.40N 73.06W
115 L17 **North Albanian Alps** Alb. Bjeshkët e Namuna, SCr. Prokletije. ▲▲ Albania/Serbia and Montenegro (Yugoslavia)
99 M15 **Northallerton** N England, UK 54.19N 1.25W
188 J12 **Northam** Western Australia 31.40S 116.40E
85 J20 **Northam** Northern, N South Africa 24.56S 27.18E
1 **North America** continent
1 N12 **North American Basin** undersea feature W Sargasso Sea
(0) C5 **North American Plate** tectonic feature
20 M11 **North Amherst** Massachusetts, NE USA 42.24N 72.31W
99 N20 **Northampton** C England, UK 52.13N 0.54W
99 M20 **Northamptonshire** cultural region C England, UK
157 P18 **North Andaman** island Andaman Islands, India, NE Indian Ocean
67 D25 **North Arm** East Falkland, Falkland Islands 52.06S 59.21W
23 Q13 **North Augusta** South Carolina, SE USA 33.30N 81.58W
181 W8 **North Australian Basin** Fr. Bassin Nord de l' Australie. undersea feature E Indian Ocean
33 R11 **North Baltimore** Ohio, N USA 41.10N 83.40W
9 T15 **North Battleford** Saskatchewan, S Canada 52.46N 108.19W
12 H11 **North Bay** Ontario, S Canada 46.19N 79.28W
10 H6 **North Belcher Islands** island group Belcher Islands, Nunavut, C Canada
31 R15 **North Bend** Nebraska, C USA 41.27N 96.46W
34 E14 **North Bend** Oregon, NW USA 43.24N 124.13W
98 K12 **North Berwick** SE Scotland, UK 56.03N 2.44W
North Beveland see Noord-Beveland
North Borneo see Sabah
191 P5 **North Bourke** New South Wales, SE Australia 30.03S 145.56E
North Brabant see Noord-Brabant
190 F2 **North Branch Neales** seasonal river South Australia
46 M6 **North Caicos** island NW Turks and Caicos Islands
28 L10 **North Canadian River** ≈ Oklahoma, C USA
33 U12 **North Canton** Ohio, N USA 40.52N 81.24W
11 R13 **North, Cape** headland Cape Breton Island, Nova Scotia, SE Canada 47.06N 60.24W
192 I1 **North Cape** headland North Island, NZ 34.23S 173.02E
195 N9 **North Cape** headland New Ireland, NE PNG 2.33S 150.48E
North Cape see Nordkapp
20 J17 **North Cape May** New Jersey, NE USA 38.59N 74.55W
10 C9 **North Caribou Lake** ⊚ Ontario, C Canada
23 U10 **North Carolina** off. State of North Carolina; also known as Old North State, Tar Heel State, Turpentine State. ◈ state SE USA
North Celebes see Sulawesi Utara
161 J24 **North Central Province** ◈ province N Sri Lanka
33 S4 **North Channel** lake channel Canada/USA
99 G14 **North Channel** strait Northern Ireland/Scotland, UK
23 S14 **North Charleston** South Carolina, SE USA 32.51N 79.58W
33 N10 **North Chicago** Illinois, N USA 42.19N 87.50W
205 Y10 **Northcliffe Glacier** glacier Antarctica
33 Q14 **North College Hill** Ohio, N USA 39.13N 84.33W
27 O8 **North Concho River** ≈ Texas, SW USA
21 O8 **North Conway** New Hampshire, NE USA 44.03N 71.06W
29 V14 **North Crossett** Arkansas, C USA 33.10N 91.56W
30 L4 **North Dakota** off. State of North Dakota; also known as Flickertail State, Peace Garden State, Sioux State. ◈ state N USA
North Devon Island see Devon Island
99 O22 **North Downs** hill range SE England, UK
20 C11 **North East** Pennsylvania, NE USA 42.13N 79.49W
85 I18 **North East** ◈ district NE Botswana
67 G15 **North East Bay** bay Ascension Island, C Atlantic Ocean
40 L10 **Northeast Cape** headland Saint Lawrence Island, Alaska, USA 63.16N 168.50W
178 Mm13 **Northeast Cay** island NW Spratly Islands
83 J17 **North Eastern** ◈ province Kenya
North East Frontier Agency/North East Frontier Agency of Assam see Arunāchal Pradesh
67 E25 **North East Island** island E Falkland Islands
201 V11 **Northeast Island** island Chuuk, C Micronesia
46 L12 **North East Point** headland E Jamaica 18.09N 76.19W
46 L6 **Northeast Point** headland Great Inagua, S Bahamas 21.18N 73.01W
46 K5 **Northeast Point** headland Acklins Island, SE Bahamas 22.43N 73.50W
203 Z2 **Northeast Point** headland Kiritimati, E Kiribati 10.22S 105.45E
46 H2 **Northeast Providence Channel** channel N Bahamas
103 J14 **Northeim** Niedersachsen, C Germany 51.42N 10.00E
31 X14 **North English** Iowa, C USA 41.30N 92.04W
144 G8 **Northern** ◈ district N Israel
84 M12 **Northern** ◈ region N Malawi
194 L15 **Northern** ◈ province S PNG
Northern see Limpopo
82 D7 **Northern** ◈ state N Sudan
84 K12 **Northern** ◈ province NE Zambia
82 B13 **Northern Bahr el Ghazal** ◈ state SW Sudan
Northern Border Region see Al Ḥudūd ash Shamālīyah
85 F24 **Northern Cape** off. Northern Cape Province, Afr. Noord-Kaap. ◈ province W South Africa
202 K14 **Northern Cook Islands** island group N Cook Islands
82 B8 **Northern Darfur** ◈ state NW Sudan
Northern Dvina see Severnaya Dvina
99 F14 **Northern Ireland** var. The Six Counties. political division UK
82 D9 **Northern Kordofan** ◈ state C Sudan
197 K14 **Northern Lau Group** island group Lau Group, NE Fiji
196 K3 **Northern Mariana Islands** ◇ US commonwealth territory W Pacific Ocean
161 J23 **Northern Province** ◈ province N Sri Lanka
Northern Rhodesia see Zambia
Northern Sporades see Vóreioi Sporádes
190 D1 **Northern Territory** ◈ territory N Australia
Northern Transvaal see Limpopo
Northern Ural Hills see Severnyye Uvaly
86 I9 **North European Plain** plain N Europe
29 V2 **North Fabius River** ≈ Missouri, C USA
67 D24 **North Falkland Sound** sound N Falkland Islands
31 V9 **Northfield** Minnesota, N USA 44.27N 93.10W
21 O9 **Northfield** New Hampshire, NE USA 43.26N 71.34W
183 Q8 **North Fiji Basin** undersea feature N Coral Sea
99 Q22 **North Foreland** headland SE England, UK 51.22N 1.26E
37 P6 **North Fork American River** ≈ California, W USA
41 R7 **North Fork Chandalar River** ≈ Alaska, USA
30 K7 **North Fork Grand River** ≈ North Dakota/South Dakota, N USA
23 O6 **North Fork Kentucky River** ≈ Kentucky, S USA
41 Q7 **North Fork Koyukuk River** ≈ Alaska, USA
41 Q10 **North Fork Kuskokwim River** ≈ Alaska, USA
28 K11 **North Fork Red River** ≈ Oklahoma/Texas, SW USA
28 K3 **North Fork Solomon River** ≈ Kansas, C USA
25 W14 **North Fort Myers** Florida, SE USA 26.40N 81.52W
33 P5 **North Fox Island** island Michigan, N USA
102 G6 **North Frisian Islands** var. Nordfriesische Inseln. island group N Germany
207 N9 **North Geomagnetic Pole** pole Arctic Ocean 78.30N 69.00W
20 M13 **North Haven** Connecticut, NE USA 41.25N 72.51W
192 J5 **North Head** headland North Island, NZ 36.23S 174.01E
20 L6 **North Hero** Vermont, NE USA 44.49N 73.14W
37 O7 **North Highlands** California, W USA 38.40N 121.25W
North Holland see Noord-Holland
83 I16 **North Horr** Eastern, N Kenya 3.17N 37.08E
157 K21 **North Huvadhu Atoll** var. Gaafu Alifu Atoll. atoll S Maldives
67 A24 **North Island** island W Falkland Islands
192 N9 **North Island** island N NZ
23 U14 **North Island** island South Carolina, SE USA
33 O11 **North Judson** Indiana, N USA 41.12N 86.44W
North Kazakhstan see Severnyy Kazakhstan
33 V10 **North Kingsville** Ohio, N USA 41.54N 80.41W
169 Y13 **North Korea** off. Democratic People's Republic of Korea, Kor. Chosŏn-minjujuŭi-inmin-kanghwaguk. ◆ republic E Asia
159 X11 **North Lakhimpur** Assam, NE India 27.10N 94.00E
192 J3 **Northland** off. Northland Region. ◈ region North Island, NZ
199 J12 **Northland Plateau** undersea feature S Pacific Ocean
37 X11 **North Las Vegas** Nevada, W USA 36.12N 115.07W
33 O11 **North Liberty** Indiana, N USA 41.36N 86.22W
31 X14 **North Liberty** Iowa, C USA 41.45N 91.36W
29 V12 **North Little Rock** Arkansas, C USA 34.46N 92.15W
30 M13 **North Loup River** ≈ Nebraska, C USA
157 K18 **North Maalhosmadulu Atoll** var. North Malosmadulu Atoll, Raa Atoll. atoll N Maldives
33 U10 **North Madison** Ohio, N USA 41.48N 81.03W
33 P12 **North Manchester** Indiana, N USA 41.00N 85.45W
33 P6 **North Manitou Island** island Michigan, N USA
31 U10 **North Mankato** Minnesota, N USA 44.11N 94.03W
25 Z15 **North Miami** Florida, SE USA 25.54N 80.11W
157 K18 **North Miladummadulu Atoll** atoll N Maldives
North Minch see Minch, The
25 W15 **North Naples** Florida, SE USA 26.13N 81.47W
183 P8 **North New Hebrides Trench** undersea feature N Coral Sea
25 Y15 **North New River Canal** ≈ Florida, SE USA
157 K20 **North Nilandhe Atoll** var. Faafu Atoll. atoll C Maldives
38 L2 **North Ogden** Utah, W USA 41.18N 111.57W
North Ossetia see Severnaya Osetiya-Alaniya, Respublika
37 S10 **North Palisade** ▲ California, W USA 37.06N 118.31W
201 U11 **North Pass** passage Chuuk Islands, C Micronesia
30 M15 **North Platte** Nebraska, C USA 41.07N 100.46W
35 X17 **North Platte River** ≈ C USA
67 G14 **North Point** headland Ascension Island, C Atlantic Ocean
180 I16 **North Point** headland Mahé, NE Seychelles 4.22S 55.28E
33 S6 **North Point** headland Michigan, N USA 45.01N 83.16W
33 R5 **North Point** headland Michigan, N USA 45.21N 83.30W
41 S9 **North Pole** Alaska, USA 64.42N 147.09W
207 R9 **North Pole** pole Arctic Ocean 90.00N 0.00W
25 O4 **Northport** Alabama, S USA 33.13N 87.34W
25 W14 **North Port** Florida, SE USA 27.03N 82.15W
34 L6 **Northport** Washington, NW USA 48.54N 117.48W
34 L12 **North Powder** Oregon, NW USA 45.00N 117.56W
31 U13 **North Raccoon River** ≈ Iowa, C USA
North Rhine-Westphalia see Nordrhein-Westfalen
99 M16 **North Riding** cultural region N England, UK
98 G5 **North Rona** island NW Scotland, UK
98 K4 **North Ronaldsay** island NE Scotland, UK
38 L2 **North Salt Lake** Utah, W USA 40.51N 111.54W
9 P15 **North Saskatchewan** ≈ Alberta/Saskatchewan, S Canada
37 X5 **North Schell Peak** ▲ Nevada, W USA 39.25N 114.34W
North Scotia Ridge see South Georgia Ridge
88 D10 **North Sea** Dan. Nordsøen, Dut. Noordzee, Fr. Mer du Nord, Ger. Nordsee, Nor. Nordsjøen; prev. German Ocean, Lat. Mare Germanicum. sea NW Europe
37 T6 **North Shoshone Peak** ▲ Nevada, W USA 39.08N 117.28W
North Siberian Lowland/North Siberian Plain see Severo-Sibirskaya Nizmennost'
31 R13 **North Sioux City** South Dakota, N USA 42.31N 96.28W
98 K4 **North Sound, The** sound N Scotland, UK
191 T4 **North Star** New South Wales, SE Australia 28.55S 150.25E
North Star State see Minnesota
191 V3 **North Stradbroke Island** island Queensland, E Australia
North Sulawesi see Sulawesi Utara
North Sumatra see Sumatera Utara
12 D17 **North Sydenham** ≈ Ontario, S Canada
20 H9 **North Syracuse** New York, NE USA 43.07N 76.07W
192 K9 **North Taranaki Bight** gulf North Island, NZ
10 H9 **North Twin Island** island Nunavut, C Canada
98 E8 **North Uist** island NW Scotland, UK
99 L14 **Northumberland** cultural region N England, UK
189 Y7 **Northumberland Isles** island group Queensland, NE Australia
11 Q14 **Northumberland Strait** strait SE Canada
34 G14 **North Umpqua River** ≈ Oregon, NW USA
47 Q13 **North Union** Saint Vincent, Saint Vincent and the Grenadines 13.15N 61.07W
8 L17 **North Vancouver** British Columbia, SW Canada 49.21N 123.04W
20 K9 **Northville** New York, NE USA 43.13N 74.08W
99 Q19 **North Walsham** E England, UK 52.49N 1.22E
41 T10 **Northway** Alaska, USA 62.57N 141.56W
85 G21 **North-West** off. North-West Province, Afr. Noordwes. ◈ province N South Africa
North-West see Nord-Ouest
66 I6 **Northwest Atlantic Mid-Ocean Canyon** undersea feature N Atlantic Ocean
188 G8 **North West Cape** headland Western Australia 21.48S 114.10E
40 J9 **Northwest Cape** headland Saint Lawrence Island, Alaska, USA 63.46N 171.45W
84 H13 **North Western** ◈ province W Zambia
161 J24 **North Western Province** ◈ province W Sri Lanka
155 U4 **North-West Frontier Province** ◈ province NW Pakistan
98 H8 **North West Highlands** ▲▲ N Scotland, UK
199 Hh4 **Northwest Pacific Basin** undersea feature NW Pacific Ocean
203 Y2 **Northwest Point** headland Kiritimati, E Kiribati 10.25S 105.34E
46 G1 **Northwest Providence Channel** channel N Bahamas
11 Q8 **North West River** Newfoundland and Labrador, E Canada 53.30N 60.10W
15 Ii5 **Northwest Territories** Fr. Territoires du Nord-Ouest. ◈ territory NW Canada
99 K18 **Northwich** C England, UK 53.16N 2.31W
27 Q5 **North Wichita River** ≈ Texas, SW USA
20 J17 **North Wildwood** New Jersey, NE USA 39.00N 74.45W
23 R9 **North Wilkesboro** North Carolina, SE USA 36.09N 81.09W
21 P8 **North Windham** Maine, NE USA 43.51N 70.25W
207 Q6 **Northwind Plain** undersea feature Arctic Ocean
31 V11 **Northwood** Iowa, C USA 43.26N 93.13W
31 Q4 **Northwood** North Dakota, N USA 47.43N 97.34W
99 M15 **North York Moors** moorland N England, UK
27 V9 **North Zulch** Texas, SW USA 30.54N 96.06W
28 K2 **Norton** Kansas, C USA 39.49N 99.53W
33 S13 **Norton** Ohio, N USA 40.25N 83.04W
23 P7 **Norton** Virginia, NE USA 36.55N 82.37W
41 N9 **Norton Bay** bay Alaska, USA
Norton de Matos see Balombo
33 O9 **Norton Shores** Michigan, N USA 43.10N 86.15W
40 M10 **Norton Sound** inlet Alaska, USA
29 Q3 **Nortonville** Kansas, C USA 39.25N 95.19W
104 I8 **Nort-sur-Erdre** Loire-Atlantique, NW France 47.27N 1.30W
205 N2 **Norvegia, Cape** headland Antarctica 71.16S 12.25W
20 L13 **Norwalk** Connecticut, NE USA 41.08N 73.28W
31 V14 **Norwalk** Iowa, C USA 41.28N 93.40W
33 S11 **Norwalk** Ohio, N USA 41.14N 82.37W
21 P7 **Norway** Maine, NE USA 44.13N 70.30W
33 N5 **Norway** Michigan, N USA 45.47N 87.54W
95 E17 **Norway** off. Kingdom of Norway, Nor. Norge. ◆ monarchy N Europe
9 X13 **Norway House** Manitoba, C Canada 53.58N 97.49W
207 R16 **Norwegian Basin** undersea feature NW Norwegian Sea
86 D6 **Norwegian Sea** Nor. Norske Havet. sea NE Atlantic Ocean
207 S17 **Norwegian Trench** undersea feature NE North Sea
12 F16 **Norwich** Ontario, S Canada 42.57N 80.37W
99 Q19 **Norwich** E England, UK 52.37N 1.18E
21 N13 **Norwich** Connecticut, NE USA 41.30N 72.02W
20 I11 **Norwich** New York, NE USA 42.31N 75.31W
31 U9 **Norwood** Minnesota, N USA 44.46N 93.55W
33 Q15 **Norwood** Ohio, N USA 39.07N 84.27W
12 H11 **Nosbonsing, Lake** ⊚ Ontario, S Canada
Nösen see Bistrița
172 P1 **Noshappu-misaki** headland Hokkaidō, NE Japan 45.26N 141.38E
171 M9 **Noshiro** var. Nosiro; prev. Noshirominato. Akita, Honshū, C Japan 40.10N 140.01E
Noshirominato/Nosiro see Noshiro
119 Q3 **Nosivka** Rus. Nosovka. Chernihivs'ka Oblast', NE Ukraine 50.55N 31.37E
69 T14 **Nosop** var. Nossob, Nossop. ≈ Botswana/Namibia
129 S4 **Nosovaya** Nenetskiy Avtonomnyy Okrug, NW Russian Federation 68.12N 54.33E
Nosovka see Nosivka
149 V11 **Noṣratābād** Sīstān va Balūchestān, E Iran 29.53N 59.57E
97 J18 **Nossebro** Västra Götaland, S Sweden 58.12N 12.42E
98 K6 **Noss Head** headland N Scotland, UK 58.29N 3.03W
Nossi-Bé see Be, Nosy
85 E20 **Nossob** ≈ E Namibia
Nossob/Nossop see Nosop
180 J2 **Nosy Be** ✈ Antsirañana, N Madagascar 23.36S 47.36E
180 J6 **Nosy Varika** Fianarantsoa, SE Madagascar 20.36S 48.31E
12 L10 **Notawassi** ≈ Quebec, SE Canada
12 M9 **Notawassi, Lac** ⊚ Quebec, SE Canada
38 J5 **Notch Peak** ▲ Utah, W USA 39.08N 113.24W
112 G10 **Noteć** Ger. Netze. ≈ NW Poland
Nóties Sporádes see Dodekánisos
117 J22 **Nótion Aigaíon** Eng. Aegean South. ◈ region E Greece
117 H18 **Nótios Evvoïkós Kólpos** gulf E Greece
117 B16 **Nótio Stenó Kérkyras** strait W Greece
109 L25 **Noto** anc. Netum. Sicilia, Italy, C Mediterranean Sea 36.52N 15.04E
171 J12 **Noto** Ishikawa, Honshū, SW Japan 37.18N 137.11E
97 G15 **Notodden** Telemark, S Norway 59.33N 9.15E
109 L25 **Noto, Golfo di** gulf Sicilia, Italy, C Mediterranean Sea
171 J12 **Noto-hantō** peninsula Honshū, SW Japan
171 J12 **Noto-jima** island SW Japan
172 Qq5 **Notoro-ko** ⊚ Hokkaidō, NE Japan
11 T11 **Notre Dame Bay** bay Newfoundland, E Canada
13 P6 **Notre-Dame-de-Lorette** Quebec, SE Canada 49.05N 72.24W
12 L11 **Notre-Dame-de-Pontmain** Quebec, SE Canada 46.18N 75.37W
13 T8 **Notre-Dame-du-Lac** Quebec, SE Canada 47.36N 68.48W
13 Q6 **Notre-Dame-du-Rosaire** Quebec, SE Canada 48.48N 71.27W
13 U8 **Notre-Dame, Monts** ▲▲ Quebec, S Canada
79 R16 **Notsé** S Togo 6.53N 1.09E
172 R7 **Notsuke-suidō** strait Japan/Russian Federation
172 R7 **Notsuke-zaki** headland Hokkaidō, NE Japan 43.33N 145.18E
12 G14 **Nottawasaga** ≈ Ontario, S Canada
12 G14 **Nottawasaga Bay** lake bay Ontario, S Canada
10 I11 **Nottaway** ≈ Quebec, SE Canada
25 S1 **Nottely Lake** ⊠ Georgia, SE USA
97 H16 **Nøtterøy** island S Norway
99 M19 **Nottingham** C England, UK 52.58N 1.10W
16 N5 **Nottingham Island** island Nunavut, NE Canada
99 N18 **Nottinghamshire** cultural region C England, UK
23 V7 **Nottoway** Virginia, NE USA 37.07N 78.03W
23 V7 **Nottoway River** ≈ Virginia, NE USA
78 G7 **Nouâdhibou** prev. Port-Étienne. Dakhlet Nouâdhibou, W Mauritania 20.54N 17.01W
78 G7 **Nouâdhibou** ✈ Dakhlet Nouâdhibou, W Mauritania 20.59N 17.02W
78 F7 **Nouâdhibou, Dakhlet** prev. Baie du Lévrier. bay W Mauritania
78 F7 **Nouâdhibou, Râs** prev. Cap Blanc. headland NW Mauritania 20.48N 17.03W
78 G9 **Nouakchott** ● (Mauritania) Nouakchott District, SW Mauritania 18.09N 15.58W
78 G9 **Nouakchott** ✈ Trarza, SW Mauritania 18.18N 15.54W
123 K13 **Noual, Sebkhet en** var. Sabkhat an Nawāl. salt flat C Tunisia
78 G8 **Nouâmghâr** var. Nouamrhar. Dakhlet Nouâdhibou, W Mauritania 19.22N 16.31W
Nouamrhar see Nouâmghâr
Nouă Sulița see Novoselytsya
197 I7 **Nouméa** ○ (New Caledonia) Province Sud, S New Caledonia 22.13S 166.29E
81 E15 **Noun** ≈ C Cameroon
79 N12 **Nouna** W Burkina 12.43N 3.54W
85 H24 **Noupoort** Northern Cape, C South Africa 31.10S 24.57E
Nouveau-Brunswick see New Brunswick
Nouveau-Comptoir see Wemindji
13 T4 **Nouvel, Lacs** ⊚ Quebec, SE Canada
13 W7 **Nouvelle** Quebec, SE Canada 48.07N 66.16W
13 W7 **Nouvelle** ≈ Quebec, SE Canada
Nouvelle-Calédonie see New Caledonia
Nouvelle Écosse see Nova Scotia
105 R3 **Nouzonville** Ardennes, N France 49.49N 4.45E

◆ Country
● Country Capital
◇ Dependent Territory
○ Dependent Territory Capital
◈ Administrative Region
✈ International Airport
▲ Mountain
▲▲ Mountain Range
Volcano
≈ River
⊚ Lake
⊠ Reservoir

153 *Q11* **Nov** *Rus.* Nau. NW Tajikistan *40.10N 69.16E*
61 *I21* **Nova Alvorada** Mato Grosso do Sul, SW Brazil *21.25S 54.19W*
Novabad *see* Navobod
113 *D19* **Nová Bystřice** *Ger.* Neubistritz. Budějovický Kraj, S Czech Republic *48.59N 15.05E*
118 *H13* **Novaci** Gorj, SW Romania *45.08N 23.39E*
Nova Civitas *see* Neustadt an der Weinstrasse
Novaesium *see* Neuss
62 *H10* **Nova Esperança** Paraná, S Brazil *23.09S 52.13W*
108 *H11* **Novafeltria** Marche, C Italy *43.54N 12.18E*
62 *Q9* **Nova Friburgo** Rio de Janeiro, SE Brazil *22.16S 42.34W*
84 *D12* **Nova Gaia** *var.* Cambundi-Catembo. Malanje, NE Angola *10.03S 17.31E*
111 *S12* **Nova Gorica** W Slovenia *45.57N 13.40E*
114 *G10* **Nova Gradiška** *Ger.* Neugradisk, *Hung.* Újgradiska. Brod-Posavina, NE Croatia *45.15N 17.23E*
62 *K7* **Nova Granada** São Paulo, S Brazil *20.33S 49.19W*
62 *O10* **Nova Iguaçu** Rio de Janeiro, SE Brazil *22.31S 44.04W*
119 *S10* **Nova Kakhovka** *Rus.* Novaya Kakhovka. Khersons'ka Oblast', SE Ukraine *46.45N 33.19E*
Nová Karvinná *see* Karviná
Nova Lamego *see* Gabú
Nova Lisboa *see* Huambo
114 *C11* **Novalja** Lika-Senj, W Croatia *44.33N 14.53E*
121 *M14* **Novalukoml'** *Rus.* Novolukoml'. Vitsyebskaya Voblasts', N Belarus *54.40N 29.09E*
Nova Mambone *see* Mambone
85 *P16* **Nova Nabúri** Zambézia, NE Mozambique *16.47S 38.55E*
119 *Q9* **Nova Odesa** *var.* Novaya Odessa. Mykolayivs'ka Oblast', S Ukraine *47.18N 31.45E*
62 *H10* **Nova Olímpia** Paraná, S Brazil *23.28S 53.12W*
63 *I15* **Nova Prata** Rio Grande do Sul, S Brazil *28.45S 51.37W*
12 *H12* **Novar** Ontario, S Canada *45.26N 79.14W*
108 *C7* **Novara** *anc.* Novaria. Piemonte, NW Italy *45.27N 8.36E*
Novaria *see* Novara
119 *P7* **Novarkanels'k** Kirovohrads'ka Oblast', C Ukraine *48.39N 30.48E*
11 *P15* **Nova Scotia** *Fr.* Nouvelle Écosse. ◈ *province* SE Canada
(0) *M9* **Nova Scotia** *physical region* SE Canada
36 *M8* **Novato** California, W USA *38.06N 122.35W*
199 *Jj8* **Nova Trough** *undersea feature* W Pacific Ocean
118 *L7* **Nova Ushtsya** Khmel'nyts'ka Oblast', W Ukraine *48.50N 27.16E*
85 *M17* **Nova Vanduzi** Manica, C Mozambique *18.54S 33.18E*
119 *U5* **Nova Vodolaha** *Rus.* Novaya Vodolaga. Kharkivs'ka Oblast', E Ukraine *49.42N 35.48E*
126 *L13* **Novaya Chara** Chitinskaya Oblast', S Russian Federation *56.45N 117.58E*
126 *J14* **Novaya Igirma** Irkutskaya Oblast', C Russian Federation *57.08N 103.52E*
Novaya Kakhovka *see* Nova Kakhovka
150 *E10* **Novaya Kazanka** Zapadnyy Kazakhstan, W Kazakhstan *48.57N 49.34E*
128 *I12* **Novaya Ladoga** Leningradskaya Oblast', NW Russian Federation *60.03N 32.15E*
125 *Ee10* **Novaya Lyalya** Sverdlovskaya Oblast, C Russian Federation *59.01N 60.37E*
131 *R5* **Novaya Malykla** Ul'yanovskaya Oblast', W Russian Federation *54.13N 49.55E*
Novaya Odessa *see* Nova Odesa
126 *M4* **Novaya Sibir', Ostrov** *island* Novosibirskiye Ostrova, NE Russian Federation
Novaya Vodolaga *see* Nova Vodolaha
121 *P17* **Novaya Yel'nya** *Rus.* Novaya Yel'nya. Mahilyowskaya Voblasts', E Belarus *53.16N 31.13E*
125 *G4* **Novaya Zemlya** *island group* N Russian Federation
Novaya Zemlya Trough *see* East Novaya Zemlya Trough
116 *K10* **Nova Zagora** Sliven, C Bulgaria *42.29N 26.00E*
107 *S12* **Novelda** País Valenciano, E Spain *38.24N 0.45W*
113 *H19* **Nové Mesto nad Váhom** *Ger.* Waagneustadtll, *Hung.* Vágújhely. Trenčiansky Kraj, W Slovakia *48.48N 17.50E*
113 *F17* **Nové Město na Moravě** *Ger.* Neustadtl in Mähren. Jihlavský Kraj, C Czech Republic *49.34N 16.04E*
Novesium *see* Neuss
113 *I21* **Nové Zámky** *Ger.* Neuhäusel, *Hung.* Érsekújvár. Nitriansky Kraj, SW Slovakia *49.00N 18.10E*
125 *C6* **Novgorod** Novgorodskaya Oblast', W Russian Federation *58.31N 31.15E*
Novgorod-Severskiy *see* Novhorod-Sivers'kyy
125 *C6* **Novgorodskaya Oblast'** ◈ *province* W Russian Federation
119 *R8* **Novhorodka** Kirovohrads'ka Oblast', C Ukraine *48.21N 32.38E*
119 *R2* **Novhorod-Sivers'kyy** *Rus.* Novgorod-Severskiy. Chernihivs'ka Oblast', NE Ukraine *52.00N 33.15E*
33 *R10* **Novi** Michigan, N USA *42.28N 83.28W*
Novi *see* Novi Vinodolski
114 *L9* **Novi Bečej** *prev.* Új-Becse, Vološinovo, *Ger.* Neubetsche, *Hung.* Törökbecse. Serbia, N Serbia and Montenegro (Yugoslavia) *45.36N 20.09E*
27 *Q8* **Novice** Texas, SW USA *32.00N 99.38W*
114 *A9* **Novigrad** Istra, NW Croatia *45.19N 13.33E*
Novi Grad *see* Bosanski Novi
116 *G9* **Novi Iskŭr** Sofiya-Grad, W Bulgaria *42.46N 23.19E*
108 *C9* **Novi Ligure** Piemonte, NW Italy *44.46N 8.46E*
101 *L22* **Noville** Luxembourg, SE Belgium *50.04N 5.46E*
204 *I10* **Noville Peninsula** *peninsula* Thurston Island, Antarctica
Noviodunum *see* Soissons, Aisne, France
Noviodunum *see* Nevers, Nièvre, France
Noviodunum *see* Nyon, Vaud, Switzerland
Noviomagus *see* Lisieux, France
Noviomagus *see* Nijmegen, Netherlands
116 *M8* **Novi Pazar** Shumen, NE Bulgaria *43.21N 27.13E*
115 *M15* **Novi Pazar** *Turk.* Yenipazar. Serbia, S Serbia and Montenegro (Yugoslavia) *43.09N 20.31E*
114 *K10* **Novi Sad** *Ger.* Neusatz, *Hung.* Újvidék. Serbia, N Serbia and Montenegro (Yugoslavia) *45.16N 19.49E*
119 *T6* **Novi Sanzhary** Poltavs'ka Oblast', C Ukraine *49.21N 34.18E*
114 *H12* **Novi Travnik** *prev.* Pučarevo. Federacija Bosna I Hercegovina, C Bosnia and Herzegovina *44.12N 17.39E*
114 *B10* **Novi Vinodolski** *var.* Novi. Primorje-Gorski Kotar, NW Croatia *45.08N 14.46E*
60 *F12* **Novo Airão** Amazonas, N Brazil *2.06S 61.19W*
131 *N14* **Novoaleksandrovsk** Stavropol'skiy Kray, SW Russian Federation *44.41N 43.01E*
Novoalekseyevka *see* Zhobda
126 *H14* **Novoaltaysk** Altayskiy Kray, S Russian Federation *53.22N 83.58E*
131 *N9* **Novoanninskiy** Volgogradskaya Oblast', SW Russian Federation *50.31N 42.43E*
60 *F13* **Novo Aripuanã** Amazonas, N Brazil *5.04S 60.19W*
119 *Y6* **Novoaydar** Luhans'ka Oblast', E Ukraine *49.00N 39.00E*
119 *X9* **Novoazovs'k** *Rus.* Novoazovsk. Donets'ka Oblast', E Ukraine *47.07N 38.06E*
126 *Mm16* **Novobureyskiy** Amurskaya Oblast', SE Russian Federation *49.42N 129.46E*
131 *Q3* **Novocheboksarsk** Chavash Respubliki, W Russian Federation *56.07N 47.32E*
131 *R5* **Novocheremshansk** Ul'yanovskaya Oblast', W Russian Federation *54.23N 50.08E*
130 *L12* **Novocherkassk** Rostovskaya Oblast', SW Russian Federation *47.23N 40.00E*
131 *R6* **Novodevich'ye** Samarskaya Oblast', W Russian Federation *53.33N 48.51E*
128 *M8* **Novodvinsk** Arkhangel'skaya Oblast', NW Russian Federation *64.22N 40.48E*
Novograd-Volynskiy *see* Novohrad-Volyns'kyy
Novogrudok *see* Navahrudak
63 *I15* **Novo Hamburgo** Rio Grande do Sul, S Brazil *29.42S 51.07W*
61 *H16* **Novo Horizonte** Mato Grosso, W Brazil *11.19S 57.11W*
62 *K8* **Novo Horizonte** São Paulo, S Brazil *21.27S 49.14W*
118 *M4* **Novohrad-Volyns'kyy** *Rus.* Novograd-Volynskiy. Zhytomyrs'ka Oblast', N Ukraine *50.33N 27.31E*
150 *L14* **Novokazalinsk** *see* Ayteke Bi
130 *M8* **Novokhopersk** Voronezhskaya Oblast', W Russian Federation *51.09N 41.34E*
131 *R6* **Novokuybyshevsk** Samarskaya Oblast', W Russian Federation *53.06N 49.56E*
126 *H14* **Novokuznetsk** *prev.* Stalinsk. Kemerovskaya Oblast', S Russian Federation *53.45N 87.12E*
205 *R1* **Novolazarevskaya** *Russian research station* Antarctica *70.42S 11.31E*
Novolukoml' *see* Novalukoml'
111 *V12* **Novo mesto** *Ger.* Rudolfswert; *prev. Ger.* Neustadtl. SE Slovenia *45.48N 15.09E*
130 *K15* **Novomikhaylovskiy** Krasnodarskiy Kray, SW Russian Federation *44.18N 38.49E*
114 *L8* **Novo Miloševo** Serbia, N Serbia and Montenegro (Yugoslavia) *45.43N 20.20E*
Novomirgorod *see* Novomyrhorod
130 *L5* **Novomoskovsk** Tul'skaya Oblast', W Russian Federation *54.04N 38.22E*
119 *U7* **Novomoskovs'k** *Rus.* Novomoskovsk. Dnipropetrovs'ka Oblast', E Ukraine *48.37N 35.13E*
119 *V8* **Novomykolayivka** Zaporiz'ka Oblast', SE Ukraine *47.58N 35.54E*
119 *Q7* **Novomyrhorod** *Rus.* Novomirgorod. Kirovohrads'ka Oblast', S Ukraine *48.46N 31.39E*
126 *I12* **Novonazimovo** Krasnoyarskiy Kray, C Russian Federation *59.30N 90.45E*
131 *N8* **Novonikolayevskiy** Volgogradskaya Oblast', SW Russian Federation *50.55N 42.24E*
131 *P10* **Novonikol'skoye** Volgogradskaya Oblast', SW Russian Federation *49.23N 45.06E*
131 *X7* **Novoorsk** Orenburgskaya Oblast', W Russian Federation *51.21N 59.03E*
130 *M13* **Novopokrovskaya** Krasnodarskiy Kray, SW Russian Federation *45.58N 40.43E*
Novopolotsk *see* Navapolatsk
119 *Y5* **Novopskov** Luhans'ka Oblast', E Ukraine *49.33N 39.07E*
Novoradomsk *see* Radomsko
Novo Redondo *see* Sumbe
131 *R8* **Novorepnoye** Saratovskaya Oblast', W Russian Federation *51.04N 48.34E*
130 *K14* **Novorossiysk** Krasnodarskiy Kray, SW Russian Federation *44.49N 37.37E*
Novorossiyskiy *see* Novorossiyskoye
150 *J10* **Novorossiyskoye** *prev.* Novorossiyskiy. Aktyubinsk, NW Kazakhstan *50.13N 57.57E*
126 *Jj6* **Novorybnaya** Taymyrskiy (Dolgano-Nenetskiy) Avtonomnyy Okrug, N Russian Federation *72.48N 105.49E*
128 *F15* **Novorzhev** Pskovskaya Oblast', W Russian Federation *57.01N 29.19E*
Novoselitsa *see* Novoselytsya
119 *S12* **Novoselivs'ke** Respublika Krym, S Ukraine *45.26N 33.37E*
Novosëlki *see* Navasyolki
116 *G6* **Novo Selo** Vidin, NW Bulgaria *44.08N 22.48E*
115 *M14* **Novo Selo** Serbia, C Serbia and Montenegro (Yugoslavia) *43.39N 20.54E*
118 *K8* **Novoselytsya** *Rom.* Nouă Sulița, *Rus.* Novoselitsa. Chernivets'ka Oblast', W Ukraine *48.13N 26.18E*
131 *U7* **Novosergiyevka** Orenburgskaya Oblast', W Russian Federation *52.04N 53.40E*
130 *L11* **Novoshakhtinsk** Rostovskaya Oblast', SW Russian Federation *47.48N 39.51E*
126 *Gg14* **Novosibirsk** Novosibirskaya Oblast', C Russian Federation *55.04N 83.04E*
125 *G13* **Novosibirskaya Oblast'** ◈ *province* C Russian Federation
126 *M4* **Novosibirskiye Ostrova** *Eng.* New Siberian Islands. *island group* N Russian Federation
130 *K6* **Novosil'** Orlovskaya Oblast', W Russian Federation *53.00N 37.59E*
128 *G16* **Novosokol'niki** Pskovskaya Oblast', W Russian Federation *56.21N 30.07E*
131 *Q6* **Novospasskoye** Ul'yanovskaya Oblast', W Russian Federation *53.08N 47.48E*
131 *X8* **Novotroitsk** Orenburgskaya Oblast', W Russian Federation *51.09N 58.18E*
Novotroitskoye *see* Brlik, Kazakhstan
Novotroitskoye *see* Novotroyits'ke, Ukraine
119 *T11* **Novotroyits'ke** *Rus.* Novotroitskoye. Khersons'ka Oblast', S Ukraine *46.21N 34.21E*
Novoukrainka *see* Novoukrayinka
119 *Q8* **Novoukrayinka** *Rus.* Novoukrainka. Kirovohrads'ka Oblast', C Ukraine *48.19N 31.33E*
131 *Q5* **Novoul'yanovsk** Ul'yanovskaya Oblast', W Russian Federation *54.10N 48.19E*
125 *Ee10* **Novoural'ske** Sverdlovkaya Oblast', W Russian Federation *56.58N 59.50E*
131 *W8* **Novouralets** Orenburgskaya Oblast', W Russian Federation *51.19N 56.57E*
Novo-Urgench *see* Urganch
118 *I4* **Novovolyns'k** *Rus.* Novovolynsk. Volyns'ka Oblast', NW Ukraine *50.46N 24.09E*
119 *S9* **Novovorontsovka** Khersons'ka Oblast', S Ukraine *47.28N 33.55E*
153 *Y7* **Novovoznesenovka** Issyk-Kul'skaya Oblast', E Kyrgyzstan *42.36N 78.44E*
129 *R14* **Novovyatsk** Kirovskaya Oblast', NW Russian Federation *58.30N 49.42E*
Novoyel'nya *see* Navayel'nya
128 *I7* **Novoye Yushkozero** Respublika Kareliya, NW Russian Federation *64.46N 32.13E*
119 *O6* **Novozhyvotiv** Vinnyts'ka Oblast', C Ukraine *49.16N 29.31E*
130 *H6* **Novozybkov** Bryanskaya Oblast', W Russian Federation *52.36N 31.58E*
114 *F9* **Novska** Sisak-Moslavina, NE Croatia *45.20N 16.58E*
Nový Bohumín *see* Bohumín
113 *D15* **Nový Bor** *Ger.* Haida; *prev.* Bor u České Lípy, Hajda. Liberecký Kraj, N Czech Republic *50.46N 14.32E*
113 *E16* **Nový Bydžov** *Ger.* Neubidschow. Hradecký Kraj, N Czech Republic *50.15N 15.27E*
121 *G18* **Novy Dvor** *Rus.* Novyy Dvor. Hrodzyenskaya Voblasts', W Belarus *52.49N 24.22E*
113 *I17* **Nový Jičín** *Ger.* Neutitschein. Ostravský Kraj, E Czech Republic *49.36N 18.00E*
120 *K12* **Novy Pahost** *Rus.* Novyy Pogost. Vitsyebskaya Voblasts', NW Belarus *55.30N 27.28E*
Novyy Bug *see* Novyy Buh
119 *R9* **Novyy Buh** *Rus.* Novyy Bug. Mykolayivs'ka Oblast', S Ukraine *47.39N 32.31E*
119 *Q4* **Novyy Bykiv** Chernihivs'ka Oblast', N Ukraine *50.36N 31.39E*
Novyy Dvor *see* Novy Dvor
Novyye Aneny *see* Anenii Noi
131 *P7* **Novyye Burasy** Saratovskaya Oblast', W Russian Federation *52.10N 46.00E*
Novyy Margilan *see* Farghona
130 *K8* **Novyy Oskol** Belgorodskaya Oblast', W Russian Federation *50.43N 37.55E*
Novyy Pogost *see* Novy Pahost
131 *R2* **Novyy Tor"yal** Respublika Mariy El, W Russian Federation *56.59N 48.53E*
126 *K14* **Novyy Uoyan** Respublika Buryatiya, S Russian Federation *56.06N 111.27E*
126 *Gg9* **Novyy Urengoy** Yamalo-Nenetskiy Avtonomnyy Okrug, N Russian Federation *66.06N 76.25E*
127 *N15* **Novyy Urgal** Khabarovskiy Kray, E Russian Federation *51.02N 132.45E*
Novyy Uzen' *see* Zhanaozen
125 *G12* **Novyy Vasyugan** Tomskaya Oblast', C Russian Federation *58.28N 76.19E*
113 *N16* **Nowa Dęba** Podkarpackie, SE Poland *50.31N 21.53E*
113 *G15* **Nowa Ruda** *Ger.* Neurode. Dolnośląskie, SW Poland *50.34N 16.30E*
112 *F12* **Nowa Sól** *var.* Nowasól, *Ger.* Neusalz an der Oder. Lubuskie, W Poland *51.47N 15.42E*
29 *Q8* **Nowata** Oklahoma, C USA *36.42N 95.38W*
148 *M6* **Nowbarān** Markazī, W Iran *35.07N 49.51E*
112 *J8* **Nowe** Kujawski-pomorskie, C Poland *53.39N 18.44E*
112 *K9* **Nowe Miasto Lubawskie** *Ger.* Neumark. Warmińsko-Mazurskie, NE Poland *53.24N 19.36E*
112 *L13* **Nowe Miasto nad Pilicą** Mazowieckie, C Poland *51.37N 20.34E*
112 *D8* **Nowe Warpno** *Ger.* Neuwarp. Zachodniopomorskie, NW Poland *53.52N 14.12E*
Nowgong *see* Nagaon
112 *E8* **Nowogard** *var.* Nowógard, *Ger.* Naugard. Zachodniopomorskie, NW Poland *53.41N 15.09E*
112 *N9* **Nowogród** Podlaskie, NE Poland *53.14N 21.52E*
Nowogródek *see* Navahrudak
113 *E14* **Nowogrodziec** *Ger.* Naumburg am Queis. Dolnośląskie, SW Poland *51.12N 15.24E*
Nowojelnia *see* Navayel'nya
Nowo-Minsk *see* Mińsk Mazowiecki
35 *V13* **Nowood River** ≈ Wyoming, C USA
Nowo-Święciany *see* Švenčionėliai
191 *S10* **Nowra-Bomaderry** New South Wales, SE Australia *34.51S 150.41E*
155 *T5* **Nowshera** *var.* Naushahra, Naushara. North-West Frontier Province, NE Pakistan *34.00N 72.00E*
112 *J7* **Nowy Dwór Gdański** *Ger.* Tiegenhof. Pomorskie, N Poland *54.12N 19.03E*
112 *L11* **Nowy Dwór Mazowiecki** Mazowieckie, C Poland *52.25N 20.43E*
113 *M17* **Nowy Sącz** *Ger.* Neu Sandec. Małopolskie, S Poland *49.36N 20.41E*
113 *L18* **Nowy Targ** *Ger.* Neumark. Małopolskie, S Poland *49.28N 20.00E*
112 *F11* **Nowy Tomyśl** *var.* Nowy Tomysl. Wielkolpolskie, C Poland *52.18N 16.07E*
154 *M7* **Now Zād** *var.* Nauzad. Helmand, S Afghanistan *32.22N 64.31E*
25 *N4* **Noxubee River** ≈ Alabama/Mississippi, S USA
126 *Gg10* **Noyabr'sk** Yamalo-Nenetskiy Avtonomnyy Okrug, N Russian Federation *63.08N 75.19E*
104 *L8* **Noyant** Maine-et-Loire, NW France *47.28N 0.08W*
41 *X14* **Noyes Island** *island* Alexander Archipelago, Alaska, USA
105 *O3* **Noyon** Oise, N France *49.35N 3.00E*
104 *I7* **Nozay** Loire-Atlantique, NW France *47.34N 1.36W*
84 *L12* **Nsando** Northern, NE Zambia *10.22S 31.14E*
85 *N16* **Nsanje** Southern, S Malawi *16.57S 35.10E*
79 *Q17* **Nsawam** SE Ghana *5.46N 0.19W*
81 *E16* **Nsimalen** ✕ Centre, C Cameroon *19.15N 81.22W*
84 *K12* **Nsombo** Northern, NE Zambia *10.35S 29.58E*
84 *H13* **Ntambu** North Western, NW Zambia *12.22S 24.57E*
85 *N14* **Ntcheu** *var.* Ncheu. Central, S Malawi *14.49S 34.37E*
81 *D17* **Ntem** *prev.* Campo, Kampo. ≈ Cameroon/Equatorial Guinea
85 *I14* **Ntemwa** North Western, NW Zambia *14.03S 26.13E*
Ntlenyana, Mount *see* Thabana Ntlenyana
81 *I19* **Ntomba, Lac** *var.* Lac Tumba. ◎ NW Dem. Rep. Congo
83 *E19* **Ntungamo** SW Uganda *0.54S 30.16E*
83 *E18* **Ntusi** SW Uganda *0.03N 31.11E*
85 *H18* **Ntwetwe Pan** *salt lake* NE Botswana
95 *M15* **Nuasjärvi** ◎ C Finland
82 *F11* **Nuba Mountains** ▲▲ C Sudan
70 *I9* **Nubian Desert** *desert* NE Sudan
118 *G10* **Nucet** *Hung.* Diófás. Bihor, W Romania *46.28N 22.34E*
Nu Chiang *see* Salween
151 *U9* **Nuclear Testing Ground** *nuclear site* Pavlodar, E Kazakhstan
58 *E9* **Nucuray, Río** ≈ N Peru
27 *R14* **Nueces River** ≈ Texas, SW USA
9 *V9* **Nueltin Lake** ◎ Manitoba/Nunavut, C Canada
101 *K15* **Nuenen** Noord-Brabant, S Netherlands *51.29N 5.36E*
64 *G6* **Nuestra Señora, Bahía** *bay* N Chile
63 *D14* **Nuestra Señora Rosario de Caa Catí** Corrientes, NE Argentina *27.48S 57.42W*
56 *J9* **Nueva Antioquia** Vichada, E Colombia *6.04N 69.30W*
Nueva Caceres *see* Naga
43 *O7* **Nueva Ciudad Guerrera** Tamaulipas, C Mexico *26.32N 99.13W*
57 *N4* **Nueva Esparta** *off.* Estado Nueva Esparta. ◈ *state* NE Venezuela
46 *C5* **Nueva Gerona** Isla de la Juventud, S Cuba *21.49N 82.49W*
44 *H8* **Nueva Guadalupe** San Miguel, E El Salvador *13.30N 88.21W*
44 *M11* **Nueva Guinea** Región Autónoma Atlántico Sur, SE Nicaragua *11.40N 84.22W*
63 *D19* **Nueva Helvecia** Colonia, SW Uruguay *34.16S 57.52W*
65 *J25* **Nueva, Isla** *island* S Chile
42 *M14* **Nueva Italia** Michoacán de Ocampo, SW Mexico *19.01N 102.06W*
58 *D6* **Nueva Loja** *var.* Lago Agrio. Sucumbíos, NE Ecuador
44 *F6* **Nueva Ocotepeque** *prev.* Ocotepeque. Ocotepeque, W Honduras *14.25N 89.11W*
63 *D19* **Nueva Palmira** Colonia, SW Uruguay *33.52S 58.25W*
43 *N6* **Nueva Rosita** Coahuila de Zaragoza, NE Mexico *27.58N 101.10W*
44 *E7* **Nueva San Salvador** *prev.* Santa Tecla. La Libertad, SW El Salvador *13.42N 89.18W*
44 *J8* **Nueva Segovia** ◈ *department* NW Nicaragua
Nueva Tabarca *see* Plana, Isla
Nueva Villa de Padilla *see* Nuevo Padilla
63 *B21* **Nueve de Julio** Buenos Aires, E Argentina *35.29S 60.52W*
46 *H6* **Nuevitas** Camagüey, E Cuba *21.34N 77.18W*
63 *D18* **Nuevo Berlin** Río Negro, W Uruguay *32.58S 58.03W*
42 *I4* **Nuevo Casas Grandes** Chihuahua, N Mexico *30.23N 107.53W*
45 *T14* **Nuevo Chagres** Colón, C Panama *9.13N 80.03W*
43 *W15* **Nuevo Coahuila** Campeche, E Mexico *17.52N 90.46W*
65 *K17* **Nuevo, Golfo** *gulf* S Argentina
43 *O7* **Nuevo Laredo** Tamaulipas, NE Mexico *27.27N 99.31W*
43 *N8* **Nuevo León** ◈ *state* NE Mexico
43 *P10* **Nuevo Padilla** *var.* Nueva Villa de Padilla. Tamaulipas, C Mexico *24.01N 98.48W*
58 *E6* **Nuevo Rocafuerte** Napo, E Ecuador *0.55S 75.25W*
168 *G6* **Nuga** Dzavhan, W Mongolia *48.17N 95.07E*
82 *O13* **Nugaal** *off.* Gobolka Nugaal. ◈ *region* N Somalia
193 *E24* **Nugget Point** *headland* South Island, NZ *46.26S 169.49E*
195 *R9* **Nuguria Islands** *island group* E PNG
192 *P10* **Nuhaka** Hawke's Bay, North Island, NZ *39.03S 177.43E*
144 *M10* **Nuhaydayn, Wādī an** *dry watercourse* W Iraq
202 *E7* **Nui Atoll** *atoll* W Tuvalu
Nu Jiang *see* Salween
Nûk *see* Nuuk
190 *G7* **Nukey Bluff** *hill* South Australia *32.34S 135.36E*
Nukha *see* Şäki
127 *O9* **Nukh Yablonevyy, Gora** ▲ E Russian Federation *60.26N 151.45E*
195 *T13* **Nukiki** Choiseul Island, NW Solomon Islands *6.45S 94.30E*
194 *F10* **Nuku** Sandaun, NW PNG *3.40S 142.29E*
200 *R15* **Nuku** *island* Tongatapu Group, NE Tonga
200 *Qq15* **Nuku'alofa** Tongatapu, S Tonga *21.09S 175.13W*
200 *Qq15* **Nuku'alofa** ● (Tonga) Tongatapu, S Tonga *21.07S 175.13W*
202 *G12* **Nukuatea** *island* N Wallis and Futuna
202 *F7* **Nukufetau Atoll** *atoll* C Tuvalu
202 *G12* **Nukuhifala** *island* E Wallis and Futuna
203 *W7* **Nuku Hiva** *island* Îles Marquises, NE French Polynesia
199 *Ll9* **Nuku Hiva Island** *island* Îles Marquises, N French Polynesia
202 *F9* **Nukulaelae Atoll** *var.* Nukulailai. *atoll* E Tuvalu
Nukulailai *see* Nukulaelae Atoll
202 *G11* **Nukuloa** *island* N Wallis and Futuna
195 *W10* **Nukumanu Islands** *prev.* Tasman Group. *island group* NE PNG
Nukunau *see* Nikunau
202 *J9* **Nukunonu Atoll** *island* C Tokelau
202 *J9* **Nukunonu Village** Nukunonu Atoll, C Tokelau
201 *S18* **Nukuoro Atoll** *atoll* Caroline Islands, S Micronesia
152 *H8* **Nukus** Qoraqalpog'iston Respublikasi, W Uzbekistan *42.28N 59.32E*
202 *G11* **Nukutapu** *island* N Wallis and Futuna
41 *O9* **Nulato** Alaska, USA *64.43N 158.06W*
41 *O10* **Nulato Hills** ▲▲ Alaska, USA
107 *T9* **Nules** País Valenciano, E Spain *39.52N 0.10W*
Nuling *see* Sultan Kudarat
190 *C6* **Nullarbor** South Australia *31.28S 130.57E*
188 *M11* **Nullarbor Plain** *plateau* South Australia/Western Australia
169 *S12* **Nulu'erhu Shan** ▲▲ N China
79 *X14* **Numan** Adamawa, E Nigeria *9.26N 11.58E*
171 *K14* **Numata** Gunma, Honshū, S Japan *36.39N 139.00E*
172 *Oo4* **Numata** Hokkaidō, NE Japan *43.48N 141.55E*
83 *C15* **Numatinna** ≈ W Sudan
171 *J17* **Numazu** Shizuoka, Honshū, S Japan *35.05N 138.52E*
97 *F14* **Numedalen** *valley* S Norway
97 *G14* **Numedalslågen** *var.* Laagen. ≈ S Norway
95 *L19* **Nummela** Etelä-Suomi, S Finland *60.21N 24.19E*
125 *G9* **Numto** Khanty-Mansiyskiy Avtonomnyy Okrug, N Russian Federation *63.33N 70.53E*
191 *O11* **Numurkah** Victoria, SE Australia *36.04S 145.28E*
206 *L16* **Nunap Isua** *var.* Uummannarsuaq, *Dan.* Kap Farvel, *Eng.* Cape Farewell. *headland* S Greenland *59.57N 44.27W*
15 *K5* **Nunavut** ◈ *Territory* N Canada
56 *H9* **Nunchia** Casanare, C Colombia *5.37N 72.13W*
99 *M20* **Nuneaton** C England, UK *52.31N 1.28W*
159 *W14* **Nungba** Manipur, NE India *24.46N 93.25E*
40 *L12* **Nunivak Island** *island* Alaska, USA
158 *I5* **Nun Kun** ▲ NW India *34.01N 76.04E*
100 *L10* **Nunspeet** Gelderland, E Netherlands *52.21N 5.45E*
109 *C18* **Nuoro** Sardegna, Italy, C Mediterranean Sea *40.19N 9.19E*
77 *R12* **Nuqayy, Jabal** *hill range* S Libya
56 *C9* **Nuquí** Chocó, W Colombia *5.43N 77.16W*
149 *O4* **Nūr** Māzandarān, N Iran *36.34N 52.01E*
151 *Q9* **Nura** ≈ N Kazakhstan
149 *N11* **Nūrābād** Fārs, C Iran *30.07N 51.30E*
Nurakita *see* Niulakita
Nurata *see* Nurota
Nuratau, Khrebet *see* Nurota Tizmasi
142 *L17* **Nur Dağları** ▲▲ S Turkey
Nurek *see* Norak
Nuremberg *see* Nürnberg
142 *M15* **Nurhak** Kahramanmaraş, S Turkey *37.57N 37.21E*
190 *J9* **Nuriootpa** South Australia *34.28S 139.00E*
131 *S5* **Nurlat** Respublika Tatarstan, W Russian Federation *54.26N 50.48E*
95 *N15* **Nurmes** Itä-Suomi, E Finland *63.31N 29.10E*
103 *K20* **Nürnberg** *Eng.* Nuremberg. Bayern, S Germany *49.27N 11.04E*
103 *K20* **Nürnberg** ✕ Bayern, SE Germany *49.29N 11.04E*
152 *M10* **Nurota** *Rus.* Nurata. Navoiy Viloyati, C Uzbekistan *40.40N 65.43E*
153 *N10* **Nurota Tizmasi** *Rus.* Khrebet Nuratau. ▲▲ C Uzbekistan
155 *T8* **Nūrpur** Punjab, E Pakistan *31.54N 71.55E*
191 *P6* **Nurri, Mount** *hill* New South Wales, SE Australia *31.42S 146.03E*
27 *T13* **Nursery** Texas, SW USA *28.55N 97.04W*
175 *P16* **Nusa Tenggara** *Eng.* Lesser Sunda Islands. *island group* East Timor/ Indonesia
175 *O15* **Nusa Tenggara Barat** *off.* Propinsi Nusa Tenggara Barat, *Eng.* West Nusa Tenggara. ◈ *province* S Indonesia
175 *Q17* **Nusa Tenggara Timur** *off.* Propinsi Nusa Tenggara Timur, *Eng.* East Nusa Tenggara. ◈ *province* S Indonesia
176 *Vv12* **Nusawulan** Papua, E Indonesia *4.03S 132.56E*
143 *Q16* **Nusaybin** *var.* Nisibin. Manisa, SE Turkey *37.07N 41.10E*
41 *O14* **Nushagak Bay** *bay* Alaska, USA
41 *O13* **Nushagak Peninsula** *headland* Alaska, USA *58.39N 159.03W*
41 *O13* **Nushagak River** ≈ Alaska, USA
166 *E11* **Nu Shan** ▲▲ SW China
155 *N11* **Nushki** Baluchistān, SW Pakistan *29.33N 66.01E*
Nussdorf *see* Năsăud
114 *J9* **Nuštar** Vukovar-Srijem, E Croatia *45.20N 18.48E*
101 *L18* **Nuth** Limburg, SE Netherlands *50.55N 5.52E*
102 *N13* **Nuthe** ≈ NE Germany
Nutmeg State *see* Connecticut
41 *T10* **Nutzotin Mountains** ▲▲ Alaska, USA
66 *I5* **Nuuk** *var.* Nûk, *Dan.* Godthaab, Godthåb. ○ (Greenland). Kitaa, SW Greenland *64.15N 51.34W*
94 *L13* **Nuupas** Lappi, NW Finland *66.01N 26.19E*
203 *O7* **Nuupere, Pointe** *headland* Moorea, W French Polynesia *17.34S 149.46W*
203 *O7* **Nuuroa, Pointe** *headland* Tahiti, W French Polynesia
168 *M8* **Nüürst** Töv, C Mongolia *47.44N 108.22E*
Nuwara *see* Nuwara Eliya
161 *K25* **Nuwara Eliya** *var.* Nuwara. Central Province, S Sri Lanka *6.58N 80.46E*
190 *E7* **Nuyts Archipelago** *island group* South Australia
85 *F17* **Nxaunxau** Ngamiland, NW Botswana *18.57S 21.18E*
41 *N12* **Nyac** Alaska, USA *61.00N 159.56W*
125 *Ff10* **Nyagan'** Khanty-Mansiyskiy Avtonomnyy Okrug, N Russian Federation *62.10N 65.32E*
Nyagassola *see* Niagassola
83 *I18* **Nyahururu** Central, W Kenya *0.04N 36.22E*
190 *M10* **Nyah West** Victoria, SE Australia *35.14S 143.18E*
164 *M15* **Nyainqêntanglha Feng** ▲ W China *30.20N 90.28E*
165 *N15* **Nyainqêntanglha Shan** ▲▲ W China
82 *B11* **Nyala** Southern Darfur, W Sudan *12.01N 24.49E*
85 *M16* **Nyamapanda** Mashonaland East, NE Zimbabwe *16.57S 32.51E*
83 *H25* **Nyamtumbo** Ruvuma, S Tanzania *10.33S 36.07E*
Nyanda *see* Masvingo
128 *M11* **Nyandoma** Arkhangel'skaya Oblast', NW Russian Federation *61.39N 40.09E*
85 *M16* **Nyanga** *prev.* Inyanga. Manicaland, E Zimbabwe *18.14S 32.42E*
81 *D20* **Nyanga** *off.* Province de la Nyanga, *var.* La Nyanga. ◈ *province* SW Gabon
81 *E20* **Nyanga** ≈ Congo/Gabon
83 *F20* **Nyantakara** Kagera, NW Tanzania *3.04S 31.22E*
83 *G19* **Nyanza** ◈ *province* W Kenya
83 *E21* **Nyanza-Lac** S Burundi *4.16S 29.38E*
70 *J14* **Nyasa, Lake** *var.* Lake Malawi; *prev.* Lago Nyassa. ◎ E Africa
Nyasaland/Nyasaland Protectorate *see* Malawi
Nyassa, Lago *see* Nyasa, Lake
121 *J17* **Nyasvizh** *Pol.* Nieśwież, *Rus.* Nesvizh. Minskaya Voblasts', C Belarus *53.13N 26.40E*
177 *G8* **Nyaunglebin** Pegu, SW Myanmar *17.58N 96.43E*
177 *G5* **Nyaung-u** Magwe, C Myanmar *21.03N 95.43E*
97 *H24* **Nyborg** Fyn, C Denmark *55.19N 10.48E*
97 *N21* **Nybro** Kalmar, S Sweden *56.45N 15.54E*
121 *J16* **Nyeharelaye** *Rus.* Negoreloye. Minskaya Voblasts', C Belarus *53.36N 27.05E*
205 *W3* **Nye Mountains** ▲▲ Antarctica
83 *I19* **Nyeri** Central, C Kenya *0.25S 36.55E*
120 *M11* **Nyeshcharda, Vozyera** ◎ N Belarus
94 *O2* **Ny-Friesland** *physical region* N Svalbard
97 *L14* **Nyhammar** Dalarna, C Sweden *60.19N 14.55E*
166 *F7* **Nyikog Qu** ≈ C China
164 *L14* **Nyima** Xizang Zizhiqu, W China *31.53N 87.50E*
85 *L14* **Nyimba** Eastern, E Zambia *14.33S 30.49E*
165 *P16* **Nyingchi** Xizang Zizhiqu, W China *29.34N 94.22E*
113 *O21* **Nyírbátor** Szabolcs-Szatmár-Bereg, E Hungary *47.49N 22.06E*
113 *N21* **Nyíregyháza** Szabolcs-Szatmár-Bereg, NE Hungary *47.57N 21.43E*
Nyiro *see* Ewaso Ng'iro
Nyitra *see* Nitra
Nyitrabánya *see* Handlová
95 *K16* **Nykarleby** *Fin.* Uusikaarlepyy. Länsi-Suomi, W Finland *63.22N 22.30E*
97 *I25* **Nykøbing** Storstrøm, SE Denmark *54.46N 11.52E*
97 *I22* **Nykøbing** Vestsjælland, C Denmark *55.55N 11.40E*
97 *F21* **Nykøbing** Viborg, NW Denmark *56.48N 8.52E*
97 *N17* **Nyköping** Södermanland, S Sweden *58.45N 17.03E*
97 *L15* **Nykroppa** Värmland, C Sweden *59.37N 14.18E*
Nylstroom *see* Modimolle
191 *P7* **Nymagee** New South Wales, SE Australia *32.06S 146.19E*
191 *V5* **Nymboida** New South Wales, SE Australia *29.57S 152.45E*
191 *U5* **Nymboida River** ≈ New South Wales, SE Australia
113 *D16* **Nymburk** *var.* Neuenburg an der Elbe, *Ger.* Nimburg. Středočeský Kraj, C Czech Republic *50.12N 15.00E*
97 *O16* **Nynäshamn** Stockholm, C Sweden *58.54N 17.55E*
191 *Q6* **Nyngan** New South Wales, SE Australia *31.36S 147.07E*
Nyoman *see* Neman
110 *A10* **Nyon** *Ger.* Neuss; *anc.* Noviodunum. Vaud, SW Switzerland *46.22N 6.15E*
81 *D16* **Nyong** ≈ SW Cameroon
105 *S14* **Nyons** Drôme, E France *44.22N 5.06E*
81 *D14* **Nyos, Lac** *Eng.* Lake Nyos. ◎ NW Cameroon
Nyos, Lake *see* Nyos, Lac
129 *U11* **Nyrob** *var.* Nyrov. Permskaya Oblast', NW Russian Federation *60.41N 56.42E*
Nyrov *see* Nyrob
113 *H15* **Nysa** *Ger.* Neisse. Opolskie, S Poland *50.28N 17.20E*
Nysa Łużycka *see* Neisse
Nyslott *see* Savonlinna
34 *M13* **Nyssa** Oregon, NW USA *43.52N 116.59W*
Nystad *see* Uusikaupunki
97 *I25* **Nysted** Storstrøm, SE Denmark *54.40N 11.41E*
129 *U14* **Nytva** Permskaya Oblast', NW Russian Federation *57.56N 55.22E*
171 *Ll9* **Nyūdō-zaki** *headland* Honshū, C Japan *39.59N 139.40E*
129 *P9* **Nyukhcha** Arkhangel'skaya Oblast', NW Russian Federation *63.24N 46.34E*
128 *H8* **Nyuk, Ozero** *var.* Ozero Njuk. ◎ NW Russian Federation
129 *O12* **Nyuksenitsa** *var.* Njuksenica. Vologodskaya Oblast', NW Russian Federation *60.25N 44.12E*
81 *O22* **Nyunzu** Katanga, SE Dem. Rep. Congo *5.55S 28.00E*
126 *Kk11* **Nyurba** Respublika Sakha (Yakutiya), NE Russian Federation *63.17N 118.14E*
126 *Kk12* **Nyuya** Respublika Sakha (Yakutiya), NE Russian Federation *60.33N 116.10E*
126 *K12* **Nyuya** ≈ NE Russian Federation
119 *T10* **Nyzhni Sirohozy** Khersons'ka Oblast', S Ukraine *46.49N 34.21E*
119 *U12* **Nyzhn'ohirs'kyy** *Rus.* Nizhnegorskiy. Respublika Krym, S Ukraine *45.26N 34.42E*
83 *G21* **Nzega** Tabora, C Tanzania *4.13S 33.10E*
78 *K15* **Nzérékoré** Guinée-Forestière, SE Guinea *7.45N 8.49W*
84 *A10* **N'Zeto** *prev.* Ambrizete. Zaire, NW Angola *7.13S 12.52E*
81 *M24* **Nzilo, Lac** *prev.* Lac Delcommune. ◎ SE Dem. Rep. Congo

O

31 *O11* **Oacoma** South Dakota, N USA *43.49N 99.25W*
31 *N9* **Oahe Dam** *dam* South Dakota, N USA *44.27N 100.24W*
30 *M9* **Oahe, Lake** ▣ North Dakota/South Dakota, N USA
40 *C9* **Oahu** *Haw.* O'ahu. *island* Hawaii, USA, C Pacific Ocean
172 *Qq6* **O-Akan-dake** ▲ Hokkaidō, NE Japan *43.26N 144.09E*
190 *K8* **Oakbank** South Australia *33.07S 140.36E*
21 *P13* **Oak Bluffs** Martha's Vineyard, New York, NE USA *41.25N 70.32W*
38 *K4* **Oak City** Utah, W USA *39.22N 112.19W*
39 *R3* **Oak Creek** Colorado, C USA *40.16N 106.57W*
37 *P8* **Oakdale** California, W USA *37.46N 120.51W*
24 *H8* **Oakdale** Louisiana, S USA *30.49N 92.39W*
31 *P7* **Oakes** North Dakota, N USA *46.08N 98.05W*
24 *J4* **Oak Grove** Louisiana, S USA *32.51N 91.25W*
99 *N19* **Oakham** C England, UK *52.40N 0.45W*
34 *H7* **Oak Harbor** Washington, NW USA *48.17N 122.38W*
23 *R5* **Oak Hill** West Virginia, NE USA *37.59N 81.09W*
37 *N8* **Oakland** California, W USA *37.48N 122.16W*
31 *T15* **Oakland** Iowa, C USA *41.18N 95.22W*

◆ Country
● Country Capital
◇ Dependent Territory
○ Dependent Territory Capital
◈ Administrative Region
✕ International Airport
▲ Mountain
▲▲ Mountain Range
Volcano
≈ River
◎ Lake
▣ Reservoir

21 Q7 **Oakland** Maine, NE USA 44.32N 69.43W
23 T3 **Oakland** Maryland, NE USA 39.24N 79.24W
31 R14 **Oakland** Nebraska, C USA 41.50N 96.28W
33 N11 **Oak Lawn** Illinois, N USA 41.43N 87.45W
35 P16 **Oakley** Idaho, NW USA 42.13N 113.54W
28 I4 **Oakley** Kansas, C USA 39.06N 100.51W
33 N10 **Oak Park** Illinois, N USA 41.53N 87.46W
9 X16 **Oak Point** Manitoba, S Canada 50.23N 97.00W
34 G13 **Oakridge** Oregon, NW USA 43.45N 122.27W
22 M9 **Oak Ridge** Tennessee, S USA 36.01N 84.12W
192 K10 **Oakura** Taranaki, North Island, NZ 39.07S 173.58E
24 L7 **Oak Vale** Mississippi, S USA 31.26N 89.57W
12 G16 **Oakville** Ontario, S Canada 43.27N 79.40W
27 V8 **Oakwood** Texas, SW USA 31.34N 95.51W
193 F22 **Oamaru** Otago, South Island, NZ 45.10S 170.51E
98 F13 **Oa, Mull of** *headland* W Scotland, UK 55.35N 6.20W
175 Q7 **Oan** Sulawesi, N Indonesia 1.16N 121.25E
193 J17 **Oaro** Canterbury, South Island, NZ 42.29S 173.30E
37 X2 **Oasis** Nevada, W USA 41.01N 114.29W
205 S15 **Oates Land** *physical region* Antarctica
191 P17 **Oatlands** Tasmania, SE Australia 42.21S 147.23E
38 I11 **Oatman** Arizona, SW USA 35.03N 114.19W
43 R16 **Oaxaca** *var.* Oaxaca de Juárez; *prev.* Antequera. Oaxaca, SE Mexico 17.04N 96.40W
43 Q16 **Oaxaca** ◆ *state* SE Mexico
Oaxaca de Juárez *see* Oaxaca
125 G8 **Ob'** ≈ C Russian Federation
12 G9 **Obabika Lake** ◎ Ontario, S Canada
Obagan *see* Ubagan
120 M12 **Obal'** *Rus.* Obol'. Vitsyebskaya Voblasts', N Belarus 55.22N 29.16E
81 E16 **Obala** Centre, SW Cameroon 4.09N 11.31E
12 C6 **Oba Lake** ◎ Ontario, S Canada
171 H14 **Obama** Fukui, Honshū, SW Japan 35.29N 135.42E
98 H11 **Oban** W Scotland, UK 56.25N 5.28W
Oban *see* Halfmoon Bay
171 Ll12 **Obanazawa** Yamagata, Honshū, C Japan 38.40N 140.21E
Obando *see* Puerto Inírida
106 I4 **O Barco** *var.* El Barco, El Barco de Valdeorras, O Barco de Valdeorras. Galicia, NW Spain 42.24N 7.00W
O Barco de Valdeorras *see* O Barco
Obbia *see* Hobyo
95 J16 **Obbola** Västerbotten, N Sweden 63.42N 20.18E
Obbrovazzo *see* Obrovac
Obchuga *see* Abchuha
Obdorsk *see* Salekhard
Óbecse *see* Bečej
120 I11 **Obeliai** Rokiškis, NE Lithuania 55.57N 25.47E
62 F13 **Oberá** Misiones, NE Argentina 27.28S 55.07W
110 E8 **Oberburg** Bern, W Switzerland 47.00N 7.37E
111 Q9 **Oberdrauburg** Salzburg, S Austria 46.45N 12.59E
Oberglogau *see* Głogówek
111 W4 **Ober Grafendorf** Niederösterreich, NE Austria 48.09N 15.33E
103 E15 **Oberhausen** Nordrhein-Westfalen, W Germany 51.28N 6.52E
Oberhollabrunn *see* Tulln
Oberlaibach *see* Vrhnika
103 Q15 **Oberlausitz** *physical region* E Germany
28 J2 **Oberlin** Kansas, C USA 39.48N 100.31W
24 H8 **Oberlin** Louisiana, S USA 30.37N 92.45W
33 T11 **Oberlin** Ohio, N USA 41.17N 82.13W
105 U5 **Obernai** Bas-Rhin, NE France 48.28N 7.30E
111 R4 **Obernberg-am-Inn** Oberösterreich, N Austria 48.19N 13.20E
Oberndorf *see* Oberndorf am Neckar
103 G23 **Oberndorf am Neckar** *var.* Oberndorf. Baden-Württemberg, SW Germany 48.18N 8.32E
111 Q5 **Oberndorf bei Salzburg** Salzburg, W Austria 47.57N 12.57E
Oberneustadtl *see* Kysucké Nové Mesto
191 S8 **Oberon** New South Wales, SE Australia 33.42S 149.50E
111 Q4 **Oberösterreich** *off.* Land Oberösterreich, *Eng.* Upper Austria. ◆ *state* NW Austria
Oberpahlen *see* Põltsamaa
103 M19 **Oberpfälzer Wald** ▲▲ SE Germany
111 Y6 **Oberpullendorf** Burgenland, E Austria 47.32N 16.30E
Oberradkersburg *see* Gornja Radgona
103 G18 **Oberursel** Hessen, W Germany 50.12N 8.34E
111 Q8 **Obervellach** Salzburg, S Austria 46.56N 13.10E
111 X7 **Oberwart** Burgenland, SE Austria 47.18N 16.12E
Oberwischau *see* Vişeu de Sus
111 T7 **Oberwölz** *var.* Oberwölz-Stadt. Steiermark, SE Austria 47.12N 14.20E
Oberwölz-Stadt *see* Oberwölz
33 S13 **Obetz** Ohio, N USA 39.52N 82.57W
Ob', Gulf of *see* Obskaya Guba
56 G8 **Obia** Santander, C Colombia 6.16N 73.18W
60 H12 **Óbidos** Pará, NE Brazil 1.52S 55.30W
106 F10 **Óbidos** Leiria, C Portugal 39.21N 9.09W
Obidovichi *see* Abidavichy
153 Q13 **Obigarm** W Tajikistan 38.42N 69.34E
172 P7 **Obihiro** Hokkaidō, NE Japan 42.55N 143.09E
Obi-Khingou *see* Khingov
153 P13 **Obikiik** SW Tajikistan 38.07N 68.36E
115 N16 **Obilić** Serbia, S Serbia and Montenegro (Yugoslavia) 42.50N 20.57E
131 O12 **Obil'noye** Respublika Kalmykiya, SW Russian Federation 47.31N 44.24E
22 F8 **Obion** Tennessee, S USA 36.15N 89.11W
22 F8 **Obion River** ≈ Tennessee, S USA
175 T9 **Obi, Pulau** *island* Maluku, E Indonesia
172 Oo4 **Obira** Hokkaidō, NE Japan 44.01N 141.39E
175 T9 **Obi, Selat** *strait* Maluku, E Indonesia
131 N11 **Oblivskaya** Rostovskaya Oblast', SW Russian Federation 48.34N 42.31E
127 N16 **Obluch'ye** Yevreyskaya Avtonomnaya Oblast', SE Russian Federation 48.59N 131.18E
130 K4 **Obninsk** Kaluzhskaya Oblast', W Russian Federation 55.06N 36.40E
116 J8 **Obnova** Pleven, N Bulgaria 43.26N 25.04E
81 N15 **Obo** Haut-Mbomou, E Central African Republic 5.20N 26.28E
82 M11 **Obock** E Djibouti 11.57N 43.09E
Obol' *see* Obal'
Obolyanka *see* Abalyanka
176 Vv11 **Obome** Papua, E Indonesia 3.42S 133.21E
112 G11 **Oborniki** Wielkolpolskie, C Poland 52.38N 16.48E
81 G19 **Obouya** Cuvette, C Congo 0.55S 15.40E
130 J8 **Oboyan'** Kurskaya Oblast', W Russian Federation 51.12N 36.15E
128 M9 **Obozerskiy** Arkhangel'skaya Oblast', NW Russian Federation 63.26N 40.20E
114 L11 **Obrenovac** Serbia, N Serbia and Montenegro (Yugoslavia) 44.39N 20.12E
114 D12 **Obrovac** *It.* Obbrovazzo. Zadar, SW Croatia 44.12N 15.40E
Obrovo *see* Abrova
37 Q3 **Observation Peak** ▲ California, W USA 40.48N 120.07W
126 H7 **Obskaya Guba** *Eng.* Gulf of Ob'. *gulf* N Russian Federation
181 N13 **Ob' Tablemount** *undersea feature* S Indian Ocean 50.16S 51.59E
181 T10 **Ob' Trench** *undersea feature* E Indian Ocean
79 P16 **Obuasi** S Ghana 6.15N 1.36W
119 P5 **Obukhiv** *Rus.* Obukhov. Kyyivs'ka Oblast', N Ukraine 50.05N 30.37E
Obukhov *see* Obukhiv
129 U14 **Obva** ≈ NW Russian Federation
119 V10 **Obytichna Kosa** *spit* SE Ukraine
119 V10 **Obytichna Zatoka** *gulf* SE Ukraine
107 O3 **Oca** ≈ N Spain
25 W10 **Ocala** Florida, SE USA 29.11N 82.08W
42 M7 **Ocampo** Coahuila de Zaragoza, NE Mexico 27.18N 102.24W
56 G7 **Ocaña** Norte de Santander, N Colombia 8.16N 73.21W
107 N9 **Ocaña** Castilla-La Mancha, C Spain 39.57N 3.30W
106 H4 **O Carballiño** *Cast.* Carballiño Galicia, NW Spain 42.25N 8.04W
39 T9 **Ocate** New Mexico, SW USA 36.09N 105.03W
Ocavango *see* Okavango
56 D14 **Occidental, Cordillera** ▲▲ W Colombia
59 D14 **Occidental, Cordillera** ▲▲ W S America
23 Q6 **Oceana** West Virginia, NE USA 37.41N 81.37W
23 Z4 **Ocean City** Maryland, NE USA 38.20N 75.05W
20 J17 **Ocean City** New Jersey, NE USA 39.15N 74.33W
8 K15 **Ocean Falls** British Columbia, SW Canada 52.24N 127.42W
Ocean Island *see* Kure Atoll
Ocean Island *see* Banaba
66 J9 **Oceanographer Fracture Zone** *tectonic feature* NW Atlantic Ocean
37 U17 **Oceanside** California, W USA 33.12N 117.22W
24 M9 **Ocean Springs** Mississippi, S USA 30.24N 88.49W
Ocean State *see* Rhode Island
27 O9 **O C Fisher Lake** ▣ Texas, SW USA
119 Q10 **Ochakiv** *Rus.* Ochakov. Mykolayivs'ka Oblast', S Ukraine 46.36N 31.33E
Ochakov *see* Ochakiv
Ochamchira *see* Och'amch'ire
143 Q9 **Och'amch'ire** *Rus.* Ochamchira. W Georgia 42.45N 41.30E
Ochansk *see* Okhansk
129 T15 **Ocher** Permskaya Oblast', NW Russian Federation 57.54N 54.40E
117 I19 **Óchi** ▲ Évvoia, C Greece 38.03N 24.27E
172 R8 **Ochiishi-misaki** *headland* Hokkaidō, NE Japan 43.10N 145.29E
25 S9 **Ochlockonee River** ≈ Florida/Georgia, SE USA
46 K12 **Ocho Rios** C Jamaica 18.24N 77.06W
Ochrida *see* Ohrid
Ochrida, Lake *see* Ohrid, Lake
103 J19 **Ochsenfurt** Bayern, C Germany 49.39N 10.03E
25 U7 **Ocilla** Georgia, SE USA 31.35N 83.15W
96 N13 **Ockelbo** Gävleborg, C Sweden 60.51N 16.46E
Ocker *see* Oker
97 I19 **Öckerö** Västra Götaland, S Sweden 57.43N 11.39E
25 U6 **Ocmulgee River** ≈ Georgia, SE USA
118 H11 **Ocna Mureş** *Hung.* Marosújvár; *prev.* Ocna Mureşului; *prev. Hung.* Marosújvárakna. Alba, C Romania 46.25N 23.52E
Ocna Mureşului *see* Ocna Mureş
118 H11 **Ocna Sibiului** *Ger.* Salzburg, *Hung.* Vizakna. Sibiu, C Romania 45.52N 23.59E
118 H13 **Ocnele Mari** *prev.* Vioara. Vâlcea, S Romania 45.03N 24.18E
118 L7 **Ocniţa** *Rus.* Oknitsa. N Moldova 48.25N 27.30E
25 U4 **Oconee, Lake** ▣ Georgia, SE USA
25 U5 **Oconee River** ≈ Georgia, SE USA
32 M9 **Oconomowoc** Wisconsin, N USA 43.06N 88.29W
32 M6 **Oconto** Wisconsin, N USA 44.55N 87.52W
32 M6 **Oconto Falls** Wisconsin, N USA 44.52N 88.06W
32 M6 **Oconto River** ≈ Wisconsin, N USA
106 I3 **O Corgo** Galicia, NW Spain 42.55N 7.25W
43 V16 **Ocosingo** Chiapas, SE Mexico 16.51N 92.06W
44 J8 **Ocotal** Nueva Segovia, NW Nicaragua 13.38N 86.27W
44 F6 **Ocotepeque** ◆ *department* W Honduras
Ocotepeque *see* Nueva Ocotepeque
42 L13 **Ocotlán** Jalisco, SW Mexico 20.18N 102.45W
43 R16 **Ocotlán** *var.* Ocotlán de Morelos. Oaxaca, SE Mexico 16.49N 96.49W
Ocotlán de Morelos *see* Ocotlán
43 U16 **Ocozocuautla** Chiapas, SE Mexico 16.43N 93.19W
23 Y10 **Ocracoke Island** *island* North Carolina, SE USA
104 I3 **Octeville** Manche, N France 49.37N 1.39W
October Revolution Island *see* Oktyabr'skoy Revolyutsii, Ostrov
45 R17 **Ocú** Herrera, S Panama 7.55N 80.47W
85 Q14 **Ocua** Cabo Delgado, NE Mozambique 13.37S 39.44E
Ocumare *see* Ocumare del Tuy
56 M5 **Ocumare del Tuy** *var.* Ocumare. Miranda, N Venezuela 10.07N 66.46W
79 P17 **Oda** SE Ghana 5.54N 1.01W
170 F12 **Ōda** *var.* Oda. Shimane, Honshū, SW Japan 35.09N 132.31E
94 K3 **Ódáðahraun** *lava flow* C Iceland
176 Y14 **Odammun** ≈ Papua, E Indonesia
171 Mm9 **Ōdate** Akita, Honshū, C Japan 40.18N 140.34E
171 J16 **Odawara** Kanagawa, Honshū, S Japan 35.15N 139.07E
97 D14 **Odda** Hordaland, S Norway 60.03N 6.34E
97 G22 **Odder** Århus, C Denmark 55.58N 10.10E
Oddur *see* Xuddur
31 T13 **Odebolt** Iowa, C USA 42.18N 95.15W
106 H14 **Odeleite** Faro, S Portugal 37.01N 7.28W
27 Q4 **Odell** Texas, SW USA 34.19N 99.24W
27 T14 **Odem** Texas, SW USA 27.57N 97.34W
106 F13 **Odemira** Beja, S Portugal 37.34N 8.37W
142 C14 **Ödemiş** İzmir, SW Turkey 38.10N 27.58E
Ödenburg *see* Sopron
85 I22 **Odendaalsrus** Free State, C South Africa 27.52S 26.42E
Odenpäh *see* Otepää
97 H23 **Odense** Fyn, C Denmark 55.24N 10.22E
103 H19 **Odenwald** ▲▲ W Germany
86 H10 **Oder** *Cz./Pol.* Odra. ≈ C Europe
Oderberg *see* Bohumín
102 P11 **Oderbruch** *wetland* Germany/Poland
Oderhaff *see* Szczeciński, Zalew
102 O11 **Oder-Havel-Kanal** *canal* NE Germany
Oderhellen *see* Odorheiu Secuiesc
102 P13 **Oder-Spree-Kanal** *canal* NE Germany
Odertal *see* Zdzieszowice
108 I7 **Oderzo** Veneto, NE Italy 45.48N 12.33E
124 Pp4 **Odesa** *Rus.* Odessa. Odes'ka Oblast', SW Ukraine 46.28N 30.43E
Odesa *see* Odes'ka Oblast'
97 L18 **Ödeshög** Östergötland, S Sweden 58.13N 14.40E
119 O9 **Odes'ka Oblast'** *var.* Odesa, *Rus.* Odesskaya Oblast'. ◆ *province* SW Ukraine
26 M8 **Odessa** Texas, SW USA 31.51N 102.22W
34 K8 **Odessa** Washington, NW USA 47.19N 118.41W
Odessa *see* Odesa
Odesskaya Oblast' *see* Odes'ka Oblast'
125 Ff13 **Odesskoye** Omskaya Oblast', C Russian Federation 54.15N 72.45E
Odessus *see* Varna
104 F6 **Odet** ≈ NW France
106 I14 **Odiel** ≈ SW Spain
78 L14 **Odienné** NW Ivory Coast 9.32N 7.34W
179 Pp12 **Odiongan** Tablas Island, C Philippines 12.23N 122.01E
118 L12 **Odobeşti** Vrancea, E Romania 45.46N 27.06E
112 H13 **Odolanów** *Ger.* Adelnau. Wielkopolskie, C Poland 51.35N 17.42E
178 J13 **Ŏdŏngk** Kâmpóng Spoe, S Cambodia 11.48N 104.45E
27 N6 **O'donnell** Texas, SW USA 32.57N 101.49W
100 O7 **Odoorn** Drenthe, NE Netherlands 52.52N 6.49E
Odorhei *see* Odorheiu Secuiesc
118 J11 **Odorheiu Secuiesc** *Ger.* Oderhellen, *Hung.* Vámosudvarhely; *prev.* Odorhei; *Ger.* Hofmarkt. Harghita, C Romania 46.18N 25.17E
Odra *see* Oder
114 J9 **Odžaci** *Ger.* Hodschag, *Hung.* Hodság. Serbia, NW Serbia and Montenegro (Yugoslavia) 45.31N 19.15E
61 N14 **Oeiras** Piauí, E Brazil 07.00S 42.07W
106 F11 **Oeiras** Lisboa, C Portugal 38.40N 9.18W
103 G14 **Oelde** Nordrhein-Westfalen, W Germany 51.49N 8.09E
30 J11 **Oelrichs** South Dakota, N USA 43.08N 103.13W
Oels/Oels in Schlesien *see* Oleśnica
103 M17 **Oelsnitz** Sachsen, E Germany 50.22N 12.12E
31 X12 **Oelwein** Iowa, C USA 42.40N 91.54W
Oeniadae *see* Oiniádes
203 N17 **Oeno Island** *atoll* Pitcairn Islands, C Pacific Ocean
Oesel *see* Saaremaa
110 L7 **Oetz** *var.* Ötz. Tirol, W Austria 47.15N 10.56E
143 P11 **Of** Trabzon, NE Turkey 40.57N 40.16E
32 K15 **O'Fallon** Illinois, N USA 38.35N 89.54W
29 W4 **O'Fallon** Missouri, C USA 38.54N 90.31W
109 N16 **Ofanto** ≈ S Italy
99 D18 **Offaly** *Ir.* Ua Uíbh Fhailí; *prev.* King's County. *cultural region* C Ireland
103 H18 **Offenbach** *var.* Offenbach am Main. Hessen, W Germany 50.06N 8.46E
Offenbach am Main *see* Offenbach
103 F22 **Offenburg** Baden-Württemberg, SW Germany 48.28N 7.57E
190 C2 **Officer Creek** *seasonal river* South Australia
Oficina María Elena *see* María Elena
Oficina Pedro de Valdivia *see* Pedro de Valdivia
117 K22 **Ofidoússa** *island* Kykládes, Greece, Aegean Sea
Ofiral *see* Sharm el Sheikh
94 H10 **Ofotfjorden** *fjord* N Norway
198 D8 **Ofu** *island* Manua Islands, E American Samoa
171 Mm12 **Ōfunato** Iwate, Honshū, C Japan 39.04N 141.41E
171 M10 **Oga** Akita, Honshū, C Japan 39.54N 139.48E
Ogaadeen *see* Ogadēn
171 M11 **Ogachi** Akita, Honshū, C Japan 39.03N 140.26E
171 M11 **Ogachi-tōge** *pass* Honshū, C Japan 39.00N 140.20E
83 N14 **Ogadēn** *Som.* Ogaadeen. *plateau* Ethiopia/Somalia
171 M10 **Oga-hantō** *peninsula* Honshū, C Japan
171 Hh14 **Ōgaki** Gifu, Honshū, SW Japan 35.21N 136.35E
30 L15 **Ogallala** Nebraska, C USA 41.09N 101.43W
174 I12 **Ogan, Air** ≈ Sumatera, W Indonesia
172 T16 **Ogasawara-shotō** *Eng.* Bonin Islands. *island group* SE Japan
12 I9 **Ogascanane, Lac** ◎ Quebec, SE Canada
172 N9 **Ogawara-ko** ◎ Honshū, C Japan
79 T15 **Ogbomosho** Oyo, W Nigeria 8.10N 4.16E
31 U13 **Ogden** Iowa, C USA 42.03N 94.01W
38 L2 **Ogden** Utah, W USA 41.09N 111.58W
20 I6 **Ogdensburg** New York, NE USA 44.42N 75.25W
197 L16 **Ogea Driki** *island* Lau Group, E Fiji
197 L16 **Ogea Levu** *island* Lau Group, E Fiji
25 W5 **Ogeechee River** ≈ Georgia, SE USA
Oger *see* Ogre
171 K12 **Ogi** Niigata, Sado, C Japan 37.49N 138.16E
8 H5 **Ogilvie** Yukon Territory, NW Canada 63.34N 139.43W
8 H4 **Ogilvie** ≈ Yukon Territory, NW Canada
8 H5 **Ogilvie Mountains** ▲▲ Yukon Territory, NW Canada
Oginskiy Kanal *see* Ahinski Kanal
152 F6 **Og'iyon Sho'rxogi** *wetland* NW Uzbekistan
152 B10 **Oglanly** Balkanskiy Velayat, W Turkmenistan 39.56N 54.25E
25 T5 **Oglethorpe** Georgia, SE USA 32.17N 84.03W
25 T2 **Oglethorpe, Mount** ▲ Georgia, SE USA 34.29N 84.19W
108 F7 **Oglio** *anc.* Ollius. ≈ N Italy
105 T8 **Ognon** ≈ E France
175 Pp7 **Ogoamas, Pegunungan** ▲▲ Sulawesi, N Indonesia
127 N14 **Ogodzha** Amurskaya Oblast', S Russian Federation 52.51N 132.49E
79 W16 **Ogoja** Cross River, S Nigeria 6.37N 8.48E
10 C10 **Ogoki** ≈ Ontario, S Canada
10 D11 **Ogoki Lake** ◎ Ontario, C Canada
168 K10 **Ögöömör** Ömnögovĭ, S Mongolia 43.47N 104.31E
81 F19 **Ogooué** ≈ Congo/Gabon
81 E18 **Ogooué-Ivindo** *off.* Province de l'Ogooué-Ivindo, *var.* L'Ogooué-Ivindo. ◆ *province* N Gabon
81 E19 **Ogooué-Lolo** *off.* Province de l'Ogooué-Lolo, *var.* L'Ogooué-Lolo. ◆ *province* C Gabon
81 C19 **Ogooué-Maritime** *off.* Province de l'Ogooué-Maritime, *var.* L'Ogooué-Maritime. ◆ *province* W Gabon
170 Cc13 **Ogōri** Fukuoka, Kyūshū, SW Japan 33.25N 130.30E
170 Dd13 **Ogōri** Yamaguchi, Honshū, SW Japan 34.05N 131.20E
116 H7 **Ogosta** ≈ NW Bulgaria
114 Q9 **Ogražden** *Bul.* Ograzhden. ▲▲ Bulgaria/FYR Macedonia *see also* Ograzhden
116 G12 **Ograzhden** *Mac.* Ogražden. ▲▲ Bulgaria/FYR Macedonia *see also* Ogražden
120 G9 **Ogre** *Ger.* Oger. Ogre, C Latvia 56.49N 24.36E
120 H9 **Ogre** ≈ C Latvia
114 C10 **Ogulin** Karlovac, NW Croatia 45.15N 15.13E
79 S16 **Ogun** ◆ *state* SW Nigeria
152 A12 **Ogurdzhaly, Ostrov** *Turkm.* Ogurjaly Adasy. *island* W Turkmenistan
Ogurjaly Adasy *see* Ogurdzhaly, Ostrov
79 U16 **Ogwashi-Uku** Delta, S Nigeria 6.08N 6.38E
193 B23 **Ohai** Southland, South Island, NZ 45.56S 167.59E
153 Q10 **Ohangaron** *Rus.* Akhangaran. Toshkent Viloyati, E Uzbekistan 40.56N 69.37E
153 Q10 **Ohangaron** *Rus.* Akhangaran. ≈ E Uzbekistan
85 C16 **Ohangwena** ◆ *district* N Namibia
171 K17 **Ōhara** Chiba, Honshū, S Japan 35.14N 140.19E
32 M10 **O'Hare** ✕ (Chicago) Illinois, N USA 41.59N 87.56W
172 Nn8 **Ōhata** Aomori, Honshū, C Japan 41.23N 141.09E
192 L13 **Ohau** Manawatu-Wanganui, North Island, NZ 40.40S 175.15E
193 E20 **Ohau, Lake** ◎ South Island, NZ
Ohcejohka *see* Utsjoki
101 J20 **Ohey** Namur, SE Belgium 50.26N 5.07E
203 X15 **O'Higgins, Cabo** *headland* Easter Island, Chile, E Pacific Ocean 27.04S 109.15W
O'Higgins, Lago *see* San Martín, Lago
33 S12 **Ohio** *off.* State of Ohio; also known as The Buckeye State. ◆ *state* N USA
(0) L10 **Ohio River** ≈ N USA
Ohlau *see* Oława
103 H16 **Ohm** ≈ C Germany
200 R16 **Ohonua** 'Eua, E Tonga 21.20S 174.57W
25 V5 **Ohoopee River** ≈ Georgia, SE USA
102 L12 **Ohre** *Ger.* Eger. ≈ Czech Republic/Germany
Ohri *see* Ohrid
115 M20 **Ohrid** *Turk.* Ochrida, Ohri. SW FYR Macedonia 41.07N 20.48E
115 M20 **Ohrid, Lake** *var.* Lake Ochrida, *Alb.* Liqeni i Ohrit, *Mac.* Ohridsko Ezero. ◎ Albania/FYR Macedonia
Ohridsko Ezero/Ohrit, Liqeni i *see* Ohrid, Lake
192 L9 **Ohura** Manawatu-Wanganui, North Island, NZ 38.51S 174.58E
60 J9 **Oiapoque** Amapá, E Brazil 3.54N 51.46W
60 J10 **Oiapoque, Rio** *var.* Fleuve l'Oyapok, Oyapock. ≈ Brazil/French Guiana *see also* Oyapok, Fleuve l'
13 O9 **Oies, Île aux** *island* Quebec, SE Canada
94 L13 **Oijärvi** Oulu, C Finland 65.37N 26.04E
94 L12 **Oikarainen** Lappi, N Finland 66.30N 25.46E
196 F10 **Oikuul** Babeldaob, N Palau
20 C13 **Oil City** Pennsylvania, NE USA 41.25N 79.42W
20 C12 **Oil Creek** ≈ Pennsylvania, NE USA
37 R13 **Oildale** California, W USA 35.25N 119.01W
Oileán Ciarral *see* Castleisland
Oil Islands *see* Chagos Archipelago
117 D18 **Oiniádes** *anc.* Oeniadae. *site of ancient city* Dytikí Ellás, W Greece 38.23N 21.13E
117 L18 **Oinoússes** *island* E Greece
Oírr, Inis *see* Inisheer
101 J15 **Oirschot** Noord-Brabant, S Netherlands 51.30N 5.18E
105 N4 **Oise** ◆ *department* N France
105 P3 **Oise** ≈ N France
101 J14 **Oisterwijk** Noord-Brabant, S Netherlands 51.34N 5.12E
47 O14 **Oistins** S Barbados 13.04N 59.33W
170 D14 **Ōita** Ōita, Kyūshū, SW Japan 33.15N 131.34E
170 D14 **Ōita** *off.* Ōita-ken. ◆ *prefecture* Kyūshū, SW Japan
117 E17 **Oíti** ▲ C Greece 38.48N 22.12E
172 Oo6 **Oiwake** Hokkaidō, NE Japan 42.54N 141.49E
37 R14 **Ojai** California, W USA 34.25N 119.15W
96 K13 **Öje** Dalarna, C Sweden 60.49N 13.54E
95 J14 **Öjebyn** Norrbotten, N Sweden 65.20N 21.26E
170 Bb12 **Ojika-jima** *island* SW Japan
42 K5 **Ojinaga** Chihuahua, N Mexico 29.30N 104.25W
171 K13 **Ojiya** *var.* Oziya. Niigata, Honshū, C Japan 37.18N 138.47E
42 M11 **Ojo Caliente** *var.* Ojocaliente. Zacatecas, C Mexico 22.39N 102.17W
42 D6 **Ojo de Liebre, Laguna** *var.* Laguna Scammon, Scammon Lagoon. *lagoon* W Mexico
64 I7 **Ojos del Salado, Cerro** ▲ W Argentina 27.04S 68.34W
107 R7 **Ojos Negros** Aragón, NE Spain 40.43N 1.30W
42 M12 **Ojuelos de Jalisco** Aguascalientes, C Mexico 21.52N 101.40W
131 N4 **Oka** ≈ W Russian Federation
85 D19 **Okahandja** Otjozondjupa, C Namibia 21.58S 16.55E
192 L9 **Okahukura** Manawatu-Wanganui, North Island, NZ 38.48S 175.13E
192 J3 **Okaihau** Northland, North Island, NZ 35.19S 173.45E
85 D18 **Okakarara** Otjozondjupa, N Namibia 20.34S 17.24E
11 P5 **Okak Islands** *island group* Newfoundland and Labrador, E Canada
8 M17 **Okanagan** ≈ British Columbia, SW Canada
9 N17 **Okanagan Lake** ◎ British Columbia, SW Canada
Ōkanizsa *see* Kanjiža
85 C16 **Okankolo** Otjikoto, N Namibia 17.57S 16.28E
34 K6 **Okanogan River** ≈ Washington, NW USA
194 I13 **Okapa** Eastern Highlands, C PNG 6.22S 145.29E
85 D18 **Okaputa** Otjozondjupa, N Namibia 20.09S 16.55E
155 V9 **Okāra** Punjab, E Pakistan 30.49N 73.31E
28 M10 **Okarche** Oklahoma, C USA 35.43N 97.58W
152 B13 **Okarem** *Turkm.* Ekerem. Balkanskiy Velayat, W Turkmenistan 38.06N 53.52E
201 X14 **Okat Harbor** *harbor* Kosrae, E Micronesia
24 M5 **Okatibbee Creek** ≈ Mississippi, S USA
85 C17 **Okaukuejo** Kunene, N Namibia 19.09S 15.57E
Okavanggo *see* Cubango/Okavango
85 E17 **Okavango** ◆ *district* NW Namibia
85 G17 **Okavango** *var.* Cubango, Kavango, Kavengo, Kubango, Okavanggo, *Port.* Ocavango. ≈ S Africa *see also* Cubango
85 G17 **Okavango Delta** *wetland* N Botswana
171 J15 **Okaya** Nagano, Honshū, S Japan 36.04N 138.02E
170 Ff14 **Okayama** Okayama, Honshū, SW Japan 34.40N 133.54E
170 F13 **Okayama** *off.* Okayama-ken. ◆ *prefecture* Honshū, SW Japan
171 I16 **Okazaki** Aichi, Honshū, C Japan 34.58N 137.10E
112 M12 **Okęcie** ✕ (Warszawa) Mazowieckie, C Poland 52.08N 20.57E
25 Y13 **Okeechobee** Florida, SE USA 27.14N 80.49W
25 Y14 **Okeechobee, Lake** ◎ Florida, SE USA
28 M9 **Okeene** Oklahoma, C USA 36.07N 98.19W
25 V8 **Okefenokee Swamp** *wetland* Georgia, SE USA
99 J24 **Okehampton** SW England, UK 50.44N 4.00W
29 P10 **Okemah** Oklahoma, C USA 35.25N 96.18W
79 U16 **Okene** Kogi, S Nigeria 7.31N 6.15E
102 K13 **Oker** *var.* Ocker. ≈ NW Germany
103 J14 **Oker-Stausee** ◎ C Germany
127 O13 **Okha** Ostrov Sakhalin, Sakhalinskaya Oblast', SE Russian Federation 53.33N 142.55E
129 U15 **Okhansk** *var.* Ochansk. Permskaya Oblast', NW Russian Federation 57.44N 55.20E
127 N10 **Okhota** ≈ E Russian Federation
127 Nn11 **Okhotsk** Khabarovskiy Kray, E Russian Federation 59.21N 143.14E
199 J2 **Okhotsk, Sea of** *sea* NW Pacific Ocean
119 T4 **Okhtyrka** *Rus.* Akhtyrka. Sums'ka Oblast', NE Ukraine 50.19N 34.54E
199 Gg6 **Oki-Daitō Ridge** *undersea feature* W Pacific Ocean
85 E23 **Okiep** Northern Cape, W South Africa 29.39S 17.53E
Oki-guntō *see* Oki-shotō
170 Ff11 **Oki-kaikyō** *strait* SW Japan
172 P15 **Okinawa** Okinawa, SW Japan 26.19N 127.46E
172 Oo14 **Okinawa** *off.* Okinawa-ken. ◆ *prefecture* Okinawa, SW Japan
172 Oo14 **Okinawa** *island* SW Japan
172 Q14 **Okinoerabu-jima** *island* Nansei-shotō, SW Japan
170 Dd15 **Okino-shima** *island* SW Japan
170 Ff11 **Oki-shotō** *var.* Oki-guntō. *island group* SW Japan
79 T16 **Okitipupa** Ondo, SW Nigeria 6.33N 4.43E
177 G8 **Okkan** Pegu, SW Myanmar 17.31N 95.51E
29 N10 **Oklahoma** *off.* State of Oklahoma; also known as The Sooner State. ◆ *state* C USA
29 N11 **Oklahoma City** *state capital* Oklahoma, C USA 35.28N 97.31W
27 Q4 **Oklaunion** Texas, SW USA 34.07N 99.07W
25 W10 **Oklawaha River** ≈ Florida, SE USA
29 P10 **Okmulgee** Oklahoma, C USA 35.37N 95.57W
Oknitsa *see* Ocniţa
24 M3 **Okolona** Mississippi, S USA 34.00N 88.45W
172 Q4 **Okoppe** Hokkaidō, NE Japan 44.27N 143.06E
9 Q16 **Okotoks** Alberta, SW Canada 50.46N 113.57W
82 H6 **Oko, Wadi** ≈ NE Sudan
81 G19 **Okoyo** Cuvette, W Congo 1.28S 15.04E
79 S15 **Okpara** ≈ Benin/Nigeria
94 J8 **Øksfjord** Finnmark, N Norway 70.13N 22.22E
176 Z12 **Oksibil** Papua, E Indonesia 4.52S 140.32E
129 R4 **Oksino** Nenetskiy Avtonomnyy Okrug, NW Russian Federation 67.33N 52.15E
94 G13 **Oksskolten** ▲ C Norway 66.00N 14.18E
Oksu *see* Oqsu
150 M8 **Oktaybr'skiy** Kostanay, N Kazakhstan
194 E11 **Ok Tedi** Western, W PNG
Oktemberyan *see* Armavir
177 G7 **Oktwin** Pegu, C Myanmar 18.46N 96.21E
131 R6 **Oktyabr'sk** Samarskaya Oblast', W Russian Federation 53.13N 48.36E
Oktyabr'sk *see* Kandyagash
129 N12 **Oktyabr'skiy** Arkhangel'skaya Oblast', NW Russian Federation 61.03N 43.16E
127 Pp12 **Oktyabr'skiy** Kamchatskaya Oblast', E Russian Federation 52.35N 94.18E
131 T5 **Oktyabr'skiy** Respublika Bashkortostan, W Russian Federation 54.28N 53.29E
131 O11 **Oktyabr'skiy** Volgogradskaya Oblast', SW Russian Federation 48.00N 43.35E
Oktyabr'skiy *see* Aktsyabrski
131 V7 **Oktyabr'skoye** Orenburgskaya Oblast', W Russian Federation 52.22N 55.39E
126 J3 **Oktyabr'skoy Revolyutsii, Ostrov** *Eng.* October Revolution Island. *island* Severnaya Zemlya, N Russian Federation
170 C15 **Ōkuchi** *var.* Ōkuti. Kagoshima, Kyūshū, SW Japan 32.03N 130.36E
Okulovka *see* Uglovka
171 Mm5 **Okushiri-tō** *var.* Okusiri Tô. *island* NE Japan
Okusiri Tô *see* Okushiri-tō
79 S15 **Okuta** Kwara, W Nigeria 9.18N 3.09E
Ōkuti *see* Ōkuchi
85 F19 **Okwa** *var.* Chapman's. ≈ Botswana/Namibia
127 O10 **Ola** Magadanskaya Oblast', E Russian Federation 59.36N 151.18E
29 T11 **Ola** Arkansas, C USA 35.01N 93.13W
Ola *see* Ala
37 T11 **Olacha Peak** ▲ California, W USA 36.15N 118.07W
94 J1 **Ólafsfjörður** Nordhurland Eystra, N Iceland 66.04N 18.36W
94 H3 **Ólafsvík** Vesturland, W Iceland 64.52N 23.45W
Oláhbrettye *see* Bretea-Română
Oláhszentgyörgy *see* Sângeorz-Băi
Oláh-Toplicza *see* Topliţa
37 T11 **Olancha** California, W USA 36.16N 118.00W
44 J5 **Olanchito** Yoro, C Honduras 15.27N 86.37W
44 J6 **Olancho** ◆ *department* E Honduras
97 O20 **Öland** *island* S Sweden
97 O19 **Ölands norra udde** *headland* S Sweden 57.21N 17.06E
97 N22 **Ölands södra udde** *headland* S Sweden 56.12N 16.26E
190 K7 **Olary** South Australia 32.18S 140.16E
29 R4 **Olathe** Kansas, C USA 38.52N 94.49W
63 C22 **Olavarría** Buenos Aires, E Argentina 36.57S 60.19W
94 O2 **Olav V Land** *physical region* C Svalbard
113 H14 **Oława** *Ger.* Ohlau. Dolnośląskie, SW Poland 50.57N 17.18E
109 D17 **Olbia** *prev.* Terranova Pausania. Sardegna, Italy, C Mediterranean Sea 40.55N 9.30E
46 G5 **Old Bahama Channel** *channel* Bahamas/Cuba
Old Bay State/Old Colony State *see* Massachusetts
8 H2 **Old Crow** Yukon Territory, NW Canada 67.34N 139.55W
Old Dominion *see* Virginia
Oldeberkeap *see* Oldeberkoop
100 M7 **Oldeberkoop** *Fris.* Oldeberkeap. Friesland, N Netherlands 52.55N 6.07E
100 L10 **Oldebroek** Gelderland, E Netherlands 52.27N 5.54E
100 L8 **Oldemarkt** Overijssel, N Netherlands 52.49N 5.58E
96 E11 **Olden** Sogn og Fjordane, C Norway 61.52N 6.44E
102 G10 **Oldenburg** Niedersachsen, NW Germany 53.09N 8.13E
102 K8 **Oldenburg** Schleswig-Holstein, N Germany 54.17N 10.55E
100 P10 **Oldenzaal** Overijssel, E Netherlands 52.19N 6.52E
94 K8 **Olderfjord** Finnmark, N Norway 70.29N 24.58E
20 J8 **Old Forge** New York, NE USA 43.42N 74.59W
Old Goa *see* Goa
99 L17 **Oldham** NW England, UK 53.36N 2.00W
41 Q14 **Old Harbor** Kodiak Island, Alaska, USA 57.12N 153.18W
46 J13 **Old Harbour** C Jamaica 17.55N 77.06W
99 C22 **Old Head of Kinsale** *Ir.* An Seancheann. *headland* SW Ireland 51.37N 8.33W
22 J8 **Old Hickory Lake** ▣ Tennessee, S USA
Old Line State *see* Maryland
Old North State *see* North Carolina
83 I17 **Ol Doinyo Lengeyo** ▲▲ C Kenya
9 Q16 **Olds** Alberta, SW Canada 51.49N 114.06W
21 O7 **Old Speck Mountain** ▲ Maine, NE USA 44.34N 70.55W
21 S6 **Old Town** Maine, NE USA 44.55N 68.39W
9 T17 **Old Wives Lake** ◎ Saskatchewan, S Canada
168 J7 **Öldziyt** Arhangay, C Mongolia 48.30N 101.25E
169 N10 **Öldziyt** Dornogovĭ, SE Mongolia 44.42N 109.10E
196 H6 **Oleai** *var.* San Jose. Saipan, S Northern Mariana Islands
20 E11 **Olean** New York, NE USA 42.04N 78.24W
112 O7 **Olecko** *Ger.* Treuburg. Warmińsko-Mazurskie, NE Poland 54.01N 22.28E
108 C7 **Oleggio** Piemonte, NE Italy 45.36N 8.37E
126 L13 **Olëkma** Amurskaya Oblast', SE Russian Federation 57.00N 120.27E
126 L13 **Olëkma** ≈ C Russian Federation
126 L13 **Olëkminsk** Respublika Sakha (Yakutiya), NE Russian Federation 60.25N 120.25E
119 W7 **Oleksandrivka** Donets'ka Oblast', E Ukraine 48.42N 36.56E
119 R7 **Oleksandrivka** *Rus.* Aleksandrovka. Kirovohrads'ka Oblast', C Ukraine 48.58N 32.13E
119 Q9 **Oleksandrivka** Mykolayivs'ka Oblast', S Ukraine 47.42N 31.17E
119 S7 **Oleksandriya** *Rus.* Aleksandriya. Kirovohrads'ka Oblast', C Ukraine 48.42N 33.07E
95 B20 **Ølen** Hordaland, S Norway 59.36N 5.48E
128 J4 **Olenegorsk** Murmanskaya Oblast', NW Russian Federation 68.06N 33.15E
126 K8 **Olenëk** Respublika Sakha (Yakutiya), NE Russian Federation 68.28N 112.18E

◆ Country ● Country Capital ◇ Dependent Territory ○ Dependent Territory Capital ◆ Administrative Region ✕ International Airport ▲ Mountain ▲▲ Mountain Range Volcano ≈ River ◎ Lake ▣ Reservoir

126 Jj9 Olenëk ≈ NE Russian Federation
126 Kk6 Olenëkskiy Zaliv bay N Russian Federation
128 K6 Olenitsa Murmanskaya Oblast', NW Russian Federation 66.27N 35.21E
104 I11 Oléron, Île d' island W France
113 H14 Oleśnica Ger. Oels, Oels in Schlesien. Dolnośląskie, SW Poland 51.13N 17.19E
113 I15 Olesno Ger. Rosenberg. Opolskie, S Poland 50.53N 18.23E
118 M3 Olevs'k Rus. Olevsk. Zhytomyrs'ka Oblast', N Ukraine 51.12N 27.38E
127 Nn18 Ol'ga Primorskiy Kray, SE Russian Federation 43.41N 135.06E
Olga, Mount see Kata Tjuta
94 P2 Olgastretet strait E Svalbard
168 D5 Ölgiy Bayan-Ölgiy, W Mongolia 48.57N 89.59E
97 F23 Ølgod Ribe, W Denmark 55.43N 8.37E
106 H14 Olhão Faro, S Portugal 37.01N 7.49W
95 L14 Olhava Oulu, C Finland 65.28N 25.25E
114 B12 Olib It. Ulbo. island W Croatia
85 B16 Olifa Kunene, NW Namibia 17.25S 14.27E
85 E20 Olifants var. Elephant River. ≈ E Namibia
85 E25 Olifants var. Elefantes. ≈ SW South Africa
85 G22 Olifantshoek Northern Cape, N South Africa 27.52S 22.46E
196 L15 Olimarao Atoll atoll Caroline Islands, C Micronesia
Ólimbos see Ólympos
Olimpo see Fuerte Olimpo
61 Q15 Olinda Pernambuco, E Brazil 08.00S 34.51W
Olinthos see Ólynthos
85 I20 Oliphants Drift Kgatleng, SE Botswana 24.13S 26.52E
Olisipo see Lisboa
Olita see Alytus
107 Q4 Olite Navarra, N Spain 42.28N 1.40W
64 K10 Oliva Córdoba, C Argentina 32.03S 63.34W
107 T11 Oliva País Valenciano, E Spain 38.55N 0.09W
106 I12 Oliva de la Frontera Extremadura, W Spain 38.16N 6.54W
Olivares see Olivares de Júcar
64 H9 Olivares, Cerro de ▲ N Chile 30.25S 69.52W
107 P9 Olivares de Júcar var. Olivares. Castilla-La Mancha, C Spain 39.45N 2.21W
24 L1 Olive Branch Mississippi, S USA 34.58N 89.49W
23 O5 Olive Hill Kentucky, S USA 38.18N 83.10W
37 O6 Olivehurst California, W USA 39.05N 121.33W
106 G7 Oliveira de Azeméis Aveiro, N Portugal 40.49N 8.28W
106 I11 Olivenza Extremadura, W Spain 38.40N 7.06W
9 N17 Oliver British Columbia, SW Canada 49.10N 119.37W
105 N7 Olivet Loiret, C France 47.52N 1.53E
31 Q12 Olivet South Dakota, N USA 43.13N 97.40W
31 T9 Olivia Minnesota, N USA 44.46N 94.59W
193 C20 Olivine Range ▲▲ South Island, NZ
110 H10 Olivone Ticino, S Switzerland 46.32N 8.55E
Ölkeyek see Ul'kayak
131 O9 Ol'khovka Volgogradskaya Oblast', SW Russian Federation 49.54N 44.36E
113 K16 Olkusz Małopolskie, S Poland 50.16N 19.31E
24 I6 Olla Louisiana, S USA 31.54N 92.14W
64 I4 Ollagüe, Volcán var. Oyahue, Volcán Oyahue. ▲ N Chile 21.25S 68.10W
201 U13 Ollan island Chuuk, C Micronesia
196 F7 Ollei Babeldaob, N Palau 7.43N 134.37E
Ollius see Oglio
110 C10 Ollon Vaud, W Switzerland 46.19N 7.00E
153 Q10 Olmaliq Rus. Almalyk. Toshkent Viloyati, E Uzbekistan 40.51N 69.39E
106 M6 Olmedo Castilla-León, N Spain 41.16N 4.40W
58 B10 Olmos Lambayeque, W Peru 6.00S 79.43W
Olmütz see Olomouc
32 M15 Olney Illinois, N USA 38.43N 88.05W
27 R5 Olney Texas, SW USA 33.22N 98.45W
97 L22 Olofström Blekinge, S Sweden 56.16N 14.33E
195 Y15 Olomburi Malaita, N Solomon Islands 9.00S 161.09E
113 H17 Olomouc Ger. Olmütz, Pol. Ołomuniec. Olomoucký Kraj, E Czech Republic 49.36N 17.13E
113 H18 Olomoucký Kraj ◈ region E Czech Republic
Ołomuniec see Olomouc
125 Cc6 Olonets Respublika Kareliya, NW Russian Federation 60.58N 33.01E
179 P10 Olongapo off. Olongapo City. Luzon, N Philippines 14.52N 120.16E
104 J16 Oloron-Ste-Marie Pyrénées-Atlantiques, SW France 43.12N 0.34W
198 Dd8 Olosega island Manua Islands, E American Samoa
107 W4 Olot Cataluña, NE Spain 42.10N 2.30E
152 K12 Olot Rus. Alat. Buxoro Viloyati, C Uzbekistan 39.22N 63.42E
114 I12 Olovo Federacija Bosna I Hercegovina, E Bosnia and Herzegovina 44.08N 18.35E
126 Kk16 Olovyannaya Chitinskaya Oblast', S Russian Federation 50.58N 115.24E
127 Oo6 Oloy ≈ NE Russian Federation
103 F16 Olpe Nordrhein-Westfalen, W Germany 51.01N 7.51E
111 N8 Olperer ▲ SW Austria 47.03N 11.36E
Olshanka see Vil'shanka
Ol'shany see Al'shany
Olsnitz see Murska Sobota
100 M10 Olst Overijssel, E Netherlands 52.19N 6.06E
112 L8 Olsztyn Ger. Allenstein. Warmińsko-Mazurskie, NE Poland, 53.46N 20.28E
112 L8 Olsztynek Ger. Hohenstein in Ostpreussen. Warmińsko-Mazurskie, NE Poland, 53.34N 20.16E
118 I14 Olt ◈ county SW Romania
118 I14 Olt var. Oltul, Ger. Alt. ≈ S Romania
110 E7 Olten Solothurn, NW Switzerland 47.20N 7.51E
118 K14 Oltenița prev. Eng. Oltenitsa, anc. Constantiola. Călărași, SE Romania 44.04N 26.40E
Oltenitsa see Oltenița
118 H14 Olteț ≈ S Romania
26 M4 Olton Texas, SW USA 34.10N 102.07W
143 R12 Oltu Erzurum, NE Turkey 40.34N 41.58E
Oltul see Olt
152 G7 Oltynko'l Qoraqalpog'iston Respublikasi, NW Uzbekistan 43.04N 58.51E
167 S15 Oluan Pi Eng. Cape Olwanpi. headland S Taiwan 21.57N 120.48E
Ólubló see Stará Ľubovňa
143 R11 Olur Erzurum, NE Turkey 40.49N 42.07E
106 L15 Olvera Andalucía, S Spain 36.55N 5.15W
Ol'viopol' see Pervomays'k
Olwanpi, Cape see Oluan Pi
17 G2 Olympia state capital Washington, NW USA 47.02N 122.54W
117 D20 Olympía Dytikí Ellás, S Greece 37.39N 21.36E
190 H5 Olympic Dam South Australia 30.25S 136.56E
34 F7 Olympic Mountains ▲▲ Washington, NW USA
124 R12 Ólympos var. Troodos, Eng. Mount Olympus. ▲ C Cyprus 34.55N 32.49E
117 F15 Ólympos var. Ólimbos, Eng. Mount Olympus. ▲ N Greece 40.04N 22.24E
117 L17 Ólympos ▲ Lésvos, E Greece 39.03N 26.20E
17 G1 Olympus, Mount ▲ Washington, NW USA 47.48N 123.42W
Olympus, Mount see Ólympos
117 G14 Ólynthos var. Olinthos; anc. Olynthus. site of ancient city Kentrikí Makedonía, N Greece 40.16N 23.21E
Olynthus see Ólynthos
119 Q3 Olyshivka Chernihivs'ka Oblast', N Ukraine 51.13N 31.19E
127 Q7 Olyutorskiy, Mys headland E Russian Federation 59.56N 170.22E
127 Pp8 Olyutorskiy Zaliv bay E Russian Federation
194 F11 Om ≈ W PNG
133 S6 Om' ≈ N Russian Federation
164 I13 Oma Xizang Zizhiqu, W China 32.30N 83.13E
172 N8 Ōma Aomori, Honshū, C Japan 41.31N 140.54E
129 P6 Oma ≈ NW Russian Federation
171 J14 Ōmachi var. Ōmati. Nagano, Honshū, S Japan 36.33N 137.49E
171 Ii17 Omae-zaki headland Honshū, S Japan 34.36N 138.12E
171 M11 Ōmagari Akita, Honshū, C Japan 39.27N 140.28E
99 E15 Omagh Ir. An Ómaigh. W Northern Ireland, UK 54.36N 7.18W
31 S15 Omaha Nebraska, C USA 41.14N 95.57W
85 E19 Omaheke ◈ district W Namibia
147 W10 Oman off. Sultanate of Oman, Ar. Salṭanat 'Umān; prev. Muscat and Oman. ◆ monarchy SW Asia
133 O10 Oman Basin var. Bassin d'Oman. undersea feature N Indian Ocean
Oman, Bassin d' see Oman Basin
133 N10 Oman, Gulf of Ar. Khalīj 'Umān. gulf N Arabian Sea
192 J3 Omapere Northland, North Island, NZ 35.32S 173.24E
193 E20 Omarama Canterbury, South Island, NZ 44.29S 169.57E
114 F11 Omarska Republika Srpska, NW Bosnia and Herzegovina 44.53N 16.52E
85 C18 Omaruru Erongo, NW Namibia 21.25S 15.57E
85 C19 Omaruru ≈ W Namibia
85 E17 Omatako ≈ NE Namibia
Ōmati see Ōmachi
85 E18 Omawewozonyanda Omaheke, E Namibia 21.30S 19.34E
172 N7 Ōma-zaki headland Honshū, C Japan 41.32N 140.53E
Omba see Ambae
Ombai see Alor, Pulau
175 Rr16 Ombai, Selat strait Nusa Tenggara, S Indonesia
85 C16 Ombalantu Omusati, N Namibia 17.33S 14.58E
81 H15 Ombella-Mpoko ◈ prefecture S Central African Republic
Ombetsu see Onbetsu
85 B17 Ombombo Kunene, NW Namibia 18.43S 13.55E
81 D19 Omboué Ogooué-Maritime, W Gabon 1.37S 9.19E
108 G13 Ombrone ≈ C Italy
82 F9 Omdurman var. Umm Durmān. Khartoum, C Sudan 15.37N 32.28E
171 Jj16 Ōme Tōkyō, Honshū, S Japan 35.48N 139.10E
108 C6 Omegna Piemonte, NE Italy 45.54N 8.25E
191 P12 Omeo Victoria, SE Australia 37.09S 147.36E
144 F11 'Omer Southern, C Israel 31.16N 34.51E
43 P16 Ometepec Guerrero, S Mexico 16.39N 98.22W
44 K11 Ometepe, Isla de island S Nicaragua
Om Hager see Om Hajer
82 I10 Om Hajer var. Om Hager. SW Eritrea 14.19N 36.46E
171 H14 Ōmi-Hachiman var. Ōmihachiman. Shiga, Honshū, SW Japan 35.09N 136.04E
8 L12 Omineca Mountains ▲▲ British Columbia, W Canada
115 F14 Omiš It. Almissa. Split-Dalmacija, S Croatia 43.27N 16.41E
114 B10 Omišalj Primorje-Gorski Kotar, NW Croatia 45.10N 14.33E
170 Dd12 Ōmi-shima island SW Japan
85 D19 Omitara Khomas, C Namibia 22.18S 18.01E
43 O16 Omitlán, Río ≈ S Mexico
41 X14 Ommaney, Cape headland Baranof Island, Alaska, USA 56.10N 134.40W
100 N9 Ommen Overijssel, E Netherlands 52.31N 6.25E
168 K11 Ömnögovĭ ◈ province S Mongolia
203 X7 Omoa Fatu Hiva, NE French Polynesia 10.30S 138.40E
Omo Botego see Omo Wenz
Ómoldova see Moldova Veche
127 O6 Omolon Chukotskiy Avtonomnyy Okrug, NE Russian Federation 65.11N 96.33E
127 O7 Omolon ≈ NE Russian Federation
126 Ll8 Omoloy ≈ NE Russian Federation
171 M10 Omono-gawa ≈ Honshū, C Japan
83 I14 Omo Wenz var. Omo Botego. ≈ Ethiopia/Kenya
125 Ff13 Omsk Omskaya Oblast', C Russian Federation 55.00N 73.22E
125 Ff12 Omskaya Oblast' ◈ province C Russian Federation
127 O8 Omsukchan Magadanskaya Oblast', E Russian Federation 62.25N 155.22E
172 Q4 Ōmu Hokkaidō, NE Japan 44.36N 142.55E
112 M9 Omulew ≈ NE Poland
118 J12 Omul, Vârful prev. Virful Omu. ▲ C Romania 45.24N 25.26E
85 D16 Omundaungilo Ohangwena, N Namibia 17.28S 16.39E
170 C13 Ōmura Nagasaki, Kyūshū, SW Japan 32.55N 129.54E
85 B17 Omusati ◈ district N Namibia
170 Cc13 Ōmuta Fukuoka, Kyūshū, SW Japan 33.02N 130.26E
129 S14 Omutninsk Kirovskaya Oblast', NW Russian Federation 58.37N 52.08E
Omu, Vîrful see Omul, Vârful
31 V7 Onamia Minnesota, N USA 46.04N 93.40W
23 Y5 Onancock Virginia, NE USA 37.42N 75.45W
12 E10 Onaping Lake ◎ Ontario, S Canada
32 M12 Onarga Illinois, N USA 40.39N 88.00W
13 R6 Onatchiway, Lac ◎ Quebec, SE Canada
31 S14 Onawa Iowa, C USA 42.01N 96.06W
172 Pp7 Onbetsu var. Ombetsu. Hokkaidō, NE Japan 42.52N 143.54E
85 B16 Oncócua Cunene, SW Angola 16.37S 13.23E
107 S9 Onda País Valenciano, E Spain 39.58N 0.17W
113 N18 Ondava ≈ NE Slovakia
Ondjiva see N'Giva
79 T16 Ondo Ondo, SW Nigeria 7.07N 4.50E
79 T16 Ondo ◈ state SW Nigeria
169 N8 Öndörhaan Hentiy, E Mongolia 47.20N 110.42E
85 D18 Ondundazongonda Otjozondjupa, N Namibia 20.28S 18.00E
157 K21 One and Half Degree Channel channel S Maldives
197 L15 Oneata island Lau Group, E Fiji
128 L9 Onega Arkhangel'skaya Oblast', NW Russian Federation 63.54N 37.58E
125 Dd6 Onega ≈ NW Russian Federation
Onega Bay see Onezhskaya Guba
Onega, Lake see Onezhskoye Ozero
20 I10 Oneida New York, NE USA 43.05N 75.39W
22 M8 Oneida Tennessee, S USA 36.30N 84.30W
20 H9 Oneida Lake ◎ New York, NE USA
31 P13 O'Neill Nebraska, C USA 42.28N 98.37W
127 Pp13 Onekotan, Ostrov island Kuril'skiye Ostrova, SE Russian Federation
25 P3 Oneonta Alabama, S USA 33.57N 86.28W
20 J11 Oneonta New York, NE USA 42.27N 75.03W
202 I16 Oneroa island S Cook Islands
118 K11 Onești Hung. Onyest; prev. Gheorghe Gheorghiu-Dej. Bacău, E Romania 46.13N 26.46E
200 Qq15 Onevai island Tongatapu Group, S Tonga
110 A11 Onex Genève, SW Switzerland 46.11N 6.04E
128 K8 Onezhskaya Guba Eng. Onega Bay. bay NW Russian Federation
125 D6 Onezhskoye Ozero Eng. Lake Onega. ◎ NW Russian Federation
85 C16 Ongandjera Omusati, N Namibia 17.49S 15.06E
192 N12 Ongaonga Hawke's Bay, North Island, NZ 39.57S 176.21E
168 K9 Ongi Dundgovĭ, C Mongolia 45.27N 103.58E
168 J8 Ongi Övörhangay, C Mongolia 46.30N 102.18E
169 W14 Ongjin SW North Korea 37.55N 125.21E
161 J17 Ongole Andhra Pradesh, E India 15.33N 80.03E
168 K8 Ongon Övörhangay, C Mongolia 46.58N 103.45E
Ongtüstik Qazaqstan Oblysy see Yuzhnyy Kazakhstan
101 I21 Onhaye Namur, S Belgium 50.15N 4.51E
177 G8 Onhne Pegu, SW Myanmar 17.02N 96.28E
143 S9 Oni N Georgia 42.36N 43.13E
31 N9 Onida South Dakota, N USA 44.42N 100.03W
170 E15 Onigajō-yama ▲ Shikoku, SW Japan 33.10N 132.37E
180 H7 Onilahy ≈ S Madagascar
79 U16 Onitsha Anambra, S Nigeria 6.09N 6.48E
171 Gg14 Ono Hyōgo, Honshū, SW Japan 34.51N 134.56E
197 I15 Ono island SW Fiji
171 I14 Ōno Fukui, Honshū, SW Japan 35.59N 136.29E
170 D12 Onoda Yamaguchi, Honshū, SW Japan 33.59N 131.10E
197 L17 Ono-i-lau island SE Fiji
170 Cc13 Ōnojō var. Ōnozyō. Fukuoka, Kyūshū, SW Japan 33.30N 130.30E
126 K16 Onokhoy Respublika Buryatiya, S Russian Federation 51.51N 108.17E
170 F14 Onomichi var. Onomiti. Hiroshima, Honshū, SW Japan 34.25N 133.13E
Onomiti see Onomichi
169 O7 Onon Gol ≈ N Mongolia
Ononte see Orontes
57 N6 Onoto Anzoátegui, NE Venezuela 9.36N 65.10W
203 O3 Onotoa prev. Clerk Island. atoll Tungaru, W Kiribati
Ōnozyō see Ōnojō
97 I19 Onsala Halland, S Sweden 57.25N 12.00E
85 E23 Onseepkans Northern Cape, W South Africa 28.44S 19.18E
106 F4 Ons, Illa de island NW Spain
188 H7 Onslow Western Australia 21.42S 115.07E
23 W11 Onslow Bay bay North Carolina, E USA
100 P6 Onstwedde Groningen, NE Netherlands 53.01N 7.04E
170 Bb16 On-take ▲ Kyūshū, SW Japan 31.35N 130.39E
171 Ii15 Ontake-san ▲ Honshū, S Japan 35.54N 137.28E
37 T15 Ontario California, W USA 34.03N 117.39W
34 M13 Ontario Oregon, NW USA 44.01N 116.57W
10 D10 Ontario ◈ province S Canada
15 Gg2 Ontario, Lake ◎ Canada/USA
(0) L9 Ontario Peninsula peninsula Canada/USA
Onteniente see Ontinyent
107 S11 Ontinyent var. Onteniente. País Valenciano, E Spain 38.49N 0.37W
95 N15 Ontojärvi ◎ E Finland
32 L3 Ontonagon Michigan, N USA 46.52N 89.18W
32 L3 Ontonagon River ≈ Michigan, N USA
195 W11 Ontong Java Atoll prev. Lord Howe Island. atoll N Solomon Islands
183 N5 Ontong Java Rise undersea feature W Pacific Ocean
Onuba see Huelva
57 W9 Onverwacht Para, N Suriname 5.36N 55.12W
Onyest see Onești
190 J7 Oodla Wirra South Australia 32.52S 139.05E
190 F2 Oodnadatta South Australia 27.34S 135.27E
190 C5 Ooldea South Australia 30.29S 131.50E
29 Q8 Oologah Lake ⊠ Oklahoma, C USA
Oos-Kaap see Eastern Cape
Oos-Londen see East London
101 E17 Oostakker Oost-Vlaanderen, NW Belgium 51.06N 3.46E
101 D15 Oostburg Zeeland, SW Netherlands 51.19N 3.30E
100 K9 Oostelijk-Flevoland polder C Netherlands
101 B16 Oostende Eng. Ostend, Fr. Ostende. West-Vlaanderen, NW Belgium 51.13N 2.55E
101 B16 Oostende ✈ West-Vlaanderen, NW Belgium 51.12N 2.55E
100 L12 Oosterbeek Gelderland, SE Netherlands 51.58N 5.51E
101 I14 Oosterhout Noord-Brabant, S Netherlands 51.37N 4.51E
100 O6 Oostermoers Vaart var. Hunze. ≈ NE Netherlands
101 F14 Oosterschelde Eng. Eastern Scheldt. inlet SW Netherlands
101 E14 Oosterscheldedam dam SW Netherlands 51.38N 3.45E
100 M7 Oosterwolde Fris. Easterwâlde. Friesland, N Netherlands 53.00N 6.15E
100 I9 Oosthuizen Noord-Holland, NW Netherlands 52.34N 5.00E
101 H16 Oostmalle Antwerpen, N Belgium 51.18N 4.44E
Oos-Transvaal see Mpumalanga
101 E15 Oost-Souburg Zeeland, SW Netherlands 51.28N 3.36E
101 E17 Oost-Vlaanderen Eng. East Flanders. ◈ province NW Belgium
100 J5 Oost-Vlieland Friesland, N Netherlands 53.19N 5.02E
100 F12 Oostvoorne Zuid-Holland, SW Netherlands 51.55N 4.06E
Ootacamund see Udagamandalam
100 O10 Ootmarsum Overijssel, E Netherlands 52.25N 6.55E
8 K14 Ootsa Lake ◎ British Columbia, SW Canada
116 L8 Opaka Tŭrgovishte, N Bulgaria 43.26N 26.12E
81 M18 Opala Orientale, C Dem. Rep. Congo 0.40S 24.19E
129 Q13 Oparino Kirovskaya Oblast', NW Russian Federation 59.52N 48.14E
12 H8 Opasatica, Lac ◎ Quebec, SE Canada
114 B9 Opatija It. Abbazia. Primorje-Gorski Kotar, NW Croatia 45.18N 14.15E
113 N15 Opatów Świętokrzyskie, C Poland 50.45N 21.27E
113 I17 Opava Ger. Troppau. Ostravský Kraj, E Czech Republic 49.55N 17.53E
113 H16 Opava Ger. Oppa. ≈ NE Czech Republic
Opazova see Stara Pazova
194 L14 Ope ≈ S PNG
Ópécska see Pecica
12 E8 Opeepeesway Lake ◎ Ontario, S Canada
25 R5 Opelika Alabama, S USA 32.39N 85.22W
24 I8 Opelousas Louisiana, S USA 30.31N 92.04W
195 O11 Open Bay bay New Britain, E PNG
12 I12 Opeongo Lake ◎ Ontario, SE Canada
101 K17 Opglabbeek Limburg, NE Belgium 51.04N 5.39E
35 W6 Opheim Montana, NW USA 48.50N 106.24W
41 P10 Ophir Alaska, USA 63.08N 94.31W
Ophiusa see Formentera
81 N18 Opienge Orientale, E Dem. Rep. Congo 0.15N 27.25E
193 G20 Opihi ≈ South Island, NZ
10 J9 Opinaca ≈ Quebec, C Canada
10 J10 Opinaca, Réservoir ⊠ Quebec, E Canada
119 T5 Opishnya Rus. Oposhnya. Poltavs'ka Oblast', NE Ukraine 49.56N 34.36E
100 I8 Opmeer Noord-Holland, NW Netherlands 52.43N 4.55E
79 V17 Opobo Akwa Ibom, S Nigeria 4.36N 7.37E
128 F16 Opochka Pskovskaya Oblast', W Russian Federation 56.42N 28.39E
112 L13 Opoczno Łodzkie, C Poland 51.24N 20.18E
113 I15 Opole Ger. Oppeln. Opolskie, S Poland 50.40N 17.55E
113 H15 Opolskie ◈ province S Poland
150 G13 Opornyy Mangistau, SW Kazakhstan 46.09N 54.32E
Oporto see Porto
Oposhnya see Opishnya
192 P8 Opotiki Bay of Plenty, North Island, NZ 38.02S 177.18E
25 Q7 Opp Alabama, S USA 31.16N 86.14W
Oppa see Opava
96 G9 Oppdal Sør-Trøndelag, S Norway 62.36N 9.41E
Oppeln see Opole
109 N23 Oppido Mamertina Calabria, SW Italy 38.17N 15.58E
Oppidum Ubiorum see Köln
96 F12 Oppland ◈ county S Norway
120 J12 Opsa Rus. Opsa. Vitsyebskaya Voblasts', NW Belarus 55.31N 26.49E
28 I8 Optima Lake ⊠ Oklahoma, C USA
192 J11 Opunake Taranaki, North Island, NZ 39.27S 173.51E
203 N6 Opunohu, Baie d' bay Moorea, W French Polynesia
85 B17 Opuwo Kunene, NW Namibia 18.06S 13.52E
152 H6 Oqqal'a var. Akkala, Rus. Karakala. Qoraqalpog'iston Respublikasi, NW Uzbekistan 43.43N 59.25E
153 V13 Oqsu Rus. Oksu. ≈ SE Tajikistan
153 P14 Oqtogh, Qatorkŭhi Rus. Khrebet Aktau. ▲▲ SW Tajikistan
152 M11 Oqtosh Rus. Aktash. Samarqand Viloyati, C Uzbekistan 39.23N 65.45E
153 N11 Oqtov Tizmasi Rus. Khrebet Aktau. ▲▲ C Uzbekistan
32 J12 Oquawka Illinois, N USA 40.55N 90.55W
150 J10 Or' Kaz. Or. ≈ Kazakhstan/Russian Federation
38 M15 Oracle Arizona, SW USA 32.36N 110.46W
153 N13 O'radaryo Rus. Uradar'ya. ≈ S Uzbekistan
118 F9 Oradea prev. Oradea Mare, Ger. Grosswardein, Hung. Nagyvárad. Bihor, NW Romania 47.02N 21.55E
Oradea Mare see Oradea
115 M17 Orahovac Alb. Rahovec. Serbia, S Serbia and Montenegro (Yugoslavia) 42.24N 20.40E
114 H9 Orahovica Virovitica-Podravina, NE Croatia 45.33N 17.54E
158 K13 Orai Uttar Pradesh, N India 26.00N 79.26E
94 K12 Orajärvi Lappi, NW Finland 66.54N 24.04E
Or Akiva see Or 'Aqiva
Oral see Ural'sk
76 I5 Oran var. Ouahran, Wahran. NW Algeria 35.42N 0.37W
191 R8 Orange New South Wales, SE Australia 33.16S 149.06E
105 R14 Orange anc. Arausio. Vaucluse, SE France 44.06N 4.52E
27 Y10 Orange Texas, SW USA 30.05N 93.44W
23 V5 Orange Virginia, NE USA 38.15N 78.06W
23 R13 Orangeburg South Carolina, SE USA 33.29N 80.51W
60 J9 Orange, Cabo headland NE Brazil 4.24N 51.33W
31 S12 Orange City Iowa, C USA 43.00N 96.03W
Orange Cone see Orange Fan
180 J10 Orange Fan var. Orange Cone. undersea feature SW Indian Ocean
Orange Free State see Free State
27 S14 Orange Grove Texas, SW USA 27.57N 97.56W
20 K13 Orange Lake New York, NE USA 41.32N 74.06W
25 V10 Orange Lake ◎ Florida, SE USA
Orange Mouth/Orangemund see Oranjemund
25 W9 Orange Park Florida, SE USA 30.10N 81.42W
194 M17 Orangerie Bay bay SE PNG
85 E23 Orange River Afr. Oranjerivier. ≈ S Africa
12 G15 Orangeville Ontario, S Canada 43.55N 80.06W
38 M5 Orangeville Utah, W USA 39.14N 111.03W
44 G1 Orange Walk Orange Walk, N Belize 18.06N 88.30W
44 F1 Orange Walk ◈ district NW Belize
102 N11 Oranienburg Brandenburg, NE Germany 52.46N 13.15E
100 O7 Oranjekanaal canal NE Netherlands
85 D23 Oranjemund var. Orangemund; prev. Orange Mouth. Karas, SW Namibia 28.33S 16.27E
Oranjerivier see Orange River
47 N16 Oranjestad ○ (Aruba) W Aruba 12.31N 70.00W
Oranje Vrystaat see Free State
176 W9 Oransbari Papua, E Indonesia 1.18S 134.16E
Orany see Varėna
85 H18 Orapa Central, C Botswana 21.18S 25.22E
144 F9 Or 'Aqiva var. Or Akiva. Haifa, W Israel 32.40N 34.58E
114 I10 Orašje Federacija Bosna I Hercegovina, N Bosnia and Herzegovina 45.01N 18.42E
118 G11 Orăștie Ger. Broos, Hung. Szászváros. Hunedoara, W Romania 45.49N 23.10E
Orașul Stalin see Brașov
113 K18 Orava Hung. Árva, Pol. Orawa. ≈ N Slovakia
Oravainen see Oravais
95 K16 Oravais Fin. Oravainen. Länsi-Suomi, W Finland 63.18N 22.25E
Oravicabánya see Oravița
118 F13 Oravița Ger. Orawitza, Hung. Oravicabánya. Caraș-Severin, SW Romania 45.01N 21.43E
Orawa see Orava
193 B24 Orawia Southland, South Island, NZ 46.03S 167.49E
Orawitza see Oravița
105 P16 Orb ≈ S France
108 C9 Orba ≈ NW Italy
164 H12 Orba Co ◎ W China
110 B9 Orbe Vaud, W Switzerland 46.42N 6.28E
109 G14 Orbetello Toscana, C Italy 42.27N 11.14E
106 K3 Orbigo ≈ NW Spain
191 Q12 Orbost Victoria, SE Australia 37.44S 148.28E
97 O14 Örbyhus Uppsala, C Sweden 60.15N 17.43E
204 I1 Orcadas Argentinian research station South Orkney Islands, Antarctica 60.37S 44.48W
107 P12 Orcera Andalucía, S Spain 38.20N 2.36W
35 P9 Orchard Homes Montana, NW USA 46.52N 114.01W
39 P5 Orchard Mesa Colorado, C USA 39.02N 108.33W
20 D10 Orchard Park New York, NE USA 42.46N 78.44W
Orchid Island see Lan Yü
117 G18 Orchómenos var. Orhomenos, Orkhómenos; prev. Skripón, anc. Orchomenus. Stereá Ellás, C Greece 38.29N 22.58E
Orchomenus see Orchómenos
108 B7 Orco ≈ NW Italy
105 R8 Or, Côte d' physical region C France
31 O14 Ord Nebraska, C USA 41.36N 98.55W
Ordat' see Ordats'
121 O15 Ordats' Rus. Ordat'. Mahilyowskaya Voblasts', E Belarus 54.09N 30.42E
38 K8 Orderville Utah, W USA 37.16N 112.38W
106 H2 Ordes Galicia, NW Spain 43.04N 8.25W
37 V14 Ord Mountain ▲ California, W USA 34.41N 116.46W
Ordos Desert see Mu Us Shamo
196 B16 Ordot C Guam
143 N11 Ordu anc. Cotyora. Ordu, N Turkey 41.00N 37.52E
142 M11 Ordu ◈ province N Turkey
143 V14 Ordubad SW Azerbaijan 38.55N 46.00E
107 O3 Orduña País Vasco, N Spain 43.00N 3.00W
39 U6 Ordway Colorado, C USA 38.13N 103.45W
Ordzhonikidze see Denisovka
119 T9 Ordzhonikidze Dnipropetrovs'ka Oblast', E Ukraine 47.39N 34.09E
Ordzhonikidze see Vladikavkaz, Russian Federation
Ordzhonikidze see Yenakiyeve, Ukraine
Ordzhonikidzeabad see Kofarnihon
57 U9 Orealla E Guyana 5.13N 57.17W
115 G15 Orebić It. Sabbioncello. Dubrovnik-Neretva, S Croatia 42.58N 17.12E
97 M16 Örebro Örebro, C Sweden 59.18N 15.12E
97 L16 Örebro ◈ county C Sweden
27 W6 Ore City Texas, SW USA 32.48N 94.43W
32 L10 Oregon Illinois, N USA 42.00N 89.19W
29 Q2 Oregon Missouri, C USA 39.59N 95.08W
33 R11 Oregon Ohio, N USA 41.38N 83.29W
34 H13 Oregon off. State of Oregon; also known as Beaver State, Sunset State, Valentine State, Webfoot State. ◈ state NW USA
34 G11 Oregon City Oregon, NW USA 45.21N 122.36W
97 P14 Öregrund Uppsala, C Sweden 60.19N 18.30E
Orekhov see Orikhiv
130 J3 Orekhovo-Zuyevo Moskovskaya Oblast', W Russian Federation 55.46N 39.01E
Orekhovsk see Arekhawsk
Orel see Oril'
130 J6 Orël Orlovskaya Oblast', W Russian Federation 52.57N 36.06E
58 E11 Orellana Loreto, N Peru 6.55S 75.10W
106 L11 Orellana, Embalse de ⊠ W Spain
38 L3 Orem Utah, W USA 40.18N 111.41W
Ore Mountains see Erzgebirge/Krušné Hory
131 V7 Orenburg prev. Chkalov. Orenburgskaya Oblast', W Russian Federation 51.45N 55.11E
131 V7 Orenburg ✈ Orenburgskaya Oblast', W Russian Federation 51.54N 55.15E
131 T7 Orenburgskaya Oblast' ◈ province W Russian Federation
Orense see Ourense
196 C8 Oreor var. Koror. ● (Palau) Oreor, N Palau 7.21N 134.28E
196 C8 Oreor var. Koror. island N Palau
193 B24 Orepuki Southland, South Island, NZ 46.17S 167.46E
116 L12 Orestiáda prev. Orestiás. Anatolikí Makedonía kai Thráki, NE Greece 41.30N 26.31E
Orestiás see Orestiáda
Öresund/Øresund see Sound, The
193 C23 Oreti ≈ South Island, NZ
192 L5 Orewa Auckland, North Island, NZ 36.36S 174.42E
176 Y14 Oreyabo Papua, E Indonesia 6.57S 139.05E
67 A25 Orford, Cape headland West Falkland, Falkland Islands 52.00S 61.04W
46 B5 Órganos, Sierra de los ▲▲ W Cuba
39 R15 Organ Peak ▲ New Mexico, SW USA 32.17N 106.35W
107 N9 Orgaz Castilla-La Mancha, C Spain 39.39N 3.52W
Orgeyev see Orhei
168 I6 Orgil Hövsgöl, C Mongolia 48.31N 99.19E
107 O15 Orgiva var. Orjiva. Andalucía, S Spain 36.54N 3.25W
168 I9 Örgön Bayanhongor, C Mongolia 44.43N 100.23E
119 N9 Orhei var. Orheiu, Rus. Orgeyev. N Moldova 47.25N 28.48E
Orheiu see Orhei
107 R3 Orhi var. Orhy, Pico de Orhy, Pic d'Orhy. ▲ France/Spain see also Orhy 42.55N 1.01W
Orhomenos see Orchómenos
168 L6 Orhon Gol ≈ N Mongolia
104 J16 Orhy var. Orhi, Pico de Orhy, Pic d'Orhy. ▲ France/Spain see also Orhi 43.00N 1.00W
Orhy, Pic d'/Orhy, Pico de see Orhi/Orhy
36 L2 Orick California, W USA 41.16N 124.03W
34 L6 Orient Washington, NW USA 48.51N 118.14W
50 D6 Oriental, Cordillera ▲▲ Bolivia/Peru
50 D6 Oriental, Cordillera ▲▲ C Colombia
59 H16 Oriental, Cordillera ▲▲ C Peru
65 M15 Oriente Buenos Aires, E Argentina 38.45S 60.37W
107 R12 Orihuela País Valenciano, E Spain 38.04N 0.55W
119 V9 Orikhiv Rus. Orekhov. Zaporiz'ka Oblast', SE Ukraine 47.32N 35.48E
115 K22 Orikum var. Orikumi. Vlorë, SW Albania 40.20N 19.28E
Orikumi see Orikum
119 V6 Oril' Rus. Orel. ≈ E Ukraine
12 H14 Orillia Ontario, S Canada 44.36N 79.25W
95 M19 Orimattila Etelä-Suomi, S Finland 60.51N 25.46E
35 Y15 Orin Wyoming, C USA 42.39N 105.10W
49 R4 Orinoco, Río ≈ Colombia/Venezuela
194 G15 Oriomo Western, SW PNG 8.53S 143.13E
32 K11 Orion Illinois, N USA 41.21N 90.22W
31 Q5 Oriska North Dakota, N USA 46.54N 97.46W
159 P17 Orissa ◈ state NE India
Orissaar see Orissaare
120 E5 Orissaare Ger. Orissaar. Saaremaa, W Estonia 58.33N 23.05E
109 B19 Oristano Sardegna, Italy, C Mediterranean Sea 39.54N 8.34E
109 A19 Oristano, Golfo di gulf Sardegna, Italy, C Mediterranean Sea
56 D13 Orito Putumayo, SW Colombia 0.41N 76.48W
95 L18 Orivesi Häme, SW Finland 61.39N 24.21E
95 N17 Orivesi ◎ Länsi-Suomi, SE Finland
60 H12 Oriximiná Pará, NE Brazil 1.45S 55.49W
43 Q14 Orizaba Veracruz-Llave, E Mexico 18.55N 97.57W
43 Q14 Orizaba, Volcán Pico de var. Citlaltépetl. ▲ S Mexico 19.00N 97.15W
97 I16 Ørje Østfold, S Norway 59.28N 11.39E
115 I16 Orjen ▲ Bosnia and Herzegovina/Serbia and Montenegro (Yugoslavia)
Orjiva see Orgiva
96 G8 Orkanger Sør-Trøndelag, S Norway 63.18N 9.51E
96 G8 Orkdalen valley S Norway
97 K22 Örkelljunga Skåne, S Sweden 56.16N 13.19E
Orkhaniye see Botevgrad
Orkhómenos see Orchómenos
96 H9 Orkla ≈ S Norway
Orkney see Orkney Islands
67 J22 Orkney Deep undersea feature Scotia Sea/Weddell Sea
98 J4 Orkney Islands var. Orkney, Orkneys. island group N Scotland, UK
Orkneys see Orkney Islands
26 K8 Orla Texas, SW USA 31.48N 103.55W
37 N5 Orland California, W USA 39.43N 122.12W
25 X11 Orlando Florida, SE USA 28.32N 81.22W
25 X12 Orlando ✈ Florida, SE USA 28.24N 81.16W
109 K23 Orlando, Capo d' headland Sicilia, Italy, C Mediterranean Sea 38.10N 14.44E
Orlau see Orlová
105 N6 Orléanais cultural region C France
36 L2 Orleans California, W USA 41.16N 123.36W
21 Q12 Orleans Massachusetts, NE USA 41.48N 69.57W
105 N7 Orléans anc. Aurelianum. Loiret, C France 47.54N 1.52E
13 R10 Orléans, Île d' island Quebec, SE Canada
Orléansville see Chlef
113 F16 Orlice Ger. Adler. ≈ NE Czech Republic
126 Ii15 Orlik Respublika Buryatiya, S Russian Federation 52.32N 99.36E
129 Q14 Orlov prev. Khalturin. Kirovskaya Oblast', NW Russian Federation 58.34N 48.57E

◆ Country ● Country Capital ◇ Dependent Territory ○ Dependent Territory Capital ◈ Administrative Region ✈ International Airport ▲ Mountain ▲▲ Mountain Range Volcano ≈ River ◎ Lake ⊠ Reservoir

113 I17 **Orlová** *Ger.* Orlau, *Pol.* Orłowa. Ostravský Kraj, E Czech Republic *49.52N 18.25E*
Orlov, Mys *see* Orlovskiy, Mys
130 I6 **Orlovskaya Oblast'** ◆ *province* W Russian Federation
128 M5 **Orlovskiy, Mys** *var.* Mys Orlov. *headland* NW Russian Federation *67.14N 41.17E*
Orłowa *see* Orlová
105 O5 **Orly** ✕ (Paris) Essonne, N France *48.43N 2.24E*
121 G16 **Orlya** *Rus.* Orlya. Hrodzyenskaya Voblasts', W Belarus *53.30N 24.58E*
116 M7 **Orlyak** *prev.* Makenzen, Trubchular, *Rom.* Trupcilar. Dobrich, NE Bulgaria *43.39N 27.21E*
154 L16 **Ormāra** Baluchistān, SW Pakistan *25.14N 64.36E*
179 Qq13 **Ormoc** *off.* Ormoc City, *var.* MacArthur. Leyte, C Philippines *11.02N 124.35E*
25 X10 **Ormond Beach** Florida, SE USA *29.16N 81.04W*
111 X10 **Ormož** *Ger.* Friedau. NE Slovenia *46.24N 16.09E*
12 J13 **Ormsby** Ontario, SE Canada *44.52N 77.45W*
99 K17 **Ormskirk** NW England, UK *53.34N 2.54W*
Ormsö *see* Vormsi
13 N13 **Ormstown** Quebec, SE Canada *45.08N 73.57W*
Ormuz, Strait of *see* Hormuz, Strait of
105 T8 **Ornans** Doubs, E France *47.06N 6.06E*
104 K5 **Orne** ◆ *department* N France
104 K5 **Orne** ↝ N France
94 G12 **Ørnes** Nordland, C Norway *66.51N 13.43E*
112 L7 **Orneta** Warmińsko-Mazurskie, NE Poland *54.07N 20.10E*
97 P16 **Ornö** Stockholm, C Sweden *59.03N 18.28E*
39 Q3 **Orno Peak** ▲ Colorado, C USA *40.06N 107.06W*
95 I16 **Örnsköldsvik** Västernorrland, C Sweden *63.16N 18.45E*
169 X13 **Oro** E North Korea *39.59N 127.27E*
47 T6 **Orocovis** C Puerto Rico *18.13N 66.22W*
56 H10 **Orocué** Casanare, E Colombia *4.46N 71.22W*
79 N13 **Orodara** SW Burkina *11.00N 4.54W*
107 S4 **Oroel, Peña de** ▲ N Spain *42.30N 0.31W*
35 N10 **Orofino** Idaho, NW USA *46.28N 116.15W*
168 I9 **Orog Nuur** ◎ S Mongolia
37 U14 **Oro Grande** California, W USA *34.36N 117.19W*
39 S15 **Orogrande** New Mexico, SW USA *32.24N 106.04W*
203 Q7 **Orohena, Mont** ⛰ Tahiti, W French Polynesia *17.37S 149.27W*
Orolaunum *see* Arlon
Orol Dengizi *see* Aral Sea
201 S15 **Oroluk Atoll** *atoll* Caroline Islands, C Micronesia
82 J13 **Oromo** ◆ *region* C Ethiopia
11 O15 **Oromocto** New Brunswick, SE Canada *45.49N 66.28W*
203 S4 **Orona** *prev.* Hull Island. *atoll* Phoenix Islands, C Kiribati
203 V17 **Orongo** *ancient monument* Easter Island, Chile, E Pacific Ocean *27.10S 109.27W*
144 I3 **Orontes** *var.* Ononte, *Ar.* Nahr el Aassi, Nahr al 'Aṣī. ↝ SW Asia
106 L9 **Oropesa** Castilla-La Mancha, C Spain *39.55N 5.10W*
107 T8 **Oropesa** País Valenciano, E Spain *40.06N 0.07E*
Oropeza *see* Cochabamba
169 U5 **Oroqen Zizhiqi** Nei Mongol Zizhiqu, N China *50.34N 123.40E*
179 Qq15 **Oroquieta** *var.* Oroquieta City. Mindanao, S Philippines *8.27N 123.46E*
42 J8 **Oro, Río del** ↝ C Mexico
61 O14 **Orós, Açude** ⊠ E Brazil
109 D18 **Orosei, Golfo di** *gulf* Tyrrhenian Sea, C Mediterranean Sea
113 M24 **Orosháza** Békés, SE Hungary *46.33N 20.40E*
Orosirá Rodhópis *see* Rhodope Mountains
113 I22 **Oroszlány** Komárom-Esztergom, W Hungary *47.31N 18.19E*
196 B16 **Orote Peninsula** *peninsula* W Guam
127 O9 **Orotukan** Magadanskaya Oblast', E Russian Federation *62.18N 150.46E*
37 O5 **Oroville** California, W USA *39.29N 121.35W*
34 K6 **Oroville** Washington, NW USA *48.56N 119.25W*
37 O5 **Oroville, Lake** ⊠ California, W USA
(0) G15 **Orozco Fracture Zone** *tectonic feature* E Pacific Ocean
66 I7 **Orphan Knoll** *undersea feature* NW Atlantic Ocean *51.00N 47.00W*
31 V3 **Orr** Minnesota, N USA *48.03N 92.48W*
97 M21 **Orrefors** Kalmar, S Sweden *56.48N 15.45E*
190 I7 **Orroroo** South Australia *32.46S 138.38E*
33 T12 **Orrville** Ohio, N USA *40.50N 81.45W*
96 L12 **Orsa** Dalarna, C Sweden *61.07N 14.40E*
Orschowa *see* Orşova
Orschütz *see* Orzyc
121 O14 **Orsha** *Rus.* Orsha. Vitsyebskaya Voblasts', NE Belarus *54.30N 30.25E*
131 Q2 **Orshanka** Respublika Mariy El, W Russian Federation *56.54N 47.54E*
110 C11 **Orsières** Valais, SW Switzerland *46.00N 7.09E*
125 Dd13 **Orsk** Orenburgskaya Oblast', W Russian Federation *51.13N 58.34E*
118 F13 **Orşova** *Ger.* Orschowa, *Hung.* Orsova. Mehedinți, SW Romania *44.42N 22.22E*
96 D10 **Ørsta** Møre og Romsdal, S Norway *62.12N 6.07E*
97 O15 **Örsundsbro** Uppsala, C Sweden *59.45N 17.19E*
142 D16 **Ortaca** Muğla, SW Turkey *36.49N 28.43E*
109 M16 **Orta Nova** Puglia, SE Italy *41.19N 15.43E*
142 I17 **Orta Toroslar** ▲ S Turkey
56 E11 **Ortega** Tolima, W Colombia *3.57N 75.10W*
106 H1 **Ortegal, Cabo** *headland* NW Spain *43.46N 7.54W*
Ortelsburg *see* Szczytno
104 J15 **Orthez** Pyrénées-Atlantiques, SW France *43.28N 0.46W*
59 K14 **Orthon, Río** ↝ N Bolivia
62 J10 **Ortigueira** Paraná, S Brazil *24.10S 50.55W*
106 H1 **Ortigueira** Galicia, NW Spain *43.40N 7.50W*
108 H5 **Ortisei** *Ger.* Sankt-Ulrich. Trentino-Alto Adige, N Italy *46.35N 11.42E*
42 F6 **Ortiz** Sonora, NW Mexico *28.18N 110.40W*
56 L5 **Ortiz** Guárico, N Venezuela *9.37N 67.17W*
Ortler *see* Ortles
108 F5 **Ortles** *Ger.* Ortler. ▲ N Italy *46.29N 10.33E*
109 K14 **Ortona** Abruzzo, C Italy *42.21N 14.24E*
31 R8 **Ortonville** Minnesota, N USA *45.18N 96.26W*
153 W8 **Orto-Tokoy** Issyk-Kul'skaya Oblast', NE Kyrgyzstan *42.20N 76.03E*
95 I15 **Örträsk** Västerbotten, N Sweden *64.10N 19.00E*
102 J12 **Örtze** ↝ NW Germany
Oruba *see* Aruba
148 I3 **Orūmīyeh** *var.* Rizaiyeh, Urmia, Urmiyeh; *prev.* Reẓā'īyeh. Āzarbāyjān-e Bākhtarī, NW Iran *37.33N 45.06E*
148 J3 **Orūmīyeh, Daryācheh-ye** *var.* Matianus, Sha Hi, Urumi Yeh, *Eng.* Lake Urmia; *prev.* Daryācheh-ye Reẓā'īyeh. ◎ NW Iran
59 K19 **Oruro** Oruro, W Bolivia *17.57S 67.05W*
59 J19 **Oruro** ◆ *department* W Bolivia
97 I18 **Orust** *island* S Sweden
Oruzgān/Orūzgān *see* Ūrūzgān
108 H13 **Orvieto** *anc.* Velsuna. Umbria, C Italy *42.43N 12.07E*
204 K7 **Orville Coast** *physical region* Antarctica
116 H7 **Oryakhovo** Vratsa, NW Bulgaria *43.43N 23.58E*
Oryokko *see* Yalu
119 R5 **Orzhytsya** Poltavs'ka Oblast', C Ukraine *49.48N 32.40E*
112 M9 **Orzyc** *Ger.* Orschütz. ↝ NE Poland
112 N8 **Orzysz** *Ger.* Arys. Warmińsko-Mazurskie, NE Poland *53.49N 21.54E*
96 I10 **Os** Hedmark, S Norway *62.29N 11.14E*
97 C14 **Os** Hordaland, S Norway *60.10N 5.30E*
129 U15 **Osa** Permskaya Oblast', NW Russian Federation *57.16N 55.22E*
31 W11 **Osage** Iowa, C USA *43.16N 92.48W*
29 U5 **Osage Beach** Missouri, C USA *38.09N 92.37W*
29 P5 **Osage City** Kansas, C USA *38.37N 95.49W*
29 U7 **Osage Fork River** ↝ Missouri, C USA
29 U5 **Osage River** ↝ Missouri, C USA
171 Gg15 **Ōsaka** *hist.* Naniwa. Ōsaka, Honshū, SW Japan *34.38N 135.27E*
171 Gg15 **Ōsaka** *off.* Ōsaka-fu, *var.* Ōsaka Hu. ◆ *urban prefecture* Honshū, SW Japan
Ōsaka-fu/Ōsaka Hu *see* Ōsaka
151 R10 **Osakarovka** Karaganda, C Kazakhstan *50.27N 72.43E*
170 G15 **Ōsaka-wan** *bay* SW Japan
31 T7 **Osakis** Minnesota, N USA *45.51N 95.08W*
45 N16 **Osa, Península de** *peninsula* S Costa Rica
62 M10 **Osasco** São Paulo, S Brazil *23.31S 46.46W*
29 R5 **Osawatomie** Kansas, C USA *38.30N 94.57W*
28 L3 **Osborne** Kansas, C USA *39.26N 98.41W*
181 S8 **Osborn Plateau** *undersea feature* E Indian Ocean
97 L21 **Osby** Skåne, S Sweden *56.24N 14.00E*
Osca *see* Huesca
94 N2 **Oscar II Land** *physical region* W Svalbard
29 Y10 **Osceola** Arkansas, C USA *35.40N 89.58W*
31 V15 **Osceola** Iowa, C USA *41.01N 93.45W*
29 S6 **Osceola** Missouri, C USA *38.03N 93.42W*
31 Q15 **Osceola** Nebraska, C USA *41.09N 97.28W*
103 N15 **Oschatz** Sachsen, E Germany *51.17N 13.10E*
102 K13 **Oschersleben** Sachsen-Anhalt, C Germany *52.02N 11.14E*
33 R7 **Oscoda** Michigan, N USA *44.25N 83.19W*
Ösel *see* Saaremaa
96 H6 **Osen** Sør-Trøndelag, S Norway *64.17N 10.29E*
170 Aa12 **Ōse-zaki** *headland* Fukue-jima, SW Japan *32.36N 128.37E*
153 T10 **Osh** Oshskaya Oblast', SW Kyrgyzstan *40.34N 72.46E*
85 C16 **Oshakati** Oshana, N Namibia *17.45S 15.42E*
172 Nn6 **Oshamanbe** Hokkaidō, NE Japan *42.31N 140.22E*
85 C16 **Oshana** ◆ *district* N Namibia
126 Ii12 **Osharovo** Evenkiyskiy Avtonomnyy Okrug, N Russian Federation *60.16N 98.20E*
12 H15 **Oshawa** Ontario, SE Canada *43.54N 78.50W*
171 Mm13 **Oshika-hantō** *peninsula* Honshū, C Japan
85 C16 **Oshikango** Ohangwena, N Namibia *17.28S 15.54E*
Oshikoto *see* Otjikoto
170 Cc12 **Ō-shima** *island* SW Japan
171 M7 **Ō-shima** *island* NE Japan
171 Jj17 **Ō-shima** *island* S Japan
170 G17 **Ō-shima** *island* SW Japan
172 N6 **Oshima-hantō** ▲ Hokkaidō, NE Japan
85 D17 **Oshivelo** Otjikoto, N Namibia *18.37S 17.10E*
30 K14 **Oshkosh** Nebraska, C USA *41.25N 102.21W*
32 M7 **Oshkosh** Wisconsin, N USA *44.01N 88.31W*
Oshmyany *see* Ashmyany
Osh Oblasty *see* Oshskaya Oblast'
79 T16 **Oshogbo** Osun, W Nigeria *7.42N 4.31E*
153 S11 **Oshskaya Oblast'** *Kir.* Osh Oblasty. ◆ *province* SW Kyrgyzstan
81 J20 **Oshwe** Bandundu, C Dem. Rep. Congo *3.24S 19.31E*
Osiek *see* Osijek
114 I9 **Osijek** *prev.* Osiek, Osjek, *Ger.* Esseg, *Hung.* Eszék. Osijek-Baranja, E Croatia *45.33N 18.40E*
114 I9 **Osijek-Baranja** *off.* Osječko-Baranjska Županija. ◆ *province* E Croatia
108 J12 **Osimo** Marche, C Italy *43.28N 13.28E*
126 H15 **Osinniki** Kemerovskaya Oblast', S Russian Federation *53.30N 87.25E*
126 J14 **Osinovka** Irkutskaya Oblast', C Russian Federation *56.19N 101.55E*
Osintorf *see* Asintorf
114 N11 **Osipaonica** Serbia, NE Serbia and Montenegro (Yugoslavia) *44.34N 21.00E*
Osipenko *see* Berdyans'k
Osipovichi *see* Asipovichy
Osječko-Baranjska Županija *see* Osijek-Baranja
Osjek *see* Osijek
31 W15 **Oskaloosa** Iowa, C USA *41.17N 92.38W*
29 Q4 **Oskaloosa** Kansas, C USA *39.13N 95.18W*
97 N20 **Oskarshamn** Kalmar, S Sweden *57.16N 16.25E*
97 J21 **Oskarström** Halland, S Sweden *56.48N 13.00E*
12 M8 **Oskélanéo** Quebec, SE Canada *48.06N 75.12W*
Öskemen *see* Ust'-Kamenogorsk
Oskil *see* Oskol
119 W5 **Oskol** *Ukr.* Oskil. ↝ Russian Federation/Ukraine
95 D20 **Oslo** *prev.* Christiania, Kristiania. ● (Norway) Oslo, S Norway *59.54N 10.43E*
95 D20 **Oslo** ◆ *county* S Norway
95 D21 **Oslofjorden** *fjord* S Norway
161 G15 **Osmānābād** Mahārāshtra, C India *18.09N 76.06E*
142 J11 **Osmancık** Çorum, N Turkey *40.58N 34.49E*
142 L16 **Osmaniye** Osmaniye, S Turkey *37.04N 36.15E*
142 L16 **Osmaniye** ◆ *province* S Turkey
97 O16 **Ösmo** Stockholm, C Sweden *58.58N 17.55E*
120 E3 **Osmussaar** *island* W Estonia
102 G13 **Osnabrück** Niedersachsen, NW Germany *52.08N 7.42E*
112 D11 **Ośno Lubuskie** *Ger.* Drossen. Lubuskie, W Poland *52.28N 14.51E*
115 P19 **Osogov Mountains** *var.* Osogovske Planine, Osogovski Planina, *Mac.* Osogovski Planini. ▲ Bulgaria/FYR Macedonia
Osogovske Planine/ Osogovski Planina/ Osogovski Planini *see* Osogov Mountains
172 N8 **Osore-yama** ▲ Honshū, C Japan *41.18N 141.06E*
Oşorhei *see* Târgu Mureş
63 J16 **Osório** Rio Grande do Sul, S Brazil *29.52S 50.16W*
65 G16 **Osorno** Los Lagos, C Chile *40.38S 73.04W*
106 M4 **Osorno** Castilla-León, N Spain *42.24N 4.22W*
9 N17 **Osoyoos** British Columbia, SW Canada *49.01N 119.31W*
56 J6 **Ospino** Portuguesa, N Venezuela *9.16N 69.25W*
100 K13 **Oss** Noord-Brabant, S Netherlands *51.46N 5.31E*
106 H11 **Ossa** ▲ S Portugal *38.43N 7.33W*
117 F15 **Óssa** ▲ C Greece
25 X6 **Ossabaw Island** *island* Georgia, SE USA
25 X6 **Ossabaw Sound** *sound* Georgia, SE USA
191 O16 **Ossa, Mount** ▲ Tasmania, SE Australia *41.55S 146.03E*
106 H11 **Ossa, Serra d'** ▲ SE Portugal
79 U16 **Osse** ↝ S Nigeria
32 J6 **Osseo** Wisconsin, N USA *44.33N 91.13W*
111 S9 **Ossiacher See** ◎ S Austria
20 K13 **Ossining** New York, NE USA *41.10N 73.50W*
96 I12 **Ossjøen** ◎ S Norway
127 P9 **Ossora** Koryakskiy Avtonomnyy Okrug, E Russian Federation *59.16N 163.01E*
128 I15 **Ostashkov** Tverskaya Oblast', W Russian Federation *57.08N 33.10E*
102 H9 **Oste** ↝ NW Germany
Ostee *see* Baltic Sea
Ostend/Ostende *see* Oostende
119 P3 **Oster** Chernihivs'ka Oblast', N Ukraine *50.57N 30.55E*
97 O14 **Österbybruk** Uppsala, C Sweden *60.13N 17.55E*
97 M19 **Österbymo** Östergotland, S Sweden *57.49N 15.15E*
96 K12 **Österdalälven** ↝ C Sweden
96 I12 **Østerdalen** *valley* S Norway
97 L18 **Östergötland** ◆ *county* S Sweden
102 H10 **Osterholz-Scharmbeck** Niedersachsen, NW Germany *53.13N 8.46E*
Östermark *see* Teuva
Östermyra *see* Seinäjoki
Osterode/Osterode in Ostpreussen *see* Ostróda
103 J14 **Osterode am Harz** Niedersachsen, C Germany *51.43N 10.15E*
96 C13 **Osterøy** *island* S Norway
Österreich *see* Austria
95 G16 **Östersund** Jämtland, C Sweden *63.10N 14.44E*
97 N14 **Östervåla** Västmanland, C Sweden *60.10N 17.13E*
103 H22 **Ostfildern** Baden-Württemberg, SW Germany *48.43N 9.16E*
97 H16 **Østfold** ◆ *county* S Norway
102 E9 **Ostfriesische Inseln** *Eng.* East Frisian Islands. *island group* NW Germany
102 F10 **Ostfriesland** *historical region* NW Germany
97 P14 **Östhammar** Uppsala, C Sweden *60.16N 18.25E*
Ostia Aterni *see* Pescara
108 G8 **Ostiglia** Lombardia, N Italy *45.03N 11.09E*
97 J14 **Östmark** Värmland, C Sweden *60.15N 12.45E*
97 K22 **Östra Ringsjön** ◎ S Sweden
113 I17 **Ostrava** Ostravský Kraj, E Czech Republic *49.49N 18.15E*
113 H17 **Ostravský Kraj** ◆ *region* E Czech Republic
96 J11 **Østrehogna** *Swe.* Härjahågnen, Härjehågna. ▲ Norway/Sweden *61.43N 12.07E*
112 K8 **Ostróda** *Ger.* Osterode, Osterode in Ostpreussen. Warmińsko-Mazurskie, NE Poland *53.42N 19.58E*
Ostrog/Ostróg *see* Ostroh
Ostrogozhsk Voronezhskaya Oblast', W Russian Federation *50.52N 39.00E*
118 L4 **Ostroh** *Pol.* Ostróg, *Rus.* Ostrog. Rivnens'ka Oblast', NW Ukraine *50.19N 26.30E*
112 N9 **Ostrołęka** *Ger.* Wiesenhof, *Rus.* Ostrolenka. Mazowieckie, C Poland *53.06N 21.33E*
113 A16 **Ostrov** *Ger.* Schlackenwerth. Karlovarský Kraj, W Czech Republic *50.18N 12.53E*
128 F15 **Ostrov** *Latv.* Austrava. Pskovskaya Oblast', W Russian Federation *57.21N 28.18E*
Ostrovets *see* Ostrowiec Świętokrzyski
115 M21 **Ostrovicës, Mali i** ▲ SE Albania *40.36N 20.25E*
172 T6 **Ostrov Iturup** *island* NE Russian Federation
128 M4 **Ostrovnoy** Murmanskaya Oblast', NW Russian Federation *68.00N 39.40E*
116 L7 **Ostrovo** *prev.* Golema Ada. Razgrad, N Bulgaria *43.40N 26.37E*
129 N15 **Ostrovskoye** Kostromskaya Oblast', NW Russian Federation *57.46N 42.18E*
Ostrów *see* Ostrów Wielkopolski
Ostrowiec *see* Ostrowiec Świętokrzyski
113 M14 **Ostrowiec Świętokrzyski** *var.* Ostrowiec, *Rus.* Ostrovets. Świętokrzyskie, C Poland *50.54N 21.22E*
112 P13 **Ostrów Lubelski** Lubelskie, E Poland *51.29N 22.57E*
112 N10 **Ostrów Mazowiecka** *var.* Ostrów Mazowiecki. Mazowieckie, C Poland *52.48N 21.53E*
Ostrów Mazowiecki *see* Ostrów Mazowiecka
Ostrowo *see* Ostrów Wielkopolski
112 H13 **Ostrów Wielkopolski** *var.* Ostrów, *Ger.* Ostrowo. Wielkopolskie, C Poland *51.40N 17.47E*
Ostryna *see* Astryna
112 I13 **Ostrzeszów** Wielkopolskie, C Poland *51.26N 17.54E*
109 P18 **Ostuni** Puglia, SE Italy *40.43N 17.34E*
Ostyako-Voguls'k *see* Khanty-Mansiysk
Osum *see* Osumit, Lumi i
116 I9 **Osūm** ↝ N Bulgaria
170 Bb17 **Ōsumi-hantō** ▲ Kyūshū, SW Japan
170 Bb17 **Ōsumi-kaikyō** *strait* SW Japan
115 L22 **Osumit, Lumi i** *var.* Osum. ↝ SE Albania
79 T16 **Osun** ◆ *state* SW Nigeria
106 L14 **Osuna** Andalucía, S Spain *37.13N 5.06W*
62 J8 **Osvaldo Cruz** São Paulo, S Brazil *21.49S 50.52W*
Osveya *see* Asvyeya
20 J7 **Oswegatchie River** ↝ New York, NE USA
29 Q7 **Oswego** Kansas, C USA *37.08N 95.07W*
20 H9 **Oswego** New York, NE USA *43.27N 76.13W*
99 K19 **Oswestry** W England, UK *52.50N 3.06W*
113 J16 **Oświęcim** *Ger.* Auschwitz. Małopolskie, S Poland *50.02N 19.11E*
171 K15 **Ōta** Gunma, Honshū, S Japan *36.19N 139.20E*
193 E22 **Otago** *off.* Otago Region. ◆ *region* South Island, NZ
193 F23 **Otago Peninsula** *peninsula* South Island, NZ
170 E13 **Ōtake** Hiroshima, Honshū, SW Japan *34.13N 132.13E*
192 L13 **Otaki** Wellington, North Island, NZ *40.46S 175.08E*
171 L14 **Ōtakine-yama** ▲ Honshū, C Japan *37.23N 140.42E*
95 M15 **Otanmäki** Oulu, C Finland *64.07N 27.04E*
151 T15 **Otar** Zhambyl, SE Kazakhstan *43.34N 75.13E*
172 O5 **Otaru** Hokkaidō, NE Japan *43.13N 140.58E*
193 C24 **Otatara** Southland, South Island, NZ *46.26S 168.18E*
193 C24 **Otautau** Southland, South Island, NZ *46.10S 168.01E*
95 M18 **Otava** Isä-Suomi, E Finland *61.37N 27.07E*
113 B18 **Otava** *Ger.* Wottawa. ↝ SW Czech Republic
58 C6 **Otavalo** Imbabura, N Ecuador *0.13N 78.15W*
85 D17 **Otavi** Otjozondjupa, N Namibia *19.34S 17.25E*
171 Kk15 **Ōtawara** Tochigi, Honshū, S Japan *36.52N 140.01E*
85 B16 **Otchinjau** Cunene, SW Angola *16.31S 13.54E*
118 F12 **Oţelu Roşu** *Ger.* Ferdinandsberg, *Hung.* Nándorhgy. Caras-Severin, SW Romania *45.30N 22.22E*
193 E21 **Otematata** Canterbury, South Island, NZ *44.37S 170.12E*
120 I6 **Otepää** *Ger.* Odenpäh. Valgamaa, SE Estonia *58.04N 26.31E*
34 K9 **Othello** Washington, NW USA *46.49N 119.10W*
117 A15 **Othonoí** *island* Iónioi Nísoi, Greece, C Mediterranean Sea
Othris *see* Óthrys
117 F17 **Óthrys** *var.* Othris. ▲ C Greece
79 Q14 **Oti** ↝ N Togo
42 K10 **Otinapa** Durango, C Mexico *24.01N 104.58W*
193 G17 **Otira** West Coast, South Island, NZ *42.51S 171.32E*
39 V3 **Otis** Colorado, C USA *40.09N 102.57W*
10 L10 **Otish, Monts** ▲ Quebec, E Canada
85 C17 **Otjikondo** Kunene, N Namibia *19.48S 15.28E*
85 C17 **Otjikoto** *var.* Oshikoto. ◆ *district* N Namibia
85 E18 **Otjinene** Omaheke, NE Namibia *21.10S 18.43E*
85 D18 **Otjiwarongo** Otjozondjupa, N Namibia *20.28S 16.36E*
85 D18 **Otjosondu** *var.* Otjosundu. Otjozondjupa, C Namibia *21.19S 17.51E*
Otjosundu *see* Otjosondu
85 D18 **Otjozondjupa** ◆ *district* C Namibia
114 C11 **Otočac** Lika-Senj, W Croatia *44.52N 15.13E*
172 Pp6 **Otofuke-gawa** ↝ Hokkaidō, NE Japan
168 M14 **Otog Qi** Nei Mongol Zizhiqu, N China *39.05N 107.58E*
172 Pp3 **Otoineppu** Hokkaidō, NE Japan *44.43N 142.13E*
114 J10 **Otok** Vukovar-Srijem, E Croatia *45.10N 18.52E*
118 K14 **Otopeni** ✕ (Bucureşti) Bucureşti, S Romania *44.34N 26.09E*
192 L8 **Otorohanga** Waikato, North Island, NZ *38.10S 175.13E*
10 D9 **Otoskwin** ↝ Ontario, C Canada
170 F15 **Ōtoyo** Kōchi, Shikoku, SW Japan *33.45N 133.42E*
97 E16 **Otra** ↝ S Norway
109 R19 **Otranto** Puglia, SE Italy *40.08N 18.28E*
Otranto, Canale d' *see* Otranto, Strait of
109 Q18 **Otranto, Strait of** *It.* Canale d'Otranto. *strait* Albania/Italy
113 H18 **Otrokovice** *Ger.* Otrokowitz. Zlínský Kraj, E Czech Republic *49.13N 17.32E*
Otrokowitz *see* Otrokovice
33 P10 **Otsego** Michigan, N USA *42.27N 85.42W*
33 Q6 **Otsego Lake** ◎ Michigan, N USA
20 I11 **Otselic River** ↝ New York, NE USA
171 H15 **Ōtsu** *var.* Ōtu. Shiga, Honshū, SW Japan *35.03N 135.49E*
171 Jj16 **Ōtsuki** *var.* Otuki. Yamanashi, Honshū, S Japan *35.35N 138.53E*
96 G11 **Otta** Oppland, S Norway *61.46N 9.31E*
201 U13 **Otta** *island* Chuuk, C Micronesia
96 F11 **Otta** ↝ S Norway
201 U13 **Otta Pass** *passage* Chuuk Islands, C Micronesia
97 J22 **Ottarp** Skåne, S Sweden *55.55N 12.55E*
12 L12 **Ottawa** ● (Canada) Ontario, SE Canada *45.24N 75.40W*
32 L11 **Ottawa** Illinois, N USA *41.21N 88.50W*
29 Q5 **Ottawa** Kansas, C USA *38.37N 95.16W*
33 R12 **Ottawa** Ohio, N USA *41.01N 84.03W*
12 L12 **Ottawa** *var.* Uplands. ✕ Ontario, SE Canada *45.19N 75.39W*
12 M12 **Ottawa** *Fr.* Outaouais. ↝ Ontario/Quebec, SE Canada
10 I4 **Ottawa Islands** *island group* Nunavut, C Canada
20 L8 **Otter Creek** ↝ Vermont, NE USA
38 L6 **Otter Creek Reservoir** ⊠ Utah, W USA
100 L11 **Otterlo** Gelderland, E Netherlands *52.06N 5.46E*
96 D9 **Otterøya** *island* S Norway
31 S6 **Otter Tail Lake** ◎ Minnesota, N USA
31 R7 **Otter Tail River** ↝ Minnesota, C USA
97 H23 **Otterup** Fyn, C Denmark *55.31N 10.25E*
101 H19 **Ottignies** Wallon Brabant, C Belgium *50.40N 4.34E*
103 L23 **Ottobrunn** Bayern, SE Germany *48.02N 11.40E*
194 I12 **Otto, Mount** ▲ C PNG *5.54S 145.24E*
31 X15 **Ottumwa** Iowa, C USA *41.00N 92.24W*
Otu *see* Ōtsu
85 B16 **Otuazuma** Kunene, NW Namibia *17.52S 13.16E*
Otuki *see* Ōtsuki
79 V16 **Oturkpo** Benue, S Nigeria *7.12N 8.06E*
200 Ss14 **Otu Tolu Group** *island group* SE Tonga
190 M13 **Otway, Cape** *headland* Victoria, SE Australia *38.52S 143.31E*
65 H24 **Otway, Seno** *inlet* S Chile
Ötz *see* Oetz
110 L8 **Ötztaler Ache** ↝ W Austria
110 L9 **Ötztaler Alpen** *It.* Alpi Venoste. ▲ SW Austria
29 T12 **Ouachita, Lake** ⊠ Arkansas, C USA
29 R11 **Ouachita Mountains** ▲ Arkansas/Oklahoma, C USA
29 U13 **Ouachita River** ↝ Arkansas/Louisiana, C USA
Ouadaï *see* Ouaddaï
78 J7 **Ouadâne** *var.* Ouadane. Adrar, C Mauritania *20.57N 11.34W*
80 K13 **Ouadda** Haute-Kotto, N Central African Republic *8.02N 22.22E*
80 J10 **Ouaddaï** *off.* Préfecture du Ouaddaï, *var.* Ouadaï, Wadai. ◆ *prefecture* SE Chad
79 P13 **Ouagadougou** *var.* Wagadugu. ● (Burkina) C Burkina *12.20N 1.31W*
79 P13 **Ouagadougou** ✕ C Burkina *12.21N 1.27W*
79 O12 **Ouahigouya** NW Burkina *13.31N 2.19W*
Ouahran *see* Oran
81 J14 **Ouaka** ◆ *prefecture* C Central African Republic
81 J15 **Ouaka** ↝ S Central African Republic
Oualam *see* Ouallam
78 M9 **Oualâta** *var.* Oualata. Hodh ech Chargui, SE Mauritania *17.18N 7.00W*
79 R11 **Ouallam** *var.* Oualam. Tillabéri, W Niger *14.13N 2.07E*
180 H14 **Ouanani** Mohéli, S Comoros *12.19S 94.37E*
57 Z10 **Ouanary** E French Guiana *4.10N 51.40W*
80 L13 **Ouanda Djallé** Vakaga, NE Central African Republic *8.53N 22.47E*
81 N14 **Ouando** Haut-Mbomou, SE Central African Republic *5.57N 25.57E*
81 L15 **Ouango** Mbomou, S Central African Republic *4.19N 22.30E*
79 N14 **Ouangolodougou** *var.* Wangolodougou. N Ivory Coast *9.58N 5.09W*
180 I13 **Ouani** Anjouan, SE Comoros
81 M15 **Ouara** ↝ E Central African Republic
78 K7 **Ouarâne** *desert* C Mauritania
13 O11 **Ouareau** ↝ Quebec, SE Canada
76 K7 **Ouargla** *var.* Wargla. NE Algeria *32.00N 5.16E*
76 F8 **Ouarzazate** S Morocco *30.54N 6.55W*
79 Q11 **Ouatagouna** Gao, E Mali *15.06N 0.41E*
76 G6 **Ouazzane** *var.* Ouezzane, *Ar.* Wazan, Wazzan. N Morocco *34.52N 5.34W*
Oubangui *see* Ubangi
Oubangui-Chari *see* Central African Republic
Oubari, Edeyen d' *see* Awbāri, Idhān
100 G13 **Oud-Beijerland** Zuid-Holland, SW Netherlands *51.49N 4.25E*
100 F13 **Ouddorp** Zuid-Holland, SW Netherlands *51.49N 3.55E*
79 P9 **Oudeïka** *oasis* C Mali *17.16N 1.42W*
100 G13 **Oude Maas** ↝ SW Netherlands
101 E18 **Oudenaarde** *Fr.* Audenarde. Oost-Vlaanderen, SW Belgium *50.49N 3.37E*
101 H14 **Oudenbosch** Noord-Brabant, S Netherlands *51.34N 4.31E*
100 P6 **Oude Pekela** Groningen, NE Netherlands *53.06N 7.00E*
Ouderkerk *see* Ouderkerk aan den Amstel
100 I10 **Ouderkerk aan den Amstel** *var.* Ouderkerk. Noord-Holland, C Netherlands *52.18N 4.54E*
100 I6 **Oudeschild** Noord-Holland, NW Netherlands *53.01N 4.51E*
101 G14 **Oude-Tonge** Zuid-Holland, SW Netherlands *51.40N 4.13E*
100 I12 **Oudewater** Utrecht, C Netherlands *52.01N 4.54E*
Oudjda *see* Oujda
100 L5 **Oudkerk** Friesland, N Netherlands *53.16N 5.52E*
104 J7 **Oudon** ↝ NW France
100 I9 **Oudorp** Noord-Holland, NW Netherlands *52.39N 4.46E*
85 G25 **Oudtshoorn** Western Cape, SW South Africa *33.32S 22.12E*
101 I16 **Oud-Turnhout** Antwerpen, N Belgium *51.19N 5.01E*
76 F7 **Oued-Zem** C Morocco *32.53N 6.30W*
197 H5 **Ouégoa** Province Nord, C New Caledonia *20.22S 164.25E*
78 L13 **Ouéléssébougou** *var.* Ouolossébougou. Koulikoro, SW Mali *11.58N 7.51W*
79 N16 **Ouellé** E Ivory Coast *7.18N 4.01W*
79 R16 **Ouémé** ↝ C Benin
197 J7 **Ouen, Île** *island* S New Caledonia
79 O13 **Ouessa** S Burkina *11.02N 2.44W*
104 D5 **Ouessant, Île d'** *Eng.* Ushant. *island* NW France
81 H17 **Ouésso** La Sangha, NW Congo *1.37N 16.03E*
81 D15 **Ouest** *Eng.* West. ◆ *province* W Cameroon
202 G11 **Ouest, Baie de l'** *bay* Îles Wallis, Wallis and Futuna
13 Y7 **Ouest, Pointe de l'** *headland* Quebec, SE Canada *48.08N 64.57W*
Ouezzane *see* Ouazzane
101 K20 **Ouffet** Liège, E Belgium *50.30N 5.31E*
81 H14 **Ouham** ◆ *prefecture* NW Central African Republic
80 I13 **Ouham** ↝ Central African Republic/Chad
81 G14 **Ouham-Pendé** ◆ *prefecture* W Central African Republic
79 R16 **Ouidah** *Eng.* Whydah, Wida. S Benin *6.22N 2.07E*
76 H6 **Oujda** *Ar.* Oudjda, Ujda. NE Morocco *34.45N 1.53W*
78 I7 **Oujeft** Adrar, C Mauritania *20.05N 13.00W*
95 L15 **Oulainen** Oulu, C Finland *64.14N 24.50E*
Ould Yanja *see* Ould Yenjé
78 J10 **Ould Yenjé** *var.* Ould Yanja. Guidimaka, S Mauritania *15.33N 11.43W*
95 L14 **Oulu** *Swe.* Uleåborg. Oulu, C Finland *65.01N 25.28E*
95 M14 **Oulu** *Swe.* Uleåborg. ◆ *province* N Finland
95 L15 **Oulujärvi** *Swe.* Uleträsk. ◎ C Finland
95 M14 **Oulujoki** *Swe.* Uleälv. ↝ C Finland
95 L14 **Oulunsalo** Oulu, C Finland *64.55N 25.19E*
108 A8 **Oulx** Piemonte, NE Italy *45.05N 6.41E*
80 J9 **Oum-Chalouba** Borkou-Ennedi-Tibesti, NE Chad *15.48N 20.46E*
78 M16 **Oumé** C Ivory Coast *6.23N 5.25W*
76 F7 **Oum er Rbia** ↝ C Morocco
80 J10 **Oum-Hadjer** Batha, E Chad *13.18N 19.40E*
94 K10 **Ounasjoki** ↝ N Finland
80 J7 **Ounianga Kébir** Borkou-Ennedi-Tibesti, N Chad *19.06N 20.28E*
Ouolossébougou *see* Ouéléssébougou
Oup *see* Auob
101 K19 **Oupeye** Liège, E Belgium *50.42N 5.37E*
101 N21 **Our** ↝ NW Europe
39 Q7 **Ouray** Colorado, C USA *38.01N 107.40W*
105 R7 **Ource** ↝ C France
106 G9 **Ourém** Santarém, C Portugal *39.40N 8.32W*
106 H4 **Ourense** *Cast.* Orense; *Lat.* Aurium. Galicia, NW Spain *42.19N 7.52W*
106 I4 **Ourense** *Cast.* Orense ◆ *province* Galicia, NW Spain
61 O15 **Ouricuri** Pernambuco, E Brazil *7.51S 40.04W*
62 J9 **Ourinhos** São Paulo, S Brazil *22.58S 49.52W*
106 G13 **Ourique** Beja, S Portugal *37.37N 8.13W*
61 M20 **Ouro Preto** Minas Gerais, NE Brazil *20.25S 43.30W*
Ours, Grand Lac de l' *see* Great Bear Lake
101 K20 **Ourthe** ↝ E Belgium
171 Mm11 **Ōu-sanmyaku** ▲ Honshū, C Japan
99 M17 **Ouse** ↝ N England, UK
Ouse *see* Great Ouse
104 H7 **Oust** ↝ NW France
Outaouais *see* Ottawa
13 T4 **Outardes Quatre, Réservoir** ⊠ Quebec, SE Canada
13 T5 **Outardes, Rivière aux** ↝ Quebec, SE Canada
98 E8 **Outer Hebrides** *var.* Western Isles. *island group* NW Scotland, UK
32 K3 **Outer Island** *island* Apostle Islands, Wisconsin, N USA
37 S16 **Outer Santa Barbara Passage** *passage* California, SW USA
106 G3 **Outes** Galicia, NW Spain *42.50N 8.54W*
85 C18 **Outjo** Kunene, N Namibia *20.06S 16.06E*
9 T16 **Outlook** Saskatchewan, S Canada *51.30N 107.03W*
95 N16 **Outokumpu** Itä-Suomi, E Finland *62.43N 29.04E*
98 M2 **Out Skerries** *island group* NE Scotland, UK
197 J5 **Ouvéa** *island* Îles Loyauté, NE New Caledonia
105 S14 **Ouvèze** ↝ SE France
190 L9 **Ouyen** Victoria, SE Australia *35.06S 142.18E*
41 Q14 **Ouzinkie** Kodiak Island, Alaska, USA *57.54N 152.27W*
143 O13 **Ovacık** Tunceli, E Turkey *39.22N 39.13E*
108 C9 **Ovada** Piemonte, NE Italy *44.41N 8.39E*
197 I14 **Ovalau** *island* C Fiji
64 G9 **Ovalle** Coquimbo, N Chile *30.33S 71.16W*
85 C17 **Ovamboland** *physical region* N Namibia
56 L10 **Ovana, Cerro** ▲ S Venezuela *4.41N 66.54W*
106 G7 **Ovar** Aveiro, N Portugal *40.52N 8.37W*
116 L10 **Ovcharitsa, Yazovir** ⊠ SE Bulgaria
56 E6 **Ovejas** Sucre, NW Colombia *9.30N 75.15W*
103 E16 **Overath** Nordrhein-Westfalen, W Germany *50.55N 7.16E*
100 F13 **Overflakkee** *island* SW Netherlands
101 H19 **Overijse** Vlaams Brabant, C Belgium *50.46N 4.31E*
100 N10 **Overijssel** ◆ *province* E Netherlands
100 M9 **Overijssels Kanaal** *canal* E Netherlands
94 K13 **Överkalix** Norrbotten, N Sweden *66.19N 22.49E*
29 R4 **Overland Park** Kansas, C USA *38.57N 94.40W*
101 L14 **Overloon** Noord-Brabant, SE Netherlands *51.35N 5.54E*
101 K16 **Overpelt** Limburg, NE Belgium *51.13N 5.24E*
37 Y10 **Overton** Nevada, W USA *36.32N 114.25W*
27 W7 **Overton** Texas, SW USA *32.16N 94.58W*
94 K13 **Övertorneå** Norrbotten, N Sweden *66.22N 23.38E*
97 N18 **Överum** Kalmar, S Sweden *57.58N 16.19E*
94 G13 **Överuman** ◎ N Sweden
168 H6 **Övgödiy** Dzavhan, C Mongolia *48.38N 97.39E*
119 P11 **Ovidiopol'** Odes'ka Oblast', SW Ukraine *46.15N 30.27E*
118 M14 **Ovidiu** Constanța, SE Romania *44.16N 28.34E*
47 N10 **Oviedo** SW Dominican Republic *17.46N 71.22W*
106 K2 **Oviedo** *anc.* Asturias. Asturias, NW Spain *43.21N 5.49W*
106 K2 **Oviedo** ✕ Asturias, N Spain *43.21N 5.49W*
Ovilava *see* Wels
120 D7 **Oviši** Ventspils, W Latvia *57.34N 21.43E*
152 K10 **Ovminzatovo Tog'lari** *Rus.* Gory Auminzatau. ▲ N Uzbekistan
169 P10 **Ovoot** Sühbaatar, SE Mongolia *45.18N 113.51E*
163 O4 **Övörhangay** ◆ *province* C Mongolia
96 E12 **Øvre Årdal** Sogn og Fjordane, S Norway *61.17N 7.44E*
97 J14 **Övre Fryken** ◎ C Sweden
94 J11 **Övre Soppero** Norrbotten, N Sweden *68.07N 21.40E*
119 N3 **Ovruch** Zhytomyrs'ka Oblast', N Ukraine *51.19N 28.50E*
168 J8 **Övt** Övörhangay, C Mongolia *46.50N 102.15E*
193 E24 **Owaka** Otago, South Island, NZ *46.27S 169.42E*
81 H18 **Owando** *prev.* Fort-Rousset. Cuvette, C Congo *0.28S 15.55E*
171 Gg17 **Owase** Mie, Honshū, SW Japan *34.04N 136.10E*
29 P9 **Owasso** Oklahoma, C USA *36.16N 95.51W*
31 V10 **Owatonna** Minnesota, N USA *44.04N 93.13W*
181 O4 **Owen Fracture Zone** *tectonic feature* W Arabian Sea
193 H15 **Owen, Mount** ▲ South Island, NZ *41.32S 172.33E*

193 *H15* **Owen River** Tasman, South Island, NZ *41.40S 172.28E*
46 *D8* **Owen Roberts** ✈ Grand Cayman, Cayman Islands *19.15N 81.22W*
22 *I6* **Owensboro** Kentucky, S USA *37.46N 87.06W*
37 *T11* **Owens Lake** *salt flat* California, W USA
12 *F14* **Owen Sound** Ontario, S Canada *44.34N 80.55W*
12 *F13* **Owen Sound** ◎ Ontario, S Canada
37 *T10* **Owens River** ≈ California, W USA
194 *K15* **Owen Stanley Range** ⛰ S PNG
29 *V5* **Owensville** Missouri, C USA *38.21N 91.30W*
22 *M4* **Owenton** Kentucky, S USA *38.33N 84.51W*
79 *U17* **Owerri** Imo, S Nigeria *5.19N 7.07E*
192 *M10* **Owhango** Manawatu-Wanganui, North Island, NZ *39.01S 175.22E*
23 *N5* **Owingsville** Kentucky, S USA *38.10N 83.42W*
79 *T16* **Owo** Ondo, SW Nigeria *7.10N 5.31E*
33 *R9* **Owosso** Michigan, N USA *43.00N 84.10W*
37 *V1* **Owyhee** Nevada, W USA *41.57N 116.07W*
34 *L14* **Owyhee, Lake** ◎ Oregon, NW USA
34 *L15* **Owyhee River** ≈ Idaho/Oregon, NW USA
94 *K1* **Öxarfjördhur** *var.* Axarfjördhur. *fjord* N Iceland
96 *K12* **Oxberg** Dalarna, C Sweden *61.07N 14.10E*
9 *V17* **Oxbow** Saskatchewan, S Canada *49.16N 102.12W*
97 *O17* **Oxelösund** Södermanland, S Sweden *58.40N 17.10E*
193 *H18* **Oxford** Canterbury, South Island, NZ *43.18S 172.10E*
99 *M21* **Oxford** ***Lat.*** Oxonia. S England, UK *51.46N 1.15W*
25 *Q3* **Oxford** Alabama, S USA *33.36N 85.50W*
24 *L2* **Oxford** Mississippi, S USA *34.23N 89.30W*
31 *N16* **Oxford** Nebraska, C USA *40.15N 99.37W*
20 *I11* **Oxford** New York, NE USA *42.21N 75.39W*
23 *U8* **Oxford** North Carolina, SE USA *36.18N 78.35W*
33 *Q14* **Oxford** Ohio, N USA *39.30N 84.45W*
20 *H16* **Oxford** Pennsylvania, NE USA *39.46N 75.57W*
9 *X12* **Oxford House** Manitoba, C Canada *54.55N 95.13W*
31 *Y13* **Oxford Junction** Iowa, C USA *41.58N 90.57W*
9 *X12* **Oxford Lake** ◎ Manitoba, C Canada
99 *M21* **Oxfordshire** *cultural region* S England, UK
Oxia *see* Oxyá
43 *X12* **Oxkutzcab** Yucatán, SE Mexico *20.14N 89.20W*
37 *R15* **Oxnard** California, W USA *34.12N 119.10W*
Oxonia *see* Oxford
12 *I12* **Oxtongue** ≈ Ontario, SE Canada
Oxus *see* Amu Darya
117 *E15* **Oxyá** *var.* Oxia. ▲ C Greece *39.46N 21.56E*
171 *Ii13* **Oyabe** Toyama, Honshū, SW Japan *36.41N 136.53E*
Oyahue/Oyahue, Volcán *see* Ollagüe, Volcán
171 *K16* **Oyama** Tochigi, Honshū, S Japan *36.19N 139.46E*
49 *U5* **Oyapock** ≈ E French Guiana
Oyapock *see* Oiapoque, Rio
57 *Z10* **Oyapok, Baie de L'** *bay* Brazil/French Guiana
57 *Z11* **Oyapok, Fleuve l'** *var.* Oyapock, Rio Oiapoque. ≈ Brazil/French Guiana ***see also*** Oiapoque, Rio
81 *E17* **Oyem** Woleu-Ntem, N Gabon *1.34N 11.31E*
9 *R16* **Oyen** Alberta, SW Canada *51.19N 110.28W*
97 *I15* **Øyeren** ◎ S Norway
168 *G6* **Oygon** Dzavhan, N Mongolia *48.57N 96.33E*
98 *I7* **Oykel** ≈ N Scotland, UK
127 *N9* **Oymyakon** Respublika Sakha (Yakutiya), NE Russian Federation *63.28N 142.22E*
81 *H19* **Oyo** Cuvette, C Congo *1.05S 15.55E*
79 *S15* **Oyo** Oyo, W Nigeria *7.51N 3.57E*
79 *S15* **Oyo** ◈ *state* SW Nigeria
58 *D13* **Oyón** Lima, C Peru *10.39S 76.46W*
105 *S10* **Oyonnax** Ain, E France *46.16N 5.39E*
152 *L10* **Oyoqogʻitma** ***Rus.*** Ayakagytma. Buxoro Viloyati, C Uzbekistan *40.37N 64.26E*
152 *M9* **Oyoqquduq** ***Rus.*** Ayakkuduk. Navoiy Viloyati, N Uzbekistan *41.16N 65.12E*
34 *F9* **Oysterville** Washington, NW USA *46.33N 124.03W*
97 *D14* **Øystese** Hordaland, S Norway *60.22N 6.13E*
153 *U10* **Oy-Tal** Oshskaya Oblast', SW Kyrgyzstan *40.23N 74.04E*
153 *T10* **Oy-Tal** ≈ SW Kyrgyzstan
151 *S16* **Oytal** Zhambyl, S Kazakhstan *42.50N 73.21E*
Oyyl *see* Uil
179 *Qq15* **Ozamiz** Mindanao, S Philippines *8.09N 123.51E*
Ozarichi *see* Azarychy
25 *R7* **Ozark** Alabama, S USA *31.27N 85.38W*
29 *S10* **Ozark** Arkansas, C USA *35.29N 93.49W*
29 *T8* **Ozark** Missouri, C USA *37.01N 93.12W*
29 *T8* **Ozark Plateau** *plain* Arkansas/Missouri, C USA
29 *T6* **Ozarks, Lake of the** ▣ Missouri, C USA
199 *Jj11* **Ozbourn Seamount** *undersea feature* W Pacific Ocean *26.00S 174.49W*
113 *L20* **Ózd** Borsod-Abaúj-Zemplén, NE Hungary *48.14N 20.18E*
114 *D11* **Ozeblin** ▲ C Croatia *44.37N 15.52E*
127 *Pp12* **Ozernovskiy** Kamchatskaya Oblast', E Russian Federation *51.28N 94.32E*
150 *M7* **Ozërnoye** *var.* Ozërnyy. Kostanay, N Kazakhstan *53.27N 63.10E*
Ozërnyy *see* Ozërnoye
128 *I15* **Ozërnyy** Tverskaya Oblast', W Russian Federation *57.55N 33.45E*
117 *D18* **Ozerós, Límni** ◎ W Greece
121 *D14* **Ozersk** ***prev.*** Darkehnen, ***Ger.*** Angerapp. Kaliningradskaya Oblast', W Russian Federation *54.23N 21.59E*
124 *Ee11* **Ozërsk** Chelyabinskaya Oblast', C Russian Federation *55.44N 60.59E*
130 *L4* **Ozery** Moskovskaya Oblast', W Russian Federation *54.51N 38.37E*
Özgön *see* Uzgen
109 *C17* **Ozieri** Sardegna, Italy, C Mediterranean Sea *40.34N 9.01E*
113 *I15* **Ozimek** ***Ger.*** Malapane. Opolskie, S Poland *50.41N 18.16E*
131 *R8* **Ozinki** Saratovskaya Oblast', W Russian Federation *51.16N 49.45E*
Oziya *see* Ojiya
27 *O10* **Ozona** Texas, SW USA *30.42N 101.12W*
Ozorkov *see* Ozorków
112 *J12* **Ozorków** ***Rus.*** Ozorkov. Łódź, C Poland *51.58N 19.16E*
170 *E14* **Ōzu** Ehime, Shikoku, SW Japan *33.31N 132.31E*
143 *R10* **Ozurget'i** ***prev.*** Makharadze. W Georgia *41.57N 42.01E*

P

101 *J17* **Paal** Limburg, NE Belgium *51.03N 5.08E*
197 *C13* **Paama** *island* C Vanuatu
206 *M14* **Paamiut** *var.* Pâmiut, ***Dan.*** Frederikshåb. Kitaa, S Greenland *62.22N 49.52W*
178 *Gg9* **Pa-an** Karen State, S Myanmar *16.51N 97.37E*
103 *L22* **Paar** ≈ SE Germany
85 *E26* **Paarl** Western Cape, SW South Africa *33.45S 18.58E*
95 *L15* **Paavola** Oulu, C Finland *64.34N 25.15E*
98 *E8* **Pabbay** *island* NW Scotland, UK
175 *P12* **Pabbiring, Kepulauan** *island group* C Indonesia
159 *T15* **Pabna** Rajshahi, W Bangladesh *24.02N 89.15E*
111 *U4* **Pabneukirchen** Oberösterreich, N Austria *48.19N 14.49E*
120 *H13* **Pabradė** ***Pol.*** Podbrodzie. Švenčionys, SE Lithuania *54.58N 25.43E*
58 *L13* **Pacahuaras, Río** ≈ N Bolivia
Pacaraima, Sierra/Pacaraim, Serra *see* Pakaraima Mountains
58 *B11* **Pacasmayo** La Libertad, W Peru *7.27S 79.34W*
44 *D6* **Pacaya, Volcán de** ♨ S Guatemala *14.19N 90.36W*
117 *K23* **Pachía** *island* Kykládes, Greece, Aegean Sea
109 *L26* **Pachino** Sicilia, Italy, C Mediterranean Sea *36.43N 15.06E*
58 *F12* **Pachitea, Río** ≈ C Peru
160 *I11* **Pachmarhi** Madhya Pradesh, C India *22.36N 78.18E*
124 *N4* **Páchna** *var.* Pakhna. SW Cyprus *34.47N 32.48E*
117 *H25* **Páchnes** ▲ Kríti, Greece, E Mediterranean Sea *35.19N 24.00E*
56 *F9* **Pacho** Cundinamarca, C Colombia *5.07N 74.11W*
160 *F12* **Pāchora** Mahārāshtra, C India *20.52N 75.28E*
43 *P13* **Pachuca** *var.* Pachuca de Soto. Hidalgo, C Mexico *20.05N 98.46W*
Pachuca de Soto *see* Pachuca
29 *W5* **Pacific** Missouri, C USA *38.28N 90.44W*
199 *Jj15* **Pacific-Antarctic Ridge** *undersea feature* S Pacific Ocean
34 *F8* **Pacific Beach** Washington, NW USA *47.09N 124.12W*
37 *N10* **Pacific Grove** California, W USA *36.35N 121.54W*
31 *S15* **Pacific Junction** Iowa, C USA *41.01N 95.48W*
198-199 **Pacific Ocean** *ocean*
133 *Z10* **Pacific Plate** *tectonic feature*
115 *J15* **Pačir** ▲ SW Serbia and Montenegro (Yugoslavia) *43.19N 19.07E*
190 *L5* **Packsaddle** New South Wales, SE Australia *30.42S 141.55E*
34 *H9* **Packwood** Washington, NW USA *46.37N 121.38W*
Padalung *see* Phatthalung
175 *Q12* **Padamarang, Pulau** *island* C Indonesia
173 *G9* **Padang** Sumatera, W Indonesia *01.00S 100.21E*
174 *Hh5* **Padang Endau** Pahang, Peninsular Malaysia *2.38N 103.37E*
Padangpandjang *see* Padangpanjang
173 *G8* **Padangpanjang** ***prev.*** Padangpandjang. Sumatera, W Indonesia *0.30S 100.25E*
173 *Ff7* **Padangsidempuan** ***prev.*** Padangsidimpoean. Sumatera, W Indonesia *1.22N 99.14E*
Padangsidimpoean *see* Padangsidempuan
128 *I9* **Padany** Respublika Kareliya, NW Russian Federation *63.18N 33.20E*
95 *M18* **Padasjoki** Etelä-Suomi, S Finland *61.20N 25.20E*
59 *M22* **Padcaya** Tarija, S Bolivia *21.52S 64.46W*
103 *H14* **Paderborn** Nordrhein-Westfalen, NW Germany *51.43N 8.45E*
Padeșul/Padeș, Vîrful *see* Padeș, Vârful
118 *F12* **Padeș, Vârful** *var.* Padeșul; ***prev.*** Vîrful Padeș. ▲ W Romania *45.39N 22.19E*
114 *L10* **Padinska Skela** Serbia, N Serbia and Montenegro (Yugoslavia) *44.58N 20.25E*
Padma *see* Brahmaputra
159 *S14* **Padma** *var.* Ganges. ≈ Bangladesh/India ***see also*** Ganges
108 *H8* **Padova** ***Eng.*** Padua; ***anc.*** Patavium. Veneto, NE Italy *45.24N 11.52E*
84 *A10* **Padrão, Ponta do** *headland* NW Angola *6.06S 12.18E*
27 *T16* **Padre Island** *island* Texas, SW USA
106 *G3* **Padrón** Galicia, NW Spain *42.43N 8.40W*
120 *K13* **Padsvillye** ***Rus.*** Podsvil'ye. Vitsyebskaya Voblasts', N Belarus *55.10N 27.58E*
190 *K11* **Padthaway** South Australia *36.39S 140.30E*
Padua *see* Padova
22 *G7* **Paducah** Kentucky, S USA *37.09N 88.52W*
27 *P4* **Paducah** Texas, SW USA *33.59N 100.19W*
107 *N15* **Padul** Andalucía, S Spain *37.01N 3.37W*
203 *P8* **Paea** Tahiti, W French Polynesia *17.40S 149.34W*
193 *L14* **Paekakariki** Wellington, North Island, NZ *41.00S 174.58E*
169 *X11* **Paektu-san** *var.* Baitou Shan. ▲ China/North Korea *42.00N 128.03W*
169 *V15* **Paengnyŏng-do** *island* NW South Korea
192 *M7* **Paeroa** Waikato, North Island, NZ *37.22S 175.39E*
56 *D12* **Páez** Cauca, SW Colombia *2.37N 76.00W*
123 *Mm4* **Páfos** *var.* Paphos. W Cyprus *34.46N 32.25E*
123 *Mm4* **Páfos** ✈ SW Cyprus *34.46N 32.25E*
85 *L19* **Pafúri** Gaza, SW Mozambique *22.24S 31.27E*
114 *C12* **Pag** ***It.*** Pago. Lika-Senj, W Croatia *44.26N 15.01E*
114 *B11* **Pag** ***It.*** Pago. *island* Zadar, SW Croatia
179 *Qq16* **Pagadian** Mindanao, S Philippines *7.47N 123.22E*
173 *G11* **Pagai Selatan, Pulau** *island* Kepulauan Mentawai, W Indonesia
173 *Ff10* **Pagai Utara, Pulau** *island* Kepulauan Mentawai, W Indonesia
196 *K4* **Pagan** *island* C Northern Mariana Islands
117 *G16* **Pagasitikós Kólpos** *gulf* E Greece
38 *L8* **Page** Arizona, SW USA *36.54N 111.28W*
31 *Q5* **Page** North Dakota, N USA *47.09N 97.33W*
120 *D13* **Pagėgiai** ***Ger.*** Pogegen. Šilutė, SW Lithuania *55.08N 21.54E*
23 *S11* **Pageland** South Carolina, SE USA *34.46N 80.23W*
83 *G16* **Pager** ≈ NE Uganda
155 *Q5* **Paghmān** Kābul, E Afghanistan *34.33N 68.55E*
Pago *see* Pag
196 *C16* **Pago Bay** *bay* E Guam, W Pacific Ocean
117 *M20* **Pagóndas** *var.* Pagóndhas. Sámos, Dodekánisos, Greece, Aegean Sea *37.40N 26.49E*
Pagóndhas *see* Pagóndas
198 *C8* **Pago Pago** ○ (American Samoa) Tutuila, W American Samoa *14.16S 170.43W*
39 *R8* **Pagosa Springs** Colorado, C USA *37.13N 107.01W*
40 *H12* **Pahala** *var.* Pāhala. Hawaii, USA, C Pacific Ocean *19.12N 155.28W*
174 *H4* **Pahang** ***off.*** Negeri Pahang Darul Makmur. ◈ *state* Peninsular Malaysia
Pahang *see* Pahang, Sungai
174 *Hh5* **Pahang, Sungai** *var.* Pahang, Sungei Pahang. ≈ Peninsular Malaysia
155 *S8* **Pahārpur** North-West Frontier Province, NW Pakistan *32.06N 71.00E*
193 *B24* **Pahia Point** *headland* South Island, NZ *46.19S 167.42E*
192 *M13* **Pahiatua** Manawatu-Wanganui, North Island, NZ *40.30S 175.48E*
40 *H12* **Pahoa** ***Haw.*** Pāhoa. Hawaii, USA, C Pacific Ocean *19.28N 154.55W*
25 *Y14* **Pahokee** Florida, SE USA *26.49N 80.40W*
37 *X9* **Pahranagat Range** ⛰ Nevada, W USA
37 *W11* **Pahrump** Nevada, W USA *36.11N 115.58W*
Pahsien *see* Chongqing
37 *V9* **Pahute Mesa** ⛰ Nevada, W USA
178 *H7* **Pai** Mae Hong Son, NW Thailand *19.24N 98.25E*
40 *F10* **Paia** ***Haw.*** Pāʻia. Maui, Hawaii, USA, C Pacific Ocean *20.54N 94.22W*
Pai-ch'eng *see* Baicheng
120 *H4* **Paide** ***Ger.*** Weissenstein. Järvamaa, N Estonia *58.54N 25.36E*
99 *J24* **Paignton** SW England, UK *50.25N 3.34W*
192 *K3* **Paihia** Northland, North Island, NZ *35.18S 174.06E*
95 *M18* **Päijänne** ◎ S Finland
116 *F13* **Páïko** ⛰ N Greece
59 *M17* **Paila, Río** ≈ C Bolivia
178 *I12* **Pailĭn** Bătdâmbâng, W Cambodia *12.51N 102.34E*
56 *F6* **Pailitas** Cesar, N Colombia *8.58N 73.37W*
40 *F9* **Pailolo Channel** *channel* Hawaii, USA, C Pacific Ocean
95 *K19* **Paimio** ***Swe.*** Pemar. Länsi-Suomi, W Finland *60.27N 22.42E*
172 *O17* **Paimi-saki** *var.* Yaeme-saki. *headland* Iriomote-jima, SW Japan *24.18N 123.40E*
104 *G5* **Paimpol** Côtes d'Armor, NW France *48.46N 3.03W*
174 *Gg9* **Painan** Sumatera, W Indonesia *1.22S 100.33E*
65 *G23* **Paine, Cerro** ▲ S Chile *51.01S 72.57W*
33 *U11* **Painesville** Ohio, N USA *41.43N 81.15W*
33 *S14* **Paint Creek** ≈ Ohio, N USA
38 *L10* **Painted Desert** *desert* Arizona, SW USA
Paint Hills *see* Wemindji
32 *M4* **Paint River** ≈ Michigan, N USA
27 *P8* **Paint Rock** Texas, SW USA *31.30N 99.55W*
23 *O6* **Paintsville** Kentucky, S USA *37.48N 82.48W*
Paisance *see* Piacenza
98 *I12* **Paisley** W Scotland, UK *55.49N 4.25W*
34 *I15* **Paisley** Oregon, NW USA *42.40N 120.31W*
107 *R10* **País Valenciano** *var.* Valencia, ***Cat.*** València; ***anc.*** Valentia. ◈ *autonomous community* NE Spain
107 *O3* **País Vasco** ***Basq.*** Euskadi, ***Eng.*** The Basque Country, ***Sp.*** Provincias Vascongadas. ◈ *autonomous community* N Spain
58 *A9* **Paita** Piura, NW Peru *5.07S 81.07W*
197 *J7* **Païta** Province Sud, S New Caledonia *22.06S 166.18E*
175 *O1* **Paitan, Teluk** *bay* Sabah, East Malaysia
106 *H7* **Paiva, Rio** ≈ N Portugal
94 *K12* **Pajala** Norrbotten, N Sweden *67.12N 23.19E*
106 *K3* **Pajares, Puerto de** *pass* NW Spain *43.00N 5.53W*
56 *G9* **Pajárito** Boyacá, C Colombia *5.18N 72.43W*
56 *G4* **Pajaro** La Guajira, S Colombia *11.41N 72.37W*
Pakanbaru *see* Pekanbaru
57 *Q10* **Pakaraima Mountains** ***var.*** Serra Pacaraim, Sierra Pacaraima. ⛰ N South America
178 *Hh11* **Pak Chong** Nakhon Ratchasima, C Thailand *14.38N 101.22E*
127 *Pp7* **Pakhachi** Koryakskiy Avtonomnyy Okrug, E Russian Federation *60.36N 168.59E*
Pakhna *see* Páchna
201 *U16* **Pakin Atoll** *atoll* Caroline Islands, E Micronesia
155 *Q12* **Pakistan** ***off.*** Islamic Republic of Pakistan, ***var.*** Islami Jamhuriya e Pakistan. ◆ *republic* S Asia
Pakistan, Islami Jamhuriya e *see* Pakistan
178 *I8* **Pak Lay** *var.* Muang Pak Lay. Xaignabouli, C Laos *18.06N 101.21E*
Paknam *see* Samut Prakan
177 *Ff5* **Pakokku** Magwe, C Myanmar *21.19N 95.04E*
112 *I10* **Pakość** ***Ger.*** Pakosch. Kujawski-pomorskie, C Poland *52.47N 18.03E*
Pakosch *see* Pakość
155 *V10* **Pākpattan** Punjab, E Pakistan *30.19N 73.27E*
178 *H16* **Pak Phanang** *var.* Ban Pak Phanang. Nakhon Si Thammarat, SW Thailand *8.19N 100.10E*
114 *G9* **Pakrac** ***Hung.*** Pakrácz. Požega-Slavonija, NE Croatia *45.26N 17.09E*
Pakrácz *see* Pakrac
120 *F11* **Pakruojis** Pakruojis, N Lithuania *55.59N 23.50E*
113 *J24* **Paks** Tolna, S Hungary *46.37N 18.51E*
Pak Sane *see* Pakxan
Paksé *see* Pakxé
178 *I11* **Pak Thong Chai** Nakhon Ratchasima, C Thailand *14.43N 102.01E*
155 *R6* **Paktīā** ◈ *province* SE Afghanistan
155 *Q7* **Paktīkā** ◈ *province* SE Afghanistan
175 *Pp9* **Pakuli** Sulawesi, C Indonesia *1.14S 119.55E*
83 *F17* **Pakwach** NW Uganda *2.28N 31.28E*
178 *Ii8* **Pakxan** *var.* Muang Pakxan, Pak Sane. Bolikhamxai, C Laos *18.27N 103.38E*
178 *Jj10* **Pakxé** *var.* Paksé. Champasak, S Laos *15.09N 105.49E*
80 *G12* **Pala** Mayo-Kébbi, SW Chad *9.22N 14.54E*
63 *A17* **Palacios** Santa Fe, C Argentina *30.43S 61.37W*
27 *V13* **Palacios** Texas, SW USA *28.42N 96.13W*
107 *X5* **Palafrugell** Cataluña, NE Spain *41.55N 3.10E*
109 *L24* **Palagonia** Sicilia, Italy, C Mediterranean Sea *37.19N 14.45E*
115 *E17* **Palagruža** ***It.*** Pelagosa. *island* SW Croatia
117 *G20* **Palaiá Epídavros** Pelopónnisos, S Greece *37.38N 23.09E*
124 *Nn3* **Palaichóri** *var.* Palekhori. C Cyprus *34.55N 33.06E*
117 *H25* **Palaiochóra** Kríti, Greece, E Mediterranean Sea *35.14N 23.37E*
117 *A15* **Palaiolastrítsa** *religious building* Kérkyra, Iónioi Nísoi, Greece, C Mediterranean Sea *39.41N 19.42E*
117 *J19* **Palaiópoli** Ándros, Kykládes, Greece, Aegean Sea *37.49N 24.49E*
105 *N5* **Palaiseau** Essonne, N France *48.40N 2.13E*
Palakkad *see* Pālghāt
160 *N11* **Pāla Laharha** Orissa, E India *21.27N 85.14E*
85 *G19* **Palamakoloi** Ghanzi, C Botswana *23.10S 22.22E*
117 *E16* **Palamás** Thessalía, C Greece *39.28N 22.04E*
107 *X5* **Palamós** Cataluña, NE Spain *41.51N 3.06E*
120 *J5* **Palamuse** ***Ger.*** Sankt-Bartholomäi. Jõgevamaa, E Estonia *58.40N 26.34E*
191 *Q14* **Palana** Tasmania, SE Australia *39.48S 147.54E*
127 *P9* **Palana** Koryakskiy Avtonomnyy Okrug, E Russian Federation *59.04N 159.58E*
120 *C11* **Palanga** ***Ger.*** Polangen. Palanga, NW Lithuania *5.54N 21.05E*
149 *V10* **Palangān, Kūh-e** ⛰ E Iran
Palangkaraja *see* Palangkaraya
174 *Mm10* **Palangkaraya** ***prev.*** Palangkaraja. Borneo, C Indonesia *2.16S 113.55E*
161 *H22* **Palani** Tamil Nādu, SE India *10.30N 77.24E*
Palanka *see* Bačka Palanka
160 *D9* **Pālanpur** Gujarāt, W India *24.12N 72.28E*
Palantia *see* Palencia
85 *I19* **Palapye** Central, SE Botswana *22.37S 27.06E*
161 *J19* **Pālār** ≈ SE India
106 *H3* **Palas de Rei** Galicia, NW Spain *42.52N 7.51W*
127 *O10* **Palatka** Magadanskaya Oblast', E Russian Federation *60.09N 150.33E*
25 *W10* **Palatka** Florida, SE USA *29.39N 81.38W*
196 *B9* **Palau** *var.* Belau. ◆ *republic* W Pacific Ocean
133 *Y14* **Palau Islands** *var.* Palau. *island group* N Palau
198 *Aa8* **Palauli Bay** *bay* Savai'i, Samoa, C Pacific Ocean
178 *Gg12* **Palaw** Tenasserim, S Myanmar *12.57N 98.39E*
179 *Oo15* **Palawan** *island* W Philippines
179 *Oo15* **Palawan Passage** *passage* W Philippines
198 *F7* **Palawan Trough** *undersea feature* S South China Sea
179 *P10* **Palayan City** Luzon, N Philippines *15.34N 121.34E*
161 *H23* **Pālayankottai** Tamil Nādu, SE India *8.44N 77.45E*
109 *L25* **Palazzola Acreide** ***anc.*** Acrae. Sicilia, Italy, C Mediterranean Sea *37.04N 14.54E*
120 *G3* **Paldiski** ***prev.*** Baltiski, ***Eng.*** Baltic Port, ***Ger.*** Baltischport. Harjumaa, NW Estonia *59.20N 24.04E*
114 *I13* **Pale** Republika Srpska, E Bosnia and Herzegovina *43.49N 18.35E*
Palekhori *see* Palaichóri
175 *Q7* **Paleleh, Pegunungan** ⛰ Sulawesi, N Indonesia
175 *Qq7* **Paleleh, Teluk** *bay* Sulawesi, N Indonesia
174 *I11* **Palembang** Sumatera, W Indonesia *2.58S 104.45E*
65 *G18* **Palena** Los Lagos, S Chile *43.40S 71.49W*
65 *G18* **Palena, Río** ≈ S Chile
106 *M5* **Palencia** ***anc.*** Palantia, Pallantia. Castilla-León, NW Spain *41.01N 4.31W*
106 *M3* **Palencia** ◈ *province* Castilla-León, N Spain
37 *X15* **Palen Dry Lake** ◎ California, W USA
43 *V15* **Palenque** Chiapas, SE Mexico *17.37N 92.03W*
43 *V15* **Palenque** ***var.*** Ruinas de Palenque. *ruins* Chiapas, SE Mexico *17.31N 91.58W*
47 *O9* **Palenque, Punta** *headland* S Dominican Republic *18.13N 70.08W*
Palenque, Ruinas de *see* Palenque
Palerme *see* Palermo
109 *I23* **Palermo** ***Fr.*** Palerme; ***anc.*** Panhormus, Panormus. Sicilia, Italy, C Mediterranean Sea *38.07N 13.22E*
27 *V8* **Palestine** Texas, SW USA *31.44N 95.38W*
27 *V7* **Palestine, Lake** ▣ Texas, SW USA
109 *I15* **Palestrina** Lazio, C Italy *41.49N 12.53E*
177 *F5* **Paletwa** Chin State, W Myanmar *21.21N 92.51E*
161 *G21* **Pālghāt** *var.* Palakkad; ***prev.*** Pulicat. Kerala, SW India *10.46N 76.42E*
158 *F13* **Pāli** Rājasthān, N India *25.48N 73.21E*
178 *Gg16* **Palian** Trang, SW Thailand
201 *O12* **Palikir** ● (Micronesia) Pohnpei, E Micronesia *6.58N 158.13E*
179 *R17* **Palimbang** Mindanao, S Philippines *6.16N 124.10E*
Palimé *see* Kpalimé
109 *L19* **Palinuro, Capo** *headland* S Italy *40.02N 15.16E*
117 *H15* **Palioúri, Akrotírio** *var.* Akra Kanestron. *headland* N Greece *39.55N 23.45E*
35 *R14* **Palisades Reservoir** ▣ Idaho, NW USA
101 *J23* **Paliseul** Luxembourg, SE Belgium *49.55N 5.09E*
160 *C11* **Pālitāna** Gujarāt, W India *21.30N 71.49E*
120 *F4* **Palivere** Läänemaa, W Estonia *58.59N 23.58E*
43 *V14* **Palizada** Campeche, SE Mexico *18.15N 92.03W*
95 *L18* **Pälkäne** Länsi-Suomi, W Finland *61.21N 24.15E*
161 *J22* **Palk Strait** *strait* India/Sri Lanka
161 *J23* **Pallai** Northern Province, NW Sri Lanka *9.34N 80.19E*
Pallantia *see* Palencia
108 *C6* **Pallanza** Piemonte, NE Italy *45.57N 8.32E*
131 *Q9* **Pallasovka** Volgogradskaya Oblast', SW Russian Federation *50.06N 46.52E*
Pallene/Pallíni *see* Kassándra
193 *L15* **Palliser Bay** *bay* North Island, NZ
193 *L15* **Palliser, Cape** *headland* North Island, NZ *41.37S 175.16E*
203 *U9* **Palliser, Îles** *island group* Îles Tuamotu, C French Polynesia
107 *X9* **Palma** *var.* Palma de Mallorca. Mallorca, Spain, W Mediterranean Sea *39.34N 2.39E*
107 *X9* **Palma** ✈ Mallorca, Spain, W Mediterranean Sea
84 *Q12* **Palma** Cabo Delgado, N Mozambique *10.46S 40.30E*
107 *X10* **Palma, Badia de** *bay* Mallorca, Spain, W Mediterranean Sea
106 *L13* **Palma del Río** Andalucía, S Spain *37.42N 5.16W*
Palma de Mallorca *see* Palma
109 *J25* **Palma di Montechiaro** Sicilia, Italy, C Mediterranean Sea *37.12N 13.46E*
108 *J7* **Palmanova** Friuli-Venezia Giulia, NE Italy *45.54N 13.20E*
56 *J7* **Palmarito** Apure, C Venezuela *7.36N 70.11W*
45 *N15* **Palmar Sur** Puntarenas, SE Costa Rica *8.54N 83.27W*
62 *I12* **Palmas** Paraná, S Brazil *26.29S 52.00W*
61 *K16* **Palmas** *var.* Palmas do Tocantins, C Brazil *10.24S 48.19W*
Palmas do Tocantins *see* Palmas
56 *D11* **Palmaseca** ✈ (Cali) Valle del Cauca, SW Colombia *3.31N 76.27W*
109 *B21* **Palmas, Golfo di** *gulf* Sardegna, Italy, C Mediterranean Sea
46 *I7* **Palma Soriano** Santiago de Cuba, E Cuba *20.10N 76.00W*
25 *Y12* **Palm Bay** Florida, SE USA *28.01N 80.35W*
37 *T14* **Palmdale** California, W USA *34.34N 118.07W*
63 *H14* **Palmeira das Missões** Rio Grande do Sul, S Brazil *27.54S 53.19W*
84 *A11* **Palmeirinhas, Ponta das** *headland* NW Angola *9.04S 13.02E*
41 *R11* **Palmer** Alaska, USA *61.36N 149.06W*
21 *N11* **Palmer** Massachusetts, NE USA *42.09N 72.19W*
27 *U7* **Palmer** Texas, SW USA *32.25N 96.40W*
204 *H4* **Palmer** *US research station* Antarctica *64.37S 64.01W*
13 *R11* **Palmer** ≈ Quebec, SE Canada
39 *T5* **Palmer Lake** Colorado, C USA *39.07N 104.55W*
204 *J6* **Palmer Land** *physical region* Antarctica
12 *F15* **Palmerston** Ontario, SE Canada *43.51N 80.49W*
193 *F22* **Palmerston** Otago, South Island, NZ *45.27S 170.42E*
202 *K15* **Palmerston** *island* S Cook Islands
Palmerston *see* Darwin
192 *M12* **Palmerston North** Manawatu-Wanganui, North Island, NZ *40.19S 175.52E*
78 *L18* **Palmés, Cap des** *headland* SW Ivory Coast *4.18N 7.31W*
25 *V13* **Palmetto** Florida, SE USA *27.31N 82.34W*
Palmetto State *see* South Carolina
109 *M22* **Palmi** Calabria, SW Italy *38.21N 15.51E*
56 *D11* **Palmira** Valle del Cauca, W Colombia *3.33N 76.16W*
58 *F8* **Palmira, Río** ≈ N Peru
63 *D19* **Palmitas** Soriano, SW Uruguay *33.27S 57.48W*
Palmnicken *see* Yantarnyy
37 *V15* **Palm Springs** California, W USA *33.48N 116.33W*
29 *V2* **Palmyra** Missouri, C USA *39.47N 91.31W*
20 *G10* **Palmyra** New York, NE USA *43.02N 77.13W*
20 *G15* **Palmyra** Pennsylvania, NE USA *40.18N 76.35W*
23 *V5* **Palmyra** Virginia, NE USA *37.53N 78.15W*
Palmyra *see* Tudmur
199 *K7* **Palmyra Atoll** ◇ *US privately owned unincorporated territory* C Pacific Ocean
160 *P12* **Palmyras Point** *headland* E India *20.46N 87.00E*
37 *N9* **Palo Alto** California, W USA *37.26N 122.08W*
27 *O1* **Palo Duro Creek** ≈ Texas, SW USA
Paloe *see* Palu
Paloe *see* Denpasar, Bali, C Indonesia
174 *Hh6* **Paloh** Johor, Peninsular Malaysia *2.10N 103.10E*
82 *F12* **Paloich** Upper Nile, SE Sudan *10.28N 32.31E*
42 *I3* **Palomas** Chihuahua, N Mexico *31.45N 107.38W*
109 *I15* **Palombara Sabina** Lazio, C Italy *42.04N 12.45E*
107 *S13* **Palos, Cabo de** *headland* SE Spain *37.38N 0.42W*
106 *I14* **Palos de la Frontera** Andalucía, S Spain *37.13N 6.52W*
62 *G11* **Palotina** Paraná, S Brazil *24.16S 53.49W*
34 *M9* **Palouse** Washington, NW USA *46.54N 117.04W*
34 *L9* **Palouse River** ≈ Washington, NW USA
37 *Y16* **Palo Verde** California, W USA *33.25N 114.43W*
59 *E16* **Palpa** Ica, W Peru *14.33S 75.09W*
97 *M16* **Pålsboda** Örebro, C Sweden *59.04N 15.21E*
95 *M15* **Paltamo** Oulu, C Finland *64.25N 27.49E*
175 *Pp9* **Palu** ***prev.*** Paloe. Sulawesi, C Indonesia *0.54S 119.52E*
143 *P14* **Palu** Elâzığ, E Turkey *38.43N 39.55E*
175 *Q16* **Palu, Pulau** *island* S Indonesia
175 *P8* **Palu, Teluk** *bay* Sulawesi, C Indonesia
158 *I11* **Palwal** Haryāna, N India *28.15N 77.18E*
127 *Oo4* **Palyavaam** ≈ NE Russian Federation
79 *Q13* **Pama** SE Burkina *11.13N 0.46E*
180 *J14* **Pamandzi** ✈ (Mamoudzou) Petite-Terre, E Mayotte
Pamangkat *see* Pemangkat
149 *R11* **Pā Mazār** Kermān, C Iran
85 *N19* **Pambarra** Inhambane, SE Mozambique *21.57S 35.06E*
176 *Xx10* **Pamdai** Papua, E Indonesia *1.58S 137.19E*
176 *X10* **Pami** Papua, E Indonesia *2.45S 136.02E*
105 *N16* **Pamiers** Ariège, S France *43.07N 1.36E*
153 *T14* **Pamir** *var.* Daryā-ye Pāmīr, ***Taj.*** Dar"yoi Pomir. ≈ Afghanistan/Tajikistan ***see also*** Pāmīr, Daryā-ye
Pamir/Pāmīr, Daryā-ye *see* Pamirs
155 *U1* **Pāmīr, Daryā-ye** *var.* Pamir, ***Taj.*** Dar"yoi Pomir. ≈ Afghanistan/Tajikistan ***see also*** Pamir
Pāmīr-e Khord *see* Little Pamir
133 *Q8* **Pamirs** ***Pash.*** Daryā-ye Pāmīr, ***Rus.*** Pamir. ⛰ C Asia
Pâmiut *see* Paamiut
23 *X10* **Pamlico River** ≈ North Carolina, SE USA
23 *Y10* **Pamlico Sound** *sound* North Carolina, SE USA
27 *O2* **Pampa** Texas, SW USA *35.31N 100.58W*
Pampa Aullagas, Lago *see* Poopó, Lago
63 *B21* **Pampa Húmeda** *grassland* E Argentina
58 *A10* **Pampa las Salinas** *salt lake* NW Peru
59 *F15* **Pampas** Huancavelica, C Peru *12.22S 74.52W*
64 *K13* **Pampas** *plain* C Argentina
57 *O4* **Pampatar** Nueva Esparta, NE Venezuela *10.58N 63.49W*
Pampeluna *see* Pamplona
106 *H8* **Pampilhosa da Serra** ***var.*** Pampilhosa de Serra. Coimbra, N Portugal *40.03N 7.58W*
181 *Y15* **Pamplemousses** N Mauritius *20.06S 57.34E*
56 *G7* **Pamplona** Norte de Santander, N Colombia *7.24N 72.37W*
107 *Q3* **Pamplona** ***Basq.*** Iruña; ***prev.*** Pampeluna, ***anc.*** Pompaelo. Navarra, N Spain *42.49N 1.39W*
116 *I11* **Pamporovo** ***prev.*** Vasil Kolarov. Smolyan, S Bulgaria *41.39N 24.45E*
142 *D15* **Pamukkale** Denizli, W Turkey *37.51N 29.13E*
23 *W5* **Pamunkey River** ≈ Virginia, NE USA
158 *K5* **Pamzal** Jammu and Kashmir, NW India *34.16N 78.49E*
32 *L14* **Pana** Illinois, N USA *39.23N 89.04W*
43 *Y11* **Panabá** Yucatán, SE Mexico *21.18N 88.15W*
37 *Y8* **Panaca** Nevada, W USA *37.47N 114.24W*
117 *E19* **Panachaikó** ⛰ S Greece
12 *F11* **Panache Lake** ◎ Ontario, S Canada
116 *I10* **Panagyurishte** Pazardzhik, C Bulgaria *42.30N 24.10E*
174 *I14* **Panaitan, Pulau** *island* S Indonesia
174 *Ii14* **Panaitan, Selat** *strait* Jawa, SW Indonesia
117 *D18* **Panaitolikó** ⛰ C Greece
161 *E17* **Panaji** *var.* Pangim, Panjim, New Goa. Goa, W India *15.31N 73.52E*
45 *T14* **Panama** ***off.*** Republic of Panama. ◆ *republic* Central America
45 *T15* **Panamá** *var.* Ciudad de Panamá, ***Eng.*** Panama City. ● (Panama) Panamá, C Panama *8.57N 79.33W*
45 *U14* **Panamá** ***off.*** Provincia de Panamá. ◈ *province* E Panama
45 *U15* **Panamá, Bahía de** *bay* N Gulf of Panama
200 *Oo8* **Panama Basin** *undersea feature* E Pacific Ocean
45 *T15* **Panama Canal** *canal* E Panama
25 *R9* **Panama City** Florida, SE USA *30.09N 85.39W*
45 *T14* **Panama City** ✈ Panamá, C Panama *9.02N 79.24W*
Panama City *see* Panamá
25 *Q9* **Panama City Beach** Florida, SE USA *30.10N 85.48W*
45 *T17* **Panamá, Golfo de** ***var.*** Gulf of Panama. *gulf* S Panama
Panama, Gulf of *see* Panamá, Golfo de
Panama, Isthmus of *see* Panamá, Istmo de
45 *T15* **Panamá, Istmo de** ***Eng.*** Isthmus of Panama; ***prev.*** Isthmus of Darien. *isthmus* E Panama
37 *U11* **Panamint Range** ⛰ California, W USA
109 *L22* **Panarea, Isola** *island* Isole Eolie, S Italy
108 *G9* **Panaro** ≈ N Italy
179 *Q14* **Panay Gulf** *gulf* C Philippines
179 *Pp13* **Panay Island** *island* C Philippines
37 *W7* **Pancake Range** ⛰ Nevada, W USA
114 *M11* **Pančevo** ***Ger.*** Pantschowa, ***Hung.*** Pancsova. Serbia, N Serbia and Montenegro (Yugoslavia) *44.52N 20.39E*
115 *M15* **Pančićev Vrh** ▲ SW Serbia and Montenegro (Yugoslavia) *43.16N 20.49E*
118 *L12* **Panciu** Vrancea, E Romania *45.54N 27.07E*
118 *F10* **Pâncota** ***Hung.*** Pankota; ***prev.*** Pîncota. Arad, W Romania *46.19N 21.45E*
Pancsova *see* Pančevo
85 *N20* **Panda** Inhambane, SE Mozambique *24.04S 34.44E*
176 *X9* **Pandaidori, Kepulauan** *island group* E Indonesia
27 *N11* **Pandale** Texas, SW USA *30.09N 101.34W*
174 *H7* **Pandang, Pulau** *island* W Indonesia
174 *Kk9* **Pandang Tikar, Pulau** *island* N Indonesia
63 *F20* **Pan de Azúcar** Maldonado, S Uruguay *34.45S 55.13W*
120 *H11* **Pandėlys** Rokiškis, NE Lithuania *56.04N 25.18E*
161 *F15* **Pandharpur** Mahārāshtra, W India *17.42N 75.24E*
190 *J1* **Pandie Pandie** South Australia *26.06S 139.26E*
175 *Pp9* **Pandiri** Sulawesi, C Indonesia *1.32S 120.47E*
63 *F20* **Pando** Canelones, S Uruguay *34.43S 55.58W*
59 *J14* **Pando** ◈ *department* N Bolivia
199 *Ii10* **Pandora Bank** *undersea feature* W Pacific Ocean
97 *G20* **Pandrup** Nordjylland, N Denmark *57.13N 9.42E*
159 *V12* **Pandu** Assam, NE India *26.08N 91.37E*
81 *J15* **Pandu** Equateur, NW Dem. Rep. Congo *5.03N 19.14E*
Paneas *see* Bāniyās
61 *F15* **Panelas** Mato Grosso, W Brazil *9.06S 60.41W*
120 *G12* **Panevėžys** Panevėžys, C Lithuania *55.44N 24.21E*
Panfilov *see* Zharkent
131 *N9* **Panfilovo** Volgogradskaya Oblast', SW Russian Federation *50.25N 42.55E*
81 *N17* **Panga** Orientale, N Dem. Rep. Congo *1.52N 26.18E*
200 *Ss13* **Pangai** Lifuka, C Tonga *19.49S 174.22W*
116 *H13* **Pangaío** ⛰ N Greece
81 *G20* **Pangala** Le Pool, S Congo *3.26S 14.38E*
83 *J22* **Pangani** Tanga, E Tanzania *5.27S 39.00E*
83 *I21* **Pangani** ≈ NE Tanzania
195 *U13* **Panggoe** Choiseul Island, NW Solomon Islands *7.00S 95.05E*
81 *N20* **Pangi** Maniema, E Dem. Rep. Congo *3.12S 26.39E*
194 *H12* **Pangia** Southern Highlands, W PNG *6.18S 144.12E*
Pangim *see* Panaji
173 *F4* **Pangkalanbrandan** Sumatera, W Indonesia *4.00N 98.15E*
Pangkalanbun *see* Pangkalanbuun
174 *Ll10* **Pangkalanbuun** ***var.*** Pangkalanbun. Borneo, C Indonesia *2.43S 111.37E*
174 *J10* **Pangkalpinang** Pulau Bangka, W Indonesia *2.04S 106.09E*

◆ Country
● Country Capital
◇ Dependent Territory
○ Dependent Territory Capital
◈ Administrative Region
✈ International Airport
▲ Mountain
⛰ Mountain Range
♨ Volcano
≈ River
◎ Lake
▣ Reservoir

9 U17 **Pangman** Saskatchewan, S Canada 49.37N 104.33W
Pang-Nga see Phang-Nga
16 Nn2 **Pangnirtung** Baffin Island, Nunavut, NE Canada 66.04N 65.45W
158 K6 **Pangong Tso** var. Bangong Co. ◎ China/India see also Bangong Co
38 K7 **Panguitch** Utah, W USA 37.49N 112.26W
195 S12 **Panguna** Bougainville Island, NE PNG 6.22S 155.19E
179 Pp17 **Pangutaran Group** island group Sulu Archipelago, SW Philippines
27 N2 **Panhandle** Texas, SW USA 35.18N 101.23W
Panhormus see Palermo
176 X12 **Paniai, Danau** ◎ Papua, E Indonesia
81 L21 **Pania-Mutombo** Kasai Oriental, C Dem. Rep. Congo 5.09S 23.49E
Panicherevo see Dolno Panicherevo
197 H5 **Panié, Mont** ▲ C New Caledonia 20.33S 164.41E
158 I10 **Pānīpat** Haryāna, N India 29.18N 77.00E
153 Q14 **Panj** Rus. Pyandzh; prev. Kirovabad. SW Tajikistan 37.39N 69.55E
153 P15 **Panj** Rus. Pyandzh. ≈ Afghanistan/Tajikistan
155 O5 **Panjāb** Bāmīān, C Afghanistan 34.21N 67.00E
153 O12 **Panjakent** Rus. Pendzhikent. W Tajikistan 39.28N 67.33E
154 L14 **Panjgūr** Baluchistān, SW Pakistan 26.58N 64.05E
Panjim see Panaji
169 U12 **Panjin** Liaoning, NE China 41.11N 122.05E
153 P14 **Panji Poyon** Rus. Nizhniy Pyandzh. SW Tajikistan 37.14N 68.32E
155 Q4 **Panjshīr** ≈ E Afghanistan
Pankota see Pâncota
79 W14 **Pankshin** Plateau, C Nigeria 9.21N 9.27E
169 Y10 **Pan Ling** ▲ N China
Panlong Jiang see Lô, Sông
160 J9 **Panna** Madhya Pradesh, C India 24.43N 80.10E
101 M16 **Panningen** Limburg, SE Netherlands 51.19N 5.58E
155 R13 **Pāno Āqil** Sind, SE Pakistan 27.56N 69.16E
124 Nn3 **Páno Léfkara** S Cyprus 34.52N 33.18E
124 N3 **Páno Panayia** var. Pano Panayia. W Cyprus 34.55N 32.38E
Pano Panayia see Páno Panagiá
Panopolis see Akhmīm
31 U14 **Panora** Iowa, C USA 41.41N 94.21W
62 I8 **Panorama** São Paulo, S Brazil 21.22S 51.51W
117 I24 **Pánormos** Kríti, Greece, E Mediterranean Sea 35.24N 24.42E
Panormus see Palermo
169 W11 **Panshi** Jilin, NE China 42.50N 126.06E
61 H19 **Pantanal** var. Pantanalmato-Grossense. swamp SW Brazil
Pantanalmato-Grossense see Pantanal
63 H16 **Pântano Grande** Rio Grande do Sul, S Brazil 30.12S 52.24W
175 R16 **Pantar, Pulau** island Kepulauan Alor, S Indonesia
23 X9 **Pantego** North Carolina, SE USA 35.34N 76.39E
109 G25 **Pantelleria** anc. Cossyra, Cosyra. Sicilia, Italy, C Mediterranean Sea 36.47N 12.00E
109 G25 **Pantelleria, Isola di** island SW Italy
Pante Macassar/Pante Makassar see Pante Makasar
175 Rr17 **Pante Makasar** var. Pante Macassar, Pante Makassar. W East Timor 9.10S 124.27E
158 K10 **Pantnagar** Uttar Pradesh, N India 29.00N 79.28E
117 A15 **Pantokrátoras** ▲ Kérkyra, Iónioi Nísoi, Greece, C Mediterranean Sea 39.45N 19.51E
Pantschowa see Pančevo
179 Rr16 **Pantukan** Mindanao, S Philippines 7.10N 125.55E
43 P11 **Pánuco** Veracruz-Llave, E Mexico 22.01N 98.10W
43 P11 **Pánuco, Río** ≈ C Mexico
166 I12 **Panxian** Guizhou, S China 25.45N 104.28E
173 G7 **Panyabungan** Sumatera, N Indonesia 0.55N 99.30E
79 W14 **Panyam** Plateau, C Nigeria 9.28N 9.13E
163 N13 **Panzhihua** prev. Dukou, Tu-k'ou. Sichuan, C China 26.35N 101.41E
81 I22 **Panzi** Bandundu, SW Dem. Rep. Congo 7.10S 17.55E
44 E5 **Panzós** Alta Verapaz, E Guatemala 15.21N 89.40W
Pao-chi/Paoki see Baoji
Pao-king see Shaoyang
109 N20 **Paola** Calabria, SW Italy 39.21N 16.03E
123 Jj17 **Paola** E Malta 35.52N 14.30E
29 R5 **Paola** Kansas, C USA 38.34N 94.52W
33 O15 **Paoli** Indiana, N USA 38.31N 86.26W
197 D14 **Paonangisu** Éfaté, C Vanuatu 17.33S 168.23E
175 Tt11 **Paoni** var. Pauni. Pulau Seram, E Indonesia 2.48S 129.03E
39 Q5 **Paonia** Colorado, C USA 38.52N 107.35W
203 O7 **Paopao** Moorea, W French Polynesia 17.28S 149.48W
Pao-shan see Baoshan
Pao-ting see Baoding
Pao-t'ou/Paotow see Baotou
81 H14 **Paoua** Ouham-Pendé, W Central African Republic 7.22N 16.25E
Pap see Pop
113 H23 **Pápa** Veszprém, W Hungary 47.19N 17.27E
44 J12 **Papagayo, Golfo de** gulf NW Costa Rica
40 H11 **Papaikou** var. Pāpa'ikou. Hawaii, USA, C Pacific Ocean 19.45N 155.06W
43 R15 **Papaloapan, Río** ≈ S Mexico
192 L6 **Papakura** Auckland, North Island, NZ 37.03S 174.57E
43 Q13 **Papantla** var. Papantla de Olarte. Veracruz-Llave, E Mexico 20.27N 97.21W
Papantla de Olarte see Papantla
203 P8 **Papara** Tahiti, W French Polynesia 17.45S 149.33W
192 K4 **Paparoa** Northland, North Island, NZ 36.06S 174.12E
193 G16 **Paparoa Range** ▲▲ South Island, NZ
117 K20 **Pápas, Akrotírio** headland Ikaría, Dodekánisos, Greece, Aegean Sea 37.31N 25.58E
98 L2 **Papa Stour** island NE Scotland, UK
192 L6 **Papatoetoe** Auckland, North Island, NZ 36.58S 174.52E
193 E25 **Papatowai** Otago, South Island, NZ 46.33S 169.33E
98 K4 **Papa Westray** island NE Scotland, UK
203 T10 **Papeete** ○ (French Polynesia) Tahiti, W French Polynesia 17.31S 149.34W
102 F11 **Papenburg** Niedersachsen, NW Germany 53.04N 7.24E
100 H13 **Papendrecht** Zuid-Holland, SW Netherlands 51.49N 4.42E
203 Q7 **Papenoo** Tahiti, W French Polynesia 17.28S 149.25W
203 Q7 **Papenoo Rivière** ≈ Tahiti, W French Polynesia
203 N7 **Papetoai** Moorea, W French Polynesia 17.28S 149.52W
94 L3 **Papey** island E Iceland
Paphos see Páfos
42 H5 **Papigochic, Río** ≈ NW Mexico
120 E10 **Papilė** Akmenė, NW Lithuania 56.08N 22.51E
31 S15 **Papillion** Nebraska, C USA 41.09N 96.02W
13 T5 **Papinachois** ≈ Quebec, SE Canada
176 Y13 **Papua** var. Irian Barat, West Irian, West New Guinea, West Papua ; prev. Dutch New Guinea, Irian Jaya, Netherlands New Guinea. ◈ province E Indonesia
194 I15 **Papua, Gulf of** gulf S PNG
194 H13 **Papua New Guinea** off. Independent State of Papua New Guinea; prev. Territory of Papua and New Guinea, abbrev. PNG. ◆ commonwealth republic NW Melanesia
199 H10 **Papua Plateau** undersea feature N Coral Sea
114 G9 **Papuk** ▲▲ NE Croatia
177 G8 **Papun** Karen State, S Myanmar 18.04N 97.25E
44 L14 **Paquera** Puntarenas, W Costa Rica 9.52N 84.55W
57 V9 **Para** ◈ district N Suriname
60 I13 **Pará** off. Estado do Pará. ◈ state NE Brazil
Pará see Belém
126 H12 **Parabel'** Tomskaya Oblast', C Russian Federation 58.54N 80.45E
188 I8 **Paraburdoo** Western Australia 23.07S 117.40E
59 E16 **Paracas, Península de** peninsula W Peru
61 L19 **Paracatu** Minas Gerais, NE Brazil 17.13S 46.52W
198 F7 **Paracel Islands** ◇ disputed territory SE Asia
190 I6 **Parachilna** South Australia 31.09S 138.23E
155 R6 **Pārachinār** North-West Frontier Province, NW Pakistan 33.55N 70.04E
114 N13 **Paraćin** Serbia, C Serbia and Montenegro (Yugoslavia) 43.51N 21.25E
12 K8 **Paradis** Quebec, SE Canada 48.13N 76.36W
41 N11 **Paradise** var. Paradise Hill. Alaska, USA 62.28N 96.09W
37 O5 **Paradise** California, W USA 39.42N 121.39W
37 X11 **Paradise** Nevada, W USA 36.05N 115.10W
Paradise Hill see Paradise
39 R11 **Paradise Hills** New Mexico, SW USA 35.12N 106.42W
Paradise of the Pacific see Hawaii
38 L13 **Paradise Valley** Arizona, SW USA 33.31N 111.56W
37 T2 **Paradise Valley** Nevada, W USA 41.30N 117.30W
117 O22 **Paradisi** ✕ (Ródos) Ródos, Dodekánisos, Greece, Aegean Sea 36.24N 28.08E
176 X10 **Paradoi** Papua, E Indonesia 2.10S 136.25E
160 P12 **Pārādwīp** Orissa, E India 20.18N 86.39E
Paraetonium see Maţrūḩ
119 R4 **Parafiyivka** Chernihivs'ka Oblast', N Ukraine 50.53N 32.40E
38 K7 **Paragonah** Utah, W USA 37.53N 112.46W
29 X9 **Paragould** Arkansas, C USA 36.03N 90.30W
49 X8 **Paraguaçu** var. Paraguassú. ≈ E Brazil
62 J9 **Paraguaçu Paulista** São Paulo, S Brazil 22.22S 50.35W
56 H4 **Paraguaipoa** Zulia, NW Venezuela 11.21N 71.58W
64 O6 **Paraguarí** Paraguarí, S Paraguay 25.38S 57.09W
64 O7 **Paraguarí** off. Departamento de Paraguarí. ◈ department S Paraguay
57 O8 **Paragua, Río** ≈ SE Venezuela
59 O16 **Paraguá, Río** ≈ NE Bolivia
Paraguassú see Paraguaçu
64 N5 **Paraguay** ◆ republic C South America
49 U10 **Paraguay** var. Río Paraguay. ≈ C South America
Parahiba/Parahyba see Paraíba
61 P15 **Paraíba** off. Estado da Paraíba; prev. Parahiba, Parahyba. ◈ state E Brazil
Paraíba see João Pessoa
62 P9 **Paraíba do Sul, Rio** ≈ SE Brazil
Parainen see Pargas
45 N14 **Paraíso** Cartago, C Costa Rica 9.50N 83.51W
43 U14 **Paraíso** Tabasco, SE Mexico 18.23N 93.03W
59 O17 **Paraíso, Río** ≈ E Bolivia
Parajd see Praid
79 S14 **Parakou** C Benin 9.22N 2.40E
124 O3 **Paralimni** E Cyprus 35.01N 34.01E
117 G18 **Paralímni, Límni** ◎ C Greece
194 G15 **Parama Island** island SW PNG
57 W8 **Paramaribo** ● (Suriname) Paramaribo, N Suriname 5.52N 55.13W
57 W9 **Paramaribo** ◈ district N Suriname
57 W9 **Paramaribo** ✕ Paramaribo, N Suriname 5.52N 55.13W
Paramithiá see Paramythiá
58 C13 **Paramonga** Lima, W Peru 10.40S 77.51W
127 Pp13 **Paramushir, Ostrov** island SE Russian Federation
117 C16 **Paramythiá** var. Paramithiá. Ípeiros, W Greece 39.28N 20.31E
64 M10 **Paraná** Entre Ríos, E Argentina 31.48S 60.29W
62 H11 **Paraná** off. Estado do Paraná. ◈ state S Brazil
49 U11 **Paraná** var. Alto Paraná. ≈ C South America
62 K12 **Paranaguá** Paraná, S Brazil 25.31S 48.36W
61 J20 **Paranaíba, Rio** ≈ E Brazil
61 C19 **Paraná Ibicuy, Río** ≈ E Argentina
61 H15 **Paranaíta** Mato Grosso, W Brazil 9.35S 57.01W
62 H9 **Paranapanema, Rio** ≈ S Brazil
62 K11 **Paranapiacaba, Serra do** ▲▲ S Brazil
62 H9 **Paranavaí** Paraná, S Brazil 23.03S 52.25W
149 N5 **Parandak** Markazī, W Iran 35.19N 50.40E
116 I12 **Paranéstio** Anatolikí Makedonía kai Thráki, NE Greece 41.16N 24.31E
203 W11 **Paraoa** atoll Îles Tuamotu, C French Polynesia
192 L13 **Paraparaumu** Wellington, North Island, NZ 40.55S 175.01E
59 N20 **Parapetí, Río** ≈ SE Bolivia
56 L10 **Paraque, Cerro** ▲ W Venezuela 6.00S 67.00W
160 I11 **Parasiya** Madhya Pradesh, C India 22.11N 78.47E
117 M23 **Paraspóri, Akrotírio** headland Kárpathos, SE Greece 35.54N 27.15E
62 O10 **Parati** Rio de Janeiro, SE Brazil 23.15S 44.42W
61 K14 **Parauapebas** Pará, N Brazil 6.03S 49.48W
105 Q10 **Paray-le-Monial** Saône-et-Loire, C France 46.27N 4.07E
Parbatsar see Parvatsar
160 G13 **Parbhani** Mahārāshtra, C India 19.16N 76.51E
102 L10 **Parchim** Mecklenburg-Vorpommern, N Germany 53.25N 11.51E
Parchwitz see Prochowice
112 P13 **Parczew** Lubelskie, E Poland 51.39N 22.59E
62 L8 **Pardo, Rio** ≈ S Brazil
113 E16 **Pardubice** Ger. Pardubitz. Pardubický Kraj, C Czech Republic 50.01N 15.46E
113 E17 **Pardubický Kraj** ◈ region C Czech Republic
Pardubitz see Pardubice
121 F16 **Parechcha** Pol. Porzecze, Rus. Porech'ye. Hrodzyenskaya Voblasts', W Belarus 53.51N 24.07E
61 F17 **Parecis, Chapada dos** var. Serra dos Parecis. ▲▲ W Brazil
Parecis, Serra dos see Parecis, Chapada dos
106 M4 **Paredes de Nava** Castilla-León, N Spain 42.09N 4.42W
201 U12 **Parem** island Chuuk, C Micronesia
201 O12 **Parem Island** island E Micronesia
192 I1 **Parengarenga Harbour** inlet North Island, NZ
13 N8 **Parent** Quebec, SE Canada 47.55N 74.36W
104 J14 **Parentis-en-Born** Landes, SW France 44.22N 1.04W
Parenzo see Poreč
193 G20 **Pareora** Canterbury, South Island, NZ 44.28S 171.12E
175 P12 **Parepare** Sulawesi, C Indonesia 4.00S 119.40E
117 B16 **Párga** Ípeiros, W Greece 39.18N 20.19E
95 K20 **Pargas** Swe. Parainen. Länsi-Suomi, W Finland 60.18N 22.19E
66 O5 **Pargo, Ponta do** headland Madeira, Portugal, NE Atlantic Ocean 32.48N 17.16W
Paria, Golfo de see Paria, Gulf of
57 N6 **Pariaguán** Anzoátegui, NE Venezuela 8.51N 64.43W
47 X17 **Paria, Gulf of** var. Golfo de Paria. gulf Trinidad and Tobago/Venezuela
59 I15 **Pariamanu, Río** ≈ E Peru
38 L8 **Paria River** ≈ Utah, W USA
Parichi see Parychy
42 M14 **Paricutín, Volcán** ⊼ C Mexico 19.25N 102.20W
45 S16 **Parida, Isla** island SW Panama
57 T8 **Parika** NE Guyana 6.51N 58.25W
95 O18 **Parikkala** Etelä-Suomi, S Finland 61.33N 29.33E
60 E10 **Parima, Serra** var. Sierra Parima. ▲▲ Brazil/Venezuela see also Parima, Sierra
57 N11 **Parima, Sierra** var. Serra Parima. ▲▲ Brazil/Venezuela see also Parima, Serra
59 F17 **Parinacochas, Laguna** ◎ SW Peru
58 A9 **Pariñas, Punta** headland NW Peru 4.45S 81.22W
60 H12 **Parintins** Amazonas, N Brazil 2.37S 56.45W
105 O5 **Paris** anc. Lutetia, Lutetia Parisiorum, Parisii. ● (France) Paris, N France 48.52N 2.19E
203 Y2 **Paris** Kiritimati, E Kiribati 1.55N 95.30W
29 S11 **Paris** Arkansas, C USA 35.17N 93.43W
35 S16 **Paris** Idaho, NW USA 42.14N 111.24W
33 N14 **Paris** Illinois, N USA 39.36N 87.42W
22 M5 **Paris** Kentucky, S USA 38.12N 84.15W
29 V3 **Paris** Missouri, C USA 39.28N 92.00W
22 H8 **Paris** Tennessee, S USA 36.18N 88.19W
27 V5 **Paris** Texas, SW USA 33.40N 95.33W
Parisii see Paris
45 S16 **Parita** Herrera, S Panama 7.59N 80.31W
45 S16 **Parita, Bahía de** bay S Panama
Parkan/Párkány see Štúrovo
95 K18 **Parkano** Länsi-Suomi, W Finland 62.03N 23.00E
29 N6 **Park City** Kansas, C USA 37.48N 97.19W
38 L3 **Park City** Utah, W USA 40.39N 111.30W
38 I12 **Parker** Arizona, SW USA 34.07N 114.16W
25 R9 **Parker** Florida, SE USA 30.07N 85.36W
31 R11 **Parker** South Dakota, N USA 43.24N 97.08W
37 Z14 **Parker Dam** California, W USA 34.17N 114.08W
31 W13 **Parkersburg** Iowa, C USA 42.34N 92.47W
23 Q3 **Parkersburg** West Virginia, NE USA 39.15N 81.33W
31 T7 **Parkers Prairie** Minnesota, N USA 46.09N 95.19W
179 R17 **Parker Volcano** ⊼ Mindanao, S Philippines 6.09N 124.52E
189 W13 **Parkes** New South Wales, SE Australia 33.09S 148.10E
32 K4 **Park Falls** Wisconsin, N USA 45.57N 90.25W
Parkhar see Farkhor
12 E16 **Parkhill** Ontario, S Canada 43.11N 81.39W
31 T5 **Park Rapids** Minnesota, N USA 46.55N 95.03W
31 Q3 **Park River** North Dakota, N USA 48.24N 97.44W
31 Q11 **Parkston** South Dakota, N USA 43.24N 97.58W
8 L17 **Parksville** Vancouver Island, British Columbia, SW Canada 49.13N 124.13W
39 S3 **Parkview Mountain** ▲ Colorado, C USA 40.19N 106.08W
107 N8 **Parla** Madrid, C Spain 40.13N 3.48W
31 S8 **Parle, Lac qui** ⊠ Minnesota, N USA
117 F20 **Parlía Tyroú** Pelopónnisos, S Greece 37.17N 22.50E
161 G14 **Parli Vaijnāth** Mahārāshtra, C India 18.52N 76.36E
108 F9 **Parma** Emilia-Romagna, N Italy 44.49N 10.19E
33 T11 **Parma** Ohio, N USA 41.24N 81.43W
Parnahyba see Parnaíba
60 N13 **Parnaíba** var. Parnahyba. Piauí, E Brazil 2.58S 41.46W
67 J14 **Parnaíba Ridge** undersea feature C Atlantic Ocean
60 N13 **Parnaíba, Rio** ≈ NE Brazil
117 F18 **Parnassós** ▲ C Greece
193 J17 **Parnassus** Canterbury, South Island, NZ 42.41S 173.18E
190 H10 **Parndana** South Australia 35.48S 137.13E
117 H19 **Párnitha** ▲ C Greece
117 F21 **Párnon** ▲▲ S Greece
120 G5 **Pärnu** Ger. Pernau, Latv. Pērnava; prev. Rus. Pernov. Pärnumaa, SW Estonia 58.23N 24.31E
120 G6 **Pärnu** var. Parnu Jōgi, Ger. Pernau. ≈ SW Estonia
120 G5 **Pärnu-Jaagupi** Ger. Sankt-Jakobi. Pärnumaa, SW Estonia 58.36N 24.30E
Parnu Jōgi see Pärnu
120 G5 **Pärnu Laht** Ger. Pernauer Bucht. bay SW Estonia
120 F5 **Pärnumaa** off. Pärnu Maakond. ◈ province SW Estonia
159 T11 **Paro** W Bhutan 27.22N 89.31E
159 T11 **Paro** ✕ (Thimphu) W Bhutan 27.22N 89.31E
193 G17 **Paroa** West Coast, South Island, NZ 42.31S 171.10E
169 X14 **P'aro-ho** var. Hwach'ŏn-chŏsuji. ⊠ N South Korea
191 N6 **Paroo River** seasonal river New South Wales/Queensland, SE Australia
Paropamisus Range see Sefīdkūh, Selseleh-ye
117 J21 **Páros** Páros, Kykládes, Greece, Aegean Sea 37.04N 25.09E
117 J21 **Páros** island Kykládes, Greece, Aegean Sea
38 K7 **Parowan** Utah, W USA 37.50N 112.49W
105 U13 **Parpaillon** ▲▲ SE France
110 I9 **Parpan** Graubünden, S Switzerland 46.46N 9.32E
64 G13 **Parral** Maule, C Chile 36.07S 71.47W
Parral see Hidalgo del Parral
191 T9 **Parramatta** New South Wales, SE Australia 33.49S 150.58E
23 Y6 **Parramore Island** island Virginia, NE USA
42 M8 **Parras** var. Parras de la Fuente. Coahuila de Zaragoza, NE Mexico 25.26N 102.07W
Parras de la Fuente see Parras
44 M14 **Parrita** Puntarenas, S Costa Rica 9.33N 84.20W
12 G13 **Parry Island** island Ontario, S Canada
207 O9 **Parry Islands** island group Nunavut, NW Canada
12 G12 **Parry Sound** Ontario, S Canada 45.21N 80.03W
112 F7 **Parsęta** Ger. Persante. ≈ NW Poland
30 L3 **Parshall** North Dakota, N USA 47.57N 102.07W
29 Q7 **Parsons** Kansas, C USA 37.20N 95.15W
22 H9 **Parsons** Tennessee, S USA 35.39N 88.07W
23 T3 **Parsons** West Virginia, NE USA 39.06N 79.40W
Parsonstown see Birr
102 P11 **Parsteiner See** ◎ NE Germany
109 I24 **Partanna** Sicilia, Italy, C Mediterranean Sea 37.43N 12.54E
110 J8 **Partenen** Graubünden, E Switzerland 46.58N 10.01E
104 K9 **Parthenay** Deux-Sèvres, W France 46.39N 0.13W
97 J19 **Partille** Västra Götaland, S Sweden 57.43N 12.12E
109 I23 **Partinico** Sicilia, Italy, C Mediterranean Sea 38.03N 13.07E
113 I20 **Partizánske** prev. Šimonovany; Hung. Simony. Trenčiansky Kraj, W Slovakia 48.39N 18.22E
60 H11 **Paru de Oeste, Rio** ≈ N Brazil
190 K9 **Paruna** South Australia 34.45S 140.43E
60 I11 **Paru, Rio** ≈ N Brazil
Parvān see Parwān
161 M14 **Pārvatīpuram** Andhra Pradesh, E India 17.01N 81.47E
158 G12 **Parvatsar** prev. Parbatsar. Rājasthān, N India 26.52N 74.49E
155 Q5 **Parwān** Per. Parvān. ◈ province E Afghanistan
164 I15 **Paryang** Xizang Zizhiqu, W China 30.04N 83.28E
121 M18 **Parychy** Rus. Parichi. Homyel'skaya Voblasts', SE Belarus 52.48N 29.25E
85 J21 **Parys** Free State, C South Africa 26.51S 27.28E
37 T15 **Pasadena** California, W USA 34.09N 118.09W
27 W11 **Pasadena** Texas, SW USA 29.41N 95.12W
58 B8 **Pasaje** El Oro, SW Ecuador 3.17S 79.45W
143 T9 **P'asanauri** N Georgia 42.21N 44.40E
173 G10 **Pasapuat** Pulau Pagai Utara, W Indonesia 2.36S 99.58E
178 Gg7 **Pasawng** Kayah State, C Myanmar 18.50N 97.16E
116 L13 **Paşayiğit** Edirne, NW Turkey 40.58N 26.38E
25 N9 **Pascagoula** Mississippi, S USA 30.21N 88.31W
24 M8 **Pascagoula River** ≈ Mississippi, S USA
118 F12 **Paşcani** Hung. Páskán. Iaşi, NE Romania 47.13N 26.46E
111 T4 **Pasching** Oberösterreich, N Austria 48.16N 14.10E
34 K10 **Pasco** Washington, NW USA 46.13N 119.06W
58 E13 **Pasco** off. Departamento de Pasco. ◈ department C Peru
203 N11 **Pascua, Isla de** var. Rapa Nui, Eng. Easter Island. island E Pacific Ocean
65 G21 **Pascua, Río** ≈ S Chile
105 N1 **Pas-de-Calais** ◈ department N France
102 P10 **Pasewalk** Mecklenburg-Vorpommern, NE Germany 53.30N 13.58E
9 T10 **Pasfield Lake** ◎ Saskatchewan, C Canada
Pa-shih Hai-hsia see Bashi Channel
Pashkeni see Bolyarovo
Pashmakli see Smolyan
179 P10 **Pasig** Luzon, N Philippines 14.34N 121.04E
159 X10 **Pāsighāt** Arunāchel Pradesh, NE India 28.08N 95.13E
143 Q12 **Pasinler** Erzurum, NE Turkey 39.58N 41.40E
Pasi Oloy, Qatorkŭhi see Zaalayskiy Khrebet
44 E3 **Pasión, Río de la** ≈ N Guatemala
174 Gg10 **Pasirganting** Sumatera, W Indonesia 2.04S 100.51E
Pasirpangarayan see Bagansiapiapi
174 H2 **Pasir Puteh** var. Pasir Putih. Kelantan, Peninsular Malaysia 5.49N 102.24E
174 L6 **Pasir, Tanjung** headland East Malaysia 2.24N 111.12E
97 N20 **Påskallavik** Kalmar, S Sweden 57.10N 16.25E
Páskán see Paşcani
112 K7 **Pasłęk** Ger. Preußisch Holland. Warmińsko-Mazurskie, NE Poland 54.03N 19.39E
112 K7 **Pasłęka** Ger. Passarge. ≈ N Poland
154 K16 **Pasni** Baluchistān, SW Pakistan 25.13N 63.30E
65 I18 **Paso de Indios** Chubut, S Argentina 43.52S 69.06W
56 L7 **Paso del Caballo** Guárico, N Venezuela 8.19N 67.07W
63 E15 **Paso de los Libres** Corrientes, NE Argentina 29.39S 57.04W
63 E18 **Paso de los Toros** Tacuarembó, C Uruguay 32.45S 56.30W
37 P12 **Paso Robles** California, W USA 35.37N 120.42W
13 Y7 **Paspébiac** Quebec, SE Canada 48.03N 65.10W
9 U14 **Pasquia Hills** ▲▲ Saskatchewan, S Canada
155 W7 **Pasrūr** Punjab, E Pakistan 32.12N 74.42E
32 M1 **Passage Island** island Michigan, N USA
67 B24 **Passage Islands** island group W Falkland Islands
15 I1 **Passage Point** headland Banks Island, Northwest Territories, NW Canada 73.31N 115.12W
Passarge see Pasłęka
117 C15 **Passarón** ancient monument Ípeiros, W Greece 39.41N 20.43E
Passarowitz see Požarevac
103 O22 **Passau** Bayern, SE Germany 48.34N 13.28E
24 M9 **Pass Christian** Mississippi, S USA 30.19N 89.15W
109 L26 **Passero, Capo** headland Sicilia, Italy, C Mediterranean Sea 36.40N 15.09E
179 Q13 **Passi** Panay Island, C Philippines 11.05N 122.37E
63 H14 **Passo Fundo** Rio Grande do Sul, S Brazil 28.16S 52.19W
62 H13 **Passo Fundo, Barragem de** ⊠ S Brazil
63 H15 **Passo Real, Barragem de** ⊠ S Brazil
61 L20 **Passos** Minas Gerais, NE Brazil 20.45S 46.37W
178 M11 **Passu Keah** island S Paracel Islands
120 J13 **Pastavy** Pol. Postawy, Rus. Postavy. Vitsyebskaya Voblasts', NW Belarus 55.07N 26.50E
58 D7 **Pastaza** ◈ province E Ecuador
58 D9 **Pastaza, Río** ≈ Ecuador/Peru
63 A21 **Pasteur** Buenos Aires, E Argentina 35.10S 62.13W
13 V3 **Pasteur** ≈ Quebec, SE Canada
153 Q12 **Pastigav** Rus. Pastigov. W Tajikistan 39.27N 69.16E
Pastigov see Pastigav
56 C13 **Pasto** Nariño, SW Colombia 1.12N 77.16W
40 M10 **Pastol Bay** bay Alaska, USA
39 O8 **Pastora Peak** ▲ Arizona, SW USA 36.48N 109.10W
107 O8 **Pastrana** Castilla-La Mancha, C Spain 40.24N 2.55W
174 M15 **Pasuruan** prev. Pasoeroean. Jawa, C Indonesia 7.37S 112.43E
120 F11 **Pasvalys** Pasvalys, N Lithuania 56.03N 24.24E
113 K21 **Pásztó** Nógrád, N Hungary 47.57N 19.41E
201 U12 **Pata** var. Patta. atoll Chuuk Islands, C Micronesia
38 M16 **Patagonia** Arizona, SW USA 31.32N 110.45W
65 H20 **Patagonia** physical region Argentina/Chile
Patalung see Phatthalung
160 D9 **Pātan** Gujarāt, W India 23.51N 72.10E
160 J10 **Pātan** Madhya Pradesh, C India 23.19N 79.41E
175 Tt8 **Patani** Pulau Halmahera, E Indonesia 0.19N 128.46E
Patani see Pattani
13 V7 **Patapédia Est** ≈ Quebec, SE Canada
118 K13 **Pătârlagele** prev. Pătîrlagele. Buzău, SE Romania 45.19N 26.21E
Patavium see Padova
190 I5 **Patawarta Hill** ▲ South Australia 30.57S 138.42E
190 L10 **Patchewollock** Victoria, SE Australia 35.24S 142.11E
192 K11 **Patea** Taranaki, North Island, NZ 39.48S 174.35E
192 K11 **Patea** ≈ North Island, NZ
79 U15 **Pategi** Kwara, C Nigeria 8.39N 5.46E
83 K20 **Pate Island** var. Patta Island. island SE Kenya
107 S10 **Paterna** País Valenciano, E Spain 39.30N 0.24W
111 R9 **Paternion** Slvn. Špatrjan. Kärnten, S Austria 46.40N 13.43E
109 L24 **Paternò** anc. Hybla, Hybla Major. Sicilia, Italy, C Mediterranean Sea 37.34N 14.55E
34 J7 **Pateros** Washington, NW USA 48.01N 119.55W
20 J14 **Paterson** New Jersey, NE USA 40.54N 74.11W
34 J10 **Paterson** Washington, NW USA 45.56N 119.37W
193 C25 **Paterson Inlet** inlet Stewart Island, NZ
100 N6 **Paterswolde** Drenthe, NE Netherlands 53.07N 6.32E
158 H7 **Pathānkot** Himāchal Pradesh, N India 32.16N 75.43E
Pathein see Bassein
35 W15 **Pathfinder Reservoir** ⊠ Wyoming, C USA
178 Hh11 **Pathum Thani** var. Patumdhani, Prathum Thani, Pathum Thani. C Thailand 14.03N 100.28E
174 L14 **Pati** Jawa, C Indonesia 6.45S 111.00E
56 C12 **Patía** var. El Bordo. Cauca, SW Colombia 2.06N 77.02W
158 I9 **Patiāla** var. Puttiala. Punjab, NW India 30.21N 76.27E
56 B12 **Patía, Río** ≈ SW Colombia
175 T8 **Patinti, Selat** strait Maluku, E Indonesia
196 D15 **Pati Point** headland NE Guam 13.36N 144.39E
Pătîrlagele see Pătârlagele
58 C13 **Pativilca** Lima, W Peru 10.40S 77.52W
178 Gg1 **Pātkai Bum** var. Patkai Range. ▲▲ Myanmar/India
Patkai Range see Pātkai Bum
117 L20 **Pátmos** Pátmos, Dodekánisos, Greece, Aegean Sea 37.18N 26.32E
117 L20 **Pátmos** island Dodekánisos, Greece, Aegean Sea
159 P13 **Patna** var. Azimabad. Bihār, N India 25.36N 85.11E
160 M12 **Patnāgarh** Orissa, E India 20.42N 83.12E
179 Pp13 **Patnongon** Panay Island, C Philippines 10.56N 122.03E
143 S13 **Patnos** Ağrı, E Turkey 39.13N 42.52E
62 H12 **Pato Branco** Paraná, S Brazil 26.15S 52.40W
33 O16 **Patoka Lake** ◎ Indiana, N USA
94 L9 **Patoniva** Lapp. Buoddobohki. Lappi, N Finland 69.44N 27.01E
115 K21 **Patos** var. Patosi. Fier, SW Albania 40.40N 19.37E
Patos see Patos de Minas
61 K19 **Patos de Minas** var. Patos. Minas Gerais, NE Brazil 18.34S 46.31W
Patosi see Patos
63 I17 **Patos, Lagoa dos** lagoon S Brazil
64 J9 **Patquía** La Rioja, C Argentina 30.01S 66.54W
117 E19 **Pátra** Eng. Patras; prev. Pátrai. Dytikí Ellás, S Greece 38.13N 21.45E
Pátrai/Patras see Pátra
117 D18 **Patraïkós Kólpos** gulf S Greece
94 G2 **Patreksfjördhur** Vestfirdhir, W Iceland 65.33N 23.54W
26 M7 **Patricia** Texas, SW USA 32.34N 102.00W
65 F21 **Patricio Lynch, Isla** island S Chile
Patta see Pata
Patta Island see Pate Island
178 Hh17 **Pattani** var. Patani. Pattani, SW Thailand 6.50N 101.18E
178 Hh12 **Pattaya** Chon Buri, S Thailand 12.55N 100.55E
21 S4 **Patten** Maine, NE USA 45.58N 68.27W
37 O9 **Patterson** California, W USA 37.27N 121.07W
24 J10 **Patterson** Louisiana, S USA 29.41N 91.18W
37 R7 **Patterson, Mount** ▲ California, W USA 38.27N 119.16W
33 P4 **Patterson, Point** headland Michigan, N USA 45.58N 85.39W
109 L23 **Patti** Sicilia, Italy, C Mediterranean Sea 38.07N 14.59E
109 L23 **Patti, Golfo di** gulf Sicilia, Italy, C Mediterranean Sea
95 L14 **Pattijoki** Oulu, W Finland 64.41N 24.40E
199 Mm5 **Patton Escarpment** undersea feature E Pacific Ocean
29 S2 **Pattonsburg** Missouri, C USA 40.03N 94.08W
(0) D6 **Patton Seamount** undersea feature NE Pacific Ocean 54.40N 150.30W
8 J12 **Pattullo, Mount** ▲ British Columbia, W Canada 56.18N 129.43W
Patuakhali see Patukhali
44 M5 **Patuca, Río** ≈ E Honduras
159 U16 **Patukhali** var. Patuakhali. Khulna, S Bangladesh 22.19N 90.19E
Patumdhani see Pathum Thani
42 M14 **Pátzcuaro** Michoacán de Ocampo, SW Mexico 19.30N 101.36W
44 C6 **Patzicía** Chimaltenango, S Guatemala 14.37N 90.54W
104 K16 **Pau** Pyrénées-Atlantiques, SW France 43.18N 0.22W
104 J12 **Pauillac** Gironde, SW France 45.12N 0.44W
177 Ff5 **Pauk** Magwe, W Myanmar 21.25N 94.30E
15 H3 **Paulatuk** Northwest Territories, NW Canada 69.23N 124.00W
44 K5 **Paulaya, Río** ≈ NE Honduras
24 M6 **Paulding** Mississippi, S USA 32.01N 89.01W
33 Q12 **Paulding** Ohio, N USA 41.08N 84.34W
31 S12 **Paullina** Iowa, C USA 42.58N 95.41W
61 P15 **Paulo Afonso** Bahia, E Brazil 9.21S 38.13W
40 M16 **Pauloff Harbor** var. Pavlor Harbour. Sanak Island, Alaska, USA 54.26N 162.43W
29 N12 **Pauls Valley** Oklahoma, C USA 34.44N 97.13W
177 Ff7 **Paungde** Pegu, C Myanmar 18.30N 95.30E
Pauni see Paoni
158 K9 **Pauri** Uttar Pradesh, N India 30.07N 78.48E
Pautalia see Kyustendil
176 Z11 **Pauwasi** ≈ Papua, E Indonesia
148 J5 **Pāveh** Kermānshāh, NW Iran 35.01N 46.15E
130 L5 **Pavelets** Ryazanskaya Oblast', W Russian Federation 53.47N 39.22E
108 D8 **Pavia** anc. Ticinum. Lombardia, N Italy 45.10N 9.10E
120 C9 **Pāvilosta** Liepāja, W Latvia 56.52N 21.12E
129 P14 **Pavino** Kostromskaya Oblast', NW Russian Federation 59.10N 46.09E
116 J8 **Pavlikeni** Veliko Tŭrnovo, N Bulgaria 43.15N 25.20E
151 T8 **Pavlodar** Pavlodar, NE Kazakhstan 52.21N 76.58E
151 S9 **Pavlodar** off. Pavlodarskaya Oblast', Kaz. Pavlodar Oblysy. ◈ province NE Kazakhstan
Pavlodar Oblysy/Pavlodarskaya Oblast' see Pavlodar
Pavlograd see Pavlohrad
119 U7 **Pavlohrad** Rus. Pavlograd. Dnipropetrovs'ka Oblast', E Ukraine 48.32N 35.50E
Pavlor Harbour see Pauloff Harbor
151 R9 **Pavlovka** Akmola, C Kazakhstan 51.22N 72.35E
131 V4 **Pavlovka** Respublika Bashkortostan, W Russian Federation 55.28N 56.36E
131 Q7 **Pavlovka** Ul'yanovskaya Oblast', W Russian Federation 52.40N 47.08E
131 N3 **Pavlovo** Nizhegorodskaya Oblast', W Russian Federation 55.59N 43.03E
130 L9 **Pavlovsk** Voronezhskaya Oblast', W Russian Federation 50.26N 40.08E
130 L13 **Pavlovskaya** Krasnodarskiy Kray, SW Russian Federation 46.06N 39.52E
119 S7 **Pavlysh** Kirovohrads'ka Oblast', C Ukraine 48.54N 33.20E
108 F10 **Pavullo nel Frignano** Emilia-Romagna, C Italy 44.19N 10.52E
29 P8 **Pawhuska** Oklahoma, C USA 36.40N 96.20W
23 U13 **Pawleys Island** South Carolina, SE USA 33.27N 79.07W
178 Gg6 **Pawn** ≈ C Myanmar
32 K14 **Pawnee** Illinois, N USA 39.35N 89.34W
29 O9 **Pawnee** Oklahoma, C USA 36.18N 96.47W
39 U2 **Pawnee Buttes** ▲ Colorado, C USA 40.49N 103.58W
31 S17 **Pawnee City** Nebraska, C USA 40.06N 96.09W
28 K5 **Pawnee River** ≈ Kansas, C USA
33 O10 **Paw Paw** Michigan, N USA 42.12N 86.09W
33 O10 **Paw Paw Lake** Michigan, N USA 42.12N 86.16W
21 O12 **Pawtucket** Rhode Island, NE USA 41.52N 71.22W
Pax Augusta see Badajoz
117 I25 **Paximádia** island SE Greece
Pax Julia see Beja
117 B16 **Paxoí** island Iónioi Nísoi, Greece, C Mediterranean Sea
41 S10 **Paxson** Alaska, USA 62.58N 145.27W
153 O11 **Paxtakor** Jizzax Viloyati, C Uzbekistan 40.21N 67.54E
32 M13 **Paxton** Illinois, N USA 40.27N 88.06W
128 J11 **Pay** Respublika Kareliya, NW Russian Federation 61.10N 34.24E
177 G8 **Payagyi** Pegu, SW Myanmar 17.28N 96.31E
110 C9 **Payerne** Ger. Peterlingen. Vaud, W Switzerland 46.49N 6.57E
34 M13 **Payette** Idaho, NW USA 44.04N 116.55W
34 M13 **Payette River** ≈ Idaho, NW USA
129 V2 **Pay-Khoy, Khrebet** ▲▲ NW Russian Federation

◆ Country ● Country Capital ◇ Dependent Territory ○ Dependent Territory Capital ◈ Administrative Region ✕ International Airport ▲ Mountain ▲▲ Mountain Range ⊼ Volcano ≈ River ◎ Lake ⊠ Reservoir

Payne see Kangirsuk
10 K4 Payne, Lac ◎ Quebec, NE Canada
31 T8 Paynesville Minnesota, N USA 45.22N 94.42W
174 M4 Payong, Tanjung headland East Malaysia 3.46N 113.27E
Payo Obispo see Chetumal
63 D18 Paysandú Paysandú, W Uruguay 32.21S 58.04W
63 D17 Paysandú ◆ department W Uruguay
104 I7 Pays de la Loire ◆ region NW France
38 L12 Payson Arizona, SW USA 34.13N 111.19W
38 L4 Payson Utah, W USA 40.02N 111.43W
129 W4 Payyer, Gora ▲ NW Russian Federation 66.49N 64.33E
Payzawat see Jiashi
143 Q11 Pazar Rize, NE Turkey 41.10N 40.52E
142 F10 Pazarbaşı Burnu headland NW Turkey 41.12N 30.18E
142 M16 Pazarcık Kahramanmaraş, S Turkey 37.31N 37.19E
116 I10 Pazardzhik prev. Tatar Pazardzhik.Pazardzhik, C Bulgaria 42.11N 24.21E
66 H11 Pazardzhik ◆ province C Bulgaria 42.11N 24.21E
56 H9 Paz de Ariporo Casanare, E Colombia 5.51N 71.52W
114 A10 Pazin Ger. Mitterburg, It. Pisino. Istra, NW Croatia 45.14N 13.56E
44 D7 Paz, Río ≈ El Salvador/Guatemala
115 O18 Pčinja ≈ N FYR Macedonia
200 Qq15 Pea Tongatapu, S Tonga 21.10S 175.14W
29 O6 Peabody Kansas, C USA 38.10N 97.06W
9 O12 Peace ≈ Alberta/British Columbia, W Canada
Peace Garden State see North Dakota
9 Q10 Peace Point Alberta, C Canada 59.11N 112.12W
9 O12 Peace River Alberta, W Canada 56.15N 117.18W
25 W13 Peace River ≈ Florida, SE USA
9 N17 Peachland British Columbia, SW Canada 49.49N 119.48W
38 J10 Peach Springs Arizona, SW USA 35.33N 113.27W
Peach State see Georgia
25 S4 Peachtree City Georgia, SE USA 33.24N 84.36W
201 Y13 Peacock Point point SE Wake Island 19.16N 166.39E
99 M18 Peak District physical region C England, UK
191 Q7 Peak Hill New South Wales, SE Australia 32.39S 148.12E
67 G15 Peak, The ▲ C Ascension Island
107 O13 Peal de Becerro Andalucía, S Spain 37.55N 3.07W
201 X11 Peale Island island N Wake Island
39 O6 Peale, Mount ▲ Utah, W USA 38.26N 109.13W
41 O4 Peard Bay bay Alaska, USA
25 Q7 Pea River ≈ Alabama/Florida, S USA
27 W11 Pearland Texas, SW USA 29.33N 95.17W
40 D9 Pearl City Oahu, Hawaii, USA, C Pacific Ocean 21.24N 95.58W
40 D9 Pearl Harbor inlet Oahu, Hawaii, USA, C Pacific Ocean
Pearl Islands see Perlas, Archipiélago de las
Pearl Lagoon see Perlas, Laguna de
24 M5 Pearl River ≈ Louisiana/Mississippi, S USA
27 Q13 Pearsall Texas, SW USA 28.53N 99.05W
25 U7 Pearson Georgia, SE USA 31.18N 82.51W
27 P4 Pease River ≈ Texas, SW USA
10 F7 Peawanuk Ontario, C Canada 54.55N 85.31W
85 P16 Pebane Zambézia, NE Mozambique 17.13S 38.10E
67 C23 Pebble Island island N Falkland Islands
67 C23 Pebble Island Settlement Pebble Island, N Falkland Islands 51.19S 59.40W
115 L16 Peć Alb. Pejë, Turk. Ipek. Serbia, S Serbia and Montenegro (Yugoslavia) 42.40N 20.19E
27 R8 Pecan Bayou ≈ Texas, SW USA
24 H10 Pecan Island Louisiana, S USA 29.39N 92.26W
62 L12 Peças, Ilha das island S Brazil
32 L10 Pecatonica River ≈ Illinois/Wisconsin, N USA
110 G10 Peccia Ticino, S Switzerland 46.24N 8.39E
Pechenegi see Pechenihy
Pechenezhskoye Vodokhranilishche see Pecheniz'ke Vodoskhovyshche
128 I2 Pechenga Fin. Petsamo. Murmanskaya Oblast', NW Russian Federation 69.34N 31.14E
119 V5 Pechenihy Rus. Pechenegi. Kharkivs'ka Oblast', E Ukraine 49.49N 36.57E
119 V5 Pecheniz'ke Vodoskhovyshche Rus. Pechenezhskoye Vodokhranilishche. ⊠ E Ukraine
129 U7 Pechora Respublika Komi, NW Russian Federation 65.08N 57.09E
129 R6 Pechora ≈ NW Russian Federation
Pechora Bay see Pechorskaya Guba
Pechora Sea see Pechorskoye More
129 S3 Pechorskaya Guba Eng. Pechora Bay. bay NW Russian Federation
125 Ff6 Pechorskoye More Eng. Pechora Sea. sea NW Russian Federation
118 E11 Pecica Ger. Petschka, Hung. Ópécska. Arad, W Romania 46.09N 21.06E
26 K8 Pecos Texas, SW USA 31.25N 103.30W
27 N11 Pecos River ≈ New Mexico/Texas, SW USA
113 I25 Pécs Ger. Fünfkirchen; Lat. Sopianae. Baranya, SW Hungary 46.04N 18.11E
45 T17 Pedasí Los Santos, S Panama 7.30N 80.02W
Pedde see Pedja
191 O17 Pedder, Lake ◎ Tasmania, SE Australia
46 M10 Pedernales SW Dominican Republic 17.59N 71.42W
57 Q5 Pedernales Delta Amacuro, NE Venezuela 9.58N 62.15W
27 R10 Pedernales River ≈ Texas, SW USA
64 H6 Pedernales, Salar de salt lake N Chile
Pedhoulas see Pedoulás
57 X11 Pédima var. Malavate. SW French Guiana 3.15N 54.07W
190 F1 Pedirka South Australia 26.41S 135.11E
175 T7 Pedjwang Pulau Halmahera, E Indonesia 1.29N 127.57E
120 I5 Pedja var. Pedja Jõgi, Ger. Pedde. ≈ E Estonia
Pedja Jõgi see Pedja
124 N3 Pedoulás var. Pedhoulas. W Cyprus 34.58N 32.51E
61 N18 Pedra Azul Minas Gerais, NE Brazil 16.01S 41.16W
106 I3 Pedrafita, Porto de var. Puerto de Piedrafita. pass NW Spain 42.43N 7.01W
78 E9 Pedra Lume Sal, NE Cape Verde 16.46N 22.54W
45 P16 Pedregal Chiriquí, W Panama 8.21N 82.26W
56 J4 Pedregal Falcón, N Venezuela 11.01N 70.06W
42 L9 Pedriceña Durango, C Mexico 25.08N 103.46W
62 L11 Pedro Barros São Paulo, S Brazil 24.12S 47.22W
41 Q13 Pedro Bay Alaska, USA 59.47N 154.06W
64 H4 Pedro de Valdivia var. Oficina Pedro de Valdivia. Antofagasta, N Chile 22.33S 69.37W
64 P4 Pedro Juan Caballero Amambay, E Paraguay 22.33S 55.40W
65 L15 Pedro Luro Buenos Aires, E Argentina 39.26S 62.40W
107 O10 Pedro Muñoz Castilla-La Mancha, C Spain 39.25N 2.55W
161 J22 Pedro, Point headland NW Sri Lanka 9.54N 80.08E
190 K9 Peebinga South Australia 34.56S 140.56E
98 J13 Peebles SE Scotland, UK 55.39N 3.14W
33 S15 Peebles Ohio, N USA 38.57N 83.23W
98 J12 Peebles cultural region SE Scotland, UK
20 K13 Peekskill New York, NE USA 41.17N 73.54W
99 I16 Peel W Isle of Man 54.13N 4.04W
14 Ff4 Peel ≈ Northwest Territories/Yukon Territory, NW Canada
15 I1 Peel Point headland Victoria Island, Northwest Territories, NW Canada 73.22N 114.33W
15 K1 Peel Sound passage Nunavut, N Canada
102 N9 Peene ≈ NE Germany
101 K17 Peer Limburg, NE Belgium 51.08N 5.28E
12 H14 Pefferlaw Ontario, S Canada 44.18N 79.11W
193 I18 Pegasus Bay bay South Island, NZ
123 Mm3 Pégeia var. Peyia. SW Cyprus 34.52N 32.24E
111 V7 Peggau Steiermark, SE Austria 47.10N 15.20E
103 L19 Pegnitz Bayern, SE Germany 49.45N 11.33E
103 L19 Pegnitz ≈ SE Germany
107 T11 Pego País Valenciano, E Spain 38.51N 0.07W
177 G8 Pegu var. Bago. Pegu, SW Myanmar 17.18N 96.31E
177 G7 Pegu ◆ division S Myanmar
176 W7 Pegun, Pulau island Kepulauan Mapia, E Indonesia
201 N13 Pehleng Pohnpei, E Micronesia
116 M12 Pehlivanköy Kırklareli, NW Turkey 41.21N 26.56E
79 R14 Péhonko C Benin 10.14N 1.57E
63 B21 Pehuajó Buenos Aires, E Argentina 35.48S 61.52W
Pei-ching see Beijing/Beijing Shi
102 J13 Peine Niedersachsen, C Germany 52.19N 10.13E
Pei-p'ing see Beijing/Beijing Shi
Peipsi Järv/Peipus-See see Peipus, Lake
120 J5 Peipus, Lake Est. Peipsi Järv, Ger. Peipus-See, Rus. Chudskoye Ozero. ◎ Estonia/Russian Federation
117 H19 Peiraías prev. Piraiévs, Eng. Piraeus. Attikí, C Greece 37.56N 23.39E
Peisern see Pyzdry
62 J8 Peixe, Rio do ≈ S Brazil
61 I16 Peixoto de Azevedo Mato Grosso, W Brazil 10.18S 55.03W
174 J8 Pejantan, Pulau island W Indonesia
Pejë see Peć
114 N11 Pek ≈ E Serbia and Montenegro (Yugoslavia)
178 Ii7 Pèk var. Xieng Khouang; prev. Xiangkhoang. Xiangkhoang, N Laos 19.19N 103.22E
174 Kk14 Pekalongan Jawa, C Indonesia 6.54S 109.37E
174 Gg7 Pekanbaru var. Pakanbaru. Sumatera, W Indonesia 0.31N 101.27E
32 L12 Pekin Illinois, N USA 40.34N 89.38W
Peking see Beijing/Beijing Shi
Pelabohan Kelang/Pelabuhan Kelang see Pelabuhan Klang
173 G5 Pelabuhan Klang var. Kuala Pelabohan Kelang, Pelabohan Kelang, Pelabuhan Kelang, Port Klang, Port Swettenham. Selangor, Peninsular Malaysia 2.57N 101.24E
174 J15 Pelabuhan Ratu, Teluk bay Jawa, SW Indonesia
123 L12 Pelagie, Isole island group SW Italy
Pelagosa see Palagruža
24 L5 Pelahatchie Mississippi, S USA 32.19N 89.48W
175 N11 Pelaihari var. Pleihari. Borneo, C Indonesia 3.48S 114.45E
105 U14 Pelat, Mont ▲ SE France 44.16N 6.46E
118 F12 Peleaga, Vârful prev. Vîrful Peleaga. ▲ W Romania 45.23N 22.52E
Peleaga, Vîrful see Peleaga, Vârful
126 K12 Peleduy Respublika Sakha (Yakutiya), NE Russian Federation 59.39N 112.36E
12 C18 Pelee Island island Ontario, S Canada
47 Q11 Pelée, Montagne ▲ N Martinique 14.47N 61.10W
12 D18 Pelee, Point headland Ontario, S Canada 41.56N 82.30W
175 R9 Pelei Pulau Peleng, N Indonesia 1.26S 123.27E
Peleliu see Beliliou
175 R9 Peleng, Pulau island Kepulauan Banggai, N Indonesia
175 Qq9 Peleng, Selat strait Sulawesi, C Indonesia
25 T7 Pelham Georgia, SE USA 31.07N 84.09W
113 E18 Pelhřimov Ger. Pilgram. Jihlavský Kraj, C Czech Republic 49.25N 15.13E
41 W13 Pelican Chichagof Island, Alaska, USA 57.52N 136.05W
203 Z3 Pelican Lagoon ◎ Kiritimati, E Kiribati
31 U6 Pelican Lake ◎ Minnesota, N USA
31 V3 Pelican Lake ◎ Minnesota, N USA
32 L5 Pelican Lake ◎ Wisconsin, N USA
46 G1 Pelican Point Grand Bahama Island, N Bahamas 26.39N 78.09W
85 B19 Pelican Point headland W Namibia 22.55S 14.25E
31 S6 Pelican Rapids Minnesota, N USA 46.34N 96.04W
Pelican State see Louisiana
9 U13 Pelikan Narrows Saskatchewan, C Canada 55.11N 102.51W
117 L18 Pelinaío ▲ Chíos, E Greece 38.31N 26.01E
Pelinnaeum see Pelinnaío
117 E16 Pelinnaío anc. Pelinnaeum. ruins Thessalía, C Greece 39.33N 21.45E
115 N20 Pelister ▲ SW FYR Macedonia 41.00N 21.12E
115 G15 Pelješac peninsula S Croatia
94 M12 Pelkosenniemi Lappi, NE Finland 67.06N 27.30E
31 W15 Pella Iowa, C USA 41.24N 92.55W
116 F13 Pélla site of ancient city Kentrikí Makedonía, N Greece 40.46N 22.35E
25 Q3 Pell City Alabama, S USA 33.35N 86.17W
63 A22 Pellegrini Buenos Aires, E Argentina 36.16S 63.07W
94 K12 Pello Lappi, NW Finland 66.47N 24.00E
102 G7 Pellworm island N Germany
8 H6 Pelly ≈ Yukon Territory, NW Canada
15 L3 Pelly Bay Nunavut, N Canada 68.37N 89.45W
8 I8 Pelly Mountains ▲ Yukon Territory, W Canada
Pélmonostor see Beli Manastir
39 P13 Pelona Mountain ▲ New Mexico, SW USA 33.40N 108.06W
Peloponnese/Peloponnesus see Pelopónnisos
117 E20 Pelopónnisos Eng. Peloponnese. ◆ region S Greece
117 E20 Pelopónnisos var. Morea, Eng. Peloponnese; anc. Peloponnesus. peninsula S Greece
109 L23 Peloritani, Monti anc. Pelorus and Neptunius. ▲ Sicilia, Italy, C Mediterranean Sea
109 M22 Peloro, Capo var. Punta del Faro. headland S Italy 38.15N 15.39E
Pelorus and Neptunius see Peloritani, Monti
63 H17 Pelotas Rio Grande do Sul, S Brazil 31.45S 52.19W
63 I14 Pelotas, Rio ≈ S Brazil
94 K10 Peltovuoma Lapp. Bealdovuopmi. Lappi, N Finland 68.23N 24.11E
125 F10 Pelym ≈ C Russian Federation
21 R4 Pemadumcook Lake ◎ Maine, NE USA
174 Kk14 Pemalang Jawa, C Indonesia 6.52S 109.07E
174 K7 Pemangkat var. Pamangkat. Borneo, C Indonesia 1.11N 109.00E
Pemar see Paimio
173 Ff5 Pematangsiantar Sumatera, W Indonesia 2.58N 99.01E
85 Q14 Pemba prev. Port Amelia, Porto Amélia. Cabo Delgado, NE Mozambique 13.00S 40.30E
83 J22 Pemba ◆ region E Tanzania
83 K21 Pemba island E Tanzania
85 Q14 Pemba, Baia de inlet NE Mozambique
83 J21 Pemba Channel channel E Tanzania
188 J14 Pemberton Western Australia 34.27S 116.09E
8 M16 Pemberton British Columbia, SW Canada 50.19N 122.49W
31 Q2 Pembina North Dakota, N USA 48.58N 97.14W
31 Q2 Pembina ≈ Canada/USA
9 P15 Pembina ≈ Alberta, SW Canada
176 Xx15 Pembre Papua, E Indonesia 7.49S 138.01E
12 K12 Pembroke Ontario, SE Canada 45.49N 77.07W
99 H21 Pembroke SW Wales, UK 51.40N 4.55W
25 W6 Pembroke Georgia, SE USA 32.09N 81.35W
23 U11 Pembroke North Carolina, SE USA 34.40N 79.12W
23 R7 Pembroke Virginia, NE USA 37.19N 80.38W
99 H21 Pembroke cultural region SW Wales, UK
Pembuang, Sungai see Seruyan, Sungai
45 S15 Peña Blanca, Cerro ▲ C Panama 8.39N 80.39W
106 K8 Peña de Francia, Sierra de la ▲ W Spain
106 G6 Penafiel var. Peñafiel. Porto, N Portugal 41.12N 8.16W
107 N6 Peñafiel Castilla-León, N Spain 41.36N 4.07W
107 S8 Peñagolosa ▲ E Spain 40.10N 0.15W
107 N7 Peñalara, Pico de ▲ C Spain 40.52N 3.55W
175 Nn5 Penambo, Banjaran var. Banjaran Tama Abu, Penambo Range. ▲ Indonesia/Malaysia
Penambo Range see Penambo, Banjaran
43 O10 Peña Nevada, Cerro ▲ C Mexico 23.46N 99.52W
Penang see Pinang, Pulau, Peninsular Malaysia
Penang see Pinang
Penang see George Town
62 J8 Penápolis São Paulo, S Brazil 21.23S 50.02W
106 L7 Peñaranda de Bracamonte Castilla-León, N Spain 40.54N 5.13W
107 S8 Peñarroya ▲ E Spain 40.24N 0.42W
106 L12 Peñarroya-Pueblonuevo Andalucía, S Spain 38.21N 5.18W
99 K22 Penarth S Wales, UK 51.27N 3.10W
106 K1 Peñas, Cabo de headland N Spain 43.39N 5.52W
65 F20 Penas, Golfo de gulf S Chile
Pen-ch'i see Benxi
81 H14 Pendé var. Logone Oriental. ≈ Central African Republic/Chad
78 I14 Pendembu E Sierra Leone 9.06N 12.12W
31 R13 Pender Nebraska, C USA 42.06N 96.42W
Penderma see Bandırma
34 K11 Pendleton Oregon, NW USA 45.40N 118.47W
34 M7 Pend Oreille, Lake ◎ Idaho, NW USA
34 M7 Pend Oreille River ≈ Idaho/Washington, NW USA
Pendzhikent see Panjakent
Peneius see Pineiós
106 G8 Penela Coimbra, N Portugal 40.01N 8.22W
12 G13 Penetanguishene Ontario, S Canada 44.45N 79.55W
157 H15 Penganga ≈ C India
167 T12 P'engchia Yu island N Taiwan
81 M21 Penge Kasai Oriental, C Dem. Rep. Congo 5.29S 24.38E
Penghu Archipelago/P'enghu Ch'üntao/Penghu Islands see P'enghu Liehtao
167 R14 P'enghu Liehtao var. P'enghu Ch'üntao, Penghu Islands, Eng. Penghu Archipelago, Pescadores, Jap. Hoko-guntō, Hoko-shotō. island group W Taiwan
Penghu Shuidao/P'enghu Shuitao see Pescadores Channel
167 R4 Penglai var. Dengzhou. Shandong, E China 37.48N 120.43E
Peng-pu see Bengbu
Penhsihu see Benxi
Penibético, Sistema see Béticos, Sistemas
106 F10 Peniche Leiria, W Portugal 39.21N 9.22W
175 Nn16 Penida, Nusa island S Indonesia
Peninsular State see Florida
107 T8 Peñíscola País Valenciano, E Spain 40.22N 0.24E
42 M13 Pénjamo Guanajuato, C Mexico 20.20N 101.35W
Penki see Benxi
104 F7 Penmarch, Pointe de headland NW France 47.46N 4.34W
109 L15 Penna, Punta della headland C Italy 42.10N 14.43E
109 K14 Penne Abruzzo, C Italy 42.28N 13.57E
Penner see Penneru
161 J18 Penneru var. Penner. ≈ C India
190 I10 Penneshaw South Australia 35.45S 137.57E
20 C14 Penn Hills Pennsylvania, NE USA 40.28N 79.52W
Penninae, Alpes/Pennine, Alpi see Pennine Alps
110 D11 Pennine Alps Fr. Alpes Pennines, It. Alpi Pennine; Lat. Alpes Penninae. ▲ Italy/Switzerland
Pennine Chain see Pennines
99 L15 Pennines var. Pennine Chain. ▲ N England, UK
Pennines, Alpes see Pennine Alps
23 O8 Pennington Gap Virginia, NE USA 36.45N 83.01W
20 I16 Penns Grove New Jersey, NE USA 39.42N 75.27W
20 I16 Pennsville New Jersey, NE USA 39.37N 75.29W
20 E14 Pennsylvania off. Commonwealth of Pennsylvania; also known as The Keystone State. ◆ state NE USA
20 G10 Penn Yan New York, NE USA 42.39N 77.02W
128 H16 Peno Tverskaya Oblast', W Russian Federation 56.55N 32.44E
21 R7 Penobscot Bay bay Maine, NE USA
21 S5 Penobscot River ≈ Maine, NE USA
190 K12 Penola South Australia 37.24S 140.50E
42 K9 Peñón Blanco Durango, C Mexico 25.12N 100.50W
190 E7 Penong South Australia 31.57S 133.01E
45 S16 Penonomé Coclé, C Panama 8.29N 80.21W
202 L13 Penrhyn atoll N Cook Islands
199 Kk10 Penrhyn Basin undersea feature C Pacific Ocean
191 S9 Penrith New South Wales, SE Australia 33.45S 150.48E
99 K15 Penrith NW England, UK 54.40N 2.43W
25 O9 Pensacola Florida, SE USA 30.25N 87.13W
25 O9 Pensacola Bay bay Florida, SE USA
205 N7 Pensacola Mountains ▲ Antarctica
190 L12 Penshurst Victoria, SE Australia 37.54S 142.19E
197 C12 Pentecost Fr. Pentecôte. island C Vanuatu
13 V4 Pentecôte ≈ Quebec, SE Canada
Pentecôte see Pentecost
13 V4 Pentecôte, Lac ◎ Quebec, SE Canada
15 Gg16 Penticton British Columbia, SW Canada 49.28N 119.37W
98 J6 Pentland Firth strait N Scotland, UK
98 J12 Pentland Hills hill range S Scotland, UK
175 Rr10 Penu Pulau Taliabu, E Indonesia 1.43S 125.09E
161 H18 Penukonda Andhra Pradesh, E India 14.04N 77.38E
177 G7 Penwegon Pegu, C Myanmar 18.13N 96.34E
26 M8 Penwell Texas, SW USA 31.45N 102.32W
99 J21 Pen y Fan ▲ SE Wales, UK 51.52N 3.25W
99 L16 Pen-y-ghent ▲ N England, UK 54.11N 2.15W
175 T12 Penyu, Kepulauan island group E Indonesia
131 O6 Penza Penzenskaya Oblast', W Russian Federation 53.11N 45.00E
99 G25 Penzance SW England, UK 50.07N 5.33W
131 N6 Penzenskaya Oblast' ◆ province W Russian Federation
127 P7 Penzhina ≈ E Russian Federation
127 N17 Penzhinskaya Guba bay E Russian Federation
Penzig see Pieńsk
38 K13 Peoria Arizona, SW USA 33.34N 112.14W
32 L12 Peoria Illinois, N USA 40.41N 89.35W
32 L12 Peoria Heights Illinois, N USA 40.45N 89.34W
33 N11 Peotone Illinois, N USA 41.19N 87.47W
20 J11 Pepacton Reservoir ⊠ New York, NE USA
78 I15 Pepel W Sierra Leone 8.39N 13.04W
32 I6 Pepin, Lake ⊠ Minnesota/Wisconsin, N USA
101 L20 Pepinster Liège, E Belgium 50.34N 5.49E
115 L20 Peqin var. Peqini. Elbasan, C Albania 41.03N 19.46E
Peqini see Peqin
42 D7 Pequeña, Punta headland W Mexico 26.13N 112.34W
174 I11 Perabumulih var. Prabumulih. Sumatera, W Indonesia 3.27S 104.15E
174 Gg4 Perak ◆ state Peninsular Malaysia
174 Gg4 Perak, Sungai ≈ Peninsular Malaysia
107 R7 Perales del Alfambra Aragón, NE Spain 40.38N 1.00W
117 C15 Pérama var. Perama. Ípeiros, W Greece 39.42N 20.51E
94 M13 Perä-Posio Lappi, NE Finland 66.10N 27.56E
13 Z6 Percé Quebec, SE Canada 48.31N 64.15W
13 Z6 Percé, Rocher island Quebec, S Canada
104 L5 Perche, Collines de ▲ N France
111 X4 Perchtoldsdorf Niederösterreich, NE Austria 48.06N 16.16E
188 L6 Percival Lakes lakes Western Australia
107 T3 Perdido, Monte ▲ NE Spain 42.41N 0.01E
25 O8 Perdido River ≈ Alabama/Florida, S USA
Perece Vela Basin see West Mariana Basin
118 G7 Perechyn Zakarpats'ka Oblast', W Ukraine 48.45N 22.28E
56 E10 Pereira Risaralda, W Colombia 4.52N 75.48W
62 I7 Pereira Barreto São Paulo, S Brazil 20.37S 51.07W
61 G15 Pereirinha Pará, N Brazil 8.18S 57.30W
131 N10 Perelazovskiy Volgogradskaya Oblast', SW Russian Federation 49.10N 42.30E
131 S7 Perelyub Saratovskaya Oblast', W Russian Federation 51.52N 50.19E
33 P7 Pere Marquette River ≈ Michigan, N USA
Peremyshl see Podkarpackie
118 I5 Peremyshlyany L'vivs'ka Oblast', W Ukraine 49.42N 24.33E
Pereshchepino see Pereshchepyne
118 L9 Pereshchepyne Rus. Pereshchepino. Dnipropetrovs'ka Oblast', E Ukraine 48.59N 35.21E
128 L16 Pereslavl'-Zalesskiy Yaroslavskaya Oblast', W Russian Federation 56.42N 38.45E
119 Y7 Pereval's'k Luhans'ka Oblast', E Ukraine 48.28N 38.54E
131 U7 Perevolotskiy Orenburgskaya Oblast', W Russian Federation 51.54N 54.05E
127 Nn16 Pereyaslavka Khabarovskiy Kray, SE Russian Federation 47.49N 134.56E
Pereyaslav-Khmel'nitskiy see Pereyaslav-Khmel'nyts'kyy
119 Q5 Pereyaslav-Khmel'nyts'kyy Rus. Pereyaslav-Khmel'nitskiy. Kyyivs'ka Oblast', N Ukraine 50.04N 31.28E
111 U4 Perg Oberösterreich, N Austria 48.15N 14.39E
63 B19 Pergamino Buenos Aires, E Argentina 33.55S 60.37W
108 G6 Pergine Valsugana Ger. Persen. Trentino-Alto Adige, N Italy 46.04N 11.13E
31 S6 Perham Minnesota, N USA 46.35N 95.34W
95 L16 Perho Länsi-Suomi, W Finland 63.15N 24.25E
118 E11 Periam Ger. Perjamosch, Hung. Perjámos. Timiş, W Romania 46.01N 20.54E
13 Q6 Péribonca ≈ Quebec, SE Canada
10 L11 Péribonca, Lac ◎ Quebec, SE Canada
13 Q6 Péribonca, Petite Rivière ≈ Quebec, SE Canada
13 Q7 Péribonka Quebec, SE Canada 48.45N 72.01W
42 I9 Pericos Sinaloa, C Mexico 25.04N 107.40W
174 Kk7 Perigi Borneo, C Indonesia
104 L12 Périgueux anc. Vesuna. Dordogne, SW France 45.12N 0.41E
56 G5 Perijá, Serranía de ▲ Columbia/Venezuela
117 H17 Peristéra island Vóreioi Sporádes, Greece, Aegean Sea
65 H20 Perito Moreno Santa Cruz, S Argentina 46.35S 71.00W
161 G22 Periyal var. Periyār. ≈ SW India
Periyār see Periyal
161 G23 Periyār Lake ◎ S India
Perjámos/Perjamosch see Periam
29 O9 Perkins Oklahoma, C USA 35.58N 97.01W
118 L7 Perkivtsi Chernivets'ka Oblast', W Ukraine 48.28N 26.48E
45 U15 Perlas, Archipiélago de las Eng. Pearl Islands. island group SE Panama
45 O10 Perlas, Cayos de reef SE Nicaragua
45 N9 Perlas, Laguna de Eng. Pearl Lagoon. lagoon E Nicaragua
45 N10 Perlas, Punta de headland E Nicaragua 12.22N 83.30W
102 L11 Perleberg Brandenburg, N Germany 53.04N 11.51E
Perlepe see Prilep
173 G2 Perlis ◆ state Peninsular Malaysia
129 U14 Perm' prev. Molotov. Permskaya Oblast', NW Russian Federation 58.01N 56.10E
115 M22 Përmet var. Përmeti, Prëmet. Gjirokastër, S Albania 40.12N 20.24E
Përmeti see Përmet
129 U15 Permskaya Oblast' ◆ province NW Russian Federation
61 P15 Pernambuco off. Estado de Pernambuco. ◆ state E Brazil
Pernambuco see Recife
Pernambuco Abyssal Plain see Pernambuco Plain
49 Y6 Pernambuco Plain var. Pernambuco Abyssal Plain. undersea feature E Atlantic Ocean
67 K15 Pernambuco Seamounts undersea feature C Atlantic Ocean
190 H6 Pernatty Lagoon salt lake South Australia
Pernau see Pärnu
Pernauer Bucht see Pärnu Laht
Pērnava see Pärnu
116 G9 Pernik prev. Dimitrovo. Pernik, W Bulgaria 42.36N 23.01E
116 G10 Pernik ◆ province W Bulgaria
95 K20 Perniö Swe. Bjärnå. Länsi-Suomi, W Finland 60.13N 23.10E
111 X5 Pernitz Niederösterreich, E Austria 47.54N 15.58E
Pernov see Pärnu
105 O3 Péronne Somme, N France 49.55N 2.57E
12 L8 Péronne, Lac ◎ Quebec, SE Canada
108 A8 Perosa Argentina Piemonte, NE Italy 45.02N 7.10E
43 Q14 Perote Veracruz-Llave, E Mexico 19.31N 97.16W
Pérouse see Perugia
203 W15 Pérouse, Bahía de la bay Easter Island, Chile, E Pacific Ocean
Perovsk see Kyzylorda
105 O17 Perpignan Pyrénées-Orientales, S France 42.40N 2.52E
115 M20 Përrenjas var. Përrenjasi, Prenjas, Prenjasi. Elbasan, E Albania 41.04N 20.34E
Përrenjasi see Përrenjas
94 O2 Perriertoppen ▲ C Svalbard 79.10N 17.01E
27 S6 Perrin Texas, SW USA 32.59N 98.03W
25 Y16 Perrine Florida, SE USA 25.36N 80.21W
39 S12 Perro, Laguna del ◎ New Mexico, SW USA
104 G5 Perros-Guirec Côtes d'Armor, NW France 48.49N 3.28W
25 T9 Perry Florida, SE USA 30.07N 83.34W
25 T5 Perry Georgia, SE USA 32.27N 83.43W
31 U14 Perry Iowa, C USA 41.50N 94.06W
20 E10 Perry New York, NE USA 42.43N 78.00W
29 N9 Perry Oklahoma, C USA 36.17N 97.17W
29 Q3 Perry Lake ⊠ Kansas, C USA
33 R11 Perrysburg Ohio, N USA 41.33N 83.37W
27 O1 Perryton Texas, SW USA 36.24N 100.48W
41 O15 Perryville Alaska, USA 55.55N 159.08W
29 U11 Perryville Arkansas, C USA 35.00N 92.48W
29 Y6 Perryville Missouri, C USA 37.43N 89.51W
Persante see Parsęta
Persen see Pergine Valsugana
Pershay see Pyarshai
119 V7 Pershotravens'k Dnipropetrovs'ka Oblast', E Ukraine 48.19N 36.22E
119 W9 Pershotravneve Donets'ka Oblast', E Ukraine 47.03N 37.20E
Persia see Iran
147 T5 Persian Gulf var. Gulf, The, Ar. Khalīj al 'Arabī, Per. Khalīj-e Fars. gulf SW Asia
Persis see Fārs
97 K22 Perstorp Skåne, S Sweden 56.07N 13.22E
143 O14 Pertek Tunceli, C Turkey 38.52N 39.19E
191 P16 Perth Tasmania, SE Australia 41.39S 147.11E
188 I13 Perth state capital Western Australia 31.58S 115.49E
12 L13 Perth Ontario, SE Canada 44.54N 76.15W
98 J11 Perth C Scotland, UK 56.24N 3.28W
188 I12 Perth ✖ Western Australia 31.51S 116.06E
98 J10 Perth cultural region C Scotland, UK
181 V10 Perth Basin undersea feature SE Indian Ocean
105 S15 Pertuis Vaucluse, SE France 43.42N 5.30E
105 Y16 Pertusato, Capo headland Corse, France, C Mediterranean Sea 41.22N 9.10E
32 L11 Peru Illinois, N USA 41.18N 89.09W
33 P12 Peru Indiana, N USA 40.45N 86.04W
59 E13 Peru off. Republic of Peru. ◆ republic W South America
Peru see Beru
200 Oo10 Peru Basin undersea feature E Pacific Ocean
200 Oo9 Peru-Chile Trench undersea feature E Pacific Ocean
114 F13 Perućko Jezero ◎ S Croatia
108 H13 Perugia Fr. Pérouse; anc. Perusia. Umbria, C Italy 43.06N 12.24E
Perugia, Lake of see Trasimeno, Lago
63 D15 Perugorría Corrientes, NE Argentina 29.21S 58.34W
62 M11 Peruíbe São Paulo, S Brazil 24.18S 47.01W
161 B21 Perumalpār reef India, N Indian Ocean
Perusia see Perugia
101 D20 Péruwelz Hainaut, SW Belgium 50.30N 3.34E
143 R15 Pervari Siirt, SE Turkey 37.58N 42.30E
131 O4 Pervomaysk Nizhegorodskaya Oblast', W Russian Federation 54.52N 43.49E
119 X7 Pervomays'k Luhans'ka Oblast', E Ukraine 48.37N 38.36E
119 P8 Pervomays'k prev. Ol'viopol'. Mykolayivs'ka Oblast', S Ukraine 48.01N 30.51E
119 S12 Pervomays'ke Respublika Krym, S Ukraine 45.43N 33.49E
129 R14 Pervomayskiy Kirovskaya Oblast', NW Russian Federation 59.15N 49.20E
131 V7 Pervomayskiy Orenburgskaya Oblast', W Russian Federation 51.32N 54.58E
130 M6 Pervomayskiy Tambovskaya Oblast', W Russian Federation 53.15N 40.20E
119 V6 Pervomays'kyy Kharkivs'ka Oblast', E Ukraine 49.24N 36.12E
125 E10 Pervoural'sk Sverdlovskaya Oblast', C Russian Federation 56.58N 59.50E
127 Pp12 Pervyy Kuril'skiy Proliv strait E Russian Federation
101 I19 Perwez Wallon Brabant, C Belgium 50.39N 4.49E
108 I11 Pesaro anc. Pisaurum. Marche, C Italy 43.55N 12.52E
37 N9 Pescadero California, W USA 37.15N 122.23W
Pescadores see P'enghu Liehtao
167 S14 Pescadores Channel var. Penghu Shuidao, P'enghu Shuitao. channel W Taiwan
109 K14 Pescara anc. Aternum, Ostia Aterni. Abruzzo, C Italy 42.28N 14.13E
109 K15 Pescara ≈ C Italy
108 F11 Pescia Toscana, C Italy 43.54N 10.40E
110 C8 Peseux Neuchâtel, W Switzerland 46.58N 6.52E
129 P6 Pesha ≈ NW Russian Federation
155 T5 Peshāwar North-West Frontier Province, N Pakistan 34.00N 71.33E
155 T6 Peshāwar ✖ North-West Frontier Province, N Pakistan 34.01N 71.40E
115 M19 Peshkopi var. Peshkopia, Peshkopija. Dibër, NE Albania 41.40N 20.25E
Peshkopia/Peshkopija see Peshkopi
116 I11 Peshtera Pazardzhik, C Bulgaria 42.01N 24.18E
33 N6 Peshtigo Wisconsin, N USA 45.04N 87.43W
33 N6 Peshtigo River ≈ Wisconsin, N USA
Peski see Pyeski
129 S13 Peskovka Kirovskaya Oblast', NW Russian Federation 59.04N 52.17E
105 S8 Pesmes Haute-Saône, E France 47.17N 5.33E
106 H6 Peso da Régua var. Pêso da Regua. Vila Real, N Portugal 41.10N 7.46W
42 F5 Pesqueira Sonora, NW Mexico 29.22N 110.52W
104 J13 Pessac Gironde, SW France 44.46N 0.42W
113 J23 Pest off. Pest Megye. ◆ county C Hungary
128 J14 Pestovo Novgorodskaya Oblast', W Russian Federation 58.37N 35.48E
42 M15 Petacalco, Bahía bay W Mexico
Petach-Tikva/Petah Tiqva see Petah Tiqwa
144 F10 Petah Tiqwa var. Petach-Tikva, Petah Tiqva, Petakh Tikva. Tel Aviv, C Israel 32.04N 34.52E
Petakh Tikva see Petah Tiqwa
95 L17 Petäjävesi Länsi-Suomi, W Finland 62.16N 25.10E
24 M7 Petal Mississippi, S USA 31.21N 89.15W
117 I19 Petalioí island C Greece
117 H19 Petalión, Kólpos gulf E Greece
117 J19 Pétalo ▲ Ándros, Kykládes, Greece, Aegean Sea 37.51N 24.50E
36 M8 Petaluma California, W USA 38.15N 122.37W
101 L25 Pétange Luxembourg, SW Luxembourg 49.33N 5.52E
56 M5 Petare Miranda, N Venezuela 10.29N 66.47W
43 N16 Petatlán Guerrero, S Mexico 17.31N 101.16W
85 L14 Petauke Eastern, E Zambia 14.12S 31.16E
12 J12 Petawawa Ontario, SE Canada 45.53N 77.16W
12 J11 Petawawa ≈ Ontario, SE Canada
Petchaburi see Phetchaburi
44 D2 Petén off. Departamento del Petén. ◆ department N Guatemala
44 D2 Petén Itzá, Lago var. Lago de Flores. ◎ N Guatemala

◆ Country ● Country Capital ◇ Dependent Territory ○ Dependent Territory Capital ◆ Administrative Region ✖ International Airport ▲ Mountain ▲ Mountain Range ▲ Volcano ≈ River ◎ Lake ⊠ Reservoir

32 K7 **Petenwell Lake** ⊟ Wisconsin, N USA
12 D6 **Peterbell** Ontario, S Canada 48.34N 83.19W
190 I7 **Peterborough** South Australia 32.59S 138.50E
12 I14 **Peterborough** Ontario, SE Canada 44.19N 78.19W
99 N20 **Peterborough** *prev.* Medeshamstede. E England, UK 52.34N 0.15W
21 N10 **Peterborough** New Hampshire, NE USA 42.51N 71.54W
98 L8 **Peterhead** NE Scotland, UK 57.30N 1.46W
Peterhof *see* Luboń
199 Mm16 **Peter I Island** ◇ Norwegian dependency Antarctica
204 H9 **Peter I Island** *var.* Peter I øy. *island* Antarctica
Peter I øy *see* Peter I Island
99 M14 **Peterlee** N England, UK 54.45N 1.18W
Peterlingen *see* Payerne
207 P14 **Petermann Bjerg** ▲ C Greenland 73.16N 27.59W
9 S12 **Peter Pond Lake** ◎ Saskatchewan, C Canada
41 X13 **Petersburg** Mytkof Island, Alaska, USA 56.43N 132.51W
32 K13 **Petersburg** Illinois, N USA 40.01N 89.52W
33 N16 **Petersburg** Indiana, N USA 38.30N 87.16W
31 Q3 **Petersburg** North Dakota, N USA 47.59N 97.59W
27 N5 **Petersburg** Texas, SW USA 33.52N 101.36W
23 V7 **Petersburg** Virginia, NE USA 37.13N 77.24W
23 T4 **Petersburg** West Virginia, NE USA 38.59N 79.07W
102 H12 **Petershagen** Nordrhein-Westfalen, NW Germany 52.22N 8.58E
57 S9 **Peters Mine** *var.* Peter's Mine. N Guyana 6.13N 59.18W
109 O21 **Petilia Policastro** Calabria, SW Italy 39.07N 16.48E
46 M9 **Pétionville** S Haiti 18.29N 72.16W
47 X6 **Petit-Bourg** Basse Terre, C Guadeloupe 16.11N 61.34W
13 Y5 **Petit-Cap** Quebec, SE Canada 49.00N 64.26W
47 Y6 **Petit Cul-de-Sac Marin** *bay* C Guadeloupe
10 K7 **Petite Rivière de la Baleine** ≈ Quebec, NE Canada
46 M9 **Petite-Rivière-de-l'Artibonite** C Haiti 19.06N 72.28W
181 X16 **Petite Rivière Noire, Piton de la** ▲ C Mauritius
13 R9 **Petite-Rivière-St-François** Quebec, SE Canada 47.18N 70.34W
46 L9 **Petit-Goâve** S Haiti 18.23N 72.51W
Petitjean *see* Sidi-Kacem
11 N10 **Petit Lac Manicouagan** ◎ Quebec, E Canada
21 T7 **Petit Manan Point** *headland* Maine, NE USA 44.23N 67.54W
Petit Mécatina, Rivière du *see* Little Mecatina
9 N10 **Petitot** ≈ Alberta/British Columbia, W Canada
47 S12 **Petit Piton** ▲ SW Saint Lucia 13.49N 61.03W
Petit-Popo *see* Aného
Petit St-Bernard, Col du *see* Little Saint Bernard Pass
11 O8 **Petitsikapau Lake** ◎ Newfoundland and Labrador, E Canada
94 L11 **Petkula** Lappi, N Finland 67.40N 26.43E
43 X12 **Peto** Yucatán, SE Mexico 20.09N 88.55W
64 G10 **Petorca** Valparaíso, C Chile 32.13S 70.49W
33 Q5 **Petoskey** Michigan, N USA 45.51N 88.03W
144 G14 **Petra** *archaeological site* Ma'ān, W Jordan 30.19N 35.25E
Petra *see* Wādī Mūsā
117 F14 **Pétras, Sténa** *pass* N Greece 40.12N 22.15E
127 Nn18 **Petra Velikogo, Zaliv** *bay* SE Russian Federation
Petrel *see* Petrer
12 K15 **Petre, Point** *headland* Ontario, SE Canada 43.49N 77.07W
107 S12 **Petrer** *var.* Petrel. País Valenciano, E Spain 38.28N 0.46W
129 U11 **Petretsovo** Permskaya Oblast', NW Russian Federation 61.22N 57.21E
116 G12 **Petrich** Blagoevgrad, SW Bulgaria 41.24N 23.12E
197 H3 **Petrie, Récif** *reef* N New Caledonia
39 N11 **Petrified Forest** *prehistoric site* Arizona, SW USA 35.10N 109.49W
Petrikau *see* Piotrków Trybunalski
Petrikov *see* Pyetrykaw
118 H12 **Petrila** *Hung.* Petrilla. Hunedoara, W Romania 45.27N 23.25E
Petrilla *see* Petrila
114 E9 **Petrinja** Sisak-Moslavina, C Croatia 45.27N 16.14E
Petroaleksandrovsk *see* To'rtkok'l
Petrőcz *see* Bački Petrovac
128 G12 **Petrodvorets** *Fin.* Pietarhovi. Leningradskaya Oblast', NW Russian Federation 59.52N 29.52E
Petrograd *see* Sankt-Peterburg
Petrokov *see* Piotrków Trybunalski
56 G6 **Petrólea** Norte de Santander, NE Colombia 8.30N 72.34W
12 D16 **Petrolia** Ontario, S Canada 42.54N 82.07W
27 S4 **Petrolia** Texas, SW USA 34.00N 98.13W
61 O15 **Petrolina** Pernambuco, E Brazil 9.22S 40.30W
47 T6 **Petrona, Punta** *headland* C Puerto Rico 17.57N 66.23W
Petropavel *see* Petropavlovsk
119 V7 **Petropavlivka** Dnipropetrovs'ka Oblast', E Ukraine 48.28N 36.28E
151 P6 **Petropavlovsk** *Kaz.* Petropavl. Severnyy Kazakhstan, N Kazakhstan 54.46N 69.06E
127 Pp11 **Petropavlovsk-Kamchatskiy** Kamchatskaya Oblast', E Russian Federation 53.03N 158.43E
62 P9 **Petrópolis** Rio de Janeiro, SE Brazil 22.30S 43.28W
118 H12 **Petroşani** *var.* Petroşeni, *Ger.* Petroschen, *Hung.* Petrozsény. Hunedoara, W Romania 45.25N 23.22E
Petroschen/Petroşeni *see* Petroşani
Petroskoi *see* Petrozavodsk
Petrovac/Petrovácz *see* Bački Petrovac
115 J17 **Petrovac na Moru** Montenegro, SW Serbia and Montenegro (Yugoslavia) 42.11N 19.00E
119 S8 **Petrove** Kirovohrads'ka Oblast', C Ukraine 48.22N 33.12E
115 O18 **Petrovec** C FYR Macedonia 41.57N 21.37E
Petrovgrad *see* Zrenjanin
131 P7 **Petrovsk** Saratovskaya Oblast', W Russian Federation 52.20N 45.23E
128 J9 **Petrovskiy Yam** Respublika Kareliya, NW Russian Federation 63.19N 35.14E
Petrovsk-Port *see* Makhachkala
126 K16 **Petrovsk-Zabaykal'skiy** Chitinskaya Oblast', S Russian Federation 51.15N 108.36E
131 P9 **Petrov Val** Volgogradskaya Oblast', SW Russian Federation 50.10N 45.16E
128 J11 **Petrozavodsk** *Fin.* Petroskoi. Respublika Kareliya, NW Russian Federation 61.46N 34.19E
Petrozsény *see* Petroşani
85 D20 **Petrusdal** Hardap, C Namibia 23.42S 17.23E
119 T7 **Petrykivka** Dnipropetrovs'ka Oblast', E Ukraine 48.44N 34.42E
Petsamo *see* Pechenga
Petschka *see* Pecica
Pettau *see* Ptuj
111 S5 **Pettenbach** Oberösterreich, C Austria 47.58N 14.03E
27 S13 **Pettus** Texas, SW USA 28.34N 97.49W
125 F13 **Petukhovo** Kurganskaya Oblast', C Russian Federation 55.04N 67.49E
Petuna *see* Songyuan
111 R4 **Peuerbach** Oberösterreich, N Austria 48.19N 13.45E
64 G12 **Peumo** Libertador, C Chile 34.22S 71.58W
173 Ee3 **Peusangan, Krueng** ≈ Sumatera, NW Indonesia
127 O4 **Pevek** Chukotskiy Avtonomnyy Okrug, NE Russian Federation 69.40N 170.19E
29 X5 **Pevely** Missouri, C USA 38.16N 90.24W
Peyia *see* Pégeia
104 J15 **Peyrehorade** Landes, SW France 43.33N 1.04W
128 J14 **Peza** ≈ NW Russian Federation
105 P16 **Pézenas** Hérault, S France 43.28N 3.25E
113 H20 **Pezinok** *Ger.* Bösing, *Hung.* Bazin. Bratislavský Kraj, W Slovakia 48.16N 17.15E
103 L22 **Pfaffenhofen an der Ilm** Bayern, SE Germany 48.31N 11.30E
110 G7 **Pfäffikon** Schwyz, C Switzerland 47.11N 8.46E
103 F20 **Pfälzer Wald** *hill range* W Germany
103 N22 **Pfarrkirchen** Bayern, SE Germany 48.25N 12.56E
103 G21 **Pforzheim** Baden-Württemberg, SW Germany 48.52N 8.42E
103 H24 **Pfullendorf** Baden-Württemberg, S Germany 47.55N 9.16E
110 K8 **Pfunds** Tirol, W Austria 46.56N 10.30E
103 G19 **Pfungstadt** Hessen, W Germany 49.48N 8.36E
85 L20 **Phalaborwa** Limpopo, NE South Africa 23.50S 31.08E
158 E11 **Phalodi** Rājasthān, NW India 27.06N 72.22E
158 E12 **Phalsund** Rājasthān, NW India 26.22N 71.55E
161 E15 **Phaltan** Mahārāshtra, W India 18.01N 74.31E
178 Hh7 **Phan** *var.* Muang Phan. Chiang Rai, NW Thailand 19.34N 99.43E
178 H14 **Phangan, Ko** *island* SW Thailand
178 Gg15 **Phang-Nga** *var.* Pang-Nga, Phangnga. Phangnga, SW Thailand 8.28N 98.31E
Phan Rang/Phanrang *see* Phan Rang-Thap Cham
178 Kk13 **Phan Rang-Thap Cham** *var.* Phanrang, Phan Rang, Phan Rang Thap Cham. Ninh Thuân, S Vietnam 11.34N 109.00E
178 Kk14 **Phan Ri** Binh Thuân, S Vietnam 11.11N 108.31E
178 K14 **Phan Thiêt** Binh Thuân, S Vietnam 10.55N 108.06E
Pharnacia *see* Giresun
27 S17 **Pharr** Texas, SW USA 26.11N 98.10W
Pharus *see* Hvar
178 H16 **Phatthalung** *var.* Padalung, Patalung. Phatthalung, SW Thailand 7.37N 100.04E
178 Hh7 **Phayao** *var.* Muang Phayao. Phayao, NW Thailand 19.10N 99.55E
9 U10 **Phelps Lake** ◎ Saskatchewan, C Canada
23 X9 **Phelps Lake** ◎ North Carolina, SE USA
25 R5 **Phenix City** Alabama, S USA 32.28N 85.00W
178 Jj8 **Pheo** Quang Binh, C Vietnam 17.42N 105.58E
Phet Buri *see* Phetchaburi
178 H12 **Phetchaburi** *var.* Bejraburi, Petchaburi, Phet Buri. Phetchaburi, SW Thailand 13.04N 99.58E
178 Hh9 **Phichit** *var.* Bichitra, Muang Phichit, Pichit. Phichit, C Thailand 16.28N 100.21E
24 M5 **Philadelphia** Mississippi, S USA 32.45N 89.06W
20 I7 **Philadelphia** New York, NE USA 44.10N 75.40W
20 I16 **Philadelphia** Pennsylvania, NE USA 40.00N 75.10W
20 I16 **Philadelphia** ✕ Pennsylvania, NE USA 39.51N 75.13W
Philadelphia *see* 'Ammān
30 L10 **Philip** South Dakota, N USA 44.02N 101.39W
101 H22 **Philippeville** Namur, S Belgium 50.12N 4.33E
Philippeville *see* Skikda
23 S3 **Philippi** West Virginia, NE USA 39.09N 80.02W
Philippi *see* Fílippoi
205 Y9 **Philippi Glacier** *glacier* Antarctica
198 G7 **Philippine Basin** *undersea feature* W Pacific Ocean
133 X12 **Philippine Plate** *tectonic feature*
179 Q13 **Philippines** *off.* Republic of the Philippines. ◆ *republic* SE Asia
133 X13 **Philippines** *island group* W Pacific Ocean
179 S12 **Philippine Sea** *sea* W Pacific Ocean
198 G7 **Philippine Trench** *undersea feature* W Philippine Sea
85 H23 **Philippolis** Free State, C South Africa 30.16S 25.16E
Philippopolis *see* Plovdiv, Bulgaria
Philippopolis *see* Shahbā', Syria
47 V9 **Philipsburg** Sint Maarten, N Netherlands Antilles 17.58N 63.02W
35 P10 **Philipsburg** Montana, NW USA 46.19N 113.17W
41 R6 **Philip Smith Mountains** ▲▲ Alaska, USA
158 H8 **Phillaur** Punjab, N India 31.01N 75.49E
191 N13 **Phillip Island** *island* Victoria, SE Australia
27 N2 **Phillips** Texas, SW USA 35.39N 101.21W
32 K5 **Phillips** Wisconsin, N USA 45.42N 90.22W
28 K3 **Phillipsburg** Kansas, C USA 39.45N 99.19W
20 I14 **Phillipsburg** New Jersey, NE USA 40.39N 75.09W
23 S7 **Philpott Lake** ⊟ Virginia, NE USA
Phintias *see* Licata
178 Hh9 **Phitsanulok** *var.* Bisnulok, Muang Phitsanulok, Pitsanulok. Phitsanulok, C Thailand 16.49N 100.15E
Phlórina *see* Flórina
Phnom Penh *see* Phnum Penh
178 J13 **Phnum Penh** *var.* Phnom Penh. ● (Cambodia) Phnum Penh, S Cambodia 11.34N 104.55E
178 J12 **Phnum Tbêng Meanchey** Preăh Vihéar, N Cambodia 13.45N 104.58E
38 K13 **Phoenix** *state capital* Arizona, SW USA 33.27N 112.04W
Phoenix Island *see* Rawaki
203 R3 **Phoenix Islands** *island group* C Kiribati
20 I15 **Phoenixville** Pennsylvania, NE USA 40.07N 75.31W
85 K22 **Phofung** *var.* Mont-aux-Sources. ▲ N Lesotho 28.47S 28.52E
178 I10 **Phon** Khon Kaen, E Thailand 15.47N 102.35E
178 I5 **Phôngsali** *var.* Phong Saly. Phôngsali, N Laos 21.40N 102.04E
Phong Saly *see* Phôngsali
178 I8 **Phônhông** C Laos 18.29N 102.26E
178 J5 **Phô Rang** Lao Cai, N Vietnam 22.12N 104.27E
Phort Láirge, Cuan *see* Waterford Harbour
178 Gg10 **Phra Chedi Sam Ong** Kanchanaburi, W Thailand 15.18N 98.26E
178 Hh8 **Phrae** *var.* Muang Phrae, Prae. Phrae, NW Thailand 18.07N 100.09E
Phra Nakhon Si Ayutthaya *see* Ayutthaya
177 G15 **Phra Thong, Ko** *island* SW Thailand
Phu Cương *see* Thu Dâu Môt
177 G16 **Phuket** *var.* Bhuket, Puket, *Mal.* Ujung Salang; *prev.* Junkseylon, Salang. Phuket, SW Thailand 7.52N 98.22E
177 G16 **Phuket** ✕ Phuket, SW Thailand 8.03N 98.16E
177 G16 **Phuket, Ko** *island* SW Thailand
160 N12 **Phulabāni** *prev.* Phulbani. Orissa, E India 20.30N 84.18E
Phulbani *see* Phulabāni
178 K10 **Phu Lôc** Th,a Thiên-Huê, C Vietnam 16.13N 107.53E
178 J14 **Phumĭ Banam** Prey Vêng, S Cambodia 11.14N 105.18E
178 Ii13 **Phumĭ Chŏâm** Kâmpóng Spœ, SW Cambodia 11.42N 103.58E
178 Jj11 **Phumĭ Kalêng** Stœng Trêng, NE Cambodia 13.57N 106.17E
178 J12 **Phumĭ Kâmpóng Trâbêk** *prev.* Phum Kompong Trabek. Kâmpóng Thum, C Cambodia 13.06N 105.16E
178 Ii12 **Phumĭ Koŭk Kduŏch** Bătdâmbâng, NW Cambodia 13.16N 103.08E
178 K12 **Phumĭ Labăng** Rôtânôkiri, NE Cambodia 13.51N 107.01E
178 J11 **Phumĭ Mlu Prey** Preăh Vihéar, N Cambodia 13.48N 105.16E
178 Ii11 **Phumĭ Moŭng** Siĕmréab, NW Cambodia 13.45N 103.35E
178 Ii13 **Phumĭ Prâmaôy** Poŭthĭsăt, W Cambodia 12.13N 103.05E
178 I14 **Phumĭ Samĭt** Kaôh Kông, SW Cambodia 10.54N 103.09E
178 Ii11 **Phumĭ Sâmraông** *prev.* Phum Samrong. Siĕmréab, NW Cambodia 14.09N 103.30E
178 Jj12 **Phumĭ Siĕmbok** Stœng Trêng, N Cambodia 13.28N 105.59E
178 Jj12 **Phumĭ Thalabârĭvăt** Stœng Trêng, N Cambodia 13.34N 105.57E
178 Ii14 **Phumĭ Veal Renh** Kâmpôt, SW Cambodia 10.43N 103.49E
178 Ii13 **Phumĭ Yeay Sên** Kaôh Kông, SW Cambodia 11.09N 103.09E
Phum Kompong Trabek *see* Phumĭ Kâmpóng Trâbêk
Phum Samrong *see* Phumĭ Sâmraông
178 Kk11 **Phu My** Binh Đinh, C Vietnam 14.07N 109.05E
178 J15 **Phung Hiêp** Cân Thơ, S Vietnam 9.49N 105.48E
159 T12 **Phuntsholing** SW Bhutan 26.52N 89.25E
178 J15 **Phươc Long** Minh Hai, S Vietnam 9.27N 105.25E
178 Ii14 **Phu Quôc, Đao** *var.* Phu Quoc Island. *island* S Vietnam
Phu Quoc Island *see* Phu Quôc, Đao
178 J6 **Phu Tho** Vinh Phu, N Vietnam 21.22N 105.13E
Phu Vinh *see* Tra Vinh
201 T13 **Piaanu Pass** *passage* Chuuk Islands, C Micronesia
108 E8 **Piacenza** *Fr.* Paisance; *anc.* Placentia. Emilia-Romagna, N Italy 45.01N 9.42E
109 K14 **Pianella** Abruzzo, C Italy 42.23N 14.04E
109 M15 **Pianosa, Isola** *island* Archipelago Toscano, C Italy
176 Vv11 **Piar** Papua, E Indonesia 2.49S 132.46E
47 U14 **Piarco** *var.* Port of Spain. ✕ (Port-of-Spain) Trinidad, Trinidad and Tobago 10.36N 61.21W
112 M12 **Piaseczno** Mazowieckie, C Poland 52.04N 21.05E
118 I15 **Piatra** Teleorman, S Romania 43.49N 25.10E
118 L10 **Piatra-Neamţ** *Hung.* Karácsonkő. Neamţ, NE Romania 46.54N 26.23E
Piauhy *see* Piauí
61 N15 **Piauí** *off.* Estado do Piauí; *prev.* Piauhy. ◈ *state* E Brazil
108 I7 **Piave** ≈ NE Italy
109 K24 **Piazza Armerina** *var.* Chiazza. Sicilia, Italy, C Mediterranean Sea 37.22N 14.22E
83 G14 **Pibor** *Amh.* Pībor Wenz. ≈ Ethiopia/Sudan
83 G14 **Pibor Post** Jonglei, SE Sudan 6.49N 33.06E
Pībor Wenz *see* Pibor
Pibrans *see* Příbram
38 K11 **Picacho Butte** ▲ Arizona, SW USA 35.12N 112.44W
42 D4 **Picachos, Cerro** ▲ NW Mexico 29.15N 114.04W
105 O4 **Picardie** *Eng.* Picardy. ◈ *region* N France
Picardy *see* Picardie
24 L8 **Picayune** Mississippi, S USA 30.31N 89.40W
Piccolo San Bernardo, Colle di *see* Little Saint Bernard Pass
64 K5 **Pichanal** Salta, N Argentina 23.22S 64.11W
153 P12 **Pichandar** W Tajikistan 38.44N 68.51E
29 R8 **Picher** Oklahoma, C USA 36.59N 94.49W
64 G12 **Pichilemu** Libertador, C Chile 34.25S 72.00W
42 F9 **Pichilingue** Baja California Sur, W Mexico 24.19N 110.16W
58 B6 **Pichincha** ◈ *province* N Ecuador
58 C6 **Pichincha** ▲ N Ecuador 0.12S 78.39W
Pichit *see* Phichit
43 U15 **Pichucalco** Chiapas, SE Mexico 17.32N 93.07W
24 L5 **Pickens** Mississippi, S USA 32.52N 89.58W
23 O11 **Pickens** South Carolina, SE USA 34.52N 82.42W
12 G11 **Pickerel** ≈ Ontario, S Canada
12 H15 **Pickering** Ontario, S Canada 43.50N 79.03W
99 N16 **Pickering** N England, UK 54.14N 0.46W
33 S13 **Pickerington** Ohio, N USA 39.52N 82.45W
10 C10 **Pickle Lake** Ontario, C Canada 51.30N 90.10W
31 P12 **Pickstown** South Dakota, N USA 43.02N 98.31W
27 V6 **Pickton** Texas, SW USA 33.01N 95.19W
25 N1 **Pickwick Lake** ⊟ S USA
66 N2 **Pico** *var.* Ilha do Pico. *island* Azores, Portugal, NE Atlantic Ocean
65 J19 **Pico de Salamanca** Chubut, SE Argentina 45.26S 67.26W
1 P9 **Pico Fracture Zone** *tectonic feature* NW Atlantic Ocean
Pico, Ilha do *see* Pico
61 O14 **Picos** Piauí, E Brazil 7.04S 41.24W
65 I20 **Pico Truncado** Santa Cruz, SE Argentina 46.49S 68.01W
191 S9 **Picton** New South Wales, SE Australia 34.12S 150.36E
12 K15 **Picton** Ontario, SE Canada 43.59N 77.09W
193 K14 **Picton** Marlborough, South Island, NZ 41.18S 174.00E
65 H15 **Picún Leufú, Arroyo** ≈ SW Argentina
Pidálion *see* Gkréko, Akrotíri
161 K25 **Pidurutalagala** ▲ S Sri Lanka 7.03N 80.47E
118 K6 **Pidvolochys'k** Ternopil's'ka Oblast', W Ukraine 49.31N 26.09E
109 K16 **Piedimonte Matese** Campania, S Italy 41.20N 14.30E
29 X7 **Piedmont** Missouri, C USA 37.09N 90.42W
23 P11 **Piedmont** South Carolina, SE USA 34.42N 82.27W
19 Q12 **Piedmont** *escarpment* E USA
Piedmont *see* Piemonte
33 U13 **Piedmont Lake** ⊟ Ohio, N USA
106 M11 **Piedrabuena** Castilla-La Mancha, C Spain 39.01N 4.10W
Piedrafita, Puerto de *see* Pedrafita, Porto de
106 L8 **Piedrahita** Castilla-León, N Spain 40.27N 5.19W
43 N6 **Piedras Negras** *var.* Ciudad Porfirio Díaz. Coahuila de Zaragoza, NE Mexico 28.40N 100.31W
63 E21 **Piedras, Punta** *headland* E Argentina 35.27S 57.04W
59 I14 **Piedras, Río de las** ≈ E Peru
113 J16 **Piekary Śląskie** Śląskie, S Poland 50.23N 19.01E
95 M17 **Pieksämäki** Isä-Suomi, E Finland 62.18N 27.10E
111 V5 **Pielach** ≈ NE Austria
95 N16 **Pielavesi** Itä-Suomi, C Finland 63.13N 26.45E
95 N16 **Pielinen** *var.* Pielisjärvi. ◎ E Finland
Pielisjärvi *see* Pielinen
108 A8 **Piemonte** *Eng.* Piedmont. ◈ *region* NW Italy
113 L18 **Pieniny** ▲▲ Poland/Slovakia
113 E14 **Pieńsk** *Ger.* Penzig. Dolnośląskie, SW Poland 51.14N 15.03E
31 Q13 **Pierce** Nebraska, C USA 42.12N 97.31W
9 R14 **Pierceland** Saskatchewan, C Canada
117 E14 **Piéria** ▲▲ N Greece
31 N10 **Pierre** *state capital* South Dakota, N USA 44.22N 100.21W
104 K16 **Pierrefitte-Nestalas** Hautes-Pyrénées, S France 42.58N 0.04W
105 R14 **Pierrelatte** Drôme, E France 44.22N 4.40E
13 P11 **Pierreville** Quebec, SE Canada 46.05N 72.48W
13 O7 **Pierriche** ≈ Quebec, SE Canada
113 H20 **Piešt'any** *Ger.* Pistyan, *Hung.* Pöstyén. Trnavský, W Slovakia 48.36N 17.48E
111 X5 **Piesting** ≈ E Austria
Pietarhovi *see* Petrodvorets
Pietari *see* Sankt-Peterburg
Pietarsaari *see* Jakobstad
85 K23 **Pietermaritzburg** *var.* Maritzburg. KwaZulu/Natal, E South Africa 29.34S 30.23E
Pietersburg *see* Polokwane
109 K24 **Pietraperzia** Sicilia, Italy, C Mediterranean Sea 37.25N 14.07E
109 N22 **Pietra Spada, Passo della** *pass* SW Italy 38.30N 16.20E
85 K22 **Piet Retief** Mpumalanga, E South Africa 27.00S 30.49E
118 I9 **Pietrosul, Vârful** *prev.* Vîrful Pietrosu. ▲ N Romania 47.36N 24.39E
118 J10 **Pietrosul, Vârful** *prev.* Vîrful Pietrosu. ▲ N Romania 47.06N 25.09E
Pietrosu, Vîrful *see* Pietrosul, Vârful
108 I6 **Pieve di Cadore** Veneto, NE Italy 46.27N 12.22E
12 C18 **Pigeon Bay** *lake bay* Ontario, S Canada
29 X8 **Piggott** Arkansas, C USA 36.22N 90.11W
85 L21 **Piggs Peak** NW Swaziland 25.58S 31.16E
Pigs, Bay of *see* Cochinos, Bahía de
63 A23 **Pigüé** Buenos Aires, E Argentina 37.37S 62.24W
43 O12 **Piguícas** ▲ C Mexico 21.08N 99.37W
200 Qq15 **Piha Passage** *passage* S Tonga
Pihkva Järv *see* Pskov, Lake
95 N18 **Pihlajavesi** ◎ SE Finland
95 J18 **Pihlava** Länsi-Suomi, W Finland 61.33N 21.36E
95 L16 **Pihtipudas** Länsi-Suomi, W Finland 63.20N 25.37E
42 L14 **Pihuamo** Jalisco, SW Mexico 19.16N 103.21W
201 U11 **Piis Moen** *var.* Pis. *atoll* Chuuk Islands, C Micronesia
43 U17 **Pijijiapán** Chiapas, SE Mexico 15.39N 93.13W
100 G12 **Pijnacker** Zuid-Holland, W Netherlands 52.01N 4.25E
44 H5 **Pijol, Pico** ▲ NW Honduras 15.07N 87.39W
Pikaar *see* Bikar Atoll
128 I13 **Pikalevo** Leningradskaya Oblast', NW Russian Federation 59.33N 34.04E
196 M15 **Pikelot** *island* Caroline Islands, C Micronesia
32 M5 **Pike River** ≈ Wisconsin, N USA
39 T5 **Pikes Peak** ▲ Colorado, C USA 38.51N 105.06W
23 P6 **Pikeville** Kentucky, S USA 37.28N 82.31W
22 L9 **Pikeville** Tennessee, S USA 35.36N 85.11W
Pikinni *see* Bikini Atoll
81 H18 **Pikounda** La Sangha, C Congo 0.30N 16.43E
112 G9 **Piła** *Ger.* Schneidemühl. Wielkopolskie, C Poland 53.09N 16.43E
64 N6 **Pilagá, Riacho** ≈ NE Argentina
63 D20 **Pilar** Buenos Aires, E Argentina 34.28S 58.55W
64 N7 **Pilar** *var.* Villa del Pilar. Neembucú, S Paraguay 26.55S 58.19W
64 N6 **Pilcomayo, Río** ≈ C South America
153 R12 **Pildon** *Rus.* Pil'don. C Tajikistan 39.10N 71.00E
Piles *see* Pylés
Pilgram *see* Pelhřimov
179 Q11 **Pili** Luzon, N Philippines 13.31N 123.15E
158 L10 **Pīlībhīt** Uttar Pradesh, N India 28.37N 79.48E
112 M13 **Pilica** ≈ C Poland
117 G16 **Pílio** ▲ C Greece
113 J22 **Pilisvörösvár** Pest, N Hungary 47.37N 18.55E
67 G15 **Pillar Bay** *bay* Ascension Island, C Atlantic Ocean
191 P17 **Pillar, Cape** *headland* Tasmania, SE Australia 43.13S 147.58E
Pillau *see* Baltiysk
191 R5 **Pilliga** New South Wales, SE Australia 30.22S 148.53E
46 H8 **Pilón** Granma, E Cuba 19.54N 77.20W
Pilos *see* Pýlos
9 W17 **Pilot Mound** Manitoba, S Canada 49.12N 98.49W
23 S8 **Pilot Mountain** North Carolina, SE USA 36.23N 80.28W
41 O14 **Pilot Point** Alaska, USA 57.33N 95.34W
27 T5 **Pilot Point** Texas, SW USA 33.24N 96.57W
34 K11 **Pilot Rock** Oregon, NW USA 45.28N 118.49W
40 M11 **Pilot Station** Alaska, USA 61.56N 162.52W
Pilsen *see* Plzeň
113 K18 **Pilsko** ▲ N Slovakia 49.31N 19.21E
Pilten *see* Piltene
120 D8 **Piltene** *Ger.* Pilten. Ventspils, W Latvia 57.14N 21.41E
113 M16 **Pilzno** Podkarpackie, SE Poland 49.58N 21.18E
Pilzno *see* Plzeň
39 N14 **Pima** Arizona, SW USA 32.49N 109.50W
60 H13 **Pimenta** Pará, N Brazil 4.32S 56.17W
61 F16 **Pimenta Bueno** Rondônia, W Brazil 11.40S 61.13W
58 B11 **Pimentel** Lambayeque, W Peru 6.51S 79.52W
107 S6 **Pina** Aragón, NE Spain 41.28N 0.31W
121 I20 **Pina** *Rus.* Pina. ≈ SW Belarus
42 E2 **Pinacate, Sierra del** ▲ NW Mexico 31.49N 113.30W
65 H22 **Pináculo, Cerro** ▲ S Argentina 50.46S 72.07W
203 X11 **Pinaki** *atoll* Îles Tuamotu, E French Polynesia
39 N15 **Pinaleno Mountains** ▲▲ Arizona, SW USA
179 Pp12 **Pinamalayan** Mindoro, N Philippines 13.00N 121.30E
174 Kk8 **Pinang** Borneo, C Indonesia 0.36N 109.10W
173 G3 **Pinang** *var.* Penang. ◈ *state* Peninsular Malaysia
Pinang *see* Pinang, Pulau, Peninsular Malaysia
Pinang *see* George Town
173 G3 **Pinang, Pulau** *var.* Penang, Pinang; *prev.* Prince of Wales Island. *island* Peninsular Malaysia
46 B5 **Pinar del Río** Pinar del Río, W Cuba 22.23N 83.42W
116 N11 **Pınarhisar** Kırklareli, NW Turkey 41.37N 27.30E
179 P10 **Pinatubo, Mount** (volcano) Luzon, N Philippines 15.07N 120.21E
9 Y16 **Pinawa** Manitoba, S Canada 50.09N 95.52W
9 Q17 **Pincher Creek** Alberta, SW Canada 49.31N 113.52W
32 L16 **Pinckneyville** Illinois, N USA 38.04N 89.22W
Pincota *see* Pâncota
113 L15 **Pińczów** Świętokrzyskie, C Poland 50.30N 20.31E
155 U7 **Pind Dādan Khān** Punjab, E Pakistan 32.36N 73.07E
Píndhos/Píndhos Óros *see* Píndos
155 V8 **Pindi Bhattiān** Punjab, E Pakistan 31.54N 73.19E
155 U6 **Pindi Gheb** Punjab, E Pakistan 33.15N 72.16E
117 D15 **Píndos** *var.* Píndhos Óros, *Eng.* Pindus Mountains; *prev.* Píndhos. ▲▲ C Greece
Pindus Mountains *see* Píndos
20 J16 **Pine Barrens** *physical region* New Jersey, NE USA
29 V12 **Pine Bluff** Arkansas, C USA 34.13N 92.01W
25 X11 **Pine Castle** Florida, SE USA 28.28N 81.22W
31 V7 **Pine City** Minnesota, N USA 45.49N 92.55W
189 P2 **Pine Creek** Northern Territory, N Australia 13.51S 131.51E
37 V4 **Pine Creek** ≈ Nevada, W USA
20 F13 **Pine Creek** ≈ Pennsylvania, NE USA
29 Q13 **Pine Creek Lake** ⊟ Oklahoma, C USA
35 T15 **Pinedale** Wyoming, C USA 42.52N 109.51W
9 X15 **Pine Dock** Manitoba, S Canada 51.34N 96.47W
9 Y16 **Pine Falls** Manitoba, S Canada 50.29N 96.12W
37 R10 **Pine Flat Lake** ⊟ California, W USA
129 N8 **Pinega** Arkhangel'skaya Oblast', NW Russian Federation 64.40N 43.24E
129 N8 **Pinega** ≈ NW Russian Federation
13 N12 **Pine Hill** Quebec, SE Canada 45.44N 74.30W
9 T12 **Pinehouse Lake** ◎ Saskatchewan, C Canada
23 T10 **Pinehurst** North Carolina, SE USA 35.12N 79.28W
117 D19 **Pineiós** ≈ S Greece
117 E16 **Pineiós** *var.* Piniós; *anc.* Peneius. ≈ C Greece
31 W10 **Pine Island** Minnesota, N USA 44.12N 92.39W
25 V15 **Pine Island** *island* Florida, SE USA
204 K10 **Pine Island Glacier** *glacier* Antarctica
27 X9 **Pineland** Texas, SW USA 31.15N 93.58W
25 V13 **Pinellas Park** Florida, SE USA 27.50N 82.42W
8 M13 **Pine Pass** *pass* British Columbia, W Canada 55.21N 122.43W
15 I9 **Pine Point** Northwest Territories, W Canada 60.52N 114.30W
30 K12 **Pine Ridge** South Dakota, N USA 43.01N 102.33W
31 U6 **Pine River** Minnesota, N USA 46.43N 94.24W
33 Q8 **Pine River** ≈ Michigan, N USA
32 M4 **Pine River** ≈ Wisconsin, N USA
108 A8 **Pinerolo** Piemonte, NE Italy 44.56N 7.21E
27 W6 **Pines, Lake O' the** ⊟ Texas, SW USA
Pines, The Isle of the *see* Juventud, Isla de la
Pine Tree State *see* Maine
23 N7 **Pineville** Kentucky, S USA 36.45N 83.42W
24 H7 **Pineville** Louisiana, S USA 31.19N 92.25W
29 R8 **Pineville** Missouri, C USA 36.35N 94.22W
23 R10 **Pineville** North Carolina, SE USA 35.04N 80.53W
23 Q6 **Pineville** West Virginia, NE USA 37.34N 81.32W
35 V8 **Piney Buttes** *physical region* Montana, NW USA
169 W9 **Ping'an** Jilin, NE China 44.36N 127.13E
166 H14 **Pingbian** *var.* Pingbian Miaozu Zizhixian. Yunnan, SW China 22.51N 103.28E
163 S9 **Pingdingshan** Henan, C China 33.52N 113.19E
167 R4 **Pingdu** Shandong, E China 36.48N 119.56E
201 W16 **Pingelap Atoll** *atoll* Caroline Islands, E Micronesia
166 K14 **Pingguo** Guangxi Zhuangzu Zizhiqu, S China 23.22N 107.34E
167 Q13 **Pinghe** Fujian, SE China 24.30N 117.19E
P'ing-hsiang *see* Pingxiang
167 N10 **Pingjiang** Hunan, S China 28.44N 113.33E
Pingkiang *see* Harbin
166 L8 **Pingli** Shaanxi, C China 32.24N 109.17E
165 W10 **Pingliang** *var.* P'ing-liang. Gansu, C China 35.31N 106.46E
165 W8 **Pingluo** Ningxia, N China 38.55N 106.31E
Pingma *see* Tiandong
178 H9 **Ping, Mae Nam** ≈ W Thailand
167 Q1 **Pingquan** Hebei, E China 41.01N 118.34E
31 P5 **Pingree** North Dakota, N USA 47.07N 98.54W
Pingsiang *see* Pingxiang
167 S14 **P'ingtung** *Jap.* Heitō. S Taiwan 22.43N 120.26E
166 I8 **Pingwu** Sichuan, C China 32.33N 104.32E
166 J15 **Pingxiang** Guangxi Zhuangzu Zizhiqu, S China 22.03N 106.43E
167 O11 **Pingxiang** *var.* P'ing-hsiang; *prev.* Pingsiang. Jiangxi, S China 27.42N 113.49E
167 S11 **Pingyang** Zhejiang, SE China 27.46N 120.37E
167 P5 **Pingyi** Shandong, E China 35.30N 117.37E
167 P5 **Pingyin** Shandong, E China 36.18N 116.24E
62 H13 **Pinhalzinho** Santa Catarina, S Brazil 26.53S 52.57W
62 I12 **Pinhão** Paraná, S Brazil 25.46S 51.32W
63 H17 **Pinheiro Machado** Rio Grande do Sul, S Brazil 31.34S 53.22W
106 I7 **Pinhel** Guarda, N Portugal 40.46N 7.03W
Piniós *see* Pineiós
195 R10 **Pinipel Island** *island* Green Islands, NE PNG
173 Ff8 **Pini, Pulau** *island* Kepulauan Batu, W Indonesia
111 Y7 **Pinka** ≈ SE Austria
111 X7 **Pinkafeld** Burgenland, SE Austria 47.18N 16.09E
Pinkiang *see* Harbin
8 M12 **Pink Mountain** British Columbia, W Canada 57.01N 122.26W
177 G3 **Pinlebu** Sagaing, N Myanmar 24.02N 95.21E
40 J12 **Pinnacle Island** *island* Alaska, USA
188 I12 **Pinnacles, The** *tourist site* Western Australia
190 K10 **Pinnaroo** South Australia 35.17S 140.54E
Pinne *see* Pniewy
102 I9 **Pinneberg** Schleswig-Holstein, N Germany 53.40N 9.48E
117 I15 **Pínnes, Akrotírio** *headland* N Greece 40.06N 24.19E
Pinos, Isla de *see* Juventud, Isla de la
37 R14 **Pinos, Mount** ▲ California, W USA 34.48N 119.09W
107 R12 **Pinoso** País Valenciano, E Spain 38.25N 1.01W
107 N14 **Pinos-Puente** Andalucía, S Spain 37.16N 3.46W
43 Q17 **Pinotepa Nacional** *var.* Santiago Pinotepa Nacional. Oaxaca, SE Mexico 16.19N 98.02W
116 F13 **Pínovo** ▲ N Greece 41.06N 22.19E
197 K7 **Pins, Île des** *var.* Kunyé. *island* E New Caledonia
121 I20 **Pinsk** *Pol.* Pińsk. Brestskaya Voblasts', SW Belarus 52.07N 26.07E
12 D18 **Pins, Pointe aux** *headland* Ontario, S Canada 42.14N 81.53W
59 B16 **Pinta, Isla** *var.* Abingdon. *island* Galapagos Islands, Ecuador, E Pacific Ocean
129 Q12 **Pinyug** Kirovskaya Oblast', NW Russian Federation 60.12N 47.45E
59 B17 **Pinzón, Isla** *var.* Duncan Island. *island* Galapagos Islands, Ecuador, E Pacific Ocean
37 Y8 **Pioche** Nevada, W USA 37.54N 114.27W
108 F13 **Piombino** Toscana, C Italy 42.54N 10.30E
(0) C9 **Pioneer Fracture Zone** *tectonic feature* NE Pacific Ocean
126 Ii2 **Pioner, Ostrov** *island* Severnaya Zemlya, N Russian Federation
120 A13 **Pionerskiy** *Ger.* Neukuhren. Kaliningradskaya Oblast', W Russian Federation 54.57N 20.16E
112 N13 **Pionki** Mazowieckie, C Poland 51.28N 21.27E
192 L9 **Piopio** Waikato, North Island, NZ 38.27S 175.00E
112 K13 **Piotrków Trybunalski** *Ger.* Petrikau, *Rus.* Petrokov. Łodzkie, C Poland 51.25N 19.42E
158 F12 **Pipār Road** Rājasthān, N India 26.25N 73.28E
117 I16 **Pipéri** *island* Vóreioi Sporádes, Greece, Aegean Sea
31 S10 **Pipestone** Minnesota, N USA 44.00N 96.19W
10 C9 **Pipestone** ≈ Ontario, C Canada
63 E21 **Pipinas** Buenos Aires, E Argentina 35.31S 57.19W
155 T7 **Piplān** *prev.* Liaqatabad. Punjab, E Pakistan 32.19N 71.21E
13 R5 **Pipmuacan, Réservoir** ⊟ Quebec, SE Canada
Piqan *see* Shanshan
33 R13 **Piqua** Ohio, N USA 40.08N 84.14W
107 P5 **Piqueras, Puerto de** *pass* N Spain 42.04N 2.35W
62 H11 **Piquiri, Rio** ≈ S Brazil
62 L9 **Piracicaba** São Paulo, S Brazil 22.44S 47.33W
Piraeus/Piraiévs *see* Peiraías
62 K10 **Piraju** São Paulo, S Brazil 23.12S 49.24W
62 K9 **Pirajuí** São Paulo, S Brazil 21.58S 49.27W
65 G21 **Pirámide, Cerro** ▲ S Chile 49.06S 73.32W
Piramiva *see* Pyramíva
111 R13 **Piran** *It.* Pirano. SW Slovenia 45.31N 13.36E
64 N6 **Pirané** Formosa, N Argentina 25.42S 59.06W
61 J18 **Piranhas** Goiás, S Brazil 16.24S 51.51W
Pirano *see* Piran
148 I4 **Pirānshahr** Āżarbāyjān-e Bākhtarī, NW Iran 36.41N 45.10E
61 M19 **Pirapora** Minas Gerais, NE Brazil 17.19S 44.54W

◆ Country ● Country Capital ◇ Dependent Territory ○ Dependent Territory Capital ◈ Administrative Region ✕ International Airport ▲ Mountain ▲▲ Mountain Range (volcano) Volcano ≈ River ◎ Lake ⊟ Reservoir

62 I9 **Pirapòzinho** São Paulo, S Brazil 22.17S 51.31W
63 G19 **Piraraja** Lavalleja, S Uruguay 33.43S 54.45W
62 L9 **Pirassununga** São Paulo, S Brazil 21.58S 47.23W
47 V6 **Pirata, Monte** ▲ E Puerto Rico 18.06N 65.33W
62 I13 **Piratuba** Santa Catarina, S Brazil 27.26S 51.47W
116 I9 **Pirdop** prev. Srednogorie. Sofiya, W Bulgaria 42.44N 24.09E
203 P7 **Pirea** Tahiti, W French Polynesia
61 K18 **Pirenópolis** Goiás, S Brazil 15.48S 49.00W
159 S13 **Pirganj** Rajshahi, NW Bangladesh 25.51N 88.25E
Pirgi see Pyrgí
Pírgos see Pýrgos
63 F20 **Piriápolis** Maldonado, S Uruguay 34.51S 55.15W
116 G11 **Pirin** ▲ SW Bulgaria
Pirineos see Pyrenees
60 N13 **Piripiri** Piauí, E Brazil 4.15S 41.46W
120 H4 **Pirita** var. Pirita Jõgi. ≈ NW Estonia
Pirita Jõgi see Pirita
56 J6 **Píritu** Portuguesa, N Venezuela 9.21N 69.16W
95 L18 **Pirkkala** Länsi-Suomi, W Finland 61.27N 23.47E
103 F20 **Pirmasens** Rheinland-Pfalz, SW Germany 49.12N 7.36E
103 P16 **Pirna** Sachsen, E Germany 50.57N 13.56E
Piroe see Piru
115 Q15 **Pirot** Serbia, SE Serbia and Montenegro (Yugoslavia) 43.12N 22.34E
158 H6 **Pīr Panjāl Range** ▲ NE India
45 W16 **Pirre, Cerro** ▲ SE Panama 7.54N 77.42W
143 Y11 **Pirsaat** Rus. Pirsagat. ≈ E Azerbaijan
Pirsagat see Pirsaat
149 V11 **Pīr Shūrān, Selseleh-ye** ▲ SE Iran
94 M12 **Pirttikoski** Lappi, N Finland 66.20N 27.08E
Pirttikylä see Pörtom
175 T11 **Piru** prev. Piroe. Pulau Seram, E Indonesia 3.01S 128.10E
Piryatin see Pyryatyn
Pis see Piis Moen
108 F11 **Pisa** var. Pisae. Toscana, C Italy 43.43N 10.22E
Pisae see Pisa
176 Uu10 **Pisang, Kepulauan** island group E Indonesia
176 Xx11 **Pisapa** Papua, E Indonesia 3.25S 137.04E
201 V12 **Pisar** atoll Chuuk Islands, C Micronesia
Pisaurum see Pesaro
12 M10 **Piscatosine, Lac** ◎ Quebec, SE Canada
111 W7 **Pischeldorf** Steiermark, SE Austria 47.11N 15.48E
Pischk see Simeria
109 L19 **Pisciotta** Campania, S Italy 40.07N 15.13E
59 E16 **Pisco** Ica, SW Peru 13.46S 76.12W
118 G9 **Pişcolt** Hung. Piskolt. Satu Mare, NW Romania 47.34N 22.18E
59 E16 **Pisco, Río** ≈ E Peru
113 C18 **Písek** Budějovický Kraj, S Czech Republic 49.18N 14.07E
33 R14 **Pisgah** Ohio, N USA 39.19N 84.22W
164 F9 **Pishan** var. Guma. Xinjiang Uygur Zizhiqu, NW China 37.36N 78.45E
119 N8 **Pishchanka** Vinnyts'ka Oblast', C Ukraine 48.12N 28.52E
115 K21 **Pishë** Fier, SW Albania 40.40N 19.22E
149 X14 **Pishin** Sīstān va Balūchestān, SE Iran 26.05N 61.46E
155 O9 **Pishin** North-West Frontier Province, NW Pakistan 30.39N 66.52E
155 N11 **Pishin Lora** var. Psein Lora, Pash. Pseyn Bowr. ≈ SW Pakistan
Pishma see Pizhma
Pishpek see Bishkek
175 Q13 **Pising** Pulau Kabaena, C Indonesia 5.07S 121.50E
Pisino see Pazin
Piski see Simeria
Piskolt see Pişcolt
153 Q9 **Piskom** Rus. Pskem. ≈ E Uzbekistan
Piskom Tizmasi see Pskemskiy Khrebet
37 P13 **Pismo Beach** California, W USA 35.08N 120.38W
79 P12 **Pissila** C Burkina 13.07N 0.51W
64 H8 **Pissis, Monte** ▲ N Argentina 27.45S 68.43W
43 X12 **Piste** Yucatán, E Mexico 20.40N 88.34W
109 O18 **Pisticci** Basilicata, S Italy 40.22N 16.33E
108 F11 **Pistoia** anc. Pistoria, Pistoriæ. Toscana, C Italy 43.57N 10.52E
34 E15 **Pistol River** Oregon, NW USA 42.13N 124.23W
Pistoria/Pistoriæ see Pistoia
13 U5 **Pistuacanis** ≈ Quebec, SE Canada
Pistyan see Piešt'any
106 M5 **Pisuerga** ≈ N Spain
112 N8 **Pisz** Ger. Johannisburg. Warmińsko-Mazurskie, NE Poland 53.37N 21.49E
78 I13 **Pita** Moyenne-Guinée, NW Guinea 11.04N 12.15W
56 D12 **Pitalito** Huila, S Colombia 1.51N 76.01W
62 I11 **Pitanga** Paraná, S Brazil 24.45S 51.43W
190 M9 **Pitarpunga Lake** salt lake New South Wales, SE Australia
199 M11 **Pitcairn Island** island S Pitcairn Islands
199 M11 **Pitcairn Islands** ◇ UK dependent territory C Pacific Ocean
95 J14 **Piteå** Norrbotten, N Sweden 65.19N 21.30E
94 I13 **Piteälven** ≈ N Sweden
118 I13 **Pitești** Argeș, S Romania 44.53N 24.49E
Pithagorio see Pythagóreio
188 I12 **Pithara** Western Australia 30.31S 116.38E
105 N6 **Pithiviers** Loiret, C France 48.10N 2.15E
158 L9 **Pithorāgarh** Uttar Pradesh, N India 29.34N 80.12E
196 B16 **Piti** W Guam 13.28N 144.42E
108 G13 **Pitigliano** Toscana, C Italy 42.38N 11.40E
42 F3 **Pitiquito** Sonora, NW Mexico 30.39N 112.00W
Pitkäranta see Pitkyaranta
40 M11 **Pitkas Point** Alaska, USA 62.01N 163.17W
128 H11 **Pitkyaranta** Fin. Pitkäranta. Respublika Kareliya, NW Russian Federation 61.34N 31.27E
98 J10 **Pitlochry** C Scotland, UK 56.46N 3.48W
20 I16 **Pitman** New Jersey, NE USA 39.43N 75.06W
152 I9 **Pitnak** Var. Drujba, Rus. Druzhba. Xorazm Viloyati, W Uzbekistan 41.14N 61.13E
114 G8 **Pitomača** Virovitica-Podravina, NE Croatia 45.57N 17.14E
37 O2 **Pit River** ≈ California, W USA
65 G15 **Pitrufquén** Araucanía, S Chile 38.58S 72.40W
Pitsanulok see Phitsanulok
Pitschen see Byczyna
Pitsunda see Bichvint'a
111 X6 **Pitten** ≈ E Austria
8 J14 **Pitt Island** island British Columbia, W Canada
Pitt Island see Makin
24 M3 **Pittsboro** Mississippi, S USA 33.55N 89.20W
23 T9 **Pittsboro** North Carolina, SE USA 35.46N 79.21W
29 R7 **Pittsburg** Kansas, C USA 37.24N 94.42W
27 W6 **Pittsburg** Texas, SW USA 33.00N 94.58W
20 B14 **Pittsburgh** Pennsylvania, NE USA 40.26N 80.00W
32 J14 **Pittsfield** Illinois, N USA 39.36N 90.48W
21 R6 **Pittsfield** Maine, NE USA 44.46N 69.22W
20 L11 **Pittsfield** Massachusetts, NE USA 42.27N 73.15W
191 U3 **Pittsworth** Queensland, E Australia 27.43S 151.36E
64 I8 **Pituil** La Rioja, NW Argentina 28.33S 67.24W
58 A10 **Piura** Piura, NW Peru 5.11S 80.41W
58 A9 **Piura** off. Departamento de Piura. ◈ department NW Peru
37 S13 **Piute Peak** ▲ California, W USA 35.27N 118.24W
115 J15 **Piva** ≈ SW Serbia and Montenegro (Yugoslavia)
119 V5 **Pivdenne** Kharkivs'ka Oblast', E Ukraine 49.52N 36.04E
119 P8 **Pivdennyy Buh** Rus. Yuzhnyy Bug. ≈ S Ukraine
56 F5 **Pivijay** Magdalena, N Colombia 10.28N 74.37W
111 T13 **Pivka** prev. Šent Peter, Ger. Sankt Peter, It. San Pietro del Carso. SW Slovenia 45.41N 14.12E
119 U13 **Pivnichno-Kryms'kyy Kanal** canal S Ukraine
115 J15 **Pivsko Jezero** ◎ SW Serbia and Montenegro (Yugoslavia)
113 M18 **Piwniczna** Małopolskie, S Poland 49.26N 20.43E
37 R12 **Pixley** California, W USA 35.58N 119.18W
129 Q15 **Pizhma** var. Pishma. ≈ NW Russian Federation
11 U13 **Placentia** Newfoundland and Labrador, SE Canada 47.12N 53.58W
Placentia see Piacenza
11 U13 **Placentia Bay** inlet Newfoundland and Labrador, SE Canada
179 Qq12 **Placer** Masbate, N Philippines 11.54N 123.54E
37 P7 **Placerville** California, W USA 38.42N 120.48W
46 F5 **Placetas** Villa Clara, C Cuba 22.18N 79.40W
115 Q18 **Plačkovica** ▲ E FYR Macedonia
38 L2 **Plain City** Utah, W USA 41.18N 112.05W
24 G4 **Plain Dealing** Louisiana, S USA 32.54N 93.42W
33 O14 **Plainfield** Indiana, N USA 39.42N 86.18W
20 K14 **Plainfield** New Jersey, NE USA 40.37N 74.25W
35 O8 **Plains** Montana, NW USA 47.27N 114.52W
26 L6 **Plains** Texas, SW USA 33.11N 102.49W
31 X10 **Plainview** Minnesota, N USA 44.10N 92.10W
31 Q13 **Plainview** Nebraska, C USA 42.21N 97.47W
27 N4 **Plainview** Texas, SW USA 34.12N 101.43W
28 K4 **Plainville** Kansas, C USA 39.13N 99.18W
117 L25 **Pláka, Akrotírio** headland Kríti, Greece, E Mediterranean Sea 35.10N 26.19E
117 J15 **Pláka, Akrotírio** headland Límnos, E Greece 40.02N 25.25E
115 N19 **Plakenska Planina** ▲ SW FYR Macedonia
46 K5 **Plana Cays** islets SE Bahamas
107 S12 **Plana, Isla** var. Nueva Tabarca. island E Spain
61 L18 **Planaltina** Goiás, S Brazil 15.34S 47.28W
85 O14 **Planalto Moçambicano** plateau N Mozambique
114 N10 **Plandište** Serbia, NE Serbia and Montenegro (Yugoslavia) 45.13N 21.07E
102 N13 **Plane** ≈ NE Germany
56 E6 **Planeta Rica** Córdoba, NW Colombia 8.24N 75.39W
31 P11 **Plankinton** South Dakota, N USA 43.43N 98.28W
32 M11 **Plano** Illinois, N USA 41.39N 88.32W
27 U6 **Plano** Texas, SW USA 33.01N 96.42W
25 W12 **Plant City** Florida, SE USA 28.01N 82.06W
24 J9 **Plaquemine** Louisiana, S USA 30.17N 91.13W
106 K9 **Plasencia** Extremadura, W Spain 40.01N 6.04W
112 P7 **Płaska** Podlaskie, NE Poland 53.55N 23.18E
114 C10 **Plaški** Karlovac, C Croatia 45.04N 15.21E
115 N19 **Plasnica** SW FYR Macedonia 41.28N 21.07E
125 E12 **Plast** Chelyabinskaya Oblast', C Russian Federation 54.24N 60.51E
11 N14 **Plaster Rock** New Brunswick, SE Canada 46.55N 67.24W
109 J24 **Platani** anc. Halycus. ≈ Sicilia, Italy, C Mediterranean Sea
117 G17 **Plataniá** Thessalía, C Greece 39.09N 23.15E
117 G24 **Plátanos** Kríti, Greece, E Mediterranean Sea 35.27N 23.34E
67 H18 **Plata, Río de la** var. River Plate. estuary Argentina/Uruguay
79 V15 **Plateau** ◈ state C Nigeria
81 G19 **Plateaux** var. Région des Plateaux. ◈ province C Congo
94 P1 **Platen, Kapp** headland NE Svalbard 80.30N 22.46E
Plate, River see Plata, Río de la
101 G22 **Plate Taille, Lac de la** var. L'Eau d'Heure. ◎ SE Belgium
Plathe see Płoty
41 N13 **Platinum** Alaska, USA 59.00N 161.49W
56 F5 **Plato** Magdalena, N Colombia 9.47N 74.46W
31 O11 **Platte** South Dakota, N USA 43.20N 98.51W
29 R3 **Platte City** Missouri, C USA 39.22N 94.46W
Plattensee see Balaton
29 R3 **Platte River** ≈ Iowa/Missouri, USA
31 Q15 **Platte River** ≈ Nebraska, C USA
39 T3 **Platteville** Colorado, C USA 40.13N 104.49W
32 K9 **Platteville** Wisconsin, N USA 42.44N 90.27W
103 N21 **Plattling** Bayern, SE Germany 48.45N 12.52E
29 R3 **Plattsburg** Missouri, C USA 39.34N 94.27W
20 L6 **Plattsburgh** New York, NE USA 44.42N 73.28W
31 S15 **Plattsmouth** Nebraska, C USA 41.00N 95.52W
103 M17 **Plauen** var. Plauen im Vogtland. Sachsen, E Germany 50.30N 12.08E
Plauen im Vogtland see Plauen
102 M10 **Plauer See** ◎ NE Germany
115 L16 **Plav** Montenegro, SW Serbia and Montenegro (Yugoslavia) 42.36N 19.57E
120 I10 **Pļaviņas** Ger. Stockmannshof. Aizkraukle, S Latvia 56.37N 25.40E
130 K5 **Plavsk** Tul'skaya Oblast', W Russian Federation 53.42N 37.21E
43 Z12 **Playa del Carmen** Quintana Roo, E Mexico 20.37N 87.04W
42 J12 **Playa Los Corchos** Nayarit, SW Mexico 22.31N 105.28W
39 P16 **Playas Lake** ◎ New Mexico, SW USA
43 S15 **Playa Vicente** Veracruz-Llave, SE Mexico 17.42N 95.01W
178 K11 **Plây Cu** var. Pleiku. Gia Lai, C Vietnam 13.57N 108.01E
30 L3 **Plaza** North Dakota, N USA 48.00N 102.00W
65 I15 **Plaza Huincul** Neuquén, C Argentina 38.54S 69.10W
38 L3 **Pleasant Grove** Utah, W USA 40.21N 111.44W
31 V14 **Pleasant Hill** Iowa, C USA 41.34N 93.31W
29 R4 **Pleasant Hill** Missouri, C USA 38.47N 94.16W
Pleasant Island see Nauru
38 K13 **Pleasant, Lake** ⊠ Arizona, SW USA
21 P8 **Pleasant Mountain** ▲ Maine, NE USA 44.01N 70.47W
29 R5 **Pleasanton** Kansas, C USA 38.09N 94.43W
27 R12 **Pleasanton** Texas, SW USA 28.58N 98.28W
193 G20 **Pleasant Point** Canterbury, South Island, NZ 44.16S 171.09E
21 R5 **Pleasant River** ≈ Maine, NE USA
20 J17 **Pleasantville** New Jersey, NE USA 39.22N 74.31W
105 N12 **Pléaux** Cantal, C France 45.08N 2.10E
113 B19 **Plechý** Ger. Plöckenstein. ▲ Austria/Czech Republic 48.45N 13.50E
Pleebo see Plibo
Pleihari see Pelaihari
Pleiku see Plây Cu
103 M16 **Pleisse** ≈ E Germany
Plencia see Plentzia
192 O7 **Plenty, Bay of** bay North Island, NZ
35 Y6 **Plentywood** Montana, NW USA 48.46N 104.33W
107 O2 **Plentzia** var. Plencia. País Vasco, N Spain 43.25N 2.56W
104 H5 **Plérin** Côtes d'Armor, NW France 48.33N 2.46W
128 M10 **Plesetsk** Arkhangel'skaya Oblast', NW Russian Federation 62.40N 40.14E
Pleshchenitsy see Plyeshchanitsy
Pleskau see Pskov
Pleskauer See see Pskov, Lake
Pleskava see Pskov
114 E8 **Pleso International** ✕ (Zagreb) Zagreb, NW Croatia 45.45N 16.00E
Pless see Pszczyna
13 Q11 **Plessisville** Quebec, SE Canada 46.14N 71.45W
112 H12 **Pleszew** Wielkopolskie, C Poland 51.54N 17.46E
10 L10 **Plétipi, Lac** ◎ Quebec, SE Canada
103 F15 **Plettenberg** Nordrhein-Westfalen, W Germany 51.13N 7.52E
116 I8 **Pleven** prev. Plevna. Pleven, N Bulgaria 43.25N 24.36E
116 I8 **Pleven** ◈ province N Bulgaria
Plevlja/Plevlje see Pljevlja
Plevna see Pleven
Plezzo see Bovec
Pliberk see Bleiburg
78 L17 **Plibo** var. Pleebo. SE Liberia 4.37N 7.40W
124 Oo13 **Pliny Trench** undersea feature C Mediterranean Sea
120 K13 **Plisa** Rus. Plissa. Vitsyebskaya Voblasts', N Belarus 55.12N 27.58E
Plissa see Plisa
114 D11 **Plitvica Selo** Lika-Senj, W Croatia 44.53N 15.36E
114 D11 **Plješevica** ▲ C Croatia
115 K14 **Pljevlja** prev. Plevlja, Plevlje. Montenegro, N Serbia and Montenegro (Yugoslavia) 43.21N 19.21E
Ploça see Ploçë
Plocce see Ploče
115 G15 **Ploče** It. Plocce; prev. Kardeljevo. Dubrovnik-Neretva, SE Croatia 43.02N 17.25E
115 K22 **Ploçë** var. Ploça. Vlorë, SW Albania 40.24N 19.41E
112 K11 **Płock** Ger. Plozk. Mazowieckie, C Poland 52.31N 19.40E
111 Q10 **Plöcken Pass** Ger. Plöckenpass, It. Passo di Monte Croce Carnico. pass SW Austria 46.36N 12.55E
Plöckenstein see Plechý
101 B19 **Ploegsteert** Hainaut, W Belgium 50.45N 2.52E
104 H6 **Ploërmel** Morbihan, NW France 47.57N 2.24W
Ploești see Ploiești
118 K13 **Ploiești** prev. Ploești. Prahova, SE Romania 44.56N 26.03E
117 L17 **Plomári** prev. Plomárion. Lésvos, E Greece 38.58N 26.24E
Plomárion see Plomári
105 O12 **Plomb du Cantal** ▲ C France 45.03N 2.48E
191 V6 **Plomer, Point** headland New South Wales, SE Australia 31.19S 153.00E
102 J8 **Plön** Schleswig-Holstein, N Germany 54.10N 10.25E
112 L11 **Płońsk** Mazowieckie, C Poland 52.37N 20.22E
121 J20 **Plotnitsa** Rus. Plotnitsa. Brestskaya Voblasts', SW Belarus 52.03N 26.39E
112 E8 **Płoty** Ger. Plathe. Zachodniopomorskie, NW Poland 53.48N 15.16E
104 G7 **Plouay** Morbihan, NW France 47.54N 3.14W
113 D15 **Ploučnice** Ger. Polzen. ≈ NE Czech Republic
116 I10 **Plovdiv** prev. Eumolpias, anc. Evmolpia, Philippopolis, Lat. Trimontium. Plovdiv, C Bulgaria 42.08N 24.47
116 J11 **Plovdiv** ◈ province C Bulgaria
32 L6 **Plover** Wisconsin, N USA 44.30N 89.33W
Plozk see Płock
29 U11 **Plumerville** Arkansas, C USA 35.09N 92.38W
21 P10 **Plum Island** island Massachusetts, NE USA
34 M9 **Plummer** Idaho, NW USA 47.19N 116.54W
85 J18 **Plumtree** Matabeleland South, SW Zimbabwe 20.27S 27.49E
120 D11 **Plungė** Plungė, W Lithuania 55.55N 21.53E
115 J15 **Plužine** Montenegro, SW Serbia and Montenegro (Yugoslavia) 43.08N 18.49E
121 K14 **Plyeshchanitsy** Rus. Pleshchenitsy. Minskaya Voblasts', N Belarus 54.25N 27.49E
47 V10 **Plymouth** ○ (Montserrat) SW Montserrat 16.39N 62.11W
99 I24 **Plymouth** SW England, UK 50.22N 4.10W
33 O11 **Plymouth** Indiana, N USA 41.19N 86.19W
21 P12 **Plymouth** Massachusetts, NE USA 41.57N 70.40W
21 N8 **Plymouth** New Hampshire, NE USA 43.43N 71.39W
23 X9 **Plymouth** North Carolina, SE USA 35.52N 76.45W
32 M8 **Plymouth** Wisconsin, N USA 43.48N 87.58W
99 J20 **Plynlimon** ▲ C Wales, UK 52.27N 3.48W
128 G14 **Plyussa** Pskovskaya Oblast', W Russian Federation 58.27N 29.21E
113 B17 **Plzeň** Ger. Pilsen, Pol. Pilzno. Plzeňský Kraj, W Czech Republic 49.44N 13.22E
113 B17 **Plzeňský Kraj** ◈ region W Czech Republic
112 F11 **Pniewy** Ger. Pinne. Wielkolpolskie, C Poland 52.31N 16.14E
108 D8 **Po** ≈ N Italy
79 P13 **Pô** S Burkina 11.10N 1.10W
44 M13 **Poás, Volcán** ▲ NW Costa Rica 10.12N 84.12W
79 S16 **Pobè** S Benin 7.00N 2.41E
127 N8 **Pobeda, Gora** ▲ NE Russian Federation 65.28N 145.44E
Pobeda Peak see Pobedy, Pik/Tomur Feng
153 Z7 **Pobedy, Pik** var. Pobeda Peak, Chin. Tomur Feng. ▲ China/Kyrgyzstan see also Tomur Feng 42.02N 80.02E
112 H11 **Pobiedziska** Ger. Pudewitz. Wielkolpolskie, C Poland 52.30N 17.19E
Po, Bocche del see Po, Foci del
29 W9 **Pocahontas** Arkansas, C USA 36.15N 90.58W
31 U12 **Pocahontas** Iowa, C USA 42.44N 94.40W
35 Q15 **Pocatello** Idaho, NW USA 42.52N 112.27W
178 J13 **Pochentong** ✕ (Phnum Penh) Phnum Penh, S Cambodia 11.24N 104.52E
130 I6 **Pochep** Bryanskaya Oblast', W Russian Federation 52.56N 33.20E
130 H4 **Pochinok** Smolenskaya Oblast', W Russian Federation 54.20N 32.29E
43 R17 **Pochutla** var. San Pedro Pochutla. Oaxaca, SE Mexico 15.44N 96.27W
64 I6 **Pocitos, Salar** var. Salar Quiróm. salt lake NW Argentina
103 O22 **Pocking** Bayern, SE Germany 48.22N 13.17E
195 R17 **Pocklington Reef** reef SE PNG
199 Hh9 **Pocklington Trough** undersea feature W Pacific Ocean
29 R11 **Pocola** Oklahoma, C USA 35.13N 94.28W
23 Y5 **Pocomoke City** Maryland, NE USA 38.04N 75.34W
61 L21 **Poços de Caldas** Minas Gerais, NE Brazil 21.48S 46.33W
128 H14 **Podberez'ye** Novgorodskaya Oblast', NW Russian Federation 58.42N 31.22E
Podbrodzie see Pabradė
129 U8 **Podcher'ye** Respublika Komi, NW Russian Federation 63.55N 57.34E
113 E16 **Poděbrady** Ger. Podiebrad. Středočeský Kraj, C Czech Republic 50.09N 15.06E
176 Yy10 **Podena, Kepulauan** island group E Indonesia
130 L9 **Podgorenskiy** Voronezhskaya Oblast', W Russian Federation 50.22N 39.43E
115 J17 **Podgorica** prev. Titograd. Montenegro, SW Serbia and Montenegro (Yugoslavia) 42.25N 19.16E
115 K17 **Podgorica** ✕ Montenegro, SW Serbia and Montenegro (Yugoslavia) 42.22N 19.16E
111 T13 **Podgrad** SW Slovenia 45.31N 14.09E
Podiebrad see Poděbrady
118 M5 **Podil's'ka Vysochina** plateau W Ukraine
Podium Anicensis see le Puy
126 Ii11 **Podkamennaya Tunguska** Eng. Stony Tunguska. ≈ C Russian Federation
113 N17 **Podkarpackie** ◈ province SE Poland
Pod Klošter see Arnoldstein
112 O9 **Podlaskie** ◈ province NE Poland
131 Q8 **Podlesnoye** Saratovskaya Oblast', W Russian Federation 51.51N 47.03E
130 K4 **Podol'sk** Moskovskaya Oblast', W Russian Federation 55.24N 37.30E
78 H10 **Podor** N Senegal 16.40N 14.57W
129 P12 **Podosinovets** Kirovskaya Oblast', NW Russian Federation 60.15N 47.06E
128 I12 **Podporozh'ye** Leningradskaya Oblast', NW Russian Federation 60.52N 34.00E
Podravska Slatina see Slatina, Croatia
114 J13 **Podromanlja** Republika Srpska, SE Bosnia & Herzegovina 43.55N 18.46E
Podsvil'ye see Padsvillye
118 L9 **Podu Iloaiei** prev. Podul Iloaiei. Iaşi, NE Romania 47.13N 27.16E
115 N15 **Podujevo** Serbia, S Serbia and Montenegro (Yugoslavia) 42.56N 21.13E
Podul Iloaiei see Podu Iloaiei
Podunajská Rovina see Little Alföld
128 M12 **Podyuga** Arkhangel'skaya Oblast', NW Russian Federation 61.04N 40.46E
58 A9 **Poechos, Embalse** ◎ NW Peru
57 W10 **Poeketi** Sipaliwini, E Suriname
102 L8 **Poel** island N Germany
85 M20 **Poelela, Lagoa** ◎ S Mozambique
Poerwodadi see Purwodadi
Poetovio see Ptuj
85 E23 **Pofadder** Northern Cape, W South Africa 29.03S 19.25E
108 I9 **Po, Foci del** var. Bocche del Po. ≈ NE Italy
118 E12 **Pogăniș** ≈ W Romania
Pogegen see Pagėgiai
108 G12 **Poggibonsi** Toscana, C Italy 43.28N 11.09E
109 I14 **Poggio Mirteto** Lazio, C Italy 42.17N 12.42E
111 V4 **Pöggstall** Niederösterreich, N Austria 48.19N 15.10E
118 L13 **Pogoanele** Buzău, SE Romania 44.55N 27.00E
Pogónion see Delvináki
115 M21 **Pogradec** var. Pogradeci. Korçë, SE Albania 40.54N 20.40E
Pogradeci see Pogradec
127 N18 **Pogranichnyy** Primorskiy Kray, SE Russian Federation 44.18N 131.33E
40 M16 **Pogromni Volcano** ▲ Unimak Island, Alaska, USA 54.34N 164.41W
169 Z15 **P'ohang** Jap. Hokō. E South Korea 36.01N 129.20E
13 T9 **Pohénégamook, Lac** ◎ Quebec, SE Canada
95 L20 **Pohja** Swe. Pojo. Etelä-Suomi, SW Finland 60.07N 23.30E
Pohjanlahti see Bothnia, Gulf of
201 U16 **Pohnpei** ◈ state E Micronesia
201 O12 **Pohnpei** ✕ Pohnpei, E Micronesia
201 O12 **Pohnpei** prev. Ponape Ascension Island. island E Micronesia
113 F19 **Pohořelice** Ger. Pohrlitz. Brněnský Kraj, SE Czech Republic 48.58N 16.30E
111 V10 **Pohorje** Ger. Bacher. ▲ N Slovenia
119 N6 **Pohrebyshche** Vinnyts'ka Oblast', C Ukraine 49.31N 29.16E
Pohrlitz see Pohořelice
175 Qq9 **Poh, Teluk** bay Sulawesi, C Indonesia
167 P9 **Po Hu** ⊠ E China
118 G15 **Poiana Mare** Dolj, S Romania 43.55N 23.01E
Poictiers see Poitiers
131 N6 **Poim** Penzenskaya Oblast', W Russian Federation 53.03N 43.11E
197 I6 **Poindimié** Province Nord, C New Caledonia 20.55S 165.18E
Poindo see Lhünzhub
205 Y13 **Poinsett, Cape** headland Antarctica 65.35S 113.00E
31 R9 **Poinsett, Lake** ◎ South Dakota, N USA
24 I10 **Point Au Fer Island** island Louisiana, S USA
41 X14 **Point Baker** Prince of Wales Island, Alaska, USA 56.19N 133.31W
27 U13 **Point Comfort** Texas, SW USA 28.40N 96.33W
Point de Galle see Galle
46 K10 **Pointe à Gravois** headland SW Haiti 18.00N 73.53W
24 L10 **Pointe a la Hache** Louisiana, S USA 29.34N 89.48W
47 Y6 **Pointe-à-Pitre** Grande Terre, C Guadeloupe 16.15N 61.31W
13 U7 **Pointe-au-Père** Quebec, SE Canada 48.31N 68.27W
13 V5 **Pointe-aux-Anglais** Quebec, SE Canada 49.40N 67.09W
47 T10 **Pointe du Cap** headland N Saint Lucia 14.06N 60.56W
81 E21 **Pointe-Noire** Le Kouilou, S Congo 4.46S 11.52E
47 X6 **Pointe Noire** Basse Terre, W Guadeloupe 16.13N 61.47W
81 E21 **Pointe-Noire** ✕ Le Kouilou, S Congo 4.45S 11.55E
47 U15 **Point Fortin** Trinidad, Trinidad and Tobago 10.09N 61.41W
40 M6 **Point Hope** Alaska, USA 68.21N 166.48W
41 N5 **Point Lay** Alaska, USA 69.42N 162.57W
20 B16 **Point Marion** Pennsylvania, NE USA 39.44N 79.53W
20 K16 **Point Pleasant** New Jersey, NE USA 40.04N 74.00W
23 P4 **Point Pleasant** West Virginia, NE USA 38.50N 82.08W
47 R14 **Point Salines** ✕ (St.George's) SW Grenada 12.00N 61.47W
104 L9 **Poitiers** prev. Poictiers, anc. Limonum. Vienne, W France 46.34N 0.19E
104 K9 **Poitou** cultural region W France
104 K10 **Poitou-Charentes** ◈ region W France
105 N3 **Poix-de-Picardie** Somme, N France 49.47N 1.58E
Pojo see Pohja
39 S10 **Pojoaque** New Mexico, SW USA 35.52N 106.01W
158 E11 **Pokaran** Rājasthān, NW India 26.55N 71.55E
191 R4 **Pokataroo** New South Wales, SE Australia 29.37S 148.43E
121 P18 **Pokats'** Rus. Pokot'. ≈ SE Belarus
31 V5 **Pokegama Lake** ◎ Minnesota, N USA
192 L6 **Pokeno** Waikato, North Island, NZ 37.15S 175.01E
159 O11 **Pokhara** Western, C Nepal 28.13N 84.00E
131 T6 **Pokhvistnevo** Samarskaya Oblast', W Russian Federation 53.38N 52.07E
57 W10 **Pokigron** Sipaliwini, C Suriname 4.25N 55.24W
94 L10 **Pokka** Lapp. Bohkká. Lappi, N Finland 68.10N 25.45E
81 N16 **Poko** Orientale, NE Dem. Rep. Congo 3.07N 26.51E
Pokot' see Pokats'
Po-ko-to Shan see Bogda Shan
153 S7 **Pokrovka** Talasskaya Oblast', NW Kyrgyzstan 42.45N 71.33E
Pokrovka see Kyzyl-Suu
126 M11 **Pokrovsk** Respublika Sakha (Yakutiya), NE Russian Federation 61.40N 129.25E
119 V8 **Pokrovs'ke** Rus. Pokrovskoye. Dnipropetrovs'ka Oblast', E Ukraine 47.58N 36.15E
Pokrovskoye see Pokrovs'ke
Pola see Pula
39 N10 **Polacca** Arizona, SW USA 35.49N 110.21W
106 L2 **Pola de Laviana** Asturias, N Spain 43.15N 5.33W
106 K2 **Pola de Lena** Asturias, N Spain 43.10N 5.49W
106 L2 **Pola de Siero** Asturias, N Spain 43.24N 5.39W
203 Y3 **Poland** Kiritimati, E Kiribati 1.52N 95.33W
112 H12 **Poland** off. Republic of Poland, var. Polish Republic, Pol. Polska, Rzeczpospolita Polska; prev. Pol. Polska Rzeczpospolita Ludowa, Polish People's Republic. ◆ republic C Europe
Polangen see Palanga
112 G7 **Polanów** Ger. Pollnow. Zachodniopomorskie, NW Poland 54.07N 16.38E
142 H13 **Polatlı** Ankara, C Turkey 39.34N 32.07E
120 L12 **Polatsk** Rus. Polotsk. Vitsyebskaya Voblasts', N Belarus 55.28N 28.46E
112 F8 **Połczyn-Zdrój** Ger. Bad Polzin. Zachodniopomorskie, NW Poland 53.43N 16.02E
152 I16 **Polekhatum** prev. Pul'-I-Khatum. Akhalskiy Velayat, S Turkmenistan 36.01N 61.08E
155 Q3 **Pol-e Khomrī** var. Pul-i-Khumri. Baghlān, NE Afghanistan 35.55N 68.45E
207 S10 **Pole Plain** undersea feature Arctic Ocean
149 P5 **Pol-e Safid** var. Pol-e-Sefid, Pul-i-Sefid. Māzandarān, N Iran 36.10N 53.03E
Pol-e-Sefid see Pol-e Safid
120 B13 **Polessk** Ger. Labiau. Kaliningradskaya Oblast', W Russian Federation 54.52N 21.06E
Polesskoye see Polis'ke
175 P11 **Polewali** Sulawesi, C Indonesia 3.25S 119.22E
116 G11 **Polezhan** ▲ SW Bulgaria 41.42N 23.28E
80 F13 **Poli** Nord, N Cameroon 8.42N 13.09E
Poli see Pólis
109 M19 **Policastro, Golfo di** gulf S Italy
112 D8 **Police** Ger. Pölitz. Zachodniopomorskie, NW Poland 53.34N 14.34E
180 I17 **Police, Pointe** headland Mahé, NE Seychelles 4.48S 55.31E
117 L17 **Polichnítos** var. Polihnitos, Políkhnitos. Lésvos, E Greece 39.04N 26.10E
Poligiros see Polýgyros
109 P17 **Polignano a Mare** Puglia, SE Italy 40.58N 17.13E
105 S9 **Poligny** Jura, E France 46.51N 5.42E
Polihnitos see Polichnítos
Polikastro/Políkastron see Polýkastro
Políkhnitos see Polichnítos
116 K8 **Polikrayshte** Veliko Tŭrnovo, N Bulgaria 43.12N 25.38E
179 Pp10 **Polillo Islands** island group N Philippines
111 Q9 **Polinik** ▲ SW Austria 46.54N 13.10E
123 Mm3 **Pólis** var. Poli. W Cyprus 35.02N 32.27E
Polish People's Republic see Poland
Polish Republic see Poland
119 O3 **Polis'ke** Rus. Polesskoye. Kyyivs'ka Oblast', N Ukraine 51.15N 29.27E
109 N22 **Polistena** Calabria, SW Italy 38.25N 16.04E
Politz see Police
Políyiros see Polýgyros
31 V14 **Polk City** Iowa, C USA 41.46N 93.42W
112 F13 **Polkowice** Ger. Heerwegen. Dolnośląskie, SW Poland 51.31N 16.04E
161 G22 **Pollāchi** Tamil Nādu, SE India 10.38N 77.00E
111 W7 **Pöllau** Steiermark, SE Austria 47.18N 15.46E
201 T13 **Polle** atoll Chuuk Islands, C Micronesia
Pollnow see Polanów
31 N7 **Pollock** South Dakota, N USA 45.53N 100.15W
94 L8 **Polmak** Finnmark, N Norway 70.01N 28.04E
32 L10 **Polo** Illinois, N USA 41.59N 89.34W
200 Qq15 **Poloa** island Tongatapu Group, N Tonga
44 E5 **Polochic, Río** ≈ C Guatemala
Pologi see Polohy
119 V9 **Polohy** Rus. Pologi. Zaporiz'ka Oblast', SE Ukraine 47.29N 36.18E
85 K20 **Polokwane** prev. Pietersburg. Limpopo, NE South Africa 23.54S 29.22E
12 M10 **Polonais, Lac des** ◎ Quebec, SE Canada
63 G20 **Polonio, Cabo** headland E Uruguay 34.22S 53.46W
161 K24 **Polonnaruwa** North Central Province, C Sri Lanka 7.55N 81.01E
118 L5 **Polonne** Rus. Polonnoye. Khmel'nyts'ka Oblast', NW Ukraine 50.10N 27.30E
Polonnoye see Polonne
Polotsk see Polatsk
111 T7 **Pöls** var. Pölsbach. ≈ E Austria
Pölsbach see Pöls
Polska/Polska, Rzeczpospolita/Polska Rzeczpospolita Ludowa see Poland
116 L10 **Polski Gradets** Stara Zagora, C Bulgaria 42.12N 26.06E
116 K8 **Polsko Kosovo** Ruse, N Bulgaria 43.26N 25.40E
35 P8 **Polson** Montana, NW USA 47.41N 114.09W
119 T6 **Poltava** Poltavs'ka Oblast', NE Ukraine 49.33N 34.32E
Poltava see Poltavs'ka Oblast'
119 R5 **Poltavs'ka Oblast'** var. Poltava, Rus. Poltavskaya Oblast'. ◈ province NE Ukraine
Poltavskaya Oblast' see Poltavs'ka Oblast'
Poltoratsk see Ashgabat
120 I5 **Põltsamaa** Ger. Oberpahlen. Jõgevamaa, E Estonia 58.40N 25.58E
120 I4 **Põltsamaa** var. Põltsamaa Jõgi. ≈ C Estonia
Põltsamaa Jõgi see Põltsamaa
125 F10 **Polunochnoye** Sverdlovskaya Oblast', C Russian Federation 60.56N 60.15E
125 G8 **Poluy** ≈ N Russian Federation
120 J6 **Põlva** Ger. Pölwe. Põlvamaa, SE Estonia 58.03N 27.05E
95 N16 **Polvijärvi** Itä-Suomi, E Finland 62.52N 29.19E
Pölwe see Põlva
117 I22 **Polýaigos** island Kykládes, Greece, Aegean Sea
117 I22 **Polyaígou Folégandrou, Stenó** strait Kykládes, Greece, Aegean Sea
128 J3 **Polyarnyy** Murmanskaya Oblast', NW Russian Federation 69.10N 33.21E
129 W5 **Polyarnyy Ural** ▲ NW Russian Federation
117 G14 **Polýgyros** var. Poligiros, Políyiros. Kentrikí Makedonía, N Greece 40.21N 23.27E
116 F13 **Polýkastro** var. Polikastro; prev. Políkastron. Kentrikí Makedonía, N Greece 41.01N 22.33E
199 Kk9 **Polynesia** island group C Pacific Ocean
117 J15 **Políochni** site of ancient city Límnos, E Greece 39.51N 25.21E
43 Y13 **Polyuc** Quintana Roo, E Mexico
111 V10 **Polzela** C Slovenia 46.18N 15.04E
Polzen see Ploučnice
176 Ww9 **Pom** Papua, E Indonesia 1.34S 135.39E
58 D12 **Pomabamba** Ancash, C Peru 8.51S 77.13W
193 D23 **Pomahaka** ≈ South Island, NZ
108 F12 **Pomarance** Toscana, C Italy 43.19N 10.53E
106 G9 **Pombal** Leiria, C Portugal 39.55N 8.37W
78 D9 **Pombas** Santo Antão, NW Cape Verde 17.09N 25.02W
85 N19 **Pomene** Inhambane, SE Mozambique 22.57S 35.34E
112 G8 **Pomerania** cultural region Germany/Poland
112 D7 **Pomeranian Bay** Ger. Pommersche Bucht, Pol. Zatoka Pomorska. bay Germany/Poland
33 T15 **Pomeroy** Ohio, N USA 39.01N 82.01W
34 L10 **Pomeroy** Washington, NW USA 46.28N 117.36W
119 Q8 **Pomichna** Kirovohrads'ka Oblast', C Ukraine 48.07N 31.25E
195 O12 **Pomio** New Britain, E PNG 5.28S 151.29E
Pomir, Dar"yoi see Pamir/Pāmīr, Daryā-ye
29 T6 **Pomme de Terre Lake** ⊠ Missouri, C USA
31 S8 **Pomme de Terre River** ≈ Minnesota, N USA
Pommersche Bucht see Pomeranian Bay

37 T15 **Pomona** California, W USA 34.03N 117.45W
116 N9 **Pomorie** Burgas, E Bulgaria 42.31N 27.39E
Pomorska, Zatoka *see* Pomeranian Bay
112 H8 **Pomorskie** ◆ *province* N Poland
129 Q4 **Pomorskiy Proliv** *strait* NW Russian Federation
129 T10 **Pomozdino** Respublika Komi, NW Russian Federation 62.11N 54.13E
Pompaelo *see* Pamplona
175 Q9 **Pompangeo, Pegunungan** ▲ Sulawesi, C Indonesia
25 Z15 **Pompano Beach** Florida, SE USA 26.14N 80.06W
109 K18 **Pompei** Campania, S Italy 40.45N 14.27E
35 V10 **Pompeys Pillar** Montana, NW USA 45.58N 107.55W
Ponape Ascension Island *see* Pohnpei
31 R13 **Ponca** Nebraska, C USA 42.34N 96.42W
29 O8 **Ponca City** Oklahoma, C USA 36.42N 97.05W
47 T6 **Ponce** C Puerto Rico 18.01N 66.36W
25 X10 **Ponce de Leon Inlet** *inlet* Florida, SE USA
24 K8 **Ponchatoula** Louisiana, S USA 30.26N 90.26W
28 M8 **Pond Creek** Oklahoma, C USA 36.40N 97.48W
161 J20 **Pondicherry** *var.* Puduchcheri, *Fr.* Pondichéry. Pondicherry, SE India 11.58N 79.49E
157 I20 **Pondicherry** *var.* Puduchcheri, *Fr.* Pondichéry. ◆ *union territory* India
Pondichéry *see* Pondicherry
207 N11 **Pond Inlet** Baffin Island, Nunavut, NE Canada 72.37N 77.56W
197 I6 **Ponérihouen** Province Nord, C New Caledonia 21.04S 165.24E
106 J4 **Ponferrada** Castilla-León, NW Spain 42.33N 6.34W
192 N13 **Pongaroa** Manawatu-Wanganui, North Island, NZ 40.36S 176.08E
178 I12 **Pong Nam Ron** Chantaburi, S Thailand 12.55N 102.15E
83 C14 **Pongo** ⚡ S Sudan
158 I7 **Pong Reservoir** ⊠ N India
113 N14 **Poniatowa** Lubelskie, E Poland 51.10N 22.04E
178 J13 **Pônley** Kâmpóng Chhnăng, C Cambodia 12.26N 104.25E
161 I20 **Ponnaiyār** ⚡ SE India
9 Q15 **Ponoka** Alberta, SW Canada 52.42N 113.33W
131 U6 **Ponomarevka** Orenburgskaya Oblast', W Russian Federation 53.16N 54.10E
174 L15 **Ponorogo** Jawa, C Indonesia 7.51S 111.30E
128 M5 **Ponoy** Murmanskaya Oblast', NW Russian Federation 67.00N 41.06E
125 E5 **Ponoy** ⚡ NW Russian Federation
104 K11 **Pons** Charente-Maritime, W France 45.31N 0.31W
Pons *see* Ponts
Pons Aelii *see* Newcastle upon Tyne
Pons Vetus *see* Pontevedra
101 G20 **Pont-à-Celles** Hainaut, S Belgium 50.31N 4.21E
104 K16 **Pontacq** Pyrénées-Atlantiques, SW France 43.10N 0.07W
66 P3 **Ponta Delgada** São Miguel, Azores, Portugal, NE Atlantic Ocean 37.28N 25.40W
66 P3 **Ponta Delgado** ✕ São Miguel, Azores, Portugal, NE Atlantic Ocean
66 N2 **Ponta do Pico** ▲ Pico, Azores, Portugal, NE Atlantic Ocean 38.28N 28.25W
62 J11 **Ponta Grossa** Paraná, S Brazil 25.07S 50.09W
105 S5 **Pont-à-Mousson** Meurthe-et-Moselle, NE France 48.55N 6.03E
105 T9 **Pontarlier** Doubs, E France 46.54N 6.19E
108 G11 **Pontassieve** Toscana, C Italy 43.46N 11.28E
104 L4 **Pont-Audemer** Eure, N France 49.22N 0.31E
24 K9 **Pontchartrain, Lake** ◎ Louisiana, S USA
104 I8 **Pontchâteau** Loire-Atlantique, NW France 47.26N 2.04W
105 R10 **Pont-de-Vaux** Ain, E France 46.25N 4.57E
106 G4 **Ponteareas** Galicia, NW Spain 42.10N 8.29W
108 J6 **Pontebba** Friuli-Venezia Giulia, NE Italy 46.32N 13.18E
106 G4 **Ponte Caldelas** Galicia, NW Spain 42.22N 8.30W
109 J16 **Pontecorvo** Lazio, C Italy 41.27N 13.40E
106 G5 **Ponte da Barca** Viana do Castelo, N Portugal 41.48N 8.25W
106 G5 **Ponte de Lima** Viana do Castelo, N Portugal 41.46N 8.34W
108 F11 **Pontedera** Toscana, C Italy 43.40N 10.37E
106 H10 **Ponte de Sor** Portalegre, C Portugal 39.15N 8.01W
106 H2 **Pontedeume** Galicia, NW Spain 43.22N 8.09W
108 F6 **Ponte di Legno** Lombardia, N Italy 46.16N 10.31E
9 T17 **Ponteix** Saskatchewan, S Canada 49.43N 107.22W
61 N20 **Ponte Nova** Minas Gerais, NE Brazil 20.25S 42.54W
61 G18 **Pontes e Lacerda** Mato Grosso, W Brazil 15.13S 59.21W
106 G4 **Pontevedra** *anc.* Pons Vetus. Galicia, NW Spain 42.25N 8.39W
106 G3 **Pontevedra** ◆ *province* Galicia, NW Spain
106 G4 **Pontevedra, Ría de** *estuary* NW Spain
32 M12 **Pontiac** Illinois, N USA 40.51N 88.37W
33 R9 **Pontiac** Michigan, N USA 42.38N 83.17W
174 Kk8 **Pontianak** Borneo, C Indonesia 0.04S 109.16E
109 I16 **Pontino, Agro** *plain* C Italy
Pontisarae *see* Pontoise
104 H6 **Pontivy** Morbihan, NW France 48.04N 2.58W
104 F6 **Pont-l'Abbé** Finistère, NW France 47.52N 4.13W
105 N4 **Pontoise** *anc.* Briva Isarae, Cergy-Pontoise, Pontisarae. Val-d'Oise, N France 49.03N 2.04E
9 W13 **Ponton** Manitoba, C Canada 54.36N 99.02W
104 J5 **Pontorson** Manche, N France 48.33N 1.31W
24 M2 **Pontotoc** Mississippi, S USA 34.15N 89.00W
27 R9 **Pontotoc** Texas, SW USA 30.52N 98.57W
108 E10 **Pontremoli** Toscana, C Italy 44.24N 9.55E
110 J10 **Pontresina** Graubünden, S Switzerland 46.29N 9.52E
107 U5 **Ponts** *var.* Pons. Cataluña, NE Spain 41.55N 1.12E
105 R14 **Pont-St-Esprit** Gard, S France 44.15N 4.37E
99 K21 **Pontypool** *Wel.* Pontypŵl. SE Wales, UK 51.43N 3.01W
99 J22 **Pontypridd** S Wales, UK 51.37N 3.22W
Pontypŵl *see* Pontypool
45 R17 **Ponuga** Veraguas, SE Panama 7.50N 80.58W
192 L6 **Ponui Island** *island* N NZ
121 K14 **Ponya** *Rus.* Ponya. ⚡ N Belarus
109 I17 **Ponza, Isola di** *island* Isole Ponziane, S Italy
109 I17 **Ponziane, Isole** *island* C Italy
190 F7 **Poochera** South Australia 32.45S 134.51E
99 L24 **Poole** S England, UK 50.43N 1.58W
27 S6 **Poolville** Texas, SW USA 33.00N 97.55W
Poona *see* Pune
190 M8 **Pooncarie** New South Wales, SE Australia 33.26S 142.37E
191 N6 **Poopelloe Lake** *seasonal lake* New South Wales, SE Australia
59 K19 **Poopó** Oruro, C Bolivia 18.22S 66.58W
59 K19 **Poopó, Lago** *var.* Lago Pampa Aullagas. ◎ W Bolivia
192 L3 **Poor Knights Islands** *island* N NZ
41 P10 **Poorman** Alaska, USA 64.05N 155.34W
190 E3 **Pootnoura** South Australia 28.31S 134.09E
153 R10 **Pop** *Rus.* Pap. Namangan Viloyati, E Uzbekistan 40.49N 71.06E
119 X7 **Popasna** *Rus.* Popasnaya. Luhans'ka Oblast', E Ukraine 48.37N 38.24E
Popasnaya *see* Popasna
56 D12 **Popayán** Cauca, SW Colombia 2.27N 76.31W
101 B18 **Poperinge** West-Vlaanderen, W Belgium 50.52N 2.43E
126 K7 **Popigay** Taymyrskiy (Dolgano-Nenetskiy) Avtonomnyy Okrug, N Russian Federation 71.54N 110.45E
126 Jj7 **Popigay** ⚡ N Russian Federation
119 O5 **Popil'nya** Zhytomyrs'ka Oblast', N Ukraine 49.57N 29.24E
190 K8 **Popiltah Lake** *seasonal lake* New South Wales, SE Australia
35 X7 **Poplar** Montana, NW USA 48.06N 105.12W
9 Y14 **Poplar** ⚡ Manitoba, C Canada
29 X8 **Poplar Bluff** Missouri, C USA 36.45N 90.23W
35 X6 **Poplar River** ⚡ Montana, NW USA
43 P14 **Popocatépetl** ⚠ S Mexico 18.59N 98.37W
174 Ll16 **Popoh** Jawa, S Indonesia 8.13S 111.50E
81 H21 **Popokabaka** Bandundu, SW Dem. Rep. Congo 5.43S 16.35E
109 J15 **Popoli** Abruzzo, C Italy 42.09N 13.51E
195 X16 **Popomanaseu, Mount** ▲ Guadalcanal, C Solomon Islands 9.40S 96.01E
194 L15 **Popondetta** Northern, S PNG 8.45S 148.15E
114 F9 **Popovača** Sisak-Moslavina, NE Croatia 45.35N 16.37E
116 J10 **Popovitsa** Türgovishte, C Bulgaria 42.08N 25.04E
116 L8 **Popovo** Türgovishte, N Bulgaria 43.19N 26.13E
Popovo *see* Iskra
Popper *see* Poprad
32 M5 **Popple River** ⚡ Wisconsin, N USA
113 L19 **Poprad** *Ger.* Deutschendorf, *Hung.* Poprád. Prešovský Kraj, E Slovakia 49.03N 20.16E
113 L18 **Poprad** *Ger.* Popper, *Hung.* Poprád. ⚡ Poland/Slovakia
113 L19 **Poprad-Tatry** ✕ (Poprad) Prešovský Kraj, E Slovakia 49.04N 20.21E
23 X7 **Poquoson** Virginia, NE USA 37.07N 76.21W
155 O15 **Porāli** ⚡ SW Pakistan
192 N12 **Porangahau** Hawke's Bay, North Island, NZ 40.19S 176.36E
61 K17 **Porangatu** Goiás, C Brazil 13.28S 49.13W
121 G18 **Porazava** *Pol.* Porozow, *Rus.* Porozovo. Hrodzyenskaya Voblasts', W Belarus 52.57N 24.24E
160 A11 **Porbandar** Gujarāt, W India 21.40N 69.40E
8 I13 **Porcher Island** *island* British Columbia, SW Canada
106 M13 **Porcuna** Andalucía, S Spain 37.52N 4.12W
12 F7 **Porcupine** Ontario, S Canada 48.31N 81.07W
66 M6 **Porcupine Bank** *undersea feature* N Atlantic Ocean
9 V15 **Porcupine Hills** ▲ Manitoba/Saskatchewan, S Canada
32 L3 **Porcupine Mountains** *hill range* Michigan, N USA
66 M7 **Porcupine Plain** *undersea feature* E Atlantic Ocean
14 F4 **Porcupine River** ⚡ Canada/USA
108 I7 **Pordenone** *anc.* Portenau. Friuli-Venezia Giulia, NE Italy 45.58N 12.39E
56 H9 **Pore** Casanare, E Colombia 5.42N 71.58W
114 A9 **Poreč** *It.* Parenzo. Istra, NW Croatia 45.16N 13.36E
62 I9 **Porecatu** Paraná, S Brazil 22.46S 51.22W
Porech'ye *see* Parechcha
131 P4 **Poretskoye** Chavash Respubliki, W Russian Federation 55.12N 46.20E
79 Q13 **Porga** N Benin 11.04N 0.58E
194 G12 **Porgera** Enga, W PNG 5.27S 143.09E
95 K18 **Pori** *Swe.* Björneborg. Länsi-Suomi, W Finland 61.28N 21.49E
193 L14 **Porirua** Wellington, North Island, NZ 41.08S 174.50E
94 I12 **Porjus** Norrbotten, N Sweden 66.55N 19.55E
128 G14 **Porkhov** Pskovskaya Oblast', W Russian Federation 57.46N 29.26E
57 O4 **Porlamar** Nueva Esparta, NE Venezuela 10.56N 63.53W
104 I8 **Pornic** Loire-Atlantique, NW France 47.07N 2.07W
194 G12 **Poroma** Southern Highlands, W PNG 6.15S 143.34E
127 Oo15 **Poronaysk** Ostrov Sakhalin, Sakhalinskaya Oblast', SE Russian Federation 49.15N 143.00E
117 G20 **Póros** Póros, S Greece 37.30N 23.29E
117 C19 **Póros** Kefallinía, Iónioi Nísoi, Greece, C Mediterranean Sea 38.09N 20.45E
117 G20 **Póros** *island* S Greece
83 G24 **Poroto Mountains** ▲ SW Tanzania
114 B10 **Porozina** Primorje-Gorski Kotar, NW Croatia 45.07N 14.17E
Porozovo/Porozow *see* Porazava
205 X15 **Porpoise Bay** *bay* Antarctica
67 G15 **Porpoise Point** *headland* NE Ascension Island 7.54S 14.22W
67 C25 **Porpoise Point** *headland* East Falkland, Falkland Islands 52.19S 59.18W
110 C6 **Porrentruy** Jura, NW Switzerland 47.25N 7.06E
108 F10 **Porretta Terme** Emilia-Romagna, C Italy 44.10N 11.01E
106 G4 **Porriño** Galicia, NW Spain 42.10N 8.37W
94 L7 **Porsangerfjorden** *fjord* N Norway
94 K8 **Porsangerhalvøya** *peninsula* N Norway
97 G16 **Porsgrunn** Telemark, S Norway 59.07N 9.37E
142 E13 **Porsuk Çayı** ⚡ C Turkey
Porsy *see* Boldumsaz
59 N18 **Portachuelo** Santa Cruz, C Bolivia 17.20S 63.24W
190 I9 **Port Adelaide** South Australia 34.49S 138.31E
99 F15 **Portadown** *Ir.* Port An Dúnáin. S Northern Ireland, UK 54.25N 6.27W
33 P10 **Portage** Michigan, N USA 42.12N 85.34W
20 D15 **Portage** Pennsylvania, NE USA 40.23N 78.40W
32 K8 **Portage** Wisconsin, N USA 43.33N 89.28W
32 M3 **Portage Lake** ◎ Michigan, N USA
9 X16 **Portage la Prairie** Manitoba, S Canada 49.58N 98.19W
33 R11 **Portage River** ⚡ Ohio, N USA
29 Y8 **Portageville** Missouri, C USA 36.25N 89.42W
30 L2 **Portal** North Dakota, N USA 48.57N 102.33W
8 L17 **Port Alberni** Vancouver Island, British Columbia, SW Canada 49.10N 124.49W
12 E15 **Port Albert** Ontario, S Canada 43.51N 81.42W
106 I10 **Portalegre** *anc.* Ammaia, Amoea. Portalegre, E Portugal 39.16N 7.25W
106 H10 **Portalegre** ◆ *district* C Portugal
39 V12 **Portales** New Mexico, SW USA 34.11N 103.19W
41 X14 **Port Alexander** Baranof Island, Alaska, USA 56.15N 134.38W
85 I25 **Port Alfred** Eastern Cape, S South Africa 33.30S 26.55E
8 J16 **Port Alice** Vancouver Island, British Columbia, SW Canada 50.22N 127.24W
24 J8 **Port Allen** Louisiana, S USA 30.27N 91.12W
Port Amelia *see* Pemba
Port An Dúnáin *see* Portadown
34 G7 **Port Angeles** Washington, NW USA 48.07N 123.25W
46 L12 **Port Antonio** NE Jamaica 18.10N 76.27W
117 D16 **Pórta Panagiá** *religious building* Thessalía, C Greece 39.28N 21.37E
27 T14 **Port Aransas** Texas, SW USA 27.49N 97.03W
99 E18 **Portarlington** *Ir.* Cúil an tSúdaire. C Ireland 53.10N 7.10W
191 P17 **Port Arthur** Tasmania, SE Australia 43.09S 147.51E
27 Y11 **Port Arthur** Texas, SW USA 29.55N 93.55W
98 G12 **Port Askaig** W Scotland, UK 55.51N 6.06W
190 I7 **Port Augusta** South Australia 32.29S 137.48E
46 M9 **Port-au-Prince** ● (Haiti) C Haiti 18.33N 72.19W
46 M9 **Port-au-Prince** ✕ E Haiti 18.38N 72.13W
24 I8 **Port Barre** Louisiana, S USA 30.33N 91.57W
157 Q19 **Port Blair** Andaman and Nicobar Islands, SE India 11.40N 92.43E
27 X12 **Port Bolivar** Texas, SW USA 29.21N 94.45W
107 X4 **Portbou** Cataluña, NE Spain 42.26N 3.10E
79 N17 **Port Bouet** ✕ (Abidjan) SE Ivory Coast 5.17N 3.55W
190 I8 **Port Broughton** South Australia 33.39S 137.55E
12 F17 **Port Burwell** Ontario, S Canada 42.37N 80.47W
10 G17 **Port Burwell** Quebec, NE Canada 60.25N 64.49W
190 M13 **Port Campbell** Victoria, SE Australia 38.37S 143.00E
13 V4 **Port-Cartier** Quebec, SE Canada 50.00N 66.55W
193 F23 **Port Chalmers** Otago, South Island, NZ 45.46S 170.37E
25 W14 **Port Charlotte** Florida, SE USA 27.00N 82.07W
40 L9 **Port Clarence** Alaska, USA 65.15N 166.51W
8 I13 **Port Clements** Graham Island, British Columbia, SW Canada 53.37N 132.12W
33 S11 **Port Clinton** Ohio, N USA 41.30N 82.56W
12 H17 **Port Colborne** Ontario, S Canada 42.51N 79.16W
13 Y7 **Port-Daniel** Quebec, SE Canada 48.10N 64.58W
Port Darwin *see* Darwin
191 O17 **Port Davey** *headland* Tasmania, SE Australia 43.19S 145.54E
46 K8 **Port-de-Paix** NW Haiti 19.53N 72.50W
189 W4 **Port Douglas** Queensland, NE Australia 16.32S 145.27E
8 J13 **Port Edward** British Columbia, SW Canada 54.10N 130.16W
85 K24 **Port Edward** KwaZulu/Natal, SE South Africa 31.03S 30.13E
60 J12 **Portel** Pará, NE Brazil 1.58S 50.45W
106 H12 **Portel** Évora, S Portugal 38.18N 7.42W
12 E14 **Port Elgin** Ontario, S Canada 44.26N 81.22W
47 Y14 **Port Elizabeth** Bequia, Saint Vincent and the Grenadines 13.01N 61.15W
85 I26 **Port Elizabeth** Eastern Cape, S South Africa 33.58S 25.36E
98 G13 **Port Ellen** W Scotland, UK 55.37N 6.12W
Portenau *see* Pordenone
99 H16 **Port Erin** SW Isle of Man 54.05N 4.47W
47 Q13 **Porter Point** *headland* Saint Vincent, Saint Vincent and the Grenadines 13.22N 61.10W
193 G18 **Porters Pass** *pass* South Island, NZ 43.18S 171.45E
85 E25 **Porterville** Western Cape, SW South Africa 33.03S 19.00E
37 R12 **Porterville** California, W USA 36.03N 119.03W
Port-Étienne *see* Nouâdhibou
190 L13 **Port Fairy** Victoria, SE Australia 38.24S 142.13E
192 M4 **Port Fitzroy** Great Barrier Island, Auckland, NE NZ 36.10S 175.21E
Port Florence *see* Kisumu
Port-Francqui *see* Ilebo
81 C18 **Port-Gentil** Ogooué-Maritime, W Gabon 0.40S 8.49E
190 I7 **Port Germein** South Australia 33.02S 138.01E
24 J6 **Port Gibson** Mississippi, S USA 31.57N 90.58W
41 Q13 **Port Graham** Alaska, USA 59.21N 151.49W
79 U17 **Port Harcourt** Rivers, S Nigeria 4.43N 7.02E
8 J16 **Port Hardy** Vancouver Island, British Columbia, SW Canada 50.40N 127.30W
Port Harrison *see* Inukjuak
11 R14 **Port Hawkesbury** Cape Breton Island, Nova Scotia, SE Canada 45.36N 61.22W
188 I6 **Port Hedland** Western Australia 20.22S 118.40E
41 O15 **Port Heiden** Alaska, USA 56.54N 158.40W
99 I19 **Porthmadog** *var.* Portmadoc. NW Wales, UK 52.55N 4.07W
12 I15 **Port Hope** Ontario, SE Canada 43.56N 78.16W
11 S9 **Port Hope Simpson** Newfoundland and Labrador, E Canada 52.30N 56.18W
67 C24 **Port Howard Settlement** West Falkland, Falkland Islands
33 T9 **Port Huron** Michigan, N USA 42.58N 82.25W
109 K17 **Portici** Campania, S Italy 40.48N 14.19E
143 Y13 **Port-İliç** *Rus.* Port Il'ich. SE Azerbaijan 38.54N 48.49E
Port Il'ich *see* Port-İliç
106 G14 **Portimão** *var.* Vila Nova de Portimão. Faro, S Portugal 37.07N 8.31W
27 T17 **Port Isabel** Texas, SW USA 26.04N 97.13W
20 J13 **Port Jervis** New York, NE USA 41.22N 74.39W
57 S7 **Port Kaituma** NW Guyana 7.42N 59.52W
130 K12 **Port-Katon** Rostovskaya Oblast', SW Russian Federation 46.52N 38.46E
191 S9 **Port Kembla** New South Wales, SE Australia 34.29S 150.53E
190 F8 **Port Kenny** South Australia 33.09S 134.38E
Port Klang *see* Pelabuhan Klang
Port Láirge *see* Waterford
191 S8 **Portland** New South Wales, SE Australia 33.24S 150.00E
190 L13 **Portland** Victoria, SE Australia 38.21S 141.37E
192 K4 **Portland** Northland, North Island, NZ 35.48S 174.19E
33 Q13 **Portland** Indiana, N USA 40.25N 84.58W
21 P8 **Portland** Maine, NE USA 43.40N 70.16W
33 Q9 **Portland** Michigan, N USA 42.51N 84.52W
31 Q4 **Portland** North Dakota, N USA 47.28N 97.22W
34 G11 **Portland** Oregon, NW USA 45.31N 122.40W
22 J8 **Portland** Tennessee, S USA 36.34N 86.31W
27 T14 **Portland** Texas, SW USA 27.52N 97.19W
34 G11 **Portland** ✕ Oregon, NW USA 45.36N 122.34W
190 L13 **Portland Bay** *bay* Victoria, SE Australia
46 K13 **Portland Bight** *bay* S Jamaica
99 L24 **Portland Bill** *var.* Bill of Portland. *headland* S England, UK 50.31N 2.28W
Portland, Bill of *see* Portland Bill
191 P15 **Portland, Cape** *headland* Tasmania, SE Australia 40.46S 147.58E
8 J12 **Portland Inlet** *inlet* British Columbia, W Canada
192 P11 **Portland Island** *island* E NZ
67 F15 **Portland Point** *headland* SW Ascension Island
46 J13 **Portland Point** *headland* C Jamaica 17.42N 77.10W
105 P16 **Port-la-Nouvelle** Aude, S France 43.01N 3.04E
Portlaoighise *see* Port Laoise
99 E18 **Port Laoise** *var.* Portlaoise, *Ir.* Portlaoighise; *prev.* Maryborough. C Ireland 53.01N 7.16W
27 U13 **Port Lavaca** Texas, SW USA 28.36N 96.39W
190 G9 **Port Lincoln** South Australia 34.43S 135.49E
41 Q14 **Port Lions** Kodiak Island, Alaska, USA 57.55N 152.48W
78 I15 **Port Loko** W Sierra Leone 8.49N 12.49W
67 E24 **Port Louis** East Falkland, Falkland Islands 51.31S 58.07W
47 Y5 **Port-Louis** Grande Terre, N Guadeloupe 16.25N 61.31W
181 X16 **Port Louis** ● (Mauritius) NW Mauritius 20.10S 57.30E
Port Louis *see* Scarborough
Port-Lyautey *see* Kénitra
190 K12 **Port MacDonnell** South Australia 38.04S 140.40E
191 U7 **Port Macquarie** New South Wales, SE Australia 31.25S 152.55E
Portmadoc *see* Porthmadog
Port Mahon *see* Mahón
46 K12 **Port Maria** C Jamaica 18.21N 76.53W
8 K16 **Port McNeill** Vancouver Island, British Columbia, SW Canada 50.34N 127.06W
11 P11 **Port-Menier** Île d'Anticosti, Quebec, E Canada 49.49N 64.19W
41 N15 **Port Moller** Alaska, USA 56.00N 96.31W
46 L13 **Port Morant** E Jamaica 17.52N 76.19W
46 K13 **Portmore** C Jamaica 17.58N 76.52W
194 I16 **Port Moresby** ● (PNG) Central/National Capital District, SW PNG 9.28S 147.11E
Port Natal *see* Durban
27 Y11 **Port Neches** Texas, SW USA 29.59N 93.57W
190 G9 **Port Neill** South Australia 34.06S 136.19E
13 S6 **Portneuf** ⚡ Quebec, SE Canada
13 R6 **Portneuf, Lac** ◎ Quebec, SE Canada
85 D23 **Port Nolloth** Northern Cape, W South Africa 29.18S 16.58E
20 J17 **Port Norris** New Jersey, NE USA 39.13N 75.00W
Port-Nouveau-Québec *see* Kangiqsualujjuaq
106 G6 **Porto** *Eng.* Oporto; *anc.* Portus Cale. Porto, NW Portugal 41.09N 8.37W
106 G6 **Porto** *var.* Pôrto. ◆ *district* N Portugal
106 G6 **Porto** ✕ Porto, W Portugal 41.15N 8.45W
63 I16 **Porto Alegre** *var.* Pôrto Alegre. *state capital* Rio Grande do Sul, S Brazil 30.03S 51.10W
Porto Alexandre *see* Tombua
84 B12 **Porto Amboim** Cuanza Sul, NW Angola 10.43S 13.49E
Porto Amélia *see* Pemba
Porto Bello *see* Portobelo
45 T14 **Portobelo** *var.* Porto Bello, Puerto Bello. Colón, N Panama 9.32N 79.40W
62 G10 **Pôrto Camargo** Paraná, S Brazil 23.23S 53.47W
27 U13 **Port O'Connor** Texas, SW USA 28.26N 96.26W
Pôrto de Mós *see* Porto de Moz
60 J12 **Porto de Moz** *var.* Pôrto de Mós. Pará, NE Brazil 1.45S 52.15W
66 O5 **Porto do Moniz** Madeira, Portugal, NE Atlantic Ocean
61 H16 **Porto dos Gaúchos** Mato Grosso, W Brazil 11.31S 57.16W
Porto Edda *see* Sarandë
109 J24 **Porto Empedocle** Sicilia, Italy, C Mediterranean Sea 37.16N 13.31E
61 H20 **Porto Esperança** Mato Grosso do Sul, SW Brazil 19.36S 57.24W
108 E13 **Portoferraio** Toscana, C Italy 42.48N 10.18E
98 G6 **Port of Ness** NW Scotland, UK 58.29N 6.15W
47 U14 **Port-of-Spain** ● (Trinidad and Tobago) Trinidad, Trinidad and Tobago 10.39N 61.30W
Port of Spain *see* Piarco
105 X15 **Porto, Golfe de** *gulf* Corse, France, C Mediterranean Sea
Porto Grande *see* Mindelo
108 I7 **Portogruaro** Veneto, NE Italy 45.46N 12.49E
37 P5 **Portola** California, W USA 39.48N 120.28W
197 B12 **Port-Olry** Espiritu Santo, C Vanuatu 15.03S 167.04E
95 J17 **Pörtom** *Fin.* Pirttikylä. Länsi-Suomi, W Finland 62.42N 21.40E
Port Omna *see* Portumna
61 G21 **Porto Murtinho** Mato Grosso do Sul, SW Brazil 21.42S 57.52W
61 K16 **Porto Nacional** Tocantins, C Brazil 10.40S 48.19W
79 S16 **Porto-Novo** ● (Benin) S Benin 6.28N 2.37E
25 X10 **Port Orange** Florida, SE USA 29.06N 80.59W
34 G8 **Port Orchard** Washington, NW USA 47.32N 122.38W
Porto Re *see* Kraljevica
34 E15 **Port Orford** Oregon, NW USA 42.45N 124.30W
Porto Rico *see* Puerto Rico
108 J13 **Porto San Giorgio** Marche, C Italy 43.10N 13.47E
109 F14 **Porto San Stefano** Toscana, C Italy 42.26N 11.09E
66 P5 **Porto Santo** *var.* Vila Baleira. Porto Santo, Madeira, Portugal, NE Atlantic Ocean 33.04N 16.19W
66 Q5 **Porto Santo** ✕ Porto Santo, Madeira, Portugal, NE Atlantic Ocean 33.04N 16.19W
66 P5 **Porto Santo** *var.* Ilha do Porto Santo. *island* Madeira, Portugal, NE Atlantic Ocean
62 H9 **Porto São José** Paraná, S Brazil 22.43S 53.10W
61 O19 **Porto Seguro** Bahia, E Brazil 16.25S 39.07W
109 B17 **Porto Torres** Sardegna, Italy, C Mediterranean Sea 40.49N 8.22E
61 J23 **Porto União** Santa Catarina, S Brazil 26.15S 51.04W
105 Y16 **Porto-Vecchio** Corse, France, C Mediterranean Sea 41.35N 9.17E
61 E15 **Porto Velho** *var.* Velho. *state capital* Rondônia, W Brazil 8.45S 63.54W
58 A6 **Portoviejo** *var.* Puertoviejo. Manabí, W Ecuador 1.02S 80.31W
193 B26 **Port Pegasus** *bay* Stewart Island, NZ
12 H15 **Port Perry** Ontario, SE Canada 44.08N 78.57W
191 N12 **Port Phillip Bay** *harbor* Victoria, SE Australia
190 I8 **Port Pirie** South Australia 33.10S 138.01E
98 G9 **Portree** N Scotland, UK 57.25N 6.11W
Port Rex *see* East London
Port Rois *see* Portrush
46 K13 **Port Royal** E Jamaica 17.56N 76.49W
23 R15 **Port Royal** South Carolina, SE USA 32.22N 80.41W
23 R15 **Port Royal Sound** *inlet* South Carolina, SE USA
99 F14 **Portrush** *Ir.* Port Rois. N Northern Ireland, UK 55.12N 6.40W
77 W7 **Port Said** *Ar.* Būr Sa'īd. N Egypt 31.16N 32.18E
25 R9 **Port Saint Joe** Florida, SE USA 29.49N 85.18W
25 Y11 **Port Saint John** Florida, SE USA 28.28N 80.46W
85 K24 **Port St.Johns** Eastern Cape, SE South Africa 31.34S 29.30E
105 R16 **Port-St-Louis-du-Rhône** Bouches-du-Rhône, SE France 43.22N 4.48E
46 K10 **Port Salut** SW Haiti 18.04N 73.55W
67 E24 **Port Salvador** *inlet* East Falkland, Falkland Islands
67 D24 **Port San Carlos** East Falkland, Falkland Islands 51.30S 58.58W
11 S10 **Port Saunders** Newfoundland and Labrador, SE Canada 50.40N 57.17W
85 K24 **Port Shepstone** KwaZulu/Natal, E South Africa 30.40S 30.24E
47 O11 **Portsmouth** *var.* Grand-Anse. NW Dominica 15.33N 61.27W
99 N24 **Portsmouth** S England, UK 50.48N 1.04W
21 P10 **Portsmouth** New Hampshire, NE USA 43.04N 70.46W
33 S15 **Portsmouth** Ohio, N USA 38.43N 83.00W
23 X7 **Portsmouth** Virginia, NE USA 36.50N 76.18W
12 E17 **Port Stanley** Ontario, S Canada 42.39N 81.12W
67 B25 **Port Stephens** *inlet* West Falkland, Falkland Islands
67 B25 **Port Stephens Settlement** West Falkland, Falkland Islands
99 F14 **Portstewart** *Ir.* Port Stíobhaird. N Northern Ireland, UK 55.10N 6.43W
Port Stíobhaird *see* Portstewart
82 I7 **Port Sudan** Red Sea, NE Sudan 19.37N 37.13E
24 L10 **Port Sulphur** Louisiana, S USA 29.28N 89.41W
Port Swettenham *see* Klang/Pelabuhan Klang
99 J22 **Port Talbot** S Wales, UK 51.36N 3.46W
94 L11 **Porttipahdan Tekojärvi** ◎ N Finland
34 G7 **Port Townsend** Washington, NW USA 48.07N 122.45W
106 H9 **Portugal** *off.* Republic of Portugal. ◆ *republic* SW Europe
107 O2 **Portugalete** País Vasco, N Spain 43.19N 3.01W
56 J6 **Portuguesa** *off.* Estado Portuguesa. ◆ *state* N Venezuela
Portuguese East Africa *see* Mozambique
Portuguese Guinea *see* Guinea-Bissau
Portuguese Timor *see* East Timor
Portuguese West Africa *see* Angola
99 D18 **Portumna** *Ir.* Port Omna. W Ireland 53.06N 8.13W
Portus Cale *see* Porto
Portus Magnus *see* Almería
Portus Magonis *see* Mahón
105 P17 **Port-Vendres** *var.* Port Vendres. Pyrénées-Orientales, S France 42.31N 3.06E
190 H9 **Port Victoria** South Australia 34.34S 137.31E
197 C14 **Port-Vila** *var.* Vila. ● (Vanuatu) Éfaté, C Vanuatu 17.45S 168.21E
190 I9 **Port Wakefield** South Australia 34.13S 138.10E
33 N8 **Port Washington** Wisconsin, N USA 43.22N 87.54W
59 J14 **Porvenir** Pando, NW Bolivia 11.15S 68.43W
65 I24 **Porvenir** Magallanes, S Chile 53.18S 70.22W
63 D18 **Porvenir** Paysandú, W Uruguay 32.22S 57.58W
95 M19 **Porvoo** *Swe.* Borgå. Etelä-Suomi, S Finland 60.25N 25.40E
Porzecze *see* Parechcha
106 M10 **Porzuna** Castilla-La Mancha, C Spain 39.10N 4.10W
63 E14 **Posadas** Misiones, NE Argentina 27.27S 55.52W
106 L13 **Posadas** Andalucía, S Spain 37.48N 5.06W
Poschega *see* Požega
110 J11 **Poschiavino** ⚡ Italy/Switzerland
110 J10 **Poschiavo** *Ger.* Puschlav. Graubünden, S Switzerland 46.19N 10.02E
114 D12 **Posedarje** Zadar, SW Croatia 44.12N 15.27E
Posen *see* Poznań
128 L14 **Poshekhon'ye** Yaroslavskaya Oblast', W Russian Federation 58.31N 39.07E
94 M13 **Posio** Lappi, NE Finland 66.06N 28.16E
Poskam *see* Zepu
Posnania *see* Poznań
175 Pp9 **Poso** Sulawesi, C Indonesia 1.22S 120.45E
61 P15 **Poço da Cruz, Açude** ⊠ E Brazil
175 Pp10 **Poso, Danau** ◎ Sulawesi, C Indonesia
143 R10 **Posof** Ardahan, NE Turkey 41.31N 42.44E
175 Pp9 **Poso, Sungai** ⚡ Sulawesi, C Indonesia
27 R6 **Possum Kingdom Lake** ⊠ Texas, SW USA
27 N6 **Post** Texas, SW USA 33.11N 101.22W
Postavy/Postawy *see* Pastavy
10 I7 **Poste-de-la-Baleine** Quebec, NE Canada 55.13N 77.54W
101 M17 **Posterholt** Limburg, SE Netherlands 51.07N 6.01E
85 G22 **Postmasburg** Northern Cape, N South Africa 28.19S 23.04E
Pôsto Diuarum *see* Campo de Diauarum
61 I16 **Pôsto Jacaré** Mato Grosso, W Brazil 11.59S 53.27W
111 T12 **Postojna** *Ger.* Adelsberg, *It.* Postumia. SW Slovenia 45.48N 14.12E
Postumia *see* Postojna
31 X12 **Postville** Iowa, C USA 43.04N 91.34W
Pöstyén *see* Piešt'any
115 G14 **Posušje** Federacija Bosna I Herzegovina, SE Bosnia & Herzegovina 43.28N 17.20E
175 Pp16 **Pota** Flores, C Indonesia 8.21S 120.49E
117 G23 **Potamós** Antikýthira, S Greece 35.53N 23.17E
57 S9 **Potaru River** ⚡ C Guyana
85 I21 **Potchefstroom** North-West, N South Africa 26.42S 27.06E
29 R11 **Poteau** Oklahoma, C USA 35.03N 94.37W
27 R12 **Poteet** Texas, SW USA 29.02N 98.34W
117 G14 **Poteídaia** *site of ancient city* Kentrikí Makedonía, N Greece 40.12N 23.21E
Potentia *see* Potenza
109 M18 **Potenza** *anc.* Potentia. Basilicata, S Italy 40.40N 15.49E
193 A24 **Poteriteri, Lake** ◎ South Island, NZ
106 M2 **Potes** Cantabria, N Spain 43.10N 4.40W
Potgietersrus *see* Mokopane
27 S12 **Poth** Texas, SW USA 29.04N 98.04W
34 J9 **Potholes Reservoir** ⊠ Washington, NW USA
143 Q9 **P'ot'i** W Georgia 42.10N 41.42E
79 X13 **Potiskum** Yobe, NE Nigeria 11.38N 11.07E
Potkozarje *see* Ivanjska
34 M9 **Potlatch** Idaho, NW USA 46.55N 116.51W
35 N9 **Pot Mountain** ▲ Idaho, NW USA 46.44N 115.24W
115 H14 **Potoci** Federacija Bosna I Hercegovina, SE Bosnia & Herzegovina 43.24N 17.52E
23 V3 **Potomac River** ⚡ NE USA
29 W6 **Potosi** Missouri, C USA 37.56N 90.47W
59 L20 **Potosí** Potosí, S Bolivia 19.34S 65.51W
44 H9 **Potosí** Chinandega, NW Nicaragua 12.58N 87.30W
59 K21 **Potosí** ◆ *department* SW Bolivia
64 H7 **Potrerillos** Atacama, N Chile 26.25S 70.09W
44 H5 **Potrerillos** Cortés, NW Honduras 15.12N 87.57W
64 H8 **Potro, Cerro del** ▲ N Chile 28.22S 69.34W
102 N12 **Potsdam** Brandenburg, NE Germany 52.24N 13.04E
20 J7 **Potsdam** New York, NE USA 44.40N 74.58W
111 X5 **Pottendorf** Niederösterreich, E Austria 47.53N 16.22E
111 X5 **Pottenstein** Niederösterreich, E Austria 47.55N 16.06E
197 G4 **Pott, Île** *island* Îles Belep, W New Caledonia
20 I15 **Pottstown** Pennsylvania, NE USA 40.15N 75.39W
20 H14 **Pottsville** Pennsylvania, NE USA 40.40N 76.10W
161 L25 **Pottuvil** Eastern Province, SE Sri Lanka 6.52N 81.49E
155 U6 **Potwar Plateau** *plateau* NE Pakistan
104 J7 **Pouancé** Maine-et-Loire, W France 47.46N 1.11W
197 H5 **Pouébo** Province Nord, C New Caledonia 20.40S 164.02E
197 H6 **Pouembout** Province Nord, W New Caledonia 21.09S 164.52E
13 R6 **Poulin de Courval, Lac** ◎ Quebec, SE Canada
20 L9 **Poultney** Vermont, NE USA 43.31N 73.12W
197 H5 **Poum** Province Nord, W New Caledonia 20.15S 164.03E
61 L21 **Pouso Alegre** Minas Gerais, NE Brazil 22.13S 45.55W
198 Bb8 **Poutasi** Upolu, SE Samoa 14.00S 171.43W
178 Ii12 **Poŭthĭsăt** *prev.* Pursat. Poŭthĭsăt, W Cambodia 12.31N 103.55E
178 Ii13 **Poŭthĭsăt, Stœng** *prev.* Pursat. ⚡ W Cambodia
104 J9 **Pouzauges** Vendée, NW France 46.47N 0.54W
Po, Valle del *see* Po Valley
108 F8 **Po Valley** *It.* Valle del Po. *valley* N Italy
113 I19 **Považská Bystrica** *Ger.* Waagbistritz, *Hung.* Vágbeszterce. Trenčiansky Kraj, W Slovakia 49.07N 18.26E
128 J10 **Povenets** Respublika Kareliya, NW Russian Federation 62.50N 34.47E
192 Q9 **Poverty Bay** *inlet* North Island, NZ
114 K12 **Povlen** ▲ W Serbia and Montenegro (Yugoslavia)
106 G6 **Póvoa de Varzim** Porto, NW Portugal 41.22N 8.46W
131 N8 **Povorino** Voronezhskaya Oblast', W Russian Federation 51.10N 42.16E
Povungnituk *see* Puvirnituq

◆ Country ● Country Capital ◇ Dependent Territory ○ Dependent Territory Capital ◆ Administrative Region ✕ International Airport ▲ Mountain ▲ Mountain Range ⚠ Volcano ⚡ River ◎ Lake ⊠ Reservoir

10 J3 **Povungnituk, Rivière de** ≈ Quebec, NE Canada
12 H11 **Powassan** Ontario, S Canada 46.04N 79.21W
37 U17 **Poway** California, W USA 32.57N 117.02W
35 W14 **Powder River** Wyoming, C USA 43.01N 106.57W
35 Y10 **Powder River** ≈ Montana/Wyoming, NW USA
34 L12 **Powder River** ≈ Oregon, NW USA
35 W13 **Powder River Pass** *pass* Wyoming, C USA 44.08N 107.03W
35 U12 **Powell** Wyoming, C USA 44.45N 108.45W
67 I22 **Powell Basin** *undersea feature* NW Weddell Sea
38 M8 **Powell, Lake** ◎ Utah, W USA
39 R4 **Powell, Mount** ▲ Colorado, C USA 39.25N 106.20W
8 L17 **Powell River** British Columbia, SW Canada 49.54N 124.34W
33 N5 **Powers** Michigan, N USA 45.40N 87.29W
30 K2 **Powers Lake** North Dakota, N USA 48.33N 102.37W
23 V6 **Powhatan** Virginia, NE USA 37.32N 77.55W
33 V13 **Powhatan Point** Ohio, N USA 39.49N 80.49W
99 J20 **Powys** *cultural region* E Wales, UK
197 I6 **Poya** Province Nord, C New Caledonia 21.19S 165.07E
167 P10 **Poyang Hu** ◎ S China
126 Mm16 **Poyarkovo** Amurskaya Oblast', SE Russian Federation 49.37N 128.40E
32 L7 **Poygan, Lake** ◎ Wisconsin, N USA
111 Y2 **Poysdorf** Niederösterreich, NE Austria 48.40N 16.37E
114 N11 **Požarevac** *Ger.* Passarowitz. Serbia, NE Serbia and Montenegro (Yugoslavia) 44.37N 21.11E
43 Q13 **Poza Rica** *var.* Poza Rica de Hidalgo. Veracruz-Llave, E Mexico 20.33N 97.27W
Poza Rica de Hidalgo *see* Poza Rica
114 L13 **Požega** *Prev.* Slavonska Požega; *Ger.* Poschega, *Hung.* Pozsega. Požega-Slavonija, NE Croatia 43.19N 17.42E
114 H9 **Požega-Slavonija** *off.* Požeško-Slavonska Županija. ◈ *province* NE Croatia
129 U13 **Pozhva** Komi-Permyatskiy Avtonomnyy Okrug, NW Russian Federation 59.07N 56.04E
112 G11 **Poznań** *Ger.* Posen, Posnania. Wielkolpolskie, C Poland 52.24N 16.56E
107 O13 **Pozo Alcón** Andalucía, S Spain 37.43N 2.55W
64 H3 **Pozo Almonte** Tarapacá, N Chile 20.13S 69.48W
106 L12 **Pozoblanco** Andalucía, S Spain 38.22N 4.47W
107 Q11 **Pozo Cañada** Castilla-La Mancha, C Spain 38.49N 1.45W
64 N5 **Pozo Colorado** Presidente Hayes, C Paraguay 23.25S 58.51W
65 J20 **Pozos, Punta** *headland* S Argentina 47.55S 65.46W
Pozsega *see* Požega
Pozsony *see* Bratislava
57 N5 **Pozuelos** Anzoátegui, NE Venezuela 10.10N 64.39W
109 L26 **Pozzallo** Sicilia, Italy, C Mediterranean Sea 36.43N 14.51E
109 K17 **Pozzuoli** *anc.* Puteoli. Campania, S Italy 40.49N 14.07E
79 P17 **Pra** ≈ S Ghana
Prabumulih *see* Perabumulih
113 C19 **Prachatice** *Ger.* Prachatitz. Budějovický Kraj, S Czech Republic 49.01N 14.00E
Prachatitz *see* Prachatice
178 Hh11 **Prachin Buri** *var.* Prachinburi. Prachin Buri, C Thailand 14.05N 101.19E
Prachuab Girikhand *see* Prachuap Khiri Khan
178 H13 **Prachuap Khiri Khan** *var.* Prachuab Girikhand. Prachuap Khiri Khan, SW Thailand 11.50N 99.45E
113 H16 **Praděd** *Ger.* Altvater. ▲ NE Czech Republic 50.06N 17.14E
56 D11 **Pradera** Valle del Cauca, SW Colombia 3.24N 76.19W
105 O17 **Prades** Pyrénées-Orientales, S France 42.36N 2.22E
61 O19 **Prado** Bahia, SE Brazil 17.13S 39.15W
56 E11 **Prado** Tolima, C Colombia 3.38N 74.57W
Prado del Ganso *see* Goose Green
Prae *see* Phrae
Prag/Praga/Prague *see* Praha
29 O10 **Prague** Oklahoma, C USA 35.29N 96.40W
113 D16 **Praha** *Eng.* Prague, *Ger.* Prag, *Pol.* Praga. ● (Czech Republic) Středočeský Kraj, NW Czech Republic 50.06N 14.25E
118 J13 **Prahova** ◈ *county* SE Romania
118 J13 **Prahova** ≈ S Romania
78 E10 **Praia** ● (Cape Verde) Santiago, S Cape Verde 14.55N 23.31W
85 M21 **Praia do Bilene** Gaza, S Mozambique 25.18S 33.10E
85 M20 **Praia do Xai-Xai** Gaza, S Mozambique 25.04S 33.43E
118 J10 **Praid** *Hung.* Parajd. Harghita, C Romania 46.33N 25.06E
28 J3 **Prairie Dog Creek** ≈ Kansas/Nebraska, C USA
32 J9 **Prairie du Chien** Wisconsin, N USA 43.01N 91.07W
29 S9 **Prairie Grove** Arkansas, C USA 35.58N 94.19W
33 P10 **Prairie River** ≈ Michigan, N USA
Prairie State *see* Illinois
27 V11 **Prairie View** Texas, SW USA 30.05N 95.59W
178 Ii11 **Prakhon Chai** Buri Ram, E Thailand 14.36N 103.04E
111 R4 **Pram** ≈ N Austria
111 S4 **Prambachkirchen** Oberösterreich, N Austria 48.18N 13.50E
120 H2 **Prangli** *island* N Estonia
160 J13 **Prānhita** ≈ C India
180 I15 **Praslin** *island* Inner Islands, NE Seychelles
117 O23 **Prasonísi, Akrotírio** *headland* Ródos, Dodekánisos, Greece, Aegean Sea 35.53N 27.46E
113 I14 **Praszka** Opolskie, S Poland 51.05N 18.29E
121 M18 **Pratasy** *Rus.* Protasy. Homyel'skaya Voblasts', SE Belarus 52.48N 29.04E
178 I10 **Prathai** Nakhon Ratchasima, E Thailand 15.31N 102.42E
Prathet Thai *see* Thailand
Prathum Thani *see* Pathum Thani
65 F21 **Prat, Isla** *island* S Chile
108 G11 **Prato** Toscana, C Italy 43.52N 11.04E
105 O17 **Prats-de-Mollo-la-Preste** Pyrénées-Orientales, S France 42.25N 2.28E
28 L6 **Pratt** Kansas, C USA 37.38N 98.44W
110 E6 **Pratteln** Basel-Land, NW Switzerland 47.31N 7.42E
199 L2 **Pratt Seamount** *undersea feature* N Pacific Ocean 56.09N 142.30W
25 P5 **Prattville** Alabama, S USA 32.27N 86.27W
Praust *see* Pruszcz Gdański
116 M7 **Pravda** *prev.* Dogrular. Silistra, NE Bulgaria 43.53N 26.58E
121 B14 **Pravdinsk** *Ger.* Friedland. Kaliningradskaya Oblast', W Russian Federation 54.26N 21.01E
106 K2 **Pravia** Asturias, N Spain 43.29N 6.06W
120 L12 **Prazaroki** *Rus.* Prozoroki. Vitsyebskaya Voblasts', N Belarus 55.16N 28.11E
Prázsmár *see* Prejmer
178 J11 **Preăh Vihéar** Preăh Vihéar, N Cambodia 13.57N 104.48E
118 J12 **Predeal** *Hung.* Predeál. Brașov, C Romania 45.30N 25.31E
111 S8 **Predlitz** Steiermark, SE Austria 47.04N 13.54E
9 V15 **Preeceville** Saskatchewan, S Canada 51.58N 102.40W
Preenkuln *see* Priekule
104 K6 **Pré-en-Pail** Mayenne, NW France 48.27N 0.15W
111 T4 **Pregarten** Oberösterreich, N Austria 48.21N 14.31E
56 H7 **Pregonero** Táchira, NW Venezuela 8.01N 71.45W
120 J10 **Preiļi** *Ger.* Preli. Preiļi, SE Latvia 56.17N 26.52E
118 J12 **Prejmer** *Ger.* Tartlau, *Hung.* Prázsmár. Brașov, S Romania 45.42N 25.49E
115 J16 **Prekornica** ▲▲ SW Serbia and Montenegro (Yugoslavia)
Preli *see* Preiļi
Prëmet *see* Përmet
102 M12 **Premnitz** Brandenburg, NE Germany 52.33N 12.22E
27 S15 **Premont** Texas, SW USA 27.21N 98.07W
115 H14 **Prenj** ▲▲ S Bosnia and Herzegovina
Prenjas/Prenjasi *see* Përrenjas
24 L7 **Prentiss** Mississippi, S USA 31.36N 89.52W
Preny *see* Prienai
102 O10 **Prenzlau** Brandenburg, NE Germany 53.19N 13.52E
126 Jj12 **Preobrazhenka** Irkutskaya Oblast', C Russian Federation 60.01N 108.00E
177 Ee9 **Preparis Island** *island* SW Myanmar
Prerau *see* Přerov
113 H18 **Přerov** *Ger.* Prerau. Olomoucký Kraj, E Czech Republic 49.27N 17.27E
Preschau *see* Prešov
12 M14 **Prescott** Ontario, SE Canada 44.43N 75.33W
38 K12 **Prescott** Arizona, SW USA 34.33N 112.26W
29 T13 **Prescott** Arkansas, C USA 33.48N 93.22W
34 L10 **Prescott** Washington, NW USA 46.17N 118.21W
32 H6 **Prescott** Wisconsin, N USA 44.46N 92.45W
193 A24 **Preservation Inlet** *inlet* South Island, NZ
114 O7 **Preševo** Serbia, SE Serbia and Montenegro (Yugoslavia) 42.20N 21.38E
31 N10 **Presho** South Dakota, N USA 43.54N 100.03W
60 M13 **Presidente Dutra** Maranhão, E Brazil 5.16S 44.30W
62 I8 **Presidente Epitácio** São Paulo, S Brazil 21.45S 52.07W
64 N5 **Presidente Hayes** *off.* Departamento de Presidente Hayes. ◈ *department* C Paraguay
62 I9 **Presidente Prudente** São Paulo, S Brazil 22.09S 51.24W
Presidente Stroessner *see* Ciudad del Este
Presidente Vargas *see* Itabira
62 I8 **Presidente Venceslau** São Paulo, S Brazil 21.52S 51.51W
199 L11 **President Thiers Seamount** *undersea feature* C Pacific Ocean 24.39S 145.50W
26 J11 **Presidio** Texas, SW USA 29.33N 104.22W
Preslav *see* Veliki Preslav
113 M19 **Prešov** *var.* Preschau, *Ger.* Eperies, *Hung.* Eperjes. Prešovský Kraj, E Slovakia 49.00N 21.13E
113 M19 **Prešovský Kraj** ◈ *region* E Slovakia
115 N20 **Prespa, Lake** *Alb.* Liqen i Prespës, *Gk.* Límni Megáli Préspa, Límni Prespa, *Mac.* Prespansko Ezero, *Serb.* Prespansko Jezero. ◎ SE Europe
Prespa, Limni/Prespansko Ezero/Prespansko Jezero/Prespës, Liqen i *see* Prespa, Lake
21 S2 **Presque Isle** Maine, NE USA 46.40N 68.01W
20 B11 **Presque Isle** *headland* Pennsylvania, NE USA 42.09N 80.06W
Pressburg *see* Bratislava
79 P17 **Prestea** SW Ghana 5.22N 2.07W
113 B17 **Přeštice** *Ger.* Pschestitz. Plzeňský Kraj, W Czech Republic 49.36N 13.19E
99 K17 **Preston** NW England, UK 53.46N 2.42W
25 S6 **Preston** Georgia, SE USA 32.08N 84.35W
35 R16 **Preston** Idaho, NW USA 42.06N 111.52W
31 Z13 **Preston** Iowa, C USA 42.03N 90.24W
31 X11 **Preston** Minnesota, N USA 43.41N 92.06W
23 O6 **Prestonsburg** Kentucky, S USA 37.40N 82.46W
98 I13 **Prestwick** W Scotland, UK 55.30N 4.39W
85 J21 **Pretoria** *var.* Epitoli, Tshwane. ● (South Africa-administrative capital) Gauteng, NE South Africa 25.40S 28.11E
Pretoria-Witwatersrand-Vereeniging *see* Gauteng
Pretusha *see* Pretushë
115 M21 **Pretushë** *var.* Pretusha. Korçë, SE Albania 40.50N 20.45E
Preussisch Eylau *see* Bagrationovsk
Preussisch-Stargard *see* Starogard Gdański
Preußisch Holland *see* Pasłęk
117 C17 **Préveza** Ípeiros, W Greece 38.58N 20.43E
39 V3 **Prewitt Reservoir** ⊠ Colorado, C USA
178 J13 **Prey Vêng** Prey Vêng, S Cambodia 11.30N 105.19E
150 M12 **Priaral'skiye Karakumy, Peski** *desert* SW Kazakhstan
126 L16 **Priargunsk** Chitinskaya Oblast', S Russian Federation 50.25N 119.12E
40 K14 **Pribilof Islands** *island group* Alaska, USA
115 K14 **Priboj** Serbia, W Serbia and Montenegro (Yugoslavia) 43.34N 19.33E
113 C17 **Příbram** *Ger.* Pibrans. Středočeský Kraj, W Czech Republic 49.40N 14.01E
38 M4 **Price** Utah, W USA 39.34N 110.48W
39 N5 **Price River** ≈ Utah, W USA
25 N8 **Prichard** Alabama, S USA 30.44N 88.04W
27 R8 **Priddy** Texas, SW USA 31.39N 98.30W
107 P8 **Priego** Castilla-La Mancha, C Spain 40.25N 2.19W
106 M14 **Priego de Córdoba** Andalucía, S Spain 37.27N 4.12W
120 C10 **Priekule** *Ger.* Preenkuln. Liepāja, SW Latvia 56.26N 21.36E
120 C12 **Priekulė** *Ger.* Prökuls. Gargždai, W Lithuania 55.36N 21.16E
121 F14 **Prienai** *Pol.* Preny. Prienai, S Lithuania 54.37N 23.56E
85 G23 **Prieska** Northern Cape, C South Africa 29.40S 22.45E
34 M7 **Priest Lake** ⊠ Idaho, NW USA
34 M7 **Priest River** Idaho, NW USA 48.10N 117.02W
106 M3 **Prieta, Peña** ▲ N Spain 43.01N 4.42W
42 J10 **Prieto, Cerro** ▲ C Mexico 24.10N 105.21W
113 J19 **Prievidza** *var.* Priewitz, *Ger.* Priwitz, *Hung.* Privigye. Trenčiansky Kraj, C Slovakia 48.48N 18.37E
Priewitz *see* Prievidza
114 F10 **Prijedor** Republika Srpska, NW Bosnia & Herzegovina 45.00N 16.43E
115 K14 **Prijepolje** Serbia, W Serbia and Montenegro (Yugoslavia) 43.24N 19.39E
Prikaspiyskaya Nizmennost' *see* Caspian Depression
115 O19 **Prilep** *Turk.* Perlepe. S FYR Macedonia 41.21N 21.33E
110 B9 **Prilly** Vaud, SW Switzerland 46.32N 6.36E
Priluki *see* Pryluky
64 L10 **Primero, Río** ≈ C Argentina
31 S12 **Primghar** Iowa, C USA 43.05N 95.37W
114 B9 **Primorje-Gorski Kotar** *off.* Primorsko-Goranska Županija. ◈ *province* NW Croatia
120 A13 **Primorsk** *Ger.* Fischhausen. Kaliningradskaya Oblast', W Russian Federation 54.45N 20.00E
128 G12 **Primorsk** *Fin.* Koivisto. Leningradskaya Oblast', NW Russian Federation 60.20N 28.39E
Primorsk/Primorskoye *see* Prymors'k
127 Nn17 **Primorskiy Kray** *prev. Eng.* Maritime Territory. ◈ *territory* SE Russian Federation
116 N10 **Primorsko** *prev.* Keupriya. Burgas, E Bulgaria 42.15N 27.45E
130 K13 **Primorsko-Akhtarsk** Krasnodarskiy Kray, SW Russian Federation 46.03N 38.44E
119 U13 **Primors'kyy** Respublika Krym, S Ukraine 45.09N 35.33E
115 D14 **Primošten** Šibenik-Knin, S Croatia 43.34N 15.57E
9 R13 **Primrose Lake** ◎ Saskatchewan, C Canada
9 T14 **Prince Albert** Saskatchewan, S Canada 53.08N 105.43W
85 G25 **Prince Albert** Western Cape, SW South Africa 33.13S 22.03E
15 I1 **Prince Albert Peninsula** *peninsula* Victoria Island, Northwest Territories, NW Canada
15 I3 **Prince Albert Sound** *inlet* Northwest Territories, N Canada
15 Mm2 **Prince Charles Island** *island* Nunavut, NE Canada
205 W6 **Prince Charles Mountains** ▲▲ Antarctica
Prince-Édouard, Île-du *see* Prince Edward Island
180 M13 **Prince Edward Fracture Zone** *tectonic feature* SW Indian Ocean
11 P14 **Prince Edward Island** *Fr.* Île-du Prince-Édouard. ◈ *province* SE Canada
11 Q14 **Prince Edward Island** *Fr.* Île-du Prince-Édouard. *island* SE Canada
181 M12 **Prince Edward Islands** *island group* S South Africa
23 X4 **Prince Frederick** Maryland, NE USA 38.32N 76.33W
8 M14 **Prince George** British Columbia, SW Canada 53.55N 122.49W
23 W6 **Prince George** Virginia, NE USA 37.13N 77.13W
207 O8 **Prince Gustaf Adolf Sea** *sea* Nunavut, N Canada
207 Q3 **Prince of Wales, Cape** *headland* Alaska, USA 65.39N 168.12W
189 V1 **Prince of Wales Island** *island* Queensland, E Australia
15 Jj1 **Prince of Wales Island** *island* Queen Elizabeth Islands, Nunavut, NW Canada
41 Y14 **Prince of Wales Island** *island* Alexander Archipelago, Alaska, USA
Prince of Wales Island *see* Pinang, Pulau
15 I1 **Prince of Wales Strait** *strait* Northwest Territories, N Canada
207 O8 **Prince Patrick Island** *island* Parry Islands, Northwest Territories, NW Canada
15 Kk1 **Prince Regent Inlet** *channel* Nunavut, N Canada
8 J13 **Prince Rupert** British Columbia, SW Canada 54.18N 130.16W
Prince's Island *see* Príncipe
23 Y5 **Princess Anne** Maryland, NE USA 38.12N 75.48W
205 R1 **Princess Astrid Kyst** *physical region* Antarctica
189 W2 **Princess Charlotte Bay** *bay* Queensland, NE Australia
205 W7 **Princess Elizabeth Land** *physical region* Antarctica
8 J14 **Princess Royal Island** *island* British Columbia, SW Canada
47 U15 **Princes Town** Trinidad, Trinidad and Tobago 10.16N 61.22W
9 N17 **Princeton** British Columbia, SW Canada 49.25N 120.34W
32 L11 **Princeton** Illinois, N USA 41.22N 89.27W
33 N16 **Princeton** Indiana, N USA 38.21N 87.33W
31 Z14 **Princeton** Iowa, C USA 41.40N 90.21W
22 H7 **Princeton** Kentucky, S USA 37.06N 87.52W
31 V8 **Princeton** Minnesota, N USA 45.34N 93.34W
29 S1 **Princeton** Missouri, C USA 40.24N 93.34W
20 J15 **Princeton** New Jersey, NE USA 40.21N 74.39W
23 R6 **Princeton** West Virginia, NE USA 37.22N 81.06W
41 S12 **Prince William Sound** *inlet* Alaska, USA
69 P9 **Príncipe** *var.* Príncipe Island, *Eng.* Prince's Island. *island* N Sao Tome and Principe
Príncipe Island *see* Príncipe
34 I13 **Prineville** Oregon, NW USA 44.18N 120.50W
30 J11 **Pringle** South Dakota, N USA 43.34N 103.34W
27 N1 **Pringle** Texas, SW USA 35.55N 101.28W
101 H14 **Prinsenbeek** Noord-Brabant, S Netherlands 51.36N 4.42E
100 L6 **Prinses Margriet Kanaal** *canal* N Netherlands
205 T2 **Prinsesse Ragnhild Kyst** *physical region* Antarctica
205 U2 **Prins Harald Kyst** *physical region* Antarctica
94 N2 **Prins Karls Forland** *island* W Svalbard
45 N8 **Prinzapolka** Región Autónoma Atlántico Norte, NE Nicaragua 13.19N 83.34W
44 L8 **Prinzapolka, Río** ≈ NE Nicaragua
125 Ff9 **Priob'ye** Khanty-Mansiyskiy Avtonomnyy Okrug, N Russian Federation 62.25N 65.36E
106 H1 **Prior, Cabo** *headland* NW Spain 43.33N 8.21W
31 V9 **Prior Lake** Minnesota, N USA 44.42N 93.25W
128 H11 **Priozersk** *Fin.* Käkisalmi. Leningradskaya Oblast', NW Russian Federation 61.02N 30.07E
121 J20 **Pripet** *Bel.* Prypyats', *Ukr.* Pryp"yat'. ≈ Belarus/Ukraine
121 J20 **Pripet Marshes** *wetland* Belarus/Ukraine
Prishtinë *see* Priština
130 J8 **Pristen'** Kurskaya Oblast', W Russian Federation 51.15N 36.47E
115 N16 **Priština** *Alb.* Prishtinë. Serbia, S Serbia and Montenegro (Yugoslavia) 42.39N 21.09E
102 M10 **Pritzwalk** Brandenburg, NE Germany 53.10N 12.11E
105 R13 **Privas** Ardèche, E France 44.45N 4.34E
109 I16 **Priverno** Lazio, C Italy 41.28N 13.10E
Privigye *see* Prievidza
114 C12 **Privlaka** Zadar, SW Croatia 44.15N 15.07E
128 M15 **Privolzhsk** Ivanovskaya Oblast', NW Russian Federation 57.24N 41.16E
131 P7 **Privolzhskaya Vozvyshennost'** *var.* Volga Uplands. ▲▲ W Russian Federation
131 P8 **Privolzhskoye** Saratovskaya Oblast', W Russian Federation 51.08N 45.57E
Priwitz *see* Prievidza
131 N13 **Priyutnoye** Respublika Kalmykiya, SW Russian Federation 46.08N 43.33E
115 M17 **Prizren** *Alb.* Prizreni. Serbia, S Serbia and Montenegro (Yugoslavia) 42.13N 20.46E
Prizreni *see* Prizren
109 I24 **Prizzi** Sicilia, Italy, C Mediterranean Sea 37.43N 13.25E
115 P18 **Probištip** NE FYR Macedonia 42.00N 22.06E
174 M15 **Probolinggo** Jawa, C Indonesia 7.45S 113.12E
Probstberg *see* Wyszków
113 F14 **Prochowice** *Ger.* Parchwitz. Dolnośląskie, SW Poland 51.15N 16.22E
31 W5 **Proctor** Minnesota, N USA 46.46N 92.13W
27 R8 **Proctor** Texas, SW USA 31.57N 98.25W
27 R8 **Proctor Lake** ⊠ Texas, SW USA
161 I18 **Proddatūr** Andhra Pradesh, E India 14.46N 78.39E
106 H9 **Proença-a-Nova** Castelo Branco, C Portugal 39.45N 7.55W
97 I24 **Præstø** Storstrøm, SE Denmark 55.07N 12.03E
101 I21 **Profondeville** Namur, SE Belgium 50.22N 4.52E
43 W11 **Progreso** Yucatán, SE Mexico 21.14N 89.40W
126 Mm16 **Progress** Amurskaya Oblast', SE Russian Federation 49.40N 129.30E
131 O15 **Prokhladnyy** Kabardino-Balkarskaya Respublika, SW Russian Federation 43.48N 44.02E
Prokletije *see* North Albanian Alps
126 H14 **Prokop'yevsk** Kemerovskaya Oblast', S Russian Federation 53.56N 86.48E
Prökuls *see* Priekulė
115 O15 **Prokuplje** Serbia, SE Serbia and Montenegro (Yugoslavia) 43.15N 21.35E
128 H14 **Proletariy** Novgorodskaya Oblast', W Russian Federation 58.24N 31.40E
130 M12 **Proletarsk** Rostovskaya Oblast', SW Russian Federation 46.42N 41.48E
130 J8 **Proletarskiy** Belgorodskaya Oblast', W Russian Federation 50.48N 35.46E
177 Ff7 **Prome** *var.* Pyè. Pegu, C Myanmar 18.49N 95.13E
62 J8 **Promissão** São Paulo, S Brazil 21.33S 49.51W
62 J8 **Promissão, Represa de** ⊠ S Brazil
129 V4 **Promyshlennyy** Respublika Komi, NW Russian Federation 67.36N 63.59E
121 O16 **Pronya** *Rus.* Pronya. ≈ E Belarus
8 M11 **Prophet River** British Columbia, W Canada 58.07N 122.39W
32 K11 **Prophetstown** Illinois, N USA 41.40N 89.56W
61 P16 **Propriá** Sergipe, E Brazil 10.15S 36.51W
105 X16 **Propriano** Corse, France, C Mediterranean Sea 41.41N 8.54E
Prościejów *see* Prostějov
Proskurov *see* Khmel'nyts'kyy
116 H12 **Prosotsáni** Anatolikí Makedonía kai Thráki, NE Greece 41.10N 23.58E
179 Rr15 **Prosperidad** Mindanao, S Philippines 8.36N 125.54E
34 J10 **Prosser** Washington, NW USA 46.12N 119.46W
Prossnitz *see* Prostějov
113 G18 **Prostějov** *Ger.* Prossnitz, *Pol.* Prościejów. Olomoucký Kraj, E Czech Republic 49.28N 17.07E
119 V8 **Prosyana** Dnipropetrovs'ka Oblast', E Ukraine 48.07N 36.22E
113 L16 **Proszowice** Małopolskie, S Poland 50.12N 20.15E
Protasy *see* Pratasy
180 J11 **Protea Seamount** *undersea feature* SW Indian Ocean 36.49S 18.04E
117 D21 **Próti** *island* S Greece
116 N8 **Provadiya** Varna, E Bulgaria 43.10N 27.28E
105 S15 **Provence** *prev.* Marseille-Marignane. ✈ (Marseille) Bouches-du-Rhône, SE France 43.25N 5.15E
105 T14 **Provence** *cultural region* SE France
105 T14 **Provence-Alpes-Côte d'Azur** ◈ *region* SE France
22 H6 **Providence** Kentucky, S USA 37.23N 87.47W
21 N12 **Providence** *state capital* Rhode Island, NE USA 41.50N 71.26W
38 L1 **Providence** Utah, W USA 41.42N 111.49W
Providence *see* Fort Providence
69 X10 **Providence Atoll** *var.* Providence. *atoll* S Seychelles
12 D12 **Providence Bay** Manitoulin Island, Ontario, S Canada 45.39N 82.16W
25 R6 **Providence Canyon** *valley* Alabama/Georgia, S USA
24 I5 **Providence, Lake** ◎ Louisiana, S USA
37 X13 **Providence Mountains** ▲▲ California, W USA
46 L6 **Providenciales** *island* W Turks and Caicos Islands
127 Q4 **Provideniya** Chukotskiy Avtonomnyy Okrug, NE Russian Federation 64.22N 173.14W
21 Q12 **Provincetown** Massachusetts, NE USA 42.01N 70.10W
105 P5 **Provins** Seine-et-Marne, N France 48.34N 3.18E
38 L3 **Provo** Utah, W USA 40.13N 111.39W
9 R15 **Provost** Alberta, SW Canada 52.24N 110.16W
114 G13 **Prozor** Federacija Bosna I Hercegovina, SW Bosnia & Herzegovina 43.46N 17.38E
Prozoroki *see* Prazaroki
62 I11 **Prudentópolis** Paraná, S Brazil 25.12S 50.58W
41 R5 **Prudhoe Bay** Alaska, USA 70.16N 148.18W
41 R4 **Prudhoe Bay** *bay* Alaska, USA
113 H16 **Prudnik** *Ger.* Neustadt, Neustadt in Oberschlesien. Opolskie, S Poland 50.19N 17.34E
121 J16 **Prudy** *Rus.* Prudy. Minskaya Voblasts', C Belarus 53.48N 26.32E
103 D18 **Prüm** Rheinland-Pfalz, W Germany 50.15N 6.27E
103 D18 **Prüm** ≈ W Germany
Prusa *see* Bursa
112 J7 **Pruszcz Gdański** *Ger.* Praust. Pomorskie, N Poland 54.16N 18.36E
112 M12 **Pruszków** *Ger.* Kaltdorf. Mazowieckie, C Poland 52.09N 20.49E
118 K8 **Prut** *Ger.* Pruth. ≈ E Europe
Pruth *see* Prut
110 L8 **Prutz** Tirol, W Austria 47.07N 10.42E
Pružana *see* Pruzhany
121 G19 **Pruzhany** *Pol.* Prużana. Brestskaya Voblasts', SW Belarus 52.33N 24.28E
128 I11 **Pryazha** Respublika Kareliya, NW Russian Federation 61.42N 33.39E
119 U10 **Pryazovs'ke** Zaporiz'ka Oblast', SE Ukraine 46.43N 35.39E
Prychornomors'ka Nyzovyna *see* Black Sea Lowland
Prydniprovs'ka Nyzovyna/Prydnyaprowskaya Nizina *see* Dnieper Lowland
205 Y7 **Prydz Bay** *bay* Antarctica
119 R4 **Pryluky** *Rus.* Priluki. Chernihivs'ka Oblast', NE Ukraine 50.34N 32.23E
119 V10 **Prymors'k** *Rus.* Primorsk; *prev.* Primorskoye. Zaporiz'ka Oblast', SE Ukraine 46.43N 36.19E
29 Q9 **Pryor** Oklahoma, C USA 36.18N 95.18W
35 U11 **Pryor Creek** ≈ Montana, NW USA
Pryp"yat'/Prypyats' *see* Pripet
112 M10 **Przasnysz** Mazowieckie, C Poland 53.01N 20.53E
113 K14 **Przedbórz** Łodzkie, S Poland 51.04N 19.51E
113 P17 **Przemyśl** *Rus.* Peremyshl. Podkarpackie, SE Poland 49.46N 22.46E
113 O16 **Przeworsk** Podkarpackie, SE Poland 50.04N 22.30E
Przheval'sk *see* Karakol
112 L13 **Przysucha** Mazowieckie, SE Poland 51.22N 20.36E
117 H18 **Psachná** *var.* Psahna, Psakhná. Évvoia, C Greece 38.34N 23.40E
Psahna/Psakhná *see* Psachná
117 K18 **Psará** *island* E Greece
117 I16 **Psathoúra** *island* Vóreioi Sporádes, Greece, Aegean Sea
Pschestitz *see* Přeštice
Psein Lora *see* Pishin Lora
119 S5 **Psël** ≈ Russian Federation/Ukraine
117 M21 **Psérimos** *island* Dodekánisos, Greece, Aegean Sea
Pseyn Bowr *see* Pishin Lora
Pskem *see* Piskom
153 R8 **Pskemskiy Khrebet** *Uzb.* Piskom Tizmasi. ▲▲ Kyrgyzstan/Uzbekistan
128 F14 **Pskov** *Ger.* Pleskau, *Latv.* Pleskava. Pskovskaya Oblast', W Russian Federation 58.31N 31.15E
120 K6 **Pskov, Lake** *Est.* Pihkva Järv, *Ger.* Pleskauer See, *Rus.* Pskovskoye Ozero. ◎ Estonia/Russian Federation
128 F15 **Pskovskaya Oblast'** ◈ *province* W Russian Federation
Pskovskoye Ozero *see* Pskov, Lake
114 G9 **Psunj** ▲▲ NE Croatia
113 J17 **Pszczyna** *Ger.* Pless. Śląskie, S Poland 49.58N 18.56E
Ptačnik/Ptacsnik *see* Vtáčnik
117 D17 **Ptéri** ▲ C Greece 39.08N 21.32E
Ptich' *see* Ptsich
117 E14 **Ptolemaïda** *prev.* Ptolemaïs. Dytikí Makedonía, N Greece 40.31N 21.40E
Ptolemaïs *see* Ptolemaïda, Greece
Ptolemaïs *see* 'Akko, Israel
123 Gg10 **Ptolemy Seamounts** *undersea feature* C Mediterranean Sea
121 M19 **Ptsich** *Rus.* Ptich'. Homyel'skaya Voblasts', SE Belarus 52.10N 28.49E
121 M18 **Ptsich** *Rus.* Ptich'. ≈ SE Belarus
111 X10 **Ptuj** *Ger.* Pettau; *anc.* Poetovio. NE Slovenia 46.26N 15.53E
194 E9 **Pua** ≈ NW PNG
63 A23 **Puán** Buenos Aires, E Argentina 37.34S 62.45W
198 B7 **Pu'apu'a** Savai'i, C Samoa 13.31S 172.09W
198 A7 **Puava, Cape** *headland* Savai'i, NW Samoa
58 F12 **Pucallpa** Ucayali, C Peru 8.21S 74.33W
59 J17 **Pucarani** La Paz, NW Bolivia 16.18S 68.28W
Pučarevo *see* Novi Travnik
163 U12 **Pucheng** Fujian, SE China 27.54N 118.34E
166 L6 **Pucheng** Shaanxi, C China 34.55N 109.28E
129 N16 **Puchezh** Ivanovskaya Oblast', W Russian Federation 56.58N 41.08E
113 I19 **Púchov** *Hung.* Puhó. Trenčiansky Kraj, W Slovakia 49.06N 18.19E
118 J13 **Pucioasa** Dâmbovița, S Romania 45.04N 25.22E
112 I6 **Puck** Pomorskie, N Poland 54.43N 18.24E
32 L8 **Puckaway Lake** ◎ Wisconsin, N USA
65 G15 **Pucón** Araucanía, S Chile 39.18S 71.52W
95 M14 **Pudasjärvi** Oulu, C Finland 65.19N 27.01E
154 L8 **Pūdeh Tal, Shelleh-ye** ≈ SW Afghanistan
131 S1 **Pudem** Udmurtskaya Respublika, NW Russian Federation 58.18N 52.08E
Pudewitz *see* Pobiedziska
128 K11 **Pudozh** Respublika Kareliya, NW Russian Federation 61.48N 36.30E
99 M17 **Pudsey** N England, UK 53.48N 1.40W
Puduchcheri *see* Pondicherry
157 H21 **Pudukkottai** Tamil Nādu, SE India 10.22N 78.46E
176 Z10 **Pue** Papua, E Indonesia 2.42S 140.36E
43 P14 **Puebla** *var.* Puebla de Zaragoza. Puebla, S Mexico 19.02N 98.12W
43 P15 **Puebla** ◈ *state* S Mexico
106 L11 **Puebla de Alcocer** Extremadura, W Spain 38.58N 5.13W
Puebla de Don Fabrique *see* Puebla de Don Fadrique
107 P13 **Puebla de Don Fadrique** *var.* Puebla de Don Fabrique. Andalucía, S Spain 37.58N 2.25W
106 J11 **Puebla de la Calzada** Extremadura, W Spain 38.54N 6.37W
106 J5 **Puebla de Sanabria** Castilla-León, N Spain 42.04N 6.37W
106 I4 **Puebla de Trives** *see* A Pobla de Trives
Puebla de Zaragoza *see* Puebla
39 T6 **Pueblo** Colorado, C USA 38.15N 104.36W
39 N10 **Pueblo Colorado Wash** *valley* Arizona, SW USA
63 C16 **Pueblo Libertador** Corrientes, NE Argentina 30.13S 59.22W
42 J10 **Pueblo Nuevo** Durango, C Mexico 23.24N 105.21W
44 J8 **Pueblo Nuevo** Estelí, NW Nicaragua 13.24N 86.26W
56 J3 **Pueblo Nuevo** Falcón, N Venezuela 11.58N 69.57W
44 B6 **Pueblo Nuevo Tiquisate** *var.* Tiquisate. Escuintla, SW Guatemala 14.16N 91.21W
43 Q11 **Pueblo Viejo, Laguna de** *lagoon* E Mexico
65 J14 **Puelches** La Pampa, C Argentina 38.08S 65.56W
106 L14 **Puente-Genil** Andalucía, S Spain 37.23N 4.45W
107 Q3 **Puente la Reina** Navarra, N Spain 42.40N 1.49W
106 L12 **Puente Nuevo, Embalse de** ⊠ S Spain
59 D14 **Puente Piedra** Lima, W Peru 11.49S 77.01W
166 F14 **Pu'er** Yunnan, SW China 23.09N 100.57E
47 V6 **Puerca, Punta** *headland* E Puerto Rico 18.13N 65.36W
39 R12 **Puerco, Rio** ≈ New Mexico, SW USA
59 J17 **Puerto Acosta** La Paz, W Bolivia 15.33S 69.15W
65 G19 **Puerto Aisén** Aisén, S Chile 45.24S 72.42W
43 R17 **Puerto Ángel** Oaxaca, SE Mexico 15.39N 96.29W
Puerto Argentino *see* Stanley
43 T17 **Puerto Arista** Chiapas, SE Mexico 15.55N 93.47W
45 O16 **Puerto Armuelles** Chiriquí, SW Panama 8.16N 82.51W
Puerto Arrecife *see* Arrecife
56 D14 **Puerto Asís** Putumayo, SW Colombia 0.27N 76.27W
56 L9 **Puerto Ayacucho** Amazonas, SW Venezuela 5.44N 67.36W
59 C18 **Puerto Ayora** Galapagos Islands, Ecuador, E Pacific Ocean 0.45S 90.19W
59 C18 **Puerto Baquerizo Moreno** *var.* Baquerizo Moreno. Galapagos Islands, Ecuador, E Pacific Ocean 0.54S 89.37W
44 G4 **Puerto Barrios** Izabal, E Guatemala 15.42N 88.34W
Puerto Bello *see* Portobelo
56 F8 **Puerto Berrío** Antioquia, C Colombia 6.25N 74.27W
56 F9 **Puerto Boyacá** Boyacá, C Colombia 5.58N 74.36W
56 K4 **Puerto Cabello** Carabobo, N Venezuela 10.27N 68.02W
45 N7 **Puerto Cabezas** *var.* Bilwi. Región Autónoma Atlántico Norte, NE Nicaragua 14.04N 83.22W
56 L9 **Puerto Carreño** Vichada, E Colombia 6.08N 67.30W
56 E4 **Puerto Colombia** Atlántico, N Colombia 10.58N 74.57W
44 H4 **Puerto Cortés** Cortés, NW Honduras 15.49N 87.55W
56 J4 **Puerto Cumarebo** Falcón, N Venezuela 11.28N 69.21W
Puerto de Cabras *see* Puerto del Rosario
57 Q5 **Puerto de Hierro** Sucre, NE Venezuela 10.40N 62.03W
66 O11 **Puerto de la Cruz** Tenerife, Islas Canarias, Spain, NE Atlantic Ocean 28.24N 16.33W
66 Q11 **Puerto del Rosario** *var.* Puerto de Cabras. Fuerteventura, Islas Canarias, Spain, NE Atlantic Ocean 28.28N 13.52W
65 J20 **Puerto Deseado** Santa Cruz, SE Argentina 47.46S 65.52W
42 F8 **Puerto Escondido** Baja California Sur, W Mexico 25.49N 111.20W
43 R17 **Puerto Escondido** Oaxaca, SE Mexico 15.48N 96.57W
62 G12 **Puerto Esperanza** Misiones, NE Argentina 26.01S 54.39W
58 D6 **Puerto Francisco de Orellana** *var.* Coca. Napo, N Ecuador 0.27S 76.57W
56 H10 **Puerto Gaitán** Meta, C Colombia 4.19N 72.07W
Puerto Gallegos *see* Río Gallegos
62 G12 **Puerto Iguazú** Misiones, NE Argentina 25.39S 54.34W
58 F12 **Puerto Inca** Huánuco, N Peru 9.21S 74.55W
56 L11 **Puerto Inírida** *var.* Obando. Guainía, E Colombia 3.48N 67.54W
44 K13 **Puerto Jesús** Guanacaste, NW Costa Rica 10.08N 85.26W
43 Z11 **Puerto Juárez** Quintana Roo, SE Mexico 21.06N 86.46W
57 N5 **Puerto La Cruz** Anzoátegui, NE Venezuela 10.13N 64.40W
56 E14 **Puerto Leguízamo** Putumayo, S Colombia 0.07S 74.51W
45 N5 **Puerto Lempira** Gracias a Dios, E Honduras 15.13N 83.48W
Puerto Libertad *see* La Libertad
56 I11 **Puerto Limón** Meta, E Colombia 4.00N 71.09W
56 D13 **Puerto Limón** Putumayo, SW Colombia 1.01N 76.30W
Puerto Limón *see* Limón
107 N11 **Puertollano** Castilla-La Mancha, C Spain 38.40N 4.07W
65 K17 **Puerto Lobos** Chubut, SE Argentina 42.00S 64.58W
56 I3 **Puerto López** La Guajira, N Colombia 11.54N 71.21W
107 Q14 **Puerto Lumbreras** Murcia, SE Spain 37.34N 1.49W
43 V17 **Puerto Madero** Chiapas, SE Mexico 14.43N 92.25W
65 K17 **Puerto Madryn** Chubut, S Argentina 42.45S 65.01W
Puerto Magdalena *see* Bahía Magdalena
59 J15 **Puerto Maldonado** Madre de Dios, E Peru 12.37S 69.10W
Puerto Masachapa *see* Masachapa
Puerto México *see* Coatzacoalcos

◆ Country
● Country Capital
◇ Dependent Territory
○ Dependent Territory Capital
◈ Administrative Region
✈ International Airport
▲ Mountain
▲▲ Mountain Range
Volcano
≈ River
◎ Lake
⊠ Reservoir

65 G17 **Puerto Montt** Los Lagos, C Chile 41.28S 72.57W
43 Z12 **Puerto Morelos** Quintana Roo, SE Mexico 20.47N 86.54W
56 L10 **Puerto Nariño** Vichada, E Colombia 4.57N 67.51W
65 H23 **Puerto Natales** Magallanes, S Chile 51.42S 72.28W
45 X15 **Puerto Obaldía** San Blas, NE Panama 8.37N 77.25W
46 H6 **Puerto Padre** Las Tunas, E Cuba 21.13N 76.34W
56 L9 **Puerto Páez** Apure, C Venezuela 6.10N 67.30W
42 E3 **Puerto Peñasco** Sonora, NW Mexico 31.21N 113.32W
57 N5 **Puerto Píritu** Anzoátegui, NE Venezuela 10.02N 65.02W
47 N8 **Puerto Plata** var. San Felipe de Puerto Plata. N Dominican Republic 19.46N 70.42W
47 N8 **Puerto Plata** ✈ N Dominican Republic 19.43N 70.43W
Puerto Presidente Stroessner see Ciudad del Este
179 Oo14 **Puerto Princesa** off. Puerto Princesa City. Palawan, W Philippines 9.48N 118.43E
Puerto Princesa City see Puerto Princesa
Puerto Príncipe see Camagüey
Puerto Quellón see Quellón
62 F13 **Puerto Rico** Misiones, NE Argentina 26.48S 54.58W
59 K14 **Puerto Rico** Pando, N Bolivia 11.09S 67.28W
56 E12 **Puerto Rico** Caquetá, S Colombia 1.53N 75.08W
47 U5 **Puerto Rico** off. Commonwealth of Puerto Rico; prev. Porto Rico. ◇ US commonwealth territory C West Indies
66 F11 **Puerto Rico** island C West Indies
66 G11 **Puerto Rico Trench** undersea feature NE Caribbean Sea
56 I8 **Puerto Rondón** Arauca, E Colombia 6.16N 71.05W
Puerto San José see San José
65 J21 **Puerto San Julián** var. San Julián. Santa Cruz, SE Argentina 49.14S 67.40W
65 I22 **Puerto Santa Cruz** var. Santa Cruz. Santa Cruz, SE Argentina 50.05S 68.31W
Puerto Sauce see Juan L.Lacaze
59 Q20 **Puerto Suárez** Santa Cruz, E Bolivia 18.58S 57.47W
56 D13 **Puerto Umbría** Putumayo, SW Colombia 0.52N 76.31W
42 J13 **Puerto Vallarta** Jalisco, SW Mexico 20.36N 105.15W
65 G16 **Puerto Varas** Los Lagos, C Chile 41.24S 72.55W
44 M13 **Puerto Viejo** Heredia, NE Costa Rica 10.27N 84.00W
Puertoviejo see Portoviejo
59 B18 **Puerto Villamil** var. Villamil. Galapagos Islands, Ecuador, E Pacific Ocean 0.57S 91.00W
56 F8 **Puerto Wilches** Santander, N Colombia 7.19N 73.55W
65 H20 **Pueyrredón, Lago** var. Lago Cochrane. ◎ S Argentina
131 R7 **Pugachëv** Saratovskaya Oblast', W Russian Federation 52.06N 48.50E
131 T3 **Pugachëvo** Udmurtskaya Respublika, NW Russian Federation 56.38N 53.03E
34 H8 **Puget Sound** sound Washington, NW USA
109 O17 **Puglia** var. Le Puglie, Eng. Apulia. ◈ region SE Italy
109 N17 **Puglia, Canosa di** anc. Canusium. Puglia, SE Italy 41.13N 16.04E
120 I6 **Puhja** Ger. Kawelecht. Tartumaa, SE Estonia 58.19N 26.19E
Puhó see Púchov
107 V4 **Puigcerdà** Cataluña, NE Spain 42.25N 1.53E
Puigmal see Puigmal d'Err
105 N17 **Puigmal d'Err** var. Puigmal. ▲ S France 42.24N 2.07E
78 I16 **Pujehun** S Sierra Leone 7.22N 11.43W
Puka see Pukë
193 E20 **Pukaki, Lake** ◎ South Island, NZ
40 F10 **Pukalani** Maui, Hawaii, USA, C Pacific Ocean 20.50N 94.20W
202 J13 **Pukapuka** atoll N Cook Islands
203 X9 **Pukapuka** atoll Îles Tuamotu, E French Polynesia
Pukari Neem see Purekkari Neem
203 X11 **Pukarua** var. Pukaruha. atoll Îles Tuamotu, E French Polynesia
Pukaruha see Pukarua
12 A7 **Pukaskwa** ≈ Ontario, S Canada
9 V12 **Pukatawagan** Manitoba, C Canada 55.46N 101.13W
203 X16 **Pukatikei, Maunga** ※ Easter Island, Chile, E Pacific Ocean
190 C1 **Pukatja** var. Ernabella. South Australia 26.18S 132.13E
169 Y12 **Pukch'ŏng** E North Korea 40.13N 128.19E
115 L18 **Pukë** var. Puka. Shkodër, N Albania 42.03N 19.53E
192 L6 **Pukekohe** Auckland, North Island, NZ 37.12S 174.54E
192 L7 **Pukemiro** Waikato, North Island, NZ 37.37S 175.02E
202 D12 **Puke, Mont** ▲ Île Futuna, W Wallis and Futuna
Puket see Phuket
193 C20 **Puketeraki Range** ⛰ South Island, NZ
192 N13 **Puketoi Range** ⛰ North Island, NZ
193 F21 **Pukeuri Junction** Otago, South Island, NZ 45.01S 171.01E
121 L16 **Pukhavichy** Rus. Pukhovichi. Minskaya Voblasts', C Belarus 53.30N 28.15E
Pukhovichi see Pukhavichy
128 M10 **Puksoozero** Arkhangel'skaya Oblast', NW Russian Federation 62.37N 40.29E
114 A10 **Pula** It. Pola; prev. Pulj. Istra, NW Croatia 44.53N 13.51E
169 U14 **Pulandian** var. Xinjin. Liaoning, NE China 39.25N 121.58E
169 T14 **Pulandian Wan** bay NE China
179 Rr15 **Pulangi** ≈ Mindanao, S Philippines
201 O15 **Pulap Atoll** atoll Caroline Islands, C Micronesia
20 H9 **Pulaski** New York, NE USA 43.34N 76.06W
22 I10 **Pulaski** Tennessee, S USA 35.11N 87.00W
23 R7 **Pulaski** Virginia, NE USA 37.03N 80.46W
176 Yy13 **Pulau, Sungai** ≈ Papua, E Indonesia
112 N13 **Puławy** Ger. Neu Amerika. Lubelskie, E Poland 51.25N 21.56E
103 E16 **Pulheim** Nordrhein-Westfalen, W Germany 51.00N 6.48E
Pulicat see Pālghāt
161 J19 **Pulicat Lake** lagoon SE India
194 M12 **Pulie** ≈ New Britain, C PNG
Pul'-I-Khatum see Polekhatum
Pul-i-Khumri see Pol-e Khomrī
Pul-i-Sefid see Pol-e Safīd
Pulj see Pula
111 W2 **Pulkau** ≈ NE Austria
95 L15 **Pulkkila** Oulu, C Finland 64.14N 25.52E
125 Cc6 **Pul'kovo** ✈ (Sankt-Peterburg) Leningradskaya Oblast', NW Russian Federation 60.06N 30.23E
34 M9 **Pullman** Washington, NW USA 46.43N 117.10W
110 B10 **Pully** Vaud, SW Switzerland 46.31N 6.40E
42 F7 **Púlpita, Punta** headland W Mexico 26.30N 111.28W
112 M10 **Pułtusk** Mazowieckie, C Poland 52.41N 21.04E
164 H10 **Pulu** Xinjiang Uygur Zizhiqu, W China 36.10N 81.28E
143 P13 **Pülümür** Tunceli, E Turkey 39.30N 39.54E
201 N16 **Pulusuk** island Caroline Islands, C Micronesia
201 N16 **Puluwat Atoll** atoll Caroline Islands, C Micronesia
27 N11 **Pumpville** Texas, SW USA 39.55N 101.43W
203 P7 **Punaauia** var. Hakapehi. Tahiti, W French Polynesia 17.37S 149.37W
58 B8 **Puná, Isla** island SW Ecuador
193 G16 **Punakaiki** West Coast, South Island, NZ 42.07S 171.21E
159 T11 **Punakha** C Bhutan 27.37N 89.49E
59 L18 **Punata** Cochabamba, C Bolivia 17.33S 65.52W
161 E14 **Pune** prev. Poona. Mahārāshtra, W India 18.31N 73.52E
85 M17 **Pungoè, Rio** var. Púnguè, Pungwe. ≈ C Mozambique
23 X10 **Pungo River** ≈ North Carolina, SE USA
Púnguè/Pungwe see Pungoè, Rio
81 N19 **Punia** Maniema, E Dem. Rep. Congo 1.28S 26.25E
64 H8 **Punilla, Sierra de la** ⛰ W Argentina
167 P14 **Puning** Guangdong, S China 23.18N 116.12E
64 G10 **Punitaqui** Coquimbo, C Chile 30.49S 71.13W
158 H8 **Punjab** ◈ state NW India
155 T9 **Punjab** prev. West Punjab, Western Punjab. ◈ province E Pakistan
133 Q9 **Punjab Plains** plain N India
95 O17 **Punkaharju** var. Punkasalmi. Isä-Suomi, E Finland 61.45N 29.21E
Punkasalmi see Punkaharju
59 I17 **Puno** Puno, SE Peru 15.52S 70.03W
59 H17 **Puno** off. Departamento de Puno. ◈ department S Peru
63 B24 **Punta Alta** Buenos Aires, E Argentina 38.53S 62.00W
65 H24 **Punta Arenas** prev. Magallanes. Magallanes, S Chile 53.10S 70.55W
47 T6 **Punta, Cerro de** ▲ C Puerto Rico 18.10N 66.36W
45 T15 **Punta Chame** Panamá, C Panama 8.39N 79.42W
59 G17 **Punta Colorada** Arequipa, SW Peru 16.17S 72.31W
42 F9 **Punta Coyote** Baja California Sur, W Mexico
64 G8 **Punta de Díaz** Atacama, N Chile 28.03S 70.36W
63 G20 **Punta del Este** Maldonado, S Uruguay 34.58S 54.58W
65 K17 **Punta Delgada** Chubut, SE Argentina 42.46S 63.40W
57 O5 **Punta de Mata** Monagas, NE Venezuela 9.43N 63.39W
57 O4 **Punta de Piedras** Nueva Esparta, NE Venezuela 10.54N 64.06W
44 F4 **Punta Gorda** Toledo, SE Belize 16.07N 88.47W
45 N11 **Punta Gorda** Región Autónoma Atlántico Sur, SE Nicaragua 11.31N 83.46W
25 W14 **Punta Gorda** Florida, SE USA 26.55N 82.03W
44 M11 **Punta Gorda, Río** ≈ SE Nicaragua
64 H6 **Punta Negra, Salar de** salt lake N Chile
42 D5 **Punta Prieta** Baja California, NW Mexico 28.55N 114.10W
44 L13 **Puntarenas** Puntarenas, W Costa Rica 9.57N 84.49W
44 L13 **Puntarenas** off. Provincia de Puntarenas. ◈ province W Costa Rica
56 J4 **Punto Fijo** Falcón, N Venezuela 11.42N 70.13W
107 S4 **Puntón de Guara** ▲ N Spain 42.18N 0.13W
20 D14 **Punxsutawney** Pennsylvania, NE USA 40.55N 78.57W
95 M14 **Puolanka** Oulu, C Finland 64.51N 27.42E
59 J17 **Pupuya, Nevado** ▲ W Bolivia 15.04S 69.01W
167 O10 **Puqi** Hubei, C China 29.45N 113.51E
59 F16 **Puquio** Ayacucho, S Peru 14.43S 74.06W
126 H9 **Pur** ≈ N Russian Federation
194 I13 **Purari** ≈ S PNG
29 N11 **Purcell** Oklahoma, C USA 35.00N 97.21W
9 O16 **Purcell Mountains** ⛰ British Columbia, SW Canada
107 P14 **Purchena** Andalucía, S Spain 37.21N 2.21W
29 S8 **Purdy** Missouri, C USA 36.49N 93.55W
120 I2 **Purekkari Neem** prev. Pukari Neem. headland N Estonia 59.33N 24.49E
39 U7 **Purgatoire River** ≈ Colorado, C USA
Purgstall see Purgstall an der Erlauf
111 V5 **Purgstall an der Erlauf** var. Purgstall. Niederösterreich, NE Austria 48.01N 15.08E
160 O13 **Puri** var. Jagannath. Orissa, E India 19.52N 85.49E
Puriramya see Buriram
111 X4 **Purkersdorf** Niederösterreich, NE Austria 48.13N 16.12E
100 I9 **Purmerend** Noord-Holland, C Netherlands 52.30N 4.55E
157 G16 **Pūrna** ≈ C India
Purnea see Pūrnia
159 R13 **Pūrnia** prev. Purnea. Bihār, NE India 25.46N 87.28E
Pursat see Poŭthĭsăt, Poŭthĭsăt, W Cambodia
Pursat see Poŭthĭsăt, Stœ̆ng, W Cambodia
Purulia see Puruliya
156 L13 **Puruliya** prev. Purulia. West Bengal, NE India 23.19N 86.24E
49 G7 **Purus, Rio** Sp. Río Purús. ≈ Brazil/Peru
194 G15 **Purutu Island** island SW PNG
95 N17 **Puruvesi** ◎ SE Finland
24 L7 **Purvis** Mississippi, S USA 31.08N 89.24W
116 J11 **Pŭrvomay** prev. Borisovgrad. Plovdiv, C Bulgaria 42.06N 25.14E
174 J14 **Purwakarta** prev. Poerwakarta. Jawa, C Indonesia 6.30S 107.25E
174 L15 **Purwodadi** prev. Poerwodadi. Jawa, C Indonesia 7.04S 110.52E
174 K15 **Purwokerto** prev. Poerwokerto. Jawa, C Indonesia 7.25S 109.13E
174 Kk15 **Purworejo** prev. Poerworedjo. Jawa, C Indonesia 7.45S 110.04E
22 H8 **Puryear** Tennessee, S USA 36.25N 88.21W
160 H13 **Pusad** Mahārāshtra, C India 19.56N 77.40E
169 Z16 **Pusan** off. Pusan-gwangyŏksi, var. Busan, Jap. Fusan. SE South Korea 35.11N 129.04E
173 Ee4 **Pusatgajo, Pegunungan** ⛰ Sumatera, NW Indonesia
Puschlav see Poschiavo
Pushkin see Tsarskoye Selo
131 Q8 **Pushkino** Saratovskaya Oblast', W Russian Federation 51.09N 47.00E
Pushkino see Biläsuvar
113 M22 **Püspökladány** Hajdú-Bihar, E Hungary 47.19N 21.04E
120 J3 **Püssi** Ger. Isenhof. Ida-Virumaa, NE Estonia 59.21N 27.05E
118 I5 **Pustomyty** L'vivs'ka Oblast', W Ukraine 49.43N 23.55E
128 F16 **Pustoshka** Pskovskaya Oblast', W Russian Federation 56.21N 29.16E
Pusztakalán see Călan
178 H1 **Putao** prev. Fort Hertz. Kachin State, N Myanmar 27.22N 97.24E
192 M8 **Putaruru** Waikato, North Island, NZ 38.02S 175.46E
Puteoli see Pozzuoli
167 R12 **Putian** Fujian, SE China 25.28N 119.01E
109 O17 **Putignano** Puglia, SE Italy 40.51N 17.07E
Putivl' see Putyvl'
43 Q16 **Putla** var. Putla de Guerrero. Oaxaca, SE Mexico 16.54N 97.55W
Putla de Guerrero see Putla
21 N12 **Putnam** Connecticut, NE USA 41.56N 71.52W
27 Q7 **Putnam** Texas, SW USA 32.22N 99.11W
20 M10 **Putney** Vermont, NE USA 42.59N 72.30W
113 L20 **Putnok** Borsod-Abaúj-Zemplén, NE Hungary 48.18N 20.25E
Putorana, Gory/Putorana Mountains see Putorana, Plato
126 Ii8 **Putorana, Plato** var. Gory Putorana, Eng. Putorana Mountains. ⛰ N Russian Federation
64 H2 **Putre** Tarapacá, N Chile 18.11S 69.30W
161 J24 **Puttalam** North Western Province, W Sri Lanka 8.01N 79.54E
161 J24 **Puttalam Lagoon** lagoon W Sri Lanka
101 H17 **Putte** Antwerpen, C Belgium 51.04N 4.39E
100 K11 **Putten** Gelderland, C Netherlands 52.15N 5.36E
102 K7 **Puttgarden** Schleswig-Holstein, N Germany 54.30N 11.12E
Puttiala see Patiāla
103 D20 **Püttlingen** Saarland, SW Germany 49.16N 6.52E
56 D14 **Putumayo** off. Intendencia del Putumayo. ◈ province S Colombia
50 E7 **Putumayo, Río** var. Rio Içá. ≈ NW South America see also Içá, Rio
174 K8 **Putus, Tanjung** headland Borneo, N Indonesia 0.27S 109.04E
118 J8 **Putyla** Chernivets'ka Oblast', W Ukraine 47.59N 25.04E
119 S3 **Putyvl'** Rus. Putivl'. Sums'ka Oblast', NE Ukraine 51.21N 33.52E
95 M18 **Puula** ◎ SE Finland
95 N18 **Puumala** Isä-Suomi, E Finland 61.31N 28.12E
120 I5 **Puurmani** Ger. Talkhof. Jõgevamaa, E Estonia 58.36N 26.17E
101 G17 **Puurs** Antwerpen, N Belgium 51.04N 4.16E
Pu'uUla'ula see Red Hill
40 A8 **Puuwai** Niihau, Hawaii, USA, C Pacific Ocean 21.54N 96.11W
10 J4 **Puvirnituq** prev. Povungnituk. Quebec, NE Canada 60.10N 77.19W
34 H8 **Puyallup** Washington, NW USA 47.11N 122.17W
167 O5 **Puyang** Henan, C China 35.42N 115.03E
167 R9 **Puyang Jiang** var. Tsien Tang. ≈ SE China
105 O11 **Puy-de-Dôme** ◈ department C France
105 N15 **Puylaurens** Tarn, S France 43.33N 2.01E
104 M13 **Puy-l'Evêque** Lot, S France 44.31N 1.10E
105 N17 **Puymorens, Col de** pass S France 42.33N 1.50E
58 C7 **Puyo** Pastaza, C Ecuador 1.30S 77.58W
193 A24 **Puysegur Point** headland South Island, NZ 46.09S 166.38E
154 J8 **Pūzak, Hāmūn-e** Pash. Hāmūn-i-Puzak. ◎ SW Afghanistan
Puzak, Hāmūn-i- see Pūzak, Hāmūn-e
83 J23 **Pwani** Eng. Coast. ◈ region E Tanzania
81 O23 **Pweto** Katanga, SE Dem. Rep. Congo 8.29S 28.57E
99 I19 **Pwllheli** NW Wales, UK 52.53N 4.22W
201 O14 **Pwok** Pohnpei, E Micronesia
126 Gg10 **Pyakupur** ≈ N Russian Federation
128 M6 **Pyalitsa** Murmanskaya Oblast', NW Russian Federation 66.16N 39.55E
128 K10 **Pyal'ma** Respublika Kareliya, NW Russian Federation 62.24N 35.56E
Pyandzh see Panj
128 I6 **Pyaozero, Ozero** ◎ NW Russian Federation
177 Ff9 **Pyapon** Irrawaddy, SW Myanmar 16.15N 95.40E
121 J15 **Pyarshai** Rus. Pershay. Minskaya Voblasts', C Belarus 54.02N 26.44E
126 I6 **Pyasina** ≈ N Russian Federation
116 I10 **Pyasŭchnik, Yazovir** ⊠ C Bulgaria
125 B13 **Pyatigorsk** Stavropol'skiy Kray, SW Russian Federation 44.01N 43.06E
Pyatikhatki see P"yatykhatky
119 S7 **P"yatykhatky** Rus. Pyatikhatki. Dnipropetrovs'ka Oblast', E Ukraine 48.22N 33.43E
177 G6 **Pyawbwe** Mandalay, C Myanmar 20.39N 96.04E
131 T3 **Pychas** Udmurtskaya Respublika, NW Russian Federation 56.30N 52.33E
Pyè see Prome
177 F6 **Pyechin** Chin State, W Myanmar 20.01N 93.36E
121 G17 **Pyeski** Rus. Peski. Hrodzyenskaya Voblasts', W Belarus 53.22N 24.37E
121 L19 **Pyetrykaw** Rus. Petrikov. Homyel'skaya Voblasts', SE Belarus 52.07N 28.30E
95 M16 **Pyhajärvi** ◎ C Finland
95 O17 **Pyhäjärvi** ◎ SE Finland
95 L15 **Pyhäjoki** Oulu, W Finland 64.28N 24.15E
95 L15 **Pyhäjoki** ≈ W Finland
95 M15 **Pyhäntä** Oulu, C Finland 64.07N 26.19E
95 M16 **Pyhäsalmi** Oulu, C Finland 63.38N 26.00E
95 O17 **Pyhäselkä** ◎ SE Finland
95 M19 **Pyhtää** Swe. Pyttis. Etelä-Suomi, S Finland 60.29N 26.40E
177 G6 **Pyinmana** Mandalay, C Myanmar 19.45N 96.12E
117 N24 **Pylés** var. Piles. Kárpathos, SE Greece 35.31N 27.08E
117 D21 **Pýlos** var. Pilos. Pelopónnisos, S Greece 36.55N 21.42E
20 B12 **Pymatuning Reservoir** ⊠ Ohio/Pennsylvania, NE USA
169 X15 **P'yŏngt'aek** NW South Korea 37.00N 127.04E
169 V14 **P'yŏngyang** var. P'yŏngyang-si, Eng. Pyongyang. ● (North Korea) SW North Korea 39.04N 125.46E
P'yŏngyang-si see P'yŏngyang
37 Q4 **Pyramid Lake** ◎ Nevada, W USA
39 P15 **Pyramid Mountains** ⛰ New Mexico, SW USA
39 R5 **Pyramid Peak** ▲ Colorado, C USA 39.04N 106.57W
117 D17 **Pyramíva** var. Piramiva. ▲ C Greece 39.08N 21.18E
Pyrenaei Montes see Pyrenees
88 B12 **Pyrenees** Fr. Pyrénées, Sp. Pirineos; anc. Pyrenaei Montes. ⛰ SW Europe
104 J16 **Pyrénées-Atlantiques** ◈ department SW France
105 N17 **Pyrénées-Orientales** ◈ department S France
117 L19 **Pyrgí** var. Pirgi. Chíos, E Greece 38.13N 26.01E
117 D20 **Pýrgos** var. Pírgos. Dytikí Ellás, S Greece 37.40N 21.27E
Pyritz see Pyrzyce
117 E19 **Pýrros** ≈ S Greece
119 R4 **Pyryatyn** Rus. Piryatin. Poltavs'ka Oblast', NE Ukraine 50.13N 32.31E
112 D9 **Pyrzyce** Ger. Pyritz. Zachodniopomorskie, NW Poland 53.09N 14.52E
128 F15 **Pytalovo** Latv. Abrene; prev. Jaunlatgale. Pskovskaya Oblast', W Russian Federation 57.06N 27.55E
117 M20 **Pythagóreio** var. Pithagorio. Sámos, Dodekánisos, Greece, Aegean Sea 37.42N 26.57E
12 L11 **Pythonga, Lac** ◎ Quebec, SE Canada
96 E10 **Pyttegga** ▲ S Norway 62.13N 7.40E
Pyttis see Pyhtää
177 G7 **Pyu** Pegu, C Myanmar 18.28N 96.25E
177 G8 **Pyuntaza** Pegu, SW Myanmar 17.51N 96.43E
159 N11 **Pyuthan** Mid Western, W Nepal 28.09N 82.50E
112 H12 **Pyzdry** Ger. Peisern. Wielkopolskie, C Poland 52.10N 17.42E

Q

144 H13 **Qā' al Jafr** ◎ S Jordan
207 O11 **Qaanaaq** var. Qânâq, Dan. Thule. Avannaarsua, N Greenland 77.34N 69.44W
144 G7 **Qabb Eliâs** E Lebanon 33.46N 35.49E
Qabil see Al Qābil
Qabırrı see Iori
Qābis see Gabès
Qābis, Khalīj see Gabès, Golfe de
147 S14 **Qabr Hūd** C Yemen 16.02N 49.36E
Qacentina see Constantine
154 L4 **Qādes** Bādghīs, NW Afghanistan 34.52N 63.25E
145 T11 **Qādisīyah** S Iraq 31.43N 44.28E
149 O4 **Qā'emshahr** prev. 'Alīābad, Shāhī. Māzandarān, N Iran 36.31N 52.49E
149 U7 **Qā'en** var. Qain, Qāyen. Khorāsān, E Iran 33.43N 59.07E
147 U13 **Qafa** spring/well SW Oman 17.46N 52.55E
Qafṣah see Gafsa
169 V9 **Qagan Nur** ◎ NE China
169 Q11 **Qagan Nur** ◎ N China
Qagan Us see Dulan
164 H13 **Qagcaka** Xizang Zizhiqu, W China 32.31N 81.52E
Qahremānshahr see Bākhtarān
165 Q10 **Qaidam He** ≈ C China
162 L8 **Qaidam Pendi** basin C China
Qain see Qā'en
Qala Āhangarān see Chaghcharān
145 U3 **Qaḷā Diza** var. Qal 'at Dīzah. NE Iraq 36.10N 45.07E
Qal'ah Sālih see Qal'at Ṣāliḥ
153 R13 **Qal'aikhum** Rus. Kalaikhum. S Tajikistan 38.28N 70.49E
Qala Nau see Qal'eh-ye Now
147 V17 **Qalansīyah** Suquṭrā, W Yemen 12.40N 53.30E
Qala Panja see Qal'eh-ye Panjeh
Qala Shāhar see Qal'eh Shahr
Qalāt see Kalāt
145 W9 **Qal'at Aḥmad** E Iraq 32.24N 46.46E
147 N11 **Qal'at Bīshah** 'Asīr, SW Saudi Arabia 19.59N 42.38E
144 H4 **Qal'at Burzay** Ḥamāh, W Syria 35.37N 36.16E
Qal 'at Dīzah see Qaḷā Diza
145 W9 **Qal'at Ḥusayh** E Iraq 32.19N 46.46E
145 V10 **Qal'at Majnūnah** S Iraq 31.39N 45.44E
145 X11 **Qal'at Ṣāliḥ** var. Qal'ah Sālih. E Iraq 31.30N 47.24E
145 V10 **Qal'at Sukkar** SE Iraq 31.52N 46.04E
Qalba Zhotasy see Kalbinskiy Khrebet
149 Q12 **Qal'eh Biābān** Fārs, S Iran
155 N4 **Qal'eh Shahr** Pash. Qala Shāhar. Sar-e Pol, N Afghanistan 35.34N 65.38E
154 L4 **Qal'eh-ye Now** var. Qala Nau. Bādghīs, NW Afghanistan 34.59N 63.07E
155 T2 **Qal'eh-ye Panjeh** var. Qala Panja. Badakhshān, NE Afghanistan 36.56N 72.15E
Qamar Bay see Qamar, Ghubbat al
147 U14 **Qamar, Ghubbat al** Eng. Qamar Bay. bay Oman/Yemen
147 V13 **Qamar, Jabal al** ⛰ SW Oman
153 N12 **Qamashi** Qashqadaryo Viloyati, S Uzbekistan 38.52N 66.30E
Qambar see Kambar
165 R14 **Qamdo** Xizang Zizhiqu, W China 31.09N 97.09E
197 K13 **Qamea** prev. Nggamea. island N Fiji
77 R7 **Qamīnis** NE Libya 31.48N 20.04E
Qamishly see Al Qāmishlī
Qânâq see Qaanaaq
Qandahār see Kandahār
82 Q11 **Qandala** Bari, NE Somalia 11.30N 50.00E
Qandyaghash see Kandyagash
144 L2 **Qanṭārī** Ar Raqqah, N Syria 36.24N 39.16E
143 V13 **Qapiciğ Dağı** Rus. Gora Kapydzhik. ▲ SW Azerbaijan 39.18N 46.00E
164 H5 **Qapqal** var. Qapqal Xibe Zizhixian. Xinjiang Uygur Zizhiqu, NW China 43.46N 81.09E
Qapqal Xibe Zizhixian see Qapqal
Qapshagay Böyeni see Kapchagayskoye Vodokhranilishche
206 M15 **Qaqortoq** Dan. Julianehåb. Kitaa, S Greenland 60.51N 46.01W
77 U8 **Qâra** var. Qārah. NW Egypt 29.34N 26.28E
145 T4 **Qara Anjīr** N Iraq 35.30N 44.37E
Qarabāgh see Qarah Bāgh
Qaraböget see Karaboget
Qarabulaq see Karabulak
Qarabutaq see Karabutak
Qaraghandy/Qaraghandy Oblysy see Karaganda
Qaraghayly see Karagayly
145 U4 **Qara Gol** NE Iraq 35.21N 45.38E
Qārah see Qâra
154 J4 **Qarah Bāgh** var. Qarabāgh. Herāt, NW Afghanistan 35.06N 61.33E
144 G7 **Qaraoun, Lac de** var. Buḥayrat al Qir'awn. ◎ S Lebanon
Qaraoy see Karaoy
Qaraqoyyn see Karakoyyn, Ozero
Qara Qum see Garagumy
Qarasū see Karasu
Qaratal see Karatal
Qarataū see Karatau, Khrebet, Kazakhstan
Qarataū see Karatau, Zhambyl, Kazakhstan
Qaraton see Karaton
82 P13 **Qardho** var. Kardh, It. Gardo. Bari, N Somalia 9.34N 49.30E
148 M6 **Qareh Chāy** ≈ N Iran
148 K2 **Qareh Sū** ≈ NW Iran
Qariateïne see Al Qaryatayn
Qarkilik see Ruoqiang
153 O13 **Qarluq** Rus. Karluk. Surkhondaryo Viloyati, S Uzbekistan 38.17N 67.39E
153 U12 **Qarokŭl** Rus. Karakul'. E Tajikistan 39.07N 73.33E
153 T12 **Qarokŭl** Rus. Ozero Karakul'. ◎ E Tajikistan
Qarqan see Qiemo
164 K9 **Qarqan He** ≈ NW China
Qarqannah, Juzur see Kerkenah, Îles de
Qarqaraly see Karkaralinsk
155 O1 **Qarqīn** Jowzjān, N Afghanistan 37.25N 66.03E
Qars see Kars
Qarsaqbay see Karsakpay
152 M12 **Qarshi** Rus. Karshi; prev. Bek-Budi. Qashqadaryo Viloyati, S Uzbekistan 38.54N 65.48E
152 L12 **Qarshi Cho'li** Rus. Karshinskaya Step. grassland S Uzbekistan
152 M13 **Qarshi Kanali** Rus. Karshinskiy Kanal. canal Turkmenistan/Uzbekistan
Qaryatayn see Al Qaryatayn
152 M12 **Qashqadaryo Viloyati** Rus. Kashkadar'inskaya Oblast'. ◈ province S Uzbekistan
Qasigianguit see Qasigiannguit
207 N13 **Qasigiannguit** var. Qasigianguit, Dan. Christianshåb. Kitaa, C Greenland 68.42N 50.49W
Qaşīm, Minţaqat see Al Qaşīm
145 P8 **Qaşr 'Amīj** C Iraq 33.30N 41.52E
145 R9 **Qaşr Darwīshāh** C Iraq 32.36N 43.27E
148 J6 **Qaşr-e Shīrīn** Kermānshāh, W Iran 34.33N 45.37E
77 V10 **Qasr Farâfra** W Egypt 27.00N 27.58E
Qassim see Al Qaşīm
147 O16 **Qa'ṭabah** SW Yemen 13.51N 44.42E
144 H7 **Qaṭanā** var. Katana. Dimashq, S Syria 33.27N 36.04E
149 N15 **Qatar** off. State of Qatar, Ar. Dawlat Qaṭar. ◆ monarchy SW Asia
Qatrana see Al Qaṭrānah
149 Q12 **Qaṭrūyeh** Fārs, S Iran
Qattara Depression/Qaṭṭārah, Munkhafaḍ al see Qaṭṭâra, Monkhafad el
77 U8 **Qaṭṭâra, Monkhafad el** var. Munkhafaḍ al Qaṭṭārah, Eng. Qattara Depression. desert NW Egypt
Qaṭṭīnah, Buḥayrat see Ḥimş, Buḥayrat
Qaydār see Qeydār
Qāyen see Qā'en
153 Q11 **Qayroqqum** Rus. Kayrakkum. NW Tajikistan 40.16N 69.46E
153 Q10 **Qayroqqum, Obanbori** Rus. Kayrakkumskoye Vodokhranilishche. ⊠ NW Tajikistan
145 U7 **Qazānīyah** var. Dhū Shaykh. E Iraq 33.39N 45.33E
Qazaqstan/Qazaqstan Respublikasy see Kazakhstan
143 T9 **Qazbegi** Rus. Kazbegi. NE Georgia 42.39N 44.36E
155 P15 **Qāzi Ahmad** var. Kazi Ahmad. Sind, SE Pakistan 26.19N 68.06E
143 Y12 **Qazimämmäd** Rus. Kazi Magomed. SE Azerbaijan 40.03N 48.56E
Qazris see Cáceres
148 M4 **Qazvīn** var. Kazvin. Qazvīn, N Iran 36.16N 50.00E
148 M5 **Qazvīn** ◈ province N Iran
197 K12 **Qelelevu Lagoon** lagoon NE Fiji
77 X10 **Qena** var. Qinā; anc. Caene, Caenepolis. E Egypt 26.12N 32.49E
115 L23 **Qeparo** Vlorë, S Albania 40.04N 19.49E
Qeqertarssuaq see Qeqertarsuaq
207 N13 **Qeqertarsuaq** var. Qeqertarssuaq, Dan. Godhavn. Kitaa, Greenland 69.27N 52.54W
206 M13 **Qeqertarsuaq** island W Greenland
207 N13 **Qeqertarsuup Tunua** Dan. Disko Bugt. inlet W Greenland
Qerveh see Qorveh
149 S14 **Qeshm** Hormozgān, S Iran 26.58N 56.16E
149 R14 **Qeshm** var. Jazīreh-ye Qeshm, Qeshm Island. island S Iran
Qeshm Island/Qeshm, Jazīreh-ye see Qeshm
148 L4 **Qeydār** var. Qaydār. Zanjān, NW Iran 36.50N 47.40E
148 K5 **Qezel Owzan** var. Ki Zil Uzen, Qi Zil Uzun. ≈ NW Iran
148 L5 **Qezel Owzan, Rūd-e** ≈ NW Iran
Qian see Guizhou
Qian Gorlo see Qian Gorlos
169 V9 **Qian Gorlos** var. Qian Gorlo, Qian Gorlos Mongolzu Zizhixian, Qianguozhen. Jilin, NE China 45.06N 124.48E
Qian Gorlos Mongolzu Zizhixian/Qianguozhen see Qian Gorlos
167 N9 **Qianjiang** Hubei, C China 30.26N 112.55E
166 K10 **Qianjiang** Sichuan, C China 29.30N 108.45E
166 L14 **Qian Jiang** ≈ S China
166 G9 **Qianning** var. Gartar. Sichuan, C China 30.33N 101.22E
169 U13 **Qian Shan** ⛰ NE China
166 H10 **Qianwei** Sichuan, C China 29.15N 103.52E
166 J11 **Qianxi** Guizhou, S China 27.00N 106.01E
165 Q7 **Qiaowan** Gansu, N China 40.37N 96.43E
Qibilī see Kebili
164 K9 **Qiemo** var. Qarqan. Xinjiang Uygur Zizhiqu, NW China 38.09N 85.30E
166 J10 **Qijiang** Chongqing Shi, C China 29.06N 106.35E
165 N5 **Qijiaojing** Xinjiang Uygur Zizhiqu, NW China 43.28N 91.34E
155 P9 **Qila Saifullāh** Baluchistān, SW Pakistan 30.45N 68.08E
165 S9 **Qilian** Qinghai, C China 38.09N 100.08E
139 Nn10 **Qilian Shan** var. Kilien Mountains. ⛰ N China
207 O11 **Qimusseriarsuaq** Dan. Melville Bugt, Eng. Melville Bay. bay NW Greenland
Qinā see Qena
165 W11 **Qin'an** Gansu, C China 34.49N 105.50E
Qing see Qinghai
169 W7 **Qing'an** Heilongjiang, NE China 46.53N 127.29E
167 R5 **Qingdao** var. Ching-Tao, Ch'ing-tao, Tsingtao, Tsintao, Ger. Tsingtau. Shandong, E China 36.30N 120.55E
169 V8 **Qinggang** Heilongjiang, NE China 46.40N 126.04E
Qinggil see Qinghe
165 P11 **Qinghai** var. Chinghai, Koko Nor, Qing, Qinghai Sheng, Tsinghai. ◈ province C China
165 S10 **Qinghai Hu** var. Ch'ing Hai, Tsing Hai, Mong. Koko Nor. ◎ C China
Qinghai Sheng see Qinghai
164 M3 **Qinghe** var. Qinggil. Xinjiang Uygur Zizhiqu, NW China 46.42N 90.19E
166 L4 **Qingjian** Shaanxi, C China 37.10N 110.09E
166 L9 **Qing Jiang** ≈ C China
Qingjiang see Huaiyin
Qingkou see Ganyu
166 I12 **Qinglong** var. Liancheng. Guizhou, S China 25.49N 105.10E
167 Q2 **Qinglong** Hebei, E China 40.24N 118.57E
Qingshan see Dedu
165 R12 **Qingshuihe** Qinghai, C China 33.08N 97.19E
Qingyang see Jinjiang
169 V11 **Qingyuan** Liaoning, NE China 42.08N 124.55E
164 L13 **Qingzang Gaoyuan** var. Xizang Gaoyuan, Eng. Plateau of Tibet. plateau W China
167 Q4 **Qingzhou** prev. Yidu. Shandong, E China 36.46N 118.23E
163 R9 **Qin He** ≈ C China
167 Q2 **Qinhuangdao** Hebei, E China 39.57N 119.31E
166 K7 **Qin Ling** ⛰ C China
Qin Xian see Qinxian
167 N5 **Qinxian** var. Qin Xian. Shanxi, C China 36.46N 112.42E
167 N6 **Qinyang** Henan, C China 35.04N 112.55E
166 K15 **Qinzhou** Guangxi Zhuangzu Zizhiqu, S China 22.09N 108.36E
Qiong see Hainan
166 L17 **Qionghai** prev. Jiaji. Hainan, S China 19.12N 110.26E
166 H9 **Qionglai** Sichuan, C China 30.24N 103.28E
166 H8 **Qionglai Shan** ⛰ C China
166 L17 **Qiongzhou Haixia** var. Hainan Strait. strait S China
169 U7 **Qiqihar** var. Ch'i-ch'i-ha-erh, Tsitsihar; prev. Lungkiang. Heilongjiang, NE China 47.23N 124.00E
149 P12 **Qīr** Fārs, S Iran 28.27N 53.04E
164 H10 **Qira** Xinjiang Uygur Zizhiqu, NW China 37.04N 80.45E
Qir'awn, Buḥayrat al see Qaraoun, Lac de
144 F11 **Qiryat Gat** var. Kiryat Gat. Southern, C Israel 31.37N 34.46E
144 G8 **Qiryat Shemona** Northern, N Israel 33.13N 35.34E
Qishlaq see Garmsār
147 U14 **Qishn** SE Yemen 15.28N 51.43E
144 G9 **Qishon, Naḥal** ≈ N Israel
Qita Ghazzah see Gaza Strip
162 K5 **Qitai** Xinjiang Uygur Zizhiqu, NW China 44.00N 89.33E
169 Y8 **Qitaihe** Heilongjiang, NE China 45.45N 130.53E
147 W12 **Qitbīt, Wādī** dry watercourse S Oman
167 O5 **Qixian** var. Qi Xian, Zhaoge. Henan, C China 35.34N 114.10E
Qīzān see Jīzān
Qizil Orda see Kyzylorda
Qizil Qum/Qizilqum see Kyzyl Kum
153 V14 **Qizilrabot** Rus. Kyzylrabot. SE Tajikistan 37.28N 74.43E
152 J10 **Qizilravot** Rus. Kyzylrabat. Buxoro Viloyati, C Uzbekistan 40.35N 62.09E
Qi Zil Uzun see Qezel Owzan
145 S4 **Qizil Yār** N Iraq 35.26N 44.12E
Qoghaly see Kugaly
Qogir Feng see K2
149 N6 **Qom** var. Kum, Qum. Qom, N Iran 34.43N 50.53E
149 N6 **Qom** ◈ province N Iran
Qomisheh see Shahreẕā
Qomolangma Feng see Everest, Mount
148 M7 **Qom, Rūd-e** ≈ C Iran
Qomsheh see Shahreẕā
Qomul see Hami
Qondūz see Kunduz
152 G7 **Qo'ng'irot** Rus. Kungrad. Qoraqalpog'iston Respublikasi, NW Uzbekistan 43.01N 58.49E
Qongyrat see Konyrat
Qoqek see Tacheng
153 R10 **Qo'qon** var. Khokand, Rus. Kokand. Farg'ona Viloyati, E Uzbekistan 40.34N 70.55E
Qorabowur Kirlari see Karabaur', Uval
Qoradaryo see Karadar'ya
152 G6 **Qorajar** Rus. Karadzhar. Qoraqalpog'iston Respublikasi, NW Uzbekistan 43.34N 58.35E
152 K12 **Qorako'l** Rus. Karakul'. Buxoro Viloyati, C Uzbekistan 39.27N 63.45E
152 E5 **Qoraqalpog'iston** Rus. Karakalpakya. Qoraqalpog'iston Respublikasi, NW Uzbekistan 44.45N 56.06E
152 G7 **Qoraqalpog'iston Respublikasi** Rus. Respublika Karakalpakstan. ◈ autonomous republic NW Uzbekistan
152 H7 **Qorao'zak** Rus. Karauzyak. Qoraqalpog'iston Respublikasi, NW Uzbekistan 43.07N 60.03E
Qorghazhyn see Korgalzhyn
144 H6 **Qornet es Saouda** ▲ NE Lebanon 36.06N 34.06E
152 L12 **Qorovulbozor** Rus. Karaulbazar. Buxoro Viloyati, C Uzbekistan 39.28N 64.49E
148 K5 **Qorveh** var. Qerveh, Qurveh. Kordestān, W Iran 35.13N 47.46E
153 N11 **Qo'shrabot** Rus. Kushrabat. Samarqand Viloyati, C Uzbekistan 40.15N 66.40E
Qosshaghyl see Koschagyl
Qostanay/Qostanay Oblysy see Kostanay
149 P12 **Qoṭbābād** Fārs, S Iran 28.52N 53.40E
149 R13 **Qoṭbābād** Hormozgān, S Iran 27.49N 56.00E
144 H6 **Qoubaïyât** var. Al Qubayyāt. N Lebanon 37.00N 34.30E
Qoussantîna see Constantine
164 K16 **Qowowuyag** see Cho Oyu
153 O11 **Qo'ytosh** Rus. Koytash. Jizzax Viloyati, C Uzbekistan 40.13N 67.19E

◆ Country
● Country Capital
◇ Dependent Territory
○ Dependent Territory Capital
◈ Administrative Region
✈ International Airport
▲ Mountain
⛰ Mountain Range
※ Volcano
≈ River
◎ Lake
⊠ Reservoir

152 G7 Qozonketkan Rus. Kazanketken. Qoraqalpog'iston Respublikasi, W Uzbekistan 42.59N 59.21E
152 H6 Qozoqdaryo Rus. Kazakdar'ya. Qoraqalpog'iston Respublikasi, NW Uzbekistan 43.26N 59.47E
21 N11 Quabbin Reservoir ⊠ Massachusetts, NE USA
102 F12 Quakenbrück Niedersachsen, NW Germany 52.41N 7.57E
20 I15 Quakertown Pennsylvania, NE USA 40.26N 75.17W
190 M10 Quambatook Victoria, SE Australia 35.52S 143.28E
27 Q4 Quanah Texas, SW USA 34.19N 99.45W
178 Kk11 Quang Ngai var. Quangngai, Quang Nghia. Quang Ngai, C Vietnam 15.09N 108.49E
Quang Nghia see Quang Ngai
178 K9 Quang Tri Quang Tri, C Vietnam 16.42N 107.15E
Quan Long see Ca Mau
158 L4 Quanshuigou China/India 35.40N 79.28E
167 R13 Quanzhou var. Ch'uan-chou, Tsinkiang; prev. Chin-chiang. Fujian, SE China 24.56N 118.31E
166 M12 Quanzhou Guangxi Zhuangzu Zizhiqu, S China 25.59N 111.01E
9 V16 Qu'Appelle ≈ Saskatchewan, S Canada
10 M3 Quaqtaq prev. Koartac. Quebec, NE Canada 60.49N 69.30W
63 E16 Quaraí Rio Grande do Sul, S Brazil 30.24S 56.24W
61 H24 Quaraí, Rio Sp. Río Cuareim. ≈ Brazil/Uruguay see also Cuareim, Río
175 P10 Quarles, Pegunungan ▲ Sulawesi, C Indonesia
Quarnero see Kvarner
109 C20 Quartu Sant' Elena Sardegna, Italy, C Mediterranean Sea 39.15N 9.12E
31 X13 Quasqueton Iowa, C USA 42.23N 91.45W
181 X16 Quatre Bornes W Mauritius 20.15S 57.28E
180 I17 Quatre Bornes Mahé, NE Seychelles
143 X10 Quba Rus. Kuba. N Azerbaijan 41.22N 48.30E
Qubba see Ba'qūbah
149 T3 Qūchān var. Kuchan. Khorāsān, NE Iran 37.12N 58.28E
191 R10 Queanbeyan New South Wales, SE Australia 35.24S 149.16E
13 Q10 Québec var. Quebec. Quebec, SE Canada 46.49N 71.15W
12 K10 Quebec var. Québec. ◈ province SE Canada
63 D17 Quebracho Paysandú, W Uruguay 31.58S 57.52W
103 K14 Quedlinburg Sachsen-Anhalt, C Germany 51.48N 11.09E
144 H10 Queen Alia ✈ ('Ammān) Al 'Āşimah, C Jordan
8 L16 Queen Bess, Mount ▲ British Columbia, SW Canada 51.15N 124.29W
8 I14 Queen Charlotte British Columbia, SW Canada 53.18N 132.04W
67 B24 Queen Charlotte Bay bay West Falkland, Falkland Islands
8 H14 Queen Charlotte Islands Fr. Îles de la Reine-Charlotte. island group British Columbia, SW Canada
8 I15 Queen Charlotte Sound sea area British Columbia, W Canada
8 J16 Queen Charlotte Strait strait British Columbia, W Canada
29 U1 Queen City Missouri, C USA 40.24N 92.34W
27 X5 Queen City Texas, SW USA 33.09N 94.09W
207 O9 Queen Elizabeth Islands Fr. Îles de la Reine-Elisabeth. island group Nunavut, N Canada
205 Y10 Queen Mary Coast physical region Antarctica
67 N24 Queen Mary's Peak ▲ C Tristan da Cunha
206 M8 Queen Maud Gulf gulf Arctic Ocean
205 P11 Queen Maud Mountains ▲ Antarctica
Queen's County see Laois
189 U7 Queensland ◈ state N Australia
199 Hh10 Queensland Plateau undersea feature N Coral Sea
191 O16 Queenstown Tasmania, SE Australia 42.06S 145.33E
193 C22 Queenstown Otago, South Island, NZ 45.03S 168.41E
85 I24 Queenstown Eastern Cape, S South Africa 31.52S 26.50E
Queenstown see Cobh
34 F8 Queets Washington, NW USA 47.31N 124.19W
63 D18 Queguay Grande, Río ≈ W Uruguay
61 O16 Queimadas Bahia, E Brazil 10.58S 39.37W
84 D11 Quela Malanje, NW Angola 9.18S 17.07E
85 O16 Quelimane var. Kilimane, Kilmain, Quilimane. Zambézia, NE Mozambique 17.52S 36.51E
65 G18 Quellón var. Puerto Quellón. Los Lagos, S Chile 43.05S 73.38W
Quelpart see Cheju-do
39 P12 Quemado New Mexico, SW USA 34.18N 108.29W
27 O12 Quemado Texas, SW USA 28.58N 100.36W
46 K7 Quemado, Punta de headland E Cuba 20.13N 74.07W
Quemoy see Chinmen Tao
64 K13 Quemú Quemú La Pampa, E Argentina 36.03S 63.30W
161 E17 Quepem Goa, W India 15.13N 74.03E
44 M14 Quepos Puntarenas, S Costa Rica 9.28N 84.10W
Que Que see Kwekwe
63 D23 Quequén Buenos Aires, E Argentina 38.30S 58.43W
63 D23 Quequén Grande, Río ≈ E Argentina
63 C23 Quequén Salado, Río ≈ E Argentina
Quera see Chur
43 N13 Querétaro Querétaro de Arteaga, C Mexico 20.36N 100.24W
42 F4 Querobabi Sonora, NW Mexico 30.03N 111.02W
44 M13 Quesada var. Ciudad Quesada, San Carlos. Alajuela, N Costa Rica 10.17N 84.24W
107 O13 Quesada Andalucía, S Spain 37.52N 3.05W
167 O7 Queshan Henan, C China 32.48N 114.03E
8 M15 Quesnel British Columbia, SW Canada 52.58N 122.30W
39 S9 Questa New Mexico, SW USA 36.41N 105.37W
104 H7 Questembert Morbihan, NW France 47.39N 2.24W
59 K22 Quetena, Río ≈ SW Bolivia
155 O10 Quetta Baluchistān, SW Pakistan 30.15N 67.00E
Quetzalcoalco see Coatzacoalcos
Quetzaltenango see Quezaltenango
58 B6 Quevedo Los Ríos, C Ecuador 1.01S 79.27W
44 B6 Quezaltenango var. Quetzaltenango. Quezaltenango, W Guatemala 14.48N 91.27W
44 A2 Quezaltenango off. Departamento de Quezaltenango, var. Quetzaltenango. ◈ department SW Guatemala
44 E6 Quezaltepeque Chiquimula, SE Guatemala 14.38N 89.25W
179 O15 Quezon Palawan, W Philippines 9.13N 118.01E
179 P10 Quezon City Luzon, N Philippines 14.39N 121.01E
167 P5 Qufu Shandong, E China 35.37N 117.05E
84 B12 Quibala Cuanza Sul, NW Angola 10.44S 14.58E
84 B11 Quibaxe var. Quibaxi. Cuanza Norte, NW Angola 8.30S 14.36E
Quibaxi see Quibaxe
56 D9 Quibdó Chocó, W Colombia 5.40N 76.37W
104 G7 Quiberon Morbihan, NW France 47.30N 3.07W
104 G7 Quiberon, Baie de bay NW France
56 J5 Quíbor Lara, N Venezuela 9.55N 69.34W
44 C4 Quiché off. Departamento del Quiché. ◈ department W Guatemala
101 E21 Quiévrain Hainaut, S Belgium 50.25N 3.40E
42 I9 Quila Sinaloa, C Mexico 24.24N 107.11W
85 B14 Quilengues Huíla, SW Angola 14.03S 14.03E
Quilimane see Quelimane
59 G15 Quillabamba Cusco, C Peru 12.48S 72.42W
59 L18 Quillacollo Cochabamba, C Bolivia 17.23S 66.15W
64 H4 Quillagua Antofagasta, N Chile 21.33S 69.32W
105 N17 Quillan Aude, S France 42.52N 2.10E
9 U15 Quill Lakes ◎ Saskatchewan, S Canada
64 G11 Quillota Valparaíso, C Chile 32.54S 71.16W
161 G23 Quilon var. Kolam, Kollam. Kerala, SW India 8.57N 76.36E
189 V9 Quilpie Queensland, C Australia 26.39S 144.15E
155 O4 Quil-Qala Bāmiān, N Afghanistan 35.13N 67.02E
64 L7 Quimilí Santiago del Estero, C Argentina 27.38S 62.25W
59 O19 Quimome Santa Cruz, E Bolivia 17.45S 61.15W
104 F6 Quimper anc. Quimper Corentin. Finistère, NW France 48.00N 4.05W
Quimper Corentin see Quimper
104 G7 Quimperlé Finistère, NW France 47.52N 3.33W
34 F8 Quinault Washington, NW USA 47.27N 123.53W
34 F8 Quinault River ≈ Washington, NW USA
37 P5 Quincy California, W USA 39.55N 120.57W
25 S8 Quincy Florida, SE USA 30.35N 84.34W
32 I13 Quincy Illinois, N USA 39.56N 91.24W
21 O11 Quincy Massachusetts, NE USA 42.15N 71.00W
34 J9 Quincy Washington, NW USA 47.13N 119.51W
56 E10 Quindío off. Departamento del Quindío. ◈ province C Colombia
56 E10 Quindío, Nevado del ▲ C Colombia 4.42N 75.25W
64 J10 Quines San Luis, C Argentina 32.15S 65.46W
41 N13 Quinhagak Alaska, USA 59.45N 161.55W
78 G13 Quinhámel W Guinea-Bissau 11.52N 15.52W
Qui Nhon/Quinhon see Quy Nhơn
Quinindé see Rosa Zárate
27 U6 Quinlan Texas, SW USA 32.54N 96.08W
63 H17 Quinta Rio Grande do Sul, S Brazil 32.05S 52.18W
107 O10 Quintanar de la Orden Castilla-La Mancha, C Spain 39.36N 3.03W
43 X13 Quintana Roo ◈ state SE Mexico
107 S6 Quinto Aragón, NE Spain 41.25N 0.31W
110 G10 Quinto Ticino, S Switzerland 46.32N 8.44E
29 Q11 Quinton Oklahoma, C USA 35.07N 95.22W
64 K12 Quinto, Río ≈ C Argentina
84 A10 Quinzau Zaire, NW Angola 6.50S 12.48E
12 H8 Quinze, Lac des ◎ Quebec, SE Canada
85 B15 Quipungo Huíla, C Angola 14.49S 14.29E
64 G13 Quirihue Bío Bío, C Chile 36.15S 72.34W
84 D12 Quirima Malanje, NW Angola 10.51S 18.06E
191 T6 Quirindi New South Wales, SE Australia 31.29S 150.40E
57 P5 Quiriquire Monagas, NE Venezuela 9.58N 63.13W
12 D10 Quirke Lake ◎ Ontario, S Canada
63 B21 Quiroga Buenos Aires, E Argentina 35.18S 61.22W
106 I4 Quiroga Galicia, NW Spain 42.28N 7.15W
Quiróm, Salar see Pocitos, Salar
58 B9 Quiroz, Río ≈ NW Peru
84 Q13 Quissanga Cabo Delgado, NE Mozambique 12.21S 40.31E
85 M20 Quissico Inhambane, S Mozambique 24.42S 34.43E
27 O4 Quitaque Texas, SW USA 34.22N 101.03W
84 Q13 Quiterajo Cabo Delgado, NE Mozambique 11.37S 40.22E
25 T6 Quitman Georgia, SE USA 30.46N 83.33W
24 M6 Quitman Mississippi, S USA 32.02N 88.43W
27 V6 Quitman Texas, SW USA 32.48N 95.27W
58 C6 Quito ● (Ecuador) Pichincha, N Ecuador 0.13S 78.30W
Quito see Mariscal Sucre
60 P13 Quixadá Ceará, E Brazil 4.57S 39.04W
85 Q15 Quixaxe Nampula, NE Mozambique 15.15S 40.07E
166 J9 Qu Jiang ≈ C China
167 R10 Qu Jiang ≈ SE China
167 N13 Qujiang prev. Maba. Guangdong, S China 24.47N 113.34E
166 H12 Qujing Yunnan, SW China 25.39N 103.52E
Qulan see Kulan
152 L10 Quljuqtov Tog'lari Rus. Gory Kul'dzhuktau. ▲ C Uzbekistan
Qulsary see Kul'sary
Qulyndy Zhazyghy see Kulunda Steppe
Qum see Qom
Qumälisch see Lubartów
165 P11 Qumar He ≈ C China
165 Q12 Qumarlêb Qinghai, C China 34.06N 95.54E
Qumisheh see Shahrezā
153 O14 Qumqo'rg'on Rus. Kumkurgan. Surkhondaryo Viloyati, S Uzbekistan 37.54N 67.31E
Qunaytirah/Qunayṭirah, Muḥāfaẓat al/Qunaytra see Al Qunayṭirah
201 V12 Quoi island Chuuk, C Micronesia
15 Kk6 Quoich ≈ Nunavut, NE Canada
85 E26 Quoin Point headland SW South Africa 34.48S 19.39E
190 I7 Quorn South Australia 32.22S 138.03E
Qurein see Al Kuwayt
153 P14 Qŭrghonteppa Rus. Kurgan-Tyube. SW Tajikistan 37.51N 68.42E
Qurlurtuuq see Kugluktuk
Qurveh see Qorveh
Qusair see Quseir
143 X10 Qusar Rus. Kusary. NE Azerbaijan 41.26N 48.27E
Quşayr see Al Quşayr
77 Y10 Quseir var. Al Quşayr, Qusair. E Egypt 26.05N 34.16E
148 I2 Qūshchī Āzarbāyjān-e Bākhtarī, N Iran 37.58N 45.04E
Qusmuryn see Kushmurun, Kostanay, Kazakhstan
Qusmuryn see Kushmurun, Ozero, Kazakhstan
Quṭayfah/Qutayfe/Quteife see Al Quṭayfah
Quthing see Moyeni
153 S10 Quvasoy Rus. Kuvasay. Farg'ona Viloyati, E Uzbekistan 40.17N 71.53E
Quwair see Guwēr
Qu Xian see Quzhou
165 N16 Qüxü Xizang Zizhiqu, W China 29.25N 90.48E
178 Kk13 Quy Chanh Ninh Thuân, S Vietnam 11.28N 108.53E
178 Kk12 Quy Nhơn var. Quinhon, Qui Nhon. Bình Định, C Vietnam 13.46N 109.10E
167 R10 Quzhou var. Qu Xian. Zhejiang, SE China 28.55N 118.54E
Qyteti Stalin see Kuçovë
Qyzylorda/Qyzylorda Oblysy see Kyzylorda
Qyzyltū see Kishkenekol'
Qyzylzhar see Kyzylzhar

R

111 R4 Raab Oberösterreich, N Austria 48.19N 13.40E
111 X8 Raab Hung. Rába. ≈ Austria/Hungary see also Rába
Raab see Győr
111 V2 Raabs an der Thaya Niederösterreich, E Austria 48.51N 15.28E
95 L14 Raahe Swe. Brahestad. Oulu, W Finland 64.42N 24.30E
100 M10 Raalte Overijssel, E Netherlands 52.22N 6.16E
101 I14 Raamsdonksveer Noord-Brabant, S Netherlands 51.42N 4.54E
94 L12 Raanujärvi Lappi, NW Finland 66.39N 24.40E
98 G9 Raasay island NW Scotland, UK
120 H3 Raasiku Ger. Rasik. Harjumaa, NW Estonia 59.22N 25.12E
114 B11 Rab It. Arbe. Primorje-Gorski Kotar, NW Croatia 44.46N 14.46E
114 B11 Rab It. Arbe. island NW Croatia
175 P16 Raba Sumbawa, S Indonesia 8.30S 118.46E
113 G22 Rába Ger. Raab. ≈ Austria/Hungary see also Raab
114 A10 Rabac Istra, NW Croatia 45.03N 14.09E
106 I2 Rábade Galicia, NW Spain 42.07N 7.37W
82 F10 Rabak White Nile, C Sudan 13.12N 32.43E
194 M16 Rabaraba Milne Bay, SE PNG 10.02S 149.53E
104 K16 Rabastens-de-Bigorre Hautes-Pyrénées, S France 43.22N 0.10E
123 Jj17 Rabat W Malta 35.51N 14.25E
76 F6 Rabat var. al Dar al Baida. ● (Morocco) NW Morocco 34.01N 6.51W
Rabat see Victoria
195 P10 Rabaul New Britain, E PNG 4.13S 152.10E
Rabbah Ammon/Rabbath Ammon see 'Ammān
30 K8 Rabbit Creek ≈ South Dakota, N USA
12 H10 Rabbit Lake ◎ Ontario, S Canada
197 K13 Rabi prev. Rambi. island N Fiji
146 K9 Rābigh Makkah, W Saudi Arabia 22.51N 39.00E
44 D5 Rabinal Baja Verapaz, C Guatemala 15.05N 90.23W
173 Ee6 Rabi, Pulau island NW Indonesia, East Indies
113 L17 Rabka Małopolskie, S Poland 49.37N 20.00E
161 F16 Rabkavi Karnātaka, W India 16.40N 75.03E
Râbniţa see Ribniţa
111 Y6 Rabnitz ≈ E Austria
128 J7 Rabocheostrovsk Respublika Kareliya, NW Russian Federation 64.58N 34.46E
25 U1 Rabun Bald ▲ Georgia, SE USA 34.58N 83.18W
77 S11 Rabyānah SE Libya 24.07N 21.58E
77 S11 Rabyānah, Ramlat var. Rebiana Sand Sea, Şahrā' Rabyānah. desert SE Libya
Rabyānah, Şahrā' see Rabyānah, Ramlat
118 L11 Răcăciuni Bacău, E Romania 46.20N 27.00E
109 J24 Racalmuto Sicilia, Italy, C Mediterranean Sea 37.25N 13.43E
118 J14 Răcari Dâmboviţa, SE Romania 44.37N 25.43E
Răcari see Durankulak
118 F13 Răcăşdia Hung. Rakasd. Caraş-Severin, SW Romania 44.58N 21.36E
108 B9 Racconigi Piemonte, NE Italy 44.45N 7.41E
33 T15 Raccoon Creek ≈ Ohio, N USA
11 V13 Race, Cape headland Newfoundland and Labrador, E Canada 46.40N 53.05W
24 K10 Raceland Louisiana, S USA 29.43N 90.36W
21 Q12 Race Point headland Massachusetts, NE USA 42.03N 70.14W
178 J15 Rach Gia Kiên Giang, S Vietnam 10.01N 105.04E
178 J14 Rach Gia, Vinh bay S Vietnam
78 J8 Rachid Tagant, C Mauritania 18.48N 11.40W
112 L10 Raciąż Mazowieckie, C Poland 52.46N 20.04E
113 I16 Racibórz Ger. Ratibor. Śląskie, S Poland 50.06N 18.13E
33 N9 Racine Wisconsin, N USA 42.42N 87.49W
12 D7 Racine Lake ◎ Ontario, S Canada
113 J23 Ráckeve Pest, C Hungary 47.07N 18.57E
Rácz-Becse see Bečej
147 O15 Radā' var. Ridā'. W Yemen 14.24N 44.49E
115 O15 Radan ▲ SE Serbia and Montenegro (Yugoslavia) 42.59N 21.31E
65 J19 Rada Tilly Chubut, SE Argentina 45.54S 67.33W
118 K8 Rădăuţi Ger. Radautz, Hung. Rádóc. Suceava, N Romania 47.49N 25.58E
118 L8 Rădăuţi-Prut Botoşani, NE Romania 48.14N 26.47E
Radautz see Rădăuţi
Radbusa see Radbuza
113 A17 Radbuza Ger. Radbusa. ≈ SE Czech Republic
22 K6 Radcliff Kentucky, S USA 37.50N 85.57W
145 O2 Radd, Wādī ar dry watercourse N Syria
97 H16 Råde Østfold, S Norway 59.21N 10.52E
111 V11 Radeče Ger. Ratschach. C Slovenia 46.01N 15.10E
Radein see Radenci
118 J4 Radekhiv Pol. Radziechów, Rus. Radekhov. L'vivs'ka Oblast', W Ukraine 50.17N 24.39E
Radekhov see Radekhiv
111 X9 Radenci Ger. Radein; prev. Radinci. NE Slovenia 46.36N 16.02E
111 S9 Radenthein Kärnten, S Austria 46.48N 13.42E
23 R7 Radford Virginia, NE USA 37.07N 80.34W
160 C9 Rādhanpur Gujarāt, W India 23.52N 71.49E
Radinci see Radenci
131 Q6 Radishchevo Ul'yanovskaya Oblast', W Russian Federation 52.49N 47.54E
10 I9 Radisson Quebec, E Canada 53.47N 77.35W
9 P16 Radium Hot Springs British Columbia, SW Canada 50.39N 116.09W
118 F11 Radna Hung. Máriaradna. Arad, W Romania 46.04N 21.40E
116 K10 Radnevo Stara Zagora, C Bulgaria 42.18N 25.57E
99 J20 Radnor cultural region E Wales, UK
Radnót see Iernut
Radóc see Rădăuţi
103 H24 Radolfzell am Bodensee Baden-Württemberg, S Germany 47.43N 8.58E
112 M13 Radom Mazowieckie, C Poland 51.23N 21.07E
118 I14 Radomireşti Olt, S Romania 44.06N 25.00E
113 K14 Radomsko Rus. Novoradomsk. Łodzkie, C Poland 51.04N 19.25E
119 N4 Radomyshl' Zhytomyrs'ka Oblast', N Ukraine 50.30N 29.16E
115 P19 Radoviš prev. Radovište. E FYR Macedonia 41.39N 22.26E
Radovište see Radoviš
96 B13 Radøy island S Norway
111 R7 Radstadt Salzburg, NW Austria 47.24N 13.31E
190 E8 Radstock, Cape headland South Australia 33.11S 134.18E
121 G15 Radun' Rus. Radun'. Hrodzyenskaya Voblasts', W Belarus 54.03N 25.00E
126 Gg11 Raduzhnyy Khanty-Mansiyskiy Avtonomnyy Okrug, C Russian Federation 62.03N 77.28E
130 M3 Raduzhnyy Vladimirskaya Oblast', W Russian Federation 55.59N 40.15E
120 F11 Radviliškis Radviliškis, N Lithuania 55.48N 23.32E
9 U17 Radville Saskatchewan, S Canada 49.28N 104.19W
146 K7 Raḍwá, Jabal ▲ W Saudi Arabia 24.31N 38.21E
113 P16 Radymno Podkarpackie, SE Poland 49.57N 22.49E
118 J5 Radyvyliv Rivnens'ka Oblast', NW Ukraine 50.07N 25.12E
Radziechów see Radekhiv
112 I11 Radziejów Kujawsko-pomorskie, C Poland 52.36N 18.33E
112 O12 Radzyń Podlaski Lubelskie, E Poland 51.48N 22.36E
15 Hh4 Rae ≈ Nunavut, NW Canada
158 M13 Rāe Bareli Uttar Pradesh, N India 26.13N 81.13E
Rae-Edzo see Edzo
23 T11 Raeford North Carolina, SE USA 34.58N 79.13W
101 M19 Raeren Liège, E Belgium 50.42N 6.06E
15 Kk3 Rae Strait strait Nunavut, N Canada
192 L11 Raetihi Manawatu-Wanganui, North Island, NZ 39.28S 175.16E
203 U13 Raevavae var. Raivavae. island Îles Australes, SW French Polynesia
Rafa see Rafah
64 M10 Rafaela Santa Fe, E Argentina 31.16S 61.25W
144 E11 Rafah var. Rafa, Rafaḥ, Heb. Rafiaḥ, Raphiah. SW Gaza Strip 31.17N 34.18E
81 L15 Rafaï Mbomou, SE Central African Republic 5.01N 23.51E
147 O4 Rafḥah Al Ḥudūd ash Shamālīyah, N Saudi Arabia 29.40N 43.28E
Rafiaḥ see Rafah
149 R10 Rafsanjān Kermān, C Iran 30.25N 56.00E
82 B13 Raga Western Bahr el Ghazal, SW Sudan 8.28N 25.40E
21 S8 Ragged Island island Maine, NE USA
46 I5 Ragged Island Range island group S Bahamas
192 L7 Raglan Waikato, North Island, NZ 37.49S 174.52E
24 G8 Ragley Louisiana, S USA 30.31N 93.13W
Ragnit see Neman
109 K25 Ragusa Sicilia, Italy, C Mediterranean Sea 36.55N 14.42E
Ragusa see Dubrovnik
Ragusavecchia see Cavtat
175 Qq12 Raha Pulau Muna, C Indonesia 4.49S 122.43E
121 N17 Rahachow Rus. Rogachëv. Homyel'skaya Voblasts', SE Belarus 53.03N 30.04E
69 U6 Rahad var. Nahr ar Rahad. ≈ W Sudan
Rahad, Nahr ar see Rahad
Rahaeng see Tak
144 F11 Rahat Southern, C Israel 31.20N 34.43E
146 L8 Rahaṭ, Ḥarrat lavaflow W Saudi Arabia
155 S12 Rahīmyār Khān Punjab, SE Pakistan 28.27N 70.21E
97 I14 Råholt Akershus, S Norway 60.16N 11.10E
Rahovec see Orahovac
203 S10 Raiatea island Îles Sous le Vent, W French Polynesia
161 H16 Rāichūr Karnātaka, C India 16.15N 77.19E
Raidestos see Tekirdağ
159 S13 Rāiganj West Bengal, NE India 25.37N 88.10E
160 M11 Raigarh Madhya Pradesh, C India 21.55N 83.24E
175 Q18 Raijua, Selat strait Nusa Tenggara, S Indonesia
191 O16 Railton Tasmania, SE Australia 41.24S 146.28E
38 L8 Rainbow Bridge natural arch Utah, W USA
25 Q3 Rainbow City Alabama, S USA 33.57N 86.02W
9 N11 Rainbow Lake Alberta, W Canada 58.30N 119.24W
23 R5 Rainelle West Virginia, NE USA 37.57N 80.46W
34 G10 Rainier Oregon, NW USA 46.05N 122.55W
34 H9 Rainier, Mount ▲ Washington, NW USA 46.51N 121.45W
25 Q2 Rainsville Alabama, S USA 34.29N 85.51W
10 B11 Rainy Lake ◎ Canada/USA
10 A11 Rainy River Ontario, C Canada 48.43N 94.33W
Raippaluoto see Replot
160 K12 Raipur Madhya Pradesh, C India 21.16N 81.42E
160 H10 Raisen Madhya Pradesh, C India 23.21N 77.49E
13 N13 Raisin ≈ Ontario, SE Canada
33 R11 Raisin, River ≈ Michigan, N USA
Raivavae see Raevavae
155 W9 Rāiwind Punjab, E Pakistan 31.13N 74.10E
176 U9 Raja Ampat, Kepulauan island group E Indonesia
161 L16 Rājahmundry Andhra Pradesh, E India 17.05N 81.42E
161 I18 Rājampet Andhra Pradesh, E India 14.09N 79.10E
Rajang see Rajang, Batang
174 Mm6 Rajang, Batang var. Rajang. ≈ East Malaysia
155 S11 Rājanpur Punjab, E Pakistan 29.07N 70.19E
161 H23 Rājapālaiyam Tamil Nādu, SE India 9.25N 77.36E
158 E12 Rājasthān ◈ state NW India
159 T15 Rājbari Dhaka, C Bangladesh 23.46N 89.39E
159 R12 Rājbiraj Eastern, E Nepal 26.34N 86.52E
160 G9 Rājgarh Madhya Pradesh, C India 24.01N 76.42E
158 H10 Rājgarh Rājasthān, NW India 28.38N 75.21E
159 P14 Rājgīr Bihār, N India 25.01N 85.25E
112 O8 Rajgród Podlaskie, NE Poland 53.43N 22.40E
160 L12 Rājim Madhya Pradesh, C India 20.57N 81.58E
114 C11 Rajinac, Mali ▲ W Croatia 44.47N 15.04E
160 B10 Rājkot Gujarāt, W India 22.18N 70.46E
159 R14 Rājmahal Bihār, NE India 25.03N 87.49E
159 Q14 Rājmahāl Hills hill range N India
160 K12 Rāj Nāndgaon Madhya Pradesh, C India 21.06N 81.01E
158 I8 Rājpura Punjab, NW India 30.30N 76.36E
159 S14 Rajshahi prev. Rampur Boalia. Rajshahi, W Bangladesh 24.24N 88.40E
159 S13 Rajshahi ◈ division NW Bangladesh
202 K13 Rakahanga atoll N Cook Islands
193 H19 Rakaia Canterbury, South Island, NZ 43.45S 172.02E
193 G19 Rakaia ≈ South Island, NZ
158 H3 Rakaposhi ▲ N India 36.06N 74.31E
Rakasd see Răcăşdia
174 Ii14 Rakata, Pulau var. Pulau Krakatau. island S Indonesia
164 K16 Raka Zangbo ≈ W China
147 U10 Rakbah, Qalamat ar well SE Saudi Arabia 20.37N 52.45E
Rakhine State see Arakan State
118 I8 Rakhiv Zakarpats'ka Oblast', W Ukraine 48.05N 24.15E
147 V13 Rakhyūt SW Oman 16.41N 53.09E
197 I14 Rakiraki Viti Levu, W Fiji 17.21S 178.11E
Rakka see Ar Raqqah
120 I4 Rakke Lääne-Virumaa, NE Estonia 58.58N 26.14E
97 I16 Rakkestad Østfold, S Norway 59.25N 11.19E
112 F12 Rakoniewice Ger. Rakwitz. Wielkolpolskie, C Poland 52.09N 16.10E
Rakonitz see Rakovník
85 H18 Rakops Central, C Botswana 21.01S 24.23E
113 C16 Rakovník Ger. Rakonitz. Středočeský Kraj, W Czech Republic 50.07N 13.43E
116 J10 Rakovski Plovdiv, C Bulgaria 42.16N 24.58E
Rakutō-kō see Naktong-gang
120 I3 Rakvere Ger. Wesenberg. Lääne-Virumaa, N Estonia 59.21N 26.19E
Rakwitz see Rakoniewice
24 L6 Raleigh Mississippi, S USA 32.01N 89.30W
23 U9 Raleigh state capital North Carolina, SE USA 35.46N 78.38W
23 Y11 Raleigh Bay bay North Carolina, SE USA
23 U9 Raleigh-Durham ✈ North Carolina, SE USA 35.54N 78.45W
201 S6 Ralik Chain island group Ralik Chain, W Marshall Islands
27 N5 Ralls Texas, SW USA 33.40N 101.23W
20 G13 Ralston Pennsylvania, NE USA 41.29N 76.57W
147 O16 Ramādah W Yemen 13.35N 43.50E
Ramadi see Ar Ramādī
107 N2 Ramales de la Victoria Cantabria, N Spain 43.15N 3.28W
144 F10 Ramallah C West Bank 31.53N 34.49E
63 C19 Ramallo Buenos Aires, E Argentina 33.30S 60.01W
161 H20 Rāmanagaram Karnātaka, E India 12.45N 77.16E
161 I23 Rāmanāthapuram Tamil Nādu, SE India 9.22N 78.52E
160 N12 Rāmapur Orissa, E India 21.48N 84.00E
161 I14 Rāmāreddi var. Kāmāreddi, Kamareddy. Andhra Pradesh, C India 18.19N 78.23E
144 F10 Ramat Gan Tel Aviv, W Israel 32.04N 34.48E
105 T6 Rambervillers Vosges, NE France 48.15N 6.50E
Rambi see Rabi
105 N5 Rambouillet Yvelines, N France 48.39N 1.49E
194 L8 Rambutyo Island island N PNG
159 Q12 Ramechhap Central, C Nepal 27.19N 86.04E
191 R12 Rame Head headland Victoria, SE Australia 37.48S 149.30E
130 L4 Ramenskoye Moskovskaya Oblast', W Russian Federation 55.31N 38.24E
128 J15 Rameshki Tverskaya Oblast', W Russian Federation 57.21N 36.05E
159 P14 Rāmgarh Bihār, N India 23.37N 85.31E
158 D11 Rāmgarh Rājasthān, NW India 27.26N 70.35E
148 M9 Rāmhormoz var. Ram Hormuz, Ramuz. Khūzestān, SW Iran 31.17N 49.37E
Ram Hormuz see Rāmhormoz
Ram, Jebel see Ramm, Jabal
144 F10 Ramla var. Ramle, Ramleh, Ar. Er Ramle. Central, C Israel 31.55N 34.52E
Ramle/Ramleh see Ramla
144 F14 Ramm, Jabal var. Jebel Ram. ▲ SW Jordan 29.34N 35.24E
158 K10 Rāmnagar Uttar Pradesh, N India 29.22N 79.07E
97 N15 Ramnäs Västmanland, C Sweden 59.46N 16.16E
Râmnicul-Sărat see Râmnicu Sărat
118 L12 Râmnicu Sărat prev. Râmnicul-Sărat, Rîmnicu-Sărat. Buzău, E Romania 45.24N 27.06E
118 I13 Râmnicu Vâlcea prev. Rîmnicu Vîlcea. Vâlcea, C Romania 45.04N 24.32E
Ramokgwebana see Ramokgwebane
85 J18 Ramokgwebane var. Ramokgwebana. Central, NE Botswana 20.36S 27.39E
130 L7 Ramon' Voronezhskaya Oblast', W Russian Federation 51.51N 39.18E
37 V17 Ramona California, W USA 33.02N 116.52W
58 A10 Ramón, Laguna ◎ NW Peru
12 G7 Ramore Ontario, S Canada 48.26N 80.19W
42 M11 Ramos San Luis Potosí, C Mexico 22.48N 101.55W
43 N8 Ramos Arizpe Coahuila de Zaragoza, NE Mexico 25.34N 100.58W
42 J9 Ramos, Río de ≈ C Mexico
41 R8 Rampart Alaska, USA 65.30N 150.10W
14 G5 Ramparts ≈ Northwest Territories, NW Canada
158 K10 Rāmpur Uttar Pradesh, N India 28.48N 79.03E
160 F9 Rāmpura Madhya Pradesh, C India 24.34N 75.25E
Rampur Boalia see Rajshahi
177 F6 Ramree Island island W Myanmar
147 W6 Rams var. Ar Rams. Ra's al Khaymah, NE UAE 25.52N 56.01E
149 N4 Rāmsar prev. Sakhtsar. Māzandarān, N Iran 36.55N 50.39E
95 H16 Ramsele Västernorrland, N Sweden 63.33N 16.35E
23 T9 Ramseur North Carolina, SE USA 35.43N 79.39W
99 I16 Ramsey NE Isle of Man 54.19N 4.24W
99 I16 Ramsey Bay bay NE Isle of Man
12 E9 Ramsey Lake ◎ Ontario, S Canada
99 Q22 Ramsgate SE England, UK 51.19N 1.25E
96 M10 Ramsjö Gävleborg, C Sweden 62.10N 15.40E
160 I12 Rāmtek Mahārāshtra, C India 21.28N 79.28E
Ramtha see Ar Ramthā
194 H11 Ramu ≈ N PNG
Ramuz see Rāmhormoz
120 G12 Ramygala Panevėžys, C Lithuania 55.30N 24.18E
158 H14 Rāna Pratāp Sāgar ◎ N India
175 O2 Ranau Sabah, East Malaysia 5.55N 116.43E
174 I12 Ranau, Danau ◎ Sumatera, W Indonesia
64 H12 Rancagua Libertador, C Chile 34.10S 70.45W
101 G22 Rance Hainaut, S Belgium 50.09N 4.16E
104 H6 Rance ≈ NW France
62 J9 Rancharia São Paulo, S Brazil 22.13S 50.53W
159 P15 Rānchi Bihār, N India 23.22N 85.19E
63 D21 Ranchos Buenos Aires, E Argentina 35.31S 58.22W
39 S9 Ranchos De Taos New Mexico, SW USA 36.21N 105.36W
65 G16 Ranco, Lago ◎ C Chile
97 C16 Randaberg Rogaland, S Norway 59.00N 5.38E
31 U7 Randall Minnesota, N USA 46.05N 94.30W
94 G12 Randalen ≈ C Norway
109 L23 Randazzo Sicilia, Italy, C Mediterranean Sea 37.52N 14.57E
97 G21 Randers Århus, C Denmark 56.28N 10.03E
94 I12 Randijaure ◎ N Sweden
23 T9 Randleman North Carolina, SE USA 35.49N 79.48W
21 O11 Randolph Massachusetts, NE USA 42.09N 71.02W
31 Q13 Randolph Nebraska, C USA 42.25N 97.05W
38 M1 Randolph Utah, W USA 41.40N 111.10W
102 P9 Randow ≈ NE Germany
97 H14 Randsfjorden ◎ S Norway
94 K13 Råneå Norrbotten, N Sweden 65.52N 22.17E
95 F15 Ranemsletta Nord-Trøndelag, C Norway 64.36N 11.55E
78 H10 Ranérou C Senegal 15.17N 14.00W
193 E22 Ranfurly Otago, South Island, NZ 45.07S 170.06E
178 Hh17 Rangae Narathiwat, SW Thailand 6.19N 101.45E
159 V16 Rangamati Chittagong, SE Bangladesh 22.40N 92.10E
192 I2 Rangaunu Bay bay North Island, NZ
21 P6 Rangeley Maine, NE USA 44.58N 70.37W
39 O4 Rangely Colorado, C USA 40.05N 108.48W
27 R7 Ranger Texas, SW USA 32.28N 98.40W
12 C9 Ranger Lake Ontario, S Canada 46.51N 83.34W
12 C9 Ranger Lake ◎ Ontario, S Canada
159 V12 Rangia Assam, NE India 26.27N 91.34E
193 I18 Rangiora Canterbury, South Island, NZ 43.19S 172.33E
203 T9 Rangiroa atoll Îles Tuamotu, W French Polynesia
192 N9 Rangitaiki ≈ North Island, NZ
193 F19 Rangitata ≈ South Island, NZ
192 M12 Rangitikei ≈ North Island, NZ
192 L6 Rangitoto Island island N NZ
Rangkasbitoeng see Rangkasbitung
174 Ii14 Rangkasbitung prev. Rangkasbitoeng. Jawa, SW Indonesia 6.21S 106.12E
178 Hh9 Rang, Khao ▲ C Thailand 16.13N 99.03E
153 V13 Rangkŭl Rus. Rangkul'. SE Tajikistan 38.30N 74.24E
Rangkul' see Rangkŭl
Rangoon see Yangon
159 T13 Rangpur Rajshahi, N Bangladesh 25.46N 89.20E
174 Hh7 Rangsang, Pulau island W Indonesia
161 F18 Rānībennur Karnātaka, W India 14.36N 75.39E
159 R15 Rāniganj West Bengal, NE India 23.34N 87.13E
155 Q13 Rānīpur Sind, SE Pakistan 27.16N 68.34E
Rāniyah see Rānya
27 N9 Rankin Texas, SW USA 31.12N 101.56W
15 L7 Rankin Inlet Nunavut, C Canada 62.52N 92.13W
191 P8 Rankins Springs New South Wales, SE Australia 33.51S 146.16E
Rankovićevo see Kraljevo
110 I7 Rankweil Vorarlberg, W Austria 47.16N 9.40E
Rann see Brežice
131 T8 Ranneye Orenburgskaya Oblast', W Russian Federation 51.28N 52.29E
98 I10 Rannoch, Loch ◎ C Scotland, UK
203 U17 Rano Kau var. Rano Kao. crater Easter Island, Chile, E Pacific Ocean 27.10S 109.25W

◆ Country ● Country Capital ◇ Dependent Territory ○ Dependent Territory Capital ◈ Administrative Region ✈ International Airport ▲ Mountain ▲ Mountain Range Volcano ≈ River ◎ Lake ⊠ Reservoir

178 *Gg14* **Ranong** Ranong, SW Thailand *9.58N 98.40E*
195 *T14* **Ranongga** ***var.*** Ghanongga. *island* NW Solomon Islands
203 *W16* **Rano Raraku** *ancient monument* Easter Island, Chile, E Pacific Ocean *27.07S 109.18W*
176 *W9* **Ransiki** Papua, E Indonesia *1.27S 134.12E*
94 *K12* **Rantajärvi** Norrbotten, N Sweden *66.45N 23.39E*
95 *N17* **Rantasalmi** Isä-Suomi, SE Finland *62.02N 28.22E*
175 *N11* **Rantau** Borneo, C Indonesia *2.55S 115.09E*
174 *Hh7* **Rantau, Pulau** ***var.*** Pulau Tebingtinggi. *island* W Indonesia
175 *Pp11* **Rantepao** Sulawesi, C Indonesia *2.58S 119.58E*
32 *M13* **Rantoul** Illinois, N USA *40.19N 88.08W*
95 *L15* **Rantsila** Oulu, C Finland *64.31N 25.40E*
94 *L13* **Ranua** Lappi, NW Finland *65.55N 26.34E*
145 *T3* **Ŗānya** ***var.*** Rāniyah. NE Iraq *36.15N 44.52E*
163 *X3* **Raohe** Heilongjiang, NE China *46.49N 134.00E*
76 *H9* **Raoui, Erg er** *desert* W Algeria
199 *L11* **Rapa** *island* Îles Australes, S French Polynesia
203 *V14* **Rapa Iti** *island* Îles Australes, SW French Polynesia
108 *D10* **Rapallo** Liguria, NW Italy *44.21N 9.13E*
Rapa Nui *see* Pascua, Isla de
Raphiah *see* Rafah
23 *V5* **Rapidan River** ≈ Virginia, NE USA
30 *J10* **Rapid City** South Dakota, N USA *44.04N 103.13W*
13 *P8* **Rapide-Blanc** Quebec, SE Canada *47.48N 72.57W*
12 *I8* **Rapide-Deux** Quebec, SE Canada *47.56N 78.33W*
120 *K6* **Räpina** ***Ger.*** Rappin. Põlvamaa, SE Estonia *58.06N 27.27E*
120 *G4* **Rapla** ***Ger.*** Rappel. Raplamaa, NW Estonia *59.00N 24.46E*
120 *G4* **Raplamaa** ***off.*** Rapla Maakond. ⬖ *province* NW Estonia
23 *X6* **Rappahonnock River** ≈ Virginia, NE USA
Rappel *see* Rapla
110 *G7* **Rapperswil** Sankt Gallen, NE Switzerland *47.13N 8.49E*
Rappin *see* Räpina
159 *N12* **Rāpti** ≈ N India
59 *K16* **Rapulo, Río** ≈ E Bolivia
Raqqah/Raqqah, Muḩāfaẓat al *see* Ar Raqqah
20 *J8* **Raquette Lake** ◎ New York, NE USA
20 *J6* **Raquette River** ≈ New York, NE USA
203 *V10* **Raraka** *atoll* Îles Tuamotu, C French Polynesia
203 *V10* **Raroia** *atoll* Îles Tuamotu, C French Polynesia
202 *H15* **Rarotonga** ✈ Rarotonga, S Cook Islands, C Pacific Ocean *21.15S 159.45W*
202 *H16* **Rarotonga** *island* S Cook Islands, C Pacific Ocean
153 *P12* **Rarz** W Tajikistan *39.23N 68.43E*
Ras al 'Ain *see* Ra's al 'Ayn
145 *N2* **Ra's al 'Ayn** ***var.*** Ras al 'Ain. Al Ḩasakah, N Syria *36.52N 40.04E*
144 *H3* **Ra's al Basīţ** Al Lādhiqīyah, W Syria *35.57N 35.55E*
Ra's al-Hafgī *see* Ra's al Khafjī
147 *R5* **Ra's al Khafjī** ***var.*** Ra's al-Hafgī. Ash Sharqīyah, NE Saudi Arabia *28.22N 48.29E*
Ras al-Khaimah/Ras al Khaimah *see* Ra's al Khaymah
149 *R15* **Ra's al Khaymah** ***var.*** Ras al Khaimah. Ra's al Khaymah, NE UAE *25.44N 55.54E*
149 *R15* **Ra's al Khaymah** ***var.*** Ras al-Khaimah. ✈ Ra's al Khaymah, NE UAE *25.37N 55.51E*
144 *G13* **Ra's an Naqb** Ma'ān, S Jordan *30.00N 35.29E*
63 *B26* **Rasa, Punta** *headland* E Argentina *40.50S 62.15W*
176 *W10* **Rasawi** Papua, E Indonesia *2.04S 134.02E*
Râşcani *see* Rîşcani
82 *J10* **Ras Dashen Terara** ▲ N Ethiopia *13.12N 38.09E*
157 *K19* **Rasdu Atoll** *atoll* C Maldives
120 *E12* **Raseiniai** Raseiniai, C Lithuania *55.23N 23.06E*
77 *X8* **Râs Ghârib** E Egypt *28.16N 33.01E*
168 *D6* **Rashaant** Bayan-Ölgiy, W Mongolia *47.48N 90.45E*
168 *L10* **Rashaant** Dundgovĭ, C Mongolia *44.54N 106.32E*
168 *J6* **Rashaant** Hövsgöl, N Mongolia *49.08N 101.27E*
145 *Y11* **Rashīd** E Iraq *31.15N 47.31E*
77 *V7* **Rashîd** ***Eng.*** Rosetta. N Egypt *31.24N 30.25E*
148 *M3* **Rasht** ***var.*** Resht. Gīlān, NW Iran *37.18N 49.37E*
145 *S2* **Rashwān** N Iraq *36.28N 43.54E*
Rasik *see* Raasiku
115 *M15* **Raška** Serbia, C Serbia and Montenegro (Yugoslavia) *43.18N 20.37E*
121 *P15* **Rasna** ***Rus.*** Ryasna. Mahilyowskaya Voblasts', E Belarus *54.01N 31.12E*
118 *J12* **Râşnov** ***prev.*** Rîşno, Rozsnyó, ***Hung.*** Barcarozsnyó. Braşov, C Romania *45.34N 25.27E*
120 *L11* **Rasony** ***Rus.*** Rossony. Vitsyebskaya Voblasts', N Belarus *55.55N 28.51E*
Ra's Shamrah *see* Ugarit
131 *N7* **Rasskazovo** Tambovskaya Oblast', W Russian Federation *52.42N 41.45E*
121 *O16* **Rasta** ≈ E Belarus
Rastadt *see* Rastatt
Rastâne *see* Ar Rastān
147 *S6* **Ra's Tannūrah** ***Eng.*** Ras Tanura. Ash Sharqīyah, NE Saudi Arabia *26.44N 50.04E*
Ras Tanura *see* Ra's Tannūrah
103 *G21* **Rastatt** ***var.*** Rastadt. Baden-Württemberg, SW Germany *48.52N 8.12E*
Rastenburg *see* Kętrzyn
155 *V7* **Rasūlnagar** Punjab, E Pakistan *32.19N 73.51E*
201 *U6* **Ratak Chain** *island group* Ratak Chain, E Marshall Islands
121 *K15* **Ratamka** ***Rus.*** Ratomka. Minskaya Voblasts', C Belarus *53.57N 27.23E*
95 *G17* **Ratan** Jämtland, C Sweden *62.28N 14.34E*
158 *G11* **Ratangarh** Rājasthān, NW India *28.01N 74.39E*
Rat Buri *see* Ratchaburi
178 *H11* **Ratchaburi** ***var.*** Rat Buri. Ratchaburi, W Thailand *13.30N 99.49E*
31 *W15* **Rathbun Lake** ▨ Iowa, C USA
Ráth Caola *see* Rathkeale
177 *F5* **Rathedaung** Arakan State, W Myanmar *20.30N 92.48E*
102 *M12* **Rathenow** Brandenburg, NE Germany *52.34N 12.20E*
99 *C19* **Rathkeale** ***Ir.*** Ráth Caola. SW Ireland *52.31N 8.55W*
98 *F13* **Rathlin Island** ***Ir.*** Reachlainn. *island* N Northern Ireland, UK
99 *C20* **Ráthluirc** ***Ir.*** An Ráth. SW Ireland *52.22N 8.44W*
Ratibor *see* Racibórz
Ratisbon/Ratisbona/Ratisbonne *see* Regensburg
Rätische Alpen *see* Rhaetian Alps
40 *E17* **Rat Island** *island* Aleutian Islands, Alaska, USA
40 *E17* **Rat Islands** *island group* Aleutian Islands, Alaska, USA
160 *F10* **Ratlām** ***prev.*** Rutlam. Madhya Pradesh, C India *23.23N 75.03E*
161 *D15* **Ratnāgiri** Mahārāshtra, W India *17.00N 73.20E*
161 *K26* **Ratnapura** Sabaragamuwa Province, S Sri Lanka *6.40N 80.25E*
118 *J2* **Ratne** ***Rus.*** Ratno. Volyns'ka Oblast', NW Ukraine *51.40N 24.33E*
Ratno *see* Ratne
Ratomka *see* Ratamka
39 *U8* **Raton** New Mexico, SW USA *36.54N 104.27W*
145 *O7* **Ratqah, Wādī ar** *dry watercourse* W Iraq
Ratschach *see* Radeče
178 *H17* **Rattaphum** Songkhla, SW Thailand *7.07N 100.16E*
28 *L6* **Rattlesnake Creek** ≈ Kansas, C USA
96 *L13* **Rättvik** Dalarna, C Sweden *60.53N 15.12E*
102 *K9* **Ratzeburg** Mecklenburg-Vorpommern, N Germany *53.41N 10.48E*
102 *K9* **Ratzeburger See** ◎ N Germany
8 *J10* **Ratz, Mount** ▲ British Columbia, SW Canada *57.22N 132.17W*
63 *D22* **Rauch** Buenos Aires, E Argentina *36.47S 59.06W*
43 *U16* **Raudales** Chiapas, SE Mexico
Raudhatain *see* Ar Rawḑatayn
Raudnitz an der Elbe *see* Roudnice nad Labem
94 *K1* **Raufarhöfn** Nordhurland Eystra, NE Iceland *66.26N 15.57W*
96 *H13* **Raufoss** Oppland, S Norway *60.43N 10.36E*
Raukawa *see* Cook Strait
192 *Q8* **Raukumara** ▲ North Island, NZ *37.46S 178.07E*
199 *J12* **Raukumara Plain** *undersea feature* N Coral Sea
192 *P8* **Raukumara Range** ▲▲ North Island, NZ
160 *N11* **Rāulakela** ***var.*** Raurkela; ***prev.*** Rourkela. Orissa, E. India *22.13N 84.52E*
97 *F15* **Rauland** Telemark, S Norway *59.41N 7.57E*
95 *J19* **Rauma** ***Swe.*** Raumo. Länsi-Suomi, W Finland *61.09N 21.30E*
96 *F10* **Rauma** ≈ S Norway
Raumo *see* Rauma
120 *H8* **Rauna** Cēsis, C Latvia *57.19N 25.34E*
174 *Mm16* **Raung, Gunung** ▲ Jawa, S Indonesia *8.00S 114.07E*
Rāurkela *see* Rāulakela
97 *J22* **Raus** Skåne, S Sweden *56.01N 12.48E*
172 *R6* **Rausu** Hokkaidō, NE Japan *44.00N 145.06E*
172 *R6* **Rausu-dake** ▲ Hokkaidō, NE Japan *44.06N 145.04E*
95 *M17* **Rautalampi** Itä-Suomi, C Finland *62.37N 26.48E*
95 *N16* **Rautavaara** Itä-Suomi, C Finland *63.30N 28.19E*
118 *M9* **Raŭtel** ≈ C Moldova
95 *O18* **Rautjärvi** Etelä-Suomi, S Finland *61.21N 29.20E*
Rautu *see* Sosnovo
203 *V11* **Ravahere** *atoll* Îles Tuamotu, C French Polynesia
109 *J25* **Ravanusa** Sicilia, Italy, C Mediterranean Sea *37.16N 13.57E*
149 *S9* **Rāvar** Kermān, C Iran *31.15N 56.51E*
153 *Q11* **Ravat** Oshskaya Oblast', SW Kyrgyzstan *39.54N 70.06E*
20 *K11* **Ravena** New York, NE USA *42.28N 73.49W*
108 *H10* **Ravenna** Emilia-Romagna, N Italy *44.28N 12.15E*
31 *O15* **Ravenna** Nebraska, C USA *41.01N 98.54W*
33 *U11* **Ravenna** Ohio, N USA *41.09N 81.14W*
103 *I24* **Ravensburg** Baden-Württemberg, S Germany *47.46N 9.37E*
189 *W4* **Ravenshoe** Queensland, NE Australia *17.29S 145.28E*
188 *K13* **Ravensthorpe** Western Australia *33.37S 120.03E*
23 *Q4* **Ravenswood** West Virginia, NE USA *38.57N 81.45W*
155 *U9* **Rāvi** ≈ India/Pakistan
114 *C9* **Ravna Gora** Primorje-Gorski Kotar, NW Croatia *45.20N 14.54E*
111 *U10* **Ravne na Koroškem** ***Ger.*** Gutenstein. N Slovenia *46.33N 14.57E*
145 *P6* **Rāwah** W Iraq *34.32N 41.54E*
203 *T4* **Rawaki** ***prev.*** Phoenix Island. *atoll* Phoenix Islands, C Kiribati
155 *U6* **Rāwalpindi** Punjab, NE Pakistan *33.38N 73.06E*
112 *L13* **Rawa Mazowiecka** Łódzkie, C Poland *51.46N 20.15E*
145 *T2* **Ŗawāndiz** ***var.*** Rawandoz, Rawāndūz. N Iraq *36.37N 44.31E*
Rawandoz/Rawāndūz *see* Ŗawāndiz
176 *Vv9* **Rawarra** ≈ Papua, E Indonesia
176 *V9* **Rawas** Papua, E Indonesia *1.07S 132.12E*
145 *O4* **Rawḑah** ◎ E Syria
112 *G13* **Rawicz** ***Ger.*** Rawitsch. Wielkopolskie, C Poland *51.37N 16.51E*
Rawitsch *see* Rawicz
188 *M11* **Rawlinna** Western Australia *31.00S 125.35E*
35 *W16* **Rawlins** Wyoming, C USA *41.47N 107.14W*
65 *K17* **Rawson** Chubut, SE Argentina *43.22S 65.01W*
165 *R16* **Rawu** Xizang Zizhiqu, W China *29.30N 96.42E*
159 *P12* **Raxaul** Bihār, N India *26.58N 84.51E*
30 *K3* **Ray** North Dakota, N USA *48.19N 103.11W*
174 *M9* **Raya, Bukit** ▲ Borneo, C Indonesia *0.40S 112.40E*
161 *I18* **Rāyachoti** Andhra Pradesh, E India *14.03N 78.43E*
Rāyadrug *see* Rāyagarha
161 *M14* **Rāyagarha** ***prev.*** Rāyadrug. Orissa, E India *19.11N 83.22E*
144 *H7* **Rayak** ***var.*** Rayaq, Riyāq. E Lebanon *33.51N 36.03E*
Rayaq *see* Rayak
145 *T2* **Ŗāyat** E Iraq *36.39N 44.56E*
174 *J10* **Raya, Tanjung** *headland* Pulau Bangka, W Indonesia *1.49S 106.04E*
11 *R13* **Ray, Cape** *headland* Newfoundland and Labrador, E Canada *47.38N 59.15W*
126 *Mm16* **Raychikhinsk** Amurskaya Oblast', SE Russian Federation *49.47N 129.19E*
131 *U5* **Rayevskiy** Respublika Bashkortostan, W Russian Federation *54.04N 54.58E*
9 *Q17* **Raymond** Alberta, SW Canada *49.30N 112.40W*
24 *K6* **Raymond** Mississippi, S USA *32.15N 90.25W*
34 *F9* **Raymond** Washington, NW USA *46.41N 123.43W*
191 *T8* **Raymond Terrace** New South Wales, SE Australia *32.46S 151.45E*
27 *T17* **Raymondville** Texas, SW USA *26.27N 97.45W*
9 *U16* **Raymore** Saskatchewan, S Canada *51.24N 104.34W*
41 *Q8* **Ray Mountains** ▲▲ Alaska, USA
24 *H9* **Rayne** Louisiana, S USA *30.13N 92.15W*
43 *O12* **Rayón** San Luis Potosí, C Mexico *21.54N 99.33W*
42 *G4* **Rayón** Sonora, NW Mexico *29.45N 110.33W*
178 *Hh12* **Rayong** Rayong, S Thailand *12.42N 101.16E*
27 *T5* **Ray Roberts, Lake** ◎ Texas, SW USA
20 *E15* **Raystown Lake** ▨ Pennsylvania, NE USA
147 *V13* **Raysūt** SW Oman *16.58N 54.01E*
29 *R4* **Raytown** Missouri, C USA *39.00N 94.27W*
24 *I5* **Rayville** Louisiana, S USA *32.29N 91.45W*
148 *L5* **Razan** Hamadān, W Iran *35.22N 48.58E*
145 *S9* **Razāzah, Buḩayrat ar** ***var.*** Baḩr al Milḩ. ◎ C Iraq
116 *L9* **Razboyna** ▲ E Bulgaria *42.54N 26.31E*
Razdan *see* Hrazdan
Razdolnoye *see* Rozdol'ne
Razelm, Lacul *see* Razim, Lacul
145 *U2* **Ŗazga** E Iraq *36.25N 45.06E*
116 *L8* **Razgrad** Razgrad, N Bulgaria *43.33N 26.31E*
116 *L8* **Razgrad** ⬖ *province* N Bulgaria
119 *N13* **Razim, Lacul** ***prev.*** Lacul Razelm. *lagoon* NW Black Sea
116 *G11* **Razlog** Blagoevgrad, SW Bulgaria *41.52N 23.28E*
120 *K10* **Rāznas Ezers** ◎ SE Latvia
104 *E6* **Raz, Pointe du** *headland* NW France *48.06N 4.52W*
Reachlainn *see* Rathlin Island
Reachrainn *see* Lambay Island
99 *N22* **Reading** S England, UK *51.28N 0.58W*
20 *H15* **Reading** Pennsylvania, NE USA *40.19N 75.55W*
50 *C7* **Real, Cordillera** ▲▲ C Ecuador
64 *K12* **Realicó** La Pampa, C Argentina *35.01S 64.13W*
27 *R15* **Realitos** Texas, SW USA *27.26N 98.31W*
110 *G9* **Realp** Uri, C Switzerland *46.36N 8.32E*
178 *Ii12* **Reăng Kesei** Bătdâmbâng, W Cambodia *12.57N 103.15E*
203 *Y11* **Reao** *atoll* Îles Tuamotu, E French Polynesia
Reate *see* Rieti
188 *L11* **Rebecca, Lake** ◎ Western Australia
Rebiana Sand Sea *see* Rabyānah, Ramlat
128 *H8* **Reboly** Respublika Kareliya, NW Russian Federation *63.51N 30.49E*
172 *P1* **Rebun** Rebun-tō, NE Japan *45.19N 141.02E*
172 *P1* **Rebun-suidō** *strait* E Sea of Japan
172 *P1* **Rebun-tō** *island* NE Japan
108 *J12* **Recanati** Marche, C Italy *43.23N 13.34E*
Rechitsa *see* Rechytsa
111 *Y7* **Rechnitz** Burgenland, SE Austria *47.18N 16.26E*
121 *J20* **Rechytsa** ***Rus.*** Rechitsa. Brestskaya Voblasts', SW Belarus *51.51N 26.49E*
121 *O19* **Rechytsa** ***Rus.*** Rechitsa. Homyel'skaya Voblasts', SE Belarus *52.22N 30.22E*
61 *Q15* **Recife** ***prev.*** Pernambuco. *state capital* Pernambuco, E Brazil *8.06S 34.52W*
85 *I26* **Recife, Cape** ***Afr.*** Kaap Recife. *headland* S South Africa *34.03S 25.37E*
Recife, Kaap *see* Recife, Cape
180 *I16* **Récifs, Îles aux** *island* Inner Islands, NE Seychelles
103 *E14* **Recklinghausen** Nordrhein-Westfalen, W Germany *51.37N 7.12E*
102 *M8* **Recknitz** ≈ NE Germany
101 *K23* **Recogne** Luxembourg, SE Belgium *49.56N 5.20E*
63 *C15* **Reconquista** Santa Fe, C Argentina *29.10S 59.41W*
205 *O6* **Recovery Glacier** *glacier* Antarctica
61 *G15* **Recreio** Mato Grosso, W Brazil *8.13S 58.15W*
29 *X9* **Rector** Arkansas, C USA *36.15N 90.17W*
112 *E9* **Recz** ***Ger.*** Reetz Neumark. Zachodniopomorskie, NW Poland *53.16N 15.32E*
101 *L24* **Redange** ***var.*** Redange-sur-Attert. Diekirch, W Luxembourg *49.46N 5.52E*
Redange-sur-Attert *see* Redange
20 *C13* **Redbank Creek** ≈ Pennsylvania, NE USA
11 *S9* **Red Bay** Quebec, E Canada *51.40N 56.37W*
25 *N2* **Red Bay** Alabama, S USA *34.26N 88.08W*
37 *N4* **Red Bluff** California, W USA *40.09N 122.14W*
26 *J8* **Red Bluff Reservoir** ◎ New Mexico/Texas, SW USA
32 *K16* **Red Bud** Illinois, N USA *38.12N 89.59W*
32 *J5* **Red Cedar River** ≈ Wisconsin, N USA
9 *R17* **Redcliff** Alberta, SW Canada *50.06N 110.48W*
85 *K17* **Redcliff** Midlands, C Zimbabwe *19.01S 29.43E*
190 *L9* **Red Cliffs** Victoria, SE Australia *34.21S 142.12E*
31 *P17* **Red Cloud** Nebraska, C USA *40.05N 98.31W*
24 *L8* **Red Creek** ≈ Mississippi, S USA
9 *P15* **Red Deer** Alberta, SW Canada *52.15N 113.48W*
9 *Q16* **Red Deer** ≈ Alberta, SW Canada
41 *O11* **Red Devil** Alaska, USA *61.45N 95.18W*
37 *N3* **Redding** California, W USA *40.33N 122.26W*
99 *L20* **Redditch** W England, UK *52.19N 1.55W*
31 *P9* **Redfield** South Dakota, N USA *44.51N 98.31W*
26 *J12* **Redford** Texas, SW USA *29.31N 104.19W*
47 *V13* **Redhead** Trinidad, Trinidad and Tobago *10.48N 60.56W*
190 *I8* **Red Hill** South Australia *33.34S 138.13E*
40 *F10* **Red Hill** ***Haw.*** Pu'uUla'ula. ▲ Maui, Hawaii, USA, C Pacific Ocean *20.42N 94.16W*
28 *K7* **Red Hills** *hill range* Kansas, C USA
11 *T12* **Red Indian Lake** ◎ Newfoundland and Labrador, E Canada
128 *J16* **Redkino** Tverskaya Oblast', W Russian Federation *56.41N 36.07E*
10 *A10* **Red Lake** Ontario, C Canada *51.00N 93.55W*
38 *I10* **Red Lake** *salt flat* Arizona, SW USA
31 *S4* **Red Lake Falls** Minnesota, N USA *47.52N 96.16W*
31 *R4* **Red Lake River** ≈ Minnesota, N USA
37 *U15* **Redlands** California, W USA *34.03N 117.10W*
20 *G16* **Red Lion** Pennsylvania, NE USA *39.53N 76.36W*
35 *U11* **Red Lodge** Montana, NW USA *45.11N 109.15W*
34 *H13* **Redmond** Oregon, NW USA *44.16N 121.10W*
38 *L5* **Redmond** Utah, W USA *39.00N 111.51W*
34 *H8* **Redmond** Washington, NW USA *47.40N 122.07W*
Rednitz *see* Regnitz
31 *T15* **Red Oak** Iowa, C USA *41.00N 95.10W*
20 *K12* **Red Oaks Mill** New York, NE USA *41.39N 73.52W*
104 *I7* **Redon** Ille-et-Vilaine, NW France *47.39N 2.04W*
47 *W10* **Redonda** *island* SW Antigua and Barbuda
106 *G4* **Redondela** Galicia, NW Spain *42.16N 8.36W*
106 *H11* **Redondo** Évora, S Portugal *38.37N 7.31W*
41 *Q12* **Redoubt Volcano** ▲ Alaska, USA *60.29N 152.44W*
9 *Y16* **Red River** ≈ Canada/USA
133 *U12* **Red River** ***var.*** Yuan, ***Chin.*** Yuan Jiang, ***Vtn.*** Sông Hông Hà. ≈ China/Vietnam
27 *W4* **Red River** ≈ S USA
24 *H7* **Red River** ≈ Louisiana, S USA
32 *M6* **Red River** ≈ Wisconsin, N USA
Red Rock, Lake *see* Red Rock Reservoir
31 *W14* **Red Rock Reservoir** ***var.*** Lake Red Rock. ▨ Iowa, C USA
194 *J15* **Redscar Bay** *bay* S PNG
82 *H7* **Red Sea** ⬖ *state* NE Sudan
77 *Y9* **Red Sea** ***anc.*** Sinus Arabicus. *sea* Africa/Asia
23 *T11* **Red Springs** North Carolina, SE USA *34.49N 79.10W*
15 *Gg6* **Redstone** ≈ Northwest Territories, NW Canada
9 *V17* **Redvers** Saskatchewan, S Canada *49.31N 101.33W*
79 *P13* **Red Volta** ***var.*** Nazinon, ***Fr.*** Volta Rouge. ≈ Burkina/Ghana
9 *Q14* **Redwater** Alberta, SW Canada *53.57N 113.06W*
30 *M16* **Red Willow Creek** ≈ Nebraska, C USA
31 *W9* **Red Wing** Minnesota, N USA *44.33N 92.31W*
37 *N9* **Redwood City** California, W USA *37.29N 122.13W*
31 *T9* **Redwood Falls** Minnesota, N USA *44.33N 95.07W*
198 *Ff7* **Reed Bank** *undersea feature* C South China Sea
33 *P7* **Reed City** Michigan, N USA *43.52N 85.30W*
30 *K6* **Reeder** North Dakota, N USA *46.03N 102.55W*
37 *R11* **Reedley** California, W USA *36.35N 119.27W*
35 *T11* **Reedpoint** Montana, NW USA *45.41N 109.33W*
32 *K8* **Reedsburg** Wisconsin, N USA *43.33N 90.03W*
34 *E13* **Reedsport** Oregon, NW USA *43.42N 124.06W*
195 *X8* **Reef Islands** *island group* Santa Cruz Islands, E Solomon Islands
193 *H16* **Reefton** West Coast, South Island, NZ *42.07S 171.52E*
22 *F8* **Reelfoot Lake** ◎ Tennessee, S USA
99 *D17* **Ree, Lough** ***Ir.*** Loch Rí. ◎ C Ireland
Reengus *see* Rīngas
37 *U4* **Reese River** ≈ Nevada, W USA
100 *M8* **Reest** ≈ E Netherlands
Reetz Neumark *see* Recz
143 *N13* **Refahiye** Erzincan, C Turkey *39.54N 38.45E*
25 *N4* **Reform** Alabama, S USA *33.22N 88.01W*
97 *K20* **Reftele** Jönköping, S Sweden *57.10N 13.34E*
27 *T14* **Refugio** Texas, SW USA *28.18N 97.16W*
112 *E8* **Rega** ≈ NW Poland
Regar *see* Tursunzoda
103 *O21* **Regen** Bayern, SE Germany *48.57N 13.10E*
103 *M20* **Regen** ≈ SE Germany
103 *M21* **Regensburg** ***Eng.*** Ratisbon, ***Fr.*** Ratisbonne; ***hist.*** Ratisbona, ***anc.*** Castra Regina, Reginum. Bayern, SE Germany *49.01N 12.06E*
103 *M21* **Regenstauf** Bayern, SE Germany *49.06N 12.07E*
76 *I10* **Reggane** C Algeria *26.45N 0.10E*
100 *N9* **Regge** ≈ E Netherlands
Reggio *see* Reggio nell' Emilia
Reggio Calabria *see* Reggio di Calabria
109 *M23* **Reggio di Calabria** ***var.*** Reggio Calabria, ***Gk.*** Rhegion; ***anc.*** Regium, Rhegium. Calabria, SW Italy *38.06N 15.39E*
Reggio Emilia *see* Reggio nell' Emilia
108 *F9* **Reggio nell' Emilia** ***var.*** Reggio Emilia, ***abbrev.*** Reggio; ***anc.*** Regium Lepidum. Emilia-Romagna, N Italy *44.42N 10.37E*
118 *I10* **Reghin** ***Ger.*** Sächsisch-Reen, ***Hung.*** Szászrégen; ***prev.*** Reghinul Săsesc, ***Ger.*** Sächsisch-Regen. Mureş, C Romania *46.46N 24.40E*
Reghinul Săsesc *see* Reghin
9 *U16* **Regina** Saskatchewan, S Canada *50.25N 104.39W*
9 *U16* **Regina** ✈ Saskatchewan, S Canada *50.21N 104.43W*
57 *Z10* **Régina** E French Guiana *4.19N 52.07W*
9 *U16* **Regina Beach** Saskatchewan, S Canada *50.44N 105.03W*
Reginum *see* Regensburg
Registan *see* Rīgestān
62 *L11* **Registro** São Paulo, S Brazil *24.30S 47.49W*
Regium *see* Reggio di Calabria
Regium Lepidum *see* Reggio nell' Emilia
103 *K19* **Regnitz** ***var.*** Rednitz. ≈ SE Germany
42 *K10* **Regocijo** Durango, W Mexico *23.34N 105.10W*
106 *H12* **Reguengos de Monsaraz** Évora, S Portugal *38.25N 7.31W*
103 *M18* **Rehau** Bayern, E Germany *50.15N 12.03E*
85 *D19* **Rehoboth** Hardap, C Namibia *23.18S 17.03E*
Rehoboth/Rehovoth *see* Reẖovot
23 *Z4* **Rehoboth Beach** Delaware, NE USA *38.42N 75.03W*
144 *F10* **Reẖovot** ***var.*** Rehoboth, Rekhovot, Rehovoth. Central, C Israel *31.54N 34.49E*
83 *J20* **Rei** *spring/well* S Kenya *3.24S 39.18E*
Reichenau *see* Rychnov nad Kněžnou, Czech Republic
Reichenau *see* Bogatynia, Poland
103 *M17* **Reichenbach** ***var.*** Reichenbach im Vogtland. Sachsen, E Germany *50.36N 12.18E*
Reichenbach *see* Dzierżoniów
Reichenbach im Vogtland *see* Reichenbach
Reichenberg *see* Liberec
189 *O11* **Reid** Western Australia *30.48S 128.24E*
25 *V6* **Reidsville** Georgia, SE USA *32.05N 82.07W*
23 *T8* **Reidsville** North Carolina, SE USA *36.21N 79.39W*
Reifnitz *see* Ribnica
99 *O22* **Reigate** SE England, UK *51.13N 0.13W*
Reikjavik *see* Reykjavík
104 *I10* **Ré, Île de** *island* W France
39 *N15* **Reiley Peak** ▲ Arizona, SW USA *32.24N 110.09W*
105 *Q4* **Reims** ***Eng.*** Rheims; ***anc.*** Durocortorum, Remi. Marne, N France *49.16N 4.01E*
65 *G23* **Reina Adelaida, Archipiélago** *island group* S Chile
47 *O16* **Reina Beatrix** ✈ (Oranjestad) C Aruba *12.30N 69.57W*
110 *F7* **Reinach** Aargau, W Switzerland *47.15N 8.12E*
110 *E6* **Reinach** Basel-Land, NW Switzerland *47.30N 7.36E*
66 *O11* **Reina Sofía** ✈ (Tenerife) Tenerife, Islas Canarias, Spain, NE Atlantic Ocean
31 *W13* **Reinbeck** Iowa, C USA *42.19N 92.36W*
102 *J10* **Reinbek** Schleswig-Holstein, N Germany *53.31N 10.15E*
9 *U12* **Reindeer** ≈ Saskatchewan, C Canada
9 *U11* **Reindeer Lake** ◎ Manitoba/Saskatchewan, C Canada
Reine-Charlotte, Îles de la *see* Queen Charlotte Islands
Reine-Élisabeth, Îles de la *see* Queen Elizabeth Islands
96 *F13* **Reineskarvet** ▲ S Norway *60.38N 7.48E*
192 *H1* **Reinga, Cape** *headland* North Island, NZ *34.24S 172.40E*
107 *N3* **Reinosa** Cantabria, N Spain *43.01N 4.09W*
111 *R8* **Reisseck** ▲ S Austria *46.57N 13.21E*
23 *W3* **Reisterstown** Maryland, NE USA *39.27N 76.46W*
Reisui *see* Yŏsu
100 *N5* **Reitdiep** ≈ NE Netherlands
203 *V10* **Reitoru** *atoll* Îles Tuamotu, C French Polynesia
97 *M17* **Rejmyre** Östergötland, S Sweden *58.49N 15.55E*
Reka *see* Rijeka
Reka Ili *see* Ili
97 *N16* **Rekarne** Västmanland, C Sweden *59.25N 16.04*
Rekhovot *see* Reẖovot
15 *Ii7* **Reliance** Northwest Territories, C Canada *62.45N 109.07W*
35 *U16* **Reliance** Wyoming, C USA *41.42N 109.13W*
76 *I5* **Relizane** ***var.*** Ghelîzâne, Ghilizane. NW Algeria *35.45N 0.39E*
190 *I7* **Remarkable, Mount** ▲ South Australia *32.46S 138.08E*
56 *E8* **Remedios** Antioquia, N Colombia *7.01N 74.42W*
45 *Q16* **Remedios** Veraguas, W Panama *8.12N 81.49W*
44 *D8* **Remedios, Punta** *headland* SW El Salvador *13.31N 89.48W*
Remi *see* Reims
101 *N25* **Remich** Grevenmacher, SE Luxembourg *49.33N 6.22E*
101 *J19* **Remicourt** Liège, E Belgium *50.40N 5.19E*
12 *H8* **Rémigny, Lac** ◎ Quebec, SE Canada
57 *Z10* **Rémire** NE French Guiana *4.52N 52.16W*
131 *N13* **Remontnoye** Rostovskaya Oblast', SW Russian Federation *46.35N 43.38E*
176 *V13* **Remoon** Pulau Kur, E Indonesia *5.18S 131.59E*
101 *L20* **Remouchamps** Liège, E Belgium *50.29N 5.43E*
105 *R15* **Remoulins** Gard, S France *43.56N 4.34E*
181 *X16* **Rempart, Mont du** ***var.*** Mount Rempart. *hill* W Mauritius
103 *E15* **Remscheid** Nordrhein-Westfalen, W Germany *51.10N 7.10E*
31 *S12* **Remsen** Iowa, C USA *42.48N 95.58W*
96 *I12* **Rena** Hedmark, S Norway *61.07N 11.21E*
96 *I11* **Rena** ≈ S Norway
Renaix *see* Ronse
120 *H7* **Rencēni** Valmiera, N Latvia *57.43N 25.25E*
120 *D9* **Renda** Kuldīga, W Latvia *57.04N 22.18E*
109 *N20* **Rende** Calabria, SW Italy *39.19N 16.10E*
101 *K21* **Rendeux** Luxembourg, SE Belgium *50.15N 5.28E*
Rendina *see* Rentína
32 *L16* **Rend Lake** ▨ Illinois, N USA
195 *U15* **Rendova** *island* New Georgia Islands, NW Solomon Islands
102 *I8* **Rendsburg** Schleswig-Holstein, N Germany *54.18N 9.40E*
110 *B9* **Renens** Vaud, SW Switzerland *46.31N 6.36E*
12 *K12* **Renfrew** Ontario, SE Canada *45.28N 76.42W*
98 *I12* **Renfrew** *cultural region* SW Scotland, UK
174 *H8* **Rengat** Sumatera, W Indonesia *0.25S 102.38E*
159 *W12* **Rengma Hills** ▲▲ NE India
64 *H12* **Rengo** Libertador, C Chile *34.26S 70.53W*
118 *M12* **Reni** Odes'ka Oblast', SW Ukraine *45.30N 28.24E*
82 *F11* **Renk** Upper Nile, E Sudan *11.48N 32.49E*
95 *L19* **Renko** Etelä-Suomi, S Finland *60.52N 24.16E*
100 *L12* **Renkum** Gelderland, SE Netherlands *51.58N 5.43E*
190 *K9* **Renmark** South Australia *34.12S 140.43E*
195 *W17* **Rennell** ***var.*** Mu Nggava. *island* S Solomon Islands
189 *Q4* **Renner Springs Roadhouse** Northern Territory, N Australia *18.12S 133.48E*
104 *I6* **Rennes** ***Bret.*** Roazon; ***anc.*** Condate. Ille-et-Vilaine, NW France *48.07N 1.40W*
205 *S16* **Rennick Glacier** *glacier* Antarctica
9 *Y16* **Rennie** Manitoba, S Canada *49.51N 95.28W*
37 *Q5* **Reno** Nevada, W USA *39.31N 119.48W*
108 *H10* **Reno** ≈ N Italy
37 *Q5* **Reno-Cannon** ✈ Nevada, W USA *39.26N 119.42W*
85 *F24* **Renoster** ≈ SW South Africa
13 *T5* **Renouard, Lac** ◎ Quebec, SE Canada
20 *F13* **Renovo** Pennsylvania, NE USA *41.19N 77.42W*
167 *O3* **Renqiu** Hebei, E China *38.49N 116.02E*
166 *I9* **Renshou** Sichuan, C China *29.58N 104.06E*
33 *N12* **Rensselaer** Indiana, N USA *40.55N 87.10W*
20 *L11* **Rensselaer** New York, NE USA *42.38N 73.44W*
107 *Q2* **Rentería** ***Basq.*** Errenteria. País Vasco, N Spain *43.17N 1.54W*
117 *E17* **Rentína** ***var.*** Rendina. Thessalía, C Greece *39.04N 21.58E*
31 *T9* **Renville** Minnesota, N USA *44.48N 95.13W*
79 *O13* **Réo** W Burkina *12.19N 2.28W*
13 *O12* **Repentigny** Quebec, SE Canada *45.42N 73.28W*
152 *K13* **Repetek** Lebapskiy Velayat, E Turkmenistan *38.40N 63.12E*
95 *J16* **Replot** ***Fin.*** Raippaluoto. *island* W Finland
Reppen *see* Rzepin
Reps *see* Rupea
29 *T7* **Republic** Missouri, C USA *37.07N 93.28W*
34 *K7* **Republic** Washington, NW USA *48.39N 118.44W*
29 *N3* **Republican River** ≈ Kansas/Nebraska, C USA
15 *Ll4* **Repulse Bay** Northwest Territories, N Canada *66.34N 86.19W*
58 *F9* **Requena** Loreto, NE Peru *5.02S 73.47W*
107 *R10* **Requena** País Valenciano, E Spain *39.28N 1.07W*
105 *O14* **Réquista** Aveyron, S France *44.00N 2.31E*
142 *M12* **Reşadiye** Tokat, N Turkey *40.24N 37.19E*
Reschenpass *see* Resia, Passo di
Reschitza *see* Reşiţa
115 *N20* **Resen** ***Turk.*** Resne. SW FYR Macedonia *41.07N 21.00E*
62 *J11* **Reserva** Paraná, S Brazil *24.40S 50.52W*
9 *V15* **Reserve** Saskatchewan, S Canada *52.24N 102.37W*
39 *P13* **Reserve** New Mexico, SW USA *33.42N 108.45W*
Reshetilovka *see* Reshetylivka
119 *S6* **Reshetylivka** ***Rus.*** Reshetilovka. Poltavs'ka Oblast', NE Ukraine *49.34N 34.04E*
Resht *see* Rasht
108 *F5* **Resia, Passo di** ***Ger.*** Reschenpass. *pass* Austria/Italy *46.51N 10.32E*
Resicabánya *see* Reşiţa
64 *N7* **Resistencia** Chaco, NE Argentina *27.27S 58.55W*
118 *F12* **Reşiţa** ***Ger.*** Reschitza, ***Hung.*** Resicabánya. Caraş-Severin, W Romania *45.13N 21.58E*
Resne *see* Resen
207 *N9* **Resolute** Cornwallis Island, Nunavut, N Canada *74.40N 94.54W*
Resolution *see* Fort Resolution
16 *P4* **Resolution Island** *island* Nunavut, NE Canada
193 *A23* **Resolution Island** *island* SW NZ
13 *W7* **Restigouche** Quebec, SE Canada *48.01N 66.42W*
9 *W17* **Reston** Manitoba, S Canada *49.33N 101.03W*
12 *H11* **Restoule Lake** ◎ Ontario, S Canada
56 *F10* **Restrepo** Meta, C Colombia *4.20N 73.29W*
44 *B6* **Retalhuleu** Retalhuleu, SW Guatemala *14.30N 91.41W*
44 *A1* **Retalhuleu** ***off.*** Departamento de Retalhuleu. ⬖ *department* SW Guatemala
99 *N18* **Retford** C England, UK *53.18N 0.52W*
105 *Q3* **Rethel** Ardennes, N France *49.31N 4.22E*
Rethimno/Réthimnon *see* Réthymno
117 *I25* **Réthymno** ***var.*** Rethimno; ***prev.*** Réthimnon. Kríti, Greece, E Mediterranean Sea *35.21N 24.28E*
Retiche, Alpi *see* Rhaetian Alps
101 *J16* **Retie** Antwerpen, N Belgium *51.18N 5.05E*
113 *J21* **Rétság** Nógrád, N Hungary *47.57N 19.07E*
111 *W2* **Retz** Niederösterreich, NE Austria *48.46N 15.58E*
181 *N15* **Réunion** ***off.*** La Réunion. ◇ *French overseas department* W Indian Ocean
132 *L17* **Réunion** *island* W Indian Ocean
107 *U6* **Reus** Cataluña, E Spain *41.10N 1.06E*
101 *J15* **Reusel** Noord-Brabant, S Netherlands *51.21N 5.10E*
110 *F7* **Reuss** ≈ NW Switzerland
Reuţel *see* Ciuhuru
103 *H22* **Reutlingen** Baden-Württemberg, S Germany *48.30N 9.13E*
110 *L7* **Reutte** Tirol, W Austria *47.30N 10.43E*
101 *M16* **Reuver** Limburg, SE Netherlands *51.16N 6.04E*
30 *K7* **Reva** South Dakota, N USA *45.30N 103.03W*
Reval/Revel' *see* Tallinn
128 *J4* **Revda** Murmanskaya Oblast', NW Russian Federation *67.57N 34.29E*
125 *Ee11* **Revda** Sverdlovskaya Oblast', C Russian Federation *56.48N 59.42E*
105 *N16* **Revel** Haute-Garonne, S France *43.27N 1.58E*
9 *O16* **Revelstoke** British Columbia, SW Canada *51.01N 118.12W*
45 *N13* **Reventazón, Río** ≈ E Costa Rica
108 *G9* **Revere** Lombardia, N Italy *45.03N 11.07E*
41 *Y14* **Revillagigedo Island** *island* Alexander Archipelago, Alaska, USA
199 *Mm7* **Revillagigedo Islands** *island group* NW Mexico
105 *R3* **Revin** Ardennes, N France *49.57N 4.39E*
94 *O3* **Revnosa** *headland* C Svalbard *78.03N 18.52E*
Revolyutsii, Pik *see* Revolyutsiya, Qullai
153 *T13* **Revolyutsiya, Qullai** ***Rus.*** Pik Revolyutsii. ▲ SE Tajikistan *38.40N 72.26E*
113 *L19* **Revúca** ***Ger.*** Grossrauschenbach, ***Hung.*** Nagyrőce. Banskobystrický Kraj, C Slovakia *48.40N 20.10E*
160 *K9* **Rewa** Madhya Pradesh, C India *24.31N 81.18E*
158 *I11* **Rewāri** Haryāna, N India *28.13N 76.37E*
35 *R14* **Rexburg** Idaho, NW USA *43.49N 111.47W*
80 *G13* **Rey Bouba** Nord, NE Cameroon *8.40N 14.10E*
94 *L3* **Reydharfjördhur** Austurland, E Iceland *65.02N 14.12W*
59 *K16* **Reyes** Beni, NW Bolivia *14.17S 67.18W*
36 *L8* **Reyes, Point** *headland* California, W USA *37.58N 123.01W*
56 *B12* **Reyes, Punta** *headland* SW Colombia *2.43N 78.07W*
142 *L17* **Reyhanlı** Hatay, S Turkey *36.16N 36.33E*
45 *U16* **Rey, Isla del** *island* Archipiélago de las Perlas, SE Panama
94 *H2* **Reykhólar** Vestfirdhir, W Iceland *65.28N 22.12W*
94 *K2* **Reykjahlídh** Nordhurland Eystra, NE Iceland *65.37N 16.54W*
94 *I4* **Reykjanes** ⬖ *region* SW Iceland
207 *O16* **Reykjanes Basin** ***var.*** Irminger Basin. *undersea feature* N Atlantic Ocean

◆ Country ● Country Capital ◇ Dependent Territory ○ Dependent Territory Capital ⬖ Administrative Region ✈ International Airport ▲ Mountain ▲▲ Mountain Range Volcano ≈ River ◎ Lake ▨ Reservoir

207 N17 **Reykjanes Ridge** *undersea feature* N Atlantic Ocean
94 H4 **Reykjavík** *var.* Reikjavik. ● (Iceland) Höfudhborgarsvaedhi, W Iceland 64.07N 21.54W
20 D13 **Reynoldsville** Pennsylvania, NE USA 41.04N 78.51W
43 P8 **Reynosa** Tamaulipas, C Mexico 26.03N 98.19W
Reẕā'īyeh *see* Orūmīyeh
Reẕā'īyeh, Daryācheh-ye *see* Orūmīyeh, Daryācheh-ye
104 I8 **Rezé** Loire-Atlantique, NW France 47.10N 1.36W
120 K10 **Rēzekne** *Ger.* Rositten; *prev. Rus.* Rezhitsa. Rēzekne, SE Latvia 56.31N 27.22E
Rezhitsa *see* Rēzekne
119 N9 **Rezina** NE Moldova 47.44N 28.58E
116 N11 **Rezovo** *Turk.* Rezve. Burgas, E Bulgaria 42.00N 28.00E
116 N11 **Rezovska Reka** *Turk.* Rezve Deresi. ≈ Bulgaria/Turkey *see also* Rezve Deresi
Rezve *see* Rezovo
116 N11 **Rezve Deresi** *Bul.* Rezovska Reka. ≈ Bulgaria/Turkey *see also* Rezovska Reka
Rhadames *see* Ghadāmis
Rhaedestus *see* Tekirdağ
110 J10 **Rhaetian Alps** *Fr.* Alpes Rhétiques, *Ger.* Rätische Alpen, *It.* Alpi Retiche. ▲▲ C Europe
110 I8 **Rhätikon** ▲▲ C Europe
103 G14 **Rheda-Wiedenbrück** Nordrhein-Westfalen, W Germany 51.51N 8.19E
100 M12 **Rheden** Gelderland, E Netherlands 52.01N 6.03E
Rhegion/Rhegium *see* Reggio di Calabria
Rheims *see* Reims
Rhein *see* Rhine
103 E17 **Rheinbach** Nordrhein-Westfalen, W Germany 50.37N 6.57E
102 F13 **Rheine** *var.* Rheine in Westfalen. Nordrhein-Westfalen, NW Germany 52.16N 7.27E
Rheine in Westfalen *see* Rheine
Rheinfeld *see* Rheinfelden
103 F24 **Rheinfelden** Baden-Württemberg, S Germany 47.34N 7.46E
110 E6 **Rheinfelden** *var.* Rheinfeld. Aargau, N Switzerland 47.33N 7.46E
103 E17 **Rheinisches Schiefergebirge** *var.* Rhine State Uplands, *Eng.* Rhenish Slate Mountains. ▲▲ W Germany
103 D18 **Rheinland-Pfalz** *Eng.* Rhineland-Palatinate, *Fr.* Rhénanie-Palatinat. ⬖ *state* W Germany
103 G18 **Rhein/Main** ✕ (Frankfurt am Main) Hessen, W Germany 50.03N 8.33E
Rhénanie du Nord-Westphalie *see* Nordrhein-Westfalen
Rhénanie-Palatinat *see* Rheinland-Pfalz
100 K12 **Rhenen** Utrecht, C Netherlands 51.57N 5.34E
Rhenish Slate Mountains *see* Rheinisches Schiefergebirge
Rhétiques, Alpes *see* Rhaetian Alps
102 N10 **Rhin** ≈ NE Germany
Rhin *see* Rhine
86 F10 **Rhine** *Dut.* Rijn, *Fr.* Rhin, *Ger.* Rhein. ≈ W Europe
32 L5 **Rhinelander** Wisconsin, N USA 45.39N 89.22W
Rhineland-Palatinate *see* Rheinland-Pfalz
Rhine State Uplands *see* Rheinisches Schiefergebirge
102 N11 **Rhinkanal** *canal* NE Germany
83 F17 **Rhino Camp** NW Uganda 2.58N 31.24E
76 D7 **Rhir, Cap** *headland* W Morocco 30.40N 9.54W
108 D7 **Rho** Lombardia, N Italy 45.31N 9.01E
21 N12 **Rhode Island** *off.* State of Rhode Island and Providence Plantations; also known as Little Rhody, Ocean State. ⬖ *state* NE USA
21 O13 **Rhode Island** *island* Rhode Island, NE USA
21 O13 **Rhode Island Sound** *sound* Maine/Rhode Island, NE USA
Rhodes *see* Ródos
Rhode-Saint-Genèse *see* Sint-Genesius-Rode
86 L14 **Rhodes Basin** *undersea feature* E Mediterranean Sea
Rhodesia *see* Zimbabwe
116 I12 **Rhodope Mountains** *var.* Rodhópi Óri, *Bul.* Rhodope Planina, Rodopi, *Gk.* Orosirá Rodhópis, *Turk.* Dospad Dagh. ▲▲ Bulgaria/Greece
Rhodope Planina *see* Rhodope Mountains
Rhodos *see* Ródos
103 I18 **Rhön** ▲▲ C Germany
105 Q10 **Rhône** ⬖ *department* E France
88 C12 **Rhône** ≈ France/Switzerland
105 R12 **Rhône-Alpes** ⬖ *region* E France
123 J6 **Rhône Fan** *undersea feature* W Mediterranean Sea
100 G13 **Rhoon** Zuid-Holland, SW Netherlands 51.52N 4.25E
98 G9 **Rhum** *var.* Rum. *island* W Scotland, UK
Rhuthun *see* Ruthin
99 J18 **Rhyl** NE Wales, UK 53.19N 3.28W
61 K18 **Rialma** Goiás, S Brazil 15.22S 49.35W
106 L3 **Riaño** Castilla-León, N Spain 42.59N 5.00W
107 O9 **Riansáres** ≈ C Spain
158 H6 **Riāsi** Jammu and Kashmir, NW India 33.03N 74.51E
174 Gg7 **Riau** *off.* Propinsi Riau. ⬖ *province* W Indonesia
Riau Archipelago *see* Riau, Kepulauan
174 I8 **Riau, Kepulauan** *var.* Riau Archipelago, *Dut.* Riouw-Archipel. *island group* W Indonesia
107 O6 **Riaza** Castilla-León, N Spain 41.17N 3.29W
107 N6 **Riaza** ≈ N Spain
83 K17 **Riba** *spring/well* NE Kenya 1.56N 40.38E
106 H4 **Ribadavia** Galicia, NW Spain 42.16N 8.07W
106 J2 **Ribadeo** Galicia, NW Spain 43.31N 7.04W
106 L2 **Ribadesella** Asturias, N Spain 43.27N 5.04W
106 G10 **Ribatejo** *former province* C Portugal
149 Q8 **Ribaṭ-e Rīzāb** Yazd, C Iran
85 P15 **Ribáuè** Nampula, N Mozambique 14.56S 38.19E
99 K17 **Ribble** ≈ NW England, UK
97 F23 **Ribe** Ribe, W Denmark 55.19N 8.46E
97 F23 **Ribe** *off.* Ribe Amt, *var.* Ripen. ⬖ *county* W Denmark
106 G3 **Ribeira** Galicia, NW Spain 42.33N 9.01W
66 O5 **Ribeira Brava** Madeira, Portugal, NE Atlantic Ocean 32.39N 17.04W
66 P3 **Ribeira Grande** São Miguel, Azores, Portugal, NE Atlantic Ocean 37.34N 25.31W
62 L8 **Ribeirão Preto** São Paulo, S Brazil 21.09S 47.48W
62 L11 **Ribeira, Rio** ≈ S Brazil
109 I24 **Ribera** Sicilia, Italy, C Mediterranean Sea 37.31N 13.16E
59 L14 **Riberalta** Beni, N Bolivia 11.00S 66.04W
107 W4 **Ribes de Freser** Cataluña, NE Spain 42.18N 2.11E
32 L6 **Rib Mountain** ▲ Wisconsin, N USA 44.55N 89.41W
111 U12 **Ribnica** *Ger.* Reifnitz. S Slovenia 45.46N 14.40E
119 N9 **Rîbniţa** *var.* Râbniţa, *Rus.* Rybnitsa. NE Moldova 47.46N 29.01E
102 M8 **Ribnitz-Damgarten** Mecklenburg-Vorpommern, NE Germany 54.14N 12.25E
113 D16 **Říčany** *Ger.* Ritschan. Středočeský Kraj, W Czech Republic 49.58N 14.39E
31 U7 **Rice** Minnesota, N USA 45.42N 94.10W
32 J5 **Rice Lake** Wisconsin, N USA 45.33N 91.43W
12 I15 **Rice Lake** ◎ Ontario, SE Canada
12 E8 **Rice Lake** ◎ Ontario, S Canada
25 V3 **Richard B.Russell Lake** ⊡ Georgia, SE USA
27 U6 **Richardson** Texas, SW USA 32.57N 96.43W
9 R11 **Richardson** ≈ Alberta, C Canada
8 I3 **Richardson Mountains** ▲▲ Yukon Territory, NW Canada
193 C21 **Richardson Mountains** ▲▲ South Island, NZ
44 F3 **Richardson Peak** ▲ SE Belize 16.34N 88.46W
78 G10 **Richard Toll** N Senegal 16.27N 15.44W
30 L5 **Richardton** North Dakota, N USA 46.52N 102.19W
12 F13 **Rich, Cape** *headland* Ontario, S Canada 44.42N 80.37W
104 L8 **Richelieu** Indre-et-Loire, C France 47.01N 0.18E
35 P15 **Richfield** Idaho, NW USA 43.03N 114.11W
38 K5 **Richfield** Utah, W USA 38.46N 112.06W
20 J10 **Richfield Springs** New York, NE USA 42.52N 74.57W
20 M6 **Richford** Vermont, NE USA 44.59N 72.37W
29 R6 **Rich Hill** Missouri, C USA 38.06N 94.22W
11 P14 **Richibucto** New Brunswick, SE Canada 46.42N 64.54W
110 G8 **Richisau** Glarus, NE Switzerland 47.00N 8.54E
25 S6 **Richland** Georgia, SE USA 32.05N 84.40W
29 U6 **Richland** Missouri, C USA 37.51N 92.24W
27 U8 **Richland** Texas, SW USA 31.55N 96.25W
34 K10 **Richland** Washington, NW USA 46.17N 119.16W
32 K8 **Richland Center** Wisconsin, N USA 43.18N 90.22W
23 W11 **Richlands** North Carolina, SE USA 34.52N 77.33W
23 Q7 **Richlands** Virginia, NE USA 37.05N 81.47W
27 R9 **Richland Springs** Texas, SW USA 31.16N 98.56W
191 S8 **Richmond** New South Wales, SE Australia 33.36S 150.43E
8 L17 **Richmond** British Columbia, SW Canada 49.07N 123.09W
12 L13 **Richmond** Ontario, SE Canada 45.12N 75.49W
13 Q12 **Richmond** Quebec, SE Canada 45.39N 72.07W
193 I14 **Richmond** Tasman, South Island, NZ 41.24S 173.04E
37 N8 **Richmond** California, W USA 37.57N 122.22W
33 Q14 **Richmond** Indiana, N USA 39.48N 84.52W
22 M6 **Richmond** Kentucky, S USA 37.45N 84.17W
29 S4 **Richmond** Missouri, C USA 39.16N 93.58W
27 V11 **Richmond** Texas, SW USA 29.34N 95.45W
38 L1 **Richmond** Utah, W USA 41.55N 111.51W
23 W6 **Richmond** *state capital* Virginia, NE USA 37.33N 77.27W
12 H15 **Richmond Hill** Ontario, S Canada 43.51N 79.24W
193 J15 **Richmond Range** ▲▲ South Island, NZ
29 S12 **Rich Mountain** ▲ Arkansas, C USA 34.37N 94.17W
33 S13 **Richwood** Ohio, N USA 40.25N 83.18W
23 R5 **Richwood** West Virginia, NE USA 38.13N 80.31W
106 K5 **Ricobayo, Embalse de** ⊡ NW Spain
Ricomagus *see* Riom
Ridā' *see* Radā'
100 H13 **Ridderkerk** Zuid-Holland, SW Netherlands 51.52N 4.34E
35 N16 **Riddle** Idaho, NW USA 42.07N 116.09W
34 F14 **Riddle** Oregon, NW USA 42.57N 123.21W
12 L13 **Rideau** ≈ Ontario, SE Canada
37 T12 **Ridgecrest** California, W USA 35.37N 117.40W
20 L13 **Ridgefield** Connecticut, NE USA 41.16N 73.30W
24 K5 **Ridgeland** Mississippi, S USA 32.25N 90.07W
23 R15 **Ridgeland** South Carolina, SE USA 32.28N 80.58W
22 F8 **Ridgely** Tennessee, S USA 36.15N 89.29W
12 D17 **Ridgetown** Ontario, S Canada 42.27N 81.52W
Ridgeway *see* Ridgway
23 R12 **Ridgeway** South Carolina, SE USA 34.17N 80.56W
20 D13 **Ridgway** *var.* Ridgeway. Pennsylvania, NE USA 41.24N 78.40W
9 W16 **Riding Mountain** ▲▲ Manitoba, S Canada
Ried *see* Ried im Innkreis
111 R4 **Ried im Innkreis** *var.* Ried. Oberösterreich, NW Austria 48.13N 13.28E
111 X8 **Riegersburg** Steiermark, SE Austria 47.03N 15.52E
110 E6 **Riehen** Basel-Stadt, NW Switzerland 47.34N 7.39E
94 J9 **Riehppegáisá** *var.* Rieppe. ▲ N Norway 69.38N 21.31E
101 K18 **Riemst** Limburg, NE Belgium 50.49N 5.35E
Rieppe *see* Riehppegáisá
103 O15 **Riesa** Sachsen, E Germany 51.18N 13.18E
65 H24 **Riesco, Isla** *island* S Chile
109 K25 **Riesi** Sicilia, Italy, C Mediterranean Sea 37.16N 14.04E
85 F25 **Riet** ≈ SW South Africa
85 I23 **Riet** ≈ SW South Africa
120 D11 **Rietavas** Plungė, W Lithuania 55.43N 21.56E
85 F19 **Rietfontein** Omaheke, E Namibia 21.54S 20.57E
109 I14 **Rieti** *anc.* Reate. Lazio, C Italy 42.22N 12.49E
86 D14 **Rif** *var.* Er Rif, Er Riff, Riff. ▲▲ N Morocco
Riff *see* Rif
39 Q4 **Rifle** Colorado, C USA 39.30N 107.46W
33 R7 **Rifle River** ≈ Michigan, N USA
83 H18 **Rift Valley** ⬖ *province* Kenya
Rift Valley *see* Great Rift Valley
120 F9 **Rīga** *Eng.* Riga. ● (Latvia) Rīga, C Latvia 56.57N 24.07E
Rigaer Bucht *see* Riga, Gulf of
120 F6 **Riga, Gulf of** *Est.* Liivi Laht, *Ger.* Rigaer Bucht, *Latv.* Rīgas Jūras Līcis, *Rus.* Rizhskiy Zaliv; *prev. Est.* Riia Laht. *gulf* Estonia/Latvia
149 U12 **Rīgān** Kermān, SE Iran 28.39N 59.01E
Rīgas Jūras Līcis *see* Riga, Gulf of
13 N12 **Rigaud** ≈ Ontario/Quebec, SE Canada
35 R14 **Rigby** Idaho, NW USA 43.40N 111.54W
154 M10 **Rīgestān** *var.* Registan. *desert region* S Afghanistan
34 M11 **Riggins** Idaho, NW USA 45.24N 116.18W
11 R8 **Rigolet** Newfoundland and Labrador, NE Canada 51.10N 58.25W
80 G9 **Rig-Rig** Kanem, W Chad 14.19N 14.19E
120 F4 **Riguldi** Läänemaa, W Estonia 59.07N 23.34E
Riia Laht *see* Riga, Gulf of
95 L19 **Riihimäki** Etelä-Suomi, S Finland 60.45N 24.45E
205 O2 **Riiser-Larsen Ice Shelf** *ice shelf* Antarctica
205 U2 **Riiser-Larsen Peninsula** *peninsula* Antarctica
67 P22 **Riiser-Larsen Sea** *sea* Antarctica
42 D2 **Riíto** Sonora, NW Mexico 32.06N 114.57W
114 B9 **Rijeka** *Ger.* Sankt Veit am Flaum, *It.* Fiume, *Slvn.* Reka; *anc.* Tarsatica. Primorje-Gorski Kotar, NW Croatia 45.20N 14.25E
101 I14 **Rijen** Noord-Brabant, S Netherlands 51.34N 4.55E
101 H15 **Rijkevorsel** Antwerpen, N Belgium 51.23N 4.43E
Rijn *see* Rhine
100 G11 **Rijnsburg** Zuid-Holland, W Netherlands 52.12N 4.27E
Rijssel *see* Lille
100 N10 **Rijssen** Overijssel, E Netherlands 52.19N 6.30E
100 G12 **Rijswijk** *Eng.* Ryswick. Zuid-Holland, W Netherlands 52.04N 4.22E
94 I10 **Riksgränsen** Norrbotten, N Sweden 68.24N 18.15E
172 Q6 **Rikubetsu** Hokkaidō, NE Japan 43.30N 143.43E
171 Mm12 **Rikuzen-Takata** Iwate, Honshū, C Japan 39.01N 141.37E
29 O4 **Riley** Kansas, C USA 39.18N 96.49W
101 I17 **Rillaar** Vlaams Brabant, C Belgium 50.58N 4.58E
Rí, Loch *see* Ree, Lough
116 G11 **Rilska Reka** ≈ W Bulgaria
79 T12 **Rima** ≈ N Nigeria
147 N7 **Rimah, Wādī ar** *var.* Wādī ar Rummah. *dry watercourse* C Saudi Arabia
Rimaszombat *see* Rimavská Sobota
203 R12 **Rimatara** *island* Îles Australes, SW French Polynesia
113 L20 **Rimavská Sobota** *Ger.* Gross-Steffelsdorf, *Hung.* Rimaszombat. Banskobystrický Kraj, C Slovakia 48.24N 20.01E
9 Q15 **Rimbey** Alberta, SW Canada 52.39N 114.10W
97 P15 **Rimbo** Stockholm, C Sweden 59.43N 18.21E
97 M18 **Rimforsa** Östergötland, S Sweden 58.06N 15.40E
108 I11 **Rimini** *anc.* Ariminum. Emilia-Romagna, N Italy 44.03N 12.33E
Rîmnicu-Sărat *see* Râmnicu Sărat
Rîmnicu Vîlcea *see* Râmnicu Vâlcea
155 Y3 **Rimo Muztāgh** ▲▲ India/Pakistan
13 U7 **Rimouski** Quebec, SE Canada 48.25N 68.31W
164 M16 **Rinbung** Xizang Zizhiqu, W China 29.15N 89.40E
168 I5 **Rinchinlhümbe** Hövsgöl, N Mongolia 51.06N 99.40E
64 I5 **Rincón, Cerro** ▲ N Chile 24.01S 67.19W
106 M15 **Rincón de la Victoria** Andalucía, S Spain 36.43N 4.18W
Rincón del Bonete, Lago Artificial de *see* Río Negro, Embalse del
107 Q4 **Rincón de Soto** La Rioja, N Spain 42.15N 1.49W
96 G8 **Rindal** Møre og Romsdal, S Norway 63.02N 9.09E
117 J20 **Ríneia** *island* Kykládes, Greece, Aegean Sea
158 H11 **Rīngas** *prev.* Reengus, Rīngus. Rājasthān, N India 27.18N 75.27E
97 H24 **Ringe** Fyn, C Denmark 55.13N 10.30E
96 H11 **Ringebu** Oppland, S Norway 61.31N 10.09E
Ringen *see* Rõngu
195 U14 **Ringgi** Kolombangara, NW Solomon Islands 8.03S 95.08E
25 R1 **Ringgold** Georgia, SE USA 34.55N 85.06W
24 G5 **Ringgold** Louisiana, S USA 32.19N 93.16W
27 S5 **Ringgold** Texas, SW USA 33.47N 97.56W
97 E22 **Ringkøbing** Ringkøbing, W Denmark 56.04N 8.22E
97 E21 **Ringkøbing** *off.* Ringkøbing Amt. ⬖ *county* W Denmark
97 E22 **Ringkøbing Fjord** *fjord* W Denmark
35 S10 **Ringling** Montana, NW USA 46.15N 110.48W
29 N13 **Ringling** Oklahoma, C USA 34.12N 97.35W
96 H13 **Ringsaker** Hedmark, S Norway 60.54N 10.45E
97 I23 **Ringsted** Vestsjælland, E Denmark 55.28N 11.48E
Rīngus *see* Rīngas
94 I9 **Ringvassøya** *island* N Norway
20 K13 **Ringwood** New Jersey, NE USA 41.06N 74.15W
Rinn Duáin *see* Hook Head
102 H13 **Rinteln** Niedersachsen, NW Germany 52.10N 9.04E
Rio *see* Rio de Janeiro
117 E18 **Río** Dytikí Ellás, S Greece 38.18N 21.48E
58 C7 **Riobamba** Chimborazo, C Ecuador 1.38S 78.40W
62 P9 **Rio Bonito** Rio de Janeiro, SE Brazil 22.42S 42.38W
61 C16 **Rio Branco** *state capital* Acre, W Brazil 9.58S 67.49W
63 H18 **Río Branco** Cerro Largo, NE Uruguay 32.34S 53.21W
Rio Branco, Território de *see* Roraima
43 P8 **Río Bravo** Tamaulipas, C Mexico 25.57N 98.03W
65 G16 **Río Bueno** Los Lagos, C Chile 40.19S 72.55W
57 P5 **Río Caribe** Sucre, NE Venezuela 10.40N 63.07W
56 M5 **Río Chico** Miranda, N Venezuela 10.18N 66.00W
65 H18 **Río Cisnes** Aisén, S Chile 44.29S 71.15W
62 L9 **Rio Claro** São Paulo, S Brazil 22.22S 47.31W
47 V14 **Rio Claro** Trinidad, Trinidad and Tobago 10.18N 61.10W
56 J5 **Río Claro** Lara, N Venezuela 9.54N 69.22W
65 K15 **Rio Colorado** Río Negro, E Argentina 39.04S 64.04W
64 K11 **Río Cuarto** Córdoba, C Argentina 33.06S 64.20W
62 P10 **Rio de Janeiro** *var.* Rio. *state capital* Rio de Janeiro, SE Brazil 22.52S 43.16W
62 P9 **Rio de Janeiro** *off.* Estado do Rio de Janeiro. ⬖ *state* SE Brazil
45 R17 **Río de Jesús** Veraguas, S Panama 7.57N 81.09W
36 K3 **Rio Dell** California, W USA 40.30N 124.07W
62 K13 **Rio do Sul** Santa Catarina, S Brazil 27.15S 49.37W
65 I23 **Río Gallegos** *var.* Gallegos, Puerto Gallegos. Santa Cruz, S Argentina 51.39S 69.21W
63 I18 **Rio Grande** *var.* São Pedro do Rio Grande do Sul. Rio Grande do Sul, S Brazil 32.03S 52.07W
26 I9 **Rio Grande** ≈ Texas, SW USA
65 J24 **Río Grande** Tierra del Fuego, S Argentina 53.45S 67.46W
42 L10 **Río Grande** Zacatecas, C Mexico 23.48N 103.03W
44 J9 **Río Grande** León, NW Nicaragua 12.57N 86.31W
47 V5 **Río Grande** E Puerto Rico 18.22N 65.49W
27 R17 **Rio Grande City** Texas, SW USA 26.22N 98.49W
61 P14 **Rio Grande do Norte** *off.* Estado do Rio Grande do Norte. ⬖ *state* E Brazil
63 G15 **Rio Grande do Sul** *off.* Estado do Rio Grande do Sul. ⬖ *state* S Brazil
67 M17 **Rio Grande Fracture Zone** *tectonic feature* C Atlantic Ocean
67 J18 **Rio Grande Gap** *undersea feature* S Atlantic Ocean
Rio Grande Plateau *see* Rio Grande Rise
67 J18 **Rio Grande Rise** *var.* Rio Grande Plateau. *undersea feature* SW Atlantic Ocean
56 G4 **Ríohacha** La Guajira, N Colombia 11.22N 72.46W
45 S16 **Río Hato** Coclé, C Panama 8.22N 80.09W
27 T17 **Rio Hondo** Texas, SW USA 26.14N 97.34W
58 D10 **Rioja** San Martín, N Peru 6.03S 77.05W
43 Y11 **Río Lagartos** Yucatán, SE Mexico 21.34N 88.07W
105 P11 **Riom** *anc.* Ricomagus. Puy-de-Dôme, C France 45.54N 3.06E
106 F10 **Rio Maior** Santarém, C Portugal 39.19N 8.55W
105 O12 **Riom-ès-Montagnes** Cantal, C France 45.15N 2.39E
62 J12 **Rio Negro** Paraná, S Brazil 26.06S 49.46W
65 I15 **Río Negro** *off.* Provincia de Río Negro. ⬖ *province* C Argentina
63 D18 **Río Negro** ⬖ *department* W Uruguay
49 V12 **Río Negro, Embalse del** *var.* Lago Artificial de Rincón del Bonete. ⊡ C Uruguay
109 M17 **Rionero in Vulture** Basilicata, S Italy 40.55N 15.40E
143 S9 **Rioni** ≈ W Georgia
107 P12 **Riópar** Castilla-La Mancha, C Spain 38.31N 2.27W
63 H16 **Rio Pardo** Rio Grande do Sul, S Brazil 29.41S 52.25W
39 R11 **Rio Rancho Estates** New Mexico, SW USA 35.14N 106.40W
44 L11 **Río San Juan** ⬖ *department* S Nicaragua
56 E9 **Ríosucio** Caldas, W Colombia 5.25N 75.43W
56 C7 **Ríosucio** Chocó, NW Colombia 7.24N 77.09W
64 K10 **Río Tercero** Córdoba, C Argentina 32.12S 64.03W
56 J5 **Río Tocuyo** Lara, N Venezuela 10.12N 69.58W
Riouw-Archipel *see* Riau, Kepulauan
61 J19 **Rio Verde** Goiás, C Brazil 17.49S 50.55W
43 O12 **Río Verde** *var.* Rioverde. San Luis Potosí, C Mexico 21.58N 100.00W
37 O8 **Rio Vista** California, W USA 38.09N 121.42W
114 M11 **Ripanj** Serbia, N Serbia and Montenegro (Yugoslavia) 44.37N 20.30E
108 J13 **Ripatransone** Marche, C Italy 43.00N 13.45E
Ripen *see* Ribe
24 M2 **Ripley** Mississippi, S USA 34.43N 88.57W
33 R15 **Ripley** Ohio, N USA 38.45N 83.51W
22 F9 **Ripley** Tennessee, S USA 35.45N 89.31W
23 Q4 **Ripley** West Virginia, NE USA 38.49N 81.42W
107 W4 **Ripoll** Cataluña, NE Spain 42.12N 2.12E
99 M16 **Ripon** N England, UK 54.07N 1.31W
32 M7 **Ripon** Wisconsin, N USA 43.52N 88.48W
109 L24 **Riposto** Sicilia, Italy, C Mediterranean Sea 37.43N 15.13E
101 L14 **Rips** Noord-Brabant, SE Netherlands 51.31N 5.49E
56 D9 **Risaralda** *off.* Departamento de Risaralda. ⬖ *province* C Colombia
118 L8 **Rîşcani** *var.* Râşcani, *Rus.* Ryshkany. NW Moldova 47.55N 27.31E
158 J9 **Rishikesh** Uttar Pradesh, N India 30.06N 78.16E
172 P2 **Rishiri-suidō** *strait* E Sea of Japan
172 Oo2 **Rishiri-tō** *var.* Risiri Tô. *island* NE Japan
172 P2 **Rishiri-yama** Ѫ Rishiri-tō, NE Japan 45.11N 141.11E
27 R7 **Rising Star** Texas, SW USA 32.06N 98.57W
33 Q15 **Rising Sun** Indiana, N USA 38.58N 84.52W
Risiri Tô *see* Rishiri-tō
104 L4 **Risle** ≈ N France
Rîşno *see* Râşnov
29 V13 **Rison** Arkansas, C USA 33.57N 92.11W
97 G17 **Risør** Aust-Agder, S Norway 58.43N 9.13E
94 H10 **Risøyhamn** Nordland, C Norway 69.00N 15.37E
103 I23 **Riss** ≈ S Germany
120 G4 **Risti** *Ger.* Kreuz. Läänemaa, W Estonia 59.03N 24.11E
13 V8 **Ristigouche** ≈ Quebec, SE Canada
95 N18 **Ristiina** Isä-Suomi, E Finland 61.31N 27.15E
95 N14 **Ristijärvi** Oulu, C Finland 64.30N 28.15E
196 C14 **Ritidian Point** *headland* N Guam 13.39N 144.51E
Ritschan *see* Říčany
37 R9 **Ritter, Mount** ▲ California, W USA 37.40N 119.10W
33 T12 **Rittman** Ohio, N USA 40.58N 81.46W
34 L9 **Ritzville** Washington, NW USA 47.07N 118.22W
Riva *see* Riva del Garda
63 A21 **Rivadavia** Buenos Aires, E Argentina 35.28S 62.58W
108 F7 **Riva del Garda** *var.* Riva. Trentino-Alto Adige, N Italy 45.54N 10.50E
108 B8 **Rivarolo Canavese** Piemonte, W Italy 45.21N 7.42E
44 K11 **Rivas** Rivas, SW Nicaragua 11.25N 85.49W
44 J11 **Rivas** ⬖ *department* SW Nicaragua
105 R11 **Rive-de-Gier** Loire, E France 45.31N 4.36E
63 A22 **Rivera** Buenos Aires, E Argentina 37.13S 63.13W
63 F16 **Rivera** Rivera, NE Uruguay 30.54S 55.31W
63 F17 **Rivera** ⬖ *department* NE Uruguay
37 P9 **Riverbank** California, W USA 37.43N 120.59W
78 K17 **River Cess** SW Liberia 5.28N 9.31W
30 M4 **Riverdale** North Dakota, N USA 47.29N 101.22W
32 I6 **River Falls** Wisconsin, N USA 44.52N 92.38W
9 T16 **Riverhurst** Saskatchewan, S Canada 50.52N 106.49W
191 O10 **Riverina** *physical region* New South Wales, SE Australia
82 G8 **River Nile** ⬖ *state* NE Sudan
65 F19 **Rivero, Isla** *island* Archipiélago de los Chonos, S Chile
9 W16 **Rivers** Manitoba, S Canada 50.01N 100.13W
79 U17 **Rivers** ⬖ *state* S Nigeria
193 D23 **Riversdale** Southland, South Island, NZ 45.54S 168.44E
85 F26 **Riversdale** Western Cape, SW South Africa 34.04S 21.15E
37 U15 **Riverside** California, W USA 33.57N 117.24W
27 W9 **Riverside** Texas, SW USA 30.51N 95.24W
39 U3 **Riverside Reservoir** ⊡ Colorado, C USA
8 K15 **Rivers Inlet** British Columbia, SW Canada 51.43N 127.19W
8 K15 **Rivers Inlet** *inlet* British Columbia, SW Canada
9 X15 **Riverton** Manitoba, S Canada 51.00N 97.00W
193 C24 **Riverton** Southland, South Island, NZ 46.19S 168.02E
32 L13 **Riverton** Illinois, N USA 39.50N 89.31W
38 L3 **Riverton** Utah, W USA 40.32N 111.57W
35 V15 **Riverton** Wyoming, C USA 43.01N 108.22W
12 G10 **River Valley** Ontario, S Canada 46.36N 80.09W
11 P14 **Riverview** New Brunswick, SE Canada 46.03N 64.46W
105 O17 **Rivesaltes** Pyrénées-Orientales, S France 42.46N 2.48E
38 H11 **Riviera** Arizona, SW USA 35.06N 114.36W
27 S15 **Riviera** Texas, SW USA 27.15N 97.48W
25 Z14 **Riviera Beach** Florida, SE USA 26.46N 80.03W
13 Q10 **Rivière-à-Pierre** Quebec, SE Canada 46.59N 72.12W
13 T9 **Rivière-Bleue** Quebec, SE Canada 47.25N 69.01W
13 T8 **Rivière-du-Loup** Quebec, SE Canada 47.49N 69.31W
181 Y15 **Rivière du Rempart** NE Mauritius 20.06S 57.40E
47 R12 **Rivière-Pilote** S Martinique 14.29N 60.54W
181 O17 **Rivière St-Etienne, Point de la** *headland* SW Réunion
11 S10 **Rivière-St-Paul** Quebec, E Canada 51.26N 57.52W
Rivière Sèche *see* Bel Air
118 K4 **Rivne** *Pol.* Równe, *Rus.* Rovno. Rivnens'ka Oblast', NW Ukraine 50.37N 26.15E
Rivne *see* Rivnens'ka Oblast'
118 K3 **Rivnens'ka Oblast'** *var.* Rivne, *Rus.* Rovenskaya Oblast'. ⬖ *province* NW Ukraine
108 B8 **Rivoli** Piemonte, NW Italy 45.04N 7.31E
165 Q14 **Riwoqê** Xizang Zizhiqu, W China 31.10N 96.25E
101 H19 **Rixensart** Wallon Brabant, C Belgium 50.43N 4.31E
Riyadh/Riyāḍ, Minṭaqat ar *see* Ar Riyāḍ
Riyāq *see* Rayak
Rizaiyeh *see* Orūmīyeh
143 P11 **Rize** Rize, NE Turkey 41.02N 40.33E
143 P11 **Rize** *prev.* Çoruh. ⬖ *province* NE Turkey
167 R5 **Rizhao** Shandong, E China 35.23N 119.31E
Rizhskiy Zaliv *see* Riga, Gulf of
Rizokarpaso/Rizokárpason *see* Dipkarpaz
109 O21 **Rizzuto, Capo** *headland* S Italy 38.54N 17.05E
97 F15 **Rjukan** Telemark, S Norway 59.52N 8.37E
97 D16 **Rjuven** ▲▲ S Norway
78 H9 **Rkîz** Trarza, W Mauritania 16.49N 15.19W
97 H14 **Roa** Oppland, S Norway 60.16N 10.38E
107 N5 **Roa** Castilla-León, N Spain 41.42N 3.55W
47 T9 **Road Town** ○ (British Virgin Islands) Tortola, C British Virgin Islands 18.24N 64.38W
98 F6 **Roag, Loch** *inlet* NW Scotland, UK
39 O5 **Roan Cliffs** *cliff* Colorado/Utah, W USA
23 P9 **Roan High Knob** *var.* Roan Mountain. ▲ North Carolina/Tennessee, SE USA 36.09N 82.07W
Roan Mountain *see* Roan High Knob
105 Q10 **Roanne** *anc.* Rodunma. Loire, E France 46.03N 4.04E
25 R4 **Roanoke** Alabama, S USA 33.09N 85.22W
23 S7 **Roanoke** Virginia, NE USA 37.16N 79.56W
23 Z9 **Roanoke Island** *island* North Carolina, SE USA
23 W8 **Roanoke Rapids** North Carolina, SE USA 36.27N 77.39W
23 X9 **Roanoke River** ≈ North Carolina/Virginia, SE USA
39 O4 **Roan Plateau** *plain* Utah, W USA
39 R5 **Roaring Fork River** ≈ Colorado, C USA
27 O5 **Roaring Springs** Texas, SW USA 33.54N 100.51W
44 J4 **Roatán** *var.* Coxen Hole, Coxin Hole. Islas de la Bahía, N Honduras 16.18N 86.32W
44 I4 **Roatán, Isla de** *island* Islas de la Bahía, N Honduras
Roat Kampuchea *see* Cambodia
Roazon *see* Rennes
149 T7 **Robāṭ-e Chāh Gonbad** Khorāsān, E Iran
149 R7 **Robāṭ-e Khān** Khorāsān, C Iran 33.24N 56.04E
149 T7 **Robāṭ-e Khvosh Āb** Khorāsān, E Iran
149 R8 **Robāṭ-e Posht-e Bādām** Khorāsān, NE Iran 33.01N 55.34E
183 S8 **Robbie Ridge** *undersea feature* W Pacific Ocean
23 T10 **Robbins** North Carolina, SE USA 35.25N 79.35W
191 N15 **Robbins Island** *island* Tasmania, SE Australia
23 N10 **Robbinsville** North Carolina, SE USA 35.19N 83.48W
190 J12 **Robe** South Australia 37.11S 139.48E
23 W9 **Robersonville** North Carolina, SE USA 35.49N 77.15W
27 P8 **Robert Lee** Texas, SW USA 31.54N 100.26W
37 V5 **Roberts Creek Mountain** ▲ Nevada, W USA 39.52N 116.16W
95 J15 **Robertsfors** Västerbotten, N Sweden 64.12N 20.49E
29 R11 **Robert S.Kerr Reservoir** ⊡ Oklahoma, C USA
40 L12 **Roberts Mountain** ▲ Nunivak Island, Alaska, USA 60.01N 166.15W
85 F26 **Robertson** Western Cape, SW South Africa 33.48S 19.52E
204 H4 **Robertson Island** *island* Antarctica
78 J16 **Robertsport** W Liberia 6.45N 11.15W
190 J8 **Robertstown** South Australia 34.00S 139.04E
Robert Williams *see* Caála
13 P7 **Roberval** Quebec, SE Canada 48.31N 72.16W
33 N15 **Robinson** Illinois, N USA 39.00N 87.44W
200 Oo12 **Róbinson Crusoe, Isla** *island* Islas Juan Fernández, Chile, E Pacific Ocean
188 J9 **Robinson Range** ▲▲ Western Australia
194 L16 **Robinson River** Central, S PNG 10.06S 148.51E
190 M9 **Robinvale** Victoria, SE Australia 34.37S 142.45E
107 P11 **Robledo** Castilla-La Mancha, C Spain 38.45N 2.27W
56 G5 **Robles** *var.* La Paz, Robles La Paz. Cesar, N Colombia 10.24N 73.10W
Robles La Paz *see* Robles
9 V15 **Roblin** Manitoba, S Canada 51.15N 101.19W
195 U13 **Rob Roy** *island* NW Solomon Islands
9 S17 **Robsart** Saskatchewan, S Canada 49.22N 109.15W
9 N15 **Robson, Mount** ▲ British Columbia, SW Canada 53.09N 119.16W
27 T14 **Robstown** Texas, SW USA 27.47N 97.40W
27 P6 **Roby** Texas, SW USA 32.43N 100.22W
106 E11 **Roca, Cabo da** *headland* C Portugal 38.47N 9.32W
Rocadas *see* Xangongo
43 S14 **Roca Partida, Punta** *headland* C Mexico 18.43N 95.11W
49 X6 **Rocas, Atol das** *island* E Brazil
109 L18 **Roccadaspide** *var.* Rocca d'Aspide. Campania, S Italy 40.25N 15.12E
109 K15 **Roccaraso** Abruzzo, C Italy 41.49N 14.01E
108 H10 **Rocca San Casciano** Emilia-Romagna, C Italy 44.06N 11.51E
108 G13 **Roccastrada** Toscana, C Italy 43.00N 11.09E
63 G20 **Rocha** Rocha, E Uruguay 34.30S 54.22W
63 G19 **Rocha** ⬖ *department* E Uruguay
99 L17 **Rochdale** NW England, UK 53.37N 2.09W
104 L11 **Rochechouart** Haute-Vienne, C France 45.49N 0.49E
101 J22 **Rochefort** Namur, SE Belgium 50.10N 5.13E
104 J11 **Rochefort** *var.* Rochefort sur Mer. Charente-Maritime, W France 45.57N 0.58W
Rochefort sur Mer *see* Rochefort
129 N10 **Rochegda** Arkhangel'skaya Oblast', NW Russian Federation 62.37N 43.21E
32 L10 **Rochelle** Illinois, N USA 41.54N 89.03W
27 Q9 **Rochelle** Texas, SW USA 31.13N 99.10W
11 P13 **Rocher Percé** *island* Rocher Percé, Quebec, E Canada
13 V3 **Rochers Ouest, Rivière aux** ≈ Quebec, SE Canada
99 O22 **Rochester** *anc.* Durobrivae. SE England, UK 51.24N 0.30E
33 O12 **Rochester** Indiana, N USA 41.03N 86.13W
31 W10 **Rochester** Minnesota, N USA 44.01N 92.28W
21 O9 **Rochester** New Hampshire, NE USA 43.18N 70.58W
20 F9 **Rochester** New York, NE USA 43.09N 77.37W
27 P5 **Rochester** Texas, SW USA 33.19N 99.51W
33 S9 **Rochester Hills** Michigan, N USA 42.39N 83.04W
Rocheuses, Montagnes/Rockies *see* Rocky Mountains
66 M6 **Rockall** *island* UK, N Atlantic Ocean
66 L6 **Rockall Bank** *undersea feature* N Atlantic Ocean
86 B8 **Rockall Rise** *undersea feature* N Atlantic Ocean
86 C9 **Rockall Trough** *undersea feature* N Atlantic Ocean
37 U2 **Rock Creek** ≈ Nevada, W USA
27 T10 **Rockdale** Texas, SW USA 30.39N 96.58W
205 N12 **Rockefeller Plateau** *plateau* Antarctica
32 K11 **Rock Falls** Illinois, N USA 41.46N 89.41W
25 Q5 **Rockford** Alabama, S USA 32.53N 86.11W
32 L10 **Rockford** Illinois, N USA 42.16N 89.05W
13 Q12 **Rock Forest** Quebec, SE Canada 45.21N 71.58W
9 T17 **Rockglen** Saskatchewan, S Canada 49.10N 105.57W
189 Y8 **Rockhampton** Queensland, E Australia 23.31S 150.31E
23 R11 **Rock Hill** South Carolina, SE USA 34.55N 80.59W
188 I13 **Rockingham** Western Australia 32.16S 115.21E
23 T11 **Rockingham** North Carolina, SE USA 34.56N 79.46W
32 J11 **Rock Island** Illinois, N USA 41.30N 90.34W
27 U12 **Rock Island** Texas, SW USA 29.31N 96.33W
12 C10 **Rock Lake** Ontario, S Canada 46.25N 83.49W
31 O2 **Rock Lake** North Dakota, N USA 48.45N 99.12W
12 I12 **Rock Lake** ◎ Ontario, SE Canada
12 M12 **Rockland** Ontario, SE Canada 45.33N 75.16W
21 R7 **Rockland** Maine, NE USA 44.08N 69.06W
190 L11 **Rocklands Reservoir** ⊡ Victoria, SE Australia

◆ Country
● Country Capital
◇ Dependent Territory
○ Dependent Territory Capital
⬖ Administrative Region
✕ International Airport
▲ Mountain
▲▲ Mountain Range
Ѫ Volcano
≈ River
◎ Lake
⊡ Reservoir

37 O7 **Rocklin** California, W USA 38.48N 121.13W
25 R3 **Rockmart** Georgia, SE USA 34.00N 85.02W
33 N16 **Rockport** Indiana, N USA 37.52N 87.04W
29 Q1 **Rock Port** Missouri, C USA 40.26N 95.30W
27 T14 **Rockport** Texas, SW USA 28.01N 97.03W
34 I7 **Rockport** Washington, NW USA 48.28N 121.36W
31 S11 **Rock Rapids** Iowa, C USA 43.25N 96.10W
32 K11 **Rock River** ≈ Illinois/Wisconsin, N USA
46 I3 **Rock Sound** Eleuthera Island, C Bahamas 24.51N 76.09W
35 U17 **Rock Springs** Wyoming, C USA 41.35N 109.12W
27 P11 **Rocksprings** Texas, SW USA 30.01N 100.12W
57 T9 **Rockstone** C Guyana 5.58N 58.33W
31 S12 **Rock Valley** Iowa, C USA 43.12N 96.17W
33 N14 **Rockville** Indiana, N USA 39.45N 87.13W
23 W3 **Rockville** Maryland, NE USA 39.04N 77.04W
27 U6 **Rockwall** Texas, SW USA 32.55N 96.27W
31 U13 **Rockwell City** Iowa, C USA 42.24N 94.37W
33 S10 **Rockwood** Michigan, N USA 42.04N 83.15W
22 M9 **Rockwood** Tennessee, S USA 35.52N 84.41W
27 Q8 **Rockwood** Texas, SW USA 31.29N 99.23W
39 U6 **Rocky Ford** Colorado, C USA 38.03N 103.45W
12 D9 **Rocky Island Lake** ◎ Ontario, S Canada
23 V9 **Rocky Mount** North Carolina, SE USA 35.56N 77.47W
23 S7 **Rocky Mount** Virginia, NE USA 37.00N 79.53W
35 Q8 **Rocky Mountain** ▲ Montana, NW USA 47.45N 112.46W
9 P15 **Rocky Mountain House** Alberta, SW Canada 52.24N 114.52W
39 T3 **Rocky Mountain National Park** *national park* Colorado, C USA
2 E12 **Rocky Mountains** *var.* Rockies, *Fr.* Montagnes Rocheuses. ▲▲ Canada/USA
44 H1 **Rocky Point** *headland* NE Belize 18.21N 88.04W
85 A17 **Rocky Point** *headland* NW Namibia 19.01S 12.27E
97 F14 **Rødberg** Buskerud, S Norway 60.16N 9.00E
97 I25 **Rødby** Storstrøm, SE Denmark 54.42N 11.24E
97 I25 **Rødbyhavn** Storstrøm, SE Denmark 54.39N 11.24E
11 T10 **Roddickton** Newfoundland and Labrador, SE Canada 50.51N 56.03W
97 F23 **Rødding** Sønderjylland, SW Denmark 55.22N 9.04E
97 M22 **Rödeby** Blekinge, S Sweden 56.16N 15.34E
100 N6 **Roden** Drenthe, NE Netherlands 53.07N 6.25E
64 H9 **Rodeo** San Juan, W Argentina 30.12S 69.06W
105 O14 **Rodez** *anc.* Segodunum. Aveyron, S France 44.21N 2.34E
Rodholívos *see* Rodolívos
Rodhópi Óri *see* Rhodope Mountains
Ródhos/Rodi *see* Ródos
109 N15 **Rodi Garganico** Puglia, SE Italy 41.54N 15.51E
103 N20 **Roding** Bayern, SE Germany 49.12N 12.30E
115 J19 **Rodinit, Kepi i** *headland* W Albania 41.35N 19.27E
118 I9 **Rodnei, Munții** ▲▲ N Romania
192 L4 **Rodney, Cape** *headland* North Island, NZ 36.16S 174.48E
40 L9 **Rodney, Cape** *headland* Alaska, USA 64.39N 166.24W
128 M16 **Rodniki** Ivanovskaya Oblast', W Russian Federation 57.04N 41.45E
121 Q16 **Rodnya** *Rus.* Rodnya. Mahilyowskaya Voblasts', E Belarus 53.30N 32.12E
Rodó *see* José Enrique Rodó
116 H13 **Rodolívos** *var.* Rodholívos. Kentrikí Makedonía, NE Greece 40.55N 23.59E
Rodopi *see* Rhodope Mountains
117 O22 **Ródos** *var.* Ródhos, *Eng.* Rhodes, *It.* Rodi. Ródos, Dodekánisos, Greece, Aegean Sea 36.25N 28.13E
117 O22 **Ródos** *var.* Ródhos, *Eng.* Rhodes, *It.* Rodi; *anc.* Rhodos. *island* Dodekánisos, Greece, Aegean Sea
Rodosto *see* Tekirdağ
61 A14 **Rodrigues** Amazonas, W Brazil 6.50S 73.45W
181 P8 **Rodrigues** *var.* Rodriquez. *island* E Mauritius
Rodriquez *see* Rodrigues
Rodunma *see* Roanne
188 I7 **Roebourne** Western Australia 20.49S 117.04E
85 J20 **Roedtan** Limpopo, NE South Africa 24.37S 29.04E
100 H11 **Roelofarendsveen** Zuid-Holland, W Netherlands 52.12N 4.37E
Roepat *see* Rupat, Pulau
Roer *see* Rur
101 M16 **Roermond** Limburg, SE Netherlands 51.12N 6.00E
101 C18 **Roeselare** *Fr.* Roulers; *prev.* Rousselaere. West-Vlaanderen, W Belgium 50.57N 3.07E
15 L15 **Roes Welcome Sound** *strait* Nunavut, N Canada
Roeteng *see* Ruteng
Rofreit *see* Rovereto
Rogachëv *see* Rahachow
59 L15 **Rogagua, Laguna** ◎ NW Bolivia
97 C16 **Rogaland** ◆ *county* S Norway
27 Y9 **Roganville** Texas, SW USA 30.49N 93.54W
111 W11 **Rogaška Slatina** *Ger.* Rohitsch-Sauerbrunn; *prev.* Rogatec-Slatina. E Slovenia 46.13N 15.38E
Rogatec-Slatina *see* Rogaška Slatina
114 J13 **Rogatica** Republica Srpska, SE Bosnia & Herzegovina 43.50N 18.55E
Rogatin *see* Rohatyn
95 F17 **Rogen** ◎ C Sweden
29 S9 **Rogers** Arkansas, C USA 36.19N 94.07W
31 P5 **Rogers** North Dakota, N USA 47.03N 98.12W
27 T9 **Rogers** Texas, SW USA 30.53N 97.10W
33 R5 **Rogers City** Michigan, N USA 45.25N 83.49W
Roger Simpson Island *see* Abemama
37 T14 **Rogers Lake** *salt flat* California, W USA
23 Q8 **Rogers, Mount** ▲ Virginia, NE USA 36.39N 81.32W
35 O16 **Rogerson** Idaho, NW USA 42.11N 114.36W
9 O16 **Rogers Pass** *pass* British Columbia, SW Canada 51.18N 117.36W
23 O8 **Rogersville** Tennessee, S USA 36.26N 83.01W
101 L16 **Roggel** Limburg, SE Netherlands 51.16N 5.55E
Roggeveen *see* Roggewein, Cabo
200 Nn12 **Roggeveen Basin** *undersea feature* E Pacific Ocean
203 X16 **Roggewein, Cabo** *var.* Roggeveen. *headland* Easter Island, Chile, E Pacific Ocean 27.07S 109.15W
105 Y13 **Rogliano** Corse, France, C Mediterranean Sea 42.58N 9.25E
109 N21 **Rogliano** Calabria, SW Italy 39.09N 16.18E
94 G12 **Rognan** Nordland, C Norway 67.04N 15.21E
102 K10 **Rögnitz** ≈ N Germany
Rogozhina/Rogozhinë *see* Rrogozhinë
112 G10 **Rogoźno** Wielkopolskie, C Poland 52.46N 16.57E
34 E15 **Rogue River** ≈ Oregon, NW USA
118 I6 **Rohatyn** *Rus.* Rogatin. Ivano-Frankivs'ka Oblast', W Ukraine 49.25N 24.35E
201 O14 **Rohi** Pohnpei, E Micronesia
Rohitsch-Sauerbrunn *see* Rogaška Slatina
155 Q13 **Rohri** Sind, SE Pakistan 27.40N 68.52E
158 I10 **Rohtak** Haryāna, N India 28.55N 76.32E
Roi Ed *see* Roi Et
178 Ii10 **Roi Et** *var.* Muang Roi Et, Roi Ed. Roi Et, E Thailand 16.04N 103.37E
203 U9 **Roi Georges, Îles du** *island group* Îles Tuamotu, C French Polynesia
159 Y10 **Roing** Arunāchal Pradesh, NE India 28.06N 95.46E
120 E7 **Roja** Talsi, NW Latvia 57.31N 22.44E
63 B20 **Rojas** Buenos Aires, E Argentina 34.13S 60.41W
155 R12 **Rojhān** Punjab, E Pakistan 28.44N 70.01E
43 Q12 **Rojo, Cabo** *headland* C Mexico 21.33N 97.19W
47 Q10 **Rojo, Cabo** *headland* W Puerto Rico 17.57N 67.10W
173 G7 **Rokan Kanan, Sungai** ≈ Sumatera, W Indonesia
173 G7 **Rokan Kiri, Sungai** ≈ Sumatera, W Indonesia
Rokha *see* Rokhah
155 R4 **Rokhah** *var.* Rokha. Kāpīsā, E Afghanistan 35.16N 69.28E
120 I11 **Rokiškis** Rokiškis, NE Lithuania 55.58N 25.34E
172 Nn9 **Rokkasho** Aomori, Honshū, C Japan 40.59N 141.22E
113 B17 **Rokycany** *Ger.* Rokytzan. Plzeňský Kraj, NW Czech Republic 49.45N 13.36E
119 P6 **Rokytne** Kyyivs'ka Oblast', N Ukraine 49.40N 30.29E
118 L3 **Rokytne** Rivnens'ka Oblast', NW Ukraine 51.19N 27.09E
Rokytzan *see* Rokycany
164 L11 **Rola Co** ◎ W China
31 V13 **Roland** Iowa, C USA 42.10N 93.30W
97 D15 **Røldal** Hordaland, S Norway 59.52N 6.49E
100 O7 **Rolde** Drenthe, NE Netherlands 52.58N 6.39E
31 O2 **Rolette** North Dakota, N USA 48.39N 99.50W
29 V6 **Rolla** Missouri, C USA 37.57N 91.46W
31 O2 **Rolla** North Dakota, N USA 48.51N 99.37W
110 A10 **Rolle** Vaud, W Switzerland 46.27N 6.19E
189 X8 **Rolleston** Queensland, E Australia 24.30S 148.36E
193 H19 **Rolleston** Canterbury, South Island, NZ 43.34S 172.24E
193 G18 **Rolleston Range** ▲▲ South Island, NZ
12 H8 **Rollet** Quebec, SE Canada 47.56N 79.14W
24 J4 **Rolling Fork** Mississippi, S USA 32.54N 90.52W
22 L6 **Rolling Fork** ≈ Kentucky, S USA
12 J11 **Rolphton** Ontario, SE Canada 46.09N 77.43W
Röm *see* Rømø
189 X10 **Roma** Queensland, E Australia 26.36S 148.53E
109 I15 **Roma** *Eng.* Rome. ● (Italy) Lazio, C Italy 41.52N 12.30E
97 P19 **Roma** Gotland, SE Sweden 57.31N 18.28E
23 T14 **Romain, Cape** *headland* South Carolina, SE USA 33.00N 79.21W
11 P11 **Romaine** ≈ Newfoundland and Labrador/Quebec, E Canada
27 R17 **Roma Los Saenz** Texas, SW USA 26.24N 99.01W
116 H8 **Roman** Vratsa, NW Bulgaria 43.09N 23.56E
118 L10 **Roman** *Hung.* Románvásár. Neamț, NE Romania 46.46N 26.55E
66 M13 **Romanche Fracture Zone** *tectonic feature* E Atlantic Ocean
63 C15 **Romang** Santa Fe, C Argentina 29.30S 59.46W
175 T15 **Romang, Pulau** *var.* Pulau Roma. *island* Kepulauan Damar, E Indonesia
175 Ss15 **Romang, Selat** *strait* Nusa Tenggara, S Indonesia
118 J11 **Romania** *Bul.* Rumŭniya, *Ger.* Rumänien, *Hung.* Románia, *Rom.* România, *SCr.* Rumunjska, *Ukr.* Rumuniya; *prev.* Republica Socialistă România, Roumania, Rumania, Socialist Republic of Romania, *Rom.* Romînia. ◆ *republic* SE Europe
119 T14 **Roman-Kash** ▲ S Ukraine 44.37N 34.13E
25 W16 **Romano, Cape** *headland* Florida, SE USA 25.51N 81.40W
46 G5 **Romano, Cayo** *island* C Cuba
126 Kk15 **Romanovka** Respublika Buryatiya, S Russian Federation 53.10N 112.34E
131 N8 **Romanovka** Saratovskaya Oblast', W Russian Federation 51.45N 42.45E
110 I6 **Romanshorn** Thurgau, NE Switzerland 47.33N 9.21E
105 R12 **Romans-sur-Isère** Drôme, E France 45.03N 5.03E
201 U12 **Romanum** *island* Chuuk, C Micronesia
Románvásár *see* Roman
41 S5 **Romanzof Mountains** ▲▲ Alaska, USA
Roma, Pulau *see* Romang, Pulau
105 S4 **Rombas** Moselle, NE France 49.15N 6.04E
176 Xx10 **Rombebai, Danau** ◎ Papua, E Indonesia
25 R2 **Rome** Georgia, SE USA 34.01N 85.01W
20 I9 **Rome** New York, NE USA 43.13N 75.28W
Rome *see* Roma
33 S9 **Romeo** Michigan, N USA 42.48N 83.00W
Römerstadt *see* Rýmařov
Rometan *see* Romiton
105 P5 **Romilly-sur-Seine** Aube, N France 48.31N 3.43E
Rominia *see* Romania
152 L11 **Romiton** *Rus.* Rometan. Buxoro Viloyati, C Uzbekistan 39.56N 64.21E
23 U3 **Romney** West Virginia, NE USA 39.20N 78.45W
119 S4 **Romny** Sums'ka Oblast', NE Ukraine 50.45N 33.30E
97 E24 **Rømø** *Ger.* Röm. *island* SW Denmark
119 S5 **Romodan** Poltavs'ka Oblast', NE Ukraine 50.00N 33.20E
131 P5 **Romodanovo** Respublika Mordoviya, W Russian Federation 54.25N 45.24E
Romorantin *see* Romorantin-Lanthenay
105 N8 **Romorantin-Lanthenay** *var.* Romorantin. Loir-et-Cher, C France 47.22N 1.43E
174 Hh5 **Rompin, Sungai** ≈ Peninsular Malaysia
96 F10 **Romsdal** *physical region* S Norway
96 F10 **Romsdalen** *valley* S Norway
96 E9 **Romsdalsfjorden** *fjord* S Norway
35 P8 **Ronan** Montana, NW USA 47.31N 114.06W
61 M14 **Roncador** Maranhão, E Brazil 5.48S 45.08W
195 W12 **Roncador Reef** *reef* N Solomon Islands
61 J17 **Roncador, Serra do** ▲▲ C Brazil
23 S6 **Ronceverte** West Virginia, NE USA 37.45N 80.27W
109 H14 **Ronciglione** Lazio, C Italy 42.16N 12.15E
106 L15 **Ronda** Andalucía, S Spain 36.45N 5.10W
96 G11 **Rondane** ▲ S Norway
106 L15 **Ronda, Serranía de** ▲▲ S Spain
97 H22 **Rønde** Århus, C Denmark 56.18N 10.28E
Rōn̄dik *see* Rongrik Atoll
61 E16 **Rondônia** *off.* Estado de Rondônia; *prev.* Território de Rondônia. ⬖ *state* W Brazil
61 I18 **Rondonópolis** Mato Grosso, W Brazil 16.28S 54.37W
96 G11 **Rondslottet** ▲ S Norway 61.54N 9.48E
97 P20 **Ronehamn** Gotland, SE Sweden 57.10N 18.30E
166 L13 **Rong'an** *var.* Chang'an, Rongan. Guangxi Zhuangzu Zizhiqu, S China 25.13N 109.19E
201 R4 **Rongelap Atoll** *var.* Rōn̄ļap. *atoll* Ralik Chain, NW Marshall Islands
Rongerik *see* Rongrik Atoll
166 L13 **Rong Jiang** ≈ S China
166 K12 **Rongjiang** *prev.* Guzhou. Guizhou, S China 25.59N 108.27E
Rong, Kas *see* Rŭng, Kaôh
178 Hh8 **Rong Kwang** Phrae, NW Thailand 18.19N 100.18E
201 T4 **Rongrik Atoll** *var.* Rōn̄dik, Rongerik. *atoll* Ralik Chain, N Marshall Islands
201 X2 **Rongrong** *island* SE Marshall Islands
166 L13 **Rongshui** *var.* Rongshui Miaozu Zizhixian. Guangxi Zhuangzu Zizhiqu, S China 25.08N 109.15E
Rongshui Miaozu Zizhixian *see* Rongshui
120 I6 **Rõngu** *Ger.* Ringen. Tartumaa, SE Estonia 58.10N 26.17E
166 L15 **Rongxian** *var.* Rong Xian. Guangxi Zhuangzu Zizhiqu, S China 22.52N 110.33E
Roniu *see* Ronui, Mont
201 N13 **Ronkiti** Pohnpei, E Micronesia 6.48N 158.10E
Rōn̄ļap *see* Rongelap Atoll
97 L24 **Rønne** Bornholm, E Denmark 55.07N 14.43E
97 M22 **Ronneby** Blekinge, S Sweden 56.12N 15.18E
204 J7 **Ronne Entrance** *inlet* Antarctica
204 L6 **Ronne Ice Shelf** *ice shelf* Antarctica
101 E19 **Ronse** *Fr.* Renaix. Oost-Vlaanderen, SW Belgium 50.45N 3.36E
203 R8 **Ronui, Mont** *var.* Roniu. ⛰ Tahiti, W French Polynesia 17.49S 149.12W
32 K14 **Roodhouse** Illinois, N USA 39.28N 90.22W
85 C19 **Rooibank** Erongo, W Namibia 23.04S 14.34E
Rooke Island *see* Umboi Island
67 N24 **Rookery Point** *headland* NE Tristan da Cunha 37.03S 12.15W
176 W10 **Roon, Pulau** *island* E Indonesia
181 V7 **Roo Rise** *undersea feature* E Indian Ocean
158 J9 **Roorkee** Uttar Pradesh, N India 29.51N 77.54E
101 H15 **Roosendaal** Noord-Brabant, S Netherlands 51.31N 4.28E
27 P10 **Roosevelt** Texas, SW USA 30.28N 100.06W
39 N3 **Roosevelt** Utah, W USA 40.18N 109.59W
49 T8 **Roosevelt** ≈ W Brazil
205 O13 **Roosevelt Island** *island* Antarctica
8 L10 **Roosevelt, Mount** ▲ British Columbia, W Canada 58.28N 125.22W
9 P17 **Roosville** British Columbia, SW Canada 48.59N 115.03W
31 X10 **Root River** ≈ Minnesota, N USA
113 N16 **Ropczyce** Podkarpackie, SE Poland 50.03N 21.36E
189 Q3 **Roper Bar** Northern Territory, N Australia 14.45S 134.30E
26 M5 **Ropesville** Texas, SW USA 33.24N 102.09W
104 K14 **Roquefort** Landes, SW France 44.01N 0.18W
63 C21 **Roque Pérez** Buenos Aires, E Argentina 35.25S 59.24W
60 E10 **Roraima** *off.* Estado de Roraima; *prev.* Território de Rio Branco, Território de Roraima. ⬖ *state* N Brazil
60 F9 **Roraima, Mount** ▲ N South America 5.10N 60.36W
176 X10 **Rori** Papua, E Indonesia 1.44S 136.49E
Ro Ro Reef *see* Malolo Barrier Reef
96 I9 **Røros** Sør-Trøndelag, S Norway 62.37N 11.25E
110 I7 **Rorschach** Sankt Gallen, NE Switzerland 47.28N 9.30E
95 E14 **Rørvik** Nord-Trøndelag, C Norway 64.52N 11.13E
121 G17 **Ros'** *Rus.* Ross'. Hrodzyenskaya Voblasts', W Belarus 53.20N 24.25E
121 G17 **Ros'** *Rus.* Ross'. ≈ W Belarus
119 O6 **Ros'** ≈ N Ukraine
46 K7 **Rosa, Lake** ◎ Great Inagua, S Bahamas
34 M9 **Rosalia** Washington, NW USA 47.14N 117.22W
203 W15 **Rosalia, Punta** *headland* Easter Island, Chile, E Pacific Ocean 27.04S 109.19W
47 P12 **Rosalie** E Dominica 15.22N 61.15W
37 T14 **Rosamond** California, W USA 34.51N 118.09W
37 S14 **Rosamond Lake** *salt flat* California, W USA
63 B18 **Rosario** Santa Fe, C Argentina 32.56S 60.38W
42 J11 **Rosario** Sinaloa, C Mexico 23.00N 105.51W
42 G6 **Rosario** Sonora, NW Mexico 27.53N 109.18W
64 O6 **Rosario** San Pedro, C Paraguay 24.26S 57.06W
63 E20 **Rosario** Colonia, SW Uruguay 34.19S 57.18W
56 H5 **Rosario** Zulia, NW Venezuela 10.18N 72.19W
Rosario *see* Rosarito
42 B4 **Rosario, Bahía del** *bay* NW Mexico
64 K6 **Rosario de la Frontera** Salta, N Argentina 25.50S 65.00W
63 C18 **Rosario del Tala** Entre Ríos, E Argentina 32.19S 59.10W
63 F16 **Rosário do Sul** Rio Grande do Sul, S Brazil 30.15S 54.55W
61 H18 **Rosário Oeste** Mato Grosso, W Brazil 14.49S 56.25W
42 E7 **Rosarito** Baja California, NW Mexico 26.27N 111.37W
42 B1 **Rosarito** *var.* Rosario. Baja California, NW Mexico 32.25N 117.03W
42 E7 **Rosarito** Baja California Sur, W Mexico 26.28N 111.40W
106 L9 **Rosarito, Embalse del** ▣ W Spain
109 N22 **Rosarno** Calabria, SW Italy 38.28N 15.58E
58 B5 **Rosa Zárate** *var.* Quinindé. Esmeraldas, SW Ecuador 0.18N 79.28W
Roscianum *see* Rossano
31 O8 **Roscoe** South Dakota, N USA 45.24N 99.19W
27 P7 **Roscoe** Texas, SW USA 32.27N 100.32W
104 F5 **Roscoff** Finistère, NW France 48.43N 4.00W
Ros Comáin *see* Roscommon
99 C17 **Roscommon** *Ir.* Ros Comáin. C Ireland 53.37N 8.10W
33 Q7 **Roscommon** Michigan, N USA 44.30N 84.34W
99 C17 **Roscommon** *Ir.* Ros Comáin. *cultural region* C Ireland
Ros. Cré *see* Roscrea
99 D19 **Roscrea** *Ir.* Ros. Cré. C Ireland 52.57N 7.46W
47 X12 **Roseau** *prev.* Charlotte Town. ● (Dominica) SW Dominica 15.16N 61.22W
31 S2 **Roseau** Minnesota, N USA 48.51N 95.45W
181 Y16 **Rose Belle** SE Mauritius 20.24S 57.36E
191 O16 **Rosebery** Tasmania, SE Australia 41.51S 145.33E
23 U11 **Roseboro** North Carolina, SE USA 34.58N 78.31W
27 T9 **Rosebud** Texas, SW USA 31.04N 96.58W
35 W10 **Rosebud Creek** ≈ Montana, NW USA
34 F14 **Roseburg** Oregon, NW USA 43.13N 123.20W
24 J3 **Rosedale** Mississippi, S USA 33.51N 91.01W
101 H21 **Rosée** Namur, S Belgium 50.15N 4.43E
57 U8 **Rose Hall** E Guyana 6.14N 57.30W
181 X16 **Rose Hill** W Mauritius 20.13S 57.28E
82 H12 **Roseires, Reservoir** *var.* Lake Rusayris. ▣ E Sudan
Rosenau *see* Rožnov pod Radhoštěm, Czech Republic
Rosenau *see* Rožňava, Slovakia
27 V11 **Rosenberg** Texas, SW USA 29.33N 95.48W
Rosenberg *see* Olesno, Poland
Rosenberg *see* Ružomberok, Slovakia
102 I10 **Rosengarten** Niedersachsen, N Germany 53.24N 9.53E
103 M24 **Rosenheim** Bayern, S Germany 47.51N 12.07E
Rosenhof *see* Zilupe
107 X4 **Roses** Cataluña, NE Spain 42.15N 3.10E
107 X4 **Roses, Golf de** *gulf* NE Spain
109 K14 **Roseto degli Abruzzi** Abruzzo, C Italy 42.39N 14.01E
9 S16 **Rosetown** Saskatchewan, S Canada 51.34N 107.58W
Rosetta *see* Rashîd
37 O7 **Roseville** California, W USA 38.44N 121.16W
32 J12 **Roseville** Illinois, N USA 40.42N 90.40W
31 V8 **Roseville** Minnesota, N USA 45.00N 93.09W
31 R7 **Rosholt** South Dakota, N USA 45.51N 96.42W
108 F12 **Rosignano Marittimo** Toscana, C Italy 43.24N 10.28E
118 I14 **Roșiori de Vede** Teleorman, S Romania 44.06N 25.00E
116 K8 **Rositsa** ≈ N Bulgaria
Rositten *see* Rēzekne
97 J23 **Roskilde** Roskilde, E Denmark 55.39N 12.07E
97 I23 **Roskilde** *off.* Roskilde Amt. ⬖ *county* E Denmark
Ros Láir *see* Rosslare
130 H5 **Roslavl'** Smolenskaya Oblast', W Russian Federation 53.59N 32.57E
34 I8 **Roslyn** Washington, NW USA 47.13N 120.52W
101 K14 **Rosmalen** Noord-Brabant, S Netherlands 51.43N 5.21E
Ros Mhic Thriúin *see* New Ross
115 P19 **Rosoman** C FYR Macedonia 41.31N 21.55E
104 F6 **Rosporden** Finistère, NW France 47.58N 3.54W
193 F17 **Ross** West Coast, South Island, NZ 42.54S 170.51E
8 J7 **Ross** ≈ Yukon Territory, W Canada
Ross' *see* Ros'
98 H8 **Ross and Cromarty** *cultural region* N Scotland, UK
109 O20 **Rossano** *anc.* Roscianum. Calabria, SW Italy 39.34N 16.37E
24 L5 **Ross Barnett Reservoir** ▣ Mississippi, S USA
9 W16 **Rossburn** Manitoba, S Canada 50.42N 100.49W
12 H13 **Rosseau** Ontario, S Canada 45.15N 79.38W
12 H13 **Rosseau, Lake** ◎ Ontario, S Canada
195 R17 **Rossel Island** *prev.* Yela Island. *island* SE PNG
205 P12 **Ross Ice Shelf** *ice shelf* Antarctica
11 P16 **Rossignol, Lake** ◎ Nova Scotia, SE Canada
85 C19 **Rössing** Erongo, W Namibia 22.27S 14.52E
205 Q14 **Ross Island** *island* Antarctica
Rossitten *see* Rybachiy
Rossiyskaya Federatsiya *see* Russian Federation
9 N17 **Rossland** British Columbia, SW Canada 49.03N 117.49W
99 F20 **Rosslare** *Ir.* Ros Láir. SE Ireland 52.15N 6.22W
99 F20 **Rosslare Harbour** Wexford, SE Ireland 52.15N 6.19W
103 M14 **Rosslau** Sachsen-Anhalt, E Germany 51.52N 12.15E
78 G10 **Rosso** Trarza, SW Mauritania 16.36N 15.49W
105 X14 **Rosso, Cap** *headland* Corse, France, C Mediterranean Sea 42.25N 8.22E
95 H16 **Rosson** Jämtland, C Sweden 63.54N 16.21E
99 K21 **Ross-on-Wye** W England, UK 51.55N 2.34W
Rossony *see* Rasony
130 L9 **Rossosh'** Voronezhskaya Oblast', W Russian Federation 50.09N 39.34E
189 Q7 **Ross River** Northern Territory, N Australia 23.36S 134.30E
8 J7 **Ross River** Yukon Territory, W Canada 61.57N 132.26W
205 O15 **Ross Sea** *sea* Antarctica
94 G13 **Røssvatnet** ◎ C Norway
25 R1 **Rossville** Georgia, SE USA 34.59N 85.22W
Rostak *see* Ar Rustāq
149 P14 **Rostāq** Hormozgān, S Iran 26.48N 53.50E
119 N5 **Rostavytsya** ≈ N Ukraine
9 T15 **Rosthern** Saskatchewan, S Canada 52.40N 106.19W
102 M8 **Rostock** Mecklenburg-Vorpommern, NE Germany 54.04N 12.07E
128 L16 **Rostov** Yaroslavskaya Oblast', W Russian Federation 57.11N 39.19E
Rostov *see* Rostov-na-Donu
130 L12 **Rostov-na-Donu** *var.* Rostov, *Eng.* Rostov-on-Don. Rostovskaya Oblast', SW Russian Federation 47.16N 39.45E
Rostov-on-Don *see* Rostov-na-Donu
130 L10 **Rostovskaya Oblast'** ⬖ *province* SW Russian Federation
95 J14 **Rosvik** Norrbotten, N Sweden 65.26N 21.48E
25 S3 **Roswell** Georgia, SE USA 34.01N 84.21W
39 U14 **Roswell** New Mexico, SW USA 33.23N 104.31W
96 K12 **Rot** Dalarna, C Sweden 61.16N 14.04E
103 I23 **Rot** ≈ S Germany
106 J15 **Rota** Andalucía, S Spain 36.39N 6.20W
196 K9 **Rota** *island* S Northern Mariana Islands
27 P6 **Rotan** Texas, SW USA 32.51N 100.28W
Rotcher Island *see* Tamana
102 I11 **Rotenburg** Niedersachsen, NW Germany 53.06N 9.25E
Rotenburg *see* Rotenburg an der Fulda
103 I16 **Rotenburg an der Fulda** *var.* Rotenburg. Thüringen, C Germany 51.00N 9.43E
103 L18 **Roter Main** ≈ E Germany
103 K20 **Roth** Bayern, SE Germany 49.15N 11.06E
103 G16 **Rothaargebirge** ▲▲ W Germany
Rothenburg *see* Rothenburg ob der Tauber
103 J20 **Rothenburg ob der Tauber** *var.* Rothenburg. Bayern, S Germany 49.23N 10.10E
204 H6 **Rothera** *UK research station* Antarctica 67.28S 68.31W
193 I17 **Rotherham** Canterbury, South Island, NZ 42.42S 172.56E
99 M17 **Rotherham** N England, UK 53.25N 1.19W
98 H12 **Rothesay** W Scotland, UK 55.49N 5.03W
110 E7 **Rothrist** Aargau, N Switzerland 47.18N 7.54E
204 H6 **Rothschild Island** *island* Antarctica
175 Qq18 **Roti, Pulau** *island* S Indonesia
175 R18 **Roti, Selat** *strait* Nusa Tenggara, S Indonesia
191 O8 **Roto** New South Wales, SE Australia 33.04S 145.27E
192 N8 **Rotoiti, Lake** ◎ North Island, NZ
Rotomagus *see* Rouen
109 N19 **Rotondella** Basilicata, S Italy 40.12N 16.30E
105 X15 **Rotondo, Monte** ▲ Corse, France, C Mediterranean Sea 42.15N 9.03E
193 I15 **Rotoroa, Lake** ◎ South Island, NZ
192 N8 **Rotorua** Bay of Plenty, North Island, NZ 38.09S 176.13E
192 N8 **Rotorua, Lake** ◎ North Island, NZ
103 N22 **Rott** ≈ SE Germany
110 F10 **Rotten** ≈ S Switzerland
111 T6 **Rottenmann** Steiermark, E Austria 47.31N 14.18E
100 H12 **Rotterdam** Zuid-Holland, SW Netherlands 51.55N 4.30E
20 K10 **Rotterdam** New York, NE USA 42.46N 73.57W
97 M21 **Rottnen** ◎ S Sweden
100 N4 **Rottumeroog** *island* Waddeneilanden, NE Netherlands
100 N4 **Rottumerplaat** *island* Waddeneilanden, NE Netherlands
103 G23 **Rottweil** Baden-Württemberg, S Germany 48.10N 8.37E
203 O7 **Rotui, Mont** ⛰ Moorea, W French Polynesia 17.30S 149.49W
105 P1 **Roubaix** Nord, N France 50.42N 3.10E
113 C15 **Roudnice nad Labem** *Ger.* Raudnitz an der Elbe. Ústecký Kraj, NW Czech Republic 50.25N 14.13E
104 M4 **Rouen** *anc.* Rotomagus. Seine-Maritime, N France 49.25N 1.04E
176 Y11 **Rouffaer Reserves** *reserve* Papua, E Indonesia
13 N10 **Rouge, Rivière** ≈ Quebec, SE Canada
22 J6 **Rough River** ≈ Kentucky, S USA
22 J6 **Rough River Lake** ▣ Kentucky, S USA
Rouhaïbé *see* Ar Ruḩaybah
104 K11 **Rouillac** Charente, W France 45.46N 0.04W
Roulers *see* Roeselare
Roumania *see* Romania
181 Y15 **Round Island** *var.* Île Ronde. *island* NE Mauritius
12 J12 **Round Lake** ◎ Ontario, SE Canada
37 U7 **Round Mountain** Nevada, W USA 38.42N 117.04W
27 R10 **Round Mountain** Texas, SW USA 30.25N 98.20W
191 U5 **Round Mountain** ▲ New South Wales, SE Australia 30.22S 152.13E
27 S10 **Round Rock** Texas, SW USA 30.30N 97.40W
35 U10 **Roundup** Montana, NW USA 46.27N 108.32W
57 Y10 **Roura** NE French Guiana 4.45N 52.18W
Rourkela *see* Rāulakela
98 J4 **Rousay** *island* N Scotland, UK
Rousselaere *see* Roeselare
105 O17 **Roussillon** *cultural region* S France
13 V7 **Routhierville** Quebec, SE Canada 48.09N 67.07W
101 K25 **Rouvroy** Luxembourg, SE Belgium 49.33N 5.28E
12 I7 **Rouyn-Noranda** Quebec, SE Canada 48.16N 79.01W
Rouyuanchengzi *see* Huachi
94 L12 **Rovaniemi** Lappi, N Finland 66.28N 25.40E
108 E7 **Rovato** Lombardia, N Italy 45.34N 10.03E
129 N11 **Rovdino** Arkhangel'skaya Oblast', NW Russian Federation 61.36N 42.28E
Roven'ki *see* Roven'ky
119 Y8 **Roven'ky** *var.* Roven'ki. Luhans'ka Oblast', E Ukraine 48.04N 39.19E
Rovenskaya Oblast' *see* Rivnens'ka Oblast'
Rovenskaya Sloboda *see* Rovyenskaya Slabada
108 G7 **Rovereto** *Ger.* Rofreit. Trentino-Alto Adige, N Italy 45.52N 11.03E
178 J12 **Rôviĕng Tbong** Preăh Vihéar, N Cambodia 13.18N 105.06E
Rovigno *see* Rovinj
108 H8 **Rovigo** Veneto, NE Italy 45.04N 11.48E
114 A10 **Rovinj** *It.* Rovigno. Istra, NW Croatia 45.06N 13.39E
56 E10 **Rovira** Tolima, C Colombia 4.15N 75.15W
Rovno *see* Rivne
131 P9 **Rovnoye** Saratovskaya Oblast', W Russian Federation 50.43N 46.03E
84 Q12 **Rovuma, Rio** *var.* Ruvuma. ≈ Mozambique/Tanzania *see also* Ruvuma
121 O19 **Rovyenskaya Slabada** *Rus.* Rovenskaya Sloboda. Homyel'skaya Voblasts', SE Belarus 52.12N 30.19E
191 R5 **Rowena** New South Wales, SE Australia 29.51S 148.55E
23 T11 **Rowland** North Carolina, SE USA 34.32N 79.17W
15 M1 **Rowley** ≈ Baffin Island, Nunavut, NE Canada
15 M2 **Rowley Island** *island* Nunavut, NE Canada
181 W8 **Rowley Shoals** *reef* NW Australia
179 Pp12 **Roxas** Mindoro, N Philippines 12.36N 121.29E
179 Q13 **Roxas City** Panay Island, C Philippines 11.33N 122.43E
23 U8 **Roxboro** North Carolina, SE USA 36.23N 78.58W
193 D23 **Roxburgh** Otago, South Island, NZ 45.32S 169.18E
98 K13 **Roxburgh** *cultural region* SE Scotland, UK
190 H5 **Roxby Downs** South Australia 30.29S 136.56E
97 M17 **Roxen** ◎ S Sweden
27 V5 **Roxton** Texas, SW USA 33.33N 95.43W
13 P12 **Roxton-Sud** Quebec, SE Canada 45.30N 72.35W
35 U8 **Roy** Montana, NW USA 47.19N 108.55W
39 U10 **Roy** New Mexico, SW USA 35.56N 104.12W
99 E17 **Royal Canal** *Ir.* An Chanáil Ríoga. *canal* C Ireland
32 L1 **Royale, Isle** *island* Michigan, N USA
39 S6 **Royal Gorge** *valley* Colorado, C USA
99 M20 **Royal Leamington Spa** *var.* Leamington, Leamington Spa. C England, UK 52.18N 1.31W
99 O23 **Royal Tunbridge Wells** *var.* Tunbridge Wells. SE England, UK 51.07N 0.16E
26 L9 **Royalty** Texas, SW USA 31.21N 102.51W
104 J11 **Royan** Charente-Maritime, W France 45.37N 1.01W
67 B24 **Roy Cove Settlement** West Falkland, Falkland Islands 51.31S 60.22W
105 O3 **Roye** Somme, N France 49.42N 2.46E
97 H15 **Røyken** Buskerud, S Norway 59.47N 10.21E
95 F14 **Røyrvik** Nord-Trøndelag, C Norway 64.53N 13.30E
27 U6 **Royse City** Texas, SW USA 32.58N 96.19W
99 O21 **Royston** E England, UK 52.05N 0.01W
25 U2 **Royston** Georgia, SE USA 34.17N 83.06W
116 L10 **Roza** *prev.* Gyulovo. Yambol, E Bulgaria 42.29N 26.30E
115 L16 **Rožaje** Montenegro, SW Serbia and Montenegro (Yugoslavia) 42.51N 20.11E
112 M10 **Różan** Mazowieckie, C Poland 52.36N 21.27E
119 O10 **Rozdil'na** Odes'ka Oblast', SW Ukraine 46.51N 30.03E
119 S12 **Rozdol'ne** *Rus.* Razdolnoye. Respublika Krym, S Ukraine 45.45N 33.27E
151 Q9 **Rozhdestvenka** Akmola, C Kazakhstan 50.51N 71.25E
118 I6 **Rozhnyativ** Ivano-Frankivs'ka Oblast', W Ukraine 48.58N 24.07E
118 J3 **Rozhyshche** Volyns'ka Oblast', NW Ukraine 50.54N 25.16E
Roznau am Radhost *see* Rožnov pod Radhoštěm
113 L19 **Rožňava** *Ger.* Rosenau, *Hung.* Rozsnyó. Košický Kraj, E Slovakia 48.40N 20.31E
118 K10 **Roznov** Neamț, NE Romania 46.46N 26.33E
113 I18 **Rožnov pod Radhoštěm** *Ger.* Rosenau, Roznau am Radhost. Zlínský Kraj, E Czech Republic 49.28N 18.09E
Rózsahegy *see* Ružomberok
Rozsnyó *see* Râșnov, Romania
Rozsnyó *see* Rožňava, Slovakia
115 K18 **Rranxë** Shkodër, NW Albania 41.58N 19.27E
115 L18 **Rrëshen** *var.* Rresheni, Rrshen. Lezhë, C Albania 41.46N 19.54E
Rresheni *see* Rrëshen
Rrogozhina *see* Rrogozhinë
115 K20 **Rrogozhinë** *var.* Rogozhina, Rogozhinë, Rrogozhina. Tiranë, W Albania 41.04N 19.40E
Rrshen *see* Rrëshen
114 O13 **Rtanj** ▲ E Serbia and Montenegro (Yugoslavia) 43.45N 21.54E
131 O7 **Rtishchevo** Saratovskaya Oblast', W Russian Federation 52.16N 43.46E
192 N12 **Ruahine Range** *var.* Ruarine. ▲▲ North Island, NZ
193 L14 **Ruamahanga** ≈ North Island, NZ
Ruanda *see* Rwanda
192 M10 **Ruapehu, Mount** ▲ North Island, NZ 39.15S 175.33E
193 C25 **Ruapuke Island** *island* SW NZ
Ruarine *see* Ruahine Range
192 O9 **Ruatahuna** Bay of Plenty, North Island, NZ 38.38S 176.56E
192 Q8 **Ruatoria** Gisborne, North Island, NZ 37.54S 178.18E
192 K4 **Ruawai** Northland, North Island, NZ 36.08S 174.03E
13 N8 **Ruban** ≈ Quebec, SE Canada
81 I22 **Rubeho Mountains** ▲▲ C Tanzania
172 Q5 **Rubeshibe** Hokkaidō, NE Japan 43.49N 143.37E
Rubezhnoye *see* Rubizhne
115 L18 **Rubik** Lezhë, C Albania 41.46N 19.48E
56 H7 **Rubio** Táchira, W Venezuela 7.42N 72.23W
119 X6 **Rubizhne** *Rus.* Rubezhnoye. Luhans'ka Oblast', E Ukraine 49.01N 38.22E
83 F20 **Rubondo Island** *island* N Tanzania
126 Gg15 **Rubtsovsk** Altayskiy Kray, S Russian Federation 51.34N 81.10E

◆ Country ● Country Capital ◇ Dependent Territory ○ Dependent Territory Capital ⬖ Administrative Region ✈ International Airport ▲ Mountain ▲▲ Mountain Range ⛰ Volcano ≈ River ◎ Lake ▣ Reservoir

41 P9 **Ruby** Alaska, USA 64.44N 155.29W
37 W3 **Ruby Dome** ▲ Nevada, W USA 40.35N 115.25W
37 W4 **Ruby Lake** ◎ Nevada, W USA
37 W4 **Ruby Mountains** ▲ Nevada, W USA
35 Q12 **Ruby Range** ▲ Montana, NW USA
120 C10 **Rucava** Liepāja, SW Latvia 56.09N 21.10E
Rūdān see Dehbārez
Rudelstadt see Ciechanowiec
Rudensk see Rudzyensk
121 G14 **Rūdiškės** Trakai, S Lithuania 54.31N 24.49E
97 H24 **Rudkøbing** Fyn, C Denmark 54.57N 10.43E
127 Nn17 **Rudnaya Pristan'** Primorskiy Kray, SE Russian Federation 44.19N 135.42E
151 V14 **Rudnichnyy** Kaz. Rūdnīchnyy. Almaty, SE Kazakhstan 44.39N 78.57E
129 S13 **Rudnichnyy** Kirovskaya Oblast', NW Russian Federation 59.37N 52.28E
116 N9 **Rudnik** Varna, E Bulgaria 42.57N 27.46E
Rudny see Rudnyy
130 H4 **Rudnya** Smolenskaya Oblast', W Russian Federation 54.55N 31.10E
131 O8 **Rudnya** Volgogradskaya Oblast', SW Russian Federation 50.54N 44.27E
150 M7 **Rudnyy** var. Rudny. Kostanay, N Kazakhstan 53.00N 63.05E
126 Hh1 **Rudol'fa, Ostrov** island Zemlya Frantsa-Iosifa, NW Russian Federation
Rudolf, Lake see Lake Turkana
Rudolfswert see Novo mesto
103 L17 **Rudolstadt** Thüringen, C Germany 50.43N 11.19E
33 Q4 **Rudyard** Michigan, N USA 46.15N 84.36W
35 S7 **Rudyard** Montana, NW USA 48.33N 110.37W
121 K16 **Rudzyensk** Rus. Rudensk. Minskaya Voblasts', C Belarus 53.36N 27.52E
106 L6 **Rueda** Castilla-León, N Spain 41.24N 4.58W
116 F10 **Ruen** ▲ Bulgaria/FYR Macedonia 42.10N 22.31E
82 G10 **Rufa'a** Gezira, C Sudan 14.49N 33.21E
104 L10 **Ruffec** Charente, W France 46.01N 0.10E
23 R14 **Ruffin** South Carolina, SE USA 33.00N 80.48W
83 J23 **Rufiji** ∽ E Tanzania
63 A20 **Rufino** Santa Fe, C Argentina 34.15S 62.40W
78 F11 **Rufisque** W Senegal 14.44N 17.18W
85 K14 **Rufunsa** Lusaka, C Zambia 15.03S 29.36E
120 J9 **Rugāji** Balvi, E Latvia 57.01N 27.07E
167 R7 **Rugao** Jiangsu, E China 32.25N 120.39E
99 M20 **Rugby** C England, UK 52.22N 1.18W
31 N3 **Rugby** North Dakota, N USA 48.24N 100.00W
102 N7 **Rügen** headland NE Germany 54.25N 13.21E
Ruhaybeh see Ar Ruḩaybah
167 N7 **Ru He** ∽ C China
83 E19 **Ruhengeri** NW Rwanda 1.39S 29.16E
Ruhja see Rūjiena
102 M10 **Ruhner Berg** hill N Germany 53.17N 12.00E
120 F7 **Ruhnu** var. Ruhnu Saar, Swe. Runö. island SW Estonia
Ruhnu Saar see Ruhnu
103 G15 **Ruhr** ∽ W Germany
93 W6 **Ruhr Valley** industrial region W Germany
167 S11 **Rui'an** var. Rui an. Zhejiang, SE China 27.48N 120.36E
167 P10 **Ruichang** Jiangxi, S China 29.46N 115.37E
26 J11 **Ruidosa** Texas, SW USA 30.00N 104.40W
39 S14 **Ruidoso** New Mexico, SW USA 33.19N 105.40W
167 P12 **Ruijin** Jiangxi, S China 25.52N 116.01E
166 D13 **Ruili** Yunnan, SW China 24.04N 97.49E
100 N8 **Ruinen** Drenthe, NE Netherlands 52.46N 6.19E
101 D17 **Ruiselede** West-Vlaanderen, W Belgium 51.03N 3.21E
66 P5 **Ruivo de Santana, Pico** ▲ Madeira, Portugal, NE Atlantic Ocean 32.46N 16.57W
42 J12 **Ruiz** Nayarit, SW Mexico 22.00N 105.09W
56 E10 **Ruiz, Nevado del** ⛰ W Colombia 4.52N 75.22W
144 J9 **Rujaylah, Ḩarrat ar** salt lake N Jordan
Rujen see Rūjiena
120 H7 **Rūjiena** Est. Ruhja, Ger. Rujen. Valmiera, N Latvia 57.54N 25.22E
81 I18 **Ruki** ∽ W Dem. Rep. Congo (Zaire)
83 E22 **Rukwa** ◆ region SW Tanzania
83 F23 **Rukwa, Lake** ◎ SE Tanzania
27 P6 **Rule** Texas, SW USA 33.10N 99.53W
24 K3 **Ruleville** Mississippi, S USA 33.43N 90.33W
Rum see Rhum
114 K10 **Ruma** Serbia, N Yugoslavia 45.02N 19.51E
Rumadiya see Ar Ramādī
147 Q7 **Rumāḩ** Ar Riyāḑ, C Saudi Arabia 25.35N 47.09E
Rumaitha see Ar Rumaythah
Rumania/Rumänien see Romania
Rumänisch-Sankt-Georgen see Sângeorz-Băi
145 Y13 **Rumaylah** SE Iraq 30.16N 47.22E
145 P2 **Rumaylah, Wādī** dry watercourse NE Syria
176 V10 **Rumbati** Papua, E Indonesia 2.44S 132.04E
83 E14 **Rumbek** El Buhayrat, S Sudan 6.49N 29.42E
176 W10 **Rumberpon, Pulau** island E Indonesia
Rumburg see Rumburk
113 D14 **Rumburk** Ger. Rumburg. Ústecký Kraj, NW Czech Republic 50.59N 14.31E
46 J4 **Rum Cay** island C Bahamas
101 M26 **Rumelange** Luxembourg, S Luxembourg 49.28N 6.01E
101 D20 **Rumes** Hainaut, SW Belgium 50.33N 3.19E
21 P7 **Rumford** Maine, NE USA 44.31N 70.31W
112 I6 **Rumia** Pomorskie, N Poland 54.35N 18.21E
115 J17 **Rumija** ▲ SW Yugoslavia
105 T11 **Rumilly** Haute-Savoie, E France 45.52N 5.57E
145 O6 **Rūmiyah** W Iraq 34.28N 41.17E
Rummah, Wādī ar see Rimah, Wādī ar
Rummelsburg in Pommern see Miastko
172 Oo4 **Rumoi** Hokkaidō, NE Japan 43.55N 141.37E
84 M12 **Rumphi** var. Rumpi. Northern, N Malawi 11.00S 33.51E
Rumpi see Rumphi
31 V7 **Rum River** ∽ Minnesota, N USA
196 F16 **Rumung** island Caroline Islands, W Micronesia
Rumuniya/Rumŭniya/Rumunjska see Romania
193 G16 **Runanga** West Coast, South Island, NZ 42.24S 171.15E
192 P7 **Runaway, Cape** headland North Island, NZ 37.33S 177.59E
99 K18 **Runcorn** C England, UK 53.19N 2.43W
120 K10 **Rundāni** Ludza, E Latvia 56.19N 27.51E
85 L18 **Runde** var. Lundi. ∽ SE Zimbabwe
85 E16 **Rundu** var. Runtu. Okavango, NE Namibia 17.55S 19.45E
95 I16 **Rundvik** Västerbotten, N Sweden 63.31N 19.22E
83 G20 **Runere** Mwanza, N Tanzania 3.06S 33.18E
27 S13 **Runge** Texas, SW USA 28.52N 97.42W
178 I14 **Rŭng, Kaôh** prev. Kas Rong. island SW Cambodia
81 O16 **Rungu** Orientale, NE Dem. Rep. Congo (Zaire) 3.09N 27.58E
83 F23 **Rungwa** Rukwa, W Tanzania 7.18S 31.40E
83 G22 **Rungwa** Singida, C Tanzania 6.54S 33.33E
96 M13 **Runn** ◎ C Sweden
26 M4 **Running Water Draw** valley New Mexico/Texas, SW USA
Runö see Ruhnu
Runtu see Rundu
201 V12 **Ruo** island Caroline Islands, C Micronesia
164 L9 **Ruoqiang** var. Jo-ch'iang, Uigh. Charkhlik, Charkhliq, Qarkilik. Xinjiang Uygur Zizhiqu, NW China 38.59N 88.07E
165 S7 **Ruo Shui** ∽ N China
94 L8 **Ruostekfielbmá** var. Rustefjelbma Finnmark. Finnmark, N Norway 70.25N 28.10E
95 L18 **Ruovesi** Länsi-Suomi, W Finland 61.58N 24.04E
114 B9 **Rupa** Primorje-Gorski Kotar, NW Croatia 45.29N 14.15E
190 M11 **Rupanyup** Victoria, SE Australia 36.38S 142.37E
174 H6 **Rupat, Pulau** prev. Roepat. island W Indonesia
174 Gg6 **Rupat, Selat** strait Sumatera, W Indonesia
118 J11 **Rupea** Ger. Reps, Hung. Kőhalom; prev. Cohalm. Braşov, C Romania 46.01N 25.13E
101 G17 **Rupel** ∽ N Belgium
Rupella see la Rochelle
35 P15 **Rupert** Idaho, NW USA 42.37N 113.40W
23 R5 **Rupert** West Virginia, NE USA 37.57N 80.40W
Rupert House see Fort Rupert
10 J10 **Rupert, Rivière de** ∽ Quebec, C Canada
204 M13 **Ruppert Coast** physical region Antarctica
102 N11 **Ruppiner Kanal** canal NE Germany
57 S11 **Rupununi River** ∽ S Guyana
103 D16 **Rur** Dut. Roer. ∽ Germany/Netherlands
60 H13 **Rurópolis Presidente Medici** Pará, N Brazil 4.05S 55.26W
203 S12 **Rurutu** island Îles Australes, SW French Polynesia
Rusaddir see Melilla
85 L17 **Rusape** Manicaland, E Zimbabwe 18.31S 32.07E
Rusayris, Lake see Roseires, Reservoir
Ruschuk/Rusçuk see Ruse
116 K7 **Ruse** var. Ruschuk, Rustchuk, Turk. Rusçuk. Ruse, N Bulgaria 43.49N 25.58E
116 L7 **Ruse** ◆ province N Bulgaria
111 W10 **Ruše** NE Slovenia 46.31N 15.30E
116 K7 **Rusenski Lom** ∽ N Bulgaria
99 G17 **Rush** Ir. An Ros. E Ireland 53.31N 6.06W
167 S4 **Rushan** var. Xiacun. Shandong, E China 36.57N 121.33E
Rushan see Rŭshon
Rushanskiy Khrebet see Rushon, Qatorkŭhi
31 V7 **Rush City** Minnesota, N USA 45.41N 92.56W
39 V5 **Rush Creek** ∽ Colorado, C USA
31 X10 **Rushford** Minnesota, N USA 43.48N 91.45W
160 N13 **Rushikulya** ∽ E India
12 D8 **Rush Lake** ◎ Ontario, S Canada
32 M7 **Rush Lake** ◎ Wisconsin, N USA
30 J10 **Rushmore, Mount** ▲ South Dakota, N USA 43.52N 103.27W
153 S13 **Rŭshon** Rus. Rushan. S Tajikistan 37.58N 71.31E
153 S14 **Rushon, Qatorkŭhi** Rus. Rushanskiy Khrebet. ▲ SE Tajikistan
28 M12 **Rush Springs** Oklahoma, C USA 34.46N 97.57W
47 V15 **Rushville** Trinidad, Trinidad and Tobago 10.07N 61.03W
32 J13 **Rushville** Illinois, N USA 40.07N 90.33W
30 K12 **Rushville** Nebraska, C USA 42.41N 102.28W
191 O11 **Rushworth** Victoria, SE Australia 36.36S 145.03E
27 W8 **Rusk** Texas, SW USA 31.48N 95.09W
95 I14 **Ruskele** Västerbotten, N Sweden 64.49N 18.55E
120 C12 **Rusnė** Šilutė, W Lithuania 55.18N 21.19E
116 M10 **Rusokastrenska Reka** ∽ E Bulgaria
Russadir see Melilla
111 X3 **Russbach** ∽ NE Austria
9 V16 **Russell** Manitoba, S Canada 50.46N 101.16W
192 K2 **Russell** Northland, North Island, NZ 35.17S 174.07E
28 L4 **Russell** Kansas, C USA 38.54N 98.51W
23 O4 **Russell** Kentucky, S USA 38.30N 82.43W
195 W15 **Russell Islands** island group C Solomon Islands
22 L7 **Russell Springs** Kentucky, S USA 37.02N 85.03W
25 O2 **Russellville** Alabama, S USA 34.30N 87.43W
29 T11 **Russellville** Arkansas, C USA 35.16N 93.07W
22 J7 **Russellville** Kentucky, S USA 36.51N 86.53W
103 G18 **Rüsselsheim** Hessen, W Germany 50.00N 8.25E
Russia see Russian Federation
Russian America see Alaska
127 N17 **Russian Federation** off. Russian Federation, var. Russia, Latv. Krievija, Rus. Rossiyskaya Federatsiya. ◆ republic Asia/Europe
41 N11 **Russian Mission** Alaska, USA 61.48N 161.23W
36 M7 **Russian River** ∽ California, W USA
204 L13 **Russkaya** Russian research station Antarctica 74.45S 135.24W
126 H3 **Russkaya Gavan'** Novaya Zemlya, Arkhangel'skaya Oblast', N Russian Federation 76.13N 62.48E
126 J4 **Russkiy, Ostrov** island N Russian Federation
111 Y5 **Rust** Burgenland, E Austria 47.48N 16.42E
Rustaq see Ar Rustāq
143 U10 **Rust'avi** SE Georgia 41.36N 45.00E
23 T7 **Rustburg** Virginia, NE USA 37.16N 79.04W
Rustchuk see Ruse
Rustefjelbma see Ruostekfielbmá
85 I21 **Rustenburg** North-West, N South Africa 25.40S 27.15E
24 H5 **Ruston** Louisiana, S USA 32.31N 92.38W
83 E21 **Rutana** SE Burundi 4.01S 30.01E
64 I4 **Rutana, Volcán** ▲ N Chile 22.43S 67.52W
Rutanzige, Lake see Edward, Lake
Rutba see Ar Ruṭbah
106 M14 **Rute** Andalucía, S Spain 37.19N 4.23W
175 Pp16 **Ruteng** prev. Roeteng. Flores, C Indonesia 8.34S 120.28E
204 L8 **Rutford Ice Stream** ice feature Antarctica
37 X6 **Ruth** Nevada, W USA 39.15N 115.00W
103 G15 **Rüthen** Nordrhein-Westfalen, W Germany 51.30N 8.28E
12 D17 **Rutherford** Ontario, S Canada 42.39N 82.06W
23 Q10 **Rutherfordton** North Carolina, SE USA 35.22N 81.57W
99 J18 **Ruthin** Wel. Rhuthun. NE Wales, UK 53.05N 3.18W
110 G7 **Rüti** Zürich, N Switzerland 47.16N 8.51E
Rutlam see Ratlām
20 M9 **Rutland** Vermont, NE USA 43.37N 72.58W
99 N19 **Rutland** cultural region C England, UK
23 N8 **Rutledge** Tennessee, S USA 36.16N 83.31W
164 G12 **Rutog** var. Rutok. Xizang Zizhiqu, W China 33.27N 79.43E
Rutok see Rutog
81 P19 **Rutshuru** Nord Kivu, E Dem. Rep. Congo (Zaire) 1.13S 29.27E
100 L8 **Rutten** Flevoland, N Netherlands 52.49N 5.44E
131 Q17 **Rutul** Respublika Dagestan, SW Russian Federation 41.35N 47.30E
95 L14 **Ruukki** Oulu, C Finland 64.40N 25.35E
100 N11 **Ruurlo** Gelderland, E Netherlands 52.04N 6.27E
149 S15 **Ru'ūs al Jibāl** headland Oman/UAE 26.13N 56.23E
144 I7 **Ru'ūs aṭ Ṭiwāl, Jabal** ▲ W Syria
83 H23 **Ruvuma** ◆ region SE Tanzania
83 I25 **Ruvuma** var. Rio Rovuma. ∽ Mozambique/Tanzania see also Rovuma, Rio
Ruwais see Ar Ruways
144 L9 **Ruwayshid, Wadi ar** dry watercourse NE Jordan
147 Z10 **Ruways, Ra's ar** headland E Oman 20.58N 59.00E
81 P18 **Ruwenzori** ▲ Uganda/Dem. Rep. Congo (Zaire)
147 Y8 **Ruwī** NE Oman 23.33N 58.31E
116 F8 **Ruy** ▲ Bulgaria/Yugoslavia 42.52N 22.35E
Ruya see Luia, Rio
83 E20 **Ruyigi** E Burundi 3.28S 30.19E
131 P5 **Ruzayevka** Respublika Mordoviya, W Russian Federation 54.04N 44.56E
121 G18 **Ruzhany** Rus. Ruzhany. Brestskaya Voblasts', SW Belarus 52.52N 24.52E
116 I10 **Rŭzhevo Konare** var. Rŭzhevo Konare. Plovdiv, C Bulgaria 42.16N 24.58E
Ruzhin see Ruzhyn
116 G7 **Ruzhintsi** Vidin, NW Bulgaria 43.38N 22.50E
119 N5 **Ruzhyn** Rus. Ruzhin. Zhytomyrs'ka Oblast', N Ukraine 49.42N 29.01E
113 K19 **Ružomberok** Ger. Rosenberg, Hung. Rózsahegy. Žilinský Kraj, N Slovakia 49.03N 19.18E
113 C16 **Ruzyně** ✕ (Praha) Praha, C Czech Republic 50.06N 14.16E
83 D19 **Rwanda** off. Rwandese Republic; prev. Ruanda. ◆ republic C Africa
Rwandese Republic see Rwanda
97 G22 **Ry** Århus, C Denmark 56.06N 9.46E
Ryasna see Rasna
130 L5 **Ryazan'** Ryazanskaya Oblast', W Russian Federation 54.37N 39.37E
130 L5 **Ryazanskaya Oblast'** ◆ province W Russian Federation
130 M6 **Ryazhsk** Ryazanskaya Oblast', W Russian Federation 53.42N 40.09E
120 B13 **Rybachiy** Ger. Rossitten. Kaliningradskaya Oblast', W Russian Federation 55.09N 20.49E
128 J2 **Rybachiy, Poluostrov** peninsula NW Russian Federation
Rybach'ye see Balykchy
128 L15 **Rybinsk** prev. Andropov. Yaroslavskaya Oblast', W Russian Federation 58.03N 38.52E
128 K14 **Rybinskoye Vodokhranilishche** Eng. Rybinsk Reservoir, Rybinsk Sea. ⊞ W Russian Federation
Rybinsk Reservoir/Rybinsk Sea see Rybinskoye Vodokhranilishche
113 I16 **Rybnik** Śląskie, S Poland 50.05N 18.30E
Rybnitsa see Rîbniţa
113 F16 **Rychnov nad Kněžnou** Ger. Reichenau. Hradecký Kraj, N Czech Republic 50.09N 16.15E
112 I12 **Rychwał** Wielkopolskie, C Poland 52.04N 18.09E
9 O13 **Rycroft** Alberta, W Canada 55.45N 118.42W
97 L21 **Ryd** Kronoberg, S Sweden 56.27N 14.44E
97 L20 **Rydaholm** Jönköping, S Sweden 56.57N 14.19E
204 I8 **Rydberg Peninsula** peninsula Antarctica
99 P23 **Rye** SE England, UK 50.57N 0.42E
35 T10 **Ryegate** Montana, NW USA 46.21N 109.12W
37 S3 **Rye Patch Reservoir** ⊞ Nevada, W USA
97 D15 **Ryfylke** physical region S Norway
97 H16 **Rygge** Østfold, S Norway 59.22N 10.45E
112 N13 **Ryki** Lubelskie, E Poland 51.37N 21.57E
Rykovo see Yenakiyeve
130 I7 **Ryl'sk** Kurskaya Oblast', W Russian Federation 51.34N 34.41E
191 S8 **Rylstone** New South Wales, SE Australia 32.48S 149.58E
113 H17 **Rýmařov** Ger. Römerstadt. Ostravský Kraj, E Czech Republic 49.57N 17.13E
150 E11 **Ryn-Peski** desert W Kazakhstan
171 K12 **Ryōtsu** var. Ryôtu. Niigata, Sado, C Japan 38.02N 138.23E
Ryôtu see Ryōtsu
112 K10 **Rypin** Kujawsko-pomorskie, C Poland 53.03N 19.25E
Ryshkany see Rîşcani
Ryssel see Lille
Ryswick see Rijswijk
97 M24 **Rytterknægten** hill E Denmark 55.07N 14.53E
171 Kk16 **Ryūgasaki** Ibaraki, Honshū, S Japan 35.54N 140.11E
198 G5 **Ryukyu Trench** var. Nansei Syotō Trench. undersea feature S East China Sea
112 D11 **Rzepin** Ger. Reppen. Lubuskie, W Poland 52.20N 14.48E
113 N16 **Rzeszów** Podkarpackie, SE Poland 50.04N 22.00E
128 I16 **Rzhev** Tverskaya Oblast', W Russian Federation 56.16N 34.21E
Rzhishchev see Rzhyshchiv
119 P5 **Rzhyshchiv** Rus. Rzhishchev. Kyyivs'ka Oblast', N Ukraine 49.58N 31.01E

S

144 E11 **Sa'ad** Southern, W Israel 31.27N 34.31E
111 P7 **Saalach** ∽ W Austria
103 L14 **Saale** ∽ C Germany
103 L17 **Saalfeld** var. Saalfeld an der Saale. Thüringen, C Germany 50.39N 11.22E
Saalfeld see Zalewo
Saalfeld an der Saale see Saalfeld
110 C8 **Saane** ∽ W Switzerland
103 D19 **Saar** Fr. Sarre. ∽ France/Germany
103 E20 **Saarbrücken** Fr. Sarrebruck. Saarland, SW Germany 49.13N 7.01E
Saarburg see Sarrebourg
Saare see Saaremaa
120 D6 **Sääre** var. Sjar. Saaremaa, W Estonia 57.55N 22.03E
120 D5 **Saaremaa** off. Saare Maakond. ◆ province W Estonia
120 E6 **Saaremaa** Ger. Oesel, Ösel; prev. Saare. island W Estonia
94 L12 **Saarenkylä** Lappi, N Finland 66.31N 25.51E
Saargemund see Sarreguemines
95 L17 **Saarijärvi** Länsi-Suomi, W Finland 62.42N 25.16E
Saar in Mähren see Žďár nad Sázavou
94 M10 **Saariselkä** Lapp. Suoločielgi. Lappi, N Finland 68.26N 27.28E
94 L10 **Saariselkä** hill range NE Finland
103 D20 **Saarland** Fr. Sarre. ◆ state SW Germany
Saarlautern see Saarlouis
103 D20 **Saarlouis** prev. Saarlautern. Saarland, SW Germany 49.18N 6.49E
110 E11 **Saaser Vispa** ∽ S Switzerland
143 X12 **Saatlı** Rus. Saatly. C Azerbaijan 39.57N 48.24E
Saatly see Saatlı
Saaz see Žatec
176 X9 **Saba** Papua, E Indonesia 1.04S 136.15E
47 V9 **Saba** island N Netherlands Antilles
144 J7 **Sab' Ābār** var. Sab'a Biyar, Sa'b Bi'ār. Ḩimş, C Syria 33.46N 37.40E
Sab'a Biyar see Sab' Ābār
114 K11 **Šabac** Serbia, W Yugoslavia 44.45N 19.42E
107 W5 **Sabadell** Cataluña, E Spain 41.33N 2.07E
171 Hh13 **Sabae** Fukui, Honshū, SW Japan 36.00N 136.12E
175 O3 **Sabah** prev. British North Borneo, North Borneo. ◆ state East Malaysia
174 Gg4 **Sabak** var. Sabak Bernam. Selangor, Peninsular Malaysia 3.45N 100.58E
Sabak Bernam see Sabak
40 D16 **Sabak, Cape** headland Agattu Island, Alaska, USA 52.21N 173.43E
83 J20 **Sabaki** ∽ S Kenya
175 P14 **Sabalana, Kepulauan** var. Kepulauan Liukang Tenggaya. island group C Indonesia
148 L2 **Sabalān, Kuhhā-ye** ▲ NW Iran 38.21N 47.47E
160 H7 **Sabalgarh** Madhya Pradesh, C India 26.18N 77.28E
46 E4 **Sabana, Archipiélago de** island group C Cuba
44 H7 **Sabanagrande** var. Sabana Grande. Francisco Morazán, S Honduras 13.48N 87.15W
56 E5 **Sabanalarga** Atlántico, N Colombia 10.37N 74.55W
43 W14 **Sabancuy** Campeche, SE Mexico 18.56N 91.08W
47 N8 **Sabaneta** NW Dominican Republic 19.27N 71.22W
56 J4 **Sabaneta** Falcón, N Venezuela 11.15N 70.04W
196 H4 **Sabaneta, Puntan** prev. Ushi Point. headland Saipan, S Northern Mariana Islands 15.17N 145.49E
176 Y12 **Sabang** Papua, E Indonesia 4.33S 138.42E
118 L10 **Săbăoani** Neamţ, NE Romania 47.01N 26.51E
161 J26 **Sabaragamuwa Province** ◆ province C Sri Lanka
Sabaria see Szombathely
160 D10 **Sābarmati** ∽ NW India
175 T6 **Sabatai** Pulau Morotai, E Indonesia 2.04N 128.23E
147 Q15 **Sab'atayn, Ramlat as** desert C Yemen
109 I16 **Sabaudia** Lazio, C Italy 41.17N 13.02E
59 J19 **Sabaya** Oruro, S Bolivia 19.09S 68.20W
Sa'b Bi'ār see Sab' Ābār
Sabbioncello see Orebić
154 I8 **Šāberī, Hāmūn-e** var. Daryācheh-ye Hāmūn, Daryācheh-ye Sīstān. ◎ Afghanistan/Iran see also Sīstān, Daryācheh-ye
29 P2 **Sabetha** Kansas, C USA 39.54N 95.48W
77 P10 **Sabhā** C Libya 27.01N 14.25E
69 V13 **Sabi** var. Rio Save. ∽ Mozambique/Zimbabwe see also Save, Rio
120 E8 **Sabile** Ger. Zabeln. Talsi, NW Latvia 57.03N 22.33E
33 R14 **Sabina** Ohio, N USA 39.29N 83.38W
42 I3 **Sabinal** Chihuahua, N Mexico 30.59N 107.29W
27 Q12 **Sabinal** Texas, SW USA 29.19N 99.28W
27 Q11 **Sabinal River** ∽ Texas, SW USA
107 S4 **Sabiñánigo** Aragón, NE Spain 42.31N 0.22W
43 N6 **Sabinas** Coahuila de Zaragoza, NE Mexico 27.52N 101.04W
43 O8 **Sabinas Hidalgo** Nuevo León, NE Mexico 26.28N 100.08W
43 N6 **Sabinas, Río** ∽ NE Mexico
24 F9 **Sabine Lake** ◎ Louisiana/Texas, S USA
94 O3 **Sabine Land** physical region C Svalbard
27 W7 **Sabine River** ∽ Louisiana/Texas, SW USA
143 X12 **Sabirabad** C Azerbaijan 40.00N 48.27E
Sabkha see As Sabkhah
179 P12 **Sablayan** Mindoro, N Philippines 12.48N 120.48E
11 P16 **Sable, Cape** headland Newfoundland and Labrador, SE Canada 43.21N 65.40W
25 X17 **Sable, Cape** headland Florida, SE USA 25.12N 81.06W
11 R16 **Sable Island** island Nova Scotia, SE Canada
12 L11 **Sables, Lac des** ◎ Quebec, SE Canada
12 E10 **Sables, Rivière aux** ∽ Ontario, S Canada
104 K7 **Sable-sur-Sarthe** Sarthe, NW France 47.49N 0.19W
129 U7 **Sablya, Gora** ▲ NW Russian Federation 64.46N 58.52E
79 U14 **Sabon Birnin Gwari** Kaduna, C Nigeria 10.43N 6.39E
79 V11 **Sabon Kafi** Zinder, C Niger 14.37N 8.46E
106 I6 **Sabor, Rio** ∽ N Portugal
12 J8 **Sabourin, Lac** ◎ Quebec, SE Canada
104 J14 **Sabres** Landes, SW France 44.07N 0.46W
205 X13 **Sabrina Coast** physical region Antarctica
146 M11 **Sabt al Ulayā** 'Asīr, SW Saudi Arabia 19.33N 41.58E
106 I8 **Sabugal** Guarda, N Portugal 40.19N 7.04W
31 Z13 **Sabula** Iowa, C USA 42.04N 90.10W
147 N13 **Şabyā** Jīzān, SW Saudi Arabia 17.49N 42.49E
Sabzawar see Sabzevār
Sabzawaran see Sabzvārān
149 S4 **Sabzevār** var. Sabzawar. Khorāsān, NE Iran 36.13N 57.37E
149 T12 **Sabzvārān** var. Sabzawaran; prev. Jiroft. Kermān, SE Iran 28.40N 57.40E
Sacajawea Peak see Matterhorn
84 C9 **Sacandica** Uíge, NW Angola 6.01S 15.57E
44 A2 **Sacatepéquez** off. Departamento de Sacatepéquez. ◆ department S Guatemala
106 F11 **Sacavém** Lisboa, W Portugal 38.46N 9.06W
31 T13 **Sac City** Iowa, C USA 42.25N 94.59W
107 P8 **Sacedón** Castilla-La Mancha, C Spain 40.28N 2.43W
118 J12 **Săcele** Ger. Vierdörfer, Hung. Négyfalu; prev. Ger. Sieben Dörfer, Hung. Hétfalu. Braşov, C Romania 45.36N 25.40E
10 C8 **Sachigo** Ontario, C Canada 53.52N 92.16W
10 C7 **Sachigo** ∽ Ontario, C Canada
10 C8 **Sachigo Lake** ◎ Ontario, C Canada
169 Y16 **Sach'ŏn** Jap. Sansenhō; prev. Samch'ŏnpŏ. S South Korea 34.55N 128.07E
103 O15 **Sachsen** Eng. Saxony, Fr. Saxe. ◆ state E Germany
103 K14 **Sachsen-Anhalt** Eng. Saxony-Anhalt. ◆ state C Germany
111 R9 **Sachsenburg** Salzburg, S Austria 46.49N 13.23E
Sachsenfeld see Žalec
15 H1 **Sachs Harbour** Banks Island, Northwest Territories, N Canada 72.00N 125.13W
Sächsisch-Reen/Sächsisch-Regen see Reghin
20 H8 **Sackets Harbor** New York, NE USA 43.57N 76.06W
11 P14 **Sackville** New Brunswick, SE Canada 45.54N 64.22W
21 P9 **Saco** Maine, NE USA 43.32N 70.25W
21 P8 **Saco River** ∽ Maine/New Hampshire, NE USA
37 O7 **Sacramento** state capital California, W USA 38.34N 121.29W
39 T14 **Sacramento Mountains** ▲ New Mexico, SW USA
37 N6 **Sacramento River** ∽ California, W USA
37 N5 **Sacramento Valley** valley California, W USA
38 I10 **Sacramento Wash** valley Arizona, SW USA
107 N15 **Sacratif, Cabo** headland S Spain 36.41N 3.30W
118 F9 **Săcueni** prev. Săcuieni, Hung. Székelyhíd. Bihor, W Romania 47.19N 22.04E
Săcuieni see Săcueni
107 R4 **Sádaba** Aragón, NE Spain 42.15N 1.16W
Sá da Bandeira see Lubango
144 I6 **Şadad** Ḩimş, W Syria 34.19N 36.52E
147 O13 **Şa'dah** NW Yemen 16.59N 43.45E
170 Dd14 **Sadamisaki-hantō** peninsula Shikoku, SW Japan
175 P12 **Sadang, Sungai** ∽ Sulawesi, C Indonesia
178 H17 **Sadao** Songkhla, SW Thailand 6.34N 100.22E
148 L8 **Sadd-e Dez, Daryācheh-ye** ◎ W Iran
21 S3 **Saddleback Mountain** hill Maine, NE USA 46.25N 68.00W
21 P6 **Saddleback Mountain** ▲ Maine, NE USA 44.57N 70.27W
178 J14 **Sa Dec** Đông Thap, S Vietnam 10.19N 105.45E
147 W13 **Sadḩ** S Oman 17.10N 55.07E
78 J11 **Sadiola** Kayes, W Mali 13.48N 11.47W
155 R12 **Sādiqābād** Punjab, E Pakistan 28.16N 70.10E
159 Y10 **Sadiya** Assam, NE India 27.49N 95.37E
145 W9 **Sa'diyah, Hawr as** ◎ E Iraq
171 K12 **Sado** var. Sadoga-shima. island C Japan
Sadoga-shima see Sado
106 F12 **Sado, Rio** ∽ S Portugal
116 I8 **Sadovets** Pleven, N Bulgaria 43.19N 24.21E
131 O11 **Sadovoye** Respublika Kalmykiya, SW Russian Federation 47.51N 44.34E
107 W9 **Sa Dragonera** var. Isla Dragonera. island Islas Baleares, Spain, W Mediterranean Sea
97 H20 **Sæby** Nordjylland, N Denmark 57.19N 10.33E
107 P9 **Saelices** Castilla-La Mancha, C Spain 39.55N 2.49W
Saena Julia see Siena
Saetabicula see Alzira
116 O12 **Safaalan** Tekirdağ, NW Turkey 41.26N 28.07E
Safad see Zefat
Şafāqis see Sfax
198 B8 **Safata Bay** bay Upolu, Samoa, C Pacific Ocean
Safed see Zefat
Safed, Āb-i- see Sefīd, Darya-ye
145 X11 **Şaffāf, Ḩawr aş** wetland S Iraq
97 J16 **Säffle** Värmland, C Sweden 59.07N 12.55E
39 N15 **Safford** Arizona, SW USA 32.46N 109.41W
76 E7 **Safi** W Morocco 32.19N 9.14W
149 V9 **Safīdābeh** Khorāsān, E Iran 31.04N 60.30E
148 M4 **Safīd, Rūd-e** ∽ NW Iran
130 I4 **Safonovo** Smolenskaya Oblast', W Russian Federation 55.05N 33.12E
142 H11 **Safranbolu** Karabük, N Turkey 41.16N 32.40E
145 Y13 **Safwān** SE Iraq 30.06N 47.43E
164 J16 **Saga** var. Gya'gya. Xizang Zizhiqu, W China 29.22N 85.19E
170 Cc13 **Saga** Saga, Kyūshū, SW Japan 33.14N 130.16E
170 Cc13 **Saga** off. Saga-ken. ◆ prefecture Kyūshū, SW Japan
171 Ll12 **Sagae** Yamagata, Honshū, C Japan 38.22N 140.13E
177 G5 **Sagaing** Sagaing, C Myanmar 21.55N 95.55E
177 G3 **Sagaing** ◆ division N Myanmar
171 Jj16 **Sagamihara** Kanagawa, Honshū, S Japan 35.32N 139.23E
171 Jj17 **Sagami-nada** inlet SW Japan
171 Jj17 **Sagami-wan** bay SW Japan
Sagan see Żagań
31 Y3 **Saganaga Lake** ◎ Minnesota, N USA
161 F18 **Sāgar** Karnātaka, W India 14.09N 75.02E
160 I9 **Sāgar** prev. Saugor. Madhya Pradesh, C India 23.52N 78.46E
13 S8 **Sagard** Quebec, SE Canada 48.01N 70.03W
Sagarmatha see Everest, Mount
179 Qq13 **Sagay** Negros, C Philippines 10.54N 123.26E
Sagebrush State see Nevada
149 V11 **Sāghand** Yazd, C Iran 32.33N 55.12E
21 N14 **Sag Harbor** Long Island, New York, NE USA 40.59N 72.15W
Saghez see Saqqez
33 R8 **Saginaw** Michigan, N USA 43.25N 83.57W
33 R8 **Saginaw Bay** lake bay Michigan, N USA
150 H11 **Sagiz** Atyrau, W Kazakhstan 48.12N 54.55E
66 H6 **Saglek Bank** undersea feature W Labrador Sea
11 P5 **Saglek Bay** bay SW Labrador Sea
Saglouc/Sagluk see Salluit
105 X15 **Sagonne, Golfe de** gulf Corse, France, C Mediterranean Sea
107 P13 **Sagra** ▲ S Spain 37.59N 2.33W
106 F14 **Sagres** Faro, S Portugal 37.01N 8.55W
39 S7 **Saguache** Colorado, C USA 38.05N 106.05W
46 J7 **Sagua de Tánamo** Holguín, E Cuba 20.34N 75.14W
46 E5 **Sagua la Grande** Villa Clara, C Cuba 22.48N 80.06W
13 R7 **Saguenay** ∽ Quebec, SE Canada
76 C9 **Saguia al Hamra** var. As Saqia al Hamra. ∽ N Western Sahara
Sagunt/Saguntum see Sagunto
107 S9 **Sagunto** var. Sagunt, Ar. Murviedro; anc. Saguntum. País Valenciano, E Spain 39.40N 0.16W
144 H10 **Saḩāb** Al 'Āşimah, NW Jordan 31.52N 36.00E
56 E6 **Sahagún** Córdoba, NW Colombia 8.57N 75.26W
106 L4 **Sahagún** Castilla-León, N Spain 42.22N 5.01W
147 X8 **Saḩam** N Oman 24.06N 56.52E
70 F9 **Sahara** desert Libya/Algeria
77 U9 **Sahara el Gharbîya** var. Aş Şaḩrā' al Gharbīyah, Eng. Western Desert. desert C Egypt
77 X9 **Sahara el Sharqîya** var. Aş Şaḩrā' ash Sharqīyah, Eng. Arabian Desert, Eastern Desert. desert E Egypt
Saharan Atlas see Atlas Saharien
158 J9 **Sahāranpur** Uttar Pradesh, N India 29.58N 77.33E
66 L10 **Saharan Seamounts** var. Saharian Seamounts. undersea feature E Atlantic Ocean 25.00N 20.00W
159 Q13 **Saharsa** Bihār, NE India 25.54N 86.36E
69 O7 **Sahel** physical region C Africa
159 R14 **Sāhibganj** Bihār, NE India 25.15N 87.40E
145 Q7 **Sahīlīyah** C Iraq 33.43N 42.42E
144 H4 **Şāḩilīyah, Jibāl as** ▲ NW Syria
116 M13 **Şahin** Tekirdağ, NW Turkey 41.01N 26.51E
155 U8 **Sāhīwāl** Punjab, E Pakistan 31.57N 72.22E
155 U9 **Sāhīwāl** prev. Montgomery. Punjab, E Pakistan 30.40N 73.04E
147 W11 **Saḩmah, Ramlat as** desert C Oman
145 T13 **Şaḩrā' al Ḩijārah** desert S Iraq
42 H5 **Sahuaripa** Sonora, NW Mexico 29.02N 109.14W
38 M16 **Sahuarita** Arizona, SW USA 31.24N 110.55W
42 L13 **Sahuayo** var. Sahuayo de José María Morelos; prev. Sahuayo de Díaz, Sahuayo de Porfirio Díaz. Michoacán de Ocampo, SW Mexico 20.04N 102.44W
Sahuayo de Díaz/Sahuayo de José María Morelos/Sahuayo de Porfirio Díaz see Sahuayo
181 W8 **Sahul Shelf** undersea feature N Timor Sea
178 Hh17 **Sai Buri** Pattani, SW Thailand 6.42N 101.37E
76 I6 **Saïda** NW Algeria 34.49N 0.10E
144 G7 **Saïda** var. Şaydā, Sayida; anc. Sidon. W Lebanon 33.20N 35.24E
Sa'īdābād see Sīrjān
82 B13 **Sa'id Bundas** Western Bahr el Ghazal, SW Sudan 8.24N 24.53E
194 J12 **Saidor** Madang, N PNG 5.37S 146.28E
159 S13 **Saidpur** var. Syedpur. Rajshahi, NW Bangladesh 25.48N 89.00E
110 C7 **Saignelégier** Jura, NW Switzerland 47.18N 7.03E
170 G11 **Saigō** Shimane, Dōgo, SW Japan 36.12N 133.18E
Saigon see Hô Chi Minh
168 I12 **Saihan Toroi** Nei Mongol Zizhiqu, N China 41.44N 100.29E
Saihon Tal see Sonid Youqi
Sai Hun see Syr Darya
94 M11 **Saija** Lappi, NE Finland 67.07N 28.46E
170 Ee14 **Saijō** Ehime, Shikoku, SW Japan 33.55N 133.10E
170 Dd15 **Saiki** Ōita, Kyūshū, SW Japan 32.57N 131.52E
176 Uu9 **Saileen** Papua, E Indonesia 1.14S 130.56E
95 N18 **Saimaa** ◎ SE Finland
95 N18 **Saimaa Canal** Fin. Saimaan Kanava, Rus. Saymenskiy Kanal. canal Finland/Russian Federation
Saimaan Kanava see Saimaa Canal
42 L10 **Saín Alto** Zacatecas, C Mexico 23.38N 103.13W
98 L12 **St Abb's Head** headland SE Scotland, UK 55.54N 2.07W
9 Y16 **St.Adolphe** Manitoba, S Canada 49.39N 96.55W
105 O15 **St-Affrique** Aveyron, S France 43.57N 2.52E
13 Q10 **St-Agapit** Quebec, SE Canada 46.33N 71.25W
99 O21 **St Albans** anc. Verulamium. E England, UK 51.46N 0.21W
20 L6 **Saint Albans** Vermont, NE USA 44.49N 73.07W
23 Q5 **Saint Albans** West Virginia, NE USA 38.21N 81.47W
St Alban's Head see St.Aldhelm's Head
9 Q14 **St.Albert** Alberta, SW Canada 53.37N 113.37W
99 M24 **St. Aldhelm's Head** var. St.Alban's Head. headland S England, UK 50.34N 2.04W
13 S8 **St-Alexandre** Quebec, SE Canada 47.39N 69.36W

◆ Country · ● Country Capital · ◇ Dependent Territory · ○ Dependent Territory Capital · ◆ Administrative Region · ✕ International Airport · ▲ Mountain · ▲ Mountain Range · ⛰ Volcano · ∽ River · ◎ Lake · ⊞ Reservoir

13 O11 **St-Alexis-des-Monts** Quebec, SE Canada 46.30N 73.08W
105 P2 **St-Amand-les-Eaux** Nord, N France 50.27N 3.25E
105 O9 **St-Amand-Montrond** *var.* St-Amand-Mont-Rond. Cher, C France 46.43N 2.28E
13 Q7 **St-Ambroise** Quebec, SE Canada 48.35N 71.19W
181 P16 **St-André** NE Réunion
12 M12 **St-André-Avellin** Quebec, SE Canada 45.45N 75.04W
104 K12 **St-André-de-Cubzac** Gironde, SW France 45.01N 0.26W
98 K11 **St Andrews** E Scotland, UK 56.20N 2.48W
25 Q9 **Saint Andrews Bay** *bay* Florida, SE USA
25 W7 **Saint Andrew Sound** *sound* Georgia, SE USA
Saint Anna Trough *see* Svyataya Anna Trough
46 J11 **St.Ann's Bay** C Jamaica 18.25N 77.12W
11 T10 **St.Anthony** Newfoundland and Labrador, SE Canada 51.21N 55.34W
35 R13 **Saint Anthony** Idaho, NW USA 43.56N 111.38W
190 M11 **Saint Arnaud** Victoria, SE Australia 36.39S 143.15E
193 I15 **St.Arnaud Range** ▲ South Island, NZ
13 T8 **St-Arsène** Quebec, SE Canada 47.55N 69.21W
11 R10 **St-Augustin** Quebec, E Canada 51.13N 58.39W
25 X9 **Saint Augustine** Florida, SE USA 29.54N 81.19W
99 H24 **St Austell** SW England, UK 50.21N 4.46W
105 T4 **St-Avold** Moselle, NE France 49.06N 6.43E
105 N17 **St-Barthélemy** ▲ S France
104 L17 **St-Béat** Haute-Garonne, S France 42.55N 0.39E
99 I15 **St Bees Head** *headland* NW England, UK 54.30N 3.39W
181 P16 **St-Benoit** E Réunion
105 T13 **St-Bonnet** Hautes-Alpes, SE France 44.41N 6.04E
St.Botolph's Town *see* Boston
99 G21 **St Brides Bay** *inlet* SW Wales, UK
104 H5 **St-Brieuc** Côtes d'Armor, NW France 48.31N 2.45W
104 H5 **St-Brieuc, Baie de** *bay* NW France
104 L7 **St-Calais** Sarthe, NW France 47.55N 0.48E
13 Q10 **St-Casimir** Quebec, SE Canada 46.40N 72.05W
12 H16 **St.Catharines** Ontario, S Canada 43.10N 79.15W
47 S14 **St.Catherine, Mount** ▲ N Grenada 12.10N 61.41W
66 C11 **St Catherine Point** *headland* E Bermuda
25 X6 **Saint Catherines Island** *island* Georgia, SE USA
99 M24 **St Catherine's Point** *headland* S England, UK 50.34N 1.17W
105 N13 **St-Céré** Lot, S France 44.50N 1.53E
110 A10 **St.Cergue** Vaud, W Switzerland 46.25N 6.10E
105 R11 **St-Chamond** Loire, E France 45.28N 4.31E
35 S16 **Saint Charles** Idaho, NW USA 42.05N 111.23W
29 X4 **Saint Charles** Missouri, C USA 38.48N 90.28W
105 P13 **St-Chély-d'Apcher** Lozère, S France 44.51N 3.16E
Saint Christopher-Nevis *see* Saint Kitts and Nevis
33 S9 **Saint Clair** Michigan, N USA 42.49N 82.29W
12 D17 **St.Clair** ⇝ Canada/USA
191 O17 **St.Clair, Lake** ◎ Tasmania, SE Australia
12 C17 **St.Clair, Lake** *var.* Lac à L'eau Claire. ◎ Canada/USA
33 S10 **Saint Clair Shores** Michigan, N USA 42.30N 82.53W
105 S10 **St-Claude** *anc.* Condate. Jura, E France 46.22N 5.52E
47 X6 **St-Claude** Basse Terre, SW Guadeloupe 16.01N 61.41W
25 X12 **Saint Cloud** Florida, SE USA 28.15N 81.15W
31 U8 **Saint Cloud** Minnesota, N USA 45.33N 94.09W
47 T9 **Saint Croix** *island* S Virgin Islands (US)
32 J4 **Saint Croix Flowage** ▣ Wisconsin, N USA
21 T5 **Saint Croix River** ⇝ Canada/USA
31 W7 **Saint Croix River** ⇝ Minnesota/Wisconsin, N USA
47 S14 **St.David's** SE Grenada 12.01N 61.40W
99 H21 **St David's** SW Wales, UK 51.53N 5.16W
99 G21 **St David's Head** *headland* SW Wales, UK 51.54N 5.19W
66 C12 **St David's Island** *island* E Bermuda
181 O16 **St-Denis** ○ (Réunion) NW Réunion 20.55S 14.33E
105 U6 **St-Dié** Vosges, NE France 48.16N 6.57E
105 R5 **St-Dizier** *anc.* Desiderii Fanum. Haute-Marne, N France 48.39N 5.00E
13 N11 **St-Donat** Quebec, SE Canada 46.16N 74.12W
13 N11 **Ste-Adèle** Quebec, SE Canada 45.58N 74.10W
13 N11 **Ste-Agathe-des-Monts** Quebec, SE Canada 46.03N 74.19W
180 I16 **Sainte Anne** *island* Inner Islands, NE Seychelles
9 Y16 **Ste.Anne** Manitoba, S Canada 49.40N 96.40W
47 R12 **Ste-Anne** Grande Terre, E Guadeloupe 16.13N 61.22W
47 Y6 **Ste-Anne** SE Martinique 14.25N 60.53W
13 Q10 **Ste-Anne** ⇝ Quebec, SE Canada
13 W6 **Ste-Anne-des-Monts** Quebec, SE Canada 49.07N 66.28W
12 M10 **Ste-Anne-du-Lac** Quebec, SE Canada 46.51N 75.20W
13 U4 **Ste-Anne, Lac** ◎ Quebec, SE Canada
13 S10 **Ste-Apolline** Quebec, SE Canada 46.47N 70.15W
13 U7 **Ste-Blandine** Quebec, SE Canada 48.22N 68.27W
13 R10 **Ste-Claire** Quebec, SE Canada 46.30N 70.40W
13 Q10 **Ste-Croix** Quebec, SE Canada 46.36N 71.42W
110 B8 **Ste.Croix** Vaud, SW Switzerland 46.49N 6.31E
105 P14 **Ste-Énimie** Lozère, S France 44.21N 3.26E
29 Y6 **Sainte Genevieve** Missouri, C USA 37.57N 90.01W
105 S12 **St-Egrève** Isère, E France 45.15N 5.40E
41 T12 **Saint Elias, Cape** *headland* Kayak Island, Alaska, USA 59.48N 144.36W
41 U11 **Saint Elias, Mount** ▲ Alaska, USA 60.18N 140.57W
8 G8 **Saint Elias Mountains** ▲ Canada/USA
57 Y10 **St-Élie** N French Guiana 4.49N 53.21W
105 O10 **St-Eloy-les-Mines** Puy-de-Dôme, C France 46.07N 2.50E
13 S7 **Ste-Marguerite Nord-Est** ⇝ Quebec, SE Canada
13 R7 **Ste-Marguerite** ⇝ Quebec, SE Canada
13 V4 **Ste-Marguerite, Pointe** *headland* Quebec, SE Canada 50.01N 66.43W
13 V3 **Ste-Marguesite** ⇝ Quebec, SE Canada
13 R10 **Ste-Marie** Quebec, SE Canada 46.28N 71.00W
47 Q11 **Ste-Marie** NE Martinique 14.48N 61.01W
181 P16 **Ste-Marie** NE Réunion
105 U6 **Ste-Marie-aux-Mines** Haut-Rhin, NE France 48.16N 7.12E
10 J14 **Ste-Marie, Lac** ▣ Quebec, S Canada
180 K4 **Sainte Marie, Nosy** *island* E Madagascar
104 L8 **Ste-Maure-de-Touraine** Indre-et-Loire, C France 47.06N 0.38E
105 R4 **Ste-Menehould** Marne, NE France 49.06N 4.54E
Ste-Perpétue *see* Ste-Perpétue-de-l'Islet
13 S9 **Ste-Perpétue-de-l'Islet** *var.* Ste-Perpétue. Quebec, SE Canada 47.02N 69.54W
47 X11 **Ste-Rose** Basse Terre, N Guadeloupe 16.20N 61.41W
181 P16 **Ste-Rose** E Réunion
9 W15 **Ste.Rose du Lac** Manitoba, S Canada 51.04N 99.31W
104 J11 **Saintes** *anc.* Mediolanum. Charente-Maritime, W France 45.45N 0.37W
47 X7 **Saintes, Canal des** *channel* SW Guadeloupe
Saintes, Îles des *see* les Saintes
181 P16 **Ste-Suzanne** N Réunion
13 P10 **Ste-Thècle** Quebec, SE Canada 46.48N 72.31W
105 Q12 **St-Étienne** Loire, E France 45.25N 4.22E
104 M4 **St-Étienne-du-Rouvray** Seine-Maritime, N France 49.22N 1.07E
Saint Eustatius *see* Sint Eustatius
12 M11 **Ste-Véronique** Quebec, SE Canada 46.30N 74.58W
13 T7 **St-Fabien** Quebec, SE Canada 48.19N 68.51W
13 P7 **St-Félicien** Quebec, SE Canada 48.38N 72.28W
13 O11 **St-Félix-de-Valois** Quebec, SE Canada 46.10N 73.25W
105 Y14 **St-Florent** Corse, France, C Mediterranean Sea 42.41N 9.19E
105 Y14 **St-Florent, Golfe de** *gulf* Corse, France, C Mediterranean Sea
105 P6 **St-Florentin** Yonne, C France 48.00N 3.46E
105 N9 **St-Florent-sur-Cher** Cher, C France 47.00N 2.13E
105 P12 **St-Flour** Cantal, C France 45.01N 3.04E
28 H2 **Saint Francis** Kansas, C USA 39.45N 101.31W
85 H26 **St.Francis, Cape** *headland* S South Africa 34.11S 24.45E
29 X10 **Saint Francis River** ⇝ Arkansas/Missouri, C USA
24 J8 **Saint Francisville** Louisiana, S USA 30.46N 91.22W
13 Q12 **St-François** ⇝ Quebec, SE Canada
47 Y6 **St-François** Grande Terre, E Guadeloupe 16.15N 61.16W
13 R11 **St-François, Lac** ◎ Quebec, SE Canada
29 X7 **Saint Francois Mountains** ▲ Missouri, C USA
St-Gall/Saint Gall/St.Gallen *see* Sankt Gallen
104 L16 **St-Gaudens** Haute-Garonne, S France 43.07N 0.43E
13 R12 **St-Gédéon** Quebec, SE Canada 45.51N 70.36W
189 X10 **Saint George** Queensland, E Australia 28.04S 148.29E
66 B12 **St George** N Bermuda 32.24N 64.42W
40 K15 **Saint George** Saint George Island, Alaska, USA 56.34N 169.30W
23 S14 **Saint George** South Carolina, SE USA 33.10N 80.34W
38 J8 **Saint George** Utah, W USA 37.06N 113.35W
11 R12 **St.George, Cape** *headland* Newfoundland and Labrador, E Canada 48.26N 59.17W
195 P11 **St.George, Cape** *headland* New Ireland, NE PNG 4.49S 152.52E
40 J15 **Saint George Island** *island* Pribilof Islands, Alaska, USA
25 S10 **Saint George Island** *island* Florida, SE USA
101 J19 **Saint-Georges** Liège, E Belgium 50.36N 5.20E
13 R11 **St-Georges** Quebec, SE Canada 46.07N 70.40W
57 Z11 **St-Georges** E French Guiana 3.55N 51.49W
47 R14 **St.George's** ● (Grenada) SW Grenada 12.03N 61.45W
11 R12 **St.George's Bay** *inlet* Newfoundland and Labrador, E Canada
99 G21 **Saint George's Channel** *channel* Ireland/Wales, UK
195 P10 **St.George's Channel** *channel* NE PNG
66 B11 **St George's Island** *island* E Bermuda
101 I21 **Saint-Gérard** Namur, S Belgium 50.20N 4.47E
St-Germain *see* St-Germain-en-Laye
13 P12 **St-Germain-de-Grantham** Quebec, SE Canada 45.49N 72.32W
105 N5 **St-Germain-en-Laye** *var.* St-Germain. Yvelines, N France 48.52N 2.04E
104 H8 **St-Gildas, Pointe du** *headland* NW France 47.09N 2.25W
105 R15 **St-Gilles** Gard, S France 43.41N 4.24E
104 I9 **St-Gilles-Croix-de-Vie** Vendée, NW France 46.41N 1.55W
181 O16 **St-Gilles-les-Bains** W Réunion 21.01S 55.13E
104 M16 **St-Girons** Ariège, S France 42.58N 1.07E
Saint Gotthard *see* Szentgotthárd
110 G9 **St.Gotthard Tunnel** *tunnel* Ticino, S Switzerland
99 H22 **St Govan's Head** *headland* SW Wales, UK 51.35N 4.55W
36 M7 **Saint Helena** California, W USA 38.29N 122.30W
67 F24 **Saint Helena** ◇ *UK dependent territory* C Atlantic Ocean
69 O12 **Saint Helena** *island* C Atlantic Ocean
85 E25 **St.Helena Bay** *bay* SW South Africa
67 M16 **Saint Helena Fracture Zone** *tectonic feature* C Atlantic Ocean
36 M7 **Saint Helena, Mount** ▲ California, W USA 38.40N 122.39W
23 S15 **Saint Helena Sound** *inlet* South Carolina, SE USA
33 Q7 **Saint Helen, Lake** ◎ Michigan, N USA
191 Q16 **Saint Helens** Tasmania, SE Australia 41.21S 148.15E
99 K18 **St Helens** NW England, UK 53.28N 2.43W
34 G10 **Saint Helens** Oregon, NW USA 45.55N 122.51W
34 H10 **Saint Helens, Mount** ℞ Washington, NW USA 46.24N 121.49W
99 L26 **St Helier** ○ (Jersey) S Jersey, Channel Islands 49.12N 2.07W
13 S9 **St-Hilarion** Quebec, SE Canada 47.34N 70.24W
101 K22 **Saint-Hubert** Luxembourg, SE Belgium 50.02N 5.23E
13 T8 **St-Hubert** Quebec, SE Canada 47.46N 69.15W
13 P12 **St-Hyacinthe** Quebec, SE Canada 45.37N 72.57W
St.Iago de la Vega *see* Spanish Town
33 Q4 **Saint Ignace** Michigan, N USA 45.52N 84.43W
13 O10 **St-Ignace-du-Lac** Quebec, SE Canada 46.43N 73.49W
10 D12 **St.Ignace Island** *island* Ontario, S Canada
110 C7 **St.Imier** Bern, W Switzerland 47.09N 6.55E
99 G25 **St Ives** SW England, UK 50.12N 5.28W
31 U10 **Saint James** Minnesota, N USA 43.58N 94.40W
8 I15 **St.James, Cape** *headland* Graham Island, British Columbia, SW Canada 51.57N 131.04W
13 O13 **St-Jean** *var.* St-Jean-sur-Richelieu. Quebec, SE Canada 45.15N 73.16W
57 X9 **St-Jean** NW French Guiana 5.21N 54.09W
13 R8 **St-Jean** ⇝ Quebec, SE Canada
Saint-Jean-d'Acre *see* 'Akko
104 K11 **St-Jean-d'Angély** Charente-Maritime, W France 45.57N 0.31W
105 N7 **St-Jean-de-Braye** Loiret, C France 47.54N 1.58E
104 I16 **St-Jean-de-Luz** Pyrénées-Atlantiques, SW France 43.24N 1.40W
105 T12 **St-Jean-de-Maurienne** Savoie, E France 45.16N 6.21E
104 I9 **St-Jean-de-Monts** Vendée, NW France 46.45N 2.00W
105 Q14 **St-Jean-du-Gard** Gard, S France 44.06N 3.49E
13 Q7 **St-Jean, Lac** ◎ Quebec, SE Canada
104 I16 **St-Jean-Pied-de-Port** Pyrénées-Atlantiques, SW France 43.10N 1.13W
13 S9 **St-Jean-Port-Joli** Quebec, SE Canada 47.13N 70.16W
St-Jean-sur-Richelieu *see* St-Jean
13 N12 **St-Jérôme** Quebec, SE Canada 45.46N 74.01W
27 T5 **Saint Jo** Texas, SW USA 33.42N 97.33W
11 O15 **St.John** New Brunswick, SE Canada 45.16N 66.03W
28 L6 **Saint John** Kansas, C USA 37.59N 98.44W
78 K16 **Saint John** ⇝ C Liberia
47 T9 **Saint John** *island* C Virgin Islands (US)
24 I6 **Saint John, Lake** ◎ Louisiana, S USA
21 Q2 **Saint John** *Fr.* Saint-John. ⇝ Canada/USA
47 W10 **St John's** ● (Antigua and Barbuda) Antigua, Antigua and Barbuda 17.06N 61.50W
11 V12 **St.John's** Newfoundland and Labrador, E Canada 47.34N 52.40W
39 O12 **Saint Johns** Arizona, SW USA 34.28N 109.22W
33 Q9 **Saint Johns** Michigan, N USA 42.58N 84.31W
11 V12 **St.John's** ✖ Newfoundland and Labrador, E Canada 47.22N 52.45W
25 X11 **Saint Johns River** ⇝ Florida, SE USA
47 N12 **St.Joseph** W Dominica 15.24N 61.25W
181 P17 **St-Joseph** S Réunion
24 J6 **Saint Joseph** Louisiana, S USA 31.56N 91.14W
33 O10 **Saint Joseph** Michigan, N USA 42.04N 86.30W
29 R3 **Saint Joseph** Missouri, C USA 39.45N 94.49W
22 I10 **Saint Joseph** Tennessee, S USA 35.02N 87.29W
24 R9 **Saint Joseph Bay** *bay* Florida, SE USA
13 R11 **St-Joseph-de-Beauce** Quebec, SE Canada 46.20N 70.52W
10 C10 **St.Joseph, Lake** ◎ Ontario, C Canada
33 Q11 **Saint Joseph River** ⇝ N USA
12 C11 **Saint Joseph's Island** *island* Ontario, S Canada
13 N11 **St-Jovite** Quebec, SE Canada 46.07N 74.35W
123 Jj16 **St Julian's** N Malta 35.55N 14.29E
St-Julien *see* St-Julien-en-Genevois
105 T10 **St-Julien-en-Genevois** *var.* St-Julien. Haute-Savoie, E France 46.07N 6.06E
104 M11 **St-Junien** Haute-Vienne, C France 45.52N 0.54E
105 Q11 **St-Just-St-Rambert** Loire, E France 45.30N 4.13E
98 D8 **St Kilda** *island* NW Scotland, UK
47 V10 **Saint Kitts** *island* Saint Kitts and Nevis
47 U10 **Saint Kitts and Nevis** *off.* Federation of Saint Christopher and Nevis, *var.* Saint Christopher-Nevis. ◆ *commonwealth republic* E West Indies
9 X16 **St.Laurent** Manitoba, S Canada 50.20N 97.55W
St-Laurent *see* St-Laurent-du-Maroni
57 X9 **St-Laurent-du-Maroni** *var.* St-Laurent. NW French Guiana 5.28N 54.03W
St-Laurent, Fleuve *see* St.Lawrence
104 J12 **St-Laurent-Médoc** Gironde, SW France 45.11N 0.50W
11 N12 **St.Lawrence** *Fr.* Fleuve St-Laurent. ⇝ Canada/USA
11 Q12 **St.Lawrence, Gulf of** *gulf* NW Atlantic Ocean
40 K10 **Saint Lawrence Island** *island* Alaska, USA
12 M14 **Saint Lawrence River** ⇝ Canada/USA
101 L25 **Saint-Léger** Luxembourg, SE Belgium 49.36N 5.39E
11 N14 **St.Léonard** New Brunswick, SE Canada 47.10N 67.55W
13 P11 **St-Léonard** Quebec, SE Canada 46.06N 72.18W
181 O17 **St-Leu** W Réunion 21.09S 55.16E
104 J4 **St-Lô** *anc.* Briovera, Laudus. Manche, N France 49.07N 1.08W
9 T15 **St.Louis** Saskatchewan, S Canada 52.50N 105.43W
105 V7 **St-Louis** Haut-Rhin, NE France 47.34N 7.34E
181 O17 **St-Louis** S Réunion
78 G10 **Saint Louis** NW Senegal 15.58N 16.30W
29 X4 **Saint Louis** Missouri, C USA 38.38N 90.15W
31 W5 **Saint Louis River** ⇝ Minnesota, N USA
105 T7 **St-Loup-sur-Semouse** Haute-Saône, E France 47.53N 6.15E
13 O12 **St-Luc** Quebec, SE Canada 45.19N 73.18W
85 L22 **St.Lucia** KwaZulu/Natal, E South Africa 28.22S 32.25E
47 X13 **Saint Lucia** ◆ *commonwealth republic* SE West Indies
49 S3 **Saint Lucia** *island* SE West Indies
85 L22 **St.Lucia, Cape** *headland* E South Africa 28.29S 32.26E
47 Y13 **Saint Lucia Channel** *channel* Martinique/Saint Lucia
25 Y14 **Saint Lucie Canal** *canal* Florida, SE USA
25 Z13 **Saint Lucie Inlet** *inlet* Florida, SE USA
98 L2 **St Magnus Bay** *bay* N Scotland, UK
104 K10 **St-Maixent-l'École** Deux-Sèvres, W France 46.24N 0.13W
9 Y16 **St.Malo** Manitoba, S Canada 49.16N 96.58W
104 I5 **St-Malo** Ille-et-Vilaine, NW France 48.39N 2.00W
104 H4 **St-Malo, Golfe de** *gulf* NW France
46 L9 **St-Marc** C Haiti 19.05N 72.42W
46 L9 **St-Marc, Canal de** *channel* W Haiti
57 Y12 **Saint-Marcel, Mont** ▲ S French Guiana 2.32N 53.00W
105 S12 **St-Marcellin-le-Mollard** Isère, E France 45.12N 5.18E
98 K5 **St Margaret's Hope** NE Scotland, UK 58.49N 2.57W
34 M9 **Saint Maries** Idaho, NW USA 47.19N 116.37W
25 T9 **Saint Marks** Florida, SE USA 30.09N 84.12W
110 D11 **St.Martin** Valais, SW Switzerland 46.09N 7.27E
Saint Martin *see* Sint Maarten
33 O5 **Saint Martin Island** *island* Michigan, N USA
24 I9 **Saint Martinville** Louisiana, S USA 30.09N 91.51W
193 E20 **St.Mary, Mount** ▲ South Island, NZ 44.16S 169.42E
194 K14 **St.Mary, Mount** ▲ S PNG 8.06S 147.00E
190 I6 **Saint Mary Peak** ▲ South Australia 31.25S 138.39E
191 Q16 **Saint Marys** Tasmania, SE Australia 41.34S 148.13E
12 E16 **St.Marys** Ontario, S Canada 43.15N 81.08W
40 M11 **Saint Marys** Alaska, USA 62.03N 163.10W
25 W8 **Saint Marys** Georgia, SE USA 30.44N 81.30W
29 P4 **Saint Marys** Kansas, C USA 39.09N 96.00W
33 Q4 **Saint Marys** Ohio, N USA 40.31N 84.22W
23 R3 **Saint Marys** West Virginia, NE USA 39.23N 81.11W
25 W8 **Saint Marys River** ⇝ Florida/Georgia, SE USA
33 Q4 **Saint Marys River** ⇝ Michigan, N USA
104 D6 **St-Mathieu, Pointe** *headland* NW France 48.17N 4.56W
40 J12 **Saint Matthew Island** *island* Alaska, USA
23 R13 **Saint Matthews** South Carolina, SE USA 33.40N 80.46W
St.Matthew's Island *see* Zadetkyi Kyun
194 M8 **St.Matthias Group** *island group* NE PNG
110 C11 **St.Maurice** Valais, SW Switzerland 46.09N 7.28E
13 P9 **St-Maurice** ⇝ Quebec, SE Canada
104 J13 **St-Médard-en-Jalles** Gironde, SW France 44.54N 0.43W
41 N10 **Saint Michael** Alaska, USA 63.28N 162.02W
St.Michel *see* Mikkeli
13 N10 **St-Michel-des-Saints** Quebec, SE Canada 46.39N 73.54W
105 S5 **St-Mihiel** Meuse, NE France 48.57N 5.33E
110 J10 **St.Moritz** *Ger.* Sankt Moritz, *Rmsch.* San Murezzan. Graubünden, SE Switzerland 46.30N 9.50E
104 H8 **St-Nazaire** Loire-Atlantique, NW France 47.16N 2.12W
Saint Nicholas *see* São Nicolau
Saint-Nicolas *see* Sint-Niklaas
105 N1 **St-Omer** Pas-de-Calais, N France 50.45N 2.15E
Saintonge *cultural region* W France
13 S9 **St-Pacôme** Quebec, SE Canada 47.22N 69.56W
13 S10 **St-Pamphile** Quebec, SE Canada 46.57N 69.46W
13 S9 **St-Pascal** Quebec, SE Canada 47.25N 69.51W
12 J11 **St-Patrice, Lac** ◎ Quebec, SE Canada
9 R14 **St.Paul** Alberta, SW Canada 54.00N 111.18W
181 O16 **St-Paul** NW Réunion
40 K14 **Saint Paul** Saint Paul Island, Alaska, USA 57.08N 170.13W
31 V8 **Saint Paul** *state capital* Minnesota, N USA 45.00N 93.10W
31 P15 **Saint Paul** Nebraska, C USA 41.12N 98.26W
23 P7 **Saint Paul** Virginia, NE USA 36.53N 82.18W
79 Q17 **Saint Paul, Cape** *headland* S Ghana 5.44N 0.55E
105 O17 **St-Paul-de-Fenouillet** Pyrénées-Orientales, S France 42.49N 2.28E
67 K14 **Saint Paul Fracture Zone** *tectonic feature* E Atlantic Ocean
40 J14 **Saint Paul Island** *island* Pribilof Islands, Alaska, USA
104 J15 **St-Paul-les-Dax** Landes, SW France 43.45N 1.01W
23 U11 **Saint Pauls** North Carolina, SE USA 34.45N 78.56W
Saint Paul's Bay *see* San Pawl il-Bahar
203 R16 **St Paul's Point** *headland* Pitcairn Island, Pitcairn Islands
31 U10 **Saint Peter** Minnesota, N USA 44.18N 93.59W
99 L26 **St Peter Port** ○ (Guernsey) C Guernsey, Channel Islands 49.28N 2.33W
25 V13 **Saint Petersburg** Florida, SE USA 27.46N 82.37W
Saint Petersburg *see* Sankt-Peterburg
25 V13 **Saint Petersburg Beach** Florida, SE USA 27.43N 82.43W
181 P17 **St-Philippe** SE Réunion 21.21S 55.46E
47 Q11 **St-Pierre** NW Martinique 14.44N 61.10W
181 O17 **St-Pierre** SW Réunion
11 S13 **St-Pierre and Miquelon** *Fr.* Îles St-Pierre et Miquelon. ◇ *French territorial collectivity* NE North America
13 P11 **St-Pierre, Lac** ◎ Quebec, SE Canada
104 F5 **St-Pol-de-Léon** Finistère, NW France 48.42N 4.00W
105 O2 **St-Pol-sur-Ternoise** Pas-de-Calais, N France 50.22N 2.21E
St. Pons *see* St-Pons-de-Thomières
105 O16 **St-Pons-de-Thomières** *var.* St.Pons. Hérault, S France 43.28N 2.48E
105 P10 **St-Pourçain-sur-Sioule** Allier, C France 46.19N 3.16E
13 S11 **St-Prosper** Quebec, SE Canada 46.14N 70.28W
105 P3 **St-Quentin** Aisne, N France 49.51N 3.16E
13 R10 **St-Raphaël** Quebec, SE Canada 46.47N 70.46W
105 U15 **St-Raphaël** Var, SE France 43.25N 6.46E
13 Q10 **St-Raymond** Quebec, SE Canada 46.53N 71.49W
35 O9 **Saint Regis** Montana, NW USA 47.18N 115.06W
20 J7 **Saint Regis River** ⇝ New York, NE USA
105 R15 **St-Rémy-de-Provence** Bouches-du-Rhône, SE France 43.48N 4.49E
13 V6 **St-René-de-Matane** Quebec, SE Canada 48.42N 67.22W
104 M9 **St-Savin** Vienne, W France 46.34N 0.53E
13 S8 **St-Siméon** Quebec, SE Canada 47.49N 69.55W
25 X7 **Saint Simons Island** *island* Georgia, SE USA
203 Y2 **Saint Stanislas Bay** *bay* Kiritimati, E Kiribati
11 O15 **St.Stephen** New Brunswick, SE Canada 45.12N 67.18W
41 X12 **Saint Terese** Alaska, USA 58.28N 134.46W
12 E17 **St.Thomas** Ontario, S Canada 42.46N 81.12W
31 Q2 **Saint Thomas** North Dakota, N USA 48.37N 97.28W
47 T9 **Saint Thomas** *island* W Virgin Islands (US)
Saint Thomas *see* São Tomé, Sao Tome and Principe
Saint Thomas *see* Charlotte Amalie, Virgin Islands (US)
13 P10 **St-Tite** Quebec, SE Canada 46.42N 72.32W
Saint-Trond *see* Sint-Truiden
105 U16 **St-Tropez** Var, SE France 43.16N 6.39E
Saint Ubes *see* Setúbal
104 L3 **St-Valéry-en-Caux** Seine-Maritime, N France 49.53N 0.42E
105 Q9 **St-Vallier** Saône-et-Loire, C France 46.39N 4.19E
108 B7 **St-Vincent** Valle d'Aosta, NW Italy 45.47N 7.42E
47 Q14 **Saint Vincent** *island* N Saint Vincent and the Grenadines
Saint Vincent *see* São Vicente
47 W14 **Saint Vincent and the Grenadines** ◆ *commonwealth republic* SE West Indies
Saint Vincent, Cape *see* São Vicente, Cabo de
104 I15 **St-Vincent-de-Tyrosse** Landes, SW France 43.39N 1.16W
190 I9 **Saint Vincent, Gulf** *gulf* South Australia
25 R10 **Saint Vincent Island** *island* Florida, SE USA
47 T12 **Saint Vincent Passage** *passage* Saint Lucia/Saint Vincent and the Grenadines
191 N18 **Saint Vincent, Point** *headland* Tasmania, SE Australia 43.19S 145.50E
Saint-Vith *see* Sankt-Vith
9 S14 **St.Walburg** Saskatchewan, S Canada 53.37N 109.12W
St Wolfgangsee *see* Wolfgangsee
104 M11 **St-Yrieix-la-Perche** Haute-Vienne, C France 45.31N 1.12E
Saint Yves *see* Setúbal
13 Y5 **St-Yvon** Quebec, SE Canada 49.09N 64.51W
196 H5 **Saipan** *island* ● (Northern Mariana Islands) S Northern Mariana Islands
196 H6 **Saipan Channel** *channel* S Northern Mariana Islands
196 H6 **Saipan International Airport** ✖ Saipan, S Northern Mariana Islands
76 G6 **Sais** ✖ (Fès) C Morocco 33.58N 4.48W
Saishū *see* Cheju
Saishū *see* Cheju-do
104 J16 **Saison** ⇝ SW France
174 L7 **Sai, Sungai** ⇝ Borneo, N Indonesia
171 Jj16 **Saitama** *off.* Saitama-ken. ◈ *prefecture* Honshū, S Japan
170 Cc16 **Saito** Miyazaki, Kyūshū, SW Japan 32.07N 131.22E
Saiyid Abid *see* Sayyid 'Abid
59 J19 **Sajama, Nevado** ▲ W Bolivia 17.57S 68.51W
147 V13 **Sājir, Ras** *headland* S Oman 16.42N 53.40E
113 M20 **Sajószentpéter** Borsod-Abaúj-Zemplén, NE Hungary 48.13N 20.43E
85 F24 **Sak** ⇝ SW South Africa
83 J18 **Saka** Coast, E Kenya 0.11S 39.27E
178 I11 **Sa Kaeo** Prachin Buri, C Thailand 13.47N 102.03E
171 Gg15 **Sakai** Ōsaka, Honshū, SW Japan 34.34N 135.28E
170 F14 **Sakaide** Kagawa, Shikoku, SW Japan 34.19N 133.49E
170 Ff12 **Sakaiminato** Tottori, Honshū, SW Japan 35.34N 133.12E
146 M3 **Sakākah** Al Jawf, NW Saudi Arabia 29.55N 40.10E
30 L4 **Sakakawea, Lake** ▣ North Dakota, N USA
10 J9 **Sakami, Lac** ◎ Quebec, C Canada
81 O26 **Sakania** Katanga, SE Dem. Rep. Congo (Zaire) 12.43S 28.34E
152 K12 **Sakar** Lebapskiy Velayat, E Turkmenistan 38.57N 63.46E
180 H7 **Sakaraha** Toliara, SW Madagascar 22.54S 44.31E
152 I14 **Sakar-Chaga** *Turkm.* Sakarchäge. Maryyskiy Velayat, C Turkmenistan 37.40N 61.33E
Sakarchäge *see* Sakar-Chaga
Sak'art'velo *see* Georgia
142 F11 **Sakarya** ◈ *province* NW Turkey
142 F11 **Sakarya Nehri** ⇝ NW Turkey
150 K13 **Saksaul'skiy** *var.* Saksaul'skoye *Kaz.* Sekseüil. Kyzylorda, S Kazakhstan 47.07N 61.06E
Saksaul'skoye *see* Saksaul'skiy
171 Ll11 **Sakata** Yamagata, Honshū, C Japan 38.54N 139.51E
126 L9 **Sakha (Yakutiya), Respublika** *var.* Respublika Yakutiya, Yakutiya, *Eng.* Yakutia. ◈ *autonomous republic* NE Russian Federation
Sakhalin *see* Sakhalin, Ostrov
127 Oo14 **Sakhalin, Ostrov** *var.* Sakhalin. *island* SE Russian Federation
127 P14 **Sakhalinskaya Oblast'** ◈ *province* SE Russian Federation
127 Nn13 **Sakhalinskiy Zaliv** *gulf* E Russian Federation
Sakhnovshchina *see* Sakhnovshchyna
119 U6 **Sakhnovshchyna** *Rus.* Sakhnovshchina. Kharkivs'ka Oblast', E Ukraine 49.08N 35.51E
Sakhon Nakhon *see* Sakon Nakhon
Sakhtsar *see* Rāmsar
Saki *see* Saky
143 W10 **Şäki** *Rus.* Sheki; *prev.* Nukha. NW Azerbaijan 41.09N 47.10E
120 E13 **Šakiai** *Ger.* Schaken. Šakiai, S Lithuania 54.57N 23.04E
176 Z16 **Sakiramke** Papua, E Indonesia 8.36S 140.55E
172 Oo16 **Sakishima-shotō** *var.* Sakisima Syotō. *island group* SW Japan
Sakiz *see* Saqqez
Sakiz-Adasi *see* Chíos
161 F19 **Sakleshpur** Karnātaka, E India 12.58N 75.45E
178 J9 **Sakon Nakhon** *var.* Muang Sakon Nakhon, Sakhon Nakhon. Sakon Nakhon, E Thailand 17.10N 104.07E
155 P15 **Sakrand** Sind, SE Pakistan 26.10N 68.13E
85 F24 **Sak River** *Afr.* Sakrivier. Northern Cape, W South Africa 30.49S 20.24E
Sakrivier *see* Sak River
Saksaul'skiy *see* Saksaul'skoye
150 K13 **Saksaul'skoye** *prev.* Saksaul'skiy, *Kaz.* Sekseüil. Kzylorda, S Kazakhstan 47.07N 61.06E
97 I25 **Sakskøbing** Storstrøm, SE Denmark 54.48N 11.39E
171 Jj15 **Saku** Nagano, Honshū, S Japan 36.15N 138.28E
171 K16 **Sakura** Chiba, Honshū, S Japan 35.42N 140.10E
119 S13 **Saky** *Rus.* Saki. Respublika Krym, S Ukraine 45.08N 33.36E
78 E9 **Sal** *island* Ilhas de Barlavento, NE Cape Verde
131 N12 **Sal** ⇝ SW Russian Federation
113 I21 **Sal'a** *Hung.* Sellye, Vágsellye. Nitrianský Kraj, SW Slovakia 48.08N 17.55E
97 N15 **Sala** Västmanland, C Sweden 59.55N 16.37E
175 Qq11 **Salabangka, Kepulauan** *island group* N Indonesia
13 N13 **Salaberry-de-Valleyfield** *var.* Valleyfield. Quebec, SE Canada 45.15N 74.07W
120 G7 **Salacgrīva** *Est.* Salatsi. Limbaži, N Latvia 57.45N 24.21E
109 M18 **Sala Consilina** Campania, S Italy 40.22N 15.34E
42 C2 **Salada, Laguna** ◎ NW Mexico
63 D14 **Saladas** Corrientes, NE Argentina 28.15S 58.40W
63 C21 **Saladillo** Buenos Aires, E Argentina 35.40S 59.49W
63 B16 **Saladillo, Río** ⇝ C Argentina
27 T9 **Salado** Texas, SW USA 30.57N 97.32W
65 J16 **Salado, Arroyo** ⇝ SE Argentina
39 Q12 **Salado, Rio** ⇝ New Mexico, SW USA
63 D21 **Salado, Río** ⇝ E Argentina
64 J12 **Salado, Río** ⇝ C Argentina
43 N7 **Salado, Río** ⇝ NE Mexico
149 N6 **Salafchegān** *var.* Sarafjagān. Qom, N Iran 34.28N 50.28E
79 Q15 **Salaga** C Ghana 8.31N 0.37W
198 Aa7 **Sala'ilua** Savai'i, W Samoa 13.39S 172.33W
118 G9 **Sălaj** ◈ *county* NW Romania
85 H20 **Salajwe** Kweneng, SE Botswana 23.40S 24.46E
80 H9 **Salal** Kanem, W Chad 14.48N 17.12E
82 I6 **Salala** Red Sea, NE Sudan 21.16N 36.16E
147 V13 **Şalālah** SW Oman 17.01N 54.03E
44 D5 **Salamá** Baja Verapaz, C Guatemala 15.06N 90.18W
44 J6 **Salamá** Olancho, C Honduras 14.48N 86.34W
64 G10 **Salamanca** Coquimbo, C Chile 31.49S 70.58W
43 N13 **Salamanca** Guanajuato, C Mexico 20.33N 101.06W
106 K7 **Salamanca** *anc.* Helmantica, Salmantica. Castilla-León, NW Spain 40.58N 5.40W
20 D11 **Salamanca** New York, NE USA 42.09N 78.43W
106 J7 **Salamanca** ◈ *province* Castilla-León, W Spain
65 J19 **Salamanca, Pampa de** *plain* S Argentina
80 J12 **Salamat** *off.* Préfecture du Salamat. ◈ *prefecture* SE Chad
80 I12 **Salamat, Bahr** ⇝ S Chad
56 F5 **Salamina** Magdalena, N Colombia 10.28N 74.46W
117 G19 **Salamína** *var.* Salamís. Salamína, C Greece 37.58N 23.28E
117 G19 **Salamína** *island* C Greece
Salamís *see* Salamína
144 I5 **Salamīyah** *var.* As Salamīyah. Ḩamāh, W Syria 35.01N 37.01E
33 P12 **Salamonie Lake** ▣ Indiana, N USA
33 P12 **Salamonie River** ⇝ Indiana, N USA
Salang *see* Phuket
198 Bb8 **Salani** Upolu, SE Samoa 14.00S 171.35W
120 C11 **Salantai** Kretinga, NW Lithuania 56.05N 21.36E
106 K2 **Salas** Asturias, N Spain 43.25N 6.15W
107 O5 **Salas de los Infantes** Castilla-León, N Spain 42.01N 3.16W
104 M16 **Salat** ⇝ S France
201 V13 **Salat** *island* Chuuk, C Micronesia
174 L15 **Salatiga** Jawa, C Indonesia 7.15S 110.34E
201 V13 **Salat Pass** *passage* W Pacific Ocean
Salatsi *see* Salacgrīva
178 Jj10 **Salavan** *var.* Saravan, Saravane. Salavan, S Laos 15.43N 106.26E
131 V6 **Salavat** Respublika Bashkortostan, W Russian Federation 53.20N 55.54E
58 C12 **Salaverry** La Libertad, N Peru 8.15S 78.57W
176 Uu9 **Salawati, Pulau** *island* E Indonesia
200 Nn11 **Sala y Gomez** *island* Chile, E Pacific Ocean
Sala y Gomez Fracture Zone *see* Sala y Gomez Ridge
200 O11 **Sala y Gomez Ridge** *var.* Sala y Gomez Fracture Zone. *tectonic feature* SE Pacific Ocean
63 A22 **Salazar** Buenos Aires, E Argentina 36.19S 62.10W
56 G7 **Salazar** Norte de Santander, N Colombia 7.46N 72.46W
Salazar *see* N'Dalatando
181 P16 **Salazie** C Réunion 21.01S 55.33E
105 N8 **Salbris** Loir-et-Cher, C France 47.26N 2.01E
59 G15 **Salcantay, Nevado** ▲ C Peru 13.21S 72.31W
47 O8 **Salcedo** N Dominican Republic 19.21N 70.23W
41 S9 **Salcha River** ⇝ Alaska, USA
121 H15 **Šalčininkai** Šalčininkai, SE Lithuania 54.19N 25.26E
Saldae *see* Béjaïa
56 E11 **Saldaña** Tolima, C Colombia 3.57N 75.01W
106 M4 **Saldaña** Castilla-León, N Spain 42.31N 4.43W
85 E25 **Saldanha** Western Cape, SW South Africa 33.00S 17.56E
Salduba *see* Zaragoza
63 B23 **Saldungaray** Buenos Aires, E Argentina 38.15S 61.45W
120 D9 **Saldus** *Ger.* Frauenburg. Saldus, W Latvia 56.40N 22.29E
191 P13 **Sale** Victoria, SE Australia 38.06S 147.06E
76 F6 **Salé** NW Morocco 34.07N 6.40W
76 F6 **Salé** ✖ (Rabat) W Morocco 34.09N 6.30W
Salehābād *see* Andīmeshk
174 Ii10 **Saleh, Air** ⇝ Sumatera, W Indonesia
175 Oo16 **Saleh, Teluk** *bay* Nusa Tenggara, S Indonesia
125 G8 **Salekhard** *prev.* Obdorsk. Yamalo-Nenetskiy Avtonomnyy Okrug, N Russian Federation 66.33N 66.34E

◆ Country ● Country Capital ◇ Dependent Territory ○ Dependent Territory Capital ◈ Administrative Region ✖ International Airport ▲ Mountain ▲ Mountain Range ℞ Volcano ⇝ River ◎ Lake ▣ Reservoir

198 B7 **Sāleloga** Savai'i, C Samoa 13.42S 172.10W
161 H21 **Salem** Tamil Nādu, SE India 11.37N 78.07E
29 V9 **Salem** Arkansas, C USA 36.21N 91.49W
32 L15 **Salem** Illinois, N USA 38.37N 88.57W
33 P15 **Salem** Indiana, N USA 38.37N 86.06W
21 P11 **Salem** Massachusetts, NE USA 42.30N 70.51W
29 V6 **Salem** Missouri, C USA 37.39N 91.32W
20 I16 **Salem** New Jersey, NE USA 39.33N 75.26W
33 U12 **Salem** Ohio, N USA 40.52N 80.51W
34 G12 **Salem** *state capital* Oregon, NW USA 44.57N 123.01W
31 Q11 **Salem** South Dakota, N USA 43.43N 97.23W
38 L4 **Salem** Utah, W USA 40.03N 111.40W
23 S7 **Salem** Virginia, NE USA 37.16N 80.00W
23 R3 **Salem** West Virginia, NE USA 39.15N 80.32W
109 H23 **Salemi** Sicilia, Italy, C Mediterranean Sea 37.48N 12.48E
Salemy *see* As Sālimī
96 K12 **Sälen** Dalarna, C Sweden 61.11N 13.14E
109 Q18 **Salentina, Campi** Puglia, SE Italy 40.22N 18.01E
109 Q18 **Salentina, Penisola** *peninsula* SE Italy
109 L18 **Salerno** *anc.* Salernum. Campania, S Italy 40.40N 14.43E
109 L18 **Salerno, Golfo di** *Eng.* Gulf of Salerno. *gulf* S Italy
Salerno, Gulf of *see* Salerno, Golfo di
Salernum *see* Salerno
99 K17 **Salford** NW England, UK 53.30N 2.16W
Salgir *see* Salhyr
113 K21 **Salgótarján** Nógrád, N Hungary 48.06N 19.46E
61 O15 **Salgueiro** Pernambuco, E Brazil 8.04S 39.04W
96 C13 **Salhus** Hordaland, S Norway 60.30N 5.15E
119 T12 **Salhyr** *Rus.* Salgir. ≈ S Ukraine
175 S4 **Salibabu, Pulau** *island* N Indonesia
39 S6 **Salida** Colorado, C USA 38.29N 105.57W
104 J15 **Salies-de-Béarn** Pyrénées-Atlantiques, SW France 43.28N 0.55W
142 C14 **Salihli** Manisa, W Turkey 38.28N 28.07E
121 K18 **Salihorsk** *Rus.* Soligorsk. Minskaya Voblasts', S Belarus 52.48N 27.31E
121 K18 **Salihorskaye Vodaskhovishcha** ⊠ C Belarus
85 N14 **Salima** Central, C Malawi 13.44S 34.21E
177 Ff5 **Salin** Magwe, W Myanmar 20.30N 94.40E
29 N4 **Salina** Kansas, C USA 38.50N 97.36W
38 L5 **Salina** Utah, W USA 38.57N 111.54W
43 S17 **Salina Cruz** Oaxaca, SE Mexico 16.10N 95.12W
109 L22 **Salina, Isola** *island* Isole Eolie, S Italy
46 J5 **Salina Point** *headland* Acklins Island, SE Bahamas 22.10N 74.16W
58 A7 **Salinas** Guayas, W Ecuador 2.15S 80.54W
42 M11 **Salinas** *var.* Salinas de Hidalgo. San Luis Potosí, C Mexico 22.36N 101.41W
47 T6 **Salinas** C Puerto Rico 17.58N 66.18W
37 O10 **Salinas** California, W USA 36.40N 121.40W
Salinas, Cabo de *see* Salines, Cap de ses
Salinas de Hidalgo *see* Salinas
84 A13 **Salinas, Ponta das** *headland* W Angola 12.50S 12.57E
47 O10 **Salinas, Punta** *headland* S Dominican Republic 18.11N 70.32W
Salinas, Río *see* Chixoy, Río
37 O11 **Salinas River** ≈ California, W USA
24 H6 **Saline Lake** ⊗ Louisiana, S USA
27 R17 **Salineno** Texas, SW USA 26.29N 99.06W
29 V14 **Saline River** ≈ Arkansas, C USA
32 M17 **Saline River** ≈ Illinois, N USA
107 X10 **Salines, Cap de ses** *var.* Cabo de Salinas. *headland* Mallorca, Spain, W Mediterranean Sea 39.15N 3.03E
Salisburg *see* Mazsalaca
47 O12 **Salisbury** *var.* Baroui. W Dominica 15.25N 61.27W
99 M23 **Salisbury** *var.* New Sarum. S England, UK 51.04N 1.48W
23 Y4 **Salisbury** Maryland, NE USA 38.21N 75.36W
29 T3 **Salisbury** Missouri, C USA 39.25N 92.48W
23 S9 **Salisbury** North Carolina, SE USA 35.40N 80.28W
Salisbury *see* Harare
16 N5 **Salisbury Island** *island* Nunavut, NE Canada
Salisbury, Lake *see* Bisina, Lake
99 L23 **Salisbury Plain** *plain* S England, UK
23 R14 **Salkehatchie River** ≈ South Carolina, SE USA
144 I9 **Şalkhad** As Suwaydā', SW Syria 32.28N 36.42E
94 M12 **Salla** Lappi, NE Finland 66.49N 28.40E
105 U11 **Sallanches** Haute-Savoie, E France 45.55N 6.37E
107 V5 **Sallent** Cataluña, NE Spain 41.48N 1.52E
63 A22 **Salliqueló** Buenos Aires, E Argentina 36.42S 62.52W
29 R10 **Sallisaw** Oklahoma, C USA 35.29N 94.47W
82 I7 **Sallom** Red Sea, NE Sudan 19.30N 37.11E
10 J2 **Salluit** *prev.* Saglouc, Sagluk. Quebec, NE Canada 62.10N 75.40W
Sallūm, Khalīj as *see* Salûm, Gulf of
11 S11 **Sally's Cove** Newfoundland and Labrador, E Canada 49.43N 58.00W
145 W9 **Salmān Bin 'Arāzah** E Iraq 32.33N 46.36E
Salmantica *see* Salamanca
148 I2 **Salmās** *prev.* Dilman, Shāpūr. Āzarbāyjān-e Bākhtarī, NW Iran 38.13N 44.49E
128 I11 **Salmi** Respublika Kareliya, NW Russian Federation 61.21N 31.55E
35 P12 **Salmon** Idaho, NW USA 45.10N 113.54W
9 N16 **Salmon Arm** British Columbia, SW Canada 50.40N 119.18W
199 Jj5 **Salmon Bank** *undersea feature* N Pacific Ocean 26.55N 176.28W
Salmon Leap *see* Leixlip
36 L2 **Salmon Mountains** ▲ California, W USA
12 J15 **Salmon Point** *headland* Ontario, SE Canada 43.51N 77.15W
35 N11 **Salmon River** ≈ Idaho, NW USA
20 K6 **Salmon River** ≈ New York, NE USA
35 N12 **Salmon River Mountains** ▲ Idaho, NW USA
20 I9 **Salmon River Reservoir** ⊠ New York, NE USA
95 K19 **Salo** Länsi-Suomi, W Finland 60.22N 23.10E
108 F7 **Salò** Lombardia, N Italy 45.37N 10.30E
Salona/Salonae *see* Solin
105 S15 **Salon-de-Provence** Bouches-du-Rhône, SE France 43.39N 5.04E
Salonica/Salonika *see* Thessaloníki
117 I14 **Salonikós, Akrotírio** *headland* Thásos, E Greece 40.34N 24.39E
118 F10 **Salonta** *Hung.* Nagyszalonta. Bihor, W Romania 46.47N 21.37E
106 I9 **Salor** ≈ W Spain
107 U6 **Salou** Cataluña, NE Spain 41.04N 1.07E
78 H11 **Saloum** ≈ C Senegal
44 H4 **Sal, Punta** *headland* NW Honduras 15.55N 87.36W
94 N3 **Salpynten** *headland* W Svalbard 78.12N 12.11E
144 I3 **Salqīn** Idlib, W Syria 36.09N 36.27E
95 F14 **Salsbruket** Nord-Trøndelag, C Norway 64.49N 11.48E
130 M13 **Sal'sk** Rostovskaya Oblast', SW Russian Federation 46.30N 41.30E
109 K25 **Salso** ≈ Sicilia, Italy, C Mediterranean Sea
109 J25 **Salso** ≈ Sicilia, Italy, C Mediterranean Sea
108 E9 **Salsomaggiore Terme** Emilia-Romagna, N Italy 44.49N 9.58E
Salt *see* As Salṭ
64 J6 **Salta** Salta, NW Argentina 24.47S 65.23W
64 K6 **Salta** *off.* Provincia de Salta. ◆ *province* N Argentina
99 I24 **Saltash** SW England, UK 50.26N 4.13W
26 I8 **Salt Basin** *basin* Texas, SW USA
9 V16 **Saltcoats** Saskatchewan, S Canada 51.06N 102.12W
32 L13 **Salt Creek** ≈ Illinois, N USA
26 J9 **Salt Draw** ≈ Texas, SW USA
99 F21 **Saltee Islands** *island group* SE Ireland
94 G12 **Saltfjorden** *inlet* C Norway
26 I8 **Salt Flat** Texas, SW USA 31.43N 105.05W
29 N8 **Salt Fork Arkansas River** ≈ Oklahoma, C USA
33 T13 **Salt Fork Lake** ⊗ Ohio, N USA
28 J11 **Salt Fork Red River** ≈ Oklahoma/Texas, C USA
97 J23 **Saltholm** *island* E Denmark
42 N8 **Saltillo** Coahuila de Zaragoza, NE Mexico 25.30N 101.00W
190 L5 **Salt Lake** *salt lake* New South Wales, SE Australia
39 U15 **Salt Lake** ⊗ New Mexico, SW USA
38 K2 **Salt Lake City** *state capital* Utah, W USA 40.44N 111.54W
63 C20 **Salto** Buenos Aires, E Argentina 34.18S 60.17W
63 D17 **Salto** Salto, N Uruguay 31.22S 57.58W
63 E17 **Salto** ◆ *department* N Uruguay
109 I14 **Salto** ≈ C Italy
64 Q6 **Salto del Guairá** Canindeyú, E Paraguay 24.06S 54.22W
63 D17 **Salto Grande, Embalse de** *var.* Lago de Salto Grande. ⊠ Argentina/Uruguay
Salto Grande, Lago de *see* Salto Grande, Embalse de
37 W16 **Salton Sea** ⊗ California, W USA
62 I12 **Salto Santiago, Represa de** ⊠ S Brazil
155 U7 **Salt Range** ▲ E Pakistan
38 M13 **Salt River** ≈ Arizona, SW USA
22 L5 **Salt River** ≈ Kentucky, S USA
29 V3 **Salt River** ≈ Missouri, C USA
97 F17 **Saltrød** Aust-Agder, S Norway 58.28N 8.49E
97 P16 **Saltsjöbaden** Stockholm, C Sweden 59.15N 18.19E
94 G12 **Saltstraumen** Nordland, C Norway 67.16N 14.42E
23 Q7 **Saltville** Virginia, NE USA 36.52N 81.48W
Saluces/Saluciae *see* Saluzzo
23 Q12 **Saluda** South Carolina, SE USA 34.00N 81.47W
23 X6 **Saluda** Virginia, NE USA 37.36N 76.36W
23 Q12 **Saluda River** ≈ South Carolina, SE USA
175 R10 **Salue Timpaus, Selat** *var.* Selat Banggai. *strait* N Banda Sea
77 T7 **Salûm** *var.* As Sallūm. NW Egypt 31.31N 25.09E
158 F14 **Sālūmbar** Rājasthān, N India 24.16N 74.04E
77 T7 **Salûm, Gulf of** *Ar.* Khalīj as Sallūm. *gulf* Egypt/Libya
175 Q7 **Salumpaga** Sulawesi, N Indonesia 1.18N 120.58E
161 M14 **Sālūr** Andhra Pradesh, E India 18.31N 83.16E
57 Y9 **Salut, Îles du** *island group* N French Guiana
108 A9 **Saluzzo** *Fr.* Saluces; *anc.* Saluciae. Piemonte, NW Italy 44.39N 7.28E
65 F23 **Salvación, Bahía** *bay* S Chile
61 P17 **Salvador** *prev.* São Salvador. Bahia, E Brazil 12.58S 38.28W
67 E24 **Salvador** East Falkland, Falkland Islands 51.28S 58.22W
24 K10 **Salvador, Lake** ⊗ Louisiana, S USA
Salvaleón de Higüey *see* Higüey
106 F10 **Salvaterra de Magos** Santarém, C Portugal 39.01N 8.46W
43 N13 **Salvatierra** Guanajuato, C Mexico 20.13N 100.52W
107 P3 **Salvatierra** *Basq.* Agurain. País Vasco, N Spain 42.52N 2.22W
Salwa/Salwah *see* As Salwā
178 H5 **Salween** *Bur.* Thanlwin, *Chin.* Nu Chiang, Nu Jiang. ≈ SE Asia
143 Y12 **Salyan** *Rus.* Sal'yany. SE Azerbaijan 39.36N 48.57E
159 N11 **Salyan** *var.* Sallyana. Mid Western, W Nepal 28.22N 82.10E
Sal'yany *see* Salyan
23 O6 **Salyersville** Kentucky, S USA 37.44N 83.01W
111 V6 **Salza** ≈ E Austria
111 Q7 **Salzach** ≈ Austria/Germany
111 Q6 **Salzburg** *anc.* Juvavum. Salzburg, N Austria 47.48N 13.03E
111 O8 **Salzburg** *off.* Land Salzburg. ◆ *state* C Austria
Salzburg *see* Ocna Sibiului
Salzburg Alps *see* Salzburger Kalkalpen
111 Q7 **Salzburger Kalkalpen** *Eng.* Salzburg Alps. ▲ C Austria
102 J13 **Salzgitter** *prev.* Watenstedt-Salzgitter. Niedersachsen, C Germany 52.06N 10.24E
103 G14 **Salzkotten** Nordrhein-Westfalen, W Germany 51.40N 8.36E
102 K11 **Salzwedel** Sachsen-Anhalt, N Germany 52.51N 11.10E
158 D11 **Sām** Rājasthān, NW India 26.49N 70.30E
Šamac *see* Bosanski Šamac
56 G9 **Samacá** Boyacá, C Colombia 5.26N 73.30W
42 I7 **Samachique** Chihuahua, N Mexico 27.16N 107.28W
147 Y8 **Şamad** NE Oman 22.45N 58.07E
Sama de Langreo *see* Sama
Samadan *see* Samedan
59 M19 **Samaipata** Santa Cruz, C Bolivia 18.09S 63.49W
178 Jj11 **Samakhixai** *var.* Attapu, Attopeu. Attapu, S Laos 14.48N 106.51E
Samakov *see* Samokov
44 B6 **Samalá, Río** ≈ SW Guatemala
42 J3 **Samalayuca** Chihuahua, N Mexico 31.14N 106.28W
179 Q17 **Samales Group** *island group* Sulu Archipelago, SW Philippines
161 L16 **Sāmalkot** Andhra Pradesh, E India 17.03N 82.15E
47 P8 **Samaná** *var.* Santa Bárbara de Samaná. E Dominican Republic 19.11N 69.19W
47 P8 **Samaná, Bahía de** *bay* E Dominican Republic
46 K4 **Samana Cay** *island* SE Bahamas
142 K17 **Samandağı** Hatay, S Turkey 36.06N 35.56E
155 P3 **Samangān** ◆ *province* N Afghanistan
Samangān *see* Āybak
172 P8 **Samani** Hokkaidō, NE Japan 42.07N 142.57E
56 C13 **Samaniego** Nariño, SW Colombia 1.22N 77.34W
179 R12 **Samar** *island* C Philippines
131 S6 **Samara** *prev.* Kuybyshev. Samarskaya Oblast', W Russian Federation 53.15N 50.15E
131 S6 **Samara** ✈ Samarskaya Oblast', W Russian Federation 53.11N 50.27E
131 T7 **Samara** ≈ W Russian Federation
119 V7 **Samara** ≈ E Ukraine
195 N17 **Samarai** Milne Bay, SE PNG 10.37S 150.39E
Samarang *see* Semarang
144 G9 **Samarian Hills** *hill range* N Israel
56 L9 **Samariapo** Amazonas, C Venezuela 5.13N 67.47W
175 O8 **Samarinda** Borneo, C Indonesia 0.30S 117.09E
Samarkand *see* Samarqand
Samarkandskaya Oblast' *see* Samarqand Viloyati
Samarkandski/Samarkandskoye *see* Temirtau
Samarobriva *see* Amiens
153 N11 **Samarqand** *Rus.* Samarkand. Samarqand Viloyati, C Uzbekistan 39.39N 66.55E
152 M11 **Samarqand Viloyati** *Rus.* Samarkandskaya Oblast'. ◆ *province* C Uzbekistan
145 S6 **Sāmarrā'** C Iraq 34.13N 43.52E
131 R7 **Samarskaya Oblast'** *prev.* Kuybyshevskaya Oblast'. ◆ *province* W Russian Federation
159 Q13 **Samastīpur** Bihār, N India 25.52N 85.46E
78 L14 **Samatiguila** NW Ivory Coast 9.51N 7.36W
121 Q17 **Samatsevichy** *Rus.* Samotevichi. Mahilyowskaya Voblasts', E Belarus 53.12N 31.49E
Samawa *see* As Samāwah
143 Y11 **Şamaxı** *Rus.* Shemakha. C Azerbaijan 40.31N 48.54E
158 H6 **Samba** Jammu and Kashmir, NW India 32.31N 75.07E
81 K18 **Samba** Equateur, NW Dem. Rep. Congo (Zaire) 0.13N 21.16E
81 N21 **Samba** Maniema, E Dem. Rep. Congo (Zaire) 4.40S 26.22E
175 O6 **Sambaliung, Pegunungan** ▲ Borneo, N Indonesia
160 M11 **Sambalpur** Orissa, E India 21.28N 84.04E
69 X12 **Sambao** ≈ W Madagascar
174 Kk7 **Sambas, Sungai** ≈ Borneo, N Indonesia
180 K2 **Sambava** Antsirañana, NE Madagascar 14.16S 50.10E
176 Ww9 **Samberi** Papua, E Indonesia 1.07S 135.54E
158 J10 **Sambhal** Uttar Pradesh, N India 28.34N 78.34E
158 H12 **Sāmbhar Salt Lake** ⊗ N India
109 N21 **Sambiase** Calabria, SW Italy 38.58N 16.16E
118 H5 **Sambir** *Rus.* Sambor. L'vivs'ka Oblast', NW Ukraine 49.29N 23.09E
84 C13 **Sambo** Huambo, C Angola 13.07S 16.06E
Sambor *see* Sambir
63 E21 **Samborombón, Bahía** *bay* NE Argentina
101 H20 **Sambre** ≈ Belgium/France
45 V16 **Sambú, Río** ≈ SE Panama
169 Z14 **Samch'ŏk** *Jap.* Sanchoku. NE South Korea 37.21N 129.12E
Samch'ŏnpŏ *see* Sach'ŏn
83 I21 **Same** Kilimanjaro, NE Tanzania 4.02S 37.46E
110 J10 **Samedan** *Ger.* Samaden. Graubünden, S Switzerland 46.31N 9.51E
84 K12 **Samfya** Luapula, N Zambia 11.25S 29.30E
147 W13 **Samḥān, Jabal** ▲ SW Oman
117 C18 **Sámi** Kefallinía, Iónioi Nísoi, Greece, C Mediterranean Sea 38.15N 20.39E
58 F10 **Samiria, Río** ≈ N Peru
Samirum *see* Semirom
143 V11 **Şämkir** *Rus.* Shamkhor. NW Azerbaijan 40.51N 46.03E
178 J7 **Sam, Nam** *Vtn.* Sông Chu. ≈ Laos/Vietnam
Samnān *see* Semnān
Sam Neua *see* Xam Nua
77 P10 **Samnū** C Libya 27.19N 15.01E
198 Bb7 **Samoa** *off.* Independent State of Samoa, *var.* Sāmoa; *prev.* Western Samoa. ◆ *monarchy* W Polynesia
198 C8 **Sāmoa** *island group* American /Samoa
183 T9 **Samoa Basin** *undersea feature* W Pacific Ocean
Sāmoa-i-Sisifo *see* Samoa
114 D8 **Samobor** Zagreb, N Croatia 45.48N 15.38E
116 H10 **Samokov** *var.* Samakov. Sofiya, W Bulgaria 42.19N 23.34E
113 H21 **Šamorín** *Ger.* Sommerein, *Hung.* Somorja. Trnavský Kraj, W Slovakia 48.01N 17.18E
117 M19 **Sámos** *prev.* Limín Vathéos. Sámos, Dodekánisos, Greece, Aegean Sea 37.46N 26.58E
117 M20 **Sámos** *island* Dodekánisos, Greece, Aegean Sea
Samosch *see* Szamos
173 Ff5 **Samosir, Pulau** *island* W Indonesia
Samotevichi *see* Samatsevichy
Samothrace *see* Samothráki
117 K14 **Samothráki** Samothráki, NE Greece 40.28N 25.31E
117 J14 **Samothráki** *anc.* Samothrace. *island* NE Greece
117 A15 **Samothráki** *island* Iónioi Nísoi, Greece, C Mediterranean Sea
Samotschin *see* Szamocin
174 M10 **Sampit** Borneo, C Indonesia 2.30S 112.30E
174 M10 **Sampit, Sungai** ≈ Borneo, N Indonesia
Sampoku *see* Sanpoku
195 P11 **Sampun** New Britain, E PNG 5.19S 152.06E
81 N24 **Sampwe** Katanga, SE Dem. Rep. Congo (Zaire) 9.17S 27.22E
27 X8 **Sam Rayburn Reservoir** ⊠ Texas, SW USA
178 Ii6 **Sam Sao, Phou** ▲ Laos/Thailand
97 H22 **Samsø** *island* E Denmark
97 H23 **Samsø Bælt** *channel* E Denmark
178 Jj7 **Sâm Sơn** Thanh Hoa, N Vietnam 19.43N 105.52E
142 L11 **Samsun** *anc.* Amisus. Samsun, N Turkey 41.16N 36.22E
142 K11 **Samsun** ◆ *province* N Turkey
143 R9 **Samtredia** W Georgia 42.09N 42.20E
61 E15 **Samuel, Represa de** ⊠ W Brazil
178 H15 **Samui, Ko** *island* SW Thailand
Samundari *see* Samundri
155 U9 **Samundri** *var.* Samundari. Punjab, E Pakistan 31.04N 72.58E
143 X10 **Samur** ≈ Azerbaijan/Russian Federation
143 Y11 **Samur-Abşeron Kanalı** *Rus.* Samur-Apsheronskiy Kanal. *canal* E Azerbaijan
Samur-Apsheronskiy Kanal *see* Samur-Abşeron Kanalı
178 Hh11 **Samut Prakan** *var.* Muang Samut Prakan, Paknam. Samut Prakan, C Thailand 13.33N 100.13E
178 H11 **Samut Sakhon** *var.* Maha Chai, Samut Sakorn, Tha *Chin.* Samut Sakhon, C Thailand 13.31N 100.15E
Samut Sakorn *see* Samut Sakhon
178 H11 **Samut Songhram** *prev.* Meklong. Samut Songkhram, SW Thailand 13.25N 100.01E
79 N12 **San** Ségou, C Mali 13.18N 4.51W
113 O15 **San** ≈ SE Poland
147 O15 **Şan'ā'** *Eng.* Sana. ● (Yemen) W Yemen 15.24N 44.14E
114 F11 **Sana** ≈ NW Bosnia and Herzegovina
82 O12 **Sanaag** *off.* Gobolka Sanaag. ◆ *region* N Somalia
116 J8 **Sanadinovo** Pleven, N Bulgaria 43.33N 25.00E
205 P1 **Sanae** *South African research station* Antarctica 70.19S 1.31W
145 Y10 **Sanāf, Hawr as** ⊗ S Iraq
81 E15 **Sanaga** ≈ C Cameroon
56 D12 **San Agustín** Huila, SW Colombia 1.52N 76.13W
179 S16 **San Agustin, Cape** *headland* Mindanao, S Philippines 6.17N 126.12E
39 Q13 **San Agustin, Plains of** *plain* New Mexico, SW USA
40 M16 **Sanak Islands** *island group* Aleutian Islands, Alaska, USA
200 P11 **San Ambrosio, Isla** *Eng.* San Ambrosio Island. *island* W Chile
San Ambrosio Island *see* San Ambrosio, Isla
175 S10 **Sanana** Pulau Sanana, E Indonesia 2.04S 125.58E
175 S10 **Sanana, Pulau** *island* Maluku, E Indonesia
148 K5 **Sanandaj** *prev.* Sinneh. Kordestān, W Iran 35.18N 47.01E
37 P8 **San Andreas** California, W USA 38.10N 120.40W
2 C13 **San Andreas Fault** *fault* W USA
56 G8 **San Andrés** Santander, C Colombia 6.52N 72.52W
63 C20 **San Andrés de Giles** Buenos Aires, E Argentina 34.27S 59.27W
39 R14 **San Andres Mountains** ▲ New Mexico, SW USA
43 S15 **San Andrés Tuxtla** *var.* Tuxtla. Veracruz-Llave, E Mexico 18.27N 95.18W
27 P8 **San Angelo** Texas, SW USA 31.27N 100.26W
109 A20 **San Antioco, Isola di** *island* W Italy
44 F4 **San Antonio** Toledo, S Belize 16.13N 89.02W
64 G11 **San Antonio** Valparaíso, C Chile 33.35S 71.34W
196 H6 **San Antonio** Saipan, S Northern Mariana Islands
39 R13 **San Antonio** New Mexico, SW USA 33.53N 106.52W
27 R12 **San Antonio** Texas, SW USA 29.25N 98.29W
56 M11 **San Antonio** Amazonas, S Venezuela 3.31N 66.46W
56 I7 **San Antonio** Barinas, C Venezuela 7.24N 71.28W
57 O5 **San Antonio** Monagas, NE Venezuela 10.03N 63.45W
27 S12 **San Antonio** ✈ Texas, SW USA 29.31N 98.11W
San Antonio *see* San Antonio del Táchira
107 V11 **San Antonio Abad** Eivissa, Spain, W Mediterranean Sea 38.58N 1.18E
27 U13 **San Antonio Bay** *inlet* Texas, SW USA
63 E22 **San Antonio, Cabo** *headland* E Argentina 36.45S 56.40W
46 A5 **San Antonio, Cabo de** *headland* W Cuba 21.51N 84.58W
107 T11 **San Antonio, Cabo de** *headland* E Spain 38.50N 0.09E
56 H7 **San Antonio de Caparo** Táchira, W Venezuela 7.34N 71.28W
64 J5 **San Antonio de los Cobres** Salta, NE Argentina 24.15S 66.17W
56 H7 **San Antonio del Táchira** *var.* San Antonio. Táchira, W Venezuela 7.49N 72.27W
37 T15 **San Antonio, Mount** ▲ California, W USA 34.18N 117.37W
65 K16 **San Antonio Oeste** Río Negro, E Argentina 40.45S 64.58W
27 T13 **San Antonio River** ≈ Texas, SW USA
56 J5 **Sanare** Lara, N Venezuela 9.45N 69.39W
105 T16 **Sanary-sur-Mer** Var, SE France 43.07N 5.48E
27 X8 **San Augustine** Texas, SW USA 31.31N 94.06W
147 T13 **Sanāw** *var.* Sanaw. NE Yemen 18.00N 51.00E
43 O11 **San Bartolo** San Luis Potosí, C Mexico 22.19N 100.04W
109 L16 **San Bartolomeo in Galdo** Campania, S Italy 41.24N 15.01E
108 K13 **San Benedetto del Tronto** Marche, C Italy 42.57N 13.52E
44 E3 **San Benito** Petén, N Guatemala 16.55N 89.58W
27 T17 **San Benito** Texas, SW USA 26.07N 97.37W
56 E6 **San Benito Abad** Sucre, N Colombia 8.55N 75.01W
37 P11 **San Benito Mountain** ▲ California, W USA 36.21N 120.37W
37 O10 **San Benito River** ≈ California, W USA
110 H10 **San Bernardino** Graubünden, S Switzerland 46.21N 9.13E
37 U15 **San Bernardino** California, W USA 34.06N 117.15W
64 H11 **San Bernardo** Santiago, C Chile 33.36S 70.40W
42 J8 **San Bernardo** Durango, C Mexico 25.58N 105.27W
170 F12 **Sanbe-san** ▲ Kyūshū, SW Japan 35.09N 132.36E
42 J12 **San Blas** Nayarit, C Mexico 21.33N 105.17W
42 H8 **San Blas** Sinaloa, C Mexico 26.05N 108.44W
45 V14 **San Blas** *off.* Comarca de San Blas. ◆ *special territory* NE Panama
45 U14 **San Blas, Archipiélago de** *island group* NE Panama
25 Q10 **San Blas, Cape** *headland* Florida, SE USA 29.39N 85.21W
45 V14 **San Blas, Cordillera de** ▲ NE Panama
64 J8 **San Blas de los Sauces** Catamarca, NW Argentina 28.18S 67.12W
108 G8 **San Bonifacio** Veneto, NE Italy 45.22N 11.14E
31 S12 **Sanborn** Iowa, C USA 43.10N 95.39W
42 M7 **San Buenaventura** Coahuila de Zaragoza, NE Mexico 27.03N 101.33W
107 S5 **San Caprasio** ▲ N Spain 41.45N 0.26W
64 G13 **San Carlos** Bío Bío, C Chile 36.25S 71.58W
42 E9 **San Carlos** Baja California Sur, W Mexico 24.52N 112.15W
43 N5 **San Carlos** Coahuila de Zaragoza, NE Mexico 29.00N 100.51W
San Carlos, Estrecho de *see* Falkland Sound
43 P9 **San Carlos** Tamaulipas, C Mexico 24.36N 98.42W
44 L12 **San Carlos** Río San Juan, S Nicaragua 11.06N 84.46W
45 T16 **San Carlos** Panamá, C Panama 8.28N 79.58W
179 P9 **San Carlos** *off.* San Carlos City. Luzon, N Philippines 15.57N 120.18E
38 M14 **San Carlos** Arizona, SW USA 33.21N 110.27W
63 G20 **San Carlos** Maldonado, S Uruguay 34.46S 54.58W
56 K5 **San Carlos** Cojedes, N Venezuela 9.39N 68.34W
San Carlos *see* Quesada, Costa Rica
San Carlos *see* Luba, Equatorial Guinea
63 B17 **San Carlos Centro** Santa Fe, C Argentina 31.45S 61.04W
179 Q13 **San Carlos City** Negros, C Philippines 10.34N 123.24E
San Carlos de Ancud *see* Ancud
65 H16 **San Carlos de Bariloche** Río Negro, SW Argentina 41.07S 71.15W
63 B21 **San Carlos de Bolívar** Buenos Aires, E Argentina 36.15S 61.06W
56 H6 **San Carlos del Zulia** Zulia, W Venezuela 9.01N 71.58W
56 L12 **San Carlos de Río Negro** Amazonas, S Venezuela 1.54N 67.54W
San Carlos, Estrecho de *see* Falkland Sound
38 M14 **San Carlos Reservoir** ⊠ Arizona, SW USA
44 M12 **San Carlos, Río** ≈ N Costa Rica
67 D24 **San Carlos Settlement** East Falkland, Falkland Islands
63 C23 **San Cayetano** Buenos Aires, E Argentina 38.19S 59.37W
105 O8 **Sancerre** Cher, C France 47.19N 2.53E
164 G7 **Sanchakou** Xinjiang Uygur Zizhiqu, NW China 39.58N 78.26E
Sanchoku *see* Samch'ŏk
43 O12 **San Ciro** San Luis Potosí, C Mexico 21.40N 99.49W
107 P10 **San Clemente** Castilla-La Mancha, C Spain 39.24N 2.25W
37 T16 **San Clemente** California, W USA 33.25N 117.36W
63 E21 **San Clemente del Tuyú** Buenos Aires, E Argentina 36.25S 56.45W
37 S17 **San Clemente Island** *island* Channel Islands, California, W USA
105 O9 **Sancoins** Cher, C France 46.49N 3.00E
195 Z17 **San Cristobal** *var.* Makira. *island* SE Solomon Islands
63 B16 **San Cristóbal** Santa Fe, C Argentina 30.19S 61.13W
46 B4 **San Cristóbal** Pinar del Río, W Cuba 22.43N 83.03W
47 O9 **San Cristóbal** *var.* Benemérita de San Cristóbal. S Dominican Republic 18.26N 70.07W
56 H7 **San Cristóbal** Táchira, W Venezuela 7.46N 72.15W
San Cristóbal *see* San Cristóbal de Las Casas
43 U16 **San Cristóbal de Las Casas** *var.* San Cristóbal. Chiapas, SE Mexico 16.43N 92.40W
200 Oo8 **San Cristóbal, Isla** *var.* Chatham Island. *island* Galapagos Islands, Ecuador, E Pacific Ocean
44 D5 **San Cristóbal Verapaz** Alta Verapaz, C Guatemala 15.22N 90.25W
46 F6 **Sancti Spíritus** Sancti Spíritus, C Cuba 21.54N 79.27W
105 O11 **Sancy, Puy de** ▲ C France 45.33N 2.48E
97 D15 **Sand** Rogaland, S Norway 59.28N 6.16E
175 Oo2 **Sandakan** Sabah, East Malaysia 5.52N 118.04E
190 K9 **Sandalwood** South Australia 34.51S 140.13E
Sandalwood Island *see* Sumba, Pulau
96 D11 **Sandane** Sogn og Fjordane, S Norway 61.46N 6.13E
116 G12 **Sandanski** *prev.* Sveti Vrach. Blagoevgrad, SW Bulgaria 41.36N 23.18E
78 J11 **Sandaré** Kayes, W Mali 14.36N 10.22W
97 J19 **Sandared** Västra Götaland, S Sweden 57.43N 12.46E
96 N12 **Sandarne** Gävleborg, C Sweden 61.15N 17.15E
194 E10 **Sandaun** *prev.* West Sepik. ◆ *province* NW PNG
98 K4 **Sanday** *island* NE Scotland, UK
179 N14 **Sand Cay** *island* W Spratly Islands
33 P15 **Sand Creek** ≈ Indiana, N USA
97 H15 **Sande** Vestfold, S Norway 59.34N 10.13E
97 H16 **Sandefjord** Vestfold, S Norway 59.07N 10.13E
79 O15 **Sandégué** E Ivory Coast 7.58N 3.33W
79 P14 **Sandema** N Ghana 10.42N 1.17W
39 O11 **Sanders** Arizona, SW USA 35.13N 109.21W
26 M11 **Sanderson** Texas, SW USA 30.08N 102.23W
25 U4 **Sandersville** Georgia, SE USA 32.58N 82.48W
94 H4 **Sandgerdhi** Sudhurland, SW Iceland 64.01N 22.42W
30 K14 **Sand Hills** ▲ Nebraska, C USA
27 S14 **Sandia** Texas, SW USA 27.59N 97.52W
37 T17 **San Diego** California, W USA 32.43N 117.09W
27 S14 **San Diego** Texas, SW USA 27.45N 98.14W
142 F14 **Sandıklı** Afyon, W Turkey 38.28N 30.16E
158 L12 **Sandila** Uttar Pradesh, N India 27.05N 80.37E
123 J15 **San Dimitri, Ras** *var.* San Dimitri Point. *headland* Gozo, NW Malta 36.04N 14.12E
174 Gg11 **Sanding, Selat** *strait* W Indonesia
32 J3 **Sand Island** *island* Apostle Islands, Wisconsin, N USA
97 C16 **Sandnes** Rogaland, S Norway 58.51N 5.45E
94 F13 **Sandnessjøen** Nordland, C Norway 66.00N 12.37E
81 L24 **Sandoa** Katanga, S Dem. Rep. Congo (Zaire) 9.39S 22.58E
113 N15 **Sandomierz** *Rus.* Sandomir. Świętokrzyskie, C Poland 50.42N 21.44E
Sandomir *see* Sandomierz
56 C13 **Sandoná** Nariño, SW Colombia 1.13N 77.29W
108 I7 **San Donà di Piave** Veneto, NE Italy 45.37N 12.34E
128 K14 **Sandovo** Tverskaya Oblast', W Russian Federation 58.26N 36.30E
177 Ff7 **Sandoway** Arakan State, W Myanmar 18.28N 94.19E
99 M24 **Sandown** S England, UK 50.39N 1.11W
97 B19 **Sandoy** *Dan.* Sandø *Island* Faeroe Islands 61.52N 6.51W
41 N16 **Sand Point** Popof Island, Alaska, USA 55.20N 160.30W
67 N24 **Sand Point** *headland* E Tristan da Cunha
33 R7 **Sand Point** *headland* Michigan, N USA 43.54N 83.24W
34 M7 **Sandpoint** Idaho, NW USA 48.16N 116.33W
95 H14 **Sandsele** Västerbotten, N Sweden 65.16N 17.40E
8 I14 **Sandspit** Moresby Island, British Columbia, SW Canada 53.13N 131.49W
29 P9 **Sand Springs** Oklahoma, C USA 36.08N 96.06W
31 W7 **Sandstone** Minnesota, N USA 46.07N 92.51W
38 K15 **Sand Tank Mountains** ▲ Arizona, SW USA
33 S8 **Sandusky** Michigan, N USA 43.24N 82.47W
33 S11 **Sandusky** Ohio, N USA 41.27N 82.42W
33 S12 **Sandusky River** ≈ Ohio, N USA
85 D22 **Sandverhaar** Karas, S Namibia 26.49S 17.25E
97 L24 **Sandvig** Bornholm, E Denmark 55.15N 14.45E
97 H15 **Sandvika** Akershus, S Norway 59.54N 10.28E
96 N13 **Sandviken** Gävleborg, C Sweden 60.37N 16.49E
32 M11 **Sandwich** Illinois, N USA 41.39N 88.37W
Sandwich Island *see* Efaté
Sandwich Islands *see* Hawaiian Islands
159 V16 **Sandwip Island** *island* SE Bangladesh
9 U12 **Sandy Bay** Saskatchewan, C Canada 55.31N 102.14W
191 N16 **Sandy Cape** *headland* Tasmania, SE Australia 41.27S 144.43E
178 Mm14 **Sandy Cay** *island* NW Spratly Islands
38 L3 **Sandy City** Utah, W USA 40.36N 111.53W
33 U12 **Sandy Creek** ≈ Ohio, N USA
23 O5 **Sandy Hook** Kentucky, S USA 38.09N 83.05W
20 K15 **Sandy Hook** *headland* New Jersey, NE USA 40.27N 73.59W
152 J15 **Sandykachi** *Turkm.* Sandykgachy. Maryyskiy Velayat, S Turkmenistan 36.34N 62.28E
Sandykgachy *see* Sandykachi
152 L13 **Sandykly, Peski** *desert* E Turkmenistan
9 Q13 **Sandy Lake** Alberta, W Canada 55.50N 113.30W
10 B8 **Sandy Lake** Ontario, C Canada 53.00N 93.25W
10 B8 **Sandy Lake** ⊗ Ontario, C Canada
25 S3 **Sandy Springs** Georgia, SE USA 33.57N 84.23W
26 H8 **San Elizario** Texas, SW USA 31.35N 106.16W
101 L25 **Sanem** Luxembourg, SW Luxembourg 49.33N 5.55E
44 K5 **San Esteban** Olancho, C Honduras 15.18N 85.45W
107 O6 **San Esteban de Gormaz** Castilla-León, N Spain 41.34N 3.13W
42 E5 **San Esteban, Isla** *island* NW Mexico
San Eugenio/San Eugenio del Cuareim *see* Artigas
64 H11 **San Felipe** *var.* San Felipe de Aconcagua. Valparaíso, C Chile 32.45S 70.42W
42 D3 **San Felipe** Baja California, NW Mexico 31.02N 114.55W
42 N12 **San Felipe** Guanajuato, C Mexico 21.27N 101.12W
56 K5 **San Felipe** Yaracuy, NW Venezuela 10.25N 68.40W
46 B5 **San Felipe, Cayos de** *island group* W Cuba
San Felipe de Aconcagua *see* San Felipe
San Felipe de Puerto Plata *see* Puerto Plata
39 R11 **San Felipe Pueblo** New Mexico, SW USA 35.25N 106.27W
San Feliú de Guixols *see* Sant Feliu de Guíxols
200 Oo11 **San Félix, Isla** *Eng.* San Felix Island. *island* W Chile
San Felix Island *see* San Félix, Isla
56 L11 **San Fernando de Atabapo** Amazonas, S Venezuela 4.00N 67.42W
42 C4 **San Fernando** *var.* Misión San Fernando. Baja California, NW Mexico 29.58N 115.14W
43 P9 **San Fernando** Tamaulipas, C Mexico 24.51N 98.09W
179 P9 **San Fernando** Luzon, N Philippines 16.45N 120.21E
179 P10 **San Fernando** Luzon, N Philippines 15.01N 120.41E
106 J16 **San Fernando** *prev.* Isla de León. Andalucía, S Spain 36.28N 6.12W
47 U14 **San Fernando** Trinidad, Trinidad and Tobago 10.16N 61.27W
37 S15 **San Fernando** California, W USA 34.16N 118.26W
56 L7 **San Fernando** *var.* San Fernando de Apure. Apure, C Venezuela 7.54N 67.28W
San Fernando de Apure *see* San Fernando
64 L8 **San Fernando del Valle de Catamarca** *var.* Catamarca. Catamarca, NW Argentina 28.28S 65.46W
San Fernando de Monte Cristi *see* Monte Cristi
43 P9 **San Fernando, Río** ≈ C Mexico
25 X11 **Sanford** Florida, SE USA 28.48N 81.16W
21 P9 **Sanford** Maine, NE USA 43.26N 70.46W
23 T10 **Sanford** North Carolina, SE USA 35.28N 79.10W
27 N2 **Sanford** Texas, SW USA 35.42N 101.31W

◆ Country ● Country Capital ◇ Dependent Territory ○ Dependent Territory Capital ◆ Administrative Region ✈ International Airport ▲ Mountain ▲ Mountain Range Volcano ≈ River ⊗ Lake ⊠ Reservoir

41 T10 **Sanford, Mount** ▲ Alaska, USA *62.21N 144.12W*
44 G8 **San Francisco** *var.* Gotera, San Francisco Gotera. Morazán, E El Salvador *13.40N 88.06W*
45 R16 **San Francisco** Veraguas, C Panama *8.14N 80.58W*
179 Pp11 **San Francisco** *var.* Aurora. Luzon, N Philippines *13.22N 122.31E*
37 L8 **San Francisco** California, W USA *37.46N 122.25W*
56 H5 **San Francisco** Zulia, NW Venezuela *10.36N 71.39W*
36 M8 **San Francisco** ✕ California, W USA *37.37N 122.23W*
37 N9 **San Francisco Bay** *bay* California, W USA
63 C24 **San Francisco de Bellocq** Buenos Aires, E Argentina *38.42S 60.01W*
42 I6 **San Francisco de Borja** Chihuahua, N Mexico *27.57N 106.42W*
44 J6 **San Francisco de la Paz** Olancho, C Honduras *14.55N 86.13W*
42 J7 **San Francisco del Oro** Chihuahua, N Mexico *26.52N 105.49W*
42 M12 **San Francisco del Rincón** Jalisco, SW Mexico *20.57N 101.54W*
47 O8 **San Francisco de Macorís** C Dominican Republic *19.15N 70.15W*
San Francisco de Satipo *see* Satipo
San Francisco Gotera *see* San Francisco
San Francisco Telixtlahuaca *see* Telixtlahuaca
109 K23 **San Fratello** Sicilia, Italy, C Mediterranean Sea *38.00N 14.35E*
San Fructuoso *see* Tacuarembó
84 C12 **Sanga** Cuanza Sul, NW Angola *11.10S 15.27E*
58 C5 **San Gabriel** Carchi, N Ecuador *0.37N 77.49W*
165 S15 **Sa'ngain** Xizang Zizhiqu, W China *30.46N 98.45E*
160 E13 **Sangamner** Mahārāshtra, W India *19.37N 74.18E*
158 H12 **Sāngāner** Rājasthān, N India *26.48N 75.48E*
Sangan, Koh-i- *see* Sangān, Kūh-e
155 N6 **Sangān, Kūh-e** *Pash.* Koh-i-Sangan. ▲▲ C Afghanistan
126 Ll10 **Sangar** Respublika Sakha (Yakutiya), NE Russian Federation *63.48N 127.37E*
175 O8 **Sangasanga** Borneo, C Indonesia *0.36S 117.12E*
105 N1 **Sangatte** Pas-de-Calais, N France *50.56N 1.41E*
109 B19 **San Gavino Monreale** Sardegna, Italy, C Mediterranean Sea *39.33N 8.47E*
59 D16 **Sangayan, Isla** *island* W Peru
32 L14 **Sangchris Lake** ⊡ Illinois, N USA
175 P15 **Sangeang, Pulau** *island* S Indonesia
118 I10 **Sângeorgiu de Pădure** *prev.* Erdăt-Sângeorz, Sîngeorgiu de Pădure, *Hung.* Erdőszentgyörgy. Mureș, C Romania *46.27N 24.49E*
118 I9 **Sângeorz-Băi** *var.* Singeroz Băi, *Ger.* Rumänisch-Sankt-Georgen, *Hung.* Oláhszentgyörgy; *prev.* Sîngeorz-Băi. Bistrița-Năsăud, N Romania *47.24N 24.40E*
37 R10 **Sanger** California, W USA *36.42N 119.33W*
27 T5 **Sanger** Texas, SW USA *33.21N 97.10W*
Sângerei *see* Sîngerei
103 L15 **Sangerhausen** Sachsen-Anhalt, C Germany *51.28N 11.18E*
47 S6 **San Germán** W Puerto Rico *18.05N 67.02W*
San Germano *see* Cassino
167 N2 **Sanggan He** ≈ E China
175 Oo16 **Sanggar, Teluk** *bay* Nusa Tenggara, S Indonesia
174 L8 **Sanggau** Borneo, C Indonesia *0.07N 110.34E*
81 H16 **Sangha** ≈ Central African Republic/Congo
81 G16 **Sangha-Mbaéré** ◈ *prefecture* SW Central African Republic
155 Q15 **Sānghar** Sind, SE Pakistan *26.10N 68.58E*
117 F22 **Sangiás** ▲ S Greece *36.39N 22.24E*
Sangihe, Kepulauan *see* Sangir, Kepulauan
175 S4 **Sangihe, Pulau** *var.* Sangir. *island* N Indonesia
56 G8 **San Gil** Santander, C Colombia *6.34N 73.07W*
108 F12 **San Gimignano** Toscana, C Italy *43.30N 11.00E*
154 M8 **Sangīn** *var.* Sangin. Helmand, S Afghanistan *32.03N 64.49E*
109 O21 **San Giovanni in Fiore** Calabria, SW Italy *39.16N 16.42E*
109 M16 **San Giovanni Rotondo** Puglia, SE Italy *41.43N 15.43E*
108 G12 **San Giovanni Valdarno** Toscana, C Italy *43.34N 11.31E*
Sangir *see* Sangihe, Pulau
175 Rr6 **Sangir, Kepulauan** *var.* Kepulauan Sangihe. *island group* N Indonesia
168 K9 **Sangiyn Dalay** Dundgovĭ, C Mongolia *45.59N 104.58E*
168 H9 **Sangiyn Dalay** Govĭ-Altay, C Mongolia *45.12N 97.51E*
168 K11 **Sangiyn Dalay** Ömnögovĭ, S Mongolia *42.50N 105.04E*
168 K8 **Sangiyn Dalay** Övörhangay, C Mongolia *46.35N 103.18E*
169 Y15 **Sangju** *Jap.* Shōshū. C South Korea *36.26N 128.09E*
178 Ii11 **Sangkha** Surin, E Thailand *14.36N 103.43E*
175 Oo7 **Sangkulirang** Borneo, N Indonesia *1.00N 117.56E*
175 Oo7 **Sangkulirang, Teluk** *bay* Borneo, N Indonesia
161 E16 **Sāngli** Mahārāshtra, W India *16.55N 74.37E*
81 E16 **Sangmélima** Sud, S Cameroon *2.57N 11.55E*
37 V15 **San Gorgonio Mountain** ▲ California, W USA *34.06N 116.50W*
39 T8 **Sangre de Cristo Mountains** ▲▲ Colorado/New Mexico, C USA
63 A20 **San Gregorio** Santa Fe, C Argentina *34.18S 62.01W*
63 F18 **San Gregorio de Polanco** Tacuarembó, C Uruguay *32.37S 55.49W*
47 V14 **Sangre Grande** Trinidad, Trinidad and Tobago *10.35N 61.07W*
165 N16 **Sangri** Xizang Zizhiqu, W China *29.17N 92.01E*
158 H9 **Sangrūr** Punjab, NW India *30.16N 75.52E*
46 I11 **Sangster** *off.* Sir Donald Sangster International Airport, *var.* Montego Bay. ✕ (Montego Bay) W Jamaica *18.30N 77.54W*
61 G17 **Sangue, Rio do** ≈ W Brazil
107 R4 **Sangüesa** Navarra, N Spain *42.34N 1.16W*
63 C16 **San Gustavo** Entre Ríos, E Argentina *30.40S 59.22W*
Sangyuan *see* Wuqiao
42 C6 **San Hipólito, Punta** *headland* W Mexico *26.57N 114.00W*
25 W15 **Sanibel** Sanibel Island, Florida, SE USA *26.27N 82.01W*
25 V15 **Sanibel Island** *island* Florida, SE USA
62 F13 **San Ignacio** Misiones, NE Argentina *27.13S 55.29W*
44 F2 **San Ignacio** *prev.* Cayo, El Cayo. Cayo, W Belize *17.09N 89.02W*
59 L16 **San Ignacio** Beni, N Bolivia *14.54S 65.34W*
59 O18 **San Ignacio** Santa Cruz, E Bolivia *16.27S 60.57W*
44 M14 **San Ignacio** *var.* San Ignacio de Acosta. San José, W Costa Rica *9.46N 84.10W*
42 E6 **San Ignacio** Baja California Sur, W Mexico *27.18N 112.51W*
42 J10 **San Ignacio** Sinaloa, W Mexico *23.55N 106.25W*
58 B9 **San Ignacio** Cajamarca, N Peru *5.03S 79.03W*
San Ignacio de Acosta *see* San Ignacio
42 D7 **San Ignacio, Laguna** *lagoon* W Mexico
10 I6 **Sanikiluaq** Belcher Islands, Nunavut, C Canada *55.16N 77.44W*
179 Pp9 **San Ildefonso Peninsula** *peninsula* Luzon, N Philippines
Saniquillie *see* Sanniquellie
63 D20 **San Isidro** Buenos Aires, E Argentina *34.28S 58.31W*
45 N14 **San Isidro** *var.* San Isidro de El General. San José, SE Costa Rica *9.21N 83.42W*
San Isidro de El General *see* San Isidro
56 E5 **San Jacinto** Bolívar, N Colombia *9.52N 75.10W*
37 U16 **San Jacinto** California, W USA *33.47N 116.58W*
37 V15 **San Jacinto Peak** ▲ California, W USA *33.48N 116.40W*
63 F14 **San Javier** Misiones, NE Argentina *27.49S 55.06W*
63 C16 **San Javier** Santa Fe, C Argentina *30.34S 59.58W*
107 S13 **San Javier** Murcia, SE Spain *37.49N 0.49W*
63 D18 **San Javier** Río Negro, W Uruguay *32.40S 58.07W*
63 C16 **San Javier, Río** ≈ C Argentina
Sanjiang *see* Jinping
166 L12 **Sanjiang** *var.* Guyi, Sanjiang Dongzu Zizhixian. Guangxi Zhuangzu Zizhiqu, S China *25.49N 109.31E*
Sanjiang Dongzu Zizhixian *see* Sanjiang
171 Kk13 **Sanjō** *var.* Sanzyô. Niigata, Honshū, C Japan *37.39N 139.00E*
59 M15 **San Joaquín** Beni, N Bolivia *13.03S 64.47W*
57 O6 **San Joaquín** Anzoátegui, NE Venezuela *9.21N 64.30W*
37 O9 **San Joaquin River** ≈ California, W USA
37 P10 **San Joaquin Valley** *valley* California, W USA
63 A18 **San Jorge** Santa Fe, C Argentina *31.49S 61.49W*
195 W15 **San Jorge** *island* N Solomon Islands
42 D3 **San Jorge, Bahía de** *bay* NW Mexico
San Jorge, Isla de *see* Weddell Island
65 J19 **San Jorge, Golfo** *var.* Gulf of San Jorge. *gulf* S Argentina
San Jorge, Gulf of *see* San Jorge, Golfo
196 K8 **San Jose** Tinian, S Northern Mariana Islands *15.00S 145.38E*
179 Pp12 **San Jose** Mindoro, N Philippines *12.20N 121.07E*
37 N9 **San Jose** California, W USA *37.18N 121.53W*
63 F14 **San José** Misiones, NE Argentina *27.46S 55.46W*
59 P19 **San José** *var.* San José de Chiquitos. Santa Cruz, E Bolivia *14.13S 68.04W*
44 M14 **San José** ● (Costa Rica) San José, C Costa Rica *9.55N 84.05W*
44 C7 **San José** *var.* Puerto San José. Escuintla, S Guatemala *13.55N 90.48W*
42 G6 **San José** Sonora, NW Mexico *27.31N 110.09W*
107 U11 **San José** Eivissa, Spain, W Mediterranean Sea *38.55N 1.18E*
56 H5 **San José** Zulia, NW Venezuela *9.58N 72.22W*
44 M14 **San José** *off.* Provincia de San José. ◈ *province* W Costa Rica
63 E19 **San José** ◈ *department* S Uruguay
44 M13 **San José** ✕ Alajuela, C Costa Rica *10.03N 84.12W*
San José *see* San José del Guaviare, Colombia
San José *see* San José de Mayo, S Uruguay
179 P9 **San Jose City** Luzon, N Philippines *15.49N 120.57E*
179 Pp13 **San Jose de Buenavista** Panay Island, C Philippines *10.44N 122.00E*
San José de Cúcuta *see* Cúcuta
63 D16 **San José de Feliciano** Entre Ríos, E Argentina *30.21S 58.47W*
57 O6 **San José de Guanipa** *var.* El Tigrito. Anzoátegui, NE Venezuela *8.54N 64.10W*
64 I9 **San José de Jáchal** San Juan, W Argentina *30.15S 68.46W*
42 G10 **San José del Cabo** Baja California Sur, W Mexico *23.01N 109.40W*
56 G12 **San José del Guaviare** *var.* San José. Guaviare, S Colombia *2.34N 72.37W*
63 E20 **San José de Mayo** *var.* San José. San José, S Uruguay *34.19S 56.42W*
56 I10 **San José de Ocuné** Vichada, E Colombia *4.10N 70.21W*
43 O9 **San José de Raíces** Nuevo León, NE Mexico *24.32N 100.15W*
65 K17 **San José, Golfo** *gulf* E Argentina
42 F9 **San José, Isla** *island* W Mexico
45 U16 **San José, Isla** *island* SE Panama
27 U14 **San Jose Island** *island* Texas, SW USA
64 I10 **San Juan** San Juan, W Argentina *31.36S 68.26W*
47 N9 **San Juan** *var.* San Juan de la Maguana. C Dominican Republic *18.46N 71.13W*
59 E17 **San Juan** Ica, S Peru *15.22S 75.08W*
47 U5 **San Juan** ○ (Puerto Rico) NE Puerto Rico *18.28N 66.06W*
64 H10 **San Juan** *off.* Provincia de San Juan. ◈ *province* W Argentina
47 U5 **San Juan** *var.* Luis Muñoz Marin. ✕ NE Puerto Rico *18.27N 66.05W*
San Juan *see* San Juan de los Morros
62 O7 **San Juan Bautista** Misiones, S Paraguay *26.39S 57.08W*
37 O10 **San Juan Bautista** California, W USA *36.50N 121.34W*
San Juan Bautista *see* Villahermosa
San Juan Bautista Cuicatlán *see* Cuicatlán
San Juan Bautista Tuxtepec *see* Tuxtepec
81 C17 **San Juan, Cabo** *headland* S Equatorial Guinea *1.09N 9.25E*
107 S12 **San Juan de Alicante** País Valenciano, E Spain *38.25N 0.27W*
56 H7 **San Juan de Colón** Táchira, NW Venezuela *8.01N 72.16W*
42 L9 **San Juan de Guadalupe** Durango, C Mexico *25.12N 100.50W*
San Juan de la Maguana *see* San Juan
56 G4 **San Juan del Cesar** La Guajira, N Colombia *10.45N 73.00W*
42 L15 **San Juan de Lima, Punta** *headland* SW Mexico *18.34N 103.40W*
44 I8 **San Juan de Limay** Estelí, NW Nicaragua *13.10N 86.36W*
45 N12 **San Juan del Norte** *var.* Greytown. Río San Juan, SE Nicaragua *10.54N 83.42W*
56 K4 **San Juan de los Cayos** Falcón, N Venezuela *11.06N 68.25W*
42 M12 **San Juan de los Lagos** Jalisco, C Mexico *21.15N 102.15W*
56 L5 **San Juan de los Morros** *var.* San Juan. Guárico, N Venezuela *9.52N 67.22W*
42 K9 **San Juan del Río** Durango, C Mexico *25.12N 100.50W*
43 O13 **San Juan del Río** Querétaro de Arteaga, C Mexico *20.21N 100.01W*
44 J11 **San Juan del Sur** Rivas, SW Nicaragua *11.14N 85.52W*
56 M9 **San Juan de Manapiare** Amazonas, S Venezuela *5.15N 66.04W*
42 E7 **San Juanico** Baja California Sur, W Mexico
42 D7 **San Juanico, Punta** *headland* W Mexico *26.01N 112.17W*
34 G6 **San Juan Islands** *island group* Washington, NW USA
42 I6 **San Juanito** Chihuahua, N Mexico
42 I12 **San Juanito, Isla** *island* C Mexico
39 R8 **San Juan Mountains** ▲▲ Colorado, C USA
56 E5 **San Juan Nepomuceno** Bolívar, NW Colombia *9.57N 75.06W*
46 E5 **San Juan, Pico** ▲ C Cuba *21.58N 80.10W*
203 W15 **San Juan, Punta** *headland* Easter Island, Chile, E Pacific Ocean *27.03S 109.22W*
44 M12 **San Juan, Río** ≈ Costa Rica/Nicaragua
43 S15 **San Juan, Río** ≈ SE Mexico
39 O8 **San Juan River** ≈ Colorado/Utah, W USA
San Julián *see* Puerto San Julián
63 B17 **San Justo** Santa Fe, C Argentina *30.46S 60.31W*
111 W5 **Sankt Aegyd-am-Neuwalde** Niederösterreich, E Austria *47.51N 15.34E*
111 U9 **Sankt Andrä** *Slvn.* Šent Andraž. Kärnten, S Austria *46.46N 14.49E*
Sankt Andrä *see* Szentendre
Sankt Anna *see* Sântana
110 K8 **Sankt Anton-am-Arlberg** Vorarlberg, W Austria *47.08N 10.11E*
103 E16 **Sankt Augustin** Nordrhein-Westfalen, W Germany *50.46N 7.10E*
Sankt-Bartholomäi *see* Palamuse
103 F24 **Sankt Blasien** Baden-Württemberg, SW Germany *47.43N 8.09E*
111 R3 **Sankt Florian am Inn** Oberösterreich, N Austria *48.24N 13.27E*
110 I7 **Sankt Gallen** *var.* St.Gallen, *Eng.* Saint Gall, *Fr.* St-Gall. Sankt Gallen, NE Switzerland *47.25N 9.22E*
110 H8 **Sankt Gallen** *var.* St.Gallen, Eng, Saint Gall, *Fr.* St-Gall. ◈ *canton* NE Switzerland
110 J8 **Sankt Gallenkirch** Vorarlberg, W Austria *47.00N 10.59E*
111 Q5 **Sankt Georgen** Salzburg, N Austria *47.59N 12.57E*
Sankt Georgen *see* Đurđevac, Croatia
Sankt-Georgen *see* Sfântu Gheorghe, Romania
111 R6 **Sankt Gilgen** Salzburg, NW Austria *47.46N 13.21E*
Sankt Gotthard *see* Szentgotthárd
103 E20 **Sankt Ingbert** Saarland, SW Germany *49.16N 7.07E*
Sankt-Jakobi *see* Viru-Jaagupi, Lääne-Virumaa, Estonia
Sankt-Jakobi *see* Pärnu-Jaagupi, Pärnumaa, Estonia
Sankt Johann *see* Sankt Johann in Tirol
111 T7 **Sankt Johann am Tauern** Steiermark, E Austria *47.20N 14.27E*
111 Q7 **Sankt Johann im Pongau** Salzburg, NW Austria *47.22N 13.13E*
111 P6 **Sankt Johann in Tirol** *var.* Sankt Johann. Tirol, W Austria *47.31N 12.25E*
Sankt-Johannis *see* Järva-Jaani
110 L8 **Sankt Leonhard** Tirol, W Austria *47.05N 10.53E*
Sankt Margarethen *see* Sankt Margarethen im Burgenland
111 Y5 **Sankt Margarethen im Burgenland** *var.* Sankt Margarethen. Burgenland, E Austria *47.49N 16.37E*
Sankt Martin *see* Martin
111 X8 **Sankt Martin an der Raab** Burgenland, SE Austria *46.59N 16.12E*
111 U7 **Sankt Michael in Obersteiermark** Steiermark, SE Austria *47.21N 14.59E*
Sankt Michel *see* Mikkeli
Sankt Moritz *see* St.Moritz
110 E11 **Sankt Niklaus** Valais, S Switzerland *46.09N 7.48E*
111 S7 **Sankt Nikolai** *var.* Sankt Nikolai im Sölktal. Steiermark, SE Austria *47.18N 14.04E*
Sankt Nikolai im Sölktal *see* Sankt Nikolai
111 U9 **Sankt Paul** *var.* Sankt Paul im Lavanttal. Kärnten, S Austria *46.42N 14.53E*
Sankt Paul im Lavanttal *see* Sankt Paul
Sankt Peter *see* Pivka
111 W9 **Sankt Peter am Ottersbach** Steiermark, SE Austria *46.49N 15.48E*
128 J13 **Sankt-Peterburg** *prev.* Leningrad, Petrograd, *Eng.* Saint Petersburg, *Fin.* Pietari. Leningradskaya Oblast', NW Russian Federation *59.55N 30.25E*
102 H8 **Sankt Peter-Ording** Schleswig-Holstein, N Germany *54.18N 8.37E*
111 V4 **Sankt Pölten** Niederösterreich, N Austria *48.14N 15.37E*
111 W7 **Sankt Ruprecht** *var.* Sankt Ruprecht an der Raab. Steiermark, SE Austria *47.10N 15.41E*
Sankt Ruprecht an der Raab *see* Sankt Ruprecht
Sankt-Ulrich *see* Ortisei
111 T4 **Sankt Valentin** Niederösterreich, C Austria *48.09N 14.30E*
Sankt Veit am Flaum *see* Rijeka
111 T9 **Sankt Veit an der Glan** *Slvn.* Šent Vid. Kärnten, S Austria *46.46N 14.22E*
101 M21 **Sankt-Vith** *var.* Saint-Vith. Liège, E Belgium *50.16N 6.07E*
103 E20 **Sankt Wendel** Saarland, SW Germany *49.28N 7.10E*
111 R6 **Sankt Wolfgang** Salzburg, NW Austria *47.43N 13.30E*
81 K21 **Sankuru** ≈ C Dem. Rep. Congo
42 D8 **San Lázaro, Cabo** *headland* W Mexico *24.46N 112.15W*
143 O16 **Şanlıurfa** *prev.* Sanli Urfa, Urfa, *anc.* Edessa. Şanlıurfa, S Turkey *37.07N 38.45E*
143 O16 **Şanlıurfa** *prev.* Urfa. ◈ *province* SE Turkey
143 O16 **Şanlıurfa Yaylası** *plateau* SE Turkey
63 B18 **San Lorenzo** Santa Fe, C Argentina *32.37S 60.48W*
59 M21 **San Lorenzo** Tarija, S Bolivia *21.27S 64.47W*
58 C5 **San Lorenzo** Esmeraldas, N Ecuador *1.15N 78.51W*
44 H8 **San Lorenzo** Valle, S Honduras *13.25N 87.27W*
107 N8 **San Lorenzo de El Escorial** *var.* El Escorial. Madrid, C Spain *40.36N 4.07W*
42 E5 **San Lorenzo, Isla** *island* NW Mexico
59 C14 **San Lorenzo, Isla** *island* W Peru
65 G20 **San Lorenzo, Monte** ▲ S Argentina *47.40S 72.12W*
42 I9 **San Lorenzo, Río** ≈ C Mexico
106 J15 **Sanlúcar de Barrameda** Andalucía, S Spain *36.46N 6.21W*
106 J14 **Sanlúcar la Mayor** Andalucía, S Spain *37.24N 6.13W*
42 F11 **San Lucas** Baja California Sur, NW Mexico *22.49N 109.52W*
42 E6 **San Lucas** *var.* Cabo San Lucas. Baja California Sur, W Mexico *27.13N 112.15W*
42 G11 **San Lucas, Cabo** *var.* San Lucas Cape. *headland* W Mexico *22.52N 109.55W*
San Lucas Cape *see* San Lucas, Cabo
64 J11 **San Luis** San Luis, C Argentina *33.18S 66.18W*
44 E4 **San Luis** Petén, NE Guatemala *16.16N 89.27W*
42 D2 **San Luis** *var.* San Luis Río Colorado. Sonora, NW Mexico *32.25N 114.48W*
44 M7 **San Luis** Región Autónoma Atlántico Norte, NE Nicaragua *13.58N 84.10W*
38 H15 **San Luis** Arizona, SW USA *32.27N 114.45W*
39 T8 **San Luis** Colorado, C USA *37.09N 105.24W*
56 J4 **San Luis** Falcón, N Venezuela *11.08N 69.36W*
64 J11 **San Luis** *off.* Provincia de San Luis. ◈ *province* C Argentina
43 N12 **San Luis de la Paz** Guanajuato, C Mexico *21.15N 100.33W*
42 K8 **San Luis del Cordero** Durango, C Mexico *25.25N 104.09W*
42 D4 **San Luis, Isla** *island* NW Mexico
44 E6 **San Luis Jilotepeque** Jalapa, SE Guatemala *14.36N 89.40W*
59 M16 **San Luis, Laguna de** ◎ NW Bolivia
37 P13 **San Luis Obispo** California, W USA *35.16N 120.39W*
39 R7 **San Luis Peak** ▲ Colorado, C USA *37.59N 106.55W*
43 N11 **San Luis Potosí** San Luis Potosí, C Mexico *22.09N 100.57W*
43 N11 **San Luis Potosí** ◈ *state* C Mexico
37 O10 **San Luis Reservoir** ⊡ California, W USA
San Luis Río Colorado *see* San Luis
39 S8 **San Luis Valley** *basin* Colorado, C USA
109 C19 **Sanluri** Sardegna, Italy, C Mediterranean Sea *39.34N 8.54E*
63 D23 **San Manuel** Buenos Aires, E Argentina *37.46S 58.49W*
38 M15 **San Manuel** Arizona, SW USA *32.36N 110.37W*
108 F11 **San Marcello Pistoiese** Toscana, C Italy *44.03N 10.46E*
109 N20 **San Marco Argentano** Calabria, SW Italy *39.31N 16.07E*
56 E6 **San Marcos** Sucre, N Colombia *8.37N 75.12W*
44 M14 **San Marcos** San José, C Costa Rica *9.39N 84.00W*
44 B5 **San Marcos** San Marcos, W Guatemala *14.57N 91.46W*
44 F6 **San Marcos** Ocotepeque, SW Honduras *14.23N 88.57W*
43 O16 **San Marcos** Guerrero, S Mexico *16.47N 99.29W*
27 S11 **San Marcos** Texas, SW USA *29.52N 97.56W*
44 A5 **San Marcos** *off.* Departamento de San Marcos. ◈ *department* W Guatemala
San Marcos de Arica *see* Arica
42 E6 **San Marcos, Isla** *island* W Mexico
108 H11 **San Marino** ● (San Marino) C San Marino *43.53N 12.27E*
108 I11 **San Marino** *off.* Republic of San Marino. ◆ *republic* S Europe
64 I11 **San Martín** Mendoza, C Argentina *33.04S 68.28W*
56 F11 **San Martín** Meta, C Colombia *3.43N 73.42W*
58 D11 **San Martín** *off.* Departamento de San Martín. ◈ *department* C Peru
204 I5 **San Martín** *Argentinian research station* Antarctica *68.18S 67.03W*
65 H16 **San Martín de los Andes** Neuquén, W Argentina *40.10S 71.22W*
106 M8 **San Martín de Valdeiglesias** Madrid, C Spain *40.21N 4.24W*
65 G21 **San Martín, Lago** *var.* Lago O'Higgins. ◎ S Argentina
108 H6 **San Martino di Castrozza** Trentino-Alto Adige, N Italy *46.16N 11.50E*
59 N16 **San Martín, Río** ≈ N Bolivia
San Martín Texmelucan *see* Texmelucan
37 N9 **San Mateo** California, W USA *37.33N 122.19W*
57 O6 **San Mateo** Anzoátegui, NE Venezuela *9.34N 64.30W*
44 B4 **San Mateo Ixtatán** Huehuetenango, W Guatemala *15.48N 91.30W*
59 Q18 **San Matías** Santa Cruz, E Bolivia *16.19S 58.23W*
65 K16 **San Matías, Golfo** *var.* Gulf of San Matías. *gulf* E Argentina
San Matías, Gulf of *see* San Matías
13 O8 **Sanmaur** Quebec, SE Canada *47.52N 73.47W*
167 T10 **Sanmen Wan** *bay* E China
166 M6 **Sanmenxia** *var.* Shan Xian. Henan, C China *34.46N 111.16E*
Sânmiclăuș Mare *see* Sânnicolau Mare
63 D14 **San Miguel** Corrientes, NE Argentina *28.02S 57.38W*
59 L16 **San Miguel** Beni, N Bolivia *16.43S 61.06W*
44 G8 **San Miguel** San Miguel, SE El Salvador *13.27N 88.10W*
42 L6 **San Miguel** Coahuila de Zaragoza, N Mexico *29.10N 101.28W*
42 J9 **San Miguel** *var.* San Miguel de Cruces. Durango, C Mexico *24.25N 105.55W*
45 U16 **San Miguel** Panamá, SE Panama *8.26N 78.57W*
37 P12 **San Miguel** California, W USA *35.45N 120.42W*
44 B9 **San Miguel** ◈ *department* E El Salvador
43 N13 **San Miguel de Allende** Guanajuato, C Mexico *20.54N 100.46W*
San Miguel de Cruces *see* San Miguel
San Miguel de Ibarra *see* Ibarra
63 D21 **San Miguel del Monte** Buenos Aires, E Argentina *35.25S 58.49W*
64 J7 **San Miguel de Tucumán** *var.* Tucumán. Tucumán, N Argentina *26.46S 65.15W*
45 V16 **San Miguel, Golfo de** *gulf* S Panama
37 P15 **San Miguel Island** *island* California, W USA
44 L11 **San Miguelito** Río San Juan, S Nicaragua *11.22N 84.52W*
45 T15 **San Miguelito** Panamá, C Panama *8.58N 79.31W*
59 N18 **San Miguel, Río** ≈ E Bolivia
58 D6 **San Miguel, Río** ≈ Colombia/Ecuador
42 I7 **San Miguel, Río** ≈ N Mexico
44 G8 **San Miguel, Volcán de** ▲ SE El Salvador *13.27N 88.18W*
167 Q12 **Sanming** Fujian, SE China *26.10N 117.37E*
108 F11 **San Miniato** Toscana, C Italy *43.40N 10.53E*
San Murezzan *see* St.Moritz
Sannār *see* Sennar
109 M15 **Sannicandro Garganico** Puglia, SE Italy *41.49N 15.31E*
42 H6 **San Nicolás** Sonora, NW Mexico *28.31N 109.24W*
63 C19 **San Nicolás de los Arroyos** Buenos Aires, E Argentina *33.17S 60.12W*
37 R16 **San Nicolas Island** *island* Channel Islands, California, W USA
Sânnicolaul-Mare *see* Sânnicolau Mare
118 E11 **Sânnicolau Mare** *var.* Sânnicolaul-Mare, *Hung.* Nagyszentmiklós; *prev.* Sânmiclăuș Mare, Sînnicolau Mare. Timiș, W Romania *46.05N 20.37E*
126 Ll5 **Sannikova, Proliv** *strait* NE Russian Federation
78 K16 **Sanniquellie** *var.* Saniquillie. NE Liberia *7.24N 8.45W*
172 N9 **Sannohe** Aomori, Honshū, C Japan *40.23N 141.16E*
Sanntaler Alpen *see* Kamniško-Savinjske Alpe
171 K15 **Sano** Tochigi, Honshū, S Japan *36.19N 139.26E*
113 O17 **Sanok** Podkarpackie, SE Poland *49.31N 22.14E*
56 E5 **San Onofre** Sucre, NW Colombia *9.45N 75.33W*
59 K21 **San Pablo** Potosí, S Bolivia *21.43S 66.37W*
179 P11 **San Pablo** *off.* San Pablo City. Luzon, N Philippines *14.04N 121.16E*
San Pablo Balleza *see* Balleza
37 N8 **San Pablo Bay** *bay* California, W USA
42 C6 **San Pablo, Punta** *headland* W Mexico *27.12N 114.30W*
45 R16 **San Pablo, Río** ≈ C Panama
179 Q11 **San Pascual** Burias Island, C Philippines *13.06N 122.59E*
123 Jj16 **San Pawl il-Bahar** *Eng.* Saint Paul's Bay. E Malta *35.57N 14.24E*
63 C19 **San Pedro** Buenos Aires, E Argentina *33.37S 59.42W*
64 K5 **San Pedro** Jujuy, N Argentina *24.13S 64.51W*
62 G13 **San Pedro** Misiones, NE Argentina *26.37S 54.12W*
44 H1 **San Pedro** Corozal, NE Belize *17.58N 87.55W*
42 L8 **San Pedro** *var.* San Pedro de las Colonias. Coahuila de Zaragoza, NE Mexico *25.47N 102.57W*
64 O5 **San Pedro** San Pedro, SE Paraguay *24.04S 57.03W*
64 O6 **San Pedro** *off.* Departamento de San Pedro. ◈ *department* C Paraguay
79 N16 **San Pedro** ✕ (Yamoussoukro) C Ivory Coast *6.49N 5.14W*
46 G6 **San Pedro** ≈ C Cuba
San Pedro *see* San Pedro del Pinatar
78 M17 **San-Pédro** S Ivory Coast *4.45N 6.37W*
44 D5 **San Pedro Carchá** Alta Verapaz, C Guatemala *15.30N 90.12W*
37 S16 **San Pedro Channel** *channel* California, W USA
64 I5 **San Pedro de Atacama** Antofagasta, N Chile *22.52S 68.10W*
San Pedro de Durazno *see* Durazno
42 G5 **San Pedro de la Cueva** Sonora, NW Mexico *29.16N 109.46W*
San Pedro de las Colonias *see* San Pedro
58 B11 **San Pedro de Lloc** La Libertad, NW Peru *7.27S 79.34W*
107 S13 **San Pedro del Pinatar** *var.* San Pedro. Murcia, SE Spain *37.49N 0.46W*
47 P9 **San Pedro de Macorís** SE Dominican Republic *18.28N 69.19W*
42 C3 **San Pedro Mártir, Sierra** ▲▲ NW Mexico
San Pedro Pochutla *see* Pochutla
44 D2 **San Pedro, Río** ≈ Guatemala/Mexico
42 K10 **San Pedro, Río** ≈ C Mexico
106 J10 **San Pedro, Sierra de** ▲▲ W Spain
44 G5 **San Pedro Sula** Cortés, NW Honduras *15.25N 88.01W*
San Pedro Tapanatepec *see* Tapanatepec
64 I4 **San Pedro, Volcán** ▲ N Chile *21.46S 68.13W*
108 E7 **San Pellegrino Terme** Lombardia, N Italy *45.53N 9.42E*
27 T16 **San Perlita** Texas, SW USA *26.30N 97.38W*
San Pietro *see* Supetar
San Pietro del Carso *see* Pivka
109 A20 **San Pietro, Isola di** *island* W Italy
34 K7 **Sanpoil River** ≈ Washington, NW USA
171 L12 **Sanpoku** *var.* Sampoku. Niigata, Honshū, C Japan *38.32N 139.33E*
42 C3 **San Quintín** Baja California, NW Mexico *30.21N 115.58W*
42 B3 **San Quintín, Bahía de** *bay* NW Mexico
42 B3 **San Quintín, Cabo** *headland* NW Mexico *30.22N 116.01W*
64 I12 **San Rafael** Mendoza, W Argentina *34.43S 68.15W*
43 N9 **San Rafael** Nuevo León, NE Mexico *25.01N 100.33W*
36 M8 **San Rafael** California, W USA *37.58N 122.31W*
39 Q11 **San Rafael** New Mexico, SW USA *35.03N 107.52W*
56 H4 **San Rafael** *var.* El Moján. Zulia, NW Venezuela *10.58N 71.45W*
44 J8 **San Rafael del Norte** Jinotega, NW Nicaragua *13.10N 86.10W*
44 J10 **San Rafael del Sur** Managua, SW Nicaragua *11.51N 86.24W*
38 M5 **San Rafael Knob** ▲ Utah, W USA *38.46N 110.45W*
37 Q14 **San Rafael Mountains** ▲▲ California, W USA
44 M13 **San Ramón** Alajuela, C Costa Rica *10.04N 84.27W*
59 E14 **San Ramón** Junín, C Peru *11.08S 75.19W*
63 F19 **San Ramón** Canelones, S Uruguay *34.18S 55.55W*
64 K5 **San Ramón de la Nueva Orán** Salta, N Argentina *23.07S 64.19W*
59 O16 **San Ramón, Río** ≈ E Bolivia
108 B11 **San Remo** Liguria, NW Italy *43.48N 7.46E*
56 J3 **San Román, Cabo** *headland* NW Venezuela *12.10N 70.01W*
63 C15 **San Roque** Corrientes, NE Argentina *28.34S 58.45W*
196 I4 **San Roque** Saipan, S Northern Mariana Islands *15.15S 85.46E*
106 K16 **San Roque** Andalucía, S Spain *36.13N 5.22W*
27 R9 **San Saba** Texas, SW USA *31.12N 98.43W*
27 Q9 **San Saba River** ≈ Texas, SW USA
63 D17 **San Salvador** Entre Ríos, E Argentina *31.37S 58.30W*
44 F7 **San Salvador** ● (El Salvador) San Salvador, SW El Salvador *13.42N 89.12W*
44 A10 **San Salvador** ◈ *department* C El Salvador
44 F8 **San Salvador** ✕ La Paz, S El Salvador *13.27N 89.04W*
46 K4 **San Salvador** *prev.* Watlings Island. *island* E Bahamas
64 J5 **San Salvador de Jujuy** *var.* Jujuy. Jujuy, N Argentina *24.10S 65.19W*
44 F7 **San Salvador, Volcán de** ▲ C El Salvador *13.58N 89.14W*
79 Q14 **Sansanné-Mango** *var.* Mango. N Togo *10.21N 0.28E*
47 S5 **San Sebastián** W Puerto Rico *18.21N 67.00W*
65 J24 **San Sebastián, Bahía** *bay* S Argentina
Sansenhō *see* Sach'ŏn
108 H12 **Sansepolcro** Toscana, C Italy *43.34N 12.12E*
109 M16 **San Severo** Puglia, SE Italy *41.40N 15.22E*
114 F11 **Sanski Most** Federacija Bosna I Hercegovina, NW Bosnia & Herzegovina *44.43N 16.40E*
176 Ww9 **Sansundi** Papua, E Indonesia *0.42S 135.48E*
106 K11 **Santa Amalia** Extremadura, W Spain *39.00N 6.01W*
62 F13 **Santa Ana** Misiones, NE Argentina *27.22S 55.34W*
59 L16 **Santa Ana** Beni, N Bolivia *13.43S 65.37W*
44 E7 **Santa Ana** Santa Ana, NW El Salvador *13.58N 89.34W*
42 F4 **Santa Ana** Sonora, NW Mexico *30.33N 111.07W*
37 T16 **Santa Ana** California, W USA *33.45N 117.52W*
57 N6 **Santa Ana** Nueva Esparta, NE Venezuela *9.15N 64.39W*
44 A9 **Santa Ana** ◈ *department* NW El Salvador
Santa Ana de Coro *see* Coro
44 E7 **Santa Ana, Volcán de** *var.* La Matepec. ▲ W El Salvador *13.49N 89.36W*
42 J7 **Santa Barbara** Chihuahua, N Mexico *26.46N 105.46W*
37 Q14 **Santa Barbara** California, W USA *34.24N 119.40W*
44 G6 **Santa Bárbara** Santa Bárbara, W Honduras *14.57N 88.15W*
56 L11 **Santa Bárbara** Amazonas, S Venezuela *3.55N 67.06W*
56 I7 **Santa Bárbara** Barinas, W Venezuela *7.48N 71.10W*
44 F5 **Santa Bárbara** ◈ *department* NW Honduras
Santa Bárbara *see* Iscuandé
37 Q15 **Santa Barbara Channel** *channel* California, W USA
Santa Bárbara de Samaná *see* Samaná
37 R16 **Santa Barbara Island** *island* Channel Islands, California, W USA
56 E5 **Santa Catalina** Bolívar, N Colombia *10.34N 75.22W*
45 R15 **Santa Catalina** Bocas del Toro, W Panama *8.46N 81.18W*
37 T17 **Santa Catalina, Gulf of** *gulf* California, W USA
42 F8 **Santa Catalina, Isla** *island* W Mexico
37 S16 **Santa Catalina Island** *island* Channel Islands, California, W USA
43 N8 **Santa Catarina** Nuevo León, NE Mexico *25.39N 100.30W*
62 H13 **Santa Catarina** *off.* Estado de Santa Catarina. ◈ *state* S Brazil
Santa Catarina de Tepehuanes *see* Tepehuanes
62 L13 **Santa Catarina, Ilha de** *island* S Brazil
47 Q16 **Santa Catherina** Curaçao, C Netherlands Antilles *12.07N 68.46W*
46 E5 **Santa Clara** Villa Clara, C Cuba *22.25N 78.00W*
37 N9 **Santa Clara** California, W USA *37.20N 121.57W*
38 J8 **Santa Clara** Utah, W USA *37.07N 113.39W*
Santa Clara *see* Santa Clara de Olimar
63 F18 **Santa Clara de Olimar** *var.* Santa Clara. Cerro Largo, NE Uruguay *32.54S 54.55W*
63 A17 **Santa Clara de Saguier** Santa Fe, C Argentina *31.21S 61.49W*
Santa Coloma *see* Santa Coloma de Gramanet
107 X5 **Santa Coloma de Farners** *var.* Santa Coloma de Farnés. Cataluña, NE Spain *41.52N 2.39E*
Santa Coloma de Farnés *see* Santa Coloma de Farners
107 W6 **Santa Coloma de Gramanet** *var.* Santa Coloma. Cataluña, NE Spain *41.28N 2.13E*
106 G2 **Santa Comba** Galicia, NW Spain *43.01N 8.49W*
Santa Comba *see* Uaco Cungo
106 H8 **Santa Comba Dão** Viseu, N Portugal *40.22N 8.07W*
84 C10 **Santa Cruz** Uíge, NW Angola *6.56S 16.25E*
59 N19 **Santa Cruz** *var.* Santa Cruz de la Sierra. Santa Cruz, C Bolivia *17.49S 63.10W*
64 G12 **Santa Cruz** Libertador, C Chile *34.39S 71.16W*
44 K13 **Santa Cruz** Guanacaste, W Costa Rica *10.15N 85.34W*
46 I12 **Santa Cruz** W Jamaica *18.03N 77.41W*
66 P6 **Santa Cruz** Madeira, Portugal, NE Atlantic Ocean *32.43N 16.46W*
37 N10 **Santa Cruz** California, W USA *36.58N 122.01W*
65 H20 **Santa Cruz** *off.* Provincia de Santa Cruz. ◈ *province* S Argentina

◆ Country ● Country Capital ◇ Dependent Territory ○ Dependent Territory Capital ◈ Administrative Region ✕ International Airport ▲ Mountain ▲▲ Mountain Range ▲ Volcano ≈ River ◎ Lake ⊡ Reservoir

59 O18 **Santa Cruz** ◈ *department* E Bolivia
Santa Cruz *see* Viru-Viru
Santa Cruz *see* Puerto Santa Cruz
Santa Cruz Barillas *see* Barillas
61 O18 **Santa Cruz Cabrália** Bahia, E Brazil *16.16S 39.03W*
Santa Cruz de El Seibo *see* El Seibo
66 N11 **Santa Cruz de la Palma** La Palma, Islas Canarias, Spain, NE Atlantic Ocean *28.40N 17.46W*
Santa Cruz de la Sierra *see* Santa Cruz
107 O9 **Santa Cruz de la Zarza** Castilla-La Mancha, C Spain *39.59N 3.10W*
44 C5 **Santa Cruz del Quiché** Quiché, W Guatemala *15.01N 91.08W*
107 N8 **Santa Cruz del Retamar** Castilla-La Mancha, C Spain *40.07N 4.13W*
Santa Cruz del Seibo *see* El Seibo
46 G7 **Santa Cruz del Sur** Camagüey, C Cuba *20.44N 78.00W*
107 O11 **Santa Cruz de Mudela** Castilla-La Mancha, C Spain *38.37N 3.27W*
66 Q11 **Santa Cruz de Tenerife** Tenerife, Islas Canarias, Spain, NE Atlantic Ocean *28.28N 16.15W*
66 P11 **Santa Cruz de Tenerife** ◈ *province* Islas Canarias, Spain, NE Atlantic Ocean
62 K9 **Santa Cruz do Rio Pardo** São Paulo, S Brazil *22.52S 49.37W*
63 H15 **Santa Cruz do Sul** Rio Grande do Sul, S Brazil *29.42S 52.25W*
59 C17 **Santa Cruz, Isla** *var.* Indefatigable Island, Isla Chávez. *island* Galapagos Islands, Ecuador, E Pacific Ocean
42 F8 **Santa Cruz, Isla** *island* W Mexico
37 Q15 **Santa Cruz Island** *island* California, W USA
195 X8 **Santa Cruz Islands** *island group* E Solomon Islands
65 I22 **Santa Cruz, Río** ≈ S Argentina
38 L15 **Santa Cruz River** ≈ Arizona, SW USA
63 C17 **Santa Elena** Entre Ríos, E Argentina *30.58S 59.46W*
44 F2 **Santa Elena** Cayo, W Belize *17.08N 89.04W*
27 R16 **Santa Elena** Texas, SW USA *26.43N 98.30W*
58 A7 **Santa Elena, Bahía de** *bay* W Ecuador
57 R10 **Santa Elena de Uairén** Bolívar, E Venezuela *4.40N 61.03W*
44 K12 **Santa Elena, Península** *peninsula* NW Costa Rica
58 A7 **Santa Elena, Punta** *headland* W Ecuador *2.11S 81.00W*
106 L11 **Santa Eufemia** Andalucía, S Spain *38.36N 4.54W*
109 N21 **Santa Eufemia, Golfo di** *gulf* S Italy
109 N21 **Santa Eufemia Lamezia Terme** Calabria, SE Italy *38.54N 16.13E*
107 S4 **Santa Eulalia de Gállego** Aragón, NE Spain *42.16N 0.46W*
107 V11 **Santa Eulalia del Río** Eivissa, Spain, W Mediterranean Sea *39.00N 1.33E*
63 B17 **Santa Fe** Santa Fe, C Argentina *31.36S 60.46W*
107 N14 **Santa Fe** Andalucía, S Spain *37.10N 3.43W*
39 S10 **Santa Fe** *state capital* New Mexico, SW USA *35.41N 105.56W*
63 B15 **Santa Fe** *off.* Provincia de Santa Fe. ◈ *province* C Argentina
Santa Fe *see* Bogotá
46 C6 **Santa Fé** *var.* La Fe. Isla de la Juventud, W Cuba *21.39N 82.45W*
45 R16 **Santa Fé** Veraguas, C Panama *8.28N 81.03W*
Santa Fe de Bogotá *see* Bogotá
62 J7 **Santa Fé do Sul** São Paulo, S Brazil *20.13S 50.55W*
59 B18 **Santa Fe, Isla** *var.* Barrington Island. *island* Galapagos Islands, Ecuador, E Pacific Ocean
25 V9 **Santa Fe River** ≈ Florida, SE USA
61 M15 **Santa Filomena** Piauí, E Brazil *9.06S 45.52W*
42 G10 **Santa Genoveva** ▲ W Mexico *23.07N 109.56W*
159 S14 **Santahar** Rajshahi, NW Bangladesh *24.45N 89.03E*
62 G11 **Santa Helena** Paraná, S Brazil *24.53S 54.19W*
56 J5 **Santa Inés** Lara, N Venezuela *10.37N 69.18W*
65 G24 **Santa Inés, Isla** *island* S Chile
64 J13 **Santa Isabel** La Pampa, C Argentina *36.11S 66.59W*
45 U14 **Santa Isabel** Colón, N Panama *9.31N 79.12W*
195 W14 **Santa Isabel** *var.* Bughotu. *island* N Solomon Islands
Santa Isabel *see* Malabo
60 D11 **Santa Isabel do Rio Negro** Amazonas, NW Brazil *0.40S 64.55W*
63 C15 **Santa Lucia** Corrientes, NE Argentina *28.58S 59.05W*
59 I17 **Santa Lucía** Puno, S Peru *15.45S 70.34W*
63 F20 **Santa Lucía** *var.* Santa Lucia. Canelones, S Uruguay *34.25S 56.25W*
44 B6 **Santa Lucía Cotzumalguapa** Escuintla, SW Guatemala *14.20N 91.00W*
109 L23 **Santa Lucia del Mela** Sicilia, Italy, C Mediterranean Sea *38.07N 15.16E*
37 O11 **Santa Lucia Range** ▲▲ California, W USA
42 D9 **Santa Margarita, Isla** *island* W Mexico
63 G15 **Santa Maria** Rio Grande do Sul, S Brazil *29.40S 53.48W*
37 P13 **Santa Maria** California, W USA *34.56N 120.25W*
66 Q4 **Santa Maria** ✕ Santa Maria, Azores, Portugal, NE Atlantic Ocean
66 P3 **Santa Maria** *island* Azores, Portugal, NE Atlantic Ocean
Santa Maria *see* Gaua.
64 J7 **Santa María** Catamarca, N Argentina *26.38S 66.01W*
Santa María Asunción Tlaxiaco *see* Tlaxiaco
42 G9 **Santa María, Bahía** *bay* W Mexico
85 L21 **Santa Maria, Cabo de** *headland* S Mozambique *26.05S 32.58E*
106 G15 **Santa Maria, Cabo de** *headland* S Portugal *36.57N 7.55W*
46 J4 **Santa Maria, Cape** *headland* Long Island, C Bahamas *23.40N 75.20W*
109 J17 **Santa Maria Capua Vetere** Campania, S Italy *41.04N 14.15E*
61 M17 **Santa Maria da Vitória** Bahia, E Brazil *13.25S 44.09W*
57 N9 **Santa Maria de Erebato** Bolívar, SE Venezuela *5.09N 64.49W*
106 G7 **Santa Maria da Feira** Aveiro, N Portugal *40.55N 8.31W*
57 N6 **Santa María de Ipire** Guárico, C Venezuela *8.51N 65.21W*
Santa Maria del Buen Aire *see* Buenos Aires
42 J8 **Santa María del Oro** Durango, C Mexico *25.57N 105.22W*
43 N12 **Santa María del Río** San Luis Potosí, C Mexico *21.48N 100.42W*
Santa Maria di Castellabate *see* Castellabate
109 Q20 **Santa Maria di Leuca, Capo** *headland* SE Italy *39.48N 18.21E*
110 K10 **Santa Maria-im-Münstertal** Graubünden, SE Switzerland *46.36N 10.25E*
59 B18 **Santa María, Isla** *var.* Isla Floreana, Charles Island. *island* Galapagos Islands, Ecuador, E Pacific Ocean
42 J3 **Santa María, Laguna de** ◎ N Mexico
63 G16 **Santa Maria, Rio** ≈ S Brazil
45 R16 **Santa María, Río** ≈ C Panama
38 J12 **Santa Maria River** ≈ Arizona, SW USA
109 G15 **Santa Marinella** Lazio, C Italy *42.01N 11.51E*
56 F4 **Santa Marta** Magdalena, N Colombia *11.13N 74.13W*
106 J11 **Santa Marta** Extremadura, W Spain *38.37N 6.39W*
Santa Maura *see* Lefkáda
37 S15 **Santa Monica** California, W USA *34.01N 118.29W*
118 F10 **Sântana** *Ger.* Sankt Anna, ***Hung.*** Újszentanna; ***prev.*** Sîntana. Arad, W Romania *46.19N 21.30E*
63 F16 **Santana, Coxilha de** *hill range* S Brazil
63 H16 **Santana da Boa Vista** Rio Grande do Sul, S Brazil *30.52S 53.03W*
63 F16 **Santana do Livramento** *prev.* Livramento. Rio Grande do Sul, S Brazil *30.52S 55.30W*
107 N2 **Santander** Cantabria, N Spain *43.28N 3.48W*
56 F8 **Santander** *off.* Departamento de Santander. ◈ *province* C Colombia
Santander Jiménez *see* Jiménez
Sant'Andrea *see* Svetac
109 B20 **Sant'Antioco** Sardegna, Italy, C Mediterranean Sea *39.03N 8.28E*
106 J13 **Santa Olalla del Cala** Andalucía, S Spain *37.54N 6.13W*
37 R15 **Santa Paula** California, W USA *34.21N 119.03W*
38 L4 **Santaquin** Utah, W USA *39.58N 111.46W*
60 I12 **Santarém** Pará, N Brazil *2.25S 54.40W*
106 G10 **Santarém** *anc.* Scalabis. Santarém, W Portugal *39.13N 8.40W*
106 G10 **Santarém** ◈ *district* C Portugal
46 F4 **Santaren Channel** *channel* W Bahamas
56 K10 **Santa Rita** Vichada, E Colombia *4.51N 68.27W*
196 B16 **Santa Rita** SW Guam
44 H5 **Santa Rita** Cortés, NW Honduras *15.10N 87.54W*
42 E9 **Santa Rita** Baja California Sur, W Mexico *27.28N 100.33W*
56 H5 **Santa Rita** Zulia, NW Venezuela *10.33N 71.31W*
61 I19 **Santa Rita de Araguaia** Goiás, S Brazil *17.17S 53.13W*
Santa Rita de Cassia *see* Cássia
63 D14 **Santa Rosa** Corrientes, NE Argentina *28.18S 58.04W*
64 K13 **Santa Rosa** La Pampa, C Argentina *36.37S 64.15W*
63 G14 **Santa Rosa** Rio Grande do Sul, S Brazil *27.49S 54.28W*
60 E10 **Santa Rosa** Roraima, N Brazil *3.41N 62.29W*
58 B8 **Santa Rosa** El Oro, SW Ecuador *3.27S 79.57W*
59 I16 **Santa Rosa** Puno, S Peru *14.38S 70.48W*
36 M7 **Santa Rosa** California, W USA *38.26N 122.42W*
39 U11 **Santa Rosa** New Mexico, SW USA *34.54N 104.43W*
57 O6 **Santa Rosa** Anzoátegui, NE Venezuela *9.36N 64.16W*
44 A3 **Santa Rosa** *off.* Departamento de Santa Rosa. ◈ *department* SE Guatemala
Santa Rosa *see* Santa Rosa de Copán
65 J15 **Santa Rosa, Bajo de** *basin* E Argentina
44 F6 **Santa Rosa de Copán** *var.* Santa Rosa. Copán, W Honduras *14.46N 88.48W*
56 E8 **Santa Rosa de Osos** Antioquia, C Colombia *6.40N 75.27W*
37 Q15 **Santa Rosa Island** *island* California, W USA
25 O9 **Santa Rosa Island** *island* Florida, SE USA
42 E6 **Santa Rosalía** Baja California Sur, W Mexico *27.19N 112.16W*
56 K6 **Santa Rosalía** Portuguesa, NW Venezuela *9.01N 69.02W*
196 C15 **Santa Rosa, Mount** ▲ NE Guam
37 V16 **Santa Rosa Mountains** ▲▲ California, W USA
37 T2 **Santa Rosa Range** ▲▲ Nevada, W USA
64 M8 **Santa Sylvina** Chaco, N Argentina *27.49S 61.07W*
Santa Tecla *see* Nueva San Salvador
63 B19 **Santa Teresa** Santa Fe, C Argentina *33.30S 60.45W*
61 O20 **Santa Teresa** Espírito Santo, SE Brazil *19.51S 40.49W*
109 M23 **Santa Teresa di Riva** Sicilia, Italy, C Mediterranean Sea *38.00N 15.25E*
63 E21 **Santa Teresita** Buenos Aires, E Argentina *36.34S 56.43W*
63 H19 **Santa Vitória do Palmar** Rio Grande do Sul, S Brazil *33.31S 53.25W*
37 Q14 **Santa Ynez River** ≈ California, W USA
Sant Carles de la Rápida *see* Sant Carles de la Ràpita
107 U7 **Sant Carles de la Ràpita** *var.* Sant Carles de la Rápida. Cataluña, NE Spain *40.37N 0.36E*
107 W5 **Sant Celoni** Cataluña, NE Spain *41.39N 2.25E*
37 U17 **Santee** California, W USA *32.50N 116.58W*
23 T13 **Santee River** ≈ South Carolina, SE USA
42 K15 **San Telmo, Punta** *headland* SW Mexico *18.19N 103.30W*
109 O17 **Santeramo in Colle** Puglia, SE Italy *40.46N 16.45E*
107 X5 **Sant Feliu de Guíxols** *var.* San Feliú de Guixols. Cataluña, NE Spain *41.46N 3.01E*
107 W6 **Sant Feliu de Llobregat** Cataluña, NE Spain *41.22N 2.00E*
108 C7 **Santhià** Piemonte, NE Italy *45.21N 8.11E*
63 F15 **Santiago** Rio Grande do Sul, S Brazil *29.10S 54.52W*
64 H11 **Santiago** *var.* Gran Santiago. ● (Chile) Santiago, C Chile *33.30S 70.40W*
47 N8 **Santiago** *var.* Santiago de los Caballeros. N Dominican Republic *19.27N 70.42W*
42 G10 **Santiago** Baja California Sur, W Mexico *23.32N 109.45W*
43 O8 **Santiago** Nuevo León, NE Mexico *25.22N 100.09W*
45 R16 **Santiago** Veraguas, S Panama *8.06N 80.58W*
59 E16 **Santiago** Ica, SW Peru *14.13S 75.43W*
106 G3 **Santiago** *var.* Santiago de Compostela, ***Eng.*** Compostella; ***anc.*** Campus Stellae. Galicia, NW Spain *42.52N 8.33W*
64 H11 **Santiago** *off.* Región Metropolitana de Santiago, *var.* Metropolitan. ◈ *region* C Chile
64 H11 **Santiago** ✕ Santiago, C Chile *33.27S 70.40W*
106 G3 **Santiago** ✕ Galicia, NW Spain
78 D10 **Santiago** *var.* São Tiago. *island* Ilhas de Sotavento, S Cape Verde
Santiago *see* Santiago de Cuba, Cuba
Santiago *see* Grande de Santiago, Río, Mexico
44 B6 **Santiago Atitlán** Sololá, SW Guatemala *14.36N 91.13W*
45 Q16 **Santiago, Cerro** ▲ W Panama *8.27N 81.42W*
Santiago de Compostela *see* Santiago
46 I8 **Santiago de Cuba** *var.* Santiago. Santiago de Cuba, E Cuba *20.01N 75.50W*
Santiago de Guayaquil *see* Guayaquil
64 K8 **Santiago del Estero** Santiago del Estero, C Argentina *27.51S 64.15W*
63 A15 **Santiago del Estero** *off.* Provincia de Santiago del Estero. ◈ *province* N Argentina
42 I8 **Santiago de los Caballeros** Sinaloa, W Mexico *25.33N 107.22W*
Santiago de los Caballeros *see* Santiago, Dominican Republic
Santiago de los Caballeros *see* Guatemala, Guatemala
44 F8 **Santiago de María** Usulután, SE El Salvador *13.28N 88.28W*
106 F12 **Santiago do Cacém** Setúbal, S Portugal *38.01N 8.42W*
42 J12 **Santiago Ixcuintla** Nayarit, C Mexico *21.49N 105.07W*
Santiago Jamiltepec *see* Jamiltepec
26 L11 **Santiago Mountains** ▲▲ Texas, SW USA
42 J9 **Santiago Papasquiaro** Durango, C Mexico *25.03N 105.25W*
Santiago Pinotepa Nacional *see* Pinotepa Nacional
58 C8 **Santiago, Río** ≈ N Peru
42 M10 **San Tiburcio** Zacatecas, C Mexico *24.07N 101.28W*
107 N2 **Santillana** Cantabria, N Spain *43.24N 4.06W*
56 I5 **San Timoteo** Zulia, NW Venezuela *9.49N 71.04W*
Santi Quaranta *see* Sarandë
Santissima Trinidad *see* Chilung
107 O12 **Santisteban del Puerto** Andalucía, S Spain *38.15N 3.10W*
107 U7 **Sant Jordi, Golf de** *gulf* NE Spain
107 T8 **Sant Mateu** País Valenciano, E Spain *40.28N 0.10E*
27 S7 **Santo** Texas, SW USA *32.35N 98.06W*
Santo *see* Espiritu Santo
62 M10 **Santo Amaro, Ilha de** *island* SE Brazil
63 G14 **Santo Ângelo** Rio Grande do Sul, S Brazil *28.16S 54.15W*
78 C9 **Santo Antão** *island* Ilhas de Barlavento, N Cape Verde
62 J10 **Santo Antônio da Platina** Paraná, S Brazil *23.20S 50.05W*
60 C13 **Santo Antônio do Içá** Amazonas, N Brazil *3.04S 67.55W*
59 Q18 **Santo Corazón, Río** ≈ E Bolivia
46 E5 **Santo Domingo** Villa Clara, C Cuba *22.34N 80.15W*
47 O9 **Santo Domingo** *prev.* Ciudad Trujillo. ● (Dominican Republic) SE Dominican Republic *18.30N 69.57W*
42 E8 **Santo Domingo** Baja California Sur, W Mexico *25.31N 111.54W*
42 M10 **Santo Domingo** San Luis Potosí, C Mexico *23.18N 101.42W*
44 L10 **Santo Domingo** Chontales, S Nicaragua *12.15N 85.06W*
107 P4 **Santo Domingo de la Calzada** La Rioja, N Spain *42.25N 2.57W*
58 B6 **Santo Domingo de los Colorados** Pichincha, NW Ecuador *0.16S 79.11W*
Santo Domingo Tehuantepec *see* Tehuantepec
57 O6 **San Tomé** Anzoátegui, NE Venezuela *8.54N 64.14W*
San Tomé de Guayana *see* Ciudad Guayana
107 R13 **Santomera** Murcia, SE Spain *38.03N 1.05W*
107 O2 **Santoña** Cantabria, N Spain *43.27N 3.28W*
Santorin/Santoríni *see* Thíra
62 M10 **Santos** São Paulo, S Brazil *23.55S 46.22W*
67 J17 **Santos Plateau** *undersea feature* SW Atlantic Ocean
106 G6 **Santo Tirso** Porto, N Portugal *41.20N 8.25W*
42 B2 **Santo Tomás** Baja California, NW Mexico *31.31N 116.25W*
44 L10 **Santo Tomás** Chontales, S Nicaragua *12.04N 85.01W*
44 G5 **Santo Tomás de Castilla** Izabal, E Guatemala *15.40N 88.36W*
42 B2 **Santo Tomás, Punta** *headland* NW Mexico *31.30N 116.40W*
59 H16 **Santo Tomás, Río** ≈ C Peru
59 B18 **Santo Tomás, Volcán** ⛰ Galapagos Islands, Ecuador, E Pacific Ocean *0.46S 91.01W*
63 F14 **Santo Tomé** Corrientes, NE Argentina *28.31S 56.03W*
Santo Tomé de Guayana *see* Ciudad Guayana
100 H10 **Santpoort** Noord-Holland, W Netherlands *52.25N 4.37E*
Santurce *see* Santurtzi
107 O2 **Santurtzi** *var.* Santurce, Santurzi. País Vasco, N Spain *43.19N 3.03W*
Santurzi *see* Santurtzi
65 G20 **San Valentín, Cerro** ▲ S Chile *46.36S 73.17W*
44 F8 **San Vicente** San Vicente, C El Salvador *13.37N 88.44W*
42 C2 **San Vicente** Baja California, NW Mexico *31.18N 116.12W*
196 H6 **San Vicente** Saipan, S Northern Mariana Islands
44 B9 **San Vicente** ◈ *department* E El Salvador
106 I10 **San Vicente de Alcántara** Extremadura, W Spain *39.21N 7.07W*
107 N2 **San Vicente de Barakaldo** *var.* Baracaldo. País Vasco, N Spain *43.16N 2.58W*
59 E15 **San Vicente de Cañete** *var.* Cañete. Lima, W Peru *13.04S 76.25W*
106 M2 **San Vicente de la Barquera** Cantabria, N Spain *43.22N 4.24W*
56 E12 **San Vicente del Caguán** Caquetá, S Colombia *2.07N 74.46W*
44 F8 **San Vicente, Volcán de** ⛰ C El Salvador *13.34N 88.50W*
45 O15 **San Vito** Puntarenas, SE Costa Rica *8.49N 82.58W*
108 I7 **San Vito al Tagliamento** Friuli-Venezia Giulia, NE Italy *45.54N 12.55E*
109 H23 **San Vito, Capo** *headland* Sicilia, Italy, C Mediterranean Sea *38.11N 12.41E*
109 P18 **San Vito dei Normanni** Puglia, SE Italy *40.40N 17.42E*
166 L17 **Sanya** *var.* Ya Xian. Hainan, S China *18.17N 109.32E*
85 J16 **Sanyati** ≈ N Zimbabwe
27 Q16 **San Ygnacio** Texas, SW USA *27.04N 99.25W*
166 L6 **Sanyuan** Shaanxi, C China *34.40N 108.55E*
126 Ll12 **Sanyyakhtakh** Respublika Sakha (Yakutiya), NE Russian Federation *60.34N 124.09E*
84 C10 **Sanza Pombo** Uíge, NW Angola *07.20S 16.00E*
Sanzyô *see* Sanjō
106 G14 **São Bartolomeu de Messines** Faro, S Portugal *37.12N 8.16W*
62 M10 **São Bernardo do Campo** São Paulo, S Brazil *23.41S 46.29W*
63 F15 **São Borja** Rio Grande do Sul, S Brazil *28.34S 56.01W*
106 H14 **São Brás de Alportel** Faro, S Portugal *37.09N 7.55W*
62 M10 **São Caetano do Sul** São Paulo, S Brazil *23.37S 46.34W*
62 L9 **São Carlos** São Paulo, S Brazil *22.01S 47.52W*
61 P16 **São Cristóvão** Sergipe, E Brazil *10.58S 37.10W*
63 F15 **São Francisco de Assis** Rio Grande do Sul, S Brazil *29.31S 55.07W*
60 K13 **São Félix** Pará, NE Brazil *6.43S 51.55W*
São Félix *see* São Félix do Araguaia
61 J16 **São Félix do Araguaia** *var.* São Félix. Mato Grosso, W Brazil *11.36S 50.40W*
61 J14 **São Félix do Xingu** Pará, NE Brazil *6.37S 51.58W*
62 Q9 **São Fidélis** Rio de Janeiro, SE Brazil *21.37S 41.40W*
78 D10 **São Filipe** Fogo, S Cape Verde *14.52N 24.28W*
62 K12 **São Francisco do Sul** Santa Catarina, S Brazil *26.16S 48.39W*
62 K12 **São Francisco, Ilha de** *island* S Brazil
61 P16 **São Francisco, Rio** ≈ E Brazil
63 G16 **São Gabriel** Rio Grande do Sul, S Brazil *30.17S 54.17W*
62 P10 **São Gonçalo** Rio de Janeiro, SE Brazil *22.48S 43.02W*
83 H23 **Sao Hill** Iringa, S Tanzania *8.19S 35.10E*
62 R9 **São João da Barra** Rio de Janeiro, SE Brazil *21.39S 41.04W*
106 G7 **São João da Madeira** Aveiro, N Portugal *40.52N 8.28W*
60 M12 **São João de Cortês** Maranhão, E Brazil *2.30S 44.27W*
61 M21 **São João del Rei** Minas Gerais, NE Brazil *21.07S 44.15W*
61 N15 **São João do Piauí** Piauí, E Brazil *8.21S 42.13W*
61 N14 **São João dos Patos** Maranhão, E Brazil *6.28S 43.43W*
60 C11 **São Joaquim** Amazonas, NW Brazil *0.08S 67.10W*
63 J14 **São Joaquim** Santa Catarina, S Brazil *28.20S 49.55W*
62 L7 **São Joaquim da Barra** São Paulo, S Brazil *20.36S 47.50W*
66 N2 **São Jorge** *island* Azores, Portugal, NE Atlantic Ocean
63 K14 **São José** Santa Catarina, S Brazil *27.34S 48.39W*
62 M8 **São José do Rio Pardo** São Paulo, S Brazil *21.37S 46.52W*
62 K8 **São José do Rio Preto** São Paulo, S Brazil *20.49S 49.19W*
62 N10 **São Jose dos Campos** São Paulo, S Brazil *23.07S 45.52W*
63 I17 **São Lourenço do Sul** Rio Grande do Sul, S Brazil *31.25S 52.00W*
60 F11 **São Luís** Roraima, N Brazil *1.11N 60.15W*
60 M12 **São Luís** *state capital* Maranhão, NE Brazil *2.34S 44.16W*
60 M12 **São Luís, Ilha de** *island* NE Brazil
63 F14 **São Luiz Gonzaga** Rio Grande do Sul, S Brazil *28.24S 54.58W*
106 I10 **São Mamede** ▲ C Portugal *39.18N 7.19W*
São Mandol *see* São Manuel, Rio
49 U8 **Sao Manuel** ≈ C Brazil
61 H15 **São Manuel, Rio** *var.* São Mandol, Teles Pirés. ≈ C Brazil
60 C11 **São Marcelino** Amazonas, NW Brazil *0.53N 67.16W*
60 N12 **São Marcos, Baía de** *bay* N Brazil
61 O20 **São Mateus** Espírito Santo, SE Brazil *18.43S 39.52W*
62 J12 **São Mateus do Sul** Paraná, S Brazil *25.51S 50.24W*
66 P3 **São Miguel** *island* Azores, Portugal, NE Atlantic Ocean
62 G13 **São Miguel d'Oeste** Santa Catarina, S Brazil *26.45S 53.34W*
47 P9 **Saona, Isla** *island* SE Dominican Republic
180 H12 **Saondzou** ▲ Grande Comore, NW Comoros
105 R10 **Saône** ≈ E France
105 Q9 **Saône-et-Loire** ◈ *department* C France
78 D9 **São Nicolau** *Eng.* Saint Nicholas. *island* Ilhas de Barlavento, N Cape Verde
62 M10 **São Paulo** *state capital* São Paulo, S Brazil *23.33S 46.39W*
62 K9 **São Paulo** *off.* Estado de São Paulo. ◈ *state* S Brazil
São Paulo de Loanda *see* Luanda
São Pedro do Rio Grande do Sul *see* Rio Grande
106 H7 **São Pedro do Sul** Viseu, N Portugal *40.46N 7.58W*
66 K13 **São Pedro e São Paulo** *undersea feature* C Atlantic Ocean *1.25N 28.54W*
61 M14 **São Raimundo das Mangabeiras** Maranhão, E Brazil *07.00S 45.30W*
61 Q14 **São Roque, Cabo de** *headland* E Brazil *5.28S 35.16W*
São Salvador/São Salvador do Congo *see* M'Banza Congo, Angola
São Salvador *see* Salvador, Brazil
62 N10 **São Sebastião, Ilha de** *island* S Brazil
85 N19 **São Sebastião, Ponta** *headland* C Mozambique *22.09S 35.33E*
106 F13 **São Teotónio** Beja, S Portugal *37.30N 8.41W*
São Tiago *see* Santiago
81 B18 **São Tomé** ● (Sao Tome and Principe) São Tomé, S Sao Tome and Principe *0.19N 5.18E*
81 B18 **São Tomé** ✕ São Tomé, S Sao Tome and Principe *0.24N 6.39E*
81 B18 **São Tomé** *Eng.* Saint Thomas. *island* S Sao Tome and Principe
81 B17 **Sao Tome and Principe** *off.* Democratic Republic of Sao Tome and Principe. ◆ *republic* E Atlantic Ocean
76 H9 **Saoura, Oued** ≈ NW Algeria
62 M10 **São Vicente** *Eng.* Saint Vincent. São Paulo, S Brazil *23.55S 46.25W*
66 O5 **São Vicente** Madeira, Portugal, NE Atlantic Ocean *32.48N 17.03W*
78 C9 **São Vicente** *Eng.* Saint Vincent. *island* Ilhas de Barlavento, N Cape Verde
São Vicente, Cabo de *see* São Vicente, Cabo de
106 F14 **São Vicente, Cabo de** *Eng.* Cape Saint Vincent, ***Port.*** Cabo de São Vicente. *headland* S Portugal *37.01N 9.01W*
Sápai *see* Sápes
Sapaleri, Cerro *see* Zapaleri, Cerro
175 Tt11 **Saparau, Pulau** *island* C Indonesia
Saparoea *see* Saparua
175 Tt11 **Saparua** *prev.* Saparoea. Pulau Saparau, C Indonesia *3.34S 128.37E*
174 Hh8 **Sapat** Sumatera, W Indonesia *0.18S 103.18E*
79 U17 **Sapele** Delta, S Nigeria *5.54N 5.43E*
25 X7 **Sapelo Island** *island* Georgia, SE USA
25 X7 **Sapelo Sound** *sound* Georgia, SE USA
116 K13 **Sápes** *var.* Sápai. Anatolikí Makedonía kai Thráki, NE Greece *41.01N 25.42E*
175 P16 **Sape, Selat** *strait* Nusa Tenggara, S Indonesia
117 D22 **Sapiéntza** *island* S Greece
Sapir *see* Sappir
63 I15 **Sapiranga** Rio Grande do Sul, S Brazil *29.39S 50.58W*
116 K13 **Sápka** ▲▲ NE Greece
58 D11 **Saposoa** San Martín, N Peru *6.58S 76.40W*
121 F16 **Sapotskino** *Pol.* Sopockinie, ***Rus.*** Sopotskin. Hrodzyenskaya Voblasts', W Belarus *53.50N 23.41E*
79 P13 **Sapoui** *var.* Sapouy. S Burkina *11.34N 1.43W*
Sapouy *see* Sapoui
144 F12 **Sappir** *var.* Sapir. Southern, S Israel *30.43N 35.11E*
172 O5 **Sapporo** Hokkaidō, NE Japan *43.04N 141.21E*
109 M19 **Sapri** Campania, S Italy *40.04N 15.35E*
174 Mm15 **Sapudi, Pulau** *island* S Indonesia
29 P9 **Sapulpa** Oklahoma, C USA *36.00N 96.06W*
148 J4 **Saqqez** *var.* Saghez, Sakiz, Saqqiz. Kordestān, NW Iran *36.30N 46.16E*
Saqqiz *see* Saqqez
145 U8 **Sarābādī** E Iraq *33.00N 44.52E*
178 Hh11 **Sara Buri** *var.* Saraburi. Saraburi, C Thailand *14.30N 100.54E*
26 K9 **Saragosa** Texas, SW USA *31.03N 103.39W*
Saragossa *see* Zaragoza
Saragt *see* Serakhs
58 B8 **Saraguro** Loja, S Ecuador *3.42S 79.16W*
130 M6 **Sarai** Ryazanskaya Oblast', W Russian Federation *53.43N 39.59E*
Sarāi *see* Sarāy
160 M12 **Saraipāli** Madhya Pradesh, C India *21.21N 83.01E*
155 T9 **Sarāi Sidhu** Punjab, E Pakistan *30.34N 71.58E*
95 M15 **Säräisniemi** Oulu, C Finland *64.25N 26.50E*
115 I14 **Sarajevo** ● (Bosnia and Herzegovina) Federacija Bosna I Hercegovina, SE Bosnia and Herzegovina *43.52N 18.24E*
114 I13 **Sarajevo** ✕ Federacija Bosna I Hercegovina, C Bosnia and Herzegovina *43.49N 18.21E*
149 V4 **Sarakhs** Khorāsān, NE Iran *36.41N 61.06E*
117 H17 **Sarakíniko, Akrotírio** *headland* Évvoia, C Greece *38.46N 23.43E*
117 I18 **Sarakinó** *island* Vóreioi Sporádes, Greece, Aegean Sea
131 V7 **Saraktash** Orenburgskaya Oblast', W Russian Federation *51.45N 56.23E*
32 L15 **Sara, Lake** ⊠ Illinois, N USA
25 N8 **Saraland** Alabama, S USA *30.49N 88.04W*
57 V9 **Saramacca** ◈ *district* N Suriname
57 V10 **Saramacca Rivier** ≈ C Suriname
177 G2 **Saramati** ▲ N Myanmar *25.46N 95.01E*
151 R10 **Saran'** *Kaz.* Saran. Karaganda, C Kazakhstan *49.46N 73.01E*
20 K7 **Saranac Lake** New York, NE USA *44.18N 74.06W*
20 K7 **Saranac River** ≈ New York, NE USA
Saranda *see* Sarandë
115 L23 **Sarandë** *var.* Saranda, ***It.*** Porto Edda; ***prev.*** Santi Quaranta. Vlorë, S Albania *39.53N 19.59E*
63 H14 **Sarandi** Rio Grande do Sul, S Brazil *27.57S 52.58W*
63 F19 **Sarandí del Yí** Durazno, C Uruguay *33.18S 55.37W*
63 F19 **Sarandí Grande** Florida, S Uruguay *33.43S 56.19W*
179 Rr17 **Sarangani Islands** *island group* S Philippines
131 P5 **Saransk** Respublika Mordoviya, W Russian Federation *54.10N 45.09E*
117 C14 **Sarantáporos** ≈ N Greece
116 H9 **Sarantsi** Sofiya, W Bulgaria *42.43N 23.46E*
131 T3 **Sarapul** Udmurtskaya Respublika, NW Russian Federation *56.26N 53.52E*
Sarâqeb *see* Sarāqib
144 I3 **Sarāqib** *Fr.* Sarâqeb. Idlib, N Syria *35.52N 36.48E*
56 J5 **Sarare** Lara, N Venezuela *9.46N 69.10W*
57 O10 **Sarariña** Amazonas, S Venezuela *4.10N 64.31W*
149 S10 **Sar Ashk** Kermān, C Iran
25 V13 **Sarasota** Florida, SE USA *27.20N 82.31W*
119 O11 **Sarata** Odes'ka Oblast', SW Ukraine *46.01N 29.40E*
118 I10 **Sărăţel** *Hung.* Szeretfalva. Bistriţa-Năsăud, N Romania *47.02N 24.24E*
27 X10 **Saratoga** Texas, SW USA *30.15N 94.31W*
20 K10 **Saratoga Springs** New York, NE USA *43.04N 73.47W*
131 P8 **Saratov** Saratovskaya Oblast', W Russian Federation *51.33N 45.57E*
131 P8 **Saratovskaya Oblast'** ◈ *province* W Russian Federation
131 Q7 **Saratovskoye Vodokhranilishche** ⊠ W Russian Federation
Saravan/Saravane *see* Salavan
194 K12 **Sarawaget Range** *var.* Saruwaged Range. ▲▲ C PNG
174 M5 **Sarawak** ◈ *state* East Malaysia
Sarawak *see* Kuching
145 U6 **Sarāy** *var.* Sarāi. E Iraq *34.06N 45.06E*
142 D10 **Saray** Tekirdağ, NW Turkey *41.27N 27.54E*
78 J12 **Saraya** SE Senegal *12.49N 11.45W*
149 W14 **Sarbāz** Sīstān va Balūchestān, SE Iran *26.37N 61.13E*
149 U8 **Sarbīsheh** Khorāsān, E Iran *32.34N 59.49E*
113 J24 **Sárbogárd** Fejér, C Hungary *46.53N 18.36E*
Şărcad *see* Sarkad
29 S7 **Sarcoxie** Missouri, C USA *37.04N 94.07W*
158 L11 **Sārda** *Nep.* Kali. ≈ India/Nepal
158 G10 **Sardārshahr** Rājasthān, NW India *28.24N 74.32E*
109 C18 **Sardegna** *Eng.* Sardinia. ◈ *region* Italy, C Mediterranean Sea
109 A18 **Sardegna** *Eng.* Sardinia. *island* Italy, C Mediterranean Sea
44 K13 **Sardinal** Guanacaste, NW Costa Rica *10.30N 85.38W*
56 G7 **Sardinata** Norte de Santander, N Colombia *8.05N 72.50W*
Sardinia *see* Sardegna
123 K8 **Sardinia-Corsica Trough** *undersea feature* Tyrrhenian Sea, C Mediterranean Sea
24 L2 **Sardis** Mississippi, S USA *34.25N 89.55W*
24 L2 **Sardis Lake** ⊠ Mississippi, S USA
29 P12 **Sardis Lake** ⊠ Oklahoma, C USA
94 H12 **Sarek** ▲▲ N Sweden
94 H11 **Sarektjåhkkå** ▲ N Sweden *67.28N 17.56E*
155 N3 **Sar-e Pol** *var.* Sar-i-Pul. Sar-e Pol, N Afghanistan *36.16N 65.55E*
155 O3 **Sar-e Pol** ◈ *province* N Afghanistan
Sar-e Pol *see* Sar-e Pol-e Żahāb
148 J6 **Sar-e Pol-e Żahāb** *var.* Sar-e Pol, Sar-i Pul. Kermānshāh, W Iran *34.28N 45.52E*
153 T13 **Sarez, Kŭli** *Rus.* Sarezskoye Ozero. ◎ SE Tajikistan
Sarezskoye Ozero *see* Sarez, Kŭli
66 G10 **Sargasso Sea** *sea* W Atlantic Ocean
155 U8 **Sargodha** Punjab, NE Pakistan *32.06N 72.47E*
80 I13 **Sarh** *prev.* Fort-Archambault. Moyen-Chari, S Chad *9.07N 18.22E*
149 P4 **Sārī** *var.* Sari, Sāri. Māzandarān, N Iran *36.36N 53.04E*
117 N23 **Sarία** *island* SE Greece
Sariasiya *see* Sariosiyo
42 F3 **Saric** Sonora, NW Mexico *31.07N 111.22W*
196 K6 **Sarigan** *island* C Northern Mariana Islands
142 D14 **Sarıgöl** Manisa, SW Turkey *38.13N 28.40E*
145 T6 **Sārihah** E Iraq *34.34N 44.38E*
143 R12 **Sarıkamış** Kars, NE Turkey *40.18N 42.36E*
174 L6 **Sarikei** Sarawak, East Malaysia *2.07N 111.30E*
153 U12 **Sarikol Range** *Rus.* Sarykol'skiy Khrebet. ▲▲ China/Tajikistan
189 Y7 **Sarina** Queensland, NE Australia *21.34S 149.12E*
Sarine *see* La Sarine
107 S5 **Sariñena** Aragón, NE Spain *41.46N 0.10W*
153 O13 **Sariosiyo** *Rus.* Sariasiya. Surkhondaryo Viloyati, S Uzbekistan *38.25N 67.51E*
Sar-i-Pul *see* Sar-e Pol, Afghanistan
Sar-i Pul *see* Sar-e Pol-e Żahāb, Iran
Sariqamish Kŭli *see* Sarykamyshkoye Ozero
155 V1 **Sarī Qūl** *Rus.* Ozero Zurkul', ***Taj.*** Zŭrkŭl. ◎ Afghanistan/Tajikistan ***see also*** Zŭrkŭl
77 Q12 **Sarīr Tībistī** *var.* Serir Tibesti. *desert* S Libya
27 S15 **Sarita** Texas, SW USA *27.12N 97.48W*
169 W14 **Sariwŏn** SW North Korea *38.30N 125.52E*
116 P12 **Sarıyer** İstanbul, NW Turkey *41.10N 29.03E*
99 L26 **Sark** *Fr.* Sercq. *island* Channel Islands
113 N24 **Sarkad** *Rom.* Şărcad. Békés, SE Hungary *46.42N 21.21E*
151 W14 **Sarkand** Almaty, SW Kazakhstan *45.25N 79.53E*
Sarkaṇi *see* Krasnogorskoye
158 D11 **Sarkāri Tala** Rājasthān, NW India *27.39N 70.52E*
142 G15 **Şarkîkaraağaç** *var.* Şarki Karaağaç. Isparta, SW Turkey *38.04N 31.22E*
142 L13 **Şarkışla** Sivas, C Turkey *39.21N 36.27E*
142 C11 **Şarköy** Tekirdağ, NW Turkey *40.37N 27.07E*
Sárköz *see* Livada
Sarlat *see* Sarlat-la-Canéda
104 M13 **Sarlat-la-Canéda** *var.* Sarlat. Dordogne, SW France *44.54N 1.12E*
111 S3 **Sarleinsbach** Oberösterreich, N Austria *48.33N 13.55E*
176 Y10 **Sarmi** Papua, E Indonesia *1.51S 138.45E*
65 I19 **Sarmiento** Chubut, S Argentina *45.37S 69.06W*
65 H25 **Sarmiento, Monte** ▲ S Chile *54.28S 70.49W*
96 J11 **Särna** Dalarna, C Sweden *61.40N 13.10E*
110 F8 **Sarnen** Obwalden, C Switzerland *46.54N 8.15E*
110 F9 **Sarner See** ◎ C Switzerland
12 D16 **Sarnia** Ontario, S Canada *42.57N 82.22W*
118 L3 **Sarny** Rivnens'ka Oblast', NW Ukraine *51.20N 26.34E*
175 Q10 **Saroako** Sulawesi, C Indonesia *2.31S 121.18E*
120 L13 **Sarochyna** *Rus.* Sorochino. Vitsyebskaya Voblasts', N Belarus *55.12N 28.45E*
174 Hh10 **Sarolangun** Sumatera, W Indonesia *2.17S 102.39E*
172 Q5 **Saroma** Hokkaidō, NE Japan *44.01N 143.43E*
172 Q5 **Saroma-ko** ◎ Hokkaidō, NE Japan
Saronic Gulf *see* Saronikós Kólpos
117 H20 **Saronikós Kólpos** *Eng.* Saronic Gulf. *gulf* S Greece
108 D7 **Saronno** Lombardia, N Italy *45.37N 9.01E*
142 B11 **Saros Körfezi** *gulf* NW Turkey
113 N20 **Sárospatak** Borsod-Abaúj-Zemplén, NE Hungary *48.18N 21.30E*
131 O4 **Sarov** Respublika Mordoviya, SW Russian Federation *54.39N 43.09E*
131 P12 **Sarpa** Respublika Kalmykiya, SW Russian Federation *47.00N 45.42E*
131 P12 **Sarpa, Ozero** ◎ SW Russian Federation
115 M18 **Šar Planina** ▲▲ FYR Macedonia/Serbia and Montenegro (Yugoslavia)
97 I16 **Sarpsborg** Østfold, S Norway *59.16N 11.07E*
145 U5 **Sarqalā** N Iraq
105 U4 **Sarralbe** Moselle, NE France *49.02N 7.01E*
Sarre *see* Saar, France/Germany
Sarre *see* Saarland, Germany
105 U5 **Sarrebourg** *Ger.* Saarburg. Moselle, NE France *48.43N 7.03E*
Sarrebruck *see* Saarbrücken
105 U4 **Sarreguemines** *prev.* Saargemund. Moselle, NE France *49.06N 7.04E*
106 I3 **Sarria** Galicia, NW Spain *42.46N 7.25W*
107 S8 **Sarrión** Aragón, NE Spain *40.09N 0.49W*
44 F4 **Sarstoon** *Sp.* Río Sarstún. ≈ Belize/Guatemala
Sarstún, Río *see* Sarstoon

◆ Country
● Country Capital
◇ Dependent Territory
○ Dependent Territory Capital
◈ Administrative Region
✕ International Airport
▲ Mountain
▲▲ Mountain Range
⛰ Volcano
≈ River
◎ Lake
⊠ Reservoir

126 M9 Sartang ≈ NE Russian Federation
105 X16 Sartène Corse, France, C Mediterranean Sea 41.37N 8.58E
104 K7 Sarthe ◈ department NW France
104 K7 Sarthe ≈ N France
117 H15 Sárti Kentrikí Makedonía, N Greece 40.04N 23.59E
172 Pp2 Sarufutsu Hokkaidō, NE Japan 45.20N 142.03E
172 Oo7 Saru-gawa ≈ Hokkaidō, NE Japan
Saruhan see Manisa
158 G9 Sarūpsar Rājasthān, NW India 29.25N 73.49E
143 U13 Şärur prev. Il'ichevsk. SW Azerbaijan 39.30N 44.59E
Saruwaged Range see Sarawaget Range
Sarvani see Marneuli
113 G23 Sárvár Vas, W Hungary 47.14N 16.57E
149 P11 Sarvestān Fārs, S Iran 29.16N 53.13E
176 X9 Sarwon Papua, E Indonesia 0.58S 136.08E
151 P17 Saryagach Kaz. Saryaghash. Yuzhnyy Kazakhstan, S Kazakhstan 41.28N 69.10E
Saryaghash see Saryagach
Saryarqa see Kazakhskiy Melkosopochnik
153 W8 Sary-Bulak Narynskaya Oblast', C Kyrgyzstan 41.56N 75.44E
153 U10 Sary-Bulak Oshskaya Oblast', SW Kyrgyzstan 40.49N 73.44E
119 S14 Sarych, Mys headland S Ukraine 44.23N 33.44E
153 Z7 Sary-Dzhaz var. Aksu He. ≈ China/Kyrgyzstan see also Aksu He
151 T14 Saryesik-Atyrau, Peski desert E Kazakhstan
150 G13 Sarykamys Kaz. Saryqamys. Mangistau, SW Kazakhstan 45.58N 53.30E
152 F8 Sarykamyshkoye Ozero Uzb. Sariqamish Kŭli. salt lake Kazakhstan/Uzbekistan
Sarykol'skiy Khrebet see Sarikol Range
150 M10 Sarykopa, Ozero ◎ C Kazakhstan
151 V15 Saryozek Kaz. Saryözek. Almaty, SE Kazakhstan 44.22N 77.57E
Saryqamys see Sarykamys
151 S13 Saryshagan Kaz. Saryshahan. Zhezkazgan, SE Kazakhstan 46.03N 73.36E
Saryshahan see Saryshagan
151 O13 Sarysu ≈ S Kazakhstan
153 T11 Sary-Tash Oshskaya Oblast', SW Kyrgyzstan 39.43N 73.13E
152 J15 Saryyazynskoye Vodokhranilishche ▣ S Turkmenistan
108 E10 Sarzana Liguria, NW Italy 44.07N 9.59E
196 B17 Sasalaguan, Mount ▲ S Guam
159 O14 Sasarām Bihār, N India 24.58N 84.01E
195 W14 Sasari, Mount ▲ Santa Isabel, N Solomon Islands 8.09S 159.32E
170 C12 Sasebo Nagasaki, Kyūshū, SW Japan 33.10N 129.42E
12 I9 Saseginaga, Lac ◎ Quebec, SE Canada
Saseno see Sazan
9 R13 Saskatchewan ◈ province SW Canada
9 U14 Saskatchewan ≈ Manitoba/Saskatchewan, C Canada
9 T15 Saskatoon Saskatchewan, S Canada 52.10N 106.40W
9 T15 Saskatoon ✕ Saskatchewan, S Canada 52.15N 107.05W
126 K7 Saskylakh Respublika Sakha (Yakutiya), NE Russian Federation 71.56N 114.07E
44 L7 Saslaya, Cerro ▲ N Nicaragua 13.52N 85.06W
40 G17 Sasmik, Cape headland Tanaga Island, Alaska, USA 51.36N 105.55W
121 N19 Sasnovy Bor Rus. Sosnovyy Bor. Homyel'skaya Voblasts', SE Belarus 52.31N 29.37E
131 N5 Sasovo Ryazanskaya Oblast', W Russian Federation 54.19N 41.54E
27 S12 Saspamco Texas, SW USA 29.13N 98.18W
111 W9 Sass var. Sassbach. ≈ SE Austria
78 M17 Sassandra S Ivory Coast 4.58N 6.07W
78 M17 Sassandra var. Ibo, Sassandra Fleuve. ≈ S Ivory Coast
Sassandra Fleuve see Sassandra
109 B17 Sassari Sardegna, Italy, C Mediterranean Sea 40.43N 8.33E
Sassbach see Sass
100 H11 Sassenheim Zuid-Holland, W Netherlands 52.13N 4.31E
Sassmacken see Valdemārpils
102 O7 Sassnitz Mecklenburg-Vorpommern, NE Germany 54.32N 13.39E
101 E16 Sas van Gent Zeeland, SW Netherlands 51.13N 3.48E
151 W12 Sasykkol', Ozero ◎ E Kazakhstan
119 O12 Sasyk Kunduk, Ozero ◎ SW Ukraine
78 J12 Satadougou Kayes, SW Mali 12.40N 11.25W
107 V11 Sa Talaiassa ▲ Eivissa, Spain, W Mediterranean Sea 38.55N 1.17E
170 B17 Sata-misaki headland Kyūshū, SW Japan 31.00N 130.39E
28 I7 Satanta Kansas, C USA 37.23N 102.00W
161 E15 Sātāra Mahārāshtra, W India 17.40N 73.58E
198 Aa7 Sātaua Savai'i, NW Samoa 13.25S 172.40W
196 M16 Satawal island Caroline Islands, C Micronesia
201 R17 Satawan Atoll atoll Mortlock Islands, C Micronesia
25 Y12 Satellite Beach Florida, SE USA 28.10N 80.35W
97 M14 Säter Dalarna, C Sweden 60.21N 15.45E
Sathmar see Satu Mare
25 V7 Satilla River ≈ Georgia, SE USA
59 F14 Satipo var. San Francisco de Satipo. Junín, C Peru 11.13S 74.40W
125 E11 Satka Chelyabinskaya Oblast', C Russian Federation 55.08N 58.54E
159 T16 Satkhira Khulna, SW Bangladesh 22.43N 89.06E
160 K9 Satna prev. Sutna. Madhya Pradesh, C India 24.33N 80.49E
105 R11 Satolas ✕ (Lyon) Rhône, E France 45.44N 5.01E
113 N20 Sátoraljaújhely Borsod-Abaúj-Zemplén, NE Hungary 48.24N 21.39E
151 O12 Satpayev prev. Nikol'skiy. Zhezkazgan, C Kazakhstan 47.59N 67.27E
160 G11 Sātpura Range ⛰ C India
170 Bb16 Satsuma-hantō peninsula Kyūshū, SW Japan
178 Hh12 Sattahip var. Ban Sattahip, Ban Sattahipp. Chon Buri, S Thailand 12.41N 100.55E
94 L11 Sattanen Lappi, NE Finland 67.31N 26.35E
Satul see Satun
118 H9 Satulung Hung. Kővárhosszúfalu. Maramureş, N Romania 47.34N 23.25E
Satul-Vechi see Staro Selo
118 G8 Satu Mare Ger. Sathmar, Hung. Szatmárnémeti. Satu Mare, NW Romania 47.46N 22.54E
118 G8 Satu Mare ◈ county NW Romania
178 H17 Satun var. Satul, Setul. Satun, SW Thailand 6.34N 100.02E
198 Aa8 Satupaiteau Savai'i, W Samoa 13.46S 172.26W
Sau see Sava
12 F14 Sauble ≈ Ontario, S Canada
12 F13 Sauble Beach Ontario, S Canada 44.36N 81.15W
63 C16 Sauce Corrientes, NE Argentina 30.07S 58.50W
Sauce see Juan L.Lacaze
38 K15 Sauceda Mountains ⛰ Arizona, SW USA
63 C17 Sauce de Luna Entre Ríos, E Argentina 31.15S 59.09W
65 L15 Sauce Grande, Río ≈ E Argentina
42 K6 Saucillo Chihuahua, N Mexico 28.01N 105.17W
97 D15 Sauda Rogaland, S Norway 59.39N 6.21E
151 Q16 Saudakent Kaz. Saūdakent; prev. Baykadam. Zhambyl, S Kazakhstan 43.45N 69.52E
94 J2 Saudhárkrókur Nordhurland Vestra, N Iceland 65.45N 19.39W
147 P9 Saudi Arabia off. Kingdom of Saudi Arabia, Ar. Al 'Arabīyah as Su'ūdīyah, Al Mamlakah al 'Arabīyah as Su'ūdīyah. ◆ monarchy SW Asia
103 D19 Sauer var. Sûre. ≈ NW Europe see also Sûre
103 F15 Sauerland forest W Germany
12 F14 Saugeen ≈ Ontario, S Canada
20 K12 Saugerties New York, NE USA 42.04N 73.55W
Saugor see Sāgar
8 K15 Saugstad, Mount ▲ British Columbia, SW Canada 52.12N 126.35W
Sāūjbulāgh see Mahābād
104 J11 Saujon Charente-Maritime, W France 45.40N 0.54W
31 T7 Sauk Centre Minnesota, N USA 45.44N 94.57W
32 L8 Sauk City Wisconsin, N USA 43.16N 89.43W
176 Vv8 Sau Korem Papua, E Indonesia 0.30S 133.10E
31 U7 Sauk Rapids Minnesota, N USA 45.35N 94.09W
57 Y11 Saül C French Guiana 3.37N 53.12W
105 O7 Sauldre ≈ C France
103 I23 Saulgau Baden-Württemberg, SW Germany 48.03N 9.28E
105 Q8 Saulieu Côte d'Or, C France 47.15N 4.15E
120 G8 Saulkrasti Rīga, C Latvia 57.13N 24.25E
13 S6 Sault-aux-Cochons, Rivière du ≈ Quebec, SE Canada
33 Q4 Sault Sainte Marie Michigan, N USA 46.29N 84.22W
12 F14 Sault Ste.Marie Ontario, S Canada 46.30N 84.16W
151 P7 Saumalkol' prev. Volodarskoye. Severnyy Kazakhstan, N Kazakhstan 53.19N 68.04E
202 E13 Sauma, Pointe headland Île Alofi, W Wallis and Futuna 14.21S 105.58W
176 Uu15 Saumlaki var. Saumlakki. Pulau Yamdena, E Indonesia 7.53S 131.18E
Saumlakki see Saumlaki
13 R12 Saumon, Rivière au ≈ Quebec, SE Canada
104 K8 Saumur Maine-et-Loire, NW France 47.16N 0.04W
193 F23 Saunders, Cape headland South Island, NZ 45.53S 170.40E
205 N13 Saunders Coast physical region Antarctica
67 B23 Saunders Island island NW Falkland Islands
67 C24 Saunders Island Settlement Saunders Island, NW Falkland Islands 51.22S 60.04W
84 F11 Saurimo Port. Henrique de Carvalho, Vila Henrique de Carvalho. Lunda Sul, NE Angola 9.39S 20.24E
57 S11 Sauriwaunawa S Guyana 3.10N 59.51W
176 V8 Sausapor Papua, E Indonesia 0.28S 132.09E
84 D12 Sautar Malanje, NW Angola 11.10S 18.26E
47 S13 Sauteurs N Grenada 12.13N 61.38W
104 K13 Sauveterre-de-Guyenne Gironde, SW France 44.43N 0.02W
121 O14 Sava Rus. Sava. Mahilyowskaya Voblasts', E Belarus 54.22N 30.47E
86 H11 Sava Eng. Save, Ger. Sau, Hung. Száva. ≈ SE Europe
44 J5 Savá Colón, N Honduras 15.30N 86.12W
35 Y8 Savage Montana, NW USA 47.28N 104.17W
191 N16 Savage River Tasmania, SE Australia 41.34S 145.15E
198 Aa7 Savai'i island NW Samoa
79 R15 Savalou S Benin 7.58N 1.58E
32 K10 Savanna Illinois, N USA 42.05N 90.09W
25 X6 Savannah Georgia, SE USA 32.01N 81.00W
29 R2 Savannah Missouri, C USA 39.56N 94.49W
22 H10 Savannah Tennessee, S USA 35.13N 88.15W
23 O12 Savannah River ≈ Georgia/South Carolina, SE USA
Savannakhét see Khanthabouli
46 H12 Savanna-La-Mar W Jamaica 18.13N 78.07W
10 B10 Savant Lake ◎ Ontario, S Canada
161 F17 Savanūr Karnātaka, W India 14.58N 75.19E
95 J16 Sävar Västerbotten, N Sweden 63.52N 20.33E
Savaria see Szombathely
160 C11 Sāvarkundla var. Kundla. Gujarāt, W India 21.21N 71.20E
118 F11 Săvârşin Hung. Soborsin; prev. Săvirşin. Arad, W Romania 46.00N 22.15E
142 C13 Savaştepe Balıkesir, W Turkey 39.19N 27.37E
Savat see Savot
85 N18 Save Inhambane, E Mozambique 21.07S 34.35E
104 L16 Save ≈ S France
85 L17 Save var. Sabi. ≈ Mozambique/Zimbabwe see also Sabi
Save see Sava
79 R15 Savè SE Benin 8.04N 2.28E
148 M6 Sāveh Markazī, W Iran 35.03N 50.21E
118 L8 Săveni Botoşani, NE Romania 47.57N 26.49E
105 N16 Saverdun Ariège, S France 43.15N 1.34E
105 U5 Saverne var. Zabern; anc. Tres Tabernae. Bas-Rhin, NE France 48.45N 7.22E
Savichi see Savichy
121 O21 Savichy Rus. Savichi. Homyel'skaya Voblasts', SE Belarus 51.37N 30.19E
108 B9 Savigliano Piemonte, NW Italy 44.39N 7.39E
Savigsivik see Savissivik
Savinichi see Savinichy
121 Q16 Savinichy Rus. Savinichi. Mahilyowskaya Voblasts', E Belarus 53.28N 31.46E
111 U10 Savinja ≈ N Slovenia
Savinski see Savinskiy
125 Dd6 Savinskiy var. Savinski. Arkhangel'skaya Oblast', NW Russian Federation 62.54N 40.07E
108 H11 Savio ≈ C Italy
Săvirşin see Săvârşin
207 O11 Savissivik var. Savigsivik. Avannaarsua, S Greenland 76.09N 65.24W
95 N18 Savitaipale Etelä-Suomi, S Finland 61.12N 27.43E
115 J15 Šavnik Montenegro, SW Serbia and Montenegro (Yugoslavia) 42.57N 19.04E
195 W15 Savo island C Solomon Islands
110 I9 Savognin Graubünden, S Switzerland 46.34N 9.35E
105 T12 Savoie ◈ department E France
108 C10 Savona Liguria, NW Italy 44.18N 8.28E
95 N17 Savonlinna Swe. Nyslott. Itä-Suomi, SE Finland 61.51N 28.55E
95 N17 Savonranta Itä-Suomi, SE Finland 62.10N 29.10E
40 K10 Savoonga Saint Lawrence Island, Alaska, USA 63.40N 170.29W
153 P11 Savot Rus. Savat. Sirdaryo Viloyati, E Uzbekistan 40.03N 68.35E
32 M13 Savoy Illinois, N USA 40.03N 88.15W
119 O8 Savran' Odes'ka Oblast', SW Ukraine 48.07N 30.00E
143 R11 Şavşat Artvin, NE Turkey 41.15N 42.30E
97 L19 Sävsjö Jönköping, S Sweden 57.25N 14.40E
Savu, Kepulauan see Sawu, Kepulauan
94 M11 Savukoski Lappi, NE Finland 67.17N 28.14E
Savu, Pulau see Sawu, Pulau
197 J13 Savusavu Vanua Levu, N Fiji 16.47S 179.21E
175 Q17 Savu Sea Ind. Laut Sawu. sea S Indonesia
85 H17 Savute Chobe, N Botswana 18.33S 24.06E
145 N7 Şawāb 'Uqlat well W Iraq 33.57N 40.04E
144 M7 Sawāb, Wādī as dry watercourse W Iraq
158 H13 Sawāi Mādhopur Rājasthān, N India 26.00N 76.22E
175 Tt10 Sawai, Teluk bay Pulau Seram, E Indonesia
Sawakin see Suakin
178 Ii9 Sawang Daen Din Sakon Nakhon, E Thailand 17.28N 103.27E
178 H8 Sawankhalok var. Swankalok. Sukhothai, NW Thailand 17.19N 99.49E
171 Kk17 Sawara Chiba, Honshū, S Japan 35.52N 140.29E
171 Jj12 Sawasaki-bana headland Sado, C Japan 37.48N 138.11E
39 R5 Sawatch Range ⛰ Colorado, C USA
147 N12 Sawdā', Jabal ⛰ SW Saudi Arabia 18.15N 42.26E
77 P9 Sawdā', Jabal as ⛰ C Libya
Sawdiri see Sodiri
176 W9 Saweba, Tanjung headland Papua, E Indonesia 0.41S 133.59E
99 F14 Sawel Mountain ▲ C Northern Ireland, UK 54.49N 7.04W
Sawhāj see Sohâg
79 O15 Sawla N Ghana 9.14N 2.26W
147 X12 Şawqirah var. Suqrah. S Oman 18.16N 56.34E
147 X12 Şawqirah, Dawḩat var. Ghubbat Sawqirah, Sukra Bay, Suqrah Bay. bay S Oman
Sawqirah, Ghubbat see Şawqirah, Dawḩat
191 V5 Sawtell New South Wales, SE Australia 30.22S 153.04E
144 K7 Şawt, Wādī aş dry watercourse S Syria
175 Q18 Sawu, Kepulauan var. Kepulauan Savu. island group S Indonesia
Sawu, Laut see Savu Sea
175 Qq18 Sawu, Pulau var. Pulau Savu. island Kepulauan Sawu, S Indonesia
107 S12 Sax País Valenciano, E Spain 38.33N 0.49W
Saxe see Sachsen
110 C11 Saxon Valais, SW Switzerland 46.07N 7.09E
Saxony see Sachsen
Saxony-Anhalt see Sachsen-Anhalt
79 R12 Say Niamey, SW Niger 13.02N 2.22E
13 V7 Sayabec Quebec, SE Canada 48.33N 67.42W
Sayaboury see Xaignabouli
151 U12 Sayak Kaz. Sayaq. Zhezkazgan, E Kazakhstan 46.54N 77.17E
59 D14 Sayán Lima, W Peru 11.06S 77.09W
126 Hh15 Sayanogorsk Respublika Khakasiya, S Russian Federation 53.07N 91.08E
126 J15 Sayansk Irkutskaya Oblast', S Russian Federation 54.06N 102.10E
133 T6 Sayanskiy Khrebet ⛰ S Russian Federation
Sayaq see Sayak
152 K13 Sayat Lebapskiy Velayat, E Turkmenistan 38.44N 63.51E
44 D3 Sayaxché Petén, N Guatemala 16.31N 90.10W
Şaydā/Sayida see Saïda
147 T15 Sayḩūt E Yemen 15.18N 51.15E
31 U14 Saylorville Lake ▣ Iowa, C USA
Saymenskiy Kanal see Saimaa Canal
169 N10 Saynshand Dornogovĭ, SE Mongolia 44.51N 110.07E
168 J11 Saynshand Ömnögovĭ, S Mongolia 43.30N 102.08E
168 F7 Sayn-Ust Govĭ-Altay, W Mongolia 47.23N 94.19E
Say-Ötesh see Say-Utës
144 J7 Şayqal, Baḩr ◎ S Syria
Sayrab see Sayrob
164 H4 Sayram Hu ◎ NW China
28 K11 Sayre Oklahoma, C USA 35.17N 99.38W
20 H12 Sayre Pennsylvania, NE USA 41.57N 76.30W
20 K15 Sayreville New Jersey, NE USA 40.27N 74.19W
153 N13 Sayrob Rus. Sayrab. Surkhondaryo Viloyati, S Uzbekistan 38.03N 66.54E
42 L13 Sayula Jalisco, SW Mexico 19.52N 103.36W
147 R14 Say'ūn var. Saywūn. C Yemen 15.52N 48.31E
150 G14 Say-Utës Kaz. Say-Ötesh. Mangistau, SW Kazakhstan 44.20N 53.32E
8 K16 Sayward Vancouver Island, British Columbia, SW Canada 50.20N 126.01W
Saywūn see Say'ūn
Sayyāl see As Sayyāl
145 U8 Sayyid 'Abīd var. Saiyid Abid. E Iraq 32.51N 45.07E
115 J22 Sazan var. Ishulli i Sazanit, It. Saseno. island SW Albania
Sazanit, Ishulli i see Sazan
Sazau/Sazawa see Sázava
113 E17 Sázava var. Sazau, Ger. Sazawa. ≈ C Czech Republic
128 J14 Sazonovo Vologodskaya Oblast', NW Russian Federation 59.04N 35.10E
104 G6 Scaër Finistère, NW France 48.00N 3.40W
99 J15 Scafell Pike ▲ NW England, UK 54.26N 3.10W
Scalabis see Santarém
98 M2 Scalloway N Scotland, UK 60.10N 1.17W
40 M11 Scammon Bay Alaska, USA 61.50N 165.34W
Scammon Lagoon/Scammon, Laguna see Ojo de Liebre, Laguna
86 F7 Scandinavia geophysical region NW Europe
Scania see Skåne
98 K5 Scapa Flow sea basin N Scotland, UK
109 K26 Scaramia, Capo headland Sicilia, Italy, C Mediterranean Sea 36.46N 14.29E
12 H15 Scarborough Ontario, SE Canada 43.46N 79.14W
47 Z16 Scarborough prev. Port Louis. Tobago, Trinidad and Tobago 11.10N 60.45W
99 N16 Scarborough N England, UK 54.16N 0.24W
193 I17 Scargill Canterbury, South Island, NZ 42.57S 172.57E
98 E7 Scarp island NW Scotland, UK
Scarpanto see Karpathos
Scarpanto Strait see Karpathou, Stenó
109 G25 Scauri Sicilia, Italy, C Mediterranean Sea 36.45N 12.06E
Scealg, Bá na see Ballinskelligs Bay
Scebeli see Shebeli
102 K10 Schaale ≈ N Germany
102 K9 Schaalsee ◎ N Germany
101 G18 Schaerbeek Brussels, C Belgium 50.51N 4.21E
110 G6 Schaffhausen Fr. Schaffhouse. Schaffhausen, N Switzerland 47.42N 8.37E
110 G6 Schaffhausen Fr. Schaffhouse. ◈ canton N Switzerland
Schaffhouse see Schaffhausen
100 I8 Schagen Noord-Holland, NW Netherlands 52.46N 4.46E
Schaken see Šakiai
100 M10 Schalkhaar Overijssel, E Netherlands 52.16N 6.10E
111 R3 Schärding Oberösterreich, N Austria 48.27N 13.26E
102 G9 Scharhörn island NW Germany
Schässburg see Sighişoara
Schaulen see Šiauliai
32 M10 Schaumburg Illinois, N USA 42.01N 88.04W
Schebschi Mountains see Shebshi Mountains
100 P6 Scheemda Groningen, NE Netherlands 53.10N 6.58E
102 I10 Scheessel Niedersachsen, NW Germany 53.11N 9.32E
11 N8 Schefferville Quebec, E Canada 54.50N 67.00W
Schelde see Scheldt
101 D18 Scheldt Dut. Schelde, Fr. Escaut. ≈ W Europe
37 X5 Schell Creek Range ⛰ Nevada, W USA
20 K10 Schenectady New York, NE USA 42.48N 73.57W
101 I17 Scherpenheuvel Fr. Montaigu. Vlaams Brabant, C Belgium 51.00N 4.57E
100 K11 Scherpenzeel Gelderland, C Netherlands 52.07N 5.30E
27 S12 Schertz Texas, SW USA 29.33N 98.16W
100 G11 Scheveningen Zuid-Holland, W Netherlands 52.07N 4.18E
100 G12 Schiedam Zuid-Holland, SW Netherlands 51.55N 4.25E
101 M24 Schieren Diekirch, NE Luxembourg 49.49N 6.06E
100 M4 Schiermonnikoog Fris. Skiermûntseach. Friesland, N Netherlands 53.28N 6.09E
100 M4 Schiermonnikoog Fris. Skiermûntseach. island Waddeneilanden, N Netherlands
101 K14 Schijndel Noord-Brabant, S Netherlands 51.37N 5.27E
Schil see Jiu
101 H16 Schilde Antwerpen, N Belgium 51.13N 4.34E
Schillen see Zhilino
105 V5 Schiltigheim Bas-Rhin, NE France 48.37N 7.46E
108 G7 Schio Veneto, NE Italy 45.42N 11.21E
100 H10 Schiphol ✕ (Amsterdam) Noord-Holland, C Netherlands 52.18N 4.48E
Schippenbeil see Sępopol
Schiria see Şiria
Schivelbein see Świdwin
117 D22 Schíza island S Greece
183 U3 Schjetman Reef reef Antarctica
Schlackenwerth see Ostrov
111 R7 Schladming Steiermark, SE Austria 47.23N 13.37E
Schlan see Slaný
Schlanders see Silandro
102 I7 Schlei inlet N Germany
103 D17 Schleiden Nordrhein-Westfalen, W Germany 50.31N 6.30E
195 P9 Schleinitz Range ⛰ New Ireland, N PNG
Schlelau see Szydłowiec
102 I7 Schleswig Schleswig-Holstein, N Germany 54.31N 9.34E
31 T13 Schleswig Iowa, C USA 42.10N 95.27W
102 H8 Schleswig-Holstein ◈ state N Germany
Schlettstadt see Sélestat
110 F7 Schlieren Zürich, N Switzerland 47.22N 8.27E
Schlochau see Człuchów
Schloppe see Człopa
103 I18 Schlüchtern Hessen, C Germany 50.19N 9.27E
103 J17 Schmalkalden Thüringen, C Germany 50.42N 10.26E
111 W2 Schmida ≈ NE Austria
67 P19 Schmidt-Ott Seamount var. Schmitt-Ott Seamount, Schmitt-Ott Tablemount. undersea feature SW Indian Ocean 39.37S 13.00E
Schmiegel see Śmigiel
Schmitt-Ott Seamount/Schmitt-Ott Tablemount see Schmidt-Ott Seamount
13 V3 Schmon ≈ Quebec, SE Canada
103 M18 Schneeberg ▲ W Germany 50.03N 11.51E
Schneeberg see Veliki Snežnik
Schnee-Eifel see Schneifel
Schneekoppe see Sněžka
Schneidemühl see Piła
103 D18 Schneifel var. Schnee-Eifel. plateau W Germany
Schnelle Körös/Schnelle Kreisch see Crişul Repede
102 I11 Schneverdingen var. Schneverdingen (Wümme). Niedersachsen, NW Germany 53.07N 9.48E
Schneverdingen (Wümme) see Schneverdingen
Schoden see Skuodas
20 K10 Schoharie New York, NE USA 42.40N 74.19W
20 K11 Schoharie Creek ≈ New York, NE USA
117 J21 Schoinoússa island Kykládes, Greece, Aegean Sea
102 L13 Schönebeck Sachsen-Anhalt, C Germany 52.01N 11.45E
Schöneck see Skarszewy
102 O12 Schönefeld ✕ (Berlin) Berlin, NE Germany 52.23N 13.29E
103 K24 Schongau Bayern, S Germany 47.49N 10.54E
102 K13 Schöningen Niedersachsen, C Germany 52.07N 10.58E
Schönlanke see Trzcianka
Schönsee see Kowalewo Pomorskie
33 P10 Schoolcraft Michigan, N USA 42.05N 85.39W
100 O8 Schoonebeek Drenthe, NE Netherlands 52.39N 6.57E
100 I12 Schoonhoven Zuid-Holland, C Netherlands 51.57N 4.51E
100 H8 Schoorl Noord-Holland, NW Netherlands 52.42N 4.40E
Schooten see Schoten
103 F24 Schopfheim Baden-Württemberg, SW Germany 47.39N 7.49E
103 I21 Schorndorf Baden-Württemberg, S Germany 48.48N 9.31E
102 F10 Schortens Niedersachsen, NW Germany 53.31N 7.57E
101 H16 Schoten var. Schooten. Antwerpen, N Belgium 51.15N 4.30E
191 Q17 Schouten Island island Tasmania, SE Australia
194 H9 Schouten Islands island group NW PNG
100 E13 Schouwen island SW Netherlands
47 Q12 Schœlcher W Martinique 14.37N 61.06W
Schreiberhau see Szklarska Poręba
111 U2 Schrems Niederösterreich, E Austria 48.49N 15.01E
103 L22 Schrobenhausen Bayern, SE Germany 48.33N 11.14E
20 L8 Schroon Lake ◎ New York, NE USA
110 J8 Schruns Vorarlberg, W Austria 47.04N 9.54E
Schubin see Szubin
27 U11 Schulenburg Texas, SW USA 29.40N 96.54W
Schuls see Scuol
110 E8 Schüpfheim Luzern, C Switzerland 47.02N 7.23E
37 S6 Schurz Nevada, W USA 38.55N 118.48W
103 I24 Schussen ≈ S Germany
Schüttenhofen see Sušice
31 R15 Schuyler Nebraska, C USA 41.25N 97.04W
20 L10 Schuylerville New York, NE USA 43.05N 73.34W
103 K20 Schwabach Bayern, SE Germany 49.19N 11.01E
Schwabenalb see Schwäbische Alb
103 I23 Schwäbische Alb var. Schwabenalb, Eng. Swabian Jura. ⛰ S Germany
103 I22 Schwäbisch Gmünd var. Gmünd. Baden-Württemberg, SW Germany 48.48N 9.48E
103 I21 Schwäbisch Hall var. Hall. Baden-Württemberg, SW Germany 49.07N 9.43E
103 H16 Schwalm ≈ C Germany
111 V9 Schwanberg Steiermark, SE Austria 46.46N 15.12E
110 H8 Schwanden Glarus, E Switzerland 47.02N 9.04E
103 M20 Schwandorf Bayern, SE Germany 49.19N 12.07E
111 S5 Schwanenstadt Oberösterreich, NW Austria 48.03N 13.45E
174 M9 Schwaner, Pegunungan ⛰ Borneo, N Indonesia
111 W5 Schwarza ≈ E Austria
111 P9 Schwarzach ≈ S Austria
103 M20 Schwarzach Cz. Černice. ≈ Czech Republic/Germany
Schwarzach see Schwarzach im Pongau, Austria
Schwarzach see Svratka, Czech Republic
111 Q7 Schwarzach im Pongau var. Schwarzach. Salzburg, NW Austria 47.19N 13.09E
Schwarzawa see Svratka
103 N14 Schwarze Elster ≈ E Germany
Schwarze Körös see Crişul Negru
110 D9 Schwarzenburg Bern, W Switzerland 46.51N 7.28E
85 D21 Schwarzrand ⛰ S Namibia
103 G23 Schwarzwald Eng. Black Forest. ⛰ SW Germany
Schwarzwasser see Wda
41 P7 Schwatka Mountains ⛰ Alaska, USA
111 N7 Schwaz Tirol, W Austria 47.21N 11.43E
111 Y4 Schwechat Niederösterreich, NE Austria 48.09N 16.29E
111 Y4 Schwechat ✕ (Wien) Wien, E Austria 48.04N 16.31E
102 P11 Schwedt Brandenburg, NE Germany 53.04N 14.16E
103 D19 Schweich Rheinland-Pfalz, SW Germany 49.49N 6.44E
Schweidnitz see Świdnica
103 J18 Schweinfurt Bayern, SE Germany 50.03N 10.13E
Schweiz see Switzerland
102 L9 Schwerin Mecklenburg-Vorpommern, N Germany 53.37N 11.25E
Schwerin see Skwierzyna
102 L9 Schweriner See ◎ N Germany
Schwertberg see Świecie
103 F15 Schwerte Nordrhein-Westfalen, W Germany 51.27N 7.34E
Schwiebus see Świebodzin
102 P13 Schwielochsee ◎ NE Germany
Schwihau see Švihov
Schwiz see Schwyz
110 G8 Schwyz var. Schwiz. Schwyz, C Switzerland 47.01N 8.39E
110 G8 Schwyz var. Schwiz. ◈ canton C Switzerland
12 J11 Schyan ≈ Quebec, SE Canada
Schyl see Jiu
109 I24 Sciacca Sicilia, Italy, C Mediterranean Sea 37.30N 13.05E
Sciasciamana see Shashemenē
109 L26 Scicli Sicilia, Italy, C Mediterranean Sea 36.48N 14.43E
99 F25 Scilly, Isles of island group SW England, UK
113 H17 Ścinawa Ger. Steinau an der Elbe. Dolnośląskie, SW Poland 51.22N 16.27E
Scio see Chíos
33 S14 Scioto River ≈ Ohio, N USA
38 L5 Scipio Utah, W USA 39.15N 112.06W
35 X6 Scobey Montana, NW USA 48.47N 105.25W
191 T7 Scone New South Wales, SE Australia 32.02S 150.51E
Scoresby Sound/Scoresbysund see Ittoqqortoormiit
Scoresby Sund see Kangertittivaq
Scorno, Punta dello see Caprara, Punta
36 K3 Scotia California, W USA 40.04N 124.07W
49 Y14 Scotia Plate tectonic feature
49 V15 Scotia Ridge undersea feature S Atlantic Ocean
204 H2 Scotia Sea sea SW Atlantic Ocean
31 Q12 Scotland South Dakota, N USA 43.09N 97.43W
27 R5 Scotland Texas, SW USA 33.37N 98.27W
98 H11 Scotland national region UK
23 W8 Scotland Neck North Carolina, SE USA 36.07N 77.25W
205 R13 Scott Base NZ research station Antarctica 77.52S 167.18E
8 J16 Scott, Cape headland Vancouver Island, British Columbia, SW Canada 50.43N 128.24W
28 I5 Scott City Kansas, C USA 38.28N 100.54W
29 Y7 Scott City Missouri, C USA 37.13N 89.31W
205 R14 Scott Coast physical region Antarctica
20 C15 Scottdale Pennsylvania, NE USA 40.05N 79.35W
205 Y11 Scott Glacier glacier Antarctica
205 Q17 Scott Island island Antarctica
28 L11 Scott, Mount ▲ Oklahoma, USA 34.52N 98.34W
34 G15 Scott, Mount ▲ Oregon, NW USA 42.53N 122.06W
36 M1 Scott River ≈ California, W USA
30 I13 Scottsbluff Nebraska, C USA 41.52N 103.40W
25 Q2 Scottsboro Alabama, S USA 34.40N 86.01W
33 P15 Scottsburg Indiana, N USA 38.42N 85.46W
191 P16 Scottsdale Tasmania, SE Australia 41.13S 147.30E
38 L13 Scottsdale Arizona, SW USA 33.30N 111.54W
47 O12 Scotts Head Village var. Cachacrou. S Dominica 15.12N 61.22W
199 Jj17 Scott Shoal undersea feature S Pacific Ocean
22 K7 Scottsville Kentucky, S USA 36.45N 86.11W
31 U14 Scranton Iowa, C USA 42.01N 94.33W
20 I13 Scranton Pennsylvania, NE USA 41.25N 75.40W
194 G10 Screw ≈ NW PNG
31 R14 Scribner Nebraska, C USA 41.40N 96.40W
Scrobesbyrig' see Shrewsbury
12 I14 Scugog ≈ Ontario, SE Canada
12 I14 Scugog, Lake ◎ Ontario, SE Canada
99 N17 Scunthorpe E England, UK 53.34N 0.39W
110 K9 Scuol Ger. Schuls. Graubünden, E Switzerland 46.51N 10.21E
Scupi see Skopje
Scutari see Shkodër
115 K17 Scutari, Lake Alb. Liqeni i Shkodrës, SCr. Skadarsko Jezero. ◎ Albania/Serbia and Montenegro (Yugoslavia)
Scyros see Skýros
Scythopolis see Bet She'an
27 U13 Seadrift Texas, SW USA 28.25N 96.42W
23 Y4 Seaford var. Seaford City. Delaware, NE USA 38.38N 75.36W
Seaford City see Seaford
12 E15 Seaforth Ontario, S Canada 43.33N 81.25W
26 M6 Seagraves Texas, SW USA 32.56N 102.33W
9 X9 Seal ≈ Manitoba, C Canada
190 M10 Sea Lake Victoria, SE Australia 35.34S 142.51E
85 G26 Seal, Cape headland S South Africa 34.06S 23.18E
67 D26 Sea Lion Islands island group SE Falkland Islands
21 S8 Seal Island island Maine, NE USA
27 V11 Sealy Texas, SW USA 29.46N 96.09W
37 X12 Searchlight Nevada, W USA 35.27N 114.54W
29 V11 Searcy Arkansas, C USA 35.15N 91.44W
21 R7 Searsport Maine, NE USA 44.28N 68.54W
37 N10 Seaside California, W USA 36.36N 121.51W
34 F10 Seaside Oregon, NW USA 45.57N 123.55W
20 K16 Seaside Heights New Jersey, NE USA 39.56N 74.03W
34 H8 Seattle Washington, NW USA 47.34N 122.19W
34 H9 Seattle-Tacoma ✕ Washington, NW USA 47.04N 122.27W
193 J16 Seaward Kaikoura Range ⛰ South Island, NZ
44 J9 Sébaco Matagalpa, W Nicaragua 12.50N 86.04W
21 P8 Sebago Lake ◎ Maine, NE USA
176 V11 Sebakor, Teluk bay Papua, E Indonesia
Sebangan, Sungai see Sebangau Besar, Sungai
174 M11 Sebangan, Teluk bay Borneo, C Indonesia
174 Mm11 Sebanganu, Teluk bay Borneo, C Indonesia
174 Mm11 Sebangau Besar, Sungai var. Sungai Sebangan. ≈ Borneo, N Indonesia
174 I8 Sebanglea, Pulau island W Indonesia
Sebaste/Sebastia see Sivas
25 Y12 Sebastian Florida, SE USA 27.55N 80.31W
42 C5 Sebastián Vizcaíno, Bahía bay NW Mexico
21 R6 Sebasticook Lake ◎ Maine, NE USA
36 M7 Sebastopol California, W USA 38.22N 122.50W
Sebastopol see Sevastopol'
175 Oo4 Sebatik, Pulau island N Indonesia
21 R5 Sebec Lake ◎ Maine, NE USA
78 K12 Sébékoro Kayes, W Mali 13.00N 9.03W
Sebenico see Šibenik
42 G6 Seberi, Cerro ▲ NW Mexico 27.49N 110.18W
118 H11 Sebeş Ger. Mühlbach, Hung. Szászsebes; prev. Sebeşu Săsesc. Alba, W Romania 45.57N 23.34E
Sebes-Körös see Crişul Repede
Sebeşu Săsesc see Sebeş
33 R8 Sebewaing Michigan, N USA 43.43N 83.27W
128 F16 Sebezh Pskovskaya Oblast', W Russian Federation 56.19N 28.31E

◆ Country ● Country Capital ◇ Dependent Territory ○ Dependent Territory Capital ◈ Administrative Region ✕ International Airport ▲ Mountain ⛰ Mountain Range Volcano ≈ River ◎ Lake ▣ Reservoir

143 N12 **Şebinkarahisar** Giresun, N Turkey *40.19N 38.25E*
118 F11 **Sebiş** *Hung.* Borossebes. Arad, W Romania *46.21N 22.09E*
Sebkra Azz el Matti *see* Azzel Matti, Sebkha
21 Q4 **Seboomook Lake** ◎ Maine, NE USA
76 G6 **Sebou** *var.* Sebu. ≈ N Morocco
22 I6 **Sebree** Kentucky, S USA *37.34N 87.30W*
25 X13 **Sebring** Florida, SE USA *27.30N 81.26W*
Sebta *see* Ceuta
Sebu *see* Sebou
175 Nn11 **Sebuku, Pulau** *island* N Indonesia
175 Oo4 **Sebuku, Teluk** *bay* Borneo, N Indonesia
176 Vv10 **Sebyar** ≈ Papua, E Indonesia
108 F10 **Secchia** ≈ N Italy
8 L17 **Sechelt** British Columbia, SW Canada *49.25N 123.37W*
58 C12 **Sechin, Río** ≈ W Peru
58 A10 **Sechura, Bahía de** *bay* NW Peru
193 A22 **Secretary Island** *island* SW NZ
161 I15 **Secunderābād** *var.* Sikandarabad. Andhra Pradesh, C India *17.30N 78.33E*
59 L17 **Sécure, Río** ≈ C Bolivia
120 D10 **Seda** Mažeikiai, NW Lithuania *56.10N 22.04E*
29 T5 **Sedalia** Missouri, C USA *38.42N 93.13W*
105 R3 **Sedan** Ardennes, N France *49.42N 4.55E*
29 P7 **Sedan** Kansas, C USA *37.07N 96.11W*
107 N3 **Sedano** Castilla-León, N Spain *42.43N 3.43W*
106 H10 **Seda, Ribeira de** *stream* C Portugal
193 K15 **Seddon** Marlborough, South Island, NZ *41.41S 174.04E*
193 H15 **Seddonville** West Coast, South Island, NZ *41.34S 171.59E*
149 U7 **Sedeh** Khorāsān, E Iran *33.18N 59.12E*
125 G12 **Sedel'nikovo** Omskaya Oblast', C Russian Federation *56.54N 75.24E*
144 E11 **Sederot** Southern, S Israel *31.31N 34.34E*
67 B23 **Sedge Island** *island* NW Falkland Islands
78 G12 **Sédhiou** SW Senegal *12.39N 15.33W*
9 U16 **Sedley** Saskatchewan, S Canada *50.06N 103.51W*
Sedlez *see* Siedlce
119 Q2 **Sedniv** Chernihivs'ka Oblast', N Ukraine *51.39N 31.34E*
38 L11 **Sedona** Arizona, SW USA *34.52N 111.45W*
Sedunum *see* Sion
120 F12 **Šeduva** Radviliškis, N Lithuania *55.45N 23.46E*
147 Y8 **Seeb** *var.* Muscat Sīb Airport. ✕ (Masqaṭ) NE Oman *23.36N 58.27E*
Seeb *see* As Sīb
110 M7 **Seefeld-in-Tirol** Tirol, W Austria *47.19N 11.16E*
85 E22 **Seeheim Noord** Karas, S Namibia *26.49S 17.50E*
Seeland *see* Sjælland
205 N9 **Seelig, Mount** ▲ Antarctica *81.45S 102.15W*
Seeonee *see* Seoni
168 E6 **Seer** Hovd, W Mongolia *48.18N 92.37E*
104 L5 **Sées** Orne, N France *48.36N 0.11E*
103 J14 **Seesen** Niedersachsen, C Germany *51.54N 10.10E*
Seesker Höhe *see* Szeskie Wzgórza
102 J10 **Seevetal** Niedersachsen, N Germany *53.24N 10.01E*
111 V6 **Seewiesen** Steiermark, E Austria *47.37N 15.16E*
142 J13 **Şefaatli** *var.* Kızılkoca. Yozgat, C Turkey *39.31N 34.45E*
155 N3 **Sefīd, Darya-ye** *Pash.* Āb-i-Safed. ≈ N Afghanistan
154 K5 **Sefīd Kūh, Selseleh-ye** *Eng.* Paropamisus Range. ▲▲ W Afghanistan
76 G6 **Sefrou** N Morocco *33.51N 4.49W*
193 E19 **Sefton, Mount** ▲ South Island, NZ *43.43S 169.58E*
176 U10 **Segaf, Kepulauan** *island group* E Indonesia
175 Oo3 **Segama, Sungai** ≈ East Malaysia
174 Hh6 **Segamat** Johor, Peninsular Malaysia *2.30N 102.48E*
79 S13 **Ségbana** NE Benin *10.55N 3.42E*
Segestica *see* Sisak
Segesvár *see* Sighişoara
176 Uu9 **Seget** Papua, E Indonesia *1.21S 131.04E*
Segewold *see* Sigulda
128 J9 **Segezha** Respublika Kareliya, NW Russian Federation *63.39N 34.24E*
Seghedin *see* Szeged
Segna *see* Senj
109 I16 **Segni** Lazio, C Italy *41.41N 13.02E*
Segodunum *see* Rodez
107 S9 **Segorbe** País Valenciano, E Spain *39.51N 0.30W*
78 M12 **Ségou** *var.* Segu. Ségou, C Mali *13.25N 6.12W*
78 M12 **Ségou** ◈ *region* SW Mali
56 E8 **Segovia** Antioquia, N Colombia *7.06N 74.42W*
107 N7 **Segovia** Castilla-León, C Spain *40.57N 4.07W*
106 M6 **Segovia** ◈ *province* Castilla-León, N Spain
Segoviao Wangkí *see* Coco, Río
128 J9 **Segozero, Ozero** ◎ NW Russian Federation
107 U5 **Segre** ≈ NE Spain
104 J7 **Segré** Maine-et-Loire, NW France *47.40N 0.51W*
Segu *see* Ségou
40 I17 **Seguam Island** *island* Aleutian Islands, Alaska, USA
40 I17 **Seguam Pass** *strait* Aleutian Islands, Alaska, USA
79 Y7 **Séguédine** Agadez, NE Niger *20.12N 13.03E*
78 M15 **Séguéla** W Ivory Coast *8.01N 6.38W*
27 S11 **Seguin** Texas, SW USA *29.34N 97.58W*
40 E17 **Segula Island** *island* Aleutian Islands, Alaska, USA
64 K10 **Segundo, Río** ≈ C Argentina
107 Q12 **Segura** ≈ S Spain
107 P13 **Sierra de Segura** ▲▲ S Spain
85 G18 **Sehithwa** Ngamiland, N Botswana *20.28S 22.43E*
160 H10 **Sehore** Madhya Pradesh, C India *23.12N 77.07E*
195 O16 **Sehulea** Normanby Island, S PNG *9.55S 151.10E*
155 P15 **Sehwān** Sind, SE Pakistan *26.27N 67.46E*
111 V8 **Seiersberg** Steiermark, SE Austria *47.01N 15.22E*
28 L9 **Seiling** Oklahoma, C USA *36.09N 98.55W*
105 S9 **Seille** ≈ E France
101 J20 **Seilles** Namur, SE Belgium *50.31N 5.12E*
95 K17 **Seinäjoki** *Swe.* Östermyra. Länsi-Suomi, W Finland *62.45N 22.54E*
10 B12 **Seine** ≈ Ontario, S Canada
104 M4 **Seine** ≈ N France
104 K4 **Seine, Baie de la** *bay* N France
Seine, Banc de la *see* Seine Seamount
105 O5 **Seine-et-Marne** ◈ *department* N France
104 L3 **Seine-Maritime** ◈ *department* N France
86 B14 **Seine Plain** *undersea feature* E Atlantic Ocean
86 B15 **Seine Seamount** *var.* Banc de la Seine. *undersea feature* E Atlantic Ocean *33.45N 14.25W*
104 E6 **Sein, Île de** *island* NW France
176 Y12 **Seinma** Papua, E Indonesia *4.10S 138.54E*
Seisbierrum *see* Sexbierum
111 U5 **Seitenstetten Markt** Niederösterreich, C Austria *48.03N 14.41E*
Seiyu *see* Chŏnju
97 H22 **Sejerø** *island* E Denmark
112 P7 **Sejny** Podlaskie, NE Poland *54.09N 23.21E*
174 Ii13 **Sekampung, Way** ≈ Sumatera, SW Indonesia
83 G20 **Seke** Shinyanga, N Tanzania *3.16S 33.31E*
171 I15 **Seki** Gifu, Honshū, SW Japan *35.25N 136.51E*
167 U12 **Sekibi-sho** *island* China/Japan/Taiwan
172 Pp5 **Sekihoku-tōge** *pass* Hokkaidō, NE Japan *43.40N 143.10E*
Sekondi *see* Sekondi-Takoradi
79 P17 **Sekondi-Takoradi** *var.* Sekondi. S Ghana *4.55N 1.45W*
82 J11 **Sek'ot'a** Amhara, N Ethiopia *12.41N 39.05E*
Sekseūil *see* Saksaul'skiy
34 I9 **Selah** Washington, NW USA *46.39N 120.31W*
174 Gg5 **Selangor** *var.* Negeri Selangor Darul Ehsan. ◈ *state* Peninsular Malaysia
Selânik *see* Thessaloníki
174 Hh7 **Selapanjang** Pulau Rantau, W Indonesia *1.00N 102.44E*
178 Ii10 **Selaphum** Roi Et, E Thailand *16.00N 103.54E*
176 Uu16 **Selaru, Pulau** *island* Kepulauan Tanimbar, E Indonesia
176 Vv11 **Selassi** Papua, E Indonesia *3.16S 132.50E*
173 G3 **Selatan, Selat** *strait* Peninsular Malaysia
41 N8 **Selawik** Alaska, USA *66.36N 160.00W*
41 N8 **Selawik Lake** ◎ Alaska, USA
175 Pp13 **Selayar, Selat** *strait* Sulawesi, C Indonesia
97 C14 **Selbjørnsfjorden** *fjord* S Norway
96 H8 **Selbusjøen** ◎ S Norway
99 M17 **Selby** N England, UK *53.49N 1.06W*
31 N8 **Selby** South Dakota, N USA *45.30N 100.01W*
23 Z4 **Selbyville** Delaware, NE USA *38.28N 75.12W*
142 B15 **Selçuk** *var.* Akıncılar. İzmir, SW Turkey *37.55N 27.21E*
41 Q13 **Seldovia** Alaska, USA *59.26N 151.42W*
109 M18 **Sele** *anc.* Silarius. ≈ S Italy
44 B5 **Selegua, Río** ≈ W Guatemala
133 X7 **Selemdzha** ≈ SE Russian Federation
133 U7 **Selenga** *Mong.* Selenge Mörön. ≈ Mongolia/Russian Federation
168 K6 **Selenge** Bulgan, N Mongolia *49.34N 104.18E*
168 J6 **Selenge** Hövsgöl, N Mongolia *49.25N 101.30E*
81 I19 **Selenge** Bandundu, W Dem. Rep. Congo *1.58S 18.10E*
168 L6 **Selenge** ◈ *province* N Mongolia
Selenge Mörön *see* Selenga
126 Jj16 **Selenginsk** Respublika Buryatiya, S Russian Federation *52.00N 106.40E*
Selenica *see* Selenicë
115 K22 **Selenicë** *var.* Selenica. Vlorë, SW Albania *40.32N 19.38E*
126 M7 **Selennyakh** ≈ NE Russian Federation
102 J8 **Selenter See** ◎ N Germany
Sele Sound *see* Soela Väin
105 U6 **Sélestat** *Ger.* Schlettstadt. Bas-Rhin, NE France *48.16N 7.28E*
Selety *see* Sileti
Seleucia *see* Silifke
94 I4 **Selfoss** Sudhurland, SW Iceland *63.56N 20.59W*
30 M7 **Selfridge** North Dakota, N USA *46.01N 100.52W*
78 I15 **Seli** ≈ N Sierra Leone
78 I11 **Sélibabi** *var.* Sélibaby. Guidimaka, S Mauritania *15.13N 12.10W*
Sélibaby *see* Sélibabi
Selidovka/Selidovo *see* Selydove
128 I15 **Seliger, Ozero** ◎ W Russian Federation
38 J11 **Seligman** Arizona, SW USA *35.20N 112.56W*
29 S8 **Seligman** Missouri, C USA *36.31N 93.56W*
82 E6 **Selima Oasis** *oasis* N Sudan *21.22N 29.19E*
78 L13 **Sélingué, Lac de** ⊠ S Mali
Selinoús *see* Kréstena
20 G14 **Selinsgrove** Pennsylvania, NE USA *40.47N 76.51W*
Selishche *see* Syelishcha
128 I16 **Selizharovo** Tverskaya Oblast', W Russian Federation *56.50N 33.24E*
96 C10 **Selje** Sogn og Fjordane, S Norway *62.02N 5.22E*
9 X16 **Selkirk** Manitoba, S Canada *50.10N 96.52W*
98 K13 **Selkirk** SE Scotland, UK *55.35N 2.48W*
98 K13 **Selkirk** *cultural region* SE Scotland, UK
9 O16 **Selkirk Mountains** ▲▲ British Columbia, SW Canada
200 Oo12 **Selkirk Rise** *undersea feature* SE Pacific Ocean
117 F21 **Sellasía** Pelopónnisos, S Greece *37.14N 22.24E*
46 M9 **Selle, Pic de la** *var.* La Selle. ▲ SE Haiti *18.18N 71.55W*
104 M8 **Selles-sur-Cher** Loir-et-Cher, C France *47.16N 1.31E*
38 K16 **Sells** Arizona, SW USA *31.54N 111.52W*
Sellye *see* Sal'a
25 P5 **Selma** Alabama, S USA *32.24N 87.01W*
37 Q11 **Selma** California, W USA *36.33N 119.37W*
22 G10 **Selmer** Tennessee, S USA *35.10N 88.35W*
181 N17 **Sel, Pointe au** *headland* W Réunion
Selseleh-ye Kūh-e Vākhān *see* Nicholas Range
131 S2 **Selty** Udmurtskaya Respublika, NW Russian Federation *57.19N 52.09E*
Selukwe *see* Shurugwi
64 L9 **Selva** Santiago del Estero, N Argentina *29.46S 62.01W*
9 T9 **Selwyn Lake** ◎ Northwest Territories/Saskatchewan, C Canada
8 K6 **Selwyn Mountains** ▲▲ Yukon Territory, NW Canada
189 T6 **Selwyn Range** ▲▲ Queensland, C Australia
119 W8 **Selydove** *var.* Selidovka, *Rus.* Selidovo. Donets'ka Oblast', SE Ukraine *48.06N 37.16E*
Selzaete *see* Zelzate
Seman *see* Semanit, Lumi i
174 Ii13 **Semangka, Teluk** *bay* Sumatera, SW Indonesia
174 I13 **Semangka, Way** ≈ Sumatera, SW Indonesia
115 D22 **Semanit, Lumi i** *var.* Seman. ≈ W Albania
174 Kk14 **Semarang** *var.* Samarang. Jawa, C Indonesia *6.58S 110.28E*
174 Kk6 **Sematan** Sarawak, East Malaysia *1.49N 109.43E*
175 Qq17 **Semau, Pulau** *island* S Indonesia
175 Nn8 **Semayang, Danau** ◎ Borneo, N Indonesia
175 O4 **Sembakung, Sungai** ≈ Borneo, N Indonesia
81 G17 **Sembé** La Sangha, NW Congo *1.37N 14.34E*
Semberong *see* Semberong, Sungai
174 Hh6 **Semberong, Sungai** *var.* Semberong. ≈ Peninsular Malaysia
174 M10 **Sembulu, Danau** ◎ Borneo, N Indonesia
Semendria *see* Smederevo
119 R1 **Semenivka** Chernihivs'ka Oblast', N Ukraine *52.10N 32.37E*
119 S6 **Semenivka** *Rus.* Semenovka. Poltavs'ka Oblast', NE Ukraine *49.36N 33.11E*
131 O3 **Semenov** Nizhegorodskaya Oblast', W Russian Federation *56.47N 44.27E*
Semenovka *see* Semenivka
174 M16 **Semeru, Gunung** *var.* Mahameru. ▲ Jawa, S Indonesia *8.01S 112.53E*
Semey *see* Semipalatinsk
Semezhevo *see* Syemyezhava
130 L7 **Semiluki** Voronezhskaya Oblast', W Russian Federation *51.46N 39.00E*
35 W16 **Seminoe Reservoir** ⊠ Wyoming, C USA
29 O11 **Seminole** Oklahoma, C USA *35.13N 96.40W*
26 M6 **Seminole** Texas, SW USA *32.43N 102.38W*
25 S8 **Seminole, Lake** ⊠ Florida/Georgia, SE USA
150 M8 **Semiozernoye** Kostanay, N Kazakhstan *52.22N 64.06E*
151 V9 **Semipalatinsk** *Kaz.* Semey. Vostochnyy Kazakhstan, E Kazakhstan *50.25N 80.16E*
149 O9 **Semīrom** *var.* Samirum. Eşfahān, C Iran *31.19N 51.49E*
40 F17 **Semisopochnoi Island** *island* Aleutian Islands, Alaska, USA
174 Ll7 **Semitau** Borneo, C Indonesia *0.30N 111.58E*
83 E18 **Semliki** ≈ Uganda/Dem. Rep. Congo
149 P5 **Semnān** *var.* Samnān. Semnān, N Iran *35.37N 53.21E*
149 Q5 **Semnān** *off.* Ostān-e Semnān. ◈ *province* N Iran
101 K24 **Semois** ≈ SE Belgium
110 E8 **Sempacher See** ◎ C Switzerland
Sena *see* Vila de Sena
32 L12 **Senachwine Lake** ◎ Illinois, N USA
61 O14 **Senador Pompeu** Ceará, E Brazil *5.30S 39.25W*
Sena Gallica *see* Senigallia
61 C15 **Sena Madureira** Acre, W Brazil *9.04S 68.40W*
161 L25 **Senanayake Samudra** ◎ E Sri Lanka
85 G15 **Senanga** Western, SW Zambia *16.09S 23.16E*
29 Y9 **Senath** Missouri, C USA *36.07N 90.09W*
24 L2 **Senatobia** Mississippi, S USA *34.37N 89.58W*
170 C15 **Sendai** Kagoshima, Kyūshū, SW Japan *31.48N 130.16E*
171 M13 **Sendai** Miyagi, Honshū, C Japan *38.16N 140.52E*
170 Bb15 **Sendai-gawa** ≈ Kyūshū, SW Japan
171 M14 **Sendai-wan** *bay* E Japan
103 J23 **Senden** Bayern, S Germany *48.18N 10.04E*
160 F11 **Sendhwa** Madhya Pradesh, C India *21.38N 75.04E*
113 H21 **Senec** *Ger.* Wartberg, *Hung.* Szenc; *prev.* Szempcz. Bratislavský Kraj, W Slovakia *48.14N 17.24E*
29 P3 **Seneca** Kansas, C USA *39.47N 96.04W*
29 R8 **Seneca** Missouri, C USA *36.50N 94.36W*
34 K13 **Seneca** Oregon, NW USA *44.06N 118.57W*
23 O11 **Seneca** South Carolina, SE USA *34.41N 82.57W*
20 G11 **Seneca Lake** ◎ New York, NE USA
33 U13 **Senecaville Lake** ⊠ Ohio, N USA
78 G11 **Senegal** *off.* Republic of Senegal, *Fr.* Sénégal. ◆ *republic* W Africa
78 H9 **Senegal** *Fr.* Sénégal. ≈ W Africa
33 O4 **Seney Marsh** *wetland* Michigan, N USA
103 P14 **Senftenberg** Brandenburg, E Germany *51.31N 14.01E*
84 L11 **Senga Hill** Northern, NE Zambia *9.26S 31.12E*
164 G13 **Sênggê Zangbo** ≈ W China
176 Z11 **Senggi** Papua, E Indonesia *3.26S 140.46E*
131 R5 **Sengiley** Ul'yanovskaya Oblast', W Russian Federation *53.54N 48.51E*
65 I19 **Senguerr, Río** ≈ S Argentina
85 J16 **Sengwa** ≈ C Zimbabwe
Senia *see* Senj
113 H19 **Senica** *Ger.* Senitz, *Hung.* Szenice. Trnavský Kraj, W Slovakia *48.40N 17.22E*
Seniça *see* Sjenica
108 J11 **Senigallia** *anc.* Sena Gallica. Marche, C Italy *43.43N 13.13E*
142 F15 **Senirkent** Isparta, SW Turkey *38.07N 30.34E*
Senitz *see* Senica
114 C10 **Senj** *Ger.* Zengg, *It.* Segna; *anc.* Senia. Lika-Senj, NW Croatia *44.58N 14.55E*
169 O10 **Senj** Dornogovĭ, SE Mongolia *44.34N 110.58E*
94 H9 **Senja** *prev.* Senjen. *island* N Norway
Senjen *see* Senja
167 U12 **Senkaku-shotō** *island group* SW Japan
143 R12 **Şenkaya** Erzurum, NE Turkey *40.33N 42.16E*
85 I16 **Senkobo** Southern, S Zambia *17.34S 25.57E*
105 O4 **Senlis** Oise, N France *49.13N 2.33E*
178 K13 **Senmonorom** Môndól Kiri, E Cambodia *12.27N 107.12E*
82 G10 **Sennar** *var.* Sannār. Sinnar, C Sudan *13.31N 33.37E*
Senno *see* Syanno
Senones *see* Sens
111 W11 **Senovo** E Slovenia *46.01N 15.24E*
105 P6 **Sens** *anc.* Agendicum, Senones. Yonne, C France *48.12N 3.16E*
Sensburg *see* Mrągowo
178 J12 **Sên, Stœng** ≈ C Cambodia
44 F7 **Sensuntepeque** Cabañas, NE El Salvador *13.52N 88.37W*
114 L8 **Senta** *Hung.* Zenta. Serbia, N Serbia and Montenegro (Yugoslavia) *45.57N 20.04E*
Šent Andraž *see* Sankt Andrä
176 Z10 **Sentani, Danau** ◎ Papua, E Indonesia
30 J5 **Sentinel Butte** ▲ North Dakota, N USA *46.52N 103.50W*
8 M13 **Sentinel Peak** ▲ British Columbia, W Canada *54.51N 122.02W*
61 N16 **Sento Sé** Bahia, E Brazil *9.51S 41.56W*
Šent Peter *see* Pivka
Šent Vid *see* Sankt Veit an der Glan
194 E10 **Senu** ≈ NW PNG
Seo de Urgel *see* La See d'Urgel
160 I7 **Seondha** Madhya Pradesh, C India *26.09N 78.46E*
160 J11 **Seoni** *prev.* Seeonee. Madhya Pradesh, C India *22.07N 79.33E*
Seoul *see* Sŏul
192 I13 **Separation Point** *headland* South Island, NZ *40.46S 172.58E*
175 O7 **Sepasu** Borneo, N Indonesia *0.44N 117.38E*
194 F10 **Sepik** ≈ Indonesia/PNG
Sepone *see* Muang Xépôn
112 M7 **Sępopol** *Ger.* Schippenbeil. Warmińsko-Mazurskie, NE Poland, *54.16N 21.09E*
118 F10 **Şepreuş** *Hung.* Seprős. Arad, W Romania *46.34N 21.44E*
Seprős *see* Şepreuş
Şepşi-Sângeorz/Sepsiszentgyőrgy *see* Sfântu Gheorghe
13 W4 **Sept-Îles** Quebec, SE Canada *50.11N 66.18W*
107 N6 **Sepúlveda** Castilla-León, N Spain *41.18N 3.45W*
174 Ii12 **Seputih, Way** ≈ Sumatera, SW Indonesia
106 K8 **Sequeros** Castilla-León, N Spain *40.31N 6.04W*
106 L5 **Sequillo** ≈ NW Spain
37 G7 **Sequim** Washington, NW USA *48.04N 123.06W*
37 S11 **Sequoia National Park** *national park* California, W USA
143 Q14 **Şerafettin Dağları** ▲▲ E Turkey
131 N10 **Serafimovich** Volgogradskaya Oblast', SW Russian Federation *49.34N 42.43E*
175 Rr6 **Serai** Sulawesi, N Indonesia *1.45N 124.58E*
101 K19 **Seraing** Liège, E Belgium *50.37N 5.31E*
Sêraitang *see* Baima
Serajgonj *see* Shirajganj Ghat
152 I15 **Serakhs** *var.* Saragt. Akhalskiy Velayat, S Turkmenistan *36.33N 61.10E*
176 X10 **Serami** Papua, E Indonesia *2.11S 136.46E*
Seram, Laut *see* Ceram Sea
Serampore/Serampur *see* Shrīrāmpur
175 Tt11 **Seram, Pulau** *var.* Serang, *Eng.* Ceram. *island* Maluku, E Indonesia
174 J14 **Serang** Jawa, C Indonesia *6.07S 106.09E*
Serang *see* Seram, Pulau
174 Kk6 **Serasan, Pulau** *island* Kepulauan Natuna, W Indonesia
174 Kk6 **Serasan, Selat** *strait* Indonesia/Malaysia
114 M12 **Serbia** *Ger.* Serbien, *Serb.* Srbija. ◈ *republic* Serbia and Montenegro (Yugoslavia)
114 M13 **Serbia and Montenegro (Yugoslavia)** *off.* Federal Republic of Serbia and Montenegro, *Prev.* Yugoslavia, *SCr.* Jugoslavija, Savezna Republika Jugoslavija. ◆ *federal republic* SE Europe
Serbien *see* Serbia
Sercq *see* Sark
Serdica *see* Sofiya
131 O7 **Serdobsk** Penzenskaya Oblast', W Russian Federation *52.30N 44.16E*
151 X9 **Serebryansk** Vostochnyy Kazakhstan, E Kazakhstan *49.43N 83.16E*
126 Ll13 **Serebryanyy Bor** Respublika Sakha (Yakutiya), NE Russian Federation *56.40N 124.46E*
113 H20 **Sered'** *Hung.* Szered. Trnavský Kraj, SW Slovakia *48.17N 17.44E*
119 S1 **Seredyna-Buda** Sums'ka Oblast', NE Ukraine *52.09N 34.00E*
120 E13 **Seredžius** Jurbarkas, C Lithuania *55.04N 23.24E*
142 I14 **Şereflikoçhisar** Ankara, C Turkey *38.55N 33.31E*
108 D7 **Seregno** Lombardia, N Italy *45.39N 9.12E*
105 P7 **Serein** ≈ C France
174 H5 **Seremban** Negeri Sembilan, Peninsular Malaysia *2.42N 101.54E*
83 H20 **Serengeti Plain** *plain* N Tanzania
84 K13 **Serenje** Central, E Zambia *13.12S 30.15E*
Seres *see* Sérres
118 J5 **Seret** ≈ W Ukraine
Seret/Sereth *see* Siret
117 I21 **Serfopoúla** *island* Kykládes, Greece, Aegean Sea
131 P4 **Sergach** Nizhegorodskaya Oblast', W Russian Federation *55.31N 45.29E*
31 S13 **Sergeant Bluff** Iowa, C USA *42.24N 96.19W*
169 P7 **Sergelen** Dornod, NE Mongolia *48.31N 114.01E*
169 O9 **Sergelen** Sühbaatar, E Mongolia *46.12N 111.48E*
173 F4 **Sergeulangit, Pegunungan** ▲▲ Sumatera, NW Indonesia
126 I4 **Sergeya Kirova, Ostrova** *island* N Russian Federation
Sergeyevichi *see* Syarhyeyevichy
151 O7 **Sergeyevka** Severnyy Kazakhstan, N Kazakhstan *53.51N 67.17E*
Sergiopol *see* Ayagoz
61 P16 **Sergipe** *off.* Estado de Sergipe. ◈ *state* E Brazil
130 L3 **Sergiyev Posad** Moskovskaya Oblast', W Russian Federation *56.21N 38.10E*
128 K5 **Sergozero, Ozero** ◎ NW Russian Federation
174 L7 **Serian** Sarawak, East Malaysia *1.10N 110.34E*
174 J13 **Seribu, Kepulauan** *island group* S Indonesia
117 I21 **Sérifos** *anc.* Seriphos. *island* Kykládes, Greece, Aegean Sea
117 I21 **Sérifou, Stenó** *strait* SE Greece
142 F16 **Serik** Antalya, SW Turkey *36.55N 31.06E*
108 E7 **Serio** ≈ N Italy
Seriphos *see* Sérifos
Serir Tibesti *see* Sarīr Tibistī
131 S5 **Sernovodsk** Samarskaya Oblast', W Russian Federation *53.56N 51.16E*
131 R2 **Sernur** Respublika Mariy El, W Russian Federation *56.55N 49.09E*
112 M11 **Serock** Mazowieckie, C Poland *52.30N 21.03E*
63 B18 **Serodino** Santa Fe, C Argentina *32.33S 60.52W*
Seroei *see* Serui
107 P14 **Serón** Andalucía, S Spain *37.20N 2.28W*
101 E14 **Serooskerke** Zeeland, SW Netherlands *51.42N 3.52E*
107 T6 **Seròs** Cataluña, NE Spain *41.27N 0.24E*
125 F10 **Serov** Sverdlovskaya Oblast', C Russian Federation *59.42N 60.31E*
85 I19 **Serowe** Central, SE Botswana *22.25S 26.43E*
106 H13 **Serpa** Beja, S Portugal *37.55N 7.36W*
Serpa Pinto *see* Menongue
190 A4 **Serpentine Lakes** *salt lake* South Australia
47 T15 **Serpent's Mouth, The** *Sp.* Boca de la Serpiente. *strait* Trinidad and Tobago/Venezuela
Serpiente, Boca de la *see* Serpent's Mouth, The
130 K4 **Serpukhov** Moskovskaya Oblast', W Russian Federation *54.54N 37.25E*
62 K13 **Serra do Mar** ▲▲ S Brazil
Sérrai *see* Sérres
109 N22 **Serra San Bruno** Calabria, SW Italy *38.32N 16.18E*
105 S14 **Serres** Hautes-Alpes, SE France *44.26N 5.42E*
116 H13 **Sérres** *var.* Seres; *prev.* Sérrai. Kentrikí Makedonía, NE Greece *41.04N 23.34E*
64 J9 **Serrezuela** Córdoba, C Argentina *30.37S 65.25W*
61 O16 **Serrinha** Bahia, E Brazil *11.37S 38.55W*
61 M19 **Serro** *var.* Sêrro. Minas Gerais, NE Brazil *18.37S 43.22W*
Sêrro *see* Serro
Sert *see* Siirt
Sertá *see* Sertã
106 H9 **Sertã** *var.* Sertá. Castelo Branco, C Portugal *39.48N 8.04W*
62 L8 **Sertãozinho** São Paulo, S Brazil *21.04S 47.55W*
166 F7 **Sêrtar** Sichuan, C China *32.18N 100.18E*
176 X10 **Serui** *prev.* Seroei. Papua, E Indonesia *1.52S 136.15E*
85 J19 **Serule** Central, E Botswana *21.58S 27.18E*
174 Ll10 **Seruyan, Sungai** *var.* Sungai Pembuang. ≈ Borneo, N Indonesia
117 E14 **Sérvia** Dytikí Makedonía, N Greece *40.12N 22.01E*
166 E7 **Sêrxü** Sichuan, C China *32.54N 98.06E*
126 Mm15 **Seryshevo** Amurskaya Oblast', SE Russian Federation *51.03N 128.16E*
Sesana *see* Sežana
175 Nn5 **Sesayap, Sungai** ≈ Borneo, N Indonesia
Sesdlets *see* Siedlce
81 N17 **Sese** Orientale, N Dem. Rep. Congo *2.13N 25.52E*
83 F18 **Sese Islands** *island group* S Uganda
175 T9 **Sesepe** Pulau Obi, E Indonesia *1.26S 127.55E*
85 H16 **Sesheke** *var.* Sesheko. Western, SE Zambia *17.27S 24.19E*
Sesheko *see* Sesheke
108 C8 **Sesia** *anc.* Sessites. ≈ NW Italy
106 F11 **Sesimbra** Setúbal, S Portugal *38.25N 9.06W*
117 N22 **Seskló** *island* Dodekánisos, Greece, Aegean Sea
32 L16 **Sesser** Illinois, N USA *38.05N 89.03W*
Sessites *see* Sesia
108 G11 **Sesto Fiorentino** Toscana, C Italy *43.49N 11.12E*
108 E7 **Sesto San Giovanni** Lombardia, N Italy *45.31N 9.13E*
108 A8 **Sestriere** Piemonte, NE Italy *45.00N 6.54E*
108 D10 **Sestri Levante** Liguria, NW Italy *44.16N 9.22E*
109 C20 **Sestu** Sardegna, Italy, C Mediterranean Sea *39.15N 9.06E*
114 E8 **Sesvete** Zagreb, N Croatia *45.50N 16.03E*
120 G12 **Šeta** Kėdainiai, C Lithuania *55.17N 24.16E*
Setabis *see* Xátiva
172 N5 **Setana** Hokkaidō, NE Japan *42.27N 139.52E*
105 Q16 **Sète** *prev.* Cette. Hérault, S France *43.24N 3.42E*
60 J11 **Sete Ilhas** Amapá, NE Brazil *1.06N 52.06W*
61 L20 **Sete Lagoas** Minas Gerais, NE Brazil *19.28S 44.15W*
62 G10 **Sete Quedas, Ilha das** *island* S Brazil
94 I10 **Setermoen** Troms, N Norway *68.51N 18.19E*
97 E17 **Setesdal** *valley* S Norway
45 W16 **Setetule, Cerro** ▲ SE Panama *7.51N 77.37W*
23 Q5 **Seth** West Virginia, NE USA *38.06N 81.40W*
Setia *see* Sezze
76 K5 **Sétif** *var.* Stif. N Algeria *36.10N 5.24E*
171 I15 **Seto** Aichi, Honshū, SW Japan *35.13N 137.03E*
170 F14 **Seto-naikai** *Eng.* Inland Sea. *sea* S Japan
172 Qq13 **Setouchi** *var.* Setoushi. Kagoshima, Amami-Ō-shima, SW Japan *44.19N 142.58E*
76 F6 **Settat** W Morocco *33.03N 7.37W*
81 D20 **Setté Cama** Ogooué-Maritime, SW Gabon *2.31S 9.46E*
9 W13 **Setting Lake** ◎ Manitoba, C Canada
99 L16 **Settle** N England, UK *54.04N 2.17W*
201 Y12 **Settlement** E Wake Island *19.16N 166.37E*
106 F11 **Setúbal** *Eng.* Saint Ubes, Saint Yves. Setúbal, W Portugal *38.31N 8.54W*
106 F11 **Setúbal** ◈ *district* S Portugal
106 F12 **Setúbal, Baía de** *bay* W Portugal
Setul *see* Satun
10 B10 **Seul, Lac** ◎ Ontario, S Canada
105 R8 **Seurre** Côte d'Or, C France *47.00N 5.09E*
143 U11 **Sevan** C Armenia *40.31N 44.55E*
143 V12 **Sevana Lich** *Eng.* Lake Sevan, *Rus.* Ozero Sevan. ◎ E Armenia
Sevan, Lake/Sevan, Ozero *see* Sevana Lich
79 N11 **Sévaré** Mopti, C Mali *14.30N 4.08W*
119 S14 **Sevastopol'** *Eng.* Sebastopol. Respublika Krym, S Ukraine *44.36N 33.33E*
27 R14 **Seven Sisters** Texas, SW USA *27.57N 98.34W*
8 K13 **Seven Sisters Peaks** ▲ British Columbia, SW Canada *54.57N 128.10W*
101 M15 **Sevenum** Limburg, SE Netherlands *51.25N 6.01E*
105 P14 **Séverac-le-Château** Aveyron, S France *44.18N 3.03E*
12 H13 **Severn** ≈ Ontario, S Canada
99 L21 **Severn** *Wel.* Hafren. ≈ England/Wales, UK
129 O11 **Severnaya Dvina** *var.* Northern Dvina. ≈ NW Russian Federation
131 N16 **Severnaya Osetiya-Alaniya, Respublika** *Eng.* North Ossetia; *prev.* Respublika Severnaya Osetiya, Severo-Osetinskaya SSR. ◈ *autonomous republic* SW Russian Federation
Severnaya Osetiya, Respublika *see* Severnaya Osetiya-Alaniya Respublika
125 F9 **Severnaya Sos'va** ≈ N Russian Federation
126 J2 **Severnaya Zemlya** *var.* Nicholas II Land. *island group* N Russian Federation
131 T5 **Severnoye** Orenburgskaya Oblast', W Russian Federation *54.03N 52.31E*
37 S3 **Severn Troughs Range** ▲▲ Nevada, W USA
129 W3 **Severnyy** Respublika Komi, NW Russian Federation *67.37N 64.12E*
150 I13 **Severnyy Chink Ustyurta** ▲ W Kazakhstan
129 Q13 **Severnyye Uvaly** *var.* Northern Ural Hills. *hill range* NW Russian Federation
151 O6 **Severnyy Kazakhstan** *off.* Severo-Kazakhstanskaya Oblast', *var.* North Kazakhstan, *Kaz.* Soltüstik Qazaqstan Oblysy. ◈ *province* N Kazakhstan
129 V9 **Severnyy Ural** ▲▲ NW Russian Federation
Severo-Alichurskiy Khrebet *see* Alichuri Shimolí, Qatorkŭhi
126 K14 **Severobaykal'sk** Respublika Buryatiya, S Russian Federation *55.39N 109.17E*
Severodonetsk *see* Syeverodonets'k
128 M8 **Severodvinsk** *prev.* Molotov, Sudostroy. Arkhangel'skaya Oblast', NW Russian Federation *64.31N 39.50E*
Severo-Kazakhstanskaya Oblast' *see* Severnyy Kazakhstan
127 Pp13 **Severo-Kuril'sk** Sakhalinskaya Oblast', SE Russian Federation *50.38N 155.57E*
128 J3 **Severomorsk** Murmanskaya Oblast', NW Russian Federation *69.00N 33.15E*
Severo-Osetinskaya SSR *see* Severnaya Osetiya-Alaniya, Respublika
126 J6 **Severo-Sibirskaya Nizmennost'** *var.* North Siberian Plain, *Eng.* North Siberian Lowland. *lowlands* N Russian Federation
125 Ee10 **Severoural'sk** Sverdlovskaya Oblast', C Russian Federation *60.09N 59.58E*
126 I12 **Severo-Yeniseyskiy** Krasnoyarskiy Kray, C Russian Federation *60.29N 93.13E*
126 H13 **Seversk** Tomskaya Oblast', C Russian Federation *53.37N 84.47E*
130 M11 **Severskiy Donets** *Ukr.* Sivers'kyy Donets'. ≈ Russian Federation/Ukraine *see also* Sivers'kyy Donets'
94 M9 **Sevettijärvi** Lappi, N Finland *69.31N 28.40E*
38 M5 **Sevier Bridge Reservoir** ⊠ Utah, W USA
38 J4 **Sevier Desert** *plain* Utah, W USA
38 J5 **Sevier Lake** ◎ Utah, W USA
23 N9 **Sevierville** Tennessee, S USA *35.52N 83.33W*
106 J14 **Sevilla** *Eng.* Seville; *anc.* Hispalis. Andalucía, SW Spain *37.24N 5.58W*
106 J13 **Sevilla** ◈ *province* Andalucía, SW Spain
Sevilla de Niefang *see* Niefang
45 O16 **Sevilla, Isla** *island* SW Panama
Seville *see* Sevilla
116 J9 **Sevlievo** Gabrovo, N Bulgaria *43.01N 25.07E*
Sevluš/Sevlyush *see* Vynohradiv
111 V11 **Sevnica** *Ger.* Lichtenwald. E Slovenia *46.00N 15.20E*
130 I7 **Sevsk** Bryanskaya Oblast', W Russian Federation *52.03N 34.31E*
78 J15 **Sewa** ≈ E Sierra Leone
41 R12 **Seward** Alaska, USA *60.06N 149.26W*
31 R15 **Seward** Nebraska, C USA *40.52N 97.06W*
8 G8 **Seward Glacier** *glacier* Yukon Territory, W Canada
207 Q3 **Seward Peninsula** *peninsula* Alaska, USA
Seward's Folly *see* Alaska
64 H12 **Sewell** Libertador, C Chile *34.03S 70.16W*
100 K5 **Sexbierum** *Fris.* Seisbierrum. Friesland, N Netherlands *53.13N 5.28E*
9 O13 **Sexsmith** Alberta, W Canada *55.18N 118.45W*
43 W13 **Seybaplaya** Campeche, SE Mexico *19.39N 90.36W*
181 N6 **Seychelles** *off.* Republic of Seychelles. ◆ *republic* W Indian Ocean
69 Z9 **Seychelles** *island group* NE Seychelles
181 N6 **Seychelles Bank** *var.* Le Banc des Seychelles. *undersea feature* W Indian Ocean
Seychelles, Le Banc des *see* Seychelles Bank
180 H17 **Seychellois, Morne** ▲ Mahé, NE Seychelles
94 L2 **Seydhisfjördhur** Austurland, E Iceland *65.15N 14.00W*
152 J12 **Seydi** *prev.* Neftezavodsk. Lebapskiy Velayat, E Turkmenistan *39.30N 62.52E*
142 G16 **Seydişehir** Konya, SW Turkey *37.25N 31.51E*
142 J13 **Seyfe Gölü** ◎ C Turkey
Seyhan *see* Adana
142 K16 **Seyhan Barajı** ⊠ S Turkey
142 K17 **Seyhan Nehri** ≈ S Turkey
142 F13 **Seyitgazi** Eskişehir, W Turkey *39.27N 30.42E*
130 J7 **Seym** ≈ W Russian Federation
119 S3 **Seym** ≈ N Ukraine
127 O9 **Seymchan** Magadanskaya Oblast', E Russian Federation *62.54N 152.27E*
116 N12 **Seymen** Tekirdağ, NW Turkey *41.06N 27.56E*
191 O11 **Seymour** Victoria, SE Australia *37.01S 145.10E*
85 I25 **Seymour** Eastern Cape, S South Africa *32.31S 26.48E*
31 W16 **Seymour** Iowa, C USA *40.40N 93.07W*
29 6U7 **Seymour** Missouri, C USA *37.09N 92.46W*
27 Q5 **Seymour** Texas, SW USA *33.35N 99.15W*
116 M12 **Şeytan Deresi** ≈ NW Turkey
111 S12 **Sežana** *It.* Sesana. SW Slovenia *45.42N 13.52E*
105 P5 **Sézanne** Marne, N France *48.43N 3.41E*
109 I16 **Sezze** *anc.* Setia. Lazio, C Italy *41.28N 13.04E*
117 H25 **Sfákia** Kríti, Greece, E Mediterranean Sea *35.12N 24.05E*
117 D21 **Sfaktiría** *island* S Greece
118 J11 **Sfântu Gheorghe** *Ger.* Sankt-Georgen, *Hung.* Sepsiszentgyőrgy; *prev.* Şepşi-Sângeorz, Sfîntu Gheorghe. Covasna, C Romania *45.52N 25.49E*

◆ Country
● Country Capital
◇ Dependent Territory
○ Dependent Territory Capital
◈ Administrative Region
✕ International Airport
▲ Mountain
▲▲ Mountain Range
Volcano
≈ River
◎ Lake
⊠ Reservoir

119 N13 **Sfântu Gheorghe, Braţul** var. Gheorghe Braţul. ≈ E Romania
77 N6 **Sfax** Ar. Şafāqis. E Tunisia 34.45N 10.45E
77 N6 **Sfax** ✕ E Tunisia 34.43N 10.37E
Sfîntu Gheorghe see Sfântu Gheorghe
100 H13 **'s-Gravendeel** Zuid-Holland, SW Netherlands 51.48N 4.36E
100 F11 **'s-Gravenhage** var. Den Haag, Eng. The Hague, Fr. La Haye. ● (Netherlands-seat of government) Zuid-Holland, W Netherlands 52.07N 4.16E
100 G12 **'s-Gravenzande** Zuid-Holland, W Netherlands 52.00N 4.10E
Shaan/Shaanxi Sheng see Shaanxi
165 X11 **Shaanxi** var. Shaan, Shaanxi Sheng, Shan-hsi, Shenshi, Shensi. ◆ province C China
Shaartuz see Shahrtuz
Shabani see Zvishavane
83 N17 **Shabeellaha Dhexe** off. Gobolka Shabeellaha Dhexe. ◆ region E Somalia
83 L17 **Shabeellaha Hoose** off. Gobolka Shabeellaha Hoose. ◆ region S Somalia
Shabeelle, Webi see Shebeli
116 O7 **Shabla** Dobrich, NE Bulgaria 43.33N 28.31E
116 O7 **Shabla, Nos** headland NE Bulgaria 43.30N 28.36E
11 N9 **Shabogama Lake** ⊙ Newfoundland and Labrador, E Canada
81 N20 **Shabunda** Sud Kivu, E Dem. Rep. Congo 2.42S 27.19E
147 Q15 **Shabwah** C Yemen 15.09N 46.46E
164 F8 **Shache** var. Yarkant. Xinjiang Uygur Zizhiqu, NW China 38.27N 77.16E
Shacheng see Huailai
205 R12 **Shackleton Coast** physical region Antarctica
205 Z10 **Shackleton Ice Shelf** ice shelf Antarctica
Shaddādī see Ash Shadādah
30 K7 **Shadehill Reservoir** ⊞ South Dakota, N USA
125 Ee12 **Shadrinsk** Kurganskaya Oblast', C Russian Federation 56.08N 63.18E
33 O12 **Shafer, Lake** ⊞ Indiana, N USA
37 R13 **Shafter** California, W USA 35.27N 119.15W
26 J11 **Shafter** Texas, SW USA 29.49N 104.18W
99 L23 **Shaftesbury** S England, UK 51.01N 2.12W
193 F22 **Shag** ≈ South Island, NZ
151 V9 **Shagan** ≈ E Kazakhstan
41 O11 **Shageluk** Alaska, USA 62.40N 159.33W
126 I16 **Shagonar** Respublika Tyva, S Russian Federation 51.31N 93.06E
193 F22 **Shag Point** headland South Island, NZ 45.28S 170.50E
150 J12 **Shagyray, Plato** plain SW Kazakhstan
Shāhābād see Eslāmābād
174 H5 **Shah Alam** Selangor, Peninsular Malaysia 3.01N 101.31E
119 O12 **Shahany, Ozero** ⊙ SW Ukraine
144 H9 **Shahbā'** anc. Philippopolis. As Suwaydā', S Syria 32.49N 36.37E
Shahbān see Ad Dayr
155 P17 **Shāhbandar** Sind, SE Pakistan 23.59N 67.54E
155 P13 **Shāhdād Kot** Sind, SW Pakistan 27.49N 67.49E
149 T10 **Shahdād, Namakzār-e** salt pan E Iran
155 Q15 **Shāhdādpur** Sind, SE Pakistan 25.55N 68.40E
160 K10 **Shahdol** Madhya Pradesh, C India 23.19N 81.25E
167 N7 **Sha He** ≈ C China
Shahepu see Linze
159 N13 **Shāhganj** Uttar Pradesh, N India 26.03N 82.40E
158 C11 **Shāhgarh** Rājasthān, NW India 27.07N 69.55E
Sha Hi see Orūmīyeh, Daryācheh-ye, Iran
Shāhī see Qā'emshahr, Māzandarān, Iran
145 Q6 **Shāhimah** var. Shahma. C Iraq 34.21N 42.19E
Shāhjahanabad see Delhi
158 L11 **Shāhjahānpur** Uttar Pradesh, N India 27.52N 79.55E
Shahma see Shāhimah
155 U7 **Shāhpur** Punjab, E Pakistan 32.15N 72.31E
Shāhpur see Shāhpur Chākar
158 G13 **Shāhpura** Rājasthān, N India 25.37N 75.01E
155 Q15 **Shāhpur Chākar** var. Shāhpur. Sind, SE Pakistan 26.09N 68.40E
154 M5 **Shahrak** Ghowr, C Afghanistan 34.09N 64.16E
149 Q11 **Shahr-e Bābak** Kermān, C Iran 30.07N 55.04E
149 N8 **Shahr-e Kord** var. Shahr Kord. Chahār Maḩall va Bakhtīārī, C Iran 32.19N 50.52E
149 O9 **Shahreẕā** var. Qomisheh, Qumisheh, Shahriza; prev. Qomsheh. Eşfahān, C Iran 32.01N 51.51E
153 S10 **Shahrikhon** Rus. Shakhrikhan. Andijon Viloyati, E Uzbekistan 40.42N 72.03E
153 P11 **Shahriston** Rus. Shakhristan. NW Tajikistan 39.45N 68.47E
Shahriza see Shahreẕā
Shahr-i-Zabul see Zābol
Shahr Kord see Shahr-e Kord
153 P14 **Shahrtuz** Rus. Shaartuz. SW Tajikistan 37.13N 68.05E
149 Q4 **Shāhrūd** prev. Emāmrūd, Emāmshahr. Semnān, N Iran 36.30N 54.59E
Shahsavār/Shahsawar see Tonekābon
Shaidara see Step' Nardara
Shaikh Ābid see Shaykh 'Ābid
Shaikh Fāris see Shaykh Fāris
Shaikh Najm see Shaykh Najm
144 K5 **Shā'ir, Jabal** ▲ C Syria 34.51N 37.49E
160 G10 **Shājāpur** Madhya Pradesh, C India 23.27N 76.21E
82 J8 **Shakal, Ras** headland NE Sudan 18.04N 38.34E
Shakhdarinskiy Khrebet see Shokhdara, Qatorkŭhi
Shakhrikhan see Shahrikhon
Shakhrisabz see Sharixon
Shakhristan see Shahriston
119 X8 **Shakhtars'k** Rus. Shakhtërsk. Donets'ka Oblast', SE Ukraine 48.02N 38.18E
127 O15 **Shakhtërsk** Ostrov Sakhalin, Sakhalinskaya Oblast', SE Russian Federation 49.10N 142.09E
Shakhtërsk see Shakhtars'k
151 R10 **Shakhtinsk** Karaganda, C Kazakhstan 49.40N 72.37E
130 L11 **Shakhty** Rostovskaya Oblast', SW Russian Federation 47.45N 40.14E
131 P2 **Shakhun'ya** Nizhegorodskaya Oblast', W Russian Federation 57.42N 46.36E
79 S15 **Shaki** Oyo, W Nigeria 8.37N 3.25E
83 J15 **Shakīso** Oromo, C Ethiopia 5.33N 38.48E
119 X8 **Shakmars'k** Donets'ka Oblast', E Ukraine 48.04N 38.22E
31 V9 **Shakopee** Minnesota, N USA 44.48N 93.31W
172 Nn5 **Shakotan-hantō** peninsula Hokkaidō, NE Japan
172 O4 **Shakotan-misaki** headland Hokkaidō, NE Japan 43.22N 140.28E
41 N9 **Shaktoolik** Alaska, USA 64.19N 161.05W
83 J14 **Shala Hāyk'** ⊙ C Ethiopia
128 M10 **Shalakusha** Arkhangel'skaya Oblast', NW Russian Federation 62.16N 40.16E
151 U8 **Shalday** Pavlodar, NE Kazakhstan 51.57N 78.51E
131 P16 **Shali** Chechenskaya Respublika, SW Russian Federation 43.03N 45.55E
147 W12 **Shalīm** var. Shelim. S Oman 18.07N 55.39E
Shaliuhe see Gangca
150 F9 **Shalkar, Ozero** prev. Chelkar, Ozero. ⊙ W Kazakhstan
23 V12 **Shallotte** North Carolina, SE USA 33.58N 78.21W
27 N5 **Shallowater** Texas, SW USA 33.41N 102.00W
128 K11 **Shal'skiy** Respublika Kareliya, NW Russian Federation 61.45N 36.02E
166 F9 **Shaluli Shan** ▲▲ C China
83 F22 **Shama** ≈ C Tanzania
9 Z11 **Shamattawa** Manitoba, C Canada 55.52N 92.04W
10 F8 **Shamattawa** ≈ Ontario, C Canada
Shām, Bādiyat ash see Syrian Desert
Shamiya see Ash Shāmīyah
147 X8 **Shām, Jabal ash** var. Jebel Sham. ▲ NW Oman 23.21N 57.08E
Sham, Jebel see Shām, Jabal ash
Shamkhor see Şämkir
20 G14 **Shamokin** Pennsylvania, NE USA 40.47N 76.33W
27 P2 **Shamrock** Texas, SW USA 35.12N 100.15W
Sha'nabī, Jabal ash see Chambi, Jebel
145 Y12 **Shanāwah** E Iraq 30.57N 47.25E
165 T8 **Shandan** Gansu, N China 38.43N 101.12E
Shandī see Shendi
167 Q5 **Shandong** var. Lu, Shandong Sheng, Shantung. ◆ province E China
167 R4 **Shandong Bandao** var. Shantung Peninsula. peninsula E China
Shandong Peninsula see Shandong Bandao
Shandong Sheng see Shandong
145 U8 **Shandrūkh** E Iraq 33.20N 45.19E
85 J17 **Shangani** ≈ W Zimbabwe
167 O15 **Shangchuan Dao** island S China
Shangchuankou see Minhe
169 P12 **Shangdu** Nei Mongol Zizhiqu, N China 41.32N 113.33E
167 O11 **Shanggao** Jiangxi, S China 28.16N 114.52E
167 S8 **Shanghai** var. Shang-hai. Shanghai Shi, E China 31.13N 121.28E
Shanghai see Shanghai Shi
167 S8 **Shanghai Shi** var. Hu, Shanghai. ◆ municipality E China
167 P13 **Shanghang** Fujian, SE China 25.02N 116.21E
166 K14 **Shanglin** Guangxi Zhuangzu Zizhiqu, S China 23.25N 108.31E
85 G15 **Shangombo** Western, W Zambia 16.21S 22.12E
167 O6 **Shangqiu** var. Zhuji. Henan, C China 34.29N 115.39E
167 Q10 **Shangrao** Jiangxi, S China 28.27N 117.57E
167 S9 **Shangyu** var. Baiguan. Zhejiang, SE China 30.03N 120.52E
169 X9 **Shangzhi** Heilongjiang, NE China 45.11N 127.58E
166 L7 **Shangzhou** var. Shang Xian. Shaanxi, C China 33.51N 109.55E
169 W9 **Shanhetun** Heilongjiang, NE China 44.42N 127.12E
Shan-hsi see Shaanxi, China
Shan-hsi see Shanxi, China
165 O6 **Shankou** Xinjiang Uygur Zizhiqu, W China 42.01N 94.07E
192 M13 **Shannon** Manawatu-Wanganui, North Island, NZ 40.33S 175.25E
99 B19 **Shannon** ✕ W Ireland 52.42N 8.57W
99 C17 **Shannon** Ir. An tSionainn. ≈ W Ireland
178 H6 **Shan Plateau** plateau E Myanmar
164 M6 **Shanshan** var. Piqan. Xinjiang Uygur Zizhiqu, NW China 42.53N 90.18E
Shansi see Shanxi
178 Gg5 **Shan State** ◆ state E Myanmar
Shantar Islands see Shantarskiye Ostrova
127 N13 **Shantarskiye Ostrova** Eng. Shantar Islands. island group E Russian Federation
167 Q14 **Shantou** var. Shan-t'ou, Swatow. Guangdong, S China 23.22N 116.39E
Shantung see Shandong
Shantung Peninsula see Shandong Bandao
169 O14 **Shanxi** var. Jin, Shan-hsi, Shansi, Shanxi Sheng. ◆ province C China
Shan Xian see Sanmenxia
167 P6 **Shanxian** var. Shan Xian. Shandong, E China 34.51N 116.05E
Shanxi Sheng see Shanxi
166 L7 **Shanyang** Shaanxi, C China 33.35N 109.48E
167 O13 **Shaoguan** var. Shao-kuan, Cant. Kukong; prev. Ch'u-chiang. Guangdong, S China 24.56N 113.37E
Shao-kuan see Shaoguan
167 Q11 **Shaowu** Fujian, SE China 27.24N 117.26E
167 S9 **Shaoxing** Zhejiang, SE China 30.01N 120.34E
166 M12 **Shaoyang** prev. Tangdukou. Hunan, S China 26.54N 111.14E
166 M11 **Shaoyang** var. Baoqing, Shao-yang; prev. Pao-king. Hunan, S China 27.18N 111.33E
98 K5 **Shapinsay** island NE Scotland, UK
129 S4 **Shapkina** ≈ NW Russian Federation
Shāpūr see Salmās
164 M4 **Shaqiuhe** Xinjiang Uygur Zizhiqu, W China 45.00N 88.52E
145 T2 **Shaqlāwa** var. Shaqlāwah. E Iraq 36.24N 44.21E
Shaqlāwah see Shaqlāwa
144 I8 **Shaqqā** As Suwaydā', S Syria 32.53N 36.42E
147 P7 **Shaqrā'** Ar Riyāḑ, C Saudi Arabia 25.10N 45.08E
Shaqrā see Shuqrah
151 W10 **Shar** var. Charsk. Vostochnyy Kazakhstan, E Kazakhstan 49.33N 81.03E
155 O6 **Sharan** Urūzgān, SE Afghanistan 33.28N 66.19E
Sharaqpur see Sharqpur
Sharbaqty see Shcherbakty
147 X12 **Sharbatāt** S Oman 17.57N 56.14E
147 X12 **Sharbithāt, Ras** var. Ra's Sharbatāt. headland S Oman 17.55N 56.30E
12 K14 **Sharbot Lake** Ontario, SE Canada 44.45N 76.46W
151 P17 **Shardara** var. Chardara. Yuzhnyy Kazakhstan, S Kazakhstan 41.17N 68.03E
Shardara Dalasy see Step' Nardara
168 F8 **Sharga** Govĭ-Altay, W Mongolia 46.16N 95.32E
168 H6 **Sharga** Hövsgöl, N Mongolia 49.33N 98.36E
118 M7 **Sharhorod** Vinnyts'ka Oblast', C Ukraine 48.46N 28.05E
168 K10 **Sharhulsan** Ömnögovĭ, S Mongolia 44.43N 104.06E
172 Qq6 **Shari** Hokkaidō, NE Japan 43.54N 144.42E
Shari see Chari
145 T6 **Shārī, Buḩayrat** ⊙ C Iraq
153 R12 **Sharixon** Rus. Shakhrisabz. Qashqadaryo Viloyati, S Uzbekistan 39.01N 66.45E
Sharjah see Ash Shāriqah
120 K12 **Sharkawshchyna** var. Sharkowshchyna, Pol. Szarkowszczyzna, Rus. Sharkovshchina. Vitsyebskaya Voblasts', NW Belarus 55.27N 27.28E
188 G9 **Shark Bay** bay Western Australia
147 Y9 **Sharkh** E Oman 21.19N 59.04E
Sharkovshchina/Sharkowshchyna see Sharkawshchyna
131 U6 **Sharlyk** Orenburgskaya Oblast', W Russian Federation 52.52N 54.45E
Sharm ash Shaykh see Sharm el Sheikh
77 Y9 **Sharm el Sheikh** var. Ofiral, Sharm ash Shaykh. E Egypt 27.51N 34.16E
20 B13 **Sharon** Pennsylvania, NE USA 41.12N 80.28W
28 H4 **Sharon Springs** Kansas, C USA 38.54N 101.45W
33 Q14 **Sharonville** Ohio, N USA 39.16N 84.24W
Sharourah see Sharūrah
31 O10 **Sharpe, Lake** ⊞ South Dakota, N USA
Sharqī, Al Jabal ash/Sharqi, Jebel esh see Anti-Lebanon
Sharqīyah, Al Minţaqah ash see Ash Sharqīyah
144 I6 **Sharqīyat an Nabk, Jabal** ▲▲ W Syria
155 W8 **Sharqpur** var. Sharaqpur. Punjab, E Pakistan 31.27N 74.10E
147 Q13 **Sharūrah** var. Sharourah. Najrān, S Saudi Arabia 17.29N 47.04E
129 O14 **Shar'ya** Kostromskaya Oblast', NW Russian Federation 58.22N 45.30E
151 V15 **Sharyn** var. Charyn. ≈ SE Kazakhstan
Sharyn see Charyn
85 J18 **Shashe** Central, NE Botswana 21.25S 27.28E
85 J18 **Shashe** var. Shashi. ≈ Botswana/Zimbabwe
83 J14 **Shashemenē** var. Shashemenne, Shashhamana, It. Sciasciamana. Oromo, C Ethiopia 7.16N 38.38E
Shashemenne/Shashhamana see Shashemenē
Shashi see Shashe
Shashi/Sha-shih/Shasi see Jingzhou
37 N3 **Shasta Lake** ⊞ California, W USA
37 N2 **Shasta, Mount** ▲ California, W USA 41.24N 122.11W
131 O4 **Shatki** Nizhegorodskaya Oblast', W Russian Federation 55.09N 44.04E
152 J13 **Shatlyk** Maryyskiy Velayat, C Turkmenistan 37.55N 61.00E
Shatra see Ash Shaţrah
121 K17 **Shatsk** Rus. Shatsk. Minskaya Voblasts', C Belarus 53.25N 27.44E
131 N5 **Shatsk** Ryazanskaya Oblast', W Russian Federation 54.02N 41.38E
28 J9 **Shattuck** Oklahoma, C USA 36.16N 99.52W
151 P16 **Shaul'der** Yuzhnyy Kazakhstan, S Kazakhstan 42.49N 68.22E
9 S17 **Shaunavon** Saskatchewan, S Canada 49.37N 108.22W
Shavat see Shovot
164 K4 **Shawan** Xinjiang Uygur Zizhiqu, NW China 44.19N 85.34E
12 G12 **Shawanaga** Ontario, S Canada 45.29N 80.16W
32 M6 **Shawano** Wisconsin, N USA 44.46N 88.36W
32 M6 **Shawano Lake** ⊙ Wisconsin, N USA
13 P10 **Shawinigan** prev. Shawinigan Falls. Quebec, SE Canada 46.35N 72.45W
Shawinigan Falls see Shawinigan
13 P10 **Shawinigan-Sud** Quebec, SE Canada 46.30N 72.43W
144 J5 **Shawmarīyah, Jabal ash** ▲▲ C Syria
29 O11 **Shawnee** Oklahoma, C USA 35.20N 96.55W
12 K12 **Shawville** Quebec, SE Canada 45.37N 76.31W
Shaykh see Ash Shakk
145 W9 **Shaykh 'Ābid** var. Shaikh Ābid. E Iraq 32.40N 46.09E
145 Y10 **Shaykh Fāris** var. Shaikh Fāris. E Iraq 32.06N 47.39E
145 T7 **Shaykh Ḩātim** E Iraq 33.28N 44.15E
Shaykh, Jabal ash see Hermon, Mount
145 X10 **Shaykh Najm** var. Shaikh Najm. E Iraq 32.04N 46.54E
145 W9 **Shaykh Sa'd** E Iraq 32.35N 46.16E
153 T14 **Shazud** SE Tajikistan 37.45N 72.22E
121 N18 **Shchadryn** Rus. Shchedrin. Homyel'skaya Voblasts', SE Belarus 52.55N 29.32E
121 H18 **Shchara** ≈ SW Belarus
Shchedrin see Shchadryn
Shcheglovsk see Kemerovo
130 K5 **Shchëkino** Tul'skaya Oblast', W Russian Federation 53.57N 37.33E
129 S7 **Shchel'yayur** Respublika Komi, NW Russian Federation 65.19N 53.27E
151 U8 **Shcherbakty** Kaz. Sharbaqty. Pavlodar, E Kazakhstan 52.28N 78.00E
130 K7 **Shchigry** Kurskaya Oblast', W Russian Federation 51.53N 36.49E
Shchitkovichi see Shchytkavichy
119 Q2 **Shchors** Chernihivs'ka Oblast', N Ukraine 51.49N 31.58E
119 T8 **Shchors'k** Dnipropetrovs'ka Oblast', E Ukraine 48.20N 34.10E
Shchuchin see Shchuchyn
151 Q7 **Shchuchinsk** prev. Shchuchye. Akmola, N Kazakhstan 52.56N 70.09E
Shchuchye see Shchuchinsk
121 G16 **Shchuchyn** Pol. Szczuczyn Nowogródzki, Rus. Shchuchin. Hrodzyenskaya Voblasts', W Belarus 53.38N 24.48E
121 K17 **Shchytkavichy** Rus. Shchitkovichi. Minskaya Voblasts', C Belarus 53.13N 27.58E
126 H15 **Shebalino** Respublika Altay, S Russian Federation 51.16N 85.41E
130 J9 **Shebekino** Belgorodskaya Oblast', W Russian Federation 50.25N 36.54E
Shebelē Wenz, Wabē see Shebeli
83 L14 **Shebeli** Amh. Wabē Shebelē Wenz, It. Scebeli, Som. Webi Shabeelle. ≈ Ethiopia/Somalia
115 M20 **Shebenikut, Maja e** ▲ E Albania 41.13N 20.27E
155 N2 **Sheberghān** var. Shibarghān, Shiberghan, Shiberghān. Jowzjān, N Afghanistan 36.40N 65.45E
150 F14 **Shebir** Mangistau, SW Kazakhstan 44.52N 52.01E
33 N8 **Sheboygan** Wisconsin, N USA 43.46N 87.43W
79 X15 **Shebshi Mountains** var. Schebschi Mountains. ▲▲ E Nigeria
Shechem see Nablus
Shedadi see Ash Shadādah
11 P14 **Shediac** New Brunswick, SE Canada 46.13N 64.34W
130 L15 **Shedok** Krasnodarskiy Kray, SW Russian Federation 44.12N 40.49E
82 N12 **Sheekh** Woqooyi Galbeed, N Somalia 10.01N 45.21E
40 M11 **Sheenjek River** ≈ Alaska, USA
98 D13 **Sheep Haven** Ir. Cuan na gCaorach. inlet N Ireland
37 X10 **Sheep Range** ▲▲ Nevada, W USA
100 M13 **'s-Heerenberg** Gelderland, E Netherlands 51.52N 6.15E
99 P22 **Sheerness** SE England, UK 51.27N 0.45E
11 Q15 **Sheet Harbour** Nova Scotia, SE Canada 44.55N 62.31W
193 H18 **Sheffield** Canterbury, South Island, NZ 43.22S 172.01E
99 M18 **Sheffield** N England, UK 53.22N 1.30W
25 O2 **Sheffield** Alabama, S USA 34.46N 87.42W
31 V12 **Sheffield** Iowa, C USA 42.53N 93.13W
27 N10 **Sheffield** Texas, SW USA 30.42N 101.49W
65 H22 **Shehuen, Río** ≈ S Argentina
Shekhem see Nablus
155 V8 **Shekhūpura** Punjab, NE Pakistan 31.43N 73.58E
Sheki see Şäki
128 L14 **Sheksna** Vologodskaya Oblast', NW Russian Federation 59.11N 38.32E
127 O4 **Shelagskiy, Mys** headland NE Russian Federation 70.04N 170.39E
29 V3 **Shelbina** Missouri, C USA 39.41N 92.02W
11 P16 **Shelburne** Nova Scotia, SE Canada 43.46N 65.19W
12 G14 **Shelburne** Ontario, S Canada 44.04N 80.12W
35 R7 **Shelby** Montana, NW USA 48.30N 111.52W
23 Q10 **Shelby** North Carolina, SE USA 35.17N 81.32W
33 S12 **Shelby** Ohio, N USA 40.52N 82.39W
32 L14 **Shelbyville** Illinois, N USA 39.24N 88.47W
33 P14 **Shelbyville** Indiana, N USA 39.31N 85.46W
22 L5 **Shelbyville** Kentucky, S USA 38.12N 85.13W
29 V2 **Shelbyville** Missouri, C USA 39.48N 92.02W
22 J10 **Shelbyville** Tennessee, S USA 35.28N 86.27W
27 X8 **Shelbyville** Texas, SW USA 31.42N 94.03W
32 L14 **Shelbyville, Lake** ⊞ Illinois, N USA
31 S12 **Sheldon** Iowa, C USA 43.10N 95.51W
40 M11 **Sheldons Point** Alaska, USA 62.31N 165.03W
126 J16 **Shelekhov** Irkutskaya Oblast', C Russian Federation 52.04N 104.03E
Shelekhov Gulf see Shelikhova, Zaliv
127 Oo9 **Shelikhova, Zaliv** Eng. Shelekhov Gulf. gulf E Russian Federation
41 P14 **Shelikof Strait** strait Alaska, USA
Shelim see Shalīm
9 T14 **Shellbrook** Saskatchewan, S Canada 53.13N 106.24W
30 L3 **Shell Creek** ≈ North Dakota, N USA
Shellif see Chelif, Oued
24 I10 **Shell Keys** island group Louisiana, S USA
32 I4 **Shell Lake** Wisconsin, N USA 45.43N 91.55W
31 W12 **Shell Rock** Iowa, C USA 42.42N 92.34W
193 C26 **Shelter Point** headland Stewart Island, NZ 47.04S 168.13E
20 L13 **Shelton** Connecticut, NE USA 41.19N 73.06W
34 G8 **Shelton** Washington, NW USA 47.13N 123.06W
Shemakha see Şamaxı
151 W9 **Shemonaikha** Vostochnyy Kazakhstan, E Kazakhstan 50.39N 81.51E
131 Q4 **Shemursha** Chavash Respubliki, W Russian Federation 54.57N 47.27E
40 D16 **Shemya Island** island Aleutian Islands, Alaska, USA
31 T16 **Shenandoah** Iowa, C USA 40.46N 95.23W
23 U4 **Shenandoah** Virginia, NE USA 38.26N 78.34W
23 U4 **Shenandoah Mountains** ridge West Virginia, NE USA
23 V3 **Shenandoah River** ≈ West Virginia, NE USA
79 W15 **Shendam** Plateau, C Nigeria 8.52N 9.30E
82 G8 **Shendi** var. Shandī. River Nile, NE Sudan 16.40N 33.22E
78 I15 **Shenge** SW Sierra Leone 7.54N 12.54W
152 L10 **Shengeldi** Rus. Chingildi. Navoiy Viloyati, N Uzbekistan 40.59N 64.13E
151 U15 **Shengel'dy** Almaty, SE Kazakhstan 44.04N 77.31E
115 K18 **Shëngjin** var. Shëngjini. Lezhë, NW Albania 41.49N 19.34E
Shëngjini see Shëngjin
Shengking see Liaoning
Sheng Xian/Shengxian see Shengzhou
167 S9 **Shengzhou** var. Shengxian, Sheng Xian. Zhejiang, SE China 29.36N 120.47E
Shenking see Liaoning
129 N11 **Shenkursk** Arkhangel'skaya Oblast', NW Russian Federation 62.10N 42.58E
166 L3 **Shenmu** Shaanxi, C China 38.49N 110.27E
115 L19 **Shën Noj i Madh** ▲ C Albania 41.23N 20.07E
Shenshi/Shensi see Shaanxi
169 V12 **Shenyang** Chin. Shen-yang, Eng. Moukden, Mukden; prev. Fengtien. Liaoning, NE China 41.49N 123.25E
167 O15 **Shenzhen** Guangdong, S China 22.39N 114.02E
160 G8 **Sheopur** Madhya Pradesh, C India 25.40N 76.42E
118 L5 **Shepetivka** Rus. Shepetovka. Khmel'nyts'ka Oblast', NW Ukraine 50.12N 27.01E
Shepetovka see Shepetivka
27 W10 **Shepherd** Texas, SW USA 30.30N 95.00W
197 D14 **Shepherd Islands** island group C Vanuatu
22 K5 **Shepherdsville** Kentucky, S USA 37.59N 85.43W
191 O11 **Shepparton** Victoria, SE Australia 36.25S 145.25E
99 P22 **Sheppey, Isle of** island SE England, UK
Sherabad see Sherobod
99 L23 **Sherborne** S England, UK 50.57N 2.30W
78 H16 **Sherbro Island** island SW Sierra Leone
13 Q12 **Sherbrooke** Quebec, SE Canada 45.23N 71.54W
31 T11 **Sherburn** Minnesota, N USA 43.39N 94.43W
80 H6 **Sherda** Borkou-Ennedi-Tibesti, N Chad 20.04N 16.48E
82 G7 **Shereik** River Nile, N Sudan 18.43N 33.37E
130 K3 **Sheremet'yevo** ✕ (Moskva) Moskovskaya Oblast', W Russian Federation 56.05N 37.10E
159 P14 **Shergāti** Bihār, N India 24.35N 84.51E
29 U12 **Sheridan** Arkansas, C USA 34.18N 92.24W
35 W12 **Sheridan** Wyoming, C USA 44.47N 106.59W
190 G8 **Sheringa** South Australia 33.51S 135.13E
126 L16 **Sherlovaya Gora** Chitinskaya Oblast', S Russian Federation 50.26N 116.09E
27 U5 **Sherman** Texas, SW USA 33.39N 96.34W
204 J10 **Sherman Island** island Antarctica
21 S4 **Sherman Mills** Maine, NE USA 45.51N 68.23W
31 O15 **Sherman Reservoir** ⊞ Nebraska, C USA
153 N14 **Sherobod** Rus. Sherabad. Surkhondaryo Viloyati, S Uzbekistan 37.43N 66.59E
153 O13 **Sherobod** Rus. Sherabad. ≈ S Uzbekistan
159 T14 **Sherpur** Dhaka, N Bangladesh 25.00N 90.01E
39 T4 **Sherrelwood** Colorado, C USA 39.49N 105.00W
101 J14 **'s-Hertogenbosch** Fr. Bois-le-Duc, Ger. Herzogenbusch. Noord-Brabant, S Netherlands 51.40N 5.19E
30 M2 **Sherwood** North Dakota, N USA 48.55N 101.36W
9 Q14 **Sherwood Park** Alberta, SW Canada 53.34N 113.04W
58 F13 **Sheshea, Río** ≈ E Peru
149 T5 **Sheshtamad** Khorāsān, NE Iran 36.03N 57.45E
31 S10 **Shetek, Lake** ⊙ Minnesota, N USA
98 M2 **Shetland Islands** island group NE Scotland, UK
150 F14 **Shetpe** Mangistau, SW Kazakhstan 44.06N 52.03E
160 C11 **Shetrunji** ≈ W India
Shevchenko see Aktau
119 W5 **Shevchenkove** Kharkivs'ka Oblast', E Ukraine 49.40N 37.13E
83 H14 **Shewa Gimira** Southern, S Ethiopia 7.12N 35.49E
167 Q9 **Shexian** var. Huicheng, She Xian. Anhui, E China 29.52N 118.27E
167 R6 **Sheyang** prev. Hede. Jiangsu, E China 33.49N 120.13E
31 O4 **Sheyenne** North Dakota, N USA 47.49N 99.08W
31 P4 **Sheyenne River** ≈ North Dakota, N USA
98 G7 **Shiant Islands** island group NW Scotland, UK
127 Pp14 **Shiashkotan, Ostrov** island Kuril'skiye Ostrova, SE Russian Federation
33 R9 **Shiawassee River** ≈ Michigan, N USA
147 R14 **Shibām** C Yemen 15.49N 48.24E
Shibarghān see Sheberghān
171 Kk12 **Shibata** var. Sibata. Niigata, Honshū, C Japan 37.57N 139.19E
172 Qq7 **Shibecha** Hokkaidō, NE Japan 43.19N 144.34E
Shiberghan/Shiberghān see Sheberghān
172 Qq6 **Shibetsu** Hokkaidō, N Japan 43.40N 145.10E
172 Pp4 **Shibetsu** var. Sibetu. Hokkaidō, NE Japan 44.12N 142.23E
172 P5 **Shibetsu** var. Sibetu. Hokkaidō, NE Japan 43.57N 142.13E
Shibh Jazīrat Sīnā' see Sinai
Shibīn al Kawm see Shibīn el Kôm
77 W8 **Shibīn el Kôm** var. Shibīn al Kawm. N Egypt 30.33N 30.59E
149 O13 **Shīb, Kūh-e** ▲ S Iran
10 D8 **Shibogama Lake** ⊙ Ontario, C Canada
Shibotsu-jima see Zelënyy, Ostrov
171 K14 **Shibukawa** var. Sibukawa. Gunma, Honshū, S Japan 36.31N 138.58E
170 Bb16 **Shibushi** Kagoshima, Kyūshū, SW Japan 31.27N 131.05E
170 C17 **Shibushi-wan** bay SW Japan
172 N9 **Shichinohe** Aomori, Honshū, C Japan 40.40N 141.07E
201 U13 **Shichiyo Islands** island group Chuuk, C Micronesia
Shickshock Mountains see Chic-Chocs, Monts
151 S9 **Shiderti** ≈ N Kazakhstan
151 S8 **Shiderty** Pavlodar, NE Kazakhstan 51.43N 74.34E
98 G10 **Shiel, Loch** ⊙ N Scotland, UK
171 H15 **Shiga** off. Shiga-ken, var. Siga. ◆ prefecture Honshū, SW Japan
Shigatse see Xigazê
147 U13 **Shiḩan** oasis NE Yemen 17.46N 52.25E
Shih-chia-chuang/Shihmen see Shijiazhuang
164 K4 **Shihezi** Xinjiang Uygur Zizhiqu, NW China 44.20N 85.59E
Shiichi see Shyichy
115 K19 **Shijak** var. Shijaku. Durrës, W Albania 41.21N 19.34E
Shijaku see Shijak
167 O4 **Shijiazhuang** var. Shih-chia-chuang; prev. Shihmen. Hebei, E China 38.04N 114.28E
172 Nn7 **Shikabe** Hokkaidō, NE Japan 42.03N 140.45E
155 Q13 **Shikārpur** Sind, S Pakistan 27.59N 68.39E
131 Q7 **Shikhany** Saratovskaya Oblast', W Russian Federation 52.07N 47.13E
201 V12 **Shiki Islands** island group Chuuk, C Micronesia
170 Ee15 **Shikoku** var. Sikoku. island SW Japan
199 Gg6 **Shikoku Basin** var. Sikoku Basin. undersea feature N Philippine Sea
170 Ee15 **Shikoku-sanchi** ▲▲ Shikoku, SW Japan
172 S7 **Shikotan, Ostrov** Jap. Shikotan-tō. island NE Russian Federation
Shikotan-tō see Shikotan, Ostrov
172 O6 **Shikotsu-ko** var. Sikotu Ko. ⊙ Hokkaidō, NE Japan
83 N15 **Shilabo** Somali, E Ethiopia 6.05N 44.48E
131 X7 **Shil'da** Orenburgskaya Oblast', W Russian Federation 51.46N 59.48E
145 V3 **Shilēr, Āw-e** ≈ E Iraq
159 S12 **Shiliguri** prev. Siliguri. West Bengal, NE India 26.45N 88.24E
126 Kk16 **Shilka** Chitinskaya Oblast', S Russian Federation 51.52N 115.49E
133 V7 **Shilka** ≈ S Russian Federation
20 H15 **Shillington** Pennsylvania, NE USA 40.18N 75.57W
159 V13 **Shillong** Meghālaya, NE India 25.36N 91.54E
130 M5 **Shilovo** Ryazanskaya Oblast', W Russian Federation 54.18N 40.53E
170 C14 **Shimabara** var. Simabara. Nagasaki, Kyūshū, SW Japan 32.48N 130.20E
170 C14 **Shimabara-wan** bay SW Japan
171 Ii17 **Shimada** var. Simada. Shizuoka, Honshū, S Japan 34.49N 138.10E
170 Ee12 **Shimane** off. Shimane-ken, var. Simane. ◆ prefecture Honshū, SW Japan
170 F11 **Shimane-hantō** peninsula Honshū, SW Japan
126 M15 **Shimanovsk** Amurskaya Oblast', SE Russian Federation 52.00N 127.36E
Shimbir Berris see Shimbiris
82 O12 **Shimbiris** var. Shimbir Berris. ▲ N Somalia 10.43N 47.10E
172 P6 **Shimizu** Hokkaidō, NE Japan 42.58N 142.54E
171 Ii16 **Shimizu** var. Simizu. Shizuoka, Honshū, S Japan 35.01N 138.28E
158 I8 **Shimla** prev. Simla. Himāchal Pradesh, N India 31.07N 77.09E
Shimminato see Shinminato
171 J18 **Shimoda** var. Simoda. Shizuoka, Honshū, S Japan 34.49N 138.09E
171 Kk16 **Shimodate** var. Simodate. Ibaraki, Honshū, S Japan 36.18N 139.57E
161 F18 **Shimoga** Karnātaka, W India 13.55N 75.31E
170 Bb14 **Shimo-jima** island SW Japan
170 B15 **Shimo-Koshiki-jima** island SW Japan
83 J21 **Shimoni** Coast, S Kenya 4.40S 39.22E
170 D12 **Shimonoseki** var. Simonoseki; hist. Akamagaseki, Bakan. Yamaguchi, Honshū, SW Japan 33.57N 130.54E
171 Kk16 **Shimotsuma** var. Simotuma. Ibaraki, Honshū, S Japan 36.10N 139.58E
128 G14 **Shimsk** Novgorodskaya Oblast', NW Russian Federation 58.12N 30.43E
171 Jj14 **Shinano-gawa** var. Sinano Gawa. ≈ Honshū, C Japan
147 W7 **Shināş** N Oman 24.45N 56.24E
154 J6 **Shīndand** Farāh, W Afghanistan 33.19N 62.09E
Shinei see Hsinying
27 T12 **Shiner** Texas, SW USA 29.25N 97.10W
178 Gg1 **Shingbwiyang** Kachin State, N Myanmar 26.40N 96.14E
151 W11 **Shingozha** Vostochnyy Kazakhstan, E Kazakhstan 47.46N 80.38E
171 Gg17 **Shingū** var. Singû. Wakayama, Honshū, SW Japan 33.40N 135.57E
12 F8 **Shining Tree** Ontario, S Canada 47.36N 81.12W
170 F12 **Shinji-ko** var. Sinzi-ko. ⊙ Honshū, SW Japan
171 Ll12 **Shinjō** var. Sinzyô. Yamagata, Honshū, C Japan 38.46N 140.16E
98 I7 **Shin, Loch** ⊙ N Scotland, UK
171 Ii13 **Shinminato** var. Shimminato, Sinminato. Toyama, Honshū, SW Japan 36.46N 137.04E
170 Dd12 **Shinnanyō** var. Shin-Nan'yō, Sinn'anyô. Yamaguchi, Honshū, SW Japan 34.04N 131.43E
23 S3 **Shinnston** West Virginia, NE USA 39.22N 80.19W
144 I6 **Shinshār** Fr. Chinnchār. Ḩimş, W Syria 34.36N 36.45E
171 I16 **Shinshiro** var. Sinsiro. Aichi, Honshū, SW Japan 34.52N 137.29E
Shinshū see Chinju
172 P6 **Shintoku** Hokkaidō, NE Japan 43.03N 142.50E
83 G20 **Shinyanga** Shinyanga, NW Tanzania 3.40S 33.25E
83 G20 **Shinyanga** ◆ region N Tanzania
171 M13 **Shiogama** var. Siogama. Miyagi, Honshū, C Japan 38.19N 140.59E
171 J15 **Shiojiri** var. Sioziri. Nagano, Honshū, S Japan 36.07N 137.57E
170 G17 **Shiono-misaki** headland Honshū, SW Japan 33.25N 135.45E
171 Ll15 **Shioya-zaki** headland Honshū, C Japan 37.00N 140.57E
116 J9 **Shipchenski Prokhod** pass C Bulgaria 42.46N 25.21E
166 G14 **Shiping** Yunnan, SW China 23.45N 102.23E
11 P13 **Shippagan** var. Shippegan. New Brunswick, SE Canada 47.45N 64.43W
Shippegan see Shippagan
20 F15 **Shippensburg** Pennsylvania, NE USA 40.03N 77.31W
39 O9 **Ship Rock** ▲ New Mexico, SW USA 36.41N 108.50W
39 P9 **Shiprock** New Mexico, SW USA 36.47N 108.41W
13 R6 **Shipshaw** ≈ Quebec, SE Canada
127 Pp11 **Shipunskiy, Mys** headland E Russian Federation 53.04N 159.57E
166 K7 **Shiquan** Shaanxi, C China 33.05N 108.10E
126 Hh14 **Shira** Respublika Khakasiya, S Russian Federation 54.35N 89.58E
170 G16 **Shirahama** Wakayama, Honshū, SW Japan 33.40N 135.21E
159 T14 **Shirajganj Ghat** var. Serajgonj, Sirajganj. Rajshahi, C Bangladesh 24.25N 89.40E
171 Mm7 **Shirakami-misaki** headland Hokkaidō, NE Japan 41.26N 140.10E
171 L14 **Shirakawa** var. Sirakawa. Fukushima, Honshū, C Japan 37.07N 140.11E
171 Ii13 **Shirakawa** Gifu, Honshū, SW Japan 36.17N 136.52E
171 K14 **Shirane-san** ▲ Honshū, S Japan 36.44N 139.21E
171 J16 **Shirane-san** ▲ Honshū, S Japan 35.39N 138.13E
172 Pp7 **Shiranuka** Hokkaidō, NE Japan 42.57N 144.01E
172 O6 **Shiraoi** Hokkaidō, NE Japan 42.34N 141.24E
205 N12 **Shirase Coast** physical region Antarctica
172 Pp5 **Shirataki** Hokkaidō, NE Japan 43.55N 143.14E
149 O11 **Shīrāz** var. Shīrāz. Fārs, S Iran 29.37N 52.34E
85 N15 **Shire** var. Chire. ≈ Malawi/Mozambique

◆ Country ● Country Capital ◇ Dependent Territory ○ Dependent Territory Capital ◆ Administrative Region ✕ International Airport ▲ Mountain ▲▲ Mountain Range Volcano ≈ River ⊙ Lake ⊞ Reservoir

168 G7 **Shiree** Dzavhan, W Mongolia 47.30N 96.48E
169 O9 **Shireet** Sühbaatar, SE Mongolia 45.33N 112.19E
172 R6 **Shiretoko-hantō** headland Hokkaidō, NE Japan 44.06N 145.07E
172 R5 **Shiretoko-misaki** headland Hokkaidō, NE Japan 44.20N 145.19E
131 N5 **Shiringushi** Respublika Mordoviya, W Russian Federation 53.50N 42.49E
154 M3 **Shīrīn Tagāb** Fāryāb, N Afghanistan 36.49N 65.01E
155 N2 **Shīrīn Tagāb** ≈ N Afghanistan
172 Nn8 **Shiriya-zaki** headland Honshū, C Japan 41.24N 141.27E
150 I12 **Shirkala, Gryada** plain W Kazakhstan
171 Ll13 **Shiroishi** var. Siroisi. Miyagi, Honshū, C Japan 38.01N 140.37E
Shirokoye see Shyroke
171 K12 **Shirone** var. Sirone. Niigata, Honshū, C Japan 37.46N 139.00E
171 I14 **Shirotori** Gifu, Honshū, SW Japan 35.53N 136.52E
171 J13 **Shirouma-dake** ▲ Honshū, S Japan 36.46N 137.46E
207 T1 **Shirshov Ridge** undersea feature W Bering Sea
Shirshütür see Shirshyutyur, Peski
152 K12 **Shirshyutyur, Peski** Turkm. Shirshütür. desert E Turkmenistan
149 T3 **Shīrvān** var. Shirwān. Khorāsān, NE Iran 37.25N 57.55E
Shirwa, Lake see Chilwa, Lake
Shirwān see Shīrvān
165 N5 **Shisanjianfang** Xinjiang Uygur Zizhiqu, W China 43.10N 91.15E
40 M16 **Shishaldin Volcano** ▲ Unimak Island, Alaska, USA 54.45N 163.58W
Shishchitsy see Shyshchytsy
40 M8 **Shishmaref** Alaska, USA 66.15N 166.04W
Shisur see Ash Shişar
171 I16 **Shitara** Aichi, Honshū, SW Japan 35.06N 137.33E
158 D12 **Shiv** Rājasthān, NW India 26.10N 71.13E
157 E15 **Shivāji Sāgar** prev. Konya Reservoir ⊠ W India
160 H8 **Shivpuri** Madhya Pradesh, C India 25.28N 77.41E
38 J9 **Shivwits Plateau** plain Arizona, SW USA
Shiwālik Range see Siwalik Range
166 M8 **Shiyan** Hubei, C China 32.39N 110.48E
166 H13 **Shizong** Yunnan, SW China 24.49N 103.59E
171 Mm13 **Shizugawa** Miyagi, Honshū, NE Japan 38.40N 141.26E
165 W8 **Shizuishan** var. Dawukou. Ningxia, N China 39.04N 106.22E
172 Oo7 **Shizunai** Hokkaidō, NE Japan 42.20N 142.24E
171 Ii16 **Shizuoka** var. Sizuoka. Shizuoka, Honshū, S Japan 34.58N 138.20E
171 Ii16 **Shizuoka** off. Shizuoka-ken, var. Sizuoka. ◈ prefecture Honshū, S Japan
Shklov see Shklow
121 N15 **Shklow** Rus. Shklov. Mahilyowskaya Voblasts', E Belarus 54.13N 30.16E
115 K18 **Shkodër** var. Shkodra, It. Scutari, SCr. Skadar. Shkodër, NW Albania 42.03N 19.31E
115 K17 **Shkodër** ◈ district NW Albania
Shkodra see Shkodër
Shkodrës, Liqeni i see Scutari, Lake
Shkumbî/Shkumbin see Shkumbinit, Lumi i
115 L20 **Shkumbinit, Lumi i** var. Shkumbî, Shkumbin. ≈ C Albania
Shligigh, Cuan see Sligo Bay
126 Ii2 **Shmidta, Ostrov** island Severnaya Zemlya, N Russian Federation
191 S10 **Shoalhaven River** ≈ New South Wales, SE Australia
9 W16 **Shoal Lake** Manitoba, S Canada 50.28N 100.36W
33 O15 **Shoals** Indiana, N USA 38.40N 86.46W
170 F13 **Shōbara** var. Syôbara. Hiroshima, Honshū, SW Japan 34.50N 132.58E
170 Ff14 **Shōdo-shima** island SW Japan
171 Ii13 **Shō-gawa** ≈ Honshū, SW Japan
Shōka see Changhua
126 J3 **Shokal'skogo, Proliv** strait N Russian Federation
172 Oo4 **Shokanbetsu-dake** 🌋 Hokkaidō, NE Japan 43.43N 141.33E
153 T14 **Shokhdara, Qatorkŭhi** Rus. Shakhdarinskiy Khrebet. ⛰ SE Tajikistan
151 N9 **Sholaksay** Kostanay, N Kazakhstan 51.45N 64.45E
Sholāpur see Solāpur
Sholdaneshty see Şoldăneşti
151 P17 **Shollakorgan** var. Chulakkurgan. Yuzhnyy Kazakhstan, S Kazakhstan 43.48N 69.12E
Shoqpar see Chokpar
161 G21 **Shoranūr** Kerala, SW India 10.53N 76.06E
161 G16 **Shorāpur** Karnātaka, C India 16.34N 76.48E
153 O14 **Sho'rchi** Rus. Shurchi. Surkhondaryo Viloyati, S Uzbekistan 37.58N 67.40E
32 M11 **Shorewood** Illinois, N USA 41.31N 88.12W
Shorkazakhly, Solonchak see Kazakhlyshor, Solonchak
151 Q9 **Shortandy** Akmola, C Kazakhstan 51.47N 70.55E
Shortepa/Shor Tepe see Shūr Tappeh
195 S13 **Shortland Island** var. Alu. island Shortland Islands, NW Solomon Islands
195 T13 **Shortland Islands** island group NW Solomon Islands
Shosambetsu see Shosanbetsu
172 P3 **Shosanbetsu** var. Shosambetsu. Hokkaidō, NE Japan 44.31N 141.47E
35 O15 **Shoshone** Idaho, NW USA 42.56N 114.24W
37 T6 **Shoshone Mountains** ⛰ Nevada, W USA
35 U12 **Shoshone River** ≈ Wyoming, C USA
85 I19 **Shoshong** Central, SE Botswana 23.03S 26.33E
35 V14 **Shoshoni** Wyoming, C USA 43.13N 108.06W
Shōshū see Sangju
119 S2 **Shostka** Sums'ka Oblast', NE Ukraine 51.51N 33.30E
193 C21 **Shotover** ≈ South Island, NZ
152 H9 **Shovot** Rus. Shavat. Xorazm Viloyati, W Uzbekistan 41.41N 60.13E
39 N12 **Show Low** Arizona, SW USA 34.15N 110.01W
Show Me State see Missouri
129 O4 **Shoyna** Nenetskiy Avtonomnyy Okrug, NW Russian Federation 67.50N 44.09E
128 M11 **Shozhma** Arkhangel'skaya Oblast', NW Russian Federation 61.57N 40.10E
119 Q7 **Shpola** Cherkas'ka Oblast', N Ukraine 49.00N 31.27E
Shqipëria/Shqipërisë, Republika e see Albania
24 G5 **Shreveport** Louisiana, S USA 32.31N 93.45W
99 K19 **Shrewsbury** hist. Scrobesbyrig'. W England, UK 52.43N 2.45W
158 D11 **Shri Mohangarh** prev. Sri Mohangorh. Rājasthān, NW India 27.16N 71.18E
159 S16 **Shrīrāmpur** prev. Serampore, Serampur. West Bengal, NE India 22.43N 88.19E
99 K19 **Shropshire** cultural region W England, UK
151 S16 **Shu** Kaz. Shū. Zhambyl, SE Kazakhstan 43.34N 73.40E
Shū see Chu
166 G13 **Shuangbai** Yunnan, SW China 24.45N 101.38E
169 W9 **Shuangcheng** Heilongjiang, NE China 45.20N 126.21E
166 E14 **Shuangjiang** Yunnan, SW China 23.28N 99.43E
169 U10 **Shuangliao** var. Zhengjiatun. Jilin, NE China 43.31N 123.32E
Shuang-liao see Liaoyuan
169 Y7 **Shuangyashan** var. Shuang-ya-shan. Heilongjiang, NE China 46.37N 131.10E
Shu'aymiah see Shu'aymīyah
147 W12 **Shu'aymīyah** var. Shu'aymiah. S Oman 17.55N 55.39E
150 I10 **Shubarkuduk** Kaz. Shubarqudyq. Aktyubinsk, W Kazakhstan 49.10N 56.28E
Shubarqudyq see Shubarkuduk
151 N12 **Shubar-Tengiz, Ozero** ◎ C Kazakhstan
41 S5 **Shublik Mountains** ⛰ Alaska, USA
Shubrā al Khaymah see Shubrâ el Kheima
124 Qq16 **Shubrâ el Kheima** var. Shubrā al Khaymah. N Egypt 30.06N 31.15E
164 E8 **Shufu** Xinjiang Uygur Zizhiqu, NW China 39.18N 75.43E
153 S14 **Shughnon, Qatorkŭhi** Rus. Shugnanskiy Khrebet. ⛰ SE Tajikistan
Shugnanskiy Khrebet see Shughnon, Qatorkŭhi
167 Q6 **Shu He** ≈ E China
Shuiding see Huocheng
Shuiji see Laixi
Shū-Ile Taūlary see Chu-Iliyskiye Gory
155 T10 **Shujāābād** Punjab, E Pakistan 29.52N 71.22E
169 W9 **Shulan** Jilin, NE China 44.28N 126.57E
164 E8 **Shule** Xinjiang Uygur Zizhiqu, NW China 39.19N 76.06E
Shuleh see Shule He
165 Q8 **Shule He** var. Shuleh, Sulo. ≈ C China
32 K9 **Shullsburg** Wisconsin, N USA 42.37N 90.12W
41 N16 **Shumagin Islands** island group Alaska, USA
152 G7 **Shumanay** Qoraqalpog'iston Respublikasi, W Uzbekistan 42.42N 58.56E
116 M8 **Shumen** Shumen, NE Bulgaria 43.17N 26.57E
116 M8 **Shumen** ◈ province NE Bulgaria
131 P4 **Shumerlya** Chavash Respubliki, W Russian Federation 55.31N 46.24E
125 Ee12 **Shumikha** Kurganskaya Oblast', C Russian Federation 55.12N 63.09E
120 M12 **Shumilina** Rus. Shumilino. Vitsyebskaya Voblasts', NE Belarus 55.19N 29.33E
Shumilino see Shumilina
127 Pp12 **Shumshu, Ostrov** island SE Russian Federation
118 K5 **Shums'k** Ternopil's'ka Oblast', W Ukraine 50.06N 26.04E
41 O7 **Shungnak** Alaska, USA 66.53N 157.08W
Shunsen see Ch'unch'ŏn
166 M3 **Shuo Xian** Shanxi, NE China 39.19N 112.25E
Shuo Xian/Shuoxian see Shuozhou
167 N3 **Shuozhou** var. Shuoxian; prev. Shuo Xian. Shanxi, C China 39.19N 112.25E
147 P16 **Shuqrah** var. Shaqrā. SW Yemen 13.25N 45.43E
Shurab see Shŭrob
153 R11 **Shŭrob** Rus. Shurab. NW Tajikistan 40.02N 70.31E
149 T10 **Shūr, Rūd-e** ≈ E Iran
155 O2 **Shūr Tappeh** var. Shortepa, Shor Tepe. Balkh, N Afghanistan 37.22N 66.49E
85 K17 **Shurugwi** prev. Selukwe. Midlands, C Zimbabwe 19.40S 30.00E
148 L8 **Shūsh** anc. Susa, Bibl. Shushan. Khūzestān, SW Iran 32.11N 48.13E
Shushan see Shūsh
148 L9 **Shūshtar** var. Shustar, Shushter. Khūzestān, SW Iran 32.03N 48.51E
Shushter/Shustar see Shūshtar
147 T9 **Shuţfah, Qalamat** well E Saudi Arabia 22.46N 52.50E
145 V9 **Shuwayjah, Hawr ash** var. Hawr as Suwayqiyah. ◎ E Iraq
128 M16 **Shuya** Ivanovskaya Oblast', W Russian Federation 56.51N 41.24E
41 Q14 **Shuyak Island** island Alaska, USA
177 G4 **Shwebo** Sagaing, C Myanmar 22.34N 95.42E
177 Ff7 **Shwedaung** Pegu, W Myanmar 18.43N 95.15E
177 G8 **Shwegyin** Pegu, SW Myanmar 17.55N 96.58E
178 Gg4 **Shweli** Chin. Longchuan Jiang. ≈ Myanmar/China
177 G6 **Shwemyo** Mandalay, C Myanmar 20.04N 96.13E
Shyghys Qazagastan Oblysy see Vostochnyy Kazakhstan
Shyghys Qongyrat see Shygys Konyrat
151 T12 **Shygys Konyrat** var. Vostochno-Kounradskiy, Kaz. Shyghys Qongyrat. Karaganda, C Kazakhstan 47.01N 75.05E
121 M19 **Shyichy** Rus. Shiichi. Homyel'skaya Voblasts', SE Belarus 52.15N 29.13E
151 Q17 **Shymkent** prev. Chimkent. Yuzhnyy Kazakhstan, S Kazakhstan 42.19N 69.36E
Shyngghyrlaū see Chingirlau
158 J5 **Shyok** Jammu and Kashmir, NW India 34.13N 78.12E
119 S9 **Shyroke** Rus. Shirokoye. Dnipropetrovs'ka Oblast', E Ukraine 47.37N 33.15E
119 O9 **Shyryayeve** Odes'ka Oblast', SW Ukraine 47.21N 30.11E
119 S5 **Shyshaky** Poltavs'ka Oblast', C Ukraine 49.54N 34.00E
121 K17 **Shyshchytsy** Rus. Shishchitsy. Minskaya Voblasts', C Belarus 53.12N 27.33E
155 Y3 **Siachen Muztāgh** ⛰ NE Pakistan
Siadehan see Tākestān
154 M13 **Siāhān Range** ⛰ W Pakistan
148 I1 **Sīāh Chashmeh** Āžarbāyjān-e Bākhtarī, N Iran 39.01N 44.22E
155 W7 **Siālkot** Punjab, NE Pakistan 32.31N 74.33E
194 K12 **Sialum** Morobe, C PNG 6.05S 147.33E
Siam see Thailand
Siam, Gulf of see Thailand, Gulf of
Sian see Xi'an
Siang see Brahmaputra
Siangtan see Xiangtan
174 J5 **Siantan, Pulau** island Kepulauan Anambas, W Indonesia
56 H11 **Siare, Río** ≈ C Colombia
179 Rr13 **Siargao Island** island S Philippines
194 K12 **Siassi** Umboi Island, C PNG 5.34S 147.50E
117 D14 **Siátista** Dytikí Makedonía, N Greece 40.16N 21.34E
177 Ff4 **Siatlai** Chin State, W Myanmar 22.05N 93.36E
179 Q15 **Siaton** Negros, C Philippines 9.03N 123.03E
179 Q15 **Siaton Point** headland Negros, C Philippines 9.03N 123.00E
120 F11 **Šiauliai** Ger. Schaulen. Šiauliai, N Lithuania 55.54N 23.21E
175 S5 **Siau, Pulau** island N Indonesia
85 J15 **Siavonga** Southern, SE Zambia 16.28S 28.45E
Siazan' see Siyäzän
Sibah see As Sībah
109 N20 **Sibari** Calabria, S Italy 39.45N 16.26E
Sibata see Shibata
131 X6 **Sibay** Respublika Bashkortostan, W Russian Federation 52.39N 58.39E
95 M19 **Sibbo** Fin. Sipoo. Etelä-Suomi, S Finland 60.22N 25.19E
114 D13 **Šibenik** It. Sebenico. Šibenik-Knin, S Croatia 43.43N 15.54E
Šibenik see Šibenik-Knin
114 E13 **Šibenik-Knin** off. Šibenska Županija. var. Šibenik ◈ province S Croatia
Šibenska Županija see Šibenik-Knin
Siberia see Sibir'
Siberoet see Siberut, Pulau
173 Ff9 **Siberut, Pulau** prev. Siberoet. island Kepulauan Mentawai, W Indonesia
173 Ff9 **Siberut, Selat** strait W Indonesia
Sibetu see Shibetsu
155 P11 **Sibi** Baluchistān, SW Pakistan 29.31N 67.54E
194 F15 **Sibidiri** Western, SW PNG 8.58S 142.14E
126 K10 **Sibir'** var. Siberia. physical region NE Russian Federation
126 H14 **Sibirskiy** Altayskiy Oblast', S Russian Federation 53.45N 84.00E
81 F20 **Sibiti** La Lékoumou, S Congo 3.40S 13.19E
83 G21 **Sibiti** ≈ C Tanzania
118 I12 **Sibiu** Ger. Hermannstadt, Hung. Nagyszeben. Sibiu, C Romania 45.48N 24.08E
118 I11 **Sibiu** ◈ county C Romania
31 S11 **Sibley** Iowa, C USA 43.24N 95.45W
173 Ff6 **Sibolga** Sumatera, W Indonesia 1.42N 98.48E
173 Ff6 **Sibolga, Teluk** var. Teluk Tapanuli. bay Sumatera, W Indonesia
174 Ll6 **Sibu** Sarawak, East Malaysia 2.18N 111.49E
Sibukawa see Shibukawa
44 G2 **Sibun** ≈ E Belize
81 I15 **Sibut** prev. Fort-Sibut. Kémo, S Central African Republic 5.44N 19.07E
179 P17 **Sibutu** island SW Philippines
179 P17 **Sibutu Passage** passage SW Philippines
179 Q12 **Sibuyan Island** island C Philippines
179 Q12 **Sibuyan Sea** sea C Philippines
201 U1 **Sibylla Island** island N Marshall Islands
9 N16 **Sicamous** British Columbia, SW Canada 50.49N 118.52W
Sichelburger Gebirge see Gorjanci/Žumberačko Gorje
178 H15 **Sichon** var. Ban Sichon, Si Chon. Nakhon Si Thammarat, SW Thailand 9.03N 99.51E
166 H9 **Sichuan** var. Chuan, Sichuan Sheng, Ssu-ch'uan, Szechuan, Szechwan. ◈ province C China
166 I9 **Sichuan Pendi** basin C China
Sichuan Sheng see Sichuan
105 S16 **Sicie, Cap** headland SE France 43.03N 5.50E
109 J24 **Sicilia** Eng. Sicily; anc. Trinacria. ◈ region Italy, C Mediterranean Sea
109 M24 **Sicilia** Eng. Sicily; anc. Trinacria. island Italy, C Mediterranean Sea
Sicilian Channel see Sicily, Strait of
Sicily see Sicilia
109 H24 **Sicily, Strait of** var. Sicilian Channel. strait C Mediterranean Sea
44 K5 **Sico Tinto, Río** var. Río Negro. ≈ NE Honduras
59 H16 **Sicuani** Cusco, S Peru 14.18S 71.16W
114 J10 **Šid** Serbia, NW Serbia and Montenegro (Yugoslavia) 45.07N 19.13E
117 A15 **Sidári** Kérkyra, Iónioi Nísoi, Greece, C Mediterranean Sea 39.47N 19.43E
174 Kk8 **Sidas** Borneo, C Indonesia 0.24N 109.46E
100 O5 **Siddeburen** Groningen, NE Netherlands 53.15N 6.52E
160 D9 **Siddhapur** prev. Siddhpur, Sidhpur. Gujarāt, W India 23.57N 72.28E
Siddhpur see Siddhapur
161 I15 **Siddipet** Andhra Pradesh, C India 18.10N 78.54E
195 O17 **Sideia Island** island SE PNG
175 Pp12 **Sidenreng, Danau** ◎ Sulawesi, C Indonesia
79 N14 **Sidéradougou** SW Burkina 10.39N 4.16W
109 N23 **Siderno** Calabria, SW Italy 38.17N 16.19E
Siders see Sierre
160 L9 **Sidhi** Madhya Pradesh, C India 24.24N 81.54E
Sidhirókastron see Sidirókastro
Sidhpur see Siddhapur
Sīdī al Hānī', Sabkhat see Sidi el Hani, Sebkhet de
77 U7 **Sîdi Barrâni** NW Egypt 31.33N 25.54E
76 I6 **Sidi Bel Abbès** var. Sidi bel Abbès, Sidi-Bel-Abbès. NW Algeria 35.12N 0.42W
76 E7 **Sidi-Bennour** W Morocco 32.39N 8.28W
76 M6 **Sidi Bouzid** var. Gammouda, Sīdī Bu Zayd. C Tunisia 35.05N 9.20E
123 K12 **Sidi el Hani, Sebkhet de** var. Sabkhat Sīdī al Hānī'. salt flat NE Tunisia
76 D8 **Sidi-Ifni** SW Morocco 29.33N 10.04W
76 G6 **Sidi-Kacem** prev. Petitjean. N Morocco 34.21N 5.46W
116 G12 **Sidirókastro** prev. Sidhirókastron. Kentrikí Makedonía, NE Greece 41.13N 23.24E
204 L12 **Sidley, Mount** ▲ Antarctica 76.39S 124.48W
31 S16 **Sidney** Iowa, C USA 40.45N 95.39W
35 Y7 **Sidney** Montana, NW USA 47.42N 104.10W
30 J15 **Sidney** Nebraska, C USA 41.09N 102.57W
20 I11 **Sidney** New York, NE USA 42.18N 75.21W
33 R13 **Sidney** Ohio, N USA 40.16N 84.09W
25 T2 **Sidney Lanier, Lake** ⊠ Georgia, SE USA
Sidon see Saïda
126 Hh9 **Sidorovsk** Yamalo-Nenetskiy Avtonomnyy Okrug, N Russian Federation 66.34N 82.12E
Sidra/Sidra, Gulf of see Surt, Khalīj, N Libya
Sidra see Surt, N Libya
Sīdī Bu Zayd see Sidi Bouzid
Siebenbürgen see Transylvania
Sieben Dörfer see Săcele
112 O12 **Siedlce** Ger. Sedlez, Rus. Sesdlets. Mazowieckie, C Poland 52.10N 22.18E
103 E16 **Sieg** ≈ W Germany
103 F16 **Siegen** Nordrhein-Westfalen, W Germany 50.52N 8.01E
111 X4 **Sieghartskirchen** Niederösterreich, E Austria 48.13N 16.01E
112 O11 **Siemiatycze** Podlaskie, NE Poland 52.27N 22.51E
178 Jj11 **Siĕmpang** Stœng Trêng, NE Cambodia 14.07N 106.24E
178 Ii12 **Siĕmréab** prev. Siemreap. Siĕmréab, NW Cambodia 13.21N 103.49E
Siemreap see Siĕmréab
108 G12 **Siena** Fr. Sienne; anc. Saena Julia. Toscana, C Italy 43.19N 11.19E
Sienne see Siena
94 K12 **Sieppijärvi** Lappi, NW Finland 67.09N 23.58E
112 J13 **Sieradz** Sieradz, C Poland 51.36N 18.42E
112 K10 **Sierpc** Mazowieckie, C Poland 52.51N 19.43E
26 I9 **Sierra Blanca** Texas, SW USA 31.10N 105.21W
39 S14 **Sierra Blanca Peak** ▲ New Mexico, SW USA 33.22N 105.48W
37 P5 **Sierra City** California, W USA 39.34N 120.35W
65 I16 **Sierra Colorada** Río Negro, S Argentina 40.37S 67.48W
64 I13 **Sierra del Nevado** ⛰ W Argentina
65 J16 **Sierra Grande** Río Negro, E Argentina 41.40S 65.22W
78 G15 **Sierra Leone** off. Republic of Sierra Leone. ◆ republic W Africa
66 M13 **Sierra Leone Basin** undersea feature E Atlantic Ocean
68 K8 **Sierra Leone Fracture Zone** tectonic feature E Atlantic Ocean
Sierra Leone Ridge see Sierra Leone Rise
66 L13 **Sierra Leone Rise** var. Sierra Leone Ridge, Sierra Leone Schwelle. undersea feature E Atlantic Ocean
Sierra Leone Schwelle see Sierra Leone Rise
43 U17 **Sierra Madre** var. Sierra de Soconusco. ⛰ Guatemala/Mexico
179 Pp9 **Sierra Madre** ⛰ Luzon, N Philippines
39 R2 **Sierra Madre** ⛰ Colorado/Wyoming, C USA
(0) H15 **Sierra Madre del Sur** ⛰ S Mexico
(0) G13 **Sierra Madre Occidental** var. Western Sierra Madre. ⛰ C Mexico
(0) H13 **Sierra Madre Oriental** var. Eastern Sierra Madre. ⛰ C Mexico
46 H8 **Sierra Maestra** ⛰ E Cuba
42 L7 **Sierra Mojada** Coahuila de Zaragoza, NE Mexico 27.13N 103.42W
107 O14 **Sierra Nevada** ⛰ S Spain
37 P6 **Sierra Nevada** ⛰ W USA
56 F4 **Sierra Nevada de Santa Marta** ⛰ NE Colombia
44 K5 **Sierra Río Tinto** ⛰ NE Honduras
26 J10 **Sierra Vieja** ⛰ Texas, SW USA
39 N16 **Sierra Vista** Arizona, SW USA 31.33N 110.18W
110 D10 **Sierre** Ger. Siders. Valais, SW Switzerland 46.18N 7.33E
38 L16 **Sierrita Mountains** ⛰ Arizona, SW USA
Siete Moai see Ahu Akivi
78 M15 **Sifié** W Ivory Coast 7.58N 6.55W
117 I21 **Sífnos** anc. Siphnos. island Kykládes, Greece, Aegean Sea
117 I21 **Sífnou, Stenó** strait SE Greece
Siga see Shiga
197 H15 **Sigatoka** prev. Singatoka. Viti Levu, W Fiji 18.10S 105.30E
105 P16 **Sigean** Aude, S France 43.01N 2.58E
Sighet see Sighetu Marmaţiei
Sighetul Marmaţiei see Sighetu Marmaţiei
118 I8 **Sighetu Marmaţiei** var. Sighet, Sighetul Marmaţiei, Hung. Máramarossziget. Maramureş, N Romania 47.55N 23.52E
118 I11 **Sighişoara** Ger. Schässburg, Hung. Segesvár. Mureş, C Romania 46.12N 24.48E
173 E3 **Sigli** Sumatera, W Indonesia 5.21N 95.55E
94 J1 **Siglufjördhur** Nordhurland Vestra, N Iceland 66.09N 18.55W
103 H23 **Sigmaringen** Baden-Württemberg, S Germany 48.04N 9.12E
103 N20 **Signalberg** ▲ SE Germany 49.30N 12.34E
38 I13 **Signal Peak** ▲ Arizona, SW USA 33.20N 114.03W
Signan see Xi'an
204 H1 **Signy** UK research station South Orkney Islands, Antarctica 60.27S 45.35W
31 X15 **Sigourney** Iowa, C USA 41.19N 92.12W
117 K17 **Sígri, Akrotírio** headland Lésvos, E Greece 39.12N 25.49E
Sigsbee Deep see Mexico Basin
49 N2 **Sigsbee Escarpment** undersea feature N Gulf of Mexico
58 C8 **Sigsig** Azuay, S Ecuador 3.04S 78.49W
97 O15 **Sigtuna** Stockholm, C Sweden 59.36N 17.43E
44 H6 **Siguatepeque** Comayagua, W Honduras 14.38N 87.52W
107 P7 **Sigüenza** Castilla-La Mancha, C Spain 41.04N 2.37W
107 R4 **Sigües** Aragón, NE Spain 42.39N 1.01W
78 K13 **Siguiri** Haute-Guinée, NE Guinea 11.25N 9.07W
120 G8 **Sigulda** Ger. Segewold. Rīga, C Latvia 57.08N 24.51E
Sihanoukville see Kâmpóng Saôm
110 G8 **Sihlsee** ◎ NW Switzerland
95 K18 **Siikainen** Länsi-Suomi, W Finland 61.52N 21.49E
95 M16 **Siilinjärvi** Itä-Suomi, C Finland 63.04N 27.40E
143 R15 **Siirt** var. Sert; anc. Tigranocerta. Siirt, SE Turkey 37.55N 41.55E
143 R15 **Siirt** var. Sert. ◈ province SE Turkey
195 Z15 **Sikaiana** var. Stewert Islands. island group W Solomon Islands
Sikandarabad see Secunderābād
158 J11 **Sikandra Rao** Uttar Pradesh, N India 27.42N 78.22E
8 M11 **Sikanni Chief** British Columbia, W Canada 57.16N 122.44W
8 M11 **Sikanni Chief** ≈ British Columbia, W Canada
158 H11 **Sīkar** Rājasthān, N India 27.39N 75.09E
78 M13 **Sikasso** Sikasso, S Mali 11.21N 5.42W
78 L13 **Sikasso** ◈ region SW Mali
178 Gg3 **Sikaw** Kachin State, C Myanmar 23.50N 97.04E
85 H14 **Sikelenge** Western, W Zambia 14.51S 24.13E
29 Y7 **Sikeston** Missouri, C USA 36.52N 89.35W
95 J14 **Sikfors** Norrbotten, N Sweden 65.29N 21.17E
127 O16 **Sikhote-Alin', Khrebet** ⛰ SE Russian Federation
Siking see Xi'an
117 J22 **Síkinos** island Kykládes, Greece, Aegean Sea
159 S11 **Sikkim** Tib. Denjong. ◈ state N India
113 I26 **Siklós** Baranya, SW Hungary 45.51N 18.18E
Sikoku see Shikoku
Sikoku Basin see Shikoku Basin
85 G14 **Sikongo** Western, W Zambia 15.03S 22.07E
Sikotu Ko see Shikotsu-ko
Sikouri/Sikoúrion see Sykoúri
126 L7 **Siktyakh** Respublika Sakha (Yakutiya), NE Russian Federation 69.45N 124.42E
120 D12 **Šilalė** Šilalė, W Lithuania 55.29N 22.10E
108 G5 **Silandro** Ger. Schlanders. Trentino-Alto Adige, N Italy 46.39N 10.55E
43 N12 **Silao** Guanajuato, C Mexico 20.55N 101.24W
Silarius see Sele
179 Q13 **Silay** off. Silay City. Negros, C Philippines 10.49N 122.58E
159 W14 **Silchar** Assam, NE India 24.49N 92.48E
110 G9 **Silenen** Uri, C Switzerland 46.49N 8.39E
23 T9 **Siler City** North Carolina, SE USA 35.43N 79.27W
35 U11 **Silesia** Montana, NW USA 45.32N 108.52W
112 F13 **Silesia** physical region SW Poland
76 K12 **Silet** S Algeria 22.45N 4.51E
151 R8 **Sileti** var. Selety. ≈ N Kazakhstan
Siletitengiz see Siletiteniz, Ozero
151 R7 **Siletiteniz, Ozero** Kaz. Siletitengiz. ◎ N Kazakhstan
180 H16 **Silhouette** island Inner Islands, SE Seychelles
142 I17 **Silifke** anc. Seleucia. İçel, S Turkey 36.22N 33.57E
Siliguri see Shiliguri
162 J10 **Siling Co** ◎ W China
Silinhot see Xilinhot
198 Aa7 **Silisili** ▲ Savai'i, C Samoa 13.37S 172.26W
116 M6 **Silistra** var. Silistria; anc. Durostorum. Silistra, NE Bulgaria 44.07N 27.16E
116 M7 **Silistra** ◈ province NE Bulgaria
Silistria see Silistra
142 D10 **Silivri** İstanbul, NW Turkey 41.04N 28.15E
96 L13 **Siljan** ◎ C Sweden
97 G22 **Silkeborg** Århus, C Denmark 56.10N 9.34E
110 M8 **Sill** ≈ W Austria
107 S10 **Silla** País Valenciano, E Spain 39.22N 0.25W
64 H3 **Sillajguay, Cordillera** ▲ N Chile 19.45S 68.39W
120 K3 **Sillamäe** Ger. Sillamäggi. Ida-Virumaa, NE Estonia 59.23N 27.45E
Sillamäggi see Sillamäe
Sillein see Žilina
111 P9 **Sillian** Tirol, W Austria 46.45N 12.25E
114 B10 **Šilo** Primorje-Gorski Kotar, NW Croatia 45.09N 14.39E
29 R9 **Siloam Springs** Arkansas, C USA 36.11N 94.32W
27 X10 **Silsbee** Texas, SW USA 30.21N 94.10W
149 W15 **Sīlūp, Rūd-e** ≈ SE Iran
120 C12 **Šilutė** Ger. Heydekrug. Šilutė, W Lithuania 55.20N 21.29E
143 Q15 **Silvan** Dıyarbakır, SE Turkey 38.08N 41.00E
110 J10 **Silvaplana** Graubünden, S Switzerland 46.27N 9.45E
Silva Porto see Kuito
60 M12 **Silva, Recife do** reef E Brazil
160 D12 **Silvassa** Dādra and Nagar Haveli, W India 20.13N 73.03E
31 X4 **Silver Bay** Minnesota, N USA 47.17N 91.15W
39 P15 **Silver City** New Mexico, SW USA 32.46N 108.16W
20 D10 **Silver Creek** New York, NE USA 42.32N 79.10W
39 N12 **Silver Creek** ≈ Arizona, SW USA
29 P4 **Silver Lake** Kansas, C USA 39.06N 95.51W
34 I14 **Silver Lake** Oregon, NW USA 43.07N 121.04W
37 T9 **Silver Peak Range** ⛰ Nevada, W USA
23 W3 **Silver Spring** Maryland, NE USA 38.59N 77.01W
Silver State see Nevada
Silver State see Colorado
39 Q7 **Silverton** Colorado, C USA 37.48N 107.39W
20 K16 **Silverton** New Jersey, NE USA 40.00N 74.09W
34 G11 **Silverton** Oregon, NW USA 45.00N 122.46W
27 N4 **Silverton** Texas, SW USA 34.26N 101.19W
106 G14 **Silves** Faro, S Portugal 37.10N 8.25W
56 D12 **Silvia** Cauca, SW Colombia 2.36N 76.20W
110 J9 **Silvrettagruppe** ⛰ Austria/Switzerland
Sily-Vajdej see Vulcan
110 L7 **Silz** Tirol, W Austria 47.17N 11.00E
180 I13 **Sima** Anjouan, SE Comoros 12.10S 44.18E
Simabara see Shimabara
Simada see Shimada
85 H15 **Simakando** Western, W Zambia 16.43S 24.46E
Simane see Shimane
121 L20 **Simanichy** Rus. Simonichi. Homyel'skaya Voblasts', SE Belarus 51.53N 28.04E
166 F14 **Simao** Yunnan, SW China 22.30N 101.06E
159 P12 **Simara** Central, C Nepal 27.14N 85.00E
12 I8 **Simard, Lac** ◎ Quebec, SE Canada
142 D13 **Simav** Kütahya, W Turkey 39.04N 28.58E
142 D13 **Simav Çayı** ≈ NW Turkey
81 L18 **Simba** Orientale, N Dem. Rep. Congo 0.46N 22.54E
194 H11 **Simbai** Madang, N PNG 5.12S 144.33E
195 O9 **Simberi Island** island Tabar Islands, N PNG
Simbirsk see Ul'yanovsk
12 F17 **Simcoe** Ontario, S Canada 42.50N 80.16W
12 H14 **Simcoe, Lake** ◎ Ontario, S Canada
82 J11 **Sīmēn** ⛰ N Ethiopia
116 K11 **Simeonovgrad** prev. Maritsa. Khaskovo, S Bulgaria 42.03N 25.36E
118 G11 **Simeria** Ger. Pischk, Hung. Piski. Hunedoara, W Romania 45.51N 23.00E
109 L24 **Simeto** ≈ Sicilia, Italy, C Mediterranean Sea
173 E5 **Simeulue, Pulau** island NW Indonesia
119 T13 **Simferopol'** Respublika Krym, S Ukraine 44.55N 33.05E
119 T13 **Simferopol'** ✕ Respublika Krym, S Ukraine 44.55N 34.04E
Simi see Sými
158 M9 **Simikot** Far Western, NW Nepal 30.02N 81.49E
56 F7 **Simití** Bolívar, N Colombia 7.57N 73.57W
116 G11 **Simitla** Blagoevgrad, SW Bulgaria 41.57N 23.06E
37 S15 **Simi Valley** California, W USA 34.17N 118.52W
Simizu see Shimizu
Simla see Shimla
Şimlăul Silvaniei/Şimleul Silvaniei see Şimleu Silvaniei
118 G9 **Şimleu Silvaniei** Hung. Szilágsomlyó; prev. Şimlăul Silvaniei, Şimleul Silvaniei. Sălaj, NW Romania 47.12N 22.49E
Simmer see Simmerbach
103 E19 **Simmerbach** var. Simmer. ≈ W Germany
103 F18 **Simmern** Rheinland-Pfalz, W Germany 50.00N 7.30E
24 I7 **Simmesport** Louisiana, S USA 30.58N 91.48W
121 F14 **Simnas** Alytus, S Lithuania 54.23N 23.40E
94 L13 **Simo** Lappi, NW Finland 65.40N 25.04E
Simoda see Shimoda
Simodate see Shimodate
94 M13 **Simojärvi** ◎ N Finland
94 L13 **Simojoki** ≈ NW Finland
43 U15 **Simojovel** var. Simojovel de Allende. Chiapas, SE Mexico 17.12N 92.42W
Simojovel de Allende see Simojovel
58 B7 **Simon Bolivar** var. Guayaquil. ✕ (Quayaquil) Guayas, W Ecuador 2.16S 79.54W
56 L5 **Simon Bolívar** ✕ (Caracas) Distrito Federal, N Venezuela
Simonichi see Simanichy
12 M12 **Simon, Lac** ◎ Quebec, SE Canada
Simonoseki see Shimonoseki
Šimonovany see Partizánske
Simonstad see Simon's Town
85 E26 **Simon's Town** var. Simonstad. Western Cape, SW South Africa 34.12S 18.25E
Simony see Partizánske
Simotuma see Shimotsuma
173 F6 **Simpangkaman, Sungai** ≈ Sumatera, NW Indonesia
173 F5 **Simpangkiri, Sungai** ≈ Sumatera, NW Indonesia
Simpeln see Simplon
101 M18 **Simpelveld** Limburg, SE Netherlands 50.49N 5.58E
110 E11 **Simplon** var. Simpeln. Valais, SW Switzerland 46.13N 8.01E
110 E11 **Simplon Pass** pass S Switzerland 46.18N 8.01E
108 C6 **Simplon Tunnel** tunnel Italy/Switzerland
Simpson see Fort Simpson
190 G1 **Simpson Desert** desert Northern Territory/South Australia
8 J9 **Simpson Peak** ▲ British Columbia, W Canada 59.43N 131.29W
15 L3 **Simpson Peninsula** peninsula Nunavut, NE Canada
23 P11 **Simpsonville** South Carolina, SE USA 34.44N 82.15W
97 L23 **Simrishamn** Skåne, S Sweden 55.34N 14.20E
127 Pp15 **Simushir, Ostrov** island Kuril'skiye Ostrova, SE Russian Federation
Sīnā'/Sinai Peninsula see Sinai
173 Ee6 **Sinabang** Sumatera, W Indonesia 2.27N 96.24E
83 N15 **Sina Dhaqa** Galguduud, C Somalia 5.21N 46.21E
77 X8 **Sinai** var. Sinai Peninsula, Ar. Shibh Jazīrat Sīnā', Sīnā'. physical region NE Egypt
118 J12 **Sinaia** Prahova, SE Romania 45.19N 25.33E
196 B16 **Sinajana** C Guam 13.28N 144.45E
42 H8 **Sinaloa** ◈ state C Mexico
56 H4 **Sinamaica** Zulia, NW Venezuela 11.06N 71.52W
169 X14 **Sinan-ni** SE North Korea 38.37N 127.43E
Sinano Gawa see Shinano-gawa
Sīnāwan see Sīnāwin
77 N8 **Sīnāwin** var. Sīnāwan. NW Libya 31.00N 10.37E
85 J16 **Sinazongwe** Southern, S Zambia 17.11S 27.20E
177 Ff6 **Sinbaungwe** Magwe, W Myanmar 19.43N 95.10E
177 Ff5 **Sinbyugyun** Magwe, W Myanmar 20.37N 94.40E
56 E6 **Since** Sucre, NW Colombia 9.15N 75.12W
56 E6 **Sincelejo** Sucre, NW Colombia 9.16N 75.22W
177 F5 **Sinchaingbyin** var. Zullapara. Arakan State, W Myanmar 20.51N 92.23E
25 U4 **Sinclair, Lake** ⊠ Georgia, SE USA
8 M14 **Sinclair Mills** British Columbia, SW Canada 54.03N 121.37W
178 Mm15 **Sin Cowe East Island** island S Spratly Islands
178 Mm15 **Sin Cowe Island** island SW Spratly Islands
155 Q14 **Sind** var. Sindh. ◈ province SE Pakistan
160 I8 **Sind** ≈ N India
97 H19 **Sindal** Nordjylland, N Denmark 57.28N 10.13E
179 Q15 **Sindañgan** Mindanao, S Philippines 8.09N 122.59E
81 D19 **Sindara** Ngounié, W Gabon 1.07S 10.40E
158 E13 **Sindari** prev. Sindri. Rājasthān, N India 25.34N 71.57E
175 Q16 **Sindeh, Teluk** bay Nusa Tenggara, C Indonesia
116 N8 **Sindel** Varna, E Bulgaria 43.07N 27.35E
103 H22 **Sindelfingen** Baden-Württemberg, SW Germany 48.43N 9.01E
161 G16 **Sindgi** Karnātaka, C India 17.01N 76.22E
Sindh see Sind
120 G5 **Sindi** Ger. Zintenhof. Pärnumaa, SW Estonia 58.25N 24.40E

◆ Country
● Country Capital
◇ Dependent Territory
○ Dependent Territory Capital
◈ Administrative Region
✕ International Airport
▲ Mountain
⛰ Mountain Range
🌋 Volcano
≈ River
◎ Lake
⊠ Reservoir

142 C13 **Sındırgı** Balıkesir, W Turkey 39.15N 28.10E
79 N14 **Sindou** SW Burkina 10.34N 5.04W
Sindri see Sindari
155 T9 **Sind Sāgar Doāb** desert E Pakistan
130 M11 **Sinegorskiy** Rostovskaya Oblast', SW Russian Federation 48.01N 40.52E
127 O9 **Sinegor'ye** Magadanskaya Oblast', E Russian Federation 62.04N 150.33E
116 O12 **Sinekli** İstanbul, NW Turkey 41.13N 28.13E
106 F12 **Sines** Setúbal, S Portugal 37.58N 8.52W
106 F12 **Sines, Cabo de** headland S Portugal 37.57N 8.55W
94 L12 **Sinettä** Lappi, NW Finland 66.39N 25.25E
195 P11 **Sinewit, Mount** ▲ New Britain, C PNG 4.42S 151.58E
82 G11 **Singa** var. Sinja, Sinjah. Sinnar, E Sudan 13.07N 33.54E
80 J12 **Singako** Moyen-Chari, S Chad 9.52N 19.31E
Singan see Xi'an
174 I7 **Singapore** ● (Singapore) S Singapore 1.17N 103.48E
174 I7 **Singapore** off. Republic of Singapore. ◆ republic SE Asia
174 I7 **Singapore Strait** var. Strait of Singapore, Mal. Selat Singapura. strait Indonesia/Singapore
Singapore, Strait of/Singapura, Selat see Singapore Strait
175 N16 **Singaraja** Bali, C Indonesia 8.06S 115.04E
Singatoka see Sigatoka
178 H10 **Sing Buri** var. Singhaburi. Sing Buri, C Thailand 14.55N 100.21E
103 H24 **Singen** Baden-Württemberg, S Germany 47.46N 8.49E
Singeorgiu de Pădure see Sângeorgiu de Pădure
Singeorz-Băi/Singeroz Băi see Sângeorz-Băi
118 M9 **Sîngerei** var. Sângerei; prev. Lazovsk. N Moldova 47.38N 28.08E
Singhaburi see Sing Buri
83 H21 **Singida** Singida, C Tanzania 4.45S 34.48E
83 G22 **Singida** ◈ region C Tanzania
Singidunum see Beograd
177 G2 **Singkaling Hkamti** Sagaing, N Myanmar 26.00N 95.43E
175 Pp12 **Singkang** Sulawesi, C Indonesia 4.09S 119.58E
174 Gg8 **Singkarak, Danau** ◎ Sumatera, W Indonesia
174 K7 **Singkawang** Borneo, C Indonesia 0.57N 108.57E
174 I8 **Singkep, Pulau** island Kepulauan Lingga, W Indonesia
173 F6 **Singkilbaru** Sumatera, W Indonesia 2.18N 97.47E
191 T7 **Singleton** New South Wales, SE Australia 32.36S 151.10E
Singora see Songkhla
Singû see Shingū
Sining see Xining
109 D17 **Siniscola** Sardegna, Italy, C Mediterranean Sea 40.34N 9.42E
115 F14 **Sinj** Split-Dalmacija, SE Croatia 43.41N 16.37E
Sinja/Sinjah see Singa
Sinjajevina see Sinjavina
145 P3 **Sinjār** NW Iraq 36.19N 41.51E
145 P2 **Sinjār, Jabal** ▲▲ N Iraq
115 K15 **Sinjavina** var. Sinjajevina. ▲▲ SW Serbia and Montenegro (Yugoslavia)
82 I7 **Sinkat** Red Sea, NE Sudan 18.52N 36.51E
Sinkiang/Sinkiang Uighur Autonomous Region see Xinjiang Uygur Zizhiqu
Sinmartin see Târnăveni
169 V13 **Sinmi-do** island NW North Korea
Sinminato see Shinminato
103 I18 **Sinn** ≈ C Germany
Sinnamarie see Sinnamary
57 Y9 **Sinnamary** var. Sinnamarie. N French Guiana 5.23N 52.57W
Sinn'anyô see Shinnanyō
82 G11 **Sinnar** ◈ state E Sudan
Sinneh see Sanandaj
20 E13 **Sinnemahoning Creek** ≈ Pennsylvania, NE USA
Sinnicolau Mare see Sânnicolau Mare
Sino/Sinoe see Greenville
Sinoe, Lacul see Sinoie, Lacul
Sinoia see Chinhoyi
119 N14 **Sinoie, Lacul** prev. Lacul Sinoe. lagoon SE Romania
61 H16 **Sinop** Mato Grosso, W Brazil 11.38S 55.27W
142 K10 **Sinop** anc. Sinope. Sinop, N Turkey 42.01N 35.09E
142 J10 **Sinop** ◈ province N Turkey
142 K10 **Sinop Burnu** headland N Turkey 42.02N 35.12E
Sinope see Sinop
169 Y12 **Sinp'o** E North Korea 40.01N 128.09E
103 H20 **Sinsheim** Baden-Württemberg, SW Germany 49.15N 8.52E
Sinsiro see Shinshiro
Sîntana see Sântana
174 L8 **Sintang** Borneo, C Indonesia 0.03N 111.31E
101 F14 **Sint Annaland** Zeeland, SW Netherlands 51.36N 4.07E
100 L5 **Sint Annaparochie** Friesland, N Netherlands 53.20N 5.46E
47 V9 **Sint Eustatius** Eng. Saint Eustatius. island N Netherlands Antilles
101 G19 **Sint-Genesius-Rode** Fr. Rhode-Saint-Genèse. Vlaams Brabant, C Belgium 50.45N 4.21E
101 F16 **Sint-Gillis-Waas** Oost-Vlaanderen, N Belgium 51.14N 4.08E
101 H17 **Sint-Katelijne-Waver** Antwerpen, C Belgium 51.05N 4.31E
101 E18 **Sint-Lievens-Houtem** Oost-Vlaanderen, NW Belgium 50.55N 3.52E
47 V9 **Sint Maarten** Eng. Saint Martin. island N Netherlands Antilles
101 F14 **Sint Maartensdijk** Zeeland, SW Netherlands 51.33N 4.05E
101 L19 **Sint-Martens-Voeren** Fr. Fouron-Saint-Martin. Limburg, NE Belgium 50.46N 5.49E
101 J14 **Sint-Michielsgestel** Noord-Brabant, S Netherlands 51.37N 5.21E
Sint-Miclăuş see Gheorgheni
47 O16 **Sint Nicholaas** S Aruba 12.25N 69.52W
101 F16 **Sint-Niklaas** Fr. Saint-Nicolas. Oost-Vlaanderen, N Belgium 51.10N 4.09E
101 K14 **Sint-Oedenrode** Noord-Brabant, S Netherlands 51.34N 5.28E
27 T14 **Sinton** Texas, SW USA 28.02N 97.30W
101 G14 **Sint Philipsland** Zeeland, SW Netherlands 51.37N 4.11E
101 G19 **Sint-Pieters-Leeuw** Vlaams Brabant, C Belgium 50.46N 4.16E
106 E11 **Sintra** prev. Cintra. Lisboa, W Portugal 38.48N 9.22W
101 J18 **Sint-Truiden** Fr. Saint-Trond. Limburg, NE Belgium 50.48N 5.13E
101 H14 **Sint Willebrord** Noord-Brabant, S Netherlands 51.33N 4.34E
169 V13 **Sinŭiju** W North Korea 40.08N 124.33E
82 P13 **Sinujiif** Nugaal, NE Somalia 8.33N 49.05E
Sinus Aelaniticus see Aqaba, Gulf of
Sinus Gallicus see Lion, Golfe du
Sinyang see Xinyang
Sinyavka see Sinyawka
121 I18 **Sinyawka** Rus. Sinyavka. Minskaya Voblasts', SW Belarus 52.57N 26.29E
126 Ll11 **Sinyaya** ≈ NE Russian Federation
Sinying see Hsinying
Sinyukha see Synyukha
Sinzi-ko see Shinji-ko
Sinzyô see Shinjō
113 I24 **Sió** ≈ W Hungary
179 Q16 **Siocon** Mindanao, S Philippines 7.37N 122.09E
113 I24 **Siófok** Somogy, C Hungary 46.54N 18.03E
Sioghanbiri see Shiogama
85 G15 **Sioma** Western, SW Zambia 16.41S 23.34E
110 D11 **Sion** Ger. Sitten; anc. Sedunum. Valais, SW Switzerland 46.15N 7.23E
105 O11 **Sioule** ≈ C France
31 S12 **Sioux Center** Iowa, C USA 43.04N 96.10W
31 R13 **Sioux City** Iowa, C USA 42.30N 96.24W
31 R11 **Sioux Falls** South Dakota, N USA 43.33N 96.45W
10 B11 **Sioux Lookout** Ontario, S Canada 49.27N 94.06W
31 T12 **Sioux Rapids** Iowa, C USA 42.53N 95.09W
Sioux State see North Dakota
Siozira see Shiojiri
179 Q14 **Sipalay** Negros, C Philippines 9.46N 122.25E
57 V11 **Sipaliwini** ◈ district S Suriname
47 U15 **Siparia** Trinidad, Trinidad and Tobago 10.07N 61.33W
Siphnos see Sífnos
169 V11 **Siping** var. Ssu-p'ing, Szeping; prev. Ssu-p'ing-chieh. Jilin, NE China 43.09N 124.22E
9 X12 **Sipiwesk** Manitoba, C Canada 55.28N 97.16W
9 W13 **Sipiwesk Lake** ◎ Manitoba, C Canada
205 O11 **Siple Coast** physical region Antarctica
204 K12 **Siple Island** island Antarctica
204 K13 **Siple, Mount** ▲ Siple Island, Antarctica 73.25S 126.24W
Sipoo see Sibbo
114 G12 **Šipovo** Republika Srpska, W Bosnia and Herzegovina 44.16N 17.05E
25 O4 **Sipsey River** ≈ Alabama, S USA
173 Ff10 **Sipura, Pulau** island W Indonesia
(0) G16 **Siqueiros Fracture Zone** tectonic feature E Pacific Ocean
44 L10 **Siquia, Río** ≈ SE Nicaragua
179 Qq14 **Siquijor Island** island C Philippines
45 N13 **Siquirres** Limón, E Costa Rica 10.06N 83.33W
56 J5 **Siquisique** Lara, N Venezuela 10.36N 69.38W
161 G19 **Sira** Karnātaka, W India 13.46N 76.54E
97 D16 **Sira** ≈ S Norway
178 Hh12 **Siracha** var. Ban Si Racha, Si Racha. Chon Buri, S Thailand 13.10N 100.57E
109 L25 **Siracusa** Eng. Syracuse. Sicilia, Italy, C Mediterranean Sea 37.04N 15.16E
Sirajganj see Shirajganj Ghat
Sirakawa see Shirakawa
9 N14 **Sir Alexander, Mount** ▲ British Columbia, W Canada 54.00N 120.33W
143 O12 **Şiran** Gümüşhane, NE Turkey 40.12N 39.07E
79 Q12 **Sirba** ≈ E Burkina
149 O17 **Şīr Banī Yās** island W UAE
97 D17 **Sirdalsvatnet** ◎ S Norway
Sir Darya/Sirdaryo see Syr Darya
153 P10 **Sirdaryo** Sirdaryo Viloyati, E Uzbekistan 40.46N 68.34E
153 O11 **Sirdaryo Viloyati** Rus. Syrdar'inskaya Oblast'. ◈ province E Uzbekistan
Sir Donald Sangster International Airport see Sangster
194 H13 **Sirebi** ≈ S PNG
189 S3 **Sir Edward Pellew Group** island group Northern Territory, NE Australia
118 K8 **Siret** Ger. Sereth, Hung. Szeret. Suceava, N Romania 47.55N 26.04E
118 K8 **Siret** var. Siretul, Ger. Sereth, Rus. Seret, Ukr. Siret. ≈ Romania/Ukraine
Siretul see Siret
146 K3 **Sirḩān, Wādī as** dry watercourse Jordan/Saudi Arabia
158 I8 **Sirhind** Punjab, N India 30.39N 76.28E
118 F11 **Şiria** Ger. Schiria. Arad, W Romania 46.16N 21.37E
Siria see Syria
149 S14 **Sīrīk** Hormozgān, SE Iran 26.31N 57.06E
178 Hh8 **Sirikit Reservoir** ▣ N Thailand
60 K12 **Sirituba, Ilha** island NE Brazil
176 Ww11 **Siriwo** ≈ Papua, E Indonesia
149 R11 **Sīrjān** prev. Sa'īdābād. Kermān, S Iran 29.28N 55.39E
190 H9 **Sir Joseph Banks Group** island group South Australia
94 K11 **Sirkka** Lappi, N Finland 67.49N 24.48E
Sirna see Sýrna
143 R16 **Şırnak** Şırnak, SE Turkey 37.33N 42.27E
143 S16 **Şırnak** ◈ province SE Turkey
Siroisi see Shiroishi
161 J14 **Sironcha** Mahārāshtra, C India 18.51N 80.03E
Sirone see Shirone
Síros see Sýros
Sirotino see Sirotsina
120 M12 **Sirotsina** Rus. Sirotino. Vitsyebskaya Voblasts', N Belarus 55.22N 29.34E
158 H9 **Sirsa** Haryāna, NW India 29.31N 75.04E
181 Y17 **Sir Seewoosagur Ramgoolam** ✕ (Port Louis) SE Mauritius
161 E18 **Sirsi** Karnātaka, W India 14.46N 74.49E
Sirte see Surt
190 A2 **Sir Thomas, Mount** ▲ South Australia 27.09S 129.49E
Sirti, Gulf of see Surt, Khalīj
148 J5 **Sīrvān, Rūdkhāneh-ye** var. Nahr Diyālá, Sirwan. ≈ Iran/Iraq see also Diyālá, Nahr
120 H13 **Širvintos** Širvintos, SE Lithuania 55.01N 24.58E
Sirwan see Diyālá, Nahr/Sīrvān, Rūdkhāneh-ye
9 N15 **Sir Wilfrid Laurier, Mount** ▲ British Columbia, SW Canada 52.45N 119.51W
12 M10 **Sir-Wilfrid, Mont** ▲ Quebec, SE Canada 46.57N 75.33W
Sisačko-Moslavačka Županija see Sisak-Moslavina
114 E9 **Sisak** var. Siscia, Ger. Sissek, Hung. Sziszek; anc. Segestica. Sisak-Moslavina, C Croatia 45.28N 16.21E
178 J10 **Si Sa Ket** var. Sisaket, Sri Saket. Si Sa Ket, E Thailand 15.07N 104.18E
114 E9 **Sisak-Moslavina** off. Sisačko-Moslavačka Županija. ◈ province C Croatia
178 H8 **Si Satchanala** Sukhothai, NW Thailand
Siscia see Sisak
176 W10 **Sisember** Papua, E Indonesia 1.51S 134.09E
85 G22 **Sishen** Northern Cape, NW South Africa 27.46S 22.58E
143 V13 **Sisian** SE Armenia 39.31N 46.03E
207 N13 **Sisimiut** var. Holsteinborg, Holsteinsborg, Holstenborg, Holstensborg. Kitaa, S Greenland 67.07N 53.42W
32 M1 **Siskiwit Bay** lake bay Michigan, N USA
36 L1 **Siskiyou Mountains** ▲▲ California/Oregon, W USA
178 I12 **Sisŏphŏn** Bătdâmbâng, NW Cambodia 13.37N 102.58E
110 E7 **Sissach** Basel-Land, NW Switzerland 47.27N 7.48E
194 F9 **Sissano** Sandaun, NW PNG 3.01S 142.01E
Sissek see Sisak
31 R7 **Sisseton** South Dakota, N USA 45.39N 97.03W
149 W9 **Sistān, Daryācheh-ye** var. Daryācheh-ye Hāmūn, Hāmūn-e Şāberī. ◎ Afghanistan/Iran see also Şāberī, Hāmūn-e
149 V12 **Sīstān va Balūchestān** off. Ostān-e Sīstān va Balūchestān, var. Balūchestān va Sīstān. ◈ province SE Iran
105 T14 **Sisteron** Alpes-de-Haute-Provence, SE France 44.12N 5.55E
34 H13 **Sisters** Oregon, NW USA 44.17N 121.33W
67 G15 **Sisters Peak** ▲ N Ascension Island 7.55S 14.22W
23 R3 **Sistersville** West Virginia, NE USA 39.33N 81.00W
Sistova see Svishtov
Sitakund see Sitakunda
159 V16 **Sitakunda** var. Sitakund. Chittagong, SE Bangladesh 22.35N 91.40E
159 P12 **Sītāmarhi** Bihār, N India 26.36N 85.30E
158 L11 **Sītāpur** Uttar Pradesh, N India 27.33N 80.40E
Sitaş Cristuru see Cristuru Secuiesc
117 L25 **Siteía** var. Sitía. Kríti, Greece, E Mediterranean Sea 35.13N 26.06E
107 V6 **Sitges** Cataluña, NE Spain 41.13N 1.49E
117 H15 **Sithoniá** peninsula NE Greece
Sitía see Siteía
56 F4 **Sitionuevo** Magdalena, N Colombia 10.41N 74.42W
41 X13 **Sitka** Baranof Island, Alaska, USA 57.03N 135.19W
41 Q15 **Sitkinak Island** island Trinity Islands, Alaska, USA
177 G7 **Sittang** var. Sittoung. ≈ S Myanmar
101 L17 **Sittard** Limburg, SE Netherlands 51.00N 5.52E
Sitten see Sion
110 H7 **Sitter** ≈ NW Switzerland
111 U10 **Sittersdorf** Kärnten, S Austria 46.31N 14.34E
Sittoung see Sittang
177 F6 **Sittwe** var. Akyab. Arakan State, W Myanmar 22.09N 92.51E
174 Mm15 **Situbondo** prev. Sitoebondo. Jawa, C Indonesia 7.40S 114.01E
44 L8 **Siuna** Región Autónoma Atlántico Norte, NE Nicaragua 13.43N 84.46W
159 R15 **Siuri** West Bengal, NE India 23.54N 87.31E
Siut see Asyūt
126 M15 **Sivaki** Amurskaya Oblast', SE Russian Federation 52.39N 126.43E
142 M13 **Sivas** anc. Sebastia, Sebaste. Sivas, C Turkey 39.43N 37.01E
142 M13 **Sivas** ◈ province C Turkey
143 O15 **Siverek** Şanlıurfa, S Turkey 37.46N 39.19E
119 X6 **Sivers'k** Donets'ka Oblast', E Ukraine 48.52N 38.07E
128 G13 **Siverskiy** Leningradskaya Oblast', NW Russian Federation 59.21N 30.01E
119 X6 **Sivers'kyy Donets'** Rus. Severskiy Donets. ≈ Russian Federation/Ukraine see also Severskiy Donets
129 W5 **Sivomaskinskiy** Respublika Komi, NW Russian Federation 66.42N 62.33E
142 G13 **Sivrihisar** Eskişehir, W Turkey 39.28N 31.29E
101 F22 **Sivry** Hainaut, S Belgium 50.10N 4.11E
127 Pp9 **Sivuchiy, Mys** headland E Russian Federation 56.45N 163.13E
77 U9 **Siwa** var. Sīwah. NW Egypt 29.11N 25.32E
Sīwah see Siwa
158 J9 **Siwalik Range** var. Shiwālik Range. ▲▲ India/Nepal
159 O13 **Siwān** Bihār, N India 26.13N 84.21E
45 O14 **Sixaola, Río** ≈ Costa Rica/Panama
Six Counties, The see Northern Ireland
105 T16 **Six-Fours-les-Plages** Var, SE France 43.04N 5.49E
167 Q7 **Sixian** var. Si Xian. Anhui, E China 33.28N 117.52E
24 J9 **Six Mile Lake** ◎ Louisiana, S USA
145 V3 **Siyāh Gūz** E Iraq 35.49N 45.45E
161 L25 **Siyambalanduwa** Uva Province, SE Sri Lanka 6.54N 81.31E
143 Y10 **Siyäzän** Rus. Siazan'. NE Azerbaijan 41.04N 49.04E
Sizebolu see Sozopol
Sizuoka see Shizuoka
Sjar see Sääre
115 L15 **Sjenica** Turk. Seniça. Serbia, SW Serbia and Montenegro (Yugoslavia) 43.16N 20.01E
96 G11 **Sjoa** ≈ S Norway
97 K23 **Sjöbo** Skåne, S Sweden 55.37N 13.45E
97 I24 **Sjælland** Eng. Zealand, Ger. Seeland. island E Denmark
96 E9 **Sjøholt** Møre og Romsdal, S Norway 62.28N 6.49E
94 O1 **Sjuøyane** island group N Svalbard
Skadar see Shkodër
Skadarsko Jezero see Scutari, Lake
119 R11 **Skadovs'k** Khersons'ka Oblast', S Ukraine 46.07N 32.53E
94 I2 **Skagaströnd** prev. Höfdhakaupstadhur. Nordhurland Vestra, N Iceland 65.49N 20.18W
97 H19 **Skagen** Nordjylland, N Denmark 57.43N 11.36E
Skagerak see Skagerrak
97 L16 **Skagern** ◎ C Sweden
207 T17 **Skagerrak** var. Skagerak. channel N Europe
96 G12 **Skaget** ▲ S Norway 61.19N 9.07E
34 H7 **Skagit River** ≈ Washington, NW USA
41 W12 **Skagway** Alaska, USA 59.27N 135.18W
94 K8 **Skáidi** Finnmark, N Norway 70.26N 24.31E
117 F21 **Skála** Pelopónnisos, S Greece 36.51N 22.39E
118 K6 **Skalat** Pol. Skałat. Ternopil's'ka Oblast', W Ukraine 49.27N 25.59E
97 J22 **Skälderviken** inlet Denmark/Sweden
128 J3 **Skalistyy** Murmanskaya Oblast', NW Russian Federation 69.16N 33.20E
94 I12 **Skalka** ◎ N Sweden
116 I12 **Skalotí** Anatolikí Makedonía kai Thráki, NE Greece 41.24N 24.16E
97 G22 **Skanderborg** Århus, C Denmark 56.01N 9.57E
97 K22 **Skåne** prev. Eng. Scania. ◈ county S Sweden
77 N6 **Skanès** ✕ (Sousse) E Tunisia 35.36N 10.56E
97 C15 **Skånevik** Hordaland, S Norway 59.43N 6.35E
97 M18 **Skänninge** Östergötland, S Sweden 58.24N 15.04E
97 J23 **Skanör** Skåne, S Sweden 55.24N 12.48E
117 H17 **Skantzoúra** island Vóreioi Sporádes, Greece, Aegean Sea
97 K18 **Skara** Västra Götaland, S Sweden 58.22N 13.25E
97 M17 **Skärblacka** Östergötland, S Sweden 58.34N 15.54E
97 I18 **Skärhamn** Västra Götaland, S Sweden 57.58N 11.33E
97 I14 **Skarnes** Hedmark, S Norway 60.13N 11.40E
121 M21 **Skarodnaye** Rus. Skorodnoye. Homyel'skaya Voblasts', SE Belarus 51.38N 28.50E
112 I8 **Skarszewy** Ger. Schöneck. Pomorskie, NW Poland 54.04N 18.25E
113 M14 **Skarżysko-Kamienna** Świętokrzyskie, C Poland 51.07N 20.52E
97 K16 **Skattkärr** Värmland, C Sweden 59.25N 13.42E
120 D12 **Skaudvilė** Tauragė, SW Lithuania 55.25N 22.33E
94 J12 **Skaulo** Norrbotten, N Sweden 67.21N 21.03E
113 K17 **Skawina** Małopolskie, S Poland 49.56N 19.49E
8 K12 **Skeena** ≈ British Columbia, SW Canada
8 J11 **Skeena Mountains** ▲▲ British Columbia, W Canada
99 O18 **Skegness** E England, UK 53.10N 0.21E
94 J4 **Skeidharársandur** coast S Iceland
95 J15 **Skellefteå** Västerbotten, N Sweden 64.45N 20.58E
95 I14 **Skellefteälven** ≈ N Sweden
95 J15 **Skelleftehamn** Västerbotten, N Sweden 64.41N 21.13E
27 O2 **Skellytown** Texas, SW USA 35.34N 101.10W
97 J19 **Skene** Västra Götaland, S Sweden 57.30N 12.34E
99 G17 **Skerries** Ir. Na Sceirí. E Ireland 53.34N 6.07W
97 H15 **Ski** Akershus, S Norway 59.43N 10.49E
117 G17 **Skíathos** Skíathos, Vóreioi Sporádes, Greece, Aegean Sea 39.10N 23.30E
117 G17 **Skíathos** island Vóreioi Sporádes, Greece, Aegean Sea
29 P9 **Skiatook** Oklahoma, C USA 36.22N 96.00W
29 P9 **Skiatook Lake** ▣ Oklahoma, C USA
99 B22 **Skibbereen** Ir. An Sciobairín. SW Ireland 51.33N 9.15W
94 I9 **Skibotn** Troms, N Norway 69.22N 20.18E
121 F16 **Skidal'** Rus. Skidel'. Hrodzyenskaya Voblasts', W Belarus 53.34N 24.12E
99 K15 **Skiddaw** ▲ NW England, UK 54.37N 3.07W
Skidel' see Skidal'
27 T14 **Skidmore** Texas, SW USA 28.13N 97.40W
97 G16 **Skien** Telemark, S Norway 59.12N 9.36E
Skiermûntseach see Schiermonnikoog
112 L12 **Skierniewice** Łodzkie, C Poland 51.58N 20.10E
76 L5 **Skikda** prev. Philippeville. NE Algeria 36.51N 7.00E
32 M16 **Skillet Fork** ≈ Illinois, N USA
97 L19 **Skillingaryd** Jönköping, S Sweden 57.27N 14.04E
117 B19 **Skinári, Akrotírio** headland Zákynthos, Iónioi Nísoi, Greece, C Mediterranean Sea 37.55N 20.57E
97 M15 **Skinnskatteberg** Västmanland, C Sweden 59.49N 15.40E
190 M12 **Skipton** Victoria, SE Australia 37.44S 143.21E
99 L16 **Skipton** N England, UK 53.56N 1.59W
Skiropoula see Skyropoúla
Skíros see Skýros
97 F21 **Skive** Viborg, NW Denmark 56.34N 9.01E
96 F11 **Skjåk** Oppland, S Norway 61.52N 8.21E
94 K2 **Skjálfandafljót** ≈ C Iceland
97 F22 **Skjern** Ringkøbing, W Denmark 55.55N 8.30E
97 F22 **Skjern Å** var. Skjern Aa. ≈ W Denmark
Skjern Aa see Skjern Å
94 G12 **Skjerstad** Nordland, C Norway 67.14N 15.00E
94 I8 **Skjervøy** Troms, N Norway 70.01N 20.57E
94 I10 **Skjold** Troms, N Norway 69.03N 19.18E
113 I17 **Skoczów** Śląskie, S Poland 49.47N 18.46E
97 I24 **Skælskør** Vestsjælland, E Denmark 55.16N 11.18E
111 T11 **Škofja Loka** Ger. Bischoflack. NW Slovenia 46.12N 14.16E
96 N12 **Skog** Gävleborg, C Sweden 61.10N 16.49E
97 K16 **Skoghall** Värmland, C Sweden 59.19N 13.30E
33 N10 **Skokie** Illinois, N USA 42.01N 87.43W
118 H6 **Skole** L'vivs'ka Oblast', W Ukraine 49.04N 23.29E
117 D19 **Skóllis** ▲ S Greece 37.58N 21.33E
178 J13 **Skon** Kâmpóng Cham, C Cambodia 12.56N 104.36E
117 H17 **Skópelos** Skópelos, Vóreioi Sporádes, Greece, Aegean Sea 39.07N 23.44E
117 H17 **Skópelos** island Vóreioi Sporádes, Greece, Aegean Sea
130 L5 **Skopin** Ryazanskaya Oblast', W Russian Federation 53.46N 39.37E
115 N18 **Skopje** var. Üsküb, Turk. Üsküp; prev. Skoplje, anc. Scupi. ● (FYR Macedonia) N FYR Macedonia 42.01N 21.27E
115 O18 **Skopje** ✕ N FYR Macedonia 41.58N 21.35E
Skoplje see Skopje
112 I8 **Skórcz** Ger. Skurz. Pomorskie, N Poland 53.46N 18.43E
Skorodnoye see Skarodnaye
95 H16 **Skorped** Västernorrland, C Sweden 63.22N 17.55E
97 G21 **Skørping** Nordjylland, N Denmark 56.49N 9.55E
97 K18 **Skövde** Västra Götaland, S Sweden 58.24N 13.52E
126 Ll14 **Skovorodino** Amurskaya Oblast', SE Russian Federation 54.02N 123.47E
21 Q6 **Skowhegan** Maine, NE USA 44.46N 69.41W
9 W15 **Skownan** Manitoba, S Canada 51.55N 99.34W
96 H13 **Skreia** Oppland, S Norway 60.37N 11.00E
Skripón see Orchómenos
120 H9 **Skrīveri** Aizkraukle, S Latvia 56.39N 25.07E
120 J11 **Skrudaliena** Daugvapils, SE Latvia 55.50N 26.42E
120 D9 **Skrunda** Kuldīga, W Latvia 56.39N 22.01E
97 C16 **Skudeneshavn** Rogaland, S Norway 59.09N 5.16E
85 L20 **Skukuza** Mpumalanga, NE South Africa 24.54S 31.33E
99 B22 **Skull** Ir. An Scoil. SW Ireland 51.32N 9.33W
24 L3 **Skuna River** ≈ Mississippi, S USA
31 X15 **Skunk River** ≈ Iowa, C USA
120 C10 **Skuodas** Ger. Schoden, Pol. Szkudy. Skuodas, NW Lithuania 56.16N 21.30E
97 K23 **Skurup** Skåne, S Sweden 55.28N 13.30E
Skurz see Skórcz
116 H8 **Skŭt** ≈ NW Bulgaria
96 O13 **Skutskär** Uppsala, C Sweden 60.38N 17.29E
97 B19 **Skúvoy** Dan. Skuø Island Faeroe Islands 61.46N 6.49W
Skvira see Skvyra
119 O5 **Skvyra** Rus. Skvira. Kyyivs'ka Oblast', N Ukraine 49.44N 29.42E
41 Q11 **Skwentna** Alaska, USA 61.56N 151.03W
112 E11 **Skwierzyna** Ger. Schwerin. Lubuskie, W Poland 52.36N 15.27E
38 K13 **Sky Harbour** ✕ (Phoenix) Arizona, SW USA 33.26N 112.00W
98 G9 **Skye, Isle of** island NW Scotland, UK
34 I8 **Skykomish** Washington, NW USA 47.40N 121.20W
Skylge see Terschelling
65 F19 **Skyring, Peninsula** peninsula S Chile
65 H24 **Skyring, Seno** inlet S Chile
117 H17 **Skyropoúla** var. Skiropoula. island Vóreioi Sporádes, Greece, Aegean Sea
117 I17 **Skýros** var. Skíros. Skýros, Vóreioi Sporádes, Greece, Aegean Sea 38.55N 24.34E
117 I17 **Skýros** var. Skíros; anc. Scyros. island Vóreioi Sporádes, Greece, Aegean Sea
120 J12 **Slabodka** Rus. Slobodka. Vitsyebskaya Voblasts', NW Belarus 55.42N 27.10E
97 I23 **Slagelse** Vestsjælland, E Denmark 55.25N 11.21E
95 I14 **Slagnäs** Norrbotten, N Sweden 65.36N 18.10E
174 Kk15 **Slamet, Gunung** ▲ Jawa, S Indonesia 7.12S 109.13E
41 T10 **Slana** Alaska, USA 62.46N 144.00W
99 F20 **Slaney** Ir. An tSláine. ≈ SE Ireland
118 J13 **Slănic** Prahova, SE Romania 45.13N 25.58E
118 K11 **Slănic Moldova** Bacău, E Romania 46.12N 26.23E
115 H16 **Slano** Dubrovnik-Neretva, SE Croatia 42.47N 17.54E
128 F13 **Slantsy** Leningradskaya Oblast', NW Russian Federation 59.06N 28.00E
113 C16 **Slaný** Ger. Schlan. Střední Čechy, NW Czech Republic 50.13N 14.04E
113 I16 **Śląskie** ◈ province S Poland
10 C10 **Slate Falls** Ontario, S Canada 51.11N 91.32W
29 T4 **Slater** Missouri, C USA 39.13N 93.04W
114 H9 **Slatina** Hung. Szlatina prev. Podravska Slatina. Virovitica-Podravina, NE Croatia 45.40N 17.46E
118 I14 **Slatina** Olt, S Romania 45.27N 24.21E
27 N5 **Slaton** Texas, SW USA 33.26N 101.38W
97 H14 **Slattum** Akershus, S Norway 60.00N 10.55E
9 R10 **Slave** ≈ Alberta/Northwest Territories, C Canada
70 E11 **Slave Coast** coastal region W Africa
9 P13 **Slave Lake** Alberta, SW Canada 55.16N 114.46W
125 G14 **Slavgorod** Altayskiy Kray, S Russian Federation 52.55N 78.46E
Slavgorod see Slawharad
Slavonia see Slavonija
114 G9 **Slavonija** Eng. Slavonia, Ger. Slawonien, Hung. Szlavonia, Szlavonország. cultural region NE Croatia
Slavonska Požega see Požega
114 H10 **Slavonski Brod** Ger. Brod, Hung. Bród; prev. Brod, Brod na Savi. Brod-Posavina, NE Croatia 45.09N 18.00E
118 L4 **Slavuta** Khmel'nyts'ka Oblast', NW Ukraine 50.17N 26.52E
119 P2 **Slavutych** Chernihivs'ka Oblast', N Ukraine 51.31N 30.47E
127 N18 **Slavyanka** Primorskiy Kray, SE Russian Federation 42.46N 131.19E
116 J8 **Slavyanovo** Pleven, N Bulgaria 43.28N 24.52E
Slavyansk see Slov"yans'k
130 K14 **Slavyansk-na-Kubani** Krasnodarskiy Kray, SW Russian Federation 45.16N 38.09E
121 N20 **Slavyechna** Rus. Slovechna. ≈ Belarus/Ukraine
121 O16 **Slawharad** Rus. Slavgorod. Mahilyowskaya Voblasts', E Belarus 53.27N 31.00E
112 G7 **Sławno** Zachodniopomorskie, NW Poland 54.22N 16.43E
Slawonien see Slavonija
31 S10 **Slayton** Minnesota, N USA 43.59N 95.45W
99 N18 **Sleaford** E England, UK 52.58N 0.27W
99 A20 **Slea Head** Ir. Ceann Sléibhe. headland SW Ireland 52.05N 10.25W
98 G9 **Sleat, Sound of** strait NW Scotland, UK
Sledyuki see Slyedzyuki
10 I5 **Sleeper Islands** island group Nunavut, C Canada
33 O6 **Sleeping Bear Point** headland Michigan, N USA 44.54N 86.02W
31 T10 **Sleepy Eye** Minnesota, N USA 44.18N 94.43W
41 O11 **Sleetmute** Alaska, USA 61.42N 157.10W
Sléibhe, Ceann see Slea Head
Slēmānī see As Sulaymānīyah
205 O5 **Slessor Glacier** glacier Antarctica
24 L9 **Slidell** Louisiana, S USA 30.16N 89.46W
20 K12 **Slide Mountain** ▲ New York, NE USA 42.00N 74.23W
100 I13 **Sliedrecht** Zuid-Holland, C Netherlands 51.49N 4.45E
123 Jj16 **Sliema** N Malta 35.54N 14.31E
99 G16 **Slieve Donard** ▲ SE Northern Ireland, UK 54.10N 5.57W
Sligeach see Sligo
99 D16 **Sligo** Ir. Sligeach. NW Ireland 54.16N 8.28W
99 C16 **Sligo** Ir. Sligeach. cultural region NW Ireland
99 C15 **Sligo Bay** Ir. Cuan Shligigh. inlet NW Ireland
20 B13 **Slippery Rock** Pennsylvania, NE USA 41.02N 80.02W
97 P19 **Slite** Gotland, SE Sweden 57.37N 18.46E
116 L9 **Sliven** var. Slivno. Sliven, C Bulgaria 42.42N 26.20E
116 L10 **Sliven** ◈ province C Bulgaria
116 G9 **Slivnitsa** Sofiya, W Bulgaria 42.51N 23.01E
Slivno see Sliven
116 L7 **Slivo Pole** Ruse, N Bulgaria 43.57N 26.15E
31 S13 **Sloan** Iowa, C USA 42.13N 96.13W
37 X12 **Sloan** Nevada, W USA 35.56N 115.13W
Slobodka see Slabodka
129 R14 **Slobodskoy** Kirovskaya Oblast', NW Russian Federation 58.43N 50.12E
Slobodzeya see Slobozia
119 O10 **Slobozia** Rus. Slobodzeya. E Moldova 46.45N 29.42E
118 L14 **Slobozia** Ialomiţa, SE Romania 44.34N 27.22E
100 O5 **Slochteren** Groningen, NE Netherlands 53.13N 6.48E
121 H17 **Slonim** Pol. Słonim, Rus. Slonim. Hrodzyenskaya Voblasts', W Belarus 53.04N 25.21E
100 K7 **Sloter Meer** ◎ N Netherlands
Slot, The see New Georgia Sound
99 N22 **Slough** S England, UK 51.31N 0.36W
113 J20 **Slovakia** off. Slovenská Republika, Ger. Slowakei, Hung. Szlovákia, Slvk. Slovensko. ◆ republic C Europe
Slovak Ore Mountains see Slovenské rudohorie
Slovechna see Slavyechna
111 S12 **Slovenia** off. Republic of Slovenia, Ger. Slowenien, Slvn. Slovenija. ◆ republic SE Europe
Slovenija see Slovenia
111 V10 **Slovenj Gradec** Ger. Windischgraz. N Slovenia 46.29N 15.05E
111 W10 **Slovenska Bistrica** Ger. Windischfeistritz. NE Slovenia 46.21N 15.27E
Slovenská Republika see Slovakia
111 W10 **Slovenske Konjice** E Slovenia 46.21N 15.28E
113 K20 **Slovenské rudohorie** Eng. Slovak Ore Mountains, Ger. Slowakisches Erzgebirge, Ungarisches Erzgebirge. ▲▲ C Slovakia
Slovensko see Slovakia
119 Y7 **Slov"yanoserbs'k** Luhans'ka Oblast', E Ukraine 48.41N 39.00E
119 W6 **Slov"yans'k** Rus. Slavyansk. Donets'ka Oblast', E Ukraine 48.51N 37.38E
Slowakei see Slovakia
Slowakisches Erzgebirge see Slovenské rudohorie
Slowenien see Slovenia
112 D11 **Słubice** Ger. Frankfurt. Lubuskie, W Poland 52.19N 14.34E
121 K19 **Sluch** Rus. Sluch'. ≈ C Belarus
118 L4 **Sluch** ≈ NW Ukraine
101 D16 **Sluis** Zeeland, SW Netherlands 51.18N 3.22E
114 D10 **Slunj** Hung. Szluin. Karlovac, C Croatia 45.06N 15.35E
112 I11 **Słupca** Wielkolpolskie, C Poland 52.16N 17.54E
112 G6 **Słupia** Ger. Stolpe. ≈ NW Poland
112 G6 **Słupsk** Ger. Stolp. Pomorskie, N Poland 54.27N 17.01E
121 K18 **Slutsk** Rus. Slutsk. Minskaya Voblasts', S Belarus 53.01N 27.31E
121 O16 **Slyedzyuki** Rus. Sledyuki. Mahilyowskaya Voblasts', E Belarus 53.35N 30.31E
99 A17 **Slyne Head** Ir. Ceann Léime. headland W Ireland 53.25N 10.11W
126 J16 **Slyudyanka** Irkutskaya Oblast', S Russian Federation 51.36N 103.28E
29 U14 **Smackover** Arkansas, C USA 33.21N 92.43W
97 L20 **Småland** cultural region S Sweden
97 K20 **Smålandsstenar** Jönköping, S Sweden 57.10N 13.24E
Small Malaita see Maramasike
11 O8 **Smallwood Reservoir** ▣ Newfoundland and Labrador, S Canada
121 N14 **Smalyany** Rus. Smolyany. Vitsyebskaya Voblasts', NE Belarus 54.36N 30.04E
121 L15 **Smalyavichy** Rus. Smolevichi. Minskaya Voblasts', C Belarus 54.01N 28.09E
76 C9 **Smara** var. Es Semara. N Western Sahara 26.45N 11.43W
121 I14 **Smarhon'** Pol. Smorgonie, Rus. Smorgon'. Hrodzyenskaya Voblasts', W Belarus 54.28N 26.24E
114 M11 **Smederevo** Ger. Semendria. Serbia, N Serbia and Montenegro (Yugoslavia) 44.40N 20.55E
114 M12 **Smederevska Palanka** Serbia, C Serbia and Montenegro (Yugoslavia) 44.23N 20.55E
97 M14 **Smedjebacken** Dalarna, C Sweden 60.07N 15.25E
118 L13 **Smeeni** Buzău, SE Romania 45.00N 26.52E
Smela see Smila
109 D16 **Smeralda, Costa** cultural region Sardegna, Italy, C Mediterranean Sea
113 J22 **Šmigiel** Ger. Schmiegel. Wielkolpolskie, C Poland 52.02N 16.33E
119 Q6 **Smila** Rus. Smela. Cherkas'ka Oblast', C Ukraine 49.15N 31.54E
100 N7 **Smilde** Drenthe, NE Netherlands 52.57N 6.28E
9 S16 **Smiley** Saskatchewan, S Canada 51.40N 109.24W
27 T12 **Smiley** Texas, SW USA 29.16N 97.38W
Smilten see Smiltene
120 I8 **Smiltene** Ger. Smilten. Valka, N Latvia 57.25N 25.53E
127 O14 **Smirnykh** Ostrov Sakhalin, Sakhalinskaya Oblast', SE Russian Federation 49.43N 142.48E
9 Q13 **Smith** Alberta, W Canada 55.06N 113.57W
41 P4 **Smith Bay** bay Alaska, USA
10 I3 **Smith, Cape** headland Quebec, NE Canada 60.50N 78.06W
28 L3 **Smith Center** Kansas, C USA 39.46N 98.46W
8 K13 **Smithers** British Columbia, SW Canada 54.45N 127.10W

◆ Country ● Country Capital ◇ Dependent Territory ○ Dependent Territory Capital ◈ Administrative Region ✕ International Airport ▲ Mountain ▲▲ Mountain Range Volcano ≈ River ◎ Lake ▣ Reservoir

23 V10 Smithfield North Carolina, SE USA 35.30N 78.20W
38 L1 Smithfield Utah, W USA 41.50N 111.49W
23 X7 Smithfield Virginia, NE USA 36.41N 76.38W
10 I3 Smith Island island Nunavut, C Canada
Smith Island see Sumisu-jima
22 H7 Smithland Kentucky, S USA 37.06N 88.24W
23 T7 Smith Mountain Lake var. Leesville Lake. ⊠ Virginia, NE USA
36 L1 Smith River California, W USA 41.54N 124.09W
35 R9 Smith River ↝ Montana, NW USA
12 L13 Smiths Falls Ontario, SE Canada 44.54N 76.01W
35 N13 Smiths Ferry Idaho, NW USA 44.19N 116.04W
22 K7 Smiths Grove Kentucky, S USA 37.01N 86.14W
191 N15 Smithton Tasmania, SE Australia 40.54S 145.06E
20 L14 Smithtown Long Island, New York, NE USA 40.52N 73.13W
22 K9 Smithville Tennessee, S USA 35.57N 85.48W
27 T11 Smithville Texas, SW USA 30.04N 97.32W
Šmohor see Hermagor
37 Q4 Smoke Creek Desert desert Nevada, W USA
9 O14 Smoky ↝ Alberta, W Canada
190 E7 Smoky Bay South Australia 32.22S 133.57E
191 V6 Smoky Cape headland New South Wales, SE Australia 30.54S 153.06E
28 L4 Smoky Hill River ↝ Kansas, C USA
28 L4 Smoky Hills hill range Kansas, C USA
9 Q14 Smoky Lake Alberta, SW Canada 54.07N 112.25W
96 E8 Smøla island W Norway
130 H4 Smolensk Smolenskaya Oblast', W Russian Federation 54.48N 32.07E
130 H4 Smolenskaya Oblast' ◈ province W Russian Federation
Smolensk-Moscow Upland see Smolensko-Moskovskaya Vozvyshennost'
130 J3 Smolensko-Moskovskaya Vozvyshennost' var. Smolensk-Moscow Upland. ▲▲ W Russian Federation
Smolevichi see Smalyavichy
117 C15 Smólikás ▲ W Greece 40.06N 20.54E
116 I12 Smolyan prev. Pashmakli. Smolyan, S Bulgaria 41.33N 24.46E
116 I12 Smolyan ◈ province S Bulgaria
Smolyany see Smalyany
35 S15 Smoot Wyoming, C USA 42.37N 110.55W
10 G12 Smooth Rock Falls Ontario, S Canada 49.16N 81.37W
Smorgon'/Smorgonie see Smarhon'
97 K23 Smygehamn Skåne, S Sweden 55.19N 13.25E
204 I7 Smyley Island island Antarctica
23 Y3 Smyrna Delaware, NE USA 39.18N 75.36W
25 S3 Smyrna Georgia, SE USA 33.52N 84.30W
22 J9 Smyrna Tennessee, S USA 36.00N 86.30W
Smyrna see İzmir
176 W10 Snabai Papua, E Indonesia 1.45S 134.14E
99 I16 Snaefell ▲ C Isle of Man 54.15N 4.29W
94 H3 Snaefellsjökull ▲ W Iceland 64.51N 23.51W
8 J4 Snake ↝ Yukon Territory, NW Canada
31 O8 Snake Creek ↝ South Dakota, N USA
191 P13 Snake Island island Victoria, SE Australia
37 Y6 Snake Range ▲▲ Nevada, W USA
34 K10 Snake River ↝ NW USA
31 V6 Snake River ↝ Minnesota, N USA
30 L12 Snake River ↝ Nebraska, C USA
35 Q14 Snake River Plain plain Idaho, NW USA
15 I7 Snare ↝ Northwest Territories, NW Canada
95 F15 Snåsa Nord-Trøndelag, C Norway 64.16N 12.25E
23 O8 Sneedville Tennessee, S USA 36.31N 83.13W
100 K6 Sneek Friesland, N Netherlands 53.01N 5.40E
Sneeuw-gebergte see Maoke, Pegunungan
97 F22 Snejbjerg Ringkøbing, C Denmark 56.07N 8.55E
128 J3 Snezhnogorsk Murmanskaya Oblast', NW Russian Federation 69.12N 33.20E
126 I8 Snezhnogorsk Taymyrskiy (Dolgano-Nenetskiy) Avtonomnyy Okrug, N Russian Federation 68.06N 87.37E
Snezhnoye see Snizhne
113 G15 Sněžka Ger. Schneekoppe. ▲ N Czech Republic 50.42N 15.55E
112 N8 Śniardwy, Jezioro Ger. Spirdingsee. ◎ NE Poland
Sniečkus see Visaginas
119 R10 Snihurivka Mykolayivs'ka Oblast', S Ukraine 47.05N 32.48E
118 I5 Snilov ✈ (L'viv) L'vivs'ka Oblast', W Ukraine 49.45N 23.59E
113 O19 Snina Hung. Szinna. Prešovský Kraj, E Slovakia 49.00N 22.10E
119 Y8 Snizhne Rus. Snezhnoye. Donets'ka Oblast', SE Ukraine 48.01N 38.46E
94 J3 Snækollur ▲ C Iceland 64.38N 19.18W
96 G10 Snøhetta var. Snohetta. ▲ S Norway 62.22N 9.08E
94 G12 Snøtinden ▲ C Norway 66.39N 13.50E
99 I18 Snowdon ▲ NW Wales, UK 53.04N 4.04W
99 I18 Snowdonia ▲▲ NW Wales, UK
15 I8 Snowdrift ↝ Northwest Territories, NW Canada
Snowdrift see Łutsel'k'e
39 N12 Snowflake Arizona, SW USA 34.30N 110.04W
23 Y5 Snow Hill Maryland, NE USA 38.10N 75.23W
23 W10 Snow Hill North Carolina, SE USA 35.25N 77.40W
204 H3 Snowhill Island island Antarctica
9 V13 Snow Lake Manitoba, C Canada 54.55N 100.01W
39 R5 Snowmass Mountain ▲ Colorado, C USA 39.07N 107.04W
20 M10 Snow, Mount ▲ Vermont, NE USA 42.56N 72.52W
36 M5 Snow Mountain ▲ California, W USA 39.44N 123.01W
Snow Mountains see Maoke, Pegunungan
35 N7 Snowshoe Peak ▲ Montana, NW USA 48.15N 115.44W
190 I8 Snowtown South Australia 33.49S 138.13E
38 K1 Snowville Utah, W USA 41.59N 112.42W
37 X3 Snow Water Lake ◎ Nevada, W USA
191 Q11 Snowy Mountains ▲▲ New South Wales/Victoria, SE Australia
191 Q12 Snowy River ↝ New South Wales/Victoria, SE Australia
46 K5 Snug Corner Acklins Island, SE Bahamas 22.31N 73.51W
178 Jj13 Snuŏl Krâchéh, E Cambodia 12.04N 106.25E
118 J7 Snyatyn Rus. Snyatyn. Ivano-Frankivs'ka Oblast', W Ukraine 48.28N 25.33E
28 L12 Snyder Oklahoma, C USA 34.37N 98.56W
27 O6 Snyder Texas, SW USA 32.43N 100.54W
180 H3 Soalala Mahajanga, W Madagascar 16.04S 45.21E
180 J4 Soanierana-Ivongo Toamasina, E Madagascar 16.52S 49.34E
175 Ss7 Soasiu var. Tidore. Pulau Tidore, E Indonesia 0.40N 127.25E
56 G8 Soatá Boyacá, C Colombia 6.14N 72.42W
180 I5 Soavinandriana Antananarivo, C Madagascar 19.09S 46.43E
176 Yy12 Soba Papua, E Indonesia 4.18S 139.11E
79 V13 Soba Kaduna, C Nigeria 10.58N 8.06E
169 Y16 Sobaek-sanmaek ▲▲ S South Korea
82 F13 Sobat ↝ E Sudan
176 Z12 Sobger, Sungai ↝ Papua, E Indonesia
176 W10 Sobiei Papua, E Indonesia 2.31S 134.30E
130 M3 Sobinka Vladimirskaya Oblast', W Russian Federation 56.00N 39.55E
131 S7 Sobolevo Orenburgskaya Oblast', W Russian Federation 51.57N 51.42E
Soborsin see Săvârşin
170 D15 Sobo-san ▲ Kyūshū, SW Japan 32.50N 131.16E
113 G14 Sobótka Dolnośląskie, SW Poland 50.53N 16.48E
61 O15 Sobradinho Bahia, E Brazil 9.33S 40.56W
Sobradinho, Barragem de see Sobradinho, Represa de
61 O16 Sobradinho, Represa de var. Barragem de Sobradinho. ⊠ E Brazil
60 O13 Sobral Ceará, E Brazil 3.45S 40.19W
107 T4 Sobrarbe physical region NE Spain
111 R10 Soča It. Isonzo. ↝ Italy/Slovenia
112 L11 Sochaczew Mazowieckie, C Poland 52.15N 20.15E
130 L15 Sochi Krasnodarskiy Kray, SW Russian Federation 43.34N 39.46E
116 G13 Sochós var. Sohos, Sokhós. Kentrikí Makedonía, N Greece 40.49N 23.22E
203 R11 Société, Archipel de la var. Archipel de Tahiti, Îles de la Société, Eng. Society Islands. island group W French Polynesia
Société, Îles de la/Society Islands see Société, Archipel de la
23 T11 Society Hill South Carolina, SE USA 34.28N 79.54W
183 W9 Society Ridge undersea feature C Pacific Ocean
64 I5 Socompa, Volcán ▲ N Chile 24.18S 68.03W
Soconusco, Sierra de see Sierra Madre
56 G8 Socorro Santander, C Colombia 6.25N 73.13W
39 R13 Socorro New Mexico, SW USA 33.58N 106.55W
Socotra see Suquţrā
178 Jj15 Soc Trăng var. Khanh Hung. Soc Trăng, S Vietnam 9.36N 105.58E
107 P10 Socuéllamos Castilla-La Mancha, C Spain 39.18N 2.48W
37 W13 Soda Lake salt flat California, W USA
94 L11 Sodankylä Lappi, N Finland 67.25N 26.34E
Sodari see Sodiri
35 R15 Soda Springs Idaho, NW USA 42.39N 111.36W
Soddo/Soddu see Sodo
22 L10 Soddy Daisy Tennessee, S USA 35.14N 85.11W
97 N14 Söderfors Uppsala, C Sweden 60.23N 17.19E
96 N12 Söderhamn Gävleborg, C Sweden 61.19N 17.10E
97 N17 Söderköping Östergötland, S Sweden 58.28N 16.19E
97 N17 Södermanland ◈ county C Sweden
97 O16 Södertälje Stockholm, C Sweden 59.10N 17.39E
82 D10 Sodiri var. Sawdirī, Sodari. Northern Kordofan, C Sudan 14.22N 29.06E
83 I14 Sodo var. Soddo, Soddu. Southern, S Ethiopia 6.49N 37.43E
96 N11 Södra Dellen ◎ C Sweden
97 M19 Södra Vi Kalmar, S Sweden 57.45N 15.45E
20 G9 Sodus Point headland New York, NE USA 43.16N 76.59W
175 Rr17 Soe prev. Soë. Timor, C Indonesia 9.51S 124.28E
174 J14 Soekarno-Hatta ✈ (Jakarta) Jawa, S Indonesia
Soëla-Sund see Soela Väin
120 E5 Soela Väin prev. Eng. Sele Sound, Ger. Dagden-Sund, Soëla-Sund. strait W Estonia
Soemba see Sumba, Pulau
Soembawa see Sumbawa
Soemenep see Sumenep
Soengaipenoeh see Sungaipenuh
Soerabaja see Surabaya
103 G14 Soest Nordrhein-Westfalen, W Germany 51.34N 8.07E
100 J11 Soest Utrecht, C Netherlands 52.10N 5.19E
102 F11 Soeste ↝ NW Germany
100 J11 Soesterberg Utrecht, C Netherlands 52.07N 5.16E
117 E16 Sofádes var. Sofádhes. Thessalía, C Greece 39.19N 22.06E
Sofádhes see Sofádes
85 N18 Sofala Sofala, C Mozambique 20.04S 34.43E
85 N17 Sofala ◈ province C Mozambique
85 N18 Sofala, Baia de bay E Mozambique
180 J3 Sofia seasonal river NW Madagascar
Sofia see Sofiya
117 G19 Sofikó Pelopónnisos, S Greece 37.46N 23.04E
Sofi-Kurgan see Sopu-Korgon
116 G10 Sofiya var. Sophia, Eng. Sofia; Lat. Serdica. ● (Bulgaria) Sofiya-Grad, W Bulgaria 42.42N 23.20E
116 G9 Sofiya ✈ Sofiya-Grad, W Bulgaria 42.42N 23.26E
116 H9 Sofiya ◈ province W Bulgaria
116 G9 Sofiya-Grad ◈ municipality W Bulgaria
Sofiyevka see Sofiyivka
119 S8 Sofiyivka Rus. Sofiyevka. Dnipropetrovs'ka Oblast', E Ukraine 48.03N 33.52E
127 Nn14 Sofiysk Khabarovskiy Kray, SE Russian Federation 51.31N 139.46E
127 N14 Sofiysk Khabarovskiy Kray, SE Russian Federation 52.20N 133.37E
128 I6 Sofporog Respublika Kareliya, NW Russian Federation 65.48N 31.30E
172 Ss15 Sōfu-gan island Izu-shotō, SE Japan
Sog see Sog Xian
56 G9 Sogamoso Boyacá, C Colombia 5.43N 72.55W
142 I11 Soğanlı Çayı ↝ N Turkey
96 E12 Sogn physical region S Norway
96 E12 Sogndalsfjør var. Sogndal. Sogn Og Fjordane, S Norway 61.13N 7.06E
Sogndal see Sogndalsfjøra
97 E18 Søgne Vest-Agder, S Norway 58.04N 7.48E
96 D12 Sognefjorden fjord NE North Sea
96 C12 Sogn Og Fjordane ◈ county S Norway
179 R13 Sogod Leyte, C Philippines 10.25N 125.00E
168 I11 Sogo Nur ◎ N China
165 T12 Sogruma Qinghai, W China 32.31N 100.52E
169 X17 Sŏgwip'o S South Korea 33.13N 126.33E
162 K10 Sog Xian var. Sog. Xizang Zizhiqu, W China 31.52N 93.40E
77 X10 Sohâg var. Sawhāj, Suliag. C Egypt 26.27N 31.43E
Sohar see Şuḩār
66 H9 Sohm Plain undersea feature NW Atlantic Ocean
102 H7 Soholmer Au ↝ N Germany
Sohos see Sochós
Sohrau see Żory
101 F20 Soignies Hainaut, SW Belgium 50.34N 4.04E
165 R15 Soila Xizang Zizhiqu, W China 30.40N 97.07E
105 P4 Soissons anc. Augusta Suessionum, Noviodunum. Aisne, N France 49.22N 3.19E
170 Ff14 Sōja Okayama, Honshū, SW Japan 34.41N 133.45E
158 F13 Sojat Rājasthān, N India 25.55N 73.43E
169 W13 Sŏjosŏn-man inlet W North Korea
118 I4 Sokal' Rus. Sokal. L'vivs'ka Oblast', NW Ukraine 50.28N 24.16E
169 Y14 Sokch'o N South Korea 38.07N 128.33E
142 B15 Söke Aydın, SW Turkey 37.45N 27.24E
201 N12 Sokehs Island island E Micronesia
81 M24 Sokele Katanga, SE Dem. Rep. Congo 9.54S 24.38E
153 R11 Sokh Uzb. Sŭkh. ↝ Kyrgyzstan/Uzbekistan
Sokh see So'x
Sokhós see Sochós
143 Q8 Sokhumi Rus. Sukhumi. NW Georgia 43.01N 41.01E
115 O14 Sokobanja Serbia, E Serbia and Montenegro (Yugoslavia) 43.39N 21.51E
79 R15 Sokodé C Togo 8.58N 1.10E
127 O10 Sokol Magadanskaya Oblast', E Russian Federation 59.51N 150.56E
128 M13 Sokol Vologodskaya Oblast', NW Russian Federation 59.26N 40.09E
112 P9 Sokółka Podlaskie, NE Poland 53.24N 23.30E
78 M11 Sokolo Ségou, W Mali 14.43N 6.02W
113 A16 Sokolov Ger. Falkenau an der Eger; prev. Falknov nad Ohří. Karlovarský Kraj, W Czech Republic 50.10N 12.38E
113 O16 Sokołów Małopolski Podkarpackie, SE Poland 50.12N 22.07E
112 O11 Sokołów Podlaski Mazowieckie, E Poland 52.25N 22.14E
78 G11 Sokone W Senegal 13.52N 16.22W
79 T12 Sokoto Sokoto, NW Nigeria 13.05N 5.15E
79 T12 Sokoto ◈ state NW Nigeria
79 S12 Sokoto ↝ NW Nigeria
Sokotra see Suquţrā
153 U7 Sokuluk Chuyskaya Oblast', N Kyrgyzstan 42.53N 74.19E
118 L7 Sokyryany Chernivets'ka Oblast', W Ukraine 48.28N 27.25E
97 C16 Sola Rogaland, S Norway 58.52N 5.37E
197 C10 Sola Vanua Lava, N Vanuatu 13.51S 167.34E
97 C17 Sola ✈ (Stavanger) Rogaland, S Norway 58.54N 5.36E
83 H18 Solai Rift Valley, W Kenya 0.02N 36.03E
176 Y15 Solaka Papua, E Indonesia 7.52S 138.45E
158 I8 Solan Himāchal Pradesh, N India 30.54N 77.06E
193 A25 Solander Island island SW NZ
Solano see Bahía Solano
161 F15 Solāpur var. Sholāpur. Mahārāshtra, W India 17.42N 75.54E
95 H16 Solberg Västernorrland, C Sweden 63.48N 17.40E
118 K9 Solca Ger. Solka. Suceava, N Romania 47.40N 25.49E
107 O16 Sol, Costa del coastal region S Spain
108 F5 Solda Trentino-Alto Adige, N Italy 46.33N 10.35E
119 N9 Şoldăneşti Rus. Sholdaneshty. N Moldova 47.49N 28.45E
Soldau see Wkra
110 L8 Sölden Tirol, W Austria 46.58N 11.01E
29 P3 Soldier Creek ↝ Kansas, C USA
41 R12 Soldotna Alaska, USA 60.29N 151.03W
112 I10 Solec Kujawski Kujawsko-pomorskie, C Poland 53.04N 18.09E
63 B16 Soledad Santa Fe, C Argentina 30.37S 60.52W
57 E4 Soledad Atlántico, N Colombia 10.54N 74.48W
37 O11 Soledad California, W USA 36.25N 121.19W
57 O7 Soledad Anzoátegui, NE Venezuela 8.10N 63.31W
Soledad see East Falkland
Soledad, Isla see East Falkland
63 H15 Soledade Rio Grande do Sul, S Brazil 28.49S 52.30W
105 Y15 Solenzara Corse, France, C Mediterranean Sea 41.55N 9.24E
Soleure see Solothurn
96 C12 Solheim Hordaland, S Norway 60.54N 5.30E
129 N14 Soligalich Kostromskaya Oblast', NW Russian Federation 59.05N 42.15E
Soligorsk see Salihorsk
99 L20 Solihull C England, UK 52.25N 1.45W
129 U13 Solikamsk Permskaya Oblast', NW Russian Federation 59.37N 56.46E
131 V8 Sol'-Iletsk Orenburgskaya Oblast', W Russian Federation 51.08N 55.05E
59 G17 Solimana, Nevado ▲ S Peru 15.24S 72.49W
60 E13 Solimões, Rio ↝ C Brazil
115 E14 Solin It. Salona; anc. Salonae. Split-Dalmacija, S Croatia 43.33N 16.29E
103 E15 Solingen Nordrhein-Westfalen, W Germany 51.10N 7.04E
Solka see Solca
95 H16 Sollefteå Västernorrland, C Sweden 63.09N 17.15E
97 O15 Sollentuna Stockholm, C Sweden 59.25N 17.55E
96 L13 Sollerön Dalarna, C Sweden 60.55N 14.34E
103 I14 Solling hill range C Germany
97 O16 Solna Stockholm, C Sweden 59.22N 17.58E
130 K3 Solnechnogorsk Moskovskaya Oblast', W Russian Federation 56.07N 37.04E
127 Nn15 Solnechnyy Khabarovskiy Kray, SE Russian Federation 50.41N 136.42E
126 Hh13 Solnechnyy Krasnoyarskiy Kray, C Russian Federation 55.15N 89.48E
127 N11 Solnechnyy Respublika Sakha (Yakutiya), NE Russian Federation 60.13N 137.42E
96 H11 Sølnkletten ▲ S Norway 61.52N 11.32E
109 L17 Solofra Campania, S Italy 40.49N 14.48E
174 Gg9 Solok Sumatera, W Indonesia 0.45S 100.42E
44 C6 Sololá Sololá, W Guatemala 14.46N 91.09W
44 A2 Sololá off. Departamento de Sololá. ◈ department SW Guatemala
83 J16 Sololo Eastern, N Kenya 3.31N 38.39E
44 C4 Soloma Huehuetenango, W Guatemala 15.38N 91.25W
40 M9 Solomon Alaska, USA 64.33N 164.26W
29 N4 Solomon Kansas, C USA 38.55N 97.22W
195 U16 Solomon Islands prev. British Solomon Islands Protectorate. ◆ commonwealth republic W Pacific Ocean
195 T12 Solomon Islands island group PNG/Solomon Islands
28 M3 Solomon River ↝ Kansas, C USA
199 Hh9 Solomon Sea sea W Pacific Ocean
33 U11 Solon Ohio, N USA 41.23N 81.26W
119 T8 Solone Dnipropetrovs'ka Oblast', E Ukraine 48.12N 34.49E
175 R16 Solor, Kepulauan island group S Indonesia
130 M4 Solotcha Ryazanskaya Oblast', W Russian Federation 54.43N 39.50E
110 D7 Solothurn Fr. Soleure. Solothurn, NW Switzerland 47.12N 7.28E
110 D7 Solothurn Fr. Soleure. ◈ canton NW Switzerland
128 J7 Solovetskiye Ostrova island group NW Russian Federation
107 V5 Solsona Cataluña, NE Spain 42.00N 1.31E
115 E14 Šolta It. Solta. island S Croatia
Solţānābād see Kāshmar
148 L4 Solţānīyeh Zanjān, NW Iran 36.24N 48.49E
102 I11 Soltau Niedersachsen, NW Germany 52.58N 9.49E
128 G14 Sol'tsy Novgorodskaya Oblast', W Russian Federation 58.09N 30.22E
Soltüstik Qazaqstan Oblysy see Severnyy Kazakhstan
Solun see Thessaloníki
115 O19 Solunska Glava ▲ C FYR Macedonia 41.43N 21.24E
97 L22 Sölvesborg Blekinge, S Sweden 56.04N 14.34E
99 J15 Solway Firth inlet England/Scotland, UK
84 I13 Solwezi North Western, NW Zambia 12.10S 26.22E
171 Ll14 Sōma Fukushima, Honshū, C Japan 37.49N 140.52E
142 C13 Soma Manisa, W Turkey 39.11N 27.34E
83 M14 Somali ◈ region E Ethiopia
83 O15 Somalia off. Somali Democratic Republic, Som. Jamuuriyada Demuqraadiga Soomaaliyeed, Soomaaliya; prev. Italian Somaliland, Somaliland Protectorate. ◆ republic E Africa
181 N6 Somali Basin undersea feature W Indian Ocean
69 Y8 Somali Plain undersea feature W Indian Ocean
114 J8 Sombor Hung. Zombor. Serbia, NW Serbia and Montenegro (Yugoslavia) 45.46N 19.07E
101 H20 Sombreffe Namur, S Belgium 50.32N 4.39E
42 L10 Sombrerete Zacatecas, C Mexico 23.36N 103.46W
47 V8 Sombrero island N Anguilla
157 Q21 Sombrero Channel channel Nicobar Islands, India
118 H9 Şomcuta Mare Hung. Nagysomkút; prev. Somcuța Mare. Maramureş, N Romania 47.28N 23.30E
178 Ii9 Somdet Kalasin, E Thailand 16.41N 103.44E
101 L15 Someren Noord-Brabant, SE Netherlands 51.22N 5.42E
95 L19 Somero Länsi-Suomi, W Finland 60.37N 23.30E
35 P7 Somers Montana, NW USA 48.04N 114.16W
66 A12 Somerset var. Somerset Village. W Bermuda 32.18N 64.52W
39 Q5 Somerset Colorado, C USA 38.55N 107.27W
22 M7 Somerset Kentucky, S USA 37.05N 84.36W
21 O12 Somerset Massachusetts, NE USA 41.46N 71.07W
99 K23 Somerset cultural region SW England, UK
Somerset East see Somerset-Oos
66 A12 Somerset Island island W Bermuda
207 N9 Somerset Island island Queen Elizabeth Islands, Nunavut, NW Canada
Somerset Nile see Victoria Nile
85 I25 Somerset-Oos Eng. Somerset East. Eastern Cape, S South Africa 32.43S 25.34E
85 E26 Somerset-Wes Eng. Somerset West. Western Cape, SW South Africa 34.01S 18.51E
Somerset West see Somerset-Wes
Somers Islands see Bermuda
20 J17 Somers Point New Jersey, NE USA 39.18N 74.34W
21 P9 Somersworth New Hampshire, NE USA 43.15N 70.52W
38 H15 Somerton Arizona, SW USA 32.36N 114.42W
20 J14 Somerville New Jersey, NE USA 40.34N 74.36W
22 F10 Somerville Tennessee, S USA 35.14N 89.21W
27 U10 Somerville Texas, SW USA 30.21N 96.31W
27 T10 Somerville Lake ⊠ Texas, SW USA
Someş/Somesch/Someşul see Szamos
105 N2 Somme ◈ department N France
105 N2 Somme ↝ N France
97 L18 Sommen Jönköping, S Sweden 58.07N 14.58E
97 M18 Sommen ◎ S Sweden
103 K16 Sömmerda Thüringen, C Germany 51.10N 11.07E
Sommerein see Šamorín
Sommerfeld see Lubsko
57 Y11 Sommet Tabulaire var. Mont Itoupé. ▲ S French Guiana
113 H25 Somogy off. Somogy Megye. ◈ county SW Hungary
Somorja see Šamorín
107 N7 Somosierra, Puerto de pass N Spain 41.07N 3.36W
197 J13 Somosomo Taveuni, N Fiji 16.46S 179.57W
44 I9 Somotillo Chinandega, NW Nicaragua 13.01N 86.54W
44 I8 Somoto Madriz, NW Nicaragua 13.28N 86.36W
112 I11 Sompolno Wielkopolskie, C Poland 52.24N 18.30E
107 S3 Somport var. Puerto de Somport, Fr. Col du Somport; anc. Summus Portus. pass France/Spain see also Somport, Col du 42.48N 0.33W
104 J17 Somport, Col du var. Puerto de Somport, Sp. Somport; anc. Summus Portus. pass France/Spain see also Somport 42.47N 0.33W
Somport, Puerto de see Somport/Somport, Col du
101 K15 Son Noord-Brabant, S Netherlands 51.32N 5.34E
97 H15 Son Akershus, S Norway 59.31N 10.42E
160 L9 Son var. Sone. ↝ C India
45 R16 Soná Veraguas, W Panama 08.00N 81.20W
160 M12 Sonapur prev. Sonepur. Orissa, E India 20.49N 83.52E
176 Vv10 Sonar Papua, E Indonesia 2.31S 133.01E
97 G24 Sønderborg Ger. Sonderburg. Sønderjylland, SW Denmark 54.55N 9.48E
Sonderburg see Sønderborg
97 F24 Sønderjylland off. Sønderjyllands Amt. ◈ county SW Denmark
103 K15 Sondershausen Thüringen, C Germany 51.22N 10.52E
Søndre Strømfjord see Kangerlussuaq
108 E6 Sondrio Lombardia, N Italy 46.10N 9.52E
Sone see Son
Sonepur see Sonapur
59 K22 Sonequera ▲ S Bolivia 22.06S 67.10W
178 Kk12 Sông Câu Phu Yên, C Vietnam 13.25N 109.12E
178 J15 Sông Đôc Minh Hai, S Vietnam 9.03N 104.51E
83 H25 Songea Ruvuma, S Tanzania 10.42S 35.39E
176 Z11 Songgato, Sungai ↝ Papua, E Indonesia
169 X10 Songhua Hu ◎ NE China
169 Y7 Songhua Jiang var. Sungari. ↝ NE China
167 S8 Songjiang Shanghai Shi, E China 31.01N 121.13E
Sŏngjin see Kimch'aek
178 H17 Songkhla var. Songkla, Mal. Singora. Songkhla, SW Thailand 7.12N 100.34E
Songkla see Songkhla
169 T13 Song Ling ▲▲ NE China
169 W14 Songnim SW North Korea 38.43N 125.40E
84 B10 Songo Uíge, NW Angola 7.30S 14.55E
85 M15 Songo Tete, NW Mozambique 15.35S 32.43E
81 F21 Songololo Bas-Congo, SW Dem. Rep. Congo 5.40S 14.04E
166 H7 Songpan prev. Sungqu. Sichuan, C China 32.49N 103.39E
169 Y17 Sŏngsan S South Korea
167 R11 Songxi Fujian, SE China 27.33N 118.46E
166 M6 Songxian var. Song Xian. Henan, C China 34.11N 112.04E
167 R10 Songyin Zhejiang, SE China 28.29N 119.27E
169 V9 Songyuan var. Fu-yü, Petuna; prev. Fuyu. Jilin, NE China 45.10N 124.52E
169 P11 Sonid Youqi var. Saihon Tal. Nei Mongol Zizhiqu, N China 42.45N 112.36E
169 P11 Sonid Zuoqi Nei Mongol Zizhiqu, N China 43.49N 113.36E
158 I10 Sonīpat Haryāna, N India 29.00N 77.01E
95 M15 Sonkajärvi Itä-Suomi, C Finland 63.40N 27.30E
178 J6 Sơn La Sơn La, N Vietnam 21.19N 103.55E
155 O16 Sonmiāni Balūchistān, S Pakistan 25.24N 66.37E
155 O16 Sonmiāni Bay bay S Pakistan
103 K18 Sonneberg Thüringen, C Germany 50.22N 11.10E
103 N24 Sonntagshorn ▲ Austria/Germany 47.40N 12.42E
Sonoita see Sonoyta
42 E3 Sonoita, Rio var. Río Sonoyta. ↝ Mexico/USA
37 N7 Sonoma California, W USA 38.16N 122.28W
37 T3 Sonoma Peak ▲ Nevada, W USA 40.50N 117.34W
37 P8 Sonora California, W USA 37.58N 120.22W
27 O10 Sonora Texas, SW USA 30.31N 100.40W
42 F5 Sonora ◈ state NW Mexico
37 X17 Sonoran Desert var. Desierto de Altar. desert Mexico/USA see also Altar, Desierto de
42 G5 Sonora, Río ↝ NW Mexico
42 E2 Sonoyta var. Sonoita. Sonora, NW Mexico 31.49N 112.50W
Sonoyta, Río see Sonoita, Rio
148 K6 Sonqor var. Sunqur. Kermānshāh, W Iran 34.45N 47.39E
107 N9 Sonseca var. Sonseca con Casalgordo. Castilla-La Mancha, C Spain 39.40N 3.58W
Sonseca con Casalgordo see Sonseca
56 E9 Sonsón Antioquia, W Colombia 5.41N 75.15W
44 E7 Sonsonate Sonsonate, W El Salvador 13.43N 89.43W
44 A9 Sonsonate ◈ department SW El Salvador
196 A10 Sonsorol Islands island group S Palau
114 J9 Sonta Hung. Szond; prev. Szonta. Serbia, NW Serbia and Montenegro (Yugoslavia) 45.34N 19.06E
178 Jj6 Sơn Tây var. Sontay. Ha Tây, N Vietnam 21.06N 105.31E
103 J25 Sonthofen Bayern, S Germany 47.31N 10.16E
Soochow see Suzhou
Soomaaliya/Soomaaliyeed, Jamuuriyada Demuqraadiga see Somalia
Soome Laht see Finland, Gulf of
Sooner State see Oklahoma
25 V5 Soperton Georgia, SE USA 32.22N 82.35W
178 J6 Sop Hao Houaphan, N Laos 20.33N 104.25E
Sophia see Sofiya
175 Tt5 Sopi Pulau Morotai, E Indonesia 2.36N 128.32E
Sopianae see Pécs
176 Vv11 Sopinusa Papua, E Indonesia 3.31S 132.55E
175 Tt5 Sopi, Tanjung headland Pulau Morotai, N Indonesia 2.39N 128.34E
83 B14 Sopo ↝ W Sudan
Sopockinie/Sopotskin see Sapotskino
116 I9 Sopot Plovdiv, C Bulgaria 42.40N 24.45E
112 I7 Sopot Ger. Zoppot. Pomorskie, N Poland 54.25N 18.33E
178 H8 Sop Prap var. Ban Sop Prap. Lampang, NW Thailand 17.55N 99.19E
113 G22 Sopron Ger. Ödenburg. Győr-Moson-Sopron, NW Hungary 47.40N 16.34E
153 U11 Sopu-Korgon var. Sofi-Kurgan. Oshskaya Oblast', SW Kyrgyzstan 40.03N 73.30E
158 H5 Sopur Jammu and Kashmir, NW India 34.19N 74.28E
109 J15 Sora Lazio, C Italy 41.43N 13.37E
160 N13 Sorada Orissa, E India 19.46N 84.28E
95 H17 Söråker Västernorrland, C Sweden 62.31N 17.31E
59 J17 Sorata La Paz, W Bolivia 15.49S 68.39W
Sorau/Sorau in der Niederlausitz see Żary
107 Q14 Sorbas Andalucía, S Spain 37.06N 2.06W
Sord/Sórd Choluim Chille see Swords
13 O11 Sorel Quebec, SE Canada 46.02N 73.06W
191 P17 Sorell Tasmania, SE Australia 42.49S 147.34E
191 O17 Sorell, Lake ◎ Tasmania, SE Australia
108 E8 Soresina Lombardia, N Italy 45.16N 9.51E
97 D14 Sørfjorden fjord S Norway
96 N11 Sörforsa Gävleborg, C Sweden 61.45N 17.00E
105 R14 Sorgues Vaucluse, SE France 44.00N 4.52E
142 K13 Sorgun Yozgat, C Turkey 39.49N 35.10E
107 P5 Soria Castilla-León, N Spain 41.46N 2.26W
107 P6 Soria ◈ province Castilla-León, N Spain
63 D19 Soriano Soriano, SW Uruguay 33.25S 58.21W
63 D19 Soriano ◈ department SW Uruguay
94 O4 Sørkapp headland SW Svalbard 76.34N 16.33E
149 T5 Sorkh, Kūh-e ▲▲ NE Iran
97 I23 Sorø Vestsjælland, E Denmark 55.25N 11.34E
118 M8 Soroca Rus. Soroki. N Moldova 48.10N 28.18E
62 L10 Sorocaba São Paulo, S Brazil 23.28S 47.27W
Sorochino see Sarochyna
131 T7 Sorochinsk Orenburgskaya Oblast', W Russian Federation 52.26N 53.10E
Soroki see Soroca
196 H15 Sorol atoll Caroline Islands, W Micronesia
176 Uu9 Sorong Papua, E Indonesia 0.49S 131.16E
83 G17 Soroti C Uganda 1.42N 33.37E
Sørøy see Sørøya
94 J8 Sørøya var. Sørøy. island N Norway
106 G11 Sorraia, Rio ↝ C Portugal
94 I10 Sørreisa Troms, N Norway 69.08N 18.09E
109 K18 Sorrento anc. Surrentum. Campania, S Italy 40.37N 14.22E
106 H10 Sor, Ribeira de stream C Portugal
205 T3 Sør Rondane Mountains ▲▲ Antarctica
95 H14 Sorsele Västerbotten, N Sweden 65.31N 17.34E
109 B17 Sorso Sardegna, Italy, C Mediterranean Sea 40.46N 8.33E
179 Qq11 Sorsogon Luzon, N Philippines 12.57N 124.04E
107 U4 Sort Cataluña, NE Spain 42.25N 1.07E
128 H11 Sortavala Respublika Kareliya, NW Russian Federation 61.45N 30.36E
109 L25 Sortino Sicilia, Italy, C Mediterranean Sea 37.10N 15.01E
94 G10 Sortland Nordland, C Norway 68.40N 15.22E
96 G9 Sør-Trøndelag ◈ county S Norway
97 I15 Sørumsand Akershus, S Norway 59.58N 11.13E
120 D6 Sörve Säär headland SW Estonia 57.54N 22.02E
97 K22 Sösdala Skåne, S Sweden 56.00N 13.36E
107 R4 Sos del Rey Católico Aragón, NE Spain 42.30N 1.13W
95 F15 Sösjöfjällen ▲ C Sweden 63.51N 13.15E
130 K7 Sosna ↝ W Russian Federation
64 H12 Sosneado, Cerro ▲ W Argentina 34.44S 69.52W
129 S9 Sosnogorsk Respublika Komi, NW Russian Federation 63.33N 53.55E
128 J8 Sosnovets Respublika Kareliya, NW Russian Federation 64.25N 34.23E
Sosnovets see Sosnowiec
131 Q3 Sosnovka Chavash Respubliki, W Russian Federation 56.18N 47.14E
129 S16 Sosnovka Kirovskaya Oblast', NW Russian Federation 56.15N 51.20E
128 M6 Sosnovka Murmanskaya Oblast', NW Russian Federation 66.28N 40.31E
130 M6 Sosnovka Tambovskaya Oblast', W Russian Federation 53.14N 41.19E
128 H12 Sosnovo Fin. Rautu. Leningradskaya Oblast', NW Russian Federation 60.30N 30.13E
126 K15 Sosnovo-Ozerskoye Respublika Buryatiya, S Russian Federation 52.34N 111.36E
Sosnovyy Bor see Sasnovy Bor
113 J16 Sosnowiec Ger. Sosnowitz, Rus. Sosnovets. Śląskie, S Poland 50.16N 19.07E
Sosnowitz see Sosnowiec
119 R2 Sosnytsya Chernihivs'ka Oblast', N Ukraine 51.31N 32.30E
111 V10 Šoštanj N Slovenia 46.23N 15.03E
125 F10 Sos'va Sverdlovskaya Oblast', C Russian Federation 59.13N 61.58E
56 D12 Sotará, Volcán ▲ S Colombia 2.04N 76.40W
78 D10 Sotavento, Ilhas de var. Leeward Islands. island group S Cape Verde

◆ Country
● Country Capital
◇ Dependent Territory
○ Dependent Territory Capital
◈ Administrative Region
✈ International Airport
▲ Mountain
▲▲ Mountain Range
Volcano
↝ River
◎ Lake
⊠ Reservoir

95 N15 **Sotkamo** Oulu, C Finland 64.05N 28.30E
111 W11 **Sotla** ♒ E Slovenia
43 P10 **Soto la Marina** Tamaulipas, C Mexico 23.46N 98.12W
43 P10 **Soto la Marina, Río** ♒ C Mexico
43 X12 **Sotuta** Yucatán, SE Mexico 20.34N 89.00W
81 F17 **Souanké** La Sangha, NW Congo 2.03N 14.01E
78 M17 **Soubré** S Ivory Coast 5.49N 6.34W
117 H24 **Soúda** *var.* Soúdha, *Eng.* Suda. Kríti, Greece, E Mediterranean Sea 35.28N 24.04E
Soúdha *see* Soúda
Soueida *see* As Suwaydā'
116 L12 **Souflí** *prev.* Souflíon. Anatolikí Makedonía kai Thrákí, NE Greece 41.12N 26.17E
Souflíon *see* Souflí
47 S11 **Soufrière** W Saint Lucia 13.51N 61.03W
47 X6 **Soufrière** ⛰ Basse Terre, S Guadeloupe 16.03N 61.39W
104 M13 **Souillac** Lot, S France 44.53N 1.29E
181 Y17 **Souillac** S Mauritius 20.31S 57.31E
76 M5 **Souk Ahras** NE Algeria 36.14N 8.00E
76 E6 **Souk-el-Arba-Rharb** *var.* Souk el Arba du Rharb, Souk-el-Arba-du-Rharb, Souk-el-Arba-el-Rhab. NW Morocco 34.38N 6.00W
Soukhné *see* As Sukhnah
169 X14 **Sŏul** *off.* Sŏul-t'ŭkpyŏlsi, *Eng.* Seoul, *Jap.* Keijō; *prev.* Kyŏngsŏng. ● (South Korea) NW South Korea 37.30N 126.57E
104 J11 **Soulac-sur-Mer** Gironde, SW France 45.31N 1.06W
101 L19 **Soumagne** Liège, E Belgium 50.36N 5.48E
20 M14 **Sound Beach** Long Island, New York, NE USA 40.56N 72.58W
97 J22 **Sound, The** *Dan.* Øresund, *Swe.* Öresund. *strait* Denmark/Sweden
117 H20 **Soúnio, Akrotírio** *headland* C Greece 37.39N 24.01E
144 F8 **Soûr** *var.* Şūr; *anc.* Tyre. SW Lebanon 33.18N 35.30E
Sources, Mont-aux- *see* Phofung
106 G8 **Soure** Coimbra, N Portugal 40.04N 8.37W
9 W17 **Souris** Manitoba, S Canada 49.37N 100.16W
11 Q14 **Souris** Prince Edward Island, SE Canada 46.22N 62.16W
30 L2 **Souris River** *var.* Mouse River. ♒ Canada/USA
27 X10 **Sour Lake** Texas, SW USA 30.08N 94.24W
117 F17 **Sourpi** Thessalía, C Greece 39.07N 22.54E
106 H11 **Sousel** Portalegre, C Portugal 38.57N 7.40W
77 N6 **Sousse** *var.* Sūsah. NE Tunisia 35.45N 10.37E
12 H11 **South** ♒ Ontario, S Canada
South *see* Sud
85 G23 **South Africa** *off.* Republic of South Africa, *Afr.* Suid-Afrika. ◆ *republic* S Africa
48-49 **South America** *continent*
2 J17 **South American Plate** *tectonic feature*
99 M23 **Southampton** *hist.* Hamwih, *Lat.* Clausentum. S England, UK 50.54N 1.22W
21 N14 **Southampton** Long Island, New York, NE USA 40.52N 72.22W
15 M5 **Southampton Island** *island* Nunavut, NE Canada
157 P20 **South Andaman** *island* Andaman Islands, India, NE Indian Ocean
11 Q6 **South Aulatsivik Island** *island* Newfoundland and Labrador, E Canada
190 E4 **South Australia** ◆ *state* S Australia
South Australian Abyssal Plain *see* South Australian Plain
199 Gg13 **South Australian Basin** *undersea feature* SW Indian Ocean
181 X12 **South Australian Plain** *var.* South Australian Abyssal Plain. *undersea feature* SE Indian Ocean
39 R13 **South Baldy** ▲ New Mexico, SW USA 33.59N 107.11W
25 Y14 **South Bay** Florida, SE USA 26.39N 80.43W
12 E12 **South Baymouth** Manitoulin Island, Ontario, S Canada 45.33N 82.01W
32 L10 **South Beloit** Illinois, N USA 42.29N 89.02W
33 O11 **South Bend** Indiana, N USA 41.40N 86.15W
27 R6 **South Bend** Texas, SW USA 32.58N 98.39W
34 F9 **South Bend** Washington, NW USA 46.38N 123.48W
South Beveland *see* Zuid-Beveland
South Borneo *see* Kalimantan Selatan
23 U7 **South Boston** Virginia, NE USA 36.42N 78.54W
190 F2 **South Branch Neales** *seasonal river* South Australia
23 U3 **South Branch Potomac River** ♒ West Virginia, NE USA
193 H19 **Southbridge** Canterbury, South Island, NZ 43.49S 172.17E
21 N12 **Southbridge** Massachusetts, NE USA 42.03N 72.00W
197 P17 **South Bruny Island** *island* Tasmania, SE Australia
20 L7 **South Burlington** Vermont, NE USA 44.27N 73.08W
46 M6 **South Caicos** *island* S Turks and Caicos Islands
South Cape *see* Ka Lae
25 V3 **South Carolina** *off.* State of South Carolina; also known as The Palmetto State. ◆ *state* SE USA
South Carpathians *see* Carpaţii Meridionali
South Celebes *see* Sulawesi Selatan
23 Q5 **South Charleston** West Virginia, NE USA 38.22N 81.42W
198 F7 **South China Basin** *undersea feature* SE South China Sea
198 F7 **South China Sea** *Chin.* Nan Hai, *Ind.* Laut Cina Selatan, *Vtn.* Biên Đông. *sea* SE Asia
35 Z10 **South Dakota** *off.* State of South Dakota; also known as The Coyote State, Sunshine State. ◆ *state* N USA
25 X10 **South Daytona** Florida, SE USA 29.09N 81.01W
39 R10 **South Domingo Pueblo** New Mexico, SW USA 35.28N 106.24W
99 N23 **South Downs** *hill range* SE England, UK
85 I21 **South East** ◆ *district* SE Botswana
67 H15 **South East Bay** *bay* Ascension Island, C Atlantic Ocean
191 O17 **South East Cape** *headland* Tasmania, SE Australia 43.36S 146.52E
40 K10 **Southeast Cape** *headland* Saint Lawrence Island, Alaska, USA 62.56N 169.39W
South-East Celebes *see* Sulawesi Tenggara
198 G14 **Southeast Indian Ridge** *undersea feature* Indian Ocean/Pacific Ocean
Southeast Island *see* Tagula Island
199 Mm16 **Southeast Pacific Basin** *var.* Belling Hausen Mulde. *undersea feature* SE Pacific Ocean
67 H15 **South East Point** *headland* SE Ascension Island
191 O14 **South East Point** *headland* Victoria, S Australia 39.10S 146.21E
203 Z3 **South East Point** *headland* Kiritimati, NE Kiribati 1.42N 157.10W
46 L5 **Southeast Point** *headland* Mayaguana, SE Bahamas 22.15N 72.44W
South-East Sulawesi *see* Sulawesi Tenggara
9 U12 **Southend** Saskatchewan, C Canada 56.19N 103.13W
99 P22 **Southend-on-Sea** E England, UK 51.33N 0.43E
85 H20 **Southern** *var.* Bangwaketse, Ngwaketze. ◆ *district* SE Botswana
83 I15 **Southern** ◆ *region* S Ethiopia
144 E13 **Southern** ◆ *district* S Israel
85 N15 **Southern** ◆ *region* S Malawi
85 I15 **Southern** ◆ *province* S Zambia
193 E19 **Southern Alps** ▲ South Island, NZ
202 K15 **Southern Cook Islands** *island group* S Cook Islands
188 K12 **Southern Cross** Western Australia 31.17S 119.15E
82 A12 **Southern Darfur** ◆ *state* W Sudan
194 F13 **Southern Highlands** ◆ *province* W PNG
9 V11 **Southern Indian Lake** ◎ Manitoba, C Canada
82 E11 **Southern Kordofan** ◆ *state* C Sudan
197 L15 **Southern Lau Group** *island group* Lau Group, SE Fiji
181 S13 **Southern Ocean** *ocean*
23 T10 **Southern Pines** North Carolina, SE USA 35.10N 79.23W
161 J26 **Southern Province** ◆ *province* S Sri Lanka
98 I13 **Southern Uplands** ▲ S Scotland, UK
Southern Urals *see* Yuzhnyy Ural
191 P16 **South Esk River** ♒ Tasmania, SE Australia
9 U16 **Southey** Saskatchewan, S Canada 50.53N 104.27W
29 V2 **South Fabius River** ♒ Missouri, C USA
33 S10 **Southfield** Michigan, N USA 42.28N 83.12W
199 J11 **South Fiji Basin** *undersea feature* S Pacific Ocean
99 Q22 **South Foreland** *headland* SE England, UK 51.08N 1.22E
37 P7 **South Fork American River** ♒ California, W USA
30 K7 **South Fork Grand River** ♒ South Dakota, N USA
37 T12 **South Fork Kern River** ♒ California, W USA
41 Q7 **South Fork Koyukuk River** ♒ Alaska, USA
41 Q11 **South Fork Kuskokwim River** ♒ Alaska, USA
28 H2 **South Fork Republican River** ♒ C USA
28 L3 **South Fork Solomon River** ♒ Kansas, C USA
33 P5 **South Fox Island** *island* Michigan, N USA
22 G8 **South Fulton** Tennessee, S USA 36.28N 88.53W
205 U10 **South Geomagnetic Pole** *pole* Antarctica 78.30S 111.00E
67 J20 **South Georgia** *island* South Georgia and the South Sandwich Islands, SW Atlantic Ocean
67 K21 **South Georgia and the South Sandwich Islands** ◇ *UK dependent territory* SW Atlantic Ocean
49 Y14 **South Georgia Ridge** *var.* North Scotia Ridge. *undersea feature* SW Atlantic Ocean
189 Q1 **South Goulburn Island** *island* Northern Territory, N Australia
159 U16 **South Hatia Island** *island* SE Bangladesh
33 O10 **South Haven** Michigan, N USA 42.24N 86.16W
23 V7 **South Hill** Virginia, NE USA 36.43N 78.07W
South Holland *see* Zuid-Holland
23 P8 **South Holston Lake** ⊠ Tennessee/Virginia, S USA
183 N1 **South Honshu Ridge** *undersea feature* W Pacific Ocean
28 M6 **South Hutchinson** Kansas, C USA 38.01N 97.56W
157 K21 **South Huvadhu Atoll** *var.* Gaafu Dhaalu Atoll. *atoll* S Maldives
181 U14 **South Indian Basin** *undersea feature* Indian Ocean/Pacific Ocean
9 W11 **South Indian Lake** Manitoba, C Canada 56.48N 98.55W
83 I17 **South Island** *island* NW Kenya
193 C20 **South Island** *island* S NZ
67 B23 **South Jason** *island* Jason Islands, NW Falkland Islands
South Kalimantan *see* Kalimantan Selatan
South Kazakhstan *see* Yuzhnyy Kazakhstan
169 X15 **South Korea** *off.* Republic of Korea, *Kor.* Taehan Min'guk. ◆ *republic* E Asia
37 Q6 **South Lake Tahoe** California, W USA 38.56N 119.57W
27 N6 **Southland** Texas, SW USA 33.16N 101.31W
193 B23 **Southland** *off.* Southland Region. ◆ *region* South Island, NZ
31 N15 **South Loup River** ♒ Nebraska, C USA
157 K19 **South Maalhosmadulu Atoll** *var.* Baa Atoll. *atoll* N Maldives
12 E15 **South Maitland** ♒ Ontario, S Canada
198 Ff9 **South Makassar Basin** *undersea feature* E Java Sea
33 O6 **South Manitou Island** *island* Michigan, N USA
157 K18 **South Miladummadulu Atoll** *atoll* N Maldives
23 X8 **South Mills** North Carolina, SE USA 36.28N 76.18W
14 G7 **South Nahanni** ♒ Northwest Territories, NW Canada
41 P13 **South Naknek** Alaska, USA 58.39N 157.01W
12 M13 **South Nation** ♒ Ontario, SE Canada
46 F9 **South Negril Point** *headland* W Jamaica 18.14N 78.21W
157 K20 **South Nilandhe Atoll** *var.* Dhaalu Atoll. *atoll* C Maldives
38 L2 **South Ogden** Utah, W USA 41.09N 111.58W
20 M14 **Southold** Long Island, New York, NE USA 41.03N 72.24W
204 H1 **South Orkney Islands** *island group* Antarctica
143 S9 **South Ossetia** *former autonomous region* SW Georgia
South Pacific Basin *see* Southwest Pacific Basin
21 P7 **South Paris** Maine, NE USA 44.14N 70.29W
35 U15 **South Pass** *pass* Wyoming, C USA 42.20N 108.55W
201 U13 **South Pass** *passage* Chuuk Islands, C Micronesia
22 K10 **South Pittsburg** Tennessee, S USA 35.00N 85.42W
30 K15 **South Platte River** ♒ Colorado/Nebraska, C USA
33 T16 **South Point** Ohio, N USA 38.25N 82.35W
67 G15 **South Point** *headland* S Ascension Island
33 R6 **South Point** *headland* Michigan, N USA 44.51N 83.17W
South Point *see* Ka Lae
205 P9 **South Pole** *pole* Antarctica 90.00S 0.00E
191 P17 **Southport** Tasmania, SE Australia 43.26S 146.57E
99 K17 **Southport** NW England, UK 53.39N 3.01W
23 V12 **Southport** North Carolina, SE USA 33.55N 78.01W
21 P8 **South Portland** Maine, NE USA 43.38N 70.14W
12 H12 **South River** Ontario, S Canada 45.48N 79.21W
23 U11 **South River** ♒ North Carolina, SE USA
98 K5 **South Ronaldsay** *island* NE Scotland, UK
38 L2 **South Salt Lake** Utah, W USA 40.42N 111.52W
67 L21 **South Sandwich Islands** *island group* SE South Georgia and South Sandwich Islands
67 K21 **South Sandwich Trench** *undersea feature* SW Atlantic Ocean
9 S16 **South Saskatchewan** ♒ Alberta/Saskatchewan, S Canada
67 I21 **South Scotia Ridge** *undersea feature* S Scotia Sea
9 V10 **South Seal** ♒ Manitoba, C Canada
204 G4 **South Shetland Islands** *island group* Antarctica
67 H22 **South Shetland Trough** *undersea feature* Atlantic Ocean/Pacific Ocean
99 M14 **South Shields** NE England, UK 55.00N 1.25W
31 R13 **South Sioux City** Nebraska, C USA 42.28N 96.24W
199 I10 **South Solomon Trench** *undersea feature* W Pacific Ocean
191 V3 **South Stradbroke Island** *island* Queensland, E Australia
South Sulawesi *see* Sulawesi Selatan
South Sumatra *see* Sumatera Selatan
192 K11 **South Taranaki Bight** *bight* SE Tasman Sea
South Tasmania Plateau *see* Tasman Plateau
38 M15 **South Tucson** Arizona, SW USA 32.11N 110.56W
10 H9 **South Twin Island** *island* Nunavut, C Canada
98 E9 **South Uist** *island* NW Scotland, UK
South-West *see* Sud-Ouest
South-West Africa/South West Africa *see* Namibia
67 F15 **South West Bay** *bay* Ascension Island, C Atlantic Ocean
191 N18 **South West Cape** *headland* Tasmania, SE Australia 43.34S 146.01E
193 B26 **South West Cape** *headland* Stewart Island, NZ 47.15S 167.28E
40 J10 **Southwest Cape** *headland* Saint Lawrence Island, Alaska, USA 63.19N 171.27W
178 Mm13 **Southwest Cay** *island* NW Spratly Islands
Southwest Indian Ocean Ridge *see* Southwest Indian Ridge
181 N11 **Southwest Indian Ridge** *var.* Southwest Indian Ocean Ridge. *undersea feature* SW Indian Ocean
199 Kk13 **Southwest Pacific Basin** *var.* South Pacific Basin. *undersea feature* SE Pacific Ocean
46 H2 **Southwest Point** *headland* Great Abaco, N Bahamas 25.50N 77.12W
203 X3 **South West Point** *headland* Kiritimati, NE Kiribati 1.52N 157.34E
67 G25 **South West Point** *headland* SW Saint Helena 16.00S 5.48W
27 P5 **South Wichita River** ♒ Texas, SW USA
99 Q20 **Southwold** E England, UK 52.15N 1.36E
21 Q12 **South Yarmouth** Massachusetts, NE USA 41.38N 70.09W
118 J10 **Sovata** *Hung.* Szováta. Mureş, C Romania 46.36N 25.04E
109 N22 **Soverato** Calabria, SW Italy 38.40N 16.31E
Sovetabad *see* Ghafurov
130 C2 **Sovetsk** *Ger.* Tilsit. Kaliningradskaya Oblast', W Russian Federation 53.04N 21.52E
129 Q15 **Sovetsk** Kirovskaya Oblast', NW Russian Federation 57.37N 49.02E
131 N10 **Sovetskaya** Rostovskaya Oblast', SW Russian Federation 49.00N 42.09E
127 O15 **Sovetskaya Gavan'** Khabarovskiy Kray, SE Russian Federation 48.54N 140.19E
125 F10 **Sovetskiy** Khanty-Mansiyskiy Avtonomnyy Okrug, C Russian Federation 61.20N 63.34E
Sovetskoye *see* Ketchenery
152 I15 **Sovet"yab** *prev.* Sovet"yap. Akhalskiy Velayat, S Turkmenistan 36.29N 61.13E
Sovet"yap *see* Sovet"yab
119 U12 **Sovyets'kyy** Respublika Krym, S Ukraine 45.20N 34.54E
85 I18 **Sowa** *var.* Sua. Central, NE Botswana 20.33S 26.18E
85 I18 **Sowa Pan** *salt lake* NE Botswana
176 Ww9 **Sowek** Papua, E Indonesia 0.46S 135.31E
85 J21 **Soweto** Gauteng, NE South Africa 26.08S 27.53E
153 R11 **So'x** *Rus.* Sokh. Farg'ona Viloyati, E Uzbekistan 39.56N 71.10E
Sōya-kaikyō *see* La Perouse Strait
172 Pp1 **Sōya-misaki** *headland* Hokkaidō, NE Japan 45.31N 141.55E
129 N7 **Soyana** ♒ NW Russian Federation
152 A8 **Soye, Mys** *var.* Mys Suz. *headland* NW Turkmenistan 41.47N 52.27E
84 A10 **Soyo** Zaire, NW Angola 6.07S 12.19E
82 J10 **Soyra** ▲ C Eritrea 14.46N 39.29E
Sozaq *see* Suzak
121 P16 **Sozh** *Rus.* Sozh. ♒ NE Europe
116 N10 **Sozopol** *prev.* Sizebolu *anc.* Apollonia. Burgas, E Bulgaria 42.25N 27.42E
180 J15 **Sœurs, Les** *island group* Inner Islands, W Seychelles
101 L20 **Spa** Liège, E Belgium 50.28N 5.52E
204 I7 **Spaatz Island** *island* Antarctica
150 M14 **Space Launching Centre** *space station* Kzylorda, S Kazakhstan 45.50N 63.20E
107 O7 **Spain** *off.* Kingdom of Spain, *Sp.* España; *anc.* Hispania, Iberia, *Lat.* Hispana. ◆ *monarchy* SW Europe
Spalato *see* Split
99 O19 **Spalding** E England, UK 52.48N 0.06W
12 D11 **Spanish** Ontario, S Canada 46.12N 82.21W
38 L3 **Spanish Fork** Utah, W USA 40.09N 111.40W
66 B12 **Spanish Point** *headland* C Bermuda 32.18N 64.49W
12 E9 **Spanish River** ♒ Ontario, S Canada
46 K13 **Spanish Town** *hist.* St.Iago de la Vega. C Jamaica 18.00N 76.57W
117 H24 **Spánta, Akrotírio** *headland* Kríti, Greece, E Mediterranean Sea 35.40N 23.44E
37 Q5 **Sparks** Nevada, W USA 39.32N 119.45W
Sparnacum *see* Épernay
97 N16 **Sparreholm** Södermanland, C Sweden 59.04N 16.51E
25 U4 **Sparta** Georgia, SE USA 33.16N 82.58W
32 K16 **Sparta** Illinois, N USA 38.07N 89.42W
33 P9 **Sparta** Michigan, N USA 43.09N 85.42W
23 R8 **Sparta** North Carolina, SE USA 36.34N 81.21W
22 L9 **Sparta** Tennessee, S USA 35.55N 85.27W
32 J7 **Sparta** Wisconsin, N USA 43.57N 90.49W
Sparta *see* Spárti
23 Q11 **Spartanburg** South Carolina, SE USA 34.57N 81.55W
122 F10 **Spartel, Cap** *headland* N Morocco 35.49N 5.55W
117 F21 **Spárti** *Eng.* Sparta. Pelopónnisos, S Greece 37.04N 22.25E
109 B21 **Spartivento, Capo** *headland* Sardegna, Italy, C Mediterranean Sea 38.52N 8.50E
9 P17 **Sparwood** British Columbia, SW Canada 49.45N 114.45W
130 I4 **Spas-Demensk** Kaluzhskaya Oblast', W Russian Federation 54.22N 34.16E
130 M4 **Spas-Klepiki** Ryazanskaya Oblast', W Russian Federation 55.08N 40.15E
Spasovo *see* Kulen Vakuf
127 N17 **Spassk-Dal'niy** Primorskiy Kray, SE Russian Federation 44.34N 132.52E
130 M5 **Spassk-Ryazanskiy** Ryazanskaya Oblast', W Russian Federation 54.25N 40.21E
117 H19 **Spáta** Attikí, C Greece 37.58N 23.55E
124 O12 **Spátha, Akrotírio** *headland* Kríti, Greece, E Mediterranean Sea 35.42N 23.43E
Špatrjan *see* Paternion
30 I9 **Spearfish** South Dakota, N USA 44.29N 103.51W
27 O1 **Spearman** Texas, SW USA 36.12N 101.11W
67 C25 **Speedwell Island** *island* S Falkland Islands
67 C25 **Speedwell Island Settlement** S Falkland Islands 52.13S 59.40W
67 G25 **Speery Island** *island* S Saint Helena
47 N14 **Speightstown** NW Barbados 13.13N 59.37W
108 I13 **Spello** Umbria, C Italy 43.00N 12.41E
41 R12 **Spenard** Alaska, USA 61.09N 150.03W
Spence Bay *see* Taloyoak
33 O14 **Spencer** Indiana, N USA 39.18N 86.46W
31 T12 **Spencer** Iowa, C USA 43.09N 95.07W
31 P12 **Spencer** Nebraska, C USA 42.52N 98.42W
23 S9 **Spencer** North Carolina, SE USA 35.41N 80.26W
22 L9 **Spencer** Tennessee, S USA 35.46N 85.27W
23 Q4 **Spencer** West Virginia, NE USA 38.48N 81.21W
32 K6 **Spencer** Wisconsin, N USA 44.46N 90.17W
190 G10 **Spencer, Cape** *headland* South Australia 35.17S 136.52E
41 V13 **Spencer, Cape** *headland* Alaska, USA 58.12N 136.39W
190 H9 **Spencer Gulf** *gulf* South Australia
20 F9 **Spencerport** New York, NE USA 43.11N 77.48W
33 Q12 **Spencerville** Ohio, N USA 40.42N 84.21W
117 E17 **Sperchеiáda** *var.* Sperhiada, Sperkhiás. Stereá Ellás, C Greece 38.54N 22.07E
117 E17 **Sperchеiós** ♒ C Greece
Sperhiada *see* Sperchеiáda
97 G14 **Sperillen** ◎ S Norway
Sperkhiás *see* Sperchеiáda
103 I18 **Spessart** *hill range* C Germany
Spétsai *see* Spétses
117 G21 **Spétses** *prev.* Spétsai. Spétses, S Greece 37.16N 23.09E
117 G21 **Spétses** *island* S Greece
98 J8 **Spey** ♒ NE Scotland, UK
103 G20 **Speyer** *Eng.* Spires; *anc.* Civitas Nemetum, Spira. Rheinland-Pfalz, SW Germany 49.19N 8.25E
103 G20 **Speyerbach** ♒ W Germany
109 N20 **Spezzano Albanese** Calabria, SW Italy 39.40N 16.17E
Spice Islands *see* Maluku
102 F9 **Spiekeroog** *island* NW Germany
111 W9 **Spielfeld** Steiermark, SE Austria 46.43N 15.36E
67 N21 **Spiess Seamount** *undersea feature* S Atlantic Ocean 53.00S 2.00W
110 E9 **Spiez** Bern, W Switzerland 46.42N 7.40E
100 G13 **Spijkenisse** Zuid-Holland, SW Netherlands 51.52N 4.19E
41 T6 **Spike Mountain** ▲ Alaska, USA 67.42N 141.39W
117 I25 **Spíli** Kríti, Greece, E Mediterranean Sea 35.12N 24.33E
110 D10 **Spillgerten** ▲ W Switzerland 46.34N 7.25E
120 F9 **Spilva** ✈ (Rīga) Rīga, C Latvia 56.55N 24.03E
109 N17 **Spinazzola** Puglia, SE Italy 40.58N 16.06E
155 O9 **Spīn Būldak** Kandahār, S Afghanistan 31.01N 66.22E
Spira *see* Speyer
Spirdingsee *see* Śniardwy, Jezioro
Spires *see* Speyer
31 T11 **Spirit Lake** Iowa, C USA 43.25N 95.06W
31 T11 **Spirit Lake** ◎ Iowa, C USA
9 N13 **Spirit River** Alberta, W Canada 55.46N 118.51W
9 S14 **Spiritwood** Saskatchewan, S Canada 53.18N 107.33W
29 R11 **Spiro** Oklahoma, C USA 35.14N 94.37W
113 L19 **Spišská Nová Ves** *Ger.* Neudorf, Zipser Neudorf, *Hung.* Igló. Košický Kraj, E Slovakia 48.58N 20.34E
143 T11 **Spitak** NW Armenia 40.51N 44.17E
94 O2 **Spitsbergen** *island* NW Svalbard
Spittal *see* Spittal an der Drau
111 R9 **Spittal an der Drau** *var.* Spittal. Kärnten, S Austria 46.48N 13.30E
111 V3 **Spitz** Niederösterreich, NE Austria 48.24N 15.22E
96 D9 **Spjelkavik** Møre og Romsdal, S Norway 62.28N 6.22E
27 W10 **Splendora** Texas, SW USA 30.13N 95.09W
115 E14 **Split** *It.* Spalato. Split-Dalmacija, S Croatia 43.31N 16.27E
115 E14 **Split** ✈ Split-Dalmacija, S Croatia 43.33N 16.19E
115 E14 **Split-Dalmacija** *off.* Splitsko-Dalmatinska Županija. ◆ *province* S Croatia
9 X12 **Split Lake** ◎ Manitoba, C Canada
Splitsko-Dalmatinska Županija *see* Split-Dalmacija
110 H10 **Splügen** Graubünden, S Switzerland 46.33N 9.18E
Spodnji Dravograd *see* Dravograd
27 P12 **Spofford** Texas, SW USA 29.10N 100.24W
120 J11 **Špoģi** Daugvapils, SE Latvia 56.03N 26.47E
34 L8 **Spokane** Washington, NW USA 47.39N 117.25W
34 L8 **Spokane River** ♒ Washington, NW USA
108 I13 **Spoleto** Umbria, C Italy 42.43N 12.43E
32 I4 **Spooner** Wisconsin, N USA 45.51N 91.49W
32 K12 **Spoon River** ♒ Illinois, N USA
23 W5 **Spotsylvania** Virginia, NE USA 38.13N 77.31W
34 L8 **Sprague** Washington, NW USA 47.19N 117.55W
178 Ll16 **Spratly Island** *island* SW Spratly Islands
198 Ff7 **Spratly Islands** *Chin.* Nansha Qundao. ◇ *disputed territory* SE Asia
34 J12 **Spray** Oregon, NW USA 44.30N 119.38W
114 I11 **Spreča** ♒ N Bosnia and Herzegovina
102 P13 **Spree** ♒ E Germany
102 P13 **Spreewald** *wetland* NE Germany
103 P14 **Spremberg** Brandenburg, E Germany 51.34N 14.22E
27 W11 **Spring** Texas, SW USA 30.03N 95.24W
33 Q10 **Spring Arbor** Michigan, N USA 42.12N 84.33W
85 E23 **Springbok** Northern Cape, W South Africa 29.38S 17.56E
20 I15 **Spring City** Pennsylvania, NE USA 40.10N 75.33W
22 L9 **Spring City** Tennessee, S USA 35.41N 84.51W
38 L4 **Spring City** Utah, W USA 39.28N 111.30W
37 W3 **Spring Creek** Nevada, W USA 40.45N 115.40W
29 S9 **Springdale** Arkansas, C USA 36.11N 94.07W
33 Q14 **Springdale** Ohio, N USA 39.17N 84.29W
102 I13 **Springe** Niedersachsen, N Germany 52.13N 9.33E
39 U9 **Springer** New Mexico, SW USA 36.21N 104.35W
39 W7 **Springfield** Colorado, C USA 37.24N 102.36W
25 W5 **Springfield** Georgia, SE USA 32.21N 81.20W
32 K14 **Springfield** *state capital* Illinois, N USA 39.48N 89.38W
22 L6 **Springfield** Kentucky, S USA 37.41N 85.13W
20 M12 **Springfield** Massachusetts, NE USA 42.06N 72.32W
31 T10 **Springfield** Minnesota, N USA 44.15N 94.58W
29 T7 **Springfield** Missouri, C USA 37.13N 93.18W
33 R13 **Springfield** Ohio, N USA 39.55N 83.48W
34 G13 **Springfield** Oregon, NW USA 44.03N 123.01W
31 Q12 **Springfield** South Dakota, N USA 42.51N 97.54W
22 J8 **Springfield** Tennessee, S USA 36.30N 86.53W
20 M9 **Springfield** Vermont, NE USA 43.18N 72.27W
32 K14 **Springfield, Lake** ⊠ Illinois, N USA
57 T8 **Spring Garden** NE Guyana 6.58N 58.34W
32 K8 **Spring Green** Wisconsin, N USA 43.10N 90.02W
31 X11 **Spring Grove** Minnesota, N USA 43.33N 91.38W
24 G4 **Springhill** Louisiana, S USA 33.01N 93.27W
25 V12 **Spring Hill** Florida, SE USA 28.28N 82.36W
29 R4 **Spring Hill** Kansas, C USA 38.44N 94.49W
11 P15 **Springhill** Nova Scotia, SE Canada 45.40N 64.04W
22 I9 **Spring Hill** Tennessee, S USA 35.46N 86.55W
23 U10 **Spring Lake** North Carolina, SE USA 35.10N 78.58W
26 M4 **Springlake** Texas, SW USA 34.13N 102.18W
37 W11 **Spring Mountains** ▲ Nevada, W USA
67 B24 **Spring Point** West Falkland, Falkland Islands 51.49S 60.27W
29 W9 **Spring River** ♒ Arkansas/Missouri, C USA
29 S7 **Spring River** ♒ Missouri/Oklahoma, C USA
85 J21 **Springs** Gauteng, NE South Africa 26.13S 28.32E
193 H16 **Springs Junction** West Coast, South Island, NZ 42.20S 172.10E
189 X8 **Springsure** Queensland, E Australia 24.09S 148.06E
31 W11 **Spring Valley** Minnesota, N USA 43.41N 92.23W
20 K13 **Spring Valley** New York, NE USA 41.10N 73.58W
31 N12 **Springview** Nebraska, C USA 42.48N 99.45W
20 D11 **Springville** New York, NE USA 42.27N 78.52W
38 L3 **Springville** Utah, W USA 40.10N 111.36W
Sprottau *see* Szprotawa
13 V4 **Sproule, Pointe** *headland* Quebec, SE Canada 49.47N 67.02W
9 Q14 **Spruce Grove** Alberta, SW Canada 53.36N 113.55W
23 T4 **Spruce Knob** ▲ West Virginia, NE USA 38.40N 79.37W
37 X3 **Spruce Mountain** ▲ Nevada, W USA 40.33N 114.46W
23 P9 **Spruce Pine** North Carolina, SE USA 35.55N 82.03W
100 G13 **Spui** ♒ SW Netherlands
109 O19 **Spulico, Capo** *headland* S Italy 39.57N 16.38E
27 O5 **Spur** Texas, SW USA 33.28N 100.51W
99 O17 **Spurn Head** *headland* E England, UK 53.34N 0.06E
101 H20 **Spy** Namur, S Belgium 50.29N 4.43E
97 I15 **Spydeberg** Østfold, S Norway 59.36N 11.04E
193 J17 **Spy Glass Point** *headland* South Island, NZ 42.33S 173.31E
8 L17 **Squamish** British Columbia, SW Canada 49.40N 123.10W
21 O8 **Squam Lake** ◎ New Hampshire, NE USA
21 S2 **Squa Pan Mountain** ▲ Maine, NE USA 46.36N 68.09W
41 N16 **Squaw Harbor** Unga Island, Alaska, USA 55.12N 160.41W
12 E11 **Squaw Island** *island* Ontario, S Canada
109 O22 **Squillace, Golfo di** *gulf* S Italy
109 Q18 **Squinzano** Puglia, SE Italy 40.25N 18.03E
174 L15 **Sragen** Jawa, C Indonesia 7.24S 111.00E
Sráid na Cathrach *see* Milltown Malbay
178 Jj11 **Srâlau** Stœng Trêng, N Cambodia 14.03N 105.46E
Srath an Urláir *see* Stranorlar
114 G10 **Srbac** Republika Srpska, N Bosnia & Herzegovina 45.06N 17.33E
Srbinje *see* Foča
Srbija *see* Serbia
Srbobran *see* Donji Vakuf
114 K9 **Srbobran** *var.* Bácsszenttamás, *Hung.* Szenttamás. Serbia, N Serbia and Montenegro (Yugoslavia) 45.33N 19.46E
178 Ii14 **Srê Âmběl** Kaôh Kông, SW Cambodia 11.07N 103.46E
114 K13 **Srebrenica** Republika Srpska, E Bosnia & Herzegovina 44.04N 19.18E
114 I11 **Srebrenik** Federacija Bosna I Hercegovina, E Bosnia & Herzegovina 44.42N 18.30E
116 M10 **Sredets** *prev.* Grudovo. Burgas, E Bulgaria 42.21N 27.13E
116 K10 **Sredets** *prev.* Syulemeshlii. Stara Zagora, C Bulgaria 42.16N 25.40E
116 M10 **Sredetska Reka** ♒ SE Bulgaria
127 P9 **Sredinnyy Khrebet** ▲ E Russian Federation
116 N7 **Sredishte** *Rom.* Beibunar; *prev.* Knyazhevo. Dobrich, NE Bulgaria 43.51N 27.30E
116 I10 **Sredna Gora** ▲ C Bulgaria
127 N7 **Srednekolymsk** Respublika Sakha (Yakutiya), NE Russian Federation 67.28N 153.52E
130 K7 **Srednerusskaya Vozvyshennost'** *Eng.* Central Russian Upland. ▲ W Russian Federation
126 Ii9 **Srednesibirskoye Ploskogor'ye** *var.* Central Siberian Uplands, *Eng.* Central Siberian Plateau. ▲ N Russian Federation
129 V13 **Sredniy Ural** ▲ NW Russian Federation
178 Jj13 **Srê Khtŭm** Môndól Kiri, E Cambodia 12.10N 106.52E
112 G12 **Śrem** Wielkopolskie, C Poland 52.07N 17.00E
114 K10 **Sremska Mitrovica** *prev.* Mitrovica, *Ger.* Mitrowitz. Serbia, NW Serbia and Montenegro (Yugoslavia) 44.58N 19.37E
178 Ii11 **Srêng, Stœng** ♒ NW Cambodia
178 Ii11 **Srê Noy** Siĕmréab, NW Cambodia 13.47N 104.03E
Srepok, Sông *see* Srêpôk, Tônle
178 K12 **Srêpôk, Tônle** *var.* Sông Srepok. ♒ Cambodia/Vietnam
126 L15 **Sretensk** Chitinskaya Oblast', S Russian Federation 52.14N 117.33E
174 Ll7 **Sri Aman** Sarawak, East Malaysia 1.13N 111.25E
119 R4 **Sribne** Chernihivs'ka Oblast', N Ukraine 50.40N 32.55E
161 I25 **Sri Jayawardanapura** *var.* Sri Jayawardenepura; *prev.* Kotte. Western Province, W Sri Lanka 6.54N 79.58E
161 M14 **Srīkākulam** Andhra Pradesh, E India 18.18N 83.54E
161 I25 **Sri Lanka** *off.* Democratic Socialist Republic of Sri Lanka; *prev.* Ceylon. ◆ *republic* S Asia
138 Mm15 **Sri Lanka** *island* S Asia
159 V14 **Srimangal** Chittagong, E Bangladesh 24.19N 91.40E
Sri Mohangorh *see* Shri Mohangarh
158 H5 **Srīnagar** Jammu and Kashmir, N India 34.06N 74.50E
178 H10 **Srinagarind Reservoir** ◎ W Thailand
161 F19 **Sringeri** Karnātaka, W India 13.25N 75.13E
161 K25 **Sri Pada** *Eng.* Adam's Peak. ▲ S Sri Lanka 6.49N 80.25E
Sri Saket *see* Si Sa Ket
113 G14 **Środa Śląska** *Ger.* Neumarkt. Dolnośląskie, SW Poland 51.10N 16.30E
112 H12 **Środa Wielkopolska** Wielkopolskie, C Poland 52.13N 17.16E
Srpska Kostajnica *see* Bosanska Kostajnica
115 G14 **Srpska, Republika** ◆ *republic* Bosnia & Herzegovina
Srpski Brod *see* Bosanski Brod
Ssu-ch'uan *see* Sichuan
Ssu-p'ing/Ssu-p'ing-chieh *see* Siping
Stablo *see* Stavelot
101 G15 **Stabroek** Antwerpen, N Belgium 51.21N 4.22E
Stackeln *see* Strenči
98 I5 **Stack Skerry** *island* N Scotland, UK
96 C10 **Stad** *peninsula* S Norway
102 I9 **Stade** Niedersachsen, NW Germany 53.36N 9.28E
111 R5 **Stadl-Paura** Oberösterreich, NW Austria 48.04N 13.52E
121 L20 **Stadolichy** *Rus.* Stodolichi. Homyel'skaya Voblasts', SE Belarus 51.43N 28.30E
100 P7 **Stadskanaal** Groningen, NE Netherlands 53.00N 6.55E
103 H16 **Stadtallendorf** Hessen, C Germany 50.49N 9.01E
103 K23 **Stadtbergen** Bayern, S Germany 48.21N 10.50E
110 G7 **Stäfa** Zürich, NE Switzerland 47.14N 8.42E
97 K23 **Staffanstorp** Skåne, S Sweden 55.37N 13.13E
103 K18 **Staffelstein** Bayern, C Germany 50.05N 11.00E
99 L19 **Stafford** C England, UK 52.48N 2.07W
28 L6 **Stafford** Kansas, C USA 37.57N 98.36W
23 W4 **Stafford** Virginia, NE USA 38.24N 77.22W
99 L19 **Staffordshire** *cultural region* C England, UK
21 N12 **Stafford Springs** Connecticut, NE USA 41.57N 72.18W
117 H14 **Stágira** Kentrikí Makedonía, N Greece 40.31N 23.46E
120 G7 **Staicele** Limbaži, N Latvia 57.52N 24.48E
Ştaierdorf-Anina *see* Anina
111 V8 **Stainz** Steiermark, SE Austria 46.55N 15.18E
Stájerlakanina *see* Anina
119 Y7 **Stakhanov** Luhans'ka Oblast', E Ukraine 48.30N 38.42E
110 E11 **Stalden** Valais, SW Switzerland 46.12N 7.55E
Stalin *see* Varna
Stalinabad *see* Dushanbe

◆ Country
● Country Capital
◇ Dependent Territory
○ Dependent Territory Capital
◆ Administrative Region
✈ International Airport
▲ Mountain
▲ Mountain Range
⛰ Volcano
♒ River
◎ Lake
⊠ Reservoir

Stalingrad *see* Volgograd
Staliniri *see* Ts'khinvali
Stalino *see* Donets'k
Stalinobod *see* Dushanbe
Stalinov Štít *see* Gerlachovský štít
Stalinsk *see* Novokuznetsk
Stalinskaya Oblast' *see* Donets'ka Oblast'
Stalinski Zaliv *see* Varnenski Zaliv
Stalin, Yazovir *see* Iskŭr, Yazovir
113 *N15* **Stalowa Wola** Podkarpackie, SE Poland *50.34N 22.01E*
116 *I11* **Stamboliyski** Plovdiv, C Bulgaria *42.08N 24.36E*
116 *J8* **Stamboliyski, Yazovir** ⊠ N Bulgaria
99 *N19* **Stamford** E England, UK *52.39N 0.32W*
20 *L14* **Stamford** Connecticut, NE USA *41.03N 73.31W*
27 *P6* **Stamford** Texas, SW USA *32.55N 99.49W*
27 *Q6* **Stamford, Lake** ⊠ Texas, SW USA
110 *I10* **Stampa** Graubünden, SE Switzerland *46.21N 9.35E*
Stampalia *see* Astypálaia
29 *T14* **Stamps** Arkansas, C USA *33.22N 93.30W*
94 *G11* **Stamsund** Nordland, C Norway *68.07N 13.49E*
29 *R2* **Stanberry** Missouri, C USA *40.12N 94.33W*
205 *O3* **Stancomb-Wills Glacier** *glacier* Antarctica
85 *K21* **Standerton** Mpumalanga, E South Africa *26.54S 29.15E*
33 *R7* **Standish** Michigan, N USA *43.58N 83.58W*
22 *M6* **Stanford** Kentucky, S USA *37.30N 84.39W*
35 *S9* **Stanford** Montana, NW USA *47.08N 110.15W*
97 *P19* **Stånga** Gotland, SE Sweden *57.16N 18.30E*
96 *I13* **Stange** Hedmark, S Norway *60.43N 11.12E*
85 *L23* **Stanger** KwaZulu/Natal, E South Africa *29.18S 31.17E*
Stanimaka *see* Asenovgrad
Stanislau *see* Ivano-Frankivs'k
37 *P8* **Stanislaus River** ~ California, W USA
Stanislav *see* Ivano-Frankivs'k
Stanislavskaya Oblast' *see* Ivano-Frankivs'ka Oblast'
Stanisławów *see* Ivano-Frankivs'k
Stanke Dimitrov *see* Dupnitsa
191 *O15* **Stanley** Tasmania, SE Australia *40.48S 145.18E*
67 *E24* **Stanley** *var.* Port Stanley, Puerto Argentino ○ (Falkland Islands) East Falkland, Falkland Islands *51.45S 57.55W*
35 *O13* **Stanley** Idaho, NW USA *44.12N 114.58W*
30 *L3* **Stanley** North Dakota, N USA *48.19N 102.23W*
23 *U4* **Stanley** Virginia, NE USA *38.34N 78.30W*
32 *J6* **Stanley** Wisconsin, N USA *44.58N 90.54W*
81 *G21* **Stanley Pool** *var.* Pool Malebo. ◎ Congo/Dem. Rep. Congo
161 *H20* **Stanley Reservoir** ⊠ S India
Stanleyville *see* Kisangani
44 *G3* **Stann Creek** ◈ *district* SE Belize
Stann Creek *see* Dangriga
127 *N17* **Stanovoy Khrebet** ▲▲ SE Russian Federation
110 *F8* **Stans** Unterwalden, C Switzerland *46.57N 8.22E*
99 *O21* **Stansted** ✈ (London) Essex, E England, UK *51.53N 0.16E*
191 *U4* **Stanthorpe** Queensland, E Australia *28.35S 151.52E*
23 *N6* **Stanton** Kentucky, S USA *37.51N 83.51W*
33 *Q8* **Stanton** Michigan, N USA *43.17N 85.01W*
31 *Q14* **Stanton** Nebraska, C USA *41.57N 97.13W*
30 *L5* **Stanton** North Dakota, N USA *47.19N 101.22W*
27 *N7* **Stanton** Texas, SW USA *32.07N 101.47W*
34 *H7* **Stanwood** Washington, NW USA *48.14N 122.22W*
119 *Y7* **Stanychno-Luhans'ke** Luhans'ka Oblast', E Ukraine *48.39N 39.30E*
110 *K7* **Stanzach** Tirol, W Austria *47.24N 10.36E*
100 *M9* **Staphorst** Overijssel, E Netherlands *52.37N 6.12E*
12 *D18* **Staples** Ontario, S Canada *42.09N 82.34W*
31 *T6* **Staples** Minnesota, N USA *46.21N 94.47W*
30 *M14* **Stapleton** Nebraska, C USA *41.28N 100.30W*
27 *S8* **Star** Texas, SW USA *31.27N 98.16W*
113 *M14* **Starachowice** Świętokrzyskie, C Poland *51.04N 21.02E*
Stara Kanjiža *see* Kanjiža
113 *M18* **Stará Ľubovňa** *Ger.* Altlublau, *Hung.* Prešovský Kraj, E Slovakia *49.18N 20.40E*
114 *L10* **Stara Pazova** *Ger.* Altpasua, *Hung.* Ópazova. Serbia, N Serbia and Montenegro (Yugoslavia) *44.59N 20.10E*
Stara Planina *see* Balkan Mountains
116 *L9* **Stara Reka** ~ C Bulgaria
118 *M5* **Stara Synyava** Khmel'nyts'ka Oblast', W Ukraine *49.39N 27.39E*
118 *I2* **Stara Vyzhivka** Volyns'ka Oblast', NW Ukraine *51.27N 24.25E*
Staraya Belitsa *see* Staraya Byelitsa
121 *M14* **Staraya Byelitsa** *Rus.* Staraya Belitsa. Vitsyebskaya Voblasts', NE Belarus *54.42N 29.37E*
131 *R5* **Staraya Mayna** Ul'yanovskaya Oblast', W Russian Federation *54.36N 48.57E*
121 *O18* **Staraya Rudnya** *Rus.* Staraya Rudnya. Homyel'skaya Voblasts', SE Belarus *52.50N 30.15E*
128 *H14* **Staraya Russa** Novgorodskaya Oblast', W Russian Federation *57.59N 31.18E*
116 *K10* **Stara Zagora** *Lat.* Augusta Trajana. Stara Zagora, C Bulgaria *42.26N 25.39E*
116 *K10* **Stara Zagora** ◈ *province* C Bulgaria
31 *S8* **Starbuck** Minnesota, N USA *45.36N 95.31W*
203 *W4* **Starbuck Island** *prev.* Volunteer Island. *island* E Kiribati
29 *V13* **Star City** Arkansas, C USA *33.56N 91.50W*
114 *F13* **Staretina** ▲▲ W Bosnia and Herzegovina
Stargard in Pommern *see* Stargard Szczeciński
112 *E9* **Stargard Szczeciński** *Ger.* Stargard in Pommern. Zachodniopomorskie, NW Poland *53.19N 15.01E*
195 *Z17* **Star Harbour** *harbor* San Cristobal, SE Solomon Islands
Stari Bečej *see* Bečej
115 *F15* **Stari Grad** *It.* Cittavecchia. Split-Dalmacija, S Croatia *43.11N 16.36E*
175 *Qq12* **Staring, Teluk** *var.* Teluk Wawosungu. *bay* Sulawesi, C Indonesia
128 *J16* **Staritsa** Tverskaya Oblast', W Russian Federation *56.28N 34.51E*
25 *V9* **Starke** Florida, SE USA *29.56N 82.07W*
24 *M4* **Starkville** Mississippi, S USA *33.27N 88.49W*
194 *E11* **Star Mountains** *Ind.* Pegunungan Sterren. ▲▲ Indonesia/PNG
103 *L23* **Starnberg** Bayern, SE Germany *48.00N 11.19E*
103 *L24* **Starnberger See** ◎ SE Germany
Starobel'sk *see* Starobil's'k
119 *X8* **Starobesheve** Donets'ka Oblast', E Ukraine *47.45N 38.01E*
119 *Y6* **Starobil's'k** *Rus.* Starobel'sk. Luhans'ka Oblast', E Ukraine *49.16N 38.55E*
Starobin *see* Starobyn
121 *K18* **Starobyn** *Rus.* Starobin. Minskaya Voblasts', S Belarus *52.43N 27.28E*
130 *H6* **Starodub** Bryanskaya Oblast', W Russian Federation *52.30N 32.56E*
112 *I8* **Starogard Gdański** *Ger.* Preussisch-Stargard. Pomorskie, N Poland *53.57N 18.29E*
151 *P16* **Staroikan** Yuzhnyy Kazakhstan, S Kazakhstan *43.09N 68.34E*
Starokonstantinov *see* Starokostyantyniv
118 *L5* **Starokostyantyniv** *Rus.* Starokonstantinov. Khmel'nyts'ka Oblast', NW Ukraine *49.43N 27.12E*
130 *K12* **Starominskaya** Krasnodarskiy Kray, SW Russian Federation *46.31N 39.03E*
116 *L7* **Staro Selo** *Rom.* Satul-Vechi; *prev.* Star-Smil. Silistra, NE Bulgaria *43.58N 26.32E*
130 *K12* **Staroshcherbinovskaya** Krasnodarskiy Kray, SW Russian Federation *46.36N 38.42E*
131 *V6* **Starosubkhangulovo** Respublika Bashkortostan, W Russian Federation *53.05N 57.22E*
37 *S4* **Star Peak** ▲ Nevada, W USA *40.31N 118.09W*
Star-Smil *see* Staro Selo
99 *J25* **Start Point** *headland* SW England, UK *50.13N 3.38W*
Startsy *see* Kirawsk
Starum *see* Stavoren
121 *L18* **Staryya Darohi** *Rus.* Staryye Dorogi. Minskaya Voblasts', S Belarus *53.01N 28.12E*
Staryye Dorogi *see* Staryya Darohi
131 *T2* **Staryye Zyattsy** Udmurtskaya Respublika, NW Russian Federation *57.22N 52.42E*
119 *U13* **Staryy Krym** Respublika Krym, S Ukraine *45.03N 35.06E*
130 *K8* **Staryy Oskol** Belgorodskaya Oblast', W Russian Federation *51.21N 37.52E*
118 *H6* **Staryy Sambir** L'vivs'ka Oblast', W Ukraine *49.27N 23.00E*
103 *L14* **Stassfurt** *var.* Staßfurt. Sachsen-Anhalt, C Germany *51.51N 11.34E*
113 *M15* **Staszów** Świętokrzyskie, C Poland *50.34N 21.08E*
31 *W13* **State Center** Iowa, C USA *42.01N 93.09W*
20 *E14* **State College** Pennsylvania, NE USA *40.48N 77.52W*
20 *K15* **Staten Island** *island* New York, NE USA
Staten Island *see* Estados, Isla de los
25 *U8* **Statenville** Georgia, SE USA *30.42N 83.00W*
25 *W5* **Statesboro** Georgia, SE USA *32.28N 81.46W*
States, The *see* United States of America
23 *R9* **Statesville** North Carolina, SE USA *35.46N 80.53W*
97 *G16* **Stathelle** Telemark, S Norway *59.01N 9.40E*
32 *K15* **Staunton** Illinois, N USA *39.00N 89.47W*
23 *T5* **Staunton** Virginia, NE USA *38.09N 79.04W*
97 *C16* **Stavanger** Rogaland, S Norway *58.58N 5.43E*
101 *L21* **Stavelot** *Dut.* Stablo. Liège, E Belgium *50.24N 5.55E*
97 *G16* **Stavern** Vestfold, S Norway *58.58N 10.01E*
Stavers Island *see* Vostok Island
100 *J7* **Stavoren** *Fris.* Starum. Friesland, N Netherlands *52.52N 5.22E*
130 *M14* **Stavropol'** *prev.* Voroshilovsk. Stavropol'skiy Kray, SW Russian Federation *45.02N 41.57E*
Stavropol' *see* Tol'yatti
130 *M14* **Stavropol'skaya Vozvyshennost'** ▲▲ SW Russian Federation
130 *M14* **Stavropol'skiy Kray** ◈ *territory* SW Russian Federation
117 *H14* **Stavrós** Kentrikí Makedonía, N Greece *40.39N 23.43E*
117 *J24* **Stavrós, Akrotírio** *headland* Kríti, Greece, E Mediterranean Sea *35.25N 24.57E*
117 *K21* **Stavrós, Akrotírio** *headland* Náxos, Kykládes, Greece, Aegean Sea *37.12N 25.32E*
116 *I12* **Stavroúpoli** *prev.* Stavroúpolis. Anatolikí Makedonía kai Thráki, NE Greece *41.12N 24.42E*
Stavroúpolis *see* Stavroúpoli
119 *O6* **Stavyshche** Kyyivs'ka Oblast', N Ukraine *49.23N 30.10E*
190 *M11* **Stawell** Victoria, SE Australia *37.05S 142.47E*
112 *N9* **Stawiski** Podlaskie, NE Poland *53.22N 22.08E*
12 *G14* **Stayner** Ontario, S Canada *44.25N 80.05W*
39 *R3* **Steamboat Springs** Colorado, C USA *40.28N 106.51W*
22 *M8* **Stearns** Kentucky, S USA *36.39N 84.27W*
41 *N10* **Stebbins** Alaska, USA *63.30N 162.15W*
110 *K7* **Steeg** Tirol, W Austria *47.15N 10.18E*
29 *Y9* **Steele** Missouri, C USA *36.04N 89.49W*
31 *N5* **Steele** North Dakota, N USA *46.51N 99.55W*
204 *J5* **Steele Island** *island* Antarctica
32 *K16* **Steeleville** Illinois, N USA *38.00N 89.39W*
29 *W6* **Steelville** Missouri, C USA *37.58N 91.21W*
101 *G14* **Steenbergen** Noord-Brabant, S Netherlands *51.34N 4.13E*
Steenkool *see* Bintuni
9 *O10* **Steen River** Alberta, W Canada *59.37N 117.16W*
100 *M8* **Steenwijk** Overijssel, N Netherlands *52.46N 6.07E*
67 *A23* **Steeple Jason** *island* Jason Islands, NW Falkland Islands
182 *J8* **Steep Point** *headland* Western Australia *26.09S 113.10E*
118 *L9* **Ştefăneşti** Botoşani, NE Romania *47.43N 27.15E*
Stefanie, Lake *see* Ch'ew Bahir
15 *J1* **Stefansson Island** *island* Nunavut, N Canada
119 *O10* **Ştefan Vodă** *Rus.* Suvorovo. SE Moldova *46.33N 29.39E*
65 *H18* **Steffen, Cerro** ▲ S Chile *44.27S 71.42W*
110 *D9* **Steffisburg** Bern, C Switzerland *46.46N 7.37E*
97 *J24* **Stege** Storstrøm, SE Denmark *54.58N 12.18E*
118 *G10* **Ştei** *Hung.* Vaskohsziklás. Bihor, W Romania *46.33N 22.28E*
Steier *see* Steyr
Steierdorf/Steierdorf-Anina *see* Anina
111 *T7* **Steiermark** *off.* Land Steiermark, *Eng.* Styria. ◈ *state* C Austria
103 *J19* **Steigerwald** *hill range* C Germany
101 *L17* **Stein** Limburg, SE Netherlands *50.58N 5.45E*
Stein *see* Stein an der Donau, Austria
Stein *see* Kamnik, Slovenia
110 *M8* **Steinach** Tirol, W Austria *47.07N 11.30E*
Steinamanger *see* Szombathely
111 *W3* **Stein an der Donau** *var.* Stein. Niederösterreich, NE Austria *48.24N 15.35E*
Steinau an der Elbe *see* Ścinawa
9 *Y16* **Steinbach** Manitoba, S Canada *49.31N 96.40W*
Steiner Alpen *see* Kamniško-Savinjske Alpe
101 *L24* **Steinfort** Luxembourg, W Luxembourg *49.39N 5.55E*
102 *H12* **Steinhuder Meer** ◎ NW Germany
95 *E15* **Steinkjer** Nord-Trøndelag, C Norway *64.01N 11.28E*
Stejarul *see* Karapelit
101 *F16* **Stekene** Oost-Vlaanderen, NW Belgium *51.13N 4.04E*
85 *E26* **Stellenbosch** Western Cape, SW South Africa *33.48S 18.49E*
100 *F13* **Stellendam** Zuid-Holland, SW Netherlands *51.48N 4.01E*
41 *T12* **Steller, Mount** ▲ Alaska, USA *60.36N 142.49W*
105 *Y14* **Stello, Monte** ▲ Corse, France, C Mediterranean Sea *42.49N 9.24E*
108 *F5* **Stelvio, Passo dello** *pass* Italy/Switzerland *46.32N 10.27E*
105 *R3* **Stenay** Meuse, NE France *49.29N 5.12E*
102 *L12* **Stendal** Sachsen-Anhalt, C Germany *52.36N 11.52E*
120 *E8* **Stende** Talsi, NW Latvia *57.09N 22.33E*
190 *H10* **Stenhouse Bay** South Australia *35.15S 136.58E*
97 *J23* **Stenløse** Frederiksborg, E Denmark *55.46N 12.13E*
97 *L19* **Stensjön** Jönköping, S Sweden *57.36N 14.42E*
97 *K18* **Stenstorp** Västra Götaland, S Sweden *58.15N 13.45E*
97 *I18* **Stenungsund** Västra Götaland, S Sweden *58.04N 11.55E*
Stepanakert *see* Xankändi
143 *T11* **Step'anavan** N Armenia *41.00N 44.27E*
102 *K9* **Stepenitz** ~ N Germany
31 *O10* **Stephan** South Dakota, N USA *44.12N 99.25W*
31 *R3* **Stephen** Minnesota, N USA *48.27N 96.54W*
29 *T14* **Stephens** Arkansas, C USA *33.25N 93.04W*
192 *J13* **Stephens, Cape** *headland* D'Urville Island, Marlborough, SW New Zealand *40.42S 173.56E*
23 *V3* **Stephens City** Virginia, NE USA *39.03N 78.10W*
190 *L6* **Stephens Creek** New South Wales, SE Australia *31.51S 141.30E*
192 *K13* **Stephens Island** *island* C NZ
33 *N5* **Stephenson** Michigan, N USA *45.27N 87.36W*
11 *S12* **Stephenville** Newfoundland and Labrador, SE Canada *48.33N 58.29W*
27 *S7* **Stephenville** Texas, SW USA *32.12N 98.13W*
151 *P17* **Step' Nardara** *Kaz.* Shardara Dalasy; *prev.* Shaidara. *grassland* S Kazakhstan
151 *R8* **Stepnogorsk** Akmola, C Kazakhstan *52.04N 72.18E*
131 *O15* **Stepnoye** Stavropol'skiy Kray, SW Russian Federation *44.18N 44.34E*
151 *Q8* **Stepnyak** Akmola, N Kazakhstan *52.52N 70.49E*
198 *C9* **Steps Point** *headland* Tutuila, W American Samoa *14.22S 170.46W*
117 *F17* **Stereá Ellás** *Eng.* Greece Central. ◈ *region* C Greece
85 *J24* **Sterkspruit** Eastern Cape, SE South Africa *30.28S 27.24E*
131 *U6* **Sterlibashevo** Respublika Bashkortostan, W Russian Federation *53.19N 55.12E*
41 *R12* **Sterling** Alaska, USA *60.32N 150.51W*
39 *V3* **Sterling** Colorado, C USA *40.37N 103.12W*
32 *K11* **Sterling** Illinois, N USA *41.47N 89.42W*
28 *M5* **Sterling** Kansas, C USA *38.12N 98.12W*
27 *O8* **Sterling City** Texas, SW USA *31.50N 100.58W*
33 *S9* **Sterling Heights** Michigan, N USA *42.34N 83.01W*
23 *W3* **Sterling Park** Virginia, NE USA *39.00N 77.24W*
39 *V2* **Sterling Reservoir** ⊠ Colorado, C USA
24 *I5* **Sterlington** Louisiana, S USA *32.42N 92.05W*
131 *U6* **Sterlitamak** Respublika Bashkortostan, W Russian Federation *53.39N 56.00E*
Sternberg *see* Šternberk
113 *H17* **Šternberk** *Ger.* Sternberg. Olomoucký Kraj, E Czech Republic *49.45N 17.19E*
147 *V17* **Stēroh** Suquţrā, S Yemen *12.21N 53.50E*
112 *G11* **Stęszew** Wielkopolskie, C Poland *52.16N 16.41E*
Stettin *see* Szczecin
Stettiner Haff *see* Szczeciński, Zalew
9 *Q15* **Stettler** Alberta, SW Canada *52.21N 112.40W*
33 *V13* **Steubenville** Ohio, N USA *40.21N 80.37W*
99 *O21* **Stevenage** E England, UK *51.55N 0.13W*
25 *Q1* **Stevenson** Alabama, S USA *34.52N 85.50W*
34 *H11* **Stevenson** Washington, NW USA *45.43N 121.54W*
190 *E1* **Stevenson Creek** *seasonal river* South Australia
41 *Q13* **Stevenson Entrance** *strait* Alaska, USA
32 *L6* **Stevens Point** Wisconsin, N USA *44.31N 89.33W*
41 *R8* **Stevens Village** Alaska, USA *66.01N 149.02W*
35 *P10* **Stevensville** Montana, NW USA *46.30N 114.05W*
95 *E25* **Stevns Klint** *headland* E Denmark *55.15N 12.25E*
8 *J12* **Stewart** British Columbia, W Canada *55.58N 129.52W*
8 *J6* **Stewart** ~ Yukon Territory, NW Canada
8 *I6* **Stewart Crossing** Yukon Territory, NW Canada *63.22N 136.37W*
65 *H25* **Stewart, Isla** *island* S Chile
193 *B25* **Stewart Island** *island* S NZ
189 *W6* **Stewart, Mount** ▲ Queensland, E Australia *20.11S 145.29E*
8 *H6* **Stewart River** Yukon Territory, NW Canada *63.17N 139.24W*
29 *R3* **Stewartsville** Missouri, C USA *39.45N 94.30W*
9 *S16* **Stewart Valley** Saskatchewan, S Canada *50.34N 107.47W*
31 *W10* **Stewartville** Minnesota, N USA *43.51N 92.29W*
Steyerlak-Anina *see* Anina
111 *T5* **Steyr** *var.* Steier. Oberösterreich, N Austria *48.02N 14.26E*
111 *T5* **Steyr** ~ NW Austria
31 *P11* **Stickney** South Dakota, N USA *43.24N 98.23W*
100 *L5* **Stiens** Friesland, N Netherlands *53.15N 5.45E*
Stif *see* Sétif
29 *Q11* **Stigler** Oklahoma, C USA *35.15N 95.07W*
109 *N18* **Stigliano** Basilicata, S Italy *40.24N 16.13E*
97 *N17* **Stigtomta** Södermanland, C Sweden *58.48N 16.46E*
8 *I11* **Stikine** ~ British Columbia, W Canada
Stilida/Stilís *see* Stylída
97 *G22* **Stilling** Århus, C Denmark *56.04N 10.00E*
31 *W8* **Stillwater** Minnesota, N USA *45.03N 92.48W*
29 *O9* **Stillwater** Oklahoma, C USA *36.07N 97.02W*
37 *S5* **Stillwater Range** ▲▲ Nevada, W USA
20 *I8* **Stillwater Reservoir** ⊠ New York, NE USA
109 *O22* **Stilo, Punta** *headland* S Italy *38.27N 16.36E*
29 *R10* **Stilwell** Oklahoma, C USA *35.48N 94.37W*
115 *N17* **Štimlje** Serbia, S Serbia and Montenegro (Yugoslavia) *42.27N 21.03E*
27 *N1* **Stinnett** Texas, SW USA *35.49N 101.26W*
115 *P18* **Štip** E FYR Macedonia *41.45N 22.10E*
Stira *see* Stýra
98 *J12* **Stirling** C Scotland, UK *56.07N 3.57W*
98 *I12* **Stirling** *cultural region* C Scotland, UK
188 *J14* **Stirling Range** ▲▲ Western Australia
95 *E16* **Stjørdalshalsen** Nord-Trøndelag, C Norway *63.27N 10.57E*
Stochód *see* Stokhid
103 *H24* **Stockach** Baden-Württemberg, S Germany *47.51N 9.01E*
27 *S12* **Stockdale** Texas, SW USA *29.14N 97.57W*
111 *X3* **Stockerau** Niederösterreich, NE Austria *48.24N 16.13E*
95 *H20* **Stockholm** ● (Sweden) Stockholm, C Sweden *59.16N 18.03E*
97 *O15* **Stockholm** ◈ *county* C Sweden
Stockmannshof *see* Pļaviņas
99 *L18* **Stockport** NW England, UK *53.25N 2.10W*
67 *K15* **Stocks Seamount** *undersea feature* C Atlantic Ocean *11.42S 33.48W*
37 *O8* **Stockton** California, W USA *37.55N 121.19W*
28 *L3* **Stockton** Kansas, C USA *39.25N 99.17W*
29 *S6* **Stockton** Missouri, C USA *37.42N 93.48W*
32 *K3* **Stockton Island** *island* Apostle Islands, Wisconsin, N USA
29 *S7* **Stockton Lake** ⊠ Missouri, C USA
99 *M15* **Stockton-on-Tees** *var.* Stockton on Tees. N England, UK *54.34N 1.19W*
26 *M10* **Stockton Plateau** *plain* Texas, SW USA
30 *M16* **Stockville** Nebraska, C USA *40.30N 100.21W*
95 *H17* **Stöde** Västernorrland, C Sweden *62.27N 16.34E*
Stodolichi *see* Stadolichy
178 *Jj12* **Stœng Trêng** *prev.* Stung Treng. Stœng Trêng, NE Cambodia *13.31N 105.58E*
115 *M19* **Stogovo Karaorman** ▲▲ W FYR Macedonia
Stoke *see* Stoke-on-Trent
99 *L19* **Stoke-on-Trent** *var.* Stoke. C England, UK *53.00N 2.10W*
190 *M15* **Stokes Point** *headland* Tasmania, SE Australia *40.09S 143.55E*
118 *J2* **Stokhid** *Pol.* Stochód, *Rus.* Stokhod. ~ NW Ukraine
Stokhod *see* Stokhid
94 *I4* **Stokkseyri** Sudhurland, SW Iceland *63.49N 21.00W*
94 *G10* **Stokmarknes** Nordland, C Norway *68.33N 14.54E*
Stol *see* Veliki Krš
115 *H15* **Stolac** Federacija Bosna I Hercegovina, S Bosnia and Herzegovina *43.04N 17.58E*
Stolbce *see* Stowbtsy
103 *D16* **Stolberg** *var.* Stolberg im Rheinland. Nordrhein-Westfalen, W Germany *50.46N 6.13E*
Stolberg im Rheinland *see* Stolberg
126 *L5* **Stolbovoy, Ostrov** *island* NE Russian Federation
Stolbtsy *see* Stowbtsy
121 *J20* **Stolin** *Rus.* Stolin. Brestskaya Voblasts', SW Belarus *51.52N 26.51E*
97 *K14* **Stöllet** *var.* Norra Ny. Värmland, C Sweden *60.24N 13.15E*
Stolp *see* Słupsk
Stolpe *see* Słupia
Stolpmünde *see* Ustka
117 *F15* **Stómio** Thessalía, C Greece *39.51N 22.45E*
12 *J11* **Stonecliffe** Ontario, SE Canada *46.12N 77.58W*
98 *L10* **Stonehaven** NE Scotland, UK *56.58N 2.13W*
99 *M23* **Stonehenge** *ancient monument* Wiltshire, S England, UK *51.12N 1.54W*
25 *T3* **Stone Mountain** ▲ Georgia, SE USA *33.48N 84.10W*
9 *X16* **Stonewall** Manitoba, S Canada *50.07N 97.19W*
23 *S3* **Stonewood** West Virginia, NE USA *39.15N 80.18W*
12 *D17* **Stoney Point** Ontario, S Canada *42.18N 82.32W*
94 *H10* **Stonglandseidet** Troms, N Norway *69.03N 17.06E*
67 *N25* **Stonybeach Bay** *bay* Tristan da Cunha, SE Atlantic Ocean
37 *N5* **Stony Creek** ~ California, W USA
67 *N25* **Stonyhill Point** *headland* S Tristan da Cunha
12 *I14* **Stony Lake** ◎ Ontario, SE Canada
9 *Q14* **Stony Plain** Alberta, SW Canada *53.31N 114.04W*
23 *R9* **Stony Point** North Carolina, SE USA *35.51N 81.04W*
20 *G8* **Stony Point** *headland* New York, NE USA *43.50N 76.18W*
9 *T10* **Stony Rapids** Saskatchewan, C Canada *59.13N 105.48W*
41 *P11* **Stony River** Alaska, USA *61.48N 156.37W*
Stony Tunguska *see* Podkamennaya Tunguska
10 *G10* **Stooping** ~ Ontario, C Canada
102 *I9* **Stör** ~ N Germany
97 *M15* **Storå** Örebro, S Sweden *59.43N 15.10E*
97 *J16* **Stora Gla** ◎ C Sweden
97 *I16* **Stora Le** *Nor.* Store Le. ◎ Norway/Sweden
94 *I12* **Stora Lulevatten** ◎ N Sweden
94 *H13* **Storavan** ◎ N Sweden
95 *I20* **Storby** Åland, SW Finland *60.12N 19.33E*
96 *E10* **Stordalen** Møre og Romsdal, S Norway *62.22N 7.00E*
Storebelt *see* Storebælt
97 *H23* **Storebælt** *var.* Store Bælt, *Eng.* Great Belt, Storebelt. *channel* Baltic Sea/Kattegat
97 *M19* **Storebro** Kalmar, S Sweden *57.36N 15.30E*
97 *J24* **Store Heddinge** Storstrøm, SE Denmark *55.19N 12.24E*
Store Le *see* Stora Le
95 *E16* **Støren** Sør-Trøndelag, S Norway *63.01N 10.16E*
97 *B14* **Store Sotra** *island* S Norway
94 *O4* **Storfjorden** *fjord* S Norway
97 *L15* **Storfors** Värmland, C Sweden *59.33N 14.16E*
94 *G13* **Storforshei** Nordland, C Norway *66.25N 14.25E*
Storhammer *see* Hamar
102 *L10* **Störkanal** *canal* N Germany
95 *F16* **Storlien** Jämtland, C Sweden *63.18N 12.10E*
191 *P17* **Storm Bay** *inlet* Tasmania, SE Australia
31 *T12* **Storm Lake** Iowa, C USA *42.38N 95.12W*
31 *S13* **Storm Lake** ◎ Iowa, C USA
98 *G7* **Stornoway** NW Scotland, UK *58.13N 6.22W*
Storojineţ *see* Storozhynets'
94 *P1* **Storøya** *island* NE Svalbard
129 *S10* **Storozhevsk** Respublika Komi, NW Russian Federation *61.56N 52.18E*
Storozhinets *see* Storozhynets'
118 *K8* **Storozhynets'** *Ger.* Storozynetz, *Rom.* Storojineţ, *Rus.* Storozhinets. Chernivets'ka Oblast', W Ukraine *48.09N 25.46E*
Storozynetz *see* Storozhynets'
94 *H11* **Storriten** ▲ C Norway *68.09N 17.12E*
21 *N12* **Storrs** Connecticut, NE USA *41.48N 72.15W*
96 *I11* **Storsjøen** ◎ S Norway
96 *N13* **Storsjön** ◎ C Sweden
95 *F16* **Storsjön** ◎ C Sweden
94 *J9* **Storslett** Troms, N Norway *69.45N 21.03E*
94 *I9* **Storsteinnes** Troms, N Norway *69.13N 19.14E*
97 *I24* **Storstrøm** *off.* Storstrøms Amt. ◈ *county* SE Denmark
95 *J14* **Storsund** Norrbotten, N Sweden *65.36N 20.40E*
95 *F16* **Storsylen** ▲ S Norway *63.07N 12.10E*
95 *H14* **Storuman** Västerbotten, N Sweden *65.04N 17.10E*
95 *H14* **Storuman** ◎ N Sweden
96 *N13* **Storvik** Gävleborg, C Sweden *60.37N 16.30E*
97 *O14* **Storvreta** Uppsala, C Sweden *59.58N 17.42E*
31 *V13* **Story City** Iowa, C USA *42.10N 93.36W*
9 *V17* **Stoughton** Saskatchewan, S Canada *49.40N 103.01W*
21 *O11* **Stoughton** Massachusetts, NE USA *42.07N 71.06W*
32 *L9* **Stoughton** Wisconsin, N USA *42.56N 89.12W*
99 *L23* **Stour** ~ E England, UK
99 *P21* **Stour** ~ S England, UK
29 *T5* **Stover** Missouri, C USA *38.26N 92.59W*
97 *G21* **Støvring** Nordjylland, N Denmark *56.52N 9.52E*
121 *J17* **Stowbtsy** *Pol.* Stolbce, *Rus.* Stolbtsy. Minskaya Voblasts', C Belarus *53.27N 26.44E*
27 *X11* **Stowell** Texas, SW USA *29.47N 94.22W*
99 *P20* **Stowmarket** E England, UK *52.04N 0.54E*
116 *N8* **Stozher** Dobrich, NE Bulgaria *43.27N 27.49E*
99 *E14* **Strabane** *Ir.* An Srath Bán. W Northern Ireland, UK *54.49N 7.27W*
123 *Gg10* **Strabo Trench** *undersea feature* C Mediterranean Sea
29 *T7* **Strafford** Missouri, C USA *37.16N 93.07W*
191 *N17* **Strahan** Tasmania, SE Australia *42.10S 145.18E*
113 *C18* **Strakonice** *Ger.* Strakonitz. Budějovický Kraj, S Czech Republic *49.13N 13.55E*
Strakonitz *see* Strakonice
102 *N8* **Stralsund** Mecklenburg-Vorpommern, NE Germany *54.18N 13.06E*
101 *L16* **Stramproy** Limburg, SE Netherlands *51.12N 5.43E*
85 *E26* **Strand** Western Cape, SW South Africa *34.06S 18.49E*
96 *E10* **Stranda** Møre og Romsdal, S Norway *62.18N 6.55E*
99 *G15* **Strangford Lough** *Ir.* Loch Cuan. *inlet* E Northern Ireland, UK
97 *N16* **Strängnäs** Södermanland, C Sweden *59.22N 17.01E*
99 *E14* **Stranorlar** *Ir.* Srath an Urláir. NW Ireland *54.48N 7.46W*
99 *H14* **Stranraer** S Scotland, UK *54.54N 5.01W*
9 *U16* **Strasbourg** Saskatchewan, S Canada *51.04N 104.58W*
105 *V5* **Strasbourg** *Ger.* Strassburg; *anc.* Argentoratum. Bas-Rhin, NE France *48.34N 7.45E*
39 *U4* **Strasburg** Colorado, C USA *39.42N 104.13W*
31 *N7* **Strasburg** North Dakota, N USA *46.07N 100.10W*
33 *U12* **Strasburg** Ohio, N USA *40.35N 81.31W*
23 *U3* **Strasburg** Virginia, NE USA *38.59N 78.21W*
119 *N10* **Străşeni** *var.* Strasheny. C Moldova *47.07N 28.37E*
Strasheny *see* Străşeni
111 *T8* **Strassburg** Kärnten, S Austria *46.54N 14.21E*
Strassburg *see* Strasbourg, France
Strassburg *see* Aiud, Romania
101 *M25* **Strassen** Luxembourg, S Luxembourg *49.37N 6.04E*
111 *R5* **Strasswalchen** Salzburg, C Austria *47.59N 13.19E*
12 *F16* **Stratford** Ontario, S Canada *43.22N 81.00W*
192 *K10* **Stratford** Taranaki, North Island, NZ *39.20S 174.16E*
37 *Q11* **Stratford** California, W USA *36.10N 119.47W*
31 *V13* **Stratford** Iowa, C USA *42.16N 93.55W*
29 *O12* **Stratford** Oklahoma, C USA *34.48N 96.57W*
27 *N1* **Stratford** Texas, SW USA *36.20N 102.04W*
32 *K6* **Stratford** Wisconsin, N USA *44.53N 90.13W*
Stratford *see* Stratford-upon-Avon
99 *M20* **Stratford-upon-Avon** *var.* Stratford. C England, UK *52.12N 1.40W*
191 *O17* **Strathgordon** Tasmania, SE Australia *42.49S 146.04E*
9 *Q16* **Strathmore** Alberta, SW Canada *51.04N 113.19W*
37 *R11* **Strathmore** California, W USA *36.07N 119.04W*
12 *E16* **Strathroy** Ontario, S Canada *42.57N 81.40W*
98 *I6* **Strathy Point** *headland* N Scotland, UK *58.36N 4.04W*
39 *W4* **Stratton** Colorado, C USA *39.16N 102.34W*
21 *P6* **Stratton** Maine, NE USA *45.08N 70.25W*
20 *M10* **Stratton Mountain** ▲ Vermont, NE USA *43.05N 72.55W*
103 *N21* **Straubing** Bayern, SE Germany *48.52N 12.34E*
102 *O12* **Strausberg** Brandenburg, E Germany *52.34N 13.52E*
34 *K13* **Strawberry Mountain** ▲ Oregon, NW USA *44.18N 118.43W*
31 *X12* **Strawberry Point** Iowa, C USA *42.40N 91.31W*
38 *M3* **Strawberry Reservoir** ⊠ Utah, W USA
38 *M4* **Strawberry River** ~ Utah, W USA
27 *R7* **Strawn** Texas, SW USA *32.33N 98.30W*
115 *P17* **Straža** ▲ Bulgaria/FYR Macedonia *42.16N 22.13E*
113 *I19* **Strážov** *Hung.* Sztrazsó. ▲ NW Slovakia *48.59N 18.29E*
190 *F7* **Streaky Bay** South Australia *32.49S 134.13E*
190 *E7* **Streaky Bay** *bay* South Australia
32 *L12* **Streator** Illinois, N USA *41.07N 88.50W*
Streckenbach *see* Świdnik
113 *C17* **Středočeský Kraj** ◈ *region* C Czech Republic
Strednogorie *see* Pirdop
31 *O6* **Streeter** North Dakota, N USA *46.37N 99.23W*
27 *U8* **Streetman** Texas, SW USA *31.52N 96.19W*
118 *G13* **Strehaia** Mehedinţi, SW Romania *44.37N 23.10E*
Strehlen *see* Strzelin
116 *I10* **Strelcha** Pazardzhik, C Bulgaria *42.28N 24.21E*
126 *I13* **Strelka** Krasnoyarskiy Kray, C Russian Federation *58.04N 92.54E*
128 *L6* **Strel'na** ~ NW Russian Federation
120 *H7* **Strenči** *Ger.* Stackeln. Valka, N Latvia *57.38N 25.42E*
110 *K8* **Strengen** Tirol, W Austria *47.07N 10.25E*
108 *C6* **Stresa** Piemonte, NE Italy *45.52N 8.32E*
Streshin *see* Streshyn
121 *N18* **Streshyn** *Rus.* Streshin. Homyel'skaya Voblasts', SE Belarus *52.42N 30.08E*
97 *B18* **Streymoy** *Dan.* Strømø *Island* Faeroe Islands *62.10N 7.05W*
126 *Gg11* **Strezhevoy** Tomskaya Oblast', C Russian Federation *60.39N 77.37E*
97 *G23* **Strib** Fyn, C Denmark *55.33N 9.46E*
113 *A17* **Stříbro** *Ger.* Mies. Plzeňský Kraj, W Czech Republic *49.44N 12.55E*
194 *E13* **Strickland** ~ SW PNG
Striegau *see* Strzegom
Strigonium *see* Esztergom
100 *H13* **Strijen** Zuid-Holland, SW Netherlands *51.45N 4.34E*
65 *H21* **Strobel, Lago** ◎ S Argentina
63 *B25* **Stroeder** Buenos Aires, E Argentina *40.10S 62.34W*
117 *C20* **Strofádes** *island* Iónioi Nísoi, Greece, C Mediterranean Sea
Strofilia *see* Strofyliá
117 *G17* **Strofyliá** *var.* Strofilia. Évvoia, C Greece *38.49N 23.25E*
102 *O10* **Strom** ~ NE Germany
109 *L22* **Stromboli** ▲ Isola Stromboli, SW Italy *38.48N 15.13E*
109 *L22* **Stromboli, Isola** *island* Isole Eolie, S Italy
98 *H9* **Stromeferry** N Scotland, UK *57.20N 5.34W*
98 *J5* **Stromness** N Scotland, UK *58.57N 3.18W*
96 *N11* **Strömsbruk** Gävleborg, C Sweden *61.52N 17.19E*
31 *Q15* **Stromsburg** Nebraska, C USA *41.06N 97.36W*
97 *K21* **Strömsnäsbruk** Kronoberg, S Sweden *56.34N 13.45E*
97 *I17* **Strömstad** Västra Götaland, S Sweden *58.55N 11.10E*
95 *G16* **Strömsund** Jämtland, C Sweden *63.51N 15.34E*
95 *G15* **Ströms Vattudal** *valley* N Sweden
29 *V14* **Strong** Arkansas, C USA *33.06N 92.19W*
Strongilí *see* Strongylí
109 *O21* **Strongoli** Calabria, SW Italy *39.17N 17.03E*
33 *T11* **Strongsville** Ohio, N USA *41.18N 81.50W*
117 *Q23* **Strongylí** *var.* Strongilí. *island* SE Greece
98 *K5* **Stronsay** *island* NE Scotland, UK
99 *L21* **Stroud** C England, UK *51.45N 2.15W*
29 *O10* **Stroud** Oklahoma, C USA *35.45N 96.39W*
20 *I14* **Stroudsburg** Pennsylvania, NE USA *40.59N 75.12W*
97 *F21* **Struer** Ringkøbing, W Denmark *56.28N 8.37E*
115 *M20* **Struga** SW FYR Macedonia *41.11N 20.40E*
Strugi-Kranyse *see* Strugi-Krasnyye
128 *G14* **Strugi-Krasnyye** *var.* Strugi-Kranyse. Pskovskaya Oblast', W Russian Federation *58.19N 29.09E*
116 *G11* **Struma** *Gk.* Strymónas. ~ Bulgaria/Greece ***see also*** Strymónas
99 *G21* **Strumble Head** *headland* SW Wales, UK *52.01N 5.05W*
115 *Q19* **Strumeshnitsa** | Mac. Strumica. ~ Bulgaria/FYR Macedonia
115 *Q19* **Strumica** E FYR Macedonia *41.27N 22.39E*
Strumica *see* Strumeshnitsa
116 *G11* **Strumyani** Blagoevgrad, SW Bulgaria *41.41N 23.13E*
33 *V12* **Struthers** Ohio, N USA *41.03N 80.36W*
116 *I10* **Stryama** ~ C Bulgaria
116 *G13* **Strymónas** *Bul.* Struma. ~ Bulgaria/Greece ***see also*** Struma
117 *H14* **Strymonikós Kólpos** *gulf* N Greece
118 *I6* **Stryy** L'vivs'ka Oblast', NW Ukraine *49.16N 23.51E*
118 *H6* **Stryy** ~ W Ukraine
113 *F14* **Strzegom** *Ger.* Striegau. Walbrzych, SW Poland *50.58N 16.19E*

◆ Country ● Country Capital ◇ Dependent Territory ○ Dependent Territory Capital ◈ Administrative Region ✈ International Airport ▲ Mountain ▲▲ Mountain Range ▲ Volcano ~ River ◎ Lake ⊠ Reservoir

112 E10 **Strzelce Krajeńskie** *Ger.* Friedeberg Neumark. Lubuskie, W Poland *52.52N 15.30E*
113 I15 **Strzelce Opolskie** *Ger.* Gross Strehlitz. Opolskie, S Poland *50.31N 18.19E*
190 K3 **Strzelecki Creek** *seasonal river* South Australia
190 J3 **Strzelecki Desert** *desert* South Australia
113 G15 **Strzelin** *Ger.* Strehlen. Dolnośląskie, SW Poland *50.46N 17.03E*
112 I11 **Strzelno** Kujawsko-pomorskie, C Poland *52.38N 18.11E*
113 N17 **Strzyżów** Podkarpackie, SE Poland *49.52N 21.46E*
Stua Laighean *see* Leinster, Mount
25 Y13 **Stuart** Florida, SE USA *27.12N 80.15W*
31 U14 **Stuart** Iowa, C USA *41.30N 94.19W*
31 O13 **Stuart** Nebraska, C USA *42.36N 99.08W*
23 S8 **Stuart** Virginia, NE USA *36.38N 80.16W*
8 L13 **Stuart** ≈ British Columbia, SW Canada
41 N10 **Stuart Island** *island* Alaska, USA
8 L13 **Stuart Lake** ◎ British Columbia, SW Canada
193 B22 **Stuart Mountains** ▲▲ South Island, NZ
190 F3 **Stuart Range** *hill range* South Australia
Stubaital *see* Neustift im Stubaital
97 I24 **Stubbekøbing** Storstrøm, SE Denmark *54.52N 12.04E*
47 P14 **Stubbs** Saint Vincent, Saint Vincent and the Grenadines *13.08N 61.09W*
111 V6 **Stübming** ≈ E Austria
116 J11 **Studen Kladenets, Yazovir** ▣ S Bulgaria
193 G21 **Studholme** Canterbury, South Island, NZ *44.44S 171.07E*
Stuhlweissenberg *see* Székesfehérvár
Stuhm *see* Sztum
10 C7 **Stull Lake** ◎ Ontario, C Canada
Stung Treng *see* Stŏeng Trêng
130 L4 **Stupino** Moskovskaya Oblast', W Russian Federation *54.54N 38.06E*
29 U4 **Sturgeon** Missouri, C USA *39.13N 92.16W*
12 G10 **Sturgeon** ≈ Ontario, S Canada
33 N6 **Sturgeon Bay** Wisconsin, N USA *44.51N 87.21W*
12 G11 **Sturgeon Falls** Ontario, S Canada *46.22N 79.57W*
10 C11 **Sturgeon Lake** ◎ Ontario, S Canada
32 M3 **Sturgeon River** ≈ Michigan, N USA
22 H6 **Sturgis** Kentucky, S USA *37.33N 87.58W*
33 P11 **Sturgis** Michigan, N USA *41.48N 85.25W*
30 J9 **Sturgis** South Dakota, N USA *44.24N 103.30W*
114 D10 **Šturlić** Federacija Bosna I Hercegovina, NW Bosnia and Herzegovina *45.03N 15.47E*
113 J22 **Štúrovo** *Hung.* Párkány; *prev.* Parkan. Nitriansky Kraj, W Slovakia *47.49N 18.44E*
190 L4 **Sturt, Mount** *hill* New South Wales, SE Australia *29.30S 141.41E*
189 P4 **Sturt Plain** *plain* Northern Territory, N Australia
189 T9 **Sturt Stony Desert** *desert* South Australia
85 J25 **Stutterheim** Eastern Cape, S South Africa *32.34S 27.25E*
103 H21 **Stuttgart** Baden-Württemberg, SW Germany *48.47N 9.12E*
29 W12 **Stuttgart** Arkansas, C USA *34.30N 91.33W*
94 H2 **Stykkishólmur** Vesturland, W Iceland *65.03N 22.43W*
117 F17 **Stylída** *var.* Stilida, Stilís. Stereá Ellás, C Greece *38.55N 22.37E*
118 K2 **Styr** *Rus.* Styr'. ≈ Belarus/Ukraine
117 I19 **Stýra** *var.* Stira. Évvoia, C Greece *38.10N 24.13E*
Styria *see* Steiermark
Su *see* Jiangsu
Sua *see* Sowa
175 S17 **Suai** W East Timor *9.19S 125.16E*
56 G9 **Suaita** Santander, C Colombia *6.07N 73.30W*
82 I7 **Suakin** *var.* Sawakin. Red Sea, NE Sudan *19.06N 37.17E*
167 T13 **Suao** *Jap.* Suō. N Taiwan *24.33N 121.48E*
Suao *see* Suau
42 G6 **Suaqui Grande** Sonora, NW Mexico *28.22N 109.52W*
63 A16 **Suardi** Santa Fe, C Argentina *30.31S 61.58W*
56 D11 **Suárez** Cauca, SW Colombia *2.55N 76.40W*
195 N17 **Suau** *var.* Suao. Suaul Island, SE PNG *10.44S 150.18E*
120 G12 **Subačius** Kupiškis, NE Lithuania *55.46N 24.45E*
174 Jj14 **Subang** *prev.* Soebang. Jawa, C Indonesia *6.31S 107.45E*
174 Gg5 **Subang** ✈ (Kuala Lumpur) Pahang, Peninsular Malaysia
133 S10 **Subansiri** ≈ NE India
120 I11 **Subate** Daugvapils, SE Latvia *56.00N 25.54E*
145 N5 **Subaykhān** Dayr az Zawr, E Syria *34.47N 40.38E*
165 P8 **Subei** *var.* Dangchengwan, Subei Mongolzu Zizhixian. Gansu, N China *39.33N 94.50E*
Subei Mongolzu Zizhixian *see* Subei
174 K5 **Subi Besar, Pulau** *island* Kepulauan Natuna, W Indonesia
Subiyah *see* Aş Şubayḩīyah
28 I7 **Sublette** Kansas, C USA *37.26N 100.48W*
114 K8 **Subotica** *Ger.* Maria-Theresiopel, *Hung.* Szabadka. Serbia, N Serbia and Montenegro (Yugoslavia) *46.06N 19.40E*
118 K9 **Suceava** *Ger.* Suczawa, *Hung.* Szucsava. Suceava, NE Romania *47.40N 26.15E*
118 J9 **Suceava** ◈ *county* NE Romania
118 K9 **Suceava** *Ger.* Suczawa. ≈ N Romania
114 E12 **Sučevići** Zadar, SW Croatia *44.13N 16.04E*
113 K17 **Sucha Beskidzka** Małopolskie, S Poland *49.39N 19.11E*
113 M14 **Suchedniów** Świętokrzyskie, C Poland *51.01N 20.49E*
44 A2 **Suchitepéquez** *off.* Departamento de Suchitepéquez. ◈ *department* SW Guatemala
Su-chou *see* Suzhou
Suchow *see* Suzhou, Jiangsu, China
Suchow *see* Xuzhou, Jiangsu, China
99 D17 **Suck** ≈ C Ireland
Sucker State *see* Illinois
194 M16 **Suckling, Mount** ▲ S PNG *9.36S 149.00E*
59 L19 **Sucre** *hist.* Chuquisaca, La Plata. ● (Bolivia-legal capital) Chuquisaca, S Bolivia *18.52S 65.24W*
56 E6 **Sucre** Santander, N Colombia *8.50N 74.22W*
58 A7 **Sucre** Manabí, W Ecuador *1.21S 80.27W*
56 E6 **Sucre** *off.* Departamento de Sucre. ◈ *province* N Colombia
57 O5 **Sucre** *off.* Estado Sucre. ◈ *state* NE Venezuela
58 D6 **Sucumbíos** ◈ *province* NE Ecuador
115 G15 **Sućuraj** Split-Dalmacija, S Croatia *43.07N 17.10E*
60 K10 **Sucuriju** Amapá, NE Brazil *1.30N 50.00W*
Suczawa *see* Suceava
81 E16 **Sud** *Eng.* South. ◈ *province* S Cameroon
128 K13 **Suda** ≈ NW Russian Federation
Suda *see* Soúda
119 U13 **Sudak** Respublika Krym, S Ukraine *44.51N 34.55E*
26 M4 **Sudan** Texas, SW USA *34.04N 102.31W*
82 C10 **Sudan** *off.* Republic of Sudan, *Ar.* Jumhuriyat as-Sudan; *prev.* Anglo-Egyptian **Sudan.** ◆ *republic* N Africa
Sudanese Republic *see* Mali
Sudan, Jumhuriyat as- *see* Sudan
12 F10 **Sudbury** Ontario, S Canada *46.29N 80.59W*
99 P20 **Sudbury** E England, UK *52.04N 0.43E*
Sud, Canal de *see* Gonâve, Canal de la
82 E13 **Sudd** *swamp region* S Sudan
102 K10 **Sude** ≈ N Germany
Sudest Island *see* Tagula Island
113 E15 **Sudeten** *var.* Sudetes, Sudetic Mountains, *Cz./Pol.* Sudety. ▲▲ Czech Republic/Poland
Sudetes/Sudetic Mountains/Sudety *see* Sudeten
94 G1 **Sudhureyri** Vestfirdhir, NW Iceland *66.08N 23.31W*
94 J4 **Sudhurland** ◈ *region* S Iceland
97 B19 **Sudhuroy** *Dan.* Suderø *Island* Faeroe Islands *61.60N 6.29W*
176 Xx12 **Sudirman, Pegunungan** ▲▲ Papua, E Indonesia
128 M15 **Sudislavl'** Kostromskaya Oblast', NW Russian Federation *57.55N 41.45E*
Südkarpaten *see* Carpații Meridionali
81 N20 **Sud Kivu** *off.* Région Sud Kivu. ◈ *region* E Dem. Rep. Congo
Südliche Morava *see* Južna Morava
102 E12 **Süd-Nord-Kanal** *canal* NW Germany
130 M3 **Sudogda** Vladimirskaya Oblast', W Russian Federation *55.58N 40.57E*
Sudostroy *see* Severodvinsk
81 C15 **Sud-Ouest** *Eng.* South-West. ◈ *province* W Cameroon
181 X17 **Sud Ouest, Pointe** *headland* SW Mauritius *20.27S 57.18E*
197 J7 **Sud, Province** ◈ *province* S New Caledonia
130 J8 **Sudzha** Kurskaya Oblast', W Russian Federation *51.12N 35.19E*
83 D15 **Sue** ≈ S Sudan
107 S10 **Sueca** País Valenciano, E Spain *39.13N 0.19W*
116 I10 **Sŭedinenie** Plovdiv, C Bulgaria *42.14N 24.36E*
Suero *see* Alzira
77 X8 **Suez** *Ar.* As Suways, El Suweis. NE Egypt *29.58N 32.33E*
77 W7 **Suez Canal** *Ar.* Qanāt as Suways. *canal* NE Egypt
77 X8 **Suez, Gulf of** *Ar.* Khalīj as Suways. *gulf* NE Egypt
9 R17 **Suffield** Alberta, SW Canada *50.15N 111.05W*
23 X7 **Suffolk** Virginia, NE USA *36.43N 76.34W*
99 P20 **Suffolk** *cultural region* E England, UK
148 J2 **Şūfiān** Āżarbāyjān-e Khāvarī, N Iran *38.15N 45.58E*
33 N12 **Sugar Creek** ≈ Illinois, N USA
32 L13 **Sugar Creek** ≈ Illinois, N USA
33 R3 **Sugar Island** *island* Michigan, N USA
27 V11 **Sugar Land** Texas, SW USA *29.37N 95.37W*
21 P6 **Sugarloaf Mountain** ▲ Maine, NE USA *45.01N 70.18W*
67 G24 **Sugar Loaf Point** *headland* N Saint Helena *15.54S 5.43W*
142 G16 **Suğla Gölü** ◎ SW Turkey
127 O8 **Sugoy** ≈ E Russian Federation
164 F7 **Sugun** Xinjiang Uygur Zizhiqu, W China *39.46N 76.45E*
153 U11 **Sugut, Gora** ▲ SW Kyrgyzstan *39.52N 73.36E*
175 O2 **Sugut, Sungai** ≈ East Malaysia
165 O9 **Suhai Hu** ◎ C China
168 K14 **Suhait** Nei Mongol Zizhiqu, N China *39.29N 105.11E*
147 X7 **Şuḩār** *var.* Sohar. N Oman *24.20N 56.43E*
168 L6 **Sühbaatar** Selenge, N Mongolia *50.11N 106.14E*
169 P9 **Sühbaatar** ◈ *province* E Mongolia
103 K17 **Suhl** Thüringen, C Germany *50.37N 10.43E*
110 F7 **Suhr** Aargau, N Switzerland *47.22N 8.04E*
167 O12 **Suichuan** Jiangxi, S China *26.18N 114.31E*
Suid-Afrika *see* South Africa
166 L4 **Suide** Shaanxi, C China *37.30N 110.10E*
Suidwes-Afrika *see* Namibia
169 Y9 **Suifenhe** Heilongjiang, NE China *44.22N 131.12E*
Suigen *see* Suwŏn
169 W8 **Suihua** Heilongjiang, NE China *46.40N 127.00E*
Súilí, Loch *see* Swilly, Lough
167 Q6 **Suining** Jiangsu, E China *33.54N 117.58E*
166 I9 **Suining** Sichuan, C China *30.31N 105.33E*
105 Q4 **Suippes** Marne, N France *49.08N 4.31E*
99 E20 **Suir** *Ir.* An tSiúir. ≈ S Ireland
171 Gg15 **Suita** Ōsaka, Honshū, SW Japan *34.39N 135.27E*
166 L16 **Suixi** Guangdong, S China *21.22N 110.13E*
Sui Xian *see* Suizhou
169 T13 **Suizhong** Liaoning, NE China *40.19N 120.20E*
167 N8 **Suizhou** *prev.* Sui Xian. Hubei, C China *31.46N 113.20E*
155 P17 **Sujāwal** Sind, SE Pakistan *24.36N 68.06E*
174 Jj14 **Sukabumi** *prev.* Soekaboemi. Jawa, C Indonesia *6.55S 106.55E*
174 Kk9 **Sukadana, Teluk** *bay* Borneo, W Indonesia
171 Ll14 **Sukagawa** Fukushima, Honshū, C Japan *37.16N 140.19E*
Sukarnapura *see* Jayapura
Sukarno, Puntjak *see* Jaya, Puncak
Sŭkh *see* Sokh
116 N8 **Sukha Reka** ≈ NE Bulgaria
130 J5 **Sukhinichi** Kaluzhskaya Oblast', W Russian Federation *54.06N 35.22E*
Sukhne *see* As Sukhnah
133 Q4 **Sukhona** *var.* Tot'ma. ≈ NW Russian Federation
178 H9 **Sukhothai** *var.* Sukotai. Sukhothai, W Thailand *17.00N 99.51E*
Sukhumi *see* Sokhumi
Sukkertoppen *see* Maniitsoq
155 Q13 **Sukkur** Sind, SE Pakistan *27.44N 68.46E*
Sukotai *see* Sukhothai
Sukra Bay *see* Şawqirah, Dawḩat
129 V15 **Suksun** Permskaya Oblast', NW Russian Federation *57.10N 57.27E*
170 E16 **Sukumo** Kōchi, Shikoku, SW Japan *32.55N 132.42E*
96 B12 **Sula** *island* S Norway
129 Q5 **Sula** ≈ NW Russian Federation
119 R5 **Sula** ≈ N Ukraine
44 H6 **Sulaco, Río** ≈ NW Honduras
Sulaimaniya *see* As Sulaymānīyah
155 S10 **Sulaimān Range** ▲▲ C Pakistan
131 Q16 **Sulak** Respublika Dagestan, SW Russian Federation *43.19N 47.28E*
131 Q16 **Sulak** ≈ SW Russian Federation
175 Rr10 **Sula, Kepulauan** *island group* C Indonesia
142 I12 **Sulakyurt** *var.* Konur. Kırıkkale, N Turkey *40.10N 33.42E*
175 R17 **Sulamu** Timor, S Indonesia *9.57S 123.33E*
98 F5 **Sula Sgeir** *island* NW Scotland, UK
175 Pp10 **Sulawesi** *Eng.* Celebes. *island* C Indonesia
Sulawesi, Laut *see* Celebes Sea
175 P11 **Sulawesi Selatan** *off.* Propinsi Sulawesi Selatan, *Eng.* South Celebes, South Sulawesi. ◈ *province* C Indonesia
175 Q9 **Sulawesi Tengah** *off.* Propinsi Sulawesi Tengah, *Eng.* Central Celebes, Central Sulawesi. ◈ *province* N Indonesia
175 Q11 **Sulawesi Tenggara** *off.* Propinsi Sulawesi Tenggara, *Eng.* South-East Celebes, South-East Sulawesi. ◈ *province* C Indonesia
175 Qq7 **Sulawesi Utara** *off.* Propinsi Sulawesi Utara, *Eng.* North Celebes, North Sulawesi. ◈ *province* N Indonesia
145 T5 **Sulaymān Beg** N Iraq
97 D15 **Suldalsvatnet** ◎ S Norway
112 E12 **Sulechów** *Ger.* Züllichau. Lubuskie, W Poland *52.04N 15.37E*
112 E11 **Sulęcin** Lubuskie, W Poland *52.29N 15.06E*
79 U14 **Suleja** Niger, C Nigeria *9.15N 7.10E*
113 K14 **Sulejów** Łodzkie, S Poland *51.21N 19.57E*
98 I5 **Sule Skerry** *island* N Scotland, UK
Suliag *see* Sohâg
78 J16 **Sulima** S Sierra Leone *6.58N 11.34W*
119 O13 **Sulina** Tulcea, SE Romania *45.07N 29.40E*
119 N13 **Sulina Braţul** ≈ SE Romania
102 H12 **Sulingen** Niedersachsen, NW Germany *52.40N 8.48E*
94 H12 **Suliskongen** ▲ C Norway *67.10N 16.16E*
94 H12 **Sulitjelma** Nordland, C Norway *67.09N 15.59E*
58 A9 **Sullana** Piura, NW Peru *4.54S 80.42W*
25 N3 **Sulligent** Alabama, S USA *33.54N 88.07W*
32 M14 **Sullivan** Illinois, N USA *39.36N 88.36W*
33 N15 **Sullivan** Indiana, N USA *39.04N 87.24W*
29 W5 **Sullivan** Missouri, C USA *38.12N 91.09W*
Sullivan Island *see* Lanbi Kyun
98 M1 **Sullom Voe** NE Scotland, UK *60.24N 1.09W*
105 O7 **Sully-sur-Loire** Loiret, C France *47.46N 2.21E*
Sulmo *see* Sulmona
109 K15 **Sulmona** *anc.* Sulmo. Abruzzo, C Italy *42.03N 13.55E*
Sulo *see* Shule He
116 M11 **Süloğlu** Edirne, NW Turkey *41.46N 26.55E*
24 G9 **Sulphur** Louisiana, S USA *30.14N 93.22W*
29 O12 **Sulphur** Oklahoma, C USA *34.30N 96.58W*
30 K9 **Sulphur Creek** ≈ South Dakota, N USA
26 M5 **Sulphur Draw** ≈ Texas, SW USA
27 W5 **Sulphur River** ≈ Arkansas/Texas, SW USA
27 V6 **Sulphur Springs** Texas, SW USA *33.09N 95.36W*
26 M6 **Sulphur Springs Draw** ≈ Texas, SW USA
12 D8 **Sultan** Ontario, S Canada *47.34N 82.45W*
Sultānābād *see* Arāk
Sultan Alonto, Lake *see* Lanao, Lake
142 G15 **Sultan Dağları** ▲▲ C Turkey
116 N13 **Sultanköy** Tekirdağ, NW Turkey *41.01N 27.58E*
179 R16 **Sultan Kudarat** *var.* Nuling. Mindanao, S Philippines *7.20N 124.16E*
158 M13 **Sultānpur** Uttar Pradesh, N India *26.15N 82.04E*
179 Pp17 **Sulu Archipelago** *island group* SW Philippines
198 Ff7 **Sulu Basin** *undersea feature* SE South China Sea
Sülüktü *see* Sulyukta
Sulu, Laut *see* Sulu Sea
175 Pp1 **Sulu Sea** *Ind.* Laut Sulu. *sea* SW Philippines
151 O15 **Sulutobe** *Kaz.* Sulūtöbe. Kzylorda, S Kazakhstan *44.31N 66.17E*
153 Q11 **Sulyukta** *Kir.* Sülüktü. Oshskaya Oblast', SW Kyrgyzstan *39.57N 69.30E*
Sulz *see* Sulz am Neckar
103 G22 **Sulz am Neckar** *var.* Sulz. Baden-Württemberg, SW Germany *48.22N 8.37E*
103 L20 **Sulzbach-Rosenberg** Bayern, SE Germany *49.30N 11.43E*
205 N13 **Sulzberger Bay** *bay* Antarctica
Sumail *see* Summēl
115 F15 **Sumartin** Split-Dalmacija, S Croatia *43.17N 16.52E*
34 H6 **Sumas** Washington, NW USA *49.00N 122.15W*
174 Gg7 **Sumatera** *Eng.* Sumatra. *island* W Indonesia
173 G9 **Sumatera Barat** *off.* Propinsi Sumatera Barat, *Eng.* West Sumatra. ◈ *province* W Indonesia
174 Hh11 **Sumatera Selatan** *off.* Propinsi Sumatera Selatan, *Eng.* South Sumatra. ◈ *province* W Indonesia
173 Ff6 **Sumatera Utara** *off.* Propinsi Sumatera Utara, *Eng.* North Sumatra. ◈ *province* W Indonesia
Sumatra *see* Sumatera
Šumava *see* Bohemian Forest
Sumayl *see* Summēl
145 U7 **Sumayr al Muḩammad** E Iraq *33.34N 45.06E*
175 P17 **Sumba, Pulau** *Eng.* Sandalwood Island; *prev.* Soemba. *island* Nusa Tenggara, C Indonesia
152 D12 **Sumbar** ≈ W Turkmenistan
175 P16 **Sumba, Selat** *strait* Nusa Tenggara, S Indonesia
175 Oo16 **Sumbawa** *prev.* Soembawa. *island* Nusa Tenggara, C Indonesia
175 O16 **Sumbawabesar** Sumbawa, S Indonesia *8.30S 117.25E*
83 F23 **Sumbawanga** Rukwa, W Tanzania *7.57S 31.36E*
84 B12 **Sumbe** *prev.* N'Gunza, *Port.* Novo Redondo. Cuanza Sul, W Angola *11.13S 13.52E*
98 M3 **Sumburgh Head** *headland* NE Scotland, UK *59.51N 1.16W*
113 H23 **Sümeg** Veszprém, W Hungary *47.00N 17.13E*
82 C12 **Sumeih** Southern Darfur, S Sudan *9.49N 27.39E*
174 Mm14 **Sumenep** *prev.* Soemenep. Pulau Madura, C Indonesia *7.01S 113.51E*
Sumgait *see* Sumqayıt, Azerbaijan
Sumgait *see* Sumqayıtçay, Azerbaijan
172 Ss14 **Sumisu-jima** *Eng.* Smith Island. *island* SE Japan
145 Q2 **Summēl** *var.* Sumail, Sumayl. N Iraq *36.52N 42.51E*
33 O5 **Summer Island** *island* Michigan, N USA
34 H15 **Summer Lake** ◎ Oregon, NW USA
9 N17 **Summerland** British Columbia, SW Canada *49.34N 119.45W*
11 P14 **Summerside** Prince Edward Island, SE Canada *46.24N 63.46W*
23 R5 **Summersville** West Virginia, NE USA *38.16N 80.51W*
23 R5 **Summersville Lake** ▣ West Virginia, NE USA
23 S13 **Summerton** South Carolina, SE USA *33.36N 80.21W*
25 R2 **Summerville** Georgia, SE USA *34.28N 85.21W*
23 S14 **Summerville** South Carolina, SE USA *33.01N 80.10W*
41 R10 **Summit** Alaska, USA *63.21N 148.50W*
37 V6 **Summit Mountain** ▲ Nevada, W USA *39.23N 116.25W*
39 R8 **Summit Peak** ▲ Colorado, C USA *37.21N 106.42W*
Summus Portus *see* Somport, Col du
31 X12 **Sumner** Iowa, C USA *42.51N 92.05W*
24 K3 **Sumner** Mississippi, S USA *33.58N 90.22W*
193 H17 **Sumner, Lake** ◎ South Island, NZ
39 U12 **Sumner, Lake** ▣ New Mexico, SW USA
171 Kk13 **Sumon-dake** ▲ Honshū, C Japan *37.24N 139.07E*
170 G15 **Sumoto** Hyōgo, Awaji-shima, SW Japan *34.18N 134.52E*
113 G17 **Šumperk** *Ger.* Mährisch-Schönberg. Olomoucký Kraj, E Czech Republic *49.59N 16.58E*
44 F7 **Sumpul, Río** ≈ El Salvador/Honduras
143 Z11 **Sumqayıt** *Rus.* Sumgait. E Azerbaijan *40.33N 49.41E*
143 Y11 **Sumqayıtçay** *Rus.* Sumgait. ≈ E Azerbaijan
153 R9 **Sumsar** Dzhalal-Abadskaya Oblast', W Kyrgyzstan *41.12N 71.16E*
119 S3 **Sums'ka Oblast'** *var.* Sumy, *Rus.* Sumskaya Oblast'. ◈ *province* NE Ukraine
Sumskaya Oblast' *see* Sums'ka Oblast'
128 J8 **Sumskiy Posad** Respublika Kareliya, NW Russian Federation *64.12N 35.22E*
23 S12 **Sumter** South Carolina, SE USA *33.55N 80.20W*
119 T3 **Sumy** Sums'ka Oblast', NE Ukraine *50.54N 34.48E*
Sumy *see* Sums'ka Oblast'
165 Q15 **Sumzom** Xizang Zizhiqu, W China *29.45N 96.13E*
129 R15 **Suna** Kirovskaya Oblast', NW Russian Federation *57.53N 50.04E*
128 I10 **Suna** ≈ NW Russian Federation
172 Oo5 **Sunagawa** Hokkaidō, NE Japan *43.30N 141.55E*
159 V13 **Sunamganj** Chittagong, NE Bangladesh *25.04N 91.24E*
165 S8 **Sunan** *var.* Hongwan, Sunan Yugurzu Zizhixian. Gansu, N China *38.55N 99.29E*
169 W14 **Sunan** ✈ (P'yŏngyang) SW North Korea *39.12N 125.40E*
Sunan Yugurzu Zizhixian *see* Sunan
21 N9 **Sunapee Lake** ◎ New Hampshire, NE USA
145 P4 **Sunaysilah** *salt marsh* N Iraq
22 M8 **Sunbright** Tennessee, S USA *36.12N 84.39W*
35 R6 **Sunburst** Montana, NW USA *48.51N 111.54W*
191 N12 **Sunbury** Victoria, SE Australia *37.36S 144.42E*
23 X8 **Sunbury** North Carolina, SE USA *36.27N 76.34W*
20 G14 **Sunbury** Pennsylvania, NE USA *40.51N 76.47W*
63 A17 **Sunchales** Santa Fe, C Argentina *30.58S 61.34W*
169 W13 **Sunch'ŏn** SW North Korea *39.28N 125.58E*
169 Y16 **Sunch'ŏn** *Jap.* Junten. S South Korea *34.56N 127.28E*
38 K13 **Sun City** Arizona, SW USA *33.36N 112.16W*
21 O9 **Suncook** New Hampshire, NE USA *43.07N 71.25W*
Sunda Islands *see* Greater Sunda Islands
35 Z12 **Sundance** Wyoming, C USA *44.24N 104.22W*
159 T17 **Sundarbans** *wetland* Bangladesh/India
160 M11 **Sundargarh** Orissa, E India *22.07N 84.01E*
174 Ii14 **Sunda, Selat** *strait* Jawa/Sumatera, SW Indonesia
133 U15 **Sunda Shelf** *undersea feature* S South China Sea
Sunda Trench *see* Java Trench
133 U17 **Sunda Trough** *undersea feature* E Indian Ocean
97 O16 **Sundbyberg** Stockholm, C Sweden *59.22N 17.58E*
99 M14 **Sunderland** *var.* Wearmouth. NE England, UK *54.55N 1.22W*
103 F15 **Sundern** Nordrhein-Westfalen, W Germany *51.19N 8.00E*
142 F12 **Sündiken Dağları** ▲▲ C Turkey
26 M5 **Sundown** Texas, SW USA *33.27N 102.29W*
9 P16 **Sundre** Alberta, SW Canada *51.49N 114.46W*
12 H12 **Sundridge** Ontario, S Canada *45.45N 79.25W*
95 H17 **Sundsvall** Västernorrland, C Sweden *62.22N 17.19E*
28 H4 **Sunflower, Mount** ▲ Kansas, C USA *39.01N 102.02W*
Sunflower State *see* Kansas
174 Gg4 **Sungai Bernam** ≈ Peninsular Malaysia
174 Ii12 **Sungaibuntu** Sumatera, SW Indonesia *4.04S 105.37E*
174 Gg9 **Sungaidareh** Sumatera, W Indonesia *0.58S 101.30E*
178 Hh17 **Sungai Kolok** *var.* Sungai Ko-Lok. Narathiwat, SW Thailand *6.01N 101.58E*
174 Gg10 **Sungaipenuh** *prev.* Soengaipenoeh. Sumatera, W Indonesia *2.00S 101.28E*
174 Kk8 **Sungaipinyuh** Borneo, C Indonesia *0.16N 109.06E*
Sungari *see* Songhua Jiang
Sungaria *see* Dzungaria
Sungei Pahang *see* Pahang, Sungai
178 Hh8 **Sung Men** Phrae, NW Thailand *17.59N 100.07E*
85 M15 **Sungo** Tete, NW Mozambique *16.31S 33.58E*
174 Ii10 **Sungsang** Sumatera, W Indonesia *2.22S 104.50E*
116 M9 **Sungurlare** Burgas, E Bulgaria *42.47N 26.46E*
142 J12 **Sungurlu** Çorum, N Turkey *40.10N 34.22E*
114 F9 **Sunja** Sisak-Moslavina, C Croatia *45.21N 16.33E*
159 Q12 **Sun Koshi** ≈ E Nepal
96 F9 **Sunndalen** *valley* S Norway
96 F9 **Sunndalsøra** Møre og Romsdal, S Norway *62.40N 8.34E*
97 K15 **Sunne** Värmland, C Sweden *59.52N 14.30E*
97 O15 **Sunnersta** Uppsala, C Sweden *59.46N 17.40E*
96 C11 **Sunnfjord** *physical region* S Norway
97 C15 **Sunnhordland** *physical region* S Norway
96 D10 **Sunnmøre** *physical region* S Norway
39 N4 **Sunnyside** Utah, W USA *39.33N 110.23W*
34 J10 **Sunnyside** Washington, NW USA *46.01N 119.58W*
37 N9 **Sunnyvale** California, W USA *37.22N 122.02W*
32 L8 **Sun Prairie** Wisconsin, N USA *43.12N 89.12W*
Sunqur *see* Sonqor
27 N1 **Sunray** Texas, SW USA *36.01N 101.49W*
24 I8 **Sunset** Louisiana, S USA *30.24N 92.04W*
27 S5 **Sunset** Texas, SW USA *33.24N 97.45W*
Sunset State *see* Oregon
189 Z10 **Sunshine Coast** *cultural region* Queensland, E Australia
Sunshine State *see* Florida, USA
Sunshine State *see* New Mexico, USA
Sunshine State *see* South Dakota, USA
126 Kk11 **Suntar** Respublika Sakha (Yakutiya), NE Russian Federation *62.09N 117.34E*
41 R10 **Suntrana** Alaska, USA *63.51N 148.51W*
154 J15 **Suntsar** Baluchistān, SW Pakistan *25.30N 62.03E*
169 W15 **Sunwi-do** *island* SW North Korea
169 W6 **Sunwu** Heilongjiang, NE China *49.23N 127.17E*
79 O16 **Sunyani** W Ghana *7.22N 2.18W*
Suō *see* Suao
95 M17 **Suolahti** Länsi-Suomi, W Finland *62.32N 25.51E*
Suoločielgi *see* Saariselkä
Suomenlahti *see* Finland, Gulf of
Suomen Tasavalta/Suomi *see* Finland
95 N14 **Suomussalmi** Oulu, E Finland *64.54N 29.05E*
170 D13 **Suō-nada** *sea* SW Japan
95 M17 **Suonenjoki** Itä-Suomi, C Finland *62.36N 27.06E*
178 Jj13 **Suŏng** Kâmpóng Cham, C Cambodia *11.53N 105.41E*
128 I10 **Suoyarvi** Respublika Kareliya, NW Russian Federation *62.01N 32.24E*
Supanburi *see* Suphan Buri
59 D14 **Supe** Lima, W Peru *10.49S 77.42W*
13 V7 **Supérieur, Lac** ◎ Quebec, SE Canada
Supérieur, Lac *see* Superior, Lake
38 M14 **Superior** Arizona, SW USA *33.17N 111.06W*
35 O9 **Superior** Montana, NW USA *47.11N 114.53W*
31 P17 **Superior** Nebraska, C USA *40.01N 98.04W*
32 I3 **Superior** Wisconsin, N USA *46.41N 92.03W*
43 S17 **Superior, Laguna** *lagoon* S Mexico
33 N2 **Superior, Lake** *Fr.* Lac Supérieur. ◎ Canada/USA
38 L13 **Superstition Mountains** ▲▲ Arizona, SW USA
115 F14 **Supetar** *It.* San Pietro. Split-Dalmacija, S Croatia *43.22N 16.34E*
178 H11 **Suphan Buri** *var.* Supanburi. Suphan Buri, W Thailand *14.28N 100.10E*
176 W9 **Supiori, Pulau** *island* E Indonesia
196 K2 **Supply Reef** *reef* N Northern Mariana Islands
205 O7 **Support Force Glacier** *glacier* Antarctica
143 R10 **Sup'sa** *var.* Supsa. ≈ W Georgia
Sūq 'Abs *see* 'Abs
145 W12 **Sūq ash Shuyūkh** SE Iraq *30.52N 46.28E*
144 H4 **Şuqaylibīyah** Ḩamāh, W Syria *35.21N 36.24E*
167 Q6 **Suqian** Jiangsu, E China *33.57N 118.18E*
Suqrah *see* Şawqirah
Suqrah Bay *see* Şawqirah, Dawḩat
147 V16 **Suquṭrā** *var.* Sokotra, *Eng.* Socotra. *island* SE Yemen
147 Z8 **Şūr** NE Oman *22.32N 59.33E*
Şūr *see* Soûr
131 P5 **Sura** Penzenskaya Oblast', W Russian Federation *53.23N 45.03E*
131 P4 **Sura** ≈ W Russian Federation
155 N12 **Sūrāb** Baluchistān, SW Pakistan *28.28N 66.15E*
Surabaja *see* Surabaya
174 M15 **Surabaya** *prev.* Soerabaja, Surabaja. Jawa, C Indonesia *7.13S 112.45E*
97 N15 **Surahammar** Västmanland, C Sweden *59.43N 16.13E*
174 L15 **Surakarta** *Eng.* Solo; *prev.* Soerakarta. Jawa, S Indonesia *7.31S 110.49E*
Surakhany *see* Suraxanı
179 R17 **Surallah** Mindanao, S Philippines *6.16N 124.46E*
143 S10 **Surami** C Georgia *41.59N 43.36E*
149 X13 **Sūrān** Sīstān va Balūchestān, SE Iran *27.18N 61.58E*
113 I21 **Šurany** *Hung.* Nagysurány. Nitriansky Kraj, SW Slovakia *48.05N 18.10E*
160 D12 **Sūrat** Gujarāt, W India *21.10N 72.54E*
Suratdhani *see* Surat Thani
158 G9 **Sūratgarh** Rājasthān, NW India *29.19N 73.58E*
178 Gg15 **Surat Thani** *var.* Suratdhani. Surat Thani, SW Thailand *9.09N 99.19E*
121 Q16 **Suraw** *Rus.* Surov. ≈ E Belarus
143 Z11 **Suraxanı** *Rus.* Surakhany. E Azerbaijan *40.25N 49.59E*
147 Y11 **Surayr** E Oman *19.55N 57.46E*
144 K2 **Suraysāt** Ḩalab, N Syria *36.42N 38.01E*
120 O12 **Surazh** *Rus.* Surazh. Vitsyebskaya Voblasts', NE Belarus *55.24N 30.46E*
130 H6 **Surazh** Bryanskaya Oblast', W Russian Federation *53.04N 32.29E*
203 V17 **Sur, Cabo** *headland* Easter Island, Chile, E Pacific Ocean *27.10S 109.25W*
114 L11 **Surčin** Serbia, N Serbia and Montenegro (Yugoslavia) *44.48N 20.19E*
118 H9 **Surduc** *Hung.* Szurduk. Sălaj, NW Romania *47.13N 23.19E*
115 P16 **Surdulica** Serbia, SE Serbia and Montenegro (Yugoslavia) *42.43N 22.10E*
101 L24 **Sûre** *var.* Sauer. ≈ W Europe *see also* Sauer
160 C10 **Surendranagar** Gujarāt, W India *22.43N 71.43E*
20 K16 **Surf City** New Jersey, NE USA *39.21N 74.24W*
191 V3 **Surfers Paradise** Queensland, E Australia *27.54S 153.18E*
23 U13 **Surfside Beach** South Carolina, SE USA *33.36N 78.58W*
104 J10 **Surgères** Charente-Maritime, W France *46.07N 0.44W*
125 G11 **Surgut** Khanty-Mansiyskiy Avtonomnyy Okrug, C Russian Federation *61.13N 73.28E*
126 Hh10 **Surgutikha** Krasnoyarskiy Kray, N Russian Federation *64.44N 87.13E*
100 M6 **Surhuisterveen** Friesland, N Netherlands *53.10N 6.10E*
107 V5 **Súria** Cataluña, NE Spain *41.49N 1.45E*
149 P10 **Sūriān** Fārs, S Iran
161 J15 **Suriāpet** Andhra Pradesh, C India *17.10N 79.42E*
179 R14 **Surigao** Mindanao, S Philippines *9.43N 125.31E*
178 Ii11 **Surin** Surin, E Thailand *14.52N 103.28E*
Surinam *see* Suriname
57 U11 **Suriname** *off.* Republic of Suriname, *var.* Surinam; *prev.* Dutch Guiana, Netherlands Guiana. ◆ *republic* N South America
Sūrīya/Sūrīyah, Al-Jumhūrīyah al-'Arabīyah as - *see* Syria
Surkhab, Darya-i- *see* Kahmard, Daryā-ye
Surkhandar'inskaya Oblast' *see* Surkhondaryo Viloyati
Surkhandar'ya *see* Surxondaryo
Surkhet *see* Birendranagar
153 R12 **Surkhob** ≈ C Tajikistan
153 N13 **Surkhondaryo Viloyati** *Rus.* Surkhandar'inskaya Oblast'. ◈ *province* S Uzbekistan
143 P11 **Sürmene** Trabzon, NE Turkey *40.55N 40.03E*
Surov *see* Suraw
131 N11 **Surovikino** Volgogradskaya Oblast', SW Russian Federation *48.39N 42.46E*
126 Jj14 **Surovo** Irkutskaya Oblast', S Russian Federation *55.45N 105.31E*
37 N11 **Sur, Point** *headland* California, W USA *36.18N 121.54W*
197 F3 **Surprise, Île** *island* N New Caledonia
63 E22 **Sur, Punta** *headland* E Argentina *50.58S 69.10W*
Surrentum *see* Sorrento
30 M3 **Surrey** North Dakota, N USA *48.13N 101.05W*
99 O22 **Surrey** *cultural region* SE England, UK
23 X7 **Surry** Virginia, NE USA *37.08N 76.48W*
110 F8 **Sursee** Luzern, W Switzerland *47.10N 8.07E*
131 P6 **Sursk** Penzenskaya Oblast', W Russian Federation *53.06N 45.46E*
131 P5 **Surskoye** Ul'yanovskaya Oblast', W Russian Federation *54.28N 46.47E*
77 P8 **Surt** *var.* Sidra, Sirte. N Libya *31.13N 16.34E*
97 I19 **Surte** Västra Götaland, S Sweden *57.49N 12.01E*
77 Q8 **Surt, Khalīj** *Eng.* Gulf of Sidra, Gulf of Sirti, Sidra. *gulf* N Libya
94 I5 **Surtsey** *island* S Iceland
143 N17 **Suruç** Şanlıurfa, S Turkey *36.58N 38.24E*
171 Ii17 **Suruga-wan** *bay* SE Japan
174 Hh10 **Surulangun** Sumatera, W Indonesia *2.36S 102.43E*
153 P13 **Surxondaryo** *Rus.* Surkhandar'ya. ≈ Tajikistan/Uzbekistan
Süs *see* Susch
108 A8 **Susa** Piemonte, NE Italy *45.09N 7.01E*
170 E12 **Susa** Yamaguchi, Honshū, SW Japan *34.35N 131.34E*
Susa *see* Shūsh
115 E16 **Sušac** *It.* Cazza. *island* SW Croatia
Sūsah *see* Sousse
170 Ee15 **Susaki** Kōchi, Shikoku, SW Japan *33.22N 133.13E*
170 G17 **Susami** Wakayama, Honshū, SW Japan *33.32N 135.32E*
148 K9 **Sūsangerd** *var.* Susangird. Khūzestān, SW Iran *31.40N 48.06E*
Susangird *see* Sūsangerd
37 P4 **Susanville** California, W USA *40.25N 120.39W*
110 J9 **Susch** *var.* Süs. Graubünden, SE Switzerland *46.45N 10.04E*
143 N12 **Suşehri** Sivas, N Turkey *40.10N 38.06E*
Susiana *see* Khūzestān
113 B18 **Sušice** *Ger.* Schüttenhofen. Plzeňský Kraj, W Czech Republic *49.13N 13.31E*
41 R11 **Susitna** Alaska, USA *61.32N 150.30W*
41 R11 **Susitna River** ≈ Alaska, USA
131 Q3 **Suslonger** Respublika Mariy El, W Russian Federation *56.18N 48.16E*
107 N14 **Suspiro del Moro, Puerto del** *pass* S Spain *37.04N 3.39W*
20 H16 **Susquehanna River** ≈ New York/Pennsylvania, NE USA
11 O15 **Sussex** New Brunswick, SE Canada *45.43N 65.31W*
20 J13 **Sussex** New Jersey, NE USA *41.12N 74.34W*
23 W7 **Sussex** Virginia, NE USA *36.54N 77.16W*
99 O23 **Sussex** *cultural region* S England, UK
191 S10 **Sussex Inlet** New South Wales, SE Australia *35.10S 150.35E*
101 L17 **Susteren** Limburg, SE Netherlands *51.04N 5.49E*
8 K12 **Sustut Peak** ▲ British Columbia, W Canada *56.25N 126.34W*
127 Nn9 **Susuman** Magadanskaya Oblast', E Russian Federation *62.46N 148.07E*
196 H6 **Susupe** Saipan, S Northern Mariana Islands
142 D12 **Susurluk** Balıkesir, NW Turkey *39.55N 28.10E*
116 M13 **Susuzmüsellim** Tekirdağ, NW Turkey *41.04N 27.03E*

◆ Country
● Country Capital
◇ Dependent Territory
○ Dependent Territory Capital
◈ Administrative Region
✈ International Airport
▲ Mountain
▲▲ Mountain Range
Volcano
≈ River
◎ Lake
▣ Reservoir

142 F15 **Sütçüler** Isparta, SW Turkey 37.31N 31.00E
118 L13 **Şuţeşti** Brăila, SE Romania 45.13N 27.26E
85 F25 **Sutherland** Western Cape, SW South Africa 32.22S 20.42E
30 L15 **Sutherland** Nebraska, C USA 41.09N 101.07W
98 I7 **Sutherland** cultural region N Scotland, UK
193 B21 **Sutherland Falls** waterfall South Island, NZ 44.49S 167.32E
34 F14 **Sutherlin** Oregon, NW USA 43.23N 123.18W
155 V10 **Sutlej** ≈ India/Pakistan
Sutna see Satna
37 P7 **Sutter Creek** California, W USA 38.22N 120.49W
41 R11 **Sutton** Alaska, USA 61.42N 148.53W
31 Q16 **Sutton** Nebraska, C USA 40.36N 97.52W
23 R4 **Sutton** West Virginia, NE USA 38.39N 80.42W
10 F8 **Sutton** ≈ Ontario, C Canada
99 M19 **Sutton Coldfield** C England, UK 52.34N 1.48W
23 R4 **Sutton Lake** ⊠ West Virginia, NE USA
13 P13 **Sutton, Monts** hill range Quebec, SE Canada
10 F8 **Sutton Ridges** ▲▲ Ontario, C Canada
172 Nn5 **Suttsu** Hokkaidō, NE Japan 42.46N 140.12E
41 P15 **Sutwik Island** island Alaska, USA
168 K7 **Süüj** Bulgan, C Mongolia 47.49N 104.06E
120 H5 **Suure-Jaani** Ger. Gross-Sankt-Johannis. Viljandimaa, S Estonia 58.34N 25.26E
120 J7 **Suur Munamägi** var. Munamägi, Ger. Eier-Berg. ▲ SE Estonia 57.42N 27.03E
120 F5 **Suur Väin** Ger. Grosser Sund. strait W Estonia
153 U8 **Suusamyr** Chuyskaya Oblast', C Kyrgyzstan 42.07N 73.55E
197 I13 **Suva** ● (Fiji) Viti Levu, W Fiji 18.07S 178.26E
197 I13 **Suva** ✈ Viti Levu, C Fiji 18.01S 178.30E
115 N18 **Suva Gora** ▲▲ W FYR Macedonia
120 H11 **Suvainiškis** Rokiškis, NE Lithuania 56.09N 25.15E
Suvalkai/Suvalki see Suwałki
115 P15 **Suva Planina** ▲▲ SE Serbia and Montenegro (Yugoslavia)
115 M17 **Suva Reka** Serbia, S Serbia and Montenegro (Yugoslavia) 42.23N 20.50E
130 K5 **Suvorov** Tul'skaya Oblast', W Russian Federation 54.08N 36.33E
119 N12 **Suvorove** Odes'ka Oblast', SW Ukraine 45.35N 28.58E
Suvorovo see Ştefan Vodă
171 J15 **Suwa** Nagano, Honshū, S Japan 36.01N 138.07E
Suwaik see As Suwayq
Suwaira see Aş Şuwayrah
112 O7 **Suwałki** Lith. Suvalkai, Rus. Suvalki. Podlaskie, NE Poland 54.06N 22.55E
178 Ii10 **Suwannaphum** Roi Et, E Thailand 15.36N 103.46E
25 V8 **Suwannee River** ≈ Florida/Georgia, SE USA
Şuwār see Aş Şuwār
202 K14 **Suwarrow** atoll N Cook Islands
Suwaydá/Suwaydā', Muḩāfaẓat as see As Suwaydā'
149 R16 **Suwaydān** var. Sweiham. Abū Ẓaby, E UAE 24.30N 55.18E
Suwayqiyah, Hawr as see Shuwayjah, Hawr ash
Suways, Khalīj as see Suez, Gulf of
Suways, Qanāt as see Suez Canal
Suweida see As Suwaydā'
Suweon see Suwŏn
169 X15 **Suwŏn** var. Suweon, Jap. Suigen. NW South Korea 37.17N 127.03E
Su Xian see Suzhou
149 R14 **Sūzā** Hormozgān, S Iran 26.49N 56.04E
151 P15 **Suzak** Kaz. Sozaq. Yuzhnyy Kazakhstan, S Kazakhstan 44.09N 68.28E
Suzaka see Suzuka
130 M3 **Suzdal'** Vladimirskaya Oblast', W Russian Federation 56.27N 40.29E
167 P7 **Suzhou** var. Su Xian. Anhui, E China 33.39N 116.56E
167 R8 **Suzhou** var. Soochow, Su-chou, Suchow; prev. Wuhsien. Jiangsu, E China 31.22N 120.34E
Suz, Mys see Soye, Mys
171 J12 **Suzu** Ishikawa, Honshū, SW Japan 37.24N 137.12E
171 Hh16 **Suzuka** Mie, Honshū, SW Japan 34.51N 136.31E
171 Jj14 **Suzuka** var. Suzaka. Nagano, Honshū, S Japan 36.39N 138.16E
171 J12 **Suzu-misaki** headland Honshū, SW Japan 37.31N 137.19E
Svågälv see Svågan
96 M10 **Svågan** var. Svågälv. ≈ C Sweden
Svalava/Svaljava see Svalyava
94 O2 **Svalbard** ◇ Norwegian dependency Arctic Ocean
94 J2 **Svalbardhseyri** Nordhurland Eystra, N Iceland 65.43N 18.03W
97 K22 **Svalöv** Skåne, S Sweden 55.55N 13.06E
118 H7 **Svalyava** Cz. Svalava, Svaljava, Hung. Szolyva. Zakarpats'ka Oblast', W Ukraine 48.33N 23.00E
94 O2 **Svanbergfjellet** ▲ C Svalbard 78.40N 18.10E
97 M24 **Svaneke** Bornholm, E Denmark 55.07N 15.08E
97 L22 **Svängsta** Blekinge, S Sweden 56.16N 14.46E
97 J16 **Svanskog** Värmland, C Sweden 59.10N 12.34E
97 L16 **Svartå** Örebro, C Sweden 59.13N 14.07E
97 L15 **Svartälven** ≈ C Sweden
94 G12 **Svartisen** glacier C Norway
119 X6 **Svatove** Rus. Svatovo. Luhans'ka Oblast', E Ukraine 49.24N 38.10E
Svatovo see Svatove
Sväty Kríž nad Hronom see Žiar nad Hronom
178 Ii12 **Svay Chék, Stœng** ≈ Cambodia/Thailand
178 Jj14 **Svay Riĕng** Svay Riĕng, S Cambodia 11.04N 105.48E
94 O3 **Sveagruva** Spitsbergen, W Svalbard 77.53N 16.42E
97 K23 **Svedala** Skåne, S Sweden 55.30N 13.15E
120 H12 **Svėdesai** Anykščiai, NE Lithuania 55.42N 25.22E
95 G18 **Sveg** Jämtland, C Sweden 62.01N 14.19E
120 C12 **Švėkšna** Šilutė, W Lithuania 55.31N 21.37E
96 C11 **Svelgen** Sogn og Fjordane, S Norway 61.46N 5.18E
97 H15 **Svelvik** Vestfold, S Norway 59.36N 10.22E
120 I13 **Švenčionėliai** Pol. Nowo-Święciany. Švenčionys, SE Lithuania 55.10N 26.00E
120 I13 **Švenčionys** Pol. Swięciany. Švenčionys, SE Lithuania 55.08N 26.08E
97 H24 **Svendborg** Fyn, C Denmark 55.04N 10.37E
97 K19 **Svenljunga** Västra Götaland, S Sweden 57.30N 13.04E
94 P2 **Svenskøya** island E Svalbard
95 G17 **Svenstavik** Jämtland, C Sweden 62.39N 14.24E
97 G20 **Svenstrup** Nordjylland, N Denmark 56.58N 9.52E
120 H12 **Šventoji** ≈ C Lithuania
119 Z8 **Sverdlovs'k** Rus. Sverdlovsk; prev. Imeni Sverdlova Rudnik. Luhans'ka Oblast', E Ukraine 48.05N 39.37E
Sverdlovsk see Yekaterinburg
131 W2 **Sverdlovskaya Oblast'** ⬖ province C Russian Federation
126 Hh5 **Sverdrup, Ostrov** island N Russian Federation
Sverige see Sweden
115 D15 **Svetac** prev. Sveti Andrea, It. Sant'Andrea. island SW Croatia
Sveti Andrea see Svetac
Sveti Nikola see Sveti Nikole
115 O18 **Sveti Nikole** prev. Sveti Nikola. C FYR Macedonia 41.54N 21.55E
Sveti Vrach see Sandanski
127 O16 **Svetlaya** Primorskiy Kray, SE Russian Federation 46.33N 138.20E
130 B2 **Svetlogorsk** Kaliningradskaya Oblast', W Russian Federation 54.56N 20.09E
126 I9 **Svetlogorsk** Krasnoyarskiy Kray, N Russian Federation 66.51N 88.29E
Svetlogorsk see Svyetlahorsk
131 N14 **Svetlograd** Stavropol'skiy Kray, SW Russian Federation 45.19N 42.52E
Svetlovodsk see Svitlovods'k
121 A14 **Svetlyy** Ger. Zimmerbude. Kaliningradskaya Oblast', W Russian Federation 54.42N 20.07E
131 Y8 **Svetlyy** Orenburgskaya Oblast', W Russian Federation 50.34N 60.42E
131 P7 **Svetlyy** Saratovskaya Oblast', W Russian Federation 51.42N 45.40E
128 G11 **Svetogorsk** Fin. Enso. Leningradskaya Oblast', NW Russian Federation 61.06N 28.52E
Svetozarevo see Jagodina
113 B18 **Švihov** Ger. Schwihau. Plzeňský Kraj, W Czech Republic 49.31N 13.18E
114 E13 **Svilaja** ▲▲ SE Croatia
114 N12 **Svilajnac** Serbia, C Serbia and Montenegro (Yugoslavia) 44.15N 21.12E
116 L11 **Svilengrad** prev. Mustafa-Pasha. Khaskovo, S Bulgaria 41.46N 26.13E
Svinecea Mare, Munte see Svinecea Mare, Vârful
118 F13 **Svinecea Mare, Vârful** var. Munte Svinecea Mare. ▲ SW Romania 44.47N 22.10E
97 B18 **Svínoy** Dan. Svinø Island Faeroe Islands 62.17N 6.17W
153 N14 **Svintsovyy Rudnik** Turkm. Swintsowyy Rudnik. Lebapskiy Velayat, E Turkmenistan 37.54N 66.25E
120 I13 **Svir** Rus. Svir'. Minskaya Voblasts', NW Belarus 54.51N 26.24E
128 I12 **Svir'** canal NW Russian Federation
Svir', Ozero see Svir, Vozyera
121 I14 **Svir, Vozyera** Rus. Ozero Svir'. ◎ C Belarus
116 J7 **Svishtov** prev. Sistova. Veliko Tŭrnovo, N Bulgaria 43.37N 25.22E
121 F18 **Svislach** Pol. Świsłocz, Rus. Svisloch'. Hrodzyenskaya Voblasts', W Belarus 53.01N 24.06E
121 M17 **Svislach** Rus. Svisloch'. Mahilyowskaya Voblasts', E Belarus 53.25N 28.56E
121 L17 **Svislach** Rus. Svisloch'. ≈ E Belarus
Svisloch' see Svislach
113 F17 **Svitavy** Ger. Zwittau. Pardubický Kraj, C Czech Republic 49.44N 16.27E
119 S6 **Svitlovods'k** Rus. Svetlovodsk. Kirovohrads'ka Oblast', C Ukraine 49.04N 33.15E
Svizzera see Switzerland
127 Mm15 **Svobodnyy** Amurskaya Oblast', SE Russian Federation 51.24N 128.05E
116 G9 **Svoge** Sofiya, W Bulgaria 42.58N 23.20E
94 G11 **Svolvær** Nordland, C Norway 68.15N 14.29E
113 F18 **Svratka** Ger. Schwarzach, Schwarzawa. ≈ SE Czech Republic
115 P14 **Svrljig** Serbia, E Serbia and Montenegro (Yugoslavia) 43.26N 22.07E
207 U10 **Svyataya Anna Trough** var. Saint Anna Trough. undersea feature N Kara Sea
128 M4 **Svyatoy Nos, Mys** headland NW Russian Federation 68.07N 39.49E
126 M5 **Svyatoy Nos, Mys** headland NE Russian Federation 72.49N 140.45E
121 N18 **Svyetlahorsk** Rus. Svetlogorsk. Homyel'skaya Voblasts', SE Belarus 52.39N 29.43E
Swabian Jura see Schwäbische Alb
99 P19 **Swaffham** E England, UK 52.38N 0.40E
25 V5 **Swainsboro** Georgia, SE USA 32.36N 82.19W
85 C19 **Swakop** ≈ W Namibia
85 C19 **Swakopmund** Erongo, W Namibia 22.40S 14.34E
99 M15 **Swale** ≈ N England, UK
Swallow Island see Nendö
101 M16 **Swalmen** Limburg, SE Netherlands 51.13N 6.01E
10 G8 **Swan** ≈ Ontario, C Canada
99 L24 **Swanage** S England, UK 50.37N 1.59W
190 M10 **Swan Hill** Victoria, SE Australia 35.21S 143.34E
9 P13 **Swan Hills** Alberta, W Canada 54.40N 116.19W
67 D24 **Swan Island** island C Falkland Islands
Swankalok see Sawankhalok
31 U10 **Swan Lake** ◎ Minnesota, N USA
23 Y10 **Swanquarter** North Carolina, SE USA 35.23N 76.17W
190 J9 **Swan Reach** South Australia 34.39S 139.35E
9 V15 **Swan River** Manitoba, S Canada 52.06N 101.16W
191 P17 **Swansea** Tasmania, SE Australia 42.09S 148.03E
99 J22 **Swansea** Wel. Abertawe. S Wales, UK 51.37N 3.57W
23 R13 **Swansea** South Carolina, SE USA 33.47N 81.06W
21 S7 **Swans Island** island Maine, NE USA
30 L17 **Swanson Lake** ⊠ Nebraska, C USA
33 R11 **Swanton** Ohio, N USA 41.35N 83.53W
112 G11 **Swarzędz** Poznań, C Poland 52.24N 17.05E
Swatow see Shantou
85 L22 **Swaziland** off. Kingdom of Swaziland. ◆ monarchy S Africa
95 G18 **Sweden** off. Kingdom of Sweden, Swe. Sverige. ◆ monarchy N Europe
Swedru see Agona Swedru
27 V12 **Sweeny** Texas, SW USA 29.02N 95.42W
35 R6 **Sweetgrass** Montana, NW USA 48.58N 111.58W
34 G12 **Sweet Home** Oregon, NW USA 44.24N 122.44W
27 T12 **Sweet Home** Texas, SW USA 29.21N 97.04W
29 T4 **Sweet Springs** Missouri, C USA 38.57N 93.24W
22 M10 **Sweetwater** Tennessee, S USA 35.36N 84.27W
27 P7 **Sweetwater** Texas, SW USA 32.28N 100.24W
35 V15 **Sweetwater River** ≈ Wyoming, C USA
Sweiham see Suwaydān
85 F26 **Swellendam** Western Cape, SW South Africa 34.01S 20.25E
113 G15 **Świdnica** Ger. Schweidnitz. Wałbrzych, SW Poland 50.51N 16.28E
113 O14 **Świdnik** Ger. Streckenbach. Lubelskie, E Poland 51.13N 22.39E
112 F8 **Świdwin** Ger. Schivelbein. Zachodniopomorskie, NW Poland 53.46N 15.43E
113 F15 **Świebodzice** Ger. Freiburg in Schlesien, Swiebodzice. Wałbrzych, SW Poland 50.54N 16.22E
112 E11 **Świebodzin** Ger. Schwiebus. Lubuskie, W Poland 52.15N 15.30E
Święciany see Švenčionys
112 I9 **Świecie** Ger. Schwertberg. Kujawsko-pomorskie, N Poland 53.24N 18.24E
113 L15 **Świętokrzyskie** ⬖ province C Poland
9 T16 **Swift Current** Saskatchewan, S Canada 50.16N 107.49W
100 K9 **Swifterbant** Flevoland, C Netherlands 52.36N 5.33E
191 Q12 **Swifts Creek** Victoria, SE Australia 37.17S 147.41E
98 E13 **Swilly, Lough** Ir. Loch Súilí. inlet N Ireland
99 M22 **Swindon** S England, UK 51.34N 1.46W
Swinemünde see Świnoujście
112 D8 **Świnoujście** Ger. Swinemünde. Zachodniopomorskie, NW Poland 53.54N 14.12E
Swintsowyy Rudnik see Svintsovyy Rudnik
Świsłocz see Svislach
Swiss Confederation see Switzerland
110 E9 **Switzerland** off. Swiss Confederation, Fr. La Suisse, Ger. Schweiz, It. Svizzera; anc. Helvetia. ◆ federal republic C Europe
99 F17 **Swords** Ir. Sord, Sórd Choluim Chille. E Ireland 53.28N 6.13W
20 H13 **Swoyersville** Pennsylvania, NE USA 41.18N 75.48W
128 I10 **Syamozero, Ozero** ◎ NW Russian Federation
128 M13 **Syamzha** Vologodskaya Oblast', NW Russian Federation 60.02N 41.09E
120 N13 **Syanno** Rus. Senno. Vitsyebskaya Voblasts', NE Belarus 54.48N 29.44E
121 K16 **Syarhyeyevichy** Rus. Sergeyevichi. Minskaya Voblasts', C Belarus 53.30N 27.45E
128 I12 **Syas'stroy** Leningradskaya Oblast', NW Russian Federation 60.05N 32.37E
Sycaminum see Hefa
32 M10 **Sycamore** Illinois, N USA 41.59N 88.41W
130 J3 **Sychëvka** Smolenskaya Oblast', W Russian Federation 55.52N 34.19E
113 H14 **Syców** Ger. Gross Wartenberg. Dolnośląskie, SW Poland 51.18N 17.42E
12 E17 **Sydenham** ≈ Ontario, S Canada
Sydenham Island see Nonouti
191 T9 **Sydney** state capital New South Wales, SE Australia 33.55S 151.10E
11 R14 **Sydney** Cape Breton Island, Nova Scotia, SE Canada 46.10N 60.10W
Sydney Island see Manra
11 R14 **Sydney Mines** Cape Breton Island, Nova Scotia, SE Canada 46.14N 60.19W
Syedpur see Saidpur
121 K18 **Syelishcha** Rus. Selishche. Minskaya Voblasts', C Belarus 53.01N 27.25E
121 J18 **Syemyezhava** Rus. Semezhevo. Minskaya Voblasts', C Belarus 52.57N 27.01E
Syene see Aswân
119 X6 **Syeverodonets'k** Rus. Severodonetsk. Luhans'ka Oblast', E Ukraine 48.58N 38.28E
167 T6 **Sÿiao Shan** island SE China
102 H11 **Syke** Niedersachsen, NW Germany 52.55N 8.49E
96 D10 **Sykkylven** Møre og Romsdal, S Norway 62.22N 6.34E
117 F15 **Sykoúri** var. Sikouri; prev. Sikoúrion. Thessalía, C Greece 39.46N 22.34E
129 R11 **Syktyvkar** prev. Ust'-Sysol'sk. Respublika Komi, NW Russian Federation 61.42N 50.45E
25 Q4 **Sylacauga** Alabama, S USA 33.10N 86.15W
Sylarna see Sylene
96 J9 **Sylene** Swe. Sylarna. ▲ Norway/Sweden 63.00N 12.14E
159 V14 **Sylhet** Chittagong, NE Bangladesh 24.52N 91.51E
102 G6 **Sylt** island NW Germany
23 O10 **Sylva** North Carolina, SE USA 35.22N 83.13W
129 V15 **Sylva** ≈ NW Russian Federation
25 W5 **Sylvania** Georgia, SE USA 32.45N 81.38W
33 R11 **Sylvania** Ohio, N USA 41.43N 83.42W
9 Q15 **Sylvan Lake** Alberta, SW Canada 52.18N 114.02W
35 T13 **Sylvan Pass** pass Wyoming, C USA 44.29N 110.03W
25 T7 **Sylvester** Georgia, SE USA 31.31N 83.50W
27 P6 **Sylvester** Texas, SW USA 32.42N 100.15W
8 L11 **Sylvia, Mount** ▲ British Columbia, W Canada 58.03N 124.26W
126 Hh12 **Sym** ≈ C Russian Federation
117 N22 **Sými** var. Simi. island Dodekánisos, Greece, Aegean Sea
119 U8 **Synel'nykove** Dnipropetrovs'ka Oblast', E Ukraine 48.18N 35.31E
129 U6 **Synya** Respublika Komi, NW Russian Federation 65.21N 58.01E
119 P7 **Synyukha** Rus. Sinyukha. ≈ S Ukraine
Syôbara see Shōbara
205 V2 **Syowa** Japanese research station Antarctica 68.58S 40.07E
28 H6 **Syracuse** Kansas, C USA 38.00N 101.43W
31 S16 **Syracuse** Nebraska, C USA 40.39N 96.11W
20 H10 **Syracuse** New York, NE USA 43.03N 76.09W
Syracuse see Siracusa
Syrdar'inskaya Oblast' see Sirdaryo Viloyati
Syrdariya see Syr Darya
150 L14 **Syr Darya** var. Sai Hun, Sir Darya, Syrdarya, Kaz. Syrdariya, Rus. Syrdar'ya, Uzb. Sirdaryo; anc. Jaxartes. ≈ C Asia
144 J6 **Syria** off. Syrian Arab Republic, var. Siria, Syrie, Ar. Al-Jumhūrīyah al-'Arabīyah as-Sūrīyah, Sūrīya. ◆ republic SW Asia
144 L9 **Syrian Desert** Ar. Al Hamad, Bādiyat ash Shām. desert SW Asia
Syrie see Syria
117 L22 **Sýrna** var. Sirna. island Kykládes, Greece, Aegean Sea
117 I20 **Sýros** var. Síros. island Kykládes, Greece, Aegean Sea
95 M18 **Sysmä** Etelä-Suomi, S Finland 61.28N 25.37E
129 R12 **Sysola** ≈ NW Russian Federation
Syulemeshlii see Sredets
131 S2 **Syumsi** Udmurtskaya Respublika, NW Russian Federation 57.07N 51.35E
116 K10 **Syuyutliyka** ≈ C Bulgaria
Syvash, Zaliv see Syvash, Zatoka
119 U12 **Syvash, Zatoka** Rus. Zaliv Syvash. inlet S Ukraine
131 Q6 **Syzran'** Samarskaya Oblast', W Russian Federation 53.10N 48.22E
Szabadka see Subotica
113 N21 **Szabolcs-Szatmár-Bereg** off. Szabolcs-Szatmár-Bereg Megye. ⬖ county E Hungary
112 G10 **Szamocin** Ger. Samotschin. Wielkolpolskie, C Poland 53.02N 17.04E
118 H8 **Szamos** var. Someş, Someşul, Ger. Samosch, Somesch. ≈ Hungary/Romania
Szamosújvár see Gherla
112 G11 **Szamotuły** Poznań, C Poland 52.35N 16.35E
Szarkowszczyzna see Sharkawshchyna
113 M24 **Szarvas** Békés, SE Hungary 46.52N 20.32E
Szászmagyarós see Măieruş
Szászrégen see Reghin
Szászsebes see Sebeş
Szászváros see Orăştie
Szatmárrnémeti see Satu Mare
Száva see Sava
113 P15 **Szczebrzeszyn** Lubelskie, E Poland 50.43N 23.00E
112 D9 **Szczecin** Eng./Ger. Stettin. Zachodniopomorskie, NW Poland 53.25N 14.31E
112 G8 **Szczecinek** Ger. Neustettin. Zachodniopomorskie, NW Poland 53.42N 16.39E
112 D8 **Szczeciński, Zalew** var. Stettiner Haff, Ger. Oderhaff. bay Germany/Poland
113 K15 **Szczekociny** Śląskie, S Poland 50.38N 19.46E
112 N8 **Szczuczyn** Podlaskie, NE Poland 53.34N 22.17E
Szczuczyn Nowogródzki see Shchuchyn
112 M8 **Szczytno** Ger. Ortelsburg. Warmińsko-Mazurskie, NE Poland, 53.33N 21.00E
Szechuan/Szechwan see Sichuan
113 K21 **Szécsény** Nógrád, N Hungary 48.04N 19.31E
113 L25 **Szeged** Ger. Szegedin, Rom. Seghedin. Csongrád, SE Hungary 46.16N 20.06E
Szegedin see Szeged
113 N23 **Szeghalom** Békés, SE Hungary 47.02N 21.09E
Székelyhid see Săcueni
Székelykeresztúr see Cristuru Secuiesc
113 I23 **Székesfehérvár** Ger. Stuhlweissenberg; anc. Alba Regia. Fejér, W Hungary 47.13N 18.24E
Szeklerburg see Miercurea-Ciuc
Szekler Neumarkt see Târgu Secuiesc
113 J25 **Szekszárd** Tolna, S Hungary 46.21N 18.40E
Szempcz/Szenc see Senec
Szenice see Senica
Szentágota see Agnita
113 J22 **Szentendre** Ger. Sankt Andrä. Pest, N Hungary 47.40N 19.04E
113 L24 **Szentes** Csongrád, SE Hungary 46.40N 20.16E
113 F23 **Szentgotthárd** Eng. Saint Gotthard, Ger. Sankt Gotthard. Vas, W Hungary 46.57N 16.18E
Szentgyörgy see Đurđevac
Szenttamás see Srbobran
Széphely see Jebel
Szeping see Siping
Szered see Sered'
113 N21 **Szerencs** Borsod-Abaúj-Zemplén, NE Hungary 48.10N 21.10E
Szeret see Siret
Szeretfalva see Sărăţel
112 N7 **Szeskie Wzgórza** Ger. Seesker Höhe. hill NE Poland 54.15N 22.19E
113 H25 **Szigetvár** Baranya, SW Hungary 46.03N 17.47E
Szilágşomlyó see Şimleu Silvaniei
Szinna see Snina
Sziszek see Sisak
Szitás-Keresztúr see Cristuru Secuiesc
113 E15 **Szklarska Poręba** Ger. Schreiberhau. Dolnośląskie, SW Poland 50.50N 15.30E
Szkudy see Skuodas
Szlatina see Slatina, Croatia
Szlavonia/Szlavonország see Slavonija
Szlovákia see Slovakia
Szluin see Slunj
113 L23 **Szolnok** Jász-Nagykun-Szolnok, C Hungary 47.10N 20.12E
Szolyva see Svalyava
113 G23 **Szombathely** Ger. Steinamanger; anc. Sabaria, Savaria. Vas, W Hungary 47.13N 16.37E
Szond/Szonta see Sonta
Szováta see Sovata
112 F13 **Szprotawa** Ger. Sprottau. Lubuskie, W Poland 51.33N 15.31E
Sztálinváros see Dunaújváros
Sztrazsó see Strážov
112 J8 **Sztum** Ger. Stuhm. Pomorskie, N Poland 53.54N 19.01E
112 H10 **Szubin** Ger. Schubin. Kujawsko-pomorskie, W Poland 53.04N 17.49E
Szucsava see Suceava
Szurduk see Surduc
113 M14 **Szydłowiec** Ger. Schlelau. Mazowieckie, C Poland 51.15N 20.51E

T

Taalintehdas see Dalsbruk
179 P11 **Taal, Lake** ◎ Luzon, NW Philippines
97 J23 **Taastrup** var. Tåstrup. København, E Denmark 55.39N 12.19E
113 I24 **Tab** Somogy, W Hungary 46.40N 18.01E
179 Q11 **Tabaco** Luzon, N Philippines 13.22N 123.42E
194 M7 **Tabalo** Mussau Island, NE PNG 1.22S 149.37E
106 K5 **Tábara** Castilla-León, N Spain 41.49N 5.57W
195 P9 **Tabar Island** island Tabar Islands, N PNG
195 P9 **Tabar Islands** island group NE PNG
Tabariya, Bahrat see Tiberias, Lake
149 S7 **Ţabas** var. Golshan. Khorāsān, C Iran 33.37N 56.54E
45 P15 **Tabasará, Serranía de** ▲▲ W Panama
43 U15 **Tabasco** ⬖ state SE Mexico
Tabasco see Grijalva, Río
131 Q2 **Tabashino** Respublika Mariy El, W Russian Federation 57.00N 47.47E
60 B13 **Tabatinga** Amazonas, N Brazil 4.13S 69.43W
76 G9 **Tabelbala** W Algeria 29.22N 3.01W
9 Q17 **Taber** Alberta, SW Canada 49.48N 112.09W
176 W14 **Taberfane** Pulau Trangan, E Indonesia 6.14S 134.08E
97 L19 **Taberg** Jönköping, S Sweden 57.42N 14.04E
Tabibug see Tabibuga
194 H12 **Tabibuga** var. Tabibug. Western Highlands, C PNG 5.32S 144.37E
203 O3 **Tabiteuea** prev. Drummond Island. atoll Tungaru, W Kiribati
179 Q12 **Tablas Island** island C Philippines
179 Pp12 **Tablas Strait** strait C Philippines
194 M16 **Table Bay** bay SE PNG
192 Q10 **Table Cape** headland North Island, NZ 39.07S 178.00E
11 S13 **Table Mountain** ▲ Newfoundland and Labrador, E Canada 47.39N 59.15W
181 P17 **Table, Pointe de la** headland SE Réunion 21.19S 55.49E
29 S8 **Table Rock Lake** ⊠ Arkansas/Missouri, C USA
38 K14 **Table Top** ▲ Arizona, SW USA 32.45N 112.07W
194 J13 **Tabletop, Mount** ▲ C PNG 6.51S 146.00E
126 Mm5 **Tabor** Respublika Sakha (Yakutiya), NE Russian Federation 71.14N 150.23E
31 S15 **Tabor** Iowa, C USA 40.54N 95.40W
113 D18 **Tábor** Budějovický Kraj, S Czech Republic 49.25N 14.40E
83 F21 **Tabora** Tabora, W Tanzania 5.04S 32.49E
83 F21 **Tabora** ⬖ region C Tanzania
23 U12 **Tabor City** North Carolina, SE USA 34.09N 78.52W
153 Q10 **Taboshar** NW Tajikistan 40.37N 69.33E
78 L18 **Tabou** var. Tabu. S Ivory Coast 4.28N 7.19W
148 J2 **Tabrīz** var. Tebriz; anc. Tauris. Āžarbāyjān-e Khāvarī, NW Iran 38.04N 46.18E
Tabu see Tabou
203 W1 **Tabuaeran** prev. Fanning Island. atoll Line Islands, E Kiribati
194 E11 **Tabubil** Western, SW PNG 5.13S 141.13E
179 P8 **Tabuk** Luzon, N Philippines 17.26N 121.25E
146 J4 **Tabūk** Tabūk, NW Saudi Arabia 28.25N 36.33E
146 J5 **Tabūk** off. Minţaqat Tabūk. ⬖ province NW Saudi Arabia
197 B12 **Tabwemasana, Mount** ▲ Espiritu Santo, W Vanuatu 15.22S 166.44E
97 O15 **Täby** Stockholm, C Sweden 59.28N 18.04E
43 N14 **Tacámbaro** Michoacán de Ocampo, SW Mexico 19.12N 101.27W
44 A5 **Tacaná, Volcán** ⛰ Guatemala/Mexico 15.07N 92.06W
45 X16 **Tacarcuna, Cerro** ▲ SE Panama 8.08N 77.15W
Tachau see Tachov
164 J3 **Tacheng** var. Qoqek. Xinjiang Uygur Zizhiqu, NW China 46.45N 82.55E
56 H7 **Táchira** off. Estado Táchira. ⬖ state W Venezuela
167 T13 **Tachoshui** N Taiwan 24.26N 121.43E
113 A17 **Tachov** Ger. Tachau. Plzeňský Kraj, W Czech Republic 49.48N 12.37E
179 R13 **Tacloban** off. Tacloban City. Leyte, C Philippines 11.15N 124.59E
59 I19 **Tacna** Tacna, SE Peru 18.00S 70.15W
59 H18 **Tacna** off. Departamento de Tacna. ⬖ department S Peru
34 H8 **Tacoma** Washington, NW USA 47.15N 122.26W
20 L11 **Taconic Range** ▲▲ NE USA
64 L6 **Taco Pozo** Formosa, N Argentina 25.35S 63.15W
59 M20 **Tacsara, Cordillera de** ▲▲ S Bolivia
63 F17 **Tacuarembó** prev. San Fructuoso. Tacuarembó, C Uruguay 31.42S 56.00W
63 E18 **Tacuarembó** ⬖ department C Uruguay
63 F17 **Tacuarembó, Río** ≈ C Uruguay
85 I14 **Taculi** North Western, NW Zambia 14.17S 26.51E
179 R16 **Tacurong** Mindanao, S Philippines 6.42N 124.40E
171 Kk13 **Tadamu-gawa** ≈ Honshū, C Japan
79 V8 **Tadek** ≈ NW Niger
76 J9 **Tademaït, Plateau du** plateau C Algeria
197 K6 **Tadine** Province des Îles Loyauté, E New Caledonia 21.33S 167.54E
82 L11 **Tadjoura** E Djibouti 11.47N 42.51E
82 M11 **Tadjoura, Golfe de** Eng. Gulf of Tajura. inlet E Djibouti
Tadmor/Tadmur see Tudmur
9 W10 **Tadoule Lake** ◎ Manitoba, C Canada
13 S8 **Tadoussac** Quebec, SE Canada 48.07N 69.55W
161 H18 **Tādpatri** Andhra Pradesh, E India 14.55N 77.58E
Tadzhikabad see Tojikobod
Tadzhikistan see Tajikistan
169 Y14 **T'aebaek-sanmaek** ▲▲ E South Korea
169 V15 **Taechŏng-do** island NW South Korea
169 X13 **Taedong-gang** ≈ C North Korea
169 Y16 **Taegu** off. Taegu-gwangyŏksi, var. Daegu, Jap. Taikyū. SE South Korea 35.55N 128.32E
Taehan-haehyŏp see Korea Strait
Taehan Min'guk see South Korea
169 Y15 **Taejŏn** off. Taejŏn-gwangyŏksi, Jap. Taiden. C South Korea 36.19N 127.28E
200 T11 **Tafahi** island N Tonga
107 Q4 **Tafalla** Navarra, N Spain 42.31N 1.40W
77 M12 **Tafassâsset, Oued** ≈ SE Algeria
79 W7 **Tafassâsset, Ténéré du** desert N Niger
57 U11 **Tafelberg** ▲ S Suriname 3.55N 56.09W
99 J21 **Taff** ≈ SE Wales, UK
Tafila/Ţafīlah, Muḩāfaẓat aţ see Aţ Ţafīlah
79 N15 **Tafiré** N Ivory Coast 9.04N 5.10W
148 M6 **Tafresh** Markazī, W Iran 34.40N 50.00E
149 Q9 **Taft** Yazd, C Iran 31.48N 54.10E
37 R13 **Taft** California, W USA 35.08N 119.27W
27 T14 **Taft** Texas, SW USA 27.58N 97.24W
149 W12 **Taftān, Kūh-e** ▲ SE Iran 28.38N 61.06E
37 R13 **Taft Heights** California, W USA 35.06N 119.29W
201 Y14 **Tafunsak** Kosrae, E Micronesia 5.21N 162.58E
198 Aa8 **Tāga** Savai'i, SW Samoa 13.46S 172.31W
155 O6 **Tagāb** Kāpīsā, E Afghanistan 33.52N 66.22E
41 O8 **Tagagawik River** ≈ Alaska, USA
171 M13 **Tagajō** var. Tagazyô. Miyagi, Honshū, C Japan 38.21N 141.02E
130 K12 **Taganrog** Rostovskaya Oblast', SW Russian Federation 47.10N 38.54E
130 K12 **Taganrog, Gulf of** Rus. Taganrogskiy Zaliv, Ukr. Tahanroz'ka Zatoka. gulf Russian Federation/Ukraine
Taganrogskiy Zaliv see Taganrog, Gulf of
78 J8 **Tagant** ⬖ region C Mauritania
154 M14 **Tagas** Baluchistān, SW Pakistan 27.09N 64.36E
170 D13 **Tagawa** Fukuoka, Kyūshū, SW Japan 33.37N 130.46E
179 P11 **Tagaytay** Luzon, N Philippines 14.04N 120.55E
Tagazyô see Tagajō
179 Qq14 **Tagbilaran** var. Tagbilaran City. Bohol, C Philippines 9.41N 123.54E
108 B10 **Taggia** Liguria, NW Italy 43.51N 7.48E
79 V9 **Taghouaji, Massif de** ▲ C Niger 17.13N 8.37E
109 J15 **Tagliacozzo** Lazio, C Italy 42.03N 13.15E
108 J7 **Tagliamento** ≈ NE Italy
179 R15 **Tagoloan** Mindanao, S Philippines 8.30N 124.45E
155 N3 **Tagow Bāy** var. Bai. Sar-e Pol, N Afghanistan 35.41N 66.01E
Tagtabazar see Takhtabazar
61 L17 **Taguatinga** Tocantins, C Brazil 12.16S 46.25W
195 Q17 **Tagula** Tagula Island, SE PNG 11.21S 153.13E
195 P17 **Tagula Island** prev. Southeast Island, Sudest Island. island SE PNG
179 Rr15 **Tagum** Mindanao, S Philippines 7.22N 125.51E
56 C7 **Tagún, Cerro** elevation Colombia/Panama 7.57N 77.13W
107 P7 **Tagus** Port. Rio Tejo, Sp. Río Tajo. ≈ Portugal/Spain
66 M9 **Tagus Plain** undersea feature E Atlantic Ocean
203 S10 **Tahaa** island Îles Sous le Vent, W French Polynesia
203 U10 **Tahanea** atoll Îles Tuamotu, C French Polynesia
Tahanroz'ka Zatoka see Taganrog, Gulf of
171 I16 **Tahara** Aichi, Honshū, SW Japan 34.40N 137.15E
76 K12 **Tahat** ▲ SE Algeria 23.15N 5.34E
169 V12 **Ta He** ≈ NE China
169 U4 **Tahe** Heilongjiang, NE China 52.21N 124.42E
168 G9 **Tahilt** Govĭ-Altay, W Mongolia 45.20N 96.42E
203 T10 **Tahiti** island Îles du Vent, W French Polynesia
Tahiti, Archipel de see Société, Archipel de la
120 E4 **Tahkuna nina** headland W Estonia 59.06N 22.35E
154 K12 **Tāhlāb** ≈ W Pakistan
154 K12 **Tāhlāb, Dasht-i** desert SW Pakistan
29 R10 **Tahlequah** Oklahoma, C USA 35.55N 94.58W
37 Q6 **Tahoe City** California, W USA 39.09N 120.09W
37 P6 **Tahoe, Lake** ◎ California/Nevada, W USA
Tahoena see Tahuna
27 N6 **Tahoka** Texas, SW USA 33.10N 101.47W
34 F8 **Taholah** Washington, NW USA 47.19N 124.17W
79 T11 **Tahoua** Tahoua, W Niger 14.52N 5.18E
79 T11 **Tahoua** ⬖ department W Niger
33 P3 **Tahquamenon Falls** waterfall Michigan, N USA 46.34N 85.14W
33 P4 **Tahquamenon River** ≈ Michigan, N USA
145 V10 **Taḩrīr** S Iraq 31.58N 45.34E
8 K17 **Tahsis** Vancouver Island, British Columbia, SW Canada 49.42N 126.31W
Tahta see Takhta
77 W9 **Ţahta** C Egypt 26.40N 31.27E
142 L15 **Tahtalı Dağları** ▲▲ C Turkey
59 I14 **Tahuamanu, Río** ≈ Bolivia/Peru
58 F13 **Tahuanía, Río** ≈ E Peru
203 X7 **Tahuata** island Îles Marquises, NE French Polynesia
175 S6 **Tahulandang, Pulau** island N Indonesia
175 S5 **Tahuna** prev. Tahoena. Pulau Sangihe, N Indonesia 3.33N 125.33E
176 Yy10 **Tahun, Danau** see Tahun, Danau
78 L17 **Taï** SW Ivory Coast 5.53N 7.28W
167 P5 **Tai'an** Shandong, E China 36.13N 117.12E
203 R8 **Taiarapu, Presqu'île de** peninsula Tahiti, W French Polynesia
Taibad see Tāybād
166 K7 **Taibai Shan** ▲ C China 33.57N 107.31E
107 Q12 **Taibilla, Sierra de** ▲▲ S Spain
169 Q12 **Taibus Qi** var. Baochang. Nei Mongol Zizhiqu, N China 41.55N 115.22E
Taichū see T'aichung
167 S13 **T'aichung** Jap. Taichū; prev. Taiwan. C Taiwan 24.09N 120.40E
Taiden see Taejŏn
193 E23 **Taieri** ≈ South Island, NZ
117 E21 **Taïgetos** ▲▲ S Greece
167 N4 **Taihang Shan** ▲▲ C China
192 M11 **Taihape** Manawatu-Wanganui, North Island, NZ 39.41S 175.46E
167 O7 **Taihe** Anhui, E China 33.14N 115.35E
167 O12 **Taihe** Jiangxi, S China 26.50N 114.49E
Taihoku see T'aipei
167 R8 **Tai Hu** ◎ E China
167 P9 **Taihu** Anhui, E China 30.26N 116.13E
167 O6 **Taikang** Henan, C China 34.06N 114.53E
172 P7 **Taiki** Hokkaidō, NE Japan 42.29N 143.15E
177 Ff8 **Taikkyi** Yangon, SW Myanmar 17.16N 95.55E
Taikyū see Taegu
169 U8 **Tailai** Heilongjiang, NE China 46.25N 123.25E
173 Ff10 **Taileleo** Pulau Siberut, W Indonesia 1.45S 99.06E
190 J10 **Tailem Bend** South Australia 35.20S 139.33E
98 I8 **Tain** N Scotland, UK 57.49N 4.04W

◆ Country
● Country Capital
◇ Dependent Territory
○ Dependent Territory Capital
⬖ Administrative Region
✈ International Airport
▲ Mountain
▲▲ Mountain Range
⛰ Volcano
≈ River
◎ Lake
⊠ Reservoir

167 S14 **T'ainan** *Jap.* Tainan; *prev.* Dainan. S Taiwan 23.00N 120.05E
117 E22 **Taínaro, Akrotírio** *headland* S Greece 36.41N 22.28E
167 Q11 **Taining** Fujian, SE China 26.55N 117.13E
203 W7 **Taiohae** *prev.* Madisonville. Nuku Hiva, NE French Polynesia 8.55S 140.04W
167 T13 **T'aipei** *Jap.* Taihoku; *prev.* Daihoku. ● (Taiwan) N Taiwan 25.01N 121.28E
174 Gg3 **Taiping** Perak, Peninsular Malaysia 4.54N 100.42E
169 S8 **Taiping Ling** ▲ NE China 47.27N 120.27E
172 N6 **Taisei** Hokkaidō, NE Japan 42.13N 139.52E
170 F12 **Taisha** Shimane, Honshū, SW Japan 35.23N 132.40E
111 R4 **Taiskirchen** Oberösterreich, NW Austria 48.15N 13.33E
65 F20 **Taitao, Peninsula de** *peninsula* S Chile
Taitō *see* T'aitung
167 T14 **T'aitung** *Jap.* Taitō. S Taiwan 22.49N 121.04E
94 M13 **Taivalkoski** Oulu, E Finland 65.34N 28.19E
95 K19 **Taivassalo** Länsi-Suomi, W Finland 60.35N 21.36E
167 T14 **Taiwan** *off.* Republic of China, *var.* Formosa, Formo'sa. ◆ *republic* E Asia
139 Q11 **Taiwan** *var.* Formosa. *island* E Asia
Taiwan *see* T'aichung
T'aiwan Haihsia/Taiwan Haixia *see* Taiwan Strait
Taiwan Shan *see* Chungyang Shanmo
167 R13 **Taiwan Strait** *var.* Formosa Strait, *Chin.* T'aiwan Haihsia, Taiwan Haixia. *strait* China/Taiwan
167 N4 **Taiyuan** *prev.* T'ai-yuan, T'ai-yüan, Yangku. Shanxi, C China 37.48N 112.33E
167 R7 **Taizhou** Jiangsu, E China 32.36N 119.52E
167 S10 **Taizhou** *prev.* Haimen, Jiaojiang. Zhejiang, SE China 28.36N 121.19E
Taizhou *see* Linhai
147 O16 **Ta'izz** SW Yemen 13.36N 44.04E
147 O16 **Ta'izz** ✈ SW Yemen 13.40N 44.10E
77 P12 **Tajarhī** SW Libya 24.21N 14.28E
153 P13 **Tajikistan** *off.* Republic of Tajikistan, *Rus.* Tadzhikistan, *Taj.* Jumhurii Tojikiston; *prev.* Tajik S.S.R. ◆ *republic* C Asia
Tajik S.S.R *see* Tajikistan
171 Kk14 **Tajima** Fukushima, Honshū, C Japan 37.10N 139.46E
Tajoe *see* Tayu
Tajo, Río *see* Tagus
44 B5 **Tajumulco, Volcán** ▲ W Guatemala 15.04N 91.50W
107 P7 **Tajuña** ~ C Spain
Tajura, Gulf of *see* Tadjoura, Golfe de
178 H9 **Tak** *var.* Rahaeng. Tak, W Thailand 16.51N 99.07E
201 U4 **Taka Atoll** *var.* Tōke. *atoll* Ratak Chain, N Marshall Islands
171 L16 **Takahagi** Ibaraki, Honshū, S Japan 36.43N 140.40E
170 Ff13 **Takahashi** *var.* Takahasi. Okayama, Honshū, SW Japan 34.48N 133.37E
170 F13 **Takahashi-gawa** ~ Honshū, SW Japan
Takahasi *see* Takahashi
201 P12 **Takaieu Island** *island* E Micronesia
192 I13 **Takaka** Tasman, South Island, NZ 40.52S 172.49E
175 P13 **Takalar** Sulawesi, C Indonesia 5.28S 119.24E
170 Ff14 **Takamatsu** *var.* Takamatu. Kagawa, Shikoku, SW Japan 34.18N 133.58E
Takamatu *see* Takamatsu
170 Cc14 **Takamori** Kumamoto, Kyūshū, SW Japan 32.50N 131.08E
170 Cc16 **Takanabe** Miyazaki, Kyūshū, SW Japan 32.13N 131.31E
175 O16 **Takan, Gunung** ▲ Pulau Sumba, S Indonesia 8.52S 117.32E
171 M9 **Takanosu** Akita, Honshū, C Japan 40.13N 140.23E
Takao *see* Kaohsiung
171 Ii13 **Takaoka** Toyama, Honshū, SW Japan 36.43N 137.01E
192 N12 **Takapau** Hawke's Bay, North Island, NZ 40.01S 176.21E
203 U9 **Takapoto** *atoll* Îles Tuamotu, C French Polynesia
192 L5 **Takapuna** Auckland, North Island, NZ 36.48S 174.45E
171 Gg14 **Takarazuka** Hyōgo, Honshū, SW Japan 34.48N 135.18E
203 U9 **Takaroa** *atoll* Îles Tuamotu, C French Polynesia
171 Jj15 **Takasaki** Gunma, Honshū, S Japan 36.20N 139.00E
171 Gg15 **Takatsuki** *var.* Takatuki. Ōsaka, Honshū, SW Japan 34.50N 135.36E
Takatuki *see* Takatsuki
171 Ii14 **Takayama** Gifu, Honshū, SW Japan 36.09N 137.17E
171 Hh13 **Takefu** *var.* Takehu. Fukui, Honshū, SW Japan 35.55N 136.11E
170 F14 **Takehara** Hiroshima, Honshū, SW Japan 34.19N 132.52E
Takehu *see* Takefu
170 C13 **Takeo** Saga, Kyūshū, SW Japan 33.12N 130.01E
Takeo *see* Takêv
170 B17 **Take-shima** *island* Nansei-shotō, SW Japan
148 M5 **Tākestān** *var.* Takistan; *prev.* Siadehan. Qazvin, N Iran 36.02N 49.36E
170 D14 **Taketa** Ōita, Kyūshū, SW Japan 32.56N 131.21E
178 J14 **Takêv** *prev.* Takeo. Takêv, S Cambodia 10.58N 104.46E
178 Hh10 **Tak Fah** Nakhon Sawan, C Thailand
145 T13 **Takhādīd** *well* S Iraq 29.56N 44.33E
155 R3 **Takhār** ⬖ *province* NE Afghanistan
Takhiatash *see* Taxiatosh
178 J13 **Ta Khmau** Kândal, S Cambodia 11.30N 104.59E
152 H9 **Takhta** *Turkm.* Tahta. Dashkhovuzskiy Velayat, N Turkmenistan 41.40N 59.51E
152 J16 **Takhtabazar** *var.* Tagtabazar. Maryyskiy Velayat, S Turkmenistan 35.57N 62.49E
151 O8 **Takhtabrod** Severnyy Kazakhstan, N Kazakhstan 52.35N 67.37E
Takhtakupyr *see* Taxtako'pir
148 M8 **Takht-e Shāh, Kūh-e** ⛰ C Iran
79 V12 **Takiéta** Zinder, S Niger 13.43N 8.33E
15 I5 **Takijuq Lake** ◎ Nunavut, NW Canada
172 P4 **Takikawa** Hokkaidō, NE Japan 43.34N 141.54E
172 Pp4 **Takinoue** Hokkaidō, NE Japan 44.10N 143.09E
Takistan *see* Tākestān
193 B23 **Takitimu Mountains** ⛰ South Island, NZ
Takkaze *see* Tekezē
172 N10 **Takko** Aomori, Honshū, C Japan 40.19N 141.11E
8 L13 **Takla Lake** ◎ British Columbia, SW Canada
Takla Makan Desert *see* Taklimakan Shamo
164 H9 **Taklimakan Shamo** *Eng.* Takla Makan Desert. *desert* NW China
178 Jj12 **Takôk** Môndól Kiri, E Cambodia 12.37N 106.30E
175 P9 **Takolekaju, Pegunungan** ⛰ Sulawesi, N Indonesia
41 P10 **Takotna** Alaska, USA 62.59N 156.03W
Takow *see* Kaohsiung
126 Kk14 **Taksimo** Respublika Buryatiya, S Russian Federation 56.18N 114.53E
170 Cc13 **Taku** Saga, Kyūshū, SW Japan 33.17N 130.07E
8 I10 **Taku** ~ British Columbia, W Canada
177 G15 **Takua Pa** *var.* Ban Takua Pa. Phangnga, SW Thailand 8.47N 98.16E
79 W16 **Takum** Taraba, E Nigeria 7.16N 10.00E
203 V10 **Takume** *atoll* Îles Tuamotu, C French Polynesia
202 L16 **Takutea** *island* S Cook Islands
195 U11 **Takuu Islands** *prev.* Mortlock Group. *island group* NE PNG
121 L18 **Tal'** *Rus.* Tal'. Minskaya Voblasts', S Belarus 52.52N 27.59E
42 L13 **Tala** Jalisco, C Mexico 20.39N 103.45W
63 F19 **Tala** Canelones, S Uruguay 34.24S 55.45W
Talabriga *see* Aveiro, Portugal
Talabriga *see* Talavera de la Reina, Spain
121 N14 **Talachyn** *Rus.* Tolochin. Vitsyebskaya Voblasts', NE Belarus 54.25N 29.42E
155 U7 **Talagang** Punjab, E Pakistan 32.55N 72.23E
161 J23 **Talaimannar** Northern Province, NW Sri Lanka 9.07N 79.45E
119 R3 **Talalayivka** Chernihivs'ka Oblast', N Ukraine 50.51N 33.09E
45 O15 **Talamanca, Cordillera de** ⛰ S Costa Rica
58 A9 **Talara** Piura, NW Peru 4.31S 81.17W
106 L11 **Talarrubias** Extremadura, W Spain 39.03N 5.13W
153 S8 **Talas** Talasskaya Oblast', NW Kyrgyzstan 42.29N 72.21E
153 S8 **Talas** ~ NW Kyrgyzstan
195 N11 **Talasea** New Britain, E PNG 5.19S 150.02E
Talas Oblasty *see* Talasskaya Oblast'
153 S8 **Talasskaya Oblast'** *Kir.* Talas Oblasty. ⬖ *province* NW Kyrgyzstan
153 S8 **Talasskiy Alatau, Khrebet** ⛰ Kazakhstan/Kyrgyzstan
79 U12 **Talata Mafara** Zamfara, NW Nigeria 12.33N 6.01E
175 Ss4 **Talaud, Kepulauan** *island group* E Indonesia
106 M9 **Talavera de la Reina** *anc.* Caesarobriga, Talabriga. Castilla-La Mancha, C Spain 39.58N 4.49W
106 J11 **Talavera la Real** Extremadura, W Spain 38.52N 6.46W
194 L12 **Talawe, Mount** ▲ New Britain, C PNG 5.30S 148.24E
25 S5 **Talbotton** Georgia, SE USA 32.40N 84.32W
191 R7 **Talbragar River** ~ New South Wales, SE Australia
64 G13 **Talca** Maule, C Chile 35.28S 71.42W
64 F13 **Talcahuano** Bío Bío, C Chile 36.43S 73.07W
160 N12 **Tālcher** Orissa, E India 20.57N 85.13E
27 W5 **Talco** Texas, SW USA 33.21N 95.06W
151 V14 **Taldykorgan** *Kaz.* Taldyqorghan; *prev.* Taldy-Kurgan. Almaty, SE Kazakhstan 45.00N 78.23E
Taldy-Kurgan/Taldyqorghan *see* Taldykorgan
153 Y7 **Taldy-Suu** Issyk-Kul'skaya Oblast', E Kyrgyzstan 42.49N 78.33E
153 U10 **Taldy-Suu** Oshskaya Oblast', SW Kyrgyzstan 40.33N 73.52E
Tal-e Khosravī *see* Yāsūj
200 Ss14 **Taleki Tonga** *island* Otu Tolu Group, C Tonga
200 Ss13 **Taleki Vavu'u** *island* Otu Tolu Group, C Tonga
104 J13 **Talence** Gironde, SW France 44.49N 0.35W
151 U16 **Talgar** *Kaz.* Talghar. Almaty, SE Kazakhstan 43.25N 77.07E
Talghar *see* Talgar
175 Rr10 **Taliabu, Pulau** *island* Kepulauan Sula, C Indonesia
117 L22 **Taliarós, Akrotírio** *headland* Astypálaia, Kykládes, Greece, Aegean Sea 36.31N 26.18E
Ta-lien *see* Dalian
29 Q12 **Talihina** Oklahoma, C USA 34.45N 95.03W
Talimardzhan *see* Tollimarjon
Talin *see* T'alin
143 T12 **T'alin** *Rus.* Talin; *prev.* Verin T'alin. W Armenia 40.23N 43.51E
83 E15 **Tali Post** Bahr el Gabel, S Sudan 5.55N 30.43E
Taliq-an *see* Tāloqān
Talış Dağları *see* Talish Mountains
148 L2 **Talish Mountains** *Az.* Talış Dağları, *Per.* Kūhhā-ye Ţavālesh, *Rus.* Talyshskiye Gory. ⛰ Azerbaijan/Iran
125 F11 **Talitsa** Sverdlovskaya Oblast', C Russian Federation 56.58N 63.34E
175 O16 **Taliwang** Sumbawa, C Indonesia 8.45S 116.55E
121 L17 **Tal'ka** *Rus.* Tal'ka. Minskaya Voblasts', C Belarus 53.22N 28.22E
Talkang *see* Dorbod
41 R11 **Talkeetna** Alaska, USA 62.19N 150.06W
41 R11 **Talkeetna Mountains** ⛰ Alaska, USA
Talkhof *see* Puurmani
94 H2 **Tálknafjördhur** Vestfirdhir, W Iceland 65.38N 23.51W
145 Q3 **Tall 'Abţah** N Iraq 35.52N 42.40E
144 M2 **Tall Abyaḑ** *var.* Tell Abiad. Ar Raqqah, N Syria 36.42N 38.56E
25 Q4 **Talladega** Alabama, S USA 33.26N 86.06W
145 Q2 **Tall 'Afar** N Iraq 36.22N 42.27E
25 S8 **Tallahassee** *prev.* Muskogean. *state capital* Florida, SE USA 30.26N 84.16W
24 L2 **Tallahatchie River** ~ Mississippi, S USA
Tall al Abyaḑ *see* At Tall al Abyaḑ
145 W12 **Tall al Laḩm** S Iraq 30.46N 46.22E
191 P11 **Tallangatta** Victoria, SE Australia 36.15S 147.13E
25 R4 **Tallapoosa River** ~ Alabama/Georgia, S USA
105 T13 **Tallard** Hautes-Alpes, SE France 44.30N 6.04E
145 Q3 **Tall ash Sha'īr** N Iraq 36.11N 42.26E
25 Q5 **Tallassee** Alabama, S USA 32.32N 85.53W
145 R4 **Tall 'Azbah** NW Iraq 35.47N 43.13E
144 I5 **Tall Bīsah** Ḩimş, W Syria 34.49N 36.43E
145 R3 **Tall Ḩassūnah** N Iraq 36.05N 43.10E
145 Q2 **Tall Ḩuqnah** *var.* Tell Huqnah. N Iraq 36.33N 42.34E
Tallin *see* Tallinn
120 G3 **Tallinn** *Ger.* Reval, *Rus.* Tallin; *prev.* Revel. ● (Estonia) Harjumaa, NW Estonia 59.25N 24.42E
120 H3 **Tallinn** ✈ Harjumaa, NW Estonia 59.23N 24.52E
144 H5 **Tall Kalakh** *var.* Tell Kalakh. Ḩimş, C Syria 34.40N 36.18E
145 R2 **Tall Kayf** NW Iraq 36.30N 43.07E
Tall Kūchak *see* Tall Kūshik
145 P2 **Tall Kūshik** *var.* Tall Kūchak. Al Ḩasakah, E Syria 36.48N 42.01E
33 U12 **Tallmadge** Ohio, N USA 41.06N 81.26W
24 J5 **Tallulah** Louisiana, S USA 32.22N 91.12W
145 Q2 **Tall 'Uwaynāt** NW Iraq 36.43N 42.18E
145 Q2 **Tall Ẕāhir** N Iraq 36.51N 42.29E
126 H14 **Tal'menka** Altayskiy Kray, S Russian Federation 53.55N 83.26E
126 I8 **Talnakh** Taymyrskiy (Dolgano-Nenetskiy) Avtonomnyy Okrug, N Russian Federation 69.26N 88.26E
119 P7 **Tal'ne** *Rus.* Tal'noye. Cherkas'ka Oblast', C Ukraine 48.54N 30.39E
Tal'noye *see* Tal'ne
82 E12 **Talodi** Southern Kordofan, C Sudan 10.40N 30.25E
196 B16 **Talofofo** SE Guam 13.21N 144.45E
196 B16 **Talofofo Bay** *bay* SE Guam
28 L9 **Taloga** Oklahoma, C USA 36.01N 98.58W
127 O10 **Talon** Magadanskaya Oblast', E Russian Federation 59.47N 148.46E
12 H11 **Talon, Lake** ◎ Ontario, S Canada
155 R2 **Tāloqān** *var.* Taliq-an. Takhār, NE Afghanistan 36.43N 69.33E
130 M8 **Talovaya** Voronezhskaya Oblast', W Russian Federation 51.07N 40.46E
175 Qq10 **Talowa, Teluk** *bay* Sulawesi, C Indonesia
15 Kk3 **Taloyoak** *prev.* Spence Bay. Nunavut, N Canada 69.30N 93.25W
27 Q8 **Talpa** Texas, SW USA 31.46N 99.42W
42 K13 **Talpa de Allende** Jalisco, C Mexico 20.22N 104.51W
25 S9 **Talquin, Lake** ▣ Florida, SE USA
Talsen *see* Talsi
168 H9 **Talshand** Govĭ-Altay, C Mongolia 45.21N 98.00E
120 E8 **Talsi** *Ger.* Talsen. Talsi, NW Latvia 57.14N 22.34E
149 V11 **Tal Sīāh** Sīstān va Balūchestān, SE Iran 28.19N 57.43E
64 G6 **Taltal** Antofagasta, N Chile 25.22S 70.27W
15 Ii8 **Taltson** ~ Northwest Territories, NW Canada
174 H8 **Taluk** Sumatera, W Indonesia 0.30S 101.36E
94 J8 **Talvik** Finnmark, N Norway 70.02N 22.58E
190 M7 **Talyawalka Creek** ~ New South Wales, SE Australia
Talyshskiye Gory *see* Talish Mountains
31 W14 **Tama** Iowa, C USA 41.58N 92.34W
Tama Abu, Banjaran *see* Penambo, Banjaran
175 N5 **Tamabo, Banjaran** ⛰ East Malaysia
202 B16 **Tamakautoga** SW Niue 19.04S 169.55W
131 N7 **Tamala** Penzenskaya Oblast', W Russian Federation 52.32N 43.18E
79 P15 **Tamale** C Ghana 9.21N 0.54W
170 Cc13 **Tamana** Kumamoto, Kyūshū, SW Japan 32.54N 130.34E
203 P3 **Tamana** *prev.* Rotcher Island. *atoll* Tungaru, W Kiribati
170 Ff14 **Tamano** Okayama, Honshū, SW Japan 34.28N 133.53E
76 K12 **Tamanrasset** *var.* Tamenghest. S Algeria 22.49N 5.31E
76 J13 **Tamanrasset** *wadi* Algeria/Mali
177 G2 **Tamanthi** Sagaing, N Myanmar 25.17N 95.18E
99 I24 **Tamar** ~ SW England, UK
Tamar *see* Tudmur
56 H9 **Támara** Casanare, C Colombia 5.51N 72.10W
56 F7 **Tamar, Alto de** ▲ C Colombia 7.25N 74.28W
181 X16 **Tamarin** E Mauritius 20.19S 57.22E
107 T5 **Tamarite de Litera** *var.* Tararite de Llitera. Aragón, NE Spain 41.52N 0.25E
113 I24 **Tamási** Tolna, S Hungary 46.39N 18.16E
Tamatave *see* Toamasina
43 O9 **Tamaulipas** ⬖ *state* C Mexico
43 P10 **Tamaulipas, Sierra de** ⛰ C Mexico
58 F12 **Tamaya, Río** ~ E Peru
42 I9 **Tamazula** Durango, C Mexico 24.43N 106.33W
42 L14 **Tamazula** Jalisco, C Mexico 19.41N 103.18W
Tamazulápam *see* Tamazulapán
43 Q15 **Tamazulapán** *var.* Tamazulápam. Oaxaca, SE Mexico 17.40N 97.33W
43 P12 **Tamazunchale** San Luis Potosí, C Mexico 21.17N 98.45W
78 H11 **Tambacounda** SE Senegal 13.43N 13.43W
85 M16 **Tambara** Manica, C Mozambique 16.45S 34.14E
175 Pp9 **Tambarana** Sulawesi, N Indonesia 1.09S 120.30E
79 T13 **Tambawel** Sokoto, NW Nigeria 12.24N 4.42E
195 W15 **Tambea** Guadalcanal, C Solomon Islands 9.19S 159.42E
174 Jj7 **Tambelan, Kepulauan** *island group* W Indonesia
59 E15 **Tambo de Mora** Ica, W Peru 13.43S 76.12W
175 Oo15 **Tambora, Gunung** ⋀ Sumbawa, S Indonesia 8.16S 117.59E
63 E17 **Tambores** Paysandú, W Uruguay 31.49S 56.16W
59 F14 **Tambo, Río** ~ C Peru
58 F7 **Tamboryacu, Río** ~ N Peru
130 M7 **Tambov** Tambovskaya Oblast', W Russian Federation 52.43N 41.28E
130 L6 **Tambovskaya Oblast'** ⬖ *province* W Russian Federation
106 H3 **Tambre** ~ NW Spain
175 Nn3 **Tambunan** Sabah, East Malaysia 5.40N 116.22E
83 C15 **Tambura** Western Equatoria, SW Sudan 5.37N 27.30E
175 P8 **Tambu, Teluk** *bay* Sulawesi, C Indonesia
Tamchaket *see* Tâmchekkeţ
78 J9 **Tâmchekkeţ** *var.* Tamchaket. Hodh el Gharbi, S Mauritania 17.12N 10.36W
178 Jj7 **Tam Điệp** Ninh Bình, N Vietnam 20.09N 105.54E
Tamdybulak *see* Tomdibuloq
56 H8 **Tame** Arauca, C Colombia 6.27N 71.44W
106 H6 **Tâmega, Rio** *Sp.* Río Támega. ~ Portugal/Spain
117 H20 **Tamélos, Akrotírio** *headland* Kéa, Kykládes, Greece, Aegean Sea 37.31N 24.16E
Tamenghest *see* Tamanrasset
79 V8 **Tamgak, Adrar** ▲ C Niger 19.10N 8.39E
78 I13 **Tamgue** ▲ NW Guinea 12.14N 12.18W
43 Q12 **Tamiahua** Veracruz-Llave, E Mexico 21.15N 97.27W
43 Q12 **Tamiahua, Laguna de** *lagoon* E Mexico
25 Y16 **Tamiami Canal** *canal* Florida, SE USA
196 F17 **Tamil Harbor** *harbor* Yap, W Micronesia
161 H21 **Tamil Nādu** *prev.* Madras. ⬖ *state* SE India
101 H20 **Tamines** Namur, S Belgium 50.27N 4.37E
118 E12 **Tamiš** *Ger.* Temesch, *Hung.* Temes, *SCr.* Tamiš. ~ Romania/Serbia and Montenegro (Yugoslavia)
178 Kk10 **Tam Ky** Quang Nam-Đa Nẵng, C Vietnam 15.31N 108.30E
Tammerfors *see* Tampere
Tammisaari *see* Ekenäs
97 N14 **Tämnaren** ◎ C Sweden
203 Q7 **Tamotoe, Passe** *passage* Tahiti, W French Polynesia
25 V12 **Tampa** Florida, SE USA 27.57N 82.27W
25 V12 **Tampa** ✈ Florida, SE USA 27.57N 82.29W
25 V13 **Tampa Bay** *bay* Florida, SE USA
95 L18 **Tampere** *Swe.* Tammerfors. Länsi-Suomi, W Finland 61.30N 23.45E
43 Q11 **Tampico** Tamaulipas, C Mexico 22.18N 97.52W
175 Qq12 **Tampo** Pulau Muna, C Indonesia 4.38S 122.40E
178 Kk11 **Tam Quan** Bình Định, C Vietnam 14.34N 109.00E
176 V9 **Tamrau, Pegunungan** ⛰ Papua, E Indonesia
168 J13 **Tamsag Muchang** Nei Mongol Zizhiqu, N China 40.28N 102.34E
Tamsal *see* Tamsalu
120 I4 **Tamsalu** *Ger.* Tamsal. Lääne-Virumaa, NE Estonia 59.10N 26.07E
111 S8 **Tamsweg** Salzburg, SW Austria 47.07N 13.49E
177 Ff3 **Tamu** Sagaing, N Myanmar 24.11N 94.21E
43 P12 **Tamuín** San Luis Potosí, C Mexico 21.57N 98.46W
196 C15 **Tamuning** NW Guam 13.29N 144.47E
191 T6 **Tamworth** New South Wales, SE Australia 31.07S 150.54E
99 M19 **Tamworth** C England, UK 52.39N 1.40W
94 M8 **Tana** *var.* Tenojoki, *Fin.* Teno, *Lapp.* Dealnu. ~ Finland/Norway *see also* Teno
83 K19 **Tana** ~ SE Kenya
170 G17 **Tanabe** Wakayama, Honshū, SW Japan 33.43N 135.22E
94 L8 **Tana Bru** Finnmark, N Norway 70.10N 28.06E
41 T10 **Tanacross** Alaska, USA 63.30N 143.21W
94 L7 **Tanafjorden** *fjord* N Norway
40 G17 **Tanaga Island** *island* Aleutian Islands, Alaska, USA
40 G17 **Tanaga Volcano** ▲ Tanaga Island, Alaska, USA 51.53N 178.08W
109 M18 **Tanagro** ~ S Italy
82 H11 **T'ana Hāyk'** *Eng.* Lake Tana. ◎ NW Ethiopia
173 F8 **Tanahbela, Pulau** *island* Kepulauan Batu, W Indonesia
175 Pp15 **Tanahjampea, Pulau** *island* W Indonesia
173 Ff8 **Tanahmasa, Pulau** *island* Kepulauan Batu, W Indonesia
Tanais *see* Don
158 L10 **Tanakpur** Uttar Pradesh, N India 29.04N 80.06E
Tana, Lake *see* T'ana Hāyk'
189 P5 **Tanami Desert** *desert* Northern Territory, N Australia
178 Jj14 **Tân An** Long An, S Vietnam 10.31N 106.24E
41 Q9 **Tanana** Alaska, USA 65.12N 152.00W
Tananarive *see* Antananarivo
41 Q9 **Tanana River** ~ Alaska, USA
97 C16 **Tananger** Rogaland, S Norway 58.55N 5.34E
196 H5 **Tanapag** Saipan, S Northern Mariana Islands 15.13S 145.45E
196 H5 **Tanapag, Puetton** *bay* Saipan, S Northern Mariana Islands
108 C9 **Tanaro** ~ N Italy
169 Y12 **Tanch'ŏn** E North Korea 40.22N 128.49E
42 M14 **Tancitaro, Cerro** ⋀ C Mexico 19.16N 102.25W
159 N12 **Tānda** Uttar Pradesh, N India 26.36N 82.39E
79 O15 **Tanda** E Ivory Coast 7.48N 3.10W
179 Rr14 **Tandag** Mindanao, S Philippines 9.00N 126.13E
118 L14 **Ţăndărei** Ialomiţa, SE Romania 44.39N 27.40E
65 N14 **Tandil** Buenos Aires, E Argentina 37.18S 59.10W
80 H12 **Tandjilé** *off.* Préfecture du Tandjilé. ⬖ *prefecture* SW Chad
Tandjoeng *see* Tanjung
Tandjoengpandan *see* Tanjungpandan
Tandjoengpinang *see* Tanjungpinang
Tandjoengredeb *see* Tanjungredeb
155 Q16 **Tando Allāhyār** Sind, SE Pakistan 25.30N 68.43E
155 Q17 **Tando Bāgo** Sind, SE Pakistan 24.48N 68.58E
155 Q16 **Tando Muhammad Khān** Sind, SE Pakistan 25.07N 68.34E
190 L7 **Tandou Lake** *seasonal lake* New South Wales, SE Australia
96 L11 **Tandsjöborg** Gävleborg, C Sweden 61.40N 14.40E
161 H15 **Tāndūr** Andhra Pradesh, C India 17.16N 77.37E
170 Bb17 **Tanega-shima** *island* Nansei-shotō, SW Japan
172 N10 **Taneichi** Iwate, Honshū, C Japan 40.23N 141.42E
Tanen Taunggyi *see* Tane Range
178 H8 **Tane Range** *Bur.* Tanen Taunggyi. ⛰ W Thailand
113 P15 **Tanew** ~ SE Poland
23 W2 **Taneytown** Maryland, NE USA 39.39N 77.10W
76 H12 **Tanezrouft** *desert* Algeria/Mali
144 L7 **Ţanf, Jabal aţ** ▲ SE Syria 33.31N 38.43E
83 J21 **Tanga** Tanga, E Tanzania 5.07S 39.04E
83 I22 **Tanga** ⬖ *region* E Tanzania
159 T14 **Tangail** Dhaka, C Bangladesh 24.15N 89.55E
195 Q9 **Tanga Islands** *island group* NE PNG
161 K26 **Tangalla** Southern Province, S Sri Lanka 6.01N 80.46E
Tanganyika and Zanzibar *see* Tanzania
70 I13 **Tanganyika, Lake** ◎ E Africa
58 E7 **Tangarana, Río** ~ N Peru
195 W16 **Tangarare** Guadalcanal, C Solomon Islands 9.37S 159.40E
203 V16 **Tangaroa, Maunga** ⋀ Easter Island, Chile, E Pacific Ocean
76 G5 **Tanger** *var.* Tangiers, Tangier, *Fr./Ger.* Tangerk, *Sp.* Tánger; *anc.* Tingis. NW Morocco 35.49N 5.48W
174 J14 **Tangerang** Jawa, C Indonesia 6.13S 106.36E
Tangerk *see* Tanger
102 M12 **Tangermünde** Sachsen-Anhalt, C Germany 52.35N 11.57E
162 K10 **Tanggula Shan** *var.* Dangla, Tangla Range. ⛰ W China
165 N13 **Tanggula Shan** ▲ W China 33.18N 91.10E
Tanggulashan *see* Tuotuoheyan
162 K10 **Tanggula Shankou** *pass* W China 32.52N 91.59E
167 N7 **Tanghe** Henan, C China 32.40N 112.49E
155 T5 **Tāngi** North-West Frontier Province, NW Pakistan 34.18N 71.42E
Tangier *see* Tanger
23 Y5 **Tangier Island** *island* Virginia, NE USA
Tangiers *see* Tanger
24 K8 **Tangipahoa River** ~ Louisiana, S USA
Tangla Range *see* Tanggula Shan
171 H13 **Tango-hantō** *peninsula* Honshū, SW Japan
162 I10 **Tangra Yumco** *var.* Tangro Tso. ◎ W China
Tangro Tso *see* Tangra Yumco
163 T7 **Tangshan** *var.* T'ang-shan. Hebei, E China 39.38N 118.14E
179 Qq15 **Tangub** *var.* Tangub City. Mindanao, S Philippines 8.07N 123.42E
79 R14 **Tanguiéta** NW Benin 10.34N 1.19E
169 X7 **Tangwang He** ~ NE China
169 X7 **Tangyuan** Heilongjiang, NE China 46.45N 129.52E
94 M11 **Tanhua** Lappi, N Finland 67.31N 27.30E
176 Uu16 **Tanimbar, Kepulauan** *island group* Maluku, E Indonesia
Tanintharyi *see* Tenasserim
145 U4 **Tānjarō** ~ E Iraq
133 T15 **Tanjong Piai** *headland* Peninsular Malaysia
Tanjore *see* Thanjāvūr
175 N10 **Tanjung** *prev.* Tandjoeng. Borneo, C Indonesia 2.07S 115.22E
175 Oo6 **Tanjungbatu** Borneo, N Indonesia 2.19N 118.03E
Tanjungkarang *see* Bandarlampung
174 J11 **Tanjunglabu** Pulau Lepar, W Indonesia 2.57S 106.51E
174 J10 **Tanjungpandan** *prev.* Tandjoengpandan. Pulau Belitung, W Indonesia 2.43S 107.36E
174 I7 **Tanjungpinang** *prev.* Tandjoengpinang. Pulau Bintan, W Indonesia 0.55N 104.28E
175 O6 **Tanjungredeb** *var.* Tanjungredep; *prev.* Tandjoengredeb. Borneo, C Indonesia 2.09N 117.28E
Tanjungredep *see* Tanjungredeb
155 S8 **Tānk** North-West Frontier Province, NW Pakistan 32.13N 70.28E
197 D16 **Tanna** *island* S Vanuatu
95 F17 **Tännäs** Jämtland, C Sweden 62.27N 12.40E
Tannenhof *see* Krynica
110 K7 **Tannheim** Tirol, W Austria 47.30N 10.32E
Tannu-Tuva *see* Tyva, Respublika
175 Rr10 **Tano** Pulau Taliabu, E Indonesia 1.51S 124.55E
79 O17 **Tano** ~ S Ghana
158 D10 **Tanot** Rājasthān, NW India 27.49N 70.21E
79 V11 **Tanout** Zinder, C Niger 14.58N 8.54E
43 P12 **Tanquián** San Luis Potosí, C Mexico 21.38N 98.39W
79 R13 **Tansarga** E Burkina 11.51N 1.51E
178 Jj14 **Tan Son Nhat** ✈ (Hồ Chí Minh) Tây Ninh, S Vietnam 10.52N 106.38E
77 V8 **Tanta** *var.* Tantā, Tantâ. N Egypt 30.42N 31.00E
76 D9 **Tan-Tan** SW Morocco 28.30N 11.10W
43 P12 **Tantoyuca** Veracruz-Llave, E Mexico 21.18N 98.12W
158 J12 **Tāntpur** Uttar Pradesh, N India 26.51N 77.28E
Tan-tung *see* Dandong
40 M12 **Tanunak** Alaska, USA 60.35N 165.15W
177 Ff5 **Ta-nyaung** Magwe, W Myanmar 20.49N 94.40E
178 J5 **Tân Yên** Tuyên Quang, N Vietnam 22.08N 104.58E
83 F22 **Tanzania** *off.* United Republic of Tanzania, *Swa.* Jamhuri ya Muungano wa Tanzania; *prev.* German East Africa, Tanganyika and Zanzibar. ◆ *republic* E Africa
Tanzania, Jamhuri ya Muungano wa *see* Tanzania
169 U9 **Tao'an** *var.* Taoan, Taonan. Jilin, NE China 45.19N 122.46E
169 T8 **Tao'er He** ~ NE China
165 U11 **Tao He** ~ C China
T'aon-an *see* Baicheng
Taongi *see* Bokaak Atoll
109 M23 **Taormina** *anc.* Tauromenium. Sicilia, Italy, C Mediterranean Sea 37.54N 15.18E
39 S9 **Taos** New Mexico, SW USA 36.24N 105.34W
Taoudenit *see* Taoudenni
79 O6 **Taoudenni** *var.* Taoudenit. Tombouctou, N Mali 22.46N 3.54W
76 G6 **Taounate** N Morocco 34.34N 4.35W
167 S13 **T'aoyüan** *Jap.* Tōen. N Taiwan 25.00N 121.15E
120 I3 **Tapa** *Ger.* Taps. Lääne-Virumaa, NE Estonia 59.15N 26.00E
43 V17 **Tapachula** Chiapas, SE Mexico 14.53N 92.18W
Tapaiu *see* Gvardeysk
61 H14 **Tapajós, Rio** *var.* Tapajóz. ~ NW Brazil
Tapajóz *see* Tapajós, Rio
63 C21 **Tapalqué** *var.* Tapalquén. Buenos Aires, E Argentina 36.21S 60.01W
Tapalquén *see* Tapalqué
Tapanahoni *see* Tapanahony Rivier
57 W11 **Tapanahony Rivier** *var.* Tapanahoni. ~ E Suriname
43 T16 **Tapanatepec** *var.* San Pedro Tapanatepec. Oaxaca, SE Mexico 16.23N 94.09W
193 D23 **Tapanui** Otago, South Island, NZ 45.55S 169.16E
Tapanuli, Teluk *see* Sibolga, Teluk
61 E14 **Tapauá** Amazonas, N Brazil 5.42S 64.15W
49 R7 **Tapauá, Rio** ~ W Brazil
193 I14 **Tapawera** Tasman, South Island, NZ 41.24S 172.50E
63 I16 **Tapes** Rio Grande do Sul, S Brazil 30.40S 51.25W
78 K16 **Tapeta** C Liberia 6.30N 8.53W
160 H11 **Tāpi** *prev.* Tāpti. ~ W India
106 J2 **Tapia de Casariego** Asturias, N Spain 43.34N 6.55W
58 F10 **Tapiche, Río** ~ N Peru
178 Gg15 **Tapi, Mae Nam** *var.* Luang. ~ SW Thailand
194 K14 **Tapini** Central, S PNG 8.20S 146.57E
Tapirapecó, Serra *see* Tapirapecó, Sierra
57 N13 **Tapirapecó, Sierra** *Port.* Serra Tapirapecó. ⛰ Brazil/Venezuela
79 R13 **Tapoa** ~ Benin/Niger
196 H5 **Tapochau, Mount** ▲ Saipan, S Northern Mariana Islands
113 H24 **Tapolca** Veszprém, W Hungary 46.54N 17.28E
23 X5 **Tappahannock** Virginia, NE USA 37.55N 76.51W
33 U13 **Tappan Lake** ▣ Ohio, N USA
171 Mm7 **Tappi-zaki** *headland* Honshū, C Japan 41.15N 140.19E
Taps *see* Tapa
Tāpti *see* Tāpi
193 J16 **Tapuaenuku** ▲ South Island, NZ 42.00S 173.39E
179 Pp17 **Tapul Group** *island group* Sulu Archipelago, SW Philippines
60 E11 **Tapurmcuará** *var.* Tapuruquara. Amazonas, NW Brazil 0.17S 65.00W
Tapuruquara *see* Tapurmcuará
198 C9 **Taputapu, Cape** *headland* Tutuila, W American Samoa 14.19S 170.51W
147 W13 **Ţāqah** S Oman 17.04N 54.24E
145 T3 **Taqtaq** N Iraq 35.54N 44.36E
63 J15 **Taquara** Rio Grande do Sul, S Brazil 29.40S 50.46W
61 H19 **Taquari, Rio** ~ C Brazil
62 L8 **Taquaritinga** São Paulo, S Brazil 21.22S 48.29W
125 G12 **Tara** Omskaya Oblast', C Russian Federation 56.54N 74.17E
85 I16 **Tara** Southern, S Zambia 16.54S 26.47E
115 J15 **Tara** ~ SW Serbia and Montenegro (Yugoslavia)
114 K13 **Tara** ⛰ W Serbia and Montenegro (Yugoslavia)
79 W15 **Taraba** ⬖ *state* E Nigeria
79 X15 **Taraba** ~ E Nigeria
77 O7 **Ţarābulus** *var.* Ţarābulus al Gharb, *Eng.* Tripoli. ● (Libya) NW Libya 32.54N 13.10E
77 O7 **Tarābulus** ✈ NW Libya 32.37N 13.07E
Tarābulus/Ţarābulus ash Shām *see* Tripoli
Ţarābulus al Gharb *see* Ţarābulus
107 O7 **Taracena** Castilla-La Mancha, C Spain 40.39N 3.07W
119 N12 **Taraclia** *Rus.* Tarakilya. S Moldova 45.55N 28.40E
145 V10 **Tarād al Kahf** SE Iraq 31.58N 45.58E
191 R10 **Tarago** New South Wales, SE Australia 35.04S 149.40E
174 Jj15 **Taraju** Jawa, S Indonesia 7.27S 107.58E
176 Vv11 **Tarak** Papua, E Indonesia 3.21S 132.43E
175 O5 **Tarakan** Borneo, C Indonesia 3.19N 117.37E
175 O5 **Tarakan, Pulau** *island* N Indonesia
Tarakilya *see* Taraclia
172 Pp16 **Tarama-jima** *island* Sakishima-shotō, SW Japan
192 K10 **Taranaki** *off.* Taranaki Region. ⬖ *region* North Island, NZ
192 K10 **Taranaki, Mount** *var.* Egmont. ▲ North Island, NZ 39.16S 174.04E
107 O9 **Tarancón** Castilla-La Mancha, C Spain 40.01N 3.01W
196 M15 **Tarang Reef** *reef* C Micronesia
98 E7 **Taransay** *island* NW Scotland, UK
109 P18 **Taranto** *var.* Tarentum. Puglia, SE Italy 40.30N 17.10E
109 O19 **Taranto, Golfo di** *Eng.* Gulf of Taranto. *gulf* S Italy
Taranto, Gulf of *see* Taranto, Golfo di
64 G3 **Tarapacá** *off.* Región de Tarapacá. ⬖ *region* N Chile
195 Y16 **Tarapaina** Maramasike Island, N Solomon Islands 9.28S 161.24E
58 D10 **Tarapoto** San Martín, N Peru 6.31S 76.24W
144 M6 **Ţaraq an Na'jah** *hill range* E Syria
144 M6 **Ţaraq Sidāwī** *hill range* E Syria
105 Q11 **Tarare** Rhône, E France 45.54N 4.25E
Tararite de Llitera *see* Tamarite de Litera
192 M13 **Tararua Range** ⛰ North Island, NZ
157 Q22 **Tarāsa Dwīp** *island* Nicobar Islands, India, NE Indian Ocean
105 Q15 **Tarascon** Bouches-du-Rhône, SE France 43.48N 4.39E
104 M17 **Tarascon-sur-Ariège** Ariège, S France 42.51N 1.36E
119 P6 **Tarashcha** Kyyivs'ka Oblast', N Ukraine 49.34N 30.31E
59 L18 **Tarata** Cochabamba, C Bolivia 17.34S 66.04W
59 I18 **Tarata** Tacna, SW Peru 17.30S 70.00W
202 H2 **Taratai** *atoll* Tungaru, W Kiribati
61 B15 **Tarauacá** Acre, W Brazil 8.06S 70.45W
61 B15 **Tarauacá, Rio** ~ NW Brazil
203 Q8 **Taravao** Tahiti, W French Polynesia 17.43S 149.19W
203 R8 **Taravao, Baie de** *bay* Tahiti, W French Polynesia
203 Q8 **Taravao, Isthme de** *isthmus* Tahiti, W French Polynesia
105 X16 **Taravo** ~ Corse, France, C Mediterranean Sea
202 J3 **Tarawa** ✈ Tarawa, W Kiribati 0.52S 169.31E
202 H2 **Tarawa** *atoll* Tungaru, W Kiribati
192 N10 **Tarawera** Hawke's Bay, North Island, NZ 39.03S 176.34E
192 N8 **Tarawera, Lake** ◎ North Island, NZ
192 N8 **Tarawera, Mount** ▲ North Island, NZ 38.13S 176.29E
107 S8 **Tarayuela** ▲ N Spain 40.28N 0.22W
151 R16 **Taraz** *prev.* Aulie Ata, Auliye-Ata, Dzhambul, Zhambyl. Zhambyl, S Kazakhstan. 42.55N 71.27E
107 Q5 **Tarazona** Aragón, NE Spain 41.54N 1.43W
107 Q10 **Tarazona de la Mancha** Castilla-La Mancha, C Spain 39.16N 1.55W
151 X12 **Tarbagatay, Khrebet** ⛰ China/Kazakhstan
98 J8 **Tarbat Ness** *headland* N Scotland, UK 57.51N 3.48W
155 U5 **Tarbela Reservoir** ▣ N Pakistan
98 H12 **Tarbert** W Scotland, UK 55.52N 5.25W
98 F7 **Tarbert** Western Isles, NW Scotland, UK 57.53N 6.48W
104 K16 **Tarbes** *anc.* Bigorra. Hautes-Pyrénées, S France 43.13N 0.04E
23 W9 **Tarboro** North Carolina, SE USA 35.54N 77.32W
Tarca *see* Torysa
108 J6 **Tarcento** Friuli-Venezia Giulia, NE Italy 46.13N 13.13E
190 F5 **Tarcoola** South Australia 30.44S 134.33E
107 S5 **Tardienta** Aragón, NE Spain 41.58N 0.31W
104 L11 **Tardoire** ~ W France
191 U7 **Taree** New South Wales, SE Australia 31.55S 152.28E
94 K12 **Tärendö** Norrbotten, N Sweden 67.10N 22.40E
Tarentum *see* Taranto

◆ Country
● Country Capital
◇ Dependent Territory
○ Dependent Territory Capital
⬖ Administrative Region
✈ International Airport
▲ Mountain
⛰ Mountain Range
⋀ Volcano
~ River
◎ Lake
▣ Reservoir

76 C9 **Tarfaya** SW Morocco 27.56N 12.55W
118 J13 **Târgovişte** *prev.* Tîrgovişte. Dâmboviţa, S Romania 44.54N 25.28E
118 M12 **Târgu Bujor** *prev.* Tîrgu Bujor. Galaţi, E Romania 45.52N 27.55E
118 H13 **Târgu Cărbuneşti** *prev.* Tîrgu. Gorj, SW Romania 44.57N 23.31E
118 L9 **Târgu Frumos** *prev.* Tîrgu Frumos. Iaşi, NE Romania 47.12N 27.00E
118 H13 **Targu Jui** *prev.* Tîrgu Jiu. Gorj, W Romania 45.02N 23.19E
118 H9 **Târgu Lăpuş** *prev.* Tîrgu Lăpuş. Maramureş, N Romania 47.28N 23.54E
Târgul-Neamţ *see* Târgu-Neamţ
Târgul-Săcuiesc *see* Târgu Secuiesc
118 I10 **Târgu Mureş** *prev.* Oşorhei, Tîrgu Mures, *Ger.* Neumarkt, *Hung.* Marosvásárhely. Mureş, C Romania 46.33N 24.36E
118 K9 **Târgu-Neamţ** *var.* Târgul-Neamţ; *prev.* Tîrgu-Neamţ. Neamţ, NE Romania 47.12N 26.25E
118 K11 **Târgu Ocna** *Hung.* Aknavásár; *prev.* Tîrgu Ocna. Bacău, E Romania 46.16N 26.37E
118 K11 **Târgu Secuiesc** *Ger.* Neumarkt, Szekler Neumarkt, *Hung.* Kezdivásárhely; *prev.* Chezdi-Oşorheiu, Târgul-Săcuiesc, Tîrgu Secuiesc. Covasna, E Romania 46.00N 26.08E
151 X10 **Targyn** Vostochnyy Kazakhstan, E Kazakhstan 49.31N 82.46E
Tar Heel State *see* North Carolina
194 G12 **Tari** Southern Highlands, W PNG 5.52S 142.58E
149 P17 **Ţarīf** Abū Ẓaby, C UAE 24.01N 53.46E
106 K16 **Tarifa** Andalucía, S Spain 36.01N 5.36W
86 C14 **Tarifa, Punta de** *headland* SW Spain 36.01N 5.39W
59 M21 **Tarija** Tarija, S Bolivia 21.33S 64.42W
59 M21 **Tarija** ◈ *department* S Bolivia
147 R14 **Tarīm** C Yemen 16.00N 48.50E
Tarim Basin *see* Tarim Pendi
83 G19 **Tarime** Mara, N Tanzania 1.19S 34.24E
133 S8 **Tarim He** ≈ NW China
165 H8 **Tarim Pendi** *Eng.* Tarim Basin. *basin* NW China
155 N7 **Tarīn Kowt** *var.* Terinkot. Urūzgān, C Afghanistan 32.37N 65.52E
175 Pp10 **Taripa** Sulawesi, C Indonesia 1.51S 120.46E
176 Z11 **Taritatu, Sungai** *prev.* Idenburg-rivier. ≈ Papua, E Indonesia
119 Q12 **Tarkhankut, Mys** *headland* S Ukraine 45.20N 32.32E
29 Q1 **Tarkio** Missouri, C USA 40.25N 95.24W
126 H9 **Tarko-Sale** Yamalo-Nenetskiy Avtonomnyy Okrug, N Russian Federation 64.55N 77.34E
79 P17 **Tarkwa** S Ghana 5.16N 1.58W
179 P10 **Tarlac** Luzon, N Philippines 15.29N 120.34E
97 F22 **Tarm** Ringkøbing, W Denmark 55.55N 8.31E
59 E14 **Tarma** Junín, C Peru 11.25S 75.43W
105 N15 **Tarn** ◈ *department* S France
104 M15 **Tarn** ≈ S France
113 L22 **Tarna** ≈ C Hungary
94 G13 **Tärnaby** Västerbotten, N Sweden 65.43N 15.19E
155 P8 **Tarnak Rūd** ≈ SE Afghanistan
118 J11 **Târnava Mare** *Ger.* Grosse Kokel, *Hung.* Nagy-Küküllő; *prev.* Tîrnava Mare. ≈ S Romania
118 I11 **Târnava Mică** *Ger.* Kleine Kokel, *Hung.* Kis-Küküllo; *prev.* Tîrnava Mică. ≈ C Romania
118 I11 **Târnăveni** *Ger.* Marteskirch, Martinskirch, *Hung.* Dicsőszentmárton; *prev.* Sînmartin, Tîrnăveni. Mureş, C Romania 46.19N 24.16E
104 L14 **Tarn-et-Garonne** ◈ *department* S France
113 P18 **Tarnica** ▲ SE Poland 49.05N 22.43E
113 N15 **Tarnobrzeg** Podkarpackie, SE Poland 50.34N 21.40E
129 N12 **Tarnogskiy Gorodok** Vologodskaya Oblast', NW Russian Federation 60.28N 43.45E
Tarnopol *see* Ternopil'
113 M16 **Tarnów** Małopolskie, SE Poland 50.01N 20.58E
Tarnowice/Tarnowitz *see* Tarnowskie Góry
113 J16 **Tarnowskie Góry** *var.* Tarnowice, Tarnowskie Gory, *Ger.* Tarnowitz. Śląskie, S Poland 50.27N 18.52E
97 N14 **Tärnsjö** Västmanland, C Sweden 60.10N 16.57E
108 E9 **Taro** ≈ NW Italy
195 Q10 **Taron** New Ireland, NE PNG 4.22S 153.04E
76 E8 **Taroudannt** *var.* Taroudant. SW Morocco 30.31N 8.50W
Taroudant *see* Taroudannt
25 V12 **Tarpon, Lake** ◎ Florida, SE USA
25 V12 **Tarpon Springs** Florida, SE USA 28.09N 82.45W
109 G14 **Tarquinia** *anc.* Tarquinii; *hist.* Corneto. Lazio, C Italy 42.22N 11.45E
Tarquinii *see* Tarquinia
Tarraco *see* Tarragona
78 D10 **Tarrafal** Santiago, S Cape Verde 15.16N 23.45W
107 V6 **Tarragona** *anc.* Tarraco. Cataluña, E Spain 41.07N 1.15E
107 T7 **Tarragona** ◈ *province* Cataluña, NE Spain
191 O17 **Tarraleah** Tasmania, SE Australia 42.11S 146.29E
25 P3 **Tarrant City** Alabama, S USA 33.34N 86.45W
193 D21 **Tarras** Otago, South Island, NZ 44.48S 169.25E
Tarrasa *see* Terrassa
107 U5 **Tàrrega** *var.* Tarrega. Cataluña, NE Spain 41.39N 1.09E
23 W9 **Tar River** ≈ North Carolina, SE USA
Tarsatica *see* Rijeka
142 J17 **Tarsus** İçel, S Turkey 36.52N 34.52E
64 K4 **Tartagal** Salta, N Argentina 22.31S 63.49W
143 V12 **Tärtär** *Rus.* Terter. ≈ SW Azerbaijan
104 J15 **Tartas** Landes, SW France 43.52N 0.45W
145 Q6 **Tārtasah** C Iraq 34.18N 42.21E
Tartlau *see* Prejmer
Tartous/Tartouss *see* Ţarţūs
120 J5 **Tartu** *Ger.* Dorpat; *prev. Rus.* Yurev, Yur'yev. Tartumaa, SE Estonia 58.19N 26.43E
120 I5 **Tartumaa** *off.* Tartu Maakond. ◈ *province* E Estonia
144 H5 **Ţarţūs** *Fr.* Tartouss; *anc.* Tortosa. Ţarţūs, W Syria 34.55N 35.52E
144 H5 **Ţarţūs** *off.* Muḩāfaẓat Ţarţūs, *var.* Tartous, Tartus. ◈ *governorate* W Syria
170 Bb16 **Tarumizu** Kagoshima, Kyūshū, SW Japan 31.30N 130.40E
130 K4 **Tarusa** Kaluzhskaya Oblast', W Russian Federation 54.45N 37.10E
173 G9 **Tarusan** Sumatera, W Indonesia 1.13S 100.22E
119 N11 **Tarutyne** Odes'ka Oblast', SW Ukraine 46.11N 29.09E
168 I7 **Tarvagatyn Nuruu** ▲▲ N Mongolia
108 J6 **Tarvisio** Friuli-Venezia Giulia, NE Italy 46.31N 13.33E
Tarvisium *see* Treviso
59 O16 **Tarvo, Río** ≈ E Bolivia
12 G8 **Tarzwell** Ontario, S Canada 48.00N 79.58W
42 K5 **Tasajera, Sierra de la** ▲▲ N Mexico
151 S13 **Tasaral** Zhezkazgan, C Kazakhstan 46.17N 73.54E
Tasböget *see* Tasbuget
151 N15 **Tasbuget** *Kaz.* Tasböget. Kzylorda, S Kazakhstan 44.49N 65.34E
110 E11 **Tasch** Valais, SW Switzerland 46.04N 7.43E
Tasek Kenyir *see* Kenyir, Tasik
126 Hh16 **Tashanta** Respublika Altay, S Russian Federation 49.42N 89.15E
Tashauz *see* Dashkhovuz
Tashi Chho Dzong *see* Thimphu
159 U11 **Tashigang** E Bhutan 27.19N 91.33E
143 T11 **Tashir** *prev.* Kalinino. N Armenia 41.07N 44.16E
149 Q11 **Ţashk, Daryācheh-ye** ◎ C Iran
Tashkent *see* Toshkent
Tashkentskaya Oblast' *see* Toshkent Viloyati
152 J16 **Tashkepri** *Turkm.* Dashköpri. Maryyskiy Velayat, S Turkmenistan 36.15N 62.37E
Tash-Kömür *see* Tash-Kumyr
153 S9 **Tash-Kumyr** *Kir.* Tash-Kömür. Dzhalal-Abadskaya Oblast', W Kyrgyzstan 41.22N 72.08E
131 T7 **Tashla** Orenburgskaya Oblast', W Russian Federation 51.42N 52.33E
Tashqurghan *see* Kholm
126 H15 **Tashtagol** Kemerovskaya Oblast', S Russian Federation 52.49N 88.00E
174 Jj15 **Tasikmalaya** *prev.* Tasikmalaja. Jawa, C Indonesia 7.19S 108.16E
97 H24 **Tåsinge** *island* C Denmark
10 M5 **Tasiujaq** Quebec, E Canada 58.43N 69.58W
127 Nn9 **Taskan** Magadanskaya Oblast', E Russian Federation 63.00N 150.03E
79 W11 **Tasker** Zinder, C Niger 15.06N 10.42E
151 W12 **Taskesken** Vostochnyy Kazakhstan, E Kazakhstan 47.15N 80.42E
142 J10 **Taşköprü** Kastamonu, N Turkey 41.30N 34.12E
Taskuduk, Peski *see* Tosquduq Qumlari
195 N9 **Taskul** New Ireland, NE PNG 2.30S 150.22E
143 S13 **Taşlıçay** Ağrı, E Turkey 39.37N 43.22E
193 H14 **Tasman** *off.* Tasman District. ◈ *unitary authority* South Island, NZ
199 I14 **Tasman Basin** *var.* East Australian Basin. *undersea feature* S Tasman Sea
193 I14 **Tasman Bay** *inlet* South Island, NZ
199 Hh14 **Tasman Fracture Zone** *tectonic feature* S Indian Ocean
193 E19 **Tasman Glacier** *glacier* South Island, NZ
Tasman Group *see* Nukumanu Islands
191 N15 **Tasmania** *prev.* Van Diemen's Land. ◈ *state* SE Australia
191 Q16 **Tasmania** *island* SE Australia
193 H14 **Tasman Mountains** ▲▲ South Island, NZ
191 P17 **Tasman Peninsula** *peninsula* Tasmania, SE Australia
199 Hh13 **Tasman Plain** *undersea feature* W Tasman Sea
199 Hh14 **Tasman Plateau** *var.* South Tasmania Plateau. *undersea feature* SW Tasman Sea
199 Ii14 **Tasman Sea** *sea* SW Pacific Ocean
118 G9 **Tăşnad** *Ger.* Trestenberg, Trestendorf, *Hung.* Tasnád. Satu Mare, NW Romania 47.30N 22.33E
142 L11 **Taşova** Amasya, N Turkey 40.45N 36.19E
79 T10 **Tassara** Tahoua, W Niger 16.40N 5.34E
10 K4 **Tassialouc, Lac** ◎ Quebec, C Canada
Tassili du Hoggar *see* Tassili ta-n-Ahaggar
76 L11 **Tassili-n-Ajjer** *plateau* E Algeria
76 K14 **Tassili ta-n-Ahaggar** *var.* Tassili du Hoggar. *plateau* S Algeria
61 M15 **Tasso Fragoso** Maranhão, E Brazil 8.22S 45.53W
Tåstrup *see* Taastrup
151 O9 **Tasty-Taldy** Akmola, C Kazakhstan 50.45N 66.35E
149 W10 **Tāsūkī** Sīstān va Balūchestān, SE Iran
113 I22 **Tata** *Ger.* Totis. Komárom-Esztergom, NW Hungary 47.39N 18.19E
76 E8 **Tata** SW Morocco 29.38N 8.04W
Tataaihoa, Pointe *see* Vénus, Pointe
113 I22 **Tatabánya** Komárom-Esztergom, NW Hungary 47.33N 18.22E
203 X10 **Tatakoto** *atoll* Îles Tuamotu, E French Polynesia
77 N7 **Tataouine** *var.* Taţāwīn. SE Tunisia 32.48N 10.27E
57 O5 **Tataracual, Cerro** ▲ NE Venezuela 10.13N 64.20W
119 O12 **Tatarbunary** Odes'ka Oblast', SW Ukraine 45.50N 29.37E
121 M17 **Tatarka** *Rus.* Tatarka. Mahilyowskaya Voblasts', E Belarus 53.15N 28.49E
Tatar Pazardzhik *see* Pazardzhik
125 G13 **Tatarsk** Novosibirskaya Oblast', C Russian Federation 55.08N 75.58E
Tatarskaya ASSR *see* Tatarstan, Respublika
127 O15 **Tatarskiy Proliv** *Eng.* Tatar Strait. *strait* SE Russian Federation
131 R4 **Tatarstan, Respublika** *prev.* Tatarskaya ASSR. ◈ *autonomous republic* W Russian Federation
Tatar Strait *see* Tatarskiy Proliv
195 O9 **Tatau Island** *island* Tabar Islands, N PNG
Taţāwīn *see* Tataouine
175 P8 **Tate** Sulawesi, N Indonesia 0.12S 119.44E
171 Jj17 **Tateyama** Chiba, Honshū, S Japan 35.00N 139.51E
171 J14 **Tate-yama** ▲ Honshū, S Japan 36.27N 137.32E
147 N11 **Tathlīth** 'Asīr, S Saudi Arabia 19.37N 43.31E
147 O11 **Tathlīth, Wādī** *dry watercourse* S Saudi Arabia
191 R11 **Tathra** New South Wales, SE Australia 36.46S 149.58E
131 P8 **Tatishchevo** Saratovskaya Oblast', W Russian Federation 51.43N 45.35E
41 S12 **Tatitlek** Alaska, USA 60.49N 146.29W
8 L15 **Tatla Lake** British Columbia, SW Canada 51.54N 124.39W
124 O2 **Tatlısu** *Gk.* Akanthoú. N Cyprus 35.21N 33.45E
9 Z10 **Tatnam, Cape** *headland* Manitoba, C Canada 57.16N 91.03W
Tatra/Tátra *see* Tatra Mountains
113 K18 **Tatra Mountains** *Ger.* Tatra, *Hung.* Tátra, *Pol./Slvk.* Tatry. ▲▲ Poland/Slovakia
Tatry *see* Tatra Mountains
170 G14 **Tatsuno** *var.* Tatuno. Hyōgo, Honshū, SW Japan 34.51N 134.33E
151 S16 **Tatti** *var.* Tatty. Zhambyl, S Kazakhstan 43.10N 73.22E
Tatty *see* Tatti
62 L10 **Tatuí** São Paulo, S Brazil 23.21S 47.49W
39 V14 **Tatum** New Mexico, SW USA 33.15N 103.19W
27 X7 **Tatum** Texas, SW USA 32.19N 94.31W
Ta-t'ung/Tatung *see* Datong
Tatuno *see* Tatsuno
143 R14 **Tatvan** Bitlis, SE Turkey 38.31N 42.15E
97 C16 **Tau** Rogaland, S Norway 59.04N 5.55E
198 Dd8 **Ta'ū** *var.* Tau. *island* Manua Islands, E American Samoa
200 R14 **Tau** *island* Tongatapu Group, N Tonga
61 O14 **Tauá** Ceará, E Brazil 6.04S 40.25W
62 N10 **Taubaté** São Paulo, S Brazil 23.00S 45.36W
103 I19 **Tauber** ≈ SW Germany
103 I19 **Tauberbiscofsheim** Baden-Württemberg, C Germany 49.37N 9.39E
150 E14 **Tauchik** *Kaz.* Taūshyq. Mangistau, SW Kazakhstan 44.17N 51.22E
203 W10 **Tauere** *atoll* Îles Tuamotu, C French Polynesia
103 H17 **Taufstein** ▲ C Germany 50.31N 9.18E
202 I17 **Taukoka** *island* SE Cook Islands
151 T15 **Taukum, Peski** *desert* SE Kazakhstan
192 L10 **Taumarunui** Manawatu-Wanganui, North Island, NZ 38.52S 175.14E
61 A15 **Taumaturgo** Acre, W Brazil 8.54S 72.48W
29 X6 **Taum Sauk Mountain** ▲ Missouri, C USA 37.34N 90.43W
85 H22 **Taung** North-West, N South Africa 27.31S 24.47E
177 G6 **Taungdwingyi** Magwe, C Myanmar 20.01N 95.34E
178 Gg6 **Taunggyi** Shan State, C Myanmar 20.46N 97.00E
177 G5 **Taungtha** Mandalay, C Myanmar 21.16N 95.25E
177 F7 **Taungup** Arakan State, W Myanmar 18.49N 94.13E
155 S9 **Taunsa** Punjab, E Pakistan 30.43N 70.40E
99 K23 **Taunton** SW England, UK 51.01N 3.06W
21 O12 **Taunton** Massachusetts, NE USA 41.54N 71.03W
103 F18 **Taunus** ▲▲ W Germany
103 G18 **Taunusstein** Hessen, W Germany 50.09N 8.09E
192 N9 **Taupo** Waikato, North Island, NZ 38.42S 176.05E
192 M9 **Taupo, Lake** ◎ North Island, NZ
111 R8 **Taurach** *var.* Taurachbach. ≈ E Austria
Taurachbach *see* Taurach
120 D12 **Tauragė** *Ger.* Tauroggen. Tauragė, SW Lithuania 55.15N 22.17E
56 G10 **Tauramena** Casanare, C Colombia 5.01N 72.48W
192 N7 **Tauranga** Bay of Plenty, North Island, NZ 37.41S 176.09E
13 O10 **Taureau, Réservoir** ⊠ Quebec, SE Canada
109 N22 **Taurianova** Calabria, SW Italy 38.22N 16.01E
Tauris *see* Tabrīz
192 I2 **Tauroa Point** *headland* North Island, NZ 35.09S 173.02E
Tauroggen *see* Tauragė
Tauromenium *see* Taormina
Taurus Mountains *see* Toros Dağları
Taus *see* Domažlice
Taūshyq *see* Tauchik
107 R5 **Tauste** Aragón, NE Spain 41.55N 1.15W
203 V16 **Tautara, Motu** *island* Easter Island, Chile, E Pacific Ocean
203 R8 **Tautira** Tahiti, W French Polynesia 17.45S 149.10W
Tauz *see* Tovuz
Ţavālesh, Kūhhā-ye *see* Talish Mountains
142 D15 **Tavas** Denizli, SW Turkey 37.33N 29.04E
Tavastehus *see* Hämeenlinna
Tavau *see* Davos
125 F11 **Tavda** Sverdlovskaya Oblast', C Russian Federation 58.01N 65.07E
125 F11 **Tavda** ≈ C Russian Federation
107 T11 **Tavernes de la Valldigna** País Valenciano, E Spain 39.03N 0.13W
83 I20 **Taveta** Coast, S Kenya 3.24S 37.46E
197 J13 **Taveuni** *island* N Fiji
153 R13 **Tavildara** *Rus.* Tavil'dara, Tovil'-Dora. C Tajikistan 38.42N 70.27E
168 L8 **Tavin** Dundgovĭ, C Mongolia 46.27N 105.43E
106 H14 **Tavira** Faro, S Portugal 37.07N 7.39W
99 I24 **Tavistock** SW England, UK 50.33N 4.07W
178 Gg11 **Tavoy** *var.* Dawei. Tenasserim, S Myanmar 14.01N 98.12E
Tavoy Island *see* Mali Kyun
125 Ff13 **Tavricheskoye** Omskaya Oblast', C Russian Federation 54.34N 73.33E
117 E16 **Tavropoú, Techníti Límni** ⊠ C Greece
142 E13 **Tavşanlı** Kütahya, NW Turkey 39.34N 29.28E
197 H14 **Tavua** Viti Levu, W Fiji 17.26S 105.53E
197 I16 **Tavuki** Kadavu, SW Fiji 19.05S 178.06E
99 J23 **Taw** ≈ SW England, UK
193 L14 **Tawa** Wellington, North Island, NZ 41.11S 174.48E
27 V6 **Tawakoni, Lake** ⊠ Texas, SW USA
159 V11 **Tawang** Arunāchal Pradesh, NE India 27.34N 91.54E
174 L16 **Tawang, Teluk** *bay* Jawa, S Indonesia
33 R7 **Tawas Bay** ◎ Michigan, N USA
33 R7 **Tawas City** Michigan, N USA 44.16N 83.33W
175 Oo4 **Tawau** Sabah, East Malaysia 4.16N 117.54E
147 U10 **Ţawīl, Qalamat aţ** *well* SE Saudi Arabia 21.07N 52.11E
179 P17 **Tawitawi** *island* Tawitawi Group, SW Philippines
179 Pp17 **Tawitawi Group** *island group* Sulu Archipelago, SW Philippines
Ţawkar *see* Tokar
Tāwūq *see* Dāqūq
Tawzar *see* Tozeur
43 O15 **Taxco** *var.* Taxco de Alarcón. Guerrero, S Mexico 18.32N 99.37W
Taxco de Alarcón *see* Taxco
152 H8 **Taxiatosh** *Rus.* Takhiatash. Qoraqalpog'iston Respublikasi, W Uzbekistan 42.27N 59.26E
164 D9 **Taxkorgan** *var.* Taxkorgan Tajik Zizhixian. Xinjiang Uygur Zizhiqu, NW China 37.43N 75.13E
Taxkorgan Tajik Zizhixian *see* Taxkorgan
152 H7 **Taxtako'pir** *Rus.* Takhtakupyr. Qoraqalpog'iston Respublikasi, NW Uzbekistan 43.04N 60.23E
98 J10 **Tay** ≈ C Scotland, UK
176 V13 **Tayandu, Kepulauan** *island group* E Indonesia
149 V6 **Tāybād** *var.* Taibad, Tāyybād, Tayyebāt. Khorāsān, NE Iran 34.48N 60.46E
Taybert at Turkz *see* Ţayyibat at Turkī
128 J3 **Taybola** Murmanskaya Oblast', NW Russian Federation 68.30N 33.18E
83 M16 **Tayeeglow** Bakool, C Somalia 4.01N 44.25E
98 K11 **Tay, Firth of** *inlet* E Scotland, UK
126 H13 **Tayga** Kemerovskaya Oblast', S Russian Federation 56.02N 85.26E
168 G8 **Taygan** Govĭ-Altay, C Mongolia 46.20N 97.22E
127 Oo9 **Taygonos, Mys** *headland* E Russian Federation 60.36N 160.09E
98 I11 **Tay, Loch** ◎ C Scotland, UK
9 N12 **Taylor** British Columbia, W Canada 56.09N 120.43W
31 O14 **Taylor** Nebraska, C USA 41.45N 99.22W
20 I13 **Taylor** Pennsylvania, NE USA 41.22N 75.41W
27 T10 **Taylor** Texas, SW USA 30.34N 97.24W
39 Q11 **Taylor, Mount** ▲ New Mexico, SW USA 35.14N 107.36W
39 R5 **Taylor Park Reservoir** ⊠ Colorado, C USA
39 R6 **Taylor River** ≈ Colorado, C USA
23 P11 **Taylors** South Carolina, SE USA 34.55N 82.18W
22 L5 **Taylorsville** Kentucky, S USA 38.01N 85.21W
23 R6 **Taylorsville** North Carolina, SE USA 35.55N 81.10W
32 L14 **Taylorville** Illinois, N USA 39.33N 89.17W
146 K5 **Taymā'** Tabūk, NW Saudi Arabia 27.39N 38.32E
126 J11 **Taymura** ≈ C Russian Federation
126 Kk6 **Taymylyr** Respublika Sakha (Yakutiya), NE Russian Federation 72.32N 121.54E
126 J5 **Taymyr, Ozero** ◎ N Russian Federation
126 J5 **Taymyr, Poluostrov** *peninsula* N Russian Federation
126 Ii7 **Taymyrskiy (Dolgano-Nenetskiy) Avtonomnyy Okrug** *var.* Taymyrskiy Avtonomnyy Okrug. ◈ *autonomous district* N Russian Federation
178 Jj13 **Tây Ninh** Tây Ninh, S Vietnam 11.20N 106.03E
126 Ii14 **Tayshet** Irkutskaya Oblast', S Russian Federation 55.51N 98.04E
179 Oo13 **Taytay** Palawan, W Philippines 10.49N 119.30E
174 L14 **Tayu** *prev.* Tajoe. Jawa, C Indonesia 6.31S 111.01E
Tāyybād/Tayyebāt *see* Tāybād
144 L5 **Ţayyibah** *var.* At Taybé. Ḩimş, C Syria 35.13N 38.51E
144 I4 **Ţayyibat at Turkī** *var.* Taybert at Turkz. Ḩamāh, W Syria 35.16N 36.55E
151 P7 **Tayynsha** *prev.* Krasnoarmeysk. Severnyy Kazakhstan, N Kazakhstan 53.52N 69.51E
126 H9 **Taz** ≈ N Russian Federation
76 G6 **Taza** NE Morocco 34.13N 4.06W
145 T4 **Tāza Khurmātū** E Iraq 35.18N 44.21E
171 M10 **Tazawa-ko** ◎ Honshū, C Japan
Taz, Bay of *see* Tazovskaya Guba
23 N8 **Tazewell** Tennessee, S USA 36.27N 83.34W
23 Q7 **Tazewell** Virginia, NE USA 37.06N 81.31W
77 S11 **Tāzirbū** SE Libya 25.43N 21.16E
41 S11 **Tazlina Lake** ◎ Alaska, USA
126 H7 **Tazovskaya Guba** *Eng.* Bay of Taz. *bay* N Russian Federation
126 H8 **Tazovskiy** Yamalo-Nenetskiy Avtonomnyy Okrug, N Russian Federation 67.33N 78.21E
143 U10 **T'bilisi** *Eng.* Tiflis. ● (Georgia) SE Georgia 41.40N 44.54E
143 T10 **T'bilisi** ✈ S Georgia 41.43N 44.49E
81 E14 **Tchabal Mbabo** ▲ NW Cameroon 7.12N 12.16E
Tchad *see* Chad
Tchad, Lac *see* Chad, Lake
79 S15 **Tchaourou** E Benin 8.55N 2.39E
81 E20 **Tchibanga** Nyanga, S Gabon 02.49S 11.00E
Tchien *see* Zwedru
79 Z6 **Tchigaï, Plateau du** ▲▲ NE Niger
79 V9 **Tchighozérine** Agadez, C Niger 17.15N 7.48E
79 T10 **Tchin-Tabaradene** Tahoua, W Niger 15.57N 5.49E
80 G13 **Tcholliré** Nord, NE Cameroon 8.48N 14.00E
Tchongking *see* Chongqing
24 K4 **Tchula** Mississippi, S USA 33.10N 90.13W
112 I7 **Tczew** *Ger.* Dirschau. Pomorskie, N Poland 54.05N 18.46E
118 I10 **Teaca** *Ger.* Tekendorf, *Hung.* Teke; *prev. Ger.* Teckendorf. Bistriţa-Năsăud, N Romania 46.55N 24.30E
42 J11 **Teacapán** Sinaloa, C Mexico 22.33N 105.44W
202 A10 **Teafuafou** *island* Funafuti Atoll, C Tuvalu
27 U8 **Teague** Texas, SW USA 31.37N 96.16W
203 R9 **Teahupoo** Tahiti, W French Polynesia 17.51S 149.15W
202 H15 **Te Aiti Point** *headland* Rarotonga, S Cook Islands 21.10S 59.46W
67 D24 **Teal Inlet** East Falkland, Falkland Islands 51.34S 58.25W
193 B22 **Te Anau** Southland, South Island, NZ 45.24S 167.44E
193 B22 **Te Anau, Lake** ◎ South Island, NZ
43 U15 **Teapa** Tabasco, SE Mexico 17.36N 92.57W
192 Q7 **Te Araroa** Gisborne, North Island, NZ 37.37S 178.21E
192 M7 **Te Aroha** Waikato, North Island, NZ 37.33S 175.41E
Teate *see* Chieti
202 A9 **Te Ava Fuagea** *channel* Funafuti Atoll, SE Tuvalu
202 B8 **Te Ava I Te Lape** *channel* Funafuti Atoll, SE Tuvalu
202 B9 **Te Ava Pua Pua** *channel* Funafuti Atoll, SE Tuvalu
192 M8 **Te Awamutu** Waikato, North Island, NZ 37.59S 175.19E
176 Xx9 **Teba** Papua, E Indonesia 1.27S 137.54E
106 L15 **Teba** Andalucía, S Spain 36.59N 4.54W
130 M15 **Teberda** Karachayevo-Cherkesskaya Respublika, SW Russian Federation 43.28N 41.45E
76 M6 **Tébessa** NE Algeria 35.21N 8.06E
64 O7 **Tebicuary, Río** ≈ S Paraguay
174 Hh11 **Tebingtinggi** Sumatera, W Indonesia 3.33S 103.00E
173 Ff5 **Tebingtinggi** Sumatera, N Indonesia 3.19N 99.07E
Tebingtinggi, Pulau *see* Rantau, Pulau
Tebriz *see* Tabrīz
143 U9 **Tebulos Mt'a** *Rus.* Gora Tebulosmta. ▲ Georgia/Russian Federation 42.33N 45.21E
Tebulosmta, Gora *see* Tebulos Mt'a
43 Q14 **Tecamachalco** Puebla, S Mexico 18.52N 97.43W
42 B1 **Tecate** Baja California, NW Mexico 32.33N 116.37W
142 M13 **Tecer Dağları** ▲▲ C Turkey
105 O17 **Tech** ≈ S France
79 P16 **Techiman** W Ghana 7.35N 1.56W
119 N15 **Techirghiol** Constanţa, SE Romania 44.03N 28.37E
76 A12 **Techla** *var.* Techlé. SW Western Sahara 21.39N 14.57W
Techlé *see* Techla
65 H18 **Tecka, Sierra de** ▲▲ SW Argentina
Teckendorf *see* Teaca
42 K13 **Tecolotlán** Jalisco, SW Mexico 20.14N 104.01W
42 K14 **Tecomán** Colima, SW Mexico 18.52N 103.54W
37 V12 **Tecopa** California, W USA 35.51N 116.14W
42 G5 **Tecoripa** Sonora, NW Mexico 28.36N 109.57W
43 N16 **Tecpan** *var.* Tecpan de Galeana. Guerrero, S Mexico 17.11N 100.39W
Tecpan de Galeana *see* Tecpan
42 J11 **Tecuala** Nayarit, C Mexico 22.24N 105.30W
118 L12 **Tecuci** Galaţi, E Romania 45.49N 27.27E
33 R10 **Tecumseh** Michigan, N USA 42.00N 83.57W
31 S16 **Tecumseh** Nebraska, C USA 40.22N 96.12W
29 O11 **Tecumseh** Oklahoma, C USA 35.15N 96.56W
194 E12 **Tedi** ≈ W PNG
152 H14 **Tedzhen** *Turkm.* Tejen. Akhalskiy Velayat, S Turkmenistan 37.23N 60.28E
152 I15 **Tedzhen** *Per.* Harīrūd, *Turkm.* Tejen. ≈ Afghanistan/Iran *see also* Harīrūd
152 H15 **Tedzhenstroy** *Turkm.* Tejenstroy. Akhalskiy Velayat, S Turkmenistan 36.57N 60.49E
168 I7 **Teel** Arhangay, C Mongolia 48.01N 100.30E
99 L15 **Tees** ≈ N England, UK
12 E15 **Teeswater** Ontario, S Canada 44.00N 81.17W
202 A10 **Tefala** *island* Funafuti Atoll, C Tuvalu
60 D13 **Tefé** Amazonas, N Brazil 3.24S 64.45W
76 K11 **Tefedest** ▲▲ S Algeria
142 E16 **Tefenni** Burdur, SW Turkey 37.19N 29.45E
60 D13 **Tefé, Rio** ≈ NW Brazil
174 Kk14 **Tegal** Jawa, C Indonesia 6.52S 109.07E
102 O12 **Tegel** ✈ (Berlin) Berlin, NE Germany 52.33N 13.16E
101 M15 **Tegelen** Limburg, SE Netherlands 51.19N 6.09E
103 L24 **Tegernsee** ◎ SE Germany
109 M18 **Teggiano** Campania, S Italy 40.25N 15.28E
79 U14 **Tegina** Niger, C Nigeria 10.06N 6.10E
197 B10 **Tegua** *island* Torres Islands, N Vanuatu
44 I7 **Tegucigalpa** ● (Honduras) Francisco Morazán, SW Honduras 14.04N 87.10W
44 H7 **Tegucigalpa** ✈ Central District, C Honduras 14.03N 87.20W
Tegucigalpa *see* Central District, Honduras
Tegucigalpa *see* Francisco Morazán, Honduras
79 U9 **Teguidda-n-Tessoumt** Agadez, C Niger 17.27N 6.40E
66 Q11 **Teguise** Lanzarote, Islas Canarias, Spain, NE Atlantic Ocean 29.04N 13.37W
126 Hh13 **Tegul'det** Tomskaya Oblast', C Russian Federation 57.16N 87.58E
37 S13 **Tehachapi** California, W USA 35.07N 118.27W
37 S13 **Tehachapi Mountains** ▲▲ California, W USA
Tehama *see* Tihāmah
Teheran *see* Tehrān
79 O14 **Téhini** NE Ivory Coast 9.36N 3.40W
149 N5 **Tehrān** *var.* Teheran. ● (Iran) Tehrān, N Iran 35.43N 51.26E
149 N6 **Tehrān** *off.* Ostān-e Tehrān, *var.* Tehran. ◈ *province* N Iran
158 K9 **Tehri** Uttar Pradesh, N India 30.12N 78.28E
Tehri *see* Tīkamgarh
43 Q15 **Tehuacán** Puebla, S Mexico 18.28N 97.24W
43 S17 **Tehuantepec** *var.* Santo Domingo Tehuantepec. Oaxaca, SE Mexico 16.18N 95.13W
43 S17 **Tehuantepec, Golfo de** *var.* Gulf of Tehuantepec. *gulf* S Mexico
Tehuantepec, Gulf of *see* Tehuantepec, Golfo de
Tehuantepec, Isthmus of *see* Tehuantepec, Istmo de
43 T16 **Tehuantepec, Istmo de** *var.* Isthmus of Tehuantepec. *isthmus* SE Mexico
(0) I16 **Tehuantepec Ridge** *undersea feature* E Pacific Ocean
43 S16 **Tehuantepec, Río** ≈ SE Mexico
203 W10 **Tehuata** *atoll* Îles Tuamotu, C French Polynesia
66 O11 **Teide, Pico de** ▲ Gran Canaria, Islas Canarias, Spain, NE Atlantic Ocean 28.16N 16.39W
99 I21 **Teifi** ≈ SW Wales, UK
82 B9 **Teiga Plateau** *plateau* W Sudan
99 J24 **Teignmouth** SW England, UK 50.34N 3.29W
Teisen *see* Chech'ŏn
118 H1 **Teiuş** *Ger.* Dreikirchen, *Hung.* Tövis. Alba, C Romania 46.12N 23.40E
175 N16 **Tejakula** Bali, C Indonesia 8.09S 115.19E
Tejen *see* Harīrūd/Tedzhen
Tejenstroy *see* Tedzhenstroy
37 S14 **Tejon Pass** *pass* California, W USA 34.46N 118.49W
Tejo, Rio *see* Tagus
43 O14 **Tejupilco** *var.* Tejupilco de Hidalgo. México, S Mexico 18.55N 100.10W
Tejupilco de Hidalgo *see* Tejupilco
192 P7 **Te Kaha** Bay of Plenty, North Island, NZ 37.45S 105.42E
31 S14 **Tekamah** Nebraska, C USA 41.46N 96.13W
192 I1 **Te Kao** Northland, North Island, NZ 34.39S 172.57E
193 F20 **Tekapo** ≈ South Island, NZ
193 F19 **Tekapo, Lake** ◎ South Island, NZ
192 P9 **Te Karaka** Gisborne, North Island, NZ 38.30S 105.52E
192 L7 **Te Kauwhata** Waikato, North Island, NZ 37.22S 175.07E
43 X12 **Tekax** *var.* Tekax de Álvaro Obregón. Yucatán, SE Mexico 20.07N 89.10W
Tekax de Álvaro Obregón *see* Tekax
Teke/Tekendorf *see* Teaca
142 A14 **Teke Burnu** *headland* W Turkey 38.06N 26.35E
116 M12 **Teke Deresi** ≈ NW Turkey
152 D10 **Tekedzhik, Gory** *hill range* NW Turkmenistan
151 V14 **Tekeli** Almaty, SE Kazakhstan 44.49N 78.46E
151 R7 **Teke, Ozero** ◎ N Kazakhstan
164 I5 **Tekes** Xinjiang Uygur Zizhiqu, NW China 43.15N 81.43E
151 W16 **Tekes** Almaty, SE Kazakhstan 42.40N 80.01E
Tekes *see* Tekes He
164 H5 **Tekes He** *Rus.* Tekes. ≈ China/Kazakhstan
82 I10 **Tekezē** *var.* Takkaze. ≈ Eritrea/Ethiopia
Tekhtin *see* Tsyakhtsin
142 C10 **Tekirdağ** *It.* Rodosto; *anc.* Bisanthe, Raidestos, Rhaedestus. Tekirdağ, NW Turkey 40.58N 27.31E
142 C10 **Tekirdağ** ◈ *province* NW Turkey
161 N14 **Tekkali** Andhra Pradesh, E India 18.37N 84.15E
117 K15 **Tekke Burnu** *Turk.* İlyasbaba Burnu. *headland* NW Turkey 40.03N 26.12E
143 Q13 **Tekman** Erzurum, NE Turkey 39.39N 41.31E
34 M9 **Tekoa** Washington, NW USA 47.13N 117.05W
202 H16 **Te Kou** ▲ Rarotonga, S Cook Islands 21.13S 159.46W
Tekrit *see* Tikrīt
175 R9 **Teku** Sulawesi, N Indonesia 0.46S 123.25E
192 L9 **Te Kuiti** Waikato, North Island, NZ 38.21S 175.09E
44 H4 **Tela** Atlántida, NW Honduras 15.43N 87.27W
144 F12 **Telalim** Southern, S Israel 30.58N 34.47E
Telanaipura *see* Jambi
143 U10 **T'elavi** E Georgia 41.55N 45.29E
144 F10 **Tel Aviv** ◈ *district* W Israel
Tel Aviv-Jaffa *see* Tel Aviv-Yafo
144 F10 **Tel Aviv-Yafo** *var.* Tel Aviv-Jaffa. Tel Aviv, C Israel 32.04N 34.46E
144 F10 **Tel Aviv-Yafo** ✈ Tel Aviv, C Israel 32.04N 34.45E
113 E18 **Telč** *Ger.* Teltsch. Jihnlavský Kraj, C Czech Republic 49.10N 15.28E
194 E11 **Telefomin** Sandaun, NW PNG 5.05S 141.40E
8 J10 **Telegraph Creek** British Columbia, W Canada 57.55N 131.10W
202 B10 **Telele** *island* Funafuti Atoll, C Tuvalu
62 J11 **Telêmaco Borba** Paraná, S Brazil 24.21S 50.39W
97 E15 **Telemark** ◈ *county* S Norway
64 J13 **Telén** La Pampa, C Argentina 36.16S 65.24W
Teleneshty *see* Teleneşti
118 M9 **Teleneşti** *Rus.* Teleneshty. C Moldova 47.35N 28.20E
106 J4 **Teleno, El** ▲ NW Spain 42.19N 6.21W
175 O8 **Telen, Sungai** ≈ Borneo, C Indonesia
118 I15 **Teleorman** ◈ *county* S Romania
118 I14 **Teleorman** ≈ S Romania
27 V5 **Telephone** Texas, SW USA 33.48N 96.00W
37 U11 **Telescope Peak** ▲ California, W USA 36.09N 117.03W
Teles Pirés *see* São Manuel, Rio
99 L19 **Telford** C England, UK 52.42N 2.28W
110 L7 **Telfs** Tirol, W Austria 47.19N 11.04E
44 I9 **Telica** León, NW Nicaragua 12.29N 86.51W
44 J6 **Telica, Río** ≈ C Honduras
78 I13 **Télimélé** Guinée-Maritime, W Guinea 10.45N 13.01W
45 O14 **Telire, Río** ≈ Costa Rica/Panama
116 I8 **Telish** *prev.* Azizie. Pleven, N Bulgaria 43.20N 24.16E
43 R16 **Telixtlahuaca** *var.* San Francisco Telixtlahuaca. Oaxaca, SE Mexico 17.18N 96.54W
8 K13 **Telkwa** British Columbia, SW Canada 54.39N 126.51W
27 P4 **Tell** Texas, SW USA 34.18N 100.20W
Tell Abiad *see* Tall Abyaḑ
Tell Abiad/Tell Abyad *see* At Tall al Abyaḑ
33 O16 **Tell City** Indiana, N USA 37.56N 86.47W
40 M9 **Teller** Alaska, USA 65.15N 166.21W
Tell Huqnah *see* Tall Ḩuqnah
161 F20 **Tellicherry** *var.* Thalassery. Kerala, SW India 11.48N 75.30E
22 M10 **Tellico Plains** Tennessee, S USA 35.19N 84.18W
Tell Kalakh *see* Tall Kalakh
Tell Mardīkh *see* Ebla
56 E11 **Tello** Huila, C Colombia 3.06N 75.07W
Tell Shedadi *see* Ash Shadādah
39 Q7 **Telluride** Colorado, C USA 37.56N 107.48W
Tel'man/Tel'mansk *see* Gubadag
119 X9 **Tel'manove** Donets'ka Oblast', E Ukraine 47.24N 38.03E
168 H6 **Telmen Nuur** ◎ NW Mongolia
Teloekbetoeng *see* Bandarlampung
43 O15 **Teloloapán** Guerrero, S Mexico 18.21N 99.54W
Telo Martius *see* Toulon
129 V8 **Telposiz, Gora** ▲ NW Russian Federation 63.52N 59.15E
Telschen *see* Telšiai
65 J17 **Telsen** Chubut, S Argentina 42.27S 66.59W
120 D11 **Telšiai** *Ger.* Telschen. Telšiai, NW Lithuania 55.59N 22.21E
Teltsch *see* Telč
Telukbetung *see* Bandarlampung
173 F7 **Telukdalam** Pulau Nias, W Indonesia 0.34N 97.47E
12 H9 **Temagami** Ontario, S Canada 47.03N 79.47W
12 G9 **Temagami, Lake** ◎ Ontario, S Canada
202 H16 **Te Manga** ▲ Rarotonga, S Cook Islands 21.13S 159.45W
Temanggoeng *see* Temanggung
174 Kk15 **Temanggung** *prev.* Temanggoeng. Jawa, S Indonesia 0.22S 110.12E
203 W12 **Tematangi** *atoll* Îles Tuamotu, S French Polynesia
43 X11 **Temax** Yucatán, SE Mexico 21.10N 88.55W
176 X12 **Tembagapura** Papua, E Indonesia 4.10S 137.18E
133 U5 **Tembenchi** ≈ N Russian Federation
174 Hh10 **Tembesi, Sungai** ≈ Sumatera, W Indonesia
57 P6 **Temblador** Monagas, NE Venezuela 9.01N 62.38W
107 N9 **Tembleque** Castilla-La Mancha, C Spain 39.40N 3.30W
Temboni *see* Mitemele, Río
37 U16 **Temecula** California, W USA 33.29N 117.09W

◆ Country
● Country Capital
◇ Dependent Territory
○ Dependent Territory Capital
◈ Administrative Region
✈ International Airport
▲ Mountain
▲▲ Mountain Range
Volcano
≈ River
◎ Lake
⊠ Reservoir

174 Gg3 **Temengor, Tasik** ◎ Peninsular Malaysia
114 L9 **Temerin** Serbia, N Serbia and Montenegro (Yugoslavia) 45.25N 19.54E
Temes/Temesch see Tamiš
Temeschburg/Temeschwar see Timişoara
Temes-Kubin see Kovin
Temesvár/Temeswar see Timişoara
Teminaboean see Teminabuan
176 V9 **Teminabuan** prev. Teminaboean. Papua, E Indonesia 1.30S 131.58E
151 P17 **Temirlanovka** Yuzhnyy Kazakhstan, S Kazakhstan 42.36N 69.15E
151 R10 **Temirtau** prev. Samarkandski, Samarkandskoye. Karaganda, C Kazakhstan 50.04N 72.55E
12 H10 **Témiscaming** Quebec, SE Canada 46.40N 79.04W
Témiscamingue, Lac see Timiskaming, Lake
13 T8 **Témiscouata, Lac** ◎ Quebec, SE Canada
131 N5 **Temnikov** Respublika Mordoviya, W Russian Federation 54.39N 43.09E
203 Y13 **Temoe** island Îles Gambier, E French Polynesia
191 Q9 **Temora** New South Wales, SE Australia 34.28S 147.33E
42 H7 **Témoris** Chihuahua, W Mexico 27.16N 108.15W
42 I5 **Temósachic** Chihuahua, N Mexico 28.55N 107.42W
195 W8 **Temotu** off. Temotu Province. ◆ province E Solomon Islands
38 L14 **Tempe** Arizona, SW USA 33.24N 111.54W
175 P12 **Tempe, Danau** ◎ Sulawesi, C Indonesia
Tempelburg see Czaplinek
109 C17 **Tempio Pausania** Sardegna, Italy, C Mediterranean Sea 40.55N 9.07E
44 K12 **Tempisque, Río** ∽ NW Costa Rica
27 T9 **Temple** Texas, SW USA 31.06N 97.22W
102 O12 **Templehof** ✕ (Berlin) Berlin, NE Germany 52.28N 13.24E
99 D19 **Templemore** Ir. An Teampall Mór. C Ireland 52.48N 7.49W
102 O11 **Templin** Brandenburg, NE Germany 53.07N 13.31E
43 P12 **Tempoal** var. Tempoal de Sánchez. Veracruz-Llave, E Mexico 21.27N 98.21W
Tempoal de Sánchez see Tempoal
43 P13 **Tempoal, Río** ∽ C Mexico
85 E14 **Tempué** Moxico, C Angola 13.36S 18.56E
130 J14 **Temryuk** Krasnodarskiy Kray, SW Russian Federation 45.15N 37.26E
101 G17 **Temse** Oost-Vlaanderen, N Belgium 51.07N 4.13E
65 F15 **Temuco** Araucanía, C Chile 38.45S 72.37W
193 G20 **Temuka** Canterbury, South Island, NZ 44.13S 171.16E
201 P13 **Temwen Island** island E Micronesia
58 C6 **Tena** Napo, C Ecuador 01.00S 77.48W
43 W13 **Tenabo** Campeche, E Mexico 20.01N 90.12W
Tenaghau see Aola
27 X7 **Tenaha** Texas, SW USA 31.56N 94.14W
41 X13 **Tenake** Chichagof Island, Alaska, USA 57.46N 135.13W
161 K16 **Tenāli** Andhra Pradesh, E India 16.13N 80.36E
Tenan see Ch'ŏnan
43 O14 **Tenancingo** var. Tenencingo de Degollado. México, S Mexico 18.57N 99.39W
203 X12 **Tenararo** island Groupe Actéon, SE French Polynesia
178 Gg12 **Tenasserim** Tenasserim, S Myanmar 12.06N 98.55E
178 H11 **Tenasserim** var. Tanintharyi. ◆ division S Myanmar
100 O5 **Ten Boer** Groningen, NE Netherlands 53.16N 6.42E
99 I21 **Tenby** SW Wales, UK 51.40N 4.43W
82 K11 **Tendaho** Afar, NE Ethiopia 11.39N 40.59E
105 V14 **Tende** Alpes Maritimes, SE France 44.04N 7.34E
157 Q20 **Ten Degree Channel** strait Andaman and Nicobar Islands, India, E Indian Ocean
82 F11 **Tendelti** White Nile, E Sudan 13.01N 31.55E
78 G8 **Te-n-Dghâmcha, Sebkhet** var. Sebkha de Ndrhamcha, Sebkra de Ndaghamcha. salt lake W Mauritania
171 Ll12 **Tendō** Yamagata, Honshū, C Japan 38.22N 140.22E
76 H7 **Tendrara** NE Morocco 33.06N 1.58W
119 Q11 **Tendrivs'ka Kosa** spit S Ukraine
119 Q11 **Tendrivs'ka Zatoka** gulf S Ukraine
Tenencingo de Degollado see Tenancingo
79 N11 **Ténenkou** Mopti, C Mali 14.28N 4.55W
79 W9 **Ténéré** physical region C Niger
79 W9 **Ténére, Erg du** desert C Niger
66 O11 **Tenerife** island Islas Canarias, Spain, NE Atlantic Ocean
76 J5 **Ténès** NW Algeria 36.30N 1.18E
175 Oo15 **Tengah, Kepulauan** island group C Indonesia
175 O8 **Tenggarong** Borneo, C Indonesia 0.23S 117.00E
168 J15 **Tengger Shamo** desert N China
174 I4 **Tenggul, Pulau** island Peninsular Malaysia
Tengiz Köl see Tengiz, Ozero
151 P9 **Tengiz, Ozero** Kaz. Tengiz Köl. salt lake C Kazakhstan
78 M14 **Tengréla** var. Tingréla. N Ivory Coast 10.25N 6.25W
166 M14 **Tengxian** var. Teng Xian. Guangxi Zhuangzu Zizhiqu, S China 23.24N 110.49E
204 H2 **Teniente Rodolfo Marsh** Chilean research station South Shetland Islands, Antarctica 61.57S 58.23W
34 G9 **Tenino** Washington, NW USA 46.51N 122.51W
114 I9 **Tenja** Osijek-Baranja, E Croatia 45.30N 18.45E
196 B16 **Tenjo, Mount** ▲ W Guam
161 H23 **Tenkāsi** Tamil Nādu, SE India 8.58N 77.22E
81 N24 **Tenke** Katanga, SE Dem. Rep. Congo 10.34S 26.12E
Tenke see Tinca
126 M7 **Tenkeli** Respublika Sakha (Yakutiya), NE Russian Federation 70.09N 140.39E
29 R10 **Tenkiller Ferry Lake** ▣ Oklahoma, C USA
79 Q13 **Tenkodogo** S Burkina 11.43N 0.19W
189 Q5 **Tennant Creek** Northern Territory, C Australia 19.40S 134.16E
22 G9 **Tennessee** off. State of Tennessee; also known as The Volunteer State. ◆ state SE USA
39 R5 **Tennessee Pass** pass Colorado, C USA 39.21N 106.18W
22 H10 **Tennessee River** ∽ S USA
25 N2 **Tennessee Tombigbee Waterway** canal Alabama/Mississippi, S USA
101 K22 **Tenneville** Luxembourg, SE Belgium 50.05N 5.31E
94 M11 **Tenniöjoki** ∽ NE Finland
94 L9 **Teno** var. Tenojoki, Lapp. Dealnu, Nor. Tana. ∽ Finland/Norway see also Tana
Tenojoki see Tana/Teno
175 Nn3 **Tenom** Sabah, East Malaysia 5.07N 115.57E
Tenos see Tínos
43 V15 **Tenosique** var. Tenosique de Pino Suárez. Tabasco, SE Mexico 17.30N 91.24W
Tenosique de Pino Suárez see Tenosique
171 H15 **Tenri** Nara, Honshū, SW Japan 34.36N 135.51E
171 I16 **Tenryū** Shizuoka, Honshū, SW Japan 34.49N 137.48E
172 ii15 **Tenryū-gawa** ∽ Honshū, C Japan
24 I6 **Tensas River** ∽ Louisiana, S USA
25 O8 **Tensaw River** ∽ Alabama, S USA
76 E7 **Tensift** seasonal river W Morocco
175 Pp10 **Tentena** var. Tenteno. Sulawesi, C Indonesia 1.46S 120.40E
Tenteno see Tentena
191 U4 **Tenterfield** New South Wales, SE Australia 29.04S 152.02E
25 X16 **Ten Thousand Islands** island group Florida, SE USA
62 H9 **Teodoro Sampaio** São Paulo, S Brazil 22.30S 52.13W
61 N19 **Teófilo Otoni** var. Theophilo Ottoni. Minas Gerais, NE Brazil 17.52S 41.31W
118 K5 **Teofipol'** Khmel'nyts'ka Oblast', W Ukraine 50.00N 26.22E
203 Q8 **Teohatu** Tahiti, W French Polynesia
43 P14 **Teotihuacán** ruins México, S Mexico 19.49N 98.48W
Teotilán see Teotitlán del Camino
43 Q15 **Teotitlán del Camino** var. Teotilán. Oaxaca, S Mexico 18.05N 97.04W
202 G12 **Tepa** Île Uvea, E Wallis and Futuna 13.19S 176.09W
203 P8 **Tepaee, Récif** reef Tahiti, W French Polynesia
42 L14 **Tepalcatepec** Michoacán de Ocampo, SW Mexico 19.10N 102.49W
202 A16 **Tepa Point** headland SW Niue 19.07S 169.55E
42 L13 **Tepatitlán** var. Tepatitlán de Morelos. Jalisco, SW Mexico 20.54N 102.45W
Tepatitlán de Morelos see Tepatitlán
42 J9 **Tepehuanes** var. Santa Catarina de Tepehuanes. Durango, C Mexico 25.18N 105.43W
Tepelena see Tepelenë
115 L22 **Tepelenë** var. Tepelena, It. Tepeleni. Gjirokastër, S Albania 40.18N 20.00E
Tepeleni see Tepelenë
42 K12 **Tepic** Nayarit, C Mexico 21.29N 104.54W
113 C15 **Teplice** Ger. Teplitz; prev. Teplice-Šanov, Teplitz-Schönau. Ústecký Kraj, NW Czech Republic 50.37N 13.48E
Teplice-Šanov/Teplitz/Teplitz-Schönau see Teplice
119 O7 **Teplyk** Vinnyts'ka Oblast', C Ukraine 48.40N 29.46E
126 Mm10 **Teplyy Klyuch** Respublika Sakha (Yakutiya), NE Russian Federation 62.46N 137.01E
42 E5 **Tepoca, Cabo** headland NW Mexico 29.19N 112.24W
203 W9 **Tepoto** island Îles du Désappointement, C French Polynesia
94 L11 **Tepsa** Lappi, N Finland 67.34N 25.36E
202 B8 **Tepuka** atoll Funafuti Atoll, C Tuvalu
192 N7 **Te Puke** Bay of Plenty, North Island, NZ 37.48S 176.19E
42 L13 **Tequila** Jalisco, SW Mexico 20.52N 103.48W
43 O13 **Tequisquiapan** Querétaro de Arteaga, C Mexico 20.34N 99.52W
106 J5 **Tera** ∽ NW Spain
79 Q12 **Téra** Tillabéri, W Niger 14.01N 0.48E
203 V1 **Teraina** prev. Washington Island. atoll Line Islands, E Kiribati
83 F15 **Terakeka** Bahr el Gabel, S Sudan 5.25N 31.45E
109 J14 **Teramo** anc. Interamna. Abruzzo, C Italy 42.40N 13.43E
100 P7 **Ter Apel** Groningen, NE Netherlands 52.52N 7.04E
106 H11 **Tera, Ribeira de** ∽ S Portugal
193 K14 **Terawhiti, Cape** headland North Island, NZ 41.17S 174.36E
100 N12 **Terborg** Gelderland, E Netherlands 51.55N 6.22E
143 P13 **Tercan** Erzincan, NE Turkey 39.46N 40.22E
66 O2 **Terceira** ✕ Terceira, Azores, Portugal, NE Atlantic Ocean 38.43N 27.13W
66 O2 **Terceira** var. Ilha Terceira. island Azores, Portugal, NE Atlantic Ocean
Terceira, Ilha see Terceira
118 K6 **Terebovlya** Ternopil's'ka Oblast', W Ukraine 49.18N 25.43E
131 O15 **Terek** ∽ SW Russian Federation
Terekhovka see Tsyerakhowka
153 R9 **Terek-Say** Dzhalal-Abadskaya Oblast', W Kyrgyzstan 41.28N 71.06E
151 Z10 **Terekty** Kaz. Alekseevka, prev. Alekseyevka.Vostochnyy Kazakhstan, E Kazakhstan 48.25N 85.38E
174 Hh3 **Terengganu** var. Trengganu. ◆ state Peninsular Malaysia
131 X7 **Terensay** Orenburgskaya Oblast', W Russian Federation 51.35N 59.28E
60 N13 **Teresina** var. Therezina. state capital Piauí, NE Brazil 5.09S 42.46W
62 P9 **Teresópolis** Rio de Janeiro, SE Brazil 22.25S 42.59W
112 P12 **Terespol** Lubelskie, E Poland 52.05N 23.37E
203 V16 **Terevaka, Maunga** ▲ Easter Island, Chile, E Pacific Ocean 27.04S 109.22W
105 P3 **Tergnier** Aisne, N France 49.39N 3.18E
45 O14 **Teribe, Río** ∽ NW Panama
128 K3 **Teriberka** Murmanskaya Oblast', NW Russian Federation 69.10N 35.18E
Terijoki see Zelenogorsk
Terinkot see Tarīn Kowt
Terisaqqan see Tersakkan
26 K12 **Terlingua** Texas, SW USA 29.18N 103.36W
26 K11 **Terlingua Creek** ∽ Texas, SW USA
64 K7 **Termas de Río Hondo** Santiago del Estero, N Argentina 27.28S 64.52W
142 M11 **Terme** Samsun, N Turkey 41.11N 36.58E
Termez see Termiz
Termia see Kýthnos
109 J23 **Termini Imerese** anc. Thermae Himerenses. Sicilia, Italy, C Mediterranean Sea 38.01N 13.55E
43 V14 **Términos, Laguna de** lagoon SE Mexico
79 X10 **Termit-Kaoboul** Zinder, C Niger 15.34N 11.31E
153 O14 **Termiz** Rus. Termez. Surkhondaryo Viloyati, S Uzbekistan 37.17N 67.12E
109 L15 **Termoli** Molise, C Italy 42.00N 14.58E
Termonde see Dendermonde
100 P5 **Termunten** Groningen, NE Netherlands 53.18N 7.02E
175 T7 **Ternate** Pulau Ternate, E Indonesia 0.50N 127.20E
175 Ss7 **Ternate, Pulau** island E Indonesia
111 T5 **Ternberg** Oberösterreich, N Austria 47.57N 14.22E
101 E15 **Terneuzen** var. Neuzen. Zeeland, SW Netherlands 51.19N 3.49E
127 O17 **Terney** Primorskiy Kray, SE Russian Federation 45.03N 136.43E
109 I14 **Terni** anc. Interamna Nahars. Umbria, C Italy 42.34N 12.37E
111 X6 **Ternitz** Niederösterreich, E Austria 47.43N 16.01E
119 V7 **Ternivka** Dnipropetrovs'ka Oblast', E Ukraine 48.30N 36.05E
118 K6 **Ternopil'** Pol. Tarnopol, Rus. Ternopol'. Ternopil's'ka Oblast', W Ukraine 49.32N 25.37E
Ternopil' see Ternopil's'ka Oblast'
118 I6 **Ternopil's'ka Oblast'** var. Ternopil', Rus. Ternopol'skaya Oblast'. ◆ province NW Ukraine
Ternopol' see Ternopil'
Ternopol'skaya Oblast' see Ternopil's'ka Oblast'
127 Oo15 **Terpeniya, Mys** headland Ostrov Sakhalin, SE Russian Federation 48.37N 144.40E
127 Oo15 **Terpeniya, Zaliv** inlet Ostrov Sakhalin, SE Russian Federation
Térraba, Río see Grande de Térraba, Río
8 J13 **Terrace** British Columbia, W Canada 54.34N 128.31W
10 D12 **Terrace Bay** Ontario, S Canada 48.46N 87.06W
109 I16 **Terracina** Lazio, C Italy 41.17N 13.13E
95 F14 **Terråk** Troms, N Norway 65.03N 12.22E
28 M13 **Terral** Oklahoma, C USA 33.55N 97.54W
109 B19 **Terralba** Sardegna, Italy, C Mediterranean Sea 39.47N 8.35E
Terranova di Sicilia see Gela
Terranova Pausania see Olbia
107 W5 **Terrassa** Cast. Tarrasa. Cataluña, E Spain 41.34N 2.01E
13 O12 **Terrebonne** Quebec, SE Canada 45.42N 73.37W
24 J11 **Terrebonne Bay** bay Louisiana, SE USA
33 N14 **Terre Haute** Indiana, N USA 39.27N 87.24W
27 U6 **Terrell** Texas, SW USA 32.44N 96.16W
Terre Neuve see Newfoundland and Labrador
35 Q14 **Terreton** Idaho, NW USA 43.49N 112.25W
105 T7 **Territoire-de-Belfort** ◆ department E France
35 X9 **Terry** Montana, NW USA 46.46N 105.16W
30 I9 **Terry Peak** ▲ South Dakota, N USA 44.19N 103.49W
142 H14 **Tersakan Gölü** ◎ C Turkey
151 O10 **Tersakkan** Kaz. Terisaqqan. ∽ C Kazakhstan
100 J4 **Terschelling** Fris. Skylge. island Waddeneilanden, N Netherlands
80 H10 **Tersef** Chari-Baguirmi, C Chad 12.55N 16.49E
153 X8 **Terskey Ala-Too, Khrebet** ⛰ Kazakhstan/Kyrgyzstan
Terter see Tărtăr
107 R8 **Teruel** anc. Turba. Aragón, E Spain 40.21N 1.06W
107 R7 **Teruel** ◆ province Aragón, E Spain
116 M7 **Tervel** prev. Kurtbunar, Rom. Curtbunar. Dobrich, NE Bulgaria 43.45N 27.25E
95 M16 **Tervo** Itä-Suomi, C Finland 62.57N 26.48E
94 L13 **Tervola** Lappi, NW Finland 66.04N 24.49E
Tervueren see Tervuren
101 H18 **Tervuren** var. Tervueren. Vlaams Brabant, C Belgium 50.48N 4.28E
114 H11 **Tešanj** Federacija Bosna I Hercegovina, N Bosnia and Herzegovina 44.37N 18.00E
Teschen see Cieszyn
85 M19 **Tesenane** Inhambane, S Mozambique 22.48S 34.02E
82 I9 **Teseney** var. Tessenei. W Eritrea 15.05N 36.42E
41 P5 **Teshekpuk Lake** ◎ Alaska, USA
168 K6 **Teshig** Bulgan, N Mongolia 49.51N 102.45E
172 Q6 **Teshikaga** Hokkaidō, NE Japan 43.29N 144.27E
172 P2 **Teshio** Hokkaidō, NE Japan 44.49N 141.46E
172 P2 **Teshio-gawa** var. Tesio Gawa. ∽ Hokkaidō, NE Japan
172 P3 **Teshio-sanchi** ⛰ Hokkaidō, NE Japan
Těšín see Cieszyn
Tesio Gawa see Teshio-gawa
168 F5 **Tesiyn Gol** var. Tes-Khem. ∽ Mongolia/Russian Federation see also Tes-Khem
133 T7 **Tes-Khem** var. Tesiyn Gol. ∽ Mongolia/Russian Federation see also Tesiyn Gol
114 H11 **Teslić** Republika Srpska, N Bosnia and Herzegovina 44.35N 17.50E
8 I9 **Teslin** Yukon Territory, W Canada 60.12N 132.44W
8 I8 **Teslin** ∽ British Columbia/Yukon Territory, W Canada
79 Q8 **Tessalit** Kidal, NE Mali 20.11N 0.58E
79 V12 **Tessaoua** Maradi, S Niger 13.43N 7.59E
101 J17 **Tessenderlo** Limburg, NE Belgium 51.04N 5.04E
Tessenei see Teseney
12 L7 **Tessier, Lac** ◎ Quebec, SE Canada
Tessin see Ticino
99 M23 **Test** ∽ S England, UK
Testama see Tõstamaa
57 P4 **Testigos, Islas los** island group N Venezuela
39 S10 **Tesuque** New Mexico, SW USA 35.45N 105.55W
105 O17 **Têt** var. Tet. ∽ S France
56 G5 **Tetas, Cerro de las** ▲ NW Venezuela 9.58N 73.00W
85 M15 **Tete** Tete, NW Mozambique 16.14S 33.34E
85 M15 **Tete** off. Província de Tete. ◆ province NW Mozambique
9 N15 **Tête Jaune Cache** British Columbia, SW Canada 52.52N 119.22W
192 O8 **Te Teko** Bay of Plenty, North Island, NZ 38.03S 176.48E
195 U15 **Tetepare** island New Georgia Islands, NW Solomon Islands
Teterev see Teteriv
118 M5 **Teteriv** Rus. Teterev. ∽ N Ukraine
102 M9 **Teterow** Mecklenburg-Vorpommern, NE Germany 53.46N 12.34E
116 I9 **Teteven** Lovech, N Bulgaria 42.54N 24.19E
203 T10 **Tetiaroa** atoll Îles du Vent, W French Polynesia
107 P14 **Tetica de Bacares** ▲ S Spain 37.15N 2.31W
Tetiyev see Tetiyiv
119 O6 **Tetiyiv** Rus. Tetiyev. Kyyivs'ka Oblast', N Ukraine 49.21N 29.40E
41 T10 **Tetlin** Alaska, USA 63.08N 142.31W
35 R8 **Teton River** ∽ Montana, NW USA
76 G5 **Tétouan** var. Tetouan, Tetuán. N Morocco 35.33N 5.22W
Tetova/Tetovë see Tetovo
116 L7 **Tetovo** Razgrad, N Bulgaria 43.49N 26.21E
115 N18 **Tetovo** Alb. Tetova, Tetovë, Turk. Kalkandelen. NW FYR Macedonia 42.01N 20.58E
117 E20 **Tetrázio** ⛰ S Greece
Tetschen see Děčín
Tetuán see Tétouan
203 Q8 **Tetufera, Mont** ▲ Tahiti, W French Polynesia 17.40S 149.25W
131 R4 **Tetyushi** Respublika Tatarstan, W Russian Federation 54.55N 48.46E
110 I7 **Teufen** Sankt Gallen, NE Switzerland 47.24N 9.24E
42 L12 **Teul** var. Teul de Gonzáles Ortega. Zacatecas, C Mexico 21.30N 103.28W
109 B21 **Teulada** Sardegna, Italy, C Mediterranean Sea 38.58N 8.46E
Teul de Gonzáles Ortega see Teul
9 X16 **Teulon** Manitoba, S Canada 50.20N 97.14W
44 I7 **Teupasenti** El Paraíso, S Honduras 14.14N 86.43W
172 Oo3 **Teuri-tō** island NE Japan
103 G13 **Teutoburger Wald** Eng. Teutoburg Forest. hill range NW Germany
Teutoburg Forest see Teutoburger Wald
95 K17 **Teuva** Swe. Östermark. Länsi-Suomi, W Finland 62.28N 21.45E
109 H15 **Tevere** Eng. Tiber. ∽ C Italy
144 G9 **Teverya** var. Tiberias, Tverya. Northern, N Israel 32.48N 35.31E
98 K13 **Teviot** ∽ SE Scotland, UK
Tevli see Tewli
125 Ff12 **Tevriz** Omskaya Oblast', C Russian Federation 57.30N 72.13E
193 B24 **Te Waewae Bay** bay South Island, NZ
99 L21 **Tewkesbury** C England, UK 51.58N 2.09W
121 F19 **Tewli** Rus. Tevli. Brestskaya Voblasts', SW Belarus 52.20N 24.15E
165 U12 **Têwo** var. Dêngkagoin. Gansu, C China 34.05N 103.15E
27 U12 **Texana, Lake** ◎ Texas, SW USA
29 S14 **Texarkana** Arkansas, C USA 33.26N 94.02W
27 X5 **Texarkana** Texas, SW USA 33.25N 94.03W
27 N9 **Texas** off. State of Texas; also known as The Lone Star State. ◆ state S USA
27 W12 **Texas City** Texas, SW USA 29.22N 94.54W
43 P14 **Texcoco** México, C Mexico 19.31N 98.52W
100 I6 **Texel** island Waddeneilanden, NW Netherlands
28 H8 **Texhoma** Oklahoma, C USA 36.30N 101.46W
27 N1 **Texhoma** Texas, SW USA 36.30N 101.46W
39 W12 **Texico** New Mexico, SW USA 34.23N 103.03W
26 L1 **Texline** Texas, SW USA 36.22N 103.01W
43 P14 **Texmelucan** var. San Martín Texmelucan. Puebla, S Mexico 19.13N 98.25W
29 O13 **Texoma, Lake** ▣ Oklahoma/Texas, C USA
27 N9 **Texon** Texas, SW USA 31.13N 101.42W
126 I12 **Teya** Krasnoyarskiy Kray, C Russian Federation 60.27N 92.46E
85 J23 **Teyateyaneng** NW Lesotho 29.04S 27.51E
128 M16 **Teykovo** Ivanovskaya Oblast', W Russian Federation 56.49N 40.31E
128 M16 **Teza** ∽ W Russian Federation
43 Q13 **Teziutlán** Puebla, S Mexico 19.49N 97.22W
159 W12 **Tezpur** Assam, NE India 26.39N 92.47E
15 L8 **Tha-Anne** ∽ Nunavut, NE Canada
85 K23 **Thabana Ntlenyana** var. Thabantshonyana, Mount Ntlenyana. ▲ E Lesotho 29.26S 29.16E
Thabantshonyana see Thabana Ntlenyana
85 J23 **Thaba Putsoa** ▲ C Lesotho 29.48S 27.46E
178 I8 **Tha Bo** Nong Khai, E Thailand 17.52N 102.34E
105 T12 **Thabor, Pic du** ▲ E France 45.07N 6.34E
Tha Chin see Samut Sakhon
177 G7 **Thagaya** Pegu, C Myanmar 19.19N 96.16E
Thai, Ao see Thailand, Gulf of
178 Jj6 **Thai Binh** Thai Binh, N Vietnam 20.27N 106.19E
178 Jj7 **Thai Hoa** Nghê An, N Vietnam 19.21N 105.26E
178 Hh10 **Thailand** off. Kingdom of Thailand, Th. Prathet Thai; prev. Siam. ◆ monarchy SE Asia
178 Hh13 **Thailand, Gulf of** var. Gulf of Siam, Th. Ao Thai, Vtn. Vinh Thai Lan. gulf SE Asia
Thai Lan, Vinh see Thailand, Gulf of
178 Jj6 **Thai Nguyên** Bắc Thai, N Vietnam 21.36N 105.49E
178 J9 **Thakhèk** prev. Muang Khammouan. Khammouan, C Laos 17.24N 104.50E
159 S13 **Thakurgaon** Rajshahi, NW Bangladesh 26.04N 88.34E
155 S6 **Thal** North-West Frontier Province, NW Pakistan 33.24N 70.31E
177 G16 **Thalang** Phuket, SW Thailand 08.00N 98.21E
Thalassery see Tellicherry
178 I10 **Thalat Khae** Nakhon Ratchasima, C Thailand 15.15N 102.24E
111 Q5 **Thalgau** Salzburg, NW Austria 47.49N 13.19E
110 G7 **Thalwil** Zürich, NW Switzerland 47.16N 8.34E
85 I20 **Thamaga** Kweneng, SE Botswana 24.40S 25.31E
Thamarīd see Thamarīt
147 V13 **Thamarīt** var. Thamarīd, Thumrayt. SW Oman 17.39N 54.01E
147 P16 **Thamar, Jabal** ▲ SW Yemen 13.46N 45.32E
192 M6 **Thames** Waikato, North Island, NZ 37.10S 175.33E
12 D17 **Thames** ∽ Ontario, S Canada
99 O22 **Thames** ∽ S England, UK
192 M6 **Thames, Firth of** gulf North Island, NZ
12 D17 **Thamesville** Ontario, S Canada 42.33N 81.58W
147 S13 **Thamūd** N Yemen 17.17N 49.57E
178 Gg9 **Thanbyuzayat** Mon State, S Myanmar 15.58N 97.43E
158 I9 **Thānesar** Haryāna, NW India 29.58N 76.51E
178 Jj7 **Thanh Hoa** Thanh Hoa, N Vietnam 19.49N 105.48E
Thanintari Taungdan see Bilauktaung Range
161 I21 **Thanjāvūr** prev. Tanjore. Tamil Nādu, SE India 10.46N 79.09E
Thanlwin see Salween
105 U7 **Thann** Haut-Rhin, NE France 47.51N 7.04E
178 H16 **Tha Nong Phrom** Phatthalung, SW Thailand 7.24N 100.04E
178 H13 **Thap Sakae** var. Thap Sakau. Prachuap Khiri Khan, SW Thailand 11.30N 99.34E
Thap Sakau see Thap Sakae
100 L10 **'t Harde** Gelderland, E Netherlands 52.25N 5.52E
158 D11 **Thar Desert** var. Great Indian Desert, Indian Desert. desert India/Pakistan
189 V10 **Thargomindah** Queensland, C Australia 28.00S 143.47E
156 D11 **Thar Pārkar** desert SE Pakistan
145 S7 **Tharthār al Furāt, Qanāt ath** canal C Iraq
145 R7 **Tharthār, Buḩayrat ath** ◎ C Iraq
145 R5 **Tharthār, Wādī ath** dry watercourse N Iraq
178 Gg14 **Tha Sae** Chumphon, SW Thailand
178 H15 **Tha Sala** Nakhon Si Thammarat, SW Thailand 8.43N 99.54E
116 I13 **Thásos** Thásos, E Greece 40.46N 24.43E
117 I14 **Thásos** island E Greece
39 N14 **Thatcher** Arizona, SW USA 32.47N 109.46W
178 Jj5 **Thât Khê** var. Trâng Dinh. Lang Sơn, N Vietnam 22.15N 106.26E
178 Gg9 **Thaton** Mon State, S Myanmar 16.55N 97.19E
178 J9 **That Phanom** Nakhon Phanom, E Thailand 16.52N 104.41E
178 Ii10 **Tha Tum** Surin, E Thailand 15.18N 103.39E
105 P16 **Thau, Bassin de** var. Étang de Thau. ◎ S France
Thau, Étang de see Thau, Bassin de
177 G3 **Thaungdut** Sagaing, N Myanmar 24.25N 94.45E
178 Gg8 **Thaungyin** Th. Mae Nam Moei. ∽ Myanmar/Thailand
178 J9 **Tha Uthen** Nakhon Phanom, E Thailand 17.31N 104.34E
111 W2 **Thaya** var. Dyje. ∽ Austria/Czech Republic see also Dyje
29 V8 **Thayer** Missouri, C USA 36.31N 91.34W
177 Ff7 **Thayetmyo** Magwe, C Myanmar 19.19N 95.10E
35 S15 **Thayne** Wyoming, C USA 42.54N 111.01W
177 G6 **Thazi** Mandalay, C Myanmar 20.49N 96.04E
Thebes see Thíva
46 L5 **The Carlton** var. Abraham Bay. Mayaguana, SE Bahamas 22.21N 72.56W
47 O14 **The Crane** var. Crane. S Barbados 13.06N 59.26W
34 I11 **The Dalles** Oregon, NW USA 45.36N 121.10W
30 M14 **Thedford** Nebraska, C USA 41.58N 100.34W
The Hague see 's-Gravenhage
Theiss see Tisa/Tisza
15 Jj6 **Thelon** ∽ Northwest Territories/Nunavut, N Canada
9 V15 **Theodore** Saskatchewan, S Canada 51.25N 103.01W
25 N8 **Theodore** Alabama, S USA 30.33N 88.10W
38 L13 **Theodore Roosevelt Lake** ▣ Arizona, SW USA
Theodosia see Feodosiya
Theophilo Ottoni see Teófilo Otoni
15 K13 **The Pas** Manitoba, C Canada 53.49N 101.09W
33 T14 **The Plains** Ohio, N USA 39.22N 82.07W
Thera see Thíra
180 H17 **Thérèse, Île** island Inner Islands, NE Seychelles
Therezina see Teresina
117 L20 **Thérma** Ikaría, Dodekánisos, Greece, Aegean Sea 37.37N 26.18E
Thermae Himerenses see Termini Imerese
Thermae Pannonicae see Baden
Thermaic Gulf/Thermaicus Sinus see Thermaïkós Kólpos
123 Gg10 **Thermaïkós Kólpos** Eng. Thermaic Gulf; anc. Thermaicus Sinus. gulf N Greece
Thermiá see Kýthnos
117 L17 **Thermís** Lésvos, E Greece 39.08N 26.32E
117 E18 **Thérmo** Dytikí Ellás, C Greece 38.32N 21.42E
35 V14 **Thermopolis** Wyoming, C USA 43.39N 108.12W
191 P10 **The Rock** New South Wales, SE Australia 35.18S 147.07E
205 O5 **Theron Mountains** ⛰ Antarctica
117 G18 **Thespiés** Stereá Ellás, C Greece 38.18N 23.08E
117 E16 **Thessalía** Eng. Thessaly. ◆ region C Greece
12 C10 **Thessalon** Ontario, S Canada 46.15N 83.32W
117 G14 **Thessaloníki** Eng. Salonica, Salonika, SCr. Solun, Turk. Selânik. Kentrikí Makedonía, N Greece 40.37N 22.58E
117 G14 **Thessaloníki** ✕ Kentrikí Makedonía, N Greece 40.30N 22.58E
Thessaly see Thessalía
86 B12 **Theta Gap** undersea feature E Atlantic Ocean
99 P20 **Thetford** E England, UK 52.25N 0.45E
13 R11 **Thetford-Mines** Quebec, SE Canada 46.07N 71.16W
115 K17 **Theth** var. Thethi. Shkodër, N Albania 42.25N 19.45E
Thethi see Theth
101 L20 **Theux** Liège, E Belgium 50.33N 5.48E
47 V9 **The Valley** ○ (Anguilla) E Anguilla 18.12N 63.00W
29 N10 **The Village** Oklahoma, C USA 35.33N 97.33W
27 W10 **The Woodlands** Texas, SW USA 30.09N 95.27E
Thiamis see Thýamis
Thian Shan see Tien Shan
24 J9 **Thibodaux** Louisiana, S USA 29.48N 90.49W
31 S3 **Thief Lake** ◎ Minnesota, N USA
31 S3 **Thief River** ∽ Minnesota, C USA
31 S3 **Thief River Falls** Minnesota, N USA 48.07N 96.10W
Thièle see La Thielle
34 G14 **Thielsen, Mount** ▲ Oregon, NW USA 43.09N 122.04W
Thielt see Tielt
108 G7 **Thiene** Veneto, NE Italy 45.43N 11.28E
Thienen see Tienen
105 P11 **Thiers** Puy-de-Dôme, C France 45.51N 3.33E
78 F11 **Thiès** W Senegal 14.51N 16.51W
83 I19 **Thika** Central, S Kenya 1.03S 37.04E
Thikombia see Cikobia
157 K18 **Thiladhunmathi Atoll** var. Tiladummati Atoll. atoll N Maldives
Thimbu see Thimphu
159 T11 **Thimphu** var. Thimbu; prev. Tashi Chho Dzong. ● (Bhutan) W Bhutan 27.28N 89.37E
94 H2 **Thingeyri** Vestfirdhir, NW Iceland 65.52N 23.28W
94 I3 **Thingvellir** Sudhurland, SW Iceland 64.15N 21.06W
197 J6 **Thio** Province Sud, C New Caledonia 21.37S 166.13E
105 T4 **Thionville** Ger. Diedenhofen. Moselle, NE France 49.22N 6.10E
117 K22 **Thíra** Thíra, Kykládes, Greece, Aegean Sea 36.25N 25.26E
117 K22 **Thíra** prev. Santorin, Santoríni, anc. Thera. island Kykládes, Greece, Aegean Sea
117 J22 **Thirasía** island Kykládes, Greece, Aegean Sea
99 M16 **Thirsk** N England, UK 54.06N 1.16W
12 F12 **Thirty Thousand Islands** island group Ontario, S Canada
Thiruvanathapuram see Trivandrum
97 F20 **Thisted** Viborg, NW Denmark 56.58N 8.42E
Thistil Fjord see Thistilfjördhur
94 L1 **Thistilfjördhur** var. Thistil Fjord. fjord NE Iceland
190 G9 **Thistle Island** island South Australia
Thithia see Cicia
179 N14 **Thitu Island** island NW Spratly Islands
Thiukhaoluang Phrahang see Luang Prabang Range
117 G18 **Thíva** Eng. Thebes; prev. Thívai. Stereá Ellás, C Greece 38.19N 23.19E
Thívai see Thíva
104 M12 **Thiviers** Dordogne, SW France 45.24N 0.54E
94 J4 **Thjórsá** ∽ C Iceland
15 L9 **Thlewiaza** ∽ Nunavut, NE Canada
15 J9 **Thoa** ∽ Northwest Territories, NW Canada
101 G14 **Tholen** Zeeland, SW Netherlands 51.31N 4.13E
101 F14 **Tholen** island SW Netherlands
28 L10 **Thomas** Oklahoma, C USA 35.44N 98.45W
23 T3 **Thomas** West Virginia, NE USA 39.09N 79.28W
29 U3 **Thomas Hill Reservoir** ▣ Missouri, C USA
25 S5 **Thomaston** Georgia, SE USA 32.53N 84.19W
21 R7 **Thomaston** Maine, NE USA 44.06N 69.10W
27 T12 **Thomaston** Texas, SW USA 28.56N 97.07W
25 O6 **Thomasville** Alabama, S USA 31.54N 87.42W
25 T8 **Thomasville** Georgia, SE USA 30.49N 83.57W
23 S9 **Thomasville** North Carolina, SE USA 35.52N 80.04W
37 N5 **Thomes Creek** ∽ California, W USA
9 W12 **Thompson** Manitoba, C Canada 55.45N 97.54W
31 R4 **Thompson** North Dakota, N USA 47.45N 97.07W
(0) F8 **Thompson** ∽ Alberta/British Columbia, SW Canada
35 O8 **Thompson Falls** Montana, NW USA 47.36N 115.20W
31 Q10 **Thompson, Lake** ◎ South Dakota, N USA
36 M3 **Thompson Peak** ▲ California, W USA 41.00N 123.01W
29 S2 **Thompson River** ∽ Missouri, C USA
193 A22 **Thompson Sound** sound South Island, NZ
15 Hh1 **Thomsen** ∽ Banks Island, Northwest Territories, NW Canada
25 V4 **Thomson** Georgia, SE USA 33.28N 82.30W
105 T10 **Thonon-les-Bains** Haute-Savoie, E France 46.22N 6.30E
105 O15 **Thoré** var. Thore. ∽ S France
39 P11 **Thoreau** New Mexico, SW USA 35.24N 108.13W
Thorenburg see Turda
94 J3 **Thórisvatn** ◎ C Iceland
94 P4 **Thor, Kapp** headland S Svalbard 76.25N 25.01E
94 I4 **Thorlákshöfn** Sudhurland, SW Iceland 63.51N 21.24W
Thorn see Toruń
27 T10 **Thorndale** Texas, SW USA 30.36N 97.12W
12 H10 **Thorne** Ontario, S Canada 46.38N 79.04W
99 J14 **Thornhill** S Scotland, UK 55.13N 3.46W
27 U8 **Thornton** Texas, SW USA 31.24N 96.34W
Thornton Island see Millennium Island
12 H16 **Thorold** Ontario, S Canada 43.07N 79.15W
34 I9 **Thorp** Washington, NW USA 47.03N 120.40W
205 S3 **Thorshavnheiane** physical region Antarctica
94 L1 **Thórshöfn** Nordhurland Eystra, NE Iceland 66.09N 15.18W
Thospitis see Van Gölü
178 J14 **Thôt Nôt** Cân Thơ, S Vietnam 10.16N 105.31E
104 K8 **Thouars** Deux-Sèvres, W France 46.58N 0.13W
159 X14 **Thoubal** Manipur, NE India 24.40N 94.00E
104 K9 **Thouet** ∽ W France
Thoune see Thun
20 H7 **Thousand Islands** island Canada/USA
37 S15 **Thousand Oaks** California, W USA 34.10N 118.50W
116 L12 **Thrace** cultural region SE Europe
116 J13 **Thracian Sea** Gk. Thrakikó Pélagos; anc. Thracium Mare. sea Greece/Turkey
Thracium Mare/Thrakikó Pélagos see Thracian Sea
Thrá Lí, Bá see Tralee Bay
35 R11 **Three Forks** Montana, NW USA 45.53N 111.34W
9 Q16 **Three Hills** Alberta, SW Canada 51.43N 113.15W

◆ Country ● Country Capital ◇ Dependent Territory ○ Dependent Territory Capital ◆ Administrative Region ✕ International Airport ▲ Mountain ⛰ Mountain Range ▲ Volcano ∽ River ◎ Lake ▣ Reservoir

191 N15 **Three Hummock Island** *island* Tasmania, SE Australia
192 H1 **Three Kings Islands** *island group* N NZ
183 P10 **Three Kings Rise** *undersea feature* W Pacific Ocean
79 O18 **Three Points, Cape** *headland* S Ghana 4.43N 2.03W
33 P10 **Three Rivers** Michigan, N USA 41.56N 85.37W
27 S13 **Three Rivers** Texas, SW USA 28.27N 98.10W
85 G24 **Three Sisters** Northern Cape, SW South Africa 31.51S 23.04E
34 H13 **Three Sisters** ▲ Oregon, NW USA 44.08N 121.46W
195 Z16 **Three Sisters Islands** *island group* SE Solomon Islands
Thrissur *see* Trichūr
27 Q6 **Throckmorton** Texas, SW USA 33.10N 99.10W
188 M10 **Throssell, Lake** *salt lake* Western Australia
117 K25 **Thrýptis** ▲ Kríti, Greece, E Mediterranean Sea 35.06N 25.51E
178 Jj14 **Thu Dâu Môt** *var.* Phu Cương. Sông Be, S Vietnam 10.58N 106.40E
178 Jj6 **Thu Do** ✕ (Ha Nôi) Ha Nôi, N Vietnam 21.13N 105.46E
101 G21 **Thuin** Hainaut, S Belgium 50.21N 4.18E
155 Q12 **Thul** Sind, SE Pakistan 28.13N 68.49E
Thule *see* Qaanaaq
85 J18 **Thuli** *var.* Tuli. ⩩ S Zimbabwe
Thumrayt *see* Thamarīt
110 D9 **Thun** *Fr.* Thoune. Bern, W Switzerland 46.46N 7.37E
10 C12 **Thunder Bay** Ontario, S Canada 48.27N 89.12W
32 M1 **Thunder Bay** *lake bay* S Canada
33 R6 **Thunder Bay** *lake bay* Michigan, N USA
33 R6 **Thunder Bay River** ⩩ Michigan, N USA
29 N11 **Thunderbird, Lake** ⊠ Oklahoma, C USA
30 L8 **Thunder Butte Creek** ⩩ South Dakota, N USA
110 E9 **Thuner See** ◎ C Switzerland
178 H16 **Thung Song** *var.* Cha Mai. Nakhon Si Thammarat, SW Thailand 8.10N 99.40E
110 H7 **Thur** ⩩ N Switzerland
110 G6 **Thurgau** *Fr.* Thurgovie. ◆ *canton* NE Switzerland
Thurgovie *see* Thurgau
Thuringe *see* Thüringen
110 J7 **Thüringen** Vorarlberg, W Austria 47.12N 9.48E
103 J17 **Thüringen** *Eng.* Thuringia, *Fr.* Thuringe. ◆ *state* C Germany
103 J17 **Thüringer Wald** *Eng.* Thuringian Forest. ▲ C Germany
Thuringia *see* Thüringen
Thuringian Forest *see* Thüringer Wald
99 D19 **Thurles** *Ir.* Durlas. S Ireland 52.40N 7.49W
23 W2 **Thurmont** Maryland, NE USA 39.36N 77.22W
Thurø *see* Thurø By
97 H24 **Thurø By** *var.* Thurø. Fyn, C Denmark 55.03N 10.43E
12 M12 **Thurso** Quebec, SE Canada 45.36N 75.13W
98 J6 **Thurso** N Scotland, UK 58.34N 3.31W
204 I10 **Thurston Island** *island* Antarctica
110 I9 **Thusis** Graubünden, S Switzerland 46.40N 9.27E
117 C15 **Thýamis** *var.* Thiamis. ⩩ W Greece
97 E21 **Thyborøn** *var.* Tyborøn. Ringkøbing, W Denmark 56.40N 8.12E
205 U3 **Thyer Glacier** *glacier* Antarctica
117 L20 **Thýmaina** *island* Dodekánisos, Greece, Aegean Sea
85 N15 **Thyolo** *var.* Cholo. Southern, S Malawi 16.03S 35.11E
191 U6 **Tia** New South Wales, SE Australia 31.14S 151.51E
56 H5 **Tía Juana** Zulia, NW Venezuela 10.18N 71.22W
166 J14 **Tiandong** *var.* Pingma. Guangxi Zhuangzu Zizhiqu, S China 23.37N 107.06E
167 O3 **Tianjin** *var.* Tientsin. Tianjin Shi, E China 39.12N 117.06E
Tianjin *see* Tianjin Shi
167 P3 **Tianjin Shi** *var.* Jin, Tianjin, T'ien-ching, Tientsin. ◆ *municipality* E China
165 S10 **Tianjun** *var.* Xinyuan. Qinghai, C China 37.16N 99.03E
166 J13 **Tianlin** *prev.* Leli. Guangxi Zhuangzu Zizhiqu, S China 24.27N 106.03E
Tian Shan *see* Tien Shan
165 W11 **Tianshui** Gansu, C China 34.33N 105.51E
156 I7 **Tianshuihai** Xinjiang Uygur Zizhiqu, W China 35.16N 79.30E
167 S10 **Tiantai** Zhejiang, SE China 29.11N 121.01E
166 J14 **Tianyang** Guangxi Zhuangzu Zizhiqu, S China 23.45N 106.54E
165 U9 **Tianzhu** *var.* Tianzhu Zangzu Zizhixian. Gansu, C China 37.01N 103.04E
Tianzhu Zangzu Zizhixian *see* Tianzhu
203 Q7 **Tiarei** Tahiti, W French Polynesia 17.31S 149.19W
76 J6 **Tiaret** *var.* Tihert. NW Algeria 35.23N 1.18E
79 N17 **Tiassalé** S Ivory Coast 5.54N 4.49W
198 Bb8 **Ti'avea** Upolu, SE Samoa 13.58S 171.30W
Tiba *see* Chiba
62 J11 **Tibagi** *var.* Tibaji. Paraná, S Brazil 24.28S 50.28W
62 J10 **Tibagi, Rio** *var.* Rio Tibají. ⩩ S Brazil
Tibaji *see* Tibagi
Tibají, Rio *see* Tibagi, Rio
145 Q9 **Tibal, Wādī** *dry watercourse* S Iraq
56 G9 **Tibaná** Boyacá, C Colombia 5.19N 73.25W
81 F14 **Tibati** Adamaoua, N Cameroon 6.28N 12.37E
78 K15 **Tibé, Pic de** ▲ SE Guinea 8.39N 8.58W
Tiber *see* Tivoli, Italy
Tiber *see* Tevere, Italy
Tiberias *see* Teverya
144 G8 **Tiberias, Lake** *var.* Chinnereth, Sea of Bahr Tabariya, Sea of Galilee, *Ar.* Bahrat Tabariya, *Heb.* Yam Kinneret. ◎ N Israel
69 Q5 **Tibesti** *var.* Tibesti Massif, *Ar.* Tibistī. ▲ N Africa
Tibesti Massif *see* Tibesti
Tibetan Autonomous Region *see* Xizang Zizhiqu
Tibet, Plateau of *see* Qingzang Gaoyuan
Tibistī *see* Tibesti
12 K7 **Tiblemont, Lac** ◎ Quebec, SE Canada
145 X9 **Ţīb, Nahr aţ** ⩩ S Iraq
Tibnī *see* At Tibnī
190 L4 **Tibooburra** New South Wales, SE Australia 29.24S 142.01E
97 L18 **Tibro** Västra Götaland, S Sweden 58.25N 14.10E
42 E5 **Tiburón, Isla** *var.* Isla del Tiburón. *island* NW Mexico
Tiburón, Isla del *see* Tiburón, Isla
25 W14 **Tice** Florida, SE USA 26.40N 81.49W
Tichau *see* Tychy
116 L8 **Ticha, Yazovir** ◎ NE Bulgaria
78 K9 **Tichît** *var.* Tichitt. Tagant, C Mauritania 18.25N 9.31W
Tichitt *see* Tichît
110 G11 **Ticino** *Fr./Ger.* Tessin. ◆ *canton* S Switzerland
108 D8 **Ticino** ⩩ Italy/Switzerland
110 H11 **Ticino** *Ger.* Tessin. ⩩ SW Switzerland
Ticinum *see* Pavia
43 X12 **Ticul** Yucatán, SE Mexico 20.21N 89.29W
97 K18 **Tidaholm** Västra Götaland, S Sweden 58.12N 13.55E
Tidjikdja *see* Tidjikja
78 J8 **Tidjikja** *var.* Tidjikdja; *prev.* Fort-Cappolani. Tagant, C Mauritania 18.30N 11.24W
Tidore *see* Soasiu
175 Ss7 **Tidore, Pulau** *island* E Indonesia
Tidra, Ile *see* Et Tîdra
79 N16 **Tiébissou** *var.* Tiebissou. C Ivory Coast 7.10N 5.10W
169 V11 **Tiefa** Liaoning, NE China 42.25N 123.29E
110 I9 **Tiefencastel** Graubünden, S Switzerland 46.40N 9.33E
Tiegenhof *see* Nowy Dwór Gdański
T'ieh-ling *see* Tieling
100 K13 **Tiel** Gelderland, C Netherlands 51.54N 5.04E
169 W7 **Tieli** Heilongjiang, NE China 46.57N 128.01E
169 V11 **Tieling** *var.* T'ieh-ling. Liaoning, NE China 42.19N 123.52E
158 L4 **Tielongtan** China/India 35.10N 79.31E
101 D17 **Tielt** *var.* Thielt. West-Vlaanderen, W Belgium 51.00N 3.20E
T'ien-ching *see* Tianjin Shi
101 I18 **Tienen** *var.* Thienen, *Fr.* Tirlemont. Vlaams Brabant, C Belgium 50.48N 4.55E
Tiên Giang, Sông *see* Mekong
153 X9 **Tien Shan** *Chin.* Thian Shan, Tian Shan, T'ien Shan, *Rus.* Tyan'-Shan'. ▲ C Asia
Tientsin *see* Tianjin
Tientsin *see* Tianjin Shi
178 K6 **Tiên Yên** Quang Ninh, N Vietnam 21.19N 107.24E
97 O14 **Tierp** Uppsala, C Sweden 60.19N 17.30E
64 H7 **Tierra Amarilla** Atacama, N Chile 27.28S 70.16W
39 R9 **Tierra Amarilla** New Mexico, SW USA 36.42N 106.31W
43 R15 **Tierra Blanca** Veracruz-Llave, E Mexico 18.28N 96.21W
43 O16 **Tierra Colorada** Guerrero, S Mexico 17.10N 99.36W
65 J17 **Tierra Colorada, Bajo de la** *basin* SE Argentina
65 I25 **Tierra del Fuego** *off.* Provincia de la Tierra del Fuego. ◆ *province* S Argentina
65 J24 **Tierra del Fuego** *island* Argentina/Chile
56 D7 **Tierralta** Córdoba, NW Colombia 8.10N 76.04W
106 K9 **Tiétar** ⩩ W Spain
62 L10 **Tietê** São Paulo, S Brazil 23.04S 47.40W
62 J8 **Tietê, Rio** ⩩ S Brazil
34 I9 **Tieton** Washington, NW USA 46.41N 120.43W
34 J6 **Tiffany Mountain** ▲ Washington, NW USA 48.40N 119.55W
33 S12 **Tiffin** Ohio, N USA 41.06N 83.10W
33 Q11 **Tiffin River** ⩩ Ohio, N USA
Tiflis *see* T'bilisi
25 U7 **Tifton** Georgia, SE USA 31.27N 83.31W
175 Ss11 **Tifu** Pulau Buru, E Indonesia 3.46S 126.36E
197 K6 **Tiga, Île** *island* Îles Loyauté, W New Caledonia
40 L17 **Tigalda Island** *island* Aleutian Islands, Alaska, USA
117 I15 **Tigáni, Akrotírio** *headland* Límnos, E Greece 39.50N 25.03E
175 O1 **Tiga Tarok** Sabah, East Malaysia 6.57N 117.07E
119 O10 **Tighina** *Rus.* Bendery; *prev.* Bender. E Moldova 46.51N 29.27E
127 P10 **Tigil'** Koryakskiy Avtonomnyy Okrug, E Russian Federation 57.43N 158.39E
151 X9 **Tigiretskiy Khrebet** ▲ E Kazakhstan
81 F14 **Tignère** Adamaoua, N Cameroon 7.25N 12.49E
11 P14 **Tignish** Prince Edward Island, SE Canada 46.58N 64.03W
Tigranocerta *see* Siirt
82 I11 **Tigray** ◆ *province* N Ethiopia
43 O11 **Tigre, Cerro del** ▲ C Mexico 23.06N 99.13W
58 F8 **Tigre, Río** ⩩ N Peru
145 X10 **Tigris** *Ar.* Dijlah, *Turk.* Dicle. ⩩ Iraq/Turkey
78 G9 **Tiguent** Trarza, SW Mauritania 17.15N 16.00W
76 M10 **Tiguentourine** E Algeria 27.59N 9.16E
79 V10 **Tiguidit, Falaise de** *ridge* C Niger
147 N13 **Tihāmah** *var.* Tehama. *plain* Saudi Arabia/Yemen
Tihert *see* Tiaret
Ti-hua/Tihwa *see* Ürümqi
43 Q13 **Tihuatlán** Veracruz-Llave, E Mexico 20.44N 97.30W
42 B1 **Tijuana** Baja California, NW Mexico 32.31N 117.01W
44 E2 **Tikal** Petén, N Guatemala 17.11N 89.36W
160 I9 **Tīkamgarh** *prev.* Tehri. Madhya Pradesh, C India 24.43N 78.49E
164 L7 **Tikanlik** Xinjiang Uygur Zizhiqu, NW China 40.34N 87.37E
79 P12 **Tikaré** N Burkina 13.16N 1.39W
41 O12 **Tikchik Lakes** *lakes* Alaska, USA
203 T9 **Tikehau** *atoll* Îles Tuamotu, C French Polynesia
203 V9 **Tikei** *island* Îles Tuamotu, C French Polynesia
125 B12 **Tikhoretsk** Krasnodarskiy Kray, SW Russian Federation 45.50N 40.07E
128 I13 **Tikhvin** Leningradskaya Oblast', NW Russian Federation 59.37N 33.29E
199 Ll10 **Tiki Basin** *undersea feature* S Pacific Ocean
78 K13 **Tikinsso** ⩩ NE Guinea
192 Q8 **Tikitiki** Gisborne, North Island, NZ 37.49S 178.23E
81 D16 **Tiko** Sud-Ouest, SW Cameroon 4.01N 9.19E
145 S6 **Tikrīt** *var.* Tekrit. N Iraq 34.36N 43.42E
128 I8 **Tiksha** Respublika Kareliya, NW Russian Federation 64.07N 32.31E
128 I6 **Tikshozero, Ozero** ◎ NW Russian Federation
126 L7 **Tiksi** Respublika Sakha (Yakutiya), NE Russian Federation 71.40N 128.46E
173 G8 **Tiku** Sumatera, W Indonesia 0.24S 99.55E
44 A6 **Tilapa** San Marcos, SW Guatemala 14.31N 92.11W
44 L13 **Tilarán** Guanacaste, NW Costa Rica 10.28N 84.57W
101 J14 **Tilburg** Noord-Brabant, S Netherlands 51.34N 5.04E
12 D17 **Tilbury** Ontario, S Canada 42.15N 82.25W
190 K4 **Tilcha** South Australia 29.37S 140.52E
Tilcha Creek *see* Callabonna Creek
31 Q14 **Tilden** Nebraska, C USA 42.03N 97.49W
27 R13 **Tilden** Texas, SW USA 28.26N 98.32W
12 H10 **Tilden Lake** Ontario, S Canada 46.35N 79.36W
118 G9 **Tileagd** *Hung.* Mezőtelegd. Bihor, W Romania 47.03N 22.10E
79 Q8 **Tilemsi, Vallée de** ⩩ C Mali
127 Pp8 **Tilichiki** Koryakskiy Avtonomnyy Okrug, E Russian Federation 60.25N 165.55E
Tiligul *see* Tilihul
Tiligul'skiy Liman *see* Tilihul's'kyy Lyman
119 P9 **Tilihul** *Rus.* Tiligul. ⩩ SW Ukraine
119 P10 **Tilihul's'kyy Lyman** *Rus.* Tiligul'skiy Liman. ◎ S Ukraine
Tilimsen *see* Tlemcen
Tilio Martius *see* Toulon
79 R11 **Tillabéri** *var.* Tillabéry. Tillabéri, W Niger 14.12N 1.25E
79 R11 **Tillabéri** ◆ *department* SW Niger
Tillabéry *see* Tillabéri
34 F11 **Tillamook** Oregon, NW USA 45.27N 123.50W
34 E11 **Tillamook Bay** *inlet* Oregon, NW USA
157 Q22 **Tillanchāng Dwīp** *island* Nicobar Islands, India, NE Indian Ocean
97 N15 **Tillberga** Västmanland, C Sweden 59.52N 16.39E
Tillenberg *see* Dyleń
23 S10 **Tillery, Lake** ⊠ North Carolina, SE USA
79 T10 **Tillia** Tahoua, W Niger 16.13N 4.51E
25 N8 **Tillmans Corner** Alabama, S USA 30.35N 88.10W
12 F17 **Tillsonburg** Ontario, S Canada 42.51N 80.41W
117 N22 **Tílos** *island* Dodekánisos, Greece, Aegean Sea
191 N5 **Tilpa** New South Wales, SE Australia 30.56S 144.24E
Tilsit *see* Sovetsk
33 N13 **Tilton** Illinois, N USA 40.06N 87.39W
130 K7 **Tim** Kurskaya Oblast', W Russian Federation 51.39N 37.11E
56 D12 **Timaná** Huila, S Colombia 1.56N 75.57W
Timan Ridge *see* Timanskiy Kryazh
129 Q6 **Timanskiy Kryazh** *Eng.* Timan Ridge. *ridge* NW Russian Federation
193 G20 **Timaru** Canterbury, South Island, NZ 44.22S 171.15E
131 S6 **Timashevo** Samarskaya Oblast', W Russian Federation 53.22N 51.13E
130 K13 **Timashevsk** Krasnodarskiy Kray, SW Russian Federation 45.37N 38.57E
Timbaki/Timbákion *see* Tympáki
24 K10 **Timbalier Bay** *bay* Louisiana, S USA
24 K11 **Timbalier Island** *island* Louisiana, S USA
194 K12 **Timbe** ⩩ C Papua New Guinea
78 L10 **Timbedgha** *var.* Timbédra. Hodh ech Chargui, SE Mauritania 16.16N 8.13W
Timbédra *see* Timbedgha
34 G10 **Timber** Oregon, NW USA 45.42N 123.19W
189 O3 **Timber Creek** Northern Territory, N Australia 15.35S 130.21E
30 M8 **Timber Lake** South Dakota, N USA 45.25N 101.01W
56 D12 **Timbío** Cauca, SW Colombia 2.22N 76.41W
56 C12 **Timbiquí** Cauca, SW Colombia 2.41N 77.41W
85 O17 **Timbue, Ponta** *headland* C Mozambique 18.49S 36.22E
Timbuktu *see* Tombouctou
176 Vv10 **Timbuni, Sungai** ⩩ Papua, E Indonesia
175 Oo4 **Timbun Mata, Pulau** *island* E Malaysia
79 P8 **Timétrine** *var.* Ti-n-Kâr. *oasis* C Mali 19.18N 0.09W
Timfi *see* Týmfi
Timfristos *see* Tymfristós
79 V9 **Timia** Agadez, C Niger 18.07N 8.49E
176 X12 **Timika** Papua, E Indonesia 4.39S 137.15E
76 I9 **Timimoun** C Algeria 29.18N 0.21E
Timiris, Cap *see* Timirist, Râs
78 F8 **Timirist, Râs** *var.* Cap Timiris. *headland* NW Mauritania 19.18N 16.28W
151 O7 **Timiryazevo** Severnyy Kazakhstan, N Kazakhstan 53.45N 66.33E
118 E11 **Timiş** ◆ *county* SW Romania
12 H9 **Timiskaming, Lake** *Fr.* Lac Témiscamingue. ◎ Ontario/Quebec, SE Canada
118 E11 **Timişoara** *Ger.* Temeschwar, Temeswar, *Hung.* Temesvár; *prev.* Temeschburg. Timiş, W Romania 45.46N 21.16E
118 E11 **Timişoara** ✕ Timiş, W Romania 45.50N 21.21E
Timkovichi *see* Tsimkavichy
79 U8 **Ti-m-Meghsoï** ⩩ NW Niger
102 K8 **Timmerdorfer Strand** Schleswig-Holstein, N Germany 53.59N 10.50E
12 F7 **Timmins** Ontario, S Canada 48.09N 80.01W
23 S12 **Timmonsville** South Carolina, SE USA 34.07N 79.56W
32 K5 **Timms Hill** ▲ Wisconsin, N USA 45.27N 90.12W
176 Vv9 **Timoforo** ⩩ Papua, E Indonesia
114 P12 **Timok** ⩩ E Serbia and Montenegro (Yugoslavia)
60 N13 **Timon** Maranhão, E Brazil 5.07S 42.52W
175 Rr17 **Timor** *island* East Timor/Indonesia
175 S17 **Timor Sea** *sea* E Indian Ocean
Timor Timur *see* East Timor
Timor Trench *see* Timor Trough
198 G9 **Timor Trough** *var.* Timor Trench. *undersea feature* NE Timor Sea
63 A21 **Timote** Buenos Aires, E Argentina 35.22S 62.13W
56 I6 **Timotes** Mérida, NW Venezuela 8.57N 70.46W
27 X8 **Timpson** Texas, SW USA 31.54N 94.24W
126 Ll13 **Timpton** ⩩ NE Russian Federation
95 H17 **Timrå** Västernorrland, C Sweden 62.28N 17.19E
22 J10 **Tims Ford Lake** ⊠ Tennessee, S USA
174 Hh7 **Timun** Pulau Kundur, C Indonesia 0.49N 103.23E
174 H3 **Timur, Banjaran** ▲ Peninsular Malaysia
179 R17 **Tinaca Point** *headland* Mindanao, S Philippines 5.35N 125.18E
56 K5 **Tinaco** Cojedes, N Venezuela 9.42N 68.27W
66 Q11 **Tinajo** Lanzarote, Islas Canarias, Spain, NE Atlantic Ocean 29.03N 13.40W
195 W8 **Tinakula** *island* Santa Cruz Islands, E Solomon Islands
56 K5 **Tinaquillo** Cojedes, N Venezuela 9.52N 68.19W
118 F10 **Tinca** *Hung.* Tenke. Bihor, W Romania 46.46N 21.58E
161 J20 **Tindivanam** Tamil Nādu, SE India 12.15N 79.40E
76 E9 **Tindouf** W Algeria 27.43N 8.09W
76 E9 **Tindouf, Sebkha de** *salt lake* W Algeria
106 J2 **Tineo** Asturias, N Spain 43.19N 6.25W
79 R9 **Ti-n-Essako** Kidal, E Mali 18.30N 2.27E
191 T5 **Tingha** New South Wales, SE Australia 29.56S 151.13E
Tingis *see* Tanger
Tinglett *see* Tinglev
97 F24 **Tinglev** *Ger.* Tinglett. Sønderjylland, SW Denmark 54.57N 9.15E
58 E12 **Tingo María** Huánuco, C Peru 9.19S 75.56W
Tingréla *see* Tengréla
164 K16 **Tingri** *var.* Xêgar. Xizang Zizhiqu, W China 28.40N 87.04E
97 M21 **Tingsryd** Kronoberg, S Sweden 56.30N 15.00E
97 P19 **Tingstäde** Gotland, SE Sweden 57.45N 18.36E
64 H12 **Tinguiririca, Volcán** ▲ C Chile 34.52S 70.24W
96 F9 **Tingvoll** Møre og Romsdal, S Norway 62.55N 8.13E
194 M9 **Tingwon Island** *island* N PNG
196 K8 **Tinian** *island* S Northern Mariana Islands
Ti-n-Kâr *see* Timétrine
Tinnevelly *see* Tirunelveli
97 G15 **Tinnoset** Telemark, S Norway 59.43N 9.03E
97 F15 **Tinnsjø** ◎ S Norway
Tino *see* Chino
117 J20 **Tínos** Tínos, Kykládes, Greece, Aegean Sea 37.32N 25.10E
117 J20 **Tínos** *anc.* Tenos. *island* Kykládes, Greece, Aegean Sea
159 R14 **Tinpahar** Bihār, NE India 25.00N 87.43E
124 O14 **Tin, Ra's al** *headland* N Libya 32.36N 23.10E
159 X11 **Tinsukia** Assam, NE India 27.28N 95.19E
78 K10 **Tîntâne** Hodh el Gharbi, S Mauritania 16.25N 10.08W
64 L7 **Tintina** Santiago del Estero, N Argentina 27.03S 62.42W
190 K10 **Tintinara** South Australia 35.54S 140.04E
106 I14 **Tinto** ⩩ SW Spain
79 S8 **Ti-n-Zaouâtene** Kidal, NE Mali 19.56N 2.45E
Tiobraid Árann *see* Tipperary
30 K3 **Tioga** North Dakota, N USA 48.24N 102.56W
20 G12 **Tioga** Pennsylvania, NE USA 41.54N 77.07W
27 T5 **Tioga** Texas, SW USA 33.28N 96.55W
37 Q8 **Tioga Pass** *pass* California, W USA 37.53N 119.15W
20 G12 **Tioga River** ⩩ New York/Pennsylvania, NE USA
176 Y11 **Tiom** Papua, E Indonesia 3.49S 138.22E
Tioman Island *see* Tioman, Pulau
174 I5 **Tioman, Pulau** *var.* Tioman Island. *island* Peninsular Malaysia
20 C12 **Tionesta** Pennsylvania, NE USA 41.31N 79.30W
20 D12 **Tionesta Creek** ⩩ Pennsylvania, NE USA
173 G11 **Tiop** Pulau Pagai Selatan, W Indonesia 3.12S 100.21E
175 Qq12 **Tioro, Selat** *var.* Tiworo. *strait* Sulawesi, C Indonesia
79 O12 **Tiou** NW Burkina 13.42N 2.34W
20 H11 **Tioughnioga River** ⩩ New York, NE USA
176 U10 **Tip** Papua, E Indonesia 1.50S 130.04E
76 J5 **Tipasa** *var.* Tipaza. N Algeria 36.34N 2.27E
Tipaza *see* Tipasa
44 J10 **Tipitapa** Managua, W Nicaragua 12.10N 86.04W
33 R13 **Tipp City** Ohio, N USA 39.57N 84.10W
33 O12 **Tippecanoe River** ⩩ Indiana, N USA
99 D20 **Tipperary** *Ir.* Tiobraid Árann. S Ireland 52.28N 8.10W
99 D19 **Tipperary** *Ir.* Tiobraid Árann. *cultural region* S Ireland
37 R12 **Tipton** California, W USA 36.02N 119.19W
33 P13 **Tipton** Indiana, N USA 40.19N 86.00W
31 Y14 **Tipton** Iowa, C USA 41.46N 91.07W
29 U5 **Tipton** Missouri, C USA 38.39N 92.46W
38 I10 **Tipton, Mount** ▲ Arizona, SW USA 35.32N 114.11W
22 F8 **Tiptonville** Tennessee, S USA 36.22N 89.28W
10 E12 **Tip Top Mountain** ▲ Ontario, S Canada 48.18N 86.06W
161 G19 **Tiptūr** Karnātaka, W India 13.17N 76.31E
Tiquisate *see* Pueblo Nuevo Tiquisate
60 L13 **Tiracambu, Serra do** ▲ E Brazil
Tirana *see* Tiranë
115 K19 **Tirana Rinas** ✕ Durrës, W Albania 41.25N 19.41E
115 L20 **Tiranë** *var.* Tirana. ● (Albania) Tiranë, C Albania 41.19N 19.49E
115 K20 **Tiranë** ◆ *district* W Albania
146 I5 **Tirān, Jazīrat** *island* Egypt/Saudi Arabia
108 F6 **Tirano** Lombardia, N Italy 46.13N 10.10E
190 I2 **Tirari Desert** *desert* South Australia
119 O10 **Tiraspol** *Rus.* Tiraspol'. E Moldova 46.50N 29.34E
192 M8 **Tirau** Waikato, North Island, NZ 37.59S 175.44E
142 C14 **Tire** İzmir, SW Turkey 38.04N 27.45E
143 O11 **Tirebolu** Giresun, N Turkey 41.01N 38.49E
98 F11 **Tiree** *island* W Scotland, UK
Tîrgovişte *see* Târgovişte
Tîrgu *see* Târgu Cărbuneşti
Tîrgu Bujor *see* Târgu Bujor
Tîrgu Frumos *see* Târgu Frumos
Tîrgu Jiu *see* Târgu Jiu
Tîrgu Lăpuş *see* Târgu Lăpuş
Tîrgu Mures *see* Târgu Mureş
Tîrgu-Neamţ *see* Târgu-Neamţ
Tîrgu Ocna *see* Târgu Ocna
Tîrgu Secuiesc *see* Târgu Secuiesc
155 T3 **Tirich Mīr** ▲ NW Pakistan 36.12N 71.51E
78 J5 **Tiris Zemmour** ◆ *region* N Mauritania
Tirlemont *see* Tienen
131 W5 **Tirlyanskiy** Respublika Bashkortostan, W Russian Federation 54.09N 58.32E
Tîrnava Mare *see* Târnava Mare
Tîrnava Mică *see* Târnava Mică
Tîrnăveni *see* Târnăveni
Tírnavos *see* Týrnavos
Tirnovo *see* Veliko Tŭrnovo
160 J11 **Tirodi** Madhya Pradesh, C India 21.40N 79.43E
110 K8 **Tirol** *off.* Land Tirol, *var.* Tyrol, *It.* Tirolo. ◆ *state* W Austria
Tirolo *see* Tirol
Tirreno, Mare *see* Tyrrhenian Sea
109 B19 **Tirso** ⩩ Sardegna, Italy, C Mediterranean Sea
97 H22 **Tirstrup** ✕ (Århus) Århus, C Denmark 56.17N 10.36E
161 I21 **Tiruchchirāppalli** *prev.* Trichinopoly. Tamil Nādu, SE India 10.49N 78.43E
161 H23 **Tirunelveli** *var.* Tinnevelly. Tamil Nādu, SE India 8.45N 77.43E
161 J19 **Tirupati** Andhra Pradesh, E India 13.39N 79.25E
161 I20 **Tiruppattūr** Tamil Nādu, SE India 12.28N 78.31E
161 H21 **Tiruppūr** Tamil Nādu, SW India 11.04N 77.19E
161 I20 **Tiruvannāmalai** Tamil Nādu, SE India 12.13N 79.07E
114 L10 **Tisa** *Ger.* Theiss, *Hung.* Tisza, *Rus.* Tissa, *Ukr.* Tysa. ⩩ SE Europe *see also* Tisza
Tischnowitz *see* Tišnov
9 U14 **Tisdale** Saskatchewan, S Canada 52.51N 104.01W
29 O13 **Tishomingo** Oklahoma, C USA 34.14N 96.40W
97 M17 **Tisnaren** ◎ S Sweden
113 F18 **Tišnov** *Ger.* Tischnowitz. Brnenský Kraj, SE Czech Republic 49.21N 16.24E
Tissa *see* Tisa/Tisza
76 J6 **Tissemsilt** N Algeria 35.37N 1.48E
159 S12 **Tista** ⩩ NE India
114 L8 **Tisza** *Ger.* Theiss, *Rom./Slvn./SCr.* Tisa, *Rus.* Tissa, *Ukr.* Tysa. ⩩ SE Europe *see also* Tisa
113 L23 **Tiszaföldvár** Jász-Nagykun-Szolnok, E Hungary 47.00N 20.16E
113 M22 **Tiszafüred** Jász-Nagykun-Szolnok, E Hungary 47.34N 20.45E
113 L23 **Tiszakécske** Bács-Kiskun, C Hungary 46.55N 20.04E
113 M21 **Tiszaújváros** *prev.* Leninváros. Borsod-Abaúj-Zemplén, NE Hungary 47.55N 21.03E
113 N21 **Tiszavasvári** Szabolcs-Szatmár-Bereg, NE Hungary 47.57N 21.24E
Titibu *see* Chichibu
59 I17 **Titicaca, Lake** ◎ Bolivia/Peru
202 H17 **Titikaveka** Rarotonga, S Cook Islands 21.16S 159.45W
160 M13 **Titilāgarh** Orissa, E India 20.18N 83.09E
174 Gg4 **Titiwangsa, Banjaran** ▲ Peninsular Malaysia
Titograd *see* Podgorica
Titose *see* Chitose
Titova Mitrovica *see* Kosovska Mitrovica
Titovo Užice *see* Užice
115 M18 **Titov Vrv** ▲ NW FYR Macedonia 41.58N 20.49E
96 F7 **Titran** Sør-Trøndelag, S Norway 63.40N 8.20E
33 Q8 **Tittabawassee River** ⩩ Michigan, N USA
118 J13 **Titu** Dâmboviţa, S Romania 44.40N 25.31E
81 M16 **Titule** Orientale, N Dem. Rep. Congo 3.19N 25.23E
25 X11 **Titusville** Florida, SE USA 28.34N 80.48W
20 C12 **Titusville** Pennsylvania, NE USA 41.36N 79.39W
78 G11 **Tivaouane** W Senegal 14.59N 16.50W
115 I17 **Tivat** Montenegro, SW Serbia and Montenegro (Yugoslavia) 42.25N 18.43E
12 E14 **Tiverton** Ontario, S Canada 44.15N 81.31W
99 J23 **Tiverton** SW England, UK 50.54N 3.30W
21 O12 **Tiverton** Rhode Island, NE USA 41.38N 71.10W
109 I15 **Tivoli** *anc.* Tiber. Lazio, C Italy 41.58N 12.45E
27 U13 **Tivoli** Texas, SW USA 28.26N 96.54W
176 W11 **Tiwarra** Papua, E Indonesia 2.54S 133.52E
147 Z8 **Ţīwī** NE Oman 22.43N 59.20E
Tiworo *see* Tioro, Selat
176 Ww12 **Tiyo, Pegunungan** ▲ Papua, E Indonesia
43 Y11 **Tizimín** Yucatán, SE Mexico 21.10N 88.09W
76 K5 **Tizi Ouzou** *var.* Tizi-Ouzou. N Algeria 36.44N 4.06E
76 D8 **Tiznit** SW Morocco 29.43N 9.39W
115 I14 **Tjentište** Republika Srpska, SE Bosnia and Herzegovina 43.23N 18.42E
Tjepoe/Tjepu *see* Cepu
100 L7 **Tjeukemeer** ◎ N Netherlands
Tjiamis *see* Ciamis
Tjiandjoer *see* Cianjur
Tjilatjap *see* Cilacap
Tjiledoeg *see* Ciledug
97 F23 **Tjæreborg** Ribe, W Denmark 55.28N 8.34E
97 I18 **Tjörn** *island* S Sweden
94 O3 **Tjuvfjorden** *fjord* S Svalbard
Tkvarcheli *see* Tqvarch'eli
42 L8 **Tlahualillo** Durango, N Mexico 26.06N 103.25W
43 P14 **Tlalnepantla** México, C Mexico 19.37N 99.09W
43 Q13 **Tlapacoyán** Veracruz-Llave, E Mexico 19.57N 97.18W
43 P16 **Tlapa de Comonfort** Guerrero, S Mexico 17.33N 98.33W
42 L13 **Tlaquepaque** Jalisco, C Mexico 20.36N 103.19W
Tlascala *see* Tlaxcala
43 P14 **Tlaxcala** *var.* Tlascala, Tlaxcala de Xicohténcatl. Tlaxcala, C Mexico 19.17N 98.15W
43 P14 **Tlaxcala** ◆ *state* S Mexico
Tlaxcala de Xicohténcatl *see* Tlaxcala
43 P14 **Tlaxco** *var.* Tlaxco de Morelos. Tlaxcala, S Mexico 19.37N 98.07W
Tlaxco de Morelos *see* Tlaxco
43 Q16 **Tlaxiaco** *var.* Santa María Asunción Tlaxiaco. Oaxaca, S Mexico 17.18N 97.42W
76 I6 **Tlemcen** *var.* Tilimsen, Tlemsen. NW Algeria 34.52N 1.21W
Tlemsen *see* Tlemcen
144 L4 **Tlété Ouâte Rharbi, Jebel** ▲ N Syria
118 J7 **Tlumach** Ivano-Frankivs'ka Oblast', W Ukraine 48.53N 25.00E
131 P17 **Tlyarata** Respublika Dagestan, SW Russian Federation 42.10N 46.30E
118 K10 **Toaca, Vârful** *prev.* Vîrful Toaca. ▲ NE Romania 46.58N 25.55E
Toaca, Vîrful *see* Toaca, Vârful
197 C13 **Toak** Ambrym, C Vanuatu 16.21S 168.16E
180 J4 **Toamasina** *var.* Tamatave. Toamasina, E Madagascar 18.10S 49.22E
180 J4 **Toamasina** ◆ *province* E Madagascar
180 J4 **Toamasina** ✕ Toamasina, E Madagascar 18.10S 49.22E
23 X6 **Toano** Virginia, NE USA 37.22N 76.46W
203 U10 **Toau** *atoll* Îles Tuamotu, C French Polynesia
47 T6 **Toa Vaca, Embalse** ⊠ C Puerto Rico
64 K13 **Toay** La Pampa, C Argentina 36.43S 64.22W
165 R14 **Toba** Xizang Zizhiqu, W China 31.16N 97.37E
171 Hh16 **Toba** Mie, Honshū, SW Japan 34.28N 136.49E
173 Ff5 **Toba, Danau** ◎ Sumatera, W Indonesia
47 Y16 **Tobago** *island* NE Trinidad and Tobago
155 Q9 **Toba Kākar Range** ▲ NW Pakistan
175 T10 **Tobalai, Selat** *strait* Maluku, E Indonesia
175 Q9 **Tobamawu** Sulawesi, N Indonesia 1.16S 121.42E
107 Q12 **Tobarra** Castilla-La Mancha, C Spain 38.36N 1.40W
155 U9 **Toba Tek Singh** Punjab, E Pakistan 30.54N 72.30E
175 T6 **Tobelo** Pulau Halmahera, E Indonesia 1.45N 127.58E
12 E12 **Tobermory** Ontario, S Canada 45.13N 81.39W
98 G10 **Tobermory** W Scotland, UK 56.37N 6.12W
172 Oo5 **Tōbetsu** Hokkaidō, NE Japan 43.12N 141.28E
188 M6 **Tobin Lake** ◎ Western Australia
9 U14 **Tobin Lake** ◎ Saskatchewan, C Canada
37 T4 **Tobin, Mount** ▲ Nevada, W USA 40.25N 117.28W
171 L10 **Tobi-shima** *island* C Japan
174 J11 **Toboali** Pulau Bangka, W Indonesia 2.57S 106.25E
150 M8 **Tobol** *Kaz.* Tobyl. Kostanay, N Kazakhstan 52.42N 62.36E
150 L8 **Tobol** *Kaz.* Tobyl. ⩩ Kazakhstan/Russian Federation
125 F11 **Tobol'sk** Tyumenskaya Oblast', C Russian Federation 58.15N 68.12E
Tobruch/Tobruk *see* Ţubruq
129 R3 **Tobseda** Nenetskiy Avtonomnyy Okrug, NW Russian Federation 68.37N 52.24E
Tobyl *see* Tobol
129 Q6 **Tobysh** ⩩ NW Russian Federation
56 F10 **Tocaima** Cundinamarca, C Colombia 4.30N 74.37W
61 K16 **Tocantins** *off.* Estado do Tocantins. ◆ *state* C Brazil
61 K15 **Tocantins, Rio** ⩩ N Brazil
25 T2 **Toccoa** Georgia, SE USA 34.34N 83.19W
171 K15 **Tochigi** *var.* Totigi. Tochigi, Honshū, S Japan 36.24N 139.42E
171 Kk15 **Tochigi** *off.* Tochigi-ken, *var.* Totigi. ◆ *prefecture* Honshū, S Japan
171 K13 **Tochio** *var.* Totio. Niigata, Honshū, C Japan 37.27N 139.00E
97 I15 **Töcksfors** Värmland, C Sweden 59.30N 11.49E
44 J5 **Tocoa** Colón, N Honduras 15.36N 86.01W
64 H4 **Tocopilla** Antofagasta, N Chile 22.06S 70.08W
64 I4 **Tocorpuri, Cerro de** ▲ Bolivia/Chile 22.25S 67.52W
191 O10 **Tocumwal** New South Wales, SE Australia 35.53S 145.35E
56 K4 **Tocuyo de La Costa** Falcón, NW Venezuela 11.02N 68.29W
158 H13 **Toda Rāisingh** Rājasthān, N India 26.01N 75.34E
108 H13 **Todi** Umbria, C Italy 42.46N 12.25E
110 G9 **Tödi** ▲ NE Switzerland 46.52N 8.53E
176 Uu9 **Todlo** Papua, E Indonesia 0.46S 130.50E
172 N12 **Todoga-saki** *headland* Honshū, C Japan 39.33N 142.02E
61 P17 **Todos os Santos, Baía de** *bay* E Brazil
42 F10 **Todos Santos** Baja California Sur, W Mexico 23.26N 110.14W
42 B2 **Todos Santos, Bahía de** *bay* NW Mexico
Toeban *see* Tuban
Toekang Besi Eilanden *see* Tukangbesi, Kepulauan
Tōen *see* T'aoyüan
193 D25 **Toetoes Bay** *bay* South Island, NZ
9 Q14 **Tofield** Alberta, SW Canada 53.22N 112.39W
8 K17 **Tofino** Vancouver Island, British Columbia, SW Canada 49.04N 125.51W
201 X17 **Tofol** Kosrae, E Micronesia
97 J20 **Tofta** Halland, S Sweden 57.10N 12.19E
97 H15 **Tofte** Buskerud, S Norway 59.31N 10.33E
97 F24 **Toftlund** Sønderjylland, SW Denmark 55.12N 9.04E
200 S13 **Tofua** *island* Ha'apai Group, C Tonga
197 B10 **Toga** *island* Torres Islands, N Vanuatu
171 Kk17 **Tōgane** Chiba, Honshū, S Japan 35.32N 140.22E
82 N13 **Togdheer** *off.* Gobolka Togdheer. ◆ *region* NW Somalia
Toghyzaq *see* Toguzak
171 Ii12 **Togi** Ishikawa, Honshū, SW Japan 37.06N 136.43E
41 N13 **Togiak** Alaska, USA 59.03N 160.31W
175 Qq8 **Togian, Kepulauan** *island group* C Indonesia
79 Q15 **Togo** *off.* Togolese Republic; *prev.* French Togoland. ◆ *republic* W Africa
168 F8 **Tögrög** Govĭ-Altay, SW Mongolia 45.51N 95.04E
168 E7 **Tögrög** Hovd, W Mongolia 47.24N 92.06E
Togton-heyan *see* Tuotuoheyan
150 L7 **Toguzak** *Kaz.* Toghyzaq. ⩩ Kazakhstan/Russian Federation
39 P10 **Tohatchi** New Mexico, SW USA 35.51N 108.45W
203 O7 **Tohiea, Mont** ⩕ Moorea, W French Polynesia 17.33S 149.48W
95 O17 **Tohmajärvi** Itä-Suomi, E Finland 62.12N 30.19E
143 N14 **Tohma Çayı** ⩩ C Turkey
95 L16 **Toholampi** Länsi-Suomi, W Finland 63.46N 24.15E
168 M10 **Töhöm** Dornogovĭ, SE Mongolia 44.25N 108.18E
25 X12 **Tohopekaliga, Lake** ◎ Florida, SE USA
171 J17 **Toi** Shizuoka, Honshū, S Japan 34.55N 138.45E
202 B15 **Toi** N Niue 18.57S 169.51W
95 L19 **Toijala** Länsi-Suomi, W Finland 61.09N 23.51E

◆ Country
● Country Capital
◇ Dependent Territory
○ Dependent Territory Capital
◈ Administrative Region
✕ International Airport
▲ Mountain
▲ Mountain Range
⩕ Volcano
⩩ River
◎ Lake
⊠ Reservoir

175 Qq9 Toima Sulawesi, N Indonesia 0.48S 122.21E
170 C17 Toi-misaki headland Kyūshū, SW Japan 31.21N 131.18E
175 Rr17 Toineke Timor, S Indonesia 10.06S 124.22E
Toirc, Inis see Inishturk
37 U6 Toiyabe Range ▲ Nevada, W USA
Tojikiston, Jumhurii see Tajikistan
153 R12 Tojikobod Rus. Tadzhikabad. C Tajikistan 39.08N 70.54E
170 F13 Tōjō Hiroshima, Honshū, SW Japan 34.54N 133.15E
41 T10 Tok Alaska, USA 63.20N 142.59W
172 P5 Tokachi-dake ▲ Hokkaidō, NE Japan 43.24N 142.41E
172 Pp7 Tokachi-gawa var. Tokati Gawa. ~ Hokkaidō, NE Japan
171 Hh16 Tōkai Aichi, Honshū, SW Japan 35.01N 136.51E
113 N21 Tokaj Borsod-Abaúj-Zemplén, NE Hungary 48.07N 21.25E
171 Jj13 Tōkamachi Niigata, Honshū, C Japan 37.08N 138.46E
193 D25 Tokanui Southland, South Island, NZ 46.33S 169.01E
82 I7 Tokar var. Ţawkar. Red Sea, NE Sudan 18.27N 37.40E
142 L12 Tokat Tokat, N Turkey 40.19N 36.34E
142 L12 Tokat ◆ province N Turkey
Tokati Gawa see Tokachi-gawa
169 X15 Tŏkchŏk-gundo island group NW South Korea
Tōke see Taka Atoll
202 J9 Tokelau ◇ NZ overseas territory W Polynesia
Tőketerebes see Trebišov
Tokhtamyshbek see Tŭkhtamish
26 M6 Tokio Texas, SW USA 33.09N 102.31W
Tokio see Tōkyō
201 W11 Toki Point point NW Wake Island 19.19N 166.36E
Tokkuztara see Gongliu
153 V7 Tokmak Kir. Tokmok. Chuyskaya Oblast', N Kyrgyzstan 42.49N 75.18E
119 V9 Tokmak var. Velykyy Tokmak. Zaporiz'ka Oblast', SE Ukraine 47.13N 35.42E
Tokmok see Tokmak
192 Q8 Tokomaru Bay Gisborne, North Island, NZ 38.10S 178.18E
171 Hh16 Tokoname Aichi, Honshū, SW Japan 34.54N 136.49E
172 Qq5 Tokoro Hokkaidō, NE Japan 44.06N 144.03E
192 M8 Tokoroa Waikato, North Island, NZ 38.14S 175.52E
172 Q6 Tokoro-gawa ~ Hokkaidō, NE Japan
78 K14 Tokounou Haute-Guinée, C Guinea 9.43N 9.46W
40 M12 Toksook Bay Alaska, USA 60.33N 165.01W
Toksu see Xinhe
Toksum see Toksun
164 L6 Toksun var. Toksum. Xinjiang Uygur Zizhiqu, NW China 42.46N 88.37E
153 T8 Toktogul Talasskaya Oblast', NW Kyrgyzstan 41.51N 72.56E
153 T9 Toktogul'skoye Vodokhranilishche ▣ W Kyrgyzstan
Toktomush see Tŭkhtamish
200 Ss12 Toku island Vava'u Group, N Tonga
172 Qq14 Tokunoshima Kagoshima, Tokuno-shima, SW Japan
172 Q14 Tokuno-shima island Nansei-shotō, SW Japan
170 Ff15 Tokushima var. Tokusima. Tokushima, Shikoku, SW Japan 34.04N 134.28E
170 F15 Tokushima off. Tokushima-ken, var. Tokusima. ◆ prefecture Shikoku, SW Japan
Tokusima see Tokushima
170 E13 Tokuyama Yamaguchi, Honshū, SW Japan 34.04N 131.48E
171 Jj16 Tōkyō var. Tokio. ● (Japan) Tōkyō, Honshū, S Japan 35.40N 139.45E
171 J15 Tōkyō off. Tōkyō-to. ◆ capital district Honshū, S Japan
171 K17 Tōkyō-wan bay S Japan
151 T12 Tokyrau ~ C Kazakhstan
155 O3 Tokzār Pash. Tukzār. Sar-e Pol, N Afghanistan 35.47N 66.28E
151 W13 Tokzhaylau prev. Dzerzhinskoye. Almaty, SE Kazakhstan 45.49N 81.04E
201 U12 Tol atoll Chuuk Islands, C Micronesia
192 Q9 Tolaga Bay Gisborne, North Island, NZ 38.22S 178.17E
180 I7 Tôlañaro prev. Faradofay, Fort-Dauphin. Toliara, SE Madagascar
168 D6 Tolbo Bayan-Ölgiy, W Mongolia 48.22N 90.22E
Tolbukhin see Dobrich
62 G11 Toledo Paraná, S Brazil 24.45S 53.41W
56 G8 Toledo Norte de Santander, N Colombia 7.16N 72.28W
179 Qq13 Toledo off. Toledo City. Cebu, C Philippines 10.23N 123.39E
107 N9 Toledo anc. Toletum. Castilla-La Mancha, C Spain 39.52N 4.01W
32 M14 Toledo Illinois, N USA 39.16N 88.15W
31 W13 Toledo Iowa, C USA 42.00N 92.34W
33 R11 Toledo Ohio, N USA 41.39N 83.33W
34 F12 Toledo Oregon, NW USA 44.37N 123.56W
34 G9 Toledo Washington, NW USA 46.27N 122.49W
44 F3 Toledo ◆ district S Belize
106 M9 Toledo ◆ province Castilla-La Mancha, C Spain
27 Y7 Toledo Bend Reservoir ▣ Louisiana/Texas, SW USA
106 M10 Toledo, Montes de ▲ C Spain
108 J12 Tolentino Marche, C Italy 43.08N 13.17E
Toletum see Toledo
96 H10 Tolga Hedmark, S Norway 62.25N 11.00E
164 J3 Toli Xinjiang Uygur Zizhiqu, NW China 45.55N 83.33E
180 H7 Toliara var. Toliary; prev. Tuléar. Toliara, SW Madagascar 23.19S 43.40E
180 H7 Toliara ◆ province SW Madagascar
Toliary see Toliara
56 D11 Tolima off. Departamento del Tolima. ◆ province C Colombia
175 Pp7 Tolitoli Sulawesi, C Indonesia 1.04N 120.49E
97 K22 Tollarp Skåne, S Sweden 55.55N 14.00E
102 N9 Tollense ~ NE Germany
102 N10 Tollensesee ◎ NE Germany
38 K13 Tolleson Arizona, SW USA 33.25N 112.15W
152 M13 Tollimarjon Rus. Talimardzhan. Qashqadaryo Viloyati, S Uzbekistan 38.22N 65.31E
Tolmein see Tolmin
108 J6 Tolmezzo Friuli-Venezia Giulia, NE Italy 46.27N 13.01E
111 S11 Tolmin Ger. Tolmein, It. Tolmino. W Slovenia 46.12N 13.39E
Tolmino see Tolmin
113 J25 Tolna Ger. Tolnau. Tolna, S Hungary 46.25N 18.46E
113 I24 Tolna off. Tolna Megye. ◆ county SW Hungary
Tolnau see Tolna
81 I20 Tolo Bandundu, W Dem. Rep. Congo 2.57S 18.35E
Tolochin see Talachyn
202 D12 Toloke Île Futuna, W Wallis and Futuna
32 M13 Tolono Illinois, N USA 39.59N 88.16W
107 Q3 Tolosa País Vasco, N Spain 43.09N 2.04W
Tolosa see Toulouse
175 Qq10 Tolo, Teluk bay Sulawesi, C Indonesia
41 R9 Tolovana River ~ Alaska, USA
127 Oo10 Tolstoy, Mys headland E Russian Federation 59.12N 155.04E
65 G15 Toltén Araucanía, C Chile 39.13S 73.10W
65 G15 Toltén, Río ~ S Chile
56 E6 Tolú Sucre, NW Colombia 9.31N 75.34W
43 O14 Toluca var. Toluca de Lerdo. México, S Mexico 19.19N 99.40W
Toluca de Lerdo see Toluca
43 O14 Toluca, Nevado de ▲ C Mexico 19.05N 99.45W
131 R6 Tol'yatti prev. Stavropol'. Samarskaya Oblast', W Russian Federation 53.31N 49.27E
126 H14 Tom' ~ S Russian Federation
79 O12 Toma NW Burkina 12.46N 2.51W
32 K7 Tomah Wisconsin, N USA 43.59N 90.31W
32 L5 Tomahawk Wisconsin, N USA 45.27N 89.40W
119 T8 Tomakivka Dnipropetrovs'ka Oblast', E Ukraine 47.47N 34.45E
172 O6 Tomakomai Hokkaidō, NE Japan 42.38N 141.32E
172 P3 Tomamae Hokkaidō, NE Japan 44.18N 141.38E
106 G9 Tomar Santarém, W Portugal 39.36N 8.25W
127 O15 Tomari Ostrov Sakhalin, Sakhalinskaya Oblast', SE Russian Federation 47.47N 142.09E
117 C16 Tómaros ▲ W Greece 39.31N 20.45E
Tomaschow see Tomaszów Lubelski, Poland
Tomaschow see Tomaszów Mazowiecki, Poland
63 E16 Tomás Gomensoro Artigas, N Uruguay 30.28S 57.28W
119 N7 Tomashpil' Vinnyts'ka Oblast', C Ukraine 48.32N 28.31E
Tomaszów see Tomaszów Mazowiecki
113 P15 Tomaszów Lubelski Ger. Tomaschow. Lubelskie, E Poland 50.28N 23.22E
Tomaszów Mazowiecka see Tomaszów Mazowiecki
112 L13 Tomaszów Mazowiecki var. Tomaszów Mazowiecka; prev. Tomaszów, Ger. Tomaschow. Łodzkie, C Poland 51.33N 20.00E
42 J13 Tomatlán Jalisco, C Mexico 19.53N 105.18W
170 F12 Tombara Shimane, Honshū, SW Japan 35.04N 132.46E
83 F15 Tombe Jonglei, S Sudan 5.52N 31.40E
25 N4 Tombigbee River ~ Alabama/Mississippi, S USA
84 A10 Tomboco Zaire, NW Angola 6.47S 13.18E
79 O10 Tombouctou Eng. Timbuktu. Tombouctou, N Mali 16.47N 3.03W
79 N9 Tombouctou ◆ region W Mali
39 N16 Tombstone Arizona, SW USA 31.42N 110.04W
85 A15 Tombua Port. Porto Alexandre. Namibe, SW Angola 15.49S 11.52E
85 J19 Tom Burke Limpopo, NE South Africa 23.07S 28.01E
152 L9 Tomdibuloq Rus. Tamdybulak. Navoiy Viloyati, N Uzbekistan 41.48N 64.33E
152 L9 Tomditov-Tog'lari ▲ N Uzbekistan
64 G13 Tomé Bío Bío, C Chile 36.39S 72.53W
60 L12 Tomé-Açu Pará, NE Brazil 2.25S 48.09W
97 L23 Tomelilla Skåne, S Sweden 55.33N 14.00E
107 O10 Tomelloso Castilla-La Mancha, C Spain 39.09N 3.01W
12 H10 Tomiko Lake ◎ Ontario, S Canada
79 N12 Tominian Ségou, C Mali 13.18N 4.39W
175 Pp8 Tomini, Gulf of var. Teluk Tomini; prev. Teluk Gorontalo. bay Sulawesi, C Indonesia
Tomini, Teluk see Tomini, Gulf of
172 Il15 Tomioka Fukushima, Honshū, C Japan 37.19N 140.57E
172 Jj15 Tomioka Gunma, Honshū, S Japan 36.15N 138.51E
115 G14 Tomislavgrad Federacija Bosna I Hercegovina, SW Bosnia and Herzegovina 43.43N 17.15E
189 O9 Tomkinson Ranges ▲ South Australia/Western Australia
126 Ll12 Tommot Respublika Sakha (Yakutiya), NE Russian Federation 58.56N 126.24E
175 Rr7 Tomohon Sulawesi, N Indonesia 1.19N 124.49E
56 K9 Tomo, Río ~ E Colombia
115 L21 Tomorrit, Mali i ▲ S Albania 40.43N 20.12E
9 S17 Tompkins Saskatchewan, S Canada 50.03N 108.49W
22 K8 Tompkinsville Kentucky, S USA 36.42N 85.41W
175 Pp7 Tompo Sulawesi, N Indonesia 0.56N 120.16E
188 I8 Tom Price Western Australia 22.48S 117.49E
126 H13 Tomsk Tomskaya Oblast', C Russian Federation 56.30N 85.04E
126 Gg12 Tomskaya Oblast' ◆ province C Russian Federation
20 K16 Toms River New Jersey, NE USA 39.56N 74.09W
Tom Steed Lake see Tom Steed Reservoir
28 L12 Tom Steed Reservoir var. Tom Steed Lake. ▣ Oklahoma, C USA
176 Vv10 Tomu Papua, E Indonesia 2.07S 133.01E
194 F13 Tomu ~ W PNG
164 H6 Tomur Feng var. Pik Pobedy, Pobeda Peak. ▲ China/Kyrgyzstan see also Pobedy, Pik 42.02N 80.07E
201 N13 Tomworoahlang Pohnpei, E Micronesia
43 U17 Tonalá Chiapas, SE Mexico 16.03N 93.43W
108 F6 Tonale, Passo del pass N Italy 46.16N 10.37E
171 I13 Tonami Toyama, Honshū, SW Japan 36.39N 136.57E
60 C12 Tonantins Amazonas, W Brazil 2.58S 67.30W
34 K6 Tonasket Washington, NW USA 48.41N 119.27W
57 Y9 Tonate var. Macouria. N French Guiana 05.00N 52.28W
20 D10 Tonawanda New York, NE USA 43.00N 78.51W
175 Rr7 Tondano Sulawesi, C Indonesia 1.19N 124.55E
175 Rr7 Tondano, Danau ◎ Sulawesi, N Indonesia
106 H7 Tondela Viseu, N Portugal 40.31N 8.04W
97 F24 Tønder Ger. Tondern. Sønderjylland, SW Denmark 54.57N 8.52E
Tondern see Tønder
171 K16 Tone-gawa ~ Honshū, S Japan
149 N4 Tonekābon var. Shahsawar, Tonkābon; prev. Shahsavār. Māzandarān, N Iran 36.49N 51.51E
Tonezh see Tonyezh
200 S15 Tonga off. Kingdom of Tonga, var. Friendly Islands. ◆ monarchy SW Pacific Ocean
183 R9 Tonga island group SW Pacific Ocean
85 K23 Tongaat KwaZulu/Natal, E South Africa 29.31S 31.09E
167 Q13 Tong'an var. Tong an. Fujian, SE China 24.43N 118.07E
29 Q4 Tonganoxie Kansas, C USA 39.06N 95.05W
41 Y13 Tongass National Forest reserve Alaska, USA
200 Qq16 Tongatapu ✈ Tongatapu, S Tonga 21.10S 175.10W
200 R15 Tongatapu island Tongatapu Group, S Tonga
200 S14 Tongatapu Group island group S Tonga
183 S9 Tonga Trench undersea feature S Pacific Ocean
167 N8 Tongbai Shan ▲ C China
167 P8 Tongcheng Anhui, E China 31.16N 117.00E
166 L6 Tongchuan Shaanxi, C China 35.10N 109.03E
166 L12 Tongdao var. Tongdao Dongzu Zizhixian; prev. Shuangjiang. Hunan, S China 26.06N 109.46E
165 T11 Tongde Qinghai, C China 35.13N 100.39E
101 K19 Tongeren Fr. Tongres. Limburg, NE Belgium 50.46N 5.28E
Tonggou see Tongyu
169 Y14 Tonghae NE South Korea 37.25N 129.08E
166 G13 Tonghai Yunnan, SW China 24.06N 102.45E
169 X8 Tonghe Heilongjiang, NE China 46.00N 128.45E
169 W11 Tonghua Jilin, NE China 41.43N 125.56E
194 L8 Tong Island island N PNG
169 Z6 Tongjiang Heilongjiang, NE China 47.39N 132.29E
169 Y13 Tongjosŏn-man prev. Broughton Bay. bay E North Korea
169 V7 Tongken He ~ NE China
178 K7 Tongking, Gulf of Chin. Beibu Wan, Vtn. Vinh Bắc Bộ. gulf China/Vietnam
169 U10 Tongliao Nei Mongol Zizhiqu, N China 43.37N 122.15E
167 Q9 Tongling Anhui, E China 30.54N 117.51E
167 R9 Tonglu Zhejiang, SE China 29.49N 119.37E
197 D14 Tongoa island Shepherd Islands, S Vanuatu
64 G9 Tongoy Coquimbo, C Chile 30.20S 71.28W
166 L11 Tongren Guizhou, S China 27.43N 109.10E
165 T11 Tongren Qinghai, C China 35.31N 101.58E
Tongres see Tongeren
159 U11 Tongsa var. Tongsa Dzong. C Bhutan 27.33N 90.30E
Tongsa Dzong see Tongsa
Tongshan see Xuzhou
Tongshi see Wuzhishan
165 P12 Tongtian He ~ C China
98 I6 Tongue N Scotland, UK 58.29N 4.24W
46 H3 Tongue of the Ocean strait C Bahamas
35 X10 Tongue River ~ Montana, NW USA
35 W11 Tongue River Resevoir ▣ Montana, NW USA
165 V11 Tongwei Gansu, C China 35.09N 105.15E
165 W9 Tongxin Ningxia, N China 37.00N 105.41E
169 U9 Tongyu var. Tonggou. Jilin, NE China 44.49N 123.08E
166 J11 Tongzi Guizhou, S China 28.07N 106.49E
42 G5 Tónichi Sonora, NW Mexico 28.30N 109.33W
83 D14 Tonj Warab, SW Sudan 7.18N 28.40E
158 H13 Tonk Rājasthān, N India 26.10N 75.49E
Tonkābon see Tonekābon
29 N8 Tonkawa Oklahoma, C USA 36.40N 97.18W
178 Ii12 Tônlé Sap Eng. Great Lake. ◎ W Cambodia
104 L14 Tonneins Lot-et-Garonne, SW France 44.21N 0.21E
105 Q7 Tonnerre Yonne, C France 47.50N 4.00E
Tonoas see Dublon
37 U8 Tonopah Nevada, W USA 38.04N 117.13W
170 Ff14 Tonoshō Okayama, Shōdo-shima, SW Japan 34.29N 134.10E
45 S17 Tonosí Los Santos, S Panama 7.23N 80.25W
97 H16 Tønsberg Vestfold, S Norway 59.16N 10.25E
41 T11 Tonsina Alaska, USA 61.39N 145.10W
97 D17 Tonstad Vest-Agder, S Norway 58.40N 6.42E
200 S14 Tonumea island Nomuka Group, W Tonga
143 O11 Tonya Trabzon, NE Turkey 40.52N 39.16E
121 K20 Tonyezh Rus. Tonezh. Homyel'skaya Voblasts', SE Belarus 51.49N 27.48E
38 L3 Tooele Utah, W USA 40.31N 112.18W
126 Ii15 Toora-Khem Respublika Tyva, S Russian Federation 52.25N 96.01E
191 O5 Toorale East New South Wales, SE Australia 30.29S 145.25E
85 H25 Toorberg ▲ S South Africa 32.02S 24.02E
120 G5 Tootsi Pärnumaa, SW Estonia 58.35N 24.46E
191 U3 Toowoomba Queensland, E Australia 27.34S 151.54E
29 Q4 Topeka state capital Kansas, C USA 39.03N 95.40W
113 M18 Topla Hung. Toplya. ~ NE Slovakia
126 H14 Topki Kemerovskaya Oblast', S Russian Federation 55.12N 85.40E
Toplicza see Toplița
118 J10 Toplița Ger. Töplitz, Hung. Maroshévíz; prev. Toplița Română, Hung. Oláh-Toplicza, Toplicza. Harghita, C Romania 46.57N 25.22E
Toplița Română/Töplitz see Toplița
Toplya see Topla
113 I20 Topoľčany Hung. Nagytapolcsány. Nitriansky Kraj, SW Slovakia 48.33N 18.10E
42 G8 Topolobampo Sinaloa, C Mexico 25.37N 109.02W
118 I13 Topoloveni Argeș, S Romania 44.49N 25.01E
116 L11 Topolovgrad prev. Kavakli. Khaskovo, S Bulgaria 42.06N 26.20E
Topolya see Bačka Topola
128 I6 Topozero, Ozero ◎ NW Russian Federation
34 J10 Toppenish Washington, NW USA 46.22N 120.18W
189 P4 Top Springs Roadhouse Northern Territory, N Australia 16.37S 131.49E
201 U11 Tora island Chuuk, C Micronesia
Toraigh see Tory Island
201 U11 Tora Island Pass passage Chuuk Islands, C Micronesia
149 U5 Torbat-e Ḩeydarīyeh var. Turbat-i-Haidari. Khorāsān, NE Iran 35.18N 59.12E
149 V5 Torbat-e Jām var. Turbat-i-Jam. Khorāsān, NE Iran 35.16N 60.36E
41 Q11 Torbert, Mount ▲ Alaska, USA 61.30N 152.15W
33 P6 Torch Lake ◎ Michigan, N USA
Törcsvár see Bran
Torda see Turda
106 L6 Tordesillas Castilla-León, N Spain 41.30N 5.00W
94 K13 Töre Norrbotten, N Sweden 65.55N 22.40E
97 L17 Töreboda Västra Götaland, S Sweden 58.40N 14.07E
97 J21 Torekov Skåne, S Sweden 56.25N 12.39E
92 O3 Torell Land physical region SW Svalbard
119 Y8 Torez Donets'ka Oblast', SE Ukraine 48.02N 38.45E
103 N14 Torgau Sachsen, E Germany 51.34N 13.01E
Torgay Üstirti see Turgayskaya Stolovaya Strana
Torghay see Turgay
97 N22 Torhamn Blekinge, S Sweden 56.04N 15.49E
101 C17 Torhout West-Vlaanderen, W Belgium 51.04N 3.06E
108 B8 Torino Eng. Turin. Piemonte, NW Italy 45.03N 7.39E
172 Q13 Tori-shima island Izu-shotō, SE Japan
83 F16 Torit Eastern Equatoria, S Sudan 4.27N 32.31E
195 O11 Toriu New Britain, E PNG 4.39S 151.42E
154 M4 Torkestān, Selseleh-ye Band-e var. Bandi-i Turkistan. ▲ NW Afghanistan
106 L7 Tormes ~ W Spain
Tornacum see Tournai
Torneå see Tornio
94 K12 Torneälven | var.Torniojoki, Fin. Tornionjoki. ~ Finland/Sweden
94 I11 Torneträsk ◎ N Sweden
11 O4 Torngat Mountains ▲ Newfoundland and Labrador, NE Canada
26 H8 Tornillo Texas, SW USA 31.26N 106.06W
94 K13 Tornio Swe. Torneå. Lappi, NW Finland 65.50N 24.17E
Torniojoki/Tornionjoki see Torneälven
63 B23 Tornquist Buenos Aires, E Argentina 38.05S 62.13W
106 L6 Toro Castilla-León, N Spain 41.31N 5.24W
64 H9 Toro, Cerro del ▲ N Chile 29.10S 69.43W
79 R12 Torodi Tillabéri, SW Niger 13.05N 1.46E
Törökbecse see Novi Bečej
195 S12 Torokina Bougainville Island, NE PNG 6.12S 155.04E
113 L23 Törökszentmiklós Jász-Nagykun-Szolnok, E Hungary 47.10N 20.25E
44 G7 Torola, Río ~ El Salvador/Honduras
Toronaíos, Kólpos see Kassándras, Kólpos
12 H15 Toronto Ontario, S Canada 43.42N 79.25W
33 V12 Toronto Ohio, N USA 40.27N 80.36W
Toronto see Lester B.Pearson
29 P6 Toronto Lake ▣ Kansas, C USA
37 V16 Toro Peak ▲ California, W USA 33.31N 116.25W
128 H16 Toropets Tverskaya Oblast', W Russian Federation 56.29N 31.37E
83 G18 Tororo E Uganda 0.46N 34.12E
142 H16 Toros Dağları Eng. Taurus Mountains. ▲ S Turkey
191 N13 Torquay Victoria, SE Australia 38.21S 144.18E
99 J24 Torquay SW England, UK 50.28N 3.30W
106 M5 Torquemada Castilla-León, N Spain 42.02N 4.17W
37 S16 Torrance California, W USA 33.49N 118.19W
106 G12 Torrão Setúbal, S Portugal 38.18N 8.13W
106 H8 Torre, Alto da ▲ C Portugal 40.21N 7.31W
109 K18 Torre Annunziata Campania, S Italy 40.45N 14.27E
107 T8 Torreblanca País Valenciano, E Spain 40.13N 0.12E
106 L15 Torrecilla ▲ S Spain 36.38N 4.54W
107 P4 Torrecilla en Cameros La Rioja, N Spain 42.18N 2.33W
107 N13 Torredelcampo Andalucía, S Spain 37.45N 3.52W
109 K17 Torre del Greco Campania, S Italy 40.46N 14.22E
106 I6 Torre de Moncorvo var. Moncorvo, Tôrre de Moncorvo. Bragança, N Portugal 41.10N 7.03W
106 J9 Torrejoncillo Extremadura, W Spain 39.54N 6.28W
107 O8 Torrejón de Ardoz Madrid, C Spain 40.27N 3.28W
107 N7 Torrelaguna Madrid, C Spain 40.49N 3.33W
107 N2 Torrelavega Cantabria, N Spain 43.21N 4.03W
109 M16 Torremaggiore Puglia, SE Italy 41.42N 15.17E
106 M15 Torremolinos Andalucía, S Spain 36.37N 4.30W
190 I6 Torrens, Lake salt lake South Australia
Torrent/Torrent de l'Horta see Torrente
107 S10 Torrente var. Torrent, Torrent de l'Horta. País Valenciano, E Spain 39.27N 0.28W
42 L8 Torreón Coahuila de Zaragoza, NE Mexico 25.47N 103.21W
107 R13 Torre Pacheco Murcia, SE Spain 37.43N 0.57W
108 A8 Torre Pellice Piemonte, NE Italy 44.49N 7.12E
107 O13 Torreperogil Andalucía, S Spain 38.01N 3.16W
63 J15 Torres Rio Grande do Sul, S Brazil 29.19S 49.46W
Torrès, Îles see Torres Islands
197 B10 Torres Islands Fr. Îles Torrès. island group N Vanuatu
106 G9 Torres Novas Santarém, C Portugal 39.28N 8.31W
189 V1 Torres Strait strait Australia/PNG
106 F10 Torres Vedras Lisboa, C Portugal 39.04N 9.15W
107 S13 Torrevieja País Valenciano, E Spain 37.58N 0.40W
194 F9 Torricelli Mountains ▲ NW PNG
98 G8 Torridon, Loch inlet NW Scotland, UK
108 D9 Torriglia Liguria, NW Italy 44.31N 9.08E
106 M9 Torrijos Castilla-La Mancha, C Spain 39.58N 4.18W
20 L12 Torrington Connecticut, NE USA 41.48N 73.07W
35 Z15 Torrington Wyoming, C USA 42.04N 104.10W
95 F16 Torröjen var. Torrön. ◎ C Sweden
Torrön see Torröjen
107 N15 Torrox Andalucía, S Spain 36.45N 3.58W
96 N13 Torsåker Gävleborg, C Sweden 60.31N 16.30E
97 N21 Torsås Kalmar, S Sweden 56.24N 16.00E
97 J14 Torsby Värmland, C Sweden 60.07N 13.00E
97 N16 Torshälla Södermanland, C Sweden 59.25N 16.28E
97 B19 Tórshavn Dan. Thorshavn Dependent territory capital Faeroe Islands 62.02N 6.47W
Torshiz see Kāshmar
152 I9 To'rtkok'l var. Tŭrtkŭl, Rus. Turtkul'; prev. Petroaleksandrovsk. Qoraqalpog'iston Respublikasi, W Uzbekistan 41.34N 61.00E
47 T9 Tortola island C British Virgin Islands
108 D9 Tortona anc. Dertona. Piemonte, NW Italy 44.54N 8.52E
109 L23 Tortorici Sicilia, Italy, C Mediterranean Sea 38.01N 14.49E
107 U7 Tortosa anc. Dertosa. Cataluña, E Spain 40.49N 0.31E
Tortosa see Ţarţūs
107 U7 Tortosa, Cap headland E Spain 40.43N 0.52E
46 L8 Tortue, Île de la var. Tortuga Island. island N Haiti
57 Y10 Tortue, Montagne ▲ C French Guiana
Tortuga, Isla see La Tortuga, Isla
Tortuga Island see Tortue, Île de la
56 C11 Tortugas, Golfo gulf W Colombia
47 T5 Tortuguero, Laguna lagoon N Puerto Rico
143 Q12 Tortum Erzurum, NE Turkey 40.15N 41.30E
Torugart, Pereval see Turugart Shankou
143 O12 Torul Gümüşhane, NE Turkey 40.34N 39.18E
112 J10 Toruń Ger. Thorn. Toruń, Kujawsko-pomorskie, C Poland 53.01N 18.36E
97 K20 Torup Halland, S Sweden 56.57N 13.04E
120 I6 Tõrva Ger. Törwa. Valgamaa, S Estonia 58.00N 25.54E
Törwa see Tõrva
98 D13 Tory Island Ir. Toraigh. island NW Ireland
113 N19 Torysa Hung. Tarca. ~ NE Slovakia
Torzburg see Bran
128 J16 Torzhok Tverskaya Oblast', W Russian Federation 57.04N 34.55E
170 Ee15 Tosa Kōchi, Shikoku, SW Japan 33.28N 133.25E
170 E16 Tosa-Shimizu var. Tosasimizu. Kōchi, Shikoku, SW Japan 32.46N 132.55E
Tosasimizu see Tosa-Shimizu
170 Ee16 Tosa-wan bay SW Japan
85 H21 Tosca North-West, N South Africa 25.51S 23.56E
108 F12 Toscana Eng. Tuscany. ◆ region C Italy
109 E14 Toscano, Archipelago Eng. Tuscan Archipelago. island group C Italy
108 G10 Tosco-Emiliano, Appennino Eng. Tuscan-Emilian Mountains. ▲ C Italy
Tōsei see Tungshih
171 J18 To-shima island Izu-shotō, SE Japan
153 Q9 Toshkent Eng./Rus. Tashkent. ● (Uzbekistan) Toshkent Viloyati, E Uzbekistan 41.19N 69.17E
153 Q9 Toshkent ✈ Toshkent Viloyati, E Uzbekistan 41.13N 69.15E
153 P9 Toshkent Viloyati Rus. Tashkentskaya Oblast'. ◆ province E Uzbekistan
128 H13 Tosno Leningradskaya Oblast', NW Russian Federation 59.34N 30.48E
165 Q10 Toson Hu ◎ C China
168 H6 Tosontsengel Dzavhan, NW Mongolia 48.42N 98.14E
152 I8 Tosquduq Qumlari prev. Goshquduq Qum, Rus. Peski Taskuduk. desert W Uzbekistan
107 U4 Tossal de l'Orri var. Llorri. ▲ NE Spain 42.24N 1.15E
63 A15 Tostado Santa Fe, C Argentina 29.14S 61.43W
120 F6 Tõstamaa Ger. Testama. Pärnumaa, SW Estonia 58.19N 23.58E
102 I10 Tostedt Niedersachsen, NW Germany 53.16N 9.42E
142 J11 Tosya Kastamonu, N Turkey 41.01N 34.01E
97 F15 Totak ◎ S Norway
107 R13 Totana Murcia, SE Spain 37.45N 1.30W
96 H13 Toten physical region S Norway
85 G18 Toteng Ngamiland, C Botswana 20.19S 22.57E
104 M3 Tôtes Seine-Maritime, N France 49.40N 1.02E
Totigi see Tochigi
Totio see Tochio
Totis see Tata
201 U13 Totiw island Chuuk, C Micronesia
129 N13 Tot'ma var. Totma. Vologodskaya Oblast', NW Russian Federation 59.58N 42.42E
Tot'ma see Sukhona
57 V9 Totness Coronie, N Suriname 5.51N 56.19W
44 C5 Totonicapán Totonicapán, W Guatemala 14.54N 91.18W
44 A2 Totonicapán off. Departamento de Totonicapán. ◆ department W Guatemala
63 B18 Totoras Santa Fe, C Argentina 32.34S 61.10W
197 K15 Totoya island S Fiji
191 Q7 Tottenham New South Wales, SE Australia 32.16S 147.23E
171 Gg13 Tottori Tottori, Honshū, SW Japan 35.29N 134.14E
170 Ff13 Tottori off. Tottori-ken. ◆ prefecture Honshū, SW Japan
78 I6 Touâjil Tiris Zemmour, N Mauritania 22.03N 12.39W
78 L15 Touba W Ivory Coast 8.16N 7.40W
78 G11 Touba W Senegal 14.55N 15.53W
76 E7 Toubkal, Jbel ▲ W Morocco 31.00N 7.50W
34 K10 Touchet Washington, NW USA 46.03N 118.40W
105 P7 Toucy Yonne, C France 47.45N 3.18E
79 O12 Tougan W Burkina 13.06N 3.03W
76 L7 Touggourt NE Algeria 33.07N 6.04E
79 Q12 Tougouri N Burkina 13.22N 0.25W
78 J13 Tougué Moyenne-Guinée, NW Guinea 11.28N 11.48W
78 K12 Toukoto Kayes, W Mali 13.24N 9.52W
105 S5 Toul Meurthe-et-Moselle, NE France 48.40N 5.54E
78 L16 Touléplеu var. Toulobli. W Ivory Coast 6.37N 8.27W
167 S14 Touliu C Taiwan 23.44N 120.27E
13 U3 Toulnustouc ~ Quebec, SE Canada
Toulobli see Touléplеu
105 T16 Toulon anc. Telo Martius, Tilio Martius. Var, SE France 43.07N 5.55E
32 K12 Toulon Illinois, N USA 41.04N 89.54W
104 M15 Toulouse anc. Tolosa. Haute-Garonne, S France 43.36N 1.24E
104 M15 Toulouse ✈ Haute-Garonne, S France 43.38N 1.19E
79 N16 Toumodi C Ivory Coast 6.34N 5.01W
76 G9 Tounassine, Hamada hill range W Algeria
177 G7 Toungoo Pegu, C Myanmar 18.57N 96.25E
104 L8 Touraine cultural region C France
Tourane see Đà Nẵng
105 P1 Tourcoing Nord, N France 50.43N 3.10E
106 F2 Touriñán, Cabo headland NW Spain 43.02N 9.20W
78 J6 Tourine Tiris Zemmour, N Mauritania 22.22N 11.49W
104 J3 Tourlaville Manche, N France 49.39N 1.34W
101 D19 Tournai var. Tournay, Dut. Doornik; anc. Tornacum. Hainaut, SW Belgium 50.36N 3.24E
104 L16 Tournay Hautes-Pyrénées, S France 43.10N 0.16E
Tournay see Tournai
105 R12 Tournon Ardèche, E France 45.04N 4.49E
105 R9 Tournus Saône-et-Loire, C France 46.33N 4.53E
61 Q14 Touros Rio Grande do Norte, E Brazil 5.10S 35.28W
104 L8 Tours anc. Caesarodunum, Turoni. Indre-et-Loire, C France 47.22N 0.40E
191 Q17 Tourville, Cape headland Tasmania, SE Australia 42.09S 148.20E
168 L8 Töv ◆ province C Mongolia
56 H7 Tovar Mérida, NW Venezuela 8.21N 71.45W
130 L5 Tovarkovskiy Tul'skaya Oblast', W Russian Federation 53.41N 38.18E
Tovil'-Dora see Tavildara
Tövis see Teiuș
143 V11 Tovuz Rus. Tauz. W Azerbaijan 40.58N 45.41E
172 N9 Towada Aomori, Honshū, C Japan 40.36N 141.11E
172 N9 Towada-ko var. Towada Ko. ◎ Honshū, C Japan
192 K3 Towai Northland, North Island, NZ 35.29S 174.06E
20 H12 Towanda Pennsylvania, NE USA 41.45N 76.25W
31 W4 Tower Minnesota, N USA 47.48N 92.16W
175 Pp8 Towera Sulawesi, N Indonesia 0.29S 120.01E
Tower Island see Genovesa, Isla
188 M13 Tower Peak ▲ Western Australia 33.23S 123.27E
37 U11 Towne Pass pass California, W USA
31 N3 Towner North Dakota, N USA 48.20N 100.27W
35 R10 Townsend Montana, NW USA 46.19N 111.31W
189 X6 Townsville Queensland, NE Australia 19.24S 146.52E
Towoeti Meer see Towuti, Danau
175 Q10 Towori, Teluk bay Sulawesi, C Indonesia
154 K4 Towraghoudī Herāt, NW Afghanistan 35.12N 62.19E
23 X3 Towson Maryland, NE USA 39.22N 76.33W
175 Q11 Towuti, Danau Dut. Towoeti Meer. ◎ Sulawesi, C Indonesia
Toxkan He see Ak-say
26 K9 Toyah Texas, SW USA 31.18N 103.47W
172 Nn6 Tōya-ko ◎ Hokkaidō, NE Japan
171 Ii13 Toyama Toyama, Honshū, SW Japan 36.41N 137.12E
171 Ii13 Toyama off. Toyama-ken. ◆ prefecture Honshū, SW Japan
171 J13 Toyama-wan bay W Japan
170 F16 Tōyo Ehime, Shikoku, SW Japan 33.57N 133.02E
170 Ee14 Tōyo Kōchi, Shikoku, SW Japan 33.28N 134.13E
Toyohara see Yuzhno-Sakhalinsk
171 Hh16 Toyohashi var. Toyohasi. Aichi, Honshū, SW Japan 34.45N 137.22E
Toyohasi see Toyohashi
171 I16 Toyokawa Aichi, Honshū, SW Japan 34.49N 137.22E
171 Gg13 Toyooka Hyōgo, Honshū, SW Japan 35.33N 134.48E
171 Kk12 Toyosaka Niigata, Honshū, C Japan 37.54N 139.12E
171 I16 Toyota Aichi, Honshū, SW Japan 35.04N 137.09E
172 Pp2 Toyotomi Hokkaidō, NE Japan 45.07N 141.45E
170 Dd12 Toyoura Yamaguchi, Honshū, SW Japan 34.09N 130.55E
Toytepa see To'ytepa
153 Q10 To'ytepa Rus. Toytepa. Toshkent Viloyati, E Uzbekistan 41.04N 69.22E
76 M6 Tozeur var. Tawzar. W Tunisia 34.00N 8.09E
41 Q8 Tozi, Mount ▲ Alaska, USA 65.45N 151.01W
143 Q9 Tqvarch'eli Rus. Tkvarcheli. NW Georgia 42.51N 41.42E
Trāblous see Tripoli
143 O11 Trabzon Eng. Trebizond; anc. Trapezus. Trabzon, NE Turkey 41.00N 39.43E
143 O11 Trabzon Eng. Trebizond. ◆ province NE Turkey
11 P13 Tracadie New Brunswick, SE Canada 47.31N 64.57W
Trachenberg see Żmigród
13 O11 Tracy Quebec, SE Canada 45.59N 73.07W
37 O8 Tracy California, W USA 37.43N 121.27W
31 S10 Tracy Minnesota, N USA 44.14N 95.37W
22 K10 Tracy City Tennessee, S USA 35.15N 85.44W
108 D7 Tradate Lombardia, N Italy 45.43N 8.57E
86 F6 Traena Bank undersea feature E Norwegian Sea
31 W13 Traer Iowa, C USA 42.11N 92.28W
106 J16 Trafalgar, Cabo de headland SW Spain 36.10N 6.03W

◆ Country ● Country Capital ◇ Dependent Territory ○ Dependent Territory Capital ◆ Administrative Region ✈ International Airport ▲ Mountain ▲ Mountain Range ▲ Volcano ~ River ◎ Lake ▣ Reservoir

Traiectum ad Mosam/Traiectum Tungorum *see* Maastricht
Tráigh Mhór *see* Tramore
9 *O17* **Trail** British Columbia, SW Canada *49.04N 117.46W*
60 *B11* **Traíra, Serra do** ⛰ NW Brazil
111 *V5* **Traisen** Niederösterreich, NE Austria *48.03N 15.37E*
111 *W4* **Traisen** ≈ NE Austria
111 *X4* **Traiskirchen** Niederösterreich, NE Austria *48.01N 16.18E*
Trajani Portus *see* Civitavecchia
Trajectum ad Rhenum *see* Utrecht
121 *H14* **Trakai** *Ger.* Traken, *Pol.* Troki. Trakai, SE Lithuania *54.39N 24.58E*
Traken *see* Trakai
99 *B20* **Tralee** *Ir.* Trá Lí. SW Ireland *52.16N 9.42W*
99 *A20* **Tralee Bay** *Ir.* Bá Thrá Lí. *bay* SW Ireland
Trá Lí *see* Tralee
Trälleborg *see* Trelleborg
Tralles *see* Aydın
63 *J16* **Tramandaí** Rio Grande do Sul, S Brazil *30.01S 50.11W*
110 *C7* **Tramelan** Bern, W Switzerland *47.13N 7.07E*
Trá Mhór *see* Tramore
99 *E20* **Tramore** *Ir.* Tráigh Mhór, Trá Mhór. S Ireland *52.10N 7.10W*
97 *L18* **Tranås** Jönköping, S Sweden *58.03N 15.00E*
64 *J7* **Trancas** Tucumán, N Argentina *26.10S 65.19W*
106 *I7* **Trancoso** Guarda, N Portugal *40.46N 7.21W*
97 *H22* **Tranebjerg** Århus, C Denmark *55.51N 10.36E*
97 *K19* **Tranemo** Västra Götaland, S Sweden *57.30N 13.19E*
178 *Gg16* **Trang** Trang, S Thailand *7.33N 99.36E*
176 *W14* **Trangan, Pulau** *island* Kepulauan Aru, E Indonesia
Trâng Dinh *see* Thât Khê
191 *Q7* **Trangie** New South Wales, SE Australia *32.01S 147.58E*
96 *K12* **Trängslet** Dalarna, C Sweden *61.22N 13.43E*
109 *N16* **Trani** Puglia, SE Italy *41.16N 16.24E*
63 *F17* **Tranqueras** Rivera, NE Uruguay *31.13S 55.45W*
65 *G17* **Tranqui, Isla** *island* S Chile
41 *V6* **Trans-Alaska pipeline** *oil pipeline* Alaska, USA
205 *Q10* **Transantarctic Mountains** ⛰ Antarctica
Transcarpathian Oblast *see* Zakarpats'ka Oblast'
Transilvania *see* Transylvania
Transilvaniei, Alpi *see* Carpații Meridionali
Transjordan *see* Jordan
180 *L11* **Transkei Basin** *undersea feature* SW Indian Ocean
127 *N17* **Trans-Siberian Railway** *Railroad* Russian Federation
Transsylvanische Alpen/Transylvanian Alps *see* Carpații Meridionali
96 *K12* **Transtrand** Dalarna, C Sweden *61.06N 13.19E*
118 *G10* **Transylvania** *Eng.* Ardeal, Transilvania, *Ger.* Siebenbürgen, *Hung.* Erdély. *cultural region* NW Romania
178 *Jj15* **Tra Ôn** Vinh Long, S Vietnam *9.58N 105.58E*
109 *H23* **Trapani** *anc.* Drepanum. Sicilia, Italy, C Mediterranean Sea *38.02N 12.31E*
178 *J12* **Trâpeăng Vêng** Kâmpóng Thum, C Cambodia *12.37N 104.58E*
Trapezus *see* Trabzon
116 *L9* **Trapoklovo** Sliven, C Bulgaria *42.40N 26.36E*
191 *P13* **Traralgon** Victoria, SE Australia *38.15S 146.35E*
78 *H9* **Trarza** ◈ *region* SW Mauritania
Trasimenischersee *see* Trasimeno, Lago
108 *H12* **Trasimeno, Lago** *Eng.* Lake of Perugia, *Ger.* Trasimenischersee. ◎ C Italy
97 *J20* **Träslövsläge** Halland, S Sweden *57.02N 12.18E*
Trás-os-Montes *see* Cucumbi
106 *I6* **Trás-os-Montes e Alto Douro** *former province* N Portugal
178 *I13* **Trat** *var.* Bang Phra. Trat, S Thailand *12.16N 102.30E*
Trá Tholl, Inis *see* Inishtrahull
Traù *see* Trogir
111 *T4* **Traun** Oberösterreich, N Austria *48.14N 14.13E*
111 *S5* **Traun** ≈ N Austria
Traun, Lake *see* Traunsee
103 *N23* **Traunreut** Bayern, SE Germany *47.58N 12.36E*
111 *S5* **Traunsee** *var.* Gmundner See, *Eng.* Lake Traun. ◎ N Austria
Trautenau *see* Trutnov
23 *P11* **Travelers Rest** South Carolina, SE USA *34.58N 82.26W*
190 *L8* **Travellers Lake** *seasonal lake* New South Wales, SE Australia
33 *P6* **Traverse City** Michigan, N USA *44.45N 85.37W*
1 *R7* **Traverse, Lake** ◎ Minnesota/South Dakota, N USA
193 *I16* **Travers, Mount** ▲ South Island, NZ *42.01S 172.46E*
9 *P17* **Travers Reservoir** ⊠ Alberta, SW Canada
8 *Jj15* **Tra Vinh** *var.* Phu Vinh. Tra Vinh, S Vietnam *9.57N 106.19E*
27 *S10* **Travis, Lake** ⊠ Texas, SW USA
114 *H12* **Travnik** Federacija Bosna I Hercegovina, C Bosnia and Herzegovina *44.14N 17.40E*
111 *V11* **Trbovlje** *Ger.* Trifail. C Slovenia *46.09N 15.03E*
25 *V13* **Treasure Island** Florida, SE USA *27.46N 82.46W*
Treasure State *see* Montana
195 *S14* **Treasury Islands** *island group* NW Solomon Islands
108 *D9* **Trebbia** *anc.* Trebia. ≈ NW Italy
102 *N8* **Trebel** ≈ NE Germany
105 *O16* **Trèbes** Aude, S France *43.12N 2.25E*
Trebia *see* Trebbia
113 *F18* **Třebíč** *Ger.* Trebitsch. Jihlavský Kraj, S Czech Republic *49.13N 15.52E*
115 *I16* **Trebinje** Republika Srpska, S Bosnia and Herzegovina *42.42N 18.19E*
Trebišnica *see* Trebišnjica
115 *H16* **Trebišnjica** *var.* Trebišnica. ≈ S Bosnia and Herzegovina
113 *N20* **Trebišov** *Hung.* Tőketerebes. Košický Kraj, E Slovakia *48.36N 21.44E*
Trebitsch *see* Třebíč
Trebizond *see* Trabzon
Trebnitz *see* Trzebnica
111 *V12* **Trebnje** SE Slovenia *45.54N 15.01E*
113 *D19* **Třeboň** *Ger.* Wittingau. Budějovický Kraj, S Czech Republic *49.00N 14.46E*
106 *J15* **Trebujena** Andalucía, S Spain *36.52N 6.10W*
102 *I7* **Treene** ≈ N Germany
Tree Planters State *see* Nebraska
111 *S9* **Treffen** Kärnten, S Austria *46.40N 13.51E*
Trefynwy *see* Monmouth
104 *G5* **Tréguier** Côtes d'Armor, NW France *48.50N 3.12W*
63 *G18* **Treinta y Tres** Treinta y Tres, E Uruguay *33.12S 54.19W*
63 *F18* **Treinta y Tres** ◈ *department* E Uruguay
125 *E11* **Trëkhgornyy** Chelyabinskaya Oblast', C Russian Federation *54.42N 58.25E*
116 *F9* **Treklyanska Reka** ≈ W Bulgaria
175 *R10* **Treko, Kepulauan** *island group* N Indonesia
104 *K8* **Trélazé** Maine-et-Loire, NW France *47.27N 0.28W*
65 *K17* **Trelew** Chubut, SE Argentina *43.13S 65.15W*
97 *K23* **Trelleborg** *var.* Trälleborg. Skåne, S Sweden *55.22N 13.10E*
115 *P15* **Trem** ▲ SE Serbia and Montenegro (Yugoslavia) *43.10N 22.12E*
13 *N11* **Tremblant, Mont** ▲ Quebec, SE Canada *46.13N 74.34W*
101 *H17* **Tremelo** Vlaams Brabant, C Belgium *50.59N 4.34E*
109 *M15* **Tremiti, Isole** *island group* SE Italy
32 *K12* **Tremont** Illinois, N USA *40.30N 89.31W*
38 *L1* **Tremonton** Utah, W USA *41.42N 112.09W*
107 *U4* **Tremp** Cataluña, NE Spain *42.09N 0.53E*
32 *J7* **Trempealeau** Wisconsin, N USA *44.00N 91.25W*
13 *P8* **Trenche** ≈ Quebec, SE Canada
13 *O7* **Trenche, Lac** ◎ Quebec, SE Canada
113 *I20* **Trenčiansky Kraj** ◈ *region* W Slovakia
113 *I19* **Trenčín** *Ger.* Trentschin, *Hung.* Trencsén. Trenčiansky Kraj, W Slovakia *48.54N 18.03E*
Trencsén *see* Trenčín
Trengganu *see* Terengganu
63 *A21* **Trenque Lauquen** Buenos Aires, E Argentina *36.00S 62.46W*
12 *J14* **Trent** ≈ Ontario, SE Canada
99 *N18* **Trent** ≈ C England, UK
Trent *see* Trento
108 *F5* **Trentino-Alto Adige** *prev.* Venezia Tridentina. ◈ *region* N Italy
108 *G6* **Trento** *Eng.* Trent, *Ger.* Trient; anc.Tridentum. Trentino-Alto Adige, N Italy *46.04N 11.07E*
12 *J15* **Trenton** Ontario, SE Canada *44.06N 77.36W*
25 *V10* **Trenton** Florida, SE USA *29.36N 82.49W*
25 *R1* **Trenton** Georgia, SE USA *34.52N 85.27W*
33 *S10* **Trenton** Michigan, N USA *42.08N 83.10W*
29 *S2* **Trenton** Missouri, C USA *40.04N 93.37W*
30 *M17* **Trenton** Nebraska, C USA *40.10N 101.00W*
20 *J15* **Trenton** *state capital* New Jersey, NE USA *40.13N 74.44W*
23 *W10* **Trenton** North Carolina, SE USA *35.03N 77.20W*
22 *G9* **Trenton** Tennessee, S USA *35.58N 88.56W*
38 *L1* **Trenton** Utah, W USA *41.53N 111.57W*
Trentschin *see* Trenčín
Treptow an der Rega *see* Trzebiatów
63 *C23* **Tres Arroyos** Buenos Aires, E Argentina *38.21S 60.16W*
63 *J15* **Três Cachoeiras** Rio Grande do Sul, S Brazil *29.21S 49.48W*
108 *E7* **Trescore Balneario** Lombardia, N Italy *45.43N 9.52E*
43 *V17* **Tres Cruces, Cerro** ▲ SE Mexico *15.28N 92.27W*
59 *K18* **Tres Cruces, Cordillera** ⛰ W Bolivia
115 *N18* **Treska** ≈ NW FYR Macedonia
115 *I14* **Treskavica** ⛰ SE Bosnia and Herzegovina
61 *J20* **Três Lagoas** Mato Grosso do Sul, SW Brazil *20.46S 51.43W*
42 *H12* **Tres Marías, Islas** *island group* C Mexico
61 *M19* **Três Marias, Represa** ⊠ SE Brazil
65 *F20* **Tres Montes, Península** *headland* S Chile *46.49S 75.29W*
107 *O3* **Trespaderne** Castilla-León, N Spain *42.46N 3.24W*
62 *G13* **Três Passos** Rio Grande do Sul, S Brazil *27.28S 53.55W*
63 *A23* **Tres Picos, Cerro** ▲ E Argentina *38.10S 61.54W*
65 *G17* **Tres Picos, Cerro** ▲ SW Argentina *42.22S 71.51W*
62 *I12* **Três Pinheiros** Paraná, S Brazil *25.25S 51.57W*
61 *M21* **Três Pontas** Minas Gerais, SE Brazil *21.33S 45.18W*
Tres Puntas, Cabo *see* Manabique, Punta
62 *P9* **Três Rios** Rio de Janeiro, SE Brazil *22.06S 43.15W*
Tres Tabernae *see* Saverne
Trestenberg/Trestendorf *see* Tăşnad
43 *R15* **Tres Valles** Veracruz-Llave, SE Mexico *18.14N 96.03W*
96 *H12* **Tretten** Oppland, S Norway *61.19N 10.19E*
Treuburg *see* Olecko
103 *K21* **Treuchtlingen** Bayern, S Germany *48.57N 10.55E*
102 *N13* **Treuenbrietzen** Brandenburg, E Germany *52.06N 12.52E*
97 *F16* **Treungen** Telemark, S Norway *59.00N 8.34E*
65 *H17* **Trevelín** Chubut, SW Argentina *43.02S 71.27W*
Treves/Trèves *see* Trier
108 *I13* **Trevi** Umbria, C Italy *42.52N 12.46E*
108 *E7* **Treviglio** Lombardia, N Italy *45.31N 9.34E*
106 *J4* **Trevinca, Peña** ▲ NW Spain *42.10N 6.49W*
107 *P3* **Treviño** Castilla-León, N Spain *42.45N 2.41W*
108 *I7* **Treviso** *anc.* Tarvisium. Veneto, NE Italy *45.40N 12.15E*
99 *G24* **Trevose Head** *headland* SW England, UK *50.33N 5.03W*
Trg *see* Feldkirchen in Kärnten
191 *P17* **Triabunna** Tasmania, SE Australia *42.33S 147.55E*
23 *W4* **Triangle** Virginia, NE USA *38.30N 77.17W*
85 *L18* **Triangle** Masvingo, SE Zimbabwe *20.58S 31.28E*
117 *L23* **Tría Nisía** *island* Kykládes, Greece, Aegean Sea
Triberg *see* Triberg im Schwarzwald
103 *G23* **Triberg im Schwarzwald** *var.* Triberg. Baden-Württemberg, SW Germany *48.07N 8.13E*
159 *P11* **Tribhuvan** ✈ (Kathmandu) Central, C Nepal
56 *C9* **Tribugá, Golfo de** *gulf* W Colombia
189 *W4* **Tribulation, Cape** *headland* Queensland, NE Australia *16.14S 145.48E*
110 *M8* **Tribulaun** ▲ SW Austria *46.59N 11.18E*
9 *U17* **Tribune** Saskatchewan, S Canada *49.16N 103.50W*
28 *H5* **Tribune** Kansas, C USA *38.28N 101.45W*
109 *N18* **Tricarico** Basilicata, S Italy *40.37N 16.09E*
109 *Q19* **Tricase** Puglia, SE Italy *39.56N 18.21E*
Trichinopoly *see* Tiruchchirāppalli
117 *D18* **Trichonída, Límni** ◎ C Greece
161 *G22* **Trichūr** *var.* Thrissur. Kerala, SW India *10.31N 76.13E*
Tricorno *see* Triglav
191 *O8* **Trida** New South Wales, SE Australia *33.02S 145.03E*
37 *S1* **Trident Peak** ▲ Nevada, W USA *41.52N 118.22W*
Tridentum/Trient *see* Trento
111 *T6* **Trieben** Steiermark, SE Austria *47.29N 14.27E*
103 *D19* **Trier** *Eng.* Treves, *Fr.* Trèves; *anc.* Augusta Treverorum. Rheinland-Pfalz, SW Germany *49.45N 6.39E*
108 *K7* **Trieste** *Slvn.* Trst. Friuli-Venezia Giulia, NE Italy *45.39N 13.45E*
Trieste, Golfo di/Triest, Golf von *see* Trieste, Gulf of
108 *J8* **Trieste, Gulf of** *Cro.* Tršćanski Zaljev, *Ger.* Golf von Triest, *It.* Golfo di Trieste, *Slvn.* Tržaški Zaliv. *gulf* S Europe
111 *W4* **Triesting** ≈ W Austria
Trifail *see* Trbovlje
118 *L9* **Trifeşti** Iaşi, NE Romania *47.30N 27.31E*
111 *S10* **Triglav** *It.* Tricorno. ▲ NW Slovenia *46.22N 13.40E*
106 *I14* **Trigueros** Andalucía, S Spain *37.24N 6.49W*
117 *E16* **Tríkala** *prev.* Trikkala. Thessalía, C Greece *39.33N 21.46E*
117 *E17* **Trikeriótis** ≈ C Greece
Trikkala *see* Tríkala
Trikomo/Tríkomon *see* İskele
99 *F17* **Trim** *Ir.* Baile Átha Troim. E Ireland *53.34N 6.46W*
110 *E7* **Trimbach** Solothurn, NW Switzerland *47.21N 7.49E*
111 *Q5* **Trimmelkam** Oberösterreich, N Austria *48.02N 12.55E*
31 *U11* **Trimont** Minnesota, N USA *43.45N 94.42W*
Trimontium *see* Plovdiv
Trinacria *see* Sicilia
161 *K24* **Trincomalee** *var.* Trinkomali. Eastern Province, NE Sri Lanka *8.34N 81.13E*
67 *K16* **Trindade, Ilha da** *island* Brazil, W Atlantic Ocean
49 *Y9* **Trindade Spur** *undersea feature* SW Atlantic Ocean
113 *J17* **Třinec** *Ger.* Trzynietz. Ostravský Kraj, E Czech Republic *49.42N 18.37E*
59 *M16* **Trinidad** Beni, N Bolivia *14.52S 64.54W*
56 *H9* **Trinidad** Casanare, E Colombia *5.25N 71.39W*
46 *E6* **Trinidad** Sancti Spíritus, C Cuba *21.48N 80.00W*
39 *U8* **Trinidad** Colorado, C USA *37.10N 104.31W*
63 *E19* **Trinidad** Flores, S Uruguay *33.34S 56.54W*
47 *Y17* **Trinidad** *island* C Trinidad and Tobago
Trinidad *see* Jose Abad Santos
47 *Y16* **Trinidad and Tobago** *off.* Republic of Trinidad and Tobago. ◆ *republic* SE West Indies
65 *F22* **Trinidad, Golfo** *gulf* S Chile
63 *B24* **Trinidad, Isla** *island* E Argentina
109 *N16* **Trinitapoli** Puglia, SE Italy *41.22N 16.06E*
57 *X10* **Trinité, Montagnes de la** ⛰ C French Guiana
27 *W9* **Trinity** Texas, SW USA *30.57N 95.22W*
11 *U12* **Trinity Bay** *inlet* Newfoundland and Labrador, E Canada
41 *P15* **Trinity Islands** *island group* Alaska, USA
37 *N2* **Trinity Mountains** ⛰ California, W USA
37 *S4* **Trinity Peak** ▲ Nevada, W USA *40.13N 118.43W*
37 *S5* **Trinity Range** ⛰ Nevada, W USA
37 *N2* **Trinity River** ≈ California, W USA
27 *V8* **Trinity River** ≈ Texas, SW USA
Trinkomali *see* Trincomalee
181 *Y15* **Triolet** NW Mauritius *20.04S 57.31E*
109 *O20* **Trionto, Capo** *headland* S Italy *39.37N 16.46E*
173 *Ee4* **Tripa, Krueng** ≈ Sumatera, NW Indonesia
117 *J16* **Tripití, Akrotírio** *headland* Ágios Efstrátios, E Greece *39.28N 24.58E*
144 *G6* **Tripoli** *var.* Tarābulus, Ţarābulus ash Shām, Trâblous; *anc.* Tripolis. N Lebanon *34.30N 35.42E*
31 *X12* **Tripoli** Iowa, C USA *42.48N 92.15W*
Tripoli *see* Ţarābulus
117 *F20* **Trípoli** *prev.* Trípolis. Pelopónnisos, S Greece *37.31N 22.22E*
Tripolis *see* Tripoli, Lebanon
Trípolis *see* Trípoli, Greece
31 *Q12* **Tripp** South Dakota, N USA *43.12N 97.57W*
159 *V15* **Tripura** *var.* Hill Tippera. ◈ *state* NE India
110 *K8* **Trisanna** ≈ W Austria
102 *H8* **Trischen** *island* NW Germany
67 *M24* **Tristan da Cunha** ◇ *dependency of Saint Helena* SE Atlantic Ocean
69 *P15* **Tristan da Cunha** *island* SE Atlantic Ocean
67 *L18* **Tristan da Cunha Fracture Zone** *tectonic feature* S Atlantic Ocean
178 *J14* **Tri Tôn** An Giang, S Vietnam *10.25N 105.01E*
178 *Ll11* **Triton Island** *island* S Paracel Islands
161 *G24* **Trivandrum** *var.* Thiruvanathapuram. Kerala, SW India *8.30N 76.57E*
113 *H20* **Trnava** *Ger.* Tyrnau, *Hung.* Nagyszombat. Trnavský Kraj, W Slovakia *48.22N 17.36E*
113 *H20* **Trnavský Kraj** ◈ *region* W Slovakia
Trnovo *see* Veliko Tŭrnovo
Trobriand Island *see* Kiriwina Island
Trobriand Islands *see* Kiriwina Islands
9 *Q16* **Trochu** Alberta, SW Canada *51.48N 113.12W*
111 *U7* **Trofaiach** Steiermark, SE Austria *47.24N 14.56E*
95 *F14* **Trofors** Troms, N Norway *65.31N 13.19E*
115 *E14* **Trogir** *It.* Traù. Split-Dalmacija, S Croatia *43.32N 16.13E*
114 *F13* **Troglav** ▲ Bosnia and Herzegovina/Croatia *44.00N 16.36E*
109 *M16* **Troia** Puglia, SE Italy *41.21N 15.19E*
109 *K24* **Troina** Sicilia, Italy, C Mediterranean Sea *37.48N 14.33E*
181 *O16* **Trois-Bassins** W Réunion *21.04S 55.18E*
103 *E17* **Troisdorf** Nordrhein-Westfalen, W Germany *50.49N 7.09E*
76 *H5* **Trois Fourches, Cap des** *headland* NE Morocco *35.27N 2.58W*
13 *T8* **Trois-Pistoles** Quebec, SE Canada *48.07N 69.10W*
101 *L21* **Trois-Ponts** Liège, E Belgium *50.22N 5.52E*
13 *P11* **Trois-Rivières** Quebec, SE Canada *46.21N 72.34W*
57 *Y12* **Trois Sauts** S French Guiana *2.15N 52.52W*
101 *M22* **Troisvierges** Diekirch, N Luxembourg *50.07N 6.00E*
125 *Ee12* **Troitsk** Chelyabinskaya Oblast', S Russian Federation *54.04N 61.31E*
129 *T9* **Troitsko-Pechorsk** Respublika Komi, NW Russian Federation *62.39N 56.06E*
131 *V7* **Troitskoye** Orenburgskaya Oblast', W Russian Federation *52.23N 56.24E*
Troki *see* Trakai
96 *F9* **Trolla** ▲ S Norway *62.41N 9.47E*
97 *J18* **Trollhättan** Västra Götaland, S Sweden *58.16N 12.19E*
96 *G9* **Trollheimen** ⛰ S Norway
96 *E9* **Trolltindane** ▲ S Norway *62.30N 7.43E*
60 *H11* **Trombetas, Rio** ≈ NE Brazil
132 *L16* **Tromelin, Île** *island* N Réunion
94 *I9* **Troms** ◈ *county* N Norway
94 *I9* **Tromsø** *Fin.* Tromssa. Troms, N Norway *69.42N 19.00E*
86 *F5* **Tromsøflaket** *undersea feature* W Barents Sea
Tromssa *see* Tromsø
96 *H10* **Tron** ▲ S Norway *62.12N 10.46E*
37 *U12* **Trona** California, W USA *35.46N 117.21W*
65 *G16* **Tronador, Cerro** ▲ S Chile *41.12S 71.51W*
96 *H8* **Trondheim** *Ger.* Drontheim; *prev.* Nidaros, Trondhjem. Sør-Trøndelag, S Norway *63.25N 10.24E*
96 *H7* **Trondheimsfjorden** *fjord* S Norway
Trondhjem *see* Trondheim
109 *J14* **Tronto** ≈ C Italy
Troodos *see* Ólympos
124 *N3* **Troódos** *var.* Troodos Mountains. ⛰ C Cyprus
Troodos Mountains *see* Troódos
98 *I13* **Troon** W Scotland, UK *55.32N 4.41W*
109 *M22* **Tropea** Calabria, SW Italy *38.40N 15.52E*
38 *L7* **Tropic** Utah, W USA *37.37N 112.04W*
66 *L10* **Tropic Seamount** *var.* Banc du Tropique. *undersea feature* E Atlantic Ocean *23.49N 20.40W*
Tropique, Banc du *see* Tropic Seamount
Tropoja *see* Tropojë
115 *L17* **Tropojë** *var.* Tropoja. Kukës, N Albania *42.25N 20.09E*
Troppau *see* Opava
97 *O16* **Trosa** Södermanland, C Sweden *58.54N 17.34E*
120 *H12* **Troškūnai** Anykščiai, E Lithuania *55.36N 24.55E*
103 *G23* **Trossingen** Baden-Württemberg, SW Germany *48.04N 8.37E*
119 *T4* **Trostyanets'** *Rus.* Trostyanets. Sums'ka Oblast', NE Ukraine *50.29N 34.58E*
119 *N7* **Trostyanets'** *Rus.* Trostyanets. Vinnyts'ka Oblast', C Ukraine *48.35N 29.10E*
118 *L11* **Trotuş** ≈ E Romania
46 *M8* **Trou-du-Nord** N Haiti *19.34N 71.57W*
27 *W7* **Troup** Texas, SW USA *32.08N 95.07W*
15 *H8* **Trout** ≈ Northwest Territories, NW Canada
35 *N8* **Trout Creek** Montana, NW USA *47.51N 115.40W*
34 *H10* **Trout Lake** Washington, NW USA *45.59N 121.33W*
10 *B9* **Trout Lake** ◎ Ontario, S Canada
35 *T12* **Trout Peak** ▲ Wyoming, C USA *44.36N 109.33W*
104 *L4* **Trouville** Calvados, N France *49.21N 0.07E*
99 *L22* **Trowbridge** S England, UK *51.19N 2.13W*
25 *Q6* **Troy** Alabama, S USA *31.48N 85.58W*
29 *Q3* **Troy** Kansas, C USA *39.46N 95.05W*
29 *W4* **Troy** Missouri, C USA *38.58N 90.58W*
20 *L10* **Troy** New York, NE USA *42.43N 73.37W*
23 *S10* **Troy** North Carolina, SE USA *35.21N 79.53W*
33 *R13* **Troy** Ohio, N USA *40.02N 84.12W*
27 *T9* **Troy** Texas, SW USA *31.12N 97.18W*
116 *I9* **Troyan** Lovech, N Bulgaria *42.53N 24.43E*
116 *I9* **Troyanski Prokhod** *pass* N Bulgaria *42.48N 24.38E*
151 *N6* **Troyebratskiy** Severnyy Kazakhstan, N Kazakhstan *54.21N 66.07E*
105 *Q6* **Troyes** *anc.* Augustobona Tricassium. Aube, N France *48.18N 4.04E*
119 *X5* **Troyits'ke** Luhans'ka Oblast', E Ukraine *49.55N 38.18E*
37 *W7* **Troy Peak** ▲ Nevada, W USA *38.18N 115.27W*
115 *G15* **Trpanj** Dubrovnik-Neretva, S Croatia *43.00N 17.18E*
Tršćanski Zaljev *see* Trieste, Gulf of
Trst *see* Trieste
115 *N14* **Trstenik** Serbia, C Serbia and Montenegro (Yugoslavia) *43.38N 21.01E*
130 *I6* **Trubchevsk** Bryanskaya Oblast', W Russian Federation *52.33N 33.45E*
Trubchular *see* Orlyak
39 *S10* **Truchas Peak** ▲ New Mexico, SW USA *35.57N 105.38W*
149 *P16* **Trucial Coast** *physical region* C UAE
Trucial States *see* United Arab Emirates
37 *Q6* **Truckee** California, W USA *39.18N 120.10W*
37 *R5* **Truckee River** ≈ Nevada, W USA
131 *Q13* **Trudfront** Astrakhanskaya Oblast', SW Russian Federation *45.56N 47.42E*
12 *I9* **Truite, Lac à la** ◎ Quebec, SE Canada
44 *K4* **Trujillo** Colón, NE Honduras *15.59N 85.54W*
58 *C12* **Trujillo** La Libertad, NW Peru *8.04S 79.02W*
106 *K10* **Trujillo** Extremadura, W Spain *39.28N 5.52W*
56 *I6* **Trujillo** Trujillo, NW Venezuela *9.19N 70.37W*
56 *I6* **Trujillo** *off.* Estado Trujillo. ◈ *state* W Venezuela
Truk *see* Chuuk
Truk Islands *see* Chuuk Islands
31 *U10* **Truman** Minnesota, N USA *43.49N 94.26W*
29 *X10* **Trumann** Arkansas, C USA *35.40N 90.30W*
38 *J9* **Trumbull, Mount** ▲ Arizona, SW USA *36.22N 113.09W*
116 *F9* **Trŭn** Pernik, W Bulgaria *42.51N 22.37E*
191 *Q8* **Trundle** New South Wales, SE Australia *32.55S 147.43E*
133 *U13* **Trung Phân** *physical region* S Vietnam
Trupcilar *see* Orlyak
11 *Q15* **Truro** Nova Scotia, SE Canada *45.20N 63.14W*
99 *H25* **Truro** SW England, UK *50.16N 5.03W*
27 *P5* **Truscott** Texas, SW USA *33.43N 99.48W*
118 *K9* **Truşeşti** Botoşani, NE Romania *47.45N 27.01E*
118 *H6* **Truskavets'** L'vivs'ka Oblast', W Ukraine *49.15N 23.30E*
97 *H22* **Trustrup** Århus, C Denmark *56.20N 10.46E*
8 *M11* **Trutch** British Columbia, W Canada *57.42N 123.00W*
39 *Q14* **Truth Or Consequences** New Mexico, SW USA *33.07N 107.15W*
113 *F15* **Trutnov** *Ger.* Trautenau. Hradecký Kraj, NE Czech Republic *50.34N 15.52E*
105 *P13* **Truyère** ≈ C France
116 *K9* **Tryavna** Lovech, N Bulgaria *42.52N 25.30E*
30 *M14* **Tryon** Nebraska, C USA *41.31N 100.56W*
96 *I11* **Trysilelva** ≈ S Norway
114 *D10* **Tržac** Federacija Bosna I Hercegovina, NW Bosnia and Herzegovina *44.58N 15.48E*
Tržaški Zaliv *see* Trieste, Gulf of
112 *G10* **Trzcianka** *Ger.* Schönlanke. Piła, Wielkopolskie, C Poland *53.01N 16.24E*
112 *E7* **Trzebiatów** *Ger.* Treptow an der Rega. Zachodniopomorskie, NW Poland *54.04N 15.14E*
113 *G14* **Trzebnica** *Ger.* Trebnitz. Dolnośląskie, SW Poland *51.18N 17.03E*
111 *T10* **Tržič** *Ger.* Neumarktl. NW Slovenia *46.22N 14.17E*
Trzynietz *see* Třinec
Tsabong *see* Tshabong
168 *G7* **Tsagaanchuluut** Dzavhan, C Mongolia *47.06N 96.40E*
169 *P7* **Tsagaanders** Dornod, NE Mongolia *48.03N 114.16E*
169 *S8* **Tsagaannuur** Dornod, E Mongolia *47.30N 118.45E*
168 *G8* **Tsagaan-Olom** Govĭ-Altay, C Mongolia *46.42N 96.30E*
168 *J8* **Tsagaan-Ovoo** Övörhangay, C Mongolia *45.57N 101.25E*
168 *D5* **Tsagaantüngi** Bayan-Ölgiy, NW Mongolia *49.06N 90.26E*
131 *P12* **Tsagan Aman** Respublika Kalmykiya, SW Russian Federation *47.37N 46.43E*
25 *V11* **Tsala Apopka Lake** ◎ Florida, SE USA
Tsamkong *see* Zhanjiang
Tsangpo *see* Brahmaputra
168 *L9* **Tsant** Dundgovĭ, C Mongolia *46.16N 106.55E*
85 *G17* **Tsao** Ngamiland, NW Botswana *20.08S 22.29E*
180 *I4* **Tsaratanana** Mahajanga, C Madagascar *16.46S 47.40E*
116 *N10* **Tsarevo** *prev.* Michurin. Burgas, E Bulgaria *42.10N 27.51E*
Tsarigrad *see* İstanbul
Tsaritsyn *see* Volgograd
128 *G13* **Tsarskoye Selo** *prev.* Pushkin. Leningradskaya Oblast', NW Russian Federation *59.42N 30.24E*
119 *T7* **Tsarychanka** Dnipropetrovs'ka Oblast', E Ukraine *48.56N 34.29E*
85 *H21* **Tsatsu** Southern, S Botswana *25.21S 24.45E*
83 *J20* **Tsavo** Coast, S Kenya *2.58S 38.28E*
85 *E21* **Tsawisis** Karas, S Namibia *26.18S 18.07E*
Tschakathurn *see* Čakovec
Tschaslau *see* Čáslav
Tschenstochau *see* Częstochowa
Tschernembl *see* Črnomelj
30 *K6* **Tschida, Lake** ⊠ North Dakota, N USA
Tschorna *see* Mustvee
85 *I17* **Tsebanana** Central, NE Botswana *19.50S 26.29E*
Tsefat *see* Ẕefat
168 *G8* **Tseel** Govĭ-Altay, SW Mongolia *45.45N 95.54E*
130 *M13* **Tselina** Rostovskaya Oblast', SW Russian Federation *46.31N 41.01E*
Tselinograd *see* Astana
Tselinogradskaya Oblast' *see* Akmola
168 *J6* **Tsengel** Hövsgöl, N Mongolia *49.29N 101.09E*
168 *E7* **Tsenher** Hovd, W Mongolia *47.07N 92.04E*
152 *E12* **Tsentral'nyye Nizmennyye Garagumy** *Turkm.* Mencezi Garagum. *desert* C Turkmenistan
85 *E21* **Tses** Karas, S Namibia *25.54S 18.09E*
Tseshevlya *see* Tsyeshawlya
168 *E7* **Tsetsegnuur** Hovd, W Mongolia *46.30N 93.16E*
168 *J7* **Tsetserleg** Arhangay, C Mongolia *47.28N 101.19E*
79 *R16* **Tsévié** S Togo *6.25N 1.13E*
85 *G21* **Tshabong** *var.* Tsabong. Kgalagadi, SW Botswana *26.01S 22.24E*
85 *G20* **Tshane** Kgalagadi, SW Botswana *24.02S 21.54E*
Tshangalele, Lac *see* Lufira, Lac de Retenue de la
85 *H17* **Tshauxaba** Central, C Botswana *19.56S 25.09E*
81 *F21* **Tshela** Bas-Congo, W Dem. Rep. Congo *4.55S 13.01E*
81 *K22* **Tshibala** Kasai Occidental, S Dem. Rep. Congo *6.53S 22.01E*
81 *J22* **Tshikapa** Kasai Occidental, SW Dem. Rep. Congo *6.23S 20.47E*
81 *L22* **Tshilenge** Kasai Oriental, S Dem. Rep. Congo *6.16S 23.48E*
81 *L24* **Tshimbalanga** Katanga, S Dem. Rep. Congo *9.42S 23.04E*
81 *L22* **Tshimbulu** Kasai Occidental, S Dem. Rep. Congo *6.27S 22.54E*
Tshiumbe *see* Chiumbe
81 *M21* **Tshofa** Kasai Oriental, C Dem. Rep. Congo *5.13S 25.13E*
81 *K18* **Tshuapa** ≈ C Dem. Rep. Congo
Tshwane *see* Pretoria
116 *G7* **Tsibritsa** ≈ NW Bulgaria
Tsien Tang *see* Puyang Jiang
116 *I12* **Tsigansko Gradishte** ▲ Bulgaria/Greece *41.24N 24.41E*
14 *G3* **Tsiigehtchic** *prev.* Arctic Red River. Northwest Territories, NW Canada *67.24N 133.40W*
129 *Q7* **Tsil'ma** ≈ NW Russian Federation
121 *J17* **Tsimkavichy** *Rus.* Timkovichi. Minskaya Voblasts', C Belarus *53.04N 26.58E*
130 *M11* **Tsimlyansk** Rostovskaya Oblast', SW Russian Federation *47.39N 42.05E*
131 *N11* **Tsimlyanskoye Vodokhranilishche** *var.* Tsimlyansk Vodoskhovshche, *Eng.* Tsimlyansk Reservoir ⊠ SW Russian Federation
Tsimlyansk Reservoir *see* Tsimlyanskoye Vodokhranilishche
Tsimlyansk Vodoskhovshche *see* Tsimlyanskoye Vodokhranilishche
Tsinan *see* Jinan
Tsing Hai *see* Qinghai Hu, China
Tsinghai *see* Qinghai, China
Tsingtao/Tsingtau *see* Qingdao
Tsingyuan *see* Baoding
Tsinkiang *see* Quanzhou
Tsintao *see* Qingdao
85 *D17* **Tsintsabis** Otjikoto, N Namibia *18.44S 17.57E*
180 *H8* **Tsiombe** *var.* Tsihombe. Toliara, S Madagascar
126 *Kk14* **Tsipa** ≈ S Russian Federation
180 *H5* **Tsiribihina** ≈ W Madagascar
180 *I5* **Tsiroanomandidy** Antananarivo, C Madagascar *18.43S 46.01E*
201 *U13* **Tsis** *island* Chuuk, C Micronesia
Tsitsihar *see* Qiqihar
131 *Q3* **Tsivil'sk** Chavash Respubliki, W Russian Federation *55.51N 47.30E*
143 *T9* **Ts'khinvali** *prev.* Staliniri. C Georgia *42.12N 43.58E*
121 *J19* **Tsna** ≈ SW Belarus
128 *I15* **Tsna** *var.* Zna. ≈ W Russian Federation
168 *K11* **Tsoohor** Ömnögovĭ, S Mongolia *43.15N 104.04E*
171 *H16* **Tsu** *var.* Tu. Mie, Honshū, SW Japan *34.40N 136.30E*
171 *K13* **Tsubame** *var.* Tubame. Niigata, Honshū, C Japan *37.39N 138.55E*
171 *Ii13* **Tsubata** Ishikawa, Honshū, SW Japan *36.33N 136.42E*
172 *Q6* **Tsubetsu** Hokkaidō, NE Japan *43.43N 144.01E*
171 *Kk16* **Tsuchiura** *var.* Tutiura. Ibaraki, Honshū, S Japan *36.03N 140.09E*
172 *N7* **Tsugaru-kaikyō** *strait* N Japan
171 *Kk13* **Tsugawa** Niigata, Honshū, C Japan *37.40N 139.26E*
172 *Oo5* **Tsukigata** Hokkaidō, NE Japan *43.18N 141.37E*
170 *Dd15* **Tsukumi** *var.* Tukumi. Ōita, Kyūshū, SW Japan *33.02N 131.51E*
168 *E5* **Tsul-Ulaan** Bayan-Ölgiy, W Mongolia *48.51N 91.13E*
85 *D17* **Tsumeb** Otjikoto, N Namibia *19.13S 17.42E*
85 *F17* **Tsumkwe** Otjozondjupa, NE Namibia *19.35S 20.26E*
170 *Cc16* **Tsuno** Miyazaki, Kyūshū, SW Japan *32.43N 131.32E*
170 *D11* **Tsuno-shima** *island* SW Japan
171 *H14* **Tsuruga** *var.* Turuga. Fukui, Honshū, SW Japan *35.38N 136.01E*
170 *F15* **Tsurugi-san** ▲ Shikoku, SW Japan *33.50N 134.04E*
170 *Dd15* **Tsurumi-zaki** *headland* Kyūshū, SW Japan *32.55N 132.03E*
171 *L11* **Tsuruoka** *var.* Turuoka. Yamagata, Honshū, C Japan *38.43N 139.48E*
171 *Hh15* **Tsushima** *var.* Tusima. Aichi, Honshū, SW Japan *35.10N 136.45E*
170 *C10* **Tsushima** *var.* Tsushima-tō, Tusima. *island group* SW Japan
Tsushima-tō *see* Tsushima
170 *E12* **Tsuwano** Shimane, Honshū, SW Japan *34.28N 131.43E*
170 *Ff13* **Tsuyama** *var.* Tuyama. Okayama, Honshū, SW Japan *35.03N 133.57E*
85 *G19* **Tswaane** Ghanzi, W Botswana *22.21S 21.52E*
121 *N16* **Tsyakhtsin** *Rus.* Tekhtin. Mahilyowskaya Voblasts', E Belarus *53.52N 29.43E*
121 *P19* **Tsyerakhowka** *Rus.* Terekhovka. Homyel'skaya Voblasts', SE Belarus *52.13N 31.24E*
121 *I17* **Tsyeshawlya** *Rus.* Cheshevlya, Tseshevlya. Brestskaya Voblasts', SW Belarus *53.13N 25.49E*
Tsyurupinsk *see* Tsyurupyns'k
119 *R10* **Tsyurupyns'k** *Rus.* Tsyurupinsk. Khersons'ka Oblast', S Ukraine *46.34N 32.42E*
Tu *see* Tsu
194 *H13* **Tua** ≈ C PNG
Tuaim *see* Tuam
192 *L6* **Tuakau** Waikato, North Island, NZ *37.16S 174.56E*
99 *C17* **Tuam** *Ir.* Tuaim. W Ireland *53.31N 8.49W*
193 *K14* **Tuamarina** Marlborough, South Island, NZ *41.27S 174.00E*
Tuamotu, Archipel des *see* Tuamotu, Îles
199 *M10* **Tuamotu Fracture Zone** *tectonic feature* E Pacific Ocean
203 *W9* **Tuamotu, Îles** *var.* Archipel des Tuamotu, Dangerous Archipelago, Tuamotu Islands. *island group* N French Polynesia
Tuamotu Islands *see* Tuamotu, Îles
183 *X10* **Tuamotu Ridge** *undersea feature* C Pacific Ocean
178 *Ii5* **Tuân Giao** Lai Châu, N Vietnam *21.34N 103.24E*
179 *P8* **Tuao** Luzon, N Philippines *17.42N 121.25E*
202 *B15* **Tuapa** NW Niue *18.57S 169.58W*
45 *N7* **Tuapi** Región Autónoma Atlántico Norte, NE Nicaragua *14.10N 83.18W*
130 *K15* **Tuapse** Krasnodarskiy Kray, SW Russian Federation *44.07N 39.07E*
175 *Nn2* **Tuaran** Sabah, East Malaysia *6.12N 116.12E*
106 *I6* **Tua, Rio** ≈ N Portugal
198 *B7* **Tuasivi** Savai'i, C Samoa *13.37S 172.07W*
193 *B24* **Tuatapere** Southland, South Island, NZ *46.09S 167.43E*
38 *M9* **Tuba City** Arizona, SW USA *36.08N 111.14W*
144 *H11* **Ţūbah, Qaşr aţ** *castle* Ma'ān, C Jordan *31.22N 36.39E*
Tubame *see* Tsubame
174 *Ll14* **Tuban** *prev.* Toeban. Jawa, C Indonesia *6.55S 112.01E*
147 *O16* **Tuban, Wādī** *dry watercourse* SW Yemen
63 *K14* **Tubarão** Santa Catarina, S Brazil *28.29S 49.00W*
100 *O10* **Tubbergen** Overijssel, E Netherlands *52.25N 6.46E*
Tubeke *see* Tubize
103 *H22* **Tübingen** *var.* Tuebingen. Baden-Württemberg, SW Germany *48.31N 9.04E*
131 *W6* **Tubinskiy** Respublika Bashkortostan, W Russian Federation *52.48N 58.18E*
101 *G19* **Tubize** *Dut.* Tubeke. Wallon Brabant, C Belgium *50.43N 4.14E*
78 *J16* **Tubmanburg** NW Liberia *6.50N 10.53W*
179 *Qq15* **Tubod** Mindanao, S Philippines *7.58N 123.46E*
77 *T7* **Ţubruq** *Eng.* Tobruk, *It.* Tobruch. NE Libya *32.04N 23.58E*
203 *T13* **Tubuai** *island* Îles Australes, SW French Polynesia
Tubuai, Îles/Tubuai Islands *see* Australes, Îles
42 *F3* **Tubutama** Sonora, NW Mexico *30.51N 111.31W*
56 *K4* **Tucacas** Falcón, N Venezuela *10.46N 68.19W*
61 *P16* **Tucano** Bahia, E Brazil *10.52S 38.48W*
59 *P19* **Tucavaca, Río** ≈ E Bolivia
112 *H8* **Tuchola** Kujawsko-pomorskie, C Poland *53.36N 17.49E*

◆ Country
● Country Capital
◇ Dependent Territory
○ Dependent Territory Capital
◈ Administrative Region
✈ International Airport
▲ Mountain
⛰ Mountain Range
Volcano
≈ River
◎ Lake
⊠ Reservoir

113 M17 **Tuchów** Małopolskie, S Poland 49.53N 21.04E
25 S3 **Tucker** Georgia, SE USA 33.53N 84.10W
29 W10 **Tuckerman** Arkansas, C USA 35.43N 91.12W
66 B12 **Tucker's Town** E Bermuda 32.19N 64.42W
Tuckum see Tukums
38 M15 **Tucson** Arizona, SW USA 32.13N 111.00W
64 J7 **Tucumán** off. Provincia de Tucumán. ◈ province N Argentina
Tucumán see San Miguel de Tucumán
39 V11 **Tucumcari** New Mexico, SW USA 35.10N 103.43W
60 H13 **Tucunaré** Pará, N Brazil 5.15S 55.49W
57 Q6 **Tucupita** Delta Amacuro, NE Venezuela 9.01N 62.04W
60 K13 **Tucuruí, Represa de** ⊠ NE Brazil
112 F9 **Tuczno** Zachodniopomorskie, NW Poland 53.12N 16.08E
Tuddo see Tudu
107 Q5 **Tudela** Basq. Tutera; anc. Tutela. Navarra, N Spain 42.04N 1.37W
106 M6 **Tudela de Duero** Castilla-León, N Spain 41.35N 4.34W
144 K6 **Tudmur** var. Tadmur, Tamar, Gk. Palmyra; Bibl. Tadmor. Ḥimṣ, C Syria 34.36N 38.15E
120 J4 **Tudu** Ger. Tuddo. Lääne-Virumaa, NE Estonia 59.12N 26.52E
Tuebingen see Tübingen
126 H16 **Tuekta** Respublika Altay, S Russian Federation 50.51N 85.52E
106 I5 **Tuela, Rio** ↝ N Portugal
159 X12 **Tuensang** Nāgāland, NE India 26.16N 94.45E
142 L15 **Tufanbeyli** Adana, C Turkey 38.15N 36.13E
Tüffer see Laško
194 M15 **Tufi** Northern, S PNG 9.04S 149.15E
199 L3 **Tufts Plain** undersea feature N Pacific Ocean
Tugalan see Kolkhozobod
69 V14 **Tugela** ↝ SE South Africa
23 P6 **Tug Fork** ↝ S USA
41 P15 **Tugidak Island** island Trinity Islands, Alaska, USA
179 P8 **Tuguegarao** Luzon, N Philippines 17.36N 121.47E
127 N13 **Tugur** Khabarovskiy Kray, SE Russian Federation 53.43N 137.00E
167 P4 **Tuhai He** ↝ E China
106 G4 **Tui** Galicia, NW Spain 42.02N 8.37W
79 O13 **Tui** var. Grand Balé. ↝ W Burkina
59 J16 **Tuichi, Río** ↝ W Bolivia
66 Q11 **Tuineje** Fuerteventura, Islas Canarias, Spain, NE Atlantic Ocean 28.18N 14.03W
45 X16 **Tuira, Río** ↝ SE Panama
Tuisarkan see Tūysarkān
Tujiabu see Yongxiu
131 W5 **Tukan** Respublika Bashkortostan, W Russian Federation 53.58N 57.29E
175 R13 **Tukangbesi, Kepulauan** Dut. Toekang Besi Eilanden. island group C Indonesia
153 V13 **Tŭkhtamish** Rus. Toktomush, prev. Tokhtamyshbek. SE Tajikistan 37.51N 74.41E
192 O12 **Tukituki** ↝ North Island, NZ
Tu-k'ou see Panzhihua
124 N15 **Tūkrah** NE Libya 32.28N 20.36E
14 G2 **Tuktoyaktuk** Northwest Territories, NW Canada 69.27N 133.00W
173 Ff6 **Tuktuk** Pulau Samosir, W Indonesia 2.32N 98.43E
Tukumi see Tsukumi
120 E9 **Tukums** Ger. Tuckum. Tukums, W Latvia 56.58N 23.12E
83 G24 **Tukuyu** prev. Neu-Langenburg. Mbeya, S Tanzania 9.13S 33.39E
Tukzār see Tokzār
43 O13 **Tula** var. Tula de Allende. Hidalgo, C Mexico 20.01N 99.17W
43 O11 **Tula** Tamaulipas, C Mexico 22.59N 99.43W
130 K5 **Tula** Tul'skaya Oblast', W Russian Federation 54.10N 37.39E
Tulach Mhór see Tullamore
Tula de Allende see Tula
165 N10 **Tulage Ar Gol** ↝ W China
195 X15 **Tulaghi** var. Tulagi. Florida Islands, C Solomon Islands 9.04S 160.09E
Tulagi see Tulaghi
43 P13 **Tulancingo** Hidalgo, C Mexico 20.34N 98.24W
37 R11 **Tulare** California, W USA 36.12N 119.21W
31 P9 **Tulare** South Dakota, N USA 44.43N 98.29W
37 Q12 **Tulare Lake Bed** salt flat California, W USA
39 S14 **Tularosa** New Mexico, SW USA 33.04N 106.01W
39 P13 **Tularosa Mountains** ▲▲ New Mexico, SW USA
39 S15 **Tularosa Valley** basin New Mexico, SW USA
85 E25 **Tulbagh** Western Cape, SW South Africa 33.16S 19.09E
58 C5 **Tulcán** Carchi, N Ecuador 0.44N 77.43W
119 N13 **Tulcea** Tulcea, E Romania 45.11N 28.48E
119 N13 **Tulcea** ◈ county SE Romania
Tul'chin see Tul'chyn
119 N7 **Tul'chyn** Rus. Tul'chin. Vinnyts'ka Oblast', C Ukraine 48.40N 28.48E
Tuléar see Toliara
37 O1 **Tulelake** California, W USA 41.57N 121.30W
118 J10 **Tulgheș** Hung. Gyergyótölgyes. Harghita, C Romania 46.57N 25.46E
Tul'govichi see Tul'havichy
121 N20 **Tul'havichy** Rus. Tul'govichi. Homyel'skaya Voblasts', SE Belarus 51.45N 29.41E
Tuli see Thuli
27 N4 **Tulia** Texas, SW USA 34.32N 101.45W
15 Gg6 **Tulita** prev. Fort Norman, Norman. Northwest Territories, NW Canada 64.55N 125.25W
22 J10 **Tullahoma** Tennessee, S USA 35.21N 86.12W
191 N12 **Tullamarine** ✕ (Melbourne) Victoria, SE Australia 37.40S 144.46E
191 Q7 **Tullamore** New South Wales, SE Australia 32.39S 147.35E
99 E18 **Tullamore** Ir. Tulach Mhór. C Ireland 53.16N 7.30W
105 N12 **Tulle** anc. Tutela. Corrèze, C France 45.16N 1.46E
111 X3 **Tulln** var. Oberhollabrunn. Niederösterreich, NE Austria 48.19N 16.01E
111 W4 **Tulln** ↝ NE Austria
24 H6 **Tullos** Louisiana, S USA 31.48N 92.19W
99 F19 **Tullow** Ir. An Tullach. SE Ireland 52.48N 6.43W
189 W5 **Tully** Queensland, NE Australia 18.03S 145.55E
128 J3 **Tuloma** ↝ NW Russian Federation
116 K10 **Tulovo** Stara Zagora, C Bulgaria 42.34N 25.34E
29 P9 **Tulsa** Oklahoma, C USA 36.09N 95.59W
159 N11 **Tulsipur** Mid Western, W Nepal 28.01N 82.22E
130 K6 **Tul'skaya Oblast'** ◈ province W Russian Federation
130 L14 **Tul'skiy** Respublika Adygeya, SW Russian Federation 44.26N 40.12E
194 K8 **Tulu** Manus Island, N PNG 1.58S 146.50E
56 D10 **Tuluá** Valle del Cauca, W Colombia 4.01N 76.16W
118 M12 **Tulucești** Galați, E Romania 45.35N 28.01E
41 N12 **Tuluksak** Alaska, USA 61.06N 160.57W
43 Z12 **Tulum, Ruinas de** ruins Quintana Roo, SE Mexico 20.13N 87.24W
126 Ii15 **Tulun** Irkutskaya Oblast', S Russian Federation 54.28N 100.18E
174 Ll15 **Tulungagung** prev. Toeloengagoeng. Jawa, C Indonesia 8.03S 111.54E
195 S11 **Tulun Islands** var. Kilinailau Islands; prev. Carteret Islands. island group NE PNG
130 M4 **Tuma** Ryazanskaya Oblast', W Russian Federation 55.09N 40.27E
56 B12 **Tumaco** Nariño, SW Colombia 1.51N 78.46W
56 B12 **Tumaco, Bahía de** bay SW Colombia
Tuman-gang see Tumen
44 L8 **Tuma, Río** ↝ N Nicaragua
97 O16 **Tumba** Stockholm, C Sweden 59.12N 17.49E
Tumba, Lac see Ntomba, Lac
174 M9 **Tumbangsenamang** Borneo, C Indonesia 1.16S 112.21E
191 Q10 **Tumbarumba** New South Wales, SE Australia 35.47S 148.03E
58 A8 **Tumbes** Tumbes, NW Peru 3.33S 80.27W
58 A9 **Tumbes** off. Departamento de Tumbes. ◈ department NW Peru
21 P5 **Tumbledown Mountain** ▲ Maine, NE USA 45.27N 70.28W
9 N13 **Tumbler Ridge** British Columbia, W Canada 55.06N 120.51W
178 I12 **Tumbŏt, Phnum** ▲ W Cambodia 12.23N 102.57E
190 G9 **Tumby Bay** South Australia 34.22S 136.05E
169 Y10 **Tumen** Jilin, NE China 42.58N 129.52E
169 Y11 **Tumen** Chin. Tumen Jiang, Kor. Tuman-gang, Rus. Tumyn'tszyan. ↝ E Asia
Tumen Jiang see Tumen
57 Q8 **Tumeremo** Bolívar, E Venezuela 7.19N 61.28W
161 G19 **Tumkūr** Karnātaka, W India 13.19N 77.06E
98 I10 **Tummel** ↝ C Scotland, UK
196 B15 **Tumon Bay** bay W Guam
79 P14 **Tumu** NW Ghana 10.51N 1.58W
60 I10 **Tumuc Humac Mountains** var. Serra Tumucumaque. ▲▲ N South America
Tumucumaque, Serra see Tumuc Humac Mountains
191 Q10 **Tumut** New South Wales, SE Australia 35.19S 148.12E
Tumyn'tszyan see Tumen
Tūn see Ferdows
47 U14 **Tunapuna** Trinidad, Trinidad and Tobago 10.38N 61.23W
62 K11 **Tunas** Paraná, S Brazil 24.57S 49.05W
Tunbridge Wells see Royal Tunbridge Wells
116 L11 **Tunca Nehri** Bul. Tundzha. ↝ Bulgaria/Turkey see also Tundzha
143 O14 **Tunceli** var. Kalan. Tunceli, E Turkey 39.07N 39.34E
143 O14 **Tunceli** ◈ province C Turkey
158 J12 **Tūndla** Uttar Pradesh, N India 27.13N 78.13E
83 I25 **Tunduru** Ruvuma, S Tanzania 11.07S 37.21E
116 L10 **Tundzha** Turk. Tunca Nehri. ↝ Bulgaria/Turkey see also Tunca Nehri
161 H17 **Tungabhadra** ↝ S India
161 G17 **Tungabhadra Reservoir** ◎ S India
203 P2 **Tungaru** prev. Gilbert Islands. island group W Kiribati
179 Q16 **Tungawan** Mindanao, S Philippines 7.33N 122.22E
174 Hh9 **Tungkal** ↝ Sumatera, W Indonesia
T'ung-shan see Xuzhou
167 Q16 **Tungsha Tao** Chin. Dongsha Qundao, Eng. Pratas Island. island S Taiwan
167 S13 **Tungshih** Jap. Tōsei. N Taiwan 24.13N 120.54E
14 G7 **Tungsten** Northwest Territories, W Canada 62.00N 128.09W
Tung-t'ing Hu see Dongting Hu
58 A13 **Tungurahua** ◈ province C Ecuador
97 F14 **Tunhovdfjorden** ◎ S Norway
24 K2 **Tunica** Mississippi, S USA 34.40N 90.22W
77 N5 **Tunis** var. Tūnis. ● (Tunisia) NE Tunisia 36.53N 10.10E
77 N5 **Tunis, Golfe de** Ar. Khalīj Tūnis. gulf NE Tunisia
77 N6 **Tunisia** off. Republic of Tunisia, Ar. Al Jumhūrīyah at Tūnisīyah, Fr. République Tunisienne. ◆ republic N Africa
Tūnisīyah, Al Jumhūrīyah at see Tunisia
Tūnis, Khalīj see Tunis, Golfe de
56 G9 **Tunja** Boyacá, C Colombia 5.33N 73.22W
95 F14 **Tunnsjøen** ◎ C Norway
41 N12 **Tuntutuliak** Alaska, USA 60.21N 162.40W
153 U8 **Tunuk** Chuyskaya Oblast', C Kyrgyzstan 42.11N 73.55E
11 Q6 **Tunungayualok Island** island Newfoundland and Labrador, E Canada
64 H11 **Tunuyán** Mendoza, W Argentina 33.28S 69.01W
207 P14 **Tunu** ◈ province E Greenland
64 I11 **Tunuyán, Río** ↝ W Argentina
Tunxi see Huangshan
37 P9 **Tuolumne River** ↝ California, W USA
Tuong Buong see Tương Đương
178 J7 **Tương Đương** var. Tuong Buong. Nghệ An, N Vietnam 19.14N 104.30E
166 I13 **Tuoniang Jiang** ↝ S China
165 N12 **Tuotuo He** ↝ C China
165 O12 **Tuotuoheyan** var. Tanggulashan, Togton-heyan. Qinghai, C China 34.13N 92.25E
Tüp see Tyup
62 J9 **Tupã** São Paulo, S Brazil 21.57S 50.28W
203 S10 **Tupai** var. Motu Iti. atoll Îles Sous le Vent, W French Polynesia
63 G15 **Tupanciretã** Rio Grande do Sul, S Brazil 29.06S 53.48W
24 M2 **Tupelo** Mississippi, S USA 34.15N 88.42W
126 L14 **Tupik** Chitinskaya Oblast', S Russian Federation 54.21N 119.56E
61 K18 **Tupiraçaba** Goiás, S Brazil 14.33S 48.40W
59 L21 **Tupiza** Potosí, S Bolivia 21.27S 65.45W
9 N13 **Tupper** British Columbia, W Canada 55.30N 119.59W
20 J8 **Tupper Lake** ◎ New York, NE USA
152 J10 **Tuproqqal'a** Rus. Turpakkla. Xorazm Viloyati, W Uzbekistan 40.52N 62.00E
64 H11 **Tupungato, Volcán** ▲ W Argentina 33.27S 69.42W
169 T9 **Tuquan** Nei Mongol Zizhiqu, N China 45.21N 121.36E
56 C13 **Túquerres** Nariño, SW Colombia 1.06N 77.37W
159 U13 **Tura** Meghālaya, NE India 25.33N 90.14E
126 J10 **Tura** Evenkiyskiy Avtonomnyy Okrug, N Russian Federation 64.19N 100.16E
125 F11 **Tura** ↝ C Russian Federation
146 M10 **Turabah** Makkah, W Saudi Arabia 21.27N 41.40E
57 O8 **Turagua, Cerro** ▲ C Venezuela 6.59N 64.34W
192 L12 **Turakina** Manawatu-Wanganui, North Island, NZ 40.03S 175.13E
193 K15 **Turakirae Head** headland North Island, NZ 41.26S 174.54E
194 G13 **Turama** ↝ S PNG
126 I15 **Turan** Respublika Tyva, S Russian Federation 52.11N 93.40E
192 M10 **Turangi** Waikato, North Island, NZ 39.01S 175.46E
152 F11 **Turan Lowland** var. Turan Plain, Kaz. Turan Oypaty, Rus. Turanskaya Nizmennost', Turk. Turan Pesligi, Uzb. Turon Pasttekisligi. plain C Asia
Turan Oypaty/Turan Pesligi/Turan Plain/Turanskaya Nizmennost' see Turan Lowland
144 K7 **Ţurāq al 'Ilab** hill range S Syria
121 K20 **Turaw** Rus. Turov. Homyel'skaya Voblasts', SE Belarus 52.04N 27.41E
146 L2 **Ţurayf** Al Ḥudūd ash Shamālīyah, NW Saudi Arabia 31.43N 38.39E
Turba see Teruel
56 E5 **Turbaco** Bolívar, N Colombia 10.19N 75.25W
154 K15 **Turbat** Baluchistān, SW Pakistan 26.02N 62.56E
Turbat-i-Haidari see Torbat-e Ḩeydarīyeh
Turbat-i-Jam see Torbat-e Jām
56 D7 **Turbo** Antioquia, NW Colombia 8.06N 76.43W
Turčianský Svätý Martin see Martin
118 H10 **Turda** Ger. Thorenburg, Hung. Torda. Cluj, NW Romania 46.34N 23.49E
148 M7 **Ţūreh** Markazī, W Iran
203 X12 **Tureia** atoll Îles Tuamotu, SE French Polynesia
112 I12 **Turek** Wielkopolskie, C Poland 52.01N 18.30E
95 L19 **Turenki** Etelä-Suomi, S Finland 60.55N 24.37E
Turfan see Turpan
151 R8 **Turgay** Kaz. Torghay. Akmola, W Kazakhstan 51.43N 72.46E
151 N10 **Turgay** Kaz. Torgay. ↝ C Kazakhstan
150 M8 **Turgayskaya Stolovaya Strana** Kaz. Torgay Üstirti. plateau Kazakhstan/Russian Federation
Turgel see Türi
116 L8 **Tŭrgovishte** prev. Eski Dzhumaya. Tŭrgovishte, N Bulgaria 43.15N 26.33E
116 L8 **Tŭrgovishte** ◈ province N Bulgaria
142 C14 **Turgutlu** Manisa, W Turkey 38.30N 27.43E
142 L12 **Turhal** Tokat, N Turkey 40.22N 36.04E
120 H4 **Türi** Ger. Turgel. Järvamaa, N Estonia 58.49N 25.25E
107 S9 **Turia** ↝ E Spain
60 M12 **Turiaçu** Maranhão, E Brazil 1.40S 45.22W
Turin see Torino
118 I3 **Turiys'k** Volyns'ka Oblast', NW Ukraine 51.05N 24.31E
Turja see Tur"ya
126 K15 **Turka** Respublika Buryatiya, S Russian Federation 53.02N 108.19E
118 H6 **Turka** L'vivs'ka Oblast', W Ukraine 49.07N 23.01E
83 H16 **Turkana, Lake** var. Lake Rudolf. ◎ N Kenya
151 P16 **Turkestan** Kaz. Türkistan. Yuzhnyy Kazakhstan, S Kazakhstan 43.18N 68.18E
153 Q12 **Turkestan Range** Rus. Turkestanskiy Khrebet. ▲▲ C Asia
Turkestanskiy Khrebet see Turkestan Range
113 M23 **Túrkeve** Jász-Nagykun-Szolnok, E Hungary 47.07N 20.48E
27 O4 **Turkey** Texas, SW USA 34.23N 100.54W
142 H14 **Turkey** off. Republic of Turkey, Turk. Türkiye Cumhuriyeti. ◆ republic SW Asia
189 N4 **Turkey Creek** Western Australia 16.54S 128.12E
28 M9 **Turkey Creek** ↝ Oklahoma, C USA
39 T9 **Turkey Mountains** ▲▲ New Mexico, SW USA
31 X11 **Turkey River** ↝ Iowa, C USA
131 N7 **Turki** Saratovskaya Oblast', W Russian Federation 52.00N 43.16E
124 Nn2 **Turkish Republic of Northern Cyprus** ◇ disputed territory Cyprus
Türkistan see Turkestan
Turkistan, Bandi-i see Torkestān, Selseleh-ye Band-e
Türkiye Cumhuriyeti see Turkey
Türkmen Aylagy see Turkmenskiy Zaliv
152 A10 **Turkmenbashi** prev. Krasnovodsk. Balkanskiy Velayat, W Turkmenistan 40.00N 53.04E
Türkmengala see Turkmen-kala
152 G13 **Turkmenistan** off. Turkmenistan; prev. Turkmenskaya Soviet Socialist Republic. ◆ republic C Asia
152 J14 **Turkmen-kala** Turkm. Türkmengala; prev. Turkmen-Kala. Maryyskiy Velayat, S Turkmenistan 37.25N 62.19E
Turkmenskaya Soviet Socialist Republic see Turkmenistan
152 A11 **Turkmenskiy Zaliv** Turkm. Türkmen Aylagy. lake gulf W Turkmenistan
142 L16 **Türkoğlu** Kahramanmaraş, S Turkey 37.24N 36.49E
46 L6 **Turks and Caicos Islands** ◇ UK dependent territory N West Indies
66 G10 **Turks and Caicos Islands** island group N West Indies
47 N6 **Turks Islands** island group SE Turks and Caicos Islands
95 K19 **Turku** Swe. Åbo. Länsi-Suomi, W Finland 60.27N 22.16E
83 H17 **Turkwel** seasonal river NW Kenya
29 P9 **Turley** Oklahoma, C USA 36.14N 95.58W
37 P9 **Turlock** California, W USA 37.29N 120.52W
120 I12 **Turmantas** Zarasai, NE Lithuania 55.41N 26.27E
56 L5 **Turmero** Aragua, N Venezuela 10.14N 66.40W
Turnberg see Wieżyca
192 N13 **Turnagain, Cape** headland North Island, NZ 40.30S 176.36E
Turnau see Turnov
44 H2 **Turneffe Islands** island group E Belize
20 M11 **Turners Falls** Massachusetts, NE USA 42.36N 72.31W
9 P16 **Turner Valley** Alberta, SW Canada 50.43N 114.19W
101 I16 **Turnhout** Antwerpen, N Belgium 51.19N 4.57E
111 V5 **Turnitz** Niederösterreich, E Austria 47.56N 15.26E
9 S12 **Turnor Lake** ◎ Saskatchewan, C Canada
113 E15 **Turnov** Ger. Turnau. Liberecký Kraj, N Czech Republic 50.36N 15.10E
Tŭrnovo see Veliko Tŭrnovo
118 I15 **Turnu Măgurele** var. Turnu-Măgurele. Teleorman, S Romania 43.43N 24.52E
Turnu Severin see Drobeta-Turnu Severin
Turócszentmárton see Martin
Turoni see Tours
Turon Pasttekisligi see Turan Lowland
Turov see Turaw
Turpakkla see Tuproqqal'a
164 M6 **Turpan** var. Turfan. Xinjiang Uygur Zizhiqu, NW China 42.54N 89.06E
Turpan Depression see Turpan Pendi
164 M6 **Turpan Pendi** Eng. Turpan Depression. depression NW China
164 M5 **Turpan Zhan** Xinjiang Uygur Zizhiqu, W China 43.10N 89.06E
Turpentine State see North Carolina
46 H8 **Turquino, Pico** ▲ E Cuba 19.54N 76.55W
29 Y10 **Turrell** Arkansas, C USA 35.22N 90.13W
45 N14 **Turrialba** Cartago, E Costa Rica 9.52N 83.40W
98 K8 **Turriff** NE Scotland, UK 57.32N 2.28W
145 V7 **Tursāq** E Iraq 33.27N 45.47E
Turshiz see Kāshmar
Tursunzade see Tursunzoda
153 P13 **Tursunzoda** Rus. Tursunzade; prev. Regar. W Tajikistan 38.30N 68.10E
168 J4 **Turt** Hövsgöl, N Mongolia 51.30N 100.40E
Türtkül see To'rtkok'l
31 O9 **Turtle Creek** ↝ South Dakota, N USA
32 K4 **Turtle Flambeau Flowage** ⊠ Wisconsin, N USA
9 S14 **Turtleford** Saskatchewan, S Canada 53.21N 108.48W
30 M4 **Turtle Lake** North Dakota, N USA 47.31N 100.53W
94 K12 **Turtola** Lappi, NW Finland 66.39N 23.55E
126 Jj10 **Turu** ↝ N Russian Federation
Turuga see Tsuruga
153 V10 **Turugart Pass** pass China/Kyrgyzstan 40.33N 74.04E
164 E7 **Turugart Shankou** var. Pereval Torugart. pass China/Kyrgyzstan 40.33N 75.21E
126 Hh9 **Turukhan** ↝ N Russian Federation
126 I9 **Turukhansk** Krasnoyarskiy Kray, N Russian Federation 65.50N 87.48E
145 N3 **Ţurumbah** well NE Syria 36.09N 40.24E
Turuoka see Tsuruoka
150 H14 **Turush** Mangistau, SW Kazakhstan 45.24N 56.02E
62 K7 **Turvo, Rio** ↝ S Brazil
118 J2 **Tur"ya** Pol. Turja, Rus. Tur'ya. ↝ NW Ukraine
25 O4 **Tuscaloosa** Alabama, S USA 33.12N 87.34W
25 O4 **Tuscaloosa, Lake** ◎ Alabama, S USA
Tuscan Archipelago see Toscano, Archipelago
Tuscan-Emilian Mountains see Tosco-Emiliano, Appennino
Tuscany see Toscana
37 V2 **Tuscarora** Nevada, W USA 41.16N 116.13W
20 F15 **Tuscarora Mountain** ridge Pennsylvania, NE USA
32 M14 **Tuscola** Illinois, N USA 39.46N 88.19W
27 P7 **Tuscola** Texas, SW USA 32.12N 99.48W
25 O2 **Tuscumbia** Alabama, S USA 34.43N 87.42W
94 O4 **Tusenøyane** island group S Svalbard
150 K13 **Tushybas, Zaliv** prev. Zaliv Paskevicha. lake gulf SW Kazakhstan
Tusima see Tsushima
176 Z14 **Tusirah** Papua, E Indonesia 6.46S 140.19E
25 Q5 **Tuskegee** Alabama, S USA 32.25N 85.41W
96 E8 **Tustna** island S Norway
41 R12 **Tustumena Lake** ◎ Alaska, USA
112 K13 **Tuszyn** Łodzkie, C Poland 51.36N 19.31E
143 S13 **Tutak** Ağrı, E Turkey 39.34N 42.48E
193 C20 **Tutamoe Range** ▲▲ North Island, NZ
Tutasev see Tutayev
128 L15 **Tutayev** var. Tutasev. Yaroslavskaya Oblast', W Russian Federation 57.51N 39.29E
Tutela see Tulle, France
Tutela see Tudela, Spain
Tutera see Tudela
161 H23 **Tuticorin** Tamil Nādu, SE India 8.48N 78.10E
115 L15 **Tutin** Serbia, S Serbia and Montenegro (Yugoslavia) 43.00N 20.20E
192 O10 **Tutira** Hawke's Bay, North Island, NZ 39.14S 176.53E
Tutiura see Tsuchiura
126 Ii10 **Tutonchany** Evenkiyskiy Avtonomnyy Okrug, N Russian Federation 64.12N 93.52E
116 L6 **Tutrakan** Silistra, NE Bulgaria 44.03N 26.38E
31 N5 **Tuttle** North Dakota, N USA 47.07N 99.58W
28 M11 **Tuttle** Oklahoma, C USA 35.17N 97.48W
29 O3 **Tuttle Creek Lake** ⊠ Kansas, C USA
103 H23 **Tuttlingen** Baden-Württemberg, S Germany 47.58N 8.49E
175 Ss16 **Tutuala** W East Timor 8.23S 127.12E
198 Cc9 **Tutuila** island W American Samoa
85 I18 **Tutume** Central, E Botswana 20.27S 26.58E
41 N7 **Tututalak Mountain** ▲ Alaska, USA 67.51N 161.27W
24 K3 **Tutwiler** Mississippi, S USA 34.00N 90.25W
168 L8 **Tuul Gol** ↝ N Mongolia
95 O16 **Tuupovaara** Itä-Suomi, E Finland 62.30N 30.40E
Tuva see Tyva, Respublika
202 E7 **Tuvalu** prev. Ellice Islands. ◆ commonwealth republic SW Pacific Ocean
197 L17 **Tuvana-i-colo** prev. Tuvana-i-tholo. island Lau Group, SE Fiji
197 L18 **Tuvana-i-ra** island Lau Group, SE Fiji
Tuvana-i-tholo see Tuvana-i-colo
Tuvinskaya ASSR see Tyva, Respublika
197 L14 **Tuvuca** prev. Tuvutha. island Lau Group, E Fiji
Tuvutha see Tuvuca
147 P9 **Ţuwayq, Jabal** ▲▲ C Saudi Arabia
144 H13 **Ţuwayyil ash Shihāq** desert S Jordan
9 U16 **Tuxford** Saskatchewan, S Canada 50.33N 105.32W
178 K13 **Tu Xoay** Đắc Lắc, S Vietnam 12.18N 107.33E
42 L14 **Tuxpan** Jalisco, C Mexico 19.33N 103.21W
42 J12 **Tuxpan** Nayarit, C Mexico 21.57N 105.12W
43 Q12 **Tuxpán** var. Tuxpán de Rodríguez Cano. Veracruz-Llave, E Mexico 20.58N 97.22W
Tuxpán de Rodríguez Cano see Tuxpán
43 R15 **Tuxtepec** var. San Juan Bautista Tuxtepec. Oaxaca, S Mexico 18.01N 96.05W
43 U16 **Tuxtla** var. Tuxtla Gutiérrez. Chiapas, SE Mexico 16.43N 93.03W
Tuxtla see San Andrés Tuxtla
Tuxtla Gutiérrez see Tuxtla
Tuyama see Tsuyama
178 Jj5 **Tuyên Quang** Tuyên Quang, N Vietnam 21.48N 105.10E
178 K14 **Tuy Hoa** Binh Thuân, S Vietnam 11.03N 108.12E
178 Kk12 **Tuy Hoa** Phu Yên, S Vietnam 13.01N 109.15E
131 U5 **Tuymazy** Respublika Bashkortostan, W Russian Federation 54.36N 53.40E
148 L6 **Tūysarkān** var. Tuisarkan, Tuyserkān. Hamadān, W Iran 34.31N 48.30E
Tuyserkān see Tūysarkān
151 W16 **Tuyuk** Kaz. Tuyyq. Almaty, SE Kazakhstan 43.07N 79.24E
Tuyyq see Tuyuk
142 I14 **Tuz Gölü** ◎ C Turkey
129 Q15 **Tuzha** Kirovskaya Oblast', NW Russian Federation 57.37N 48.02E
115 K17 **Tuzi** Montenegro, SW Serbia and Montenegro (Yugoslavia) 42.22N 19.21E
145 T5 **Tūz Khurmātū** N Iraq 34.55N 44.37E
114 I11 **Tuzla** Federacija Bosna I Hercegovina, NE Bosnia and Herzegovina 44.33N 18.40E
119 N15 **Tuzla** Constanța, SE Romania 43.58N 28.38E
143 T12 **Tuzluca** Iğdır, NE Turkey 40.01N 43.39E
97 J20 **Tvååker** Halland, S Sweden 57.04N 12.25E
97 F17 **Tvedestrand** Aust-Agder, S Norway 58.37N 8.55E
128 J16 **Tver'** prev. Kalinin. Tverskaya Oblast', W Russian Federation 56.52N 35.52E
Tverya see Teverya
130 I15 **Tverskaya Oblast'** ◈ province W Russian Federation
128 I15 **Tvertsa** ↝ W Russian Federation
112 H13 **Twardogóra** Ger. Festenberg. Dolnośląskie, SW Poland 51.21N 17.27E
12 J14 **Tweed** Ontario, SE Canada 44.28N 77.19W
98 K13 **Tweed** ↝ England/Scotland, UK
100 O7 **Tweede-Exloërmond** Drenthe, NE Netherlands 52.55N 6.55E
191 V3 **Tweed Heads** New South Wales, SE Australia 28.10S 153.32E
100 M11 **Twello** Gelderland, E Netherlands 52.13N 6.07E
37 W15 **Twentynine Palms** California, W USA 34.08N 116.03W
27 P9 **Twin Buttes Reservoir** ⊠ Texas, SW USA
35 O15 **Twin Falls** Idaho, NW USA 42.33N 114.27W
41 N13 **Twin Hills** Alaska, USA 59.06N 160.21W
9 O11 **Twin Lakes** Alberta, W Canada 57.46N 117.30W
35 O12 **Twin Peaks** ▲ Idaho, NW USA 44.37N 114.24W
193 I14 **Twins, The** ▲ South Island, NZ 41.14S 172.38E
31 S5 **Twin Valley** Minnesota, N USA 47.15N 96.15W
102 G11 **Twistringen** Niedersachsen, NW Germany 52.48N 8.39E
193 E20 **Twizel** Canterbury, South Island, NZ 44.15S 170.06E
31 X5 **Two Harbors** Minnesota, N USA 47.01N 91.40W
9 R14 **Two Hills** Alberta, SW Canada 53.40N 111.43W
33 N7 **Two Rivers** Wisconsin, N USA 44.10N 87.33W
118 H8 **Tyachiv** Zakarpats'ka Oblast', W Ukraine 48.02N 23.35E
Tyan'-Shan' see Tien Shan
177 Ff3 **Tyao** ↝ Myanmar/India
119 R6 **Tyas'myn** ↝ N Ukraine
25 X6 **Tybee Island** Georgia, SE USA 32.00N 80.51W
Tyborøn see Thyborøn
113 J16 **Tychy** Ger. Tichau. Śląskie, S Poland 50.12N 19.01E
113 O16 **Tyczyn** Podkarpackie, SE Poland 49.58N 22.03E
96 I8 **Tydal** Sør-Trøndelag, S Norway 63.01N 11.36E
117 H24 **Tyflós** ↝ Kríti, Greece, E Mediterranean Sea
23 S3 **Tygart Lake** ⊠ West Virginia, NE USA
126 M15 **Tygda** Amurskaya Oblast', SE Russian Federation 53.07N 126.12E
23 Q11 **Tyger River** ↝ South Carolina, SE USA
34 I11 **Tygh Valley** Oregon, NW USA 45.15N 121.12W
96 F12 **Tyin** ◎ S Norway
31 S10 **Tyler** Minnesota, N USA 44.16N 96.07W
27 W7 **Tyler** Texas, SW USA 32.21N 95.18W
27 W7 **Tyler, Lake** ⊠ Texas, SW USA
24 K7 **Tylertown** Mississippi, S USA 31.07N 90.08W
119 P10 **Tylihuls'kyy Lyman** ◎ SW Ukraine
Tylos see Bahrain
126 Gg12 **Tym** ↝ C Russian Federation
117 C15 **Týmfi** var. Timfi. ▲ W Greece 39.58N 20.51E
117 E17 **Tymfristós** var. Timfristos. ▲ C Greece 38.57N 21.49E
127 O14 **Tymovskoye** Ostrov Sakhalin, Sakhalinskaya Oblast', SE Russian Federation 50.36N 142.45E
117 J25 **Tympáki** var. Timbaki; prev. Timbákion. Kríti, Greece, E Mediterranean Sea 35.04N 24.46E
126 Ll14 **Tynda** Amurskaya Oblast', SE Russian Federation 55.09N 124.43E
31 Q12 **Tyndall** South Dakota, N USA 42.57N 97.52W
99 L14 **Tyne** ↝ N England, UK
99 M14 **Tynemouth** NE England, UK 55.01N 1.24W
99 L14 **Tyneside** cultural region NE England, UK
96 H10 **Tynset** Hedmark, S Norway 61.45N 10.48E
41 Q12 **Tyonek** Alaska, USA 61.04N 151.08W
Tyôsi see Chōshi
Tyras see Dniester, Moldova/Ukraine
Tyras see Bilhorod-Dnistrovs'kyy, Ukraine
Tyre see Soûr
97 G14 **Tyrifjorden** ◎ S Norway
97 K22 **Tyringe** Skåne, S Sweden 56.09N 13.34E
127 N15 **Tyrma** Khabarovskiy Kray, SE Russian Federation 50.00N 132.04E
Tyrnau see Trnava
117 F15 **Týrnavos** var. Tírnavos. Thessalía, C Greece 39.45N 22.18E
131 N16 **Tyrnyauz** Kabardino-Balkarskaya Respublika, SW Russian Federation 43.19N 42.55E
Tyrol see Tirol
20 E14 **Tyrone** Pennsylvania, NE USA 40.41N 78.12W
99 E15 **Tyrone** cultural region W Northern Ireland, UK
190 M10 **Tyrrell, Lake** salt lake Victoria, SE Australia
86 H14 **Tyrrhenian Basin** undersea feature Tyrrhenian Sea, C Mediterranean Sea
123 L9 **Tyrrhenian Sea** It. Mare Tirreno. sea N Mediterranean Sea
96 J12 **Tyrsil** ↝ Hedmark, S Norway 61.18N 12.16E
Tysa see Tisa/Tisza
118 J7 **Tysmenytsya** Ivano-Frankivs'ka Oblast', W Ukraine 48.54N 24.50E
97 C14 **Tysnesøya** island S Norway
97 C14 **Tysse** Hordaland, S Norway 60.23N 5.46E
97 D14 **Tyssedal** Hordaland, S Norway 60.07N 6.36E
97 O17 **Tystberga** Södermanland, C Sweden 58.51N 17.15E
120 E12 **Tytuvėnai** Kelmė, C Lithuania 55.36N 23.14E
150 D14 **Tyub-Karagan, Mys** headland SW Kazakhstan 44.40N 50.19E
153 V8 **Tyugel'-Say** Narynskaya Oblast', C Kyrgyzstan 41.57N 74.40E
125 Ff13 **Tyukalinsk** Omskaya Oblast', C Russian Federation 55.56N 72.02E
131 V7 **Tyul'gan** Orenburgskaya Oblast', W Russian Federation 52.27N 56.08E
125 F11 **Tyumen'** Tyumenskaya Oblast', C Russian Federation 57.10N 65.28E
125 Ff10 **Tyumenskaya Oblast'** ◈ province C Russian Federation
126 Kk10 **Tyung** ↝ NE Russian Federation
153 Y7 **Tyup** Kir. Tüp. Issyk-Kul'skaya Oblast', NE Kyrgyzstan 42.43N 78.18E
126 I16 **Tyva, Respublika** prev. Tannu-Tuva, Tuva, Tuvinskaya ASSR. ◈ autonomous republic C Russian Federation
119 N7 **Tyvriv** Vinnyts'ka Oblast', C Ukraine 49.01N 28.28E
99 J21 **Tywi** ↝ S Wales, UK
99 I19 **Tywyn** W Wales, UK 52.34N 4.06W
85 K20 **Tzaneen** Limpopo, NE South Africa 23.49S 30.09E
Tzekung see Zigong
43 X12 **Tzucacab** Yucatán, SE Mexico 20.04N 89.03W

U

84 B12 **Uaco Cungo** var. Waku Kungo, Port. Santa Comba. Cuanza Sul, C Angola 11.21S 15.04E
UAE see United Arab Emirates
203 X7 **Ua Huka** island Îles Marquises, NE French Polynesia
60 E10 **Uaiacás** Roraima, N Brazil 3.28N 63.13W
Uamba see Wamba
Uanle Uen see Wanlaweyn
203 W7 **Ua Pu** island Îles Marquises, NE French Polynesia
83 L17 **Uar Garas** spring/well SW Somalia 1.19N 41.22E
60 G12 **Uatumã, Rio** ↝ C Brazil
Ua Uíbh Fhailí see Offaly
60 C11 **Uaupés, Rio** var. Río Vaupés. ↝ Brazil/Colombia see also Vaupés, Río
151 X9 **Uba** ↝ E Kazakhstan
151 N6 **Ubagan** Kaz. Obagan. ↝ Kazakhstan/Russian Federation
195 N12 **Ubai** New Britain, E PNG 5.38S 150.45E
81 J15 **Ubangi** Fr. Oubangui. ↝ C Africa
Ubangi-Shari see Central African Republic
118 M3 **Ubarts'** Ukr. Ubort'. ↝ Belarus/Ukraine see also Ubort'
56 F9 **Ubaté** Cundinamarca, C Colombia 5.19N 73.49W
62 N10 **Ubatuba** São Paulo, S Brazil 23.24S 45.06W
155 R12 **Ubauro** Sind, SE Pakistan 28.07N 69.43E
179 Qq14 **Ubay** Bohol, C Philippines 10.02N 124.29E
105 U14 **Ubaye** ↝ SE France
Ubayid, Wadi al see Ubayyiḍ, Wādī al
145 N8 **Ubaylah** W Iraq 33.06N 40.13E
145 O10 **Ubayyiḍ, Wādī al** var. Wadi al Ubayid. dry watercourse SW Iraq
100 L13 **Ubbergen** Gelderland, E Netherlands 51.49N 5.54E
170 Dd13 **Ube** Yamaguchi, Honshū, SW Japan 33.56N 131.14E
107 O13 **Úbeda** Andalucía, S Spain 38.01N 3.22W
111 V7 **Übelbach** var. Markt-Übelbach. Steiermark, SE Austria 47.13N 15.15E
61 L20 **Uberaba** Minas Gerais, SE Brazil 19.46S 47.57W
59 Q19 **Uberaba, Laguna** ◎ E Bolivia
61 K19 **Uberlândia** Minas Gerais, SE Brazil 18.16S 48.16W
103 H24 **Überlingen** Baden-Württemberg, S Germany 47.46N 9.10E
79 U16 **Ubiaja** Edo, S Nigeria 6.39N 6.23E
106 K3 **Ubiña, Peña** ▲ NW Spain 43.01N 5.58W
59 H17 **Ubinas, Volcán** ▲ S Peru 16.16S 70.49W
Ubol Rajadhani/Ubol Ratchathani see Ubon Ratchathani
178 Ii9 **Ubolratna Reservoir** ⊠ C Thailand
178 J10 **Ubon Ratchathani** var. Muang Ubon, Ubol Rajadhani, Ubol Ratchathani, Udon Ratchathani. Ubon Ratchathani, E Thailand 15.15N 104.49E

◆ Country ● Country Capital ◇ Dependent Territory ○ Dependent Territory Capital ◈ Administrative Region ✕ International Airport ▲ Mountain ▲▲ Mountain Range ▲ Volcano ↝ River ◎ Lake ⊠ Reservoir

121 L20 **Ubort'** *Bel.* Ubarts'. ≈ Belarus/Ukraine *see also* Ubarts'
106 K15 **Ubrique** Andalucía, S Spain *36.42N 5.27W*
Ubsu-Nur, Ozero *see* Uvs Nuur
81 M18 **Ubundu** Orientale, C Dem. Rep. Congo *0.24S 25.30E*
143 X11 **Ucar** *Rus.* Udzhary. C Azerbaijan *40.31N 47.40E*
58 G13 **Ucayali** *off.* Departamento de Ucayali. ◇ *department* E Peru
58 F10 **Ucayali, Río** ≈ C Peru
Uccle *see* Ukkel
152 J13 **Uch-Adzhi** *Turkm.* Üchaji. Maryyskiy Velayat, C Turkmenistan *38.06N 62.44E*
Üchaji *see* Uch-Adzhi
131 X4 **Uchaly** Respublika Bashkortostan, W Russian Federation *54.19N 59.33E*
151 W13 **Ucharal** *Kaz.* Üsharal. Almaty, E Kazakhstan *46.07N 80.55E*
170 C17 **Uchinoura** Kagoshima, Kyūshū, SW Japan *31.16N 131.04E*
172 Nn6 **Uchiura-wan** *bay* NW Pacific Ocean
Uchkuduk *see* Uchquduq
Uchkurghan *see* Uchqo'rg'on
153 S9 **Uchqo'rg'on** *Rus.* Uchkurghan. Namangan Viloyati, E Uzbekistan *41.06N 72.04E*
152 K8 **Uchquduq** *Rus.* Uchkuduk. Navoiy Viloyati, N Uzbekistan *42.12N 63.27E*
Uchsay *see* Uchsoy
152 G6 **Uchsoy** *Rus.* Uchsay. Qoraqalpog'iston Respublikasi, NW Uzbekistan *43.51N 58.51E*
Uchtagan Gumy *see* Uchtagan, Peski
152 D10 **Uchtagan, Peski** *Turkm.* Uchtagan Gumy. *desert* NW Turkmenistan
126 Mm12 **Uchur** ≈ E Russian Federation
102 O10 **Uckermark** *cultural region* E Germany
8 K17 **Ucluelet** Vancouver Island, British Columbia, SW Canada *48.58N 125.28W*
126 Ii14 **Uda** ≈ S Russian Federation
126 Mm13 **Uda** ≈ E Russian Federation
126 K9 **Udachnyy** Respublika Sakha (Yakutiya), NE Russian Federation *66.27N 112.18E*
161 G21 **Udagamandalam** *var.* Udhagamandalam; *prev.* Ootacamund. Tamil Nādu, SW India *11.28N 76.42E*
158 F14 **Udaipur** *prev.* Oodeypore. Rājasthān, N India *24.34N 73.40E*
Udayadhani *see* Uthai Thani
149 N16 **'Udayd, Khawr al** *var.* Khor al Udeid. *inlet* Qatar/Saudi Arabia
114 D11 **Udbina** Lika-Senj, W Croatia *44.33N 15.46E*
97 I18 **Uddevalla** Västra Götaland, S Sweden *58.19N 11.55E*
Uddjaur *see* Uddjaure
94 H13 **Uddjaure** *var.* Uddjaur. ◎ N Sweden
Udeid, Khor al *see* 'Udayd, Khawr al
101 K14 **Uden** Noord-Brabant, SE Netherlands *51.40N 5.37E*
Uden *see* Udenhout
101 J14 **Udenhout** *var.* Uden. Noord-Brabant, S Netherlands *51.37N 5.09E*
161 H14 **Udgīr** Mahārāshtra, C India *18.23N 77.06E*
Udhagamandalam *see* Udagamandalam
158 H6 **Udhampur** Jammu and Kashmir, NW India *32.55N 75.07E*
145 X14 **'Udhaybah, 'Uqlat al** *well* S Iraq *29.46N 46.50E*
108 J7 **Udine** *anc.* Utina. Friuli-Venezia Giulia, NE Italy *46.04N 13.10E*
183 T14 **Udintsev Fracture Zone** *tectonic feature* S Pacific Ocean
Udipi *see* Udupi
Udmurtia *see* Udmurtskaya Respublika
131 S2 **Udmurtskaya Respublika** *Eng.* Udmurtia. ◇ *autonomous republic* NW Russian Federation
128 J15 **Udomlya** Tverskaya Oblast', W Russian Federation *57.53N 34.59E*
Udon Ratchathani *see* Ubon Ratchathani
178 Ii9 **Udon Thani** *var.* Ban Mak Khaeng, Udorndhani. Udon Thani, N Thailand *17.25N 102.45E*
Udorndhani *see* Udon Thani
201 U12 **Udot** *atoll* Chuuk Islands, C Micronesia
127 N13 **Udskaya Guba** *bay* E Russian Federation
161 E19 **Udupi** *var.* Udipi. Karnātaka, SW India *13.18N 74.46E*
Udzhary *see* Ucar
175 Q9 **Uebonti, Teluk** *bay* Sulawesi, C Indonesia
103 L17 **Uecker** ≈ NE Germany
102 P9 **Ueckermünde** Mecklenburg-Vorpommern, NE Germany *53.43N 14.03E*
171 J14 **Ueda** *var.* Uyeda. Nagano, Honshū, S Japan *36.25N 138.14E*
81 L16 **Uele** *var.* Welle. ≈ NE Dem. Rep. Congo
Uele (upper course) *see* Uolo, Río, Equatorial Guinea/Gabon
Uele (upper course) *see* Kibali, Dem. Rep. Congo
127 Q3 **Uelen** Chukotskiy Avtonomnyy Okrug, NE Russian Federation *66.01N 169.52W*
102 J11 **Uelzen** Niedersachsen, N Germany *52.58N 10.34E*
171 H15 **Ueno** Mie, Honshū, SW Japan *34.45N 136.09E*
131 V4 **Ufa** Respublika Bashkortostan, W Russian Federation *54.46N 56.02E*
131 V4 **Ufa** ≈ W Russian Federation
152 A10 **Ufra** Balkanskiy Velayat, NW Turkmenistan *40.00N 53.05E*
85 C18 **Ugab** ≈ C Namibia
120 D8 **Ugāle** Ventspils, NW Latvia *57.16N 21.58E*
83 F17 **Uganda** *off.* Republic of Uganda. ◆ *republic* E Africa
144 G4 **Ugarit** *Ar.* Ra's Shamrah. *site of ancient city* Al Lādhiqīyah, NW Syria *35.34N 35.45E*
41 O14 **Ugashik** Alaska, USA *57.30N 157.24W*
109 Q19 **Ugento** Puglia, SE Italy *39.53N 18.09E*
107 O15 **Ugíjar** Andalucía, S Spain *36.58N 3.03W*
105 T11 **Ugine** Savoie, E France *45.45N 6.25E*
126 M14 **Uglegorsk** Amurskaya Oblast', S Russian Federation *51.40N 128.05E*
127 O15 **Uglegorsk** Ostrov Sakhalin, Sakhalinskaya Oblast', SE Russian Federation *49.05N 142.06E*
129 V13 **Ugleural'sk** Permskaya Oblast', NW Russian Federation *58.57N 57.37E*
128 L15 **Uglich** Yaroslavskaya Oblast', W Russian Federation *57.33N 38.23E*
128 I14 **Uglovka** *var.* Okulovka. Novgorodskaya Oblast', W Russian Federation *58.24N 33.15E*
127 Pp5 **Ugol'nyye Kopi** Chukotskiy Avtonomnyy Okrug, NE Russian Federation *64.43N 105.46E*
130 I4 **Ugra** ≈ W Russian Federation
153 V9 **Ugyut** Narynskaya Oblast', C Kyrgyzstan *41.22N 74.49E*
113 H19 **Uherské Hradiště** *Ger.* Ungarisch-Hradisch. Zlínský kraj, E Czech Republic *49.04N 17.26E*
113 H19 **Uherský Brod** *Ger.* Ungarisch-Brod. Zlínský kraj, E Czech Republic *49.01N 17.37E*
113 B17 **Úhlava** *Ger.* Angel. ≈ W Czech Republic
Uhorshchyna *see* Hungary
33 T13 **Uhrichsville** Ohio, N USA *40.23N 81.21W*
Uhuru Peak *see* Kilimanjaro
98 G8 **Uig** N Scotland, UK *57.35N 6.22W*
84 B10 **Uíge** *Port.* Carmona, Vila Marechal Carmona. Uíge, NW Angola *7.37S 15.02E*
84 B10 **Uíge** ◇ *province* N Angola
200 Ss13 **Uiha** *island* Ha'apai Group, C Tonga
201 U13 **Uijec** *island* Chuuk, C Micronesia
169 X14 **Ŭijŏngbu** *Jap.* Giseifu. NW South Korea *37.42N 127.02E*
150 H10 **Uil** *Kaz.* Oyyl. Aktyubinsk, W Kazakhstan *49.06N 54.41E*
150 H10 **Uil** *Kaz.* Oyyl. ≈ W Kazakhstan
38 M3 **Uinta Mountains** ▲▲ Utah, W USA
85 C18 **Uis** Erongo, NW Namibia *21.15S 14.54E*
85 I25 **Uitenhage** Eastern Cape, S South Africa *33.43S 25.27E*
100 H9 **Uitgeest** Noord-Holland, W Netherlands *52.31N 4.43E*
100 I11 **Uithoorn** Noord-Holland, C Netherlands *52.13N 4.49E*
100 O4 **Uithuizen** Groningen, NE Netherlands *53.24N 6.40E*
100 O4 **Uithuizermeeden** Groningen, NE Netherlands *53.25N 6.43E*
201 R6 **Ujae Atoll** *var.* Wūjae. *atoll* Ralik Chain, W Marshall Islands
Ujain *see* Ujjain
113 I16 **Ujazd** Opolskie, S Poland *50.22N 18.20E*
Új-Becse *see* Novi Bečej
Ujda *see* Oujda
201 N5 **Ujelang Atoll** *var.* Wujlān. *atoll* Ralik Chain, W Marshall Islands
113 N21 **Újfehértó** Szabolcs-Szatmár-Bereg, E Hungary *47.48N 21.41E*
Újgradiska *see* Nova Gradiška
171 H15 **Uji** *var.* Uzi. Kyōto, Honshū, SW Japan *34.52N 135.47E*
170 Aa16 **Uji-guntō** *island* Nansei-shotō, SW Japan
83 E21 **Ujiji** Kigoma, W Tanzania *4.55S 29.39E*
160 G10 **Ujjain** *prev.* Ujain. Madhya Pradesh, C India *23.10N 75.49E*
Újlak *see* Ilok
'Ujmān *see* 'Ajmān
Újmoldova *see* Moldova Nouă
Újszentanna *see* Sântana
175 P13 **Ujungpandang** *var.* Macassar, Makassar; *prev.* Makasar. Sulawesi, C Indonesia *5.09S 119.28E*
Ujung Salang *see* Phuket
Újvidék *see* Novi Sad
160 E11 **Ukāi Reservoir** ⊠ W India
83 G19 **Ukara Island** *island* N Tanzania
'Ukash, Wādī *see* 'Akāsh, Wādī
83 F19 **Ukerewe Island** *island* N Tanzania
145 S9 **Ukhaydhir** C Iraq *32.28N 43.36E*
159 X13 **Ukhrul** Manipur, NE India *25.07N 94.24E*
129 S9 **Ukhta** Respublika Komi, NW Russian Federation *63.30N 53.47E*
36 L6 **Ukiah** California, W USA *39.07N 123.14W*
34 K12 **Ukiah** Oregon, NW USA *45.06N 118.57W*
101 G18 **Ukkel** *Fr.* Uccle. Brussels, C Belgium *50.47N 4.19E*
120 G13 **Ukmergė** *Pol.* Wiłkomierz. Ukmergė, C Lithuania *55.16N 24.46E*
Ukraina *see* Ukraine
118 L6 **Ukraine** *off.* Ukraine, *Rus.* Ukraina, *Ukr.* Ukrayina; *prev.* Ukrainian Soviet Socialist Republic, Ukrainskay S.S.R. ◆ *republic* SE Europe
Ukrainskay S.S.R/Ukrayina *see* Ukraine
84 B13 **Uku** Cuanza Sul, NW Angola *11.25S 14.18E*
170 Bb12 **Uku-jima** *island* Gotō-rettō, SW Japan
85 F20 **Ukwi** Kgalagadi, SW Botswana *23.41S 20.26E*
120 M13 **Ula** *Rus.* Ulla. Vitsyebskaya Voblasts', N Belarus *55.13N 29.15E*
142 C16 **Ula** Muğla, SW Turkey *37.07N 28.25E*
120 M13 **Ula** *Rus.* Ulla. ≈ N Belarus
168 L7 **Ulaanbaatar** *Eng.* Ulan Bator. ● (Mongolia) Töv, C Mongolia *47.54N 106.57E*
169 N8 **Ulaan-Ereg** Hentiy, E Mongolia *46.50N 109.39E*
168 E5 **Ulaangom** Uvs, NW Mongolia *49.56N 92.06E*
168 E7 **Ulaantolgoy** Hovd, W Mongolia *46.39N 92.50E*
168 I8 **Ulaan-Uul** Bayanhongor, C Mongolia *46.03N 100.52E*
169 O10 **Ulaan-Uul** Dornogovĭ, SE Mongolia *44.21N 111.06E*
165 R10 **Ulan** Qinghai, C China *36.59N 98.21E*
Ulan Bator *see* Ulaanbaatar
168 L13 **Ulan Buh Shamo** *desert* N China
Ulanhad *see* Chifeng
169 T8 **Ulanhot** Nei Mongol Zizhiqu, N China *46.02N 122.00E*
131 Q14 **Ulan Khol** Respublika Kalmykiya, SW Russian Federation *45.27N 46.48E*
168 M13 **Ulansuhai Nur** ◎ N China
126 Jj16 **Ulan-Ude** *prev.* Verkhneudinsk. Respublika Buryatiya, S Russian Federation *51.55N 107.40E*
165 N12 **Ulan Ul Hu** ◎ C China
195 Z16 **Ulawa Island** *island* SE Solomon Islands
144 J7 **'Ulayyānīyah, Bi'r al** *var.* Al Hilbeh. *well* S Syria *34.01N 38.06E*
127 Nn13 **Ul'banskiy Zaliv** *strait* E Russian Federation
Ulbo *see* Olib
115 J18 **Ulcinj** Montenegro, SW Serbia and Montenegro (Yugoslavia) *41.56N 19.14E*
169 O7 **Uldz** Hentiy, NE Mongolia *48.47N 112.01E*
Uleåborg *see* Oulu
Uleälv *see* Oulujoki
97 G16 **Ulefoss** Telemark, S Norway *59.16N 9.16E*
Uleträsk *see* Oulujärvi
115 L19 **Ulëz** *var.* Ulëza. Dibër, C Albania *41.42N 19.52E*
Ulëza *see* Ulëz
97 F22 **Ulfborg** Ringkøbing, W Denmark *56.16N 8.21E*
100 N13 **Ulft** Gelderland, E Netherlands *51.52N 6.22E*
168 G7 **Uliastay** Dzavhan, W Mongolia *47.46N 96.53E*
196 F8 **Ulimang** Babeldaob, N Palau
69 T10 **Ulindi** ≈ W Dem. Rep. Congo
196 H14 **Ulithi Atoll** *atoll* Caroline Islands, W Micronesia
114 N10 **Uljma** Serbia, NE Serbia and Montenegro (Yugoslavia) *45.04N 21.08E*
150 L11 **Ul'kayak** *Kaz.* Ölkeyek. ≈ C Kazakhstan
151 Q7 **Ul'ken-Karoy, Ozero** ◎ N Kazakhstan
Ülkenözen *see* Bol'shoy Uzen'
Ülkenqobda *see* Bol'shaya Khobda
106 G3 **Ulla** ≈ NW Spain
Ulla *see* Ula
191 S10 **Ulladulla** New South Wales, SE Australia *35.22S 150.28E*
159 T14 **Ullapara** Rajshahi, W Bangladesh *24.19N 89.34E*
98 H7 **Ullapool** N Scotland, UK *57.54N 5.10W*
97 J20 **Ullared** Halland, S Sweden *57.07N 12.45E*
107 T7 **Ulldecona** Cataluña, NE Spain *40.36N 0.27E*
94 I9 **Ullsfjorden** *fjord* N Norway
99 K15 **Ullswater** ◎ NW England, UK
103 I22 **Ulm** Baden-Württemberg, S Germany *48.24N 9.58E*
35 R8 **Ulm** Montana, NW USA *47.27N 111.32W*
191 V5 **Ulmarra** New South Wales, SE Australia *29.37S 153.06E*
118 K13 **Ulmeni** Buzău, C Romania *45.08N 26.43E*
118 K14 **Ulmeni** Călăraşi, S Romania *44.08N 26.43E*
44 L7 **Ulmukhuás** Región Autónoma Atlántico Norte, NE Nicaragua *14.21N 84.34W*
196 C8 **Ulong** *var.* Aulong. *island* Palau Islands, N Palau
85 N14 **Ulongue** *var.* Ulongwé. Tete, NW Mozambique *14.42S 34.21E*
Ulongwé *see* Ulongue
97 K19 **Ulricehamn** Västra Götaland, S Sweden *57.57N 13.25E*
100 N5 **Ulrum** Groningen, NE Netherlands *53.24N 6.20E*
169 Z16 **Ulsan** *Jap.* Urusan. SE South Korea *35.33N 129.19E*
96 D10 **Ulsteinvik** Møre og Romsdal, S Norway *62.19N 5.52E*
99 D15 **Ulster** ◇ *province* Northern Ireland, UK/Ireland
175 S5 **Ulu** Pulau Siau, N Indonesia *2.46N 125.22E*
126 Ll12 **Ulu** Respublika Sakha (Yakutiya), NE Russian Federation *60.18N 127.27E*
44 H5 **Ulúa, Río** ≈ NW Honduras
142 D12 **Ulubat Gölü** ◎ NW Turkey
142 E12 **Uludağ** ▲ NW Turkey *40.08N 29.13E*
Ulugh Muztag *see* Muztag Feng
164 D7 **Ulugqat** Xinjiang Uygur Zizhiqu, W China *39.45N 74.10E*
142 J16 **Ulukışla** Niğde, S Turkey *37.33N 34.28E*
201 O15 **Ulul** *island* Caroline Islands, C Micronesia
85 L22 **Ulundi** KwaZulu/Natal, E South Africa *28.18S 31.25E*
164 M3 **Ulungur He** ≈ NW China
164 K2 **Ulungur Hu** ◎ NW China
189 P8 **Uluru** *var.* Ayers Rock. *rocky outcrop* Northern Territory, C Australia *25.20S 130.59E*
Ulveah *see* Lopevi
99 K16 **Ulverston** NW England, UK *54.12N 3.07W*
191 O16 **Ulverstone** Tasmania, SE Australia *41.13S 146.09E*
96 D13 **Ulvik** Hordaland, S Norway *60.34N 6.53E*
95 J18 **Ulvila** Länsi-Suomi, W Finland *61.25N 21.55E*
119 O8 **Ulyanivka** *Rus.* Ul'yanovka. Kirovohrads'ka Oblast', C Ukraine *48.18N 30.15E*
Ul'yanovka *see* Ulyanivka
131 Q5 **Ul'yanovsk** *prev.* Simbirsk. Ul'yanovskaya Oblast', W Russian Federation *54.16N 48.21E*
131 Q5 **Ul'yanovskaya Oblast'** ◇ *province* W Russian Federation
151 S10 **Ul'yanovskiy** Karaganda, C Kazakhstan *50.04N 73.45E*
Ul'yanovskiy Kanal *see* Ul'yanow Kanali
152 M13 **Ul'yanow Kanali** *Rus.* Ul'yanovskiy Kanal. *canal* Turkmenistan/Uzbekistan
Ulyshylanshyq *see* Uly-Zhylanshyk
28 H6 **Ulysses** Kansas, C USA *37.34N 101.21W*
151 O12 **Ulytau, Gory** ▲▲ C Kazakhstan
126 K14 **Ulyunkhan** Respublika Buryatiya, S Russian Federation *54.48N 111.01E*
151 N11 **Uly-Zhylanshyk** *Kaz.* Ulyshylanshyq. ≈ C Kazakhstan
114 A9 **Umag** *It.* Umago. Istra, NW Croatia *45.25N 13.32E*
Umago *see* Umag
201 V13 **Uman** *atoll* Chuuk Islands, C Micronesia
119 O7 **Uman'** *Rus.* Uman. Cherkas'ka Oblast', C Ukraine *48.45N 30.10E*
43 W12 **Umán** Yucatán, SE Mexico *20.51N 89.45W*
Umanak/Umanaq *see* Uummannaq
'Umān, Khalīj *see* Oman, Gulf of
'Umān, Salṭanat *see* Oman
176 Ww12 **Umari** Papua, E Indonesia *4.18S 135.22E*
160 K10 **Umaria** Madhya Pradesh, C India *23.34N 80.49E*
155 R16 **Umar Kot** Sind, SE Pakistan *25.19N 69.45E*
196 B17 **Umatac** SW Guam *13.17N 144.40E*
196 A17 **Umatac Bay** *bay* SW Guam
145 S6 **Umayqah** C Iraq *34.32N 43.45E*
128 J5 **Umba** Murmanskaya Oblast', NW Russian Federation *66.39N 34.24E*
144 I8 **Umbāshī, Khirbat al** *ruins* As Suwaydā', S Syria *33.05N 37.00E*
82 A12 **Umbelasha** ≈ W Sudan
108 H12 **Umbertide** Umbria, C Italy *43.16N 12.21E*
63 B17 **Umberto** *var.* Humberto. Santa Fe, C Argentina *30.52S 61.19W*
194 K11 **Umboi Island** *var.* Rooke Island. *island* C PNG
128 J4 **Umbozero, Ozero** ◎ NW Russian Federation
108 H13 **Umbria** ◇ *region* C Italy
Umbrian-Machigian Mountains *see* Umbro-Marchigiano, Appennino
108 I12 **Umbro-Marchigiano, Appennino** *Eng.* Umbrian-Machigian Mountains. ▲▲ C Italy
95 J16 **Umeå** Västerbotten, N Sweden *63.49N 20.15E*
95 H14 **Umeälven** ≈ N Sweden
41 Q5 **Umiat** Alaska, USA *69.22N 152.08W*
85 K23 **Umlazi** KwaZulu/Natal, E South Africa *29.58S 30.50E*
145 X10 **Umm al Baqar, Hawr** *var.* Birkat ad Dawaymah. *spring* S Iraq *31.43N 46.50E*
147 U12 **Umm al Ḥayt, Wādī** *var.* Wādī Amilḥayt. *seasonal river* SW Oman
Umm al Qaiwain *see* Umm al Qaywayn
149 R15 **Umm al Qaywayn** *var.* Umm al Qaiwain. Umm al Qaywayn, NE UAE *25.43N 55.54E*
145 Q5 **Umm al Tūz** C Iraq *34.53N 42.42E*
144 J3 **Umm 'Āmūd** Ḥalab, N Syria *35.57N 37.39E*
147 Y10 **Umm ar Ruṣāṣ** *var.* Umm Ruṣayṣ. W Oman *20.26N 58.48E*
147 X9 **Ummas Samīn** *salt flat* C Oman
147 V7 **Umm az Zumūl** *oasis* E Saudi Arabia *22.39N 54.45E*
82 A9 **Umm Buru** Western Darfur, W Sudan *15.01N 23.36E*
82 A12 **Umm Dafag** Southern Darfur, W Sudan *10.28N 23.19E*
Umm Durmān *see* Omdurman
144 F9 **Umm el Fahm** Haifa, N Israel *32.30N 35.06E*
82 F9 **Umm Inderab** Northern Kordofan, C Sudan *15.18N 31.56E*
82 C10 **Umm Keddada** Northern Darfur, W Sudan *13.36N 26.42E*
146 J7 **Umm Lajj** Tabūk, W Saudi Arabia *25.01N 37.19E*
144 L10 **Umm Maḥfur** ≈ N Jordan
145 Y13 **Umm Qaṣr** SE Iraq *30.01N 47.55E*
Umm Ruṣayṣ *see* Umm ar Ruṣāṣ
82 F11 **Umm Ruwaba** *var.* Umm Ruwābah, Um Ruwāba. Northern Kordofan, C Sudan *12.54N 31.13E*
Umm Ruwābah *see* Umm Ruwaba
149 N16 **Umm Sa'īd** *var.* Musay'īd. S Qatar *24.57N 51.31E*
144 K10 **Umm Ṭuways, Wādī** *dry watercourse* N Jordan
40 J17 **Umnak Island** *island* Aleutian Islands, Alaska, USA
34 F13 **Umpqua River** ≈ Oregon, NW USA
84 D13 **Umpulo** Bié, C Angola *12.43S 17.42E*
160 I12 **Umred** Mahārāshtra, C India *20.54N 79.19E*
145 Y10 **Umr Sawān, Hawr** ◎ S Iraq
Um Ruwāba *see* Umm Ruwaba
Umtali *see* Mutare
85 J24 **Umtata** Eastern Cape, SE South Africa *31.33S 28.47E*
79 V17 **Umuahia** Abia, SW Nigeria *5.30N 7.33E*
62 H10 **Umuarama** Paraná, S Brazil *23.45S 53.19W*
Umvuma *see* Mvuma
85 K18 **Umzingwani** ≈ S Zimbabwe
114 D11 **Una** ≈ Bosnia and Herzegovina/Croatia
114 E12 **Unac** ≈ W Bosnia and Herzegovina
25 T6 **Unadilla** Georgia, SE USA *32.15N 83.44W*
20 I10 **Unadilla River** ≈ New York, NE USA
61 L18 **Unaí** Minas Gerais, SE Brazil *16.24S 46.49W*
41 N10 **Unalakleet** Alaska, USA *63.52N 160.47W*
40 K17 **Unalaska Island** *island* Aleutian Islands, Alaska, USA
193 I16 **Una, Mount** ▲ South Island, NZ *42.12S 172.34E*
84 N13 **Unango** Niassa, N Mozambique *12.45S 35.28E*
Unao *see* Unnāo
94 L12 **Unari** Lappi, N Finland *67.07N 25.37E*
147 O6 **'Unayzah** *var.* Anaiza. Al Qaṣīm, C Saudi Arabia *26.03N 44.00E*
144 L10 **'Unayzah, Jabal** ▲ Jordan/Saudi Arabia *32.09N 39.10E*
Unci *see* Almería
59 K19 **Uncía** Potosí, C Bolivia *18.30S 66.29W*
39 Q7 **Uncompahgre Peak** ▲ Colorado, C USA *38.04N 107.27W*
39 P6 **Uncompahgre Plateau** *plain* Colorado, C USA
97 L17 **Unden** ◎ S Sweden
30 M4 **Underwood** North Dakota, N USA *47.25N 101.09W*
176 Uu11 **Undur** Pulau Seram, E Indonesia *3.41S 130.38E*
194 M11 **Unea Island** *island* C PNG
130 H6 **Unecha** Bryanskaya Oblast', W Russian Federation *52.51N 32.38E*
41 N16 **Unga** Unga Island, Alaska, USA *55.14N 160.34W*
Ungaria *see* Hungary
191 P8 **Ungarie** New South Wales, SE Australia *33.39S 146.54E*
Ungarisch-Brod *see* Uherský Brod
Ungarisches Erzgebirge *see* Slovenské rudohorie
Ungarisch-Hradisch *see* Uherské Hradiště
Ungarn *see* Hungary
10 M4 **Ungava Bay** *bay* Quebec, E Canada
10 J2 **Ungava, Péninsule d'** *peninsula* Quebec, SE Canada
Ungeny *see* Ungheni
118 M9 **Ungheni** *Rus.* Ungeny. W Moldova *47.13N 27.48E*
Unguja *see* Zanzibar
Üngüz Angyrsyndaky Garagum *see* Zaunguzskiye Garagumy
152 H11 **Unguz, Solonchakovyye Vpadiny** *salt marsh* C Turkmenistan
Ungvár *see* Uzhhorod
62 I12 **União da Vitória** Paraná, S Brazil *26.13S 51.04W*
113 G17 **Uničov** *Ger.* Mährisch-Neustadt. Olomoucký Kraj, E Czech Republic *49.46N 17.05E*
112 J12 **Uniejów** Łódzkie, C Poland *51.58N 18.46E*
114 A11 **Unije** *island* W Croatia
40 L16 **Unimak Island** *island* Aleutian Islands, Alaska, USA
40 L16 **Unimak Pass** *strait* Aleutian Islands, Alaska, USA
29 W5 **Union** Missouri, C USA *38.27N 91.01W*
34 L12 **Union** Oregon, NW USA *45.12N 117.51W*
23 Q11 **Union** South Carolina, SE USA *34.40N 81.35W*
23 R6 **Union** West Virginia, NE USA *37.33N 80.33W*
64 J12 **Unión** San Luis, C Argentina *35.09S 65.55W*
63 B25 **Unión, Bahía** *bay* E Argentina
33 Q13 **Union City** Indiana, N USA *40.12N 84.50W*
33 Q10 **Union City** Michigan, N USA *42.03N 85.06W*
20 C12 **Union City** Pennsylvania, NE USA *41.54N 79.51W*
22 G8 **Union City** Tennessee, S USA *36.25N 89.01W*
34 G14 **Union Creek** Oregon, NW USA *42.54N 122.26W*
85 G25 **Uniondale** Western Cape, SW South Africa *33.40S 23.07E*
42 K13 **Unión de Tula** Jalisco, SW Mexico *19.58N 104.20W*
32 M9 **Union Grove** Wisconsin, N USA *42.39N 88.03W*
47 Y15 **Union Island** *island* S Saint Vincent and the Grenadines
48 K5 **Union Reefs** *reef* SW Mexico
(0) D7 **Union Seamount** *undersea feature* NE Pacific Ocean *49.34N 132.45W*
25 Q6 **Union Springs** Alabama, S USA *32.08N 85.43W*
22 H6 **Uniontown** Kentucky, S USA *37.46N 87.55W*
20 C16 **Uniontown** Pennsylvania, NE USA *39.54N 79.43W*
29 T1 **Unionville** Missouri, C USA *40.28N 93.00W*
147 V8 **United Arab Emirates** *Ar.* Al Imārāt al 'Arabīyah al Muttaḥidah, *abbrev.* UAE; *prev.* Trucial States. ◆ *federation* SW Asia
United Arab Republic *see* Egypt
99 H14 **United Kingdom** *off.* UK of Great Britain and Northern Ireland, *abbrev.* UK. ◆ *monarchy* NW Europe
United Mexican States *see* Mexico
United Provinces *see* Uttar Pradesh
18 L9 **United States of America** *off.* United States of America, *var.* America, The States, *abbrev.* U.S., USA. ◆ *federal republic*
128 J10 **Unitsa** Respublika Kareliya, NW Russian Federation *62.31N 34.31E*
9 S15 **Unity** Saskatchewan, S Canada *52.27N 109.10W*
Unity State *see* Wahda
107 Q8 **Universales, Montes** ▲▲ C Spain
29 X4 **University City** Missouri, C USA *38.40N 90.19W*
197 B13 **Unmet** Malekula, C Vanuatu *16.09S 167.16E*
103 F15 **Unna** Nordrhein-Westfalen, W Germany *51.31N 7.40E*
158 L12 **Unnāo** *prev.* Unao. Uttar Pradesh, N India *26.31N 80.30E*
197 D15 **Unpongkor** Erromango, S Vanuatu *18.48S 169.01E*
Unruhstadt *see* Kargowa
98 M1 **Unst** *island* NE Scotland, UK
103 K16 **Unstrut** ≈ C Germany
Unterdrauburg *see* Dravograd
Unterlimbach *see* Lendava
103 L23 **Unterschleissheim** Bayern, SE Germany *48.16N 11.34E*
103 H24 **Untersee** ◎ Germany/Switzerland
102 O10 **Unterueckersee** ◎ NE Germany
110 F9 **Unterwalden** ◇ *canton* C Switzerland
57 N12 **Unturán, Sierra de** ▲▲ Brazil/Venezuela
165 N11 **Unuli Horog** Qinghai, W China *35.10N 91.49E*
142 M11 **Ünye** Ordu, W Turkey *41.07N 37.14E*
Unza *see* Unzha
129 O14 **Unzha** *var.* Unza. ≈ NW Russian Federation
81 E17 **Uolo, Río** *var.* Eyo (lower course), Mbini, Uele (upper course), Woleu; *prev.* Benito. ≈ Equatorial Guinea/Gabon
57 Q10 **Uonán** Bolívar, SE Venezuela *4.33N 62.10W*
167 T12 **Uotsuri-shima** *island* China/Japan/Taiwan
171 J13 **Uozu** Toyama, Honshū, SW Japan *36.48N 137.23E*
44 L12 **Upala** Alajuela, NW Costa Rica *10.52N 85.00W*
57 P7 **Upata** Bolívar, E Venezuela *8.01N 62.25W*
81 M23 **Upemba, Lac** ◎ SE Dem. Rep. Congo
207 O12 **Upernavik** *var.* Upernivik. Kitaa, C Greenland *73.06N 55.42W*
Upernivik *see* Upernavik
85 F22 **Upington** Northern Cape, W South Africa *28.24S 21.13E*
Uplands *see* Ottawa
198 Bb8 **Upolu** *island* SE Samoa
40 G11 **Upolu Point** *headland* Hawaii, USA, C Pacific Ocean *20.15N 155.51W*
Upper Austria *see* Oberösterreich
Upper Bann *see* Bann
12 M13 **Upper Canada Village** *tourist site* Ontario, SE Canada *44.57N 75.04W*
20 I16 **Upper Darby** Pennsylvania, NE USA *39.57N 75.15W*
30 L2 **Upper Des Lacs Lake** ⊠ North Dakota, N USA
193 L14 **Upper Hutt** Wellington, North Island, NZ *41.08S 174.58E*
31 X11 **Upper Iowa River** ≈ Iowa, C USA
34 H15 **Upper Klamath Lake** ◎ Oregon, NW USA
36 M6 **Upper Lake** California, W USA *39.07N 122.53W*
37 Q1 **Upper Lake** ◎ California, W USA
8 K9 **Upper Liard** Yukon Territory, W Canada *60.01N 128.59W*
99 E16 **Upper Lough Erne** ◎ SW Northern Ireland, UK
82 F12 **Upper Nile** ◇ *state* E Sudan
31 T3 **Upper Red Lake** ◎ Minnesota, N USA
33 S12 **Upper Sandusky** Ohio, N USA *40.49N 83.16W*
Upper Volta *see* Burkina
97 O15 **Upplandsväsby** *var.* Upplands Väsby. Stockholm, C Sweden *59.28N 17.49E*
97 O15 **Uppsala** Uppsala, C Sweden *59.52N 17.37E*
97 O14 **Uppsala** ◇ *county* C Sweden
40 J12 **Upright Cape** *headland* Saint Matthew Island, Alaska, USA *60.19N 172.15W*
22 K6 **Upton** Kentucky, S USA *37.25N 85.53W*
35 Y13 **Upton** Wyoming, C USA *44.06N 104.37W*
147 N7 **'Uqlat aṣ Ṣuqūr** Al Qaṣīm, W Saudi Arabia *25.51N 42.12E*
Uqturpan *see* Wushi
56 C7 **Urabá, Golfo de** *gulf* NW Colombia
Uracas *see* Farallon de Pajaros
Uradar'ya *see* O'radaryo
168 M13 **Urad Qianqi** *var.* Xishanzui. Nei Mongol Zizhiqu, N China *40.40N 108.36E*
171 Jj17 **Uraga-suidō** *strait* S Japan
172 Pp7 **Urahoro** Hokkaidō, NE Japan *42.47N 143.41E*
172 Oo8 **Urakawa** Hokkaidō, NE Japan *42.11N 142.42E*
131 X6 **Ural** *Kaz.* Zayyq. ≈ Kazakhstan/Russian Federation
191 T6 **Uralla** New South Wales, SE Australia *30.39S 151.30E*
Ural Mountains *see* Ural'skiye Gory
150 F8 **Ural'sk** *Kaz.* Oral. Zapadnyy Kazakhstan, NW Kazakhstan *51.12N 51.17E*
Ural'skaya Oblast' *see* Zapadnyy Kazakhstan
131 W5 **Ural'skiye Gory** *var.* Ural'skiy Khrebet, *Eng.* Ural Mountains. ▲▲ Kazakhstan/Russian Federation
Ural'skiy Khrebet *see* Ural'skiye Gory
144 I3 **Urām aṣ Ṣughrá** Ḥalab, N Syria *36.10N 36.55E*
191 P10 **Urana** New South Wales, SE Australia *35.22S 146.16E*
9 S10 **Uranium City** Saskatchewan, C Canada *59.30N 108.46W*
60 F10 **Uraricoera** Roraima, N Brazil *3.26N 60.54W*
49 S5 **Uraricoera, Rio** ≈ N Brazil
Ura-Tyube *see* Üroteppa
171 K16 **Urawa** Saitama, Honshū, S Japan *35.51N 139.37E*
125 F10 **Uray** Khanty-Mansiyskiy Avtonomnyy Okrug, C Russian Federation *60.07N 64.38E*
147 R7 **'Uray'irah** Ash Sharqīyah, E Saudi Arabia *25.59N 48.51E*
32 M13 **Urbana** Illinois, N USA *40.06N 88.12W*
33 R13 **Urbana** Ohio, N USA *40.04N 83.46W*
31 V14 **Urbandale** Iowa, C USA *41.37N 93.42W*
108 I11 **Urbania** Marche, C Italy *43.40N 12.33E*
176 Uu8 **Urbinasopon** Papua, E Indonesia *0.19S 131.12E*
108 I11 **Urbino** Marche, C Italy *43.45N 12.38E*
59 H16 **Urcos** Cusco, S Peru *13.45S 71.37W*
150 D10 **Urda** Zapadnyy Kazakhstan, W Kazakhstan *48.52N 47.31E*
107 N10 **Urda** Castilla-La Mancha, C Spain *39.25N 3.43W*
168 E7 **Urdgol** Hovd, W Mongolia *47.39N 92.46E*
Urdunn *see* Jordan
151 X12 **Urdzhar** *Kaz.* Ürzhar. Vostochnyy Kazakhstan, E Kazakhstan *47.06N 81.37E*
99 L16 **Ure** ≈ N England, UK
121 K18 **Urechcha** *Rus.* Urech'ye. Minskaya Voblasts', S Belarus *52.57N 27.54E*
Urech'ye *see* Urechcha
131 P2 **Uren'** Nizhegorodskaya Oblast', W Russian Federation *57.29N 45.47E*
126 H9 **Urengoy** Yamalo-Nenetskiy Avtonomnyy Okrug, N Russian Federation *65.52N 78.42E*
192 K10 **Urenui** Taranaki, North Island, NZ *38.59S 174.25E*
197 B10 **Ureparapara** *island* Banks Islands, N Vanuatu
42 G5 **Ures** Sonora, NW Mexico *29.25N 110.24W*
Urfa *see* Şanlıurfa
152 H9 **Urganch** *Rus.* Urgench; *prev.* Novo-Urgench. Xorazm Viloyati, W Uzbekistan *41.39N 60.32E*
Urgench *see* Urganch
142 J14 **Ürgüp** Nevşehir, C Turkey *38.39N 34.55E*
153 O12 **Urgut** Samarqand Viloyati, C Uzbekistan *39.25N 67.15E*
164 K3 **Urho** Xinjiang Uygur Zizhiqu, W China *46.04N 84.51E*
158 G5 **Uri** Jammu and Kashmir, NW India *34.04N 74.03E*
110 G9 **Uri** ◇ *canton* C Switzerland
56 F11 **Uribe** Meta, C Colombia *3.01N 74.33W*
56 H4 **Uribia** La Guajira, N Colombia *11.45N 72.19W*
118 G12 **Uricani** *Hung.* Hobicaurikány. Hunedoara, SW Romania *45.18N 23.03E*
59 M21 **Uriondo** Tarija, S Bolivia *21.40S 64.37W*
42 I7 **Urique** Chihuahua, N Mexico *27.16N 107.51W*
42 I7 **Urique, Río** ≈ N Mexico
58 E9 **Urituyacu, Río** ≈ N Peru
151 N7 **Uritskiy** Kostanay, N Kazakhstan *53.21N 65.27E*
100 K8 **Urk** Flevoland, N Netherlands *52.40N 5.34E*
142 B14 **Urla** İzmir, W Turkey *38.19N 26.46E*
118 K13 **Urlaţi** Prahova, SE Romania *44.58N 26.15E*
131 V4 **Urman** Respublika Bashkortostan, W Russian Federation *54.53N 56.52E*
153 P12 **Urmetan** W Tajikistan *39.27N 68.13E*
Urmia *see* Orūmīyeh
Urmia, Lake *see* Orūmīyeh, Daryācheh-ye
Urmiyeh *see* Orūmīyeh
115 N17 **Uroševac** *Alb.* Ferizaj. Serbia, S Serbia and Montenegro (Yugoslavia) *42.23N 21.09E*
153 P11 **Üroteppa** *Rus.* Ura-Tyube. NW Tajikistan *39.54N 68.57E*
56 D8 **Urrao** Antioquia, W Colombia *6.16N 76.10W*
Ursat'yevskaya *see* Xovos
168 I11 **Urt** Ömnögovĭ, S Mongolia *42.36N 101.00E*
131 X7 **Urtazym** Orenburgskaya Oblast', W Russian Federation *52.12N 58.48E*
61 K18 **Uruaçu** Goiás, C Brazil *14.37S 49.06W*
42 M14 **Uruapan** *var.* Uruapan del Progreso. Michoacán de Ocampo, SW Mexico *19.25N 102.04W*
Uruapan del Progreso *see* Uruapan
59 G15 **Urubamba, Cordillera** ▲▲ C Peru
59 G14 **Urubamba, Río** ≈ C Peru
60 G12 **Urucará** Amazonas, N Brazil *2.30S 57.45W*
63 E16 **Uruguaiana** Rio Grande do Sul, S Brazil *29.45S 57.04W*
Uruguai, Rio *see* Uruguay
63 E18 **Uruguay** *off.* Oriental Republic of Uruguay; *prev.* La Banda Oriental. ◆ *republic* E South America
63 E15 **Uruguay** *var.* Rio Uruguai, Río Uruguay. ≈ E South America
Uruguay, Río *see* Uruguay
Urumchi *see* Ürümqi
164 L5 **Ürümqi** *var.* Tihwa, Urumchi, Urumqi, Urumtsi, Wu-lu-k'o-mu-shi, Wu-lu-mu-ch'i; *prev.* Ti-hua. *autonomous region capital* Xinjiang Uygur Zizhiqu, NW China *43.52N 87.31E*
Urumtsi *see* Ürümqi
Urundi *see* Burundi
191 V6 **Urunga** New South Wales, SE Australia *30.33S 152.58E*
196 C15 **Uruno Point** *headland* NW Guam *13.37N 144.49E*
127 P15 **Urup, Ostrov** *island* Kuril'skiye Ostrova, SE Russian Federation
147 P11 **'Uruq al Mawārid** *desert* S Saudi Arabia
Urusan *see* Ulsan
131 T5 **Urussu** Respublika Tatarstan, W Russian Federation *54.34N 53.23E*
192 K10 **Uruti** Taranaki, North Island, NZ *38.57S 174.32E*
59 K19 **Uru Uru, Lago** ◎ W Bolivia
57 P9 **Uruyén** Bolívar, SE Venezuela *5.40N 62.25W*
155 O7 **Urūzgān** *var.* Oruzgān, Orūzgān. Urūzgān, C Afghanistan *32.58N 66.39E*
155 N6 **Urūzgān** *Per.* Orūzgān. ◇ *province* C Afghanistan
172 P6 **Uryū-gawa** ≈ Hokkaidō, NE Japan
172 P4 **Uryū-ko** ◎ Hokkaidō, NE Japan
131 N8 **Uryupinsk** Volgogradskaya Oblast', SW Russian Federation *50.51N 41.59E*
Ürzhar *see* Urdzhar
129 R16 **Urzhum** Kirovskaya Oblast', NW Russian Federation *57.09N 49.56E*
118 K13 **Urziceni** Ialomiţa, SE Romania *44.43N 26.39E*

U.S./USA see United States of America
170 D13 **Usa** Ōita, Kyūshū, SW Japan 33.32N 131.20E
121 L16 **Usa** *Rus.* Usa. ≈ C Belarus
129 T6 **Usa** ≈ NW Russian Federation
142 E14 **Uşak** *prev.* Ushak. Uşak, W Turkey 38.42N 29.25E
142 D14 **Uşak** *var.* Ushak. ◈ province W Turkey
85 C19 **Usakos** Erongo, W Namibia 22.01S 15.31E
83 J21 **Usambara Mountains** ▲▲ NE Tanzania
83 G23 **Usangu Flats** wetland SW Tanzania
67 D24 **Usborne, Mount** ▲ East Falkland, Falkland Islands 51.34S 58.57W
102 O8 **Usedom** island NE Germany
101 M24 **Useldange** Diekirch, C Luxembourg 49.46N 5.58E
120 L12 **Ushacha** *Rus.* Ushacha. Vitsyebskaya Voblasts', N Belarus 55.31N 28.30E
Ushachi see Ushachy
120 L13 **Ushachy** *Rus.* Ushachi. Vitsyebskaya Voblasts', N Belarus 55.09N 28.37E
Ushak see Uşak
126 I2 **Ushakova, Ostrov** island Severnaya Zemlya, N Russian Federation
Ushant see Ouessant, Île d'
Üsharal see Ucharal
170 Bb14 **Ushibuka** *var.* Usibuka. Kumamoto, Shimo-jima, SW Japan 32.13N 130.01E
Ushi Point see Sabaneta, Puntan
151 V14 **Ushtobe** *Kaz.* Üshtöbe. Almaty, SE Kazakhstan 45.15N 77.58E
65 I25 **Ushuaia** Tierra del Fuego, S Argentina 54.48S 68.19W
41 R10 **Usibelli** Alaska, USA 63.54N 148.41W
Usibuka see Ushibuka
194 I12 **Usino** Madang, N PNG 5.40S 145.31E
129 U6 **Usinsk** Respublika Komi, NW Russian Federation 66.00N 57.37E
99 K22 **Usk** *Wel.* Wysg. ≈ SE Wales, UK
Uskočke Planine/Uskokengebirge see Gorjanci/Žumberačko Gorje
Uskoplje see Gornji Vakuf
Üsküb see Skopje
116 M11 **Üsküpdere** Kırklareli, NW Turkey 41.41N 27.21E
130 L7 **Usman'** Lipetskaya Oblast', W Russian Federation 52.04N 39.41E
120 D8 **Usmas Ezers** ◎ NW Latvia
129 U13 **Usol'ye** Permskaya Oblast', NW Russian Federation 59.27N 56.33E
126 J15 **Usol'ye-Sibirskoye** Irkutskaya Oblast', C Russian Federation 52.48N 103.40E
43 T16 **Uspanapa, Río** ≈ SE Mexico
151 R11 **Uspenskiy** Zhezkazgan, C Kazakhstan 48.45N 72.46E
105 O11 **Ussel** Corrèze, C France 45.33N 2.18E
169 Z6 **Ussuri** *var.* Usuri, Wusuri, *Chin.* Wusuli Jiang. ≈ China/Russian Federation
127 Nn18 **Ussuriysk** *prev.* Nikol'sk, Nikol'sk-Ussuriyskiy, Voroshilov. Primorskiy Kray, SE Russian Federation 43.48N 131.58E
142 J10 **Usta Burnu** headland N Turkey 41.58N 34.30E
155 P13 **Usta Muhammad** Baluchistān, SW Pakistan 28.07N 68.00E
126 K15 **Ust'-Barguzin** Respublika Buryatiya, S Russian Federation 53.28N 109.00E
127 P12 **Ust'-Bol'sheretsk** Kamchatskaya Oblast', E Russian Federation 52.48N 156.12E
131 N9 **Ust'-Buzulukskaya** Volgogradskaya Oblast', SW Russian Federation 50.12N 42.06E
113 C16 **Ústecký Kraj** ◈ region NW Czech Republic
110 G7 **Uster** Zürich, NE Switzerland 47.20N 8.40E
109 I22 **Ustica, Isola d'** island S Italy
126 J13 **Ust'-Ilimsk** Irkutskaya Oblast', C Russian Federation 57.57N 102.30E
113 C15 **Ústí nad Labem** *Ger.* Aussig. Ústecký Kraj, NW Czech Republic 50.40N 14.04E
113 F17 **Ústí nad Orlicí** *Ger.* Wildenschwert. Pardubický Kraj, E Czech Republic 49.58N 16.24E
Ustinov see Izhevsk
115 J14 **Ustiprača** Republika Srpska, SE Bosnia and Herzegovina 43.42N 19.03E
125 Ff12 **Ust'-Ishim** Omskaya Oblast', C Russian Federation 57.42N 70.58E
112 G6 **Ustka** *Ger.* Stolpmünde. Pomorskie, N Poland 54.34N 16.50E
127 Pp10 **Ust'-Kamchatsk** Kamchatskaya Oblast', E Russian Federation 56.13N 162.28E
151 X9 **Ust'-Kamenogorsk** *Kaz.* Öskemen. Vostochnyy Kazakhstan, E Kazakhstan 49.58N 82.36E
127 Oo10 **Ust'-Khayryuzovo** Koryakskiy Avtonomnyy Okrug, E Russian Federation 57.07N 156.37E
126 H16 **Ust'-Koksa** Respublika Altay, S Russian Federation 50.15N 85.45E
129 S11 **Ust'-Kulom** Respublika Komi, NW Russian Federation 61.42N 53.42E
126 Jj14 **Ust'-Kut** Irkutskaya Oblast', C Russian Federation 56.49N 105.31E
126 M7 **Ust'-Kuyga** Respublika Sakha (Yakutiya), NE Russian Federation 69.59N 135.27E
130 L14 **Ust'-Labinsk** Krasnodarskiy Kray, SW Russian Federation 44.40N 40.46E
126 Mm11 **Ust'-Maya** Respublika Sakha (Yakutiya), NE Russian Federation 60.27N 134.28E
127 N9 **Ust'-Nera** Respublika Sakha (Yakutiya), NE Russian Federation 64.28N 143.01E
126 Ll13 **Ust'-Nyukzha** Amurskaya Oblast', S Russian Federation 56.30N 121.32E
126 Kk6 **Ust'-Olenëk** Respublika Sakha (Yakutiya), NE Russian Federation 73.03N 119.34E
127 O10 **Ust'-Omchug** Magadanskaya Oblast', E Russian Federation 61.07N 149.17E
126 Jj15 **Ust'-Ordynskiy** Ust'-Ordynskiy Buryatskiy Avtonomnyy Okrug, S Russian Federation 52.49N 104.42E
126 J15 **Ust'-Ordynskiy Buryatskiy Avtonomnyy Okrug** ◈ autonomous district S Russian Federation
129 N8 **Ust'-Pinega** Arkhangel'skaya Oblast', NW Russian Federation 64.09N 41.55E
126 Hh8 **Ust'-Port** Taymyrskiy (Dolgano-Nenetskiy) Avtonomnyy Okrug, N Russian Federation 69.42N 84.25E
116 L11 **Ustrem** *prev.* Vakav. Yambol, E Bulgaria 42.01N 26.28E
113 O18 **Ustrzyki Dolne** Podkarpackie, SE Poland 49.26N 22.36E
Ust'-Sysol'sk see Syktyvkar
129 R7 **Ust'-Tsil'ma** Respublika Komi, NW Russian Federation 65.25N 52.09E
Ust Urt see Ustyurt Plateau
129 O11 **Ust'ya** ≈ NW Russian Federation
127 P12 **Ust'yevoye** Kamchatskaya Oblast', E Russian Federation 54.06N 155.48E
119 R8 **Ustynivka** Kirovohrads'ka Oblast', C Ukraine 47.58N 32.32E
150 H15 **Ustyurt Plateau** *var.* Ust Urt, *Uzb.* Ustyurt Platosi. plateau Kazakhstan/Uzbekistan
Ustyurt Platosi see Ustyurt Plateau
128 K14 **Ustyuzhna** Vologodskaya Oblast', NW Russian Federation 58.50N 36.25E
164 J4 **Usu** Xinjiang Uygur Zizhiqu, NW China 44.27N 84.37E
175 Q10 **Usu** Sulawesi, C Indonesia 2.34S 120.58E
170 Dd14 **Usuki** Ōita, Kyūshū, SW Japan 33.07N 131.46E
44 G8 **Usulután** Usulután, SE El Salvador 13.19N 88.26W
44 B9 **Usulután** ◈ department SE El Salvador
43 W16 **Usumacinta, Río** ≈ Guatemala/Mexico
Usumbura see Bujumbura
Usuri see Ussuri
176 X12 **Uta** Papua, E Indonesia 4.28S 136.03E
38 K5 **Utah** *off.* State of Utah; also known as Beehive State, Mormon State. ◈ state W USA
38 L3 **Utah Lake** ◎ Utah, W USA
Utaidhani see Uthai Thani
95 M14 **Utajärvi** Oulu, C Finland 64.45N 26.25E
Utamboni see Mitemele, Río
Utaradit see Uttaradit
173 G3 **Utara, Selat** strait Peninsular Malaysia
172 P5 **Utashinai** *var.* Utasinai. Hokkaidō, NE Japan 43.32N 142.03E
Utasinai see Utashinai
176 X12 **Uta, Sungai** ≈ Papua, E Indonesia
200 Ss12 **'Uta Vava'u** island Vava'u Group, N Tonga
39 V9 **Ute Creek** ≈ New Mexico, SW USA
120 H12 **Utena** Utena, E Lithuania 55.30N 25.34E
39 V10 **Ute Reservoir** ⊠ New Mexico, SW USA
178 H10 **Uthai Thani** *var.* Muang Uthai Thani, Udayadhani, Utaidhani. Uthai Thani, W Thailand 15.22N 100.03E
155 O15 **Uthal** Baluchistān, SW Pakistan 25.53N 66.37E
20 I10 **Utica** New York, NE USA 43.06N 75.15W
107 R10 **Utiel** País Valenciano, E Spain 39.33N 1.13W
9 O13 **Utikuma Lake** ◎ Alberta, W Canada
44 I4 **Utila, Isla de** island Islas de la Bahía, N Honduras
Utina see Udine
61 O17 **Utinga** Bahia, E Brazil 12.05S 41.07W
Utirik see Utrik Atoll
97 M22 **Utlängan** island S Sweden
119 U11 **Utlyuts'kyy Lyman** bay S Ukraine
170 Cc14 **Uto** Kumamoto, Kyūshū, SW Japan 32.40N 130.37E
97 P16 **Utö** Stockholm, C Sweden 58.55N 18.19E
27 Q12 **Utopia** Texas, SW USA 29.30N 99.31W
100 J11 **Utrecht** *Lat.* Trajectum ad Rhenum. Utrecht, C Netherlands 52.06N 5.07E
85 K22 **Utrecht** KwaZulu/Natal, E South Africa 27.34S 30.19E
100 I11 **Utrecht** ◈ province C Netherlands
106 K14 **Utrera** Andalucía, S Spain 37.10N 5.46W
201 V4 **Utrik Atoll** *var.* Utirik, Utrōk, Utrōnk. atoll Ratak Chain, N Marshall Islands
Utrōk/Utrōnk see Utrik Atoll
97 B16 **Utsira** island SW Norway
94 L8 **Utsjoki** *var.* Ohcejohka. Lappi, N Finland 69.54N 27.01E
171 Kk15 **Utsunomiya** *var.* Utunomiya. Tochigi, Honshū, S Japan 36.36N 139.52E
131 P13 **Utta** Respublika Kalmykiya, SW Russian Federation 46.22N 46.03E
178 Hh8 **Uttaradit** *var.* Utaradit. Uttaradit, N Thailand 17.37N 100.04E
158 J8 **Uttarkāshi** Uttar Pradesh, N India 30.45N 78.19E
158 K11 **Uttar Pradesh** *prev.* United Provinces, United Provinces of Agra and Oudh. ◈ state N India
47 T5 **Utuado** C Puerto Rico 18.16N 66.43W
164 K3 **Utubulak** Xinjiang Uygur Zizhiqu, W China 46.49N 86.15E
41 N5 **Utukok River** ≈ Alaska, USA
Utunomiya see Utsunomiya
195 X9 **Utupua** island Santa Cruz Islands, E Soloman Islands
150 G9 **Utva** ≈ NW Kazakhstan
201 Y15 **Utwe** Kosrae, E Micronesia
201 X15 **Utwe Harbor** harbor Kosrae, E Micronesia
168 J7 **Uubulan** Arhangay, C Mongolia 48.37N 101.58E
120 G6 **Uulu** Pärnumaa, SW Estonia 58.15N 24.31E
207 N13 **Uummannaq** *var.* Umanak, Umanaq. Kitaa, C Greenland 70.37N 52.25W
Uummannarsuaq see Nunap Isua
168 E4 **Üüreg Nuur** ◎ NW Mongolia
Uusikaarlepyy see Nykarleby
95 J19 **Uusikaupunki** *Swe.* Nystad. Länsi-Suomi, W Finland 60.48N 21.25E
131 S2 **Uva** Udmurtskaya Respublika, NW Russian Federation 56.41N 52.15E
115 L14 **Uvac** ≈ W Serbia and Montenegro (Yugoslavia)
27 Q12 **Uvalde** Texas, SW USA 29.13N 99.49W
161 K25 **Uva Province** ◈ province SE Sri Lanka
121 O18 **Uvaravichy** *Rus.* Uvarovichi. Homyel'skaya Voblasts', SE Belarus 52.36N 30.43E
56 J11 **Uvá, Río** ≈ E Colombia
Uvarovichi see Uvaravichy
131 N7 **Uvarovo** Tambovskaya Oblast', W Russian Federation 51.58N 42.13E
125 Ff11 **Uvat** Tyumenskaya Oblast', C Russian Federation 59.11N 68.37E
202 G12 **Uvea, Île** island N Wallis and Futuna
83 E21 **Uvinza** Kigoma, W Tanzania 5.04S 30.24E
81 O20 **Uvira** Sud Kivu, E Dem. Rep. Congo 3.24S 29.04E
168 E5 **Uvs** ◈ province NW Mongolia
168 F5 **Uvs Nuur** *var.* Ozero Ubsu-Nur. ◎ Mongolia/Russian Federation
170 E15 **Uwa** Ehime, Shikoku, SW Japan 33.22N 132.29E
170 E15 **Uwajima** *var.* Uwazima. Ehime, Shikoku, SW Japan 33.13N 132.32E
82 B5 **'Uwaynāt, Jabal al** *var.* Jebel Uweinat. ▲ Libya/Sudan 21.51N 25.01E
Uwazima see Uwajima
Uweinat, Jebel see 'Uwaynāt, Jabal al
176 Z14 **Uwimmerah, Sungai** ≈ Papua, E Indonesia
12 H14 **Uxbridge** Ontario, S Canada 44.07N 79.07W
Uxellodunum see Issoudun
168 M15 **Uxin Qi** Nei Mongol Zizhiqu, N China 38.29N 108.48E
43 X12 **Uxmal, Ruinas** ruins Yucatán, SE Mexico 20.20N 89.46W
133 Q5 **Uy** ≈ Kazakhstan/Russian Federation
150 K15 **Uyaly** Kzylorda, S Kazakhstan 44.22N 61.16E
126 Mm7 **Uyandina** ≈ NE Russian Federation
168 L10 **Üydzen** Ömnögovĭ, S Mongolia 44.08N 106.48E
Uyeda see Ueda
126 Hh3 **Uyedineniya, Ostrov** island N Russian Federation
79 V17 **Uyo** Akwa Ibom, S Nigeria 5.00N 7.57E
168 D8 **Üyönch** Hovd, W Mongolia 46.04N 92.05E
151 Q15 **Uyuk** Zhambyl, S Kazakhstan 43.46N 70.55E
147 V13 **'Uyūn** SW Oman 17.12N 53.46E
59 K20 **Uyuni** Potosí, W Bolivia 20.26S 66.48W
59 J20 **Uyuni, Salar de** wetland SW Bolivia
152 I9 **Uzbekistan** *off.* Republic of Uzbekistan. ◆ republic C Asia
164 D8 **Uzbel Shankou** *Rus.* Pereval Kyzyl-Dzhiik. pass China/Tajikistan 38.33N 73.46E
121 J17 **Uzda** *Rus.* Uzda. Minskaya Voblasts', C Belarus 53.29N 27.10E
105 N12 **Uzerche** Corrèze, C France 45.24N 1.35E
105 R14 **Uzès** Gard, S France 44.00N 4.25E
153 T10 **Uzgen** *Kir.* Özgön. Oshskaya Oblast', SW Kyrgyzstan 40.42N 73.17E
119 O3 **Uzh** ≈ N Ukraine
Uzhgorod see Uzhhorod
118 G7 **Uzhhorod** *Rus.* Uzhgorod; *prev.* Ungvár. Zakarpats'ka Oblast', W Ukraine 48.36N 22.19E
126 Hh14 **Uzhur** Krasnoyarskiy Kray, S Russian Federation 55.18N 89.36E
Uzi see Uji
114 K13 **Užice** *prev.* Titovo Užice. Serbia, W Serbia and Montenegro (Yugoslavia) 43.52N 19.51E
Uzin see Uzyn
130 L5 **Uzlovaya** Tul'skaya Oblast', W Russian Federation 54.01N 38.15E
110 H7 **Uznach** Sankt Gallen, NE Switzerland 47.12N 9.00E
151 U16 **Uzunagach** Almaty, SE Kazakhstan 43.07N 76.19E
142 B10 **Uzunköprü** Edirne, NW Turkey 41.15N 26.42E
120 D11 **Užventis** Kelmė, C Lithuania 55.49N 22.38E
119 P5 **Uzyn** *Rus.* Uzin. Kyyivs'ka Oblast', N Ukraine 49.52N 30.28E

V

Vääksy see Asikkala
85 H23 **Vaal** ≈ C South Africa
95 M14 **Vaala** Oulu, C Finland 64.34N 26.49E
95 N19 **Vaalimaa** Etelä-Suomi, SE Finland 60.34N 27.49E
101 M19 **Vaals** Limburg, SE Netherlands 50.46N 6.01E
95 J16 **Vaasa** *Swe.* Vasa; *prev.* Nikolainkaupunki. Vaasa, W Finland 63.07N 21.39E
100 L10 **Vaassen** Gelderland, E Netherlands 52.18N 5.58E
120 G11 **Vabalninkas** Biržai, NE Lithuania 55.59N 24.45E
Vabkent see Vobkent
113 J22 **Vác** *Ger.* Waitzen. Pest, N Hungary 47.46N 19.07E
63 I14 **Vacaria** Rio Grande do Sul, S Brazil 28.30S 50.57W
37 N7 **Vacaville** California, W USA 38.21N 121.59W
105 R15 **Vaccarès, Étang de** ◎ SE France
46 L10 **Vache, Île à** island SW Haiti
181 Y16 **Vacoas** W Mauritius 20.18S 57.28E
34 G10 **Vader** Washington, NW USA 46.23N 122.58W
96 D12 **Vadheim** Sogn og Fjordane, S Norway 61.12N 5.48E
124 O3 **Vadili** *Gk.* Vatilí. C Cyprus 35.09N 33.39E
160 D11 **Vadodara** *prev.* Baroda. Gujarāt, W India 22.19N 73.13E
94 M8 **Vadsø** *Fin.* Vesisaari. Finnmark, N Norway 70.07N 29.47E
97 L17 **Vadstena** Östergötland, S Sweden 58.25N 14.55E
110 I8 **Vaduz** ● (Liechtenstein) W Liechtenstein 47.07N 9.31E
Vág see Váh
129 N12 **Vaga** ≈ NW Russian Federation
96 G11 **Vågåmo** Oppland, S Norway 61.52N 9.06E
114 D12 **Vaganski Vrh** ▲ W Croatia 44.24N 15.32E
97 A19 **Vágar** *Dan.* Vågø Island Faeroe Islands 62.03N 7.19W
Vágbeszterce see Považská Bystrica
97 L19 **Vaggeryd** Jönköping, S Sweden 57.30N 14.10E
195 U14 **Vaghena** *var.* Wagina. island NW Solomon Islands
97 O16 **Vagnhärad** Södermanland, C Sweden 58.57N 17.31E
106 G7 **Vagos** Aveiro, N Portugal 40.33N 8.42W
Vágsellye see Sal'a
94 H10 **Vågsfjorden** fjord N Norway
96 C10 **Vågsøy** island S Norway
Vágújhely see Nové Mesto nad Váhom
113 I21 **Váh** *Ger.* Waag, *Hung.* Vág. ≈ W Slovakia
95 K16 **Vähäkyrö** Länsi-Suomi, W Finland 63.04N 22.04E
203 X11 **Vahitahi** atoll Îles Tuamotu, E French Polynesia
Vaidei see Vulcan
24 L4 **Vaiden** Mississippi, S USA 33.19N 89.42W
161 I23 **Vaigai** ≈ SE India
203 V16 **Vaihu** Easter Island, Chile, E Pacific Ocean 27.10S 109.22W
120 I6 **Väike Emajõgi** ≈ S Estonia
120 I4 **Väike-Maarja** *Ger.* Klein-Marien. Lääne-Virumaa, NE Estonia 59.07N 26.13E
Väike-Salatsi see Mazsalaca
39 R4 **Vail** Colorado, C USA 39.36N 106.20W
200 Qq15 **Vaina** Tongatapu, S Tonga 21.12S 175.10W
120 E5 **Väinameri** *prev.* Muhu Väin, *Ger.* Moon-Sund. sea E Baltic Sea
95 N18 **Vainikkala** Etelä-Suomi, SE Finland 60.54N 28.18E
120 D10 **Vaiņode** Liepāja, SW Latvia 56.25N 21.52E
161 H23 **Vaippār** ≈ SE India
203 W11 **Vairaatea** atoll Îles Tuamotu, C French Polynesia
203 R8 **Vairao** Tahiti, W French Polynesia 17.48S 149.16W
105 R14 **Vaison-la-Romaine** Vaucluse, SE France 44.15N 5.04E
202 G11 **Vaitupu** Île Uvea, E Wallis and Futuna 13.13S 176.09W
202 F7 **Vaitupu** atoll C Tuvalu
Vajdahunyad see Hunedoara
Vajdej see Vulcan
80 K12 **Vakaga** ◈ prefecture NE Central African Republic
116 H10 **Vakarel** Sofiya, W Bulgaria 42.34N 23.43E
Vakav see Ustrem
143 O11 **Vakfıkebir** Trabzon, NE Turkey 41.03N 39.19E
126 H11 **Vakh** ≈ C Russian Federation
Vakhon, Qatorkŭhi see Nicholas Range
153 P14 **Vakhsh** SW Tajikistan 37.46N 68.48E
153 Q12 **Vakhsh** ≈ SW Tajikistan
131 P1 **Vakhtan** Nizhegorodskaya Oblast', W Russian Federation 58.00N 46.43E
96 C13 **Vaksdal** Hordaland, S Norway 60.28N 5.45E
129 O8 **Vashka** ≈ NW Russian Federation
195 O15 **Vakuta Island** island Kiriwina Islands, SE PNG
Valachia see Wallachia
110 D11 **Valais** *Ger.* Wallis. ◈ canton SW Switzerland
115 M21 **Valamarës, Mali i** ▲ SE Albania 40.48N 20.31E
131 S2 **Valamaz** Udmurtskaya Respublika, NW Russian Federation 57.36N 52.07E
115 Q19 **Valandovo** SE FYR Macedonia 41.20N 22.33E
113 I18 **Valašské Meziříčí** *Ger.* Wallachisch-Meseritsch, *Pol.* Wałeckie Międzyrzecze. Zlínský Kraj, E Czech Republic 49.28N 17.57E
117 I17 **Valáxa** island Vóreioi Sporádes, Greece, Aegean Sea
97 K16 **Vålberg** Värmland, C Sweden 59.24N 13.12E
118 H12 **Vâlcea** *prev.* Vîlcea. ◈ county SW Romania
65 J16 **Valcheta** Río Negro, E Argentina 40.42S 66.07W
13 P12 **Valcourt** Quebec, SE Canada 45.28N 72.18W
Valdai Hills see Valdayskaya Vozvyshennost'
106 M3 **Valdavia** ≈ N Spain
128 I15 **Valday** Novgorodskaya Oblast', W Russian Federation 57.56N 33.19E
128 I15 **Valdayskaya Vozvyshennost'** *var.* Valdai Hills. hill range W Russian Federation
106 L9 **Valdecañas, Embalse de** ⊠ W Spain
120 E8 **Valdemārpils** *Ger.* Sassmacken. Talsi, NW Latvia 57.23N 22.36E
97 N18 **Valdemarsvik** Östergötland, S Sweden 58.13N 16.34E
107 N8 **Valdemoro** Madrid, C Spain 40.12N 3.40W
107 O11 **Valdepeñas** Castilla-La Mancha, C Spain 38.46N 3.24W
106 L5 **Valderaduey** ≈ NE Spain
106 L5 **Valderas** Castilla-León, N Spain 42.04N 5.27W
107 T7 **Valderrobres** *var.* Vall-de-roures. Aragón, NE Spain 40.52N 0.07E
65 K17 **Valdés, Península** peninsula SE Argentina
41 S11 **Valdez** Alaska, USA 61.07N 146.21W
58 C5 **Valdéz** *var.* Limones. Esmeraldas, NW Ecuador 1.17N 78.56W
Valdia see Weldiya
105 U11 **Val d'Isère** Savoie, E France 45.23N 7.03E
65 G15 **Valdivia** Los Lagos, C Chile 39.49S 73.12W
Valdivia Bank see Valdivia Seamount
67 P17 **Valdivia Seamount** *var.* Valdivia Bank. undersea feature E Atlantic Ocean 26.15S 6.25E
105 N4 **Val-d'Oise** ◈ department N France
12 J8 **Val-d'Or** Quebec, SE Canada 48.05N 77.42W
25 U8 **Valdosta** Georgia, SE USA 30.49N 83.16W
96 G13 **Valdres** physical region S Norway
34 L13 **Vale** Oregon, NW USA 43.58N 117.14W
118 F9 **Valea lui Mihai** *Hung.* Érmihályfalva. Bihor, NW Romania 47.31N 22.08E
9 N15 **Valemount** British Columbia, SW Canada 52.46N 119.17W
61 O17 **Valença** Bahia, E Brazil 13.22S 39.06W
106 F4 **Valença do Minho** Viana do Castelo, N Portugal 42.01N 8.37W
61 N14 **Valença do Piauí** Piauí, E Brazil 6.25S 41.46W
105 N8 **Valençay** Indre, C France 47.10N 1.31E
105 R13 **Valence** *anc.* Valentia, Valentia Julia, Ventia. Drôme, E France 44.55N 4.54E
107 S10 **Valencia** País Valenciano, E Spain 39.28N 0.24W
56 K5 **Valencia** Carabobo, N Venezuela 10.11N 68.02W
107 R10 **Valencia** *Cat.* València. ◈ province País Valenciano, E Spain
107 S10 **Valencia** ✕ Valencia, E Spain
València/Valencia see País Valenciano
106 I10 **Valencia de Alcántara** Extremadura, W Spain 39.25N 7.13W
106 L4 **Valencia de Don Juan** Castilla-León, N Spain 42.16N 5.31W
107 U9 **Valencia, Golfo de** *var.* Gulf of Valencia. gulf E Spain
Valencia, Gulf of see Valencia, Golfo de
99 A21 **Valencia Island** *Ir.* Dairbhre. island SW Ireland
105 P2 **Valenciennes** Nord, N France 50.21N 3.31E
118 K13 **Vălenii de Munte** Prahova, SE Romania 45.10N 26.01E
Valentia see Valence, France
Valentia see País Valenciano
Valentia Julia see Valence
105 T8 **Valentigney** Doubs, E France 47.27N 6.49E
30 M12 **Valentine** Nebraska, C USA 42.52N 100.31W
26 J10 **Valentine** Texas, SW USA 30.35N 104.30W
Valentine State see Oregon
108 C8 **Valenza** Piemonte, NW Italy 45.01N 8.37E
96 I13 **Våler** Hedmark, S Norway 60.39N 11.52E
56 I6 **Valera** Trujillo, NW Venezuela 9.21N 70.37W
199 K13 **Valerie Guyot** undersea feature S Pacific Ocean 33.00S 164.00W
Valetta see Valletta
120 I7 **Valga** *Ger.* Walk, *Latv.* Valka. Valgamaa, S Estonia 57.48N 26.04E
120 I7 **Valgamaa** *off.* Valga Maakond. ◈ province S Estonia
45 Q15 **Valiente, Península** peninsula NW Panama
105 X16 **Valinco, Golfe de** gulf Corse, France, C Mediterranean Sea
114 L12 **Valjevo** Serbia, W Serbia and Montenegro (Yugoslavia) 44.16N 19.54E
Valjok see Válljohka
120 I7 **Valka** *Ger.* Walk. Valka, N Latvia 57.48N 26.01E
Valka see Valga
95 L18 **Valkeakoski** Länsi-Suomi, W Finland 61.16N 24.04E
95 M19 **Valkeala** Etelä-Suomi, S Finland 60.55N 26.49E
101 L18 **Valkenburg** Limburg, SE Netherlands 50.52N 5.46E
101 K15 **Valkenswaard** Noord-Brabant, S Netherlands 51.21N 5.28E
121 G15 **Valkininkai** Varėna, S Lithuania 54.22N 24.51E
119 U5 **Valky** Kharkivs'ka Oblast', E Ukraine 49.51N 35.40E
43 Y12 **Valladolid** Yucatán, SE Mexico 20.39N 88.13W
106 M5 **Valladolid** Castilla-León, NW Spain 41.39N 4.45W
106 L5 **Valladolid** ◈ province Castilla-León, N Spain
105 U15 **Vallauris** Alpes-Maritimes, SE France 43.34N 7.03E
Vall-de-roures see Valderrobres
107 S9 **Vall d'Uxó** País Valenciano, E Spain 39.49N 0.15W
97 E16 **Valle** Aust-Agder, S Norway 59.13N 7.33E
107 N2 **Valle** Cantabria, N Spain 43.14N 4.16W
44 H8 **Valle** ◈ department S Honduras
107 N8 **Vallecas** Madrid, C Spain 40.22N 3.37W
39 Q8 **Vallecito Reservoir** ⊠ Colorado, C USA
108 A7 **Valle d'Aosta** ◈ region NW Italy
43 O14 **Valle de Bravo** México, S Mexico 19.19N 100.08W
57 N5 **Valle de Guanape** Anzoátegui, N Venezuela 9.49N 65.34W
56 M6 **Valle de La Pascua** Guárico, N Venezuela 09.15N 66.00W
56 B11 **Valle del Cauca** *off.* Departamento del Valle del Cauca. ◈ province W Colombia
43 N13 **Valle de Santiago** Guanajuato, C Mexico 20.21N 101.13W
42 J7 **Valle de Zaragoza** Chihuahua, N Mexico 27.25N 105.50W
56 G5 **Valledupar** Cesar, N Colombia 10.31N 73.16W
78 G10 **Vallée de Ferlo** ≈ NW Senegal
59 M19 **Vallegrande** Santa Cruz, C Bolivia 18.30S 64.06W
43 P8 **Valle Hermoso** Tamaulipas, C Mexico 25.39N 97.49W
37 N8 **Vallejo** California, W USA 38.07N 122.16W
64 G8 **Vallenar** Atacama, N Chile 28.35S 70.44W
97 O15 **Vallentuna** Stockholm, C Sweden 59.31N 18.04E
123 Ll12 **Valletta** *prev.* Valetta. ● (Malta) E Malta 35.54N 14.30E
29 N6 **Valley Center** Kansas, C USA 37.49N 97.22W
31 Q5 **Valley City** North Dakota, N USA 46.57N 97.58W
34 I15 **Valley Falls** Oregon, NW USA 42.28N 120.16W
Valleyfield see Salaberry-de-Valleyfield
23 S4 **Valley Head** West Virginia, NE USA 38.33N 80.01W
27 T8 **Valley Mills** Texas, SW USA 31.36N 97.27W
77 W10 **Valley of the Kings** ancient monument E Egypt 25.41N 32.30E
31 R11 **Valley Springs** South Dakota, N USA 43.34N 96.28W
22 K5 **Valley Station** Kentucky, S USA 38.06N 85.52W
9 O13 **Valleyview** Alberta, W Canada 55.01N 117.16W
27 T5 **Valley View** Texas, SW USA 33.27N 97.08W
63 C21 **Vallimanca, Arroyo** ≈ E Argentina
94 L9 **Válljohka** *var.* Valjok Finnmark, N Norway 69.39N 25.52E
109 M19 **Vallo della Lucania** Campania, S Italy 40.13N 15.15E
110 B9 **Vallorbe** Vaud, W Switzerland 46.43N 6.21E
107 V6 **Valls** Cataluña, NE Spain 41.18N 1.15E
96 N11 **Vallsta** Gävleborg, C Sweden 61.30N 16.25E
96 N12 **Vallvik** Gävleborg, C Sweden 61.10N 17.15E
9 T17 **Val Marie** Saskatchewan, S Canada 49.15N 107.43W
120 H7 **Valmiera** *Est.* Volmari, *Ger.* Wolmar. Valmiera, N Latvia 57.33N 25.26E
107 N3 **Valnera** ▲ N Spain 43.08N 3.39W
104 J3 **Valognes** Manche, N France 49.31N 1.28W
Valona see Vlorë
Valona Bay see Vlorës, Gjiri i
106 G6 **Valongo** *var.* Valongo de Gaia. Porto, N Portugal 41.10N 8.30W
Valongo de Gaia see Valongo
106 M5 **Valoria la Buena** Castilla-León, N Spain 41.48N 4.33W
121 J15 **Valozhyn** *Pol.* Wołożyn, *Rus.* Volozhin. Minskaya Voblasts', C Belarus 54.07N 26.31E
106 I5 **Valpaços** Vila Real, N Portugal 41.36N 7.16W
25 P8 **Valparaiso** Florida, SE USA 30.30N 86.28W
33 N11 **Valparaiso** Indiana, N USA 41.28N 87.04W
64 G11 **Valparaíso** Valparaíso, C Chile 33.04S 71.18W
42 L11 **Valparaíso** Zacatecas, C Mexico 22.49N 103.28W
64 G11 **Valparaíso** *off.* Región de Valparaíso. ◈ region C Chile
Valpo see Valpovo
114 I9 **Valpovo** *Hung.* Valpo. Osijek-Baranja, E Croatia 45.40N 18.25E
105 R14 **Valréas** Vaucluse, SE France 44.22N 5.00E
Vals see Vals-Platz
160 D12 **Valsād** *prev.* Bulsar. Gujarāt, W India 20.40N 72.55E
Valsbaai see False Bay
176 Uu10 **Valse Pisang, Kepulauan** island group E Indonesia
110 H9 **Vals-Platz** *var.* Vals. Graubünden, S Switzerland 46.39N 9.09E
176 Xx16 **Vals, Tanjung** headland Papua, SE Indonesia 8.25S 137.34E
95 N15 **Valtimo** Itä-Suomi, E Finland 63.39N 28.49E
117 D17 **Váltou** ▲▲ C Greece
131 O12 **Valuyevka** Rostovskaya Oblast', SW Russian Federation 46.48N 43.49E
130 K9 **Valuyki** Belgorodskaya Oblast', W Russian Federation 50.11N 38.07E
38 L2 **Val Verda** Utah, W USA 40.51N 111.53W
66 N12 **Valverde** Hierro, Islas Canarias, Spain, NE Atlantic Ocean 27.48N 17.55W
106 I13 **Valverde del Camino** Andalucía, S Spain 37.34N 6.45W
97 G23 **Vamdrup** Vejle, C Denmark 55.25N 9.18E
96 L12 **Våmhus** Dalarna, C Sweden 61.07N 14.30E
95 K18 **Vammala** Länsi-Suomi, W Finland 61.19N 22.55E
Vámosudvarhely see Odorheiu Secuiesc
143 S14 **Van** Van, E Turkey 38.30N 43.22E
27 V7 **Van** Texas, SW USA 32.31N 95.38W
143 T14 **Van** ◈ province E Turkey
143 T11 **Vanadzor** *prev.* Kirovakan. N Armenia 40.49N 44.28E
27 U5 **Van Alstyne** Texas, SW USA 33.25N 96.34W
35 W10 **Vananda** Montana, NW USA 46.22N 106.58W
118 I11 **Vânători** *Hung.* Héjjasfalva; *prev.* Vînători. Mureş, C Romania 46.13N 24.56E
203 W12 **Vanavana** atoll Îles Tuamotu, SE French Polynesia
Vana-Vändra see Vändra
126 J12 **Vanavara** Evenkiyskiy Avtonomnyy Okrug, C Russian Federation 60.19N 102.19E
13 Q8 **Van Bruyssel** Quebec, SE Canada 47.56N 72.08W
29 R10 **Van Buren** Arkansas, C USA 35.26N 94.21W
21 S1 **Van Buren** Maine, NE USA 47.07N 67.57W
29 W7 **Van Buren** Missouri, C USA 37.00N 91.00W
21 T5 **Vanceboro** Maine, NE USA 45.31N 67.25W
23 W10 **Vanceboro** North Carolina, SE USA 35.16N 77.06W
23 O4 **Vanceburg** Kentucky, S USA 38.32N 83.18W
Vanch see Vanj
8 L17 **Vancouver** British Columbia, SW Canada 49.13N 123.06W
34 G11 **Vancouver** Washington, NW USA 45.38N 122.39W
8 L17 **Vancouver** ✕ British Columbia, SW Canada 49.03N 123.00W
8 K16 **Vancouver Island** island British Columbia, SW Canada
Vanda see Vantaa
176 Xx11 **Van Daalen** ≈ Papua, E Indonesia
32 L15 **Vandalia** Illinois, N USA 38.57N 89.05W
29 V3 **Vandalia** Missouri, C USA 39.18N 91.29W
33 R13 **Vandalia** Ohio, N USA 39.53N 84.12W
27 U13 **Vanderbilt** Texas, SW USA 28.45N 96.37W
33 Q10 **Vandercook Lake** Michigan, N USA 42.11N 84.23W
8 L14 **Vanderhoof** British Columbia, SW Canada 53.54N 124.00W
20 K8 **Vanderwhacker Mountain** ▲ New York, NE USA 43.54N 74.06W
189 P1 **Van Diemen Gulf** gulf Northern Territory, N Australia
Van Diemen's Land see Tasmania
120 H5 **Vändra** *Ger.* Fennern; *prev.* Vana-Vändra. Pärnumaa, SW Estonia 58.40N 25.01E
Vandsburg see Więcbork
36 L4 **Van Duzen River** ≈ California, W USA
120 F13 **Vandžiogala** Kaunas, C Lithuania 55.07N 23.55E
43 N10 **Vanegas** San Luis Potosí, C Mexico 23.53N 100.55W
Vaner, Lake see Vänern
97 K17 **Vänern** *Eng.* Lake Vaner; *prev.* Lake Vener. ◎ S Sweden
97 J18 **Vänersborg** Västra Götaland, S Sweden 58.16N 12.22E
96 F12 **Vang** Oppland, S Norway 61.07N 8.34E
180 I7 **Vangaindrano** Fianarantsoa, SE Madagascar 23.21S 47.34E
143 S14 **Van Gölü** *Eng.* Lake Van; *anc.* Thospitis. salt lake E Turkey
195 V15 **Vangunu** island New Georgia Islands, NW Solomon Islands
26 J9 **Van Horn** Texas, SW USA 31.03N 104.51W
195 X9 **Vanikolo** *var.* Vanikoro. island Santa Cruz Islands, E Solomon Islands
Vanikoro see Vanikolo
194 E9 **Vanimo** Sandaun, NW PNG 2.43S 141.22E
127 O15 **Vanino** Khabarovskiy Kray, SE Russian Federation 49.10N 140.18E
161 G19 **Vānīvilāsa Sāgara** ◎ SW India
153 S13 **Vanj** *Rus.* Vanch. S Tajikistan 38.22N 71.27E
118 G14 **Vânju Mare** *prev.* Vînju Mare. Mehedinţi, SW Romania 44.25N 22.52E
127 P3 **Vankarem** Chukotskiy Avtonomnyy Okrug, NE Russian Federation 67.48N 176.11W
13 N12 **Vankleek Hill** Ontario, SE Canada 45.32N 74.39W
Van, Lake see Van Gölü
95 I16 **Vännäs** Västerbotten, N Sweden 63.54N 19.43E
95 I15 **Vännäsby** Västerbotten, N Sweden 63.55N 19.53E
104 H7 **Vannes** *anc.* Dariorigum. Morbihan, NW France 47.40N 2.45W
94 I8 **Vannøya** island N Norway
105 T12 **Vanoise, Massif de la** ▲▲ E France
176 Xx10 **Van Rees, Pegunungan** ▲▲ Papua, E Indonesia
85 E24 **Vanrhynsdorp** Western Cape, SW South Africa 31.33S 18.42E
23 P7 **Vansant** Virginia, NE USA 37.13N 82.03W
96 L13 **Vansbro** Dalarna, C Sweden 60.31N 14.15E
97 D18 **Vanse** Vest-Agder, S Norway 58.04N 6.40E
15 M4 **Vansittart Island** island Nunavut, NE Canada
95 M20 **Vantaa** *Swe.* Vanda. Etelä-Suomi, S Finland 60.18N 25.01E
95 L19 **Vantaa** ✕ (Helsinki) Etelä-Suomi, S Finland 60.18N 25.01E
34 J9 **Vantage** Washington, NW USA 46.55N 119.55W
197 K14 **Vanua Balavu** *prev.* Vanua Mbalavu. island Lau Group, E Fiji
197 C10 **Vanua Lava** island Banks Islands, N Vanuatu
197 J12 **Vanua Levu** island N Fiji
197 I12 **Vanua Levu Barrier Reef** reef C Fiji
Vanua Mbalavu see Vanua Balavu

◆ Country
● Country Capital
◇ Dependent Territory
○ Dependent Territory Capital
◈ Administrative Region
✕ International Airport
▲ Mountain
▲▲ Mountain Range
Volcano
≈ River
◎ Lake
⊠ Reservoir

197 B10 Vanuatu off. Republic of Vanuatu; prev. New Hebrides. ◆ republic SW Pacific Ocean
183 P8 Vanuatu island group SW Pacific Ocean
197 K15 Vanua Vatu island Lau Group, E Fiji
33 Q12 Van Wert Ohio, N USA 40.52N 84.34W
197 K7 Vao Province Sud, S New Caledonia 22.40S 167.29E
Vapincum see Gap
119 N7 Vapnyarka Vinnyts'ka Oblast', C Ukraine 48.32N 28.44E
105 T15 Var ◆ department SE France
105 U14 Var ⁓ SE France
97 J18 Vara Västra Götaland, S Sweden 58.16N 12.57E
Varadinska Županija see Varaždin
120 J10 Varakļani Madona, C Latvia 56.36N 26.40E
108 C7 Varallo Piemonte, NE Italy 45.51N 8.16E
149 O5 Varāmīn var. Veramin. Tehrān, N Iran 35.19N 51.40E
159 N14 Vārānasi prev. Banaras, Benares, hist. Kasi. Uttar Pradesh, N India 25.20N 83.00E
129 T3 Varandey Nenetskiy Avtonomnyy Okrug, NW Russian Federation 68.48N 57.54E
94 M8 Varangerbotn Finnmark, N Norway 70.09N 28.28E
94 M8 Varangerfjorden fjord N Norway
94 M8 Varangerhalvøya peninsula N Norway
Varannó see Vranov nad Topľou
109 M15 Varano, Lago di ⊚ SE Italy
120 J13 Varapayeva Rus. Voropayevo. Vitsyebskaya Voblasts', NW Belarus 55.09N 27.13E
Varasd see Varaždin
114 E7 Varaždin Ger. Warasdin, Hung. Varasd. Varaždin, N Croatia 46.18N 16.20E
114 E7 Varaždin off. Varadinska Županija. ◆ province N Croatia
108 C10 Varazze Liguria, NW Italy 44.21N 8.35E
97 J20 Varberg Halland, S Sweden 57.06N 12.15E
Vardak see Wardag
115 Q19 Vardar Gk. Axiós. ⁓ FYR Macedonia/Greece see also Axiós
97 F23 Varde Ribe, W Denmark 55.37N 8.31E
143 V12 Vardenis E Armenia 40.11N 45.43E
94 N8 Vardø Fin. Vuoreija. Finnmark, N Norway 70.22N 31.04E
117 E18 Vardoúsia ▲ C Greece
Vareia see Logroño
102 G10 Varel Niedersachsen, NW Germany 53.24N 8.07E
121 G15 Varėna Pol. Orany. Varėna, S Lithuania 54.13N 24.35E
13 O12 Varennes Quebec, SE Canada 45.42N 73.25W
105 P10 Varennes-sur-Allier Allier, C France 46.17N 3.24E
114 I12 Vareš Federacija Bosna I Hercegovina, E Bosnia and Herzegovina 44.12N 18.19E
108 D7 Varese Lombardia, N Italy 45.49N 8.49E
118 J12 Vârful Moldoveanu var. Moldoveanul; prev. Vîrful Moldoveanu. ▲ C Romania 45.35N 24.48E
Varganzi see Warganza
97 J18 Vårgårda Västra Götaland, S Sweden 58.00N 12.49E
125 F12 Vargashi Kurganskaya Oblast', C Russian Federation 55.22N 65.39E
97 J18 Vargön Västra Götaland, S Sweden 58.21N 12.22E
97 C17 Varhaug Rogaland, S Norway 58.37N 5.39E
95 N17 Varkaus Itä-Suomi, C Finland 62.19N 27.49E
94 J2 Varmahlidh Nordhurland Vestra, N Iceland 65.32N 19.33W
97 J15 Värmland ◆ county C Sweden
97 K16 Värmlandsnäs peninsula S Sweden
116 N8 Varna prev. Stalin, anc. Odessus. Varna, E Bulgaria 43.13N 27.55E
116 N8 Varna ✕ Varna, E Bulgaria 43.16N 27.52E
116 N8 Varna ◆ province E Bulgaria
97 L20 Värnamo Jönköping, S Sweden 57.10N 14.03E
116 N8 Varnenski Zaliv prev. Stalinski Zaliv. bay E Bulgaria
116 N8 Varnensko Ezero estuary E Bulgaria
120 D11 Varniai Telšiai, W Lithuania 55.45N 22.22E
Varnoús see Baba
113 D14 Varnsdorf Ger. Warnsdorf. Ústecký Kraj, N Czech Republic 50.55N 14.34E
113 I23 Várpalota Veszprém, W Hungary 47.13N 18.07E
Varshava see Warszawa
120 K6 Värska Põlvamaa, SE Estonia 57.58N 27.37E
100 N12 Varsseveld Gelderland, E Netherlands 51.55N 6.28E
117 D19 Vartholomió prev. Vartholomión. Dytikí Ellás, S Greece 37.52N 21.12E
Vartholomión see Vartholomió
143 Q14 Varto Muş, E Turkey 39.10N 41.28E
97 K18 Vartofta Västra Götaland, S Sweden 58.06N 13.40E
95 O17 Värtsilä Itä-Suomi, E Finland 62.10N 30.35E
Värtsilä see Vyartsilya
119 R4 Varva Chernihivs'ka Oblast', NE Ukraine 50.31N 32.43E
61 H18 Várzea Grande Mato Grosso, SW Brazil 15.39S 56.07W
108 D9 Varzi Lombardia, N Italy 44.51N 9.13E
Varzimanor Ayni see Ayní
128 K5 Varzuga ⁓ NW Russian Federation
105 P8 Varzy Nièvre, C France 47.22N 3.22E
113 G23 Vas off. Vas Megye. ◆ county W Hungary
Vasa see Vaasa
202 A9 Vasafua island Funafuti Atoll, C Tuvalu
113 O21 Vásárosnamény Szabolcs-Szatmár-Bereg, E Hungary 48.07N 22.19E
106 H13 Vascão, Ribeira de ⁓ S Portugal
118 G10 Vaşcău Hung. Vaskoh. Bihor, NE Romania 46.26N 22.30E
Vascongadas, Provincias see País Vasco
Vashess Bay see Vaskess Bay
Vāsht see Khāsh
Vasilevichi see Vasilyevichy
117 G14 Vasiliká Kentrikí Makedonía, NE Greece 40.28N 23.07E
117 C18 Vasilikí Lefkáda, Iónioi Nísoi, Greece, C Mediterranean Sea 38.36N 20.37E
117 K25 Vasilikí Kríti, Greece, E Mediterranean Sea 35.04N 25.49E
121 G16 Vasilishki Pol. Wasiliszki, Rus. Vasilishki. Hrodzyenskaya Voblasts', W Belarus 53.46N 24.51E
Vasil Kolarov see Pamporovo
Vasil'kov see Vasyl'kiv
121 N19 Vasilyevichy Rus. Vasilevichi. Homyel'skaya Voblasts', SE Belarus 52.15N 29.49E
203 Y3 Vaskess Bay var. Vashess Bay. bay Kiritimati, E Kiribati
Vaskoh see Vaşcău
Vaskohsziklás see Ştei
118 M10 Vaslui Vaslui, C Romania 46.38N 27.44E
118 L11 Vaslui ◆ county NE Romania
33 R8 Vassar Michigan, N USA 43.22N 83.34W
97 E15 Vassdalseggi ▲ S Norway 59.47N 7.07E
62 P9 Vassouras Rio de Janeiro, SE Brazil 22.24S 43.38W
94 H11 Vastenjaure ⊚ N Sweden
97 N15 Västerås Västmanland, C Sweden 59.37N 16.33E
95 G15 Västerbotten ◆ county N Sweden
96 K12 Västerdalälven ⁓ C Sweden
97 O16 Västerhaninge Stockholm, C Sweden 59.07N 18.06E
96 M10 Västernorrland ◆ county C Sweden
97 N19 Västervik Kalmar, S Sweden 57.44N 16.40E
97 M15 Västmanand ◆ county C Sweden
109 L15 Vasto anc. Histonium. Abruzzo, C Italy 42.07N 14.40E
97 J19 Västra Götaland ◆ county S Sweden
97 J16 Västra Silen ⊚ S Sweden
113 G23 Vasvár Ger. Eisenburg. Vas, W Hungary 47.04N 16.46E
119 U9 Vasylivka Zaporiz'ka Oblast', SE Ukraine 47.26N 35.18E
119 O5 Vasyl'kiv Rus. Vasil'kov. Kyyivs'ka Oblast', N Ukraine 50.10N 30.18E
126 Gg12 Vasyugan ⁓ C Russian Federation
105 N8 Vatan Indre, C France 47.06N 1.49E
Vaté see Efate
109 G15 Vatican City off. Vatican City State. ◆ papal state S Europe
109 M22 Vaticano, Capo headland S Italy 38.37N 15.49E
Vatilî see Vadili
94 K3 Vatnajökull glacier SE Iceland
97 P15 Vätö Stockholm, C Sweden 59.48N 18.55E
197 L16 Vatoa island Lau Group, SE Fiji
180 J5 Vatomandry Toamasina, E Madagascar 19.19S 48.58E
118 J9 Vatra Dornei Ger. Dorna Watra. Suceava, NE Romania 47.19N 25.21E
118 J9 Vatra Moldoviței Suceava, NE Romania 47.37N 25.36E
Vatter, Lake see Vättern
97 L18 Vättern Eng. Lake Vatter; prev. Lake Vetter. ⊚ S Sweden
197 H14 Vatukoula Viti Levu, W Fiji 17.33S 105.49E
197 H15 Vatulele island SW Fiji
119 P7 Vatutine Cherkas'ka Oblast', C Ukraine 49.01N 31.04E
197 J14 Vatu Vara island Lau Group, E Fiji
105 R14 Vaucluse ◆ department SE France
105 S5 Vaucouleurs Meuse, NE France 48.37N 5.38E
110 B9 Vaud Ger. Waadt. ◆ canton SW Switzerland
13 N12 Vaudreuil Quebec, SE Canada 45.24N 74.01W
39 T12 Vaughn New Mexico, SW USA 34.36N 105.12W
56 I14 Vaupés off. Comisaría del Vaupés. ◆ province SE Colombia
56 J13 Vaupés, Río var. Rio Uaupés. ⁓ Brazil/Colombia see also Uaupés, Rio
105 Q15 Vauvert Gard, S France 43.42N 4.16E
9 R17 Vauxhall Alberta, SW Canada 50.04N 112.09W
101 K23 Vaux-sur-Sûre Luxembourg, SE Belgium 49.55N 5.34E
180 J4 Vavatenina Toamasina, E Madagascar 17.25S 49.10E
200 Ss12 Vava'u Group island group N Tonga
78 M16 Vavoua W Ivory Coast 7.22N 6.28W
131 S2 Vavozh Udmurtskaya Respublika, NW Russian Federation 56.48N 51.53E
161 K23 Vavuniya Northern Province, N Sri Lanka 8.45N 80.30E
121 G17 Vawkavysk Pol. Wołkowysk, Rus. Volkovysk. Hrodzyenskaya Voblasts', W Belarus 53.10N 24.28E
121 F17 Vawkavyskaye Wzvyshsha Rus. Volkovyskiye Vysoty. hill range W Belarus
97 P15 Vaxholm Stockholm, C Sweden 59.43N 18.57E
97 L21 Växjö var. Vexiö. Kronoberg, S Sweden 56.52N 14.49E
129 T1 Vaygach, Ostrov island NW Russian Federation
143 V13 Vayk' prev. Azizbekov. SE Armenia 39.41N 45.28E
129 P8 Vazhgort prev. Chasovo. Respublika Komi, NW Russian Federation 64.06N 46.44E
47 V10 V.C.Bird ✕ (St John's) Antigua, Antigua and Barbuda 17.07N 61.49W
97 C16 Veavågen Rogaland, S Norway 59.18N 5.13E
31 Q7 Veblen South Dakota, N USA 45.50N 97.17W
100 N9 Vecht Ger. Vechte. ⁓ Germany/Netherlands see also Vechte
102 G12 Vechta Niedersachsen, NW Germany 52.44N 8.16E
102 E12 Vechte Dut. Vecht. ⁓ Germany/Netherlands see also Vecht
120 I8 Vecpiebalga Cēsis, C Latvia 57.03N 25.47E
120 G9 Vecumnieki Bauska, C Latvia 56.36N 24.30E
Vedāvati see Hagari
97 J20 Veddige Halland, S Sweden 57.16N 12.19E
118 J15 Vedea ⁓ S Romania
131 P16 Vedeno Chechenskaya Respublika, SW Russian Federation 42.57N 46.02E
197 H14 Ve Drala Reef reef N Fiji
100 O6 Veendam Groningen, NE Netherlands 53.04N 6.52E
100 K12 Veenendaal Utrecht, C Netherlands 52.03N 5.33E
101 E14 Veere Zeeland, SW Netherlands 51.33N 3.40E
26 M2 Vega Texas, SW USA 35.14N 102.25W
94 E13 Vega island C Norway
47 T5 Vega Baja C Puerto Rico 18.27N 66.23W
40 D17 Vega Point headland Kiska Island, Alaska, USA 51.49N 105.19E
97 F17 Vegår ⊚ S Norway
101 K14 Veghel Noord-Brabant, S Netherlands 51.37N 5.33E
Veglia see Krk
116 E13 Vegorítis, Límni ⊚ N Greece
9 Q14 Vegreville Alberta, SW Canada 53.30N 112.01W
97 K21 Veinge Halland, S Sweden 56.33N 13.04E
63 B21 Veinticinco de Mayo var. 25 de Mayo. Buenos Aires, E Argentina 35.27S 60.11W
65 I14 Veinticinco de Mayo La Pampa, C Argentina 37.45S 67.40W
121 F15 Veisiejai Lazdijai, S Lithuania 54.06N 23.41E
97 F23 Vejen Ribe, W Denmark 55.28N 9.09E
106 K16 Vejer de la Frontera Andalucía, S Spain 36.15N 5.58W
97 G23 Vejle Vejle, C Denmark 55.43N 9.33E
97 F23 Vejle off. Vejle Amt. ◆ county C Denmark
116 M7 Vekilski Shumen, NE Bulgaria 43.33N 27.19E
56 G3 Vela, Cabo de la headland NE Colombia 12.13N 72.13W
Vela Goa see Goa
115 F15 Vela Luka Dubrovnik-Neretva, S Croatia 42.57N 16.43E
63 G19 Velázquez Rocha, E Uruguay 34.04S 54.16W
103 E15 Velbert Nordrhein-Westfalen, W Germany 51.19N 7.03E
111 S9 Velden Kärnten, S Austria 46.37N 13.59E
Veldes see Bled
101 K15 Veldhoven Noord-Brabant, S Netherlands 51.24N 5.24E
114 C11 Velebit ▲ C Croatia
116 N11 Veleka ⁓ SE Bulgaria
111 V10 Velenje Ger. Wöllan. N Slovenia 46.21N 15.07E
202 E12 Vele, Pointe headland Île Futuna, S Wallis and Futuna
115 O18 Veles Turk. Köprülü. C FYR Macedonia 41.43N 21.49E
115 M20 Velešta SW FYR Macedonia 41.16N 20.37E
117 F16 Velestíno prev. Velestínon. Thessalía, C Greece 39.22N 22.43E
Velestínon see Velestíno
Velevshchina see Vyelyewshchyna
56 F9 Vélez Santander, C Colombia 6.01N 73.37W
107 Q13 Vélez Blanco Andalucía, S Spain 37.43N 2.07W
106 M17 Vélez de la Gomera, Peñon de island group S Spain
107 N15 Vélez-Málaga Andalucía, S Spain 36.46N 4.06W
107 Q13 Vélez Rubio Andalucía, S Spain 37.39N 2.04W
Velha Goa see Goa
Velho see Porto Velho
114 E8 Velika Gorica Zagreb, N Croatia 45.43N 16.03E
114 C9 Velika Kapela ▲ NW Croatia
Velika Kikinda see Kikinda
114 D10 Velika Kladuša Federacija Bosna I Hercegovina, NW Bosnia and Herzegovina 45.10N 15.48E
114 N11 Velika Morava var. Glavn'a Morava, Morava, Ger. Grosse Morava. ⁓ C Serbia and Montenegro (Yugoslavia)
114 N12 Velika Plana Serbia, C Serbia and Montenegro (Yugoslavia) 44.20N 21.01E
111 U10 Velika Raduha ▲ N Slovenia 46.24N 14.46E
127 Pp5 Velikaya ⁓ NE Russian Federation
128 F15 Velikaya ⁓ W Russian Federation
Velikaya Berestovitsa see Vyalikaya Byerastavitsa
Velikaya Lepetikha see Velyka Lepetykha
Veliki Bečkerek see Zrenjanin
114 P12 Veliki Krš var. Stol. ▲ E Serbia and Montenegro (Yugoslavia) 44.10N 22.09E
116 L8 Veliki Preslav prev. Preslav. Shumen, NE Bulgaria 43.09N 26.46E
114 B9 Veliki Risnjak ▲ NW Croatia 45.30N 14.31E
111 T13 Veliki Snežnik Ger. Schneeberg, It. Monte Nevoso. ▲ SW Slovenia 45.36N 14.25E
114 J13 Veliki Stolac ▲ E Bosnia and Herzegovina 43.55N 19.15E
Velikiy Bor see Vyaliki Bor
128 G16 Velikiye Luki Pskovskaya Oblast', W Russian Federation 56.19N 30.27E
129 P12 Velikiy Ustyug Vologodskaya Oblast', NW Russian Federation 60.46N 46.18E
114 N11 Veliko Gradište Serbia, NE Serbia and Montenegro (Yugoslavia) 44.46N 21.28E
161 I18 Velikonda Range ▲ SE India
116 K9 Veliko Tŭrnovo prev. Tirnovo, Trnovo, Tŭrnovo. Veliko Tŭrnovo, N Bulgaria 43.04N 25.40E
116 K8 Veliko Tŭrnovo ◆ province N Bulgaria
Velikovec see Völkermarkt
129 R5 Velikovisochnoye Nenetskiy Avtonomnyy Okrug, NW Russian Federation 67.13N 52.00E
78 H12 Vélingara C Senegal 15.00N 14.39W
78 H11 Vélingara S Senegal 13.12N 14.04W
116 H11 Velingrad Pazardzhik, C Bulgaria 42.01N 24.00E
130 H3 Velizh Smolenskaya Oblast', W Russian Federation 55.30N 31.06E
113 F16 Velká Deštná var. Deštná, Grossķoppe, Ger. Deschnaer Koppe. ▲ NE Czech Republic 50.18N 16.25E
113 F18 Velké Meziříčí Ger. Grossmeseritsch. Jihlavský Kraj, C Czech Republic 49.22N 16.01E
94 N1 Velkomstpynten headland NW Svalbard 79.51N 11.37E
113 K21 Veľký Krtíš Banskobystrický Kraj, C Slovakia 48.13N 19.21E
195 T14 Vella Lavella var. Mbilua. island New Georgia Islands, NW Solomon Islands
109 I15 Velletri Lazio, C Italy 41.43N 12.43E
97 K23 Vellinge Skåne, S Sweden 55.29N 13.00E
161 I19 Vellore Tamil Nādu, SE India 12.55N 79.09E
Velobriga see Viana do Castelo
117 G21 Velopoúla island S Greece
100 M12 Velp Gelderland, SE Netherlands 52.00N 5.59E
Velsen see Velsen-Noord
100 H9 Velsen-Noord var. Velsen. Noord-Holland, W Netherlands 52.27N 4.40E
129 N12 Vel'sk var. Velsk. Arkhangel'skaya Oblast', NW Russian Federation 61.02N 42.00E
Velsuna see Orvieto
100 K10 Veluwemeer lake channel C Netherlands
30 M3 Velva North Dakota, N USA 48.03N 100.55W
117 E14 Velvendós var. Velvendos. Dytikí Makedonía, N Greece 40.15N 22.04E
119 S5 Velyka Bahachka Poltavs'ka Oblast', C Ukraine 49.46N 33.44E
119 S9 Velyka Lepetykha Rus. Velikaya Lepetikha. Khersons'ka Oblast', S Ukraine 47.10N 33.55E
119 O10 Velyka Mykhaylivka Odes'ka Oblast', SW Ukraine 47.07N 29.49E
119 W8 Velyka Novosilka Donets'ka Oblast', E Ukraine 47.49N 36.49E
119 S9 Velyka Oleksandrivka Khersons'ka Oblast', S Ukraine 47.17N 33.16E
119 T4 Velyka Pysanivka Sums'ka Oblast', NE Ukraine 50.25N 35.28E
118 G6 Velykyy Bereznyy Zakarpats'ka Oblast', W Ukraine 48.54N 22.27E
119 W4 Velykyy Burluk Kharkivs'ka Oblast', E Ukraine 50.04N 37.25E
Velykyy Tokmak see Tokmak
181 P7 Vema Fracture Zone tectonic feature W Indian Ocean
67 P18 Vema Seamount undersea feature SW Indian Ocean 31.37S 8.19E
95 F17 Vemdalen Jämtland, C Sweden 62.26N 13.50E
97 N19 Vena Kalmar, S Sweden 57.31N 16.00E
43 N11 Venado San Luis Potosí, C Mexico 22.54N 101.06W
64 L11 Venado Tuerto Entre Ríos, E Argentina 33.45S 61.56W
63 A19 Venado Tuerto Santa Fe, C Argentina 33.46S 61.57W
109 K16 Venafro Molise, C Italy 41.28N 14.03E
57 Q9 Venamo, Cerro ▲ E Venezuela 5.56N 61.25W
108 B8 Venaria Piemonte, NW Italy 45.09N 7.40E
105 U15 Vence Alpes-Maritimes, SE France 43.45N 7.07E
106 H5 Venda Nova Vila Real, N Portugal 41.40N 7.58W
106 G11 Vendas Novas Évora, S Portugal 38.40N 8.27W
104 J9 Vendée ◆ department NW France
105 Q6 Vendeuvre-sur-Barse Aube, NE France 48.08N 4.17E
104 M7 Vendôme Loir-et-Cher, C France 47.48N 1.04E
Venedig see Venezia
Vener, Lake see Vänern
108 I8 Veneta, Laguna lagoon NE Italy
Venetia see Venezia
41 S7 Venetie Alaska, USA 67.00N 146.25W
108 H8 Veneto var. Venezia Euganea. ◆ region NE Italy
116 M7 Venets Shumen, NE Bulgaria 43.33N 26.56E
130 L5 Venev Tul'skaya Oblast', W Russian Federation 54.18N 38.16E
108 I8 Venezia Eng. Venice, Fr. Venise, Ger. Venedig; anc. Venetia. Veneto, NE Italy 45.25N 12.19E
Venezia Euganea see Veneto
Venezia, Golfo di see Venice, Gulf of
Venezia Tridentina see Trentino-Alto Adige
56 K8 Venezuela off. Republic of Venezuela; prev. Estados Unidos de Venezuela, United States of Venezuela. ◆ republic N South America
Venezuela, Cordillera de see Costa, Cordillera de la
56 I4 Venezuela, Golfo de Eng. Gulf of Maracaibo, Gulf of Venezuela. gulf NW Venezuela
Venezuela, Gulf of see Venezuela, Golfo de
66 F11 Venezuelan Basin undersea feature E Caribbean Sea
161 D16 Vengurla Mahārāshtra, W India 15.55N 73.39E
41 O15 Veniaminof, Mount ▲ Alaska, USA 56.12N 159.24W
25 V14 Venice Florida, SE USA 27.06N 82.27W
24 L10 Venice Louisiana, S USA 29.15N 89.20W
Venice see Venezia
108 J8 Venice, Gulf of It. Golfo di Venezia, Slvn. Beneški Zaliv. gulf N Adriatic Sea
Venise see Venezia
96 K13 Venjan Dalarna, C Sweden 60.58N 13.55E
96 K13 Venjansjön ⊚ C Sweden
161 J18 Venkatagiri Andhra Pradesh, E India 14.00N 79.39E
101 M15 Venlo prev. Venloo. Limburg, SE Netherlands 51.22N 6.10E
Venloo see Venlo
97 E18 Vennesla Vest-Agder, S Norway 58.15N 7.58E
109 M17 Venosa anc. Venusia. Basilicata, S Italy 40.57N 15.49E
Venoste, Alpi see Ötztaler Alpen
Venraij see Venray
101 M14 Venray var. Venraij. Limburg, SE Netherlands 51.31N 5.58E
120 C8 Venta Ger. Windau. ⁓ Latvia/Lithuania
Venta Belgarum see Winchester
42 G9 Ventana, Punta Arena de la var. Punta de la Ventana. headland W Mexico 24.03N 109.49W
Ventana, Punta de la see Ventana, Punta Arena de la
63 B23 Ventana, Sierra de la hill range E Argentina
Ventia see Valence
203 S11 Vent, Îles du var. Windward Islands. island group Archipel de la Société, W French Polynesia
203 R10 Vent, Îles Sous le var. Leeward Islands. island group Archipel de la Société, W French Polynesia
108 B11 Ventimiglia Liguria, NW Italy 43.46N 7.37E
99 M24 Ventnor S England, UK 50.36N 1.10W
20 J17 Ventnor City New Jersey, NE USA 39.19N 74.27W
105 S14 Ventoux, Mont ▲ SE France 44.12N 5.21E
120 C8 Ventspils Ger. Windau. Ventspils, NW Latvia 57.22N 21.34E
56 M10 Ventuari, Río ⁓ S Venezuela
37 R15 Ventura California, W USA 34.15N 119.14W
190 F8 Venus Bay South Australia 33.15S 134.42E
Venusia see Venosa
203 P7 Vénus, Pointe var. Pointe Tataaihoa. headland Tahiti, W French Polynesia 17.28S 149.28W
43 V16 Venustiano Carranza Chiapas, SE Mexico 16.24N 92.04W
43 N7 Venustiano Carranza, Presa ⊠ NE Mexico
63 B15 Vera Santa Fe, C Argentina 29.28S 60.10W
107 Q14 Vera Andalucía, S Spain 37.15N 1.51W
65 K18 Vera, Bahía bay E Argentina
43 R14 Veracruz var. Veracruz Llave. Veracruz-Llave, E Mexico 19.09N 96.09W
43 Q13 Veracruz-Llave var. Veracruz. ◆ state E Mexico
45 Q16 Veraguas off. Provincia de Veraguas. ◆ province W Panama
Veramin see Varāmīn
160 B12 Verāval Gujarāt, W India 20.54N 70.22E
108 C6 Verbania Piemonte, NW Italy 45.55N 8.34E
109 N20 Verbicaro Calabria, SW Italy 39.44N 15.51E
110 D11 Verbier Valais, SW Switzerland 46.06N 7.14E
Vercellae see Vercelli
108 C8 Vercelli anc. Vercellae. Piemonte, NW Italy 45.19N 8.25E
105 S13 Vercors physical region E France
95 E16 Verdal Nord-Trøndelag, C Norway 63.46N 11.27E
Verde, Cabo see Cape Verde
46 J5 Verde, Cape headland Long Island, C Bahamas 22.51N 75.50W
106 M2 Verde, Costa coastal region N Spain
Verde Grande, Río/Verde Grande y de Belem, Río see Verde, Río
102 H11 Verden Niedersachsen, NW Germany 52.55N 9.13E
61 J19 Verde, Rio ⁓ SE Brazil
59 P16 Verde, Río ⁓ Bolivia/Brazil
42 M12 Verde, Río var. Río Verde Grande, Río Verde Grande y de Belem. ⁓ C Mexico
43 Q16 Verde, Río ⁓ SE Mexico
38 L13 Verde River ⁓ Arizona, SW USA
Verdhikoúsa/Verdhikoússa see Verdikoússa
29 Q8 Verdigris River ⁓ Kansas/Oklahoma, C USA
117 E15 Verdikoússa var. Verdhikoúsa, Verdhikoússa. Thessalía, C Greece 39.46N 21.58E
105 S15 Verdon ⁓ SE France
13 O12 Verdun Quebec, SE Canada 45.27N 73.36W
105 S4 Verdun var. Verdun-sur-Meuse; anc. Verodunum. Meuse, NE France 49.09N 5.25E
Verdun-sur-Meuse see Verdun
85 J21 Vereeniging Gauteng, NE South Africa 26.40S 27.55E
Veremeyki see Vyeramyeyki
129 T14 Vereshchagino Permskaya Oblast', NW Russian Federation 58.06N 54.38E
78 G14 Verga, Cap headland W Guinea 10.12N 14.27W
63 G18 Vergara Treinta y Tres, E Uruguay 32.58S 53.54W
110 G11 Vergeletto Ticino, S Switzerland 46.13N 8.34E
20 L8 Vergennes Vermont, NE USA 44.09N 73.13W
Veria see Véroia
106 I5 Verín Galicia, NW Spain 41.55N 7.25W
Verin T'alin see T'alin
120 K6 Veriora Põlvamaa, SE Estonia 57.57N 27.23E
119 T7 Verkhivtseve Dnipropetrovs'ka Oblast', E Ukraine 48.27N 34.15E
Verkhnedvinsk see Vyerkhnyadzvinsk
126 Hh11 Verkhneimbatsk Krasnoyarskiy Kray, N Russian Federation 63.06N 88.03E
128 I3 Verkhnetulomskiy Murmanskaya Oblast', NW Russian Federation 68.37N 31.46E
128 I3 Verkhnetulomskoye Vodokhranilishche ⊠ NW Russian Federation
Verkhneudinsk see Ulan-Ude
126 L11 Verkhnevilyuysk Respublika Sakha (Yakutiya), NE Russian Federation 63.44N 119.59E
131 W3 Verkhniye Kigi Respublika Bashkortostan, W Russian Federation 55.25N 58.40E
131 W5 Verkhniy Avzyan Respublika Bashkortostan, W Russian Federation 53.31N 57.26E
131 Q11 Verkhniy Baskunchak Astrakhanskaya Oblast', SW Russian Federation 48.14N 46.43E
119 T9 Verkhniy Rohachyk Khersons'ka Oblast', S Ukraine 47.16N 34.16E
126 Ll12 Verkhnyaya Amga Respublika Sakha (Yakutiya), NE Russian Federation 59.34N 127.07E
129 V6 Verkhnyaya Inta Respublika Komi, NW Russian Federation 65.55N 60.07E
126 Ii6 Verkhnyaya Taymyra ⁓ N Russian Federation
129 O10 Verkhnyaya Toyma Arkhangel'skaya Oblast', NW Russian Federation 62.12N 44.57E
130 K6 Verkhov'ye Orlovskaya Oblast', W Russian Federation 52.49N 37.20E
118 I8 Verkhovyna Ivano-Frankivs'ka Oblast', W Ukraine 48.09N 24.48E
126 M8 Verkhoyansk Respublika Sakha (Yakutiya), NE Russian Federation 67.27N 133.27E
126 L8 Verkhoyanskiy Khrebet ▲ NE Russian Federation
119 T7 Verkhn'odniprovs'k Dnipropetrovs'ka Oblast', E Ukraine 48.40N 34.17E
103 G14 Verl Nordrhein-Westfalen, NW Germany 51.52N 8.30E
94 N1 Verlegenhuken headland N Svalbard 80.03N 16.15E
84 A9 Vermelha, Ponta headland NW Angola 5.40S 12.09E
105 P7 Vermenton Yonne, C France 47.40N 3.43E
9 R14 Vermilion Alberta, SW Canada 53.21N 110.52W
33 T11 Vermilion Ohio, N USA 41.25N 82.21W
24 I10 Vermilion Bay bay Louisiana, S USA
31 V4 Vermilion Lake ⊚ Minnesota, N USA
12 F9 Vermilion River ⁓ Ontario, S Canada
32 L12 Vermilion River ⁓ Illinois, N USA
31 R12 Vermillion South Dakota, N USA 42.46N 96.55W
31 R12 Vermillion River ⁓ South Dakota, N USA
13 O9 Vermillon, Rivière ⁓ Quebec, SE Canada
117 E14 Vérmio ▲ N Greece
20 L8 Vermont off. State of Vermont; also known as The Green Mountain State. ◆ state NE USA
115 K16 Vermosh var. Vermoshi. Shkodër, N Albania 42.37N 19.42E
Vermoshi see Vermosh
39 O3 Vernal Utah, W USA 40.27N 109.31W
12 G11 Verner Ontario, S Canada 46.24N 80.04W
104 M5 Verneuil-sur-Avre Eure, N France 48.44N 0.55E
116 D13 Vérno ▲ N Greece
9 N17 Vernon British Columbia, SW Canada 50.16N 119.19W
104 M4 Vernon Eure, N France 49.04N 1.28E
25 N3 Vernon Alabama, S USA 33.45N 88.06W
33 P15 Vernon Indiana, N USA 38.58N 85.39W
27 Q4 Vernon Texas, SW USA 34.10N 99.16W
34 G10 Vernonia Oregon, NW USA 45.51N 123.11W
12 G12 Vernon, Lake ⊚ Ontario, S Canada
24 G7 Vernon Lake ⊠ Louisiana, S USA
25 Y13 Vero Beach Florida, SE USA 27.38N 80.24W
Verőcze see Virovitica
Verodunum see Verdun
117 E14 Véroia var. Veria, Vérroia, Turk. Karaferiye. Kentrikí Makedonía, N Greece 40.31N 22.14E
108 E8 Verolanuova Lombardia, N Italy 45.20N 10.06E
12 K14 Verona Ontario, SE Canada 44.30N 76.42W
108 G8 Verona Veneto, NE Italy 45.26N 11.00E
31 P6 Verona North Dakota, N USA 46.19N 98.03W
32 L9 Verona Wisconsin, N USA 42.59N 89.33W
63 E20 Verónica Buenos Aires, E Argentina 35.25S 57.16W
24 J9 Verret, Lake ⊚ Louisiana, S USA
Vérroia see Véroia
195 P10 Verron Range ▲ New Ireland, NE PNG
105 N5 Versailles Yvelines, N France 48.48N 2.07E
33 P15 Versailles Indiana, N USA 39.04N 85.15W
22 M5 Versailles Kentucky, S USA 38.03N 84.43W
29 U5 Versailles Missouri, C USA 38.25N 92.50W
33 Q13 Versailles Ohio, N USA 40.13N 84.28W
Versecz see Vršac
110 A10 Versoix Genève, SW Switzerland 46.16N 6.10E
13 Z6 Verte, Pointe headland Quebec, SE Canada 48.36N 64.10W
113 I22 Vértes ▲ NW Hungary
46 G6 Vertientes Camagüey, C Cuba 21.15N 78.09W
116 G13 Vertískos ▲ N Greece
104 I8 Vertou Loire-Atlantique, NW France 47.10N 1.28W
Verulamium see St Albans
101 L19 Verviers Liège, E Belgium 50.36N 5.52E
105 Y14 Vescovato Corse, France, C Mediterranean Sea 42.30N 9.27E
101 L20 Vesdre ⁓ E Belgium
119 U10 Vesele Rus. Veseloye. Zaporiz'ka Oblast', S Ukraine 47.00N 34.52E
113 D18 Veselí nad Lužnicí var. Weseli an der Lainsitz, Ger. Frohenbruck. Budějovický Kraj, S Czech Republic 49.11N 14.40E
116 M9 Veselinovo Shumen, E Bulgaria 43.01N 27.02E
130 L12 Veselovskoye Vodokhranilishche ⊠ SW Russian Federation
Veseloye see Vesele
119 Q9 Veselynove Mykolayivs'ka Oblast', S Ukraine 47.21N 31.15E
Veseya see Vyasyeya
130 M10 Veshenskaya Rostovskaya Oblast', SW Russian Federation 49.37N 41.43E
131 Q5 Veshkayma Ul'yanovskaya Oblast', W Russian Federation 54.04N 47.06E
Vesisaari see Vadsø
Vesontio see Besançon
105 T7 Vesoul anc. Vesulium, Vesulum. Haute-Saône, E France 47.37N 6.09E
97 J20 Vessigebro Halland, S Sweden 56.58N 12.40E
97 D17 Vest-Agder ◆ county S Norway
25 P4 Vestavia Hills Alabama, S USA 33.27N 86.47W
86 F6 Vesterålen island NW Norway
94 G10 Vesterålen island group N Norway
89 V3 Vestervig Viborg, NW Denmark 56.46N 8.19E
94 H2 Vestfirdhir ◆ region NW Iceland
94 G11 Vestfjorden fjord C Norway
97 G16 Vestfold ◆ county S Norway
97 B18 Vestmanna Dan. Vestmanhavn Faeroe Islands 62.09N 7.11W
94 I4 Vestmannaeyjar Sudhurland, S Iceland 63.26N 20.13W
96 E9 Vestnes Møre og Romsdal, S Norway 62.39N 7.00E
97 I23 Vestsjælland off. Vestsjællands Amt. ◆ county E Denmark
94 H3 Vesturland ◆ region W Iceland
94 G11 Vestvågøya island C Norway
Vesulium/Vesulum see Vesoul
Vesuna see Périgueux
109 K17 Vesuvio Eng. Vesuvius. ⛰ S Italy 40.48N 14.29E
Vesuvius see Vesuvio
128 K14 Ves'yegonsk Tverskaya Oblast', W Russian Federation 58.40N 37.13E
113 I23 Veszprém Ger. Veszprim. Veszprém, W Hungary 47.06N 17.54E
113 H23 Veszprém off. Veszprém Megye. ◆ county W Hungary
Veszprim see Veszprém
Vetka see Vyetka
97 M19 Vetlanda Jönköping, S Sweden 57.25N 15.04E
131 P1 Vetluga Nizhegorodskaya Oblast', W Russian Federation 57.51N 45.45E
129 P14 Vetluga ⁓ NW Russian Federation
129 O14 Vetluzhskiy Kostromskaya Oblast', NW Russian Federation 58.21N 45.25E
131 P2 Vetluzhskiy Nizhegorodskaya Oblast', W Russian Federation 57.10N 45.07E
109 H14 Vetralla Lazio, C Italy 42.18N 12.03E
116 M9 Vetren prev. Zhitarovo. Burgas, E Bulgaria 42.38N 27.22E
116 M8 Vetrino Varna, E Bulgaria 43.19N 27.26E
Vetrino see Vyetryna
126 Ii6 Vetrovaya, Gora ▲ N Russian Federation 73.54N 95.00E
Vetter, Lake see Vättern
108 J13 Vettore, Monte ▲ C Italy 42.49N 13.15E
101 A17 Veurne var. Furnes. West-Vlaanderen, W Belgium 51.04N 2.40E
33 Q15 Vevay Indiana, N USA 38.45N 85.07W
110 C10 Vevey Ger. Vivis; anc. Vibiscum. Vaud, SW Switzerland 46.28N 6.51E
Vexiö see Växjö
105 S13 Veynes Hautes-Alpes, SE France 44.33N 5.51E
105 N11 Vézère ⁓ W France
116 I9 Vezhen ▲ C Bulgaria 42.45N 24.22E
142 K11 Vezirköprü Samsun, N Turkey 41.09N 35.27E
59 J18 Viacha La Paz, W Bolivia 16.40S 68.16W
29 R10 Vian Oklahoma, C USA 35.30N 94.56W
Viana de Castelo see Viana do Castelo
106 H12 Viana do Alentejo Évora, S Portugal 38.20N 8.00W
106 I4 Viana do Bolo Galicia, NW Spain 42.10N 7.06W
106 G5 Viana do Castelo var. Viana de Castelo; anc. Velobriga. Viana do Castelo, NW Portugal 41.40N 8.49W
106 G5 Viana do Castelo var. Viana de Castelo. ◆ district N Portugal
100 J12 Vianen Zuid-Holland, C Netherlands 52.00N 5.06E

◆ Country
● Country Capital
◇ Dependent Territory
○ Dependent Territory Capital
◆ Administrative Region
✕ International Airport
▲ Mountain
▲ Mountain Range
⛰ Volcano
⁓ River
⊚ Lake
⊠ Reservoir

178 Ii8 Viangchan Eng./Fr. Vientiane. ● (Laos) C Laos 17.57N 102.38E
178 I6 Viangphoukha var. Vieng Pou Kha. Louang Namtha, N Laos 20.41N 101.03E
106 K13 Viar ≈ SW Spain
108 E11 Viareggio Toscana, C Italy 43.52N 10.15E
105 O14 Viaur ≈ S France
Vibiscum see Vevey
97 G21 Viborg Viborg, NW Denmark 56.28N 9.25E
31 R12 Viborg South Dakota, N USA 43.10N 97.04W
97 F21 Viborg off. Viborg Amt. ⬖ county NW Denmark
109 N22 Vibo Valentia prev. Monteleone di Calabria; anc. Hipponium. Calabria, SW Italy 38.40N 16.06E
107 W5 Vic var. Vich; anc. Ausa, Vicus Ausonensis. Cataluña, NE Spain 41.55N 2.16E
104 K16 Vic-en-Bigorre Hautes-Pyrénées, S France 43.22N 0.03E
42 K10 Vicente Guerrero Durango, C Mexico 23.30N 104.24W
43 P10 Vicente Guerrero, Presa var. Presa de las Adjuntas. ⊠ NE Mexico
Vicentia see Vicenza
108 G8 Vicenza anc. Vicentia. Veneto, NE Italy 45.31N 11.31E
Vich see Vic
56 J10 Vichada off. Comisaría del Vichada. ⬖ province E Colombia
56 K10 Vichada, Río ≈ E Colombia
63 G17 Vichadero Rivera, NE Uruguay 31.45S 54.40W
Vichegda see Vychegda
128 M16 Vichuga Ivanovskaya Oblast', W Russian Federation 57.13N 41.51E
105 P10 Vichy Allier, C France 46.08N 3.26E
28 K9 Vici Oklahoma, C USA 36.09N 99.18W
33 P10 Vicksburg Michigan, N USA 42.07N 85.31W
24 J5 Vicksburg Mississippi, S USA 32.21N 90.52W
105 O12 Vic-sur-Cère Cantal, C France 45.00N 2.36E
31 X14 Victor Iowa, C USA 41.45N 92.18W
61 I21 Víctor Mato Grosso do Sul, SW Brazil 21.39S 53.21W
190 I10 Victor Harbor South Australia 35.33S 138.37E
63 C18 Victoria Entre Ríos, E Argentina 32.36S 60.12W
8 L17 Victoria Vancouver Island, British Columbia, SW Canada 48.25N 123.22W
47 R14 Victoria NW Grenada 12.11N 61.42W
44 H6 Victoria Yoro, NW Honduras 15.01N 87.28W
123 J16 Victoria var. Rabat. Gozo, NW Malta 36.02N 14.14E
118 I12 Victoria Ger. Viktoriastadt. Braşov, C Romania 45.43N 24.40E
180 H17 Victoria ● (Seychelles) Mahé, SW Seychelles 4.37S 28.28E
27 U13 Victoria Texas, SW USA 28.47N 96.58W
191 N12 Victoria ⬖ state SE Australia
182 K7 Victoria ≈ Western Australia
Victoria see Labuan, East Malaysia
Victoria see Masvingo, Zimbabwe
Victoria Bank see Vitória Seamount
9 Y15 Victoria Beach Manitoba, S Canada 50.40N 96.30W
Victoria de Durango see Durango
Victoria de las Tunas see Las Tunas
85 I16 Victoria Falls Matabeleland North, W Zimbabwe 17.55S 25.48E
85 I16 Victoria Falls ✕ Matabeleland North, W Zimbabwe 18.03S 25.48E
85 I16 Victoria Falls waterfall Zambia/Zimbabwe 18.03S 25.50E
Victoria Falls see Iguaçu, Salto do
65 F19 Victoria, Isla island Archipiélago de los Chonos, S Chile
15 J2 Victoria Island island Northwest Territories/Nunavut, NW Canada
190 L8 Victoria, Lake ◎ New South Wales, SE Australia
70 I12 Victoria, Lake var. Victoria Nyanza. ◎ E Africa
205 S13 Victoria Land physical region Antarctica
177 F5 Victoria, Mount ▲ W Myanmar 21.13N 93.53E
197 I14 Victoria, Mount ▲ Viti Levu, W Fiji 17.37S 178.00E
194 K15 Victoria, Mount ▲ S PNG 8.51S 147.36E
83 F17 Victoria Nile var. Somerset Nile. ≈ C Uganda
Victoria Nyanza see Victoria, Lake
44 G3 Victoria Peak ▲ SE Belize 16.50N 88.38W
193 H16 Victoria Range ▲▲ South Island, NZ
189 O3 Victoria River ≈ Northern Territory, N Australia
189 P3 Victoria River Roadhouse Northern Territory, N Australia 15.37S 131.07E
13 Q11 Victoriaville Québec, SE Canada 46.03N 71.55W
Victoria-Wes see Victoria West
85 G24 Victoria West Afr. Victoria-Wes. Northern Cape, W South Africa 31.22S 23.06E
64 J13 Victorica La Pampa, C Argentina 36.14S 65.21W
205 T3 Victor, Mount ▲ Antarctica 72.49S 33.01E
37 U14 Victorville California, W USA 34.32N 117.17W
64 G9 Vicuña Coquimbo, N Chile 30.00S 70.44W
64 K11 Vicuña Mackenna Córdoba, C Argentina 33.52S 64.25W
Vicus Ausonensis see Vic
Vicus Elbii see Viterbo
35 X7 Vida Montana, NW USA 47.52N 105.30W
25 V6 Vidalia Georgia, SE USA 32.13N 82.24W
24 J7 Vidalia Louisiana, S USA 31.34N 91.25W
97 F22 Videbæk Ringkøbing, C Denmark 56.07N 8.37E
62 I13 Videira Santa Catarina, S Brazil 27.00S 51.08W
118 J14 Videle Teleorman, S Romania 44.15N 25.27E
Videm-Krško see Krško
Viden' see Wien
106 H12 Vidigueira Beja, S Portugal 38.12N 7.48W
116 J9 Vidima ≈ N Bulgaria
116 G7 Vidin anc. Bononia. Vidin, NW Bulgaria 44.00N 22.50E
116 F8 Vidin ⬖ province NW Bulgaria
160 H10 Vidisha Madhya Pradesh, C India 23.30N 77.49E
27 Y10 Vidor Texas, SW USA 30.07N 94.01W
97 L20 Vidöstern ◎ S Sweden
94 J13 Vidsel Norrbotten, N Sweden 65.49N 20.31E
120 H9 Vidzemes Augstiene ▲▲ C Latvia
120 J12 Vidzy Rus. Vidzy. Vitsyebskaya Voblasts', NW Belarus 55.22N 26.37E
65 L16 Viedma Río Negro, E Argentina 40.50S 62.57W
65 H22 Viedma, Lago ◎ S Argentina
47 O11 Vieille Case var. Itassi. N Dominica 15.36N 61.24W
106 M2 Vieja, Peña ▲ N Spain 43.09N 4.47W
42 E4 Viejo, Cerro ▲ NW Mexico 30.16N 112.18W
58 B9 Viejo, Cerro ▲ N Peru 4.54S 79.24W
120 E10 Viekšniai Akmenė, NW Lithuania 56.14N 22.33E
107 U3 Vielha var. Viella. Cataluña, NE Spain 42.40N 0.46E
Viella see Vielha
101 L21 Vielsalm Luxembourg, E Belgium 50.16N 5.55E
Vieng Pou Kha see Viangphoukha
25 T6 Vienna Georgia, SE USA 32.05N 83.48W
32 L17 Vienna Illinois, N USA 37.22N 88.51W
29 V5 Vienna Missouri, C USA 38.11N 91.57W
23 Q3 Vienna West Virginia, NE USA 39.19N 81.33W
Vienna see Wien, Austria
Vienna see Vienne, France
105 R11 Vienne anc. Vienna. Isère, E France 45.31N 4.52E
104 L10 Vienne ⬖ department W France
104 L9 Vienne ≈ W France
Vientiane see Viangchan
Vientos, Paso de los see Windward Passage
47 V6 Vieques var. Isabel Segunda. E Puerto Rico 18.08N 65.27W
47 V6 Vieques, Isla de island E Puerto Rico
47 V6 Vieques, Pasaje de passage E Puerto Rico
47 V5 Vieques, Sonda de sound E Puerto Rico
Vierdörfer see Săcele
95 M15 Vieremä Itä-Suomi, C Finland 63.42N 27.02E
101 M14 Vierlingsbeek Noord-Brabant, SE Netherlands 51.36N 6.01E
103 G20 Viernheim Hessen, W Germany 49.31N 8.34E
103 D15 Viersen Nordrhein-Westfalen, W Germany 51.15N 6.24E
110 G8 Vierwaldstätter See Eng. Lake of Lucerne. ◎ C Switzerland
105 N8 Vierzon Cher, C France 47.13N 2.04E
42 L8 Viesca Coahuila de Zaragoza, NE Mexico 25.25N 102.45W
120 H10 Viesīte Ger. Eckengraf. Jēkabpils, S Latvia 56.21N 25.30E
109 N15 Vieste Puglia, SE Italy 41.52N 16.10E
178 Jj9 Vietnam off. Socialist Republic of Vietnam, Vtn. Công Hoa Xã Hôi Chu Nghia Viêt Nam. ◆ republic SE Asia
178 J5 Viêt Quang Ha Giang, N Vietnam 22.24N 104.48E
Vietri see Viêt Tri
178 Jj6 Viêt Tri var. Vietri. Vinh Phu, N Vietnam 21.19N 105.25E
32 L4 Vieux Desert, Lac ◎ Michigan/Wisconsin, N USA
47 Y13 Vieux Fort S Saint Lucia 13.43N 60.57W
47 X6 Vieux-Habitants Basse Terre, SW Guadeloupe 16.03N 61.45W
121 G14 Vievis Kaišiadorys, S Lithuania 54.46N 24.51E
179 P8 Vigan Luzon, N Philippines 17.34N 102.21E
108 D8 Vigevano Lombardia, N Italy 45.19N 8.51E
109 N18 Viggiano Basilicata, S Italy 40.21N 15.54E
60 L12 Vigia Pará, NE Brazil 0.49S 48.07W
43 Y12 Vigía Chico Quintana Roo, SE Mexico 19.49N 87.31W
Vigie see George F L Charles
104 K17 Vignemale var. Pic de Vignemale. ▲ France/Spain 42.48N 0.06W
Vignemale, Pic de see Vignemale
108 G10 Vignola Emilia-Romagna, C Italy 44.28N 11.00E
106 G4 Vigo Galicia, NW Spain 42.15N 8.43W
106 G4 Vigo, Ría de estuary NW Spain
96 D9 Vigra island S Norway
97 C17 Vigrestad Rogaland, S Norway 58.34N 5.42E
95 L15 Vihanti Oulu, C Finland 64.28N 25.00E
155 U10 Vihāri Punjab, E Pakistan 30.03N 72.31E
104 K8 Vihiers Maine-et-Loire, NW France 47.09N 0.37W
113 O19 Vihorlat ▲ E Slovakia 48.54N 22.09E
95 L19 Vihti Etelä-Suomi, S Finland 60.25N 24.16E
Viipuri see Vyborg
95 M16 Viitasaari Länsi-Suomi, W Finland 63.05N 25.52E
120 K3 Viivikonna Ida-Virumaa, NE Estonia 59.19N 27.40E
161 K16 Vijayawāda prev. Bezwada. Andhra Pradesh, SE India 16.34N 80.40E
Vijosa/Vijosë see Aóos, Albania/Greece
Vijosa/Vijosë see Vjosës, Lumi i, Albania/Greece
Vik see Vikøyri
94 J4 Vík Sudhurland, S Iceland 63.25N 18.58W
96 L13 Vika Dalarna, C Sweden 60.55N 14.30E
94 L12 Vikajärvi Lappi, N Finland 66.37N 26.10E
96 L13 Vikarbyn Dalarna, C Sweden 60.57N 15.00E
97 J22 Viken Skåne, S Sweden 56.09N 12.36E
97 L17 Viken ◎ C Sweden
97 G15 Vikersund Buskerud, S Norway 59.58N 9.58E
126 J14 Vikhorevka Irkutskaya Oblast', S Russian Federation 56.09N 99.09E
116 G11 Vikhren ▲ SW Bulgaria 41.45N 23.24E
9 R15 Viking Alberta, SW Canada 53.07N 111.49W
86 E7 Viking Bank undersea feature N North Sea
97 M14 Vikmanshyttan Dalarna, C Sweden 60.19N 15.55E
96 D12 Vikøyri var. Vik. Sogn og Fjordane, S Norway 61.04N 6.34E
95 H17 Viksjö Västernorrland, C Sweden 62.45N 17.30E
Viktoriastadt see Victoria
Vila see Port-Vila
Vila Arriaga see Bibala
Vila Artur de Paiva see Cubango
Vila Bela da Santissima Trindade see Mato Grosso
60 B12 Vila Bittencourt Amazonas, NW Brazil 1.25S 69.24W
Vila da Ponte see Cubango
66 O2 Vila da Praia da Vitória Terceira, Azores, Portugal, NE Atlantic Ocean 38.43N 27.04W
Vila de Aljustrel see Cangamba
Vila de Almoster see Chiange
Vila de João Belo see Xai-Xai
Vila de Macia see Macia
Vila de Manhiça see Manhiça
Vila de Manica see Manica
Vila de Mocímboa da Praia see Mocímboa da Praia
85 N16 Vila de Sena var. Sena. Sofala, C Mozambique 17.25S 34.59E
106 F14 Vila do Bispo Faro, S Portugal 37.04N 8.52W
106 G6 Vila do Conde Porto, NW Portugal 41.21N 8.45W
Vila do Maio see Maio
66 P3 Vila do Porto Santa Maria, Azores, Portugal, NE Atlantic Ocean 36.57N 25.10W
85 K15 Vila do Zumbo prev. Vila do Zumbu, Zumbo. Tete, NW Mozambique 15.36S 30.30E
Vila do Zumbu see Vila do Zumbo
106 I6 Vila Flor var. Vila Flôr. Bragança, N Portugal 41.18N 7.09W
107 V6 Vilafranca del Penedès var. Villafranca del Panadés. Cataluña, NE Spain 41.21N 1.42E
106 F10 Vila Franca de Xira var. Vilafranca de Xira. Lisboa, C Portugal 38.57N 8.58W
Vila Gago Coutinho see Lumbala N'Guimbo
106 G3 Vilagarcía de Arousa var. Villagarcía de Arosa. Galicia, NW Spain 42.34N 8.45W
Vila General Machado see Camacupa
Vila Henrique de Carvalho see Saurimo
104 I7 Vilaine ≈ NW France
Vila João de Almeida see Chibia
120 K8 Viļaka Ger. Marienhausen. Balvi, NE Latvia 57.11N 27.42E
106 I2 Vilalba Galicia, NW Spain 43.16N 7.40W
Vila Marechal Carmona see Uíge
Vila Mariano Machado see Ganda
180 G3 Vilanandro, Tanjona headland W Madagascar 16.10S 44.27E
Vilanculos see Vilankulo
120 J10 Viļāni Rēzekne, E Latvia 56.33N 26.55E
85 N19 Vilankulo var. Vilanculos. Inhambane, E Mozambique 22.01S 35.19E
Vila Norton de Matos see Balombo
106 G6 Vila Nova de Famalicão var. Vila Nova de Famalicão. Braga, N Portugal 41.24N 8.31W
106 I6 Vila Nova de Foz Côa var. Vila Nova de Fozcôa. Guarda, N Portugal 41.04N 7.09W
106 F6 Vila Nova de Gaia Porto, NW Portugal 41.07N 8.37W
Vila Nova de Portimão see Portimão
107 V6 Vilanova i La Geltrú Cataluña, NE Spain 41.15N 1.42E
Vila Pereira de Eça see N'Giva
106 H6 Vila Pouca de Aguiar Vila Real, N Portugal 41.30N 7.37W
106 H6 Vila Real var. Vila Rial. Vila Real, N Portugal 41.16N 7.45W
106 H6 Vila Real ⬖ district N Portugal
107 T9 Vila-real de los Infantes var. Villarreal. País Valenciano, E Spain 39.55N 0.07W
106 H14 Vila Real de Santo António Faro, S Portugal 37.12N 7.25W
106 J7 Vilar Formoso Guarda, N Portugal 40.37N 6.49W
Vila Rial see Vila Real
61 J15 Vila Rica Mato Grosso, W Brazil 9.52S 50.44W
Vila Robert Williams see Caála
Vila Salazar see N'Dalatando
Vila Serpa Pinto see Menongue
Vila Teixeira da Silva see Bailundo
Vila Teixeira de Sousa see Luau
106 H9 Vila Velha de Ródão Castelo Branco, C Portugal 39.39N 7.40W
106 G5 Vila Verde Braga, N Portugal 41.39N 8.27W
106 H11 Vila Viçosa Évora, S Portugal 38.46N 7.25W
59 G15 Vilcabamba, Cordillera de ▲▲ C Peru
Vîlcea see Vâlcea
126 Hh1 Vil'cheka, Zemlya Eng. Wilczek Land. island Zemlya Frantsa-Iosifa, NW Russian Federation
97 F22 Vildbjerg Ringkøbing, C Denmark 56.12N 8.46E
Vileyka see Vilyeyka
95 H15 Vilhelmina Västerbotten, N Sweden 64.37N 16.40E
61 F17 Vilhena Rondônia, W Brazil 12.40S 60.07W
117 G19 Vília Attikí, C Greece 38.09N 23.21E
Viliya see Viliya
121 I14 Viliya Lith. Neris, Rus. Viliya. ≈ W Belarus
Viliya see Neris
120 H5 Viljandi Ger. Fellin. Viljandimaa, S Estonia 58.22N 25.34E
120 H5 Viljandimaa off. Viljandi Maakond. ⬖ province SW Estonia
121 E14 Vilkaviškis Pol. Wyłkowyszki. Vilkaviškis, SW Lithuania 54.39N 23.03E
120 F13 Vilkija Kaunas, C Lithuania 55.02N 23.36E
207 V9 Vil'kitskogo, Proliv strait N Russian Federation
Vilkovo see Vylkove
59 L21 Villa Abecia Chuquisaca, S Bolivia 21.01S 65.12W
43 N5 Villa Acuña var. Ciudad Acuña. Coahuila de Zaragoza, NE Mexico 29.17N 100.57W
42 J4 Villa Ahumada Chihuahua, N Mexico 30.37N 106.30W
47 O9 Villa Altagracia C Dominican Republic 18.37N 70.11W
58 L13 Villa Bella Beni, N Bolivia 10.21S 65.25W
106 J3 Villablino Castilla-León, N Spain 42.55N 6.21W
56 K6 Villa Bruzual Portuguesa, N Venezuela 9.19N 69.06W
107 O9 Villacañas Castilla-La Mancha, C Spain 39.37N 3.19W
107 O12 Villacarrillo Andalucía, S Spain 38.07N 3.04W
106 M7 Villacastín Castilla-León, N Spain 40.46N 4.25W
Villa Cecilia see Ciudad Madero
111 S9 Villach Slvn. Beljak. Kärnten, S Austria 46.36N 13.49E
109 B20 Villacidro Sardegna, Italy, C Mediterranean Sea 39.27N 8.43E
Villa Concepción see Concepción
106 L4 Villada Castilla-León, N Spain 42.15N 4.58W
42 M10 Villa de Cos Zacatecas, C Mexico 23.20N 102.20W
56 L5 Villa de Cura var. Cura. Aragua, N Venezuela 10.00N 67.30W
Villa del Nevoso see Ilirska Bistrica
Villa del Pilar see Pilar
106 M13 Villa del Río Andalucía, S Spain 37.58N 4.16W
Villa de Méndez see Méndez
44 H6 Villa de San Antonio Comayagua, W Honduras 14.24N 87.37W
107 N4 Villadiego Castilla-León, N Spain 42.31N 4.01W
107 T8 Villafames País Valenciano, E Spain 40.07N 0.03W
43 U16 Villa Flores Chiapas, SE Mexico 16.12N 93.16W
106 J3 Villafranca del Bierzo Castilla-León, N Spain 42.36N 6.49W
107 S8 Villafranca del Cid País Valenciano, E Spain 40.25N 0.15W
106 J11 Villafranca de los Barros Extremadura, W Spain 38.34N 6.19W
107 N10 Villafranca de los Caballeros Castilla-La Mancha, C Spain 39.25N 3.21W
Villafranca del Panadés see Vilafranca del Penedès
108 F8 Villafranca di Verona Veneto, NE Italy 45.22N 10.51E
109 J23 Villafrati Sicilia, Italy, C Mediterranean Sea 37.53N 13.30E
Villagarcía de Arosa see Vilagarcía de Arousa
43 O9 Villagrán Tamaulipas, C Mexico 24.28N 99.30W
63 C17 Villaguay Entre Ríos, E Argentina 31.55S 59.01W
64 O6 Villa Hayes Presidente Hayes, S Paraguay 25.04S 57.25W
43 U15 Villahermosa prev. San Juan Bautista. Tabasco, SE Mexico 17.56N 92.50W
107 O11 Villahermosa Castilla-La Mancha, C Spain 38.46N 2.52W
66 O11 Villahermoso Gomera, Islas Canarias, Spain, NE Atlantic Ocean 38.46N 2.52W
Villa Hidalgo see Hidalgo
107 T12 Villajoyosa var. La Vila Jojosa. País Valenciano, E Spain 38.31N 0.13W
Villa Juárez see Juárez
Villalba see Collado Villalba
43 N8 Villaldama Nuevo León, NE Mexico 26.29N 100.27W
106 L5 Villalón de Campos Castilla-León, N Spain 42.04N 5.03W
63 A25 Villalonga Buenos Aires, E Argentina 39.55S 62.34W
106 L5 Villalpando Castilla-León, N Spain 41.51N 5.25W
42 K9 Villa Madero var. Francisco I.Madero. Durango, C Mexico 24.27N 104.11W
43 O9 Villa Mainero Tamaulipas, C Mexico 24.32N 99.39W
Villamaña see Villamañán
106 L4 Villamañán var. Villamaña. Castilla-León, N Spain 42.19N 5.34W
64 L10 Villa María Córdoba, C Argentina 32.22S 63.15W
63 C17 Villa María Grande Entre Ríos, E Argentina 31.39S 59.54W
59 K21 Villa Martín Potosí, SW Bolivia 20.48S 67.36W
106 K15 Villamartin Andalucía, S Spain 36.50N 5.39W
64 J8 Villa Mazán La Rioja, NW Argentina 28.43S 66.25W
Villa Mercedes see Mercedes
Villamil see Puerto Villamil
Villa Nador see Nador
56 G5 Villanueva La Guajira, N Colombia 10.37N 72.58W
44 H5 Villanueva Cortés, NW Honduras 15.17N 87.58W
42 L11 Villanueva Zacatecas, C Mexico 22.24N 102.52W
44 I9 Villa Nueva Chinandega, NW Nicaragua 12.58N 86.46W
39 T11 Villanueva New Mexico, SW USA 35.18N 105.20W
106 M12 Villanueva de Córdoba Andalucía, S Spain 38.19N 4.37W
107 O12 Villanueva del Arzobispo Andalucía, S Spain 38.10N 3.00W
106 K11 Villanueva de la Serena Extremadura, W Spain 38.58N 5.48W
106 L5 Villanueva del Campo Castilla-León, N Spain 41.58N 5.25W
107 O11 Villanueva de los Infantes Castilla-La Mancha, C Spain 38.45N 3.01W
63 C14 Villa Ocampo Santa Fe, C Argentina 28.28S 59.22W
42 J8 Villa Ocampo Durango, C Mexico 26.26N 105.28W
42 J7 Villa Orestes Pereyra Durango, C Mexico 26.30N 105.38W
107 N3 Villarcayo Castilla-León, N Spain 42.55N 3.34W
106 L5 Villardefrades Castilla-León, N Spain 41.43N 5.15W
107 S9 Villar del Arzobispo País Valenciano, E Spain 39.43N 0.49W
107 Q6 Villaroya de la Sierra Aragón, NE Spain 41.28N 1.46W
Villarreal see Vila-real de los Infantes
64 P6 Villarrica Guairá, SE Paraguay 25.45S 56.28W
65 G15 Villarrica, Volcán ⩙ S Chile 39.28S 71.57W
107 P10 Villarrobledo Castilla-La Mancha, C Spain 39.16N 2.36W
107 N10 Villarrubia de los Ojos Castilla-La Mancha, C Spain 39.13N 3.36W
20 J17 Villas New Jersey, NE USA 39.01N 74.54W
107 O3 Villasana de Mena Castilla-León, N Spain 43.04N 3.16W
109 M23 Villa San Giovanni Calabria, S Italy 38.12N 15.39E
63 D18 Villa San José Entre Ríos, E Argentina 32.12S 58.15W
Villa Sanjurjo see Al-Hoceïma
107 P6 Villasayas Castilla-León, N Spain 41.19N 2.36W
109 C20 Villasimius Sardegna, Italy, C Mediterranean Sea 39.10N 9.30E
43 N6 Villa Unión Coahuila de Zaragoza, NE Mexico 28.18N 100.43W
42 K10 Villa Unión Durango, C Mexico 23.58N 104.01W
42 J10 Villa Unión Sinaloa, C Mexico 23.13N 106.10W
64 K12 Villa Valeria Córdoba, C Argentina 34.21S 64.55W
107 N8 Villaverde Madrid, C Spain 40.21N 3.43W
56 F10 Villavicencio Meta, C Colombia 4.09N 73.37W
106 L2 Villaviciosa Asturias, N Spain 43.28N 5.25W
106 L12 Villaviciosa de Córdoba Andalucía, S Spain 38.04N 5.00W
59 L22 Villazón Potosí, S Bolivia 22.04S 65.34W
12 J8 Villebon, Lac ◎ Quebec, SE Canada
Ville de Kinshasa see Kinshasa
104 J5 Villedieu-les-Poêles Manche, N France 48.51N 1.12W
Villefranche see Villefranche-sur-Saône
105 N16 Villefranche-de-Lauragais Haute-Garonne, S France 43.24N 1.42E
105 N14 Villefranche-de-Rouergue Aveyron, S France 44.21N 2.01E
105 R10 Villefranche-sur-Saône var. Villefranche. Rhône, E France 46.00N 4.40E
12 H9 Ville-Marie Quebec, SE Canada 47.21N 79.25W
104 M15 Villemur-sur-Tarn Haute-Garonne, S France 43.50N 1.32E
107 S11 Villena País Valenciano, E Spain 38.39N 0.52W
Villeneuve-d'Agen see Villeneuve-sur-Lot
104 L13 Villeneuve-sur-Lot var. Villeneuve-d'Agen; hist. Gajac. Lot-et-Garonne, SW France 44.24N 0.43E
105 P6 Villeneuve-sur-Yonne Yonne, C France 48.04N 3.21E
24 H8 Ville Platte Louisiana, S USA 30.41N 92.16W
105 R11 Villeurbanne Rhône, E France 45.46N 4.54E
103 G23 Villingen-Schwenningen Baden-Württemberg, S Germany 48.04N 8.27E
31 T15 Villisca Iowa, C USA 40.55N 94.58W
Villmanstrand see Lappeenranta
Vilna see Vilnius
121 H14 Vilnius Pol. Wilno, Ger. Wilna; prev. Rus. Vilna. ● (Lithuania) Vilnius, SE Lithuania 54.41N 25.19E
121 H14 Vilnius ✕ Vilnius, SE Lithuania 54.33N 25.17E
119 S7 Vil'nohirs'k Dnipropetrovs'ka Oblast', E Ukraine 48.31N 34.01E
119 U8 Vil'nyans'k Zaporiz'ka Oblast', SE Ukraine 47.56N 35.22E
95 L17 Vilppula Länsi-Suomi, W Finland 62.01N 24.30E
103 M20 Vils ≈ SE Germany
120 C5 Vilsandi Saar island W Estonia
119 P8 Vil'shanka Rus. Olshanka. Kirovohrads'ka Oblast', C Ukraine 48.12N 30.54E
103 O22 Vilshofen Bayern, SE Germany 48.36N 13.10E
161 J20 Viluppuram Tamil Nādu, SE India 12.54N 79.40E
115 I16 Vilusi Montenegro, SW Serbia and Montenegro (Yugoslavia) 42.44N 18.34E
101 G18 Vilvoorde Fr. Vilvorde. Vlaams Brabant, C Belgium 50.55N 4.25E
Vilvorde see Vilvoorde
121 J14 Vilyeyka Pol. Wilejka, Rus. Vileyka. Minskaya Voblasts', NW Belarus 54.30N 26.54E
126 Kk11 Vilyuy ≈ NE Russian Federation
127 P11 Vilyuchinsk Kamchatskaya Oblast', E Russian Federation 52.55N 158.28E
126 L10 Vilyuysk Respublika Sakha (Yakutiya), NE Russian Federation 63.42N 121.20E
126 K11 Vilyuyskoye Vodokhranilishche ⊠ NE Russian Federation
106 G2 Vimianzo Galicia, NW Spain 43.06N 9.03W
97 M19 Vimmerby Kalmar, S Sweden 57.40N 15.49E
104 L5 Vimoutiers Orne, N France 48.56N 0.10E
95 L16 Vimpeli Länsi-Suomi, W Finland 63.10N 23.49E
81 G14 Vina ≈ Cameroon/Chad
64 G11 Viña del Mar Valparaíso, C Chile 33.01S 71.34W
21 R8 Vinalhaven Island island Maine, NE USA
107 T8 Vinaròs País Valenciano, E Spain 40.28N 0.28E
Vînători see Vânători
33 N15 Vincennes Indiana, N USA 38.42N 87.30W
205 Y12 Vincennes Bay bay Antarctica
27 O7 Vincent Texas, SW USA 32.30N 101.10W
97 H24 Vindeby Fyn, C Denmark 54.55N 11.09E
95 I15 Vindeln Västerbotten, N Sweden 64.10N 19.45E
97 F21 Vinderup Ringkøbing, C Denmark 56.28N 8.48E
Vindhya Mountains see Vindhya Range
159 N14 Vindhya Range var. Vindhya Mountains. ▲▲ N India
Vindobona see Wien
22 K6 Vine Grove Kentucky, S USA 37.48N 85.58W
20 J17 Vineland New Jersey, NE USA 39.28N 75.01W
118 E11 Vinga Arad, W Romania 46.00N 21.14E
97 M16 Vingåker Södermanland, C Sweden 59.01N 15.52E
178 Jj8 Vinh Nghê An, N Vietnam 18.42N 105.40E
106 I5 Vinhais Bragança, N Portugal 41.50N 7.00W
178 K9 Vinh Linh Quang Tri, C Vietnam 17.02N 107.03E
Vinh Loi see Bac Liêu
178 Jj14 Vinh Long var. Vinhlong. Vinh Long, S Vietnam 10.15N 105.58E
115 Q18 Vinica NE FYR Macedonia 41.53N 22.30E
111 V13 Vinica SE Slovenia 45.28N 15.12E
116 G8 Vinishte Montana, NW Bulgaria 43.30N 23.04E
29 Q8 Vinita Oklahoma, C USA 36.38N 95.09W
Vinju Mare see Vânju Mare
100 I11 Vinkeveen Utrecht, C Netherlands 52.13N 4.55E
118 L6 Vin'kivtsi Khmel'nyts'ka Oblast', W Ukraine 49.02N 27.13E
114 I10 Vinkovci Ger. Winkowitz, Hung. Vinkovcze. Vukovar-Srijem, E Croatia 45.18N 18.45E
Vinkovcze see Vinkovci
Vinnitsa see Vinnytsya
Vinnitskaya Oblast'/Vinnytsya see Vinnyts'ka Oblast'
118 M7 Vinnyts'ka Oblast' var. Vinnytsya, Rus. Vinnitskaya Oblast'. ⬖ province C Ukraine
119 N6 Vinnytsya Rus. Vinnitsa. Vinnyts'ka Oblast', C Ukraine 49.14N 28.30E
119 N6 Vinnytsya ✕ Vinnyts'ka Oblast', N Ukraine 49.13N 28.40E
Vinogradov see Vynohradiv
204 L8 Vinson Massif ▲ Antarctica 78.45S 85.19W
96 G11 Vinstra Oppland, S Norway 61.36N 9.44E
118 K12 Vintilă Vodă Buzău, SE Romania 45.28N 26.44E
31 X13 Vinton Iowa, C USA 42.10N 92.01W
24 F9 Vinton Louisiana, S USA 30.10N 93.37W
161 J17 Vinukonda Andhra Pradesh, E India 16.03N 79.41E
Vioara see Ocnele Mari
85 E23 Vioolsdrif Northern Cape, SW South Africa 28.50S 17.38E
111 S12 Vipava ≈ SW Slovenia
84 M13 Viphya Mountains ▲▲ C Malawi
179 Qq11 Virac Catanduanes Island, N Philippines 13.39N 124.17E
128 K8 Virandozero Respublika Kareliya, NW Russian Federation 63.59N 36.00E
143 P16 Viranşehir Şanlıurfa, SE Turkey 37.13N 39.31E
160 D13 Virār Mahārāshtra, W India 19.30N 72.48E
9 W16 Virden Manitoba, S Canada 49.49N 100.57W
32 K14 Virden Illinois, N USA 39.30N 89.46W
Virdois see Virrat
104 J5 Vire Calvados, N France 48.49N 0.52W
104 J4 Vire ≈ N France
85 A15 Virei Namibe, SW Angola 15.43S 12.54E
Virful Moldoveanu see Vârful Moldoveanu
37 R5 Virgina Peak ▲ Nevada, W USA 39.46N 119.26W
47 U9 Virgin Gorda island C British Virgin Islands
85 I22 Virginia Free State, C South Africa 28.04S 26.51E
32 K13 Virginia Illinois, N USA 39.57N 90.12W
31 W4 Virginia Minnesota, N USA 47.31N 92.32W
23 T6 Virginia off. Commonwealth of Virginia; also known as Mother of Presidents, Mother of States, Old Dominion. ⬖ state NE USA
23 Y7 Virginia Beach Virginia, NE USA 36.51N 75.58W
35 R11 Virginia City Montana, NW USA 45.17N 111.54W
37 Q6 Virginia City Nevada, W USA 39.19N 119.39W
12 H8 Virginiatown Ontario, S Canada 48.09N 79.35W
Virgin Islands see British Virgin Islands
47 T9 Virgin Islands (US) var. Virgin Islands of the United States; prev. Danish West Indies. ◇ US unincorporated territory E West Indies
47 T9 Virgin Passage passage Puerto Rico/Virgin Islands (US)
37 Y10 Virgin River ≈ Nevada/Utah, W USA
Virihaure see Virihaure
94 H12 Virihaure var. Virihaur. ◎ N Sweden
178 Jj11 Virôchey Rôtânôkiri, NE Cambodia 13.58N 106.49E
95 N19 Virolahti Etelä-Suomi, S Finland 60.33N 27.37E
32 J8 Viroqua Wisconsin, N USA 43.33N 90.54W
114 G8 Virovitica Ger. Virovititz, Hung. Verőcze; prev. Ger. Werowitz. Virovitica-Podravina, NE Croatia 45.49N 17.25E
114 G8 Virovitica-Podravina off. Virovitičko-Podravska Županija. ⬖ province NE Croatia
Virovititz see Virovitica
115 J17 Virpazar Montenegro, SW Serbia and Montenegro (Yugoslavia) 42.15N 19.06E
95 L17 Virrat Swe. Virdois. Länsi-Suomi, SW Finland 62.13N 23.49E
97 M20 Virserum Kalmar, S Sweden 57.17N 15.18E
101 K25 Virton Luxembourg, SE Belgium 49.34N 5.31E
120 F5 Virtsu Ger. Werder. Läänemaa, W Estonia 58.35N 23.32E
58 C12 Virú La Libertad, C Peru 8.27S 78.44W
Virudhunagar see Virudunagar
161 H23 Virudunagar var. Virudhunagar. Tamil Nādu, SE India 9.34N 77.57E
120 I3 Viru-Jaagupi Ger. Sankt-Jakobi. Lääne-Virumaa, NE Estonia 59.13N 26.28E
59 N19 Viru-Viru var. Santa Cruz. ✕ (Santa Cruz) Santa Cruz, C Bolivia 17.49S 63.12W
115 E15 Vis It. Lissa; anc. Issa. island S Croatia
Vis see Fish
120 I12 Visaginas prev. Sniečkus. Ignalina, E Lithuania 55.36N 26.22E
161 M15 Visākhapatnam Andhra Pradesh, SE India 17.45N 83.19E
37 R11 Visalia California, W USA 36.19N 119.19W
Višău see Vişeu
179 Qq12 Visayan Sea sea C Philippines
97 P19 Visby Ger. Wisby. Gotland, SE Sweden 57.37N 18.19E
207 N9 Viscount Melville Sound prev. Melville Sound. sound Northwest Territories/Nunavut, N Canada
101 L19 Visé Liège, E Belgium 50.43N 5.42E
114 K13 Višegrad Republika Srpska, E Bosnia and Herzegovina 43.46N 19.18E
60 L12 Viseu Pará, NE Brazil 1.10S 46.09W
106 H7 Viseu prev. Vizeu. Viseu, N Portugal 40.40N 7.55W
106 H7 Viseu var. Vizeu. ⬖ district N Portugal
118 I8 Vişeu Hung. Visó; prev. Višău. ≈ NW Romania
118 I8 Vişeu de Sus var. Vişeul de Sus, Ger. Oberwischau, Hung. Felsővisó. Maramureş, N Romania 47.43N 24.24E
Vişeul de Sus see Vişeu de Sus
129 R10 Vishera ≈ NW Russian Federation
97 J19 Viskafors Västra Götaland, S Sweden 57.37N 12.49E
97 J20 Viskan ≈ SW Sweden
97 L21 Vislanda Kronoberg, S Sweden 56.46N 14.30E
Vislinskiy Zaliv see Vistula Lagoon
Visó see Vişeu
114 H13 Visoko Federacija Bosna I Hercegovina, C Bosnia and Herzegovina 43.58N 18.12E
108 A9 Viso, Monte ▲ NW Italy 44.42N 7.04E
110 E10 Visp Valais, SW Switzerland 46.18N 7.52E
110 E10 Vispa ≈ S Switzerland
97 M21 Vissefjärda Kalmar, S Sweden 56.31N 15.34E
102 I11 Visselhövede Niedersachsen, NW Germany 52.58N 9.36E
97 G23 Vissenbjerg Fyn, C Denmark 55.22N 10.07E
37 U17 Vista California, W USA 33.12N 117.14W
60 C11 Vista Alegre Amazonas, NW Brazil 1.23N 68.13W
116 J13 Vistonída, Límni ◎ NE Greece
94 K12 Visttasjohka ≈ N Sweden
Vistula see Wisła
121 A14 Vistula Lagoon Ger. Frisches Haff, Pol. Zalew Wiślany, Rus. Vislinskiy Zaliv. lagoon Poland/Russian Federation
116 I8 Vit ≈ NW Bulgaria
Vitebsk see Vitsyebsk
Vitebskaya Oblast' see Vitsyebskaya Voblasts'
109 H14 Viterbo anc. Vicus Elbii. Lazio, C Italy 42.25N 12.07E
114 H12 Vitez Federacija Bosna I Hercegovina, C Bosnia and Herzegovina 44.08N 17.47E
178 J15 Vi Thanh Cân Thơ, S Vietnam 9.45N 105.28E
Viti see Fiji

◆ Country ● Country Capital ◇ Dependent Territory ○ Dependent Territory Capital ⬖ Administrative Region ✕ International Airport ▲ Mountain ▲▲ Mountain Range ⩙ Volcano ≈ River ◎ Lake ⊠ Reservoir

194 K12 **Vitiaz Strait** strait NE PNG
106 J7 **Vitigudino** Castilla-León, N Spain 41.00N 6.26W
197 H15 **Viti Levu** island W Fiji
126 Kk14 **Vitim** ≈ C Russian Federation
126 Kk13 **Vitimskiy** Irkutskaya Oblast', C Russian Federation 58.12N 113.10E
111 V2 **Vitis** Niederösterreich, N Austria 48.45N 15.09E
Vitoria see Vitoria-Gasteiz
61 O20 **Vitória** Espírito Santo, SE Brazil 20.19S 40.21W
Vitoria Bank see Vitória Seamount
61 N18 **Vitória da Conquista** Bahia, E Brazil 14.52S 40.52W
107 P3 **Vitoria-Gasteiz** var. Vitoria, Eng. Vittoria. País Vasco, N Spain 42.51N 2.40W
67 J16 **Vitória Seamount** var. Victoria Bank, Vitoria Bank. undersea feature C Atlantic Ocean 18.48S 37.24W
114 F13 **Vitorog** ▲ SW Bosnia and Herzegovina 44.06N 17.03E
104 J6 **Vitré** Ille-et-Vilaine, NW France 48.07N 1.12W
105 R5 **Vitry-le-François** Marne, N France 48.43N 4.36E
116 D13 **Vítsoi** ▲ N Greece 40.39N 21.23E
120 N13 **Vitsyebsk** Rus. Vitebsk. Vitsyebskaya Voblasts', NE Belarus 55.11N 30.10E
120 K13 **Vitsyebskaya Voblasts'** prev. Rus. Vitebskaya Oblast'. ◈ province N Belarus
94 J11 **Vittangi** Norrbotten, N Sweden 67.40N 21.39E
105 R8 **Vitteaux** Côte d'Or, C France 47.24N 4.31E
105 S6 **Vittel** Vosges, NE France 48.13N 5.57E
97 N15 **Vittinge** Västmanland, C Sweden 59.52N 17.04E
109 K25 **Vittoria** Sicilia, Italy, C Mediterranean Sea 36.55N 14.30E
Vittoria see Vitoria-Gasteiz
108 I7 **Vittorio Veneto** Veneto, NE Italy 45.58N 12.18E
183 Q9 **Vitu Levu** island W Fiji
199 Jj7 **Vityaz Seamount** undersea feature C Pacific Ocean 13.30N 173.15W
183 Q7 **Vityaz Trench** undersea feature W Pacific Ocean
110 G8 **Vitznau** Luzern, W Switzerland 47.01N 8.28E
106 I1 **Viveiro** Galicia, NW Spain 43.39N 7.34W
107 S9 **Viver** País Valenciano, E Spain 39.55N 0.36W
105 Q13 **Viverais, Monts du** ▲▲ C France
126 Ii10 **Vivi** ≈ N Russian Federation
24 F4 **Vivian** Louisiana, S USA 32.52N 93.59W
31 N10 **Vivian** South Dakota, N USA 43.53N 100.16W
105 R13 **Viviers** Ardèche, E France 44.31N 4.40E
Vivis see Vevey
85 K19 **Vivo** Limpopo, NE South Africa 22.58S 29.13E
104 L10 **Vivonne** Vienne, W France 46.25N 0.15E
197 G14 **Viwa** island Yasawa Group, NW Fiji
Vizakna see Ocna Sibiului
107 O2 **Vizcaya** Basq. Bizkaia. ◈ province País Vasco, N Spain
Vizcaya, Golfo de see Biscay, Bay of
142 C10 **Vize** Kırklareli, NW Turkey 41.33N 27.49E
126 I2 **Vize, Ostrov** island Severnaya Zemlya, N Russian Federation
Vizeu see Viseu
161 M15 **Vizianagaram** var. Vizianagram. Andhra Pradesh, E India 18.07N 83.25E
Vizianagram see Vizianagaram
105 S12 **Vizille** Isère, E France 45.05N 5.46E
129 R11 **Vizinga** Respublika Komi, NW Russian Federation 61.06N 50.09E
118 M13 **Viziru** Brăila, SE Romania 45.00N 27.43E
115 K21 **Vjosës, Lumi i** var. Vijosa, Vijosë, Gk. Aóos. ≈ Albania/Greece see also Aóos
101 H18 **Vlaams Brabant** ◈ province C Belgium
Vlaanderen see Flanders
100 G12 **Vlaardingen** Zuid-Holland, SW Netherlands 51.55N 4.21E
118 F10 **Vlădeasa, Vârful** prev. Vîrful Vlădeasa. ▲ NW Romania 46.45N 22.46E
Vlădeasa, Vîrful see Vlădeasa, Vârful
115 P16 **Vladičin Han** Serbia, SE Serbia and Montenegro (Yugoslavia) 42.44N 22.04E
131 O16 **Vladikavkaz** prev. Dzaudzhikau, Ordzhonikidze. Respublika Severnaya Osetiya, SW Russian Federation 42.58N 44.41E
130 M3 **Vladimir** Vladimirskaya Oblast', W Russian Federation 56.09N 40.21E
150 M7 **Vladimirovka** Kostanay, N Kazakhstan 53.28N 64.01E
Vladimirovka see Yuzhno-Sakhalinsk
130 L3 **Vladimirskaya Oblast'** ◈ province W Russian Federation
130 I3 **Vladimirskiy Tupik** Smolenskaya Oblast', W Russian Federation 55.45N 33.25E
Vladimir-Volynskiy see Volodymyr-Volyns'kyy
127 Nn18 **Vladivostok** Primorskiy Kray, SE Russian Federation 43.09N 131.52E
119 U13 **Vladyslavivka** Respublika Krym, S Ukraine 45.09N 35.25E
100 P6 **Vlagtwedde** Groningen, NE Netherlands 53.01N 7.07E
Vlajna see Kukavica
114 J12 **Vlasenica** Republika Srpska, E Bosnia and Herzegovina 44.10N 18.57E
114 G12 **Vlašić** ▲ C Bosnia and Herzegovina 44.18N 17.40E
113 D17 **Vlašim** Ger. Wlaschim. Středočeský Kraj, C Czech Republic 49.42N 14.54E
115 P15 **Vlasotince** Serbia, SE Serbia and Montenegro (Yugoslavia) 42.58N 22.07E
126 Ll7 **Vlasovo** Respublika Sakha (Yakutiya), NE Russian Federation 70.41N 134.49E
100 I11 **Vleuten** Utrecht, C Netherlands 52.07N 5.01E
100 I5 **Vlieland** Fris. Flylân. island Waddeneilanden, N Netherlands
100 I5 **Vliestroom** strait NW Netherlands
101 J14 **Vlijmen** Noord-Brabant, S Netherlands 51.42N 5.13E
101 E15 **Vlissingen** Eng. Flushing, Fr. Flessingue. Zeeland, SW Netherlands 51.25N 3.34E
Vlodava see Włodawa
Vlonë/Vlora see Vlorë
115 K22 **Vlorë** prev. Vlonë, It. Valona, Vlora. Vlorë, SW Albania 40.27N 19.31E
115 K22 **Vlorë** ◈ district SW Albania
115 K22 **Vlorës, Gjiri i** var. Valona Bay. bay SW Albania
Vlotslavsk see Włocławek
113 C16 **Vltava** Ger. Moldau. ≈ W Czech Republic
130 K3 **Vnukovo** ✕ (Moskva) Gorod Moskva, W Russian Federation 55.30N 36.52E
152 L11 **Vobkent** Rus. Vabkent. Buxoro Viloyati, C Uzbekistan 40.01N 64.25E
27 Q9 **Voca** Texas, SW USA 30.58N 99.09W
111 R5 **Vöcklabruck** Oberösterreich, NW Austria 48.01N 13.37E
114 D13 **Vodice** Šibenik-Knin, S Croatia 43.46N 15.46E
128 K10 **Vodlozero, Ozero** ◎ NW Russian Federation
114 A10 **Vodnjan** It. Dignano d'Istria. Istra, NW Croatia 44.57N 13.51E
129 S9 **Vodnyy** Respublika Komi, NW Russian Federation 63.31N 53.21E
97 G20 **Vodskov** Nordjylland, N Denmark 57.07N 10.01E
94 H4 **Vogar** Sudhurland, SW Iceland 63.58N 22.20W
195 N16 **Vogel, Cape** headland SE PNG 9.42S 150.04E
Vogelkop see Doberai, Jazirah
79 X15 **Vogel Peak** prev. Dim lang. ▲ E Nigeria 8.16N 11.44E
103 H17 **Vogelsberg** ▲▲ C Germany
108 D8 **Voghera** Lombardia, N Italy 44.58N 9.01E
114 I13 **Vogošća** Federacija Bosna I Hercegovina, SE Bosnia and Herzegovina 43.55N 18.20E
103 M17 **Vogtland** historical region E Germany
129 V12 **Vogul'skiy Kamen', Gora** ▲ NW Russian Federation 60.10N 58.41E
197 H6 **Voh** Province Nord, C New Caledonia 20.57S 164.41E
Vohémar see Iharaña
180 H8 **Vohimena, Tanjona** Fr. Cap Sainte Marie. headland S Madagascar 25.20S 45.06E
180 J6 **Vohipeno** Fianarantsoa, SE Madagascar 22.21S 47.51E
120 H5 **Võhma** Ger. Wöchma. Viljandimaa, S Estonia 58.37N 25.34E
83 J20 **Voi** Coast, S Kenya 3.22S 38.34E
78 K15 **Voinjama** N Liberia 8.23N 9.48W
105 S12 **Voiron** Isère, E France 45.22N 5.34E
111 V8 **Voitsberg** Steiermark, SE Austria 47.04N 15.09E
97 F24 **Vojens** Ger. Woyens. Sønderjylland, SW Denmark 55.15N 9.19E
114 K9 **Vojvodina** Ger. Wojwodina. Region N Serbia and Montenegro (Yugoslavia)
13 S6 **Volant** ≈ Quebec, SE Canada
Volaterrae see Volterra
45 P15 **Volcán** var. Hato del Volcán. Chiriquí, W Panama 8.45N 82.38W
Volchansk see Vovchans'k
Volchya see Vovcha
96 D10 **Volda** Møre og Romsdal, S Norway 62.07N 6.04E
100 J9 **Volendam** Noord-Holland, C Netherlands 52.30N 5.04E
128 L15 **Volga** Yaroslavskaya Oblast', W Russian Federation 57.56N 38.23E
31 R10 **Volga** South Dakota, N USA 44.19N 96.55W
125 Cc11 **Volga** ≈ NW Russian Federation
Volga-Baltic Waterway see Volgo-Baltiyskiy Kanal
Volga Hills/Volga Uplands see Privolzhskaya Vozvyshennost'
128 L13 **Volgo-Baltiyskiy Kanal** Eng. Volga-Baltic Waterway. canal NW Russian Federation
130 M12 **Volgodonsk** Rostovskaya Oblast', SW Russian Federation 47.34N 42.03E
131 O10 **Volgograd** prev. Stalingrad, Tsaritsyn. Volgogradskaya Oblast', SW Russian Federation 48.42N 44.28E
131 N9 **Volgogradskaya Oblast'** ◈ province SW Russian Federation
131 P10 **Volgogradskoye Vodokhranilishche** ⊠ SW Russian Federation
103 J19 **Volkach** Bayern, C Germany 49.51N 10.15E
111 U9 **Völkermarkt** Slvn. Velikovec. Kärnten, S Austria 46.39N 14.37E
128 I12 **Volkhov** Leningradskaya Oblast', NW Russian Federation 59.56N 32.19E
103 D20 **Völklingen** Saarland, SW Germany 49.15N 6.51E
Volkovysk see Vawkavysk
Volkovyskiye Vysoty see Vawkavyskaye Wzvyshsha
85 K22 **Volksrust** Mpumalanga, E South Africa 27.18S 29.53E
100 L8 **Vollenhove** Overijssel, N Netherlands 52.40N 5.58E
121 L16 **Volma** Rus. Volma. ≈ C Belarus
Volmari see Valmiera
119 W9 **Volnovakha** Donets'ka Oblast', SE Ukraine 47.36N 37.31E
118 K6 **Volochys'k** Khmel'nyts'ka Oblast', W Ukraine 49.32N 26.14E
119 O6 **Volodarka** Kyyivs'ka Oblast', N Ukraine 49.31N 29.55E
119 W9 **Volodars'ke** Donets'ka Oblast', E Ukraine 47.11N 37.19E
131 R13 **Volodarskiy** Astrakhanskaya Oblast', SW Russian Federation 46.23N 48.39E
Volodarskoye see Saumalkol'
119 N8 **Volodars'k-Volyns'kyy** Zhytomyrs'ka Oblast', N Ukraine 50.37N 28.28E
118 K3 **Volodymerets'** Rivnens'ka Oblast', NW Ukraine 51.24N 25.52E
118 I3 **Volodymyr-Volyns'kyy** Pol. Włodzimierz, Rus. Vladimir-Volynskiy. Volyns'ka Oblast', NW Ukraine 50.51N 24.19E
128 L14 **Vologda** Vologodskaya Oblast', W Russian Federation 59.10N 39.55E
128 L12 **Vologodskaya Oblast'** ◈ province NW Russian Federation
130 K3 **Volokolamsk** Moskovskaya Oblast', W Russian Federation 56.03N 35.57E
130 K9 **Volokonovka** Belgorodskaya Oblast', W Russian Federation 50.30N 37.54E
117 G16 **Vólos** Thessalía, C Greece 39.21N 22.58E
128 M11 **Voloshka** Arkhangel'skaya Oblast', NW Russian Federation 61.19N 40.06E
Vološinovo see Novi Bečej
118 H7 **Volovets'** Zakarpats'ka Oblast', W Ukraine 48.42N 23.12E
116 K7 **Volovo** Ruse, N Bulgaria 43.33N 25.49E
Volozhin see Valozhyn
131 Q7 **Vol'sk** Saratovskaya Oblast', W Russian Federation 52.04N 47.19E
79 Q17 **Volta** ≈ SE Ghana
Volta Blanche see White Volta
79 P16 **Volta, Lake** ⊠ SE Ghana
Volta Noire see Black Volta
62 O9 **Volta Redonda** Rio de Janeiro, SE Brazil 22.31S 44.04W
Volta Rouge see Red Volta
108 F12 **Volterra** anc. Volaterrae. Toscana, C Italy 43.25N 10.51E
109 K17 **Volturno** ≈ S Italy
115 I15 **Volujak** ▲▲ SW Serbia and Montenegro (Yugoslavia)
Volunteer Island see Starbuck Island
67 F24 **Volunteer Point** headland East Falkland, Falkland Islands 51.31S 57.43W
Volunteer State see Tennessee
116 H13 **Vólvi, Límni** ◎ N Greece
Volyn see Volyns'ka Oblast'
118 I3 **Volyns'ka Oblast'** var. Volyn, Rus. Volynskaya Oblast'. ◈ province NW Ukraine
Volynskaya Oblast' see Volyns'ka Oblast'
131 Q3 **Volzhsk** Respublika Mariy El, W Russian Federation 55.53N 48.21E
131 O10 **Volzhskiy** Volgogradskaya Oblast', SW Russian Federation 48.48N 44.40E
180 I7 **Vondrozo** Fianarantsoa, SE Madagascar 22.49S 47.19E
116 K9 **Voneshta Voda** Veliko Tŭrnovo, N Bulgaria 42.55N 25.40E
41 P10 **Von Frank Mountain** ▲ Alaska, USA 63.36N 154.29W
117 C17 **Vónitsa** Dytikí Ellás, W Greece 38.55N 20.52E
120 J6 **Võnnu** Ger. Wendau. Tartumaa, SE Estonia 58.15N 27.04E
100 G12 **Voorburg** Zuid-Holland, W Netherlands 52.04N 4.22E
100 H11 **Voorschoten** Zuid-Holland, W Netherlands 52.07N 4.25E
100 M11 **Voorst** Gelderland, E Netherlands 52.10N 6.10E
100 K11 **Voorthuizen** Gelderland, C Netherlands 52.12N 5.36E
94 L2 **Vopnafjördhur** Austurland, E Iceland 65.45N 14.51W
94 L2 **Vopnafjördhur** bay E Iceland
Vora see Vorë
121 H15 **Voranava** Pol. Werenów, Rus. Voronovo. Hrodzyenskaya Voblasts', W Belarus 54.10N 25.21E
110 I8 **Vorarlberg** off. Land Vorarlberg. ◈ state W Austria
111 X7 **Vorau** Steiermark, E Austria 47.22N 15.55E
100 N11 **Vorden** Gelderland, E Netherlands 52.07N 6.18E
110 H9 **Vorderrhein** ≈ SE Switzerland
94 J2 **Vordhufell** ▲ N Iceland 65.42N 18.45W
97 I24 **Vordingborg** Storstrøm, SE Denmark 55.01N 11.55E
115 K19 **Vorë** var. Vora. Tiranë, W Albania 41.23N 19.37E
117 H17 **Vóreioi Sporádes** var. Vórioi Sporádhes, Eng. Northern Sporades. island group E Greece
117 J17 **Vóreion Aigaíon** Eng. Aegean North. ◈ region SE Greece
117 G18 **Voreiós Evvoïkós Kólpos** gulf E Greece
207 S16 **Voring Plateau** undersea feature N Norwegian Sea
Vórioi Sporádhes see Vóreioi Sporádes
129 W4 **Vorkuta** Respublika Komi, NW Russian Federation 67.27N 64.00E
97 I14 **Vorma** ≈ S Norway
120 E4 **Vormsi** var. Vormsi Saar, Ger. Worms, Swed. Ormsö. island W Estonia
Vormsi Saar see Vormsi
126 Hh12 **Vorogovo** Krasnoyarskiy Kray, C Russian Federation 61.01N 89.25E
131 N7 **Vorona** ≈ W Russian Federation
130 L7 **Voronezh** Voronezhskaya Oblast', W Russian Federation 51.39N 39.13E
130 L7 **Voronezh** ≈ W Russian Federation
130 K8 **Voronezhskaya Oblast'** ◈ province W Russian Federation
Voronovitsya see Voronovytsya
Voronovo see Voranava
119 N6 **Voronovytsya** Rus. Voronovitsya. Vinnyts'ka Oblast', C Ukraine 49.06N 28.49E
126 Hh7 **Vorontsovo** Taymyrskiy (Dolgano-Nenetskiy) Avtonomnyy Okrug, N Russian Federation 71.45N 83.31E
128 K3 **Voron'ya** ≈ NW Russian Federation
Voropayevo see Varapayeva
Voroshilov see Ussuriysk
Voroshilovgrad see Luhans'k, Ukraine
Voroshilovgrad see Luhans'ka Oblast', Ukraine
Voroshilovgradskaya Oblast' see Luhans'ka Oblast'
Voroshilovsk see Stavropol', Russian Federation
Voroshilovsk see Alchevs'k, Ukraine
143 V13 **Vorotan** Az. Bärguşad. ≈ Armenia/Azerbaijan
131 P3 **Vorotynets** Nizhegorodskaya Oblast', W Russian Federation 56.06N 46.06E
119 S3 **Vorozhba** Sums'ka Oblast', NE Ukraine 51.09N 34.16E
119 T5 **Vorskla** ≈ Russian Federation/Ukraine
101 I17 **Vorst** Antwerpen, N Belgium 51.06N 5.01E
85 G21 **Vorstershoop** North-West, N South Africa 25.46S 22.57E
120 H6 **Võrtsjärv** Ger. Wirz-See. ◎ SE Estonia
120 J7 **Võru** Ger. Werro. Võrumaa, SE Estonia 57.51N 27.00E
153 R11 **Vorukh** N Tajikistan 39.51N 70.34E
120 I7 **Võrumaa** off. Võru Maakond. ◈ province SE Estonia
85 G24 **Vosburg** Northern Cape, W South Africa 30.33S 22.49E
153 Q14 **Vose'** Rus. Vose; prev. Aral. SW Tajikistan 37.51N 69.31E
105 S6 **Vosges** ◈ department NE France
105 U6 **Vosges** ▲▲ NE France
128 K13 **Voskresenskoye** Vologodskaya Oblast', NW Russian Federation 59.25N 37.56E
130 L4 **Voskresensk** Moskovskaya Oblast', W Russian Federation 55.19N 38.42E
131 P2 **Voskresenskoye** Nizhegorodskaya Oblast', W Russian Federation 57.00N 45.33E
131 V6 **Voskresenskoye** Respublika Bashkortostan, W Russian Federation 53.07N 56.07E
96 D13 **Voss** Hordaland, S Norway 60.37N 6.25E
96 D13 **Voss** physical region S Norway
101 I16 **Vosselaar** Antwerpen, N Belgium 51.19N 4.55E
96 D13 **Vosso** ≈ S Norway
Vostochno-Kazakhstanskaya Oblast' see Shygys Konyrat
151 T12 **Vostochno-Kounradskiy** Kaz. Shyghys Qongyrat. Zhezkazgan, C Kazakhstan 47.01N 75.05E
127 N4 **Vostochno-Sibirskoye More** Eng. East Siberian Sea. sea Arctic Ocean
151 X10 **Vostochnyy Kazakhstan** off. Vostochno-Kazakhstanskaya Oblast', var. East Kazakhstan, Kaz. Shyghys Qazagastan Oblysy. ◈ province E Kazakhstan
Vostochnyy Sayan see Eastern Sayans
Vostock Island see Vostok Island
205 U10 **Vostok** Russian research station Antarctica 77.18S 105.32E
203 X5 **Vostok Island** var. Vostock Island; prev. Stavers Island. island Line Islands, SE Kiribati
131 T2 **Votkinsk** Udmurtskaya Respublika, NW Russian Federation 57.04N 54.00E
129 U15 **Votkinskoye Vodokhranilishche** var. Votkinsk Reservoir. ⊠ NW Russian Federation
Votkinsk Reservoir see Votkinskoye Vodokhranilishche
62 J7 **Votuporanga** São Paulo, S Brazil 20.25S 49.52W
106 H7 **Vouga, Rio** ≈ N Portugal
117 E14 **Voúrinos** ▲▲ N Greece
117 G24 **Voúxa, Akrotírio** headland Kríti, Greece, E Mediterranean Sea 35.37N 23.34E
105 R4 **Vouziers** Ardennes, N France 49.24N 4.42E
119 V7 **Vovcha** Rus. Volchya. ≈ E Ukraine
119 V4 **Vovchans'k** Rus. Volchansk. Kharkivs'ka Oblast', E Ukraine 50.19N 36.54E
105 N6 **Voves** Eure-et-Loir, C France 48.18N 1.39E
81 M14 **Vovodo** ≈ S Central Africa Republic
96 M12 **Voxna** Gävleborg, C Sweden 61.20N 15.34E
96 L11 **Voxnan** ≈ C Sweden
116 F7 **Voynishka Reka** ≈ NW Bulgaria
129 T9 **Voyvozh** Respublika Komi, NW Russian Federation 62.54N 54.52E
128 M12 **Vozhega** Vologodskaya Oblast', NW Russian Federation 60.27N 40.11E
128 L12 **Vozhe, Ozero** ◎ NW Russian Federation
119 Q9 **Voznesens'k** Rus. Voznesensk. Mykolayivs'ka Oblast', S Ukraine 47.33N 31.22E
128 J12 **Voznesen'ye** Leningradskaya Oblast', NW Russian Federation 61.00N 35.24E
150 J14 **Vozrozhdeniya, Ostrov** Uzb. Wozrojdeniye Oroli. island Kazakhstan/Uzbekistan
97 G20 **Vrå** var. Vraa. Nordjylland, N Denmark 57.21N 9.57E
Vraa see Vrå
116 H9 **Vrachesh** Sofiya, NW Bulgaria 42.52N 23.45E
117 C19 **Vrachíonas** ▲ Zákynthos, Iónioi Nísoi, Greece, C Mediterranean Sea 37.49N 20.43E
119 P8 **Vradiyivka** Mykolayivs'ka Oblast', S Ukraine 47.51N 30.37E
115 G14 **Vran** ▲ SW Bosnia and Herzegovina 43.35N 17.30E
118 K12 **Vrancea** ◈ county E Romania
153 T14 **Vrang** SE Tajikistan 37.03N 72.26E
127 Oo2 **Vrangelya, Ostrov** Eng. Wrangel Island. island NE Russian Federation
114 H13 **Vranica** ▲ C Bosnia and Herzegovina 43.57N 17.43E
115 O16 **Vranje** Serbia, SE Serbia and Montenegro (Yugoslavia) 42.33N 21.55E
Vranov see Vranov nad Topl'ou
113 N19 **Vranov nad Topl'ou** var. Vranov, Hung. Varannó. Prešovský Kraj, E Slovakia 48.54N 21.40E
116 H8 **Vratsa** Vratsa, NW Bulgaria 43.13N 23.33E
116 H8 **Vratsa** ◈ province NW Bulgaria
116 F10 **Vrattsa** prev. Mirovo. Kyustendil, W Bulgaria 42.16N 22.39E
114 G11 **Vrbanja** ≈ NW Bosnia and Herzegovina
114 K9 **Vrbas** Serbia, NW Serbia and Montenegro (Yugoslavia) 45.34N 19.39E
114 G13 **Vrbas** ≈ N Bosnia and Herzegovina
114 E8 **Vrbovec** Zagreb, N Croatia 45.53N 16.24E
114 C9 **Vrbovsko** Primorje-Gorski Kotar, NW Croatia 45.22N 15.06E
113 E15 **Vrchlabí** Ger. Hohenelbe. Hradecký Kraj, NE Czech Republic 50.37N 15.37E
85 J22 **Vrede** Free State, E South Africa 27.25S 29.10E
102 E13 **Vreden** Nordrhein-Westfalen, NW Germany 52.01N 6.50E
85 E25 **Vredenburg** Western Cape, SW South Africa 32.55S 18.00E
101 I23 **Vresse-sur-Semois** Namur, SE Belgium 49.52N 4.56E
97 L16 **Vretstorp** Örebro, C Sweden 59.03N 14.51E
115 G15 **Vrgorac** prev. Vrhgorac. Split-Dalmacija, SE Croatia 43.10N 17.24E
Vrhgorac see Vrgorac
111 T12 **Vrhnika** Ger. Oberlaibach. W Slovenia 45.57N 14.18E
161 I21 **Vriddhāchalam** Tamil Nādu, SE India 11.33N 79.18E
100 N6 **Vries** Drenthe, NE Netherlands 53.04N 6.34E
100 O10 **Vriezenveen** Overijssel, E Netherlands 52.25N 6.39E
97 L20 **Vrigstad** Jönköping, S Sweden 57.19N 14.30E
110 H9 **Vrin** Graubünden, S Switzerland 46.40N 9.06E
114 E13 **Vrlika** Split-Dalmacija, S Croatia 43.54N 16.24E
115 M14 **Vrnjačka Banja** Serbia, C Serbia and Montenegro (Yugoslavia) 43.36N 20.55E
Vrondádhes/Vrondados see Vrontádos
117 L18 **Vrontádos** var. Vrondados; prev. Vrondádhes. Chíos, E Greece 38.25N 26.07E
100 N9 **Vroomshoop** Overijssel, E Netherlands 52.28N 6.34E
114 N10 **Vršac** Ger. Werschetz, Hung. Versecz. Serbia, NE Serbia and Montenegro (Yugoslavia) 45.08N 21.17E
114 M10 **Vršački Kanal** canal N Serbia and Montenegro (Yugoslavia)
85 H21 **Vryburg** North-West, N South Africa 26.57S 24.43E
85 K22 **Vryheid** KwaZulu/Natal, E South Africa 27.45S 30.48E
113 I18 **Vsetín** Ger. Wsetin. Zlínský Kraj, E Czech Republic 49.21N 17.57E
113 J20 **Vtáčnik** Hung. Madaras, Ptacsnik; prev. Ptačnik. ▲ W Slovakia 48.38N 18.38E
Vuadil' see Wodil
Vuanggava see Vuaqava
197 K15 **Vuaqava** prev. Vuanggava. island Lau Group, SE Fiji
116 I11 **Vŭcha** ≈ SW Bulgaria
115 N16 **Vučitrn** Serbia, S Serbia and Montenegro (Yugoslavia) 42.49N 21.00E
101 J14 **Vught** Noord-Brabant, S Netherlands 51.37N 5.19E
119 W8 **Vuhledar** Donets'ka Oblast', E Ukraine 47.48N 37.11E
114 I9 **Vuka** ≈ E Croatia
115 K17 **Vukël** var. Vukli. Shkodër, N Albania 42.29N 19.39E
Vukli see Vukël
114 J9 **Vukovar** Hung. Vukovár. Vukovar-Srijem, E Croatia 45.18N 18.45E
114 I10 **Vukovar-Srijem** off. Vukovarsko-Srijemska Županija. ◈ province E Croatia
129 U8 **Vuktyl** Respublika Komi, NW Russian Federation 63.49N 57.07E
9 Q17 **Vulcan** Alberta, SW Canada 50.27N 113.12W
118 G12 **Vulcan** Ger. Wulkan, Hung. Zsilyvajdevulkán; prev. Crivadia Vulcanului, Vaidei, Hung. Sily-Vajdej, Vajdej. Hunedoara, W Romania 45.22N 23.16E
118 M12 **Vulcănești** Rus. Vulkaneshty. S Moldova 45.41N 28.25E
109 L22 **Vulcano, Isola** island Isole Eolie, S Italy
116 G7 **Vŭlchedrŭm** Montana, NW Bulgaria 43.42N 23.25E
116 N8 **Vŭlchidol** prev. Kurt-Dere. Varna, NE Bulgaria 43.25N 27.33E
Vulkaneshty see Vulcănești
127 P11 **Vulkannyy** Kamchatskaya Oblast', E Russian Federation 53.01N 158.26E
38 J13 **Vulture Mountains** ▲▲ Arizona, SW USA
178 K14 **Vung Tau** prev. Fr. Cape Saint Jacques, Cap Saint-Jacques. Ba Ria-Vung Tau, S Vietnam 10.21N 107.04E
197 I15 **Vunisea** Kadavu, SE Fiji 19.04S 178.09E
Vuohčču see Vuotso
95 N15 **Vuokatti** Oulu, C Finland 64.08N 28.16E
95 M15 **Vuolijoki** Oulu, C Finland 64.09N 27.00E
94 J13 **Vuollerim** Norrbotten, N Sweden 66.24N 20.36E
Vuoreija see Vardø
94 L10 **Vuotso** Lapp. Vuohčču. Lappi, N Finland 68.04N 27.05E
116 J11 **Vŭrbitsa** prev. Filevo. Khaskovo, S Bulgaria 42.02N 25.25E
116 J12 **Vŭrbitsa** ≈ S Bulgaria
131 Q4 **Vurnary** Chavash Respubliki, W Russian Federation 55.30N 46.59E
116 G8 **Vŭrshets** Montana, NW Bulgaria 43.14N 23.20E
121 F17 **Vyalikaya Byerastavitsa** Pol. Brzostowica Wielka, Rus. Bol'shaya Berëstovitsa; prev. Velikaya Berestovitsa. Hrodzyenskaya Voblasts', SW Belarus 53.12N 24.03E
121 N20 **Vyaliki Bor** Rus. Velikiy Bor. Homyel'skaya Voblasts', SE Belarus 52.01N 29.54E
121 J18 **Vyaliki Rozhan** Rus. Bol'shoy Rozhan. Minskaya Voblasts', S Belarus 52.46N 27.07E
128 H10 **Vyartsilya** Fin. Värtsilä. Respublika Kareliya, NW Russian Federation 62.07N 30.43E
121 K17 **Vyasyeya** Rus. Veseya. Minskaya Voblasts', C Belarus 53.04N 27.40E
129 R15 **Vyatka** ≈ NW Russian Federation
Vyatka see Kirov
129 S16 **Vyatskiye Polyany** Kirovskaya Oblast', NW Russian Federation 56.15N 51.06E
127 Nn16 **Vyazemskiy** Khabarovskiy Kray, SE Russian Federation 47.28N 134.39E
130 I4 **Vyaz'ma** Smolenskaya Oblast', W Russian Federation 55.09N 34.20E
131 N3 **Vyazniki** Vladimirskaya Oblast', W Russian Federation 56.15N 42.06E
131 O8 **Vyazovka** Volgogradskaya Oblast', SW Russian Federation 50.57N 43.57E
121 J14 **Vyazyn'** Rus. Vyazyn'. Minskaya Voblasts', NW Belarus 54.25N 27.10E
128 G11 **Vyborg** Fin. Viipuri. Leningradskaya Oblast', NW Russian Federation 60.44N 28.47E
129 P11 **Vychegda** var. Vichegda. ≈ NW Russian Federation
126 Jj16 **Vydrino** Respublika Buryatiya, S Russian Federation 51.22N 104.34E
121 L14 **Vyelyewshchyna** Rus. Velevshchina. Vitsyebskaya Voblasts', N Belarus 54.44N 28.33E
121 P16 **Vyeramyeyki** Rus. Veremeyki. Mahilyowskaya Voblasts', E Belarus 53.46N 31.18E
120 K11 **Vyerkhnyadzvinsk** Rus. Verkhnedvinsk. Vitsyebskaya Voblasts', N Belarus 55.46N 27.55E
121 P18 **Vyetka** Rus. Vetka. Homyel'skaya Voblasts', SE Belarus 52.34N 31.13E
120 L12 **Vyetryna** Rus. Vetrino. Vitsyebskaya Voblasts', N Belarus 55.24N 28.28E
Vygonovskoye, Ozero see Vyhanawskaye, Vozyera
128 J9 **Vygozero, Ozero** ◎ NW Russian Federation
Vyhanashchanskaye Vozyera see Vyhanawskaye, Vozyera
121 I18 **Vyhanawskaye, Vozyera** var. Vyhanashchanskaye Vozyera, Rus. Ozero Vygonovskoye. ◎ SW Belarus
131 N4 **Vyksa** Nizhegorodskaya Oblast', W Russian Federation 55.21N 42.10E
119 O12 **Vylkove** Rus. Vilkovo. Odes'ka Oblast', SW Ukraine 45.24N 29.37E
129 R9 **Vym'** ≈ NW Russian Federation
118 H8 **Vynohradiv** Cz. Sevluš, Hung. Nagyszöllös, Rus. Vinogradov; prev. Sevlyush. Zakarpats'ka Oblast', W Ukraine 48.09N 23.01E
128 G13 **Vyritsa** Leningradskaya Oblast', NW Russian Federation 59.25N 30.20E
99 J19 **Vyrnwy** Wel. Afon Efyrnwy. ≈ E Wales, UK
151 X9 **Vyshe Ivanovskiy Belak, Gora** ▲ E Kazakhstan 50.16N 83.46E
119 P4 **Vyshhorod** Kyyivs'ka Oblast', N Ukraine 50.36N 30.28E
128 I15 **Vyshniy Volochek** Tverskaya Oblast', W Russian Federation 57.37N 34.33E
113 G18 **Vyškov** Ger. Wischau. Brněnský Kraz, SE Czech Republic 49.16N 16.58E
113 F17 **Vysoké Mýto** Ger. Hohenmauth. Pardubický Kraj, C Czech Republic 49.58N 16.08E
119 S9 **Vysokopillya** Khersons'ka Oblast', S Ukraine 47.28N 33.30E
130 K3 **Vysokovsk** Moskovskaya Oblast', W Russian Federation 56.12N 36.42E
128 K12 **Vytegra** Vologodskaya Oblast', NW Russian Federation 60.59N 36.27E
118 J8 **Vyzhnytsya** Chernivets'ka Oblast', W Ukraine 48.14N 25.10E

W

79 O14 **Wa** NW Ghana 10.07N 2.28W
Waadt see Vaud
Waag see Váh
Waagbistritz see Považská Bystrica
Waagneustadtl see Nové Mesto nad Váhom
83 M16 **Waajid** Gedo, SW Somalia 3.37N 43.19E
100 L13 **Waal** ≈ S Netherlands
197 G4 **Waala** Province Nord, W New Caledonia 19.46S 163.41E
101 I14 **Waalwijk** Noord-Brabant, S Netherlands 51.42N 5.04E
101 E16 **Waarschoot** Oost-Vlaanderen, NW Belgium 51.09N 3.35E
194 G12 **Wabag** Enga, W PNG 5.28S 143.40E
13 N7 **Wabano** ≈ Quebec, SE Canada
9 P11 **Wabasca** ≈ Alberta, SW Canada
33 P12 **Wabash** Indiana, N USA 40.46N 85.48W
31 X9 **Wabasha** Minnesota, N USA 44.22N 92.01W
33 N13 **Wabash River** ≈ N USA
12 C7 **Wabatongushi Lake** ◎ Ontario, S Canada
83 L15 **Wabē Gestro Wenz** ≈ SE Ethiopia
12 B9 **Wabos** Ontario, S Canada 46.48N 84.06W
9 W13 **Wabowden** Manitoba, C Canada 54.57N 98.37W
112 J9 **Wąbrzeźno** Kujawsko-pomorskie, N Poland 53.18N 18.55E
194 G14 **Wabuda Island** island SW PNG
23 U12 **Waccamaw River** ≈ South Carolina, SE USA
25 U11 **Waccasassa Bay** bay Florida, SE USA
101 F16 **Wachtebeke** Oost-Vlaanderen, NW Belgium 51.10N 3.52E
27 T8 **Waco** Texas, SW USA 31.33N 97.09W
28 M3 **Waconda Lake** var. Great Elder Reservoir. ⊠ Kansas, C USA
Wadai see Ouaddaï
Wad Al-Hajarah see Guadalajara
171 Gg13 **Wadayama** Hyōgo, Honshū, SW Japan 35.19N 134.51E
82 D10 **Wad Banda** Western Kordofan, C Sudan 13.07N 27.55E
77 P9 **Waddān** NW Libya 29.10N 16.07E
100 J4 **Waddeneilanden** Eng. West Frisian Islands. island group N Netherlands
100 J6 **Waddenzee** var. Wadden Zee. sea SE North Sea
8 L16 **Waddington, Mount** ▲ British Columbia, SW Canada 51.17N 125.16W
100 H12 **Waddinxveen** Zuid-Holland, C Netherlands 52.03N 4.37E
9 U15 **Wadena** Saskatchewan, S Canada 51.57N 103.48W
31 T6 **Wadena** Minnesota, N USA 46.27N 95.07W
110 G7 **Wädenswil** Zürich, N Switzerland 47.13N 8.39E
23 S11 **Wadesboro** North Carolina, SE USA 34.58N 80.04W
161 G16 **Wādi** Karnātaka, C India 17.00N 76.58E
144 G10 **Wādī as Sīr** var. Wadi es Sir. Al 'Āşimah, NW Jordan 31.57N 35.49E
Wadi es Sir see Wādī as Sīr
82 F5 **Wadi Halfa** var. Wādī Ḩalfā'. Northern, N Sudan 21.46N 31.16E
144 G13 **Wādī Mūsā** var. Petra. Ma'ān, S Jordan 30.19N 35.28E
25 V4 **Wadley** Georgia, SE USA 32.52N 82.24W
Wad Madanī see Wad Medani
82 G10 **Wad Medani** var. Wad Madanī. Gezira, C Sudan 14.24N 33.30E
82 F10 **Wad Nimr** White Nile, C Sudan 14.31N 32.10E
172 Q14 **Wadomari** Kagoshima, Okinoerabu-jima, SW Japan 27.25N 128.40E
113 K17 **Wadowice** Małopolskie, S Poland 49.52N 19.30E
37 R5 **Wadsworth** Nevada, W USA 39.39N 119.16W
33 T12 **Wadsworth** Ohio, N USA 41.01N 81.43W
27 T11 **Waelder** Texas, SW USA 29.42N 97.16W
Waereghem see Waregem
169 U13 **Wafangdian** var. Fuxian, Fu Xian. Liaoning, NE China 39.36N 122.00E
175 S11 **Waflia** Pulau Buru, E Indonesia 3.09S 126.05E
Wagadugu see Ouagadougou
100 K12 **Wageningen** Gelderland, SE Netherlands 51.58N 5.40E
57 V9 **Wageningen** Nickerie, NW Suriname 5.43N 56.45W
15 Ll5 **Wager Bay** inlet Nunavut, N Canada
176 Y10 **Wageseri** Papua, E Indonesia 1.48S 138.19E
191 P10 **Wagga Wagga** New South Wales, SE Australia 35.10S 147.22E
188 J13 **Wagin** Western Australia 33.16S 117.25E
Wagina see Vaghena
110 H8 **Wägitaler See** ◎ SW Switzerland
31 P12 **Wagner** South Dakota, N USA 43.04N 98.17W
29 Q9 **Wagoner** Oklahoma, C USA 35.57N 95.22W
39 U10 **Wagon Mound** New Mexico, SW USA 36.00N 104.42W
34 J14 **Wagontire** Oregon, NW USA 43.15N 119.51W
112 H10 **Wągrowiec** Wielkopolskie, NW Poland 52.49N 17.10E
155 U6 **Wāh** Punjab, NE Pakistan 33.49N 72.43E
176 U10 **Wahai** Pulau Seram, E Indonesia 2.48S 129.28E
175 O7 **Wahau, Sungai** ≈ Borneo, C Indonesia
Wahaybah, Ramlat Al see Wahībah, Ramlat Āl
82 D13 **Wahda** var. Unity State. ◈ state S Sudan
40 D9 **Wahiawa** Haw. Wahiawā. Oahu, Hawaii, USA, C Pacific Ocean 21.30N 158.01W
Wahībah, Ramlat Ahl see Wahībah, Ramlat Āl
147 Y9 **Wahībah, Ramlat Āl** var. Ramlat Ahl Wahībah, Ramlat Al Wahaybah, Eng. Wahibah Sands. desert N Oman
Wahibah Sands see Wahībah, Ramlat Āl
103 E16 **Wahn** ✕ (Köln) Nordrhein-Westfalen, W Germany 50.51N 7.09E
31 R15 **Wahoo** Nebraska, C USA 41.12N 96.37W
31 R6 **Wahpeton** North Dakota, N USA 46.16N 96.36W
Wahran see Oran

◆ Country
● Country Capital
◇ Dependent Territory
○ Dependent Territory Capital
◈ Administrative Region
✕ International Airport
▲ Mountain
▲▲ Mountain Range
Volcano
≈ River
◎ Lake
⊠ Reservoir

38 J6 **Wah Wah Mountains** ▲▲ Utah, W USA
40 D9 **Waialua** Oahu, Hawaii, USA, C Pacific Ocean 21.34N 158.07W
40 D9 **Waianae** *Haw.* Wai'anae. Oahu, Hawaii, USA, C Pacific Ocean 21.26N 158.11W
192 Q8 **Waiapu** ≈ North Island, NZ
193 I17 **Waiau** Canterbury, South Island, NZ 42.39S 173.03E
193 I17 **Waiau** ≈ South Island, NZ
193 B23 **Waiau** ≈ South Island, NZ
103 H21 **Waiblingen** Baden-Württemberg, S Germany 48.49N 9.19E
Waidhofen *see* Waidhofen an der Ybbs, Niederösterreich, Austria
Waidhofen *see* Waidhofen an der Thaya, Niederösterreich, Austria
111 V2 **Waidhofen an der Thaya** *var.* Waidhofen. Niederösterreich, NE Austria 48.49N 15.16E
111 U5 **Waidhofen an der Ybbs** *var.* Waidhofen. Niederösterreich, E Austria 47.57N 14.47E
176 Uu8 **Waigeo, Pulau** *island* Maluku, E Indonesia
192 L5 **Waiheke Island** *island* N NZ
192 M7 **Waihi** Waikato, North Island, NZ 37.24S 175.49E
193 C20 **Waihou** ≈ North Island, NZ
Waikaboebak *see* Waikabubak
175 P17 **Waikabubak** *prev.* Waikaboebak. Pulau Sumba, C Indonesia 9.40S 119.25E
193 D23 **Waikaia** ≈ South Island, NZ
193 D23 **Waikaka** Southland, South Island, NZ 45.55S 168.59E
192 L13 **Waikanae** Wellington, North Island, NZ 40.52S 175.04E
192 M7 **Waikare, Lake** ◎ North Island, NZ
192 O9 **Waikaremoana, Lake** ◎ North Island, NZ
193 I17 **Waikari** Canterbury, South Island, NZ 42.50S 172.41E
192 L8 **Waikato** *off.* Waikato Region. ◈ *region* North Island, NZ
192 M8 **Waikato** ≈ North Island, NZ
190 J9 **Waikerie** South Australia 34.12S 139.57E
193 F23 **Waikouaiti** Otago, South Island, NZ 45.36S 170.39E
40 H11 **Wailea** Hawaii, USA, C Pacific Ocean 19.53N 155.07W
40 F10 **Wailuku** Maui, Hawaii, USA, C Pacific Ocean 20.53N 156.30W
193 H18 **Waimakariri** ≈ South Island, NZ
40 D9 **Waimanalo Beach** Oahu, Hawaii, USA, C Pacific Ocean 21.20N 157.42W
193 G15 **Waimangaroa** West Coast, South Island, NZ 41.41S 171.49E
193 G21 **Waimate** Canterbury, South Island, NZ 44.44S 171.03E
40 G11 **Waimea** *var.* Kamuela. Hawaii, USA, C Pacific Ocean 20.01N 155.39W
40 D9 **Waimea** *var.* Maunawai. Oahu, Hawaii, USA, C Pacific Ocean 21.38N 158.03W
40 B8 **Waimea** Kauai, Hawaii, USA, C Pacific Ocean 21.57N 159.39W
101 M20 **Waimes** Liège, E Belgium 50.25N 6.10E
160 J11 **Wainganga** *var.* Wain River. ≈ C India
Waingapoe *see* Waingapu
175 Pp17 **Waingapu** *prev.* Waingapoe. Pulau Sumba, C Indonesia 9.40S 120.16E
57 S7 **Waini** ≈ N Guyana
57 S7 **Waini Point** *headland* NW Guyana 8.24N 59.48W
Wain River *see* Wainganga
9 R15 **Wainwright** Alberta, SW Canada 52.49N 110.51W
41 O5 **Wainwright** Alaska, USA 70.38N 160.02W
192 K4 **Waiotira** Northland, North Island, NZ 35.56S 174.11E
192 M11 **Waiouru** Manawatu-Wanganui, North Island, NZ 39.27S 175.40E
176 X11 **Waipa** Papua, E Indonesia 3.47S 136.16E
192 L8 **Waipa** ≈ North Island, NZ
192 P9 **Waipaoa** ≈ North Island, NZ
193 D25 **Waipapa Point** *headland* South Island, NZ 46.39S 168.51E
193 I18 **Waipara** Canterbury, South Island, NZ 43.03S 172.44E
192 N12 **Waipawa** Hawke's Bay, North Island, NZ 39.57S 176.35E
192 K4 **Waipu** Northland, North Island, NZ 35.58S 174.25E
192 N12 **Waipukurau** Hawke's Bay, North Island, NZ 40.01S 176.34E
176 Vv13 **Wair** Pulau Kai Besar, E Indonesia 5.16S 133.09E
Wairakai *see* Wairakei
192 N9 **Wairakei** *var.* Wairakai. Waikato, North Island, NZ 38.37S 176.05E
193 M14 **Wairarapa, Lake** ◎ North Island, NZ
193 J15 **Wairau** ≈ South Island, NZ
192 P10 **Wairoa** Hawke's Bay, North Island, NZ 39.03S 105.25E
192 P10 **Wairoa** ≈ North Island, NZ
192 J4 **Wairoa** ≈ North Island, NZ
192 N9 **Waitahanui** Waikato, North Island, NZ 38.48S 176.04E
192 M6 **Waitakaruru** Waikato, North Island, NZ 37.14S 175.22E
193 F21 **Waitaki** ≈ South Island, NZ
192 K10 **Waitara** Taranaki, North Island, NZ 39.01S 174.14E
192 M7 **Waitoa** Waikato, North Island, NZ 37.36S 175.37E
192 L8 **Waitomo Caves** Waikato, North Island, NZ 38.17S 175.06E
192 L11 **Waitotara** Taranaki, North Island, NZ 39.49S 174.43E
192 L11 **Waitotara** ≈ North Island, NZ
34 L10 **Waitsburg** Washington, NW USA 46.16N 118.09W
Waitzen *see* Vác
192 L6 **Waiuku** Auckland, North Island, NZ 37.15S 174.44E
171 J12 **Wajima** *var.* Wazima. Ishikawa, Honshū, SW Japan 37.21N 136.53E
83 K17 **Wajir** North Eastern, NE Kenya 1.43N 40.04E
83 I14 **Waka** Southern, SW Ethiopia 7.12N 37.19E
81 J17 **Waka** Equateur, NW Dem. Rep. Congo 1.04N 20.11E
12 D9 **Wakami Lake** ◎ Ontario, S Canada
170 G13 **Wakasa** Tottori, Honshū, SW Japan 35.18N 134.25E
171 H13 **Wakasa-wan** *bay* C Japan
193 C22 **Wakatipu, Lake** ◎ South Island, NZ
9 T15 **Wakaw** Saskatchewan, S Canada 52.40N 105.45W
197 I14 **Wakaya** *island* C Fiji
170 Ff15 **Wakayama** Wakayama, Honshū, SW Japan 34.12N 135.09E
170 G16 **Wakayama** *off.* Wakayama-ken. ◈ *prefecture* Honshū, SW Japan
28 K4 **Wa Keeney** Kansas, C USA 39.01N 99.52W
193 I14 **Wakefield** Tasman, South Island, NZ 41.24S 173.03E
99 M17 **Wakefield** N England, UK 53.42N 1.28W
29 O4 **Wakefield** Kansas, C USA 39.12N 97.00W
32 L4 **Wakefield** Michigan, N USA 46.27N 89.55W
23 U9 **Wake Forest** North Carolina, SE USA 35.58N 78.30W
Wakeham Bay *see* Kangiqsujuaq
201 Y11 **Wake Island** ◇ *US unincorporated territory* NW Pacific Ocean
201 Y12 **Wake Island** ✕ NW Pacific Ocean
201 Y12 **Wake Island** *atoll* NW Pacific Ocean
201 X12 **Wake Lagoon** *lagoon* Wake Island, NW Pacific Ocean
177 Ff9 **Wakema** Irrawaddy, SW Myanmar 16.36N 95.10E
Wakhan *see* Khandūd
170 Ff15 **Waki** Tokushima, Shikoku, SW Japan 34.04N 134.10E
172 N8 **Wakinosawa** Aomori, Honshū, C Japan 41.08N 140.47E
172 Pp1 **Wakkanai** Hokkaidō, NE Japan 45.24N 141.39E
85 K22 **Wakkerstroom** Mpumalanga, E South Africa 27.21S 30.10E
12 C10 **Wakomata Lake** ◎ Ontario, S Canada
191 N10 **Wakool** New South Wales, SE Australia 35.30S 144.22E
Wakra *see* Al Wakrah
Waku Kungo *see* Uaco Cungo
195 S12 **Wakunai** Bougainville Island, NE PNG 5.52S 155.13E
Walachei/Walachia *see* Wallachia
175 Pp12 **Walanae, Sungai** ≈ Sulawesi, C Indonesia
161 K26 **Walawe Ganga** ≈ S Sri Lanka
113 F15 **Wałbrzych** *Ger.* Waldenburg, Waldenburg in Schlesien. Dolnośląskie, SW Poland 50.44N 16.19E
191 T6 **Walcha** New South Wales, SE Australia 31.01S 151.38E
103 K24 **Walchensee** ◎ SE Germany
101 D14 **Walcheren** *island* SW Netherlands
31 Z14 **Walcott** Iowa, C USA 41.34N 90.46W
35 W16 **Walcott** Wyoming, C USA 41.46N 106.46W
101 G21 **Walcourt** Namur, S Belgium 50.15N 4.26E
112 G9 **Wałcz** *Ger.* Deutsch Krone. Zachodniopomorskie, NW Poland 53.16N 16.28E
110 H7 **Wald** Zürich, N Switzerland 47.16N 8.54E
111 U3 **Waldaist** ≈ N Austria
188 I9 **Waldburg Range** ▲▲ Western Australia
39 R3 **Walden** Colorado, C USA 40.43N 106.16W
20 K13 **Walden** New York, NE USA 41.35N 74.09W
Waldenburg/Waldenburg in Schlesien *see* Wałbrzych
9 T15 **Waldheim** Saskatchewan, S Canada 52.38N 106.35W
Waldia *see* Weldiya
103 M23 **Waldkraiburg** Bayern, SE Germany 48.10N 12.23E
29 T14 **Waldo** Arkansas, C USA 33.21N 93.18W
25 V9 **Waldo** Florida, SE USA 29.47N 82.07W
21 R7 **Waldoboro** Maine, NE USA 44.06N 69.22W
23 W4 **Waldorf** Maryland, NE USA 38.36N 76.54W
34 F12 **Waldport** Oregon, NW USA 44.25N 124.04W
29 S11 **Waldron** Arkansas, C USA 34.54N 94.05W
205 Y13 **Waldron, Cape** *headland* Antarctica 66.08S 116.00E
103 F24 **Waldshut-Tiengen** Baden-Württemberg, S Germany 47.37N 8.13E
175 Qq9 **Walea, Selat** *strait* Sulawesi, C Indonesia
Wałeckie Międzyrzecze *see* Valašské Meziříčí
110 H8 **Walensee** ◎ NW Switzerland
40 L8 **Wales** Alaska, USA 65.36N 168.02W
99 J20 **Wales** *Wel.* Cymru. *national region* UK
15 Ll3 **Wales Island** *island* Nunavut, NE Canada
79 P14 **Walewale** N Ghana 10.21N 0.48W
101 M24 **Walferdange** Luxembourg, C Luxembourg 49.39N 6.07E
191 Q5 **Walgett** New South Wales, SE Australia 30.02S 148.13E
204 K10 **Walgreen Coast** *physical region* Antarctica
31 Q2 **Walhalla** North Dakota, N USA 48.55N 97.55W
23 O11 **Walhalla** South Carolina, SE USA 34.45N 83.03W
81 O19 **Walikale** Nord Kivu, E Dem. Rep. Congo 1.28S 28.04E
194 G9 **Walis Island** *island* NW PNG
Walk *see* Valga, Estonia
Walk *see* Valka, Latvia
31 U5 **Walker** Minnesota, N USA 47.06N 94.35W
13 V4 **Walker, Lac** ◎ Quebec, SE Canada
37 S7 **Walker Lake** ◎ Nevada, W USA
37 R6 **Walker River** ≈ Nevada, W USA
30 K10 **Wall** South Dakota, N USA 43.58N 102.12W
181 U9 **Wallaby Plateau** *undersea feature* E Indian Ocean
35 N8 **Wallace** Idaho, NW USA 47.28N 115.55W
23 V11 **Wallace** North Carolina, SE USA 34.42N 77.59W
12 D17 **Wallaceburg** Ontario, S Canada 42.36N 82.22W
24 F5 **Wallace Lake** ▣ Louisiana, S USA
9 P13 **Wallace Mountain** ▲ Alberta, W Canada 54.50N 115.57W
118 J14 **Wallachia** *var.* Walachia, *Ger.* Walachei, *Rom.* Valachia. *cultural region* S Romania
Wallachisch-Meseritsch *see* Valašské Meziříčí
191 U4 **Wallangarra** New South Wales, SE Australia 28.56S 151.57E
190 I8 **Wallaroo** South Australia 33.56S 137.38E
34 L10 **Walla Walla** Washington, NW USA 46.03N 118.20W
47 V9 **Wallblake** ✕ (The Valley) C Anguilla 18.12N 63.02W
103 H19 **Walldürn** Baden-Württemberg, SW Germany 49.34N 9.22E
102 F12 **Wallenhorst** Niedersachsen, NW Germany 52.21N 8.01E
Wallenthal *see* Hațeg
111 S4 **Wallern** Oberösterreich, N Austria 48.13N 13.58E
Wallern *see* Wallern im Burgenland
111 Z5 **Wallern im Burgenland** *var.* Wallern. Burgenland, E Austria 47.43N 16.56E
20 M9 **Wallingford** Vermont, NE USA 43.27N 72.56W
27 V11 **Wallis** Texas, SW USA 29.37N 96.04W
Wallis *see* Valais
199 Jj10 **Wallis and Futuna** *Fr.* Territoire de Wallis et Futuna. ◇ *French overseas territory* C Pacific Ocean
110 G7 **Wallisellen** Zürich, N Switzerland 47.27N 8.33E
202 H11 **Wallis, Îles** *island group* N Wallis and Futuna
101 H19 **Wallon Brabant** ◈ *province* C Belgium
33 Q5 **Walloon Lake** ◎ Michigan, N USA
34 K10 **Wallula** Washington, NW USA 46.03N 118.54W
34 K10 **Wallula, Lake** ◎ Washington, NW USA
23 S8 **Walnut Cove** North Carolina, SE USA 36.18N 80.08W
37 N8 **Walnut Creek** California, W USA 37.52N 122.04W
28 K5 **Walnut Creek** ≈ Kansas, C USA
29 W9 **Walnut Ridge** Arkansas, C USA 36.06N 90.56W
27 S7 **Walnut Springs** Texas, SW USA 32.05N 97.42W
190 L10 **Walpeup** Victoria, SE Australia 35.09S 142.01E
197 L7 **Walpole, Île** *island* SE New Caledonia
41 N13 **Walrus Islands** *island group* Alaska, USA
99 L19 **Walsall** C England, UK 52.34N 1.58W
39 T7 **Walsenburg** Colorado, C USA 37.37N 104.46W
9 S17 **Walsh** Alberta, SW Canada 49.58N 110.03W
39 W7 **Walsh** Colorado, C USA 37.20N 102.17W
102 I11 **Walsrode** Niedersachsen, NW Germany 52.52N 9.36E
Waltenberg *see* Zalău
23 R14 **Walterboro** South Carolina, SE USA 32.54N 80.40W
Walter F. George Lake *see* Walter F. George Reservoir
25 R6 **Walter F. George Reservoir** *var.* Walter F. George Lake. ▣ Alabama/Georgia, SE USA
28 M12 **Walters** Oklahoma, C USA 34.21N 98.18W
103 J16 **Waltershausen** Thüringen, C Germany 50.53N 10.33E
181 N10 **Walters Shoal** *var.* Walters Shoals. *reef* S Madagascar
Walters Shoals *see* Walters Shoal
24 M3 **Walthall** Mississippi, S USA 33.36N 89.16W
22 M4 **Walton** Kentucky, S USA 38.52N 84.36W
20 J11 **Walton** New York, NE USA 42.10N 75.07W
81 O20 **Walungu** Sud Kivu, E Dem. Rep. Congo 2.40S 28.37E
Walvisbaai *see* Walvis Bay
85 C19 **Walvis Bay** *Afr.* Walvisbaai. Erongo, NW Namibia 22.59S 14.33E
85 B19 **Walvis Bay** *bay* NW Namibia
Walvish Ridge *see* Walvis Ridge
67 O17 **Walvis Ridge** *var.* Walvish Ridge. *undersea feature* E Atlantic Ocean
176 Yy15 **Wamal** Papua, E Indonesia 8.00S 139.06E
176 W13 **Wamar, Pulau** *island* Kepulauan Aru, E Indonesia
79 V15 **Wamba** Nassarawa, C Nigeria 8.57N 8.35E
81 O17 **Wamba** Orientale, NE Dem. Rep. Congo 2.10N 27.58E
81 H22 **Wamba** *var.* Uamba. ≈ Angola/Dem. Rep. Congo
29 P4 **Wamego** Kansas, C USA 39.12N 96.18W
20 I10 **Wampsville** New York, NE USA 43.03N 75.40W
44 K6 **Wampú, Río** ≈ E Honduras
176 Xx16 **Wan** Papua, E Indonesia 8.15S 138.00E
Wan *see* Anhui
191 N4 **Wanaaring** New South Wales, SE Australia 29.42S 144.07E
193 D21 **Wanaka** Otago, South Island, NZ 44.42S 169.09E
193 D20 **Wanaka, Lake** ◎ South Island, NZ
176 Ww12 **Wanapiri** Papua, E Indonesia 4.21S 135.52E
12 F9 **Wanapitei** ≈ Ontario, S Canada
12 F10 **Wanapitei Lake** ◎ Ontario, S Canada
20 K14 **Wanaque** New Jersey, NE USA 41.02N 74.17W
176 V9 **Wanau** Papua, E Indonesia 1.20S 132.40E
193 F22 **Wanbrow, Cape** *headland* South Island, NZ 45.07S 170.59E
Wanchuan *see* Zhangjiakou
176 X11 **Wandai** *var.* Komeyo. Papua, E Indonesia 3.35S 136.15E
169 Z8 **Wanda Shan** ▲▲ NE China
207 R11 **Wandel Sea** *sea* Arctic Ocean
166 D13 **Wanding** *var.* Wandingzhen. Yunnan, SW China 24.12N 98.05E
Wandingzhen *see* Wanding
176 Z14 **Wandip** Papua, E Indonesia 6.08S 140.47E
101 H20 **Wanfercée-Baulet** Hainaut, S Belgium 50.27N 4.37E
192 L12 **Wanganui** Manawatu-Wanganui, North Island, NZ 39.56S 175.02E
192 L11 **Wanganui** ≈ North Island, NZ
191 P11 **Wangaratta** Victoria, SE Australia 36.22S 146.16E
166 J8 **Wangcang** *prev.* Fengjiaba. Sichuan, C China 32.15N 106.16E
Wangda *see* Zogang
103 I24 **Wangen im Allgäu** Baden-Württemberg, S Germany 47.40N 9.49E
Wangerin *see* Węgorzyno
102 F9 **Wangerooge** *island* NW Germany
176 Ww11 **Wanggar** Papua, E Indonesia 3.22S 135.15E
166 J13 **Wangmo** *var.* Fuxing. Guizhou, S China 25.10N 106.07E
Wangolodougou *see* Ouangolodougou
167 S9 **Wangpan Yang** *sea* E China
169 Y10 **Wangqing** Jilin, NE China 43.19N 129.42E
178 I9 **Wang Saphung** Loei, C Thailand 17.18N 101.45E
178 H6 **Wan Hsa-la** Shan State, E Myanmar 20.27N 98.39E
57 W9 **Wanica** ◈ *district* N Suriname
81 M18 **Wanie-Rukula** Orientale, C Dem. Rep. Congo 0.12N 25.31E
Wankie *see* Hwange
Wanki, Río *see* Coco, Río
83 N17 **Wanlaweyn** *var.* Wanle Weyn, *It.* Uanle Uen. Shabeellaha Hoose, SW Somalia 2.36N 44.47E
Wanle Weyn *see* Wanlaweyn
188 I12 **Wanneroo** Western Australia 31.37S 115.43E
166 L17 **Wanning** Hainan, S China 18.55N 110.27E
178 Ii8 **Wanon Niwat** Sakon Nakhon, E Thailand 17.39N 103.45E
161 H16 **Wanparti** Andhra Pradesh, C India 16.19N 78.06E
Wansen *see* Wiązów
166 L11 **Wanshan** Guizhou, S China 27.45N 109.12E
101 M14 **Wanssum** Limburg, SE Netherlands 51.31N 6.04E
192 N12 **Wanstead** Hawke's Bay, North Island, NZ 40.09S 176.31E
166 K9 **Wanxian** Chongqing Shi, C China 30.48N 108.21E
196 F16 **Wanyaan** Yap, Micronesia
166 K8 **Wanyuan** Sichuan, C China 32.04N 108.07E
167 O11 **Wanzai** Jiangxi, S China 28.06N 114.27E
101 J20 **Wanze** Liège, E Belgium 50.32N 5.16E
33 R12 **Wapakoneta** Ohio, N USA 40.34N 84.11W
10 D7 **Wapaseese** ≈ Ontario, C Canada
34 I10 **Wapato** Washington, NW USA 46.27N 120.25W
31 Y15 **Wapello** Iowa, C USA 41.10N 91.13W
194 H12 **Wapenamanda** Enga, W PNG 5.36S 143.51E
9 N13 **Wapiti** ≈ Alberta/British Columbia, SW Canada
29 X7 **Wappapello Lake** ▣ Missouri, C USA
20 K13 **Wappingers Falls** New York, NE USA 41.36N 73.54W
31 X13 **Wapsipinicon River** ≈ Iowa, C USA
194 G14 **Wapumba Island** *island* SW PNG
12 L9 **Wapus** ≈ Quebec, SE Canada
166 H7 **Waqên** Sichuan, C China 33.04N 102.41E
23 Q7 **War** West Virginia, NE USA 37.18N 81.39W
82 D13 **Warab** Warab, SW Sudan 8.13N 28.52E
83 D14 **Warab** ◈ *state* SW Sudan
161 J15 **Warangal** Andhra Pradesh, C India 18.00N 79.35E
Warasdin *see* Varaždin
191 O16 **Waratah** Tasmania, SE Australia 41.28S 145.34E
191 O14 **Waratah Bay** *bay* Victoria, SE Australia
103 H15 **Warburg** Nordrhein-Westfalen, W Germany 51.30N 9.10E
188 M9 **Warburton** Western Australia 26.17S 126.18E
190 I1 **Warburton Creek** *seasonal river* South Australia 101 M20
Warche ≈ E Belgium
155 P5 **Wardag** *var.* Wardak, *Per.* Vardak. ◈ *province* E Afghanistan
Wardak *see* Wardag
34 K9 **Warden** Washington, NW USA 46.58N 119.02W
160 I12 **Wardha** Mahārāshtra, W India 20.40N 78.40E
194 L14 **Ward Hunt, Cape** *headland* S PNG 8.03S 148.15E
195 N16 **Ward Hunt Strait** *strait* S PNG
123 J16 **Wardija, Ras il-** *var.* Wardija Point. *headland* Gozo, NW Malta 36.03N 14.11E
145 P3 **Wardīyah** N Iraq 36.18N 41.45E
193 E19 **Ward, Mount** ▲ South Island, NZ 43.49S 169.54E
176 Ww9 **Wardo** Papua, E Indonesia 0.54S 135.52E
8 L11 **Ware** British Columbia, W Canada 57.25N 125.40W
101 D18 **Waregem** *var.* Waereghem. West-Vlaanderen, W Belgium 50.52N 3.25E
101 J19 **Waremme** Liège, E Belgium 50.40N 5.15E
102 N10 **Waren** Mecklenburg-Vorpommern, NE Germany 53.31N 12.42E
176 X10 **Waren** Papua, E Indonesia 2.13S 136.21E
103 F14 **Warendorf** Nordrhein-Westfalen, W Germany 51.57N 8.00E
23 P12 **Ware Shoals** South Carolina, SE USA 34.24N 82.15W
100 N4 **Warffum** Groningen, NE Netherlands 53.22N 6.34E
83 O15 **Wargalo** Mudug, E Somalia 6.06N 47.40E
152 M12 **Warganza** *Rus.* Varganzi. Qashqadaryo Viloyati, S Uzbekistan 39.18N 66.00E
Wargla *see* Ouargla
194 K14 **Waria** ≈ S PNG
191 T4 **Warialda** New South Wales, SE Australia 29.34S 150.35E
160 F13 **Wāri Godri** Mahārāshtra, C India 19.28N 75.43E
176 W11 **Warika** Papua, E Indonesia 3.45S 134.16E
176 W13 **Warilau** Pulau Warilau, E Indonesia 5.19S 134.33E
176 Ww13 **Warilau, Pulau** *island* Kepulauan Aru, E Indonesia
178 J10 **Warin Chamrap** Ubon Ratchathani, E Thailand 15.10N 104.51E
27 R11 **Waring** Texas, SW USA 29.56N 98.48W
41 O8 **Waring Mountains** ▲▲ Alaska, USA
112 M12 **Warka** Mazowieckie, E Poland 51.45N 21.12E
192 L5 **Warkworth** Auckland, North Island, NZ 36.24S 174.39E
176 V8 **Warmandi** Papua, E Indonesia 0.21S 132.38E
85 E22 **Warmbad** Karas, S Namibia 28.28S 18.40E
100 H8 **Warmenhuizen** Noord-Holland, NW Netherlands 52.43N 4.45E
112 L8 **Warmińsko-Mazurskie** ◈ *province* NW Poland
99 L22 **Warminster** S England, UK 51.13N 2.12W
20 I15 **Warminster** Pennsylvania, NE USA 40.11N 75.04W
37 V8 **Warm Springs** Nevada, W USA 38.10N 116.21W
34 H12 **Warm Springs** Oregon, NW USA 44.51N 121.24W
23 S5 **Warm Springs** Virginia, NE USA 38.02N 79.46W
102 M8 **Warnemünde** Mecklenburg-Vorpommern, NE Germany 54.10N 12.03E
29 Q10 **Warner** Oklahoma, C USA 35.29N 95.18W
37 Q2 **Warner Mountains** ▲▲ California, W USA
25 T5 **Warner Robins** Georgia, SE USA 32.38N 83.38W
59 N18 **Warnes** Santa Cruz, C Bolivia 17.30S 63.07W
102 M9 **Warnow** ≈ NE Germany
Warnsdorf *see* Varnsdorf
100 M11 **Warnsveld** Gelderland, E Netherlands 52.07N 6.13E
176 Uu10 **Waromge, Teluk** *bay* Papua, E Indonesia
160 I13 **Warora** Mahārāshtra, C India 20.12N 79.01E
190 L11 **Warracknabeal** Victoria, SE Australia 36.17S 142.26E
191 O13 **Warragul** Victoria, SE Australia 38.10S 145.55E
191 O4 **Warrego River** *seasonal river* New South Wales/Queensland, E Australia
191 Q6 **Warren** New South Wales, SE Australia 31.41S 147.51E
9 X16 **Warren** Manitoba, S Canada 50.05N 97.33W
29 V14 **Warren** Arkansas, C USA 33.36N 92.03W
33 S10 **Warren** Michigan, N USA 42.28N 83.01W
31 R3 **Warren** Minnesota, N USA 48.12N 96.46W
33 U11 **Warren** Ohio, N USA 41.14N 80.49W
20 D12 **Warren** Pennsylvania, NE USA 41.52N 79.09W
27 X10 **Warren** Texas, SW USA 30.33N 94.24W
99 G16 **Warrenpoint** *Ir.* An Pointe. SE Northern Ireland, UK 54.07N 6.15W
29 S4 **Warrensburg** Missouri, C USA 38.45N 93.44W
85 H22 **Warrenton** Northern Cape, N South Africa 28.06S 24.49E
25 U4 **Warrenton** Georgia, SE USA 33.24N 82.39W
29 W4 **Warrenton** Missouri, C USA 38.48N 91.08W
23 V8 **Warrenton** North Carolina, SE USA 36.22N 78.09W
23 V4 **Warrenton** Virginia, NE USA 38.42N 77.48W
79 U17 **Warri** Delta, S Nigeria 5.26N 5.34E
99 L18 **Warrington** C England, UK 53.24N 2.37W
25 O9 **Warrington** Florida, SE USA 30.22N 87.16W
25 P3 **Warrior** Alabama, S USA 33.49N 86.49W
190 L13 **Warrnambool** Victoria, SE Australia 38.22S 142.30E
31 T2 **Warroad** Minnesota, N USA 48.55N 95.18W
191 S6 **Warrumbungle Range** ▲▲ New South Wales, SE Australia
160 J12 **Wārsa** Mahārāshtra, C India 20.42N 79.58E
33 P11 **Warsaw** Indiana, N USA 41.13N 85.52W
22 L4 **Warsaw** Kentucky, S USA 38.45N 84.51W
29 T5 **Warsaw** Missouri, C USA 38.14N 93.22W
20 E10 **Warsaw** New York, NE USA 42.44N 78.06W
23 V10 **Warsaw** North Carolina, SE USA 35.00N 78.05W
23 X5 **Warsaw** Virginia, NE USA 37.57N 76.45W
Warsaw/Warschau *see* Warszawa
83 N17 **Warshiikh** Shabeellaha Dhexe, C Somalia 2.22N 45.52E
103 G15 **Warstein** Nordrhein-Westfalen, W Germany 51.27N 8.21E
112 M11 **Warszawa** *Eng.* Warsaw, *Ger.* Warschau, *Rus.* Varshava. ● (Poland) Mazowieckie, C Poland 52.15N 21.00E
112 J13 **Warta** Sieradz, C Poland 51.43N 18.37E
112 D11 **Warta** *Ger.* Warthe. ≈ W Poland
Wartberg *see* Senec
22 M9 **Wartburg** Tennessee, S USA 36.06N 84.34W
110 J7 **Warth** Vorarlberg, NW Austria 47.16N 10.11E
Warthe *see* Warta
175 O9 **Waru** Borneo, C Indonesia 1.24S 116.37E
176 Uu11 **Waru** Pulau Seram, E Indonesia 3.24S 130.38E
145 N6 **Wa'r, Wādī al** *dry watercourse* E Syria
191 U3 **Warwick** Queensland, E Australia 28.12S 152.00E
13 Q11 **Warwick** Quebec, SE Canada 45.55N 72.00W
99 M20 **Warwick** C England, UK 52.16N 1.34W
20 K13 **Warwick** New York, NE USA 41.15N 74.21W
31 P4 **Warwick** North Dakota, N USA 47.49N 98.42W
21 O12 **Warwick** Rhode Island, NE USA 41.40N 71.21W
99 L20 **Warwickshire** *cultural region* C England, UK
12 G14 **Wasaga Beach** Ontario, S Canada 44.30N 80.00W
79 U13 **Wasagu** Kebbi, NW Nigeria 11.25N 5.48E
38 M2 **Wasatch Range** ▲▲ W USA
37 R12 **Wasco** California, W USA 35.34N 119.20W
31 V10 **Waseca** Minnesota, N USA 44.04N 93.30W
12 H13 **Washago** Ontario, S Canada 44.46N 78.48W
21 S2 **Washburn** Maine, NE USA 46.46N 68.08W
30 M5 **Washburn** North Dakota, N USA 47.15N 101.02W
32 K3 **Washburn** Wisconsin, N USA 46.40N 90.52W
33 S14 **Washburn Hill** *hill* Ohio, N USA 39.10N 83.25W
160 H13 **Wāshīm** Mahārāshtra, C India 20.06N 77.08E
99 M14 **Washington** NE England, UK 54.54N 1.31W
25 U3 **Washington** Georgia, SE USA 33.44N 82.44W
32 L12 **Washington** Illinois, N USA 40.42N 89.24W
33 N15 **Washington** Indiana, N USA 38.40N 87.10W
31 X15 **Washington** Iowa, C USA 41.18N 91.41W
29 O3 **Washington** Kansas, C USA 39.46N 97.03W
29 W5 **Washington** Missouri, C USA 38.31N 91.01W
23 X9 **Washington** North Carolina, SE USA 35.33N 77.03W
20 B15 **Washington** Pennsylvania, NE USA 40.10N 80.16W
27 V10 **Washington** Texas, SW USA 30.18N 96.08W
38 J8 **Washington** Utah, W USA 37.07N 113.30W
23 V4 **Washington** Virginia, NE USA 38.40N 78.10W
34 I9 **Washington** *off.* State of Washington; also known as Chinook State, Evergreen State. ◈ *state* NW USA
Washington *see* Washington Court House
33 S14 **Washington Court House** *var.* Washington. Ohio, NE USA 39.31N 83.25W
23 W4 **Washington DC** ● (USA) District of Columbia, NE USA 38.54N 77.02W
33 O5 **Washington Island** *island* Wisconsin, N USA
Washington Island *see* Teraina
21 O7 **Washington, Mount** ▲ New Hampshire, NE USA 44.16N 71.18W
28 M11 **Washita River** ≈ Oklahoma/Texas, C USA
99 O18 **Wash, The** *inlet* E England, UK
34 L9 **Washtucna** Washington, NW USA 46.44N 118.19W
Wasiliszki *see* Vasilishki
112 P9 **Wasilków** Podlaskie, NE Poland 53.12N 23.15E
41 R11 **Wasilla** Alaska, USA 61.34N 149.26W
57 U9 **Wasjabo** Sipaliwini, NW Suriname 5.09N 57.09W
9 X11 **Waskaiowaka Lake** ◎ Manitoba, C Canada
9 T14 **Waskesiu Lake** Saskatchewan, C Canada 53.55N 106.04W
27 X7 **Waskom** Texas, SW USA 32.28N 94.03W
112 G13 **Wąsosz** Dolnośląskie, SW Poland 51.36N 16.30E
44 M6 **Waspam** *var.* Waspán. Región Autónoma Atlántico Norte, NE Nicaragua 14.40N 84.04W
Waspán *see* Waspam
172 P4 **Wassamu** Hokkaidō, NE Japan 44.01N 142.25E
110 G9 **Wassen** Uri, C Switzerland 46.42N 8.34E
100 G11 **Wassenaar** Zuid-Holland, W Netherlands 52.07N 4.24E
101 N24 **Wasserbillig** Grevenmacher, E Luxembourg 49.43N 6.30E
Wasserburg *see* Wasserburg am Inn
103 M23 **Wasserburg am Inn** *var.* Wasserburg. Bayern, SE Germany 48.02N 12.12E
103 I17 **Wasserkuppe** ▲ C Germany 50.30N 9.55E
105 R5 **Wassy** Haute-Marne, N France 48.32N 4.54E
175 Pp12 **Watampone** *var.* Bone. Sulawesi, C Indonesia 4.31S 120.15E
175 Ss11 **Watawa** Pulau Buru, E Indonesia 3.36S 127.13E
Watenstedt-Salzgitter *see* Salzgitter
20 M13 **Waterbury** Connecticut, NE USA 41.33N 73.01W
23 R11 **Wateree Lake** ▣ South Carolina, SE USA
23 R12 **Wateree River** ≈ South Carolina, SE USA
99 E20 **Waterford** *Ir.* Port Láirge. S Ireland 52.15N 7.07W
33 S9 **Waterford** Michigan, N USA 42.42N 83.24W
99 E20 **Waterford** *Ir.* Port Láirge. *cultural region* S Ireland
99 E21 **Waterford Harbour** *Ir.* Cuan Phort Láirge. *inlet* S Ireland
100 G12 **Wateringen** Zuid-Holland, W Netherlands 52.01N 4.16E
101 G19 **Waterloo** Wallon Brabant, C Belgium 50.43N 4.24E
12 F16 **Waterloo** Ontario, S Canada 43.28N 80.31W
13 P12 **Waterloo** Quebec, SE Canada 45.20N 72.28W
32 K16 **Waterloo** Illinois, N USA 38.20N 90.09W
31 X13 **Waterloo** Iowa, C USA 42.31N 92.16W
20 G10 **Waterloo** New York, NE USA 42.54N 76.51W
32 L4 **Watersmeet** Michigan, N USA 46.16N 89.10W
25 V9 **Watertown** Florida, SE USA 30.11N 82.36W
20 I8 **Watertown** New York, NE USA 43.37N 75.55W
31 R9 **Watertown** South Dakota, N USA 44.54N 97.06W
32 M8 **Watertown** Wisconsin, N USA 43.12N 88.44W
24 L3 **Water Valley** Mississippi, S USA 34.09N 89.37W
29 O3 **Waterville** Kansas, C USA 39.41N 96.45W
19 Ss4 **Waterville** Maine, NE USA 44.34N 69.40W
31 V10 **Waterville** Minnesota, N USA 44.13N 93.34W
20 I10 **Waterville** New York, NE USA 42.55N 75.18W
12 E16 **Watford** Ontario, S Canada 42.57N 81.51W
99 N21 **Watford** SE England, UK 51.39N 0.24W
30 K4 **Watford City** North Dakota, N USA 47.48N 103.16W
147 X12 **Wāṭif** S Oman 18.34N 56.31E
20 G11 **Watkins Glen** New York, NE USA 42.22N 76.52W
Watlings Island *see* San Salvador
176 V13 **Watnil** Pulau Kai Kecil, E Indonesia 5.45S 132.39E
28 M10 **Watonga** Oklahoma, C USA 35.50N 98.24W
9 T16 **Watrous** Saskatchewan, S Canada 51.40N 105.28W
39 T10 **Watrous** New Mexico, SW USA 35.48N 104.58W
81 P16 **Watsa** Orientale, NE Dem. Rep. Congo 3.00N 29.31E
33 N12 **Watseka** Illinois, N USA 40.46N 87.44W
81 J19 **Watsikengo** Equateur, C Dem. Rep. Congo 0.49S 20.34E
190 C5 **Watson** South Australia 30.32S 131.28E
9 U15 **Watson** Saskatchewan, S Canada 52.13N 104.30W
205 O10 **Watson Escarpment** ▲▲ Antarctica
8 K9 **Watson Lake** Yukon Territory, W Canada 60.04N 128.46W
37 N10 **Watsonville** California, W USA 36.53N 121.43W
178 I8 **Wattay** ✕ (Viangchan) Viangchan, C Laos 18.03N 102.36E
111 N7 **Wattens** Tirol, W Austria 47.18N 11.37E
22 M9 **Watts Bar Lake** ▣ Tennessee, S USA
110 H7 **Wattwil** Sankt Gallen, NE Switzerland 47.19N 9.04E
176 Uu12 **Watubela, Kepulauan** *island group* E Indonesia
103 N24 **Watzmann** ▲ SE Germany 47.32N 12.56E
194 J13 **Wau** Morobe, C PNG 7.18S 146.38E
83 D14 **Wau** *var.* Wāw. Western Bahr el Ghazal, S Sudan 7.43N 28.01E
31 Q8 **Waubay** South Dakota, N USA 45.19N 97.18W
31 Q8 **Waubay Lake** ◎ South Dakota, N USA
191 U7 **Wauchope** New South Wales, SE Australia 31.30S 152.46E
25 W13 **Wauchula** Florida, SE USA 27.33N 81.48W
32 M10 **Wauconda** Illinois, N USA 42.15N 88.08W
190 J7 **Waukaringa** South Australia 32.19S 139.27E
33 N10 **Waukegan** Illinois, N USA 42.21N 87.50W
32 M9 **Waukesha** Wisconsin, N USA 43.01N 88.13W
31 X11 **Waukon** Iowa, C USA 43.16N 91.28W
32 L8 **Waunakee** Wisconsin, N USA 43.13N 89.28W
32 L7 **Waupaca** Wisconsin, N USA 44.22N 89.04W
32 M8 **Waupun** Wisconsin, N USA 43.40N 88.43W
28 M13 **Waurika** Oklahoma, C USA 34.10N 98.00W
28 M12 **Waurika Lake** ▣ Oklahoma, C USA
32 L6 **Wausau** Wisconsin, N USA 44.58N 89.40W
33 R11 **Wauseon** Ohio, N USA 41.33N 84.08W
32 L7 **Wautoma** Wisconsin, N USA 44.04N 89.16W
32 M9 **Wauwatosa** Wisconsin, N USA 43.03N 88.03W
24 L9 **Waveland** Mississippi, S USA 30.17N 89.22W
99 Q20 **Waveney** ≈ E England, UK
192 L11 **Waverley** Taranaki, North Island, NZ 39.46S 174.37E
31 W12 **Waverly** Iowa, C USA 42.43N 92.28W
29 T4 **Waverly** Missouri, C USA 39.12N 93.31W
31 R15 **Waverly** Nebraska, C USA 40.56N 96.27W
20 G12 **Waverly** New York, NE USA 42.00N 76.33W
22 H8 **Waverly** Tennessee, S USA 36.04N 87.47W
23 W7 **Waverly** Virginia, NE USA 37.02N 77.06W
101 H19 **Wavre** Wallon Brabant, C Belgium 50.43N 4.37E

◆ Country ● Country Capital ◇ Dependent Territory ○ Dependent Territory Capital ◈ Administrative Region ✕ International Airport ▲ Mountain ▲▲ Mountain Range Volcano ≈ River ◎ Lake ▣ Reservoir

177 G8 **Waw** Pegu, SW Myanmar 17.25N 96.40E
Wāw see Wau
12 B7 **Wawa** Ontario, S Canada 47.59N 84.43W
79 T14 **Wawa** Niger, W Nigeria 9.52N 4.33E
77 Q11 **Wāw al Kabīr** S Libya 25.21N 16.40E
45 N7 **Wawa, Río** var. Rio Huahua. ≈ NE Nicaragua
194 G13 **Wawoi** ≈ SW PNG
Wawosungu, Teluk see Staring, Teluk
27 T7 **Waxahachie** Texas, SW USA 32.23N 96.51W
164 L9 **Waxxari** Xinjiang Uygur Zizhiqu, NW China 38.43N 87.11E
197 H14 **Waya** island Yasawa Group, NW Fiji
25 V7 **Waycross** Georgia, SE USA 31.12N 82.21W
188 K10 **Way, Lake** ◎ Western Australia
33 P9 **Wayland** Michigan, N USA 42.40N 85.38W
31 R13 **Wayne** Nebraska, C USA 42.13N 97.01W
20 K14 **Wayne** New Jersey, NE USA 40.57N 74.16W
23 P5 **Wayne** West Virginia, NE USA 38.13N 82.26W
25 V4 **Waynesboro** Georgia, SE USA 33.04N 82.01W
24 M7 **Waynesboro** Mississippi, S USA 31.40N 88.39W
22 H10 **Waynesboro** Tennessee, S USA 35.19N 87.45W
23 U5 **Waynesboro** Virginia, NE USA 38.04N 78.53W
20 B16 **Waynesburg** Pennsylvania, NE USA 39.51N 80.10W
29 U6 **Waynesville** Missouri, C USA 37.49N 92.12W
23 O10 **Waynesville** North Carolina, SE USA 35.29N 82.59W
28 L8 **Waynoka** Oklahoma, C USA 36.36N 98.53W
Wazan see Ouazzane
Wazima see Wajima
155 V7 **Wazīrābād** Punjab, NE Pakistan 32.28N 74.04E
Wazzan see Ouazzane
112 I8 **Wda** var. Czarna Woda, Ger. Schwarzwasser. ≈ N Poland
197 K6 **Wé** Province des Îles Loyauté, E New Caledonia 20.55S 167.15E
99 O23 **Weald, The** lowlands SE England, UK
194 E15 **Weam** Western, SW PNG 8.33S 141.10E
99 L15 **Wear** ≈ N England, UK
Wearmouth see Sunderland
28 L10 **Weatherford** Oklahoma, C USA 35.31N 98.42W
27 S6 **Weatherford** Texas, SW USA 32.45N 97.48W
36 M3 **Weaverville** California, W USA 40.42N 122.57W
29 R7 **Webb City** Missouri, C USA 37.07N 94.28W
198 G9 **Weber Basin** undersea feature S Ceram Sea
Webfoot State see Oregon
20 F9 **Webster** New York, NE USA 43.12N 77.25W
31 Q8 **Webster** South Dakota, N USA 45.19N 97.31W
31 V13 **Webster City** Iowa, C USA 42.28N 93.49W
29 X5 **Webster Groves** Missouri, C USA 38.32N 90.20W
23 S4 **Webster Springs** var. Addison. West Virginia, NE USA 38.27N 80.24W
175 T8 **Weda, Teluk** bay Pulau Halmahera, E Indonesia
67 B25 **Weddell Island** var. Isla San José. Island W Falkland Islands
67 K22 **Weddell Plain** undersea feature SW Atlantic Ocean
67 K23 **Weddell Sea** sea SW Atlantic Ocean
67 B25 **Weddell Settlement** Weddell Island, W Falkland Islands 52.52S 60.54W
190 M11 **Wedderburn** Victoria, SE Australia 36.26S 143.37E
102 I9 **Wedel** Schleswig-Holstein, N Germany 53.35N 9.42E
94 N3 **Wedel Jarlsberg Land** physical region SW Svalbard
102 I12 **Wedemark** Niedersachsen, NW Germany 52.33N 9.43E
8 M17 **Wedge Mountain** ▲ British Columbia, SW Canada 50.10N 122.43W
25 R4 **Wedowee** Alabama, S USA 33.16N 85.28W
176 Vv13 **Weduar** Pulau Kai Besar, E Indonesia 5.55S 132.51E
176 Vv14 **Weduar, Tanjung** headland Pulau Kai Besar, SE Indonesia 5.58S 132.49E
37 N2 **Weed** California, W USA 41.26N 122.24W
13 Q12 **Weedon Centre** Quebec, SE Canada 45.40N 71.28W
20 E13 **Weedville** Pennsylvania, NE USA 41.15N 78.28W
102 F10 **Weener** Niedersachsen, NW Germany 53.09N 7.19E
31 S16 **Weeping Water** Nebraska, C USA 40.52N 96.08W
101 L16 **Weert** Limburg, SE Netherlands 51.15N 5.43E
100 I10 **Weesp** Noord-Holland, C Netherlands 52.18N 5.03E
191 S5 **Wee Waa** New South Wales, SE Australia 30.16S 149.27E
112 N7 **Węgorzewo** Ger. Angerburg. Warmińsko-Mazurskie, NE Poland 54.12N 21.49E
112 E9 **Węgorzyno** Ger. Wangerin. Zachodniopomorskie, NW Poland 53.34N 15.35E
112 N11 **Węgrów** Ger. Bingerau. Mazowieckie, E Poland 52.22N 22.00E
100 N5 **Wehe-Den Hoorn** Groningen, NE Netherlands 53.20N 6.29E
100 M12 **Wehl** Gelderland, E Netherlands 51.58N 6.13E
Wehlau see Znamensk
173 E2 **Weh, Pulau** island NW Indonesia
Wei see Weifang
167 P1 **Weichang** prev. Zhuizishan. Hebei, E China 41.55N 117.45E
Weichsel see Wisła
103 M16 **Weida** Thüringen, C Germany 50.46N 12.05E
Weiden see Weiden in der Oberpfalz
103 M19 **Weiden in der Oberpfalz** var. Weiden. Bayern, SE Germany 49.40N 12.10E
167 Q4 **Weifang** var. Wei, Wei-fang; prev. Weihsien. Shandong, E China 36.43N 119.10E
167 S4 **Weihai** Shandong, E China 37.30N 122.04E
166 K6 **Wei He** ≈ C China
Weihsien see Weifang
103 G17 **Weilburg** Hessen, W Germany 50.31N 8.18E
103 K24 **Weilheim** Bayern, SE Germany 47.50N 11.09E
191 P4 **Weilmoringle** New South Wales, SE Australia 29.13S 146.51E
103 L16 **Weimar** Thüringen, C Germany 50.58N 11.19E
27 U11 **Weimar** Texas, SW USA 29.42N 96.46W
166 L6 **Weinan** Shaanxi, C China 34.30N 109.30E
110 H6 **Weinfelden** Thurgau, NE Switzerland 47.33N 9.09E
103 I24 **Weingarten** Baden-Württemberg, S Germany 47.49N 9.37E
103 G20 **Weinheim** Baden-Württemberg, SW Germany 49.33N 8.40E
166 H11 **Weining** var. Weining Yizu Huizu Miaozu Zizhixian. Guizhou, S China 26.51N 104.16E
Weining Yizu Huizu Miaozu Zizhixian see Weining
189 V2 **Weipa** Queensland, NE Australia 12.43S 142.01E
9 Y11 **Weir River** Manitoba, C Canada 56.44N 94.06W
23 R1 **Weirton** West Virginia, NE USA 40.25N 80.35W
34 M13 **Weiser** Idaho, NW USA 44.15N 116.58W
166 F12 **Weishan** Yunnan, SW China 25.22N 100.19E
167 P6 **Weishan Hu** ◎ E China
103 M15 **Weisse Elster** Eng. White Elster. ≈ Czech Republic/Germany
Weisse Körös/Weisse Kreisch see Crişul Alb
110 L7 **Weissenbach am Lech** Tirol, W Austria 47.27N 10.39E
103 K21 **Weissenburg** Bayern, SE Germany 49.02N 10.58E
Weissenburg see Wissembourg, France
Weissenburg see Alba Iulia, Romania
103 M15 **Weissenfels** var. Weißenfels. Sachsen-Anhalt, C Germany 51.12N 11.58E
111 R9 **Weissensee** ◎ S Austria
Weissenstein see Paide
110 E11 **Weisshorn** var. Flüela Wisshorn. ▲ SW Switzerland 46.06N 7.43E
Weisskirchen see Bela Crkva
25 R3 **Weiss Lake** ⊡ Alabama, S USA
103 Q14 **Weisswasser** Lus. Běla Woda. Sachsen, E Germany 51.30N 14.37E
101 M22 **Weiswampach** Diekirch, N Luxembourg 50.07N 6.04E
111 U2 **Weitra** Niederösterreich, N Austria 48.41N 14.54E
167 O4 **Weixian** var. Wei Xian. Hebei, E China 36.58N 115.15E
165 V11 **Weiyuan** Gansu, C China 35.07N 104.12E
166 F14 **Weiyuan Jiang** ≈ SW China
111 W7 **Weiz** Steiermark, SE Austria 47.13N 15.37E
166 K16 **Weizhou Dao** island S China
112 I6 **Wejherowo** Pomorskie, NW Poland 54.36N 18.12E
29 Q8 **Welch** Oklahoma, C USA 36.52N 95.06W
26 M6 **Welch** Texas, SW USA 32.52N 102.06W
23 Q6 **Welch** West Virginia, NE USA 37.25N 81.34W
47 O14 **Welchman Hall** C Barbados 13.10N 59.34W
82 J11 **Weldiya** var. Waldia, It. Valdia. Amhara, N Ethiopia 11.45N 39.39E
23 W8 **Weldon** North Carolina, SE USA 36.25N 77.36W
27 V9 **Weldon** Texas, SW USA 31.00N 95.33W
101 M19 **Welkenraedt** Liège, E Belgium 50.40N 5.58E
199 L2 **Welker Seamount** undersea feature N Pacific Ocean 55.07N 140.18W
85 I22 **Welkom** Free State, C South Africa 27.58S 26.43E
12 H16 **Welland** Ontario, S Canada 43.58N 79.13W
12 G16 **Welland** ≈ Ontario, S Canada
99 O19 **Welland** ≈ C England, UK
12 H17 **Welland Canal** canal Ontario, S Canada
161 K25 **Wellawaya** Uva Province, SE Sri Lanka 6.43N 81.07E
Welle see Uele
189 T4 **Wellesley Islands** island group Queensland, N Australia
101 J22 **Wellin** Luxembourg, SE Belgium 50.06N 5.05E
99 N20 **Wellingborough** C England, UK 52.19N 0.42W
191 R7 **Wellington** New South Wales, SE Australia 32.34S 148.55E
12 J15 **Wellington** Ontario, SE Canada 43.57N 77.24W
193 L14 **Wellington** ● (NZ) Wellington, North Island, NZ 41.16S 174.46E
85 E26 **Wellington** Western Cape, SW South Africa 33.39S 19.00E
39 T2 **Wellington** Colorado, C USA 40.42N 105.00W
29 N7 **Wellington** Kansas, C USA 37.16N 97.22W
37 R7 **Wellington** Nevada, W USA 38.45N 119.22W
33 T11 **Wellington** Ohio, N USA 41.10N 82.13W
27 P3 **Wellington** Texas, SW USA 34.51N 100.12W
38 M4 **Wellington** Utah, W USA 39.31N 110.45W
193 M14 **Wellington** off. Wellington Region. ◆ region North Island, NZ
193 L14 **Wellington** ✕ Wellington, North Island, NZ 41.19S 174.48E
Wellington see Wellington, Isla
65 F22 **Wellington, Isla** var. Wellington. island S Chile
191 P12 **Wellington, Lake** ◎ Victoria, SE Australia
31 X14 **Wellman** Iowa, C USA 41.27N 91.50W
26 M6 **Wellman** Texas, SW USA 33.03N 102.25W
99 K22 **Wells** SW England, UK 51.13N 2.39W
31 V11 **Wells** Minnesota, N USA 43.45N 93.43W
37 X2 **Wells** Nevada, W USA 41.06N 114.57W
27 W8 **Wells** Texas, SW USA 31.28N 94.54W
20 F12 **Wellsboro** Pennsylvania, NE USA 41.43N 77.39W
23 R1 **Wellsburg** West Virginia, NE USA 40.16N 80.36W
192 K4 **Wellsford** Auckland, North Island, NZ 36.17S 174.30E
188 L9 **Wells, Lake** ◎ Western Australia
189 N4 **Wells, Mount** ▲ Western Australia 17.39S 127.08E
99 P18 **Wells-next-the-Sea** E England, UK 52.58N 0.48E
33 T15 **Wellston** Ohio, N USA 39.07N 82.31W
29 O10 **Wellston** Oklahoma, C USA 35.41N 97.03W
20 E11 **Wellsville** New York, NE USA 42.06N 77.55W
33 V12 **Wellsville** Ohio, N USA 40.36N 80.39W
38 L1 **Wellsville** Utah, W USA 41.38N 111.55W
38 I14 **Wellton** Arizona, SW USA 32.40N 114.09W
111 S4 **Wels** anc. Ovilava. Oberösterreich, N Austria 48.10N 14.01E
101 K15 **Welschap** ✕ (Eindhoven) Noord-Brabant, S Netherlands 51.27N 5.22E
102 P10 **Welse** ≈ NE Germany
24 H9 **Welsh** Louisiana, S USA 30.12N 92.49W
99 K19 **Welshpool** Wel. Y Trallwng. E Wales, UK 52.38N 3.06W
99 O21 **Welwyn Garden City** SE England, UK 51.48N 0.13W
81 K18 **Wema** Equateur, NW Dem. Rep. Congo 0.25S 21.33E
83 G21 **Wembere** ≈ C Tanzania
9 N13 **Wembley** Alberta, W Canada 55.07N 119.12W
10 I9 **Wemindji** prev. Nouveau-Comptoir, Paint Hills. Quebec, C Canada 53.00N 78.42W
101 G18 **Wemmel** Vlaams Brabant, C Belgium 50.54N 4.18E
34 J8 **Wenatchee** Washington, NW USA 47.49N 120.48W
166 M17 **Wenchang** Hainan, S China 19.34N 110.46E
167 R11 **Wencheng** prev. Daxue. Zhejiang, SE China 27.48N 120.01E
79 P16 **Wenchi** W Ghana 7.45N 2.01W
Wen-chou/Wenchow see Wenzhou
166 H8 **Wenchuan** prev. Weizhou. Sichuan, C China 31.29N 103.39E
Wendau see Võnnu
Wenden see Cēsis
167 S4 **Wendeng** Shandong, E China 37.14N 122.06E
83 J14 **Wendo** Southern, S Ethiopia 6.34N 38.28E
38 J2 **Wendover** Utah, W USA 40.41N 114.00W
12 D9 **Wenebegon** ≈ Ontario, S Canada
12 D8 **Wenebegon Lake** ◎ Ontario, S Canada
110 E9 **Wengen** Bern, W Switzerland 46.38N 7.57E
167 O13 **Wengyuan** prev. Longxian. Guangdong, S China 24.22N 114.06E
201 P15 **Weno** prev. Moen. Chuuk, C Micronesia
201 V12 **Weno** prev. Moen. atoll Chuuk Islands, C Micronesia
164 N13 **Wenquan** Qinghai, C China 33.16N 91.43E
165 H4 **Wenquan** var. Arixang. Xinjiang Uygur Zizhiqu, NW China 45.00N 81.02E
166 H14 **Wenshan** Yunnan, SW China 23.22N 104.21E
164 H6 **Wensu** Xinjiang Uygur Zizhiqu, W China 41.15N 80.10E
190 L8 **Wentworth** New South Wales, SE Australia 34.04S 141.53E
29 W4 **Wentzville** Missouri, C USA 38.48N 90.51W
165 V12 **Wenxian** var. Wen Xian. Gansu, C China 32.57N 104.42E
167 S10 **Wenzhou** var. Wen-chou, Wenchow. Zhejiang, SE China 28.02N 120.36E
36 L4 **Weott** California, W USA 40.19N 123.57W
101 I20 **Wépion** Namur, SE Belgium 50.24N 4.53E
102 O11 **Werbellinsee** ◎ NE Germany
101 L21 **Werbomont** Liège, E Belgium 50.22N 5.43E
85 G20 **Werda** Kgalagadi, S Botswana 25.13S 23.16E
Werder see Virtsu
83 N14 **Werdēr** Somalil, E Ethiopia 6.59N 45.20E
Werenów see Voranava
176 V11 **Weri** Papua, E Indonesia 3.10S 132.39E
100 I13 **Werkendam** Noord-Brabant, S Netherlands 51.48N 4.54E
103 M20 **Wernberg-Köblitz** Bayern, SE Germany 49.31N 12.10E
103 J18 **Werneck** Bayern, C Germany 50.00N 10.06E
103 K14 **Wernigerode** Sachsen-Anhalt, C Germany 51.51N 10.48E
Werowitz see Virovitica
103 J16 **Werra** ≈ C Germany
191 N12 **Werribee** Victoria, SE Australia 37.55S 144.39E
191 T6 **Werris Creek** New South Wales, SE Australia 31.22S 150.40E
Werro see Võru
Werschetz see Vršac
103 K23 **Wertach** ≈ S Germany
103 I19 **Wertheim** Baden-Württemberg, SW Germany 49.45N 9.31E
100 J8 **Wervershoof** Noord-Holland, NW Netherlands 52.43N 5.09E
Wervicq see Wervik
101 C18 **Wervik** var. Wervicq, Werwick. West-Vlaanderen, W Belgium 50.46N 3.03E
Werwick see Wervik
103 D14 **Wesel** Nordrhein-Westfalen, W Germany 51.40N 6.37E
Weseli an der Lainsitz see Veselí nad Lužnicí
Wesenberg see Rakvere
102 H12 **Weser** ≈ NW Germany
Wes-Kaap see Western Cape
27 S17 **Weslaco** Texas, SW USA 26.09N 97.59W
12 J13 **Weslemkoon Lake** ◎ Ontario, SE Canada
189 R1 **Wessel Islands** island group Northern Territory, N Australia
31 P9 **Wessington** South Dakota, N USA 44.27N 98.40W
31 P10 **Wessington Springs** South Dakota, N USA 44.02N 98.33W
27 T8 **West** Texas, SW USA 31.48N 97.05W
West see Ouest
32 M9 **West Allis** Wisconsin, N USA 43.01N 88.00W
190 E8 **Westall, Point** headland South Australia 32.54S 134.04E
West Antarctica see Lesser Antarctica
12 G11 **West Arm** Ontario, S Canada 46.16N 80.25W
West Azerbaijan see Āzarbāyjān-e Gharbī
144 F10 **West Bank** disputed region SW Asia
9 N17 **Westbank** British Columbia, SW Canada 49.50N 119.37W
12 E11 **West Bay** Manitoulin Island, Ontario, S Canada 45.48N 82.09W
24 L11 **West Bay** bay Louisiana, S USA
32 M8 **West Bend** Wisconsin, N USA 43.25N 88.13W
159 R16 **West Bengal** ◆ state NE India
West Borneo see Kalimantan Barat
31 Y14 **West Branch** Iowa, C USA 41.40N 91.21W
33 R7 **West Branch** Michigan, N USA 44.16N 84.13W
20 F13 **West Branch Susquehanna River** ≈ Pennsylvania, NE USA
99 L20 **West Bromwich** C England, UK 52.28N 1.59W
21 P8 **Westbrook** Maine, NE USA 43.42N 70.21W
31 T10 **Westbrook** Minnesota, N USA 44.02N 95.26W
31 Y15 **West Burlington** Iowa, C USA 40.49N 91.09W
98 L2 **West Burra** island NE Scotland, UK
32 J8 **Westby** Wisconsin, N USA 43.39N 90.52W
46 L6 **West Caicos** island W Turks and Caicos Islands
193 A24 **West Cape** headland South Island, NZ 45.51S 166.26E
182 L4 **West Caroline Basin** undersea feature SW Pacific Ocean
20 I16 **West Chester** Pennsylvania, NE USA 39.56N 75.35W
193 E18 **West Coast** off. West Coast Region. ◆ region South Island, NZ
27 V12 **West Columbia** Texas, SW USA 29.08N 95.39W
31 W10 **West Concord** Minnesota, N USA 44.09N 92.54W
31 V14 **West Des Moines** Iowa, C USA 41.33N 93.42W
39 Q6 **West Elk Peak** ▲ Colorado, C USA 38.43N 107.12W
46 F1 **West End** Grand Bahama Island, N Bahamas 26.36N 78.55W
46 F1 **West End Point** headland Grand Bahama Island, N Bahamas 26.40N 78.58W
100 O7 **Westerbork** Drenthe, NE Netherlands 52.49N 6.36E
100 N3 **Westereems** strait Germany/Netherlands
100 O9 **Westerhaar-Vriezenveensewijk** Overijssel, E Netherlands 52.28N 6.38E
102 G6 **Westerland** Schleswig-Holstein, N Germany 54.54N 8.19E
101 I17 **Westerlo** Antwerpen, N Belgium 51.05N 4.55E
21 N13 **Westerly** Rhode Island, NE USA 41.22N 71.45W
83 G18 **Western** ◆ province W Kenya
159 N11 **Western** ◆ zone C Nepal
194 E14 **Western** ◆ province SW PNG
195 T14 **Western** off. Western Province. ◆ province NW Solomon Islands
85 G15 **Western** ◆ province SW Zambia
188 K8 **Western Australia** ◆ state W Australia
82 A13 **Western Bahr el Ghazal** ◆ state SW Sudan
Western Bug see Bug
85 F25 **Western Cape** off. Western Cape Province, Afr. Wes-Kaap. ◆ province SW South Africa
82 A11 **Western Darfur** ◆ state W Sudan
Western Desert see Sahara el Gharbîya
120 G9 **Western Dvina** Bel. Dzvina, Ger. Düna, Latv. Daugava, Rus. Zapadnaya Dvina. ≈ W Europe
83 D15 **Western Equatoria** ◆ state SW Sudan
161 E16 **Western Ghats** ▲▲ SW India
194 G12 **Western Highlands** ◆ province C PNG
Western Isles see Outer Hebrides
82 C12 **Western Kordofan** ◆ state C Sudan
23 T3 **Westernport** Maryland, NE USA 39.29N 79.03W
161 J26 **Western Province** ◆ province SW Sri Lanka
76 B10 **Western Sahara** ◇ disputed territory N Africa
Western Samoa see Samoa
Western Sayans see Zapadnyy Sayan
Western Scheldt see Westerschelde
Western Sierra Madre see Madre Occidental, Sierra
101 E15 **Westerschelde** Eng. Western Scheldt; prev. Honte. inlet S North Sea
33 S13 **Westerville** Ohio, N USA 40.07N 82.55W
103 F17 **Westerwald** ▲▲ W Germany
67 C25 **West Falkland** var. Gran Malvina, Isla Gran Malvina. island W Falkland Islands
31 R5 **West Fargo** North Dakota, N USA 46.49N 96.51W
196 M15 **West Fayu Atoll** atoll Caroline Islands, C Micronesia
20 C11 **Westfield** New York, NE USA 42.18N 79.34W
32 L7 **Westfield** Wisconsin, N USA 43.56N 89.31W
West Flanders see West-Vlaanderen
29 S10 **West Fork** Arkansas, C USA 35.55N 94.11W
31 P16 **West Fork Big Blue River** ≈ Nebraska, C USA
31 U12 **West Fork Des Moines River** ≈ Iowa/Minnesota, C USA
27 S5 **West Fork Trinity River** ≈ Texas, SW USA
32 L16 **West Frankfort** Illinois, N USA 37.54N 88.55W
100 I8 **West-Friesland** physical region NW Netherlands
West Frisian Islands see Waddeneilanden
21 T5 **West Grand Lake** ◎ Maine, NE USA
20 M12 **West Hartford** Connecticut, NE USA 41.44N 72.45W
20 M13 **West Haven** Connecticut, NE USA 41.16N 72.57W
29 X12 **West Helena** Arkansas, C USA 34.33N 90.38W
30 M2 **Westhope** North Dakota, N USA 48.54N 101.01W
205 Y8 **West Ice Shelf** ice shelf Antarctica
49 R2 **West Indies** island group SE North America
West Irian see Papua
West Java see Jawa Barat
38 L3 **West Jordan** Utah, W USA 40.37N 111.55W
West Kalimantan see Kalimantan Barat
101 D14 **Westkapelle** Zeeland, SW Netherlands 51.32N 3.26E
33 O13 **West Lafayette** Indiana, N USA 40.24N 86.54W
33 T13 **West Lafayette** Ohio, N USA 40.16N 81.45W
West Lake see Kagera
31 Y14 **West Liberty** Iowa, C USA 41.34N 91.15W
23 O5 **West Liberty** Kentucky, S USA 38.04N 83.22W
Westliche Morava see Zapadna Morava
15 I13 **Westlock** Alberta, SW Canada 54.12N 113.49W
12 E17 **West Lorne** Ontario, S Canada 42.36N 81.34W
98 J12 **West Lothian** cultural region S Scotland, UK
101 H16 **Westmalle** Antwerpen, N Belgium 51.18N 4.40E
199 H6 **West Mariana Basin** var. Perece Vela Basin. undersea feature W Pacific Ocean
99 E17 **Westmeath** Ir. An Iarmhí, Na h-Iarmhidhe. cultural region C Ireland
29 Y11 **West Memphis** Arkansas, C USA 35.09N 90.11W
23 W2 **Westminster** Maryland, NE USA 39.34N 77.00W
23 O11 **Westminster** South Carolina, SE USA 34.39N 83.06W
24 I5 **West Monroe** Louisiana, S USA 32.31N 92.09W
20 D15 **Westmont** Pennsylvania, NE USA 40.16N 78.55W
29 O3 **Westmoreland** Kansas, C USA 39.23N 96.30W
37 W17 **Westmorland** California, W USA 33.02N 115.37W
194 L11 **West New Britain** ◆ province E PNG
West New Guinea see Papua
85 K18 **West Nicholson** Matabeleland South, S Zimbabwe 21.06S 29.23E
31 T14 **West Nishnabotna River** ≈ Iowa, C USA
183 P11 **West Norfolk Ridge** undersea feature W Pacific Ocean
27 P12 **West Nueces River** ≈ Texas, SW USA
West Nusa Tenggara see Nusa Tenggara Barat
31 T11 **West Okoboji Lake** ◎ Iowa, C USA
35 R16 **Weston** Idaho, NW USA 42.01N 119.29W
23 R4 **Weston** West Virginia, NE USA 39.02N 80.28W
99 J22 **Weston-super-Mare** SW England, UK 51.21N 2.58W
25 Z14 **West Palm Beach** Florida, SE USA 26.43N 80.03W
West Papua see Papua
196 E9 **West Passage** passage Babeldaob, N Palau
25 O9 **West Pensacola** Florida, SE USA 30.25N 87.16W
29 V8 **West Plains** Missouri, C USA 36.43N 91.51W
37 P7 **West Point** California, W USA 38.21N 120.33W
25 R5 **West Point** Georgia, SE USA 32.52N 85.10W
24 M3 **West Point** Mississippi, S USA 33.36N 88.39W
31 R14 **West Point** Nebraska, C USA 41.50N 96.42W
23 X6 **West Point** Virginia, NE USA 37.31N 76.48W
190 G10 **West Point** headland South Australia 35.01S 135.58E
67 B24 **Westpoint Island Settlement** Westpoint Island, NW Falkland Islands 51.21S 60.40W
25 R4 **West Point Lake** ⊡ Alabama/Georgia, SE USA
99 B16 **Westport** Ir. Cathair na Mart. W Ireland 53.48N 9.31W
193 G15 **Westport** West Coast, South Island, NZ 41.46S 171.37E
34 F10 **Westport** Oregon, NW USA 46.07N 123.22W
34 F9 **Westport** Washington, NW USA 46.53N 124.06W
33 S15 **West Portsmouth** Ohio, N USA 38.45N 83.01W
West Punjab see Punjab
9 V14 **Westray** Manitoba, C Canada 53.30N 101.19W
98 J4 **Westray** island NE Scotland, UK
12 F9 **Westree** Ontario, S Canada 47.25N 81.32W
99 L16 **West Riding** cultural region N England, UK
West River see Xi Jiang
32 J7 **West Salem** Wisconsin, N USA 43.54N 91.04W
67 H21 **West Scotia Ridge** undersea feature W Scotia Sea
West Sepik see Sandaun
181 N4 **West Sheba Ridge** undersea feature W Indian Ocean
West Siberian Plain see Zapadno-Sibirskaya Ravnina
33 S11 **West Sister Island** island Ohio, N USA
West-Skylge see West-Terschelling
West Sumatra see Sumatera Barat
100 J5 **West-Terschelling** Fris. West-Skylge. Friesland, N Netherlands 53.22N 5.14E
66 J7 **West Thulean Rise** undersea feature N Atlantic Ocean
31 X12 **West Union** Iowa, C USA 42.57N 91.48W
33 R15 **West Union** Ohio, N USA 38.47N 83.33W
23 R3 **West Union** West Virginia, NE USA 39.18N 80.46W
33 N13 **Westville** Illinois, N USA 40.02N 87.38W
23 R3 **West Virginia** off. State of West Virginia; also known as The Mountain State. ◆ state NE USA
101 A17 **West-Vlaanderen** Eng. West Flanders. ◆ province W Belgium
37 R7 **West Walker River** ≈ California/Nevada, W USA
37 P4 **Westwood** California, W USA 40.18N 121.02W
191 P9 **West Wyalong** New South Wales, SE Australia 33.56S 147.10E
179 N14 **West York Island** island N Spratly Islands
175 S15 **Wetar, Pulau** island Kepulauan Damar, E Indonesia
175 Ss16 **Wetar, Selat** var. Wetar Strait. strait Nusa Tenggara, S Indonesia
Wetar Strait see Wetar, Selat
9 Q15 **Wetaskiwin** Alberta, SW Canada 52.57N 113.19W
83 K21 **Wete** Pemba, E Tanzania 5.03S 39.40E
177 G4 **Wetlet** Sagaing, C Myanmar 22.21N 95.49E
39 T6 **Wet Mountains** ▲▲ Colorado, C USA
103 E15 **Wetter** Nordrhein-Westfalen, W Germany 51.22N 7.24E
103 H17 **Wetter** ≈ W Germany
101 F17 **Wetteren** Oost-Vlaanderen, NW Belgium 51.06N 3.58E
110 F7 **Wettingen** Aargau, N Switzerland 47.30N 8.14E
29 P11 **Wetumka** Oklahoma, C USA 35.14N 96.14W
25 Q5 **Wetumpka** Alabama, S USA 32.32N 86.12W
110 G7 **Wetzikon** Zürich, N Switzerland 47.19N 8.48E
103 G17 **Wetzlar** Hessen, W Germany 50.33N 8.30E
101 C18 **Wevelgem** West-Vlaanderen, W Belgium 50.48N 3.12E
40 M6 **Wevok** var. Wewuk. Alaska, USA 68.52N 166.05W
25 R9 **Wewahitchka** Florida, SE USA 30.06N 85.12W
194 G10 **Wewak** East Sepik, NW PNG 3.32S 143.36E
29 O11 **Wewoka** Oklahoma, C USA 35.09N 96.29W
Wewuk see Wevok
99 F20 **Wexford** Ir. Loch Garman. SE Ireland 52.21N 6.31W
99 F20 **Wexford** Ir. Loch Garman. cultural region SE Ireland
32 L7 **Weyauwega** Wisconsin, N USA 44.16N 88.54W
9 U17 **Weyburn** Saskatchewan, S Canada 49.39N 103.51W
Weyer see Weyer Markt
111 U5 **Weyer Markt** var. Weyer. Oberösterreich, N Austria 47.52N 14.39E
102 H11 **Weyhe** Niedersachsen, NW Germany 53.00N 8.52E
99 L24 **Weymouth** S England, UK 50.36N 2.28W
21 P11 **Weymouth** Massachusetts, NE USA 42.13N 70.56W
101 H18 **Wezembeek-Oppem** Vlaams Brabant, C Belgium 50.51N 4.28E
100 M9 **Wezep** Gelderland, E Netherlands 52.28N 6.00E
192 M9 **Whakamaru** Waikato, North Island, NZ 38.27S 175.48E
192 O8 **Whakatane** Bay of Plenty, North Island, NZ 37.58S 105.00E
192 O8 **Whakatane** ≈ North Island, NZ
15 L7 **Whale Cove** Nunavut, C Canada 62.13N 92.10W
98 M2 **Whalsay** island NE Scotland, UK
192 L11 **Whangaehu** ≈ North Island, NZ
192 M6 **Whangamata** Waikato, North Island, NZ 37.13S 175.51E
192 Q9 **Whangara** Gisborne, North Island, NZ 38.34S 178.12E
192 K3 **Whangarei** Northland, North Island, NZ 35.44S 174.18E
192 K3 **Whangaruru Harbour** inlet North Island, NZ
27 V12 **Wharton** Texas, SW USA 29.19N 96.08W
181 U8 **Wharton Basin** var. West Australian Basin. undersea feature E Indian Ocean
193 E18 **Whataroa** West Coast, South Island, NZ 43.16S 170.19E
15 Hh7 **Wha Ti** prev. Lac La Martre. Northwest Territories, W Canada 63.10N 117.12W
192 K6 **Whatipu** Auckland, North Island, NZ 37.17S 174.44E
35 Y16 **Wheatland** Wyoming, C USA 42.03N 104.57W
12 D18 **Wheatley** Ontario, S Canada 42.06N 82.27W
32 M10 **Wheaton** Illinois, N USA 41.52N 88.06W
31 R7 **Wheaton** Minnesota, N USA 45.48N 96.30W
39 T4 **Wheat Ridge** Colorado, C USA 39.44N 105.06W
27 P2 **Wheeler** Texas, SW USA 35.26N 100.16W
25 O2 **Wheeler Lake** ⊡ Alabama, S USA
37 Y6 **Wheeler Peak** ▲ Nevada, W USA 39.00N 114.17W
39 T9 **Wheeler Peak** ▲ New Mexico, SW USA 36.34N 105.25W
33 S15 **Wheelersburg** Ohio, N USA 38.43N 82.51W
23 R2 **Wheeling** West Virginia, NE USA 40.03N 80.43W
99 L16 **Whernside** ▲ N England, UK 54.13N 2.27W
190 F9 **Whidbey, Point** headland South Australia 34.36S 135.08E
188 I7 **Whim Creek** Western Australia 20.51S 117.54E
8 L17 **Whistler** British Columbia, SW Canada 50.07N 122.57W
23 W8 **Whitakers** North Carolina, SE USA 36.06N 77.43W
12 H15 **Whitby** Ontario, S Canada 43.53N 78.54W
99 N15 **Whitby** N England, UK 54.28N 0.37W
8 G6 **White** ≈ Yukon Territory, W Canada
11 T11 **White Bay** bay Newfoundland and Labrador, E Canada
22 I8 **White Bluff** Tennessee, S USA 36.06N 87.13W
30 J6 **White Butte** ▲ North Dakota, N USA 46.23N 103.18W
21 R5 **White Cap Mountain** ▲ Maine, NE USA 45.33N 69.15W
24 J9 **White Castle** Louisiana, S USA 30.10N 91.09W
190 M5 **White Cliffs** New South Wales, SE Australia 30.52S 143.04E
33 P8 **White Cloud** Michigan, N USA 43.34N 85.46W
9 P14 **Whitecourt** Alberta, SW Canada 54.10N 115.37W
27 O2 **White Deer** Texas, SW USA 35.26N 101.10W
White Elster see Weisse Elster
26 M5 **Whiteface** Texas, SW USA 33.36N 102.36W
20 K7 **Whiteface Mountain** ▲ New York, NE USA 44.22N 73.54W
31 W5 **Whiteface Reservoir** ⊡ Minnesota, N USA
35 O7 **Whitefish** Montana, NW USA 48.24N 114.20W
33 N9 **Whitefish Bay** Wisconsin, N USA 43.09N 87.54W
33 Q3 **Whitefish Bay** lake bay Canada/USA
12 E11 **Whitefish Falls** Ontario, S Canada 46.06N 81.42W
12 B7 **Whitefish Lake** ◎ Ontario, S Canada
31 U6 **Whitefish Lake** ◎ Minnesota, C USA
33 Q3 **Whitefish Point** headland Michigan, N USA 46.46N 84.57W
33 O4 **Whitefish River** ≈ Michigan, N USA
27 O4 **Whiteflat** Texas, SW USA 34.06N 100.55W
29 V12 **White Hall** Arkansas, C USA 34.18N 92.05W
32 K14 **White Hall** Illinois, N USA 39.26N 90.24W
33 O8 **Whitehall** Michigan, N USA 43.24N 86.21W
20 L9 **Whitehall** New York, NE USA 43.33N 73.24W
33 S13 **Whitehall** Ohio, N USA 39.58N 82.53W
32 J7 **Whitehall** Wisconsin, N USA 44.22N 91.19W
99 J15 **Whitehaven** NW England, UK 54.33N 3.34W
8 I8 **Whitehorse** territory capital Yukon Territory, W Canada 60.40N 135.07W
192 O7 **White Island** island NE NZ
12 K13 **White Lake** ◎ Ontario, SE Canada
24 H10 **White Lake** ◎ Louisiana, S USA
195 N12 **Whiteman Range** ▲▲ New Britain, E PNG
191 Q15 **Whitemark** Tasmania, SE Australia 40.10S 148.01E
37 S9 **White Mountains** ▲▲ California/Nevada, W USA
21 N7 **White Mountains** ▲▲ Maine/New Hampshire, NE USA
82 F11 **White Nile** ◆ state C Sudan
69 U7 **White Nile** var. Bahr el Jebel. ≈ S Sudan
83 E14 **White Nile** Ar. Al Baḥr al Abyaḍ, An Nīl al Abyaḍ, Bahr el Jebel. ≈ SE Sudan
27 W5 **White Oak Creek** ≈ Texas, SW USA
8 H9 **White Pass** pass Canada/USA 59.35N 135.05W
34 I9 **White Pass** pass Washington, NW USA 46.38N 121.23W
23 O9 **White Pine** Tennessee, S USA 36.06N 83.17W
20 K14 **White Plains** New York, NE USA 41.01N 73.45W
27 O5 **White River** ≈ Texas, SW USA
30 M11 **White River** South Dakota, N USA 43.34N 100.45W
29 W12 **White River** ≈ Arkansas, SE USA
39 P3 **White River** ≈ Colorado/Utah, C USA
33 N15 **White River** ≈ Indiana, N USA
33 O8 **White River** ≈ Michigan, N USA
30 K11 **White River** ≈ South Dakota, N USA
20 M8 **White River** ≈ Vermont, NE USA
39 N13 **Whiteriver** Arizona, SW USA 33.50N 109.57W
27 O5 **White River Lake** ⊡ Texas, SW USA

◆ Country
● Country Capital
◇ Dependent Territory
○ Dependent Territory Capital
◆ Administrative Region
✕ International Airport
▲ Mountain
▲▲ Mountain Range
Volcano
≈ River
◎ Lake
⊡ Reservoir

34 H11 **White Salmon** Washington, NW USA 45.43N 121.29W
20 I10 **Whitesboro** New York, NE USA 43.07N 75.17W
27 T5 **Whitesboro** Texas, SW USA 33.39N 96.54W
23 O7 **Whitesburg** Kentucky, S USA 37.16N 82.55W
White Sea *see* Beloye More
White Sea-Baltic Canal/White Sea Canal *see* Belomorsko-Baltiyskiy Kanal
65 I25 **Whiteside, Canal** *channel* S Chile
35 S10 **White Sulphur Springs** Montana, NW USA 46.33N 110.54W
23 R6 **White Sulphur Springs** West Virginia, NE USA 37.48N 80.18W
22 J6 **Whitesville** Kentucky, S USA 37.40N 86.48W
34 I10 **White Swan** Washington, NW USA 46.22N 120.46W
23 U12 **Whiteville** North Carolina, SE USA 34.20N 78.42W
22 F10 **Whiteville** Tennessee, S USA 35.19N 89.09W
79 Q13 **White Volta** *var.* Nakambé, *Fr.* Volta Blanche. ⟿ Burkina/Ghana
32 M9 **Whitewater** Wisconsin, N USA 42.51N 88.43W
39 P14 **Whitewater Baldy** ▲ New Mexico, SW USA 33.19N 108.38W
25 X17 **Whitewater Bay** *bay* Florida, SE USA
33 Q14 **Whitewater River** ⟿ Indiana/Ohio, N USA
9 V16 **Whitewood** Saskatchewan, S Canada 50.19N 102.16W
30 J9 **Whitewood** South Dakota, N USA 44.27N 103.38W
27 U5 **Whitewright** Texas, SW USA 33.30N 96.23W
99 I15 **Whithorn** S Scotland, UK 54.43N 4.26W
192 M6 **Whitianga** Waikato, North Island, NZ 36.49S 175.42E
21 N11 **Whitinsville** Massachusetts, NE USA 42.06N 71.40W
22 M8 **Whitley City** Kentucky, S USA 36.40N 84.28W
23 Q11 **Whitmire** South Carolina, SE USA 34.30N 81.36W
33 R10 **Whitmore Lake** Michigan, N USA 42.26N 83.44W
205 N9 **Whitmore Mountains** ▲▲ Antarctica
12 I12 **Whitney** Ontario, SE Canada 45.29N 78.11W
27 T8 **Whitney** Texas, SW USA 31.56N 97.20W
27 S8 **Whitney, Lake** ▣ Texas, SW USA
37 S11 **Whitney, Mount** ▲ California, W USA 37.45N 119.55W
189 Y6 **Whitsunday Group** *island group* Queensland, E Australia
27 S6 **Whitt** Texas, SW USA 32.55N 98.01W
31 U12 **Whittemore** Iowa, C USA 43.03N 94.25W
41 R12 **Whittier** Alaska, USA 60.46N 148.40W
37 T15 **Whittier** California, W USA 33.58N 118.01W
85 I25 **Whittlesea** Eastern Cape, S South Africa 32.08S 26.51E
22 K10 **Whitwell** Tennessee, S USA 35.12N 85.31W
15 J9 **Wholdaia Lake** ◎ Northwest Territories, NW Canada
190 H7 **Whyalla** South Australia 33.04S 137.34E
Whydah *see* Ouidah
12 F13 **Wiarton** Ontario, S Canada 44.44N 81.09W
175 Q11 **Wiau** Sulawesi, C Indonesia 3.08S 121.22E
113 H15 **Wiązów** *Ger.* Wansen. Dolnośląskie, SW Poland 50.49N 17.13E
35 Y8 **Wibaux** Montana, NW USA 46.57N 104.11W
29 N6 **Wichita** Kansas, C USA 37.41N 97.20W
27 R5 **Wichita Falls** Texas, SW USA 33.54N 98.29W
28 L11 **Wichita Mountains** ▲▲ Oklahoma, C USA
27 R5 **Wichita River** ⟿ Texas, SW USA
98 K6 **Wick** N Scotland, UK 58.25N 3.06W
38 K13 **Wickenburg** Arizona, SW USA 33.57N 112.41W
26 L8 **Wickett** Texas, SW USA 31.34N 103.00W
188 I7 **Wickham** Western Australia 20.40S 117.11E
190 M14 **Wickham, Cape** *headland* Tasmania, SE Australia 39.36S 143.55E
22 G7 **Wickliffe** Kentucky, S USA 37.14N 89.16W
99 G19 **Wicklow** *Ir.* Cill Mhantáin. E Ireland 52.58N 6.03W
99 F19 **Wicklow** *Ir.* Cill Mhantáin. *cultural region* E Ireland
99 G19 **Wicklow Head** *Ir.* Ceann Chill Mhantáin. *headland* E Ireland 52.57N 6.00W
99 F18 **Wicklow Mountains** *Ir.* Sléibhte Chill Mhantáin. ▲▲ E Ireland
12 H10 **Wicksteed Lake** ◎ Ontario, S Canada
Wida *see* Ouidah
67 G15 **Wideawake Airfield** ✈ (Georgetown) SW Ascension Island
195 P11 **Wide Bay** *bay* New Britain, PNG
175 T19 **Widi, Kepulauan** *island group* E Indonesia
99 K18 **Widnes** C England, UK 53.22N 2.43W
112 H9 **Więcbork** *Ger.* Vandsburg. Kujawsko-pomorskie, C Poland 53.21N 17.31E
103 E17 **Wied** ⟿ W Germany
103 F16 **Wiehl** Nordrhein-Westfalen, W Germany 50.57N 7.33E
113 L17 **Wieliczka** Małopolskie, S Poland 50.00N 20.02E
112 G12 **Wielkopolskie** ◈ *province* C Poland
113 J14 **Wieluń** Sieradz, C Poland 51.13N 18.33E
111 X4 **Wien** *Eng.* Vienna, *Hung.* Bécs, *Slvk.* Vídeň, *Slvn.* Dunaj; *anc.* Vindobona. ● (Austria) Wien, NE Austria 48.13N 16.22E
111 X4 **Wien** *off.* Land Wien, *Eng.* Vienna. ◈ *state* NE Austria
111 X5 **Wiener Neustadt** Niederösterreich, E Austria 47.49N 16.07E
112 G7 **Wieprza** *Ger.* Wipper. ⟿ NW Poland
100 O10 **Wierden** Overijssel, E Netherlands 52.22N 6.34E
100 I7 **Wieringerwerf** Noord-Holland, NW Netherlands 52.51N 5.01E
Wieruschow *see* Wieruszów
113 I14 **Wieruszów** *Ger.* Wieruschow. Łódzkie, C Poland 51.18N 18.09E
111 V9 **Wies** Steiermark, SE Austria 46.40N 15.16E
Wiesbachhorn *see* Grosses Wiesbachhorn
103 G18 **Wiesbaden** Hessen, W Germany 50.06N 8.13E
Wieselburg and Ungarisch-Altenburg/Wieselburg-Ungarisch-Altenburg *see* Mosonmagyaróvár
Wiesenhof *see* Ostrołęka
103 G20 **Wiesloch** Baden-Württemberg, SW Germany 49.18N 8.42E
102 F10 **Wiesmoor** Niedersachsen, NW Germany 53.22N 7.46E
112 I7 **Wieżyca** *Ger.* Turmberg. *hill* Pomorskie, N Poland 54.13N 18.06E
99 L17 **Wigan** NW England, UK 53.33N 2.37W
39 U3 **Wiggins** Colorado, C USA 40.11N 104.03W
24 M8 **Wiggins** Mississippi, S USA 30.50N 89.09W
Wigorna Ceaster *see* Worcester
99 I14 **Wigtown** S Scotland, UK 54.52N 4.26W
99 H14 **Wigtown** *cultural region* SW Scotland, UK
99 I15 **Wigtown Bay** *bay* SW Scotland, UK
100 L13 **Wijchen** Gelderland, SE Netherlands 51.48N 5.43E
94 N1 **Wijdefjorden** *fjord* NW Svalbard
100 M10 **Wijhe** Overijssel, E Netherlands 52.22N 6.07E
100 J12 **Wijk bij Duurstede** Utrecht, C Netherlands 51.58N 5.21E
100 J13 **Wijk en Aalburg** Noord-Brabant, S Netherlands 51.46N 5.06E
101 H16 **Wijnegem** Antwerpen, N Belgium 51.13N 4.31E
12 E11 **Wikwemikong** Manitoulin Island, Ontario, S Canada 45.46N 81.43W
110 H7 **Wil** Sankt Gallen, NE Switzerland 47.28N 9.03E
31 R16 **Wilber** Nebraska, C USA 40.28N 96.57W
34 K8 **Wilbur** Washington, NW USA 47.45N 118.42W
29 Q11 **Wilburton** Oklahoma, C USA 34.55N 95.18W
190 M6 **Wilcannia** New South Wales, SE Australia 31.34S 143.23E
20 D12 **Wilcox** Pennsylvania, NE USA 41.34N 78.40W
Wilczek Land *see* Vil'cheka, Zemlya
111 U6 **Wildalpen** Steiermark, E Austria 47.40N 14.54E
33 O13 **Wildcat Creek** ⟿ Indiana, N USA
110 L9 **Wilde Kreuzspitze** *It.* Picco di Croce. ▲ Austria/Italy 46.53N 10.51E
Wildenschwert *see* Ústí nad Orlicí
100 O6 **Wildervank** Groningen, NE Netherlands 53.04N 6.52E
102 G11 **Wildeshausen** Niedersachsen, NW Germany 52.54N 8.26E
110 D10 **Wildhorn** ▲ SW Switzerland 46.21N 7.22E
9 R17 **Wild Horse** Alberta, SW Canada 49.00N 110.19W
29 N12 **Wildhorse Creek** ⟿ Oklahoma, C USA
30 L14 **Wild Horse Hill** ▲ Nebraska, C USA 41.52N 101.56W
111 W8 **Wildon** Steiermark, SE Austria 46.53N 15.29E
26 M2 **Wildorado** Texas, SW USA 35.12N 102.10W
31 R6 **Wild Rice River** ⟿ Minnesota/North Dakota, N USA
Wilejka *see* Vilyeyka
205 Y9 **Wilhelm II Coast** *physical region* Antarctica
205 X9 **Wilhelm II Land** *physical region* Antarctica
57 U11 **Wilhelmina Gebergte** ▲▲ C Suriname
20 B13 **Wilhelm, Lake** ▣ Pennsylvania, NE USA
194 I12 **Wilhelm, Mount** ▲ C PNG 5.51S 147.25E
94 O2 **Wilhelmøya** *island* C Svalbard
Wilhelm-Pieck-Stadt *see* Guben
111 W4 **Wilhelmsburg** Niederösterreich, E Austria 48.07N 15.36E
102 G10 **Wilhelmshaven** Niedersachsen, NW Germany 53.31N 8.07E
Wilia/Wilja *see* Neris
20 H13 **Wilkes Barre** Pennsylvania, NE USA 41.15N 75.49W
23 R9 **Wilkesboro** North Carolina, SE USA 36.09N 81.09W
205 W15 **Wilkes Coast** *physical region* Antarctica
201 W12 **Wilkes Island** *island* N Wake Island
205 X12 **Wilkes Land** *physical region* Antarctica
9 S15 **Wilkie** Saskatchewan, S Canada 52.27N 108.42W
204 I6 **Wilkins Ice Shelf** *ice shelf* Antarctica
190 D4 **Wilkinsons Lakes** *salt lake* South Australia
Wiłkomierz *see* Ukmergė
190 K11 **Willalooka** South Australia 36.24S 140.20E
34 G11 **Willamette River** ⟿ Oregon, NW USA
191 O8 **Willandra Billabong Creek** *seasonal river* New South Wales, SE Australia
34 F9 **Willapa Bay** *inlet* Washington, NW USA
29 T7 **Willard** Missouri, C USA 37.18N 93.25W
39 S12 **Willard** New Mexico, SW USA 34.36N 106.01W
33 S12 **Willard** Ohio, N USA 41.03N 82.43W
38 L1 **Willard** Utah, W USA 41.23N 112.01W
195 N11 **Willaumez Peninsula** *headland* New Britain, E PNG 5.03S 150.04E
39 N15 **Willcox** Arizona, SW USA 32.13N 109.49W
39 N16 **Willcox Playa** *salt flat* Arizona, SW USA
101 G17 **Willebroek** Antwerpen, C Belgium 51.04N 4.22E
47 P16 **Willemstad** ○ (Netherlands Antilles) Curaçao, Netherlands Antilles 12.06N 68.54W
101 G14 **Willemstad** Noord-Brabant, S Netherlands 51.40N 4.27E
9 S11 **William** ⟿ Saskatchewan, C Canada
25 O6 **William "Bill" Dannelly Reservoir** ▣ Alabama, S USA
190 G3 **William Creek** South Australia 28.55S 136.23E
189 T15 **William, Mount** ▲ South Australia
38 K11 **Williams** Arizona, SW USA 35.15N 112.11W
31 X14 **Williamsburg** Iowa, C USA 41.39N 92.00W
22 M8 **Williamsburg** Kentucky, S USA 36.43N 84.06W
33 R15 **Williamsburg** Ohio, N USA 39.00N 84.02W
23 X6 **Williamsburg** Virginia, NE USA 37.16N 76.41W
8 M15 **Williams Lake** British Columbia, SW Canada 52.07N 122.09W
23 P6 **Williamson** West Virginia, NE USA 37.40N 82.16W
33 N13 **Williamsport** Indiana, N USA 40.18N 87.18W
20 G13 **Williamsport** Pennsylvania, NE USA 41.13N 76.59W
23 W9 **Williamston** North Carolina, SE USA 35.51N 77.03W
23 P11 **Williamston** South Carolina, SE USA 34.37N 82.28W
22 M4 **Williamstown** Kentucky, S USA 38.38N 84.33W
20 L10 **Williamstown** Massachusetts, NE USA 42.41N 73.11W
20 J16 **Willingboro** New Jersey, NE USA 40.01N 74.52W
9 Q14 **Willingdon** Alberta, SW Canada 53.49N 112.08W
27 W10 **Willis** Texas, SW USA 30.25N 95.28W
110 F8 **Willisau** Luzern, W Switzerland 47.07N 8.00E
85 F24 **Williston** Northern Cape, W South Africa 31.19S 20.52E
25 V10 **Williston** Florida, SE USA 29.23N 82.27W
30 J3 **Williston** North Dakota, N USA 48.07N 103.37W
23 Q13 **Williston** South Carolina, SE USA 33.24N 81.25W
8 L12 **Williston Lake** ▣ British Columbia, W Canada
36 L5 **Willits** California, W USA 39.24N 123.22W
31 T8 **Willmar** Minnesota, N USA 45.07N 95.02W
8 K11 **Will, Mount** ▲ British Columbia, W Canada 57.31N 128.48W
33 T11 **Willoughby** Ohio, N USA 41.38N 81.24W
9 U17 **Willow Bunch** Saskatchewan, S Canada 49.30N 105.40W
34 J11 **Willow Creek** ⟿ Oregon, NW USA
41 R11 **Willow Lake** Alaska, USA 61.44N 150.02W
15 H7 **Willowlake** ⟿ Northwest Territories, NW Canada
85 H25 **Willowmore** Eastern Cape, S South Africa 33.18S 23.30E
32 L5 **Willow Reservoir** ▣ Wisconsin, N USA
37 N5 **Willows** California, W USA 39.28N 122.12W
29 V7 **Willow Springs** Missouri, C USA 36.59N 91.58W
190 I7 **Wilmington** South Australia 32.42S 138.08E
23 Y2 **Wilmington** Delaware, NE USA 39.45N 75.33W
23 V12 **Wilmington** North Carolina, SE USA 34.13N 77.57W
33 R14 **Wilmington** Ohio, N USA 39.27N 83.49W
22 M6 **Wilmore** Kentucky, S USA 37.51N 84.39W
31 R8 **Wilmot** South Dakota, N USA 45.24N 96.51W
Wilna/Wilno *see* Vilnius
103 G16 **Wilnsdorf** Nordrhein-Westfalen, W Germany 50.49N 8.06E
101 G16 **Wilrijk** Antwerpen, N Belgium 51.10N 4.24E
102 I10 **Wilseder Berg** *hill* NW Germany 53.10N 9.56E
69 Z12 **Wilshaw Ridge** *undersea feature* W Indian Ocean
23 V9 **Wilson** North Carolina, SE USA 35.42N 77.54W
27 N5 **Wilson** Texas, SW USA 33.21N 101.44W
190 A7 **Wilson Bluff** *headland* South Australia/Western Australia 31.41S 129.01E
37 Y7 **Wilson Creek Range** ▲▲ Nevada, W USA
25 O1 **Wilson Lake** ▣ Alabama, S USA
28 M4 **Wilson Lake** ▣ Kansas, SE USA
39 P7 **Wilson, Mount** ▲ Colorado, C USA 37.50N 107.59W
191 P13 **Wilsons Promontory** *peninsula* Victoria, SE Australia
31 Y14 **Wilton** Iowa, C USA 41.35N 91.01W
21 P7 **Wilton** Maine, NE USA 44.35N 70.15W
30 M5 **Wilton** North Dakota, N USA 47.09N 100.46W
99 L22 **Wiltshire** *cultural region* S England, UK
101 M23 **Wiltz** Diekirch, NW Luxembourg 49.58N 5.55E
188 K9 **Wiluna** Western Australia 26.34S 120.14E
101 M23 **Wilwerwiltz** Diekirch, NE Luxembourg 49.59N 6.00E
31 P5 **Wimbledon** North Dakota, N USA 47.08N 98.25W
44 K7 **Wina** *var.* Güina. Jinotega, N Nicaragua 13.58N 85.14W
33 O12 **Winamac** Indiana, N USA 41.03N 86.37W
83 G19 **Winam Gulf** *var.* Kavirondo Gulf. *gulf* SW Kenya
85 I22 **Winburg** Free State, C South Africa 28.31S 27.01E
21 N10 **Winchendon** Massachusetts, NE USA 42.41N 72.01W
12 M13 **Winchester** Ontario, SE Canada 45.07N 75.19W
99 M23 **Winchester** *hist.* Wintanceaster, *Lat.* Venta Belgarum. S England, UK 51.04N 1.19W
34 M10 **Winchester** Idaho, NW USA 46.13N 116.35W
32 J14 **Winchester** Illinois, N USA 39.37N 90.28W
33 Q13 **Winchester** Indiana, N USA 40.09N 84.58W
22 M5 **Winchester** Kentucky, S USA 37.59N 84.10W
20 M10 **Winchester** New Hampshire, NE USA 42.46N 72.21W
22 K10 **Winchester** Tennessee, S USA 35.11N 86.06W
23 V3 **Winchester** Virginia, NE USA 39.11N 78.09W
101 L22 **Wincrange** Diekirch, NW Luxembourg 50.03N 5.55E
8 I5 **Wind** ⟿ Yukon Territory, NW Canada
191 S8 **Windamere, Lake** ◎ New South Wales, SE Australia
Windau *see* Ventspils, Latvia
Windau *see* Venta, Latvia/Lithuania
20 D15 **Windber** Pennsylvania, NE USA 40.12N 78.47W
25 T3 **Winder** Georgia, SE USA 33.59N 83.43W
99 K15 **Windermere** NW England, UK 54.24N 2.54W
12 C7 **Windermere Lake** ◎ Ontario, S Canada
33 U11 **Windham** Ohio, N USA 41.14N 81.03W
85 D19 **Windhoek** *Ger.* Windhuk. ● (Namibia) Khomas, C Namibia 22.34S 17.06E
85 D20 **Windhoek** ✈ Khomas, C Namibia 22.31S 17.04E
Windhuk *see* Windhoek
13 O8 **Windigo** Quebec, SE Canada 47.45N 73.19W
13 O8 **Windigo** ⟿ Quebec, SE Canada
Windischfeistritz *see* Slovenska Bistrica
111 T6 **Windischgarsten** Oberösterreich, W Austria 47.42N 14.21E
Windischgraz *see* Slovenj Gradec
39 T16 **Wind Mountain** ▲ New Mexico, SW USA 32.01N 105.35W
31 T10 **Windom** Minnesota, N USA 43.52N 95.07W
39 Q7 **Windom Peak** ▲ Colorado, C USA 37.37N 107.35W
189 U9 **Windorah** Queensland, C Australia 25.25S 142.40E
39 O10 **Window Rock** Arizona, SW USA 35.40N 109.03W
33 N9 **Wind Point** *headland* Wisconsin, N USA 42.46N 87.46W
35 U14 **Wind River** ⟿ Wyoming, C USA
11 P15 **Windsor** Nova Scotia, SE Canada 44.58N 64.13W
12 C17 **Windsor** Ontario, S Canada 42.18N 83.00W
13 Q12 **Windsor** Quebec, SE Canada 45.34N 72.00W
99 N22 **Windsor** S England, UK 51.29N 0.39W
39 T3 **Windsor** Colorado, C USA 40.28N 104.54W
20 M12 **Windsor** Connecticut, NE USA 41.51N 72.38W
29 T5 **Windsor** Missouri, C USA 38.31N 93.31W
23 X9 **Windsor** North Carolina, SE USA 36.00N 76.57W
20 M12 **Windsor Locks** Connecticut, NE USA 41.55N 72.37W
27 R5 **Windthorst** Texas, SW USA 33.34N 98.26W
47 Z14 **Windward Islands** *island group* E West Indies
Windward Islands *see* Vent, Îles du, Archipel de la Société, French Polynesia
Windward Islands *see* Barlavento, Ilhas de, Cape Verde
46 K8 **Windward Passage** *Sp.* Paso de los Vientos. *channel* Cuba/Haiti
57 T9 **Wineperu** C Guyana 6.10N 58.34W
25 O3 **Winfield** Alabama, S USA 33.55N 87.49W
31 Y15 **Winfield** Iowa, C USA 41.07N 91.26W
29 O7 **Winfield** Kansas, C USA 37.14N 97.00W
27 W6 **Winfield** Texas, SW USA 33.10N 95.06W
23 Q4 **Winfield** West Virginia, NE USA 38.30N 81.54W
31 N5 **Wing** North Dakota, N USA 47.06N 100.16W
191 U7 **Wingham** New South Wales, SE Australia 31.52S 152.24E
10 G16 **Wingham** Ontario, S Canada 43.54N 81.19W
35 T8 **Winifred** Montana, NW USA 47.33N 109.26W
10 E9 **Winisk** ⟿ Ontario, S Canada
10 E8 **Winisk Lake** ◎ Ontario, C Canada
26 L8 **Wink** Texas, SW USA 31.45N 103.09W
38 M14 **Winkelman** Arizona, SW USA 32.59N 110.46W
9 X17 **Winkler** Manitoba, S Canada 49.12N 97.55W
111 Q9 **Winklern** Tirol, W Austria 46.54N 12.54E
Winkowitz *see* Vinkovci
34 G9 **Winlock** Washington, NW USA 46.29N 122.56W
79 P17 **Winneba** SE Ghana 5.22N 0.37W
31 U11 **Winnebago** Minnesota, N USA 43.46N 94.10W
31 R13 **Winnebago** Nebraska, C USA 42.14N 96.28W
32 M7 **Winnebago, Lake** ◎ Wisconsin, N USA
32 M7 **Winneconne** Wisconsin, N USA 44.07N 88.44W
37 T3 **Winnemucca** Nevada, W USA 40.58N 117.43W
37 R4 **Winnemucca Lake** ◎ Nevada, W USA
103 H21 **Winnenden** Baden-Württemberg, SW Germany 48.52N 9.22E
31 N11 **Winner** South Dakota, N USA 43.22N 99.51W
35 U9 **Winnett** Montana, NW USA 47.00N 108.18W
12 I9 **Winneway** Quebec, SE Canada 47.35N 78.33W
24 H6 **Winnfield** Louisiana, S USA 31.55N 92.38W
31 U4 **Winnibigoshish, Lake** ◎ Minnesota, N USA
27 X11 **Winnie** Texas, SW USA 29.49N 94.22W
9 Y16 **Winnipeg** Manitoba, S Canada 49.52N 97.10W
9 X16 **Winnipeg** ✈ Manitoba, S Canada 49.56N 97.16W
(0) J8 **Winnipeg** ⟿ Manitoba, S Canada
9 X16 **Winnipeg Beach** Manitoba, S Canada 50.25N 96.59W
9 W14 **Winnipeg, Lake** ◎ Manitoba, C Canada
9 W15 **Winnipegosis** Manitoba, S Canada 51.36N 99.59W
9 W15 **Winnipegosis, Lake** ◎ Manitoba, C Canada
21 O8 **Winnipesaukee, Lake** ◎ New Hampshire, NE USA
24 I6 **Winnsboro** Louisiana, S USA 32.09N 91.43W
23 R12 **Winnsboro** South Carolina, SE USA 34.22N 81.05W
27 W6 **Winnsboro** Texas, SW USA 33.01N 95.16W
31 X10 **Winona** Minnesota, N USA 44.03N 91.37W
24 L4 **Winona** Mississippi, S USA 33.30N 89.42W
29 W7 **Winona** Missouri, C USA 37.00N 91.19W
27 W7 **Winona** Texas, SW USA 32.29N 95.10W
20 M7 **Winooski River** ⟿ Vermont, NE USA
100 P6 **Winschoten** Groningen, NE Netherlands 53.09N 7.03E
102 J10 **Winsen** Niedersachsen, N Germany 53.22N 10.13E
38 M11 **Winslow** Arizona, SW USA 35.01N 110.42W
21 Q7 **Winslow** Maine, NE USA 44.33N 69.35W
20 M12 **Winsted** Connecticut, NE USA 41.55N 73.03W
34 F14 **Winston** Oregon, NW USA 43.07N 123.24W
23 S9 **Winston Salem** North Carolina, SE USA 36.06N 80.14W
100 N5 **Winsum** Groningen, NE Netherlands 53.19N 5.37E
Wintanceaster *see* Winchester
25 W11 **Winter Garden** Florida, SE USA 28.34N 81.35W
8 J16 **Winter Harbour** Vancouver Island, British Columbia, SW Canada 50.28N 128.03W
25 W12 **Winter Haven** Florida, SE USA 28.01N 81.43W
25 X11 **Winter Park** Florida, SE USA 28.36N 81.20W
27 P8 **Winters** Texas, SW USA 31.57N 99.57W
31 U15 **Winterset** Iowa, C USA 41.19N 94.00W
100 O12 **Winterswijk** Gelderland, E Netherlands 51.58N 6.43E
110 G6 **Winterthur** Zürich, NE Switzerland 47.30N 8.43E
31 U9 **Winthrop** Minnesota, N USA 44.32N 94.22W
34 J7 **Winthrop** Washington, NW USA 48.28N 120.13W
189 V7 **Winton** Queensland, E Australia 22.22S 143.04E
193 C24 **Winton** Southland, South Island, NZ 46.08S 168.19E
23 X8 **Winton** North Carolina, SE USA 36.22N 76.56W
103 K15 **Wipper** ⟿ C Germany
103 K14 **Wipper** ⟿ C Germany
Wipper *see* Wieprza
176 Vv9 **Wiriagar, Sungai** ⟿ Papua, E Indonesia
190 G6 **Wirraminna** South Australia 31.10S 136.13E
190 F4 **Wirrida** South Australia 29.34S 134.33E
190 F7 **Wirrulla** South Australia 32.27S 134.32E
Wirsitz *see* Wyrzysk
Wirz-See *see* Võrtsjärv
99 O19 **Wisbech** E England, UK 52.39N 0.08E
Wisby *see* Visby
21 Q8 **Wiscasset** Maine, NE USA 44.01N 69.40W
Wischau *see* Vyškov
32 J5 **Wisconsin** *off.* State of Wisconsin; also known as The Badger State. ◈ *state* N USA
32 L8 **Wisconsin Dells** Wisconsin, N USA 43.37N 89.43W
32 L8 **Wisconsin, Lake** ▣ Wisconsin, N USA
32 L7 **Wisconsin Rapids** Wisconsin, N USA 44.24N 89.49W
32 L7 **Wisconsin River** ⟿ Wisconsin, N USA
35 P11 **Wisdom** Montana, NW USA 45.36N 113.27W
23 P7 **Wise** Virginia, NE USA 36.58N 82.34W
41 Q7 **Wiseman** Alaska, USA 67.24N 150.06W
98 J12 **Wishaw** W Scotland, UK 55.46N 3.55W
31 O6 **Wishek** North Dakota, N USA 46.12N 99.33W
34 I11 **Wishram** Washington, NW USA 45.40N 120.53W
113 J17 **Wisła** Śląskie, S Poland 49.39N 18.49E
112 K11 **Wisła** *Eng.* Vistula, *Ger.* Weichsel. ⟿ C Poland
Wiślany, Zalew *see* Vistula Lagoon
113 M16 **Wisłoka** ⟿ SE Poland
102 L9 **Wismar** Mecklenburg-Vorpommern, N Germany 53.54N 11.28E
31 R14 **Wisner** Nebraska, C USA 41.59N 96.54W
105 V4 **Wissembourg** *var.* Weissenburg. Bas-Rhin, NE France 49.03N 7.57E
32 J6 **Wissota, Lake** ▣ Wisconsin, N USA
99 O18 **Witham** ⟿ E England, UK
99 O17 **Withernsea** E England, UK 53.45N 0.00W
39 Q13 **Withington, Mount** ▲ New Mexico, SW USA 33.52N 107.29W
25 U8 **Withlacoochee River** ⟿ Florida/Georgia, SE USA
112 H11 **Witkowo** Wielkopolskie, C Poland 52.27N 17.49E
99 M21 **Witney** S England, UK 51.47N 1.30W
103 E15 **Witten** Nordrhein-Westfalen, W Germany 51.25N 7.19E
103 N14 **Wittenberg** Sachsen-Anhalt, E Germany 51.52N 12.39E
32 L6 **Wittenberg** Wisconsin, N USA 44.53N 89.20W
102 L11 **Wittenberge** Brandenburg, N Germany 52.58N 11.45E
105 U7 **Wittenheim** Haut-Rhin, NE France 47.49N 7.19E
188 I7 **Wittenoom** Western Australia 22.17S 118.22E
Wittingau *see* Třeboň
102 K12 **Wittingen** Niedersachsen, C Germany 52.42N 10.43E
103 E18 **Wittlich** Rheinland-Pfalz, SW Germany 49.59N 6.54E
102 F9 **Wittmund** Niedersachsen, NW Germany 53.34N 7.46E
102 M10 **Wittstock** Brandenburg, NE Germany 53.09N 12.28E
194 M11 **Witu Islands** *island group* E PNG
112 O7 **Wiżajny** Podlaskie, NE Poland 54.21N 22.51E
57 W10 **W.J. van Blommesteinmeer** ▣ E Suriname
112 L11 **Wkra** *Ger.* Soldau. ⟿ C Poland
112 I6 **Władysławowo** Pomorskie, N Poland 54.48N 18.25E
Wlaschim *see* Vlašim
113 E14 **Wleń** *Ger.* Lähn. Dolnośląskie, SW Poland 51.00N 15.39E
112 J11 **Włocławek** *Ger./Rus.* Vlotslavsk. Kujawsko-pomorskie, C Poland 52.39N 19.02E
112 P13 **Włodawa** *Rus.* Vlodava. Lubelskie, SE Poland 51.33N 23.31E
Włodzimierz *see* Volodymyr-Volyns'kyy
113 K15 **Włoszczowa** Świętokrzyskie, C Poland 50.51N 19.58E
85 C19 **Wlotzkasbaken** Erongo, W Namibia 22.25S 14.30E
13 R12 **Woburn** Quebec, SE Canada 45.22N 70.52W
21 O11 **Woburn** Massachusetts, NE USA 42.28N 71.09W
Wocheiner Feistritz *see* Bohinjska Bistrica
Wöchma *see* Võhma
153 S11 **Wodil** *var.* Vuadil'. Farg'ona Viloyati, E Uzbekistan 40.10N 71.43E
189 V14 **Wodonga** Victoria, SE Australia 36.10S 146.55E
113 I17 **Wodzisław Śląski** *Ger.* Loslau. Śląskie, S Poland 49.59N 18.27E
100 I11 **Woerden** Zuid-Holland, C Netherlands 52.06N 4.54E
100 I8 **Wognum** Noord-Holland, NW Netherlands 52.40N 5.01E
Wohlau *see* Wołów
110 F7 **Wohlen** Aargau, NW Switzerland 47.21N 8.16E
205 R2 **Wohlthat Mountains** ▲▲ Antarctica
176 W9 **Woinui, Selat** *strait* Papua, E Indonesia
194 K15 **Woitape** Central, S PNG 8.35S 147.15E
Wōjjā *see* Wotje Atoll
Wojwodina *see* Vojvodina
176 W13 **Wokam, Pulau** *island* Kepulauan Aru, E Indonesia
99 N22 **Woking** SE England, UK 51.19N 0.34W
Woldenberg Neumark *see* Dobiegniew
196 K15 **Woleai Atoll** *atoll* Caroline Islands, W Micronesia
Woleu *see* Uolo, Río
81 E17 **Woleu-Ntem** *off.* Province du Woleu-Ntem, *var.* Le Woleu-Ntem. ◈ *province* W Gabon
34 F15 **Wolf Creek** Oregon, NW USA 42.40N 123.22W
28 K9 **Wolf Creek** ⟿ Oklahoma/Texas, SW USA
39 R7 **Wolf Creek Pass** *pass* Colorado, C USA 37.28N 106.48W
21 O9 **Wolfeboro** New Hampshire, NE USA 43.34N 71.10W
27 U5 **Wolfe City** Texas, SW USA 33.22N 96.04W
12 L15 **Wolfe Island** *island* Ontario, SE Canada
103 M14 **Wolfen** Sachsen-Anhalt, E Germany 51.40N 12.16E
102 J13 **Wolfenbüttel** Niedersachsen, C Germany 52.10N 10.31E
111 T4 **Wolfern** Oberösterreich, N Austria 48.06N 14.16E
111 Q6 **Wolfgangsee** *var.* Abersee, St Wolfgangsee. ◎ N Austria
41 P9 **Wolf Mountain** ▲ Alaska, USA 65.20N 154.08W
35 X7 **Wolf Point** Montana, NW USA 48.04N 105.40W
24 L8 **Wolf River** ⟿ Mississippi, S USA
32 M7 **Wolf River** ⟿ Wisconsin, N USA
111 U9 **Wolfsberg** Kärnten, SE Austria 46.49N 14.49E
102 K12 **Wolfsburg** Niedersachsen, N Germany 52.25N 10.46E
59 B17 **Wolf, Volcán** ⛰ Galapagos Islands, Ecuador, E Pacific Ocean 0.01N 91.22W
102 O8 **Wolgast** Mecklenburg-Vorpommern, NE Germany 54.03N 13.47E
110 F8 **Wolhusen** Luzern, W Switzerland 47.04N 8.06E
112 D8 **Wolin** *Ger.* Wollin. Zachodniopomorskie, NW Poland 53.52N 14.34E
111 Y3 **Wolkersdorf** Niederösterreich, NE Austria 48.24N 16.31E
Wołkowysk *see* Vawkavysk
Wöllan *see* Velenje
15 I2 **Wollaston, Cape** *headland* Victoria Island, Northwest Territories, NW Canada 71.00N 118.21W
65 J25 **Wollaston, Isla** *island* S Chile
9 U11 **Wollaston Lake** Saskatchewan, C Canada 58.04N 103.37W
9 T10 **Wollaston Lake** ◎ Saskatchewan, C Canada
15 I3 **Wollaston Peninsula** *peninsula* Victoria Island, Northwest Territories/Nunavut, NW Canada
Wollin *see* Wolin
191 S9 **Wollongong** New South Wales, SE Australia 34.25S 150.52E
Wolmar *see* Valmiera
102 L13 **Wolmirstedt** Sachsen-Anhalt, C Germany 52.15N 11.37E
112 M11 **Wołomin** Mazowieckie, C Poland 52.21N 21.15E
112 G13 **Wołów** *Ger.* Wohlau. Dolnośląskie, SW Poland 51.21N 16.39E
Wołożyn *see* Valozhyn
12 G11 **Wolseley Bay** Ontario, S Canada 46.05N 80.16W
31 P10 **Wolsey** South Dakota, N USA 44.22N 98.28W
112 F12 **Wolsztyn** Wielkopolskie, W Poland 52.06N 16.06E
100 M7 **Wolvega** *Fris.* Wolvegea. Friesland, N Netherlands 52.53N 6.00E
Wolvegea *see* Wolvega
99 K19 **Wolverhampton** C England, UK 52.36N 2.07W
Wolverine State *see* Michigan
101 G18 **Wolvertem** Vlaams Brabant, C Belgium 50.55N 4.19E
101 H16 **Wommelgem** Antwerpen, N Belgium 51.12N 4.31E
176 W11 **Wondiwoi, Pegunungan** ▲▲ Papua, E Indonesia
194 J13 **Wonenara** *var.* Wonerara. Eastern Highlands, C PNG 6.46S 145.54E
Wonerara *see* Wonenara
Wongalara Lake *see* Wongalarroo Lake
191 N6 **Wongalarroo Lake** *var.* Wongalara Lake. *seasonal lake* New South Wales, SE Australia
169 Y15 **Wŏnju** *Jap.* Genshū. N South Korea 37.21N 127.57E
8 M12 **Wonowon** British Columbia, W Canada 56.46N 121.54W
169 X13 **Wŏnsan** SE North Korea 39.11N 127.21E
191 O13 **Wonthaggi** Victoria, SE Australia 38.37S 145.39E
25 N2 **Woodall Mountain** ▲ Mississippi, S USA 34.47N 88.14W
25 W7 **Woodbine** Georgia, SE USA 30.58N 81.43W
31 S14 **Woodbine** Iowa, C USA 41.44N 95.42W
20 J17 **Woodbine** New Jersey, NE USA 39.12N 74.47W
23 W4 **Woodbridge** Virginia, NE USA 38.39N 77.14W
191 V4 **Woodburn** New South Wales, SE Australia 29.07S 153.23E
34 G11 **Woodburn** Oregon, NW USA 45.08N 122.51W
22 K9 **Woodbury** Tennessee, S USA 35.49N 86.04W
191 V5 **Wooded Bluff** *headland* New South Wales, SE Australia 29.24S 153.22E
191 V3 **Woodenbong** New South Wales, SE Australia 28.24S 152.39E
37 R11 **Woodlake** California, W USA 36.24N 119.06W
37 N7 **Woodland** California, W USA 38.39N 121.46W
21 T5 **Woodland** Maine, NE USA 45.10N 67.25W
34 G10 **Woodland** Washington, NW USA 45.54N 122.44W
39 T5 **Woodland Park** Colorado, C USA 38.59N 105.03W
195 P15 **Woodlark Island** *var.* Murua Island. *island* SE PNG
Woodle Island *see* Kuria
9 T17 **Wood Mountain** ▲▲ Saskatchewan, S Canada
32 K15 **Wood River** Illinois, N USA 38.51N 90.06W
31 P16 **Wood River** Nebraska, C USA 40.48N 98.33W
41 R9 **Wood River** ⟿ Alaska, USA
41 O13 **Wood River Lakes** *lakes* Alaska, USA
190 C1 **Woodroffe, Mount** ▲ South Australia 26.19S 131.42E
23 P11 **Woodruff** South Carolina, SE USA 34.44N 82.02W
32 K4 **Woodruff** Wisconsin, N USA 45.55N 89.41W
27 T14 **Woodsboro** Texas, SW USA 28.14N 97.19W
33 U13 **Woodsfield** Ohio, N USA 39.45N 81.07W
189 P4 **Woods, Lake** ◎ Northern Territory, N Australia
9 Z16 **Woods, Lake of the** *Fr.* Lac des Bois. ◎ Canada/USA
27 Q6 **Woodson** Texas, SW USA 33.00N 99.01W
11 N14 **Woodstock** New Brunswick, SE Canada 46.10N 67.37W
12 F16 **Woodstock** Ontario, S Canada 43.07N 80.46W
32 M10 **Woodstock** Illinois, N USA 42.18N 88.27W
20 M9 **Woodstock** Vermont, NE USA 43.37N 72.33W

◆ COUNTRY
● COUNTRY CAPITAL
◇ DEPENDENT TERRITORY
○ DEPENDENT TERRITORY CAPITAL
◈ ADMINISTRATIVE REGION
✈ INTERNATIONAL AIRPORT
▲ MOUNTAIN
▲▲ MOUNTAIN RANGE
⛰ VOLCANO
⟿ RIVER
◎ LAKE
▣ RESERVOIR

23 U4 **Woodstock** Virginia, NE USA 38.51N 78.28W
21 N8 **Woodsville** New Hampshire, NE USA 44.07N 72.01W
192 M12 **Woodville** Manawatu-Wanganui, North Island, NZ 40.21S 175.58E
24 J7 **Woodville** Mississippi, S USA 31.06N 91.18W
27 X9 **Woodville** Texas, SW USA 30.46N 94.25W
28 K9 **Woodward** Oklahoma, C USA 36.25N 99.23W
31 O5 **Woodworth** North Dakota, N USA 47.06N 99.19W
176 Y12 **Woogi** Papua, E Indonesia 3.59S 138.45E
176 Ww9 **Wool** Papua, E Indonesia 1.38S 135.34E
191 V5 **Woolgoolga** New South Wales, E Australia 30.04S 153.09E
190 H6 **Woomera** South Australia 31.12S 136.52E
21 O12 **Woonsocket** Rhode Island, NE USA 41.58N 71.27W
31 P10 **Woonsocket** South Dakota, N USA 44.03N 98.16W
33 T12 **Wooster** Ohio, N USA 40.48N 81.56W
82 L12 **Woqooyi Galbeed** off. Gobolka Woqooyi Galbeed. ◈ region NW Somalia
110 E8 **Worb** Bern, C Switzerland 46.54N 7.36E
85 F26 **Worcester** Western Cape, SW South Africa 33.40S 19.22E
99 L20 **Worcester** hist. Wigorna Ceaster. W England, UK 52.10N 2.13W
21 N11 **Worcester** Massachusetts, NE USA 42.17N 71.48W
99 L20 **Worcestershire** cultural region C England, UK
34 H16 **Worden** Oregon, NW USA 42.04N 121.50W
111 O6 **Wörgl** Tirol, W Austria 47.28N 12.04E
176 Ww14 **Workai, Pulau** island Kepulauan Aru, E Indonesia
99 J15 **Workington** NW England, UK 54.39N 3.33W
100 K7 **Workum** Friesland, N Netherlands 52.58N 5.25E
35 V13 **Worland** Wyoming, C USA 44.01N 107.57W
Wormatia see Worms
101 N25 **Wormeldange** Grevenmacher, E Luxembourg 49.37N 6.25E
100 I9 **Wormer** Noord-Holland, C Netherlands 52.30N 4.49E
103 G19 **Worms** anc. Augusta Vangionum, Borbetomagus, Wormatia. Rheinland-Pfalz, SW Germany 49.37N 8.22E
Worms see Vormsi
103 K21 **Wörnitz** ~ S Germany
103 G21 **Wörth** Rheinland-Pfalz, SW Germany 49.04N 8.16E
27 U8 **Wortham** Texas, SW USA 31.47N 96.27W
111 S9 **Wörther See** ◎ S Austria
99 O23 **Worthing** SE England, UK 50.48N 0.22W
31 S11 **Worthington** Minnesota, N USA 43.37N 95.36W
33 S13 **Worthington** Ohio, N USA 40.05N 83.01W
37 W8 **Worthington Peak** ▲ Nevada, W USA 37.57N 115.32W
176 Y12 **Wosi** Papua, E Indonesia 3.55S 138.54E
176 W11 **Wosimi** Papua, E Indonesia 2.44S 134.34E
201 R5 **Wotho Atoll** var. Wōtto. atoll Ralik Chain, W Marshall Islands
201 V5 **Wotje Atoll** var. Wōjjā. atoll Ratak Chain, E Marshall Islands
Wotoe see Wotu
Wottawa see Otava
Wōtto see Wotho Atoll
175 Pp10 **Wotu** prev. Wotoe. Sulawesi, C Indonesia 2.34S 120.46E
100 K11 **Woudenberg** Utrecht, C Netherlands 52.04N 5.25E
100 I13 **Woudrichem** Noord-Brabant, S Netherlands 51.49N 5.00E
45 N8 **Wounta** var. Huaunta. Región Autónoma Atlántico Norte, NE Nicaragua 13.33N 83.31W
175 R12 **Wowoni, Pulau** island C Indonesia
175 Qq12 **Wowoni, Selat** strait Sulawesi, C Indonesia
83 J17 **Woyamdero Plain** plain E Kenya
Woyens see Vojens
Wozrojdeniye Oroli see Vozrozhdeniya, Ostrov
Wrangel Island see Vrangelya, Ostrov
41 Y13 **Wrangell** Wrangell Island, Alaska, USA 56.28N 132.22W
40 C15 **Wrangell, Cape** headland Attu Island, Alaska, USA 52.55N 172.28E
41 S11 **Wrangell, Mount** ▲ Alaska, USA 62.00N 144.01W
41 T11 **Wrangell Mountains** ▲▲ Alaska, USA
207 S7 **Wrangel Plain** undersea feature Arctic Ocean
98 H6 **Wrath, Cape** headland N Scotland, UK 58.37N 5.01W
39 W3 **Wray** Colorado, C USA 40.01N 102.12W
46 K13 **Wreck Point** headland C Jamaica 17.50N 76.55W
85 C23 **Wreck Point** headland W South Africa 28.52S 16.17E
25 V4 **Wrens** Georgia, SE USA 33.12N 82.23W
99 K18 **Wrexham** NE Wales, UK 53.03N 3.00W
29 R13 **Wright City** Oklahoma, C USA 34.03N 95.00W
204 J12 **Wright Island** island Antarctica
11 N9 **Wright, Mont** ▲ Quebec, E Canada 52.36N 67.40W
27 X5 **Wright Patman Lake** ◎ Texas, SW USA
38 M16 **Wrightson, Mount** ▲ Arizona, SW USA 31.42N 110.51W
25 U5 **Wrightsville** Georgia, SE USA 32.43N 82.43W
23 W12 **Wrightsville Beach** North Carolina, SE USA 34.12N 77.48W
37 T15 **Wrightwood** California, W USA 34.21N 117.37W
15 Gg7 **Wrigley** Northwest Territories, W Canada 63.16N 123.39W
113 G14 **Wrocław** Eng./Ger. Breslau. Dolnośląskie, SW Poland 51.06N 17.01E
112 F10 **Wronki** Ger. Fronicken. Wielkopolskie, NW Poland 52.42N 16.21E
112 H11 **Września** Wielkolpolskie, C Poland 52.19N 17.33E
112 F12 **Wschowa** Lubuskie, W Poland 51.48N 16.18E
Wsetin see Vsetín
188 I12 **Wubin** Western Australia 30.05S 116.43E
169 W9 **Wuchang** Heilongjiang, NE China 44.55N 127.13E
Wuchang see Wuhan
Wu-chou/Wuchow see Wuzhou
166 M16 **Wuchuan** var. Meilu. Guangdong, S China 21.30N 110.40E
166 K10 **Wuchuan** prev. Duru. Guizhou, S China 28.40N 108.04E
169 O13 **Wuchuan** Nei Mongol Zizhiqu, N China 41.04N 111.28E
169 V6 **Wudalianchi** Heilongjiang, NE China 48.40N 126.06E
165 O11 **Wudaoliang** Qinghai, C China 35.16N 93.03E
147 Q13 **Wuday'ah** spring/well S Saudi Arabia 17.03N 47.06E
79 V13 **Wudil** Kano, N Nigeria 11.46N 8.49E
166 G12 **Wuding** Yunnan, SW China 25.31N 102.24E
166 L4 **Wuding He** ~ C China
190 G8 **Wudinna** South Australia 33.06S 135.30E
163 P10 **Wudu** Gansu, C China 33.22N 105.01E
166 L9 **Wufeng** Hubei, C China 30.09N 110.31E
167 O11 **Wugong Shan** ▲▲ S China
163 P7 **Wuhai** Nei Mongol Zizhiqu, N China 39.40N 106.48E
167 O9 **Wuhan** var. Han-kou, Han-k'ou, Hanyang, Wuchang, Wu-han; prev. Hankow. Hubei, C China 30.34N 114.19E
167 Q7 **Wuhe** Anhui, E China 33.10N 117.50E
Wuhsi/Wu-hsi see Wuxi
Wuhsien see Suzhou
167 Q8 **Wuhu** var. Wu-na-mu. Anhui, E China 31.22N 118.25E
Wūjae see Ujae Atoll
166 K11 **Wu Jiang** ~ C China
Wujlān see Ujelang Atoll
79 W15 **Wukari** Taraba, E Nigeria 7.51N 9.49E
166 H11 **Wulian Feng** ▲▲ SW China
166 F13 **Wuliang Shan** ▲▲ SW China
176 U15 **Wuliaru, Pulau** island Kepulauan Tanimbar, E Indonesia
166 K11 **Wuling Shan** ▲▲ S China
111 Y5 **Wulka** ~ E Austria
Wulkan see Vulcan
111 T3 **Wullowitz** Oberösterreich, N Austria 48.37N 14.27E
Wu-lu-k'o-mu-shi/Wu-lu-mu-ch'i see Ürümqi
81 D14 **Wum** Nord-Ouest, NE Cameroon 6.24N 10.04E
166 H12 **Wumeng Shan** ▲▲ SW China
166 K14 **Wuming** Guangxi Zhuangzu Zizhiqu, S China 23.12N 108.16E
102 I10 **Wümme** ~ NW Germany
Wu-na-mu see Wuhu
176 Y11 **Wunen** Papua, E Indonesia 3.40S 138.31E
10 D9 **Wunnummin Lake** ◎ Ontario, C Canada
82 D13 **Wun Rog** Warab, S Sudan 09.00N 28.20E
103 M18 **Wunsiedel** Bayern, E Germany 50.02N 12.00E
102 I12 **Wunstorf** Niedersachsen, NW Germany 52.25N 9.25E
177 G3 **Wuntho** Sagaing, N Myanmar 23.52N 95.43E
103 F15 **Wupper** ~ W Germany
103 E15 **Wuppertal** prev. Barmen-Elberfeld. Nordrhein-Westfalen, W Germany 51.16N 7.12E
166 K5 **Wuqi** Shaanxi, C China 36.55N 108.13E
167 P4 **Wuqiao** var. Sangyuan. Hebei, E China 37.40N 116.21E
103 L23 **Würm** ~ SE Germany
79 T12 **Wurno** Sokoto, NW Nigeria 13.15N 5.24E
103 I19 **Würzburg** Bayern, SW Germany 49.48N 9.55E
103 N15 **Wurzen** Sachsen, E Germany 51.21N 12.48E
166 L9 **Wu Shan** ▲▲ C China
164 G7 **Wushi** var. Uqturpan. Xinjiang Uygur Zizhiqu, NW China 41.07N 79.09E
Wusih see Wuxi
67 N18 **Wüst Seamount** undersea feature S Atlantic Ocean 32.00S 0.06E
Wusuli Jiang/Wusuri see Ussuri
167 N3 **Wutai Shan** ▲ C China 39.00N 114.00E
166 H10 **Wutongqiao** Sichuan, C China 29.24N 103.54E
165 P6 **Wutongwozi Quan** spring NW China 42.30N 95.21E
194 E9 **Wutung** Sandaun, NW PNG 2.39S 141.01E
101 H15 **Wuustwezel** Antwerpen, N Belgium 51.24N 4.34E
194 G8 **Wuvulu Island** island NW PNG
165 U9 **Wuwei** var. Liangzhou. Gansu, C China 38.02N 102.30E
167 R8 **Wuxi** var. Wuhsi, Wu-hsi, Wusih. Jiangsu, E China 31.34N 120.19E
Wuxing see Huzhou
166 L14 **Wuxuan** Guangxi Zhuangzu Zizhiqu, S China 23.40N 109.41E
166 K11 **Wuyang He** ~ S China
169 X6 **Wuyiling** Heilongjiang, NE China 48.36N 129.24E
167 Q12 **Wuyi Shan** ▲▲ SE China
167 Q11 **Wuyishan** prev. Chong'an. Fujian, SE China 27.48N 118.03E
168 M13 **Wuyuan** Nei Mongol Zizhiqu, N China 41.04N 108.15E
166 L17 **Wuzhishan** prev. Tongshi. Hainan, S China 18.37N 109.34E
166 L17 **Wuzhi Shan** ▲ S China 18.52N 109.36E
165 W8 **Wuzhong** Ningxia, N China 37.58N 106.09E
166 M14 **Wuzhou** var. Wu-chou, Wuchow. Guangxi Zhuangzu Zizhiqu, S China 23.30N 111.19E
20 H12 **Wyalusing** Pennsylvania, NE USA 41.40N 76.13W
190 M10 **Wycheproof** Victoria, SE Australia 36.06S 143.13E
99 K21 **Wye** Wel. Gwy. ~ England/Wales, UK
Wyłkowyszki see Vilkaviškis
99 P19 **Wymondham** E England, UK 52.29N 1.10E
31 R17 **Wymore** Nebraska, C USA 40.07N 96.39W
190 E5 **Wynbring** South Australia 30.34S 133.27E
189 N3 **Wyndham** Western Australia 15.28S 128.07E
31 R6 **Wyndmere** North Dakota, N USA 46.16N 97.07W
29 X11 **Wynne** Arkansas, C USA 35.13N 90.47W
29 N12 **Wynnewood** Oklahoma, C USA 34.39N 97.09W
191 O15 **Wynyard** Tasmania, SE Australia 40.57S 145.33E
9 U15 **Wynyard** Saskatchewan, S Canada 51.46N 104.10W
35 V11 **Wyola** Montana, NW USA 45.07N 107.23W
190 A4 **Wyola Lake** salt lake South Australia
33 P9 **Wyoming** Michigan, N USA 42.54N 85.42W
35 V14 **Wyoming** off. State of Wyoming; also known as The Equality State. ◈ state C USA
35 S15 **Wyoming Range** ▲▲ Wyoming, C USA
191 T8 **Wyong** New South Wales, SE Australia 33.18S 151.27E
112 G9 **Wyrzysk** Ger. Wirsitz. Wielkopolskie, C Poland 53.09N 17.15E
Wysg see Usk
112 O10 **Wysokie Mazowieckie** Łomża, E Poland 52.54N 22.34E
112 M11 **Wyszków** Ger. Probstberg. Mazowieckie, C Poland 52.36N 21.27E
112 L11 **Wyszogród** Mazowieckie, C Poland 52.24N 20.14E
23 R7 **Wytheville** Virginia, NE USA 36.57N 81.05W

X

82 Q12 **Xaafuun** It. Hafun. Bari, NE Somalia 10.25N 51.17E
82 Q12 **Xaafuun, Raas** var. Ras Hafun. headland NE Somalia 10.36N 51.09E
Xábia see Jávea
44 C4 **Xaclbal, Río** var. Xalbal. ~ Guatemala/Mexico
143 Y10 **Xaçmaz** Rus. Khachmas. N Azerbaijan 41.26N 48.46E
82 O12 **Xadeed** var. Haded. physical region N Somalia
165 O14 **Xagquka** Xizang Zizhiqu, W China 31.46N 92.46E
178 I6 **Xai** var. Muang Xay, Muong Sai. Oudômxai, N Laos 20.41N 102.00E
164 F10 **Xaidulla** Xinjiang Uygur Zizhiqu, W China 36.27N 77.46E
178 I7 **Xaignabouli** prev. Muang Xaignabouri, Fr. Sayaboury. Xaignabouli, N Laos 19.16N 101.43E
178 J7 **Xai Lai Leng, Phou** ▲ Laos/Vietnam 19.13N 104.09E
164 L15 **Xainza** Xizang Zizhiqu, W China 30.54N 88.36E
164 L16 **Xaitongmoin** Xizang Zizhiqu, W China 29.27N 88.13E
85 M20 **Xai-Xai** prev. João Belo, Vila de João Bel. Gaza, S Mozambique 25.00S 33.37E
Xalbal see Xaclbal, Río
82 P13 **Xalin** Nugaal, N Somalia 9.16N 49.00E
152 H7 **Xalqobod** Rus. Khalkabad. Qoraqalpog'iston Respublikasi, W Uzbekistan 42.42N 59.46E
178 J6 **Xam Nua** var. Sam Neua. Houaphan, N Laos 20.24N 104.03E
84 D11 **Xá-Muteba** Port. Cinco de Outubro. Lunda Norte, NE Angola 9.31S 17.46E
85 C16 **Xangongo** Port. Rocadas. Cunene, SW Angola 16.41S 14.58E
143 W12 **Xankändi** Rus. Khankendi; prev. Stepanakert. SW Azerbaijan 39.50N 46.44E
143 V11 **Xanlar** Rus. Khanlar. NW Azerbaijan 40.37N 46.18E
116 J13 **Xánthi** Anatolikí Makedonía kai Thráki, NE Greece 41.09N 24.54E
62 H13 **Xanxerê** Santa Catarina, S Brazil 26.52S 52.25W
83 O15 **Xarardheere** Mudug, E Somalia 4.45N 47.54E
133 W8 **Xar Moron** ~ NE China
Xarra see Xarrë
115 L23 **Xarrë** var. Xarra. Vlorë, S Albania 39.45N 20.01E
84 D12 **Xassengue** Lunda Sul, NW Angola 10.28S 18.32E
107 S11 **Xàtiva** var. Jativa; anc. Setabis. País Valenciano, E Spain 39.00N 0.32W
Xauen see Chefchaouen
62 K10 **Xavantes, Represa de** var. Represa de Chavantes. ⊠ S Brazil
164 I7 **Xayar** Xinjiang Uygur Zizhiqu, W China 41.16N 82.52E
Xäzär Dänizi see Caspian Sea
178 Jj9 **Xé Bangfai** ~ C Laos
178 Jj10 **Xé Banghiang** var. Bang Hieng. ~ S Laos
Xégar see Tingri
33 R14 **Xenia** Ohio, N USA 39.40N 83.55W
Xeres see Jeréz de la Frontera
117 E15 **Xeriás** ~ C Greece
117 G17 **Xeró** ▲ Évvoia, C Greece 38.52N 23.18E
85 H18 **Xhumo** Central, C Botswana 21.13S 24.37E
167 N15 **Xiachuan Dao** island S China
Xiacun see Rushan
Xiaguan see Dali
165 U11 **Xiahe** var. Labrang. Gansu, C China 35.12N 102.28E
167 Q13 **Xiamen** var. Hsia-men; prev. Amoy. Fujian, SE China 24.28N 118.04E
166 L6 **Xi'an** var. Changan, Sian, Signan, Siking, Singan, Xian. Shaanxi, C China 34.16N 108.54E
166 L10 **Xianfeng** Hubei, C China 29.39N 109.07E
Xiang see Hunan
167 N7 **Xiangcheng** Henan, C China 33.52N 113.29E
166 F10 **Xiangcheng** prev. Qagchêng. Sichuan, C China 28.52N 99.45E
166 M8 **Xiangfan** var. Xiangyang. Hubei, C China 32.07N 112.00E
167 N10 **Xiang Jiang** ~ S China
Xiangkhoang see Pèk
178 Ii7 **Xiangkhoang, Plateau de** var. Plain of Jars. plateau N Laos
167 N11 **Xiangtan** var. Hsiang-t'an, Siangtan. Hunan, S China 27.52N 112.54E
167 N11 **Xiangxiang** Hunan, S China 27.50N 112.31E
Xiangyang see Xiangfan
167 S10 **Xianju** Zhejiang, SE China 28.53N 120.41E
166 F8 **Xianshui He** ~ C China
167 N9 **Xiantao** var. Mianyang. Hubei, C China 30.19N 113.31E
167 R10 **Xianxia Ling** ▲▲ SE China
166 K6 **Xianyang** Shaanxi, C China 34.23N 118.40E
164 L5 **Xiaocaohu** Xinjiang Uygur Zizhiqu, W China 43.43N 90.07E
169 W6 **Xiao Hinggan Ling** Eng. Lesser Khingan Range. ▲▲ NE China
166 M6 **Xiao Shan** ▲▲ C China
166 M12 **Xiao Shui** ~ S China
167 P6 **Xiaoxian** var. Xiao Xian. Anhui, E China 34.12N 116.55E
166 G11 **Xichang** Sichuan, C China 27.52N 102.16E
43 P11 **Xicoténcatl** Tamaulipas, C Mexico 22.59N 98.54W
Xieng Khouang see Pèk
Xieng Ngeun see Muong Xiang Ngeun
165 X10 **Xifeng** Gansu, C China 35.46N 107.35E
166 J11 **Xifeng** Guizhou, S China 27.15N 106.44E
Xigang see Helan
164 L16 **Xigazê** var. Jih-k'a-tse, Shigatse, Xigaze. Xizang Zizhiqu, W China 29.18N 88.49E
166 I8 **Xi He** ~ C China
165 W11 **Xihe** Gansu, C China 34.00N 105.24E
Xihuachi see Heshui
165 Q7 **Xijan Quan** spring NW China 40.52N 96.31E
165 W10 **Xiji** Ningxia, N China 36.02N 105.33E
166 M14 **Xi Jiang** var. Hsi Chiang, Eng. West River. ~ S China
166 K15 **Xijin Shuiku** ⊠ S China
Xilagani see Xylagani
166 I13 **Xilin** prev. Bada. Guangxi Zhuangzu Zizhiqu, S China 24.30N 105.00E
169 Q10 **Xilinhot** var. Silinhot. Nei Mongol Zizhiqu, N China 43.58N 116.06E
Xilokastro see Xylókastro
Xin see Xinjiang Uygur Zizhiqu
167 R10 **Xin'anjiang Shuiku** ⊠ SE China
Xin'anzhen see Xinyi
169 Q7 **Xin Barag Youqi** var. Altan Emel. Nei Mongol Zizhiqu, N China 48.37N 116.40E
169 R7 **Xin Barag Zuoqi** var. Amgalang. Nei Mongol Zizhiqu, N China 48.12N 118.15E
169 W12 **Xinbin** Liaoning, NE China 41.39N 125.04E
167 O7 **Xincai** Henan, C China 32.46N 114.54E
165 V8 **Xincheng** var. Yinchuanzhan. Ningxia, N China 38.27N 106.04E
167 O13 **Xinfeng** Jiangxi, S China 25.30N 114.52E
167 O14 **Xinfengjiang Shuiku** ⊠ S China
169 T13 **Xingcheng** Liaoning, NE China 40.38N 120.47E
84 E11 **Xinge** Lunda Norte, NE Angola 9.44S 19.10E
167 P12 **Xingguo** Jiangxi, S China 26.25N 115.22E
165 S11 **Xinghai** Qinghai, C China 35.12N 102.28E
167 R7 **Xinghua** Jiangsu, E China 32.54N 119.48E
Xingkai Hu see Khanka, Lake
167 P13 **Xingning** Guangdong, S China 24.13N 115.38E
166 I13 **Xingren** Guizhou, S China 25.25N 105.07E
167 O4 **Xingtai** Hebei, E China 37.07N 114.28E
61 J14 **Xingu, Rio** ~ C Brazil
165 P6 **Xingxingxia** Xinjiang Uygur Zizhiqu, NW China 41.48N 95.01E
166 I13 **Xingyi** Guizhou, S China 25.04N 104.51E
164 I6 **Xinhe** var. Toksu. Xinjiang Uygur Zizhiqu, NW China 41.34N 82.30E
Xin Hot see Abag Qi
165 T10 **Xining** var. Hsining, Hsi-ning, Sining. province capital Qinghai, C China 36.37N 101.46E
167 O4 **Xinji** prev. Shulu. Hebei, E China 37.55N 115.14E
167 P10 **Xinjian** Jiangxi, S China 28.42N 115.43E
Xinjiang see Xinjiang Uygur Zizhiqu
168 D8 **Xinjiang Uygur Zizhiqu** var. Sinkiang, Sinkiang Ughur Autonomous Region, Xin, Xinjiang. ◈ autonomous region NW China
166 H9 **Xinjin** Sichuan, C China 30.24N 103.48E
Xinjin see Pulandian
169 U12 **Xinmin** Liaoning, NE China 41.58N 122.51E
166 M12 **Xinning** Hunan, S China 26.34N 110.57E
Xinpu see Lianyungang
167 P5 **Xinwen** prev. Suncun. Shandong, E China 35.49N 117.36E
Xin Xian see Xinzhou
167 N6 **Xinxiang** Henan, C China 35.13N 113.48E
167 O8 **Xinyang** var. Hsin-yang, Sinyang. Henan, C China 32.09N 114.04E
167 Q6 **Xinyi** var. Xin'anzhen. Jiangsu, E China 34.25N 118.19E
167 Q6 **Xinyi He** ~ E China
167 O11 **Xinyu** Jiangxi, S China 27.51N 115.00E
164 I5 **Xinyuan** var. Künes. Xinjiang Uygur Zizhiqu, NW China 43.25N 83.12E
Xinyuan see Tianjun
168 M14 **Xinzhao Shan** ▲ N China 39.37N 107.51E
167 N3 **Xinzhou** var. Xin Xian. Shanxi, C China 38.24N 112.43E
106 H4 **Xinzo de Limia** Galicia, NW Spain 42.04N 7.45W
Xions see Książ Wielkopolski
167 O7 **Xiping** Henan, C China 33.22N 114.00E
165 T11 **Xiqing Shan** ▲▲ C China
61 N16 **Xique-Xique** Bahia, E Brazil 10.46S 42.43W
117 E14 **Xirovoúni** ▲ N Greece 40.31N 21.58E
Xishanzui see Urad Qianqi
166 J11 **Xishui** Guizhou, S China 28.24N 106.09E
167 O9 **Xishui** Hubei, E China 30.29N 115.13E
169 R10 **Xi Ujimqin Qi** var. Bayan Ul Hot. Nei Mongol Zizhiqu, N China 44.31N 117.36E
166 K11 **Xiushan** Sichuan, C China 28.23N 108.52E
167 O10 **Xiu Shui** ~ S China
152 H9 **Xiva** var. Khiwa, Rus. Khiva. Xorazm Viloyati, W Uzbekistan 41.22N 60.21E
164 J16 **Xixabangma Feng** ▲ W China 28.25N 85.47E
166 M7 **Xixia** Henan, C China 33.19N 111.25E
Xixón see Gijón
Xixona see Jijona
Xizang see Xizang Zizhiqu
Xizang Gaoyuan see Qingzang Gaoyuan
166 E9 **Xizang Zizhiqu** var. Thibet, Tibetan Autonomous Region, Xizang, Eng. Tibet. ◈ autonomous region W China
169 U14 **Xizhong Dao** island N China
152 H8 **Xo'jayli** Rus. Khodzheyli. Qoraqalpog'iston Respublikasi, W Uzbekistan 42.23N 59.27E
Xolotlán see Managua, Lago de
152 I9 **Xonqa** var. Khonqa, Rus. Khanka. Xorazm Viloyati, W Uzbekistan 41.31N 60.39E
152 H9 **Xorazm Viloyati** Rus. Khorezmskaya Oblast'. ◈ province W Uzbekistan
165 N9 **Xorkol** Xinjiang Uygur Zizhiqu, NW China 38.45N 91.07E
153 P11 **Xovos** var. Ursat'yevskaya, Rus. Khavast. Sirdaryo Viloyati, E Uzbekistan 40.14N 68.46E
43 X14 **Xpujil** Quintana Roo, E Mexico 18.30N 89.24W
Xuancheng see Xuanzhou
178 Jj9 **Xuân Đuc** Quang Binh, C Vietnam 17.19N 106.38E
166 L9 **Xuan'en** Hubei, C China 30.03N 109.26E
166 K8 **Xuanhan** Sichuan, C China 31.25N 107.41E
167 O2 **Xuanhua** Hebei, E China 40.37N 115.04E
167 P4 **Xuanhui He** ~ E China
167 Q8 **Xuanzhou** var. Xuancheng. Anhui, E China 30.59N 118.43E
167 N7 **Xuchang** Henan, C China 34.03N 113.48E
143 X10 **Xudat** Rus. Khudat. NE Azerbaijan 41.37N 48.39E
83 M16 **Xuddur** var. Hudur, It. Oddur. Bakool, SW Somalia 4.06N 43.47E
82 O13 **Xudun** Nugaal, N Somalia 9.12N 47.34E
166 L11 **Xuefeng Shan** ▲▲ S China
44 F2 **Xunantunich** ruins Cayo, W Belize 17.06N 89.10W
169 W6 **Xun He** ~ NE China
166 L7 **Xun He** ~ C China
166 L14 **Xun Jiang** ~ S China
169 W5 **Xunke** Heilongjiang, NE China 49.36N 128.25E
167 P13 **Xunwu** Jiangxi, S China 24.58N 115.37E
167 O3 **Xushui** Hebei, E China 39.01N 115.37E
166 L16 **Xuwen** Guangdong, S China 20.20N 110.09E
166 I11 **Xuyong** var. Yongning. Sichuan, C China 28.16N 105.21E
167 P6 **Xuzhou** var. Hsu-chou, Suchow, Tongshan; prev. T'ung-shan. Jiangsu, E China 34.16N 117.09E
116 K13 **Xylaganí** var. Xilagani. Anatolikí Makedonía kai Thráki, NE Greece 40.58N 25.27E
117 F19 **Xylókastro** var. Xilokastro. Pelopónnisos, S Greece 38.04N 22.36E

Y

166 H9 **Ya'an** var. Yaan. Sichuan, C China 30.00N 102.57E
190 L10 **Yaapeet** Victoria, SE Australia 35.48S 142.03E
81 D15 **Yabassi** Littoral, W Cameroon 4.30N 9.58E
83 J15 **Yabēlo** Oromo, C Ethiopia 4.53N 38.00E
172 Pp5 **Yabetsu-gawa** var. Yūbetsu-gawa. ~ Hokkaidō, NE Japan
116 H9 **Yablanitsa** Lovech Oblast, W Bulgaria 43.02N 24.04E
45 N7 **Yablis** Región Autónoma Atlántico Norte, NE Nicaragua 14.02N 83.44W
126 Kk16 **Yablonovyy Khrebet** ▲▲ S Russian Federation
168 J14 **Yabrai Shan** ▲▲ NE China
47 U6 **Yabucoa** E Puerto Rico 18.03N 65.53W
197 K14 **Yacata** island Lau Group, E Fiji
166 J11 **Yachi He** ~ S China
34 H10 **Yacolt** Washington, NW USA 45.49N 122.22W
56 M10 **Yacuaray** Amazonas, S Venezuela 4.12N 66.30W
59 M22 **Yacuiba** Tarija, S Bolivia 22.03S 63.40W
59 K16 **Yacuma, Río** ~ C Bolivia
161 H16 **Yādgīr** Karnātaka, C India 16.46N 77.09E
23 R8 **Yadkin River** ~ North Carolina, SE USA
23 R9 **Yadkinville** North Carolina, SE USA 36.07N 80.39W
131 P3 **Yadrin** Chavash Respubliki, W Russian Federation 55.55N 46.10E
197 I13 **Yadua** prev. Yandua. island NW Fiji
172 Oo17 **Yaeyama-shotō** var. Yaegama-shotō. island group SW Japan
77 O8 **Yafran** NW Libya 32.04N 12.31E
197 L15 **Yagasa Cluster** island group Lau Group, E Fiji
172 Oo3 **Yagashiri-tō** island NE Japan
67 H21 **Yaghan Basin** undersea feature SE Pacific Ocean
127 Nn9 **Yagodnoye** Magadanskaya Oblast', E Russian Federation 62.37N 149.18E
Yagotin see Yahotyn
80 G12 **Yagoua** Extrême-Nord, NE Cameroon 10.22N 15.13E
165 Q11 **Yagradagzê Shan** ▲ C China 35.06N 95.41E
Yaguachi see Yaguachi Nuevo
58 B7 **Yaguachi Nuevo** var. Yaguachi. Guayas, W Ecuador 2.06S 79.43W
Yaguarón, Río see Jaguarão, Rio
171 I16 **Yahagi-gawa** ~ Honshū, SW Japan
119 Q11 **Yahorlyts'kyy Lyman** bay S Ukraine
119 Q5 **Yahotyn** Rus. Yagotin. Kyyivs'ka Oblast', N Ukraine 50.15N 31.48E
42 L12 **Yahualica** Jalisco, SW Mexico 21.12N 102.52W
81 L17 **Yahuma** Orientale, N Dem. Rep. Congo 1.12N 23.00E
142 K15 **Yahyalı** Kayseri, C Turkey 38.07N 35.22E
178 Gg15 **Yai, Khao** ▲ SW Thailand 8.45N 99.32E
171 Kk15 **Yaita** Tochigi, Honshū, S Japan 36.47N 139.54E
171 Ii17 **Yaizu** Shizuoka, Honshū, S Japan 34.52N 138.19E
166 G9 **Yajiang** Sichuan, C China 30.05N 100.57E
121 O14 **Yakawlyevichi** Rus. Yakovlevichi. Vitsyebskaya Voblasts', NE Belarus 54.21N 30.29E
169 S6 **Yakeshi** Nei Mongol Zizhiqu, N China 49.16N 120.42E
34 I9 **Yakima** Washington, NW USA 46.36N 120.30W
34 J10 **Yakima River** ~ Washington, NW USA
116 G7 **Yakimovo** Montana, NW Bulgaria 43.39N 23.21E
Yakkabag see Yakkabog'
153 N12 **Yakkabog'** Rus. Yakkabag. Qashqadaryo Viloyati, S Uzbekistan 38.57N 66.35E
154 L12 **Yakmach** Baluchistān, SW Pakistan 28.48N 63.48E
79 O12 **Yako** W Burkina 12.58N 2.15W
41 W13 **Yakobi Island** island Alexander Archipelago, Alaska, USA
81 K16 **Yakoma** Equateur, N Dem. Rep. Congo 4.04N 22.22E
116 H11 **Yakoruda** Blagoevgrad, SW Bulgaria 42.01N 23.40E
Yakovlevichi see Yakawlyevichi
131 T2 **Yakshur-Bod'ya** Udmurtskaya Respublika, NW Russian Federation 57.10N 53.10E
172 N6 **Yakumo** Hokkaidō, NE Japan 42.18N 140.15E
170 B17 **Yaku-shima** island Nansei-shotō, SW Japan
41 V12 **Yakutat** Alaska, USA 59.33N 139.43W
41 U12 **Yakutat Bay** inlet Alaska, USA
Yakutia/Yakutiya/Yakutiya, Respublika see Sakha (Yakutiya), Respublika
126 M11 **Yakutsk** Respublika Sakha (Yakutiya), NE Russian Federation 62.10N 129.49E
178 Hh17 **Yala** Yala, SW Thailand 6.31N 101.19E
190 D6 **Yalata** South Australia 31.30S 131.53E
33 S9 **Yale** Michigan, N USA 43.07N 82.45W
188 I11 **Yalgoo** Western Australia 28.23S 116.43E
116 O12 **Yalıköy** İstanbul, NW Turkey 41.29N 28.19E
81 L14 **Yalinga** Haute-Kotto, C Central African Republic 6.47N 23.09E
121 M17 **Yalizava** Rus. Yelizovo. Mahilyowskaya Voblasts', E Belarus 53.24N 29.01E
46 L13 **Yallahs Hill** ▲ E Jamaica 17.53N 76.31W
24 L3 **Yalobusha River** ~ Mississippi, S USA
81 H15 **Yaloké** Ombella-Mpoko, W Central African Republic 5.15N 17.12E
166 E7 **Yalong Jiang** ~ C China
142 E11 **Yalova** Yalova, NW Turkey 40.40N 29.16E
142 E11 **Yalova** ◈ province NW Turkey
Yaloveny see Ialoveni
Yalpug see Ialpug
Yalpug, Ozero see Yalpuh, Ozero
119 N12 **Yalpuh, Ozero** Rus. Ozero Yalpug. ◎ SW Ukraine
119 T14 **Yalta** Respublika Krym, S Ukraine 44.30N 34.09E
169 W12 **Yalu** Chin. Yalu Jiang, Jap. Oryokko, Kor. Amnok-kang. ~ China/North Korea
Yalu Jiang see Yalu
125 F12 **Yalutorovsk** Tyumenskaya Oblast', C Russian Federation 56.36N 66.09E
142 F14 **Yalvaç** Isparta, SW Turkey 38.16N 31.09E
172 N12 **Yamada** Iwate, Honshū, C Japan 39.27N 141.56E
170 Cc14 **Yamaga** Kumamoto, Kyūshū, SW Japan 33.01N 130.42E
171 L12 **Yamagata** Yamagata, Honshū, C Japan 38.15N 140.19E
171 Ll12 **Yamagata** off. Yamagata-ken. ◈ prefecture Honshū, C Japan
170 Bb16 **Yamagawa** Kagoshima, Kyūshū, SW Japan 31.12N 130.37E
170 Dd12 **Yamaguchi** var. Yamaguti. Yamaguchi, Honshū, SW Japan 34.10N 131.26E
170 Dd12 **Yamaguchi** off. Yamaguchi-ken, var. Yamaguti. ◈ prefecture Honshū, SW Japan
Yamaguti see Yamaguchi
129 X5 **Yamalo-Nenetskiy Avtonomnyy Okrug** ◈ autonomous district N Russian Federation
126 Gg6 **Yamal, Poluostrov** peninsula N Russian Federation
171 J16 **Yamanashi** off. Yamanashi-ken, var. Yamanasi. ◈ prefecture Honshū, S Japan
Yamanasi see Yamanashi
Yamanīyah, Al Jumhūrīyah al see Yemen
131 W5 **Yamantau** ▲ W Russian Federation 53.11N 57.30E
126 K16 **Yamarovka** Chitinskaya Oblast', S Russian Federation 50.36N 110.25E
Yamasaki see Yamazaki
13 P12 **Yamaska** ~ Quebec, SE Canada
171 Jj17 **Yamato** Kanagawa, Honshū, S Japan 35.30N 139.25E
199 Gg4 **Yamato Ridge** undersea feature S Sea of Japan
170 G14 **Yamazaki** var. Yamasaki. Hyōgo, Honshū, SW Japan 35.00N 134.31E
191 V5 **Yamba** New South Wales, SE Australia 29.28S 153.22E
83 D16 **Yambio** var. Yambiyo. Western Equatoria, S Sudan 4.34N 28.21E
Yambiyo see Yambio
116 L10 **Yambol** Turk. Yanboli. Yambol, E Bulgaria 42.28N 26.30E
116 M11 **Yambol** ◈ province E Bulgaria
81 M17 **Yambuya** Orientale, N Dem. Rep. Congo 1.22N 24.21E
176 Uu15 **Yamdena, Pulau** prev. Jamdena. island Kepulauan Tanimbar, E Indonesia
170 Cc13 **Yame** Fukuoka, Kyūshū, SW Japan 33.12N 130.31E
177 G6 **Yamethin** Mandalay, C Myanmar 20.25N 96.08E
194 G11 **Yaminbot** East Sepik, NW PNG 4.30S 143.44E
171 L15 **Yamizo-san** ▲ Honshū, C Japan 36.56N 140.14E
189 U9 **Yamma Yamma, Lake** ◎ Queensland, C Australia
78 M16 **Yamoussoukro** ● (Ivory Coast) C Ivory Coast 6.51N 5.21W
39 P3 **Yampa River** ~ Colorado, C USA
119 S2 **Yampil'** Sums'ka Oblast', NE Ukraine 51.57N 33.49E
118 M8 **Yampil'** Vinnyts'ka Oblast', C Ukraine 48.15N 28.18E
127 Oo10 **Yamsk** Magadanskaya Oblast', E Russian Federation 59.33N 154.04E
158 J8 **Yamuna** prev. Jumna. ~ N India
158 I9 **Yamunānagar** Haryāna, N India 30.07N 77.16E
Yamundá see Nhamundá, Rio
151 U8 **Yamyshevo** Pavlodar, NE Kazakhstan 51.49N 77.28E
165 N16 **Yamzho Yumco** ◎ W China
126 Ll6 **Yana** ~ NE Russian Federation
195 P15 **Yanaba Island** island SE PNG
170 C13 **Yanagawa** Fukuoka, Kyūshū, SW Japan 33.08N 130.23E
170 E13 **Yanai** Yamaguchi, Honshū, SW Japan 33.56N 132.05E
161 L16 **Yanam** var. Yanaon. Pondicherry, E India 16.45N 82.16E
166 L5 **Yan'an** var. Yanan. Shaanxi, C China 36.34N 109.26E
Yanaon see Yanam
131 U3 **Yanaul** Respublika Bashkortostan, W Russian Federation 56.15N 54.57E
120 O12 **Yanavichy** Rus. Yanovichi. Vitsyebskaya Voblasts', NE Belarus 55.16N 30.42E
Yanboli see Yambol
146 K8 **Yanbu' al Baḩr** Al Madīnah, W Saudi Arabia 24.06N 38.03E
23 T8 **Yanceyville** North Carolina, SE USA 36.24N 79.20W
167 R7 **Yancheng** Jiangsu, E China 33.27N 120.10E
165 W8 **Yanchi** Ningxia, N China 37.49N 107.24E
166 L5 **Yanchuan** Shaanxi, C China 36.54N 110.04E
191 O10 **Yanco Creek** seasonal river New South Wales, SE Australia
191 O6 **Yanda Creek** seasonal river New South Wales, SE Australia
190 K4 **Yandama Creek** seasonal river New South Wales/South Australia
167 S11 **Yandang Shan** ▲▲ SE China
197 G5 **Yandé, Île** island Îles Belep, W New Caledonia
Yandua see Yadua
165 O6 **Yandun** Xinjiang Uygur Zizhiqu, W China 42.24N 94.07E
78 L13 **Yanfolila** Sikasso, SW Mali 11.08N 8.12W
81 M18 **Yangambi** Orientale, N Dem. Rep. Congo 0.46N 24.24E
164 M15 **Yangbajain** Xizang Zizhiqu, W China 30.04N 90.34E
Yangchow see Yangzhou
166 M15 **Yangchun** Guangdong, S China 22.16N 111.49E
167 N2 **Yanggao** Shanxi, C China 40.24N 113.51E
Yanggeta see Yaqeta
Yangiabad see Yangiobod
Yangibazar see Dzhany-Bazar, Kyrgyzstan
Yangi-Bazar see Kofarnihon, Tajikistan
Yangikishlak see Yangiqishloq
152 M13 **Yangi-Nishon** Rus. Yang-Nishan. Qashqadaryo Viloyati, S Uzbekistan 38.37N 65.39E
153 Q9 **Yangiobod** Rus. Yangiabad. Toshkent Viloyati, E Uzbekistan 41.10N 70.10E
153 O10 **Yangiqishloq** Rus. Yangikishlak. Jizzax Viloyati, C Uzbekistan 40.27N 67.06E
153 P11 **Yangiyer** Sirdaryo Viloyati, E Uzbekistan 40.19N 68.48E

◆ Country ● Country Capital ◇ Dependent Territory ○ Dependent Territory Capital ◈ Administrative Region ✈ International Airport ▲ Mountain ▲▲ Mountain Range Volcano ~ River ◎ Lake ⊠ Reservoir

153 P9 **Yangiyo'l** *Rus.* Yangiyul'. Toshkent Viloyati, E Uzbekistan *41.12N 69.05E*
166 M15 **Yangjiang** Guangdong, S China *21.52N 111.55E*
Yangku *see* Taiyuan
Yang-Nishan *see* Yangi-Nishon
177 G9 **Yangon** *Eng.* Rangoon. ● (Myanmar) Yangon, S Myanmar *16.49N 96.10E*
177 G8 **Yangon** *Eng.* Rangoon. ◈ *division* SW Myanmar
166 K17 **Yangpu Gang** *harbour* Hainan, S China
167 N4 **Yangquan** Shanxi, C China *37.52N 113.28E*
167 N13 **Yangshan** Guangdong, S China *24.32N 112.36E*
178 Kk13 **Yang Sin, Chu** ▲ S Vietnam *12.23N 108.25E*
Yangtze *see* Chang Jiang, C China
Yangtze Kiang *see* Chang Jiang
167 R7 **Yangzhou** *var.* Yangchow. Jiangsu, E China *32.22N 119.22E*
166 L5 **Yan He** ≈ C China
169 Y10 **Yanji** Jilin, NE China *42.53N 129.31E*
Yanji *see* Longjing
31 Q12 **Yankton** South Dakota, N USA *42.52N 97.24W*
Yannina *see* Ioánnina
126 M6 **Yano-Indigirskaya Nizmennost'** *plain* NE Russian Federation
Yanovichi *see* Yanavichy
161 K24 **Yan Oya** ≈ N Sri Lanka
164 K6 **Yanqi** *var.* Yanqi Huizu Zizhixian. Xinjiang Uygur Zizhiqu, NW China *42.04N 86.32E*
Yanqi Huizu Zizhixian *see* Yanqi
167 P2 **Yan Shan** ▲▲ E China
167 Q10 **Yanshan** Jiangxi, S China *28.17N 117.47E*
166 H14 **Yanshan** *prev.* Hekou. Yunnan, SW China *23.36N 104.20E*
169 X8 **Yanshou** Heilongjiang, NE China *45.27N 128.19E*
126 Ll6 **Yanskiy Zaliv** *bay* N Russian Federation
191 O4 **Yantabulla** New South Wales, SE Australia *29.22S 145.00E*
167 R4 **Yantai** *var.* Yan-t'ai; *prev.* Chefoo, Chih-fu. Shandong, E China *37.30N 121.22E*
120 A13 **Yantarnyy** *Ger.* Palmnicken. Kaliningradskaya Oblast', W Russian Federation *54.53N 19.59E*
116 J9 **Yantra** Gabrovo, N Bulgaria *42.58N 25.19E*
116 K9 **Yantra** ≈ N Bulgaria
166 G11 **Yanyuan** Sichuan, C China *27.30N 101.22E*
167 P5 **Yanzhou** Shandong, E China *35.34N 116.52E*
81 E16 **Yaoundé** *var.* Yaunde. ● (Cameroon) Centre, S Cameroon *3.51N 11.31E*
196 I14 **Yap** ◈ *state* W Micronesia
196 F16 **Yap** *island* Caroline Islands, W Micronesia
59 M18 **Yapacani, Río** ≈ C Bolivia
176 Ww12 **Yapa Kopra** Papua, E Indonesia *4.18S 135.05E*
Yapan *see* Yapen, Selat
Yapanskoye More *see* Japan, Sea of
79 P15 **Yapei** N Ghana *9.10N 1.08W*
10 M10 **Yapeitso, Mont** ▲ Quebec, E Canada *52.18N 70.24W*
176 X10 **Yapen, Pulau** *prev.* Japen. *island* E Indonesia
176 X9 **Yapen, Selat** *var.* Yapan. *strait* Papua, E Indonesia
63 E15 **Yapeyú** Corrientes, NE Argentina *29.28S 56.49W*
142 I11 **Yapraklı** Çankırı, N Turkey *40.45N 33.46E*
182 M3 **Yap Trench** *var.* Yap Trough. *undersea feature* SE Philippine Sea
Yap Trough *see* Yap Trench
Yapurá *see* Caquetá, Río, Brazil/Colombia
Yapurá *see* Japurá, Rio, Brazil/Colombia
176 U11 **Yaputih** Pulau Seram, E Indonesia *3.16S 129.29E*
197 I13 **Yaqaga** *island* N Fiji
197 H13 **Yaqeta** *prev.* Yanggeta. *island* Yasawa Group, NW Fiji
42 G6 **Yaqui** Sonora, NW Mexico *27.21N 109.59W*
34 E12 **Yaquina Bay** *bay* Oregon, NW USA
42 G6 **Yaqui, Río** ≈ NW Mexico
176 Y14 **Yar** *channel* Papua, E Indonesia
56 K5 **Yaracuy** *off.* Estado Yaracuy. ◈ *state* NW Venezuela
152 E13 **Yaradzhi** *Turkm.* Yarajy. Akhalskiy Velayat, C Turkmenistan *38.12N 57.40E*
Yarajy *see* Yaradzhi
129 Q15 **Yaransk** Kirovskaya Oblast', NW Russian Federation *57.18N 47.52E*
142 F17 **Yardımcı Burnu** *headland* SW Turkey *36.10N 30.25E*
99 Q19 **Yare** ≈ E England, UK
129 S9 **Yarega** Respublika Komi, NW Russian Federation *63.27N 53.28E*
118 I7 **Yaremcha** Ivano-Frankivs'ka Oblast', W Ukraine *48.27N 24.34E*
201 Q9 **Yaren** SW Nauru *0.33S 166.54E*
129 Q10 **Yarensk** Arkhangel'skaya Oblast', NW Russian Federation *62.09N 49.03E*
161 F16 **Yargatti** Karnātaka, W India *16.07N 75.11E*
171 Ii14 **Yariga-take** ▲ Honshū, S Japan *36.20N 137.38E*
147 O15 **Yarīm** W Yemen *14.15N 44.22E*
56 F14 **Yarí, Río** ≈ SW Colombia
56 K5 **Yaritagua** Yaracuy, N Venezuela *10.04N 69.07W*
Yarkand *see* Yarkant He
Yarkant *see* Shache
164 E9 **Yarkant He** *var.* Yarkand. ≈ NW China
155 U3 **Yarkhūn** ≈ NW Pakistan
Yarlung Zangbo Jiang *see* Brahmaputra
118 L6 **Yarmolyntsi** Khmel'nyts'ka Oblast', W Ukraine *49.13N 26.53E*
169 T11 **Yar Moron** ≈ N China
11 O16 **Yarmouth** Nova Scotia, SE Canada *43.53N 66.08W*
Yarmouth *see* Great Yarmouth
Yaroslav *see* Jarosław
128 L15 **Yaroslavl'** Yaroslavskaya Oblast', W Russian Federation *57.38N 39.52E*
128 K14 **Yaroslavskaya Oblast'** ◈ *province* W Russian Federation
126 Kk12 **Yaroslavskiy** Respublika Sakha (Yakutiya), NE Russian Federation *60.10N 114.12E*
191 P13 **Yarram** Victoria, SE Australia *38.36S 146.40E*
191 O11 **Yarrawonga** Victoria, SE Australia *36.04S 145.58E*
190 L4 **Yarriarraburra Swamp** *wetland* New South Wales, SE Australia
126 Gg8 **Yar-Sale** Yamalo-Nenetskiy Avtonomnyy Okrug, N Russian Federation *66.52N 70.42E*
126 I12 **Yartsevo** Krasnoyarskiy Kray, C Russian Federation *60.15N 90.09E*
130 I4 **Yartsevo** Smolenskaya Oblast', W Russian Federation *55.03N 32.46E*
56 E8 **Yarumal** Antioquia, NW Colombia *6.58N 75.25W*
197 H13 **Yasawa** *island* Yasawa Group, NW Fiji
197 G13 **Yasawa Group** *island group* NW Fiji
79 V12 **Yashi** Katsina, N Nigeria *12.21N 7.56E*
79 S14 **Yashikera** Kwara, W Nigeria *9.40N 3.19E*
153 T14 **Yashilkŭl** *Rus.* Ozero Yashil'kul'. ◎ SE Tajikistan
Yashil'kul', Ozero *see* Yashilkŭl
171 Ll11 **Yashima** Akita, Honshū, C Japan *39.10N 140.10E*
170 Dd14 **Ya-shima** *island* SW Japan
170 E14 **Yashiro-jima** *island* SW Japan
131 P13 **Yashkul'** Respublika Kalmykiya, SW Russian Federation *46.09N 45.22E*
152 F13 **Yashlyk** Akhalskiy Velayat, C Turkmenistan *37.46N 58.51E*
Yasinovataya *see* Yasynuvata
116 N10 **Yasna Polyana** Burgas, SE Bulgaria *42.18N 27.35E*
126 M14 **Yasnyy** Amurskaya Oblast', SE Russian Federation *53.03N 127.52E*
178 J10 **Yasothon** Yasothon, E Thailand *15.46N 104.12E*
191 R10 **Yass** New South Wales, SE Australia *34.52S 148.55E*
Yassy *see* Iaşi
170 Ff12 **Yasugi** Shimane, Honshū, SW Japan *35.25N 133.14E*
149 N10 **Yāsūj** *var.* Yesuj; *prev.* Tal-e Khosravī. Kohkīlūyeh va Būyer Aḩmadī, C Iran *30.40N 51.34E*
142 M11 **Yasun Burnu** *headland* N Turkey *41.07N 37.40E*
119 X8 **Yasynuvata** *Rus.* Yasinovataya. Donets'ka Oblast', SE Ukraine *48.04N 37.56E*
142 C15 **Yatağan** Muğla, SW Turkey *37.22N 28.07E*
171 M9 **Yatate-tōge** *pass* Honshū, C Japan *40.25N 140.36E*
197 J7 **Yaté** Province Sud, S New Caledonia *22.10S 166.56E*
29 P6 **Yates Center** Kansas, C USA *37.52N 95.43W*
193 B21 **Yates Point** *headland* South Island, NZ *44.30S 167.49E*
15 Kk7 **Yathkyed Lake** ◎ Nunavut, NE Canada
176 U15 **Yatoke** Pulau Babar, E Indonesia *7.51S 129.49E*
81 M18 **Yatolema** Orientale, N Dem. Rep. Congo *0.25N 24.34E*
171 J15 **Yatsuga-take** ▲ Honshū, S Japan *35.58N 138.22E*
170 C14 **Yatsushiro** *var.* Yatusiro. Kumamoto, Kyūshū, SW Japan *32.30N 130.34E*
170 C15 **Yatsushiro-kai** *bay* SW Japan
144 F11 **Yatta** *var.* Yuta. S West Bank *31.29N 35.10E*
83 J20 **Yatta Plateau** *plateau* SE Kenya
Yatusiro *see* Yatsushiro
59 F17 **Yauca, Río** ≈ SW Peru
47 S6 **Yauco** W Puerto Rico *18.02N 66.51W*
176 Xx9 **Yauke** Papua, E Indonesia *1.34S 137.56E*
Yaunde *see* Yaoundé
Yavan *see* Yovon
Yavarí *see* Javari, Rio
58 G9 **Yavari Mirim, Río** ≈ NE Peru
42 G7 **Yavaros** Sonora, NW Mexico *26.40N 109.32W*
160 I13 **Yavatmāl** Mahārāshtra, C India *20.22N 78.10E*
56 M9 **Yaví, Cerro** ▲ C Venezuela *5.43N 65.51W*
45 W16 **Yaviza** Darién, SE Panama *8.09N 77.40W*
144 F10 **Yavne** Central, W Israel *31.52N 34.45E*
118 H5 **Yavoriv** *Pol.* Jaworów, *Rus.* Yavorov. L'vivs'ka Oblast', NW Ukraine *49.57N 23.21E*
Yavorov *see* Yavoriv
170 E15 **Yawatahama** Ehime, Shikoku, SW Japan *33.27N 132.24E*
Ya Xian *see* Sanya
142 L17 **Yayladağı** Hatay, S Turkey *35.55N 36.03E*
129 V13 **Yayva** Permskaya Oblast', NW Russian Federation *59.19N 57.15E*
129 V12 **Yayva** ≈ NW Russian Federation
149 Q9 **Yazd** *var.* Yezd. Yazd, C Iran *31.55N 54.22E*
149 Q8 **Yazd** *off.* Ostān-e Yazd, *var.* Yezd. ◈ *province* C Iran
Yazgulemskiy Khrebet *see* Yazgulom, Qatorkŭhi
153 S13 **Yazgulom, Qatorkŭhi** *Rus.* Yazgulemskiy Khrebet. ▲▲ S Tajikistan
24 K5 **Yazoo City** Mississippi, S USA *32.51N 90.24W*
24 K5 **Yazoo River** ≈ Mississippi, S USA
131 Q5 **Yazykovo** Ul'yanovskaya Oblast', W Russian Federation *54.19N 47.22E*
111 U4 **Ybbs** Niederösterreich, NE Austria *48.10N 15.03E*
111 U4 **Ybbs** ≈ C Austria
97 G22 **Yding Skovhøj** *hill* C Denmark *55.58N 9.45E*
117 G20 **Ýdra** *var.* Ídhra, Idra. Ýdra, S Greece *37.20N 23.27E*
117 G21 **Ýdra** *var.* Ídhra. *island* S Greece
117 G20 **Ýdras, Kólpos** *strait* S Greece
178 Gg10 **Ye** Mon State, S Myanmar *15.15N 97.49E*
191 O12 **Yea** Victoria, SE Australia *37.15S 145.27E*
80 I5 **Yebbi-Bou** Borkou-Ennedi-Tibesti, N Chad *21.12N 17.55E*
164 F9 **Yecheng** *var.* Kargilik. Xinjiang Uygur Zizhiqu, NW China *37.54N 77.25E*
107 R11 **Yecla** Murcia, SE Spain *38.36N 1.07W*
42 H6 **Yécora** Sonora, NW Mexico *28.20N 108.55W*
Yedintsy *see* Edineţ
128 J13 **Yefimovskiy** Leningradskaya Oblast', NW Russian Federation *59.32N 34.34E*
176 Uu9 **Yeflio** Papua, E Indonesia *1.01S 131.17E*
130 K6 **Yefremov** Tul'skaya Oblast', W Russian Federation *53.09N 38.02E*
Yēgainnyin *see* Henan
143 U12 **Yeghegis** *Rus.* Yekhegis. ≈ C Armenia
151 T10 **Yegindybulak** *Kaz.* Egindibulaq. Karaganda, C Kazakhstan *49.45N 75.45E*
130 L4 **Yegor'yevsk** Moskovskaya Oblast', W Russian Federation *55.29N 39.03E*
Yehuda, Haré *see* Judaean Hills
83 E15 **Yei** ≈ S Sudan
167 P8 **Yeji** *var.* Yejiaji. Anhui, E China *31.52N 115.58E*
Yejiaji *see* Yeji
125 Ee11 **Yekaterinburg** *prev.* Sverdlovsk. Sverdlovskaya Oblast', C Russian Federation *56.52N 60.34E*
Yekaterinodar *see* Krasnodar
Yekaterinoslav *see* Dnipropetrovs'k
126 Mm15 **Yekaterinoslavka** Amurskaya Oblast', SE Russian Federation *50.23N 129.03E*
131 O7 **Yekaterinovka** Saratovskaya Oblast', W Russian Federation *52.01N 44.11E*
78 K16 **Yekepa** NE Liberia *7.34N 8.31W*
131 T3 **Yelabuga** Respublika Tatarstan, W Russian Federation *55.46N 52.07E*
Yela Island *see* Rossel Island
131 O8 **Yelan'** Volgogradskaya Oblast', SW Russian Federation *51.00N 43.40E*
119 Q9 **Yelanets'** *Rus.* Yelanets. Mykolayivs'ka Oblast', S Ukraine *47.40N 31.51E*
125 G13 **Yelanka** Novosibirskaya Oblast', C Russian Federation *55.38N 75.23E*
130 L7 **Yelets** Lipetskaya Oblast', W Russian Federation *52.37N 38.29E*
129 W4 **Yeletskiy** Respublika Komi, NW Russian Federation *67.03N 64.05E*
78 J11 **Yélimané** Kayes, W Mali *15.06N 10.43W*
Yelisavetpol *see* Gäncä
Yelizavetgrad *see* Kirovohrad
127 O13 **Yelizavety, Mys** *headland* SE Russian Federation *54.20N 142.39E*
127 Pp11 **Yelizovo** Kamchatskaya Oblast', E Russian Federation *53.12N 158.18E*
Yelizovo *see* Yalizava
131 S5 **Yelkhovka** Samarskaya Oblast', W Russian Federation *53.51N 50.16E*
98 M1 **Yell** *island* NE Scotland, UK
161 E17 **Yellāpur** Karnātaka, W India *15.06N 74.50E*
9 U17 **Yellow Grass** Saskatchewan, S Canada *49.51N 104.09W*
Yellowhammer State *see* Alabama
9 O15 **Yellowhead Pass** *pass* Alberta/British Columbia, SW Canada *52.54N 118.44W*
15 Hh8 **Yellowknife** *territory capital* Northwest Territories, W Canada *62.30N 114.28W*
15 I7 **Yellowknife** ≈ Northwest Territories, NW Canada
194 F10 **Yellow River** ≈ NW PNG
25 P8 **Yellow River** ≈ Alabama/Florida, S USA
32 I4 **Yellow River** ≈ Wisconsin, N USA
32 J6 **Yellow River** ≈ Wisconsin, N USA
32 K7 **Yellow River** ≈ Wisconsin, N USA
Yellow River *see* Huang He
163 V8 **Yellow Sea** *Chin.* Huang Hai, *Kor.* Hwang-Hae. *sea* E Asia
35 S13 **Yellowstone Lake** ◎ Wyoming, C USA
35 T13 **Yellowstone National Park** *national park* Wyoming, NW USA
35 Y8 **Yellowstone River** ≈ Montana/Wyoming, NW USA
98 L1 **Yell Sound** *strait* N Scotland, UK
29 U9 **Yellville** Arkansas, C USA *36.13N 92.40W*
126 Hh11 **Yeloguy** ≈ C Russian Federation
152 J14 **Yëloten** *prev.* Iolotan', *Turkm.* Yolöten. Maryyskiy Velayat, S Turkmenistan *37.15N 62.18E*
121 M20 **Yel'sk** *Rus.* Yel'sk. Homyel'skaya Voblasts', SE Belarus *51.49N 29.09E*
79 T13 **Yelwa** Kebbi, W Nigeria *10.52N 4.46E*
125 Ee12 **Yemanzhelinsk** Chelyabinskaya Oblast', C Russian Federation *54.43N 61.08E*
23 R15 **Yemassee** South Carolina, SE USA *32.41N 80.51W*
147 O15 **Yemen** *off.* Republic of Yemen, *Ar.* Al Jumhūrīyah al Yamanīyah, Al Yaman. ◆ *republic* SW Asia
118 M4 **Yemil'chyne** Zhytomyrs'ka Oblast', N Ukraine *50.51N 27.49E*
128 M10 **Yemtsa** Arkhangel'skaya Oblast', NW Russian Federation *63.04N 40.18E*
128 M10 **Yemtsa** ≈ NW Russian Federation
129 R10 **Yemva** *prev.* Zheleznodorozhnyy. Respublika Komi, NW Russian Federation *62.38N 50.58E*
79 U17 **Yenagoa** Bayelsa, S Nigeria *4.58N 6.16E*
119 X7 **Yenakiyeve** *Rus.* Yenakiyevo; *prev.* Ordzhonikidze, Rykovo. Donets'ka Oblast', E Ukraine *48.13N 38.13E*
Yenakiyevo *see* Yenakiyeve
177 Ff6 **Yenangyaung** Magwe, W Myanmar *20.28N 94.54E*
178 Jj5 **Yên Bai** Yên Bai, N Vietnam *21.43N 104.54E*
191 P9 **Yenda** New South Wales, SE Australia *34.16S 146.15E*
176 W10 **Yende** Papua, E Indonesia *2.19S 134.34E*
79 Q14 **Yendi** NE Ghana *9.23N 0.02W*
164 E8 **Yengisar** Xinjiang Uygur Zizhiqu, NW China *38.50N 76.10E*
124 O3 **Yeniboğaziçi** *var.* Ayios Seryios, *Gk.* Ágios Sérgios. E Cyprus *35.10N 33.53E*
124 Oo2 **Yenierenköy** *var.* Yialousa, *Gk.* Agialoúsa. NE Cyprus *35.32N 34.12E*
Yenipazar *see* Novi Pazar
142 E12 **Yenişehir** Bursa, NW Turkey *40.16N 29.37E*
Yenisei Bay *see* Yeniseyskiy Zaliv
126 Hh8 **Yenisey** ≈ Mongolia/Russian Federation
126 I13 **Yeniseysk** Krasnoyarskiy Kray, C Russian Federation *58.23N 92.06E*
207 W10 **Yeniseyskiy Zaliv** *var.* Yenisei Bay. *bay* N Russian Federation
131 Q12 **Yenotayevka** Astrakhanskaya Oblast', SW Russian Federation *47.16N 47.01E*
128 L4 **Yenozero, Ozero** ◎ NW Russian Federation
Yenping *see* Nanping
41 Q11 **Yentna River** ≈ Alaska, USA
188 M10 **Yeo, Lake** *salt lake* Western Australia
191 R7 **Yeoval** New South Wales, SE Australia *32.45S 148.39E*
99 K23 **Yeovil** SW England, UK *50.57N 2.39W*
42 H6 **Yepachic** Chihuahua, N Mexico *28.27N 108.25W*
189 Y8 **Yeppoon** Queensland, E Australia *23.04S 150.42E*
130 M5 **Yerakhtur** Ryazanskaya Oblast', W Russian Federation *54.45N 41.09E*
Yeraliyev *see* Kuryk
152 F12 **Yerbent** Akhalskiy Velayat, C Turkmenistan *39.19N 58.34E*
126 Jj12 **Yerbogachen** Irkutskaya Oblast', C Russian Federation *61.07N 108.03E*
143 T12 **Yerevan** *Eng.* Erivan. ● (Armenia) C Armenia *40.12N 44.31E*
143 U12 **Yerevan** ✈ C Armenia *40.07N 44.34E*
151 R9 **Yereymentau** *var.* Jermentau, Yermentau, *Kaz.* Ereymentaū. Akmola, C Kazakhstan *51.37N 73.10E*
131 O12 **Yergeni** *hill range* SW Russian Federation
Yeriho *see* Jericho
37 R6 **Yerington** Nevada, W USA *38.58N 119.10W*
142 J13 **Yerköy** Yozgat, C Turkey *39.39N 34.28E*
116 L13 **Yerlisu** Edirne, NW Turkey *40.45N 26.38E*
Yermak *see* Aksu
151 R9 **Yermentau** *Kaz.* Ereymentaū. Akmola, C Kazakhstan *51.37N 73.10E*
151 R9 **Yermentau, Gory** ▲▲ C Kazakhstan
129 R5 **Yermitsa** Respublika Komi, NW Russian Federation *66.57N 52.15E*
37 V14 **Yermo** California, W USA *34.54N 116.49W*
126 Ll14 **Yerofey Pavlovich** Amurskaya Oblast', SE Russian Federation *53.58N 121.49E*
101 F15 **Yerseke** Zeeland, SW Netherlands *51.30N 4.03E*
131 Q8 **Yershov** Saratovskaya Oblast', W Russian Federation *51.18N 48.16E*
129 P9 **Yërtom** Respublika Komi, NW Russian Federation *63.27N 47.52E*
58 D13 **Yerupaja, Nevado** ▲ C Peru *10.23S 76.58W*
Yerushalayim *see* Jerusalem
107 R4 **Yesa, Embalse de** ⊞ NE Spain
151 V15 **Yesik** *Kaz.* Esik; *prev.* Issyk. Almaty, SE Kazakhstan *43.23N 77.31E*
151 O8 **Yesil'** *Kaz.* Esil. Akmola, C Kazakhstan *51.58N 66.22E*
142 K15 **Yeşilhisar** Kayseri, C Turkey *38.22N 35.07E*
142 L11 **Yeşilırmak** *anc.* Iris. ≈ N Turkey
39 U12 **Yeso** New Mexico, SW USA *34.25N 104.36W*
Yeso *see* Hokkaidō
131 N15 **Yessentuki** Stavropol'skiy Kray, SW Russian Federation *44.06N 42.51E*
126 J9 **Yessey** Evenkiyskiy Avtonomnyy Okrug, N Russian Federation *68.18N 101.49E*
107 P12 **Yeste** Castilla-La Mancha, C Spain *38.21N 2.18W*
Yesuj *see* Yāsūj
191 T4 **Yetman** New South Wales, SE Australia *28.56S 150.47E*
78 L4 **Yetti** *physical region* N Mauritania
177 G4 **Ye-u** Sagaing, C Myanmar *22.49N 95.25E*
104 H9 **Yeu, Île d'** *island* NW France
Yevlakh *see* Yevlax
143 W11 **Yevlax** *Rus.* Yevlakh. C Azerbaijan *40.36N 47.09E*
119 S13 **Yevpatoriya** Respublika Krym, S Ukraine *45.12N 33.22E*
125 B17 **Yevreyskaya Avtonomnaya Oblast'** *Eng.* Jewish Autonomous Oblast. ◈ *autonomous province* SE Russian Federation
130 K12 **Yeya** ≈ SW Russian Federation
164 I10 **Yeyik** Xinjiang Uygur Zizhiqu, W China *36.43N 83.13E*
130 K12 **Yeysk** Krasnodarskiy Kray, SW Russian Federation *46.41N 38.15E*
Yezd *see* Yazd
Yezerishche *see* Yezyaryshcha
120 N11 **Yezyaryshcha** *Rus.* Yezerishche. Vitsyebskaya Voblasts', NE Belarus *55.49N 29.58E*
Yialí *see* Gyalí
Yialousa *see* Yenierenköy
169 V7 **Yi'an** Heilongjiang, NE China *47.52N 125.13E*
Yiannitsá *see* Giannitsá
166 I10 **Yibin** Sichuan, C China *28.47N 104.36E*
164 K13 **Yibug Caka** ◎ W China
166 M9 **Yichang** Hubei, C China *30.37N 111.02E*
166 L5 **Yichuan** Shaanxi, C China *36.05N 110.02E*
163 W3 **Yichun** Heilongjiang, NE China *47.40N 129.10E*
169 X6 **Yichun** *var.* I-ch'un. Heilongjiang, NE China *47.39N 128.54E*
167 O11 **Yichun** Jiangxi, S China *27.45N 114.22E*
Yidu *see* Qingzhou
196 C15 **Yigo** NE Guam *13.33N 144.52E*
167 Q5 **Yi He** ≈ E China
169 X8 **Yilan** Heilongjiang, NE China *46.18N 129.36E*
142 C9 **Yıldız Dağları** ▲▲ NW Turkey
142 L13 **Yıldızeli** Sivas, N Turkey *39.52N 36.37E*
169 U4 **Yilehuli Shan** ▲▲ NE China
169 S7 **Yimin He** ≈ NE China
165 W8 **Yinchuan** *var.* Yinch'uan, Yin-ch'uan, Yinchwan. Ningxia, N China *38.30N 106.19E*
Yinchuanzhan *see* Xincheng
Yinchwan *see* Yinchuan
Yindu He *see* Indus
167 N14 **Yingde** Guangdong, S China *24.08N 113.21E*
167 O7 **Ying He** ≈ C China
169 U13 **Yingkou** *var.* Ying-k'ou, Yingkow; *prev.* Newchwang, Niuchwang. Liaoning, NE China *40.38N 122.17E*
Yingkow *see* Yingkou
167 P9 **Yingshan** Hubei, C China *30.45N 115.41E*
Yingshan *see* Guangshui
167 Q10 **Yingtan** Jiangxi, S China *28.17N 117.03E*
Yin-hsien *see* Ningbo
164 H5 **Yining** *var.* I-ning, *Uigh.* Gulja, Kuldja. Xinjiang Uygur Zizhiqu, NW China *43.53N 81.18E*
166 K11 **Yinjiang** Guizhou, S China *28.22N 108.07E*
177 Ff4 **Yinmabin** Sagaing, C Myanmar *22.04N 94.57E*
169 N13 **Yin Shan** ▲▲ N China
Yin-tu Ho *see* Indus
165 P15 **Yi'ong Zangbo** ≈ W China
Yioúra *see* Gyáros
83 J14 **Yirga 'Alem** *It.* Irgalem. Southern, S Ethiopia *6.43N 38.24E*
63 E19 **Yí, Río** ≈ C Uruguay
83 E14 **Yirol** El Buhayrat, S Sudan *6.34N 30.33E*
Yirshi *see* Yirxie
169 S8 **Yirxie** *prev.* Yirshi. Nei Mongol Zizhiqu, N China *47.16N 119.51E*
167 Q5 **Yishui** Shandong, E China *35.49N 118.39E*
Yisrael/Yisra'el *see* Israel
Yíthion *see* Gýtheio
Yitiaoshan *see* Jingtai
169 W10 **Yitong** Jilin, NE China *43.22N 125.19E*
165 P5 **Yiwu** *var.* Aratürük. Xinjiang Uygur Zizhiqu, NW China *43.16N 94.38E*
169 U12 **Yiwulü Shan** ▲▲ N China
169 T12 **Yi Xian** Liaoning, NE China *41.29N 121.21E*
167 N10 **Yiyang** Hunan, S China *28.39N 112.19E*
167 Q10 **Yiyang** Jiangxi, S China *28.23N 117.24E*
167 N13 **Yizhang** Hunan, S China *25.24N 112.55E*
95 K19 **Yläne** Länsi-Suomi, W Finland *60.50N 22.26E*
95 L14 **Yli-Ii** Oulu, C Finland *65.21N 25.55E*
95 L14 **Ylikiiminki** Oulu, C Finland *65.00N 26.10E*
94 N13 **Yli-Kitka** ◎ NE Finland
95 K17 **Ylistaro** Länsi-Suomi, W Finland *62.58N 22.30E*
94 K13 **Ylitornio** Lappi, NW Finland *66.16N 23.39E*
95 L15 **Ylivieska** Oulu, W Finland *64.04N 24.30E*
95 L18 **Ylöjärvi** Länsi-Suomi, W Finland *61.31N 23.37E*
97 N17 **Yngaren** ◎ C Sweden
27 T12 **Yoakum** Texas, SW USA *29.17N 97.09W*
79 X13 **Yobe** ◈ *state* NE Nigeria
172 Nn4 **Yobetsu-dake** ▲ Hokkaidō, NE Japan *43.15N 140.27E*
176 Xx10 **Yobi** Papua, E Indonesia *1.42S 138.09E*
82 L11 **Yoboki** C Djibouti *11.30N 42.04E*
170 C12 **Yobuko** Saga, Kyūshū, SW Japan *33.31N 129.50E*
24 M4 **Yockanookany River** ≈ Mississippi, S USA
24 L2 **Yocona River** ≈ Mississippi, S USA
176 Yy15 **Yodom** Papua, E Indonesia *7.12S 139.24E*
174 Kk15 **Yogyakarta** *prev.* Djokjakarta, Jogjakarta, Jokyakarta. Jawa, C Indonesia *7.48S 110.24E*
174 Kk16 **Yogyakarta** *off.* Daerah Istimewa Yogyakarta, *var.* Djokjakarta, Jogjakarta, Jokyakarta. ◈ *autonomous district* S Indonesia
172 O5 **Yoichi** Hokkaidō, NE Japan *43.11N 140.45E*
44 G6 **Yojoa, Lago de** ◎ NW Honduras
81 G16 **Yokadouma** Est, SE Cameroon *3.25N 15.06E*
171 H15 **Yōkaichi** *var.* Yôkaiti. Shiga, Honshū, SW Japan *35.07N 136.10E*
Yōkaiti *see* Yōkaichi
171 H15 **Yokkaichi** *var.* Yokkaiti. Mie, Honshū, SW Japan *34.58N 136.36E*
Yokkaiti *see* Yokkaichi
81 E15 **Yoko** Centre, C Cameroon *5.28N 12.19E*
172 Qq12 **Yokoate-jima** *island* Nansei-shotō, SW Japan
172 N9 **Yokohama** Aomori, Honshū, C Japan *41.04N 141.14E*
171 Jj16 **Yokohama** Kanagawa, Honshū, S Japan *35.26N 139.37E*
171 Jj17 **Yokosuka** Kanagawa, Honshū, S Japan *35.15N 139.39E*
170 F12 **Yokota** Shimane, Honshū, SW Japan *35.10N 133.03E*
171 M11 **Yokote** Akita, Honshū, C Japan *39.19N 140.33E*
172 Nn7 **Yokotsu-dake** ▲ Hokkaidō, NE Japan *41.54N 140.48E*
79 Y14 **Yola** Adamawa, E Nigeria *9.07N 12.24E*
81 L19 **Yolombo** Equateur, C Dem. Rep. Congo *1.36S 23.13E*
Yolöten *see* Yëloten
176 W10 **Yomber** Papua, E Indonesia *2.04S 134.22E*
172 T16 **Yome-jima** *island* Ogasawara-shotō, SE Japan
78 K16 **Yomou** Guinée-Forestière, SE Guinea *7.30N 9.13W*
176 Y15 **Yomuka** Papua, E Indonesia *7.25S 138.36E*
196 C16 **Yona** E Guam *13.24N 144.46E*
170 Ff12 **Yonago** Tottori, Honshū, SW Japan *35.30N 134.15E*
172 O17 **Yonaguni** Okinawa, SW Japan *24.29N 123.00E*
172 Nn16 **Yonaguni-jima** *island* Nansei-shotō, SW Japan
172 Pp14 **Yonaha-dake** ▲ Okinawa, SW Japan *26.43N 128.13E*
169 X14 **Yonan** SW North Korea *37.50N 126.15E*
171 L13 **Yonezawa** Yamagata, Honshū, C Japan *37.54N 140.06E*
167 Q12 **Yong'an** *var.* Yongan. Fujian, SE China *25.58N 117.25E*
165 T9 **Yongchang** Gansu, N China *38.15N 101.55E*
167 P7 **Yongcheng** Henan, C China *33.55N 116.21E*
169 Z15 **Yŏngch'ŏn** *Jap.* Eisen. SE South Korea *35.56N 128.55E*
166 J10 **Yongchuan** Chongqing Shi, C China *29.27N 105.56E*
165 U10 **Yongdeng** Gansu, C China *35.58N 103.27E*
133 W9 **Yongding He** ≈ E China
167 P11 **Yongfeng** Jiangxi, S China *27.19N 115.22E*
164 L5 **Yongfengqu** Xinjiang Uygur Zizhiqu, W China *43.28N 87.09E*
166 L13 **Yongfu** Guangxi Zhuangzu Zizhiqu, S China *24.57N 109.59E*
169 X13 **Yŏnghŭng** E North Korea *39.30N 127.13E*
165 U10 **Yongjing** Gansu, C China *36.00N 103.30E*
169 Y15 **Yŏngju** *Jap.* Eishū. C South Korea *36.48N 128.37E*
Yongning *see* Xuyong
166 E12 **Yongping** Yunnan, SW China *25.30N 99.28E*
166 G12 **Yongren** Yunnan, SW China *26.11N 101.49E*
166 L10 **Yongshun** *var.* Lingxi. Hunan, S China *29.01N 109.48E*
167 P10 **Yongxiu** *var.* Tujiabu. Jiangxi, S China *29.08N 115.47E*
166 M12 **Yongzhou** Hunan, S China *26.12N 111.36E*
20 K14 **Yonkers** New York, NE USA *40.56N 73.51W*
105 Q7 **Yonne** ◈ *department* C France
105 P6 **Yonne** ≈ C France
56 H9 **Yopal** *var.* El Yopal. Casanare, C Colombia *5.19N 72.19W*
164 E8 **Yopurga** *var.* Yukuriawat. Xinjiang Uygur Zizhiqu, NW China *39.13N 76.44E*
153 S11 **Yordan** *var.* Iordan, *Rus.* Jardan. Farg'ona Viloyati, E Uzbekistan *39.58N 71.43E*
188 J12 **York** Western Australia *31.55S 116.52E*
99 M16 **York** *anc.* Eboracum, Eburacum. N England, UK *53.58N 1.04W*
25 N5 **York** Alabama, S USA *32.29N 88.18W*
31 Q15 **York** Nebraska, C USA *40.52N 97.35W*
20 G16 **York** Pennsylvania, NE USA *39.55N 76.42W*
23 R11 **York** South Carolina, SE USA *34.59N 81.14W*
12 J13 **York** ≈ Ontario, SE Canada
13 X6 **York** ≈ Quebec, SE Canada
189 V1 **York, Cape** *headland* Queensland, NE Australia *10.40S 142.36E*
190 I9 **Yorke Peninsula** *peninsula* South Australia
190 I9 **Yorketown** South Australia *35.01S 137.38E*
21 P9 **York Harbor** Maine, NE USA *43.10N 70.37W*
23 X6 **York River** ≈ Virginia, NE USA
99 M16 **Yorkshire** *cultural region* N England, UK
99 L16 **Yorkshire Dales** *physical region* N England, UK
9 V16 **Yorkton** Saskatchewan, S Canada *51.12N 102.28W*
27 T12 **Yorktown** Texas, SW USA *28.58N 97.30W*
23 X6 **Yorktown** Virginia, NE USA *37.13N 76.29W*
32 M11 **Yorkville** Illinois, N USA *41.38N 88.27W*
44 I5 **Yoro** Yoro, C Honduras *15.06N 87.09W*
44 H5 **Yoro** ◈ *department* N Honduras
172 Pp14 **Yoron-jima** *island* Nansei-shotō, SW Japan
79 N13 **Yorosso** Sikasso, S Mali *12.18N 4.44W*
37 R8 **Yosemite National Park** *national park* California, W USA
170 Ff14 **Yoshii-gawa** ≈ Honshū, SW Japan
170 Ff15 **Yoshino-gawa** *var.* Yosino Gawa. ≈ Shikoku, SW Japan
131 Q3 **Yoshkar-Ola** Respublika Mariy El, W Russian Federation *56.37N 47.53E*
Yosino Gawa *see* Yoshino-gawa
176 Y15 **Yos Sudarso, Pulau** *var.* Pulau Dolak, Pulau Kolepom; *prev.* Jos Sudarso. *island* E Indonesia
176 Z10 **Yos Sudarso, Teluk** *bay* Papua, E Indonesia
169 Y17 **Yŏsu** *Jap.* Reisui. S South Korea *34.45N 127.40E*
172 Nn5 **Yotei-zan** ▲ Hokkaidō, NE Japan *42.50N 140.46E*
99 D21 **Youghal** *Ir.* Eochaill. S Ireland *51.57N 7.49W*
99 D21 **Youghal Bay** *Ir.* Cuan Eochaille. *inlet* S Ireland
20 C15 **Youghiogheny River** ≈ Pennsylvania, NE USA
166 K14 **You Jiang** ≈ S China
191 Q9 **Young** New South Wales, SE Australia *34.19S 148.19E*
9 T15 **Young** Saskatchewan, S Canada *51.44N 105.44W*
63 E18 **Young** Río Negro, W Uruguay *32.43S 57.36W*
190 G5 **Younghusband, Lake** *salt lake* South Australia
190 J10 **Younghusband Peninsula** *peninsula* South Australia
192 Q10 **Young Nicks Head** *headland* North Island, NZ *39.38S 105.03E*
193 D20 **Young Range** ▲▲ South Island, NZ
203 Q15 **Young's Rock** *island* Pitcairn Island, Pitcairn Islands
9 R16 **Youngstown** Alberta, SW Canada *51.31N 111.12W*
33 V12 **Youngstown** Ohio, N USA *41.06N 80.39W*
165 N9 **Youshashan** Qinghai, C China *38.12N 90.58E*
Youth, Isle of *see* Juventud, Isla de la
79 N11 **Youvarou** Mopti, C Mali *15.19N 4.15W*
166 K10 **Youyang** Sichuan, C China *28.48N 108.48E*
169 Y7 **Youyi** Heilongjiang, NE China *46.51N 131.54E*
153 P13 **Yovon** *Rus.* Yavan. SW Tajikistan *38.19N 69.02E*
142 J13 **Yozgat** Yozgat, C Turkey *39.49N 34.48E*
142 K13 **Yozgat** ◈ *province* C Turkey
64 O6 **Ypacaraí** *var.* Ypacaray. Central, S Paraguay *25.22S 57.16W*
Ypacaray *see* Ypacaraí
64 P5 **Ypané, Río** ≈ C Paraguay
Ypres *see* Ieper
116 I13 **Ypsário** *var.* Ipsario. ▲ Thásos, E Greece *40.43N 24.39E*
33 R10 **Ypsilanti** Michigan, N USA *42.12N 83.36W*
36 M1 **Yreka** California, W USA *41.43N 122.38W*
Yrendagüé *see* General Eugenio A. Garay
195 N8 **Ysabel Channel** *channel* N PNG
12 K8 **Yser, Lac** ◎ Quebec, SE Canada
153 Y8 **Yshtyk** Issyk-Kul'skaya Oblast', E Kyrgyzstan *41.34N 78.21E*
Yssel *see* IJssel
105 Q12 **Yssingeaux** Haute-Loire, C France *45.09N 4.07E*
97 K23 **Ystad** Skåne, S Sweden *55.25N 13.51E*
Ysyk-Köl *see* Balykchy, Kyrgyzstan
Ysyk-Köl *see* Issyk-Kul', Ozero, Kyrgyzstan
Ysyk-Köl Oblasty *see* Issyk-Kul'skaya Oblast'
98 L8 **Ythan** ≈ NE Scotland, UK
Y Trallwng *see* Welshpool
96 C13 **Ytre Arna** Hordaland, S Norway *60.28N 5.25E*
96 B12 **Ytre Sula** *island* S Norway
95 G17 **Ytterhogdal** Jämtland, C Sweden *62.10N 14.55E*
126 M10 **Ytyk-Kyuyel'** Respublika Sakha (Yakutiya), NE Russian Federation *62.22N 133.37E*
Yu *see* Henan
Yuan Jiang *see* Red River
167 S13 **Yüanlin** *Jap.* Inrin. C Taiwan *23.57N 120.33E*
167 N3 **Yuanping** Shanxi, C China *38.26N 112.42E*
167 O11 **Yuan Shui** ≈ S China
170 G16 **Yuasa** Wakayama, Honshū, SW Japan *34.00N 135.08E*
194 H10 **Yuat** ≈ N PNG
37 O6 **Yuba City** California, W USA *39.07N 121.40W*
172 Oo6 **Yūbari** Hokkaidō, NE Japan *43.09N 141.00E*
172 P6 **Yūbari-sanchi** ▲▲ Hokkaidō, NE Japan
37 O6 **Yuba River** ≈ California, W USA
82 H13 **Yubdo** Oromo, C Ethiopia *9.05N 35.28E*
172 Q5 **Yūbetsu** Hokkaidō, NE Japan *44.12N 143.34E*
Yūbetsu-gawa *see* Yubetsu-gawa
130 L3 **Yubileynyy** Moskovskaya Oblast', W Russian Federation *55.56N 37.47E*
43 X12 **Yucatán** ◈ *state* SE Mexico
49 O3 **Yucatan Basin** *var.* Yucatan Deep. *undersea feature* N Caribbean Sea
Yucatán, Canal de *see* Yucatan Channel
43 Y10 **Yucatan Channel** *Sp.* Canal de Yucatán. *channel* Cuba/Mexico
Yucatan Deep *see* Yucatan Basin
Yucatan Peninsula *see* Yucatán, Península de
43 X13 **Yucatán, Península de** *Eng.* Yucatan Peninsula. *peninsula* Guatemala/Mexico
38 I11 **Yucca** Arizona, SW USA *34.49N 114.06W*
37 V15 **Yucca Valley** California, W USA *34.06N 116.30W*
167 P4 **Yucheng** Shandong, E China *37.01N 116.37E*
167 N4 **Yuci** Shanxi, C China *37.34N 112.45E*
133 X5 **Yudoma** ≈ E Russian Federation
167 P12 **Yudu** Jiangxi, C China *26.02N 115.24E*
Yue *see* Guangdong
166 M12 **Yuecheng Ling** ▲▲ S China

◆ Country ● Country Capital ◇ Dependent Territory ○ Dependent Territory Capital ◈ Administrative Region ✈ International Airport ▲ Mountain ▲▲ Mountain Range Volcano ≈ River ◎ Lake ⊞ Reservoir

189 P7 **Yuendumu** Northern Territory, N Australia 22.19S 131.51E
166 H10 **Yuexi** Sichuan, C China 28.50N 102.36E
167 N10 **Yueyang** Hunan, S China 29.24N 113.08E
129 U14 **Yug** Permskaya Oblast', NW Russian Federation 57.49N 56.08E
129 P13 **Yug** ≈ NW Russian Federation
127 N11 **Yugorenok** Respublika Sakha (Yakutiya), NE Russian Federation 59.46N 137.36E
125 F10 **Yugorsk** Khanty-Mansiyskiy Avtonomnyy Okrug, C Russian Federation 61.17N 63.25E
125 G6 **Yugorskiy Poluostrov** *peninsula* NW Russian Federation
Yugoslavia *see* Serbia and Montenegro (Yugoslavia)
152 K14 **Yugo-Vostochnyye Garagumy** *prev.* Yugo-Vostochnyye Karakumy. *desert* E Turkmenistan
Yugo-Vostochnyye Karakumy *see* Yugo-Vostochnyye Garagumy
167 S10 **Yuhuan Dao** *island* SE China
166 L14 **Yu Jiang** ≈ S China
127 Nn7 **Yukagirskoye Ploskogor'ye** *plateau* NE Russian Federation
120 L11 **Yukhavichy** *Rus.* Yukhovichi. Vitsyebskaya Voblasts', N Belarus 56.02N 28.39E
130 J4 **Yukhnov** Kaluzhskaya Oblast', W Russian Federation 54.43N 35.15E
Yukhovichi *see* Yukhavichy
81 J20 **Yuki** *var.* Yuki Kengunda. Bandundu, W Dem. Rep. Congo 3.52S 19.32E
Yuki Kengunda *see* Yuki
28 M10 **Yukon** Oklahoma, C USA 35.30N 97.45W
(0) F4 **Yukon** ≈ Canada/USA
Yukon *see* Yukon Territory
41 S7 **Yukon Flats** *salt flat* Alaska, USA
14 F5 **Yukon Territory** *var.* Yukon, *Fr.* Territoire du Yukon. ◆ *territory* NW Canada
143 T16 **Yüksekova** Hakkâri, SE Turkey 37.34N 44.16E
126 Jj11 **Yukta** Evenkiyskiy Avtonomnyy Okrug, C Russian Federation 63.16N 106.04E
170 Dd13 **Yukuhashi** *var.* Yukuhasi. Fukuoka, Kyūshū, SW Japan 33.41N 131.00E
Yukuhasi *see* Yukuhashi
Yukuriawat *see* Yopurga
129 O9 **Yula** ≈ NW Russian Federation
189 P8 **Yulara** Northern Territory, N Australia 25.15S 130.57E
131 W6 **Yuldybayevo** Respublika Bashkortostan, W Russian Federation 52.22N 57.55E
25 W8 **Yulee** Florida, SE USA 30.37N 81.36W
164 K7 **Yuli** *var.* Lopnur. Xinjiang Uygur Zizhiqu, NW China 41.24N 86.12E
167 T14 **Yüli** C Taiwan 23.23N 121.18E
166 L15 **Yulin** Guangxi Zhuangzu Zizhiqu, S China 22.37N 110.07E
166 L4 **Yulin** Shaanxi, C China 38.22N 109.47E
167 T14 **Yüli Shan** ▲ E Taiwan 23.22N 121.13E
166 F11 **Yulongxue Shan** ▲ SW China 27.09N 100.10E
38 H14 **Yuma** Arizona, SW USA 32.40N 114.38W
39 W3 **Yuma** Colorado, C USA 40.07N 102.43W
56 K5 **Yumare** Yaracuy, N Venezuela 10.37N 68.40W
65 G14 **Yumbel** Bío Bío, C Chile 37.07S 72.33W
81 N19 **Yumbi** Maniema, E Dem. Rep. Congo 1.13S 26.13E
165 R8 **Yumen** *var.* Laojunmiao, Yümen. Gansu, N China 39.49N 97.46E
165 Q7 **Yumenzhen** Gansu, N China 40.15N 97.03E
164 J3 **Yumin** Xinjiang Uygur Zizhiqu, NW China 46.14N 82.52E
Yun *see* Yunnan
142 G14 **Yunak** Konya, W Turkey 38.49N 31.42E
47 O8 **Yuna, Río** ≈ E Dominican Republic
40 I17 **Yunaska Island** *island* Aleutian Islands, Alaska, USA
166 M6 **Yuncheng** Shanxi, C China 35.07N 110.45E
59 L18 **Yungas** *physical region* E Bolivia
Yungki *see* Jilin
Yung-ning *see* Nanning
166 I12 **Yun Gui Gaoyuan** *plateau* SW China
Yunjinghong *see* Jinghong
166 M15 **Yunkai Dashan** ▲▲ S China
Yunki *see* Jilin
166 E11 **Yun Ling** ▲▲ SW China
167 N9 **Yunmeng** Hubei, C China 30.59N 113.44E
163 N14 **Yunnan** *var.* Yun, Yunnan Sheng, Yünnan, Yun-nan. ◆ *province* SW China
Yunnan *see* Kunming
Yunnan Sheng *see* Yunnan
170 Cc15 **Yunomae** Kumamoto, Kyūshū, SW Japan 32.16N 131.00E
167 N8 **Yun Shui** ≈ C China
190 J7 **Yunta** South Australia 32.37S 139.33E
167 Q14 **Yunxiao** Fujian, SE China 23.56N 117.16E
166 K9 **Yunyang** Sichuan, C China 31.03N 109.43E
200 Nn10 **Yupanqui Basin** *undersea feature* E Pacific Ocean
Yuratishki *see* Yuratsishki
121 I15 **Yuratsishki** *Pol.* Juraciszki, *Rus.* Yuratishki. Hrodzyenskaya Voblasts', W Belarus 54.01N 25.55E
Yurev *see* Tartu
126 H14 **Yurga** Kemerovskaya Oblast', S Russian Federation 55.42N 84.59E
58 E10 **Yurimaguas** Loreto, N Peru 5.54S 76.07W
131 P3 **Yurino** Respublika Mariy El, W Russian Federation 56.19N 46.15E
43 N13 **Yuriria** Guanajuato, C Mexico 20.12N 101.09W
129 T13 **Yurla** Komi-Permyatskiy Avtonomnyy Okrug, NW Russian Federation 59.18N 54.19E
Yuruá, Río *see* Juruá, Rio
116 M13 **Yürük** Tekirdağ, NW Turkey 40.58N 27.09E
164 G10 **Yurungkax He** ≈ W China
129 Q14 **Yur'ya** *var.* Jarja. Kirovskaya Oblast', NW Russian Federation 59.01N 49.22E
Yur'yev *see* Tartu
129 N16 **Yur'yevets** Ivanovskaya Oblast', W Russian Federation 57.19N 43.01E
130 M3 **Yur'yev-Pol'skiy** Vladimirskaya Oblast', W Russian Federation 56.28N 39.39E
119 V7 **Yur"yivka** Dnipropetrovs'ka Oblast', E Ukraine 48.45N 36.01E
126 K6 **Yuryung-Khaya** Respublika Sakha (Yakutiya), NE Russian Federation 72.45N 113.32E
44 I7 **Yuscarán** El Paraíso, S Honduras 13.58N 86.48W
167 P12 **Yu Shan** ▲▲ S China
165 R13 **Yushu** Qinghai, C China 33.03N 97.00E
131 P12 **Yusta** Respublika Kalmykiya, SW Russian Federation 47.06N 46.16E
128 I10 **Yustozero** Respublika Kareliya, NW Russian Federation 62.44N 33.31E
143 Q11 **Yusufeli** Artvin, NE Turkey 40.49N 41.31E
170 E15 **Yusuhara** Kōchi, Shikoku, SW Japan 33.22N 132.52E
129 T14 **Yus'va** Permskaya Oblast', NW Russian Federation 58.48N 54.59E
Yuta *see* Yatta
167 P2 **Yutian** Hebei, E China 39.52N 117.43E
164 H10 **Yutian** *var.* Keriya. Xinjiang Uygur Zizhiqu, NW China 36.49N 81.31E
64 K5 **Yuto** Jujuy, NW Argentina 23.35S 64.28W
64 P7 **Yuty** Caazapá, S Paraguay 26.28S 56.11W
166 G13 **Yuxi** Yunnan, SW China 24.22N 102.28E
167 O2 **Yuxian** *prev.* Yu Xian. Hebei, E China 39.50N 114.33E
171 M11 **Yuzawa** Akita, Honshū, C Japan 39.11N 140.29E
129 N16 **Yuzha** Ivanovskaya Oblast', W Russian Federation 56.34N 42.00E
Yuzhno-Alichurskiy Khrebet *see* Alichuri Janubí, Qatorkŭhi
Yuzhno-Kazakhstanskaya Oblast' *see* Yuzhnyy Kazakhstan
127 Oo15 **Yuzhno-Sakhalinsk** *Jap.* Toyohara; *prev.* Vladimirovka. Ostrov Sakhalin, Sakhalinskaya Oblast', SE Russian Federation 46.58N 142.45E
131 P14 **Yuzhno-Sukhokumsk** Respublika Dagestan, SW Russian Federation 44.43N 45.32E
125 Ee12 **Yuzhnoural'sk** Chelyabinskaya Oblast', C Russian Federation 54.28N 61.13E
126 I13 **Yuzhno-Yeniseyskiy** Krasnoyarskiy Kray, C Russian Federation 58.40N 94.49E
151 Z10 **Yuzhnyy Altay, Khrebet** ▲▲ E Kazakhstan
Yuzhnyy Bug *see* Pivdennyy Buh
151 O15 **Yuzhnyy Kazakhstan** *off.* Yuzhno-Kazakhstanskaya Oblast', *Eng.* South Kazakhstan, *Kaz.* Ongtüstik Qazaqstan Oblysy; *prev.* Chimkentskaya Oblast'. ◆ *province* S Kazakhstan
127 Oo10 **Yuzhnyy, Mys** *headland* E Russian Federation 57.44N 156.49E
131 W6 **Yuzhnyy Ural** *var.* Southern Urals. ▲▲ W Russian Federation
165 V10 **Yuzhong** Gansu, C China 35.52N 104.09E
Yuzhou *see* Chongqing
105 N5 **Yvelines** ◆ *department* N France
110 B9 **Yverdon** *var.* Yverdon-les-Bains, *Ger.* Iferten; *anc.* Eborodunum. Vaud, W Switzerland 46.46N 6.37E
Yverdon-les-Bains *see* Yverdon
104 M3 **Yvetot** Seine-Maritime, N France 49.37N 0.48E
Ylanly *see* Il'yaly

Z

153 T12 **Zaalayskiy Khrebet** *Taj.* Qatorkŭhi Pasi Oloy. ▲▲ Kyrgyzstan/Tajikistan
Zaamin *see* Zomin
Zaandam *see* Zaanstad
100 I10 **Zaanstad** *prev.* Zaandam. Noord-Holland, C Netherlands 52.27N 4.49E
Zabadani *see* Az Zabdānī
121 L18 **Zabalatstsye** *Rus.* Zabolot'ye. Homyel'skaya Voblasts', SE Belarus 52.38N 28.35E
114 L9 **Žabalj** *Ger.* Josefsdorf, *Hung.* Zsablya; *prev.* Józseffalva;. Serbia, N Serbia and Montenegro (Yugoslavia) 45.22N 20.01E
Zāb aş Şaghīr, Nahraz *see* Little Zab
126 L16 **Zabaykal'sk** Chitinskaya Oblast', S Russian Federation 49.37N 117.19E
Zāb-e Kūchek, Rūdkhāneh-ye *see* Little Zab
Zabeln *see* Sabile
Zabéré *see* Zabré
Zabern *see* Saverne
147 N16 **Zabīd** W Yemen 14.00N 43.00E
147 O16 **Zabīd, Wādī** *dry watercourse* SW Yemen
Żabinka *see* Zhabinka
Ząbkowice *see* Ząbkowice Śląskie
113 G15 **Ząbkowice Śląskie** *var.* Ząbkowice, *Ger.* Frankenstein, Frankenstein in Schlesien. Dolnośląskie, SW Poland 50.34N 16.48E
112 P10 **Zabłudów** Podlaskie, NE Poland 53.00N 23.21E
114 D8 **Zabok** Krapina-Zagorje, N Croatia 46.00N 15.48E
149 W9 **Zābol** *var.* Shahr-i-Zabul, Zabul; *prev.* Nasratabad. Sīstān va Balūchestān, E Iran 31.00N 61.32E
Zābol *see* Zābul
149 W13 **Zābolī** Sīstān va Balūchestān, SE Iran 27.09N 61.31E
Zabolot'ye *see* Zabalatstsye
79 Q13 **Zabré** *var.* Zabéré. S Burkina 11.13N 0.34W
113 G17 **Zábřeh** *Ger.* Hohenstadt. Olomoucký Kraj, E Czech Republic 49.52N 16.52E
113 J16 **Zabrze** *Ger.* Hindenburg, Hindenburg in Oberschlesien. Śląskie, S Poland 50.19N 18.52E
155 O7 **Zābul** *Per.* Zābol. ◆ *province* SE Afghanistan
Zabul *see* Zābol
44 E6 **Zacapa** Zacapa, E Guatemala 14.59N 89.32W
44 A3 **Zacapa** *off.* Departamento de Zacapa. ◆ *department* E Guatemala
42 M14 **Zacapú** Michoacán de Ocampo, SW Mexico 19.49N 101.52W
43 V14 **Zacatal** Campeche, SE Mexico 18.37N 91.52W
42 M11 **Zacatecas** Zacatecas, C Mexico 22.45N 102.33W
42 L10 **Zacatecas** ◆ *state* C Mexico
44 F8 **Zacatecoluca** La Paz, S El Salvador 13.28N 88.51W
43 P15 **Zacatepec** Morelos, S Mexico 18.40N 99.11W
43 Q13 **Zacatlán** Puebla, S Mexico 19.54N 97.59W
150 F8 **Zachagansk** Zapadnyy Kazakhstan, NW Kazakhstan 51.04N 51.13E
117 D20 **Zacháro** *var.* Zaharo, Zakháro. Dytikí Ellás, S Greece 37.28N 21.40E
24 J8 **Zachary** Louisiana, S USA 30.39N 91.09W
119 U6 **Zachepylivka** Kharkivs'ka Oblast', E Ukraine 49.13N 35.15E
Zachist'ye *see* Zachystsye
112 E9 **Zachodniopomorskie** ◆ *province* NW Poland
121 L14 **Zachystsye** *Rus.* Zachist'ye. Minskaya Voblasts', NW Belarus 54.24N 28.45E
42 L13 **Zacoalco** *var.* Zacoalco de Torres. Jalisco, SW Mexico 20.12N 103.31W
Zacoalco de Torres *see* Zacoalco
43 P13 **Zacualtipán** Hidalgo, C Mexico 20.39N 98.42W
114 C12 **Zadar** *It.* Zara; *anc.* Iader. Zadar, W Croatia 44.06N 15.14E
114 C12 **Zadar** *off.* Zadarsko-Kninska Županija *prev.* Zadar-Knin. ◆ *province* SW Croatia
Zadar-Knin *see* Zadar
177 G14 **Zadetkyi Kyun** *var.* St. Matthew's Island. *island* Mergui Archipelago, S Myanmar
69 Q9 **Zadié** *var.* Djadié. ≈ NE Gabon
165 Q13 **Zadoi** Qinghai, C China 32.56N 95.21E
130 L7 **Zadonsk** Lipetskaya Oblast', W Russian Federation 52.25N 38.55E
77 X8 **Za'farâna** E Egypt 29.06N 32.34E
155 W7 **Zafarwāl** Punjab, E Pakistan 32.19N 74.52E
124 P1 **Zafer Burnu** *var.* Cape Andreas, Cape Apostolas Andreas, *Gk.* Akrotíri Apostólou Andréa. *headland* NE Cyprus 35.42N 34.34E
109 J23 **Zafferano, Capo** *headland* Sicilia, Italy, C Mediterranean Sea 38.06N 13.31E
116 M7 **Zafirovo** Silistra, NE Bulgaria 44.00N 26.51E
117 L23 **Zaforá** *island* Kykládes, Greece, Aegean Sea
106 J12 **Zafra** Extremadura, W Spain 38.25N 6.27W
112 E13 **Żagań** *var.* Zagań, Żegań, *Ger.* Sagan. Lubuskie, W Poland 51.37N 15.18E
120 F10 **Žagarė** *Pol.* Żagory. Joniškis, N Lithuania 56.22N 23.16E
77 W7 **Zagazig** *var.* Az Zaqāzīq. N Egypt 30.35N 31.31E
76 M5 **Zaghouan** *var.* Zaghwān. NE Tunisia 36.26N 10.05E
Zaghwān *see* Zaghouan
117 G16 **Zagorá** Thessalía, C Greece 39.27N 23.06E
Zagorod'ye *see* Zaharoddzye
Żagory *see* Žagarė
Zágráb *see* Zagreb
114 E8 **Zagreb** *Ger.* Agram, *Hung.* Zágráb. ● (Croatia) Zagreb, N Croatia 45.48N 15.57E
114 E8 **Zagreb** *prev.* Grad Zagreb. ◆ *province* NC Croatia
148 L7 **Zāgros, Kūhhā-ye** *Eng.* Zagros Mountains. ▲▲ W Iran
Zagros Mountains *see* Zāgros, Kūhhā-ye
114 O12 **Žagubica** Serbia, E Serbia and Montenegro (Yugoslavia) 44.13N 21.47E
113 L22 **Zagyva** ≈ N Hungary
Zaharo *see* Zacháro
121 G19 **Zaharoddzye** *Rus.* Zagorod'ye. *physical region* SW Belarus
149 W11 **Zāhedān** *var.* Zahidan; *prev.* Duzdab. Sīstān va Balūchestān, SE Iran 29.31N 60.51E
Zahidan *see* Zāhedān
Zaḥlah *see* Zahlé
144 H7 **Zahlé** *var.* Zaḥlah. C Lebanon 33.51N 35.54E
Zähmet *see* Zakhmet
113 O20 **Záhony** Szabolcs-Szatmár-Bereg, NE Hungary 48.26N 22.10E
147 N13 **Zahrān** 'Asīr, S Saudi Arabia 17.47N 43.27E
145 R12 **Zahrat al Baṭn** *hill range* S Iraq
123 I12 **Zahrez Chergui** *var.* Zahrez Chergúi. *marsh* N Algeria
131 S4 **Zainsk** Respublika Tatarstan, W Russian Federation 55.12N 52.01E
84 A10 **Zaire** *prev.* Congo. ◆ *province* NW Angola
Zaire *see* Congo (Democratic Republic of)
Zaire *see* Congo (river)
114 P13 **Zaječar** Serbia, E Serbia and Montenegro (Yugoslavia) 43.54N 22.16E
85 L18 **Zaka** Masvingo, E Zimbabwe 20.19S 31.27E
126 J16 **Zakamensk** Respublika Buryatiya, S Russian Federation 50.18N 102.57E
118 G7 **Zakarpats'ka Oblast'** *Eng.* Transcarpathian Oblast, *Rus.* Zakarpatskaya Oblast'. ◆ *province* W Ukraine
Zakarpatskaya Oblast' *see* Zakarpats'ka Oblast'
Zakataly *see* Zaqatala
Zakháro *see* Zacháro
Zakhidnyy Buh/Zakhodni Buh *see* Bug
152 J14 **Zakhmet** *Turkm.* Zähmet. Maryyskiy Velayat, C Turkmenistan 37.48N 62.33E
145 Q1 **Zākhō** *var.* Zākhū. N Iraq 37.09N 42.40E
Zākhū *see* Zākhō
Zákinthos *see* Zákynthos
113 L18 **Zakopane** Małopolskie, S Poland 49.17N 19.57E
80 J12 **Zakouma** Salamat, S Chad 10.47N 19.51E
117 L25 **Zákros** Kríti, Greece, E Mediterranean Sea 35.06N 26.12E
117 C19 **Zákynthos** *var.* Zákinthos. Zákynthos, W Greece 37.46N 20.54E
117 C20 **Zákynthos** *var.* Zákinthos, *It.* Zante. *island* Iónioi Nísoi, Greece, C Mediterranean Sea
117 C19 **Zakýnthou, Porthmós** *strait* SW Greece
113 G24 **Zala** *off.* Zala Megye. ◆ *county* W Hungary
113 G24 **Zala** ≈ W Hungary
144 M4 **Zalābiyah** Dayr az Zawr, C Syria 35.39N 39.51E
113 G24 **Zalaegerszeg** Zala, W Hungary 46.51N 16.49E
106 K11 **Zalamea de la Serena** Extremadura, W Spain 38.38N 5.37W
106 J13 **Zalamea la Real** Andalucía, S Spain 37.40N 6.40W
169 U7 **Zalantun** *var.* Butha Qi. Nei Mongol Zizhiqu, N China 47.57N 122.43E
126 J15 **Zalari** Irkutskaya Oblast', S Russian Federation 53.31N 102.10E
113 G23 **Zalaszentgrót** Zala, SW Hungary 46.57N 17.04E
Zalatna *see* Zlatna
118 G9 **Zalău** *Ger.* Waltenberg, *Hung.* Zilah; *prev. Ger.* Zillenmarkt. Sălaj, NW Romania 47.10N 23.03E
111 V10 **Žalec** *Ger.* Sachsenfeld. C Slovenia 46.15N 15.08E
119 S9 **Zalenodol's'k** Dnipropetrovs'ka Oblast', E Ukraine 47.31N 33.56E
112 K8 **Zalewo** *Ger.* Saalfeld. Warmińsko-Mazurskie, NE Poland 53.54N 19.39E
147 N9 **Zalim** Makkah, W Saudi Arabia 22.46N 42.12E
82 A11 **Zalingei** *var.* Zalinje. Western Darfur, W Sudan 12.51N 23.28E
Zalinje *see* Zalingei
118 K7 **Zalishchyky** Ternopil's'ka Oblast', W Ukraine 48.40N 25.43E
Zallah *see* Zillah
100 J13 **Zaltbommel** Gelderland, C Netherlands 51.49N 5.15E
128 H15 **Zaluch'ye** Novgorodskaya Oblast', NW Russian Federation 57.40N 31.45E
Zamak *see* Zamakh
147 Q14 **Zamakh** *var.* Zamak. N Yemen 16.25N 47.35E
142 K15 **Zamantı Irmağı** ≈ C Turkey
Zambesi/Zambeze *see* Zambezi
85 G14 **Zambezi** North Western, W Zambia 13.33S 23.07E
85 K15 **Zambezi** *var.* Zambesi, *Port.* Zambeze. ≈ S Africa
85 O15 **Zambézia** *off.* Província da Zambézia. ◆ *province* C Mozambique
85 I14 **Zambia** *off.* Republic of Zambia; *prev.* Northern Rhodesia. ◆ *republic* S Africa
179 Q16 **Zamboanga** *off.* Zamboanga City. Mindanao, S Philippines 6.56N 122.03E
56 E5 **Zambrano** Bolívar, N Colombia 9.45N 74.49W
112 N10 **Zambrów** Łomża, E Poland 52.59N 22.14E
85 L14 **Zambué** Tete, NW Mozambique 15.03S 30.49E
79 T13 **Zamfara** ≈ NW Nigeria
58 C9 **Zamora** Zamora Chinchipe, S Ecuador 4.05S 78.58W
106 K6 **Zamora** Castilla-León, NW Spain 41.30N 5.45W
106 K5 **Zamora** ◆ *province* Castilla-León, NW Spain
Zamora *see* Barinas
58 A13 **Zamora Chinchipe** ◆ *province* S Ecuador
42 M13 **Zamora de Hidalgo** Michoacán de Ocampo, SW Mexico 20.00N 102.18W
113 P15 **Zamość** *Rus.* Zamoste. Lubelskie, E Poland 50.43N 23.16E
Zamoste *see* Zamość
166 G7 **Zamtang** *prev.* Gamda. Sichuan, C China 32.19N 100.55E
77 O8 **Zamzam, Wādī** *dry watercourse* NW Libya
81 F20 **Zanaga** La Lékoumou, S Congo 2.49S 13.52E
43 T16 **Zanatepec** Oaxaca, SE Mexico 16.28N 94.24W
107 P9 **Záncara** ≈ C Spain
Zancle *see* Messina
164 G14 **Zanda** Xizang Zizhiqu, W China 31.28N 79.49E
100 H10 **Zandvoort** Noord-Holland, W Netherlands 52.22N 4.31E
41 P8 **Zane Hills** *hill range* Alaska, USA
33 T13 **Zanesville** Ohio, N USA 39.55N 82.01W
Zanga *see* Hrazdan
148 L4 **Zanjān** *var.* Zenjan, Zinjan. Zanjān, NW Iran 36.40N 48.30E
148 L4 **Zanjān** *off.* Ostān-e Zanjān, *var.* Zenjan, Zinjan. ◆ *province* NW Iran
Zante *see* Zákynthos
83 J22 **Zanzibar** Zanzibar, E Tanzania 6.10S 39.12E
83 J22 **Zanzibar** ◆ *region* E Tanzania
83 J22 **Zanzibar** *Swa.* Unguja. *island* E Tanzania
83 J22 **Zanzibar Channel** *channel* E Tanzania
171 Ll13 **Zaō-san** ▲ Honshū, C Japan 38.06N 140.27E
167 N8 **Zaoyang** Hubei, C China 32.11N 112.42E
126 I14 **Zaozernyy** Krasnoyarskiy Kray, S Russian Federation 55.53N 94.37E
128 J2 **Zaozërsk** Murmanskaya Oblast', NW Russian Federation 69.25N 32.25E
167 Q6 **Zaozhuang** Shandong, E China 34.52N 117.37E
30 L4 **Zap** North Dakota, N USA 47.18N 101.55W
114 L13 **Zapadna Morava** *Ger.* Westliche Morava. ≈ C Serbia and Montenegro (Yugoslavia)
128 H16 **Zapadnaya Dvina** Tverskaya Oblast', W Russian Federation 56.16N 32.03E
Zapadnaya Dvina *see* Western Dvina
126 H10 **Zapadno-Sibirskaya Ravnina** *Eng.* West Siberian Plain. *plain* C Russian Federation
Zapadnyy Bug *see* Bug
150 E9 **Zapadnyy Kazakhstan** *off.* Zapadno-Kazakhstanskaya Oblast', *Eng.* West Kazakhstan, *Kaz.* Batys Qazaqstan Oblysy; *prev.* Ural'skaya Oblast'. ◆ *province* NW Kazakhstan
126 Hh15 **Zapadnyy Sayan** *Eng.* Western Sayans. ▲▲ S Russian Federation
65 H15 **Zapala** Neuquén, W Argentina 38.54S 70.06W
64 I4 **Zapaleri, Cerro** *var.* Cerro Sapaleri. ▲ N Chile 22.51S 67.10W
27 Q16 **Zapata** Texas, SW USA 26.54N 99.16W
46 D5 **Zapata, Península de** *peninsula* W Cuba
63 G19 **Zapicán** Lavalleja, S Uruguay 33.31S 54.55W
67 J19 **Zapiola Ridge** *undersea feature* SW Atlantic Ocean
67 L19 **Zapiola Seamount** *undersea feature* S Atlantic Ocean 38.15S 26.15W
128 I2 **Zapolyarnyy** Murmanskaya Oblast', NW Russian Federation 69.24N 30.53E
119 U8 **Zaporizhzhya** *Rus.* Zaporozh'ye; *prev.* Aleksandrovsk. Zaporiz'ka Oblast', SE Ukraine 47.46N 35.12E
Zaporizhzhya *see* Zaporiz'ka Oblast'
119 U9 **Zaporiz'ka Oblast'** *var.* Zaporizhzhya, *Rus.* Zaporozhskaya Oblast'. ◆ *province* SE Ukraine
Zaporozhskaya Oblast' *see* Zaporiz'ka Oblast'
Zaporozh'ye *see* Zaporizhzhya
42 L14 **Zapotiltic** Jalisco, SW Mexico 19.35N 103.25W
164 G13 **Zapung** Xizang Zizhiqu, W China
143 V10 **Zaqatala** *Rus.* Zakataly. NW Azerbaijan 41.38N 46.37E
165 P13 **Zaqên** Qinghai, W China 33.22N 94.31E
165 Q13 **Za Qu** ≈ C China
142 M13 **Zara** Sivas, C Turkey 39.55N 37.43E
Zara *see* Zadar
Zarafshan *see* Zarafshon
153 P12 **Zarafshon** *Rus.* Zeravshan. W Tajikistan 39.12N 68.36E
152 L9 **Zarafshon** *Rus.* Zarafshan. Navoiy Viloyati, N Uzbekistan 41.33N 64.09E
Zarafshon *see* Zeravshan
153 O12 **Zarafshon, Qatorkŭhi** *Rus.* Zeravshanskiy Khrebet, *Uzb.* Zarafshon Tizmasi. ▲▲ Tajikistan/Uzbekistan
Zarafshon Tizmasi *see* Zarafshon, Qatorkŭhi
56 E7 **Zaragoza** Antioquia, N Colombia 7.30N 74.52W
42 I5 **Zaragoza** Chihuahua, N Mexico 29.36N 107.41W
43 N6 **Zaragoza** Coahuila de Zaragoza, NE Mexico 28.30N 100.52W
43 O10 **Zaragoza** Nuevo León, NE Mexico 23.59N 99.49W
107 R5 **Zaragoza** *Eng.* Saragossa; *anc.* Caesaraugusta, Salduba. Aragón, NE Spain 41.39N 0.54W
107 R6 **Zaragoza** ◆ *province* Aragón, NE Spain
107 R5 **Zaragoza** ✈ Aragón, NE Spain 41.37N 0.52W
149 S10 **Zarand** Kermān, C Iran 30.49N 56.34E
154 J9 **Zaranj** Nīmrūz, SW Afghanistan 30.59N 61.54E
120 I11 **Zarasai** Zarasai, E Lithuania 55.44N 26.17E
64 N12 **Zárate** *prev.* General José F.Uriburu. Buenos Aires, E Argentina 34.06S 59.03W
107 Q2 **Zarautz** *var.* Zarauz. País Vasco, N Spain 43.16N 2.10W
Zarauz *see* Zarautz
Zaravecchia *see* Biograd na Moru
Zarāyīn *see* Zarēn
130 L4 **Zaraysk** Moskovskaya Oblast', W Russian Federation 54.48N 38.54E
57 N6 **Zaraza** Guárico, N Venezuela 9.21N 65.19W
Zarbdar *see* Zarbdor
153 P11 **Zarbdor** *Rus.* Zarbdar. Jizzax Viloyati, C Uzbekistan 40.04N 68.10E
148 M8 **Zard Kūh** ▲ SW Iran 32.19N 50.03E
128 I5 **Zarechensk** Murmanskaya Oblast', NW Russian Federation 66.39N 31.27E
131 P6 **Zarechnyy** Penzenskaya Oblast', W Russian Federation 53.12N 45.12E
155 Q7 **Zareh Sharan** Paktīkā, E Afghanistan 33.07N 68.46E
41 Y14 **Zarembo Island** *island* Alexander Archipelago, Alaska, USA
145 V4 **Zarēn** *var.* Zarāyīn. E Iraq 35.16N 45.43E
155 Q7 **Zarghūn Shahr** *var.* Katawaz. Paktīkā, SE Afghanistan 32.40N 68.19E
79 V13 **Zaria** Kaduna, C Nigeria 11.06N 7.42E
118 K2 **Zarichne** Rivnens'ka Oblast', NW Ukraine 51.49N 26.09E
126 H14 **Zarinsk** Altayskiy Kray, S Russian Federation 53.34N 85.22E
118 J12 **Zărneşti** *Hung.* Zernest. Braşov, C Romania 45.34N 25.18E
117 J25 **Zarós** Kríti, Greece, E Mediterranean Sea 35.07N 24.54E
102 O9 **Zarow** ≈ NE Germany
Zarqa/Zarqā', Muḥāfaẓat az *see* Az Zarqā'
113 G20 **Záruby** ▲ W Slovakia 48.30N 17.24E
58 B8 **Zaruma** El Oro, SW Ecuador 3.41S 79.32W
112 E13 **Żary** *Ger.* Sorau, Sorau in der Niederlausitz. Lubuskie, W Poland 51.43N 15.09E
56 D10 **Zarzal** Valle del Cauca, W Colombia 4.22N 76.03W
44 I7 **Zarzalar, Cerro** ▲ S Honduras 14.15N 86.49W
158 I5 **Zāskār** ≈ NE India
158 I5 **Zāskār Range** ▲▲ NE India
121 K15 **Zaslawye** Minskaya Voblasts', C Belarus 54.01N 27.16E
118 K7 **Zastavna** Chernivets'ka Oblast', W Ukraine 48.30N 25.51E
113 B16 **Žatec** *Ger.* Saaz. Ústecký Kraj, NW Czech Republic 50.19N 13.32E
Zaumgarten *see* Chrzanów
152 G10 **Zaungukskiye Garagumy** *Turkm.* Üngüz Angyrsyndaky Garagum. *desert* N Turkmenistan
27 X9 **Zavalla** Texas, SW USA 31.09N 94.25W
101 H18 **Zaventem** Vlaams Brabant, C Belgium 50.52N 4.28E
101 H18 **Zaventem** ✈ (Brussel/Bruxelles) Vlaams Brabant, C Belgium 50.55N 4.28E
Zavertse *see* Zawiercie
116 L7 **Zavet** Razgrad, NE Bulgaria 43.46N 26.40E
131 O12 **Zavetnoye** Rostovskaya Oblast', SW Russian Federation 47.10N 43.54E
162 M3 **Zavhan Gol** ≈ W Mongolia
114 H12 **Zavidovići** Federacija Bosna I Hercegovina, N Bosnia and Herzegovina 44.26N 18.07E
126 Mm16 **Zavitinsk** Amurskaya Oblast', SE Russian Federation 50.23N 128.57E
125 F12 **Zavodoukovsk** Tyumenskaya Oblast', C Russian Federation 56.27N 66.37E
Zawia *see* Az Zāwiyah
113 K15 **Zawiercie** *Rus.* Zavertse. Śląskie, S Poland 50.28N 19.24E
77 P11 **Zawīlah** *var.* Zuwaylah, *It.* Zueila. C Libya 26.10N 15.07E
144 I4 **Zāwīyah, Jabal az** ▲▲ NW Syria
111 Y3 **Zaya** ≈ NE Austria
177 G8 **Zayatkyi** Pegu, C Myanmar 17.48N 96.27E
151 Y11 **Zaysan** Vostochnyy Kazakhstan, E Kazakhstan 47.28N 84.48E
Zaysan Köl *see* Zaysan, Ozero
151 Y11 **Zaysan, Ozero** *Kaz.* Zaysan Köl. ◎ E Kazakhstan
165 R16 **Zayü** *var.* Gyigang. Xizang Zizhiqu, W China 28.36N 97.25E
Zayyq *see* Ural
46 F6 **Zaza** ≈ C Cuba
118 K5 **Zbarazh** Ternopil's'ka Oblast', W Ukraine 49.40N 25.47E
118 J5 **Zboriv** Ternopil's'ka Oblast', W Ukraine 49.40N 25.07E
113 F18 **Zbraslav** Brněnský Kraj, SE Czech Republic 49.13N 16.19E
118 K6 **Zbruch** ≈ W Ukraine
Žďár *see* Žďár nad Sázavou
113 F17 **Žďár nad Sázavou** *Ger.* Saar in Mähren; *prev.* Žďár. Jihlavský Kraj, C Czech Republic 49.34N 15.55E
118 K4 **Zdolbuniv** *Pol.* Zdolbunów, *Rus.* Zdolbunov. Rivnens'ka Oblast', NW Ukraine 50.33N 26.15E
Zdolbunov/Zdolbunów *see* Zdolbuniv
112 J13 **Zduńska Wola** Sieradz, C Poland 51.37N 18.57E
119 O4 **Zdvizh** ≈ N Ukraine
Zdzięciół *see* Dzyatlava
113 I16 **Zdzieszowice** *Ger.* Odertal. Opolskie, S Poland 50.24N 18.06E
Zealand *see* Sjælland
196 K6 **Zealandia Bank** *undersea feature* C Pacific Ocean
65 H20 **Zeballos, Monte** ▲ S Argentina 47.04S 71.32W
85 K20 **Zebediela** Limpopo, NE South Africa 24.16S 29.21E
115 L18 **Zebë, Mal** *var.* Mali i Zebës. ▲ NE Albania 41.57N 20.16E
Zebës, Mali i *see* Zebë, Mal
23 V9 **Zebulon** North Carolina, SE USA 35.49N 78.19W
114 K8 **Žednik** *Hung.* Bácsjózseffalva. Serbia, N Serbia and Montenegro (Yugoslavia) 45.58N 19.40E
101 C15 **Zeebrugge** West-Vlaanderen, NW Belgium 51.19N 3.13E
191 N16 **Zeehan** Tasmania, SE Australia 41.54S 145.19E
101 L14 **Zeeland** Noord-Brabant, SE Netherlands 51.42N 5.40E
31 N7 **Zeeland** North Dakota, N USA 45.57N 99.49W
101 E14 **Zeeland** ◆ *province* SW Netherlands
85 I21 **Zeerust** North-West, N South Africa 25.33S 26.04E
100 K10 **Zeewolde** Flevoland, C Netherlands 52.19N 5.31E
144 G8 **Zefat** *var.* Safed, Tsefat, *Ar.* Safad. Northern, N Israel 32.57N 35.27E
Żegań *see* Żagań
Zehden *see* Cedynia
102 O11 **Zehdenick** Brandenburg, NE Germany 52.58N 13.19E
Zē-i Bādīnān *see* Great Zab
Zeiden *see* Codlea
152 M14 **Zeidskoye Vodokhranilishche** ▣ E Turkmenistan
Zē-i Kōya *see* Little Zab
189 P7 **Zeil, Mount** ▲ Northern Territory, C Australia 23.31S 132.41E
100 J12 **Zeist** Utrecht, C Netherlands 52.04N 5.15E
103 M16 **Zeitz** Sachsen-Anhalt, E Germany 51.03N 12.07E
165 T11 **Zêkog** Qinghai, C China 35.03N 101.30E
Zelaya Norte *see* Atlántico Norte, Región Autónoma
Zelaya Sur *see* Atlántico Sur, Región Autónoma
101 F17 **Zele** Oost-Vlaanderen, NW Belgium 51.04N 4.01E
112 N12 **Żelechów** Lubelskie, E Poland 51.49N 21.57E
115 H14 **Zelena Glava** ▲ SE Bosnia and Herzegovina 43.32N 17.55E
115 I14 **Zelengora** ▲▲ S Bosnia and Herzegovina
128 I5 **Zelenoborskiy** Murmanskaya Oblast', NW Russian Federation 66.52N 32.25E
131 R3 **Zelenodol'sk** Respublika Tatarstan, W Russian Federation 55.52N 48.49E
126 I13 **Zelenogorsk** Krasnoyarskiy Kray, C Russian Federation 56.08N 94.29E
128 G12 **Zelenogorsk** *Fin.* Terijoki. Leningradskaya Oblast', NW Russian Federation 60.08N 30.06E
130 K3 **Zelenograd** Moskovskaya Oblast', W Russian Federation 56.02N 37.08E
120 B13 **Zelenogradsk** *Ger.* Cranz, Kranz. Kaliningradskaya Oblast', W Russian Federation 54.57N 20.30E
131 O15 **Zelenokumsk** Stavropol'skiy Kray, SW Russian Federation 44.22N 43.48E
172 Rr7 **Zelënyy, Ostrov** *var.* Shibotsu-jima. *island* NE Russian Federation
Železna Kapela *see* Eisenkappel
Železna Vrata *see* Demir Kapija
114 L11 **Železniki** Serbia, N Serbia and Montenegro (Yugoslavia) 44.45N 20.23E
100 N12 **Zelhem** Gelderland, E Netherlands 52.00N 6.21E
115 N18 **Želino** NW FYR Macedonia 42.00N 21.06E
115 M14 **Željin** ▲▲ C Serbia and Montenegro (Yugoslavia)
103 K17 **Zella-Mehlis** Thüringen, C Germany 50.40N 10.40E
111 P7 **Zell am See** *var.* Zell-am-See. Salzburg, S Austria 47.19N 12.48E
111 N7 **Zell am Ziller** Tirol, W Austria 47.13N 11.52E
Zelle *see* Celle
111 W2 **Zellerndorf** Niederösterreich, NE Austria 48.40N 15.57E
111 U7 **Zeltweg** Steiermark, S Austria 47.10N 14.43E
121 G17 **Zel'va** *Pol.* Zelwa. Hrodzyenskaya Voblasts', W Belarus 53.09N 24.49E
120 H13 **Želva** Ukmergė, C Lithuania 55.13N 25.07E
Zelwa *see* Zel'va
101 E16 **Zelzate** *var.* Selzaete. Oost-Vlaanderen, NW Belgium 51.12N 3.49E
120 E11 **Žemaičių Aukštumas** *physical region* W Lithuania
120 C12 **Žemaičių Naumiestis** Šilutė, SW Lithuania 55.22N 21.39E
Zembin *see* Zyembin
131 N6 **Zemetchino** Penzenskaya Oblast', W Russian Federation 53.31N 42.35E
81 M15 **Zémio** Haut-Mbomou, E Central African Republic 5.04N 25.07E
43 R16 **Zempoaltepec, Cerro** ▲ SE Mexico 17.04N 95.54W
101 G17 **Zemst** Vlaams Brabant, C Belgium 50.59N 4.28E
114 L11 **Zemun** Serbia, N Serbia and Montenegro (Yugoslavia) 44.51N 20.24E
Zendajan *see* Zendeh Jan
154 J5 **Zendeh Jan** *var.* Zendajan, Zindajān. Herāt, NW Afghanistan 34.55N 61.53E
Zengg *see* Senj
114 H12 **Zenica** Federacija Bosna I Hercegovina, C Bosnia and Herzegovina 44.12N 17.52E
Zenjan *see* Zanjān
Zen'kov *see* Zin'kiv
Zenshū *see* Chŏnju
Zenta *see* Senta
170 Ff14 **Zentsūji** *var.* Zentûzi. Kagawa, Shikoku, SW Japan 34.13N 133.45E
Zentûzi *see* Zentsūji
84 B11 **Zenza do Itombe** Cuanza Norte, NW Angola 9.22S 14.10E
114 H12 **Žepče** Federacija Bosna I Hercegovina, N Bosnia and Herzegovina 44.26N 18.00E
25 W12 **Zephyrhills** Florida, SE USA 28.13N 82.10W
199 J10 **Zephyr Reef** *reef* Pacific Ocean
164 F9 **Zepu** *var.* Poskam. Xinjiang Uygur Zizhiqu, NW China 38.10N 77.18E
153 Q12 **Zeravshan** *Taj./Uzb.* Zarafshon. ≈ Tajikistan/Uzbekistan
Zeravshan *see* Zarafshon
Zeravshanskiy Khrebet *see* Zarafshon, Qatorkŭhi
103 M14 **Zerbst** Sachsen-Anhalt, E Germany 51.57N 12.05E
151 P8 **Zerenda** Akmola, N Kazakhstan 52.55N 69.09E
112 H12 **Żerków** Wielkopolskie, C Poland 52.03N 17.33E
110 E11 **Zermatt** Valais, SW Switzerland 46.00N 7.44E
Zernest *see* Zărneşti
110 J9 **Zernez** Graubünden, SE Switzerland 46.42N 10.06E
130 L12 **Zernograd** Rostovskaya Oblast', SW Russian Federation 46.52N 40.13E
Zestafoni *see* Zestap'oni
143 S9 **Zestap'oni** *Rus.* Zestafoni. C Georgia 42.09N 43.00E
100 H12 **Zestienhoven** ✈ (Rotterdam) Zuid-Holland, SW Netherlands 51.57N 4.30E
115 J16 **Zeta** ≈ SW Serbia and Montenegro (Yugoslavia)
15 J2 **Zeta Lake** ◎ Victoria Island, Nunavut, N Canada
100 L12 **Zetten** Gelderland, SE Netherlands 51.55N 5.43E
103 M17 **Zeulenroda** Thüringen, C Germany 50.40N 11.58E

◆ Country ● Country Capital ◇ Dependent Territory ○ Dependent Territory Capital ◆ Administrative Region ✈ International Airport ▲ Mountain ▲▲ Mountain Range Volcano ≈ River ◎ Lake ▣ Reservoir

102 *H10* **Zeven** Niedersachsen, NW Germany *53.17N 9.16E*
100 *M12* **Zevenaar** Gelderland, SE Netherlands *51.55N 6.04E*
101 *H14* **Zevenbergen** Noord-Brabant, S Netherlands *51.39N 4.36E*
126 *M14* **Zeya** Amurskaya Oblast', SE Russian Federation *53.51N 126.53E*
133 *X6* **Zeya** ≈ SE Russian Federation
Zeya Reservoir *see* Zeyskoye Vodokhranilishche
149 *T11* **Zeynalābād** Kermān, C Iran *29.55N 57.28E*
126 *M14* **Zeyskoye Vodokhranilishche** *Eng.* Zeya Reservoir. ⊠ SE Russian Federation
106 *H8* **Zêzere, Rio** ≈ C Portugal
Zgerzh *see* Zgierz
144 *H6* **Zgharta** N Lebanon *34.24N 35.54E*
112 *K12* **Zgierz** *Ger.* Neuhof, *Rus.* Zgerzh. Łódź, C Poland *51.55N 19.19E*
113 *E14* **Zgorzelec** *Ger.* Görlitz. Dolnośląskie, SW Poland *51.10N 15.00E*
Zhabdün *see* Zhongba
121 *F19* **Zhabinka** *Pol.* Żabinka, *Rus.* Zhabinka. Brestskaya Voblasts', SW Belarus *52.12N 24.01E*
Zhaggo *see* Luhuo
165 *R15* **Zhag'yab** Xizang Zizhiqu, W China *30.42N 97.33E*
150 *L9* **Zhailma** *Kaz.* Zhayylma. Kostanay, N Kazakhstan *51.34N 61.39E*
151 *V16* **Zhalanash** Almaty, SE Kazakhstan *43.07N 78.40E*
Zhalashash *see* Dzhalagash
151 *S7* **Zhalauly, Ozero** ◎ NE Kazakhstan
150 *E9* **Zhalpatkal** *prev.* Furmanovo. Zapadnyy Kazakhstan, W Kazakhstan *49.40N 49.27E*
121 *G16* **Zhaludok** *Rus.* Zheludok. Hrodzyenskaya Voblasts', W Belarus *53.36N 24.58E*
Zhaman-Akkol', Ozero *see* Akkol', Ozero
Zhambyl *see* Taraz
151 *Q14* **Zhambyl** *off.* Zhambylskaya Oblast', *Kaz.* Zhambyl Oblysy; *prev.* Dzhambulskaya Oblast'. ◈ *province* S Kazakhstan
Zhambyl Oblysy/Zhambylskaya Oblast' *see* Zhambyl
Zhamo *see* Bomi
151 *S12* **Zhamshy** ≈ C Kazakhstan
150 *M15* **Zhanadar'ya** Kzylorda, S Kazakhstan *44.41N 64.39E*
151 *O15* **Zhanakorgan** *Kaz.* Zhangaqorghan. Kzylorda, S Kazakhstan *43.57N 67.14E*
165 *N16* **Zhanang** Xizang Zizhiqu, W China *29.15N 91.19E*
151 *T12* **Zhanaortalyk** Zhezkazgan, C Kazakhstan *47.31N 75.42E*
150 *F15* **Zhanaozen** *Kaz.* Zhangaözen, *prev.* Novyy Uzen'. Mangistau, W Kazakhstan *43.21N 52.50E*
151 *Q16* **Zhanatas** Zhambyl, S Kazakhstan *43.33N 69.40E*
Zhangaözen *see* Zhanaozen
Zhangaqazaly *see* Ayteke Bi
Zhangaqorghan *see* Zhanakorgan
167 *O2* **Zhangbei** Hebei, E China *41.13N 114.43E*
Zhangdian *see* Zibo
169 *X9* **Zhangguangcai Ling** ▲▲ NE China
151 *W10* **Zhangiztobe** Vostochnyy Kazakhstan, E Kazakhstan *49.16N 81.16E*
165 *W11* **Zhangjiachuan** Gansu, N China *34.55N 106.25E*
166 *L10* **Zhangjiajie** *var.* Dayong. Hunan, S China *29.10N 110.22E*
167 *O2* **Zhangjiakou** *var.* Changkiakow, Zhang-chia-k'ou, *Eng.* Kalgan; *prev.* Wanchuan. Hebei, E China *40.48N 114.51E*
167 *Q13* **Zhangping** Fujian, SE China *25.21N 117.29E*
167 *Q13* **Zhangpu** Fujian, SE China *24.07N 117.36E*
169 *U11* **Zhangwu** Liaoning, NE China *42.21N 122.32E*
165 *S8* **Zhangye** Gansu, N China *38.59N 100.27E*
167 *Q13* **Zhangzhou** Fujian, SE China *24.31N 117.40E*
169 *W6* **Zhan He** ≈ NE China
150 *D9* **Zhanibek** *prev.* Dzhanybek *Kaz.* Zhänibek. Zapadnyy Kazakhstan, W Kazakhstan *49.27N 46.51E*
Zhänibek *see* Zhanibek
166 *L16* **Zhanjiang** *var.* Chanchiang, Chan-chiang, *Cant.* Tsamkong, *Fr.* Fort-Bayard. Guangdong, S China *21.10N 110.19E*
Zhansügirov *see* Dzhansugurov
169 *V8* **Zhaodong** Heilongjiang, NE China *46.03N 125.58E*
Zhaoge *see* Qixian
166 *H11* **Zhaojue** Sichuan, C China *28.03N 102.50E*
167 *N14* **Zhaoqing** Guangdong, S China *23.07N 112.26E*
164 *H5* **Zhaosu** *var.* Mongolküre. Xinjiang Uygur Zizhiqu, NW China *43.09N 81.07E*
166 *H11* **Zhaotong** Yunnan, SW China *27.17N 103.42E*
169 *V9* **Zhaoyuan** Heilongjiang, NE China *45.30N 125.04E*
169 *V9* **Zhaozhou** Heilongjiang, NE China *45.40N 125.16E*
151 *X13* **Zharbulak** Vostochnyy Kazakhstan, E Kazakhstan *46.05N 82.06E*
164 *J15* **Zhari Namco** ◎ W China
150 *I12* **Zharkamys** *Kaz.* Zharqamys. Aktyubinsk, W Kazakhstan *47.58N 56.33E*
151 *W15* **Zharkent** *prev.* Panfilov. Almaty, SE Kazakhstan *44.10N 80.01E*
128 *H17* **Zharkovskiy** Tverskaya Oblast', W Russian Federation *55.51N 32.19E*
151 *W11* **Zharma** Vostochnyy Kazakhstan, E Kazakhstan *48.48N 80.55E*
150 *F14* **Zharmysh** Mangistau, SW Kazakhstan *44.12N 52.27E*
Zharqamys *see* Zharkamys
120 *L13* **Zhary** *Rus.* Zhary. Vitsyebskaya Voblasts', N Belarus *55.04N 28.40E*
Zhaslyk *see* Jasliq
126 *Ll11* **Zhatay** Respublika Sakha (Yakutiya), NE Russian Federation *62.07N 129.42E*
164 *J14* **Zhaxi Co** ◎ W China
Zhayylma *see* Zhailma
Zhdanov *see* Beyläqan, Azerbaijan
Zhdanov *see* Mariupol', Ukraine
Zhe *see* Zhejiang
167 *R10* **Zhejiang** *var.* Che-chiang, Chekiang, Zhe, Zhejiang Sheng. ◈ *province* SE China
Zhejiang Sheng *see* Zhejiang
151 *S7* **Zhelezinka** Pavlodar, N Kazakhstan *53.35N 75.16E*
121 *C14* **Zheleznodorozhnyy** *Ger.* Gerdauen. Kaliningradskaya Oblast', W Russian Federation *54.21N 21.17E*
126 *J13* **Zheleznodorozhnyy** Irkutskaya Oblast', C Russian Federation *57.54N 102.40E*
Zheleznodorozhnyy *see* Yemva
130 *J7* **Zheleznogorsk** Kurskaya Oblast', W Russian Federation *52.22N 35.21E*
126 *Jj14* **Zheleznogorsk-Ilimskiy** Irkutskaya Oblast', S Russian Federation *56.38N 103.53E*
131 *N15* **Zheleznovodsk** Stavropol'skiy Kray, SW Russian Federation *44.12N 43.01E*
Zhëltyye Vody *see* Zhovti Vody
Zheludok *see* Zhaludok
Zhem *see* Emba
166 *K7* **Zhenba** Shaanxi, C China *32.42N 107.55E*
166 *I13* **Zhenfeng** Guizhou, S China *25.27N 105.38E*
Zhengjiatun *see* Shuangliao
165 *X10* **Zhengning** Gansu, N China *35.28N 108.21E*
169 *Q12* **Zhengxiangbai Qi** Nei Mongol Zizhiqu, N China *42.10N 114.57E*
167 *N6* **Zhengzhou** *var.* Ch'eng-chou, Chengchow; *prev.* Chenghsien. Henan, C China *34.45N 113.37E*
167 *R8* **Zhenjiang** *var.* Chenkiang. Jiangsu, E China *32.12N 119.30E*
126 *I13* **Zheleznogorsk** Krasnoyarskiy Kray, C Russian Federation *56.20N 93.36E*
169 *U9* **Zhenlai** Jilin, NE China *45.52N 123.11E*
166 *I11* **Zhenxiong** Yunnan, SW China *27.31N 104.52E*
166 *K11* **Zhenyuan** *prev.* Wuyang. Guizhou, S China *27.07N 108.33E*
167 *R11* **Zherong** Fujian, SE China *27.16N 119.54E*
151 *U15* **Zhetigen** *prev.* Nikolayevka. Almaty, SE Kazakhstan *43.39N 77.10E*
Zhetiqara *see* Zhitikara
150 *F15* **Zhetybay** Mangistau, SW Kazakhstan *43.30N 52.09E*
151 *P17* **Zhetysay** *var.* Dzhetysay. Yuzhnyy Kazakhstan *40.45N 68.18E*
166 *M11* **Zhexi Shuiku** ⊠ C China
151 *O12* **Zhezdy** Zhezkazgan, C Kazakhstan *48.06N 67.01E*
151 *O12* **Zhezkazgan** *Kaz.* Zhezqazghan; *prev.* Dzhezkazgan. Zhezkazgan, C Kazakhstan *47.48N 67.43E*
Zhezqazghan *see* Zhezkazgan
166 *M9* **Zhicheng** Hubei, C China *30.21N 111.27E*
Zhidachov *see* Zhydachiv
165 *Q12* **Zhidoi** Qinghai, C China *33.55N 95.39E*
126 *Jj15* **Zhigalovo** Irkutskaya Oblast', S Russian Federation *54.47N 105.00E*
126 *L9* **Zhigansk** Respublika Sakha (Yakutiya), NE Russian Federation *66.45N 123.20E*
131 *R6* **Zhigulevsk** Samarskaya Oblast', W Russian Federation *53.24N 49.30E*
120 *D13* **Zhilino** *Ger.* Schillen. Kaliningradskaya Oblast', W Russian Federation *54.55N 21.54E*
131 *O8* **Zhirnovsk** Volgogradskaya Oblast', SW Russian Federation *51.01N 44.49E*
Zhitarovo *see* Vetren
150 *L8* **Zhitikara** *Kaz.* Zhetiqara, *prev.* Dzhetygara. Kostanay, NW Kazakhstan *52.10N 61.12E*
Zhitkovichi *see* Zhytkavichy
131 *P10* **Zhitkur** Volgogradskaya Oblast', SW Russian Federation *49.00N 46.16E*
Zhitomir *see* Zhytomyr
Zhitomirskaya Oblast' *see* Zhytomyrs'ka Oblast'
130 *J5* **Zhizdra** Kaluzhskaya Oblast', W Russian Federation *53.38N 34.39E*
121 *N18* **Zhlobin** Homyel'skaya Voblasts', SE Belarus *52.52N 30.01E*
Zhmerinka *see* Zhmerynka
118 *M7* **Zhmerynka** *Rus.* Zhmerinka. Vinnyts'ka Oblast', C Ukraine *49.01N 28.01E*
155 *R9* **Zhob** *var.* Fort Sandeman. Baluchistān, SW Pakistan *31.22N 69.25E*
155 *R8* **Zhob** ≈ C Pakistan
150 *I10* **Zhobda** *prev.* Novoalekseyevka. Aktyubinsk, W Kazakhstan *50.10N 55.39E*
Zhodino *see* Zhodzina
121 *L15* **Zhodzina** *Rus.* Zhodino. Minskaya Voblasts', C Belarus *54.05N 28.19E*
126 *Mm3* **Zhokhova, Ostrov** *island* Novosibirskiye Ostrova, NE Russian Federation
Zholkev/Zholkva *see* Zhovkva
Zholsaly *see* Dzhusaly
Zhondor *see* Jondor
164 *I15* **Zhongba** *var.* Zhabdün. Xizang Zizhiqu, W China *29.37N 84.11E*
166 *F11* **Zhongdian** Yunnan, SW China *27.48N 99.40E*
Zhonghua Renmin Gongheguo *see* China
165 *V9* **Zhongning** Ningxia, N China *37.25N 105.40E*
167 *N15* **Zhongshan** Guangdong, S China *22.30N 113.19E*
205 *X7* **Zhongshan** *Chinese research station* Antarctica *69.23S 76.34E*
166 *M6* **Zhongtiao Shan** ▲▲ C China
165 *V9* **Zhongwei** Ningxia, N China *37.31N 105.10E*
166 *K9* **Zhongxian** *var.* Zhong Xian. Chongqing Shi, C China *30.16N 108.03E*
167 *N9* **Zhongxiang** Hubei, C China *31.12N 112.35E*
167 *O7* **Zhoukou** *var.* Zhoukouzhen. Henan, C China *33.37N 114.34E*
Zhoukouzhen *see* Zhoukou
167 *S9* **Zhoushan** Zhejiang, S China
167 *S9* **Zhoushan Qundao** *Eng.* Zhoushan Islands. *island group* SE China
118 *I5* **Zhovkva** *Pol.* Żółkiew, *Rus.* Zholkev, Zholkva; *prev.* Nesterov. L'vivs'ka Oblast', NW Ukraine *50.03N 24.00E*
119 *S7* **Zhovti Vody** *Rus.* Zhëltyye Vody. Dnipropetrovs'ka Oblast', E Ukraine *48.24N 33.30E*
119 *Q10* **Zhovtneve** *Rus.* Zhovtnevoye. Mykolayivs'ka Oblast', S Ukraine *46.50N 32.00E*
Zhovtnevoye *see* Zhovtneve
116 *K9* **Zhrebchevo, Yazovir** ⊠ C Bulgaria
169 *V13* **Zhuanghe** Liaoning, NE China *39.43N 122.57E*
165 *W11* **Zhuanglang** Gansu, C China *35.06N 106.21E*
151 *P15* **Zhuantobe** *Kaz.* Zhūantöbe. Yuzhnyy Kazakhstan, S Kazakhstan *44.45N 68.50E*
167 *Q5* **Zhucheng** Shandong, E China *35.58N 119.24E*
165 *V12* **Zhugqu** Gansu, C China *33.51N 104.14E*
167 *N15* **Zhuhai** Guangdong, S China *22.16N 113.30E*
Zhuizishan *see* Weichang
Zhuji *see* Shangqiu
130 *I5* **Zhukovka** Bryanskaya Oblast', W Russian Federation *53.33N 33.48E*
167 *O3* **Zhuozhou** *prev.* Zhuo Xian. Hebei, E China *39.22N 115.40E*
168 *L14* **Zhuozi Shan** ▲ N China *39.28N 106.58E*
Zhuravichi *see* Zhuravichy
121 *O17* **Zhuravichy** *Rus.* Zhuravichi. Homyel'skaya Voblasts', SE Belarus *53.15N 30.29E*
151 *Q8* **Zhuravlevka** Akmola, N Kazakhstan *51.56N 69.56E*
119 *Q4* **Zhurivka** Kyyivs'ka Oblast', N Ukraine *50.28N 31.48E*
150 *J11* **Zhuryn** Aktyubinsk, W Kazakhstan *49.13N 57.36E*
151 *T15* **Zhusandala, Step'** *grassland* SE Kazakhstan
166 *L8* **Zhushan** Hubei, C China *32.11N 110.05E*
167 *N11* **Zhuzhou** Hunan, S China *27.52N 112.52E*
118 *I6* **Zhydachiv** *Pol.* Żydaczów, *Rus.* Zhidachov. L'vivs'ka Oblast', NW Ukraine *49.22N 24.09E*
Zhympīty *see* Zhympity
150 *G9* **Zhympity** *Kaz.* Zhympīty, *prev.* Dzhambeyty. Zapadnyy Kazakhstan, W Kazakhstan *50.16N 52.34E*
121 *K19* **Zhytkavichy** *Rus.* Zhitkovichi. Homyel'skaya Voblasts', SE Belarus *52.13N 27.52E*
119 *N4* **Zhytomyr** *Rus.* Zhitomir. Zhytomyrs'ka Oblast', NW Ukraine *50.17N 28.39E*
Zhytomyr *see* Zhytomyrs'ka Oblast'
118 *M4* **Zhytomyrs'ka Oblast'** *var.* Zhytomyr, *Rus.* Zhitomirskaya Oblast'. ◈ *province* N Ukraine
159 *U15* **Zia** ✕ (Dhaka) Dhaka, C Bangladesh
113 *J20* **Žiar nad Hronom** *var.* Sväty Kríž nad Hronom, *Ger.* Heiligenkreuz, *Hung.* Garamszentkereszt. Banskobystrický Kraj, C Slovakia *48.36N 18.52E*
167 *Q4* **Zibo** *var.* Zhangdian. Shandong, E China *36.51N 118.01E*
166 *L4* **Zichang** *prev.* Wayaobu. Shaanxi, C China *37.08N 109.40E*
Zichenau *see* Ciechanów
113 *G15* **Ziębice** *Ger.* Münsterberg in Schlesien. Dolnośląskie, SW Poland *50.37N 17.01E*
Ziebingen *see* Cybinka
Ziegenhais *see* Głuchołazy
112 *E12* **Zielona Góra** *Ger.* Grünberg, Grünberg in Schlesien, Grüneberg. Lubuskie, W Poland *51.55N 15.30E*
101 *F14* **Zierikzee** Zeeland, SW Netherlands *51.39N 3.55E*
166 *I10* **Zigong** *var.* Tzekung. Sichuan, C China *29.19N 104.48E*
78 *G12* **Ziguinchor** SW Senegal *12.33N 16.19W*
43 *N16* **Zihuatanejo** Guerrero, S Mexico *17.39N 101.33W*
Zilah *see* Zalău
131 *W7* **Zilair** Respublika Bashkortostan, W Russian Federation *52.12N 57.15E*
142 *L12* **Zile** Tokat, N Turkey *40.18N 35.52E*
113 *J18* **Žilina** *Ger.* Sillein, *Hung.* Zsolna. Žilinský Kraj, N Slovakia *49.13N 18.43E*
113 *J19* **Žilinský Kraj** ◈ *region* N Slovakia
77 *Q9* **Zillah** *var.* Zallah. C Libya *28.30N 17.33E*
Zillenmarkt *see* Zalău
111 *N7* **Ziller** ≈ W Austria
Zillertal Alps *see* Zillertaler Alpen
111 *N8* **Zillertaler Alpen** *Eng.* Zillertal Alps, *It.* Alpi Aurine. ▲▲ Austria/Italy
120 *K10* **Zilupe** *Ger.* Rosenhof. Ludza, E Latvia *56.10N 28.06E*
126 *J15* **Zima** Irkutskaya Oblast', S Russian Federation *53.57N 101.57E*
43 *O13* **Zimapán** Hidalgo, C Mexico *20.42N 99.23W*
85 *I16* **Zimba** Southern, S Zambia *17.16S 26.10E*
85 *J17* **Zimbabwe** *off.* Republic of Zimbabwe; *prev.* Rhodesia. ◆ *republic* S Africa
118 *H10* **Zimbor** *Hung.* Magyarzsombor. Sălaj, NW Romania *47.00N 23.16E*
Zimmerbude *see* Svetlyy
118 *J15* **Zimnicea** Teleorman, S Romania *43.39N 25.21E*
116 *L9* **Zimnitsa** Yambol, E Bulgaria *42.34N 26.37E*
131 *N12* **Zimovniki** Rostovskaya Oblast', SW Russian Federation *47.07N 42.28E*
Zindajān *see* Zendeh Jan
79 *V12* **Zinder** Zinder, S Niger *13.46N 9.01E*
79 *W11* **Zinder** ◈ *department* S Niger
79 *P12* **Ziniaré** C Burkina *12.35N 1.21W*
Zinjan *see* Zanjān
147 *P16* **Zinjibār** SW Yemen *13.07N 45.22E*
119 *T4* **Zin'kiv** *var.* Zen'kov. Poltavs'ka Oblast', NE Ukraine *50.11N 34.21E*
Zinov'yevsk *see* Kirovohrad
Zintenhof *see* Sindi
33 *N10* **Zion** Illinois, N USA *42.27N 87.49W*
56 *F10* **Zipaquirá** Cundinamarca, C Colombia *5.03N 74.01W*
Zipser Neudorf *see* Spišská Nová Ves
113 *H23* **Zirc** Veszprém, W Hungary *47.16N 17.52E*
115 *D14* **Žirje** *It.* Zuri. *island* S Croatia
Zirknitz *see* Cerknica
110 *M7* **Zirl** Tirol, W Austria *47.16N 11.16E*
103 *K20* **Zirndorf** Bayern, SE Germany *49.27N 10.57E*
166 *M11* **Zi Shui** ≈ C China
111 *Y3* **Zistersdorf** Niederösterreich, NE Austria *48.31N 16.45E*
43 *O14* **Zitácuaro** Michoacán de Ocampo, SW Mexico *19.28N 100.21W*
103 *Q16* **Zittau** Sachsen, E Germany *50.53N 14.48E*
114 *I12* **Živinice** Federacija Bosna I Hercegovina, E Bosnia and Herzegovina *44.26N 18.39E*
Ziwa Magharibi *see* Kagera
83 *J14* **Ziway Hāyk'** ◎ C Ethiopia
167 *N12* **Zixing** Hunan, S China *26.01N 113.25E*
131 *W7* **Ziyanchurino** Orenburgskaya Oblast', W Russian Federation *51.36N 56.58E*
166 *K8* **Ziyang** Shaanxi, C China *32.33N 108.27E*
113 *I20* **Zlaté Moravce** *Hung.* Aranyosmarót. Nitriansky Kraj, SW Slovakia *48.22N 18.22E*
114 *K13* **Zlatibor** ▲▲ W Serbia and Montenegro (Yugoslavia)
116 *L9* **Zlati Voyvoda** Sliven, E Bulgaria *42.36N 26.13E*
118 *G11* **Zlatna** *Ger.* Kleinschlatten, *Hung.* Zalatna; *prev. Ger.* Goldmarkt. Alba, C Romania *46.07N 23.10E*
116 *I8* **Zlatna Panega** Lovech, N Bulgaria *43.07N 24.09E*
116 *N8* **Zlatni Pyasŭtsi** Dobrich, NE Bulgaria *43.19N 28.03E*
125 *E11* **Zlatoust** Chelyabinskaya Oblast', C Russian Federation *55.12N 59.33E*
113 *M19* **Zlatý Stôl** *Ger.* Goldener Tisch, *Hung.* Aranyosasztal. ▲ C Slovakia *48.45N 20.39E*
115 *P18* **Zletovo** NE FYR Macedonia *42.00N 22.14E*
113 *H18* **Zlín** *prev.* Gottwaldov. Zlínský Kraj, SE Czech Republic *49.13N 17.40E*
113 *H19* **Zlinský Kraj** ◈ *region* E Czech Republic
77 *O7* **Zlīṭan** W Libya *32.28N 14.34E*
112 *F9* **Złocieniec** *Ger.* Falkenburg in Pommern. Zachodniopomorskie, NW Poland *53.31N 16.01E*
112 *J13* **Złoczew** Sieradz, S Poland *51.24N 18.36E*
Złoczów *see* Zolochiv
113 *F14* **Złotoryja** *Ger.* Goldberg. Dolnośląskie, W Poland *51.07N 15.57E*
112 *G9* **Złotów** Wielkopolskie, NW Poland *53.22N 17.01E*
126 *Gg15* **Zmeinogorsk** Altayskiy Kray, S Russian Federation *51.07N 82.16E*
112 *G13* **Żmigród** *Ger.* Trachenberg. Dolnośląskie, SW Poland *51.31N 16.55E*
130 *J6* **Zmiyevka** Orlovskaya Oblast', W Russian Federation *52.39N 36.20E*
119 *V5* **Zmiyiv** Kharkivs'ka Oblast', E Ukraine *49.40N 36.22E*
Zna *see* Tsna
Znaim *see* Znojmo
130 *M7* **Znamenka** Tambovskaya Oblast', W Russian Federation *52.24N 42.28E*
Znamenka *see* Znam"yanka
121 *C14* **Znamens** Astrakhanskaya Oblast', SW Russian Federation *54.37N 21.13E*
131 *P10* **Znamensk** *Ger.* Wehlau. Kaliningradskaya Oblast', W Russian Federation *48.33N 46.18E*
125 *Ff12* **Znamenskoye** Omskaya Oblast', C Russian Federation *57.09N 73.40E*
119 *R7* **Znam"yanka** *Rus.* Znamenka. Kirovohrads'ka Oblast', C Ukraine *48.41N 32.39E*
112 *H10* **Żnin** Kujawsko-pomorskie, C Poland *52.50N 17.40E*
113 *F19* **Znojmo** *Ger.* Znaim. Brněnský Kraj, S Czech Republic *48.52N 16.04E*
81 *N16* **Zobia** Orientale, N Dem. Rep. Congo *2.57N 25.55E*
85 *N15* **Zóbuè** Tete, NW Mozambique *15.28S 34.25E*
100 *G12* **Zoetermeer** Zuid-Holland, W Netherlands *52.04N 4.30E*
110 *E7* **Zofingen** Aargau, N Switzerland *47.16N 7.56E*
165 *R15* **Zogang** *var.* Wangda. Xizang Zizhiqu, W China *29.41N 97.54E*
108 *E7* **Zogno** Lombardia, N Italy *45.49N 9.42E*
148 *M10* **Zohreh, Rūd-e** ≈ SW Iran
166 *H7* **Zoigê** Sichuan, C China *33.44N 102.57E*
Zółkiew *see* Zhovkva
110 *D8* **Zollikofen** Bern, W Switzerland *47.01N 7.28E*
Zolochev *see* Zolochiv
119 *U4* **Zolochiv** *Rus.* Zolochev. Kharkivs'ka Oblast', E Ukraine *50.16N 35.58E*
118 *J5* **Zolochiv** *Pol.* Złoczów, *Rus.* Zolochev. L'vivs'ka Oblast', W Ukraine *49.48N 24.51E*
119 *X7* **Zolote** *Rus.* Zolotoye. Luhans'ka Oblast', E Ukraine *48.42N 38.33E*
119 *Q6* **Zolotonosha** Cherkas'ka Oblast', C Ukraine *49.39N 32.04E*
Zolotoye *see* Zolote
Zólyom *see* Zvolen
85 *N15* **Zomba** Southern, S Malawi *15.22S 35.22E*
Zombor *see* Sombor
101 *D17* **Zomergem** Oost-Vlaanderen, NW Belgium *51.07N 3.31E*
153 *P11* **Zomin** *Rus.* Zaamin. Jizzax Viloyati, C Uzbekistan *39.56N 68.16E*
81 *I15* **Zongo** Equateur, N Dem. Rep. Congo *4.17N 18.42E*
142 *G10* **Zonguldak** Zonguldak, NW Turkey *41.25N 31.46E*
142 *H10* **Zonguldak** ◈ *province* NW Turkey
101 *K17* **Zonhoven** Limburg, NE Belgium *50.58N 5.22E*
148 *J2* **Zonūz** Āżarbāyjān-e Khāvarī, NW Iran *38.31N 45.54E*
105 *Y16* **Zonza** Corse, France, C Mediterranean Sea *41.49N 9.13E*
Zoppot *see* Sopot
Zorgho *see* Zorgo
79 *Q13* **Zorgo** *var.* Zorgho. C Burkina *12.15N 0.37W*
106 *K10* **Zorita** Extremadura, W Spain *39.18N 5.42W*
153 *U14* **Zorkŭl** *Rus.* Ozero Zorkul'. ◎ SE Tajikistan
Zorkul', Ozero *see* Zorkŭl
58 *A8* **Zorritos** Tumbes, N Peru *3.40S 80.36W*
113 *J16* **Żory** *var.* Zory, *Ger.* Sohrau. Śląskie, S Poland *50.03N 18.41E*
78 *K15* **Zorzor** N Liberia *7.46N 9.28W*
101 *E18* **Zottegem** Oost-Vlaanderen, NW Belgium *50.52N 3.49E*
79 *R15* **Zou** ≈ S Benin
80 *H6* **Zouar** Borkou-Ennedi-Tibesti, N Chad *20.24N 16.28E*
78 *J6* **Zouérat** *var.* Zouérate, Zouîrât. Tiris Zemmour, N Mauritania *22.44N 12.29W*
Zouérate *see* Zouérat
Zoug *see* Zug
Zouîrât *see* Zouérat
78 *M16* **Zoukougbeu** C Ivory Coast *9.47N 6.50W*
100 *M5* **Zoutkamp** Groningen, NE Netherlands *53.22N 6.17E*
101 *J18* **Zoutleeuw** *Fr.* Leau. Vlaams Brabant, C Belgium *50.49N 5.06E*
114 *L9* **Zrenjanin** *prev.* Petrovgrad, Veliki Bečkerek, *Ger.* Grossbetschkerek, *Hung.* Nagybecskerek. Serbia, N Serbia and Montenegro (Yugoslavia) *45.22N 20.24E*
114 *E10* **Zrinska Gora** ▲▲ C Croatia
Zsablya *see* Žabalj
103 *N16* **Zschopau** ≈ E Germany
Zsebely *see* Jebel
Zsibó *see* Jibou
Zsil/Zsily *see* Jiu
Zsilyvajdevulkán *see* Vulcan
Zsolna *see* Žilina
Zsombolya *see* Jimbolia
Zsupanya *see* Županja
57 *N7* **Zuata** Anzoátegui, NE Venezuela *8.21N 65.12W*
107 *N14* **Zubia** Andalucía, S Spain *37.10N 3.36W*
67 *P16* **Zubov Seamount** *undersea feature* E Atlantic Ocean *20.45S 8.45E*
128 *I16* **Zubtsov** Tverskaya Oblast', W Russian Federation *56.10N 34.34E*
110 *M8* **Zuckerhütl** ▲ SW Austria *46.57N 11.07E*
Zueila *see* Zawīlah
78 *M16* **Zuénoula** C Ivory Coast *7.25N 6.03W*
107 *S5* **Zuera** Aragón, NE Spain *41.52N 0.46W*
147 *V13* **Ẓufār** *Eng.* Dhofar. *physical region* SW Oman
110 *G8* **Zug** *Fr.* Zoug. Zug, C Switzerland *47.10N 8.30E*
110 *G8* **Zug** *Fr.* Zoug. ◈ *canton* C Switzerland
143 *R9* **Zugdidi** W Georgia *42.30N 41.52E*
110 *G8* **Zuger See** ◎ NW Switzerland
103 *K25* **Zugspitze** ▲ S Germany *47.25N 10.58E*
101 *E15* **Zuid-Beveland** *var.* South Beveland. *island* SW Netherlands
100 *K10* **Zuidelijk-Flevoland** *polder* C Netherlands
Zuider Zee *see* IJsselmeer
100 *G12* **Zuid-Holland** *Eng.* South Holland. ◈ *province* W Netherlands
100 *N5* **Zuidhorn** Groningen, NE Netherlands *53.15N 6.25E*
100 *O6* **Zuidlaardermeer** ◎ NE Netherlands
100 *O6* **Zuidlaren** Drenthe, NE Netherlands *53.06N 6.40E*
101 *K14* **Zuid-Willemsvaart Kanaal** *canal* S Netherlands
100 *N8* **Zuidwolde** Drenthe, NE Netherlands *52.40N 6.25E*
Zuitaizi *see* Kangxian
107 *O14* **Zújar** Andalucía, S Spain *37.33N 2.52W*
106 *L11* **Zújar** ≈ W Spain
106 *L11* **Zújar, Embalse del** ⊠ W Spain
82 *J9* **Zula** E Eritrea *15.19N 39.40E*
56 *G6* **Zulia** *off.* Estado Zulia. ◈ *state* NW Venezuela
Zullapara *see* Sinchaingbyin
Züllichau *see* Sulechów
107 *P3* **Zumárraga** País Vasco, N Spain *43.04N 2.19W*
114 *D8* **Žumberačko Gorje** *var.* Gorjanči, Uskocke Planine, Žumberak, *Ger.* Uskokengebirge; *prev.* Sichelbuger Gebirge. ▲ Croatia/Slovenia *see also* Gorjanci
Žumberak *see* Gorjanci/Žumberačko Gorje
204 *K7* **Zumberge Coast** *coastal feature* Antarctica
Zumbo *see* Vila do Zumbo
31 *W10* **Zumbro Falls** Minnesota, N USA *44.15N 92.25W*
31 *W10* **Zumbro River** ≈ Minnesota, N USA
31 *W10* **Zumbrota** Minnesota, N USA *44.18N 92.37W*
101 *H15* **Zundert** Noord-Brabant, S Netherlands *51.28N 4.40E*
Zungaria *see* Dzungaria
79 *U14* **Zungeru** Niger, C Nigeria *9.49N 6.10E*
39 *O11* **Zuni** New Mexico, SW USA *35.03N 108.52W*
39 *P11* **Zuni Mountains** ▲▲ New Mexico, SW USA
166 *J11* **Zunyi** Guizhou, S China *27.40N 106.55E*
166 *J15* **Zuo Jiang** ≈ China/Vietnam
110 *J9* **Zuoz** Graubünden, SE Switzerland *46.37N 9.58E*
114 *I10* **Županja** *Hung.* Zsupanya. Vukovar-Srijem, E Croatia *45.03N 18.42E*
115 *M17* **Žur** Serbia, S Serbia and Montenegro (Yugoslavia) *42.10N 20.37E*
131 *T2* **Zura** Udmurtskaya Respublika, NW Russian Federation *57.36N 53.19E*
145 *V8* **Zurbāṭīyah** E Iraq *33.13N 46.07E*
Zuri *see* Žirje
110 *F7* **Zürich** *Eng./Fr.* Zurich, *It.* Zurigo. Zürich, N Switzerland *47.22N 8.33E*
110 *G6* **Zürich** *Eng./Fr.* Zurich. ◈ *canton* N Switzerland
Zurich, Lake *see* Zürichsee
110 *G7* **Zürichsee** *Eng.* Lake Zurich. ◎ NE Switzerland
Zurigo *see* Zürich
155 *V1* **Zŭrkŭl** *Pash.* Sarī Qūl, *Rus.* Ozero Zurkul'. ◎ Afghanistan/Tajikistan *see also* Sarī Qūl
Zurkul', Ozero *see* Sarī Qūl/Zŭrkŭl
112 *K10* **Żuromin** Mazowieckie, N Poland *53.00N 19.54E*
110 *J8* **Zürs** Vorarlberg, W Austria *47.11N 10.11E*
79 *T13* **Zuru** Kebbi, W Nigeria *11.28N 5.13E*
110 *F6* **Zurzach** Aargau, N Switzerland *47.33N 8.21E*
103 *J22* **Zusam** ≈ S Germany
100 *M11* **Zutphen** Gelderland, E Netherlands *52.09N 6.12E*
77 *N7* **Zuwārah** NW Libya *32.55N 12.06E*
Zuwaylah *see* Zawīlah
129 *R14* **Zuyevka** Kirovskaya Oblast', NW Russian Federation *58.24N 51.08E*
167 *N10* **Zụzhou** Hunan, S China *27.52N 113.00E*
Zvenigorodka *see* Zvenyhorodka
119 *P6* **Zvenyhorodka** *Rus.* Zvenigorodka. Cherkas'ka Oblast', C Ukraine *49.05N 30.58E*
126 *Jj14* **Zvezdnyy** Irkutskaya Oblast', C Russian Federation *56.43N 106.22E*
129 *U14* **Zvëzdnyy** Permskaya Oblast', NW Russian Federation *57.45N 56.20E*
85 *K18* **Zvishavane** *prev.* Shabani. Matabeleland South, S Zimbabwe *20.19S 30.01E*
113 *J20* **Zvolen** *Ger.* Altsohl, *Hung.* Zólyom. Banskobystrický Kraj, C Slovakia *48.35N 19.06E*
114 *J12* **Zvornik** E Bosnia and Herzegovina *44.24N 19.07E*
100 *M5* **Zwaagwesteinde** *Fris.* De Westerein. Friesland, N Netherlands *53.16N 6.07E*
100 *H10* **Zwanenburg** Noord-Holland, C Netherlands *52.22N 4.43E*
100 *L8* **Zwarte Meer** ◎ N Netherlands
100 *M9* **Zwarte Water** ≈ N Netherlands
100 *M8* **Zwartsluis** Overijssel, E Netherlands *52.39N 6.04E*
78 *L17* **Zwedru** *var.* Tchien. E Liberia *6.04N 8.07W*
100 *O8* **Zweeloo** Drenthe, NE Netherlands *52.48N 6.45E*
103 *E20* **Zweibrücken** *Fr.* Deux-Ponts; *Lat.* Bipontium. Rheinland-Pfalz, SW Germany *49.15N 7.22E*
110 *D9* **Zweisimmen** Fribourg, W Switzerland *46.33N 7.22E*
103 *M15* **Zwenkau** Sachsen, E Germany *51.11N 12.19E*
111 *V3* **Zwettl** Wien, NE Austria *48.28N 14.16E*
111 *T3* **Zwettl an der Rodl** Oberösterreich, N Austria *48.28N 14.16E*
101 *D18* **Zwevegem** West-Vlaanderen, W Belgium *50.48N 3.19E*
103 *M17* **Zwickau** Sachsen, E Germany *50.43N 12.31E*
103 *O21* **Zwiesel** Bayern, SE Germany *49.02N 13.14E*
100 *H13* **Zwijndrecht** Zuid-Holland, SW Netherlands *51.49N 4.39E*
103 *N16* **Zwickauer Mulde** ≈ E Germany
Zwischenwässern *see* Medvode
Zwittau *see* Svitavy
112 *N13* **Zwoleń** Mazowieckie, SE Poland *51.21N 21.37E*
100 *M9* **Zwolle** Overijssel, E Netherlands *52.31N 6.06E*
24 *G6* **Zwolle** Louisiana, S USA *31.37N 93.38W*
112 *K12* **Żychlin** Łodzkie, C Poland *52.13N 19.43E*
Żydaczów *see* Zhydachiv
121 *L14* **Zyembin** *Rus.* Zembin. Minskaya Voblasts', C Belarus *54.25N 28.14E*
Zyôetu *see* Jōetsu
112 *L12* **Żyrardów** Mazowieckie, C Poland *52.03N 20.27E*
127 *Nn8* **Zyryanka** Respublika Sakha (Yakutiya), NE Russian Federation *65.45N 150.43E*
151 *Y9* **Zyryanovsk** Vostochnyy Kazakhstan, E Kazakhstan *49.45N 84.16E*
113 *J17* **Żywiec** *Ger.* Bäckermühle Schulzenmühle. Śląskie, S Poland *49.43N 19.10E*167 *S9*
Zhoushan Qundao *Eng.* Zhoushan Islands. *island group* SE China
118 *I5* **Zhovkva** *Pol.* Żółkiew, *Rus.* Zholkev, Zholkva; *prev.* Nesterov. L'vivs'ka Oblast', NW Ukraine *50.03N 24.00E*
119 *S7* **Zhovti Vody** *Rus.* Zhëltyye Vody. Dnipropetrovs'ka Oblast', E Ukraine *48.24N 33.30E*
119 *Q10* **Zhovtneve** *Rus.* Zhovtnevoye. Mykolayivs'ka Oblast', S Ukraine *46.50N 32.00E*
Zhovtnevoye *see* Zhovtneve
116 *K9* **Zhrebchevo, Yazovir** ⊠ C Bulgaria
169 *V13* **Zhuanghe** Liaoning, NE China *39.43N 122.57E*
165 *W11* **Zhuanglang** Gansu, C China *35.06N 106.21E*
151 *P15* **Zhuantobe** *Kaz.* Zhūantöbe. Yuzhnyy Kazakhstan, S Kazakhstan *44.45N 68.50E*
167 *Q5* **Zhucheng** Shandong, E China *35.58N 119.24E*
165 *V12* **Zhugqu** Gansu, C China *33.51N 104.14E*
167 *N15* **Zhuhai** Guangdong, S China *22.16N 113.30E*
Zhuizishan *see* Weichang
Zhuji *see* Shangqiu
130 *I5* **Zhukovka** Bryanskaya Oblast', W Russian Federation *53.33N 33.48E*
167 *O3* **Zhuozhou** *prev.* Zhuo Xian. Hebei, E China *39.22N 115.40E*
168 *L14* **Zhuozi Shan** ▲ N China *39.28N 106.58E*
Zhuravichi *see* Zhuravichy
121 *O17* **Zhuravichy** *Rus.* Zhuravichi. Homyel'skaya Voblasts', SE Belarus *53.15N 30.29E*
151 *Q8* **Zhuravlevka** Akmola, N Kazakhstan *51.56N 69.56E*
119 *Q4* **Zhurivka** Kyyivs'ka Oblast', N Ukraine *50.28N 31.48E*
150 *J11* **Zhuryn** Aktyubinsk, W Kazakhstan *49.13N 57.36E*
151 *T15* **Zhusandala, Step'** *grassland* SE Kazakhstan
166 *L8* **Zhushan** Hubei, C China *32.11N 110.05E*
167 *N11* **Zhuzhou** Hunan, S China *27.52N 112.52E*
118 *I6* **Zhydachiv** *Pol.* Żydaczów, *Rus.* Zhidachov. L'vivs'ka Oblast', NW Ukraine *49.22N 24.09E*
Zhympīty *see* Zhympity
150 *G9* **Zhympity** *Kaz.* Zhympīty, *prev.* Dzhambeyty. Zapadnyy Kazakhstan, W Kazakhstan *50.16N 52.34E*
121 *K19* **Zhytkavichy** *Rus.* Zhitkovichi. Homyel'skaya Voblasts', SE Belarus *52.13N 27.52E*
119 *N4* **Zhytomyr** *Rus.* Zhitomir. Zhytomyrs'ka Oblast', NW Ukraine *50.17N 28.39E*
Zhytomyr *see* Zhytomyrs'ka Oblast'
118 *M4* **Zhytomyrs'ka Oblast'** *var.* Zhytomyr, *Rus.* Zhitomirskaya Oblast'. ◈ *province* N Ukraine
159 *U15* **Zia** ✕ (Dhaka) Dhaka, C Bangladesh
113 *J20* **Žiar nad Hronom** *var.* Sväty Kríž nad Hronom, *Ger.* Heiligenkreuz, *Hung.* Garamszentkereszt. Banskobystrický Kraj, C Slovakia *48.36N 18.52E*
167 *Q4* **Zibo** *var.* Zhangdian. Shandong, E China *36.51N 118.01E*
166 *L4* **Zichang** *prev.* Wayaobu. Shaanxi, C China *37.08N 109.40E*
Zichenau *see* Ciechanów
113 *G15* **Ziębice** *Ger.* Münsterberg in Schlesien. Dolnośląskie, SW Poland *50.37N 17.01E*
Ziebingen *see* Cybinka
Ziegenhais *see* Głuchołazy
112 *E12* **Zielona Góra** *Ger.* Grünberg, Grünberg in Schlesien, Grüneberg. Lubuskie, W Poland *51.55N 15.30E*
101 *F14* **Zierikzee** Zeeland, SW Netherlands *51.39N 3.55E*
166 *I10* **Zigong** *var.* Tzekung. Sichuan, C China *29.19N 104.48E*
78 *G12* **Ziguinchor** SW Senegal *12.33N 16.19W*
43 *N16* **Zihuatanejo** Guerrero, S Mexico *17.39N 101.33W*
Zilah *see* Zalău
131 *W7* **Zilair** Respublika Bashkortostan, W Russian Federation *52.12N 57.15E*
142 *L12* **Zile** Tokat, N Turkey *40.18N 35.52E*
113 *J18* **Žilina** *Ger.* Sillein, *Hung.* Zsolna. Žilinský Kraj, N Slovakia *49.13N 18.43E*
113 *J19* **Žilinský Kraj** ◈ *region* N Slovakia
77 *Q9* **Zillah** *var.* Zallah. C Libya *28.30N 17.33E*
Zillenmarkt *see* Zalău
111 *N7* **Ziller** ≈ W Austria
Zillertal Alps *see* Zillertaler Alpen
111 *N8* **Zillertaler Alpen** *Eng.* Zillertal Alps, *It.* Alpi Aurine. ▲▲ Austria/Italy
120 *K10* **Zilupe** *Ger.* Rosenhof. Ludza, E Latvia *56.10N 28.06E*
126 *J15* **Zima** Irkutskaya Oblast', S Russian Federation *53.57N 101.57E*
43 *O13* **Zimapán** Hidalgo, C Mexico *20.42N 99.23W*
85 *I16* **Zimba** Southern, S Zambia *17.16S 26.10E*
85 *J17* **Zimbabwe** *off.* Republic of Zimbabwe; *prev.* Rhodesia. ◆ *republic* S Africa
118 *H10* **Zimbor** *Hung.* Magyarzsombor. Sălaj, NW Romania *47.00N 23.16E*
Zimmerbude *see* Svetlyy
118 *J15* **Zimnicea** Teleorman, S Romania *43.39N 25.21E*
116 *L9* **Zimnitsa** Yambol, E Bulgaria *42.34N 26.37E*
131 *N12* **Zimovniki** Rostovskaya Oblast', SW Russian Federation *47.07N 42.28E*
Zindajān *see* Zendeh Jan
79 *V12* **Zinder** Zinder, S Niger *13.46N 9.01E*
79 *W11* **Zinder** ◈ *department* S Niger
79 *P12* **Ziniaré** C Burkina *12.35N 1.21W*
Zinjan *see* Zanjān
147 *P16* **Zinjibār** SW Yemen *13.07N 45.22E*
119 *T4* **Zin'kiv** *var.* Zen'kov. Poltavs'ka Oblast', NE Ukraine *50.11N 34.21E*
Zinov'yevsk *see* Kirovohrad
Zintenhof *see* Sindi
33 *N10* **Zion** Illinois, N USA *42.27N 87.49W*
56 *F10* **Zipaquirá** Cundinamarca, C Colombia *5.03N 74.01W*
Zipser Neudorf *see* Spišská Nová Ves
113 *H23* **Zirc** Veszprém, W Hungary *47.16N 17.52E*
115 *D14* **Žirje** *It.* Zuri. *island* S Croatia
Zirknitz *see* Cerknica
110 *M7* **Zirl** Tirol, W Austria *47.16N 11.16E*

◆ Country
● Country Capital
◇ Dependent Territory
○ Dependent Territory Capital
◈ Administrative Region
✕ International Airport
▲ Mountain
▲▲ Mountain Range
Volcano
≈ River
◎ Lake
⊠ Reservoir

103 *K20* **Zirndorf** Bayern, SE Germany *49.27N 10.57E*
166 *M11* **Zi Shui** ≈ C China
111 *Y3* **Zistersdorf** Niederösterreich, NE Austria *48.31N 16.45E*
43 *O14* **Zitácuaro** Michoacán de Ocampo, SW Mexico *19.28N 100.21W*
103 *Q16* **Zittau** Sachsen, E Germany *50.53N 14.48E*
114 *I12* **Živinice** Federacija Bosna I Hercegovina, E Bosnia and Herzegovina *44.26N 18.39E*
Ziwa Magharibi *see* Kagera
83 *J14* **Ziway Hāyk'** ◎ C Ethiopia
167 *N12* **Zixing** Hunan, S China *26.01N 113.25E*
131 *W7* **Ziyanchurino** Orenburgskaya Oblast', W Russian Federation *51.36N 56.58E*
166 *K8* **Ziyang** Shaanxi, C China *32.33N 108.27E*
113 *I20* **Zlaté Moravce** ***Hung.*** Aranyosmarót. Nitriansky Kraj, SW Slovakia *48.22N 18.22E*
114 *K13* **Zlatibor** ▲▲ W Serbia and Montenegro (Yugoslavia)
116 *L9* **Zlati Voyvoda** Sliven, E Bulgaria *42.36N 26.13E*
118 *G11* **Zlatna** *Ger.* Kleinschlatten, ***Hung.*** Zalatna; ***prev.*** *Ger.* Goldmarkt. Alba, C Romania *46.07N 23.10E*
116 *I8* **Zlatna Panega** Lovech, N Bulgaria *43.07N 24.09E*
116 *N8* **Zlatni Pyasŭtsi** Dobrich, NE Bulgaria *43.19N 28.03E*
125 *E11* **Zlatoust** Chelyabinskaya Oblast', C Russian Federation *55.12N 59.33E*
113 *M19* **Zlatý Stôl** *Ger.* Goldener Tisch, ***Hung.*** Aranyosasztal. ▲ C Slovakia *48.45N 20.39E*
115 *P18* **Zletovo** NE FYR Macedonia *42.00N 22.14E*
113 *H18* **Zlín** ***prev.*** Gottwaldov. Zlínský Kraj, SE Czech Republic *49.13N 17.40E*
113 *H19* **Zlinský Kraj** ◐ *region* E Czech Republic
77 *O7* **Zlīţan** W Libya *32.28N 14.34E*
112 *F9* **Złocieniec** *Ger.* Falkenburg in Pommern. Zachodniopomorskie, NW Poland *53.31N 16.01E*
112 *J13* **Złoczew** Sieradz, S Poland *51.24N 18.36E*
Złoczów *see* Zolochiv
113 *F14* **Złotoryja** *Ger.* Goldberg. Dolnośląskie, W Poland *51.07N 15.57E*
112 *G9* **Złotów** Wielkopolskie, NW Poland *53.22N 17.01E*
126 *Gg15* **Zmeinogorsk** Altayskiy Kray, S Russian Federation *51.07N 82.16E*
112 *G13* **Żmigród** *Ger.* Trachenberg. Dolnośląskie, SW Poland *51.31N 16.55E*
130 *J6* **Zmiyevka** Orlovskaya Oblast', W Russian Federation *52.39N 36.20E*
119 *V5* **Zmiyiv** Kharkivs'ka Oblast', E Ukraine *49.40N 36.22E*
Zna *see* Tsna
Znaim *see* Znojmo
130 *M7* **Znamenka** Tambovskaya Oblast', W Russian Federation *52.24N 42.28E*
Znamenka *see* Znam"yanka
121 *C14* **Znamens** Astrakhanskaya Oblast', SW Russian Federation *54.37N 21.13E*
131 *P10* **Znamensk** *Ger.* Wehlau. Kaliningradskaya Oblast', W Russian Federation *48.33N 46.18E*
125 *Ff12* **Znamenskoye** Omskaya Oblast', C Russian Federation *57.09N 73.40E*
119 *R7* **Znam"yanka** ***Rus.*** Znamenka. Kirovohrads'ka Oblast', C Ukraine *48.41N 32.39E*
112 *H10* **Żnin** Kujawsko-pomorskie, C Poland *52.50N 17.40E*
113 *F19* **Znojmo** *Ger.* Znaim. Brněnský Kraj, S Czech Republic *48.52N 16.04E*
81 *N16* **Zobia** Orientale, N Dem. Rep. Congo *2.57N 25.55E*
85 *N15* **Zóbuè** Tete, NW Mozambique *15.28S 34.25E*
100 *G12* **Zoetermeer** Zuid-Holland, W Netherlands *52.04N 4.30E*
110 *E7* **Zofingen** Aargau, N Switzerland *47.16N 7.56E*
165 *R15* **Zogang** ***var.*** Wangda. Xizang Zizhiqu, W China *29.41N 97.54E*
108 *E7* **Zogno** Lombardia, N Italy *45.49N 9.42E*
148 *M10* **Zohreh, Rūd-e** ≈ SW Iran
166 *H7* **Zoigê** Sichuan, C China *33.44N 102.57E*
Zółkiew *see* Zhovkva
110 *D8* **Zollikofen** Bern, W Switzerland *47.01N 7.28E*
Zolochev *see* Zolochiv
119 *U4* **Zolochiv** ***Rus.*** Zolochev. Kharkivs'ka Oblast', E Ukraine *50.16N 35.58E*
118 *J5* **Zolochiv** ***Pol.*** Złoczów, ***Rus.*** Zolochev. L'vivs'ka Oblast', W Ukraine *49.48N 24.51E*
119 *X7* **Zolote** ***Rus.*** Zolotoye. Luhans'ka Oblast', E Ukraine *48.42N 38.33E*
119 *Q6* **Zolotonosha** Cherkas'ka Oblast', C Ukraine *49.39N 32.04E*
Zolotoye *see* Zolote
Zólyom *see* Zvolen
85 *N15* **Zomba** Southern, S Malawi *15.22S 35.22E*
Zombor *see* Sombor
101 *D17* **Zomergem** Oost-Vlaanderen, NW Belgium *51.07N 3.31E*
153 *P11* **Zomin** ***Rus.*** Zaamin. Jizzax Viloyati, C Uzbekistan *39.56N 68.16E*
81 *I15* **Zongo** Equateur, N Dem. Rep. Congo *4.17N 18.42E*
142 *G10* **Zonguldak** Zonguldak, NW Turkey *41.25N 31.46E*
142 *H10* **Zonguldak** ◐ *province* NW Turkey
101 *K17* **Zonhoven** Limburg, NE Belgium *50.58N 5.22E*
148 *J2* **Zonūz** Āżarbāyjān-e Khāvarī, NW Iran *38.31N 45.54E*
105 *Y16* **Zonza** Corse, France, C Mediterranean Sea *41.49N 9.13E*
Zoppot *see* Sopot
Zorgho *see* Zorgo
79 *Q13* **Zorgo** ***var.*** Zorgho. C Burkina *12.15N 0.37W*
106 *K10* **Zorita** Extremadura, W Spain *39.18N 5.42W*
153 *U14* **Zorkŭl** ***Rus.*** Ozero Zorkul'. ◎ SE Tajikistan
Zorkul', Ozero *see* Zorkŭl
58 *A8* **Zorritos** Tumbes, N Peru *3.40S 80.36W*
113 *J16* **Żory** ***var.*** Zory, ***Ger.*** Sohrau. Śląskie, S Poland *50.03N 18.41E*
78 *K15* **Zorzor** N Liberia *7.46N 9.28W*
101 *E18* **Zottegem** Oost-Vlaanderen, NW Belgium *50.52N 3.49E*
79 *R15* **Zou** ≈ S Benin
80 *H6* **Zouar** Borkou-Ennedi-Tibesti, N Chad *20.24N 16.28E*
78 *J6* **Zouérat** ***var.*** Zouérate, Zouîrât. Tiris Zemmour, N Mauritania *22.44N 12.29W*
Zouérate *see* Zouérat
Zoug *see* Zug
Zouîrât *see* Zouérat
78 *M16* **Zoukougbeu** C Ivory Coast *9.47N 6.50W*
100 *M5* **Zoutkamp** Groningen, NE Netherlands *53.22N 6.17E*
101 *J18* **Zoutleeuw** ***Fr.*** Leau. Vlaams Brabant, C Belgium *50.49N 5.06E*
114 *L9* **Zrenjanin** ***prev.*** Petrovgrad, Veliki Bečkerek, ***Ger.*** Grossbetschkerek, ***Hung.*** Nagybecskerek. Serbia, N Serbia and Montenegro (Yugoslavia) *45.22N 20.24E*
114 *E10* **Zrinska Gora** ▲▲ C Croatia
Zsablya *see* Žabalj
103 *N16* **Zschopau** ≈ E Germany
Zsebely *see* Jebel
Zsibó *see* Jibou
Zsil/Zsily *see* Jiu
Zsilyvajdevulkán *see* Vulcan
Zsolna *see* Žilina
Zsombolya *see* Jimbolia
Zsupanya *see* Županja
57 *N7* **Zuata** Anzoátegui, NE Venezuela *8.21N 65.12W*
107 *N14* **Zubia** Andalucía, S Spain *37.10N 3.36W*
67 *P16* **Zubov Seamount** *undersea feature* E Atlantic Ocean *20.45S 8.45E*
128 *I16* **Zubtsov** Tverskaya Oblast', W Russian Federation *56.10N 34.34E*
110 *M8* **Zuckerhütl** ▲ SW Austria *46.57N 11.07E*
Zueila *see* Zawīlah
78 *M16* **Zuénoula** C Ivory Coast *7.25N 6.03W*
107 *S5* **Zuera** Aragón, NE Spain *41.52N 0.46W*
147 *V13* **Ẓufār** ***Eng.*** Dhofar. *physical region* SW Oman
110 *G8* **Zug** ***Fr.*** Zoug. Zug, C Switzerland *47.10N 8.30E*
110 *G8* **Zug** ***Fr.*** Zoug. ◐ *canton* C Switzerland
143 *R9* **Zugdidi** W Georgia *42.30N 41.52E*
110 *G8* **Zuger See** ◎ NW Switzerland
103 *K25* **Zugspitze** ▲ S Germany *47.25N 10.58E*
101 *E15* **Zuid-Beveland** ***var.*** South Beveland. *island* SW Netherlands
100 *K10* **Zuidelijk-Flevoland** *polder* C Netherlands
Zuider Zee *see* IJsselmeer
100 *G12* **Zuid-Holland** ***Eng.*** South Holland. ◐ *province* W Netherlands
100 *N5* **Zuidhorn** Groningen, NE Netherlands *53.15N 6.25E*
100 *O6* **Zuidlaardermeer** ◎ NE Netherlands
100 *O6* **Zuidlaren** Drenthe, NE Netherlands *53.06N 6.40E*
101 *K14* **Zuid-Willemsvaart Kanaal** *canal* S Netherlands
100 *N8* **Zuidwolde** Drenthe, NE Netherlands *52.40N 6.25E*
Zuitaizi *see* Kangxian
107 *O14* **Zújar** Andalucía, S Spain *37.33N 2.52W*
106 *L11* **Zújar** ≈ W Spain
106 *L11* **Zújar, Embalse del** ⊠ W Spain
82 *J9* **Zula** E Eritrea *15.19N 39.40E*
56 *G6* **Zulia** ***off.*** Estado Zulia. ◐ *state* NW Venezuela
Zullapara *see* Sinchaingbyin
Züllichau *see* Sulechów
107 *P3* **Zumárraga** País Vasco, N Spain *43.04N 2.19W*
114 *D8* **Žumberačko Gorje** ***var.*** Gorjanči, Uskocke Planine, Žumberak, ***Ger.*** Uskokengebirge; ***prev.*** Sichelbuger Gebirge. ▲ Croatia/Slovenia *see also* Gorjanci
Žumberak *see* Gorjanci/Žumberačko Gorje
204 *K7* **Zumberge Coast** *coastal feature* Antarctica
Zumbo *see* Vila do Zumbo
31 *W10* **Zumbro Falls** Minnesota, N USA *44.15N 92.25W*
31 *W10* **Zumbro River** ≈ Minnesota, N USA
31 *W10* **Zumbrota** Minnesota, N USA *44.18N 92.37W*
101 *H15* **Zundert** Noord-Brabant, S Netherlands *51.28N 4.40E*
Zungaria *see* Dzungaria
79 *U14* **Zungeru** Niger, C Nigeria *9.49N 6.10E*
39 *O11* **Zuni** New Mexico, SW USA *35.03N 108.52W*
39 *P11* **Zuni Mountains** ▲▲ New Mexico, SW USA
166 *J11* **Zunyi** Guizhou, S China *27.40N 106.55E*
166 *J15* **Zuo Jiang** ≈ China/Vietnam
110 *J9* **Zuoz** Graubünden, SE Switzerland *46.37N 9.58E*
114 *I10* **Županja** ***Hung.*** Zsupanya. Vukovar-Srijem, E Croatia *45.03N 18.42E*
115 *M17* **Žur** Serbia, S Serbia and Montenegro (Yugoslavia) *42.10N 20.37E*
131 *T2* **Zura** Udmurtskaya Respublika, NW Russian Federation *57.36N 53.19E*
145 *V8* **Zurbāţīyah** E Iraq *33.13N 46.07E*
Zuri *see* Žirje
110 *F7* **Zürich** ***Eng./Fr.*** Zurich, ***It.*** Zurigo. Zürich, N Switzerland *47.22N 8.33E*
110 *G6* **Zürich** ***Eng./Fr.*** Zurich. ◐ *canton* N Switzerland
Zurich, Lake *see* Zürichsee
110 *G7* **Zürichsee** ***Eng.*** Lake Zurich. ◎ NE Switzerland
Zurigo *see* Zürich
155 *V1* **Zŭrkŭl** ***Pash.*** Sarī Qūl, ***Rus.*** Ozero Zurkul'. ◎ Afghanistan/Tajikistan ***see also*** Sarī Qūl
Zurkul', Ozero *see* Sarī Qūl/Zŭrkŭl
112 *K10* **Żuromin** Mazowieckie, N Poland *53.00N 19.54E*
110 *J8* **Zürs** Vorarlberg, W Austria *47.11N 10.11E*
79 *T13* **Zuru** Kebbi, W Nigeria *11.28N 5.13E*
110 *F6* **Zurzach** Aargau, N Switzerland *47.33N 8.21E*
103 *J22* **Zusam** ≈ S Germany
100 *M11* **Zutphen** Gelderland, E Netherlands *52.09N 6.12E*
77 *N7* **Zuwārah** NW Libya *32.55N 12.06E*
Zuwaylah *see* Zawīlah
129 *R14* **Zuyevka** Kirovskaya Oblast', NW Russian Federation *58.24N 51.08E*
167 *N10* **Zuzhou** Hunan, S China *27.52N 113.00E*
Zvenigorodka *see* Zvenyhorodka
119 *P6* **Zvenyhorodka** ***Rus.*** Zvenigorodka. Cherkas'ka Oblast', C Ukraine *49.05N 30.58E*
126 *Jj14* **Zvezdnyy** Irkutskaya Oblast', C Russian Federation *56.43N 106.22E*
129 *U14* **Zvëzdnyy** Permskaya Oblast', NW Russian Federation *57.45N 56.20E*
85 *K18* **Zvishavane** ***prev.*** Shabani. Matabeleland South, S Zimbabwe *20.19S 30.01E*
113 *J20* **Zvolen** *Ger.* Altsohl, ***Hung.*** Zólyom. Banskobystrický Kraj, C Slovakia *48.35N 19.06E*
114 *J12* **Zvornik** E Bosnia and Herzegovina *44.24N 19.07E*
100 *M5* **Zwaagwesteinde** ***Fris.*** De Westerein. Friesland, N Netherlands *53.16N 6.07E*
100 *H10* **Zwanenburg** Noord-Holland, C Netherlands *52.22N 4.43E*
100 *L8* **Zwarte Meer** ◎ N Netherlands
100 *M9* **Zwarte Water** ≈ N Netherlands
100 *M8* **Zwartsluis** Overijssel, E Netherlands *52.39N 6.04E*
78 *L17* **Zwedru** ***var.*** Tchien. E Liberia *6.04N 8.07W*
100 *O8* **Zweeloo** Drenthe, NE Netherlands *52.48N 6.45E*
103 *E20* **Zweibrücken** ***Fr.*** Deux-Ponts; ***Lat.*** Bipontium. Rheinland-Pfalz, SW Germany *49.15N 7.22E*
110 *D9* **Zweisimmen** Fribourg, W Switzerland *46.33N 7.22E*
103 *M15* **Zwenkau** Sachsen, E Germany *51.11N 12.19E*
111 *V3* **Zwettl** Wien, NE Austria *48.28N 14.16E*
111 *T3* **Zwettl an der Rodl** Oberösterreich, N Austria *48.28N 14.16E*
101 *D18* **Zwevegem** West-Vlaanderen, W Belgium *50.48N 3.19E*
103 *M17* **Zwickau** Sachsen, E Germany *50.43N 12.31E*
103 *O21* **Zwiesel** Bayern, SE Germany *49.02N 13.14E*
100 *H13* **Zwijndrecht** Zuid-Holland, SW Netherlands *51.49N 4.39E*
103 *N16* **Zwickauer Mulde** ≈ E Germany
Zwischenwässern *see* Medvode
Zwittau *see* Svitavy
112 *N13* **Zwoleń** Mazowieckie, SE Poland *51.21N 21.37E*
100 *M9* **Zwolle** Overijssel, E Netherlands *52.31N 6.06E*
24 *G6* **Zwolle** Louisiana, S USA *31.37N 93.38W*
112 *K12* **Żychlin** Łodzkie, C Poland *52.13N 19.43E*
Żydaczów *see* Zhydachiv
121 *L14* **Zyembin** ***Rus.*** Zembin. Minskaya Voblasts', C Belarus *54.25N 28.14E*
Zyôetu *see* Jōetsu
112 *L12* **Żyrardów** Mazowieckie, C Poland *52.03N 20.27E*
127 *Nn8* **Zyryanka** Respublika Sakha (Yakutiya), NE Russian Federation *65.45N 150.43E*
151 *Y9* **Zyryanovsk** Vostochnyy Kazakhstan, E Kazakhstan *49.45N 84.16E*
113 *J17* **Żywiec** *Ger.* Bäckermühle Schulzenmühle. Śląskie, S Poland *49.43N 19.10E*

Picture Credits

Dorling Kindersley would like to express their thanks to the following individuals, companies and institutions for their help in preparing this Atlas.

Earth Resources Mapping Ltd., *Egham, Surrey*
Brian Groombridge, World Conservation Monitoring Centre, *Cambridge*
The British Library, *London*
British Library of Political and Economic Science, *London*
The British Museum, *London*
The City Business Library, *London*
King's College, *London*
National Meteorological Library and Archive, *Bracknell, Berkshire*
The Printed Word, *London*
The Royal Geographical Society, *London*
University of London Library
Paul Beardmore
Philip Boyes
Hayley Crockford
Alistair Dougal
Nick Drake
Reg Grant
Louise Keane
Zoe Livesley
Laura Porter
Jeff Eidenshink
Chris Hornby
Rachelle Smith
Ray Pinchard
Robert Meisner
Fiona Strawbridge
Wim Jenkins

T = top, B = bottom, A=above, L = left, R = right, C = centre

Every effort has been made to trace the copyright holders and we apologize in advance for any unintentional omissions. We would be pleased to insert the appropriate acknowledgement in any subsequent edition of this publication.

Adams Picture Library: 88CLA; **G Andrews:** 194CR; **Ardea London Ltd:** K Ghana 156C; M Iljima 140TC; R Waller 154TR; **Aspect Picture Library:** P Carmichael 137CRB, 166TR; G Tompkinson 202TRB; **Axiom:** C Bradley 154CA, 165CA; J Holmes xivCRA, xxivBCR, xxviiCRB, 156TCR, 172BC, 172TL, J Morris 77TL, 77CRB, J Spaull 134BL; **Bridgeman Art Library, London / New York:** Collection of the Earl of Pembroke, Wilton House xxBC; **The J. Allan Cash Photolibrary:** xlBR, xliiCLA, xlivCL, 8BC, 62CL, 71CLB, 72CL, 74CLB, 77BR, 78BC, 89BL, 111BR, 144BCL, 147TL, 160CR, 186BR, 189TR; **Bruce Coleman Ltd:** 88BC, 100CL, 102TC; S Alden 198BR; Atlantide xxviTCR, 144BR; E Bjurstrom 147BR; S Bond 98CRB; T Buchholz xvCL, 96TR, 130TCL; J Burton xxiiiC; J Cancalosi 189TRB; B J Coates xxvBL, 198BC; B Coleman 65TL; B & C Colhoun 2TR, 38CB; A Compost xxiiiCBR; Dr S Coyne 47TL; G Cubitt xviTCL, 173BCL, 186TR, 192TR; P Davey xxviiCLB, 123BL; N Devore 201CBL; S J Doylee xxiiCRR; H Flygare xviiCRA; M P L Fogden 17CB; Jeff Foott Productions xxiiiCRB, 9CRA; M Freeman 93BRA; P van Gaalen 88TR; G Gualco 146C; B Henderson 200CR; Dr C Henneghien 71C; HPH Photography, H Van den Berg 71CR; C Hughes 71BCL; C James xxxixTC; J Johnson 41CR, 207TR; J Jurka 93CA; S C Kaufman 30C; S J Krasemann 35TR; H Lange 8TRB, 70CA; C Lockwood 34BC; L C Marigo xxiiBC, xxviiCLA, 51CRA, 61BR; M McCoy 195TR; D Meredith 3CR; J Murray xvCR, 187BR; Orion Press 172TR; Orion Services & Trading Co. Inc. 171TR; C Ott 18BL; Dr E Pott 14C, 42CL, 89C, 95TL, 204CLB; F Prenzel 197C, 200CB; M Read 44BR, 45CRB; H Reinhard xxiiCR, xxviiTR, 204BR; L Lee Rue III 157BCL; J Shaw xixTL; K N Swenson 204BC; P Terry 117CR; N Tomalin 56BCL; P Ward 80TC; S Widstrand 59TR; K Wothe 93C, 181TCL; J T Wright 131BR; **Colorific:** Black Star / L Mulvehil 162CL; Black Star / R Rogers 59BR; Black Star / J Rupp 167BCR; Camera Tres / C. Meyer 61BRA; R Caputo / Matrix 80CL; J. Hill 119CLB; M Koene 57TR; G Satterley xliiCLAR; M Yamashita 162BL, 179CA; **Comstock:** 110CRB; **D Cousens:** 153 CRA; **Sue Cunningham Photographic:** 53CR; **James Davis Travel Photography:** xxxviTCB, xxxviTR, xxxviCL, xxxiii CRA; 11CA, 21BC, 51TLB, 58BCR, 59CLA, 63BCL, 95BC, 96TC, 104TR, 122CB, 164BC, 187CRA, 203BR; **G Dunnet:** 128CA; **Environmental Picture Library:** Chris Westwood 130C; **Eye Ubiquitous:** xCA; Marcus Stone xxxiii tr; L. Fordyce 10CLA; L Johnstone 6CRA, 30BLA, 32CB; S. Miller xxiCA; M Southern 75BLA; **Chris Fairclough Colour Library:** xliBR; **Ffotograff:** C Aithie 137CL, N. Tapsell 164CL; **Geoscience Features:** xviBCR, xviBR, 104CL, 110BC, 127BR; Solar Film 66TC; **Robert Harding Picture Library:** xviiTC, xxivCR, xxxC, xxxvTC, Gavin Heller xxxiii cl; 2TLB, 3CA, 13CRB, 13CR, 39BC, 40CRA, 52BL, 97BR, 101CR, 116CR, 126BL, 138CLA, 148CB, 149TL, 153TR, 162TR, 173CA, 177BR; P G. Adam 11TCB; D Atchison-Jones 72BLA; J Bayne 74BCL; B Schuster 82CR; C Bowman 52BR, 55CA, 64CL, 72CRL; C Campbell xxiBC; G Corrigan 165CRB, 167CRB; P Craven xxxvBL; R Cundy 71BR; Delu 81BC; A Durand 113BR; Financial Times 148BR; R Frerck 53BL; T Gervis 3BCL, 7CR; I Griffiths xxxCL, 79TL; T Hall 177CRA; D Harney 148CA; S Harris xliiiBCL; G Hellier xvCRB, 135BL; F Jackson 143BCR; Jacobs xxxviiTL; P Koch 145TR; F Joseph Land 125TR; Y Marcoux 16BR; S Massif xvBC; A Mills 90CLB; L Murray 116TR; R Rainford xlivBL; G Renner 76CB, 204C; C Rennie 50CL, 118BR; R Richardson 120CL; P Van Riel 50BR; E Rooney 128TR; Sassoon xxivCL, 154CLB; P Scholey 184TR; M Short 143TL; E Simanor xxviiCR; V Southwell 145CR; J Strachan 44TR, 113BL, 136BCR; C Tokeley 140CLA; A C Waltham 167C; T Waltham xviiBL, xxiiCLLL, 144CRB; Westlight 39CR; N Wheeler 145BL; A Williams xxxviiiBR, xlTR; A Woolfitt 97BRA; **Paul Harris:** 126TR, 174TC; **Hutchison Library:** 6BL, 140BCL; P. Collomb 143CR; C. Dodwell 139TR; S Errington 72BCL; P. Hellyer 148BC; J. Horner xxxiTC; R. Ian Lloyd 134CRA; N. Durrell McKenna xxviBCR; J.Nowell 135CLB, 149TC; A Zvoznikov xxiiCL; **Image Bank:** 89BR; J Banagan 202BCA; A Becker xxivBCL; P Hendrie 174BC; M Isy-Schwart 200C, 203CL; M Khansa 124BR; K Forest 169TR; Lomeo xxivTCR; T Madison 177CR; C Molyneux xxiiCRRR; K Mori 200TC; C Navajas xviiiTR; Ocean Images Inc. 198CLB; J van Os xviiTCR; S Proehl 6CL; T Rakke xixTC, 66CL; M Reitz 206CA; M Romanelli 177BL; G A Rossi 157BCR, 184BLA; B Roussel 111TL; S Satushek xviiBCR; Stock Photos / J M Spielman xxivTRL; **Images Colour Library:** xxiiCLL, xxxixTR, xliCR, xliiiBL, 3BR, 21BR, 39TL, 46TL, 64TC, 93BR, 104CLB, 105CR, 156CL, 171CL, 172TRB, 188CA; **Impact Photos:** J & G Andrews 194BL; C. Bluntzer 162BR; Cosmos / G. Buthaud 67BC; S Franklin 130BL; A. le Garsmeur 137CRA; A Indge xxviiTC; C Jones xxxiCB, 72BL; V. Nemirousky 143BR; J Nicholl 78TCR; C. Penn 197BR; G Sweeney xviiBR, 206CB, 206TR; **JVZ Picture Library:** T Nilson 135TC; **Frank Lane Picture Agency:** xxiTCR, xxiiiBL, 95TR; A Christiansen 60CRA; J Holmes xivBL; S. McCutcheon 3C; Silvestris 181TCR; D Smith xxiiBCL; W Wisniewsli 126TL, 205BR; **Leeds Castle Foundation:** xxxviiBC; **Magnum:** Abbas 85CR, 142CA; S Franklin 134CRB; D Hurn 4BCL; P. Jones-Griffiths 203BL; H Kubota xviBCL, 162CLB; F Maver xviBL; S McCurry 75CL, 141BCR; G. Rodger 76TR; C Steele Perkins 74BL; **Mountain Camera / John Cleare:** 159TR; C Monteath 159CR; **Nature Photographers:** E.A. Janes 114CL; **Natural Science Photos:** M Andera 112C; **Network Photographers Ltd.:** C Sappa / Rapho 121BL; **N.H.P.A.:** N. J. Dennis xxiiiCL; D Heuchlin xxiiiCLA; Jane Gifford xxxiii bl; S Krasemann 13BL, 27BR, 40TC; K Schafer 51CB; R Tidman 166CLB; D Tomlinson 151CR; M Wendler 50TR; **Nottingham Trent University:** T Waltham xivCL, xvBR; **Novosti:** 150BLA; **Oxford Scientific Films:** D Allan xxiiTR; H R Bardarson xviiiBC; D Bown xxiiiCBLL; M Brown 146BL; M Colbeck 153CAR; W Faidley 3TL; L Gould xxiiiTRB; D Guravich xxiiiTR; P Hammerschmidy / Okapia 89CLA; M Hill 59TL, 205TR; C Menteath 140TR; J Netherton 2CRB; S Osolinski 84CA; R Packwood 74CA; M Pitts 187TC; N Rosing xxiiiCBL, 9TR, 207BR; D Simonson 59C; Survival Anglia / C Catton 143TR; R Toms xxiiiBR; K Wothe xxiBL, xviiCLA; **Panos Pictures:** B Aris 141C; P Barker xxivBR; T Bolstao 159BR; N Cooper 84CB, 159TC; J-L Dugast 177CB, 178BC; J Hartley 75CA, 92CL; J Holmes 155BC; J Morris 78CLB; M Rose 152TR; D Sansoni 161CL; C Stowers 169TL; **Edward Parker:** 51TL, 51CLB; **Pictor International:** xivBR, xvBRA, xixTCL, xxCL, 3CLA, 19BR, 22TR, 22CRB, 25BCA, 25CL, 28CB, 29BC, 32CA, 35TRB, 36BC, 36BR, 36CR, 40CB, 40CL, 45CL, 65BR, 67TC, 84CL, 85CLB, 101BR, 109CLA, 177TCR, 178BR, 179CR, 188CLB, 193TL; **Pictures Colour Library:** xxiBCL, xxiiBR, xxviBCL, 6BR, 13TR, 14TC, 17TR, 21TL, 22BL, 26C, 26CLA, 29TR, 34TRB, 38BC, 43CA, 45CRA, 70BL, 92TCB, 96BL, 101BL, 108CA, 109CLB, 109CR, 109BR, 119BL, 170BC, 171BR, 198CL; **Planet Earth Pictures:** 200BL; D Barrett 154CB, 192CA; R Coomber 17BL; G Douwma 180BR; E Edmonds 181BR; HC Heap 124TR; J Lythgoe 206BL; A Mounter 137BCR, 180CR; M Potts 6CA; P Scoones xxTR; J Walencik 112TR; J Waters 55BCL; **Popperfoto:** Reuters / J Drake xxxiiCLA; **Rex Features:** 170CR; Antelope xxxiiCLB; M Friedel xxiCR; I McIlgorm xxxCBR; J Shelley xxxCR; Sipa Press xxxCR; Sipa Press / Alix xxxCBL; Sipa Press / Chamussy 184BL; **Russia & Republics Photolibrary:** M Wadlow 120CR, 121CL, 128BC, 128CL, 129TL, 129BR, 130TCR; **Science Photo Library:** CNES, 1990 Distribution Spot Image 137BL; Earth Satellite Corporation xixTRB, xxxiCR, 51BCL; F Gohier xiCR; J Heseltine xviTCB; K Kent xvBLA; P Menzell xvBL; N.A.S.A. xBC; D Parker xivBC; University of Cambridge Collection Air Pictures 89CLB; RJ Wainscoat / P Arnold, Inc. xiBC; D Weintraub xiBL; **South American Pictures:** 59BL, 64TR; R Francis 54BL; Guyana Space Centre 52TR; T Morrison 51CRB, 51BL, 52CR, 54TR, 56TR, 62BL, 63C; **Southampton Oceanography:** xviiiBL; **Sovofoto / Eastfoto:** xxxiiCBR; **Spectrum Colour Library:** 52BC, 166BC; J King 151BR; **Frank Spooner Pictures / Gamma:** 28CRB; E. Baitel xxxiiBC; Bernstein xxxiCL; Contrast 114CR; Diard / Photo News 115CL; Liaison / C. Hires xxxiiTCB; Liaison / Nickelsberg xxxiiTR; Liaison / Vogel 140BL; Marleen 115TL; Novosti 118CA; P. Piel xxxCA; N Quidu 135CL; H Stucke 196CLB, 202CA; Torrengo / Figaro 80BR; A Zamur 115BL; **Still Pictures:** C Caldicott 79TC; A Crump 201CL; M & C Denis-Huot xxiiBL, 80CR, 83BL; M Edwards xxiCRL, 55BL, 66CR, 71BLA, 161BR; J Frebet 55CLB; H Giradet 55TC; M Gunther 123BC; E Parker 54CL; R Seitre 137CA, 138BL, 138TL; **Tony Stone Images:** xxviTR, 4CA, 7BL, 7CL, 11CRB, 41BR, 60C, 99BC, 103BR, 108TR, 111CL, 111CRB, 141BR, 170CLB, 171C,188CB, 189BR, 196BC, 198TR; G Allison 20TR, 33CRB, 195CRB; D Armand 12TCB; D Austen 188TR, 194CL, 195CL; J Beatty 76CL; O Benn xxviBR; K Biggs xxiTL; R Bradbury 46BR; R A Butcher xxviTL; J Callahan xxviiCRA; P Chesley 193BCL, 196C; W Clay 32BL, 33CRA; J Cornish 98BL, 109TL; C Condina 43CB; T Craddock xxivTR; P Degginger 38CLB; Demetrio 5BR; N DeVore xxivBC; A Diesendruck 62BR; S Egan 89CRA, 98BR; R Elliot xxiiBCR; S Elmore 21C; R Frerck 122TR; J Garrett 75CR; S Grandadam 12BR; R Grosskopf 30BL; D Hanson 106BC; C Harvey 71TL; G Hellier 112BL, 172CR; S Huber 105CRB; D Hughs xxxiBR; A Husmo 93TR; G Irvine 33BC; J Jangoux 60CL; G Johnson 138CLB; D Johnston xviiTR; A Kehr 115C; R Koskas xviTR; J Lamb 98CRA; J Lawrence 77CRA; L Lefkowitz 7CA; M Lewis 47CLA; S Mayman 57BR; Murray & Associates 47CR; G Norways 106CA; N Parfitt xxviiCL, 70TCR, 83TL; R Passmore 123TR; N Press xviBCA; E Pritchard 90CA, 92CLR; T Raymond 23BL, 31TR; L Resnick 76BR; M Rogers 82BR; A Sacks 30TCB; C Saule 92CR; S Schulhof xxivTC; P Seaward 36CL; M Segal 34BL; V Shenai 158CL; R Sherman 28CL; H Sitton 142CR; R Smith xxvBLA, 58C; S Studd 110CLA; H Strand 51BR, 65TR; P Tweedie 185CR; L Ulrich 19BL; M Vines 19TC; A B Wadham 62CR; J Warden 65CLB; R Wells 25CRA, 199BL; G Yeowell 36BL; **Telegraph Colour Library:** 63CRB, 63TCR, 163TL; R Antrobus xxxixBR; J Sims 28BR; **Topham Picturepoint:** xxxiCBL, 137BCL, 139CR, 168BR, 174TR, 176BC; 184BL; **Travel Ink:** A Cowin 90TR; **Trip:** 146BR, 150CA, 161CRA; B Ashe 165TR; D Cole 202BCL, 202CR; D Davis 91BL; I Deineko xxxiTR; J Dennis 24BL; Dinodia 160CL; Eye Ubiquitous / L Fordyce 2CLB; A Gasson 155CR; W Jacobs 45TL, 56BL, 185BC, 186CLA, 193BCR, 197BL; P Kingsbury 114C; K Knight 185BR; V Kolpakov 153BL; T Noorits 89TL, 121BR, 152CL; R Power 43TR; N Ray 176CA; C Rennie 118CLB; V Sidoropolev 151TR; E Smith 191BC, 191TL; **Woodfin Camp & Associates:** 94BLR; **World Pictures:** xvCRA, xviiCRA, 16CRB, 24CL, 25BC, 26BL, 37BL, 42TR, 53TR, 73BR, 82TCR, 84TR, 85BL, 88BCR, 98TC, 100BL, 102CR, 103CR, 105BC, 107TC, 123CB, 124BL, 163BL, 167BCL, 168CLB, 180CLB, 180BC, 187BL, 190CB, 191C, 192CL, 193CR; **Zefa Picture Library:** xviBLR, xviiBCL, xviiiCL, 3CL, 11BC, 12TC, 17CA, 23TL, 24CRB, 27BL, 34TCR, 38BCR, 61BCL, 67TCL, 71CLA, 81TL, 83BR, 89CRB, 94C, 100C, 101TL, 102BL, 109TR, 120CRB, 122BL, 126CB, 128CLA, 170CA, 191TR; Anatol 115BR; Barone 116BL; Brandenburg 5C; A J Brown 46TR; H J Clauss 57CLB; Damm 73BC; Evert 94BL; W Felger 3BL; J Fields 201CRA; R Frerck 4BL; G Heil 58BR; K Heibig 117BR; Heilman 30BC; Hunter 8C; Kitchen 8TR, 14CL, 14BL, 16TR; Dr H Kramarz 7BLA, 127CRA; Mehlio 161BL; J F Raga 26TR; Rossenbach 107BR, 122CA; Streichan 91TL; T Stewart 11TR, 21CR; Sunak 56BR, 168TR; D H Teuffen 97TL; B Zaunders 42BC. **Additional Photography:** Geoff Dann; Rob Reichenfeld; H Taylor; Jerry Young.

◆ Country
● Country Capital
◇ Dependent Territory
○ Dependent Territory Capital
◐ Administrative Region
✕ International Airport
▲ Mountain
▲▲ Mountain Range
Ⲁ Volcano
≈ River
◎ Lake
⊠ Reservoir

Abyssal plain A broad plain found in the depths of the ocean, more than 10,000 ft (3,000 m) below sea level.

Air mass A huge, homogeneous mass of air, within which horizontal patterns of temperature and humidity are consistent. Air masses are separated by fronts.

Alluvial fan Large fan-shaped deposit of fine sediments deposited by a river as it emerges from a narrow, mountain valley onto a broad, open plain.

Alluvium Material deposited by rivers. Nowadays usually only applied to finer particles of silt and clay.

Anticline A geological fold that forms an arch shape, curving upward in the rock strata.

Aquifer A body of rock that can absorb water. .

Arête A thin, jagged mountain ridge that divides two adjacent cirques, found in regions where glaciation has occurred.

Artesian well A naturally occurring source of underground water, stored in an aquifer.

Atoll A ring-shaped island or coral reef often enclosing a lagoon of sea water.

Badlands A landscape that has been heavily eroded and dissected by rain-water, and which has little or no vegetation.

Back slope The gentler windward slope of a sand dune or gentler slope of a cuesta.

Bajos An alluvial fan deposited by a river at the base of mountains and hills that encircle desert areas.

Bar, coastal An offshore strip of sand or shingle, either above or below the water. Usually parallel to the shore but sometimes crescent-shaped or at an oblique angle.

Barchan A crescent-shaped sand dune, formed where wind direction is very consistent. The horns of the crescent point downwind and where there is enough sand the barchan is mobile.

Base level The level below which flowing water cannot erode the land.

Basement rock A mass of ancient rock often of PreCambrian age, covered by a layer of more recent sedimentary rocks. Commonly associated with shield areas.

Bedrock Solid, consolidated and relatively unweathered rock, found on the surface of the land or just below a layer of soil or weathered rock.

Bluff The steep bank of a meander, formed by the erosive action of a river.

Breccia A type of rock composed of sharp fragments, cemented by a fine-grained material such as clay.

Butte An isolated, flat-topped hill with steep or vertical sides, buttes are the eroded remnants of a former land surface.

Calcite Hexagonal crystals of calcium carbonate.

Caldera A huge volcanic vent, often containing a number of smaller vents, and sometimes a crater lake.

Carbonation Process whereby rocks are broken down by carbonic acid. Carbon dioxide in the air dissolves in rainwater, forming carbonic acid.

Castle kopje Hill or rock outcrop, especially in southern Africa, where steep sides, and a summit composed of blocks, give a castle-like appearance.

Cataracts A series of stepped waterfalls created as a river flows over a band of hard, resistant rock.

Chernozem A fertile soil, also known as "black earth" consisting of a layer of dark topsoil, rich in decaying vegetation, overlying a lighter chalky layer.

Confluence The point at which two rivers meet.

Continental drift The theory that the continents of today are fragments of one or more prehistoric supercontinents that have moved across the Earth's surface, creating ocean basins.

Continental shelf An area of the continental crust, below sea level, which slopes gently.

Continental slope A steep slope running from the edge of the continental shelf to the ocean floor.

Core The center of the Earth, consisting of a dense mass of iron and nickel.

Coulées A US / Canadian term for a ravine formed by river erosion.

Craton A large block of the Earth's crust which has remained stable for a long period of geological time. It is made up of ancient shield rocks.

Cretaceous A period of geological time beginning about 145 million years ago and lasting until c. 65 million years ago.

Crevasse A deep crack in a glacier.

Crust The hard, thin outer shell of the Earth. It floats on the mantle, which is softer and more dense.

Crystalline rock Rocks formed when molten magma crystallizes (igneous rocks) or when heat or pressure cause re-crystallization (metamorphic rocks).

Cuesta A hill which rises into a steep slope on one side but has a gentler gradient on its other slope.

Delta Low-lying, fan-shaped area at a river mouth, formed by the deposition of successive layers of sediment.

Denudation The combined effect of weathering, erosion, and mass movement, which, over long periods, exposes underlying rocks.

Deposition The laying down of material that has accumulated: after being eroded and then transported by wind, ice, or water; as organic remains, such as coal and coral; as the result of evaporation and chemical precipitation.

Depression 1 In climatic terms it is a large low pressure system; 2 a complex fold, producing a large valley, which incorporates both a syncline and an anticline.

Detritus Piles of rock deposited by an erosive agent such as a river or glacier.

Distributary A minor branch of a river, which does not rejoin the main stream, common at deltas.

Divide A US term describing the area of high ground separating two drainage basins.

Donga A steep-sided gully, resulting from erosion by a river or by floods.

Drainage basin The area drained by a single river system, its boundary is marked by a watershed or divide.

Drumlin A long, streamlined hillock composed of material deposited by a glacier. They often occur in groups known as swarms.

Earthflow The rapid movement of soil and other loose surface material down a slope, when saturated by water.

Ephemeral A nonpermanent feature, often used in connection with seasonal rivers or lakes in dry areas.

Epicenter The point on the Earth's surface directly above the underground origin or focus of an earthquake.

Erg An extensive area of sand dunes, particularly in the Sahara Desert.

Erosion The processes which wear away the surface of the land. Glaciers, wind, rivers, waves, and currents all carry debris that causes erosion.

Escarpment A steep slope at the margin of a level, upland surface. In a landscape created by folding, escarpments (or scarps) frequently lie behind a more gentle backward slope.

Esker A narrow, winding ridge of sand and gravel deposited by streams of water flowing beneath or at the edge of a glacier.

Erratic A rock transported by a glacier and deposited some distance from its place of origin.

Eustacy A world-wide fall or rise in ocean levels.

Exfoliation A kind of weathering whereby scalelike flakes of rock are peeled or broken off by the development of salt crystals in water within the rocks.

Extrusive rock Igneous rock formed when molten material (magma) pours forth at the Earth's surface and cools rapidly. It usually has a glassy texture.

Fault A fracture or crack in rock, where strains (tectonic movement) have caused blocks to move, vertically or laterally, relative to each other.

Ferrel cell A component in the global pattern of air circulation, which rises in the colder latitudes (60° N and S) and descends in warmer latitudes (30° N and S).

Fissure A deep crack in a rock or a glacier.

Fjord A deep, narrow inlet, created when the sea inundates the U-shaped valley created by a glacier.

Flash flood A sudden, short-lived rise in the water level of a river or stream, or surge of water down a dry river channel, or wadi, caused by heavy rainfall.

Floodplain The broad, flat part of a river valley, adjacent to the river itself, formed by sediment deposited during flooding.

Fold A bend in the rock strata of the Earth's crust, resulting from compression.

Frost shattering A form of weathering where water freezes in cracks, causing expansion. As temperatures fluctuate and the ice melts and refreezes, it eventually causes the rocks to shatter.

Geosyncline A concave fold (syncline) or large depression in the Earth's crust, extending hundreds of miles.

Geothermal energy Heat derived from hot rocks within the Earth's crust and resulting in hot springs, steam, or hot rocks at the surface.

Geyser A jet of steam and hot water that intermittently erupts from vents in the ground in areas that are, or were, volcanic.

Glaciation The growth of glaciers and ice sheets, and their impact on the landscape.

Glacier A body of ice moving down-slope under the influence of gravity and consisting of compacted and frozen snow.

Glacio-eustacy A worldwide change in the level of the oceans, caused when the formation of ice sheets takes up water or when their melting returns water to the ocean.

Glaciofluvial To do with glacial meltwater, the landforms it creates and its processes; erosion, transportation, and deposition.

Glacis A gentle slope or pediment.

Gondwanaland The supercontinent thought to have existed over 200 million years ago in the southern hemisphere.

Graben A block of rock let down between two parallel faults. Where the graben occurs within a valley, the structure is known as a rift valley.

Grease ice Slicks of ice that form in Antarctic seas, when ice crystals are bonded together by wind and wave action.

Groundwater Water that has seeped into the pores, cavities, and cracks of rocks or into soil and water held in an aquifer.

Gully A deep, narrow channel eroded in the landscape by ephemeral streams.

Guyot A small, flat-topped submarine mountain, formed as a result of subsidence which occurs during sea-floor spreading.

Hadley cell A large-scale component in the global pattern of air circulation. Warm air rises over the Equator and blows at high altitude toward the poles, sinking in subtropical regions (30° N and 30° S) and creating high pressure. The air then flows at the surface toward the Equator in the form of trade winds.

Hamada An Arabic word for a plateau of bare rock in a desert.

Hanging valley A tributary valley that ends suddenly, high above the bed of the main valley.

Headwards The action of a river eroding back upstream, as opposed to the normal process of downstream erosion. Headwards erosion is often associated with gullying.

Hoodos Pinnacles of rock that have been worn away by weathering in semiarid regions.

Horst A block of the Earth's crust that has been left upstanding by the sinking of adjoining blocks along fault lines.

Hot spot A region of the Earth's crust where high thermal activity occurs, often leading to volcanic eruptions.

Hydrolysis The chemical breakdown of rocks in reaction with water, forming new compounds.

Ice Age A period in the Earth's history when surface temperatures in the temperate latitudes were much lower and ice sheets expanded considerably. There have been ice ages from Pre-Cambrian times onward.

Ice cap A permanent dome of ice in highland areas.

Ice floe A large, flat mass of ice floating free on the ocean surface. It is usually formed after the breakup of winter ice by heavy storms.

Ice sheet A continuous, very thick layer of ice and snow. The term is usually used of ice masses which are continental in extent.

Ice shelf A floating mass of ice attached to the edge of a coast. The seaward edge is usually a sheer cliff up to 100 ft (30 m) high.

Ice wedge Massive blocks of ice up to 6.5 ft (2 m) wide at the top and extending 32 ft (10 m) deep.

Iceberg A large mass of ice in a lake or a sea, which has broken off from a floating ice sheet (an ice shelf) or from a glacier.

Igneous rock Rock formed when molten material, magma, from the hot, lower layers of the Earth's crust, cools, solidifies, and crystallizes, either within the Earth's crust (intrusive) or on the surface (extrusive).

Inselberg An isolated, steep-sided hill, rising from a low plain in semiarid and savannah landscapes.

Interglacial A period of global climate, between two ice ages, when temperatures rise and ice sheets and glaciers retreat.

Intraplate volcano A volcano that lies in the center of one of the Earth's tectonic plates, rather than, as is more common, at its edge.

Intrusion (intrusive igneous rock) Rock formed when molten material, magma, penetrates existing rocks below the Earth's surface before cooling and solidifying.

Isostasy The state of equilibrium that the Earth's crust maintains as its lighter and heavier parts float on the denser underlying mantle.

Isthmus A narrow strip of land connecting two larger landmasses or islands.

Joint A crack in a rock, formed where blocks of rock have not shifted relative to each other, as is the case with a fault. Joints are created by folding; by shrinkage in igneous rock as it cools or sedimentary rock as it dries out; and by the release of pressure in a rock mass when overlying materials are removed by erosion.

Kame A mound of stratified sand and gravel with steep sides, deposited in a crevasse by meltwater running over a glacier. When the ice retreats, this forms an undulating terrain of hummocks.

Karst A barren limestone landscape created by carbonic acid in streams and rainwater, in areas where limestone is close to the surface.

Kettle hole A round hollow formed in a glacial deposit by a detached block of glacial ice, which later melted. They can fill with water to form kettle-lakes.

Lagoon A shallow stretch of coastal salt-water behind a partial barrier such as a sandbank or coral reef. Also used to describe the water encircled by an atoll.

Laterite A hard red deposit left by chemical weathering in tropical conditions, and consisting mainly of oxides of iron and aluminum.

Latitude The angular distance from the Equator, to a given point on the Earth's surface. Imaginary lines of latitude running parallel to the Equator encircle the Earth, and are measured in degrees north or south of the Equator. The Equator is 0°, the poles 90° South and North respectively. Also called parallels.

Laurasia In the theory of continental drift, the northern part of the great supercontinent of Pangaea. Laurasia is said to consist of N America, Greenland and all of Eurasia north of the Indian subcontinent.

Lava The molten rock, magma, which erupts onto the Earth's surface through a volcano, or through a fault or crack in the Earth's crust.

Leaching The process whereby water dissolves minerals and moves them down through layers of soil or rock.

Levée A raised bank alongside the channel of a river. Levées are either human-made or formed in times of flood when the river overflows its channel, slows and deposits much of its sediment load.

Lithosphere The rigid, upper layer of the Earth, comprising the crust and the upper part of the mantle..

Loess Fertile, fine-grained, yellow deposits of unstratified silts and sands.

Longitude A division of the Earth which pinpoints how far east or west a given place is from the Prime Meridian (0°) which runs through the Royal Observatory at Greenwich, England (UK). Imaginary lines of longitude are drawn around the world from pole to pole. The world is divided into 360 degrees.

Longshore drift The movement of sand and silt along the coast, carried by waves hitting the beach at an angle.

Magma Undground, molten rock, which is very hot and highly charged with gas. It is generated at great pressure, at depths 10 miles (16 km) or more below the Earth's surface.

Mantle The layer of the Earth between the crust and the core. it is about 1,800 miles (2,900 km) thick.

Massif A single very large mountain or an area of mountains with uniform characteristics and clearly-defined boundaries.

Meltwater Water resulting from the melting of a glacier or ice sheet.

Mesa A broad, flat-topped hill, characteristic of arid regions.

Metamorphic rocks Rocks that have been altered from their original form, in terms of texture, composition, and structure by intense heat, pressure, or by the introduction of new chemical substances – or a combination of more than one of these.

Milankovitch hypothesis A theory suggesting that there are a series of cycles that slightly alter the Earth's position when rotating about the Sun.

Mistral A strong, dry, cold northerly or north-westerly wind, which blows from the Massif Central of France to the Mediterranean Sea.

Mohoroviâiá discontinuity (Moho) The structural divide at the margin between the Earth's crust and the mantle. On average it is 20 miles (35 km) below the continents and 6 miles (10 km) below the oceans.

Monsoon A wind that changes direction biannually. The change is caused by the reversal of pressure over landmasses and the adjacent oceans. Because the inflowing moist winds bring rain, the term monsoon is also used to refer to the rains themselves.

Moraine Debris, transported and deposited by a glacier or ice sheet in unstratified, mixed, piles of rock, boulders, pebbles, and clay.

Mountain-building The formation of fold mountains by tectonic activity. Also known as orogeny, mountain-building often occurs on the margin where two tectonic plates collide.

Nappe A mass of rocks that has been overfolded by repeated thrust faulting.

Oasis A fertile area in the midst of a desert, usually watered by an underground aquifer.

Oceanic ridge A mid-ocean ridge formed, according to the theory of plate tectonics, when plates drift apart and hot magma pours through to form new oceanic crust.

Onion-skin weathering The weathering away or exfoliation of a rock or outcrop by the peeling off of surface layers.

Outwash plain Glaciofluvial material (typically clay, sand, and gravel) carried beyond an ice sheet by meltwater streams, forming a broad, flat deposit.

Oxbow lake A crescent-shaped lake formed on a river floodplain when a river erodes the outside bend of a meander, making the neck of the meander narrower until the river cuts across the neck. The meander is cut off and is dammed off with sediment, creating an oxbow lake.

Oxidation A form of chemical weathering where oxygen dissolved in water reacts with minerals in rocks – particularly iron to form oxides.

Pack ice Ice masses more than 10 ft (3 m) thick that form on the sea surface and are not attached to a landmass.

Pancake ice Thin discs of ice, up to 8 ft (2.4 m) wide which form when slicks of grease ice are tossed together by winds and stormy seas.

Pangaea In the theory of continental drift, Pangaea is the original great land mass which, about 190 million years ago, began to split into Gondwanaland in the south and Laurasia in the north, separated by the Tethys Sea.

Pediment A gently-sloping ramp of bedrock below a steeper slope, often found at mountain edges in desert areas, but also in other climatic zones. Pediments may include depositional elements such as alluvial fans.

Periglacial Regions on the edges of ice sheets or glaciers or, more commonly, cold regions experiencing intense frost action, permafrost or both.

Permafrost Permanently frozen ground, typical of Arctic regions.

Permeable rocks Rocks through which water can seep, because they are either porous or cracked.

Phreatic eruption A volcanic eruption which occurs when lava combines with groundwater, superheating the water and causing a sudden emission of steam at the surface.

Pingo A dome of earth with a core of ice, found in tundra regions. Pingos are formed either when groundwater freezes and expands, pushing up the land surface, or when trapped, freezing water in a lake expands and pushes up lake sediments to form the pingo dome.

Placer A belt of mineral-bearing rock strata lying at or close to the Earth's surface, from which minerals can be easily extracted.

Plate, plate tectonics The study of tectonic plates, that helps to explain continental drift, mountain formation and volcanic activity. The movement of tectonic plates may be explained by the currents of rock rising and falling from within the Earth's mantle, as it heats up and then cools. The boundaries of the plates are known as plate margins and most mountains, earthquakes, and volcanoes occur at these margins. Constructive margins are moving apart; destructive margins are crunching together and conservative margins are sliding past one another.

Pleistocene A period of geological time spanning from about 5.2 million years ago to 1.6 million years ago.

Plutonic rock Igneous rocks found deep below the surface. They are coarse-grained because they cooled and solidified slowly.

Polje A long, broad depression found in karst (limestone) regions.

Polygonal patterning Typical ground patterning, found in areas where the soil is subject to severe frost action, often in periglacial regions.

Porosity A measure of how much water can be held within a rock or a soil.

PreCambrian The earliest period of geological time dating from over 570 million years ago.

Precipitation The fall of moisture from the atmosphere onto the surface of the Earth, whether as dew, hail, rain, sleet, or snow.

Pyramidal peak A steep, isolated mountain summit, formed when the back walls of three or more cirques are cut back and move toward each other. The cliffs around such a horned peak, or horn, are divided by sharp arêtes.

Pyroclasts Fragments of rock ejected during volcanic eruptions.

Quaternary The current period of geological time, which started about 1.6 million years ago.

Reg A large area of stony desert, where tightly-packed gravel lies on top of clayey sand. A reg is formed where the wind blows away the finer sand.

Resistance The capacity of a rock to resist denudation, by processes such as weathering and erosion.

Ria A flooded V-shaped river valley or estuary, flooded by a rise in sea level (eustacy) or sinking land. It is shorter than a fjord and gets deeper as it meets the sea.

Rift valley A long, narrow depression in the Earth's crust, formed by the sinking of rocks between two faults.

Roche moutonée A rock found in a glaciated valley. The side facing the flow of the glacier has been smoothed and rounded, while the other side has been left more rugged because the glacier, as it flows over it, has plucked out frozen fragments and carried them away.

Runoff Water draining from a land surface by flowing across it.

Sabkha The floor of an isolated depression that occurs in an arid environment – usually covered by salt deposits and devoid of vegetation.

Salt plug A rounded hill produced by the upward doming of rock strata caused by the movement of salt or other evaporite deposits under intense pressure.

Sastrugi Ice ridges formed by wind action. They lie parallel to the direction of the wind.

Scree Piles of rock fragments beneath a cliff or rock face, caused by mechanical weathering, especially frost shattering, where the expansion and contraction of freezing and thawing water within the rock, gradually breaks it up.

Sea-floor spreading The process whereby tectonic plates move apart, allowing hot magma to erupt and solidify.

Seamount An isolated, submarine mountain or hill, probably of volcanic origin.

Sediment Grains of rock transported and deposited by rivers, sea, ice, or wind.

Sedimentary rocks Rocks formed from the debris of preexisting rocks or of organic material. They are found in many environments on the ocean floor, on beaches, rivers, and deserts.

Seif A sand dune which lies parallel to the direction of the prevailing wind. Seifs form steep-sided ridges, sometimes extending for miles.

Selva A region of wet forest found in the Amazon Basin.

Shale (marine shale) A compacted sedimentary rock, with fine-grained particles. Marine shale is formed on the seabed. Fuel such as oil may be extracted from it.

Sheetwash Water that runs downhill in thin sheets without forming channels. It can cause sheet erosion.

Sheet erosion The washing away of soil by a thin film or sheet of water, known as sheetwash.

Shield A vast stable block of the Earth's crust, which has experienced little or no mountain-building.

Sinkhole A circular depression in a limestone region. They are formed by the collapse of an underground cave system or the chemical weathering of the limestone.

Slip face The steep leeward side of a sand dune or slope. Opposite side to a back slope.

Soil creep The very gradual downslope movement of rock debris and soil, under the influence of gravity. This is a type of mass movement.

Solifluction A kind of soil creep, where water in the surface layer has saturated the soil and rock debris which slips slowly downhill. It often happens where frozen top-layer deposits thaw, leaving frozen layers below them.

Spit A thin linear deposit of sand or shingle extending from the sea shore.

Stack A tall, isolated pillar of rock near a coastline, created as wave action erodes away the adjacent rock.

Strike-slip fault Occurs where plates move sideways past each other and blocks of rocks move horizontally in relation to each other, not up or down as in normal faults.

Subduction zone A region where two tectonic plates collide, forcing one beneath the other.

Submarine fan Deposits of silt and alluvium, carried by large rivers forming great fan-shaped deposits on the ocean floor.

Supercontinent A large continent that breaks up to form smaller continents or that forms when smaller continents merge.

Syncline A basin-shaped downfold in rock strata, created when the strata are compressed, for example where tectonic plates collide.

Tableland A highland area with a flat or gently undulating surface.

Tectonic plates Plates, or tectonic plates, are the rigid slabs which form the Earth's outer shell, the lithosphere. Eight big plates and several smaller ones have been identified.

Thermokarst Subsidence created by the thawing of ground ice in periglacial areas, creating depressions.

Till Unstratified glacial deposits or drift left by a glacier or ice sheet. Includes mixtures of clay, sand, gravel, and boulders.

Topography The typical shape and features of a given area such as land height and terrain.

Tombolo A large sand spit which attaches part of the mainland to an island.

Transform fault In plate tectonics, a fault of continental scale, occurring where two plates slide past each other, staying close together for example, the San Andreas Fault. The jerky, uneven movement creates earthquakes but does not destroy or add to the Earth's crust

Trench (oceanic trench) A long, deep trough in the ocean floor, formed, according to the theory of plate tectonics, when two plates collide and one dives under the other, creating a subduction zone.

Tropic of Cancer A line of latitude or imaginary circle round the Earth, lying at 23° 28' N.

Tropic of Capricorn A line of latitude or imaginary circle round the Earth, lying at 23° 28' S.

U-shaped valley A river valley that has been deepened and widened by a glacier. They are characteristically flat-bottomed and steep-sided and generally much deeper than river valleys.

V-shaped valley A typical valley eroded by a river in its upper course.

Wadi The dry bed left by a torrent of water. Also classified as a ephemeral stream, found in arid and semiarid regions, which are subject to sudden and often severe flash flooding.

Watershed The dividing line between one drainage basin an area where all streams flow into a single river system – and another. In the US, watershed also means the whole drainage basin of a single river system its catchment area.

Waterspout A rotating column of water in the form of cloud, mist, and spray which form on open water. Often has the appearance of a small tornado.

Weathering The decay and breakup of rocks at or near the Earth's surface, caused by water, wind, heat, or ice, organic material, or the atmosphere. Physical weathering includes the effects of frost and temperature changes. Biological weathering includes the efects of palnt roots, burrowing animals and the acids produced by animals, especially as they decay after death. Carbonation and hydrolysis are among many kinds of chemical weathering.

NORTH AMERICA

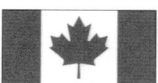

CANADA
PAGES 8–16

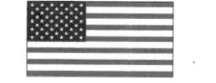

UNITED STATES OF AMERICA
PAGES 17–41

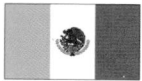

MEXICO
PAGES 42–43

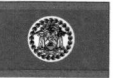

BELIZE
PAGES 44–45

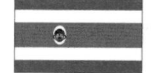

COSTA RICA
PAGES 44–45

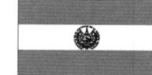

EL SALVADOR
PAGES 44–45

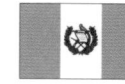

GUATEMALA
PAGES 44–45

HONDURAS
PAGES 44–45

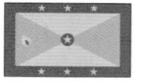

GRENADA
PAGES 46–47

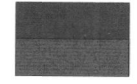

HAITI
PAGES 46–47

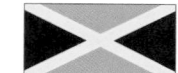

JAMAICA
PAGES 46–47

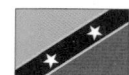

ST KITTS & NEVIS
PAGES 46–47

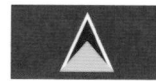

ST LUCIA
PAGES 46–47

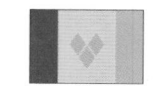

ST VINCENT & THE GRENADINES
PAGES 46–47

TRINIDAD & TOBAGO
PAGES 46–47

SOUTH AME

COLOMBIA
PAGES 56–57

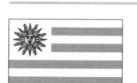

URUGUAY
PAGES 62–63

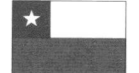

CHILE
PAGES 64–65

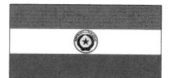

PARAGUAY
PAGES 64–65

AFRICA

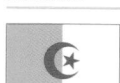

ALGERIA
PAGES 76–77

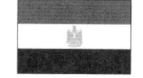

EGYPT
PAGES 76–77

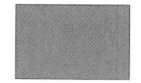

LIBYA
PAGES 76–77

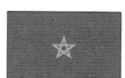

MOROCCO
PAGES 76–77

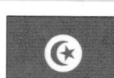

TUNISIA
PAGES 76–77

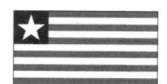

LIBERIA
PAGES 78–79

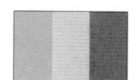

MALI
PAGES 78–79

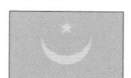

MAURITANIA
PAGES 78–79

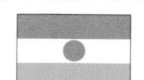

NIGER
PAGES 78–79

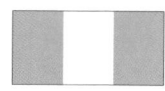

NIGERIA
PAGES 78–79

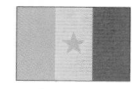

SENEGAL
PAGES 78–79

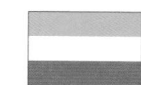

SIERRA LEONE
PAGES 78–79

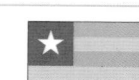

TOGO
PAGES 78–79

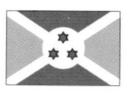

BURUNDI
PAGES 82–83

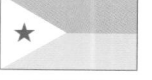

DJIBOUTI
PAGES 82–83

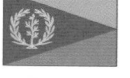

ERITREA
PAGES 82–83

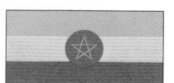

ETHIOPIA
PAGES 82–83

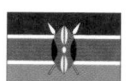

KENYA
PAGES 82–83

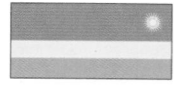

RWANDA
PAGES 82–83

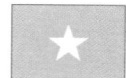

SOMALIA
PAGES 82–83

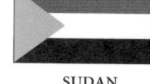

SUDAN
PAGES 82–83

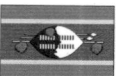

SOUTH AFRICA
PAGES 84–85

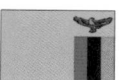

SWAZILAND
PAGES 84–85

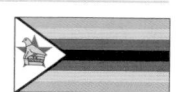

ZAMBIA
PAGES 84–85

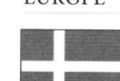

ZIMBABWE
PAGES 84–85

EUROPE

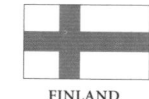

DENMARK
PAGES 94–97

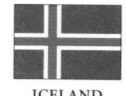

FINLAND
PAGES 94–95

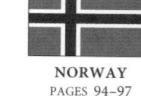

ICELAND
PAGES 94–95

NORWAY
PAGES 94–97

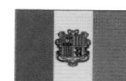

MONACO
PAGES 104–105

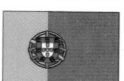

ANDORRA
PAGES 106–107

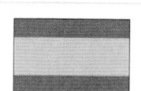

PORTUGAL
PAGES 106–107

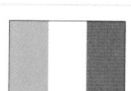

SPAIN
PAGES 106–107

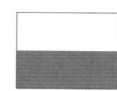

ITALY
PAGES 108–109

SAN MARINO
PAGES 108–109

VATICAN CITY
PAGES 108–109

AUSTRIA
PAGES 110–111

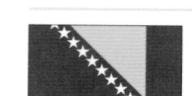

BOSNIA & HERZEGOVINA
PAGES 114–115

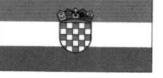

CROATIA
PAGES 114–115

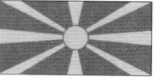

MACEDONIA
PAGES 114–115

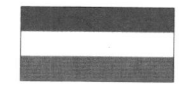

SERBIA & MONTENEGRO (YUGOSLAVIA)
PAGES 114–115

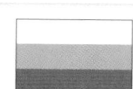

BULGARIA
PAGES 116–117

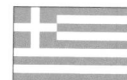

GREECE
PAGES 116–117

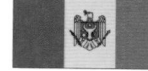

MOLDOVA
PAGES 118–119

ROMANIA
PAGES 118–119

ASIA

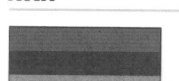

ARMENIA
PAGES 142–143

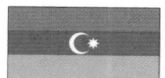

AZERBAIJAN
PAGES 142–143

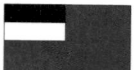

GEORGIA
PAGES 142–143

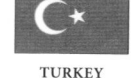

TURKEY
PAGES 142–143/116–117

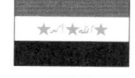

IRAQ
PAGES 144–145

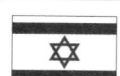

ISRAEL
PAGES 144–145

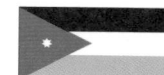

JORDAN
PAGES 144–145

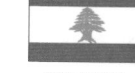

LEBANON
PAGES 144–145

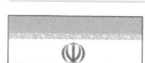

IRAN
PAGES 148–149

KAZAKHSTAN
PAGES 150–151

KYRGYZSTAN
PAGES 152–153

TAJIKISTAN
PAGES 152–153

TURKMENISTAN
PAGES 152–153

UZBEKISTAN
PAGES 152–153

AFGHANISTAN
PAGES 154–155

PAKISTAN
PAGES 154–157

TAIWAN
PAGES 166–167

JAPAN
PAGES 170–172

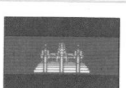

MYANMAR
PAGES 173–176

CAMBODIA
PAGES 173–176

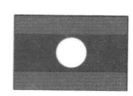

LAOS
PAGES 173–176

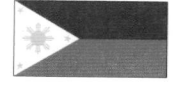

PHILIPPINES
PAGES 173–176

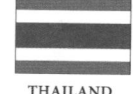

THAILAND
PAGES 177–179

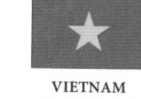

VIETNAM
PAGES 177–179

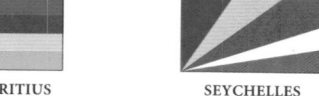

MAURITIUS
PAGES 180–181

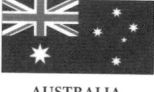

SEYCHELLES
PAGES 180–181

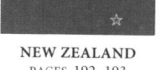

AUSTRALASIA & OCEANIA

AUSTRALIA
PAGES 188–191

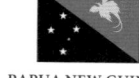

NEW ZEALAND
PAGES 192–193

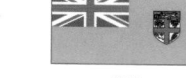

PAPUA NEW GUINEA
PAGES 194–195

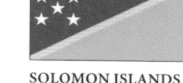

FIJI
PAGES 194–195

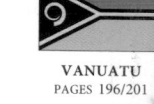

SOLOMON ISLANDS
PAGES 196/201

VANUATU
PAGES 196/201

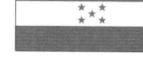

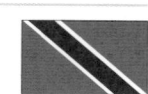

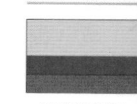

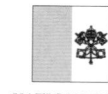

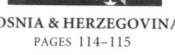

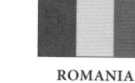

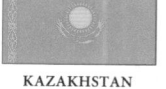

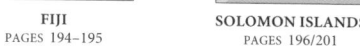